WESTMINSTER KINGSWAY COLLEGE
00021522
KU-534-484
CAMBRIDGE
PAPERBACK

THE CAMBRIDGE PAPERBACK ENCYCLOPEDIA

THIRD EDITION

Edited by
DAVID CRYSTAL

CAMBRIDGE
UNIVERSITY PRESS

PUBLISHED BY THE PRESS SYNDICATE OF THE UNIVERSITY OF CAMBRIDGE
The Pitt Building, Trumpington Street, Cambridge, United Kingdom

CAMBRIDGE UNIVERSITY PRESS
The Edinburgh Building, Cambridge CB2 2RU, UK www.cup.cam.ac.uk
40 West 20th Street, New York, NY 10011-4211, USA www.cup.org
10 Stamford Road, Oakleigh, Melbourne 3166, Australia
Ruiz de Alarcón 13, 28014 Madrid, Spain

First published in 1993
Second edition published in 1995
Third edition published in 1999

Cartography and illustrations by European Map Graphics Ltd, Finchampstead

Printed in the United Kingdom at the University Press, Cambridge

A catalogue record for this book is available from the British Library

Library of Congress Cataloguing in Publication data
The Cambridge paperback encyclopedia / edited by David Crystal. – 3rd ed.
p. cm.
ISBN 0 521 66800 X
1. Encyclopedias and dictionaries. I. Crystal, David, 1941–
AE5.C36 1999
032–dc21 98-56011 CIP

ISBN 0 521 66800 X paperback

Preface

The main aim of *The Cambridge Paperback Encyclopedia* is to provide a succinct, systematic, and readable guide to the facts, events, issues, beliefs, and achievements which make up the sum of human knowledge. Its parent volume, *The Cambridge Encyclopedia* (Third Edition) appeared in 1997 – a single-volume encyclopedia which was planned as a completely fresh venture, in terms of both coverage and treatment, with its topic entries specially commissioned from an international team of contributors. The present volume is derived from the same database, with all entries revised and updated to 1999.

Coverage

It is impossible to summarize the coverage of an encyclopedia in any simple way. Number of entries is a traditional guide, but opinion varies as to what counts as an entry, making it difficult to compare encyclopedias. In this new edition of *The Cambridge Paperback Encyclopedia*, there are nearly 21 000 entries given alphabetical treatment, and a further 8000 entries are presented in a 100-page Ready Reference section. The main entries include, additionally, 3000 bold-face head-words which are part of larger entries. An important feature of the work is the provision of 2500 headword cross-references, whose role is to anticipate the diverse routes used by readers when they are searching for information. In short, the 1080 pages of *The Cambridge Paperback Encyclopedia* provide over a million words of data on over 29 000 separately identified people, places, and topics, making it easily the most comprehensive work of its type.

Two major themes characterize the coverage of *The Cambridge Paperback Encyclopedia*: internationalism and up-to-dateness. An encyclopedia for the 2000s needs to reflect international issues, especially in history, politics, and current affairs. We have also allotted far more space than is traditional to the electronic revolution (especially computer science), space exploration, technology, economics, communications, earth sciences, environmental issues, medicine, and recreation. At the same time, we have given systematic coverage to traditionally popular areas such as flora and fauna, history, art, music, literature, theatre, religion, and mythology. For the Third Edition, 500 new entries have been added, improving the coverage of the work especially in cinema, politics, and sport, and in relation to current affairs in the USA, Northern Ireland, South Africa, and the European Union.

Treatment

Coverage is only half of the strength of any encyclopedia; the other crucial dimension is treatment. The most noticeable characteristic of *The Cambridge Paperback Encyclopedia* derives from its aim to act as a standard rapid-reference work, for use in the home, school, library, or office by both adult enquirers and young people of high-school age. The majority of entries are short and to the point – often with a simple expository structure consisting of an opening definition followed by one or two sentences of amplification or illustration. This short-entry principle allows the reader interested in a particular topic (say, a certain musical instrument) the opportunity to go directly to information on that topic, rather than to an entry in which all related topics are treated together in a single long essay.

At the same time, it is important to aid readers who do need to find out about a topic in a more comprehensive way, such as for homework assignments or course work. We have therefore retained the carefully selected system of cross-references to related topics which is such an important feature of the parent volume. For example, the cross-references at the end of the entry on **violin** will direct readers to other instruments closely associated with the violin (such as **viola** and **kit**) as well as to the family (**string instrument**), and other information (such as biographies of famous violin-makers). On the other hand, if the initial point of enquiry had been **string instrument**, the cross-references there would provide an indication of all the instruments in that family. An encyclopedia should be explored, and one way of doing this in *The Cambridge Paperback Encyclopedia* is to follow some of the many pathways provided by the cross-references, which number over 31 000.

The other important feature carried over from *The Cambridge Encyclopedia* is the commitment made by the editor to present the information in an intelligible and interesting way. All too often, encyclopedic information is put across in a dense and dull manner which creates a barrier between the enquirer and the subject being researched. The *Cambridge* family of encyclopedias aims to remove this barrier, partly by its imaginative use of typography and layout (including the use over 600 illustrations in the present edition), and partly by the use of plain English. Guidance on pronunciation is given, using a specially devised phonetic spelling, when it is not clear how a headword should be pronounced. A particular innovation is the systematic use of a specially condensed style for gazetteer, natural history, and certain other types of entry, which provides information in a clear and direct manner and increases accessibility. The principle of functional clarity has also been used in the selection of illustrations, where we have avoided the 'pretty picture' approach to encyclopedia compilation, and chosen to rely on clear, relevant line-drawings.

Interaction

As with *The Cambridge Encyclopedia*, we very much welcome feedback from readers relating to matters of coverage and treatment. Please write to the editor c/o Cambridge University Press, The Edinburgh Building, Shaftesbury Road, Cambridge, CB2 2RU, UK. In this way, our knowledge-base will grow with the times, and reflect ever more closely the interests and concerns of those wishing to benefit from it.

David Crystal

Editor
David Crystal

Editorial Administrator
Hilary Crystal

Editorial Assistants
Esther Pritchard
Tony McNicholl
Ann Rowlands
Jan Thomas

Illustrators
David Brogan
George Kilgour
John Marshall

Cartography
European Map Graphics Ltd

Design
Dale Tomlinson

For permission to reproduce copyright material we thank:
Art Directors Photo Library
Bass, Mitchells & Butler Ltd
City of Edinburgh District Council
European Space Agency
Hunting Aerofilms
National Aeronautics and Space Administration
National Gallery of Scotland
National Museums of Scotland, Dept of Geology, Edinburgh
New Scientist, London
Planet Earth Pictures
Royal Observatory, Edinburgh
Science Photo Library
Scottish National Gallery of Modern Art
South of Scotland Electricity Board
Tate Gallery, London
The Benesh Institute, London
The Telegraph Colour Library
UK Operators Offshore Association
Victory Museum, Portsmouth
Wade Cooper Associates

How to use this encyclopedia

Headword

- The order of entries follows the English alphabet, ignoring capital letters, accents, diacritics, or apostrophes.
- The ordering is letter by letter, ignoring all spaces and hyphens in compound headings, eg **seance** precedes **sea otter**, which precedes **sea perch**, which precedes **seaplane**. Exceptions include all **Mc** names, which are listed as if they were **Mac**; and all **St** names, which are listed as if they were **Saint**.
- We list phrasal names under their most specific element, eg **Japan, Sea of; Waterloo, Battle of**.
- In cases where headwords have the same spelling, the order is; (1) places, (2) people, (3) general topics.
- We list identically spelled topic headwords according to the alphabetical order of their subject areas, eg **depression** (meteorology) precedes **depression** (psychiatry).
- We list rulers chronologically, ordering them by country if titles are the same, eg **Henry II** (of England) is followed by **Henry II** (of France) then by **Henry III** (of England) and **Henry III** (of France).
- When many people have the same name (eg **John**), we list monarchs before saints and popes, followed by lay people. Compound names (eg **John of Austria**) appear later than single element names (eg **John, Elton**).
- We list places with the same name on the basis of the alphabetical order of their countries, eg **Dover** (UK) precedes **Dover** (USA).
- Parts of a person's name that are not generally used are enclosed in parentheses, eg **Wells, H(erbert) G(eorge)**. Parenthesized elements are ignored in deciding alphabetical sequence, eg **Jones, (Alfred) Ernest** follows **Jones, Daniel**.

Entry conventions

Spelling conventions

- Where alternative spellings exist in headwords, we give British usage first, then American usage, eg **colour/color television**. We give cross-references in all cases where spelling variation affects initial letters, eg **esophagus** >> **oesophagus**.
- We transliterate names in non-Roman alphabets, and add a cross-reference in cases where confusion could arise because more than one transliteration system exists. Chinese names are given in pin-yin (eg **Beijing** for **Peking**). In the case of Arabic names, we have not transliterated the alif and ain symbols. No accent is shown on French capital letters.

Cross-references

- Cross-references are generally to headwords in the encyclopedia, with a distinguishing parenthesis if required, eg **recorder** (music). We do not include personal titles in the cross-reference, and we give a distinguishing first name or initial only if entries could be confused, eg **Morgan, Henry; Morgan, J P**.
- All cross-references are listed in alphabetical order. In the case of loner entries, the references may be grouped; eg in art, cross-references to topics precede cross-references to artists.
- When several references share a common word or phrase, they are conflated, being separated by /, as in the **spacecraft** entry overleaf.
- The Ready Reference section, at the end of the book, is organized thematically, with an introductory index.

Abbreviations

AD	*Anno Domini*
BAFTA	British Academy of Film and Television Arts
BC	before Christ
c	century
c.	circa
C	Celsius (Centigrade)
C	central
cc	cubic centimetre(s)
CFA	Communauté financière africaine
Chin	Chinese
cm	centimetre(s)
Co	County
cu	cubic
cwt	hundredweight(s)
d.	died
e	estimate
E	east(ern)
eg	for example
Eng	English
EU	European Union
F	Fahrenheit
Finn	Finnish
fl.	flourished
fl oz	fluid ounce(s)
Fr	French
ft	foot/feet
g	gram(s)
Ger	German
Gr	Greek
h	hour(s)
ha	hectare(s)
Hung	Hungarian
[i]	illustration
I(s)	Island(s)
ie	that is (*id est*)
in	inch(es)
Ir	Irish
Ital	Italian
Jap	Japanese
K	Kelvin
kg	kilogram(s)
km	kilometre(s)
l	litre(s)
L	Lake
Lat	Latin
lb	pound(s)
l y	light year(s)
m	metre(s)
min	minute(s)
mi	mile(s)
Mlle	Mademoiselle
mm	millimetre(s)
Mme	Madame
m/s	metres per second
Mt(s)	Mount(ain)(s)
N	north(ern)
no.	number
oz	ounce(s)
p(p)	page(s)
pop	population
Port	Portuguese
pt	pint(s)
r.	reigned
R	River
RR	Ready Reference
Russ	Russian
S	south(ern)
s	second(s)
Span	Spanish
sq	square
St	Saint
Sta	Santa
Ste	Sainte
Swed	Swedish
trans.	translation
Turk	Turkish
UK	United Kingdom
US	United States
v.	versus
vols.	volumes
W	west(ern)
yd	yard(s)
Z	zodiac

Other conventions

- Months in parentheses are abbreviated to the first three letters
- Currency abbreviations, RR985-992
- Science abbreviations, RR1031–2, 1035–6
- Abbreviations of US states, RR994

Pronunciation guide

Symbol	Sound	Symbol	Sound	Symbol	Sound
a	hat	i	sit	r	red
ah	father	iy	lie	s	set
air	hair	j	jet	sh	ship
aw	saw	k	kit	t	tin
ay	say	l	lip	th	thin
b	big	m	man	th	this
ch	chip	n	nip	u	put
d	dig	ng	sing	uh	cup
e	set	o	hot	v	van
ee	see	oh	soul	w	will
er	bird	oo	soon	y	yes
f	fish	ow	cow	z	zoo
g	go	oy	boy	zh	leisure
h	hat	p	pin		

Non-English sounds

ã	French Nantes
hl	Welsh llan
ĩ	French Saint
õ	French bon
kh	Scots loch, German ich
oe	French soeur, German möglich
õe	French brun
ü	French tu, German müde

- Bold type is used to show stressed or accented syllables in certain languages, eg **Xerxes** [**zerk**seez]
- No distinctive symbol is used for unstressed English vowels, in cases where the pronunciation can be intuitively deduced from the spelling, eg **echidna** [e**kid**na].
- The symbol (r) is used to mark cases where an *r* in the spelling may or may not be pronounced, depending on the accent, eg Barbarossa [bah(r)**ba**rosa]. This symbol is not used when the transcription of a sound already contains an [r] symbol, as in [er].

Examples

space shuttle A re-usable crewed launch vehicle. The first-generation US shuttle launched in April 1981; it carries up to seven crew, and is capable of launching a 27 000 kg/60 000 lb payload into low Earth orbit; missions are up to 9 days' duration. It comprises a delta-winged lifting body orbiter with main engines, a jettisonable external fuel tank, and two auxiliary solid rocket boosters. The fleet comprised four vehicles: *Columbia*, *Challenger*, *Discovery*, and *Atlantis*. The *Challenger* explosion on the 25th flight (26 Jan 1986) 73 sec after launch caused the loss of the crew. The first reflight took place in September 1988, and a replacement fourth orbiter, *Endeavour*, became operational in 1992. >> launch vehicle i; spacecraft RR980

See list of abbreviations

A cross-reference to an entry which contains an illustration (a line drawing or panel) is followed by the symbol i

A cross-reference to the Ready Reference section (at the back of the encyclopedia) is preceded by RR followed by the appropriate page number, and appears after the other cross-references.

spacecraft Vehicles designed to operate in the vacuum–weightlessness–high radiation environment of space: used to convey human crew, to acquire scientific data, to conduct utilitarian operations (eg telecommunications), and to conduct research (eg microgravity experiments). The first spacecraft (Sputnik 1) was launched by the USSR in 1957 (4 Oct). >> Explorer 1; Progress/ Soyuz/ Vostok spacecraft; space exploration; Sputnik

All cross-references are preceded by the symbol >>

Vostok [vostok] ('East') **spacecraft** The first generation of Soviet crewed spacecraft, carrying a single member. Vostok 1 carried the first human into space (12 Apr 1961) – Yuri Gagarin, who orbited Earth once on a flight of 118 min. The last Vostok flight carried Valentina Tereshkova, the first woman to fly in space (Vostok 6, 16 Jun 1963). Voskhod ('Sunrise') was an intermediate-generation Soviet-crewed spacecraft following Vostok and preceding Soyuz; it made only two flights, in 1964 and 1965. >> Gagarin; Soviet space programme; spacecraft; Tereshkova

See pronunciation guide

See entry conventions (spelling)

A

Aachen [**ah**khen], Fr **Aix-La-Chapelle** 50°47N 6°04E, pop (1995e) 252 000. Manufacturing city in Cologne district, Germany; N capital of Charlemagne's empire; annexed by France, 1801; given to Prussia, 1815; badly bombed in World War 2; railway; technical college; cathedral (15th-c). >> Charlemagne; Germany [i]; Prussia

Aalto, (Hugo Henrik) Alvar [**awl**toh] (1898–1976) Architect, born in Kuortane, Finland. He was a designer of modern public and industrial buildings in Finland, and also of contemporary furniture.

aardvark [**ah(r)d**vah(r)k] A southern African mammal (*Orycteropus afer*); length, 1–1·5 m/3¼–5 ft; long ears, pig-like snout, long sticky tongue, strong claws; digs burrows; eats ants and termites; mainly nocturnal; also known as **ant bear** or **earth pig**; the only member of the order Tubulidentata. (Family: Orycteropodidae.) >> mammal [i]

aardwolf [**ah(r)d**wulf] A rare southern African carnivore (*Proteles cristatus*) of the hyena family; slender, yellow with black stripes; lives in a den; nocturnal; also known as **maned jackal**. >> carnivore [i]; hyena

Aarhus >> **Århus**

Aaron [**air**on] (15th–13th-c BC) Elder brother of Moses and the first high priest of the Israelites. He and his sons were ordained as priests after the construction of the Ark of the Covenant and the Tabernacle. >> golden calf; Levites; Moses; Zadokites

Aaron, Hank [**air**on], popular name of **Henry Lewis Aaron**, nickname **Hammerin' Hank** (1934–) Baseball player, born in Mobile, AL. In 1974 he surpassed Babe Ruth's 39-year-old record of career home runs, and retired in 1976 with a total of 755 home runs. >> baseball [i]; Ruth

abaca A fibre obtained from the leaf-stalks of a species of banana (*Musa textilis*) native to the Philippines; also called **Manila hemp**; used for cables, carpets, and ships' hawsers. (Family: Musaceae.) >> banana; fibre

abacus [**a**bakuhs] A device for performing calculations by sliding bead counters along a set of rods or in grooves, It may have originated in Babylonia, and was used in ancient China, Greece, and Rome. It became widespread in Europe in the Middle Ages, as well as in China and Japan, where it is still in use, though increasingly being replaced by the calculator.

Abadan [aba**dahn**] 30°20N 48°16E, pop (1995e) 396 000. Oil port in WC Iran at head of Persian Gulf; terminus of Iran's major oil pipelines; severely damaged in the Iran–Iraq War; airport. >> Persian Gulf; Gulf War 1; Iran [i]

abalone [aba**loh**nee] A primitive marine snail characterized by a single row of holes extending back from the front margin of its ovoid shell; collected for decoration and for human consumption; also called **ormer**. (Class: Gastropoda. Order: Archaeogastropoda.) >> algae; gastropod; snail

Abba [**a**ba] Swedish pop group, formed in 1973, with members **Bjorn Ulvaeus** (1945– , guitar, vocals), married to **Agnetha Faltskog** (1950– , vocals), and **Benny Anderson** (1945– , keyboards, vocals), married to **Anni-Frid** (known as **Frida**) **Lyngstad** (1945– , vocals). The group's name is an acronym of their first names. The group broke up at the end of the 1970s, and the couples divorced soon after.

Abbas I [**a**bas], known as **Abbas the Great** (1571–1629) Shah of Persia (1588–1628). His reign marked a peak of Persian artistic achievement, especially in painting, weaving, and manuscript illumination.

Abbas (c.566–c.652) Uncle of Mohammed, at first hostile to him, but ultimately the chief promoter of his religion. The **Abbasids** claimed descent from him, and thus a connection to the Prophet. >> Mohammed

abbey A building or group of buildings used by a religious order for worship and living. It houses a community under the direction of an abbot or abbess as head, who is elected for a term of years or for life. >> Chartreuse, La Grande; Clairvaux; Escorial, El; Fountains Abbey; monasticism

Abbey Theatre A theatre situated in Dublin's Abbey Street, the centre of the Irish dramatic movement initiated by Lady Gregory and W B Yeats. The present theatre was opened in 1966, after the earlier building had burnt down in 1951. >> O'Casey; Synge

Abbott and Costello Comedy film partners: **Bud Abbott**, originally **William A Abbott** (1896–1974), born in Asbury Park, NJ, and **Lou Costello**, originally **Louis Francis Cristillo** (1908–59), born in Paterson, NJ. They made a number of successful comedy films, beginning with *Buck Privates* (1941), Costello playing the clown and Abbott his straight man.

abdomen The lower part of the trunk, extending from within the pelvic floor to under the cover of the chest wall. It contains most of the alimentary canal (from stomach to rectum), the liver, pancreas, spleen, kidneys, and bladder, and the uterus in females. >> alimentary canal; peritoneum

Abdul-Jabbar, Kareem [abdul **ja**ber], originally **Lewis Ferdinand Alcindor**, known as **Lew Alcindor** (1947–) Basketball player, born in New York City. A 7 ft 2 in/2 m 5 cm centre, he played most of his career with the Los Angeles Lakers. When he retired in 1989, he had played more National Basketball League games (1560) than any other player, and scored more points, 38 387. >> basketball

Abel [**ay**bel] Biblical character, the second son of Adam and Eve. He is described as a shepherd, whose offering God accepts; but he was then murdered by his brother, Cain (*Gen* 4.2–16). >> Adam and Eve; Cain; Old Testament

Abelard, Peter [**a**belah(r)d] (1079–1142) Theologian, born near Nantes, France. While a lecturer at Notre-Dame, he married Héloïse, the 17-year-old niece of the canon Fulbert. Opposition to their marriage led Héloïse to enter a convent and Abelard to become a monk. He founded a monastic school, for many years defending his teaching against charges of heresy. >> Bernard of Clairvaux, St; monasticism; theology; Trinity

Aberconwy and Colwyn [aber**kon**wee, **kol**win], Welsh **Aberconwy a Cholwyn** pop (1995e) 110 700; area 1130 sq km/436 sq mi. County (unitary authority from 1996) in NC Wales, UK; drained by the R Conwy; administrative centre, Colwyn Bay; seaside resorts on north coast; part of Snowdonia National Park; castle at Conwy. >> Conwy; Snowdon; Wales [i]

Aberdeen, ancient **Devana** 57°10N 2°04W, pop (1995e) 221 000. Seaport city council (Aberdeen City), and administrative centre of Aberdeenshire council, NE Scotland; on the North Sea; royal burgh since 1179; airport; helicopter port; ferries to Orkney and Shetland; railway; universities (1494, 1992); cathedral (1131); oil supply service, granite ('Granite City'). >> Scotland [i]

Aberdeen, George Hamilton Gordon, 4th Earl of (1784–1860) British statesman and prime minister (1852–5), born in Edinburgh. He became foreign secretary (1828–30, 1841–6), and in 1852 headed a coalition ministry. Vacillating policy and mismanagement during the Crimean War led to his resignation. >> Crimean War

Aberdeen terrier >> **Scottish terrier**

Aberfan [aber**van**] 51°42N 3°21W. Village in coal-mining region, Merthyr Tydfil county, S Wales, UK; scene of major disaster in 1966, when a landslip of mining waste engulfed several houses and the school, killing 144, including 116 children. >> Wales i

Abernathy, Ralph D(avid) [**a**bernathee] (1926–90) Baptist clergyman and civil rights activist, born in Linden, AL. Pastor of the West Hunter Street Baptist Church in Atlanta, GA, he became Martin Luther King's chosen successor as head of the Southern Christian Leadership Conference (1968–77). >> civil rights; King, Martin Luther

aberrations 1 In optics, deviations in lenses from perfect images, as predicted by simple lens theory. They are consequences of the laws of refraction. > astigmatism; lens; optics i **2** In astronomy, apparent changes in the observed position of a star, because of changes in relative velocity as the Earth orbits the Sun. >> orbit; star

Aberystwyth [aber**ist**with] 52°25N 4°05W, pop (1995e) 12 600. Administrative centre of Cardiganshire county, W Wales, UK; university and resort town on Cardigan Bay; built around a castle of Edward I, 1227; railway; college of University of Wales (1872); National Library of Wales (1955). >> Wales i

Abidjan [abee**jan**] 5°19N 4°01W, pop (1995e) 2 722 000. Industrial seaport and former capital (1935–83) of Côte d'Ivoire, W Africa; airport; railway; university (1958). >> Côte d'Ivoire i; Yamoussoukro

ABM >> **antiballistic missile**

Abney level >> **clinometer**

Åbo >> **Turku**

abolitionist movement A 19th-c movement to end slavery in the US South, which crystallized around the American Anti-Slavery Society, founded in 1833. It was distinguished from earlier anti-slavery movements by its uncompromising attitude. >> civil rights

A-bomb >> **atomic bomb**

Abomey [**abo**may] 7°14N 2°00E, pop (1995e) 78 000. Town in Zou province, S Benin, W Africa; capital of old Yoruba kingdom of Dahomey; Royal Palace of Djema, including the tomb of King Gbehanzin (still guarded by women), a world heritage site. >> Benin (country) i; Dahomey; Yoruba

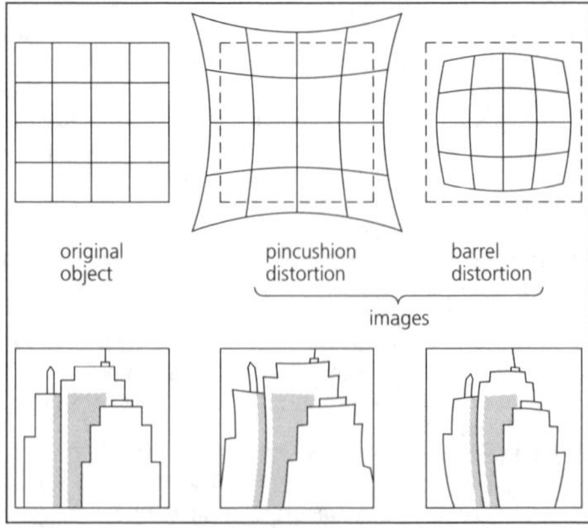

Aberration – distortion caused by variation in the lens magnifying power with an object's distance from the lens axis.

abominable snowman >> **Bigfoot; Yeti**

Aborigines [abo**ri**jineez] The indigenous inhabitants of Australia, the first of whom reached the continent c.60 000 years ago. By 1788, when European occupation began, there were c.600 territorially defined groups, subsisting on hunting and gathering, with a population of 300 000–1 million. Numbers then fell dramatically, partly through conflict with the Europeans, but mainly through European diseases, especially the smallpox epidemics of 1789 and 1829. By 1933 the population had fallen to c.66 000; it then steadily increased, and now numbers about 250 000. At first, Europeans portrayed Aboriginals as 'noble savages', but this image quickly gave way to contempt, and policies were designed to turn them into Christians with European lifestyles. Aborigines have not accepted their lot passively. In the 1950s they began moving into the cities of SE Australia and formed advancement groups; but it was not until the mid-1960s that activism became prominent. Their condition has since improved significantly, but they remain the most disadvantaged group in Australian society. >> Aranda; Australia i; Banjalang; Dieri; Dreamtime; Gunwinggu; Kngwarreye; Mabo; Pintupi; Pitjantjatjara; Tiwi; Yolngu; Yunupingu; Warlpiri

abortion The spontaneous or induced termination of pregnancy before the fetus is viable. In the UK and for legal purposes, this is taken to be the 24th week, although some fetuses expelled before then may survive. In the USA and in some European countries, the time limit may be set some weeks earlier. Spontaneous abortion (*miscarriage*) occurs in about 20% of apparently normal pregnancies, and may not be recognized. The moral issues surrounding abortion have received increasing publicity in the 1990s, with conflict between extremists from 'pro-life' (anti-abortion) and 'right-to-choose' (pro-abortion) groups leading to violent confrontation, especially in the USA. >> pregnancy i

abortion pill >> **contraception**

Aboukir Bay, Battle of 1 (Aug 1798) A naval battle during the War of the Second Coalition, in which Nelson destroyed the French fleet under Brueys off the coast of Egypt; also known as the **Battle of the Nile**. **2** (Jul 1799) The last French victory of the Egyptian campaign, in which Napoleon's Army of Egypt captured Aboukir citadel, NE of Alexandria, defeating an Ottoman Turkish force under Mustafa Pasha; also known as the **Battle of Aboukir**. >> Napoleon I; Nelson, Horatio

Abraham, Abram, or **Ibrahiz** (after 2000 BC) Biblical character revered as the ancestor of Israel and of several other nations; also an important figure in Islam. At 100 years of age he is said to have had a son Isaac by his previously barren wife, Sarah (*Gen* 21). In Judaism, Isaac was seen as the fulfilment of the divine promises, although Abraham was ordered by God to sacrifice his heir at Moriah as a test of faith (*Gen* 22). >> Bible; Isaac; Ishmael; Islam; Judaism; Sarah

Abraham, Plains / Heights of The site of a battle (1759), Quebec City, Canada, in which British forces under Wolfe defeated a French/Canadian force under Montcalm and Vaudreuil, and gained control over Quebec. Wolfe and Montcalm were both killed in the battle. >> Montcalm; Wolfe, James

abrasives Hard, rough, or sharp textured materials used to wear down, rub, or polish materials which are less hard, as in the traditional grindstone or whetstone. Naturally occurring abrasive substances include various forms of silica (sand, quartz, or flint), pumice, and emery (an aluminium oxide mineral). Artificial abrasives include silicon carbide, synthetic diamond, and boron carbide. >> emery; pumice; silica

abscess A localized collection of pus in an organ or tissue, surrounded by an inflammatory reaction which forms a well-defined wall (an abscess cavity). It is commonly due to infection, but occasionally a foreign body is responsible. >> boil; carbuncle; pus

Abse, Dannie [**ab**see] (1923–) Writer and physician, born in Cardiff. His literary output includes poetry, novels, and plays, as well as the autobiographical volumes *A Poet in the Family* (1974) and *A Strong Dose of Myself* (1983).

absolutism A theory of kingship elaborated and practised in early modern Europe, associated notably with Louis XIV of France. Absolute power was justified by the belief that monarchs were God's representatives on Earth. >> Divine Right of Kings; Louis XIV

absorbed dose >> **radioactivity units** ⓘ

abstract art A form of art in which there is no attempt to represent objects or persons, but which relies instead on lines, colours, and shapes alone for its aesthetic appeal. It seems to have emerged c.1910, and was partly a reaction against 19th-c Realism and Impressionism. Early abstract artists include Kandinsky, Miró, Pevsner, and Brancusi. The term is often used imprecisely to cover a wide range of 20th-c art. >> action painting; art; biomorphic art; concrete art; Constructivism; Cubism; *De Stijl*; figurative art; Op Art; Arp; Brancusi; Kandinsky; Miró; Mondrian; Moore, Henry; Pevsner, Antoine

abstract expressionism >> **action painting**

absurdism The expression in art of the meaninglessness of human existence. Its potential for comedy and terror has been exploited especially in the theatre (**Theatre of the Absurd**), as in the plays of Ionesco, Beckett, and Pinter. >> Beckett; Camus; Ionesco; Pinter

Abu-Bakr or **Abu-Bekr** [aboo **ba**ker] (c.573–634) Father of Mohammed's wife, Aïshah, born in Mecca. He became the prophet's most trusted follower, succeeded him as the first caliph (632), and began the compilation of the Koran. During his 2-year reign he put down a religious and political revolt, and initiated Arab conquests. >> Koran; Mohammed

Abu Dhabi or **Abu Zabi** [aboo **da**bee] pop (1995e) 883 000; area c.67 600 sq km/26 000 sq mi. Largest of the seven member states of the United Arab Emirates; capital Abu Dhabi, pop (1995e) 359 000; main oasis settlement, al-Ayn; vast areas of desert and salt flats; coastline 400 km/250 mi; a major oil region. >> United Arab Emirates ⓘ

Abuja [a**boo**ja] 9°05N 7°30E, pop (1995e) 412 000. New capital (from 1991) of Nigeria, in Federal Capital Territory, C Nigeria, at the geographical centre of the country; government offices began moving from Lagos in the 1980s. >> Nigeria ⓘ

Abu Mena [aboo **men**a] A site in NW Egypt sacred to the 3rd-c AD martyr Abu Mena (St Menas). The ruins of the early 5th-c basilica erected here by the Emperor Arcadius are a world heritage site. >> Egypt ⓘ

Abu Simbel [aboo **sim**bel] 22°22N 31°38E. The site of two huge sandstone temples carved by Pharaoh Rameses II (c.1304–1273 BC) out of the Nile bank near Aswan; now a world heritage site. They were dismantled and relocated in the 1960s when the rising waters of the newly-constructed Aswan High Dam threatened their safety. >> Aswan; Rameses II

Abyssinia >> **Ethiopia** ⓘ

Abyssinian cat A breed of domestic cat, popular in the USA (known as the **foreign short-haired**); reddish-brown, each hair with several dark bands; orange-red nose. >> cat

acacia >> **wattle** ⓘ

academy 1 A place of learning or association formed for scientific, literary, artistic, or musical purposes. From the Renaissance the term was applied in Europe to institutions of higher learning (eg the *Accademia della Crusca*, 1587) and advanced teaching (until the term 'university' became widespread in the 18th-c). >> academy of art **2** The American **Academy of Motion Picture Arts and Sciences**, widely known since 1927 for its annual awards for creative merit and craftsmanship in film production. It has been influential in establishing technical standards. >> Oscar; RR1042

Academy Award >> **Academy 2; Oscar**

Acadia [a**kay**dia] Part of France's American empire; what is today Prince Edward Island, Nova Scotia, and New Brunswick, Canada. The first settlement was established at Port Royal in 1605 by Champlain. The Treaty of Utrecht (1713) handed most of Acadia to Britain. >> Champlain

acanthus [a**kan**thuhs] A plant with thick, prickly leaves, representations of which are often used to decorate mouldings or carved parts of a building.

Acapulco [aka**pul**koh] or **Acapulco de Juárez** 16°51N 99°56W, pop (1995e) 657 000. Port and resort town in S Mexico, on the Pacific Ocean; airfield; tourism; badly damaged by hurricane Pauline in 1997. >> Mexico ⓘ

Acari [**ak**ariy] >> **mite**

ACAS [**ay**kas] Acronym for **Advisory, Conciliation and Arbitration Service**, a UK body set up in 1975. It provides facilities for conciliation, arbitration, and mediation in industrial disputes. >> industrial relations

acceleration For linear motion, the rate of change of velocity with time; equals force divided by mass; symbol a, units m/s^2; a vector quantity. For rotational motion, the rate of change of angular velocity with time; equals torque divided by moment of inertia; angular acceleration symbol α units radians/s^2; a vector quantity. >> acceleration due to gravity; force; torque ⓘ; vector (mathematics); velocity

acceleration due to gravity The acceleration on an object close to the Earth, due to the Earth's gravitational field; symbol g. Its value is usually taken as 9·81 m/s^2, but it varies over the Earth's surface and decreases with height above sea level. >> acceleration; gravitation

accent (regional) The features of pronunciation which mark a speaker's regional background or social class. Accent is to be distinguished from dialect, which involves the study of other linguistic features, such as grammar and vocabulary. >> dialectology

accentor A sparrow-like bird native to N Africa, Europe, and Asia; brownish-grey to chestnut above, often streaked; grey beneath. (Genus: *Prunella*, 12 species. Family: Prunellidae.) >> dunnock

accepting house A merchant bank which buys ('accepts') three-month bills of exchange issued by companies. In the UK, the top accepting houses in London form the Accepting Houses Committee. >> merchant bank

accordion A portable musical instrument of the reed organ type, fed with air from bellows activated by the player. In the most advanced models a treble keyboard is played with the right hand, while the left operates (usually) six rows of buttons, producing bass notes and chords. The earliest type was patented in Vienna in 1829. >> aerophone; Berg; keyboard instrument; Prokofiev; reed organ

accountancy The profession which deals with matters relating to money within an organization. It handles a wide range of activities, including financial planning, management accounting, taxation, and treasury management (managing money), as well as recording and presenting accounts for management and owners. >> audit

Accra [a**krah**] 5°33N 0°15W, pop (1995e) 1 134 000. Seaport capital of Ghana, on the Gulf of Guinea coast; founded as three forts and trading posts, 17th-c; capital of Gold Coast, 1877; capital of Ghana, 1957; airport; railway; university (1948) at Legon. >> Ghana i

accumulator A device to store electricity, by accepting a charge and later releasing it; also called a **battery**. It is a lead–acid system, with plates of lead oxides and an electrolyte of sulphuric acid. Accumulators are widely used to start car engines, and also to propel electric vehicles such as milk floats. Other systems include nickel-iron (*Nife*) and nickel-cadmium (*Nicad*) plates, with alkaline electrolytes. Some are made in small sizes, to replace torch and other batteries with rechargeable versions. >> battery (electricity); current (electricity); electricity

acetaldehyde [asi**tal**dihiyd] CH_3CHO, IUPAC **ethanal**, boiling point 21°C. The product of gentle oxidation of ethanol, intermediate in the formation of acetic acid; a colourless liquid with a sharp odour. A reducing agent, the compound is actually the one detected in the 'breathalyzer' test. >> acetic acid; aldehydes; breathalyzer; ethanol; IUPAC

acetals [**a**sitlz] Substances of the general structure $R_2C(OR)_2$, formed by the reaction of an alcohol with an aldehyde, water also being formed. Internal acetal formation gives most sugars ring structures. >> alcohols; aldehydes; glucose; ring

acetic acid [a**see**tik] CH_3COOH, IUPAC **ethanoic acid**, boiling point 118°C. The product of oxidation of ethanol. The pure substance is a viscous liquid with a strong odour. Vinegar is essentially a 5% solution of acetic acid. >> acid; ethanol; IUPAC; pH

acetone [**a**sitohn] CH_3COCH_3, IUPAC **propanone**, boiling point 56°C. A volatile liquid with an odour resembling ethers. It is a very widely used solvent, especially for plastics and lacquers. >> ether; IUPAC; ketones

acetyl [**a**sitiyl] CH_3CO-, IUPAC **ethanoyl**. A functional group in chemistry, whose addition to a name usually indicates its substitution for hydrogen in a compound. >> functional group; hydrogen; IUPAC

acetylcholine [asitiyl**koh**leen] An acetyl ester of choline ($C_7H_{16}NO_2^+$) which functions as a neurotransmitter in most animals with nervous systems. >> acetyl; choline; ester; nervous system; neurotransmitter

acetylene [a**set**ileen] $HC{\equiv}CH$, IUPAC **ethyne**, boiling point -84°C. The simplest alkyne, a colourless gas formed by the action of water on calcium carbide. It is an important starting material in organic synthesis, and is used as a fuel, especially (mixed with oxygen) in the oxyacetylene torch. >> alkynes; IUPAC; oxyacetylene welding

Achaemenids [a**kiy**menidz] The first royal house of Persia, founded by the early 7th-c BC ruler Achaemenes. Its capitals included Parsagadae and Persepolis. >> Cyrus II; Darius I; Persian Empire; Xerxes I

Achebe, Chinua [**a**chaybay], originally **Albert Chinualumogo** (1930–) Novelist, born in Ogidi, Nigeria. Four novels written between 1958 (*Things Fall Apart*) and 1966 (*A Man of the People*) describe tribal and racial tensions in pre- and post-colonial Nigerian society. After a period in politics and education, he wrote *Anthills of the Savannah* (1987).

Achenbach, Andreas [**akh**enbakh] (1815–1910) Landscape and marine painter, born in Kassel, Germany. He was regarded as the father of 19th-c German landscape painting. >> landscape painting

achene [a**keen**] A dry fruit, not splitting to release the single seed. It is usually small, often bearing hooks, spines, or other structures which aid in dispersal. >> fruit

Achernar [a**ker**na(r)] >> **Eridanus**

Acheron [**a**keron] In Greek mythology, the chasm or abyss of the Underworld, and the name of one of the rivers there. It is also the name of a river in Epirus, thought to be an entrance to Hades. >> Charon (mythology); Hades

Acheson, Dean (Gooderham) [**a**chesn] (1893–1971) US statesman and lawyer, born in Middletown, CT. Secretary of state (1949–53) in the Truman administration, he helped to establish the Marshall Plan (1947) and the North Atlantic Treaty Organization (1949). >> Marshall, George C(atlett); NATO; Truman

Acheulian [a**shoo**lian] In Europe, Africa, and Asia, a broad term for early prehistoric cultures using symmetrically-flaked stone handaxes, dating from c.1·5 million years ago. The name derives from finds made c.1850 at Saint-Acheul in the Somme Valley, N France. >> Three Age System

Achilles [a**kil**eez] A legendary Greek hero, son of Peleus and Thetis, who dipped him in the R Styx so that he was invulnerable, except for the heel where she had held him. He was killed by Paris, who shot him in the heel with a poisoned arrow.

achondroplasia [aykondro**play**zhuh] An inherited form of dwarfism, in which growth of the limb bones is disproportionately shortened. There is a characteristic bulging of the forehead, and a saddle nose. >> congenital abnormality; dwarfism

acid Usually, a substance reacting with metals to liberate hydrogen gas, or dissolving in water with dissociation and the formation of hydrogen ions. Acids are classed as strong or weak depending on the extent to which this dissociation occurs. Strong acids are corrosive. >> base (chemistry); corrosion; pH

acidic oxides >> **oxides**

acid rain A term first used in the 19th-c to describe polluted rain in Manchester, England. Colloquially it is used for polluted rainfall associated with the burning of fossil fuels. Acid pollution can be wet (rain, snow, mist) or dry (gases, particles). A number of gases are involved, particularly sulphur dioxide (SO_2) and oxides of nitrogen (NO).

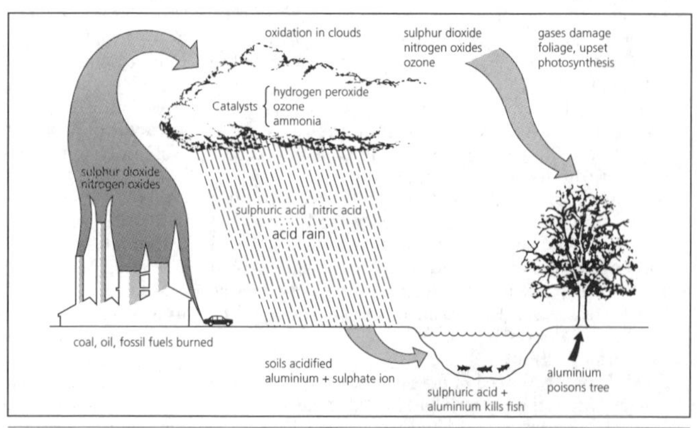

Acid rain – the chain from pollutants to acidified lakes and dying trees.

Reactions in the atmosphere lead to the production of sulphuric acid (H_2SO_4) and nitric acid (HNO_3). Acid rain is implicated in damage to forests and the acidification of soils and lakes. >> fossil fuel; greenhouse effect; nitric acid; sulphuric acid

acne [**ak**nee] A chronic inflammation of the sweat glands in the skin, notably affecting the face, upper chest, and back. It is particularly found in adolescents. >> chloracne; gland

Aconcagua, Cerro [akon**kag**wa] 32°39S 70°01W. Mountain in the Andes, rising to 6960 m/22 834 ft in W Argentina; the highest peak in the W hemisphere. >> Andes; Uspallata

aconite >> **monkshood**

acorn The fruit of the oak tree, actually a specialized nut borne in a cup-shaped structure, the cupule. >> nut; oak

acouchi [a**koo**shee] A cavy-like rodent; inhabits Amazonian forests; resembles a small agouti, but with a longer tail (white, used for signalling). (Genus: *Myoprocta*, 2 species. Family: Dasyproctidae.) >> agouti; cavy; rodent

acoustic coupler A device which allows a computer to communicate with other computers over the telephone network using a telephone handset. Digital data is transmitted as coded audio signals. >> local area network; modem; viewdata

acoustics The study of sound: the production, detection, and propagation of sound waves, and the absorption and reflection of sound. It includes the study of how electrical signals are converted into mechanical signals, as in loudspeakers, and the converse, as in microphones; also, how sound is produced in musical instruments, and perceived by audiences in concert halls; the protection of workers from damaging levels of sound; and the use of detection techniques, such as sonar and ultrasonic scanning. >> anechoic chamber; loudspeaker i; microphone i; sonar; sound; sound intensity level i

ACP countries An acronym for a grouping of c.70 developing countries from **Africa, the Caribbean, and the Pacific**. It was established in the 1970s to facilitate the making of agreements with the European Union on economic assistance and trade. >> European Union; Lomé Convention

Acre, Hebrew **Akko**, ancient **Ptolemais** 32°55N 35°04E, pop (1995e) 48 300. Ancient town in Northern district, NW Israel; resort centre on the Mediterranean Sea; capital of the Crusader kingdom after capture of Jerusalem in 1187; railway; ancient and modern harbour. >> Crusades i; Israel i

acridine [**ak**rideen] $C_{13}H_9N$, melting point 111°C. A coal-tar base structurally related to anthracene. An important class of dyestuffs is derived from it. >> anthracene i; base (chemistry); coal tar; dyestuff

acromegaly [akroh**meg**alee] An adult disorder which arises from the over-secretion of growth hormone by specific cells of the front pituitary gland. The skull, jaw, hands, and feet enlarge. >> growth hormone; pituitary gland

Acropolis, The [a**kro**polis] The citadel of ancient Athens, which contained the national treasury and many sacred sites and shrines, most of them (such as the Parthenon and the Erechtheum) associated with the worship of Athene. The present ruins date mainly from the second half of the 5th-c BC. >> Areopagus; Athens; Erechtheum; Parthenon

acrylic acid [a**kril**ik] CH_2=CH.COOH, IUPAC **prop-2-enoic acid**. The simplest unsaturated carboxylic acid. Its nitrile is the monomer of a range of polymers used as fibres and paints. Its methyl ester and the related **methylmethacrylate** form other polymers used in paints, adhesives, and safety glass. >> carboxylic acids; ester i; IUPAC; monomer

Actaeon [ak**tee**on] A hunter in Greek mythology, who came upon Artemis, the goddess of chastity, while she was bathing. She changed him into a stag, which was then killed by his own hounds. >> Artemis

actinides [**ak**tiniydz] Elements with an atomic number between 89 and 104 in which an inner electron shell is filling, the best known being uranium (92) and plutonium (94). Those heavier than uranium are known as the *transuranic elements*. All of their isotopes are radioactive, and most are artificially made. >> chemical elements; radioisotope; RR1036

action In mechanics, the difference between kinetic energy K and potential energy V ($K-V$), summed over time; symbol I or S, units J.s (joule.second). >> mechanics; quantum mechanics

action painting A form of abstract art which flourished in the USA from the late 1940s, its leading exponent being Jackson Pollock. The snappy term was introduced by the critic Harold Rosenberg in 1952 in preference to *abstract expressionism*. The physical act of applying paint to canvas is emphasized, rather than the picture as a finished artefact. >> abstract art; Pollock

Actium, Battle of [**ak**tium] (31 BC) The decisive victory of Octavian (later the Emperor Augustus) over the forces of Antony and Cleopatra off the coast of NW Greece. >> Augustus; Roman history i

Act of Congress A bill sanctioned by the US legislature, consisting of the two houses of Congress: the House of Representatives and the Senate. The bill must then be signed by the president to become law. >> Congress

act of God In law, any natural phenomenon such as an earthquake or a hurricane which, without human intervention, directly causes an accident. Heavy rain or fog to which drivers do not respond appropriately, with the result that their negligence leads to an accident, is not an act of God. >> negligence

Act of Parliament A bill which has passed five stages (first reading, second reading, committee stage, report stage, third reading) in both houses of the UK parliament, and received the royal assent. The same kind of procedure applies in other parliamentary systems.

Actors' Studio A workshop for professional actors founded in New York City by Elia Kazan, Cheryl Crawford, and Robert Lewis in 1947. Under Lee Strasberg, it was the major centre for US acting. >> Method, the; Strasberg

Acts of the Apostles A New Testament book, the second part of a narrative begun in Luke's Gospel, which traces the early progress of Jesus's followers in spreading the Christian faith. >> apostle; Jesus Christ; New Testament

actuary A statistician specializing in life expectancy, sickness, retirement, and accident matters. Actuaries are employed by insurance companies and pension funds to calculate probability and risk. >> insurance

actuator A mechanical or electrical device used to bring other equipment into operation; sometimes called a **servomotor**. It commonly refers to the equipment used for the automatic operation of brake valves in car or train brake systems. >> brake i; servo system

acuity [a**kyoo**itee] Acuteness of perception, especially of vision or hearing; the smallest visual features (usually measured in terms of angular size in the retinal image) that can be seen, or auditory difference that can be heard.

acupressure A system of treatment said to be the forerunner of acupuncture. It involves the application of pressure using thumb and fingers, but sometimes also the palms, knees, elbows, and feet, to stimulate acupuncture points and meridians. >> acupuncture; alternative medicine

acupuncture A medical practice known in China for over 3000 years, which has come to attract attention in the West. It consists of the insertion into the skin and underlying tissues of a hot or cold needle, usually made of steel, several cm long. The site of insertion of the needle is chosen in relation to the site of the tissue or organ believed to be disordered, and several hundred specific points are identified on body maps or models. It is difficult to obtain a clear idea of which disorders benefit from acupuncture, but neuralgia, migraine, sprains, and asthma are claimed to respond, while infectious disease and tumours are unlikely to do so. It is also employed as an analgesic during surgery in the Far East. Its mechanism of action is unknown. Research has shown that brain tissue contains morphine-like substances called *endorphins*, and these may be released in increased amounts when deep sensory nerves are stimulated by injury near the body surfaces. >> alternative medicine; traditional Chinese medicine

acyl [a**siyl**] In chemistry, the general name for an organic functional group R.CO–, where R represents H or an alkyl group. >> alkyl; functional group; organic chemistry

Ada A computer programming language developed for the US Department of Defense which permits the development of very large computer systems. It was named after Augusta Ada King, Countess of Lovelace, daughter of Lord Byron, who worked with Charles Babbage. >> Babbage; programming language

Adair, Red [a**dair**], popular name of **Paul Adair** (1915–) Fire-fighting specialist, born in Houston, TX, called in as a troubleshooter to deal with major oil fires. He is the subject of a film, *Hellfighter* (1968), starring John Wayne.

Adam, Adolphe (Charles) [adã] (1803–56) Composer, born in Paris. He wrote several successful operas, but is chiefly remembered for the ballet *Giselle* (1841).

Adam, James >> **Adam, Robert**

Adam, Robert (1728–92) Architect, born in Kirkcaldy, Fife. He and his brother **James Adam** (1730–94) succeeded in transforming the prevailing Palladian fashion in architecture by a series of romantically elegant variations on diverse classical originals. They also designed furniture and fittings to suit the houses they planned and decorated. >> Palladianism

Adam and Eve Biblical characters described in the Book of Genesis as the first man and woman created by God. Traditions describe their life in the garden of Eden, their disobedience and banishment, and the birth of their sons Cain, Abel, and Seth. >> Abel; Bible; Cain; Genesis, Book of

Adamov, Arthur [a**dah**mof] (1908–70) Playwright, born in Kislovodsk, Russia. His early absurdist plays, such as *L'Invasion* (1950, The Invasion) present the dislocations and cruelties of a meaningless world. Later plays show a transition to commitment.

Adams, Abigail, *née* **Smith** (1744–1818) Letter writer, born in Weymouth, MA. Her husband was the second president of the USA (1797–1801), and her correspondence became highly valued as a contemporary source of social history during the early days of the republic. >> Adams, John

Adams, Ansel (Easton) (1902–84) Photographer, born in San Francisco, CA. Famous for his landscapes of the Western States, he was also an influential writer.

Adams, Douglas (Noel) (1952–) Writer, born in Cambridge, Cambridgeshire. He is known for his humorous science fiction novels, especially *The Hitch Hiker's Guide to the Galaxy* (1979, originally a radio series, 1978, 1980, later televised).

Adams, Gerry, popular name of **Gerald Adams** (1948–) Northern Ireland politician, born in Belfast. In 1978 he became vice-president of Sinn Féin and later its president. In 1983 he was elected to the UK parliament as member for Belfast West, but declined to take up his seat at Westminster. He achieved national prominence as the chief spokesman for the IRA during the events relating to the IRA ceasefire (1994–6), and retained his seat in the 1997 general election.

Adams, John (1735–1826) US statesman and second president (1797–1801), born in Braintree (now Quincy), MA. He became the first US vice-president under Washington (1789). They were re-elected in 1792; and in 1796 Adams was chosen president by the Federalists. >> Adams, Abigail; Federalist Party

Adams, John Couch (1819–92) Astronomer, born in Laneast, Cornwall. In 1845 he and Leverrier independently predicted the existence of Neptune by analyzing irregularities in the motion of Uranus. >> astronomy; Leverrier; Neptune (astronomy)

Adams, John Quincy (1767–1848) US statesman and sixth president (1825–9), born in Quincy, MA, the son of John and Abigail Adams. As secretary of state under Monroe, he negotiated with Spain the treaty for the acquisition of Florida (1819), and was alleged to be the real author of the Monroe Doctrine (1823). >> Monroe Doctrine

Adams, Richard (George) (1920–) Novelist, born in Berkshire. He came to prominence with his first novel, *Watership Down* (1972). Later books include the novel *Shardik* (1974) and an autobiography, *The Day Gone By* (1990).

Adams, Samuel (1722–1803) American statesman, born in Boston, MA. He became governor (1794–7) of Massachusetts, helped to plan the Boston Tea Party, and was one of the signatories of the Declaration of Independence. >> Boston Tea Party; Declaration of Independence

Adams, Tony (1966–) Footballer, born in Romford, Essex. He joined Arsenal as a centre back in 1983, eventually becoming team captain. He captained England in 1994, 1995, and during the European Cup in 1996, and by mid-1998 had won 51 caps.

Adamson, Joy (Friedericke Victoria), *née* **Gessner** (1910–80) Naturalist and writer, born in Austria. Living in Kenya with her third husband, British game warden **George Adamson** (1906–89), she made her name with books about the lioness Elsa, beginning with *Born Free* (1960). She was murdered in her home by tribesmen.

Adan >> **Aden**

adaptation The process of adjustment of an individual organism to environmental conditions. It may occur by natural selection, resulting in improved survival and reproductive success, or involve physiological or behavioural changes that are not genetic. >> natural selection

adaptive suspension A pneumatic or hydro-pneumatic suspension system fitted to a motor car or a commercial vehicle that damps out the variations in road surface, and maintains the vehicle at a constant level while in use. This levelling device can be controlled electronically.

adaptogen A substance which maintains or stimulates the body's mechanisms for adapting to change. Herbs such as *Eleutherococcus senticosus* are used as general adaptogens, but the term is also applied to more specific adaptors of self-regulation, such as immune stimulants. >> immunosuppression

Adcock, Fleur (1934–) Poet, born in Papakura, New Zealand. She moved to the UK in 1963, and published her first collection, *The Eye of the Hurricane*, in 1964. Her poetry is notable for its unsentimental treatment of personal and family relationships, its psychological insights, and its interest in classical themes. She has also edited several poetry anthologies.

ADD >> attention

Addams, Charles Samuel (1912–88) Cartoonist, born in Westfield, NJ. He is known for the ghoulish group which was immortalized on television in the 1960s as *The Addams Family*.

Addams, Jane (1860–1935) Social reformer, born in Cedarville, IL. She founded Hull House in Chicago, where she worked to secure social justice, female suffrage, and the cause of pacifism. In 1931 she shared the Nobel Peace Prize. >> women's liberation movement

addax [**ad**aks] A horse-like antelope (*Addax nasomaculatus*) native to N African deserts; resembles the oryx, but has thicker, spiralling horns; pale with clump of brown hair on the forehead; never drinks. >> antelope; oryx

adder A venomous snake of family Viperidae; three species: *Vipera berus* (**European adder** or **common European viper**, the only venomous British snake) and the puff adders; also Australian **death adders** of the family Elapidae (2 species). >> puff adder; snake; viper 🛈

Addington, Henry >> **Sidmouth, 1st Viscount**

Addinsell, Richard [**ad**insel] (1904–77) Composer, born in Oxford, Oxfordshire. He composed much film music, including the popular *Warsaw Concerto* for the film *Dangerous Moonlight* (1941).

Addis Ababa or **Adis Abeba** [**ad**is **ab**aba] 9°02N 38°42E, pop (1995e) 1 943 000. Capital of Ethiopia; altitude 2400 m/7874 ft; founded by Menelik II, 1887; capital, 1889; occupied by Italy, 1936–41, declared capital of Italian East Africa; airport; railway to port of Djibouti; university (1950); cathedral. >> Ethiopia 🛈

Addison, Joseph (1672–1719) Essayist and poet, born in Milston, Wiltshire. He became a diplomat, under-secretary of state (1705–8), and an MP. Best known for his political writing, he contributed largely to the *Tatler* and the *Spectator* (which he co-founded with Steele in 1711). >> Steele, Richard

Addison, Thomas (1793–1860) Physician, born in Longbenton, Northumberland. His chief research was into the disease of the adrenal glands which has since been named after him, and into pernicious anaemia (**Addisonian anaemia**). >> Addison's disease; anaemia

Addison's disease A medical condition resulting from the destruction of the adrenal cortex. A fall in the output of corticosteroids causes physical weakness, mental apathy, low blood pressure, and increased skin pigmentation. Taking synthetic steroids by mouth restores the patient to normal health. >> Addison, Thomas; adrenal glands; corticosteroids

additives Strictly, any chemical, even a vitamin, added to a food during its processing or preparation; more usually, chemicals which have been added in order to achieve a specific aim. They include (a) *preservatives*, which reduce spoilage by bacteria, (b) *anti-oxidants*, which prevent fats from becoming rancid, (c) *emulsifiers*, which permit a stable mixture of oil and water, (d) *colouring matter*, to vary colour to specifications, (e) *sweeteners* and (f) *flavouring agents/enhancers*, to achieve a given flavour. >> antioxidants; emulsifiers; E-number; food preservation

adduct >> **addition reaction**

Adela, Princess [a**day**la] (c.1062–1137) Fourth daughter of William the Conqueror. In 1080 she married Stephen, Count of Blois, by whom she had nine children. Her third son, Stephen, became King of England in her lifetime. >> William I (of England)

Adelaide 34°56S 138°36E, pop (1995e) 1 082 000. Port capital of South Australia, on the Torrens R; founded, 1837; the first Australian municipality to be incorporated, 1840; airfield; railway; two universities (1874, 1966); two cathedrals; major wine-growing area to the S and N. >> South Australia

Adélie Land [a**day**lee] or **Adélie Coast**, Fr **Terre Adélie** area c.432 000 sq km/167 000 sq mi. Territory in Antarctica 66–67°S, 136–142°E; first seen by the French navy in 1840; French territory, 1938; research station at Base Dumont d'Urville. >> French Southern and Antarctic Territories

Aden or **Adan** [**ay**dn] 12°50N 45°00E, pop (1995e) 427 000. Port on the Gulf of Aden, at the entrance to the Red Sea; taken by British, 1839; capital of former Aden protectorate; British crown colony, 1937; scene of fighting between nationalist groups in 1960s; capital of former South Yemen, 1968–90; airport; oil refining, shipping. >> Yemen 🛈

Adenauer, Konrad [**a**denower] (1876–1967) German statesman, born in Cologne, who became the first chancellor of the Federal Republic of Germany (1949–63). He was president of the Prussian State Council 1920–33. As chancellor, he established closer post-war links with the Russians and the French. >> European Economic Community; Germany 🛈; NATO

adenine [**a**deneen] $C_4H_5N_5$. A base derived from purine; one of the five found in nucleic acids, where it is generally paired with thymine or uracil. >> base (chemistry); DNA 🛈; purines; thymine

adenoids An accumulation of lymphoid tissue, arranged as a series of folds behind the opening of the auditory tube in the nasopharynx; also known as the **pharyngeal tonsils**. When enlarged in children they can fill the nasopharynx, giving an abnormal resonance to speech. >> auditory tube; pharynx; tonsils

adenosine triphosphate (ATP) [a**den**oseen] A molecule formed by the condensation of adenine, ribose, and triphosphoric acid: HO–P(O)OH–O–P(O)OH–O–P(O)OH–OH. It is a key compound in the mediation of energy in both plants and animals. >> adenine; phosphoric acid; ribose

adhesives Materials whose function is to bind one substance to another. Examples are (1) substances of biological origin, generally water soluble, known as *glues*, which are usually proteins or carbohydrates, and (2) synthetic materials, both thermoplastic and thermosetting resins and rubbers. >> carbohydrate; protein; resin; thermoplastic; thermoset

adiabatic process [adia**bat**ik] In thermodynamics, a process in which no heat enters or leaves a system, such as in a well-insulated system, or in some process so rapid that there is not enough time for heat exchange. Sound waves in air involve adiabatic pressure changes. >> heat; sound; thermodynamics

Adie, Kate [**ay**dee], popular name of **Kathryn Adie** (1945–) News reporter and correspondent, born in Sunderland, Tyne and Wear. As a reporter for BBC TV News (1979–81), correspondent (1982), and chief correspondent (1989–), she has become a familiar figure presenting reports from the heart of war-torn countries around the world.

Adi Granth [**ah**dee **grahnt**] (Hindi 'First Book') The principal Sikh scripture, originally called the *Granth Sahib* (Hindi 'Revered Book'). The text used today is an expanded version of Guru Arjan's original compilation, and is revered by all Sikhs. >> guru; Sikhism

adipic acid [a**di**pik] HOOC–$(CH_2)_4$–COOH, IUPAC **hexanedioic acid**, melting point 153°C. It is one of the monomers for nylon, the other being 1,6-diaminohexane. >> monomer; polyamides

adipose tissue >> **fat 2**

Adirondack Mountains [adi**ron**dak] Mountain range largely in NE New York state, USA; rises to 1629 m/5344 ft at Mt Marcy; locations such as L Placid are noted winter resorts. >> United States of America 🛈

adjutant A stork native to tropical SE Asia. There are two species: the **greater adjutant stork** (*Leptoptilos dubius*), and the **lesser**, **haircrested**, or **Javan adjutant stork** (*Leptoptilos javanicus*); grey and white; head nearly naked. >> stork

Adler, Alfred (1870–1937) Pioneer psychiatrist, born in Vienna. A member of the psychoanalytical group that formed around Freud, his work led to one of the early schisms in psychoanalysis. His main contributions include the concept of the inferiority complex and his special treatment of neurosis as the exploitation of shock. >> Freud, Sigmund; inferiority complex; psychoanalysis

Admiral's Cup A yacht race for up to three boats per nation, first contested in 1957 and held biennially. Races take place in the English Channel, at Cowes, and around the Fastnet rock. >> sailing

Admiralty Court An English court which is part of the Queen's Bench Division of the High Court. Its work deals with maritime claims in civil law, such as salvage. >> High Court of Justice; sea, law of the

Admiralty Islands pop (1995e) 35 200; area 2000 sq km/ 800 sq mi. Island group in N Papua New Guinea, c.40 islands, main island, Manus; chief town, Lorengau; German protectorate, 1884; under Australian mandate, 1920. >> Bismarck Archipelago

Adonis [a**doh**nis] In Greek mythology, a beautiful young man who was loved by Aphrodite. He insisted on going hunting and was killed by a boar, but Persephone saved him on condition that he spent part of the year with her in the Underworld. >> Aphrodite; Persephone; Tammuz

adoption A legal procedure in which a civil court makes an order giving parental rights and duties over a minor to someone other than the natural parents. On adoption, the minor becomes the legal child of his or her adoptive parents. >> court of law; legitimacy; minor

Adorno, Theodor (Wiesengrund) [a**daw(r)**noh], originally **Theodor Wiesengrund** (1903–69) Social philosopher and musicologist, born in Frankfurt, Germany. Director of the Frankfurt Institute for Social Research, his works include *Philosophy of Modern Music* (1949) and *Negative Dialectics* (1966).

Adrastea [adras**tee**a] A tiny natural satellite of Jupiter, discovered in 1979 by Voyager 2; distance from the planet 129 000 km/80 000 mi; diameter 24 km/15 mi. >> Jupiter (astronomy); Voyager project [i]; RR964

adrenal glands [a**dree**nl] Paired compound endocrine glands in mammals, one situated above each kidney; also known as the **suprarenal glands**. Each comprises an outer cortex, which produces specific hormones, and an inner medulla, which secretes a specific catecholamine (either adrenaline or noradrenaline). >> Addison's disease; adrenaline; Cushing's disease; endocrine glands; hormones

adrenaline or **adrenalin** [a**dren**alin] A hormone released from the adrenal medulla in response to stress, and in some other circumstances; also known as **epinephrine** in the USA. It increases heart rate, raises blood pressure, and causes release of sugar into the blood from liver stores. It may also be a neurotransmitter in the brain. >> adrenal glands; hormones

Adrian IV, also **Hadrian**, originally **Nicholas Breakspear** (c.1100–59) The only Englishman to become pope (1154–9), born in Abbots Langley, Hertfordshire. In 1146 he was appointed Cardinal Bishop of Albano. As pope, he is said to have granted Ireland to Henry II. >> Henry II (of England); pope

Adrian, Edgar Douglas, 1st Baron Adrian (1889–1977) Neurophysiologist, born in London. A founder of modern neurophysiology, he shared the 1932 Nobel Prize for Physiology or Medicine for his work on the function of neurones. >> nervous system; neurology; Sherrington

Adriatic Sea [aydree**a**tik] Arm of the Mediterranean Sea, between the E coast of Italy and the Balkan Peninsula; length 800 km/500 mi; width 93–225 km/ 58–140 mi; maximum depth 1250 m/4100 ft; highly saline. >> Mediterranean Sea

Advaita [ad**viy**ta] (Sanskrit, 'non-dual') An influential school of Vedanta Hinduism, revived in a modern form during the 20th-c. It holds that there is only one absolute reality, Brahman. >> atman; Brahma; Hinduism; Veda

Advent In the Christian Church, a period of penitence and preparation for the celebration of the first coming of Christ at Christmas, and for his promised second coming to judge the world. It begins on **Advent Sunday**, the fourth Sunday before Christmas. >> Christmas; Jesus Christ

Adventists Those Christians whose most important belief is in the imminent and literal Second Coming of Christ. A separate movement began in the USA with William Miller (1781–1849), who predicted Christ's return (and the end of the world) in 1843–4, and whose followers eventually formed a denomination called Seventh Day Adventists. They believe that the Second Coming is delayed only by a failure to keep the Sabbath. >> Jesus Christ; millenarianism

Advisory, Conciliation, and Arbitration Service >> **ACAS**

advocate A term generally applied to lawyers practising in the courts as professional representatives of those who bring or defend a case. In Scotland, the term is used as an equivalent to an English barrister, denoting exclusive right of audience before the superior courts; however, since 1993, a hybrid form of lawyer called a **solicitor advocate** has been created from existing solicitors who, on passing further examinations, are permitted to appear in the High Court or the Court of Session. >> barrister; solicitor

aechmea [ak**may**a] A member of a genus of plants (epiphytes) native to tropical America; rosettes of succulent leaves forming a water-filled cup in the centre; inflorescence on a stout, well-developed stalk. (Genus: *Aechmea*, 172 species. Family: Bromeliaceae.) >> bromeliad; epiphyte

Aedes [ay**ee**deez] The yellow-fever mosquito, found in coastal and riverside habitats throughout the tropics and subtropics; eggs laid in stagnant water. (Order: Diptera. Family: Culicidae.) >> mosquito; yellow fever

Aegean Islands [ee**jee**an] pop (1995e) 467 000; area 9122 sq km/3521 sq mi. Island group and region of Greece; the name is generally applied to the islands of the Aegean Sea, including Lesbos, Chios, Samos, Limnos, and Thasos; a major tourist area. >> Aegean Sea; Greece [i]

Aegean Sea [ee**jee**an] Arm of the Mediterranean Sea, bounded W and N by Greece, NE and E by Turkey, S by islands of Crete and Rhodes; dotted with islands on which the Aegean civilization of 3000–1000 BC flourished; length (N–S) 645 km/400 mi; width 320 km/200 mi; greatest depth, 2013 m/6604 ft. >> Mediterranean Sea

Aegina [ee**jiy**na], Gr **Aiyna** pop (1995e) 11 800; area 83 sq km/32 sq mi. One of the largest of the Saronic Islands, Greece; chief town, Aiyna; a popular resort. >> Greece [i]

aegis [**ee**jis] Originally a goatskin, and then, in Greek mythology, a fringed piece of armour or a shield. Zeus shakes his aegis, which may possibly be the thundercloud; Athene's is equipped with the Gorgon's head. >> Athena; Gorgon; Zeus

Aegisthus [**ee**gisthuhs, **ee**jisthuhs] In Greek legend, the son of Thyestes; while Agamemnon was absent at Troy he became the lover of Clytemnestra. Together they killed Agamemnon on his return to Argos. Aegisthus was later killed by Orestes. >> Agamemnon; Clytemnestra; Orestes; Thyestes

Ælfric [alfrik, **al**frich], also known as **Ælfric Grammaticus** ('The Grammarian') (c.955–c.1020) English writer, known for his use of the Anglo-Saxon vernacular. He taught at the monastery of Cerne Abbas, later becoming abbot of Eynsham. >> Old English

Aelred of Rievaulx >> **Ailred of Rievaulx**

Aeneas [ee**nee**as] In Roman legend, the ancestor of the Romans. He was a Trojan hero, the son of Anchises and Venus, who escaped after the fall of Troy, bearing his father on his shoulders. His son founded Alba Longa, and a line of kings from whom Romulus was said to be descended. >> Romulus and Remus; Trojan War; Virgil

aeolian harp [ee**oh**lian] A wooden soundbox fitted with strings of various thicknesses, but tuned to a single pitch, which are made to vibrate freely by the surrounding air, producing an ethereal, 'disembodied' sound. It takes its name from Aeolus, god of the winds. >> Aeolus; chordophone; zither

Aeolus [**ee**olus] In Greek mythology, the god of the winds. In the *Odyssey* Aeolus lived on an island, and gave Odysseus the winds tied in a bag so that his ship would not be blown off course. Odysseus' men opened the bag, thinking it contained treasure. As a result, the ship was blown far away. >> Odysseus

Aepyornis [eepi**aw(r)**nis] >> **elephant bird**

aerial >> **antenna**

aerial photography Photography of the ground surface from an aerial viewpoint such as a balloon or aircraft. Applications include archaeology, ecology, geology, and wartime reconnaissance. >> photogrammetry; stereoscopic photography

aerobe [**air**ohb] An organism that requires the presence of oxygen for growth and reproduction. The great majority of all living organisms are aerobic, requiring oxygen for respiration. Some micro-organisms, typically bacteria, are anaerobic, able to grow only in the absence of oxygen; these are known as **anaerobes**. >> bacteria [i]; oxygen

aerobics [air**oh**biks] A system of physical training in which exercises such as walking, swimming, and running are pursued for a sufficiently long period to increase performance. In the 1980s the term was particularly used for movement exercises in time to music, which became popular among keep-fit groups of all ages. >> callisthenics

aerocapture A proposed technique for placing a spacecraft in orbit around a planet, without the expenditure of chemical propellants, by taking advantage of planetary atmosphere. The spacecraft would be equipped with an aerobrake and would be navigated into the planet's upper atmosphere, where friction would slow it down. >> Mars (astronomy); spacecraft

aerodynamics The study of the flow of air and the behaviour of objects moving relative to air; a subject which is applicable to other gases, and is part of the larger subject of fluid mechanics. Aerodynamic principles explain flight. The shape and orientation of an aircraft wing (curved upper surface, wing tilted down) mean that the air above the wing travels further than the air beneath. Air above the wing thus travels faster and so has lower pressure (Bernoulli's principle). The pressure difference provides lift to support the aircraft. The movement of an aircraft through the air produces a force which impedes motion, called *drag*, dependent on the aircraft size and shape. At velocities greater than the speed of sound (Mach 1, approximately 331·5 m/1088 ft per second) air can no longer be treated as incompressible and new rules apply, giving rise to **supersonic aerodynamics**. Passing from subsonic to supersonic speeds, aircraft cross the 'sound barrier', marked by a dramatic increase in drag. Aircraft flying at supersonic speeds produce sonic booms – shock waves in the air around the aircraft, produced because the aircraft's velocity is too great to allow the air pressure to adjust smoothly around it. >> fluid mechanics; Mach number

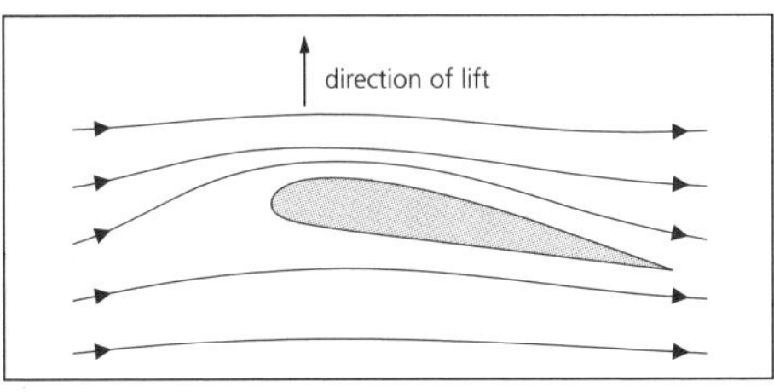

Aerodynamics – section of an aerofoil or aircraft wing, showing air flow lines

aeronautics The broad body of scientifically based knowledge describing aeroplanes as objects subject to the laws of physics. It covers such topics as the generation of lift to make the aeroplane fly, the production of thrust, the strength of the structure, and the way these elements are combined to produce a functioning vehicle. >> aeroplane; aircraft [i]

aerophone Any musical instrument in which air is the main vibrating agent. Aerophones are subdivided into types according to (a) the main material they are made of, and (b) how the air is set in motion (via a mouthpiece, a reed, or neither). >> brass / reed / woodwind instrument [i]; musical instruments; organ

aeroplane / airplane The general name given to a vehicle whose operational medium is air and which supports itself in the Earth's atmosphere by means of lift. Lift is produced through specially shaped fixed wings attached to the aeroplane's body or *fuselage*; these alter the airflow so that the pressure distribution of the air over the wing creates an upward force. The airflow is in turn produced by the aeroplane being 'pushed' or 'pulled' through the air by the propulsion device driven by a motor. By means of design, the lift produced by the wing can be made greater than the weight of the airframe and propulsive system, allowing a payload to be carried. The first truly powered flight was made by Orville Wright in December 1903, when he flew 260 m/852 ft. World War 2 saw the world's first operational jet fighter, the Me 262. In the period following the War, jet engines were applied to ever larger passenger aircraft, culminating in the introduction of the Boeing 747 Jumbo Jet in 1970. This period also saw the arrival of the supersonic Concorde in 1976. Recent developments in civilian aircraft have been away from higher speed towards more economical and quieter operation, while military and large commercial aircraft are becoming increasingly reliant upon electronics to control and keep them stable in flight. >> aircraft [i]; Concorde; jet engine [i]; propeller; turbine; Wright brothers

aerosol An airborne suspension of microscopic particles or liquid droplets, typically formed by forcing a liquid through a fine nozzle under pressure. Aerosol sprays are useful as a means of depositing fine even layers of material, such as in paint sprays. >> CFCs

Aeschines [**ees**kineez] (c.390 BC–?) Athenian orator, second only to Demosthenes. He was prominent in Athenian politics between 348 and 330 BC. Of his speeches, only three survive. >> Demosthenes; Philip II (of Macedon)

Aeschylus [**ees**kilus] (c.525–c.456 BC) Playwright, born in Eleusis, near Athens. Out of some 60 plays ascribed to him, only seven are extant, including the trilogy of the *Oresteia*: *Agamemnon*, *Choephori* (The Libation Bearers), and *Eumenides* (The Furies).

Aesculapius [eeskyu**lay**pius] The Latin form of **Asclepius**, the Greek god of healing. His cult was transferred from Epidauros to Rome in 291 BC after a plague. >> Asclepius

Aesop [**ee**sop] (? 6th-c BC) The traditional name of a Greek writer of fables. He is supposed to have been a native of Phrygia and a slave who, after being set free, travelled to Greece. The fables are anecdotes which use animals to make a moral point.

aesthetics / esthetics The philosophical investigation of art, understood to include the visual arts (painting, sculpture, photography, film), music, literature, drama, and dance. Aesthetics deals with such issues as what it is to perceive an object or a performance as a work of art; and whether there are objective standards for judging it.

aestivation >> **hibernation**

Æthel- >> **Athel-, Ethel-**

aether >> **ether**

affenpinscher [**af**enpinsher] A breed of dog; small with long dark wiry coat; usually black; face like a monkey, with short muzzle and large black eyes; very old breed, originally from Germany, now rare. >> dog

affinity A relationship by marriage. Countries generally have rules prohibiting marriage between certain people where there is an affinity – for example between parents and their step-children. Prohibitions also apply where there is *consanguinity* (a blood relationship). >> annulment; marriage

affirmative action Policies requiring institutions to act 'affirmatively' in employment practices to avoid discrimination on grounds of race, ethnic origin, or sex. They are usually found in the USA.

afforestation The planting of woodland areas. The aim may be to increase the extent of economically useful wood (eg conifer plantations in upland UK) or to protect against soil erosion and desertification by providing shelter belts and vegetation cover on bare ground. >> erosion; forestry

Afghan hound A breed of dog; large, slender, with a bouncing step; hair very long, silky (short-haired forms also exist); long thin muzzle; originated in Middle East; was used for hunting in N Afghanistan; hunts by sight. >> hound

Afghanistan, official name **Islamic Emirate of Afghanistan**, Persian **Dowlat-e-Islami-ye-Afghanestan** pop (1995e) 21 017 000, plus an estimated 2½ million nomadic tribesmen and 3 million living in Pakistan and Iran as refugees; area 647 497 sq km/249 934 sq mi. Republic in S Asia; capital, Kabul; timezone GMT +4½; Pathans the main ethnic group, with several minorities; chief religion Islam, mostly Sunni; official languages Pushtu, Dari (Persian); unit of currency the Afghani, subdivided into 100 puls; a mountainous country centred on the Hindu Kush system, reaching over 7000 m/24 000 ft; NW, the fertile valley of Herat; arid uplands to the S; desert in the SW; continental climate, winter severity increased by altitude; summers warm everywhere except on highest peaks; rain mostly during spring and autumn; nation first formed in 1747 under Ahmad Shah Durrani; seen by Britain as a bridge between India and the Middle East, but Britain failed to gain control during a series of Afghan Wars (the last in 1919); feudal monarchy survived until after World War 2, when the constitution became more liberal under several Soviet-influenced 5-year economic plans; king deposed, 1973, and a republic formed; new constitution, 1977; coup, 1979, brought to power Hafizullah Amin, which led to the invasion by USSR forces and the establishment of Babrak Karmal as head of state; new constitution, 1987, provides for an executive president, bicameral National Assembly, and council of ministers; Soviet withdrawal implemented, 1988–9; regime met heavy guerrilla resistance from the Mujahideen (Islamic fighters); resignation of President Najibullah, 1992; new Constituent Assembly, 1992; continuing unrest and disunity among Mujahideen groups; emergence of new Islamic force, the *taliban* (army of students), 1994–5; *taliban* victory imposed strict Islamic regime, with execution of Najibullah (Sep 1996), followed by counter-attack by Mujahideen alliance; over 60% of labour force engaged in agriculture; natural gas production in the N, largely for export; most sectors affected by the civil war, especially sugar and textiles. >> Hindu Kush; Kabul; Mujahideen; RR1000 political leaders

Afghan Wars A series of wars (1838–42, 1878–80, 1919) between Britain and Afghanistan, prompted by the British desire to extend control in the region to prevent the advance of Russian influence towards India. The third Afghan War resulted in the country's independence (1921). >> Afghanistan

aflatoxin [afla**tok**sin] A toxin produced by the mould *Aspergillus flavus* (from Aspergillus *flavus toxin*) commonly found in peanuts, cottonseed, soybeans, wheat, barley, sorghum, and nuts such as pistachios, almonds, and cacao, where the climate favours its growth. Symptoms of poisoning include weight loss, loss of co-ordination, convulsions, and death. >> liver; toxin

AFL/CIO >> **American Federation of Labor – Congress of Industrial Organizations**

Africa area c.30·97 million sq km/11·6 million sq mi. Second largest continent, extending S from the Mediterranean Sea; bounded W by the Atlantic Ocean and E by the Indian Ocean and the Red Sea; bisected by the Equator; maximum length, 8000 km/5000 mi; maximum width, 7200 km/4500 mi; highest point, Mt Kilimanjaro (5895 m/19 340 ft); major rivers include the Congo, Niger, Nile, Zambezi. >> Rift Valley; Sahara Desert; RR971

African marigold A misleading name for *Tagetes erecta*, a popular garden annual, originating from Mexico, with deeply cut leaves and showy yellow, orange, or red flower-heads up to 10 cm/4 in diameter. **French marigold**, also from Mexico, is very similar but has smaller flower-heads. (Family: Compositae.) >> marigold

African National Congress (ANC) The most important of the Black South African organizations opposed to the Pretoria regime. It began life in 1912. Banned by the South African government in 1961, it began a campaign of industrial and economic sabotage through its military wing, and in the 1980s it started attacking persons as well as property. It was unbanned, and suspended its armed struggle, in 1990. It dominated the first non-racial elections in 1994, taking 252 of the 400 seats in the Assembly. >> apartheid; Mandela, Nelson

African violet A perennial with hairy leaves in a dense rosette (*Saintpaulia ionantha*); white, pink, blue, purple, or red flowers; native to tropical E Africa. Their wide colour range and long flowering period make them popular house plants. (Family: Gesneriaceae.) >> violet

Afrikaans South African or Cape Dutch, the language of Dutch colonization, and a variety of West Germanic, but with many loan words from Bantu and other languages. >> Dutch; Germanic languages

Afrika Korps A German expeditionary force of two divisions under the command of Rommel, sent to N Africa (Mar 1941) to reinforce Italian troops there. It proved highly effective in desert warfare between 1941 and 1944. >> Rommel

Afrikaners An early 18th-c term to describe those Europeans who had been born in the Dutch colony at the Cape (founded 1652) and were therefore 'Africans', also known as **Boers** (Dutch 'farmers'). After 1835, groups left Cape Colony and established independent republics in the interior. Following the Union of South Africa in 1910, the Afrikaners became the dominant force in White South African politics. >> Afrikaans; apartheid; Boer Wars; Great Trek; Smuts

Afro-Asiatic languages The major language family in N Africa, the E horn of Africa, and SW Asia. It comprises more than 200 languages, spoken by 200 million people. The major subgroup is the Semitic family. >> Amhara; Arabic; Aramaic; Berber; Chadic; Egyptian; Hebrew; Tigray

Agadir [aga**deer**] 30°30N 9°40W, pop (1995e) 147 000. Seaport in W Morocco; on the Atlantic coast; named Santa Cruz by the Portuguese, 1505–41; taken by the French in 1913; extensive rebuilding after earthquake in 1960; airport. >> Morocco [i]

Aga Khan [**ah**ga **kahn**] Title of the hereditary head of the Ismailian sect of Muslims, notably **Aga Khan III** (1877–1957), in full **Aga Sultan Sir Mohammed Shah**, born at Karachi, who succeeded to the title in 1885. He owned several Derby winners. >> Ismailis

Agamemnon [aga**mem**non] King of Argos and commander of the Greek army in the Trojan War. On his return home he was murdered by his wife Clytemnestra. >> Aegisthus; Clytemnestra; Trojan War

agamid [**ag**amid] A lizard native to Africa (except Madagascar), S and SE Asia, and Australia; body usually broad, head large, scales with ridges and spines; tongue thick and fleshy; tail cannot be shed; some species able to change colour; also known as **chisel-tooth lizard**. (Family: Agamidae, 300 species.) >> bearded / frilled lizard; lizard [i]; moloch (reptile)

Agaña [a**gah**nya] 13°28N 144°45E, pop (1995e) 1300. Port and capital town of Guam, Mariana Is, W Pacific Ocean; taken by Japan, 1941; destroyed during its recapture by the USA, 1944; US naval base; university (1952); cathedral (1669). >> Guam

agar [**ay**gah(r)] A jelly-like compound produced from seaweed. It is used, after sterilization and the addition of suitable nutrients, for culture of fungi or bacteria for medicinal or research purposes. >> seaweed

Agassi, Andre [**ag**asee] (1970–) Tennis player, born in Las Vegas, NV. He turned professional in 1986, and went on to win Wimbledon (1992), the US Open (1994), the Australian Open (1995), and other titles, becoming No 1 in the world rankings for much of 1995. He is also known for his work in relation to youth community projects, notably the Andre Agassi Foundation (1994).

agate [**ag**ayt] A form of chalcedony, a fine-grained variety of the mineral quartz. Colour variations result in semi-precious stones such as onyx (white/grey), carnelian (red), and chrysoprase (apple-green). >> chalcedony; quartz; silica

Agatha, St (?–251) Christian martyr from Catania, Sicily, who is said to have rejected the love of the Prefect Quintilianus, and suffered a cruel martyrdom in 251. She is the patron saint of Catania, and is invoked against fire and lightning. Feast day 5 February.

agave [a**gah**vee] An evergreen perennial native to S USA, Central America, and N South America; stems very short, tough; leaves sword-shaped, often spiny on margins, thick, fleshy, and waxy, forming a rosette. The plant grows for many years, finally producing a huge branched inflorescence up to 7 m/23 ft high, with many flowers, after which it dies. Many species produce useful fibres, such as henequen, as well as alcoholic drinks such as pulque and mescal. (Genus: *Agave*, 300 species. Family: Agavaceae.) >> century plant

Agee, James [**ay**jee] (1909–55) Writer, born in Knoxville, TN. He is best known for *Let Us Now Praise Famous Men* (1941), in collaboration with photographer Walker Evans. His novel, *A Death in the Family* (published 1957), was awarded a posthumous Pulitzer Prize.

ageing >> **senescence**

Agence France Press (AFP) [azhãs frãs] An international news agency, with headquarters in Paris. The direct successor to Havas (established in 1832), AFP is the oldest surviving world agency, and one of the largest. >> news agency

Agent Orange (2,4,5-T or 2,4,5-trichlorophenoxy acetic acid) A herbicide used as a defoliant in jungle warfare, for example, by the British in Malaya and the USA in Vietnam. Its name derives from the orange rings painted around the containers used in Vietnam. It is toxic to humans. >> chemical warfare; dioxin; herbicide

Aggeus [**ag**ayus] >> **Haggai, Book of**

aggiornamento [ajaw(r)na**men**toh] The process of making the life, doctrine, and worship of the Roman Catholic Church effective in the modern world. This was initiated by Pope John XXIII at the Second Vatican Council (1962–5). >> John XXIII; Roman Catholicism; Vatican Councils

Agincourt, Battle of [**a**zhinkaw(r)t] (1415) A battle between France and England during the Hundred Years' War. Henry V of England was forced to fight near Hesdin (Pas-de-Calais) by the French. Though heavily outnumbered, the English won an overwhelming victory. >> Henry V; Hundred Years' War

aging >> **senescence**

Agnew, Spiro T(heodore) [**ag**nyoo] (1918–96) US Republican vice-president, born in Baltimore, MD, son of a Greek immigrant. As a compromise figure acceptable to most shades of Republican opinion, he was Nixon's running-mate in the 1968 election, and took office as vice-president in 1969. He resigned in 1973. >> Nixon; Republican Party

Agni [**uhg**ni] The Hindu god of fire. He is welcome in every home as a principle of life and because he drives away demons. >> Hinduism; Veda

Agnon, Shmuel Yosef, originally **Shmuel Josef Czaczkes** (1888–1970) Novelist, born in Buczacz, Poland, the first Israeli to win a Nobel Prize for Literature (1966). He wrote an epic trilogy of novels on Eastern European Jewry in the early 20th-c.

agnosia [agnohzia] A condition found in some brain-damaged individuals, whereby they are unable to recognize objects despite adequate basic visual and intellectual abilities; for example, a patient might be able to recognize by touch but not by sight. >> neuropsychology

agnosticism Strictly, the view that God's existence cannot be known (**theism**) nor denied (**atheism**). The term was derived from the 'unknown' God in *Acts* 17.23, and first used (by T H Huxley) in 1869: agnostics were contrasted with **gnostics**, or metaphysicians. >> atheism; God; Huxley, T H; theism

Agostini, Giacomo [agosteenee] (1944–) Motor-cyclist, born in Lovere, Italy. He won a record 15 world titles between 1966 and 1975, including the 500 cc title a record eight times (1966–72, 1975).

agouti [agootee] A cavy-like rodent, native to Central and South America and Caribbean Is; length, 500 mm/20 in; rat-like with long legs and minute black tail. (Genus: *Dasyprocta*, 11 species. Family: Dasyproctidae.) >> cavy; rodent

Agra [ahgra] 27°17N 77°58E, pop (1995e) 973 000. City in Uttar Pradesh, NE India; founded, 1566; Mughal capital until 1659; taken by the British, 1803; seat of the government of North-West Provinces, 1835–62; airfield; railway; university (1927); Taj Mahal (1632–54), Pearl Mosque of Shah Jahan, Mirror Palace (Shish Mahal), a world heritage site. >> Taj Mahal; Uttar Pradesh

agribusiness The combined businesses of: farmers, who produce commodities; input industries, which supply them with equipment, chemicals, and finance; and merchants, processors, and distributors, who convert commodities into foodstuffs, ready for sale to consumers. >> agriculture

Agricola, Georgius [agrikola], Latin name of **Georg Bauer** (1494–1555) Mineralogist, born in Glauchau, Germany. He made the first scientific classification of minerals in *De natura fossilium* (1546, On the Nature of Fossils). >> mineralogy

Agricola, Gnaeus Julius [agrikola] (40–93) Rome's longest-serving and most successful governor in Britain (78–84). He subdued N England and Lowland Scotland, and actively encouraged the development of Roman-style towns in the S.

Agricola, Johann [agrikola], originally **Schneider** or **Schnitter**, also called **Magister Islebius** (1492–1566) Reformer, born in Eisleben, Germany, one of the most zealous founders of Protestantism. He was sent by Luther to Frankfurt (1525) to institute Protestant worship there. >> Luther; Protestantism; Reformation

Agricultural Revolution The name popularly given to a series of changes in farming practice occurring first in England and later throughout W Europe. The term usually covers the period 1700–1850. The main changes included: greater intensity of productive land use; the reduction of fallow land and waste lands; the introduction of crop rotation; the development of artificial grasses; scientific animal breeding. >> agriculture; Industrial Revolution

agriculture The cultivation of crops and the keeping of domesticated animals for food, fibre, or power. Agriculture enabled primitive people, who depended on hunting, fishing, and gathering, to settle down in communities, which could then grow as their agricultural productivity grew. This was aided by the development of such implements as ploughs, hoes, and sickles – and in drier countries by the construction of irrigation systems. Agricultural production is dominated by cereals: total world cereal production in 1990 was nearly 2 thousand million tonnes. >> Agricultural Revolution; Common Agricultural Policy; soil science; subsistence agriculture

agrimony [agrimonee] An erect perennial (*Agrimonia eupatoria*) growing to 60 cm/2 ft, native to Europe, W Asia, and N Africa; leaves hairy, with pairs of small leaflets alternating with large ones; flowers 5-petalled, yellow, in a long terminal spike. (Family: Rosaceae.)

Agrippa >> **Herod Agrippa 1 / 2**

Agrippa, Marcus Vipsanius [agripa] (c.63–12 BC) Roman general and right-hand man of Octavian (later, the Emperor Augustus). He commanded the fleet at Actium (31 BC), and married Augustus's daughter, Julia. >> Augustus; Julia; Maecenas

Agrippina [agripeena], known as **Agrippina the Elder** (c.14 BC–AD 33) The granddaughter of the Roman Emperor Augustus, and mother of three potential imperial heirs. She became the focus of opposition to the Emperor Tiberius after the suspicious death of her husband, Germanicus (AD 19). Banished to the barren island of Pandateria (AD 29), she died there of starvation. >> Caligula; Germanicus Caesar; Tiberius

Agrippina [agripeena], known as **Agrippina the Younger** (15–59) The eldest daughter of Agrippina the Elder and Germanicus, and mother of the Emperor Nero. In 54 she ruthlessly engineered Nero's succession to the throne, poisoning Emperor Claudius, her husband at the time. Initially she ruled as virtual co-regent with Nero, but he tired of her influence and had her murdered. >> Claudius; Nero

agroforestry The cultivation of tree or bush crops (e.g. coffee, rubber), sometimes alternating with annual food crops, to give a sustainable and economically viable agricultural cropping system. >> forestry; sustainable agriculture

agronomy The theory and practice of field-crop production and soil management. The subject embraces several disciplines, including plant breeding, plant physiology, and soil conservation. >> soil science

Agutter, Jenny [aguhter] (1952–) Film and stage actress, born in Taunton, Somerset. She became known following her role in *The Railway Children* (1970), and later film credits include *The Snow Goose* (1971, Emmy), *Equus* (1977, BAFTA), and *Blue Juice* (1995).

Ahab [ayhab] (9th-c BC) Son and successor of Omri as King of Israel (c.873–c.852 BC). His reign was marked by frequent battles against Syria, and a religious crisis when his wife Jezebel supported the worship of Baal in opposition to Yahweh. >> Baal; Bible; Moabite Stone

Ahaggar Mountains [ahagah(r)] or **Hoggar Mountains** Mountain range in S Algeria, N Africa; rises to 2918 m/9573 ft at Mt Tahat, the highest point in Algeria. >> Algeria i

Ahern, Bertie [ahern] (1951–) Irish politician and prime minister (1997–). He became a member of the Dáil in 1977, and after holding posts as minister for labour (1987–91) and finance (1991–4), he became President of Fianna Fáil, and head of a coalition government after defeating John Bruton in 1997.

Ahimsa [ahimsa] The principle of respect for all life and the practice of non-injury to living things. It is found in certain Hindu sects, Buddhism, and especially Jainism. >> Buddhism; Hinduism; Jainism; Karma

Ahmadabad or **Ahmedabad** [ahmadabad] 23°00N 72°40E, pop (1995e) 3 110 000. Commercial centre and industrial city in Gujarat, W India; founded, 1411; fell to the Mughals, 1572; British trading post, 1619; centre of Gandhi's activities during the 1920s and 1930s; airfield; railway; university (1949). >> Gandhi; Gujarat

Ahura Mazda [ahura mazda] (Persian 'Wise Lord') The name for God used by Zoroaster and his followers. The world is the arena for the battle between Ahura Mazda and Ahriman, the spirit of evil – a battle in which Ahura Mazda will finally prevail and become fully omnipotent. >> Zoroastrianism

AI >> **artificial intelligence**

Aidan, St [**ay**dn], known as the **Apostle of Northumbria** (?–651) Irish monk who was sent from Iona in 635 to found the Northumbrian Church in England. He established the monastery at Lindisfarne. Feast day 31 August. >> monasticism; Northumbria

AIDS Acronym of **acquired immune deficiency syndrome**, the result of infection with a human immuno-deficiency virus (HIV). Groups at high risk of acquiring the disease are homosexual or bisexual men, individuals with a history of intravenous drug abuse, sufferers from haemophilia who have received many transfusions of blood or of coagulation factor VIII prior to 1986, persons who have had casual sexual relationships, especially in sub-Saharan Africa, San Francisco, or New York, and sexual partners and children of any of these. The origin of HIV virus is unknown, but it is possible that it originated from a group of African monkeys, themselves immune to the disease. In humans, transmission is by direct blood or seminal contact. The virus enters cells of the immune system, notably T-helper cells and macrophages, which engulf bacteria and cell debris. In this way the defence of the body against infection is slowly destroyed. Infected individuals may remain free from symptoms and show HIV antibodies only in the blood. Mortality is high, but during the 1990s slow progress towards a treatment was being made through the use of new combinations of drugs (AZT, 3TC, protease inhibitors) which were reducing the amount of virus in the blood. >> blood; lymphocyte; semen

Aiken, Conrad (Potter) [**ay**ken] (1889–1973) Poet, novelist, and critic, born in Savannah, GA. Much influenced by T S Eliot, his *Selected Poems* won the 1930 Pulitzer Prize. >> Eliot, T S

Aiken, Joan (Delano) [**ay**ken] (1924–) British writer, the daughter of Conrad Aiken. Her many books for children include *All You've Ever Wanted* (1953), *The Kingdom and the Cave* (1960), and *Voices Hippo* (1988). Among her adult novels are *The Silence of Herondale* (1964), *Mansfield Revisited* (1985), and *The Jewel Seed* (1997).

aikido [iy**kee**doh] An ancient Japanese art of self-defence – a combination of karate and judo deriving from ancient jujitsu. There are two main systems, *tomiki* and *uyeshiba*. >> judo; jujitsu; karate; martial arts

Ailred of Rievaulx, St [**ayl**red, ree**voh**], also **Aelred** or **Ethelred** (1109–66) Chronicler, born in Hexham, Northumberland. He became a Cistercian monk (later, abbot) at Rievaulx Abbey, Yorkshire. >> Cistercians

Ainu [**iy**noo] The caucasoid aboriginals of Japan, now intermarried with other Japanese and culturally assimilated. Traditionally hunters and fishers, today many are factory workers and labourers. >> Japan ℹ

air >> **atmosphere** ℹ

Airborne Warning and Control System (AWACS) [**ay**waks] An aircraft-mounted radar system able to detect and track hostile intruders at long range and direct friendly fighters to intercept them. The US Air Force operates the Boeing E-3 Sentry AWACS.

aircraft Any vehicle designed to operate within the Earth's atmosphere, supporting itself by means of lift generated by wings or other methods. >> aeroplane; airship; autogiro; balloon; glider; hang glider ℹ; helicopter; seaplane; STOL; VTOL; *see illustration on p 14*

aircraft carrier A naval vessel on which aircraft can take off and land, developed during World War 1. The first carrier, HMS *Furious* (1918), was a battle-cruiser with forward and after flight-decks. *Furious* was reconstructed in 1925 and fitted with an island bridge layout on the starboard side of a continuous flight-deck. This became the conventional carrier design. Later significant contributions were the steam catapult, the angled flight-deck, and the mirror landing-sight. The USS *Nimitz* (91 487 tons displacement) has 260 000 shaft horsepower, is 323 m/1092 ft long, has a crew of 5684, and carries over 90 aircraft. >> warships ℹ

air cushion vehicle (ACV) A revolutionary form of sea transport, in which the vehicle is supported on a cushion of air; also called a **ground effect machine**, or (following the principle proposed by Christopher Cockerell in 1950) a **hovercraft**. An ACV is propelled by an airscrew, and rides on a cushion of air trapped between the hull and the surface of the water by a flexible skirt, usually made of heavy-duty neoprene, which allows it to surmount obstacles. Because of delays in production, the first regular hovercraft service did not begin until 1962 (across the R Dee estuary in Britain). Hovercrafts are now in use worldwide in many varied forms. >> Cockerell, Christopher; hydrofoil

Airedale terrier The largest breed of terrier; black and tan, thick wiry coat, stiff erect tail, small ears, short beard on chin; developed in Airedale valley (England) by crossing large hunting terriers (now extinct) and foxhounds. >> terrier

air miles A consumer incentive scheme which offers the chance of free air travel in return for credits earned by frequent flyers who have joined the scheme. Credits may also be obtained through other means, such as authorized retail transactions, and flights of greater distance become possible as credits accumulate. An 'air mile' is a nautical mile as used by aircraft. >> RR1033

airplane >> **aeroplane**

airship A self-propelled steerable aircraft whose lift is generated by using lighter-than-air gases to provide buoyancy. The main body is cigar-shaped, with engines and gondolas (cabins) being suspended from it. The gas used to provide buoyancy was originally hydrogen, but its highly inflammable nature and poor safety record led to its replacement by helium. >> aircraft ℹ; dirigible; helium; hydrogen; Zeppelin

Aïshah or **Ayeshah** [**ae**esha] (c.613–78) The favourite of the nine wives of Mohammed, but who bore him no children. On Mohammed's death, she resisted Ali, the Prophet's son-in-law, and secured the caliphate for her father, Abu-Bakr. Again opposing Ali, she was defeated in 656. >> Abu-Bakr; Mohammed

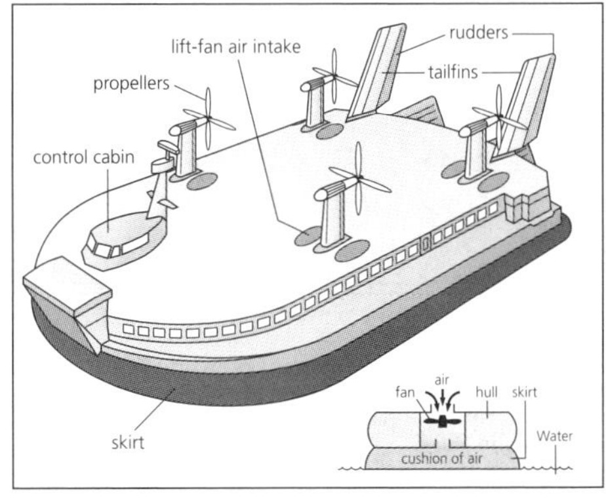

Air cushion vehicle – inset shows method of operation

Aircraft – (1) Wright Brother's Flyer of 1903: the world's first true aeroplane.
(2) Sopwith Camel: a famous fighter of World War 1.
(3) Cierva Autogiro of 1922, invented by Juan de la Cierva. The early prototype was unable to fly because its blades were not hinged.
(4) Boeing 247. A streamlined, all-metal construction, the first of the new generation of US domestic air transports, built in 1933.
(5) Supermarine S6B, the Schneider Trophy winner of 1931. It was a predecessor of the Spitfire.
(6) Me 262: the world's first operational jet aircraft. It entered service in 1944 with a maximum speed of just over 800 kph/500 mph.
(7) Boeing 747: the Jumbo Jet. It entered regular passenger service in January 1970.
(8) Convair XFY-1: Pogo. A vertical take-off aircraft of 1954 which took off and landed from its tail and wings.
(9) Concorde. A supersonic airliner, introduced in 1976, designed to travel at more than twice the speed of sound.

Aix-en-Provence [eks ã provãs] 43°31N 5°27E, pop (1995e) 128 000. Ancient city in Bouches-du-Rhône department, SW France; founded as Aquae Sextiae in 123 BC; important centre for Provençal literature since the 15th-c; airport; railway; university (1409); cathedral (11th–16th-c); archbishopric; home of Cézanne. >> Cézanne; Provence

Ajaccio [**azhak**seeoh] 41°55N 8°40E, pop (1995e) 61 800. Seaport and capital of the Island of Corsica, France; founded by the Genoese, 1492; made capital by Napoleon, 1811; Corsica's second largest port; airport; railway; car ferries to Marseille, Toulon, Nice; tourism; birthplace of Napoleon. >> Corsica; Napoleon I

Ajanta Caves [aj**an**ta] A group of 29 Buddhist cave-temples and monasteries cut into cliffs over R Wagurna, near Ajanta, Maharashtra, India; a world heritage site. The caves, built from the 2nd-c BC onwards, are particularly noted for their wall paintings. >> Buddhism; Maharashtra

Ajax [**ay**jaks], Latin form of Greek **Aias**. A legendary Greek hero during the Trojan War; the Latin form of Greek **Aias**; the son of Telamon, King of Salamis, therefore known as **Telamonian Ajax**. When the armour of the dead Achilles was not given to him, he went mad and killed himself. >> Achilles; Trojan War

Ajman [aj**man**] pop (1995e) 84 400; area c.250 sq km/ 100 sq mi. Smallest of the seven member states of the United Arab Emirates; capital, Ajman; relatively undeveloped. >> United Arab Emirates ℹ

Akabusi, Kriss (Kezie Uche-Chukwu Duru) [aka**boo**see] (1958–) Athlete, born in London. One of the leading athletes of the 1990s, his achievements include gold medals in the 400 m hurdles at the 1990 European Championships (also breaking a 22-year world record) and the 4 x 400 m relay at the 1991 World Championships. His Olympic medals include silver in the 4 x 100 m relay (1984) and bronze for the same event in 1994. Since 1993 he has been a television presenter.

Akahito, Yamabe no [aka**hee**toh] (8th-c) Japanese poet, one of the 'twin stars' (with Hitomaro) of the great anthology of classical Japanese poetry known as the *Manyoshu* (Collection of a Myriad Leaves).

Akashi-Kaikyo Bridge [**ak**ashee **kiy**kyoh] Suspension bridge across the Akashi Straits between Honshu and Shikoku, Japan, begun in 1988 and opened in 1998. With a main span of 1991 m/6532 ft (overall length 3911 m/12 831 ft) it is now the longest suspension bridge in the world.

Akbar the Great [**ak**ber], in full **Jalal ud-Din Muhammad Akbar** (1542–1605) Mughal Emperor of India, born in Umarkot, Sind. He took over the administration from his regent in 1560. Within a few years, he had gained control of the whole of India N of the Vindhya Mts. A social and economic reformer, he pursued a policy of religious tolerance, and greatly encouraged the arts. >> Mughal Empire

Akhenaton [ake**na**ton], also **Akh(e)naten** or **Amenhotep (Amenophis) IV** [amen**hoh**tep] (14th-c BC) Egyptian king of the 18th dynasty. He renounced the old gods and introduced a purified and universalized solar cult. One of his wives was Nefertiti. >> Nefertiti; pharaoh

Akhmatova, Anna [akh**mah**tofa], pseudonym of **Anna Andreeyevna Gorenko** (1889–1966) Poet, born near Odessa, Ukraine. Her works were condemned between 1922 and 1940, and again in 1946. She was 'rehabilitated' in the 1950s.

Akiba ben Joseph [a**kee**ba ben **joh**zef], also spelled **Akiva** (c.50–135) Rabbi and teacher in the formative period of rabbinic Judaism. He provided the basis for the Mishnah by his codification of the *halakhoth* (legal traditions). A supporter of bar Kokhba, he was put to death by the Romans. >> bar Kokhba; Halakhah; Judaism; Mishnah

Akihito [aki**hee**toh] (1933–) Emperor of Japan (1989–), the eldest son of Emperor Hirohito, born in Tokyo. Invested as Crown Prince in 1952, he became the first Crown Prince to marry a commoner, **Michiko Shoda** (1934–), in 1959. They have three children. >> Showa Tenno

Akkadian [a**kay**dian] One of the oldest languages in the Semitic (Afro-Asiatic) family, with a substantial literature written in cuneiform script. It is now extinct. >> Afro-Asiatic languages; cuneiform ℹ

Akmola >> **Astana**

Akrotiri [akro**tee**ree] 34°36N 32°57E. Bay on S coast of Cyprus; main port town, Limassol; British base on peninsula separating Akrotiri Bay (E) from Episkopi Bay (W). >> Cyprus ℹ

Aksum 14°08N 38°43E. Ancient city in the highlands of N Ethiopia; a world heritage site. During the 1st–7th-c AD it was the capital of a powerful kingdom dominating trade between the Sudanese Nile Valley and the Roman Mediterranean.

Aktyubinsk [ak**tyoo**byinsk] 50°16N 57°13E, pop (1995e) 267 000. Industrial city in NW Kazakhstan; established, 1869; airport; railway. >> Kazakhstan ℹ

Alabama pop (1995e) 4 283 000; area 133 911 sq km/ 51 705 sq mi. State in SE USA; the 'Heart of Dixie', the 'Camellia State', or 'Yellowhammer'; first permanent settlement by the French at Mobile, 1711; N Alabama became part of the USA in 1783, the remainder being acquired by the Louisiana Purchase in 1803; the 22nd state to be admitted to the Union, 1819; seceded, 1861; slavery abolished, 1865; re-admitted to the Union, 1868; highest point, Mt Cheaha (734 m/2 408 ft); mountainous NE, separated from the S coastal plain by the rolling plain of the Appalachian Piedmont; capital, Montgomery; diversified agriculture, after the boll weevil blight of 1915; iron and steel industry centred on Birmingham; many civil rights protests in the area in the 1950s and 1960s. >> civil rights; cotton ℹ; Montgomery (Alabama); United States of America ℹ; RR994

alabaster A fine-grained banded variety of the mineral gypsum; pale and translucent. It is soft enough to be carved and polished by hand for ornamental use. >> gypsum

Alain-Fournier, Henri [alã foornyay], pseudonym of **Henri-Alban Fournier** (1886–1914) Writer, born in Sologne, France. He was killed at St Rémy in World War 1, leaving a few short stories, and a novel, the nostalgic *Le Grand Meaulnes* (1913, trans The Lost Domain).

Alamo [**al**amoh] A battle fought during the 1836 Texan War of Independence against Mexico, when 180 Texans and US citizens held the old mission/fort of Alamo against a large number of Mexican troops. They held out for 11 days until the last survivors were overwhelmed. >> Texas

Alanbrooke (of Brookeborough), Alan Francis Brooke, 1st Viscount [**al**anbruk] (1883–1963) British field marshal, a leading strategist of World War 2, born in Bagnères-de-Bigorre, France. He commanded the 2nd corps of the British Expeditionary Force in France (1940), covering the evacuation from Dunkirk, and became Chief of the Imperial General Staff (1941–6). His war diaries presented a controversial view of Churchill and Eisenhower. >> British Expeditionary Force; World War 2

Alarcón (y Ariza), Pedro Antonio de [alah(r)**hon**] (1833–91) Writer, born in Guadix, Spain. He is best known for his *Sombrero de tres picos* (1874, The Three-Cornered Hat) on which Falla's ballet was based.

Alaric I [**al**arik] (c.370–410) King of the Visigoths from 395, and the first Germanic conqueror of Rome. The sack of Rome by his troops in 410 marks the beginning of the end of the Western Roman Empire. >> Roman history ℹ; Stilicho

Alaska pop (1995e) 647 000; area 1 518 748 sq km/ 586 412 sq mi. US state in the extreme NW corner of the continent, 'The Last Frontier' or 'The Great Land', separated from the rest of the nation by Canada; first permanent settlement by Russians on Kodiak I, 1792; bought by the USA, 1867; gold discovered in 1889 and 1902; territorial status, 1912; Aleutian islands of Attu and Kiska occupied by the Japanese (Jun 1942–Aug 1943); granted statehood as the 49th state, 1959; large oil reserves discovered in 1968 (Alaska Pipeline from Prudhoe Bay to Valdez completed in 1977); the largest state, but the least populated; highest point Mt McKinley (6194 m/20 321 ft); capital, Juneau; major city, Anchorage; oil, natural gas, wide range of minerals; balance between industrial development and landscape preservation an ongoing controversy. >> Anchorage; United States of America [i]; RR994

Alaska Highway An all-weather road which runs from Dawson Creek in British Columbia, Canada, to Fairbanks in Alaska. It was built in 1942 to supply military forces stationed in Alaska during World War 2. >> Alaska

Alaskan malamute [**mal**amyoot] A breed of dog; a spitz bred by the Malamute Eskimos of Alaska as a sledge-dog (*husky*); largest sledge-dog breed; strong and active; thick grey and white coat. >> husky; spitz

Alawi [a**lah**wee] **1** Moroccan royal family, tracing their line to the grandson of the Prophet Mohammed, Hasan bin Ali, from which they derive their name. **2** Offshoot sect of Shiite Islam, found mainly in the NW mountains of Syria, as well as in Lebanon and Turkey. Persecuted over the centuries for their heterodox beliefs, the Alawis have observed the outward forms of Sunni Islam while observing their own rites in secret. >> Shiites

Alba, Duke of >> **Alva, duque de**

albacore [**al**bakaw(r)] Large tuna fish (*Thunnus alalunga*) with long pectoral fins, widespread in open waters of tropical and warm temperate seas; length up to 1·3 m/4¼ ft, with an iridescent blue band on sides of body. (Family: Scombridae.) >> tuna

Alba Iulia [**al**ba **yool**ya], Ger **Karlsburg**, Lat **Apulum** 46°04N 23°33E, pop (1995e) 74 000. Capital of Alba county, WC Romania, on the R Mureş; founded by the Romans, 2nd-c AD; former seat of the princes of Transylvania; railway. >> Romania [i]; Transylvania

Alban, St [**awl**bn] (3rd-c) Roman soldier, who became the first British Christian martyr. Little is known about him, but he is said to have protected a Christian priest, and been converted by him. For this he was killed by the Romans in c.305. Feast day 17 or 20 June. >> Christianity

Albania, Albanian **Shqipni**, **Shqipri**, or **Shqipëri**, official name (1991) **Republic of Albania**, **Republica e Shqipërisë** pop (1995e) 3 549 000; area 28 748 sq km/11 097 sq mi. Republic in the W part of the Balkan Peninsula; capital, Tiranë; timezone GMT +1; mainly Albanians (96%), some Greeks, Vlachs, Gypsies, and Bulgarians; constitutionally an atheist state; language, Albanian; unit of currency the lek (100 qintars); a mountainous country, relatively inaccessible and untravelled; N Albanian Alps rise to 2692 m/8832 ft; many lakes throughout the country; Mediterranean-type climate; hot and dry on the plains in summer (average Jul 24–25°C), thunderstorms frequent; mild, damp, and cyclonic winters (average Jan 8–9°C); independence followed the end of Turkish rule in 1912, but Italian forces occupied the country, 1914–20; became a republic in 1925, and a monarchy in 1928, under King Zog I; occupied by Germany and Italy in World War 2; new republic in 1946, headed by Enver Hoxha (until 1985); dispute with the Soviet Union in 1961; withdrew from Warsaw Pact in 1968; maintained close links with China; Socialist People's Republic instituted in 1976; first free multi-party elections and Government of National Stability, 1991; collapse of fraudulent pyramid finance schemes, 1997, leading to rebellion in the S, arrival of UN protection force, and early elections, with unrest continuing in 1998; new constitution, 1998; supreme legislative body is the People's Assembly, which elects the Presidium, and forms the government; seventh 5-year plan, 1981–5, focused on industrial expansion, especially in oil, mining, chemicals, natural gas; main crops wheat, sugar-beet, maize, potatoes, fruit, grapes, oats; all industry is nationalized; progressive transformation of farm co-operatives into state farms. >> socialism; Tiranë; RR1000 political leaders

al-Banna, Hassan [al**ba**na] (1906–49) Islamic fundamentalist, born in Mahmudiya, near Cairo. In 1928 he founded in Egypt the Society of Muslim Brothers. Following the assassination of the Egyptian prime minister by a Brotherhood member in 1948, al-Banna was himself murdered. >> Islam; Muslim Brotherhood

Albany (Australia) 34°57S 117°54E, pop (1995e) 19 900. Resort and seaport in Western Australia; one of the oldest towns in Australia, founded in 1826; once used as a stopover point for vessels on their way to India; airfield; railway. >> Western Australia

Albany (USA) 42°39N 73°45W, pop (1995e) 103 000. Capital of New York State USA; on the Hudson R; settled by the Dutch, 1614; state capital, 1797; railway; two universities (1844, 1848); State Capitol. >> New York

Albany Congress (1754) A US colonial gathering of delegates at which Benjamin Franklin proposed a 'plan of union' for the separate British colonies. Both the colonial governments and the British authorities rejected the idea. >> Franklin, Benjamin

albatross A large, slender-winged seabird, wingspan up to 3 m/10 ft; glides near water in air currents; lands only to breed. (Order: Procellariiformes (**tubenoses**). Family: Diomedeidae, 14 species.) >> petrel; tubenose

albedo [al**bee**doh] The ratio of the radiation reflected by a surface to the total incoming solar radiation, expressed as a decimal or percentage. The degree of reflectance varies according to the type of surface: snow-covered ice has an albedo of 0·8 (80%); a tropical rainforest 0·13 (13%). >> insolation; radiation

Albee, Edward (Franklin) [**awl**bee, **al**bee] (1928–) Playwright, born near Washington, DC. His major works are *The Zoo Story* (1958), *The American Dream* (1960), and *Who's Afraid of Virginia Woolf?* (1962, filmed 1966). *A Delicate Balance* (1966) and *Seascape* (1975), and *Three Tall Women* (1991) won Pulitzer Prizes.

Albéniz, Isaac (Manuel Francisco) [al**be**nith] (1860–1909) Composer and pianist, born in Camprodón, Spain. He was especially known for his picturesque piano works based on Spanish folk music. >> folk music

Albert, Lake, Zaire **Lake Mobuto Sésé Seko** area c.6400 sq km/2500 sq mi. Lake in EC Africa; in the W Rift Valley on the frontier between the Democratic Republic of Congo and Uganda; length, c.160 km/100 mi; width, 40 km/25 mi; altitude, 619 m/2031 ft; receives the Victoria Nile (NE) and Semliki (SW) Rivers; Albert Nile flows N; European discovery by Samuel Baker, 1864; originally named after Queen Victoria's consort. >> Africa; Rift Valley

Albert, Prince, in full **Francis Albert Augustus Charles Emmanuel, Prince of Saxe-Coburg-Gotha** (1819–61) Prince Consort of Queen Victoria of Great Britain, born at Schloss Rosenau, near Coburg, Germany. He married his cousin, an infatuated Queen Victoria, in 1840, and became her chief adviser, first as Consort (1842), then as Prince Consort (1857). He died of typhoid at Windsor Castle, Berkshire. The Albert Memorial in Kensington Gardens was erected to his memory in 1871. >> Victoria

Alberta pop (1995e) 2 702 000; area 661 190 sq km/ 255 285 sq mi. Province in W Canada, bordered S by the USA; capital Edmonton; mainly a rolling plain, with edge of Rocky Mts in W; rivers, lakes, and forests in N, with much open prairie; treeless prairie in S; largest lakes, Athabasca, Claire, Lesser Slave; originally part of Rupert's Land, granted to Hudson's Bay Company, 1670; sovereignty acquired by the Dominion, 1870; status as province, 1905; governed by a lieutenant-governor and an elected Legislative Assembly; oil, natural gas, grain, cattle, timber products, coal, food processing, chemicals, fabricated metals, tourism. >> Canada [i]; Edmonton; Hudson's Bay Company

Alberti, Leon Battista [al**bair**tee] (1404–72) Architect, born in Genoa, Italy. One of the most brilliant figures of the Renaissance, his designs include the church of S Maria Novella in Florence.

Albertina An art gallery founded in 1768 by Duke Albert of Saxony-Tescha. Since 1795 it has been housed in the former Taroucca Palace in Vienna. >> Vienna

Albertus Magnus, St, Graf von (Count of) **Bollstädt**, known as **Doctor Universalis** ('Universal Doctor') (c.1200–80) Philosopher, bishop, and doctor of the church, born in Lauingen, Germany. He joined the Dominican order, becoming a teacher of theology, and did more than anyone to bring together theology and Aristotelianism. His most famous pupil was Thomas Aquinas. Feast day 15 November. >> Aquinas; Dominicans

Albigenses [albi**jen**seez] or **Albigensians** Followers of a form of Christianity which in the 11th-c and 12th-c especially had its main strength in the town of Albi, SW France; also known as **Cathari** or **Bogomils**. Condemned by the Roman Catholic Church, they were devastated in the early 13th-c crusade against them. >> Cathars; Christianity

albinism A common inherited pigmentary disorder of vertebrates: affected individuals lack pigmentation of the skin, hair, eyes (iris), feathers, or scales. It is found in all human races: the absence of pigment (or *melanin*) results in white hair, pink skin, and pink irises. >> melanins; pigments; skin [i]

Albinus >> **Alcuin**

Albright, Madeleine K(orbel) (1937–) US secretary of state (from 1997), born in Czechoslovakia. Formerly permanent US representative to the UN, in the second Clinton administration she became the first woman to head the State Department. >> Clinton, Bill

Albufeira [albu**fay**ra] 37°05N 8°15W, pop (1995e) 25 500. Fishing village and resort, S Portugal; Moorish-style architecture; Portugal's busiest seaside resort. >> Algarve; Portugal [i]

albumins [**al**byuminz] Part of a system of classification of simple proteins, usually referring to those proteins that are readily soluble in water and in dilute salt solutions. They are present in most animals and plants. >> protein

Albuquerque [**al**buhkerkee] 35°05N 106°39W, pop (1995e) 428 000. Largest city in C New Mexico, USA, on the Rio Grande; settled, 1706; city status, 1890; airport; railway; two universities (1889, 1940); base for many federal agencies; health resort; tourism. >> New Mexico

Albuquerque, Affonso d' [alboo**ker**kay], known as **Affonso the Great** (1453–1515) Portuguese viceroy of the Indies, born near Lisbon. He landed on the Malabar coast of India in 1502, and conquered Goa, Ceylon, the Sundra Is, and Malacca. >> Goa, Daman, and Diu

Alcaeus [al**see**us] (c.620–c.580 BC) Greek lyric poet, who flourished in Mitylene c.600 BC. He was the inventor of Alcaic verse, which Horace transferred into Latin. Only fragments remain of his odes. >> Horace; ode

Alcestis [al**ses**tis] In Greek mythology, the wife of Admetus; he was doomed to die, and she saved him by offering to die in his place. Heracles wrestled with the messenger of death and brought her back to life. >> Heracles

alchemy The attempt from early times to find an elixir of immortal life. The first reference is by a Chinese Taoist in 140 BC, and the practice probably spread to Europe via Arab traders, where it was taken up by such scholars as Roger Bacon. Alchemists sought to convert base metals into gold – not to create wealth, but as a step towards discovering the recipe for eternity. Because they needed accurate scales, clocks, and temperature control, their work facilitated important discoveries in chemistry, medicine, mineralogy, and pharmacology. >> Bacon, Roger; Taoism

Alcibiades [alsi**biy**adeez] (c.450–404 BC) Athenian statesman and general from the aristocratic Alcmaeonid family. He was a leader against the Spartans in the Peloponnesian War, then sided with them against Athens. After further intrigues with the Athenians and Persians, he was assassinated. >> Alcmaeonids; Peloponnesian War

Alcmaeonids [alk**miy**onidz] An aristocratic Athenian family to which many prominent Athenian politicians belonged. It was particularly influential in the period 632–415 BC. >> Alcibiades; Pericles

Alcock, Sir John William (1892–1919) Aviator, born in Manchester, who with Brown was the first to fly the Atlantic (14 Jun 1919). The trip, from Newfoundland to Ireland, was made in a Vickers-Vimy machine, and took 16 h 27 m. >> Brown, Arthur Whitten

Alcoholics Anonymous (AA) A self-help group for alcoholics trying to stop drinking. Founded in the USA in 1935, it consists of local groups where members (identified by first names only) meet to give each other support. >> self-help group

alcohols IUPAC **alkanols**. Generally organic compounds containing a hydroxyl (–OH) function bonded to a carbon atom which is not itself bonded to further atoms other than carbon or hydrogen. In everyday use, the word **alcohol** is often restricted to *ethanol* (**ethyl alcohol**), CH_3CH_2OH. >> ethanol; IUPAC

alcohol strength The measurement of the amount of ethanol (the active constituent) in alcoholic drinks, commonly expressed using either volumetric measures or proof strength. The volumetric measure declares the volume of ethanol present in a unit volume of the alcoholic beverage. *Proof spirit* is a mixture containing a standard amount of ethanol: in the UK it is 57·07% by volume, while in the USA it is 50%. Thus, a bottle of Scotch which claims to be 70° proof is in fact 70% of 57·07% (volume), or 40% ethanol by volume. >> alcohols; ethanol

alcopops [alkohpops] Soft drinks with an alcoholic content, marketed in a wide range of brand names. Known since the 1970s, they became fashionable in the late 1990s, but raised considerable public concern about the wisdom of making alcohol more accessible to young people, and (through the use of terms such as 'alcoholic soft drink') reducing their awareness of its dangers. >> alcohol strength

Alcott, Louisa M(ay) (1832–88) Writer, born in Germantown, PA. Her *Little Women* (1868–9), *An Old-fashioned Girl* (1870), *Little Men* (1871), and *Jo's Boys* (1886), are firmly established among the classics.

Alcuin [alkwin], originally **Ealhwine**, Lat **Albinus** (c.737–804) Scholar, theologian, and adviser to the emperor Charlemagne, born in York. He was a major influence on the Carolingian revival of learning. >> Charlemagne

Alcyone >> **Halcyone**

Alda, Alan [awlda] (1936–) Actor, director, and writer, born in New York City. He is best known for the award-winning television series *M*A*S*H* (1972–83). His acerbic sense of humour is evident in such films as *Canadian Bacon* (1995), and *Everyone Says I Love You* (1997).

Aldabra Islands [aldabra] 9°25S 46°20E; area 154 sq km/59 sq mi. Coral atoll nature reserve in SW Indian Ocean; outlying dependency of the Seychelles; habitat of the giant land tortoise; a world heritage site. >> Seychelles [i]

Aldebaran [aldebaran] >> **Taurus**

aldehydes [aldihiydz] IUPAC **alkanals**. Organic compounds containing a (–CHO) function. They are found in most sugars, notably glucose. >> IUPAC; sugars

alder A small deciduous N temperate tree, often growing by water or in wet soils; leaves oval or rounded; male and female flowers on separate plants; male catkins long, pendulous; females short, erect, becoming woody and cone-like in fruit. (Genus: *Alnus*, 35 species. Family: Betulaceae.) >> tree [i]

alderfly A slow, awkwardly flying insect with two pairs of large, translucent wings held over its body at rest; found around freshwater ponds and streams. (Order: Megaloptera. Family: Sialidae, c.50 species.) >> insect [i]

Alderney [awldernee], Fr **Aurigny**, ancient **Riduna** pop (1995e) 2280; area 8 sq km/3 sq mi. Third largest of the Channel Is, separated from France by the Race of Alderney; in the Bailiwick of Guernsey, with its own legislative assembly; chief town, Saint Anne; tourism, dairy farming. >> Channel Islands [i]

Aldington, Richard [awldingtn], originally **Edward Godfree** (1892–1962) Writer, editor, and biographer, born in Hampshire. He edited *The Egoist*, the periodical of the Imagist school. His best-known novel is *Death of a Hero* (1929), and his biographies include *Wellington* (1946). He married Hilda Doolittle in 1913 (divorced, 1937). >> Doolittle; Imagism

Aldiss, Brian (Wilson) [awldis] (1925–) Writer and editor, best known for his science-fiction writing, born in Dereham, Norfolk. His works include *Hothouse* (1962), *The Saliva Tree* (1966), histories of science fiction, and edited collections of short stories. >> science fiction

aldosterone [aldosterohn] A type of hormone secreted from the adrenal cortex into the blood. Its primary role in humans is to stimulate sodium reabsorption and potassium excretion by the kidneys, in order to maintain electrolyte and water balance. Excessive secretion is known as **aldosteronism**. >> adrenal glands; kidneys

Aldrin, Buzz [awldrin], popular name of **Edwin Eugene Aldrin** (1930–) Astronaut, born in Montclair, NJ. He was the second man to set foot on the Moon, after Neil Armstrong, in 1969. >> Apollo programme; Armstrong, Neil

Aldus Manutius [aldus manootius], Latin name of **Aldo Manucci** or **Manuzio** (c.1450–1515) Printer, born in Bassiano, Italy. He was the first to print Greek books, and the first to use italics on a large scale. >> printing [i]

ale An alcoholic beverage brewed from barley which has been malted (ie softened in water and allowed to germinate). It was a popular drink prior to the introduction of hops as a flavouring agent, thus creating beer. However, the term *ale* is still used to describe a hops-flavoured brew. >> barley; beer [i]; hops

alecost >> **costmary**

Alentejo [alãtezhu] Sparsely-populated agricultural area of SEC Portugal, SE of the R Tagus; low-lying plain with cork tree forests, heaths, maquis; prehistoric standing stones and chambered cairns; chief towns, Evora, Beja; noted for the Alter Real breed of horse. >> Portugal [i]

Aleppo [alepoh], Arabic **Halab** 36°12N 37°10E, pop (1995e) 1 597 000. Chief commercial and industrial centre of N Syria; airport; road and rail junction; university (1960); old city, a world heritage site. >> Syria [i]

Aletsch [alech] area 117·6 sq km/45·4 sq mi. Glacier in SC Switzerland, W and S of the Aletschhorn; length, 23·6 km/14·6 mi; the largest glacier in Europe. >> Alps

Aleutian Islands [alooshn] or **Aleutians**, formerly **Catherine Archipelago** pop (1995e) 14 000; area 18 000 sq km/7000 sq mi. Group of c.150 islands stretching c.1600 km/1000 mi from the Alaskan Peninsula, USA; many volcanic peaks over 1000 m/3000 ft; discovered by Russian explorers in 18th-c; purchased by USA, 1867; several military bases; wildlife refuge. >> Alaska

A level An abbreviation for **Advanced level**, the examination taken by British pupils, usually near the age of 18, which qualifies them for entrance to higher education and the professions. University matriculation requirements normally specify A levels in at least two subjects. One A level is deemed equivalent to two passes in the Advanced Supplementary (*A/S level*) examination.

alewife Deep-bodied herring-like fish (*Alosa pseudoharengus*), locally abundant along the American Atlantic seaboard; length up to 40 cm/16 in; migrates into rivers (Mar/Apr) to spawn in slow backwaters. (Family: Clupeidae.) >> herring

Alexander I (1777–1825) Tsar of Russia (1801–25), born in St Petersburg, the grandson of Catherine the Great. The early years of his reign were marked by the pursuit of a vigorous foreign policy. In 1805 Russia joined the coalition against Napoleon, but after a series of military defeats was forced to conclude the Treaty of Tilsit (1807) with France. When Napoleon broke the treaty by invading Russia in 1812, Alexander pursued the French back to Paris. His mysterious death at Taganrog caused a succession crisis. >> Napoleon I; Romanovs

Alexander VI, originally **Rodrigo Borgia** (1431–1503) Pope (1492–1503), born in Játiva, Spain. Father to Cesare,

Lucretia, and two other illegitimate children, he endeavoured to break the power of the Italian princes, and to gain their possessions for his own family. Under his pontificate, he apportioned the New World between Spain and Portugal. >> Borgia; pope

Alexander >> **Paris** (mythology)

Alexander of Hales, known as **Doctor Irrefragabilis** ('Irrefutable Doctor') (c.1170–1245) English theologian and philosopher, born in Hales, Gloucestershire. He became a professor of philosophy and theology in Paris, and later entered the Franciscan order. >> Franciscans; scholasticism

Alexander (of Tunis), Sir Harold (Rupert Leofric George) Alexander, 1st Earl (1891–1969) British soldier, born in London. He served in Burma, and became commander-in-chief Middle East (1942–3), and supreme allied commander, Mediterranean theatre (1944). He later held posts as Governor-General of Canada (1946–52) and minister of defence (1952–4). >> World War 2

Alexander the Great (356–323 BC) King of Macedonia (336–323 BC), born at Pella, the son of Philip II and Olympias. He was tutored by Aristotle, and ascended the throne when less than 20 years old. After crushing all opposition at home, he set out to conquer Achaemenid Persia. By 330 BC, Darius III had fled, and the capitals of Babylon, Susa, Persepolis, and Ecbatana had been taken. In the next three years, the E half of the empire followed, and Alexander set out for India. He reached the Punjab, and had set his sights on the Ganges, when his troops mutinied and forced his return. He died shortly after at Babylon. >> Achaemenids; Persian Wars; Philip II (of Macedon)

Alexander Nevski, St, also spelled **Nevsky** (c.1218–63) Russian hero and saint, born in Vladimir, Russia, who received his surname from his victory over the Swedes on the R Neva (1240). He was canonized by the Russian Orthodox Church in 1547. Feast day 30 August or 23 November. >> Eisenstein

Alexander technique A method of releasing unwanted physical and mental tension from the body by encouraging posture training and self-awareness, developed by the Australian actor Frederick Matthias Alexander (1869–1955). The technique is growing as a treatment for headache, backache, anxiety, and depression, and particularly benefits stage performers. >> alternative medicine

Alexandra, Queen (1844–1925) Eldest daughter of Christian IX of Denmark, who married the British Prince of Wales (later Edward VII) in 1863. In 1902 she founded Queen Alexandra's Imperial (now Royal) Army Nursing Corps. >> Edward VII

Alexandra, Princess, the Hon Lady Ogilvy (1936–) Daughter of George, Duke of Kent, and Princess Marina of Greece. In 1963 she married Sir **Angus James Bruce Ogilvy** (1928–). They have a son, **James Robert Bruce** (1964–), and a daughter, **Marina Victoria Alexandra** (1966–). James married Julia Rawlinson and they have a son, **Alexander Charles** (1996–); Marina married Paul Mowatt and they have a daughter, **Zenouska May** (1990–), and a son, **Christian Alexander** (1993-).

Alexandra Feodorovna [**fyod**orovna] (1872–1918) Empress of Russia upon her marriage with Nicholas II (1894), born in Darmstadt, Germany. She came under the influence of Rasputin, and meddled disastrously in politics. She was imprisoned and shot by Bolshevik revolutionaries, along with her husband and children, at Yekaterinburg. >> Bolsheviks; February Revolution (Russia); Rasputin

Alexandria, Arabic **al-Iskandariya** 31°13N 29°55E, pop (1995e) 3 631 000. Second largest city of Egypt and the country's main port; founded in 332 BC by Alexander the Great; capital of the Ptolemies 304–30 BC; noted for its famous royal libraries; airport; railway; university (1942). >> Alexander the Great; Egypt ℹ

Alexandria, Library of A library founded by Ptolemy I and greatly extended by Ptolemy II. The greatest library in the Ancient World, it was destroyed in the civil wars of the 3rd-c AD. >> Ptolemy I Soter

Alexeyev, Vasiliy [alek**say**ef] (1942–) Weightlifter, born in Pokrovo-Shishkino, Russia. He set 80 world records (1970–7), more than any other athlete in any sport. >> weightlifting

alexia >> **dyslexia**

Alexius I Comnenus [kom**nee**nus] (1048–1118) Byzantine Emperor (1081–1118), born in Constantinople, the founder of the Comnenian dynasty. His empire was invaded by the warriors of the First Crusade to Palestine (1096). >> Crusades ℹ

alfalfa >> **lucerne**

Al Fayed, Mohamed [al **fa**yed] (1933–) Businessman, born in Egypt. Owner of the Ritz Hotel in Paris in 1979, and of Harrods in London in 1985, he is one of the world's wealthiest men. One of his children, **Dodi** (1955–97), received worldwide publicity in 1997 when the press discovered his relationship with Princess Diana. A graduate of Sandhurst military academy, he became a film producer, renowned for his flamboyant lifestyle. He was killed along with Diana in a car accident in Paris while trying to escape the attentions of paparazzi. >> Diana, Princess of Wales

Alföld [**ol**fuld] Great Plain region of S Hungary, E of the R Danube, extending into adjoining countries. It is a flat area covering about half of Hungary, crossed by a system of canals which provide irrigation for grain and fruit. >> Hungary ℹ

Alfred, known as **Alfred the Great** (849–99) King of Wessex (from 871), born in Wantage, Oxfordshire, the fifth son of King Ethelwulf. He inflicted on the Danes their first major reverse at the Battle of Edington, Wiltshire (878), reorganized his forces into a standing army, built a navy, and established a network of *burhs* (fortified centres). These developments were complemented by his revival of religion and learning, and provided his successors with the means to reconquer the Danelaw and secure the unity of England. The famous story of his being scolded by a peasant woman for letting her cakes burn is first recorded in the 11th-c. >> Anglo-Saxons; Danelaw; Vikings; Wessex

Alfvén, Hannes (Olof Gösta) [al**fen**] (1908–95) Theoretical physicist, born in Norrköping, Sweden. In 1942 he predicted the existence of waves in plasmas (*Alfvén waves*), which were later observed. He shared the Nobel Prize for Physics in 1970. >> plasma (physics)

algae An informal grouping of primitive, mainly aquatic plants that have chlorophyll *a* as their primary photosynthetic pigment; body (*thallus*) not organized into root, stem, and leaf; range in form from simple unicellular plant plankton to massive seaweeds many metres in length. >> brown algae; chlorophyll; photosynthesis; plankton; plant; seaweed; yellow-green algae

Algarve [al**gah(r)v**] area 5072 sq km/1958 sq mi. Region and former province of S Portugal, bounded W and S by the Atlantic Ocean; Moorish kingdom, 1140; capital, Faro; the most popular tourist resort area in Portugal. >> Albufeira; Faro; Portugal ℹ

algebra A branch of mathematics in which unknown quantities are represented by letters or other symbols. It was developed and brought to Europe by the Moors, from whose word *al-jabr* the name of the subject is derived. In classical algebra (or **arithmetic algebra**), the operations in use are those of arithmetic; in **abstract algebra**, developed in the 19th–20th-c, different operations are defined. >> equations; mathematics

Algeciras [aljeseeras] 36°09N 5°28W, pop (1995e) 102 000. Seaport and resort in Cádiz province, Andalusia, SW Spain; founded by the Moors, 713; largely destroyed, 14th-c; rebuilt, 18th-c; railway; car ferries to Canary Is, Melilla, Tangier, Gibraltar. >> Andalusia; Spain [i]

Algeria, Fr **L'Algérie**, official name **The Democratic and Popular Republic of Algeria**, Arabic **al-Jumhuriya al-Jazairiya** pop (1995e) 28 513 000; area 2 460 500 sq km/949 753 sq mi. N African republic; capital, Algiers (Alger); timezone GMT +1; 99% of the population of Arab-Berber origin; chief religion, Islam, 99% Sunni Muslim; official language Arabic, with French also spoken; unit of currency, the dinar; mountains rise in a series of ridges and plateaux to the Atlas Saharien; 91% of population located on narrow coastal plain; Ahaggar Mts in far S, rising to 2918 m/9573 ft at Mt Tahat; typical Mediterranean climate on N coast; rainfall annual average of 400–800 mm/15·8–31·5 in (mostly Nov–Mar); rest of the country an essentially rainless Saharan climate; indigenous peoples (Berbers) driven back from the coast by many invaders, including Phoenicians, Romans, Vandals, Arabs, Turks, and French; became a province of the Roman Empire; Islam and Arabic introduced by Arabs, 8th–11th-c; Turkish invasion, 16th-c; French colonial campaign in 19th-c led to control by 1902; guerrilla war, 1954–62, with French forces by the National Liberation Front (FLN); independence gained, 1962; first president of the republic, Ahmed Ben Bella, replaced after coup in 1965; elections and a new constitution, 1976; cancellation of general election, 1991, following the likely victory of the Islamic Salvation Front; state of emergency, 1992, with continuing violence involving Islamic fundamentalists, including attacks on foreigners, from 1993; governed by a president, prime minister, and National People's Assembly; National Transitional Council, 1994; large-scale nationalization after 1963; agriculture, mainly on N coast; petroleum products account for c.30% of national income; natural gas reserves estimated to be world's fourth largest. >> Algiers; FLN; Islam; Sahara Desert; Sunnis; RR1000 political leaders

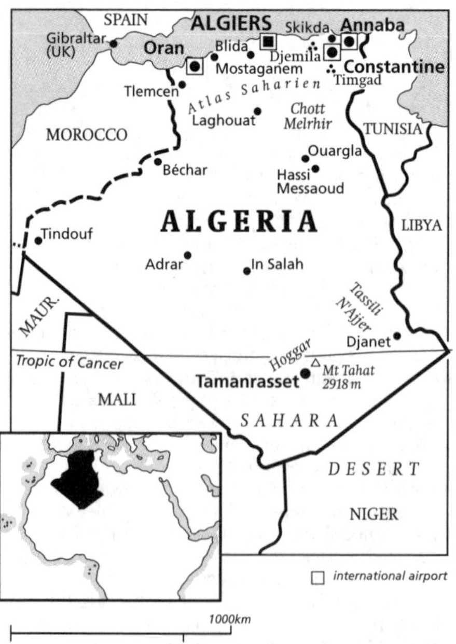

Algiers [aljeerz], Fr **Alger** [alzhay] 36°50N 3°00E, pop (1995e) 3 208 000. Seaport capital of Algeria, N Africa; founded 10th-c by Berbers on the site of Roman Icosium; Turkish rule established by Barbarossa, 1518; taken by the French, 1830; Allied headquarters in World War 2; airport; railway; cathedral; University of Algeria (1879); university of sciences and technology (1974). >> Algeria [i]; Barbarossa; Berber

ALGOL [algol] An acronym of **ALGOrithmic Language**, a high-level programming computer language. It was developed in Europe in the late 1950s for mathematical and scientific use. >> programming language

Algonkin [algongkin] or **Algonquin** Scattered small groups of American Indians speaking Algonkian languages, living in forest regions around the Ottawa R in Canada. Now only c.2000 survive. >> Blackfoot; Cree; Fox; manitou; Ojibwa; Shawnee

Algonquin >> **Algonkin**

Alhambra [alhambra] The palace-fortress of the Moorish kings built at Granada, Spain, in the 13th–14th-c; a world heritage site. >> Granada

Alhazen [alhazen], Arabic **Abu al-Hassan ibn al Haytham** (c.965–1039) Mathematician and physicist, born in Basra (now in Iraq). The best known of his many books was the *Treasury of Optics* (first published in Latin in 1270).

Ali (?–661) The first convert to Islam and the fourth caliph (656–61), the cousin of Mohammed. He was the bravest follower of Mohammed, whose daughter Fatima he married. He encountered considerable opposition to his reign, and was assassinated in the mosque at Kufa. He is held by Shiah Muslims to be the only true successor to the prophet. >> Islam; Mohammed

Ali, Muhammad, originally **Cassius (Marcellus) Clay, Jr** (1942–) Boxer, born in Louisville, KY. He won the world heavyweight title in 1964, defeating Sonny Liston in seven rounds. At that time he joined the Black Muslims and adopted the name Muhammad Ali. In 1971 he was beaten by Joe Frazier, but beat him in 1974, and went on to meet George Foreman later that year, knocking him out in eight rounds to regain his title. He was beaten by Leon Spinks (1953–) in a split decision (Feb 1978), but regained the title later that year – the first man to win the world heavyweight title three times. His slogan 'I am the greatest' became a catch phrase. He retired in 1981. >> boxing [i]

Alicante [aleekantay], Lat **Lucentum** 38°23N 0°30W, pop (1995e) 263 000. Seaport in SE Spain; airport; railway; car ferries to Marseille, Oran, Ibiza, Palma de Mallorca; popular winter resort. >> Spain [i]

Alice Springs, formerly **Stuart** (to 1933) 23°42S 133°52E, pop (1995e) 21 600. Urban centre in Northern Territory, C Australia; administrative centre for the settlements of the Outback; established, 1890; airfield; railway terminus; Flying Doctor Service regional headquarters; tourist centre for the region. >> Northern Territory

Alien and Sedition Acts (1798–1800) US laws passed to crush political opposition, led by Thomas Jefferson, then vice-president. Two Alien Acts gave the president great power over foreigners. The Sedition Act authorized fining and imprisonment for public criticism of the government. >> Jefferson; Kentucky and Virginia Resolutions

alienation Until the mid-20th-c, known mainly as a term referring either to the legal transfer of property or to progressive insanity. It then acquired currency as a key term in sociology, denoting the disorientation, depersonalization, and powerlessness of the individual in an increasingly bureaucratized industrial society. >> sociology

alimentary canal A tube in which foodstuffs are ingested, digested, and absorbed, and waste products excreted; also known as the **gut**, or the **gastro-intestinal tract**. It may exist as a simple structure with only one opening to the exterior (as in coelenterates, platyhelminths), or as a more complex structure with two openings (as in vertebrates). >> anus; cholera; Crohn's disease; digestion; duodenum; gastroenteritis; intestine; mouth

aliyah [ahl**ee**ah] (Heb 'ascend') The name given to the waves of Jewish migration to Palestine. The different waves were inspired by the push of persecution and the pull of Zionism, and drew Jews from Russia, C Europe, and the Middle East. The first two waves, spanning the years 1882–1914, brought an estimated 60–70 000 Jews to Palestine. The next three waves (1919–39) incurred opposition from Palestinian Arabs as 365 000 immigrants began to change the demographic balance. The sixth aliyah, coming mostly between 1945 and the establishment of the state of Israel, brought over 118 000 Jews, including many survivors of the Holocaust. Since statehood, numerous further waves of immigrants have reached Israel, such as emigrés from the former Soviet Union. >> Israel [i]; Judaism; Palestine

alkali [**al**kaliy] A strong base, especially sodium and potassium hydroxides. Solutions of alkalis have high values of pH, and are used as cleaning materials, as they dissolve fats. The **alkali metals** are Group I of the periodic table: lithium, sodium, potassium, rubidium, and caesium. >> base (chemistry); chemical elements; pH; potassium; sodium; RR1036

alkaline-earth Strictly, the elements calcium, strontium, barium, and radium, but often including beryllium and magnesium as well, hence Group II of the periodic table. These elements are largely responsible for the hardness of water. >> chemical elements; RR1036

alkaloids Organic, nitrogen-containing bases from plants which include complex ring structures. Many have been used as drugs, such as quinine, morphine, and cocaine. However, they may also be very toxic, as in the case of strychnine. >> base (chemistry); cocaine; morphine; opium; quinine; strychnine

alkanamides >> **amides 2**

alkanes [**al**kaynz] Saturated hydrocarbons, having a general formula C_nH_{2n+2}, derived from methane by the addition of successive $-CH_2-$ groups. Also known as **paraffins**, they make up the major components of petroleum. >> alkyl; hydrocarbons; methane; petroleum; saturated

alkanet [**al**kanet] The name given to several plants of the borage family. True alkanet (*Alkanna tinctoria*) is a bristly perennial growing to 15 cm/6 in; leaves oblong; flowers with a red tube and blue lobes; native to S Europe. The roots yield a red dye of the same name. (Family: Boraginaceae.) >> borage

alkanoic acids >> **carboxylic acids**

alkanols >> **alcohols**

alkanones >> **ketones**

alkenes [**al**keenz] Hydrocarbons containing one or more double bonds; also called **olefins**. With one double bond, their general formula is C_nH_{2n}. >> hydrocarbons

alkyl [**al**kiyl] A group $C_nH_{2n+1}-$, derived from an alkane, such as methyl (CH_3-), ethyl (C_2H_5-), and propyl (C_3H_7-). >> alkanes

alkynes [**al**kiynz] Hydrocarbons containing one or more triple bonds; also called **acetylenes**. With one triple bond, the general formula is C_nH_{2n-2}. >> acetylene; hydrocarbons

Allah [**al**ah] The Islamic name for God. Prior to Mohammed, Allah was the supreme but not the sole deity in Arabia. It was Mohammed's mission to proclaim Allah as the sole God, the creator and sustainer of all things. >> Islam; Koran; Mohammed

Allahabad [**ah**la-habahd] 25°25N 81°58E, pop (1995e) 873 000. City in Uttar Pradesh, NE India; founded, 1583; ceded to the British, 1801; airfield; railway; centre of Hindi literature. >> Hinduism; Uttar Pradesh

All Blacks The New Zealand national rugby union football team. The term was first applied to the team that toured Britain in 1905. >> football 3 [i]

Allegheny Mountains [**al**uhgenee, aluh**gay**nee] Mountain range in E USA; W part of the Appalachian Mts; extends over 800 km/500 mi, highest point Spruce Knob, 1481 m/4859 ft; rich in timber, coal, iron, and limestone. >> Appalachian Mountains

allegory A literary device by which another level of meaning is concealed within what is usually a story of some kind; also, the story itself. Myth and fable are both allegorical. Allegory has often been used for works with a religious or political bearing, such as Orwell's *Animal Farm* (1945). >> metaphor; mythology; Orwell

allele [**a**leel, a**leel**] or **allelomorph** One of the alternative forms of a gene which can occur at a given point on a chromosome. The term, introduced in 1902 to apply to Mendelian inheritance, is today increasingly applied to a short variant sequence of DNA, either within or adjacent to a functional gene. >> DNA [i]; gene; Mendel

allemande [ale**mahnd**] A dance originating in the 16th-c, probably in Germany. It is in 4/4 time and moderate tempo, and usually begins with a short note before the first main beat.

Allen, Ethan (1738–89) American soldier, revolutionary leader, and writer, born in Litchfield, CT. He led the insurgent Green Mountain Boys (1770–5), and distinguished himself early in the revolutionary war by the capture of Fort Ticonderoga (1775). He later published the deist tract known as *Ethan Allen's Bible*. >> American Revolution; Green Mountain Boys

Allen, Sir George Oswald Browning, known as **Gubby Allen** (1902–89) Cricketer, born in Sydney, New South Wales, Australia. He played for England in 25 Tests, and was captain in the Tests against India in 1936.

Allen, Woody, originally **Allen Stewart Konigsberg** (1935–) Film actor and director, born in New York City. He is best known for a series of highly successful films which explore such themes as mortality, sexual inadequacy, show-business nostalgia, psychoanalysis, and urban living. They include *Annie Hall* (1977), *Hannah and Her Sisters* (1986, Oscar), *Bullets Over Broadway* (1994, Oscar), and *Everyone Says I Love You* (1997). *Husbands and Wives* (1992) ironically coincided with the breakdown of his long-term relationship with actress **Mia Farrow** (1945–). In 1993 his private life received adverse publicity after losing a court battle for custody of three of their children, following the revelation of an affair with Farrow's adopted daughter, Soon-Yi (whom he later married).

Allenby, Edmund Henry Hynman Allenby, 1st Viscount (1861–1936) British soldier, born in Brackenhurst, Nottinghamshire. He conducted a masterly campaign against the Turks in Palestine and Syria, capturing Jerusalem (1917), Damascus and Aleppo (1918), and securing an armistice. >> World War 1

Allende (Gossens), Salvador [**ay**enday] (1908–73) Chilean statesman and president (1970–3), born in Valparaíso. A medical doctor who helped found the Chilean Socialist Party (1933), he was elected in 1970 as leader of the left-wing Unidad Popular coalition. His government was overthrown by the armed forces in 1973, and he died in the presidential palace. >> socialism

allergy A reaction of the body or tissue to contact with certain foreign substances. These substances are called **allergens**, and in sensitive individuals they react with proteins (*antibodies*) produced within the body by cells of the immune system. Many substances found in nature (eg pollen) are actual or potential allergens, capable of inducing illnesses such as asthma and dermatitis. >> anaphylaxis; desensitization; food allergy / sensitivity

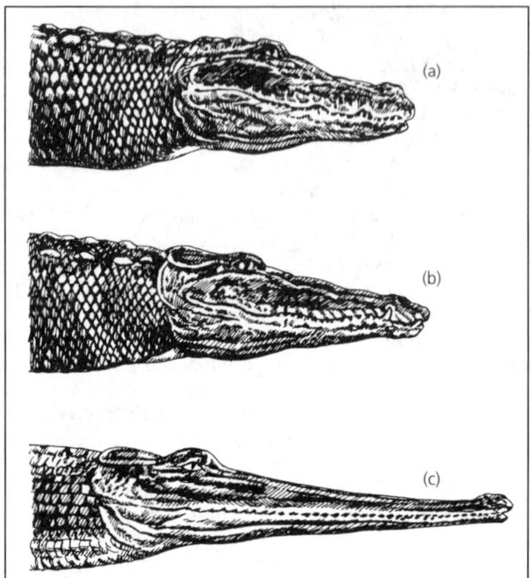

Alligator (a); crocodile (b); gharial (c)

All Fools' Day >> **April Fool**

Alliance >> **Liberal Party** (UK); **Social Democratic Party**

alligator A crocodile-like reptile of family Alligatoridae; short broad snout; fourth tooth from the front on each side of the lower jaw is hidden when the jaws are closed (unlike the crocodile); two species: **American alligator** (*Alligator mississippiensis*) from SE USA, and the rare **Chinese alligator** (*Alligator chinensis*). >> caiman; crocodile; gharial; reptile

allium A member of a large genus of perennials, all with a strong, distinctive onion smell, native to the N hemisphere; most form bulbs with a brown papery skin; leaves usually tubular; flowers have bell- or star-shaped segments in dense clusters. (Genus: *Allium*, 450 species. Family: Liliaceae.) >> chive; garlic; leek; onion; ransoms; shallot

allophone >> **phoneme**

Allosaurus [**al**osawrus] A large flesh-eating dinosaur reaching 11 m/36 ft in length and two tonnes in weight; bipedal, powerful hindlimbs, and short forelimbs, both with three claws; muscular tail assisted in balancing; teeth with serrated edges; known from the Upper Jurassic period of North America. (Order: Saurischia.) >> dinosaur [i]; Jurassic period; Saurischia

alloy A blend of a metal with one or more other metals or with a non-metallic substance. Alloys known since ancient times include bronze (copper with tin), brass (copper with zinc), and pewter (lead with tin). Modern alloys include stainless steels (iron/chromium/nickel), and high temperature-resistant alloys for use in gas turbines (containing titanium). >> amalgam

All Saints' Day A Christian festival commemorating all the Church's saints collectively; held on 1 November in the Roman Catholic and Anglican Churches, and on the first Sunday after Pentecost in the Eastern Churches; formerly known as **All Hallows**. >> Hallowe'en

All Souls' Day In the Roman Catholic Church, the day (2 Nov) set apart as a day of prayer for souls in purgatory; in the Eastern Orthodox Church celebrated about two months before Easter. >> purgatory

allspice An evergreen tree (*Pimenta dioica*) native to tropical America and the West Indies; leaves elliptical; flowers creamy; fruit small, round; also known as **pimento** or **Jamaican pepper**. Spice made from its dried, unripe fruits has a flavour like that of cinnamon, cloves, and nutmeg combined, hence the name. (Family: Myrtaceae.) >> spice

Allston, Washington [**awl**ston] (1779–1843) Artist and writer, born in Waccamaw, SC. The earliest US Romantic painter, he graduated at Harvard, then studied at the Royal Academy in London before going on to Paris and Rome. He eventually settled at Cambridgeport, MA, in 1830. He painted large canvases, particularly of religious scenes, such as 'Belshazzar's Feast', 'The Flood', and 'Elijah in the Desert'. >> Romanticism (art)

Alma-Ata >> **Almaty**

Almagro, Diego de [**al**magroh] (c.1475–1538) Conquistador and collaborator with Pizarro, born in Spain. He briefly invaded Chile in 1536. Bitter rivalry then developed between Almagro and Pizarro, who defeated him in a desperate engagement near Cuzco. Soon after, Almagro was executed. >> Pizarro, Francisco

Almaty [al**ma**tee] formerly **Alma-Ata** (to 1995), **Vernyi** (to 1921) 43°15N 76°57E, pop (1995e) 1 198 000. Former capital city of Kazakhstan (to 1997, now Astana); established in 1854 as a military fortress and trading centre; destroyed by earthquake, 1887; airport; railway; university (1934); Academy of Sciences (1968); noted tourist and athletic centre. >> Kazakhstan [i]

Almohads [**al**muhhadz] >> **Berber**

almond A small deciduous, sometimes spiny tree (*Prunus dulcis*) growing to 8 m/26 ft, native to Asia; leaves narrowly oval, toothed; flowers pink fading to white; fruit greyish, velvety, 3·5–6 cm/1½–2½ in, oval; thin, leathery flesh surrounding pitted stone. The **sweet almond** (variety *dulcis*) is the source of edible almond nuts; **bitter almond** (variety *amara*) is inedible, but provides oil of bitter almonds used in industry. (Family: Rosaceae.) >> prunus

Almoravids [almo**ra**vidz] >> **Berber**

aloe [**al**oh] A member of a large genus of shrub- or tree-like evergreens, native to Africa, especially S Africa, and Arabia; leaves sword-shaped, tough, fleshy, often waxy and toothed, in rosettes at tips of stems; flowers tubular, yellow to red; often planted for ornament. The drug **bitter aloes** is obtained from the sap. (Genus: *Aloe*, 275 species. Family: Liliaceae.)

Alonso, Dámaso [a**lon**soh] (1898–1990) Poet and philologist, born in Madrid. *Hijos de la ira* (1944, Children of Wrath) is his best-known poetic work.

alopecia [alo**pee**sha] Hair loss resulting from the failure of hair formation by the hair follicles. It may be inherited, or stem from an underlying general illness or toxin (eg a drug) which disturbs the follicular activity. >> baldness

Aloysius, St >> **Gonzaga, Luigi**

alpaca [al**pa**ka] A domesticated member of the camel family, from Peru and Bolivia (*Lama pacos*); resembles a long-haired llama, but with a shorter face, neck, and legs; kept mainly for wool. >> Camelidae; llama

Alpe Adria [**al**pay **ad**ria] A working association of 11 neighbouring regions in Austria, Germany, Italy, and Yugoslavia, linked by cultural and economic interests; established in 1978.

alphabet The most economical and versatile form of writing system yet devised, because it breaks words down into their phonic components, assigning letters or combinations of letters to represent speech sounds. The symbols of an alphabetic writing system are not tied to the meanings of the words they represent, and the need for several thousand pictograms, for instance, is avoided. Most alphabets contain less than 30 symbols. However, they differ substantially in the regularity with which they correspond to the sound system. The model for all Western alphabets

The Development of the Early Alphabet

Phoenician	Old Hebrew	Early Greek	Classical Greek	Etruscan	Early Latin	Modern Roman
			Α			Aa
			Β			Bb
			Γ			Cc
			Δ			Dd
			Ε			Ee
			Φ			Ff
						Gg
			Η			Hh
			Ι			Ii
						Jj
			Κ			Kk
			Λ			Ll
			Μ			Mm
			Ν			Nn
			Ο			Oo
			Π			Pp
						Qq
			Ρ			Rr
			Σ			Ss
			Τ			Tt
			Υ			Uu
						Vv
						Ww
			Ξ			Xx
						Yy
			Ζ			Zz

was the Etruscan (c.800 BC), itself based on the Greek alphabet, which had modified the Phoenician consonantal alphabet by adding vowel letters to it. >> graphology; i.t.a.; pictography [i]; Semitic alphabets; vowel; writing systems

Alpha Centauri [**al**fa sen**taw**ree] >> **Centaurus**

alpha decay A naturally occurring radioactive decay process in which the atomic nucleus breaks up into a lighter nucleus and an alpha particle, which is ejected. It is governed by strong nuclear force. >> alpha particle; nucleus (physics); radioactivity

alpha particle A particle emitted in alpha decay. It is composed of two neutrons plus two protons, the same as the helium nucleus, and identified as such by British physicist Ernest Rutherford in 1906; charge +2. >> alpha decay; neutron; proton; Rutherford, Ernest

Alpher, Ralph (Asher) (1921–) Physicist, born in Washington, DC. In 1948 with Hans Bethe and George Gamow he devised a theory of the processes emitting energy in the early life of the universe (the 'alpha, beta, gamma' theory). This has become part of the 'big bang' model of the universe. >> Bethe; 'big bang'; Gamow

alphorn A musical instrument found in rural communities, particularly in the Swiss Alps. Most alphorns are about 1·8 m/6 ft long, made of wood, and can sound the first five or six harmonics; but examples up to twice that length are not uncommon. >> aerophone

Alps Principal mountain range of Europe, covering 259 000 sq km/100 000 sq mi in Switzerland, France, Germany, Austria, Liechtenstein, Italy, and Yugoslavia; a series of parallel chains over 1000 km/600 mi SW–NE; originally formed by collision of African and European tectonic plates; source of many great European rivers, notably the Rhine, Po, and Rhône; Mont Blanc 4807 m/15 771 ft, highest peak in the range; notable passes include the St Bernard (Little and Greater), Simplon, St Gotthard, and Brenner; major tourist region for mountaineering and skiing. >> Brenner / Saint Bernard's / Saint Gotthard / Simplon Passes; Dolomites

Alsace [al**sas**], Ger **Elsass**, Lat **Alsatia** pop (1995e) 1 674 000; area 8280 sq km/3196 sq mi. Region of NE France; traditional scene of Franco-German conflict; formerly part of Lorraine before becoming part of German Empire; Treaty of Westphalia (1648) returned most of Alsace to France; ceded to Germany, 1871; returned to France, 1919; occupied by Germany in World War 2; chief towns, Strasbourg, Mulhouse, Colmar; fertile and industrially productive region. >> France [i]

alsatian >> **German shepherd**

alsike [**al**siyk] A species of clover (*Trifolium hybridum*), probably native to Europe, grown as a fodder crop and now occurring in many temperate countries; a variable perennial growing to 60 cm/2 ft; leaves with three-toothed leaflets; pea-flowers white or pink. (Family: Leguminosae.) >> clover

Altaic [al**tay**ik] A hypothesized family of languages extending from the Balkan peninsula to the NE of Asia; not accepted as a genetic family by many linguists. About 40 languages fall into three groups: Turkic (of which Turkish is the main member), Mongolian, and Manchu-Tungus. >> family of languages

Altai Mountains [**ahl**tiy], Chin **Altai Shan** Major mountain system of C Asia, extending from Russia SE along the border between NW China and Mongolia, into Mongolia itself; highest point, Mt Belukha (4506 m/14 783 ft); major mineral reserves. >> China [i]

Altair [al**tair**] >> **Aquila**

Altamira [alta**mee**ra] 43°18N 4°08E. A palaeolithic limestone cave of c.13 500 BC on the N Spanish coast near Santander, celebrated for its vivid ceiling paintings of game animals; a world heritage site. >> Magdalenian; Three Age System

altarpiece In a Christian church, a carved or painted screen placed above the altar facing the congregation; known as an *ancona* (Ital), *retable* (Fr), or *reredos* (Eng). The earliest examples appeared in the 10th–11th-c. An altarpiece consisting of two panels is called a *diptych*; three panels make a *triptych*. >> pala

altazimuth [al**taz**imuhth] A type of telescope in which the principal axis can be moved independently in altitude (swinging on a horizontal axis) and azimuth (swinging on a vertical axis). >> telescope [i]

Altdorfer, Albrecht [**alt**daw(r)fer] (c.1480–1538) Painter, engraver, and architect, born in Regensburg, Germany. A leading member of the Danube School of German painting, his major works are biblical and historical subjects set against atmospheric landscape backgrounds. >> Danube School

alternating current (AC) An electrical current whose direction of flow reverses periodically; the alternative is **direct current (DC)**, where the flow is in a single direction only. Household current is AC, with frequencies varying to some extent between countries, eg 50 Hz (UK), 60 Hz (USA). >> current (electricity)

alternative energy Sources of energy which do not rely on the burning of fossil fuels (eg coal, gas, oil) or nuclear power to provide energy. With the controversial nature of nuclear power, and the recognition that fossil fuels are a non-renewable resource and contribute significantly to pollution, there is considerable interest in alternative sources, such as solar, geothermal, hydroelectric, tidal, and wind power. >> biogas; energy; fossil fuel; hydroelectric power; nuclear reactor [i]; renewable resources; solar power

alternative fuel A fuel other than petrol for powering motor vehicles. These fuels include ethanol, methanol, and **biofuels** derived from organic material, such as biodiesel, obtained from various kinds of vegetable oil, and rape methyl esters (RME) from rape-oil. Such fuels are said to be environmentally friendly, but debate continues over whether they are as pollution-free as is claimed, and whether the land devoted to such crops might not be put to better use. The term often includes modifications which have been made to petrol to reduce harmful levels of lead emissions – the unleaded and superunleaded petrols (the latter giving better performance). Research continues into ways of modifying vehicle design to take advantage of such fuels (**alternative fuel vehicles**). >> ethanol; methanol; petrol; zero-emission vehicle

alternative medicine Approaches to the treatment of illness using procedures other than those recommended by orthodox medical science. There are many different approaches, and a recent publication on alternative medicine lists over 600 entries. Despite their current popularity, hardly any of the therapeutic methods used have been rigorously assessed, using the standard scientific techniques of critical assessment and refutation, or of comparison with the natural course of the ailment or with other remedies claimed to influence the ailment. At present, most of the claims for the success of alternative remedies remain anecdotal. >> acupuncture; aromatherapy; Bach flower remedies; chiropractic; healing; herbalism; holistic medicine; homeopathy; osteopathy; reflexology

Althusser, Louis [alt-hüser] (1918–90) Political philosopher, born in Algiers. He wrote influential works on the interpretation of Marxist theory. >> Marxism

Altichiero [alti**kyay**roh] (c.1330–c.1395) Painter and possible founder of the Veronese School, born near Verona, Italy. He worked in Verona, then moved to Padua, where his frescoes are in the Basilica of San Antonio (painted 1372–9) and in the Oratory of San Giorgio (1377–84). >> Venetian School

altimeter A device carried by an aircraft to measure its height above the ground. The usual type operates by sending out a radio signal, and measuring the time taken by the signal to return, since the speed at which the radio signal travels is known. >> radio waves

Altiplano [alti**plah**noh] The arid plateau of W Bolivia and S Peru between the W and E cordilleras; elevation 3000–5000 m/9800–16 400 ft. The rivers and streams of the plateau drain into L Titicaca (Bolivia/Peru) and L Poopo (Bolivia). >> Bolivia [i]; Peru [i]

altocumulus clouds Middle-level clouds of the cumulus family at altitudes of c.2000–7000 m/6500–23 000 ft. They are white and/or grey in colour, and usually indicate fine weather. Cloud symbol: Ac. >> cloud [i]; cumulus clouds

altostratus clouds Middle-level clouds of the stratus family, similar to stratus clouds but less dense and occurring at higher elevations, typically c.2000–7000 m/6500–23 000 ft. They are greyish in colour with a sheet-like appearance, and give a warning of warm, rainy weather associated with the passage of a warm front. Cloud symbol: As. >> cloud [i]; stratus clouds

alum Usually $KAl(SO_4)_2.12H_2O$. Hydrated potassium aluminium sulphate, **common alum**. Other alums have Al substituted by Fe (**iron alum**) or Cr (**chrome alum**). >> aluminium; potassium

alumina [aloo**mina**] Al_2O_3. Aluminium (III) oxide, the principal ingredient of bauxite. It occurs in various forms, including emery or corundum (used as abrasives), and the coloured forms, rubies and sapphires. >> bauxite; gemstones

aluminium [alyoo**min**yuhm] or **aluminum** [**aloo**minuhm] Al, element 13, melting point 660°C. A silvery metal, the third most abundant element in the Earth's crust, it forms a tough oxide coating and is then passive to further oxidation; with its relatively low density, 2·7 g/cm^3, this makes it a valuable structural metal. >> bauxite; chemical elements; cryolite

Alva or **Alba, Ferdinand Alvarez de Toledo, duque d'**(Duke of) (1507–82) Spanish general and statesman, born in Piedratita, Spain. Sent to quell the Revolt of the Netherlands (1567), his Council of Blood promoted a ruthless campaign of repression. Later, Holland and Zeeland renewed their efforts against him, and his fleet was destroyed. >> Blood, Council of; Revolt of the Netherlands

Alvarez Quintero [**al**vareth keen**tay**roh] Playwrights and brothers: **Serafín Alvarez Quintero** (1871–1938) and **Joaquín Alvarez Quintero** (1873–1944), born in Utrera, Spain. They were the joint authors of well over 100 modern Spanish plays, all displaying a characteristic gaiety and sentiment.

alveoli >> **lungs**

Alvey programme A UK-based collaborative research programme involving industry, government, and academic institutions which was intended to develop information technology and, in particular, fifth generation computers. It was established in 1982 through a working party chaired by John Alvey (1925–). >> computer generations; information technology

alyssum [**al**isuhm] An annual to perennial, mat-forming or bushy but low-growing, native to Europe and Asia; leaves narrow; flowers cross-shaped, white, blue, or yellow. **Golden alyssum**, a grey-leaved, yellow-flowered perennial, is often grown in gardens. (Genus: *Alyssum*, 150 species. Family: Cruciferae.) >> sweet alyssum

Alzheimer's disease [**alts**hiymer] A common form of generalized cerebral atrophy which results in slowly progressive dementia affecting all aspects of brain function. The disease was first described in 1906 by a German neurologist, Alois Alzheimer (1864–1915). >> dementia

Amado, Jorge [a**mah**doo] (1912–) Novelist, born in Ferradas, Brazil. Brought up on a cacao plantation in NE Brazil, his early writing focused on the poor social conditions of the plantation workers. Imprisoned for his political beliefs in 1935, he also spent several periods in exile. His novels include *Terras do sem-Fin* (1944, The Violent Land) and *Tenda dos milagres* (1969, Tent of Miracles).

Amal [**am**al] The first political organization of Lebanon's Shiite Muslims, the country's largest yet economically most disadvantaged community. Founded in the mid-1970s by the Imam Musa al-Sadr, the party has been led since al-Sadr's 1978 disappearance in Libya by the lawyer Nabih Berri (1939–). >> Lebanon [i]; Shiites

amalgam An alloy of mercury with some other metal(s), known since classical times. Copper, zinc, and tin amalgams are used in dentistry. >> alloy; mercury

Amalthea [amal**thee**a] The fifth natural satellite of Jupiter, discovered in 1892; distance from the planet 181 000 km/112 000 mi; diameter 270 km/168 mi. >> Jupiter (astronomy); RR964

Amanita >> **fly agaric**

amaranth [**am**aranth] An annual or perennial herb, native to tropical and temperate regions; flowers usually small and forming dense inflorescences; segments in whorls of three or five, often brightly coloured; also known as **pigweed**. Some Asian species yield a cereal substitute. (Genus: *Amaranthus*, 60 species. Family: Amaranthaceae.) >> herb

amaryllis [ama**ril**is] A large bulb, native to tropical America (Genus: *Hippeastrum*, 75 species); flowers flaring, trumpet-shaped, up to 15 cm/6 in long, in a range of bright colours on a hollow stalk. (Family: Amaryllidaceae.) >> belladonna lily

Amaterasu [amate**ra**su] The principal deity in the Shinto religion of Japan. She is both the Sun-goddess who rules all the gods and the mother-goddess who ensures fertility. >> Shinto

Amazon, River, Port **Rio Amazonas** River in N South America, the largest in the world by volume, and the second longest; flows generally W–E across Brazil, entering the Atlantic in a wide delta; drains a basin c.7 million sq km/2¾ million sq mi; more than 1100 tributaries; ocean steamers as far as Iquitos, 3680 km/2287 mi from the Atlantic; length following the Ucayali and Apurímac headwaters to the mouth via the Canal do Norte, 6449 km/4007 mi; discovered by Europeans, 1500; first descended 1541, ascended 1637; opened to world shipping 1866; free navigation guaranteed by Colombia–Brazil treaty, 1929. >> Brazil [i]; Manaus

Amazons [**am**aznz] In Greek mythology, a nation of women soldiers, located by Herodotos in Scythia (Russia). Strong and athletic, they were said to mutilate the right breast in order to use the bow. >> Herodotos

ambassador The highest ranking diplomat resident abroad, who officially represents his or her country in relations with foreign governments. Ambassadors are to be distinguished from **consuls**, whose chief functions are to protect citizens abroad, and to protect the commercial interests of these citizens. >> diplomatic service; High Commissioner

Ambler, Eric (1909–98) Novelist, born in London. He specialized in the writing of spy thrillers, such as *Epitaph for a Spy* (1938) and *The Mask of Dimitrios* (1939).

Ambrose, St (c.339–97) Roman clergyman and doctor of the Church, born in Trier, Germany. He is especially remembered for his preaching, his literary works and hymns, and the Ambrosian ritual and chant. Feast day 7 December.

ameba >> **amoeba**

Amenhotep IV >> **Akhenaton**

amenorrhoea / amenorrhea [amenor**ree**a] The absence of normal menstruation. It arises when the cyclical hormonal control (by the front pituitary gland and ovaries) of normal menstruation is disturbed by physical or psychological factors. >> Cushing's disease; menstruation

American Civil Liberties Union A US pressure group concerned to promote civil rights. It is particularly concerned with freedom of speech and maintaining an open society. >> civil rights

American Civil War (1861–5) A conflict in the USA which resolved two great issues: the nature of the Federal Union and the relative power of the states and the central government; and the existence of black slavery. The war began in the early months of Lincoln's presidency. Although Lincoln was hostile to slavery, he did not believe that he could interfere where it existed. But to Southerners, he and the Republican Party were intolerable, and 11 Southern states withdrew from the Union, establishing the Confederate States of America. War broke out (12 Apr 1861) when Southern batteries opened fire on a Union emplacement in the harbour of Charleston, SC. At first Lincoln defined the issue as the preservation of the Union, without any reference to slavery. But he broadened the war aims (1 Jan 1863), proclaiming the emancipation without compensation of all slaves in areas then under arms against the government. The winning strategy began in 1863, when Ulysses S Grant won control of the whole Mississippi Valley, isolating the W Confederate States from the rest. Meanwhile Robert E Lee was advancing into Pennsylvania, largely in the hope of winning foreign recognition for the Confederacy. His defeat at Gettysburg ended that possibility. By the autumn, the Chattanooga campaign put Northern troops in a position to bisect the Confederacy E to W, an act accomplished in late 1864 by General Sherman's march through Georgia to the sea. Grant, now the overall Northern commander, adopted a strategy of relentless pressure on Lee's forces, regardless of his own losses. The end came in the spring of 1865, as Sherman marched N through the Carolinas while Grant continued his costly siege of Richmond. Lee finally abandoned the Confederate capital (2 Apr). His capitulation at Appomattox Court House left only scattered Southern forces in the field, and the last surrender took place on 26 May. >> Chattanooga Campaign; Confederate States of America; Copperhead; Gettysburg Address; Peninsular Campaign; Reconstruction; Vicksburg; Antietam / Bull Run / Cold Harbor / Fredericksburg / Gettysburg / Seven Days' Battles; Grant, Ulysses S; Lee, Robert E; Lincoln, Abraham; Sherman, William Tecumseh

American eagle >> **bald eagle**

American Federation of Labor – Congress of Industrial Organizations (AFL/CIO) A US federation of trade unions, formed in 1955 from the merger of the AFL (mainly craft unions, founded in 1886) with the CIO (mainly industrial workers' unions, founded in 1935). It has c.14·5 million members. >> Gompers; Teamsters' Union; Trades Union Congress

American football >> **football 2** [i]

American Indians The original inhabitants of the American continent, who arrived during the last glacial period (14–40 000 years ago) from Asia, crossing from Siberia over the Bering Strait, perhaps in three waves. They settled in North America, extending into Middle America (Mesoamerica) more than 10 000 years ago, and sometime after this into South America. From the 16th-c, with the coming of European settlers, the lives of most Indians were severely disrupted. Conflict over land resulted in numerous bloody clashes, and many died from diseases introduced by Europeans. In North America, the population was very much reduced, from an estimated 1·5 million at its height, and by the 1880s most Indians had been confined to reservations. In the past generation there has been increasing political activity on the part of Indians to reclaim land rights. In Middle America, the Indian population at its height was much larger than in North America – some suggest as many as 20 million. Today most Middle Americans live in small farming and trading village communities, are Roman Catholic and Spanish-speaking, and show a high rate of admixture with the descendants of the Spanish settlers. In South America, in the century before the Spanish invasion of the region, the Inca state brought together much of the Andean area in the New World's largest empire. Following the European conquest in the 16th-c, many groups became extinct, while others were absorbed into colonial society; but in a few remote parts, there are groups which have preserved their culture virtually intact. >> Algonkin; Apache; Araucanians; Athabascan; Aztecs; Blackfoot; Cherokee; Cheyenne; Chimu; Chinook; Cree; Creek; Crow; Guaraní; Flathead; Fox; Haida; Hopi; Huron; Incas; Iroquois; Kwakiutl; Mayas; Mohawk; Navajo; Nootka; Northwest Coast Indians; Ojibwa; Olmecs; Omaha; Oneida; Paiute; Salish; Seminole; Seneca; Shawnee; Shoshoni; Sioux; Southwest Indians; Tlingit; Zapotecs; Zuni

American Legion In the USA, an association for former members of the armed forces (veterans), the largest in the world. Incorporated in 1919, its aims are to rehabilitate veterans, promote child welfare, ensure a strong national defence, and encourage patriotism. >> Royal British Legion

American Muslim Mission >> **Black Muslims**

American ostrich >> **rhea**

American Revolution (1765–88) The movement that destroyed the first British Empire, establishing the United States and, indirectly, Canada; a much larger event than the War of Independence (1775–83). It can be divided into three main phases. In the first (1764–5), relations worsened between the colonies and Britain, primarily over the issue of Parliament's right to tax the colonies without reference to the colonial assemblies. Major events included the Stamp Act crisis (1765–6), resistance to the Townshend Acts (1767–70), the Boston Massacre (1770), the burning of the customs cruiser *Gaspée* (1772), and the Boston Tea Party (1773). This phase culminated in Parliament's passage of the Intolerable Acts (1774) to punish Massachusetts for the Tea Party, and the calling of the First Continental Congress (1774). The second phase brought war and independence. Fighting began at Lexington and Concord, MA (Apr 1775), and lasted until the surrender of Lord Cornwallis to Washington at Yorktown, VA, in 1781. Military conflict centred on Boston until the British withdrew (Mar 1776). From August 1776 until the beginning of 1780, the main theatre was the states of New York, New Jersey, and Pennsylvania. The American victory at Saratoga convinced the French to enter the war officially, bringing badly-needed material support, troops, monetary credit, and a fleet. After 1780, fighting shifted southward, when Sir Henry Clinton led an invasion of S Carolina. Cornwallis, his successor, led his army gradually N until Washington and the French Admiral de Grasse trapped him on the Yorktown peninsula. The defeat resulted in the fall of Lord North, the British prime minister who had prosecuted the war. Peace was signed at Paris two years later. The third phase led to the creation of the modern United States. This process began with the writing of the first state constitutions, immediately after the Declaration of Independence (Jul 1776). At the same time, the Articles of Confederation were prepared by the Continental Congress as a basis for interstate relations, but the document was not adopted until 1781. Its weaknesses, such as an inability to enforce Congressional decisions, soon became apparent. These, together with dissatisfaction about developments in the states, led to the Federalist movement. Initially, this sought merely to reform the Articles, but its great achievement, in 1787 and 1788, was to abolish that document completely, and establish the present US Constitution. At that point, the Revolution was effectively over. >> Annapolis Convention; Boston Massacre; Constitutional Convention; Green Mountain Boys; Minutemen; Stamp Act; Thirteen Colonies; Townshend Acts; Valley Forge; Yorktown Campaign; Brandywine / Bunker Hill / Camden / Charleston / Cowpens / Monmouth / Saratoga, Battle of

American Samoa [sa**moh**a], formerly also **Loanda**, Portuguese **São Paulo de Loanda** pop (1995e) 56 400; area 197 sq km/76 sq mi. Territory of the USA, in the CS Pacific Ocean, some 3500 km/2175 mi N of New Zealand; five principal volcanic islands and two coral atolls; capital, Fagatogo; timezone GMT −11; people largely of Polynesian origin; main religion, Christianity; official language, English; main island Tutuila (109 sq km/ 42 sq mi); hilly, with large areas covered by thick bush and forest; Tutuila rises to 653 m/2142 ft; tropical maritime climate, with small annual range of temperature and plentiful rainfall (annual average, 5000 mm/200 in); US acquired rights to American Samoa in 1899, and the islands were ceded by their chiefs, 1900–25; now an unincorporated territory of the USA; bicameral legislature established in 1948 comprising the Senate and the House of Representatives; principal crops are taro, breadfruit, yams, bananas, coconuts. >> United States of America [i]

American Sign Language (ASL) A sign language widely used by the deaf in the USA; also known as **Ameslan**. The system contains over 4000 signs, and is used by over half a million deaf people. >> sign language

American Society for the Prevention of Cruelty to Animals >> **RSPCA**

American whitewood >> **tulip tree** [i]

America's Cup Yachting's most famous race, held approximately every 4 years. The trophy was originally called the One Hundred Guinea Cup, and was donated by the Royal Yacht Squadron for a race around the Isle of Wight in 1851. It was renamed when the US schooner *America* won the race six years later. Between 1870 and 1983 it remained in US ownership until the successful challenge of *Australia II*. The USA won it back in 1987. >> sailing

Ameslan >> **American Sign Language**

amethyst A violet-to-purple form of quartz. It is prized as a precious stone. >> quartz

Amhara A Semitic-speaking people of the Ethiopian C highlands who, with the Tigray, dominate the country. *Amharic* is the official language of Ethiopia. Population c.9 million. >> Ethiopia [i]; Semitic languages; Tigray

amicable numbers Two numbers such that each is the sum of all the divisors of the other. Thus 284 and 220 are amicable, for the divisors of 284 are 1, 2, 4, 71, 142, whose sum is 220, and the divisors of 220 are 1, 2, 4, 5, 10, 11, 20, 22, 44, 55, 110, whose sum is 284. Note that 1 is counted as a divisor. Pythagoras is credited with the discovery of these numbers. >> Pythagoras

Amidah [a**mee**da] (Heb 'standing') The principal component of the daily prayers of Talmudic Judaism, recited while standing, and said silently except when in a congregational service. It consists of 19 benedictions. >> Judaism; Shema

amides [**ay**miydz, **a**midz] **1** Inorganic salts of ammonia, eg sodium amide ($NaNH_2$), strongly basic and hydrolysed by water to NH_3 and OH^-. > ammonia; hydrolysis **2** Organic compounds containing the function $-CO.NR_2$, also called **alkanamides**, derived from carboxylic acids. **Polyamides** include proteins and some artificial polymers, such as nylon. >> carboxylic acids; polyamides

Amiens [amyĩ], ancient **Samarobriva** 49°54N 2°16E, pop (1995e) 136 000. Agricultural market town in N France, on left bank of R Somme; railway; university (1964); bishopric; war-time cemeteries at Arras to the E; Gothic cathedral (13th-c), a world heritage site. >> France [i]

Amies, Sir (Edwin) Hardy [**ay**meez] (1909–) Couturier, and dressmaker by appointment to Queen Elizabeth II. He became a managing designer in London in 1934, where he made his name especially with his tailored suits for women. He founded his own fashion house in 1946, and started designing for men in 1959.

amines [**ay**meenz, **a**meenz] Organic compounds derived from ammonia by the substitution of the hydrogen atoms by one, two, or three alkyl groups. Their solutions, when partially neutralized by strong acids, have pH values of about 9. >> alkyl; ammonia; pH

Amin (Dada), Idi [a**meen**] (c.1925–) President of Uganda (1971–9), born in Koboko of a peasant family. He staged a coup deposing Obote in 1971, dissolved parliament, and was proclaimed president by the army. Throughout his presidency there were continual reports of widespread atrocities. Deposed by exiled Ugandans with the help of the Tanzanian army in 1979, he fled to Libya, and eventually settled in Saudi Arabia. >> Uganda ℹ

amino acids [a**mee**noh, a**miy**noh] Aminoalkanoic acids with the general formula R–CH(NH_2)COOH. About 24 are involved in protein synthesis; 10 of these cannot be made by the human body, and thus form an essential component of the diet (**essential amino acids**). >> protein

aminobenzene >> **aniline**

aminoethanoic acid >> **glycine**

Amis, Sir Kingsley [**ay**mis] (1922–95) Novelist and poet, born in London. He achieved a reputation by his first novel, *Lucky Jim* (1954), which added a new comic hero to English fiction. Later works on wider themes include *Jake's Thing* (1978), *The Old Devils* (1986, Booker), and *The Russian Girl* (1992). He was married (1965–83) to the novelist **Elizabeth Jane Howard** (1923–). >> Amis, Martin; Angry Young Men

Amis, Martin (Louis) [**ay**mis] (1949–) Novelist and journalist, the son of Kingsley Amis. His works include the novels *The Rachel Papers* (1973), *Other People* (1981), *Time's Arrow* (1991), *The Information* (1995), and a collection of short stories, *Einstein's Monsters* (1986). >> Amis, Kingsley

Amman [a**man**] 31°57N 35°52E, pop (1995e) 1 736 000. Industrial and commercial capital city of Jordan; capital of the Ammonite kingdom in Biblical times; capital of Transjordan, 1923; many refugees after the Arab–Israeli Wars; airport; railway; university (1962); noted for its locally-quarried coloured marble. >> Arab-Israeli Wars; Jordan ℹ

ammonia NH_3, boiling point −33°C. A colourless gas with a pungent odour. It is a weak base; aqueous solutions partially neutralized with strong acid have a pH c.9·5. An important industrial chemical, it is mainly prepared by the Haber process. >> amides 1; amines; ammonium; pH

ammonia–soda process >> **Solvay process**

ammonite An extinct, nautilus-like mollusc; found extensively as fossil shells from the Devonian to the Upper Cretaceous periods. (Class: Cephalopoda. Subclass: Ammonoidea.) >> Cretaceous / Devonian period; mollusc; nautilus

ammonium NH_4^+. A cation formed by the reaction of ammonia with acid. It is found in many salts, particularly the chloride (*sal ammoniac*) and the carbonate (*sal volatile*). >> acid; ammonia; cation

amnesia Memory disability, often associated with brain damage or a traumatic event. **Retrograde amnesia** is the inability to remember material learned before the precipitating events. **Anterograde amnesia** is difficulty in learning new material.

Amnesty International A human rights organization founded in London in 1961 largely by the efforts of Peter Benenson, a Catholic lawyer. Its fundamental concern is to seek the immediate and unconditional release of prisoners of conscience, as long as they have not advocated violence. It also campaigns against torture and the death penalty, and produces independent reports on abuses of human rights. >> human rights

amniocentesis [amniohsen**tee**sis] A procedure in pregnancy which involves the withdrawal of amniotic fluid from the uterus by the insertion of a needle through the abdominal wall and the uterus. Amniotic fluid is in close contact with the fetus, and abnormalities in its development reflect many fetal abnormalities. The procedure can also reveal the sex of the fetus. >> chorionic villus sampling; pregnancy ℹ; uterus ℹ

amoeba / ameba [a**mee**ba] A naked, single-celled protozoan which moves by protoplasmic flow, changing its shape by the formation of irregular lobes (*pseudopodia*); c.0·6 mm/0·025 in across; reproduces mainly by splitting in two (*binary fission*). (Phylum: Sarcomastigophora. Class: Rhizopoda.) >> protoplasm; Protozoa

Amos, Book of One of the twelve so-called 'minor' prophetic writings in the Hebrew Bible/Old Testament; attributed to the prophet Amos, who was active in the N kingdom of Israel in the mid-8th-c BC. >> Old Testament; prophet

Amoy >> **Xiamen**

amp >> **ampere**

Ampère, André Marie [ãpair] (1775–1836) Mathematician and physicist, born in Lyon, France. The first to devise techniques for measuring electricity, his name was given to the unit of electrical current. >> ampere; electricity

ampere [**am**pair] The base SI unit of current; symbol *A*, often called **amp**. It is defined as the constant current which, if maintained in two straight parallel conductors of infinite length, of negligible cross-section, and placed 1 metre apart in vacuum, would produce a force equal to 2×10^{-7} N/m. >> Ampère; current (electricity); units (scientific)

amphetamine A powerful stimulant of the central nervous system which causes wakefulness and alertness, elevates mood, increases self-confidence, loquaciousness, and the performance of simple mental tasks, and improves physical performance. Its effects are followed by mental depression and fatigue. Prolonged use may result in paranoia or clinical psychosis. As a drug of abuse it is called **speed**; it is illegally manufactured as a powder which can be sniffed ('snorted') or injected. Amphetamine sulphate was formerly available medically under the trade name **Benzedrine**. It is now available only as dexamphetamine sulphate, an isomer, under the proprietary name **Dexedrine**. >> drug addiction; narcolepsy; psychosis; stimulants

amphibian A vertebrate animal of class Amphibia (c.4000 species), exhibiting a wide range of characters and lifestyles; usually four legs and glandular skin, lacking scales or other outgrowths; adults breathe using lungs (and partly through the skin). There are three major groups: salamanders and newts (order: Urodela or Caudata), frogs and toads (order: Anura or Salientia), and the legless caecilians (order: Gymnophiona or Apoda). >> Anura; caecilian; tadpole

amphiboles [**am**fibohlz] A group of hydrous silicate minerals of considerable chemical complexity, widely distributed in igneous and metamorphic rocks. Common varieties include hornblende, actinolite, and tremolite. Fibrous forms belong to the asbestos group of minerals. >> asbestos; horneblende; silicate minerals

amphioxus [amfi**ok**suhs] A primitive chordate; body slender, length up to 70 mm/2¾ in, tapered at both ends; notochord present, extending into head; possesses gill slits and segmented muscle blocks; 23 species found in shallow marine sediments; also known as **lancelet**. (Subphylum: Cephalochordata.) >> Chordata; notochord

amphisbaena [amfis**bee**na] A reptile native to South and Central America, Africa, SW Asia, and SW Europe; body worm-like with encircling rings; no legs or only front legs present; small eyes covered by skin; the only truly burrowing reptile; also known as **worm lizard** or **ringed lizard**. (Order: Squamata. Suborder: Amphisbaenia, 140 species.) >> reptile

amphitheatre / amphitheater An open-air theatre where tiers of seats are situated round a central circular or oval performance space. The Romans developed this form of building for gladiatorial combats, naval exhibitions, and other events. The most famous example is the Colosseum in Rome (AD 72–80).

Amphitrite [amfi**triy**tee] In Greek mythology, a goddess of the sea, married to Poseidon. She is the mother of Triton and other minor deities. >> Poseidon

amphoteric [amfo**te**rik] In chemistry, having two different properties, usually that of being an acid and a base. An example is aluminium hydroxide ($Al(OH)_3$). >> acid; base (chemistry)

amplitude In a wave or oscillation, the maximum displacement from equilibrium or rest position; symbol *A*. It is always a positive number. >> amplitude modulation; wave motion i

amplitude modulation (AM) In wave motion, the altering of wave amplitude in a systematic way, leaving frequency unchanged. In AM radio, an electrical signal is used to modulate the amplitude of the broadcast carrier radio wave. >> amplitude; modulation; radio; wave motion i

Amr ibn al-As [**am**ribnal**as**] (?–664) Arab soldier, who joined the prophet Mohammed c.629 and took part in the conquest of Palestine. In 641 he took Alexandria after a 14 months' siege, and died governor of Egypt. >> Mohammed

Amritsar [am**rit**ser] 31°35N 74°57E, pop (1995e) 768 000. City in Punjab, NW India; centre of the Sikh religion; founded in 1577 by Ram Das around a sacred tank, known as the pool of immortality; the Golden Temple contains the sacred book of the Sikhs, Adi Granth; centre of modern Sikh nationalism; massacre of Indian nationalists, 1919; battle between the Indian Army and Sikh militants inside the Golden Temple, 1984; airport; university (1969). >> Harimandir; India i; Sikhism

Amsterdam [**am**sterdam] 52°23N 4°54E, pop (1995e) 728 000. Major European port and capital city of The Netherlands; chartered, 1300; member of the Hanseatic League, 1369; capital, 1808; airport; railway; two universities (1632, 1880); harbour industry developed after World War 2; major transshipping point. >> Hanseatic League; Netherlands, The i; Rijksmuseum

amu >> **atomic mass unit**

Amudarya, River [amu**da**rya], ancient **Oxus** River forming part of the Turkmenia–Afghanistan border; flows W and NW to enter the Aral Sea in a wide delta; length 1415 km/879 mi; largest river of C Asia. >> Asia

Amun [**a**mun], also spelled **Amon**, **Ammon**, or **Amen** From the time of the Middle Kingdom, the supreme deity in Egyptian religion. Later he was given the qualities of the sun-god Re, hence the usual title **Amun-Re**. The name means 'the hidden one'. >> Re

Amundsen, Roald (Engelbregt Gravning) [**a**mundsen] (1872–1928) Explorer, born in Borge, Norway. His Antarctic expedition of 1910 reached the Pole in December 1911, one month ahead of Scott. >> Poles; Scott, Robert Falcon

Amur River [a**moor**], Chin **Heilong Jiang** River in NE China and Russia, part of the international border; flows generally E then NE to enter the Sea of Okhotsk; length, 4350 km/2700 mi.

amyl [**ay**miyl, **a**mil] $CH_3CH_2CH_2CH_2CH_2$–, IUPAC **pentyl**. A group derived from pentane by removing one hydrogen atom. **Amyl alcohol** is a fraction of fusel oil, boiling point c.130°C. **Amylose** is a low molecular weight fraction of starch. **Amyloid** is a combination of protein and polysaccharides deposited as a fibrous substance in some animal organs affected by certain diseases (e.g. kuru). >> amyl nitrite; fusel oil; IUPAC; kuru; pentane; polysaccharides; starch

amylases [**am**ilayziz] A group of enzymes which speed up the breakdown of starch and glycogen into disaccharides and small polysaccharides. They occur widely in plants and animals. >> disaccharide; enzyme

amyl nitrite ($C_5H_{11}NO_2$) A drug in the form of a volatile liquid, administered by inhalation, which acts very rapidly and very briefly. It has some use in the treatment of angina but is also sold as a sex aid ('poppers'). >> amyl; angina

Anabaptists The collective name given to groups of believers stemming from the more radical elements of the 16th-c Reformation; also known as **Rebaptizers**. They believed in the baptism of believing adults only, refusing to recognize infant baptism. They were associated with Thomas Müntzer and the Zwinglian prophets in Wittenberg (1521); the Swiss brethren in Zürich (1525); and Jan Mattys (d.1534) in Münster (1533–4). They were the forerunners of the Baptists, who are in many respects their spiritual heirs. >> baptism; Baptists; Mennonites; Müntzer; Zwingli

anabolic steroids Drugs with structures similar to the male sex hormones (*androgens*) but with reduced androgenic activity and increased anabolic activity to promote weight and muscle development. They are used clinically to accelerate recovery from protein deficiency, in muscle-wasting disorders, and sometimes in breast cancer. They are used illegally to promote the performance of athletes and racing animals, and were first used by weightlifters and bodybuilders. >> androgens; hormones; steroid

anabolism >> **metabolism**

anaconda A boa from South America (*Eunectes murinus*), the largest snake in the world; may be more than 11 m/36 ft long, weighing over 500 kg/1100 lb; dull colour with large irregular dark spots; inhabits slow-moving water; eats birds, mammals, caimans, turtles; also known as the **green anaconda**. >> boa

Anacreon [a**na**kreeon] (c.570–c.475 BC) Greek lyric poet, born in Teos, modern Turkey. Of the five books of his poems, only a few genuine fragments have been preserved.

anaemia / anemia A reduction in the amount of oxygen-carrying pigment, haemoglobin, in the red cells circulating in the blood. There are many causes, including blood loss, excessively rapid destruction of red blood cells, and failure of their normal maturation in the bone marrow. >> blood

anaerobe >> **aerobe**

anaesthetics / anesthetics, general Drugs which produce a reversible state of unconciousness deep enough to permit surgery. They may be inhaled (eg halothane) or given intravenously (eg thiopentone); intravenous anaesthetics are used for short operations only. The first of these drugs, *nitrous oxide* ('laughing gas') was discovered by Joseph Priestley in 1776, and its use in surgical operations was suggested in 1799 by Humphry Davy. The medical speciality is known as **anaesthesiology**, and the presence of a specialist (an **anaesthetist**) is required during surgical operations. >> chloroform; Davy; ether; nitrous oxide; Priestley, Joseph

anaesthetics / anesthetics, local Drugs which produce a reversible loss of sensation in a localized region of the body by blocking nerve impulses. It is achieved by topical application or by injection at the site of an operation (as in tooth extraction), near a main nerve trunk (eg to allow operations in limbs), or between spinal vertebrae (**epidural anaesthesia**). Examples include procaine, lignocaine (lidocaine), and benzocaine. >> neurone i

analgesics Drugs which relieve pain. **Narcotic analgesics** (eg codeine, morphine, heroin) act by mimicking the natural brain endorphins responsible for the subjective perception of pain. **Non-narcotic analgesics** (eg aspirin, paracetamol) act by blocking the synthesis of prostaglandins. >> aspirin; narcotics; pain; paracetamol; prostaglandins

analog computer, also spelled **analogue** Computers which accept, as inputs, continuous electrical or mechanical variables (such as voltage or the rotation rate of a shaft) and respond immediately to calculate relevant output signals. Many of their former tasks are now done using the much more versatile digital computers. >> digital computer; real-time computing; voltage

analog-to-digital (A/D) conversion, also spelled **analogue** A process of converting analog signals, such as voltage, into a digital form which can be used in a digital computer. It is usually carried out by specialized electronic circuits or discrete integrated circuits called *analog-to-digital (A–D) converters*.

analytic / analytical geometry A method of attacking geometrical problems by referring to a point by its co-ordinates in a system; also known as **Cartesian** or **co-ordinate geometry**. For the plane, the commonest system is of two perpendicular axes, when all points can be identified by a number pair, (x,y). In three-dimensional geometry a number triple is needed (x,y,z). >> Descartes; geometry

Ananda [**anan**da] (5th–6th-c BC) The cousin and favourite pupil of the Buddha. He was instrumental in establishing an order for women disciples. >> Buddhism

Ananke [a**nang**kee] The 12th natural satellite of Jupiter, discovered in 1951; distance from the planet 21 200 000 km/13 174 000 mi; diameter 30 km/19 mi. >> Jupiter (astronomy); RR964

anaphylaxis [anafuh**lak**sis] A type of hypersensitivity reaction which occurs when an individual has been previously sensitized by contact with an antigen. Examples include asthma and hay fever. >> allergy; hay fever

anarchism A generic term for political ideas and movements that reject the state and other forms of authority and coercion in favour of a society based exclusively upon voluntary co-operation between individuals. Anarchists support civil disobedience action against the state, and on occasions political violence. >> syndicalism

Anastasia [ana**stah**zia], in full **Grand Duchess Anastasia Nikolaievna Romanova** (1901–18?) Daughter of the Tsar Nicholas II of Russia, born near St Petersburg. Though she is thought to have died when the Romanov family were executed by the Bolsheviks in Yekaterinburg in 1918, several women later claimed to be Anastasia. >> Romanovs; Russian Revolution

Anatolia [ana**toh**lia], Turk **Anadolu** Asiatic region of Turkey, usually synonymous with Asia Minor; a mountainous peninsula between the Black Sea (N), Aegean Sea (W), and the Mediterranean Sea (S). >> Turkey ℹ

Anatolian [ana**toh**lian] A group of Indo-European languages, now extinct, spoken c.2000 BC in the area of present-day Turkey and Syria. The major language is Hittite, recorded on cuneiform tablets from the 17th-c BC: these are the oldest known Indo-European texts. >> cuneiform ℹ; Indo-European languages

anatomy The science concerned with the form, structure, and spatial relationships of a living organism. It originally referred to the cutting up of the body to determine the nature and organization of its parts, but nowadays it includes many other aspects of study, including *histology*, the study of the architecture of tissues and organs, and *cell biology*, concerned with the basic elements of the cell. >> cell; embryology; histology; neurology; physiology; radiography

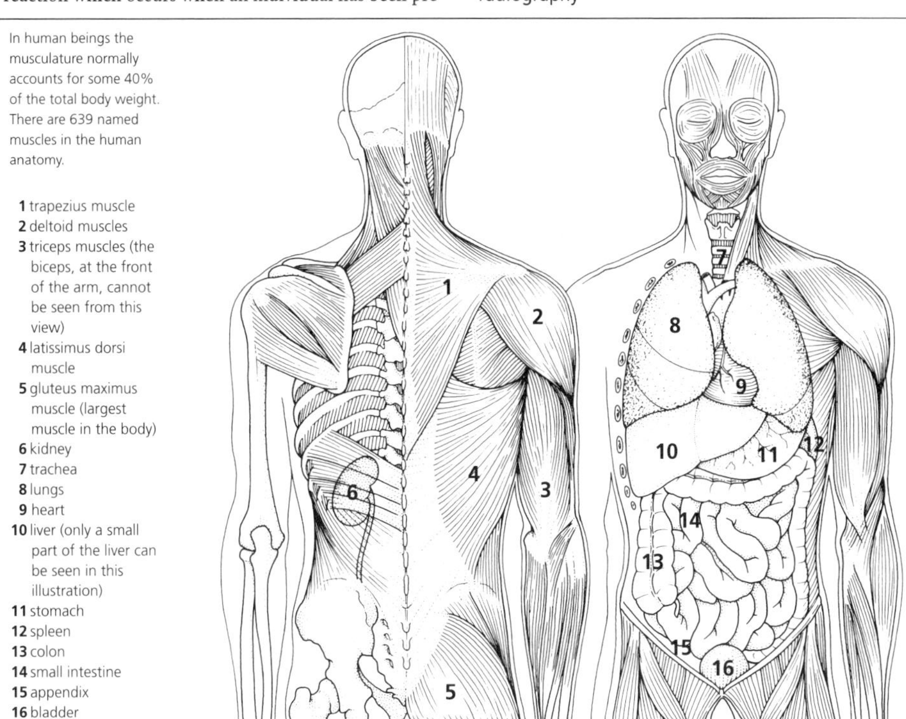

In human beings the musculature normally accounts for some 40% of the total body weight. There are 639 named muscles in the human anatomy.
1 trapezius muscle
2 deltoid muscles
3 triceps muscles (the biceps, at the front of the arm, cannot be seen from this view)
4 latissimus dorsi muscle
5 gluteus maximus muscle (largest muscle in the body)
6 kidney
7 trachea
8 lungs
9 heart
10 liver (only a small part of the liver can be seen in this illustration)
11 stomach
12 spleen
13 colon
14 small intestine
15 appendix
16 bladder

Anatomy

Anaxagoras [anak**sa**goras] (c.500–428 BC) Greek philosopher, born in Clazomenae. He taught in Athens, where he had many illustrious pupils, including Pericles. >> Pericles

Anaximander [anakzi**man**der] (c.611–547 BC) Greek philosopher, born in Miletus. He is credited with producing the first map, and with many scientific speculations, for example that the Earth is unsupported and at the centre of the universe. He was the successor and perhaps pupil of Thales. >> astronomy; Thales

Anaximenes [anak**zim**eneez] (?–c.500 BC) Greek philosopher, born in Miletus. He was the third of the great Milesian philosophers, succeeding Thales and Anaximander. He held air to be the first principle and the basis of matter from which other things were formed. >> Anaximander; Thales

anchor A device which prevents a vessel from drifting. The flukes or arms of an anchor dig into the seabed, thus resisting a horizontal pull; it is made fast to the ship by a heavy cable, usually of studded chain. >>

Anchorage 61°13N 149°54W, pop (1995e) 266 000. City and seaport in SC Alaska, USA; largest city in the state; founded, 1914; severely damaged by earthquake, 1964; important transportation hub; a vital defence centre; airport; railway; university (1957). >> Alaska

anchovy [**an**chovee] Any of the small herring-like fishes of the family Engraulidae, widespread in surface coastal waters of tropical and temperate seas; support extensive commercial fisheries. (5 genera, including *Anchoa, Engraulis*.) >> herring

ancien régime [ãsyĩ ray**zheem**] The social and political system of France existing from the late 16th-c to the outbreak of the French Revolution (1789). The term implies a hierarchical, corporative society, bound closely to the dynastic state. >> French Revolution ℹ

ancona >> **altarpiece**

Andalusia, Eng [andaloo**see**a], Span **Andalucía** [andaloo**thee**a] pop (1995e) 6 915 000; area 87 268 sq km/33 685 sq mi. Large and fertile autonomous region of S Spain; S coastal strip known for its tourist resorts on the Costa del Sol and the Costa de la Luz; chief cities, Málaga, Cádiz, Granada, Córdoba. >> Spain ℹ

andalusite [anda**loo**siyt] A variety of mineral aluminium silicate (Al_2SiO_5), found in metamorphic rocks. Its importance lies as an indicator of the pressure and temperature of metamorphism in rocks. >> silicate minerals

Andaman and Nicobar Islands [**an**daman, nikoh**bah(r)**] pop (1995e) 302 000; area 8300 sq km/3200 sq mi. Union territory of India, comprising two island groups in the Bay of Bengal; over 300 islands, stretching 725 km/450 mi N to S; occupied by Japan in World War 2; part of India, 1950; British penal colony on Andaman Is, 1858–1945; Nicobar Is 120 km/75 mi S, a mountainous group of 19 islands; occupied by Denmark, 1756–1848; annexed by Britain, 1869; chief town, Nankauri. >> India ℹ

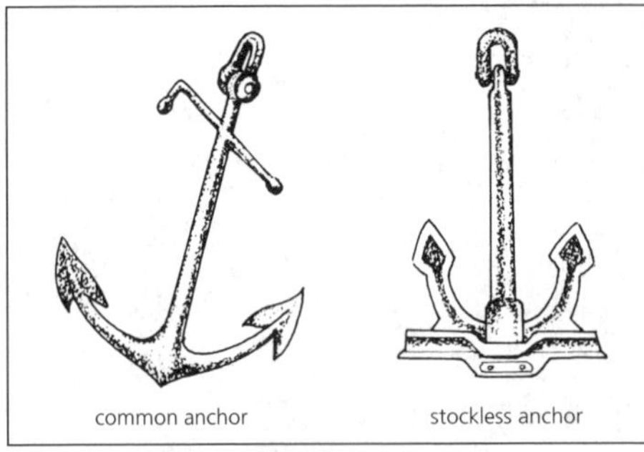

The two basic types of anchor.

Andean Community An organization modelled on the European Community, with five member countries: Bolivia, Colombia, Ecuador, Peru (announced withdrawal in 1997), and Venezuela. It was previously known as the **Andean Pact** (1969–96).

Andersen, Hans Christian (1805–75) Writer, one of the world's great story-tellers, born in Odense, Denmark. The son of a poor shoemaker, he early displayed a talent for poetry. He is mainly remembered for his fairy-tales for children, such as 'The Tin Soldier' and 'The Ugly Duckling'.

Anderson, Carl (David) (1905–91) Physicist, born in New York City. He discovered the positron (1932), did notable work on gamma and cosmic rays, and confirmed the existence of intermediate-mass particles called mesons (now muons). He shared the Nobel Prize for Physics in 1936. >> Dirac; muon

Anderson, Clive (Stuart) (1953–) Television presenter and barrister, born in London. He studied law at Cambridge, and was called to the bar in 1976. He wrote scripts for radio and television, and joined BBC Radio 4 as chairman of the popular *Whose Line Is It Anyway?* (1988). The show later transferred to Channel 4 Television, where he was also given his own chat-show *Clive Anderson Talks Back* (from 1989).

Anderson, Elizabeth Garrett, *née* **Garrett** (1836–1917) Physician, born in London, who pioneered the admission of women into medicine. She had difficulty qualifying as a doctor because of opposition to women, finally receiving an MD degree from the University of Paris (1870). She was elected Mayor of Aldeburgh in 1908 – the first woman mayor in England. >> women's liberation movement

Anderson, Gerry (1929–) British creator of puppet-character programmes for television. He enjoyed great success with adventure series that combined a range of popular puppet characters with technologically advanced hardware and special effects, such as *Thunderbirds* (1964–6), *Captain Scarlett and the Mysterons* (1967), and *Terrahawks* (1983–4). >> puppetry

Anderson, Gillian (1968–) Actor, born in Chicago, IL. Brought up in London, her family returned to the USA, where she became involved in community theatre. She moved to Los Angeles, where she was offered the part of Dana Scully in the series *The X-Files* (1993–), which has since become a cult classic. She now lives in Vancouver.

Anderson, Lindsay (Gordon) (1923–94) British stage and film director, born in Bangalore, India. He began with short documentary films, such as *Thursday's Children* (1955, Oscar), and became a leading proponent of the Free Cinema critical movement. His feature films include *This Sporting Life* (1963), *O Lucky Man!* (1973), and *The Whales of August* (1987).

Anderson, Marian (1902–93) Contralto concert and opera singer, born in Philadelphia, PA. In 1955 she became the first African-American singer at the New York Metropolitan Opera. President Eisenhower made her a delegate to the UN in 1958.

Andes [**an**deez] Major mountain range in South America, running parallel to the Pacific coast from Tierra del Fuego (S) to the Caribbean (N); extends over 6400 km/4000 mi; rises to 6960 m/22 834 ft in the Cerro Aconcagua (Argentina), the highest point in South America; several parallel ranges (*cordilleras*) and high plateaux; highest peaks on the Chile–Argentina border, with many lakes and tourist resorts; C Andes in Bolivia covers two-fifths of the country in an elevated plateau (*altiplano*) of 3000–3600 m/9800–11 800 ft; includes such active volcanoes as Chimborazo and Cotopaxi; connects via E Panama to the C American ranges. >> Aconcagua, Cerro; Chimborazo; Cotopaxi; Ojos del Salado, Cerro; South America

Andhra Pradesh [andra pra**daysh**] pop (1995e) 71 824 000; area 276 814 sq km/106 850 sq mi. State in S India, bounded E by the Bay of Bengal; capital, Hyderabad; made a separate state based on Telugu-speaking area of Madras, 1953. >> Hyderabad; India [i]

Andorra [an**do**ra] or **the Valleys of Andorra, Catalan** Valls d'Andorra, **Fr** Vallée d'Andorre, **official name** Principality of Andorra, Principat d'Andorra A small, independent, neutral state on the S slopes of the C Pyrenees between France and Spain; pop (1995e) 67 900; area 453 sq km/ 173 sq mi; capital, Andorra la Vella; timezone GMT +1; language, Catalan, also French and Spanish; currency, French francs and Spanish pesetas; a mountainous country, reaching 2946 m/9665 ft at Coma Pedrosa; cold, dry, sunny winters; one of the oldest states in Europe, under the joint protection of France and Spain since 1278; Co-Princes of the Principality are the President of France and the Bishop of Urgel; independence, 1993; the General Council of the Valleys appoints the head of the government; no restriction on currency exchange, and no direct or value-added taxes; commerce, agriculture, tourism; two airports. >> Andorra la Vella

Andorra la Vella [an**do**ra la **vel**ya], Sp **Andorra la Vieja**, Fr **Andorre la Vielle** 42°30N 1°30E, pop (1995e) 25 500. One of the seven parishes of the Principality of Andorra, with a capital town of the same name; altitude 1029 m/3376 ft; airports. >> Andorra [i]

Andrássy, Gyula, Gróf (Count) [**on**drahshee] (1823–90) Statesman and prime minister (1867–71), born in Kassa, Hungary (now Košice, Slovak Republic). A supporter of Kossuth, he was prominent in the struggle for independence (1848–9). When the Dual Monarchy was formed, he was made prime minister of Hungary (1871–9). >> Austria–Hungary, Dual Monarchy of; Kossuth

André, John [on**dray**] (1751–80) British soldier, born in London. He joined the army in Canada, and when in 1780 Benedict Arnold obtained the command of West Point, André was selected to make the arrangements for its betrayal. However, he was captured and hanged. >> American Revolution; Arnold, Benedict

Andrea del Sarto >> **Sarto, Andrea del**

andrecium [an**dree**siuhm] >> **flower**

Andress, Ursula (1936–) Film actress, born in Bern, Switzerland. She made her international debut in *Dr No* (1963), her later films including *What's New, Pussycat?* (1965), *Casino Royale* (1967), and *The Clash of the Titans* (1981).

Andrew, St (d.c.60) One of the 12 apostles, brother of Simon Peter. He is traditionally supposed to have preached the Gospel in Asia Minor and Scythia, and to have been crucified in Achaia by order of the Roman governor. He is the patron saint of Scotland and of Russia. Feast day 30 November. >> apostle; Peter, St

Andrewes, Lancelot (1555–1626) Anglican clergyman, born in Barking, Essex. Considered one of the most learned theologians and preachers of his time, he became Bishop of Chichester (1605), Ely (1609), and Winchester (1618), and took part in the translation of the Bible. >> Church of England

Andrews, Eamon (1922–87) Broadcaster, born in Dublin. He is best known as television host of *What's My Line?* (1951–63, 1984–7) and *This is Your Life* (1955–87). He was also active as a chat show host and children's programmes presenter.

Andrews, Julie, originally **Julia Elizabeth Wells** (1935–) Singer and actress, born in Walton-on-Thames, Surrey. She became internationally known through her roles in the film musicals *Mary Poppins* (1964, Oscar) and *The Sound of Music* (1965). Later films include *Victor/Victoria* (1982) and *A Fine Romace* (1992). She is married to the film director Blake Edwards (1922–).

Androcles [**an**drokleez] According to a Roman story, an escaped slave who met a lion, and extracted a thorn from its paw. When recaptured, he was made to confront a lion in the arena, and found it was the same animal, so that his life was spared.

androgens [**an**drojenz] Chemical substances, usually steroid sex hormones, which induce masculine characteristics. In men the androgens *testosterone* and *dihydrotestosterone* are secreted in the testes. They are necessary for the development of male genitalia in the fetus. During puberty they promote the development of secondary sexual characteristics (growth of the penis and testes; the appearance of pubic, facial, and body hair; an increase in muscle strength; and deepening of the voice). In adults, they are required for the production of sperm and the maintenance of libido. >> anabolic steroids; hormones; oestrogens

android >> **robotics** (cybernetics)

Andromache [an**drom**akee] In Greek legend, the wife of Hector, the hero of Troy. After the fall of the city she became the slave of the Greek Neoptolemus. >> Hector

Andromeda (mythology) [an**drom**eda] In Greek mythology, the daughter of Cepheus and Cassiopeia. To appease Poseidon, she was fastened to a rock as an offering to a sea-monster. She was rescued by Perseus, who used the Gorgon's head to change the monster to stone. >> Gorgon; Perseus; Poseidon

Andromeda (astronomy) [an**drom**ida] A constellation in the N sky. Its brightest stars are Alpheratz and Mirach. It contains the **Andromeda galaxy**, the largest of the nearby galaxies, about 700 kiloparsec away. >> constellation; galaxy; Ptolemy; RR968

Andropov, Yuri Vladimirovich [**an**dropof] (1914–84) General secretary of the Soviet Communist Party (1982–4) and president of the USSR (1983–4), born in Nagutskoye, Russia. He was head of the KGB (1967–72), and became president following the death of Brezhnev, but died soon after from illness. >> Brezhnev; KGB

Andros area 380 sq km/147 sq mi. Northernmost island of

the Cyclades, Greece; length 40 km/25 mi; chief town, Andros; rises to 994 m/3261 ft. >> Cyclades; Greece [i]

anechoic chamber [ane**koh**ik] A room or chamber in which all walls and surfaces are lined with a sound-absorbing material to minimize reflected sound; also called a **dead room**. It is important in acoustic experiments in which reflected sound would confuse results. >> acoustics

Aneirin or **Aneurin** [a**niy**rin] (fl.6th–7th-c) Welsh court poet. His principal work, the *Gododdin*, celebrates the British heroes who fell in conflict with the Saxons at Cattraeth (c.600).

anemometer A device for measuring the speed of a current of air. It is usually used to determine the speed of wind, or of a vehicle passing through air. >> Pitot tube; Venturi tube; *see illustration below*

anemone [**a**nemonee] A perennial found throughout N temperate and arctic regions, often forming large colonies; flowers with 5–9 segments ranging from white to yellow, pink, or blue, but hybrids exhibit an even greater colour range. (Genus: *Anemone*, 150 species. Family: Ranunculaceae.)

aneroid barometer >> **barometer**

anesthetics >> **anaesthetics**

Aneto, Pico de [**pee**koh thay a**nay**toh] 42°37N 0°40E. Highest peak of the Pyrenees Mts, rising to 3404 m/ 11 168 ft in Huesca province, NE Spain. >> Pyrenees

aneurysm [**an**yurizm] The abnormal enlargement of a segment of a blood vessel (usually an artery) due to the weakening or rupture of some of the layers of the wall of the vessel. Rupture of an aneurysm of the aorta or pulmonary trunk often proves fatal. >> blood vessels

angel dust The street name of the drug **phencyclidine** (l-(l-phenylcyclohexyl) piperidine, or **PCP**) which is a hallucinogen. It was originally introduced in the 1950s as a general anaesthetic, but soon withdrawn. >> hallucinogens

Angeles, Victoria de los [**an**jeles] (1923–) Soprano, born in Barcelona, Spain. She is noted particularly for her 19th-c Italian roles and for her performances of Spanish songs.

Angel Falls 5°57N 62°33W. Waterfall in SE Venezuela, on a tributary of the R Caroní; highest waterfall in the world, with a total drop of 980 m/3215 ft; named after the US aviator, Jimmy Angel, who crashed nearby in 1937. >> Venezuela [i]; RR972

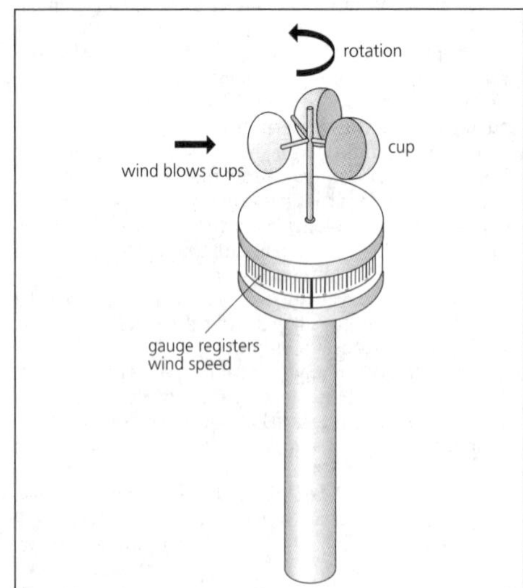

Anemometer

angelfish Any of several small brightly coloured fish found in shallow waters of warm seas; deep, flattened body; small mouth, with gill cover bearing a spine; very popular in marine aquaria; also called **butterfly fish**. The name is also used for monkfish. (Family: Chaetodontidae.) >> monkfish

angelica [an**jel**ika] A robust herb growing to 2 m/6 ft or more (*Angelica archangelica*), native from N and E Europe to C Asia; stem hollow; leaves divided into oval leaflets up to 15 cm/6 in; flowers small, greenish-white, in clusters. Aromatic oil, produced from the roots, is used in perfumes and herbal liqueurs. (Family: Umbelliferae.) >> herb

Angelico, Fra [an**je**likoh], originally **Guido di Pietro**, monastic name **Giovanni da Fiesole** (c.1400–55) Early Renaissance painter, born in Vicchio, Italy. He entered the Dominican monastery at Fiesole in 1407. His most important frescoes are those in the Convent of St Mark (now a museum) in Florence, at Orvieto, and in the Nicholas Chapel of the Vatican. The ethereal beauty of his angelic figures gave him his new name. >> fresco

Angelou, Maya [**an**jeloo] (1928–) Writer, singer, dancer, and African-American activist, born in St Louis, MO. She toured Europe and Africa in the musical *Porgy and Bess*, and in New York City joined the Harlem Writers Guild. In the 1960s she was involved in civil rights, then spent several years in Ghana as editor of *African Review*. Her multi-volume autobiography, commencing with *I Know Why the Caged Bird Sings* (1970), was a great success. >> civil rights

angelshark >> **monkfish**

Angevins [**an**jevinz] The ruling families of the mediaeval county (and later duchy) of Anjou in W France. Henry II, founder of the Angevin or Plantagenet dynasty in England, was a descendant of the earliest counts of Anjou. >> Louis IX; Plantagenets

angina [an**jiy**na] A sudden severe pain or sensation of constriction over the front of the chest resulting from inadequate blood supply to the heart muscle (**angina pectoris**). The pain is increased with exercise, and rapidly subsides with rest. It usually results from the narrowing or blockage of one or more of the arteries which supply the heart muscle with blood. It is commonly relieved by the use of drugs. >> heart [i]

angiography [anji**og**rafee] A radiological technique used to demonstrate the pathways and configuration of blood vessels in various parts of the body. A radio-opaque solution is injected into a main arterial trunk, which increases the X-ray contrast between the blood vessel and its surrounding tissues. >> blood vessels [i]; X-rays

angioplasty >> **balloon angioplasty**

Angkor Thom [**ang**kaw(r) **tom**] 13°26N 103°50E. The ancient capital of the Khmer Empire. The moated and walled city was built on a square plan, extending over 100 sq km/40 sq mi, and completed in the 12th-c. **Angkor Wat** is the largest of the temples surrounding the site. >> Cambodia [i]; Khmer Empire

anglerfish Any of about 13 families of bizarre shallow to deep-sea fishes which have a dorsal fin spine modified as a lure to attract prey; family Lophiidae includes large bottom-dwelling European species (length up to 1·5 m/5 ft) with broad flattened head, capacious mouth, and narrow tail; also called **goosefish**.

Angles A Germanic people from the S Danish peninsula and neighbourhood. With the Saxons, they formed the bulk of the invaders who, in the two centuries following the Roman withdrawal from Britain (409), conquered and colonized most of what became England. >> Anglo-Saxons

Anglesey [**ang**glsee], Welsh **Sir Fôn** or **Ynys Môn** [**uh**nis **mohn**] pop (1995e) 67 200; area 715 sq km/276 sq mi. Island unitary authority (from 1996) in NW Wales, UK; separated from Gwynedd by Menai Straits, spanned by two bridges; chief towns, Holyhead, Llangefni; linked to Holy I by an embankment; ferry link from Holyhead to Dun Laoghaire and Dublin, Ireland. >> Holyhead; Llangefni; Menai Straits; Wales ℹ

Anglesey, Henry William Paget, 1st Marquess of [**ang**glsee] (1768–1854) British field marshal, born in London. He commanded the British cavalry at the Battle of Waterloo (1815), where he lost a leg. >> Waterloo, Battle of

Anglican chant >> **chant**

Anglican Communion A fellowship of some 26 independent provincial or national Churches, several extra-provincial dioceses, and Churches resulting from unions of Anglicans with other Churches, spread throughout the world. They share a close ecclesiastical and doctrinal relationship with the Church of England. >> Church of England; Lambeth Conferences

Anglicanism >> **Church of England**

Anglican–Roman Catholic International Commission >> **ARCIC**

angling The sport of catching fish, one of the world's most popular pastimes, performed in virtually every country, practised with a rod, line, and hook. Many forms of angling exist: freshwater fishing, fly fishing, game fishing, and deep sea fishing. The oldest fishing club still in existence is the Ellem club in Scotland. >> RR1044

Anglo-Catholicism A movement within the Church of England, the term first appearing in 1838. It stresses the sacramental aspects of Christian faith, and continuity with the wider Church, especially with Roman Catholicism. >> Church of England; Roman Catholicism

Anglo-Irish Agreement A joint agreement allowing the Irish Republic to contribute to policy in Northern Ireland for the first time since 1922, signed in 1985 by the British and Irish Prime Ministers, Margaret Thatcher and Garrett Fitzgerald. It established an intergovernmental conference to discuss political, security, and legal matters affecting Northern Ireland. Both governments pledged not to change the status of Northern Ireland without the consent of the majority. The Agreement was opposed by the Republic's Opposition party, Fianna Fáil, and Unionist leaders boycotted official bodies – a boycott which did not end until 1992. >> Ireland (republic) ℹ; Northern Ireland ℹ

Anglo-Maori Wars A succession of conflicts (1843–7, 1860–70) in which Maori people attempted, unsuccessfully, to resist the occupation of New Zealand by British settlers. The main fighting finished in 1864 after the Kingite Maoris, who had led the resistance, retreated to the C North Island. >> Maoris

Anglo-Saxon >> **Old English**

Anglo-Saxons A term probably first used to distinguish the Saxons of England from those of the continent. It is now commonly employed for the entire Old English people from the incoming of Angles, Saxons, and Jutes in the 5th-c to the Norman Conquest. >> Alfred; Angles; Bede; Jutes; Old English; Saxons; Wessex

Angola [ang**goh**la], official name **Republic of Angola**, Port **República de Angola** pop (1995e) 11 539 000; area 1 245 790 sq km/480 875 sq mi. A republic of SW Africa; province of Cabinda enclosed by the Congo; capital, Luanda; timezone GMT +1; several major ethnic groups; religions Roman Catholic (68%) and Protestant (20%); official language, Portuguese, with many Bantu languages spoken; unit of currency, the new kwanza of 100 lweis; narrow coastal plain; high plateau inland, mean elevation 1200 m/4000 ft; highest point, Serro Môco (2619 m/ 8592 ft); mostly a tropical plateau climate; at Huambo on the plateau, average annual rainfall 1450 mm/57 in, average daily temperatures 24–29°C; coast is semi-desert as far N as Luanda; area became a Portuguese colony after exploration in 1482; boundaries formally defined during the Berlin West Africa Congress, 1884–5; became an Overseas Province of Portugal, 1951; civil war followed independence, 1975, with three internal factions: the Marxist MPLA (Popular Movement for the Liberation of Angola), UNITA (the National Union for the Total Independence of Angola), and the FNLA (National Front for the Liberation of Angola); Cuban combat troops arrived from 1976 at request of MPLA; at end of 1988, Geneva agreement linked arrangements for independence with withdrawal of Cuban troops, and the cessation of South African attacks and support for UNITA; peace agreement, 1991; 1992 elections brought MPLA victory, later rejected by UNITA, leading to a resumption of the conflict in 1993; Lusaka peace protocol, 1994; withdrawal of UN peace-keeping force, January, 1999 as fighting resumed between government and UNITA forces; governed by a president, Council of Ministers, and National People's Assembly; reserves of several minerals; extraction and refining of oil provides over 75% of recent export earnings. >> Cabinda; Luanda; Namibia ℹ; South West Africa People's Organization; RR1000 political leaders

Angora cat [ang**gaw**ra] A breed of domestic cat; white long-haired type originated in Turkey (*Angora* is an old name for Ankara); resembles the Persian cat, but with longer body and smaller head. >> Persian cat

Angora goat [ang**gaw**ra] A breed of domestic goat, originating in Turkey (*Angora* is an old name for Ankara); bred mainly in North America, S Africa, and Australasia for

wool; silky hair (length up to 20 cm/8 in), called *mohair*. >> goat

angostura [anggo**stoor**a] A flavouring agent used in cocktails and some fruit juices, deriving from the bark of a S American tree (*Gallipea aspuria*). It was originally used in medicines.

Angra do Heroísmo [**ang**gra duh ero**eezh**mu] 38°40N 27°14W, pop (1991) 11 672. Fortified town and seaport in the Azores; a world heritage site, on S coast of Terceira I; founded, 1464; capital of the Azores until 1832; bishopric; airport. >> Azores

Angry Brigade A left-wing group with anarchist sympathies, active in Britain in the 1960s and early 1970s. It took sporadic violent action against representatives of the establishment in the name of the working class.

Angry Young Men A term used to describe the authors of some novels and plays of the late 1950s and early 1960s in Britain, who felt a confident contempt for the (apparently) established order. They included Kingsley Amis, John Braine, John Osborne and Alan Sillitoe. The term was also applied to certain characters in their works, notably to Jimmy Porter, the hero of Osborne's *Look Back in Anger* (1957). >> Amis, Kingsley; Braine; Osborne

ångström or **angstrom** [**ang**struhm] Unit of length common in crystallography or any other subject which studies features of approximately atomic dimensions; symbol *Å*; equal to 10^{-10} m. >> Ångström

Ångström, Anders (Jonas) [**ang**struhm, **awng**stroem] (1814–74) Physicist, born in Lödgö, Sweden. He wrote on heat, magnetism, and especially spectroscopy. The unit for measuring wavelengths of light is named after him. >> ångström

Anguilla [ang**wil**a] pop (1995e) 7100; area 155 sq km/ 60 sq mi. Most northerly of the Leeward Is, E Caribbean; British overseas territory; capital, The Valley; timezone GMT −4; chief religion, Christianity; official language, English; unit of currency, the East Caribbean dollar; low-lying coral island covered in scrub; tropical climate; low and erratic annual rainfall, 550–1250 mm/22–50 in; colonized by English settlers from St Kitts, 1650; ultimately incorporated in the colony of St Kitts-Nevis–Anguilla; separated, 1980; governor appointed by the British sovereign; Legislative Assembly; tourism. >> Leeward Islands (Caribbean)

angular acceleration >> **acceleration**

angular momentum A vector quantity in rotational motion, equal to the product of moment of inertia with angular velocity; also called the **moment of momentum**; symbol *L*, units kg.m²/s. The rate of change of angular momentum is called *torque*. >> moment of inertia; momentum; torque [i]; vector (mathematics)

angular velocity >> **velocity**

angwantibo [ang**gwan**tiboh] A West African primitive primate (prosimian); golden brown with pointed face; no tail; first finger reduced to a stump, and second short; also known as **golden potto**. (*Arctocebus calabarensis*. Family: Lorisidae.) >> potto; prosimian

anhinga >> **darter** [i]

anil [**an**il] A tropical American shrub (*Indigofera anil*), but cultivated in the Old and New World as a source of the blue dye indigo; also called **indigo plant**. (Family: Leguminosae.) >> indigo

aniline [**an**ileen] $C_6H_5NH_2$, **phenylamine**, or (IUPAC) **aminobenzene**, boiling point 184°C. A liquid with an unpleasant smell, it is the starting material for many dyestuffs, known as *aniline dyes*. >> dyestuff; IUPAC

animal A living organism; one of the main kingdoms of biological classification, **Animalia**, containing all vertebrates and invertebrates. The term 'animal' is sometimes used only for four-legged creatures (mammals, reptiles, and amphibians), but correctly fish and birds are also animals, as are insects, spiders, crabs, snails, worms, starfish, sponges, corals, jellyfish, and many other groups. >> amphibian; kingdom; mammal [i]; reptile; RSPCA

Animal Protection Society of America >> **RSPCA**

animism A belief in spiritual beings thought capable of influencing human events, based on the idea that animals, plants, and even inanimate objects have souls like humans. The 19th-c anthropologist Edward Tylor (1832–1917) regarded it as the earliest form of religion, a view not accepted by modern anthropologists.

anion [**an**iyon] A negatively charged atom or group of atoms, such as Cl^- (chloride) or SO_4^{2-} (sulphate). Anions are so called because they migrate towards the anode in an electrochemical cell. >> anode; cation; ion

Aniston, Jennifer [**an**iston] (1969–) Actor, born in Sherman Oaks, CA. She worked in New York, then went to Hollywood, where she achieved success through her role as Rachel Green in the television series *Friends* (1994–). Roles in feature films include *She's the One* (1996) and *'Til There Was You* (1997).

Anjou [ãzhoo] Former province in the Paris Basin of NW France; former capital, Angers; lost provincial status in 1790. >> Angevins; Plantagenets

Ankara [**ang**kara], ancient **Ancyra** or **Angora** 39°55N 32°50E, pop (1995e) 2 854 000. Capital city of Turkey; conquered by Alexander the Great, 4th-c BC; part of Roman and Byzantine Empires; under Turkish rule, 11th-c; government transferred here from Istanbul, 1923; airport; railway; three universities (1946, 1956, 1967). >> Alexander the Great; Turkey [i]

ankh [ank] A cross with a loop for its upper vertical arm. In ancient Egypt it was an emblem of life.

ankle The region of the lower limb between the calf and the foot; specifically, the joint between the tibia and fibula and the talus (one of the tarsal bones). Movement at the joint is important during the stance phase of walking. >> fibula; sprain; tibia

ankylosaur [**ang**kilosaw(r)] A small four-legged dinosaur, heavily armoured with rectangular bony plates; head small, teeth reduced or absent; fed on vegetation; known from the Cretaceous period of North America. (Order: Ornithischia.) >> Cretaceous period; dinosaur [i]; Ornithischia

ankylosing spondylitis [angki**loh**zing spondi**liy**tis] A progressive inflammatory disease that affects mainly young adult men, giving rise to rigidity of the spine, and reduced movement of the chest and occasionally of the joints. Its cause is unknown. >> inflammation

Annan, Kofi (1938–) UN secretary-general (from 1997), born in Kumasi, Ghana. He joined the UN in 1962, and became under-secretary-general for peace-keeping operations in 1993. He is the first secretary-general from sub-Saharan Africa. >> United Nations

Annapolis [**ana**polis] 38°59N 76°30W, pop (1995e) 35 400. Capital of state, Maryland, USA; port on the Severn R; named after Princess (later Queen) Anne, 1695; US capital, 1783–4; railway; business and shipping centre; US Naval Academy (1845). >> Annapolis Convention; Maryland

Annapolis Convention (1786) In the American Revolution, a gathering at Annapolis, MD, of delegates from five states to discuss commercial problems. The main result was a call for a meeting the following year to consider changes in the Articles of Confederation. >> Articles of Confederation; Constitutional Convention

Annapurna, Mount [ana**poor**na] Mountain massif in the C Himalayas, Nepal; length c.56 km/35 mi; includes Annapurna I (8091 m/26 545 ft), Annapurna II (7937 m/ 26 040 ft), Annapurna III (7556 m/24 790 ft), Annapurna

IV (7525 m/24 688 ft), and several other peaks over 6000 m/20 000 ft. >> Himalayas

Annas [**an**as] (1st-c) Israel's high priest, appointed in AD 6 and deposed by the Romans in 15, but still described later by this title in the New Testament. He apparently questioned Jesus after his arrest (*John* 18) and Peter after his detention (*Acts* 4). >> Jesus Christ; New Testament; Peter, St

Anne (1665–1714) Queen of Great Britain and Ireland (1702–14), born in London, the second daughter of James II. She was the last Stuart sovereign. In 1683 she married Prince George of Denmark (1653–1708), and Sarah Jennings (1660–1744), the wife of Lord Churchill (afterwards Duke of Marlborough), was appointed a lady of her bedchamber. For many years Lady Churchill had supreme influence over her, exerting this in favour of her husband. Anne bore 17 children, but only William, Duke of Gloucester (1689–1700), survived infancy. >> Marlborough; Stuarts

Anne, St (fl.1st-c BC–1st-c AD) Wife of **St Joachim**, and mother of the Virgin Mary, first mentioned in the 2nd-c. She is the patron saint of carpenters. Feast day 26 July. >> Mary (mother of Jesus)

Anne (Elizabeth Alice Louise), Princess (1950–) Daughter of HM Elizabeth II and HRH Prince Philip, Duke of Edinburgh, born in London. She married **Mark Anthony Peter Phillips** (1948–) in 1973, but they were divorced in 1992. Their son is **Peter Mark Andrew** (1977–); their daughter **Zara Anne Elizabeth** (1981–). She married **Timothy Laurence** (1952–) in 1992. She was created Princess Royal in 1987, and in recent years has travelled widely on behalf of international charities. >> Elizabeth II

Anne Boleyn >> **Boleyn, Anne**

Anne of Austria (1601–66) Eldest daughter of Philip III of Spain and wife of Louis XIII of France, born in Valladolid, Spain. In 1643 she became Queen Regent for the baby Louis XIV. >> Mazarin; Richelieu

Anne of Cleves (1515–57) German princess, the fourth Queen of Henry VIII (Jan 1540). Her plainness of feature was largely responsible for the marriage being declared null and void six months afterwards. On agreeing to the divorce, Anne was given a large income, and remained in England until her death. >> Henry VIII

Anne of Denmark (1574–1619) Wife (from 1589) of James VI of Scotland, later James I of England. She became a patron of the masque and other art forms. >> James I (of England); masque

annealing The relief of internal stresses in metals after heat treatment or working (hammering, forging, or drawing), or in glass after moulding or blowing. It is effected by maintaining the object at a moderate temperature to allow for molecular or crystalline re-arrangement. >> metal

Annecy [ansee] 45°55N 6°08E, pop (1995e) 52 700. Industrial town in E France, on N shore of Lac d'Annecy; railway; bishopric; popular tourist centre. >> Alps

annelid [**an**elid] A ringed worm; a bilaterally symmetrical worm of phylum Annelida; body divided into cylindrical rings (segments) containing serially arranged organs; head typically well defined. >> bristleworm; earthworm; leech; *Tubifex*; worm

Annigoni, Pietro [ani**goh**nee] (1910–88) Painter, born in Milan, Italy. He was one of the few 20th-c artists to put into practice the technical methods of the old masters. His most usual medium was tempera. His Renaissance manner is shown at its best in his portraits, such as those of Queen Elizabeth II (1955, 1970). >> tempera

annual A plant which germinates, flowers, sets seed, and dies within one year. The definition is not strict: in mild weather some annuals may germinate late in the season, overwinter as seedlings or young plants, and complete their life-cycle in the next year. >> biennial; ephemeral; perennial

annual ring One of the concentric rings visible when the stem or root of a woody plant is cut across. Usually one ring marks one year's growth, thus providing a means of calculating the age of trees. >> xylem

annuity [**anyoo**itee] A sum of money paid to older people on a regular guaranteed basis until they die. The scheme is operated by life insurance companies. An initial lump sum is paid over, and subsequent payments are made to pensioners partly from interest on the capital invested and partly on the repayment of the capital itself. >> assurance; pension

annulment A judicial declaration of nullity of marriage. A null marriage is one that was never valid, for example because it involved parties within the prohibited degrees of affinity or consanguinity. >> affinity; bigamy

Annunciation The angel Gabriel's foretelling to Mary of the birth of Jesus and of the promise of his greatness (*Luke* 1.26–38). The feast day (25 Mar) is also known as **Lady Day**. >> Gabriel; Mary (mother of Jesus)

Annunzio, Gabriele d' >> **d'Annunzio, Gabriele**

anoa [a**noh**a] A rare member of the cattle family, from Sulawesi; height, c.80 cm/30 in; straight backward-pointing horns; two species; also known as **dwarf buffalo**, **wood ox**, **sapi-utan**, or **sapi-outan**. >> Bovidae; cattle; water buffalo

anode In electrolysis and gas discharge tubes, the positive electrode from which electrons leave the cell or tube. In a battery, the anode is the negative terminal by which electrons leave the battery. >> anion; anodizing; cathode; thermionic valve

anodizing A metal protection process, usually applied to aluminium or magnesium. The object is made the anode in an electrolytic bath which produces a thin but dense protective oxide layer. >> anode; electrolysis ℹ

anointing the sick The ritual application of oil performed in cases of (usually) serious illness or preparation for death. In the Roman Catholic and Orthodox Churches, it is recognized as a sacrament to be performed by a priest. It was formerly sometimes called **extreme unction**. >> Orthodox Church; Roman Catholicism; sacrament

anole [a**noh**lee] An iguana found from SE USA to N South America (including the West Indies); can change colour. (Genus: *Anolis*, several species.) >> chameleon; iguana

Anopheles [a**nof**ileez] The malaria mosquito, found in all major zoogeographical regions. The adult females transmit a malaria-causing agent when taking blood from vertebrates. (Order: Diptera. Family: Culicidae.) >> malaria; mosquito

anorexia nervosa [ano**rek**sia ner**voh**sa] A psychological illness which mainly affects young women, characterized by significant weight loss (usually deliberately induced), an unrealistic fear of being overweight, and a loss of normal menstrual functioning. Current views hold that there are both biological and psychological causes. >> amenorrhoea; bulimia nervosa; obesity

Anouilh, Jean (Marie Lucien Pierre) [onwee] (1910–87) Playwright, born in Bordeaux, France. He was influenced by the Neoclassical fashion inspired by Giraudoux. Among his many successful plays are *Antigone* (1944), *Becket* (1959), and *La Culotte* (1978, The Trousers). >> Giraudoux; Neoclassicism (art)

Anoura >> **Anura**

Anschluss [**an**shlus] The concept of union between Austria and Germany, expressly forbidden by the Treaty of Versailles (1919). Hitler pursued the idea once in power, and in 1938 the Germans were 'invited' to occupy Austria. >> Hitler; Schuschnigg; Versailles, Treaty of

Anselm, St (1033–1109) Theologian and philosopher, born of noble birth in Aosta, Italy. Appointed Archbishop of

Canterbury (1093), he frequently came into conflict over Church rights, first with William Rufus, then with Henry I. He was the main figure in early scholastic philosophy, remembered especially for his ontological proof for the existence of God, and his theory of atonement. Feast day 21 April. >> atonement; ontological argument; scholasticism

Anshan or **An-shan** 41°05N 122°58E, pop (1995e) 1 546 000. Town in Liaoning province, NE China; organized mining and smelting began here c.100 BC; railway; site of China's largest iron and steel complex. >> China ℹ

ant A social insect, characterized by a waist of 1–2 narrow segments, forming perennial colonies in nests made in wood, soil, plant cavities, or other constructions. The nest contains one or more fertile queens, many wingless, sterile workers, and winged males that fertilize queens during mass nuptial flights. (Order: Hymenoptera. Family: Formicidae, c.14 000 species.) >> insect ℹ; termite

Antananarivo [antananareevoh], formerly **Tananarive** or **Tananarivo** (to 1975) 18°52S 47°30E, pop (1995e) 944 000. Capital of Madagascar; altitude c.1350 m/4400 ft; airport; railway; university (1955); two cathedrals. >> Madagascar ℹ

Antarctica S Polar continent, area nearly 15·5 million sq km/6 million sq mi; mainly S of 65°S, almost entirely within the Antarctic Circle; c.22 400 km/ 14 000 mi coastline, mainly of high ice cliffs; indented by Ross and Weddell Seas; Transantarctic Mts, highest point 5140 m/ 16 863 ft at Vinson Massif; no permanent population; species of algae, moss, lichen, and sea plankton provide food for fish, birds, whales, and seals; major scientific explorations since first winter base established in 1899; Antarctic Treaty (1959), provides for international co-operation in scientific research, and prohibits military operations, nuclear explosions, and disposal of radioactive waste; 50-year ban on mining and mineral extraction, 1991; territorial claims made by the UK, Norway, France, Australia, New Zealand, Chile, and Argentina; major iceberg loss in Antarctic Peninsula, through global warming, Feb 1995. >> Adélie Land; Amundsen; Australian / British Antarctic Territory; French Southern and Antarctic Territories; Poles; Queen Maud Land; Ross Dependency; Scott, R F; RR971

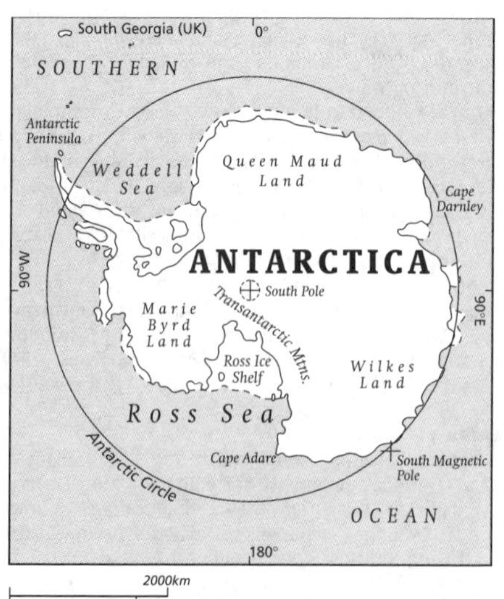

Antarctic Circle Imaginary line on the surface of the Earth at 66°30S, marking the southernmost point at which the Sun can be seen during the summer solstice, and the northernmost point at which the midnight Sun can be seen in S polar regions. >> Antarctica ℹ; Arctic Circle

Antarctic Ocean The S regions of the Atlantic, Indian, and Pacific Oceans surrounding Antarctica; narrowest point the Drake Passage between South America and the Antarctic Peninsula (1110 km/690 mi). >> Antarctica ℹ

Antares [antahreez] >> **Scorpius**

ant bear >> **aardvark**

anteater A mammal, native to Central and South America, which eats ants and termites; an edentate group, comprising four species; numbats are also known as *banded anteaters*, and pangolins as *scaly anteaters*. (Family: Myrmecophagidae.) >> Edentata; numbat; pangolin

antelope A hoofed mammal, found mainly in Africa; classified as gazelles (tribe: Antilopini), four-horned antelopes (tribe: Boselaphini), spiral-horned antelopes (tribe: Strepsicerotini), dwarf (or pygmy) antelopes (tribe: Neotragini), grazing antelopes (subfamily: Hippotraginae, including horse-like antelopes of the tribe Hippotragini, and ox-antelopes of the tribe Alcelaphini), pronghorns (subfamily: Antilocaprinae), duikers (subfamily: Cephalophinae), and goat antelopes (subfamily: Caprinae, which includes goats and sheep). (Family: Bovidae, 116 species.) >> Bovidae; duiker; gazelle ℹ; goat; horse ℹ; pronghorn

antenna (biology) One of a pair of specialized sensory appendages on the head of an invertebrate animal; insects typically have one pair, crustaceans two pairs; varies in shape and size. >> insect ℹ; invertebrate

antenna (technology) The component of a radio or television system by which electromagnetic signals are transmitted or received; also known as the **aerial**. In high-frequency practice, additional elements termed *reflectors* and *directors* are included to increase directional efficiency. >> dish

Antheil, George [**an**tiyl] (1900–59) Composer, born in Trenton, NJ. His works include the *Jazz Symphony* (1925), the *Ballet Mécanique* (1926), and the opera *Transatlantic* (1930).

anthelmintics [anthel**min**tiks] Drugs which paralyse or kill parasitic worms (*helminths*), such as ringworms, tapeworms, and schistosomes. They include mebendazole, piperazine, and niridazole. >> helminthology; worm

Anthony, St >> **Antony, St**

Anthony, Susan B(rownell) (1820–1906) Women's suffrage leader, born in Adams, MA. From 1869 she was a leader of the National Woman Suffrage Association, becoming president of the US branch in 1892. >> women's liberation movement

anthracene [**an**thraseen] $C_{14}H_{10}$, melting point 216°C. A colourless, cancer-causing, aromatic compound isolated from coal tar. Oxidized to **anthraquinone**, it is the raw material for the *alizarin* series of dyestuffs. >> coal tar; dyestuff

anthracite A hard and lustrous variety of coal, containing more than 90% carbon. It is the highest grade of coal, and burns with a very hot, virtually smokeless flame. >> coal

anthrax A disease resulting from infection with *Bacillus anthracis*. Blood poisoning, pneumonia, and death may occur.

Anthropoidea [anthro**poy**dia] A group of primates comprising monkeys and apes; face usually flat; ears small; fingers and toes with nails, not claws; live in complex social groups. >> ape; monkey ℹ; primate (biology)

anthropology The scientific study of human beings, traditionally identified as a 'four-field' discipline, encompassing **archaeology**, **social** and **cultural anthropology**,

biological anthropology, and even **linguistics**. Cultural and social anthropologists study particular living societies, and attempt through comparison to establish the range of variation in human, social, and cultural institutions, and the reasons for these differences. Physical anthropologists study local biological adaptations and human evolutionary history. >> archaeology; ethnoscience; linguistics

anthropometry The comparative study of the dimensions of the human body and their change with time. The main dimensions examined include weight, height, skinfold thickness, mid-arm circumference, and waist-to-hip ratio. The study influences the design of many products, such as clothes, car seats, and space capsules.

anti-aircraft gun (AA-gun) A gun firing a shell at high velocity at a high angle designed to shoot down aircraft. On the modern battlefield, radar-guided 'Triple A' (standing for Anti-Aircraft Artillery) has an important role in providing low-level, close-in defence against hostile aircraft, helicopters, and missiles. >> artillery; missile, guided

anti-anxiety drugs >> **benzodiazepines**

antiballistic missile (ABM) A missile capable of destroying hostile ballistic missiles or their payloads in flight at short, medium, or long ranges inside or outside the atmosphere. >> missile, guided

Antibes [ãteeb], ancient **Antipolis** 43°35N 7°07E, pop (1995e) 72 800. Fishing port and fashionable resort on the Riviera, SE France; best known for its luxurious villas and hotels sheltered by the pines of Cap d'Antibes; railway. >> Riviera

antibiotics Substances derived from one micro-organism which can selectively destroy other (infectious) organisms without harming the host. The development of penicillin (1941) was the start of the era of safe and effective antibiotics. Nearly 100 new antibiotics have since been discovered. Several are now synthesized. >> penicillin; streptomycin; sulphonamides; tetracyclines

antibodies Proteins which help protect against disease-causing micro-organisms (bacteria, viruses, parasites), present mainly in the gamma globulin fraction of serum; also known as **immunoglobulins**. The first exposure of the body to a foreign cell or molecule (an *antigen*) produces an immune response which is directed specifically against the antigen that triggered it. Antibodies are produced which eliminate the antigens by a number of mechanisms. >> gamma globulins; immunity; inflammation; lymphocyte; serum

anticoagulants Drugs which slow down or prevent the normal process of blood clotting, such as heparin and warfarin. They are used in the treatment and prevention of diseases caused by thrombi (blood clots) which block blood vessels. Warfarin is also used as a rat poison. >> blood; thrombosis

anticonvulsants Drugs used in the control of epilepsy. All sedatives are anticonvulsant at high doses, but useful drugs in current use include phenobarbitone, phenytoin, sodium valproate, and clonazepam. >> barbiturates; epilepsy

Anti-Corn-Law League An association formed in Manchester (1838), largely under the patronage of businessmen and industrialists, to repeal the British Corn Laws, which imposed protective tariffs on the import of foreign corn. The Laws were repealed by Robert Peel in 1846. >> Bright, John; Corn Laws; Peel

anticyclone A meteorological term for a high pressure system. Anticyclones are areas of generally clear skies and stable weather conditions. In the N hemisphere, surface winds blow in a clockwise direction out of an anticyclone; in the S hemisphere the direction is anticlockwise. >> atmospheric pressure; wind ℹ

antidepressants Drugs which cause elevation of mood in depressed patients. There are two major classes: *tricyclics* (eg imipramine, amitriptyline), and *Monoamine oxidase inhibitors* (eg isocarboxazid, phenelzine). >> depression (psychiatry)

Antietam, Battle of [an**tee**tam] (1862) A battle of the American Civil War, fought in Maryland. In military terms the North won a technical victory. This helped dissuade Britain and France from giving diplomatic recognition to the Confederacy. >> American Civil War

antifreeze A substance added to water in the cooling system of an engine to prevent the system freezing during cold weather. Substances used as anti-freeze include ethanol and methanol; ethylene-glycol is more reliable, but more expensive. >> engine; ethanol

antigen >> **antibodies**

Antigone [an**tig**onee] In Greek mythology, a daughter of Oedipus, King of Thebes. She is a symbol of the individual's right to defy the state over a matter of conscience. >> Polynices; Seven against Thebes; Sophocles

Antigua or **Antigua Guatemala** [an**tee**gwa] 14°33N 90°42W, pop (1995e) 35 900. City in S Guatemala; founded by the Spanish, 1543; capital, until largely destroyed by earthquake, 1773; old city now a world heritage site; cathedral (1534). >> Guatemala ℹ

Antigua and Barbuda [an**tee**ga, bah(r)**byoo**da] pop (1995e) 63 900; area 442 sq km/171 sq mi. Group of three islands in the Leeward group of the Lesser Antilles, E Caribbean; Antigua (280 sq km/108 sq mi), Barbuda (161 sq km/62 sq mi), lying 40 km/25 mi to the N, and Redonda (1 sq km/⅓ sq mi), uninhabited, lying 40 km/25 mi to the SW; capital St John's (on Antigua); other main town Codrington (on Barbuda); timezone GMT −4; people mostly of African Negro descent; dominant religion, Christianity; official language, English; unit of currency, the Eastern Caribbean dollar; W part of Antigua rises to 470 m/1542 ft at Boggy Peak; Barbuda a flat coral island reaching only 44 m/144 ft at its highest

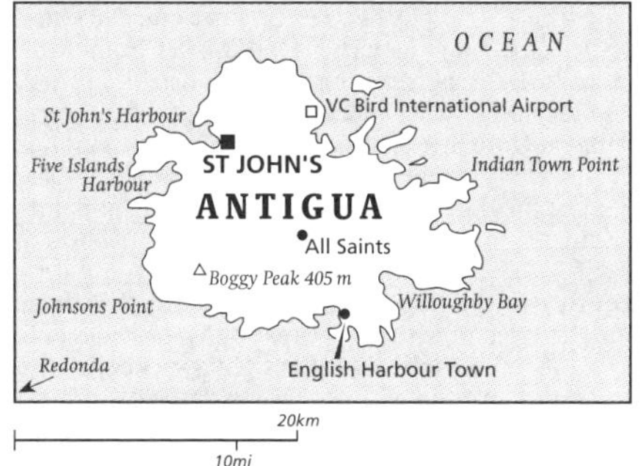

point, with a large lagoon on its W side; climate tropical (24°C, Jan, to 27°C, Aug/Sep); mean annual rainfall of 1000 mm/40 in; Antigua discovered by Columbus, 1493; colonized by English, 1632; ceded to Britain, 1667; Barbuda colonized from Antigua, 1661; administered as part of the Leeward Is Federation, 1871–1956; an associated state of the UK, 1967; independence achieved in 1981; a governor-general and a bicameral legislature; tourism, sugar, cotton. >> Antilles; Caribbean Sea; RR1000 political leaders

antihistamines Drugs used in the relief of allergic reactions, such as hay fever (but not asthma). They are so called because they act by blocking the action of the substance histamine, produced in the body during allergies. >> allergy; histamine; sedative

antiknock A chemical substance added to a spark ignition engine's fuel to improve combustion and prevent knocking. An example is tetra-ethyl lead. >> knocking; spark ignition engine

Antilles [an**til**eez] The whole of the West Indies except the Bahamas; **Greater Antilles** include Cuba, Jamaica, Hispaniola (Haiti and the Dominican Republic), and Puerto Rico; **Lesser Antilles** include the Windward Is (S), Leeward Is (N), and the Netherlands Antilles. >> Caribbean Sea

antimatter >> **antiparticles**

antimony [**an**timonee] Sb (Lat *stibium*), element 51, melting point 631°C. A metalloid in the nitrogen family; expands on solidifying. It is used in alloys, and in semiconductors. >> alloy; chemical elements; metalloids; semiconductor

Antioch [**an**teeok], Turkish **Antakya**, ancient **Hatay** or **Antiochia** 36°12N 36°10E, pop (1995e) 128 000. Town in S Turkey; founded, 300 BC; centre of early Christianity; destroyed by earthquake, 526. >> Turkey i

Antiochus I [anti**oh**kus], known as **Antiochus Soter** (Gr 'Saviour') (324–261 BC) King of Syria (281–261 BC), the son and successor of Seleucus I. He received his nickname for his victory over the Gallic invaders of Asia Minor, but fell in battle with them. >> Seleucids

Antiochus III [anti**oh**kus], known as **Antiochus the Great** (c.242–187 BC) King of Syria (223–187 BC), the greatest of the Seleucid dynasty. He restored Seleucid prestige in the East (209–204 BC), and gained possession of Palestine and Coele Syria (198 BC). He was defeated by the Romans at Thermopylae (191 BC), and Magnesia (190 BC). >> Ptolemy I Soter; Seleucids

antioxidants Substances which slow down the oxidation of others, often by being oxidized themselves. The term is usually applied to additives in foods and plastics. >> additives; oxidation

antiparticles Partners of subatomic particles having the same mass and spin but opposite charge, magnetic moment, and other quantum attributes. When antiparticles meet their particle partners the two annihilate, as predicted by British physicist Paul Dirac in 1928. The antiparticle is usually denoted by a bar over the symbol for the corresponding particle. **Antimatter** composed of antiparticles is possible, but highly unstable, and not observed naturally. >> antiproton; Dirac; particle physics

Antipater [**an**tipater] (?–43 BC) A chieftain who dominated Jewish history from the 60s BC until his death. The father of Herod the Great, he laid the foundations of his family's ascendancy in Judaea during Roman times. >> Herod the Great

antiphon In the Roman Catholic and Greek Orthodox liturgies, a chant with a prose text which precedes or follows a psalm. A collection of antiphons is known as an **antiphoner**. >> chant; liturgy; Psalms, Book of

antipodes Any two places which are on the opposite sides of the Earth when connected by a straight line passing through the centre of the Earth. The term is also loosely used by Europeans to refer to Australasia. >> latitude and longitude i

antipope In the Roman Catholic Church, a claimant to the office of pope in opposition to one regularly and canonically appointed. Antipopes featured prominently in the period of Great Schism in the Western Church (1378–1417). >> pope; RR1029

antiproton The antiparticle partner of the proton; symbol $\bar{p}$. Spin and mass are as for the proton, but the charge is −1. Discovered in 1955, antiprotons are created in particle accelerators by the collisions of protons with nuclei. >> antiparticles; particle physics; proton

antirrhinum >> **snapdragon** i

antiseptic A substance which kills or prevents the growth of micro-organisms (germs). Lister introduced the practice of antiseptic surgery (using phenol) in 1865. Commonly used antiseptics include alcohols, phenols, salts of heavy metals, and chlorine- and iodine-releasing compounds. >> Lister, Joseph; micro-organism; phenol

Antisthenes [an**tis**theneez] (c.445–c.365 BC) Greek philosopher, considered to be the co-founder, with his pupil Diogenes, of the Cynic school. Only fragments of his many works survive. >> Cynics

antlers Bone outgrowths from the head of true deer; only on males, except in reindeer; *water deer* the only species without antlers; used in display, defence, and competition for mates; shed each year (unlike the 'horns' of other ruminants), and grow larger the following year; also known as **deer-horn**. >> deer; reindeer; water deer

Antlia [ant**lee**a] (Lat 'air pump') A small S hemisphere constellation. >> constellation; RR968

antlion The larva of a nocturnal, damselfly-like insect with a long abdomen and lightly patterned wings. (Order: Neuroptera. Family: Myrmeliontidae, c.600 species.) >> damselfly; insect i

Antofagasta [antofa**gas**ta] 23°38S 70°24W, pop (1995e) 235 000. Port city in N Chile; developed with 19th-c mineral and agricultural trade; airport; railway; two universities. >> Chile i

Antonine Wall [**an**toniyn] A defensive barrier built by the Roman Emperor, Antoninus Pius, in AD 142, at the N end

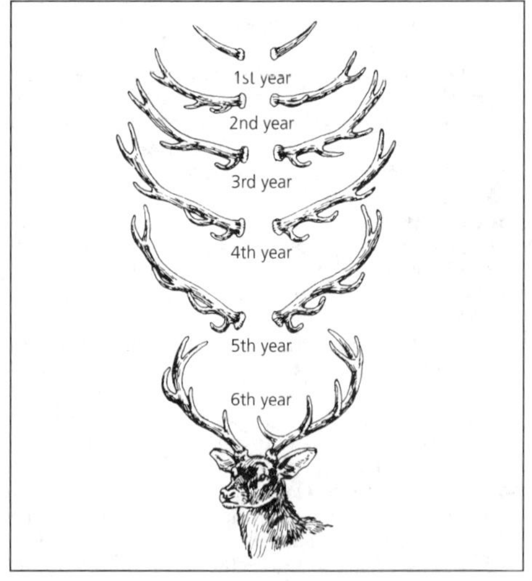

Antlers – red deer

of the British province. It ran from the Forth estuary to the Clyde.

Antonioni, Michelangelo [antoni**oh**nee] (1912–) Film director, born in Ferrara, Italy. He gained an international reputation with *L'avventura* (1959, The Adventure). Later films include *Blow-up* (1966) and *Zabriskie Point* (1969). He lost the power of speech after a stroke in 1985, but managed to make a further film, *Beyond the Clouds* (1995). He received an Academy lifetime achievement award in 1995.

Antonius, Marcus [an**toh**nius] or **Mark Antony** (c.83–30 BC) Roman statesman and soldier. After Caesar's assassination, his speeches caused the flight of the conspirators from Rome, and left him with almost absolute power. He formed a triumvirate with Octavian and Lepidus to share the Roman world among themselves. While re-organizing the E provinces, Antony met and was captivated by Queen Cleopatra, whom he followed to Egypt (41 BC). On his return to Italy in 40 BC a new division of the Roman world was made at Brundisium, with Antony taking the East. His renewed liaison with Cleopatra provided Octavian with reasons to arouse the Roman people against him. Defeat at Actium (31 BC) followed, and Antony and Cleopatra both committed suicide. >> Actium, Battle of; Augustus; Caesar; Cleopatra VII

Antony or **Anthony, St**, known as **Antony the Great**, also called **Antony of Egypt** (c.251–356) Religious hermit, one of the founders of Christian monasticism, born in Koman, Upper Egypt. Having sold his possessions for the poor, he spent 20 years in the desert, where he withstood a famous series of temptations, often represented in later art. In 305 he left his retreat and founded a monastery near Memphis and Arsinoë. In c.355, although over 100, he made a journey to Alexandria to dispute with the Arians, but retired soon after to his desert home. Feast day 17 January. >> Arius; Christianity; monasticism

Antony or **Anthony of Padua, St** (1195–1231) Friar, born in Lisbon, who became one of the most active propagators of the Franciscan order. Canonized in 1232, he is the patron saint of Portugal, the lower animals, and lost property. Feast day 13 June. >> Franciscans; friar

antonym >> **synonym**

Antrim, Ir **Aontroim** pop (1995e) 707 000; area 2831 sq km/ 1093 sq mi. County in NE Northern Ireland; rises N and E to the Antrim Mts; county town, Belfast; Giant's Causeway on N coast. >> Belfast; Giant's Causeway; Northern Ireland [i]

Antwerp, Flemish **Antwerpen**, French **Anvers** 51°13N 4°25E, pop (1995e) 474 000. City in N Belgium; on the right bank of the R Scheldt, 88 km/55 mi from the North Sea; chief port of Belgium and fourth largest port in the world; chartered, 1291; centre of the mediaeval cloth trade with England; airport; railway; colonial university (1920); cathedral (1352); major international centre of diamond trade; home of Rubens and van Dyck. >> Belgium [i]; Rubens; van Dyck

Anubis [an**yoo**bis] An Egyptian god associated with death. He has the head of a jackal or wild dog of the desert.

Anura or **Anoura** [an**oo**ra] An order of amphibians comprising the frogs and toads (3500 species); adults with no tail; move by thrusting backwards with long hind legs; larvae called *tadpoles*; also known as **Salientia**. >> amphibian; frog; tadpole

Anuradhapura [anarahda**poo**ra] 8°20N 80°25E, pop (1995e) 42 600. City in Sri Lanka; Sri Lanka's first capital; founded, 4th-c BC; Sri Mahabodhi Tree, all that remains of the Bo tree beneath which Buddha found Enlightenment, a world heritage site. >> Buddha; Sri Lanka [i]

anus The terminal part of the gastro-intestinal tract, opening into the natal cleft between the buttocks; the lower limit of the anal canal. It is guarded by internal and external sphincters under autonomic and voluntary control respectively. >> alimentary canal; haemorrhoids

Anvers [ãvayr] >> **Antwerp**

ANZAC [**an**zak] An acronym of **Australia and New Zealand Army Corps**, a unit in which troops from both countries fought during World War 1 in the Middle East and on the Western Front. **Anzac Day** (25 Apr) commemorates the Gallipoli landing in 1915. >> Gallipoli; World War 1

aorta [ay**aw(r)**ta] The largest blood vessel in the body, which conveys oxygenated blood from the left ventricle of the heart to the rest of the body. The thoracic branches supply the chest wall, and the abdominal branches supply the contents of the abdomen. >> heart [i]

Aosta [ah**os**ta], Fr **Aoste** 45°43N 7°19E, pop (1995e) 37 800. Town in NW Italy; largely French-speaking; railway; cathedral; old town surrounded by Roman walls. >> Valle d'Aosta

aoudad [**ow**dad] Wild sheep from the dry mountains of N Africa (introduced into SW USA); sandy colour, with long fringe along throat; curved horns up to 760 mm/30 in long; also known as **Barbary sheep**, **maned sheep**, **udad**, **arui**, or **fechstal**. (*Ammotragus lervia*.) >> sheep

Aozou Strip [**ow**zoo] A 100 km/60 mi-wide strip of mountainous desert in N Chad, NC Africa; area 114 000 sq km/ 44 000 sq mi; disputed territory on the frontier with Libya, which occupied the area in 1973; returned to Chad by Libya, 1994; area rich in uranium and mineral deposits. >> Chad [i]; Libya [i]

Apache [a**pah**chee] American Indians who dominated much of the SW during the 19th-c. From 1861 they fought against Federal troops in the Apache and Navajo wars, eventually surrendering in 1886. Population c.50 000 (1990 census). >> Southwest Indians

Apaloochy >> **Appaloosa**

apartheid (Afrikaans 'apartness') The former policy of separate racial development in the Republic of South Africa, supported traditionally by the Nationalist Party. Under the policy, different races were given different rights. In practice the system was one of white supremacy, blacks having no representation in the central state parliament. Many of the provisions of apartheid regarding labour, land segregation (*reserves*, *Homelands*, *Bantustans*), municipal segregation, social and educational separation, and a virtually exclusive white franchise were in place before the Nationalist victory of 1948, but after that date it was erected into a complete political, social, and economic system. The whole system was backed by extensive repression. Following widespread international condemnation, a commitment to dismantle apartheid was implemented by Frederik de Klerk in 1991. A new constitutional agreement was signed by de Klerk and Nelson Mandela in November 1993 and free elections were held in April 1994. >> Afrikaners; black consciousness; civil rights; Sharpeville Massacre; Verwoerd

apatite [**ap**atiyt] A common phosphate mineral widely distributed in many igneous and metamorphic rocks. Most varieties can be represented by the formula $Ca_5(PO_4)_3(OH,F,Cl)$. >> phosphate

Apatosaurus [a**pat**osawrus] A giant, semi-aquatic dinosaur that probably ate vegetation around swamps and lakes; four-legged, limbs pillar-like, hindlimbs longer than forelimbs; tail whip-like; neck very long; known from the Upper Jurassic period of Colorado; formerly known as *Brontosaurus*. (Order: Saurischia.) >> dinosaur [i]; Jurassic period; Saurischia

ape An anthropoid primate; comprises the **lesser apes** (*gibbons*) and **great apes** (*orang-utan, gorilla, chimpanzee*); differs from most monkeys in having no tail and in using arms to swing through trees. (Family: Pongidae,

10 species.) >> Anthropoidea; chimpanzee; gibbon; gorilla; monkey [i]; orang-utan; primate (biology)

APEC Acronym for **Asia-Pacific Economic Co-operation**, a common market founded in 1989 to promote multi-lateral trade in the Asia-Pacific region, with 21 members in 1998. It is the world's third largest free trade grouping, with c.320 million people.

Apennines [**a**peniynz], Ital **Appennino** Mountain range extending down the Italian peninsula into Sicily; length 1400 km/870 mi; width 30–150 km/20–90 mi; highest point Gran Sasso d'Italia (2914 m/9560 ft). >> Italy [i]; Vesuvius

Apgar, Virginia (1909–1974) Physician and anaesthesiologist, born in Westfield, NJ. Best known for pioneering work in anaesthesia relating to childbirth, in 1952 she developed the *Apgar Score* to evaluate newborns. >> anaesthetics, general

aphasia A disorder of language caused by brain damage; also (especially in the UK) known as **dysphasia**. **Broca's aphasia** is a disorder of production, characterized by word-finding difficulties and telegrammatic speech. **Wernicke's aphasia** is a disorder of comprehension, characterized by fluent but largely nonsensical speech. >> brain [i]; neurolinguistics

aphelion >> **periapsis**

aphid A soft-bodied bug that feeds on plant sap. About 4000 species are known, mainly from the N hemisphere, including some that are serious pests, such as blackfly and greenfly. (Order: Homoptera. Family: Aphididae.) >> blackfly; bug (entomology); greenfly

aphrodisiacs Drugs, named after Aphrodite, the goddess of love, which induce sexual desire and/or improve sexual performance. Over 500 substances have been advocated throughout history, notably Spanish fly (responsible for many deaths), rhino horn, and mandrake root. >> mandrake; Spanish fly

Aphrodite [afro**diy**tee] The Greek goddess of sexual love, said to have been born from the sea-foam at Paphos in Cyprus. This indication of an Eastern origin to her cult is borne out by resemblances to the worship of Ishtar. >> Adonis; Ishtar; Venus (mythology)

Apia [**ap**ia] 13°48S 171°45W, pop (1995e) 42 800. Capital town of Western Samoa, on N coast of Upolu I, SW Pacific Ocean. >> Western Samoa [i]

apiculture The keeping of bees in hives for honey and wax production. Bees may be also used for pollinating orchards and crops, such as oilseed rape. As a hobby, collectors (**apiarists**) keep bees both for their honey and to study their habits. >> bee

Apis [**ay**pis, **ah**pis] The Egyptian bull-god, representing or incarnating the Ptah of Memphis. An actual bull was selected from the herd, black with a triangular white patch on the forehead, and kept at Memphis; after death it was mummified and placed in a special necropolis, the Serapeum. >> Ptah

APL Abbreviation of **A Programming Language**, a scientific computer programming language, developed in the 1960s. It is of special interest to mathematicians. >> programming language

apoapsis >> **periapsis**

apocalypse (Gr 'revelation of the future') A literary genre which can be traced to post-Biblical Jewish and early Christian eras; it especially comprises works in highly symbolic language which claim to express divine disclosures about the heavenly spheres, the course of history, or the end of the world. The most famous example is the Book of Revelation in the New Testament. >> Bible; Pseudepigrapha; Revelation, Book of

Apocalypse of John >> **Revelation, Book of**

Apocrypha, New Testament [a**pok**rifa] Christian documents, largely from the early Christian centuries, which are similar in title, form, or content to many New Testament works, being called Gospels, Acts, Epistles, or Apocalypses. They are often attributed to New Testament characters, but not widely accepted as canonical. >> Apocrypha, Old Testament; Gospels

Apocrypha, Old Testament [a**pok**rifa] (Gr 'hidden things') Usually, a collection of Jewish writings found in the Greek version of the Hebrew Bible (the *Septuagint*), but not found in the Hebrew Bible itself. Most of these writings were also in the Latin version of the Christian Bible approved at the Council of Trent (the *Vulgate*), so Roman Catholics tend to consider them as authoritative, and designate them as *deuterocanonical*, while Protestants and most others attribute less authority to them, referring to them as **Apocrypha**. Modern studies prefer to limit the Apocrypha to 13 writings found in most Septuagint manuscripts, and to exclude additional works found only in the Vulgate, which are then assigned to a much larger body of writings called the Old Testament **Pseudepigrapha**. The Apocrypha would thus include: 1 Esdras, Tobit, Judith, Additions to the Book of Esther, Wisdom of Solomon, Ecclesiasticus (or Sirach), 1 Baruch, Letter of Jeremiah, Prayer of Azariah and Song of the Three Young Men, Susanna, Bel and the Dragon (the last three being Additions to the Book of Daniel), 1 and 2 Maccabees. Roman Catholics consider all of this list to be deuterocanonical except for 1 Esdras. Most of the Apocrypha were composed in the last two centuries BC. >> Baruch; Bel and the Dragon; Bible; Ecclesiasticus / Esdras / Esther / Judith / Maccabees / Tobit, Book of; Manasseh, Prayer of; Old Testament; Pseudepigrapha; Susanna, Story of; Wisdom of Solomon

apogee >> **periapsis**

Apollinaire, Guillaume [apoli**nair**, gi**yom**], pseudonym of **Wilhelm Apollinaris de Kostrowitzki** (1880–1918) Poet, born in Rome. He became a leader of the Parisian movement rejecting poetic traditions in outlook, rhythm, and language. His work is expressed chiefly in *Les Alcools* (1913) and *Calligrammes* (1918).

Apollo, (Phoebus) [a**pol**oh] In Greek mythology, the god of poetic and musical inspiration; also a destructive force, sending disease with his arrows. In historic times he was the god who spoke through the Delphic oracle. Later poetry stresses his connection with the Sun. >> Delphi; Hyperion (mythology)

Apollo asteroid An asteroid whose orbit brings it within one astronomical unit (150 million km/93 million mi) of the Sun. >> asteroids; astronomical unit

Apollonius of Perga [apo**loh**nius], known as **the Great Geometer** (280–210 BC) Greek mathematician, born in Perga, Anatolia. He is the author of a major work on conic sections which laid the foundations of modern teaching on the subject. >> analytic geometry

Apollo programme The first crewed mission to the Moon, undertaken by NASA at the direction of President Kennedy in response to the space leadership position established by the USSR. The first landing (20 Jul 1969) was made by the Apollo XI crew of Neil Armstrong and Edwin Aldrin in the spacecraft *Eagle*. Over 300 kg/660 lb of soil, cores, and rocks were returned by all six landed missions. Long duration seismology and space physics experiments were deployed near the landers. The three-man crew in each mission was launched inside a Command Module which stayed in lunar orbit, while the Lunar Module with two crew members descended to the surface. Following the surface activities, part of the Lunar Module was launched to rendezvous with the Command Module in orbit. The crew were recovered from an ocean landing after re-entry and parachute descent. >> Aldrin;

Armstrong, Neil; Collins, Michael (astronaut); Moon; NASA; space exploration; RR970

Apollo–Soyuz project [so**yoos**] A landmark joint space mission conducted by the USA and USSR in 1975, following an agreement signed by President Nixon and Chairman Kosygin in 1972. It demonstrated the capability for joint operations between the major space powers and, as such, the potential for on-orbit emergency rescue missions. The rendezvous (17 Jul 1975) lasted 48 hours. >> Apollo programme; Soyuz spacecraft; RR970

apologetics (Lat *apologia* 'defence') A branch of theology which justifies Christian faith in the light of specific criticisms or charges. An early example is Justin Martyr's *Apology* (2nd-c). >> Justin (Martyr), St; theology

apostle In its broadest sense, a missionary, envoy, or agent; more narrowly used at times in the New Testament to refer to the 12 chosen followers of Jesus (less Judas Iscariot, replaced by Matthias according to *Acts* 1) who witnessed to the resurrected Jesus and were commissioned to proclaim his gospel. At times the term also included Paul and other missionaries. >> Acts of the Apostles; Jesus Christ

Apostles' Creed A statement of Christian faith widely used in Roman Catholic and Protestant Churches, and recognized by the Orthodox Churches. In its present form, it dates from the 8th-c, but its origins go back to the 3rd-c. >> Christianity; Trinity

apothecary In most countries, an old term for a pharmacist at a time when drugs were crude and mostly derived from plants. In England, apothecaries were general medical practitioners; the Society of Apothecaries was founded by James I in 1617. As a licensing body, the examinations it sets are subject to approval by the General Medical Council. >> pharmacy

Appalachian Mountains [apa**lay**shuhn, apa**lay**chian] Mountain system in E North America extending from the Gulf of St Lawrence SW to C Alabama (2570 km/1600 mi); a series of parallel ranges separated by wide valleys; highest peak Mt Mitchell (2037 m/6683 ft), North Carolina; rich in minerals, especially coal; major barrier to westward exploration in early US history; Appalachian Trail (world's longest continuous hiking trail, 3300 km/2050 mi). >> United States of America ⓘ

Appaloosa A breed of horse; height, 14–15 hands/1·4–1·5 m/4·7–5 ft; short tail; dark with pale spots, or pale with dark spots; also called **Apaloochy** or **Palouse**. >> horse ⓘ

appeal A legal procedure whereby a superior court considers an application by a party to a case concerning the decision reached in a lower court. In criminal cases, the appeal might concern the verdict or the sentence. In civil cases, it might concern the amount of damages awarded.

appendix A blind-ended tube, also known as the **vermiform appendix**, which arises from the beginning of the large bowel on the right side of the abdomen. In humans, it is variable in length (2–20 cm/$\frac{3}{4}$–8 in) and its function is unknown. It tends to become blocked in later life, and if its single blood supply is cut off, it rapidly becomes infected and inflamed (**appendicitis**) and has to be removed as soon as possible. >> abdomen; alimentary canal; intestine

Appian Way [**ap**ian] The first of Rome's major trunk roads, constructed in 312 BC by Appius Claudius Caecus. It ran initially from Rome SE to Capua, and later was extended to the Adriatic coast. >> Roman roads ⓘ

apple A small deciduous tree; flowers white or pinkish, in clusters, appearing with the oval leaves; fruit a swollen, fleshy receptacle (or *pome*), containing a core, which is the real fruit. There are over 1000 varieties of eating and cooking apples, which all derive from the cultivated apple of gardens and orchards (*Malus domestica*). (Genus: *Malus*, 35 species. Family: Rosaceae.)

applet >> **Java**

Appleton layer A strongly ionized region of the upper part of the ionosphere, at heights of about 200–400 km/125–250 mi, which is responsible for the reflection of short radio waves back to Earth. Discovered in 1925 by Edward Appleton (1892–1965), it is also known as the **F layer**. >> ionosphere; radio waves

Appomatox Court House [apo**mat**oks] The site in Virginia, USA, of the surrender of the Confederate army under Robert E Lee to Union forces under Ulysses S Grant. It marked the end of the American Civil War (9 Apr 1865). >> American Civil War

apraxia [a**prak**sia] Difficulty in controlling voluntary movements of the limbs or vocal organs; also called **dyspraxia**. In particular, there may be an inability to control sequences of sounds or gestures. >> speech pathology

apricot A deciduous shrub or small tree (*Prunus armeniaca*) 3–10 m/10–30 ft, native to China and C Asia, and widely cultivated; flowers white or pale pink, appearing before the broadly oval, toothed leaves; fruits globose, velvety, 4–8 cm/$1\frac{1}{2}$–3 in, yellow or orange; flesh tart becoming sweet; stone ridged along one edge. (Family: Rosaceae.) >> prunus

April Fool A person tricked or made a fool of on 1 April (All Fools' Day or April Fools' Day). In origin this may have been the final day of the festivities celebrating the spring equinox, which began on Old New Year's Day (25 Mar until 1564).

April Theses A programme of revolutionary action drawn up by Lenin in April 1917 shortly after the February Revolution. In it he advocated the transformation of the Russian 'bourgeois-democratic' revolution into a 'proletarian-socialist' revolution under the slogan of 'All power to the Soviets'. >> February Revolution (Russia); Lenin

Apuleius, Lucius [apu**lay**us] (2nd-c) Latin satirist, born in Madaura, Numidia, N Africa. His romance, *Metamorphoses* or *The Golden Ass*, is a satire on the vices of the age, especially those of the priesthood and of quacks.

Apus [**ay**pus] (Lat 'bird of paradise') A rather small and inconspicuous S hemisphere constellation. >> constellation; RR968

Aqaba [**ak**aba], ancient **Aelana** 29°31N 35°00E, pop (1995e) 67 100. Seaport in SW Jordan, on the border with Israel; Jordan's only outlet to the sea; airport; railway; popular winter seaside resort. >> Jordan ⓘ

aquaculture >> **mariculture**

aquamarine A variety of the mineral beryl, used as a gemstone. It is transparent, usually sea-green or bluish-green. >> beryl

aquaplaning A phenomenon which can take place when a tyre is operating on a wet road, and a layer of water becomes interposed between the tyre and the road. The tyre 'planes' (loses adhesion), and steering and braking can become ineffective. >> car ⓘ; tyre

aquarium A building suitably equipped for the display of aquatic plant and animal life. In recent times open-air **dolphinariums** have become popular for the displaying of dolphins, and underwater **oceanariums** can be found in popular tourist resorts, such as Disney World in Florida. >> dolphin

Aquarius [**akwair**ius] (Lat 'water bearer') A constellation of the zodiac, lying between Pisces and Capricornus. It contains the Helix Nebula, the closest planetary nebula to us. >> constellation; zodiac ⓘ; RR968

aquavit A colourless spirit, distilled from potatoes or cereals, and usually flavoured with caraway seeds. It is a popular drink in Scandinavia.

aqueduct An artificial channel for the conveyance of

water. The Romans built thousands of miles of aqueducts to bring water to their towns. Many are in the form of arch bridges, such as the Pont du Gard at Nîmes, France.

aquifer Water-bearing rock strata, commonly sandstones or chalk with high porosity and permeability. They provide much of the world's water supply, which may be exploited directly by sinking wells or pumping into a reservoir. >> artesian basin; chalk; sandstone

Aquila [**ak**wila] (Lat 'eagle') A constellation on the celestial equator. Its brightest star is Altair, distance 5·2 parsec. >> constellation; RR968

aquilegia [akwi**lee**juh] >> **columbine**

Aquinas, St Thomas [a**kwiy**nas], known as **Doctor Angelicus** ('angelic doctor') (1225–74) Scholastic theologian, born near Aquino, Italy. He was the first among 13th-c metaphysicians to stress the importance of sense perception and the experimental foundation of human knowledge. His *Summa theologiae*, the first attempt at a complete theological system, remains substantially the standard authority in the Roman Catholic Church. He was canonized in 1323. Feast day 7 March. >> Dominicans; scholasticism; theology

Aquino, Cory [a**kee**noh], popular name of **(Maria) Corazon Aquino**, *née* **Cojuangco** (1933–) Philippines politician and president (1986–92), born in Tarlac province. In 1956 she married opposition leader Benigno Aquino, and lived in exile with him in the USA until 1983, when he returned to the Philippines and was assassinated. She took up her husband's cause, leading a non-violent 'people's power' movement which brought the overthrow of President Marcos. She did not stand for re-election in 1992. >> Marcos; Philippines [i]

Aquitaine [akwi**tayn**], Fr [akeeten], ancient **Aquitania** pop (1995e) 2 881 000; area 41 308 sq km/15 945 sq mi. Region of SW France; chief town, Bordeaux; noted for wines; several spas. >> France [i]

Ara (Lat 'altar') A small S hemisphere constellation. >> constellation; RR968

arabesque [ara**besk**] Flowing linear ornament, based usually on plant forms. It occurs widely throughout history, but is especially favoured by Islamic artists. >> Islam

Arabia area c.2 590 000 sq km/1 000 000 sq mi. Peninsula of SW Asia, divided politically into the states of Saudi Arabia, Yemen, Oman, United Arab Emirates, Bahrain, Qatar, and Kuwait; an important world source of petroleum. >> Persian Gulf

Arabian camel >> **dromedary**

Arabian Gulf >> **Persian Gulf**

Arabian hound >> **saluki**

Arabian Sea area 3 863 000 sq km/1 492 000 sq mi. NW part of the Indian Ocean; principal arms include the Gulf of Oman (NW) and the Gulf of Aden (W); trade route between Indian subcontinent, Persian Gulf states, and Mediterranean. >> Indian Ocean

Arabesque – detail from the Alhambra at Granada

Arabic A language of the S Semitic group within the Afro-Asiatic family, spoken by over 150 millions as a mother-tongue. *Colloquial Arabic* exists as the vernacular varieties of the major Arabic-speaking nation-states, which are not always mutually intelligible. *Classical Arabic*, the language of the Koran, provides a common, standard written form. The language is written from right to left. >> Afro-Asiatic languages; Koran

Arab–Israeli Wars Five wars (1948, 1956, 1967, 1973, 1982) fought between Israel and the Arab states over the territorial and strategic consequences of the creation of the Jewish state. In 1948, the end of the British Mandate and the declaration of Israeli statehood on 14 May led to war. By the armistice of 1949, Israel had consolidated its hold over territorial Palestine except for the Golan Heights, West Bank, and Gaza Strip. These territories, along with the Egyptian Sinai Peninsula, were occupied in the Six Day War of 1967. In all, some 800 000 Palestinians were made refugees in 1948 and another 300 000 in 1967. The wars of 1956 (the Suez Crisis) and 1973 (the Yom Kippur or Ramadan War) had no such territorial consequences, and were more opportunistic. In 1982, Israel invaded Lebanon in its only engagement primarily with Palestinian forces, and suffered domestic and international criticism for its conduct of the war. >> Gaza Strip; Golan; Israel [i]; Palestine; West Bank; Yom Kippur

Arab League A League of Arab States, founded in 1945, with the aim of encouraging Arab unity. In 1999 it had 22 member states, including Palestine. Its existence was in question following the invasion of Kuwait and the Gulf War (1990–1). >> PLO

Arabs A diverse group of people, united by their use of Arabic as a first language, who live primarily in SW Iran, Iraq, Syria, the Arabian Peninsula, the Maghreb region of N Africa, Egypt, and Mauritania. A great unifying force is Islam, the religion of 95% of all Arabs. Population c.120 million. >> Arabic; Islam; Maghreb

Arachnida [a**rak**nida] A large, diverse class of mostly terrestrial arthropods, comprising c.70 000 species; body divided into *prosoma* (fused head and thorax) and *opisthosoma* (abdomen); head lacking antennae and compound eyes; four pairs of legs present, and a pair of fangs (*chelicerae*). >> arthropod; harvestman; mite; scorpion; spider; whip scorpion

arachnodactyly [araknoh**dak**tilee] >> **Marfan's syndrome**

Arafat, Yasser [**a**rafat], originally **Mohammed Abed Ar'ouf Arafat** (1929–) Palestinian leader, born in Jerusalem or Cairo. He helped to found the Palestine Liberation Movement, or Fatah, in Kuwait in 1959. In 1969, Fatah gained control over the Palestine Liberation Organization, and he became the chairman of its executive committee. With the 1988 declaration of Palestinian statehood in the West Bank and Gaza Strip, he was elected president by the PLO Central Committee. While his support for Saddam Hussein in the 1990 Gulf Crisis hurt Arafat's international standing, he was criticized by Palestinian hardliners for his role in the negotiations which led to the recognition of a Palestinian state in 1993. He shared the Nobel Peace Prize in 1994. >> Fatah; Palestine; PLO

Aragón [ara**gon**] pop (1995e) 1 188 000; area 47 669 sq km/18 400 sq mi. Autonomous region of NE Spain; featureless upland region largely occupying the basin of the R Ebro; Pyrenees in the N; sparsely populated; former kingdom, 11th–15th-c. >> Spain [i]

Aragon, Louis [aragõ] (1897–1982) Novelist, poet and journalist, born in Paris. He was one of the most brilliant of the Surrealist group, as shown by his first novel, *Le Paysan de Paris* (1926, trans The Night-Walker). >> Surrealism

Aral Sea [**ah**ral], Russian **Aral'skoye More** Inland sea, E of the Caspian Sea, mainly in Kazakhstan; world's fourth largest lake, originally c.65 000 sq km/25 000 sq mi, but rapidly decreasing in size; shrunk by over half since 1960 and twice as saline – caused chiefly by irrigation taking too much water from its feeder rivers; originally c.420 km/ 260 mi long, 280 km/175 mi wide, maximum depth 70 m/ 230 ft; heavily polluted.

Aramaic [ara**may**ik] A Semitic language still spoken by small communities in the Middle East. A dialect of Aramaic was the language used by Jesus and his disciples. >> Afro-Asiatic languages; Jesus Christ

Araneae [a**ran**ee-ee] >> **spider**

Aran Islands Group of three islands (Inishmor, Inishmaan, Inisheer) off SW coast of Galway county, W Ireland; each has an airstrip; boat service from Rossaveel. >> Connacht; Ireland (republic) ℹ

Ararat, (Great) Mount [**a**rarat], Turkish **(Büyük) Ağri Daği** 39°44N 44°15E. Highest peak in Turkey; height 5165 m/16 945 ft; said to be the landing place of Noah's Ark; **Little Ararat** (Küçük Ağri Daği) lies to the SE, rising to 3907 m/12 818 ft. >> Noah; Turkey ℹ

Araucanians [araw**kay**nianz] South American Indian group of C Chile. They presently number c.200 000, living on reservations and in towns and cities in Chile and Argentina. >> Chile ℹ

araucaria [araw**kair**ia] An evergreen conifer, native to much of the S hemisphere except Africa; branches horizontal, in whorls; leaves usually scale-like, sometimes large; timber often sold as **parana pine**. (Genus: *Araucaria*, 18 species. Family: Araucariaceae.) >> conifer; monkey-puzzle

Arbor Day In the USA, New Zealand, and parts of Canada and Australia, a day (whose date varies from place to place) set apart each year for planting trees and increasing public awareness of the value of trees.

arboretum [ah(r)bo**ree**tum] A botanical garden, or a section of a botanical garden, used for the display and study of trees, shrubs, and vines. >> botanical garden

arbor vitae [**ah(r)**baw(r) **vee**tiy] An evergreen coniferous tree or shrub native to North America, China, Japan, and Formosa; leaves scaly, overlapping, in opposite pairs, cones urn-shaped with thin scales. Individual species are called **cedars** or **thujas**, qualified by country of origin or timber colour. (Genus: *Thuja*, 6 species. Family: Cupressaceae.) >> conifer; red cedar 1; white cedar

Arbuthnot, John [ah(r)**buhth**not] (1667–1735) Physician and writer, born in Inverbervie, Aberdeenshire. A close friend of many literary celebrities of his day, he was a founder member of the satirical Scriblerus Club. His works include *The History of John Bull* (1712).

Arc, Joan of >> **Joan of Arc, St**

Arcadia [ah(r)**kay**dia] The mountainous area in the centre of the Peloponnese. Its inhabitants claimed to be pre-Dorian, and the oldest settlers of Hellenic stock in Greece. >> Dorians

Arc de Triomphe [ah(r)k duh **tree**õf] A triumphal arch commemorating Napoleon's victories, designed by Jean Chalgrin (1739–1811) and erected (1806–35) in the Place Charles de Gaulle, Paris. It is 49 m/162 ft high and 45 m/147 ft wide. >> Napoleon I; Paris ℹ

Arcesilaus [ah(r)sesi**lay**us] (c.316–c.241 BC) Greek philosopher, born in Pitane in Aeolia. He became the sixth head of the Academy founded by Plato.

Arc-et-Senans [ah(r)k ay suhnõ] 47°02N 5°46E. A royal saltworks situated N of Arbois, France; architect, Claude-Nicolas Ledoux (1736–1806); a world heritage site. The works were abandoned by the end of the 19th-c.

arch Part of a building, or a structure in its own right, made up of wedge-shaped stones or other pieces over an opening, which support both each other and any weight above. There is a great variety of shapes. >> *illustration*

Archaean or **Archean eon** [ah(r)**kee**an] The earlier of the two geological eons into which the Precambrian is divided; the period of time from the formation of the Earth (c.4600 million years ago) to 2500 million years ago. >> geological time scale; RR976

Archaebacteria [ah(r)keebak**teer**ia] A recently established kingdom comprising the methane-producing bacteria (*Methanogens*). They possibly represent the oldest known life forms, existing more than 3 thousand million years ago. >> bacteria ℹ; kingdom; methane

archaeology / archeology The study of past peoples and societies through the systematic analysis of their material remains. The emphasis is on the study of human development over the period of more than 2 million years in which written records were non-existent (*prehistory*) or at best rudimentary (*protohistory*), and on the recovery of new data through excavation, field survey, laboratory study, and computer analysis. It now involves anthropology, ecology, and systematics alongside the more traditional preoccupations of history, art history, and taxonomy. >> anthropology; dendrochronology; ecology; palynology; potassium–argon dating; systematics; thermoluminescence dating; Three Age System

Archaeopteryx [ah(r)ki**op**teriks] The oldest fossil bird, known from the Jurassic period of Europe; characterized by feathers and a wishbone; long bony tail supported by vertebrae; three clawed fingers on wings; sharp teeth on both jaws. >> fossil; Jurassic period

Archangel, Russ **Arkhangelsk** 64°32N 40°40E, pop (1995e) 431 000. Port city in European Russia; harbour often ice-bound in winter; founded, 1584; airfield; railway. >> Russia ℹ

archbishop A bishop appointed to have jurisdiction over other bishops; often, the head of a province. In Eastern Churches, a hierarchy of archbishops is recognized. >> bishop

archdeacon A clergyman in the Anglican Church responsible for the administration of the whole or such part of a diocese as the bishop may authorize. >> Anglican Communion; clergy

Archer (of Weston-Super-Mare), Jeffrey (Howard) Archer, Baron (1940–) Writer and former parliamentarian. He was Conservative MP for Louth (1969–74), but resigned following bankruptcy. His books include *Not a Penny More, Not a Penny Less* (1975), *Kane and Abel* (1979), and *The Fourth Estate* (1996).

archerfish Any of the Asian marine and freshwater fishes renowned for their ability to dislodge or shoot down

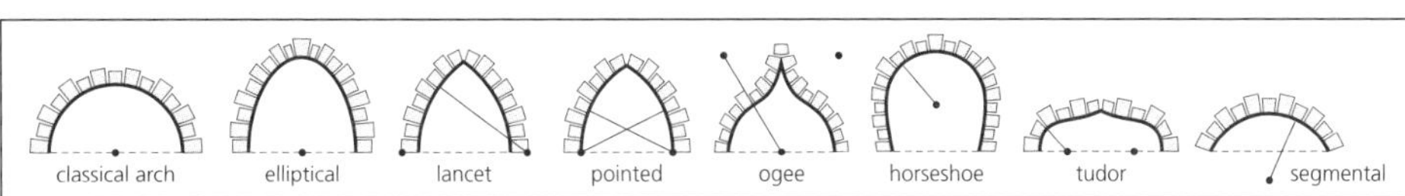

Types of arches

insect prey by spitting drops or jets of water over distances up to 3 m/10 ft; body length up to 25 cm/10 in. (Family: Toxotidae.)

archery The use of the bow and arrow, one of the first weapons used in battle. In the late 17th-c it gained popularity as a sport. The governing body, the *Fédération Internationale de Tir à l'Arc* was formed in 1931. In competition, a series of arrows is fired from 30, 50, 70, and 90 m (roughly 100–300 ft) for men, and 30, 50, 60, and 70 m (100–230 ft) for women. The circular target consists of 10 scoring zones. >> crossbow; longbow; RR1044

Archimedes [ah(r)ki**mee**deez] (c.287–212 BC) Greek scientist, the most celebrated of ancient mathematicians, born in Syracuse. He proved that a body plunged in a fluid becomes lighter by an amount equal to the weight of the fluid it displaces (**Archimedes' principle**), and in popular tradition is remembered for his cry of *eureka* ('I have found it') at the moment of discovery. >> Archimedes screw; fluid mechanics

Archimedes screw A device to raise water; named after the Greek mathematician Archimedes, who is said to have invented it. It consists of a broad threaded screw inside an inclined cylinder; as the screw is turned, the water is raised gradually between the threads and is run off at the top. >> Archimedes

architecture The art or science of building. Architecture has traditionally been thought of as an aspect of higher culture, and its study has concentrated on the work of great artist-architects such as Wren and Schinkel. It now increasingly involves a variety of skills and disciplines, ranging from the technical considerations of structural engineering, environmental services, and energy conservation, to the functional considerations of room layout, interior design, and human comfort. >> Schinkel; Wren, Christopher

archives A place where historical records and other important documents are preserved; also, the materials themselves. Such institutions are also known as Public Record Offices. The first National Archives were established in France in 1789. In recent years, the term has also come to be used for the backup storage of computer data files.

ARCIC [**ah(r)**kik] An acronym for the **Anglican–Roman Catholic International Commission**, instituted in 1966 by Pope Paul VI and Archbishop Michael Ramsey. It produces statements on areas of substantial agreement between the two Churches. >> Anglican Communion; Paul VI; Ramsey, Michael; Roman Catholicism

Arctic Area in the N hemisphere which lies N of the treeline or, more loosely, to the N of the Arctic Circle; Arctic conditions obtain in Greenland, Svalbard, and the N parts of Canada, Russia, Alaska, and Iceland. >> Antarctica ℹ; Arctic Circle; Arctic Council; Barents Euro-Arctic Council

Arctic Circle or **Polar Circle** An arbitrary boundary placed at 66°17N, but often defined as the area N of 70°N. >> Antarctic Circle; Arctic

Arctic Council An organization formed in 1996 by seven countries bordering the Arctic Ocean: Canada, Denmark (for Greenland), Iceland, Norway, Sweden, Russia, and the USA, plus Finland. Based in Ottawa for the first two years, it would advise governments on issues to do with the protection and development of the Arctic's aboriginal peoples. >> Arctic

Arctic Ocean Body of water within the Arctic Circle; world's smallest ocean, 13 986 000 sq km/5 400 000 sq mi; frozen all year except in marginal areas; hummocky icefields in winter, pack-ice during summer, carried S by surface currents; unexplored until Amundsen's flight, 1926; experiencing a period of warming. >> Arctic

Arctic tern A small tern found worldwide; migrates further than any other bird (approximately 36 000 km/22 000 mi per year); spends N summer in the Arctic, and N winter in the Antarctic. (*Sterna paradisaea*.) >> tern

Arcturus >> **Boötes**

Ardashir I [ah(r)da**sheer**] or **Artaxerxes** (c.211–42) King of Persia (224–42), destroyer of the Arsacid dynasty of Parthia, and founder of the new Persian dynasty of the Sassanids. >> Parthians; Sassanids

Arden, Elizabeth, originally **Florence Nightingale Graham** (1878–1966) Beautician and businesswoman, born in Woodbridge, Ontario, Canada. A nurse by training, she went to New York City in 1907 and opened a beauty salon on Fifth Avenue in 1910. She produced cosmetics on a large scale, and developed a worldwide chain of salons.

Arden, John (1930–) Playwright, born in Barnsley, South Yorkshire. His plays include *The Workhouse Donkey* (1963), and *Sergeant Musgrave's Dance* (1959). He has collaborated with his wife, **Margaretta D'Arcy**, in several later works.

Area of Outstanding Natural Beauty (AONB) An area in England and Wales which does not merit National Park status, but where special measures are needed to preserve its natural interest and beauty. >> National Park

areca >> **betel-nut**

Arecibo Observatory [ari**see**boh] A radio astronomy observatory in Puerto Rico, built in 1963. A natural hollow has been lined with a metallic mesh to create the world's largest single radio telescope, 305 m/1000 ft in diameter. >> observatory; radio astronomy; telescope ℹ

arena stage >> **theatre in the round**

Arendt, Hannah [**a**rent] (1906–75) Philosopher and political theorist, born in Hanover, Germany. She moved to the USA in 1940 as a refugee from the Nazis. Her writings, which attracted a readership far beyond the academic world, include *Origins of Totalitarianism* (1951) and *The Life of the Mind* (1978).

Areopagus [aray**op**agus] In ancient Greece, the name for the hill in Athens which was the seat of the oldest council of state, and also for the council whose meetings took place there. The name means 'the hill of Ares' (the god of war). >> Ares; Athens

Arequipa [aray**kee**pa] 16°25S 71°32W, pop (1995e) 692 000. City in S Peru; altitude 2380 m/7808 ft; built on the site of an ancient Inca city; main commercial centre for S Peru; airfield; railway; two universities (1828, 1964); cathedral (1612, rebuilt 19th-c). >> Peru ℹ

Ares [**air**eez] The Greek god of war, son of Zeus and Hera. He is often perceived as hostile, rather than as a national deity, as in other mythologies. >> Areopagus; Mars (mythology)

arête [**a**ret] (Fr 'edge') A sharp, jagged mountain ridge separating cirques or valleys. It is formed by glacial erosion, and often further weathered by frost shattering. >> cirque; glaciation

Arezzo [**aret**soh] 43°28N 11°53E, pop (1995e) 93 300. Town in NW Italy; on the site of an Etruscan settlement; birthplace of Petrarch; cathedral (begun 1277). >> Petrarch; Tuscany

argali [**ah(r)**galee] A wild sheep from the margins of the Gobi Desert; the largest living sheep (1·2 m/4 ft tall at the shoulder); pale brown with white rump; large curling horns on either side of head; also known as **argalis**, **Siberian argali**, or **Marco Polo's sheep**. (*Ovis ammon*.) >> sheep

Argentina, official name **The Argentine Republic**, Span **La República Argentina** pop (1995e) 34 513 000; area (American continent) 2 780 092 sq km/1 073 115 sq mi (excluding the Falkland Is). A republic of SE South America; capital, Buenos Aires; timezone GMT −3; c.85% of population of European origin, 15% of Mestizo/Indian origin; 93% Roman Catholic, with Protestant and Jewish minorities; official language, Spanish; currency, the peso of 100 centavos; Andes stretch the entire length of Argentina (N–S), forming the boundary with Chile; highest peak, Aconcagua (6960 m/22 831 ft); grassy, treeless plain (the *pampa*) to the E; uneven, arid steppes in the S; island of Tierra del Fuego, off the S tip; N Argentina drained by the Paraguay, Paraná, and Uruguay Rivers, which join in the R Plate estuary; moderately humid subtropical climate in the NE, with average annual temperature and rainfall 16°C and 500–1000 mm/20–40 in at Buenos Aires; semi-arid central *pampa*, with temperatures ranging from tropical to moderately cool; rainshadow desert plateau extends to the coast between 40°S and 50°S; S part directly influenced by strong prevailing westerlies; settled in the 16th-c by the Spanish; independence declared in 1816, and United Provinces of the Río de la Plata established; federal constitution 1853, re-established in 1983 after successive military governments; acquisition of the Gran Chaco after war with Paraguay (1865–70); attempt to control the Falkland Is in 1982 failed following war with the UK; new constitution, 1994; governed by a president and a bicameral National Congress, with a Chamber of Deputies and a Senate; considerable European settlement since the opening up of the pampas in the 19th-c; major contribution to economy from agricultural produce and meat processing; oil and gas, chiefly off the coast of Patagonia. >> Buenos Aires; Chaco War; Falklands War; Gran Chaco; pampa(s); Patagonia; Peronism; Plate, River; Tierra del Fuego; RR1000 political leaders

argon Ar, element 18, boiling point −189°C. The commonest of the noble or rare gases, with no known compounds, it makes up about 1% of the Earth's atmosphere. It is used to provide inert atmospheres, especially inside incandescent light bulbs. >> chemical elements; noble gases

argonaut >> **paper nautilus**

Argonauts [**ah(r)**gonawts] In Greek mythology, the heroes who sailed in the ship *Argo* to find the Golden Fleece, under Jason's leadership. >> Golden Fleece; Jason

Argos [**ah(r)**gohs, -gos] 37°38N 22°43E, pop (1995e) 22 000. Ancient town in Peloponnese region, S Greece, involved in wars with Sparta, 7th–4th-c BC; railway; commercial centre; many archaeological remains. >> Greece [i]; Sparta (Greek history)

Argus [**ah(r)**gus] In Greek mythology, **1** A watchman with a hundred eyes, appointed by Hera to watch over Io; after Argus was killed by Hermes, the eyes were placed in the tail of the peacock. >> Io (mythology) **2** The name of Odysseus's dog. >> Odysseus

Århus or **Aarhus** [**aw(r)**hoos] 56°08N 10°11E, pop (1995e) 266 000. Capital city in E Jutland, Denmark; cultural and educational centre; railway; university (1928); cathedral (1201). >> Denmark [i]

aria A song with an Italian text, especially one which forms part of a larger work, such as an opera, oratorio, or cantata.

Ariadne [ari**ad**nee] In Greek mythology, the daughter of the King of Crete (Minos). She enabled Theseus to escape from the labyrinth by giving him a ball of thread. She eventually became the wife of Dionysus. >> Minotaur; Theseus

Ariane >> **European Space Agency**

Arianism >> **Arius**

Arica [a**ree**ka] 18°28S 70°18W, pop (1995e) 207 000. Port city in Chile, on the Pacific coast; most northerly city in Chile; acquired from Peru, 1883; airport; railway; cathedral; major trading outlet for Bolivia. >> Chile [i]

Ariel [**air**eeuhl] The fourth-largest satellite of Uranus: distance from the planet 191 000 km/119 000 mi; diameter 1160 km/720 mi. It was discovered in 1851 by British amateur astronomer William Lassell (1799–1880). >> Uranus (astronomy); RR964

Aries [**air**eez] (Lat 'ram') A constellation in the N sky; brightest star, Hamal. It is a spring sign of the zodiac, lying between Pisces and Taurus. >> constellation; Pisces; zodiac [i]; RR968

Ariosto, Ludovico [ari**os**toh] (1474–1533) Poet, born in Reggio nell'Emilia, Italy. His greatest work was *Orlando furioso* (1516), the Roland epic that forms a continuation of Boiardo's *Orlando innamorato*. >> Boiardo; epic

Aristarchus of Samos [aris**tah(r)**kos], also spelled **Aristarchos** (c.310–230 BC) Alexandrian astronomer who proved by observation that the Sun is much further from the Earth than the Moon. He also maintained that the Sun is the centre of the planetary system.

Aristippus [aris**tip**us] (4th-c BC) Greek philosopher, born in Cyrene, a pupil of Socrates. He was founder of the Cyrenaic school of hedonism, which argued that pleasure was the highest good. >> Cyrenaics; hedonism

Aristophanes [aris**to**faneez] (c.448–c.388 BC) Greek playwright. He is said to have written 54 plays, but only 11 are extant. His most sharply satirical works belong to his early period (up to c.425 BC): *The Acharnians*, *The Knights*, *The Clouds*, *The Wasps*, and *Peace*. In later years he wrote *The Birds*, *Lysistrata*, *Thesmophoriazusae*, *Frogs*, *The Ecclesiazusae*, and *The Plutus*.

Aristotle [**a**ristotl] (384–322 BC) Greek philosopher, scientist, and physician, born in Stagira, Macedonia. At 18 he went to Athens, where he became associated with Plato's Academy for 20 years. He was for a while tutor to the young Alexander the Great. In 335 BC, he opened a school (the Lyceum). His followers were called 'Peripatetics', perhaps from his practice of walking up and down in the garden during his lectures. He wrote the first systematic treatises on logic; made major contributions to the study of natural change, psychology, and biology; and wrote some of the most influential philosophical works in the history of thought (*Metaphysics, Nicomachean Ethics, Politics, Rhetoric, Poetics*). In the Middle Ages, he was referred to simply as 'the Philosopher'. >> Alexander the Great; Plato

arithmetic The practical skill of calculating with numbers, in contrast to number theory. The four operations of addition, subtraction, multiplication, and division are defined over the set of all real numbers, and used essentially for practical results. >> mathematics; number theory

arithmetic average / mean >> **mean**

arithmetic sequence A sequence in which the difference between any one term and the next is constant; sometimes called an **arithmetic progression**. The term **arithmetic series** is now usually reserved for the sum of the terms of the arithmetic sequence. Thus the terms 1,4,7,10 form an arithmetic sequence; 1+4+7+10 is an arithmetic series. >> arithmetic; geometric sequence

Arius [**ah**rius] (Gr **Areios**) (c.250–336) Founder of **Arianism**, born in Libya. He claimed (c.319) that, in the doctrine of the Trinity, the Son was not co-equal or co-eternal with the Father, but only the first and highest of all finite beings, created out of nothing by an act of God's free will. He was excommunicated in 321. The Council of Nicaea (Nice) in 325 defined the absolute unity of the divine essence, and the equality of the three persons of the Trinity. >> Nicaea, Councils of; Trinity

Arizona pop (1995e) 4 097 000; area 295 249 sq km/114 000 sq mi. State in SW USA; the 'Grand Canyon State'; Spanish exploration, 1539; part of New Spain, 1598–1821, then included in newly-independent Mexico; acquired by the USA in the Treaty of Guadalupe Hidalgo, 1848 and the Gadsden Purchase, 1853; a separate territory, 1863; joined the Union as the 48th state, 1912; bounded S by Mexico; highest point Humphreys Peak (3862 m/12 670 ft); to the S are desert basins interspersed with bare mountain peaks, then relatively low, desert plains; capital, Phoenix; cattle on irrigated land; produces two-thirds of the nation's copper supply; tourism the most important industry (Grand Canyon, Petrified Forest, meteor craters); largest Indian population in the USA. >> American Indians; Grand Canyon; Phoenix (USA); United States of America [i]; RR994

ark >> **Ark of the Covenant; Noah**

Arkansas [**ah(r)**kansaw] pop (1995e) 2 473 000; area 137 749 sq km/53 187 sq mi. State in SC USA; the 'Land of Opportunity'; the first white settlement established by the French as part of French Louisiana, 1686; ceded to the US as part of the Louisiana Purchase, 1803; included in the Territory of Missouri, 1812; became a separate territory, 1819; joined the Union as the 25th state, 1836; seceded, 1861; re-admitted, 1868; highest point, Mt Magazine (860 m/2821 ft); the mountainous region is bisected by the Arkansas R valley; extensive plains in the S and E; over half the state covered by commercial forest; many lakes; capital, Little Rock; nation's leading producer of rice and a major tourist area; resistance to school desegregation made Little Rock a focus of world attention in 1957. >> bauxite; civil rights; Little Rock; United States of America [i]; RR994

Ark of the Covenant A portable wooden chest overlaid with gold and having a cherub with extended wings mounted at each end of the golden lid. It had many successive functions – containing the two tablets of the Decalogue, serving as a symbol of the divine presence guiding Israel, and acting as a safeguard in war. It was constructed under Moses, and housed in the Temple under Solomon, but is now lost. >> Moses; Solomon (Hebrew Bible); Ten Commandments

Arkwright, Sir Richard (1732–92) Inventor of mechanical cotton-spinning, born in Preston, Lancashire. In 1768 he set up his celebrated spinning-frame in Preston – the first machine that could produce cotton thread of sufficient strength to be used as warp. >> cotton [i]; spinning

Arles [ah(r)l] or **Arles-sur-Rhône** 43°41N 4°38E, pop (1995e) 54 200. Old town in SE France; capital of Gaul, 4th-c; formerly capital of Provence; railway; cathedral (11th-c); Roman remains, including a huge arena and theatre (a world heritage site). >> Gaul; Provence

Arlington pop (1995e) 184 000; area 68 sq km/26 sq mi. County of Virginia, USA, a suburb of Washington, DC; site of the **Arlington National Cemetery** (1920); Pentagon Building; Washington National Airport. >> Pentagon; Washington (DC)

Arlington, Henry Bennet, 1st Earl of (1618–85) English statesman, born in Arlington, Greater London. A member of the Cabal ministry under Charles II, and secretary of state (1662–74), he was created Earl of Arlington in 1672. >> Cabal; Charles II (of England)

Arlott, (Leslie Thomas) John (1914–91) Writer, journalist, and broadcaster, born in Basingstoke, Hampshire. As a BBC cricket commentator on radio and television he became one of the country's most recognizable broadcasting voices.

arm A term commonly used to denote the whole of the upper limb; more precisely, in anatomy, the region between the shoulder and elbow joints, distinguished from the *forearm* (between the elbow and wrist joints), and the *hand* (beyond the wrist joint). The bones are the *humerus* in the arm, the *radius* (on the outside) and *ulna* (on the inside) in the forearm, the *carpals* in the wrist region, and the *Metacarpals* and *phalanges* in the hand.

armadillo [ah(r)ma**dil**oh] A nocturnal mammal (an edentate), found from South America to S USA; long snout and tubular ears; head and body covered with bony plates; large front claws for digging; eats ants, termites, and other small animals. (Family: Dasypodidae, 20 species.) >> Edentata

Armageddon [ah(r)ma**ged**n] A place mentioned in the New Testament (*Rev* 16.16) as the site of the final cosmic battle between the forces of good and evil in the last days. >> eschatology; Revelation, Book of

Armagh (city) [ah(r)**mah**] 54°21N 6°39W, pop (1995e) 14 700. City in Armagh, SE Northern Ireland; seat of the kings of Ulster, 400 BC–AD 333; religious centre of Ireland in the 5th-c; Protestant and Catholic archbishoprics; city status, 1995; St Patrick's Cathedral, observatory (1791). >> Armagh (county); Patrick, St

Armagh (county) [ah(r)**mah**], Ir **Ard Mhacha** pop (1995e) 131 000; area 1254 sq km/484 sq mi. County in SE Northern Ireland; bounded S and SW by the Republic of Ireland; rises to 577 m/1893 ft at Slieve Gullion; county town, Armagh. >> Armagh (city); Northern Ireland [i]

Armani, Giorgio [ah(r)**mah**nee] (1935–) Fashion designer, born in Piacenza, Italy. He became a designer for Nino Cerruti (1930–) in 1961, then set up his own company in 1975, designing first for men, and later for women.

Armenia (republic) [ah(r)**meen**ia], official name **Republic of Armenia**, Armenian **Hayastani Hanrapetut'yun** pop (1995e) 3 671 000; area 29 800 sq km/11 500 sq mi. Republic in S Transcaucasia; capital, Yerevan; timezone GMT +3; major ethnic groups, Armenian (90%), Azer, Kurd, Russian, but ethnic conflict since 1990 makes accurate current estimates impossible; official language, Armenian; religions, Christian (Armenian Church), Russian Orthodox; unit of currency, the dram; a mountainous country, rising to 4090 m/13 418 ft at Mt Aragats (W); chief river, the Araks; climate varies with elevation; chiefly dry and continental; winter average −3°C, summer 25°C; partitioned between Turkey and Persia, 1639; ceded to Russia, 1828; proclaimed a Soviet Socialist Republic by the Soviet Union, 1920; constituent republic of the USSR, 1936; declaration of independence, 1991; governed by a president, prime minister, and Supreme Council; lays claim to Turkish Armenia; dispute with neighbouring Azerbaijan over Nagorno-Karabakh region; large mineral resources, chiefly copper; hydroelectric power on R Razdan. >> Armenia (Turkey); Russia ℹ; Transcaucasia; Yerevan; RR1001 political leaders

Armenia (Turkey) [ah(r)**mee**nia], ancient **Minni** Ancient kingdom largely occupying the present-day Van region of E Turkey and parts of NW Iran and the republic of Armenia; ruled by the Ottoman Turks from 1514; E territory ceded to Persia, 1620; further districts lost to Russia, 1828–9; today Turkish Armenia comprises the NE provinces of Turkey; chief towns, Kars, Erzurum, Erzincan; Armenian nationalist movement developed in the 19th-c. >> Armenia (republic); Armenians; Turkey ℹ

Armenians A people who came from Armenia, now in NE Turkey and the republic of Armenia. Of Indo-European origin, they speak a language of that family with some Caucasian features, and are Christians. Today 4·15 million live in the republics of the former USSR, including 2·7 million in Armenia; very few still live in Turkey. >> Armenia (republic; Turkey); Indo-European languages; Monophysites

Arminius, Jacobus [ah(r)**min**ius], Lat name of **Jakob Hermandszoon** (1560–1609) Protestant theologian, born in Oudewater, The Netherlands. He was opposed to the Calvinistic doctrine of predestination, arguing that God bestows forgiveness on all who repent and believe in Christ. **Arminianism** influenced the development of religious thought all over Europe. >> Calvin, John; predestination; Remonstrants

Armistice Day The anniversary of the day (11 Nov 1918) on which World War 1 ended, marked by a two-minute silence at 11 o'clock, the hour when the fighting stopped; replaced after World War 2 by **Remembrance Sunday**. The US equivalent is Veterans' Day. >> Remembrance Sunday; Veterans' Day; World War 1

Armory show An art exhibition, officially entitled The International Exhibition of Modern Art, held at the 69th Regiment Armory in New York, 1913. It introduced modern art to the USA. >> modern art

armoured car Typically a four-wheel-drive, light-armoured fighting vehicle with protection against small-arms fire, armed with a machine gun or small calibre cannon in a rotating turret. The first mechanical armoured cars were developed just before 1914, with the roles of reconnaissance and rear area protection. >> armoured fighting vehicle

armoured fighting vehicle (AFV) A generic term for combat vehicles such as tanks, armoured cars, armoured personnel carriers, and infantry fighting vehicles which have armour protection against hostile fire. >> armoured car; tank

arms, coats of >> **heraldry** ℹ

Armstrong, Louis, nickname **Satchmo** (1898/1900–71) Jazz trumpeter and singer, born in New Orleans, LA. He moved to Chicago in 1922 to join Joe (King) Oliver's band. His melodic inventiveness established the central role of the improvising soloist in jazz, especially in a series of recordings known as the 'Hot Fives' and 'Hot Sevens' (1925–8). He was also a popular singer and entertainer, in such films as *Pennies from Heaven* (1936), and *High Society* (1956). >> improvisation; jazz

Armstrong, Neil (Alden) (1930–) Astronaut, born in Wapakoneta, OH. In 1966 he commanded Gemini 8, and as commander of Apollo 11 in 1969 became the first man to set foot on the Moon. >> Apollo programme; astronaut

Armstrong-Jones, Antony >> **Snowdon, 1st Earl of**

army >> **Black Watch; Foreign Legion; Gurkhas; Horse Guards; janissaries; Marines; militia; Red Army** (China / USSR); **SAS; women's services**

Arnauld, Antoine [ah(r)noh], known as **the Great Arnauld** (1612–94) French theologian and philosopher, associated with the community at Port Royal, Paris. He became famous for his controversial writings against the Jesuits and in defence of the Jansenists. >> Jansen; Jesuits; Port Royal

Arne, Thomas (Augustine) (1710–78) Composer, born in London. He wrote over 50 operas and other works, notably 'Rule, Britannia' (from *The Masque of Alfred*).

Arnhem [**ah(r)**nem] 52°00N 5°53E, pop (1995e) 136 000. City in E Netherlands, on the right bank of the lower Rhine; seat of the law courts and the provincial government; charter, 1233; heavily damaged in World War 2; scene of unsuccessful airborne landing of British troops (Sep 1944); railway. >> Netherlands, The ℹ

Arnhem Land [**ah(r)**nem] The peninsular plateau in N Australia, E of Darwin; named after the Dutch ship which arrived here in 1618; chief town, Nhulunbuy; Aborigine reserve; bauxite and uranium mining. >> Aborigines; Darwin

arni >> **water buffalo**

Arnold, Benedict (1741–1801) American general and turncoat, born in Norwich, CT. In the War of Independence he joined the colonial forces, and in 1778 was placed in command of Philadelphia. He later conspired with John André (1751–80) to betray West Point. When André was captured, Arnold fled to the British lines, and was given a command in the royal army. >> American Revolution

Arnold, Sir Malcolm (Henry) (1921–) Composer, born in Northampton, Northamptonshire. His compositions include nine symphonies, 18 concertos, ballets, operas, and much film music, notably *Bridge over the River Kwai* (1957, Oscar).

Arnold, Matthew (1822–88) Poet and critic, born in Laleham, Surrey. Apart from his many poems, he wrote several works of criticism, such as *Culture and Anarchy* (1869), and of religious belief, such as *God and the Bible* (1875).

Arnold, Thomas (1795–1842) Teacher and scholar, born in East Cowes, I of Wight, the headmaster of Rugby School, and father of Matthew Arnold. He became headmaster of Rugby in 1828, reforming the school system and becoming both loved and feared (as recounted in Thomas Hughes's *Tom Brown's Schooldays*). >> Arnold, Matthew

Arnold of Brescia [**bre**shia] (c.1100–55) Clergyman and politician, born in Brescia, Italy. His preaching against the wealth and power of the Church led to his banishment from Italy (1139). He later became involved in an insurrection against the papal government, was condemned for heresy, and hanged.

aromatherapy A popular form of complementary medicine which uses concentrated essential oils extracted from plants. The application of oil to the skin is an effective way of getting active agents to be absorbed into the bloodstream, and aromatherapy treatment is often combined with massage. Cosmetic aromatherapy is offered by many beauty salons, sometimes in conjuction with facial massage, usually using proprietary brands of preblended oils. >> alternative medicine

Arp, Jean or **Hans** (1887–1966) Sculptor, painter, and poet, born in Strasbourg, France. He was one of the founders of the Dada movement in Zürich in 1916. >> Dada

arquebus [**ah(r)**kwebuhs] A firearm dating from the 15th-c, a development of the hand cannon, in outline a forerunner of the musket. Fired in action by a flame held to the touch-hole, the weapon was supported by a forked rest holding up the barrel at the operator's chest height. >> musket

Arrabal, Fernando [ara**bal**] (1932–) Playwright and novelist, born in Melilla, Spanish Morocco. Writing in the tradition of the Theatre of the Absurd, he coined the term *panic theatre*, intended to disorder the senses by shock. >> absurdism

Arran Area 430 sq km/166 sq mi. Island in North Ayrshire council, W Scotland; separated from W coast mainland by the Firth of Clyde; rises to 874 m/2867 ft at Goat Fell; chief centres, Brodick, Lamlash, Lochranza; a major tourist area. >> Scotland [i]

Arras [**a**ras] 50°17N 2°46E, pop (1995e) 44 000. Old frontier town in N France; formerly famous for its tapestries; railway; bishopric; town hall (16th-c), cathedral (18th-c); birthplace of Robespierre; many war cemeteries nearby. >> Robespierre; Vimy Ridge

Arrau, Claudio [**a**row] (1903–91) Pianist, born in Chillán, Chile. He is noted for his interpretations of the 19th-c solo repertory.

array processor A particular type of digital computer which allows arrays of numbers to be processed simultaneously. In suitable applications, this can lead to marked increases in computing speeds. >> digital computer

arrest The stopping and detaining of a person suspected of a criminal offence; referred to as **apprehension** in Scotland. Arrests are carried out mainly by the police, but a **citizen's arrest** is possible in certain circumstances. A person wrongly arrested may bring civil proceedings for false imprisonment. >> criminal law

arrhythmia [a**rith**mia] A disturbance of the normal regular rhythm of the heart. There are many types, some of which are harmless, but a few are a serious threat to life. >> heart [i]

arrow-poison frog A slender frog, native to Central and South America; often brightly coloured; inhabits woodland; skin very poisonous; also known as **poison-arrow frog**. (Family: Dendrobatidae, 116 species.) >> frog

arrowroot A type of starch obtained from the tuberous roots of several plants. The most important is probably **West Indian arrowroot** (*Maranta arundinacea*), a perennial growing to 2 m/6½ ft; sepals and petals in threes; native to South America, and cultivated in New World tropics for edible starch. >> canna; starch; tuber

Arrow War >> **Opium Wars**

arsenic As, element 33. A grey metalloid in the nitrogen family, used in some lead alloys and in semiconductors, especially gallium arsenide (GaAs). The name is commonly applied to arsenic (III) oxide (As_2O_3), the highly poisonous white arsenic of rodent control and detective novels. >> chemical elements; metalloids; nitrogen

arsine [**ah(r)**seen] AsH_3, boiling point −55°C. A gaseous hydride of arsenic, formed by reducing solutions of arsenic compounds. >> arsenic

art Originally, 'skill' (of any kind), a meaning the word still has in many everyday contexts. Modern usage referring especially to painting, drawing, or sculpture emerged by c.1700, but the modern sense of art as a uniquely significant form of creation and of the artist as a creative genius of a special kind arose somewhat later. The related concept of **fine arts**, considered as sharing common principles and distinct from science, religion, or the practical concerns of everyday life, also emerged in the 18th-c, together with a new subject, aesthetics, the philosophy of art. By the 19th-c, art was associated with the creative production of objects for abstract contemplation, with no useful function. The definition of art has become controversial again in the 20th-c. New forms, such as film, television, street theatre, pop music, and happenings, are claimed by some to be art, by others not. >> abstract / auto-destructive / biomorphic / concrete / figurative / kinetic / Minimal / modern / Op / permutational / Pop art; Art Brut / Deco / Nouveau; Baroque (art and architecture); Constructivism; Cubism; Dada; Expressionism; functionalism (art and architecture); Futurism; Impressionism (art); Mannerism; Neoclassicism (art); Neoexpressionism; Orphism; Realism (art and literature); Rococo; Romanticism; Suprematism; Surrealism; Vorticism; aesthetics

Artaud, Antonin [ah(r)toh] (1896–1948) Playwright, actor, theatre director, and theorist of the Surrealist movement, born in Marseilles, France. His chief work was *Le Théâtre et son double* (1938, The Theatre and its Double). >> Surrealism

Art Brut [ah(r) broo] A term coined by French painter Jean Dubuffet (1901–85) for the art of untrained people, especially mental patients, prisoners, and socially dispossessed persons generally. >> art

Art Deco [ah(r)t **dek**oh] A term abbreviated from the Paris *Exposition Internationale des Arts Décoratifs et Industriels Modernes* ('International Exhibition of Modern Industrial and Decorative Arts'), 1925. It has come to refer to decorative arts of the 1920s and 1930s generally, and the 'modernistic' style associated with them. >> art; Art Nouveau; Cubism

Artemis [**ah(r)**temis] In Greek mythology, the daughter of Zeus and Leto, twin sister of Apollo, and goddess of the Moon. Being connected with hunting, she is depicted with bow and arrows. >> Actaeon; Diana

arteriole >> **artery**

arteriosclerosis [ah(r)teeriohskle**roh**sis] An umbrella term covering several pathological changes in medium-sized arteries. The most important is *atheroma*, in which cholesterol and other substances are deposited on the inner layer of the vessel. >> artery; atherosclerosis

artery A vessel of the body which usually conveys blood to body tissues. Large, medium, and small arteries (**arterioles**) can be distinguished. With increasing age, arteries tend to become blocked with deposits of cholesterol-based material (*atheroma*). >> arteriosclerosis; atherosclerosis; blood vessels [i]; vein

artesian basin A shallow basin-shaped aquifer with impermeable rock strata above and below it, thus confining the groundwater under pressure. Sinking a well into the aquifer allows the water to rise to the surface without pumping. >> aquifer

art gallery >> **Hermitage; Louvre; museum; National Gallery; National Gallery of Art; National Gallery of Australia; National Portrait Gallery; Pitti Palace; Prado; Rijksmuseum; Tate Gallery; Tretyakov Gallery; Uffizi**

arthritis An inflammation of joints associated with swelling, pain, redness, and local heat. Pain and limitation of movement are characteristic. >> gout; inflammation; joint; osteoarthritis

arthropod [**ah(r)**thropod] A member of the largest and most diverse phylum of animals (Arthropoda), characterized by jointed limbs and an external chitinous skeleton. Arthropods have segmented bodies, most segments carrying a pair of limbs variously modified for locomotion, feeding, respiration, or reproduction. Size ranges from 80 μm to 3·6 m/11$\frac{3}{4}$ ft. Arthropods include the insects, arachnids, crustaceans, trilobites, centipedes, millipedes, and several minor groups. >> Arachnida; centipede; chitin; crustacean; insect [i]; millipede; phylum; trilobite

Arthur (?6th-c) A semi-legendary king of the Britons, who is represented as uniting the British tribes against the pagan invaders (5th–6th-c AD), and as the champion of Christianity. It is very doubtful if he is a historic figure. His story passed into literature and many legends became interwoven with it, including those of the Round Table and the Holy Grail (both from the 12th–13th-c). >> Camelot; Excalibur: Galahad, Sir; Guinevere; Lancelot, Sir; Malory, Thomas; Merlin; Morgan le Fay; Uther Pendragon

artichoke >> **globe artichoke; Jerusalem artichoke**

Articles of Confederation The organizing document of the USA from 1781 to 1788. It established a single-house Congress, with one vote for each state and with no executive, courts, or independent revenue. It was replaced by the present Constitution in 1788. >> Constitution of the United States; Continental Congress

artificial insemination (AI) The instrumental introduction of seminal fluid into the vagina in order to fertilize an ovum. The semen may be that of the husband (**AIH**) or of a donor (**AID**). >> infertility; semen

artificial intelligence (AI) A term applied to the study and use of computers that can simulate some of the characteristics normally ascribed to human intelligence, such as learning, deduction, intuition, and self-correction. The subject encompasses many branches of computer science, including cybernetics, knowledge-based systems, natural language processing, pattern recognition, and robotics. >> cognitive science; cybernetics; intelligence; robotics

artificial respiration A procedure to maintain the movement of air into and out of the lungs when natural breathing is inadequate or has ceased. A short-term emergency method is 'mouth-to-mouth' respiration. With the head of the patient bent backwards and the nose pinched, the resuscitator takes a deep breath and expels his or her own breath into the open mouth and lungs of the victim, either directly or via a mouthpiece, repeating the manoeuvre 10–15 times a minute. When more prolonged assistance is indicated, a mechanical ventilator supplies a predetermined volume of oxygen at given intervals, usually via a tube inserted in the trachea. >> cardiac resuscitation [i]; respiration; *see illustration above*

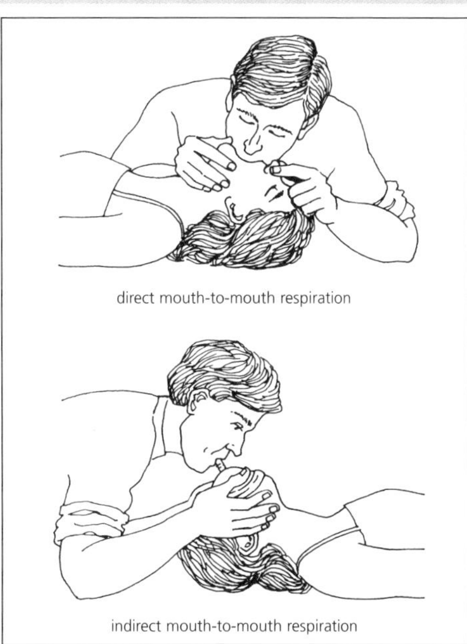

direct mouth-to-mouth respiration
indirect mouth-to-mouth respiration

Artificial respiration

artillery The heavy ordnance of an army; in particular, its longer-range weapons, as distinct from the small arms that each individual soldier carries. Modern artillery includes guns (known as 'tube' artillery) and missiles. Rocket artillery ranges from simple, unguided bombardment missiles to medium-range, nuclear-armed battlefield missiles. >> anti-aircraft gun; guided missile; howitzer

artiodactyl [ah(r)tioh**dak**til] An ungulate mammal; foot with two or four toes (first always absent, second and fifth small or absent); weight carried on the third and fourth toe, which usually form a *cloven hoof*. (Order: Artiodactyla, 192 species.) >> Bovidae; deer; perissodactyl [i]; ruminant [i]; ungulate

Art Nouveau [ah(r) noo**voh**] Literally 'new art' which flourished from c.1890 to c.1905, mainly in the decorative arts, characterized by naturalistic plant and flower motifs, and writhing patterns of sinuous, curling lines. >> art; Beardsley; Mackintosh; Gaudí; Lalique

Arts and Crafts Movement A predominantly English movement in architecture, art, and the applied arts during the second half of the 19th-c, which advocated the renewed use of handicraft and simple decoration in reaction to industrial machinery and contemporary aesthetic eclecticism. The movement centred on William Morris. >> Bauhaus; garden city; Gothic Revival; Morris, William; Pugin; Queen Anne Style; Ruskin

art therapy The use of self-expression through drawing and painting as a form of treatment for emotional problems. It was introduced to England during the 1940s as a result of a collaboration between artist Adrian Hill and psychotherapist Irene Champernowne. >> psychotherapy

Aruba [a**roo**ba] pop (1995e) 69 400; area 193 sq km/ 74 sq mi. Island of the E Caribbean, 30 km/19 mi N of Venezuela; capital, Oranjestad; airport; rises to 189 m/ 620 ft at Jamanota; formally separated from the Netherlands Antilles Federation in 1986, and became a self-governing member of the Kingdom of The Netherlands; full independence in 1996. >> Netherlands Antilles [i]

arum lily [aruhm, **air**uhm] A fleshy-stemmed perennial (*Zantedeschia aethiopica*) native to S Africa, and widely introduced elsewhere; leaves large, arrowhead-shaped, glossy; flower yellow and white; also called **calla lily**. (Family: Araceae.)

Arundel, Thomas [**a**ruhndl] (1353–1414) English clergyman and statesman, who became Archbishop of York (1388) and of Canterbury (1396). He supported the nobles opposed to Richard II, who banished him (1397), but he returned to help seat Henry of Lancaster on the throne (1399). >> Henry IV (of England); Richard II

Aryan [**air**ian] A prehistoric people and their language, an extinct member of the Indo-European language family. Aryans reputedly colonized Iran and N India, and gave rise to the Indian subcontinent's Indo-Aryan languages. >> Indo-European languages

Asad, Hafez al- [**a**sad] (1928–) Syrian general, statesman, and president (1971–), born in Qardaha, Syria. A member of the minority Alawi sect, he rose to high government office through the military and the Ba'ath Party. He instigated a coup in 1970, became prime minister, and then president. Having long enjoyed Soviet support, he was left isolated by the end of the Cold War and Russian–American co-operation in the Middle East. >> Alawi 2; Syria [i]

Asante >> **Ashanti**

ASA rating >> **ISO speed rating**

asbestos The name applied to varieties of fibrous minerals of the serpentine and amphibole groups. Fibres can be separated and woven into cloths or felted into sheets. It is an excellent insulator of heat and electricity, does not burn, and is resistant to chemical attack. The varieties used in manufacture are principally *chrysotile* (white asbestos), a form of serpentine, and *crocidolite* (blue asbestos), an amphibole. Amosite (brown asbestos) has also had fairly widespread use. All forms of asbestos cause **asbestosis**, and crocidolite and amosite are carcinogenic; as a result, several countries have banned their use, either totally or partially. >> amphiboles; serpentine

Ascaris [**as**karis] A genus of parasitic roundworm found in vertebrate hosts, typically pigs and humans; usually present in low numbers in the small intestine. (Phylum: Nematoda.) >> nematode; parasitology

Ascension, Feast of In the Christian calendar, the fifth Thursday (being 40 days – *Acts* 1) after Easter. It commemorates Jesus's last appearance to his disciples, when he was 'lifted up' from them. >> Easter; Jesus Christ

Ascension Island 7°56S 14°25W; pop (1992e) 1500; area 88 sq km/34 sq mi. Small, arid, volcanic island in the S Atlantic; highest point, Green Mountain (859 m/2818 ft); discovered by the Portuguese on Ascension Day 1501; British territory, since 1815, administered under the Admiralty; made a dependency of St Helena in 1922; British and US air bases. >> Atlantic Ocean; St Helena

asceticism [a**set**isizm] A variety of austere practices involving the renunciation or denial of ordinary bodily and sensual gratifications. These may include fasting, meditation, a life of solitude, the renunciation of possessions, denial of sexual gratification, and, in the extreme, the mortification of the flesh.

Ascham, Roger [**as**ham] (1515–68) Humanist, born in Kirby Wiske, North Yorkshire. He was tutor to Princess Elizabeth (1548–50), and later Latin secretary to Mary I. His main works were *Toxophilus* (1545), a treatise in defence of archery, and *The Scholemaster* (1570), a treatise on Classical education. >> humanism

ASCII code [**as**kee] A set of widely used binary codes, defined as the **American Standards Code for Information Interchange**. ASCII-96, an 8-bit code including a parity check bit, the most common code in use for storing text character strings in computers, allows 96 printing characters to be defined (letters, digits, arithmetic symbols, and punctuation characters) together with a number of control characters, such as printer carriage return. >> bit; EBCDIC code; parity check

Asclepios or **Asclepius** [as**klee**pius] In Greek mythology, a hero who became a god of healing, the son of Apollo and Koronis. Because he restored Hippolytus to life, he was killed by the thunderbolt of Zeus. >> Aesculapius; Hippolytus

Ascomycetes [askohmiy**seet**eez] A subdivision of the true fungi; includes cup fungi, yeasts, truffles, and many parasitic forms. (Division: Eumycota.) >> fungus; truffle; yeast

ascorbic acid Vitamin C, largely found in citrus fruits, green vegetables, and potatoes. It functions in the body to maintain tissue integrity; a deficiency causes scurvy. >> scurvy; vitamins [i]

ASDIC [**az**dik] An acronym of **Admiralty Submarine Detection Investigation Committee** (1917), an early form of submarine detection device used on warships of the Royal Navy. Its operating principle was sonar. >> sonar

asepsis [ay**sep**sis] The absence of micro-organisms from body surfaces (eg the skin) or from wounds. In surgical operations, the procedures adopted include skin sterilization, the wearing of sterile gloves and gowns, the sterilization of instruments, and the removal of contaminated air from the theatre. >> surgery

asexual reproduction >> **reproduction**

Asgard [**az**gah(r)d] In Norse mythology, the home of the gods, created by Odin in the upper branches of the World-Tree, and therefore in the approximate centre of things. >> Odin

ash A deciduous tree native to the N hemisphere; leaves pinnate; flowers borne in dense clusters appearing before leaves; seeds (*keys*) have a papery wing which aids in wind dispersal. (Genus: *Fraxinus*, 70 species. Family: Oleaceae.) >> pinnate

Ashanti or Asante [a**shan**tee] A Kwa-speaking Akan people of S Ghana and adjacent areas. They form a confederacy of chiefdoms, founded in the late 17th-c. The independent Ashanti state became a major threat to British trade on the coast, until defeated (1873) by Sir Garnet Wolseley. The state was annexed by the British in 1902. >> Ghana [i]; Wolseley

Ashbery, John (Lawrence) (1927–) Poet, born in New York City. He is recognized as the major postmodern poet of his generation. His *Selected Poems* were published in 1985, and *Hotel Lautreamont* in 1992.

Ashcan School A derisive name given to a group of US Realist painters and illustrators, also called *The Eight*. Formed in 1907, they included John Sloan (1871–1951), and George Bellows (1882–1925). They painted everyday subjects in an attempt to bring art back into direct contact with ordinary life, especially street life in New York City. >> Realism (art and literature)

Ashcroft, Dame Peggy, originally **Edith Margaret Emily Ashcroft** (1907–91) Actress, born in Croydon, Greater London. Her great roles include Juliet, in Gielgud's production (1935), Cleopatra (1935), and Hedda Gabler (1954). Her films include *A Passage to India* (1984), for which she won an Oscar as best supporting actress. >> Gielgud

Ashdod [ash**dohd**] 31°48N 34°38E, pop (1995e) 101 000. Seaport in W Israel; ancient Philistine city; modern city founded in 1956 as the major port of S Israel; railway. >> Israel [i]; Philistines

Ashdown, Paddy, popular name of **Jeremy John Durham Ashdown** (1941–) British politician, born in India.

Elected to parliament in 1983, he acted as a Liberal Party spokesman on trade and industry, and became leader of the newly constituted Social and Liberal Democratic Party, 1988–99. >> Liberal Party (UK)

Asher, Jane (1946–) Actress and cake designer, born in London. From 1957 she performed regularly in the theatre and on television, her films including *Alfie* (1966) and *Paris By Night* (1988). Among her many books on baking are *Calendar of Cakes* (1989) and *Jane Asher's Complete Book of Cake Decorating Ideas* (1993). She is married to the cartoonist Gerald Scarfe. >> Scarfe

Ashes, the A symbolic trophy contested by the cricket teams of England and Australia. It originated in 1882 after the *Sporting Times* printed an obituary to English cricket following the country's first defeat by Australia on home soil. An urn containing the ashes of a stump used in that match remains at Lord's cricket ground. >> cricket (sport) ℹ

Ashkenazim [ash**ke**nahzim] Jews of C and E European descent, as distinguished from Sephardim Jews, who are of Spanish or Portuguese descent. They have developed their own customs, traditions of interpretation of the Talmud, music, and language (Yiddish). >> Judaism; Sephardim; Yiddish

Ashkenazy, Vladimir [ashke**nah**zee] (1937–) Pianist and conductor, born in Nizhni Novgorod (formerly Gorky), Russia. After earning an international reputation as a concert pianist, he has turned increasingly to conducting, since 1987 directing the Royal Philharmonic Orchestra (1987–95) and the Radio Symphony Orchestra, Berlin (1989–).

Ashley, Laura, *née* **Mountney** (1925–85) Fashion designer, born in Merthyr Tydfil, S Wales. In 1949, she started up a business designing and producing furnishing materials, later developing this into an international chain of boutiques selling clothes, furnishing fabrics, and wallpapers. Her work was characterized by a romantic style and the use of natural fabrics, especially cotton.

Ashmolean Museum A museum at Oxford University, England. Elias Ashmole (1617–92) donated the core of the collection to the University in 1675, and the museum was opened eight years later. >> Oxford University ℹ

Ashmore and Cartier Islands Area c.3 sq km/1½ sq mi. Uninhabited Australian external territory in the Indian Ocean 320 km/200 mi off the NW coast of Australia; consists of the Ashmore Is (Middle, East and West) and Cartier I; formerly administered by the Northern Territory, it became a separate Commonwealth Territory in 1978. >> Australia ℹ; Northern Territory

ashram [**ash**ram] An Indian religious community whose members lead lives of austere self-discipline and dedicated service. A well-known ashram was that of Mahatma Gandhi. >> Gandhi

Ashton, Sir Frederick (William Mallandaine) (1906–88) British dancer and choreographer, born in Guayaquil, Ecuador. He became co-director of Sadler's Wells (later the Royal Ballet) (1952–63) and then director (1963–70). >> choreography; Royal Ballet

Ashura [a**shoo**ra] A Muslim fast day observed on the 10th of Muharram, particularly among Shiite Muslims, in commemoration of the death of Husain, grandson of Mohammed. >> Islam; Shiites

Ashurbanipal >> **Sardanapalus**

Ash Wednesday The first day of Lent. The name derives from the ritual, observed in the ancient Church and continued in Roman Catholic and some Anglican Churches, of making a cross on the forehead of Christians with blessed ashes. >> Lent; Palm Sunday

Asia area c.44·5 million sq km/17·2 million sq mi. The largest continent; maximum length, 8500 km/5300 mi; maximum width, 9600 km/6000 mi; chief mountain system, the Himalayas, rising to 8848 m/29 028 ft at Mt Everest; major rivers include the Yangtze (Chiangjiang), Yellow, Brahmaputra, Ayeyarwady (Irrawaddy), Indus, and Ganges. >> China ℹ; Commonwealth of Independent States ℹ; Himalayas; India ℹ; Ural Mountains; RR971

Asia Minor >> **Anatolia**

Asian Games A multi-sport competition first held at New Delhi, India in 1951, and since 1954 held quadrennially. The Far Eastern Games, the predecessors of the Asian Games, were first held at Manila in 1913.

Asimov, Isaac [**az**imov] (1920–92) Biochemist and a master of science-fiction writing, born in Petrovichi, Russia. His family emigrated to the USA in 1923 and he was naturalized in 1928. His many novels and story collections include *I, Robot* (1950) and *The Foundation Trilogy* (1953). Professor of biochemistry at the University of Boston, after 1958 he worked mainly on textbooks and works of popular science. >> biochemistry; science fiction

Asmara or **Asmera** [as**me**ra] 15°20N 38°58E, pop (1995e) 386 000. Capital of Eritrea region, Ethiopia; altitude 2350 m/7710 ft; occupied by Italians, 1889; regional capital, 1897; occupied by British, 1941; airport; university (1958); cathedral (1922), mosque (1937). >> Ethiopia ℹ

Asmoneans [azmo**nee**anz] >> **Maccabees**

Aśoka or **Ashoka** [a**shoh**ka] (3rd-c BC) King of India (c.264–238 BC), the last ruler of the Mauryan dynasty. He renounced armed conquest and became a convert to Buddhism, which subsequently spread throughout India. He advocated a policy called *dharma* (principles of right life), but after his death the Mauryan empire declined.

asp A venomous African snake (*Naja haje*) of family Elapidae; Cleopatra is said to have committed suicide by forcing this species to bite her; also known as the **Egyptian cobra**. The name is also used for venomous African **burrowing asps** (**atractaspid snakes** or **mole vipers**) of family Colubridae, and for the European *Vipera aspis* (**European asp**, **asp viper**, or **aspic viper**) of family Viperidae. >> snake; viper ℹ

asparagus A perennial native to Europe and Asia; erect or spreading, some species climbers, all with feathery foliage; flowers tiny, white or yellow, bell- or star-shaped; berries green, red, or black. Young shoots of *Asparagus officinalis* are prized as a vegetable. (Genus: *Asparagus*, 300 species. Family: Liliaceae.) >> vegetable

Aspel, Michael (Terence) (1933–) British broadcaster and writer. He achieved public prominence as a television newsreader (1960–8), then became a freelance broadcaster, best known for his genial interviewing style in *Aspel and Company* (1984–93) and as presenter of *This is Your Life* (from 1988).

aspen A species of poplar (*Populus tremula*), also called **trembling aspen**, because the greyish-green, rounded-to-ovoid leaves have flattened stalks, allowing the blades to flutter in the slightest breeze. (Family: Salicaceae.) >> poplar

Aspen Lodge >> **Camp David**

Aspergillus [asper**jil**us] A genus of typically asexually reproducing fungus that can cause food spoilage and produce disease in humans. (Subdivision: Ascomycetes. Order: Eurotiales.) >> fungus

asphalt A semi-solid bituminous residue of the evaporation of petroleum (formed by slow evaporation in nature or by distillation in industry). It is usually employed mixed with some solid mineral matter for roofing, road-making, etc. >> bitumen 1; petroleum

asphodel [**as**fodel] The name applied to two related genera native to the Mediterranean region and Asia, with erect stems, narrow, grass-like leaves, and spikes of flowers each with six segments. *Asphodelus* (12 species) has leaves V-shaped in cross-section, flowers white or pink.

Asphodeline (15 species) has leaves triangular in cross-section, flowers yellow. (Family: Liliaceae.)

aspidistra An evergreen perennial (*Aspidistra elatior*), native to E Asia; leaves long-stalked, elliptical, leathery, lasting several years; flowers bell-shaped, dull purple. It is much favoured as a pot-plant. (Family: Liliaceae.)

aspirin or **acetylsalicylic acid** A widely used drug effective against many types of minor pain (headache, menstruation, neuralgia), inflammation (it is frequently prescribed for rheumatoid diseases), and fever. It has more recently been discovered to prevent the formation of blood clots, and therefore to reduce the incidence of coronary and cerebral thrombosis. >> analgesics; thrombosis

Asquith, Herbert Henry Asquith, 1st Earl of Oxford (1852–1928) British Liberal statesman and prime minister (1908–16), born in Morley, West Yorkshire. He became an MP (1886), home secretary (1892–5), Chancellor of the Exchequer (1905–8), and premier. His regime was notable for the Parliament Act of 1911, suffragette troubles, the declaration of war (1914), and the Sinn Féin rebellion (1916). >> Liberal Party (UK); Sinn Féin; World War 1

ass A rare wild horse; small, long ears, short erect mane; pale grey or brown; domesticated thousands of years ago for carrying loads. The modern *donkey* (or *burro*) is a domesticated form of the African wild ass. (Genus: *Equus*. Subgenus: *Asinus*, 3 species.) >> horse [i]; mule (zoology)

Assam [**a**sam] pop (1995e) 24 132 000; area 78 523 sq km/ 30 310 sq mi. State in E India, almost completely separated from India by Bangladesh; important strategic role in World War 2; unicameral legislature; crossed by the R Brahmaputra; world's largest river island of Majuli is a pilgrimage centre; capital, Dispur; produces almost half of India's crude oil. >> India [i]

Assamese >> **Indo-Aryan languages**

assault An attack upon the person of another, causing them to fear actual injury. Contact is not an essential ingredient of assault: threatening gestures can suffice. >> battery (law); mayhem

assaying A chemical analysis which determines the amount of the principal or potent constituent of a mixture. The technique is mainly used for precious metals and for drugs. >> chemistry

assemblage Art objects formed by sticking together bits and pieces to make a three-dimensional whole. The term includes collages, readymades, and a variety of works made from crushed automobiles, old clothes, and other objects. >> collage; readymade

Assemblies of God A Christian pentecostalist denomination formed in the USA and Canada in the early 20th-c. It believes baptism by the Holy Spirit to be evidenced by speaking in tongues. >> Holy Spirit; glossolalia; Pentecostalism

assembly language A set of convenient mnemonics corresponding to the machine-code instructions of a specific central processor unit or microprocessor, defined by the manufacturer. Assembly language is more convenient for the programmer than machine code, and is translated (**assembled**) into machine code by an **assembly program**, usually known as an **assembler**. >> machine code

Assize Court A legal system in England and Wales, dating from the time of Henry II, which was abolished by the Courts Act, 1971. Assize Courts were presided over by High Court judges, who travelled on circuit to hear criminal and civil cases. >> Crown Court; Henry II (of England)

Associated Press (AP) An international news agency, with headquarters in New York City. Founded in 1848, it is the world's largest news-gathering co-operative. >> news agency

associated state A former colony that has a free and voluntary arrangement with the UK as the former colonial power. The state enjoys the right of self-government, but recognizes the British sovereign as head. The concept was introduced for states (eg Antigua, Grenada) wishing to be independent, but economically unable to support themselves. >> colony

Association football >> **football 1** [i]

Association of Caribbean States An association created by 25 Caribbean basin countries in 1994, with the aim of promoting a common approach to regional economic and political issues. It included the members of the Caribbean Community (CARICOM). >> Caribbean Community

Association of South-East Asian Nations (ASEAN) An association formed in 1967 to promote economic co-operation between Indonesia, Malaysia, the Philippines, Singapore, and Thailand. Brunei joined in 1984 and Vietnam in 1995; Laos, Cambodia, and Myanmar were formally admitted in 1997.

associative operation In mathematics, the principle that the order in which successive additions are performed does not affect the result; for example $(2 + 3) + 4 = 2 + (3 + 4)$. Over the set of real numbers, addition and multiplication are associative; subtraction and division are not.

Assumption The claim concerning the Virgin Mary, mother of Jesus Christ, that on her death she was 'assumed' (taken up, body and soul) to heaven. This was defined by Pope Pius XII as an article of Roman Catholic faith in 1950. >> Mary (mother of Jesus)

assurance Chiefly in the UK, a general term for insurance related to a person's life. In exchange for recurrent or lump-sum premiums, the insurance company guarantees a fixed sum on the policy-holder's death, or at some agreed date if they survive. Such policies may be *without profits*, ie for a fixed sum, or *with profits*, in which case the amount received reflects the company's success in investing the premiums. >> insurance

Assyria [a**si**ria] The small area around the town of Assur on the Tigris in Upper Mesopotamia, then much later the vast empire that the rulers of Assur acquired through conquering their neighbours on all sides. At its height in the 9th-c and 8th-c BC, the empire was destroyed in 612 BC. >> Nimrod; Nineveh

Astaire, Fred [as**tair**], originally **Frederick Austerlitz** (1899–1987) Actor and dancer, born in Omaha, NE. He and his elder sister Adele rose to stardom in the 1920s in *Lady be Good* and other stage shows. When Adele married, Fred continued with various partners, notably Ginger Rogers (1911–95). His many films include *Top Hat* (1935) and *Easter Parade* (1948). Later turning to straight acting, he received an Oscar nomination for *The Towering Inferno* (1974). >> vaudeville

Astana, Kazakh 'capital', formerly **Akmola** (1995–7), **Tselinograd** (1961–95), **Akmolinsk** (to 1961) 51°10N 71°30E, pop (1995e) 290 000. Capital of Kazakhstan (from 1997, as Akmola), on R Ishim; founded as a fortress, 1830; airport; railway junction. >> Kazakhstan [i]

Astarte [as**tah(r)**tay] >> **Ishtar**

aster A member of a large group of mainly perennials from America, Eurasia, and Africa; flower-heads daisy-like, usually in clusters; outer ray florets blue, purple, pink, or white, often autumn or late-summer flowering. (Genus: *Aster*, 250 species. Family: Compositae.) >> daisy; Michaelmas daisy

asteroids Rocky objects generally found in orbits lying between those of Mars and Jupiter, formerly called **minor planets**. This 'main belt' of asteroids has its inner edge c.100 million km/60 million mi outside Mars' orbit, and is c.165 million km/100 million mi wide. The orbits of c.5000 of the larger asteroids are known. The first asteroid, Ceres (diameter 940 km/580 mi) was discovered in 1801, and has an orbital period of 4·6 years. Asteroids are believed to have originated in the formation of the Solar System, when planetesimals accreted from solar nebula. The first flyby of a main-belt asteroid, Gaspra, was achieved by NASA's Galileo spacecraft, on its way to Jupiter, in October, 1991. >> meteorite; Solar System

asthenosphere [as**thee**nosfeer] The Earth's upper mantle. It extends from the base of the lithosphere at c.100 km/60 mi down to 700 km/430 mi below the surface. >> Earth i; lithosphere

asthma A condition in which there is narrowing and obstruction of the airways (bronchi and bronchioles). Narrowing results from the contraction of the bronchial muscles, and is an exaggerated response in hypersensitive individuals to various allergens. Common among these are pollen, house dust, and the detritus of house mites that inhabit mattresses, etc. Psychological factors and chest infection contribute in some cases. Attacks commonly consist of sudden episodes of breathlessness, with wheezing which may last several hours or days. In most patients, treatment involves periodic inhalation of one or more of several available drugs which relax the bronchioles or damp down any inflammation. >> allergy; bronchi

astigmatism In vision, an actual asymmetry in the optical system of the eye, so that the eye's ability to focus horizontal and vertical lines is different. In optics, the term refers to aberrations of a lens image due to the position of an object off the lens axis. >> aberrations 1 i; eye i; optics i

Aston, Francis (William) (1877–1945) Physicist, born in Birmingham, West Midlands. He invented the mass spectrograph in 1919, for which he was awarded the Nobel Prize for Chemistry in 1922. The **Aston dark space** in electronic discharges is named after him. >> isotopes; spectroscopy

Astor, John Jacob (1763–1848) Fur trader and financier, founder of the America Fur Company and the Astor family, born in Waldorf, Germany. In 1784 he moved to the USA, and rose to become one of the country's most powerful financiers.

Astor (of Hever), John Jacob Astor, Baron (1886–1971) Newspaper proprietor, born in New York City, USA. He became an MP in 1922, and chairman of the Times Publishing Company after the death of Lord Northcliffe.

Astor, Nancy (Witcher) Astor, Viscountess, *née* **Langhorne** (1879–1964) British politician, born in Danville, VA, USA. She succeeded her husband as MP for Plymouth in 1919, the first woman MP to sit in the House of Commons (1919–45), and became known for her interest in women's rights and social problems, especially temperance. >> women's liberation movement

Astrakhan [astra**khahn**], formerly **Khadzhi-Tarkhan** 46°22N 48°04E, pop (1995e) 516 000. City in SE European Russia; in the Volga delta, 22 m/72 ft below sea-level; protected from floods by dykes; founded, 13th-c; the most important port in the Volga-Caspian basin; airport; railway; university (1919); known for astrakhan fur. >> Russia i

astrobiology >> **exobiology**

astrolabe [**as**trolayb] An ancient instrument (c.200 BC) for showing the positions of the Sun and bright stars at any time and date. It was a forerunner of the sextant. >> azimuth; sextant

astrology A system of knowledge whereby human nature can be understood in terms of the heavens. It relies upon precise measurement and a body of symbolism which has come to be associated with each of the signs of the zodiac and the planets (including the Sun and Moon). It rests on the idea that the force which patterns the heavens likewise orders humanity. Today it thrives in several Eastern countries, and in the West is undergoing something of a rebirth, though the modern emphasis is on self-knowledge rather than on predicting events. >> astronomy; zodiac i

astrometry >> **astronomy**

astronaut The NASA term for a spacecraft crew member; originally applied to pilots, but now including scientists and payload specialists. Ten astronauts have lost their lives in accidents directly related to spaceflight. >> cosmonaut; space exploration

Astronomer Royal Formerly the title of the director of the Royal Greenwich Observatory, England. Since 1972, it has been an honorary title awarded to a distinguished British astronomer. >> astronomy

astronomical unit (AU) The mean distance of the Earth from the Sun, c.149·6 million km/93 million mi; a convenient measure of distance within the Solar System. There are 63 240 AU in one light year. >> light year; parsec; Solar System

astronomy The study of all classes of celestial object, such as planets, stars, and galaxies, as well as interstellar and intergalactic space, and the universe as a whole. The branch of classical astronomy concerned with the precise measurement of the positions of celestial objects is known as **astrometry**. Modern astronomy began 450 years ago with Copernicus, who set the scene for the overthrow of the Hellenistic cosmology, asserting that the Sun, not the Earth, is at the centre of the Solar System. Newton described gravitational theory in the 17th-c, and thenceforth planetary astronomy became an exact science. In the 18th-c and 19th-c, techniques to build large telescopes were developed, culminating in the construction of observatories on mountain sites in the USA. Radio astronomy emerged rapidly after World War 2, and was the first of the invisible astronomies. The use of satellites above the blanket of the Earth's atmosphere enabled ultraviolet, X-ray, and infrared astronomies to be developed from the 1960s. >> infrared / radar / radio / ultraviolet / X-ray astronomy; Aristotle; astrophysics; Copernican system; cosmology; New General Catalogue; telescope i

astrophysics The application of physical laws and theories to stars and galaxies, with the aim of deriving theoretical models to explain their behaviour. Its biggest triumph has been accounting for energy production inside stars, and there have been notable successes in explaining the properties of galaxies and quasars. >> galaxy; physics; quasar; star

Asturias [as**too**rias] pop (1995e) 1 100 000; area 10 565 sq km/4078 sq mi. Autonomous region and former principality of N Spain; largely occupied by the Cordillera Cantabrica, rising to 2646 m/8681 ft in the Picos de Europa; centre of Christian resistance to Muslim invasion, 8th–9th-c; part of Kingdom of Leon, 911; scene of unsuccessful left-wing revolution, 1934; provides nearly half of Spain's needs in coal. >> Spain i

Asturias, Miguel Angel [as**too**rias] (1899–1974) Novelist, born in Guatemala City. He is best known for his first novel, *El señor presidente* (1946, The President). Later novels include *Hombres de maíz* (1949, Men of Maize) and *Mulatta de tal* (1963, trans The Mulatta and Mr Fly). He received the Nobel Prize for Literature in 1967.

Asunción [asoon**syohn**] 25°15S 57°40W, pop (1995e) 693 000. Federal capital of Paraguay; transport and commercial centre on the E bank of the R Paraguay; established, 1537; capital of La Plata region until 1580; airport; railway; two universities (1890, 1960). >> Paraguay i

Aswan [as**wahn**], ancient **Syene** 24°05N 32°56E, pop (1995e) 234 000. Town in S Egypt, on the E bank of the R Nile;

Aswan Dam to the S (1898–1902); Aswan High Dam further S at head of L Nasser (1971); airfield; railway; winter tourism; Temple of Kalabsha (transported 55 km/34 mi from its original site and re-erected near Aswan High Dam). >> Egypt [i]

Atacama Desert [atakahma], Span **Desierto de Atacama** Arid desert area in N Chile, claimed to be the world's driest area; a series of dry salt basins, extending 960 km/596 mi S from the Peru border; average altitude 600 m/2000 ft; almost no vegetation. >> Chile [i]

Atahualpa [atawalpa] (?–1533) Last Inca ruler of Peru. On his father's death (1525) he received the kingdom of Quito, and in 1532 seized Peru. He was captured by the Spaniards, and executed. >> Pizarro

Atalanta [atalanta] In Greek mythology a heroine, nurtured by a she-bear, who grew up to be a strong huntress. She refused to marry any man who would not take part in a foot-race with her: those who lost were killed. Eventually Hippomenes (or Milanion) threw three golden apples of the Hesperides at her feet, so that her attention was diverted and she lost.

Atatürk [ataterk], originally **Mustafa Kemal** (1881–1938) Turkish army officer and president (1923–38), born in Salonika, Greece. Following a nationalist rebellion, he became virtual dictator, and launched a social and political revolution introducing Western fashions, educational reform, and the replacement of Arabic script with the Latin alphabet. >> Turkey [i]

ataxia [ataksia] Unsteadiness experienced on walking and standing, resulting from a failure of the central nervous system to control the movement of muscles in the lower limbs. >> central nervous system

Aten or **Aton** In Ancient Egypt, originally the name of the Sun's disc, and then that of the sun-god. >> Amun; monotheism

Athabascan or **Athapascan** [athabaskn] Various American Indian groups living in Alaska and NW Canada, W of Hudson Bay; also, the name of their language. Today most still live by hunting and fishing. >> hunter-gatherers

Athanasian Creed [athanayzhn] A statement of Christian faith, written in Latin probably in the 5th-c. It remains a historic statement of Trinitarian doctrine, still sometimes used liturgically. >> Athanasius, St; Christianity

Athanasius, St [athanayzius] (c.296–373) Christian leader, born in Alexandria. He led the opposition to the doctrines of Arianism, and his teaching was supported after his death at the Council of Constantinople (381). The *Athanasian Creed* (representing his beliefs) was little heard of until the 7th-c. Feast day 2 May. >> Arius; Athanasian Creed; Christianity

atheism The denial of the existence of God or gods. It includes both the rejection of any specific belief in God or gods, and the view that the only rational approach to claims about divine existence is one of scepticism. >> God; humanism; theism

Athelstan or **Æthelstan** [athelstan] (c.895–939) Son of Edward the Elder, and the grandson of Alfred the Great. Acknowledged as King of Wessex and Mercia (924), he successfully invaded Northumbria, thus establishing himself as effectively the first King of all England (927). >> Anglo-Saxons; Edward the Elder

Athene or **Athena** [atheena] The Greek goddess of wisdom. The patron of Athens, her emblem was the owl. >> Zeus

Athens, Gr **Athínai**, ancient **Athenae** 38°00N 23°44E, pop (1995e) Greater Athens 3 172 000. Capital city of Greece; ancient Greek city-state extending over Attica by the 7th-c BC; great economic and cultural prosperity under Pericles, 5th-c BC; taken by the Romans, 146 BC; part of the Ottoman Empire, 1456; capital of modern Greece, 1835; occupied by Germans in World War 2; two airports; railway; university (1837); port and main industrial area at Piraeus; tourism; hill of the Acropolis (156 m/512 ft), with the Parthenon (5th-c BC), Propylaea (437–432 BC), Temple of Athena Niki (432–421 BC), Ionic Erechtheion (421–406 BC). >> Greece [i]; Parthenon; Pericles

atherosclerosis [atherohsklerohsis] The irregular deposition of substances (lipids, mainly cholesterol and triglycerides) on the inner wall of arteries and arterioles, which causes narrowing of the affected blood vessels. Common sites are the aorta and blood vessels to the brain and heart, but no vessel is immune. Contributing causes include high animal-fat dietary intake, high blood pressure, obesity, and lack of exercise. >> artery; coronary heart disease [i]

Atherton, Mike, popular name of **Michael Andrew Atherton** (1968–) Cricketer, born in Manchester, Greater Manchester. He made his debut for Lancashire in 1987, and his first-team debut for England in 1989 against Australia. A leading batsman, he was appointed England captain (1993–8), and had played in 80 Tests by mid-1998.

athlete's foot A common form of ringworm infection (*tinea pedis*) in which a fungus causes itching and fissuring of the skin between the toes. It is usually acquired in swimming baths and from shower floors. >> foot; ringworm

athletics Tests of running, jumping, throwing, and walking skills for trained athletes; also known, especially in the USA, as **track and field** events. The track events are divided into six categories: *sprint races* (100 m, 200 m, and 400 m); *Middle distance races* (800 m and 1500 m); *long distance races* (5000 m and 10 000 m); *hurdle races* (110 m – 100 m for women – and 400 m); *relay races* (4 × 100 m and 4 × 400 m); and the *steeplechase* (3000 m). In addition there is the endurance test of the *Marathon*. The field events involve jumping and throwing. *Jumping events* consist of the high jump, long jump, triple jump, and pole vault. The *throwing events* are the discus, shot put, javelin throw and hammer throw. *Walking races* take place on either the road or the track. In addition, two multi-event competitions exist in the form of the *decathlon* (10 events) for men and the *heptathlon* (7 events) for women. The governing body is the International Amateur Athletic Federation, founded in 1912. >> decathlon; discus throw; hammer throw; heptathlon; high jump; International Amateur Athletic Federation; javelin throw; long jump; pole vault; shot put; triple jump; RR1045

Atkinson, Rowan (Sebastian) (1955–) British comic actor and writer, born in Newcastle upon Tyne, Tyne and Wear. He first appeared in Oxford University revues at the Edinburgh Festival Fringe, and in 1981 became the youngest performer to have had a one-man show in the West End. Television roles include *Not the Nine O'Clock News* (1979–82), *Blackadder* (1983–9), and *Mr Bean* (1990–4). Film credits include *Four Weddings and a Funeral* (1994) and *Bean: the Ultimate Disaster Movie* (1997).

Atlanta 33°45N 84°23W, pop (1995e) 437 000. State capital in NW Georgia, USA; founded at the end of the railway in 1837 (named Terminus); renamed Atlanta, 1845; a Confederate supply depot in the Civil War; burned by General Sherman, 1864; capital, 1887; airport; railway; four universities (1835, 1836, 1865, 1913); professional teams, Braves (baseball), Hawks (basketball), Falcons (football). >> American Civil War; Georgia; King, Martin Luther

Atlanta Campaign >> **March Through Georgia**

Atlantic, Battle of the (1940–3) The conflict arising out of German attacks on shipping in the Atlantic during World War 2. The German strategy was to cut off Britain's supplies of food and munitions by submarine action. The attacks were countered by the end of 1943. >> World War 2

Atlantic Charter A declaration of common objectives by Roosevelt and Churchill after a secret meeting off Newfoundland (Aug 1941). It agreed principles which should govern postwar settlements. The Charter was endorsed by the USSR and 14 other states at war with the Axis Powers. >> Axis Powers; Churchill, Winston; Roosevelt, Franklin D

Atlantic City 39°21N 74°27W, pop (1995e) 38 700. Town in SE New Jersey, USA, on the Atlantic coast; railway; popular seaside resort with famed boardwalk (over 9 km/5½ mi long) and piers; many casinos; convention centre. >> New Jersey

Atlantic Intracoastal Waterway >> **Intracoastal Waterway**

Atlantic Ocean Body of water extending from the Arctic to the Antarctic, separating North and South America (W) from Europe and Africa (E); area c.82 217 000 sq km/ 31 700 000 sq mi; average depth 3700 m/12 000 ft; maximum depth, Puerto Rico Trench, 8648 m/28 372 ft; principal arms (W), Labrador Sea, Gulf of Mexico, Caribbean Sea; (E), North Sea, Baltic Sea, Mediterranean and Black Sea, Bay of Biscay, Gulf of Guinea; (S), Weddell Sea; continental shelf narrow off coast of Africa and Spain, broader in NW Europe and off Americas; 'S' shaped, submarine Mid-Atlantic Ridge between Iceland and the Antarctic Circle, centre of earthquake and volcanic activity; major surface circulation, clockwise in N, counter-clockwise in S; main currents include the Gulf Stream (N Atlantic Drift), and the N Equatorial, Canary, S Equatorial, Brazil, Benguela, and Equatorial Counter Currents. >> current (oceanography); plate tectonics ℹ

Atlantic Wall An incomplete network of coastal fortifications, constructed in 1942–4 between the Pas-de-Calais and the Bay of Biscay as part of Hitler's plans for an impregnable 'Fortress Europe'. On D-Day its 'invincibility' was shown to be a myth. >> World War 2

Atlantis [at**lan**tis] According to Plato, an island in the ocean W of Spain which disappeared into the sea. Its supposed existence has generated many speculative books and expeditions. >> Plato

Atlas (astronomy) The 15th natural satellite of Saturn, discovered in 1980; distance from the planet 138 000 km/ 86 000 mi; diameter 40 km/25 mi. >> Saturn (astronomy); RR964

Atlas (mythology) In Greek mythology, a Titan who was made to hold up the heavens as a punishment for taking part in the revolt against the Olympians. When books of maps came to be published, he was often portrayed as a frontispiece, hence 'atlas'. >> Heracles; Titan (mythology)

Atlas Mountains A system of folded mountain chains in Morocco, Algeria, and Tunisia, NW Africa. Largest in the group is the **Haut Atlas** range, running SW–NE for 650 km/400 mi from Morocco's Atlantic coast, rising to Mt Toubkal (4165 m/13 665 ft). >> Morocco ℹ

atman [**aht**man] (Sanskrit, 'soul' or 'self') In Hinduism, the human soul or essential self. It is seen as being one with the absolute, and identified with Brahman. >> Brahma; Hinduism

atmosphere The layer of gas surrounding any planet or star. Earth's atmosphere is composed of air, which on average is made up of 78% nitrogen, 21% oxygen, and 1% argon, with traces of other rare gases, carbon dioxide, and hydrogen. Earth's atmosphere is divided into several concentric shells, the lowest being the *troposphere*, followed by the *stratosphere*, *mesosphere*, and *thermosphere*. The outer shell of the atmosphere, at c.400 km/250 mi, from which light gases can escape, is termed the *exosphere*. The atmosphere contains the gases vital to life, and shields the Earth from harmful ionizing radiation. >> ionosphere; ozone layer

atmospheric pressure The pressure exerted by the atmosphere on the Earth's surface; the accepted value is called one *atmosphere*, which equals 1.013 bar, 101.325 Pa (pascals), or 760 torr. Pressure is measured using a barometer. >> barometer; isobar; pascal; pressure; torr

atoll A roughly circular structure of coral reefs enclosing a lagoon. Atolls occur in warm, clear, tropical oceanic waters where corals and coralline algae can flourish. Darwin first theorized that they are the final stage in a progression of reef formations. In the first stage, a *fringing reef* grows adjacent to land with little or no lagoon separating it from the shore. The second stage, a *barrier reef*, lies offshore with a lagoon separating it from the land. An *atoll* is the third and most mature stage, where the original land is no longer present. >> coral

atom The smallest portion of a chemical element. Each atom comprises a positively charged nucleus surrounded by negatively charged electrons, whose number equals that of the protons contained within the nucleus. Electrons are attracted to the nucleus by electromagnetic force. They determine the chemistry of an atom, and are responsible for binding atoms together. >> chemical elements; electron; molecule; nucleus (physics); subatomic particles

atomic bomb A nuclear explosive device (the **A-Bomb**) which achieves its destructive effects through energy released during the fission of heavy atoms (as in uranium-235 or plutonium-239). The first atomic bombs were used to destroy the Japanese cities of Hiroshima and Nagasaki (Aug 1945). Atomic weapons have been supplanted by thermonuclear weapons, but a fission weapon trigger is an essential component of these devices. >> hydrogen bomb ℹ; Manhattan project; nuclear fission / weapons

atomic clock >> **clock** ℹ

atomic mass unit (amu) Unit of mass; symbol *u*; defined as 1/12 of the mass of the carbon-12 atom; value $1u = 1{\cdot}66 \times 10^{-27}$ kg; used to express relative atomic masses of atoms; sometimes called a **dalton**. >> atom; mass; RR1031

atomic number >> **proton number**

atomic physics >> **particle physics**

atomic spectra A set of specific frequencies of electromagnetic radiation, typically light, emitted or absorbed by atoms of a certain type. A given spectral line corresponds to the transition of an electron between two specific energy levels. The study of spectra is called

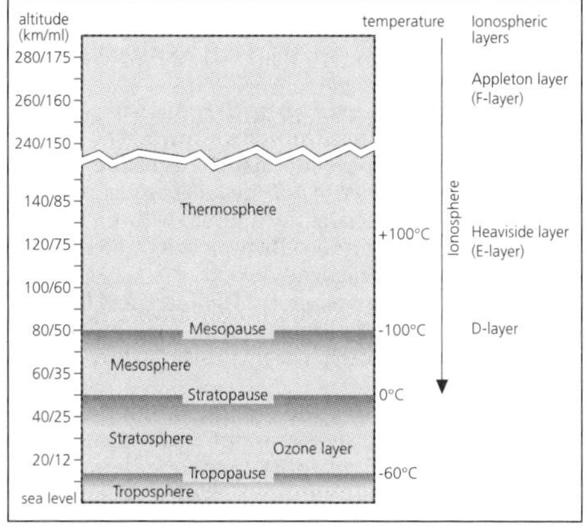

Layers of the atmosphere

spectroscopy, a major analytic technique in physics and chemistry. >> laser ℹ; nuclear magnetic resonance; spectroscopy

atomic weight >> **relative atomic mass**

atonality The property of music which is not written in a key. The term is most commonly applied to music written in the post-tonal but pre-serial style of Schoenberg's *Ewartung* (1909) and other compositions of that period. >> Schoenberg; serialism; tonality

atonement [a**tohn**mnt] In Christian theology, the process whereby sinners are made 'at one' with God, through the life, death, and resurrection of Jesus Christ. >> Christianity

Atonement, Day of >> **Yom Kippur**

atractaspid snake >> **asp**

atrium [**ay**trium] (plural **atria**) The entrance hall or open inner court of a Roman house; in mediaeval architecture, an open court in front of a church; generally, any cavity or entrance in a building. Atria have become particularly fashionable in late-20th-c hotels and office blocks.

atropine [**a**tropeen, **a**tropin] A drug extracted from deadly nightshade (*Atropa belladonna*), used as a poison during the Roman Empire and later. Safer derivatives are now used in a wide variety of disorders, commonly in motion-sickness preparations and in ophthalmology, to dilate the pupil during eye examinations. >> belladonna; ophthalmology

Atropos [atropos] >> **Moerae**

attar A fragrant essential oil distilled from plants; also called **otto**. The best known is attar of roses, obtained from the petals of the damask rose (*Rosa damascena*), cultivated in the Balkans. >> essential oil; rose

Attenborough, Sir David (Frederick) [**a**tenbruh] (1926–) Naturalist and broadcaster, born in London, the brother of Richard Attenborough. He joined the BBC in 1952 as a trainee producer. The series *Zoo Quest* (1954–64) allowed him to undertake expeditions to remote parts of the globe to record wildlife in its natural habitat. He was the controller of BBC 2 (1965–8) and director of programmes (1969–72) before returning to documentary-making with such series as *Life on Earth* (1979), *The Private Life of Plants* (1995), and *Life of Birds* (1998). He was knighted in 1985. >> Attenborough, Richard

Attenborough, Sir Richard (Samuel), Baron [**a**tenbruh] (1923–) Film actor, producer, and director, born in Cambridge, Cambridgeshire, the brother of David Attenborough. His characterization of the vicious young hooligan in *Brighton Rock* (1947) led to many varied parts. He was actor/producer of several features in the 1960s, and became a director in 1969 with *O What a Lovely War!*, followed by such major epics as *Gandhi* (1982), which won eight Oscars, and *Cry Freedom* (1987). >> Attenborough, David

attention A phenomenon where the processing capacity of the brain is directed towards a particular type of incoming, competing information. **Attention deficit (hyperactivity) disorder**, or **ADD**, includes a range of behaviour disorders, especially in children, with such symptoms as poor concentration, hyperactivity, and learning difficulties. >> hyperactivity

Attica [**at**ika] The SE promontory of C Greece, and the most easterly part of the Greek mainland. In Classical Greece, it was the territory which made up the city-state of Athens. >> Athens

Attila [atila], known as **the Scourge of God** (c.406–53) Hunnish King (434–53), whose dominion extended from the Rhine to the frontiers of China. He defeated the Emperor Theodosius, and in 451 invaded Gaul, but was defeated on the Catalaunian Plains by a joint army of Romans and Visigoths. >> Catalaunian Plains, Battle of the; Huns; Theodosius I

Attlee, Clem, popular name of **Clement Richard Attlee, 1st Earl Attlee** (1883–1967) British statesman and prime minister (1945–51), born in London. He was dominions secretary (1942–3) and deputy prime minister (1942–5) in Churchill's War Cabinet. As prime minister, he carried through a vigorous programme of nationalization, and introduced the National Health Service. >> National Health Service; nationalization; socialism

attorney A person who has power to act for another; **power of attorney** refers to the authority so given. The term is also used in some jurisdictions as a general label for lawyers.

attorney general The chief legal officer of a number of nations or states, who represents the government in its legal actions. In England and Wales, the attorney general is a member of the House of Commons and of the government. In the USA, the federal attorney general is an appointed member of the president's cabinet. >> solicitor general

Attwell, Mabel Lucie (1879–1964) Artist and writer, born in London. From 1911 onwards she drew humorous postcards for Valentine's, usually featuring chubby children. Her 'cherubic' style was continued in children's books by her daughter, working under her mother's name.

aubergine [**oh**berzheen] A bushy perennial (*Solanum meleagrum*) with funnel-shaped, violet flowers and large, edible berries, native to New World tropics; also its fruit, variable in shape and colour, but typically egg-shaped and purple; also called **egg-plant**. (Family: Solanaceae.)

aubretia [aw**bree**sha] A mat-forming perennial (*Aubretia deltoidea*); slightly greyish leaves; pink to purple or blue cross-shaped flowers; native to SE Europe. (Family: Cruciferae.)

Aubrey, John [**aw**bree] (1626–97) Antiquary and folklorist, born in Easton Percy, Wiltshire. He left a large mass of materials, some of which were later published (notably in *Letters by Eminent Persons*, 1813, commonly called *Brief Lives*). >> folklore

Aubusson, Pierre d' [ohbüsõ] (1423–1503) Grand Master of the Knights Hospitallers of St John of Jerusalem, born in Monteil-au-Vicomte, France. Mohammed II's career of conquest was halted by d'Aubusson and his small colony of Christian soldiers in Rhodes (1480). >> Hospitallers

Auchinleck, Sir Claude John Eyre [**okh**inlek] (1884–1981) British soldier. His regrouping of the 8th Army on El Alamein is now recognized as a successful defensive operation, but at the time he was made a scapegoat for the retreat, and replaced in 1942. >> World War 2

Auckland [**awk**land] 36°55S 174°43E, pop (1995e) 887 000 (urban area). Seaport city in North Island, New Zealand; principal port of New Zealand; founded, 1840; capital, 1840–65; airport; railway; university (1883); two cathedrals; Waitemata Harbour spanned by Auckland Harbour Bridge (1959). >> New Zealand ℹ

auction bridge >> **bridge** (recreation)

Auden, W(ystan) H(ugh) [**aw**den] (1907–73) Poet, born in York, North Yorkshire. His first volume of verse, *Poems* (1930), placed him in the forefront of a group of poets of left-wing sympathies, including Day-Lewis and Spender. He supported the Spanish Republic's cause, and (with Isherwood) reported on Japanese aggression in China in *Journey to a War* (1939). In 1939 he emigrated to New York, becoming a US citizen. His later conversion to Anglicanism left his writing more serious, and he developed a more reflective style, as in *City Without Walls* (1969). >> Day-Lewis, C; Isherwood; Spender

Audenarde [ohdn**ah(r)d**] >> **Oudenaarde**

audiology The study of the physiology of hearing, and of diseases that affect the ear and the associated nerve. It is specifically concerned with assessing the nature and degree of hearing loss and with the rehabilitation of people with hearing impairment. The scientific measurement of hearing is known as **audiometry**. >> ear [i]

audiometry >> **audiology**

audio-visual aids Sources other than print which are used to help people teach and learn. These may include pieces of equipment such as still, overhead, and film projectors, tape recorders, and radio or television sets, as well as pictures, graphics, charts, films, videotapes, and audiotapes. >> projector [i]; tape recorder; video; video disc

audit The process of checking that the accounts of an organization have been kept in accordance with good practice and with relevant laws, and that the accounts fairly reflect the activities of the organization and its state of affairs at a certain date. All limited companies must have accounts audited. Auditors are usually members of professional accountancy firms. >> accountancy

Audit Commission In the UK, an independent body set up by the government in 1982 to monitor local authority spending. It has also carried out reviews in the areas of education, health, and the police.

auditory tube A tube connecting the middle ear to the nasopharynx, also known as the **Eustachian tube**, after Italian physician Bartolommeo Eustachio (1520–74). It enables air to enter or leave the middle ear, so balancing the pressure on either side of the eardrum, thus allowing it to vibrate freely. >> ear [i]

Audubon, John James [**aw**duhbon] (1785–1851) Ornithologist, born in Les Cayes, Haiti. His *The Birds of America* (1827–38) contains coloured figures of 1065 birds, many natural size. The National Audubon Society, dedicated to the conservation of birds in the USA, was founded in his honour in 1866.

Augsburg [**owgs**berg], Ger [**owgs**boork], ancient **Augusta Vindelicorum** 48°22N 10°54E, pop (1995e) 263 000. Industrial and commercial city in Germany; founded by the Romans, 15 BC; seat of the famous Diets of 1530 and 1555; railway; university (1970); birthplace of Brecht and Holbein; St Ulrich's Minster (1500). >> Augsburg Confession; Augsburg, League of; Brecht; Germany [i]; Holbein

Augsburg, League of [**owgs**berg] (1686) A defensive alliance formed by the Holy Roman Emperor, Bavaria, Spain, Sweden, and several German states to challenge Louis XIV's legalistic pursuit of territory. Continuing mutual provocation between France and the League resulted in the **War of the League of Augsburg** (1689–97), also known as the **War of the Grand Alliance**. >> Louis XIV

Augsburg Confession [**owgs**berg] A statement of faith composed by Luther, Melanchthon, and others for the Diet of Augsburg (1530). It became authoritative for the Lutheran Church. >> Lutheranism; Melanchthon

augury [**awg**yuree] In ancient Rome, the principal means of divining the will of the gods. It involved observing natural phenomena such as lightning and the feeding habits of sacred chickens. The **augurs** themselves were distinguished public men who had undergone training and been admitted to the college of augurs – a select body of 16.

Augusta (Georgia) [aw**guhs**ta] 33°28N 81°58W, pop (1995e) 49 500. City in E Georgia, USA, on the Savannah R; founded as a river trading post; established in 1735; state capital, 1786–95; airfield; railway; popular resort with a notable golf club. >> Georgia

Augusta (Maine) [aw**guhs**ta] 44°17N 69°50W, pop (1995e) 21 600. State capital of Maine, USA; established as a trading post, 1628; city status, 1849; airfield. >> Maine

Augustan age The age of the Emperor Augustus in Rome (27 BC–AD 14), graced by the poets Horace, Ovid, and Virgil; hence, the classical period of any national literature. >> classicism; Horace; Ovid; Pope; Virgil

Augustine, St [aw**guhs**tin], also known as **Augustine of Canterbury** (?–604) Clergyman, the first Archbishop of Canterbury, born probably in Rome. He was prior of a Benedictine monastery at Rome, when in 596 Pope Gregory I sent him with 40 other monks to convert the Anglo-Saxons to Christianity. He was made Bishop of the English in 597. Feast day 26/27 May. >> Anglo-Saxons; Gregory I

Augustine, St [aw**guhs**tin], originally **Aurelius Augustinus**, also known as **Augustine of Hippo** (354–430) The greatest of the Latin Fathers, born in Tagaste, Numidia (modern Algeria). His mother became St Monica. He was sent to Carthage to complete his studies, but yielded to the temptation of the city, and fathered a son before he was 18. An enthusiastic student of Plato, the Neoplatonists, and the Bible, he finally became a Christian in 387. Ordained priest in 391, he proved a formidable antagonist to the heretical schools in the Donatist and Pelagian controversies. His sacred autobiography, *Confessions*, was written in 397, and *De Civitate Dei*, a vindication of the Christian Church, in 413–26. Feast day 28 August. >> Augustinians; Donatists; Fathers of the Church; Neoplatonism; Pelagius

Augustinians A religious order united in 1255 following the monastic teaching and 'rule' of St Augustine; also known as the **Augustinian** or **Austin Friars**; in full, the **Order of the Hermit Friars of St Augustine** (**OSA**). >> Augustine, St (of Hippo)

Augustus, (Gaius Julius Caesar Octavianus) (63 BC–AD 14) Founder of the Roman Empire, the son of Gaius Octavius, and great-nephew, through his mother Atia, of Julius Caesar. On Caesar's assassination (44 BC), he raised an army, defeated Antony, and extorted a consulship from the Senate (43 BC). When Antony returned from Gaul in force later that year with Lepidus, Octavian made a deal with his former enemies, joining the so-called Second Triumvirate with them, and taking Africa, Sardinia, and Sicily as his province. A later redivision of power gave him the entire western half of the Roman world, and Antony the eastern. In 31 BC, the Battle of Actium made Octavian victorious as the sole ruler of the Roman world. The Romans awarded him the title *Pater Patriae* ('Father of his Country') in 2 BC, and on his death made him a god (*divus Augustus*). >> Actium, Battle of; Antonius; Caesar; Lepidus; Livia; Roman history [i]; triumvirate

Augustusburg The 18th-c Baroque residence of the former electors of Cologne at Brühl, NW Germany; a world heritage site. It was designed by Konrad Schlaun, and later Francois Cuvillié, for Elector Clemens August (1700–61). >> Baroque (art and architecture)

auk A small, black-and-white, short-winged seabird; inhabits cool seas; excellent swimmer. (Family: Alcidae, 21 species.) >> guillemot; penguin; puffin; razorbill

Aung San Suu Kyi, Daw [owng san soo kyee] (1945–) Political leader, born in Yangon, Myanmar (formerly Rangoon, Burma), the daughter of the assassinated General Aung San, who was hailed as the father of Burmese independence. She co-founded the National League for Democracy (NLD), and in 1989 was placed under house arrest by the military government. She was awarded the Nobel Peace Prize in 1991. She was released in July 1995, but refused to leave the country (for fear she would not be allowed to return), and remained there despite the death of her husband, **Michael Aris**, in Britain in March 1999.

Aurangzeb or **Aurungzib** [**aw**rangzeb] ('ornament of the throne'), kingly title **Alamgir** (1618–1707) The last and most magnificent of the Mughal emperors of India (1658–1707), born at Dhod, Malwa. He was a fervent Muslim, which alienated the Hindus and led to war with the Marathas. >> Mughal Empire

Aurelian [aw**ree**lian], in full **Lucius Domitius Aurelianus** (c.215–75) Roman emperor (270–5), a man of outstanding military talents. He took successful action against the Goths and Carpi on the Danube, Zenobia of Palmyra in the East, and the breakaway Gallic Empire in the West. He was awarded the title 'Restorer of the World'. >> Roman history [i]; Zenobia

Aurelian Way >> **Roman roads** [i]

Aurelius [aw**reel**ius], in full **Caesar Marcus Aurelius Antoninus Augustus**, originally **Marcus Annius Verus** (121–80) Roman emperor (161–80). The adopted son of Antoninus Pius, he ruled as his junior partner from 146. His reign saw constant warfare, and he personally directed operations on the Danube frontier. >> Roman history [i]

Auric, Georges [ohrik] (1899–1983) Composer, born in Lodève, who became one of *Les Six*. His compositions ranged widely from full orchestral pieces to songs, and included many film scores. >> *Six, Les*

auricular therapy [aw**rik**yuler] A form of acupuncture which developed outside China, using points on the ear which relate to remote areas of the body. The entire body is said to be represented on the surface of the ear, and the application of needles, electronic stimulation, or laser to these points is said to cure disease in the related part. Ear acupuncture is now widely used to treat addictions and for pain relief during childbirth and dentistry. >> acupuncture

Auriga [aw**riy**ga] (Lat 'charioteer') A prominent N hemisphere constellation in the Milky Way, containing many star clusters. Its brightest star is Capella, sixth-brightest in the sky, actually a close pair of giant yellow stars, distance 14 parsec. >> constellation; star cluster; RR968

Aurignacian [awrig**nay**shn] In European prehistory, a division of Upper Palaeolithic culture. It is named after a cave site at Aurignac, Haute Garonne, SW France, excavated in 1852–60. >> Three Age System

Auriol, Vincent [ohreeol] (1884–1966) French statesman, born in Revel, France. A socialist politician, he became president of the two constituent assemblies of 1946, and the first president of the Fourth Republic (1947–54). >> France [i]

aurochs [**aw**roks] (plural, **aurochsen**) An extinct large wild ox (*Bos primigenius*), formerly widespread in Europe, Asia, and N Africa; the ancestor of domestic cattle; forward-pointing horns; last individual killed in Poland in 1627; also known as **urus**, or **wild ox**. >> bison; cattle; ox

aurora [aw**raw**ra] A diffuse coloured light in the upper atmosphere (100 km/60 mi) over polar regions, visible at night. It is caused by charged particles from the Sun colliding with oxygen and nitrogen atoms in the atmosphere. In the N it is known as the *aurora borealis* or *northern lights*; in the S as the *aurora australis*. >> geomagnetic field

Aurora [aw**raw**ra] The Roman name of the goddess of the dawn, equivalent to the Greek Eos. >> Eos

Aurungzeb(e) >> **Aurangzeb**

Auschwitz [**ow**shvitz] The largest Nazi concentration camp, on the outskirts of Oświeim, SW Poland, where 3–4 million people, mainly Jews and Poles, were murdered between 1940 and 1945; a world heritage site. >> Holocaust; Nazi Party

Ausgleich [**ows**gliykh] (Ger 'compromise') >> **Austria-Hungary, Dual Monarchy of**

Austen, Jane (1775–1817) Novelist, born in Steventon, Hampshire, where her father was rector. She later lived in Bath, Southampton, Chawton, and Winchester, where she died. Of her six great novels, four were published anonymously during her lifetime and two posthumously: *Sense and Sensibility* (1811), *Pride and Prejudice* (1813), *Mansfield Park* (1814), *Emma* (1815), *Persuasion* (1818), and *Northanger Abbey* (1818).

Auster, Paul [**aw**ster] (1947–) Novelist, born in Newark, NJ. His use of detective-story techniques to explore modern urban identity is evident in *The New York Trilogy* (1985–6). Later books include *The Music of Chance* (1990) and *Leviathan* (1992).

Austerlitz, Battle of [**ow**sterlits] Napoleon's most decisive victory, also known as **the Battle of the Three Emperors**. It was fought in Moravia against a larger combined Austro-Russian army under Kutuzov. >> Napoleonic Wars

Austin (of Longbridge), Herbert Austin, Baron (1866–1941) Car manufacturer, born in Little Missenden, Buckinghamshire. In 1895 he produced his first car, the Wolseley, and in 1905 opened his own works near Birmingham. >> car [i]

Austin, Stephen Fuller (1793–1836) Founder of the state of Texas, born in Austinville, VA. In 1822 he founded a colony on the Brazos R, and became leader of the movement for Texan independence.

Austin [**aw**stin] 30°17N 97°45W, pop (1995e) 513 000. Capital of Texas, USA, on the Colorado R; settled, 1835; capital of the Republic of Texas, 1839; airfield; railway; two universities (1876, 1881); commercial centre for an extensive agricultural region. >> Austin, Steven Fuller; Texas

Austin Friars >> **Augustinians**

Australasia A term used loosely to include Australia and the islands of Tasmania, New Zealand, New Guinea (including New Britain), New Caledonia, and Vanuatu; often described as equivalent to all of Oceania below the Equator and N of 47°S. >> Oceania

Australia, official name **Commonwealth of Australia** pop (1995e) 19 089 000; area 7 692 300 sq km/2 969 228 sq mi. An independent country; variously viewed as the smallest continent or largest island in the world, entirely in the S hemisphere; capital, Canberra; principal cities, Melbourne, Brisbane, Perth, Adelaide, Sydney; timezones GMT +8 to +10; population 1% Aborigine and Asian, 99% Caucasian; religions Anglican (under 30%), Roman Catholic (over 25%); official language, English; currency, the Australian dollar of 100 cents; consists largely of plains and plateaux, most of which average 600 m/2000 ft above sea-level; West Australian Plateau occupies nearly half the whole area; MacDonnell Ranges in the centre, highest point Mt Liebig (1525 m/5000 ft); most of the plateau dry and barren desert; Nullarbor Plain in the S, crossed by the Trans-Australian Railway; Eastern Highlands or Great Dividing Range parallel to the E seaboard, rising to 2228 m/7310 ft in Mt Kosciusko, in the Australian Alps; Great Barrier Reef off NE coast, stretching for over 1900 km/1200 mi; island of Tasmania rises to 1617 m/5305 ft at Mt Ossa, separated from the mainland by the Bass Strait; longest river is the Murray, chief tributaries the Darling, Murrumbidgee, and Lachlan; more than a third of Australia under 260 mm/10 in mean annual rainfall; less than a third over 500 mm/20 in; prolonged drought in many areas; Darwin's average daily temperature 26–34°C (Nov) and 19–31°C (Jul); rainfall from 386 mm/15·2 in (Jan) to zero (Jul); fertile land with a temperate climate and reliable rainfall only in lowlands and valleys near the E and SE coast, and a small part of the SW corner; population concentrated in these two regions; Melbourne's average daily temperature 6–13°C (Jul) and 14–26°C (Jan–Feb), with monthly rainfall averaging 48–66 mm/1·9–2·6 in; Aborigines thought to have arrived in Australia from SE Asia c.40 000 years ago; first European visitors were the Dutch, who explored the Gulf of Carpentaria in 1606 and landed in 1642; Abel Tasman charted N and W coasts 1644; arrival of Captain James

Cook in Botany Bay, 1770, and claimed the E coast for Britain; New South Wales established as a penal colony, 1788; gold discovered in New South Wales and Victoria, 1851, and in Western Australia, 1892; transportation of convicts to E Australia ended, 1840, but continued until 1853 in Tasmania and 1868 in Western Australia; during this period, the colonies drafted their own constitutions and set up governments: New South Wales (1855), Tasmania and Victoria (1856), South Australia (1857), Queensland (1860), and Western Australia (1890); Commonwealth of Australia established with Canberra chosen as the site for its capital, 1901; policy of preventing immigration by non-whites stayed in force from the end of the 19th-c until 1974; divided into six states and two territories; legislature comprises a bicameral Federal Parliament with a prime minister and cabinet; head of state is a governor-general, representing the Queen; republican movement growing since the 1980s; Northern Territory self-governing since 1978; world's largest wool producer, and a top exporter of veal and beef; most important crop is wheat; major mineral producer, with discoveries of petroleum reserves, bauxite, nickel, lead, zinc, copper, tin, uranium, iron ore, and other minerals in the early 1960s; manufacturing industry expanded rapidly since 1945, especially in engineering, shipbuilding, car manufacture, metals, textiles, clothing, chemicals, food processing, and wine. >> Aborigines; Australian Capital Territory / Labor Party / languages / republicanism / Workers' Union; Liberal Party (Australia); National Party (Australia); New South Wales; Queensland; South Australia; Tasmania; Victoria (Australia); Western Australia; White Australia Policy; RR1001 political leaders

Australia, Order of An order according recognition to Australian citizens (and others). It was established by Queen Elizabeth II in 1975.

Australia Day A public holiday in Australia commemorating the founding of the colony of New South Wales on 26 January 1788. >> Australia ℹ

Australian Alps Chain of mountains in SE Australia forming the S part of the Great Dividing Range; extends c.300 km/185 mi; rises to 2228 m/7310 ft at Mt Kosciusko; much used for winter sports. >> Great Dividing Range

Australian Antarctic Territory area 6 043 852 sq km/2 332 927 sq mi of land, 84 798 sq km/32 732 sq mi of ice shelf. Situated S of 60°S and lying between 142° and 136°E (excluding Terre Adélie); claimed by Australia, 1936; scientific station at Mawson, 1954; Davis Base, 1957. >> Antarctica ℹ; Australia ℹ

Australian Capital Territory pop (1995e) 296 000; area 2400 sq km/925 sq mi. Territory in SE Australia, created in 1911 to provide a location for the national capital, Canberra; bordered on all sides by New South Wales; Jervis Bay on the E coast ceded (1915) for its use as a port; c.50% of the workforce employed by the government. >> Australia ℹ

Australian Council of Trade Unions (ACTU) Australia's national trade union organization, formed in 1927. By 1992, there were 227 unions in the country, with a claimed total membership of 3·1 million. >> trade union

Australian East Coast Temperate and Sub-Tropical Rainforest Parks A series of national parks and nature reserves along the length of the New South Wales coast; a world heritage area. >> New South Wales

Australian Labor Party (ALP) Australia's oldest political party, founded in 1891 in New South Wales. It has always been a social democratic party, committed to evolutionary not revolutionary change.

Australian languages The aboriginal languages of Australia. About 50 survive, spoken by fewer than 50 000 people. There are now some bilingual school programmes, which will ensure the immediate survival of some languages. >> Aborigines

Australian republicanism The desire to sever ties with Britain and instal an Australian, non-hereditary head of state. An intermittent theme in Australian history since the 19th-c, republicanism has gained prominence since the late 1980s, and the Australian Republican Movement, supported by the Labor government of Paul Keating, aims for a republic by 2001, the centenary of Australian federation. In 1998 the Constitutional Convention voted in favour of a republican system and a president, the proposals being placed before the electorate in late 1999. >> Australia ℹ; Keating; republic

Australian Rules football >> **football 4** ℹ

Australian Workers' Union (AWU) The largest Australian trade union from the early 1900s to 1970, and still one of the largest. It was formed in 1894, and has always been a conservative force in trade union and labour politics. >> trade union

Australia Telescope An array of radio telescopes distributed across Australia. The most important radio telescope system in the S hemisphere, it uses aperture synthesis to achieve very high resolving power. >> radio astronomy

Austral Islands [**os**tral] >> **Tubuai Islands**

Australopithecus [ostraloh**pith**ekus] Early hominids known from fossils found in Ethiopia, Kenya, Tanzania, and South Africa; dated c.5·5–1·0 mya (million years ago); although most finds are c.4·0–1·5 mya. They were truncally erect and bipedal, narrow-chested, and pot-bellied, with long powerful arms, and short legs. Face and jaws were strongly constructed and projecting; braincases were small. Features such as erect bipedalism, reduced canines, parabolic tooth rows, and rotary chewing reveal their close evolutionary links with humans. Several species are known. Bigger-brained hominids (*Homo*), probably evolved from *A. afarensis* or *A. africanus*; later species (*A. robustus* and *A. boisei*) persist well after earliest *Homo*, showing that they are not direct ancestors. >> ape; fossil; hominid; *Homo* ℹ; Taung skull

Austria, Ger **Österreich**, official name **Republic of Austria**, Ger **Republik Österreich** pop (1995e) 8 097 000; area 83 854 sq km/32 368 sq mi. A federal republic in C Europe; capital, Vienna (Wien); timezone GMT +1; main religion (85%), Roman Catholic; official language, German; unit of currency, the Schilling of 100 Groschen; almost entirely mountainous, at E end of the Alps; highest point, Grossglockner (3797 m/12 457 ft); three climatic regions: the Alps (often sunny in winter but cloudy in summer); the Danube valley and Vienna basin (driest region); and the SE, a region of often severe winters but warmer summers; most rain in summer months; winters cold, especially with winds from the E or NE; part of Roman Empire until 5th-c, then occupied by Germanic tribes; became a duchy and passed to the Habsburg family, 1282, who made it the foundation of their Empire; Habsburg defeats in 19th-c, and Hungarian nationalism led to the Dual Monarchy of Austria–Hungary, 1867; republic established in 1918; annexed by the German Reich in 1938 (the *Anschluss*), under the name **Ostmark**; occupied by British, American, French, and Russian troops from 1945, obtaining independence in 1955; neutrality declared, since when Austria has been a haven for many refugees; governed by a Federal Assembly; a president appoints a federal chancellor; principal agricultural areas to the N of the Alps, and along both sides of the Danube; wide range of metal and mineral resources; tourism (summer and winter). >> Alps; Danube, River; Habsburgs; Vienna; RR1001 political leaders

Austria–Hungary, Dual Monarchy of A constitutional arrangement created by the Ausgleich ('compromise') of 1867. In Austria–Hungary the Habsburg emperors Francis Joseph (until 1916), and Charles (1916–18), ruled over the twin kingdoms of Austria and Hungary. It was ultimately destroyed by defeat in World War 1. >> Francis Joseph; Habsburgs

Austrian Succession, War of the (1740–8) The first phase in the struggle between Prussia and Austria for mastery of the German states, developing after 1744 into a colonial conflict between Britain and the Franco-Spanish bloc. The fighting spread from C Europe to the Austrian Netherlands, the Mediterranean, and Italy, embroiling the New World and India before peace was concluded at the Treaty of Aix-la-Chapelle (1748). >> Jenkins' Ear, War of

Austro-Asiatic languages A group of over 100 languages spoken in SE Asia. The major group is the Mon–Khmer, which has three main languages: Mon (Tailang), Khmer, and Vietnamese. >> Khmer; Mon; Vietnamese

Austronesian languages The most numerous and (after Indo-European) the most widely dispersed of the world's great language families. Extending from Taiwan to Madagascar and from Malaysia, the Philippines, and Indonesia E through the Pacific Islands, it contains over 700 separate languages. >> family of languages

Austro-Prussian War (1866) A war between Austria and Prussia occasioned by a dispute over the duchies of Schleswig and Holstein. It was declared on 14 June, decided by the Prussian victory at Königgrätz (sometimes known as Sadowa) on 3 July, and ended by the Treaty of Prague on 23 August. >> Prussia

Authorized Version of the Bible The English translation of the Bible commissioned by James I and accomplished by a panel of leading scholars of the day; widely called the **King James Bible**. It was published in 1611. >> Bible; James I (of England)

autism A condition characterized by abnormal functioning in social interaction together with repetitive behaviour and poor communication, almost always commencing before three years of age. One in 2000 children suffer from

this disorder, which is four times more common in males. The cause is unknown. >> psychiatry

auto-destructive art An artefact, typically a painting or piece of sculpture, deliberately constructed in a way guaranteed to self-destruct almost immediately. Examples include pictures executed with acid, and disintegrating kinetic machines. >> art; kinetic art

autogiro A non-fixed-wing aircraft whose lift is provided (unlike a helicopter) by non-powered horizontal blades, which are brought into action by means of an engine providing horizontal thrust propelling the aircraft forward. This type of aeroplane was popular in the 1930s, but nowadays is mainly used for sport. >> aircraft ℹ

auto-immune diseases A group of apparently unrelated disorders which are believed to possess a common underlying immunological mechanism. This involves the production by the body of antibodies which react against and damage the body's own tissues. The diseases include rheumatoid arthritis, diabetes mellitus, and Addison's disease. >> immunology

automated teller machine (ATM) The formal name for the 'service tills' now common outside most banks and building societies, through which money can be withdrawn and other transactions carried out. The ATMs are linked to the banks' computers to enable on-line monitoring of customer's accounts to take place through the machines.

automatic pilot A device that automatically controls a vehicle (aircraft, ship, land vehicle) so that it will follow a preset course. It makes suitable adjustments to the vehicle's control systems to compensate for the offsetting effects of the environment or terrain. >> automation

automation The control of a technical process without using a human being to intervene to make decisions. The result of one operation is fed back to control the next. Central heating is a simple automatic system: the thermostat is a sensor, feeding information back to the heater, which then adjusts automatically, switching on and off as necessary. Computers are the most widespread example of automation. >> control engineering; robotics

automaton [aw**tom**atn] A mechanical device that imitates the actions of a living creature, human or animal. Some are made as toys, but others are useful as research or control mechanisms, and in the remote handling of hazardous materials.

automobile >> **car** ℹ; **motor insurance**

autonomic nervous system (ANS) That part of the nervous system which supplies the glands (eg the salivary and sweat glands), heart muscle, and smooth muscle (eg the walls of blood vessels and the bladder). The *sympathetic* (S) system is distributed throughout the whole body, particularly to the blood vessels. The *parasympathetic* (P) system is distributed to the gastro-intestinal, respiratory, and urogenital systems, and to the eye. In general terms, the S system prepares the body for action, while the P is concerned with the conservation of energy. >> nervous system

autumnal equinox >> **equinox**

Auvergne [oh**vairn**] pop (1995e) 1 361 000; area 26 013 sq km/10 041 sq mi. Region and former province of C France; Roman province, later a duchy and (10th-c) principality, united to France in 1527; capital, Clermont-Ferrand. >> France ℹ

Auxerre [oh**zair**], Lat **Autissiodorum** 47°48N 3°32E, pop (1995e) 41 800. Market town in C France; on the R Yonne, surrounded by orchards and vineyards; railway; bishopric; Gothic cathedral (13th–16th-c).

auxiliary language A natural language adopted by people of different speech communities for the needs of trade, education, and communication, though it may not be the native language of any of them. English and French are used in this way in many parts of Africa. >> lingua franca

auxiliary store >> **backing store**

avahi [a**vah**hee] >> **indri**

Avalon [**av**alon] In Celtic mythology, the land of the dead, the place to which King Arthur was taken after his death. The name possibly means 'land of apples'. >> Arthur

avatar [ava**tah(r)**] In Hinduism, the descent to Earth of deity in a visible form. The idea derives from the tradition associated with the deity Vishnu, who from time to time appears on Earth in order to save it from extraordinary peril. >> Hinduism; Vishnu

Avebury [**ayv**bree] 51°27N 1°51W. Village in Wiltshire, S England; the largest megalithic monument in England, a world heritage site; in use c.2600–1600 BC; approached by a 2·4 km/1½ mi avenue of 100 paired stones; three stone circles within the enclosure, the largest of nearly 100 boulders; nearby Silbury Hill is the largest prehistoric construction in Europe. >> megalith; Silbury Hill; Three Age System

Ave Maria [**ah**vay ma**ree**a] >> **Hail Mary**

avens [**av**inz] Either of two plants from the genus *Geum*, both native to temperate regions. **Wood avens** (*Geum urbanum*), also called **herb Bennet**, is an erect perennial growing to c.60 cm/2 ft; flowers 5-petalled, erect, yellow, petals spreading. **Water avens** (*Geum rivale*) is similar, but flowers are bowl-shaped, drooping, petals pinkish. (Family: Rosaceae.) >> mountain avens

Averroës [a**ver**oheez], Latin form of **Ibn Rushd** (1126–98) The most famous of the Islamic philosophers, born in Córdoba, Spain. He wrote extensive commentaries on many of Aristotle's works. >> Aristotle

aversion therapy A process in which an unpleasant experience is induced (eg by physical or electrical means) in association with an undesirable behaviour, in an attempt to inhibit or eliminate by this conditioning the undesirable behaviour. The technique has been used in a wide range of conditions, including smoking and alcohol dependence. >> behaviour therapy; conditioning; psychiatry

Avesta [a**ves**ta] The scriptures of Zoroastrianism, written in Avestan, a language of the E branch of the Indo-European family. Traditionally believed to have been revealed to Zoroaster, few portions of the original survive. >> Indo-European languages; Zoroastrianism

Avicenna [avi**sen**a], Arabic **Ibn Sina** (980–1037) Islamic philosopher and physician, born near Bokhara, Kazakhstan. His medical system was long the standard in Europe and the Middle East.

Avignon [aveenyõ], Lat **Avenio** 43°57N 4°50E, pop (1995e) 92 200. Walled town in SE France, on left bank of R Rhône; papal residence, 1309–76; railway; archbishopric; popular tourist centre; ruins of 12th-c Pont St Benezet, subject of the folk-song 'Sur le Pont d'Avignon'. >> pope

Ávila [**av**eela], also **Avila de los Caballeros**, ancient **Avela**, **Abula**, or **Abyla** 40°39N 4°43W, pop (1995e) 46 300. Ancient walled city in C Spain; altitude, 1130 m/3707 ft; bishopric; railway; birthplace of Queen Isabella and St Teresa; cathedral (11th-c); old town and churches are a world heritage site. >> Isabella I; Spain ℹ; Teresa of Ávila, St

avocado [avoh**kah**doh] An evergreen tree growing to 18 m/60 ft (*Persea americana*), covered with aromatic oil glands, thought to be native to Central America; leaves oval, leathery; flowers greenish-white, 6-lobed; berry pear-shaped, leathery, growing to 15 cm/6 in long, green, yellow, or purplish, with thick yellowish-green edible flesh surrounding a single large stone. (Family: Lauraceae.)

avocet [**av**oset] A long-legged wading bird, found in fresh and saline waters worldwide; long, slender, up-curved bill. (Genus: *Recurvirostra*, 4 species. Family: Recurvirostridae.)

Avogadro, Amedeo [avoh**gad**roh] (1776–1856) Scientist, born in Turin, Italy. In 1811 he formulated the hypothesis, known later as **Avogadro's law**, that equal volumes of gases contain equal numbers of molecules, when at the same temperature and pressure. >> Avogadro's constant

Avogadro's constant [avoh**gad**roh] The physical quantity of molecules in a mole or of electronic charges in a faraday. Its approximate value is $6{\cdot}023 \times 10^{23}$. >> Avogadro; faraday; mole (physics)

Avon [**ay**vn] pop (1995e) 980 000; area 1347 sq km/ 520 sq mi. Former county in SW England; created in 1974 from parts of Somerset and Gloucestershire; replaced in 1996 by the unitary authorities of Bath and NE Somerset, Bristol, South Gloucestershire, and NW Somerset. >> Bath; Bristol; England ℹ

Avon, River [**ay**vn] >> **England** ℹ

Avon, 1st Earl of >> **Eden, Sir Anthony**

AWACS [**ay**waks] >> **Airborne Warning and Control System**

axis deer >> **chital**

Axis Powers The name given to the co-operation of Nazi Germany and Fascist Italy (1936–45), first used by Mussolini. In September 1940, Germany, Italy, and Japan signed a tripartite agreement, after which all three were referred to as Axis Powers. >> fascism; Nazi Party; World War 2

axolotl [**aks**olotl] A rare Mexican salamander (*Ambystoma mexicanum*) from high altitude in L Xochimilco; pale with three pairs of feathery gills; large fin around tail; family also known as **mole salamanders**. (Family: Ambystomatidae.) >> salamander ℹ

axon >> **neurone** ℹ

axonometric and isometric projection A system for producing a three-dimensional drawing of an object without perspective and in which all lines are drawn to scale. Isometric projection is a particular case of axonometric projection, in which the three axes of height, width, and depth are drawn at 120° to each other, with width and depth axes at 30° to the horizontal. The method is widely used in engineering and architectural drawings. >> section ℹ

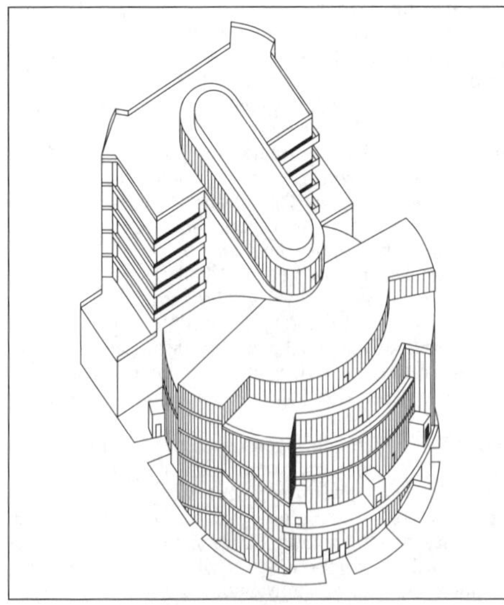

Axonometric and isometric projection – Total Theatre, design by Walter Gropius, 1926

ayatollah [iya**tol**a] A Shiite Muslim religious title meaning 'sign of God', and referring to a clergyman who has reached the third level of Shiite higher education, is recognized as a mujtahid, and is over 40. The word is particularly associated today with the Islamic Republic of Iran. >> Khomeini; mujtahid; Shiites

Ayckbourn, Sir Alan [**ayk**baw(r)n] (1939–) Playwright, born in London. The first of many West End successes was *Relatively Speaking* (1967), establishing him as a master of farce. His plays include *Absurd Person Singular* (1973), *The Norman Conquests* (1974), *Invisible Friends* (1991), and *Communicating Doors* (1995).

aye-aye [**iy**iy] A nocturnal primitive primate (prosimian) from Madagascar (*Daubentonia madagascariensis*); shaggy coat, long bushy tail, and large ears; fingers extremely long and slender; inhabits trees. (Family: Daubentoniidae.) >> prosimian

Ayer, Sir A(lfred) J(ules) [air] (1910–89) Philosopher, born in London. His antimetaphysical *Language, Truth, and Logic* (1936) was hailed as a lucid and concise rendering in English of the doctrines of the Vienna Circle of logical positivist philosophers. >> Vienna Circle

Ayers Rock [airz], Aboriginal name **Uluru** 25°18S 131°18E. A huge red rock in SW Northern Territory, Australia, 450 km/280 mi SW of Alice Springs; rises from the desert to a height of 348 m/1142 ft; 3·6 km/$2\frac{1}{4}$ mi long, 2·4 km/ $1\frac{1}{2}$ mi wide, 8·8 km/$5\frac{1}{2}$ mi in circumference; the largest monolith in the world; named after South Australia premier, Sir Henry Ayers (1821–97). >> Alice Springs

Ayeshah >> **Aïshah**

Ayeyarwady, River, formerly **Irrawaddy** Major river dissecting Myanmar N–S, formed in N Myanmar; empties into Andaman Sea through a large delta; length c.1600 km/ 1000 mi; with the Nmai Hka headstream, c.2000 km/ 1300 mi; major rice-growing region. >> Myanmar ℹ

Aykroyd, Dan (1952–) Actor, born in Ottawa, Canada. He wrote the screenplay for and starred in *The Blues Brothers* (1980), appeared in *Ghostbusters* (1984), and earned a Best Supporting Actor Oscar nomination for his first dramatic role in *Driving Miss Daisy* (1989). Later films include *Feeling Minnesota* (1996) and *Grosse Pointe Blank* (1997).

Aylesbury [**aylz**bree] 51°50N 0°50W, pop (1995e) 60 800. County town of Buckinghamshire, SC England; railway. >> Buckinghamshire

Aylward, Gladys [**ayl**werd] (1902–70) Missionary in China, born in London. She arrived in China in 1930, and helped found an inn at Yangcheng. It was from here that in 1938 she made her famous trek across the mountains leading over 100 children to safety when the war with Japan brought fighting to the area.

Ayodhya [a**yod**ya] Town in the N Indian state of Uttar Pradesh, and the location of the ancient Babri Masjid shrine. During the 1980s the shrine became the target of intense agitation by the Hindu followers of the Bharatiya Janata Paksh and related Hindu fundamentalist organizations. These asserted that the shrine lay over the birthplace of the god Rama, and that a temple should be built on the site. In 1992 a group of militant Hindus destroyed the shrine, and began to erect a temple. This sparked off intense communal violence in many parts of India. >> Bharatiya Janta Paksh; Hinduism; India ℹ

Ayr [air] 55°28N 4°38W, pop (1995e) 49 300. Administrative centre of South Ayrshire council, SW Scotland; on the Firth of Clyde, at mouth of R Ayr; railway. >> Scotland ℹ

azalea [a**zay**lia] A deciduous species of rhododendron. The name is used in horticulture to distinguish it from the evergreen species. (Genus: *Rhododendron*. Family: Ericaceae). >> rhododendron

Azerbaijan [azerbiy**jahn**], Azerbaijani **Azärbayjan Respublikasi**, official name **Republic of Azerbaijan**

pop (1995e) 7 500 000; area 86 600 sq km/33 428 sq mi. Republic in E Transcaucasia; capital, Baku; timezone GMT +3; major ethnic groups, Azerbaijani (83%), Russian (6%), Armenian (6%), though ethnic conflict since 1990 makes accurate current estimates impossible; languages, Azerbaijani (official), Russian; religion, Shiite Muslim; currency, the manat; mountainous country, crossed by the Greater Caucasus (N) and Lesser Caucasus (SW); highest peak, Mt Bazar-Dyuzi (4480 m/14 698 ft); dry and subtropical in C and E Azerbaijan, with mild winters and long hot summers (often reaching over 40°C); SE humid with annual rainfall of 1193–1396 mm/47–55 in; ruled alternately by Turkey and Persia in 18th-c; divided between Persia and Russia, 1828; proclaimed a Soviet Socialist Republic by the Soviet Union, 1920; constituent republic of the USSR, 1936; declaration of independence, 1991; governed by a president, prime minister, and National Council; ongoing conflict with Armenia over disputed enclave of Nagorno-Karabakh; oil extraction and refining, iron, steel, aluminium, copper, chemicals, cement, foodstuffs, textiles, carpets, fishing, timber, salt extraction; grain, cotton, rice, grapes, fruit, vegetables, tobacco, silk. >> Armenia (republic); Baku; Caucasus Mountains; CIS; Russia [i]; Transcaucasia; RR1001

Azhar, El [az**hah(r)**] Muslim university and mosque founded in AD 969 at Cairo, Egypt. It is said to be the oldest university in the world. >> Islam; Koran

azidothymidine >> **AZT**

azimuth The direction of an object measured in degrees clockwise around the horizon from N point to a point on the horizon vertically beneath the object. The notion is used in astronomy, navigation, gunnery, and other contexts where it is important to determine a bearing as well as an altitude. >> astrolabe

azo-dyes [**az**oh] An important class of dyes originally made (1861) by Peter Griess (1829–88), a German-born chemist who worked mainly as a brewery chemist at Burton-on-Trent, Staffordshire, UK. All have two nitrogen atoms joined: –N=N–. >> dyestuff; nitrogen

azolla [**azol**a] An aquatic, free-floating fern, native to tropical and subtropical regions; stem only a few cm long, branched with scale-like, overlapping fronds covered with non-wettable hairs, reddish in autumn. (Genus: *Azolla*, 6 species. Family: Azollaceae.) >> fern

Azores [a**zaw(r)z**], Port **(Arquipélago dos) Açôres** pop (1995e) 240 000; area 2300 sq km/900 sq mi. Island archipelago of volcanic origin, 1400–1800 km/870–1100 mi W of mainland Portugal; Portuguese autonomous region; São Miguel, the principal island (E); settled by the Portuguese, 1439; chief town, Ponta Delgada; highest point, Pico (2351 m/7713 ft). >> Ponta Delgada; Portugal [i]

Azov, Sea of [**azof**], Russ **Azovskoye More** Gulf in NE of Black Sea; shallow water, tending to freeze (Nov–Mar); important source of freshwater fish for Russia. >> Black Sea

AZT An abbreviation for **azidothymidine**, a drug which inhibits replication of viruses, including the AIDS virus, HIV. Developed as **zidovudine**, it was granted a licence unusually rapidly, in response to pressure from AIDS patients. Clinical trials have demonstrated the drug to be of limited use in therapy. It has inherent toxicity, and resistance develops rapidly. >> AIDS; drug resistance; virus

Aztecs The most powerful people of Central America during the 15th–16th-c. Their main city, Tenochtitlan (present-day Mexico City), became the most densely populated city of the region. They built up a powerful despotic state, eventually ruling 400–500 small tribute-paying states. They developed a form of hieroglyphic writing, a complex calendar system, and built famous pyramids and temples. The Aztec empire was finally destroyed by the Spanish under Cortés in 1521. >> Cortés; Montezuma II; Teotihuacan

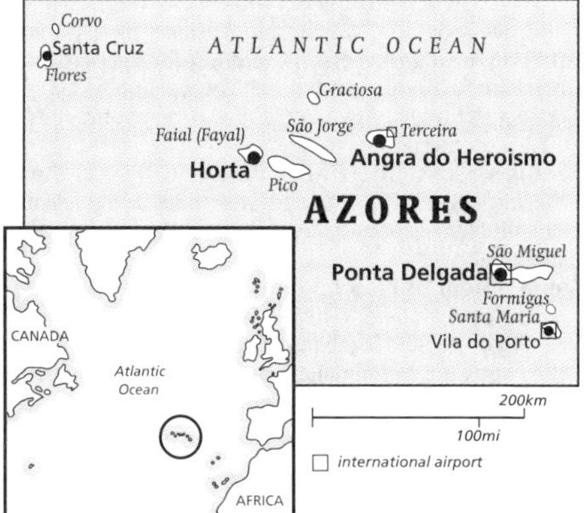

B

Baader–Meinhof [**bah**der **miyn**hof] The popular name for *Rote Armee Fraktion* (RAF), after leaders Andreas Baader (1943–77) and Ulrike Meinhof (1934–76); a left-wing German revolutionary terrorist group which carried out political bombings in Germany in the early 1970s. >> terrorism

Baal [bayl] (Heb 'lord') The Phoenician god of rain and fertility, his voice being the thunder; in the Bible, used for gods of various localities in Syria and Canaan. >> Bible; Canaan

Baalbek [**bahl**bek], ancient **Heliopolis** 34°00N 36°12E, pop (1995e) 15 600. Town in E Lebanon where the Phoenicians built a temple to the Sun-god, Baal; a world heritage site. >> Baal; Lebanon ℹ; Phoenicia

Baath or **Ba'ath** [bahth] (Arabic 'resurgence') The ideology of the Baath Arab Socialist Party, founded in 1940 by a Christian, Michel Aflaq, and a Muslim, Salah al-Din Bitar, synthesizing Marxism with a pan-Arab nationalism that aims to unite Arab nations. The party has been most prominent in Syria and Iraq. >> Marxism

Baba Malay >> **Malay** (language)

Babar or **Babur**, (Arabic 'tiger'), originally **Zahir-ud-din Muhammad** (1483–1530) First Mughal Emperor of India, born in Ferghana, Kyrgyzstan. He was a distinguished soldier, as well as a poet and diarist of note. >> Mughal Empire

Babbage, Charles (1791–1871) Mathematician and pioneer computer scientist, born in Walworth, London. He worked on the theory of logarithms, and built a 'difference machine', the forerunner of the computer, for which a system of programming was devised. His assistant was Byron's daughter, Augusta Ada, Lady Lovelace. In 1991, for the bicentenary of his birth, the Science Museum constructed a full-scale Difference Engine No 2 from original designs dating from 1847. >> Ada; computer; logarithm

Babbitt, Bruce (Edward) (1938–) US statesman, born in Flagstaff, AZ. He trained as a lawyer, served as Arizona's attorney-general (1975–8), and became state governor (1978–87). An unsuccessful candidate for the Democratic presidential nomination in 1988, he was appointed secretary of the interior in 1993, and was reappointed in the 1997 administration.

babbler A songbird native to warmer regions of the Old World; soft, fluffy plumage and short wings. (Family: Timaliidae, over 280 species.) >> chat; jay; songbird; wren babbler

Babel, Tower of Probably the site of an important temple shrine in the ancient city of Babylon. In the Bible (*Gen* 11.1–9) the legend is related of how its construction led to the confusion of languages, and the consequent dispersion of peoples, as a punishment by God for human pride. >> Babylon; Genesis, Book of

Babi >> **Baha'i**

Babington, Antony (1561–86) Conspirator, born in Dethick, Derbyshire. In 1586, he was induced to lead a conspiracy to murder Queen Elizabeth and release Queen Mary of Scotland (the **Babington Plot**). The plot was discovered, and he was executed. >> Mary, Queen of Scots

Babinski, Joseph (François Felix) [ba**bin**skee] (1857–1932) Neurologist, born in Paris. He described a reflex of the foot, symptomatic of organic disease of the motor neurones in the brain and spinal cord, and a reflex of the forearm believed to be due to a lesion in the spinal cord. Both reflexes are known as **Babinski's Sign**. >> neurone ℹ; spinal cord

babirusa [babi**roo**sa] A wild pig native to Sulawesi (*Babyrousa babyrussa*); pale, almost hairless body; long lower tusks; upper canines in the male grow from the top of the snout, and curl towards the eyes; inhabits riverbanks; swims well. >> pig

Babi Yar A huge ravine near Kiev in the Ukraine into which over 30 000 Jews were herded and massacred by Nazi German troops in 1941. >> Holocaust; Nazi Party

baboon A ground-dwelling African monkey; long dog-like muzzle with large teeth; males with swollen, naked buttocks. (Genera: *Papio*, 5 species; *Mandrillus*, 2 species; *Theropithecus*, 1 species.) >> drill; hamadryas baboon; mandrill; Old World monkey

Babylon 32°33N 44°25E. From the 18th-c BC the capital of the Babylonian Empire, situated on the R Euphrates S of Baghdad, modern Iraq. Its massive city walls and 'hanging gardens' were one of the wonders of the ancient world. >> Babylonia; Seven Wonders of the Ancient World

Babylonia [babi**loh**nia] The region in Lower Mesopotamia around the ancient city of Babylon, which formed the core twice in antiquity of extensive but short-lived empires. Under its greatest ruler Nebuchadnezzar (605–562 BC), it stretched as far E as the Mediterranean. >> Babylon; Mesopotamia

Babylonian exile The mass deportation of the Jews from Palestine to Babylonia in 587–6 BC, after the failure of their revolt against Nebuchadnezzar. >> Babylonia

Bacall, Lauren [ba**kawl**], originally **Betty Joan Perske** (1924–) Actress, born in New York City. She was given her first leading role in *To Have and Have Not* (1944), opposite Humphrey Bogart, whom she subsequently married. Later films include *The Big Sleep* (1946), *Key Largo* (1948), and *The Mirror Has Two Faces* (1996). >> Bogart

baccarat A casino card game, the most popular version being *baccarat banque*, in which the bank plays against the players. Another variant is *chemin de fer*, whereby all players take it in turn to hold the bank. >> *chemin de fer*

Bacchanalia [baka**nay**lia] The orgiastic rites of Bacchus (Dionysus), the god of nature, fertility, and wine. They were banned from Rome in 186 BC.

Bach, C(arl) P(hilipp) E(manuel), known as **the Berlin Bach** or **the Hamburg Bach** (1714–88) Composer, born in Weimar, Germany, the second surviving son of Johann Sebastian Bach. He wrote the first methodical treatment of clavier playing, and composed numerous concertos, keyboard sonatas, church music, and chamber music. >> Bach, Johann Sebastian

Bach, J(ohann) C(hristian), known as **the London Bach** or **the English Bach** (1735–82) Composer, born in Leipzig, Germany, the youngest son of Johann Sebastian Bach. In 1762 he settled in London, where he was employed at the King's Theatre and promoted an important series of subscription concerts. >> Bach, Johann Sebastian

Bach, Johann Sebastian (1685–1750) Composer, one of the world's greatest musicians, born in Eisenach, Germany. In 1707 he married a cousin, **Maria Barbara Bach** (1684–1720), and in 1711 became *Kapellmeister* to Prince Leopold of Anhalt-Cöthen, where he wrote mainly instrumental music, including the 'Brandenburg'

Concertos (1721) and *The Well-tempered Clavier* (1722). Widowed in 1720, and left with four children, he married in 1721 **Anna Magdalena Wilcke** (1701–60), and had 13 children by her, of whom six survived. In 1723 he was appointed cantor of the Thomasschule in Leipzig, where his works included perhaps c.300 church cantatas, the *St Matthew Passion* (1727), and the *Mass in B Minor*. Almost totally blind, he died in Leipzig. His main achievement was the development of polyphony, but because of his success as an organist his genius as a composer was not fully recognized until the following century. >> cantata; polyphony

Bacher, Ali [**bakh**er] (1942–) Cricketer and sports administrator, born in Roodepoort, South Africa. He captained Transvaal and South Africa with great success, but his Test career was cut short by international sports boycotts of South African teams. He was a leading figure in organizing the 'rebel' tours to South Africa in the 1980s, and in subsequent non-racial planning. >> cricket ℹ

Bach flower remedies A system of flower remedies for illnesses, and especially for disharmonies of the personality and emotional state, devised by British medical microbiologist Edward Bach (1880–1936). Bach theorized that the dew condensing on a plant would, when exposed to sunlight, absorb the energy of the plant into the water molecules. From this premise he developed a system of herbal remedies prepared from 38 different species of flower. >> alternative medicine

bacillus [ba**sil**uhs] Any rod-shaped bacterium; also a large and diverse genus of rod-shaped bacteria, typically motile by means of flagella. Some are disease-causing, including the causative agent of anthrax. (Kingdom: Monera. Family: Bacillaceae.) >> anthrax; bacteria ℹ; flagellum

backgammon A board game for two players. Introduced to Britain by the Crusaders, it became known as backgammon from c.1750. Each player has 15 round flat pieces of a particular colour, which are moved around the board on the throw of two dice. The board is divided into two halves; the inner table and the outer table. The object is to move your own pieces around the board and home to your own inner table. You win by being the first to remove all your pieces from the board.

background radiation Naturally occurring radioactivity which can be detected at any place on Earth. It results from cosmic rays reaching the Earth from outer space, and from the radioactive decay of minerals in the soil. >> cosmic rays; radioactivity

backing store A general term used in computing to describe the place where the computer stores the long term data needed to carry out its tasks; also known as **bulk store** or **secondary store**. It has a higher capacity but lower access time than the main memory of a computer, and is normally in the form of magnetic tape storage or magnetic disk storage. >> computer memory

Bacon, Francis, Viscount St Albans (1561–1626) Philosopher and statesman, born in London. He was in turn solicitor general (1607), attorney general (1613), privy counsellor (1616), Lord Keeper (1617), and Lord Chancellor (1618). His philosophy is best studied in *The Advancement of Learning* (1605) and *Novum Organum* (1620). His stress on inductive methods gave a strong impetus to subsequent scientific investigation.

Bacon, Francis (1909–92) Artist, born in Dublin. He began painting without any formal art education at the age of 19. He treated religious subjects in a highly individual manner, but made little impact until his 'Three Studies for Figures at the base of a Crucifixion' (1945). His style derives from Surrealism, often with a tendency towards the macabre. >> Surrealism

Bacon, Nathaniel (c.1642–76) American colonial leader, born in Suffolk, England. He emigrated to Virginia in 1673, and made himself prominent by his raids against the Indians. His activities prompted the English governor to declare him a rebel in 1676, whereupon Bacon captured and burned Jamestown. For a time he controlled most of Virginia, but died suddenly, and the rebellion ended.

Bacon, Roger, known as **Doctor Mirabilis** ('Wonderful Doctor') (c.1220–92) Philosopher, probably born in Ilchester, Somerset. In 1247 he began to devote himself to experimental science, and in 1266–7 compiled, at the request of Pope Clement IV, his *Opus Majus* (Great Work). In 1277 his writings were condemned, and he was imprisoned until shortly before his death. >> Franciscans

bacteria (sing **bacterium**) A diverse division of microscopic organisms that all share a *procaryotic* cellular organization, ie each cell lacks a true nucleus bounded by a nuclear membrane. The genetic information is carried on a loop of deoxyribonucleic acid (DNA) in the cytoplasm. Most bacteria are single-celled. Basic bacterial shapes are spherical (*coccus*), rod-like (*bacillus*), and spiral (*spirillum*). These may occur singly, or in chains, pairs, clusters, or other groupings. They range in size from less than 1 μ (*Chlamydia*) to about 0·5 mm (spirochaete), but most are between 1 and 10 μ. Some can grow only in the presence of oxygen (**aerobic bacteria**), while others grow only in the absence of oxygen (**anaerobic bacteria**). They occur in soil, water, and air, as well as in symbiotic associations with other organisms, and as parasites or disease-causing agents. The scientific study of bacteria is known as **bacteriology**. >> Archaebacteria; bacillus; bacteriological warfare; cell; *Chlamydia*; *Clostridium*; DNA ℹ; Escherichia; *Legionella*; micro-organism; mitosis; nucleus (biology); pneumococcus; *Proteus*; *Salmonella*; spirochaete; *Staphylococcus*; *Streptococcus*; symbiosis; *Vibrio*

bacteriological warfare A form of warfare using organic agents such as micro-organisms and viruses which cause disease and death in humans. Many such agents have been investigated, including anthrax, plague, and botulinus toxin. >> bacteria ℹ; biological warfare; chemical warfare; virus

Bactria [**bak**tria] The name given in antiquity to the area roughly corresponding to N Afghanistan and the adjacent parts of S Russia. It became an independent state in the second half of the 3rd-c BC.

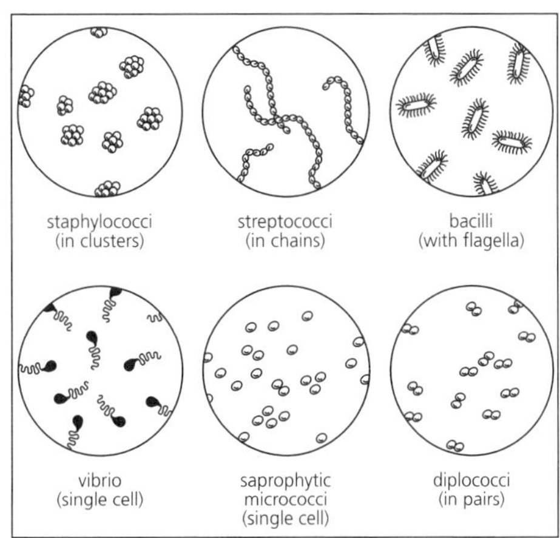

Bacteria

Badajoz [**bad**ajoz], Span [ba<u>th</u>a**hoth**], ancient **Pax Augusta** 38°50N 6°59W, pop (1995e) 123 000. City in SW Spain, on R Guadiana; bishopric; former Moorish capital; scene of a battle in the Peninsular War, 1812; airport; railway; cathedral (13th-c). >> Peninsular War; Spain ℹ

Baden [**bah**dn], ancient **Thermae Pannonicae** 48°01N 16°14E, pop (1995e) 25 700. Town in NE Austria, on the R Schwechat; connected to Vienna by tram; principal Austrian spa, with sulphurous waters, known since Roman times; tourism. >> Austria ℹ

Baden-Powell, Robert Stephenson Smyth Baden-Powell, Baron [**bay**dn **pow**el] (1857–1941) British general, born in London. He joined the army, served in India and Afghanistan, was on the staff in West Africa and Matabeleland, and won fame during the Boer War as the defender of Mafeking (1899–1900). In 1908 he founded the Boy Scout movement, and in 1910, with his sister **Agnes** (1858–1945), the Girl Guides (known as Girl Scouts in the USA after 1912). In 1916 he organized the Wolf Cubs in Britain (known as Cub Scouts in the USA) for boys under the age of 11. In 1920 he was made world chief scout at the first international Boy Scout Jamboree, and in 1929 was created Baron Baden-Powell. >> Mafeking, Siege of; scouting

Bader, Sir Douglas (Robert Stuart) [**bah**der] (1910–82) Wartime aviator, born in London. He lost both legs in a flying accident in 1931 and was invalided out of the RAF, but overcame his disability and returned to the service in 1939, commanding the first RAF Canadian Fighter Squadron. Captured in 1941, he set an example of fortitude and heroism that became a legend.

badger A nocturnal mammal, usually grey-brown with a black and white head; pointed face; length 0·5–1 m/ $1\frac{1}{2}$–$3\frac{1}{4}$ ft; lives in burrows. (Family: Mustelidae, 8 species.) >> ferret; honey badger; Mustelidae

Badlands Arid region of SW South Dakota and NW Nebraska, USA; an area of barren, eroded landscapes and fossil deposits E of the Black Hills. >> Nebraska; South Dakota

badminton An indoor court game played by two or four people using rackets and a shuttlecock. Its name derives from Badminton House, the seat of the Duke of Beaufort, where the Duke's family and guests played in the 19th-c. It developed from the children's game of *battledore and shuttlecock*. >> RR1046

Baedeker, Karl [**bay**deker] (1801–59) Publisher, born in Essen, Germany. He started his own publishing business at Koblenz in 1827, and is best known for the guidebooks which bear his name, published since 1872 at Leipzig.

Baez, Joan [biy**ez**] (1941–) Folksinger, born in Staten I, New York City. Her crystalline soprano voice first attracted critical plaudits at the Newport Folk Festival of 1960, and her recordings in the decade that followed created a mass audience for folk music. >> folk music

Baffin, William (c.1584–1622) Navigator, probably born in London. He was pilot in several expeditions in search of the Northwest Passage (1612–16). Baffin Bay is named after him.

Baffin Bay Ice-blocked Arctic gulf between Greenland (E) and Baffin, Bylot, Devon, and Ellesmere Is (W); length c.1125 km/700 mi; width 110–650 km/70–400 mi; depth over 2400 m/8100 ft; navigation only in summer; first entered by John Davis, 1585; explored by William Baffin, 1615. >> Arctic; Baffin

Baffin Island Largest island in the Canadian Arctic Archipelago, in the Arctic Ocean; area 318 186 sq km/ 122 820 sq mi; length c.1600 km/1000 mi; width 209–725 km/130–450 mi; irregular coastline, with several peninsulas and deep bays; first visited by Frobisher, 1576–8; population mainly Inuit. >> Baffin; Canada ℹ; Frobisher; Northwest Territories

bagatelle [baga**tel**] A restricted form of billiards, played on a table with nine numbered cups instead of pockets. Popular in the UK, it is played in many different forms on a rectangular table. >> billiards

Bagehot, Walter [**ba**juht] (1826–77) Economist, journalist, and political theorist, born in Langport, Somerset. His *English Constitution* (1867) is still considered a standard work. >> political science

Bagerat [bage**raht**] The former city of Khalifatabad, founded in the 15th-c by General Ulugh Khan Jahan in the S Ganges delta, present-day Bangladesh; a world heritage site. >> Bangladesh ℹ

Baghdad [bag**dad**] 33°20N 44°26E, pop (1995e) 5 385 000. Capital city of Iraq, on R Tigris; founded, 762; enclosed on three sides by ancient walls; later under Mongol, then Turkish rule; independent capital, 20th-c; badly damaged through bombing during the Gulf War, 1991; airport; railway; university (1958); Abbasid palace, Mustansiriyah law college (13th-c). >> Iraq ℹ

bagpipes A musical instrument of great antiquity consisting of a bag (usually of sheepskin) which the player fills with air through a blow-pipe or bellows, and squeezes with the arm so that the air then passes through several sounding pipes. The Highlands and Lowlands of Scotland have their different types of bagpipes, as also do Ireland, Northumberland, and several other parts of Europe. >> aerophone; reed instrument

Baguio [**bag**ioh] 16°25N 120°37E, pop (1995e) 174 000. Summer capital of the Philippines, in NW Luzon I; mountain resort town and official summer residence of the President; two universities (1911, 1948); military academy. >> Philippines ℹ

Baha'i [ba**hiy**] A religious movement arising out of the Persian Islamic sect Babi in the 1860s, when Mirza Husayn-Ali (1817–92), known as Baha'u'llah ('Glory of God'), declared himself the prophet foretold by the founder of the Babi movement, Mirza Ali-Mohammed (1819–50). Baha'ism teaches the oneness of God, the unity of all faiths, the harmony of all people, universal education, and obedience to government. Its headquarters is in Haifa, Israel. There were over 6 million adherents in 1997. >> Baha'u'llah religion

Bahamas, official name **Commonwealth of the Bahamas** pop (1995e) 274 000; area 13 934 sq km/5378 sq mi. Archipelago of c.700 low-lying islands and over 2000 cays, forming a chain extending c.800 km/500 mi SE from the coast of Florida; two oceanic banks of Little Bahama and Great Bahama; highest point 120 m/394 ft; capital, Nassau; major town, Freeport; timezone GMT −5; over 75% of the population live on New Providence or Grand Bahama; 85% black, 15% white; dominant religion, Christianity; official language, English; unit of currency, Bahamian dollar; climate subtropical, with average temperatures 21°C (winter) and 27°C (summer); mean annual rainfall 750–1500 mm/30–60 in; hurricanes frequent (Jun–Nov); visited by Columbus in 1492, but first permanent European settlement not until 1647, by English and Bermudan religious refugees; British Crown Colony, 1717; independence, 1973; a bicameral assembly; head of state, the British monarch, represented by a governor-general; tourism the mainstay of the economy, especially at New Providence (Nassau and Paradise I) and Grand Bahama; important financial centre (status as a tax haven). >> Andros (Bahamas); buccaneers; Nassau (Bahamas); New Providence; RR1001 political leaders; *see illustration on p.67*

Bahia [ba**ee**a] pop (1995e) 12 770 000; area 561 026 sq km/ 216 556 sq mi. State in NE Brazil, bounded E by the Atlantic; capital, Salvador; site of first landing by Portuguese in 1500. >> Brazil ℹ; Salvador

Bahía Blanca [baeea **blang**ka] 38°45S 62°15W, pop (1995e) 284 000. City in E Argentina; includes naval base of Puerto Belgrano; founded in 1828; university (1956); airport; railway. >> Argentina ℹ

Bahrain, official name **State of Bahrain** pop (1995e) 555 000; area 678 sq km/262 sq mi. Group of 35 islands comprising an independent state in the Persian Gulf; Saudi-Bahrain causeway (25 km/16 mi); capital, Manama; timezone GMT +3; major ethnic groups, Arab (73%) and Iranian (9%); religion, Islam (c.65% Shia); official language, Arabic; currency, Bahrain dinar; island of Bahrain c.48 km/30 mi long, 13–16 km/8–10 mi wide, area 562 sq km/217 sq mi, highest point Jabal Dukhan (135 m/443 ft); largely bare and infertile; cool N/NE winds with a little rain (Dec–Mar), average 35 mm/1·4 in, temperature 19°C (Jan); summer average temperature of 36°C and a humidity of 97% (Sep); a flourishing centre of trade, 2000–1800 BC; treaty of protection with the UK in 1861; independence in 1971; a constitutional monarchy governed by the amir, who appoints a Council of Ministers headed by a prime minister; a major centre for oil trading, banking, and commerce. >> Manama; RR1001 political leaders

Baikal or **Baykal, Lake** [biy**kal**] area 31 500 sq km/12 160 sq mi. Crescent-shaped lake in S Siberia, Russia; largest freshwater lake in Eurasia, and deepest in the world; length (SW–NE) 636 km/395 mi; width 24–80 km/15–50 mi; maximum depth 1620 m/5315 ft; freezes over (Jan–Apr); measures to control serious pollution introduced since 1971. >> Russia ℹ

Baikonur or **Baykonyr Cosmodrome** [biyko**noor**] A Russian space centre constructed in the 1950s in Kazakhstan. It was from here that the first artificial satellite and manned space flight were launched. Russia is to lease part of this complex for 20 years, and a new Cosmodrome is planned for Svobodnyy in the far East. >> Russian Space Agency

bail The freeing from custody of a person charged with a crime and awaiting trial. There are often conditions imposed to secure the person's attendance at a court on a future date. Frequently the security involves a sum of money pledged by the person or a guarantor (a *surety*) with the police or a court. This money is liable to be forfeited in the event of the accused person's non-appearance. There are several differences in the operation of the bail procedure between legal systems. Breach of any bail conditions is itself an offence.

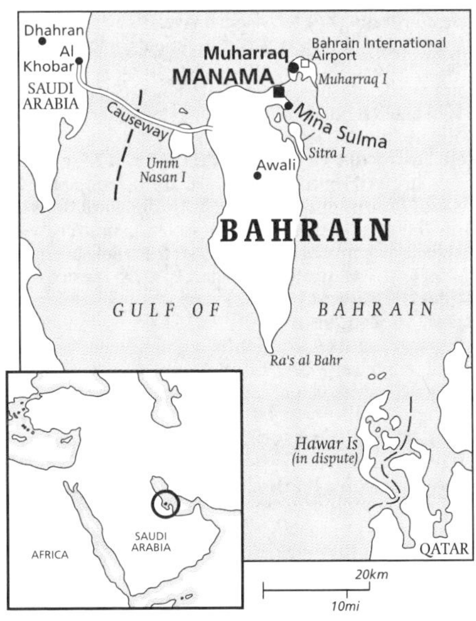

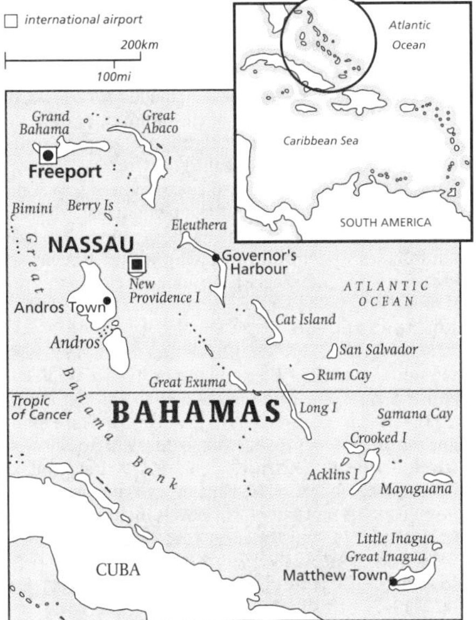

Bailey, David (Royston) (1938–) Photographer, born in London. Originally a fashion photographer, he became known for his portraits expressing the spirit of the 1960s. He has been a director of televison commercials and documentaries since the 1970s.

Bailey bridge A prefabricated bridge used by combat engineers, which can be rapidly constructed on the battlefield. The system was devised by British engineer Sir Donald Bailey (1901–85) during World War 2.

bailiff An officer of the sheriff or the county court who is responsible for executing warrants, processes, and writs. He may also seize goods as a method of obtaining payment, such as for unpaid rent. The equivalent position in Scotland is that of the Sheriff officer. >> county court; sheriff

Baillie, Dame Isobel [**bay**lee] (1895–1983) Soprano, born in Hawick, Scottish Borders. She is regarded as one of this century's greatest oratorio singers. >> oratorio

Baily, Francis (1774–1844) Astronomer, born in Newbury, West Berkshire. He described the phenomenon now known as **Baily's beads** in 1836 – a broken ring of bright points around the edge of the Moon, formed in a total solar eclipse by the Sun's rays shining through the Moon's valleys at the moment of totality. >> eclipse; Sun

Bainbridge, Beryl (Margaret) (1934–) British writer, born in Liverpool, Merseyside. She began writing in the 1960s, and became known for her terse, black comedies, such as *The Dressmaker* (1973, filmed 1979) and *Filthy Lucre* (1986). Several novels tackle historical subjects, such as *Young Adolf* (1978) and *The Birthday Boys* (1991). Later works include plays, collections of her journalistic essays (1993), and stories (1994),

Baird, John Logie (1888–1946) Television pioneer, born in Helensburgh, Argyll and Bute. In 1926 he gave the first demonstration of a television image. His 30-line mechanically scanned system was experimentally broadcast by the BBC in 1929; and during 1936, transmissions of his improved 240-line system alternated with the rival Marconi-EMI 405-line electronic system, which was adopted in 1937. >> television

Baja California [**ba**ha], Eng **Lower California** A long peninsula in NW Mexico; length 1220 km/760 mi; San Pedro Mártir Mts rise to 3095 m/10 154 ft; Colorado R flows into the N of the Gulf; geographical isolation much eased by highway completed in 1970s down the whole peninsula; chief towns, Mexicali, Ensenada, La Paz. >> Mexico ℹ

Bajazet >> **Bayezit I**

Baker, Sir Benjamin (1840–1907) Civil engineer, born in Keyford, Somerset. In 1861 he began a long association with engineer John Fowler, and together they constructed the London Metropolitan Railway, Victoria Station, and the Forth Rail Bridge (opened 1890).

Baker, James A(ddison), III (1930–) US secretary of state (1989–92), born in Houston, TX. He served President Reagan as White House chief-of-staff (1981–5) and secretary of the Treasury (1985–8) before resigning to manage George Bush's campaign for the presidency. After winning the election, Bush named him as secretary of state. In 1992 he returned to the White House as chief-of-staff, to run Bush's re-election campaign. >> Bush, George; Ford, Gerald R; Reagan

Baker, Dame Janet (Abbott) (1933–) Mezzo-soprano, born in Hatfield, South Yorkshire. She had an extensive operatic career, especially in early Italian opera and the works of Benjamin Britten; she is also a noted interpreter of Mahler and Elgar. In 1994 she became a Companion of Honour. >> Britten

Baker, Kenneth (Wilfred) (1934–) British statesman. He became an MP in 1968, and in the Thatcher administration rose to become secretary of state for the environment (1985) and for education (1986). He was later appointed chairman of the Conservative Party (1989–90) and home secretary (1990–2).

Baker, Richard (Douglas James) (1925–) Broadcaster and author, born in London. He joined the BBC as an announcer in 1950, and became known as a television newsreader (1954–82) and as a commentator on major state occasions. He also introduced the television productions of BBC Promenade Concerts (1960–95).

Bakewell, Joan (Dawson) (1933–) Broadcaster and writer, born in Stockport, Greater Manchester. She became known for her regular contributions and series on television, such as *Late Night Line Up* (1965–72), *Reports Action* (1976–8), and *The Heart of the Matter* (1988–). She won the Richard Dimbleby Award in 1994.

baking powder A mixture of sodium bicarbonate, tartaric acid, and potassium tartrate, used in baking. It is added to dough (a mixture of flour and water), and when heated, carbon dioxide is released, causing the dough to rise. >> flour

Bakst, Léon [bahkst], originally **Lev Samoilovich Rosenberg** (1866–1924) Painter, born in St Petersburg, Russia. He was associated with Diaghilev, designing the decor and costumes for numerous productions (1909–21). >> Diaghilev

Baku [ba**koo**] 40°22N 49°53E, pop (1995e) 1 140 000. Seaport capital of Azerbaijan; on the W coast of the Caspian Sea; airport; railway; university (1919). >> Azerbaijan ℹ

Balaclava, Battle of A battle fought between British and Russian forces during the early stages of the Crimean War. The Russian attack on the British base at Balaclava was unsuccessful, but the British sustained the heavier losses. >> Charge of the Light Brigade; Crimean War

Balakirev, Mili Alekseyevich [ba**la**kiryef] (1837–1910) Composer, born in Nizhni Novgorod, Russia. He became leader of the national Russian school of music. His compositions include two symphonies, many songs, and some highly individual piano music. >> folk music

balalaika [bala**liy**ka] A Russian musical instrument: a lute, with a triangular body, flat back, long neck, and three strings which are strummed by the player's fingers. >> chordophone

balance of payments The difference, for a country, between the income and expenditure arising out of its international trading activities. The *current account* handles the country's income from selling goods abroad (exporting), offset by its expenditure on goods imported. The difference between these two totals is the **trade balance**. Also included are 'invisible' services bought and sold abroad, such as banking, insurance, and tourism. The *capital account* deals with private and corporate investment abroad, borrowing and lending, and government financial transactions. A **balance of payments deficit** drains a nation's reserves of convertible currency and gold, and can lead to a devaluation of its currency. >> invisibles

Balanchine, George [**bal**uhncheen], originally **Georgi Melitonovich Balanchivadze** (1904–83) Ballet dancer and choreographer, born in St Petersburg, Russia. After a period in the Russian Ballet in Paris, he opened in 1934 the School of American Ballet in New York, and from then devoted most of his career to establishing a native American tradition of dance. In 1948 he became director of the New York City Ballet. >> ballet; Ballets Russes; choreography

Balaton, Lake [**bol**oton] area 598 sq km/231 sq mi. Lake in WC Hungary; length 77 km/48 mi; width 8–14 km/5–9 mi; largest and shallowest lake in C Europe; Hungary's largest recreation area. >> Hungary ℹ

Balboa, Vasco Núñez de [bal**boh**a] (1475–1519) Explorer, born in Jerez de los Caballeros, Spain. He joined the expedition to Darién in 1511, and became the first European to see the Pacific Ocean (1513).

bald cypress >> **swamp cypress**

bald eagle A large eagle (length 80–100 cm/30–40 in), native to North America (*Haliaeetus leucocephalus*); the name refers to the white plumage on its head and neck. The national symbol of the USA, it is also known as the **American eagle**. (Family: Accipitridae). >> eagle

Balder, Baldur, or **Baldr** [**bawl**der, **bal**der] Norse god, the most handsome and gentle of the children of Odin and Frigga; the name means 'bright'. He taught human beings the use of herbs for healing. >> Odin

baldness Commonly described as permanent loss of hair from the front and/or top of the head, usually in men, because of the degeneration and reduction in the size of hair follicles. Genetic factors, ageing, and androgens may be causative agents. There is no effective cure. >> androgens; hair

baldpate >> **wigeon**

Baldwin I (1172–c.1205) Count of Flanders (from 1194) and Hainault (from 1195), the youngest brother of Godfrey of Bouillon. He was a leader of the Fourth Crusade, and in 1204 was crowned as the first Latin Emperor of Constantinople. >> Crusades ℹ; Godfrey of Bouillon

Baldwin, James (Arthur) (1924–87) Writer, born in Harlem, New York City. He became an active member of the civil rights movement. His novels include *Go Tell it on the Mountain* (1954), *Tell Me How Long The Train's Been Gone* (1968), and *Just Above My Head* (1979). >> civil rights

Baldwin (of Bewdley), Stanley Baldwin, 1st Earl (1867–1947) British Conservative statesman, who was three times prime minister (1923–4, 1924–9, 1935–7),

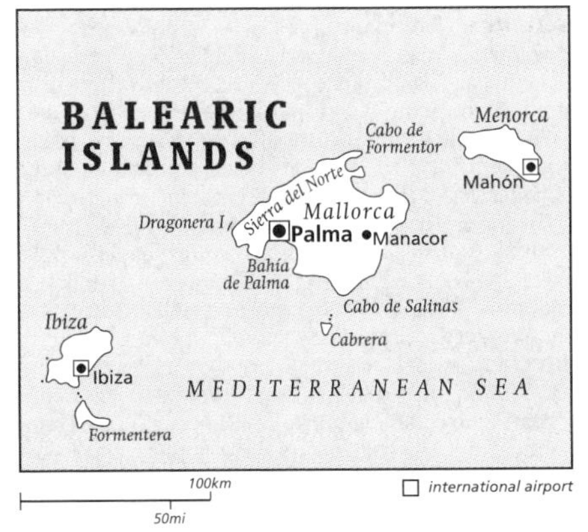

born in Bewdley, Hereford and Worcester. He was President of the Board of Trade (1921–2) and Chancellor of the Exchequer (1922–3), then unexpectedly succeeded Bonar Law as premier. His period of office included the General Strike (1926). >> Conservative Party; Edward VIII; General Strike; Law, Bonar

Balearic Islands [baliarik], Span **Islas Baleares** pop (1995e) 708 000; area 5014 sq km/1935 sq mi. Archipelago of five major islands and 11 islets in the W Mediterranean near the E coast of Spain; conquered by Aragón, 14th-c; capital, Palma de Mallorca; E group chiefly comprises Majorca, Minorca, and Cabrera; W group chiefly comprises Ibiza and Formentera; popular tourist resorts. >> Formentera; Ibiza; Majorca; Minorca; Spain ℹ

baleen A fibrous material from the mouth of some species of whale; forms a sieve during feeding; formerly used in manufacturing, when strong, light, flexible material was needed; also known as **whalebone** (though it is not in fact bone). >> humpback whale; whale ℹ

Balenciaga, Cristóbal [balenthi**ah**ga] (1895–1972) Fashion designer, born in Guetaria, Spain. He left Spain for Paris as a result of the Spanish Civil War, producing clothes noted for dramatic simplicity and elegant design.

Balfour, Arthur James Balfour, 1st Earl [**bal**fer] (1848–1930) British statesman and Conservative prime minister (1902–5), born in Whittinghame, East Lothian. He became chief secretary for Ireland (1887–91), where his policy of suppression earned him the name of 'Bloody Balfour'. As foreign secretary (1916–19) he was responsible for the **Balfour Declaration** (1917), which promised Zionists a national home in Palestine. >> Zionism

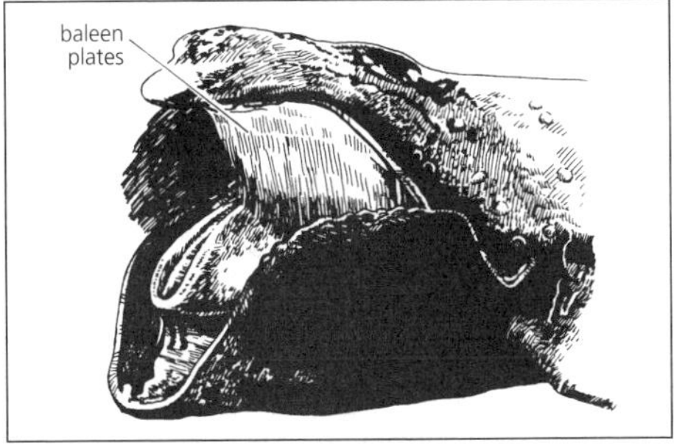

Baleen plates in the mouth of a baleen whale

Bali [**bah**lee] pop (1995e) 3 037 000; area 5561 sq km/2146 sq mi. Island province of Indonesia; mountainous, with peaks rising to 3142 m/10 308 ft at Gunung Agung (E); chiefly Hindu population; Dutch control by 1908; capital, Denpasar; major tourist area. >> Indonesia ℹ

Balkan Wars (1912–13) A series of military campaigns fought in the Balkans. In 1912, Bulgaria, Serbia, Greece, and Montenegro attacked Turkey, securing swift victories. A preliminary peace was drawn up by the Great Powers in May 1913. Disputes between the Balkan allies over the spoils of war led to a second war, in which Bulgaria attacked her former allies, and was defeated.

Balkhash, Lake [bal**kash**] area 17 000–22 300 sq km/6500–8500 sq mi. Crescent-shaped lake in SE Kazakhstan; length 605 km/376 mi; maximum width 74 km/46 mi; maximum depth 26 m/85 ft; no outlet; gradually shrinking. >> Kazakhstan ℹ

Ballantyne, R(obert) M(ichael) (1825–94) Writer of boys' books, born in Edinburgh. He joined the Hudson's Bay Company in 1841, and worked in the backwoods of N Canada until 1847. *The Coral Island* (1858) is his most famous work.

Ballarat or **Ballaarat** [**bal**arat] 37°36S 143°58E, pop (1995e) 36 500. City in SWC Victoria, Australia; railway; centre of a wool-producing district; largest gold reserves in the country discovered here, 1851; scene of the Eureka Stockade, the gold-diggers' rebellion against state authority, 1854. >> Victoria (Australia)

Ballard, J(ames) G(raham) (1930–) Writer, born in Shanghai, China. He specialized in the writing of science-fiction novels (eg his first, *The Drowned World*, 1962), later publishing an autobiographical novel *Empire of the Sun* (1984; filmed, 1987) and works on other themes.

Ballesteros, Sevvy [ba-ye**stair**os], popular name of **Severiano Ballesteros** (1957–) Golfer, born in Pedrena, Spain. His successes include the (British) Open (1979, 1984, 1988), the US Masters (1980, 1983), and the World Matchplay (1981–2, 1984–5, 1991). >> golf

ballet A theatrical form of dance typically combined with music, stage design, and costume in an integrated whole, based around a scenario. It can be divided roughly into historical periods; mid-19th-c Romantic ballets such as *Les Sylphides*, *Giselle*, and the Russian classics (eg *Swan Lake*, *The Sleeping Beauty*); neoclassical works, such as Balanchine's *Apollo*; and modern ballets, such as Ashton's *Monotones* and MacMillan's *Gloria*. The ballet technique is based on turn out from the hip socket. There are five positions of the feet and a codified system of arm positions (*port de bras*). Intensive training is required from a young age, often in specialist schools. >> Ballets Russes; Bolshoi Ballet; London Festival Ballet; Rambert; Royal Ballet

Ballet Rambert >> **Rambert**

Ballets Russes [**bal**ay **roos**] A ballet company created by Diaghilev and active in Europe 1909–29. It was famous for nurturing new talents and for collaborations between great painters (Bakst, Benois, Picasso), composers (Rimsky-Korsakov, Satie, Stravinsky), and choreographers (Fokine, Nijinsky, Massine, Nijinska, Balanchine). >> ballet

ballistic missile A missile which acquires its energy during its launch phase, flying on a trajectory dictated by its initial velocity added to the factors of gravity and aerodynamic drag, until it reaches the target. A **cruise missile**, by contrast, flies with wings through the atmosphere under continuous power. A rifle bullet is in effect a ballistic missile, but more specifically the term applies to the big intercontinental and submarine-launched ballistic missiles which carry nuclear warheads. >> antiballistic / cruise / guided / intercontinental ballistic / Trident missile

ballistics The study of what takes place when a projectile is fired from a firearm. Ballistics has three aspects: (1) *internal*, concerning the way the object is thrown into the air; (2) *external*, investigating the way it moves in flight; (3) *terminal*, analyzing its impact on the target. **Forensic ballistics** investigates gun crimes. >> firearms

balloon A flexible envelope filled with a lighter-than-air gas which provides the buoyancy force to rise upwards. A popular children's toy, large balloons are also used for meteorological and scientific research as well as for pleasure (**ballooning**). The envelope of a modern hot-air balloon is made from either nylon or Dacron, which is then coated with polyurethane applied under pressure to make the material more airtight. The first manned flight was by Pilatre de Rozier and Marquis d'Arlandes at Paris in 1783 in a balloon designed by the Montgolfier brothers. The first global circumnavigation was achieved by British balloonist Brian Jones (1948–) and Swiss balloonist Bertrand Piccard (1958–) in *Breitling Orbiter 3* in March 1999. >> Montgolfier

balloon angioplasty [**an**jiohplastee] The insertion of a catheter into an artery that has narrowed pathologically. A balloon at the tip of the catheter is expanded at the site of the constriction, causing the blood vessel to dilate. The procedure is successful in many cases of narrowing of the arteries to the limbs, kidney, and heart. >> catheter

balm A name applied to various plants, but especially to **bee balm** or **lemon balm** (*Melissa officinalis*), a member of the mint family, Labiatae. >> mint

Balmoral Castle A castle and estate of 9700 ha/24 000 acres located on Upper Deeside, Aberdeenshire, Scotland. It has been in the possession of the British Royal family since 1852, and is used by them as a holiday home. >> castle; Scotland 🛈

balsa A fast-growing tree (*Ochroma pyramidale*), reaching 25 m/80 ft or more, with very light, soft timber, native to lowland areas of tropical America; leaves broadly oval to circular, 30 cm/12 in or more in diameter; flowers 15 cm/6 in long, white. (Family: Bombacaceae.)

balsam An annual with a translucent stem; leaves alternate, opposite or in threes; flowers 2-lipped with funnel-shaped tube and curved spur, the capsule exploding to scatter seeds, especially when touched – hence the name **touch-me-not** (*Impatiens noli-tangere*) for the variety in Europe and Asia. (Family: Balsaminaceae.) >> impatiens

Baltic Exchange An abbreviation for the **Baltic Mercantile and Shipping Exchange**, a major world market for cargo space on sea and air freight, which originated in the London coffee houses, and is still found in the City of London. The Exchange also handles the market in some commodities, such as grain.

Baltic Sea [**bawl**tik], Ger **Ostsee**, ancient **Mare Suevicum** area 414 000 sq km/160 000 sq mi. An arm of the Atlantic Ocean enclosed by Denmark, Sweden, Germany, Poland, Estonia, Latvia, Lithuania, Russia, and Finland; chief arms, the Gulfs of Bothnia, Finland, Riga; mean depth 55 m/180 ft; generally shallow, with large areas frozen in winter; navigation impossible for 3–5 months yearly. >> Atlantic Ocean

Baltic Shield The geological name for the continental mass made up of Precambrian crystalline rocks exposed in parts of Norway, Sweden, and Finland, and forming the underlying basement of the continent. They are the oldest rocks in Europe. >> Precambrian era

Baltic states The countries of Estonia, Latvia, and Lithuania on the E shore of the Baltic Sea. Formed in 1918, the states remained independent until 1940, when they were annexed by the USSR. Their independence was reasserted in 1990, following the collapse of communism. >> Estonia 🛈; Latvia 🛈; Lithuania 🛈

Baltimore [**bol**timaw(r)] 39°17N 76°37W, pop (1995e) 786 000. Port in N Maryland, USA, at the upper end of Chesapeake Bay; established, 1729; developed as a seaport and shipbuilding centre (Baltimore clippers); city status, 1797; rebuilt after 1904 fire; airport; railway; six universities; centre for culture and the arts; professional team, Orioles (baseball); first Roman Catholic cathedral in the USA (1806–21). >> clipper ship; Maryland; Poe

Baluchi [ba**loo**chee] Baluchi-speaking peoples of Baluchistan (Pakistan), Iran, Afghanistan, Punjab (India), and Bahrain. They are well known for their carpets and embroidery. >> Baluchistan

Baluchistan [baloochi**stahn**] pop (1995e) 6 341 000; area 347 190 sq km/134 015 sq mi. Province in W and SW Pakistan; treaties of 1879 and 1891 brought the N section under direct British control; incorporated into Pakistan in 1947–8; capital, Quetta; mountainous terrain, with large areas of desert. >> Baluchi; Pakistan 🛈

Baluchitherium [baloochi**thee**rium] >> ***Indricotherium***

Balzac, Honoré de (1799–1850) Novelist, born in Tours, France. His *La Comédie humaine* (1827–47, The Human Comedy), a series of novels and stories which present a complete picture of modern civilization, includes such works as *Le Père Goriot* (1834, Father Goriot). He produced 85 novels in 20 years.

Bamako [bama**koh**] 12°40N 7°59E, pop (1995e) 791 000. River-port capital of Mali, on the R Niger; mediaeval centre of Islamic learning; capital of French Sudan, 1905; airport; railway. >> Mali 🛈

bamboo A giant woody grass, mostly tropical or subtropical, with a few temperate species; usually forming large clumps reaching heights of 36 m/120 ft; provides edible shoots and light timber, including garden canes. (Genera: *Bambusa* and others. Family: Gramineae.) >> grass 🛈

banana A giant perennial herb, superficially resembling a tree. The true stem lies underground, at intervals bearing buds which produce large, oar-shaped leaves. It is the closely sheathing bases of the leaves which form the soft, hollow, trunk-like 'stem' rising to a height of several metres above ground. Cultivated bananas are grown throughout the tropics as a staple food. Fruit for export is cut while still green, and ripened on the voyage. They are often sold as unblemished yellow fruits, but are not fully ripe until flecked with brown spots. (Genus: *Musa*, 35 species. Family: Musaceae.) >> abaca; herb

Banares >> **Benares**

Banda, Hastings (Kamuzu) (c.1906–97) Malawi statesman, prime minister (1963–6), and president (1966–94), born in Kasungu, Malawi. Leader of the Malawi African Congress, he was made life president in 1971. He was defeated in the 1994 elections. >> Malawi 🛈

Band Aid >> **Geldof, Bob**

Bandaranaike, S(olomon) W(est) R(idgeway) D(ias) [bandara**niy**kuh] (1899–1959) Sri Lankan statesman and prime minister (1956–9), born in Colombo. In 1951 he organized the Sri Lanka Freedom Party, which returned him to parliament as opposition leader and (1956) as prime minister on a policy of nationalization and neutralism. He was assassinated by a Buddhist monk, and succeeded by his wife **Sirimavo Ratwatte Dias Bandaranaike** (1916–), who became the world's first woman prime minister (1960–5, 1970–7). >> Sri Lanka 🛈

Bandar Seri Begawan [**bahn**dah seree begawan], formerly **Brunei Town** 4°56N 114°58E, pop (1995e) 80 900. Capital of Brunei, SE Asia; airport; town wharf used mainly for local vessels since opening of deep-water port at Muara in 1972. >> Brunei 🛈

bandicoot An Australasian marsupial (family: Peramelidae, 17 species); superficially rat-like, but larger with longer snout and ears; also includes the Australian

rabbit-eared bandicoots (or **bilbies**) of family Thylacomyidae (2 species) from dry areas. >> marsupial [i]

Bandung [ban**dung**] 0°32N 103°16E, pop (1995e) 1 921 000. City in W Java, Indonesia; founded, 1810; former administrative centre of Dutch East Indies; **Bandung Conference** (1955), at which 29 non-aligned countries met to facilitate joint diplomatic action; airport; railway; two universities (1955, 1957); nuclear research centre (1964). >> Java (country); non-aligned movement

Bangalore [bangga**law(r)**] 12°59N 77°40E, pop (1995e) 2 869 000. Capital of Karnataka, SC India; founded, 1537; airfield; railway; university (1964). >> Karnataka

Banghazi >> **Benghazi**

Bangkok [bang**kok**] 13°44N 100°30E, pop (1995e) 6 456 000. Capital city of Thailand; on Chao Praya R; capital, 1782; old city noted for its many canals; since 1955, headquarters of the SE Asia Treaty Organization; airport; railway; eight universities. >> Thailand [i]

Bangladesh [banggla**desh**], formerly **East Pakistan**, official name **People's Republic of Bangladesh**, **Gana Prajatantri Bangladesh** pop (1995e) 117 372 000; area 143 998 sq km/55 583 sq mi. Asian republic lying between the foothills of the Himalayas and the Indian Ocean; capital, Dhaka; timezone GMT +6; 98% Bengali; chief religion, Islam (mainly Sunnis); official language, Bengali (Bangla), with English as a second language; currency, the taka of 100 paisa (since 1976); mainly a vast, low-lying alluvial plain, cut by a network of rivers, canals, swamps, and marsh; main rivers the Ganges (Padma), Brahmaputra (Jamuna), and Meghna, joining in the S to form the largest delta in the world; subject to frequent flooding; major cyclone disaster in 1991; in the E, fertile valleys and peaks of Chittagong Hill Tracts, rising to 1200 m/3900 ft; lush forest vegetation; tropical monsoon climate; main rainy season June–September; part of the State of Bengal until Muslim East Bengal created in 1905, separate from Hindu West Bengal; reunited in 1911; again partitioned in 1947, with West Bengal remaining in India and E Bengal forming East Pakistan; rebellion in 1971 led to independence, helped by India; political unrest led to suspension of constitution in 1975, and assassination of first president, Sheikh Mujib; further coups in 1975, 1977, and 1982; constitution restored, 1986; unrest in 1990 led to fresh elections in 1991, and a constitutional amendment reducing presidential power; parliament has one chamber; 85% of working population employed in agriculture, especially rice; supplies 80% of world's jute. >> Brahmaputra, River; Dhaka; Ganges, River; India [i]; Pakistan [i]; RR1001 political leaders

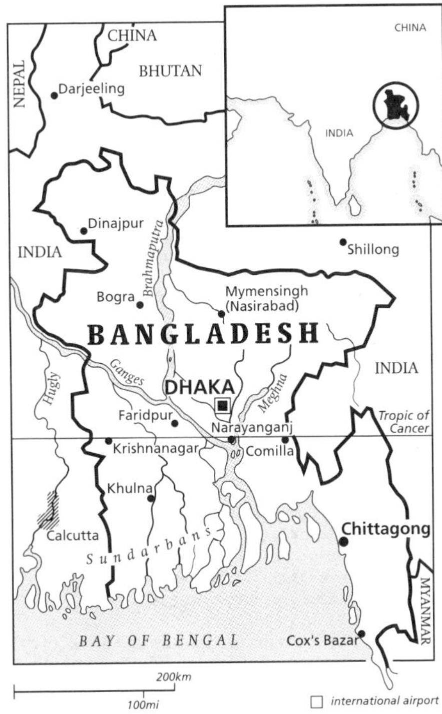

Bangor [**bang**ger] 53°13N 4°08W, pop (1995e) 48 200. City in Gwynedd, NW Wales, UK; railway; university (1884); cathedral (founded 6th-c). >> Wales [i]

Bangui [**bahn**gwee] 4°23N 18°37E, pop (1995e) 698 000. Capital of Central African Republic; on the R Ubangi; founded, 1889; airport; university (1969); handles Chad trade. >> Central African Republic [i]; Chad [i]

Bani-Sadr, Abolhassan [**ban**ee **sa**dr] (1935–) Iranian politician, who became the first president of the Islamic Republic of Iran. He was an important figure in the Iranian Revolution of 1978–9, and was elected president in 1980. Dismissed by Ayatollah Khomeini (mid-1981), he fled to France. >> Iran [i]; Khomeini

Banjalang One of the principal Aboriginal communities of NE New South Wales, Australia. The Banjalang language is currently the object of a revival programme. >> Aborigines

banjo A plucked string instrument developed in the 19th-c from earlier similar instruments used by W African slaves in the USA. It has a long neck and fingerboard, fretted like a guitar's, and five metal strings. These pass over a bridge which presses against a parchment (or plastic) membrane stretched over a circular frame. >> string instrument 2 [i]

Banjul [**ban**jul], formerly **Bathurst** (to 1973) 13°28N 16°35W, pop (1995e) 58 700. Seaport capital of The Gambia, W Africa; established in 1816 as a settlement for freed slaves; airport. >> Gambia, The [i]

bank An organization which offers a wide range of services to do with the handling of money. Most banks are *commercial banks*, which keep money on behalf of their customers, lend it to them, and offer them various facilities. A *central bank* in a country (such as the Bank of England or the Bank of America) is the banker for the government, issuing money on its behalf and setting the chief interest rate for loans; it is much involved in the country's monetary policy. There are also several types of bank with restricted functions, such as merchant banks and international banks. >> bank base rate; Bank of England; European Central Bank; International Bank for Reconstruction and Development; investment bank; merchant bank

bank base rate A base lending rate for UK clearing banks, used as the primary measure for interest rates since 1981. It is influenced by government policy through the Bank of England. >> bank; Bank of England; prime rate

Bankhead, Tallulah (1903–68) Actress, born in Huntsville, AL. She made her stage debut in 1918 and appeared in many plays and films. Her most outstanding film portrayal was in *Lifeboat* (1944).

Bank of England The central bank of Britain, founded in 1694, but in state ownership only since 1946. It controls the supply of money, prints notes, acts as a banker to the government and to other banks, and manages the gold and currency reserves. It is referred to as 'The Old Lady of Threadneedle Street', as a result of its location in the City of London. >> bank

bank rate A former interest rate at which the Bank of England would lend to discount houses, and an important instrument of government economic policy. It was abandoned in 1973, and replaced by the minimum lending rate (MLR). >> bank base rate; interest; minimum lending rate

bankruptcy The state of being reduced to financial ruin. Legally, individuals and partnerships are in this state when a court in bankruptcy proceedings declares them to be bankrupt. These proceedings are started by a creditor (or sometimes the debtor) presenting a bankruptcy petition. The analogous concept of **liquidation** applies to companies. >> company; debt

Banks, Iain (Menzies) (1954–) Novelist, born in Fife, E Scotland. He attracted equal measures of fame and notoriety with his first novel, a gruesome Gothic fantasy, *The Wasp Factory* (1984). Later books include *The Bridge* (1986) and *Whit* (1995).

Banks, Sir Joseph (1743–1820) Botanist, born in London. He accompanied Cook's expedition round the world (1768–71) and in 1772 visited the Hebrides and Iceland. As President of the Royal Society (1778–1819), he became an influential patron of science. >> Cook, James

banksia A low shrub or small tree, native to Australia; flowers commonly cream, also orange, red, or purplish, up to 1000 in spectacular globular or cylindrical heads; named after Sir Joseph Banks. (Genus: *Banksia*, 58 species. Family: Proteaceae.) >> Banks, Joseph

Banner System A system of military organization in China used by the Manchu tribes. By the early 17th-c the Manchus were organized into companies of 300 troops under at first four and then eight banners. The system survived throughout the Qing dynasty. >> Qing dynasty

Bannister, Sir Roger (Gilbert) (1929–) Athlete, born in Harrow, Greater London. He was the first man to run the mile in under 4 minutes (3 min 59·4 s), at Oxford (6 May 1954).

Bannockburn, Battle of (1314) A battle fought near Stirling between English forces under Edward II and the Scots under Robert Bruce. It resulted in a decisive victory for the Scots. >> Bruce, Robert; Edward II

Banting, Sir Frederick Grant (1891–1941) Physiologist, born in Alliston, Ontario, Canada. With J J R Macleod he discovered insulin, for which they were jointly awarded the Nobel Prize for Physiology or Medicine in 1923. >> insulin; Macleod, J J R

Bantu-speaking peoples Ethnically diverse groups who speak one of 500 Bantu languages or dialects (which belong to the Benue–Congo sub-group of the Niger–Congo family). They comprise altogether about 60 million people living in the S part of Africa, occupying a third of the continent. >> Hutu and Tutsi; Kikuyu; Kongo; Luba-Lunda Kingdoms; Mongo; Ndebele; Nguni; Niger–Congo languages; Pygmies; Shona; Swahili; Xhosa; Yao (of Africa)

Bantustans >> **apartheid**

banyan A large evergreen species of fig (*Ficus benghalensis*), native to the Old World tropics. It is notable for its aerial roots, which grow from the horizontal branches to the ground, becoming trunk-like, so that an apparent group of trees may in fact be only one. (Family: Moraceae.) >> fig

baobab [**bay**ohbab, **bow**bab] A deciduous tree (*Adansonia digitata*) native to arid parts of C Africa; its short but massive barrel- or bottle-shaped trunk 9–12 m/30–40 ft high and up to 9 m/30 ft in girth contains large stores of water. (Family: Bombacaceae.)

baptism A sacramental practice involving water. The Christian ritual is usually traced to the New Testament, where new converts were immersed in water, and where the rite is linked with the imparting of the Spirit and with repentance. Today, Church practices vary over infant and adult baptism, and over the use of immersion or sprinkling. >> Christianity; New Testament; sacrament

baptistery / baptistry A building or part of a building used to administer baptism, and containing the font. It is sometimes separate from the church. >> baptism; church i

Baptists A world-wide communion of Christians, who believe in the baptism only of believers prepared to make a personal confession of faith in Jesus Christ. They mainly derive from early 17th-c England and Wales, and late 19th-c USA. Strongly biblical, the emphasis in worship is on scripture and preaching. The Baptist World Alliance was formed in 1905. In 1999 there were over 190 member denominations, representing over 42 million baptized members. >> Anabaptists; baptism; Christianity

bar Unit of pressure; symbol bar; equal to 10^5 Pa (pascal, SI unit); 1 bar is approximately atmospheric pressure. The **millibar** (mb; 1 bar = 1000 mb) proves to be of greater use for practical measurements. >> atmospheric pressure; barometer; pascal

Barbados [bah(r)**bay**dos] pop (1995e) 261 000; area 430 sq km/166 sq mi. Most easterly of the Caribbean Is; capital, Bridgetown; timezone GMT –4; population, 80% African descent, 16% mixed race, 4% European; main religion, Protestantism; official language, English; unit of currency, Barbados dollar; island is small, triangular, length 32 km/20 mi (NW–SE), rising to 340 m/1115 ft at Mt Hillaby, ringed by a coral reef; tropical climate, with average annual temperature 26·5°C, mean annual rainfall 1420 mm/56 in; colonized by the British, 1627; self-government, 1961; independent sovereign state within the Commonwealth, 1966; executive power rests with the prime minister, appointed by a governor-general; Senate and House of Assembly; major industry, tourism. >> Bridgetown; Caribbean Sea; RR1001 political leaders

Barbarossa [bah(r)ba**ro**sa], ('Redbeard') (16th-c) **1** European name for two Turkish pirates. **Aruj** was killed fighting the Spaniards in 1518. **Khayr al-Din**, his brother, entered the service of the Ottoman Sultan, and drove the Spaniards from Algiers. >> corsairs **2** >> Frederick I (Emperor)

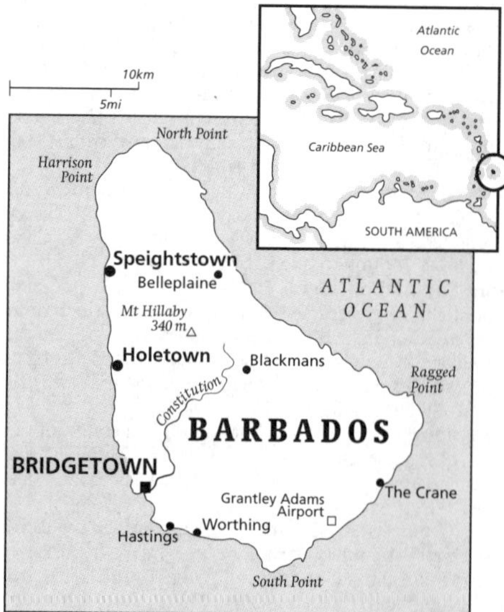

Barbary ape A monkey (macaque) native to N Africa (*Macaca sylvanus*), and maintained artificially on the Rock of Gibraltar; not an ape; stocky with no tail; also known as **magot** or **rock ape**. >> macaque

Barbary Coast The coast of N Africa from Morocco to Tripolitania (Libya). It was famous for piracy between the 16th-c and 18th-c. >> Barbarossa

Barbary sheep >> **aoudad**

barbel Slender-bodied fish (*Barbus barbus*) of the carp family Cyprinidae, widespread in European rivers on clean gravel beds; body length up to 90 cm/3 ft; lips fleshy, bearing four long barbels. >> carp

Barber, Samuel (1910–81) Composer, born in West Chester, PA. His opera *Vanessa* (1958) and piano concerto (1962) were both awarded Pulitzer Prizes.

Barbera >> **Hanna-Barbera**

barberry A deciduous or evergreen shrub, native to N temperate regions and South America; long shoots with 3-pointed spines; leaves often spiny; flowers yellow, orange, or reddish; berries red or black, globose or cylindrical. The common barberry (*Berberis vulgaris*) is a necessary host in the life-cycle of the cereal disease *black rust*. (Genus: *Berberis*, 450 species. Family: Berberidaceae.)

Barbie, Klaus, known as **the Butcher of Lyon** (1913–91) Nazi leader, born in Bad Godesberg, Germany. He worked for the Gestapo, and in Lyon sent thousands of people to Auschwitz. After the War he fled to South America, but was traced by Nazi hunters, and extradited in 1983. He was tried in France on 177 crimes against humanity, found guilty, and sentenced to life imprisonment. >> Nazi Party

Barbirolli, Sir John (Giovanni Battista) [bah(r)bi**rol**ee] (1899–1970) Conductor, born in London of French and Italian parents. He was permanent conductor (1943–58) of the Hallé Orchestra, later becoming its principal conductor (1959–68). He married the oboist **Evelyn Rothwell** (1911–) in 1939.

barbiturates Drugs derived from barbituric acid, itself first prepared on St Barbara's Day, 1863. *Barbitone* (US *barbital*) was introduced into medicine in 1903; *phenobarbitone* (US *phenobarbital*) in 1912. Over 50 different barbiturates have been used at some time as sedatives, sleep inducers, and anti-epileptic drugs. They cause severe tolerance, ie increasingly higher doses are required to produce the same effect. The doses are progressively more dangerous, and poisoning becomes a major risk; they are also addictive. >> sedative

Barbizon School [**bah(r)**bizon] A group of French landscape painters working c.1830–80 at Barbizon, a village in the Forest of Fontainbleau. Leading members included Théodore Rousseau and Charles François Daubigny. >> Daubigny; Rousseau, Théodore

Barbuda >> **Antigua and Barbuda**

barcarolle An instrumental or vocal piece in a lilting 6/8 metre, evoking the songs of the Venetian gondoliers. A well-known example is the Barcarolle in Offenbach's opera *Les Contes d'Hoffman* (Tales of Hoffman). >> Offenbach, Jacques

Barcelona [bah(r)se**loh**na], Span [barthe**loh**na], ancient **Barcino** or **Barcinona** 41°21N 2°10E, pop (1995e) 1 637 000. Major seaport in NE Spain; second largest city in Spain; airport; railway; two universities (1440, 1968); centre of Catalan art and literature, and of the separatist political movement; cathedral (13th-c); Casa Mila (1906–10), Casa Güell (1900–14), and Parque Güell (1900–14), architectural creations by Antonio Gaudí, now world heritage sites; Palau de la Música Catalana and Hospital de Sant Pau, world heritage sites; location of the 1992 Summer Olympic Games. >> Catalonia; Gaudí; Spain ℹ

Barclay, Robert (1843–1913) British banker, under whom in 1896 the merger of 20 banks took place to form Barclay & Co Ltd. In 1917 the name was changed to Barclay's Bank Ltd.

barcode A pattern of black vertical lines, with information coded in the relative widths of the lines. This type of coding is very widely used in the retail market, such as on food packages. The bar-coded labels can be read by special bar-code scanners, and the output entered into a computer to link the product with such factors as price and stock level.

bard Among ancient Celtic peoples, a poet-minstrel who held a privileged place in society, singing the praises of chiefs and celebrating heroic deeds, historical events, and the passing of laws. In Wales, bardic standards declined after the Middle Ages; however, to this day, a contestant for the Chair at the National Eisteddfod must compose a poem in classical bardic verse-form. >> eisteddfod

Bardeen, John [bah(r)**deen**] (1908–91) Physicist, the first person to receive two Nobel Prizes for Physics, born in Madison, WI. He developed in 1947 with Brattain and Shockley the point contact transistor, for which they shared the Nobel Prize in 1956. His second prize (1972) was shared for his work on the first satisfactory theory of superconductivity (the Bardeen–Cooper–Schrieffer, or *BCS* theory). >> Brattain; Shockley; superconductivity; transistor

Bardot, Brigitte [bah(r)**doh**], originally **Camille Javal** (1934–) Film actress, born in Paris. She was discovered by the director Roger Vadim, who subsequently married her, and from 1952 made her an international sex-symbol, with their greatest success in *Et Dieu créa la femme* (1956, And God Created Woman). They divorced in 1957. Her last major film was *Si Don Juan était une Femme* (1973, If Don Juan Were a Woman). In later years she has taken up the cause of endangered animal species. >> Vadim

Barebone's Parliament The British 'Parliament of Saints' (4 Jul–12 Dec 1653), nominated by the Council of Officers of the Army to succeed the Rump Parliament; named after radical member Praise-God Barebone. It collapsed after disagreements over the abolition of tithes and lay patronage in the Church. >> Rump Parliament

Barenboim, Daniel [**ba**renboym] (1942–) Pianist and conductor, born in Buenos Aires, Argentina. A noted exponent of Mozart and Beethoven, he gained his reputation as pianist/conductor with the English Chamber Orchestra. His posts include musical director of the Orchestre de Paris (1975–87). He married the cellist Jacqueline du Pré in 1967. >> du Pré

Barents, Willem [**ba**ruhnts], also spelled **Barentz** (c.1550–97) Navigator, probably born in The Netherlands. Pilot to three Dutch expeditions (1594–6) in search of the Northeast Passage, he died off Novaya Zemlya. In 1871, Captain Carlsen found his winter quarters undisturbed after 274 years. >> Barents Sea; Northeast Passage

Barents Euro-Arctic Council An organization established in 1993 to renew trade and economic co-operation in the Barents Sea region. Its members are Denmark, Finland, Iceland, Norway, Russia, and Sweden, with one Sami (Lapp) representative. >> Barents Sea

Barents Sea [**ba**rents], Russian **Barentsovo More**, Norwegian **Barents Havet** area 1 405 000 sq km/ 542 000 sq mi. Shallow arm of the Arctic Ocean, lying N of Norway and European Russia; warm North Cape Current disperses pack-ice in the S; Murmansk and Vardö ports are ice-free; fishing area. >> Arctic Ocean; Barents

Bari [**ba**ree] 41°07N 16°52E, pop (1995e) 359 000. Seaport in SE Italy; archbishopric; airport; car ferries; university (1924); cathedral (begun 1087); naval college; site of Italy's first atomic power station. >> Italy ℹ

barite [**bair**iyt] The mineral form of barium sulphate ($BaSO_4$), the chief ore of barium. Found in hydrothermal vein deposits, it is used in paints, paper making, and drilling muds; earlier known as **barytes**. >> barium

barium [**bair**ium] Ba, element 56, in Group II of the periodic table, melting point 725°C. It is a very reactive metal. Its soluble compounds are highly poisonous, but the very insoluble sulphate, $BaSO_4$, is used in the so-called **barium meal** to provide material opaque to X-rays. >> chemical elements; X-rays; RR1036

bark In its everyday sense, the rough, protective outer layer of the woody parts of trees and shrubs; in botany, the term also embraces several inner tissues, including cork and phloem. Continued growth causes the bark to stretch, often cracking, flaking, or peeling in distinctive patterns. >> cork; phloem; shrub; tree [i]

Barker, Ronnie, popular name of **Ronald William George Barker** (1929–) Comic actor, born in Bedford, Bedfordshire. He made his professional debut in 1948. Adept at characterization, tongue-twisting comic lyrics, and saucy humour, his many radio and television appearances include *Porridge* (1974–7), *Open All Hours* (1976, 1981–5) and, in partnership with Ronnie Corbett, the long-running *The Two Ronnies* (1971–87). >> Corbett

bar Kokhba, Simon [**kokh**ba], also spelled **bar Kochba** (?–135) The leader of the Jews in their great but fruitless insurrection against the Emperor Hadrian (130–5). He was killed at Bethar. In 1960 some of his letters were found in caves near the Dead Sea. >> Hadrian

bark painting A traditional product of Australian Aboriginal art: human and animal figures, sometimes geometrically stylized but occasionally naturalistic, painted on irregularly-shaped pieces of bark. They were created mainly for use in magical and initiation ceremonies. >> Aborigines

barley A cereal of Middle Eastern origin (*Hordeum vulgare*), cultivated in temperate regions; dense head with long, slender bristles; grains in 2, 4, or 6 rows. It is more tolerant of drought, cold, and poor soil than wheat, and an important crop in such regions as N Europe. Germinated grains produce malt used in brewing beer and making whisky; its flour is used in cakes and porridge. It is also an important animal feed. (Family: Gramineae.) >> beer [i]; cereals; grass [i]; whisky

Bar Mitzvah [bah(r) **mits**va] (Heb 'son [*bar*]/daughter [*bat*] of the commandment') Jewish celebrations associated with reaching the age of maturity and of legal and religious responsibility, being 13 years plus one day for boys. The child reads a passage from the Torah or the Prophets in the synagogue on the Sabbath, and is then regarded as a full member of the congregation. Non-Orthodox synagogues have a **Bat Mitzvah** ceremony for girls at 12 years plus one day. >> Judaism

Barnabas [**bah**(r)nabas] (1st-c) Christian missionary, originally a Levite from Cyprus called Joseph. He was a companion and supporter of Paul during Paul's early ministry to the Gentiles. The so-called *Letter of Barnabas* is a spurious 2nd-c work. >> Paul, St

barnacle A marine crustacean that lives attached by its base to hard substrates or to other organisms; body enclosed within a shell formed of calcareous plates; c.1000 species. (Subclass: Cirripedia.) >> calcium; crustacean; shell

Barnard, Christiaan (Neethling) (1922–) Surgeon, born in Beaufort West, South Africa. At Groote Schuur Hospital he performed the first successful human heart transplant (Dec 1967). The patient, Louis Washkansky, died of double pneumonia 18 days later. Barnard's later transplants proved to be increasingly successful. He retired from medicine in 1983.

Barnardo, Thomas John [bah(r)**nah(r)**doh] (1845–1905) Founder of homes for destitute children, born in Dublin. He founded (1867) the East End Mission for destitute children, as well as a number of homes in greater London, which came to be known as the *Dr Barnardo's Homes*.

Barnard's star One of the very few stars which is named after the astronomer who studied it, E E Barnard (1857–1923) of Yerkes Observatory, USA. The second-nearest star to the Sun, distance 1·81 parsec. It is a red dwarf, too faint to see with the naked eye.

Barnburners A faction within the US Democratic Party in New York State (1843–50), which arose through opposition to extending slavery into Western territory conquered during the Mexican War. Their name derived from the story of a Dutch farmer who burned down his barn (the Democratic Party) in order to drive out rats (slavery). >> Democratic Party; Mexican War; slavery

Barnes, William (1801–86) Pastoral poet, born in Sturminster Newton, Dorset. He was widely known for his idyllic poetry in the Dorset dialect.

barn owl An owl of worldwide distribution; legs feathered; eats small vertebrates, especially mammals and insects. (Genus: *Tyto*, 6 species. Family: Tytonidae.) >> owl

Barnum, P(hineas) T(aylor) (1810–91) Showman, born in Bethel, CT. He ran a museum in New York, introducing freak shows, at which he sponsored the famous dwarf 'General Tom Thumb' (1842). In 1881 he joined with his rival James Anthony Bailey (1847–1906) to found the Barnum and Bailey circus, 'the greatest show on earth'.

barograph >> **barometer**

Baroja (y Nessi), Pío [ba**ro**ha] (1872–1956) Writer, born in San Sebastián, Spain. His first book of short stories, *Vidas sombrías* (1900, Sombre Lives), was the prelude to more than 70 volumes with a Basque setting. >> Basques

barometer A meteorological instrument used to measure atmospheric pressure, invented in 1643 by Torricelli. It was based on the principle that the height of a column of mercury in a tube sealed at one end and inverted in a dish of mercury will change according to the atmospheric pressure exerted on the dish of mercury. The **aneroid barometer** is a metallic box containing a vacuum, with flexible sides which act as a bellows expanding and contracting with changing atmospheric pressure. Changes of pressure through time are recorded on a **barograph**. >> atmospheric pressure; bar; Torricelli

baron / baroness In the UK, a title of nobility, ranking below viscount or count. >> peerage

baronet (abbreviation **bart**) In the UK, a hereditary title, not part of the peerage and not a knighthood. The form, which was originally purchased by the holder, was created by James I in 1611 to raise money to pay the troops in Ireland. >> knight; peerage

Barons' War The wars in England during the reigns of John and Henry III. **1** (1215–17) Despite the granting of Magna Carta, many barons still defied John, and offered the crown to Prince Louis of France. After John's death, the French and baronial army was routed at Lincoln (1217). **2** (1263–7) After the Provisions of Oxford failed to achieve a settlement, barons led by Simon de Montfort captured Henry III at Lewes (1264). Earl Simon was killed at Evesham (1265), and the king was restored to power. >> Henry III (of England); John (of England); Magna Carta; Montfort; Oxford, Provisions of

Baroque (art and architecture) [ba**rok**, ba**rohk**] A style prevalent in the 17th-c and part of the 18th-c, characterized by curvilinear forms and ornate decoration arranged in dramatic compositions, often on a large scale and in a complicated fashion. Baroque art was especially associated with Louis XIV, but spread over most of W Europe until transformed into Rococo in the 18th-c. >> art; Bernini; Borromini; Caravaggio; Mannerism; Rococo; Rubens

Baroque (music) A period in musical history extending from c.1580 to c.1730. Its features include a gradual replacement of modality by tonality, a love of melodic ornamentation, and the formation of the orchestra. Genres originating in the Baroque period include the opera, oratorio, cantata, sonata, and concerto. >> Bach, Johann Sebastian; Handel; Monteverdi; Purcell; Scarlatti, Alessandro / Domenico; Vivaldi

barracuda [bara**koo**da] Any of the voracious predatory fishes widespread in tropical and warm temperate seas; body slender, length up to 1·8 m/6 ft, jaws armed with many short teeth. (Genus: *Sphyraena*. Family: Sphyraenidae.)

Barranquilla [baran**keel**ya] 11°00N 74°50W, pop (1995e) 962 000. Industrial city in N Colombia, Colombia's principal Caribbean port; founded, 1721; airport; three universities (1941, 1966, 1967). >> Colombia 🛈

Barras, Paul François Jean Nicolas, comte de (Count of) [bara] (1755–1829) French revolutionary, born in Foxemphoux, France. An original member of the Jacobin Club, and a regicide, he played the chief part in the overthrow of Robespierre. He became one of the five members of the Directory (1795), and was overthrown by Bonaparte (1799). >> French Revolution 🛈; Napoleon I

barrel A measure of volume, its value depending on the substance it contains. A barrel of alcohol is 189 litres; a barrel of petroleum is 159 litres.

barrel organ A mechanical musical instrument. By turning a handle at the side, the player both feeds a bellows and operates a rotating cylinder fitted with metal pins which allow air access to a set of pipes; the placing of the pins determines which pipes sound and when. >> organ

Barrie, Sir J(ames) M(atthew) (1860–1937) Novelist and playwright, born in Kirriemuir, Angus. His best-known plays are *The Admirable Crichton* (1902), *Dear Brutus* (1917), and *Peter Pan* (1904), for which he is chiefly remembered.

barrier reef >> **atoll**

barrigudo >> **woolly monkey**

Barringer Crater >> **Meteor Crater**

barrister A member of the legal profession in England and Wales whose work is mainly concerned with advocacy in the courts. Barristers have exclusive right of audience in the High Court and superior courts. In addition to trials and preparation for trials, they may also write advisory opinions. >> advocate; High Court of Justice; Inns of Court; solicitor

Barry, Sir Charles (1795–1860) Architect, born in London. His designs include the new Palace of Westminster (Houses of Parliament, 1840–70), completed after his death by his son **Edward Middleton Barry** (1830–80).

Barrymore, Ethel, originally **Ethel Blythe** (1879–1959) Actress, born in Philadelphia, PA, the sister of John and Lionel Barrymore. She was a leading actress in many plays and films in the early decades of the century. **John** (1882–1942) made his name in Shakespearean roles, and appeared in many films such as *Grand Hotel* (1932). **Lionel** (1878–1954) was most widely known for his role as Dr Gillespie in the original *Dr Kildare* film series.

Bart, Lionel (1930–99) Composer, born in London. His successful musicals include *Lock Up Your Daughters!* (1959) and *Oliver!* (1960).

Barth, Karl [bah(r)t] (1886–1968) Theologian, born in Basel, Switzerland. He played a leading role in the German Confessing Church. The major exponent of Reformed theology, his many works include the monumental *Church Dogmatics* (1932–67). >> Confessing Church; Protestantism

Barthes, Roland (Gérard) [bah(r)t] (1915–80) Teacher, critic, and writer on semiology and structuralism, born in Cherbourg, France. His works include *Mythologies* (1957), a semiological exploration of wrestling, children's toys, and other phenomena. From 1976 until his death he was the first professor of literary semiology at the Collège de France, Paris. >> semiotics; structuralism

Bartholdi, (Frédéric) Auguste [bah(r)**thol**dee], Fr [bah(r)toldee] (1834–1904) Sculptor, born in Colmar, France. He specialized in enormous monuments, such as the bronze Statue of Liberty, New York harbour, unveiled in 1886.

Bartlett, John (1820–1905) Publisher and bookseller, born in Plymouth, MA. He is best known as the compiler of *Bartlett's Familiar Quotations* (1855).

Bartók, Béla [**bah(r)**tok] (1881–1945) Composer, born in Nagyszentmiklós, Hungary. His compositions were greatly influenced by Hungarian and Balkan folk music. Driven into exile by World War 2, he settled in the USA, where he composed several string quartets, concertos, and other orchestral works.

Bartolommeo, Fra [bah(r)tolo**may**oh], originally **Baccio della Porta** (1472–1517) Religious painter, born near Florence, Italy. He was a follower of Savonarola, at whose death he gave up painting and became a Dominican novice; but the visit of the young Raphael to Florence in 1504 led him to resume his art. >> Raphael; Savonarola

Baruch [**ba**rukh] (7th–6th-c BC) Biblical character, described as the companion and secretary of the prophet Jeremiah (*Jer* 36). His name became attached to several Jewish works of much later date. >> Apocrypha, Old Testament; Jeremiah, Book of; Pseudepigrapha

barycentre For a group of objects composed of matter, such as the Solar System or a cluster of stars, the point at which total mass may be considered to be concentrated ('the centre of gravity') for the purposes of calculating its gravitational effect on other objects. >> gravitation

baryon [**ba**rion] In particle physics, a collective term for heavy matter particles which experience strong interactions. The least massive baryon is the proton, into which other baryons decay. >> particle physics; proton; quark

barytes >> **barite**

baryton An obsolete musical instrument resembling a bass viol, with (usually) six strings which were bowed and a further 10–15 which were plucked. Between 1765 and 1778 Haydn wrote numerous pieces for the instrument. >> chordophone; Haydn

basalt [**ba**sawlt] The most common extrusive igneous rock, characterized by low silica content, and composed essentially of plagioclase feldspar and pyroxene. It is commonly used as a building stone and road-stone aggregate. >> feldspar; igneous rock; pyroxenes

base (chemistry) A substance liberating hydroxide ions in water, an acceptor of protons, or a donor of electron pairs: each of these definitions includes the previous one. The term is thus the opposite of an acid, whatever definition of acid is used. >> acid; pH

base (mathematics) The number on which a system of counting is constructed (**number-base**). The numbers in common use are in base ten, ie numbers expressed in multiples of powers of ten; thus 'three hundred and forty two' is written 342, since it is $3 \times 10^2 + 4 \times 10 + 2$. >> binary number; logarithm; numbers

baseball A team game played on a wedge-shaped field, with a diamond-shaped infield (the *diamond*), by two sides of players with a bat and ball. One team, on offence or *at bat*, tries to score the most runs by having their players circle the bases before they are put *out* by the other team which is *in the field*. An out is made when the batter fails to hit a legally pitched ball on three successive occasions (a *strikeout*, see below), or when the fielding team catches a batted ball before it touches the ground, tags a member of the offensive team between the bases, or touches a base before an offensive player reaches that base. The defensive team is aided in stopping the offensive team by fielding batted balls with an oversized glove or *mitt*. Each game is made up of nine innings unless the score is tied, in which case the game is extended into *extra innings* until one team outscores the other in a particular inning. Each team at bat is allowed three outs in its half inning. The major confrontation of the game centres on the *pitcher* and *batter*. The pitcher hurls the ball towards the batter, who stands alongside the home plate poised to strike the ball. If the batter swings at the ball and fails to hit it, or if the pitcher throws the ball into a designated strike zone between the batter's knees and his chest, without the batter swinging at the ball, a *strike* is called. Three strikes causes a batter to be declared out. Conversely, if the pitcher fails to throw the ball into the strike zone and the batter does not swing, a *ball* is called. Four balls allow the batter to take first base. The home plate umpire, who stands behind the catcher, determines if the ball is within the strike zone. If the batter strikes the ball beyond the playing area's limits (within the foul lines), or if he circles the bases before being put out, he has hit a *home run* (or *homer*). Baseball is called the *national pastime* in the USA. Professional teams usually consist of 25 players. The *Major League* of North America is divided into the American League, each consisting of an Eastern, Western, and (since 1994) Central division and National League (12 teams of 9 players). The culmination of the season (Apr–Oct) is a best-of-seven game *World Series* between the champions of each league. The origins of the game are unclear. The person most widely cited as the game's inventor is a West Point cadet, Abner Doubleday, who in 1839 laid out a diamond at Cooperstown, NY, where the modern day Baseball Hall of Fame stands. However, there is evidence that the game was played much earlier. The first formal set of baseball rules were drawn up by Alexander Cartwright in 1845. Baseball is becoming increasingly popular in Japan and Latin America, and in 1992 a Canadian team (the Toronto Blue Jays) won the World Series for the first time. >> rounders; softball; RR1046

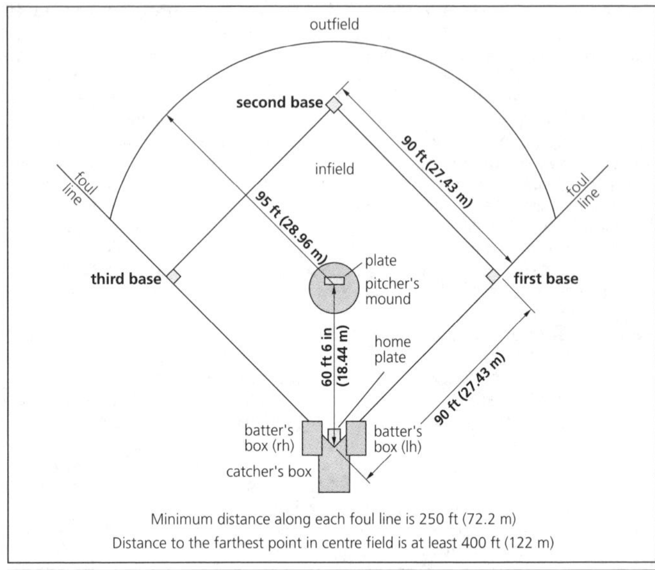

The baseball field.

Basel [**bah**zl], Eng **Basle** [bahl], Fr **Bâle** 47°35N 7°35E, pop (1995e) 177 000. City in NE Switzerland, on the R Rhine; river port at the terminus of Rhine navigation; on the site of a Roman fort; mediaeval centre for silk, dyeing, and printing; joined the Swiss Confederacy, 1501; influential centre during the Reformation; scene of the first Zionist conference, 1897; airport (on French territory, shared with France); railway junction; oldest Swiss university (1460); Switzerland's leading centre for transshipment and international commerce; Gothic minster (11th-c, largely rebuilt 14th-c); town hall (1504–14), European World Trade and Convention Centre. >> Switzerland ℹ

basenji [ba**sen**jee] A spitz breed of dog developed in C Africa for hunting; pale brown and white; short coat; cannot bark, but makes a yodelling noise. >> spitz

Basho, Matsuo (1644–94) Poet, born in Ueno (Iga), Japan. He was bred from a young age to poetry. Becoming master of the haiku, he started his own school, but later retired to a hermitage. >> haiku

BASIC [**bay**sik] Acronym of **Beginner's All-purpose Symbolic Instruction Code**, a high level computer programming language developed in the late 1950s at Dartmouth College in the USA. It has been widely adopted as a standard language by microcomputer manufacturers. >> microcomputer; programming language

Basidiomycetes [basidiohmiy**seet**eez] A subdivision of the true fungi, characterized by a sexual reproduction process that forms a club-shaped structure (*basidium*) bearing four haploid spores (*basidiospores*); includes edible mushrooms, agarics, puffballs, and many parasitic forms. (Division: Eumycota.) >> fly agaric; fungus; gametophyte; mushroom; puffball

Basie, Count [**bay**see], popular name of **William Basie** (1904–84) Bandleader and pianist, born in Red Bank, NJ. He joined Benny Moten's Kansas City Orchestra in 1929, became its leader in 1935, and took it to New York the next year. Its supple rhythmic drive propelled several brilliant soloists, elevating the band to top rank, known for such popular compositions as 'One O'Clock Jump' and 'Jumpin' at the Woodside'.

Basil, St, known as **Basil the Great** (c.329–79) One of the greatest of the Greek Fathers, born in Caesarea, Cappadocia. He was one of the leading defenders of Christian philosophy against Arianism. Feast day 1 Jan (E), 2 Jan (W). >> Fathers of the Church

basil A bushy aromatic annual or perennial (*Ocimum basilicum*), growing to 1 m/3¼ ft, but often less; stems square; leaves oval, pale, glossy, in opposite pairs; flowers 2-lipped, white or purplish, in whorls; probably native to SE Asia, but widely cultivated as a culinary herb and for use in perfumery. (Family: Labiatae.)

basilica [ba**zil**ika] Originally a royal palace or large oblong hall with double colonnades, for the administration of justice and commerce. It was later adopted by early

Christians as a similarly arranged church with two or more aisles, timber roof, and apse.

Basiliensis, Regio [**re**jioh basil**yen**sis] area 234 sq km/ 90 sq mi. Transnational 'natural region' encompassing the frontier districts of France, Switzerland, and Germany; administrative centre, Basel; co-operation between local governments, industries, and universities promoted since 1963. >> Basel; Rhine, River

basilisk (biology) An iguana native to South America; male with bony projections on head and prominent sail-like crests along back; tail long; may run upright on long hind legs. (Genus: *Basiliscus*, 5 species.) >> iguana

basilisk (mythology) A fabulous beast, a small dragon-like creature combining features of the snake and the cockerel. Its eye could freeze and kill, hence the expression 'If looks could kill'. It is equivalent to the **cockatrice**.

Basinger, Kim [**bay**sinjer] (1953–) Film actress, born in Athens, GA. She was a top model before making her feature film debut in *Hard Country* (1981). Other films include *The Real McCoy* (1993) and *The Getaway* (1994). She won an Oscar for Best Supporting Actress in *L.A. Confidential* (1997).

basketball A five-a-side team ball game, invented by James Naismith in 1891 in Springfield, MA. Played on a court, the object is to throw the ball through your opponent's basket, situated at the end of the court, and 10 ft (3·05 m) above the ground. >> Harlem Globetrotters; netball; RR1046

basking shark Extremely large, inoffensive shark (*Cetorhinus maximus*), second only to the whale shark as the largest living fish; length up to 10 m/33 ft, weight c.6000 kg/13 200 lb. (Family: Cetorhinidae.) >> shark

Basle >> **Basel**

Basque Provinces [bask], Span **País Vasco** or **Provincias Vascongadas**, Basque **Euskadi** pop (1995e) 2 110 000; area 7261 sq km/2803 sq mi. Autonomous region of N Spain, comprising the provinces of Álava, Guipúzcoa, and Vizcaya; industries centred around Bilbao and San Sebastian. >> Basques; Spain ℹ

Basques [basks] A people living in northern parts of Spain and neighbouring areas in France, and now thought to originate from local Mesolithic populations. They are physically similar to their neighbours, and are Roman Catholics, but their language, Basque, spoken by c.500 000, does not relate to any other European language. Urbanized Basques retain strong ethnic identity, and their main city Bilbao is a centre of Basque nationalism. Since the death of Franco (1975), Basques have been granted some local autonomy (1978–9), but the more militant continue to agitate for a separate Basque state, engaging in terrorism for this end. Population c.805 000 in Spain, 130 000 in France, and 170 000 elsewhere, mainly South America and the United States of America. >> Basque Provinces; Spanish Civil War

Basra [**baz**ra], Arabic **al-Basrah** 30°30N 47°50E, pop (1995e) 822 000. Port in SE Iraq, at head of the Shatt al-Arab; major centre of literature, theology, and scholarship in 8th–9th-c; badly affected in 1980s by Iran–Iraq war and again in 1991 during and after the Gulf War; modern administrative and commercial centre; airport; railway; university (1967). >> Iraq ℹ

bas-relief [bah ruh**leef**] Low relief sculpture, in which the design projects only very slightly from the background, as on a coin. >> relief sculpture

bass [bas] Marine and brackish-water fish (*Dicentrarchus labrax*) found in the surf zone around rocks and beaches of the NE Atlantic; body blue-grey with silver sides, length up to 1 m/3¼ ft. (Family: Serranidae.)

Bassae [**bas**ay] A 5th-c BC temple dedicated to Apollo Epicurius on the slopes of Mt Lykaion, SW Arcadia, Greece; a world heritage site. >> Ictinus

Bassano, Jacopo da [ba**sah**noh], also known as **Giacomo da Ponte** (c.1510–92) Painter, founder of genre painting in Europe, born in Bassano, Italy. His best paintings are of peasant life and Biblical scenes with animals. >> genre painting

basse taille enamel [bas **tiy**] A technique of enamelling on silver, or occasionally gold, where the metal is carved and engraved, and translucent coloured enamel is applied on top with the image shining through. >> enamelling

Basse-Terre [bas tair] pop (1995e) 169 000; area 848 sq km/327 sq mi. One of the two main islands of the French Overseas Department of Guadeloupe, E Caribbean; mountainous, with active volcano Grande Soufrière rising to 1484 m/4869 ft; capital, Basse-Terre, pop (1990) 14 107. >> Guadeloupe

Basseterre [bas**tair**] 17°17N 62°43W, pop (1995e) 14 300. Capital and chief port of St Kitts-Nevis, E Caribbean, on SW coast of St Kitts I; airport; cathedral. >> St Kitts-Nevis

basset-horn An 18th-c musical instrument belonging to the clarinet family, with a lower compass than that of the normal clarinet. It fell into disuse in the 19th-c. >> clarinet; reed instrument

basset hound A breed of dog formerly used in France and Belgium for hunting; long, solid body, with very short legs; muzzle long and broad; ears long and pendulous; short-haired coat of white, black, and tan. >> hound

bassoon A musical instrument consisting of a jointed wooden pipe, about 2 m 54 cm/8 ft 4 in long, doubled back on itself, and fitted with metal keys and a curved crook with a double reed. The larger **double bassoon**, or **contrabassoon**, sounds one octave lower than the standard instrument. >> reed instrument; woodwind instrument ℹ

Bass Strait [bas] A channel separating Tasmania from Victoria, Australia, maximum width 240 km/150 mi; named in 1798 after the British explorer George Bass (1771–1803). >> Tasmania; Victoria (Australia)

basswood An American species of lime (*Tilia americana*), producing useful timber; stringy inner bark used for mats and ropes. (Family: Tileaceae.) >> lime (botany)

Bastia [bas**tee**a] 42°40N 9°30E, pop (1995e) 39 900. Port in NW Corsica, France; founded by the Genoese, 1380; capital of Corsica until 1811; chief town of the island; airport; railway. >> Corsica; France ℹ

Bastille [bas**teel**] A mediaeval fortress and prison in E Paris, the symbol of Bourbon despotism, stormed by a Parisian mob on 14 July 1789. The anniversary of the day is a French national holiday. >> French Revolution ℹ

bat A nocturnal mammal, widespread in tropical and temperate regions; hibernates in winter in cold areas; usually hangs head-down at rest; the only mammal capable of sustained flight; probably evolved to exploit night-flying insects. Most members of the suborder Microchiroptera eat insects; some also eat fish, frogs, birds, or other bats. They use echolocation to detect prey and avoid obstacles, and have a nose and ears which are often complex in shape. In contrast, **fruit bats** (or *flying foxes*) of the Old World tropics (suborder: Megachiroptera, 170 species) eat fruit and flowers detected by smell. They include the largest bats, with large eyes and a dog-like head (small ears and a long muzzle). They have better vision than other bats, and few use echolocation. A quarter of living mammal species are bats. (Order: Chiroptera, 951 species.) >> echolocation; mammal ℹ; pipistrelle; vampire bat ℹ

Batak Six closely-related ethnic groups of C Sumatra, Indonesia, speaking Austronesian languages. The most literate and Christianized group are the Toba Batak, well-known for trade and their key role in national government.

They are one-third Muslim, one-third Christian, and the rest adhering to traditional religion. >> Austronesian languages; Sumatra

Batalha, Monastery of [batalya] A Dominican abbey, in Batalha, W Portugal, one of the great examples of Christian Gothic architecture; a world heritage site. It was founded in 1388 by King João I in fulfilment of a vow made at the Battle of Aljubarrota, where Portuguese independence was established. >> Portugal [i]

batch processing A defined series of tasks which are submitted to larger computers and executed only when time becomes available on the computer. This is in contrast to **interactive computing**, where the user accesses the computer in a conversational mode.

Bates, H(erbert) E(rnest) (1905–74) Writer, born in Rushden, Northamptonshire. He is one of the greatest exponents of the short-story form. His best-known novel is *Fair Stood the Wind for France* (1944). The Larkin family was introduced in *The Darling Buds of May* (1958).

Bates, H(enry) W(alter) (1825–92) Naturalist and traveller, born in Leicester, Leicestershire. In 1861 he described the phenomena of mimicry in animals (later known as **Batesian mimicry**), which contributed to the theory of natural selection. >> natural selection

Bateson, William (1861–1926) Biologist, born in Whitby, North Yorkshire. He laid the foundations of (and named) the science of genetics. >> genetics

Bath, Lat **Aquae Calidae**, Old English **Akermanceaster** 51°23N 2°22W, pop (1995e) 83 600. Spa town in Bath and North East Somerset county, SW England, on R Avon; noted since Roman times for its hot springs; chartered in 1189; railway; university (1966); Roman baths; City of Bath a world heritage site. >> England [i]; Nash, Richard

Bath, Most Honourable Order of the A British order of chivalry, formally created by George I in 1725, but traditionally founded by Henry IV in 1399 at the Tower of London, when he conferred the honour on the 46 esquires who had attended him at his bath the night before his coronation. The motto is *Tria juncta in uno* ('three joined in one').

Bathurst >> **Banjul**

bathymetry The measurement of the depths of sea-bottom features in large bodies of water. **Bathymetric charts** indicate the depths of water in feet, fathoms, or metres and are used to show the morphology of submarine topographic features. >> echo-sounding

bathyscaphe [**bath**iskayf] Any free-moving vessel designed for underwater exploration, consisting of a flotation compartment with an observation capsule underneath. Originally designed by Piccard in 1848, they have proved capable of reaching depths of over 10 000 m/32 000 ft. >> Piccard

batik [ba**teek**] A form of dyeing in which parts of the fabric are left undyed because of wax printed or painted onto it. The fabric is then crushed to crack the wax, and dyed. Removal of the wax leaves undyed areas covered in fine lines. This method, a form of *resist dyeing*, originated in Indonesia. >> dyeing

Batista (y Zaldívar), Fulgencio [ba**tee**sta] (1901–73) Cuban dictator, born in Oriente province, Cuba. In 1933, he organized a military coup (the 'sergeants' revolt'), and became president (1940–4). In 1952 he overthrew President Prio Socorras, and ruled as dictator until his overthrow by Fidel Castro (Jan 1959). >> Castro

Bat Mitzvah >> **Bar Mitzvah**

Baton Rouge [**ba**ton **roozh**] 30°27N 91°11W, pop (1995e) 228 000. Capital of state in SE Louisiana, USA; a deep-water port on the Mississippi R; founded, 1719; ceded to the USA as part of the Louisiana Purchase, 1803; declared its independence under the name Feliciana, 1810; incorporated as a town within Louisiana, 1817; state capital, 1849–61 and since 1882; airfield; railway; university (1860). >> Louisiana; Louisiana Purchase

Batten, Jean (1909–82) New Zealand pioneer aviator, born in Rotorua, New Zealand. In 1934 she made the first England–Australia 'there and back' solo flight by a woman, breaking Amy Johnson's record, and in 1936 made a record-breaking flight from England to New Zealand. >> Johnson, Amy

battered baby / child syndrome >> **child abuse**

battery (electricity) A device that converts chemical energy into electrical energy. The first battery, made by Alessandro Volta in c.1800, was the basis of the *voltaic cell* – two chemicals immersed in an electrolyte, enabling electrons to travel from one to the other along a circuit. *Primary cells* only discharge electricity, whereas *secondary cells* (or *accumulators*) can also be recharged. The batteries commonly encountered in torches, toys, cameras, etc are 'dry' primary cells, in which the electrolyte has been treated so that it will not spill out of the battery. 'Wet' primary cells are used in telephone and railway signalling systems. >> accumulator; current (electricity); electrolyte; Volta

battery (law) The use of force against another person without that person's consent. It involves physical contact (unlike assault), but not necessarily physical damage. Consent may sometimes be implied, such as in the context of lawful sporting activity. >> assault

battery farming >> **factory farming**

battleship The most powerful warship capable of engaging an enemy. The largest battleship now in service is the USS *New Jersey* (58 000 tons), mounting nine 16-inch guns. >> warships [i]

baud [bawd] A unit, named after the French inventor, J M E Baudot, which is used to measure the rate of transmission of digital data. For most purposes, one baud can be regarded as equivalent to a transmission rate of one bit per second. The **Baudot code** is a 5-bit code widely used in teleprinter-based communications systems. >> bit

Baudelaire, Charles (Pierre) [bohduhlair] (1821–67) French Symbolist poet, born in Paris. His masterpiece is a collection of poems, *Les Fleurs du mal* (1857), for which author, printer, and publisher were prosecuted for impropriety in 1864. >> Symbolism

Baudot code >> **Morse code**

Baudouin I [bohdwĩ] (1930–93) King of the Belgians (1951–93), born at Stuyvenberg Castle, near Brussels, the elder son of Leopold III and his first wife, Queen Astrid. He succeeded to the throne following the abdication of his father (Jul 1951), and in 1960 married the Spanish **Doña Fabiola de Mora y Aragón**.

Bauhaus [**bow**hows] An influential school of arts and crafts founded in the Weimar Republic by Walter Gropius in 1919. The aim was for artists and architects to work together to create a new unity in the arts. At first expressionist in style, the Bauhaus quickly championed the stark simplicity of functionalism. The school moved to Dessau in 1925, but was closed by Hitler in 1933, many members living thereafter in the USA. A new director was appointed in 1987, and the renamed Bauhaus Dessau Foundation now contains a collection, studio, academy, and workshop. >> Arts and Crafts Movement; *De Stijl*; Feininger; functionalism (art and architecture); Gropius; Kandinsky; Klee; Mies van der Rohe; Moholy-Nagy; rationalism

Baum, Vicki [bowm], originally **Vicki Hedvig** (1888–1960) Novelist, born in Vienna. Her works include *Grand Hotel* (1930), *Grand Opera* (1942), several short stories, and plays.

Bausch, Pina [bowsh], popular name of **Philippine Bausch** (1940–) Dancer, choreographer, and director, born in Solingen, Germany. She became ballet director of the Wuppertal Dance Theatre in 1973, later founding her own company. Her choreography and particularly her unusual stagings mark a turning point in contemporary dance, and have remained a powerful influence. >> Expressionism; modern dance

bauxite [**bawk**siyt] A natural mixture of hydrated aluminium oxide minerals produced by the weathering of rocks in hot, humid climates in which more soluble constituents are leached out. It is the chief ore of aluminium. >> aluminium

Bavaria, Ger **Bayern** pop (1995e) 11 677 000; area 70 553 sq km/27 233 sq mi. Largest province in former West Germany, and Europe's oldest existing political entity; capital, Munich; chief towns, Augsburg, Passau, Nuremberg, Würzburg, Regensburg; a third of the area is forested; many spas and climatic health resorts. >> Bavarian Alps / Forest; Germany ℹ

Bavarian Alps, Ger **Bayerische Alpen** Mountain range extending E and W from L Constance to Salzburg; highest peak, the Zugspitze (2962 m/9718 ft); called the **Tirol Alps** in Austria. >> Alps; Bavaria

Bavarian Forest, Ger **Bayerische Wald** Mountain range bounded SW by the Danube valley; highest peak, the Einodriegel (1126 m/3694 ft); largest continuous forest in Europe. >> Germany ℹ

Bax, Sir Arnold (Edward Trevor), pseudonym **Dermot O'Byrne** (1883–1953) Composer, born in London. His compositions include seven symphonies (1921–39), tone poems (such as *Tintagel*, 1917), choral works, chamber music, and piano concertos. In 1942 he was made Master of the King's (from 1952 Queen's) Musick.

Bayazid I >> **Bayezit I**

Bayeux Tapestry [**biy**uh, biyoe] An embroidered wall-hanging in coloured wool on linen, narrating events leading up to the invasion of England by William of Normandy, and the Battle of Hastings in 1066. Probably commissioned by William's half-brother Odo, Bishop of Bayeux in N France, and embroidered in S England c.1067–77, its length is 68 m/224 ft, and its height 46 cm–54 cm/18–21 in. >> Anglo-Saxons; Norman Conquest; Odo; tapestry

Bayezit I [baja**zet**], also spelled **Bajazet** or **Bayazid**, nickname **Yildrim** ('Thunderbolt') (c.1354–1403) Sultan in the Ottoman Empire (1389–1402). He conquered Bulgaria, parts of Serbia, Macedonia and Thessaly, and most of Asia Minor. In 1402 he was defeated near Ankara by Timur, in whose camp he died. >> Timur

Baykonyr Cosmodrome >> **Baikonur Cosmodrome**

Baylis, Lilian Mary (1874–1937) Theatrical manager, born in London. She became manager of the first Old Vic company in 1912, and in 1931 acquired Sadler's Wells Theatre for the exclusive presentation of opera and ballet.

Bay of Pigs The attempted invasion of Cuba (Apr 1961) by Cuban exiles supported by the USA. The invasion force of 1300 men landed at Bahía de Cochinos (Bay of Pigs) on the S coast, but was rapidly overwhelmed and defeated by Cuban troops commanded by Fidel Castro. >> Castro; Cuba ℹ

bayonet A steel blade, thought to have been invented in Bayonne, France, in the 17th-c, which turns an infantryman's firearm into a thrusting weapon. Originally plugging into the end of the musket, by the early 19th-c bayonets were designed to fit into a slot beneath the muzzle, allowing the weapon to be fired at will. >> musket; rifle

bayou [**biy**oo] A section of still or slow-moving marshy water cut off from a main river channel. It is often in the form of an oxbow lake. Bayous are typical of the Mississippi R delta in Louisiana, USA.

bay owl An owl native to Africa and SE Asia; inhabits wet tropical forest; eats insects and vertebrates. (Genus: *Phodilus*, 2 species. Family: Tytonidae.) >> owl

Bayreuth [biy**royt**] 49°56N 11°35E, pop (1995e) 73 500. Industrial and marketing town in Germany, on a tributary of R Main; world famous as a festival city committed to the operas of Wagner; railway; university (1975). >> Germany ℹ; Wagner

bay tree >> **sweet bay**

Bazaar Malay >> **Malay** (language)

bazooka A US infantry weapon developed during World War 2 which fires a small rocket projectile from a simple launching tube. The projectile's warhead is effective against light tank armour. >> tank

bazouka >> **kazoo**

BBC Abbreviation of the **British Broadcasting Corporation**, the UK organization responsible for making and transmitting its own television and radio programmes. It began radio broadcasts in 1922 as the British Broadcasting Company, and received a Royal Charter in 1927, thereafter maintaining a national radio service. It began its television service in 1936. Financed almost wholly by viewers' licence fees, it is formally independent of government, and committed to a public-service ethos. In the 1990s its roles and methods of operation were subjected to major review – a process which generated considerable debate both within and outside the organization. >> Birt; broadcasting; Reith

BCG An abbreviation of *Bacille Calmette-Guérin*, a vaccine named after French bacteriologists Albert Calmette (1863–1933) and Camille Guérin (1872–1961). It is a vaccine that consists of attenuated living tubercle bacteria, and in humans conveys considerable protection against tuberculosis over a number of years. >> tuberculosis; vaccination

Beach Boys, The US singing/instrumental group, formed in California in 1961, consisting orginally of brothers **Brian Wilson** (1942–, vocalist, bass guitar, keyboards, songwriter), **Carl Wilson** (1946–98, vocalist, guitar) and **Dennis Wilson** (1944–83, vocalist, drums), with cousin **Mike Love** (1941–, vocalist) and **Al(an) Jardine** (1942–, vocalist, bass guitar, guitar); later also **Bruce Johnston** (1944–) and others. They found fame in the 1960s with cheerful songs of teenage West Coast life, surfing, fast cars and motorcycles, and all-American girls, including 'I Get Around', 'California Girls', and 'Good Vibrations'. >> pop music

Beachcomber >> **Morton, John Cameron**

beach flea >> **sand hopper**

Beaconsfield, Earl of >> **Disraeli, Benjamin**

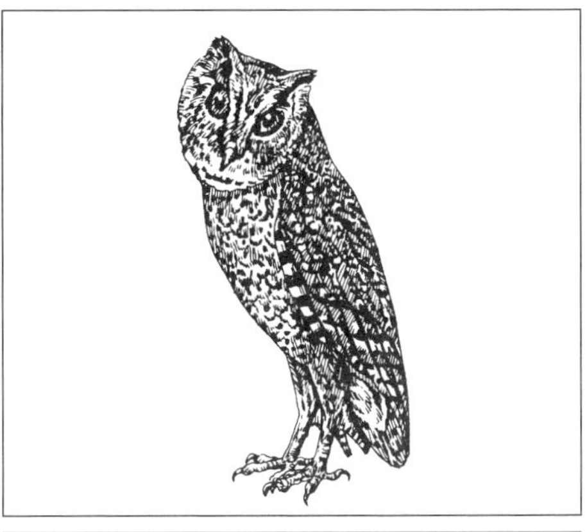

Bay owl

beagle A breed of dog developed in Britain; a medium-sized hound with a sturdy body and short coat (coarse-haired forms exist); white, tan, and black; broad pendulous ears, deep muzzle; formerly used to track hares by scent. >> hound

Beaker culture A prehistoric culture defined archaeologically by finely-made, pottery drinking vessels for mead or beer, often burnished and geometrically decorated; found in graves of the 3rd millennium BC from Spain, Czechoslovakia, and Hungary to Italy and Britain.

Beale, Dorothea (1831–1906) Pioneer of women's education, born in London. From 1858 she was principal of Cheltenham Ladies' College, and in her later years became a suffragette. >> women's liberation movement

beam weapons >> **directed energy weapons**

bean A general name applied to the seeds of many plants, but particularly those belonging to the pea family, Leguminosae, many of which are edible. >> broad bean; haricot bean; pea ℹ; runner bean

bear A carnivorous mammal, widespread in the N hemisphere; head large with short, rounded ears and long muzzle; body bulky with thick (usually shaggy) coat and very short tail. (Family: Ursidae, 7 species.) >> black / brown / polar bear; carnivore ℹ; kinkajou

Beard, Dan(iel Carter), nickname **Uncle Dan** (1850–1941) Illustrator and youth leader, born in Cincinnati, OH. He wrote *What to Do and How to Do It: The American Boy's Handy Book* (1882), the first of 16 books on handicrafts. He organized the Sons of Daniel Boone (1905) and the Boy Pioneers of America (1909), was National Scout Commissioner (1910–41), and became 'Uncle Dan' to a generation of American boys. >> scouting

bearded lizard An Australian agamid lizard; group of large spines behind each ear; body with numerous small spines; throat with deep pouch which can be enlarged as a threat display (hence 'beard'); also known as **bearded dragon**. (Genus: *Amphibolurus*, 3 species.) >> agamid

bearded vulture >> **lammergeier**

Beardsley, Aubrey (Vincent) [**beerdz**lee] (1872–98) Illustrator, born in Brighton, East Sussex. He became well known through his posters and his black and white illustrations for *Morte d'Arthur* (1893) and other books. With Oscar Wilde he is regarded as leader of the 'Decadents' of the 1890s. >> Wilde

bearings Mechanical devices supporting rotating shafts with a minimal amount of frictional resistance. In the **ball bearing**, the rotating shaft is supported by a number of balls which are interposed between it and the fixed mounting. >> camshaft; engine

bear market A stock market term which signifies that there are more sellers than buyers of stocks and shares. A **bear** is an individual who sells shares, hoping the price will then fall, so that they may be repurchased more cheaply. >> bull market; stock market

beat generation A group of US writers of the 1950s who rejected conventional society and its values for a life and writing based on authentic individual experience, according to the poet Allen Ginsberg (*Howl*, 1957), 'of God, sex, drugs, and the absurd'. Besides Ginsberg, novelist Jack Kerouac (*On the Road*, 1957) and poets Gregory Corso (1930–) and Laurence Ferlinghetti (1919–) were principal beat writers. >> absurdism; Ginsberg; Kerouac

beating the bounds In England, at Rogationtide, a traditional ceremonial walk round the boundaries of a parish, during which boundary stones are beaten with peeled willow wands, the better to fix their position in the memory. >> riding the marches; Rogation Days

Beatitudes The common name for the opening pronouncements of blessing upon the poor, the hungry, and others in Jesus's great Sermon on the Mount, reported in Matthew's gospel (nine listed in *Matt* 5.3–10) and the Sermon on the Plain in Luke's gospel (four listed in *Luke* 6.20–3). >> Jesus Christ; Sermon on the Mount

Beatles, The (1960–70) British pop group, formed in Liverpool in 1960, consisting at that time of **John Lennon** (1940–80, rhythm guitar, keyboards, vocals), **Paul McCartney** (1942–, bass guitar, vocals), **George Harrison** (1943–, lead guitar, sitar, vocals), and **Pete Best** (1941–, drums). In 1962 Best was replaced by **Ringo Starr** (1940–, originally **Richard Starkey**), and the band signed a record contract. 'Love Me Do' became a hit in the UK, and their appearances at the Cavern Club in Liverpool and elsewhere in the UK overflowed with idolizing fans. 'Beatlemania' spread around the world in 1964, buoyed by international hits such as 'She Loves You' and by the overwhelming success of a concert tour in American stadiums. Their films included *A Hard Day's Night* (1964) and *Help* (1965). In 1966 the Beatles stopped performing in public. Their first studio production was *Sergeant Pepper's Lonely Hearts Club Band* (1967). The group dissolved acrimoniously in 1970, but following Lennon's death, the others sang together again in 1994. >> Harrison, George; Lennon; McCartney; pop group; Starr

Beaton, Sir Cecil (Walter Hardy) (1904–80) Photographer and designer, born in London. In the 1920s, as a staff photographer for *Vanity Fair* and *Vogue*, he became famous for his society portraits. After World War 2, he designed scenery and costumes for many productions, including *My Fair Lady* and *Gigi*.

Beaton or **Bethune, David** (1494–1546) Scottish statesman and Roman Catholic clergyman, born in Balfour, Fife. A persecutor of the Scottish Protestants, he had the reformer George Wishart burnt at St Andrews (1546), but was murdered in revenge three months later by Protestant conspirators. >> Protestantism; Reformation; Wishart

Beatrix, in full **Beatrix Wilhelmina Armgard** (1938–) Queen of the Netherlands (1980–), born in Soestdijk, who acceded to the throne on the abdication of her mother. In 1966 she married West German diplomat **Claus-Georg Wilhelm Otto Friedrich Gerd von Amsberg** (1926–). They have three sons.

Beatty, David Beatty, 1st Earl (1871–1936) Naval commander, born in Nantwich, Cheshire. He sank the *Blücher* (Jan 1915), and took part in the Battle of Jutland (May 1916). He became commander-in-chief of the Grand Fleet in 1916 and First Sea Lord in 1919. >> World War 1

Beatty, Warren [**bay**tee], originally **Henry Warren Beaty** (1937–) Actor and film-maker, born in Richmond, VA, the younger brother of actress Shirley MacLaine (1934–). He produced *Bonnie and Clyde* (1967), co-wrote *Shampoo* (1975), and co-directed *Heaven Can Wait* (1978). He was the producer, co-writer, and star of *Reds* (1981), which won him an Oscar as Best Director. Later films include *Bulworth* (1998).

Beaufort, Henry [**boh**fert] (1377–1447) English cardinal, a major figure in English politics in the early 15th-c. He became a cardinal in 1426, and was Lord Chancellor on three occasions. During the 1430s he controlled the government of the young King Henry VI. >> Henry VI (of England); Hussites

Beaufort Scale [**byoo**fert] A scale of windspeed, ranging from 0 to 12, devised by Admiral Francis Beaufort (1774–1857) in the mid-19th-c, which uses descriptions of the way common outdoor features (eg smoke, trees) respond to different wind conditions. >> hurricane; storm; wind ℹ; RR975

Beauharnais, Alexandre, vicomte de (Viscount of) [bohah(r)nay] (1760–94) French army officer, born in Martinique. He eagerly embraced the French Revolution, and was made secretary of the National Assembly, but was guillotined (1794) for his failure to relieve Metz. In 1779 he married **Joséphine de la Pagerie**, afterwards wife of Napoleon. >> French Revolution [i]; Napoleon III

Beaujolais [**boh**zholay] Sub-division of the old province of Lyonnais in EC France, now forming part of Rhône and Loire departments; major wine-growing region; N part known as Beaujolais Villages; centre, Villefranche.

Beaumarchais, Pierre Augustin Caron de [bohmah(r)shay], originally **Pierre Augustin Caron** (1732–99) Comic playwright, born in Paris. His most successful comedies were *Le Barbier de Séville* (1775, The Barber of Seville) and *Le Mariage de Figaro* (1784, The Marriage of Figaro).

Beaumont, Francis [**boh**mont] (c.1584–1616) Playwright, born in Gracedieu, Leicestershire. He formed a close association with John Fletcher, writing many plays. *The Woman Hater* (1607) is attributed solely to him, and he had the major share in *The Knight of the Burning Pestle* (1609). >> Fletcher

Beauregard, P(ierre) G(ustave) T(outant) [**boh**regah(r)d] (1818–93) Confederate general, born near New Orleans, LA. He was appointed to the command at Charleston, where he commenced the war by the bombardment of Fort Sumter (1861). >> American Civil War

beauty >> **bottom**

Beauvais [bohvay] 49°25N 2°08E, pop (1995e) 58 000. Market town in N France, on R Thérain; railway; bishopric; former tapestry-making centre; cathedral (13th–16th-c), with highest Gothic vault in existence (48 m/156 ft).

Beauvoir, Simone de >> **de Beauvoir, Simone**

Beaux-Arts, Ecole des [bohzah(r), aykol day] The main official art school in Paris. It dates from 1648 and was installed in its present quarters on the left bank of the Seine by 1830.

beaver A large squirrel-like rodent from North America, N Europe, and Asia; semi-aquatic; hind feet webbed; tail broad, flat, and scaly; builds a 'lodge' from logs and mud in woodland ponds; often dams streams to create ponds. (Family: Castoridae, 2 species.) >> mountain beaver; rodent; squirrel

Beaverbrook (of Beaverbrook and of Cherkley), (William) Max(well) Aitken, Baron (1879–1964) Newspaper magnate and British politician, born in Maple, Ontario. In 1916 he took over the *Daily Express*, which he made into the most widely read daily newspaper in the world. He became actively involved in World War 2, and was made minister of supply (1941–2), minister of production (1942), Lord Privy Seal (1943–5), and lend-lease administrator in the USA.

bebop A jazz style, also known as **bop**, characterized by fast tempos and agitated rhythms. It was cultivated in the decade after World War 2 by small groups of musicians.

bèche de mer [besh duh **mair**] A French culinary term, referring to the food obtained from a marine animal found in the SW Pacific, also known as a **sea cucumber**. >> sea cucumber

Bechet, Sidney [**be**shay, be**shay**] (1897–1959) Jazz musician, born in New Orleans, LA. After starting on clarinet, he switched to soprano saxophone in order, he said, to dominate the brass in ensembles. Lionized in France on his first tour in 1919, he kept returning, and in 1949 became a permanent resident.

Bechstein, Karl [**bek**stiyn], Ger [**bekh**shtiyn] (1826–1900) Piano manufacturer, born in Gotha, Germany. He founded his famous factory in Berlin in 1856.

Beckenbauer, Franz [**bek**enbower], nickname **the Kaiser** (1945–) Footballer, born in Munich, Germany. He played in the West German side beaten by England in the 1966 World Cup, and led his country to World Cup success in 1974. He retired in 1983, became manager of the German national team in 1986, and is currently president of Bayern Munich.

Becker, Boris [**be**ker] (1967–) Tennis player, born in Leiman, Germany. In 1985 he was the youngest winner of the men's singles at Wimbledon (17 years 227 days). He retained the title in 1986, lost it in the 1988 final to Stefan Edberg, but regained it in 1989. In 1988 he was the World Championship Tennis champion and the Masters champion, then won the US Open (1989), the Australian Open (1991, 1996), and the Association of Tennis Professionals World Title (1992).

Becket, St Thomas (1118–70) Saint and martyr, born in London. In 1155, he became Chancellor, the first Englishman since the Conquest to hold high office. When created Archbishop of Canterbury (1162), he resigned the chancellorship, serving the Church as vigorously as he had the king, and coming into conflict with Henry II's aims to keep the clergy in subordination to the state. Henry's rashly-voiced wish to be rid of 'this turbulent priest' led to Becket's murder in Canterbury cathedral (29 Dec 1170) by four of the king's knights. He was canonized in 1173, and Henry did public penance at his tomb in 1174. Feast day 29 December. >> Henry II (of England)

Beckett, Margaret (Mary) (1943–) British stateswoman. Elected an MP in 1974, she became deputy leader of the Labour Party (1992–4, including a short term as leader in 1994). She became president of the Board of Trade and secretary of state for trade and industry in 1997, and in 1998 was appointed Leader of the House of Commons.

Beckett, Samuel (Barclay) (1906–89) Writer and playwright, born in Dublin. He settled in France in 1937. His early work was written in English, but he later wrote in French, notably the novels *Molloy* (1951) and *Malone Meurt* (1951, Malone Dies), and the play *En attendant Godot* (1954, Waiting for Godot), which later took London by storm. He was awarded the 1969 Nobel Prize for Literature. >> absurdism

Beckham, David (Robert Joseph) (1975–) Footballer, born in London. A midfield player, he joined Manchester United in 1993, and the England team in 1996. He had won 15 caps for England by mid-1998, and was a high-profile member of the 1998 World Cup team, but his popularity fell after being sent off during the match against Argentina which put England out of the competition.

becquerel [**bek**erel] The activity of a radioactive source as the number of disintegrations per second; SI unit; symbol *Bq*. >> Becquerel; radioactivity units [i]

Becquerel, (Antoine) Henri [bekerel] (1852–1908) Physicist, born in Paris. He shared the Nobel Prize with the Curies in 1903 for discovering the **Becquerel rays** emitted from uranium salts, which led to the isolation of radium. >> becquerel; Curie; radium

Bedchamber Crisis A British political crisis which occurred in May 1839, after Melbourne, Prime Minister in the Whig government, offered to resign, and advised the young Queen Victoria to appoint Peel and the Tories. The Queen refused to dismiss certain Ladies of the Bedchamber with Whig sympathies, whereupon Peel refused office and the Whig government continued. >> Melbourne, Viscount; Peel; Victoria; Whigs

Bede or **Baeda, St**, known as **the Venerable Bede** (c.673–735) Anglo-Saxon historian and theologian, born near Monkwearmouth, Durham. He wrote in the monastery at Jarrow, his most valuable work being the *Historia ecclesiastica gentis anglorum* (Ecclesiastical History of the English People). He was canonized in 1899; feast day 25 May. >> Anglo-Saxons; Benedictines

Bedford 52°08N 0°29W, pop (1995e) 80 800. County town of Bedfordshire, SC England; railway; John Bunyan was imprisoned here, during which time he wrote *The Pilgrim's Progress.* >> Bedfordshire; Bunyan, John

Bedford Level >> **Fens, the**

Bedfordshire pop (1995e) 550 000; area 1235 sq km/ 477 sq mi. County in SC England; drained W–E by the R Ouse; county town, Bedford; Luton a new unitary authority from 1997. >> Bedford; England ℹ

Bednorz, (Johannes) Georg [**bed**naw(r)ts] (1950–) Physicist, born in Germany. He worked with Swiss physicist Karl Alexander Müller (1927–) at the IBM Zürich Research Laboratory at Rüschlikon. In 1986 they demonstrated that some mixed-phase oxides would superconduct above 30 K, and by 1987 related materials were found to show the effect up to 90 K, ie at a temperature which offered novel possibilities in practical electronics. They shared the 1987 Nobel Prize for Physics. >> superconductivity

Bedouin Arabic-speaking nomads of Arabia, Syria, Jordan, Iraq, and other desert areas in the Middle East. They mainly herd animals in the desert during winter months and cultivate land in summer. Many have been forced to settle in one locality, because of political or economic moves. >> Arabs; nomadism

bedstraw An annual or perennial, found almost everywhere; weak, 4-angled stem, often with tiny hooks, narrow leaves in whorls; flowers tiny, white, yellow, or greenish, 4-petalled, in open clusters; fruits often burrs. (Genus: *Galium*, 400 species. Family: Rubiaceae.)

bee A winged insect that builds and provisions a nest for its young; the common name of several different types of hymenopteran, including solitary mining bees (Family: Andrenidae), carpenter bees (Family: Anthophoridae), bumblebees, orchid bees, stingless bees, and honeybees (all Family: Apidae). Social structure ranges from the solitary bees, in which each queen effectively raises her own brood, to honeybees, which form a complex society with a caste system and overlapping, co-operating generations. (Order: Hymenoptera.) >> apiculture; bee dancing; bumblebee; honey bee; Hymenoptera; insect ℹ; royal jelly

beech A deciduous, shallow-rooted tree native to the N hemisphere; leaves oval, margins wavy; flowers tiny, males in long-stalked clusters, females (and later, nuts) in pairs enclosed in 4-lobed, spiny case. (Genus: *Fagus*, 10 species. Family: Fagaceae.) >> roble beech; tree ℹ

Beecham, Sir Thomas (1879–1961) Conductor, born in St Helens, Merseyside. He founded the Royal Philharmonic Orchestra in 1946. A noted champion of Delius's music, he published in 1958 a study of the composer's life and works. He was also known for his candid pronouncements on musical matters, his 'Lollipop' encores, and his after-concert speeches. >> Delius

Beecher, Lyman (1775–1863) Presbyterian minister and revivalist, born in New Haven, CT, the father of Harriet Beecher Stowe. He preached in New York, Connecticut, and Massachusetts, his brand of Calvinism calling for constant church services and strong opposition to drinking. In 1832 he went to Cincinnati as head of the newly founded Lane Theological Seminary, and to serve as pastor of the Second Presbyterian Church. >> Stowe

Beecher Stowe, Harriet >> **Stowe, Harriet (Elizabeth) Beecher**

Beeching, Richard, Baron (1913–85) Engineer and administrator, born in Maidstone, Kent. As chairman of the British Railways Board (1963–5), he was responsible for the substantial contraction of the UK rail network (the **Beeching Plan**).

bee dancing The patterned movements of honey-bees used to signal the direction and distance of pollen and nectar to other members of the colony. The phenomenon was first documented by the Austrian biologist Karl von Frisch (1886–1982). >> bee

beefeater >> **Yeomen of the Guard**

bee-keeping >> **apiculture**

bee orchid The name for various species of the genus *Ophrys*, widespread throughout Europe, W Asia, and N Africa; remarkable for their flowers which mimic insects. The lower lip of the flower resembles a female insect in both colour and texture, and the flower emits a powerful pheromone-like scent to attract males of the same species. (Genus: *Ophrys*, 30 species. Family: Orchidaceae.) >> orchid ℹ

beer An alcoholic beverage made from ale (malted barley) which has been flavoured with hops. It is currently an umbrella term covering a wide range of drinks, distinguished by the type of yeast used, such as *bitter* (a beer brewed with more hops and a lighter malt than *Mild*), *lager* (a light beer which matures over a long period of time at a low temperature), and *stout* or *porter* (types of dark ale produced from the brewing of roasted malt). >> ale; brewing

Beerbohm, Sir (Henry) Max(imilian) [**beer**bohm], nickname **the Incomparable Max** (1872–1956) Writer and caricaturist, born in London. He wrote many volumes of

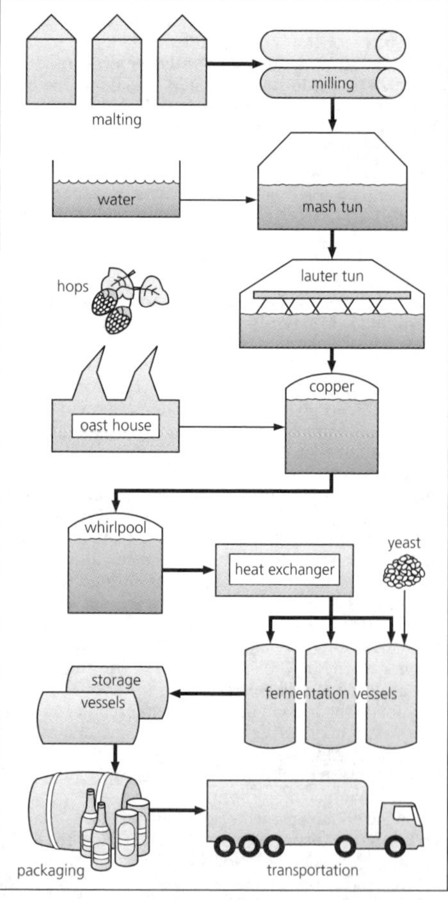

Beer – the brewing process, from malting to distribution

caricatures and parodying essays, but his best-known work was his novel on Oxford undergraduate life, *Zuleika Dobson* (1911).

Beerbohm Tree, Herbert >> **Tree, Sir Herbert (Draper) Beerbohm**

beeswax Wax secreted by bees of the family Apidae, including bumblebees, stingless bees, and honeybees. It is produced by glands beneath the abdominal body plates (*sterna* or *terga*), and used in nest construction. >> bee

beet An annual, biennial, or perennial native to Europe and Asia; leaves shiny, often tinged dark red. Cultivated beets, all derived from the wild beet (*Beta vulgaris*), are divisible into two groups: **leaf beets**, including spinach beets and chards, are grown as leaf vegetables; **root beets**, including beetroot and mangel-wurzel, are biennials grown for their edible, swollen roots. **Sugar-beet**, containing up to 20% sugar in the root, has largely replaced sugar-cane as the source of sugar in W Europe. (Genus: *Beta*, 6 species. Family: Chenopodiaceae.) >> chard; sugars

Beethoven, Ludwig van [**bay**tohvn] (1770–1827) Composer, born in Bonn, Germany. He lived and worked in Vienna from 1792. Though often in love with his noble pupils, he never married. His music is usually divided into three periods. In the first (1792–1802), which includes the first two symphonies, the first six quartets, and the 'Pathétique' and 'Moonlight' sonatas, his style gradually develops its own individuality. His second period (1803–12) begins with the 'Eroica' symphony (1803), and includes his next five symphonies, the difficult 'Kreutzer' sonata (1803), the Violin Concerto, the 'Archduke' trio (1811), and the 'Razumovsky' quartets. His third great period begins in 1813, and includes the Mass, the 'Choral' symphony (1823), and the last five quartets. His career was marred by deafness, which began in 1801 and was total by the early 1820s. >> classical music; symphony

beetle A winged insect with forewings modified as rigid, horny cases covering membranous hindwings and abdomen beneath; hindwings used in flight, sometimes missing; biting mouthparts; range in size from less than 0·5 mm/0·2 in to c.170 mm/7 in; development includes distinct larval and pupal phases; c.350 000 species known, including many pests. (Order: Coleoptera.) >> black / Colorado / deathwatch / furniture / water beetle; chafer; Dutch elm disease; firefly; ladybird; Spanish fly; weevil ℹ; whirligig

Beeton, Isabella Mary, *née* **Mayson**, known as **Mrs Beeton** (1836–65) British writer on cookery. Her *Book of Household Management* (1859–60), covering cookery and other branches of domestic science, made her name a household word.

beetroot >> **beet**

Begin, Menachem (Wolfovitch) [**bay**gin] (1913–92) Israeli statesman and prime minister (1977–83), born in Brest-Litovsk, Belarus. In 1948 he founded the Herut Freedom Movement, becoming chairman of the Herut Party. In 1973 three parties combined to form the nationalist Likud Front with Begin as its leader, and in the 1977 elections he formed a coalition government. He attended peace conferences in Jerusalem (1977) and at Camp David at the invitation of President Carter (1978), and in 1978 he and President Sadat of Egypt were jointly awarded the Nobel Peace Prize. >> Carter, Jimmy; Israel ℹ; Sadat

begonia A perennial native to warm regions, especially America; leaves asymmetric, one side larger than the other, often spotted or marked with white or red; male flowers with two large and two small petals, females with 4–5 more petals; fruit a winged capsule. (Genus: *Begonia*, 900 species. Family: Begoniaceae.)

Behan, Brendan (Francis) [**bee**an] (1923–64) Writer, born in Dublin. He was twice imprisoned for IRA activities, and had a period in hospital for alcoholism. His plays include *The Quare Fellow* (1956) and *The Hostage* (1958). His other writing includes an autobiographical novel, *Borstal Boy* (1958). >> IRA

Behar >> **Bihar**

behaviourism / behaviorism The view that psychology is most effectively pursued by analyzing the overt behaviour of people and animals, in preference to subjective states, thoughts, or hypothetical internal dynamics. It has had an important influence on modern psychology, but is now rarely held in its extreme form. >> Skinner

behaviour / behavior therapy A type of psychological treatment formulated by psychotherapist Joseph Wolpe (1915–) which emphasizes the alteration of thoughts and behaviour. It is often applied to neurotic illnesses (eg phobias) on the presumption that these are learned forms of behaviour which can be 'unlearned'. The term was coined by the British psychologist H J Eysenck in the 1950s. >> aversion therapy; Eysenck; neurosis; psychiatry

Beiderbecke, Bix [**biy**derbek], popular name of **Leon Bismarck Beiderbecke** (1903–31) Cornettist, born in Davenport, IA. When expelled from a military academy, he began the short career that made him one of the most celebrated jazz performers of the 1920s. His later career ravaged by alcoholism, he succumbed to pneumonia at the age of 28. >> jazz

Beijing [bay**zhing**] or **Peking**, formerly **Beiping (Pei-p'ing)** 39°55N 116°25E; pop (1995e) 7 892 000; administrative region 11 598 000; municipality area 17 800 sq km/ 6871 sq mi. Capital city and municipality of NE China; occupied by Japanese, 1937–45; capital of China, 1949; airport; railway; two universities (1898, 1950); Imperial Palace, formerly known as the 'Forbidden City'; Tiananmen (Gate of Heavenly Peace, built 1417, restored 1651), Niu Jie (oldest Muslim temple, 996). >> Forbidden City; Great Wall of China; Temple of Heaven; Tiananmen Square

Beira [**bay**ra] 19°46S 34°52E, pop (1995e) 337 000. Seaport capital of Mozambique, SE Africa; occupied by the Portuguese, 1506; founded as the seat of the Mozambique Company, 1891; airport; railway. >> Mozambique ℹ

Beirut [bay**root**], Arabic **Bayrut**, Fr **Beyrouth**, ancient **Berytus** 33°52N 35°30E, pop (1995e) 1 564 000. Seaport capital of Lebanon; the 'Green Line' refers to the division of the city during the 1975–6 civil war into Muslim (W) and Christian (E) sectors; Israeli attack on Palestinian and Syrian forces in 1982 led to the evacuation of Palestinians to camps such as Sabra, Chatila, and Bourj Barajneh; severely damaged by continued fighting; reduction of tension and release of foreign hostages, 1991; airport; railway; American University (1866), Lebanese University (1953), Arab University (1960); two cathedrals. >> Arab–Israeli Wars; Lebanon ℹ; PLO

Békésy, Georg von [**bay**kezee] (1899–1972) Physiologist, born in Budapest. For his studies of how the human ear analyses sounds, he was awarded the Nobel Prize for Physiology or Medicine in 1961. >> ear ℹ

Bekka, the >> **Beqaa, el**

bel >> **decibel**

Bel and the Dragon An addition to the Book of Daniel, part of the Old Testament Apocrypha, or Chapter 14 of Daniel in Catholic versions of the Bible. It includes the tale of Daniel in the lion's den. >> Apocrypha, Old Testament; Daniel, Book of

Belarus [bela**rus**], official name **Republic of Belarus**, also spelled **Byelarus**, formerly (to 1991) **Belorussian SSR** or **White Russia**, Russ **Belorusskaya** pop (1995e) 10 424 000; area 207 600 sq km/80 134 sq mi. Republic in NE Europe; capital, Minsk; timezone GMT +3; major ethnic groups,

Belorussian (78%), Russian (13%), Polish (4%), Ukrainian (3%), Jewish (1%); languages, Belorussian (official), Russian; religions, Roman Catholic, Orthodox; currency, Belorussian rouble; largely flat, with low hills in the NW rising to 346 m/1135 ft at Mt Dzyarzhynskaya; chief rivers, the Dnepr, Zapadnaya Dvina, Neman; c.11 000 lakes; a third of the area covered by forests; climate varies from maritime near Baltic to continental and humid; average annual temperature −6°C (Jan), 18°C (Jul); average annual rainfall 550–700 mm/22–28 in; formed part of Grand Duchy of Lithuania, 13th-c; under Polish control, 16th-c; partition of Poland led to Belorussia becoming part of the Russian Empire at end of 18th-c; W Belorussia ceded to Poland at Treaty of Riga, 1921; regained by Soviet Union as part of Nazi–Soviet Non-aggression Pact, and became a Soviet Socialist Republic, 1939; declaration of independence, 1991; new constitution (1994) introduces an elected president and a parliament; wide range of light and heavy industry; oil, salt, meat and dairy production, flax; farmland covers 46% of the land area. >> Commonwealth of Independent States ℹ; Minsk; RR1001 political leaders

Belau [be**low**], also **Palau** or **Pelau**, official name **Republic of Belau** 7°30N 134°30E; pop (1996e) 16 800; area 494 sq km/191 sq mi. Republic in the W Pacific Ocean, the smallest of the four political units to emerge out of the US Trust Territory of the Pacific Islands; group of c.350 small islands and islets, c.960 km/600 mi E of the Philippines; timezone GMT +10; chief ethnic group, 83% Palauan; chief languages, Palauan, English; chief religions, 66% Christianity, 25% traditional beliefs; currency, the US dollar; largest island, Babeldoab; average annual temperature, 27°C; average annual rainfall, 3810 mm/150 in; typhoons common; held by Germany, 1899–1914; mandated to Japan by League of Nations, 1920; invaded by USA, 1944; compact of free association with the USA, signed in 1982, but not confirmed until 1993; independence, 1994; member of the UN, 1995; governed by a president and a National Congress consisting of a Senate and a House of Delegates; tourism, wide range of local fruits, fishing. >> Koror; United States Trust Territory of the Pacific Islands

Belém [be**lem**], also called **Pará** 1°27S 48°29W, pop (1995e) 1 309 000. City in N Brazil; founded in 1616; airport; railway; university (1957); cathedral (1748). >> Brazil ℹ

Belfast, Ir **Beal Feirste** 54°35N 5°55W, pop (1995e) 283 000. Capital of Northern Ireland in Antrim, NE Northern Ireland; at the mouth of the Lagan R, on Belfast Lough; original settlement and castle destroyed in 1177; settled in the 17th-c by English, Scots, and Huguenots, becoming a centre of Irish Protestanism; capital, 1920; well-defined Nationalist (Catholic) and Unionist (Protestant) areas; disrupted by civil unrest since 1969; two airports; railway; university (1908); cathedral (begun 1898); Parliament House at Stormont. >> Antrim; Huguenots; Northern Ireland ℹ; Protestantism; Roman Catholicism; Stormont

Belgian Congo >> **Zaire**

Belgium, official name **Kingdom of Belgium**, Fr **Royaume de Belgique**, Flemish **Koninkrijk België** pop (1995e) 10 099 000; area 30 518 sq km/11 780 sq mi. Kingdom of NW Europe, coastline 64 km/40 mi; capital, Brussels; timezone GMT +1; a line drawn E–W just S of Brussels divides the population, by race and language, into two approximately equal parts; to the N, Flemings of Teutonic stock, speaking Flemish; to the S, French-speaking Latins, known as Walloons; languages, 56% Flemish (Dutch), 32% French, 1% (on E border) German; Brussels officially a bilingual city; religion, 75% Roman Catholic; currency, Belgian franc of 100 centimes; mostly low-lying, with some hills in the SE region (Ardennes), average elevation 300–500 m/1000–1600 ft; large areas of fertile soil, intensively cultivated for many centuries; main river systems linked by complex network of canals; low-lying, dune-fringed coastline; climate cool and temperate with strong maritime influences; part of the Roman Empire until 2nd-c AD; invasion by Germanic tribes, and part of the Frankish Empire; ruled by the Habsburgs from 1477 until the Peace of Utrecht, 1713, known as the Spanish Netherlands, 1713; conquered by the French, 1794; part of the French Republic and Empire until 1815, then united with the Netherlands; Belgian rebellion, 1830, led to recognition as an independent kingdom under Leopold of Saxe-Coburg; occupied by Germany in both World Wars; a hereditary and constitutional monarchy with a bicameral parliament; in recent decades, political ten-

sion between Walloons and Flemings has caused the collapse of several governments; new federal constitution implemented, dividing Belgium into the autonomous regions of Flanders, Wallonia, and Brussels, 1993; one of the earliest countries in Europe to industrialize, using rich coalfields of the Ardennes; famous textile industry of Flanders since Middle Ages; long-standing centre for European trade; major iron and steel industry, with wide range of metallurgical and engineering products; agriculture mainly livestock; full economic union (Benelux Economic Union) between Belgium, Netherlands, and Luxembourg in 1948; Brussels now the headquarters of several major international organizations. >> Brussels; Franks; Netherlands, The i; Zaire i; RR1001 political leaders

Belgrade, Serbo-Croatian **Beograd**, ancient **Singidunum** 44°50N 20°30E, pop (1995e) 1 574 000. Capital city of Yugoslavia and of the republic of Serbia, at the junction of the Danube and Sava Rivers; airport; railway; university (1863); arts university (1957); cathedral; damage from NATO bombing in Kosovo crisis (Apr–Jun 1999). >> Serbia; Yugoslavia i

Belgrano, General [bel**grah**noh] An Argentinian cruiser, sunk by HM submarine *Conqueror* during the Falklands conflict in 1982, with great loss of life. Her sinking proved to be one of the most controversial incidents of the war. >> Falklands War

Belize [be**leez**], formerly **British Honduras** (to 1973) pop (1995e) 212 000; area 22 963 sq km/8864 sq mi. Independent state in Central America, capital, Belmopan; timezone GMT −6; main ethnic groups, Spanish–Mayan Mestizos, Creoles, Caribs, several minorities; religion, Roman Catholic (60%); official language, English, with Spanish and local Mayan languages also spoken; currency, Belize dollar of 100 cents; extensive coastal plain, swampy in the N, more fertile in the S; Maya Mts extend almost to the E coast, rising to 1120 m/3674 ft at Victoria Peak; Belize R flows W–E; inner coastal waters protected by world's second longest barrier reef; generally subtropical climate, but tempered by trade winds; variable rainfall; often damaged by hurricanes. evidence of early Mayan settlement; colonized in the 17th-c by shipwrecked British sailors and disbanded soldiers from Jamaica; created a British colony in 1862, administered from Jamaica until 1884; internal self-government, 1964; changed name from British Honduras to Belize, 1973; full independence, 1981; Guatemalan claims over Belize territory have led to a continuing British military presence; Guatemala signed accord respecting Belize self-determination, 1991; governor-general represents British monarch, and appoints a prime minister; bicameral National Assembly; economy traditionally based on timber and forest products, more recently on agriculture; since 1980s, significant immigration from Salvadorean and Guatemalan refugees. >> Belmopan; Guatemala i; Jamaica i; Mayas; RR1002 political leaders

Belize City 17°29N 88°10W, pop (1995e) 59 400. Seaport in Belize, Central America; capital until 1970; airport. >> Belize i

bell A hollow vessel of bronze or other material which, when struck, vibrates to produce a ringing sound. If the bell is tuned, the sound may be heard as a musical note of definite pitch. The *closed* (or *crotal*) variety is a hollowed sphere, with one or more slits in the surface, which is shaken to cause a loose pellet inside to strike against the inner surface. The *open* bell is cast in the shape of an upturned cup, usually sounded by means of a clapper suspended from the inside of the bell, but sometimes struck externally with a ramrod. >> bell-ringing; carillon; change ringing; idiophone; tubular bells

Bell, Alexander Graham (1847–1922) Educationist and inventor, born in Edinburgh, the son of Alexander Melville Bell. In 1871 he moved to the USA, where he invented the telephone (1872–6), and founded the Bell Telephone Company. >> Bell, Alexander Melville; telephone

Bell, Alexander Melville (1819–1905) Educationalist, born in Edinburgh. He became a teacher of elocution, his numerous works including *Visible Speech* (1867). >> elocution; phonetics

Bell, Martin (1938–) Television journalist and politician, born in Cambridge, Cambridgeshire. He joined the BBC in 1962, becoming one of their best known foreign correspondents. He fought an 'anti-sleaze' campaign in the 1997 general election, and was returned – much to his own surprise – as Independent MP for Tatton.

belladonna (Ital 'fair lady') A liquid extract of the deadly nightshade plant (*Atropa belladonna*), so called because Italian ladies used to apply it to their eyes to make the pupils dilate, an effect deemed attractive. The main active constituent is atropine. >> atropine

belladonna lily A large bulb (*Amaryllis bella-donna*), native to S Africa; leaves strap-shaped; flowers trumpet-shaped, 7–9 cm/$2\frac{3}{4}$–$3\frac{1}{2}$ in long, white to pink, 6–12 on a solid stalk appearing in autumn after the leaves have died. (Family: Amaryllidaceae.) >> amaryllis

Bellamy, David (James) (1933–) British botanist, writer, and broadcaster. A professor at Nottingham, and the writer of numerous conservation-oriented books, he is best known for his TV programmes designed to create a greater awareness of the natural environment, such as *Bellamy's Birds' Eye View* (1988), *Bellamy's Border Raids: The Peak District* (1994), and *A Welsh Herbal* (1998–9). He established the Conservation Foundation in 1988. >> conservation (earth sciences)

Bellarmine, St Robert [**bel**ermin], originally **Roberto Francesco Romolo Bellarmino** (1542–1621) Jesuit cardinal and theologian, the chief defender of the Church in the 16th-c, born in Montepulciano, Italy. He was canonized in 1930. Feast day 17 May. >> Jesuits; theology

bell-flower A member of a large variable genus of mostly annuals and herbaceous perennials, low and spreading to tall and erect, native throughout N temperate regions; leaves very narrow to almost circular; flowers 5-lobed bells, usually large and showy, and almost always blue, sometimes pink or white. (Genus: *Campanula*, 300 species. Family: Campanulaceae.) >> Canterbury bell

Bellingshausen, Fabian Gottlieb Benjamin von [**bel**ings-howzn] (1778–1852) Explorer, born in Ösel, Estonia. In 1819–21 he led an Antarctic expedition as far south as 70°, and gave his name to the Bellingshausen Sea. >> Antarctica ℹ

Bellini [be**lee**nee] A family of 15th-c Venetian painters. **Jacopo Bellini** (c.1400–70) studied under Gentile da Fabriano; only a few of his works remain. His son **Gentile Bellini** (c.1429–1507) worked in his father's studio, and is known for his portraits. His other son, **Giovanni Bellini** (c.1430–1516), was the greatest Venetian painter of his time. His innovations of light and colour became the hallmark of Venetian art, continued by his pupils Giorgione and Titian. >> Giorgione; Titian; Venetian School

Belloc, (Joseph) Hilaire (Pierre) [**bel**ok] (1870–1953) Writer, born in St Cloud, near Paris. He became a British Liberal MP (1906–10), then continued as a writer, best known for his nonsensical verse for children, *The Bad Child's Book of Beasts* (1896) and the *Cautionary Tales* (1907). He was a leading Roman Catholic of his day. >> Newman, John; Roman Catholicism

Bellotto, Bernardo [be**lo**toh] >> **Canaletto**

Bellow, Saul (1915–) Writer, born in Lachine, Quebec, Canada. His first novel was *Dangling Man* (1944), and others include *Herzog* (1964) and *Humboldt's Gift* (1975, Pulitzer); both *A Theft* and *The Bellarosa Connection* appeared in 1989. In 1976 he was awarded the Nobel Prize for Literature.

bell-ringing The art of ringing church bells, also known as **campanology**. Its two popular forms are **change ringing**, a hand-pulled method, and the **carillon** method, performed with the use of a keyboard connected to the clappers of the bells. >> change ringing

Bell's palsy Paralysis of the muscles of one side of the face innervated by the VIIth cranial nerve (the facial nerve). The condition is named after Scottish surgeon Charles Bell (1774–1842). >> central nervous system; muscle ℹ; paralysis

Belmopan [belmoh**pan**] 17°18N 88°30W, pop (1995e) 5900. Capital of Belize, Central America; made capital in 1970, following major hurricane damage to Belize City in 1961. >> Belize ℹ

Belo, Carlos (Felipe Ximenes) (1948–) Roman Catholic bishop, born in East Timor, Indonesia. Ordained bishop in 1983, he became an outspoken critic of the Indonesian regime's actions in East Timor, and shared the Nobel Prize for Peace in 1996.

Belo Horizonte [**bel**oh oree**zon**tay] 19°54S 43°54W, pop (1995e) 2 628 000. Capital of Minas Gerais state, SE Brazil; altitude 800 m/2625 ft; Brazil's first planned modern city, founded, 1897; airport nearby; airfield; railway; three universities (1927, 1954, 1958); industrial area third largest in Brazil. >> Brazil ℹ; Minas Gerais

Belorussia >> **Belarus**

Belshazzar [bel**sha**zer], Gr **Balt(h)asar** (?–539 BC) Son of Nabonidus, King of Babylon (556–539 BC), and ruler under his father until his death at the capture of Babylon. In the Book of Daniel, mysterious writing appears on the wall of his palace, which Daniel interprets as predicting the fall of the Empire. >> Babylon; Daniel, Book of

Beltane An ancient Celtic festival held at the beginning of May, and also in late June, when bonfires were lit on the hills. Beltane was formerly a quarter-day in Scotland. >> quarter-day

beluga (fish) [be**loo**ga] Very large sturgeon (*Huso huso*) found in the Caspian Sea, Black Sea, and adjacent rivers; body length up to 5 m/16 ft; weight over 1000 kg/2200 lb; fished commercially for caviar; one of the largest freshwater fish known. (Family: Acipenseridae.) >> caviar; sturgeon

beluga (mammal) [be**loo**ga] A small toothed whale (*Delphinapterus leucas*), native to shallow Arctic seas and rivers; white when adult; no dorsal fin; also known as the **white whale** or **sea canary**. (Family: Monodontidae.) >> whale ℹ

Benares or **Banares** [be**nah**res], also **Varanasi**, ancient **Kasi** 25°22N 83°08E, pop (1995e) 1 002 000. City in N India, on N bank of R Ganges; one of the seven most sacred Hindu cities, reputed to be Shiva's capital while on Earth; also a holy city of Buddhists, Sikhs, and Jains; invaded by Afghans, 1033; ceded to Britain, 1775; airfield; railway; two universities (1916, 1958); over 1400 Hindu temples and shrines, including the Golden Temple (1777). >> Buddhism; Ganges, River; Hinduism; Jainism; Sikhism

Benaud, Richie [**ben**oh], popular name of **Richard Benaud** (1930–) Cricketer and broadcaster, born in Penrith, New South Wales, Australia. He played in 63 Test matches for Australia (captain in 28), including three successful tours of England (1953, 1956, 1961). An all-rounder, he scored 2201 Test runs and took 248 wickets. He is now a well-known cricket commentator. >> cricket (sport) ℹ

Ben Bella, (Mohammed) Ahmed [ben **be**la] (1918–) Key figure in the Algerian War of Independence against France, and Algeria's first prime minister (1962–3) and president (1963–5), born in Maghnia, Algeria. Deposed in 1965, he was imprisoned until 1980, then went into voluntary exile, returning in 1990. >> Algeria ℹ; FLN

Benbow, John (1653–1702) English naval commander, born in Shrewsbury, Shropshire. His main engagements were in the War of the League of Augsburg (1690, 1693, 1694) and the War of the Spanish Succession. >> Spanish Succession, War of the

Bendigo [**ben**digoh] 36°48S 144°21E, pop (1995e) 31 900. City in NC Victoria, Australia, NW of Melbourne; centre of a wine-producing area; gold mined here until the 1950s; railway. >> Victoria (Australia)

Benedict of Nursia, St (c.480–c.547) The founder of Western monasticism, born in Nursia, Italy. At Subiaco he founded 12 small monastic communities which followed the rule he devised (c.515). He ultimately established a monastery on Monte Cassino, which became one of the most famous in Italy. He was declared the patron saint of all Europe by Pope Paul VI in 1964. Feast day 11 July. >> Benedictines; monasticism

Benedictines A religious order following the 'rule' of St Benedict of Nursia; properly known as the **Order of St Benedict** (**OSB**). The order has a long tradition of scholarship and promotion of learning. >> Benedict, St; Maurists

Benelux A customs union between Belgium, The Netherlands, and Luxembourg which came into existence in 1947. A treaty established a more ambitious economic union between the three in 1958.

Beneš, Edvard [**ben**esh] (1884–1948) Czech statesman and president (1935–8, 1939–45 in exile, 1946–8), born in Kožlany, Czech Republic. In 1935 he succeeded Masaryk as president, but resigned in 1938, setting up a government in exile, first in France, then in England. After returning in 1945, he was re-elected president, but resigned after the Communist coup of 1948. >> Czechoslovakia ℹ; Masaryk

Benesh, Rudolph (1916–75) and **Benesh, Joan** (1920–) [**be**nesh], *née* **Rothwell** Dance notators, husband and wife, born in London and Liverpool, Merseyside, respectively. Rudolph was a painter and Joan a former member of the

Sadler's Wells Ballet. Together they copyrighted (1955) a dance notation system, called Choreology, now used to document all important Royal Ballet productions. >> dance notation

Bengal, Bay of area 2 172 000 sq km/839 000 sq mi. Arm of the Indian Ocean, on S coast of Asia; c.2000 km/1300 mi long, 1600 km/1000 mi wide; subject to heavy monsoon rains and cyclones. >> Indian Ocean

Bengali >> **Indo-Aryan languages**

Benghazi or **Banghazi** [ben**gah**zee] 32°07N 20°05E, pop (1995e) 545 000. Seaport in N Libya; first settled by Greeks; controlled by Turks, 16th-c–1911; Italian rule, 1911–42; military and naval supply base during World War 2; second largest city in Libya; airport; university (1955). >> Libya ℹ

Ben-Gurion, David [ben **gur**ion], originally **David Gruen** (1886–1973) Israeli statesman and prime minister (1948–53, 1955–63), born in Plonsk, Poland. In 1930 he became leader of the Mapai (Labour) Party, which was the ruling party in the state of Israel when the state was announced (May 1948). >> Israel ℹ; Zionism

Benidorm [**ben**idaw(r)m] 38°33N 0°09W, pop (1995e) 42 400. Resort town in E Spain, on the Mediterranean Costa Blanca; a leading centre of low-cost package holidays. >> Costa Blanca; Spain ℹ

Benin [be**neen**], formerly **Dahomey** (to 1975), official name **Republic of Benin**, Fr **République du Benin**, formerly (to 1990), **The People's Republic of Benin** pop (1995e) 5 420 000; area 112 622 sq km/43 472 sq mi. Republic in W Africa; capital, Porto Novo (nominal); political and economic capital, Cotonou; timezone GMT +1; many ethnic groups, especially the Fon, Adja, Yoruba, Bariba; religion, 70% local beliefs, remainder Christian and Muslim; official language, French, with several local languages spoken; unit of currency, CFA franc; rises from a 100 km/62 mi-long sandy coast with lagoons to low-lying plains, then to a savannah plateau at c.400 m/1300 ft; Atakora Mts rise to over 500 m/1600 ft in the NW; tropical climate; in pre-colonial times, a collection of small, warring principalities, especially the Fon Kingdom of Dahomey (founded in the 17th-c); Portuguese colonial activities centred on slave trade; subjugated by French, 1892, becoming the French Protectorate of Dahomey; territory within French West Africa, 1904; independence, 1960; name changed, 1975; Marxist-Leninist regime replaced in 1989; new constitution, 1990; governed by an elected president, who serves a 5-year term, and a single-chamber National Assembly of 64 members, serving up to 4 years; agriculture important, especially palm oil products, cashew nuts, maize, cassava, rice, cotton, coffee; important service sector. >> Cotonou; Dahomey; Porto Novo; RR1002 political leaders

Ben Macdhui [muhk**doo**ee], Gaelic **Ben Muich-Dhui** 57°04N 3°40W. Second highest mountain in the UK; in Cairngorm Mts, NC Scotland; height 1309 m/4295 ft. >> Cairngorms

Benn, Anthony (Neil) Wedgwood, known as **Tony Benn** (1925–) British statesman, son of Viscount Stansgate, born in London. He became a Labour MP (1950–60), but was debarred from the House of Commons on succeeding to his father's title. He renounced his title, and was re-elected in a by-election in 1963, since when he has held various government posts. >> Labour Party; socialism

Bennett, Alan (1934–) Playwright, actor, and director, born in Leeds, West Yorkshire. He came to prominence in the revue *Beyond the Fringe* in 1960. His stage plays include *Kafka's Dick* (1986) and a double bill, *Single Spies* (1988), and he has also written much for television, such as *Talking Heads* (1987), and *Portrait or Bust* (1994). His sense for satire, both as writer and actor, relishes the foibles and eccentricities of the English.

Bennett, (Enoch) Arnold (1867–1931) Novelist, born near Hanley, Staffordshire. Among his 30 novels are *Anna of the Five Towns* (1902), *The Old Wives' Tale* (1908), and the *Clayhanger* series, all of which reflect life in the Potteries.

Bennett, James Gordon (1795–1872) Newspaper editor, born in Keith, Moray. In 1819 he emigrated to America, where he founded the *New York Herald* (1835). His son, **James Gordon Bennett** (1841–1918), edited the paper from 1867, and financed several explorers, including Stanley's search for Livingstone (1870). >> Stanley, Henry Morton

Bennett, Michael, originally **Michael Bennet Difiglia** (1943–87) Dancer, choreographer, director, and producer, born in Buffalo, NY. His first great success came on his fourth show, *Promises, Promises* (1968). His masterpiece, *A Chorus Line*, based on transcripts of workshop interviews with dancers (1975), was highly acclaimed, and he later developed *Ballroom* (1978) and *Dreamgirls* (1981) from similar workshops. >> musical

Bennett, Sir Richard Rodney (1936–) Composer, born in Broadstairs, Kent. Well known for his music for films, he has also composed operas, orchestral works, chamber music, experimental works, and pieces involving jazz.

Bennett, William J(ohn) (1943–) US Federal official, born in Brooklyn, NY. He became secretary of education (1985–8), and as President Bush's 'drug tzar' (1989–91) co-ordinated the campaign against drugs.

Ben Nevis 56°48N 5°00W. Highest mountain in the UK; in Grampian Mts, W Scotland; height 1344 m/4409 ft. >> Grampians (Scotland)

Benny, Jack, originally **Benjamin Kubelsky** (1894–1974) Comedian, born in Waukegan, IL. A child prodigy violinist, he made his film debut in 1928. *The Jack Benny Show* (1950–65) won him the warm affection of a mass audience. A gentle, bemused, self-effacing figure, he developed an act based on his ineptitude as a fiddler, his

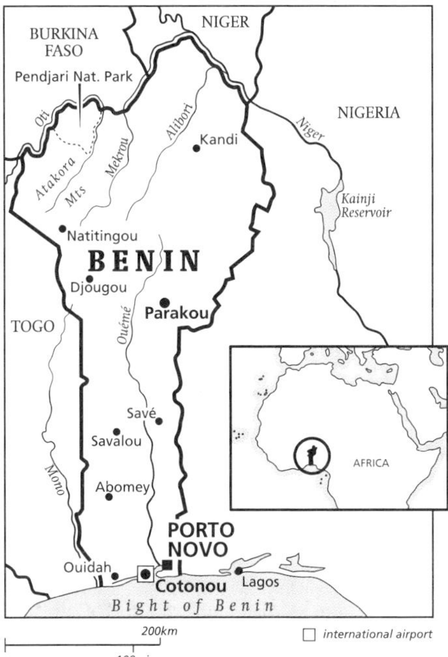

claiming of perennial youth, and an unfounded reputation as the world's cheapest man.

Bentham, Jeremy (1748–1832) Writer on jurisprudence and utilitarian ethics, born in London. He held that laws should be socially useful and not merely reflect the status quo, and that all actions are right when they promote 'the happiness of the greatest number'. He was a founder of University College, London, where his skeleton, dressed in his clothes, is preserved. >> hedonism; utilitarianism

Bentinck, William Henry Cavendish, 3rd Duke of Portland (1738–1809) British statesman and prime minister (1783, 1807–9), born in Bulstrode, Buckinghamshire. He is best remembered as home secretary under the Younger Pitt, with charge of Irish affairs (1794–1801). >> Pitt (the Younger); Whigs

Bentine, Michael [**ben**teen] >> **Goons, The**

Bentley, E(dmund) C(lerihew) (1875–1956) Journalist and novelist, born in London. He is chiefly remembered as the author of *Trent's Last Case* (1913). He also gave his name to the type of rhyming tag known as the *clerihew*.

Benton, Thomas Hart, known as **Old Bullion** (1782–1858) US statesman, born near Hillsborough, NC. He was a Missouri senator for over 30 years, and a leader of the Democratic Party. He received his byname from his opposition to paper currency.

Benton, Thomas Hart (1889–1975) Painter of large historical murals on American themes and realistic genre scenes, born in Neosho, MO. In the late 1920s he set about creating a populist American art based on ordinary Middle-Western experience – cowboys, gamblers, oil wells, and native Americans, as in 'Independence and the Opening of The West' (1959–62).

Bentsen, Lloyd Millard, Jr (1921–) US statesman, born in Mission, TX. A member of the US House of Representatives (1948–54), he became a senator for Texas in 1971, and was vice-presidential running-mate to Michael Dukakis in the Democrats' 1988 presidential challenge. In Bill Clinton's administration he served as secretary to the treasury (1993–4). >> Clinton

Benue, River [**bay**nway], Fr **Beboué** Major tributary of the R Niger in Nigeria; rises in Cameroon, and flows generally W across E and SC Nigeria; length 1295 km/805 mi. >> Niger, River

Benue–Congo languages [**bayn**way **kong**goh] >> **Niger–Congo languages**

Benz, Karl (Friedrich) (1844–1929) Engineer, born in Karlsruhe, Germany. In 1879 he constructed a two-stroke engine model and founded a factory for its manufacture. His first car – one of the earliest petrol-driven vehicles – was completed in 1885. >> car ℹ; engine

benzaldehyde [ben**zal**dihiyd] C_6H_5CHO, IUPAC **phenylmethanal**, boiling point 179°C. A colourless liquid, with the odour of almonds, used as a flavouring. It is readily oxidized to benzoic acid. >> aldehyde; IUPAC

Benzedrine >> **amphetamine**

benzene [**ben**zeen] C_6H_6, melting point 5°C, boiling point 80°C. An aromatic liquid obtained from coal tar, the simplest of the large series of aromatic compounds. It is used in dyestuffs, plastics, insecticides, detergents, and several other products. >> coal tar

benzodiazepines [benzohdiy**ay**zepeenz] A group of drugs each of which exerts, to varying degrees, anti-anxiety, anti-epilepsy, hypnotic (sleep-inducing), muscle-relaxant, and sedative properties. The two tranquillizers *chlordiazepoxide* (Librium) and *diazepam* (Valium) were the first to be introduced, in 1960 and 1962 respectively. *Nitrazepam* (Mogadon) and *temazepam* (Normison) are commonly used as hypnotics. They are very safe drugs, with fatal overdose being very uncommon, and therefore they took over from the more dangerous barbiturates. Some concern is now being expressed at their very wide use, and evidence of addiction following long-term use is accumulating. >> barbiturates

benzyl [**ben**ziyl, **ben**zil] $C_6H_5CH_2$–, IUPAC **phenylmethyl**. A functional group containing a phenyl ring, whose addition to a name usually indicates its substitution for hydrogen in a compound. >> functional group; hydrogen; IUPAC; phenyl; ring

Beqaa, al- [be**kah**], Eng **the Bekka** Governorate of E Lebanon, bounded NE and E by Syria; capital, Zahle; valley of strategic importance to both Israel and Syria, and a centre of Muslim Shiite activity. >> Lebanon ℹ

Berber Afro-Asiatic-speaking peoples of Egypt, Algeria, Libya, Tunisia, and Morocco. They were originally settled in one area, but the Bedouin Arabs who invaded N Africa in the 12th-c turned many of them into nomads. The best-known groups include the Kabyle, Shluh, and Tuareg. >> Bedouin; nomadism; Tuareg

Berberian, Cathy >> **Berio, Luciano**

berberis >> **barberry**

Beresford, Bruce (1940–) Film director, born in Sydney, New South Wales, Australia. A key figure in the revival of the Australian film industry, he won the Australian Film Institute's Best Director award for *Don's Party* (1976) and *Breaker Morant* (1979). Later films include *Driving Miss Daisy* (1989, Oscar) and *Paradise Road* (1997).

Berg, Alban (1885–1935) Composer, born in Vienna. He studied under Schoenberg, welding the 12-note system to a deeply traditional style. He is best known for his opera *Wozzeck* (1925). >> Schoenberg; serialism

Bergama [ber**gah**ma], ancient **Pergamon** or **Pergamum** 39°08N 27°10E, pop (1995e) 51 200. Town in W Turkey; former capital of Pergamum, and of the Roman province of Asia; parchment is supposed to have been invented here. >> parchment; Pergamum (Asia Minor); Turkey ℹ

Bergamo [**bair**gamoh] 45°42N 9°40E, pop (1995e) 123 000. Town in N Italy; first seat of the Republican fascist government set up by Mussolini after his fall from power, 1943; airport; railway; 15th-c cathedral. >> Mussolini

bergamot [**ber**gamot] **1** An aromatic perennial, native to North America and Mexico; stem square; leaves oval, toothed, in opposite pairs; flowers 2-lipped, hooded, purple or red, in crowded whorls around stem; leaves provide medicinal Oswego tea. (Genus: *Monarda*, 12 species. Family: Labiatae.) **2** >> orange

Bergen (Belgium) [**ber**khen] >> **Mons**

Bergen (Norway) [**ber**gn] 60°23N 5°20E, pop (1995e) 219 000. Seaport in SW Norway; second largest city in Norway; founded, 1070; capital, 12th–13th-c; occupied by Germans in World War 2; bishopric; airport; railway; university (1948); cathedral (13th-c); offshore oil services; tourist and cultural centre; birthplace of Grieg. >> Bryggen; Grieg; Norway ℹ

Berger, Samuel R, known as **Sandy Berger** (1945–) US public official and lawyer. Formerly the Deputy Assistant to the President for National Security Affairs (1993–6), he was appointed Assistant in Clinton's second administration. He is the author of *Dollar Harvest* (1971) on American rural politics.

Bergerac, Savinien Cyrano de >> **Cyrano de Bergerac, Savinien**

Bergman, (Ernst) Ingmar (1918–) Film director and writer, born in Uppsala, Sweden. His films became something of a cult for art-cinema audiences, such as *The Seventh Seal* (1956), *Wild Strawberries* (1957), *The Virgin Spring* (1960, Oscar), and *Through a Glass Darkly* (1961, Oscar), outstanding for their photographic artistry, haunting imagery, and subtle exploration of facial characteristics. Later films include *Fanny and Alexander* (1982, Oscar).

Bergman, Ingrid (1915–82) Film actress, born in Stockholm, Sweden. Her early successes included *Casablanca* (1942), *For Whom the Bell Tolls* (1943), and *Gaslight* (1944), for which she won her first Oscar. The scandal of her relationship with the Italian director Rossellini, whom she subsequently married, led to her exclusion from Hollywood for a time. She won another Oscar for *Anastasia* (1956).

Bergson, Henri (Louis) [bergsõ] (1859–1941) Philosopher and psychologist, born in Paris. He became known with his *Essai sur les données immédiates de la conscience* (1889, Time and Free Will: an Essay on the Immediate Data of Consciousness). Later works include *L'Evolution créatrice* (1907, Creative Evolution). He was awarded the Nobel Prize for Literature in 1927.

Beria, Lavrenti Pavlovich [**be**ria] (1899–1953) Soviet secret police chief, born in Mercheuli, Georgia. He became Soviet commissar for Internal Affairs in 1938, and during World War 2 was active in purging Stalin's opponents. After the death of Stalin (1953), he was shot after a brief 'treason' trial. >> Malenkov; Molotov; Stalin

beri beri A nutritional disease due primarily to an inadequate dietary intake of vitamin B_1. The disorder affects peripheral nerves (*polyneuritis*), and also causes heart failure and oedema. >> vitamins ℹ

Bering, Vitus (Jonassen) [**bay**ring], also spelled **Behring** (1681–1741) Navigator, born in Horsens, Denmark. In 1728 and again in 1741 he sailed towards the American continent, and finally sighted Alaska, but he was wrecked on the island of Avatcha (now Bering I), where he died. Bering Sea and Bering Strait are named after him. >> Bering Sea

Bering Sea [**bay**ring] area 2 304 000 sq km/890 000 sq mi. Part of the Pacific Ocean between Siberia (W) and Alaska (E); connected to the Arctic by the Bering Strait (90 km/56 mi wide at narrowest point); often ice-bound (Nov–May); contains boundary between Russia and USA. >> Bering; Pacific Ocean

Berio, Luciano [**be**rioh] (1925–) Avant-garde composer and teacher of music, born in Oneglia, Italy. He married (1950–66) the American soprano **Cathy Berberian** (1925–83), for whom he wrote several works. He is particularly interested in the combining of live and prerecorded sound, and the use of tapes and electronic music, as in the *Sequenza* series (1958–75). >> electronic music

Berkeley, Busby [**berk**lee], originally **William Berkeley Enos** (1895–1976) Film director and choreographer, born in Los Angeles, CA. He was known for his extravagant stagings of dance numbers in Hollywood films, using the camera to move among the dancers. >> choreography

Berkeley, George [**bah(r)k**lee] (1685–1753) Anglican bishop and philosopher, born near Kilkenny. His *Treatise Concerning the Principles of Human Knowledge* (1710) expounded his idealistic philosophy. >> idealism

Berkeley, Sir Lennox (Randall Francis) [**bah(r)k**lee] (1903–89) Composer, born in Boars Hill, Oxfordshire. He became professor of composition at the Royal Academy of Music, London (1946–68). His works include the operas *Nelson* (1953) and *Ruth* (1956), and several orchestral pieces. >> Boulanger

Berkowitz, David [**ber**kohvits] (c.1953–) Convicted US murderer, who dubbed himself 'Son of Sam' in a note to the New York Police Department. He terrorized the city for a year (1976–7), preying on courting couples and lone women. Finally arrested, he received a prison sentence of 365 years in 1977.

Berkshire [**bah(r)k**sheer], also known as **Royal Berkshire** pop (1996e) 774 000; area 1259 sq km/486 sq mi. Former county of S England, UK; replaced in 1998 by the unitary authorities of Windsor and Maidenhead, Wokingham, Reading, Slough, West Berkshire, and Bracknell Forest. >> England ℹ; Reading

Berlin [ber**lin**] 52°32N 13°25E, pop (1995e) 3 530 000; area 883 sq km/341 sq mi. Capital of Germany; linked to the Oder and Elbe Rivers by canals; founded in the 13th-c; former residence of the Hohenzollerns and capital of Brandenburg; later capital of Prussia, becoming an industrial and commercial centre in the 18th-c; in 1949 West Berlin became a province of the Federal Republic of Germany and East Berlin a county of the German Democratic Republic; contact between the two halves of the city was restored in 1989, following government changes in East Germany; capital of a united Germany, 1990; two airports; railway; three universities (1809, 1948, 1946); German Academies of Sciences (1700); Kaiser Wilhelm Church, Brandenburg Gate, Unter den Linden, Pergamum museum; former **East Berlin**, pop (1991) 1 272 600, area 403 sq km/156 sq mi, capital of East Germany to 1990; former **West Berlin**, pop (1991) 2 146 300, area 480 sq km/185 sq mi, enclave (city and province) lying entirely within East Germany. >> Berlin Airlift / Wall; Brandenburg Gate; Charlottenburg Palace; Germany ℹ; Hohenzollerns; Pergamum; Prussia; Tiergarten; Unter den Linden

Berlin, Irving [ber**lin**], originally **Israel Baline** (1888–1989) Composer, born in Temum, Russia. He was a child when his family emigrated to New York City. 'Alexander's Ragtime Band' became an international hit in 1911, the first of many among more than 900 songs for which he wrote both the words and music, such as 'Always' (1925), 'Easter Parade' (1933), 'God Bless America' (1939), and 'White Christmas' (1942).

Berlin, Sir Isaiah (1909–97) Philosopher, born in Riga, Latvia. His family emigrated to England in 1920, and he spent most of his academic career at Oxford. His works on political philosophy included *Historical Inevitability* (1954) and *Two Concepts of Liberty* (1959). Later works included *The Magus of the North* (1993)

Berlin Airlift A massive airlift of essential supplies flown in to postwar Berlin by British and US aircraft in round-the-clock missions. It was carried out in response to the action of the Soviet military authorities in Berlin, who had attempted to isolate the city from the West by severing all overland communication routes (Jun 1948). Stalin lifted the blockade in May 1949. >> Berlin; Stalin

Berliner Ensemble [ber**lin**er] A theatre company in East Berlin which was formed by Brecht in 1949. In its early years it had an enormous influence on Western theatre. >> Brecht

Berlin Wall A concrete wall built by the East German government in 1961 to seal off East Berlin from the part of the city occupied by the three main Western powers. Built largely to prevent mass illegal emigration to the West, which was threatening the East German economy, the wall was the scene of the shooting of many East Germans who tried to escape from the Eastern sector. The wall, seen by many as a major symbol of the denial of human rights in E Europe, was unexpectedly opened in November 1989, following increased pressure for political reform in East Germany. It has now been taken down. >> Berlin; Germany ℹ

Berlioz, (Louis-)Hector [**ber**liohz] (1803–69) Composer, born in Côte-Saint-André, France. His works include the *Symphonie Fantastique* (1830), the symphony *Harold en Italie* (1834), the *Grande messe des morts* (1837), and the operas *Les Troyens* (1856–8) and *Béatrice et Bénédict* (1860–2). >> programme music

Bermuda, formerly **Somers Is** 32°N 65°W, pop (1995e) 62 000; area 53 sq km/20 sq mi. A British overseas territory in the W Atlantic c.900 km/560 mi E of Cape Hatteras, N Carolina; c.150 low-lying coral islands and islets, 20 inhabited, seven linked by causeways and bridges; largest island (Great) Bermuda; highest point, Gibb's Hill (78 m/256 ft); capital, Hamilton; timezone GMT −4; two-thirds black population, remainder of British or Portuguese stock; main religions, Anglican (37%), Roman Catholic (14%); official language, English; unit of currency, Bermuda dollar of 100 cents; subtropical climate, generally humid, rain throughout year, summers warm to hot, winters mild; discovered by Spanish mariner, Juan Bermudez, in early 16th-c; colonized by English settlers, 1612; important naval station, and (to 1862) penal settlement; internal self-government, 1968; movement for independence caused tension in the 1970s, including assassination of the governor, 1973; British monarch represented by a governor; bicameral legislature; economy mainly year-round tourism; increasingly an international company business centre. >> Hamilton (Bermuda)

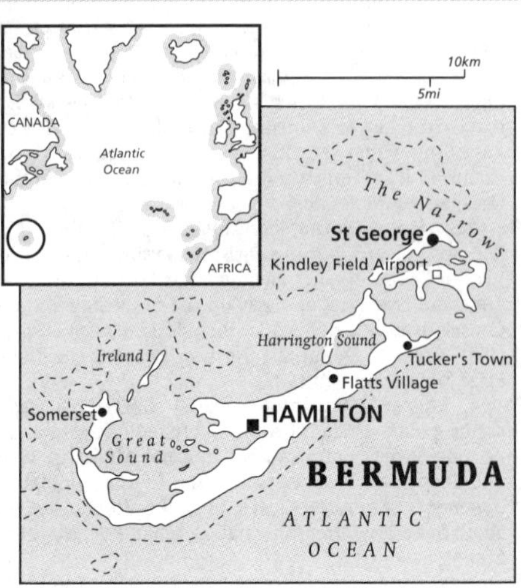

Bermuda Triangle An area of the North Atlantic Ocean, roughly delimited by Bermuda, the Greater Antilles, and the US coast, which has become part of maritime mythology. Reports of vessels which have been abandoned or disappeared, vanishing aircraft, and other inexplicable events have been known for over a century, and have attracted diverse explanations. Although objective evidence, such as wreckage, is conspicuous by its absence, the Triangle continues to attract a great deal of imaginative writing. >> Atlantic Ocean

Bern, Fr **Berne** 46°57N 7°28E, pop (1995e) 139 000. Federal capital of Switzerland; founded, 1191; joined the Swiss Confederation, 1353; capital, 1848; airport; railway junction; university (1834); Gothic cathedral (1421–1573); old city is a world heritage site; headquarters of several international organizations. >> Switzerland [i]

Bernadette of Lourdes, St, originally **Marie Bernarde Soubirous** (1844–79) Visionary, born in Lourdes, France, the daughter of a miller. She claimed in 1858 to have received 18 apparitions of the Blessed Virgin at the Massabielle Rock, near Lourdes. She was beatified in 1925, and canonized in 1933. Feast day 18 February or 16 April. >> Lourdes; Mary (mother of Jesus)

Bernadotte, Folke, Greve (Count) [berna**dot**] (1895–1948) Humanitarian and diplomat, born in Stockholm. Appointed by the UN to mediate in Palestine, he produced a partition plan, but was assassinated by Jewish terrorists in Jerusalem. >> United Nations; Zionism

Bernadottte, Jean >> **Charles XIV** (of Sweden)

Bernard of Clairvaux, St [klairvoh], known as **the Mellifluous Doctor** (1090–1153) French theologian and reformer, born of a noble family at Fontaines, near Dijon. In 1113 he entered the Cistercian monastery of Cîteaux, and in 1115 became the first abbot of Clairvaux. He was canonized in 1174. The monks of his reformed branch of the Cistercians are often called **Bernardines**. Feast day 20 August. >> Cistercians; Clairvaux; monasticism

Bernard of Menthon, St [mãtõ], known as **the Apostle of the Alps** (923–1008) Clergyman, born in Savoy, Italy. As Archdeacon of Aosta he founded the hospices in the Alpine passes that bear his name. In due course the hospices' dogs were also named after him. Feast day 28 May or 15 June. >> Alps; apostle

Bernardines >> **Bernard of Clairvaux, St**

Bernese Alps, Ger **Berner Alpen**, Fr **Alpes Bernoises** Mountain range in Switzerland, a N division of the Central Alps; highest peak, the Finsteraarhorn (4274 m/14 022 ft); also includes the Aletschhorn and Jungfrau; numerous tourist resorts. >> Alps

Bernhard Leopold [**bern**hah(r)t] (1911–) Prince of The Netherlands, born in Jena. In 1937 he married Juliana, the only daughter of Wilhelmina, Queen of The Netherlands; they have four daughters. >> Juliana

Bernhardt, Sarah [**bern**hah(r)t], originally **Henriette Rosine Bernard** (1844–1923) Actress, born in Paris. Her most famous roles included the title role in *Phèdre* (1877) and Marguerite (1884) in *La Dame aux camélias*. She founded the Théâtre Sarah Bernhardt in 1899.

Bernini, Gian Lorenzo [ber**nee**nee] (1598–1680) Baroque sculptor, architect and painter, born in Naples, Italy. In 1656 he decorated the apse of St Peter's with the so-called Cathedra Petri ('Chair of Peter'), designed the colonnade in front of the cathedral, and in 1663 the grand staircase to the Vatican. >> Baroque (art and architecture)

Bernoulli, Daniel [ber**noo**lee] (1700–82) Mathematician, born in Groningen, The Netherlands, the son of Swiss parents. He worked on trigonometrical functions, fractions, and the kinetic theory of gases, and solved an equation proposed by Jacopo Riccati, now known as 'Bernoulli's equation'. **Bernoulli's principle** (1738) states that as the speed of a moving fluid increases, its pressure decreases. >> Bernoulli disk; fluid mechanics

Bernoulli disk [ber**noo**lee] A form of computer magnetic disk storage where the disk can be removed and replaced. It is named after Daniel Bernoulli. >> Bernoulli; magnetic disk

Bernstein, Carl [**bern**stiyn] (1944–) Journalist and writer, born in Washington, DC. With Bob Woodward (1943–) he was responsible for unmasking the Watergate cover-up. They won for the *Washington Post* the 1973 Pulitzer Prize for public service, and wrote the best seller, *All the President's Men* (1974). >> Watergate

Bernstein, Leonard [**bern**stiyn] (1918–90) Conductor, pianist, and composer, born in Lawrence, MA. His compositions include three symphonies, a television opera, a Mass, a ballet, and many choral works and songs. He is most widely known for his two musicals, *On the Town* (1944) and *West Side Story* (1957).

Berra, Yogi, popular name of **Lawrence Peter Berra** (1925–) Baseball player and coach, born in St Louis, MO. He played with the New York Yankees (1946–63), including 14 World Series (a record), and set the record for most home runs by a catcher in the American League (313). He went on to manage the Yankees, the New York Mets, and the Houston Astros.

Berry, Chuck, popular name of **Charles Edward Anderson Berry** (1926–) Rock singer, guitarist, and songwriter, born in St Louis, MO. Many of his songs belong to the standard repertoire of rock and roll, usually as hits for other singers: for example, 'Roll Over Beethoven' by the Beatles, and 'Sweet Little Sixteen' by the Beach Boys.

berserker [**ber**serker] In Norse mythology, a warrior in a 'bear-shirt' who fought in such a frenzy that he was impervious to wounds. The name is the origin of the phrase 'to go berserk'.

Bertolucci, Bernardo [bertoh**loo**chee] (1940–) Film director, born in Parma, Italy. He is best known for *Last Tango in Paris* (1972) and the epic *The Last Emperor* (1987, 9 Oscars).

Bertrand, Henri Gratien, comte (Count) [bairtrã] (1773–1844) Military engineer and one of Napoleon's generals, born at Châteauroux, France. He shared the Emperor's banishment to St Helena, his shorthand diary giving a detailed account of Napoleon's life in exile. >> Napoleon I

Berwick-upon-Tweed [**be**rik] 55°46N 2°00W, pop (1995e) 13 400. Town in Northumberland, NE England; disputed by England and Scotland, changed ownership 14 times, but part of England since 1482; railway. >> Flodden, Battle of; Northumberland

beryl A beryllium, aluminium silicate mineral ($Be_3Al_2Si_6O_{18}$), occurring in granite pegmatites as greenish hexagonal prisms. Gemstone varieties are aquamarine and emerald. It is the commercial ore of beryllium. >> aquamarine; beryllium; emerald; gemstones; pegmatite

beryllium [be**ril**ium] Be, element 4, melting point 1278°C. The metal forms an unreactive coat of BeO in air, making it inert to further oxidation. Its low density (1·85 g/cm^3) makes it a valuable component of alloys, but the poisonous nature of its compounds limits its use. >> alloy; beryl; chemical elements; RR1036

Berzelius, Jöns Jakob, Baron [ber**zay**lius] (1779–1848) One of the founders of modern chemistry, born near Linköping, Sweden. His accurate determination of atomic weights established the laws of combination and the atomic theory. He also discovered the elements selenium, thorium, and cerium. >> chemical elements; chemistry; relative atomic mass

Besançon [bezãsõ], ancient **Vesontio** or **Besontium** 47°15N 6°00E, pop (1995e) 117 000. Industrial town in NE France, on R Doubs; former capital of Franche-Comté; railway; university (1485); archbishopric; cathedral (11th–13th-c), birthplace of Victor Hugo. >> Hugo

Besant, Annie [**be**znt], *née* **Wood** (1847–1933) Theosophist and social reformer, born in London. From secularism and Bradlaugh she passed in 1889 to Madame Blavatsky and theosophy, becoming its high priestess from 1891. >> Blavatsky; Bradlaugh; theosophy

Bessemer process [**bes**emer] A process for converting pig iron (high carbon iron from the blast furnace) into steel (low carbon iron alloy). Air is blown through the molten iron; the oxygen of the air converts the carbon in the iron into carbon dioxide, which escapes. This reaction produces heat which keeps the iron molten. The process is named after British engineer Henry Bessemer (1813–98), who introduced it successfully into Britain in 1856. >> iron; open-hearth process; smelting; steel

Best, George (1946–) Footballer, born in Belfast. A very talented but often tempestuous player, he made his debut for Manchester United at the age of 17 in 1963. Footballer of the Year in England and Europe in 1968, he played for Northern Ireland 37 times. Attempted come-backs with smaller clubs in England, the USA, and Scotland were unsuccessful.

best boy >> gaffer

bestiary A literary form popular in classical and mediaeval times which presents human characteristics in the guise of animal behaviour: the Greek *Physiologus* is the model. >> allegory

beta-blockers A group of drugs, introduced in the early 1960s, which lower heart rate and blood pressure. *Propranolol*, the first clinically useful beta-blocker, and *atenolol* are widely used in acute stress and panic, where they prevent symptoms such as racing of the heart, sweating, and tremor. There is current controversy over their use in some sports (eg snooker), where they may improve performance.

Betacam The trade name of a videotape cassette recorder and camera system of TV broadcast standard, introduced by Sony in 1981, initially for electronic news-gathering but widely adopted internationally for all forms of video production. **Betacam SP** is an improved version using metal-particle tape for higher bandwidth and better picture quality. >> videotape recorder

beta decay A naturally occuring radioactive decay process in which a neutron in an atomic nucleus spontaneously breaks up into a proton, which remains in the nucleus, and an electron (**beta particle**), which is emitted. The process is always accompanied by the emission of an antineutrino, and is governed by weak nuclear force. >> nucleus (physics); radioactivity; weak interaction

Betamax The trade name for a videotape cassette recorder system developed by Sony in 1975 for the domestic market. Although economical, it never achieved the popularity of the competitive VHS system. >> videotape recorder

betatron [**bay**tuhtron] A particle accelerator in which electrons are held in a circular orbit by a magnetic field, and accelerated by a varying electric field superimposed. It is used for research on high-energy electron behaviour or to produce high-energy X-rays. >> electron; particle accelerators

Betelgeuse [**bee**tlzherz, **be**tljooz] A red supergiant star, prominent in Orion, 800 times the diameter of the Sun. Distance: 180 parsec. >> Orion (astronomy); supergiant

betel-nut A slender tree (*Areca catechu*) reaching 30 m/100 ft, native to SE Asia; leaves 8 m/26 ft, feathery; seeds 4–5 cm/1½–2 in, red or orange; also called the **areca palm**. The nuts are boiled with lime, then dried, and wrapped in betel leaf from the climbing species of pepper, *Piper betle*. The 'plug' is habitually chewed in the Indian subcontinent and SE Asia for its intoxicating effects, which are similar to alcohol. The juice stains teeth and saliva bright red. (Family: Palmae.)

Bethe, Hans (Albrecht) [**bay**tuh] (1906–) Physicist, born in Strasbourg, France (formerly Germany). He held the chair of physics at Cornell (1937–75), and in 1939 proposed the first detailed theory for the generation of energy by stars through a series of nuclear reactions. He also contributed with Ralph Alpher and George Gamow to the 'alpha, beta, gamma' theory of the origin of the chemical elements during the early development of the universe. He was awarded the 1967 Nobel Prize for Physics. >> Alpher; Gamow

Bethlehem, Arabic **Beit Lahm** 31°42N 35°12E, pop (1995e) 22 300. Biblical town in Jerusalem governorate, Israeli-occupied West Bank, W Jordan; birthplace of Jesus and the home of David; trade centre; university (1973); Church of the Nativity, built by Constantine, 330. >> David; Israel i; Jesus Christ; Jordan i

Betjeman, Sir John [**bech**uhman] (1906–84) Writer and poet, born in London. He is especially known for his light verse, much of which is to be found in his *Collected Poems*

(1958) and in his verse autobiography, *Summoned by Bells* (1960). He was made Poet Laureate in 1972.

Better Business Bureau One of many local organizations, mainly in the USA and Canada, formed to protect communities against unfair or misleading advertising and selling practices. Established in the early years of this century by advertising men, they nowadays set standards for business practice, and investigate complaints.

Beuys, Joseph [boys] (1921–86) Avant-garde artist, born in Krefeld, Germany. A professor at Düsseldorf Academy (1961–71), his sculpture consisted mainly of 'assemblages' of bits and pieces of rubbish; and he also staged multimedia 'happenings'. A prominent political activist, he was one of the founders of the Green Party in Germany. >> assemblage

Bevan, Aneurin, known as **Nye Bevan** (1897–1960) British statesman, born in Tredegar, Blaenau Gwent, SE Wales. He established a reputation as a brilliant, irreverent, and often tempestuous orator. As minister of health (1945–51), he introduced the National Health Service (1948). 'Bevanism' was a left-wing movement to make the Labour Party more socialist and less 'reformist'. He married **Jennie Lee** in 1934. >> Labour Party; Lee, Jennie; National Health Service; socialism

bevatron [**bev**atron] A thousand million electron volt proton accelerator, designed and built at Berkeley Radiation Laboratory, University of California, USA. >> particle accelerators; proton

Beveridge, William Henry Beveridge, Baron (1879–1963) British economist, administrator, and social reformer, born in Rangpur, Bengal, India. He is best known as the author of the *Report on Social Insurance and Allied Services* (**The Beveridge Report**, 1942), which helped to create the welfare state. >> welfare state

Beverley 53°51N 0°26W, pop (1995e) 20 900. Administrative centre of East Riding unitary authority, NE England; railway; market town; Beverley Minster (13th-c). >> England ℹ

Beverly Hills 34°04N 118°25W, pop (1995e) 35 000. Residential city in Los Angeles County, SW California, USA; the home of many television and film celebrities. >> California; Los Angeles

Bevin, Ernest (1881–1951) British statesman, born in Winsford, Somerset. He built up the National Transport and General Workers' Union, and became its general secretary (1921–40). In 1940 he became a Labour MP, minister of labour and national service in Churchill's coalition government, and in the Labour government was foreign secretary (1945–51). >> Churchill, Winston; Labour Party; trade union

bézique [buh**zeek**] A card game believed to have originated in Spain, and brought to England in 1861. Played with at least two players, each has a pack of cards but with the twos, threes, fours, fives, and sixes taken out. The object is to win tricks, and score points on the basis of the cards won. >> pinochle

bezoar >> **goat**

Bhadgaon [**bad**gown], also **Bhaktapur** 27°41N 85°26E, pop (1995e) 163 000. City and religious centre in C Nepal, in the Kathmandu Valley; altitude 1400 m/4600 ft. >> Nepal ℹ

Bhagavadgita or **Bhagavad Gita** [bahgavad**gee**ta] (Sanskrit 'The Song of the Lord') A poem forming part of the Hindu epic, the Mahabharata, consisting of an eve of battle dialogue between the warrior prince Arjuna and Lord Krishna (in the person of his charioteer). Most Hindus regard the poem, with its teaching that there are many valid ways to salvation, but that not all are universally appropriate, as the supreme expression of their religion. >> Hinduism; Krishna; Mahabharata

Bharatiya Janata Paksh (BJP) [**bah**ratya **jan**ata **paksh**] Hindu political party, formed in 1980 with the aim of transforming a secular and multicultural India into an organic Hindu nation. From its base in the Hindi-speaking states of N India, it climbed to national prominence in the elections of 1989, capturing 12% of the popular vote. With the fundamentalist Vishwa Hindu Parishad, the Party made a disputed shrine at Ayodhya a major focus for agitation. >> Ayodhya; Hinduism

Bhopal [boh**pahl**] 23°20N 77°53E, pop (1995e) 1 151 000. Capital of Madhya Pradesh, C India; founded, 1723; scene of a major industrial disaster in December 1984, when poisonous isocyanate gas escaped from the Union Carbide factory, killing c.2500 people and leaving 100 000 homeless; airfield; railway; university (1970). >> Madhya Pradesh

Bhutan [boo**tahn**], Dzongkha **Druk-yul**, official name **Kingdom of Bhutan** pop (1995e) 1 622 000; area 46 600 sq km/18 000 sq mi. Small state in the E Himalayas; capital, Thimphu; timezone GMT +5½; 305 km/189 mi from E to W; ethnic groups include Bhote (60%), Nepalese (25%), and indigenous or migrant tribes (15%); main religions, Lamaistic Buddhism (75%) and Buddhist-influenced Hinduism (25%); official language, Dzongkha; Nepalese and English also spoken; unit of currency, the ngultrum of 100 chetrums; Indian currency also legal tender; high peaks of E Himalayas in the N, over 7000 m/23 000 ft; forested mountain ridges with fertile valleys descend to low foothills in the S; many rivers flow to meet the R Brahmaputra; permanent snowfields and glaciers in the mountains; subtropical forest in the S; torrential rain common, average 1000 mm/40 in (C valleys) and 5000 mm/200 in (S); British involvement since treaty of 1774 with the East India Company; S part of the country annexed, 1865; Britain agreed not to interfere in internal affairs, 1910; similar treaty with India, 1949; governed by a maharajah, from 1907, now addressed as King of Bhutan; absolute monarchy replaced by a form of democratic monarchy, 1969; king is head of government; unicameral National Assembly; economy largely based on agriculture, mainly rice, wheat, maize, mountain barley, potatoes, vegetables, fruit (especially oranges); large area of plantation forest. >> Buddhism; East India Company, British; Himalayas; Thimphu; RR1002 political leaders

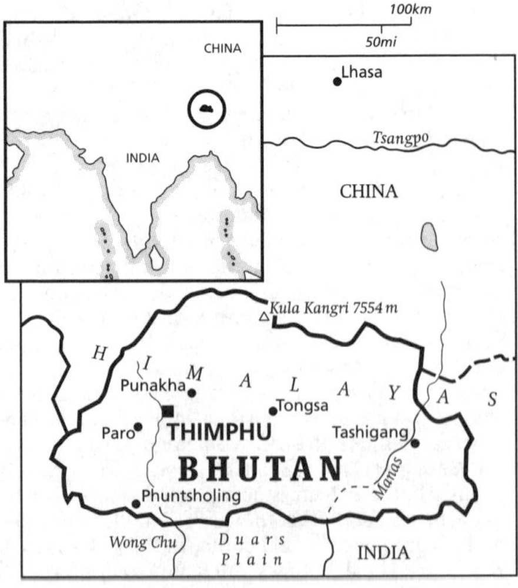

Bhutto, Benazir [**boo**toh] (1953–) Pakistani stateswoman and prime minister (1988–91, 1993–6), born in Karachi, the daughter of Zulfikar Ali Bhutto. Placed under house arrest (1977–84) by General Zia ul-Haq, she moved to England (1984–6), becoming the joint leader in exile of the Opposition Pakistan People's Party. She returned to Pakistan amid massive popular acclaim, and in 1987 was elected prime minister, but her party was defeated in 1991. She continued to be a prominent focus of Opposition discontent, and won a further election in 1993, but was replaced in 1996. In 1999, she received a 5-year jail sentance for corruption, along with her husband – a conviction which she contested from abroad. >> Bhutto, Zulfikar Ali; Zia ul-Haq

Bhutto, Zulfikar Ali [**boo**toh] (1928–79) Pakistani statesman, president (1971–3) and prime minister (1973–7), born in Larkana, Sind. He founded the Pakistan People's Party (PPP) in 1967, and after the secession of E Pakistan (now Bangladesh) in 1971, he became president. Opposition to his policies led to the army under General Zia ul-Haq seizing control after the 1977 elections. Tried for corruption and murder, he was sentenced to death in 1978. In spite of worldwide appeals for clemency, the sentence was carried out. >> Bangladesh i; Bhutto, Benazir; Pakistan i; Zia ul-Haq

Biafra [bia**fra**] The SE province of Nigeria, inhabited by the Igbo people. Under the leadership of Colonel Ojukwu, it attempted to break away from the federation, thus precipitating the civil war of 1967–70. >> Igbo; Nigeria i

Białystok [byawi**stok**] 53°09N 23°10E, pop (1995e) 267 000. Largest city in NE Poland; developed as a textile centre, 19th-c; devastated in World War 2; railway; medical academy. >> Poland i

Biarritz [**bee**arits] 43°29N 1°33W, pop (1995e) 29 800. Fashionable resort town in SW France, on Bay of Biscay; noted for its mild climate and beaches.

biathlon A combined test of cross-country skiing and rifle shooting. Men's individual competitions are over 10 km and 20 km (6·2 and 12·4 mi), while women's are over 5 km and 10 km (3·1 and 6·2 mi). At designated points on the course, competitors have to fire either standing or prone at a fixed target. >> shooting (recreation); skiing; RR1047

Bible Either the Christian Scripture or the Jewish Scripture, those works recognized as sacred and authoritative writings by the respective faiths. The Christian Scriptures are divided between two *testaments*: the Old Testament (which corresponds roughly to the canon of Jewish Scriptures), and the New Testament. The Old Testament, or **Hebrew Bible**, is a collection of writings originally composed in Hebrew, except for parts of Daniel and Ezra that are in Aramaic. These writings depict Israelite religion from its beginnings to about the 2nd-c BC. The New Testament is so-called in Christian circles because it is believed to constitute a new 'testament' or 'covenant' in the history of God's dealings with his people, centring on the ministry of Jesus and the early development of the apostolic churches. The New Testament writings were in Greek. >> Apocrypha, New Testament / Old Testament; Authorized Version of the Bible; canon (religion) 1; Christianity; Judaism; New Testament; Old Testament; Pseudepigrapha

bibliography 1 The study of the history, identification, and description of books, seen as physical objects, including the materials used and the methods of production (*critical* or *analytical* bibliography). **2** A book, or a list in a book, containing systematic details of an author's writings, or of publications on a given subject or period (*descriptive* or *enumerative* bibliography).

bicameral system A parliament of two chambers, which usually have different methods of election or selection. In some countries (such as the USA) the two chambers enjoy equal powers; but commonly one chamber enjoys supremacy over the legislative process, with the other enjoying powers of revision and delay (as in the UK). >> parliament

bicarbonate HCO_3^-, IUPAC **hydrogen carbonate**. The anion corresponding to half-neutralized carbonic acid. **Sodium bicarbonate**, or baking soda, is used with weak acids as a source of carbon dioxide. >> anion; carbon dioxide; carbonic acid

Bickerdyke, Mary Ann, *née* **Ball**, known as **Mother Bickerdyke** (1817–1901) Nurse and humanitarian, born in Knox Co, OH. When the Civil War broke out (1861) she volunteered to work as a nurse and caregiver both in battle and behind the lines, taking time out only to give speeches and gain support for the Sanitary Commission. She received a special pension from Congress in 1886. >> American Civil War

bicycle A light-framed vehicle possessing two wheels fitted with pneumatic tyres, the rear wheel being propelled by the rider through a crank, chain, and gear mechanism. It is generally held that the modern pedal bicycle was invented by Kirkpatrick Macmillan of Dumfriesshire, Scotland, and first ridden by him in 1840. The pneumatic tyre was invented by Robert William Thomson in 1845 and first successfully applied to the bicycle in 1888 by John Boyd Dunlop. >> gear; moped; motorcycle; tyre

Biennale [bee-e**nah**lay] An international art exhibition held in Venice regularly since 1895, and imitated at Paris, Tokyo, and elsewhere. Since 1948 it has been a major showcase for the avant garde.

biennial A plant which flowers, sets seed, and dies in its second year. In the first year it produces only vegetative growth, usually a rosette of leaves which build up food reserves for the onset of flowering. >> annual; perennial

Bierce, Ambrose (Gwinett) [beers] (1842–?1914) Journalist and writer, born in Meigs Co, OH. He was the author of collections of sardonically humorous tales on the theme of death, such as *In the Midst of Life* (1898).

Biffen, Sir Rowland Harry (1874–1949) Botanist and plant breeder, born in Cheltenham, Gloucestershire. The first director of the Cambridge Plant Breeding Institute in 1912, he was largely responsible for the foundation of the modern science of plant breeding.

bigamy A criminal offence committed when someone who is already married enters into 'marriage' with another person. The offence is not committed where the first marriage has been ended by divorce or death, or where it has been declared void. In some jurisdictions, there is also a good defence if the accused has, for a period of time (7 years, in England and Wales), not known that his or her first marriage partner was alive. >> annulment; divorce

'big bang' A hypothetical model of the universe which postulates that all matter and energy were once concentrated into an unimaginably dense state, or primaeval atom, from which it has been expanding since a creation event some 13–10 thousand million years ago. The main evidence favouring this model comes from cosmic background radiation and the redshifts of galaxies. Evidence of an expanding universe was announced by Edwin Hubble in 1929, and is now generally accepted. >> cosmology; Hubble; redshift; universe

Big Ben Originally the nickname of the bell in the clock tower of the Houses of Parliament, London, and now by association the clock and its tower. The bell, 2·7 m/9 ft in diameter and weighing 13 tonnes, was cast in 1858. >> Houses of Parliament

Big Dipper >> **Plough, the**

Bigfoot or **Sasquatch** In the mountaineering folklore of North America, a creature the equivalent of the abominable snowman or yeti, said to be 2–3 m/7–10 ft tall; its footprints are reported to be 43 cm/17 in long. >> yeti

Biggs, Ronald (1929–) British convicted thief, a member of the gang who perpetrated the Great Train Robbery in 1963. Sentenced to 25 years for conspiracy and 30 years (to run concurrently) for armed robbery, he escaped from Wandsworth Prison in 1965, fled to Australia, and eventually settled in Brazil. Attempts at extradition have failed.

bighorn A wild sheep, inhabiting mountains, especially cliffs; males with large curling horns; two species: **American bighorn sheep** (*Rocky Mountain sheep* or *Mountain sheep*) from North America (*Ovis canadensis*), and **Siberian bighorn** or **snow sheep** from NE Siberia (*Ovis nivicola*). >> sheep

Bihar or **Behar** [bee**hah(r)**] pop (1995e) 93 456 000; area 173 876 sq km/67 116 sq mi. State in E India, bounded N by Nepal; crossed by the R Ganges; capital, Patna; major mineral deposits, including coal, copper, mica. >> Buddh Gaya; India [i]; Patna

Bikini [bi**kee**nee] Atoll in the Marshall Is, W Pacific, 3200 km/2000 mi SW of Hawaii; site of 23 US nuclear tests, 1946–58; first H-bomb tested here (1952); inhabitants evacuated in 1946. >> atomic bomb; Marshall Islands

Biko, Stephen (Bantu) [**bee**koh], known as **Steve Biko** (1946–77) South African black activist, born in King William's Town. He was the founder and leader of the Black Consciousness Movement. In 1973 he was served with a banning order severely restricting his movements and freedom of speech and association. He died in police custody, allegedly as a result of beatings received. He was the subject of a successful film, *Cry Freedom* (1987), directed by Richard Attenborough. >> apartheid; Black Consciousness Movement

bilateralism >> **multilateralism**

Bilbao [bil**bow**] 43°16N 2°56W, pop (1995e) 372 000. Major seaport in N Spain, founded, 1300; bishopric; airport; railway; university (1886); cathedral (14th-c); commercial centre of the Basque Provinces. >> Basque Provinces; Spain [i]

bilberry A small deciduous shrub (*Vaccinium myrtillus*), native to acid soils in Europe and N Asia, especially on high ground where it may form bilberry moors; leaves oval, toothed; 1–2 flowers in leaf axils, drooping, globose, greenish-white; berry black with bluish-white bloom, sweet, edible. Alternative names are **blaeberry**, **whortleberry**, and (in the UK) **huckleberry**. (Family: Ericaceae). >> huckleberry

bilby >> **bandicoot**

bile A golden-yellow fluid produced by the liver. It is stored and concentrated in the gall bladder, until released into the duodenum in response to certain dietary substances (eg fats) in the duodenal cavity. >> alkali; cholecystitis; gallstones; jaundice; liver

bilharziasis [bilhah(r)**tsiy**asis] >> **schistosomiasis**

billiards An indoor table game played in many different forms. The most popular is that played on a standard English billiard table measuring c.12 ft × 6 ft (3·66 m × 1·83 m). It is played with three balls; one red and two white. Scoring is achieved by *potting* balls, *going in-off* another ball, and *making cannons* (hitting your white ball so that it successively strikes the two others). >> bagatelle; pool; snooker; RR1047

Billingsgate Market A fish-market in C London, dating from the 9th-c. Its name derived from a river-gate in the nearby city wall. The market was closed in 1982, and relocated further E, on the Isle of Dogs. >> London [i]

billion In earlier British usage, a million million (10^{12}); in US (and increasingly in technical international) usage, a thousand million (10^9). Because both senses are still encountered, however, many specialists avoid the term (and also *trillion* and other derivatives), preferring to state the numbers involved using superscripts, or in such a form as 'thousand million'. The latter usage is standard in this book.

bill of rights A list of citizens' rights set out in constitutional documents. Usually accompanying the document is an elaboration of the institutional means and powers by which such rights may be enforced. The best-known example is the first ten amendments to the US Constitution, adopted in 1791. >> constitution; Constitution of the United States; Declaration of Rights

Billy the Kid >> **Bonney, William H, Jr**

Biloxi [bi**lok**see] 30°24N 88°53W, pop (1995e) 48 200. Town in SE Mississippi, USA; named after an Indian tribe; settled, 1699; railway. >> Mississippi

bimetallic strip Two strips of different metals welded or riveted together face to face, which expand to different extents on heating because of their different coefficients of thermal expansion. This phenomenon can be used to actuate indicators or electric switches in response to changes in temperature. >> heat; metal

binary code A code derived from the binary number system using only two digits, 0 and 1, in comparison with the decimal system which has ten digits, 0 to 9. The advantage of the binary system for use in digital computers is that only two electronic states, off and on, are required to represent all the possible binary digits. >> ASCII code; bit

binary number A number written in base two, ie in which every number is expressed as the sum of powers of 2; thus 'seven' (in base ten) is $4 + 2 + 1 = 1 \times 2^2 + 1 \times 2^1 + 1$; thus $7_{ten} = 111_{two}$. >> base (mathematics); binary code

binary star Two stars revolving around their common centre of mass. Perhaps half of all stars in our Galaxy are members of binaries. >> black hole; eclipse 2; neutron star; star; X-rays

binary weapon An expression describing how a munition used in chemical warfare can be configured. Two individually harmless chemicals are packed separately into, for example, an artillery shell; these are combined on detonation to form a deadly toxic agent. >> chemical warfare

Binchy, Maeve [**bin**shee, mayv] (1940–) Writer, born in Dublin. She has written plays for television and the stage, but is most widely known as a romantic novelist. Her books include *Light a Penny Candle* (1982) and *The Glass Lake* (1994), and she has also written several volumes of short stories.

binding sites >> **receptors**

bindweed One of several related climbers with fleshy, rope-like roots, fast-growing twining stems, and large funnel-shaped flowers, all native to temperate regions; often pernicious weeds. *Convolvulus arvensis* is a coastal plant; leaves arrowhead-shaped; flowers pink, striped white above, maroon beneath. (Family: Convolvulaceae.) >> bract; climbing plant; sepal

Binet, Alfred [beenay] (1857–1911) Psychologist, born in Nice, France. He is principally remembered for the Binet–Simon scale (with colleague Théodore Simon) for measuring the intelligence of schoolchildren (1905) – the precursor of many of today's mental tests. >> intelligence; psychology

Binford, Lewis (Roberts) (1930–) US archaeologist, the acknowledged leader of the anthropologically-oriented school of archaeology which has powerfully influenced the discipline since the late 1960s. His works include *Bones* (1981) and *In Pursuit of the Past* (1983). >> anthropology; archaeology

bingo A game played by any number of people, using cards normally containing 15 squares numbered between 1 and 90. The caller picks numbers at random, and if players have the corresponding number on their card they eliminate it, usually by crossing it through. The first person(s) to eliminate all numbers is the winner, and is usually identified by calling out 'bingo' or 'house'. Known as **lotto** or **housey-housey** for many years, it became popularized as bingo in the 1960s.

binoculars A magnifying optical instrument for use by both eyes simultaneously; also known as **field-glasses**. Two optical systems are mounted together, each consisting of two convex lenses (an eyepiece and an object lens) plus prisms to produce an upright image. Focusing is achieved by varying the distance between eyepiece and object lens. >> lens; telescope ⓘ

binomial nomenclature The modern system of naming and classifying organisms, established by the Swedish naturalist Carl Linnaeus (1707–78) in the mid-18th-c. Every species has a unique scientific name (*binomen*) consisting of two words: a generic name and a specific name. For example, the scientific name of a lion is *Panthera leo* and that of the tiger *Panthera tigris*. They belong to the same genus, but are different species. >> systematics; taxonomy

binturong [bin**too**rong] A carnivorous mammal (*Arctictis binturong*), native to SE Asia; dense black fur, thickest on its grasping tail; tips of ears with prominent tufts; inhabits dense forests. (Family: Viverridae.) >> carnivore ⓘ; Viverridae ⓘ

Binyon, (Robert) Laurence (1869–1943) Poet and art critic, born in Lancaster, Lancashire. Extracts from his poem 'For the Fallen' (set to music by Elgar) adorn war memorials throughout the British Commonwealth.

bioassay [biyoha**say**] The measurement of amounts or activities of substances (such as the concentration of pollutants) using the responses of living organisms or cells; an abbreviation of **biological assay**. >> biological sciences; pollution

biochemistry The branch of biology dealing with the chemistry of living organisms, especially with the structure and function of their chemical components. >> biological sciences

biodegradable substance Any substance that can be decomposed by natural processes, particularly microbial decay, so that its constituents are rendered available for use within the ecosystem. >> ecosystem; micro-organism

biodiversity A term used to cover the total variety of genetic strains, species, and ecosystems in the world, which change with evolution. A treaty to preserve biodiversity, including the sustainable development of biological resources, was signed at the Earth Summit in 1992. >> Earth Summit

biofeedback A technique by which an individual can learn to control autonomic responses (ie those not usually under conscious control) by using monitoring devices to give information about the results of current and past performance. For example, training in this way using an electroencephalogram can encourage the production of alpha brain waves which are associated with well-being and relaxation. >> autonomic nervous system; electroencephalography; feedback

biogas A gas produced by the fermentation of organic waste. Decomposition of animal manure, crop residues, and food processing wastes in an airtight container produces a methane-rich gas which can be used as a source of energy. >> alternative energy; energy; waste disposal

biogeography The geographical study of the distribution of animals and plants at global, regional, and local scales. In particular it examines the factors responsible for their changing distribution in both time and space. >> ecology; geography; phytogeography; zoogeography

biography The narrative of a person's life. In classical and mediaeval times, biographical writing tended to be exemplary lives of kings, heroes, and saints, with little concern for the personal subject. But the Protestant and democratic spirit conferred greater value on the individual; Dr Johnson maintained that the narrative of any person's life would be worth reading. >> Boswell; Johnson, Samuel; literature

Bioko [bee**o**koh], formerly **Fernando Po** or **Póo** (to 1973), **Macías Nguema Bijogo** (to 1979) pop (1995e) 82 700; area 2017 sq km/779 sq mi. Island off coast of Cameroon, W Africa; province of Equatorial Guinea; volcanic origin, rising to 3007 m/9865 ft at Pico de Basilé; chief town, and capital of Equatorial Guinea, Malabo; visited by Portuguese, 1471; originally named after Portuguese navigator; coffee, cocoa, copra. >> Equatorial Guinea ⓘ; Malabo

biological assay >> **bioassay**

biological rhythm or **biorhythm** The rhythmical change in a biological function of a plant or animal. The frequency of rhythms varies from short (eg less than a second) to long (eg more than a year). Many rhythms arise from within organisms; others are entirely dependent upon external environmental factors (such as the alternation of light and dark). Examples of biological rhythms in humans are breathing, sleep, and waking. >> circadian rhythm; jet lag; menstruation

biological sciences Specialized study areas which have developed to study living organisms and systems. All biological sciences are based on *taxonomy*, the description, naming, and classification of living organisms as a means of creating order out of the diversity of the natural world. The study of the distribution of organisms throughout the world is **biogeography**. The chemical processes that occur within living systems are studied as a whole (**biochemistry**) or at the level of interactions between large organic molecules (**molecular biology**). Functional aspects of living systems are the subject of disciplines such as **physiology** and **biophysics**. The study of the comparative behaviour of animals is known as **ethology**. **Genetics** encompasses heredity and variation. The study of the relationship between organisms and their environment is **ecology**. Each major group of organisms is the basis of its own special study area, such as bacteria (**bacteriology**), plants (**botany**), and animals (**zoology**). >> amphibian; animal; bacteria ⓘ; biochemistry; biophysics; bird ⓘ; cell; crustacean; ecology; ethology; evolution; fish ⓘ; fungus; genetics; insect ⓘ; mammal ⓘ; molecular biology; palaeontology; parasitology; plant; pollen; radiobiology; reptile; seaweed; shell; sociobiology; systematics; taxonomy; virus; zoology

biological shield A protective enclosure around the radioactive core of a nuclear reactor, to prevent the escape of radiation capable of damaging biological tissue. It usually consists mainly of massive concrete walls. >> nuclear reactor ⓘ

biological value In food science, the nutritional value of a protein, which depends upon the balance of amino acids it contains. Animal proteins such as egg have a high value, while vegetable proteins such as gluten have a low value. >> amino acid; gluten; protein

biological warfare An expression that embraces *bacteriological warfare*, which uses naturally occurring micro-organisms as a weapon of war, and *toxins*, which are poisonous chemicals derived from natural sources. The manufacture and stockpiling of such agents is forbidden by a UN Convention of 1972, although research is allowed to continue. >> bacteriological warfare; chemical warfare; toxin

biology The study of living organisms and systems. The beginnings of biology as a science are the natural history observations made by all who are in contact with the natural world. Its rapid development during the 20th-c has led to the increasing subdivision of biology into a variety of specialized disciplines. >> biological sciences

bioluminescence The light produced by living organisms through a chemical reaction, and the process of emitting such biologically produced light. It can be found in some bacteria, fungi, algae, and animals such as deep-sea fishes, squid, fireflies, and glow-worms. It serves a variety of functions, such as signalling during courtship rituals and locating prey in the dark. >> biology; light; luminescence

biome [**biy**ohm] A major regional subdivision of the Earth's surface, broadly corresponding to the dominant ecological communities of the main climatic regions. Biomes are the largest recognized living communities classified on a geographical basis, such as tundra, desert, and tropical rainforest. >> ecology

biomorphic art A type of abstract art based on shapes which vaguely resemble plants and animals. The most celebrated exponent was Hans Arp. >> abstract art; Arp; art

Biondi, Matt(hew) [by**on**dee] (1965–) Swimmer, born in Morego, CA. At the 1986 world championships he won a record seven medals, including three golds, and at the 1988 Olympics won seven medals, including five golds. >> swimming

bionics The construction of artificial mechanisms, models, circuits, or programs imitating the responses or behaviour of living systems. Its purpose is to adapt observed living functions to practical purposes in useful machines. >> automation; cybernetics

bionomics The study of organisms in relation to their environment. The term is used particularly with reference to ecological studies of single species. >> ecology

biophysics The application of physics to the study of living organisms and systems. It includes the study of the mechanical properties of biological tissues and their functional significance. >> biology; physics

biopsy [**biy**opsee] The surgical removal of a small piece of tissue (eg from the skin, breast, or kidney) in order to determine the nature of any suspected disease process. >> pathology

biorhythms >> **biological rhythm**

biosphere That part of the Earth's surface and atmosphere in which living organisms are found, and with which they interact to form the global ecosystem. >> Earth [i]; ecosystem

biotechnology The application of biological and biochemical science to large-scale production. Examples include the large-scale production of penicillin in the 1940s, and research in genetic engineering. >> biochemistry; biology; genetic engineering; pharmacy

biotin One of the B vitamins, found in yeast and in the bacteria which inhabit the human gut. It acts as a co-factor in the synthesis of fatty acids and the conversion of amino acids to glucose. >> polyunsaturated fatty acids

biotite >> **micas**

birch A slender deciduous tree, occasionally a dwarf shrub, native to the N hemisphere; branches often pendulous, leaves ovoid, toothed; catkins pendulous, males long, females shorter, becoming cone-like in fruit; nutlets tiny with papery wings. (Genus: *Betula*, 60 species. Family: Betulaceae.) >> paper-bark birch; silver birch; tree [i]

bird A vertebrate animal assignable to the class Aves; any animal in which the adult bears feathers. The fore-limbs of birds are modified as wings; teeth are absent; and the projecting jaws are covered by horny sheaths to produce a bill or 'beak'. The female lays eggs with hard chalky shells. Flight has dominated the evolution of the birds, and their bodies are adapted accordingly. The bones of most birds are hollow, reducing weight; much of the wing and all of the tail is composed entirely of long feathers, these being strong but very light. The body is streamlined with a smooth covering of short overlapping feathers. Flight has also controlled size: no bird capable of horizontal flight in still air weighs more than 13 kg/30 lb. Larger birds, such as the modern ostrich (up to 150 kg/330 lb), are flightless. Birds evolved from reptiles approximately 150 million years ago. There are approximately 8600 living species of birds, and specialists indicate their relationships by grouping them into 29 orders and 181 families. >> bird of prey; dinosaur [i]; feather [i]; nest; Ratitae; *see illustration on p.97*

bird cherry >> **gean**

bird of paradise A stout-billed, strong-footed bird native to SE Asian forests. The males use spectacular plumage to attract females. (Family: Paradisaeidae, 43 species.) >> bowerbird

bird of prey Any bird that hunts large animals (especially mammals and birds) for food; also known as a **raptor**. They have a strong, curved bill and sharp claws. >> bird [i]; condor; eagle; falcon; hawk; owl; secretary bird; vulture

Birdseye, Clarence (1886–1956) Businessman and inventor, born in New York City. He is best known for developing a process for freezing food in small packages suitable for retailing. He became president of Birdseye Frosted Foods (1930–4) and of the Birdseye Electric Company (1935–8). Some 300 patents are credited to him. >> food preservation

bird's-foot trefoil A perennial growing to 40 cm/15 in (*Lotus corniculatus*), native to Europe, Asia, and Africa; leaves with five oval leaflets; pea-flowers in stalked, rather flat-topped clusters of 2–8, yellow often tinged with red; pods up to 3 cm/1¼ in long, many-seeded; also called **eggs and bacon**. (Family: Leguminosae.) >> trefoil

birefringence A property exhibited by certain crystals, in which the speed of light is different in different directions because of the crystal structure; also called **double refraction**. Birefringent crystals such as calcite and quartz have two refractive indices, and can form double images. >> liquid crystals

bireme [**biy**reem] A galley, usually Greek or Roman, propelled by two banks of oars, rowed by slaves or criminals. It was also equipped with a square sail for use with a favourable wind. >> ship [i]; trireme [i]

Birgitta, St >> **Bridget, Brigit**, or **Birgitta** (of Sweden), **St**

Birkbeck, George (1776–1841) Educationist, born in Settle, North Yorkshire. He took a leading part in the formation of the London Mechanics' or Birkbeck Institute (1824), now Birkbeck College, part of London University. >> London University [i]

Birmingham (UK) [**ber**mingm] 52°30N 1°50W, pop (1995e) 1 018 000. City in West Midlands, C England; Britain's second largest city; developed rapidly in the Industrial Revolution in an area with a large supply of iron ore and coal; heavily bombed in World War 2; railway; airport; three universities (Birmingham, 1900; Aston, 1966; Central England, 1992); National Exhibition Centre; cathedral (1839); football league teams, Aston Villa (Villa), Birmingham City (Blues), nearby West Bromwich Albion (Baggies), Walsall (Saddlers). >> West Midlands

Birmingham (USA) [**ber**mingham] 33°31N 86°48W, pop (1995e) 282 000. City in NC Alabama, USA; settled, 1813; civil rights protests in the 1960s; airfield; railway; university (1842); leading iron and steel centre in the S. >> Alabama; civil rights

Birmingham Six Six men convicted and sentenced to life imprisonment in 1975 for the bombing of two public

Birds – (1) ostrich, showing undeveloped wing and and flat sternum; (2) seagull, showing wing development and sternum with keel.
Feet adapted for (3) walking, (4) perching, (5) climbing, (6) hunting, (7) swimming.
Bills adapted for (8) preying, (9) spearing fish, (10) eating seeds and nuts, (11) nectar-feeding, (12) eating insects.

houses in Birmingham, England, in which 21 people died. After a lengthy campaign by their supporters, they were freed by the Court of Appeal for England and Wales in 1991 and had their convictions quashed.

Biró, Lazlo [bi**ro**] (1899–1985) Hungarian inventor. Realizing the advantage of quick-drying ink he developed the ballpoint pen, to which eventually his name was applied – the **biro** [**biy**roh]. >> pen

Birt, Sir John (1944–) Broadcasting executive, born in Liverpool, Merseyside. He joined Granada Television (1968), and worked on the public affairs programme *World in Action* before moving to London Weekend Television (1971). He became director-general of the BBC in 1993, and initiated a radical and controversial programme of reforms ('Birtism'), including a market-driven approach to programme-making. He received an Emmy in 1995. >> BBC; Emmy

birth control >> **contraception**

birthmark A skin blemish present at birth; also known as a **naevus/nevus**. There are two main causes: an accumulation of melanocytes (skin pigment cells) known as *moles*, which vary in colour from light brown to black; and a benign enlargement of blood and lymph vessels, the most common of which are 'strawberry marks' and 'port-wine stains'. >> lymph; melanins; mole (medicine)

Birtwistle, Sir Harrison (1934–) Composer, born in Accrington, Lancashire. Among his later works are the operas *Punch and Judy* (1966–7) and *The Mask of Orpheus* (produced 1986), and *Slow Frieze* (1996). In 1975 he became musical director of the National Theatre, and in 1993 composer in residence to the London Philharmonic Orchestra at the South Bank Centre.

Biscay, Bay of, Span **Golfe de Vizcaya**, Fr **Golfe de Gascogne** area 220 000 sq km/85 000 sq mi. Arm of the Atlantic Ocean, known for strong currents and sudden storms; major fishing region. >> Atlantic Ocean

Bishkek, formerly **Pishpek** (to 1926), **Frunze** (to 1991) 42°54N 74°46E, pop (1995e) 657 000. Capital city of Kyrgyzstan; altitude, 750–900 m/2500–3000 ft; founded, 1825; airport; railway; university (1951). >> Kyrgyzstan i

bishop An ecclesiastical office, probably equivalent to pastor or presbyter in the New Testament, and thereafter generally an ordained priest consecrated as the spiritual ruler of a diocese in Orthodox, Roman Catholic, and Episcopal Churches. The issue of whether women as well as men may be consecrated bishop aroused great controversy at the end of the 1980s, especially following the first such appointment (Rev Barbara Harris, as Bishop of Massachusetts) by the Episcopal Church of the United States in 1989. >> archbishop; Christianity; episcopacy; Reformation

Bishops' Wars Two wars between Charles I of England and the Scottish Covenanters, caused by his unpopular policies towards the Scottish Kirk. They resulted in English defeats, and bankruptcy for Charles, who was forced to call the Short and Long Parliaments in 1640. >> Charles I (of England); Covenanters; Long Parliament

Bismarck 46°48N 100°47W, pop (1995e) 49 300. Capital of state in North Dakota, USA; established, 1873 (named after the German statesman); territorial capital, 1883; state capital, 1889; airfield; railway; trade and distribution centre for agricultural region. >> North Dakota

Bismarck, Otto Eduard Leopold, Fürst von (Prince of) (1815–98) The first chancellor of the German Empire (1871–90), born in Schönhausen, Germany. Appointed prime minister in 1862, he became a guiding figure during the Schleswig-Holstein question and the war between Prussia and Austria. He was made a count in 1866, and created a prince and chancellor of the new German Empire. After the Peace of Frankfurt (1871), his policies aimed at consolidating and protecting the young Empire. In 1879, to counteract Russia and France, he formed the Austro-German Treaty of Alliance, which was later joined by Italy. Called the 'Iron Chancellor', he resigned the chancellorship in 1890, out of disapproval of Emperor William II's policy. >> Franco-Prussian War; Kulturkampf; Prussia; William II (Emperor)

Bismarck Archipelago pop (1995e) 424 000; area 49 709 sq km/19 188 sq mi. Island group, part of Papua New Guinea; main islands, New Britain, New Ireland, Admiralty Is, and Lavongai; mountainous, with several active volcanoes; annexed by Germany, 1884; mandated territory of Australia, 1920; occupied by Japan in World War 2; part of UN Trust Territory of New Guinea until 1975; chief town, Rabaul, on New Britain. >> Admiralty Islands; New Britain; New Ireland

bismuth [**biz**muhth] Bi, element 83. The heaviest element with stable isotopes, a metalloid which melts at 271°C, but forms alloys with much lower melting points. >> alloy; chemical elements; metalloids; RR1036

bison A large mammal which inhabits forest and grassland; stocky; large hairy hump on shoulders; short upcurved horns; chin with beard; two species: the **American bison**, also called **boss** or (incorrectly) **buffalo** (*Bison bison*), and the **European bison** or **wisent** (*Bison bonasus*). The American bison has been crossbred with cattle to produce the hybrid *cattalo*. (Family: Bovidae.) >> Bovidae; cattle

Bissau [bee**sow**] 11°52N 15°39W, pop (1995e) 144 000. Seaport capital of Guinea-Bissau, W Africa; established as a fortified slave-trading centre, 1687; free port, 1869; capital moved here from Bolama, 1941; airport; cathedral. >> Guinea-Bissau ℹ

bit An abbreviation of **Binary digIT**. A bit may take only one of the two possible values in the binary number system, 0 or 1. All operations in digital computers take place using the binary number system. >> binary code; byte; digital computer

BITNET [**bit**net] A data communications network linking computers in academic institutions, particularly outside Europe. The extension of BITNET in Europe is called EARN (European Academic Research Network). >> computer network; electronic mail

Bitola or **Bitolj** [**bee**tola], Turkish **Monastir** 41°01N 21°21E, pop (1995e) 159 000. Town in the Former Yugoslav Republic of Macedonia; under Turkish rule until 1912; second largest town in Macedonia; railway; carpets, textiles, tourism. >> Macedonia, Former Yugoslav Republic of ℹ

bitonality The property of music written in two keys simultaneously. The piquant dissonances that usually result were cherished particularly by *Les Six* in France during the first half of the 20th-c. >> *Six, Les*; tonality

bittern A marsh-dwelling bird, widespread; heron-like but stouter, with shorter legs and neck; mottled brown plumage. (Family: Ardeidae, 12 species.) >> heron

bittersweet >> **woody nightshade**

bitumen 1 A mixture of tar-like hydrocarbons derived from petroleum either naturally or by distillation. It is black or brown and varies from viscous to solid, when it is also known as **asphalt**. It is used in road-making. >> petroleum **2** In art, a transparent, brown pigment made from tar, popular with painters in the 18th-c. Unfortunately, it never dries, but turns black and develops wide traction-cracks which are difficult to repair. >> paint

bivalve An aquatic mollusc with a body compressed sideways and enclosed within a shell consisting of two valves joined by a flexible ligament along a hinge line; typically feeds on small particles collected by large gills covered with tiny hairs (*cilia*); class contains over 20 000 species, many of great economic importance, such as oysters, clams, and mussels; also known as **lamellibranchs** and **pelecypods**. (Class: Pelecypoda.) >> calcium; clam; larva; mollusc; mussel; oyster; plankton; shell

Bizerte or **Bizerta** [bi**zer**tuh], Lat **Hippo Diarrhytus** 37°18N 9°52E, pop (1995e) 159 000. City in N Tunisia on the Mediterranean coastline; occupied by Romans, Vandals, Arabs, Moors, Spanish, and French (1881); German base in World War 2, heavily bombed; French naval base until 1963; railway. >> Tunisia ℹ

Bizet, Georges [**bee**zay], originally **Alexandre César Léopold Bizet** (1838–75) Composer, born in Paris. His incidental music to Daudet's play *L'Arlésienne* (1872) was remarkably popular, and survived in the form of two orchestral suites. His masterpiece was the opera *Carmen* (1875).

Björling, Jussi [**byer**ling], originally **Johan Jonaton Björling** (1911–60) Tenor, born in Stora Tuna, Sweden. He sang frequently at the Metropolitan Opera, New York, and made numerous recordings.

Black, Sir James (1924–) Pharmacologist, born in Uddingston, Scotland. His work led in 1964 to the discovery of beta-blockers and in 1972 to advances in the treatment of stomach ulcers. He shared the Nobel Prize for Physiology or Medicine in 1988. >> beta-blockers; heart ℹ; pharmacology; ulcer

Black and Tans Additional members of the Royal Irish Constabulary, recruited by the British government to cope with Irish national unrest in 1920. The shortage of regulation uniforms led to the recruits being issued with khaki tunics and trousers and very dark green caps, hence their name.

black bear Either of two species of bear, usually black but sometimes brown in colour; the **American black bear** from North America (*Ursus americanus*), and the **Asiatic black bear**, **Himalayan bear**, or **moon bear** from S and E Asia, with a white chin and white 'V' on chest (Selenarctos thibetanus). >> bear

black beetle A dark beetle found in cellars and outhouses; larvae cylindrical; feeds on plant material. (Order: Coleoptera. Family: Tenebrionidae.) >> beetle; larva

blackberry A scrambling prickly shrub (*Rubus fruticosus*) with arching, biennial stems rooting at the tips; native to the Mediterranean region; flowers numerous, 5-petalled, white or pale pink; also known as **bramble**. The 'berry' is an aggregate of 1-seeded carpels, not separating from the core-like receptacle when ripe. (Family: Rosaceae.)

blackbird A thrush native to Europe, N Africa, and S and W Asia (*Turdus merula*.); male black with yellow bill; female brown. >> grackle; ouzel; thrush (bird)

black box A complete unit in an electronics or computer system whose circuitry need not be fully understood by the user. The name is commonly used for the flight data recorder in an aircraft: this collects information about the aircraft's performance during a flight, which can be used to help determine the cause of a crash. >> aircraft ℹ; computer

black bryony A perennial climber (*Tamus communis*) with a large, black tuber, related to the yam, native to Europe, W Asia, and N Africa; stems grow to 4 m/13 ft, twining; flowers tiny, 6-lobed, yellowish-green; berry red. (Family: Dioscoreaceae.) >> yam

blackbuck A gazelle native to India and Pakistan (*Antilope cervicapra*); inhabits plains and scrubland; adult males blackish-brown with white chin, white disc around eye, and white underparts; horns long, spiralling, ringed with ridges; females pale brown, hornless. >> antelope; gazelle ℹ

black consciousness An attitude, particularly in the USA, which asserts that African-Americans, by virtue of their ethnicity and history, possess a cultural tradition distinct from the wider population. Proponents aim to raise the awareness of blacks by espousing and publicizing these cultural traditions and values.

Black Consciousness Movement A movement formed by Steve Biko in 1969, when he founded the South African Students Organization. From this emerged the Black Peoples' Convention, which sought to create co-operation in social and cultural fields among all non-white peoples. Most of its leaders were imprisoned in 1977. >> apartheid; Biko; black consciousness

Black Country The industrial area of the English Midlands during and after the Industrial Revolution. It lies to the NW of Birmingham, in SW Staffordshire and N Hereford and Worcester. >> Industrial Revolution; Potteries, the

blackcurrant An aromatic species of currant (*Ribes nigrum*) native to Europe and temperate Asia. It is widely cultivated, producing edible black berries on new wood. (Family: Grossulariaceae.) >> currant

Black Death The name given to the virulent bubonic and pneumonic plague which swept through W and C Europe from Asia (1347–51). Approximately 25 million people, about a third of the population, perished. >> plague

black economy In the UK, a term used for economic activities not reported to tax and other public authorities; also referred to as the **underground economy** or (in the USA) as 'off the books' activities. This allows one or both parties to avoid paying tax and/or social security contributions, and may conceal breaches of laws concerning such matters as job security, health and safety, and work permits. >> taxation

Blackett, Patrick M(aynard) S(tuart) Blackett, Baron (1897–1974) Physicist, born in London. He was the first to photograph nuclear collisions involving transmutation (1925), and in 1932 independently discovered the positron. He pioneered research on cosmic radiation, for which he was awarded the Nobel Prize for Physics in 1948. >> cosmic rays

black-eyed Susan 1 A slender annual climber (*Thunbergia alata*) native to S Africa; stems twining to 2 m/6½ ft; leaves opposite, heart-shaped; flowers tubular with five spreading bright-yellow lobes, and a dark purplish or black central eye. (Family: Acanthaceae.) **2** In North America, members of the genus *Rudbeckia*. >> rudbeckia

blackfish >> **pilot whale**

blackfly A black-bodied aphid which feeds by sucking plant sap. (Order: Homoptera. Family: Aphididae.) >> aphid

black fly A small biting fly found near running water; larvae aquatic; also known as **buffalo gnat**. The females of some species are blood-suckers, and serious cattle pests. (Order: Diptera. Family: Simuliidae.) >> blackfly; fly; larva

Blackfoot Three Algonkin Indian Groups (Blackfoot, Blood, Piegan) originally from the E who settled in Montana, USA and Alberta, Canada. Famous hunters and trappers. Population now c.32 000 (1990 census), chiefly on reservations. >> Algonkin

Black Forest, Ger **Schwarzwald** Mountain range in Germany; extends 160 km/100 mi; highest peak, the Feldberg (1493 m/4898 ft). >> Germany ℹ

Black Friars >> **Dominicans**

black grouse A grouse native to upland areas of N Europe and N Asia (*Tetrao tetrix*); the male (**blackcock**) black with a red comb above each eye; the female (**greyhen**) brown. (Family: Phasianidae.) >> grouse

black gum >> **tupelo**

Black Hand A secret organization formed in Serbia in 1911, led by army officers, whose objective was the achievement of Serbian independence from Austria and Turkey. It planned the assassination of Archduke Francis Ferdinand of Austria in Sarajevo in June 1914. >> World War 1

black hole A region of spacetime from which matter and energy cannot escape; in origin, a star or galactic nucleus that has collapsed in on itself to the point where its escape velocity exceeds the speed of light. Its boundary is known as the *event horizon*: light generated inside the event horizon can never escape. >> binary star; light; star; X-rays

Black Hole of Calcutta A small, badly-ventilated room in which surviving British defenders were imprisoned overnight in an incident following Calcutta's capture (June 1756) by Siraj ud Daula, Nawab of Bengal. It was claimed that only 23 out of 146 prisoners survived. The incident became famous in the history of British imperialism, but its status is controversial, as the total number involved was probably much smaller.

blackjack A popular casino card game. The object is to accumulate a score of 21 with at least two cards (scoring 21 with a picture card and an ace is called a blackjack). There are several variations. >> pontoon

blackleg A debilitating disease of cattle and sheep, characterized by swollen legs; can be fatal; also known as **black legs** or **black quarter**.

black letter writing A style of writing, common in the mediaeval period, which formed the basis of early models of printers' type in Germany; sometimes called **Gothic**. It had relatively straight strokes in its letters. >> chirography; graphology

blackmail The making of an unwarranted demand with menaces. The demand must be made with a view to either personal gain or loss to someone else. In the USA, many state penal codes subsume this offence under a general theft statute as theft by *extortion* (a term also used in Scotland). >> theft

black market An illegal trade in goods or currencies. The practice is well known in countries where there is rationing or restriction on the availability of food, petrol, clothing, and other essential commodities. These may be difficult or impossible to obtain using legal channels, but may be available (at a much higher price) 'on the black market'.

black Mass A blasphemous caricature of the Roman Catholic Mass, in which terms and symbols are distorted, and Satan is worshipped instead of God. >> blasphemy; Devil; Mass

Blackmore, R(ichard) D(oddridge) (1825–1900) Novelist, born in Longworth, Oxfordshire. He wrote 15 novels, mostly with a Devonshire background, of which *Lorna Doone* (1869) is his masterpiece.

Black Mountain poetry A school of poetry started in the 1950s by Charles Olson (1910–70), one-time rector of Black Mountain College in North Carolina, USA. It included such names as Robert Creeley (1926–) and Robert Duncan (1919–88).

Black Muslims A black separatist movement in the USA, founded in 1930 by W D Fard, Elijah Mohammed (1925–75); also known at different times as the **Nation of Islam**, the **American Muslim Mission**, and the **World Community of Islam in the West**. The movement holds that black Americans are descended from an ancient Muslim tribe. Members of the movement adopted Muslim names, and demanded a separate state for blacks. Malcolm X (*né* Little) was one of their foremost preachers, while Cassius Clay (Muhammad Ali) is undoubtedly the most famous member of the movement. They now repudiate their early separatism. >> Ali, Muhammad; civil rights; Islam

Black Pagoda >> **Sun Temple**

Black Panthers A militant, revolutionary African-American organization in the USA, founded in the late 1960s after the murder of Martin Luther King, Jr. The organization preached violence and acted as a protector of blacks. It rapidly went into decline with the arrest and exile of many of its leaders. >> King, Martin Luther

Blackpool 53°50N 3°03W, pop (1995e) 156 000. Town in NW Lancashire, NW England; unitary authority from 1998; the largest holiday resort in N England; railway; conference centre; Tower (based on Eiffel Tower); football league team, Blackpool (Tangerines); illuminations (autumn). >> Lancashire

Black Prince >> **Edward the Black Prince**

Black Rod In the UK, since 1522, an official of the House of Lords. One of his chief ceremonial functions is to act as the official messenger from the Lords to the House of Commons. By tradition dating from 1643, to gain entrance to the Commons he must knock three times with his ebony staff of office (the black rod). >> Lords, House of

black rust >> **barberry**

Black Sea, ancient **Pontius Euxinus** (Euxine Sea), Bulgarian **Cherno More**, Romanian **Marea Neagra**, Russian **Chernoye More**, Turkish **Karadeniz** area 507 900 sq km/ 196 000 sq mi. Inland sea between Europe and Asia, connected to the Mediterranean (SW) by the Bosporus, Sea of Marmara, and Dardanelles; 1210 km/752 mi long by 120–560 km/75–350 mi wide, maximum depth 2246 m/ 7369 ft; largest arm, Sea of Azov; opened by Treaty of Paris, 1856, to commerce of all nations, and closed to ships of war; now increasingly polluted; states bordering Black Sea met in Istanbul, 1992, to establish a new trading zone (Black Sea Economic Co-operation Project). >> Azov, Sea of

blackshirts The colloquial name for members of Oswald Mosley's British Union of Fascists (BUF), formed in October 1932. It derived from the colour of the uniforms worn at mass rallies and demonstrations. >> fascism; Mosley

Blackstone, Sir William (1723–80) Jurist, born in London. In 1765–9 he published his influential *Commentaries on the Laws of England*, the first comprehensive description of the principles of English law.

blackthorn A deciduous spiny shrub (*Prunus spinosa*) growing to 6 m/20 ft; flowers white, appearing before ovoid, toothed leaves; fruits (**sloes**) globular, blue-black with waxy bloom, edible but very tart; native to Europe. (Family: Rosaceae.) >> prunus

Black Watch A famous Highland regiment of the British Army, first raised in 1704. The name derives from their distinctive, very dark tartan. >> army

blackwater fever An illness that has almost disappeared, but is still found among whites in the tropics; it occurs in cases of untreated or inadequately treated malaria due to *Plasmodium falciparum*. The breakdown of red blood cells in the circulation allows the passage of the pigment haemoglobin into the urine, resulting in its dark colour. >> malaria

Blackwell, Elizabeth (1821–1910) Physician and feminist, born in Bristol. She was responsible both for opening medical education to her sex and for establishing an infirmary for the poor of New York City. From 1869 she lived in England, founding the London School of Medicine for Women. >> women's liberation movement

black widow A medium-sized, dark-coloured spider, found in warm regions worldwide. Its bite is venomous, causing severe pain, nausea, and breathing difficulties. It is occasionally fatal. (Order: Araneae. Family: Theridiidae.) >> spider

Blackwood, Algernon Henry (1869–1951) Writer, born in Shooter's Hill, Kent. His novels and stories reflect his taste for the occult, such as *Tales of the Uncanny and Supernatural* (1949).

Black Zionism The term applied to quasi-nationalist, messianic movements founded among African-Americans and West Indians. Africa is held in reverence, and there is a desire to return to the land of their forefathers.

bladder A rounded muscular organ situated behind the front of the pelvis (the *symphysis pubis*), but in children extending upwards into the abdominal cavity. The bladder receives urine from the kidneys via the ureters for temporary storage and eventual expulsion via the urethra (its capacity is c.600 ml/1·05 UK pt/1·3 US pt). >> cystitis; pelvis; urinary system

bladderwort A mostly aquatic carnivorous plant with finely divided leaves, the segments bearing tiny bladders; flowers 2-lipped, spurred, borne on a slender spike projecting above the water surface. The prey are insects or crustacea such as *Daphnia*; each bladder has a trap-door triggered when sensitive hairs are touched, sucking in the prey before the door closes again. (Genus: *Utricularia*, 120 species. Family: Utriculariaceae.) >> carnivorous plant; crustacean

blaeberry >> **bilberry**

Blaenau Gwent [**bliy**niy **gwent**] pop (1995e) 73 300; area 109 sq km / 42 sq mi. County (unitary authority from 1996) in SE Wales, UK; administrative centre, Ebbw Vale; former coal mining area. >> Wales ℹ

Blainey, Geoffrey Norman (1930–) Social historian, born in Melbourne, Victoria, Australia. *The Tyranny of Distance* (1966), *Triumph of the Nomads* (1975), and *A Land Half Won* (1980) formed a trilogy, *A Vision of Australian History*. Through his books and a television programme, *The Blainey View*, he became well known in the 1980s.

Blair, Tony, popular name of **Anthony Charles Lynton Blair** (1953–) British politician and prime minister (1997–), born in Edinburgh. He became a barrister and was elected Labour MP for Sedgefield in 1983. He joined the shadow cabinet in 1988, becoming shadow secretary of state for energy (1988), employment (1989), and home affairs (1992). He became leader of the Labour Party in 1994, and led it to power in a landslide victory in 1997. His wife, **Cherie Blair** is also a barrister. >> Labour Party (UK); New Labour

Blake, Nicholas >> **Day-Lewis, Cecil**

Blake, Robert (1599–1657) English admiral, born in Bridgwater, Somerset. In 1649 he blockaded Lisbon, and in 1652–3 routed the Dutch in several battles. His greatest victory was at Santa Cruz, when he destroyed a Spanish treasure fleet off Tenerife; but he died on the return journey to England.

Blake, William (1757–1827) Poet, painter, engraver, and mystic, born in London. His first book of poems, the *Poetical Sketches* (1783), was followed by *Songs of Innocence* (1789) and *Songs of Experience* (1794), which express his ardent belief in the freedom of the imagination. These ideas found their fullest expression in his prophetic poems, especially *Jerusalem* (1804–20). His finest artistic work is to be found in the 21 *Illustrations to the Book of Job* (1826).

Blakey, Art [**blay**kee], popular name of **Arthur Blakey**, also known as **Abdulla Ibn Buhaina** (1919–90) Jazz drummmer and bandleader, born in Pittsburgh, PA. From the late 1940s he led groups under the name of the Jazz Messengers, playing 'hard bop', and introducing many future stars of jazz. >> bebop; jazz

Blanc, Mel (1908–89) Entertainer, born in Los Angeles, CA. For over fifty years he provided the voices for some of the most famous cartoon characters including Bugs Bunny, Daffy Duck, Sylvester, and Tweety Pie. He took over the voice of the stammering Porky Pig ('Th-th-th-that's all, folks') in 1937, and in 1940 created the laugh for Woody Woodpecker. He was the voice of Barney Rubble in the television cartoon series *The Flintstones* (1960–66).

Blanc, Mont >> **Mont Blanc**

Blanda, (George) Frederick (1927–) Player of American football, born in Youngwood, PA. He played for the Chicago Bears (1949), the American Football League Houston Oilers (1960), and Oakland Raiders (1967), and holds the record for the most points (2002) in any National Football League career. >> football [i]

blank verse Regular but unrhymed verse, in any metre but most usually the iambic pentameter of Shakespeare's plays, Milton's *Paradise Lost*, and Wordsworth's *Prelude*. >> metre (literature); poetry

Blanqui, (Louis) Auguste [blãkee] (1805–81) Revolutionary socialist leader, born in Puget-Théniers, France. A passionate extremist, his opposition to the Bourbon regime led to repeated periods of imprisonment. He was arrested on the eve of the Paris Commune, of which he was nevertheless elected president (1871). His supporters were known as **Blanquists**. >> Bourbon; Revolutions of 1848; socialism

Blantyre [blan**tiyr**] 14°46N 35°00E, pop (1995e) 445 000. Town in S Malawi; altitude 1040 m/3412 ft; named after David Livingstone's birthplace in Scotland; Church of Scotland mission founded here, 1876; airport; railway; two cathedrals; Malawi's main commercial and industrial centre. >> Livingstone, David; Malawi [i]

Blarney 51°56N 8°34W, pop (1995e) 2030. Small village in Cork county, S Ireland; visitors to Blarney Castle are supposed to gain the power of eloquent speech as they kiss the Blarney Stone; legend dates from the 16th-c, when Lord Blarney, by pure loquaciousness, avoided acknowledging to Queen Elizabeth's deputy that the lands of Blarney were held as a grant from the Queen and not as a chiefship. >> Cork (county); Ireland (republic) [i]

Blasco Ibáñez, Vicente [**blas**koh ee**vahn**yeth] (1867–1928) Novelist, born in Valencia, Spain. *Los cuatro jinetes del Apocalipsis* (1916, The Four Horsemen of the Apocalypse) vividly portrays World War 1, and earned him world fame.

Blasis, Carlo [**blas**ees] (1797–1878) Dancer, choreographer, and teacher, born in Naples, Italy. He was the author of several noted treatises on the codification of ballet technique.

blasphemy Any word, sign, or action which intentionally insults the goodness of or is offensive to God. Until the Enlightenment, it was punishable by death. In many Christian countries, it is technically a crime, and is extended to include the denial or ridicule of God, Christ, or the Bible; but the law is seldom if ever invoked. It is also a crime in certain non-Christian (eg Islamic) countries. The contemporary range of application of the law of blasphemy became an issue in the UK in 1989, following the publication of Salman Rushdie's book, *The Satanic Verses*. >> Enlightenment; God; heresy; Rushdie

blast furnace A furnace used for the primary reduction of iron ore to iron. Ore, coke, and limestone (which acts as a flux to remove silica) are loaded into the top of a tall furnace lined with mineral heat-resisting substances (such as fire-clay), in which the combustion of the coke is intensified by a pre-heated blast of air. At a certain temperature the iron ore is reduced to iron, which runs to the bottom of the furnace, where it is either tapped off and solidified as pig-iron, or conveyed while still molten to other plant for steel-making. >> coke; iron

blastula [**blas**tyula] An early embryonic stage in the development of multicellular animals. It typically consists of a hollow sphere of cells. >> cell; embryology; gastrula

Blattaria >> **cockroach**

Blaue Reiter, der [**blow**er **riy**ter] (Ger 'blue rider') The name adopted by a group of avant-garde artists in Munich in 1911. It was apparently inspired by a coloured illustration of a horseman on the cover of a book. >> *Brücke, die*; Kandinsky; Klee

Blavatsky, Helena Petrovna [bla**vat**skee], *née* **Hahn**, known as **Madame Blavatsky** (1831–91) Theosophist, born in Yekaterinoslav, Ukraine. She helped to found the Theosophical Society in New York (1875), and later carried on her work in India. >> theosophy

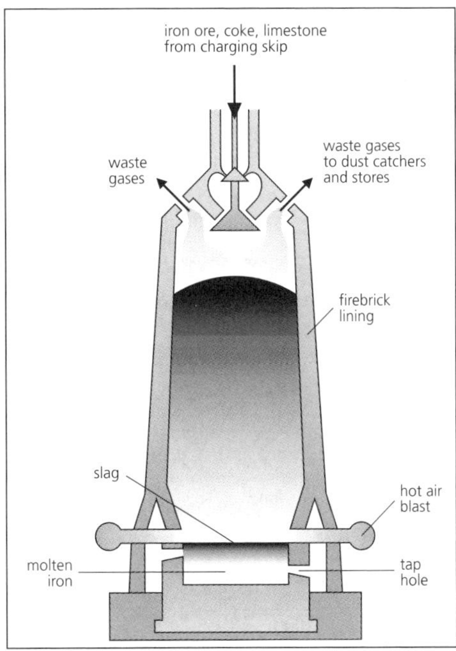

Blast furnace

blazar [**blay**zah(r)] A type of extremely luminous extragalactic object, similar to a quasar except that the optical spectrum is almost featureless. >> quasar; spectrum

blazonry The science of describing the pictorial devices used in heraldry. The basic colour (*tincture*) or background of the shield is known as the *field*, and this is overlaid with heraldic signs (*charges*). At their simplest, charges are broad bands, such as the vertical *pale*, or narrower stripes, such as the horizontal *fess*. The basic charges are called *ordinaries*. The *helm* or helmet appears above the shield, and denotes the rank of the bearer. >> heraldry ℹ

bleaching The removal of the colour of textiles or other materials, such as paper. **Bleaching powder** was used in immense quantities until its eventual replacement in the 1920s by cheap pure chlorine and sodium hypochlorite. So-called **optical bleaches** add a fluorescent emission to the basic colour of the textile. >> bleaching powder; chlorine; fluorescence

bleaching powder A crude mixture of calcium hypochlorite ($Ca(ClO)_2$) and calcium chloride ($CaCl_2$). It is used as a bleach and as a disinfectant. >> bleaching; calcium; chlorine

Bleasdale, Alan [**bleez**dayl] (1946–) Playwright, born in Liverpool, Merseyside. He became known through the popular TV series about a group of unemployed Liverpudlians, *The Boys from the Blackstuff* (1982). Later series were *GBH* (1991), and *Melissa* (1997). His stage plays include *Are You Lonesome Tonight?* (1985) and *On the Ledge* (1992).

Blenheim, Battle of [**blen**im] The greatest military triumph of Marlborough and Prince Eugene in the War of the Spanish Succession. It marked the first significant defeat of Louis XIV's armies. >> Louis XIV; Marlborough, Duke of; Spanish Succession, War of the

Blenheim Palace [**blen**im] A Baroque palace designed by Vanbrugh, and built (1705–24) at Woodstock, near Oxford, Oxfordshire; a world heritage site. The palace, with its estate of 809 ha/2000 acres, was a gift from the nation to the 1st Duke of Marlborough after the Battle of Blenheim. >> Baroque (art and architecture); Marlborough, Duke of; Vanbrugh

blenny Any of the large family Blennidae (11 genera), of mostly small bottom-dwelling fishes of coastal waters; found worldwide in tropical to temperate seas, rarely in freshwater lakes; body stout, devoid of scales; jaws bearing many small teeth.

Blériot, Louis [**blay**ryoh] (1872–1936) Airman, born in Cambrai, France. He made the first flight across the English Channel (25 Jul 1909) from Baraques to Dover in a small 24-hp monoplane. >> aircraft ℹ

blesbok >> **bontebok**

Blessed Virgin (Mary) >> **Mary** (mother of Jesus)

Bligh, William [bliy] (c.1754–c.1817) Naval officer, born in Plymouth, Devon. In 1787 he was sent as commander of HMS *Bounty* to Tahiti. On the return voyage, the men mutinied under his harsh treatment. In April 1789, Bligh and 18 men were cast adrift in an open boat without charts. In June, after great hardship, he arrived at Timor, near Java, having sailed his frail craft for 3618 miles. He was later appointed Governor of New South Wales (1805–11). >> Cook, James

blight A general term applied to any of a variety of plant diseases, especially those caused by fungal infection. >> blister blight; fungus; potato blight

blimp >> **airship**

blindness A serious or total loss of vision in both eyes. In developed countries it arises from degeneration of the retina of the eye (*Macular degeneration*), cataract, glaucoma, or diabetes. In developing countries many of the causes are infectious and preventable. >> eye ℹ

blindworm >> **slowworm**

Bliss, Sir Arthur (Edward Drummond) (1891–1975) Composer, born in London. In 1953 he became Master of the Queen's Musick. His works include the ballet *Checkmate* (1937), the opera *The Olympians* (1949), chamber music, and piano and violin works.

blister beetle A brightly coloured beetle, usually from warm, dry regions. Adults produce a chemical (*cantharidin*) that causes skin blisters. (Order: Coleoptera. Family: Meloidae, c.3000 species.) >> beetle

blister blight A serious airborne disease of tea (*Exobasidium vexans*), endemic in SE Asia. It can be controlled only by the application of expensive fungicidal sprays. (Order: Basidiomycetes.) >> blight; fungus; tea

blitzkrieg [**blitz**kreek] (Ger 'lightning war') A term coined (Sep 1939) to describe the German armed forces' use of fast-moving tanks and deep-ranging aircraft, aiming the focus of effort at the enemy's rear areas rather than making frontal attacks. >> World War 2

Bloch, Ernest [blokh] (1880–1959) Composer, born in Geneva, Switzerland. His works include the Hebrew *Sacred Service* (1930–3), and many chamber and orchestral works.

Bloch, Felix [blokh] (1905–83) Physicist, born in Zürich, Switzerland. He left Europe for the USA when Hitler came to power. He shared the 1952 Nobel Prize for Physics for developing the technique of magnetic resonance imaging. The **Bloch bands** are sets of discrete but closely adjacent energy levels rising from quantum states when a nondegenerate gas condenses to a solid. >> nuclear magnetic resonance

Bloc Québecois [kaybekwah] A separatist political organization in Quebec, Canada, formed in 1990 when Lucien Bouchard and other Conservative MPs from Quebec deserted the Mulroney government. In the 1993 federal election the *Bloc* won the second largest number of seats (all in Quebec) and became the official Opposition in Ottawa. >> Canada ℹ; *Parti Québecois*; Quebec

Bloemfontein [bloomfon**tayn**] 29°07S 26°14E, pop (1995e) 329 000. Judicial capital of South Africa, and capital of Free State province; founded as a fort, 1846; taken by Lord Roberts in Boer War, 1900; airfield; railway; university (1855); cathedral. >> Boer Wars; Free State; South Africa ℹ

Blondel or **Blondel de Nesle** [blõdel] (12th-c) French minstrel, said to have accompanied Richard I of England to Palestine, and to have found him when imprisoned in the Austrian prison of Dürrenstein (1193) by means of a song they had jointly composed. >> Richard I

Blondin, Charles [blõdĩ], originally **Jean François Gravelet** (1824–97) Tightrope walker, born in Hesdin, France. In 1859 he crossed Niagara Falls on a tightrope.

Blood, Council of A council established 1567–76 by the Duke of Alva, the Spanish Habsburg military commander in the Low Countries, on Philip II's orders, to suppress heresy and opposition during the Revolt of the Netherlands. It was also known as the **Council of Troubles**. >> Philip II (of Spain); Revolt of the Netherlands

Blood, Thomas, known as **Captain Blood** (c.1618–80) Irish adventurer, known for his activities during the English Civil War and Restoration. His most famous exploit was his attempt, disguised as a clergyman, to steal the crown jewels from the Tower of London (1671). >> crown jewels

blood An animal tissue composed of cells, cell-like bodies, and fluid plasma that circulates around the body within vascular channels or spaces by the mechanical action of the channels or their specialized parts (primarily the heart). Present in many major classes of animals, it usually contains respiratory pigment, and transports oxygen, nutrients, waste-products, and many other substances around the body. In humans, the cells (red, *erythrocytes*, and white, *leucocytes*), cell-like bodies (*platelets*), and plasma constitute about 8% of total body weight; in an average-sized adult male, blood volume is c.5·5 l/9·7 UK pt/11·6 US pt; in an equivalent female, it is c.4·5 l/7·9 UK pt/9·5 US pt. >> AIDS; anaemia; bone marrow; blood pressure / transfusion / types / vessels ℹ; embolism; erythrocytes; haematology; haemophilia; heart ℹ; inflammation; interferons; jaundice; leucocytes; leukaemia; plasma (physiology); platelets; septicaemia; uraemia

blood-bark >> **gum tree**

blood fluke A parasitic flatworm, found as an adult in the blood of some mammals, including humans; causes bilharzia. (Phylum: Platyhelminthes. Class: Trematoda. Genus *Schistosoma*.) >> flatworm; Platyhelminthes; schistosomiasis

blood group systems A series of genetically determined systems of substances on the plasma membranes of red blood cells, which act as *agglutininogens* and which, when in contact with the complementary *agglutinin* in plasma cause the red cells to stick together. In humans, the most prominent system is the ABO. Everybody belongs to four main subdivisions of this system (A, B, AB, or O) determined by the presence or the absence of A and/or B substances on the red cell membrane. The absence of A or B antigen is usually associated with the presence of corresponding natural anti-A or anti-B antibodies in the plasma. Other well-known systems are the Rh (Rhesus) and MNSs. >> antibodies; erythrocytes; rhesus factor

bloodhound A breed of dog, known for its keen sense of smell; used for tracking; large powerful body with loose-fitting skin; short coat; tan or black and tan; long pendulous ears and jowls; long, deep muzzle. >> hound

blood poisoning >> **septicaemia**

blood pressure The hydrostatic pressure of the blood within the blood vessels. It usually refers to the pressure within the arteries, the pressure within capillaries and veins being much lower. It is measured, using a sphygmomanometer, as the height in millimetres of a column of mercury (mmHg). In health the arterial blood pressure reaches a peak of about 120–130 mmHg with systole, and falls to about 70 mmHg during diastole. >> artery; blood; hypertension; sphygmomanometer

Blood River, Battle of >> **Great Trek**

blood sports The killing of animals for sport, such as fox-hunting, hare-coursing, or bullfighting; often referred to as **field sports**. They have come under increasing attack in recent years from those concerned with animal welfare. >> bullfighting; cockfighting; coursing; foxhunting

bloodstone A type of chalcedony, a fine-grained variety of the mineral quartz. It is dark-green with red flecks. >> chalcedony

blood transfusion The transfer of blood from one person to another. It was first carried out early in the 19th-c, but usually resulted in serious reactions. Clinically useful and safe blood transfusions were possible only after the discovery of blood groups. >> blood group systems

blood vessels A closed system of tubes whereby blood permeates through all the tissues of the body, comprising the arteries, arterioles, capillaries, venules, and veins. In general, arteries and arterioles carry oxygenated blood from the heart, and venules and veins return deoxygenated blood back to it. However, the pulmonary arteries convey deoxygenated blood to the lungs from the heart, while the pulmonary veins return oxygenated blood to it from the lungs. >> aneurysm; angiography; blood; capillary; catheter; circulation; embolism; haemorrhage; heart ℹ; shock; stroke; thrombosis

Bloody Assizes The name given to the western circuit assizes in England in the summer of 1685, presided over by Lord Chief Justice George Jeffreys after the defeat of the Duke of Monmouth at the Battle of Sedgemoor. About 150 of Monmouth's followers were executed, and 800 transported to the West Indies. >> Jeffreys; Monmouth, Duke of

Bloody Mary >> **Mary I**

Bloom, Claire (1931–) Actress, born in London. A distinguished Shakespearean actress, her film roles also include *Limelight* (1952) and *Look Back in Anger* (1959), and her television roles *Shadowlands* (1985, BAFTA) and *Family Money* (1997).

Bloom, Ursula, pseudonym of **Mrs Gower Robinson** (1892–1984) Novelist and playwright, born in Chelmsford, Essex. Her novels, which include *The First Elizabeth* (1953), are mainly historical romances. Most of her plays were written for radio production.

Bloomer, Amelia, *née* **Jenks** (1818–94) Champion of women's rights and dress reform, born in Homer, NY. She founded and edited the feminist paper *The Lily* (1849–55). In her pursuit of dress equality she wore her own version of trousers for women, which came to be called **bloomers**. >> feminism

Bloomsbury Group A group of writers and artists taking their name from the Bloomsbury area of London who were active around the time of World War 1: among them Virginia Woolf, Lytton Strachey, and E M Forster. In reaction against Victorian values, they had a significant influence on the Modernist movement in England. >> Forster; Modernism; Strachey; Woolf, Virginia

Bloor, Ella, *née* **Reeve**, known as **Mother Bloor** (1862–1951) Radical and feminist, born on Staten Island, New York City. Married at the age of 19, she became interested in women's rights, her political interests leading to her divorce in 1896. In 1919 she was one of the founders of the American Communist Party.

Blücher, Gebhard Leberecht von, Fürst von (Prince of) **Wahlstadt** [**bloo**cher, **bloo**ker], nickname **Marshal Forward** (1742–1819) Prussian field marshal, born in Rostock, Germany. In 1813 he defeated Napoleon at Leipzig, and entered Paris (1814). In 1815 he completed Wellington's victory at Waterloo by his timely appearance on the field. >> Napoleon I; Prussia; Waterloo, Battle of

blue In the UK, a sporting honour awarded at Oxford and Cambridge universities to students who represent their

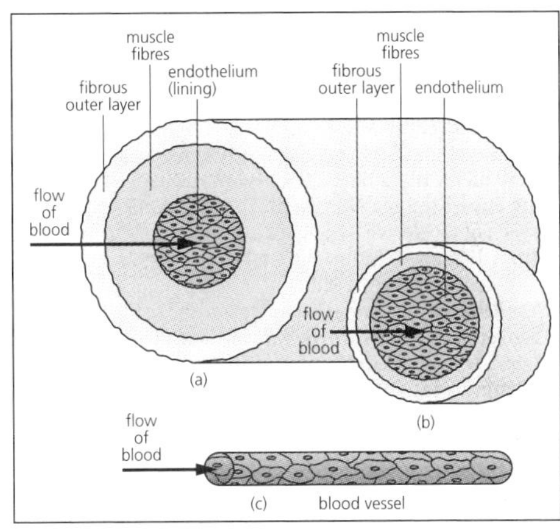

Blood vessels – artery (a); vein (b); capillary (c)

university against the other in the annual matches of certain sports. Ribbons of dark blue (Oxford) or light blue (Cambridge) were first awarded to competitors after the second Boat Race in 1836. >> Boat Race

bluebell A small herb with an annually renewed bulb (*Hyacinthoides non-scriptus*), native to W Europe; flowers bell-shaped, drooping, blue, sometimes pinkish or white. (Family: Liliaceae.) >> harebell

blueberry A deciduous shrub, native to North America, and cultivated for fruit; flowers bell-shaped; berry blue-black, edible. (Genus: *Vaccinium*, c.20 American species. Family: Ericaceae.)

bluebird A thrush native to North and Central America; male with bright blue plumage on back; nests in holes in trees. (Genus: *Sialia*, 3 species.) >> thrush (bird)

blue book A UK Government publication of official documents, presented to parliament, bound in a blue cover. Unlike other command papers, which put forward government proposals, blue books are more concerned with the provision of information. >> green paper; white paper

bluebottle >> **cornflower**

bluebottle A large fly with a metallic blue abdomen; lays eggs on decaying animal matter; legless larvae feed by liquefying food; adults feed by exuding digestive juices onto food and imbibing dissolved material. (Order: Diptera. Family: Calliphoridae.) >> fly; larva

bluebuck / blue bull >> **nilgai**

blue-green algae >> **blue-green bacteria**

blue-green bacteria Single-celled, colonial or filamentous organisms with an alga-like body and a bacterium-like (*prokaryotic*) cellular structure; photosynthetic pigment chlorophyll *a* found on a special membrane (*thylakoid*) not enclosed within chloroplasts as in true algae; very ancient organism, believed to have been responsible for enriching the Earth's atmosphere with oxygen as a by-product of its photosynthesis; over 1000 living species known, found mostly in aquatic habitats; formerly known as **blue-green algae**. (Division: Cyanophycota.) >> algae; bacteria [i]; cell; chloroplast; photosynthesis

blue moon 1 A phrase often used to refer to the second full moon in a calendar month in which two full moons occur – a rare event, only once every 2·7 years on average (though happening twice in one year in 1999 and 2018). However, research reported in 1999 suggested that this definition derives from an almanac interpretation of the 1940s, and that the phrase only makes sense in relation to a season of the year containing four (not the usual three) moons. **2** Very rarely, the Moon's disc actually appears blue. If the atmosphere has particles 0·8–1·8 microns in diameter, for example from volcanoes or forest fires, red light gets scattered out of the line of sight, but the blue is allowed through. >> month; Moon

Blue Mountains Mountain range in E New South Wales, Australia; part of the Great Dividing Range; rises to 1180 m/3871 ft at Bird Rock. >> Great Dividing Range

Blue Nile, Ethiopia **Abay Wenz**, Sudan **Bahr El Azraq** Upper reach of R Nile, NE Africa; length 1450 km/901 mi; issues from L Tana, Ethiopia; joins White Nile at Khartoum. >> Nile, River; White Nile

Blue Riband A notional honour awarded to the fastest passenger ship on the North Atlantic run. The final holder (1952) was the SS *United States* in a time of 3 days 11 hours 20 minutes at an average speed of 35·39 knots for the distance of 4745 km/2949 mi. The competition has ceased for economic reasons.

Blue Rider >> ***Blaue Reiter, der***

Blue Ridge Mountains Mountain range, SE USA; E part of the Appalachian Mts; extends NE–SW for c.1050 km/650 mi; highest point Mt Mitchell (2037 m/6683 ft). >> Appalachian Mountains

blues A style of US African-American music, related to slow jazz, originating c.1900. The singing of blues is essentially an improvisatory art, often reflecting a melancholy state of mind but also conveying the vitality of black working-class Americans. Blues songs may have a number of verses, but the standard pattern for each is one of three lines of 4 bars each, the second being a repetition of the first. The origins of the blues are associated particularly with the Mississippi region, and many of the most influential early singers, such as Bessie Smith, 'the Empress of Blues', were from the S States. Later departures were seen in the 'rhythm and blues' of the 1950s, and a great deal of rock 'n roll. Blues music is also now found in a wide range of instrumental manifestations, especially using the guitar. >> jazz; rhythm and blues; Smith, Bessie

blue shark Powerful slender-bodied shark (*Prionace glauca*) found worldwide in open tropical to temperate seas; length up to 3·8 m/12½ ft; pectoral fins elongate; deep blue dorsally, white underneath. (Family: Carcharhinidae.) >> shark

blueshift An astronomical effect observed when an object emitting electromagnetic radiation is moving towards an observer, increasing the observed frequency of its radiation. Spectral lines move to the blue end of the spectrum. Blueshifts are unusual, because almost all galaxies are moving away from us, and hence have redshifts. >> electromagnetism; light; redshift; spectrum

bluetit A small typical tit common in gardens (*Parus caeruleus*); native to Europe, N Africa, and SW Asia; nests in hole in tree or wall; also known as **tomtit**. (Family: Paridae.) >> tit

blue whale A rare baleen whale (*Balaenoptera musculus*) of the rorqual family; the largest animal that has ever existed, length up to 30 m/100 ft; blue with pale spots; also known as the **sulphur-bottom whale**. >> rorqual; whale [i]

Blunden, Edmund (Charles) (1896–1974) Poet and critic, born in Yalding, Kent. He is essentially a nature poet, as is evident in *Pastorals* (1916), but his best-known work is his prose *Undertones of War* (1928).

blunderbuss A type of firearm, dating from the late 18th-c, with a large bore and a trumpet mouth. It is able to discharge 10 or 12 balls in one shot designed for very short-range use.

Blunkett, David (1947–) British statesman. A member of Sheffield City Council from 1970, he became an MP in 1987. He held several shadow ministerial positions, was chairman of the Labour Party (1993–4), and became secretary-of-state for education in the 1997 Labour government.

Blunt, (Sir) Anthony (Frederick) (1907–83) Art historian and Soviet spy, born in Bournemouth, Dorset. Influenced by Burgess, he acted as a 'talent-spotter' at Cambridge, supplying to him the names of likely recruits to the Russian Communist cause, and during his war service in British Intelligence was in a position to pass on information to the Russian government. In 1964, after the defection of Philby, a confession was obtained from Blunt in return for immunity from prosecution, and he continued as Surveyor of the Queen's Pictures until 1972. His full involvement in espionage was made public only in 1979, when his knighthood (1956) was annulled. >> Burgess, Guy

Blyth, Chay, popular name of **Charles Blyth** (1940–) British yachtsman, the first to sail single-handed 'the hard way' round the world (1970–1). In 1966 he rowed the Atlantic from W to E with John Ridgeway (1938–), before making his epic voyage westward around the globe. With a crew of paratroopers he won the Whitbread Round the World Yacht Race (1973–4), travelling eastwards.

Blyton, Enid (Mary) (1897–1968) Children's writer, born in London. In the late 1930s she began writing her many children's stories featuring such characters as Noddy, the Famous Five, and the Secret Seven. The author of over 400 books, she is the third most translated British author, after Agatha Christie and Shakespeare.

B'nai B'rith [bniy brith] (Heb 'sons of the covenant') The oldest and largest Jewish service organization, founded in the USA in 1843. It pursues educational and community activities, and concerns itself with the rights of Jews throughout the world. >> Judaism

boa A snake native to the New World, N Africa, SW Asia, and Australasian islands; a constrictor; minute remnants of hind limbs; females give birth to live young (up to 80 at one time); includes the anaconda. (Family: Boidae, 39 species.) >> anaconda; constrictor; python; snake

Boadicea >> **Boudicca**

boar >> **pig**

Boas, Franz [**boh**as] (1858–1942) Anthropologist, born in Minden, Germany. Professor at Columbia University from 1899, he became the dominant figure in establishing modern anthropology in the USA. His approach is seen in a major collection of papers, *Race, Language and Culture* (1940). >> anthropology

Boat People Vietnamese who fled Vietnam by boat after the communist victory in 1975, travelling to Australia, Hong Kong, Japan, and several other parts of SE Asia (c.110 000 by the end of 1990). Many died on the long voyages, or were killed by pirates. Voluntary repatriation schemes gained momentum in 1989, and the first involuntary repatriation operation was carried out by the Hong Kong authorities that December. The term has since been applied to other groups who try to flee from a country using small craft. >> Vietnam [i]

Boat Race The annual rowing race between the crews of Oxford and Cambridge Universities. First held 10 June 1829 from Hambledon Lock to Henley Bridge, it is now raced over 6 km 780 m/4 mi 374 yd from Putney to Mortlake. >> rowing

bobcat A nocturnal member of the cat family native to North America (*Felis rufus*); resembles a small lynx; length up to 1 m/3¼ ft; brown with dark spots; tail very short. >> Felidae; lynx

bobolink An oriole native to North America (*Dolichonyx oryzivorus*); spends winter in South America; has the longest migration (8000 km/5000 mi) of any bird in its family. >> oriole

bobsledding The art of propelling oneself along snow or ice on a sled (or sledge). The two most popular forms of competitive bobsledding are **luge tobogganing** on a small sled, and **bobsleighing** in a sophisticated streamlined sled. >> lugeing; RR1047

Boccaccio, Giovanni [bo**kah**chioh] (1313–75) Writer, probably born in Italy. In 1358 he completed his great work, the *Decameron*, begun some 10 years before. He selected the plots of his stories from current popular fiction, and was a great influence on Chaucer, Shakespeare, and others.

Boccherini, Luigi (Rodolfo) [boke**ree**nee] (1743–1805) Composer, born in Lucca, Italy. He was a cellist and prolific composer at the courts in Madrid and Prussia, best known for his chamber music, cello concertos, and sonatas.

Boccioni, Umberto [bo**choh**nee] (1882–1916) Artist and sculptor, born in Reggio, Italy. The most original artist of the Futurist school and its principal theorist, he worked in Paris and Rome (1898–1914), and wrote a major survey of the movement. >> Futurism

Bochum [**bokh**um] 51°28N 7°12E, pop (1995e) 410 000. Industrial and commercial city in the Ruhr valley, Germany; originally developed around the coal and steel industries; railway; university (1965). >> Germany [i]; Ruhr, River

Bodensee >> **Constance, Lake**

Bode's law or **Titius–Bode law** A numerical relationship linking the distances of planets from the Sun, discovered in 1766 by German astronomer Johann Daniel Titius (1729–96), and published in 1772 by Johann Elert Bode (1747–1826), but now considered to be an interesting coincidence. The basis of this relationship is the series 0,3,6,12,...,384, in which successive numbers are obtained by doubling the previous one. If 4 is then added to create the new series 4,7,10,16,...,388, the resulting numbers correspond reasonably with the planetary distances on a scale, with the Earth's distance equal to ten units. >> Solar System

Bodh Gaya >> **Buddh Gaya**

Bodhidharma [bodhi**dah(r)**ma] (6th-c) Monk and founder of the Ch'an (or Zen) sect of Buddhism, born near Madras, India. He taught meditation as the means of return to Buddha's spiritual precepts. >> Buddhism

bodhisattva [bodhi**sat**wa] (Sanskrit, 'enlightened existence') In Mahayana Buddhism, one who has attained the enlightenment of a Buddha but chooses not to pass into Nirvana, voluntarily remaining in the world to help lesser beings attain enlightenment. >> Buddhism; Dalai Lama; Mahayana; Nirvana

bodily harm A criminal offence against the person. **Grievous bodily harm** involves serious physical injury, such as wounding with a knife. **Actual bodily harm** involves a less serious attack, such as an assault causing unconsciousness. These terms are not used in all jurisdictions.

Bodleian Library [**bod**lian] The university library and national depository at Oxford; founded in 1595 by Sir Thomas Bodley (1545–1613). >> Oxford University [i]

Body art A type of modern art which exploits the artist's – or someone else's – physical presence as a work of art in its own right. Artists may stand in the gallery like a living statue, perhaps singing; photograph themselves performing some banal action, such as smiling; or may deliberately injure themselves. A typical fad of the 1960s, it has emerged again in the 1990s, with people using paint, tattoo, rings, and a variety of attachments. >> happening; modern art

body colour >> **gouache**

body language >> **nonverbal communication**

body popping >> **street dance**

Boeing, William E(dward) [**boh**ing] (1881–1956) Aircraft manufacturer, born in Detroit, MI. He formed the Pacific Aero Products Co in 1916, renamed as the Boeing Airplane Company in 1917. It eventually became the largest manufacturer of military and civilian aircraft in the world. >> aircraft [i]

Boeotia [bee**oh**sha] In antiquity, the area in C Greece bordering on Attica. Its chief city-state was Thebes, and its inhabitants were largely of Aeolian stock. >> Attica; Thebes 2

Boers >> **Afrikaners**

Boer Wars Two wars fought by the British and the Boers for the mastery of S Africa. The first Boer War (1880–1) ended with the defeat of the British at Majuba Hill, and the signing of the Pretoria and London Conventions of 1881 and 1884. The second Boer War (1899–1902) can be divided into three phases: (1) (Oct 1899–Jan 1900) a series of Boer successes, including the sieges of Ladysmith, Kimberley, and Mafeking, as well as victories at Stormberg, Modder River, Magersfontein, Colenso, and Modersspruit; (2) (Feb–Aug 1900) counter-offensives by Lord Roberts, including the raising of the sieges, the victory at Paardeberg, and the capture of Pretoria; (3) (Sep 1900–May 1902) a period of guerrilla warfare when Kitchener attempted to prevent Boer commandos raiding isolated British units and lines of communication. The Boers effectively won the peace. They maintained control of 'native affairs', and federated South Africa on their terms in 1910. >> Great Trek; Jameson Raid; Kimberley / Ladysmith / Mafeking, Sieges of; Vereeniging, Peace of

Boesak, Allan (Aubrey) [**bu**sak] (1945–) Clergyman, born in Kakamas, South Africa. A former president of the World Alliance of Reformed Churches, he sees the Christian Gospel in terms of liberation of the oppressed. An outspoken opponent of apartheid, he became leader of the coloured (mixed-race) community in South Africa. In March 1999, after a controversial trial, he was jailed for six years for embezzlement of funds sent to his organization. >> apartheid; South Africa 🛈

Boethius, Anicius Manlius Severinus [boh**ee**thius] (c.AD 480–524) Roman statesman and philosopher, probably born in Rome. Made consul in 510, his uprightness of conduct brought him many enemies. He was accused of treason, imprisoned, and executed. During his imprisonment he wrote *De consolatione philosophiae* (The Consolation of Philosophy).

Bogarde, Sir Dirk [**boh**gah(r)d], originally **Derek Niven van den Bogaerde** (1921–99) Actor, born in London. He moved from the stage to films in 1946, playing mostly romantic or light comedy roles, such as *Doctor in the House* (1954) and its sequels. More challenging parts with varied characterization followed, as in *The Victim* (1961), *Death in Venice* (1971), and *Despair* (1981). He has published several volumes of autobiography and some novels. In 1996 he suffered a stroke, but continued to work by dictation.

Bogart, Humphrey (DeForest) [**boh**gah(r)t] (1899–1957) Actor, born in New York City. Many of his performances have become classics, notably *The Maltese Falcon* (1941), *Casablanca* (1942), *The Big Sleep* (1946), and *The African Queen* (1951, Oscar). He married Lauren Bacall as his fourth wife in 1945. >> Bacall

bog burials Ancient human bodies recovered from N European peat bogs, their soft tissues and hair remarkably preserved by waterlogged, anaerobic conditions. Notable Iron Age examples are *Tollund Man* (c.200 BC) in Denmark, and the 25–30-year-old, 1·7 m/5 ft 7 in tall *Lindow Man*, buried naked c.300 BC in Lindow Moss, Cheshire, UK, and discovered in 1984. >> peat

Bognor Regis [**bog**ner **ree**jis] 50°47N 0°41W, pop (1995e) 59 900. Coastal resort town in West Sussex, S England; the title 'Regis' dates from 1929, when King George V came here to recuperate; railway. >> Sussex, West

Bogomils [**bog**ohmilz] >> **Albigenses; Cathars**

Bogotá [bohgoh**ta**], official name **Santa Fe de Bogotá** 4°38N 74°05W, pop (1995e) 4 380 000. Federal capital of Colombia, on a plateau at 2650 m/8694 ft; founded by Spanish, 1538; former capital of Greater Colombia and of New Granada; airport; railway; several universities and colleges; cathedral. >> Colombia 🛈

Bohemia [boh**hee**mia], Czech **Čechy**, Ger **Böhmen** Historic province of W Czech Republic, a plateau enclosed by mountains; major towns include Prague; highly industrialized area; coal, iron ore, uranium; part of Moravian Empire, 9th-c; at its peak in early Middle Ages, especially in 14th-c under Charles I; Hussite religious dissension; Habsburg rule from early 16th-c; became a province of Czechoslovakia, 1918; part of Czech Republic, 1993. >> Czech Republic 🛈; Habsburgs; Huss

Bohemian Forest, Ger **Böhmerwald**, Czech **Česky Les** Forested mountain range along the boundary between Germany and Czech Republic; highest German peak, Grosser Arber (1457 m/4780 ft). >> Bohemia; Germany 🛈

Bohr, Niels (Henrik David) [baw(r)] (1885–1962) Physicist, born in Copenhagen. He greatly extended the theory of atomic structure when he explained the spectrum of hydrogen by means of an atomic model and the quantum theory (1913). During World War 2 he assisted atom bomb research in the USA. He founded the Institute of Theoretical Physics at Copenhagen, and was awarded the Nobel Prize for Physics in 1922. >> atomic bomb; quantum field theory

Boiardo, Matteo Maria, conte di (Count of) **Scandiano** [boy**ah(r)**doh] (c.1441–94) Poet, born in Scandiano, Italy. His fame rests on the *Orlando Innamorato* (1486), a long narrative poem about Roland, the greatest of Charlemagne's legendary heroes. >> Ariosto

boil An abscess in a sweat follicle, which results in a raised, reddened, and often painful swelling. It usually results from infection with *Staphylococcus aureus*. >> abscess

Boileau(-Despréaux), Nicolas [bwahloh] (1636–1711) Poet and critic, born in Paris. *L'Art poétique* (1674, The Art of Poetry), expressing the classical principles for the writing of poetry, was very influential in France and England.

boiling point The state achieved when a liquid is heated until the heat energy is no longer used to increase temperature but instead to form gas from the liquid. Formally, the boiling point temperature is reached when a liquid's vapour pressure equals external pressure. Boiling points thus decrease with altitude. >> phases of matter 🛈; vapour pressure

boiling water reactor >> **nuclear reactor** 🛈

Bois de Boulogne [bwah duh boo**loyn**] A park of 962 ha/2380 acres situated on the W outskirts of Paris. Originally a royal hunting forest, it became a popular recreation area for Parisians in the 17th-c. >> Paris 🛈

Boise [**boy**zee] 43°37N 116°13W, pop (1995e) 145 000. State capital in SW Idaho, USA, founded after the 1862 gold rush; airfield; railway; trade and transportation centre. >> Idaho

Bolden, Buddy, popular name of **Charles Joseph Bolden** (1877–1931) Jazz cornetist, born in New Orleans, LA. He is the putative founder of jazz, a figure of mythic significance; no recorded evidence survives. In 1907, his uncontrollable fits of violence led to his incarceration for life, and he died in a fire at an asylum. >> jazz

Boleyn, Anne [bo**lin**], also spelled **Bullen** (c.1507–36) English queen, the second wife of Henry VIII (1533–6). Secretly married to Henry, she was soon declared his legal wife; but within three months his passion for her had cooled. It was not revived by the birth (1533) of a princess (later Elizabeth I), still less by that of a stillborn son (1536). She was charged with treason, and beheaded. >> Henry VIII

bolide [**boh**leed] An exceptionally brilliant meteor, or fireball, which explodes in our atmosphere. It makes a very loud bang, and scatters stony debris over a wide area. >> meteor

Bolingbroke >> **Henry IV** (of England)

Bolívar, Simón [bol**ee**vah(r), **bo**livah(r)], known as **the Liberator** (1783–1830) The national hero of Venezuela, Colombia, Ecuador, Peru, and Bolivia, born in Caracas. He played the most prominent part in the wars of independence in N South America. In 1819, he proclaimed and became president of the vast Republic of Colombia, which was finally liberated in 1822. He then took charge of the last campaigns for independence in Peru (1824). >> Spanish–American Wars of Independence

Bolivia, official name **Republic of Bolivia**, Span **República de Bolivia** pop (1995e) 8 120 000; area 1 098 580 sq km/ 424 052 sq mi. Republic of WC South America; government capital, La Paz; legal and judicial capital, Sucre; timezone GMT –4; Mestizo (31%), Quechua (25%), Aymará

(17%), white (14%); religion, 92·5% Roman Catholic; official languages, Quechua, Aymará, Spanish; unit of currency, the boliviano of 100 centavos; land-locked country, bounded W by the Cordillera Occidental of the Andes, rising to 6542 m/21 463 ft at Sajama; separated from the Cordillera Real to the E by the flat, 400 km/250 mi-long Altiplano plateau, 3600 m/11 800 ft; major lakes, Titicaca and Poopó; part of Inca Empire, and evidence of earlier civilization; conquered by Spanish in 16th-c; independence after war of liberation, 1825; much territory lost after wars with neighbouring countries; several changes of government and military coups in recent decades; governed by a bicameral Congress and elected president; largely dependent on minerals for foreign exchange; silver, tin; oil and natural gas, pipelines to Argentina and Chile; illegally-produced cocaine. >> Andes; Bolívar; Incas; La Paz; Sucre; RR1002 political leaders

boll weevil A small weevil that prevents the normal development of cotton flowers by its feeding activities. It is an economically important pest of cotton. (Order: Coleoptera. Family: Curculionidae.) >> cotton ⓘ; weevil ⓘ

Bologna [bo**lohn**ya] 44°30N 11°20E, pop (1995e) 413 000. Capital city in N Italy; ancient Etruscan city, enclosed by remains of 13th–14th-c walls; archbishopric; airport; rail junction; university (11th-c). >> Italy ⓘ

Bolsheviks (Russ 'majority-ites') Members of the hard-line faction of the Marxist Russian Social Democratic Labour Party, formed by Lenin at the party's second congress in 1903; the forerunner of the Communist Party of the Soviet Union (abolished in 1991). In October 1917 the Bolsheviks led the revolution in Petrograd which established the first Soviet government. >> Mensheviks; October / Russian Revolution

Bolshoi Ballet [**bol**shoy] A Moscow-based ballet company tracing its origins to 1776 and its repertoire to the Russian classics. The main directors/choreographers are Lavrovsky and Grigorovich, who specialize in modern versions of Russian themes. >> ballet

Bolt, Robert (1924–95) Playwright, born in Sale, Greater Manchester. He worked as a teacher before achieving success with *A Man for All Seasons* (1960). He had also written screenplays, including *Lawrence of Arabia* (1962), *Dr Zhivago* (1965), and *The Mission* (1986). He was an anti-nuclear activist in the 1960s, joining the 'Committee of 100', and was jailed for a month in 1961. He continued writing, despite being partly paralysed and left with speech difficulties, following a stroke in 1979.

Boltzmann, Ludwig (Eduard) [**bolts**man] (1844–1906) Physicist, born in Vienna. He worked on the kinetic theory of gases, and helped to develop the science of statistical mechanics. **Boltzmann's law**, the principle of the equipartition of energy, and the **Boltzmann constant**, used in the study of gases, are named after him.

bomb A device used to cause an explosion, usually consisting of a container, an explosive substance, and a fuse. Generally bombs are distinguished from other explosive devices by means of delivery: they normally use gravity (when dropped from aircraft) or are placed in position (as in the case of car bombs). Gravity and release speed determine an ordinary bomb's flightpath, although so-called **smart bombs** have a target-seeking guidance package in the nose which can pick up signals from targets on the ground, and generate steering commands to guide the bomb onto a target. >> atomic bomb; hydrogen bomb ⓘ; incendiary bomb; mortar (military); neutron bomb; V-1; V-2

Bombay, official name now (1995) **Mumbai** 18°55N 72°50E, pop (1995e) 13 606 000. Port capital of Maharashtra, W India; India's largest city built on a group of islands linked by causeways; ceded to Portugal, 1534; ceded to Britain, 1661; airport; railway; two universities (1916, 1957). >> India ⓘ; Maharashtra

Bombay duck Slender-bodied fish (*Harpadon nehereus*) with large jaws and barb-like teeth; common in the tropical Indian Ocean; length up to 40 cm/16 in; flesh soft and translucent; important food fish. (Family: Harpadontidae.)

Bonaire [bon**air**] pop (1995e) 11 200; area 288 sq km/111 sq mi. Island of the S Netherlands Antilles; rises to 241 m/791 ft in the hilly NW; length 35 km/22 mi; capital, Kralendijk; airport. >> Netherlands Antilles ⓘ

Bonaparte, Jérôme [**boh**napah(r)t] (1784–1860) Youngest brother of Napoleon, born in Ajaccio, Corsica. He served in the war against Prussia, was made king and ruled Westphalia (1807–14), and fought at Waterloo (1815). >> Napoleon I / III

Bonaparte, Joseph [**boh**napah(r)t] (1768–1844) King of Naples and Spain, the eldest brother of Napoleon I, born in Corte, Corsica. He was made ruler of the Two Sicilies (1805) and King of Naples (1806). In 1808 he was transferred to the throne of Spain, but after the defeat of the French at Vittoria (1813) he abdicated. After Waterloo he escaped to the USA, but in 1832 returned to Europe. >> Napoleon I

Bonaparte [**boh**napah(r)t] >> **Napoleon I; Napoleon III**

Bonaventure or **Bonaventura, St** [**bon**avencher], known as **Doctor Seraphicus** ('Seraphic Doctor'), originally **Giovanni di Fidanza** (c.1221–74) Franciscan theologian and cardinal, born near Orvieto, Italy. He was canonized in 1482. Feast day 15 July. >> Franciscans; theology

bond A loan to a company or a government. The loan carries interest payments and is repaid after several years. It can be bought and sold on the stock market, and is a relatively secure investment often held by insurance companies and pension funds. >> insurance; pension; premium bond

Bond, Alan (1938–) Businessman, born in London. He emigrated to Fremantle, Western Australia, in 1951, where the Bond Corporation developed extensive interests in Australian newspapers and television, brewing, oil and gas, and gold mining. In 1996 he was sentenced to three years' imprisonment for failing to declare assets, and received an additional 4-year sentence for fraud in 1997.

Bond, Edward (1934–) Playwright and director, born in London. His early plays, such as *Saved* (1965), were notorious for their use of violence to portray contemporary society. Other plays include a reworking of Shakespeare's play *Lear* (1971), a trilogy *The War Plays* (1985), and *At the Inland Sea* (1996), sub-titled 'a play for young people'.

Bondi [**bon**diy] A well-known resort beach in the Sydney suburb of Waverley, New South Wales, SE Australia. >> Sydney

Bondi, Sir Hermann (1919–) Mathematical physicist and astronomer, born in Vienna. He was appointed professor of mathematics at King's College, London, in 1954, and is best known as one of the originators of the steady-state theory of the universe. >> Gold; Hoyle, Fred

bone The hard tissue component of the vertebrate skeleton. It is composed of an organic element (mainly collagen), 25% of the weight of the fully formed bone, and a mineral matrix (calcium, phosphate, and variable amounts of magnesium, sodium, carbonate, citrate, and fluoride), having a crystalline structure. It basically consists of many cylindrical units, each with a central canal, containing bone-forming cells (*osteoblasts*), blood vessels, and nerve filaments, surrounded by bony tissue. Long bones consist of a shaft (a hollow tube surrounded by compact bone) and the ends (a network of spongy bone). The growth in length occurs in the region between shaft and ends. When this region disappears (between puberty and 25 years) growth ceases, as the shaft has fused with the ends. >> bone marrow; brittle bone syndrome; callus 2; dislocation (medicine); fracture; joint; orthopaedics; osteoarthritis; osteology ℹ; osteomalacia; osteomyelitis; osteopathy; osteoporosis; Paget's disease; rickets; skeleton ℹ

bone marrow An accumulation of cells and supporting tissues found within the central cavity of all bones. **Yellow marrow** consists of fat cells, blood vessels, and a minimal framework of reticular cells and fibres. **Red marrow** consists of numerous blood cells of all kinds. The functions of red marrow include the formation of red blood cells (*erythrocytes*), blood platelets, and granulocytes, and the destruction of old (c.120 days), worn-out erythrocytes. >> blood; bone; cell; gene therapy; transplantation

Bonfire Night >> **Guy Fawkes Night**

bongos A pair of wooden conical or cylindrical drums with single heads of skin or plastic, played with the hands. Originating in Cuba c.1900, they are used throughout Latin America, and frequently elsewhere. >> rumba

Bonham-Carter, Helena [**bon**am] (1966–) Actress, born in London. Noted for playing quintessential English heroines, she made her cinematic debut as Lady Jane Grey in *Lady Jane* (1985). Later film credits include *Hamlet* (1990), *Mighty Aphrodite* (1995), *Twelfth Night* (1996), and *Portraits Chinois* (1997).

Bonhoeffer, Dietrich [**bon**hoefer] (1906–45) Lutheran pastor and theologian, born in Wrocław, Poland (formerly Breslau, Prussia). Deeply involved in the German resistance movement, he was arrested (1943), imprisoned, and hanged. His most influential works were *Ethik* (1949, Ethics) and *Widerstand und Ergebung* (1951, trans Letters and Papers from Prison). >> 'death of God' theology; Lutheranism; secular Christianity

Boniface, St [**bon**ifas], originally **Wynfrith**, known as **the Apostle of Germany** (c.680–c.754) Benedictine missionary, born in Wessex, England. He became a monk in Exeter, and in 718 was commissioned to preach the Gospel to all the tribes of Germany. He was killed at Dokkum by heathens. Feast day 5 June. >> Benedictines

Bonington, Sir Chris(tian John Storey) (1934–) Mountaineer, born in London. He was a member of the British team that took part in the first successful conquest of the N face of the Eiger (1962), a member of the expedition that climbed the S face of Annapurna (1970), and leader of the 1975 Everest expedition. >> Annapurna, Mount; Eiger; Everest, Mount

Bonin Islands, Jap **Ogasawara-shoto** area 104 sq km/40 sq mi. Group of 27 volcanic islands in the W Pacific Ocean, c.965 km/600 mi S of Tokyo, Japan; first colonized by Europeans and Hawaiians, 1830; annexed by Japanese, 1876; taken by USA, 1953; returned to Japan, 1968. >> Japan ℹ

Bonino, Emma [bo**nee**noh] (1949–) Politician, born near Turin, Italy. She became known as a radical campaigner for law reform in such areas as abortion and divorce. In 1995 she was chosen European Commissioner for fisheries, consumer affairs, and humanitarian aid, with responsibility for the controversial Common Fisheries Policy.

Bonn 50°43N 7°06E, pop (1995e) 300 000. Capital city of former West Germany, on R Rhine; early Roman fort on the Rhine; seat of Electors of Cologne (13th–16th-c); part of Prussia, 1815; badly bombed in World War 2; capital status since 1949; airport at Cologne; railway; university (1818); minster (11th–13th-c); birthplace of Beethoven. >> Beethoven; Cologne; Germany ℹ; Prussia

Bonnard, Pierre [bonah(r)] (1867–1947) Painter and lithographer, born in Paris. A member of the *Intimist* group, he painted interiors and landscapes, subordinating everything to the subtlest rendering of light and colour effects. >> *Nabis, Les*

Bonner, Neville Thomas (1922–99) Australian politician, born in Tweed Heads, New South Wales, Australia. President of the One People of Australia League (1967–73), he filled a casual Senate vacancy in 1971, becoming the first Aboriginal member of the Australian parliament. In 1972, standing for the Liberal Party, he was elected as a representative for Queensland. >> Aborigines

Bonner, Yelena (1923–) Civil rights campaigner, born in Moscow. She married **Andrei Sakharov** in 1971, and for the next 14 years she and her husband led the Soviet dissident movement. Sakharov was banished to internal exile in Gorky (Nizhni Novgorod) in 1980, and Bonner suffered a similar fate in 1984. The couple were finally released in 1986, and remained prominent campaigners for greater democratization. >> Sakharov

Bonney, William H, Jr, known as **Billy the Kid**, originally (?) **Henry McCarty** (1859–81) Bandit, born in New York. He achieved notoriety for his robberies and murders in the SW states. He was finally tracked down and shot by Sheriff Patrick F Garrett.

Bonnie and Clyde Notorious robbery partners: **Clyde Barrow** (1909–34), born in Telico, TX, and **Bonnie Parker** (1911–34), born in Rowena, TX. The pair met in 1932. With their gang, which included Barrow's brother and wife, they robbed and murdered until they were shot dead at a police road-block in Louisiana.

Bonnie Prince Charlie >> **Stuart, Charles**

bonobo >> **chimpanzee**

bonsai The technique of growing dwarfed plants in small pots, in which all parts are in proportion. It was first practised in China and Japan.

bontebok [**bon**tebok] An ox-antelope (*Damaliscus dorcas*) native to S Africa; long face; lyre-shaped horns ringed with ridges; dark brown with white face and underparts; two subspecies: **bontebok** (with white rump) and **blesbok** (with brown rump). >> antelope

bonxie >> skua

bony fish Any of the very large group Osteichthyes, comprising all true bony fishes (18 000 species; 450 families); includes both the ray-finned fishes (Actinopterygii) and the fleshy-finned fishes (Sarcopterygii); endoskeleton made of bone; with air bladder or lungs. >> cartilaginous fish; Crossopterygii

booby A bird related to gannets, native to tropical and subtropical seas; streamlined, with a colourful pointed bill. It catches fish by diving vertically into the water. (Genus: *Sula*, 6 species. Family: Sulidae.) >> gannet

booklouse A small flattened insect which typically feeds on old books or dried organic material. It can cause extensive damage in libraries. >> louse

Book of Changes, Chin **Yijing** or **I-ching** One of Chinese literature's oldest and most treasured works, possibly dating in part from the 11th-c BC, with additions in the 7th-c and 1st-c BC. It comprises 64 hexagrams, each formed by combining two out of eight trigrams of three broken (*yin*) or unbroken (*yang*) lines. The *Yijing* could yield guidance on problems and imminent decisions, since each hexagram supposedly corresponded to typical human issues and life-change patterns, and the underpinning assumption was a unification of nature and humanity in the cosmos. >> Confucius; yin and yang

Book of Common Prayer The official directory of worship or service-book of the Church of England, widely followed in churches of the Anglican Communion. Largely composed by Archbishop Cranmer, it was first introduced in 1549, and revised in 1552, 1604, and finally 1662. >> Church of England; Cranmer

book of hours A prayer book, popular in the Middle Ages, and known in England as a **primer**. It typically contained the Little Office of Our Lady, psalms of penitence, and the Office of the Dead (usually in Latin).

bookworm The common name of various larval and adult insects that damage books by feeding on the paper and binding, and by burrowing activity. It is used particularly of the booklouse and silverfish. >> booklouse; larva; silverfish

Boole, George (1815–64) Mathematician and logician, born in Lincoln, Lincolnshire. He is primarily known for his *Mathematical Analysis of Logic* (1847) and *Laws of Thought* (1854), where he employed mathematical symbolism to express logical processes (**Boolean algebra**). >> algebra; logic

boomer >> mountain beaver

boomerang A throwing stick, so shaped as to fly great distances and strike a severe blow; mainly Australian but known elsewhere. Some are made to take a curved path and return, and are used mainly for play or training.

Boone, Daniel (c.1734–1820) Pioneer, born in Berks Co, PA. Twice captured by Indians, he repeatedly repelled (1775–8) Indian attacks on his stockade fort, now Boonesboro.

Boot, Sir Jesse, Baron Trent (1850–1931) Drug manufacturer, born in Nottingham, Nottinghamshire. In 1877 he opened his first chemist's shop in Nottingham, and by mass selling at reduced prices introduced the modern chain store.

Boötes [boh**oh**teez] (Lat 'herdsman') A large N hemisphere constellation. It contains Arcturus, a red giant, the brightest star in the N sky, radius 28 times the Sun. Distance: 11 parsec. >> red giant; star

Booth, John Wilkes (1839–65) Assassin, born near Bel Air, MD. In 1865 he entered into a conspiracy to avenge the defeat of the Confederates and shot President Lincoln at Ford's Theatre, Washington, DC (14 Apr). He fled to Virginia, but was tracked down and shot. >> Lincoln, Abraham

Booth, William (1829–1912) Founder and 'general' of the Salvation Army, born in Nottingham. In 1865 he founded the Army (so named in 1878) on military lines with mission work in London's East End. His wife, **Catherine Booth** (1829–90), also helped launch the movement, and his eldest son succeeded him as general. >> Salvation Army

Boothe, Clare >> **Luce, Clare Boothe**

Booths, Feast of >> **Sukkoth**

bootlegging The illegal manufacture or distribution of alcoholic drink or other highly taxed goods, such as cigarettes. The term is mainly used with reference to the smuggling of alcohol in the USA during the Prohibition era (1920–33). >> Capone, Al; Prohibition

bop >> **bebop**

Bophuthatswana [bopootats**wah**na], locally **Bop** Former independent black homeland in South Africa; comprised seven separate units of land in Cape, Free State, and Transvaal provinces; self-government, 1971; second homeland to receive independence from South Africa (not recognized internationally), 1977; incorporated into North West province in the South African constitution of 1994. >> apartheid; North West; South Africa ℹ

borage A robust annual (*Borago officinalis*), growing to 60 cm/24 in, covered in stiff, white bristles, native to C Europe and the Mediterranean region; leaves oval, rough; flowers bright blue, drooping, with five spreading petals and black anthers; cultivated as a herb. (Family: Boraginaceae.) >> alkanet

boranes [**boh**raynz] Compounds of boron and hydrogen, the simplest being diborane (B_2H_6). They are high-energy compounds, and have been used as rocket fuels. >> boron; hydrogen

borax [**boh**raks] $Na_2B_4O_7.10H_2O$; the hydrated salt of boric acid. It forms insoluble salts with Ca^{2+} and Mg^{2+} ions, and thus is useful as a water softener and cleanser. It is an important ingredient in borosilicate (Pyrex®) glasses. >> boron

Bordeaux [baw(r)**doh**], Lat **Burdigala** 44°50N 0°36W, pop (1995e) 217 000. Inland port in SW France, on R Garonne; cultural and commercial centre for SW; 100 km/60 mi from the Atlantic; held by the English, 1154–1453, temporary seat of government in 1870, 1914, and 1940; centre of wine-growing region; airport; railway; archbishopric; university (1441); cathedral. >> Aquitaine; Frondes, the; wine

Borden, Lizzie (Andrew) (1860–1927) Alleged murderess, born in Fall River, MA. In one of the most sensational murder trials in US history, she was accused of murdering her wealthy father and hated step-mother with an axe in 1892, but was acquitted. The case is immortalized in the rhyme *Lizzie Borden took an axe...*

Border, Allan (Robert) (1955–) Cricketer, born in Sydney, New South Wales, Australia. He made his Test debut against England in 1978–9, and was captain 1984–94. A left-hander, he was Australia's most prolific batsman, and on his retirement in 1994 held Test records for the most Test appearances (156), and having captained Australia in more Tests than any other captain (93). In 1993 he became the highest run-scorer in the history of Test cricket, with 10 123 runs, and he increased this record to a final 11 174 runs. He was Australian of the Year in 1990. >> cricket ℹ

Border terrier A breed of dog, developed in the Scottish/English border hills to hunt foxes; small and active; solid, flat-ended muzzle; small ears; thick, stiff, wiry coat; usually golden or reddish brown. >> dog; terrier

bore A nearly vertical wall of water that may be produced as a result of a tide, tsunami, or seiche. Bores usually occur in funnel-shaped estuaries with sloping bottoms.

Bottom friction slows the advancing wave front, and water piles up behind to produce a nearly vertical bore face. >> seiche; tide; tsunami

boreal forests The dense, coniferous forests of North America, Europe, and Asia. Characteristic tree species include fir, hemlock, spruce, and pine in more open areas. >> conifer; taiga

borecole [**baw(r)**kohl] >> **kale**

Borg, Björn (Rune) (1956–) Tennis player, born in Södertälje, Sweden. He became Wimbledon singles champion five times (1976–80), a modern-day record, losing to McEnroe in the 1981 final. He also won the French singles title six times, and was the World Championship Tennis singles champion in 1976. >> McEnroe; tennis, lawn ℹ

Borgå >> **Porvoo**

Borge, Victor [**baw(r)**guh] (1909–) Entertainer and pianist, born in Denmark. Since 1940 he has worked in the USA, and since 1956 has performed with leading symphony orchestras on worldwide tours. He is best known for his comedy sketches combining music and narrative.

Borges, Jorge Luis [**baw(r)**khes] (1899–1986) Writer, born in Buenos Aires. From 1941 he wrote mainly short stories, including *Ficciones* (1945, Fictions) and *El Aleph* (1949, The Aleph). In 1980 he won the Cervantes Prize.

Borghese [baw(r)**gay**zay] A great 13th-c family of ambassadors and jurists of Siena, afterwards (16th-c) at Rome. The Borghese Palace still contains one of the finest collections of paintings in Rome.

Borgia [**baw(r)**ja] Italian form of **Borja**, an ancient family in the Spanish province of Valencia. **Rodrigo Borgia** (1431–1503) became pope as Alexander VI (1492). Two of his children became especially notorious. **Cesare Borgia** (1476–1507) was a brilliant general and administrator, succeeding his brother (whom he may have murdered) as Captain-General of the Church. **Lucrezia Borgia** (1480–1519) was married three times by her father, for political reasons, finally becoming the wife of Alfonso d'Este, Duke of Ferrara. She has been represented as a person of wantonness, vices, and crimes; but she died enjoying the respect of her subjects, a patroness of learning and of art.

Borglum, (John) Gutzon (de la Mothe) [**baw(r)g**luhm] (1867–1941) Sculptor, born in St Charles, ID. He won renown for works of colossal proportions, such as the Mount Rushmore National Memorial. >> Rushmore, Mount

Borlaug, Norman (Ernest) [**baw(r)**log] (1914–) Plant pathologist and geneticist, born in Cresco, IA. He developed 'dwarf' wheats which dramatically increased yields and made possible the 'green revolution', and was awarded the Nobel Peace Prize in 1970. >> wheat

Bormann, Martin (1900–?45) Nazi politician, born in Halberstadt, Germany. One of Hitler's closest advisers, he became *Reichsminister* (1941) after Hess's flight to Scotland, and was with Hitler to the last. His own fate is uncertain. >> Hitler; World War 2

Born, Max (1882–1970) Physicist, born in Wrocław, Poland (formerly Breslau, Prussia). He shared the 1954 Nobel Prize for Physics for work in the field of quantum physics. >> quantum field theory

Borneo [**baw(r)**neeoh] area 484 330 sq km/186 951 sq mi. Island in SE Asia; comprises the Malaysian states of Sarawak and Sabah and the former British protectorate of Brunei (N); remainder comprises the four provinces of Kalimantan, part of Indonesia; formerly divided between the British and the Dutch; mountainous (N), rising to 4094 m/13 432 ft at Mt Kinabalu in Sabah; interior densely forested. >> Brunei; Indonesia ℹ; Sarawak

Bornholm [baw(r)n**holm**] pop (1995e) 45 800; area 588 sq km/227 sq mi. Danish island in the Baltic Sea, 40 km/25 mi S of Sweden; length 37 km/23 mi; rises to 162 m/531 ft; taken by Sweden, 1645; returned to Denmark, 1660; administrative capital and chief port, Rønne. >> Denmark ℹ

Borobudur [**bo**rohbooder] A Buddhist sanctuary built between 750 and 850 in Java, Indonesia. The monument comprises eight stepped terraces cut into the sides of a natural mound and culminating in a central shrine (*stupa*). >> Java (country)

Borodin, Alexander Porfiryevich [boro**deen**] (1833–87) Composer and scientist, born in St Petersburg, Russia. His compositions include the unfinished opera *Prince Igor* (which contains the Polovtsian Dances) and three symphonies.

boron [**boh**ron] B, element 5; melting point 2300°C. A hard, non-metallic solid, which as a pure element does not occur free in nature. It forms many compounds in which it is bound to oxygen. >> boranes; borax; chemical elements; RR1036

borough In general terms, the second tier of local government in England and Wales, based on charters granted at different times by the monarchy. **Borough councils** were first elected in 1835, when their main function was law and order. >> local government

Borromeo, St Charles [boro**may**oh] (1538–84) Cardinal archbishop of Milan, born in Arona, Italy. He did much to bring the Council of Trent (1545–63) to a successful conclusion, and was renowned for his work for the poor. He was canonized in 1610; feast day 4 November.

Borromini, Francesco [boro**mee**nee], originally **Francesco Castello** (1599–1667) Baroque architect, born in Bissone, Italy. He spent all his working life in Rome, where his designs include San Carlo alle Quattro Fontane (1637–41). >> Baroque (art and architecture)

Borrow, George (Henry) (1803–81) Writer and traveller, born in East Dereham, Norfolk. From 1825 to 1832 he wandered in England, sometimes in gypsy company, as described in *Lavengro* and *The Romany Rye*. As agent of the Bible Society he visited many European countries. >> Rom

borstal >> **youth custody centre**

borzoi [**baw(r)**zoy] A breed of dog, developed in Russia; an athletic breed, tall and slender; long thin muzzle; long tail; coat long, straight or curly; also known as **Russian wolfhound**. >> dog; hound

Bosch, Hieronymus, originally **Jerome van Aken** (c.1450–1516) Painter, born in 's Hertogenbosch, The Netherlands. Noted for his allegorical pictures displaying macabre devils, freaks, and monsters, his best-known works include 'The Garden of Earthly Delights' (Prado) and 'The Temptation of St Anthony' (Lisbon).

Bosnia and Herzegovina [**boz**nia, hertze**go**vina], Serbo-Croatian **Bosna-Hercegovina**, official name **Republic of Bosnia and Herzegovina** pop (1996e) 4 130 000 (Muslim-Croat Federation 2 520 000; Serbian Republic 1 610 000); area 51 129 sq km/19 736 sq mi. Republic in the Balkan peninsula of SE Europe; capital, Sarajevo; timezone GMT +2; major ethnic groups Bosnians (48%), Serbian (39%), Croatian (12%); languages, Serbo-Croatian (Serbian, Croatian, Bosnian); religions, Sunni Muslim, Serbian Orthodox, Roman Catholic; currency, the convertible mark (replacing the dinar in 1998); mountainous region, including part of the Dinaric Alps, noted for its limestone gorges, lakes, rivers, and mineral springs; reaches heights of 1800 m/6000 ft; dry limestone plateau in the SW (*karst*); climate ranges from Mediterranean to mildly continental; sirocco wind brings rain from SW; strong NE wind (*bora*) affects coastal area in winter; Austrian protectorate, 1878; annexed by Austria, 1908; Serbian opposition to the annexation led to the murder of Archduke

Francis Ferdinand, and World War 1; ceded to Yugoslavia, 1918; declaration of sovereignty, 1991; Bosnian Serbs proclaimed three autonomous regions (Bosanska Krajina, Romanija, and Northern Bosnia), 1991; declaration of independence, 1992, with ongoing military conflict between formerly integrated communities of Bosnians, Croats, and Serbs; UN peace-keeping forces deployed, and air-exclusion ('no-fly') zone imposed, 1992; various political proposals rejected, 1993–4; ceasefire agreed, 1995; peace talks in Dayton, OH, created two political entities: a Bosnian Muslim-Croat Federation (c.51% of the territory, including Sarajevo) and a Bosnian-Serb republic; NATO-supervised implementation-force (I-FOR), 1995–6, followed by a stabilization-force (S-FOR), 1996–; governed by an interethnic collective presidency of three members (Muslim, Serb, Croat), with a rotating chairman; each entity has its own prime minister; bicameral Assembly; highly industrialized economy, particularly iron and steel; forestry and agricultural trade; civil war disrupted all economic activity. >> Sarajevo; Serbia; Yugoslavia ℹ; Yugoslavian Civil War; RR1002

boson [**boh**son] A subatomic particle having integer spin; named after Indian physicist **Satyendra Nath Bose** (1894–1974). Force-carrying particles, such as photons, gluons, and gravitons, are all bosons. >> meson; particle physics; spin

Bosporus or **Bosphorus** [**bos**puhruhs], Turkish **Karadeniz Boğazi** Narrow strait separating European from Asiatic Turkey, and connecting the Black Sea and the Sea of Marmara; length 32 km/20 mi; minimum width 640 m/2100 ft; an area of great strategic importance. >> Bosporus Bridge; Dardanelles; Istanbul; Turkey ℹ

Bosporus Bridge [**bos**porus] A major steel suspension bridge across the Golden Horn at Istanbul, Turkey; completed in 1973; length of main span 1074 m/3524 ft. >> Bosporus; Istanbul

Bosra Ancient Syrian city, S of Damascus; a world heritage site. Originally an Arab fortress, it flourished as capital of the province of Arabia. >> Petra; Roman history ℹ

boss >> **bison**

Bossuet, Jacques Bénigne [bosway] (1627–1704) Catholic churchman and pulpit orator, born in Dijon, France. As Bishop of Meaux (1681) he took a leading part in the Gallican controversy, asserting the king's independence from the Roman Catholic Church in secular matters.

Boston 42°22N 71°04W, pop (1995e) 579 000. Capital of Massachusetts State, USA; largest city in New England; settled, 1630; capital of the Massachusetts Bay Colony, 1632; city status, 1822; a centre of opposition to British trade restrictions and scene of the Boston Tea Party, 1773; centre of the Unitarian Church movement; airport; railway; noted for its colleges and universities (1869, 1898, 1906); large immigrant population; professional teams, Red Sox (baseball), Celtics (basketball), Bruins (ice hockey). >> Boston Massacre / Tea Party; Massachusetts; Revere; Unitarians

Boston Massacre The first bloodshed of the American Revolution. British guards at the Boston Customs House opened fire on a crowd, killing five. >> American Revolution; Boston

Boston Strangler >> **Desalvo, Albert**

Boston Tea Party During the American Revolution, the climax of resistance to British attempts at direct taxation, resulting in the destruction in 1773 of 342 chests of dutied tea by working men disguised as Mohawks. >> American Revolution; Boston; Intolerable Acts

Boston terrier A breed of dog, developed in the USA by crossing existing terriers and bulldogs; small, deep-chested; large ears, spherical head, thick neck; coat short; white and brown or white and black. >> bulldog; terrier

Boswell, James (1740–95) Man of letters and biographer of Dr Johnson, born in Edinburgh. His *Journal of a Tour to the Hebrides* (1785) appeared after Johnson's death. Its success led him to plan his masterpiece, the *Life of Samuel Johnson* (1791). >> Johnson, Samuel

Bosworth Field, Battle of The battle which put Henry Tudor on the English throne after victory over Richard III, who died in the conflict. >> Henry VII; Richard III

botanical garden A collection of living plants usually arranged by geographic or taxonomic principles, and maintained for the purposes of scientific research, education, and recreation. The first European botanical gardens were collections of medicinal plants used for study in monasteries. >> arboretum; Kew Gardens

botany The study of all aspects of plants, principally their structure, physiology, relationships, and biogeography. Important areas include genetics and plant breeding; vegetative reproduction and tissue culture; ecology and conservation, especially of endangered habitats; and the use of plants as indicators of pollution. >> biogeography; biology; conservation (earth sciences); ecology; genetics; pollution

Botany Bay A shallow inlet 8 km/5 mi S of Sydney, New South Wales, Australia; now a residential part of Sydney; Captain Cook made his first landing here in 1770, naming the bay after the number of new plants discovered there. >> Cook, James; first fleet; Sydney

bot fly A robust, hairy fly, whose larvae are parasites beneath the skin of mammals, feeding on fluids exuding from tissues. (Order: Diptera. Family: Oestridae.) >> fly; larva

Botha, Louis [**boh**ta] (1862–1919) South African statesman and soldier, the first prime minister of South Africa (1910–19), born in Greytown, Natal. He suppressed de Wet's rebellion (1914), and conquered German SW Africa (1914–15). >> Boer Wars; South Africa ℹ

Botha, P(ieter) W(illem) [**boh**ta] (1916–) South African statesman, prime minister (1978–84), and president (1984–9), born in Paul Roux, Orange Free State, South

Africa. He attempted to introduce constitutional reforms, involving limited power-sharing with non-whites. After suffering a stroke in 1989, he resigned as president later that year. In 1998 he was put on trial, and found guilty of contempt for refusing to appear before the country's Truth and Reconciliation Commission. >> apartheid; South Africa ℹ; Truth and Reconciliation Commission

Botha, Roelof Frederik [**boh**ta], known as **Pik Botha** (1932–) South African politician. He was foreign minister in the governments of P W Botha and F W de Klerk, and in 1994 was appointed minister for minerals and energy in Nelson Mandela's first cabinet. >> Botha, P W; de Klerk; Mandela, Nelson

Botham, Ian (Terence) [**boh**tham] (1955–) Cricketer, born in Heswall, Cheshire. An all-rounder, he played for England in 102 Test matches, scored 5200 runs, took 383 wickets, and held 120 catches. His all-round figures are unsurpassed in Test cricket. He is well known for his walk from John o'Groats to Lands End, and for his aborted attempt to follow Hannibal's trek across the Alps, both ventures in aid of leukaemia research. He retired from first class-cricket in 1993. >> cricket (sport) ℹ

Bothnia, Gulf of [**both**neea] N arm of Baltic, between Sweden and Finland; length c.650 km/400 mi; width 80–240 km/50–150 mi; maximum depth c.100 m/330 ft; generally freezes over in winter. >> Baltic Sea

Bothwell, James Hepburn, 4th Earl of (c.1535–78) Third husband of Mary, Queen of Scots. He was held responsible for the murder of Mary's second husband, Lord Darnley (1567). He was made Duke of Orkney, then married Mary, but fled to Denmark after Mary's surrender to rebel forces at Carberry Hill. >> Mary, Queen of Scots

bo-tree >> **peepul**

Botswana [bots**wah**na], official name **Republic of Botswana** pop (1995e) 1 540 000; area 581 730 sq km/ 224 711 sq mi. S African republic; capital, Gaborone; timezone GMT +2; population mainly Tswana; religion, mainly local beliefs, 20% Christian; languages, English, Setswana; unit of currency, the pula of 100 thebes; landlocked, undulating, sand-filled plateau, mean elevation c.1000 m/3300 ft; most live in fertile E; to the W, dry scrubland and savannah, and the sand-covered Kalahari Desert; largely subtropical climate; rainfall in N and E almost totally in summer (Oct–Apr); visited by missionaries in 19th-c; under British protection, 1885; S part became a Crown Colony, then part of Cape Colony, 1895; N part became the Bechuanaland Protectorate; self-government, 1964; independence and change of name, 1966; governed by a legislative National Assembly, president, and cabinet; there is also a House of Chiefs; mainly subsistence farming, especially livestock; continual problems of drought and disease; some crops, especially sorghum; main minerals, nickel (second largest African producer), diamonds, cobalt; tourism, especially wildlife observation. >> Gaborone; Kalahari; RR1002 political leaders

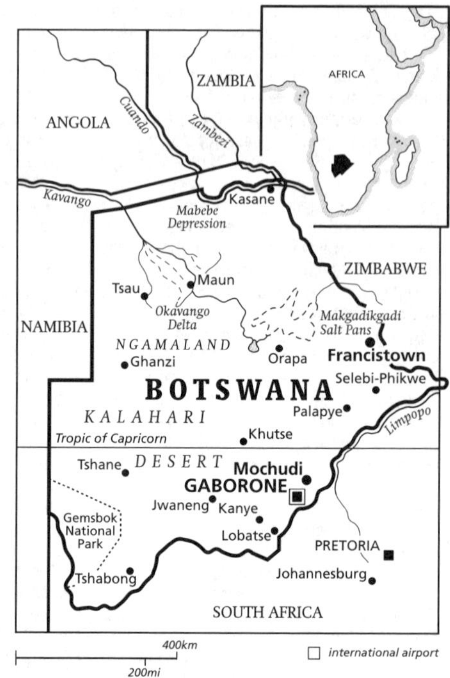

Botticelli, Sandro [boti**che**lee], originally **Alessandro Filipepi** (1445–1510) Painter of the early Renaissance, born in Florence, Italy. He produced many works on classical subjects – the finest his 'Birth of Venus' and 'Primavera' (Spring) in the Uffizi. He also painted frescoes for the Sistine Chapel at the Vatican. >> fresco

bottlebrush An evergreen shrub native to Australia; flowers small, crowded in dense cylindrical spikes, stamens red or yellow, far exceeding length of petals. (*Callistemon*, 25 species. Family: Myrtaceae.)

bottle gourd >> **calabash**

bottom or **beauty** In particle physics, an internal additive quantum number conserved in strong and electromagnetic interactions, but not in weak interactions; symbol *B*. The notion was postulated in 1977 to explain the properties of upsilon mesons, discovered that year. >> meson; particle physics; quantum numbers

botulism [**bot**yoolizm] A serious and often fatal illness resulting from the ingestion of a poisonous substance from *Clostridium botulinum*. It is one of the most severe forms of food poisoning, which affects the nervous system, and gives rise to rapidly developing paralysis and respiratory failure. The toxin is destroyed by cooking for 10 minutes at 80°C. >> clostridium; toxin

Boucher, François [booshay] (1703–70) Painter at the court of Louis XV, born in Paris. He is recognized as the purest exponent of the Rococo style in painting, known for his mythological and pastoral scenes, his female nudes, and his portraits of Madame de Pompadour. >> Rococo

Boudicca [**boo**dika, boo**di**ka], also known as **Boadicea** (1st-c) British warrior-queen, wife of Prasutagus, king of the Iceni, a tribe inhabiting what is now Norfolk and Suffolk. Her army took Londinium and Verulamium, and put to death as many as 70 000 Romans. Defeated in battle by Suetonius Paulinus, she took poison. >> Camulodunum; Verulamium

Boudin, (Louis) Eugène [boodĩ] (1824–98) Painter, born in Honfleur, France. A precursor of Impressionism, he is noted for his seascapes. >> Impressionism (art)

Bougainville [**boh**guhnvil] 6°12S 155°15E; pop (1995e) 143 000; area c.10 000 sq km/4000 sq mi. Mountainous volcanic island in Papua New Guinea, SW Pacific; length, 190 km/118 mi; width, 50 km/31 mi; rises to 2743 m/ 9000 ft at Mt Balbi; chief port, Kieta; independence movement with guerrilla fighting since 1988, badly affecting economy; copper mining, copra, cocoa, timber. >> Papua New Guinea ℹ

Bougainville, Louis Antoine, comte de (Count of)

[booganveel] (1729–1811) Navigator, born in Paris. He led the first French circumnavigation of the world (1766–9). Several places, including the largest of the Solomon Is, are named after him, as well as the plant *bougainvillea*. >> Napoleon I

bougainvillea [booguhn**vil**ia] A shrub, tree, or woody climber, native to South America; leaves oval; flowers tubular, in threes, surrounded by three lilac, purple, magenta, red, orange, pink, or white petal-like bracts. (Genus: *Bougainvillea*, 18 species. Family: Nyctaginaceae.) >> Bougainville, comte de; bract

Boulanger, Nadia [**boo**lãzhay] (1887–1979) Composer, conductor, organist, and influential teacher of music, born in Paris. Several of her pupils became well-known composers. >> Berkeley, Lennox; Copland; Milhaud

boulder clay >> **till**

Boulder Dam >> **Hoover Dam**

boules [bool] A French ball game similar to bowls, played between two players or teams; also known as *pétanque*. The object is to place the ball nearer to a target ball, or jack, than the opposing player or team. >> bowls

Boulez, Pierre [**boo**lez] (1925–) Composer and conductor, born in Montbrison, France. Known especially as an interpreter of contemporary music, he became director (1977–91) of the Institut de Recherche et de Co-ordination Acoustique Musique (Ircam) at the Pompidou Centre in Paris.

boulle >> **buhl**

Boulogne Eng [boo**loyn**], Fr [boolon] or **Boulogne-sur-Mer** 50°43N 1°37E, pop (1995e) 45 600. Seaport in NW France; principal commercial harbour and fishing port of France; ferry and hovercraft links with Dover and Folkestone. >> English Channel

Boult, Sir Adrian (Cedric) [bohlt] (1889–1983) Conductor, born in Chester, Cheshire. He became musical director of the BBC and conductor of the newly formed BBC Symphony Orchestra. He continued to conduct regularly until 1981.

***Bounty* Mutiny** The most famous of mutinies (28 Apr 1789). While HMS *Bounty* was returning to England from Tahiti, Fletcher Christian and several of the 44 crew seized control of the ship, and forced the commander, William Bligh, and 18 'loyalists' into a small boat. The 25 mutineers went back to Tahiti, 9 of whom (including Christian) travelled on to Pitcairn I. HMS *Endeavour* brought 14 surviving mutineers from Tahiti to England for trial, 3 of whom were eventually executed. >> Bligh; Christian, Fletcher

bourbon [**ber**bn] A dark-coloured American whiskey, a distillate of at least 51% maize. It originated in Bourbon Co, Kentucky. >> whisky

Bourbons [**boor**bõ] A French royal house descended from the Capetian St Louis IX (1215–70), associated with absolutist traditions at home and the extension of French influence abroad. Succeeding the last Valois, Henry IV (1589) established the dynasty. Under his son (Louis XIII) and grandson (Louis XIV), the long-standing rivalry between France and the Spanish Habsburgs came to a climax; it was concluded when a descendant, Philip of Anjou, ascended the Spanish throne (Philip V, reigned 1700–46), thereby founding the Spanish House of Bourbon. >> absolutism; Capetians; Condé; Habsburgs; Henry III / IV (of France); Louis XIV / XV / XVI; Orleans, House of; Philip V; Valois

Bourges [boorzh] 47°09N 2°25E, pop (1995e) 81 200 Ancient ducal town in C France; capital of Berry (12th-c); railway; bishopric; cathedral (13th-c).

Bourke-White, Margaret [berk], originally **Margaret White** (1906–71) Photo-journalist, born in New York City. She covered World War 2 for *Life*, and was the first woman photographer to be attached to the US armed forces, producing reports of the siege of Moscow (1941) and the opening of the concentration camps in 1944.

Bournemouth [**baw(r)n**muhth] 50°43N 1°54W, pop (1995e) 162 000. Unitary authority (from 1997) and resort town in S England, on Poole Bay; railway; university, 1992; conference centre; football league team, Bournemouth (Cherries). >> England [i]

Boutros Ghali, Boutros [**gal**ee] (1922–) Egyptian diplomat, who took office as the sixth secretary-general of the United Nations (1992–7). The former deputy prime minister of Egypt, he was the first to hold the post from the continent of Africa. He became head of La Francophonie in 1997. >> United Nations

Bouts, Dierick [bowts], also spelled **Dirk**, or **Thierry** (c.1415–75) Painter, born in Haarlem, The Netherlands. He produced austere religious paintings, with rich and gem-like colour. His best-known work is 'The Last Supper' (Louvain).

bouzouki [buh**zoo**kee] A plucked string instrument of Greece, used especially in folk music. It has a very long neck, a fretted fingerboard, and three or four courses of metal strings. >> string instrument 2 [i]

Bovidae [**boh**videe] A family of ruminant artiodactyl mammals (128 species), including cattle and antelopes; feed by grasping vegetation with their tongue, and cutting it with the lower incisor teeth; adult male (and usually female) with horns. >> antelope; artiodactyl; bison; cattle; goat; mammal [i]; ruminant [i]; water buffalo; zebu

bovine mastitis The inflammation of mammary tissue in cattle, which results in serious loss of milk production. A wide variety of micro-organisms is involved. >> cattle; mammary gland

bovine milk fever A metabolic disturbance due to a lack of circulating calcium following calving. There are muscle tremors and a general weakness leading to collapse and partial paralysis (*downer cow syndrome*) and the danger of heart changes. Most cases respond to prompt administration of calcium solutions. >> cattle

bovine spongiform encephalopathy (BSE) [**boh**viyn **spuhn**jifaw(r)m ensefa**lo**pathi] A progressive, fatal disease of the central nervous system of cattle (*encephalopathy*: disease affecting the structure of the brain); usually referred to by its abbreviation, but also widely called **mad cow disease**. BSE appeared in the UK in 1985; clinical cases peaked in late 1992–early 1993 and have declined steadily since, following control measures. Affected cattle may show behavioural changes and lack of co-ordination. There is no known treatment or cure. BSE is probably caused by a type of protein organism (a *prion*) resistant to high temperatures and disinfectants. The BSE agent is unique amongst the transmissible spongiform encephalopathies in that it may have crossed the species barrier: it is believed that cattle may have become infected by eating feed containing tissue from scrapie-infected sheep. Fear that BSE may be transmitted to humans by eating the nervous tissue of affected cattle, possibly causing the comparable spongiform encephalopathy, Creutzfeldt-Jakob disease (CJD), has led to control measures being enforced. These have included the banning of certain meat and bone meals of ruminant origin, the destruction of specified bovine offals, and the selective slaughter of cattle. The indications are that the policies adopted will see the elimination of BSE before the end of the century. >> BSE crisis; central nervous system; Creutzfeldt-Jakob disease; scrapie; virus

Bow, Clara [boh] (1905–65) Film actress, born in New York City. Having won a beauty contest, she went to Hollywood in 1921, and became a star of the silent screen, typifying the vivacious flapper of the Jazz Age. She starred in *It* (1927), and became popularly known as 'the It Girl'

bow >> crossbow; longbow

Bowdler, Thomas [**bowd**ler] (1754–1825) Man of letters, born in Ashley, Somerset. He is unhappily immortalized as the editor of *The Family Shakespeare* (1818), in which 'those words and expressions are omitted which cannot with propriety be read aloud in a family'.

bowerbird A bird native to New Guinea and Australia; related to birds of paradise. Males usually attract females by building ornate structures (*bowers*) on the ground. (Family: Ptilonorhynchidae, 18 species.) >> bird of paradise

Bowie, David [**bow**ee], originally **David Robert Jones** (1947–) Rock singer and actor, born in London. His career blossomed throughout the 1970s as he adopted a range of extreme stage images to suit a variety of musical styles. His albums include *Hunky Dory* (1971), and *Heroes* (1977). His film career includes roles in *The Man Who Fell to Earth* (1976), and *Basquiat* (1996).

Bowie, Jim [**boo**ee, **boh**ee], popular name of **James Bowie** (c.1796–1836) US pioneer, born in Logan County, KY. He is mainly remembered for his role in defending the Alamo (1836) during the Texas revolution. He was the inventor of the curved sheath knife named after him. >> Alamo; Texas

Bowles, Erskine [bowlz] (1945–) US public official, born in North Carolina. An investment banker (1975–93) and administrator of the US Small Business Administration (1993–4), he joined the White House as deputy chief-of-staff (1994–5), and after returning to his business career (1995–6) became chief-of-staff in Clinton's second administration. He left the administration in October 1998.

bowling The act of delivering a ball at pins (as opposed to a target, as in bowls); a popular indoor sport and pastime, with an ancient history. The game of **ninepins** was taken to the USA by Dutch and German immigrants in the latter part of the 19th-c. When the sport was outlawed, a 10th pin was added as a way around the legislation. **Ten-pin bowling** is now the most popular form. >> bowls; skittles; RR1047

bowls An indoor and outdoor game played as singles, pairs, triples, or fours. Glasgow solicitor William Mitchell (1803–84) drew up the rules for modern bowls in 1848. There are two main variations: **lawn bowls** (also known as **flat green bowls**) is played on a flat, level rink, whereas **crown green bowls** is played on an uneven green raised at the centre. In both varieties the object is to deliver your bowl nearer to the *jack* (a smaller target ball) than your opponent(s). Bowls have a bias which causes them to curve, imparted by flattening one side of the bowl. >> RR1047

box An evergreen shrub or small tree (*Buxus sempervirens*) growing to 10 m/30 ft, often less, native to Europe and N Africa; flowers green, lacking petals; fruit a woody capsule. (Family: Buxaceae.)

box camera The simplest form of camera for amateur photography: a rectangular box containing holders for paper-backed roll film advanced by an external winder, a fixed-focus lens, and a shutter for instantaneous exposure. Early examples are the original Kodak camera of 1888 and the Box Brownie of 1900 which popularized snapshot photography. >> camera; photography

boxer A breed of dog; large muscular body; rounded compact head; ears soft, pendulous; muzzle short and broad, with pronounced jowls and prominent lower jaw; developed from the bulldog in Germany (late 19th-c). >> bulldog; dog

Boxer Rising An anti-foreign movement in China (1898–1900). Its name derives from the secret society to which the rebels belonged, the 'Righteous and Harmonious Fists', whose members adopted boxing and other rituals, convinced by their mixture of magical beliefs that foreign weapons could not harm them. It originated in N China, as a reaction to economic distress and Western territorial seizures. Many foreigners were killed, and the foreign legations in Tianjin and Beijing were besieged. The rising was eventually suppressed, and The Boxer Protocol (1901) imposed massive indemnities on China.

boxing Fighting with fists, a sport recorded from the earliest times. The first rules were drawn up by John Broughton in 1743. Boxing was with bare knuckles, and each round lasted until one fighter was knocked down. The *Queensberry Rules*, as drawn up in 1867 by the 8th Marquess of Queensberry, laid the foundation of the modern sport. Professional championship bouts constitute 12 3-min rounds. Amateur contests are over three rounds, and all fighters must wear a vest. All fights last until one fighter is knocked out or retires, the referee halts the fight, a fighter is disqualified, or the designated number of rounds is reached. If the fight goes the distance, judges then mark the fighters according to winning punches, etc. It is possible to have a draw. Four bodies recognize world champions; the *World Boxing Council (WBC)*, founded in 1963; the *World Boxing Association (WBA)*, founded in 1927 as the National Boxing Association; the *International Boxing Federation (IBF)*, founded in 1983; and the *World Boxing Organization (WBO)*, founded in 1988. >> Lonsdale Belt; Queensberry; RR1048

Boxing Day In the UK and the Commonwealth, the day after Christmas Day. It is so called because traditionally on that day gifts from boxes placed in church were distributed to the poor, and apprentices took a box round their masters' customers in the hope of getting presents of money from them.

boyars Members of the highest stratum of the Russian feudal aristocracy from the 10th-c to the early 18th-c. The *Boyarskaya Duma* ('Boyars' Council') was a major legislative and deliberative assembly under the mediaeval tsars. >> duma; feudalism; tsar

Boycott, Charles Cunningham (1832–97) British soldier, born in Burgh St Peter, Norfolk. A land agent in Co Mayo, Ireland, he was one of the first victims in 1880 of Parnell's system of social excommunication. His name is the source of the word 'boycott' in English. >> Parnell

Boycott, Geoffrey (1940–) Cricketer and broadcaster, born in Fitzwilliam, Yorkshire. In 1981 he overtook Gary Sobers's world record of 8032 Test runs, and in 108 Tests for England scored 8114 runs (average 47·72). Captain of Yorkshire 1971–8, he was a brilliant but often controversial

The weight divisions in professional boxing

name	maximum weight
heavyweight	any weight
cruiserweight/junior-heavyweight	88 kg / 195 lb
light-heavyweight	79 kg / 175 lb
super-middleweight	77 kg / 170 lb
middleweight	73 kg / 160 lb
light-middleweight/junior-middleweight	70 kg / 154 lb
welterweight	67 kg / 147 lb
light-welterweight/junior welterweight	64 kg / 140 lb
lightweight	61 kg / 135 lb
junior-lightweight/super-featherweight	59 kg / 130 lb
featherweight	57 kg / 126 lb
super-bantamweight/junior-featherweight	55 kg / 122 lb
bantamweight	54 kg / 118 lb
super-flyweight/junior-bantamweight	52 kg / 115 lb
fly weight	51 kg / 112 lb
light-flyweight/junior-flyweight	49 kg / 108 lb
mini-flyweight/straw-weight/minimum weight	under 48 kg / 105 lb

batsman. Since retiring from first-class cricket in 1986, he has become known as a cricket commentator. >> cricket (sport) ℹ; Sobers

Boyer, Paul D (1918–) Chemist, born in Provo, UT. He graduated from the Univesity of Wisconsin in 1943, and taught at the University of California, Los Angeles. He shared the 1997 Nobel Prize for Chemistry for his contribution towards the elucidation of the enzymatic mechanism underlying the synthesis of adenosine triphosphate.

Boyer, Charles [boyay] (1899–1978) Actor, born in Figeac, France. A star of the French stage and cinema, he settled in Hollywood in 1934, and was known as the screen's 'greatest lover' from such romantic roles as *Mayerling* (1936) and *Algiers* (1938). His later appearances included *Barefoot in the Park* (1967) and *Stavisky* (1974).

Boyer, Sir Richard (James Fildes) [**boy**er] (1891–1961) Broadcasting administrator, born in Taree, New South Wales, Australia. He became chairman of the Australian Broadcasting Company in 1945. The ABC Lectures were renamed the **Boyer Lectures** in his honour after his death.

Boyle, Robert (1627–91) Physicist and chemist, born at Lismore Castle, Co Waterford. In 1661 he published his *Sceptical Chymist*, in which he criticized the current theories of matter, and in 1662 arrived at **Boyle's law**, which states that the pressure and volume of gas are inversely proportional. >> gas laws

Boyne, Battle of the A battle fought near the River Boyne, Drogheda, Ireland, between Protestant forces under William III and smaller Catholic forces led by James II. William's decisive victory marked a critical stage in the English reconquest of Ireland. >> James II (of England); William III

Boy Scouts >> **scouting**

Brabham, Jack [**bra**buhm], popular name of **Sir John Arthur Brabham** (1926–) Motor-racing driver, born in Sydney. Australia's first world champion (1959), he won further titles in 1960 and 1966. He has remained active in the motor-racing field, but no longer owns Brabham cars. >> motor racing

Brachiopoda [braki**op**oda] >> **lamp shell**

bracken A perennial fern (*Pteridium aquilinum*) with far-creeping rhizomes; fronds solitary, up to 2–4 m/6½–13 ft; tri-pinnate; common on acid soils, especially in woods and heaths. It is poisonous, and not grazed by animals such as sheep and rabbits. (Family: Polypodiaceae.) >> fern; pinnate; rhizome

bract A modified leaf immediately below a flower or inflorescence. It is usually green, but may be brightly coloured and petal-like. >> inflorescence ℹ; leaf ℹ

Bracton, Henry de (?–1268) English jurist. His *De legibus et consuetudinibus Angliae* (On the Laws and Customs of England) is the earliest attempt at a systematic treatment of English law.

Bradbury, Malcolm (1932–) Writer and critic, born in Sheffield, West Yorkshire. The travels and travails of an academic have provided material for several of his novels, such as *The History Man* (1975) and *The Atlas of Literature* (1996).

Bradbury, Ray(mond Douglas) (1920–) Science-fiction writer, born in Waukegan, IL. His collections of short stories include *The Martian Chronicles* (1950) and *The Golden Apples of the Sun* (1953). He is best known for film adaptations of two of his novels, *The Illustrated Man* (1951) and *Fahrenheit 451* (1953). >> science fiction

Bradford 53°48N 1°45W, urban area pop (1995e) 483 000. Town in West Yorkshire, N England; 19th-c development was based on the wool textile industry; railway; university (1966); cathedral (15th-c); football league team, Bradford City (Bantams); scene of major disaster (1985) when wooden stand of Bradford City Football Club caught fire, killing 56. >> Yorkshire, West

Bradford, Barbara Taylor (1933–) Journalist and novelist, born in Leeds, West Yorkshire. She worked for several newspapers and magazines, both in the UK and USA, before gaining success with her first novel, *Woman of Substance* (1980). Later books include *The Women in his Life* (1990) and *Her Own Rules* (1996).

Bradford, William (1590–1657) Colonist and religious leader, born in Austerfield, South Yorkshire. One of the moving spirits in the Pilgrim Fathers' expedition, he sailed on the *Mayflower*, and in 1621 became governor of Plymouth Colony. >> Pilgrims

Bradlaugh, Charles [**brad**law] (1833–91) Free-thinking social reformer, born in London. In 1880 he became an MP, and claimed the right as an unbeliever to make an affirmation of allegiance instead of taking the parliamentary oath, but the House refused to allow this. He was re-elected on three occasions, and was finally admitted (1886). >> Besant, Annie

Bradlee, Benjamin (Crowninshield) (1921–) Journalist and writer, born in Boston, MA. In 1965 he became managing editor of the *Washington Post*, and encouraged the investigative journalism which reached its high point in the Watergate scandal. >> Watergate

Bradley, Omar N(elson) (1893–1981) US general, born in Clark, MO. In World War 2, he played a prominent part in Tunisia and Sicily, and in 1944 led the US invading armies through France and Germany. >> World War 2

Bradman, Sir Don(ald George) (1908–) Cricketer, born in Cootamundra, New South Wales, Australia. He played for Australia 1928–48, and was captain from 1936. He set up many batting records, including the highest score (452 not out), and his Test batting average was 99·94 runs per innings. He later became chairman of the Australian Cricket Board (1960–3, 1969–72). >> cricket (sport) ℹ

Bradstreet, Anne, *née* **Dudley** (1612–72) Poet, born in Northampton, UK. She emigrated with her husband to Massachusetts in 1630, and is acknowledged as the first poet of note in British America.

Brady, Ian (1938–) Convicted murderer, born in Glasgow. In a case which horrified the public, it was revealed that Brady, with his lover **Myra Hindley** (1942–), lured young children into their home in Manchester and subjected them to torture before killing them. The lovers were described as the 'Moors Murderers' because they buried most of their victims on Saddleworth Moor in the Pennines.

Braemar [bray**mah(r)**] 57°01N 3°24W. Village in Aberdeenshire council, Scotland, 10 km/6 mi W of Balmoral Castle; Highland games (Aug). >> Balmoral Castle; Grampians (Scotland)

Braga [**brah**ga], ancient **Bracara Augusta** 41°32N 8°26W, pop (1995e) 90 200. Fourth largest city in Portugal, former capital of the old region of Entre Minho and Douro; seat of the Primate of Portugal; university; cathedral (11th-c). >> Portugal ℹ

Braganza [bra**gan**za], Port **Bragança** [bra**gan**sa], ancient **Juliobriga** 41°47N 6°46W, pop (1995e) 16 500. City in NE Portugal; original seat of the House of Braganza, rulers of Portugal, 1640–1910; castle (1187); bishopric; cathedral. >> Portugal ℹ

Bragg (of Wigton), Melvyn Bragg, Baron (1939–) Novelist and broadcaster, born in Wigton, Cumbria. His novels include *The Hired Man* (1969), *Love and Glory* (1983), and *A Time to Dance* (1990). He has been presenter and editor of ITV's *The South Bank Show* since 1978, and presenter of BBC Radio 4's *Start the Week* (1988–98). He became chairman of Border Television in 1990.

Brahe, Tycho [**brah**hoe, **tiy**koh] (1546–1601) Astronomer, born in Knudstrup, Sweden (then under the Danish crown). In 1573 he discovered serious errors in the astronomical tables, and commenced work to rectify this by observing the stars and planets with unprecedented positional accuracy. >> Copernican system; Ptolemaic system

Brahma [**brah**ma] The personified creator god of Hinduism. The deities Vishnu, Shiva, and Brahma form the *Trimurti* of classical Indian thought. As Vishnu and Shiva represent opposite forces, Brahma represents the balance between them. >> Brahmanism; Hinduism; Trimurti

Brahman cattle >> **zebu**

Brahmanism [**brah**manizm] An early religion of India (though not the earliest), to which, historically, Indians have looked as the source of their religious traditions. It came to dominance during the Vedic Period (c.1200–500 BC) and was a religion of ritual and sacrifice. >> Brahmins; Hinduism; Veda

Brahmaputra, River [brama**poo**tra], Chin **Yalu Zangbu**, Bangla **Jamuna** River in SW China and India, rising in the Chinese Himalayas; flows E then S into Assam, then S into Bangladesh, joining the R Ganges before entering the Bay of Bengal through a vast delta; length c.2900 km/1800 mi.

Brahmins [**brah**minz] The highest of the four Hindu social classes. A priestly class, the Brahmins dominated Indian society for many centuries. Many of their descendants have now taken up secular occupations. >> Brahmanism; Hinduism

Brahms, Johannes (1833–97) Composer, born in Hamburg, Germany. He earned his living as a pianist until 1853, when he was able to concentrate on composition, settling in Vienna. His main works include four symphonies, two piano concertos, a violin concerto, a large amount of chamber and piano music, and many songs. His greatest choral work is the *German Requiem* (first performed complete in 1869). >> classical music

braille [brayl] A communication system designed to enable blind people to have access to written language; devised in 1829 by French teacher Louis Braille (1809–52). It consists of a sequence of cells, each of which contains a 3 × 2 matrix of embossed dots, whose patterns can be sensed through the fingers. Computer-assisted systems are now available which can turn written text into braille.

brain The part of the central nervous system of bilaterally symmetrical animals which co-ordinates and controls many bodily activities to an extent that depends upon the species. In humans, in addition to the control of movement, sensory input, and a wide range of physiological processes, it acts as the organ of thought, with several areas being specialized for specific intellectual functions (eg language, calculation). It occupies the cranial cavity, and can be divided into the **forebrain** (the *cerebral hemispheres* and *diencephalon*), **midbrain**, and **hindbrain** (the *cerebellum*, *pons*, and *medulla oblongata*). >> brain death / stem; cerebellum; cerebral haemorrhage / palsy; cerebrospinal fluid; cerebrum; dementia; diencephalon; encephalitis; epilepsy; hydrocephalus; laterality; medulla oblongata; meningitis; paralysis; ventricles

brain death The cessation of brain activity, including in particular the death of the neurological centres in the brain stem concerned with respiration and other vital functions. It must be certified by two doctors who can demonstrate the absence of electrical impulses from the brain surface (a flat EEG), and the failure of the pupils to react to light and the eyes to oscillate (*nystagmus*) in response to the introduction of warm and cold water into the external ear canal. The diagnosis is usually made on individuals in a coma whose respirations are being artificially sustained and whose hearts have not ceased to beat. >> brain ℹ; electroencephalography

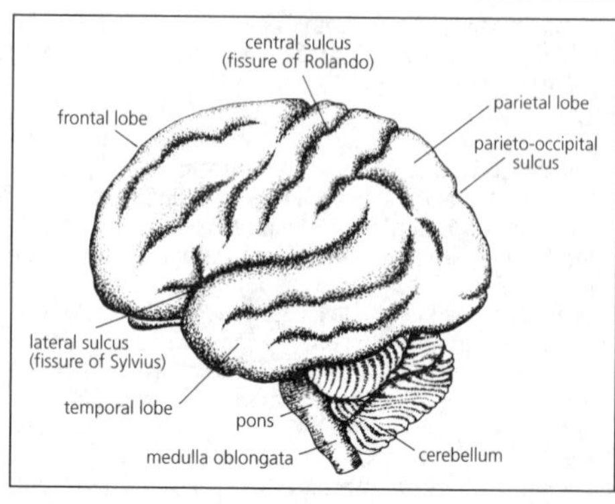

The left side of the brain (cerebrum)

Braine, John (Gerard) (1922–86) Writer, born in Bradford, West Yorkshire. The success of his first book, *Room at the Top* (1957), enabled him to embark on a career as a novelist, identified with the 'Angry Young Men' of the 1950s. His novels deal mostly with the north of England and northerners, and include *The Vodi* (1959), *Life at the Top* (1962), and *One and Last Love* (1981). >> Angry Young Men

brain stem That part of the nervous system between the spinal cord and the forebrain, consisting of a thick bundle of transversely running fibres called the *pons*, with the *midbrain* above it and the *medulla oblongata* below. The cardiac, respiratory, vasomotor, and other 'vital' physiological centres are located in the medulla. >> brain ℹ; medulla oblongata; neurone ℹ; nervous system

brake A device used to apply a force to an object to retard its motion. The most common method is to bring the moving surface into contact with a fixed surface, thereby

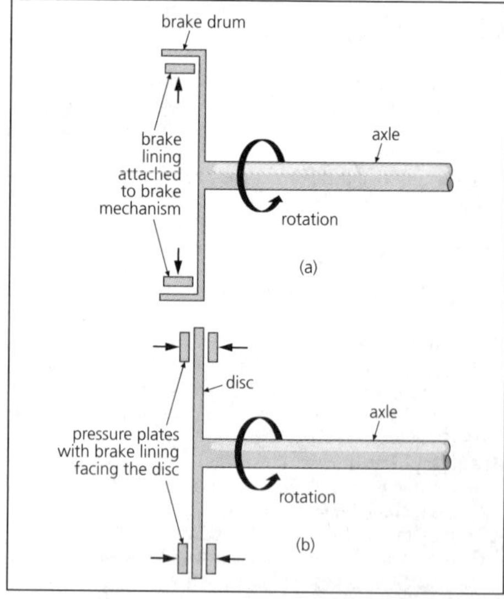

Types of brake – in a drum brake (a) the brake lining material is on the one side of a rotating drum fixed to the axle. In a disc brake (b) the brake lining is fixed on both sides of a rotating disc fixed to the axle.

generating friction which opposes the direction of movement. The two types of brake most commonly used on motor cars are **drum brakes** and **disc brakes**. >> *see illustration on p.116*

Bramah, Joseph [**bra**ma] (1748–1814) Inventor, born in Stainborough, South Yorkshire. His inventions include a hydraulic press, a machine for numbering banknotes, and a safety lock which remained pickproof for over 60 years. >> lock i

Bramante, Donato [bra**man**tay], originally **Donato di Pascuccio d'Antonio** (c.1444–1514) Architect and painter, born near Urbino, Italy. He drew up plans for the renovation of the Vatican and St Peter's (1505–6), and much influenced the development of Renaissance architecture in Italy. >> Renaissance

bramble >> **blackberry**

brambling A finch native to the N Old World (*Fringilla montifringilla*); migrates to the Mediterranean and N Africa for winter. (Family: Fringillidae.) >> finch

bran The protective coat surrounding a cereal seed which, because of its high fibre content, is becoming increasingly common as a component of human foods. It comprises about 12% of the seed. >> fibre

Branagh, Kenneth (Charles) [**bra**na] (1960–) Actor and director, born in Belfast. He joined the Royal Shakespeare Company in 1984, and in 1987 co-founded and became co-director of the Renaissance Theatre Company. He has starred in several films, such as *Henry V* (1989), *Much Ado About Nothing* (1993), and *Hamlet* (1997), all of which he directed. In 1998 he co-founded the Shakespeare Film Company. He married actress Emma Thompson in 1989 (separated, 1995). >> Thompson, Emma

Branchiopoda [brangki**op**oda] A diverse class of aquatic crustaceans found mostly in inland waters; characterized by leaf-like trunk limbs that act as food-gathering apparatus and as gills; contains c.820 living species. >> crustacean

Brancusi, Constantin [bran**koo**zee] (1876–1957) Sculptor, born in Pestisani, Romania. His 'Sleeping Muse' (1910, Muzeul de Artă, Bucharest) shows Rodin's influence, and is the first of many characteristic, highly polished, egg-shaped carvings. >> abstract art; Rodin

Brandeis, Louis (Dembitz) [**bran**diys] (1856–1941) Jurist, born in Louisville, KY. His opinions on issues of governmental power and legal procedure rank him as a major legal theoretician, and he became the first Jewish member of the Supreme Court. Brandeis University in Waltham, MA, was named after him. >> Supreme Court

Brandenburg or **Brandenburg an der Havel** [**bran**dnberg] 52°25N 12°34E, pop (1995e) 99 200. Industrial city in EC Germany, former centre of the Prussian province of Brandenburg; much rebuilding after severe damage in World War 2; railway. >> Germany i; Prussia

Brandenburg Gate An arch designed by Carl Langhans (1733–1808) and erected in Berlin in 1788–91. The monument, which was badly damaged during World War 2, was restored in 1958. >> Berlin; Unter den Linden

Brando, Marlon (1924–) Film and stage actor, born in Omaha, NE. He was a product of the New York Actors' Studio, with its emphasis on 'method' acting. His films include *The Godfather* (1972), *Apocalypse Now* (1977), and *Don Juan de Marco* (1995). His most outstanding role was in *On the Waterfront* (1954), for which he won his first Oscar, but he refused to accept a second, for *The Godfather*, in protest against the persecution of the Indians.

Brandt, Bill [brant], popular name of **William Brandt** (1904–83) Photographer, born in London. He portrayed life in London during the Blitz, and later made a striking series on the nude, in which his essays in pure form, as published in *Perspective of Nudes* (1961) and *Shadows of Light* (1966), approached the surreal.

Brandt, Willy [brant], originally **Karl Herbert Frahm** (1913–92) West German statesman and Chancellor (1969–74), born in Lübeck, Germany. In 1966 he led the Social Democratic Party into a coalition government with the Christian Democrats, and in 1969 was elected Chancellor in a coalition government with the Free Democrats. He was awarded the 1971 Nobel Peace Prize. He later chaired a commission on the world economy (the **Brandt Commission Report**, 1980). >> Germany i

brandy A spirit distilled from fruit fermentation, usually grapes, but also from stone fruits such as cherries. Cognac is produced in the Charente basin, France, from white grapes aged for a minimum of 2 years in barrels of Limousin oak. Armagnac is produced to the S of this area, and matured in 'black' oak. Calvados is made from cider in Normandy. >> fermentation

Brandywine, Battle of the A battle fought during the War of Independence, taking its name from the Brandywine Creek near Philadelphia. British forces under Howe defeated Washington's troops. >> American Revolution; Howe, William; Washington, George

Branson, Richard (Charles Nicholas) (1950–) Businessman, born in Sharnley Green, Surrey. He opened his first shop in London in 1971, under the name Virgin. This was followed by a series of highly successful business enterprises, including a recording company, various retailing operations, the travel company Voyager Group (1980), the airline Virgin Atlantic (1984), Virgin Radio (1993), Virgin Direct (1995), and V2 Music (1996). He is also known for his sporting achievements, notably the record-breaking Atlantic crossing in *Virgin Atlantic Challenger II* in 1986, and the first crossing by hot-air balloon of the Atlantic (1987) and Pacific (1991).

Braque, Georges [brak] (1882–1963) Painter, born in Argenteuil, France. He was one of the founders of classical Cubism, and worked with Picasso from 1908 to 1914. After World War 1 he developed a personal nongeometric, semi-abstract style. >> Cubism; Picasso

Brasília [bra**zil**ia] 15°45S 47°57W, pop (1995e) 1 962 000. Capital of Brazil in WC Brazil; construction began in 1956; capital moved from Rio de Janeiro in 1960; principal architect Oscar Niemeyer (1907–); laid out in the shape of a bent bow and arrow; airport; university (1961); cathedral; light industry; famous for its modern sculpture; designated a world heritage site. >> Brazil i

Braşov [bra**shov**], formerly **Kronstadt** (to 1918), **Stalin** (1950–60) 45°39N 25°35E, pop (1995e) 322 000. City in C Romania; founded, 13th-c; ceded by Hungary after World War 1; railway junction; university (1971); summer resort and winter sports centre. >> Romania i

brass An alloy composed of copper and zinc; yellowish, malleable, and ductile. Its properties and applications may be altered by varying the proportions of copper and zinc. It is the most widely used non-ferrous alloy. >> alloy; copper; zinc

brassica A member of a genus of plants containing numerous economically important vegetables, including turnip and mustard, but often in a gardening sense referring more specifically to cabbages, cauliflower, broccoli, and Brussels sprouts, all derived from the wild cabbage, *Brassica oleracea*. (Genus: *Brassica*, 30 species. Family: Cruciferae.) >> cabbage; mustard; rape (botany); swede; turnip; vegetable

brass instrument A musical instrument made of brass or other metal, in which air is made to vibrate by means of the player's lips and breath, usually through a narrow mouthpiece. In simple instruments, such as the bugle, the notes available are restricted to the lower end of a

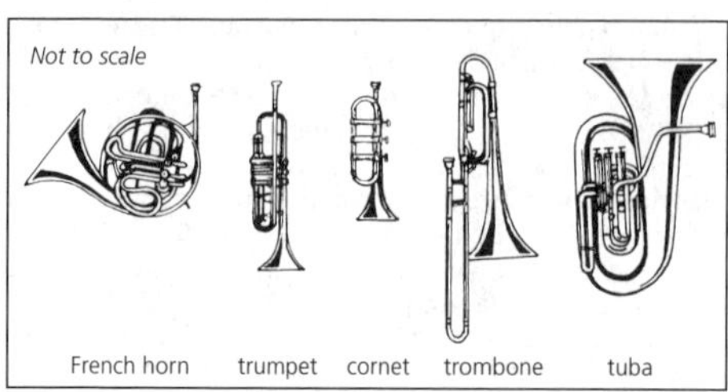

Brass instruments

single harmonic series; in others, valves or slides enable the fundamental note to be altered, and consequently a greater number of pitches to be obtained. >> aerophone; bugle (music); cornet; euphonium; flugelhorn; horn; saxhorn; sousaphone; trombone; trumpet; tuba; *see illustration above*

Bratby, John (1928–92) Artist and writer, born in London. One of the leading representatives of the English Realist School, in the mid-1950s, he was associated with the 'kitchen sink' school, as typified in 'Baby in Pram' (Liverpool). >> Realism

Bratislava [bratis**lah**va], Ger **Pressburg**, Hung **Pozsony**, ancient **Posonium** 48°10N 17°08E, pop (1995e) 450 000. River port and capital of the Slovak Republic; on R Danube; stronghold of Great Moravian Empire, 9th-c; capital of Hungary, 1541–1784; centre of emergent Slovak national revival; incorporated into Czechoslovakia in 1918; airport; railway; university (1919); technical university (1938); cathedral (13th-c). >> Slovak Republic [i]

Brattain, Walter H(ouser) (1902–87) US physicist, born in Amoy, China. In 1929 he joined Bell Telephone Laboratories, where he worked on the surface properties of semiconductors, and also helped to devise the point contact transistor, for which he shared the Nobel Prize for Physics in 1956. >> Bardeen; electronics; transistor

Braun, Eva [brown] (1910–45) The mistress of Adolf Hitler, born in Munich. She met Hitler in the early 1930s, and is said to have married him before they committed suicide together during the fall of Berlin. >> Hitler

Braun, Wernher von [brown] (1912–77) Rocket pioneer, born in Wirsitz, Germany. In 1936 he directed a rocket research station at Peenemünde, where he perfected and launched the V-2 rockets against Britain (Sep 1944). After the war, he became a naturalized American, and was chiefly responsible for the launching of the first American artificial Earth satellite (1958). >> V-2

Brazil, Port **Brasil**, official name **The Federative Republic of Brazil**, Port **República Federativa do Brasil** pop (1995e) 159 233 000; area 8 511 965 sq km/3 285 618 sq mi. Republic in E and C South America; coastline 7408 km/ 4603 mi; capital Brasília; four timezones, GMT −2 in the Atlantic islands, −3 in the E, −4 in the mid-W, and −5 in the extreme W; white (53%), mixed (34%), and black (6%); religion, 70% Roman Catholic, remainder Protestant or Spiritualist; official language, Portuguese; currency unit, the real of 100 centavos; low-lying Amazon basin in the N; where forest canopy cleared, soils susceptible to erosion; Brazilian plateau in the C and S, average height 600–900 m/2000–3000 ft; Guiana Highlands (S) contain Brazil's highest peak, Pico da Neblina (3014 m/9888 ft); eight river systems, notably the Amazon (N), the São Francisco (C), and the Paraguay, Paraná, and Uruguay (S); thin coastal strip on the Atlantic, c.100 km/325 mi wide, containing 30% of the population; climate almost entirely tropical, Equator passing through the N region, and Tropic of Capricorn through the SE; Amazon basin, annual rainfall 1500–2000 mm/60–80 in, no dry season, average midday temperatures 27–32°C; dry region in the NE, susceptible to long droughts; hot, tropical climate on narrow coastal strip, with rainfall varying greatly N–S; S states have a seasonal, temperate climate; discovered for the Portuguese by Cabral in 1500, first settlement at Salvador da Bahia; independence declared 1822, and monarchy established; republic followed 1889 coup; revolution headed by Vargas established dictatorship, 1930–45; liberal republic restored, 1946; another coup in 1964 led to a military-backed presidential regime; military junta, 1969; new elections, 1985; new constitution of 1988 allowed direct presidential elections, 1989; bicameral National Congress; one of the world's largest farming countries, agriculture employing 35% of the population; world's largest exporter of coffee, second largest exporter of cocoa and soya beans; iron ore (reserves possibly world's largest); timber reserves the third largest in the world, but continuing destruction of the Amazon rainforest is causing much concern; road network being extended through the Amazon rainforest; Carnival celebrations (weekend before Lent). >> Amazon, River; Brasília; Cabral; Minas Gerais; Rio de Janeiro; São Paulo; RR1002 political leaders

Brazil nut An evergreen tree (*Bertholletia excelsa*) growing to 30 m/100 ft, native to the jungles of Brazil; flowers white; fruit a woody or rounded capsule containing 3-sided seeds familiarly called by the same name. (Family: Lecythidaceae.) >> nut

brazing The joining of two pieces of metal (the same or different) by heating, then filling in the junction with a metal of lower melting point than those being joined. A flux is generally necessary. >> flux (technology); solder

Brazzaville [**braz**avil] 4°14S 15°14E, pop (1995e) 989 000. River-port capital of the Congo, W Africa, on right bank of R Congo; founded, 1880; capital of French Equatorial Africa, 1910; headquarters of Free French forces in World War 2; capital of Congo, 1960; airport; railway terminus from coast; university (1972); cathedral. >> Congo [i]

bread A widely used staple food made by baking a mixture of flour and water; the flour used is most commonly wheat, which may be mixed with flour from oatmeal, rye, or barley. The mix results in a dough which may be kneaded, a process that stretches and aligns the protein

molecules of the wheat. The product is then either immediately baked to give **unleavened bread**, or allowed to rise, through the production of carbon dioxide, to give **leavened bread**. The carbon dioxide can be produced either chemically or by using yeast. >> baking powder; chapati; flour; soda bread; yeast

breadfruit An evergreen tree (*Artocarpus altilis*) growing to 12–18 m/40–60 ft, probably native to Malaysia; rounded, multiple fruits, 10–20 cm/4–8 in diameter, and green to brownish when ripe, filled with a white, fibrous pulp. (Family: Moraceae.) >> achene

break dancing >> **street dance**

breaking stress >> **tensile strength**

Breakspear, Nicholas >> **Adrian IV**

bream Deep-bodied freshwater fish (*Abramis brama*) found in quiet lowland rivers and lakes of N Europe; length up to c.60 cm/2 ft. (Family: Cyprinidae.)

Bream, Julian (Alexander) [breem] (1933–) Guitarist and lutenist, born in London. Several composers, including Britten and Walton, have written works for him. He formed the Julian Bream Consort in 1961, specializing in early ensemble music. >> guitar; lute

breast The milk-producing organ of the female reproductive system; also known as the **mammary gland**. It is composed of glandular tissue supported by fibrous tissue covered by skin and a thick layer of fat. The two breasts in humans are found on the front of the chest: they are small in children, but at puberty the female breasts increase rapidly in size, whereas in males they remain rudimentary. During pregnancy the breasts enlarge, being largest during milk secretion (*lactation*). At the apex of the breast is the *nipple*, surrounded by the darker *areola*. >> breast cancer; mammary gland; thorax

breastbone >> **sternum**

breast cancer The commonest malignant tumour in women, spreading within the breast tissue and to the skin, which may ulcerate. Treatment depends on many factors, but includes surgical removal of the tumour or breast (*mastectomy*) and a combination of hormonal and anti-cancer drugs. >> breast; cancer

breathalyzer / breathalyser A device used with a driver suspected of having drunk an excessive amount of alcohol. The driver blows into a tube; crystals in the device change colour if there is alcohol present; and the extent of the change may indicate that the driver has exceeded the alcohol limit, which in the UK is 80 mg per 100 ml of blood. The initial test is given by a uniformed police officer; if positive, the driver may be arrested, and given a further blood or urine test at a police station with a doctor present. >> alcohols

breathing >> **respiration**

Brecht, (Eugene) Bertolt (Friedrich) [brekht] (1898–1956) Poet, playwright and theatre director, born in Augsburg, Germany. Popularity came with *Die Dreigroschenoper* (1928, The Threepenny Opera). Hitler's rise to power forced him to leave Germany, and he lived in exile for 15 years. During this period, he wrote some of his greatest plays, including *Mutter Courage und ihre Kinder* (1938, Mother Courage and her Children) and *Der Kaukasische Kreidekreis* (1945, The Caucasian Chalk Circle). After his return to East Berlin in 1948, his work with the Berliner Ensemble firmly established his influence as a major figure in 20th-c theatre. >> Berliner Ensemble

Breckland, The A sandy region of heathland on the border of Norfolk and Suffolk, UK. It was an important area of Neolithic flint mining. >> Three Age System

Brecon Beacons [**brek**n] National park in S Wales; area 1434 sq km/553 sq mi; established in 1957; three main peaks of 'the Beacons', Pen-y-Fan, Corn Du, and Cribyn, rise to c.900 m/2950 ft. >> Wales ℹ

Breda [**bray**da] 51°35N 4°45E, pop (1995e) 129 000. Industrial city in S Netherlands; bishopric; important cultural centre; charter, 13th-c; known for the **Compromise of Breda**, a protest against Spanish tyranny (1566); railway; cathedral (1510). >> Netherlands, The ℹ

Breeches Bible A name sometimes applied to the **Geneva Bible**, because of the rendering of *Gen* 3.7, which refers to Adam and Eve having sewn fig leaves together 'and made themselves breeches'. This translation, though, is not unique to the Geneva Bible. >> Geneva Bible

breeder reactor >> **nuclear reactor** ℹ

Bremen [**bray**men] 53°05N 8°48E, pop (1995e) 569 000. Commercial city and seaport in Germany; on the R Weser; railway; university (1970); cathedral (11th-c). >> Germany ℹ

Bremerhaven [**bray**merhahvn] 53°34N 8°35E, pop (1995e) 134 000. Seaport in Germany; on the Weser estuary; city status, 1851; united with Wesermunde, 1938; railway; Europe's largest fishing port for many years, declining in 1990s. >> Germany ℹ

Brendan, St, known as **the Navigator** (484–577) Abbot, born in Tralee, Ireland. He travelled widely, before founding the monastery of Clonfert in Co Galway (561). Feast day 16 May. >> monasticism

Bren gun A light machine-gun, the standard section weapon of the British Army during World War 2. The name derives from Brno in Czechoslovakia, where the gun was designed, and Enfield in Britain, where it was manufactured. >> machine-gun

Brenner Pass [**bren**uh], Ger **Brenner Sattel**, Ital **Passo del Brennero** 47°02N 11°32E. Mountain pass in the C Tirol Alps between Italy and Austria; altitude 1371 m/4498 ft; open all seasons of the year. >> Alps; Austria ℹ

Brentano, Clemens von [bren**tah**noh] (1778–1842) Writer, born in Ehrenbreitstein, Germany. He was a founder of the Heidelberg Romantic school. With Achim von Arnim he edited *Des Knaben Wunderhorn* (1805–8), a collection of folk songs. >> folklore; Romanticism

Brescia [**bray**sha] 45°33N 10°13E, pop (1995e) 210 000. Industrial town in N Italy; rail junction; Roman remains; cathedrals (11th-c, 17th-c). >> Lombardy

Brest (Belarus), formerly **Brest-Litovsk**, Pol **Brześć nad Bugiem** 52°08N 23°40E, pop (1995e) 281 000. River port in Belarus; on the Polish border; founded by Slavs, 1017; railway; major transportation centre. >> Belarus ℹ

Brest (France) 48°23N 4°30W, pop (1995e) 152 000. Fortified port and naval station in NW France, used as a German submarine base in World War 2; rebuilt after heavy bombing; railway; extensive dockyards, naval stores, arsenals. >> World War 2

Brest-Litovsk, Treaty of A bilateral treaty signed at Brest between Soviet Russia and the Central Powers. Under its terms, Russia withdrew from World War 1, and the new Soviet state ceded vast areas of territory to Germany. >> World War 1

Breton The Celtic language of Brittany, introduced by migration from Cornish-speaking S England in the 5th-c AD. There are no official figures for Breton speakers, but it is thought there are about half a million. There is a substantial body of literature from the mediaeval period onwards. >> Celtic languages

Breton, André [bruhtõ] (1896–1966) Poet, essayist and critic, born in Tinchebray, France. In 1919 he joined the Dadaist group, and became a founder of the Surrealist movement. His major novel, *Nadja*, was published in 1928, and his collected poems in 1948. >> Dada; Surrealism

Bretton Woods Conference An international conference held at Bretton Woods, NH, USA, in 1944. It led to the establishment of the International Monetary System, including the International Monetary Fund (IMF) and the World Bank. >> International Monetary Fund

Breughel >> **Brueghel**

breviary A book of liturgical material (psalms, hymns, lessons, prayers) used in the Daily Office, and required to be recited by all priests and clerics in major orders of the Roman Catholic Church. >> liturgy; Orders, Holy; Roman Catholicism

brewing The art and technique of producing an alcoholic beverage (most often a variety of beer) from cereals. Grain is steeped in water, and allowed to germinate. The germination is halted by heating (*malting*), and after *milling*, to crush the grain and expose the contents, the malt is *mashed* (leached with hot water to give a solution of fermentable carbohydrates (the *wort*). Sugar may be added. The wort is boiled in a *copper* with hops (to give aroma and flavour). When cool, a brewer's yeast is added. >> beer [i]; yeast

Brezhnev, Leonid Ilich [**brezh**nyef] (1906–82) Russian statesman, general secretary of the Soviet Communist Party (1964–82), and president of the Supreme Soviet (1977–82), born in Kamenskoye, Ukraine. He succeeded Khrushchev (1964), and was the first to hold simultaneously the positions of general secretary and president. >> Brezhnev Doctrine; Khrushchev

Brezhnev Doctrine [**brezh**nef] The term applied to the policies of Leonid Brezhnev, which combined strict political control internally with détente abroad. It also justified intervention in the affairs of other socialist states, as in Czechoslovakia (1968). >> Brezhnev; communism

Brian [**bree**an], known as **Brian Boroimhe** or **Boru** ('Brian of the Tribute') (c.926–1014) King of Ireland (1002–14). He became King of Leinster (984), and his rule was later acknowledged over the whole of Ireland.

Briand, Aristide [breeã] (1862–1932) French socialist statesman and prime minister, born in Nantes, France, who was 11 times French premier (1909–11, 1913, 1915–17, 1921–2, 1925–6, 1929). He shared the 1926 Nobel Peace Prize. >> Kellogg–Briand Pact

briar The woody root of two species of heath, *Erica scoparia* and *Erica arborescens*, used to make tobacco pipes. (Family: Ericaceae.) >> heath

Brickhill, Paul (Chester Jerome) (1916–91) Writer, born in Sydney, New South Wales, Australia. He served with the Royal Australian Air Force during World War 2, was shot down in North Africa, and for two years was a prisoner-of-war in Stalag Luft III, Germany. He described his escape from the camp in *The Great Escape* (1951); other books include *The Dam Busters* (1951) and *Reach for the Sky* (1954).

bricks Blocks, usually of clay or a clay mixture, baked by the Sun or by fire. Most are now made by machine, and fired in kilns. The fixing of bricks in place to provide a strong wall is called **bricklaying**. Bricks are laid in mortar, a mixture of cement or lime with sand and water.

Bride, St >> **Bridget, Brigid**, or **Bride, St**

bridge (engineering) A structure carrying a road, path, or railway over an obstacle. The principal types are **arch bridges**, **girder bridges**, and **suspension** bridges. The greatest spans are achieved by suspension bridges, the longest at present being the Akashi-Kaikyo, Japan (1991 m/6532 ft). The greatest single span arch bridge is the New River Gorge, W Virginia, USA (518 m/1700 ft). >> Bosporus / Brooklyn / Golden Gate / Humber / London / New River Gorge / Rialto / Sydney Harbour / Tower / Verrazano Narrows Bridge; Bridge of Sighs; Ponte Vecchio; pontoon bridge

bridge (recreation) A popular card game developed from whist, using the full set of 52 playing cards, and played by two pairs of players. In **auction bridge**, trumps are decided by a preliminary bid or auction that is intended to be low, because the declarer is given credit for all tricks, whether contracted or not. In the more aggressive **contract bridge**, the side winning the contract, and so naming trumps, scores towards game only the number of tricks contracted for in the bidding. Auction bridge was displaced by contract bridge in the 1920s, and is now rarely played. >> playing cards; whist; RR1049

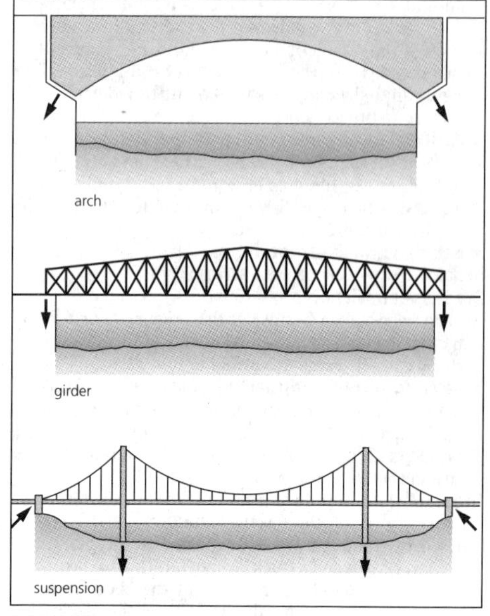

Three types of bridge – the arrows show the forces exerted by the load

Bridgend [brij**end**] pop (1995e) 130 900; area 246 sq km / 95 sq mi. County (unitary authority from 1996) in S Wales, UK; administrative centre, Bridgend; castle (12th-c). >> Wales [i]

Bridge of Sighs An enclosed 16th-c bridge in Venice, through which condemned prisoners would pass from the Doge's Palace to the Prigioni prison. >> Doge's Palace; Venice

Bridges, Robert (Seymour) (1844–1930) Poet, born in Walmer, Kent. He published three volumes of graceful lyrics (1873, 1879, 1880), and several plays, and a great deal of literary criticism. He became poet laureate in 1913. In 1929, on his 85th birthday, he issued his most ambitious poem, *The Testament of Beauty*.

Bridget, Brigid, or **Bride, St** (453–523) Patron saint of Leinster, Ireland. She founded four monasteries, the chief at Kildare. Feast day 1 February. >> monasticism

Bridget, Brigit, or **Birgitta (of Sweden), St** (c.1302–73) Patron saint of Sweden, born in Finstad, the founder of a monastic order which flourished in Sweden until the Reformation (the **Bridgettine Order**). She was canonized in 1391; feast day 23 July or 8 October >> monasticism

Bridgetown 13°06N 59°36W, pop (1995e) 6100. Port capital of Barbados, West Indies; University of the West Indies (1963); cathedral. >> Barbados [i]

Bridgewater Canal An inland waterway in England commissioned by Francis Egerton, 3rd Duke of Bridgewater (1736–1893), and constructed (1762–72) by James Brindley. The canal links Worsley to Manchester, and continues to Liverpool. It is 64 km/40 mi long. >> Brindley; canal

brig Any two-masted, square-rigged sailing vessel. Brigs became common in the mid-18th-c, and are still used as sail-training vessels. >> ship ℹ

Bright, John (1811–89) Radical British statesman and orator, born in Rochdale, Greater Manchester. He became a leading member of the Anti-Corn-Law League (1839), and was closely associated with the Reform Act of 1867. >> Anti-Corn-Law League; free trade

brightness >> **luminous intensity**

Brighton 50°50N 0°10W, pop (1995e) 143 000. Resort town in Brighton and Hove unitary authority, SE England, on the English Channel; railway; two universities (1961, 1992); conference centre; marina; Royal Pavilion (1811), designed by John Nash; football league team, Brighton and Hove Albion (Seagulls); London–Brighton veteran car run (Nov). >> England ℹ; Nash, John

Brigid, St >> **Bridget, Brigid**, or **Bride, St**

Brigit, St >> **Bridget, Brigit**, or **Birgitta (of Sweden), St**

brill Large flatfish (*Scophthalmus rhombus*) found mainly in shallow waters of NE Atlantic and Mediterranean; body length up to c.60 cm/2 ft; both eyes on left side, mouth large and curved; sandy brown with dark and light flecks. (Family: Scophthalmidae.) >> flatfish; turbot

brimstone >> **sulphur**

brimstone A wide-winged butterfly; wings lemon-yellow in male, greenish-white in female, each with an orange spot. (Order: Lepidoptera. Family: Pieridae.) >> butterfly

Brindisi [**breen**disee], ancient **Brundisium** 40°37N 17°57E, pop (1995e) 90 900. Seaport in S Italy, on the Adriatic; used by Crusaders as a naval base; archbishopric; airport; railway; cathedral (11th-c, rebuilt 18th-c). >> Italy ℹ

Brindley, James (1716–72) Engineer, born in Thornsett, Derbyshire. His inventions recommended him to the Duke of Bridgewater, who employed him (1759) to build the canal between Worsley and Manchester. >> Bridgewater Canal

Brinell hardness test [bri**nel**] A test for the hardness of metal, named after Swedish engineer, Johann August Brinell (1849–1925). A hard steel ball is pressed into the test piece with a known and reproducible force, producing a depression. The dimensions of the depression provide a measure of hardness. >> hardness; metal

Brink, André (1935–) Writer, critic, and translator, born in Vrede, South Africa. An Afrikaner dissident, he emerged as a writer in the 1950s, but it was not until his seventh novel – which he later translated into English as *Looking on Darkness* (1974) – that he began to attract international attention. Later books include *Rumours of Rain* (1978) and *States of Emergency* (1988).

Brisbane [**briz**bn] 27°30S 153°00E, pop (1995e) 1 441 000. State capital of Queensland, Australia, on the Brisbane R; founded as a penal colony, 1824; state capital, 1859; third largest city in Australia; airport; railway; two universities (1909, 1975). >> Queensland

brisling Small Norwegian fish, *Sprattus sprattus*, usually canned in oil. >> sprat

Brissot (de Warville), Jacques Pierre [breesoh] (1754–93) French revolutionary politician, born near Chartres. He established *Le Patriote français* ('The French Patriot'), the organ of the earliest Republicans, and became leader of the Girondins (or **Brissotins**). In the Convention his moderation made him suspect to Robespierre, and he was guillotined. >> French Revolution ℹ; Girondins

bristletail A primitive wingless insect with long tail filaments; the group includes the silverfish. **Two-pronged bristletails** (Order: Diplura, 660 species) are blind and found in the soil, feeding on decaying organic matter. **Three-pronged bristletails** (Order: Thysanura, 600 species) are mostly found in the soil and forest leaf litter. >> silverfish

bristleworm An aquatic annelid worm; body segments typically with paired lateral lobes bearing various bristles and scales; body length from 1 mm–3 m/0·04 in–10 ft; c.8000 species. (Class: Polychaeta.) >> annelid

Bristol, Anglo-Saxon **Bricgstow** 51°27N 2°35W, pop (1995e) 401 000. Unitary authority in SW England; former (to 1996) administrative centre of Avon county; county status 1373; major port in 17th–18th-c, much involved in the slave trade; two airports; railway; universities (1909, 1992); 12th-century cathedral, Roman Catholic cathedral (1973), Theatre Royal (1766), Clifton suspension bridge (1864); football league teams, Bristol City (Robins), Bristol Rovers (Pirates). >> Brunel, Isambard Kingdom; England ℹ; slave trade

Bristol Channel An inlet of the Atlantic Ocean and an extension of the R Severn estuary, between Wales and England; extends 128 km/79 mi E–W, with a varying width of 5–80 km/3–50 mi at its mouth; the greatest tidal range in England. >> England ℹ; Severn, River; Wales ℹ

Bristow, Eric, nickname **the Crafty Cockney** (1957–) Darts player, born in London. He was world professional champion a record five times (1980–81, 1984–6), and won several other championships during the 1980s.

Britain >> **United Kingdom** ℹ

Britain, Battle of The name given to the air war campaign of late summer 1940 in which the German Luftwaffe attempted to destroy the Royal Air Force (RAF) as a prelude to the invasion of Great Britain. British resistance proved stubborn, with the Spitfires and Hurricanes of RAF Fighter Command being directed by radar onto the incoming bomber streams. Between 1 July and 31 October the Luftwaffe lost 2848 aircraft to the RAF's 1446. >> Luftwaffe; Royal Air Force; World War 2

British >> **Celtic languages**

British Antarctic Territory British colonial territory 20–80°W and S of 60°S; includes South Orkney Is, South Shetland Is, Antarctic Graham Land Peninsula, and the land mass extending to the South Pole; area 5·7 million sq km/2·2 million sq mi; population solely of scientists of the British Antarctic Survey. >> Graham Land; South Orkney Islands; South Shetland Islands

British Association for the Advancement of Science An organization whose aims are to promote interest and progress in science. It was founded in 1831 by a group of scientists disillusioned with the elitist and conservative attitude of the Royal Society. >> Royal Society

British Athletic Federation (BAF) The former governing body for athletics in England and Wales. It was formed in 1991 as a result of a merger between the Amateur Athletic Association, founded in 1880, and the Women's Amateur Athletic Association, founded in 1922. It was replaced by **UK Athletics** in 1999. >> athletics; International Amateur Athletic Federation; UK Athletics

British Broadcasting Corporation >> **BBC**

British Columbia pop (1995e) 3 483 000; area 947 800 sq km/365 945 sq mi. Mountainous province in SW Canada, bordered S by USA and W by the Pacific; Rocky Mts in the E, Coast Mts in the W; largest islands, Queen Charlotte, Vancouver; ranges cut by fertile valleys of Fraser, Thompson, and Columbia Rivers; many lakes; capital, Victoria; Captain Cook landed at Vancouver I, 1778; sea otter fur trade flourished; border with USA settled by Oregon Treaty, 1846; gold rush to Fraser R, 1858; entered federation of Canada, 1871; Canadian Pacific Railway completed, 1885; governed by a lieutenant-governor and a Legislative Assembly. >> Canada ℹ; Cook, James; Vancouver; Victoria (Canada)

British Commonwealth >> **Commonwealth (British)**

British Council An organization founded in 1934 to spread the influence of British culture, ideas, and education. Its headquarters is in London, and in 1999 it had offices based in 109 countries throughout the world.

British Empire, Most Excellent Order of the In the UK, an order of chivalry, instituted in 1917 by George V. It has five classes: Knights and Dames Grand Cross (GBE), Knights and Dames Commanders (KBE/DBE), Commanders (CBE), Officers (OBE), and Members (MBE).

British Expeditionary Force (BEF) An army, first established in 1906, sent to France (Aug 1914 and Sep 1939) to support the left wing of the French armies against German attack. In World War 2 its total strength was 394 000, of whom 224 000 were safely evacuated, mainly from Dunkirk, in May–June 1940. >> World War 1/2

British Indian Ocean Territory pop (1995e) 2900; land area 60 sq km/23 sq mi. British territory in the Indian Ocean, 1900 km/1180 mi NE of Mauritius; islands cover c.54 400 sq km/21 000 sq mi of ocean, in six main groups; largest island, Diego Garcia; acquired by France, 18th-c; annexed by Britain, 1814; dependency of Mauritius until 1965. >> Indian Ocean

British Isles Group of islands off the NW coast of Europe. It consists of two main islands (Great Britain and Ireland) and many smaller islands, notably the Isle of Man, Isle of Wight, Channel Is, Western Is, Orkney, and Shetland. >> England [i]; Ireland (island) [i]; Scotland [i]; United Kingdom [i]; Wales [i]

British Legion >> **Royal British Legion**

British Library The national depository created by the British Library Act of 1972 through the amalgamation of the British Museum Library with two other libraries. Its reference division is based in London; its lending division in W Yorkshire. A new site for the library, in Euston Road, London, opened in 1997 after many delays. >> British Museum

British Museum The national museum of archaeology and ethnography in Bloomsbury, London. It dates from 1753, when the collection of Sir Hans Sloane was acquired for the nation. Since 1881 the natural history collection has been housed separately, and the library moved to the Euston Road site in 1997. >> British Library; Natural History Museum; Sloane, Hans

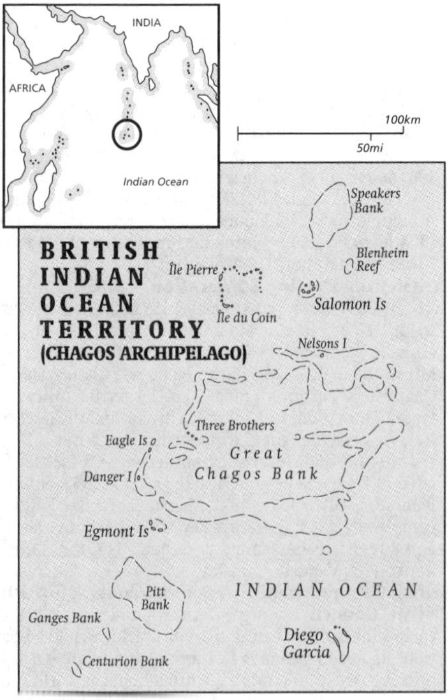

British South Africa Company A company, formed by Cecil Rhodes, which secured a Royal Charter from the British government in 1889. In 1923–4, its territories were divided into Northern Rhodesia (Zambia after 1964) and Southern Rhodesia (Zimbabwe after 1980). >> Rhodes; Zambia [i]; Zimbabwe [i]

British Sports Association for the Disabled An organization, founded in 1961, which aims to provide sports and recreation opportunities for people with disabilities throughout the UK. Its membership of c.50 000 is represented in over 500 clubs, schools, and associations, participating in over 20 different sports. >> paralympics

British Standards Institution The recognized UK body for the preparation of nationally accepted standards for engineering and industrial materials, and codes of practice. There are similar bodies in several other countries.

British Summer Time >> **Daylight Saving Time**

British thermal unit In thermodynamics, an old unit of heat; symbol *Btu*; 1 Btu = 1055 J (joule, SI unit); defined as the heat needed to raise the temperature of a pound of water from 63°F to 64°F; a *therm* is 10^5 Btu. >> heat; joule; thermodynamics; RR1031

British Virgin Islands >> **Virgin Islands, British**

Brittain, Vera (Mary) [britn] (1893–1970) Writer, born in Newcastle-under-Lyme, Staffordshire. She served as a nurse in World War 1, recording her experiences in *Testament of Youth* (1933). Her daughter is the politician, Shirley Williams. >> Williams, Shirley

Brittan, Sir Leon (1939–) British Conservative statesman, born in London, who became Home Secretary (1983–5) and secretary for trade and industry (1985–6). Following a conflict with Michael Heseltine over the takeover of Westland helicopters, he resigned from the Cabinet. He became a vice-president of the European Commission in 1989. >> Conservative Party; European Economic Community; Heseltine

Brittany, Fr **Bretagne** pop (1995e) 2 880 000; area 27 208 sq km/10 502 sq mi. Region and former province of NW France; rugged and striking coastline; rises to 391 m/1283 ft at Monts d'Arrée; arrival of Celts from Britain 5th–6th-c AD, from which came a distinctive culture and language (Breton); chief towns, Nantes, Rennes, Lorient, Quimper, Brest; high concentration of megaliths; major tourist area. >> Breton; Celts; France [i]; megalith

Britten (of Aldeburgh), (Edward) Benjamin Britten, Baron (1913–76) Composer, born in Lowestoft, Suffolk. His works were largely vocal and choral – exceptions include the famous *Variations and Fugue on a Theme of Purcell* (also known as *The Young Person's Guide to the Orchestra*). His operas include *Peter Grimes* (1945), *Billy Budd* (1951), and *Death in Venice* (1973). He was also an accomplished pianist, often accompanying Peter Pears, and helped to found (1948) the annual Aldeburgh Festival. >> Pears

brittle bone syndrome A genetically determined disease of the skeleton, characterized by the deficient formation of bone and connective tissue, resulting in excessive fragility of the skeleton. Seriously afflicted babies suffer multiple fractures and die in infancy. >> bone; dwarfism

brittle star A starfish-like marine invertebrate (echinoderm) which typically has five slender arms sharply demarcated from the central disc; arms sometimes branched; c.2000 species. (Class: Ophiuroidea.) >> echinoderm [i]; starfish

Brittonic >> **Celtic languages**

Brno [**ber**noh], Ger **Brünn** 49°11N 16°39E, pop (1995e) 390 000. Third largest city in Czech Republic; founded in 10th-c; part of Bohemia, 1229; free city, 1243; airport; railway; university (1919); technical university (1899); Špilberk fortress, 15th-c cathedral. >> Bohemia; Bren gun; Czech Republic [i]

broad bean An annual growing to 80 cm/30 in (*Vicia faba*); pea-flowers in small clusters, white with purplish-black wings; pods up to 20 cm/83 in long, hairy, black; containing few large seeds each 2–3 cm/¾–1¼ in across; also called **horse bean**. (Family: Leguminosae.) >> bean

broadcasting The provision of television and radio programmes and commercials for the general public; also, the technical transmission of television and radio signals. Starting in the 1920s, broadcasting, whether of the commercial or 'public-service' variety, quickly established itself at regional, national, and international levels as a popular source of entertainment and information. In recent years **narrowcasting** has been introduced for services geared to special interest groups. >> BBC; Caroline, Radio; International Telecommunication Union; radio; television; Voice of America

Broadmoor A special hospital for the criminally insane, established in 1863 near Camberley, Surrey Heath, UK. It is the prototype special hospital, and has lent its name to the generic description **Broadmoor institutions**.

Broads, The, also known as **The Norfolk Broads** An area (c.2000 ha/5000 acres) of low-lying and shallow lakes in East Anglia, UK. The lakes are flooded peat pits, excavated during the 11th-c and 12th-c. It is a popular holiday area.

Broadway The name of a street in New York City (25 km/15·5 mi long) which since the 1890s has become famous as a symbol of commercial theatre in the USA. In the 1950s the label **Off-Broadway** emerged to distinguish those theatrical enterprises in New York which operated outside the crippling economics of Broadway. By the mid-sixties the rising economic pressures of Off-Broadway in their turn spawned an off-Off-Broadway movement. >> Times Square

broccoli A type of cultivated cabbage (*Brassica oleracea*) grown for the immature flowers, which are edible. **Winter broccoli** has large, white heads similar to cauliflower; **sprouting broccoli** (**calabrese**) produces numerous small, purplish, green or white spears. (Family: Cruciferae.) >> cabbage

Broderick, Matthew (1963–) Actor, born in New York City. He made his film debut in *War Games* (1983), and earned Tony awards for his Broadway appearances in *Brighton Beach Memoirs* (1982–3) and *How to Succeed in Business Without Really Trying* (1995). He made his directorial debut with *Infinity* (1996).

Broglie, Louis (Victor Pierre Raymond), 7e duc de (7th Duke of) [broy, broglee] (1892–1987) Physicist, born in Dieppe, France. In 1929 he was awarded the Nobel Prize for Physics for his pioneer work on the wave nature of the electron (**de Broglie waves**). >> electron

Broken Hill 31°57S 141°30E, pop (1995e) 25 100. Mining town in New South Wales, Australia; centre of silver, lead, and zinc mining; Royal Flying Doctor Service based here (1938). >> New South Wales

bromeliad Any member of the pineapple family; typically fleshy, spiny-leaved epiphytes, especially common in the canopy of tropical forests, and notable for the reservoir of water which collects in the cup-shaped centre of the leaf rosette. (Family: Bromeliaceae.) >> aechmea; epiphyte; pineapple; succulent

bromine [**broh**meen] Br, element 35, freezing point −7°C, boiling point 58·8°C. A corrosive brown liquid with an unpleasant and irritating odour. Its main uses are in 1,2-dibromoethane, a petrol adduct, and silver bromide, used in photographic emulsions. >> chemical elements; emulsion; RR1036

bronchi [**brong**kee] A series of branching tubes which gradually decrease in size, conveying air from the trachea to the lungs. The larger bronchi contain cartilage rings to keep the tubes open. The smaller tubes, known as respiratory *bronchioles*, have sac-like dilatations (*alveoli*) where gaseous exchange occurs. >> asthma; bronchitis; cartilage; lungs; trachea

bronchitis [brong**kiy**tis] A disease marked by inflammation of the bronchial tubes. **Acute bronchitis** is a serious disease in infants, resulting from a virus which produces intense inflammation of the respiratory tract that may lead to asphyxia. **Chronic bronchitis** affects adults who smoke cigarettes. >> bronchi; pneumonia

bronchopneumonia >> **pneumonia**

Brontë, Anne [**bron**tee], pseudonym **Acton Bell** (1820–49) Poet and novelist, born in Thornton, West Yorkshire. She wrote two novels: *Agnes Grey* (1845) and *The Tenant of Wildfell Hall* (1848).

Brontë, Charlotte [**bron**tee], pseudonym **Currer Bell** (1816–55) Novelist, born in Thornton, West Yorkshire. Her first novel, *The Professor*, was not published until after her death (1857). Her masterpiece, *Jane Eyre*, apeared in 1847, and this was followed by *Shirley* (1849). *Emma* remained unfinished at her death.

Brontë, Emily (Jane) [**bron**tee], pseudonym **Ellis Bell** (1818–48) Novelist and poet, born in Thornton, West Yorkshire. Her single novel, *Wuthering Heights* (1847), remains one of the major works of English prose fiction.

Brontosaurus >> ***Apatosaurus***

Bronx or **the Bronx** 40°50N 73°52W, pop (1995e) 1 226 000, area 109 sq km/42 sq mi. A mainland borough of N New York City and County of New York State, USA; named after Jonas Bronck, an early Dutch settler. >> New York City

bronze One of the earliest known alloys; two parts copper and one part tin. Hard and resistant to corrosion, it is traditionally used in bell casting, and is the most widely used material for metal sculpture. >> alloy; copper; tin

Bronze Age >> **Three Age System**

Bronzino, Il [bron**zee**noh], originally **Agnolo di Cosimo di Mariano** (1503–72) Florentine Mannerist painter, born in Monticelli, Italy. His portraits include most of the Medici family, as well as Dante, Boccaccio, and Petrarch. >> Mannerism

Brook, Peter (Stephen Paul) (1925–) Theatre and film director, born in London. He worked with the Royal Shakespeare Company in the 1960s, his successes including *King Lear* (1962), *Marat/Sade* (1964), and *A Midsummer Night's Dream* (1970). Among his films are *Lord of the Flies* (1962), *The Mahabharata* (1989), and *The Tempest* (1990).

Brooke, Rupert (Chawner) (1887–1915) Poet, born in Rugby, Warwickshire. His *Poems* appeared in 1911, and *1914 and Other Poems* after his death. He was a favourite poet among young people in the interwar period.

Brooklyn 40°40N 73°58W, pop (1995e) 2 342 000. Borough of New York City, USA; area 182 sq km/70 sq mi; a major port, at the SW corner of Long Island. >> Brooklyn Bridge; New York City; Verrazano-Narrows Bridge

Brooklyn Bridge A suspension bridge built (1869–83) across East R from Brooklyn to Manhattan I, New York City; length of main span 486 m/1595 ft. >> New York City

Brookner, Anita (1928–) Writer and art historian, born in London. An authority on 18th-c painting, she joined the Courtauld Institute of Art in 1977. Her novels include *Hôtel du Lac* (1984, Booker Prize), *Altered States* (1996), and *Visitors* (1997).

Brooks, Mel, originally **Melvin Kaminsky** (1926–) Film actor and director, born in New York City. He is known for zany comedies satirizing established movie styles, among them *Blazing Saddles* (1974), *Silent Movie* (1976), and *Dracula: Dead and Loving It* (1995). He usually writes the script, and acts in his productions, as well as directing them.

broom A shrub (*Cytisus scoparius*) native to Europe, growing to 2·5 m/8 ft; branches numerous, green, straight, and stiff; pea-flowers golden yellow, up to 2 cm/¾ in long, pods up to 4 cm/1½ in long, black. (Family: Leguminosae.)

Broome, David (1940–) Show jumper, born in Cardiff. He won the World Championship on *Beethoven* in 1970, and was the individual bronze medallist at the 1960 and 1968 Olympics. He returned to the British Olympic team in 1988. >> equestrianism

broomrape An annual or perennial, parasitic and lacking chlorophyll; leaves reduced to scales; flowers 2-lipped, in subdued colours, mainly browns; mainly native to Old World warm temperate regions. (Genus: *Orobanche*, 140 species. Family: Orobanchaceae.) >> chlorophyll; parasitic plant

Brosnan, Pierce [**broz**nan] (1952–) Actor, born in Co Meath, E Ireland. After several stage roles in London, he moved to Los Angeles, becoming known when he took on the role of James Bond in *Goldeneye* (1995). His other film credits begin with *The Long Good Friday* (1980), and include *Mars Attacks!* (1996) and *Dante's Peak* (1997).

Brouwer or **Brauer, Adriaen** [**brow**er] (c.1605–38) Painter, born in Oudenaarde, Belgium. His favourite subjects were scenes from tavern life, country merrymakings, and all kinds of roisterers.

Brown, Sir Arthur Whitten (1886–1948) Aviator, born in Glasgow. He trained as an engineer, and was the companion of Alcock on the first transatlantic flight (1919). >> Alcock

Brown, Capability >> **Brown, Lancelot**

Brown, Charles Brockden (1771–1810) Novelist, born in Philadelphia, PA. He was the first professional American writer, and is often called 'the father of the American novel'. *Wieland* (1798), *Ormund* (1799), and *Jane Talbot* (1804) are among his Gothic Romances.

Brown, Ford Madox (1821–93) British historical painter, born in Calais, France. Among his major works are 'Manfred on the Jungfrau' (1841) and 'Chaucer reciting his poetry' (1851). He later produced designs for furniture and stained glass.

Brown, George (Alfred) >> **George-Brown, Baron**

Brown, (James) Gordon (1951–) Scottish politician, born in Glasgow. He became Opposition chief secretary to the Treasury (1987–9), Opposition trade and industry secretary (1989–92), and Shadow Chancellor (1992–97) under the leadership of John Smith, then Tony Blair, and Chancellor of the Exchequer (1997–) in the Labour government.

Brown, John (1800–59) Militant abolitionist, born in Torrington, CT. In 1859 he led a raid on the US Armory at Harper's Ferry in Virginia, trying to launch a slave insurrection. The raid failed, and he was hanged. The song 'John Brown's Body' commemorates the raid. >> American Civil War

Brown, Lancelot, known as **Capability Brown** (1715–83) Landscape gardener, born in Kirkharle, Northumberland. His gardens, such as those at Blenheim Palace and Kew are characterized by an imitation of nature. His nickname arose from his habit of saying that a place had 'capabilities'. >> landscape gardening

Brown, Robert (1773–1858) Botanist, born in Montrose, Angus. In 1831 he was the first to recognize the nucleus as the basis of a cell. He also discovered the effect later known as **Brownian motion**. >> Brownian motion; cell

brown algae A large group of predominantly marine seaweeds, characterized by their photosynthetic pigments; over 1500 species known; body form ranges from filament-like to large blades. (Class: Phaeophyceae.) >> algae; photosynthesis; seaweed

brown bear A bear widespread in the N hemisphere (*Ursus arctos*); thick brown coat and pronounced hump on shoulders; includes the **big brown bear** and **grizzly bear** from the Rocky Mts, and the **Kenai bear** and **Kodiak bear** (both from S Alaska); Kodiak bear is the largest living carnivore (length 2·7 m/9 ft; weight up to 780 kg/1720 lb). >> bear; carnivore ℹ

brown dwarf A hypothetical very large planet, which is just below the critical mass needed to ignite a stellar nuclear reaction in its own interior. There is evidence for brown dwarfs as companions to a handful of stars. >> dwarf star; planet; star

Browne, Charles Farrar, pseudonym **Artemus Ward** (1834–67) Humorist, born in Waterford, ME. He wrote a description of an imaginary travelling menagerie, followed by a series of comic letters marked by puns, grotesque spelling, and satire.

Browne, Hablot Knight, pseudonym **Phiz** (1815–82) Artist, born in London. He is best known for his Dickens illustrations, beginning with *The Pickwick Papers* (1836). >> Dickens

Browne, Sir Thomas (1605–82) Writer, born in London. His greatest work is his earliest, the *Religio medici* (c.1635), revealing a deep insight into the spiritual life.

Brownian movement or **motion** The ceaseless erratic motion of fine particles in suspension, first observed by British botanist Robert Brown in 1827, using pollen grains in water. The effect was explained by Einstein in 1905 as the result of the irregular bombardment of the suspended matter by molecules of solution. >> Brown, Robert; Einstein

Browning, Elizabeth Barrett, *née* **Barrett** (1806–61) Poet, born in Durham, Co Durham. About 1821 she seriously injured her spine, and was long an invalid. In 1845 she met Robert Browning, with whom she eloped in 1846. Her best-known work is *Sonnets from the Portuguese* (1850, 'Portuguese' being Browning's pet name for her). >> Browning, Robert

Browning, Robert (1812–89) Poet, born in London. *Bells and Pomegranates* (1841–6) included several of his best-known dramatic lyrics, such as 'How they Brought the Good News from Ghent to Aix'. In 1846 he married Elizabeth Barrett, and with her settled at Florence. After the death of his wife (1861) he settled in London, where he wrote his masterpiece, *The Ring and the Book* (1869). >> Browning, Elizabeth Barrett

Browning automatic rifle A gas-operated light machine-gun designed by US gunsmith John Moses Browning (1855–1926) in 1917, and produced until 1950. The weapon had a 20-round magazine and an effective range of 600 m/2000 ft. >> machine-gun

Brown judgment >> **civil rights**

Brownshirts German Nazi storm-troopers; officially the *Sturmabteilungen*, or *SA*. Formed in 1920, they had expanded to 500 000 by late 1932. After the Nazi accession to power (1933), they challenged the autonomy of the German army. They were crushed in the 'Night of the Long Knives' (30 Jun 1934). >> Nazi Party; Röhm; SS

Brown University >> **Ivy League** ℹ

Brubeck, Dave, popular name of **David Warren Brubeck** (1920–) Jazz pianist, bandleader, and composer, born in Concord, CA. In 1951, upon adding the alto saxophonist Paul Desmond (1924–77) to his piano–bass–drums trio, the quartet became an enormous success. Among their most famous recordings is *Time Out* (1958), featuring Desmond's 'Take Five' and Brubeck's 'Blue Rondo à la Turk'. In 1967, Brubeck and Desmond went their separate ways, though with frequent reunions. >> jazz

Bruce, James, nickname **the Abyssinian** (1730–94) Explorer, born in Larbert, Falkirk, Scotland. In 1770 he reached the source of the Blue Nile. >> Nile, River

Bruce, Lenny, originally **Leonard Alfred Schneider** (1925–66) Satirical comedian, born in New York City. The satire and 'black' humour of his largely improvised act often transgressed the conventions of respectability. In 1961 he was imprisoned for obscenity.

Bruce, Robert (1274–1329) King of Scots (1306–29), as Robert I. He joined the Scottish revolt under Wallace, was crowned king at Scone (1306), and defeated the English at Bannockburn (1314). The Treaty of Northampton (1328) recognized the independence of Scotland and his right to the throne. >> Edward I; Wallace, William

brucellosis [brooseLOHsis] A disease of animals, especially cattle, caused by micro-organisms of genus *Brucella*; can be caught by humans, when it is called **undulant fever** or **Malta fever**; named after British bacteriologist Sir David Bruce (1855–1931); also known as **contagious abortion**.

Bruch, Max [brukh] (1838–1920) Composer, born in Cologne, Germany. He is best known for his Violin Concerto in G minor and the *Scottish Fantasy*.

Brücke, die [BRÜker] (Ger 'bridge') The name adopted by a group of avant-garde artists active in Dresden, 1905–13, including Ernst Ludwig Kirchner and Emil Nolde. Their most striking works are prints, especially bold and expressive woodcuts. >> Expressionism; Kirchner; Nolde; woodcut

Bruckner, Anton [BRUKner] (1824–96) Composer and organist, born in Ansfelden, Austria. His fame chiefly rests on his nine symphonies (the last unfinished), but he also wrote four impressive masses and many choral works.

Brueghel, Pieter [BROYgl], also spelled **Bruegel** or **Breughel**, known as **the Elder** (c.1520–69) Flemish painter, probably born in the village of Brueghel, near Breda. The most original of all 16th-c Flemish painters, he settled in Brussels, where he painted his genre pictures of peasant life. His eldest son, **Pieter Brueghel**, byname **the Younger** (c.1564–1637) is known as 'Hell' Brueghel, because of his paintings of devils, hags, and robbers. His younger son, **Jan Brueghel** (1568–1625), known as 'Velvet' Brueghel painted still-life, flowers, landscapes, and religious subjects on a small scale. >> genre painting

Bruges [broozh], Flemish **Brugge** 51°13N 3°14E, pop (1995e) 119 000. Port in NW Belgium; chief market town of the Hanseatic League and a major centre of the woollen and cloth trade; railway; one of the best-preserved mediaeval European cities. >> Belgium [i]; Hanseatic League

Brugge [BROOguh] >> **Bruges**

Brummell, George Bryan, known as **Beau Brummell** (1778–1840) Dandy, a leader of early 19th-c fashion, born in London. For 20 years he had the prince regent (later George IV) as friend and admirer. They quarrelled in 1813, and gambling debts forced Brummell to flee to France (1816), where he died in a lunatic asylum.

Bruna, Dick [BROOna] (1927–) Dutch artist and writer. The creator of a highly successful series of picture books for young children, his books include such characters as Miffy the rabbit, and the small dog Snuffy.

Brundage, Avery (1887–1975) International athletics administrator, born in Detroit, MI. He was president of the US Olympic Association (1929–53) and of the International Olympic Committee (1952–72).

Brundtland, Gro Harlem [BRUNTland] (1939–) Norwegian stateswoman and first woman prime minister of Norway (1981, 1986–9, 1990–6), born in Oslo. She was appointed environment minister (1974–9) and, as leader of the Labour Party group, became prime minister for the first time. In 1987 she chaired the World Commission on Environment and Development which produced the report *Our Common Future*. She was elected director-general of the World Health Organization in 1998. >> Earth Summit

Brunei [BROOniy], official name **State of Brunei Darussalam** (Islamic Sultanate of Brunei) pop (1995e) 293 000; area 5765 sq km/2225 sq mi. State on the NW coast of Borneo, SE Asia, capital Bandar Seri Begawan (formerly Brunei Town); timezone GMT +8; ethnic groups include Malay (65%) and Chinese (15%); official religion, Islam; official language, Malay, but English widely spoken; unit of currency, the Brunei dollar of 100 sen; swampy coastal plain; equatorial rainforest covers 75% of land area; tropical climate; formerly a powerful Muslim sultanate, its name (as Borneo) being given by Europeans to the whole island; under British protection, 1888; internal self-government, 1971; independent, 1983; a constitutional monarchy with the Sultan as head of state; largely dependent on oil (discovered 1929) and gas resources. >> Bandar Seri Begawan; RR1003 political leaders

Brunel, Isambard Kingdom [brooNEL] (1806–59) Engineer, born in Portsmouth, Hampshire. He designed the *Great Western* (1837), the first steamship built to cross the Atlantic, the *Great Britain* (1843), the first ocean screw-steamer, and the *Great Eastern* (1853–8), then the largest vessel ever built.

Brunelleschi, Filippo [brooneLESkee] (1377–1446) Architect, born in Florence, Italy. He designed the dome for the Cathedral (1417–34) in Florence. The first great Renaissance architect, he had a profound influence upon his successors. >> Renaissance

Bruno, Giordano, originally **Filippo Bruno**, nickname **Il Nolano** (1548–1600) Philosopher, born in Nola, Italy. At first a Dominican, his unorthodox views caused him to leave the order. His pantheistic views and support of Copernicus caused his arrest by the Inquisition in 1593, and after a 7-year trial he was burned in Rome.

Bruno of Cologne, St (c.1030–1101) Monastic founder, born in Cologne, Germany. In 1084 he withdrew to the wild mountains of Chartreuse, near Grenoble, where he founded the austere Carthusians. Feast day 6 October. >> Carthusians; Chartreuse, La Grande

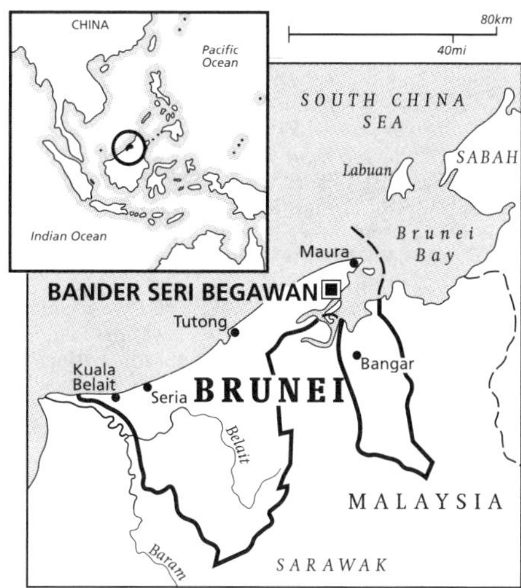

Brunswick [**brown**shviyk], Ger **Braunschweig** 52°17N 10°28E, pop (1995e) 268 000. Manufacturing and commercial city in Germany; capital of former duchy of Braunschweig; railway; technical university (1745); cathedral (12th-c), castle (12th-c). >> Germany ℹ

Brussels, Flemish **Brussel**, Fr **Bruxelles**, ancient **Broucsella** 50°50N 4°21E, pop (1995e) 1 064 000 (including suburbs). Capital of Belgium lying at the geographical mid-point of the country; inner city surrounded by 18 suburbs with independent administrations; major mediaeval wool centre; capital of Spanish and Austrian Netherlands; headquarters of many international organizations, such as the European Union and NATO; linguistic frontier between Flemings and Walloons runs just S of the city; officially Brussels is bilingual, but French predominates in the centre, Flemish in the suburbs; archbishopric; airport; railway; underground system; Free University of Brussels (1834); cathedral (13th–15th-c); industry largely outside the city, leaving the centre to the service sector. >> Belgium ℹ; European Union; NATO

Brussels, Treaty of (1948) 1 (1948) A treaty of economic, social, and cultural collaboration and collective self-defence signed by Belgium, France, Luxembourg, the Netherlands, and the UK. **2** (1973) A treaty which enabled Britain, Denmark, and Ireland to join the European Economic Community. >> European Economic Community

Brussels sprout A type of cultivated cabbage (*Brassica oleracea*) producing shoots or sprouts in all the axils of the leaves on the main stem. These sprouts resemble miniature cabbages, and can be harvested over a long period, especially in winter. (Family: Cruciferae). >> cabbage

Brutalism or **New Brutalism** An architectural concept of the 1950s, in which the buildings often have large distinct blocks of exposed concrete. It is typified by the work of Le Corbusier at Chandigarh, India. >> Le Corbusier

Brutus, Marcus Junius [**broo**tus] (c.85–42 BC) A leader of the group who assassinated Julius Caesar. Cassius prevailed on him to join the conspiracy against Caesar (44 BC). Defeated by Mark Antony and Octavian at Philippi, he killed himself. >> Caesar; Cassius; Philippi, Battle of

Bruxelles [brüksel] >> **Brussels**

Bryggen [**brüg**gen] A world heritage site in Bergen, SW Norway. Probably founded in the 11th-c, it is the best surviving example of the traditional wooden towns of N Europe. >> Bergen

bryophyte A spore-bearing, non-vascular plant belonging to the division Bryophyta, which includes some 25 000 species of moss, liverwort, and hornwort. Bryophytes have conducting cells but lack true vascular tissue; they have rhizoids, thread-like outgrowths which anchor the plant and conduct water, but no true roots. They are mainly terrestrial plants, mostly restricted to damp or humid habitats. They are increasingly regarded as important indicator plants (eg in pollution studies). >> algae; epiphyte; gametophyte; hornwort; liverwort; moss; rhizoid; sporophyte

Bryozoa [briyo**zoh**a] A phylum of small, aquatic animals that typically form colonies comprising a few to a million individuals; c.4 000 living species, mostly marine, and attached to hard substrates or seaweeds; also known as **moss animals**. >> phylum

Bryson, Bill (1951–) Writer, born in Des Moines, IA. In 1977 he moved to England and settled in North Yorkshire. His travel books include the best-sellers *The Lost Continent* and *Neither Here Nor There* (1991). *Notes From A Small Island* (1995) recounts his final trip around Britain before returning to America, when he produced *Notes From a Big Country* (1998).

Brythonic >> **Celtic languages**

Brzezinski, Zbigniew [bzhe**zin**skee] (1928–) Educator and statesman, born in Poland. He served as National Security Adviser under President Carter (1977–80). >> Carter, Jimmy

BSE >> **bovine spongiform encephalopathy**

BSE crisis A European Commission (EC) ban on the sale of British beef as a result of the discovery of bovine spongiform encephalopathy (BSE) in British cattle in the 1980s. In an attempt to stop the spread of the disease, a ban on feed derived from protein was introduced in 1988, and a decision to slaughter all BSE-affected cattle was made the same year. In 1989, the EC banned the export of cattle born before July 1988, and in 1990 restricted exports to cows under six months old. Following a British government announcement of a suspected link between BSE and CJD (Creutzfeldt-Jacob disease) in March 1996, a worldwide export ban on British beef was introduced. The British government then applied for a phased lifting of the ban, and this was agreed, with various preconditions. The ban was first removed on certified herds in Northern Ireland in March 1998, and the following November was lifted for the whole of the UK. >> bovine spongiform encephalopathy; Creutzfeldt-Jacob disease

BTU >> **British thermal unit**

bubble chamber A device for detecting the paths of nuclear particles, devised in 1952 by Donald Glaser. The chamber contains liquid hydrogen kept just above its boiling point by pressure. The pressure is briefly released. Before general boiling can take place, the passage of a particle produces a local instability which initiates evaporation, forming visible bubbles of gas along its path. >> Glaser; hydrogen; particle detectors / physics

bubble memory A type of computer memory first produced as a storage medium in the mid-1970s. These devices operate as read/write memories by circulating very small polarized magnetic bubbles which represent single bits. They have the advantage of being extremely sturdy, but they are relatively slow and expensive. >> computer memory

Buber, Martin [**boo**ber] (1878–1965) Jewish theologian and philosopher, born in Vienna. He was professor of comparative religion at Frankfurt (1923–33), then directed the Central Office for Jewish Adult Education until 1938, when he fled to Palestine. His most influential work as a figure of religious existentialism was the early *Ich und Du* (1923, I and Thou). >> existentialism; Zionism

bubonic plague >> **plague**

Bucaramanga [bookara**mang**ga] 7°08N 73°10W, pop (1995e) 367 000. City in NC Colombia; altitude, 1018 m/ 3340 ft; 'the garden city of Colombia'; founded, 1622; university (1947). >> Colombia ℹ

buccaneers Pirates and adventurers who preyed upon Spanish shipping in the West Indies and along the Spanish Main in the 17th-c; mainly Dutch, English, and French. Referred to by the Spanish as *corsarios* ('corsairs'), by the Dutch as *vrijbuiter* ('freebooters'), and by the English as *privateers*, they flourished between 1630 and 1689. >> corsairs; Spanish Main

Bucer or **Butzer, Martin** [**but**ser] (1491–1551) Protestant reformer, born in Schlettstadt, Germany. He joined the Dominicans, but in 1521 left the order. He adopted a middle course in the disputes about the Eucharist between Luther and Zwingli. >> Luther; Reformation; Zwingli

Buchan, John, Baron Tweedsmuir [**buh**kn] (1875–1940) Writer and statesman, born in Perth, Perth and Kinross. He was MP for the Scottish Universities (1927–35), and became Governor-General of Canada until 1940. Despite his busy public life, Buchan wrote over 50 books, especially fast-moving adventure stories, such as *Prester John* (1910) and *The Thirty-nine Steps* (1915).

Buchanan, James [byoo**kan**an] (1791–1868) US statesman and 15th president (1857–61), born in Stony Batter, PA. A Democratic senator from 1834, he became secretary of state in 1845. He supported the establishment of Kansas as a slave state, but his compromise failed to avert the Civil War. >> American Civil War; slavery

Bucharest [buka**rest**], Romanian **Bucureşti**, ancient **Cetatea Dambovitei** 44°25N 26°07E, pop (1995e) 2 087 000. Capital of Romania; founded, 14th-c; capital of Wallachia, 1698; capital of Romania, 1861; badly damaged by German bombing in World War 2; airport; railway; university (1864); technical university (1819). >> Romania i

Buchman, Frank (Nathan Daniel) [**buhk**man] (1878–1961) Evangelist, born in Pennsburg, PA. In 1921, believing that there was an imminent danger of the collapse of civilization, he founded at Oxford the 'Group Movement'. It was labelled the 'Oxford Group' until 1938, when it rallied under the slogan 'Moral Rearmament'. >> evangelicalism; Moral Rearmament

Buck, Pearl S(ydenstricker), pseudonym **John Sedges** (1892–1973) Novelist, born in Hillsboro, WV. *The Good Earth* (1931) earned her the Pulitzer Prize, and in 1938 she was awarded the Nobel Prize for Literature. Five novels were written under her pseudonym.

buckhound >> **deerhound**

Buckingham Palace The 600-room residence of the British sovereign in London, built for George IV on the site of his parents' home, Buckingham House. The architect was John Nash. The palace remained unused until Queen Victoria's accession in 1837. Some rooms were opened to the public for the first time in 1993. >> Nash, John

Buckinghamshire pop (1995e) 665 000; area 1883 sq km/ 727 sq mi. County in SC England; crossed in the S by the Chiltern Hills; extensive woodland; county town, Aylesbury; Milton Keynes a unitary authority from 1997. >> Aylesbury; England i

Buckley, William F(rank), Jr (1925–) Political writer and editor, born in New York City. He founded the political journal *National Review* in 1955, making it the primary voice of the intellectual US right. In the 1970s he turned to writing spy novels. >> right wing

buckminsterfullerene [buhkminster**ful**ereen] C_{60}. An almost spherical molecule, thought to be an ingredient of soots; also called **soccerene**. >> carbon; fullerenes

buckthorn A thorny, spreading, deciduous shrub or small tree (*Rhamnus catharticus*) 4–10 m/13–30 ft, native to Europe and the Mediterranean region; flowers tiny, green, parts in fours; berry black, mildly poisonous, and purgative. (Family: Rhamnaceae.)

buckwheat An erect annual (*Fagopyrum esculentum*) with spear-shaped leaves and a terminal cluster of tiny pink or white flowers; fruit a triangular nut c.6 mm/$\frac{1}{4}$ in long; native to C Asia and cultivated as a substitute for cereals. (Family: Polygonaceae.) >> cereals

Budaeus, Guglielmus [bu**day**us], Latin name of **Guillaume Budé** (1467–1540) Scholar, born in Paris. At his suggestion Francis I founded the Collège de France. As royal librarian he founded the collection which later became the Bibliothèque Nationale.

Budapest [booda**pest**] 47°29N 19°05E, pop (1995e) 1 986 000. Capital of Hungary, on R Danube; old-world Buda on W bank hills, modern Pest on E bank, unified in 1873; scene of popular uprising, crushed by Soviet troops, 1956; airport; railway; underground; Eötvös Loránd University (1635); universities of medicine (1769), economic science (1948), horticulture (1853); Hungarian Academy of Sciences; Buda castle and banks of the Danube are a world heritage site; location for World Fair (Expo) in 1996. >> Hungary i

Budd, Zola, married name **Pieterse** (1966–) Athlete, born in Bloemfontein, South Africa. She caused a controversy by obtaining British citizenship in 1984 and then being selected for the British Olympic squad. There was further controversy at the Los Angeles Games when she was involved in an incident which led to Mary Decker (USA) being tripped during the 3000 m. She set the 5000 m world record in 1984 and 1985, and was world cross-country champion in 1985 and 1986. A hip injury and public attitudes caused her to retire in 1988. >> athletics

Buddha ('the enlightened one') (c.563–c.483 BC) The founder of Buddhism, born the son of the rajah of the Sakya tribe ruling at Kapilavastu, N of Benares. His personal name was **Siddhartha**, but he was also known by his family name of **Gautama**. When about 30, he left the luxuries of the court, his beautiful wife, and all earthly ambitions for the life of an ascetic; after several years of severe austerities he saw in meditation and contemplation the way to enlightenment. For some 40 years he taught, gaining many disciples and followers, and died at Kusinagara in Oudh. >> Buddhism

Buddh Gaya or **Bodh Gaya** [bud **gah**ya] A sacred Buddhist site in Bihar, India. Since the 3rd-c BC, shrines have marked the spot where Gautama Buddha attained enlightenment. >> Bihar; Buddha

Buddhism A tradition of thought and practice originating in India c.2500 years ago, and now a world religion, deriving from the teaching of Buddha (Siddhartha Gautama), who is regarded as one of a continuing series of enlightened beings. The teaching of Buddha is summarized in the *Four Noble Truths*, the last of which affirms the existence of a path leading to deliverance from the universal human experience of suffering. A central tenet is the law of *karma*, by which good and evil deeds result in appropriate reward or punishment in this life or in a succession of rebirths. Through a proper understanding of this condition, and by obedience to the right path, human beings can break the chain of karma. The Buddha's path to deliverance is through morality (*sila*), meditation (*samadhi*), and wisdom (*panna*), as set out in the *Eightfold Path*. The goal is *Nirvana*, which means 'the blowing out' of the fires of all desires, and the absorption of the self into the infinite. There are two main traditions within Buddhism, dating from its earliest history. **Theravada Buddhism** adheres to the strict and narrow teachings of the early Buddhist writings: salvation is possible for only the few who accept the severe discipline and effort necessary to achieve it. **Mahayana Buddhism** is more liberal, and makes concessions to popular piety: it teaches that salvation is possible for everyone, and introduced the doctrine of the *bodhisattva* (or personal saviour). As Buddhism spread, other schools grew up, among which are Ch'an or Zen, Lamaism, Tendai, Nichiren, and Soka Gakkai. The only complete canon of Buddhist scripture is called the Pali canon, after the language in which it is written. >> bodhisattva; Buddha; Dalai Lama; Eightfold Path; Four Noble Truths; karma; Lamaism; Mahayana; Nichiren Buddhism; Nirvana; Theravada; Zen Buddhism

buddleia or **buddleja** [**buhd**lia] A deciduous shrub or small tree, native to warm regions; flowers small, various colours, often scented, crowded in dense spikes or globular clusters. It is very attractive to insects, especially butterflies, hence the name **butterfly bush** given to *Buddleia davidii*, the most commonly cultivated species. (Genus: *Buddleia*, 100 species. Family: Loganiaceae.)

Budé, Guillaume >> **Budaeus, Guglielmus**

budgerigar A small parrot native to C Australia, and introduced in Florida (*Melopsittacus undulatus*). It is a popular cage-bird, with many colour variations, but is usually green in the wild. (Family: Psittacidae.) >> lovebird ⓘ; parrot

Buenaventura [bwenaven**too**ra] 3°51N 77°06W, pop (1995e) 173 000. Pacific seaport in SW Colombia; founded, 1540. >> Colombia ⓘ

Buenos Aires [**bway**nos **iy**rees] 34°40S 58°30W, pop (1995e) 3 130 000 Federal capital of Argentina; on S bank of R Plate; founded in 1536 as the city of the 'Puerto de Santa Maria del Buen Aire'; destroyed by Indians, and refounded, 1580; formerly capital of the Spanish viceroyalty of La Plata; airport; railway; metro; nine universities; cathedral. >> Argentina ⓘ

Buffalo 42°53N 78°53W, pop (1995e) 334 000. Port on the Niagara R at the NE end of L Erie; second largest city in New York State, USA; railway; two universities (1846, 1867); professional teams, Bills (football), Sabres (ice hockey). >> New York

Buffalo Bill >> **Cody, William F**

buffalo >> **bison; water buffalo**

buffalo-weaver >> **weaverbird**

buffer In computing, a temporary storage area in memory for data. Buffers are often used when transmitting data between two devices with different working speeds, such as between a keyboard and the central processor. >> computer memory

buffer state A small state lying between two or more larger and potentially belligerent states, as a means of reducing border friction between them. For example, after World War 1, attempts were made to create a buffer state between Germany and France.

Buffon, Georges-Louis Leclerc, comte de (Count of) [bufõ] (1707–88) Naturalist, born in Montbard, Burgundy. In 1739 he was made director of the Jardin du Roi, with its museum, and formed the design of his *Histoire naturelle* (1749–67, Natural History). His wide-ranging ideas foreshadowed the theory of evolution. >> evolution

bug (computing) An error in a computer program or a fault in com-puter hardware. The process of detecting and correcting errors is known as **debugging**. >> computer program; hardware

bug (entomology) An insect with forewings leathery at base, membranous near the tip, and folded over membranous hindwings at rest; diverse in form and feeding habits; mouthparts modified into a snout for piercing and sucking; includes many crop pests and disease carriers. (Order: Heteroptera.) >> capsid; chinch / shield bug; Heteroptera; insect ⓘ; lac insect; pond skater; scale insect; water boatman; water scorpion; whitefly

Bugatti, Ettore (Arco Isidoro) [boo**ga**tee] (1881–1947) Car manufacturer, born in Milan, Italy. He began designing cars in 1899 and set up his works in Strasbourg in 1907. His racing cars won international fame in the 1930s. >> car ⓘ

Buginese or **Bugi** A major ethnic group of Celebes (Sulawesi), Indonesia. They live as rice cultivators, traders, and seafarers. >> Celebes

bugle A musical instrument made of brass or copper, curved elliptically and ending in a large bell. It normally has no valves and can therefore produce only those notes forming the first half-dozen harmonics above the fundamental (usually B♭). It has been used above all for sounding military calls. >> brass instrument ⓘ

bugloss [**byoo**glos] A bristly annual or biennial (*Anchusa arvensis*) growing to 50 cm/20 in, native to Europe and Asia; flowers with curved white tube, spreading bright-blue lobes, and white eye. (Family: Boraginaceae.)

buhl or **boulle** [bool] A technique of furniture decoration involving very elaborate inlays of brass, tortoiseshell, mother-of-pearl, and coloured wood. Introduced into France in the 16th-c from Italy, it was perfected by André Charles Boulle (1642–1732) and his sons. >> brass

building biology The study of the interaction between a building and its environment, especially with respect to the effects upon the health of the occupants. It deals with the location and geometry of the building, its colour scheme, lighting, and furnishings, and the selection of non-toxic and ecologically 'friendly' building materials. >> biology; environment; facilities management

building society An institution which lends money to enable people to buy property (ie a mortgage loan). Their funds are derived from investors who obtain interest on the sum deposited. Interest paid to the society by the borrower is higher than the rate paid out. In the UK there are some 150 societies which, since 1987, are permitted to provide other services. The US equivalent is the **savings and loan association**. >> mortgage

Bujumbura [bujum**boo**ra], formerly **Usumbura** 3°22S 29°21E, pop (1995e) 340 000. Port capital of Burundi, C Africa, at NE end of L Tanganyika; altitude 805 m/2641 ft; founded in 1899 by German colonists; airport; university (1960). >> Burundi ⓘ

Bukharin, Nikolay Ivanovich [boo**kha**rin] (1888–1938) Russian Marxist revolutionary and political theorist, born in Moscow. He played a leading role in the organization of the October Revolution in Moscow. In 1937 he was arrested in Stalin's Great Purge, tried on trumped-up charges, and shot. >> Lenin; October Revolution; Stalin

Bulawayo [boola**way**oh] 20°10S 28°43E, pop (1995e) 583 000. Second largest city in Zimbabwe; founded, 1893; airport; railway junction; commercial, industrial, and tourist centre. >> Matabeleland; Zimbabwe ⓘ

bulb A highly modified shoot forming an underground storage organ. It is composed of overlapping leaves or leaf bases, swollen with food reserves which nourish early growth. The bulbs usually persist from year to year, the reserves being replenished before the plant dies back. >> bulbil; corm

bulbil A small organ resembling a bulb, but produced above ground, either in a leaf axil or in the inflorescence in place of some flowers. It produces a new plant after falling from the parent. >> bulb; inflorescence ⓘ

bulbul A bird native to tropical Africa, Madagascar, and S Asia; short wings, long tail; stiff bristles at base of pointed bill. (Family: Pycnonotidae, 120 species.)

Bulfinch, Charles (1763–1844) Architect, born in Boston, MA. America's first native-born architect, he succeeded Latrobe as architect of the US Capitol (1817–30). His domed capitol buildings influenced the design of state capitals across the country throughout the 19th-c. >> Capitol; Latrobe; Neoclassicism

Bulganin, Nikolay Alexandrovich [bul**gah**nin] (1895–1975) Soviet statesman and prime minister (1955–8), born in Nizhni Novgorod, Russia. He was made premier after Malenkov resigned (1955), with Khrushchev wielding real power. 'B and K' travelled extensively abroad, conducting propaganda through lengthy letters to Western statesmen. >> communism; Khrushchev; Malenkov

Bulgaria [buhl**gair**eea], official name **Republic of Bulgaria**, Bulgarian **Republika Bulgariya**, formerly **People's Republic of Bulgaria** (1941–90) pop (1995e) 8 670 000; area 110 912 sq km/42 812 sq mi. Republic in the E of the Balkan Peninsula, SE Europe; capital, Sofia; timezone GMT +2; population c.85% Bulgarian, with several minorities; officially atheist, but religious background of people is 85% Bulgarian Orthodox and 13% Muslim; official language, Bulgarian; unit of currency, the lev of 100 stotinki; traversed W–E by the Balkan Mts, rising to heights of over 2000 m/6500 ft; Rhodope Mts in the SW rise to nearly 3000 m/9600 ft; Bulgarian lowlands stretch S from the R

Danube; largely continental climate, with hot summers and cold winters; Bulgars crossed the Danube in the 7th-c; their empire continually at war with the Byzantines until destroyed by the Turks in the 14th-c; remained under Turkish rule until 1878; full independence, 1908; a kingdom, 1908–46; aligned with Germany in World Wars; occupied by USSR, 1944; Socialist People's Republic founded, 1946; single-chamber National Assembly established, 1971; no constitutional single head of state, but a chairman of the State Council; new democratic constitution, 1991; mainly agricultural produce; coal, iron ore; offshore oil (Black Sea) and natural gas; tourism. >> Black Sea; Sofia; RR1003 political leaders

Bulgarian >> **Slavic languages**

Bulge, Battle of the The last desperate German armoured counter-offensive through the Ardennes in World War 2 (beginning 16 Dec). It achieved early success, but the Germans were then forced to retreat by the Allies by the end of January 1945. >> World War 2

bulimia nervosa [byoo**lim**ia ner**voh**sa] A condition typified by repeated episodes of binge eating and frequent vomiting and purging, associated with a preoccupation with control of body weight and a feeling of lack of control over eating behaviour. The vast majority of patients are female. >> anorexia nervosa

bulk store >> **backing store**

Bull, John (c.1562–1628) Musician, born in Somerset. A virtuoso player, he was one of the founders of contrapuntal keyboard music. He has been credited with composing the air 'God save the King'.

bull (religion) An important, formal communication or edict from a pope, originally sealed with his signet-ring (Lat *bulla*, 'seal') and identified by the opening Latin words. >> pope

bull (zoology) A male mammal belonging to one of several species; female usually called *cow*; young called *calf*; used especially for uncastrated male cattle (male castrated when young called a *bullock*, *ox*, or *steer*; if castrated when fully grown, called a *stag*). >> cattle; mammal i

bullace [**boo**lis] A type of small, wild plum (*Prunus domestica*), usually a thorny shrub with spherical black fruit with waxy bloom; native to Europe. (subspecies *institia*. Family: Rosaceae.) >> damson; plum

bulldog A breed of dog, used in mediaeval Britain for the sport of bull-baiting; heavy body with short, bowed legs and short tail; large round head with flat upturned muzzle; ears and eyes small; short brown or brown and white coat. >> boxer; dog

bulletin board A form of electronic notice board which occurs frequently in data communications networks, particularly those linking academic institutions; also called a **bulletin board system (BBS)**. The bulletin board hosts notices of meetings, technical papers, or even computer programs. Its readership is worldwide. >> BITNET; computer network; electronic mail

bullfighting The national sport in Spain, also popular in some regions of S France, and in Latin American countries. Known as the *corrida de toros* ('running of the bulls') it is regarded as an art in Spain. Leading bullfighters (*matadors*) are treated as national heroes. Picadors are sent into the bull ring to weaken the bull before the matador enters the arena to make the final killing. >> blood sports

bullfinch A bird native to Europe, Scandinavia, and Asia E to Japan and the Philippines; causes serious damage in orchards. (Genus: *Pyrrhula*, 6 species. Family Fringillidae.) >> finch

bullhead Small bottom-dwelling fish found in clear streams and lakes of N Europe; body stout, length up to 10 cm/4 in, with broad flattened head; also called **sculpin** or **miller's thumb**. (Genus: *Cottus*. Family: Cottidae.)

bull market A stock market term which signifies that the prices of stocks and shares are on a rising trend, due to buying demand. A **bull** buys shares hoping that the price will rise, so that they can be sold later at a profit. >> bear / stock market

bull-mastiff A breed of dog, developed in Britain by crossing bulldogs and mastiffs; thick-set body; brown short-haired coat; soft ears and powerful muzzle. >> bulldog; mastiff

Bull Run, Battles of Major victories by Confederate forces in the American Civil War; also known as the **Battles of Manassas**. >> American Civil War

bull terrier A breed of dog, developed for bullbaiting in Britain by crossing bulldogs and terriers; powerful body; long tail; ears pointed, erect; head broad with small eyes; coat short, usually white. The **American pit bull terrier** attracted widespread publicity during the 1980s, following several attacks on people; it became subject to controls and registration in the UK in 1991, along with the *tosa fila Brazileira* and *dogo Argentino*. >> bulldog; terrier

bulrush An aquatic, rush-like perennial (*Scirpus lacustris*), found almost everywhere; stems to 3 m/10 ft; leaves in tufts; flowers tiny, perianth reduced to six rough bristles, in oval, brown spikelets. (Family: Cyperaceae.) >> perianth; rush

bulrush millet >> **millet**

Bultmann, Rudolf (Karl) (1884–1976) Lutheran theologian and New Testament scholar, born in Wiefelstede, Germany. He is best known for his highly influential programme (1941) to 'demythologize' the New Testament and interpret it existentially, employing the categories of the earlier work of Heidegger. >> Heidegger

Bulwer-Lytton, Edward George Earle >> **Lytton, Edward George Earle Bulwer-Lytton**

bumblebee A large bee found mainly in the temperate N hemisphere. The adults transport pollen on the modified outer surface of the hindleg. (Genus: *Bombus*. Family: Apidae.) >> bee

Bunche, Ralph (Johnson) [buhnch] (1904–71) US diplomat, born in Detroit, MI. He directed the United Nations Trusteeship department (1947–54), and became UN mediator in Palestine, where he arranged for a ceasefire. He was awarded the Nobel Peace Prize in 1950. >> United Nations

Bundy, McGeorge (1919–96) US statesman and educator, born in Boston, MA. As National Security Adviser to Presidents Kennedy and Johnson he was one of the architects of the Vietnam War. >> Johnson, Lyndon B; Kennedy, John F; Vietnam War

bungee jumping The activity of jumping from a high point to which the jumper is attached by a strong rubber cable fastened to the ankles. The length and tension of the cable is calculated to ensure that the jumper bounces up before reaching the ground. The activity became popular in the early 1990s, and is now practised as a sport in several countries.

Bunin, Ivan Alexeyevich [**boo**nin] (1870–1953) Writer, born in Voronezh, Russia. His best-known work is *Gospodin iz San-Francisco* (1922, The Gentleman from San Francisco). He was the first Russian to receive the Nobel Prize for Literature (1933).

bunion A painful, inflamed hardening and thickening of the skin over the head of the metatarsal of (especially) the great toe. It is often induced by ill-fitting footwear. >> foot

Bunker Hill, Battle of The first pitched battle of the US War of Independence, fought during the siege of Boston. It was technically an American defeat, but very high British casualties forbade attempts on other American emplacements. >> American Revolution

bunraku [**bun**rakoo] The classical Japanese puppet theatre. Puppets are two-thirds life size, hand-held by a puppet master, generally with two 'invisible' assistants in black. The movements are accompanied by a singer-narrator and musicians. >> puppetry

Bunsen burner A gas burner, used mainly in chemistry laboratories. Gas enters through a jet at the lower end of a tube, and is drawn through a side tube whose aperture can be controlled. The controllable gas–air mixture makes possible a flame of quality, ranging from luminous to hot non-luminous. The idea is attributed to German scientist Robert Wilhelm Bunsen (1811–99).

bunting A small seed-eating bird, usually dull in colour with a short stout bill. It belongs to a widespread family, thought to have evolved in the Americas, spread across the Bering Straits to Asia, then colonized Europe and Africa. (Family: Emberizidae, c.290 species.) >> Darwin's finches

Buñuel, Luis [buhn**wel**] (1900–83) Film director, born in Calanda, Spain. He directed such major films as *Viridiana* (1961), *The Discreet Charm of the Bourgeoisie* (1972), and *That Obscure Object of Desire* (1977). His work is characterized by a poetic, often erotic, use of imagery, a black humour, and a hatred of Catholicism.

Bunyan, John (1628–88) Writer, born in Elstow, Bedfordshire. In 1653 he joined a Christian fellowship, preaching around Bedford. While imprisoned in the town gaol, he wrote the first part of the allegorical work *The Pilgrim's Progress* (1678). The second part was published in 1684.

Bunyan, Paul In American folklore, a lumberjack of superhuman size and strength. He could refashion geography, creating lakes, rivers, and even the Grand Canyon.

bunyip In the mythology of the Australian aborigines, the source of evil. The Rainbow Serpent, the mother of life, confined bunyip to a waterhole: he haunts dark and gloomy places. >> Aborigines

Buonaparte >> **Bonaparte**

buoyancy The upward thrust on an object immersed in liquid or gas, equal to the weight of the displaced fluid. The human body is more buoyant in salt water than in fresh water, as the former is 3% denser. >> Archimedes

Burbage, Richard [**ber**bij] (c.1569–1619) Actor, born in London. He was the leading performer with Shakespeare's company from 1594 until his death.

Burbank, Luther (1849–1926) Horticulturalist, born in Lancaster, MA. He developed the *Burbank potato* on a farm near Lunenberg, MA, and in 1875 moved to Santa Rosa, CA, where he bred over 800 new strains of fruits and flowers. >> horticulture

burbot Elongate slender-bodied fish (*Lota lota*) widespread in rivers and lakes of N Eurasia and North America; the only freshwater species in the cod family Gadidae; length up to 1 m/3¼ ft; single barbel beneath mouth; also called **eelpout**. >> cod

Burgess, Anthony, pseudonym of **John Anthony Burgess Wilson** (1917–93) Writer and critic, born in Manchester, Greater Manchester. His many novels include *A Clockwork Orange* (1962), *Earthly Powers* (1980), and *Any Old Iron* (1989). He wrote several critical studies and film scripts, including *Jesus of Nazareth* (1977), and his musical compositions include symphonies, a ballet, and an opera. In his later years, he lived in Monaco.

Burgess, Guy (Francis de Moncy) (1910–63) British traitor, born in Devonport, Devon. He studied at Cambridge, where he became a communist, and was recruited as a Soviet agent in the 1930s. Recalled from Washington in 1951 for 'serious misconduct', he and Maclean disappeared, re-emerging in the Soviet Union in 1956. >> communism; Maclean, Donald

Burgh, Hubert de [ber] (?–1243) Justiciar of England under King John and Henry III (1215–32). He is chiefly remembered as the gaoler of Prince Arthur. >> John; Henry III (of England)

burgh >> **borough**

Burghley or **Burghleigh, Lord** >> **Cecil, William**

burglary A crime which involves entering a building as a trespasser, either with the intent to commit theft, grievous bodily harm, or rape; or, having entered, stealing or attempting to steal anything, or committing or attempting to commit grievous bodily harm. The term is not used in all jurisdictions. >> theft

Burgos [**boor**gos] 42°21N 3°41W, pop (1995e) 162 000. City in N Spain; former capital of Old Castile; archbishopric; railway; cathedral (13th–16th-c), castle; a world heritage site; home and burial site of El Cid. >> El Cid; Spain ℹ

Burgoyne, John, nickname **Gentleman Johnnie** (1722–92) British general and playwright, born in Sutton, Bedfordshire. In 1777 he was sent to America, where he led an expedition from Canada, taking Ticonderoga, but was forced to surrender at Saratoga. His best-known work was his comedy, *The Heiress* (1786). >> American Revolution

Burgundy, Fr **Bourgogne** pop (1995e) 1 658 000; area 31 582 sq km/12 191 sq mi. Region and former province of EC France; former kingdom of Burgundia (5th–10th-c); famous wine-producing area (eg Beaujolais, Beaune, Chablis); chief town, Dijon; industry centred on Le Creusot. >> Dijon; France ℹ; wine

burials >> **bog burials; Kofun; Maes Howe; Mount Li; New Grange; shaft graves; Ship of Cheops; Sutton Hoo ship burial**

Burke, Edmund (1729–97) British statesman and political philosopher, born in Dublin, Ireland. His early writing includes his *Philosophical Inquiry into the Origin of Our Ideas of the Sublime and Beautiful* (1756). His *Reflections on the French Revolution* (1790) was read all over Europe. >> American Revolution

Burke, William (1792–1829) Murderer, born in Orrery, Waterford, Ireland. With his partner, **William Hare** (c.1790–c.1860), born in Londonderry, he carried out a series of infamous murders in Edinburgh in the 1820s, with the aim of supplying dissection subjects to an anatomist. Hare turned king's evidence, and died a beggar in London; Burke was hanged, to the general satisfaction of the crowd.

Burke's Peerage A reference guide to the aristocratic and titled families of Great Britain, first published by John Burke (1787–1848) in 1826 under the title *Genealogical and Heraldic Dictionary of the Peerage and Baronetage of the United Kingdom*. >> Debrett's Peerage; peerage

Burkina Faso [ber**kee**na **fa**soh], formerly **Upper Volta** (to 1984), then (Fr) **République de Haute-Volta** pop (1995e) 10 328 000; area 274 540 sq km/105 972 sq mi. Land-locked republic in W Africa; capital, Ouagadougou; timezone GMT; over 50 tribes, notably the Mossi (48%); religion, mainly local beliefs, with some Muslim (c.25%) and Christian (10%); official language, French, but many local languages; unit of currency, the CFA franc; low-lying plateau, falling away to the S; many rivers (tributaries of the Volta or Niger) unnavigable in dry season; wooded savannahs in S; semi-desert in N; tropical climate, mean temperature 27°C in dry season (Dec–May); rainy season (Jun–Oct), with violent storms (Aug); Mossi empire in 18th–19th-c; Upper Volta created by French, 1919; abolished, 1932, with most land joined to Ivory Coast; original borders reconstituted, 1947; autonomy within French community, 1958; independence, 1960, since when there have been several military coups; governed by a president and an appointed Council of Ministers; new constitution, 1991, which promulgated an Assembly of People's Deputies; an agricultural country, largely at subsistence level and subject to drought conditions. >> Ouagadougou; RR1003 political leaders

Burma >> **Myanmar**

burn A wound in which tissues are damaged or destroyed by heat; a contrast is often drawn with a **scald**, which is a burn caused by moist heat. The management of burns may now involve specialist teams composed of several medical and surgical disciplines, often housed in specialist units. >> graft (medicine); skin ℹ

Burne-Jones, Sir Edward Coley (1833–98) Painter and designer, born in Birmingham, West Midlands. His later oils, inspired by the early Italian Renaissance, are characterized by a Romantic and contrived Mannerism. He also designed stained glass and tapestries, and illustrated several books. >> Mannerism; Renaissance

burnet An erect, tuft-forming perennial, native to Europe, W Asia, or N Africa; flowers in a globular head, four sepals, petals absent. The **salad burnet** (*Sanguisorba minor*) grows to 40 cm/15 in, flowers green or purple-tinged; crushed foliage smelling of cucumber. (Family: Rosaceae.)

Burnet, Sir (Frank) Macfarlane [ber**net**] (1899–1985) Medical scientist, born in Traralgon, Victoria, Australia. A world authority on viral diseases, he shared the 1960 Nobel Prize for Physiology or Medicine for research into immunological intolerance in relation to skin and organ grafting. >> immunology; Medawar; virus

Burnett, Frances (Eliza), *née* **Hodgson** (1849–1924) Writer, born in Manchester, Greater Manchester. She wrote several plays and over 40 novels, notably *Little Lord Fauntleroy* (1886) and *The Secret Garden* (1909).

Burnett, Ivy Compton >> **Compton-Burnett, Ivy**

Burney, Fanny, popular name of **Frances Burney**, married name **Madame d'Arblay** (1752–1840) Writer and diarist, born in King's Lynn, Norfolk. Her first and best novel, *Evelina*, was published anonymously in 1778, and influenced Jane Austen. Her *Letters and Diaries* (1846) show her skill in reporting events of her time.

burning bush >> **dittany**

Burns, George, originally **Nathan Birnbaum** (1896–1996) Comedian and actor, born in New York City. He made his debut at the age of 13, and in 1923 teamed up with **Gracie Allen** (1905–64). They became a husband-and-wife comedy duo popular for over three decades in vaudeville, radio, films, and television. Well known for his omnipresent cigar, dry wit, and comic timing, he received an Oscar for his role in *The Sunshine Boys* (1975).

Burns, Robert (1759–96) Scotland's national poet, born in Alloway, South Ayrshire. On his father's death (1784) he was left in charge of the farm. At the same time his entanglement with Jean Armour (1767–1834) began, and as the farm went to ruin, his poverty, passion, and despair produced in 1785 an extraordinary output of poetry, including 'The Jolly Beggars'. Looking for money to emigrate to Jamaica, he published the famous Kilmarnock edition of his poems (1786), which brought such acclaim that he was persuaded to stay in Scotland. Going to Edinburgh, where he was feted, he began the epistolary flirtations with 'Clarinda' (Agnes Maclehose, 1759–1841). In 1788 he married Jean Armour and leased a farm near Dumfries. By 1790, when he wrote 'Tam o' Shanter', the farm was failing. He left for Dumfries, where he died. >> Burns Night

Burnside, Ambrose Everett (1824–81) US general, born in Liberty, IN. In the Civil War he was repulsed at Fredericksburg (1862), but held Knoxville (1863), and led a corps under Grant through the battles of the Wilderness and Cold Harbor (1864). He lent his name to a style of side whiskers, later known as 'sideburns'. >> American Civil War

Burns Night The evening of 25 January, anniversary of the birth of Robert Burns. It is celebrated with a special meal (**Burns Supper**) including haggis, potatoes, and swedes, followed by a set formula of toasts and performances of Burns's works. >> Burns, Robert

Burra, Edward (1905–76) Artist, born in London. Well known as a colourist, his Surrealist paintings of figures against exotic (often Spanish) backgrounds are invariably in watercolour. >> Surrealism

Burroughs, Edgar Rice [**buh**rohz] (1875–1950) Writer,

born in Chicago, IL. He had many unsuccessful jobs, before making his name with the 'Tarzan' stories, beginning with *Tarzan of the Apes* (1914).

Burroughs, William S(eward) [**buh**rohz] (1914–97) Writer, born in St Louis, MO. His novels *Naked Lunch* (1959) and *The Soft Machine* (1961) established him as a spokesman of the 'beat' movement of the late 1950s. His later work includes *The Wild Boys* (1971), and *The Western Lands* (1987). >> beat generation

Bursa [boor**sah**], ancient **Brusa** or **Prusa** 40°12N 29°04E, pop (1995e) 931 000. City in NW Turkey; founded, 3rd-c BC; airfield; railway; noted for its silk textiles. >> Turkey ℹ

Burt, Sir Cyril (Lodowic) (1883–1971) Psychologist, born in London. He was largely responsible for the theory and practice of intelligence and aptitude tests, ranging from the psychology of education to the problems of juvenile delinquency. In the 1980s, the validity of some of his techniques was called into question. >> intelligence; testing

Burton, Richard, originally **Richard Walter Jenkins** (1925–84) Stage and film actor, born in Pontrhydfen, South Wales. His early Hollywood films include *The Robe* (1953), for which he received one of his six Oscar nominations. His romance with Elizabeth Taylor during the making of *Cleopatra* (1962) and their eventual marriage (1964–74) projected them both into the 'superstar' category. Among his later films were *Becket* (1964), *Equus* (1977), and *1984* (released after his death). In his later years, interest in his social life grew, especially after his second marriage to Elizabeth Taylor (1975–6).

Burton, Sir Richard (Francis) (1821–90) Explorer, born in Torquay, Devon. In 1856 he set out on the journey which led to the discovery (1858) of L Tanganyika. He translated several Eastern works, notably, *The Arabian Nights* (1885–8). >> Speke

Burton, Robert (1577–1640) Writer, born in Lindley, Leicestershire. His great work was the *Anatomy of Melancholy* (1621), a learned miscellany on the ideas of his time.

Burundi [bu**run**dee], official name **Republic of Burundi** pop (1995e) 6 131 000; area 27 834 sq km/10 744 sq mi. Republic in C Africa; capital, Bujumbura; timezone GMT +2; population mainly Hutu (85%), with Tutsi (14%), and other tribal minorities; chief religions, Roman Catholic (62%), local beliefs (32%); official languages, Kirundi, French; unit of currency, Burundi franc; lies across the Nile-Congo watershed; average height of interior plateau c.1500 m/5000 ft; highest point, Mt Karonje (2685 m/8809 ft); equatorial climate; since 16th-c ruled by the Tutsi kingdom; German occupation in 1890, and included in German East Africa (1890); League of Nations mandated territory, administered by Belgians, 1919; joined with Rwanda to become the UN Trust Territory of Ruanda-Urundi, 1946; independence, 1962; full republic, 1966; civil war, 1972; military coup, 1976; new constitution in 1981 provided a National Assembly; Assembly dissolved and constitution suspended after 1987 coup; 1992 referendum agreed a new constitution with legalized political parties, a presidential election, and an 81-member National Assembly; political instability following assassination of president, 1993; inter-ethnic (Hutu/Tutsi) conflict, 1993–; transitional government agreed, 1994–8; economy mainly agriculture; reserves of rare-earth metals. >> Bujumbura; Hutu and Tutsi; League of Nations; mandates; RR1003 political leaders

bus A form of wiring within or between computers in which any electronic message to be transferred is sent down the wire and is taken off the wire only by the particular device to which the message is being sent. Inside a computer there are usually an **address bus**, a **data bus**, and an **input-output bus**. >> digital computer

Busan >> **Pusan**

Busby, Sir Matt(hew) (1909–94) Footballer and football manager, born in Bellshill, North Lanarkshire. He became manager of Manchester United in 1945, winning the FA Cup in 1948 and the League shortly afterwards. His side was largely wiped out in an air crash at Munich airport. He himself was severely injured, but he reconstructed the team, achieving European Cup success in 1968.

Bush, George (Herbert Walker) (1924–) US statesman and 41st President, born in Milton, MA. He entered politics in 1966, and became US permanent representative to the United Nations. Under President Ford he headed the US Mission to Beijing (Peking), then became director of the CIA. In 1980 he campaigned for the Republican nomination, but lost to Reagan, later becoming his vice-president. In 1988 he won the Republican nomination for the presidency, and defeated Governor Michael Dukakis of Massachusetts in the general election, but lost to Bill Clinton in the 1992 election. >> Ford, Gerald R; Reagan

bushbaby A primitive primate (*prosimian*), whose cry sounds like a human baby; large eyes and ears; thick coat, very long tail; long hind legs; agile; also known as **galago**. (Family; Lorisidae, 7 species.) >> prosimian

bushbuck A spiral-horned antelope (*Tragelaphus scriptus*) native to Africa S of the Sahara; reddish-brown with white spots or thin white lines; females without horns; lives in pairs; nocturnal. >> antelope

bush cat >> **genet**

bushmaster A rare pit viper (*Lachesis muta*), native to Central and South America; largest venomous snake in the New World; length, up to 3·5 m/11½ ft; the only New World viper to lay eggs; nocturnal. >> pit viper ℹ

Bushmen >> **Khoisan**

bushrangers Australian rural outlaws who operated from 1790 to 1900. Some attained folk hero status, such as Ben Hall (killed 1865), and Ned Kelly (hanged 1880). >> Kelly, Ned

☐ international airport

Busoni, Ferruccio (Benvenuto) [bu**soh**nee] (1866–1924) Composer and pianist, born in Empoli, Italy. An infant prodigy, in 1889 he became professor of pianoforte at Helsinski. The influence of Liszt is apparent in his great piano concerto.

Bussell, Darcey (Andrea) [**buh**sel] (1969–) Ballerina, born in London. She joined the Royal Ballet as soloist in 1988, and went on to become the company's youngest principal dancer. She has made guest appearances internationally for various companies, and danced leading roles in works by MacMillan and Ashton.

bussing A government policy adopted in the 1960s (particularly in the USA) to promote social integration among school children in ethnically divided urban communities. Children (especially black and Asian) were taken by bus from disadvantaged urban contexts to schools elsewhere. In the USA, bussing became controversial, and the policy was abandoned in 1972. >> ethnicity

bustard A large, long-legged, ground-living bird native to Africa, S Europe, Asia, and Australia; walks rather than flies (but flies well). (Family: Otididae, 24 species.)

busy Lizzie >> **impatiens**

butadiene [byoota**diy**een] CH_2=CH–CH=CH_2, **buta-1,3-diene**, boiling point −4°C. A gas, an important monomer of synthetic rubbers. >> gas 1; monomer

butane [**byoo**tayn] $CH_3CH_2CH_2CH_3$, boiling point 0°C. An easily liquefied alkane gas, obtained as a petroleum fraction. It is supplied as a liquid under pressure for use as a fuel, as in Calor® gas. >> alkanes

butanedioic acid >> **succinic acid**

butcherbird >> **shrike**

Buthelezi, Mangosuthu Gatsha [bootuh**lay**zee], known as **Chief Buthelezi** (1928–) South African Zulu leader and politician, born in KwaZulu Natal, South Africa. He is leader of the Zulu-based movement, Inkatha, which in the early 1990s was involved in a violent struggle for political leadership among black South Africans. In 1994 he was appointed minister for home affairs in Nelson Mandela's first cabinet. >> Inkatha; Mandela, Nelson

Butler, Joseph (1692–1752) Moral philosopher and theologian, born in Wantage, Oxfordshire. His major work, *The Analogy of Religion* (1736), argued that objections against revealed religion may also be levelled against the whole constitution of nature.

Butler, Reg(inald Cotterell) (1913–81) Sculptor, born in Buntingford, Hertfordshire. He was one of the leading exponents of 'linear' constructions in wrought iron.

Butler, R(ichard) A(usten), Baron Butler, known as **Rab Butler** (1902–82) British Conservative statesman, born in Attock Serai, India. He became minister of education (1941–5), introducing the Education Act of 1944. Later posts included Chancellor of the Exchequer (1951), home secretary (1957), deputy prime minister (1962), and foreign secretary (1963–4). He was then appointed Master of Trinity College, Cambridge (1965–78). >> Butskellism; Conservative Party

Butler, Samuel (1612–80) Satirist, baptized at Strensham, Hereford and Worcester. His great 3-part poetic work, *Hudibras* (1663, 1664, 1678), is a burlesque satire on Puritanism. >> Puritanism

Butler, Samuel (1835–1902) Writer, painter, and musician, born at Langar Rectory, Nottinghamshire. In his Utopian satire, *Erewhon* (1872) – the word is an inversion of 'nowhere' – many conventional practices and customs are reversed. He is best known for his autobiographical novel *The Way of All Flesh* (1903).

Butlin, Billy, popular name of **Sir William (Edmund) Butlin** (1899–1980) Holiday camp promoter, born in South Africa. He opened his first camp at Skegness, UK, in 1936. In World War 2 he served as director-general of hostels to the ministry of supply.

Butskellism A compound of the names of UK Conservative politician R A Butler and the Labour leader Hugh Gaitskell, used in the 1950s and early 1960s to imply a high degree of similarity between the policies of the two main parties. >> Butler, R A; Gaitskell

butte [byoot] Isolated, flat-topped, steep-sided residual hills formed by erosion of a mesa, when a remnant of hard rock protects the softer rock underneath. >> mesa

butter A pale yellow foodstuff derived from the churning of cream, typically used in baking, cooking, or for spreading on bread. It comprises c.82% fat and c.16% water. >> ghee; margarine; milk

buttercup A member of a large and diverse genus of annuals or perennials, some aquatic, especially found in the N hemisphere; flowers cup-shaped, 5-petalled, glossy yellow, sometimes white or red. (Genus: *Ranunculus*, 400 species. Family: Ranunculaceae.) >> water-crowfoot

butterfish >> **gunnel**

butterfly An insect belonging to the order Lepidoptera, which comprises the butterflies and moths. Butterflies are usually distinguished from moths by being active during the daytime, by folding their wings upright over their bodies when at rest, and by having small knobs at the tips of their antennae; but there are exceptions. >> cabbage white / nymphalid / papilionid / peacock / satyrid / swallowtail / tortoiseshell butterfly; brimstone (entomology); Camberwell beauty; fritillary (entomology); hairstreak; Lepidoptera; painted lady; red admiral; skipper

butterfly bush >> **buddleia**

butterflyfish >> **angelfish**

butterwort A small carnivorous perennial native to the N hemisphere and the mountains of South America; flowers solitary on leafless stems, 2-lipped, spurred; white, lilac, or violet. (Genus: *Pinguicula*, 46 species. Family: Lentibulariaceae.) >> carnivorous plant

buttress A mass of masonry built against a wall, usually on the outside of a building to oppose the lateral thrust of an arch, roof, or vault. Varied in form, the most notable type is the **flying buttress**, which consists of a segment of an arch, stretching from a higher wall (sometimes, from a detached pier) to an external buttress. >> arch ℹ; vault ℹ

Flying buttress

Buttrose, Ita (Clare) (1942–) Journalist, publisher, and broadcaster, born in Sydney, New South Wales, Australia. In 1981 she joined News Limited as editor-in-chief of the *Sunday Telegraph*, becoming the first woman in Australia to edit either a daily or a Sunday paper. In 1988 she was editor of that paper's opposition, *The Sun Herald*, and by 1989 had started her own magazine, called *Ita*.

butyl [**byoo**tiyl, **byoo**til] $CH_3CH_2CH_2CH_2$–. A four-carbon aliphatic group. >> carbon

Buxtehude, Diderik or **Dietrich** [**buks**tehooduh] (1637–1707) Composer and organist, born in Oldesloe or Helsingborg, Sweden (formerly in Denmark). In 1668 he was appointed organist at the Marienkirche, Lübeck, where he began the famous *Abendmusiken* – Advent evening concerts of his own sacred music and organ works.

Buys Ballot, Christoph H(endrick) D(iederick) [**biyz bal**ot] (1817–90) Meteorologist, born in Kloetinge, The Netherlands. The law relating wind direction to areas of high and low pressure (**Buys Ballot's law**, 1857) arose from his work. >> meteorology; wind 🅘

buzzard A large hawk found worldwide (except Australasia and Malaysia); brown, grey, and white; soaring flight, but spends much time perching; kills prey on ground. (Genus: *Buteo*, 25 species.) >> hawk

buzz-bomb >> **V-1**

Byatt, A(ntonia) S(usan), *née* **Drabble** (1936–) British novelist and critic, the sister of Margaret Drabble. Her novels include *Virgin in the Garden* (1978), *Still-Life* (1985), the first two parts of a projected sequence tracing English life from the mid-1950s to the present day, *Possession* (1990, Booker Prize), and *Babel Tower* (1996). >> Drabble

Byblos [**bib**los] 34°07N 35°39E. An ancient trading city on the Lebanese coast N of Beirut; a world heritage site. It was the chief supplier of papyrus to the Greeks, which they accordingly nicknamed 'byblos' – hence the word 'bible' (literally, 'the papyrus book'). >> Phoenicia

Byelarus; Byelorussia >> **Belarus**

Byng, George, 1st Viscount Torrington (1663–1733) English sailor, born in Wrotham, Kent. In 1708 he defeated the French fleet of James Stuart, the Pretender, and in 1718 destroyed the Spanish fleet off Messina. >> Stuart, James; William III

Byng (of Vimy), Julian Hedworth George Byng, 1st Viscount (1862–1935) British general, born in Wrotham Park, Middlesex. He commanded the 9th Army Corps in Gallipoli (1915), the Canadian Army Corps (1916–17), and the 3rd Army (1917–18). After World War I he became Governor-General of Canada (1921–6). >> World War 1

Byrd, Richard E(velyn) (1888–1957) Rear admiral, explorer, and aviator, born in Winchester, VA. He made the first aeroplane flight over the North Pole (1926), then flew over the South Pole (1929). >> Poles

Byrd, William (1543–1623) Composer, probably born in Lincoln, Lincolnshire. He was organist of Lincoln Cathedral until 1572, when he was made joint organist with Tallis of the Chapel Royal. He wrote music for both the Catholic and the Anglican services, as well as madrigals, songs, keyboard pieces, and music for strings. >> Tallis

Byron (of Rochdale), George (Gordon) Byron, 6th Baron, known as **Lord Byron** (1788–1824) Poet, born in London. After a grand tour of Europe, he published the popular *Childe Harold's Pilgrimage* (1812), becoming the darling of London society, and giving to Europe the concept of the 'Byronic hero'. Later works include *Don Juan* (1819–24). He gave active help to the Italian revolutionaries, and in 1823 joined the Greek insurgents who had risen against the Turks. He died of malaria at Missolonghi.

byte A fixed number of bits (binary digits), usually defined as a set of 8 bits. An 8-bit byte can therefore take 256 different values corresponding to the binary numbers 00000000, 00000001, 00000010, through to 11111111. A **kilobyte** is one thousand bytes (actually 1024); a **megabyte** is one million bytes (1024×1024); a **gigabyte** is one thousand million bytes (1024×1024×1024). >> ASCII code; bit

Byzantine Empire [bi**zan**tiyn] The E half of the Roman Empire, with its capital at Constantinople, formerly Byzantium. Founded in AD 330, Byzantium survived the collapse of the W Empire by nearly a thousand years, falling to the Ottoman Turks in 1453.

C A computer programming language, developed by AT&T in the USA to be used with the Unix operating system. It has since been adopted much more widely, and is now available on personal computers. A further development was C++. >> programming language; Unix

Cabal [ka**bal**] An acronym taken from the initials of the five leading advisers of Charles II of England between 1667 and 1673: Clifford, Arlington, Buckingham, Ashley Cooper (Shaftesbury), and Lauderdale. The name is misleading, since these five were by no means Charles's only advisers, nor did they agree on a common policy, but the overtones of intrigue found in the general use of the word *cabal* made the acronym attractive. >> Charles II (of England)

cabbage A vegetable (*Brassica oleracea*) grown for its dense leafy head, which is harvested before the flowers develop and the head elongates. There are numerous cultivars, all derived from wild cabbage, native to W Europe and the Mediterranean. (Family: Cruciferae.) >> brassica; broccoli; Brussels sprout; cauliflower; cress; cultivar; kohlrabi; vegetable

cabbage white butterfly A large butterfly, found in Europe, N Africa, and North America; wings mainly white with black markings, and yellow on undersides of hindwings. The caterpillars are pests of cabbage family crops. (Order: Lepidoptera. Family: Pieridae.) >> butterfly; caterpillar

Cabbala >> **Kabbalah**

Cabell, James (Branch) [**ka**bl] (1879–1958) Novelist and critic, born in Richmond, VA. He made his name with his novel *Jurgen* (1919), the best known of a sequence of 18 novels, collectively called *Biography of Michael*, set in the imaginary mediaeval kingdom of Poictesme.

caber tossing The art of tossing a tree trunk (**caber**), practised in Scotland. The competitor has the caber, about 3–4 m/12–18 ft in length, placed vertically into the palms of his hands. He then runs with it and tosses it; the caber should revolve longitudinally, its base landing away from him. The tradition is popular at Highland Games gatherings.

Cabinda [ka**been**da] area 7270 sq km/2800 sq mi. Province of Angola on the SW coast of Africa; surrounded by the Congo; attached to Angola in 1886 by agreement with Belgium; seaport and chief town, Cabinda. >> Angola ℹ

cabinet In a parliamentary system, a group of senior ministers usually drawn from the majority party. In Britain (where cabinet government originated), the cabinet has no constitutional status other than the conventions by which it operates. It forms the link between the executive and legislative branches of government, as its members must be drawn from the legislature. Cabinet members are bound by the doctrine of collective responsibility: ministers must publicly support decisions taken by the cabinet, or its committees, or else resign. A cabinet may also be found in a non-parliamentary system, such as that of the USA, where it provides the president with an additional consultative body. >> parliament

cable television The distribution of video programmes to subscribers by co-axial cable or fibre-optic links, rather than by broadcast transmission. It provides a wide range of choice to individual homes within a specific area. >> television; video

Cabot, John [ka**bot**], Ital **Giovanni Caboto** (1425–c.1500) Navigator, born possibly in Genoa, who discovered the mainland of North America. He set sail in 1497 with two ships, sighting Cape Breton I and Nova Scotia on 24 June. >> Cabot, Sebastian

Cabot, Sebastian [ka**bot**] (1474–1557) Explorer and navigator, born in Venice or Bristol, the son of John Cabot. In 1512 he entered the service of Ferdinand V of Spain as a cartographer, and in 1526 explored the coast of South America for Charles V. >> Cabot, John

Cabral or **Cabrera, Pedro Alvarez** [ka**bral**] (c.1467–c.1520) Explorer, born in Belmonte, Portugal. In 1500 he sailed from Lisbon bound for the East Indies, but was carried to the unknown coast of Brazil, which he claimed on behalf of Portugal.

Cabrini, St Francesca Xavier [kab**ree**nee] (1850–1917) Nun, born near Lodi, Italy. She founded the Missionary Sisters of the Sacred Heart (1886), emigrating to the USA in 1887. Canonized in 1946, she was the first American saint. Feast day 13 November.

cacao An evergreen tree native to Central America (*Theobroma cacao*), widely cultivated elsewhere; leaves oblong; flowers pink, borne in clusters directly on trunks and older branches; fruit an ovoid yellow pod, leathery and grooved, enclosing up to 100 beans. The beans are dried, roasted, and ground to produce cocoa powder, used in drinks and chocolate. (Family: Sterculiaceae.) >> chocolate

Cáceres [**kath**eres], Arabic **Qazris** 39°26N 6°23W, pop (1991) 72 000. Walled town in W Spain; railway; a world heritage site; Roman settlement, 1st-c BC. >> Spain ℹ

cachalot [**kash**alot] >> **sperm whale**

cache memory [kash] A very high-speed buffer memory which operates between the computer processor and main memory in high performance computer systems. >> buffer (computing); computer memory

cacomistle [**kak**omisl] A mammal native to S USA and Central America; pale brown with lighter underparts; long bushy tail with black bands; also known as **cacomixl** or **ringtail**. (Genus: *Bassariscus*, 2 species. Family: Procyonidae.) >> mammal ℹ

cactus A member of a large family of plants typical of arid zones but found in a number of habitats; almost all are confined to the New World. In the Old World they are paralleled by various members of the spurge family (Euphorbiaceae). Cacti exhibit a wide variety of size, form, and adaptations to dry conditions, some very sophisticated. All species are succulents and store water, sometimes in the roots but usually in swollen, often barrel-like, stems. The plants are leathery with a thick waxy cuticle. The spines can be very intricate, ranging from simple prongs to parasols and long, soft hairs; they shade or insulate the cactus, protect it from animals, reflect light, and collect and absorb droplets of dew – an important source of water. There is a wide range of flowers, often large and conspicuous. (Family: Cactaceae, c.2000 species.) >> cactus moth; spurge; succulent; *see illustration on p. 136*

cactus moth A small, dull moth with narrow forewings and broad hindwings (*Cactoblastis cactorum*); introduced successfully into Australia in 1925 as a measure to control the spread of prickly pear cactus. (Order: Lepidoptera. Family: Pyralidae.) >> cactus; moth

Cadbury, George (1839–1922) Businessman, born in

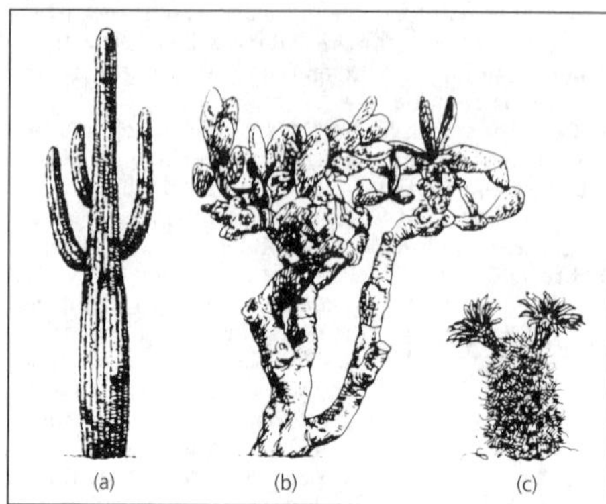

Three types of cactus – Saguaro (a); prickly pear (b); *Mamillaria tetrancistra* (76 mm/3 in) (c)

Birmingham, West Midlands. In partnership with his brother **Richard Cadbury** (1835–99), he expanded his father's cocoa and chocolate business, and established for the workers the model village of Bournville (1879), a prototype for modern methods of housing and town planning.

caddis fly A dull-coloured, moth-like insect; forewings hairy, held at oblique vertical angle at rest. (Order: Trichoptera.) >> fly; insect ℹ; moth

Cade, Jack [kayd] (?–1450) Irish leader of the insurrection of 1450 against Henry VI. Assuming the title of Captain of Kent, he marched on London with a great number of followers, and entered the city. A promise of pardon sowed dissension among the insurgents, and he was killed. >> Henry VI

cadenza An improvised (or improvisatory) passage, usually of a virtuoso and rhythmically free character, which the soloist in a concerto plays as a kind of adjunct to the main body of the piece. The orchestra is usually silent. >> improvisation

Cader Idris [**kad**er **id**ris] (Welsh 'chair of Idris') 52°42N 3°54W. Mountain ridge in NW Wales, UK; SW of Dolgellau; rises to 892 m/2928 ft at Pen-y-Gader. >> Wales ℹ

Cádiz [ka**diz**], Span [**ka**deeth], ancient **Gadier** or **Gades** 36°30N 6°20W, pop (1995e) 155 000. Seaport in SW Spain; Francis Drake burned the ships of Philip II at anchor here, 1587; bishopric; airport; railway; university; naval harbour of La Carraca; cathedral (18th-c). >> Andalusia; Drake; Spain ℹ

cadmium Cd, element 48, density 8·7 g/cm^3, melting point 321°C, colour bluish-white. A metal, normally occurring with other metals as the sulphide, CdS. The metal is recovered for use in low-melting alloys and as an absorber for neutrons in atomic reactors. Cadmium compounds (which are very toxic) are used as phosphors in colour television tubes. >> alloy; chemical elements; metal; nuclear reactor ℹ; RR1036

caecilian [see**sil**ian] An amphibian of the worldwide tropical order Gymnophiona (163 species); length, up to 1·5 m/5 ft; body worm-like with encircling rings and no legs. >> amphibian

Caedmon [**kad**mon] (?–c.680) The first English poet of known name. Bede reports that, unlearned till mature in years, Caedmon became aware in a semi-miraculous way that he was called to exercise the gift of religious poetry. He became a monk at Whitby. >> Old English

Caelum [**kiy**luhm] (Lat 'chisel') An inconspicuous S hemisphere constellation. >> constellation; RR968

Caen [kã] 49°10N 0°22W, pop (1995e) 116 000. Port in NW France; airport; railway; university (1432, refounded 1809); badly damaged in World War 2; tomb of William the Conqueror. >> William I (of England); World War 2

Caernarfon [kiyr**nar**von], Eng **Caernarvon** [kuh**nah(r)**vn] 53°08N 4°16W, pop (1995e) 9700. County town of Gwynedd, NW Wales, UK; on Menai Straits; yachting centre; castle (1284), birthplace of Edward II; investiture of Prince Charles as Prince of Wales, 1969. >> Gwynedd; Menai Straits

Caernarfonshire >> **Gwynedd**

Caerphilly [kiy(r)**fi**lee], Welsh **Caerffili** pop (1995e) 171 000; area 279 sq km / 108 sq mi. County (unitary authority from 1996) in SE Wales, UK; administrative centre, Hengoed; original home of Caerphilly cheese; Caerphilly Castle (13th-c), the largest in Wales. >> Wales ℹ

Caesar, in full **Gaius Julius Caesar** (c.101–44 BC) Roman politician of patrician origins but slender means, whose military genius enabled Rome to extend her empire to the Atlantic seaboard, but whose ruthless ambition led to the breakdown of the Republican system of government at home. In 60 BC he joined with Pompey and Crassus (the so-called First Triumvirate) to protect his interests in the state. For nine years (58–50 BC) he conducted campaigns (the Gallic Wars) which extended Roman power in the West. In 55 BC he invaded Britain, and on a second invasion in 54 BC crossed the R Thames and enforced at least the nominal submission of the SE of the island. In 49 BC, to avoid being humbled by his enemies at Rome, he led his army across the R Rubicon into Italy and plunged the state into civil war. Victory over the Pompeian forces at Pharsalus (48 BC), Zela (47 BC), Thapsus (46 BC), and Munda (45 BC) left him in sole control at Rome, taking the title 'Dictator for Life' in 44 BC. His person was declared sacred, his statue placed in temples, his portrait struck on coins, and the month Quintilis renamed Julius in his honour. He was murdered by Republican-minded Romans under the leadership of Brutus and Cassius. >> Brutus; Cassius; Gallic Wars; Pompey; Roman history ℹ; triumvirate

caesarian / cesarian section [see**zair**ian] The surgical removal of the fetus from the uterus. It is undertaken when continuing with labour and vaginal delivery causes or is likely to cause significant maternal or fetal distress. >> labour; pregnancy ℹ

caffeine $C_8H_{10}N_4O_2$. An alkaloid, also called **theine**, a weak stimulant of the central nervous system. It is found in both coffee and tea. >> alkaloids

Cage, John (1912–92) Composer, born in Los Angeles, CA. His works use such resources as electronics and the 'prepared piano' (distorting the sound of the instrument with objects placed inside). He also experimented with silence as an art form, and with musical chance, in which (for example) a dice would be thrown to determine the elements of a composition.

Cage, Nicholas, originally **Nicholas Coppola** (1964–) Film actor, born in Long Beach, CA. He became well known after his appearances in *The Cotton Club* (1984) and won critical acclaim for *Leaving Las Vegas* (1995, Oscar). Later films include *Con Air* (1997), *Face/Off* (1997), and *City of Angels* (1998).

Cagliari [kal**yah**ree], ancient **Carales** 39°13N 9°08E, pop (1995e) 237 000. Seaport in S Sardinia, Italy; archbishopric; airport; railway; university (1956); cathedral (1312), Roman amphitheatre. >> Sardinia

Cagliostro, Alessandro, conte di (Count of) [kal**yoh**stroh], originally **Giuseppe Balsamo** (1743–95) Adventurer and charlatan, born in Palermo, Italy. Successful alike as physician, philosopher, alchemist, and necromancer, he carried on a lively business in his 'elixir of immortal youth'.

Cagney, James (1899–1986) Film actor, born in New York City. His film performance as the gangster in *The Public Enemy* (1931) brought him stardom. Later films include *Angels with Dirty Faces* (1938), and *Yankee Doodle Dandy* (1942, Oscar).

Cahokia [ka**hoh**kia] A prehistoric city of Middle Mississippi Indians in E St Louis, IL, USA. It was founded c.600 and, at 13 sq km/5 sq mi, is the largest such settlement in North America; a world heritage site. >> Woodland culture

Caiaphas [**kiy**afas] (1st-c) Son-in-law of Annas, eventually appointed by the Romans to be his successor as high priest of Israel (c.18–36). In the New Testament he interrogated Jesus after his arrest. >> Annas; Jesus Christ

Caicos Islands [**kay**kos] Island group in the W Atlantic, SE of the Bahamas, forming a British overseas territory with the Turks Is. It was settled by Loyalist planters from the S States of America after the War of Independence. >> Turks and Caicos Islands

caiman or **cayman** [**kay**man] A member of the alligator family (5 species), native to Central and South America; length, up to 2 m/6½ ft; inhabits rivers and swamps. >> alligator ℹ

Cain [kayn] Biblical character, the eldest son of Adam and Eve, the brother of Abel and Seth. He is portrayed as a farmer whose offering to God was rejected, in contrast to that of his herdsman brother Abel. This led to his murder of Abel, and Cain's punishment of being banished to a nomadic life. >> Abel; Adam and Eve; Bible; Enoch

Caine, Michael [kayn], originally **Maurice Micklewhite** (1933–) Film actor, born in London. He became known with roles such as down-at-heel spy Harry Palmer in *The Ipcress File* (1965) and its two sequels, and as the Cockney Romeo in *Alfie* (1966). Later films include, *California Suite* (1978), *Educating Rita* (1983), *Hannah and Her Sisters* (1986, Oscar), and *Blood and Wine* (1996).

Cainozoic era >> **Cenozoic era**

Cairngorms or **Cairngorm Mountains** Mountain range in NEC Scotland, part of Grampian Mts; rises to 1309 m/4295 ft in Ben Macdhui; winter sports region, centre at Aviemore. >> Ben Macdhui; Grampians (Scotland) ℹ

Cairns [**kairnz**] 16°51S 145°43E, pop (1995e) 52 200. Resort and seaport on the NE coast of Queensland, Australia; starting point for tours to the Great Barrier Reef and the Cape York Peninsula; railway; airfield. >> Great Barrier Reef; Queensland

Cairo [**kiy**roh], Arabic **al-Qahira** 30°03N 31°15E, pop (1995e) 7 000 000 (Greater Cairo). Capital of Egypt, at head of R Nile delta; largest African city; originally founded as El Fustat in AD 642; occupied by British, 1882–1946; airport; railway; four universities (1908, 1919, 1950, and Muslim university in Mosque of El Azhar, 1972); Islamic Cairo a world heritage site; major archaeological sites nearby, including pyramids at El Giza. >> Egypt ℹ; pyramid

caisson [**kay**sn] A permanent structure for keeping water or soft ground from flowing into the site when building foundations. There are several types: **open caissons** open at the top and bottom; **box caissons** open at the top and closed at the bottom; and **pneumatic caissons**, containing a working chamber in which compressed air excludes the water. >> cofferdam

caisson disease [**kay**sn] >> **decompression sickness**

calabash A trailing or climbing vine (*Lagenaria siceraria*), native to warm Old World regions, with white flowers and woody, bottle-shaped fruits; also called **bottle gourd**. (Family: Cucurbitaceae.) >> climbing plant

calabash tree An evergreen tree (*Crescentia cujete*) growing to 12 m/40 ft, native to tropical America; flowers bell-shaped; fruit a woody berry up to 30 cm/12 in long or more, flask-shaped and used as a container. (Family: Bignoniaceae.)

calabrese [kala**bray**zee] >> **broccoli**

Calabria [ka**lay**bria], Ital [kala**bri**a] pop (1995e) 2 018 000; area 15 079 sq km/5820 sq mi. Region of S Italy, occupying the 'toe' of the country, capital, Catanzaro; underdeveloped area with mixed Mediterranean agriculture; subject to earthquakes, floods, and erosion. >> Italy ℹ

Calais [**ka**lay] 50°57N 1°52E, pop (1995e) 78 100. Seaport in NW France; on the Straits of Dover, at the shortest crossing to England, 34 km/21 mi SE of Dover; captured by England, 1346; retaken by France, 1558; British base in World War 1; centre of heavy fighting in World War 2; airport; railway; ferry services. >> Dover (UK)

calamine [**kal**amiyn] A mixture of zinc carbonate and ferric oxide, used as an ointment for many skin conditions. >> iron; zinc

Calamity Jane, popular name of **Martha Jane Burke**, *née* **Cannary** (c.1852–1903) Frontierswoman, possibly born in Princeton, MO. Of eccentric character, and usually dressed in man's clothes, she was celebrated for her bravery and her skill in riding and shooting. She teamed up with US marshal **Wild Bill Hickock** (1847–76) at Deadwood, SD, before he was murdered. She is said to have threatened 'calamity' for any man who tried to court her, but in 1885 she married.

calceolaria [kalsioh**lair**ia] A member of a large genus of annuals, perennials, or shrubs native to Central and South America; characteristic 2-lipped flowers with lower lip inflated and pouch-like; commonly grown ornamentals are mainly hybrids with yellow, orange, or red spotted flowers. (Genus: *Calceolaria*, 300–400 species. Family: Scrophulariaceae.)

calcite [**kal**siyt] A mineral form of calcium carbonate ($CaCO_3$), and the main constituent of limestone and marble. It can form stalactites and stalagmites, and the structure of coral reefs. Good crystals formed in vein deposits are transparent, and termed *Iceland spar*. >> chalk; limestone; marble

calcium Ca, element 20, melting point 839°C. A very reactive, silvery metal only found combined in nature; the metal is obtained by electrolysis. It is the fifth most common element in the Earth's crust, occurring mainly in fluorite (CaF_2), gypsum ($CaSO_4.2H_2O$), and limestone ($CaCO_3$). Ca^{2+} ions are largely responsible for hardness in water. Calcium is used in the structural tissue of both plants and animals; its compounds are common components of agricultural fertilizers, and are ingredients of both glass and cement. >> bleaching powder; bone; chemical elements; electrolysis ℹ; fertilizer; RR1036

calculi [**kal**kyooliy] In medicine, stone-like concretions which form within certain organs and ducts. They are formed mainly by calcium salts, most commonly in the bladder, kidneys, ureter, and bile ducts. >> colic; urinary stones

calculus >> **differential calculus**

Calcutta [kal**kuh**ta] 22°36N 88°24E, pop (1995e) 11 755 000. Port capital of West Bengal, E India; third largest city in India; founded by the British East India Company, 1690; capital of British India, 1773–1912; airport; railway; three universities; cathedral (1787), Nakhoda Mosque (1926), Jain temples (1867), Hindu Bengali Temple of Kali (1809). >> Black Hole of Calcutta; East India Company, British; West Bengal

Caldecott, Randolph [**kawl**dikot] (1846–86) Artist and illustrator, born in Chester, Cheshire. He illustrated Washington Irving's *Old Christmas* (1876) and numerous children's books, such as Aesop's Fables (1883). The **Caldecott Medal** has been awarded annually since 1938 to the best US artist-illustrator of children's books.

Calder, Alexander (Stirling) [**kawl**der] (1898–1976) Artist, born in Philadelphia. His best-known works are the abstract, hanging wire mobiles, which he began to make in 1934. >> kinetic art; mobile

caldera [kal**dair**a] A large volcanic crater formed when the remains of a volcano subside into a magma chamber, emptied after a violent eruption. The caldera may subsequently fill with water, and become a crater lake. >> Crater Lake; magma; volcano

Calderón de la Barca, Pedro [kolduh**ron** duh la **bah(r)**ka] (1600–81) Playwright, born in Madrid. He was appointed to the court of Philip IV, where he wrote over 100 plays, masques, and operas for the court, the church, and the public theatres.

Caldwell, Erskine [**kawld**wel] (1903–87) Writer, born in White Oak, GA. His best-known novels are *Tobacco Road* (1932) and *God's Little Acre* (1933). Much of his work addresses issues of social injustice in the US South.

Caledonian Canal A line of inland navigation following the Great Glen (Glen More) in Highland council, Scotland; extends from Inverness (NE) to Loch Eil near Fort William (SW), thus linking North Sea and Irish Sea; total length 96 km/60 mi; built by Telford. >> Highland; Scotland (i); Telford, Thomas

calendar >> **French Republican / Gregorian / Julian calendar**

Calgary 51°05N 114°05W, pop (1995e) 754 000. Town in S Alberta, Canada, centre of rich grain and livestock area; growth following arrival of Canadian Pacific Railway, 1883; oil found to the S, 1914; airport; university (1945); ice hockey team, Calgary Flames; Calgary Tower (1967, 190 m/623 ft). >> Alberta; Canadian Pacific Railway

Cali [**kal**ee] 3°24N 76°30W, pop (1995e) 1 426 000. City in W Colombia, at centre of rich sugar-producing region; founded, 1536; airport; two universities (1945, 1958); cathedral. >> Colombia (i)

calico bush >> **mountain laurel**

Calicut >> **Kozhikode**

California pop (1995e) 32 601 000; area 411 033 sq km/158 706 sq mi. State in SW USA; the 'Golden State'; discovered by the Spanish, 1542; colonized mid-18th-c; developed after gold discovered in the Mother Lode, 1848; ceded to the USA by the treaty of Guadalupe Hidalgo, 1848; joined the Union as the 31st state, 1850; now the most populous US state; mountainous in the N, W and E, with dry, arid depressions in the S; Coast Ranges in the W run parallel to the Pacific; Sierra Nevada in the E, rising to 4418 m/14 495 ft at Mt Whitney (state's highest point); Central Valley a major fruit-producing area; a zone of faults (the San Andreas Fault) extends S from N California along the coast; earth tremors commonplace; major earthquakes in San Francisco 1906, 1989, and in Los Angeles, 1993; capital, Sacramento; major towns, San Francisco, Los Angeles, Oakland, and San Diego; centre of the US microelectronics industry in Silicon Valley; vineyards in over 40 Californian counties; increasing Hispanic and Asian populations; a major tourist state, with several national monuments and parks (Yosemite, Kings Canyon, Sequoia, Redwood), the film industry, and Disneyland. >> earthquake; fault; Los Angeles; Sacramento; San Francisco; Silicon Valley; United States of America (i); RR994

California, Gulf of Arm of the Pacific Ocean between Mexican mainland (E) and Baja California (W); Colorado R delta (N); maximum depth 2595 m/8514 ft; 1130 km/700 mi long by 80–130 km/50–80 mi wide. >> Pacific Ocean

California redwood >> **mammoth tree**

California sorrel >> **palomino**

Caligula [ka**lig**yula], nickname of **Gaius Julius Caesar Germanicus** (12–41) Roman emperor (37–41), the youngest son of Germanicus and Agrippina, born at Antium. Brought up in an army camp, he was nicknamed Caligula from his little soldier's boots (*caligae*). Extravagant, autocratic, vicious, and mentally unstable, he wreaked havoc with the finances of the state, and terrorized those around him, until he was assassinated. >> Agrippina (the Elder); Germanicus

calimanco cat >> **tortoiseshell cat**

calisthenics The art and practice of bodily exercises designed to produce beauty and grace rather than muscular development. They are often performed with the aid of hand-held apparatus, such as rings and clubs. >> aerobics

Callaghan (of Cardiff), (Leonard) James Callaghan, Baron [**kal**ahan], known as **Jim Callaghan** (1912–) British Labour statesman and prime minister (1976–9), born in Portsmouth, Hampshire. He was Chancellor of the Exchequer (1964–7), home secretary (1967–70) and foreign secretary (1974–6), and became prime minister on Wilson's resignation. He resigned as Leader of the Opposition in 1980, and became a life peer in 1987. >> Labour Party; Wilson, Harold

Callaghan, Morley (Edward) [**kal**ahan] (1903–) Novelist, short-story writer, and memoirist, born in Toronto, Ontario, Canada. His novels include *Strange Fugitive* (1928), *The Loved and the Lost* (1951), and *A Time for Judas* (1983).

calla lily >> **arum lily**

Callao [kal**yah**oh] 12°05S 77°08W, pop (1995e) 628 000. Port in W Peru; handles 75% of Peru's imports and c.25% of its exports; occupied by Chile, 1879–84; airport. >> Peru (i)

Callas, Maria (Meneghini) [**kal**as], originally **Maria Kalogeropoulos** (1923–77) Operatic soprano, born in New York City. She sang with great authority in all the most exacting soprano roles, excelling in the intricate *bel canto* style of pre-Verdian Italian opera.

calligraphy The art of penmanship, or writing at its most formal. It is a major art form in many countries of E Asia and in Arabic-speaking countries, and there has been a revival of interest in Europe and America since the 19th-c.

Callimachus [ka**li**makus] (5th-c BC) Greek sculptor working in Athens in the late 5th-c BC. Vitruvius says he invented the Corinthian capital. >> orders of architecture (i); Vitruvius Pollio

Callimachus [ka**li**makus] (299–210 BC) Greek poet, grammarian, and critic, born in Cyrene, Libya. He became head of the Alexandrian Library, and prepared a catalogue of it, in 120 volumes.

calliope [ka**liy**opee] A steam organ patented by J C Stoddard of Worcester, MA, in 1855. Most calliopes had about 15–30 whistles, operated by a keyboard, and were fitted to the top decks of river showboats. >> organ

Calliope [ka**liy**opee] In Greek mythology, the Muse of epic poetry. She is sometimes said to be the mother of Orpheus. >> Muses

Callisto (astronomy) [ka**lis**toh] The fourth natural satellite of Jupiter, discovered in 1610 by Galileo; distance from the planet 1 883 000 km/1 170 000 mi; diameter 4800 km/3000 mi; orbital period 16·689 days. Its dark surface is a mixture of ice and rocky material, and is heavily cratered. >> Galilean moons; Jupiter (astronomy); RR964

Callisto (mythology) [ka**lis**toh] In Greek mythology, an Arcadian nymph attendant upon Artemis. Loved by Zeus, she became pregnant, and was sent away from the virgin band. She was later changed into a she-bear, and eventually into the constellation Ursa Major. >> Artemis

Calmar >> **Kalmar**

Calmette, (Léon Charles) Albert [kalmet] (1863–1933) Microbiologist, born in Nice, France. He is best known for the vaccine BCG (Bacille Calmette–Guérin), used for inoculation against tuberculosis, which he jointly developed with Dr Camille Guérin (1872–1961). >> tuberculosis; vaccination

caloric >> **thermodynamics**

calorie In thermodynamics, an old unit of heat, symbol *cal*; 1 cal = 4·184 J (joule, SI unit); defined as the quantity of heat required to raise the temperature of a gram of water from 14·5°C to 15·5°C. The calorie is an extremely small unit of energy, the average person requiring 2·5 million calories per day. To overcome the obvious problem in counting such small units, the preferred term in scientific literature is the *kilocalorie*, symbol *kcal* or *Cal*, where 1 Cal = 1000 cal, and this is the term commonly used in describing the energy content of foodstuffs. However, the public have continued to use the familiar word; so, in popular usage, 1 kilocalorie is often thought of as 1 Calorie. >> heat; joule; thermodynamics; RR1031

Calorie levels for different kinds of foods

food	Calories per 100 grams	Calories per ounce
cauliflower (boiled)	28	8
apple (flesh only)	42	12
milk (whole)	66	18
potatoes (old, boiled)	72	20
cod (poached with butter)	96	27
cheese (cottage)	98	27
rice (boiled)	138	39
roast beef (lean sirloin)	192	54
avocado	190	53
eggs (fried)	179	50
bread (white)	235	66
cornflakes	360	101
sugar	394	111
cheese (cheddar)	412	115
chocolate (plain)	525	147
butter	737	206
margarine	739	207

calorimetry The measurement of energy transferred in some physical or chemical process, such as the energy evolved by burning some substance. In nutrition, **calorimeters** are used to measure the number of calories in a given substance, or to measure the heat output of humans, equivalent to caloric expenditure. >> calorie ℹ; heat; heat capacity; latent heat

Calvary [**kal**varee] (Lat *calvaria*, 'skull', translating Semitic *Golgotha*) The site where Jesus was crucified, presumed to be a place of execution just outside Jerusalem. The term appears in the Authorized Version (*Luke* 23.33). >> crucifixion; Jesus Christ

Calvin, John (1509–64) Protestant reformer, born in Noyon, France. At Basel he issued his influential *Christianae religionis institutio* (1536, Institutes of the Christian Religion), and at Geneva was persuaded to help with the reformation. The father figure of Reformed theology, he left a double legacy to Protestantism by systematizing its doctrine and organizing its ecclesiastical discipline. >> Calvinism; Reformation

Calvinism [**kal**vinizm] A term with at least three applications. **1** The theology of the 16th-c Protestant reformer, John Calvin. **2** The principal doctrines of 17th-c Calvinist scholars, including the 'five points of Calvinism' affirmed by the Synod of Dort (1618–19). **3** More broadly, the beliefs of those Churches in the Reformed tradition which arose under the influence of Calvin. Historically, Calvinism has emphasized the sovereignty of God, the Bible as the sole rule of faith, the doctrine of predestination, and justification by faith alone. There has been a Neo-Calvinist renewal in the 20th-c under the influence of the theologian Karl Barth. >> Barth, Karl; Calvin; Church of Scotland; Knox, John; predestination; Presbyterianism; Protestantism; Reformed Churches

Calypso The 14th natural satellite of Saturn, discovered in 1980; distance from the planet 295 000 km/183 000 mi; diameter 30 km/19 mi. >> Saturn (astronomy); RR964

calyx >> **flower ℹ; sepal**

Camargue [ka**mah(r)g**] area 750 sq km/290 sq mi. District in R Rhône delta, SE France; alluvial island, mainly salt-marsh and lagoon; nature reserve for migratory birds; centre for breeding bulls and horses; chief locality, Saintes-Maries-de-la-Mer; tourism. >> France ℹ; Rhône, River

Camberwell beauty A colourful butterfly; wings velvet brown with yellow margin and line of blue spots. (Order: Lepidoptera. Family: Nymphalidae.) >> butterfly

Cambodia [kam**boh**dia], formerly **Kampuchea** (1975–89) and **Khmer Republic** (1970–5), official name (from 1993) **Kingdom of Cambodia**, Khmer **Preah Reach Ana Pak Kampuchea** pop (1995e) 9 692 000; area 181 035 sq km/ 69 879 sq mi. Kingdom in SE Asia; capital, Phnom Penh; timezone GMT +7; population mainly Khmer (93%); chief religion (to 1975), Theravada Buddhism; official language, Khmer, with French widely spoken; unit of currency, the riel of 100 sen; occupies an area surrounding the Tonlé Sap (lake); crossed by the floodplain of the Mekong R (E); highest land in the SW, where the Cardamom Mts run for 160 km/100 mi across the Thailand border, rising to 1813 m/5948 ft at Phnom Aural; tropical monsoon climate, with a wet season (May–Sep); high temperatures in lowland region throughout the year; originally part of the Kingdom of Funan, taken over by the Khmers, 6th-c; in dispute with the Vietnamese and the Thais from the 15th-c; French Protectorate, 1863; formed French Indo-Chinese Union with Laos and Vietnam; 1887; independence, 1953, with Prince Sihanouk as Prime Minister; Sihanouk deposed in 1970, and Khmer Republic formed; fighting throughout the country involved troops from N and S Vietnam and the USA; surrender of Phnom Penh to the Khmer Rouge, 1975, when the country became known as Kampuchea; attempt to reform economy on co-operative lines by Pol Pot (1975–8) caused the deaths of an estimated three million people; further fighting, 1977–8; Phnom Penh

captured by the Vietnamese, 1979, causing Khmer Rouge to flee; 1981 constitution established a Council of State and a Council of Ministers; Paris conference (1988–91) between the Phnom Penh regime, the opposition coalition led by Prince Sihanouk, and the Khmer Rouge ended with no agreement; name of Cambodia restored, 1989; Vietnamese troops completed withdrawal from Cambodia, 1989; UN peace plan agreed, with ceasefire and return of Sihanouk, 1991; further conflict following Khmer Rouge refusal to take part in 1993 elections; new constitution proclaims new Kingdom of Cambodia, 1993; a constitutional monarchy, with a prime minister and 120-member National Assembly; most of the population employed in subsistence agriculture, especially rice and corn; industrial development disrupted by the civil war. >> Khmer Empire; Khmer Rouge; Phnom Penh; Pol Pot; Sihanouk; Tonlé Sap; RR1003 political leaders

Cambodian >> **Austro-Asiatic languages; Khmer**

Cambrian period The earliest geological period of the Palaeozoic era, lasting from c.590 to 505 million years ago. Characterized by widespread seas, its rocks contain a large variety of marine invertebrate fossils. >> fossil; geological time scale; Palaeozoic era

Cambridge (UK), Lat **Cantabrigia** 52°12N 0°07E, pop (1995e) 120 000. County town of Cambridgeshire, EC England; on the R Cam (Granta); Roman settlement, AD 70; airfield; railway; one of the world's great universities, established 13th-c; football team, Cambridge United ('U's). >> Cambridge University [i]; Cambridgeshire

Cambridge (USA), formerly **New Towne** (to 1638) 42°22N 71°06W, pop (1995e) 96 500. City in E Massachusetts, USA; on the Charles R; founded, 1630; city status, 1846; railway; Harvard University (1636) is the oldest US college; Massachusetts Institute of Technology (1859) moved from Boston in 1915. >> Massachusetts

Cambridge Platonists A group of 17th-c philosophers, centred on Cambridge University, who took Plato (more than his doctrines) as their model. The movement was noted for its emphasis on reason in religion and ethics and its opposition to dogmatism. >> Cudworth; More, Henry; Plato

Cambridgeshire pop (1995e) 704 000; area 3409 sq km/ 1316 sq mi. County of EC England; flat fenland to the N; county town, Cambridge; Peterborough a unitary authority in 1998. >> Cambridge (UK); England [i]

Cambridge University The second oldest university in England, after Oxford. The first college, Peterhouse, was founded in 1284. Prestigious institutions include the Fitzwilliam Museum, the Cavendish Laboratory of experimental physics, the Cambridge University Press (founded 1534), and the University library. >> Cambridge (UK); university

Cambridge University

College	Founded	College	Founded
Peterhouse	1284	Sidney Sussex	1596
Clare	1326	Homerton*	1768
Pembroke	1347	Downing	1800
Gonville	1348	Girton	1869
(refounded as Gonville		Newnham[1]	1871
and Caius 1558)		Selwyn	1882
Trinity Hall	1350	Hughes Hall[3]	1885
Corpus Christi	1352	St Edmund's[3]	1896
King's	1441	New Hall[1]	1954
Queen's	1448	Churchill	1960
St Catharine's	1473	Lucy Cavendish[1]	1964
Jesus	1496	Darwin[2]	1964
Christ's	1505	Wolfson	1965
St John's	1511	Clare Hall[2]	1966
Magdalene	1542	Fitzwilliam	1966
Trinity	1546	Robinson	1977
Emmanuel	1584		

[1]Women's colleges
[2]Graduate colleges
[3]Graduate and affiliated graduate colleges
*Only offers education courses leading to BEd or PGCE

camcorder A small, portable video camera with an integral narrow-gauge videotape recorder, also known as the **camera cassette recorder** (CCR). It offers immediate playback through a domestic television receiver. >> videotape recorder

Camden (UK) 51°33N 0°09W, pop (1995e) 178 000. Borough of N Greater London, England; includes suburbs of Hampstead, St Pancras, and Holborn; named after an 18th-c Lord Chancellor. >> London

Camden (USA) 39°56N 75°07W, pop (1995e) 89 200. City in W New Jersey, USA; port on E bank of Delaware R; city status, 1828; railway; university (1934); home of Walt Whitman (1873–92). >> New Jersey; Philadelphia; Whitman

Camden, William (1551–1623) Scholar, antiquary, and historian, born in London. His *Britannia* (1586) was the first comprehensive topographical survey of the British Isles. The *Camden Society* (founded 1838), which promoted historical publications, was named after him. >> cartography

Camden, Battle of A battle of the US War of Independence, fought in S Carolina. Americans under Horatio Gates were defeated by British troops under Lord Cornwallis. >> American Revolution; Cornwallis; Gates

Camden Town Group A group of artists who flourished 1905–13 in London. Sickert was the leading member. They shared an enthusiasm for recent French painting. >> Postimpressionism; Sickert

camel A mammal of the family Camelidae (2 species): the **Bactrian** (or **two-humped**) **camel** (*Camelus bactrianus*) from cold deserts in C Asia, and domesticated elsewhere, and the **dromedary**; eats any vegetation; humps are stores of energy-rich fats. >> Camelidae; dromedary

Camelidae [ka**meli**dee] The camel family of mammals (6 species), found from N Africa to Mongolia (*camels*), or in the Andes (*llama, alpaca, guanaco, vicuña*); artiodactyls; unusual walk (move both right legs, then both left). >> alpaca; artiodactyl; camel; guanaco; llama; mammal [i]; ruminant [i]; vicuña

camellia [ka**mee**lia] An evergreen shrub or tree, native to China, Japan, and SE Asia; flowers usually large and showy, often scented, usually 4–7 petals, but often numerous in cultivars; white, pink, or crimson. (Genus: *Camellia*, 82 species. Family: Theaceae.) >> tea

camel(e)opard [ka**mel**uhpah(r)d] >> **giraffe**

Camelopardalis [kamelo**pah(r)**dalis] (Lat 'giraffe') A large constellation in the N hemisphere, also known as **Camelopardus**. It lacks any bright stars, so is hard to pick out except on a very clear night. >> constellation; RR968

Camelot [**kam**elot] The legendary capital of King Arthur's Britain. It is variously located at Cadbury in the West Country, Colchester (Camulodunum), and Winchester. >> Arthur

cameo A method of carving a relief image into a shell or semi-precious stone with different coloured layers. It was popular in the Roman Empire, and has been used ever since in W European art, often copied in glass and ceramic.

camera An apparatus which produces an image of an external scene. In the early **camera obscura** (literally 'darkened room'), light passing through a small hole or lens formed a picture on the opposite wall. Portable versions in boxes served as artist's guides in landscape drawing, and early 19th-c attempts to record the image led to the first photographic camera: a light-tight box containing a glass or metal plate with a light-sensitive surface on which the image was formed by a lens. In the 1880s photographic film in continuous strips revolutionized camera design. The first miniature camera to use perforated film 35 mm wide was the Leica in 1925, and this compact cassette-loaded form was widely adopted for other sizes. Camera operation has become increasingly simplified with automatic focus setting and exposure; built-in synchronized electronic flash and motor drive for film advance and repeated operation are also now available. >> camcorder; cinematography; Daguerre; film; lens; Niépce; single lens reflex; video

camera obscura >> **camera**

Cameroon [kame**roon**], official name **Republic of Cameroon**, Fr **République du Cameroon** pop (1995e) 13 986 000; area 475 442 sq km/183 569 sq mi. W African republic; capital, Yaoundé; timezone GMT +1; ethnic groups include Highlanders (31%), Equatorial Bantu (19%), Kirdi (11%), Fulani (10%); religion, Roman Catholic (35%), local beliefs (25%), Muslim (22%); official languages, French and English, with many local languages spoken; unit of currency, the CFA franc; equatorial forest on low coastal plain rising to a C plateau of over 1300 m/4200 ft; W region forested and mountainous, rising to 4070 m/13 353 ft at Mt Cameroon, active volcano, highest peak in W Africa; low savannah and semi-desert towards L Chad; rain all year in equatorial S; first explored by Portuguese navigator Fernando Po, later by traders from Spain, Netherlands, and Britain; German protectorate of Kamerun, 1884; divided into French and British Cameroon, 1919; confirmed by League of Nations mandate, 1922; UN trusteeships, 1946; French Cameroon independent as Republic of Cameroon, 1960; N sector of British Cameroon voted to become part of Nigeria, S sector part of Cameroon; Federal Republic of Cameroon, with separate parliaments, 1961; federal system abolished, 1972, and name changed to United Republic of Cameroon; change to present name, 1984; multiparty legislative and presidential elections, 1992; governed by a president, executive prime minister, cabinet, and National Assembly; agriculture employs c.80% of workforce; world's fifth largest cocoa producer; tourism, especially to national parks and reserves. >> League of Nations; Yaoundé; RR1003 political leaders

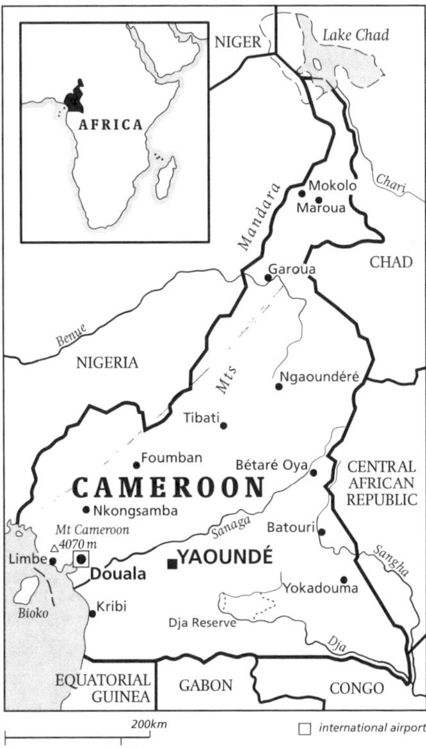

Camoens or **Camões, Luís de** [ka**moh**enz] (1524–80) Poet, born in Lisbon. He went to India (1553) and was shipwrecked while returning to Goa (1558), losing everything except his major poem, *Os Luciados* (The Lusiads, or Lusitanians). The work has since come to be regarded as the Portuguese national epic.

camomile >> **chamomile**

Campaign for Nuclear Disarmament >> **CND**

campanile [campa**nee**lay] The Italian name for a bell tower, usually tall and detached from the main building. The most famous example is the circular Leaning Tower of Pisa, with eight arcaded storeys. >> Leaning Tower

campanology >> **bell-ringing**

campanula >> **bell-flower; Canterbury bell**

Campbell, Sir Colin, Baron Clyde (1792–1863) British field marshal, born in Glasgow. In the Crimean War (1854–6) he commanded the Highland Brigade in a campaign which included the renowned repulse of the Russians by the 'thin red line' at Balaclava. During the Indian Mutiny he effected the final relief of Lucknow. >> Crimean War; Indian Mutiny

Campbell, John W(ood), Jr, pseudonym **Don A Stuart** (1910–71) Science-fiction writer, born in Newark, NJ. He developed in his stories the new idea that machines could dominate humans, notably in *Twilight* (1934). His works were highly influential, and he has come to be regarded as the father of modern science-fiction.

Campbell, Kim (Avril Phaedra Douglas) (1947–) Canadian stateswoman, and Canada's first woman prime minister (1993), born in Port Alberni, British Columbia, Canada. She was elected for British Columbia in 1988 as a federal conservative, and served in Brian Mulroney's cabinet. She became leader of her party in spring 1993, but disastrously lost the general election some months later. >> Mulroney; Progressive Conservative Party

Campbell, Sir Malcolm (1885–1948) Racing motorist, born in Chislehurst, Kent. He was the first to exceed 300 mph (483 kph) (at Bonneville Salt Flats, Utah, 1935). His son, **Donald Campbell** (1921–67), set a water speed record 444·7 kph/276·33 mph on Lake Dumbleyung, Australia, in 1964. He also set a land vehicle record in 1964 at Lake Eyre, Australia of 652·37 kph/405·45 mph. He died in an accident on Coniston Water, Cumbria while trying to break his own water speed record (achieving 528 kph/328 mph). >> motor racing

Campbell, Mrs Patrick, *née* **Beatrice Stella Tanner** (1865–1940) Actress, born in London. She went on the stage in 1888, achieving fame with *The Second Mrs Tanqueray* (1893). She played Eliza in Shaw's *Pygmalion* (1914) and formed a long friendship with the author. >> Shaw, George Bernard

Campbell-Bannerman, Sir Henry (1836–1908) British statesman and Liberal prime minister (1905–8), born in Glasgow. He was chief secretary for Ireland (1884), war secretary (1886, 1892–5), Liberal leader (1899), and prime minister. His popularity united the Liberal Party. >> Boer Wars; Liberal Party (UK)

Camp David The US presidential retreat established in 1942 by President Roosevelt in Catoctin Mountain Park, Maryland. It has been used for a number of historic meetings between heads of state. >> Camp David Accords

Camp David Accords The framework for 'a just, comprehensive, and durable settlement of the Middle East conflict', reached by Egyptian President Sadat, Israeli Prime Minister Begin, and US President Jimmy Carter at Camp David, MD, in September 1978. Based on the principle of exchanging land for peace embodied in UN Security Council Resolution 242, the accords laid the foundation for the March 1979 peace treaty between Egypt and Israel. >> Arab–Israeli Wars; Camp David; Palestine; PLO

Campese, David (Ian) [kam**pee**zee], nickname **Campo** (1962–) Rugby union player, born near Queanbeyan, New South Wales, Australia. By the end of 1990 he had a record 46 tries to his credit. A flamboyant player, he was the star of Australia's 1991 World Cup victory. He finally retired from competitive rugby in 1998 and was appointed assistant national team coach to the Singapore Rugby Union. >> football ℹ

camphor $C_{10}H_{16}O$, melting point 179°C. A colourless, waxy material (a terpene), occurring especially in the tree *Cinnamonium camphora*, and also synthesized from α-pinene. It is used in many lotions, mainly for its characteristic odour. **Camphorated oil** is a 20% solution of camphor in olive oil. >> terpene

Campi, Giulio [**kam**pee] (c.1502–72) Architect and painter, born in Cremona, Italy. He founded the Cremonese school of painting, to which his brothers **Vincenzo Campi** (1539–91) and **Antonio Campi** (1536–c.91) also belonged.

Campin, Robert [kãmpĩn] (c.1378–1444) Artist born in Tournai, Belgium. He was called **the Master of Flémalle** from his paintings in the Abbey of that name near Liège.

Campinas [kam**pee**nas] 22°54S 47°60W, pop (1995e) 1 045 000. Town in SE Brazil; NW of São Paulo; airport; railway; two universities (1941, 1962); agricultural institute; cathedral. >> Brazil ℹ

campion An annual or perennial herb, native to the temperate N hemisphere; calyx tubular, 5 petals, red or white depending on species. (Genus: *Silene*. Family: Caryophyllaceae.) >> catchfly

Campion, Edmund, St (1540–81) The first of the English Jesuit martyrs, born in London. After circulating his *Decem rationes* (Ten Reasons) against Anglicanism in 1581, he was tortured, tried on a charge of conspiracy, and hanged in London. He was beatified in 1886, and canonized in 1970; feast day 1 December. >> Jesuits; Reformation

Campion, Jane (1954–) Film director, born in Waikanae, New Zealand. Her films include *Peel* (1984), which won the 1986 Cannes Palme d'Or for best short film, *Sweetie* (1989), and *An Angel at My Table* (1990). *The Piano* (1993), which she wrote and directed, shared the Palme d'Or at the 1993 Cannes Film Festival. Later films include *Holy Smoke* (1999).

Campoli, Alfredo [**kam**pohlee] (1906–91) Violinist, born in Rome. During the 1930s he became known for his salon orchestra, disbanded at the beginning of the war. He later emerged as one of the outstanding violinists of the time.

camshaft A rotating shaft upon which **cams** are fixed. A cam is a flat plate which rotates about an axis perpendicular to the plane of the plate. The shape of the cams and their relative orientation actuate and time the lifting of valves as part of an engine's operating cycle. >> bearings; engine

Camulodunum [kamulo**doo**num] The name for ancient Colchester, the capital first of the Belgic kingdom of Cunobelinus and for a time of the Roman province of Britain. >> Cymbeline

Camus, Albert [kahmü] (1913–1960) French existentialist writer, born in Mondovi, Algeria. He earned an international reputation with his nihilistic novel, *L'Etranger* (1942, The Outsider). Later novels include *La Peste* (1947, The Plague) and *La Chute* (1956, The Fall). He received the Nobel Prize for Literature in 1957. >> existentialism

Canaan [**kay**nan, ka**nay**an] The land of the ancient Semitic-speaking peoples, living in the coastal areas of modern Israel and Syria. It was divided into various city-states during the early 2nd millennium BC, but mostly fell under the control of Israelites and other powers from the late 13th-c BC. >> Israel ℹ; Phoenicia; Semitic languages; Shiloh; Ugarit

Canada, formerly **British North America** (to 1867) pop (1995e) 28 972 000; area 9 971 500 sq km/3 848 900 sq mi. Independent country in North America, divided into 10 provinces and two territories; capital, Ottawa; several timezones (GMT W −9, to E −3); ethnic groups, 23% French origin, 20% British origin, 1.7% indigenous peoples; religion, 49% Roman Catholic, 18% United Church, 12% Anglican; official languages, English, French; currency unit, Canadian dollar of 100 cents; dominated in the NE by the Canadian Shield; fertile St Lawrence lowlands in S Quebec and Ontario; flat prairie country S and W of the Shield, stretching to the Western Cordillera, which includes the Rocky, Cassiar, and Mackenzie Mts; Coast Mts flank a rugged, heavily indented coastline, rising to 5950 m/19 521 ft at Mt Logan, highest peak in Canada; major rivers include the Mackenzie (W), and St Lawrence (E); Great Lakes in the SE; N coast permanently ice-bound or obstructed by ice floes, but for Hudson Bay (frozen c.9 months each year); mild winters and warm summers on W coast; evidence of Viking settlement c.1000; visited by Cabot, 1497; St Lawrence explored for France by Cartier, 1534; Newfoundland claimed for England, 1583; Champlain founded Quebec, 1608; Hudson's Bay Company founded, 1670; conflict between British and French in late 17th-c; Britain gained large areas from Treaty of Utrecht, 1713; after Seven Years' War, during which Wolfe captured Quebec, 1759, Treaty of Paris gave Britain almost all France's possessions in North America; province of Quebec created, 1774; migration of loyalists from USA (1783) after War of Independence led to division of Quebec into Upper and Lower Canada; reunited as Canada, 1841; Dominion of Canada created 1867 by confederation of Quebec, Ontario, Nova Scotia, and New Brunswick; Rupert's Land and Northwest Territories bought from Hudson's Bay Company, 1869–70; joined by Manitoba (1870), British Columbia (1871), Prince Edward I (1873), Alberta and Saskatchewan (1905), and Newfoundland (1949); recurring political tension in recent decades arising from French-Canadian separatist movement in Quebec; separatist referendum rejected in 1980, and again in 1995, but only by a 1% margin; Inuit territory of Nunavut created, 1999; Canada Act, 1982 gave Canada full responsibility for constitution; bicameral federal parliament includes a Senate and a House of Commons; British monarch is head of state, represented by a governor-general; economy traditionally based on natural resources and agriculture; world's second largest exporter of wheat; forest covers 44% of land area; world's largest producer of asbestos, zinc, silver, nickel; second largest producer of potash, gypsum, molybdenum, sulphur; hydroelectricity, oil (especially Alberta), natural gas; major industrial development in recent decades. >> Alberta; British Columbia; Cabot, John; Canadian Pacific Railway / Shield; Cartier; Champlain; Great Lakes; Hudson Bay; Manitoba; New Brunswick; Newfoundland (province); Northwest Territories; Nova Scotia; Nunavut; Ontario; Prince Edward Island; Quebec (province); Rocky Mountains; St Lawrence River; Saskatchewan; Seven Years' War; Yukon; RR996, 1003 political leaders; *see illustration on p. 143*

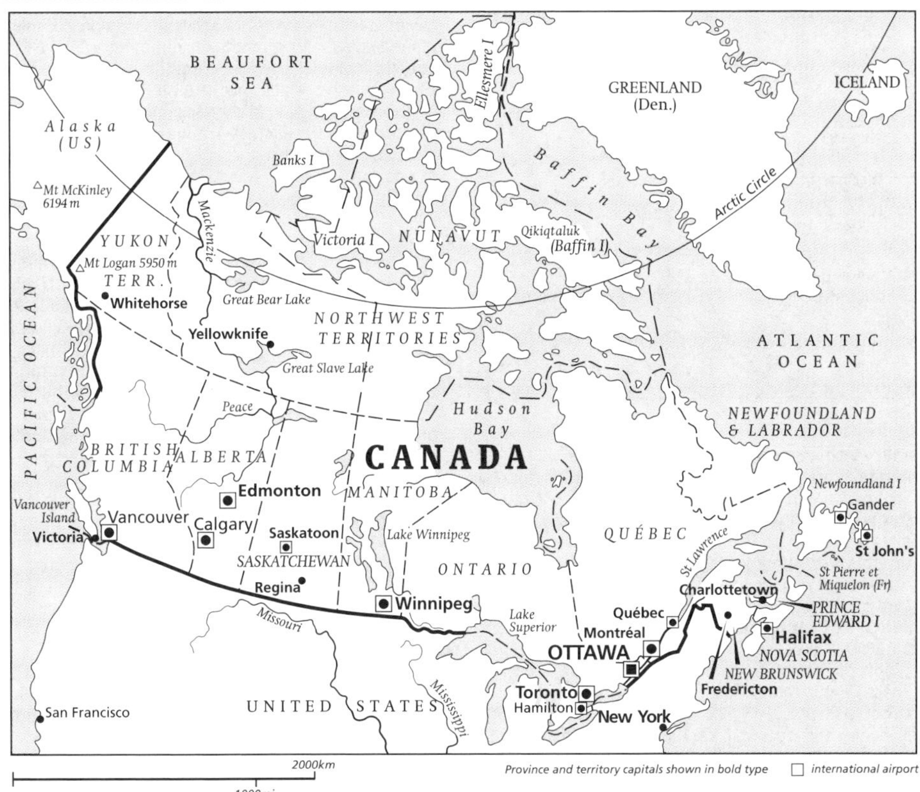

Canada Day A public holiday in Canada (observed 1 Jul), the anniversary of the union of the provinces in 1867; formerly known as **Dominion Day**.

Canada First Movement A political movement in Canada, founded in Ontario in 1868. Its objectives were to ensure that the newly-confederated Dominion of Canada would not collapse over regional disputes. >> Canada [i]

Canadian football >> **football 6**

Canadian National Tower >> **C N Tower**

Canadian Pacific Railway (CPR) A transcontinental railway, constructed 1881–5, linking the Dominion of Canada with British Columbia. It produced a chain of western railway towns terminating in Vancouver on the Pacific coast. >> Canada [i]

Canadian Rocky Mountain Parks A group of five national parks (Banff, Jasper, Waterton Lakes, Kootenay, Yoho) in Alberta and British Columbia, Canada. Together with the Burgess Shale region, these constitute a world heritage site. >> Rocky Mountains

Canadian Shield or **Laurentian Shield** Vast area of ancient pre-Cambrian rocks, forming a low plateau covering over half of Canada, extending into parts of N USA; many lakes and swamps, remnants of Pleistocene glaciation; generally infertile, but a rich source of minerals, forest products, and hydroelectricity. >> Cambrian period; Canada [i]; glaciation

canal An artificial watercourse for inland navigation. The first modern canal in the UK was the Sankey Brook from the Mersey to St Helens, built by Henry Berry between 1755 and 1772. Thousands of miles of canal were built, and they were the major method of transporting goods until the mid-19th-c, when the railways superseded them. After a long period of decline, more recently many canals have been restored, and nowadays are principally used for leisure activities. >> Bridgewater / Erie / Grand / Manchester Ship / Mittelland / Panama / Suez Canal [i]; Brindley; Intracoastal Waterway; Rhine Canals [i]; St Lawrence Seaway

Canaletto [kanal**et**oh], originally **Giovanni Antonio Canal** (1697–1768) Painter, born in Venice, Italy. He painted a renowned series of views in Venice, and his views of London and elsewhere proved extremely popular. His nephew and pupil, **Bernardo Bellotto** (1720–80), known as **Canaletto the Younger**, was also born in Venice, where he worked as a painter and engraver. >> Venetian School

canary A small finch, native to the Old World; prized as a songbird; also known as **serin**. All domestic varieties of the cage canary were developed from one species, *Serinus canaria*, from the Canary Is. (Genus: *Serinus*, 32 species. Family: Fringillidae.) >> finch; roller; siskin

Canary Islands, Span **Islas Canarias** pop (1995e) 1 468 000; area 7273 sq km/2807 sq mi. Island archipelago in the Atlantic Ocean, 100 km/60 mi off the NW coast of Africa; comprises Tenerife, Gomera, La Palma, Hierro, Lanzarote, Fuerteventura, Gran Canaria (Grand Canary), and several uninhabited islands; chief town, Las Palmas; volcanic and mountainous, the Pico de Teide rises to 3718 m/12 198 ft on Tenerife; under the control of Spain, 15th-c; the name is explained by the elder Pliny as referring to the many dogs found on Gran Canaria (Lat *canis*, 'dog'; canaries were later named after the islands); fruit and vegetables grown under irrigation; major tourist area. >> Las Palmas; Pliny (the Elder); Spain [i]; *see illustration on p. 144*

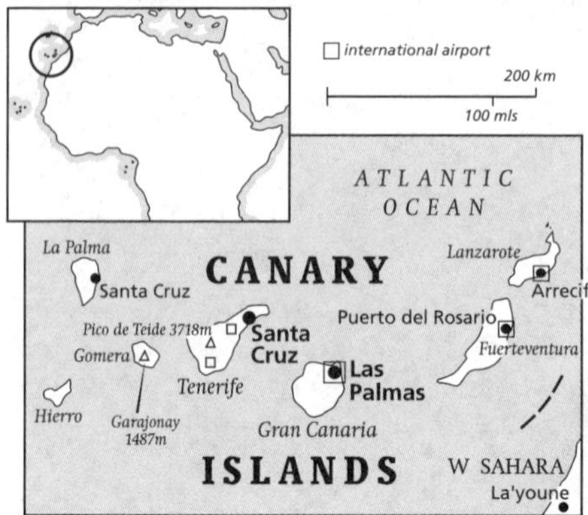

Canary whitewood >> tulip tree ℹ

canasta A card game similar to rummy. It derives from the Spanish word *canasta* ('basket'), probably referring to the tray into which cards were discarded. Its most popular form is played with two standard packs of playing cards, together with four jokers. The object is to collect as many cards of the same denomination as possible. >> playing cards; rummy

Canaveral, Cape [ka**na**veral], formerly **Cape Kennedy** 28°28N 80°28W. Cape in E Florida, USA; US crewed space flights launched from here since 1961. >> Kennedy Space Center, John F

Canberra [**kan**bera] 35°18S 149°08E, pop (1995e) 295 000. National and regional capital in Australian Capital Territory, SE Australia, on the Molonglo R; building started in 1913; Commonwealth Parliament moved from Melbourne, 1927; airport; railway; two universities (1946, 1989); Parliament House (1927, new building opened in 1988 by the Queen). >> Australian Capital Territory

Cancer (Lat 'crab') An inconspicuous N constellation of the zodiac, lying between Gemini and Leo. It contains an open star cluster, Praesepe, just visible by eye. >> constellation; star cluster; zodiac ℹ; RR968

cancer A general term to denote all forms of malignant tumour. Tumours occur when the cells of a tissue or organ multiply in an uncontrolled fashion unrelated to the biological requirements of the body and not to meet the needs of repair or of normal replacement. In contrast to *benign* tumours, which enlarge in a specific place, and cause damage by pressure on adjacent tissues, *malignant* tumours invade, destroy, and spread to other tissues. The cells of a malignant tumour may also be carried in the blood stream and lymphatics, and lodge in distant organs where they continue to spread and enlarge (*metastases*). Cancer kills by destroying vital tissues, by interfering with the performance of their functions through ulceration, bleeding, and infection, and by affecting bodily nutrition. The cause of cancer is unknown, but appears to depend upon an interplay between factors in the environment and the genetic component of body cells. Only a small number of cancers are determined solely by inherited factors. The great majority are related to exposure to one or more environmental factors which predisposes to the cancer. These factors are known as **carcinogenic** agents. >> breast / cervical cancer; carcinogen; oncology; sarcoma; tumour

candela [kan**day**la] Base SI unit of luminous intensity; symbol *cd*; defined as the luminous intensity, in a given direction, of a source that emits monochromatic radiation of frequency 540 × 10^{12} Hz, and has a radiant intensity in that direction of 1/683 watt per steradian; obsolete name **candle**. >> photometry ℹ; radiometry ℹ

Candida [**kan**dida] A genus of fungi known from its yeast-like vegetative state; parasitic in animals. (Family: Cryptococcaceae.) >> candidiasis; fungus; yeast

candidiasis [kandi**di**yasis] A disease caused by *Candida albicans*, a yeast which normally inhabits the gut and the vagina; also known as **thrush**. The organism may colonize the skin and gastro-intestinal tract, including the mouth, where white patches can be seen. >> yeast

candle A light source typically consisting of a wax cylinder (stearic acid, paraffin wax, etc) with a central fibrous wick, known from ancient times (at least 3000 BC). Light is generated by burning liquid wax melted by the flame and drawn up the wick by capillary action. >> candela; capillarity; wax

Candlemas A Christian festival (2 Feb) commemorating the purification of the Virgin Mary after the birth of Jesus, and the presentation of Jesus in the Jerusalem temple (*Luke* 2). The name is derived from the lighted candles carried in procession on that day. >> Mary (mother of Jesus)

candytuft An annual, biennial, or evergreen perennial, native to Europe and Asia; leaves narrow; flowers white or mauve, in flattened heads, cross-shaped with outer two petals of outermost flowers enlarged. (Genus: *Iberis*, 30 species. Family: Cruciferae.)

cane >> **bamboo; sugar cane**

Canea >> **Chania**

cane sugar >> **sugar cane**

Canes Venatici [**ka**neez ve**nat**isiy] (Lat 'hunting dogs') An inconspicuous constellation in the N hemisphere which includes the famous Whirlpool Galaxy. >> constellation; galaxy; RR968

Canetti, Elias [ka**ne**tee] (1905–94) Writer born in Rustschuk, Bulgaria. His interest in crowd psychology produced two important works: the novel *Die Blendung* (1936, trans as both Auto da Fé and The Tower of Babel) and the study *Masse und Macht* (1960, Crowds and Power). He was awarded the Nobel Prize for Literature in 1981.

Canidae [**kan**idee] The dog family of carnivores (36 species), usually with slender legs, lean muzzles, large erect ears, and bushy tails; four toes on hind feet, usually five on front; blunt claws not retractable; colour usually without stripes or spots. >> carnivore ℹ; coyote; dhole; dog; fox; jackal; wolf

canine parvovirus A serious viral infection of dogs and other canids, which emerged in the late 1970s. Its most characteristic feature is very severe persistent diarrhoea with blood, and there may be vomiting and a high fever. The disease is now well controlled by effective vaccines. >> dog; virus

Canis Major [**kan**is] (Lat 'great dog') A constellation in the S hemisphere, partly in the Milky Way. It is easy to see because it includes Sirius, the brightest star in our sky. >> constellation; Milky Way; Sirius; RR968

Canis Minor [**kan**is] (Lat 'little dog') A small N hemisphere constellation. Its brightest star is Procyon, just 3·5 parsec away, and the eighth brightest star in the sky. >> constellation; RR968

canker (botany) A general term for a localized disease of woody plants, in which bark formation is prevented; typically caused by bacteria or fungi. >> bacteria ℹ; bark; fungus

canker (zoology) A disease of animals, characterized by open sores or ulcers. The name is used for several conditions. >> ulcer

canna A tuberous perennial, native to Central and tropical North America; flowers in a spike, three sepals, three petals, 4–6 stamens, petal-like and brightly coloured;

fruit a warty capsule; often grown for the showy flowers. (Genus: *Canna*, 55 species. Family: Cannaceae.) >> arrowroot; sepal; stamen; tuber

cannabis A preparation of the plant *Cannabis sativa*, widely used as a recreational drug for its euphoric, relaxing properties: its extracts are found as **hashish** and **marihuana**. The plant, also called **ganja** or **hemp**, is an annual growing to 2·5 m/8 ft; its leaves have 5–7 narrow, toothed, spreading, finger-like lobes; there are tiny green flowers in terminal clusters, with males and females on separate plants. It is native to Asia, but widely cultivated elsewhere. It is a source of rope fibre and birdseed, but is best known as a narcotic resin. (Family: Cannabidaceae.) >> chemotherapy; drug addiction; resin

Cannes [kan] 43°33N 7°00E, pop (1995e) 71 500. Fashionable resort town on the French Riviera; airport; railway; major tourist centre, with many beaches and yachting harbours; International Film Festival (Apr–May). >> France ℹ; Riviera

canning A food preservation process relying on the sterilization of foods by heating in a container sealed before or immediately after the heat treatment. The idea was first applied in 1810 by Nicolas Appert (c.1750–1841) to foods sealed in bottles and heated, but since 1839 in cans. The processes are now highly automated. >> food preservation; tinplate

Canning, George (1770–1827) British statesman, born in London. He became treasurer of the Navy (1804–6), and minister for foreign affairs (1807). His disapproval of the Walcheren expedition led to a misunderstanding with Castlereagh, which resulted in a duel. As foreign secretary (1822), he was the first to recognize the free states of Spanish America, and promoted the cause of Greece (1827). In 1827 he formed an administration with the aid of the Whigs, but died the same year. >> Castlereagh; Whigs

Cannon, Annie Jump (1863–1941) Astronomer, born in Dover, DE. She reorganized the classification of stars in terms of surface temperature, and developed great skill in cataloguing them. Her classification of over 225 000 stars brighter than 9th or 10th magnitude was a major contribution. >> magnitude; star (astronomy)

Cano, Juan Sebastian del [**kah**noh] (?–1526) Navigator, born in Guetaria, Spain, the first to journey around the world. In 1519 he sailed with Magellan, after whose death he safely navigated the *Victoria* home to Spain. >> Magellan

canoe A small, double-ended open craft propelled with paddles. There are two main types: a vessel carrying three or four people, made from a light wooden framework, traditionally covered with birch bark; and the Pacific dugout canoe, often fitted with an outrigger, which could be made capable of ocean voyages. >> canoeing; kayak

canoeing A water sport practised in canoes, developed by British barrister John Macgregor (1825–92) in 1865. The Canoe Club was formed the following year. Two types of canoe are used in competition: the *kayak*, which has a keel and the canoeist sits in the boat, and the *Canadian canoe*, which has no keel and the canoeist kneels. >> canoe; RR1048

canon (music) A strictly ordered texture in which polyphony is derived from a single line by imitation of itself at fixed intervals of time and pitch. In other words, all the canonic parts are the same, but they overlap each other. >> counterpoint; Pachelbel; polyphony

canon (religion) The ecclesiastical title of clergy attached to cathedrals or certain endowed churches; either *secular* or, if living under semi-monastic rule, *regular* (eg Augustinian). In the Church of England, *residentiary* canons are the salaried staff of a cathedral, responsible for the upkeep of the building; *non-residentiary* canons are unsalaried, but have certain privileges.

canonization The culmination of a lengthy process in the Roman Catholic Church whereby, after a long process of enquiry, a deceased individual is declared a saint, or entitled to public veneration. In the Orthodox Church, there is a similar but less formal procedure. >> Orthodox Church; Roman Catholicism; saint

canon law In the Roman Catholic Church, a body of rules or laws to be observed in matters of faith, morals, and discipline. It developed out of the decisions of the Councils of the Church, and the decrees of popes and influential bishops. >> Council of the Church

Canopus [ka**noh**pus] >> **Carina**

Canova, Antonio [ka**noh**va] (1757–1822) Sculptor, born in Possagno, Italy. He is regarded as the founder of a new Neoclassicist school. In 1802 he was appointed by Pius VII curator of works of art. >> Neoclassicism (art and architecture)

Cantabria [kan**tab**ria] pop (1995e) 528 000; area 5289 sq km/ 2041 sq mi. Autonomous region of N Spain, co-extensive with the modern province of Santander; capital, Santander. >> Santander; Spain ℹ

cantata Music which is 'sung'. The Italian solo cantata of the 17th–18th-c was a setting of secular (usually amatory) verses, alternating recitative and aria. The Lutheran cantatas (eg those of Bach) were church compositions for soloists, choir, and instruments. More recent cantatas are usually choral and orchestral pieces. >> sonata

Canterbury, Lat **Durovernum**, Anglo-Saxon **Cantwaraburh** 51°17N 1°05E, pop (1995e) 42 600. Market town in Kent, SE England; St Augustine began the conversion of England to Christianity here, 597; Thomas Becket murdered in Canterbury Cathedral, 1170; seat of the Primate of the Anglican Church; railway; University of Kent (1965); cathedral (11th–15th-c). >> Augustine, St (of Canterbury); Becket; Kent

Canterbury bell A robust hairy biennial (*Campanula medium*), native to Italy; flowers 4–5 cm/1½–2 in, bell-shaped, dark blue, in long spikes; garden forms in many colours. (Family: Campanulaceae.) >> bell-flower

Canterbury Tales A series of linked narrative poems (and prose pieces) by Geoffrey Chaucer: the most important English work of literature from mediaeval times. Modelled on Boccaccio's *Decameron*, the tales are told by a group of 29 pilgrims on the road to Canterbury. Their 24 tales (the plan is incomplete) are told in a variety of poetic styles. >> Boccaccio; Chaucer

Canticles >> **Song of Solomon**

cantilever A horizontal building element where the part hidden within the building bears a downward force, and the other part projects outside without external bracing, and so appears to be self-supporting.

canton A territorial division of land. In Switzerland, cantons have their own separate governments; in France, cantons are sub-divisions of *arrondissements*, which are themselves sub-divisions of the regional *départements*.

Cantona, Eric [**kan**tona] (1966–) Footballer, born in Paris. Brought up in Marseille, he made his professional debut in 1983, and won his first French cap in 1987, moving to Leeds United in 1991 and to Manchester United in 1993. An aggressive and tempestuous player, his career has been interrupted by a series of suspensions. He announced his retirement in 1997, and began a career in films.

Cantonese >> **Chinese**

Cantor, Georg (Ferdinand Ludwig Philipp) (1845–1918) Mathematician, born in St Petersburg, Russia. He worked out a highly original arithmetic of the infinite which resulted in a theory of sets for irrational numbers. >> infinity; numbers; set

Canute or **Cnut**, sometimes known as **the Great** (c.995–1035) King of England (from 1016), Denmark (from 1019), and Norway (from 1028), the younger son of Sweyn Forkbeard. He defeated Edmund Ironside in 1016 at the Battle of Assandun, secured Mercia and Northumbria, and became King of all England after Edmund's death. The story of his failure to make the tide recede was invented by the 12th-c historian, Henry of Huntingdon, to demonstrate the frailty of earthly power compared to the might of God. >> Anglo-Saxons; Hardicanute; Harold I; Sweyn

canyon A deep valley with almost vertical sides which have been cut by a river, often in arid or semi-arid regions.

Canyon de Chelly [shay] National monument in NE Arizona, USA; established in 1931 to protect notable Indian cliff dwellings, dating from AD c.350; area 339 sq km/131 sq mi. >> Arizona

capacitance The measure of a system's ability to store electric charge; symbol *C*, units F (*farad*). For an electrical circuit, elements are usually quoted as μF (*Microfarad*, 10^{-6} F) or pF (*picofarad*, 10^{-12} F). >> dielectric

Cape Breton Island pop (1995e) 190 000; area 10 295 sq km/3974 sq mi. Island in Nova Scotia province, E Canada; almost bisected by Bras d'Or Lake (arm of the sea); chief towns, Sydney, Glace Bay, Louisburg; many people of Scottish descent, with Gaelic still spoken; originally French (Ile Royale), taken by British, 1758; joined to Nova Scotia, 1820. >> Nova Scotia

Cape Cod A sandy peninsula of SE Massachusetts, USA; length 105 km/65 mi; width up to 32 km/20 mi; crossed by the 13 km/8 mi Cape Cod Canal; pilgrims from the *Mayflower* landed near Provincetown in November 1620; airfield at Provincetown; popular resort area. >> Massachusetts; Pilgrims

Cape Coloured or **Coloured** A term used by the South African government to refer to a group of people of mixed descent, arising from the unions of Europeans with slaves or Khoikoi (Hottentots). They number about 3·2 million people (c.8·5% of the total population), mainly living in the towns and rural areas of the Western Cape province. In South Africa's racial hierarchy, they were ranked between Europeans and Black Africans. >> apartheid; South Africa [i]

Čapek, Karel [**cha**pek] (1890–1938) Writer, born in Schwadonitz, Czech Republic. His best-known work is his play *R. U. R.* (Rossum's Universal Robots), produced in 1921, showing mechanization rampant, and the comic fantasy *Ze života hmyzu* (1921, The Insect Play), written with his brother **Josef Čapek**. >> robotics

Capella [ka**pel**a] >> **Auriga**

Cape Provinces, Afrikaans **Kaapprovinsie** Former province in South Africa; founded, 1652; formally ceded to Britain (Cape Colony), 1814; separate parliament, 1850; joined Union of South Africa, 1910; since the 1994 constitution, divided into three provinces: Northern, Western, and Eastern. >> Eastern Cape; Northern Cape; South Africa [i]; Western Cape

caper A sprawling, deciduous, spiny shrub (*Capparis spinosa*), native to S Europe; flowers 5–7 cm/2–2¾ in in diameter, 4-petalled, white with numerous long purple stamens. Its pickled flower buds are eaten. (Family: Capparidaceae.)

capercaillie [kaper**kay**lee] A large grouse native to Europe and N Asia; usually solitary. (Genus: *Tetrao*, 2 species. Family: Tetraonidae.) >> grouse

Capet, Hugo or **Hugh** [**ka**pet] (c.938–96) King of France, founder of the third Frankish royal dynasty (the Capetians), which ruled France until 1328. His 40 years in power were marked by constant political intrigue and struggle. >> Capetians; Carolingians; Franks

Capetians A French ruling dynasty for over 300 years (987–1328), founded by Hugh Capet in succession to the Carolingians. Two dynamic royal descendants were Philip II Augustus (reigned 1180–1223) and Louis IX (reigned 1226–1270). The Capetians laid the foundations of the French nation-state. >> Bourbons; Capet; Louis IX

Cape Town, Afrikaans **Kaapstad** 33°56S 18°28E, pop (1995e) Greater Cape Town 1 207 000. Seaport capital of Western Cape province, South Africa; on Table Bay at the foot of Table Mt; legislative capital of South Africa; founded by the Dutch East India Company, 1652; occupied by the British, 1795; airport; railway; university (1829); cathedral; Union Houses of Parliament. >> Cape Provinces; South Africa [i]; Table Mountain; Western Cape

Cape Verde [kayp **verd**], official name **Republic of Cape Verde**, Port **República de Cabo Verde** pop (1995e) 394 000; area 4033 sq km/1557 sq mi. Island group in the Atlantic Ocean off W coast of Africa, c.500 km/310 mi W of Dakar, Senegal; Barlavento (windward) group in N; Sotavento (leeward) group in S; capital, Praia (on São Tiago I); timezone GMT −1; c.50% of population live on São Tiago I; c.70% of mixed black African and European descent; main religion, Roman Catholic; official language, Portuguese, but creole widely spoken; unit of currency, escudo Caboverdianos; islands of volcanic origin, mostly mountainous; highest peak, Cano (2829 m/9281 ft), active volcano on Fogo I; fine sandy beaches on most islands; low and unreliable rainfall (mainly Aug–Sep); small range of temperature throughout year; colonized by Portuguese in 15th-c, also used as a penal colony; administered with Portuguese Guinea until 1879; overseas province of Portugal, 1951; independence, 1975; multi-party elections for a new National Assembly, 1991; governed by a president, Council of Ministers, and People's National Assembly; economy suffered in recent years because of drought; substantial emigration in early 1970s; c.70% of workforce are farmers occupying irrigated inland valleys; increase in fishing since 1975; international airport on Sal I. >> Praia; RR1004 political leaders

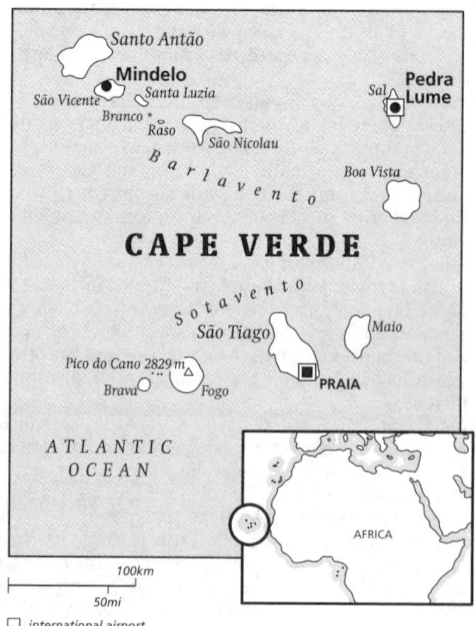

capillarity A surface tension effect in which liquids rise up narrow tubes or spread through porous solids; caused by the difference in attraction between liquid and air molecules for the material of the solid; also called **capillary action**. An example is ink soaking into blotting paper. >> chromatography; porosity; surface tension ℹ

capillary [ka**pil**aree] A minute, thin-walled blood vessel situated between arterioles and venules. It is the site of the exchange of materials (oxygen, nutrients, carbon dioxide) between capillary blood and surrounding tissues. >> blood vessels ℹ

capital (accountancy) Business sources of finance to buy assets, such as buildings, machinery, stocks, or investment in other firms. **Equity capital** is supplied by shareholders, either by buying shares or by ploughing back profits into the business. **Loan capital** or **debt** is borrowed from a financial institution or individual, and interest is paid. >> debt; equity (economics)

capital (architecture) The top part of a column, pilaster, or pier, identifiable in classical architecture as one of the five main orders. Romanesque and Gothic types include basket, bell, crocket, cushion, protomai (with animal figures), scalloped, and water-leaf. >> column; orders of architecture ℹ; pilaster

capital gains tax (CGT) A tax on the increase in the value of assets. This is usually payable only when an asset is realized by sale or bequest. CGT is levied in various countries – in the UK since 1965. In the USA it is a federal income tax. >> taxation

capitalism A set of economic arrangements which developed in the 19th-c in Western societies following the Industrial Revolution. The concept derives from the writings of Marx and rests upon the private ownership of the means of production by the capitalist class, or *bourgeoisie*. It has been the most productive economic system to date, though it has brought with it massive environmental (eg pollution) and social (eg unemployment) problems. >> Marxism; proletariat

capital punishment Sentence of death passed by a judicial body following trial. Capital punishment for murder has been abolished in the UK, though proposals for its reinstatement are regularly debated by parliament, and it remains the penalty for treason. It is still available in several states of the USA, and in many other countries. Countries employ a variety of procedures in carrying out executions, including lethal injection, electrocution, hanging, gassing, and shooting. >> murder; sentence; treason

Capitol The Assembly of the US Congress on Capitol Hill, Washington, DC. The building was designed in 1792 by William Thornton (1759–1828), but a succession of architects supervised its construction. >> Congress; Latrobe

Capitoline Hill The highest of the seven hills upon which Rome was built. Once the political and religious centre of Ancient Rome, it is now the site of the Piazza del Campidoglio. >> Rome

Capone, Al [ka**pohn**], popular name of **Alphonse Capone** (1899–1947) Gangster, born in New York City. He achieved worldwide notoriety as a racketeer during the prohibition era in Chicago. In 1931 he was sentenced to 10 years' imprisonment for tax evasion. >> Prohibition

Capote, Truman [ka**poh**tee], pseudonym of **Truman Streckfus Persons** (1924–84) Writer, born in New Orleans, LA. His novels include *Breakfast at Tiffany's* (1958), which was highly successful as a film, and *In Cold Blood* (1966), described as a 'nonfiction novel' because of the way he tells of actual events in novelistic form.

Capp, Al, originally **Alfred Gerald Caplin** (1909–79) Strip cartoonist, born in New Haven, CT. His chief comic-strip creation, the hill-billy character *L'il Abner* (1934), inspired two films, a stage musical, and an animated series.

Cappadocia [kapa**doh**shia], Turkish **Kapadokya** Ancient name for the mountainous region of C Turkey, between the Black Sea and the Taurus Mts; a province of the Roman Empire from AD 17; largest town, Nevşehir. >> Turkey ℹ

Capri [ka**pree**], Ital [**kap**ree], ancient **Capreae** area 10..5 sq km/4 sq mi. Italian island in the Tyrrhenian Sea; length 6 km/4 mi; maximum width 2·5 km/1·5 mi; rugged limestone crags rise to 589 m/1932 ft; capital, Capri; major tourist centre; home of Emperor Tiberius. >> Italy ℹ; Tiberius

capriccio [ka**prich**ioh] A short musical composition, usually of a light or fanciful kind and often (though not necessarily) for piano.

Capricornus (Lat 'goat') A S constellation of the zodiac, lying between Sagittarius and Aquarius. >> constellation; zodiac ℹ; RR968

capsid A small to medium-sized bug that typically feeds on plants; c.10 000 species, distributed worldwide. (Order: Heteroptera. Family: Miridae.)

capuchin [ka**pyoo**chin] A New World monkey, the most numerous captive monkey in the USA and Europe; tail partly adapted for grasping; acrobatic and intelligent; also known as **ring-tailed monkey** or **organ-grinder's monkey**. (Genus: *Cebus*, 4 species.) >> New World monkey

Capuchins [ka**pyoo**chinz] (Ital *capuche*, a kind of cowl) A monastic order stemming from the Franciscans; in full, the **Order of Friars Minor of St Francis Capuccinorum**; abbreviated as **OM Cap** or **OSFC**. It was formed in 1528 by Matteo di Bassi (c.1495–1552), and observes a very strict rule, stressing poverty and austerity. >> Franciscans; monasticism

capybara [kapi**bah**ra] A cavy-like rodent (*Hydrochoerus hydrochaeris*), native to Central and South America; largest living rodent (length, over 1 m/3¼ ft); dog-like with deep square snout; no tail; lives in or near water; part-webbed toes; eats vegetation. (Family: Hydrochoeridae.) >> cavy; rodent

car, also **motor car** (UK), **automobile** (USA) The general name for a passenger-carrying, self-propelled vehicle designed for normal domestic use on roads. The motive power system includes the engine (of whatever type), and its fuel supply, and the lubrication, exhaust, and cooling systems. The power developed by the engine is transmitted to the wheels by the transmission system, which includes gears, clutches, shafts, axles, and brakes. The engine and transmission are housed in the carriage unit, which also provides the compartment for the driver and passengers to sit, and in which the steering, engine controls, suspension, and electrical components can be mounted. The motor car became a reality with the invention in 1884 of the medium-speed internal combustion engine by Daimler in Germany. However, it was not until the early 1900s, and the application in the USA of mass production techniques to the motor car by Henry Ford, that mass motoring started to become a reality. >> alternative fuel; Daimler; electric car; engine; Ford, Henry; jeep; motor insurance; motor racing; transmission; tyre; *see illustration on p.148*

carabao [**ka**rabow] >> **water buffalo**

caracal [**ka**rakal] A member of the cat family, native to Africa and S Asia (*Felis caracal*); reddish-brown; slender with long legs, short tail, long tufted ears. >> Felidae

Caracas [ka**ra**kas] 10°30N 66°55W, pop (1995e) 2 035 000. Federal capital of Venezuela; altitude, 960 m/3150 ft; founded in 1567; often damaged by earthquakes; airport; airfield; railway; metro; three universities (1725, 1953, 1970); cathedral; birthplace of Bolívar. >> Bolívar; Venezuela ℹ

Caractacus [ka**rak**takus], **Caratacus**, or **Caradoc** (1st-c) A

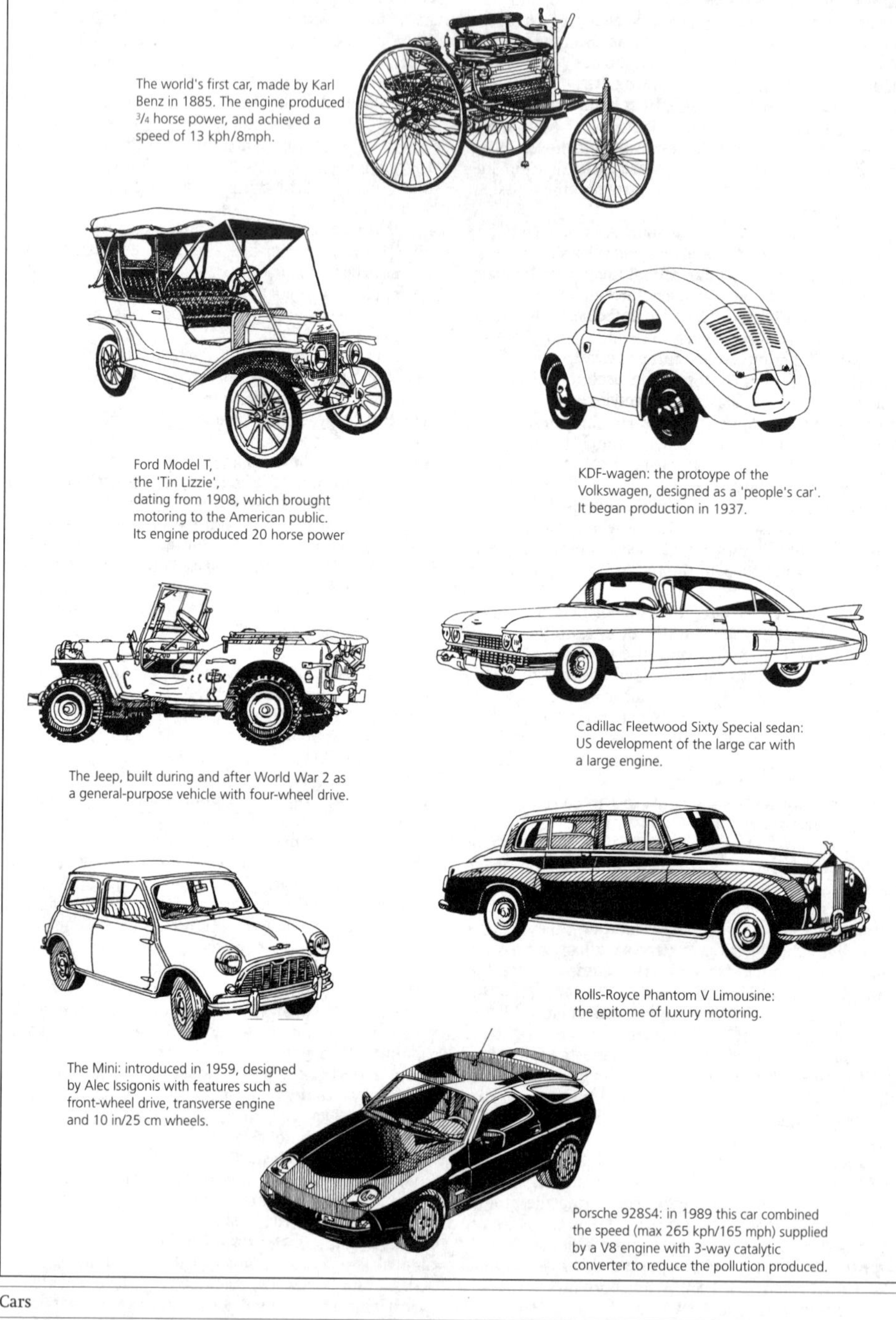

The world's first car, made by Karl Benz in 1885. The engine produced ¾ horse power, and achieved a speed of 13 kph/8mph.
Ford Model T, the 'Tin Lizzie', dating from 1908, which brought motoring to the American public. Its engine produced 20 horse power
KDF-wagen: the protoype of the Volkswagen, designed as a 'people's car'. It began production in 1937.
The Jeep, built during and after World War 2 as a general-purpose vehicle with four-wheel drive.
Cadillac Fleetwood Sixty Special sedan: US development of the large car with a large engine.
Rolls-Royce Phantom V Limousine: the epitome of luxury motoring.
The Mini: introduced in 1959, designed by Alec Issigonis with features such as front-wheel drive, transverse engine and 10 in/25 cm wheels.
Porsche 928S4: in 1989 this car combined the speed (max 265 kph/165 mph) supplied by a V8 engine with 3-way catalytic converter to reduce the pollution produced.

Cars

chief of the Catuvellauni, the son of Cunobelinus, who fought unsuccessfully against the Romans in the years following the Claudian conquest (43). He was taken to Rome (51), where he was exhibited in triumph.

caracul >> **karakul**

carat or (US) **karat 1** A measure of the purity of gold in some alloy. A gold carat is a 24th part of the whole, and the purity of a gold alloy is stated by the number of such parts it contains. Pure gold would be 24-carat gold. A 12-carat ring would be one in which half the metal is gold. >> gold **2** A unit of weight for precious stones, equal to 200 mg >> gemstones

Caratacus >> **Caractacus**

Caravaggio [kara**va**jioh], originally **Michelangelo Merisi** (1573–1610) Baroque painter, born in Caravaggio, Italy, whence his nickname. His works include several altar-pieces and religious paintings, using dramatic contrasts of light and shade, notably 'Christ at Emmaus' (c.1602–3). >> Baroque (art and architecture)

caravel [kara**vel**] A sailing vessel with up to four masts developed by the Portuguese in the 15th-c. The illustration below shows the typical lateen rig sails with the long curved spars. >> ship ℹ

caraway A much-branched annual (*Carum carvi*), growing to 1 m/3¼ ft, native to Europe; flowers small, petals whitish, deeply notched; fruit (the 'seeds') strong-smelling when crushed, used as a spice and for flavouring bread, cakes, and cheese. (Family: Umbelliferae.) >> spice

carbamide >> **urea**

carbide Any compound of carbon, especially those in which carbon is ionic. It is often used specifically for **calcium carbide**, CaC_2, a salt of acetylene. >> acetylene; carbon; ion

carbohydrate A non-nitrogen-containing compound based on carbon, hydrogen, and oxygen, generally with two hydrogen atoms per atom of oxygen. The molecules may be small (glucose) or large (cellulose, starch). Most carbohydrates comprise one or more 6-carbon units, of which glucose is by far the most abundant. >> cellulose; glucose; starch; sugars

carbolic acid >> **phenol**

carbon C, element 6. It has two main forms: **graphite** (the stable form, very soft and black with a density of c.2 g/cm^3) and **diamond** (the hardest substance known, density 3·5 g/cm^3). Both of these melt above 3500°C. Coal is mainly graphite. Carbon also occurs naturally in compounds, particularly as **carbonates**, and in the atmosphere as carbon dioxide. In virtually all its compounds, it is covalently bonded, and shows a valency of 4. Carbon compounds are the basis of all living matter, and form the subject matter of organic chemistry. There are two simple oxides, **carbon monoxide** (CO), a very poisonous gas, boiling point −191°C, formed from the incomplete combustion of carbon and hydrocarbons, and **carbon dioxide** O=C=O, the product of complete combustion. Carbon dioxide is in turn the raw material for photosynthesis, regenerating combustibles. Solid carbon dioxide, or *dry ice*, sublimes at −78°C without passing through a liquid phase. It accounts for less than 0·03% of the gases of the atmosphere. >> carbon cycle / dating / fibre; chemical elements; coal; diamond; organic chemistry; photosynthesis; sublimation (chemistry); RR1036

Carbonari [kah(r)bo**nah**ree] (Ital 'charcoal burners') Neapolitan secret societies, linked with freemasonry and probably founded under Napoleonic occupation. They played a major role in the Neapolitan revolution of 1820 and in the early stages of the Risorgimento. >> freemasonry; Risorgimento

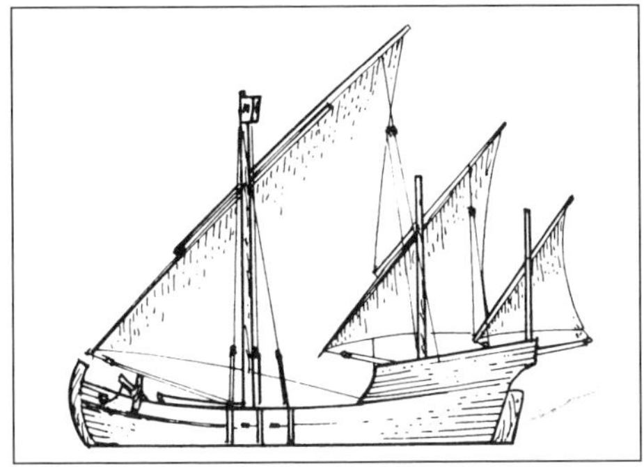

Caravel

carbonates Salts of carbonic acid, containing the ion CO_3^{2-}. Important natural carbonates include the almost insoluble **calcium carbonate** ($CaCO_3$), or limestone; **magnesium carbonate** ($MgCO_3$); and **dolomite** ($CaMg(CO_3)_2$). **Sodium carbonate**, known as 'washing soda' in its hydrated form ($Na_2CO_3.10H_2O$), is a cleansing agent and water softener. >> carbonic acid; salt

carbon cycle The cycle through which carbon is transferred between the biological and non-biological parts of the global ecosystem. It involves the fixation of gaseous carbon dioxide during photosynthesis to form complex organic molecules, as well as the process through which it returns to the atmosphere by respiration and decomposition. >> carbon; ecosystem; photosynthesis

carbon dating >> **radiocarbon dating**

carbon dioxide >> **carbon**

carbon fibre A high-strength material made by the controlled heat treatment of acrylic fibre. Woven as a fabric, it has the property of absorbing poisonous gas, and is used for protective underwear for military personnel, and for firehoods. The fibres are several times stronger than steel, and are extensively used where laminates of great strength and low weight are needed, as in components for rockets and aeroplanes.

carbonic acid H_2CO_3; the hydrated form of carbon dioxide (CO_2). It is a weak acid, dissociating in two stages to give hydrogen carbonate (HCO_3^-) and carbonate (CO_3^{2-}) ions. Rain water containing pure carbonic acid has a pH of about 5. >> carbon; pH

Carboniferous period A geological period of the Palaeozoic era, extending from 360 to 286 million years ago, and characterized by extensive swampy forests with conifers and ferns which now form most of the present-day coal deposits. It was also marked by the first appearance of reptiles and seed-bearing plants. In the USA, the period is termed the **Mississippian** (earlier) and the **Pennsylvanian** (later). >> coal; geological time scale; Palaeozoic era

carborundum The trade name for silicon carbide (SiC), a highly refractory material formed by fusing together sand and coke. It is almost as hard as diamond, and is used in grinding wheels and cutting tools. >> silicon carbide

carboxylic acids [kah(r)bok**sil**ik] Organic compounds containing the group −COOH; formed by the oxidation of alcohols or aldehydes; also called **alkanoic acids**. Many are found in nature, particularly as part of fats (*fatty acids*). >> acetic acid; alcohols; aldehyde

carbuncle A focus of infection in sweat glands and under the skin. It forms multiple confluent abscesses that discharge pus on to its surface through two or more tracts. >> abscess; sweat

carburettor / carburetor A device fitted to a spark ignition engine that mixes its fuel of air and petrol in suitable proportions for combustion. As the engine draws in its air/petrol mixture, the carburettor ensures that small droplets of petrol are carried along with the airstream. These droplets then vaporize on their way to the engine to form the highly inflammable mixture used in the engine's power stroke. >> internal combustion engine; petrol; spark ignition engine

Carcassonne [kah(r)ka**son**], ancient **Carcaso** 43°13N 2°20E, pop (1995e) 46 400. Ancient city in S France, in foothills of Pyrenees; railway; bishopric; the Cité (altitude 200 m/650 ft) is the best preserved example of a French mediaeval fortified town (world heritage site); basilica (5th-c, rebuilt 11th–13th-c), cathedral (late 13th-c, restored 1840). >> Pyrenees

Carchemish [**kah(r)**kemish] An ancient trading city in N Syria. It was ruled by the Hittites in the second millennium BC, and remained an important centre of Hittite culture until its conquest by Assyria in 716 BC. >> Assyria; Hittites

carcinogen [kah(r)**sin**ojn] An agent which is capable of inducing cancer in tissues exposed to it. Several carcinogens have been identified by studies of the frequency of specific tumours in relation to different occupations, lifestyles, exposure to injurious chemical agents, drugs, ionizing radiations, ultraviolet light, and certain tumour-inducing (*oncogenic*) viruses. Exposure to such agents does not cause cancer immediately, but only after a period which may be months or years. >> cancer

carcinoma >> **sarcoma**

cardamom [**kah(r)**damom] A perennial native to India (*Elettaria cardamomum*); stem to 3·5 m/11½ ft; flowers small, white with blue and yellow markings, in clusters 60 cm/2 ft long; fruit a capsule 2 cm/0·8 in long. The dried ripe fruits are used as spice. (Family: Zingiberaceae.) >> spice

card games >> **playing cards**

cardiac resuscitation Emergency treatment following cardiac arrest (the sudden complete cessation of heart function); also known as **external cardiac massage**. This must be given within three minutes if the brain is not to suffer irreversible damage. First-aid treatment is usually combined with mouth-to-mouth ventilation. Initially a smart blow with the closed fist should be given to the front of the chest, just to the left of the midline, and both legs elevated to 90°. If the heart does not start, forceful regular compression of the chest at about 70 times per minute should be carried out. >> artificial respiration ℹ; heart ℹ

Cardiff, Welsh **Caerdydd** 51°30N 3°13W, pop (1995e) 309 000. Capital of Wales, in Cardiff county, S Wales, UK; at the mouth of the Taff, Rhymney, and Ely Rivers, on the Bristol Channel; Roman fort, 1st-c AD; Norman castle, c.1090; city charter, 1147; capital status, 1955; airport; railway; university college (1893); registry for University of Wales; Llandaff Cathedral, Welsh National Folk Museum (St Fagans), Cardiff Castle, Cardiff Arms Park (rugby); football league team, Cardiff City (Bluebirds). >> Wales ℹ

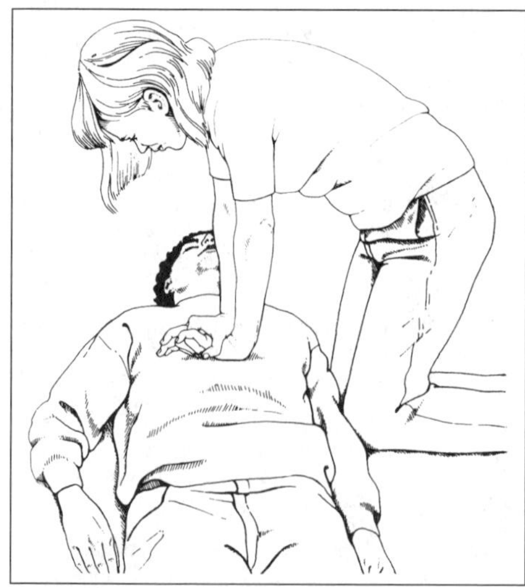

Cardiac resuscitation

Cardigan, James Thomas Brudenell, 7th Earl of (1797–1868) British general, born in Hambleden, Buckinghamshire. He led the Charge of the Light Brigade against the Russians at Balaclava (1854). The woollen jacket known as a *cardigan* is named after him. >> Crimean War

Cardiganshire, Welsh **Sir Aberteifi** pop (1995e) 69 700; area 1797 sq km / 694 sq mi. County (unitary authority from 1996) in W Wales, UK; administrative centre, Aberystwyth; Aberystwyth university and National Library of Wales. >> Wales ℹ

Cardin, Pierre [kah(r)dĩ] (1922–) French fashion designer, born in Venice, Italy. He went to Paris in 1944, opened his own house in 1953, and has since been prominent in fashion for both women and men.

cardinal (ornithology) Either of two species of bird of genus *Cardinalis*, native to the Americas: the **red** or **northern cardinal** (*Cardinalis cardinalis*), or the **vermilion cardinal** (*Cardinalis phoeniceus*); males bright red. (Family: Emberizidae.)

cardinal (religion) A name originally given to one of the parish priests, bishops, or district deacons of Rome, then applied to a senior dignitary of the Roman Catholic Church, being a priest or bishop nominated by a pope to act as counsellor. The office carries special insignia, such as the distinctive red cap. >> Cardinals, College of; Roman Curia

Cardinals, College of An institution consisting of all the cardinals of the Roman Catholic Church. It is responsible for the government of the Church during a vacancy in the papacy, and since 1179 has been responsible for the election of a pope. >> cardinal (religion); pope; Roman Catholicism

care proceedings The procedure adopted by a court or tribunal in relation to children, taken with a view to ensuring their protection and, if necessary, their reception into care. Care proceedings encompass children who are or may be the victims of abuse or neglect, those who are beyond the control of their parents, and those who are failing to receive a proper education. Many jurisdictions also include children and young persons who are committing offences in this category, though there has been an increasing tendency in some countries to separate child offenders from other children in need of care, protection, or control.

Carew, Thomas [ka**roo**] (1595–1639) Poet, born in West Wickham, Kent. He wrote polished lyrics in the Cavalier tradition, and a masque *Coelum britannicum* (1634) which was performed at court. >> Cavalier poets; masque

Carey, George Leonard [**kair**ee] (1935–) Anglican churchman, born in London. He became bishop of Bath and Wells in 1987, and in 1991 was appointed Archbishop of Canterbury.

Carey, Peter [**kair**ee] (1943–) Writer, born in Bacchus Marsh, Victoria, Australia. His first book, *The Fat Man in History* (1974), was a collection of short stories. Later books include *Bliss* (1981), *Illywhacker* (1985), *Oscar and Lucinda* (1988, Booker), and *Jack Maggs* (1997).

cargo cult The Melanesian variety of a widely occurring type of social movement (millenarianism) in which people look to some supernatural event to bring them prosperity. It is so-called because, in Melanesia, people performed rituals in an effort to obtain European material goods (referred to as 'cargo'). The movement first appeared in the late 19th-c. >> cult; Melanesia; millenarianism

Carib American Indian groups of the Lesser Antilles and neighbouring South America (the Guianas and Venezuela); also the name of the largest family of South American Indian languages. >> Antilles

Caribbean Community (CARICOM) An association chiefly of former British colonies in the Caribbean Sea. In 1968 many of the islands agreed to the establishment of the **Caribbean Free Trade Area (CARIFTA)**. >> associated state; Association of Caribbean States; Commonwealth (British)

Caribbean Sea area 2 515 900 sq km/971 100 sq mi. Arm of the Atlantic Ocean between the West Indies and Central and South America; linked to the Pacific by the Panama Canal; deepest point, Cayman Trench, 6950 m/22 802 ft; main island groups, Greater and Lesser Antilles. >> Antilles; Panama Canal

caribou >> **reindeer**

CARICOM >> **Caribbean Community**

caries [**kair**eez] A non-specific bacterial disease in which infecting organisms penetrate the enamel coating of a tooth. A high consumption of sugar predisposes to the development of caries, while an adequate amount of fluoride in drinking water (one part in a million) increases the resistance of the enamel to bacteria. >> dentistry; fluorine; teeth

CARIFTA >> **Caribbean Community**

carillon A set of bells, usually with a compass of two octaves or more, installed in a tower or other high construction, and operated mechanically or by hand to play melodies or more complex polyphonic music. Many carillons are incorporated into elaborate public clocks. >> bell; idiophone

Carina [ka**riy**na] (Lat 'keel') A S hemisphere constellation, formerly part of Argo Navis. It contains Canopus, the second brightest star in our sky, a supergiant. Distance: 30 parsec. >> constellation; supergiant; RR968

Carling, Will, popular name of **William David Charles Carling** (1965–) Player of rugby union football, born in Bradford-on-Avon, Wiltshire. He made his England debut in 1988, was appointed captain (1988–96), and played a major role in the Grand Slam victories of 1991, 1992, and 1995. He received national publicity in 1995 when the media focused on rumours of a possible relationship with Princess Diana. >> Diana, Princess of Wales

Carlisle [kah(r)**liyl**], Lat **Luguvallum** 54°54N 2°55W, pop (1995e) 73 300. County town in Cumbria, NW England; at the W end of Hadrian's Wall; important fortress in Scots–English border wars; airfield; railway junction; cathedral (11th–12th-c), castle (11th-c); football league team, Carlisle United. >> Cumbria

Carlow [**kah(r)**loh], Ir **Cheatharlach** pop (1995e) 40 600; area 896 sq km/346 sq mi. County in SE Ireland; capital, Carlow, pop (1995e) 14 100; castle (12th-c), cathedral (19th-c). >> Ireland (republic) ℹ; Leinster

Carluccio, Antonio (Mario Gaetano) [kah(r)**loo**chioh] (1937–) Restaurateur, born in Vietri Sul Mare, Italy. He joined the Neal Street Restaurant in London as restaurateur (1981), became proprietor (1989), and joint proprietor (with his wife) of Carluccio's food retailers (1992). His numerous television appearances include BBC's *Food and Drink* (from 1986) and the series *Antonio Carluccio's Italian Feasts* (1996) with accompanying book.

Carlyle, Thomas (1795–1881) Man of letters, born in Ecclefechan, Dumfriesshire. In 1826 he married **Jane Baillie Welsh** (1801–66). His best-known works are *Sartor Resartus* (1833–4), and studies on the French Revolution (3 vols, 1837) and Frederick the Great (6 vols, 1858–65). In 1866 his wife died, leaving letters and a journal showing her to have been one of the most accomplished women of her time.

Carmarthen [ka(r)**mahth**en] 51°52N 4°19W, pop (1995e) 15 600. County town of Carmarthenshire, SW Wales, UK; on R Towy; chartered, 1227; railway. >> Wales ℹ

Carmarthenshire, Welsh **Sir Caerfyrddin** pop (1995e) 169 000; area 2398 sq km / 926 sq mi. County (unitary authority from 1996) in SW Wales, UK; drained by R Teifi and R Tywi; administrative centre, Carmarthen; Laugharne (home of Dylan Thomas); Carreg Cennen and Kidwelly castles. >> Thomas, Dylan; Wales ℹ

Carme [**kah(r)**mee] The 11th natural satellite of Jupiter, discovered in 1938; distance from the planet 22 600 000 km/14 044 000 mi; diameter 40 km/25 mi. >> Jupiter (astronomy); RR964

Carmelites A Roman Catholic monastic order originating in the 12th-c from the Hermits of Mount Carmel (Israel); properly known as the **Order of the Brothers of the Blessed Virgin Mary of Mt Carmel**, or **White Friars**; abbreviated **OCarm**. Carmelite nuns were officially recognized in 1452, reformed by Teresa of Ávila in Spain (1562) as strictly cloistered **Discalced Carmelites** (**ODC**). (The term 'discalced' derives from the practice of wearing sandals.) The male order was similarly reformed by St John of the Cross, and in 1593 was recognized as a separate order. >> John of the Cross, St; monasticism; Roman Catholicism; Teresa of Ávila, St

Carmichael, Hoagy, popular name of **Howard Hoagland Carmichael** (1899–1981) Songwriter, singer, pianist, bandleader, and actor, born in Bloomington, IN. His much-loved compositions (often written with others) included 'Stardust', 'Georgia on my Mind', and '(Up a) Lazy River'.

Carmichael, Stokely, after 1969, also known as **Kwame Ture** (1941–98) Radical activist, born in Port-of-Spain, Trinidad. He popularized the phrase 'black power', and as a Black Panther came to symbolize black violence to many whites. He later favoured forging alliances with radical whites, which led to his resignation from the Panthers in 1968. He and his wife, **Miriam Makeba**, moved to Guinea in 1969, where he supported Pan-Africanism. >> Black Panthers; civil rights

Carnac A peninsula on the S coast of Brittany, N France, renowned for its megalithic alignments, stone circles, and chambered tombs of Neolithic date. About 3000 stones survive, extending over some 5 km/3 mi. >> megalith; stone circles; Three Age System

Carnap, Rudolf (1891–1970) Philosopher, born in Wuppertal, Germany. He was one of the leaders of the 'Vienna Circle' of logical positivists. His writings include *Der logische Aufbau der Welt* (1928, The Logical Construction of the World), and *Meaning and Necessity* (1947). >> logical positivism; Vienna Circle

carnation A perennial species of pink (*Dianthus caryophyllaceus*), native to the Mediterranean; leaves tufted; flowers with spreading, slightly frilly petals. Ornamental hybrids and garden cultivars are various colours and may have multiple petals. (Family: Caryophyllaceae.) >> cultivar; pink

Carneades [kah(r)**nee**adeez] (c.214–129 BC) Greek philosopher, born in Cyrene. He became head of the Academy, which under his very different, sceptical direction became known as the 'New Academy'. >> Plato

Carnegie, Andrew [kah(r)**nay**gee, or **kar**negee] (1835–1919) Industrialist and philanthropist, born in Dunfermline, Fife, UK. His family emigrated to Pittsburgh, PA, in 1848. He gave millions of dollars to libraries and other public institutions in the UK and USA, and several buildings are named after him.

carnitine A chemical substance (an *amine*) derived from the essential amino acid, lysine. Although once considered a vitamin, it is probably not an essential component of the diet. >> amines; vitamins ℹ

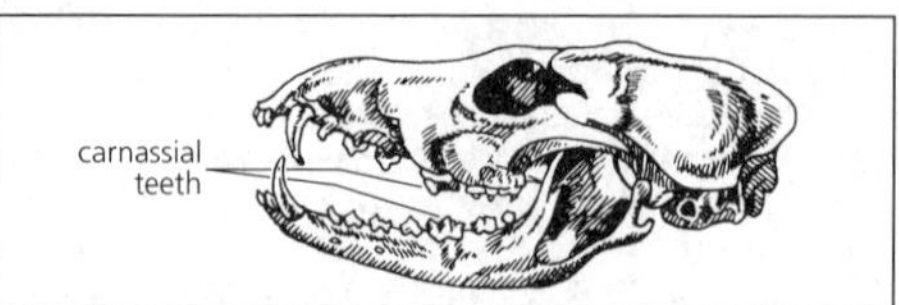

Carnivore – skull of a fox

Carnival A traditional festive period prior to Lent, celebrated in the Catholic countries of S Europe and their former colonies, and characterized by feasting, sexual licence, dancing, processions, masking, satire, and social levelling. Well known examples are those of Rome, Venice, New Orleans, and Rio de Janeiro. The term is also applied to similar festivals, such as the Notting Hill Carnival in London. >> folklore; Lent; Mardi Gras

carnivore [**kah(r)**nivaw(r)] A primarily meat-eating mammal, preying on other vertebrates; lower jaw moves only up and down; canine teeth long; some cheek teeth (*carnassials*) specialized for cutting flesh; 4–5 clawed toes on each foot. (Order: Carnivora, 7 families, 238 species.) >> bear; cat; dog; herbivore; hyena; mammal ⓘ; Mustelidae; Viverridae ⓘ; *see illustration above*

carnivorous plant A plant which traps animals, usually insects and small invertebrates, and secretes digestive enzymes which break down the prey, allowing the resulting products to be absorbed; also known as an **insectivorous plant**. >> bladderwort; butterwort; enzyme; pitcher plant; sundew; Venus's fly-trap ⓘ

Carnot, Lazare (Nicolas Marguerite) [kah(r)noh] (1753–1823) French statesman, born in Nolay, France, known as 'the organizer of victory' during the Revolutionary Wars. He was one of the Directors (1795), became minister of war (1800), helped to organize the Italian and Rhenish campaigns, and during the Hundred Days was minister of the interior. >> French Revolution ⓘ; Hundred Days

Carnot, (Nicholas Léonard) Sadi [kah(r)noh] (1796–1832) Scientist, born in Paris. He spent much of his life investigating the design of steam engines, and his findings were the foundation of the science of thermodynamics. >> Carnot cycle; thermodynamics

Carnot cycle [kah(r)noh] The fundamental thermodynamic cycle proposed in 1824 by French engineer Sadi Carnot, in an attempt to explain the working of the steam engine. A **Carnot engine** is the most efficient heat engine possible (**Carnot's law**). For intake temperature T_i and exhaust temperature T_o, thermal efficiency e is $e = (T_i - T_o)/T_i$. Because of physical and metallurgical problems, the Carnot cycle is not practical, and other cycles have been developed that meet the needs of real engines. >> Carnot, Sadi; engine; thermal efficiency; thermodynamics; *see illustration opposite*

Carnot's law >> **Carnot cycle**

carob An evergreen tree or shrub (*Ceratonia siliqua*), growing to 10 m/30 ft, native to the Mediterranean region; flowers lacking petals; pods to 20 cm/8 in long, pendent, violet-brown when ripe; also called **locust tree**. (Family: Leguminosae.)

Caroline, Radio The best-known UK pirate radio station of the 1960s. Operating illegally from a ship off the Essex coast, and financed by advertising, Radio Caroline broke the BBC's monopoly of domestic radio broadcasting and 'created' a youth audience through non-stop pop music, thus prompting the creation of Radio 1. >> BBC; broadcasting

Carolingians A Frankish ruling dynasty which rose to power as mayors of the palace, and ultimately replaced the Merovingians when Pepin II became King of the Franks in 751. The Carolingian Empire created by Charlemagne embraced most of the former territory of the Roman Empire in the West. >> Charlemagne; Charles Martel; Franks; Merovingians

carp Deep-bodied freshwater fish (*Cyprinus carpio*) native to Black Sea coasts but now introduced worldwide; length up to 1 m/$3\frac{1}{4}$ ft; two pairs of barbels on upper jaw; important food fish; broadly, any member of the large family Cyprinidae. >> barbel

Carpaccio, Vittore [kah(r)**pa**chioh] (c.1460–c.1525) Painter, born in Venice. His most characteristic work is seen in the nine subjects from the life of St Ursula (1490–5).

Carpathian Mountains Mountain system of EC Europe; extends 1400 km/870 mi in a semi-circle from Czech Republic to Romania; highest point, Mt Gerlach (2655 m/8711 ft). >> Tatra Mountains

carpel Part of the innermost whorl of a flower, collectively forming the *gynecium*: it typically consists of an ovary, style, and stigma, which together are sometimes called the **pistil**. >> flower ⓘ; ovary; stigma; style (botany)

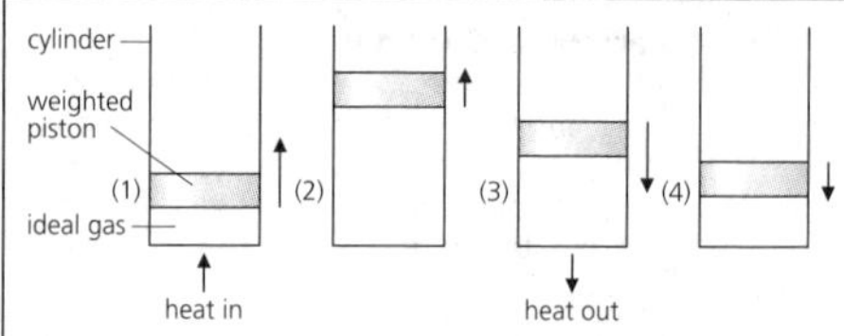

(1) A weighted piston moves in a cylinder filled with a theoretically ideal gas whose pressure, temperature, and volume are continuously measured. Heat is added to the gas at a constant temperature expanding the gas, decreasing its pressure and lifting the piston (1 & 2).

(2) The addition of heat to the gas ceases, but it continues to expand, at the same time lifting the piston whilst dropping its temperature and pressure (2 & 3).

(3) Heat is then taken out of the gas at constant temperature by means of a suitable heat sink, the volume decreases, the piston moves downwards, and the pressure of the gas increases (3 & 4).

(4) Heat ceases to be taken from the gas, the pressure and temperature increase, the volume decreases, and the piston continues to move downwards (4 to 1) until the arrangement is ready to start the cycle over again.

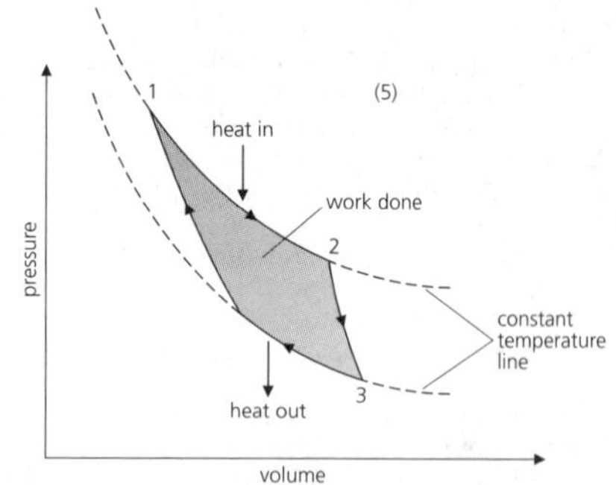

(5) The results of this cycle are plotted on a pressure / volume diagram, with the enclosed shaded area representing the useful work done. The Carnot cycle demonstrates that no engine can ever be 100% efficient.

Carnot cycle

Carpentaria, Gulf of [kah(r)pen**tay**ria] Major inlet on N coast of Australia between Cape Arnhem and Cape York; 595 km/370 mi long by 491 km/305 mi wide; named by Tasman in honour of the Governor-General of Dutch East Indies, 1642. >> Australia ℹ; Tasman

carpet A floor covering made from wool, silk, jute, mohair, or other fibres, traditionally woven but currently produced by other methods such as bonding or machine-stitching the pile to a base. The technique is thought to have originated in Persia in ancient times; in the 18th-c, it became widespread in Britain, France, and other West European countries. >> fibres

Carpetbaggers A derogatory term for US Northerners who went to the defeated South after the Civil War to aid freed blacks and take part in rebuilding. Supposedly they carried all their belongings in bags made of carpet. >> American Civil War

Carracci [ka**rah**chee] A family of Italian painters, born in Bologna. The most famous was **Annibale Carracci** (1560–1609), who with his brother, **Agostino Carracci** (1557–1602), painted the gallery of the Farnese Palace, Rome. With their cousin, **Ludovico Carracci** (1555–1619), they founded an influential academy of painting in Bologna (1582).

carrack [**ka**rak] A 15th-c development of the Portuguese caravel, distinguished by having square sails in addition to lateen sails. >> caravel ℹ; ship ℹ

Carrantuohill [karan**too**uhl] Mountain in SW Ireland in the Macgillycuddy's Reeks range, rising to 1041 m/3415 ft; highest peak in Ireland. >> Ireland (republic) ℹ

Carreras, José Maria [ka**rair**as] (1946–) Lyric tenor, born in Barcelona, Spain. He made his debut at Covent Garden and at the Metropolitan Opera in 1974. After severe illness in the mid-1980s, he returned to the stage.

Carrington, Peter (Alexander Rupert) Carrington, 6th Baron (1919–) British Conservative statesman, born in London. He served as secretary of state for defence (1970–4) and foreign secretary (1979–82), but resigned over the Argentinian invasion of the Falkland Is. He later became Secretary-General of NATO (1984–8) and Chancellor of the University of Reading. >> Conservative Party; Falklands War; NATO

Carroll, Lewis, pseudonym of **Charles Lutwidge Dodgson** (1832–98) Writer, born in Daresbury, Cheshire. He took orders in 1861, and was a lecturer in mathematics (1855–81). His nursery tale, *Alice's Adventures in Wonderland* (1865), and its sequel, *Through the Looking-Glass* (1872), quickly became classics. 'Alice', to whom the story was originally related during boating excursions, was the second daughter (who died in 1934) of Henry George Liddell, the head of his Oxford college. He wrote a great deal of humorous verse, such as *The Hunting of the Snark* (1876).

carrot A biennial herb (*Daucus carota*) growing to 1 m/3·3 ft, native to Europe, temperate Asia, and N Africa; flowers white or pink, the central flower usually dark purple; fruits spiny. The cultivated carrot (subspecies *sativus*), with a large fleshy orange or whitish tap root, is an important human dietary food. (Family: Umbelliferae.) >> herb; vegetable

Carson, Johnny, popular name of **John William Carson** (1925–) Television personality and businessman, born in Corning, IA. He starred in *The Johnny Carson Show* (1955–6), and was engaged as an occasional host of *The Tonight Show*, a position that was made permanent in 1962. Consistently top of the ratings, his breezy, relaxed manner, comic monologue, and selection of guests made him an American institution. He retired from the show in 1992.

Carson, Kit, popular name of **Christopher Carson** (1809–68) Frontiersman, born in Madison Co, KY. He was Indian agent in New Mexico (1853), and fought for the Union in the Civil War. Several places are named after him. >> American Civil War

Carson, Rachel (Louise) (1907–64) Naturalist and publicist, born in Springdale, PA. In 1962 her *Silent Spring* directed public attention to the problems caused by agricultural pesticides, and she became a pioneer in the conservationist movement of the 1960s. >> conservation (earth sciences); ecology; pesticide

Carson City 39°10N 119°46W, pop (1995e) 51 800. State capital in W Nevada, USA; founded, 1858; trade centre for a mining and agricultural area; tourism; gambling centre. >> Nevada

Cartagena (de los Indes) (Columbia) [karta**khay**na] 10°24N 75°33W, pop (1995e) 539 000. Port in NW Colombia; founded, 1533; sacked by Drake, 1586; airfield; university (1824); old colonial quarter is a world heritage site. >> Colombia ℹ; Drake, Francis

Cartagena (Spain) [kah(r)ta**jee**na], Span [karta**khay**na], Lat **Carthago Nova** 37°38N 0°59W, pop (1995e) 168 000. Fortified seaport and naval base in SE Spain; founded by the Carthaginians, 221 BC; two airports; railway. >> Spain ℹ

Carte, Richard D'Oyly >> **D'Oyly Carte, Richard**

cartel [kah(r)**tel**] An agreement by a number of companies in the same industry to fix prices and/or quantities, thus avoiding cut-price competition or overproduction. It is often seen as not being in the public interest, since it does not allow market forces to operate freely. >> OPEC

Carter, Angela (1940–92) Writer, born in Eastbourne, East Sussex. Her novels and short stories are characterized by feminist themes and fantasy narratives; they include *The Magic Toyshop* (1967), *Nights at the Circus* (1984), and *Wise Children* (1991). >> feminism

Carter, Howard (1874–1939) Archaeologist, born in Swaffham, Norfolk. His discoveries included the tombs of Hatshepsut (1907), Thutmose IV and, most notably, Tutankhamen (1922), a find on which he worked for the remainder of his life. >> Tutankhamen

Carter, Jimmy, popular name of **James (Earl) Carter** (1924–) US statesman and 39th president (1977–81), born in Plains, GA. In 1976 he won the Democratic presidential nomination, and went on to win a narrow victory over Gerald Ford. He arranged the peace treaty between Egypt and Israel (1979), and was much concerned with human rights at home and abroad. His administration ended in difficulties over the taking of US hostages in Iran, and the Soviet invasion of Afghanistan, and he was defeated by Ronald Reagan in the 1980 election. He has been much involved in international diplomacy, notably in relation to the crisis in Haiti in 1994.

Cartesian geometry >> **analytic geometry**

Carthage 36°54N 10°16E. Ancient town in Tunisia, N Africa, now a suburb of Tunis; a world heritage site; reputedly founded by the Phoenicians in 814 BC; destroyed by Rome following the Punic Wars, 146 BC; refounded by Caesar and Octavian, 29 BC; restored as capital by the Vandals, AD 439–533, but destroyed again by the Arabs, 698. >> Caesar; Phoenicia; Punic Wars; Tunisia ℹ; Vandals

Carthusians A Roman Catholic monastic order founded in 1084 by Bruno of Cologne in Chartreuse, near Grenoble, France; properly known as the **Order of Carthusians**; abbreviated **OCart**. At the mother-house, 'La Grande Chartreuse', a famous liqueur is distilled, the profits being distributed to local charities. >> Bruno of Cologne, St; liqueur; monasticism

Cartier, Jacques [ka(r)tyay] (1491–1557) Navigator, born in St-Malo, France. Between 1534 and 1542 he made three voyages of exploration to North America, surveying the coast of Canada and the St Lawrence R.

Cartier-Bresson, Henri [ka(r)tyay bresõ] (1908–) Photographer, born in Paris. His many works include *The World of Henri Cartier-Bresson* (1968). In the mid-1970s he gave up photography, and returned to his earlier interests of painting and drawing.

cartilage Tissue supplementary to bone in the skeleton, found for example in the nose, ear, and larynx; sometimes called **gristle**. It is composed of living cells surrounded by an intercellular substance containing collagen. It is not hard or strong (so can be easily cut or damaged by high pressure), and is relatively nonvascular, being nourished by tissue fluids (particularly at joint surfaces). >> bone; joint

cartilaginous fish [kah(r)ti**la**jinuhs] Any fish of the class Chondrichthyes (800 species), having a cartilaginous endoskeleton that may be calcified but not ossified (true bone), and lacking air bladder or lungs; comprises the sharks and rays (Elasmobranchii) and ratfishes (Holocephalii). >> bony fish; cartilage; fish ⓘ; ray; shark

Cartland, (Mary) Barbara (Hamilton) (1901–) Popular romantic novelist. Since her first novel, *Jigsaw* (1923), she has written over 600 books, mostly romantic novels but also biographies of 'romantic' figures, and books on food, health, and beauty. She has been active in charitable causes, and is well known for her views on health and fitness in old age.

cartography The method of construction of maps and charts. Through the use of symbols, lettering, and shading techniques, data concerning an area (eg its relief, population density) are portrayed on a map in such a way that it can be interpreted by the user to find out information about a place. Data come from many sources, such as fieldwork, surveying, and remote sensing. >> remote sensing; surveying

cartridge tape drive >> **magnetic tape 2**

Cartwright, Edmund (1743–1823) Inventor of the power loom (1785–90), born in Marnham, Nottinghamshire. Attempts to use the loom met with fierce opposition, and it was not until the 19th-c that it came into practical use. >> spinning

Caruso, Enrico [ka**roo**zoh] (1873–1921) Operatic tenor, born in Naples, where he made his debut in 1894. The extraordinary power of his voice, combined with his acting ability, won him worldwide recognition.

Carver, George Washington (c.1864–1943) Scientist, born near Diamond Grove, MO. He was born into an African-American slave family, and received little formal education in his early years. He became renowned for his research into agricultural problems and synthetic products, and was an influential teacher and humanitarian.

Cary, John [**kair**ee] (c.1754–1835) English cartographer, who began as an engraver in London. His *New and Correct English Atlas* appeared in 1787, followed by county atlases, and the *New Universal Atlas* of 1808. >> cartography

Cary, (Arthur) Joyce (Lunel) [**kair**ee] (1888–1957) Writer, born in Londonderry, Northern Ireland. His best-known work is his trilogy, *Herself Surprised* (1940), *To be a Pilgrim* (1942), and *The Horse's Mouth* (1944).

caryatid [ka**ree**atid, **ka**riatid] A sculptured female figure, used as a column or support for an entablature or other building element. The name derives from the ancient Greek women of Caryae sold into slavery. >> column; entablature

Casablanca [kasa**blang**ka], Arabic **Dar el Beida** 33°20N 71°25W, pop (1995e) 2 882 000. Seaport in W Morocco; founded by the Portuguese as Casa Branca, 1515; seriously damaged by an earthquake in 1755 and rebuilt; French occupation, 1907; meeting place of Churchill and Roosevelt, 1943; airport; railway; university; handles over 75% of Morocco's trade; world's second largest mosque (King Hassan II Mosque) opened, 1993. >> Casablanca Conference; Morocco ⓘ; World War 2

Casablanca Conference A meeting in N Africa between Roosevelt and Churchill during World War 2 (Jan 1943), at which it was decided to insist on the eventual unconditional surrender of Germany and Japan. >> Casablanca; Churchill, Sir Winston; Roosevelt, Franklin D; World War 2

Casals, Pablo [ka**sals**], Catalan **Pau** (1876–1973) Cellist, conductor, and composer, born in Vendrell, Spain. He began to appear as a soloist in 1899, and in 1919 founded the Barcelona Orchestra, which he conducted until he left Spain at the outbreak of the Civil War (1936). During his later years, he conducted many master classes.

Casanova (de Seingalt), Giacomo Girolomo [kasa**noh**va] (1725–98) Adventurer, born in Venice. By 1750 he had worked as a clergyman, secretary, soldier, and violinist in various countries. Alchemist, cabalist, and spy, he visited many parts of Europe, was everywhere introduced to the best society, and had always to 'vanish' after a brief period of felicity. His main work is his autobiography, first published in 1960, in which he emerges as one of the world's great lovers. His seductions are the first things many think of in connection with his name.

Cascade Range Mountain range in W North America; extends over 1120 km/700 mi from N California to British Columbia; named after the cascades of the Columbia R where it passes through the range in a canyon c.1200 m/4000 ft deep; highest point, Mt Rainier (4392 m/14 409 ft), Washington; Crater Lake National Park in the S. >> Crater Lake (USA); St Helens, Mount; United States of America ⓘ

casein [**kay**seen] The main protein in milk and cheese, rich in associated calcium and phosphorus. Casein is heat-stable, but is precipitated at a pH of about 4·2 (mildly acid). This is exploited in cheese-making, where the initial step is the precipitation of the curd (casein and fat) from the whey. >> cheese; milk; pH; protein; rennet

Casement, (Sir) Roger (David) [**kays**ment] (1864–1916) British consular official, born in Dun Laoghaire (formerly Kingstown), Co Dublin, Ireland. In 1916 he was arrested on landing in Ireland from a German submarine to head the Sinn Féin rebellion, and hanged for high treason in London. His controversial 'Black Diaries' were long suppressed by the government, but ultimately published in 1959. >> Sinn Féin

cashew A small evergreen tree (*Anacardium occidentale*), native to South America; flowers in terminal clusters, petals red, narrow, and reflexed; the receptacle thick, fleshy, pear-shaped in fruit, and bearing the curved nut. (Family: Anacardiaceae.)

cashmere The highly-prized fine warm undercoat fibres from the Kashmir goat; mainly produced in China and Iran. It is used principally in knitwear.

casino An establishment where gambling takes place. The first legal casino opened in Baden-Baden in 1765, and rules governing their operation are very strict in most countries. >> baccarat; blackjack; chemin de fer; craps; roulette

Casper 42°51N 106°19W, pop (1995e) 49 900. City in EC Wyoming, USA; largest city in the state; airfield; railway; trade centre of a farming, ranching, and mineral-rich area. >> Wyoming

Caspian Sea [**kas**pian], ancient **Mare Caspium** or **Mare Hyrcanium** area 371 000 sq km/143 200 sq mi. Largest inland body of water on Earth, surrounded on three sides by republics of the former USSR, and in the S by Iran; c.28 m/90 ft below sea-level, but much variation in level; maximum depth, 980 m/3215 ft in S; shallow N area; low salinity; frozen in N for several months in severe winters; no outlet and no tides; pollution an increasing problem.

Cassandra [ka**san**dra] In Greek legend, the daughter of Priam, King of Troy. She was favoured by Apollo, who gave her the gift of prophecy. Because she did not return his love, he decreed that she would never be believed. After the fall of Troy she was murdered on her arrival in Argos. >> Apollo; Trojan War

Cassatt, Mary [ka**sat**] (1844–1926) Impressionist painter, born in Allegheny, PA. A pupil and close follower of Degas, she was renowned for her etching and drypoint studies of domestic scenes. >> Degas; Impressionism

cassava A food plant (*Manihot esculenta*), also called **manioc**, important throughout the tropics. It ranges from low herbs to shrubs or slender trees, with fleshy, tuberous roots and fan-shaped, 5–9-lobed leaves. The raw roots are poisonous without treatment. It can then be made into a wide range of products, including cassava flour, bread, and tapioca. (Family: Euphorbiaceae.)

Cassegrain telescope [**kas**uhgran] A telescope designed by French scientist N Cassegrain in 1672, and now the commonest optical system for a telescope. It has a paraboloid primary mirror with a central hole, a hyperboloid secondary mounted inside the focus of the primary, and the eyepiece behind the primary. A variant of it, the Schmidt-Cassegrain, has a thin correcting lens as well, and is popular for amateur astronomy. >> telescope [i]

Cassidy, Butch, originally **Robert LeRoy Parker** (1866–?1909) Outlaw, born in Beaver, UT. He joined the infamous Wild Bunch and was partner with the Sundance Kid, robbing banks, trains, and mine stations with the law in constant pursuit. From 1901 they lived mainly in South America, where (according to one theory) they were trapped and killed. >> Sundance Kid

Cassini, Giovanni Domenico [ka**see**nee], also known as **Jean Dominique Cassini** (1625–1712) Astronomer, born in Perinaldo, Italy. In 1669 he became the first director of the observatory at Paris. **Cassini's division** (the gap between two of Saturn's rings) is named after him. **Cassini's laws**, describing the rotation of the Moon, were formulated in 1693. >> astronomy; Moon; Saturn

Cassiopeia [kasioh**pee**a] A large N constellation that includes rich star fields in the Milky Way. It contains **Cassiopeia A**, the strongest radio source in the sky after the Sun. >> constellation; Milky Way; RR968

Cassirer, Ernst [ka**see**rer] (1874–1945) Neo-Kantian philosopher, born in Wrocław, Poland (formerly Breslau, Prussia). His best-known work, *Die Philosophie der symbolischen Formen* (1923–9, The Philosophy of Symbolic Forms), analyses the symbolic functions underlying all human thought, language, and culture. >> Kant

Cassius [**ka**sius], in full **Gaius Cassius Longinus** (?–42 BC) Roman soldier and politician. Despite gaining political advancement through Caesar, he later turned against him and played a leading part in the conspiracy to murder him (44 BC). Defeated by Caesar's avengers at Philippi (42 BC), he committed suicide. >> Brutus; Caesar; Philippi, Battle of

Casson, Sir Hugh (Maxwell) [**ka**sn] (1910–) British architect. He directed the architecture of the Festival of Britain (1951), and was professor of interior design at the Royal College of Art (1953–75).

cassowary [**ka**sohwairee] A large flightless bird native to S Australasia; naked head has a bony outgrowth (*casque*), used as a shovel to uncover food; feet with long claws; its kick may be fatal. (Genus: *Casuarius*, 3 species. Family: Casuariidae.) >> emu

castanets Pairs of wooden (usually chestnut) discs, slightly concave, worn on the thumbs and clicked together rhythmically to accompany dancing, especially in Spain. >> idiophone

caste A system of inequality, most prevalent in Hindu Indian society, in which status is determined by the membership of a particular lineage and associated occupational group into which a person is born. Contact between castes is held to be polluting, and must be avoided.

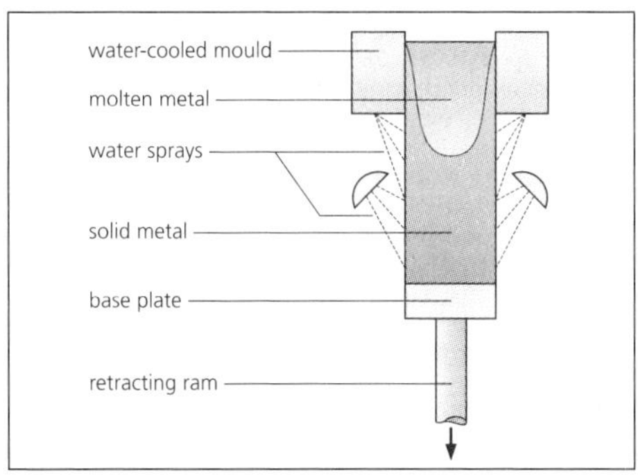

Casting process for aluminium

Castiglione, Baldassare, conte di (Count of) **Novilara** [kasteel**yoh**nay] (1478–1529) Writer and diplomat, born near Mantua, Italy. His chief work, *Il cortegiano* (1528, The Courtier), is a manual for courtiers.

casting The pouring of molten metal into a mould, where it solidifies into an ingot of manageable size for further processing, or into a desired final shape. Some metals can be **continuously cast**, solidified metal being removed at one end of a continuous length as more molten metal is added at the beginning. Some alloys (often containing zinc) can be **die-cast**, ie cast under pressure into a complex re-usable mould to give intricate shapes. >> alloy; cast iron; cire perdue; metal

cast iron The primary product of the blast furnace: iron with about 4% carbon (**pig iron**). It has a low melting point and solidifies well into the shape of the mould. It is therefore valuable for casting, but has to be purified or modified before being used for manufacture. >> blast furnace [i]; iron

Castle (of Blackburn), Barbara (Anne) Castle, Baroness, *née* **Betts** (1911–) British stateswoman, born in Bradford, West Yorkshire. She was a controversial minister of transport (1965–8), introducing a 70 mph speed limit and the 'breathalyser' test. She became secretary of state for employment and productivity (1968–70) and for social services (1974–6), and a member of the European Parliament, where she was vice-chair of the Socialist group (1979–86). She became a life peer in 1990. >> European Parliament; Labour Party

castle One of the products of feudal society as it spread across Europe and into the Crusader kingdoms. Found in France from the mid-10th-c, they reached England as a result of the Norman Conquest, where they were built in large numbers by the new Norman elite. The earliest English castles were normally earthen mounds surrounded by ditches and topped by wooden towers. In 12th-c England, castle-builders increasingly used stone for towers and walls, and in the 13th-c Edward I built a fine series of castles in Wales (eg Caernarfon, Conwy, Harlech). Castles served as residences, seats of justice, administrative centres, and symbols of lordly authority. Later, especially in England, increasing emphasis was placed on their non-military roles, with greater concessions to domestic comfort and ornamental display. >> Balmoral / Hradčany / Maiden / Nijo-jo / Windsor Castle; chateau

Castlebar [kas**lbah(r)**], Ir **Caisleán an Bharraigh** 53°52N 9°17W, pop (1995e) 7600. Capital of Mayo county, W Ireland; residential and agricultural market town; Irish Land League founded here in 1879; airfield; railway. >> Ireland (republic) i; Mayo

Castlereagh, Robert Stewart, Viscount [**kas**lray] (1769–1822) British statesman, born in Dublin. His major achievements date from 1812, when, as foreign secretary under Lord Liverpool, he was at the heart of the coalition against Napoleon (1813–14). He represented Britain at Chaumont and Vienna (1814–15), Paris (1815), and Aix-la-Chapelle (1818), advocating 'Congress diplomacy' to avoid further warfare. >> Canning; Napoleon I; Vienna, Congress of

Castor and Pollux, Gr **Kastor** and **Polydeuces** Two heroes of classical mythology, known as the **Dioscuri**, usually pictured as twin brothers on horseback. They were children of Leda, at least one being fathered by Zeus. After death they became divine beings, and were turned into the constellation Gemini. >> Gemini; Leda

castor-oil plant An evergreen plant (*Ricinus communis*), in its native tropics forming a tall shrub or tree, in temperate regions only a stout herb; flowers tiny, green, in dense clusters; processed seeds yield castor oil. (Family: Euphorbiaceae.) >> herb; ricin

castration The surgical removal of the sex glands (testes or ovaries). When carried out in children, the secondary sexual characteristics do not develop. In adults physical changes are less marked, but the individuals are sterile. In contrast with surgical castration, medical castration consists of giving a male a female sex hormone, and is usually undertaken for cancer. >> castrato; ovarian follicle; testis

castrato A male singer who underwent castration before puberty in order to preserve his treble voice. The practice probably originated at the Vatican in the 16th-c to compensate for the absence of women's voices from the choirs. Castrati took many of the leading roles in Italian opera during the 17th-c and 18th-c. >> castration

Castries [**kas**trees] 14°01N 60°59W, pop (1995e) 53 600. Port capital of St Lucia; founded, 1650; rebuilt after a fire in 1948; airport. >> St Lucia

Castro (Ruz), Fidel (1927–) Cuban revolutionary, prime minister (1959–), and president (1976–), born near Birán. He led a successful rising against Batista in 1958, proclaimed a 'Marxist–Leninist programme', and set about far-reaching reforms. His overthrow of US economic dominance, and the routing of the US-connived emigré invasion at the Bay of Pigs (1961) was balanced by his dependence on Russian aid. >> Batista; Bay of Pigs; Cuba i

cat A carnivorous mammal of the family Felidae; name popularly used for the domestic cat, *Felis catus*, other species having individual names (lion, tiger, etc); domestic cats known in Egypt 4000 years ago and may have evolved there from the **wild cat** (or **caffre cat**); numerous modern breeds; male called a *tom*, female a *queen*, young are *kittens*. >> Abyssinian / Angora / Manx / pampas / Persian / Siamese / tortoiseshell / wild cat; bobcat; carnivore i; civet; Felidae; genet; Russian blue

catabolism >> **metabolism**

catacombs Subterranean Jewish or early Christian cemeteries found in certain parts of the Roman world – notably Rome itself. The practice is believed to have been derived from ancient Jewish cave burials.

Catalan >> **Romance languages**

Catalaunian Plains, Battle of the [kata**law**nian] The decisive defeat in E France suffered by Attila the Hun at the hands of the Romans and Visigoths. >> Attila

catalepsy The adoption of a body posture which would normally be unsustainable; also referred to as **waxy flexibility**. It occurs in serious psychotic illness or as a hysterical reaction. >> catatonia; hysteria; psychosis

Çatal Hüyük [cha**tahl hoo**yuk] A prehistoric riverside settlement of c.6500–5500 BC in S Turkey, the largest Neolithic site known in the Near East. The *tell* (mound) is 20 m/65 ft high, and covers 13 ha/32 acres. >> tell; Three Age System

Catalonia [kata**loh**nia], Span **Cataluña**, Catalan **Catalunya** pop (1995e) 6 008 000 area 31 932 sq km/12 320 sq mi. Autonomous region of NE Spain, with a distinctive culture and Romance language; united with Aragon, 1137; part of Spain following union of Castilian and Aragonese crowns, 1469–79; strong separatist movement since the 17th-c; Catalan republic established, 1932; abolished by Franco during the Civil War, 1936–9; new government established, 1979; industry centred on Barcelona; major tourist resorts on the Costa Brava. >> Franco; Romance languages; Spain i; Spanish Civil War

catalysis [ka**tal**isis] The acceleration or slowing of a chemical reaction by the action of a material (**catalyst**) which is recovered unchanged at the end of the reaction. Catalysts include iron in the Haber process for ammonia, and chlorophyll in photosynthesis. >> chemical reaction; photosynthesis

catalytic converter An antipollution device often fitted to a car exhaust system. It contains a platinum catalyst for chemically converting unburned hydrocarbons and nitrogen oxides to compounds harmless to the environment. >> pollution

catamaran [**kat**amaran, katama**ran**] A twin-hulled vessel of Tamil origin, offering advantages in speed and stability. Propelled nowadays either by sail or power, it has become very popular as a yacht design in the past 25 years, and the advantages of the design have also proved attractive to firms introducing a new generation of car/passenger ferries. >> trimaran; yacht i

catamount >> **cougar**

Catania [ka**tah**nia] 37°31N 15°06E, pop (1995e) 366 000. Port in Sicily, S Italy; at foot of Mt Etna, on E coast; archbishopric; airport; railway; university (1444). >> Etna, Mount; Sicily

cataract Developing opacities in the lens of the eye which cause slowly progressive loss of vision. Senile cataract is the most common type, but cataracts may also follow excessive exposure to ultraviolet light or injury to the eye, as well as being a complication of diabetes and other conditions. When severe, the lens can be removed and the vision corrected with the aid of spectacles and a lens implantation. >> eye i; lens

catastrophe theory The mathematical study of sudden change, in contrast to continuous change. For example, in Necker's cube, the dot ● appears first either in the centre of one face or in a corner of another face, then suddenly changes. It is not possible to say in which face any one viewer will first see it, but it always changes suddenly. Catastrophe theory was created in the late 1950s by French mathematician René Thom (1923–) and developed in particular by Stephen Smale, Vladimir Arnold, Christopher Zeeman, and others. >> *see illustration on p. 157*

catatonia A psychiatric state in which there is stupor associated with catalepsy, or overactivity associated with stereotyped behaviour. This condition was first described by the German physician Karl Ludwig Kahlbaum (1828–99) in 1874, and is seen particularly in manic-depressive illnesses and schizophrenia. >> catalepsy; schizophrenia

Catch-22 The title of a novel by Joseph Heller, published in 1961. US airmen seeking to be excused bombing missions in World War 2 on grounds of mental derangement are judged ineligible to apply, since such a request proves their sanity. Hence 'Catch-22' signifies any logical trap or double bind. >> Heller

catchfly An annual or perennial herb, part of the same genus as campions, but with hairy, sticky stem; native to the temperate N hemisphere; five petals, white, pink, or yellow. (Genus: *Silene*. Family: Caryophyllaceae.) >> campion

catechism A manual of Christian doctrine, usually in question-and-answer form. It derived from the early Church period of instruction for new converts, and was later applied to the instruction of adults baptized in infancy. Some have avoided the question-and-answer format, such as the Roman Catholic 'New Catechism' of 1966 and the 'Universal Catechism' of 1992. >> Christianity

catecholamine [kate**kohl**ameen] The chemical classification of a group of biologically important components widely distributed among animals and plants. Those occurring in mammalian tissues are dopamine, noradrenaline, and adrenaline. They are crucial in the control of blood pressure, and in the 'flight or fight' response. >> adrenaline; dopamine; nervous system

caterpillar The larval stage of butterflies and moths (Order: Lepidoptera), usually feeding on plants; occasionally also used for the larvae of sawflies. (Order: Hymenoptera.) >> butterfly; moth

caterpillar bird >> **cuckoo shrike**

Catesby, Robert [**kayts**bee] (1573–1605) Chief conspirator in the Gunpowder Plot (1605), born in Lapworth, Warwickshire. A Catholic of wealth and lineage, he had suffered much as a recusant both by fines and imprisonment. He was shot dead while resisting arrest after the plot's failure. >> Gunpowder Plot

catfish Any of about 28 families of typically elongate bottom-living fishes; flattened head, smooth skin, long barbels around mouth; includes freshwater Siluridae, Bagridae, Clariidae, Ictaluridae, and marine Ariidae, Plotosidae. >> wels

cat flu A highly infectious viral disease of the upper respiratory tract of cats. Ulceration of the tongue and palate as well as obstruction of the nasal passages leads to lack of appetite and further debility. Recovered cats can remain as carriers, and may start to shed the virus when stressed. Cats may be protected by the use of vaccines, and most cat-boarding establishments require evidence of up-to-date vaccination before accepting an animal. >> cat; virus

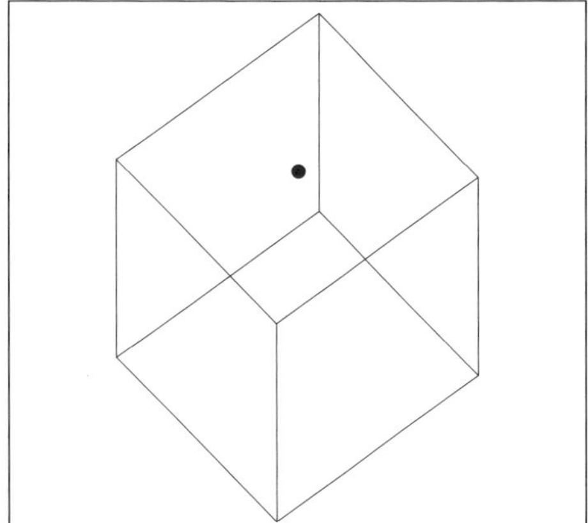

Catastrophe theory: Necker's cube

catgut A tough cord prepared from the intestines of sheep (sometimes horse or ass, but never a cat). It has been used for musical instrument strings and surgical sutures. *Cat* seems to be derived from *kit* 'fiddle'. >> kit

Cathars [**kath**ah(r)z] (Gr *kathari* 'pure ones') Originally, 3rd-c separatists from the Church, puritan and ascetic, following the teaching of the 3rd-c Roman bishop Novatian. In the Middle Ages, as a sect, they were known in Bulgaria as **Bogomils** and in France as **Albigenses**. They survived until the 14th-c. >> Albigenses

cathartid vulture >> **vulture**

cathedral (Lat *cathedra*, 'chair') The chief church of a bishop of a diocese; originally, the church which contained the throne of the bishop, then the mother church of the diocese. The most famous are the W European Gothic cathedrals built in the Middle Ages, such as those at Reims and Chartres, France (both 13th-c). >> bishop; Chartres; church ℹ; Córdoba / St Basil's / St Mark's / St Paul's Cathedral; Notre Dame; St Peter's Basilica

Catherine II, known as **Catherine the Great**, originally **Princess Sophie Friederike Auguste von Anhalt-Zerbst** (1729–96) Empress of Russia (1762–96), born in Stettin. She carried out an energetic foreign policy and extended the Russian Empire S to the Black Sea as a result of the Russo-Turkish Wars (1774, 1792), while in the W she brought about the three partitions of Poland (1772, 1793, 1795). In 1774 she suppressed the popular rebellion led by Pugachev. Her private life was dominated by a long series of lovers, most notably Potemkin. >> Potemkin; Pugachev; Romanovs; Russo-Turkish Wars

Catherine de' Medici [**may**deechee] (1519–89) Queen of France, wife of Henry II, and Regent (1560–74), born in Florence, the daughter of Lorenzo de' Medici. During the minority of her sons, Francis II (1559–60) and Charles IX (1560–3), she assumed political influence, which she retained as Queen Mother until 1588. She was drawn into political and religious intrigues, conniving in the infamous Massacre of St Bartholomew (1572). >> Henry II (of France); Huguenots

Catherine of Aragon [**a**ragon] (1485–1536) Queen of England, the first wife of Henry VIII (1509–33), and fourth daughter of Ferdinand and Isabella of Spain, born in Alcalá de Henares, Spain. She was first married in 1501 to Arthur (1486–1502), elder son of Henry VII, and following his early death was betrothed to her brother-in-law Henry, then a boy of 11. She bore him five children, but only the Princess Mary survived. Henry divorced her in 1533, and she retired to an austere religious life. >> Henry VIII (of England); Reformation

Catherine of Braganza [bra**gan**za] (1638–1705) Wife of Charles II of England, the daughter of King John IV of Portugal, born in Vila Viçosa, Portugal. She was married to Charles in 1662 as part of an alliance between England and Portugal, but failed to produce an heir. >> Charles II (of England)

Catherine of Siena, St [**syay**na], originally **Caterina Benincasa** (1347–80) Dominican nun and mystic, born in Siena, Italy. She prevailed on Pope Gregory XI to return the papacy from Avignon to Rome. Christ's stigmata were said to be imprinted on her body. She was canonized in 1461, and is the patron saint of Italy. Feast day 29 April. >> Dominicans; stigmata

catheter [**kath**eter] A fine tube made of rubber or synthetic material for insertion into body cavities, such as the bladder and blood vessels. It is used either to introduce or to withdraw fluid or blood for analysis, or to measure pressure or rates of flow. >> blood vessels ℹ

cathode The positive terminal in a battery. In cathode-ray tubes (eg television tubes) and thermionic valves, a heated cathode is a source of electrons. In electrolysis, cations (positive ions) move towards the cathode. For a battery in a completed circuit, positive current flows from the cathode through the circuit to the **anode**. >> anode; electrolysis ℹ; thermionics; valve

cathode rays >> **electron**

cathode-ray tube (CRT) An electronic device in which an image is formed on a phosphor screen in a vacuum tube by a beam of electrons deflected in electric or magnetic fields. It is used in oscilloscopes, display screens, and television receivers. >> shadow-mask tube ℹ

Catholic Church (Gr *katholikos*, 'general', 'universal') **1** As in the Apostles' Creed, the universal Church which confesses Jesus Christ as Lord. >> Apostles' Creed; Jesus Christ **2** Christian Churches with episcopal order and confessing ancient creeds. >> episcopacy **3** Specifically, the Roman Catholic Church and other Churches recognizing the primacy of the Pope. >> papacy; Roman Catholicism

Catholic Emancipation A reluctant religious concession granted by the British Tory government in 1829, following mounting agitation led by Daniel O'Connell and the Catholic Association. Roman Catholics were permitted to become MPs; and certain offices of state in Ireland were opened to Catholics. >> O'Connell; Roman Catholicism; Tories

Catiline [**kat**iliyn], in full **Lucius Sergius Catilina** (c.108–62 BC) An impoverished Roman politician who tried to exploit the economic unrest of Rome in the 60s BC for his own political ends. His conspiracy against the state was foiled by Cicero in 63 BC. >> Cicero

cation [**kat**iyon] An ion bearing a positive charge, so called because it will migrate towards the cathode in an electrochemical cell. >> anion; cathode

catmint A square-stemmed perennial (*Nepeta cataria*), growing to 1 m/40 in, native to Europe and Asia; flowers 2-lipped, white spotted with purple, in whorls forming spikes; also called **catnip**. A relative of true mints, its strong scent is attractive to cats. (Family: Labiatae.) >> mint

catnip >> **catmint**

Cato, Marcus Porcius [**kay**toh], known as **Cato the Elder** or **Cato the Censor** (234–149 BC) Roman statesman, orator, and man of letters. Sent on a mission to Carthage (c.157 BC), he was so impressed by the power of the Carthaginians that afterwards he ended every speech in the Senate with the words: 'Carthage must be destroyed'. >> Punic Wars

Cato, Marcus Porcius [**kay**toh], known as **Cato the Younger** or **Cato Uticensis** (95–46 BC) Roman statesman, the great-grandson of Cato the Censor. His career was marked by an unswerving opposition to Caesar. A supporter of Pompey in the Civil War, after Pharsalus (48 BC) he escaped to Africa. >> Caesar; Roman history ℹ

Cato Street conspiracy [**kay**toh] A plot in February 1820, formulated by Arthur Thistlewood (1770–1820) and fellow radical conspirators, to blow up the British Tory Cabinet as it attended a dinner at the house of the Earl of Harrowby. The plot was infiltrated by a government agent, and the leaders were arrested and hanged. >> radicalism; Tories

CAT scanning >> **computerized tomography**

cat's eyes Rubber road studs fitted with a pair of light reflectors, designed to mark road lanes at night by reflecting a vehicle's headlights; devised by UK inventor Percy Shaw in 1934. The device can be compressed by the vehicle's wheels without doing damage to itself or the wheel.

Catskill Mountains Mountain group in SE New York State, USA; part of the Appalachian system; rises to 1282 m/ 4206 ft at Slide Mt. >> Appalachian Mountains; New York

cat's tail >> **reedmace**

cattalo >> **bison**

cattle Domesticated mammals, developed from wild aurochs (*Bos taurus*); now worldwide with numerous breeds; kept for milk and/or meat or for hauling loads; also known as **oxen**. (Family: Bovidae.) >> anoa; aurochs; Bovidae; bovine mastitis / milk fever; bull (zoology); shorthorn; yak; zebu

cattle plague >> **rinderpest**

cattleya [**kat**lia] An orchid (mainly an epiphyte) native to the forests of Central and South America. Most kinds have swollen, bulb-like stems (*pseudobulbs*) bearing 1–3 leaves, and spikes of up to 47 large, showy flowers. They are one of the most widely used orchids of floristry. (Genus: *Cattleya*, 30 species. Family: Orchidaceae.) >> epiphyte; orchid ℹ

Catullus, Gaius Valerius [ka**tuhl**us] (c.84–c.54 BC) Lyric poet, born in Verona, Italy. He settled in Rome (c.62 BC), where he met 'Lesbia' whom he addressed in his verses. His extant works comprise 116 pieces, many of them extremely brief.

Caucasus Mountains [**kaw**kasus], Russ **Kavkaz** Major mountain system in SW Europe and Asia; comprises the **Greater Caucasus** and the **Lesser Caucasus**; extends c.1120 km/700 mi SE; in the W is Mt Elbrus (5642 m/ 18 510 ft).

caucus A meeting, public or private, restricted to persons sharing a common characteristic, usually membership of a political party, held to formulate decisions or nominate candidates in forthcoming elections. It is most often applied to the USA, where the caucus–convention system is significant in selecting presidential and vice-presidential candidates, and where caucuses are the authoritative voice of the parties in Congress. >> Congress

cauliflower A type of cultivated cabbage (*Brassica oleracea*) grown for the immature inflorescence which forms the edible white head. (Family: Cruciferae.) >> brassica; cabbage; inflorescence ℹ

Causley, Charles [**kawz**lee] (1917–) Poet, born in Launceston, Cornwall. He became known as a poet of the sea, and also as a children's poet. His *Collected Poems 1951–1997* were published in 1997.

caustic In chemistry, descriptive of substances (normally strongly alkaline) which are destructive, particularly to biological tissue. **Caustic soda** is sodium hydroxide; **caustic potash** is potassium hydroxide. >> alkali

Cavalcanti, Guido [kaval**kan**tee] (c.1230–1300) Poet, born in Florence, Italy. He was a friend of Dante, and wrote about 50 poems in the 'new style' of the period. >> Dante

Cavalier poets Poets of the mid-17th-c who supported Charles I in the Civil War. Their (mostly love) poems are characterized by urbanity, elegance, and wit. >> Carew; Herrick; Lovelace; Waller

Cavaliers Those who fought for Charles I in the English Civil War. The name was used derogatorily in 1642 by supporters of Parliament to describe swaggering courtiers with long hair and swords, who reportedly welcomed the prospect of war. Similarly, the Parliamentarians were labelled 'Roundheads' by Cavaliers, dating from the riotous assemblies in Westminster during Strafford's trial in 1641, when short-haired apprentices mobbed Charles I's supporters outside the House of Lords. >> English Civil War; Strafford

Cavan [**ka**vn] pop (1995e) 52 400; area 1891 sq km/ 730 sq mi. County in NC Ireland; capital, Cavan; pop (1995e) 5200. >> Ireland (republic) ℹ; Ulster

cave A natural cavity in the Earth's surface, generally hollowed out by the action of water, and most spectacularly developed in limestones (soluble in mildly acid rainwater), in which huge vaults and interconnected river systems may form. Caves are also made by the action of sea water against cliffs. >> Altamira; Lascaux; limestone; speleology; RR972

cave art >> **Palaeolithic art**

cavefish Small blind North American fish confined to limestone caves of SE states; body lacking pigment (Genera: *Amblyopsis, Typhlichthys*, four species); also two species (Genus: *Chologaster*) with small eyes and pigmented skin from coastal swamps. (Family: Amblyopsidae.)

Cavell, Edith [ka**vel**] (1865–1915) Nurse, born in Swardeston, Norfolk. Matron of the Berkendael Institute, Brussels, she tended friend and foe alike, yet was executed by the Germans for helping Belgian and Allied fugitives to escape capture.

Cavendish, Henry (1731–1810) Physicist and chemist, born in Nice, France. In 1760 he studied the 'inflammable air', now known as hydrogen gas; and later ascertained that water resulted from the union of two gases. The 'Cavendish Experiment' was an ingenious means of estimating the density of the Earth.

Cavendish, Spencer Compton, 8th Duke of Devonshire, known as the **Marquess of Hartington** (1858–91) (1833–1908) British statesman, born in Lower Holker, Lancashire. In 1875 he became Leader of the Liberal Opposition during Gladstone's temporary abdication, and led the breakaway from the Liberal Party, becoming head of the Liberal Unionists from 1886. His younger brother, **Lord Frederick Cavendish** (1836–82), was also a Liberal MP (1865–82). He was appointed chief secretary for Ireland, but immediately after his arrival in Dublin was murdered by 'Irish Invincibles' in Phoenix Park. >> Gladstone; Liberal Party (UK)

caviar The prepared roe (eggs) of the female sturgeon, beluga, sevruga, and starlet. These fish are caught in the winter months in the rivers flowing into the Baltic Sea and the Danube. >> sturgeon

Cavour, Camillo Benso, conte di (Count of) [ka**voor**] (1810–61) Piedmontese statesman who brought about the unification of Italy (1861), born in Turin. As premier (1852–9), he brought the Italian question before the Congress of Paris, and in 1860 secretly encouraged the expedition of Garibaldi. >> Garibaldi; Italy [i]

cavy A rodent native to South America; includes **guinea pigs** (Genus: *Cavia*), and a wide range of cavy-like rodents. (Family: Caviidae, 15 species.) >> acouchi; agouti; capybara; chinchilla; coypu; paca; porcupine; rodent; viscacha

Caxton, William (c.1422–c.1491) The first English printer, born possibly in the Weald of Kent. In Cologne (1471–2) he probably learned the art of printing, and soon after printed the first book in English, *The Recuyell of the Historyes of Troye* (1475). A year later he set up his wooden press at Westminster. Of about 100 books printed by him, over a third survive only in unique copies or fragments. >> printing [i]

Cayenne [ka**yen**] 4°55N 52°18W, pop (1995e) 51 300. Port capital of French Guiana, NE South America; founded, 1643; used as penal settlement, 1854–1938; airport; source of Cayenne pepper. >> French Guiana

cayenne >> **pepper 1**

Cayley, Sir George [**kay**lee] (1771–1857) Pioneer of aviation, born in Scarborough, North Yorkshire. In 1808 he constructed and flew a glider, probably the first heavier-than-air machine, and in 1853 made the first successful man-carrying glider. >> aircraft [i]; glider

cayman >> **caiman**

Cayman Islands [**kay**man] pop (1995e) 33 000; area 260 sq km/100 sq mi. British overseas territory in the W Caribbean, comprising the islands of Grand Cayman, Cayman Brac, and Little Cayman, c.240 km/150 mi S of Cuba; capital, George Town; timezone GMT −5; population mainly of mixed descent (c.60%); chief religion, Christianity; official language, English; unit of currency, the Cayman Is dollar of 100 cents; low-lying, rising to 42 m/138 ft on Cayman Brac plateau; tropical climate; visited by Columbus, 1503; ceded to Britain, 1670; British Crown Colony, 1962; a governor represents the British sovereign, and presides over a Legislative Assembly; economic activities mainly tourism, international finance, property development; over 450 banks and trust companies established on the islands. >> George Town

Cazaly, Roy [ka**zay**lee] (1893–1963) Legendary Australian Rules footballer, born in Melbourne, Victoria, Australia. Leaping master of the high mark (jumping above other players to catch the ball), the call 'Up there Cazaly' was chanted by South Melbourne crowds and became a rallying cry for Australian troops in World War 2. >> football [i]

CBE >> **British Empire, Order of the**

CBI >> **Confederation of British Industry**

CD >> **compact disc**

CD-ROM [seedee**rom**] An acronym of **Compact Disc Read Only Memory**, a computer storage medium based on the use of the standard 5 in (25 mm) compact disc, licensed by Sony and Philips, and usually used for digital audio. One CD-ROM disc can store more than 600 megabytes of computer information. A read-only device, the main applications have been in providing access to large volumes of information such as encyclopedias. >> byte; compact disc; magnetic disk; ROM

Ceanannus Mór, formerly **Kells** 53°44N 6°53W, pop (1995e) 3510. Urban district in Meath county, E Ireland; noted for its monastery (founded by St Columba); **Book of Kells** (now in Trinity College, Dublin) produced there c.800. >> Columba, St; Ireland (republic) [i]; Meath

Ceauşescu, Nicolae [chow**shes**koo] (1918–1989) Romanian statesman and president, born in Scorniceşti. He became general secretary of the Romanian Communist Party in 1969, and under his leadership, Romania became increasingly independent of the USSR. As the first president of the Republic in 1974, he established a strong personality cult. In 1989 he was deposed when the army joined a popular revolt against his repressive government. Following a trial by military tribunal, he and his wife, Elena, were shot. >> Romania [i]

Cech, Thomas R [chek] (1947–) Biochemist, born in Chicago, IL. He showed that RNA could have an independent catalytic function aiding a chemical reaction without being consumed or changed. This had major implications for genetic engineering, as well as for understanding how life arose, and he shared the 1989 Nobel Prize for Chemistry.

Cecil, Robert (Arthur Talbot Gascoyne), 3rd Marquess of Salisbury [**se**sil] (1830–1903) British Conservative statesman and prime minister (1885–6, 1886–92, 1895–1902), born in Hatfield, Hertfordshire. Much of the time as prime minister he served as his own foreign secretary. He was head of government during the Boer War (1899–1902). >> Boer Wars

Cecil, William, 1st Baron Burghley or **Burghleigh** [**se**sil] (1520–98) English statesman, born in Bourn, Lincolnshire. In 1558 Elizabeth appointed him chief secretary of state, and for the next 40 years he was the chief architect of Elizabethan greatness, influencing her pro-Protestant foreign policy, securing the execution of Mary, Queen of Scots, and preparing for the Spanish Armada. He used an army of spies to ensure security at home. >> Elizabeth I

Cecilia, St (2nd-c or 3rd-c) Patroness of music, especially church music. She was a convert to Christianity, and is said to have suffered martyrdom at Rome. Feast day 22 November. >> Christianity

cedar An evergreen conifer with a massive trunk and flat, wide-spreading crown, native to the mountains of N Africa, the Himalayas, and the E Mediterranean; needles sometimes bluish, in tufts; timber fragrant and oily. (Genus: *Cedrus*, 4 species. Family: Pinaceae.) >> arbor vitae; conifer

Ceefax [**see**faks] A UK teletext system operated by the British Broadcasting Corporation since 1974. The name derives from 'see facts'. >> teletext

Celebes >> **Sulawesi**

celeriac A variety of celery (*Apium graveolens* variety *rapaceum*), also called **turnip-rooted celery**, with a tuberous base to the stems, cooked as a vegetable or used in salads. (Family: Umbelliferae.) >> celery; tuber

celery A strong-smelling biennial herb (*Apium graveolens*), growing to 1 m/3$\frac{1}{4}$ ft, native to Europe, SW Asia, and N Africa; stems deeply grooved; flowers minute, greenish-white. (Family: Umbelliferae.) >> celeriac; herb; vegetable

celesta A musical instrument resembling a small upright piano, but with metal plates instead of strings and a shorter (five-octave) compass. It was invented in 1886 by French instrument maker Auguste Mustel (1842–1919). >> keyboard instrument; percussion [i]

celestial equator The great circle in which the plane of the Earth's equator cuts the celestial sphere. This is the primary circle for the co-ordinates' right ascension and declination. >> celestial sphere; Equator

celestial mechanics The study of the motions of celestial objects in gravitational fields. Founded by Isaac Newton, it deals with satellite and planetary motion within the Solar System, using Newtonian gravitational theory. >> gravity [i]; Newton, Isaac; Solar System

celestial sphere An imaginary sphere surrounding the Earth, used as a reference frame to specify the positions of celestial objects on the sky. Its N and S poles lie over those of Earth, and its equator is the projection of the terrestrial Equator. >> celestial equator; nadir

Céline, Louis-Ferdinand [sayleen], pseudonym of **Louis-Ferdinand Destouches** (1894–1961) Writer, born in Paris. His reputation is based on the two autobiographical novels he wrote during the 1930s: *Voyage au bout de la nuit* (1932, Journey to the End of the Night) and *Mort à crédit* (1936, trans Death by Instalments).

cell The basic unit of plant and animal bodies; it comprises, at least, a nucleus or nuclear material and cytoplasm enclosed within a cell membrane. Many cells contain other specialized structures (*organelles*), such as mitochondria, chloroplasts, Golgi bodies, and flagella. Many simple organisms comprise a single cell, and may lack a membrane separating nuclear material from cytoplasm. Advanced organisms consist of a variety of co-operating cells, often specialized to perform particular functions and organized into tissues and organs. Plant cells are typically surrounded by an outer cell wall containing cellulose. Cell division may occur by splitting into two parts (*fission*), by mitosis, and (in the case of reproductive cells) by meiosis. All nucleated cells contain within their nuclei the entire inherited genetic information of that individual, but in specialized cells, such as a liver or brain cell, only a minute fraction of their genetic database is operational. >> cellulose; chloroplast; cytoplasm; fission; flagellum; genetics; meiosis [i]; mitochondrion; mitosis; nucleus (biology)

Cellini, Benvenuto [che**lee**nee] (1500–71) Goldsmith, sculptor, engraver, and author, born in Florence, Italy. He is particularly known for his autobiography (1558–62). At the siege of Rome (1527), he killed the Constable de Bourbon. His best work includes the gold saltcellar made for Francis I of France, and his bronze 'Perseus'.

cello or **violoncello** [**chel**oh] The bass instrument of the violin family, with four strings tuned one octave below the viola's. The modern instrument is fitted with an adjustable endpin which rests on the floor. >> string instrument 1 [i]

cellophane >> **cellulose**

cellular radio >> **mobile communications**

cellulite According to certain beauty experts, the dimpled fat around the thighs and buttocks, which is said to resist dieting. However, available scientific evidence shows that when an individual diets, fat is lost from all fat deposits in the body. >> diet

cellulitis [selyoo**liy**tis] The bacterial infection of connective tissue, spreading between layers of tissue and adjacent organs. It is potentially dangerous, as the infection may enter the bloodstream, and is best treated by an appropriate antibiotic.

celluloid The earliest commercial plastic (c.1865–9), consisting of cellulose nitrate plasticized with camphor. It had the great virtue of dimensional stability, which kept it in vogue for photographic film in spite of its dangerous inflammability. It was eventually superseded as a film base by dimensionally stable forms of cellulose acetate. >> film; nitrocellulose

cellulose $(C_6H_{10}O_5)_n$. A structural polysaccharide found mainly in the cell walls of woody and fibrous plant material, such as cotton. It is the main raw material for paper. Important derivatives include rayon (**cellulose acetate**) and guncotton (**cellulose nitrate** or **nitrocellulose**). >> nitrocellulose; polysaccharide

celostat >> **coelostat**

Celsius A scale that takes the triple point of water to be 0·01°C, which corresponds roughly to taking the freezing point of water as 0°C and the boiling point as 100°C; named after Swedish astronomer Anders Celsius (1701–44); still often called by the old name *degrees Centigrade*. >> phases of matter [i]; temperature [i]

Celtiberia [kelti**beer**ia] The territory in NC Spain inhabited by the Celtiberians, a warlike people of mixed Celtic and Iberian ancestry. Staunch opponents of the Romans, they were pacified in 133 BC. >> Roman history [i]

Celtic languages [**kel**tik] The languages of the Celts. The dialects spoken on the continent are known as **Continental Celtic**; traces remain in several inscriptions and place-names in *Gaulish* and *Celtiberian*. **Insular Celtic** is the name given to the Celtic languages of the British Is and Brittany. There are two branches: *Goidelic* comprises the Gaelic spoken in Ireland (Irish or Erse), which spread to the Isle of Man (Manx) and Scotland (Gaelic); Welsh, Cornish, and Breton comprise the *Brythonic* (also called the *Brittonic* or *British*) branch. >> Breton; Celts; Cornish; Gaelic; Irish; Welsh

Celtic Sea [**kel**tik] Part of the Atlantic Ocean S of Ireland; separated from the Irish Sea by St George's Channel; main inlet, Bristol Channel; average depths of 100–200 m/330–650 ft. >> Atlantic Ocean

Celts Different groups of peoples who probably originated in present-day France, S Germany, and adjacent territories during the Bronze Age, and developed in the later first millennium BC. Celtic-speaking societies expanded through armed raids into the Iberian Peninsula, British Is, C Europe, Italy, Greece, Anatolia, Egypt, Bulgaria, Romania, Thrace, and Macedonia. They were finally repulsed by the Romans and Germanic tribes. They were famous for their burial sites and hill forts, and their bronze and iron art and jewellery. Their modern descendents are found chiefly in Ireland, Scotland, and Wales. >> Celtic languages

cement In general, any substance used to adhere to each of two materials which cannot themselves adhere. More usually, it refers to **Portland cement**, an artificial mineral substance used in building and engineering, made from heating clay and limestone. The addition of water produces a soft manageable substance which sets hard. It is commonly mixed with other mineral substances (sand, stone) to form various grades of concrete, or used as a mortar for joining brickwork. >> clay; limestone

Cenozoic era [seeno**zoh**ik], or **Cainozoic** [kayno**zoh**ik] The most recent of the four eras of geological time, beginning c. 65 million years ago and extending to the present day; subdivided into the *Tertiary* and *Quaternary* periods. It was characterized by widespread changes in the fauna, with the dominance of mammals and flowering plants. >> geological time scale; Quaternary period; Tertiary period; RR976

censors In Republican Rome (5th-c–1st-c BC), two officials (usually ex-consuls) elected every five years to compile a register of citizens and their property for military, legislative, electoral, and fiscal purposes. >> consul 1

census A count of the population resident in an area at a given time, together with the collection of social and economic data, made at regular intervals, often every ten years. The USA conducted its first national census in 1790, and France and the UK began to collect census data in 1801. The first Chinese census was AD 2, when the population was recorded at 59 594 978. >> demography; population ℹ

centaur [**sen**taw(r)] In Greek mythology, a creature combining the upper half of a man and the rear legs of a horse; later and more popularly imagined as having the entire body of a horse. Centaurs came from Thessaly, and most were beastly and wild. >> Chiron

Centaurus [sen**taw**rus] (Lat 'centaur') A large and rich S constellation. Its brightest star, **Alpha Centauri**, is actually three stars, the faintest of which, **Proxima Centauri**, is the closest star to the Sun, 1·31 parsec away from Earth. >> constellation; parsec

centaury An annual, sometimes perennial, found almost everywhere; flowers pink, tubular with 4–5 spreading lobes, borne in dense heads. (Genus: *Centaurium*, c.50 species. Family: Gentianaceae.)

centigrade >> **Celsius** (temperature)

centimetre >> **metre** (physics)

centipede A carnivorous, terrestrial arthropod, commonly found in soil, leaf litter, and rotting wood; body up to 30 cm/12 in long, divided into head (bearing feelers and mouthparts) and many-segmented trunk; each trunk segment has one pair of legs; c.2500 species, some venomous. (Class: Chilopoda.) >> arthropod

CENTO >> **Central Treaty Organization**

Central (Scotland) pop (1995e) 272 000; area 2631 sq km/1016 sq mi. Former (to 1996) region in C Scotland; replaced in 1996 by Stirling, Clackmannanshire, and Falkirk councils. >> Scotland ℹ; Stirling

Central African Republic, Fr **République Centrafricaine** pop (1995e) 3 422 000; area 622 984 sq km/240 535 sq mi. Republic in C Africa; capital, Bangui; timezone GMT +1; c.80 ethnic groups; religion, mainly Christianity (50%), with local and Muslim beliefs; official language, French, with Sango widely spoken; unit of currency, the franc CFA; on plateau forming watershed between Chad and Congo river basins; mean elevation, 600 m/2000 ft; single rainy season in N (May–Sep); more equatorial climate in S; part of French Equatorial Africa (Ubangi Shari); autonomous republic within the French community, 1958; independence, 1960; 1965 coup led to 1976 monarchy known as Central African Empire, under Bokassa I; Bokassa forced to flee, 1979 (returned in 1986 for trial; found guilty, 1987); military coup established Committee for National Recovery, 1981–5; National Assembly established, 1987; multiparty legislative and presidential elections, 1993; governed by a president, prime minister, and 85-member National Assembly; c.85% of working population engaged in subsistence agriculture. >> Bangui; RR1004 political leaders

Central America A geographical region that encompasses the independent states to the S of Mexico and to the N of South America; includes Guatemala, El Salvador, Belize, Honduras, Nicaragua, Costa Rica, and Panama. >> Central American Common Market; Middle America

Central American Common Market (CACM) An economic association initiated in 1960 between Guatemala, Honduras, El Salvador, Nicaragua, and (from 1963) Costa Rica. Its early apparent success was offset by growing political crisis in the late 1970s.

Central Committee Under Soviet party rules, the highest decision-making authority in the former USSR, apart from Congress, which elected it. It exercised little influence, partly because of its unwieldy size and partly because of the concentration of power in the Politburo. >> Politburo

Central Criminal Court >> **Old Bailey**

Central Intelligence Agency (CIA) The official US intelligence analysis organization responsible for external security, established under the National Security Act (1947). It suffered a loss of credibility following the investigation into the Watergate affair in the mid-1970s. >> Watergate

central nervous system (CNS) A collection of nerve cells connected in an intricate and complex manner, involved in the control of movement and the analysis of sensation, and in humans also subserving the higher-order functions of thought, language, and emotion. In vertebrates it consists of the brain and spinal cord. >> ataxia; brain ℹ; nervous system; neurone ℹ; Parkinson's / prion disease; spinal cord

Central Powers Initially, the members of the Triple Alliance (Germany, Austria–Hungary, Italy) created by Bismarck in 1882. As Italy remained neutral in 1914, the term was later used to describe Germany, Austria–Hungary, their ally Turkey, and later Bulgaria in World War 1. >> Bismarck; World War 1

central processing unit (CPU) >> **digital computer**

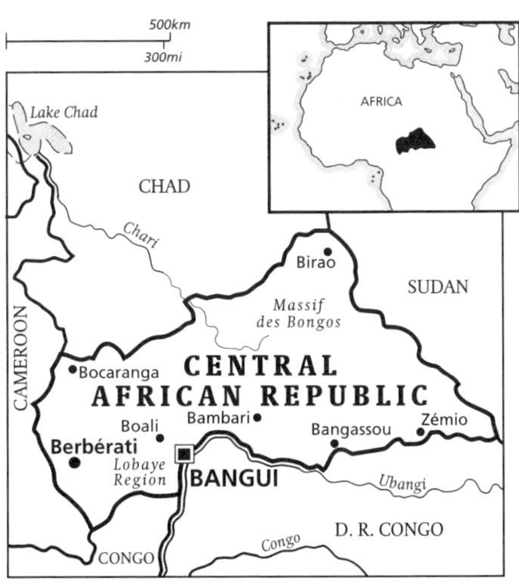

Central Treaty Organization (CENTO) A political–military alliance signed in 1955 between Iran (which withdrew after the fall of the Shah), Turkey, Pakistan, Iraq (which withdrew in 1958), and the UK, as a defence against the Soviet Union.

Central Valley or **Great Central Valley** Valley in California, USA, between the Sierra Nevada (E) and the Coast Range (W). The Central Valley Project is a series of dams and reservoirs for flood-control, irrigation, and hydroelectricity. >> California

Centre Beaubourg [sãtruh bohboorg] The popular name for the Centre National d'Art et de Culture, or **Pompidou Centre**, situated on the Plateau Beaubourg in Paris. Designed by Renzo Piano and Richard Rogers, and opened in 1977, the six-storey building houses a modern art gallery and a centre for industrial design. Display space has been maximized by placing all services on the outside of the transparent exterior walls. >> Paris; Pompidou

centrifuge A device for separating the components of a mixture (solid-in-liquid or liquid-in-liquid) by applying rapid rotation and consequent centrifugal force. It may be equipped for the technical separation of materials (eg cream) or for scientific observation (eg the **ultracentrifuge**, which separates particles of macromolecular size). >> particle physics

centrography In geography, the study of descriptive statistics for the determination and mapping of measures of central tendency. For example, the mean centre of population distribution can be mapped to show the main focus of a country's population distribution. >> statistics

century The smallest unit in a Roman legion. Probably consisting originally of 100, under the Empire there were 80 soldiers in a century. >> legion

century plant A species of agave (*Agave americana*), so-called from the length of time once thought to pass between germination and flowering – up to 100 years. In Mexico its sap is one of the sources of the national drink, pulque, as well as a spirit, mescal. (Family: Agavaceae.) >> agave

cephalic index A skull's breadth as a percentage of its length. Skulls of different relative breadths are termed *brachycephalic* (broad), *mesocephalic* (intermediate), and *dolichocephalic* (long). >> skull

Cephalonia [kefa**loh**nia], Gr **Kefallinía** pop (1995e) 33 100; area 781 sq km/301 sq mi. Largest of the Ionian Is, Greece; length 48 km/30 mi; hilly island, rising to 1628 m/ 5341 ft; capital, Argostolion. >> Ionian Islands

Cephalopoda [sefa**lop**oda] A class of carnivorous, marine molluscs characterized by the specialization of the head-foot into a ring of tentacles, typically armed with hooks or suckers, and by their method of swimming using jets of water squirted out of a funnel; mouth typically with a powerful beak; eyes usually well developed. >> cuttlefish; mollusc; nautilus; octopus; squid; *see illustration below*

Cephas [**see**fas] >> **Peter, St**

Cepheid variable [see**fee**id] A class of variable star with a period of 1–50 days, characterized by precise regularity. The observed period of a Cepheid indicates its distance from Earth, and is consequently of great importance in determining the distance scale of the universe. >> Cepheus; variable star

Cepheus [**see**fyoos] A N constellation which includes the famous star **delta Cephei**, the prototype of regular variables used for calibrating the distance scale of the universe. >> Cepheid variable; constellation; RR968

ceramics The products of the baking of clay, giving hard, strong, non-conducting, brittle, heat-resistant substances. They are useful for technical purposes (eg abrasives, cutting tools, refractory linings) and for decoration. Clays of many kinds are used, from the coarse clay used for bricks to the fine white clay used for porcelain. Ceramics may be made in stages, such as the many ways of producing a *glaze*, a coating of a second clay or glass-like substance, which confers impermeability (as in making pipes) or decorative colours. >> crystals; decorative arts; ferrites; glaze; porcelain; synroc

Ceratopsia [sera**top**sia] The horned dinosaurs; typified by enormous bony frill extending back over neck from posterior part of skull; usually with median horns in nasal region and paired horns behind eyes; evolved during the Upper Cretaceous period. (Order: Ornithischia.) >> Ornithischia; *Protoceratops*; *Triceratops*

Cephalopoda

Cerberus [**ser**berus] In Greek mythology, the dog which guards the entrance to the Underworld, originally 50-headed, later with three heads. Heracles carried him off as one of his labours. >> Hades; Heracles

cereals Grain-bearing grasses which provide staple foods for most of the world's population. The grains are much larger than those of other grass species, and are rich in protein and carbohydrates. There are eight major cereals: rice, wheat, oats, barley, rye, sorghums, millets, and maize. All derive from wild species, and their domestication in early times (c.8000 BC in the case of wheat and barley) marks a turning-point in human history. The replacement of *ramassage* (the gathering of wild grains) by a more dependable crop allowed the development of a more settled lifestyle. The development of modern cereals is very sophisticated, with strains tailored for specific purposes and conditions. (Family: Gramineae.) >> barley; buckwheat; carbohydrate; grass [i]; maize; millet; oats; protein; rice; rye; sorghum; wheat

cerebellum [sere**bel**um] A mass of neural tissue that occupies the lower back part of the cranial cavity within the skull. Its principal function is the control of posture, repetitive movements, and the geometric accuracy of voluntary movements; it also appears to have an important role in learning. >> ataxia; brain [i]; brain stem; ventricles

cerebral haemorrhage / hemorrhage An episode of acute bleeding within the substance of the brain. It tends to occur when the blood pressure is high, or when the wall of the cerebral blood vessel is weakened by degenerative change (eg atheroma) or is the site of a localized distension (*aneurysm*). The neurological disability that follows depends on the severity of the haemorrhage and the site of the bleeding. >> brain [i]; stroke

cerebral palsy A non-progressive disorder of the brain occurring in infancy or early childhood which causes weakness, paralysis, and lack of co-ordination of movement; the muscular spasms involved have led to the use of the term **spastic** for these children. A high proportion of infants also suffer from epilepsy and are retarded mentally. Several types of brain injury are responsible, but the cause is unknown in many cases. >> brain [i]; epilepsy

cerebrospinal fluid (CSF) A clear, colourless, protein-free fluid circulating through the cerebral ventricles of the brain, the central canal of the spinal cord, and the subarachnoid space in vertebrates, which provides the brain with mechanical support and nutrients. In humans, CSF is sometimes collected (by *lumbar puncture*) and analysed for diagnostic purposes. >> brain [i]; hydrocephalus; lumbar puncture; spinal cord; ventricles

cerebrum [**se**rebruhm] A large mass of neural and supporting tissue which occupies most of the cranial cavity within the skull. It is separated into right and left halves (the right and left **cerebral hemispheres**), connected by a body of nerve fibres known as the *corpus callosum*. Each hemisphere can be divided into four *lobes* which are named according to the skull bone that they are most closely related to (ie *frontal*, *parietal*, *temporal*, and *occipital*). The surface of each hemisphere is formed by a layer of *grey matter* known as the *cerebral cortex*, containing the cell bodies of the neurones responsible for the functions of the cerebrum. Within the cortex the hemispheres are formed by a large mass of *white matter* consisting largely of the axons of the neurones in the cerebral cortex. The surface of the cerebrum is thrown into a series of folds (*gyri*) separated by troughs (*sulci*): for example, the *central sulcus* separates the frontal and parietal lobes. Immediately in front of the central sulcus is the *motor cortex*, in which the opposite half of the body is represented upside down: the face lies lowest, then the hand (a very large area), then the arm, trunk, and leg. Stimulation here results in contraction of the appropriate voluntary muscles on the opposite side of the body. Below the area of the brain representing the face, on the left side, lies the speech area (*Broca's area*). Immediately behind the central sulcus is the *sensory cortex*, which receives sensory information from the opposite side of the body via the brain stem and thalamus. The occipital lobe is involved with vision. The parietal lobe is in general responsible for sensory functions such as the perception of touch, pressure, and body position, as well as three-dimensional perception, the analysis of visual images, language, and calculations. The frontal lobe subserves motor functions, and also governs the expression of the intellect and personality. The upper part of the temporal lobe is involved in the perception of sound, with the remainder being concerned with memory and various emotional functions. >> brain [i]; neurone [i]; neurophysiology

Ceres (astronomy) [**seer**eez] The first asteroid to be found, discovered on the first night of the 19th-c. Much the largest asteroid, its diameter is 1000 km/620 mi (over one-quarter of the Moon's).

Ceres (mythology) [**seer**eez] The ancient Italian corn-goddess, an early cult at Rome. She was given characteristics and stories associated with Demeter. >> Demeter; Persephone

CERN >> **Organisation Européene pour la Recherche Nucléaire**

Cervantes (Saavedra), Miguel de [ser**van**teez], Span [thair**van**tes] (1547–1616) Writer of *Don Quixote*, born in Alcalá de Henares, Spain. Tradition maintains that he wrote *Don Quixote* in prison at Argamasilla in La Mancha. When the book came out (1605), it was hugely popular. He wrote the second part in 1615, after several years writing plays and short novels.

cervical cancer [ser**viy**kl] A malignant tumour arising from the lining of the cervical canal. It occurs at all ages, and is second only to breast cancer as a cause of death from tumours in women. Its occurrence is related to frequent sexual intercourse with several partners, which has led to the view that it is possibly due to a virus. Treatment is effective if diagnosis (by the Papincolaou or 'smear' test) is made early. >> cancer; cervix; virus

cervix [**ser**viks] The lower tapering third of the uterus (womb). Its lower, blunt part projects into the vagina; its upper part communicates with the body of the uterus. >> cervical cancer; uterus [i]; vagina

cesarian section >> **caesarian section**

Cestoda [**ses**toda] >> **tapeworm**

Cetacea [see**tay**shia] >> **whale** [i]

cetane number An index defining the ignition quality of fuel for diesel internal combustion engines. The number is the cetane percentage in a mixture of cetane and alpha-methyl naphthalene, adjusted to match the characteristics of the fuel under test. >> naphthalene [i]; octane number

Cetewayo or **Cetshwayo** [kete**way**oh] (c.1826–84) Ruler of Zululand from 1873, born near Eshowe, South Africa. In 1879 he defeated the British at Isandhlwana, but was himself defeated at Ulundi. >> Zulu

Cetus [**see**tus] (Lat 'whale') The fourth largest constellation, lying on the celestial Equator, but inconspicuous because it has few bright stars. >> constellation; Mira; RR968

Ceuta [**thay**oota] 35°52N 5°18W, pop (1995e) 68 800. Freeport and military station, at E end of the Strait of Gibraltar, on the N African coast of Morocco; became Spanish in 1580; cathedral (15th-c). >> Spain [i]

Cévennes [say**ven**], ancient **Cebenna** Chief mountain range in the S of France, on the SE edge of the Massif Central; highest peak, Mt Mézenc (1754 m/5754 ft). >> France [i]

Cézanne, Paul [sayzan] (1839–1906) Postimpressionist painter, born in Aix-en-Provence, France. He abandoned his early sombre expressionism for the study of nature, and began to use his characteristic glowing colours. In his later period (after 1886), he constructed his pictures from a rhythmic series of coloured planes, thus becoming the forerunner of Cubism. Among his best-known paintings are 'The Card Players' (1890–2, Musée d'Orsay, Paris) and 'The Gardener' (1906, Tate). Picasso called him 'the father of us all'. >> Cubism; Postimpressionism

CFCs The acronym for **chlorofluorocarbons**, also called **Freons**; derivatives of methane and ethane containing both chlorine and fluorine. They are inert, volatile compounds, used as refrigerants and aerosol sprays. Their decomposition in the atmosphere damages the Earth's ozone layer. International agreements propose replacing them with less harmful substances. >> chlorine; ethane; fluorine; methane; ozone layer

Chabrier, (Alexis) Emmanuel [shabreeyay] (1841–94) Composer, born in Ambert, France. His best-known pieces were inspired by the folk music of Spain, notably his orchestral rhapsody *España* (1883).

Chabrol, Claude [shabrol] (1930–) Film critic and director, born in Paris. Identified with the French *Nouvelle Vague*, his most widely known films are dramas of abnormality in the provincial bourgeoisie, such as *Le Boucher* (1970, The Butcher), and *L'Enfer* (1993, Torment). >> *nouvelle vague*

Chaco Canyon A remote desert canyon in New Mexico, 160 km/100 mi NW of Albuquerque, the hub in AD c.950–1300 of the Anasazi Indian culture of the American SW; now a world heritage site. A National Monument since 1907, its road network links c.125 D-shaped pueblos. >> Pueblo

chaconne A dance of Latin American origin. The harmonies and basses traditionally associated with it were widely used as material for arias and instrument variations in the 17th–18th-c. >> aria; passacaglia

Chaco War A territorial struggle between Bolivia and Paraguay in the disputed Northern Chaco area. Owing to the brilliant tactics of Col José Félix Estigarribia (1888–1940), Paraguay won most of the area. >> Bolivia [i]; Gran Chaco; Paraguay [i]

Chad, Fr **Tchad**, official name **Republic of Chad**, Fr **République du Tchad** pop (1995e) 6 424 000; area 1 284 640 sq km/495 871 sq mi. Republic in NC Africa; capital, N'djamena; timezone GMT +1; c.200 ethnic groups; chief religion, Muslim (over half), with local religions and Christianity; official languages, Arabic, French, with many local languages spoken; unit of currency, the franc CFA; landlocked and mostly arid, semi-desert plateau at edge of Sahara Desert; average altitude of 200–500 m/650–1650 ft; L Chad (SW), area 10 400 sq km/4000 sq mi at low water (doubles at high water); Tibesti Mts (N) rise to 3415 m/11 204 ft at Emi Koussi; vegetation generally desert scrub or steppe; most people live in tropical S; N'djamena, average annual rainfall 744 mm/29 in; hot and arid N almost rainless; part of French Equatorial Africa in 19th-c; colonial status, 1920; independence, 1960; governed by a president with a Council of Ministers; fighting between Libyan-supported rebels and French-supported government until ceasefire agreed in 1987; National Assembly established, 1989; new constitution adopted, 1991; transitional charter, 1993; governed by a president, prime minister, Council of Ministers, and a Higher Transitional Council; Aouzou strip returned to Chad by Libya, 1994; cease-fire, 1995; elections scheduled, 1996; economy severely damaged in recent years by drought, locusts, and civil war. >> N'djamena; Tibesti Mountains; RR1004 political leaders

Chadic [chadik] A group of 100 languages, spoken by over 25 million people in parts of Ghana and the Central African Republic. It is assigned to the Afro-Asiatic family, though its position there is unclear. >> Afro-Asiatic languages; Hausa

Chadwick, John >> **Ventris, Michael**

Chadwick, Sir James (1891–1974) Physicist, born in Manchester, Greater Manchester. He discovered the neutron (1932), for which he received the Nobel Prize for Physics in 1935, and led the UK's work on the atomic bomb in World War 2. >> atomic bomb; neutron

Chadwick, Lynn (Russell) (1914–) Sculptor, born in London. He studied architecture, but after war service he began making mobiles (c.1946), then rough-finished solid metal sculptures. >> mobile

chafer A large, nocturnal beetle; adults feed on leaves; larvae fleshy, C-shaped, burrow in soil eating roots, often taking 3–4 years to develop. (Order: Coleoptera. Family: Scarabaeidae.) >> beetle; cockchafer; larva

chaffinch Either of two species of bird of genus *Fringilla*. *Fringilla coelebs* is native to Europe, N Africa, the Azores, and SW Asia; inhabits forest and human habitations; colour varies over range; N populations move S for winter. The **blue chaffinch** (*Fringilla teydea*) is from the Canary Is. (Family: Fringillidae.) >> finch

Chagall, Marc [shagal] (1887–1985) Artist, born in Vitebsk, Belarus. He moved to Paris and the USA, and became best known for his fanciful painting of animals, objects, and people from his life, dreams, and Russian folklore. The word 'Surrealist' is said to have been coined by Apollinaire to describe the work of Chagall. >> Surrealism

Chaikin, Joseph [chiykin] (1935–) Actor and theatre director, born in New York City. He acted with the Living Theater, and in 1963 founded The Open Theater, which for a decade produced some of the most original work in the US theatre. >> Living Theater; Open Theater

Chain, Sir Ernst Boris [chayn] (1906–79) Biochemist, born in Berlin. He shared the Nobel Prize for Physiology or Medicine in 1945 for the development of penicillin, and also worked on snake venoms and insulin. >> insulin; penicillin

chain reaction A nuclear reaction in which nuclear fission induced by a neutron releases further neutrons that in turn may cause further fission through some material. Nuclear power and atomic bombs rely on chain reactions in uranium or plutonium. >> atomic bomb; critical mass; neutron; nuclear fission

chakras The seven centres of energy in the yogic system. Roughly equivalent to the autonomic nervous system and endocrine glands of Western medicine, they are important for channelling vital energy and consciousness. An imbalance of energy may lead to physical, mental, emotional, or spiritual disharmony. >> autonomic nervous system; yoga

Chalcedon, Council of [kal**see**dn] A Council of the Church which agreed that Jesus Christ is truly God and truly man, two natures in one person (the *Chalcedonian definition*). >> Christology; Council of the Church

chalcedony [kal**sed**onee] A group name for the compact varieties of mineral silica (SiO_2) composed of very fine-grained crystals of quartz. Banded varieties are agate and onyx, and coloured varieties include carnelian, jasper, bloodstone, and chrysoprase. >> agate; gemstones; quartz; silica

Chalcis [**kal**sis], Gr **Khalkis**, ancient **Evripos** 38°27N 23°42E, pop (1995e) 47 600. Capital of Euboea, Greece; railway; local ferries; Aristotle died here. >> Aristotle; Euboea

Chalcolithic >> **Three Age System**

chalcopyrite [kalko**piy**riyt] A copper iron sulphide mineral ($CuFeS_2$) found in veins associated with igneous rocks; brass-coloured and metallic. It is the main ore of copper.

Chaldaeans [kal**dee**anz] **1** Originally the name of a Semitic people (*Kaldu*) from Arabia who settled in the region of Ur in Lower Mesopotamia. **2** In the 7th-c and 6th-c BC, a generic term for Babylonians. >> Babylonia; Semites; Ur

chalk A fine-grained limestone rock, mainly of calcite, formed from the shells of minute marine organisms. Often pure white in colour, it is characteristically seen in rocks of the Upper Cretaceous period of W Europe, its most famous exposures being on either side of the English Channel. Blackboard chalk is calcium sulphate. >> calcite; Cretaceous period; limestone

Challoner, Richard [**cha**loner] (1691–1781) Roman Catholic clergyman and writer, born in Lewes, East Sussex. His best-known works are the prayer book, *The Garden of the Soul* (1740), and his revision of the Douai version of the Bible (5 vols, 1750). >> Douai Bible

Chalmers, Thomas (1780–1847) Theologian and reformer, born in Anstruther, Fife. In the Disruption of 1843 he led 470 ministers out of the Established Church of Scotland to found the Free Church of Scotland. >> Church of Scotland; Reformation

Chamaeleon [ka**meel**ion] A faint S constellation. >> constellation; RR968

chambered tomb In European prehistory, megalithic monuments usually constructed of uprights (*orthostats*) and capstones beneath a cairn or mound of earth, the burial chamber sometimes being provided with a corbelled vault; also known as a **dolmen**. >> corbelling; Maes Howe; megalith; New Grange; Three Age System

Chamberlain, Sir (Joseph) Austen (1863–1937) British Conservative statesman, born in Birmingham, eldest son of Joseph Chamberlain. He was Chancellor of the Exchequer (1903–6, 1919–21), secretary for India (1915–17), Unionist leader (1921–2), foreign secretary (1924–9), and First Lord of the Admiralty (1931). He received the 1925 Nobel Peace Prize for negotiating the Locarno Pact. >> Conservative Party; Locarno Pact

Chamberlain, Joseph (1836–1914) British statesman, born in London. From 1889 he was leader of the Liberal Unionists, and in the Coalition Government of 1895 was secretary for the Colonies. >> Chamberlain, Austen / Neville; Liberal Party (UK)

Chamberlain, Lindy (Alice Lynne) (1948–) Mother of the 'dingo baby', born in Whakatane, New Zealand. The disappearance of her nine-week-old daughter, Azaria, at Uluru (Ayers Rock) in 1980 made her the subject of national obsession in Australia. Married to pastor **Michael Chamberlain** (tried with her, since divorced), she claimed the baby was taken by a dingo. She was found guilty of murder, and gaoled, but released in 1986 when a baby's jacket was found at the base of the rock. Following a judicial inquiry, all convictions against the couple were quashed, and they received A$1 million in compensation. >> dingo

Chamberlain, (Arthur) Neville (1869–1940) British statesman and Conservative prime minister (1937–40), born in Birmingham, the son of Joseph Chamberlain. He advocated 'appeasement' of Italy and Germany, returning from Munich with his claim to have found 'peace for our time' (1938). Criticism of his war leadership and initial military reverses led to his resignation (1940). >> Chamberlain, Joseph; Conservative Party; World War 2

Chamberlain, Wilt(on) Norman, nickname **Wilt the Stilt** (1936–) Basketball player, born in Philadelphia, PA, height 1·85 m/7 ft 1 in. He was seven times the National Basketball Association leading scorer (1960–6). During his career (1960–73) he scored 31 419 points at an average of 30·1 per game. >> basketball

Chamberlain, Lord In the UK, the chief official of the royal household, overseeing all aspects of its management. The office should be distinguished from the **Lord Great Chamberlain**, whose duties are largely ceremonial; in particular, at coronations, he presents the sovereign to the people.

chamber music Music for two or more players intended for performance in a room rather than a concert hall, with only one player to a part. The string quartet has been looked upon as the chamber ensemble *par excellence*, but any wind, string, or keyboard instrument might participate in chamber music. >> sonata; string quartet; trio

chamber of commerce An association of business enterprises in a district, whose aims are to promote the area and its members' businesses. The International Chamber of Commerce (ICC), based in Paris, was set up in 1920, and has the affiliation of over 40 national institutions.

Chambers, Ephraim (c.1680–1740) Encyclopedist, born in Kendal, Cumbria. While apprentice to a globemaker in London, he conceived the idea of a cyclopaedia (2 folio vols, 1728). A French translation gave rise to the great French *Encyclopédie*.

Chambers, William (1800–83) Publisher and writer, born in Peebles, Scottish Borders. In 1832 he started *Chambers's Edinburgh Journal*, and soon after united with his brother **Robert** (1802–71) in founding the printing and publishing firm of W & R Chambers.

Chambord [shãbaw(r)] 47°37N 1°31E, pop (1995e) 220. A village 18 km/11 mi E of Blois, France, noted for its chateau and estate; a world heritage site. Once a hunting lodge of the counts of Blois, the chateau was reconstructed (1519–33) as a royal residence.

chameleon [ka**meel**ion] A lizard native to Africa, the

Middle East, S Spain, India, and Sri Lanka; body flattened from side to side; can change colour rapidly; tail clasping, cannot be shed; eyes move independently of one another; tongue longer than head and body, with sticky tip that shoots out to hit insect prey. (Family: Chamaeleontidae, 85 species.) >> lizard ℹ

chamois [**sham**wah] A goat-antelope from S Europe (*Rupicapra rupicapra*) (introduced in New Zealand); brown with pale patches on face or neck; horns short, vertical, with backward-hooked tips; inhabits rugged mountains; skin formerly used to make 'shammy leather'. >> antelope; goral

chamomile or **camomile** [**kam**omiyl] A perennial growing to 30 cm/12 in (*Chamaemelum nobile*), native to W Europe and N Africa; flower-heads up to 2·5 cm/1 in across, solitary; outer ray florets spreading, white; inner disc florets yellow. It is widely used to make chamomile tea, and is a popular additive to shampoos, hair washes, etc. (Family: Compositae.) >> floret; herb

champagne A sparkling wine produced in the Champagne region of NE France, using either a mixture of black and white grapes, or white grapes only. Sweet (*sec*), slightly sweet (*demi-sec*), and dry (*brut*) varieties are made.

Champagne-Ardenne [shāpanyah(r)den] pop (1995e) 1 389 000; area 25 606 sq km/9884 sq mi. Region of NE France comprising the departments of Ardennes, Aube, Marne, and Haute-Marne; a long-standing scene of conflict between France and Germany; noted for the production of champagne wine. >> Reims; wine

Champlain, Samuel de [shāplĩ] (1567–1635) Governor of Canada, born in Brouage, France. In a series of voyages he travelled to Canada (1603), exploring the E coast (1604–7), and founding Quebec (1608). L Champlain is named after him. >> Canada ℹ

champlevé [**shom**luhvay] A technique of enamelling on metal, which involves engraving the image out of the metal surface, and filling it with vitreous pastes of different colours, which are then fired. >> enamelling

Champollion, Jean François [shāpolyõ] (1790–1832) Founder of Egyptology, born in Figeac, France. He is best known for his use of the Rosetta Stone to decipher Egyptian hieroglyphics (1822–4). >> hieroglyphics ℹ; Rosetta Stone

chancel The E end of a church, containing the altar, choir, and clergy; more generally, the body of the church to the E of the nave. >> choir (architecture); church ℹ; nave; transept

Chancellor, Lord (High) >> **Lord Chancellor**

Chancellor of the Exchequer The senior minister in charge of the UK Treasury, and a senior minister in the cabinet. The Chancellor takes responsibility for the preparation of the budget, and (in contrast to most other countries) is economic as well as finance minister. >> cabinet; treasury

Chancery Division A division of the High Court of England and Wales created by the Judicature Acts (1873–5). Its workload includes trusts and probate matters, presided over by the Lord Chancellor. In Scotland, the Court of Chancery is part of the Sheriff Court, and deals with the issue of land titles for heirs of deceased persons. >> High Court of Justice; Lord Chancellor; probate; trust

chancroid A sexually transmitted disease common in Egypt and the Middle East, resulting from infection with a *Haemophilus* organism. It causes ulceration of the genital organs. >> venereal disease

Chandigarh [**chan**digah(r)] pop (1995e) 544 000; area 114 sq km/44 sq mi. City and union territory (1966) in NW India; serves as the joint state capital of the Punjab and Haryana; airfield; railway; university (1947); city designed by Le Corbusier. >> India ℹ; Le Corbusier; Punjab

Chandler, Raymond (Thornton) (1888–1959) Writer, born in Chicago. His 'private-eye' novels include *The Big Sleep* (1939) and *Farewell, My Lovely* (1940). He is the creator of the cynical but honest detective antihero, Philip Marlowe.

Chandrasekhar, Subrahmanyan [chandra**say**ker] (1910–95) Astrophysicist, born in Lahore, Pakistan (formerly India). Working in the USA, he studied the final stages of stellar evolution, showing that the final fate of a star depends on its mass. Massive stars will be unable to evolve into white dwarfs, and this limiting stellar mass (about 1·4 solar masses) is called the **Chandrasekhar limit**. He was awarded the Nobel Prize for Physics in 1983. >> stellar evolution

Chanel, Coco [shanel], popular name of **Gabrielle Chanel** (?1883–1971) Fashion designer, born in Saumur, France. She revolutionized women's fashions during the 1920s, her designs including the 'chemise' dress and the collarless cardigan jacket. She retired in 1938, but made a surprisingly successful come-back in 1954.

Chaney, Lon [**chay**nee], originally **Alonso Chaney** (1883–1930) Film actor, born in Colorado Springs, CO. He was famous for spine-chilling deformed villains and other horrific parts, as in *The Hunchback of Notre Dame* (1923) and *The Phantom of the Opera* (1925). His son, **Lon Chaney, Jr** (1907–73), also acted in horror films.

Changchun or **Ch'ang-ch'un** [chang**chun**] 43°50N 125°20E, pop (1995e) 2 350 000. Capital of Jilin province, NE China; developed during Japanese military occupation, 1933–45, as capital of Manchukuo; airfield; railway; university (1958). >> China ℹ; Manchukuo

change ringing A British form of bell-ringing devised by 17th-c Cambridge printer Fabian Stedman. A set of differently tuned bells, usually those in a church tower, are rung in various permutations so that no sequence (**change**) is sounded more than once. A full diatonic scale of eight bells allows 40 320 changes. >> bell; bell-ringing

Changsha or **Ch'ang-sha** [chang**shah**] 28°10N 113°00E, pop (1995e) 1 477 000. River port and capital of Hunan province, SE China; founded before 1000 BC; early craft, industrial, and educational centre; foreign trade port, 1904; airfield; railway; university (1959). >> China ℹ

Chania [khan**ya**] or **Cania** 35°31N 24°01E, pop (1995e) 136 000. Town on N shore of Crete I; founded, 13th-c; capital of Crete until 1971; airport. >> Crete

Channel Islands, Fr **Iles Anglo-Normandes** pop (1995e) 147 000; area 194 sq km/75 sq mi. Island group of the British Isles in the English Channel, W of Normandy; chief islands, Jersey, Guernsey, Alderney, Sark; languages, English and Norman-French; granted to the Dukes of Normandy, 10th-c; occupied by Germany in World War 2; a dependent territory of the British Crown, with individual legislative assemblies and legal system; divided into the Bailiwick of Guernsey and the Bailiwick of Jersey; Bailiff presides over the Royal Court and the Representative Assembly (the States); used as a tax haven. >> Alderney; Guernsey; Jersey; Sark; RR999; *see illustration on p. 167*

channel swimming Swimming the English Channel, first achieved on 24–25 August 1875 by Captain Matthew Webb (1848–83), who covered the 34 km/21 mi from Dover to Calais Sands in 21 h 45 min. The record is now 7 h 40 min. >> swimming

Channel Tunnel A tunnel linking France and Britain, first proposed in 1802. In 1985 Eurotunnel, an Anglo-French consortium, was set up to finance the tunnel and operate it once it opened. Built by the Anglo-French Transmanche Link, it consists of twin rail tunnels between Cheriton near Folkestone and Fréthun near Calais. Opened in 1994, it is 50 km/31 mi long (38 km/23 mi under the sea). In

November 1996 a fire in a freight train caused serious damage and temporary closure. >> Eurostar

chansons de geste [shãsõ duh **zhest**] (Fr 'poems of action') French poems from the 12th–13th-c, celebrating historical figures and events on an epic scale. Different cycles centre on Charlemagne (including the *Chanson de Roland*) and the Crusades. >> Charlemagne; troubadours

chant A monotone or a melody, usually restricted in range, mainly stepwise in interval and free in rhythm, to which a text (especially a liturgical one) is declaimed. **Plainchant**, originally sung in unison and without accompaniment, was used for the services of the mediaeval Roman Catholic Church and later incorporated into polyphonic music. **Anglican chant** is a type of harmonized melody to which the psalms and canticles are sung in Church of England services. >> antiphon; Gregorian chant; liturgy; plainchant; Psalms, Book of; sequence (music)

chanterelle [shante**rel**] The bright yellow, edible fruiting body of the fungus *Cantharellus cibarius*; funnel-shaped, diameter up to 10 cm/4 in; gill-like ridges present on lower surface; common in Europe and North America. (Order: Agaricales.) >> fungus

Chanukah >> **Hanukkah**

chaos [**kay**os] A state of disorder and irregularity whose evolution in time, though governed by simple exact laws, is highly sensitive to starting conditions: a small variation in these conditions will produce wildly different results. Chaos is an intermediate stage between highly ordered motion and fully random motion. It is present in most real systems, such as in weather patterns and the motion of planets about the Sun. The modern theory of chaos is based on the work of US meteorologist Edward Lorenz (1917–) in 1963, arising from the study of convection in the atmosphere. >> fractals; turbulence

chaparral [shapa**ral**] (Span *chaparro* 'scrub oak') The evergreen scrub vegetation of semi-arid areas with a Mediterranean-type climate in SW USA and NW Mexico. It is a plant community adapted to frequent fires. Typical species includes evergreen scrub oak, laurel sumac, and ceanothus. >> evergreen plants; macchia

chapati [cha**pah**tee] A thin, flat, unleavened bread, made from a mixture of water and wheat flour containing c.95% of the original wheat. It is a traditional accompaniment to many Asian dishes. >> bread

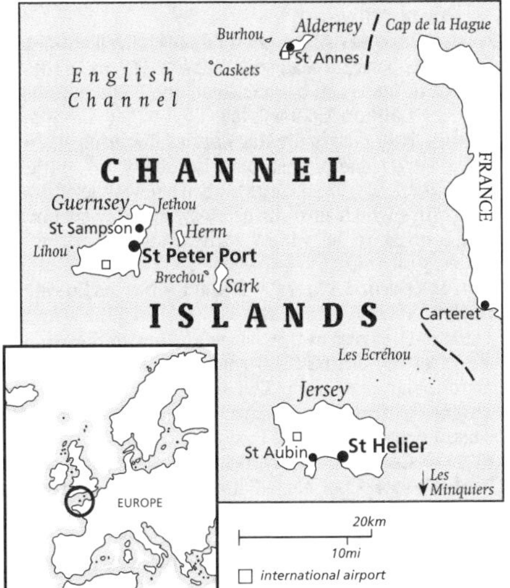

chapel Originally, a place to house sacred relics; now generally a church. In England and Wales, the term is used of Nonconformist places of worship; in N Ireland and Scotland, of Roman Catholic churches. It may also be a place of worship belonging to a college or institution, the chancel of a church or cathedral, or part of a cathedral containing a separate altar. >> church [i]; Nonconformists; Roman Catholicism

Chaplin, Charlie, popular name of **Sir Charles Spencer Chaplin** (1889–1977) Film actor and director, born in London. In his early silent comedies he adopted the bowler hat, out-turned feet, moustache and walking-cane which became his hallmark, as in *The Gold Rush* (1925), and many others. His first sound film was *The Great Dictator* (1940). In *Limelight* (1952) he acted, directed, and composed the music and dances. He was awarded an Oscar in 1972.

Chapman, George (c.1559–1634) Poet and playwright, born near Hitchin, Hertfordshire. He is best known for his translations of Homer's *Iliad* (1598–1611) and *Odyssey* (1616). He collaborated in the composition of *Eastward Ho* (1605), and in 1607 appeared *Bussy d'Ambois*, which had a sequel in 1613. >> Homer

Chappaquiddick [chapa**kwid**ik] (Algonquian 'separated-island-at') Island to the E of Martha's Vineyard I, USA; in the Nantucket Sound, off the SE coast of Massachusetts; briefly achieved worldwide fame in 1969, as the site of a car accident involving US senator Edward Kennedy. >> Kennedy, Edward M; Martha's Vineyard

Chappell, Greg(ory Stephen) (1948–) Cricketer, born in Unley, South Australia, the brother of Ian Chappell. He played 88 times for his country (1970–84), 48 as captain, and scored 24 Test centuries. >> Chappell, Ian

Chappell, Ian (Michael) (1943–) Cricketer, born in Unley, South Australia, the brother of Greg Chappell. He played 75 times for Australia (1976–80), scoring over 5000 runs and 14 Test centuries. He is now a sports commentator. >> Chappell, Greg

characin [**ka**rasin] Any of a large family of colourful carp-like freshwater fishes common in South and Central America and Africa; mostly carnivorous; 40 genera, including piranhas, tigerfish, headstanders, tetras, and penguinfish. (Family: Characidae.) >> carp; piranha; tetra; tigerfish

character recognition The technology associated with the ability of computer-based systems to recognize specific patterns; sometimes referred to as **pattern recognition**. In particular, the ability to read printed characters is known as **optical character recognition (OCR)**. Another common type is **magnetic ink character recognition (MICR)**, used worldwide to read automatically such things as account numbers on cheques. >> pattern recognition

Charadriiformes [karadriuh**faw(r)**meez] An order of essentially water-loving birds (18 families). >> auk; gull; skua; tern

charcoal An impure form of carbon made by heating animal or vegetable substances in the absence of air to drive off the volatile constituents. It burns without flame or smoke. Animal charcoal is known as *bone-black*. >> carbon; coke

chard A type of cultivated beet (*Beta vulgaris* variety *cicla*) lacking a swollen root but with swollen midribs and leaf-stalks; also called **Swiss chard**. (Family: Chenopodiaceae.) >> beet

Chardin, Pierre Teilhard de >> **Teilhard de Chardin, Pierre**

Chargaff, Erwin [**chah(r)**gaf] (1905–) Biochemist, born in Czernowitz, Czech Republic. His work on the ratio of bases present in DNA (the **Chargaff rules**) provided a fundamental contribution to the double helix structure for DNA advanced in 1953. >> DNA [i]; molecular biology

charge A quantity of electricity (**electrical charge**), the source of an electric field; symbol Q, units C (*coulombs*). The elementary unit of charge $e = 1{\cdot}602 \times 10^{-19}$ C, equal in size but opposite in sign to the electron's charge, a fundamental constant. Two types of charge are possible: **positive** and **negative**. Like-sign charges repel, opposite-sign charges attract; the force between charges is expressed by Coulomb's law. Moving charges constitute a *current*. The study of stationary charges and the forces between them is called **electrostatics**. >> capacitance; current (electricity); electricity; electron

charge card >> **credit card**

charge-coupled device (generally abbreviated **CCD**) An image sensor which in a video camera comprises a mosaic of minute photo-conductive diodes corresponding to the pixels and lines of a television system. Charges produced in each element by incident light are stored until read off in the required scanning sequence. >> camera

Charge of the Light Brigade An incident during the Battle of Balaclava (25 Oct 1854), when the Light Brigade, under the command of Lord Cardigan, charged the main Russian artillery, with massive loss of life. It resulted from the misunderstanding of an order given by the commanding officer, Lord Raglan, to stop guns captured by the Russians being carried away during their retreat. >> Balaclava, Battle of; Cardigan, Earl of; Raglan

Charing Cross An area in C London, UK, traditionally viewed as the city centre. It takes its name from a cross erected to mark the site of the resting-place of the body of Queen Eleanor, who died in 1290. >> Eleanor of Castile; London

charismatic movement [kariz**ma**tik] A movement of spiritual renewal, which takes a variety of forms in Roman Catholic, Protestant, and Eastern Orthodox Churches. It emphasizes the present reality and work of the Holy Spirit in the life of the Church and the individual. >> glossolalia; Holy Spirit; Pentecostalism

Charlemagne or **Charles the Great** [**shah(r)l**uhmayn] (742–814) King of the Franks (771–814) and Emperor of the West (800–14). He defeated the Saxons and Lombards and took control of most of Christian W Europe. In his later years he consolidated his vast empire, promoting Christianity, education, agriculture, the arts, manufacture, and commerce, so much so that the period has become known as the **Carolingian Renaissance**. >> Renaissance

Charleroi [shah(r)lrwah] 50°25N 4°27E, pop (1995e) 209 000. Town in SW Belgium; location of World War 1 German attack against the French (Aug 1914); centre of coal-mining area. >> Belgium ℹ

Charles I (1600–49) King of Britain and Ireland (1625–49), born in Dunfermline, Fife. His marriage to the French princess, Henrietta Maria (1609–69), disturbed the nation, for the marriage articles permitted her the free exercise of the Catholic religion. He warred with France (1627–9), and in 1630 made peace with Spain, but his continuing need for money led to unpopular economic policies. His attempt to anglicize the Scottish Church brought active resistance (1639). In 1642, having alienated much of the realm, Charles entered into the Civil War, which saw the annihilation of his cause at Naseby (14 Jun 1645), and he surrendered to the Scots at Newark (1646). After a second Civil War (1646–8), he came to trial at Westminster, where his dignified refusal to plead was interpreted as a confession of guilt. He was beheaded at Whitehall. >> English Civil War; Henrietta Maria; Long Parliament

Charles II (1630–85) King of Britain and Ireland (1660–85), born in London, the son of Charles I. On his father's execution (1649), he assumed the title of King, and was crowned at Scone (1651). Leading poorly organized forces into England, he met defeat at Worcester (1651). He then lived in exile until an impoverished England summoned him back as King (1660). In 1662 he married the Portuguese Princess Catherine of Braganza. His war with Holland (1665–7) was unpopular, and led to the dismissal of his adviser, Lord Clarendon (1667), who was replaced by a group of ministers (the Cabal). For the last four years of his life, he ruled without parliament. >> Cabal; Catherine of Braganza; Clarendon; Dutch Wars; English Civil War; Popish Plot

Charles V (1500–58) Holy Roman Emperor (1519–56), born in Ghent, Belgium. His rivalry with Francis I of France dominated W European affairs, and there was almost constant warfare between them, including the formation of the Holy League against Charles by Pope Clement VII, Henry VIII, Francis, and the Venetians. At the Diet of Augsburg (1530) he confirmed the 1521 Edict of Worms, which had condemned Luther, and in 1538 the pope, Francis, and Charles agreed to a truce. Charles's league with the pope drove the Protestants to rebellion, resulting in his defeat by Maurice of Saxony in 1552, and the granting of legal recognition to Protestantism. >> Francis I; Holy League; Protestantism; Reformation

Charles XIV, originally **Jean Baptiste Jules Bernadotte** (1763–1844) King of Sweden (1818–44), born a lawyer's son at Pau, France. He became marshal in the French army in 1804, fought in several Napoleonic campaigns (1805–9), then in 1810 was elected heir to the throne of Sweden. He refused to comply with Napoleon's demands, and in 1814 was rewarded with the Kingdom of Norway. >> Napoleon I

Charles (Philip Arthur George), Prince of Wales (1948–) Eldest son of Queen Elizabeth II and Prince Philip, Duke of Edinburgh, and heir apparent to the throne of Great Britain, born in London (at Buckingham Palace). Duke of Cornwall as the eldest son of the monarch, he was given the title of Prince of Wales in 1958, and invested at Caernarfon (1969). He served in the RAF and the Royal Navy (1971–6), and in 1981 married **Lady Diana Frances Spencer** (1961–97), younger daughter of the 8th Earl Spencer. They had two sons: **Prince William Arthur Philip Louis** (1982–) and **Prince Henry Charles Albert David** (1984–). The couple separated in 1992, and divorced in 1996. During this period he was, along with Princess Diana, the focus of continual media interest, attracting unprecedented attention from biographers. >> Elizabeth II

Charles, Jacques Alexandre César [shah(r)l] (1746–1823) Physicist, born in Beaugency, France. He made the first ascent by hydrogen balloon, reaching 3000 m/9800 ft in 1783. >> balloon; Charles's law

Charles, Ray, originally **Ray Charles Robinson** (1930–) Blind singer and pianist, born in Albany, GA. With 'I've got a Woman' (1955) he established a new style of rhythm and blues which introduced elements of Gospel music, and proved to be widely influential. >> rhythm and blues; soul (music)

Charles Edward Stuart >> **Stuart, Charles Edward**

Charles Martel [mah(r)**tel**] (Old French, 'the hammer') (c.688–741) Mayor of the palace for the last Merovingian kings of the Franks, and the undisputed head of the Carolingian family by 723. He conducted many campaigns against the Frisians and Saxons, and halted Muslim expansion in W Europe at the Battle of Poitiers (732). >> Carolingians; Franks; Gaul; Merovingians

Charles's law A law named after French physicist Jacques Charles (1746–1823), but first published by French physical chemist Joseph Gay-Lussac, and therefore also called **Gay-Lussac's law**: at constant pressure, the volume of a given mass of an ideal gas is directly proportional to a constant plus its temperature measured on any scale. The value of this constant fixes the zero of the absolute scale of temperature. >> gas laws; Gay-Lussac

Charleston (South Carolina) 32°46N 79°56W, pop (1995e) 87 300. Port in SE South Carolina, USA; founded in 1670; captured and held by the British, 1780–2; Confederate attack on nearby Fort Sumter (12–13 Apr 1861) began the Civil War; evacuated by Confederate forces in 1865 after a 2-year siege; devastated by an earthquake in 1886; badly damaged by hurricane Hugo in 1989; airfield; railway; US naval and air force base. >> American Civil War; South Carolina

Charleston (West Virginia) 38°21N 81°38W, pop (1995e) 58 800. Capital of state in West Virginia, USA; developed around Fort Lee in the 1780s; city status, 1870; capital, 1870–5 and from 1885; airfield; railway; an important transportation and trading centre. >> West Virginia

Charleston (dance) A jazz dance of black origin popularized in the 1920s, and first seen at Charleston, SC, USA in 1903. It can be danced either solo, with a partner, or in a group. Music is in 4/4 time and with syncopated rhythms.

Charleston, Battles of During the US War of Independence, the victorious British siege of Charleston, SC. It marked the beginning of the Southern phase of British strategy. >> American Revolution

Charlestown 17°08N 62°37W, pop (1995e) 1680. Capital and port of Nevis I, St Kitts-Nevis; formerly famous for its thermal springs. >> St Kitts-Nevis

charlock A roughly hairy annual (*Sinapis arvensis*), 30–80 cm/12–30 in, found in most temperate regions; flowers yellow, cross-shaped, capsule cylindrical, long-beaked. Once grown as a leaf vegetable, it is now a pernicious weed of arable land. (Family: Cruciferae.)

Charlotte 35°13N 80°51W, pop (1995e) 429 000. City in S North Carolina, USA; settled c.1750; incorporated, 1768; Mecklenburg Declaration of Independence was signed here, 1775; largest city in the state; airfield; railway; two universities (1867, 1946); birthplace of President Polk; professional team, Hornets (basketball). >> American Revolution; Polk

Charlotte Amalie [**shah(r)**lot a**mal**yuh], formerly **St Thomas** (1921–36) 18°22N 64°56W, pop (1995e) 12 600. Port capital of the US Virgin Is; founded by the Danes, 1672; important cruise ship port. >> Virgin Islands, United States

Charlottenburg Palace A palace in Berlin built (1695–1796) by Elector Frederick for his wife, Sophie Charlotte. The building houses a museum. >> Berlin; Frederick I (Prussia)

Charlottesville 38°02N 78°30W, pop (1995e) 43 500. City in C Virginia, USA, settled in the 1730s; named after the wife of King George III; railway; university (1819); Ash Lawn (home of James Monroe); Monticello (home of Jefferson) and University of Virginia are world heritage sites. >> Jefferson, Thomas; Monroe, James; Virginia

Charlottetown 46°14N 63°09W, pop (1991) 16 300. Principal capital of Prince Edward Island, NE Canada; founded by the French in the 1720s; capital since 1765; scene of Charlottetown Conference, 1864, which promoted plans for the union of Canada (achieved 1867); university (1969). >> Prince Edward Island

Charlottetown Accord A Canadian constitutional package for a new federal structure, put together by the prime minister (Brian Mulroney), provincial and territorial leaders, and First Nations representatives in 1992. It recognized aboriginal demands as legitimate, and promised to integrate First Nations' leadership in future constitutional discussions. It was rejected in a national referendum. >> Canada ℹ; First Nations; Meech Lake Accord; Mulroney

Charlton, Bobby, popular name of **Sir Robert Charlton** (1937–) Footballer, born in Ashington, Northumberland, the brother of Jack Charlton. He spent most of his playing career with Manchester United, surviving the Munich air disaster (1958). A member of the successful England World Cup winning team in 1966, he played for England 106 times, and scored a record 49 goals. >> Charlton, Jack; football ℹ

Charlton, Jack(ie), popular name of **John Charlton** (1935–) Footballer, born in Ashington, Northumberland, the brother of Bobby Charlton. He played for Leeds United, and also for England, later becoming manager of Middlesborough (1973), Sheffield Wednesday (1977), and Newcastle United (1984). In 1986 he was appointed manager of the Ireland team, retiring in 1996. >> Charlton, Bobby

charm In particle physics, an internal additive quantum number conserved in strong and electromagnetic interactions, but not in weak interactions; symbol *C*. It was postulated in 1974. >> particle physics; quantum numbers; quark

Charon (astronomy) [**kair**on] Pluto's only known satellite, discovered photographically in 1978; distance from the planet 19·1 million km/11·9 million mi; diameter 1200 km/745 mi. It has a surface of mainly water ice.

Charon (mythology) [**kai**ron] The ferryman of the Underworld, who carried the shades or souls of the dead across the R Acheron. The Greeks placed a small coin in the mouth of a corpse as Charon's fee. >> Styx

charr Freshwater or anadromous (ascending rivers to breed) fish in lakes and rivers of N hemisphere; length up to 1 m/3$\frac{1}{4}$ ft; includes the **Arctic charr** (*Salvelinus alpinus*) and **brook charr** or brook trout (*Salvelinus fontinalis*). (Family: Salmonidae.)

Charteris, Leslie [**chah(r)**teris], originally **Leslie Charles Bowyer Yin** (1907–93) Crime-story writer, born in Singapore. He settled in the USA (1932), becoming known as the creator of Simon Templar, 'the Saint'.

Chartism A largely working-class radical movement which achieved substantial but intermittent support in Britain between the late 1830s and the early 1850s. Its objective was democratic rights for all men, and it took its name from 'The People's Charter', first published in 1838. Its six points were: universal manhood suffrage; the abolition of property qualifications for MPs; parliamentary constituencies of equal size; a secret ballot; payment for MPs; and annual general elections. >> radicalism

Chartres [**shah(r)**truh], ancient **Autricum**, **Civitas Carnutum** 48°29N 1°30E, pop (1995e) 43 100. City in NC France; railway; bishopric; agricultural centre and wheat market; Gothic cathedral (1195–1220), a world heritage site. >> Gothic architecture

Chartreuse, La Grande [la grãd chah(r)**troez**] The principal monastery of the Carthusian order, founded in 1084 by St Bruno in the Dauphin Alps of SE France. The present structure (which is now a museum) dates from the 17th-c. Chartreuse liqueur was first distilled here in 1607. >> Bruno, St; Carthusians

Charybdis [ka**rib**dis] In Greek mythology, a whirlpool which swallowed ships whole, encountered by Odysseus on his wanderings. >> Odysseus; Scylla

Chase, James Hadley, pseudonym of **René Raymond** (1906–85) Novelist, born in London. He started the vogue for tough realism in gangster stories with his *No Orchids for Miss Blandish* (1939).

Chase, Salmon P(ortland) (1808–73) Jurist and statesman, born in Cornish, NH. He became secretary of the Treasury (1861–4), and in 1864 was appointed Chief Justice of the USA. >> Chief Justice

chat The name given to numerous birds: 51 species of thrush (Family: Turdidae), 5 species of New World warblers (Family: Parulidae), and 5 species of Australian chats (Family: Ephthianuridae). >> babbler; thrush (bird); warbler

chateau Originally, a mediaeval fortified residence in France, acting as the focus of the feudal community. By the 15th-c chateaux had become private seignoral residences, while the 16th-c saw the emergence of less fortified buildings. >> castle; Fontainebleau; Versailles

Chateaubriand, François Auguste René, vicomte de (Viscount of) [shatohbreeã] (1768–1848) Writer and French politician, born in St Malo, France. *Le Génie du christianisme* (1802, The Genius of Christianity) made him prominent among men of letters. In his later years, he wrote his celebrated autobiography, *Mémoires d'outre-tombe* (Memoirs from Beyond the Tomb), not published as a whole until 1902.

Chatham, 1st Earl of >> **Pitt, William, 1st Earl of Chatham**

Chatham Islands [**cha**tm] pop (1995e) 787; area 963 sq km/372 sq mi. Islands of New Zealand in the SW Pacific Ocean; 850 km/528 mi E of South Island; visited in 1791 by the British brig *Chatham*; chief settlement, Waitangi. >> New Zealand ℹ

Chatsworth One of the great English country houses, built (1687–1707) for the 1st Duke of Devonshire near Edensor village, Derbyshire, UK. The original design by William Talman (1650–1719) was altered and extended by successive architects.

Chattanooga Campaign A series of battles in Tennessee, during the American Civil War, leading to Southern victory at Chickamauga, and Northern victories at Lookout Mountain and Missionary Ridge. It placed Northern troops in a position to bisect the Confederacy on an E–W axis. >> American Civil War

chattels >> **property**

Chatterton, Thomas (1752–70) Poet, born in Bristol. In 1768 he hoaxed the whole city with a description, 'from an old manuscript', of the opening of Bristol Bridge in 1248. His poems, purporting to be by Thomas Rowley, a 15th-c monk, were denounced as forgeries, and the debate over their authenticity raged for 80 years.

Chaucer, Geoffrey (c.1343–1400) Poet, probably born in London. Travelling extensively abroad on the king's service, he also held royal posts at home, including that of Comptroller of the Petty Customs (1382). In 1386 he was elected a knight of the shire for Kent. During this time he wrote *Troilus and Criseyde*, and several other major works. His early writings followed French trends, but were greatly influenced by Italian authors, notably Boccaccio. His later period includes his most famous work, the unfinished *Canterbury Tales*. Chaucer was the first great poet of the English nation; and in the Middle Ages he stands supreme. >> Boccaccio; Canterbury Tales

Chautauqua movement [shuh**taw**kwuh] A late 19th-c and early 20th-c US adult education movement, organized under Methodist auspices by Lewis Miller (1829–99) and Bishop John H Vincent (1832–1920). The original centre at L Chautauqua, New York, continues its activities. >> further education

Chavez, Cesar (Estrada) [sha**vez**, **shah**vez] (1927–93) Labour leader, born in Yuma, AZ. In 1962 he started the National Farm Workers Association. He became widely known for organizing a series of national grape boycotts that helped the union to gain improved wages and working conditions for its members.

Chechnya [chech**nya**] Republic in the C Caucasus, bordered S by the main Caucasus range and Georgia; capital, Dzhoxhar Ghala (new name of Grozny, 1997); economy based on oil, with major refining centre at Grozny; population mainly Chechen (c.60%, Muslim); history of resistance to Russian rule, especially in 19th-c; became an administrative region (*oblast*) within the Soviet Union; amalgamated with Ingushetiya (**Checheno-Ingushetiya**) as an autonomous republic (ASSR) in 1934, dissolved by Stalin in 1944, with its population deported, but re-established in 1957; area 19 3000 sq km/7400 sq mi; pop (1992e) 1 300 000; Chechnya declared independence from Russia, 1991; Chechnya and Ingushetiya separated, 1992; civil war between forces loyal to Chechen president Dzhokar Dudayev and former leader of the opposition Ruslan Khasbulatov; invasion of Russian troops with aim of restoring Moscow control, 1994; Dudayev killed, peace accord signed between Yeltsin and new Chechen leadership, but hostilities renewed, 1996; Russian troops finally withdrawn by end of 1996, with fresh elections in early 1997. >> Russia ℹ

check >> **cheque**

checkers >> **draughts**

Cheddar 5°17N 2°46W, pop (1995e) 4390. Market town in Somerset, SW England; famous for the limestone features of the Cheddar Gorge and for the Cheddar cheese originally made here. >> Somerset

cheese A dairy foodstuff made from milk. Milk proteins are soluble in water at a neutral pH, but when the pH falls to a critically low level of about 4·6, the proteins precipitate out to form the curd of sour milk, which is the basis of cheese manufacture. The wide variety of cheeses is achieved by allowing particular strains of bacteria to cause the fall in pH by fermenting lactose. The curd is then processed into cheese by a variety of methods, some of which require quite lengthy maturation in the presence of moulds. Others are matured in a smoky atmosphere, and others mixed with cream to form very creamy cheeses. Many regions of Europe have produced cheeses for which they are famous. France alone has more than 400 varieties, including Brie, Camembert, and Roquefort. Other well-known cheeses include Swiss Gruyère and Emmenthal; English Cheddar, Cheshire, and Stilton; Italian Parmesan and Gorgonzola; and Dutch Gouda and Edam. Versions of these cheeses are now made in many other countries. >> casein; fermentation; milk

cheetah A member of the cat family (*Acinonyx jubatus*), native to Africa and SW Asia; fastest land animal (can reach 110 kph/70 mph); only cat unable to retract its claws completely; pale with solid dark spots; lean with long legs and tail. >> Felidae

Cheka An acronym from the Russian letters **che** + **ka**, for the All-Russian Extraordinary Commission for Combating Counter-Revolution and Sabotage, established in 1917. During the Civil War it was responsible for executing thousands of political opponents in what came to be called the 'Red Terror'. >> Bolsheviks; communism

Chekhov, Anton (Pavlovitch) [**che**kof] (1860–1904) Playwright and master of the short story, born in Taganrog, Russia. His first book of stories appeared in 1886. His early full-length plays were failures, but when *Chayka* (1896, The Seagull) was revived in 1898 it was a great success. He then wrote his masterpieces: *Dyadya Vanya* (1900, Uncle Vanya), *Tri sestry* (1901, The Three Sisters), and *Vishnyovy sad* (1904, The Cherry Orchard).

chelation therapy [kee**lay**shn] A treatment for heavy metal poisoning in which biochemical substances are given to a patient intravenously to bind the poisonous metal so that it is inactivated and can be removed from the body. The substances administered are known as **chelating agents** and vary according to the toxic substance to be inactivated. >> toxicology

Chelmsford 51°44N 0°28E, pop (1995e) 102 000. County

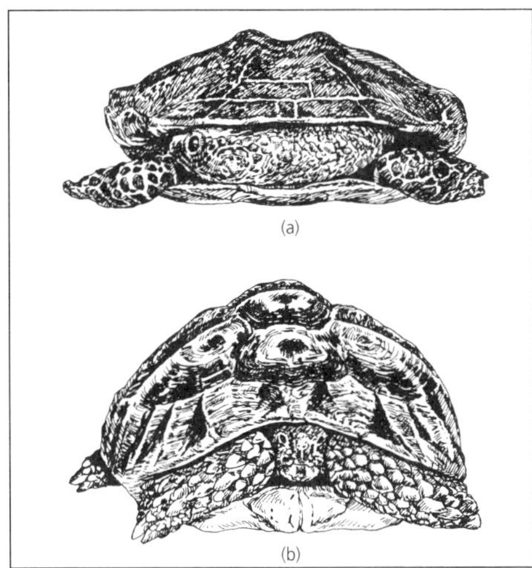

Chelonia – Side-necked turtle (a); hidden-necked turtle (b)

town of Essex, SE England; railway; university (1992); cathedral (15th-c). >> Essex

Chelonia [ke**loh**nia] An order of reptiles (244 species); body encased in a domed shell of bones covered by large horny scales; no teeth; jaws form a hard beak; most withdraw head and legs into the shell for protection. >> reptile; terrapin; tortoise; turtle (biology)

Chelsea >> **Kensington and Chelsea**

Chelsea pensioners Occupants of the hospital for old and disabled soldiers in Chelsea, London. Founded by Charles II in 1682, the Royal Hospital takes in about 420 men, usually aged over 65. Chelsea pensioners wear distinctive uniforms, navy blue in winter and scarlet in summer.

Cheltenham [**chelt**nm] 51°54N 2°04W, pop (1995e) 103 000. Residential town in Gloucestershire, SWC England; famous spa in 18th-c; railway; schools (Cheltenham College, Cheltenham Ladies' College); Cheltenham Gold Cup horse-race (Mar). >> Gloucestershire

Chelyabinsk [chil**ya**binsk], also **Tchelyabinsk** 55°12N 61°25E, pop (1995e) 1 159 000. Industrial city in W Siberian Russia; founded in 1736 as a frontier outpost; airport; road and rail junction. >> Russia ℹ

chemical bond The electric forces linking atoms in molecules and non-molecular solid phases. The energy required to break a chemical bond (eg to convert a chlorine molecule to two chlorine atoms) is called the **bond energy**. >> atom; valency

chemical elements The simplest substances into which matter can be broken without nuclear reactions. Each element is characterized by the number of protons in the nuclei of its atoms, the atomic number of the element, and is identified by a one- or two-letter symbol. There are about 90 elements which have been found in nature, and about 105 when artificially made elements are included. >> atom; RR1036

chemical engineering The theory and practice of designing, setting up, and operating apparatus for the large-scale manufacture of the products of chemical reactions. University departments, professional training, and professional institutions devoted to chemical engineering have developed in all industrialized countries since 1900. >> chemistry; engineering

chemical laser A laser in which a chemical reaction provides the energy for laser action. For example, in a laser containing carbon dioxide with hydrogen and fluorine, the laser action would take place in the carbon dioxide, powered by the reaction of hydrogen and fluorine to give hydrogen fluoride. >> chemical reaction; laser ℹ

chemical reaction A process in which one or more compounds are converted into others, usually with the gain or loss of energy by the system, by the breaking and forming of chemical bonds. >> catalysis

chemical warfare The use of deadly or disabling gases in warfare. It was forbidden by a declaration of the Hague Conference in 1899, but one of the signatories, Germany, was the first to use such weapons, the first attack being made against British troops at Ypres in April 1915. Chemical weapons are not forbidden by treaty, and large quantities were stockpiled by the USA and the former Soviet Union. Other agents of chemical warfare include non-lethal harassing and incapacitating agents, hallucinogenic substances, and herbicides. >> Agent Orange; mustard gas; nerve gas; poison gas

chemiluminescence >> **bioluminescence**

chemin de fer [shuhmĩ duh **fair**] A casino card game, often referred to as 'chemmy'. A variant of *baccarat banque*, it is played by up to 12 players. The object is to obtain a total as near as possible to 9 with two or three cards. >> baccarat

chemistry The study of the composition of substances and the changes that they undergo. Antoine Lavoisier is usually considered the father of modern chemistry, with his distinction between *elements* and *compounds* formed from elements, and his insistence that chemical reactions are quantitative in nature. With the development of the atomic theory of John Dalton, chemistry evolved rapidly in the 19th-c. **Organic chemistry** originated from the isolation of medicinal compounds from animals and plants, and **inorganic chemistry** from the study of minerals. **Physical chemistry** (studying the relationship of physical properties to chemical composition, structure, and reactivity) and **analytical chemistry** (studying the composition of material) also developed in parallel, particularly with 20th-c developments in spectroscopic and electrochemical methods. Modern chemistry has also been advanced by the elucidation of the nature of chemical bonding. Chemistry today is the basis of a worldwide industry concerned with almost every aspect of life, including food, fuel, clothing, building materials, and medicines. >> inorganic / organic / physical chemistry; assaying; chemical bond / elements / reaction; chemotherapy; Dalton, John; electrochemistry; geochemistry; histochemistry; Lavoisier; radiochemistry; stereochemistry; thermochemistry

chemoreception The perception of chemical stimuli by living organisms; usually performed by specialized receptor cells or organs. Chemoreception includes both olfaction (the perception of smells) and gustation (the perception of taste).

chemotherapy The drug treatment of infectious diseases (using antibiotics), parasitic diseases, and cancer. Cancer chemotherapy usually involves the administration of a cocktail of cytotoxic drugs (ie which kill or damage cells). These also attack normal cells (especially bone marrow) causing reduced resistance to infection, loss of hair, and sterility, though supportive therapy can now help with these problems. >> antibiotics; cancer; drug resistance; tumour

Chenab, River [**chay**nab] River in Kashmir and Pakistan; one of the five rivers of the Punjab; rises in the Himalayas and flows into Pakistan, finally joining the R Indus; length 1087 km/675 mi. >> Kashmir; Pakistan ℹ

Chengchow; Cheng-chou >> **Zhengzhou**

Chengdu or **Cheng-tu** [cheng**doo**] 30°37N 104°06E, pop (1995e) 3 168 000. Capital of Sichuan province, SWC China; founded 200 BC as Zhou dynastic capital; regional industrial base since 1949; airfield; railway; university (1931); home of Sichuan opera. >> China 🛈

Cheng-hsien >> **Zhengzhou**

Cheops, Ship of >> **Ship of Cheops**

cheque (UK) or **check** (US) An order in writing to a bank to pay the person or institution named the sum of money specified. Cheques are commonly printed by banks for the use of their customers, but may be written on anything. >> cheque card

cheque card A flexible plastic card (c.54 × 85 mm/ $2\frac{1}{8} \times 3\frac{1}{3}$ in) issued by banks to customers who have a cheque book. It shows the customer's name and account number, and guarantees that the bank will honour a cheque (up to a specified sum) where the name and number correspond. >> cheque; credit card

Chequers [**chek**erz] The official country residence of British prime ministers, located in the Chiltern Hills, Buckinghamshire. It is mentioned in the Domesday Book.

Cherbourg [**sher**boorg], Fr [shairboor], ancient **Carusbur** 49°38N 1°37W, pop (1995e) 29 600. Fortified seaport in NW France; harbour protected by a long breakwater, 1853; France's third largest naval base; shipbuilding and dockyards; ferry services to Southampton, Weymouth, Rosslare. >> France 🛈

Chernenko, Konstantin Ustinovich [cher**nyeng**ko] (1911–85) Soviet statesman and president (1984–5), born in Bolshaya Tes, Russia. Regarded as a conservative, Chernenko was a rival of Andropov in the Party leadership contest of 1982, and became Party general secretary and head of state after Andropov's death in 1984. He suffered from ill health, and died soon after, to be succeeded by Gorbachev. >> Andropov; Gorbachev

Chernobyl [cher**no**bil] 51°16N 30°15E. City in Ukraine; scene of the world's largest known nuclear disaster in 1986; nuclear power station projected to close in 2000. >> Ukraine 🛈

chernozem [**cher**nozem] A dark, rich and fertile soil found in cool, low-humidity regions. It is typical of the Russian steppes. >> soil

Cherokee [**che**rokee] North American Indian people, originally from the Great Lakes, who migrated to the SE after their defeat by the Iroquois and Delaware. They are now the largest Indian group in the USA, numbering c.308 000 (1990 census).

cherry A deciduous, mostly N temperate tree; often with distinctive, shiny, reddish-brown, banded bark; clusters of white flowers and bright red or purplish fruits which are sour or sweet, depending on the species or variety. (Genus: *Prunus*. Subgenus: *Cerasus*. Family: Rosaceae.) >> gean; prunus

chert A very fine-grained form of silica (SiO_2), in which the quartz crystals are too small to be observed by optical microscopy. It is characteristically formed on the ocean bed by the accumulation and subsequent recrystallization of the silica shells of diatoms and radiolaria. >> flint; quartz; silica

cherubim [**che**ruhbim], singular **cherub** In the Hebrew Bible/Old Testament, winged celestial creatures or beasts of various descriptions. Their roles include guarding the tree of life in the Garden of Eden (*Gen* 3.24), and accompanying the throne chariot of God (*Ezek* 1, 10). >> Eden, Garden of; seraphim

Cherubini, (Maria) Luigi (Carlo Zenobio Salvatore) [keru**bee**nee] (1760–1842) Composer, born in Florence, Italy. He wrote a succession of operas, notably *Les Deux Journées* (1880, trans The Water-Carrier). His later work was mainly ecclesiastical.

chervil A hollow-stemmed annual (*Anthriscus cerefolium*), growing to 70 cm/27 in, native to Europe and Asia; flowers small, white; fruits oblong, smooth. It is often grown for its aromatic leaves, used as a flavouring. (Family: Umbelliferae.) >> herb

Cherwell, Frederick Alexander Lindemann, 1st Viscount [**chah(r)**wel] (1886–1957) Scientist, born in Baden-Baden, Germany. In 1914 he became director of the Experimental Physics Station at Farnborough, where he evolved the mathematical theory of aircraft spin, and later became director of the Clarendon laboratory. A close friend of Winston Churchill, he became his scientific adviser in 1940.

Chesapeake Bay [**ches**apeek] 38°40N 76°25W. An inlet of the Atlantic Ocean in Virginia (S) and Maryland (N) states, USA; over 300 km/185 mi long; part of the Intracoastal Waterway; an early area of US settlement (explored 1607). >> Intracoastal Waterway; United States of America 🛈

Cheshire pop (1995e) 970 000; area 2328 sq km/899 sq mi. County of NWC England; county town, Chester; Warrington and Halton new unitary authorities from 1998. >> Chester; England 🛈

Cheshire (of Woodhall), (Geoffrey) Leonard Cheshire, Baron (1917–92) British bomber pilot and philanthropist, several times decorated (including the VC, 1944) for his bombing missions. He was one of the official British observers of the destruction caused by the atomic bomb over Nagasaki (1945). This experience, together with his new-found faith, Catholicism, made him devote the rest of his life to tending the incurably sick, by founding 'Cheshire Homes' (220, in 45 countries). In 1959 he married **Sue Ryder, Baroness Ryder** (1923–), who in 1953 founded the Sue Ryder Foundation for the sick and disabled. In several countries, projects now function under the auspices of the Ryder–Cheshire Foundation. >> atomic bomb

chess A game for two players played on a board containing 64 squares alternately black and white. Each player has 16 pieces, either black or white, consisting of eight *pawns*, two *rooks* (also known as *castles*), two *knights*, two *bishops*, a *queen*, and a *king*. The game is one of strategy, the object being to capture the opponent's king. The earliest reference to chess is from AD c.600; the current pieces have existed in standard form for more than 500 years. The international body which supervises the game is the World Chess Federation (*Fédération Internationale des Echecs*, or FIDE). It traditionally organizes the world chess championships and other international competitions, though in 1987 a disagreement between Russian grandmaster Gary Kasparov and FIDE over levels of prize funding and FIDE's alleged autocratic methods led Kasparov to promote a breakaway body (the *Professional Chess Association*). >> draughts; shogi; RR1038, RR1048

Chessman, Caryl (Whittier), nickname **The Red Light Bandit** (1921–60) Convict and writer, born in St Joseph, MI. He was sentenced to death in 1948 on 17 charges of kidnapping, robbery and sexual assault, but was granted eight stays of execution, amounting to a record period of 12 years under sentence of death without a reprieve. During this period he conducted a brilliant legal battle from prison, and wrote best-selling books against capital punishment, including *Cell 2455 Death Row* (1956).

chest >> **thorax**

Chester, Lat **Deva**, **Devana Castra**, Welsh **Caerleon**, Anglo-Saxon **Legaceaster** 53°12N 2°54W, pop (1995e) 86 700. County town of Cheshire, NWC England; on the R Dee; important Roman port and military centre; railway; cathedral (13th–15th-c); commercial centre; city walls; football league team, Chester City. >> Cheshire

Chesterton, G(ilbert) K(eith) (1874–1936) Critic, novelist and poet, born in London. The amiable detective-priest who brought him popularity with a wider public first appeared in *The Innocence of Father Brown* (1911). He became a Catholic in 1922, and thereafter wrote mainly on religious topics.

Chetniks (Serbo-Croatian *četnici*) Yugoslav, mainly Serbian, guerrillas during World War 2. Under the leadership of Drazha Mihailovic, they fought Tito's communist Partisans rather than the Axis occupiers. Abandoned by the Allies in 1944, they were defeated by the Partisans, and Mihailovic was tried and executed in 1945. Since 1990 the name has been adopted by Serb irregular forces in the former state of Yugoslavia. >> Mihailovic; Tito

Chevalier, Maurice [she**val**yay] (1888–1972) Film and vaudeville actor, born in Paris. His first Hollywood film was *The Innocents of Paris* (1929), and 30 years later his individual, straw-hatted, *bon-viveur* personality, with his distinctive French accent, was still much acclaimed, as in the musical *Gigi*. He received a special Academy Award in 1958.

Cheviot Hills [**chee**viuht] Hill range on the border between Scotland and England; extends 56 km/35 mi SW; rises to 816 m/2677 ft at The Cheviot; gives its name to a famous breed of sheep. >> England ℹ; Scotland ℹ

chevrotain [**shev**rotin] A ruminant artiodactyl mammal, native to tropical forest in Africa, India, Sri Lanka and SE Asia; small with stocky bodies and short slender legs; no horns or antlers; male with long protruding canine teeth; also known as **mouse deer** or **deerlet**. (Family: Tragulidae, 4 species.) >> antlers ℹ; artiodactyl; deer; ruminant ℹ

chewing gum A sugared and flavoured product made from the concentrated juice of latex of the sapodilla tree, especially popular in the USA. It is chewed for its flavour, but not swallowed. >> chicle

Cheyenne (Indians) [shi**yan**] North American Plains Indians, divided since the 1830s into N and S groups. They live mainly in Montana and Oklahoma, numbering c.12 000 (1990 census). >> Ojibwa; Plains Indians; Sioux

Cheyenne (Wyoming) [shi**yan**] 41°08N 104°49W, pop (1995e) 53 400. State capital in SE Wyoming, USA; founded at a railway junction, 1867; territorial capital, 1869; railway; livestock market and shipping centre. >> Wyoming

Chiang Ch'ing >> **Jiang Qing**

Chiang Kai-shek >> **Jiang Jieshi**

Chiang Mai [jee-eng miy] 18°48N 98°59E, pop (1995e) 183 000. City in NW Thailand; N Thailand's principal city since 1296, when it was founded as the capital of Lan Na Thai kingdom; airfield; railway; university. >> Thailand ℹ

chiaroscuro [keearos**koo**roh] (Ital 'light-dark') In painting, the use of strong light and shadow to define forms in space. The technique was developed in Italy by Leonardo da Vinci and Caravaggio, and perfected by Rembrandt in 17th-c Holland. >> Caravaggio; Leonardo da Vinci; Rembrandt

Chicago [shi**kah**goh] 41°53N 87°38W, pop (1995e) 2 907 000. Third largest city in the USA, in NE Illinois, on L Michigan; built on the site of Fort Dearborn; settled in the 1830s; city status, 1837; much of the city destroyed by fire, 1871; notorious gangster activity in the Prohibition years, 1920s; now the major industrial, commercial, financial and cultural centre for the US interior; a quarter of the nation's steel produced in and around the city; transport centre of the USA, with one of the busiest airports in the world; major rail network and inland port; seven universities; Sears Tower (1974), the world's second tallest building in 1999 (443 m/1454 ft); professional teams, Cubs, White Sox (baseball), Bulls (basketball), Bears (football), Black Hawks (ice hockey). >> Illinois; Michigan, Lake; Prohibition; Sears Tower

Chicago School (architecture) The name given to a group of Chicago architects and office buildings in the late 19th-c. The buildings are the forerunners of 20th-c skyscrapers, and are characterized by the pioneering use of steel frame construction, clothed in masonry and with large expanses of windows, often to a great height.

Chicago School (economics) A group of economists at Chicago University, led by Milton Friedman from 1948 to 1979. They hold the view that competition and market forces should be allowed to act freely, and with minimal government interference, for the best results. >> Friedman

Chichén Itzá [chee**chen** eet**za**] Toltec/Maya capital of the Yucatan peninsula, Mexico, AD c.1000–1200. Its monumental centre (area 3 km/1¾ mi by 2 km/1¼ mi) contains temple pyramids and the largest known Meso-American ballcourt. >> Mayas; Toltecs

Chichester [**chi**chester] 50°50N 0°48W, pop (1995e) 27 800. County town of West Sussex, S England; founded by the Romans; railway; cathedral (11th–12th-c); bishop's palace (12th-c); Chichester Festival Theatre. >> Sussex, West

Chichester, Sir Francis (Charles) [**chi**chester] (1901–72) Yachtsman, born in Barnstaple, Devon. In 1953 he took up yacht racing, winning the first solo transatlantic yacht race (1960) in *Gipsy Moth III*, sailing from Plymouth to New York in 40 days. He made a successful solo circumnavigation of the world (1966–7) in *Gipsy Moth IV*, sailing from Plymouth to Sydney in 107 days and from there back to Plymouth, via Cape Horn, in 119 days. >> sailing; yacht ℹ

chickadee A name used in the USA for certain small birds of the tit family. (Family: Paridae, 7 species.) >> tit

chickaree >> **red squirrel**

chicken >> **domestic fowl**

chickenpox A highly infectious and usually benign disease of childhood, caused by the same virus that is responsible for shingles. It has a characteristic blister-like eruption in the skin. >> shingles

chick-pea A branching annual (*Cicer arietinum*), probably native to Asia, growing to 50 cm/20 in or more; pea-flowers white or bluish, solitary on long stalks; pods inflated, usually 2-seeded; also called **garbanzos**. It has been cultivated since ancient times as a fodder plant and for its edible seeds. (Family: Leguminosae.)

chickweed A slender, spreading, often pale-green annual (*Stellaria media*); a very common weed, often flowering throughout the year; flowers tiny, white, five petals, deeply cleft into two parts. (Family: Caryophyllaceae.)

chicle An evergreen tree (*Achras zapota*) growing to 18 m/60 ft, native to Central America; flowers tiny, greenish-white, 6-petalled; fruit 5–10 cm/2–4 in, greyish to reddish-brown with yellow flesh. The copious white latex provides the elastic base for chewing gum; the edible fruit is called **sapodilla plum**. (Family: Sapotaceae.) >> chewing gum; latex; rubber

chicory A perennial growing to 120 cm/5 ft (*Cichorium intybus*), with a long stout tap root, native to Europe, W Asia, and N Africa; flower-heads nearly stalkless, bright blue, rarely pink or white. Dried and ground roots are used as a coffee substitute. (Family: Compositae.) >> coffee

Chief Justice The presiding justice of the United States Supreme Court, nominated by the US president and confirmed by a majority of the Senate. The Chief Justice serves for life, presides in both public session and at private court conferences, assigns the task of writing majority opinions, and administers the oath of office to the US president. >> Chase, Salmon P; judge; Marshall, John; Supreme Court; Warren, Earl

chiffchaff A bird belonging to a group of Old World warblers (*Phylloscopus collybita*); native to Europe, N Africa, and Asia. (Family: Silviidae.) >> warbler

chigger >> **harvest-mite**

Chihuahua [chi**wah**wa] 28°40N 106°06W, pop (1995e) 589 000. City in N Mexico; altitude 1428 m/4685 ft; centre of Pancho Villa's revolutionary activities; railway; university (1954); cathedral (18th-c). >> chihuahua; Mexico ℹ; Villa, Francisco

chihuahua [chi**wah**wa] The smallest domestic breed of dog, developed in Mexico; tiny body; head disproportionately large with bulbous forehead, large widely spaced eyes, and large ears. >> dog

chilblains Bluish and slightly swollen areas of the skin of fingers and toes, caused by exposure to excessive cold. The lesions become red and itchy on warming.

child abuse The treatment of a child by an adult in a way unacceptable in a given culture at a given time; also referred to technically as **non-accidental injury of childhood** and popularly as **battered baby/child syndrome**. Abuse may be physical (soft and bony tissue injury, burns and scalds, poisoning and suffocation), sexual, emotional, or through neglect. Most abuse is perpetrated by parents, particularly non-related cohabitants. Such activities may result in both criminal proceedings being taken against the adult concerned, and care proceedings in respect of the victim. >> care proceedings; NSPCC; social work

Childers, (Robert) Erskine [**chil**derz] (1870–1922) Irish nationalist and writer, born in London. He wrote a popular spy story, *The Riddle of the Sands* (1903), and several works of nonfiction. He later joined the Irish Republican Army, and was active in the Civil War, but was captured and executed at Dublin. His son, **Erskine Childers** (1905–74) was President of Ireland in 1973–4. >> IRA; nationalism

Children's Crusade A movement in 1212 of thousands of children from Germany and France, aiming to reach the Holy Land and recapture Jerusalem from the Turks. Some reached Genoa, Italy, but did not embark; some reached Marseille, France, whence they were shipped to N Africa and sold into slavery. >> Crusades ℹ

Child Support Agency (CSA) In the UK, a government agency responsible for assessing and collecting obligatory child maintenance payments from non-resident parents. Introduced in 1993, it took over its role from the courts, and became part of the Department of Social Security. Although its aim of alleviating single-parent poverty was welcomed, widespread complaints in the mid-1990s about its practices made its work controversial, and led to several procedural reforms.

Chile [**chi**lee], official name **Republic of Chile**, Span **República de Chile** pop (1995e) 14 263 000; area 756 626 sq km/292 058 sq mi (excluding territory claimed in Antarctica). Republic of SW South America; capital, Santiago; timezone GMT −4; mainly mixed Spanish and Indian descent; chief religions, Roman Catholic (77%), Protestant (13%); official language, Spanish; unit of currency, the peso of 100 centavos; narrow coastal belt, backed by Andean mountain ridges rising in the N to 6910 m/22 600 ft at Ojos del Salado; Atacama Desert in far NW; highly varied climate (spans 37° of latitude, with altitudes from Andean peaks to coastal plain); extreme aridity in N; cold, wet, and windy in far S; Mediterranean climate in C Chile; originally occupied by South American Indians; arrival of Spanish, 1537; part of Viceroyalty of Peru; independence from Spain declared, 1810, resulting in war until Spanish defeat in 1818; border disputes with Bolivia, Peru, and Argentina brought Chilean victory in War of the Pacific, 1879–83; Marxist coalition government of Salvador Allende ousted, 1973, and replaced by military junta under Augusto Pinochet, banning all political activity; constitution providing for eventual return to democracy came into effect in 1981; plebiscite held in 1988 resulted in a defeat for Pinochet's candidacy as president beyond 1990; National Congress restored, 1990; elections, 1993; 6-year term for president agreed in 1994; economy based on agriculture and mining; fishing in N, timber in S; oil and gas in far S. >> Atacama Desert; Easter Island; Santiago ℹ; RR1004 political leaders

Chile pine >> **monkey-puzzle**

chili >> **pepper 1**

Chilopoda [kee**lo**poda] >> **centipede**

Chiltern Hills Low chalk hill range in SE England; extends 88 km/55 mi NE between S Oxfordshire and Bedfordshire; rises to 260 m/853 ft at Coombe Hill. >> Chiltern Hundreds; England ℹ

Chiltern Hundreds In the UK, a legally fictitious office of profit under the Crown: Steward or Bailiff of Her Majesty's Chiltern Hundreds of Stoke, Desborough, and Burnham. To accept this office disqualifies an MP from the House of Commons. As an MP cannot resign, application to be appointed to the Chiltern Hundreds is the conventional manner of leaving the Commons. >> Commons, House of

Chi-lung >> **Jilong**

Chimaera >> **Chimera**

chimaera [ki**meer**a] Cartilaginous fish (*Chimaera monstrosa*) with robust body, large pelvic fins, and long tapering tail; common in deeper waters of N Atlantic and Mediterranean; length up to 1·5 m/5 ft; cream with brown patches and metallic sheen; also called **ratfish** or **rabbitfish**. (Family: Chimaeridae.) >> cartilaginous fish

Chimborazo [cheembo**ra**soh] 1°28S 78°48W. Inactive Andean volcano in C Ecuador; height 6310 m/20 702 ft. >> Andes; Ecuador ℹ

Chimbote [cheem**boh**tay] 8°59S 78°38W, pop (1995e) 325 000. Port in N Peru; one of the few natural harbours

on the W coast; a new port has been built to serve the national steel industry. >> Peru 🅸

Chimera [kiy**meer**a, ki**meer**a], also **Chimaera** In Greek mythology, a fabulous monster with the head of a lion, the body of a goat and the tail of a serpent, which breathed fire.

chimpanzee An ape native to equatorial Africa, believed to be the closest living relative to humans; height, 1–1·7 m/ $3\frac{1}{4}$–$5\frac{1}{2}$ ft; black coat; hair on head parted or directed backwards; face and ears naked; skin pale or dark; spends most time on the ground; eats fruit and some insects, but may kill small vertebrates; uses twigs, etc as tools to obtain food; two species: **chimpanzee** (*Pan troglodytes*) and the smaller, black-faced **pygmy chimpanzee** or **bonobo** (*Pan paniscus*). >> ape

Chimu [chee**moo**] A South American Indian people of Peru, the most important political and cultural group before the Incas in the 14th-c, with a highly stratified social system. They were conquered by the Incas (1465–70), who absorbed many aspects of their culture. >> Incas; Peru 🅸

China, official name **People's Republic of China**, Chin **Zhonghua Renmin Gonghe Guo** or **Zhongguo** pop (1995e) 1 215 293 000; area 9 597 000 sq km/3 704 000 sq mi; also claims island of Taiwan. Socialist state in C and E Asia; capital, Beijing; timezone GMT +8; 92% Han Chinese, with over 50 minorities; officially atheist, but widespread Confucianism, Taoism, Buddhism, and ancestor-worship; languages, standard Chinese (Putonghua) or Mandarin, also Yue (Cantonese), Wu, Minbei, Minnan, Xiang, Gan, Hakka, and minority languages; official romanized form of writing (*pinyin*); unit of currency (*renminbi*), the yuan or kuai of 100 fen (10 fen = 1 jiao); over two-thirds upland hill, mountain, and plateau; highest mountains in the W, where the Tibetan plateau rises to average altitude of 4000 m/13 000 ft; land descends to desert/semi-desert of Sinkiang and Inner Mongolia (NE); broad and fertile plains of Manchuria (NE); further E and S, prosperous Sichuan basin, drained by Yangtze R; heavily populated S plains and E coast, with rich, fertile soils; varied climate, with seven zones: (1) NE China, cold winters, with strong N winds, warm and humid summers, unreliable rainfall; (2) C China, warm and humid summers, sometimes typhoons or tropical cyclones on coast; (3) S China, partly within tropics, wettest area in summer; frequent typhoons; (4) SW China, summer temperatures moderated by altitude, winters mild with little rain; (5) Xizang autonomous region, high plateau surrounded by mountains, winters severe with frequent light snow and hard frost; (6) Xinjiang and W interior, arid desert climate, cold winters, rainfall well distributed throughout year; (7) Inner Mongolia, extreme continental-type climate, cold winters, warm summers. Site of some of the world's oldest prehistoric remains; documented Chinese history from 16th-c BC; first recorded dynasty, the Shang (1523–1028 BC) in NC and NE China; Zhou dynasty (1027–256 BC), also mainly NC and NE; disunion from 403 BC, with central power strengthened under the Qin dynasty (221–207 BC); expansion W, N, and SW under the Han dynasty (206 BC–AD 220); split into Three Kingdoms (Wei, Shu, Wu, 220–65); period of Six dynasties (221–581); from 4th-c, series of N

dynasties set up by invaders, with several dynasties in S; gradually reunited during the Sui (590–618) and Tang (618–906) dynasties; period of partition into Five Dynasties (907–60); post-Tang chaos suppressed under the Song dynasty (960–1279); Song China, Jin empire, Mongolia, and other areas united by Mongol Yuan dynasty, established by Genghis Khan (1279–1368); strong central authority under the Ming dynasty (1368–1644), first from Nanjing, then Beijing, with increased contacts with West; overthrown by Manchus, whose dynasty ruled until 1912, and who extended control over Taiwan, Outer Mongolia, Tibet, Burma, Nepal, and E Turkestan; enforcement of prohibition of opium led to Opium Wars with Britain (1839–42, 1858–60), resulting in treaties which opened certain 'treaty ports' to foreign trade; Sino–Japanese War (1895) gave control of Taiwan and Korea to Japan; Hundred Days of Reform movement, 1898; Boxer Rising (1900), attempt to oppose foreign influence; Qing dynasty overthrown, 1911; Republic of China, founded by Sun Yatsen, 1912; May Fourth Movement, 1919; unification under Jiang Jieshi, who made Nanjing capital, 1928; conflict between Nationalists and Communists led to the Long March (1934–5), with Communists moving to NW China under Mao Zedong; Nationalist defeat and withdrawal to Taiwan, 1950; People's Republic of China proclaimed 1949, with capital at Beijing; first Five-Year Plan (1953–7), period of nationalization and collectivization; Great Leap Forward (1958–9) emphasized local authority and establishment of rural communes; Cultural Revolution initiated by Mao Zedong, 1966; many policies reversed after Mao's death (1976), and a drive towards rapid industrialization, some capitalist enterprise, and wider trade relations with the West; governed by a president, an elected National People's Congress of 2 978 deputies, and a 47-minister State Council under a prime minister; since 1949, economy largely based on heavy industry; more recently, light industries; special economic zones set up to attract foreign investment; rich mineral deposits; largest oil-producing country in Far East; major subsistence crops include rice, grain, beans, potatoes, tea, sugar, cotton, oilseed; powerful philosophical, literary, artistic, scientific, technological, and medical traditions noticeable throughout all phases of Chinese history. >> Beijing; Boxer Rising; Chinese; Confucius; Cultural Revolution; Genghis Khan; Grand Canal; Great Leap Forward; Great Wall of China; Guomindang; Han; Han / Ming / Qin / Qing / Shang / Song / Sui / Tang / Yuan / Zhou dynasty; Jiang Jieshi; Lao Zi; Long March; Manchus; Mao Zedong; Opium Wars; Polo, Marco; Sino–Japanese Wars; Sun Yatsen; Taiwan [i]; Tiananmen Square; RR1004 political leaders

china clay >> **kaolin**

Chi-nan >> **Jinan**

chinch bug A small, short-winged bug that feeds by sucking juices from grasses; an important corn and grain pest in America. (Order: Heteroptera. Family: Lygaeidae.) >> bug (entomology)

chinchilla A South American cavy-like rodent; small (length, 35 cm/14 in); thick soft grey coat, bushy tail, large round ears. It is widely farmed for its fur, which is the most expensive in the world. (Genus: *Chinchilla*, 2 species. Family: Chinchillidae.) >> cavy; rodent

chinchilla cat A breed of domestic cat, of the long-haired type; round head with short face; very dense white coat; each hair tipped with black (the *blue chinchilla* has the hairs tipped with blue-grey); also known as **silver Persian** or **silver**. >> cat

chinchilla rabbit A breed of domestic rabbit with thick soft grey fur resembling that of a chinchilla. >> chinchilla; rabbit

Chindits Members of the 3rd Indian Division, raised in 1942 by Brigadier Orde Wingate for long-range guerrilla operations in Japanese-occupied Burma. High casualties were sustained in 1943 and 1944, and their military value has been questioned. >> Wingate; World War 2

Chinese The Sinitic branch of the Sino-Tibetan group of languages, comprising eight major varieties, commonly called 'dialects'. This classification is an artifact of the writing system of Chinese, which is used by all varieties. Although the orthography transfers from one variety to another, the varieties themselves are, in some cases, not mutually intelligible. The two best-known varieties are *Cantonese*, spoken in the S, and *Mandarin*, spoken in the N, C, and W, the Beijing form being the basis of the modern standard language. There have been numerous attempts to romanize the Chinese writing system, and in 1958 the *pinyin* 'phonetic spelling' system was officially adopted, with the further aim of popularizing the grammar, vocabulary, and pronunciation of the codified standard Mandarin, now known as *putonghua* ('common language'). Chinese has the largest number of mother-tongue speakers of all the world's languages, at over 1000 million. >> China [i]; ideography; romanization; Sino–Tibetan languages

Chinese block >> **wood block**

Chinese gooseberry >> **kiwi fruit**

Ching-tao >> **Qingdao**

chinoiserie [sheen**waz**eree] Silks, porcelain, and lacquer from China, which were very much admired in Europe from the time they were first imported in the late Middle Ages, and consequently much imitated. From the 17th-c a separate Western style evolved, using Chinese and Japanese motifs in an original manner. It reached its height in the 18th-c, being used throughout the decorative arts, as well as in such fields as book illustration, furniture, and gardening. >> japanning; lacquer; porcelain

Chinook A North American Indian people of Washington and Oregon, one of the NW Indian groups with an artistic tradition. White contact, dating back to 1805, eventually eroded their culture. >> Northwest Coast Indians; Plateau Indians

chinook wind >> **Föhn wind**

Chios [**kee**os], Gr **Khíos**, Ital **Scio** pop (1995e) 54 000; area 842 sq km/325 sq mi; length 48 km/30 mi. Greek island in the Aegean Sea, off the W coast of Turkey; crossed N–S by hills rising to 1298 m/4258 ft; chief town, Chios, pop (1995e) 31 800; noted for its wine and figs. >> Aegean Sea; Greece [i]

chip A commonly used name for an integrated circuit. Strictly, the term refers to the small 'chip' of silicon on which the electronic circuits reside, rather than the encapsulated package. >> integrated circuit; silicon

chipmunk A type of squirrel, all species native to North America except *Eutamias sibiricus* from W Asia; back with alternating pale and dark longitudinal stripes; cheeks with internal pouches for carrying seeds. (Genera: *Tamias*, 1 species; *Eutamias*, 22 species.) >> squirrel

Chipp, Don(ald) Leslie (1925–) Australian politician, born in Melbourne, Victoria, Australia. He founded the Australian Democrats in 1977, a centrist group, and served as their parliamentary leader from 1978 until 1986, when he retired.

Chippendale, Thomas (1718–79) Furniture-maker and designer, baptised at Otley, West Yorkshire. He made his name following publication of *The Gentleman and Cabinet-maker's Director* (1754), a comprehensive range of furniture designs in the Rococo, chinoiserie, and Gothic Revival styles. >> chinoiserie; Gothic Revival; Rococo

Chippewa >> **Ojibwa**

Chirac, Jacques (René) [shirak] (1932–) French prime

minister (1974–6, 1986–8) and president (1995–). He resigned over differences with Giscard d'Estaing and broke away to lead the Gaullist Party. Mayor of Paris since 1977, he was an unsuccessful candidate in the 1981 and 1988 presidential elections, but won in 1995. >> de Gaulle; Giscard d'Estaing

Chirico, Giorgio de [**ki**reekoh] (1888–1978) Artist, born in Volo, Greece. A major influence on the Surrealists, his whole style after 1915 is often called 'metaphysical painting', including semi-abstract geometric figures and stylized horses. In the 1930s he reverted to an academic style. >> Surrealism

chirography [kiy**rog**rafee] The various forms and styles of handwriting. Early Western styles included *majuscule*, as seen in the chiselled capital letters of early Greek and Roman inscriptions from c.300 BC; *minuscule*, the use of small letters found in Greek from the 8th-c AD; *uncial* writing, large rounded letters found in Latin and Greek manuscripts from the 4th-c AD; *cursive*, used from c.4th-c BC, in which the letters are joined together in rounded strokes to promote speed; and *italic*, developed in Italy in the 16th-c, a forerunner of italic letters in printing. >> black letter writing; graphology; majuscule; palaeography

Chiron [**kiy**ron] In Greek mythology, a good and wise centaur who kept a school for princes in Thessaly. He educated Asclepius in the art of medicine and music, Jason the Argonaut, and Achilles. >> Centaur; Heracles

chiropody [chi**rop**odee] The study of the structure and function of the foot in health, and of its disorders and deformities. It is also known as **podiatry**. >> foot

chiropractic [**kiy**rohpraktik] The study of the alignment of the bones of the skeleton and of the anatomical relations of the nerves and muscles of the body to them. The discipline was founded in 1895 by US physician Daniel David Palmer (1845–1913). It is mainly concerned with the bones of the spine. Chiropractors treat disorders by manipulation without the use of drugs or surgery. >> alternative medicine; osteopathy

Chiroptera [kiy**rop**tera] >> **bat**

Chirripó Grande [chiripoh **gran**day] 9°50N 83°25W. Highest peak of Costa Rica and S Central America; in the Cordillera de Talamanca; height 3819 m/12 529 ft. >> Costa Rica ℹ

chiru [**chi**roo] A goat-antelope (*Pantholops hodgsoni*) native to the high plateau of Tibet and China; pale-pinkish brown; nose swollen at tip; male with black face and long slender vertical horns growing apart towards tips; female without horns; also known as **Tibetan antelope**. >> antelope

chisel-tooth lizard >> **agamid**

Chisholm Trail A cattle trail in the USA, from Texas across Oklahoma to the railhead at Abilene, KS. It is named after Jesse Chisholm, who pioneered the route in 1866.

chital [**chee**tl] A true deer (*Axis axis*), native to India and Sri Lanka; pale brown with white spots; antlers long, lyre-shaped; also known as **axis deer** or **spotted deer** >> antlers ℹ; deer; langur

chitarrone [kita**roh**nay] A long-necked lute or theorbo, used in the 16th–17th-c to accompany singing. There were usually six pairs of gut or metal strings running over a fretted keyboard, and eight longer bass strings which were not stopped (ie each produced one note only). The instrument might be as long as 1 m 90 cm/6 ft 3 in. >> lute; string instrument 2 ℹ; theorbo

chitin [**kiy**tin] A long chain-like molecule (a linear homopolysaccharide of N-acetyl-D-glucosamine) found as a major constituent of the horny covering (cuticle) of insects and cell walls of fungi. When cross-linked, these chains produce a lightweight but strong material. >> molecule; polysaccharides

chiton [**kiy**tn] A marine mollusc characterized by a dorsal shell consisting of eight overlapping calcareous plates; muscular foot used for attachment to a substrate; also known as **coat-of-mail shell**. (Class: Polyplacophora.) >> calcium; mollusc

Chittagong [**chit**agong] 22°20N 91°48E, pop (1995e) 2 209 000. Principal port of Bangladesh; conquered by Nawab of Bengal, 1666; ceded to British East India Company, 1760; damaged during 1971 Indo-Pakistani War; many Hindu and Buddhist temples; university (1966). >> Bangladesh ℹ

Chittagong Hill Tracts area 8680 sq km/3350 sq mi. Region in SE Bangladesh, reaches heights of 500–1000 m/1500–3000 ft in the SE; divided into four fertile valleys, covered with thick planted forest. >> Bangladesh ℹ

Chitwin or **Royal Chitwin** area 932 sq km/360 sq mi. National park in SC Nepal; established in 1973; a world heritage site. >> Nepal ℹ

chive A perennial growing to 40 cm/15 in (*Allium schoenoprasum*); tufts of narrow, tubular leaves; pink or purple flowers; native to the N hemisphere. Its leaves are used as flavouring. (Family: Liliaceae.) >> allium

Chlamydia [kla**mid**ia] A genus of spherical, non-motile bacteria that multiply only within the cytoplasm of true nucleated (*eukaryotic*) cells. Virulent strains can cause eye, mouth, genital, and other diseases of humans and other animals. (Kingdom: Monera. Family: Chlamydiaceae.) >> bacteria ℹ; cytoplasm

chloracne [klaw**rak**nee] Acne-like lesions on the skin with pimple-like (*papular*) formations which may become infected (*pustular*). Its occurrence is linked to industrial exposure to chlorinated hydrocarbons. >> acne

chloral CCl_3CHO, IUPAC **2,2,2-trichloroethanal**, boiling point 97°C. **Chloral hydrate** is a sedative. >> IUPAC

chlorates Salts of an oxyacid of chlorine, usually a chlorate(V), containing the ion ClO_3^-, including the weed-killer **sodium chlorate** ($NaClO_3$). Chlorate(I) or **hypochlorite** is ClO^-; chlorate(VII) or **perchlorate** is ClO_4^-. >> chlorine

chlordiazepoxide >> **benzodiazepines**

Chlorella [klo**rel**a] A genus of non-motile, single-celled green algae containing a cup-shaped chloroplast; very common in a variety of freshwater habitats. >> algae; chloroplast

chlorides Compounds containing chlorine, especially those containing the ion Cl^-. Common salt is **sodium chloride** (Na^+Cl^-). >> chlorine; sodium

chlorine [**klaw**reen] Cl, element 17, boiling point −35°C. A greenish-yellow gas, containing diatomic molecules (Cl_2). It does not occur free in nature, but is recovered from deposits of NaCl or KCl by electrolysis. It may also be recovered from sea water. The gas has an intense odour and is very poisonous. Chlorine is mainly used in propellants, cleaning fluids, rubber production, and as a disinfectant, such as in swimming pools. >> chemical elements; electrolysis ℹ; gas 1; RR1036

chlorofluorocarbons >> **CFCs**

chloroform $CHCl_3$, IUPAC **trichloromethane**, boiling point 62°C. A dense liquid, used as a solvent and as an anaesthetic. >> IUPAC

Chlorophyceae [klorohf**iy**see-ee] >> **green algae**

chlorophyll [**klo**rohfil] The green pigment (a magnesium-porphyrin derivative) found in plants, which absorbs radiant energy from sunlight, mainly in blue (wavelength 435–438 nm) and red (wavelength 670–680 nm) regions of the spectrum. >> photosynthesis; spectrum

Chlorophyta [klo**ro**fita] The green algae that form zoospores or gametes having cup-shaped grass-green chloroplasts and at least two anterior flagella; classified as a phylum of the kingdom Protoctista. >> chloroplast; flagellum; gamete; green algae; Protoctista; systematics

chloroplast [**klo**rohplast] A specialized structure found within plant cells. It contains some genetic material (DNA), and partly controls the synthesis of its own proteins. >> cell; chlorophyll; DNA ℹ; protein

chlorpromazine >> **phenothiazines**

Chobham armour >> **reactive armour**

chocolate and **cocoa** A foodstuff derived from the cacao bean, cultivated mainly in W Africa. **Cocoa butter** is rich in fat, and **cocoa powder** contains a mixture of protein (25%), fat (30%), and carbohydrate (45%). **Milk chocolate** is produced by mixing finely ground cocoa powder with some cocoa butter, sugar, and dried milk. >> cacao

choir The part of a church for the singers; usually part of the chancel, and separated from the nave by a screen or a rail. >> chancel; church ℹ; nave

Choiseul(-Amboise), Etienne François, duc de (Duke of) [shwazoei] (1719–85) French statesman, minister of Louis XV, born in Lorraine. He arranged in 1756 the alliance between France and Austria against Frederick the Great, and obtained good terms for France at the end of the Seven Years' War (1763). >> Louis XV; Seven Years' War

cholecystitis [kohlesis**tiy**tis] Acute inflammation of the gall bladder, often induced by a blockage or partial blockage of the flow of bile, and stone formation. It causes severe upper right-sided abdominal pain and vomiting. >> bile; gall bladder

cholera [**kol**era] An acute infection of the gastro-intestinal tract by *Vibrio cholerae*, acquired by drinking contaminated water. It is associated with sudden profuse watery diarrhoea, which so depletes the body of water and electrolytes as to induce shock and death within 24–48 hours. If adequate treatment involving the replacement of body fluids is given, recovery should be complete. >> alimentary canal; diarrhoea; *Vibrio*

cholesterol [ko**les**terol] The most abundant steroid in animals. It is ingested in the diet as a constituent of egg-yolk, meats (particularly offal), and some shellfish; transported in the blood; and synthesized in the liver, gastro-intestinal tract, and other tissues. It is implicated as a cause of atherosclerosis. >> atherosclerosis; coronary heart disease; fatty acids; gallstones; steroid

choline [**koh**leen] The most common form of the variable part of phospholipids, which play a key role in the structure of biological membranes. It is an essential component of the diet of some species, but not humans. Phospholipids containing choline are also known as *lecithin*, commonly sold in health-food shops to reduce cholesterol absorption, a feat which it does not achieve. >> cholesterol; phospholipid

Chomsky, (Avram) Noam (1928–) Linguist and political activist, born in Philadelphia, PA. He became professor of linguistics at the Massachusetts Institute of Technology, where he introduced a new theory of language called transformational generative grammar. His opposition to the Vietnam War involved him in the radical movement, which led to such works as *American Power and the New Mandarins* (1969). >> linguistics; transformational grammar

Chongqing or **Chungking** [chungching], also **Pahsien** 31°08N 104°23E, pop (1995e) 3 352 000. City in SWC China; founded 12th-c; treaty port, 1891; capital of China, 1937–46; most important industrial city in SW; airfield; railway; river transport. >> China ℹ

Chopin, Frédéric (François) [shohpĩ] (1810–49) Composer and pianist, born in Zelazowa Wola, Poland. His works for the piano include 50 mazurkas, 27 études, 25 préludes, 19 nocturnes, 13 waltzes, and 12 polonaises. He lived with the novelist George Sand from 1838 until 1847, when they became estranged. >> piano; Sand

Chopin, Kate [**shoh**pin], *née* **Katherine O'Flaherty** (1851–1904) Novelist, short-story writer, and poet, born in St Louis, MO. She married **Oscar Chopin**, a Creole cotton trader from Louisiana, by whom she had six children. Her realistic novel of sexual passion, *The Awakening* (1899), was harshly condemned by the public, but she has since been praised for her concerns about the freedom of women.

chorale 1 A hymn of the Lutheran church. The qualities most associated with its music – harmonic strength and a firm, regular metre – are those of Bach's harmonizations. >> Bach, Johann Sebastian; hymn; Lutheranism **2** The term *chorale* is also used for a choir, especially in the USA.

chord In music, two or more notes sounded simultaneously. In tonal music of the period c.1600–1920, a chord functions as a unit in a harmonic progression related to (or diverging from) a particular key centre. In post-tonal music, chords have been formed on serial or other principles, without reference to a key centre. >> chromaticism; tonality

Chordata [kaw(r)**dah**ta] or **chordates** A phylum of animals having bilateral symmetry, a stiffening rod (*notochord*) running along the back, a hollow dorsal nerve cord, a tail extending backwards beyond the anus, and gill slits. There are three subphyla: Cephalochordata (*lancelets*), Tunicata (*sea squirts* and *salps*), and Vertebrata (*vertebrates*). Vertebrates are chordates in which the dorsal nerve cord is surrounded by *vertebrae* made from cartilage or bone. >> amphibian; bird ℹ; fish ℹ; lancelet; mammal ℹ; notochord; phylum; reptile; tunicate

chordophone Any musical instrument in which the sound is produced by the vibrations of one or more strings. Chordophones are divided into (i) those without resonators, or with resonators that can be detached while leaving the strings in place (*simple chordophones*: piano, zither, etc), and (ii) those in which an integral resonator serves to keep the strings in place (*composite chordophones*: violin, lute, etc). Each type may be further subdivided (eg according to whether the strings are bowed, plucked, or struck); but in the perception of most people the main divisions are between those with keyboards, those with bows, and those with neither. >> keyboard / musical / string instrument ℹ

chorea [ko**ree**a] A manifestation of rheumatic fever related to recent streptococcal infection; also known as **Saint Vitus' dance**. Symptoms range from periods of restlessness to exaggerated, jerky, puppet-like movements of the hands, arms, and body. >> Huntington's chorea; rheumatic fever; *Streptococcus*; Sydenham's chorea

choreography Originally, the writing of dances in notation; in its current general use, the making of dances by the selection of movements for a particular dance purpose, linked together to form a whole. The choreographic structure is often derived from music but can also be independent of it, based directly on the rhythm of movement. >> Ashton, Frederick; Balanchine; ballet; country dance; dance notation; Fokine; MacMillan, Kenneth; modern dance; Nijinsky; Petipa; postmodern dance

chorionic villus sampling [kori**on**ik **vil**uhs] A technique for obtaining samples of placental tissue, ideally at 8–11 weeks gestation. A needle introduced through the mother's abdominal and uterine walls is advanced to the edge of the placenta, a small piece of which is removed. Analysis of the tissue can identify the presence of several genetically determined disorders. >> amniocentesis; placenta (anatomy)

chorus The collective or impersonal voice in a drama (as distinct from the individual characters), which serves to introduce and comment on the action. It was an essential feature in classical drama, but less common later.

Chou En-lai >> **Zhou Enlai**

chough [chuhf] A crow-like bird, especially the **red-billed** or **Cornish chough** (*Pyrrhocorax pyrrhocorax*), native to Europe and Asia. (Family: Corvidae, 3 species.) >> crow

chow chow or **chow** A breed of dog, developed in China before 1000 BC; heavy body with thick coat and lion-like mane; blue tongue; tail curled over back; kept in temples, and bred with stern expressions to frighten away evil spirits; introduced to Europe in the 18th-c. >> dog

Chrétien, (Joseph Jacques) Jean [**kray**tyen] (1934–) Canadian statesman and prime minister (1993–), born in Shawinigan, Quebec, Canada. He served under Lester Pearson and Pierre Trudeau, and in 1990 became leader of the Liberal Party. His party won a resounding victory in the 1993 general election. >> Liberal Party (Canada); Pearson; Trudeau

Chrétien de Troyes [kraytyĩ duh trwah] (?–c.1183) Mediaeval poet, born in Troyes, France. His best-known works are the metrical Arthurian romances, such as *Lancelot* and *Perceval*, which introduce all the fantastic ingredients of Celtic legend, and add the theme of the Holy Grail. >> Arthur

Christ >> **Jesus Christ**

Christadelphians [krista**del**fianz] A Christian sect, founded by John Thomas (1805–71) in the USA, which teaches a return to primitive Christianity, and that Christ will soon come again to establish a theocracy lasting for a millennium. The name means 'Brothers of Christ'. >> millenarianism

Christchurch 43°33S 172°40E, pop (1995e) 318 000 (urban area) 300 700. City on the E coast of South Island, New Zealand; founded, 1850; airport; railway; university (1873); corn and sheep trade from the Canterbury Plains; scene of 1974 Commonwealth Games. >> New Zealand ℹ

Christian X (1870–1947) King of Denmark (1912–47), born in Charlottenlund. During the German occupation (1940–5), he attracted great acclaim by remaining in Denmark. >> Denmark ℹ; World War 2

Christian, Fletcher (18th-c) Seaman, born in Cockermouth, Cumbria. He was the ringleader in the mutiny on the *Bounty*, which sailed to Tahiti 1787–8. In 1808 his descendants were found on Pitcairn I. >> Bligh

Christian Aid A large UK-based charity supported by most Churches in Britain. It pays for development projects in the poorest countries of the world, particularly in agriculture, water supply, and health, using its own experts as advisors. >> Third World

Christian Democratic Union >> **Christian Democrats**

Christian Democrats Members of Christian Democratic political parties, most of which were formed in W Europe after 1945, and which have since become a major political force. The Christian Democratic philosophy is based upon strong links with the Catholic Church and its notions of social and economic justice. It emphasizes the traditional conservative values of the family and church, but also more progressive, liberal values such as state intervention in the economy and significant social welfare provision. >> Roman Catholicism

Christianity (Gr *christos* 'anointed') A world religion centred on the life and work of Jesus of Nazareth in Israel, and developing out of Judaism. The earliest followers were Jews who, after the death and resurrection of Jesus, believed him to be the Messiah or Christ, promised by the prophets in the Old Testament, and in unique relation to God, whose Son or 'Word' (*Logos*) he was declared to be. During his life he chose 12 men as *disciples*, who formed the nucleus of the Church as a society or communion of believers. The Gospel ('Good News') of Jesus by the end of the 1st-c was reduced to writing and accepted as authoritative scriptures of the New Testament, understood as the fulfilment of the Jewish scriptures, or Old Testament. Through the witness of the 12 earliest leaders (*Apostles*) and their successors, the Christian faith spread through the Greek and Roman world, and in 315 was declared by Emperor Constantine to be the official religion of the Roman Empire, and formed the basis of civilization in the Middle Ages in Europe. Major divisions, separated as a result of differences in doctrine and practice, are the *Eastern* or *Orthodox Churches*, the *Roman Catholic Church*, acknowledging the Bishop of Rome as head (the *Pope*), and the *Protestant Churches* stemming from the split with the Roman Church in the 16th-c Reformation. All Christians recognize the authority of the Bible, read at public worship, which takes place at least every Sunday, the first day of the week, to celebrate the resurrection of Jesus Christ. Most Churches recognize at least two sacraments (Baptism, and the Eucharist, Mass, or Lord's Supper) as essential. The impetus to spread Christianity to the non-Christian world in missionary movements, especially in the 19th-c and 20th-c, resulted in the creation of numerically very strong Churches in the developing countries of Asia, Africa, and South America. A powerful ecumenical movement in the 20th-c, promoted by, among others, the World Council of Churches, has sought to recover unity among divided Christians. >> Bible; Christology; ecumenism; Jesus Christ; Judaism; Reformation; sacrament; World Council of Churches; Adventists; Anabaptists; Anglo-Catholicism; Assemblies of God; Baptists; Calvinism; Christadelphians; Christian Science; Church of Scotland; Confessing Church; Congregationalism; Coptic Church; Dutch Reformed Church; Episcopal Church; evangelicalism; Friends, Society of; Greek Orthodox Church; Lutheranism; Methodism; millenarianism; Mormons; Nonconformists; Orthodox Church; Pentecostalism; Presbyterianism; Protestantism; Reformed Churches; Roman Catholicism; Russian Orthodox Church; Salvation Army; secular Christianity; United Church of Christ; Waldenses

Christian Science A movement, founded by Mary Baker Eddy, which seeks to reinstate the original Christian message of salvation from all evil, including sickness and disease as well as sin. The first Church of Christ, Scientist, was established in 1879 in Boston, MA, USA. Eddy's *Science and Health with Key to the Scriptures* (1875) and the Bible are the principal texts of the movement. >> Christianity; Eddy

Christian Social Union >> **Christian Democrats**

Christie, Dame Agatha (Mary Clarissa), *née* **Miller** (1890–1976) Writer, born in Torquay, Devon. She wrote more than 70 detective novels featuring the Belgian detective, Hercule Poirot, or the inquiring village lady, Miss Marple. Her play *The Mousetrap* opened in 1952 and holds the record for the longest unbroken run in a London theatre. Several of her stories have become popular films, such as *Murder on the Orient Express* (1974) and *Death on the Nile* (1978).

Christie, John Reginald Halliday (1898–1953) Murderer, born in Yorkshire. He was hanged at London for the murder of his wife, and confessed to the murder of six other women, including the wife of **Timothy John Evans**, who lived in the same house. Evans had been convicted and hanged for the murder of his infant daughter in 1950, and was also charged with his wife's murder. After a special inquiry, Evans was granted a free pardon in 1966.

Christie, Julie (1940–) Actress, born in Chukua, Assam. She became known through her role in *Billy Liar* (1963), and in 1965 won an Oscar for *Darling*. Later films include *Dr Zhivago* (1965), *The Go-Between* (1971), *Heat and Dust* (1982), *Hamlet* (1996), and *Afterglow* (1997).

Christie, Linford (1960–) Sprinter, born in Jamaica,

now living in Britain. In 1993 he held the World, Olympic, Commonwealth, and European Cup titles for the 100 m, achieving 9·87 seconds at the world championships in Stuttgart, Germany (a European record, and 0·01 seconds outside the world record).

Christmas The Christian festival commemorating the birth of Jesus, observed by most branches of the Church on 25 December but by some denominations in January. The practice of celebrating Christmas on 25 December began in the Western Church early in the 4th-c; it was a Christian substitute for the pagan festival held on that date to celebrate the birth of the unconquered Sun. The name is often abbreviated to **Xmas**, X being the first letter (*chi*) of the Greek word **Christos**. >> Jesus Christ

Christmas Island (Indian Ocean) 10°25S 105°39E, pop (1995e) 2570; area 155 sq km/60 sq mi. Island in the Indian Ocean; administered by Australia as an external territory; annexed by the UK, 1888; sovereignty passed to Australia, 1958; airport. >> Indian Ocean

Christmas Island (Kiribati) >> **Kiritimati**

Christmas tree >> **Norway spruce**

Christology The orderly study of the significance of Jesus Christ for Christian faith. Traditionally, the term was restricted to the study of the person of Christ, and in particular to the way in which he is both human and divine. Latterly, an emphasis on the inseparability of Christ's person and work has meant that Christology often encompasses enquiry into his saving significance (*soteriology*) as well. >> Christianity

Christophe, Henry [kris**tof**] (1767–1829) Haitian revolutionary, born a slave on the island of Grenada. He joined the black insurgents on Haiti against the French (1790), was appointed president in 1807, and proclaimed king in the N part of the island as Henry I in 1811. >> Toussaint L'Ouverture

Christopher, St (3rd-c) Syrian saint, said to have been 12 ft/3.6 m tall, and to have suffered martyrdom under the Emperor Decius (249–51). His name is from the Greek, 'Christ-bearer', from the legend of his carrying the Christ child across a river. He is the patron saint of wayfarers, and now motorists. Feast day 25 July. >> Jesus Christ

Christopher, Warren M(inor) (1925–) Lawyer and government official, born in Scranton, ND. Deputy attorney general (1967–9) and deputy secretary of state (1977–81), he remained a respected voice in the Democratic Party, and was appointed secretary of state in 1993. He resigned at the 1996 election.

Christ's Hospital An independent co-educational boarding school, founded in London (1552), but since 1902 at Horsham, Sussex. It is known as the **Blue Coat School**, because of the blue cloak which was part of the pupils' uniform. >> public school

chromakey An image-combination process in video production where an area of strong colour in one scene is replaced ('keyed') by the picture from another source; also termed **colour separation overlay (CSO)**.

chromaticism An attribute of music which uses notes, intervals, and chords outside the prevailing key; a note which does not belong to the diatonic scale is called a **chromatic note**. >> Schoenberg; tonality

chromatin [**kroh**matin] The network of substance in a cell nucleus that takes up stain, and which can thus be made visible under the microscope during the process of cell division. It is organized into distinct bodies (the chromosomes). >> cell; chromosome 🛈

chromatography The separation of components of a mixture (the *mobile phase*) by passing it through another phase (the *stationary phase*), making use of the different extents to which the various components are adsorbed by the stationary phase. Many systems have been developed. One is **paper chromatography**, illustrated by the separation of the constituent dyes of an ink when it is spilled on a paper tissue. Another is **gas–liquid chromatography (GLC)**, used to separate mixtures of gases.

chromatophore [kroh**mat**ofaw(r)] A pigment-bearing cell, or structure within a cell. In many animals chromatophores are cells containing pigment granules. By dispersing or contracting these granules, the animal is able to change colour. >> cell

chrominance The component of a video signal which determines the hue and saturation of a reproduced colour. The term is sometimes abbreviated to 'chroma'. >> colour television 🛈

chromium Cr, element 24, density 7·2 g/cm^3, melting point 1857°C. A hard, lustrous metal, found combined with oxygen, and generally prepared as a metal by reduction of the ore with aluminium. Its principal uses are in plating and as a component of steels, to which it gives corrosion resistance. >> aluminium; chemical elements; metal; RR1036

chromosome The threads within the nucleus of a cell which become visible during cell division. Chromosomes occur in pairs – one member of maternal and one of paternal origin. They are regarded today as the major carriers of genetic material, consisting of DNA and various types of protein (histones). The position of a particular gene on a chromosome is called its *locus*. The number of chromosomes differs from species to species. A normal human body cell has 46 chromosomes: 22 pairs of autosomes together with (in females) one matching pair of X chromosomes and (in males) one nonmatching pair, the X and Y sex chromosomes. >> cell; DNA 🛈; nucleus (biology); *see illustration on p.181*

chromosphere Part of the outer gaseous layers of the Sun, temperature 45 000K. It is visible as a thin crescent of pinkish light during a total eclipse of the Sun. >> corona (astronomy); eclipse; solar prominence; Sun

chronicle plays Plays (from any period) based upon historical events, often using the written record as both source and structure. Marlowe and Shakespeare used Holinshed's chronicles for their plays from English history. Epic theatre (after Brecht) has revived this mode of drama. >> Brecht; Marlowe; Shakespeare 🛈

Chronicles or **Paralipomenon, Books of** Two books of the Hebrew Bible/Old Testament, originally a single work, part of a history of Judah from its beginnings to its restoration under Ezra and Nehemiah. >> Ezra; Nehemiah, Book of; Old Testament

chronogram The practice of hiding a date within a series of words, by using the letters for Roman numerals (C = 100, V = 5, etc). It is often used on tombstones and foundation stones to mark the date of the event being commemorated.

chrysalis >> **pupa**

chrysanthemum A name applied in a broad sense to various members of the family Compositae. The large-flowered 'chrysanthemums' of gardens (Genus: *Dendranthema*) have a long history of cultivation, especially in China and Japan, and modern plants are derived from complex hybrids whose exact parentage is uncertain.

Chrysippus [kriy**sip**us] (c.280–c.206 BC) Stoic philosopher, born in Soli, Cilicia. The third and greatest head of the Stoa, he wrote over 700 works (only fragments remain) elaborating the Stoic system in what became its definitive and orthodox form. >> Stoicism

chrysoprase [**kri**soprayz] The apple-green form of chalcedony. >> chalcedony

Chrysostom, St John [**kris**ostom] (c.347–407) Church Father, born at Antioch. In 398 he was made Archbishop of Constantinople, but his reproof of vices moved the

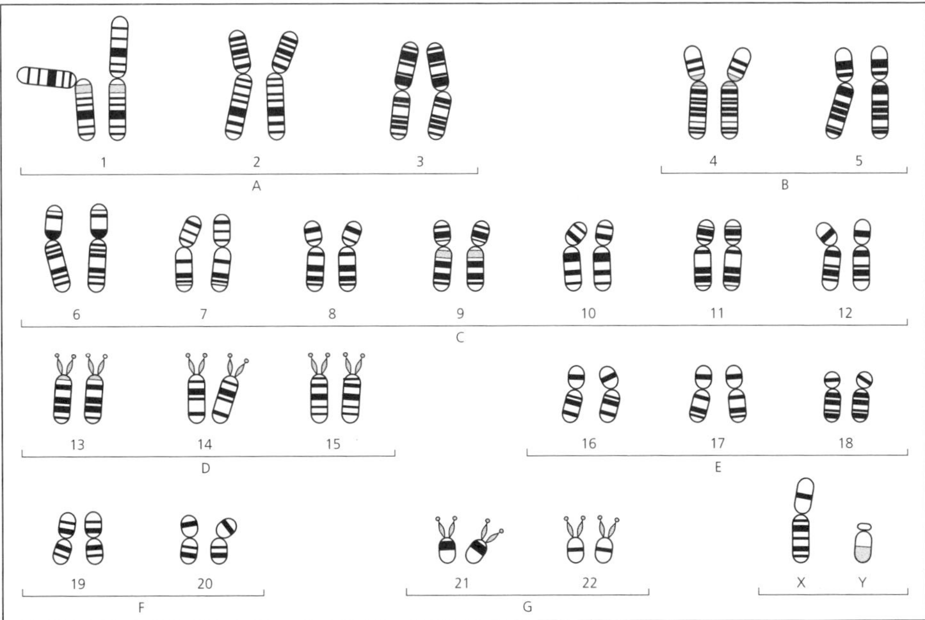

The 46 human chromosomes, showing the banding patterns characteristic of each.

Empress Eudoxia to have him deposed and banished (403). His name comes from the Greek, 'golden mouthed', on account of his eloquence. Feast day 13 September. >> Christianity; Fathers of the Church

chrysotile [**kri**sotiyl] The fibrous form of serpentine. It is a member of the asbestos group of minerals. >> asbestos; serpentine

Chu, Steven (1948–) Physicist, born in St Louis, MO. He held posts at Bell Laboratories and Stanford University, and shared the 1997 Nobel Prize for Physics for his contribution to the development of methods to cool and trap atoms with laser light.

chub Fish mainly found in European streams and rivers (*Leuciscus cephalus*); body elongate, rather cylindrical, length up to 60 cm/2 ft; greenish-grey above, sides silver, underside white. (Family: Cyprinidae.) >> dace; orfe

Chubb Crater A meteorite crater c.410 m/1350 ft deep in Quebec, Canada; occupied by Crater Lake, 260 m/850 ft deep; discovered in 1949 by a prospector, F W Chubb; also known as **Ungava–Quebec Crater**.

chuckwalla An iguana (*Sauromalus obesus*) from North America, found in rocky deserts; dark body with thick blunt yellow tail; no crest along back; eats plants. >> iguana

Chukchi or **Chuckchee** A people of NE Siberia. They are divided into **maritime Chukchi**, who are hunters and fishers of the Arctic and Bering Sea, and the previously nomadic **reindeer Chukchi**, who live inland and herd reindeer. >> Siberia

Chukchi Peninsula [**chuk**chee], Russ **Chukotskiy Poluostrov** NE extremity of Asia, in Russia; bounded N by the Chukchi Sea, E by the Bering Strait; rises to heights above 1000 m/3300 ft. >> Russia ℹ

Chu-kiang >> **Zhu Jiang**

Chungking >> **Chongqing**

church In architecture, a building used for public religious worship, especially Christian. It was developed in the Romanesque architecture of the 11th-c and 12th-c into the now more usual Latin cross plan, typically consisting of nave with side aisles, transepts, chancel, and apse. In the 20th-c, church design has become increasingly eclectic, as in the circular design of the Roman Catholic Cathedral, Liverpool, UK (1960–7), architect Frederick Gibberd. >> baptistery; basilica; cathedral; chancel; choir (architecture); nave; transept; *see illustration on p.182*

Church Army An Anglican organization of volunteer lay workers, founded in 1882. Its aims are evangelical, but it concentrates on social welfare and rehabilitation work, mainly in cities. >> Anglicanism; evangelist

Churcher, Betty, popular name of **Elizabeth Ann Churcher** (1931–) Arts administrator, born in Brisbane, Queensland, Australia. The author of the award-winning book *Understanding Art* (1974), she became director of the Australian National Gallery (1990–7).

Churchill, Lord Randolph (Henry Spencer) (1849–95) British Conservative statesman, born in Blenheim Palace, Oxfordshire, the father of Winston Churchill. He was secretary for India (1885–6), and for a short while Chancellor of the Exchequer and Leader of the House of Commons. >> Conservative Party

Churchill, Sir Winston (Leonard Spencer) (1874–1965) British statesman, prime minister (1940–5, 1951–5), and author, born in Blenheim Palace, Oxfordshire. Initially a Conservative MP (1900), he joined the Liberals in 1904, and was colonial under-secretary (1905), President of the Board of Trade (1908), home secretary (1910), and First Lord of the Admiralty (1911). After World War 1 he was secretary of state for war and air (1919–21), and Chancellor of the Exchequer (1924–9). In 1929 he returned to the Conservative fold, but remained out of step with the leadership until World War 2, when he returned to the Admiralty. On Chamberlain's defeat (May 1940) he formed a coalition government, and, holding

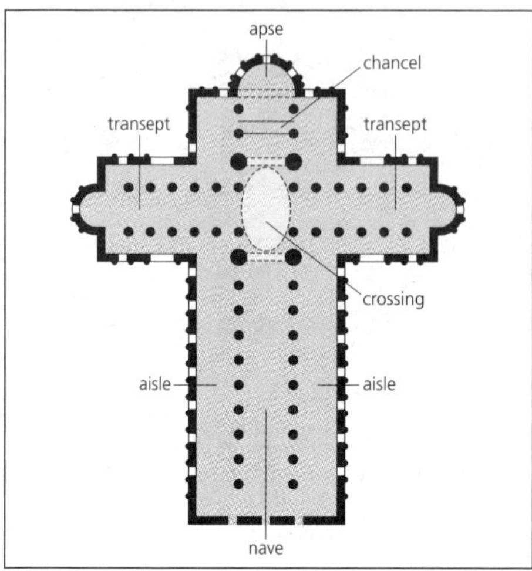

Latin cross church plan; Pisa Cathedral (1063–1118)

both the premiership and the defence portfolio, led Britain alone through the war against Germany and Italy with great oratory and steely resolution. Defeated in the July 1945 election, he became a pugnacious Leader of the Opposition. In 1951 he was prime minister again, and after 1955 remained a venerated backbencher. He was awarded the Nobel Prize for Literature in 1953. His widow, **Clementine Ogilvy Hozier**, whom he had married in 1908, was made a life peer in 1965 for her indefatigable charitable work (**Baroness Spencer-Churchill of Chartwell**). >> Boer Wars; Chamberlain, Neville; Conservative Party; Liberal Party (UK); World War 2

Church of England The official state Church of England, a national Church having both Protestant and Catholic features, based on episcopal authority, and with the monarch of England formally as its head. It originated when Henry VIII broke ties with the Roman Catholic Church (c.1532–4), its doctrine and liturgy developing in the Book of Common Prayer (1549, 1552), and the 39 Articles. The Church today consists of 44 dioceses in the two provinces of Canterbury and York, with over 16 000 churches and other places of worship. Local parishes are arranged into rural *deaneries* and dioceses, with each diocese led by a bishop. In 1970 the General Synod was established for the purpose of reaching decisions and expressing views on issues of interest to the Church. It meets three times a year, and has over 500 members, divided between the three houses: the Houses of Clergy, of Bishops, and of Laity. In 1992 it voted in favour of the ordination of women priests – an event which took place for the first time in 1994. >> Anglican Communion; Book of Common Prayer; episcopacy; Henry VIII; Lambeth Conferences; Protestantism; Reformation; Thirty-Nine Articles

Church of Scotland The national Church in Scotland, founded at the Reformation of 1560 under the leadership of John Knox. Presbyterian in its governing organization and discipline, laymen or *elders* (ordained) play a leading part with ministers in church courts at local, congregational level (in *Kirk Session*), district level (*presbyteries*, overseeing congregations in a given area), provincial synods, and the *General Assembly*. Ministers (women and men), who are ordained by presbytery, are alone authorized to administer the sacraments of baptism (of infants as well as adults) and the Lord's Supper (*communion*). >> Knox, John; Presbyterianism; Protestantism; Reformed Churches; sacrament

Church Slavonic >> **Slavic languages**

Chu-teh >> **Zhu De**

CIA >> **Central Intelligence Agency**

Cibber, Colley [**sib**er] (1671–1757) Actor and playwright, born in London. He spent most of his career at the Theatre Royal in Drury Lane. From 1730 he was Poet Laureate.

cicada [si**kah**da] A large, typically tropical insect that spends most of its long life-cycle as a nymph burrowing underground, feeding on sap from roots; adults live in trees; males typically have well-developed sound-producing organs. (Order: Homoptera. Family: Cicadidae.) >> insect ℹ

Cicero, Marcus Tullius [**sis**eroh], also known in English as **Tully** (106–43 BC) Roman orator, statesman, and man of letters, born in Arpinum, Latium. Though he foiled Catiline's revolutionary plot, he broke the law by executing Roman citizens without a trial, and fled to Thessalonica (58 BC) in exile. In 57 BC he was recalled by the people, but lost the esteem of both Caesar's and Pompey's factions by vacillating between the two. Living in retirement (46–44 BC), he wrote most of his chief works on rhetoric and philosophy. In 43 BC he delivered his famous speeches against Antony, the so-called 'Philippics', and was murdered by Antony's soldiers as he tried to escape. >> Antonius; Augustus; Caesar; Pompey; triumvirate

cichlid [**sik**lid] Any of a large family of freshwater fishes found in South and Central America, Africa, and India; body usually perch-like; feeding and breeding habits extremely diverse. (20 genera, including *Haplochromis*, *Tilapia*. Family: Cichlidae.)

CID An abbreviation of **Criminal Investigation Department**, formed in 1878 as a branch of the London Metropolitan Police, and responsible for the investigation and prevention of crime and the gathering of criminal intelligence. Most provincial forces in Scotland, England, and Wales now have their own CIDs. >> police; Scotland Yard

Cid, El [sid], Span [theed], popular name of **Rodrigo** or **Ruy Díaz de Vivar** (c.1043–99) Spanish hero, born in Burgos. He became known as the *Cid* (from the Moorish *Sidi*, 'lord'); his great achievement was the capture of Valencia (1094).

cider An alcoholic drink produced from the fermentation of apples, traditionally made in SW England and Normandy, France. Its alcoholic content varies widely, from 3% to 9% ethanol. In the USA, ciders are either 'sweet' (non-alcoholic) or 'hard' (containing alcohol). >> fermentation

Cienfuegos [syen**fway**gohs] 22°10N 80°27W, pop (1995e) 130 000. Port on S coast of Cuba; founded, 1819; important industrial centre; naval base. >> Cuba ℹ

cigar >> **cigarette**

cigarette A thin roll of finely-cut tobacco, wrapped in paper, used for smoking. The origins of the cigarette lie in Central and South America, where native Indians wrapped crushed tobacco leaves in a reed or vegetable casing. Spanish explorers then introduced the practice to Europe in the form of the *cigar*. By the 16th-c, *cigarillos* ('little cigars') had emerged, re-using the tobacco found in discarded cigar butts by wrapping it in paper. *Cigarettes* (the term is French) spread throughout Europe in the following century. >> smoking

ciliate [**sil**iuht] A microscopic, single-celled organism typically possessing short hair-like appendages (**cilia**) on its surface; commonly also with a specialized mouth region (*cytostome*); found free-living in all kinds of aquatic and terrestrial habitats, and as parasites. (Phylum: Ciliophora.) >> cell; parasitology

Cilicia [siy**lis**ia, si**lish**a] The ancient name for the S coastal part of Turkey around the Taurus Mts. It was famous for its timber and its pirates.

Cimabue [cheema**boo**ay], originally **Cenni di Peppi** (c.1240–c.1302) Painter, born in Florence, Italy. He at first adopted traditional Byzantine forms, but soon turned to nature, and led the way to the naturalism of his great pupil, Giotto. He executed several important frescoes in the Church of St Francis at Assisi; these were badly damaged in an earthquake in 1997. >> Giotto

cimbalom [**sim**balom] A kind of dulcimer, native to Hungary but found also in other E European countries. The concert cimbalom has been used as an orchestral instrument by Liszt, Kodály, Bartók, and others. >> chordophone; dulcimer

Cimbri [**kim**bree] A Germanic people from N Europe who migrated S towards the end of the 2nd-c BC in search of new lands. They were defeated and destroyed by the Romans (101 BC) in the Po valley.

Cincinnati [sinsi**na**tee] 39°06N 84°01W, pop (1995e) 378 000. City in SW Ohio, USA, on Ohio R; Fort Washington built here, 1789; city status, 1819; large numbers of German immigrants in the 1840s; airport; railway; two universities (1819, 1831); several centres for culture, music, and the arts; professional teams, Reds (baseball), Bengals (football); birthplace of William Howard Taft. >> Ohio; Taft

Cincinnatus, Lucius Quinctius [sinsi**nah**tus] (5th-c BC) Roman statesman, farmer and folk hero. Called from the plough and given absolute power to rescue the Roman army of the consul Minucius, which had been trapped by the Aequi (458 BC), he voluntarily gave up this power and returned to his farm, as soon as the crisis was over. >> Roman history ℹ

CinemaScope A system of wide-screen cinematography, based on Henri Chrétien's invention of 1927 and adopted by 20th Century Fox in 1953. A squeeze factor of 2:1 horizontally is used, resulting in a screened picture of aspect ratio (width:height) 2·35:1.

cinematography The presentation of moving pictures as a series of photographic images recorded and reproduced in rapid succession, the eye's persistence of vision giving the impression of continuous movement. Film in continuous strips provided the material for Edison's pioneer Kinetoscope camera of 1891, but projecting the image on a screen for a large audience originated with the Lumière brothers in 1895, establishing the film production and cinema industries. Pictures were exposed in the camera at a rate of 16 per second, the film being held stationary for each exposure and then advanced one frame at a time while a shutter obscured the lens. After developing this film as a negative, a positive print was made for projection, again with an intermittent mechanism and shutter. In the late 1920s synchronized sound was added to the picture presentation, after 1927 from a sound track on the film itself, the frame rate being increased to 24 pictures per second. >> IMAX; projector ℹ; sound film

cinéma vérité A style of film production stressing realistic documentary treatment even for fictional drama. The approach prefers non-professional actors and minimal script and rehearsal, using the mobile viewpoint of a hand-held camera and natural sound.

Cinerama One of the first systems of wide-screen cinema presentation in 1952, using three synchronized projectors to cover a very large curved screen in three blended panels. Its cost and complexity limited its use to showing travelogues in specially adapted theatres, and it ceased after 1962.

cineraria A dwarf shrub growing to 60 cm/2 ft or more, native to Africa and Madagascar; flower-heads numerous, daisy-like, in dense flat-topped clusters, red to deep blue-violet. (Genus: *Cineraria*, c.50 species. Family: Compositae.)

Cinna, Lucius Cornelius [**si**na] (?–84 BC) Prominent Roman politician of the turbulent 80s BC. Driven from Rome while consul in 87 BC, he recaptured the city with the help of Marius amid much bloodshed, and was all-powerful there until his murder. >> Marius; Roman history ℹ

cinnabar (entomology) [**sin**abah(r)] A medium-sized, nocturnal tiger moth; forewings dark grey with carmine patches, hindwings carmine with black margins; also called **cinnabar moth**. (Order: Lepidoptera. Family: Arctiidae.) >> tiger moth

cinnabar (metallurgy) [**sin**abah(r)] A mineral of mercury sulphide (HgS), the chief ore of mercury. It consists of small, red, soft crystals, and is used in the mineral pigment vermilion. >> mercury

cinnamon A small evergreen tree (*Cinnamomum zeylanicum*) growing to 6 m/20 ft, native to SE Asia; flowers greenish; berries black. The spice is obtained from the bark of young trees. (Family: Lauraceae). >> spice

cinquefoil [**singk**foyl] The name of various species of *Potentilla*, with 5-petalled, white, yellow, or purple flowers. (Genus: *Potentilla*. Family: Rosaceae.) >> potentilla

Cinque Ports [singk] Originally, the five S English coast ports of Dover, Hastings, Hythe, Romney, and Sandwich, associated by royal authority (under Edward the Confessor) to provide ships for naval defence; Rye and Winchelsea were added later. They received royal privileges, and were governed by a Lord Warden. Their role declined with the growth of the navy, and the status was abolished in 1835. >> Edward the Confessor

cipher A secret way of writing; also, anything written in such a manner. The letters comprising a message in ciphers are normally either replaced by others (*substitution*) or re-ordered (*transposition*) according to a frequently changing scheme. In either case the appropriate key is needed to decipher and understand the message. >> cryptanalysis; cryptography

circadian rhythm [ser**kay**dian] (Lat *circa* 'about' + *dies* 'day') A biological rhythm that has a periodicity of about one day. This periodicity can be seen, for example, in the sleep cycle in animals and the growth cycles of plants. >> biological rhythm

Circassians A people from the Caucasus, divided into Adyghians and Kabardians; they are Sunni Muslims. Most live in Russia as farmers and pastoralists. >> Caucasus Mountains; Sunnis

Circe [**ser**see] In the *Odyssey*, an enchantress who detained Odysseus and his followers on the island of Aeaea. She transformed Odysseus's men into swine with a magic drink, but he was able to defeat her charms through the protection of the herb *Moly*. >> Odysseus

Circinus [**ser**sinus] (Lat 'compasses') A small obscure S constellation. >> constellation; RR968

circle The locus of a point that is a constant distance from a fixed point. The constant distance is called the *radius*, and the fixed point the *centre*. From this definition are obtained all the properties of the circle. The area of a circle radius r is πr^2; the circumference is $2\pi r$. >> geometry; pi

circotherm oven An oven with a fan to circulate internal hot air. It is designed to achieve uniformity of heating and to economize in heating or cooking time.

circuit An administrative division of the judicial system of England and Wales. Each circuit has a circuit administrator and two presiding judges, one senior, one junior. In the USA, federal and state judicial systems have similar administrative divisions, also known as circuits. >> judge

circuit riders Early itinerant Methodist preachers on horseback who covered a circuit of churches and carried messages to new settlements. They were instrumental in the rapid expansion of early Methodism. >> Methodism

circulation In physiology, the vertebrate system in which blood is pumped intermittently from the heart and flows continuously around the body (**systemic circulation**) or to the lungs (**pulmonary circulation**) and back to the heart by a network of blood vessels. By means of the systemic circulation, tissues are provided with oxygen, nutrients, hormones, and enzymes. The pulmonary circulation is concerned with the exchange of oxygen and carbon dioxide with the environment. In mammals and birds, the circulatory system also functions in body temperature regulation. >> blood vessels i; heart i; lungs i

circumcision The widespread practice of removing all or part of the foreskin of the penis. The age of circumcision varies; male Jewish babies, for example, are circumcised eight days after birth, while other groups circumcise just before or at puberty as part of an initiation ceremony. In female circumcision, some or all external genitalia are removed. Circumcision may also be carried out for health reasons. >> penis

Circumcision, Feast of the A Christian festival (1 Jan) in honour of the circumcision of Jesus eight days after his birth (*Luke* 2). >> Jesus Christ

circumpolar star A star which never sets when viewed from a particular location. In Europe and North America the stars of Ursa Minor and Ursa Major are always visible. In Australia, Crux is a circumpolar constellation. >> Crux; star; Ursa Major / Minor

circus Historically, games in ancient Rome involving horse and chariot races, gladiatorial combat, and wild animals; in modern times, a travelling show featuring animals and feats of human endurance and skill. The modern-day circus was initiated in 1768 by trick horseback rider Philip Astley (1742–1814), who built his own 'arena' in which to display his skills. The most famous 19th-c circuses were Barnum and Bailey's, Astley's and Spengler's. In recent times the shows of Bertram Mills, Billy Smart, and David Chipperfield have been popular, though suffering a decline in recent years. European and Asian circuses, such as those of Moscow and China, continue to provide spectacular shows, and tour regularly, as does Canada's Cirque du Soleil.

Cirencester [**siy**rensester, **sis**ister], ancient **Corinium Dobunorum** 51°44N 1°59W, pop (1995e) 15 500. Market town in Gloucestershire, SWC England; second largest town in Roman Britain during 2nd-c AD; Royal Agricultural College. >> Gloucestershire

cire perdue [seer per**doo**] or **'lost wax' process** A technique for casting metals, mainly for sculpture. The desired shape is formed (eg in clay), and a mould is made, the inside of which is then coated in wax. The inside of the wax is coated with further heat-resisting material, giving a gap filled with wax. The wax is then melted out, leaving a hollow into which molten metal can be poured. >> casting i; wax

cirque [serk] A bowl-shaped, steep-sided hollow formed at the head of a mountain valley by the erosion of ice in glaciated regions; termed **corrie** or **cwm** in Scotland and Wales respectively. Two cirques cutting back into a ridge forms an *arete*, while three or more result in pyramidal peaks such as the Matterhorn in the Alps.

cirrhosis [si**roh**sis] A chronic diffuse disorder of the liver, in which liver cells are destroyed and progressively replaced by scar tissue (*fibrosis*). The commonest cause is long-continued excessive consumption of alcohol. >> liver

Cirripedia [siri**pee**dia] >> **barnacle**

cirrocumulus clouds [sirohkyoomyuluhs] High-level clouds above c.5000 m/16 000 ft, composed of ice crystals. They are white in thin sheets or layers, but have the rounded appearance of cumulus clouds. Cloud symbol: Cc. >> cloud i; cumulus clouds

cirrostratus clouds [sirohs**tra**tuhs] High-level stratus or layered clouds, in which there is a transition from supercooled water droplets to ice crystals. Found at altitudes above c.5000 m/16 000 ft, they are sheet-like and white/grey in colour. Their arrival precedes the warm front of a depression. Cloud symbol: Cs. >> cloud i; stratus clouds

cirrus clouds [**si**ruhs] High-level clouds above c.5000 m/16 000 ft, composed of ice crystals. They are white and wispy in appearance, elongated by strong winds in the upper atmosphere. They are an indication of the leading edge of a warm front at altitude. Cloud symbol: Ci. >> cloud i

CIS >> **Commonwealth of Independent States**

Cisalpine Gaul [siz**al**piyn gawl] >> **Gaul**

Cisalpine Republic [siz**al**piyn] N Italian state created by Napoleon I at the Peace of Campoformio (1797). By the Treaty of Lunéville (1802), it became the Italian Republic, with Bonaparte as president. >> Napoleon I

***cis*-butenedioic acid** >> **maleic acid**

Ciscaucasia The N Caucasus territory of Kuban, Stavropol, Terek, and the Black Sea, formed in 1924. It existed until 1934. >> Caucasus Mountains

Ciskei [**sis**kiy] pop (1995e) 1 350 000; area 7700 sq km/ 2972 sq mi. Former independent black homeland in NE Cape province, South Africa, established in 1981; military coup, 1990; incorporated into Eastern Cape province in the South African Constitution of 1994. >> apartheid; Eastern Cape; South Africa i

Cistercians [sis**ter**shnz] A religious order formed by Benedictine monks by St Robert of Molesme in Citeaux, France, in 1098, under a strict rule, with an emphasis on solitude, poverty, and simplicity. In the 17th-c it was divided into communities of **Common Observance** (now abbreviated **SOCist**) and of **Strict Observance** (in full, the **Order of the Reformed Cistercians of the Strict Observance**, abbreviated **OCSO**). The latter were revived in France after the Revolution by *Trappists* (former members of the monastery of La Trappe). >> Benedictines; Bernard of Clairvaux, St; monasticism; Trappists

cithara >> **kithara** i

Citizen's Advice Bureaux (CAB) In the UK, a national network of information offices, set up in 1939 to inform the public about the emergency wartime regulations. It has remained in operation to provide free and confidential information, particularly concerning the social services, housing, legal aid, consumer services, and family matters. Its 900 offices are staffed by trained counsellors, 90% of whom are volunteers, and each office is funded by the local authority.

citizens' band (CB) radio A short-range two-way radio communication system for use by members of the public, typically consisting of a transceiver (a combined transmitter-receiver) and aerial. CB originated in the USA in the 1940s, and is particularly associated with long-distance truck drivers, who evolved special codes and jargon to keep their messages from being understood by the police and public. In the UK, the use of CB was illegal until 1981, when a special channel was authorized. The technology has now been largely replaced by cellular phones. >> radio

Citlaltépetl [seetlal**tay**petl] or **Pico de Orizaba** 19°02N 97°02W. Highest peak in Mexico, rising to 5699 m/ 18 697 ft; a dormant volcano, inactive since 1687. >> Mexico i; volcano

citric acid cycle >> **Krebs cycle**

citron A citrus fruit (*Citrus medica*), 10–25 cm/4–10 in in diameter; ovoid, with thick, rough, yellowish-orange rind, and green or yellow flesh. (Family: Rutaceae.) >> citrus

citrus A member of a group of plants bearing distinctive juicy, acid-tasting fruits of great economic importance. The majority belong to the genus *Citrus*, but a few come from close relatives. All species are spiny evergreen shrubs or trees. The fruit is a type of berry, in which the carpels are enclosed in a thick, leathery rind. Both the foliage and rind of the fruit have numerous glands containing aromatic essential oils. The species include the orange, lemon, lime, and grapefruit, as well as more local fruits, such as the shaddock. They are now grown in the tropics and warm temperate regions throughout the world, mainly the Mediterranean, S USA, S Africa, and Australia, and have become a major export crop for several countries. (Genus: *Citrus*, 12 species. Family: Rutaceae.) >> carpel; citron; grapefruit; lemon; lime (botany); mandarin; orange; shaddock; tangerine

cittern A plucked string instrument of great antiquity, particularly popular in the 16th–17th-c. It resembled a lute, but with a smaller, pear-shaped body, a flat (or slightly convex) back, and usually four, five, or six courses of strings played with a plectrum. >> chordophone; plectrum

city A settlement larger than a town or village, the definition of which varies according to national conventions. In Britain the term is used of cathedral towns (eg Ely) and certain other towns upon which the title has been conferred by royal authority (eg Birmingham); in the USA it is used of urban centres which have a particular local government structure. >> cathedral

City, the A square mile of C London housing some of the world's major financial institutions, including the Stock Exchange, money markets, commercial and merchant banks, the insurance institutions, and commodity exchanges. The term is also used as a collective noun to denote the major British financial institutions and their interests. >> London

city-state >> **polis**

city technology college (CTC) A type of secondary school, established by the 1988 Education Act, which specializes in science and technology. It is independent of the local education authority and receives its annual grant direct from the government. >> secondary education

Ciudad Guayana [syoo**dad** gwa**ya**na] 8°22N 62°37W, pop (1995e) 605 000. New city in E Venezuela, founded in 1961; population of 1 million is planned; airfield; railway; commercial port at San Félix. >> Venezuela ℹ

civet A carnivorous mammal, found in 17 species (mostly Asian); also known as **civet cat** or **bush dog**, but the name *civet* is often used for any member of this family. (Family: Viverridae.) >> carnivore ℹ; genet; Viverridae ℹ

Civic Trust A charitable organization in the UK which exists to promote conservation and improvement of the environment in town and country. It encourages high standards in architecture and planning, and the preservation of buildings of historic and architectural interest. >> conservation (earth sciences)

civil defence (CD) The organization of civilian defences, able to limit damage and keep communications and production moving. It became a vital part of a nation's defences during the bombing campaigns of World War 2. Countries which maintain active organizations include Switzerland, Sweden, and the USA, where Civil Defense copes with natural disasters. >> Home Guard; Territorial Army

civil disobedience A political strategy adopted by M K Gandhi and his followers in India in 1930, in opposition to Britain's imperial rule: a non-violent, mass, illegal protest, intended to discredit the authority of the state. The strategy was later used by Martin Luther King Jr to good effect, and was a path sometimes advocated by opponents of nuclear weapons. >> Gandhi; King, Martin Luther

civil engineering A branch of engineering which deals with the design and construction of public works: buildings, bridges, tunnels, waterways, canals, streets, sewerage systems, railways, and airports. The subject includes structural, sanitary, and hydraulic engineering. >> engineering

civil law **1** A branch of law regulating relationships between private citizens. An aggrieved person must generally initiate proceedings personally in order to obtain a remedy. >> law **2** The term also refers to civil law systems such as those of continental Europe and Japan, where law is codified. The *Code Napoléon* is an influential example. The contrast is with **common law** systems, where the emphasis is on the development of law through individual cases under a system of precedent. >> common law **3** Domestic law, in contrast to international law. >> international law

civil liberties Individual freedoms that are thought to be essential to the operation of liberal democratic societies. These include freedom of speech, association, religion, conscience and movement, freedom before the law, and the right to a fair trial. >> civil rights

civil list In the UK, since 1760, a payment made from public funds for the maintenance of the royal household and family (except the Prince of Wales). It covers the salaries of the household staff, travel, entertaining, and public engagements at home and abroad. For 1991–2000 the civil list was fixed at £10 420 000, of which £7 900 000 was intended for the Queen. In 1992 it was decided that only the Queen, the Queen Mother and the Duke of Edinburgh would receive payments from the civil list. >> Crown Estate

civil list pension In the UK, pensions originally paid from the sovereign's civil list, but now granted separately. They are awarded by the monarch on advice from the prime minister to persons who have given service to the Crown or public. >> pension

civil rights The rights guaranteed by the state to its citizens. It incorporates the notion that governments should not arbitrarily act to infringe these rights, and that individuals and groups, through political action, have a legitimate role in determining and influencing what constitutes them. The term has become closely asssociated with movements in the USA, especially 1954–68, which aimed to secure the legal enforcement of the guarantees of racial equality contained in the 13th, 14th, and 15th Amendments to the US Constitution. Beginning as an attack on specific forms of racial segregation in the Southern states, it broadened into a massive challenge to all forms of racial subordination, and achieved considerable success, especially at the level of legal and juridical reform. >> King, Martin Luther; Jackson, Jesse; Johnson, L B; slavery

civil service Civilian personnel or officials employed on behalf of the state to administer central governmental policies, as distinct from the wider generality of public officials employed in such areas as local government, public corporations, and education, or as civilian staff of the armed forces. Most civil servants are permanent, remaining in post upon a change in government. Civil services are hierarchically organized, operate according to established rules of procedure, and are accountable through ministers to the Crown or the state.

CJD >> **Creutzfeldt-Jakob disease**

cladistics A method of classifying organisms employing evolutionary hypotheses as the basis for classification. It uses recency of common ancestry as the criterion for grouping species together, rather than data on apparent similarity between species. >> evolution; systematics

Cladocera [kla**dos**era] >> **water flea**

Clairvaux [klair**voh**] A Cistercian abbey founded in 1115 by St Bernard near Ville-sous-la-Ferté, Champagne, France. The site is now occupied by a prison. >> abbey; Bernard of Clairvaux, St

clairvoyance The gaining of information about an object or a contemporaneous external physical event by alleged paranormal means. The term **precognitive clairvoyance** is used to refer to the supposed paranormal gaining of information about an external physical source which will come into existence at some time in the future. >> extrasensory perception; paranormal

clam The common name for a variety of bivalve molluscs; includes the giant clams, soft-shelled clams, and venus clams. (Class: Pelecypoda.) >> bivalve; mollusc

clapper board In motion picture production, a board or 'slate' with subject details, photographed at the beginning of each scene for identification. A hinged arm is 'clapped' to mark a synchronization point in the separate picture and sound records.

Clapton, Eric (1945–) Rock guitarist and singer, born in Ripley, Surrey. In the 1960s he was in British rhythm-and-blues bands The Yardbirds and John Mayall's Bluesbreakers, then in Cream and Blind Faith. 'Layla' (1970) is considered a rock classic by many, as are 'I Shot the Sheriff', 'Lay Down Sally', and 'Wonderful Tonight'. >> rhythm and blues; rock music

Clare, Ir **An Chláir** pop (1995e) 90 200, area 3188 sq km/ 1231 sq mi. County in W Ireland; capital, Ennis. >> Ireland (republic) ℹ; Munster

Clare of Assisi, St (1194–1253) Abbess, born of a noble family in Assisi, Italy. In 1215 she founded with St Francis the order of Franciscan nuns known as the Poor Clares. Canonized in 1255, she is the patron saint of television. Feast day 11 August. >> Franciscans

Clare, Anthony (Ward) (1942–) British psychiatrist and broadcaster. He became professor at St Bartholomew's Hospital, London (1982–8), and at Trinity College, Dublin (1985–95), and widely known through his BBC television series, *In the Psychiatrist's Chair* (from 1982). Among his books are *Let's Talk About Me* (1981) and *Depression and How to Survive It* (1993, with Spike Milligan).

Clare, John (1793–1864) Poet, born in Helpston, Cambridgeshire. His works include *Poems Descriptive of Rural Life* (1820). He spent the last 23 years of his life in an asylum at Northampton, where he wrote some of his best poetry.

Clarendon, Edward Hyde, 1st Earl of (1609–74) English statesman and historian, born near Salisbury, Wiltshire. He headed the Royalist opposition in the Commons until 1642, and became High Chancellor in 1658. Unpopular as a statesman, in 1667 he fell victim to a court cabal. Impeached for high treason, he left the country for France. His major work is the *History of the Rebellion in England* (3 vols, 1704–7). >> English Civil War; Restoration

Clarendon Code A series of British Acts passed between 1661 and 1665 which re-asserted the supremacy of the Church of England after the collapse of the 'Puritan Revolution' in 1660. Nonconformity was recognized as lawful, but many restrictions were placed on the activities of Nonconformists. >> Nonconformists; Puritanism

Clarendon, Constitutions of A written declaration of rights claimed by Henry II of England in ecclesiastical affairs, with the purpose of restoring royal control over the English Church. Promulgated at Clarendon, near Salisbury, the Constitutions brought Thomas Becket and Henry II into open conflict. >> Becket; Henry II (of England)

claret >> **wine**

clarinet A woodwind instrument, with a cylindrical bore and a single reed. It has been in regular use as a solo and orchestral instrument since the late 18th-c. It is a transposing instrument, the most common models being pitched in A or B♭. The larger **bass clarinet** (in B♭) sounds one octave lower than the standard instrument. >> reed / transposing / woodwind instrument ℹ

Clark, Jim, popular name of **James Clark** (1936–68) Motor-racing driver, born in Kilmany, Fife. After joining the Lotus Team in 1960, he went on to become World Champion Racing Driver (1963, 1965). He won 25 Grands Prix, and was killed during a Formula Two race at Hockenheim, Germany. >> motor racing

Clark, Kenneth (Mackenzie) Clark, Baron (1903–83) Art historian, born in London. In addition to his acclaimed scholarly work on Leonardo da Vinci, he wrote many popular books on his subject, and became widely known through his television series *Civilisation* (1969).

Clark, Michael (1962–) Dancer and choreographer, born in Aberdeen, Scotland. He studied at the Royal Ballet School and formed his own company in the mid-1980s. Best known for his outlandish costumes, stage props and innovative dance technique.

Clark, William (1770–1838) Explorer, born in Caroline Co, VA. He became joint leader with Meriwether Lewis of the successful transcontinental expedition to the Pacific coast and back (1804–6). >> Lewis, Meriwether

Clarke, Sir Arthur C(harles) (1917–) Writer of science fiction, born in Minehead, Somerset. He became especially known for *2001: a Space Odyssey* (1968) which, under the direction of Stanley Kubrick, became a highly successful film. Later works include the sequels to *2001*, *2010: Space Odyssey II* (1982, film 1984), *2062: Odyssey III* (1988), and *3001: the Final Odyssey* (1997). He emigrated to Sri Lanka in the 1950s.

Clarke, Jeremiah (c.1674–1707) Composer, probably born in London. The real composer of the Trumpet Voluntary long attributed to Purcell, Clarke wrote theatre music, religious and secular choral works, and music for the harpsichord.

Clarke, Kenneth (Harry) (1940–) British statesman. He became a Conservative MP in 1970, and was appointed secretary of state for health (1988), home secretary under John Major (1992), and Chancellor of the Exchequer (1993–7).

clarkia An annual native to western North America and Chile; flowers in spikes, 4-petalled, white, pink, or violet; cultivated as ornamentals. (Genus: *Clarkia*, 36 species. Family: Onagraceae.)

class A set or group of people sharing the same socio-economic position. A **class society** is a system of social inequality based on the unequal distribution of income and wealth between different classes. >> Marxism

classical music Music which is part of a long written tradition, which lends itself to sophisticated study and analysis in conservatories and universities, and which is heard in concert halls, opera houses, and churches (rather than in dance halls, public houses, and discotheques). These days, the distinction between classical music on the one hand and folk music, light music, jazz, pop, etc on the other is felt to be largely unnecessary, and even injurious. >> Baroque (music); Neoclassicism (music); Romanticism; Bach, Johann Sebastian; Beethoven; Brahms; Haydn; Mozart; Schubert

classicism An adherence, in any period, to the standards of Greek and Roman art, traditionally understood in terms of 'correct' proportions of the figure, dignified poses and gestures (as in Raphael, Poussin), but also powerful expression of feeling (as in Donatello, David). In Western art the pendulum seems to swing between classical and non-classical (eg Gothic, Mannerist, Baroque, Romantic), although in certain periods a tension between the two is maintained. In literature, classicism is associated especially with Latin poets such as Horace and Virgil. It implies the skilful imitation and adaptation of permanent forms and themes, rather than new departures and 'originality'. >> Mannerism; Neoclassicism (art and architecture); David, Jacques Louis; Donatello; Horace; Poussin; Raphael; Virgil

Claude Lorrain [klohd], originally **Claude Gellée** (1600–82) Landscape painter, born in Champagne, France. He painted about 400 landscapes, including several with biblical or Classical themes, such as 'The Sermon on the Mount' (1656, New York). He also produced many drawings and etchings. >> landscape painting

Claudianus, Claudius [**klaw**dius] (340–410) The last of the great Latin poets, born in Alexandria, Egypt. Several of his works have survived, notably his epic poem *De raptu Proserpinae* (The Rape of Proserpine), the work for which he was famed in the Middle Ages.

Claudius [**klaw**dius], in full **Tiberius Claudius Caesar Augustus Germanicus** (10 BC–AD 54) Roman emperor (41–54), the grandson of the Empress Livia, brother of Germanicus, and nephew of the Emperor Tiberius. Kept in the background because of his physical disabilities, he devoted himself to historical studies, and thus survived the vicious in-fighting of the imperial house. Through his lavish public works and administrative reforms, he made a lasting contribution to the government of Rome and the empire, and through the annexation of Britain, Mauretania, and Thrace, a significant extension of its size. >> Germanicus; Roman history ℹ; Tiberius

Clause Four >> **New Labour**

Clausewitz, Karl (Philip Gottlieb) von [**klow**zevits] (1780–1831) General, born in Burg, Germany. His posthumously published *Vom Kriege* (1833, On War), advocating a policy of total war, revolutionized military theory. >> Gneisenau; Prussia

Clausius, Rudolf (Julius Emanuel) [**klow**zius] (1822–88) Physicist, born in Köslin, Germany. He formulated the second law of thermodynamics, and was influential in establishing thermodynamics as a science. >> thermodynamics

clavichord A keyboard instrument used from the 15th-c to the late 18th-c and revived in recent times, mainly for performing early music. The keys, when depressed, cause metal tangents to strike the strings, which run at right angles to the keys and are tuned in pairs. >> keyboard instrument

clavicle The curved bone, also known as the **collar bone**, lying almost horizontally at the base of the neck between the breastbone (*sternum*) and the shoulder blade (*scapula*); part of the pectoral girdle. >> scapula; skeleton ℹ; sternum

Clay, Cassius >> **Ali, Muhammad**

Clay, Henry (1777–1852) US statesman and orator, born in Hanover Co, VA. He was active in bringing on the war of 1812–15 with Britain. He made several attempts to hold the Union together in the face of the issue of slavery, for which he earned the title of 'the great pacificator'. >> War of 1812

clay A fine-grained sedimentary deposit composed mainly of clay minerals with some quartz, feldspar, and gypsum. Wet clay can be shaped into bricks, pottery, or sculpture, and when fired forms a durable solid. Clay-rich soils are characteristically sticky, with poor drainage when wet, or cracked and hard when dry. >> clay minerals

clay minerals Hydrous sheet silicates which form fine, flaky crystals, and which can absorb water, giving clay its characteristic plasticity when wet. They are formed as the product of the weathering of rocks, and are often deposited by rivers. They are used as fillers for paper, rubber, and paint. >> kaolin; silicate minerals; vermiculite

claymore (Gael 'great sword') A large, double-edged sword used by Scottish Highlanders in the 17th-c. It had a broad, flat blade, and was wielded with both hands. An 18th-c development was a single-edged broadsword with a basket hilt.

clay-pigeon shooting A pastime and sport in which clay targets are released into the air using an automatic machine, and are fired at with shotguns. It is also known as **trap shooting**. >> shooting (recreation)

clay tokens Small clay artifacts of several distinctive shapes, used in the Middle East since at least the 9th millennium BC as a system of accounting. Some of the symbols used on the earliest known writing tablets from the same area (c.3500 BC) show a striking resemblance in shape to those of the clay tokens. >> graphology

Clayton, Lisa (1959–) Yachtswoman, born in Birmingham, West Midlands. In 1995 she became the first British woman to circumnavigate the globe, in a single, unaided, continuous journey. Her voyage, in a 39 ft sloop, *Spirit of Birmingham*, took 285 days.

Cleanthes [klee**an**theez] (c.331–232 BC) Greek Stoic philosopher, born in Assos, Troas. He studied under Zeno of Citium, and succeeded him as head of the Stoa in 262. His own contributions to Stoicism were especially in the areas of theology and cosmology. >> Stoicism; Zeno of Citium

clearing house In economics, any institution whose function is to co-ordinate and settle the debts owed by its various members; in particular, a place where cheques from different banks are sorted, and the amounts owed by and to each bank are calculated. Since 1984, the process has been mainly automated in the UK through the Clearing House Associated Payments System (CHAPS). In the USA, the equivalent organization is the Clearing House Interbank Payments System (CHIPS).

cleavage The process by which a fertilized egg cell (*zygote*) divides to give rise to all the cells of an organism. The *deuterostomes*, which include vertebrates and echinoderms, display radial cleavage. The *protostomes*, which include molluscs and arthropods, display spiral cleavage. >> arthropod; blastula; cell; Chordata; echinoderm ℹ; mollusc

cleavers >> **goosegrass**

Cleese, John (Marwood) [kleez] (1939–) Comic actor and writer, born in Weston-super-Mare, North West

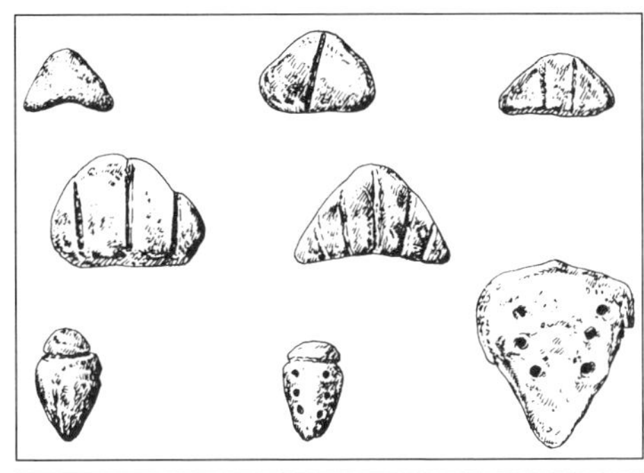

Clay tokens

Somerset. He became well known through his performances in *Monty Python's Flying Circus* (1969–74) and the films and revues which stemmed from it. He enjoyed great success as the writer and star of the series *Fawlty Towers* (1975, 1979). His films include *A Fish Called Wanda* (1988) and *Fierce Creatures* (1997). He also founded Video Arts Ltd, producing industrial training films. >> Monty Python

cleft lip and palate An abnormality of development of the lips and palate, occurring in about 1 in 1000 live births. It consists of a fissure or cleft on one or both sides of the upper lip, occurring either alone or associated with a cleft in the palate. >> congenital abnormality; palate

Cleisthenes [**kliys**theneez] (6th-c BC) Prominent Athenian politician of the Alcmaeonid family, and through his constitutional reforms (c.508 BC) the founder of Athenian democracy. >> Alcmaeonids; Pericles

Cleland, John [**klay**land] (1709–89) Novelist, born in London. He published in 1750 *Fanny Hill, or the Memoirs of a Woman of Pleasure*. A best-seller in its time, it achieved a second *succès de scandale* on its revival and prosecution under the Obscene Publications Act in 1963.

clematis [kle**may**tis] A member of a genus of woody climbers native throughout temperate regions; stalk sensitive on the lower side, acting as a tendril and bending around supports on contact; flowers with four petaloid segments, styles long and feathery. (Genus: *Clematis*, 250 species. Family: Ranunculaceae.) >> liane; style (botany)

Clemenceau, Georges [klemãsoh] (1841–1929) French statesman and prime minister (1906–9, 1917–20), born in Mouilleron-en-Pareds, France. He was a leader of the extreme left in the Chamber of Deputies. Known as 'the tiger', he presided at the Peace Conference in 1919, showing an intransigent hatred of Germany.

Clement I, St, known as **Clemens Romanus** or **Clement of Rome** (late 1st-c) One of the apostolic Fathers, reckoned variously as the second or third successor of St Peter at Rome, possibly 88–97 or 92–101. The first of two epistles attributed to him is generally accepted as his (written c.96). Feast day 23 November. >> Christianity; Fathers of the Church

Clement VII, originally **Giulio de' Medici** (1478–1534) Pope (1523–34), born in Florence, Italy. He allied himself with Francis I of France against the Holy Roman Emperor Charles V. His refusal to sanction Henry VIII's divorce from Catherine of Aragon hastened the Reformation. >> Henry VIII; pope; Reformation

Clement of Alexandria, St, Lat **Clemens Alexandrinus** (c.150–c.215) Theologian and Father of the early Church, probably born in Athens. He became head of the celebrated Catechetical school at Alexandria, where he related Greek philosophical thought to Christian belief. Feast day 5 December. >> Fathers of the Church

Clementi, Muzio [kle**men**tee] (1752–1832) Composer and pianist, born in Rome. In 1817–26 he wrote the *Gradus ad Parnassum*, on which subsequent piano methods have been based.

Cleon [**klee**on] (?–422 BC) The first Athenian of rich, bourgeois stock to play a prominent role in 5th-c BC politics. His capture of the Spartans on the island of Sphacteria (425 BC) gave Athens her trump card in the peace negotiations of the late 420s BC. >> Peloponnesian War

Cleopatra VII (69–30 BC) Queen of Egypt (51–48 BC, 47–30 BC), the daughter of Ptolemy Auletes. A woman of great intelligence, she made the most of her physical charms to strengthen her own position within Egypt, and to save the country from annexation by Rome. Thus, Julius Caesar, to whom she bore a son Caesarion, supported her claim to the throne against her brother (47 BC), while Antony, by whom she had three children, restored to her several portions of the old Ptolemaic Empire, and even gave to their joint offspring substantial areas of the Roman East (34 BC). Defeated along with Antony at Actium (31 BC), she committed suicide. >> Actium, Battle of; Antonius; Caesar

clergy >> **abbey; archbishop; archdeacon; bishop; canon** (religion)**; cardinal** (religion)**; curate; deacon; dean; priest; rector; vicar**

Clerk Maxwell, James >> **Maxwell, James**

Clermont-Ferrand [klairmõ ferã] 45°46N 3°04E, pop (1995e) 140 000. City in C France; capital of Auvergne, 16th-c; Clermont merged with Montferrand, 1630; geographical and economic centre of the Massif Central; railway; bishopric; university (1896); cathedral (begun 1248); birthplace of Pascal. >> France ℹ; Massif Central; Pascal

Cleveland (UK) [**kleev**land] pop (1995e) 562 000; area 583 sq km/225 sq mi. Former county of NE England; created in 1974 from parts of Yorkshire and Durham; replaced in 1996 by Hartlepool, Redcar and Cleveland, Middlesbrough, and Stockton-on-Tees unitary authorities. >> England ℹ

Cleveland (USA) [**kleev**land] 41°30N 81°42W, pop (1995e) 525 000. Port on L Erie, NE Ohio, USA; city status, 1836; largest city in Ohio; airfield; railway; three universities (1826, 1886, 1923); medical research centre; professional teams, Indians (baseball), Cavaliers (basketball), Browns (football). >> Erie, Lake; Ohio

Cleveland, (Stephen) Grover (1837–1908) US statesman and the 22nd and 24th president (1885–9, 1893–7), born at Caldwell, NJ. In 1895 he caused worldwide excitement by applying the Monroe Doctrine to Britain's dispute with Venezuela. >> Monroe Doctrine

Cleveland bay One of the oldest English breeds of horse; height, 15–16 hands/1·5–1·6 m/5 ft–5 ft 4 in; reddish-brown with long body, shortish legs, muscular hindquarters; also known as the **Chapman horse**. >> thoroughbred

Cleveland Way Long-distance footpath in North Yorkshire, England; length c.150 km/90 mi; stretches from Helmsley to near Filey. >> Yorkshire, North

Clewlow, Warren (Alexander Morten) (1936–) Businessman, born in KwaZulu Natal, South Africa. He became executive chairman of the Barlow Rand Group of Companies, South Africa's largest industrial corporation. He is also chairman of the State President's Economic Advisory Council, and president of the South Africa Foundation.

click beetle An elongate, usually dark-coloured beetle; an adult lying on its back can right itself with a jack-knifing movement that produces a loud click; can be serious crop pests, known as **wireworms**. (Order: Coleoptera. Family: Elateridae.) >> beetle

cliff dwellings Houses of the Pueblo Indians in SW USA from the Pueblo III cultural period (AD c.1100–1300). Made with stone blocks and adobe mortar, some were several storeys high, and built in arched recesses of cliff walls. >> Pueblo

climacteric >> **menopause**

climate The long-term prevailing weather conditions in a region or place. The climate of a place is influenced by several factors. Latitude determines the amount of solar radiation received, with the greatest in equatorial regions. Elevation affects both temperature and precipitation; mountainous areas are generally cooler and wetter. Location close to the sea or large bodies of water moderates temperature. Aspect is of local importance; in the N hemisphere, S- and W-facing slopes are warmer than N- and E-facing slopes. The scientific study of climate, describing and attempting to explain climatic differences from place to place, is known as **climatology**. >> precipitation; temperature ℹ; weather

climbing plant A plant which reaches towards the light

by clinging to neighbouring plants, walls, or other supports, sometimes referred to by the general term **vine**. Various means are used, including twining stems and leaf-stalks, tendrils, and aerial roots. **Ramblers** merely grow against and lean on their supports, but often have thorny hooks to help grip. **Lianes** have long, woody stems which reach high into the forest canopy, and are found especially in the tropics. >> liane

clinical psychology The application of psychological knowledge to the assessment, prevention, and treatment of a variety of psychological disorders, involving behavioural, emotional, or cognitive disturbances. >> behaviour therapy; psychology

clinometer A hand-held surveying instrument, also known as an **Abney level**. It is used to measure the angles of a slope by bringing a level-bubble on a graduated circle into coincidence with a wire in a sighting tube. >> surveying

Clinton, Bill, popular name of **William Jefferson Clinton**, born **William Jefferson Blythe** (1946–) US politician and 42nd president (1993–), born in Hope, AR. His father, William Blythe, died in a road accident before he was born, and he was adopted by his stepfather, Roger Clinton. He became a lawyer, then entered Arkansas politics, becoming Democratic governor (1979–81, 1983–92). Overcoming serious charges concerning extramarital affairs and questions about his draft deferment during the Vietnam War, he won the Democratic presidential nomination in 1992. His presidency was marked by a notable international profile, including intervention in several troubled parts of the world (such as the Middle East and Northern Ireland), and he was elected for a second term (defeating Bob Dole) in 1996. However, in 1997, media attention was taken up by a civil suit against him by Paula Jones, a former Arkansas state employee, who alleged sexual harassment by him in 1991. During the enquiries, which attempted to establish a pattern of behaviour by the president, a fresh series of allegations emerged in January 1998 which dominated US media for the rest of that year. These concerned Monica Lewinsky, a White House intern with whom Clinton was alleged to have had a sexual relationship. Allegations that he had committed perjury by denying the affair, and had attempted to suborn a witness, raised the issue of his resignation or impeachment. Whitewater investigator Kenneth Starr was authorized to extend his investigations, which lasted throughout 1998. However, strong support from Hillary Clinton, suggestions of a right-wing conspiracy to discredit the president, criticism of the motives and tactics of Starr (a Republican), and growing feeling among the US public that the president's private and public lives were separate, led to his continuing to receive strong popular support. Despite a campaign of personal public apology, the release of the Starr report led to the establishment of a House of Representatives judiciary committee, which voted for impeachment. A Senate trial took place in January 1999, but he was acquitted. Despite the controversy surrounding his personal life, Clinton governed from the centre of US politics. His economic policies helped produce a balanced budget, he joined Republicans in reforming the welfare system, and saw a reduction in the crime rate during his presidency. Sustained prosperity helped maintain his job ratings at a high level during his second term. >> Bush; Clinton, Hillary; Gore; Lewinsky; Starr; Whitewater affair

Clinton, Hillary (Rodham) (1947–) Lawyer and US first lady (1993–), born in Park Ridge, IL. She married fellow law graduate Bill Clinton in 1975, and emerged as a dynamic and valued partner of her husband amid the allegations of extramarital affairs which surfaced during his 1992 presidential nomination campaign. She performed an active political role following his election, heading a task force on national health reform in 1993. Her defence of her husband during the Lewinsky affair was widely admired, and her personal political presence was greatly enhanced following her effective role supporting Democratic candidates during the mid-term elections in November 1998. She was widely mentioned as a potential US Senate candidate in early 1999. >> Clinton, Bill; Lewinsky

Clio [**kliy**oh] In Greek mythology, the Muse of history, and of lyre-playing. >> Muses

clipper ship A mid-19th-c revolutionary US design of sailing ship. Its principal features were finer bow and stern lines, greater rake to the masts, and greater beam than in traditional vessels, resulting in faster ships with improved windward performance. >> ship ℹ

clitoris [**kli**toris] Part of the female external genitalia, composed of erectile tissue partly surrounded by muscle. It is the equivalent of the male penis (though it does not convey the urethra), and enlarges upon tactile stimulation. >> penis ℹ

Clive (of Plassey), Robert Clive, Baron (1725–74) Soldier and adminstrator in India, born in Styche, Shropshire. In January 1757 he recaptured Calcutta from the Nawab, and at Plassey on the 23 June defeated a large Indian–French force. For three years he was sole ruler in all but name of Bengal. >> Black Hole of Calcutta

cloaca [kloh**ay**ka] The terminal region of the gut into which the alimentary canal, urinary system, and reproductive system all open and discharge their products via a single common aperture. >> alimentary canal; reproduction; urinary system

clock A mechanism for measuring and indicating the passage of time, and for recording the duration of intervals. Its essential elements are a source of energy to drive the mechanism, and a device to maintain a regular (usually stepwise) rate of motion. The first clockwork escapement was Chinese, AD 724, and water-powered clocks are noted in China from the 760s. In mediaeval and many later clocks, the drive was a falling weight; from the 16th-c, it was the coiled mainspring; and from the late 19th-c, it was electric current from batteries or mains. From c.1670 a balance wheel was used for small clocks and watches. In modern times, clocks are powered by electric synchronous motors maintained by the mains frequency, by a maintained tuning fork, or by the oscillation of a quartz crystal. >> time; *see illustration on p.190*

Clodion [klodyõ], pseudonym of **Claude Michel** (1738–1814) Sculptor, born in Nancy, France. One of the most brilliant Rococo sculptors, he specialized in small terracottas and low reliefs of erotic dancing nymphs and satyrs. >> relief sculpture; Rococo; terracotta

cloisonné [klwazo**nay**] A method of enamelling on metal, and occasionally ceramic, in which the different fields of colour are separated by metal wires soldered to the surface to be decorated. Principally an oriental technique, it was much used in Byzantine and Mediaeval art. >> enamelling

cloisters Covered walkways around an open space or court, with a colonnade or arcaded inner side and a solid outer wall. Cloisters are used in a monastery or convent to connect the church to other parts of the building. >> colonnade

cloning The process of asexual reproduction observed in bacteria and other unicellular micro-organisms which divide by simple fission, so that the daughter cells are genetically identical to each other and to the parent, except where mutation occurs. In higher organisms, genetically identical individuals may be produced by cloning. A body (*somatic*) cell is taken from an embryo in

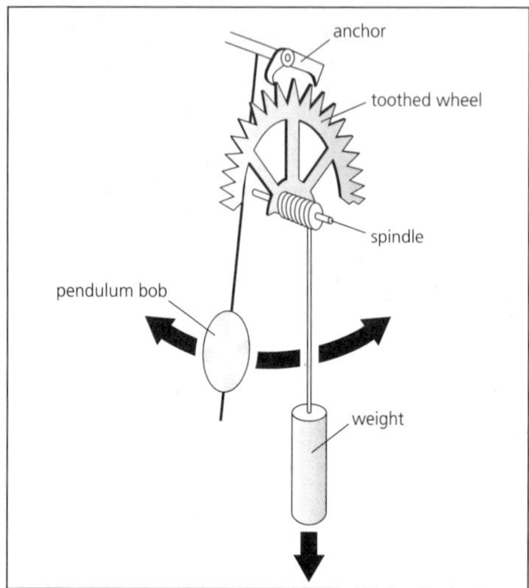

Clock – pendulum drive

an early stage of development, the nucleus transferred to an unfertilized ovum from which the nucleus has been removed, and the product grown in culture; daughter cells from the earliest divisions are removed, and grown in cell culture or implanted into host mothers to give genetically identical offspring. The successful cloning of a sheep ('Dolly') was reported by scientists from the Roslin Institute, Edinburgh, UK, in February 1997. There is considerable potential application in animal rearing, but its application to humans is extremely unlikely (except in some very rare instances of *in vitro* fertilization). In 1998, a Council of Europe protocol banning the cloning of human beings was signed in Paris by 19 states – the first international treaty on the issue. However, in 1999, predictions were being made about the application of the technique in other areas, such as bone-marrow grafting in leukaemia, and transplant medicine in general, and the controversy surrounding the ethics of human cloning continued to exercise professional and public opinion. >> cell; reproduction

Clonmel [klon**mel**], Ir **Cluain Meala** 52°21N 7°42W, pop (1995e) 15 400. Capital of Tipperary county, S Ireland; centre of Irish greyhound racing and salmon fishing; railway. >> Ireland (republic) ℹ; Tipperary

closed circuit television (CCTV) Any system of image presentation in which a video camera and its display screen are directly linked, even at a considerable distance, rather than by broadcast transmission or intermediate recording. Applications include surveillance, surgical and scientific demonstration, and industrial remote examination. >> interactive video; television

closed shop A company or works where some grades of worker are required to belong to a recognized trade union; the opposite situation is known as an **open shop**. Unions prefer the closed shop, as it gives them more members, and gives their members a better chance of getting any available jobs. Employers accept the closed shop for the sake of industrial peace, though they know it weakens their bargaining position in the event of an industrial dispute. Closed shops are banned in many US states. >> collective bargaining; trade union

Clostridium A genus of rod-shaped bacteria that are typically motile by means of flagella, and produce spores (*endospores*). They are widespread in the soil and in the intestinal tract of humans and other animals. The genus includes the causative agents of botulism, gas gangrene, and tetanus. (Kingdom: Monera. Family: Bacillaceae.) >> bacteria ℹ; intestine; spore

Clotho >> **Moerae**

cloud A visible collection of particles of ice and water held in suspension above the ground. Clouds form when air becomes saturated and water vapour condenses around nuclei of dust, smoke particles, and salt. Four main categories of clouds are recognized: **nimbus clouds**, which produce rain; **stratus clouds**, which resemble layers; **cumulus clouds**, which resemble heaps; and **cirrus clouds**, which resemble strands or filaments of hair. These names are further modified by an indication of cloud height: *strato* – low level clouds; *alto* – middle level clouds; *cirro* – high level clouds. Fog can be considered as cloud close to ground level. >> altocumulus / altostratus / cirrocumulus / cirrostratus / cirrus / cumulonimbus / cumulus / nimbostratus / nimbus / noctilucent / stratocumulus / stratus clouds; condensation (physics); dew point temperature; fog; nephanalysis; precipitation; thunderstorm; *see illustration on p.191*

cloud chamber A device for detecting subatomic particles; invented by Charles Wilson in 1912. It comprises a chamber containing vapour prone to condensing to liquid. The passage of particles forms ions, which act as centres for condensation, and the particle paths become visible as trails of mist. The device has been superseded by other particle detectors. >> bubble chamber; ion; particle detectors; Wilson, Charles

clouded tiger >> **tortoiseshell cat**

Clough, Arthur Hugh [kluhf] (1819–61) Poet, born in Liverpool, Merseyside. His works include *The Bothie* (1848) and *Amours de Voyage* (1849). His best-known poem, beginning 'Say not the struggle nought availeth', was published posthumously in 1862.

clover A low-growing annual or perennial, occurring in both temperate and subtropical regions, but mainly in the N hemisphere; leaves with three toothed leaflets; small pea-flowers, white, pink, or red, clustered into often dense, rounded heads. Several species are extensively grown as fodder for cattle, and they are also valuable pasture plants. Yellow-flowered species are generally called **trefoils**. (Genus: *Trifolium*, 250 species. Family: Leguminosae.) >> alsike; shamrock; trefoil

clove tree An evergreen tree growing to 12 m/40 ft, native to Indonesia; flowers yellow, 4-petalled, in terminal clusters. The flower buds are dried to form the spice cloves. (*Syzygium aromaticum*. Family: Myrtaceae.) >> spice

Clovis [**kloh**vis] The earliest identifiable Indian culture of North America; hunter-gatherers exploiting the mammoth herds of the plains towards the end of the last glaciation, c.10 000–9000 BC. It is characterized archaeologically by bifacially-flaked spear points found across the USA, notably near Clovis, NM, in 1963. >> hunter-gatherers

club foot A congenital deformity of one or both feet, in which the child cannot stand on the sole of the affected foot. The foot is pulled downward, and the heel turned inwards. Improvement may be achieved by the application of a series of graded splints, or in severe cases by surgical operation. >> congenital abnormality; foot

clubmoss A spore-bearing plant related to ferns and horsetails; stem long, regularly branched, clothed with numerous small leaves. It is found almost everywhere, many in heathland or similar habitats. (Genus: *Lycopodium*, 450 species. Family: Lycopodiaceae.) >> fern; horsetail; spore

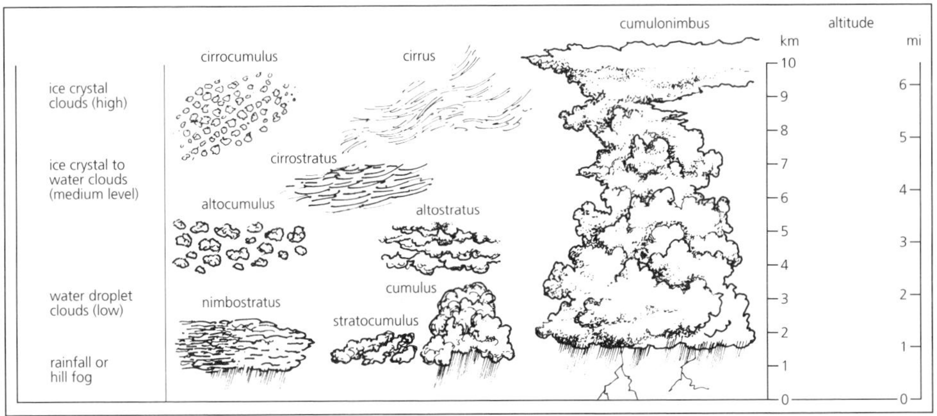

Cloud types

clubroot A disease of cabbage-family plants (the Brassicaceae) that causes gall-like swellings of roots and discoloration of leaves; caused by the parasitic slime mould *Plasmodiophora brassicae*. >> cabbage; parasitology; slime mould

Cluj-Napoca or **Cluj** [kloozh **na**poka], Ger **Klausenburg** 46°47N 23°37E, pop (1995e) 326 000. City in NEC Romania; a former capital of Transylvania; ceded from Hungary, 1920; airfield; railway; university (1872), technical university (1948). >> Romania ℹ; Transylvania

Clune, Frank [kloon], popular name of **Francis Patrick Clune** (1893–1971) Writer of biography, history, and travel, born in Sydney, New South Wales, Australia. He wrote over 60 books, often in collaboration with P R ('Inky') Stephensen, such as *Ben Hall the Bushranger* (1947), and *Wild Colonial Boys* (1948).

Cluny Abbey [klünee] A Benedictine abbey founded in 910 at Cluny, EC France, known for the monastic reforms it introduced, promoting a stricter observance of the Benedictine rule. The abbey was forced to close in 1790, during the French Revolution. >> abbey; Benedict, St

clustered wax flower >> **stephanotis; wax plant**

clutch A mechanical device that allows an engine to be connected and disconnected from its load while the engine is running. The most common application is in the motor car, where normally a plate covered with high friction material is sandwiched and held in place between a disc attached to the engine's flywheel and a disc fixed to the gear-box. >> engine; transmission

Clutha, River [**kloo**tha] Longest river of South Island, New Zealand; length c.320 km/200 mi. >> New Zealand ℹ

cluttering A disorder of speech fluency, in which the main symptom is excessive rapidity while speaking. The cause is unknown, though a physical explanation in terms of the brain's motor control of speech has been suggested. >> speech pathology; stuttering

Clwyd [**kloo**id] pop (1995e) 418 000; area 2426 sq km/ 937 sq mi. Former county in NE Wales, UK; created in 1974, and replaced in 1996 by the counties of Denbighshire, Flintshire, and Wrexham. >> Wales ℹ

Clyde, Lord >> **Campbell, Sir Colin**

Clyde, River River in S Scotland; passes through Scotland's most important industrial area, including Glasgow, then expands into the Firth of Clyde estuary leading to the Atlantic Ocean; length 170 km/100 mi. >> Clydeside; Scotland ℹ

Clydesdale A breed of horse, produced in Scotland by crossing local mares with large Flemish stallions; a heavy horse, developed in the 18th-c for hauling coal; height c.16·1 hands/1·7 m/5 ft 5 in; reddish-brown with white face and legs. >> horse ℹ

Clydeside pop (1995e) 1 608 000. Urban area in WC Scotland, focused on the R Clyde; airport; railway; major industrial area of Scotland. >> Clyde, River; Glasgow; Scotland ℹ

Clytemnestra [kliytem**nes**tra] or **Clytemestra** In Greek legend, the twin sister of Helen and the wife of Agamemnon. She murdered him on his return from Troy, assisted by her lover, Aegisthus. She was killed in revenge by her son, Orestes. >> Aegisthus; Agamemnon; Orestes

CND An acronym of the **Campaign for Nuclear Disarmament**, a mass organization founded in the UK in 1958 to mobilize public opinion against the nuclear-weapons programme and for unilateral disarmament. It organized peaceful mass marches between London and Aldermaston, where the Atomic Weapons Research Establishment was based, and was successful in securing acceptance of a resolution at the 1960 Labour Party Conference for Britain's unilateral disarmament. During the 1980s it underwent a revival, as concern over the proliferation of nuclear weapons grew. However, following disarmament agreements between the USA and USSR, the organization became less prominent. >> detente

Cnidaria [ni**da**ria] >> **coelenterate**

CNS >> **central nervous system**

C N Tower or **Canadian National Tower** The world's tallest self-supporting tower, erected in Toronto, Ontario, Canada (1973–5); 555·3 m/1822 ft high. >> Toronto

Cnut >> **Canute**

coal A black or brown sedimentary rock found in beds or seams, and formed by heat and pressure over millions of years on vegetation accumulated in shallow swamps. Successive stages in the formation of coal involve an increase in carbon content or 'rank': **peat** is the first stage, followed by **lignite** or **brown coal** (60–70% carbon), **bituminous coal** (more than 80% carbon), and **anthracite** (more than 90% carbon). >> anthracite; coal tar; coke; sedimentary rock

coalfish >> **saithe**

coalition An inter-party arrangement established to pursue a common goal, most obviously government. Coalition governments are relatively common in electoral systems using proportional representation and/or in multiparty systems. The nature of coalition is defined by those parties with seats in the cabinet.

coal mining Extracting coal from beneath the ground. In **open-cast mining**, the coal is near the surface: the overburden is stripped away, the coal removed, and the overburden restored for environmental conservation. In **drift mining**, the coal lies within a slope: a horizontal tunnel is driven into the side of the slope, and the coal removed on level railways or conveyors. **Deep mining** relies on vertical shafts with horizontal approaches to the seams. Coal is dug (mainly now by mechanical means) and removed by conveyors to the shaft bottom for haulage to the surface. World production in 1996 was c.5400 million tonnes. Reserves are estimated at around 8 million million tonnes. >> coal; firedamp

Coal Sack The finest visual example of an obscuring cloud of dust in space, 170 parsec away. It is in the constellation Crux, where it causes a gaping hole in the Milky Way. >> Milky Way

coal tar A volatile by-product of heating coal in the absence of air to form coke; a black viscous liquid consisting of a complex mixture of organic compounds. Further distillation of coal tar produces a large number of chemicals which form the basis of explosives, dyes, and drugs. >> acridine; anthracene; coal; coke

Coastal Command A separate functional Command within the British Royal Air Force (1936–69). During World War 2, it played a decisive role in winning the Battle of the Atlantic. >> Atlantic, Battle of the; World War 2

coastguard An institution whose duty is to keep watch on the coastline and organize rescue and lifeboat services to help those in trouble. The nature of these services varies widely; some nations use their naval forces, whereas others operate through voluntary organizations. The largest service is the US Coastguard, responsible for search and rescue, lighthouses and lightships, pilotage, fishery protection, security at ports, enforcement of maritime legislation, and oceanography. >> navy

Coast Range Mountain belt in W North America, extending along the coast of the Pacific Ocean from Alaska to Mexico Mts; highest point, Mt Logan (5950 m/19 521 ft). >> United States of America 🅘

coast redwood A massive evergreen conifer (*Sequoia sempervirens*), the tallest tree in the world at over 100 m/325 ft high and 8 m/26 ft thick; bark almost 1 m/3¼ ft thick, reddish, fibrous, spongy. It is now confined to the misty bottomlands of coastal California and SW Oregon. (Family: Taxodiaceae.) >> conifer

Coates, Eric (1886–1957) Composer, born in Hucknall, Nottinghamshire. Among his best-known compositions are the *London Suite* (1933), *The Three Elizabeths* (1944), and a number of popular waltzes and marches.

coati [koh**ah**tee] A raccoon-like mammal, found from S USA to South America; reddish-brown; long banded tail; long narrow muzzle with overhanging tip; solitary males called *coatimundis* (or *koatimundis*). (Genus: *Nasua*, 2 species. Family: Procyonidae.) >> raccoon

coat of arms >> **heraldry** 🅘

coat-of-mail shell >> **chiton**

coaxial cable A form of electrical wiring with relatively low loss which is used in the home as a connector from a television aerial to the television set. In computer systems it is the standard form of inter-connection wiring for local area networks. >> Ethernet; local area network

cob A type of horse, often produced when crossing a heavy cart-horse with a racehorse; height, 14·2–15·2 hands/1·5–1·6 m/4 ft 10 in–5 ft 2 in; short deep body; calm natured; also known as **rouncy** or **roncey**. >> horse 🅘

cobalt Co, element 27, density 9 g/cm^3, melting point 1495°C. A hard metal, which occurs in ores as its sulphide (CoS), along with copper and nickel. It is used mainly as a metal in steel alloys, especially for permanent magnets. >> alloy; chemical elements; metal; RR1036

Cobb, Ty(rus Raymond), nickname **the Georgia Peach** (1886–1961) Baseball player, born in Narrows, GA. An outstanding base runner and batter, in a 23-year career with Detroit and Philadelphia he hit over 4000 base hits, a record which survived 57 years until broken in 1985. >> baseball 🅘

Cobbett, William (1763–1835) Journalist and reformer, born in Farnham, Surrey. He started his famous *Weekly Political Register* in 1802, changing in 1804 from its original Toryism to an uncompromising Radicalism. His works include a *History of the Protestant Reformation* (1824–7) and *Rural Rides* (1830). >> Democratic Party; radicalism; Tories

Cobden, Richard (1804–65) Economist and politician, 'the apostle of free trade', born in Heyshott, West Sussex. In 1838 he helped to found the Anti-Corn-Law League, becoming its most prominent member. His speeches focused opinion on the Corn Laws, which were repealed in 1846. >> Anti-Corn-Law League

Coblenz [koh**blents**], Ger **Koblenz**, ancient **Confluentes** 50°21N 7°36E, pop (1995e) 113 000. City in Germany; seat of Frankish kings, 6th-c; badly bombed in World War 2; largest garrison town in former West Germany; railway; major centre of Rhine wine trade. >> Franks; Germany 🅘

COBOL [**koh**bol] An acronym of **COmmon Business Orientated Language**, a high-level computer language widely used in the business community. It uses statements written in English which are relatively easy to understand. >> programming language

cobra A venomous snake, native to S Asia and Africa; neck has loose folds of skin which can be spread as a 'hood' when alarmed; fangs short; venom attacks the nervous system; usually inhabits forests, but also open country. (Family: Elapidae, many species, most in genus *Naja*.) >> king cobra; viper 🅘

cocaine $C_{17}H_{21}NO_4$, melting point 98°C. A white alkaloid extracted from the leaves of the South American shrub *Erythroxylon coca*, and used for its stimulant properties, similar to those of amphetamine. It is widely abused; the powder is sniffed and the purified form can be smoked (*freebasing*). It causes addiction, particularly when freebased. Street names include 'Snow White', 'Charlie', and 'charge'. >> alkaloids; crack; drug addiction

coccus Any spherical bacterium. It varies in size and may occur in chains, clusters, or other groupings. >> bacteria 🅘; pneumococcus; *Staphylococcus*; *Streptococcus*

coccyx [**kok**siks] The lowest part of the vertebral column, forming the tail in many animals. In humans it is small and triangular, comprising three to five rudimentary vertebrae. >> skeleton 🅘; vertebral column

Cochabamba [kocha**bam**ba] 17°26S 66°10W, pop (1995e) 470 000. City in C Bolivia; altitude 2500 m/8200 ft; country's third largest city; founded, 1542; airfield; railway; university (1832); important agricultural centre. >> Bolivia 🅘

Cochin [**ko**chin] 9°55N 76°22E, pop (1995e) 611 000. Naval base and seaport in Kerala, SW India; Portuguese trading station, 1502; Fort Cochin, first European settlement in India; tomb of Vasco da Gama. >> Gama, Vasco da; Kerala

cochineal [kochi**neel**] A dye (**carminic acid**) obtained from the dried bodies of a female bug, *Dactylopus coccus*. The bug feeds on cacti, and is native to Peru and Mexico. (Order: Homoptera. Family: Coccidae.) >> bug (entomology); dyestuff

cockatiel [koka**teel**] An Australian parrot of the cockatoo family (*Nymphicus hollandicus*); long tapering crest on head; male with colourful facial markings. (Family: Cacatuidae.) >> cockatoo; parrot

cockatoo An Australasian parrot, separated from other parrots mainly by features of its skull, and in having an erectile crest of feathers on the head. (Family: Cacatuidae, 18 species.) >> cockatiel; parrot

cockatrice >> **basilisk** (mythology)

cockchafer A large, dark-coloured chafer; adults nocturnal, feeding on leaves; fleshy, C-shaped larvae burrow in ground for 3–4 years, feeding on roots before emerging as flying adults, typically in May, hence alternative name of **maybug**. (Order: Coleoptera. Family: Scarabaeidae.) >> chafer; larva

Cockcroft, Sir John Douglas (1897–1967) Nuclear physicist, born in Todmorden, West Yorkshire. He and E T S Walton (1903–) succeeded in disintegrating lithium by proton bombardment in 1932, pioneering the use of particle accelerators, and shared the Nobel Prize for Physics (1951). He became the first director of Britain's Atomic Energy Establishment at Harwell in 1946. >> particle physics

Cockerell, Sir Christopher (Sydney) (1910–) Engineer, born in Cambridge. He first worked on radio and radar, before turning to hydrodynamics, and in the early 1950s invented the amphibious hovercraft. >> air cushion vehicle ℹ

cocker spaniel or **American cocker spaniel** A breed of dog, developed in the USA from the **English cocker spaniel**; recognized as a separate breed in 1941; smaller than ancestral stock; longer coat; black or golden brown; popular as pets. >> dog

cockfighting A blood sport in which *gamecocks* aged 1–2 years, wearing steel spurs on their legs, were set against each other. It was a popular sport in England until 1849, when it was banned. >> blood sports

cockle A marine bivalve mollusc whose shell comprises two more or less equal valves closed by two adductor muscles; an active burrower in inter-tidal sediments; fished extensively for human consumption. (Class: Pelecypoda. Order: Veneroida.) >> bivalve; mollusc

cockroach An active, typically nocturnal insect; body depressed; legs long and adapted for running; forewings hard and leathery; hindwings membranous, sometimes lost; will eat almost any organic matter. (Order: Blattaria, c.3700 species.) >> insect ℹ

cocoa >> **chocolate**

coco de mer [**koh**koh duh **mair**] A species of palm endemic to the Seychelles (*Lodoicea maldavica*). The fruit is one of the largest known, up to 20 kg/45 lb, taking 10 years to ripen; buoyant and often washed ashore, it was well known before the tree itself was discovered. (Family: Palmae.) >> coconut palm; palm; Seychelles

coconut palm A tree with a characteristic curved trunk (*Cocos nucifera*), growing to 30 m/100 ft, with feathery leaves up to 6 m/20 ft long; the large, single-seeded fruits (coconuts) have a fibrous outer husk and a hard inner shell enclosing a layer of white flesh and a central cavity filled with milky fluid. Coconut leaves are woven into mats and baskets and are used for thatching; the outer husk of the nuts makes coir, a tough fibre used for matting. Coconut milk is a refreshing drink, and the white flesh is eaten raw or cooked, sold as desiccated coconut, or dried to form copra, the world's principal source of vegetable fat. (Family: Palmae.) >> copra; oil (botany); palm

cocoon >> **pupa**

Cocos Islands [**koh**kohs] or **Keeling Islands** 12°05S 96°53E, pop (1995e) 750, total land area 14·2 sq km/ $5\frac{1}{2}$ sq mi. Two separate groups of atolls in the Indian Ocean, 3685 km/2290 mi W of Darwin, Australia; an Australian external territory comprising 27 small, flat, palm-covered coral islands; visited in 1609 by William Keeling; first settled 1826, and developed by the Clunies-Ross family; annexed to the British Crown, 1857; granted by Queen Victoria to George Clunies-Ross, 1886; placed under Australian administration as the Territory of Cocos (Keeling) Islands, 1955; Australia purchased Clunies-Ross interests in the islands, 1978; inhabitants voted to be part of Northern Territory, 1984. >> Australia ℹ

Cocteau, Jean [kok**toh**] (1889–1963) Poet, playwright, and film director, born in Maisons-Lafitte, near Paris. His best-known works include his novel *Les Enfants terribles* (1929, trans Children of the Game), his play *Orphée* (1926, Orpheus), and his film *La Belle et la bête* (1945, Beauty and the Beast).

cod Any of the family Gadidae (15 genera; 100 species) of marine fishes, found mainly in cool temperate shelf waters of N hemisphere; body with 2–3 dorsal and 1–2 anal fins; length up to 120 cm/4 ft; greenish to reddish, freckled, with a pale lateral line; supports very important trawl and net (seine) fisheries. >> burbot; Gadidae

codec Acronym for **coder/decoder**, a device for converting the analogue signals used by audio and video equipment to digital form so that the signals can be sent over digital telecommunications networks. Pulse Code Modulation is used for the conversion.

codeine A painkiller related to morphine that is used for treating mild types of pain (eg headache); it is rarely addictive. It is also used in some cough mixtures, since it inactivates the cough reflex. >> morphine

Code Napoléon The French Civil Code, introduced (though not devised) by Napoleon Bonaparte as First Consul in 1804, to fill the void left by the abolition of the legal and social customs of pre-revolutionary France. It established the principles of equality between people, liberty of person and contract, and the inviolability of private property. From 1804 the Code was introduced into those areas of Europe under direct French control, and is still substantially extant in France, Belgium, Luxembourg, and Monaco today. >> Napoleon I

cod-liver oil An oil obtained from the fresh liver of the cod and refined. It provides a rich source of vitamins A and D. It is now believed to be protective in heart disease because of its high content of unsaturated fatty acids. >> cod; vitamins ℹ

codon [**koh**don] The sequence of three nucleotides in DNA or RNA which determine (or 'code for') the particular amino acid to be inserted into a polypeptide chain. >> amino acid; genetic code; nucleotide; peptide

Cody, William F(rederick) [**koh**dee], known as **Buffalo Bill** (1846–1917) Showman, born in Scott County, IA. He was known as 'Buffalo Bill' after killing nearly 5000 buffalo in eight months for a contract to supply workers on the Kansas Pacific Railway with meat. He served as a scout in the Sioux wars, but from 1883 toured with his Wild West Show.

Coe, Sebastian (Newbold) [koh] (1956–) Athlete, born in London. The world's most outstanding middle-distance runner of the 1980s, he broke eight world records altogether, including the mile three times. At the 1980 Olympics he won the gold medal in the 1500 m and the silver in the 800 m, repeating the achievement 4 years later. He retired from running in 1990 and became a Conservative MP in 1992, but lost his seat in the 1997 general election. >> athletics

coelacanth >> **Crossopterygii**

coelenterate [see**len**teruht] A simple, multicellular animal with a body plan comprising two primary layers separated by a layer of gelatinous material (*Mesoglea*); most are marine, and all are carnivorous; most exhibit radial symmetry, and possess stinging cells (*nematocysts*) for prey capture and defence. (Phylum: Cnidaria.) >> coral; jellyfish ℹ; sea anemone

coeliac / celiac disease [**seel**iak] A disorder of the small intestine, occurring especially in children, and characterized by reduced absorption of fat and other nutrients taken in the food. It causes failure to grow, rickets, and anaemia, and results from damage in sensitive individuals to the lining of the gut by gliaden, a protein found in wheat, barley, and rye. >> gluten; intestine; malabsorption

coelostat / celostat [**see**luhstat] A flat mirror driven by a clock mechanism in such a way as to project the same part of the heavens into a fixed telescope. This is particularly used for solar telescopes, as a means of controlling costs. >> telescope ℹ

Coelurus [see**loo**rus] A lightly built, flesh-eating dinosaur; slender neck and long tail; skull long, with large orbits; two-legged; forelimbs short with three digits, one facing the other two; known from the Upper Jurassic period of Wyoming; formerly known as *Ornitholestes*. (Order: Saurischia.) >> dinosaur ℹ; Jurassic period; Saurischia

Coetzee, John Michael [**koht**zee] (1940–) Novelist and critic, born in Cape Town, South Africa. His novels include *Dusklands* (1974), *In the Heart of the Country* (1977), *Life and Times of Michael K* (1983, Booker), and *The Master of Petersburg* (1994).

coffee An evergreen shrub; flowers white, fragrant, 5-petalled; cherry-like fruits red, fleshy, containing two seeds (the coffee beans) rich in caffeine. **Arabian coffee** (*Coffea arabica*) is native to Ethiopia, and was introduced first to Arabia, later the E Indies, W Indies, South America, and Africa. The major world producer is now Brazil. (Genus: *Coffea*, 40 species. Family: Rubiaceae.) >> caffeine

cofferdam A temporary structure designed to keep water or soft ground from flowing into a site when building foundations. A cofferdam usually consists of a dam or sheet piling. >> caisson; dam

cognitive science The formal study of mind, in which models and theories originating in artificial intelligence (AI) and in the human sciences (particularly cognitive psychology, linguistics, and philosophy) are subject to interdisciplinary development. The dominant partner in this enterprise is often the AI scientist, since the major criterion for success is usually whether a program can be written and successfully implemented on a computer. >> artificial intelligence; linguistics; psychology

Cohen, William S (1940–) US statesman. He became Republican senator for Maine in 1973, serving three terms before retiring in 1996. He was made secretary of defense in the 1997 administration, following Clinton's election promise to appoint a Republican to his cabinet.

Cohen-Tannoudji, Claude [kohĩ ta**noo**jee] (1933–) Physicist, born in Constantine, Algeria. He graduated in 1962 from the Ecole Normale Supérieure, Paris, where he went on to work. In 1997 he shared the Nobel Prize for Physics for his contribution to the development of methods to cool and trap atoms with laser light

Coimbatore [koh**im**bataw(r)] 11°00N 76°57E, pop (1995e) 924 000. City in Tamil Nadu, S India; stronghold of successive Tamil kingdoms, 9th–17th-c; ceded to Britain, 1799; airfield; railway; university (1971); agricultural centre. >> Tamil Nadu

Coimbra [**kweem**bra], ancient **Conimbriga** 40°12N 8°25W, pop (1995e) 95 800. City in C Portugal; former capital of Portugal, 12th–13th-c; oldest university in Portugal (founded at Lisbon in 1290, transferred here in 1537); bishopric; two cathedrals. >> Portugal ℹ

Coke, Thomas William >> **Leicester of Holkham, Thomas, William Coke**

Coke, Sir Edward [kook] (1552–1634) Jurist, born in Mileham, Norfolk. He brutally prosecuted Essex, Raleigh, and the Gunpowder conspirators, but after 1606 stood forth as a vindicator of national liberties against the royal prerogative. The Petition of Right (1628) was largely his doing. >> Gunpowder Plot; Petition of Right

coke A form of charcoal made by heating coal to over 1000°C in the absence of air to remove the volatile constituents. It is a brittle, porous substance consisting mainly of carbon, and used mainly in steelmaking for fuelling blast furnaces. >> charcoal; coal tar

cola >> **kola**

Colbert, Claudette [kolbair], originally **Lily Claudette Chauchoin** (1903–96) Film actress, born in Paris. She started in films with spirited comedy roles, becoming a star with *It Happened One Night* (1934, Oscar). On the stage her career continued into the 1980s.

Colbert, Jean Baptiste [kolbair] (1619–83) French statesman, born in Reims, France. In 1651 he entered the service of Mazarin, and in 1661 became the chief financial minister of Louis XIV. He introduced a series of successful reforms, reorganized the colonies, improved the civil code, and introduced a marine code. However, his successes were undone by wars and court extravagance. >> Louis XIV

Colchester, Lat **Camulodunum**, Anglo-Saxon **Colneceaster** 51°54N 0°54E, pop (1995e) 98 900. Town in Essex, SE England; railway; university (1961); claimed to be the oldest town in England, founded by Cunobelinus AD c.10; castle (12th-c); football league team, Colchester United ('U's). >> Essex

colchicine [**kol**chiseen] A drug, effective against gout, extracted from the corm and seeds of the meadow saffron, *Colchicum autumnale* ('autumn crocus'), so called because it is native to Colchis on the Black Sea. >> gout

cold An infection characterized by watering of the nose and eyes, sneezing, and nasal obstruction; also known as the **common cold** or **coryza** [ko**riy**za]. Caused by several different viruses, the condition commonly lasts for more than a week. >> cold sore; virus

cold-bloodedness >> **poikilotherm**

cold front A meteorological term for the leading edge of a parcel of cold or polar air. In a depression, the passage of a cold front is often preceded by heavy rainfall, and as it passes there is a sharp fall in temperature. >> depression (meteorology) ℹ; front

cold fusion Nuclear fusion occurring at room temperature. In March 1989, US chemist Stanley Pons and British chemist Martin Fleischmann claimed to have observed nuclear fusion in an electrolytic cell comprising platinum and titanium electrodes in heavy water. Their claims are now known to be false. The way in which Pons and Fleischmann announced their results to the media so soon, the lack of independent checking by other experimental groups, and the claims and counter-claims that followed their announcement created a scientific incident without parallel in recent times. >> electrolysis ℹ; nuclear fusion

Cold Harbor, Battles of Battles of the American Civil War, fought in Virginia as part of General Grant's strategy of unrelenting pressure on the South. Grant lost 12 000 men in one day's fighting. >> American Civil War

cold sore (*Herpes labialis*) A localized blister-like rash affecting the lips and adjoining skin around the mouth, the lining of the mouth, and the tongue. The lesions are due to a virus which usually lies dormant, but which is activated by intermittent illness or debility. >> cold; virus

cold storage Storage for perishable foodstuffs at a temperature just above freezing point. This process minimizes deterioration from chemical or biological action, but does not subject the food to damage by ice crystal formation on freezing. It is carried on in large buildings with cold air or brine circulated from a central refrigeration plant. >> food preservation

Cold War A state of tension or hostility between states that is expressed in economic and political terms, and stops short of a 'hot' or shooting war. The term is often used to describe the relationship between the USSR and the major Western non-communist powers – especially the USA – between 1945 and the mid- to late 1960s when the nuclear 'arms race' intensified. >> detente; glasnost

Cole, George (1925–) Actor, born in London. His many films include the *St Trinian's* series and other comedies, but he is probably best known in the UK as Arthur Daly from the television series, *Minder*, also *My Good Friend* (1995–6), and *An Independent Man* (1996).

Cole, Nat King, originally **Nathaniel Adams Cole**, family name formerly **Coles** (1919–65) Singer, jazz pianist, composer, and actor, born in Montgomery, AL. During the 1930s he became popular as a jazz pianist, forming his own instrumental trio of piano, guitar, and double bass in 1937. As a singer of romantic ballads, his many hit records including 'Route 66', 'Walking My Baby Back Home', and 'Unforgettable'.

Coleoptera [koli**op**tera] >> **beetle**

Coleridge, Samuel Taylor (1772–1834) Poet, born in Ottery St Mary, Devon. As a result of his friendship with William and Dorothy Wordsworth, a new poetry emerged, in reaction against Neoclassic artificiality. *Lyrical Ballads* (1798) opens with his magical 'Rime of the Ancient Mariner'. In 1800 he went to the Lake District, but his career prospects were blighted by his moral collapse, partly due to opium. In 1816 he published 'Christabel' and the fragment, 'Kubla Khan', both written in his earlier period of inspiration. >> Lake poets; Romanticism; Wordsworth, William

Colet, John [**kol**et] (c.1467–1519) Theologian and Tudor humanist, born in London. In 1505 he became Dean of St Paul's, where he delivered controversial lectures on the interpretation of Scripture, and founded St Paul's School (1509–12). >> humanism

Colette, Sidonie Gabrielle [ko**let**] (1873–1954) Novelist, born in Saint-Sauveur-en-Puisaye, France. Her novels include the *Claudine* series (1900–3), *Chéri* (1920), and *Gigi* (1945). She won many awards for her work, and died a legendary figure in Paris.

coleus A perennial native to Java (*Coleus blumei*); small flowers pale blue or white, in whorls forming slender spikes; a very popular pot-plant. (Family: Labiatae.)

coley >> **saithe**

colic [**kol**ik] Excessive contraction and spasm of smooth (involuntary) muscle, tending to occur in waves, and giving rise to severe short-lived but recurring bouts of pain. It particularly affects the smooth muscle of the gut (**intestinal colic**), the common bile duct (**biliary colic**), and the renal pelvis and ureters (**renal colic**). Calculi in the ducts are the common causes of colic. Babies are prone to develop intestinal colic as a result of feeding difficulty. >> calculi; muscle i

Coligny, Gaspard II de, seigneur de (Lord of) **Châtillon** [koleenyee] (1519–72) Huguenot leader, born in Châtillon-sur-Loing, France. In 1557 he became a Protestant, and commanded the Huguenots during the second and third Wars of Religion. He was one of the first victims in the St Bartholomew's Day massacre. >> Huguenots; Religion, Wars of

colitis [ko**liy**tis] Inflammation of the large bowel (*colon*) by micro-organisms or by immunological mechanisms. It is associated with lower abdominal pain and diarrhoea. >> inflammation; intestine

collage [ko**lahzh**] A technique of picture-making introduced by the Cubists c.1912 in which pieces of paper, fabrics, or other materials are glued to the surface of the canvas. It was much used by the Surrealists in the 1920s. >> Cubism; Surrealism

collagens [**kol**ajenz] A family of fibrous proteins found in all multicellular animals, constituting 25% of the total protein in mammals, and playing an essential role in providing tissue strength. A particularly important type is found in skin, tendon, bone, ligaments, the cornea, and internal organs. >> protein

collar bone >> **clavicle**

collateral [ko**lat**eral] A valuable item used as security for a loan – often land, shares, or an insurance policy. If the borrower fails to repay the debt, the collateral can be sold and the debt (along with any costs) deducted from the proceeds.

collective bargaining Trade union negotiations on behalf of a group of workers in relation to pay and conditions of employment. If the negotiations break down, the dispute may result in industrial action, or the matter may be referred to arbitration by another body. >> ACAS

collective farm A large co-operative farm, commonly found in socialist countries, where many small peasant holdings have been pooled to create a single unit capable of exploiting the economies of scale associated with mechanized agriculture. They were first introduced on a large scale in the USSR during Stalin's campaign for the enforced collectivization of the Russian peasantry (1928–33). >> socialism; Stalin

collectivism A set of doctrines asserting the interests of the community over the individual, and the preference for central planning over market systems. It advocates that economic and political systems should be based upon co-operation, state intervention to deal with social injustice, and central administration to ensure uniformity of treatment.

college >> **university**

College of Arms >> **heraldry** i

college of education A college specializing in the initial and in-service training of teachers. In the UK, such colleges were formerly called **training colleges**, and since the 1970s many have diversified into different fields, or merged with other colleges (as **colleges of higher education**), universities, or polytechnics. >> polytechnic; university

collie A medium-sized domestic dog; several breeds developed in Scotland as sheepdogs; **collie**, usually brown and white, with a long pointed muzzle; black and white **Border collie**, similar; **bearded collie** (or **Highland collie**), with a long shaggy coat. >> dog; lurcher; Old English sheepdog

collimator [**kol**imayter] **1** An optical device for changing a divergent beam of light (from a point source) into a parallel beam, which is required for control of the optical behaviour of the beam (as in a spectroscope). >> lens; light **2** A small telescope fixed to a large one, to help in preliminary alignment. >> telescope i

Collingwood, Cuthbert, Baron (1750–1810) British admiral, born in Newcastle upon Tyne. He fought at Brest (1794), Cape St Vincent (1797), and Trafalgar (1805), where he succeeded Nelson as commander. >> Nelson, Horatio; Trafalgar, Battle of

Collins, Joan (Henrietta) (1933–) Actress, born in London. She made her film debut in *Lady Godiva Rides Again* (1951), and used her sultry appeal and headline-catching private life to build a career as an international celebrity. She is best known for her role in the television soap opera *Dynasty* (1981–9). Her sister is the best-selling novelist **Jackie Collins** (1942–).

Collins, Michael (1890–1922) Irish politician and Sinn Féin leader, born near Clonakilty, Co Cork. He became an

MP (1918–22), and with Arthur Griffith was largely responsible for the negotiation of the treaty with Great Britain in 1921. He was killed in an ambush by his former compatriots, who had come to regard him as a traitor. >> Griffith, Arthur; Sinn Féin

Collins, Michael (1930–) US astronaut, born in Rome. He was one of the members of the Gemini 10 project, and remained in the command module during the successful Apollo 11 Moon-landing expedition. >> Apollo programme; RR970

Collins, (William) Wilkie (1824–89) Novelist, born in London. A master of the mystery story, his best-known works are *The Woman in White* (1860) and *The Moonstone* (1868).

colloid [**kol**oyd] A state midway between a suspension and a true solution. It is classified in various ways, particularly into **sols** (eg milk), in which liquid properties predominate, and **gels** (eg gelatine), which are more like solids. >> solution; suspension

colobus [**kol**obuhs] An Old World monkey, native to tropical Africa; slender with long tail; thumbs absent; also known as **guereza**. (Genus: *Colobus*, c.6 species.) >> Old World monkey

Cologne [ko**lohn**], Ger **Köln** 50°56N 6°58E, pop (1995e) 986 000. Manufacturing and commercial river port in Germany, on W bank of R Rhine; capital of N Roman Empire (3rd-c); badly bombed in World War 2; noted for its trade fairs; archbishopric; railway; university (1388); cathedral (begun 1248). >> Germany ℹ

Colombia [ko**lom**bia], official name **Republic of Colombia**, Span **República de Colombia** pop (1995e) 35 021 000; area 1 140 105 sq km/440 080 sq mi. Republic of NW South America; capital, Bogotá; timezone GMT –5; 90% of the people live in temperate Andean valleys; ethnic groups include many of mixed Spanish and Indian descent; religion, mainly Roman Catholic; official language, Spanish; unit of currency, the peso of 100 centavos; several island possessions; Andes run N–S, branching into three ranges dividing narrow coastal plains from forested lowlands of Amazon basin; Cordillera Central rises to above 5000 m/16 000 ft, highest peak Huila at 5750 m/18 865 ft; hot and humid coastal plains (NW and W) and tropical lowlands (E); Spanish occupation from early 16th-c, displacing Amerindian peoples; governed by Spain within Viceroyalty of Peru, later Viceroyalty of New Granada; independence in 1819, after campaigns of Simón Bolívar; union with Ecuador, Venezuela, and Panama as Gran Colombia; civil war 1948–57; considerable political unrest in 1980s; new constitution, 1991; governed by a president and a bicameral Congress; virtually self-sufficient in food; development of interior hampered by lack of good communications; widespread illegal cocaine trafficking. >> Andes; Bogotá; Bolívar; RR1005 political leaders

Colombo [ko**lom**boh], originally **Kalan-Totta** 6°55N 79°52E, pop (1995e) 653 000. Chief city and seaport of Sri Lanka; on the W coast; outer suburb, Sri-Jayawardenapura, the official capital since 1983; settled by the Portuguese in 1517 and by the Dutch in 1656; under British control, 1796; British defence base, 1942–5; road and rail centre; university (1972). >> Colombo Plan; Sri Lanka ℹ

Colombo Plan A plan drawn up by British Commonwealth foreign ministers in Colombo, Sri Lanka (Jan 1950), whose purpose was the co-operative development of the countries of S and SE Asia. >> Commonwealth (British)

colon >> **intestine**

Colón [ko**lon**], formerly **Aspinwall** 9°21N 79°54W, pop (1995e) 146 000. Port city in N Panama, at the Caribbean end of the Panama Canal; second largest free port in World (after Hong Kong); founded, 1850; railway. >> Panama ℹ

Colonial and Imperial Conferences A series of conferences at which representatives of the British colonies and dominions discussed matters of common imperial concern; usually held in London. The first Colonial Conference was held in 1887, and the first Imperial Conference in 1911. After World War 2 they were replaced by the Conferences of Commonwealth Prime Ministers. >> Commonwealth (British)

colonnade A series of columns in or outside a building, usually supporting an entablature, roof, or arches. The most famous example is the 284-column colonnade that forms the Piazza of St Peter's, Rome (1655–67). >> arch ℹ; cloisters; column; entablature

Colonsay [**kol**onsay] or **St Columba's Isle** Island in Argyll and Bute council, W Scotland; separated from Oronsay by a low channel which is dry at low water; rises to 142 m/468 ft at Carn Eoim; Augustinian priory. >> Columba, St; Scotland ℹ

colony An area of land or a country held and governed by another country, usually for the purpose of economic or other forms of exploitation. The present Commonwealth comprises the former colonies and the **Crown Colonies** (those still directly administered by Britain), which made up the British Empire. >> associated state; Commonwealth (British); imperialism

colophony >> **rosin**

color >> **colour** (entries)

Colorado pop (1995e) 3 753 000; area 269 585 sq km/104 091 sq mi. State in WC USA; the 'Centennial State'; E part included in the Louisiana Purchase, 1803; W part gained from Mexico by the Treaty of Guadalupe Hidalgo, 1848; settlement expanded after the gold strike of 1858; became a territory, 1861; joined the Union as the 38th state, 1876; contains the Ute Indian reservation (SW); Rocky Mts run N–S through the centre, divided into several ranges; highest point, Mt Elbert (4399 m/14 432 ft); forms part of the High Plains in the E, the centre of cattle and sheep ranching; capital, Denver; several notable national parks and monuments; world's largest deposits of molybdenum; growing tourist industry. >> Denver; Louisiana Purchase; United States of America ℹ; RR994

Colorado beetle A small, leaf beetle; yellow back with 10 longitudinal black stripes on wing cases; females lay eggs on potato plants; larvae fat, reddish-yellow with black side spots; causes great damage to potato crops. (Order: Coleoptera. Family: Chrysomelidae.) >> beetle; potato; pupa

Colorado Desert Depressed arid region in SE California and N Baja California, USA; area 5000–8000 sq km/2000–3000 sq mi. >> California; Great Basin

Colorado River River in SW USA; rises in the Continental Divide, N Colorado; empties into the Golfo de California; length c.2350 km/1450 mi; used extensively for irrigation, flood-control, and hydroelectric power. >> Grand Canyon; United States of America ℹ

Colorado Springs 38°50N 104°49W, pop (1995e) 320 000. City in C Colorado, USA; established, 1872; city status, 1886; railway; university; nearby mineral springs make it a popular health resort. >> Colorado

coloratura Florid ornamentation, or 'colouring', of a melody, especially in vocal music. A **coloratura soprano** is one with a high voice who specializes in such music.

colorization The addition of colour by electronic means to the videotape transfer of a motion picture originally photographed in black-and-white. Sometimes the former picture quality is sacrificed, and the technique has therefore proved to be controversial. >> colour photography

Colossians, Letter to the [ko**lo**shnz] New Testament writing attributed to Paul while he was in prison. It bears many similarities to the *Letter to the Ephesians*, but there is much current debate about whether the work is genuinely from Paul. >> New Testament; Pauline Letters

Colossus of Rhodes A huge, bronze statue of the Sun-god, Apollo, which bestrode the harbour entrance of the seaport of Rhodes. It was built c.280 BC. >> Seven Wonders of the Ancient World

colour / color >> **light; quark; spectrum**

colour / color blindness >> **colour / color vision**

colour / color cinematography Early attempts to show motion-pictures in colour included projecting successive frames through red and blue-green filters (Kinemacolor, 1906), or optically superimposing three separate colour images on projection (Francita, Opticolor, 1930–7, Dufay mosaic, 1931–40), but none was very successful. In 1932 Technicolor introduced a three-colour camera exposing three black-and-white separation colour negatives, with prints in three-colour dye-transfer which became the dominant medium for professional colour cinematography until Kodak produced their masked Eastmancolor negative. By 1955 the three-strip camera was obsolete, but dye-transfer printing continued into the 1970s. Eastmancolor negative/positive films opened the way to a vast expansion of colour cinematography, and similar materials are now manufactured worldwide. >> cinematography; colour photography; Technicolor; *see illustration above right*

Coloured >> **Cape Coloured**

colour / color filter A transparent material which transmits light from only a selected portion of the visible spectrum, partially or completely absorbing the remainder. Colour filters are used to provide light of a required spectral composition, or to give an overall colour balance to a colour photograph. >> colour photography

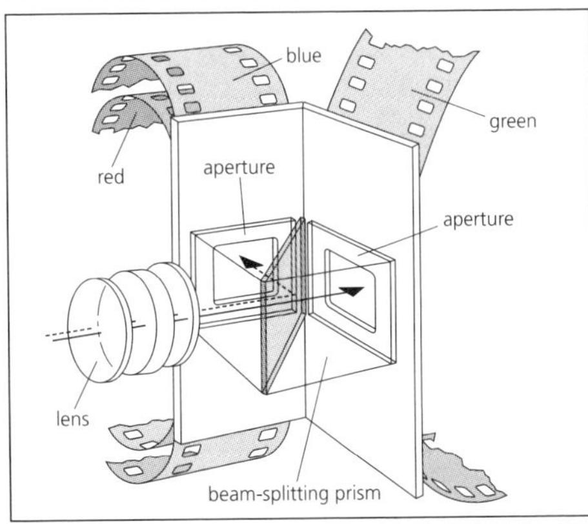

Technicolor camera – The beam-splitting prism divides the light at the two apertures. The blue, red and green components of the lightwave are recorded by three separate film strips.

colouring / coloring agents Dyes used for colouring food which are either natural, nature identical, or synthetic. Tartrazine is an example of a synthetic colouring agent, while carotene is a natural colourant. >> E-number; tartrazine

colourization >> **colorization**

colour / color photography The photographic reproduction of colour from negatives recording separately the red, green, and blue light components of a scene. A positive picture is formed by the superimposition of three corresponding images, either projected in the light of the same hues (*additive*) or printed in the complementary colours, cyan, magenta, and yellow (*subtractive*). A major advance was the integral *tripack*, recording in three separate photographic layers on a common base and developed with colour couplers. The first was Kodachrome, in 1935. >> photography

colour / color separation overlay >> **chromakey**

colour / color television A broadcasting medium, introduced in the 1950s. The image formed by the lens of a camera is divided into its components of red, green, and blue (RGB) light which are combined in the proportions of

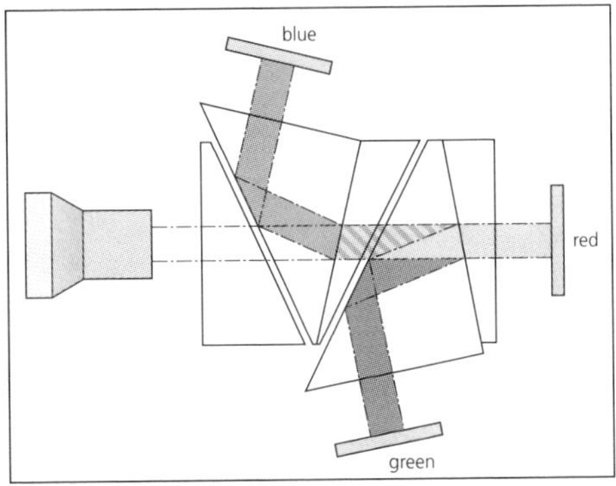

Colour television camera – light through the camera lens is divided by a beam-splitting prism system to separate red, green and blue sensors.

30% R, 59% G, and 11% B to form the *luminance* signal, Y, representing the picture in neutral tones from white to black. The colour information, *chrominance*, is handled as two colour-difference signals, B–Y and R–Y, which are coded in phase relationship and added to the luminance signal for transmission, in what is termed the *composite mode*. In the late 1980s, the alternative *component mode* was developed, in which the chrominance signals are kept separate from the luminance, but compressed in time to occupy the same period. This provides improved picture quality, and is widely used in the latest generation of videotape recorders. In a colour receiver, chrominance and luminance are decoded to give separate RGB signals controlling the three electron guns of a shadow-mask tube. As these beams are scanned across the screen they stimulate groups of minute phosphor dots which glow in the corresponding colour, red, green and blue, to form the elements of the complete picture by additive colour mixture. >> colour photography; NTSC; PAL; scanning [i]; SECAM

colour / color therapy The use of psychological and physical effects of coloured light for healing purposes. Since both infrared and ultraviolet radiation are used in orthodox medicine for healing purposes, colour therapists claim that the intervening wavelengths of visible light may also have healing properties, since the body is thought to absorb electromagnetic radiation as well as to emit it. An unhealthy body emits an unbalanced vibration pattern, and colour therapy is designed to restore balance using such methods as exposure to coloured light, wearing particular colours of clothing, or eating coloured foods. Therapists may also be asked to advise on the selection of colours in buildings. >> alternative medicine

colour / color vision The ability to detect differences between light of various wavelengths reaching the retina by converting them into colours. It is dependent on the presence of light-sensitive pigments in the cones (*retinal photoreceptors*), each being sensitive to light of a specific wavelength. In humans, the cones contain pigments most sensitive to red, green, or blue light. Absence of one or more of these pigments results in **colour blindness**: red-blindness (*protanopia*) affects the ability to distinguish red and green; blue-blindness (*deuteranopia*) affects blue and yellow; and green-blindness (*tritanopia*) affects the green range of the spectrum. Colour blindness is a sex-linked characteristic, about 20 times more common in males. >> eye [i]; light; retina; rods and cones

Colt, Samuel (1814–62) Inventor, born in Hartford, CT. In 1835 he took out his first patent for a revolver, which after the Mexican war was adopted by the US army, founding the fortunes of his company. >> revolver

Coltrane, John (William) (1926–67) Jazz tenor and soprano saxophonist, born in Hamlet, NC. He was little known in 1955 when Miles Davis chose him for his quintet. On forming his own quartet in 1960, Coltrane quickly became the most influential jazz musician of the day, with such recordings as *Giant Steps* (1959), *Africa/Brass* (1961), and *A Love Supreme* (1964). >> Davis, Miles; jazz

coltsfoot A perennial with long whitish rhizomes (*Tussilago farfara*), native to Europe, W and N Asia, and N Africa; flower-heads bright yellow, solitary on stems to 15 cm/6 in, appearing before the leaves. It is an old herbal medicine for chest complaints. (Family: Compositae.) >> rhizome

colugo [ko**loo**goh] A nocturnal mammal, native to SE Asia; face lemur-like; large gliding membrane along each side of body, extending to tips of fingers, toes, and long tail; lives in trees; only member of the order Dermoptera; also known as **flying lemur**. (Family: Cynocephalidae, 2 species.) >> lemur

Colum, Padraic (1881–1972) Poet and playwright, born in Co Longford, Ireland, a leader of the Irish literary revival. He wrote several plays for the Abbey Theatre, and helped to found the *Irish Review* (1911). >> Abbey Theatre

Columba, St, also **Columcille** or **Colm** (521–97) Missionary and abbot, born in Gartan, Donegal. He founded monasteries at Derry (546) and Durrow (553), and then at Iona, in the Inner Hebrides (c.563), from where he and his followers brought Christianity to Scotland. Feast day 9 June. >> Christianity; monasticism

Columba (Lat 'dove') A small S constellation. >> constellation; RR968

Columbae >> **Columbiformes**

Columban or **Columbanus, St** (c.543–615) Missionary and abbot, 'the younger Columba', born in Leinster, Ireland. About 585 he went to Gaul and founded the monasteries of Anegray, Luxeuil, and Fontaine in the Vosges. Feast day 23 November. >> monasticism

Columbia 34°00N 81°03W, pop (1995e) 106 000. State capital in C South Carolina, USA; settled, early 1700s; state capital, 1786; city status, 1854; burned by General Sherman, 1865; airfield; railway; two universities (1801, 1870); commercial and trading centre in a rich farming area. >> Sherman; South Carolina

Columbia River River in NW USA and SW Canada; rises in the Rocky Mts in E British Columbia, enters the Pacific at Cape Disappointment, SW of Vancouver, Washington; length 1953 km/1214 mi; source of irrigation and hydroelectric power. >> Rocky Mountains

Columbia University >> **Ivy League** [i]

Columbiformes [koluhmbi**faw(r)**meez] An order of birds encompassing the pigeons, sandgrouse, the extinct dodo, and dodo-like solitaires; also known as **Columbae**. >> dodo; pigeon; sandgrouse

columbine A perennial (*Aquilegia vulgaris*) native to Europe, N Africa, and Asia; flowers blue, rarely white, each of the five petals with a curved backward-pointing spur containing nectar. Garden forms are often called **aquilegias**. (Family: Ranunculaceae.)

Columbus 39°58N 83°00W, pop (1995e) 658 000. Capital of state in C Ohio, USA; founded, 1812; state capital, 1824; city status, 1834; railway; three universities (1850, 1870, 1902); air force base; centre for research in science and information technology. >> Ohio

Columbus, Christopher, Ital **Cristoforo Colombo**, Span **Cristóbal Colón** (1451–1506) European discoverer of the New World, born in Genoa, Italy. His plans to reach India by sailing W were supported by Ferdinand and Isabella of Spain. He set sail from Saltes (3 Aug 1492) in the *Santa Maria*, reaching the Bahamas (12 Oct), Cuba, and Hispaniola (Haiti). His second voyage (1493–6) led to the discovery of several Caribbean islands. On his third voyage (1498–1500) he discovered the S American mainland. His last great voyage (1502–4) was along the S side of the Gulf of Mexico. >> Columbus Day; Ferdinand (of Castile)

Columbus Day A national holiday in the USA, held in most states on the second Monday in October in commemoration of Christopher Columbus's discovery of America (12 Oct 1492). It is also celebrated in several countries of Central and South America. >> Columbus, Christopher

column A vertical support in a building, usually made up of a base, circular shaft, and spreading capital, and designed to carry an entablature or arch. It is also used as an aesthetic device to add ornament or to divide a space. >> capital (architecture); entablature; orders of architecture [i]

Colwyn >> **Aberconwy and Colwyn**

coly [**koh**lee] A bird native to Africa S of the Sahara, also known as **mousebird**; small, greyish; head crest, short curved bill, long tail; outer toe reversible. It is placed in a separate order (Coliiformes). (Genus: *Colius*, 6 species. Family: Coliidae.)

coma A state of unconsciousness from which individuals cannot be roused. Brain functions are progressively depressed, but the vital activities of respiration and constriction of the heart continue. The causes include trauma to the brain, meningitis, alcohol and drug overdosage, and metabolic disorders. >> metabolism

coma >> **aberrations 1** ℹ

Coma Berenices [**koh**ma bere**niy**seez] (Lat 'Berenice's hair') A faint constellation established in 1602 by Tycho Brahe. It includes the huge Coma cluster of galaxies, located 150 megaparsec away. >> Brahe; constellation; RR968

Comanche [ko**man**chee] Shoshonean-speaking North American Plains Indians who migrated S from Wyoming and became a powerful fighting group. They were settled on reservations in the 19th-c. >> Plains Indians; Shoshoni

Comaneci, Nadia [koma**neech**] (1961–) Gymnast, born in Onesti, Moldova. She was the star of the 1976 Olympic Games when, at the age of 14, she won gold medals in the beam, vault, and floor disciplines. In 1989 she defected to the USA via Hungary, amid much publicity. >> gymnastics

combassou >> **whydah**

Combination Acts British legislation passed in 1799 and 1800 which prohibited the coming together (*combination*) of workers in trade unions. The Acts were repealed in 1824–5, and trade unions legalized. >> Pitt (the Younger); trade union

Combined Operations Command A British force established in 1940 to co-ordinate British commando raids against German-occupied Europe. Combined Operations techniques were to play a crucial role in the Allied invasion of France. >> D-Day; World War 2

combine harvester A machine which cuts, threshes, and cleans all types of cereals, oilseeds, and legumes. Most combines are now self-propelled, and are equipped for handling grain and seed in bulk. >> cereals; legume; oil (botany)

combing In spinning, a post-carding process which removes unwanted short fibres, termed *noil*, and straightens and aligns the remaining fibres (*sliver*). The sliver may then be spun into fine smooth yarns. >> yarn

comb jelly >> **ctenophore**

combustion A burning, usually in a supply of oxygen to form oxides. The complete combustion of a hydrocarbon yields carbon dioxide and water. The energy associated with the combustion of a mole of a substance is called its **heat of combustion**. >> mole (physics); oxide

COMECON >> **Council for Mutual Economic Assistance**

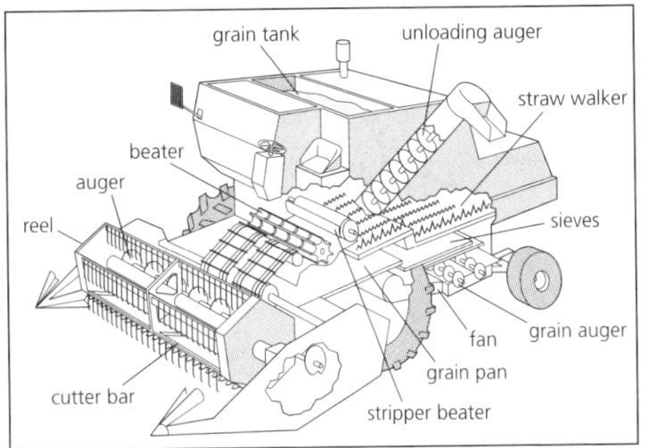

Crop flow through a self-propelled combine harvester

Comédie-Française, La [komaydee frã**sez**] The oldest surviving theatre company in France, dating officially from 1680. It is organized as a co-operative society, with its longest serving actor as the Doyen (head) of the company.

comet A small Solar System body made of ice and dust. Comets are asteroidal in appearance at distances of many astronomical units from the Sun (when they consist of a bare, inactive nucleus), and are often spectacularly active when nearer to the Sun. The characteristic bright head (*coma*) and streaming tails (both dust and ions) are created by solar heating, with emission of light from gas molecules and scattered light from the dust. The comet nucleus is a few km in size, irregularly shaped and very dark; dust in the coma contains carbon and silica; there is evidence of polymerized organic molecules; the gases of the coma include water, carbon monoxide, carbon dioxide, ammonia, methane, and hydrocarbons. The source of comets is believed to be a spherical halo cloud about the Sun called the *Oort Cloud*. Observable comets are occasionally scattered into the inner Solar System by the gravitational fields of nearby stars and giant molecular clouds. Some (eg Halley's comet) are captured into relatively short period orbits as a result of gravitational interactions with giant planets. A small 'armada' of spacecraft (Sakigake and Suisei, VEGA 1 and 2, Giotto) encountered Halley's comet in 1986. >> asteroids; cosmic dust; Giotto / Sakigake and Suisei / VEGA project; Hale-Bopp; Halley's comet; meteorite; Shoemaker–Levy 9; Solar System

comfrey A bristly perennial, native to Europe and the Mediterranean region; flowers drooping, tubular, or funnel-shaped, white, yellow, or pink in bud, and opening blue. (Genus: *Symphytum*, 25 species. Family: Boraginaceae.)

comic opera A light, amusing opera, particularly one which (like those of Gilbert and Sullivan) alternates songs and ensembles with spoken dialogue. The modern equivalent is the **musical**. >> musical; opera; Sullivan, Arthur

Cominform An abbreviation for the former USSR's **Communist Information Bureau**, and a successor to the Comintern. It was established upon Stalin's orders at a meeting in Poland (Sep 1947), its purpose being the co-ordination of the 'voice' and activities of European communist parties. It was dissolved in 1956. >> Comintern; communism; Stalin

Comino [ko**mee**noh] 36°00N 14°20E; area 2·7 sq km/ 1·04 sq mi. Smallest of the three main islands of the Maltese group, midway between Malta and Gozo; highest point, 247 m/810 ft; no cars allowed. >> Malta ℹ

Comintern An abbreviation for the **Communist International**, founded in Moscow (Mar 1919) at the behest of the Russian Communist Party, its purpose being the rallying of left-wing socialists and communists. It was disbanded in 1943. >> Cominform; Marxism-Leninism

command economy >> **market economy**

commedia dell'arte [ko**may**dia del**ah(r)**tay] (Ital 'comedy of the profession') A distinctive form of theatre which originated in Italy about the middle of the 16th-c. Its performance was the prerogative of professional troupes, and performance skills were passed on from player to player. The comedy relied on stock characters, many represented by masks. >> Harlequin; Pierrot; Punch and Judy; theatre

commodity market A market where buyers and sellers of commodities – mainly agricultural crops and metals – trade (**commodity trading**). Often prices are fixed on a bargain-by-bargain basis. The dealers who negotiate on behalf of clients are known as **commodity brokers**.

Common Agricultural Policy (CAP) The most important of the common policies of the European Community, absorbing c.65% of the total Community budget. The basic principles behind the CAP are free trade for agricultural commodities within the Community, Community preference for domestic production, control of imports from the rest of the world, and common financing. The use of high price-support measures has generated surpluses in most major commodities (eg the 'butter mountain' and 'wine lake'). >> European Community

common law A source of English law, the first source common to the entire kingdom, replacing over a period of centuries local courts and customs. It emphasizes the development of law through individual cases rather than prescriptive codes. >> civil law 2

Common Market >> **European Economic Community**

Commons, House of The lower, and effectively the ruling, chamber of the bicameral legislature of the UK. It contains 659 members, elected by universal adult suffrage, each representing a single constituency. The Commons is elected for a maximum period of five years, though the prime minister may call an election at any time within that period, and the government is drawn from the party that wins the majority of seats. >> bicameral system; Lords, House of

Commonwealth (British) A free association of independent nations formerly subject to British imperial government, and maintaining friendly and practical links with the UK. In 1931 the Statute of Westminster established the British Commonwealth of Nations; the adjective 'British' was deleted after World War 2. Most of the states granted independence, beginning with India in 1947, chose to be members of the Commonwealth. Ireland resigned from the association in 1948, South Africa in 1961, Pakistan in 1972, and Fiji in 1987; Pakistan re-entered in 1989, South Africa in 1994, and Fiji in 1997; Nigeria was suspended in 1995. >> Commonwealth Conference / Day / Games; RR1005 political leaders

Commonwealth (English history) English republican regime, established in 1649, and lasting until the Instrument of Government created a Protectorate in 1653. It failed to achieve political settlement at home, but its armies pacified Scotland and Ireland. >> English Civil War; Protectorate

Commonwealth Conference An annual meeting of prime ministers of the independent nations that now comprise the Commonwealth. It acts as a forum for maintaining political and economic links between the member countries. >> Commonwealth (British)

Commonwealth Day The second Monday in March, celebrated with receptions, educational events, etc throughout the Commonwealth; originally instituted as **Empire Day** (by which name it was known until 1960). >> Commonwealth (British)

Commonwealth Games A multi-sport gathering every 4 years by representatives of the nations of the Commonwealth. The first Games were at Hamilton, Canada in 1930. >> Commonwealth (British); RR1043

Commonwealth Institute An organization founded in 1959 to replace the Imperial Institute, itself founded in 1886 to promote commerce and industry between the countries of the British Empire. Its main activity is the promotion of the heritage and culture of its member nations. >> Commonwealth (British)

Commonwealth of Independent States (CIS), Russ **Sodruzhestvo Nezavisimykh Gosudarstv** Organization formed to replace Gorbachev's Union of Sovereign States, which was thwarted by the abortive political coup of 19–22 August 1991; administrative centre, Minsk. The initiative was taken by Belarus, the Russian Federation, and the Ukraine at a meeting in Minsk, and signed by the three parties on 8 December 1991. The Alma-Ata Declaration (21 Dec 1991) saw the original three members joined by the independent republics of Armenia, Azerbaijan, Kazakhstan, Kyrgyzstan, Moldova, Tajikistan, Turkmenistan, and Uzbekistan. Georgia joined in 1993. The aims of the CIS include: to cement historical ties; to build democracy on the rule of law; to recognize the sovereignty and territorial integrity of individual states within their existing borders; to promote mutually beneficial co-operation in the spheres of economy, transport, and communications; and to recognize the rights of the individual. There was to be an agreement on the joint command of strategic forces and the central control of nuclear weapons. >> Armenia i (republic); Azerbaijan i; Belarus i; Georgia i; Gorbachev; Kazakhstan i; Kyrgyzstan i; Moldova i; Russia i Soviet Union; Tajikistan i; Turkmenistan i; Ukraine i; Uzbekistan i; Yeltsin

Commonwealth of Independent States

Commune of Paris An uprising by Parisian Republicans (18 Mar–28 May 1871) following France's humiliating defeat in the Franco-Prussian War. The insurgents rose against the Versailles government, but were defeated, leaving an unprecedented legacy of bitterness. >> Franco-Prussian War

communicable disease A disease caused by a micro-organism which can be transmitted from infected animals or humans to non-infected individuals. The infection may be by direct contact (eg venereal diseases), via the air (eg meningitis), by ingestion (eg dysentery), or by insect transmission (eg malaria). >> infection

communication theory The application of information theory to human communication in general. Communication is seen to involve an information source encoding a message which is transmitted via a channel to a receiver, where it is decoded and has an effect. Efficient, error-free transmission is assumed to be the primary goal, especially in engineering contexts. >> information theory; semiotics

Communion, Holy >> **Eucharist**

communism A political ideology which has as its central principle the communal ownership of all property, and thereby the abolition of private property. Modern communism is specifically associated with the theories of Karl Marx, who saw the emergence of a communist society as being the final stage in a historical process that was rooted in human material needs, preceded by feudalism, capitalism, and (a transitional stage) socialism. Communism, according to Marx, would abolish class distinctions and end the exploitation of the masses inherent in the capitalist system. The working class, or proletariat, would be the instrument of a revolution that would overthrow the capitalist system and liberate human potential. The Communist Party of the Soviet Union (CPSU), first of all under Lenin's leadership and followed by Stalin, re-interpreted Marxist ideology as Marxism–Leninism–Stalinism, the major feature of which is democratic centralism. The CPSU provided the ideological lead for European communist parties. During the latter part of the 20th-c, however, its compulsory leadership was questioned. In 1989, the establishment of a non-communist Government in Poland, popular uprisings in Eastern Europe, and the decision by the Soviet Union not to intervene saw the dominant position of the Communist Party overturned and an immediate reduction in the status and influence of other communist parties. This change was symbolized best by the demolition of the Berlin Wall, a structure which had stood for the division of Europe into two ideologically opposed camps. There remain a number of countries in which communist parties continue to rule, notably the People's Republic of China, North Korea, and Cuba. However, even in these the system is showing signs of strain, and in China the aging rulers (adherents to the variant of communism known as Maoism) had to resort to force to crush demands for reform in the Tiananmen Square Massacre in 1992. Only in North Korea does a fully-blown totalitarian democratic-centralist regime continue in power.

Communism Peak, Russ **Pik Kommunizma**, formerly **Mt Garmo** (to 1933), **Mt Stalin** (1933–62) 39°00N 72°02E. Highest peak in the former USSR, in the Pamir range, N Tajikistan; height, 7495 m/24 590 ft; first climbed in 1933. >> Tajikistan ℹ

Communist Party of the Soviet Union (CPSU) The party which controlled political, economic, and social life in the former USSR. Many posts were confined to party members, who comprised only c.10% of the population. The party was ruled illegal by Boris Yeltsin following the failed 1991 coup, but Russia's constitution court reinstated the legality of at least some of their activities. >> communism

community charge A flat-rate charge on every adult resident in a particular area to contribute towards the provision of local government services. As the **poll tax**, it was first levied on each adult or 'head' (Middle English, *polle*) in 1377, and periodically reimposed (eg in 1513, 1641, and during the reign of Charles II). Most tax systems have abandoned the poll tax, but in the UK it was revived as a way of overcoming weaknesses in the domestic rating system, applying to all adults who use the services in a district, not just to those who own property. The charge came into operation in Scotland in 1989, and was introduced in England and Wales from 1990. The intention was to induce voters to impose greater financial responsibility on local authorities. In practice, the level had to be 'capped' (ie limited by central government) in some cases. The system proved to be extremely unpopular and difficult to enforce, with claims that it was unjust in its impact on the poorer members of society. Following a campaign of non-payment and increasing dissatisfaction, the tax was replaced in 1993 by a **council tax**, which reverts to the system of basing local taxation on property values. >> Peasants' Revolt; rates; taxation

community medicine A branch of medicine in which the health needs of communities, as distinct from individuals, are studied and assessed; also known as **social medicine**. >> epidemiology; industrial disease; National Health Service; occupational diseases; preventive medicine

community school / college A school or college which is open to the whole community. It may be open seven days a week, during evenings as well as through the day, and in some cases children and adults may study together.

community service order A sentence of the criminal courts whereby a convicted defendant can be required to undertake constructive unpaid work in the community, rather than being detained or paying a fine. >> sentence

Como 45°49N 9°06E, pop (1995e) 96 900. City in NW Italy, at SW end of L Como; railway; cathedral (1396). >> Como, Lake

Como, Lake (Ital **Lago di**) or **Lario**, ancient **Larius Lacus** area 146 sq km/56 sq mi. Narrow lake in N Italy, length 50 km/31 mi; maximum depth 412 m/1353 ft. >> Como; Italy ℹ

Comodoro Rivadavia [kohmoh**doh**roh reeva**dav**ia] 45°50S 67°30W, pop (1995e) 127 000. Seaport in Patagonia, S Argentina; university (1961); railway; airfield; natural gas pipeline to Buenos Aires. >> Argentina ℹ

Comoros [ko**mo**ros], official name **Federal and Islamic Republic of the Comoros, République Fédérale Islamique des Comores** pop (1995e) 600 000; area 1862 sq km/719 sq mi. Group of three volcanic islands (Njazidja, Nzwani, and Mwali, formerly Grande Comore, Anjouan, Mohéli) between Mozambique and Madagascar; capital, Moroni; timezone GMT +3; chief religion, Islam; chief languages, Arabic, French, Kiswahili; unit of currency, the franc CFA of 100 cents; tropical climate; under French control, 1843–1912; French overseas territory, 1947; internal political autonomy, 1961; unilateral independence declared, 1975; established as a Federal Islamic Republic, 1978; new constitution, 1996; a one-party state, governed by a president, a Council of Ministers, and a unicameral Federal Assembly; self-proclaimed secession of islands of Moheli and Anjouan, 1997; military coup, 1999; largely agricultural economy. >> Islam; Mayotte; Moroni; RR1005 political leaders

compact disc (CD) A plastic disc of 120 mm/4·7 in diameter, holding on a single side up to an hour of digitally encoded sound recording, stored as a succession of pits and plateaux in tracks 1·6 μm wide. The disc is coated in a reflective material (usually aluminium), which either scatters or reflects back into a photoelectric detector a laser beam used to read (play) the encoded sound when the disc is rotated at high constant linear speed. Launched in 1982–3 by Philips and Sony jointly, digital compact discs are free of stylus wear, are essentially immune to surface blemishes, and thus appear near to perfection in sound recording. >> digital recording; laser ⓘ; sound recording

Companions of Honour, Order of the (CH) In the UK, an award instituted in 1917, made to members of either sex for outstanding service to the nation. It consists of the sovereign and a maximum of 65 members.

company An association existing for a commercial or business purpose, considered to be a legal entity independent of its members. It may be formed by Act of Parliament, by Royal Charter, or by registration under company law (referred to as a **limited liability** or **joint-stock company**). *Ltd* after the company's name signifies *limited*, and *PLC* (**public limited company**) indicates that its shares are widely held. In the USA, companies are registered in a particular state – Delaware being especially favoured – and become *Incorporated (Inc)*. >> corporation tax; dividend; holding company

comparative linguistics The comparison of the features of different languages or dialects, or the different historical states of a language. In the 19th-c, the concern was exclusively historical, the field being known as **comparative philology**. >> linguistics

comparative philology >> **comparative linguistics**

compass A device for determining a horizontal geographical direction or bearing. The **magnetic compass** depends on a magnet, free to rotate in a horizontal plane, locating itself in line with the Earth's magnetic field. >> gyrocompass ⓘ; magnetic field ⓘ

compensation order In British law, an order, made by a court to someone convicted of an offence which has caused personal injury, loss, or damage, to pay a specified amount of compensation to the victim, in addition to any other sentence imposed by the court (typically a fine). Many other jurisdictions have introduced similar arrangements, some of which are restricted to financial compensation while others involve an element of service either to the victim or to the community in general. >> civil law; community service order; Criminal Injuries Compensation Scheme

competence In linguistics, an idealized conception of language, representing the system of grammatical rules which any speaker of a language subconsciously knows. It is contrasted with **performance**, the way in which sentences actually appear, containing 'imperfections' such as hesitations, and grammatical errors. >> linguistics

compiler A computer program which translates (**compiles**) the source code of a high-level computer language program, such as BASIC, into a set of machine-code instructions which can be understood by the central processing unit. Compilers are very large programs, and contain error-checking and other facilities. >> computer program

Composite order The most decorative of the five main orders of classical architecture, combining the Ionic volute with the acanthus leaves of the Corinthian order. >> acanthus; orders of architecture ⓘ

compound In chemistry, an entity with a definite composition, containing atoms of two or more elements.

comprehensive school A school catering for the whole of the ability range; opposed to a **selective school**, which takes only a section of the population. In countries such as Sweden and the USA, these schools have been commonplace for most of the 20th-c. In other places, such as the UK, the non-selective school did not become widespread until the 1960s. >> grammar school

Compton, Arthur (Holly) (1892–1962) Physicist, born in Wooster, OH. The **Compton effect**, explaining the change in the wavelength of X-rays when they collide with electrons, is named after him. He shared the Nobel Prize for Physics in 1927. >> X-rays

Compton, Denis (Charles Scott) (1918–97) Cricketer, born in London. He played cricket for England 78 times, and scored 5807 runs. During his career (1936–57) he made 38 942 runs and took 622 wickets. A winger at soccer, he won an England cap during the war years. His later career was as a journalist and broadcaster. >> cricket (sport) ⓘ

Compton-Burnett, Dame Ivy [ber**net**] (1884–1969) Novelist, born in Pinner, Middlesex. Her novels, set in upper-class Victorian or Edwardian society, include *Pastors and Masters* (1925) and *Mother and Son* (1955, James Tait Black).

computer A device which can be programmed to store and process numerical and alphabetical data. The first mechanical adding device was developed in 1642 by Pascal. In 1835, Charles Babbage formulated his concept of an 'analytical machine' which combined arithmetic processes with decisions based on the results of the computations. This was really the forerunner of the modern digital computer, in that it combined the principles of sequential control, branching, looping, and storage units. J Presper Eckert and John W Mauchly produced the first all-electronic digital computer, ENIAC (Electronic Numerical Integrator and Calculator), at the University of Pennsylvania in 1946. Very significant contributions were made around this time by Johann von Neumann, who converted the ENIAC principles to give the EDVAC computer (Electronic Discrete Variable Automatic Computer) which could modify its own programs in much the same way as suggested by Babbage. Advances were accelerated from the mid-1960s by the successful development of miniaturization techniques in the electronics industry. The first microprocessor, which might be regarded as a computer on a chip, appeared in 1971, and nowadays the power of even the most modest personal computer can equal or outstrip the early electronic computers of the 1940s. >> analog computer; Babbage; Boole; computer memory / program / science; digital computer; electronics; hacker; hypercube; mainframe computer; Neumann, Johann von; Pascal

computer game A small personal computer supplied with a computer program which allows one or more users to play some game. The game could be chess, in which case a single user plays against the computer, or it could be driving a car, in which case two users could compete against each other in a race. Many games are concerned with a series of trials (eg fighting a dragon) in which the player has to win the trial before being allowed to proceed. Increasingly, computer games require the user to wear a visor (so that the player sees only the computer display) and gloves (so that the computer can record arm and hand movements) – a technique known as *virtual reality*. >> virtual reality

computer generations Different eras of technical development of digital computers, defined as different 'generations'. **First-generation** computers were the early devices in the 1940s and 1950s, built using thermionic valves. **Second-generation** computers replaced these valves by discrete transistors. **Third-generation** computers replaced transistors by integrated circuits. **Fourth-generation** computers were built with very large integrated circuits (VLSI). **Fifth-generation** computers are those showing artificial intelligence with which we can communicate in natural language. >> artificial intelligence; integrated circuit; thermionic valve; transistor

computer graphics The use of computers to display information in graphical or pictorial form, usually on a visual display unit (VDU), a printer, or a plotter. Applications include the manipulation of highly detailed engineering drawings, computer games, high definition views in aircraft simulators, and the automatic production of animated film. >> computer; graphics tablet; X–Y plotter

computerized tomography (CT), also **computerized axial tomography (CAT)** A medical X-ray scanning technique which makes a series of pictures that are then reconstructed by computer programs to represent a 'slice' through the patient. The X-ray tube rotates round the patient and produces images in sequence on a number of detectors. These machines are especially used in setting up radiotherapy treatment for precise action on small target areas in the patient. >> computer; radiotherapy; X-rays

computer language >> **programming language**

computer memory A part of a computer which stores, either permanently or temporarily, programs and data. There are two basic types of internal memory used in digital computers: **Random Access Memory** (RAM) and **Read-Only Memory** (ROM) or variants thereof. >> backing store; bubble memory; buffer (computing); cache memory; central processing unit; EAROM; EPROM; PROM; RAM; ROM

computer network A group of computers, linked together by telecommunications lines, for the purpose of working together. During the preparation of this encyclopedia, for example, several computer terminals in one building were linked through a network to a computer containing the encyclopedia database, thus enabling different editorial tasks to be carried out simultaneously. >> BITNET; computer; Internet; JANET; USENET

computer package A computer program, or group of computer programs, sold as a 'package' for the performance of a specific function. An example is an accounting package, which contains all the routines and calculations necessary for the analysis and presentation of accounts. >> computer program; desk-top publishing

computer peripheral Any device which can be connected to a computer. Examples include printers, magnetic disks, visual display units, and plotters. The peripheral may be an input device or an output device. >> computer

computer printer A computer output device which produces characters or graphics on paper. Many different types exist, and the optimum choice for any given situation depends on the acceptable cost, printing speed, print quality, and operating noise. >> daisy-wheel / dot-matrix / golf-ball / impact / ink-jet / laser / line / thermal / xerographic printer

computer program A complete structured sequence of statements in a programming language which directs a computer to carry out a specific task. The task of writing computer programs is known as **programming**. >> programming language; systems analysis

computer science The whole area of knowledge associated with the use and study of computers and computer-based processes. It encompasses computer design and programming, and intercomputer communication. >> computer; information theory

computer terminal Any device which can be attached to a computer, possibly over a telecommunications line, to allow a user to interact with the computer. Examples are visual display units and some kinds of personal computers using appropriate software while linked to another computer. >> computer; visual display unit

computer virus A term applied to computer programs which can spread from computer to computer, usually via shared software, and damage other programs stored on the computers. The 'virus' program is often attached, by the human perpetrator, to a genuine program and is not readily detectable. >> computer program

Comte, Auguste [kõt] (1798–1857) Philosopher and sociologist, the founder of positivism, born in Montpellier, France. In his philosophy, all sciences are regarded as having passed through a theological and then a metaphysical stage into a positive or experiential stage. In positive religion, the object of reverence is humanity, and the aim the well-being and progress of the race. >> positivism

Conakry [**kon**akree] 9°30N 13°43W, pop (1995e) 992 000. Seaport capital of Guinea, W Africa; on Tumbo island; linked to the mainland by a causeway; established in 1889; airport; railway terminus; technical college (1963). >> Guinea ℹ

Conan Doyle >> **Doyle, Arthur Conan**

concentration camp A detention centre for political prisoners; first developed by the British during the Boer War, but known primarily from the camps established in Germany soon after the Nazi seizure of power. The coming of war swelled the camps with millions of Jews, Gypsies, slave workers, Soviet prisoners-of-war, and other 'enemies of the state'. The camps established in Poland, such as Auschwitz and Treblinka, became purpose-made extermination centres in which over 6 million Jews died. >> Holocaust; Nazi Party

Concepción [konsep**syohn**] 36°49S 73°03W, pop (1995e) 332 000. Industrial city in C Chile; founded, 1550; often damaged by earthquakes; airfield; railway; university (1919). >> Chile ℹ

concertina A portable reed organ similar in principle to the accordion, but hexagonal in vertical cross-section, smaller, and without a keyboard. The English type, fully chromatic, was patented in 1844: it was largely superseded by the fully developed piano accordion. >> accordion; reed organ

concertino [konsher**tee**noh] **1** A musical work for soloist(s) and orchestra, shorter than a concerto and usually with a lighter accompaniment. >> concerto **2** The solo group in a concerto grosso. >> concerto grosso

concerto A musical work for one or more solo instruments and orchestra. The early concerto with a single soloist is associated above all with Vivaldi, whose three-movement form (fast–slow–fast) was adopted by J S Bach, and remained standard in the concertos of Mozart, Beethoven, and most later composers. >> Baroque (music); cadenza; concertino; concerto grosso; movement; Bach, Johann Sebastian; Vivaldi

concerto grosso A musical work in which a small group of instruments (*concertino*: typically two violins and cello) is contrasted with the full string orchestra (*ripieno*). The Baroque concerto grosso, in four or more movements, was cultivated with particular distinction by Corelli and Handel. >> Baroque (music); concerto; Corelli, Arcangelo; Handel

conch A large marine snail found in shallow seas around coral reefs; the queen conch, *Strombus gigas*, is abundant in the Caribbean, and is gathered for food and the curio trade. (Class: Gastropoda. Order: Mesogastropoda.) >> snail

conclave (Lat *cum clave*, 'with a key') A meeting of cardinals of the Roman Catholic Church. Its original purpose was to elect a pope; by a tradition dating from 1271, the cardinals are locked into an apartment to hasten election. >> cardinal (religion); pope

Concord (Massachusetts) 42°28N 71°21W, pop (1995e) 17 200. Town in E Massachusetts, USA; 8 km/5 mi NW of Boston; in April 1775 British soldiers attempted to seize military stores in Concord but were resisted by minutemen; battles at Concord (19 Apr) and Lexington marked the start of the American War of Independence; railway. >> American Revolution

Concord (New Hampshire) 43°12N 71°32W, pop (1995e) 36 200. Capital of New Hampshire State, USA; established, 1727; city status, 1853; state capital, 1808; railway; home of Mary Baker Eddy. >> Eddy; New Hampshire

Concorde The world's first (and only remaining) supersonic airliner, built jointly by the British Aircraft Corporation and the French company, Aérospatiale. It entered full-time operational service in January 1976. Its maximum speed is 2·2 times the speed of sound, though normal cruising speed is reduced to twice the speed of sound, ie c.2000 kph/1300 mph. The maximum range is c.6400 km/4000 mi, and the time taken to cross the Atlantic is $3\frac{1}{2}$ hours. >> aircraft ℹ

concrete art An art form defined by the Dutch artist Theo van Doesburg (1883–1931) in 1930 as a totally abstract art 'constructed entirely from purely plastic elements, that is to say planes and colours'. >> abstract art; art; Constructivism

concrete music >> **musique concrète**

concrete poetry Poetry which emphasizes the visual presentation of the poem on the page. Classical inscriptions provide a model, and 17th-c emblem poems are simple examples. The French poets Mallarmé and Apollinaire considerably extended visual techniques. Later experiments include the use of different typefaces, colour, collage, and computer graphics. >> Apollinaire; computer graphics; Mallarmé

concussion A state of reversible unconsciousness which may immediately follow a severe blow to the head, but which outlasts the trauma. On regaining consciousness there is no memory of the accident or of immediately preceding events.

Condé [kõday] The junior branch of the French royal line, the House of Bourbon, which played a prominent role in French dynastic politics, particularly in the 16th–17th-c. Ten generations bore the title of **Prince de Condé**, the most eminent being Louis XIV's general, Louis II de Bourbon (1621–86), better known as the **Great Condé**. >> Bourbons

condensation The process by which water changes from a gaseous state (*water vapour*) to a liquid state. It can result from uplift of air, radiation cooling on a calm cloudless night, or when warm moist air comes into contact with a cooler surface. In such situations, vapour condenses around condensation nuclei, such as salt, dust, and smoke particles in the air. When condensation occurs at altitude, clouds form; close to the ground, it results in fog or dew. >> cloud ℹ; dew point temperature; fog; precipitation

condensed matter physics >> **solid-state physics**

Condillac, Etienne Bonnot de [kõdeeyak] (1715–80) Philosopher, born in Grenoble, France. He based all knowledge on the senses, his works including *Essai sur l'origine des connaissances humaines* (1746, Essay on the Origin of Human Knowledge) and *Traité des sensations* (1754, Treatise on Sensations).

condition In law, a relatively important term in a contract. In English law, breach of condition gives the innocent party the right to treat the contract as terminated. Contracts may also contain **warranties**, which may (eg in Scotland), in the event of a breach, justify repudiating the contract. Breach of a warranty in England is considered less important, and does not give the innocent party the right to end the contract, though a claim for damages may be possible. >> contract

conditioning An elementary associative learning process. In **Pavlovian**, **classical**, or **respondent conditioning**, a stimulus which reliably precedes another stimulus of biological significance (eg food, pain, a potential mate) comes to evoke a new pattern of reaction (a **conditioned response**) similar to that evoked by the biologically significant (**unconditioned**) stimulus. For example, salivation, normally evoked by the taste of food, comes to be evoked by the sight of food or the sound of a dinner gong. >> aversion therapy; Pavlov

condominium 1 In government, the joint rule, tenancy, or co-ownership of a territory by two or more countries, often suggested as appropriate where ownership of a territory is disputed. For example, the former New Hebrides (now the republic of Vanuatu) was, until 1980, jointly administered by Britain and France. **2** A type of co-operative ownership of a domestic dwelling. A person owns a unit (an apartment, or flat) in the building, and typically enters into an arrangement with other unit-owners to share the responsibility for the services to the building and the general upkeep of the site. The concept is particularly associated with property dealing in the USA, where the term is used both for the building as a whole and for the units within it.

condor Either of two species of New World vulture; the **Californian condor** (*Gymnogyps californianus*) and the **Andean condor** (*Vultur gryphus*). The Andean condor, which inhabits the mountains, has the largest wingspan of any living bird (up to 3 m/10 ft). The Californian condor is in danger of extinction. (Family: Cathartidae.) >> bird of prey; vulture

Condorcet, Marie Jean Antoine Nicolas de Caritat, marquis de (Marquess of) [kõdaw(r)say] (1743–94) French statesman, philosopher, and mathematician, born in Ribemont. At the Revolution he became president of the Legislative Assembly (1791), siding usually with the Girondists. Condemned by the extreme party, he was found dead in prison. In his philosophy, he proclaimed the ideal of progress, and the indefinite perfectibility of the human race. >> French Revolution ℹ; Girondins

conductance >> **resistance**

conducting The task of directing an orchestra, choir, or other musical group in the performance of a musical work. The conductor establishes a musical rhythm and interpretation, signalling this in a performance by conventional hand and arm movements, as well as by movements of the body and facial expression. A thin stick, or baton, held in the right hand, became widely used only in the mid-19th-c to give a clearly visual emphasis to the basic rhythm; but many modern conductors have dispensed with it, using only their hands. The special role of the conductor emerged only in the 19th-c; previously, the task of keeping the musicians together was performed by one of the leading players. The prestige now associated with the role developed with the emergence of composers (such as Berlioz) who also conducted, and with the serious intellectual and aesthetic demands of major works (such as those by Wagner) in which as much effort had to be devoted to the context of the work and the interpretation of the score as to the accuracy of the playing. >> music

conduction >> **electrical conduction; thermal conduction**

conductivity >> **resistivity**

condyloma [kondi**loh**ma] A localized cauliflower-like lesion or overgrowth of the epidermis in moist parts of the body, such as the vulva and around the anus. Condylomata result from infection with the virus that causes warts in drier regions of the body. >> virus; wart

cone In gymnosperms, a spike-like structure formed of woody, overlapping scales bearing seeds. Clubmosses and horsetails have similar structures bearing spores. The term is also used for the cone-like fruits of some flowering plants. >> clubmoss; gymnosperms; horsetail; seed; spore

coneflower >> **rudbeckia**

cones >> **rods and cones**

coney >> **pika; rabbit**

Coney Island [**koh**nee] (Dutch 'rabbit') 40°35N 73°59W. Resort on the S coast of Long Island in New York State, USA; developed as a pleasure resort since the 1840s. >> Long Island; New York

Confederacy >> **Confederate States of America**

Confederate States of America The official name of the states that seceded in 1860–1, precipitating the American Civil War: Virginia, N Carolina, S Carolina, Georgia, Florida, Tennessee, Alabama, Mississippi, Louisiana, Texas, and Arkansas. Its only president was Jefferson Davis of Mississippi. It never won foreign recognition, and collapsed in 1865. >> American Civil War; Davis, Jefferson; slave trade

Confederation A movement in the 1860s devoted to the unification of the British North American colonies within a federal framework. New Brunswick, Nova Scotia, Quebec, and Ontario were so joined in 1867. Confederation marked the birth of modern Canada, and it is celebrated annually on 1 July. >> Canada [i]

Confederation, Articles of >> **Articles of Confederation**

Confederation of British Industry (CBI) A federation of UK employers, founded in 1965, with a membership of some 250 000 companies. Its role is to ensure that the needs, intentions, and problems of business organizations are generally understood.

Conference on Security and Co-operation in Europe >> **Organization for Security and Co-operation in Europe (OSCE)**

Confessing Church A Church formed in Germany by Evangelical Christians opposed to Nazism. Its Synod of Barmen published the Barmen Declaration (1934), which became influential in Germany and beyond as a basis for resistance to oppressive civil authorities. >> Barth, Karl; Christianity; evangelicalism; Nazi Party

confession 1 A declaration or profession of faith, originally by an individual martyr, later by a group or church. Such a document became common after the Reformation. >> Augsburg Confession; Reformation; Westminster Confession of Faith **2** An acknowledgment of sin, made either corporately in the course of public worship or privately and individually 'into the ear' of a priest.

confessional poetry Poetry which takes as its subject the intimate details of the poet's own life. Generally considered a recent phenomenon, it has been encouraged by US poets such as Robert Lowell and Sylvia Plath. >> Lowell, Robert; Plath

confirmation The Christian sacrament of initiation. Performed only by the laying on of hands (or by anointing with oil, or both) by a bishop. Children are not usually confirmed before reaching seven years of age, and many Churches prefer them to reach adolescence. >> baptism; Christianity; sacrament

Confucius [kon**fyoo**shuhs], Lat name of **Kongfuzi** or **K'ung Fu-tse** (Chin 'Venerated Master Kong') (551–479 BC) Philosopher, born in the state of Lu (modern Shantung), China. Largely self-educated, in 531 BC he began his career as a teacher, aiming to resurrect traditional values and reinforce the structure of social obligations and behaviours which manifested them. Fundamental was benevolence, humanity or goodness, which embraced duty, loyality, and sincerity – fundamental for the maintenance at all levels of society. His precepts are preserved in the Analects (*lunyu*), probably written by some of his 22 disciples. No writings can definitely be attributed to him. His teachings later inspired a cult of veneration. Confucianism became the state religion of China, but he was denounced as a class-exploiter during the Cultural Revolution (1966–76). There are now thought to be over 5 million Confucians.

conga An Afro-Cuban dance usually performed (often with singing) in a long line, using simple and repetitive steps. It was popular in Western ballrooms in the mid-20th-c.

congenital abnormality An anatomical abnormality or malformation found at birth or within a few weeks of birth. Some disorders result from chromosome abnormalities or genetic defects. Others arise from environmental factors, such as infections (eg rubella), drugs given to the mother (eg thalidomide), or sporadic faults in development. >> achondroplasia; cleft lip and palate; club foot; spina bifida

conger eel Predatory marine fish (*Conger conger*) found in shallow coastal waters of N Europe and Mediterranean, usually within cover of rocks, jetties, or wrecks; body cylindrical, length up to 2·7 m/8¾ ft; jaws powerful, teeth conical and close-set; may be dangerous to divers. (Family: Congridae.)

conglomerate Sedimentary rock composed of rounded pebbles of pre-existing rocks and embedded in a fine matrix of sand and silt. It is commonly formed along beaches or on river beds.

Congo [**kong**goh], official name **Republic of the Congo** (1991), formerly **People's Republic of the Congo** (from 1968), Fr **République du Congo** pop (1995e) 2 954 000; area 341 945 sq km/132 047 sq mi. WC African republic; capital, Brazzaville; timezone GMT +1; c.15 main ethnic groups, notably the Kongo (51%); main religions, Christian (54% Roman Catholic, 25% Protestant) and local

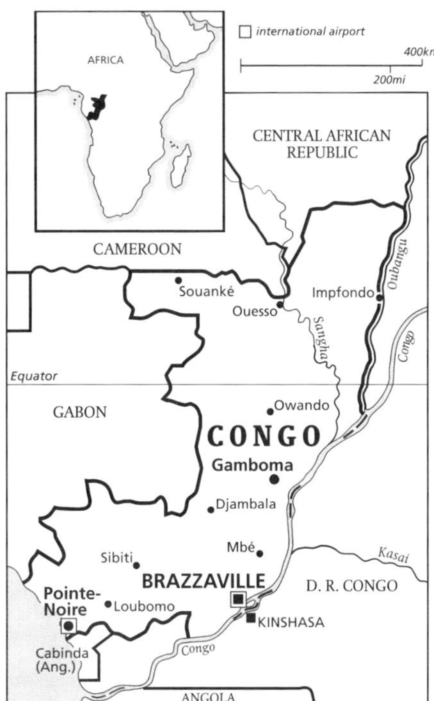

beliefs; official language, French; unit of currency, the CFA franc; rises inland to a ridge of mountains reaching 900 m/2 950 ft; beyond this ridge, Niari valley rises to 1040 m/3412 ft at Mont de la Lékéti; mainly covered by dense grassland, mangrove, and forest; hot, humid equatorial climate; visited by Portuguese, 14th-c; French established colonial presence, 19th-c; part of French Equatorial Africa, known as 'Middle Congo', 1908–58; independence as Republic of Congo, 1960; military coup created first Marxist state in Africa, renamed People's Republic of the Congo, 1968; new constitution, 1979, abrogated in 1991; following a referendum, National Assembly dissolved and principle of multi-party democracy accepted, 1992; violence following disputes over the election process, 1993; new constitution recognizes a National Assembly and Senate; a directly elected president appoints a prime minister and cabinet; economy based on agriculture and forestry. >> Brazzaville; RR1005 political leaders

Congo, Democratic Republic of, formerly **Congo Free State** (1885–1908), **Belgian Congo** (1908–60), **Democratic Republic of the Congo** (1960–71), **Republic of Zaire** [zah**eer**] (1971–97) pop (1995e) 41 837 000; area 2 234 585 sq km/905 365 sq mi. C African republic; capital, Kinshasa; timezone GMT +1 (W), +2 (E); over 200 ethnic groups, mainly of Bantu origin; chief religions, Christianity (over 70%); official language, French; unit of currency, the zaïre; land rises E from a low-lying basin to a densely-forested plateau; Ruwenzori Mts (NE) rise to 5110 m/16 765 ft in the Mt Stanley massif; chain of lakes in the Rift Valley, including Albert, Edward, Kivu, and Tanganyika; hot and humid climate; visited by the Portuguese, 1482; expeditions of Stanley, 1874–7; claimed by King Leopold II of Belgium, recognized in 1895; Congo Free State ceded to the state in 1907 and renamed the Belgian Congo; independence, 1960; mineral-rich Katanga (1971–97, Shaba) province claimed independence, leading to civil war; UN peace-keeping force present until 1964; renamed Zaire, 1971–97; further conflict, 1977–8; a one-party state, with ultimate power lying with the Popular Movement of the Revolution; national conference proposed transition to a multi-party democracy, 1991–2; conflict between president and prime minister resulted in rival cabinets, 1993–4; transitional government recognizes a president, prime minister, and single-chamber legislature, 1994; decree promulgating new assembly, 1998; presidential and legislative elections scheduled for 1999; nearly 80% of the population involved in subsistence farming; extensive mineral reserves; world's biggest producer of cobalt, industrial diamonds, copper; major source of hydroelectricity. >> Kinshasa, Rift Valley; Stanley, Henry Morton; RR1005 political leaders

Congonhas do Campo [kon**goh**nyas] 23°38S 46°38W, pop (1995e) 28 400. A town in the Brazilian highlands, noted for its 18th-c Sanctuary of Bom ('good') Jesus, an imposing church with chapels and gardens; a world heritage site and pilgrimage centre. >> Brazil ℹ

Congo, River [zah**eer**] (1971–97, known as **River Zaire**) River in C and W Africa; length c.4670 km/2900 mi, second longest in Africa; rises in SE Zaire; enters the Atlantic Ocean. >> Zaire ℹ

Congregationalism A movement which sees the Christian Church as essentially a gathered community of believers, covenanting with God, keeping God's law, and living under the Lordship of Christ. It derived from the Separatists of the 16th-c Reformation in England, of whom Robert Browne (c.1550–1633) was an early leader. Persecution drove the Congregationalists to Holland and the USA (the Pilgrim Fathers, 1620). Church affairs, including calling a minister and appointing deacons to assist, are regulated by members at a 'Church Meeting'. >> Christianity; ecumenism; Pilgrims; Presbyterianism; Reformation

Congress The national, or federal, legislature of the USA, consisting of two elected chambers: the Senate and the House of Representatives. Unusually powerful for a modern legislature, Congress can initiate legislation, and significantly amend or reject presidential legislative proposals. For a bill to become law it must be passed in identical form by both chambers and signed by the president. A presidential veto may be overturned by a two-thirds majority in both chambers. Legislation receives detailed consideration in the powerful Congressional committees. The majority party leader of the House occupies the influential position of Speaker. >> House of Representatives; Senate

Congress of Racial Equality A prominent US civil rights organization which campaigns for the rights of African-Americans, and which was particularly involved in the attack on racism in the 1960s. It is regarded as one of the more militant black rights organizations. >> civil rights

Congreve, William [**kong**greev] (1670–1729) Playwright and poet, born in Bardsey, West Yorkshire. His comedies include *The Old Bachelor*, *The Double Dealer* (1693), and *The Way of the World* (1700).

conic sections The figure in which a plane cuts a right circular double cone. Several cases arise: (1) If the plane passes through the vertex *V* of the cone, it may cut the cone in a single point *V* (*a*), or in two straight lines (*b*) through *V*, generators of the cone. (2) If the plane is at right angles perpendicular to the axis of the cone, and not through *V*, it cuts the cone in a circle (*e*). (3) If the plane is parallel to a generator of the cone, it cuts the cone in a parabola (*d*); otherwise it cuts the cone in an ellipse (*f*) or a hyperbola (*c*). >> *see illustration on p.207*

conifer A cone-bearing tree; strictly, any member of the gymnosperm order Coniferales. >> cypress; gymnosperms; monkey-puzzle; pine

Coniston Water [**kon**istn] Lake in the Lake District of Cumbria, NW England; length 9 km/6 mi; scene of world water speed record by Malcolm Campbell in 1939; Donald Campbell killed here in 1967 trying to break this record. >> Campbell, Malcolm; Lake District

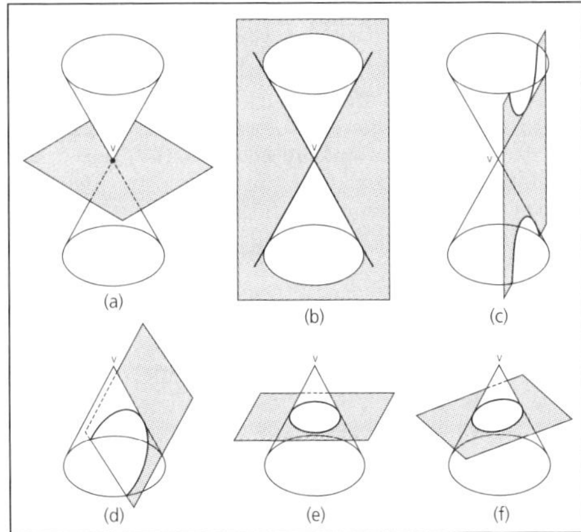

Conic sections – Cone (sometimes double) cut by a plane in (a) a single point (b) a pair of straight lines (c) a hyperbola (d) a parabola (e) a circle (f) an ellipse

conjunction The alignment of two celestial bodies seen from Earth, for example a planet with the Sun. The exact moment of conjunction occurs when the two bodies have the same celestial longitude. >> latitude and longitude; Solar System

conjunctivitis An infection of the membrane covering the inner surface of the eyelids and the front surface of the eye (the **conjunctiva**). It causes a feeling of grittiness in the eyes, and is associated with stickiness of the eyelids and a discharge. The whites of the eyes are red and infected. >> eye ℹ; ophthalmia

Connacht or **Connaught** [**ko**nawt] pop (1995e) 420 000; area 17 121 sq km/6 609 sq mi. Province in W Ireland, comprising counties of Sligo, Leitrim, Mayo, Roscommon, Galway. >> Ireland (republic) ℹ

Connaught >> **Connacht**

Connecticut [kuh**net**ikuht] pop (1995e) 3 272 000; area 12 996 sq km/5018 sq mi. A state in NE USA, the 'Constitution State', 'Nutmeg State' or 'The Insurance State'; densely populated; explored by Adriaen Block, 1614; one of the original states of the Union, fifth to ratify the Federal Constitution; highest point, Mt Frissell (725 m/2379 ft); coast largely urbanized, with many industries; interior mainly woodland and forest; capital, Hartford. >> Hartford; United States of America ℹ; RR994

connectionism A form of computer modelling in which information processing is carried out by a network of inter-connected units. It is sometimes called **parallel distributed processing**, because information is processed in many parts of the network simultaneously. >> artificial intelligence

Connemara [kone**mah**ra] Mountainous region in W Galway county, Ireland; rocky coastline with mountains rising to 765 m/2510 ft at Croagh Patrick; peat bogs; numerous lakes. >> Ireland (republic) ℹ

Connery, Sean, originally **Thomas Connery** (1930–) Film actor, born in Edinburgh. In 1963 he appeared in the highly successful *Dr No* as Ian Fleming's secret agent James Bond, a part he played in seven other films. Other films include *The Name of the Rose* (1987), *The Untouchables* (1987, Oscar), *The Russia House* (1991), and *The Rock* (1996). In 1998 he received a BAFTA Fellowship award.

Connolly, Billy (1942–) Comedian, actor, and television presenter, born in Glasgow, Scotland. After leaving school, he worked as an apprentice welder in Glasgow, then entered show business, becoming well known during the 1980s for his one-man theatre comedy performances and television appearances. His film credits include the Muppet's *Treasure Island* (1996) and *Mrs Brown* (1997).

Connolly, Maureen (Catherine), nickname **Little Mo** (1934–69) Tennis player, born in San Diego, CA. The first woman to win all four major titles in one year (1953), she won the Wimbledon singles in 1952–4, the US title in 1951–3, the French Open in 1953–4, and the Australian title in 1953. >> tennis, lawn ℹ

Connors, Jimmy, popular name of **James Scott Connors**, nickname **Jimbo** (1952–) Tennis player, born in Belleville, IL. He became Wimbledon champion in 1974 (against Ken Rosewall) and 1982 (against John McEnroe). He won the US Open in 1974, 1976, 1978, and 1982–3. In 1998 he was elected to the International Tennis Hall of Fame. >> McEnroe; tennis, lawn ℹ

conquistador [kon**kee**stadaw(r)] (Span 'conqueror') The standard term for the leaders of the Spanish expeditions of the early 16th-c that undertook the invasion and conquest of America. >> Cortés; Spain ℹ

Conrad, Joseph, originally **Józef Teodor Konrad Korzeniowski** (1857–1924) Novelist, born in Berdichev, Ukraine. His best-known works are *The Nigger of the Narcissus* (1897), *Lord Jim* (1900), *Nostromo* (1904), *The Secret Agent* (1907), *Under Western Eyes* (1911), and *Chance* (1914). He also wrote many short stories.

Conran, Jasper (1959–) Fashion designer, born in London. In 1978 he founded his own company, producing his first collection of easy-to-wear, quality clothes.

Conran, Sir Terence (Orby) (1931–) Designer and businessman, born in Esher, Surrey. He founded and ran the Habitat Company, based on his own success as a furniture designer and the virtues of good design and marketing.

conscription The practice, dating from the Napoleonic era, of compelling young men (and women, in some countries) of eligible age and fitness to serve by statute in the armed forces of a nation. Conscription was introduced in Great Britain in early 1916 and then in the USA (1917). It was again enforced in Britain from 1939–45, continuing in peacetime as **National Service**, which was finally abolished in 1962. In popular US usage, conscription is often referred to as **the draft**, last time invoked during the Vietnam war. >> women's services

conservation The protection and preservation of the Earth's resources (eg plants, animals, land, energy, minerals) or of historical artefacts (eg books, paintings, monuments) for the future. The World Conservation Strategy (1980) concluded that conservation of living resources was needed to preserve genetic diversity, to maintain essential ecological processes, and to ensure the sustainable use of species and ecosystems. >> ecology; endangered species; English Nature; environment; Nature Reserve; recycling

conservation laws Sets of rules describing quantities which are the same before and after some physical process. The identification of these laws is central to physics; all physical laws express conservation principles. A conservation law is related to a symmetry of the system. The most important such law is the **conservation of energy**, which is related to the symmetry of physical systems under translation in time. **Conservation of momentum** results from symmetry under translation in space. >> physics

conservatism A set of political ideas, attitudes, and beliefs which stress adherence to what is known and established in the political and social orders, as opposed to the innovative and untested. Generally associated with right-wing political parties, conservatives view humanity as inherently imperfect, emphasizing the need for law and order and the value of tradition. >> New Right; right-wing; Thatcher, Margaret

Conservative Party, nickname **Tories** One of the two main political parties in the UK, its full name being the **Conservative and Unionist Party**, due to its adherence to union of the countries making up the UK. It has been the most successful party electorally this century. In common with other Conservative parties, it is on the right of the political spectrum, though in the 1980s it fused conservative with radical neo-liberal ideas. It developed out of the Tory Party in the 1830s, and was almost continuously in power 1886–1905 and 1922–45. Later periods in office are 1951–64 (under Churchill, Eden, Macmillan and Home), 1970–4 (under Heath) and 1979–97 (under Thatcher and Major), when it was defeated by the Labour Party. >> conservatism; liberalism; New Right

consols [kon**solz**] Loan-stock issued by the British government, first introduced in 1751; its name derives from *consolidated fund*. It is a form of gilt-edged stock, but 'undated' – no redemption date is given for the return of the capital. >> gilt-edged securities; stocks

Constable, John (1776–1837) Landscape painter, born in East Bergholt, Suffolk. Among his best-received works were 'Haywain' (1821, National Gallery, London) and 'White Horse' (1825, New York). His work was especially popular in France. He is today considered, along with Turner, as the leading painter of the English countryside. >> landscape painting; Turner, J M

Constance, Ger **Konstanz**, ancient **Constantia** 47°39N 9°10E, pop (1995e) 77 000. Lake port in Germany, on L Constance; former episcopal see and imperial city; railway; university (1966); cathedral (15th-c). >> Constance, Lake; Germany [i]

Constance, Lake, Ger **Bodensee**, ancient **Lacus Brigantinus** area 541 sq km/209 sq mi. Lake on the N side of the Swiss Alps, forming a meeting point of Switzerland, Austria, and Germany; length, 64 km/40 mi; part of the course of the R Rhine. >> Alps

Constant (de Rebeque), (Henri) Benjamin [kõstã duh rebek] (1767–1830) Novelist and politician, born in Lausanne, Switzerland. He supported the Revolution, but was banished in 1802 for his opposition to Napoleon. His best-known work is the novel *Adolphe* (1816), based on his relationship with Mme de Staël. >> French Revolution [i]; Staël, Madame de

Constanţa [kon**stant**sa], Eng **Constantza**, ancient **Tomis** or **Constantinia** 44°10N 28°40E, pop (1995e) 310 000. Major port in SE Romania, on the W shores of the Black Sea; established as a Greek colony, 7th-c BC; under Roman rule from 72 BC; named after Constantine I (4th-c AD); ceded to Romania, 1878; airport; railway. >> Constantine I (Emperor); Romania [i]

Constantine [**kon**stanteen], ancient **Ciria**, **Qacentina** 36°22N 6°40E, pop (1995e) 497 000. Town in NE Algeria; oldest city in Algeria, important since the 3rd–4th-c BC; Roman provincial capital of Numidia; destroyed in AD 311 during a civil war, rebuilt by Constantine I; seat of successive Muslim dynasties in Middle Ages; French occupation in 1837; airport; railway; university (1969). >> Algeria [i]; Constantine I (Emperor)

Constantine I, known as **the Great**, originally **Flavius Valerius Constantinus** (c.274–337) Roman emperor, born in Naissus, Moesia. He became emperor of the West after his defeat of Maxentius at the Milvian Bridge in Rome (312), and emperor of the East after his victory over Licinius (324). Believing that his victory in 312 was the work of the Christian God, he became the first emperor to promote Christianity, whence his title 'Great'. His edict of Milan (313), issued jointly with Licinius, brought toleration to Christians throughout the empire. >> Roman history [i]

Constantine II (1940–) King of Greece (1964–73), born near Athens, who succeeded his father, Paul I. In 1964 he married **Princess Anne-Marie of Denmark** (1946–) and has two sons and a daughter. He fled to Rome (Dec 1967) after an abortive coup against the military government which had seized power, and was deposed in 1973. >> Greece [i]

constellation From ancient times, a group of stars that form a geometrical shape or picture. The stars in most constellations are not genuinely related, but lie at greatly different distances from the Solar System. The system in use by astronomers today has its origins in ancient Mesopotamia, and still includes many names from Greek mythology. It includes 88 constellations, which vary enormously in size and shape: the largest, Hydra, is 20 times bigger than the smallest, Crux. The brightest stars are named from the constellation in which they are found, using the Greek alphabet and the Latin genitive form for the constellation: *alpha Ursae Majoris* is thus the brightest star in Ursa Major. >> astronomy; star; RR968

constituency A territorial division that in many countries serves as a unit in the election of one or more political representatives to national assemblies. Population usually serves as the main criterion in determining the size of each constituency. For example, in the USA 435 people are elected to the House of Representatives from constituencies with roughly equivalent populations, while two senators are elected from each state, regardless of population size. The UK contains 650 single-member constituencies, most with electorates of c.65 000. >> House of Representatives

constitution Usually a written document which forms the rules determining the way that a country may be governed in terms of the sources, purpose, use, and limits upon the exercise of political power. The UK is one of a few exceptions in having an unwritten constitution, although in all countries the identification of constitutional principles must make reference to statute law, judicial interpretation, tradition, and other constitutional practices. >> bill of rights; Constitution of the United States

Constitutional Convention A gathering at Philadelphia during the American Revolution that produced the present US Constitution; 12 of the original 13 states were represented. >> American Revolution

Constitution of the United States A constitution founded upon the principles of the Declaration of Independence, and based on the concepts of limited and responsible government, and federalism. The constitutional document comprises a short preamble followed by seven articles which include: the organization, powers and procedures of the legislative branch (Congress); the powers of the president and executive; the powers of the judiciary, including the Supreme Court; the rights of the states; and procedures for amending the constitution. The articles are then followed by 26 amendments, the first 10 of which are known as the *bill of rights*. >> bill of rights; constitution; Declaration of Independence; federalism; Supreme Court

Constitutions of Clarendon >> **Clarendon, Constitutions of**

constrictor A snake which wraps its body tightly around its prey and, by squeezing, induces suffocation; teeth carry no venom. >> boa; python; snake

Constructivism An imprecise term usually applied to a form of abstract art that began in Russia in 1917, using machine-age materials such as steel, glass, and plastic.

Leading practitioners included Antoine Pevsner and Naum Gabo. Their ideas exerted a deep influence on abstract artists in the West (**International Constructivism**). >> abstract art; art; concrete art; Gabo

consubstantiation A theory attributed to Luther, describing the presence of Christ in the Eucharist 'under or with the elements of bread and wine'. It is to be contrasted with the Roman Catholic doctrine of transubstantiation. >> Eucharist; Luther; transubstantiation

consul 1 In Republican Rome (5th-c–1st-c BC), a chief executive officer of state, with military and judicial functions. Two consuls were elected annually. The consulship was the highest rank in the hierarchy of offices (the *cursus honorum*) and could not be held before the age of 36. >> Roman history ℹ **2** >> ambassador

consumerism The promotion of policies aimed at regulating the standards of manufacturers and sellers in the interests of buyers. The stimulus may come from a government, through legislation, from an industry itself, through setting up codes of practice, or from consumer pressure groups.

Contadora, Isla [**ees**lya konta**doh**ra] 8°40N 79°02W. Island of Panama, in the Pearl Is, Gulf of Panama; meeting place of the foreign ministers of Colombia, Mexico, Panama, and Venezuela (the Contadora Group) in 1983 to discuss the problems of Central America; their proposed solutions became known as the **Contadora process**. >> Panama ℹ

contagious abortion >> **brucellosis**

container ship A cellular ship, designed to carry 6 m/20 ft or 12 m/40 ft boxes in predetermined positions, thus largely dispensing with the lashing or stowage problems associated with traditional cargo. The first purpose-built ships were commissioned in 1966 by a British company. >> ship ℹ

containment building A steel or concrete structure enclosing a nuclear reactor, designed to withstand high pressure and high temperature and, in an emergency, to contain the escape of radiation. Such a building must also withstand external hazards, such as high winds and heavy snow. >> nuclear reactor ℹ

conté crayon [kōtay] A type of synthetic chalk named after its French inventor, Nicolas Jacques Conté (1755–1805). It is used by artists, and is available in black, white, red, and brown.

contempt of court A wide-ranging term which includes failure to comply with an order of the court, and conduct which obstructs the process of the courts (eg by intimidating witnesses or causing a disturbance in court). A person in contempt may be committed to prison or fined. >> court of law; subpoena

Conti, Tom [**kon**tee], popular name of **Thomas A Conti** (1941–) Actor and director, born in Paisley, W Scotland. He made his acting debut in 1960, and has since performed and directed regularly in London theatres, receiving a Tony Award for Best Actor in 1979. Among his films are *Merry Christmas, Mr Lawrence* (1982), *Shirley Valentine* (1989), and *Someone Else's America* (1994).

continent A term applied to the seven large land masses on the Earth's surface: Asia, Africa, North America, South America, Antarctica, Europe, and Australia, in decreasing order of size. The continents (including the submerged continental shelves) make up about 35% of the Earth's crust, the rest being made up of the oceanic plates. >> continental drift; plate tectonics ℹ

Continental Congress The gathering that declared and led the struggle for American independence. Each of the 13 colonies (states after 1776) had one vote. The First Congress met for six weeks in 1774. The Second (convened Apr 1775) did not formally dissolve until replaced by the government under the present Constitution, adopted in 1788. >> Articles of Confederation; Declaration of Independence; Ordinance of 1787

Continental Divide or **Great Divide** A line of mountain peaks in North America extending SE from NW Canada down the W USA into Mexico, Central America, and South America where it meets the N end of the Andes; a major watershed, with rivers running to the Atlantic and the Pacific; includes the Rocky Mts in Canada and the USA. >> Andes; Rocky Mountains

continental drift A theory which proposes that the present positions of the continents and oceans results from the breaking up of a single large land mass or 'supercontinent', termed *Pangaea*, c.200 million years ago. The idea is generally ascribed to Alfred Wegener (1910) but gained little support until the 1960s, when the theory of plate tectonics was established. >> continent; Pangaea; plate tectonics ℹ; Wegener

Continental System The process of economic warfare introduced by Napoleon to destroy British commercial power, after Trafalgar put paid to his invasion plans. The Decrees of Berlin (1806) and Milan (1807) established a blockade of European and neutral trade with Britain and her colonies. >> Napoleonic Wars

continuo The practice, common to most Baroque music, of filling out the harmonic texture by reference to a specially notated bass line (a *figured bass*). The continuo is usually supplied by a harmony instrument (harpsichord, organ, lute, etc) reinforced by a melodic bass instrument (cello, double bass, bassoon, etc). >> Baroque (music)

continuous assessment The appraisal of students' work on a regular basis rather than exclusively by final examination. Essays, practical work, projects, and assignments done during the course might form all or part of the final assessment, which can be based on marks, grades, or a profile.

contrabassoon >> **bassoon**

contraception The prevention of pregnancy following sexual intercourse; also known as **birth control** or **family planning**. For centuries its practice was opposed by the Church and the medical profession, but it has come to be widely advocated in order to control populations, protect against venereal disease, and regulate the size of families. Many methods are in use. The use of a 'safe period' or **rhythm method** is based on the fact that both spermatozoa and ova survive for only a day or two after release. Attractive to the Roman Catholic Church, it is fallible because of the difficulty in timing ovulation and the variability of the duration of the menstrual cycle. The condom, made of siliconed latex with an expanded part or teat on the end, is widely advocated because its mechanical protection guards not only against pregnancy but also against AIDS. Other **mechanical devices** include shields, diaphragms, or caps inserted into the vagina over the cervix. Their efficacy can be improved by the use of spermicidal agents. **Intra-uterine devices** (IUD) are empirically designed spring-like foreign bodies that are inserted by a trained person into the uterus. Made of inert plastic or metal, they act by preventing the products of conception becoming embedded in the wall of the uterus. The **contraceptive pill** contains synthetic steroids similar to the female sex hormones oestrogen and progesterone, either together or progesterone alone. Their use is based on the action of inhibiting ovulation. **Post-coital contraceptives** (the 'morning-after pill') contain the synthetic oestrogen stilboestrol. When taken after intercourse, stilboestrol prevents implantation of any fertilized egg. It is insufficiently safe to be used as an ordinary contraceptive device, and is reserved for emergencies (such as following rape). Substance RU-486 (mifepristone, often referred to as the 'abortion pill') was launched in 1988, surrounded by considerable controversy; designed for use in the early stages of pregnancy, it causes the womb lining to shed as in normal menstruation. >> abortion; DES; oestrogen; pregnancy ℹ; sterilization

contract A legally enforceable agreement. A contract has certain essential features – for example, the parties must have *legal capacity* (ie be legally able to enter into the agreement – such as by being old enough). There is no general rule that a contract must be in writing – buying something in a shop is a contractual agreement. >> condition; covenant 1; injunction

contract bridge >> **bridge** (recreation)

Contras >> **Nicaragua** ℹ

control >> **seance**

control engineering The branch of engineering concerned with the control and adjustment of systems. A human operator need not be involved. Control is achieved by using closed loop systems: when an error is detected, the information is returned to the input and used to correct the error – a system known as *feedback*. >> automation; servo system

convection The flow of heat by the actual movement of a gas or liquid. For example, air warmed by a fire expands, becomes less dense, and so rises, creating a **convection current** as fresh cool air is drawn in to replace the warmed air. >> diffusion (science); heat; thermal conduction

conversation piece A type of small group portrait which flourished in 18th-c England, representing a family and/or friends grouped informally either indoors or in a landscape or garden setting.

conveyance A legal document which, when signed, sealed, and delivered, transfers ownership of real property (eg in England and Wales) or heritable property (eg in Scotland) such as houses or land (specified in the document) from one party to another. In the USA, the document is usually a deed (a seal is no longer required in most US jurisdictions). In the UK, the Administration of Justice Act (1985) permits licensed conveyancing to be carried on for payment by a class of persons who are not solicitors. These **licensed conveyancers** are subject to the professional controls of the Council for Licensed Conveyancers. In the USA, private parties may convey land. >> land registration; solicitor

Convocation A gathering of Church of England clergy to regulate affairs of the Church. The **Upper House** consists of the archbishop and bishops; the **Lower House** of representatives of the lower clergy. The two convocations form the Church Assembly, which meets two or three times a year. >> Church of England

convolvulus >> **bindweed**

Conwy, Eng **Conway** 53°17N 3°50W, pop (1995e) 13 800. Historic market town and resort in Aberconwy and Colwyn county, NC Wales, UK; at head of R Conwy (Conway); 13th-c castle; road tunnel beneath river. >> Wales ℹ

cony >> **hyrax; pika; rabbit;**

Cook, Mount 43°37S 170°08E. Mountain in W South Island, New Zealand, in the Southern Alps; height, 3764 m/12 349 ft; highest peak in New Zealand; in Mount Cook National Park, a world heritage site; landslide in 1991 lowered its summit by 11 m to 3753 m/12 313 ft. >> New Zealand ℹ; Southern Alps

Cook, James (1728–79) Navigator, born in Marton, North Yorkshire. He surveyed the area around the St Lawrence R, Quebec, then in the *Endeavour* carried the Royal Society expedition to Tahiti to observe the transit of Venus across the Sun (1768–71), circumnavigated New Zealand, and charted parts of Australia. In his second voyage he sailed round Antarctica (1772–5), and visited several Pacific island groups. His third voyage (1776–9) aimed to find a passage round the N coast of America from the Pacific; but he was forced to turn back, and on his return voyage was killed by natives on Hawaii. >> Australia ℹ

Cook, Peter (Edward) (1937–95) Comedian and actor, born in Torquay, Devon. He became known as one of the writers and performers of *Beyond the Fringe* (1959–64), and for his collaboration with Dudley Moore in the irreverent television programme, *Not Only... But Also* (1965–71). >> Moore, Dudley

Cook, Robin, popular name of **Robert Finlayson Cook** (1946–) British statesman, born in Bellshill, North Lanarkshire, Scotland. He became an MP in 1974, held various posts in the shadow cabinet, and was chairman of the Labour Party (1996–7). He became foreign secretary in the new Labour government in 1997.

Cook, Thomas (1808–92) British railway excursion and tourist pioneer, born in Melbourne, Derbyshire. His travel agency is now a worldwide organization.

Cooke, (Alfred) Alistair (1908–) Journalist and broadcaster, born in Manchester. A sympathetic and urbane commentator on current affairs and popular culture in the USA, where he has lived since 1937, his 'Letter from America', first broadcast by the BBC in 1946, is the longest-running solo radio feature programme. His BBC TV series *America* (1972–3) also produced a best-selling book.

Cook Islands pop (1995e) 18 200; area 238 sq km/92 sq mi. Widely scattered group of 15 volcanic and coral islands, c.3200 km/2000 mi NE of New Zealand, S Pacific Ocean; self-governing country in free association with New Zealand; capital, Avarua (on Rarotonga); timezone GMT −10; mainly Polynesian population; main religion, Christianity; official language, English, with local languages widely spoken; unit of currency, New Zealand dollar; highest island, Rarotonga, rises to 650 m/2132 ft; climate damp and tropical; placed under British protection, 1888–1901; New Zealand dependency, 1901; internally self-governing, 1965; Legislative Assembly, with a premier as head of state; economy mainly agriculture and fishing. >> New Zealand ℹ; Pacific Ocean; Polynesia

Cookson, Dame Catherine (Ann) (1906–98) Novelist, born in East Jarrow, Tyne and Wear. Most of her novels are set in the NE of England, several of them belonging to a series tracing the fortunes of a single character or family, such as *Tilly Trotter* (1981). Other novels include *Rooney* (1957), *The Round Tower* (1968), and *Branded Man* (1997). In 1988 a third of all fiction borrowed from public libraries in the UK was by this author.

Cook Strait Channel of the Pacific Ocean separating North Island from South Island, New Zealand; 23–130 km/14–80 mi wide; visited by Captain Cook in 1770. >> New Zealand ℹ

Coolidge, (John) Calvin (1872–1933) US statesman and 30th president (1923–9), born in Plymouth, VT. A strong supporter of US business interests, he was triumphantly re-elected by the Republicans in 1924, but refused renomination in 1928. His economic policies led to a major stock market crash during his term of office.

Coombs, Herbert Cole, nickname **Nugget Coombs** (1906–) Australian public servant, born in Perth, Western Australia. He joined the [Australian] Commonwealth Bank, becoming its governor in 1949, and in 1959 was inaugural governor of the Reserve Bank of Australia. Pro-Chancellor of the Australian National University in 1959, he became Chancellor in 1968. He was personal adviser to seven Australian prime ministers.

Cooper, Gary (Frank) (1901–61) US film actor, born in Helena, MT. He was the archetypal hero of many Westerns, notably in *High Noon* (1952) and in the Hemingway epics

A Farewell to Arms (1932) and *For Whom the Bell Tolls* (1943). In addition to two Oscars for Best Actor he received a Special Academy Award in 1960.

Cooper, Henry (1934–) Boxer, born in Bellingham, Kent. The only man to win the Lonsdale Belt outright on three occasions, he beat Brian London to win his first British heavyweight title in 1959, but lost the title in a disputed contest against Joe Bugner in 1971. After flooring Cassius Clay at Wembley in 1963, he had his only world title fight in 1966, when a bad cut against Muhammad Ali (formerly, Cassius Clay) forced his early retirement. He is now much involved in charity work, and is a popular television personality. >> boxing ℹ

Cooper, James Fenimore (1789–1851) Novelist, born in Burlington, NJ. He is best known for his frontier adventures such as *The Last of the Mohicans* (1826) and *The Pathfinder* (1840). He also wrote novels and historical studies about the sea.

Cooper, Jilly, *née* **Sallitt** (1937–) Writer and journalist, born in Yorkshire. Her books include several general interest works, such as *Jolly Marsupial* (1982) and *Angels Rush In* (1990), and the novels *Polo* (1991), and *Appassionata* (1996).

Cooper, Leon Neil (1930–) Physicist, born in New York City. His theory of the behaviour of electron pairs (**Cooper pairs**) in certain materials at low temperatures was a major contribution to the theory of superconductivity. He shared the Nobel Prize for Physics in 1972. >> Bardeen; superconductivity

Cooper, Dame Whina (1895–1994) Maori leader, born in Hokianga, New Zealand. From the 1930s she became nationally known for her efforts to help her people recover from the problems caused by European settlement. In 1951 she became the founding president of the Maori Women's Welfare League, and in 1975 led a historic march to publicize Maori land claims.

co-operative >> **collective farm**

co-operative society A business venture owned by its members, who may be customers (in the case of a retail co-operative) or the employees (in a manufacturing company). The profits are distributed among members only. The first society was set up in 1844 in Rochdale, and soon each town had a 'co-op' store. In 1862, the retail co-operative societies set up the **Co-operative Wholesale Society (CWS)**, which manufactures and distributes goods to its members, its profits being ploughed back or distributed to member societies.

co-ordinate geometry >> **analytic geometry**

coot A bird of the rail family, inhabiting fresh water; widespread; front of head with horny shield; sides of toes lobed, to assist swimming; pelvis and legs modified for diving. (Genus: *Fulica*, 9 species.) >> moorhen; rail

Copán [ko**pahn**] 14°52N 89°10W. An ancient Mayan city in the Motagua Basin of W Honduras, noted for its three-dimensional stone carving; flourished in the 8th-c AD; area 39 sq km/15 sq mi; now a world heritage site; town of Copán (or Santa Rosa de Copán) nearby. >> Honduras ℹ; Mayas

Copenhagen [**koh**pnhaygn], Danish **København**, Lat **Hafnia** 55°43N 12°34E, pop (1995e) 469 000. Capital city of Denmark; developed around 12th-c fortifications; charter, 1254; capital, 1443; airport; railway; university (1479); technical university of Denmark (1829); shipping and commercial centre; old citadel of Frederikshavn; Tivoli amusement park (May–Sep); Amalienborg Palace (residence of Danish monarch since 1794); Christiansborg Palace; cathedral; Little Mermaid sculpture. >> Denmark ℹ

copepod [**koh**pepod] A small aquatic arthropod; free-living forms extremely abundant in most marine and freshwater habitats, forming a vital link in the food chain by feeding on minute plant plankton; the subclass contains c.9000 species. (Subphylum: Crustacea. Subclass: Copepoda.) >> arthropod; cyclops; food chain; plankton

Copernican system A model of the Solar System in which the Sun is at the centre, with the Earth and other planets moving in combinations of circular movements around it (a *heliocentric* system). Prior to the publication of this theory in 1543, it was held by European astronomers that the Earth lay at the centre of the universe. >> Copernicus; Kepler; Newton; Ptolemaic system; Solar System

Copernicus, Nicolas [ko**per**nikus], Polish **Mikolaj Kopernik** (1473–1543) The founder of modern astronomy, born in Toruń, Poland. His 400-page treatise, *De revolutionibus orbium coelestium* (completed 1530, On the Revolutions of the Celestial Spheres) had a hostile reception when it was published (1543). >> astronomy; Copernican system

Copland, Aaron [**kohp**land] (1900–90) Composer, born in New York City. Among his compositions are those tapping a deep vein of US tradition and folk music, as in the ballets *Billy the Kid* (1938) and *Appalachian Spring* (1944). He also composed film scores, two operas, and three symphonies.

Copleston, Frederick (Charles) [**koh**plston] (1907–94) Jesuit philosopher, born near Taunton, Somerset. He wrote several books on individual philosophers and movements, as well as an eight-volume *History of Philosophy* (1946–66).

copper Cu, element 29, density 9 g/cm^3, melting point 1080°C. The only brown metal, known from ancient times; its name derives from Cyprus, the main source in Roman times. It corrodes slowly, conducts electricity well, and is used mainly in electrical apparatus. >> brass; bronze; chemical elements; metal; RR1036

Copper Age >> **Three Age System**

Copperbelt pop (1995e) 1 918 000; area 31 328 sq km/ 12 093 sq mi. Province in C Zambia; economic centre of the country because of its vast copper and cobalt reserves, the world's largest known deposits; capital, Ndola. >> copper; Zambia ℹ

Copperhead A term for members of the US Democratic Party who opposed the Civil War. It is derived from the name of a poisonous snake. >> American Civil War

copperhead A pit viper (*Agkistrodon contortrix*) native to SE USA; top of head reddish-brown; bites more people in North America than any other venomous snake, but venom is weak and deaths are rare. >> pit viper ℹ

Coppola, Francis Ford [ko**poh**la] (1939–) Film director and screenwriter, born in Detroit, MI. Among his outstanding productions are *The Godfather* (1972; *Part II*, 1974; *Part III*, 1990) and his controversial study of the Vietnam War, *Apocalypse Now* (1979). Later films include *The Rainmaker* (1997).

copra The dried kernel of the coconut. In the 1860s, to supplement supplies of animal fats, manufacturers of soap, margarine, and lubricants turned to tropical vegetable oils, especially coconut oil. Plantations were set up to produce copra, from which the oil is extracted by crushing. >> coconut palm

co-processor A second computer processor, an optional extra processor on most personal computers, which allows the computer to carry out specific tasks more quickly. Examples are mathematics and graphics co-processors. >> computer graphics; digital computer

Coptic Church (Gr *aigyptos* 'Egyptian') The Christian Church in Egypt of ancient origin, claiming St Mark as founder. After the Council of Chalcedon (451), the Copts split from the rest of the Church, preserving the **Coptic language**, and observing the liturgy and sacraments of the ancient Alexandrian rite. It maintains a monastic tradition and structure, its head (called a *pope*) being elected by a religious tribunal and confirmed by the Egyptian government. >> Christianity; Mark, St

copyright Ownership of and right of control over all possible ways of reproducing a 'work', ie the product of an original creative act by one or more people, in a form which makes it possible to be copied. In particular, copyright protection is given to literary, dramatic, and artistic works (paintings, drawings, photographs, etc), sound recordings, films, television and sound broadcasts, and various productions of new technology. At some time or other the work falls into public ownership and can be copied without permission: in the UK, since 1996, the period is 70 years after the creator's death (previously, 50); in the USA, since 1978, the period is 50 years for most works (previously 28, once renewable).

coracle A small circular craft first constructed from reeds in basket form by ancient Britons. It was light enough to be carried on a man's back. The tradition mainly survives in Wales, where coracles are still used by fishermen.

coral A typically massive hydroid, found in colonies in warm shallow seas; many produce a calcareous external skeleton forming coral reefs. (Phylum: Cnidaria. Class: Hydrozoa.) >> calcium; coelenterate; Hydrozoa

Coral Sea or **Solomon Sea** area 4 791 000 sq km/ 1 850 200 sq mi. Arm of the Pacific Ocean, bounded W by NE Australia, N by Papua New Guinea and the Solomon Is, many coral islands; scene of US victory over Japanese, 1942. >> Pacific Ocean

Coral Sea Islands, Territory of the Uninhabited territory in the Coral Sea off the NE coast of Australia, administered by the Australian government since 1969; comprises scattered reefs and islands (including the Great Barrier Reef) over a sea area of about 1 million sq km. >> Australia [i]

cor anglais [kawr **ong**glay], (Fr 'English horn') A woodwind instrument with a slightly conical bore, a double reed, and a distinctive bulb-shaped bell. Neither English nor a horn, it is in effect a tenor oboe. >> reed / transposing / woodwind instrument [i]

corbelling A prehistoric method of constructing a vault, using courses of dry stone stepped successively inwards until they come close enough together to span with a single slab or capstone. The chambered tombs of Maes Howe and New Grange afford notable early examples in N Europe. >> chambered tomb; Maes Howe; New Grange

Corbett, Ronnie, popular name of **Ronald Balfour Corbett** (1930–) Comedian, born in Edinburgh. His television series include *Sorry!* (1981–8), *Small Talk* (1994–6), and a fruitful partnership with Ronnie Barker led to the long-running *The Two Ronnies* (1971–87). Film appearances comprise *Casino Royale* (1967) and *No Sex Please, We're British* (1972). >> Barker, Ronnie

Corday (d'Armont), (Marie) Charlotte [kaw(r)day] (1768–93) Noblewoman, born in St Saturnin, France. A sympathizer with the aims of the Revolution, she came to be horrified by the acts of the Jacobins. She managed to obtain an audience with Marat, while he was in his bath, and stabbed him. She was guillotined four days later. >> French Revolution [i]; Jacobins (French history); Marat

Cordeliers, Club of the [kaw(r)delyay] An extreme revolutionary club founded in Paris (1790) by Danton and Marat; also called the **Society of the Friends of the Rights of Man and Citizen**. >> Danton; French Revolution [i]; Marat

Córdoba (Argentina) [**kaw(r)**dohba], Span [**kor**thoba] 31°25S 64°11W, pop (1995e) 1 246 000. City in C Argentina; founded, 1573; renowned as a Jesuit mission centre; airport; railway; three universities (including Argentina's first, 1613); cathedral (1758). >> Argentina [i]; Jesuits

Córdoba (Spain) [**kaw(r)**dohba], Span **Cordova** [**kor**thoba] 37°50N 4°50W, pop (1995e) 303 000. City in Andalusia, S Spain; capital of Moorish Spain, 8th-c; bishopric; airport; railway; cathedral; Great Mosque (completed 990) is a world heritage site. >> Andalusia; Córdoba Cathedral; Spain [i]

Córdoba Cathedral Originally a mosque built (785–6) by Abd-er-Rahman I (731–88) in Córdoba, Spain. It has been used as a Christian cathedral since 1238, and is now a world heritage site. >> cathedral; Córdoba (Spain)

Corelli, Arcangelo [ko**re**lee] (1653–1713) Composer, born in Fusignano, Italy. His concerti grossi, and his solo and trio sonatas for violin, mark an epoch in chamber music, and influenced a whole generation of composers.

Corelli, Marie [ko**re**lee], pseudonym of **Mary Mackay** (1855–1924) Novelist, born in London. Her romantic melodramas, such as *Barabbas* (1893) and *The Sorrows of Satan* (1895), were extremely popular.

Corfu [kaw**foo**], Gr **Kérkira** pop (1995e) 105 000; area 592 sq km/228 sq mi. Northernmost and second largest of the Ionian Is, Greece, off NW coast of Greece; length 64 km/40 mi; semi-mountainous terrain (highest point 907 m/2976 ft), dense vegetation; chief town, Corfu, pop (1995e) 35 800; airport. >> Greece [i]; Ionian Islands

corgi The only British spitz breed of dog; small with short legs, pointed muzzle, large erect ears; two varieties: short-tailed **Pembroke** and long-tailed **Cardigan**; also known as **Welsh corgi**. >> dog; spitz

coriander An annual (*Coriandrum sativum*), growing to 50 cm/20 in, native to N Africa and W Asia; flowers white or pink, petals unequal; fruit globular. The leaves are used in Chinese, Indian, and Mexican cooking; the fruits are used as a spice in sausages, curries, confectionery, and liqueurs. (Family: Umbelliferae.) >> spice

Corinth, Gr **Kórinthos** 37°56N 22°55E, pop (1995e) 29 600. City in Greece, on an isthmus separating the Adriatic Sea from the Aegean; founded before 3000 BC; influential Greek city-state of Dorian origins; destroyed by Romans 146 BC; ancient Kórinthos, 7 km/4 mi SW; transferred to new site in 1858, after a severe earthquake; railway; extensive remains, including Archaic Temple of Apollo. >> Dorians; Greece [i]; Peloponnesian War

Corinthian order One of the five main orders of classical architecture, characterized by a fluted shaft and a decorative acanthus capital. It was first invented in Athens in the 5th-c BC. >> acanthus; column; orders of architecture [i]

Corinthians, Letters to the Two New Testament writings, widely accepted as genuinely from the apostle Paul to the church that he founded in Corinth. >> New Testament; Paul, St

Coriolanus, Gaius or **Gnaeus Marcius** [korio**lay**nus] (5th-c BC) Roman folk hero, so named from his capture of the Volscian town of Corioli. Banished by the Romans for tyrannical behaviour (491 BC), he took refuge with the Volscians, then led them against his native city. After entreaties from his mother and wife, he spared Rome, and was executed by the Volscians. >> Roman history [i]

Coriolis force [kori**oh**lis] An apparent force acting on objects moving across the Earth's surface; named after French mathematician Gustave Gaspard Coriolis (1792–1843). A result of the Earth's rotation, it is responsible for wind and ocean current patterns, and is applicable to rotating systems generally. >> *see illustration on p.213*

Cork, Ir **Chorcaigh** pop (1995e) 407 000; area 7459 sq km/ 2880 sq mi. County in Munster, S Ireland; capital, Cork, pop (1995e) 173 000; third largest city in Ireland; airport; railway; university (1845); two cathedrals. >> Blarney; Ireland (republic) [i]; Munster

cork A spongy, protective layer just beneath the outer bark in trees, made up of thin-walled cells impregnated with a waxy substance (*suberin*). The cork layer may be built up over several years, becoming very thick. >> bark

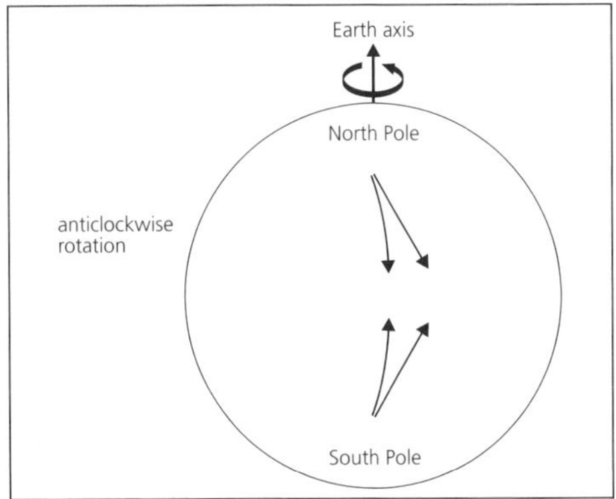

Deflections from expected paths (black lines) resulting from the Coriolis force. They are observed in the flight of missiles and artillery shells.

corm A short underground shoot containing food reserves. Early growth of foliage and flowers totally depletes the reserves, and a new corm is formed on top of the old one at the end of each year before the plant dies back. >> bulb; crocus; gladiolus

cormorant A large gregarious seabird, found worldwide; dark plumage, often with bright naked facial skin; flies fast, usually close to water surface. (Family: Phalacrocoracidae, 31 species.)

corn A generic term usually referring to the most widely cultivated cereal crop in a country or region. In North America, corn normally refers to maize, in Britain to wheat, and in Scandinavia to barley. >> barley; cereals; corn belt; cornflour; maize; wheat

corn belt The major agricultural region of the US Midwest. It is centred on the states of Iowa and Illinois, and includes parts of S Dakota, Minnesota, Nebraska, Kansas, Missouri, Ohio, and Indiana. Its main products are corn (maize) and other feed-grain. >> maize; Middle West

corncrake A bird of the rail family (*Crex crex*), native to Europe and W Asia, also known as the **landrail**; migrates to tropical Africa in winter. >> crake; rail

cornea [**kaw(r)**nia] The transparent front part of the outer protective fibrous coat of the eyeball. It is largely responsible for the fraction of light entering the eye, focusing it approximately on the retina, so that the lens can make the final fine adjustment. A large inequality in its vertical and horizontal curvatures is known as *astigmatism*. >> eye 🛈; refraction; retina; transplantation

Corneille, Pierre [kaw(r)**nay**] (1606–84) Playwright, born in Rouen, France. Among his major tragedies are *Le Cid* (1636), *Horace* (1639), *Cinna* (1639), and *Polyeucte* (1640). *Le Menteur* (1642, The Liar) entitles him to be called the father of French comedy as well as of French tragedy.

cornet A musical instrument made of brass. The modern cornet, resembling a small trumpet with three valves, is used above all in brass bands. >> brass instrument 🛈; flugelhorn

cornetfish Colourful tropical marine fish found around reefs and sea-grass beds; head and body very slender, length up to 1·8 m/6 ft; scaleless, tail bearing a whip-like process; also called **flutemouth**. (Family: Fistulariidae.)

cornett A musical instrument in use from the 15th-c to the mid-18th-c, made from two pieces of hollowed wood, glued together and covered with leather to form a tube, usually curved, with a conical bore. This was provided with finger-holes and a cup-shaped mouthpiece like that of a brass instrument. >> brass instrument 🛈; woodwind instrument 🛈

cornflour The flour of the maize seed, favoured by cooks as a thickening agent in sauces and soups.

cornflower A branched annual (*Centaurea cyanus*) growing to 80 cm/30 in, native to SE Europe; flower-heads solitary, long-stalked; outer florets bright blue, spreading, larger than the inner red-purple florets; also called **bluebottle**. (Family: Compositae.) >> floret

cornice [**kaw(r)**nis] In classical or Renaissance architecture, the crowning, projecting part of an entablature. In a general sense, it may refer to any crowning ornamental projection along the top of a building or wall. >> entablature

Cornish The Celtic language once spoken to the W of the R Tamar in Cornwall. The last speakers died in c.1800, and there is some interest in a modern revival of the language. >> Celtic languages

Corn Laws British legislation regulating the trade in corn. The most famous Corn Law was introduced in 1815, which imposed prohibitively high duties on the import of foreign corn. Following widespread criticism, the Corn Laws were amended in 1828, and repealed by Peel in 1846. >> Anti-Corn-Law League; Peel

corn poppy An erect annual (*Papaver rhoeas*), growing to 60 cm/2 ft, producing white latex, native to Europe and Asia, and introduced elsewhere; flowers round, four petals, bright scarlet; capsule pepper-pot shaped with a ring of pores around the rim. It is a poignant symbol of World War 1, when fields bloomed with poppies after being churned by battle. (Family: Papaveraceae.) >> poppy

cornucopia [kaw(r)nyu**koh**pia] A classical motif of a ram's horn overflowing with fruit and flowers, symbolizing abundance and plenty. It was much used in Renaissance and later decorative schemes to do with eating and drinking. >> Renaissance

Cornwall, Celtic **Kernow** pop (1995e) 480 000; area 3564 sq km/1376 sq mi. County in SW England; county town, Truro; Cornish nationalist movement revived the Stannary (Tinners' Parliament) in 1974, and there is renewed interest in the Cornish language. >> Cornish; Duchy of Cornwall; England 🛈; Stannaries; Truro

Cornwallis, Charles Cornwallis, 1st Marquess [kaw(r)n**wo**lis] (1738–1805) British general and statesman, born in London. He defeated Gates at Camden (1780), but was forced to surrender at Yorktown (1781). In 1786 he became Governor-General of India, where he defeated Tippoo Sahib, and introduced the series of reforms known as the **Cornwallis Code**. >> American Revolution; Tippoo Sahib

Cornwell, Patricia (Daniels) (1957–) Novelist, born in Miami, FL. In the 1990s she became one of the world's best-selling women novelists, producing a book each year, and known especially for the character of medical examiner Dr Kay Scarpetta introduced in her first novel *Postmortem* (1990). Later books include *Cause of Death* (1996) and the first non-Scarpetta mystery, *Hornet's Nest* (1997).

corolla >> **flower 🛈; petal**

Coromandel Coast [koroh**man**dl] The E coast of India, extending more than 650 km/400 mi from Point Calimere in the S to the mouth of the Krishna R in the N.

corona (astronomy) [ko**roh**na] The outermost layers of the Sun's atmosphere, visible as a pearly halo of light during a total eclipse, temperature c.1–2 million K. It is a source of strong X-rays. >> chromosphere; solar wind; Sun; X-rays

corona (botany) [ko**roh**na] An extension of the corolla (petals) of a flower, such as the central trumpet of a daffodil. >> flower 🛈

Corona Australis [ko**roh**na aw**stra**lis] (Lat 'southern crown') A small but prominent S constellation on the fringes of the Milky Way. >> constellation; Milky Way; RR968

Corona Borealis [ko**roh**na bori**a**lis] (Lat 'northern crown') A small N constellation, the stars forming a striking semicircle. >> constellation; RR968

coronary heart disease Atherosclerosis of the coronary arteries, the most important cause of death over 40 in developed countries in the West, and the commonest cause of angina pectoris and myocardial infarction; also known as **ischaemic/ischemic heart disease**. There are large differences in the prevalence of coronary artery disease between countries, and it appears to be a disorder of affluence, unbalanced diet, stress, and obesity. Smoking is known to be a contributory factor. There is a positive relationship between coronary artery disease and the level of blood cholesterol. >> angina; atherosclerosis; cholesterol; heart disease; myocardial infarction; polyunsaturated fatty acids; *see illustration below*

coroner A public officer who investigates the cause of a death, especially one where there is reason to suspect that it was not due to natural causes, in some cases holding an official inquiry, or *inquest*. Coroners are appointed by the Crown, and must be qualified as a medical doctor or a lawyer.

Corot, (Jean Baptiste) Camille [koroh] (1796–1875) Landscape painter, born in Paris. Several of his masterpieces, such as 'La Danse des nymphes' (1850) are in the Louvre. >> Barbizon School; landscape painting

corporation tax A tax levied on company profits by the UK government, created in 1966; its predecessor was the **profits tax**. The tax rate payable has been changed over the years, and small firms pay the tax at a lower rate. In the USA there are federal, state, and local taxes on corporations. >> company; taxation

Corpus Christi, Feast of [**kaw(r)**pus **kris**tee] A festival of the Roman Catholic Church in honour of the Eucharist, instituted by Pope Urban IV in 1264 and observed on the Thursday after Trinity Sunday. >> Eucharist

Correggio [ko**re**jioh], originally **Antonio Allegri** (c.1494–1534) Renaissance painter, born in Correggio, Italy. In 1518 he began his great series of mythological frescoes for the convent of San Paolo at Parma. The decoration of the cathedral of Parma was commissioned in 1522. >> fresco; Renaissance

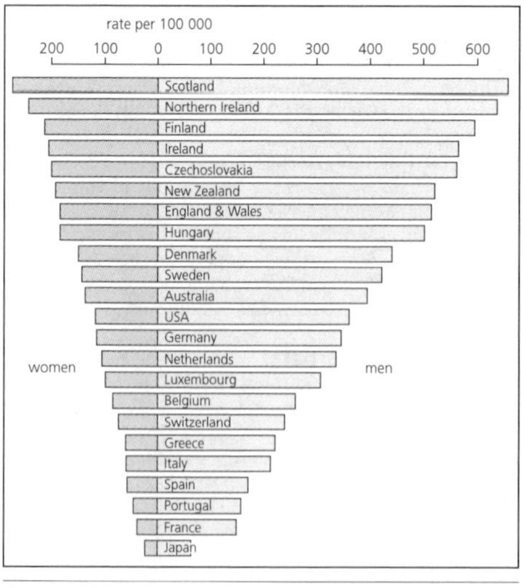

rate per 100 000

200 100 0 100 200 300 400 500 600

women men

Scotland
Northern Ireland
Finland
Ireland
Czechoslovakia
New Zealand
England & Wales
Hungary
Denmark
Sweden
Australia
USA
Germany
Netherlands
Luxembourg
Belgium
Switzerland
Greece
Italy
Spain
Portugal
France
Japan

Coronary heart disease – the chart shows age-standardized rates of mortality for men and women aged 40 to 49

corrie >> **cirque**

corrosion Destructive oxidation, usually by air in the presence of water; most marked for metals, especially iron. It is an electrochemical process, occurring most rapidly when two different metals are in contact with one another and with air and water. >> metal; oxidation; rust

corsairs Dutch, English, and French privateers licensed by governments to prey upon enemy shipping in the Channel and Atlantic during the Wars of the League of Augsburg (1689–97) and the Spanish Succession (1702–13). >> buccaneers; Kidd

Corsica [**kaw**sikuh], Fr **Corse** pop (1995e) 257 000; area 8680 sq km/3350 sq mi. Mountainous island and region of France in the Mediterranean Sea; length 183 km/114 mi; width up to 84 km/52 mi; part of France since 1768; France's largest island; mountainous interior, rising to 2710 m/8891 ft at Mont Cinto; capital, Ajaccio; airport; major scenic area, with a wide range of tourist activities. >> France [i]; maquis; Sardinia

Cort, Henry (1740–1800) Ironmaster, born in Lancaster, Lancashire. In 1784 he invented the 'puddling' process for converting pig iron into wrought iron, as well as a system of grooved rollers for the production of iron bars. >> iron

Cortés, Hernán [kaw(r)**tez**], also spelled **Cortéz** (1485–1547) The conqueror of Mexico, born in Medellín, Spain. In 1519 he commanded an expedition against Mexico, marching on the Aztec capital, and capturing the king, Montezuma; but the Mexicans rose, and Cortés was forced to flee. He then launched a successful siege of the capital, which fell in 1521. >> Aztecs; New Spain

cortex An outer layer of an organism or biological system. In the brain of vertebrates, the cerebral cortex is a layer of grey matter lying above each cerebral hemisphere. >> brain [i]; cerebrum

corticosteroids Steroid hormones produced and secreted by the adrenal glands, including **hydrocortisone**, **corticosterone**, and **aldosterone**. They have numerous effects in the body, influencing metabolism, salt and water balance, and the function of many organs. >> adrenal glands; aldosterone; cortisol; hormones; steroid

cortisol [**kaw(r)**tisol] A steroid hormone found in the adrenal cortex of vertebrates; also known as **hydrocortisone**. It promotes the conversion of protein and fat into glucose, and has an important role in the body's resistance to physical and psychological stress, especially after trauma. >> adrenal glands; corticosteroids; steroid

Cortona, Pietro (Berrettini) da [kaw(r)**toh**na] (1596–1669) Painter and architect, born in Cortona, Italy. One of the founders of the Roman High Baroque style in painting, he specialized in highly illusionistic ceiling painting, seen notably in his 'Allegory of Divine Providence' and 'Barberini Power' (1633–9) at the Palazzo Barberini in Rome. >> Baroque (art and architecture); Bernini; Guercino, Il

corundum [ko**run**dum] A mineral formed from aluminium oxide (Al_2O_3); extremely hard and used as an abrasive. Gemstone varieties are ruby and sapphire. >> emery; gemstones; ruby; sapphire

Corunna [ko**ruh**na], Span **La Coruña**, ancient **Caronium** 43°20N 8°25W, pop (1995e) 247 000. Seaport in NW Spain; base of the Spanish Armada, 1588; city sacked by Drake, 1589; scene of British victory during the Peninsular War (1809), and the death of Sir John Moore, 1809; airport; railway. >> Drake, Francis; Moore, John; Spanish Armada

corvette [kaw(r)**vet**] A small single-screw warship designed for convoy escort duties in World War 2. In former times, it was a single gun-decked, three-masted, square-rigged sailing vessel. >> warships ℹ

Corvus [**kaw(r)**vus] (Lat 'crow') A small S constellation, named in ancient times. >> constellation; RR968

coryphaena [kori**fee**na] >> **dolphinfish**

coryza [kuh**riy**za] >> **cold**

Cos, Gr **Kós**, Ital **Coo** area 290 sq km/112 sq mi. Island of the Dodecanese, E Greece, in the Aegean Sea, off the SW coast of Turkey; length 43 km/27 mi; width 2–11 km/1¼–7 mi; rises to 846 m/2776 ft at Mt Dikaios; severely damaged by earthquakes in 1933; capital, Cos, pop (1995e) 15 000; famous in antiquity for the cult of Asclepius and its doctors, notably Hippocrates. >> Asclepius; Dodecanese; Greece ℹ; Hippocrates

Cosby, Bill [**koz**bee], popular name of **William Henry Cosby** (1937–) Comedian, born in Philadelphia, PA. His television series *The Cosby Show* (1984–92, 1996) has consistently topped the ratings. His films include *Uptown Saturday Night* (1974), *California Suite* (1978), and *Leonard: Part VI* (1987).

Cosgrave, William Thomas [**koz**grayv] (1880–1965) Irish statesman and first president of the Irish Free State (1922–32), born in Dublin. His son, **Liam Cosgrave** (1920–) was prime minister (1973–7).

Cosmas and Damian, Saints (3rd-c) Arabian twin brothers, said to have been physicians at Aegaea, Cilicia, who were beheaded by Diocletian. They are the patron saints of physicians. Feast day 26 September (W), 1 July/1 November (E). >> Christianity; Diocletian

Cosmic Background Explorer (COBE) A NASA satellite launched in November 1989 to study the cosmic background radiation from the universe. COBE precisely measured the temperature of this radiation as 2·73 K. In 1992 it also discovered miniscule temperature variations in the radiation, attributed to slight fluctuations in the density of the early universe.

cosmic background radiation A weak radio signal that comes from the entire universe; also called **microwave background radiation**. It has a spectrum identical to a perfect black body a mere 2·73 degrees above absolute zero. It is a relic of an early very hot phase in the universe, a fossil of the 'big bang' itself. In 1992, satellite observations showed slight 'ripples' in the strength of this radiation, believed to be due to differences in density in the early universe which gave rise to the formation of galaxies. >> Big Bang; Penzias; spectrum; universe

cosmic dust Microscopic grains of dust of extraterrestrial origin; also called **Brownlee particles**, after the original collector. It enters Earth's atmosphere at high velocity, and is slowed down by friction in the uppermost atmosphere. The particles are a few microns in size, often with porous structure. Some are believed to be dust from comets. >> comet; meteor; meteorite

cosmic rays High energy electrons and ions moving through space, thought to be produced by exploding stars. When the particles strike the Earth's atmosphere, secondary rays comprising mostly pions and muons are produced. Cosmic rays are a useful source of high-energy particles for experiments. >> background radiation; muon; particle physics; pion

cosmic string Hypothetical massive filaments of matter (10^{19} kg/cm) predicted in supersymmetry theory as an important component of the very early universe. >> supersymmetry; universe

cosmogony [koz**mo**guhnee] >> **cosmology**

cosmological argument An argument for the existence of God as the first cause of all things, championed especially by Aquinas. The argument appeals to the intuitions that the existence of the universe cannot be explained by things *in* the universe, and that there should be only one first cause. >> Aquinas; God

cosmology The study of the universe on the largest scales of length and time, particularly the propounding of theories concerning the origin, nature, structure, and evolution of the universe. The study of the origin and mode of formation of various celestial objects is known as **cosmogony**. >> astronomy; 'big bang'; steady state theory; universe

cosmonaut The Russian term for a spacecraft crew member. Over 70 crewed flights, including three women (one British), were carried out by the Soviet (later, Russian) space programme to the beginning of 1992. >> astronaut; Soviet space programme

Cossacks Originally, members of semi-independent communities of fugitive peasants and military adventurers inhabiting the steppelands of S Russia and the Ukraine. In the 18th–19th-c they were formed into military organizations (*hosts*), and earned a reputation for ferocious fighting and skilled horsemanship.

Cossington-Smith, Grace (1892–1984) Painter, born in Sydney, New South Wales, Australia. She was instrumental in introducing Postimpressionism to her country. Her 1915 painting, 'The Sock Knitter', is seen as a key work in the Australian Modernist movement. >> Modernism; Postimpressionism

Costa Azul [**azul**] Atlantic coastline of W Portugal between the Ponta da Arrifana and the mouth of the R Sado; the name means 'blue coast'. >> Portugal ℹ

Costa Blanca [**blang**ka] The coastal resort regions of Murcia, Alicante, and part of Almería provinces, E Spain; on the Mediterranean coast; the name means 'white coast'. >> Spain ℹ

Costa Brava [**brah**va] The Mediterranean coastal resort region of Catalonia, E Spain, between Barcelona and the French border; the name means 'wild coast'. >> Spain ℹ

Costa de la Luz [**loos**] Resort region on the Atlantic coastline of Huelva and Cádiz provinces, S Spain; the name means 'coast of light'. >> Spain ℹ

Costa del Azahar [aza**khahr**] Mediterranean coastal resort region of Castellón de la Plana and Valencia provinces, E Spain; the name means 'orange-blossom coast'. >> Spain ℹ

Costa del Sol [**sol**] Mediterranean coastal resort region in Andalusia, S Spain; the name means 'coast of the sun'. >> Spain ℹ

Costa Dorada [do**rah**da] Mediterranean coastal resort region S of the Costa Brava, Barcelona, and Tarragona provinces, E Spain; the name means 'golden coast'. >> Costa Brava; Spain ℹ

Costa Dourada [**kos**ta **do**rada] Atlantic coastline of W Portugal between the Ponta da Arrifana and the mouth of the R Sado; the name means 'golden coast'. >> Portugal ℹ

Costa Rica [**kos**ta **ree**ka], official name **Republic of Costa Rica**, Span **República de Costa Rica** pop (1995e) 3 383 000; area 51 022 sq km/19 694 sq mi. Second smallest republic in Central America; capital, San José; timezone GMT −6; mainly Spanish descent; main religion, Roman Catholicism; official language, Spanish; unit of currency, the colón of 100 céntimos; crossed by Inter-American Highway; airport at San José; formed by a series of volcanic ridges; highest peak, Chirripó Grande (3819 m/12 529 ft); central plateau, altitude 800–1400 m/2600–4600 ft; much swampy land near coast, with tropical forest as land rises; tropical climate, with small temperature range and abundant rainfall; visited by Columbus, 1502; named Costa Rica (Span 'rich coast') in the belief that vast gold treasures existed; independence from Spain, 1821; member of Federation of Central America, 1824–39; governed by an executive president, Legislative Assembly, and cabinet; economy primarily agriculture, mainly coffee, bananas, sugar, cattle; Cocos I National Park, a world heritage site.

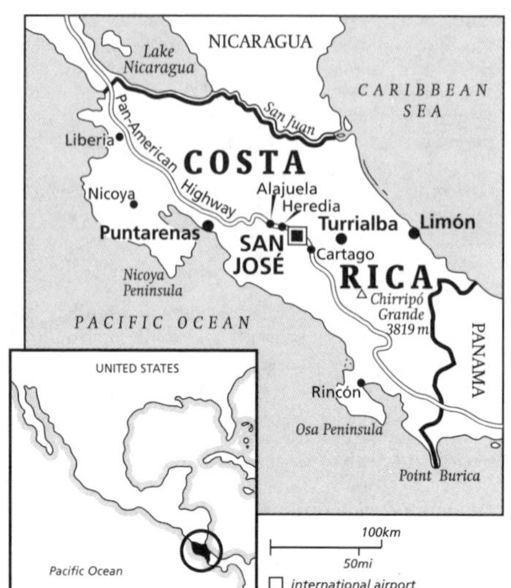

>> Pan-American Highway; San José (Costa Rica); RR1005 political leaders

Costello, Elvis, originally **Declan Patrick McManus** (1955–) Singer and songwriter, born in London. His debut album *My Aim Is True* established his reputation. For his second album, *This Year's Model* (1978), he was joined by a three-piece group, The Attractions, and they worked together on most of his recordings over the next eight years. >> pop music

Costello, Lou >> **Abbott and Costello**

costmary A sweetly aromatic perennial (*Balsamita major*) growing to 90 cm/3 ft, native to W Asia; flower-heads numerous, in flat-topped clusters; spreading outer florets white, inner disc florets yellow; also called **alecost**. Its strong-smelling foliage was formerly used for flavouring ales. (Family: Compositae.) >> floret; herb

Costner, Kevin (1955–) Motion-picture actor and director, born in Compton, CA. He established a reputation with *Bull Durham* (1988) and *Field of Dreams* (1989), then directed and starred in *Dances With Wolves* (1990, 7 Oscars). Later starring roles include *Robin Hood: Prince of Thieves* (1991), *JFK* (1991), and *The Postman* (1998).

cost of living >> **retail price index**

Cosway, Richard (1742–1821) Miniaturist, born in Tiverton, Devon. He was a fashionable painter of portraits; the use of watercolour on ivory is a notable feature of his work. In 1781 he married the artist **Maria Hadfield** (1759–1838), also a miniaturist. >> miniature painting; watercolour

cot death >> **sudden infant death syndrome**

Côte d'Ivoire [koht dee**vwah(r)**], official name **Republic of Côte d'Ivoire** (Eng **Ivory Coast**), Fr **République de Côte d'Ivoire** pop (1995e) 14 651 000; area 322 462 sq km/124 503 sq mi. Republic of W Africa, capital, Yamoussoukro; timezone GMT; wide range of ethnic groups; chief religions, local beliefs (63%), with Muslim (25%) and Christian (12%); official language, French, with many local languages; unit of currency, the franc CFA; sandy beaches and lagoons backed by broad forest-covered coastal plain; land rises towards savannah at 300–350 m/1000–1150 ft; Mt Nimba massif in NW at 1752 m/5748 ft; tropical climate, varying with distance from coast; rainfall decreases N; explored by Portuguese, 15th-c; French influence from 1842; declared French protectorate, 1889; colony, 1893; territory within French West Africa, 1904; independence, 1960; constitution provides for a multiparty system, but opposition parties allowed to function only since 1990; governed by a National Assembly, executive president, and Council of Ministers; economy largely based on agriculture, which employs c.82% of the population; world's largest cocoa producer, third largest coffee producer. >> Abidjan; Yamoussoukro; RR1005 political leaders

cotinga [ko**ting**ga] A bird native to the New World tropics; inhabits woodland. Most species eat fruit; some catch insects in flight. (Family: Cotingidae, 65 species.) >> umbrella bird

Cotman, John Sell (1782–1842) Watercolourist, born in Norwich, Norfolk. A leading member of the Norwich School, his best work shows a masterly arrangement of masses of light and shade, as in 'Greta Bridge' (c.1805, Norwich). >> landscape painting; Norwich School; watercolour

cotoneaster [kotohni**as**ter] A deciduous or evergreen shrub or small tree, native to N temperate regions; variable in size and shape, branches arching, spreading or erect; leaves oval to rounded, often with bright autumn colours; flowers usually in clusters, 5-petalled, white or pink; berries yellow, red, or black. (Genus: *Cotoneaster*, 50 species. Family: Rosaceae.)

Cotonou [kohto**noo**] 6°24N 2°31E, pop (1995e) 714 000. Port in S Benin, W Africa; largest city in Benin, and its political and economic centre, though not the official capital; airport; railway; university (1970). >> Benin [i]; Porto Novo

Cotopaxi [kohto**pak**see] 0°40S 78°26W. Active Andean volcano in NC Ecuador; height 5896 m/19 344 ft; highest active volcano in the world. >> Andes; Ecuador [i]

Cotswold Hills or **Cotswolds** [**kotz**wohld] Hill range mainly in Gloucestershire, SE England; extends 80 km/50 mi NE from Bath to Chipping Camden; rises to 333 m/1092 ft at Cleeve Cloud. >> England [i]

Cottee, Kay (1954–) Yachting record holder, born in Sydney, New South Wales, Australia. In 1988 she was the first woman to complete a solo, nonstop, unassisted circumnavigation of the world, in her sloop *First Lady*. Her time of 189 days was a women's record. She was named Australian of the Year in 1989.

Cotten, Joseph (1905–94) Film actor, born in Los Angeles, CA. A member of Orson Welles Mercury Theater radio ensemble from 1937, he starred in *Citizen Kane* (1941), *The Magnificent Ambersons* (1942), and *Journey into Fear* (1942). His many later films include *The Third Man* (1949) and *Heaven's Gate* (1980).

cotton The name of both a plant and the fibre it produces. Plants are annuals or perennials, many shrubby and growing up to 6 m/20 ft high; funnel-shaped flowers, up to 5 cm/2 in diameter, with creamy-white, yellow, or reddish petals. Ovoid seed pods (*bolls*) burst when ripe to reveal tightly packed seeds covered with creamy-white fibres which contain 87–90% cellulose. Cotton is graded according to the length (*staple*) and appearance of the fibres. The bolls are picked when ripe, either by hand or by machine. Four processes then follow: removal of the seeds (*ginning*), cleaning and separating (*carding*), stretching (*drawing*), and finally *spinning* into yarn. Major producing countries include the USA, Russia, China, India, Egypt, and Turkey. (Genus: *Gossypium*, c.20 species. Family: Malvaceae.) >> cellulose; cotton gin; mallow; mercerizing; *see illustration below*

cotton gin A machine, invented in 1793 by Eli Whitney in the USA, which separated the seeds from the cotton boll quickly and efficiently. It greatly increased productivity. >> cotton [i]; Whitney, Eli

cottonmouth A pit viper (*Agkistrodon piscivorus*) native to SE USA; inside of mouth white; lives near water; mainly nocturnal; one of the few snakes to eat carrion; venom very dangerous; also known as **water moccasin**. >> pit viper [i]

cottontail A type of rabbit, native to the New World; inhabits open country or woodland clearings. (Genus: *Sylvilagus*, 13 species.) >> myxomatosis; rabbit

cotton tree >> **kapok tree**

cottonwood >> **poplar**

cotyledons [kotileednz] Embryo leaves present in a seed. They are either fleshy and remain underground as a food store, or are thin and raised above ground to act as the first leaves of the seedling. >> dicotyledons; leaf [i]; monocotyledons

Coubertin, Pierre de [koobairtĩ] (1863–1937) Educator, born in Paris. He toured the USA and Europe to study educational methods, and visited Greece, where excavators were uncovering the ancient Olympic site. The visit inspired his proposal to revive the Olympic Games, and he became the first president (1896–1925) of the International Olympic Committee.

couch grass [kooch, kowch] A dull-green perennial grass (*Elymus repens*) with numerous creeping rhizomes, native to temperate regions; spikelets set edge-on to stem in a stiff, erect spike; a tenacious weed; also called **twitch grass**. (Family: Gramineae.) >> grass [i]; rhizome

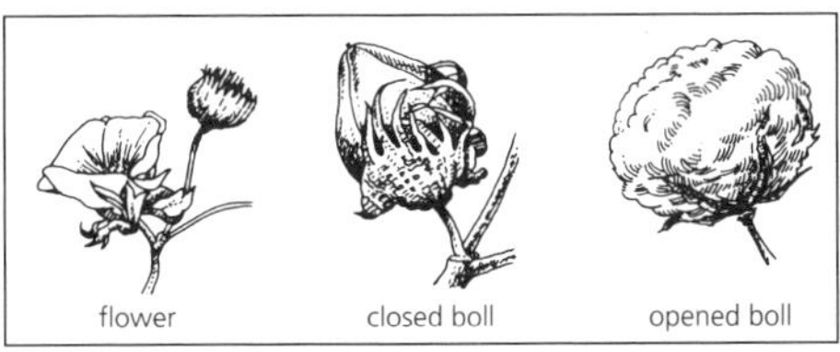

Cotton flower and boll

Coué, Emile [kooay] (1857–1926) Pharmacist, hypnotist, and pioneer of 'auto-suggestion', born in Troyes, France. His system became world-famous as *Couéism*, expressed in the famous formula 'Every day, in every way, I am becoming better and better'.

cougar A member of the cat family (*Felis concolor*), found from Canada to South America; grey or; reddish-brown; solitary; territorial; also known as **puma**, **mountain lion**, **catamount**, **panther**, **painter**. >> Felidae

coulomb [**koo**lom] SI unit of electric charge; symbol *C*; named after French physicist Charles Coulomb (1736–1806); defined as the quantity of electricity transported by a current of 1 ampere in 1 second. >> electricity

Council for Mutual Economic Assistance (COMECON) A body founded in 1949 by Stalin, and dominated by the Soviet Union; its purpose was ostensibly the economic integration of the Eastern bloc as a means of counteracting the economic power of the EEC and EFTA. It was disbanded in 1991, and replaced by the **Organization for National Economic Co-operation**. >> European Economic Community; European Free Trade Association

Council for the Protection of Rural England A pressure group founded in 1926 as the Council for the Preservation of Rural England. It aims to promote the protection and improvement of the countryside and rural amenities. The Council for the Protection of Rural Wales is a similar organization. >> conservation (earth sciences)

Council of Baltic States A grouping of 10 states established at a meeting in Copenhagen in 1992, with the aim of regional economic co-operation. Its members are Denmark, Estonia, Finland, Germany, Latvia, Lithuania, Norway, Poland, Russia, and Sweden.

Council of Europe An association of European states, established in 1949, whose representatives include the UK, France, Germany, Italy, Netherlands, and Ireland. It has a Committee of Foreign Ministers and a representative Consultative Assembly which meets at Strasbourg to discuss matters of common concern. A European Court of Human Rights was later added to this structure. There were 40 members in 1997.

Council of Ministers The body (established 1974) which allows the expression of national interest within the European Union, the minister involved depending on the subject under consideration. Agriculture and foreign affairs have the most regular meetings. >> European Council / Union

Council of the Church In the Orthodox and Roman Catholic Churches, a meeting of bishops of the whole Church to regulate doctrine and discipline. The Roman Catholic Church recognizes a Council if called by a pope, and its decisions, if approved by the pope, as infallible, and binding on the whole Church. >> Chalcedon / Lateran / Nicaea / Vatican, Councils of; bishop; infallibility; Orthodox Church; pope; Roman Catholicism

council tax >> **community charge**

count In spinning, a numerical system indicating the fineness of yarn. The *tex* unit (from *textile*), is the weight mass in grams of one kilometre of yarn, and is gradually replacing older systems such as 'cotton count' and 'denier'. >> yarn

count and **countess** The English translation of various foreign titles, such as Fr *comte/comtesse*. It is not part of the UK peerage. However, the title is used for the wife of an earl, and for female holders of earldoms. >> earl

counterfeiting Imitating some object (chiefly, currency notes and coin) in order to pass off the imitation as genuine. It is a criminal offence to counterfeit coin currently in circulation. Alterations to coins are also covered by statute. >> forgery

counter-intelligence >> **military intelligence**

counterpoint In music, the simultaneous combination of two or more melodic strands; distinct from 'harmony', which implies (in general terms) a chordal texture accompanying one or more melodic lines. >> canon (music); descant; fugue; harmony

Counter-Reformation A general movement of reform and missionary activity in the Roman Catholic Church from the mid 16th-c, stimulated in part by the Protestant Reformation. It included the revival of the monastic movement; doctrinal formulations by the Council of Trent; and liturgical and moral reforms. In a secular sense, the term also refers to the success of Roman Catholic powers in Europe in the late 16th-c and early 17th-c. >> monasticism; Reformation; Roman Catholicism

countertenor The falsetto voice of the adult male, trained and developed to sing alto parts, especially in sacred polyphony. The revival of interest in the countertenor as a solo voice has been largely due to the artistry of Alfred Deller. >> Deller

country and western A type of popular US music stemming from the hillbilly tradition of the years between the two World Wars. The country music of that time was played at barn dances, fairs, and similar gatherings, typically on a violin, banjo, and guitar. 'Country and western', a post-war fusion of the hillbilly tradition with the more jazz-orientated country music of the SW, has been popularized by such performers as Merle Haggard (1937–), Johnny Cash (1932–), and Charley Pride (1938–). The recognized centre of country and western music is Nashville, TN. >> gospel music; Nashville–Davidson; pop music

country dance Historic social dances based on John Playford's *The English Dancing Master* (1651). The emphasis was on spatial design, with couples in long or circular sets, using simple walking steps.

Country Party >> **National Party** (Australia)

Countryside Commission, formerly (to 1991) **Countryside Commission for England and Wales** A UK government amenity agency set up in 1968 to replace the National Parks Commission. It advises the government on matters of countryside interest, and formulates policy for National Parks. The Commission now covers England only; there is a separate Countryside Commission for Wales. >> National Park; Scottish National Heritage

county council The body elected to carry out such responsibilities as may be statutorily determined, within a defined geographical boundary. In non-metropolitan areas of England and Wales, it is the higher in a two-tier local government system whose powers are delegated by parliament. >> local government

county court A court system of England and Wales, concerned with civil disputes, established in 1846. It deals with certain cases of contract and tort, landlord and tenant disputes, matrimonial cases (including divorce), and the relatively informal small-claims procedure. >> contract; tort

Couperin, François [**koo**perĩ] (1668–1733) Composer, born in Paris. Known mainly as a harpsichord composer (whose influence on Bach was profound), he also composed chamber concertos and church music. >> harpsichord

courante [koo**rahnt**] A Baroque dance in triple metre; it became a standard movement of the instrumental suite. >> Baroque (music); suite

Courbet, Gustave [koorbay] (1819–77) Painter, born in Ornans, France. The founder of Realism, in 1844 he began exhibiting pictures in which everyday scenes were portrayed with complete sincerity and absence of idealism, such as 'Studio of the Painter: an Allegory of Realism' (1855, Musée d'Orsay, Paris). >> Realism

coureurs de bois [koorer duh bwah] >> **Métis**

courgette [koor**zhet**] (UK) or **zucchini** (US) A variety of marrow with small, green or yellow fruits (*Cucurbita pepo*). (Family: Cucurbitaceae.) >> marrow (botany)

Courrèges, André [koorezh] (1923–) Fashion designer, born at Pau, France. He opened his own house in 1961, and is famous for his stark, futuristic, 'Space Age' designs.

courser A long-legged, short-winged, running bird, native to Africa and SW Asia; inhabits deserts; dull-coloured plumage; long curved bill; three forward-pointing toes only on each foot; seldom flies; nests on ground. (Family: Glareolidae. Subfamily: Cursoriinae, 7 species.) >> pratincole

coursing A blood sport involving greyhounds, which seek out their prey by sight and not scent. The dogs pursue in pairs, as opposed to being in packs, and the performance of one dog against another is judged. >> blood sports

Court, Margaret (Jean) [kaw(r)t], *née* **Smith** (1942–) Lawn tennis player, born at Albury, New South Wales, Australia. She was the winner of more Grand Slam events than any other player: 10 Wimbledon titles (including the singles in 1963, 1965, 1970), 22 US titles, 13 French, and 21 Australian. >> Connolly, Maureen; tennis, lawn [i]

court martial A court which tries offences against naval, military (ie army), and air force law. The court is composed of three to five serving officers advised on the law by a judge advocate, a barrister. >> barrister

Court of Appeal An English court, with civil and criminal divisions, which hears appeals from other courts. The civil division hears appeals from the High Court and the county court; its head is the Master of the Rolls. The criminal division hears appeals from the Crown Court; its head is the Lord Chief Justice. >> county court; High Court of Justice

Court of Auditors The body within the institutions of the European Union which is responsible for overseeing the implementation of the budget. Its role is to counter fraud and inefficiency. >> European Union

Court of Justice of the European Communities The European Court which sits at Luxembourg, an institution of the European Union (EU), with its judges being appointed by the member states. Its functions involve the interpretation of EU treaties and legislation, and ruling on relevant points of law referred to it by domestic courts of member states. >> European Union

court of law A forum for settling legal disputes. There are two broad categories of courts as traditionally distinguished: **civil courts**, dealing with disputes between private persons; and **criminal courts**, dealing with offences against society generally. >> Admiralty / Assize / Divisional Court; Court of Appeal / Justice of the European Communities / Session; arbitration; civil law; tribunal

Court of Session A Scottish court, sitting in Edinburgh, which deals with civil matters. It has an Outer House and a more senior Inner House, analogous to the High Court and Court of Appeal respectively. >> Court of Appeal; High Court of Justice

Cousins, Frank [**kuh**zinz] (1904–86) Trade union leader, born in Nottingham. In 1955 he became general secretary of the Transport and General Worker's Union. He was also minister of technology (1964–6) until he resigned over the prices and incomes policy. >> prices and incomes policy; trade union

Cousins, Robin (1957–) Ice skater, born in Bristol, SW England. In 1980 he became only the second British male to win an Olympic figure-skating gold medal, and he was World freeskating champion for three successive years (1978–80). He turned professional in 1980, and has been artistic director of the Ice Castle International Training Center in California since 1989. He later returned to England and in 1997 co-founded the company, Adventure! on Ice, creating and producing programmes for television.

Cousteau, Jacques (Yves) [koos**toh**] (1910–97) Naval officer and underwater explorer, born at Saint-André, France. He invented the Aqualung diving apparatus (1943) and a process of underwater television. He wrote widely on his subject, and his films included the Oscar-winning *The Golden Fish* (1960).

covalent >> **chemical bond**

covenant 1 A term used in certain legal systems for a written document under seal; also known as a **deed**. It contains a promise to act in a certain way, which is signed, sealed, and takes effect on delivery. The term is often used in the UK for members of charities to covenant their membership subscriptions. The charity claims back from the tax authorities a sum equal to the tax paid by the member. >> contract; taxation **2** In the Hebrew Scriptures, the agreement between God and his chosen people which was the basis of Jewish religion; especially identified with the giving of the law to Moses on Mt Sinai, but preceded by a covenant with Abraham. >> Abraham; Moses; Ten Commandments

Covenanters Originally, signatories (and their successors) of the **National Covenant** (1638) in Scotland, who resisted the theory of the 'Divine Right of Kings' and the imposition of an episcopal system on the Presbyterian Church of Scotland. Until Presbyterianism was established in 1690, they were savagely persecuted. >> Church of Scotland; episcopacy; Presbyterianism

Covent Garden [**kov**nt] A square in C London, known for the fruit and vegetable market that operated there for nearly three centuries; it also gives its name to the Royal Opera House close by. Once the garden of a convent in Westminster, the site was developed in the 17th-c. The market was relocated in 1974, and the buildings restored. >> London; Royal Opera House

Coventry [**kov**ntree], Middle Eng **Couentrey** 52°25N 1°30W, pop (1995e) 302 000. Industrial city in West Midlands, C England; Benedictine priory founded in 1043, around which the town grew; important centre of clothing manufacture from 17th-c; railway; University of Warwick (1965), Coventry University (1992); old cathedral (1433) destroyed during World War 2; new cathedral designed by Sir Basil Spence (consecrated 1962); football league team, Coventry City (Sky Blues). >> West Midlands

Coverdale, Miles (1488–1568) Bible scholar, born in York, North Yorkshire. His translation of the Bible (**Coverdale's Bible**, the first complete one in English) appeared in 1535, and he then superintended the work which led to the *Great Bible* (1539). He also edited the work known as *Cranmer's Bible* (1540). >> Bible

covered wagon >> **prairie schooner**

cow >> **bull** (zoology)

Coward, Sir Noel (Pierce) (1899–1973) Actor, playwright, and composer, born in Teddington, Greater London. Among his many successes were *Hay Fever* (1925), *Private Lives* (1930), and *Blithe Spirit* (1941). He wrote the music as well as the lyrics for most of his works.

Cowes [kowz] 50°45N 1°18W, pop (1995e) 17 300. Town in the Isle of Wight, S England; a notable yachting centre; Cowes Castle (1543); Cowes Week (Aug). >> Wight, Isle of

Cowley, Abraham (1618–67) Poet, born in London. His main works were the influential *Pindarique Odes* (1656) and his unfinished epic on King David, *Davideis* (1656).

cow parsley A biennial or perennial (*Anthriscus sylvestris*), growing to 1·5 m/5 ft, native to Europe, temperate Asia, and N Africa; stems hollow, grooved; flowers small, white; fruit smooth; also called **Queen Anne's lace** and **keck**. (Family: Umbelliferae.) >> parsley

cow parsnip >> **hogweed**

Cowpens, Battle of During the US War of Independence, an engagement in S Carolina in which a small American army under Daniel Morgan (1736–1802) defeated a British force under Banastre Tarleton (1754–1833). >> American Revolution

Cowper, William [**koo**per] (1731–1800) Poet, born at Berkhamsted, Hertfordshire. His ballad of John Gilpin (1783) was highly successful, as was his long poem about rural ease, *The Task* (1785).

cow pox A virus disease of cattle characterized by small blisters (*pocks*) on the teats; also known as **kine pox**. The contents of these blisters were used by Edward Jenner in 1798 to vaccinate humans against the related *smallpox*. >> Jenner; smallpox; virus

cowrie A marine snail with a glossy, smooth, and often highly patterned shell, largely covered by lobes of mantle; used as decorations and even as currency on Pacific Islands. (Class: Gastropoda. Order: Mesogastropoda.) >> coral; gastropod; shell; snail

cowslip A perennial (*Primula veris*) with a rosette of oblong, slightly crinkled leaves, native to Europe and Asia; flowers 1–30 at the tip of a common stalk, drooping, petals yellow with orange spots at base. (Family: Primulaceae.) >> polyanthus

Cox, Courtenay (1964–) Actor, born in Birmingham, AL. She became well known through her role as Monica Geller in the acclaimed television series *Friends* (1994–). Roles in feature films began with *Down Twisted* (1986), and include *Scream* (1996) and *Commandments* (1997).

coyote [koy**oh**tee] A member of the dog family (*Canis latrans*), native to North and Central America; inhabits grassland and open woodland; also known as **prairie wolf**, **barking wolf**, **little wolf**, or (in fur trade) **cased wolf**. Coyotes have been subject to bounties, and are still often hunted by ranchers and farmers. >> Canidae

coypu [**koy**poo] A cavy-like rodent (*Myocastor coypus*), native to South America (introduced elsewhere); large (length over 1 m/3¼ ft); rat-like with broad blunt muzzle; farmed for soft underfur; also known as **nutria**. (Family: Myocastoridae.) >> cavy; rodent

CPU >> **digital computer**

crab A typically marine crustacean with a front pair of legs specialized as pincers (*chelipeds*) and used for food capture, signalling, and fighting; usually walks sideways, using four pairs of walking legs; also capable of swimming; body broad, flattened, with a hard outer covering (*carapace*); abdomen permanently tucked up beneath body; eyes usually movable on stalks; many species exploited commercially for food. (Class: Malacostraca. Order: Decapoda.) >> crustacean; Decapoda [i]; fiddler / hermit / spider crab; plankton

Crabbe, George (1754–1832) Poet, born in Aldeburgh, Suffolk. His best-known early work is *The Village* (1783). His later narrative poems include *The Parish Register* (1807) and *The Borough* (1810). >> Burke, Edmund

crabeater seal A true seal (*Lobodon carcinophagus*), native to the Antarctic and sub-Antarctic; teeth with deeply notched margins, forming a sieve when mouth is shut; eats krill (despite its name); fastest true seal on land (up to 25 kph/15 mph); one of the world's most numerous large mammals. >> krill; seal (biology)

Crab nebula The remnant of a star seen by Chinese astronomers to explode spectacularly on 4 July 1054. Photographs show a tangled web of filaments threading a luminous nebula. The explosion which triggered the nebula was a supernova, which left a dense neutron star at the centre, now observed as a pulsar rotating 30 times a second. >> nebula; neutron star; pulsar; supernova

crab-plover >> **plover**

crack A blend of cocaine, baking powder, and water. The cocaine hardens to white cinder chunks which can be smoked in a small pipe. The effect is immediate. This form of cocaine is held to be extremely addictive. >> cocaine; drug addiction

Cracow >> **Kraków**

Cradock, Fanny, *née* **Phyllis Primrose-Pechey** (1909–94) British writer and television cook. From 1955 she became known for the television programmes presented with her husband, Johnny. She wrote cookery books, children's books, novels, and press columns which were notorious for their social pretension and outspoken opinions.

Craig, Edward (Henry) Gordon (1872–1966) Stage designer, actor, director, and theorist, born in Stevenage, Hertfordshire. He published the theatre journal, *The Mask* (1908–29), which together with his scene designs and his books, *On the Art of the Theatre* (1911) and *The Theatre Advancing* (1921), had a profound influence on modern theatre practice. >> Irving, Henry

crake The name often given to any smallish rail with a short, chicken-like bill (45 species). >> corncrake; rail

Cram, Steve, popular name of **Stephen Cram** (1960–) Athlete, born in Gateshead, Tyne and Wear. He won the World Championship gold medal at 1500 m in 1983, and the Commonwealth Games gold medals at 1500 m (1982, 1986) and 800 m (1986). In 1985 he set three world records in 20 days at 1500 m, 1 mi, and 2000 m. >> athletics

Cranach, Lucas [**krah**nakh], known as **Lucas Cranach the Elder** (1472–1553) Painter, so named from Kronach, near Bamberg, Germany, where he was born. He was closely associated with the German Reformers, many of whom (including Luther) he painted. A 'Crucifixion' in the Stadtkirche, Weimar, is his masterpiece. Of three sons, all painters, the second, **Lucas Cranach the Younger** (1515–86), painted so like his father that their works are difficult to distinguish. >> Reformation

cranberry A dwarf, creeping, evergreen shrub (*Vaccinium oxycoccos*), native to N temperate regions; flowers on long, slender stalks, pink, four petals, curling backwards; berry round or pear-shaped, red- or brown-spotted, edible. (Family: Ericaceae.) >> blueberry

Crane, (Harold) Hart (1899–1932) Poet, born in Garrettsville, OH. His most important work is contained in *The White Buildings* (1926), a collection on New York life, and *The Bridge* (1930), an epic using Brooklyn Bridge as its focal point.

Crane, Stephen (1871–1900) Writer and war correspondent, born in Newark, NJ. He became known as a novelist through *Maggie: a Girl of the Streets* (1893) and *The Red Badge of Courage* (1895), a vivid story of the Civil War.

crane (engineering) A machine which can lift and position loads. It essentially consists of an arm (or *jib*) carrying a pulley, attached to a post round which it can rotate, and with a rope which can be wound round a barrel. Cranes are much used in docks (with special designs used for container traffic), in construction (**tower cranes**), and in engineering (often as **gantry cranes**). >> machine ℹ; pulley

crane (ornithology) A long-legged, long-necked bird, height 0·6–1·5 m/ 2–5 ft; worldwide except South America, New Zealand, and the Pacific; adult usually with head partly naked; inhabits flat wetlands and wet plains. (Family: Gruidae, 15 species.) >> demoiselle

cranefly A long-legged, true fly; adult body slender, legs fragile, readily discarded if trapped; larvae known as **leatherjackets**; adults also known as **daddy longlegs**; c.13 500 species. (Order: Diptera. Family: Tipulidae.) >> fly; larva

cranesbill An annual or perennial of the genus *Geranium*, native to temperate regions; flowers usually white to purple or blue, 5-petalled; fruit with long beak resembling a bird's bill, exploding when ripe. (Genus: *Geranium*, 400 species. Family: Geraniaceae.) >> geranium

Cranko, John [**krang**koh] (1927–73) Dancer, choreographer, and director, born in Rustenburg, South Africa. He choreographed for both Sadler's Wells and the Royal Ballet companies, and in 1961 became ballet director of the Stuttgart Ballet. >> ballet; choreography

Cranmer, Thomas (1489–1556) Archbishop of Canterbury, born in Aslockton, Nottinghamshire. He annulled Henry VIII's marriages to Catherine of Aragon and to Anne Boleyn (1536), and divorced him from Anne of Cleves (1540). He was largely responsible for the Book of Common Prayer (1549, 1552). On Henry's death, he agreed to the plan to divert the succession from Mary to Lady Jane Grey (1553), for which he was arraigned for treason and burned alive. >> Book of Common Prayer; Henry VIII; Protestantism; Reformation

craps A casino dice game of American origin, adapted from the game *hazard* by Bernard de Mandeville in New Orleans in 1813. Using two dice, a player loses throwing 2, 3, and 12, but wins with 7 or 11. If the player's first throw makes 4, 5, 6, 8, 9, or 10, this number is called the *point*; the player then continues to throw until the same number is rolled again (*making the point*), thus giving a win, or throws a 7 and thus loses (*craps out*). >> casino

craquelure [krakuh**lür**] The distinctive pattern of fine cracks on the surface of a painting or glazed pottery. Normally the result of aging, craquelure can be faked.

Crashaw, Richard [**kray**shaw] (c.1613–49) Religious poet, born in London. He is best known for his volume of Latin poems, *Epigrammatum sacrorum liber* (1634, A Book of Sacred Epigrams) and *Steps to the Temple* (1646).

Crassus, Marcus Licinius, nickname **Dives** (Lat 'wealthy') (c.115–53 BC) Roman politician. A friend of Caesar, he formed the First Triumvirate with him and Pompey (60 BC). In 53 BC, as Governor of Syria, he attacked the Parthians, but was killed at the Battle of Carrhae. >> Caesar; Pompey; Roman history ℹ

crater A circular depression on the surface of a planetary body. Those on Mercury, the Moon, and most of the natural satellites of planets have been formed by impacts with meteorites and comets in the remote past. The Moon, Mars, and Io (one of Jupiter's satellites) also have volcanic craters. Craters on Earth have been caused by meteorites (eg Meteor Crater, Arizona) and by volcanic explosions (eg Crater Lake, Oregon). >> meteorite; volcano

Crater (Lat 'cup') An ancient constellation in the S sky. >> constellation; RR968

Crater Lake (Canada) >> **Chubb Crater**

Crater Lake (USA) Circular crater lake in SW Oregon, USA, in the Cascade Range; 9·5 km/6 mi across; area 52 sq km/ 20 sq mi; 604 m/1982 ft deep; altitude 1879 m/6165 ft; in a large pit formed by the destruction of the summit of a prehistoric volcano. >> caldera; Oregon

Crawford, Joan, originally **Lucille Fay Le Sueur** (1904–77) Film actress, born in San Antonio, TX. She became an established star in the 1930s and 1940s, winning an Oscar for *Mildred Pierce* (1945); her last great role was in *Whatever Happened to Baby Jane?* (1962). A very critical biography, *Mommie Dearest*, by her adopted daughter Christine, was filmed in 1981.

Crawford, Michael (1942–) British actor. In the 1970s the television series *Some Mothers Do 'Ave 'Em* made him a household name in Britain, and he went on to star in musicals, such as *Billy* (1974), *Barnum* (1981), and *The Phantom of the Opera* (1986, Tony). His films include *Hello Dolly* (1968) and *Condorman* (1980).

crayfish A typically freshwater, lobster-like crustacean with a well-developed abdomen and front pair of legs modified as powerful pincers (chelipeds); many species exploited commercially for food. (Class: Malacostraca. Order: Decapoda.) >> crustacean; Decapoda ℹ; lobster

Crazy Horse, Sioux name **Tashunka Witco** (c.1842–77) Oglala Sioux Chief, born in South Dakota. Regarded as the foremost Sioux military leader, he defeated General Custer at the Battle of the Little Bighorn (1876). He is regarded as a symbol of Sioux resistance and as their greatest leader. >> Custer

cream of tartar >> **tartaric acid**

creationism Originally, the belief that God creates a soul for each human individual at conception or birth. It is now commonly applied to the belief that the Genesis account of creation in the Bible accurately describes the origins of the world and humanity. It is opposed to the theory of evolution. >> Christianity

Crécy, Battle of [**kray**see] A battle between France and England in the Hundred Years' War. Edward III routed a larger French army, mainly cavalry, near Abbeville (Somme). >> Edward III; Hundred Years' War

credit card A plastic card which is used instead of cash or cheque to pay for goods or services. The best-known companies are *Visa*, *Mastercard*, *American Express*, and *Access*. Credit cards differ from **charge cards**, in that there is a specified credit limit. Charge cards have no limit, but full repayment is to be made each month. >> cheque card

credit rating A system used to assess the ability of a company (or individual) to pay for goods and services, or the ability to borrow and repay. Popular rating systems in the USA are *Moody* and *Standard and Poor*. All companies are assigned a rating code: the highest is AAA, next is AA, and so on.

credits The recognition given to someone who has successfully completed a part of a modular course. American education is firmly based on the notion of accumulated credits. A particular advantage is that students know from the beginning how many credits they must acquire in order to obtain the qualification they seek. >> Open University

credit union A co-operative venture where members save together and lend to each other, mainly short-term consumer loans. The system is popular in North America, where there are some 50 000 credit unions.

Cree A North American Algonkin Indian group from the Canadian Subarctic region, originally hunters and fishermen.

Creek A North American Indian people, originally from Georgia and Alabama, c.44 000 (1990 census). They were forcibly moved to Oklahoma in 1837, where they became one of the Five Civilized Tribes. >> Five Civilized Tribes; Seminole

cremation Burning the remains of a dead person. The practice was recorded in ancient Greece for soldiers killed in battle. Discouraged in the past by Christians because of its pagan associations, it is the regular form of disposal by Hindus. Today cremation is becoming more common because of lack of space in cemeteries. >> sati

creodont An extinct flesh-eating mammal; known from the early Tertiary period around the world except Australia and South America; distinguished from true carnivores by shorter limbs, unfused wrist bones, cleft claw bone, and shearing teeth (*carnassials*) formed from molars. (Order: Creodonta.) >> carnivore ℹ; mammal ℹ; Tertiary period; RR976

creole A pidgin language which has become the mother-tongue of a speech community, as has happened with Jamaican creole. A creole develops a wider range of words, grammatical structures, and styles than is found in a pidgin. >> pidgin

Creon or **Kreon** [**kree**on] A name (meaning 'ruler') given to several legendary Greek kings, but especially to the brother of Jocasta, regent of Thebes, who awarded the throne to Oedipus. >> Jocasta; Oedipus

creosote [**kree**osoht] A fraction of coal tar, boiling point c.250°C, containing a variety of toxic aromatic compounds giving it strong antiseptic and preservative properties. >> coal tar

cress The name given to several different members of the cabbage family, often small weeds, some cultivated as salad plants. (Family: Cruciferae.) >> cabbage; garden cress; watercress

Cressida [**kres**ida] In mediaeval accounts of the Trojan War, the daughter of Calchas, a Trojan priest. Beloved by Troilus, a Trojan prince, she deserted him for Diomedes when transferred to the Greek camp. >> Diomedes; Troilus

Cretaceous period [kre**tay**shuhs] The last geological period of the Mesozoic era, lasting from 144 to 65 million years ago, characterized by the emergence of flowering plants and the dominance and extinction of dinosaurs. >> dinosaur ℹ; geological time scale; Mesozoic era; RR976

Crete, Gr **Kríti**, Ital **Candia**, ancient **Creta** pop (1995e) 550 000; area 8336 sq km/3218 sq mi. Island region of Greece, in the Mediterranean Sea, S of the Cyclades island group; length 256 km/159 mi; width 14–60 km/9–37 mi; largest of the Greek islands; highest point, Psiloritis (2456 m/8058 ft); evidence of settlement from c.6000 BC; important Minoan civilization, c.2000 BC; ruled at various times by Greeks, Romans, Turks, and Arabs; passed to Greece in 1913; German occupation in World War 2, after airborne invasion, 1941; capital, Heraklion; ancient sites at Knossos, Gortys, Lato, Phaistos. >> Greece ℹ; Heraklion; Knossos

cretinism A condition affecting the newly born child who suffers from the inadequate production of thyroid hormones (*thyroxine*). There is a failure of normal growth and development, with puffiness of the skin, notably of the face. >> dwarfism; thyroid hormone

Creutzfeldt-Jacob Disease [**kroyts**velt **ya**kob] A form of chronic prion disease in humans, involving the degeneration of the central nervous system; named after German neuropathologists Heinz Creutzfeldt and Andreas Jacob. The disease, which can be genetic or sporadic, is characterized by an onset typically between 45 and 60 years of age, neurological syptoms, and electroencephalographic changes. It progresses rapidly, with death occurring within 12 months. Reports in 1995 indicated the emergence of a new variant of the disease in patients under the age of 45, associated with the presence of 'kuru plaques' in the brain. The appearance of this new strain has highlighted concerns that inter-species transmission of prion disease to humans from cows with BSE has occurred in the UK. >> bovine spongiform encephalopathy; BSE crisis; central nervous system; electroencephalography; kuru

cribbage A card game popular in public houses in the UK, played by two, three, or four people with a standard pack of 52 cards and a holed board known as the **cribbage board** or *peg board*. Points are scored according to cards dropped (ie for playing a card that makes a pair, a run of three or more, etc). All scores are marked on the peg board. >> playing cards

Crick, Francis (Harry Compton) (1916–) Biophysicist, born in Northampton. With J D Watson in 1953 he constructed a molecular model of the complex genetic material DNA; and in 1958 proposed that DNA determines the sequence of amino acids in a polypeptide. He shared the Nobel Prize for Physiology or Medicine in 1962. >> DNA i; peptide; Watson, James

cricket (entomology) A large, grasshopper-like insect; forewings box-like and bent down round sides of body; many species have a well-developed sound-producing mechanism for auditory communication; c.2000 species. (Order: Orthoptera. Family: Gryllidae.) >> grasshopper; insect i

cricket (sport) A bat-and-ball team game of 11-a-side. A wicket of three stumps surmounted by a pair of bails is placed at each end of a grassy pitch 22 yd (20·1 m) in length. Each team takes it in turn to bat and bowl. The aim of the batting team is to defend the two wickets while trying to score as many runs as possible before being dismissed. Each member of the team must bat, and two batsmen are on the field at any one time, one in front of each wicket. The attacking team consists of a bowler, a wicket-keeper (who stands behind the wicket which the bowler is attacking), and nine fielders, who are placed at strategic positions around the field. A bowler delivers an 'over' of (usually) six balls to one wicket, before a different bowler attacks the other wicket. If the batsman hits a ball (and in certain other circumstances), he may decide it is safe to run between the two wickets, exchanging places with the other batsman, in which case he scores a 'run'. Several runs may be scored following a single hit, but if the ball reaches the boundary of the field, four runs are scored automatically, and six if it has not bounced on the way. A batsman can be got out by being 'bowled' (the ball from the bowler knocks his wicket down), 'caught' (the batsman hits the ball so that it is caught by a fielder), 'stumped' (the wicket-keeper knocks the wicket down with the ball while the defending batsman is standing outside his 'safe ground' or 'crease'), 'run out' (the wicket towards which one of the batsmen is running is knocked down before the batsman reaches the safe ground), and 'leg before wicket', or 'lbw' (the lower part of the batsman's leg prevents the ball from the bowler from reaching the wicket). He may also be out if he hits his own wicket while playing a shot, hits the ball twice, prevents a fielder taking a catch ('obstructing the field'), uses a hand to prevent the ball hitting the wicket ('handled the ball') or takes more than three minutes to replace the previous batsman once the wicket has fallen ('timed out'). Once ten batsmen have been dismissed, the innings comes to a close, but a team can stop its innings ('declare') at any time before that, if it thinks it has made enough runs. In first-class cricket, each team has two innings, and the one with the greater number of runs at the end of the match is the winner, provided the other side has completed – or declared – both its innings. The earliest known laws of cricket were drawn up in 1744. Test matches are normally over five days, county championship matches over four days. Limited-over competitions are normally concluded in one day, and last for a specific number of overs per side. >> Ashes, the; MCC; Sheffield Shield; RR1049

Crimea [kriy**mee**a], Russ **Krym** area 25 900 sq km/ 10 000 sq mi. Peninsula in S Ukraine; bounded S and W by the Black Sea, and E by the Sea of Azov; length, 320 km/ 200 mi; Greek colonization, 7th-c BC; autonomous Soviet republic, 1921; an oblast of the Russian SFSR, 1946; transferred to the Ukraine, 1954; tourism on coast. >> Black Sea; Crimean War; Ukraine i

Crimean War A war fought in the Crimean peninsula by Britain and France against Russia. Major battles were fought in 1854 at the R Alma (20 Sep), Balaclava (25 Oct), and Inkerman (5 Nov). The fall of the Russian fortress at Sebastopol (Sep 1855) led to peace negotiations, finally agreed at Paris (Mar 1856). >> Balaclava, Battle of; Crimea; Nightingale

Criminal Injuries Compensation Scheme A British scheme established in 1964, whereby the state pays compensation to certain victims who have suffered personal injury attributable to a crime of violence. Certain classes of victims, offences, and injuries are excluded, and any payment made is reduced by the amount of damages or compensation awarded by a civil or criminal court. The first such scheme was established in New Zealand in 1963. >> compensation order; criminal law

Criminal Investigation Department >> **CID**

criminal law A branch of law which deals with offences against society generally. Investigation of breaches of the criminal law is generally the responsibility of the police. The responsibility for prosecution varies between jurisdictions: for example, in England and Wales, it belongs to the Director of Public Prosecutions and the Crown Prosecution Service; in most US jurisdictions, to a local district attorney or county prosecutor; and in federal jurisdictions, to a US attorney. >> civil law; Crown Prosecution Service; jury; police; prosecution

crimp The waviness which occurs naturally in wool fibres, imparting a soft bulkiness to yarns. Crimping of synthetic fibres extends their range of uses into knitting and carpet yarns, and the manufacture of softer woven fabrics.

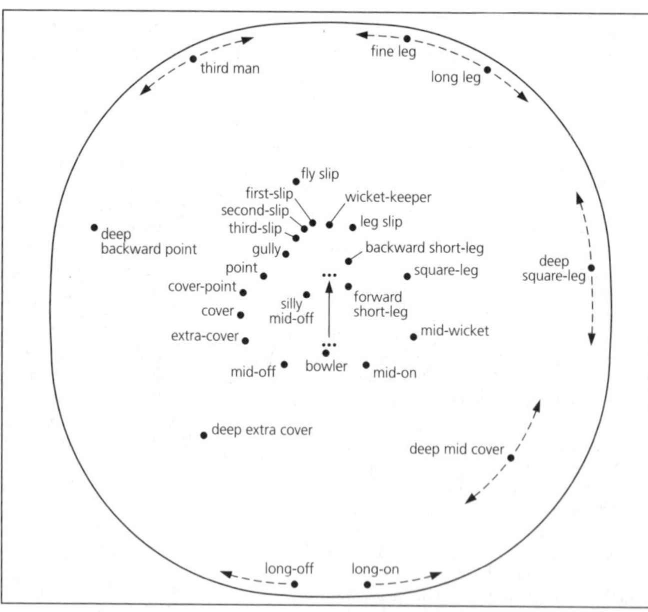

Cricket field positions

crinoid [**kriy**noyd] A primitive marine invertebrate (echinoderm), typically attached to the seabed by a long stalk; mouth and arms on upper surface; long fossil record; c.650 living species; also known as **sea lilies** and **feather stars**. (Phylum: Echinodermata. Class: Crinoidea.) >> echinoderm ℹ

Crippen, Hawley Harvey, known as **Dr Crippen** (1862–1910) Physician and murderer, born in Michigan, USA. He settled in London in 1900. After poisoning his wife, he and his mistress attempted to escape to Canada on board the *SS Montrose*. The suspicious captain contacted Scotland Yard by radiotelegraphy (the first use of radio for a murder case). They were arrested, and Crippen was hanged in London.

Cripps, Sir (Richard) Stafford (1889–1952) British Labour statesman, born in London. During the 1930s he was associated with several extreme left-wing movements, and was expelled from the Labour Party in 1939 for his 'popular front' opposing Chamberlain's policy of appeasement. In the 1945 Labour government, he was readmitted to the Party and appointed President of the Board of Trade. In 1947 he became minister of economic affairs and then Chancellor of the Exchequer, introducing a successful austerity policy. >> Chamberlain, Neville; Labour Party

Cristofori, Bartolomeo [kris**to**foree] (1655–1731) Harpsichord maker, born in Padua, Italy. He is usually credited with the invention of the pianoforte in c.1710. >> harpsichord; piano

critical mass The smallest mass of material of a given type and formed into a given shape able to sustain a nuclear-fission chain reaction. For a mass of material greater than the critical mass, large amounts of energy are released via the fission-chain reaction in a small fraction of a second. >> atomic bomb; chain reaction

Crittenden Compromise In the months preceding the American Civil War, an attempt by Senator John J Crittenden of Kentucky to resolve the crisis between North and South by formally recognizing slavery in territories S of 36°30. This proved unacceptable to Abraham Lincoln. >> American Civil War; slave trade

croaker >> **drumfish**

Croatia [kroh**ay**sha], official name **Republic of Croatia**, Serbo-Croatian **Republika Hrvatska** pop (1995e) 4 876 000; area 56 538 sq km/21 824 sq mi. Republic in the Balkan peninsula of SE Europe; capital, Zagreb; timezone GMT +1; major ethnic groups (pre-civil war), Croat (75%), Serb (12%), Slovenes (1%); language, Croatian; religions, Roman Catholic, Eastern Orthodox; currency, the kuna; fertile Pannonian Plain in C and E; mountainous, barren coastal region near Dinaric Alps; Adriatic coast to W; one third of the country forested; coastal Velebit and Velika Kapela ranges reach heights of 2200 m/7200 ft; chief rivers, the Drava, Danube, Sava; continental climate in Pannonian Basin, average temperatures −1°C (Jan), 19°C (Jul); average annual rainfall 750 mm/30 in; Mediterranean climate on Adriatic, average temperatures 6°C (Jan), 24°C (Jul); Slavic coast tribes migrated to White Russia, 6th-c; converted to Christianity, 7th–9th-c; Croat kingdom reached its peak, 11th-c; Lázló I of Hungary claimed Croatian throne, 1091; Turkish defeat of Hungary brought Pannonian Croatia under Ottoman rule, 1526; rest of Croatia elected Ferdinand of Austria as their king, and fought Turkey; joint crownland with Slovenia, 1888; formed Kingdom of Serbs, Croats and Slovenes with Montenegro and Serbia, 1918; became part of Yugoslavia, 1929; proclaimed an independent state during occupation by the Axis Powers, 1941–5; nationalist upsurges against communist rule during 1950s; declaration of independence in 1991, followed by confrontation with the National Army, and civil war; autonomy claim by Serb-dominated Krajina area, 1991; UN peace-keeping forces deployed, 1992, but fighting continued sporadically into 1993; ceasefire followed by a peace treaty, 1995; governed by a president, prime minister, and an Assembly, consisting of a Chamber of Deputies and a Chamber of Districts; chiefly an agricultural region, with tourism on Adriatic coast; natural resources include bauxite, coal, copper, iron; economy badly affected by the civil war. >> Yugoslavia ℹ; Yugoslavian Civil War; Zagreb; RR1005 political leaders

Croce, Benedetto [**kroh**chay] (1866–1952) Italian statesman, philosopher, historian, and critic, born in Pescasseroli, Italy. He founded the review *La Critica* in 1903, and made major contributions to idealistic aesthetics in his *Estetica* (1902, Aesthetic) and *La Poesia* (1936, Poetry). He was opposed to totalitarianism, and with the fall of Mussolini (1943) helped to resurrect Liberal institutions in Italy. >> idealism; totalitarianism

Crockett, Davy, popular name of **David Crockett** (1786–1836) Backwoodsman, born in Green Co, TN. He died fighting for Texas at the battle of the Alamo. Highly embellished stories of his exploits have assumed mythological proportions. >> Alamo

crocodile A reptile native to tropical rivers and estuaries worldwide; length, up to 7·5 m/25 ft; fourth tooth from the front on each side of the lower jaw is visible when the jaws are closed (unlike the alligator); eats a range of vertebrate prey; eggs have hard shells. Crocodilians (crocodiles, alligators, and the gharial) are the descendants of an ancient reptile group, the *archosaurs* (which included the extinct dinosaurs and pterodactyls). (Order: Crocodylia. Family: Crocodylidae, 14 species.) >> alligator ℹ; dinosaur ℹ; gharial; reptile

crocus A perennial producing corms, native to Europe and Asia; leaves grass-like with distinctive silvery stripe down centre; stalkless flowers, goblet-shaped with long, slender tube, mainly white, yellow, or purple, closing up at night. (Genus: *Crocus*, 75 species. Family: Iridaceae.) >> corm

Croesus [**kree**suhs] (?–c.546 BC) The last king of Lydia (c.560–546 BC), who succeeded his father, Alyattes. His conquests and mines made his wealth proverbial. Cyrus II defeated and imprisoned him (546 BC), but his death is a mystery. >> Lydia

crofting A form of small-scale subsistence farming characteristic of the Highlands and Islands of Scotland. A croft usually comprises a house, a few hectares of arable land, and grazing rights on the hill. >> subsistence agriculture

Crohn's disease [krohn] A persisting but fluctuating inflammation of any part of the alimentary canal, but especially of the small intestine. It is named after US physician Burrill Crohn (1884–1983). >> alimentary canal; inflammation

Cro-Magnon Man [kroh**man**yon] The earliest fully modern humans (*Homo sapiens sapiens*) from late Pleistocene Europe (40 000–10 000 BC), named after the 1868 discovery of fossil skeletons at Cro-Magnon in SW France. Cromagnons were specialist hunters (mammoth, reindeer) occupying rock shelters in W Europe and hut camp-ments on the steppe and tundra of C Europe and Russia. >> *Homo* ℹ

Crome, John, known as **Old Crome** (1768–1821) Landscape painter, the chief of the Norwich School, born in Norwich, Norfolk. His subjects derived from the scenery of Norfolk, such as 'Poringland Oak' and 'Mousehold Heath' (Tate, London). >> landscape painting; Norwich School

cromlech >> **megalith**

cromoglycate or **sodium cromoglycate** [krohmoh**gliy**sayt] An anti-allergy drug used especially in the prevention of asthma, also known as **cromolyn**. It is administered using a special inhaler which dispenses very fine powder into the inspired air. >> allergy; asthma

Crompton, Richmal, pseudonym of **Richmal Samuel Lamburn** (1890–1969) Writer of children's books, born in Bury, Lancashire. She wrote the first of the 'William' books (*Just William*) in 1922, and had written 40 of them before her death.

Crompton, Samuel (1753–1827) British inventor of the *spinning-mule*, born in Firwood, Greater Manchester. In 1779 he devised a machine which produced yarn of astonishing fineness, and although he was forced to sell his idea to a Bolton manufacturer he was later awarded a national grant of £5000. >> cotton ℹ; spinning; yarn

Cromwell, Oliver (1599–1658) English soldier and statesman, born in Huntingdon, Cambridgeshire. A convinced Puritan, when war broke out (1642) he fought for the parliament at Edgehill. He formed his unconquerable Ironsides, and it was his cavalry that secured the victory at Marston Moor (1644), while under Fairfax he led the New Model Army to decisive success at Naseby (1645). He brought Charles I to trial, and was one of the signatories of his death warrant (1649). Having established the Commonwealth, Cromwell suppressed the Levellers, Ireland (1649–50), and the Scots (under Charles II). He dissolved the Rump of the Long Parliament and established a Protectorate (1653). He was succeeded by his son **Richard Cromwell** (1626–1712), who was forced into French exile in 1659. >> English Civil War; Levellers; Protectorate

Cromwell, Thomas, Earl of Essex (c.1485–1540) English statesman, born in London. He arranged Henry VIII's divorce from Catherine of Aragon, and put into effect the Act of Supremacy (1534) and the dissolution of the monasteries (1536–9). He held several offices, proving himself a highly efficient adviser to the king; but Henry's aversion to Anne of Cleves, consort of Cromwell's choosing, led to his ruin. He was sent to the Tower and beheaded. >> Henry VIII; Reformation

Cronenberg, David (1943–) Film director and screenplay writer, born in Toronto, Ontario, Canada. His plots typically concern the aftermath of some disastrous biological mishap, as in the highly successful *The Dead Zone* (1983) and *The Fly* (1986), which gave him cult status, and the controversial *Crash* (1996).

Cronin, A(rchibald) J(oseph) [**kroh**nin] (1896–1981) Novelist, born in Cardross, Argyll and Bute. His books include *The Citadel* (1937) and *The Keys of the Kingdom* (1942). Several were filmed, and the television series *Dr Finlay's Casebook* was based on his stories.

Cronkite, Walter (Leland), Jr [**krong**kiyt] (1916–) Journalist and broadcaster, born in St Joseph, MO. He joined the United Press (1939–48), and provided vivid eyewitness accounts of the war in Europe. At CBS from 1950, he became a national institution as the anchorman of the *CBS Evening News* (1962–81).

Cronus [**kron**us] or **Kronos** In Greek mythology, the second ruler of the Universe, a Titan, the youngest son of Uranus, who rebelled against his father. Probably a pre-Greek deity, he is often confused with *chronos* 'time'. >> Titan

croquet [**kroh**kay] A ball-and-mallet game for two to four players, played on a lawn about 32 m/35 yd long and 25 m/28 yd wide, on which have been arranged six hoops and a central peg. The object is to strike your own ball through the hoops in a prescribed order before finally hitting the central peg. >> RR1050

Crosby, Bing, popular name of **Harry Lillis Crosby** (1904–77) Singer and film star, born in Tacoma, WA. He began to make films, specializing in light comedy roles, and his distinctive style of crooning made him one of the best-known names in the entertainment world. His recordings of 'White Christmas' and 'Silent Night' were the hits of the century. He starred in many films, notably the *Road* films with Bob Hope and Dorothy Lamour. A keen golfer, he continued to perform and give concerts until his death on a golf course in Spain.

Crosland, Tony, popular name of **(Charles) Anthony Raven Crosland** (1918–77) British Labour statesman, born in St Leonards, East Sussex. His posts include secretary for education and science (1965–7), environment secretary (1974–6), and foreign secretary (1976–7). A key member of the revisionist wing of the Labour Party, he wrote one of its seminal texts, *The Future of Socialism* (1956). >> socialism

cross The main symbol of Christianity, signifying the execution of Jesus by crucifixion, but a widespread religious symbol even in pre-Christian times. Many popular variations of the cross-symbol have appeared in Christian worship and art. >> crucifixion; Jesus Christ

cross-bencher The name given to a member of the House of Lords who sits as an independent peer rather than accepting a party whip. The name comes from the position in the Lords chamber of the benches upon which this group of peers sit. >> Lords, House of; whip

crossbill A finch native to the N hemisphere, especially N regions. The tips of its bill cross over, an adaptation for extracting seeds from pine cones. (Genus: *Loxia*, 4 species. Family: Fringillidae.) >> conifer; finch

crossbow A form of bow mounted in a stock, with a crank to wind back and tension the bow itself, and a trigger to discharge the arrow, or 'bolt'. It was much used in the Crusades. China had crossbows before the 4th-c BC. >> longbow

cross-country running An athletic running event using a pre-determined course over natural terrain. The length of race varies, but world championships are over 12 km/7·5 mi for men and 5 km/3·1 mi for women. >> RR1050

Cross Fell Highest peak of the Pennine Chain in Cumbria, NW England; rises to 893 m/2930 ft. >> Pennines

Crossman, Richard (Howard Stafford) (1907–74) British Labour statesman, born in Cropredy, Oxfordshire. He became minister of housing and local government

(1964–6), then secretary of state for social services and head of the Department of Health (1968–70). His best-known work is his series of political diaries, begun in 1952, keeping a detailed record of the day-to-day workings of government. They were published in four volumes (1975–81), despite attempts to suppress them. >> Labour Party

Crossopterygii [krosopte**rij**eeiy] A subclass of bony fishes comprising the tassel-finned (or lobe-finned) fishes, having an extensive fossil record from the Devonian to Cretaceous periods. The only living representative is the coelacanth, *Latimeria*. >> bony fish; Cretaceous / Devonian period

croup [kroop] A hollow crowing noise during respiration and on coughing which results from infection affecting the larynx and trachea. It is caused by several viruses that cause swelling and narrowing of the respiratory passages. >> larynx; trachea; virus

crow A bird of the worldwide family Corvidae. It can be a common name for the whole family, or just for the 40 species of the genus *Corvus*, or just for some species of *Corvus*. >> roller

Crow North American Sioux-speaking Plains Indians. In 1868 they were settled on reservations in Montana, where most Crow still live. >> Plains Indians; Sioux

crowberry A spreading, evergreen, heather-like shrub (*Empetrum nigrum*), native to arctic and N temperate moors; three sepals, three petals; berry black. (Family: Empetraceae.) >> sepal

Crowley, Aleister, originally **Edward Alexander Crowley** (1875–1947) British writer and 'magician'. He became interested in the occult, and founded the order known as the Silver Star. He liked to be known as 'the great beast' and 'the wickedest man alive'.

Crown Agents (for Overseas Governments and Administrations) A UK agency which provides professional, financial, and commercial services to governments and other public authorities in developing countries and to international agencies. It also acts on behalf of the World Bank. >> International Bank for Reconstruction and Development

Crown Colony >> **colony**

Crown Court A court in England and Wales, established by the Courts Act (1971), which abolished the Assizes and Quarter Sessions. Crown Courts have power to deal with indictable offences, and also hear most appeals from magistrates' courts. >> Assize Court; Central Criminal Court; indictment; recorder (law); summary trial

Crown Estate Property belonging by heredity to the British sovereign, comprising over 120 000 ha/300 000 acres in England, Scotland, and Wales. Over half of Britain's foreshore is included, together with the sea bed within territorial waters. >> New Forest

crown jewels Regalia and jewellery belonging to a sovereign. The British crown jewels have been displayed at various sites in the Tower of London for 300 years, since 1967 in the Jewel House. Most of the crown jewels date from the Restoration (1660). They include St Edward's Crown, used in most coronations since that of Charles II; the Imperial State Crown; and Queen Elizabeth the Queen Mother's crown, which is set with the Koh-i-Noor ('mountain of light') diamond. >> Tower of London

Crown Prosecution Service In England and Wales, a body of lawyers responsible for assessing the evidence collected by the police, and for deciding whether to prosecute an individual or a corporate body and what the particular charge should be. Established in 1985, it is independent of the police, and is headed by the Director of Public Prosecutions. >> police; prosecution

crucifixion A common form of capital punishment in the Roman world, in which a person was nailed or bound to a wooden cross by the wrists and feet, and left to die. The method was inflicted only upon slaves and people of low social status (*humiliores*). It was regularly preceded by flagellation. >> cross; Jesus Christ

Cruden, Alexander [**kroo**den] (1701–70) Scholar and bookseller, born in Aberdeen. In 1737 appeared his *Concordance of the Holy Scriptures*. >> Bible

Cruft, Charles (1852–1939) British showman, who organized the first dog show in London in 1886. The annual shows have since become world-famous, and have helped to improve standards of dog breeding. >> dog

Cruikshank, George [**krook**shangk] (1792–1878) Caricaturist and illustrator, born in London. His best-known work includes Grimm's *German Popular Stories* (1824–6) and Dickens's *Oliver Twist*.

Cruise, Tom [krooz] (1962–) Film actor, born in Syracuse, NY. His films include *Top Gun* (1985), *Rain Man* (1988), *Born on the Fourth of July* (1989), *Jerry Maguire* (1996), and *Eyes Wide Shut* (1998).

cruise missile A type of missile which flies continuously on wings, and is propelled continuously by an engine using air from the atmosphere as its oxidant to mix with the fuel it carries. The German V-1 of 1944 was a cruise missile. It now provides a comparatively cheap means of delivering a nuclear or conventional warhead over a long distance, using onboard computer power to provide pin-point accuracy. >> missile, guided; V-1

cruiser A medium-sized warship designed to protect trade routes and to act as a scout for a battle fleet. >> warships ℹ

crumhorn A musical instrument made from wood with a small cylindrical bore, and curved at the end like a hockey stick. It was widely used in Europe in the 16th–17th-c, and revived in the 20th-c for performing early music. >> reed instrument

Crusades Holy Wars authorized by the Pope in defence of Christendom and the Church. They were fought against the infidels in the East, Germany, and Spain, against heretics and schismatics who threatened Catholic unity, and against Christian lay powers who opposed the papacy. >> Hospitallers; Templars; Teutonic Knights; *see illustration on p.226*

crustacean [kruh**stay**shn] A typically aquatic arthropod possessing a pair of jaws (*mandibles*) and two pairs of antennae situated in front of the mouth in adults; group contains c.40 000 species. (Subphylum: Crustacea.) >> arthropod; barnacle; copepod; crab; krill; lobster; sand hopper; shrimp; water flea; woodlouse

Crutzen, Paul (1933–) Chemist, born in Amsterdam, The Netherlands. In 1970 he was among the first to draw attention to the vulnerability of the ozone layer, and demonstrated that the presence of nitrogen oxides increase the rate of ozone's decomposition. He shared the 1995 Nobel Prize for Chemistry.

Crux (Lat 'cross') The smallest constellation in the sky, and one of the most distinctive, better known as **the Southern Cross**, it features on the national flags of Australia and New Zealand. >> constellation; RR968

Cruyff, Johann [kriyf] (1947–) Footballer, born in Amsterdam. He won 11 Dutch League and Cup medals with Ajax, and helped them to three consecutive (1971–3) European Cup successes. In 1973 he joined Barcelona, and in 1974 captained Holland in the World Cup final (beaten by West Germany). He returned to Barcelona as manager in 1988, guiding the Spanish champions to the European Cup for the first time in 1992. His son, Jordi, joined Manchester United Football Club (1996–8). >> football ℹ

crwth [krooth] A Celtic (especially Welsh) lyre, played with a bow or plucked. The earliest types, known from the 12th-c onwards, had three strings, but by the 18th-c it had acquired a further three. >> lyre; string instrument 1 ℹ

cryogenics The study of physical systems at temperatures

The main Crusades to the East

	Background	Leader(s)	Outcome
First Crusade (1096–9)	Proclaimed by Urban II to aid the Greeks against the Seljuk Turks in Asia Minor, liberate Jerusalem and the Holy Land from Seljuk domination, and safeguard pilgrim routes to the Holy Sepulchre.	Bohemond I Godfrey of Bouillon Raymond, Count of Toulouse Robert, Count of Flanders Robert Curthose, Duke of Normandy Stephen, Count of Blois	Capture of Nicaea in Anatolia (Jun 1097); Turks vanquished at Battle of Dorylaeum (Jul 1097); capture of Antioch in Syria (Jun 1098), Jerusalem (Jul 1099). Godfrey of Bouillon became ruler of the new Latin Kingdom of Jerusalem, and defeated the Fatimids of Egypt near Ascalon in Palestine (Aug 1099). Three other crusader states were founded: Antioch, Edessa, Tripoli.
Second Crusade (1147–8)	Proclaimed by Eugenius III to aid the crusader states after the Muslim reconquest of Edessa (1144).	Conrad III of Germany Louis VII of France	German army heavily defeated by Turks near Dorylaeum (Oct 1147), and the French at Laodicea (Jan 1148); Damascus in Syria invested, but siege abandoned after four days (Jul 1148). The crusaders' military reputation was destroyed, and the Syrian Muslims united against the Latins.
Third Crusade (1189–92)	Proclaimed by Gregory VIII after Saladin's defeat of the Latins at the Battle of Hattin (Jul 1187) and his conquest of Jerusalem (Oct 1187). (By 1189 all that remained of the Kingdom of Jerusalem was the port of Tyre).	Frederick I Barbarossa Philip II Augustus of France Richard I of England	Cyprus conquered from Greeks (May 1191), and established as new crusader kingdom (survived until 1489); capture of Acre in Palestine (Jul 1191); Saladin defeated near Arsuf (Sept 1191); three-year truce guaranteeing safe-conduct of Christian pilgrims to Jerusalem. Most cities and castles of the Holy Land remained in Muslim hands.
Fourth Crusade (1202–4)	Proclaimed by Innocent III to recover the Holy Places.	Boniface of Montferrat	Despite papal objections, crusade diverted from Egypt or Palestine (1) to Zara, a Christian town in Dalmatia, conquered for Venetians (Nov 1202); (2) to Byzantium, where embroilment in dynastic struggles led to sack of Constantinople (Apr 1204) and foundation of Latin Empire of Constantinople (survived until 1261). The crusading movement was discredited; the Latins in Palestine and Syria were hardly helped at all; the Byzantine empire never fully recovered; and the opportunity was lost of a united front between the Latins and Greeks against the Muslims.
Fifth Crusade (1217–21)	Proclaimed by Innocent III when a six-year truce between the Kingdom of Jerusalem and Egypt expired.	Andrew II of Hungary John of Brienne, King of Jerusalem Leopold, Duke of Austria	Three indecisive expeditions against Muslims in Palestine (1217); capture of Damietta in Egypt after protracted siege (May 1218–Nov 1219); further conquests attempted, but crusaders forced to relinquish Damietta (Aug 1221) and withdraw.
Sixth Crusade (1228–9)	Emperor Frederick II, who first took the Cross in 1215, married the heiress to the Kingdom of Jerusalem in 1225. Excommunicated by Gregory IX for delaying his departure, he finally arrived at Acre in Sept 1228.	Frederick II	Negotiations with Egyptians secured Jerusalem and other places, including Bethlehem and Nazareth (Feb 1229); Frederick crowned King of Jerusalem in church of Holy Sepulchre (Mar 1229). Jerusalem was held until recaptured by the Khorezmian Turks in 1244.
Seventh Crusade (1248–54)	Proclaimed by Innocent IV after the fall of Jerusalem and defeat of the Latin army near Gaza by the Egyptians and Khorezmians (1244).	Louis IX of France	Capture of Damietta (June 1249); defeat at Mansurah (Feb 1250); surrender of crusaders during attempted withdrawal; Damietta relinquished and large ransoms paid (May 1250). Louis spent four years in Palestine, refortifying Acre, Caesarea, Joppa and Sidon, and fruitlessly attempting to regain Jerusalem by alliances with the Mameluks and Mongols.
Eighth Crusade (1270–2)	Proclaimed after the Mameluk conquest of Arsuf, Caesarea, Haifa (1265), Antioch and Joppa (1268).	Charles of Anjou, King of Naples-Sicily Edward of England (later Edward I) Louis IX of France	Attacked Tunisia in N Africa (Jul 1270); Louis died in Aug; Charles concluded treaty with Tunis and withdrew; Edward negotiated 11-years' truce with Mameluks in Palestine. By 1291 the Latins had been driven fron the Holy Land.

less than c.90 K (−183°C). Some processes can be observed only at low temperatures, either because of masking by thermal effects or because the phenomena (eg superconductivity) exist only at low temperature. >> superconductivity; superfluidity

cryolite [**kriy**oliyt] A mineral composed of sodium, aluminium, and fluorine (Na_3AlF_6), used in the smelting of aluminium ores. It occurs in important quantities in Russia and Greenland. >> aluminium

crypt Part of a building below the main floor and usually underground. In particular, it refers to the part of a church containing graves and relics. >> church [i]

cryptanalysis The deciphering or codebreaking of messages intended for others. This involves firstly intercepting a message, then analyzing it to reveal its contents. Since languages can be distinguished by the different frequencies with which the letters of the alphabet occur, the prime task is to search for such enciphered patterns. >> cipher; cryptography

cryptography The alteration of the form of a message by codes and ciphers to conceal its meaning. Codewords, normally from a code book, stand for one or more words of the *plaintext* (the original message). With ciphers, the letters of the plaintext are individually substituted or transposed (re-ordered), according to a secret key. >> cipher; cryptanalysis

Crystal, Billy (1947–) Film actor, born in Long Beach, NY. Well known for his role in the American comedy series, *Soap*, his feature films include *Throw Momma From the Train* (1987), *When Harry Met Sally* (1989), *City Slickers* and its sequel (1991, 1994), *Forget Paris* (1995), which he also directed, and *My Giant* (1998).

crystal defects Irregularities in otherwise perfectly regular crystals. Some, such as cracks and dislocations, strongly influence crystal mechanical properties, typically causing weakness. Others, such as impurities, affect electrical properties (eg the semiconductor crystals used in electronics) or give colour to crystals (eg chromium in red ruby). >> crystals; semiconductor

Crystal Palace An iron-framed, prefabricated, glass building designed by Sir Joseph Paxton to house the Great Exhibition of 1851. The structure was erected in London's Hyde Park, re-erected in S London, but destroyed by fire in 1936. >> Great Exhibition; Paxton, Joseph

crystals True solids, made up of regularly repeating groups of atoms, ions, or molecules. In contrast with liquids and other amorphous materials, the properties of crystals vary with the direction in which they are measured. A complete crystal structure is defined by giving both a lattice of points, of which only 14 types are possible, and the group of atoms associated with each lattice point. The study of crystals is called **crystallography**. >> crystal defects; liquid crystals

crystal therapy In alternative medicine, a technique which uses precious and semi-precious stones, credited with particular astrological, esoteric, and physical properties. Each stone has a particular vibration pattern which some believe can act upon the body's energy field to increase the available energy and also to correct any imbalance or blockages. >> alternative medicine

CS gas US military designation for a chlorinated compound, 1-*o*-chlorophenyl-2,2-dicyanoethylene, $Cl-C_6H_4-CH=C(C-N)_2$. It causes irritation and watering of the eyes, and is widely used in riot control. >> chlorine

ctenophore [**ten**ofaw(r)] A marine animal with a transparent, jelly-like (gelatinous) body, which swims using eight comb-like rows of plates (**ctenes**); carnivorous, using paired tentacles armed with stinging cells to catch prey; c.80 species; known as **comb jellies** or **sea gooseberries**. (Phylum: Ctenophora.)

CT scanning >> **computerized tomography**

Cuba, official name **Republic of Cuba**, Span **República de Cuba** pop (1995e) 11 089 000; area 110 860 sq km/ 42 792 sq mi. Island republic in the Caribbean Sea; capital, Havana; timezone GMT –5; people mainly Spanish and African descent; Castro regime discourages religious practices, but 40% Roman Catholic; official language, Spanish; unit of currency, the peso of 100 centavos; an archipelago, comprising the island of Cuba, Isla de la Juventud, and c.1600 islets and cays; main island 1250 km/777 mi long, varying in width from 191 km/119 mi (E) to 31 km/19 mi (W); highest peak, Pico Turquino

(2005 m/6578 ft); mostly flat, with wide, fertile valleys and plains; subtropical climate, warm and humid; visited by Columbus, 1492; Spanish colony until 1898, following revolution under José Martí, with support of USA; independence, 1902; struggle against dictatorship of General Batista led by Castro, finally successful in 1959, and communist state established; invasion of Cuban exiles with US support, defeated at Bay of Pigs, 1961; US naval blockade, after Soviet installation of missile bases, 1962; governed by a State Council, appointed by a National Assembly of People's Power; after 1959, plantation estates nationalized, and land plots distributed to peasants; world's second largest sugar producer (accounting for 75% of export earnings); world's fifth largest producer of nickel; before Castro, over half of Cuba's trade was with the USA; later, mainly with USSR; growing economic problems, following the dissolution of the USSR in 1991. >> Batista; Bay of Pigs; Castro; Havana; RR1005 political leaders

Cuban Missile Crisis A period of acute international tension between the USA and USSR in October 1962, following the USA's discovery of Soviet nuclear missile sites in Cuba. President Kennedy demanded the dismantling of the base and the return of the missiles, and threw a naval blockade around the island. The crisis ended when Soviet leader Khrushchev agreed to Kennedy's demands. >> Cuba; Kennedy, John F; Khruschev

Cubism A modern art movement out of which grew most of the early forms of abstraction. About 1907 Picasso and Braque rejected Renaissance perspective and Impressionist attention to light and atmosphere. Objects, painted in sombre shades of brown and grey, were analysed into geometrical planes with several views depicted simultaneously (**analytic cubism**). After c.1912 a flatter, more colourful and decorative hard-edged style emerged (**synthetic cubism**), using collage and painted relief constructs. >> abstract art; art; Braque; collage; Futurism; modern art; Picasso

Cubitt, Thomas (1788–1855) Builder, born in Buxton, Norfolk. With his brother **Lewis Cubitt** (1799–1883) he worked on the development of Belgravia, London; later, Thomas's buildings included Osborne House and the E front of Buckingham Palace; Lewis's best-known building is Kings Cross Station.

Cuchulain [ku**hoo**lin] Ir **Cu Chulainn** The hero of many Irish legends, the chief warrior of Ulster. He obtained his name (meaning 'the hound of Culaan') after killing a huge dog.

cuckoo A bird of the worldwide family Culculidae (130 species), mostly inhabiting woodland. About 50 species do not build nests, but lay eggs in the nests of other birds, with the young reared by 'foster' parents. >> roadrunner

cuckoo-pint >> **lords-and-ladies**

cuckoo-roller >> **roller**

cuckoo shrike A bird native to the Old World, especially the tropics; also known as the **caterpillar bird**; dull, greyish plumage. It is neither a true cuckoo nor a shrike. (Family: Campephagidae, 70 species.)

cuckoo-spit insect >> **froghopper**

cucumber A vine (*Cucumis sativa*), trailing or climbing by means of tendrils, cultivated from early times as a salad vegetable; flowers yellow, funnel-shaped; fruit up to 45 cm/18 in or more, green, fleshy, cylindrical or oval. (Family: Cucurbitaceae.) >> gherkin; gourd; squash (botany)

Cúcuta [**koo**koota] 7°55N 72°31W, pop (1995e) 403 000. City in NE Colombia; founded, 1734; destroyed by earthquake, 1875, then rebuilt; a focal point in Colombia's fight for independence; airfield; university (1962). >> Colombia i

Cudworth, Ralph (1617–88) Philosopher and theologian, born in Aller, Somerset. The leader of the 'Cambridge Platonists', his best-known work is *The True Intellectual System of the Universe* (1678). >> Cambridge Platonists

Cuenca [**kwen**ka] 2°54S 79°00W, pop (1995e) 215 000. City in SC Ecuador; founded by Spanish, 1557; airfield; railway; two universities (1868, 1970); old and new cathedrals. >> Ecuador i

Cukor, George D(ewey) [**koo**ker] (1899–1983) Film director, born in New York City. He was particularly successful with the great actresses of the star system – Garbo, Crawford, Hepburn – but his range was wide, including *Gaslight* (1944), *A Star is Born* (1954), and *My Fair Lady* (1964, Oscar).

cu lan >> **loris**

Culicidae [kyoo**lis**idee] A family containing c.3000 species of true flies, including mosquitoes and gnats. Many species are of primary medical and veterinary importance as carriers of diseases. (Order: Diptera.) >> fly; gnat; mosquito

Cullinan diamond [**kuh**linan] The largest gem diamond ever found, weight 3255 carats (650 grams/22·9 avoirdupois ounces). It was found in Premier Diamond Mine, Transvaal in 1905 and named after Sir Thomas Cullinan, who had discovered the mine. >> crown jewels; diamond

Culloden Moor, Battle of [kuh**lo**dn] A battle fought near Inverness, marking the end of the Jacobite rebellion of 1745 led by Charles Edward Stuart. His force, mainly of Scottish highlanders, was crushed by a superior force of English and lowland Scots under the Duke of Cumberland. >> Forty-five Rebellion; Stuart, Charles Edward

Culpeper, Nicholas (1616–54) Astrologer, born in London. In 1649 he published an English translation of the College of Physicians' Pharmacopoeia, *A Physical Directory*, and in 1653 appeared *The English Physician Enlarged, or the Herbal*. >> astrology

cult Any set of beliefs and practices associated with a particular god or group of gods, forming a distinctive part of a larger religious body. The focus of devotion may be an animal (eg the whale cult in Eskimo religions), a particular deity (eg the Hindu cult devoted to Shiva), or even a deified human being (eg the emperor cult in ancient Rome). >> cargo cult; religion; sect

cultivar A contraction of **cultivated variety**; in names further abbreviated to **cv**. It refers to any distinct type of plant produced in cultivation but not growing in the wild.

cultivator An agricultural implement carrying rows of prongs (*tines*); some versions carry blades. It is used for breaking up soil and creating a seed-bed before planting, and is also used in the control of weeds. >> soil

cultural anthropology >> **anthropology**

Cultural Revolution An abbreviation for the Great Proletarian Cultural Revolution, a radical Maoist mass movement initiated as a rectification campaign in 1966, which ended only with the death of Mao Zedong and the arrest of the Gang of Four in the autumn of 1976. Mao appealed directly to the masses, in particular to young students, the Red Guards, who with the support of the People's Liberation Army overthrew not only party leaders but all so-called 'bourgeois reactionaries' in authority in schools, universities, factories, and the administration. The '10 lost years' of social and political turmoil saw the closure of schools and universities, factories at a standstill, tens of thousands of deaths, and millions of people sent to undertake manual labour in the countryside as re-education. >> Gang of Four 1; Mao Zedong; Red Army (China); Red Guards

culture An artifically maintained population of micro-organisms, or of dissociated cells of a tissue, grown in a nutrient medium and reproducing by asexual division. The process is used in experimental microbiological research and also in medical applications, chiefly as part of the task of diagnosis. >> micro-organism; reproduction

Cumae [**kyoo**mee] The oldest Greek colony in Italy, founded c.750 BC near present-day Naples. It was famous in Roman times as the home of the oracular prophetess, the Sibyl.

Cumberland A former county of NW England; part of Cumbria since 1974. >> Cumbria

Cumberland, William Augustus, Duke of (1721–65) British general, the second son of George II, born in London. He crushed the Young Pretender's rebellion at Culloden (1746), and by his harsh policies afterwards earned the lasting title of 'Butcher'. >> Culloden Moor, Battle of

Cumbria pop (1995e) 493 000; area 6810 sq km/2629 sq mi. County in NW England, 40% of the county within the Lake District and Yorkshire Dales national parks; created in 1974 from the former counties of Westmorland and Cumberland; county town, Carlisle; atomic energy at Sellafield and Calder Hall. >> Carlisle; England i; Lake District

cumin A slender annual (*Cuminum cyminum*) growing to 50 cm/20 in, native to N Africa and SW Asia; flowers white or pink; fruit oblong with slender ridges. It is cultivated for the aromatic fruits, used for spice, and is an ingredient of curry powder. (Family: Umbelliferae.) >> curry; spice

Cummings, E(dward) E(stlin) (1894–1962) Writer and painter, born in Cambridge, MA. His several successful collections of poetry, starting with *Tulips and Chimneys* (1923), are striking for their unorthodox typography and linguistic style. *Complete Poems* appeared in 1968.

cumquat >> **kumquat**

cumulonimbus clouds [kyoomyulohn**nim**buhs] Clouds of the cumulus family which rise to great heights (up to 10 km/6 mi). They are often dark and threatening when seen from below, and are associated with thunderstorms and the arrival of a cold front during the passage of a depression. Cloud symbol: Cb. >> cloud i; cold front; cumulus clouds; nimbus clouds

cumulus clouds [**kyoom**yuluhs] A family of clouds with a predominantly vertical extent but relatively horizontal base. They range from small, white fluffy clouds typical of summer afternoons, to black and threatening storm or cumulonimbus clouds. Cloud symbol: Cu. >> altocumulus / cirrocumulus / cumulonimbus / stratocumulus clouds; cloud i

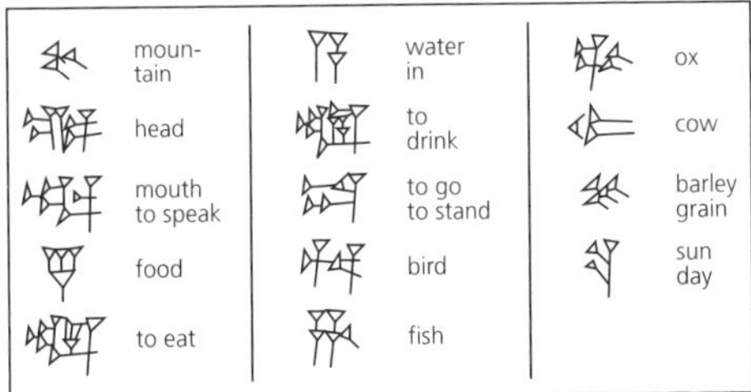

Cuneiform – symbols from the later period of cuneiform script, 1st millennium BC

Cunard, Sir Samuel [kyoo**nah(r)d**] (1787–1865) Shipowner, born in Halifax, Nova Scotia, Canada. He emigrated to Britain in 1838, and helped to found the British and North American Royal Mail Steam Packet Company, later known as the **Cunard Line**. >> ship ℹ

cuneiform A form of writing used throughout the Middle East for over 3000 years until about the 1st-c BC. Originally derived from pictograms, the symbols were later used to represent words, syllables, and phonetic elements. At first, the symbols took the form of impressions made on soft clay with a stylus, but subsequently a harder writing surface was used. >> alphabet ℹ; writing systems

Cunningham, Merce (1919–) Dancer, choreographer, teacher, and director, born in Centralia, WA. He started his own company in 1952, and is one of the major figures in the development of a concern with form and abstraction in modern dance. >> modern dance; postmodern dance

Cunobelinus >> **Cymbeline**

Cuomo, Mario [**kwoh**moh] (1932–) US politician, born in New York City. He became Governor of New York State (1983–94), and was strongly boosted for the Democratic presidency in 1984 and 1988, and 1992.

Cupid The Roman god of Love, son of Venus, depicted as a naked winged boy with bow and arrows. Apuleius tells the story of *Cupid and Psyche*. He is equivalent to Greek Eros. >> Eros (mythology); Psyche

cupola [**kyoo**pohla] A small dome over a circular, square, or polygonal part of a building, usually above a roof or turret; more loosely, a dome of any size. Good examples are found at the Royal Pavilion, Brighton, W Sussex (1815–23).

cuprite [**kyoop**riyt] A red copper oxide (Cu_2O) mineral, which is widely distributed. It is an important source of copper. >> copper

cupronickel [kyooprohn**ni**kl] An alloy of copper and nickel, silver in colour. It is used extensively for coinage. >> alloy; copper; nickel

Curaçao [koora**sah**oh] pop (1995e) 146 000; area 444 sq km/171 sq mi. Largest and most populous island of the Netherlands Antilles, E Caribbean; rises to 373 m/1224 ft in the NW; length 58 km/36 mi; width 13 km/8 mi; visited by Europeans, 1499; Dutch colony, 1634; capital, Willemstad; airport; known for its liqueur. >> Netherlands Antilles ℹ

curare [kyoo**rah**ree] An extract of the South American plants *Chondrodendron tomentosum* or *Strychnos toxifera*, used as an arrow poison for hunting by South American Indians. The active principle, tubocurarine, is widely used to induce muscle paralysis during surgery. >> strychnine

curassow [**kyoo**rasoh] A large, tree-dwelling, turkey-like bird, native to C and N South America; head with a conspicuous crest of curved feathers; legs long, strong. (Family: Cracidae, 13 species.)

curate Strictly, a Christian clergyman admitted to the 'cure of souls' and having the 'cure' or charge of a parish. Popularly, the term is used of an assistant or unbeneficed clergyman, helping or temporarily replacing the priest, rector, vicar, or other incumbent of the parish. >> priest; rector; vicar

curia In ancient Rome, the Senate house. It stood on the NW side of the forum, adjacent to the site of the legislative assembly. >> forum; Senate, Roman

Curia Romana >> **Roman Curia**

curie [**kyoo**ree] In radioactivity, defined as $3{\cdot}7 \times 10^{10}$ disintegrations per second; symbol *Ci*; 1 Ci $=3{\cdot}7 \times 10^{10}$ Bq (becquerel, SI unit); original definition related to the activity of radioactive radon; named after French physicists Pierre and Marie Curie. >> becquerel; Curie; radioactivity units ℹ

Curie, Marie [**kyoo**ree], *née* **Manya Sklodowska** (1867–1934) Physicist, born in Warsaw, who worked in Paris with her French husband **Pierre Curie** (1859–1906) on magnetism and radioactivity. Together they discovered and isolated polonium and radium (1898), and shared the 1903 Nobel Prize for Physics with Becquerel for the discovery of radioactivity. Mme Curie published her treatise on radioactivity in 1910 and was awarded the Nobel Prize for Chemistry in 1911. She died of leukaemia, probably caused by long exposure to radiation. >> Becquerel; curie; Curie's law; Curie temperature; radioactivity; radium

Curie point >> **Curie temperature**

Curie's law A law for paramagnetic materials which states that the magnetization is proportional to B/T, where B is magnetic flux density and T is temperature in kelvins; stated by French physicist Pierre Curie in 1895. >> Curie

Curie temperature In ferromagnetism, the material-dependent temperature above which a ferromagnetic material becomes merely paramagnetic; symbol T_c, units K; introduced by French physicist Pierre Curie in 1895; also called **Curie point**. For iron, $T_c = 1043$ K. >> Curie; ferromagnetism

Curitiba [kooree**chee**ba] 25°24S 49°16W, pop (1995e) 1 513 000. Industrial city in S Brazil; altitude 900 m/2950 ft; railway; airfield; two universities (1912, 1959); cathedral (1894); commercial centre. >> Brazil ℹ

Curl, Robert, Jr (1933–) Chemist, born in Alice, TX. He shared the Nobel Prize for Chemistry in 1996 for his contribution to the discovery of fullerenes (1985). >> fullerenes

curlew A long-legged sandpiper; breeds in the N hemisphere, but flies S (some as far as Australia) in N winter; long, down-curved bill; probes for food in sediments. (Genus: *Numenius*, 8 species.) >> sandpiper; whimbrel

curling A game played usually by teams of four on an ice-rink, using special stones fitted with handles. The object is similar to that of bowls, to deliver the stones nearest to a target object, known as the *tee*. The ice is swept with brooms in front of the running stone to help it to travel further. It is particularly popular in Canada, Scotland, the Nordic countries, and the USA. >> bowls

currant A deciduous shrub, native to N temperate regions and the Andes; flowers borne in clusters on short lateral shoots, 4–5 sepals and petals; berries juicy. The currants used for 'fruit' cakes are dried grapes. (Genus: *Ribes*, 150 species. Family: Grossulariaceae.) >> blackcurrant; grapevine; red currant

currency A country's money. A currency is *convertible* if it can be exchanged into other currencies without restriction. A currency *depreciates* if it becomes cheaper relative to other currencies. >> devaluation; European Monetary System; exchange rates

current (electricity) The flow of electric charge, symbol i or I, units A (amp). A current of one amp means that a charge of one coulomb flows every second. Current flows positive to negative by convention. **Current density**, symbol *j* or *J*, is the total current divided by the cross-sectional area of the conductor. >> accumulator; alternating current; charge; coulomb; direct current; electrical power

current (oceanography) Flowing water in the ocean. The surface currents depicted on atlases are long-term averages of the direction of water motion at the sea surface, driven primarily by the winds. The strong, persistent *trade winds*, blowing out of the NE in the N hemisphere and out of the SE in the S hemisphere, produce major W-flowing **equatorial currents**. These currents flow along bands of latitude until, deflected by continents, they form **boundary currents** flowing N or S. In the Atlantic and Pacific Oceans these equatorial and boundary currents are parts of semi-enclosed circulation cells called *gyres*. The W-flowing N and S equatorial currents of the N and S subtropical gyres are separated by an E-flowing equatorial countercurrent. **Counter-currents** are developed at the inter-tropical convergence, the area of weak and variable winds known as *the Doldrums*. >> Equator; Doldrums; wind ℹ

curry A spiced dish of fish, meat, poultry, or vegetables, originating in the East. Among the spices used in curries are coriander, cumin, chilli, cinnamon, cardamom, cloves, fenugreek, ginger, and turmeric.

Curtin, John (Joseph) (1885–1945) Australian statesman and Labor prime minister (1941–5), born in Creswick, Victoria. As premier, he organized national mobilization during the Japanese war. >> Australian Labor Party

Curtis, Tony, originally **Bernard Schwarz** (1925–) Actor, born in New York City. After many small film parts early in his career, he proved he could play light comedy roles as in *Some Like It Hot* (1959) while also displaying his dramatic ability in *The Boston Strangler* (1968). Other films include *The Vikings* (1958), *Spartacus* (1960), and *The Great Imposter* (1961).

Curtiss, Glenn (Hammond) (1878–1930) Engineer and aeronaut, born in Hammondsport, NY. In 1908 he won the *Scientific American* trophy for the first public flight of 1 km in the USA, and in 1911 he demonstrated the practicality of the seaplane. >> dirigible; seaplane

Curwen, John (1816–80) Music educationist, born in Heckmondwike, West Yorkshire. He devoted himself to promoting the tonic sol-fa musical system, and established a publishing house for music. >> tonic sol-fa

Curzon, Sir Clifford (1907–82) Pianist, born in London. He taught for some years at the Royal Academy of Music, later devoting himself to concert work.

Curzon (of Kedleston), George Nathaniel Curzon, Marquess (1859–1925) British statesman, born in Kedleston Hall, Derbyshire. In 1898 he was made Viceroy of India, where he introduced many social and political reforms, established the NW Frontier Province, and partitioned Bengal. He was also foreign secretary (1919–24). >> Curzon Line; Kitchener

Curzon Line A line of territorial demarcation between Russia and Poland proposed in 1920 by the British foreign secretary, Lord Curzon. It was recognized in 1945 as the frontier between Poland and the USSR. >> Curzon (of Kedleston); Poland ℹ; Yalta Conference

cuscus [**kus**kus] >> **phalanger**

Cush >> **Kush**

Cushing, Peter (1913–94) Actor, born in Kenley, Greater London. He is chiefly known for his long association with the Gothic horror films produced by Hammer, such as *The Curse of Frankenstein* (1956) and *Dracula* (1958). His numerous other films include *Dr Who and the Daleks* (1965) and *Star Wars* (1977).

Cushing's disease A disorder resulting from excessive production of the hormones secreted by the cortex of the adrenal glands; named after US neurosurgeon Harvey Williams Cushing (1869–1939). It causes profound metabolic and sexual effects. >> adrenal glands

cusp In Gothic architecture, a projecting point formed by the intersection of two or more curves in the tracery; hence, usually carved in stone. >> Gothic architecture; tracery ℹ

custard apple A deciduous tree (*Annona squamosa*) growing to 6 m/20 ft, native to tropical America; flowers with six greenish-yellow petals; fruit 10 cm/4 in, roughly heart-shaped, greenish, containing numerous seeds buried in a sweet pulp; also called **sweet sop**. (Family: Annonaceae.)

Custer, George Armstrong (1839–76) US soldier, born in New Rumley, OH. He served in the campaigns against the Indian tribes of the Great Plains. His defeat by a combined Sioux–Cheyenne force at the Little Bighorn, Montana (25 Jun 1876), shocked the nation, but did no lasting good to the Indians' cause. Although a lieutenant-colonel in the cavalry, he is often referred to by his Civil War rank of general.

custody The formal assigning of a child by a court to the care of one or other of the parents or guardian following a divorce, a separation, or the nullification of a marriage. The court can, if it sees fit, award joint custody to both parents. The non-custodial parent is usually granted access to the child. >> annulment; divorce; guardian; separation, judicial; wardship proceedings

customs and excise The government department charged with collecting taxes due on specified goods and services, and controlling imports into a country where there are tariffs or quota restrictions, or where the imports are illegal. It is most visible at airports and ports checking goods imported, and charging tax (*duty*) as appropriate. The department also handles value-added tax. >> taxation; VAT

customs union An economic agreement where nations adopt common excise duties, thereby eliminating the need for customs checks along their common frontier. They thus create a free trade area. >> Benelux; customs and excise; European Economic Community

Cuthbert, St (c.635–87) Missionary, born in Ireland or Northumbria. He became prior of Melrose (661) and of Lindisfarne (664), and in 684 became bishop of Hexham, then of Lindisfarne. Feast day 20 March. >> monasticism

Cutner, Solomon >> **Solomon** (music)

cutter A single-masted, fore-and-aft-rigged sailing vessel with more than one headsail, usually requiring a bowsprit. The term is still in use, especially in compounds (eg **revenue cutter**). In the USA it applies to vessels which would elsewhere be called **sloops**. >> ship ℹ; sloop

cutting A portion of a plant, usually a side shoot but also a leaf or root which, when removed from the parent, will grow to form a new individual. It is commonly used by gardeners as a means of propagation.

cuttlefish A squid-like marine mollusc with eight arms and two tentacles, used to capture prey; internal calcareous shell (**cuttlebone**) may be straight or curved; capable of rapid colour changes. (Class: Cephalopoda.) >> calcium; Cephalopoda ℹ; mollusc; squid

Cuvier, Georges (Léopold Chrétien Frédéric Dagobert), Baron [küvyay] (1769–1832) Anatomist, born in Montbéliard, France. Professor of natural history at the Collège de France, he originated the natural system of animal classification, and through his studies of animal and fish fossils he established the sciences of palaeontology and comparative anatomy. >> anatomy ℹ; palaeontology; systematics

Cuyp or **Cuijp, Albert** [kiyp] (1620–91) Painter, born in Dordrecht, The Netherlands. He excelled in the painting of landscapes, often suffused with golden sunlight, and containing cattle and other figures. >> landscape painting

Cuzco [**koos**koh] 13°32S 71°57W, pop (1995e) 299 000. City in S Peru; altitude 3500 m/11 500 ft; ancient capital of the Inca empire; oldest continuously occupied city in the Americas; airfield; railway; a world heritage site; university (1969); cathedral (17th-c); trade centre of an agricultural region; extensive Inca ruins. >> Incas; Peru ℹ

cwm >> **cirque**

cyanide A compound containing the group –C–N in a molecule, or salts of hydrocyanic acid containing the ion CN^-. It is a very rapidly acting poison, which can kill within minutes. Cyanide gas has been used in gas chambers. Amyl nitrite (by inhalation) can treat cyanide poisoning if administered in time. >> amyl nitrite; hydrocyanic acid

cyanocobalamin [siyanohkoh**bal**amin] The chemical name for vitamin B_{12}, involved in cell division and in the manufacture of the sheath surrounding nerve cells. It is found predominantly in animal-derived food, so that a true deficiency rarely occurs except among vegans, who eat no animal food. >> vegetarianism; vitamins ℹ

Cyanophycota [siyanoh**fiy**kuhta] >> **blue-green bacteria**

Cybele [**sib**elee] In Greek mythology, a mother-goddess, especially of wild nature, whose cult originated in Phrygia, and was taken over by the Greeks. She was depicted with a turreted mural crown, and was attended by lions.

cybernetics The study of control systems that exhibit characteristics similar to those of animal and human behaviour. The term was coined by Norbert Wiener in the 1940s, based on a Greek word meaning 'steersman'. It is a broad-based discipline which includes information, message, and noise theories. >> computer science; Wiener

cyberspace >> **Internet**

cycad [**siy**kad] A tropical or subtropical gymnosperm, palm-like in appearance, trunk usually unbranched, with a crown of tough, feathery leaves; flowers borne in separate male and female cones, the female very large. Cycads are considered to be the most primitive living seed-plants, appearing in the late Palaeozoic era. (Family: Cycadaceae, 100 species.) >> gymnosperms; Palaeozoic era

Cyclades [**sik**ladeez], Gr **Kikládhes** pop (1995e) 97 400; area 2572 sq km/993 sq mi. Island group in the Aegean Sea, Greece; capital, Siros; several now popular holiday resorts. >> Aegean Sea; Greece ℹ

cyclamate [**sik**lamayt] A derivative of cyclohexylsulphamic acid. It has c.30 times the sweetening power of sucrose, and was previously used widely in sweetening 'diet foods'. It is less used now because of possible health risks. >> sucrose

cyclamen [**sik**lamen] A perennial with leaves growing direct from a fleshy corm, native to Europe and Asia; flowers nodding, white, pink, or purple. (Genus: *Cyclamen*, 15 species. Family: Primulaceae.)

cycling The riding of a bicycle for fitness, pleasure, or as a sport. There are several popular forms of cycling as a sport. In *time trials* cyclists race against the clock. *Cyclo-cross* is a mixture of cycling and cross-country running, with the bike on the shoulder. *Track racing* takes place on purpose-built concrete or wooden velodromes. *Criteriums* are races around town or city centres. *Road races* are normally in excess of 150 km/100 mi in length, and take place either from one point to another, or involve several circuits around a predetermined road course. *Stage races* involve many days' racing, each consisting of 150 km/100 mi or more. The most famous cycle race is the *Tour de France*. >> bicycle; Tour de France; RR1050

cyclone >> **depression** (meteorology) ℹ; **hurricane**

Cyclops [**siy**klops], plural **Cyclopes** In Greek mythology, a race of one-eyed giants who worked as smiths and were associated with volcanic activity. In the *Odyssey*, the Cyclops Polyphemus is outwitted and blinded by Odysseus. >> Polyphemus

cyclostome [**siy**klohstohm] Any of a group of jawless fishes with a large sucking mouth. >> hagfish ℹ; lamprey

cyclotron A machine for accelerating charged particles, typically protons; developed by US physicist Ernest Lawrence and others in 1931, and now largely superseded by the synchrotron. Acceleration is provided by an oscillating electric field. >> Lawrence, Ernest; particle accelerators; proton

Cygnus [**sig**nus] (Lat 'swan') A large N constellation, imagined by the ancients as a swan flying along the Milky Way. Its brightest star is Deneb, a supergiant, distance 500 parsec. >> constellation; Milky Way; supergiant; RR968

cymbals Musical instruments of great antiquity. Modern orchestral cymbals are made in pairs, from an alloy of copper and tin, with a diameter of about 40–50 cm/16–20 in. They are clashed together, or suspended from a stand and played with a drumstick. An array of free-standing cymbals is also an important part of the jazz drummer's kit. >> percussion ℹ

Cymbeline [**sim**beleen], also known as **Cunobelinus** (?–c.43) Pro-Roman king of the Catuvellauni, who from his capital at Camulodunum (Colchester) ruled most of SE Britain. Shakespeare's character was based on Holinshed's half-historical Cunobelinus. >> Camulodunum

cymbidium [sim**bid**ium] A member of a genus of orchids (epiphytes) native to tropical forests from Asia to Australia. They are widely cultivated for the spikes of large, showy flowers much used in floristry and the cut-flower trade. (Genus: *Cymbidium*, 40 species. Family: Orchidaceae.) >> epiphyte; orchid ℹ

cyme [siym], **cymose** >> **inflorescence** ℹ

Cynewulf [**kin**ewulf] (8th-c) Anglo-Saxon poet, identified by some with Cynewulf, bishop of Lindisfarne (737–80). Four of his poems have his name worked into the text in runes. >> Anglo-Saxons; runes ℹ

Cynics (Gr 'dogs') A discontinuous group of philosophers, early members of which included Antisthenes and Diogenes of Sinope, influential in Greece and Rome 4th-c BC–6th-c AD. They taught by their example an ascetic life in conformity with nature. >> Antisthenes; Diogenes of Sinope

cypress An evergreen conifer, native to the temperate N hemisphere; leaves small, scale-like; cones like the head of a mace, with 4–12 woody scales joined at their margins. (Genus: *Cupressus*, 15–20 species. Family: Cupressaceae.) >> conifer; swamp cypress; tree ℹ

Cyprian, St [**si**prian], originally **Thascius Caecilius Cyprianus** (c.200–58) One of the great Fathers of the Church, probably born in Carthage. He suffered martyrdom under Valerian (reigned 253–60). At a synod in Carthage in 256 he argued for a notion of Church unity as expressed through the consensus of bishops. Feast day 16 September. >> Fathers of the Church

Cyprus [**siy**pruhs], Gr **Kypros**, Turk **Kibris**; official name **Republic of Cyprus**, Gr **Kypriaki Dimokratia**, Turk **Kibris Cumhuriyeti** pop (1995e) 600 000; area 9251 sq km/3571 sq mi. Island republic in NE Mediterranean Sea, c.80 km/50 mi S of Turkey; capital, Nicosia; airports at Larnaca, Paphos; Famagusta (chief port prior to 1974 Turkish invasion) now under Turkish occupation, and declared closed by Cyprus government; timezone GMT +2; c.77% Greek-speaking Orthodox Christians and 18% Turkish-speaking Muslims; almost all Turks now live in N sector (37% of island); official languages, Greek and

Turkish, with English widely spoken; unit of currency, Cyprus pound of 100 cents; third largest island in Mediterranean; Kyrenia Mts extend 150 km/90 mi along N coast, forest-covered Troödos Mts in SW, rising to 1951 m/6401 ft at Mt Olympus; fertile Mesaoria plain extends across island centre; indented coastline, with several long, sandy beaches; typical Mediterranean climate with hot, dry summers and warm, wet winters; recorded history of 4000 years, rulers including Greeks, Ptolemies, Persians, Romans, Byzantines, Arabs, Franks, Venetians, Turks (1571–1878), and British; British Crown Colony, 1925; Greek Cypriot demands for union with Greece (*enosis*) led to guerrilla warfare, under Grivas and Makarios, and 4-year state of emergency, 1955–9; independence, 1960, with Britain retaining sovereignty over bases at Akrotiri and Dhekelia; Greek–Turkish fighting throughout 1960s, with UN peacekeeping force sent in 1964; further terrorist campaign in 1971; Turkish invasion (1974) led to occupation of over a third of the island; island divided into two parts by the Attila Line, cutting through Nicosia where it is called the Green Line; governed by a president (head of state), elected by the Greek community, and a House of Representatives; Turkish members ceased to attend in 1983, when the Turkish community declared itself independent (as 'Turkish Republic of Northern Cyprus', recognized only by Turkey); UN-sponsored peace negotiations, 1997; Greek Cypriot area now largely recovered from the 1974 invasion, with light manufacturing a main growth sector; tourism recovering after 1974, now accounting for c.15% of national income; Turkish Cypriot economy heavily dependent on agriculture. >> enosis; EOKA; Greece ℹ; Grivas; Makarios; Nicosia; Turkey ℹ; RR1006 political leaders

Cyrano de Bergerac, Savinien [**si**ranoh duh **ber**zherak] (1619–55) Satirist and playwright, born in Paris. In his youth he fought more than a thousand duels, mostly on account of his extremely large nose. His life was the subject of the play by Edmond Rostand (1897). >> Rostand

Cyrenaics [sire**nay**iks] A school of 4th-c and 3rd-c BC Greek philosophers, whose founder was Aristippus of Cyrene. They believed that the immediate sensation of pleasure is the only good, that all such sensations are equal in worth, and that past and future pleasures have no present value. >> Aristippus

Cyrene [siy**ree**nee] 32°49N 21°52E. A prosperous Greek city-state in N Africa, famous in antiquity for the export of silphium, a plant used in ancient medicine. It is now a world heritage site, and the location of the village of Shahhat, E Libya.

Cyril, St (c.827–69) and **Methodius, St** (c.825–85) Brothers, born in Thessalonica, Greece, who became missionaries to the Slavs. Together they went to Moravia, where they prepared a Slavonic translation of the Scriptures and the chief liturgical books. Feast day 14 February (W), 11 May (E). >> Bible; Cyrillic alphabet

Cyril of Alexandria, St (376–444) Theologian, one of the Fathers of the Church, born in Alexandria. He expelled the Jews from the city (415), and relentlessly persecuted Nestorius, whose doctrine was condemned at the Council of Ephesus (431). Feast day 9 June (E) or 27 June (W). >> Fathers of the Church; Nestorians

Cyril of Jerusalem, St (c.315–86) Theologian and Bishop of Jerusalem, who took a leading part in the doctrinal controversies concerning Arianism. He spoke for the Orthodox churchmen at the Council of Constantinople (381). Feast day 18 March. >> Arius

Cyrillic alphabet [si**ril**ik] An alphabet attributed to St Cyril, and used for Slavonic languages, such as Russian and Bulgarian. It is used for many non-Slavonic languages in the republics of the former USSR. >> alphabet ℹ; Cyril and Methodius, Saints

Cyrus II [**siy**rus], known as **the Great** (?–529 BC) The founder of the Achaemenid Persian Empire, the son of Cambyses I. His empire eventually ran from the Mediterranean to the Hindu Kush. He had a policy of religious conciliation: the nations which had been carried into captivity in Babylon along with the Jews were restored to their native countries. >> Achaemenids

cyst (biology) [sist] Any relatively thick-walled resting cell formed by an organism as a means of dispersal or as a way of surviving a period of adverse conditions. Eggs and spores are often protected in cysts, but whole organisms may also encyst, to re-emerge when favourable conditions return.

cyst (medicine) [sist] A benign (non-malignant) swelling within a tissue, very often containing fluid. It is sometimes caused by the blockage of a duct (eg a sweat-gland cyst in the skin), by abnormal embryological development, or by infection. >> ganglion 2

cystic fibrosis [**sis**tik fiy**broh**sis] A widespread genetically determined disorder affecting mucous secretions in many parts of the body. The consequent blockage causes small cystic swellings behind the sites of the blockage. It results in damage to the lungs, liver, and pancreas, and obstruction in the alimentary tract. >> cyst (medicine)

cystitis [sis**tiy**tis] An infection of the wall of the urinary bladder. It induces frequency of urination, with a burning sensation on passing urine. >> bladder

cytokines [**siy**tokiynz] Messenger molecules within the immune system which are involved in modulating the immune response. Some (eg interferon) have been genetically engineered, and tested (though not with particular success) in diseases such as cancer. >> immunosuppression

cytology [siy**tol**ojee] The study of the structure and function of cells. Microscopic studies of cells, using a variety of staining techniques to identify cell types, are important in the diagnosis of some diseases, especially cancer. >> cell; electron microscope ℹ; karyology

cytoplasm [**siy**toplazm] That part of an animal or plant cell enclosed by the cell membrane (*plasma membrane*) but excluding the nucleus. The cytoplasm contains a range of organelles, each with a specialized function. >> cell

cytosine [**siy**toseen] $C_4H_5N_3O$. A base derived from pyrimidine, one of the four found in nucleic acids, where it is generally paired with guanine. >> DNA ℹ

cytotoxic drugs >> **chemotherapy**

csar >> **tsar**

Czechoslovakia [chekoslo**vah**kia], Czech **Československo**, official name **Czech and Slovak Federative Republic** pop (1992e) 15 605 000; area 127 899 sq km/49 369 sq mi. Former federal state consisting of the Czech Republic (W) and the Slovak Republic (E); capital, Prague; official languages, Czech and Slovak; population, 65% Czech, 30% Slovak, with several minorities; unit of currency, the koruna or crown of 100 haler; formerly ruled by Austrian Habsburgs; Czech lands united with Slovakia to form separate state, 1918; Mazaryk elected first president of parliamentary democracy; communist rule followed 1948 coup; attempt at liberalization by Dubček terminated by intervention of Warsaw Pact troops, 1968; strong dissident protest movement led to fall of communism in 1989, amd election of President Havel; each republic was governed by a National Council; with overall power vested in the Federal Assembly, which elected the president, and comprised the Chamber of Nations (75 Czech and 75 Slovak delegates) and Chamber of the People (200 elected deputies); agreement to divide into the two constituent republics made in 1992, effective 1 January 1993. >> Czech Republic ℹ; Dubček; Havel; Slovak Republic ℹ; RR1006 political leaders

Czech Republic [chek], Czech **Česká Republika** pop (1995e) 10 414 000; area 78 864 sq km/30 441 sq mi. Republic in C Europe; comprises former provinces of Bohemia, Silesia, Moravia; capital, Prague; other chief cities, Brno, Plzeň, Ostrava; timezone GMT +1; major ethnic groups, Czech (81%), Moravian (13%), Slovak (4%), with Hungarian, Polish, German, and Ukrainian minorities; languages, Czech (official), with several minorities; religions, Roman Catholic (39%), Protestant (2%); currency, the koruna of 100 haler; landlocked state; Bohemian massif, average height 900 m/3000 ft, surrounds the Bohemian basin in W; Elbe–Moldau river system flows N into Germany; fertile Danube plain in S Vltava valley of Moravia divides Czech from Slovak republics; c. 40% land arable; continental climate, with warm, humid summers and cold, dry winters; average annual temperatures 2° (Jan), 19° (Jul) in Prague; average annual rainfall, 483 mm/19 in; ruled by Austrian Habsburgs, early 17th-c; Czech lands united with Slovakia to form separate state of Czechoslovakia, 1918; occupied by Germany, 1938; government in exile during World War 2; independence, with some loss of territory to USSR, 1946; communist rule imposed after 1948 coup; attempt at liberalization by Dubček terminated by intervention of Warsaw Pact troops, 1968; fall from power of Communist Party, 1989; 1992 agreement to divide Czechoslovakia into its constituent republics, effective January 1993; governed by a president (elected for 5 years), prime minister, Council of Ministers, a bicameral parliament, consisting of a 200-member Chamber of Deputies (elected for 4 years) and an 81-member Senate (elected for 6 years); steel production around Ostrava coalfields; machinery, iron, glass, chemicals, motor vehicles, cement; wheat, sugar beet, potatoes, rye, corn, barley. >> Bohemia; Dubček; Havel; Moravia; Prague; Slovak Republic ℹ; RR1006 political leaders

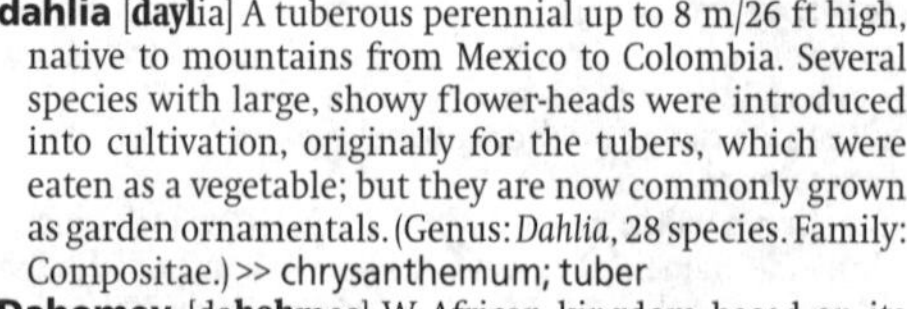

dab European flatfish (*Limanda limanda*) abundant on sandy bottoms in inshore waters; both eyes on right side of head; scales rough; body length up to 40 cm/16 in; valuable food fish. (Family: Pleuronectidae.) >> flatfish

dabchick The common name for some smaller birds of the grebe family. >> grebe

Dacca >> **Dhaka**

dace Freshwater fish (*Leuciscus leuciscus*) widespread in rivers of Europe and Russia; length up to 30 cm/1 ft, body slim; olive-green above, underside silvery white. (Family: Cyprinidae.)

dachshund A breed of dog, developed from small terriers in Germany; small, with long back, short legs; long muzzle, pendulous ears; used for hunting (sent into burrows); also known as **sausage dog**. >> dog; terrier

dactylology [dakti**lol**ojee] A means of communication in which the fingers are used to sign the different letters of the alphabet; also known as **finger-spelling**. Both two-handed and one-handed manual alphabets have been devised. >> deafness; sign language

dactyloscopy >> **fingerprint**

Dada (Fr 'rocking horse') or **Dadaism** A modern art movement founded in Zürich in 1916, which attacked traditional artistic values. The name was chosen at random from a dictionary. Important contributors included Arp, Duchamp, Ernst, Picabia, and Ray. Their deliberate shock-tactics were revived by some artists in the 1960s. >> art; collage; modern art; readymade; Arp; Duchamp; Ernst; Picabia; Ray, Man

daddy longlegs >> **cranefly**

Daedalus [**dee**dalus] A legendary Athenian inventor, who worked for King Minos in Crete and constructed the labyrinth. Any archaic work of skill was ascribed to him, and he was a patron saint of craftsmen in Ancient Greece. >> Minos

daffodil A species of narcissus (*Narcissus pseudonarcissus*), yellow, with a central trumpet up to 2·5 cm/1 in long, and darker than the six surrounding segments; native to Europe. (Family: Amaryllidaceae.) >> narcissus

Dafoe, Willem [da**foh**] (1955–) Film actor, born in Appleton, WI. He made his film debut with a small part in *Heaven's Gate* (1980), and went on to the Oscar-nominated role of Sergeant Elias in *Platoon* (1986) and the controversial title role in *The Last Temptation of Christ* (1988). Later films include *The English Patient* (1996) and *Foolish Heart* (1998).

Dafydd ap Gwilym [**dav**ith ap **gwil**im] (c.1320–c.1380) Poet, born probably in Brogynin, Cardiganshire. He wrote love songs, satirical poems, and nature poems in the complex *cywydd* metre which he perfected, much extending the range of such poetry.

daguerreotype [da**ge**ruhtiyp] An early system of photography established by Louis Daguerre (1789–1851) in France in 1839. A silver-plated sheet was sensitized by iodine vapour, and after a long exposure in the camera the image was developed over heated mercury and fixed in a solution of common salt. It became obsolete in the 1850s. >> photography

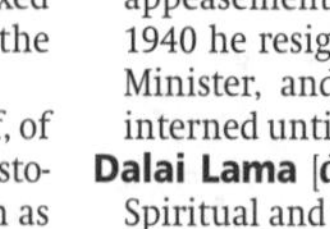

Dahl, Roald (1916–90) Writer, born in Llandaff, Cardiff, of Norwegian parents. He specialized in writing short stories of unexpected horror and macabre surprise, such as in *Someone Like You* (1953). His children's books, such as *James and the Giant Peach* (1961) and *Charlie and the Chocolate Factory* (1964), display a similar taste for the grotesque.

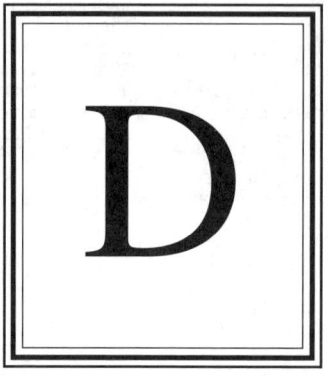

dahlia [**day**lia] A tuberous perennial up to 8 m/26 ft high, native to mountains from Mexico to Colombia. Several species with large, showy flower-heads were introduced into cultivation, originally for the tubers, which were eaten as a vegetable; but they are now commonly grown as garden ornamentals. (Genus: *Dahlia*, 28 species. Family: Compositae.) >> chrysanthemum; tuber

Dahomey [da**hoh**mee] W African kingdom based on its capital at Abomey, which in the late 17th-c extended its authority from the coast to the interior. The state was annexed by the French in 1883, and regained its independence (later renaming itself Benin) in 1960. >> Benin [i]

Dáil Éireann [**doyl air**an] (Gaelic 'Assembly of Ireland') The lower house of the parliament of the Ireland. Unlike the upper house, the Senate (*Seanad Éireann*), which is appointed, the Dáil is elected by proportional representation for a period of 5 years.

Daimler, Gottlieb (Wilhelm) [**daym**ler] (1834–1900) Engineer, born in Schorndorf, Germany. He worked from 1872 on improving the gas engine, and in 1885 designed one of the earliest roadworthy motor cars. >> car [i]; engine; gas engine

dairy farming A farming system specializing in the production of milk – usually from cows, but in some regions from sheep, goats, yaks, buffalo, or reindeer. Specialist dairy-cow breeds include Friesians, Ayrshires, and Jerseys. Farmers sell their milk to dairy manufacturers, who make butter, cheese, cream, yogurt, and skimmed milk. These foods are **dairy products**. >> cow

daisy A perennial native to Europe and W Asia (*Bellis perennis*), with a basal rosette of oval or spoon-shaped leaves; leafless flowering stems up to 20 cm/8 in, each bearing a solitary flower-head; outer ray florets white often tinged red, inner disc florets yellow. (Family: Compositae.) >> floret; immortelle

daisy-wheel printer A type of impact printer, used in computer systems and in typewriters, in which the individual print characters are carried on separate 'petals' of a segmented disc called the **daisy-wheel**. The daisy-wheel is rotated to bring the relevant character in front of a striking hammer. Daisy-wheel printers are relatively slow, but are capable of producing high quality typescript. >> computer printer

Dakar [da**kah(r)**] 14°38N 17°27W, pop (1995e) 1 874 000. Seaport capital of Senegal; founded, 1857; capital of French West Africa, 1902; part of Dakar and Dependencies, 1924–46; held by Vichy forces during World War 2; capital of Senegal, 1958; airport; railway terminus; university (1957); cathedral (consecrated, 1936). >> Senegal [i]; Vichy

Daladier, Edouard [daladyay] (1884–1970) French statesman and prime minister (1933, 1934, 1938–40), born in Carpentras, France. As premier (1938) he supported appeasement policies and signed the Munich Pact. In 1940 he resigned, became successively War and Foreign Minister, and on the fall of France was arrested and interned until 1945. >> France [i]

Dalai Lama [**da**liy **lah**ma], (Mongolian, 'ocean-like guru') Spiritual and temporal head of Tibet, regarded as a manifestation of the Bodhisattva Avalokiteshavara. Tenzin Gyatso (1935–), held to be the 14th incarnation, ruled in Tibet from 1940 to 1959. Following the Chinese invasion of the country, he escaped to India. He received the Nobel Peace Prize in 1989. >> bodhisattva; guru; Lamaism; Panchen Lama

Dalglish, Kenny [dal**gleesh**], popular name of **Kenneth Mathieson Dalglish** (1951–) Footballer and manager, born in Glasgow. He joined Glasgow Celtic in 1967, transferring to Liverpool in 1977, and won 102 caps for Scotland. Unexpectedly invited to manage Liverpool while still a player, in his first season Liverpool won both Cup and League. He joined Newcastle United as manager (1997–8). >> football

Dalhousie, James Andrew Broun Ramsay, 1st Marquess of [dal**how**zee] (1812–60) British Governor-General of India (1847–56), born at Dalhousie Castle, Midlothian. He annexed Satara (1847) and Punjab (1849), but the annexation of Oudh (1856) caused resentment which fuelled the 1857 Rebellion. >> Indian Mutiny

Dali, Salvador (Felipe Jacinto) [**dah**lee], Span **Dalí** (1904–89) Artist, born in Figueras, Spain. One of the principal figures of the Surrealist movement, his study of abnormal psychology and dream symbolism led him to represent 'paranoiac' objects in landscapes remembered from his Spanish boyhood. One of his best-known paintings is 'The Persistence of Memory' (known as 'The Limp Watches', 1931, New York). >> Surrealism

Dalian [dalyan], also **Lüda**, **Lü-ta**, **Dairen**, **Ta-lien** 38°53N 121°37E, pop (1995e) 2 663 000. Port city in NE China; port built by Japanese, 1899–1930; Soviet occupation, 1945–54; resort beaches nearby; airfield; railway; centre of fruit-growing area. >> China ℹ

Dallas 32°47N 96°49W, pop (1995e) 1 064 000. City in NE Texas, USA; commercial and financial centre of the SW; eighth largest city in the USA; founded, 1841; city status, 1871; President Kennedy assassinated here (22 Nov 1963); airport (Dallas–Fort Worth); railway; two universities (1910, 1956); scene of the television series *Dallas*; professional teams, Mavericks (basketball), Cowboys (football). >> Kennedy, John F; Texas

Dalmatia [dal**may**sha] A name applied since early times to the strip of territory bordering the Adriatic Sea in W Yugoslavia; largely mountainous and barren; formerly part of the Greek province of Illyria; occupied by Slavs, 7th-c AD. >> Adriatic Sea; Yugoslavia ℹ

dalmatian A breed of dog, officially from the Balkans W coastal region, but probably developed in India many centuries ago; large, lightly built, with long legs, tail, and muzzle; ears short, pendulous; coat short, white with black or brown spots. >> dog

Dalton, John [**dawl**tn] (1766–1844) Chemist, born in Eaglesfield, Cumbria. His chief physical researches were on mixed gases, the force of steam, the elasticity of vapours, and the expansion of gases by heat. His development of the atomic theory of matter (c.1810) elevated chemistry to a quantitative science. >> chemistry

dalton >> **atomic mass unit**

dam A barrier constructed to control the flow of water, thus forming a reservoir. Dams are built to allow storage of water, giving a controlled supply for domestic or industrial consumption, for irrigation, to generate hydro-electric power, or to prevent flooding. They are built either as **gravity dams**, where the strength is due entirely to the great weight of material; as **arch dams**, where abutments at either side support the structure; or as **arch gravity dams**, a combination of the two. The earliest known dams were in China, 6th-c BC. >> Aswan; Grand Coulee / Hoover / Itaipu / Kariba dam

daman >> **hyrax**

Daman and Diu [da**mahn**, **dee**oo] pop (1995e) 110 000; area 456 sq km/176 sq mi. Union territory in W India; chief town, Daman; island of Diu taken by Portugal, 1534; Daman area N of Bombay ceded to Portugal, 1539; occupied by India, 1961; part of Union Territory of Goa, Daman and Diu until 1987. >> India ℹ

Damascus [da**mas**kus], Arabic **Dimashq** 33°30N 36°19E, pop (1995e) 1 603 000. Capital city of Syria; claimed to be the world's oldest continuously inhabited city; a world heritage site; satellite city Dimashq ad-Jadideh; airport; railway; university (1923); famous for its crystallized fruits, brass and copper ware, silks, woodwork; Great Mosque (8th-c, burned 1893, then restored). >> Syria ℹ; Ummayyad Mosque

Damian or **Damianus, St** >> **Cosmas and Damian, Saints**

Damien, Father Joseph [damyī], originally **Joseph de Veuster** (1840–89) Missionary, born in Tremelo, Belgium. He was renowned for his great work among the lepers of the Hawaiian island of Molokai, where he lived from 1873 until his death from the disease. He became internationally known after Robert Louis Stevenson published a passionate defence of his character and work. >> Stevenson, Robert Louis

Damocles [**dam**okleez] (4th-c BC) Legendary courtier of the elder Dionysius, tyrant of Syracuse (405–367 BC), who was shown the precarious nature of fortune in a singular manner. While seated at a richly-spread table, Damocles looked up to see a keen-edged sword suspended over his head by a single horsehair. >> Dionysius the Elder

Damon and Pythias [**day**mon, **pith**ias], also found as **Phintias** (4th-c BC) Two Pythagoreans of Syracuse, remembered as the models of faithful friendship. Condemned to death by the elder Dionysius, Pythias begged to be allowed to go home to arrange his affairs, and Damon pledged his own life for his friend's. Pythias returned just in time to save Damon from death. Struck by so noble an example, Dionysius pardoned Pythias. >> Dionysius the Elder

Dampier, William [**dam**peer] (1652–1715) Navigator and buccaneer, born near Yeovil, Somerset. In 1683 he sailed across the Pacific, visiting the Philippines, China, and Australia. He then led a voyage of discovery to the South Seas (1699), exploring the NW coast of Australia, and giving his name to the *Dampier Archipelago* and *Strait*.

damping Reduction of the size of oscillations by the removal of energy. For example, the indicator needles of gauges are often immersed in oil to give frictional damping; and resistive circuit components reduce electrical oscillations. >> oscillation

damselfish Any of the family Pomacentridae; small brightly coloured marine fishes widespread in tropical and temperate seas around reefs and rocky shores; body length 10–25 cm/4–10 in. (7 genera, including *Chromis* and *Pomacentrus*.) >> anemone

damselfly A large, long-bodied insect with two pairs of slender wings typically held together over the abdomen at rest. Damselflies are powerful predators, both as aquatic larvae and as flying adults. (Order: Odonata. Suborder: Zygoptera, c.3000 species.)

damson A type of plum (*Prunus domestica*. Subspecies *insititia*) in which the small, ovoid fruit is purplish with a waxy bloom; thought to be a cultivated form of bullace. (Family: Rosaceae.) >> bullace; plum

Danae [**dan**ayee] In Greek mythology, the daughter of King Acrisius of Argos. When an oracle prophesied that her son would kill his grandfather, Acrisius imprisoned her in a bronze tower, where Zeus visited her in the form of a golden shower. She gave birth to a son, Perseus, who accidentally killed Acrisius with a discus. >> Perseus (mythology)

Danakil Depression [**dan**akil] Desert area in NE Ethiopia and Eritrea; mountainous in parts, rising to 1000 m/3000 ft; land also dips to 116 m/381 ft below sea-level;

extremely hot area, temperatures close to 60°C; major salt reserves; crossed by Djibouti–Addis Ababa railway. >> Eritrea [i]; Ethiopia [i]

Da Nang [dah **nang**], formerly **Tourane** 16°04N 108°13E, pop (1995e) 416 000. Seaport in C Vietnam; site of an important US military base during the Vietnam War. >> Vietnam [i]; Vietnam War

Dance, George, known as **George Dance the Elder** (1695–1768) Architect, born in London. He designed the Mansion House (1739) and many other London buildings. His son, **George Dance, the Younger**, (1741–1825), was also an architect. An exponent of Neoclassicism, his best-known building was Newgate Prison (1770–83). >> Neoclassicism (art and architecture)

dance notation The recording of dance movement through symbols. More than 100 systems have been created, using letter abbreviations (15th-c), track drawings (18th-c), stick figure and music note systems (19th-c), and abstract symbol systems. Three are in current use; Benesh, Eshkol, and Labanotation. >> Benesh; choreography; Laban

dance of death A common theme in late mediaeval art: the allegorical representation of a dance or procession in which the living and the dead take part. Holbein the Younger designed a famous set of woodcuts on this theme (published 1538). >> Holbein; woodcut

dance therapy A form of group psychotherapy, with or without music, which encourages spontaneous movements rather than teaching formal dance sequences. It is particularly used as a way of enabling people who have difficulty in talking about their feelings to express their emotions through body movements. >> psychotherapy

D and C >> **dilatation and curettage**

dandelion A perennial, native to Europe and W Asia; flower-heads solitary, borne on leafless hollow stems, florets yellow; fruits with a parachute of white hairs attached by a long stalk, the whole fruiting head forming the familiar 'clock'. The best-known species, *Taraxacum officinale*, is a cosmopolitan weed, its flower-heads sometimes used for wine-making, and its young leaves for salad. (Genus: *Taraxacum*, c.60 species. Family: Compositae.) >> floret

Dandie Dinmont A breed of dog, developed in Britain in the 19th-c from wire-haired hunting terriers; small terrier with long body and short legs; long soft hair, especially on the head; ears pendulous; tail long. >> dog; terrier

Dandolo, Enrico [**dan**doloh] (c.1110–1205) Italian statesman, born in Venice, Italy. He became Doge of Venice (1192), and in 1202 marched at the head of the Fourth Crusade. >> Crusades [i]

dandruff Fine dry scales which fall from an eruption of the skin of the scalp, usually noticed when the scales fall on to clothing around the shoulders. It possibly results from infection with the fungus *Pityrosporum*. >> skin [i]

Dane, Clemence, pseudonym of **Winifred Ashton** (c.1891–1965) Novelist and playwright, born in London. Her novels include *Regiment of Women* (1917), and *The Flower Girls* (1954). Many of her plays achieved long runs, notably *A Bill of Divorcement* (1921).

Danelaw That part of E England where Danish conquest and colonization in the late 9th-c left an imprint not only on legal and administrative practices, but on place-names, language, and culture. >> Vikings; Wessex

Daniel, Glyn (Edmund) (1914–86) Archaeologist, born in Barry, Vale of Glamorgan. He stimulated popular interest in archaeology through writing, editing, and broadcasting, and achieved particular popularity on British television in the 1950s as the genial chairman of the archaeological panel game, *Animal, Vegetable, Mineral*. >> archaeology

Daniel, Book of A book of the Hebrew Bible/Old Testament named after Daniel, its main character. Although some date the work in the 6th-c BC, many prefer a later date of the 3rd–2nd-c BC, with several stages of compilation. >> Old Testament

danio [**day**nioh] Colourful freshwater fish (*Danio malabaricus*) from India and Sri Lanka, extremely popular among aquarists; body with blue and golden side stripes, length up to c.13 cm/5 in. (Family: Cyprinidae.)

Danish >> **Germanic languages; Scandinavian languages**

d'Annunzio, Gabriele [da**nunt**seeoh] (1863–1938) Writer, born in Pescara, Italy. During the 1890s he wrote several novels, influenced by the philosophy of Nietzsche, notably *Il trionfo della morte* (1894, The Triumph of Death). His major plays include the tragedy *La gioconda* (1899), which he wrote for the actress Eleonora Duse. Their tempestuous relationship was exposed in his erotic novel, *Il fuoco* (1900, trans The Flame of Life). He became a national hero following his active service in World War 1, though he later supported fascism. >> Duse; Nietsche

Dante (Alighieri) (1265–1321) Poet, born in Florence, Italy. In 1274, when he was nine, a meeting with **Beatrice** (c.1265–90), possibly the daughter of the Florentine aristocrat Folco Portinari, influenced the rest of his life. The *Vita nuova*, which tells of his boyish passion for Beatrice, is probably his earliest work. By far the most celebrated is the *Divina commedia* (Divine Comedy), a vision of hell, purgatory, and heaven which gives an encyclopedic view of the highest culture and knowledge of his age. He also wrote several shorter poems, as well as treatises on government and language.

Danton, Georges (Jacques) [dãtõ] (1759–94) French revolutionary politician, born in Arcis-sur-Aube, France. He voted for the death of the king (1793), and was one of the original members of the Committee of Public Safety. He tried to abate the pitiless severity of his own Revolutionary Tribunal, but lost the leadership to Robespierre, and was guillotined. >> French Revolution [i]

Danu In Celtic religion, a mother-goddess who is associated with hills and the earth.

Danube, River, Ger **Donau**, Bulgarian **Dunav**, Russian **Dunai**, Romanian **Dunarea** River in C and SE Europe, rising in the Black Forest, SW Germany; flows generally E and S to enter the Black Sea through a wide, swampy delta; second longest river in Europe (2850 km/1770 mi); flows through Vienna, Budapest, and Belgrade.

Danube School Pioneers of imaginative landscape painting who worked in the Danube region in the early 16th-c. Their members included Altdorfer and Cranach. >> landscape painting; Altdorfer; Cranach

Danzig >> **Gdańsk**

Daoism >> **Taoism**

Daphne In Greek mythology, the daughter of a river-god, Ladon (or, in another story, Peneios). Pursued by the god Apollo, she was saved by being turned into a laurel, which became Apollo's sacred tree. >> Apollo

Daphnia [**daf**nia] A genus of water flea, commonly found in freshwater bodies. (Class: Branchiopoda. Order: Cladocera.) >> water flea

Daphnis In Greek mythology, a Sicilian shepherd, half-brother of Pan, who was loved by a nymph. He did not return her love, so she blinded him. He became the inventor of pastoral poetry. >> Pan

Dardanelles or **Hellespont** [dah(r)da**nelz**], Turkish **Çanakkale Boğazi**, ancient **Hellespontus** Narrow strait in NW Turkey, connecting the Aegean Sea (W) and the Sea of Marmara (E); length 65 km/40 mi; width varies from 1·6–6·4 km/1–4 mi; scene of an unsuccessful Allied campaign in World War 1. >> Gallipoli; Marmara, Sea of; Turkey [i]

Dar es Salaam [**dahr** es sa**lahm**] 6°51S 39°18E, pop (1995e) 1 630 000. Seaport in E Tanzania; founded, 1882; occupied by German East Africa Company, 1887; capital of German East Africa, 1891; occupied by the British in World War 1; capital of Tanganyika, 1916–64; capital of Tanzania until 1974; industrial, commercial, and financial centre; airport; university (1970). >> Tanzania [i]

Darién [da**ryen**] pop (1995e) 47 800; area 16 803 sq km/ 6 486 sq mi. Province of E Panama; capital, La Palma; attempted settlement by the Scots in the 1690s (the **Darién Scheme**). >> Panama [i]

Darío, Rubén [da**ree**oh], pseudonym of **Félix Rubén García Sarmiento** (1867–1916) Poet, born in Metapa, Nicaragua. His *Azul* (1888, Blue) and *Prosas profanas* (1896, Profane Hymns) gave new vitality to Spanish poetic modernism.

Darius I [**dah**rius], known as **the Great** (548–486 BC) King of Persia (521–486 BC), one of the greatest of the Achaemenids. He is noteworthy for his administrative reforms, military conquests, and religious toleration. His conquests, especially in the East and Europe (Thrace and Macedonia) consolidated the frontiers of the empire, but he was defeated at Marathon (490 BC). >> Achaemenids; Greek-Persian Wars [i]; Marathon, Battle of

Darjeeling or **Darjiling** [dah(r)**jee**ling] 27°02N 88°20E, pop (1995e) 74 000. Hill station in West Bengal, NE India; centre of a tea-growing region. >> West Bengal

Dark Ages A term occasionally applied to the period of European history from c.500 to c.1000, but misleading because of its negative implications. Historians usually describe the whole period c.500–c.1500 as the **Middle Ages**. >> Middle Ages

dark matter Material in space which does not emit light, and which therefore cannot be seen with conventional astronomical instruments; also known as the **missing mass**. Over 95% of the universe is thought to be composed of dark matter. According to one view, most of this matter consists of *machos* (*massive compact halo objects*) – large structures which do not emit light (such as black holes and brown dwarfs). An opposing view conceives of dark matter as consisting of new kinds of sub-atomic particle which have so far not been detected, known as *wimps* (*weakly interacting massive particles*). >> black hole; brown dwarf; interplanetary matter

Darling, Grace (1815–42) Heroine, born in Bamburgh, Northumberland. She lived with her father **William** (1795–1860), the lighthouse keeper on one of the Farne Islands. In 1838 she braved raging seas in an open rowing boat to rescue the survivors of the *Forfarshire*, which was stranded on one of the other islands in the group. >> Farne Islands

Darling Range Mountain range in Western Australia, near Perth; extends 320 km/200 mi S along the SW coast, and rises to 582 m/1909 ft at Mt Cooke. >> Western Australia

Darling River Longest tributary of the Murray R; flows generally SW to join the Murray R; length 3070 km/ 1908 mi; used for irrigation in New South Wales. >> Australia [i]; Murray River

Darnley, Henry Stewart, Lord (1545–67) Nobleman, the second husband of Mary, Queen of Scots and father of James I of England, born at Temple Newsom, Yorkshire. His part in the murder (1566) of the Queen's secretary, David Rizzio, caused his downfall. He became estranged from the Queen, and during an illness was killed at Edinburgh. >> Bothwell, Earl of; Mary, Queen of Scots

Darrow, Clarence (Seward) (1857–1938) Lawyer, born in Kinsman, OH. Known for his defences of trade union leaders, he was also involved in several notable cases, including the trial of John T Scopes (1925) for the teaching of Darwinian evolution in school. >> evolution; industrial action

Darter

Dart, Raymond (Arthur) (1893–1988) Palaeoanthropologist, born in Brisbane, Queensland, Australia. His discovery (1924) of *Australopithecus africanus* substantiated Darwin's view of Africa as the cradle of the human species. >> anthropology; Darwin, Charles

Dart, Thurston (1921–71) Keyboard player, conductor, and musical scholar, born in London. A specialist in early music, he edited several editions of 16th-c and 17th-c English works.

darter A slender bird native to warm regions worldwide; spears fish underwater with long pointed bill; swims with only head and long neck out of water; called **anhinga** in the New World, **darter** in the Old World; also known as **snake bird** and **water turkey**. (Genus: *Anhinga*, 1 or 2 species; experts disagree. Family: Anhingidae.)

Dartmoor National park in Devon, S England; area 913 sq km/352 sq mi; established in 1951; noted for its granite tors and hanging oak woods; highest point, High Willhays, 621 m/2039 ft; prison (1806–13). >> Devon; Three Age System

Dartmoor pony A small pony, developed on Dartmoor, England; tough and sure-footed; calm-natured; height, up to 12·2 hands/1·3 m/4 ft 2 in; usually brown or black; slim legs, long bushy tail and mane, short erect ears. >> Dartmoor; horse [i]

Dartmouth College >> **Ivy League** [i]

darts An indoor game played by throwing three darts (or 'arrows') at a circular board of 20 numbered segments. The throwing distance is normally 8 ft (2·4 m), and the height from the floor to the centre of the board (known as the *bull*) is 5 ft 8 in (1·7 m). The modern game is credited to a Lancashire carpenter Brian Gamlin (1852–1903) who devised the present-day board and scoring system. >> RR1051

Darwin, Charles (Robert) (1809–82) Naturalist, the discoverer of natural selection, born in Shrewsbury. In 1831 he became the naturalist on HMS *Beagle*, surveying South American waters, and returned in 1836, having travelled extensively throughout the S Pacific. From 1842 he spent his time at Downe, Kent, working in his garden and breeding pigeons and fowls, and here he devoted himself to his major work, *On the Origin of Species by Means of Natural Selection* (1859). An epoch-making work, it was given a mixed reaction throughout Europe, but in the end received widespread recognition. >> biology; Darwinism

Darwin (Australia), formerly **Palmerston** (to 1911), **Port Darwin** 12°23S 130°44E, pop (1995e) 82 600. Seaport capital of Northern Territory, Australia; first European settlement (1869) destroyed by hurricane in 1879; bombed by the Japanese, 1942; destroyed by cyclone Tracy, 1974; airport; railway; university college; cathedral (1902). >> Northern Territory

Darwin (Falkland Is) 51°48S 58°59W. Settlement on East Falkland, Falkland Is; c.70 km/43 mi from Stanley. >> Falkland Islands ℹ

Darwinism The theory of evolution proposed jointly by Charles Darwin and Alfred Russel Wallace, and later expanded upon by Darwin in *On the Origin of Species by Means of Natural Selection*. Individuals of a species show variation. On average, more offspring are produced than are needed to replace the parents, but population size remains more or less stable in nature. There must therefore be competition for survival; and it is the best adapted (the fittest) variants which survive and reproduce. Evolution occurs by means of natural selection acting on individual variation, resulting in the survival of the fittest. The discovery of the genetic mechanism causing variation has resulted in a modified version of the theory, known as **neo-Darwinism**. >> Darwin, Charles; evolution; natural selection; Wallace, Alfred Russel

Darwin's finches A closely related group of birds, native to the Galapagos Is (off Ecuador); also known as **Galapagos finches**. The classification of the group is currently uncertain; they may be put in the family Fringillidae (finches) or the family Emberizidae (buntings and their allies). Charles Darwin's observations on this group were important to his ideas about natural selection. >> bunting; finch

dasheen >> **taro**

Dassanowsky, Elfriede von [dasa**nof**skee] (1924–) Operatic singer, pianist, and music educator, born in Vienna, Austria. She promoted the rebuilding of democratic cultural institutions in postwar Austria and Germany, and was instrumental in the revival of German-language cinema. She moved to the USA in 1955, and has since come to be recognized as a leading figure of postwar European culture.

dassie >> **hyrax**

dasyure [**das**yoor] A marsupial native to Australia and New Guinea; includes quolls, dunnarts, and the Tasmanian devil. (Family: Dasyuridae, 51 species.) >> carnivore ℹ; marsupial ℹ; Tasmanian devil

data In computing, the stored facts and figures on which computers operate in order to perform their assigned task. For example, in a payroll operation the data would be the employee details, the details of the hours worked, etc, and the national insurance, pension, and taxation rules to be applied. The task of taking facts (eg names, addresses) and figures from a form and entering them into a computer system is known as **data entry**. >> character recognition; database; knowledge-based system

database A file of computer data structured in such a way that it can be of general use and is independent of any specific application. This information can be managed by a **database management system (DBMS)**, a software system or program which allows data to be modified, deleted, added to, and retrieved from one or more databases. >> computer

data processing (DP) A general term used to describe various uses of computers in business. These include clerical functions (eg scheduling and stock control), financial functions (eg salaries and budget management), and many other aspects of business management and planning. >> computer

data protection The techniques of maintaining the privacy and the integrity of computer-based information. The UK Data Protection Act (1987) requires formal registration of all computer users who store information on individuals, and there is similar legislation in several other countries.

Date Line An imaginary line, based by international agreement on the meridian of 180° (with deviations to keep certain islands in the same zone as their respective mainlands); the date is altered to compensate for the gain or loss of time (1 hour per 15°) which occurs when circumnavigating the globe. >> RR977

date palm A tree reaching 30 m/100 ft (*Phoenix dactylifera*); thick trunk covered with old, spiny leaf bases; leaves feathery; native to Near East, and widely cultivated since 6000 BC. A single tree produces up to 250 kg/550 lb of deep orange, sugary dates each year for up to 100 years or more. (Family: Palmae.) >> palm

date plum >> **persimmon**

Datong or **Ta-t'ung** [dahtoong] 40°12N 113°12E, pop (1995e) 1 369 000. City in Shanxi province, NEC China; founded in the 4th-c as capital of N Wei dynasty; railway. >> China ℹ

Daubigny, Charles François [dohbeenyee] (1817–78) Artist, born in Paris. He was a member of the Barbizon School, painting landscapes, especially moonlight and river scenes, such as 'The Banks of the Oise' (1872, Reims). >> Barbizon School

Daudet, Alphonse [dohday] (1840–97) Writer, born in Nîmes, France. He wrote several theatrical pieces, including *L'Arlésienne* (1872), for which Bizet composed incidental music. His sketches of Provençal subjects appeared as *Lettres de mon moulin* (1869, Letters from My Mill). >> Bizet

Daughters of the American Revolution A patriotic society organized in the USA in 1890; members must be directly descended from soldiers or patriots of the Revolutionary period. >> American Revolution

Daumier, Honoré (Victorin) [dohmyay] (1808–79) Painter and caricaturist, born in Marseille, France. He won contemporary fame for satirical cartoons about government corruption, and was imprisoned for caricaturing the king. >> caricature

Dauphin [**doh**fĩ] The title of the eldest son of the reigning French monarch in the period 1350–1830, acquired in 1349 when the future King Charles V purchased the lands known as Dauphiné.

daurian jackdaw >> **jackdaw**

Davao or **Davao City** [**da**vow] 7°05N 125°38E, pop (1995e) 948 000. Seaport in S Mindanao, Philippines; founded, 1849; formerly held by the Japanese; airfield; university (1965); commercial centre. >> Mindanao; Philippines ℹ

Davenant or **d'Avenant, Sir William** [**dav**enant] (1606–68) Poet and playwright, born in Oxford, Oxfordshire. His father kept the Crown, at which Shakespeare used to stop between London and Stratford – hence the rumour that he was Shakespeare's illegitimate son. His most successful work was *The Wits* (1636). He became Poet Laureate in 1638.

David (?–c.962 BC) Second King of Israel. According to Jewish tradition the author of several of the Psalms, and according to some Christian traditions the ancestor of Jesus. He was a warrior under King Saul, but his successes against the Philistines (including the killing of Goliath) caused the king's jealousy, and he was forced to become an outlaw. After Saul's death, he was chosen King of all Israel. He made Jerusalem the centre of his kingdom, building a palace for himself on its highest hill, Zion (the 'city of David'). He was succeeded by Solomon, his son by Bathsheba. >> Ark of the Covenant; Goliath; Old Testament; Samuel; Saul; Solomon (religion); Zion

David or **Dewi, St** (?–601) Patron saint of Wales, born near St Bride's Bay, Pembrokeshire. He was Bishop of Moni Judeorum, or Menevia (afterwards St David's), presided over two Welsh synods, at Brefi and Caerleon, and founded many churches in the S of Wales. Feast day 1 March. >> Christianity

David, Jacques Louis [dahveed] (1748–1825) Painter, born in Paris. He became known for his paintings of classical themes and historical events, such as 'The Oath of the Horatii' (1784, Louvre) and 'The Rape of the Sabines' (1799, Louvre), and in 1804 was appointed court painter by Napoleon. >> French Revolution ℹ

Davies, Paul (Charles William) (1946–) Physicist and popularizer of science, born in London. Professor of mathematical physics at Adelaide, Australia, his numerous popular books on science, such as *God and the New Physics* (1983) and *The Mind of God* (1992), reflect his research interests in particle physics and quantum gravity as well as in the links between science and religion. He received the Templeton Prize for Progress in Religion in 1995.

Davies, Sir Peter Maxwell (1934–) Composer, born in Manchester, Greater Manchester. He founded and co-directed the Pierrot Players (1967–70) and was founder/artistic director of The Fires of London (1971–87). His works include *Taverner* (1972) and three other operas, *Eight Songs for a Mad King* (1969), symphonies, and concertos. He was made composer laureate in 1994.

Davies, W(illiam) H(enry) (1871–1940) Poet, born in Newport, SE Wales. He lived a wandering life to raise enough money to have his poems printed (1905). Once known, he wrote several books of poetry, essays, and a prose work, *The Autobiography of a Super-tramp* (1908).

da Vinci, Leonardo >> **Leonardo da Vinci**

Davis, Andrew (Frank) (1944–) Conductor, born at Ashridge House, Hertfordshire. He became musical director of the Toronto Symphony Orchestra (1975–88), then music director of the Glyndebourne Festival Opera, and (from 1989) chief conductor of the BBC Symphony Orchestra. He becomes director of the Chicago Lyric Opera in 2000.

Davis, Bette, popular name of **Ruth Elizabeth Davis** (1908–89) Film actress, born in Lowell, MA. Her leading roles included *Of Human Bondage* (1934), *Dangerous* (1935, Oscar), *Jezebel* (1938, Oscar), *Whatever Happened to Baby Jane?* (1962), and *Death on the Nile* (1979).

Davis, Carl (1936–) Composer and conductor, born in New York City. Among his works for ballet are *Liaison Amoureuses* (1988), *The Savoy Suite* (1993), and *Alice in Wonderland* (1995). His music for television includes *The World at War* (1972, Emmy) and *Pride and Prejudice* (1995), and for film *The French Lieutenant's Woman* (1981, BAFTA) and *Waterloo* (1995).

Davis, Sir Colin (Rex) (1927–) Conductor, born in Weybridge, Surrey. He was chief conductor of the BBC Symphony Orchestra (1967–71), and musical director at Covent Garden (1971–86). He became chief conductor of the Bavarian Radio Symphony Orchestra in 1983, and principal conductor of the London Symphony Orchestra in 1995.

Davis, Geena (1957–) Film actress, born in Wareham, MA. She won an Oscar for Best Supporting Actress for *The Accidental Tourist* (1988), and critical acclaim for her role as Thelma in the controversial film *Thelma and Louise* (1991). Later films include *Angie* (1994) and *The Long Kiss Goodnight* (1996).

Davis, Jefferson (1808–89) US statesman, and president of the Confederate States during the Civil War (1861–5), born in Christian Co, KY. In the Senate he led the extreme States' Rights Party, and supported slavery. At the close of the War he was imprisoned for two years, then released on bail, and included in the amnesty of 1868. >> American Civil War

Davis, Joe, popular name of **Joseph Davis** (1901–78) Billiards and snooker champion, born in Whitwell, Derbyshire. Responsible for inaugurating the World Championship in 1927, he won every title between then and 1946, when he retired from world championship play. His brother, **Fred Davis** (1913–98), followed the same career, winning the first of his 10 world titles in 1948. >> billiards; snooker

Davis, John (c.1550–1605) Navigator, born in Sandridge, Devon. In 1585–7 he undertook three Arctic voyages in search of a Northwest Passage, in the last of which he reached 73°N, and discovered the Strait later named after him. >> Northwest Passage

Davis, Miles (Dewey) (1926–91) Trumpeter, composer, and bandleader, born in Alton, IL. He became the most admired instrumentalist of the postwar era, from 1948 leading a nonet that introduced the style known as 'cool jazz'. >> bebop; jazz; trumpet

Davis, Sammy, Jr (1925–90) Singer, actor, and dancer, born in New York City. He starred on Broadway in *Mr Wonderful* (1956) and in *Golden Boy* (1964), and his films include *Porgy and Bess* (1959), *Robin and the Seven Hoods* (1964), and *Taps* (1980).

Davis, Steve (1957–) Snooker player, born in London. He dominated snooker in the 1980s, winning the world championship six times: 1981, 1983–4, and 1987–9. In 1982, during the Lada Classic, he became the first man to compile a televised maximum 147 break. In 1997 he won the Benson & Hedges Masters tournament. >> snooker

Davis Cup An annual lawn tennis competition for international male teams, first held in 1900, named after the US public official, Dwight Filley Davis (1879–1945), who donated the trophy. >> tennis, lawn ℹ

Davis Strait Sea passage between Greenland and Baffin I, connecting Atlantic and Arctic Oceans; c.650 km/400 mi long by 290 km/180 mi wide at its narrowest point; visited by British navigator John Davis in 1587. >> Davis, John

Davos [da**vohs**], Romansch **Tavau** 46°54N 9°52E, pop (1995e) 11 000. Fashionable resort town in E Switzerland; altitude, 1560 m/5118 ft; railway; noted health resort and winter sports centre. >> Switzerland ℹ

Davy, Sir Humphry (1778–1829) Chemist, born in Penzance, Cornwall. His fame chiefly rests on his discovery that chemical compounds could be decomposed into their elements using electricity. In this way he discovered potassium, sodium, barium, strontium, calcium, and magnesium. In 1815 he invented the miner's safety lamp. In 1820 he became president of the Royal Society. >> chemistry; electricity; respiration; safety lamp

Dawes, Charles G(ates) (1865–1951) US statesman and financier, who became Republican vice-president under Coolidge (1925–9), born in Marietta, OH. He was head of the Commission which drew up the **Dawes Plan** (1924) for German reparation payments to Europe after World War 1, for which he shared the Nobel Peace Prize in 1925.

Dawkins, (Clinton) Richard (1941–) British zoologist, born in Nairobi, Kenya. One of the most successful popularizers of his subject, he became Charles Simonyi professor of public understanding of science at Oxford in 1995. His work on animal behaviour and genetics emphasizes that apparently selfish behaviour is designed to ensure survival of the gene, apparently above that of the carrier (*The Selfish Gene*, 1976), and this and wider views on behaviour and evolution have been developed in *The Blind Watchmaker* (1986), *Climbing Mount Improbable* (1996), and other works. He remains a controversial media figure, known as much for his aggressive atheism as for his scientific views on evolution.

Dayak or **Dyak** The Malayo-Polynesian-speaking indigenous inhabitants of Borneo and Sarawak. They mostly live along rivers in small village communities. >> Borneo; Sarawak

Dayan, Moshe [diyan] (1915–81) Israeli general and statesman, born in Deganya. Fighting with the Allies in World War 2, he lost his left eye, thereafter wearing his distinctive black eye patch. He formed the Rafi Party with Ben-Gurion in 1966, served as defence minister when Israel defeated Egypt, Jordan, and Syria in the Six Day War (1967), and was foreign minister when Egypt and Israel signed their historic peace treaty (1977). >> Arab–Israeli Wars; Israel ℹ

Day-Lewis, C(ecil) (1904–72) Poet, born in Ballintubber, Ireland. During the 1930s, he became known as a leading left-wing writer, but in 1939 broke away from communism. Under the pseudonym of **Nicholas Blake** he wrote detective stories. His *Collected Poems* appeared in 1954, and he became Poet Laureate in 1968. >> Day-Lewis, Daniel

Day-Lewis, Daniel (1958–) Film actor, born in London. He became well known for *My Beautiful Launderette* (1985) and *Room With A View* (1985), and won several awards for his portrayal of handicapped Irish writer Christy Brown in *My Left Foot* (1989, Oscar). Later films include *The Last of the Mohicans* (1992), *Age of Innocence* (1992), and *The Crucible* (1996). >> Day-Lewis, C

Daylight Saving Time A means of making fuller use of the hours of daylight over the summer months, usually by putting clocks forward one hour so that daylight continues longer into the evening. Adopted during World War 1 by Germany in 1917, it was retained after the war by the UK, where it is known as (British) **Summer Time**. In the USA it was enacted in a federal regulation of 1966, but states were given the choice of whether to ignore it (and some have done so). >> time

dBase IV® A widely used computer package for personal computers which allows users to design and implement their own database. Most of the features of a relational database management system are available. >> computer package; database; personal computer; relational database

D-Day The day when the Allies launched the greatest amphibious operation in history (code-named 'Overlord'), and invaded German-occupied Europe. By the end of D-Day, 130 000 troops had been landed on five beach-heads along an 80 km/50 mi stretch of the coast of Normandy, at a cost of 10 000 casualties. >> Normandy campaign; World War 2

DDT A chemical mixture, largely consisting of *d*ichloro*d*iphenyl*t*richloroethane. One of the earliest successful insecticides, it has now been largely abandoned both because new strains of insects have developed immunity to it and because its decomposition products are harmful. >> insecticide

deacon (Gr *diakonos*, 'servant') An official of the Christian Church appointed to assist the minister or priest in administrative, pastoral, and financial affairs. In the late 20th-c, ecumenical factors revived interest in an order of deacons (the **diaconate**). >> clergy; ecumenism

deadly nightshade A stout, large-leaved perennial (*Atropa belladonna*) up to 1·5 m/5 ft high, native to limestone and chalk areas of Europe, W Asia, and N Africa; dull flowers, solitary, tubular, brownish-violet; berry shiny black. All parts of the plant are narcotic and highly poisonous. (Family: Solanaceae.)

dead-nettle An annual or perennial, found almost everywhere, except in the tropics; flowers 2-lipped, the upper hooded, in whorls at the nodes. When not in flower, some species, especially white dead-nettle, resemble true nettles but lack stinging hairs; hence the name. (Genus: *Lamium*, c. 50 species. Family: Labiatae.) >> stinging nettle

dead room >> **anechoic chamber**

Dead Sea, ancient **Lacus Asphaltites**, Hebrew **Bahrat Lut** (Sea of Lot), Old Testament **Salt Sea, Sea of the Plain, East Sea** Inland lake in the Great Rift Valley on the Jordan–Israel border; lowest point on Earth, 400 m/1312 ft below sea-level; 80 km/50 mi long; up to 18 km/11 mi wide; area 900 sq km/350 sq mi; fed by Jordan R (N), but no outlet; one of the most saline lakes in the world. >> Great Rift Valley; Jordan, River

Dead Sea Scrolls Parchment scrolls in Hebrew and Aramaic, many representing books of the Old Testament, 1000 years older than previously known copies, found accidentally in 1947 and 1952–5 concealed in pottery jars in 11 caves near Qumran on the Dead Sea. They are thought to represent the library of an ascetic Jewish sect, the Essenes, concealed when their settlement was overrun by the Roman army in AD 68. >> Essenes; Old Testament; Qumran, community of

deafness Inability or reduced capacity to hear external sounds. **Conductive deafness** is caused by blockage of the entry of sound to the external canal of the ear (eg through wax in ear), or by abnormalities of the tympanic membrane or of the ossicles in the middle ear (eg through middle-ear infection). All sounds irrespective of their pitch are heard with difficulty. **Sensorineural deafness** results from a disturbance of the cochlea, auditory nerve, or neuronal pathways in the brain. Loss of hearing tends to be patchy, affecting only certain frequencies, and amplified or loud sounds are distorted. >> ear ℹ; Ménière's disease

Deák, Francis [dayak] (1803–76) Statesman, born in Zala, Hungary. He practised as an advocate, and in the restored Diet of 1861, emerged as leader of moderate liberalism and negotiated the *Ausgleich* of 1867, establishing the Dual Monarchy of Austria–Hungary. >> *Ausgleich*; Hungary ℹ

Deakin, Alfred (1856–1919) Australian Liberal statesman and prime minister (1903–4, 1905–8, 1909–10), born in Melbourne, Victoria, Australia. He helped to draft Australia's constitution, and as prime minister helped to form many of the new country's policies, notably the White Australia policy. >> Australia ℹ; White Australia Policy

Dean, Christopher >> **Torvill and Dean**

Dean, Dixie, popular name of **William Ralph Dean** (1907–80) Footballer and record goal-scorer, born in Birkenhead, Merseyside. He joined Everton in 1925, and scored 349 goals in 399 games. He still holds the scoring record of 60 League goals in one season.

Dean, James (Byron) (1931–55) Film star, born in Marion, IN. He gained overnight success in the film *East of Eden* (1955), and made only two more films, *Rebel Without a Cause* (1955) and *Giant* (released 1956), before he was killed in a car crash at Paso Robles, CA. He became a cult figure, for many years after his death remaining a symbol of youthful rebellion and self-assertion.

dean (ultimately from Lat *decem*, 'ten') Originally, in a monastery, a monk in charge of 10 novices. Later, the term denoted a senior clergyman (after the bishop) in a cathedral chapter or diocese. In lay terms, it is used for a head of a university or college faculty. >> cathedral; clergy; monasticism

Deane, Sir William (Patrick) (1931–) Governor-general of Australia, born in St Kilda, Victoria, Australia. He was made a judge in the Supreme Court of New South Wales (1977) and the Australian High Court (1982). As governor-general (1995–) he has been outspoken on the question of reconciliation with Australian's indigenous population, and other issues.

death The cessation of all cellular activity in an organism. The exact definition is controversial, and varies among legal systems. It is no longer enough to rely on such criteria as the absence of pulse or heartbeat, respiration, or corneal reflex, given that medical science can sometimes revive people who have temporarily lost these functions, and new criteria continue to be devised, notably the absence of brain waves on an EEG. The matter is of especial importance when faced with uncertainty over the state of being of a person who has been on a life-support system for some appreciable period without showing any change. >> brain death

death cap A deadly poisonous, mushroom-like fungus; cap pale greenish or white, with white gills on underside; common on the ground in broad-leaved woodland in late summer and autumn. (Order: Agaricales. Family: Amanitaceae.) >> fungus; mushroom

'death of God' theology A style of theology popular especially in the USA in the 1960s. It sought to assert the rationality of the Christian faith and belief in the uniqueness of Christ, without belief in a transcendent God. >> Christianity; theology

death's-head moth A large, nocturnal hawk-moth; wingspan up to 12 cm/4¾ in; forewings dark with yellow markings; hindwings ochre-yellow with black bands; black thorax with yellow skull-like marking. (Order: Lepidoptera. Family: Sphingidae.) >> hawk-moth

Death Valley SE California, USA; ancient rift valley lake bed beside the Nevada border; one of the hottest places in the world; contains the lowest point in North America (the Badwater River, altitude −86 m/−282 ft); 225 km/140 mi long; 6–26 km/3¾–16 mi wide; highest point Telescope Peak (3367 m/11 046 ft); less than 50 mm/2 in rainfall per year; named in 1849 by a party of gold prospectors, some of whom died while trying to cross it. >> California; desert

deathwatch beetle A small, brownish beetle, 5–9 mm/⅛–⅓ in long; now found mostly in house timbers; larvae bore into wood; adults tap on wood at mating time (Apr–May). Larvae leave large holes in timber when they emerge. (Order: Coleoptera. Family: Anobiidae.) >> beetle; larva

Deayton, (Gordon) Angus [**day**ton] (1956–) Writer and broadcaster, born in Caterham, Surrey. He became well known for his role in BBC television's *One Foot in the Grave* (from 1989), as went on to be host of *Have I Got News for You* (from 1990) and as writer/presenter of *In Search of Happiness* (1995).

de Beauvoir, Simone [duh bohvwah(r)] (1908–86) Existentialist writer and novelist, born in Paris. Closely associated with Sartre's literary activities after World War 2, she remained his companion until his death (1980). Her own works provide existentialism with an essentially feminine sensibility, notably in her masterpiece *Les Mandarins* (1954, Prix Goncourt). >> existentialism; Sartre

debenture [de**ben**cher] A loan raised by a company, usually with a fixed interest rate and possibly a definite redemption date. Debenture holders have no control over the company as long as their interest is paid, but if it is not they can take over control. >> company

de Bono, Edward (Francis Charles Publius) [duh **boh**noh] (1933–) Psychologist and writer, born in Malta. He is known for his promotion of the skills of thinking which break out of the trammels of the traditional (*lateral thinking*). He has been secretary-general of the Supranational Independent Thinking Organization since 1983.

Debrecen [**deb**retsen] 47°33N 21°42E, pop (1995e) 209 000. City in E Hungary; second largest city in Hungary; railway; three universities (1868, 1912, 1951); commercial centre for agricultural region. >> Alföld; Hungary [i]

Debrett's Peerage A reference guide to the titled aristocracy of Great Britain, named after John Debrett (c.1752–1822). It also offers information on forms of address, precedence, the wearing of decorations, and etiquette. >> Burke's Peerage; peerage

de Broglie >> **Broglie, duc de**

Debs, Eugene V(ictor) (1855–1926) US politician, born in Terre Haute, IN. He helped to establish the Socialist Party of America, was imprisoned for labour agitation, and between 1900 and 1920 stood five times as socialist candidate for president. >> socialism

debt Borrowing by individuals, companies, or governments. Interest is normally payable. Companies with high debts are 'highly geared', or 'highly leveraged', and face financial difficulties if their profits fall or interest rates rise. Individuals in debt through consumer credit or via mortgages on their house also face difficulties if interest rates rise, or if their incomes fall through unemployment. >> bankruptcy; capital (accountancy); factoring

debugging >> **bug** (computing)

Debussy, Claude (Achille) [debüsee] (1862–1918) Composer, born in St Germain-en-Laye, France. His early successes were the *Prélude à l'après-midi d'un faune* (1894), and his piano pieces, *Images* and *Préludes*, producing the pictures in sound which led to his work being described as 'musical Impressionism'.

Decalogue >> **Ten Commandments**

Decapoda [de**kap**oda] A large order of mostly marine crustaceans characterized by three pairs of thoracic legs modified as pincers for feeding, and five pairs of walking legs; horny covering fused along back to form gill chamber above leg bases; contains c.10 000 living species. (Class: Malacostraca.) >> crab; crustacean; lobster; shrimp; *see illustration on p. 242*

decathlon A multi-event track-and-field discipline consisting of 10 events, held over two days. The events, in order, are: 100 m, long jump, shot, high jump, 400 m, 110 m hurdles, discus, pole vault, javelin, and 1500 m. Points are awarded in each event based on individual performance. >> athletics; discus throw; high jump; javelin throw; long jump; pole vault; shot put

Decatur, Stephen [dee**kay**ter] (1779–1820) US naval commander, born in Sinepuxent, MD. He gained great distinction in the war with Tripoli (1801–5). In the war with England in 1812 he captured the frigate *Macedonian*, but in 1815 surrendered to the British. >> War of 1812

decay rate >> **mean life**

Deccan [**de**kan], Sanskrit **Dakshin** Eastward sloping plateau occupying most of CS India; average altitude 600 m/2000 ft; noted for cotton. >> Ghats; India [i]

Decembrists A group of progressive-minded Russian army officers who attempted a coup against the autocratic government (12 Dec 1825). They were later regarded as martyrs and founders of the 19th-c Russian revolutionary movement. >> Romanovs

decibel Unit of sound level intensity; symbol db; named after US inventor Alexander Graham Bell; defined as $10\log_{10}(I/I_0)$, where I is the sound level intensity in question and I_0 is defined as 10^{-12}W/m^2; a tenth of a **bel**. >> Bell, Alexander Graham; sound

deciduous plants Plants which shed their leaves before the onset of harsh seasons, during which they remain dormant. Leaf fall prevents excessive water loss during drought, or when water is locked up as ice, and minimizes frost damage. >> evergreen plants; leaf [i]; transpiration

decision theory A set of principles designed to enable an agent to make rational choices of self-interest in situations of uncertainty where there are various options, each of whose probable consequences must be assessed. It is used most often in economics and management studies. >> game theory; probability theory; risk analysis

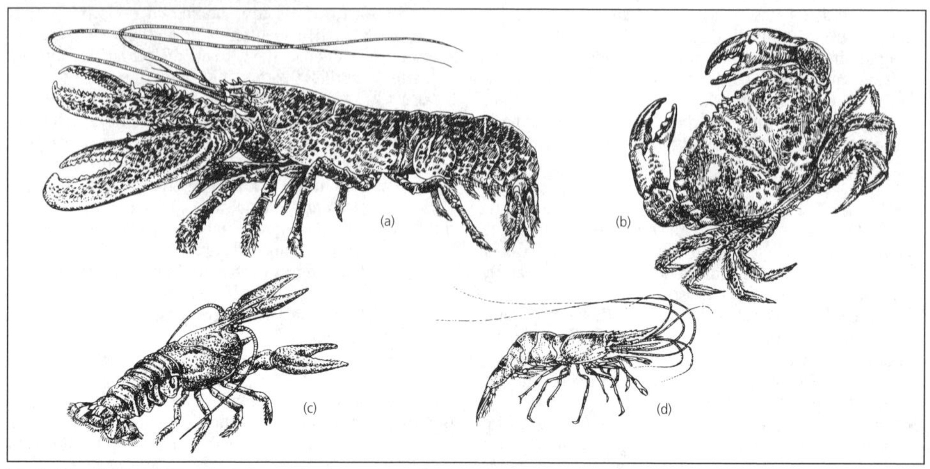

Decapoda – Lobster (a); crab (b); crayfish (c); prawn (d)

Declaration of Independence Following the American Revolution, the document adopted by the Continental Congress to proclaim the separation of the 13 colonies from Britain. It was written mainly by Thomas Jefferson. >> Continental Congress; Jefferson, Thomas

Declaration of Rights An English statute which ended the brief interregnum after James II quit the throne in December 1688, establishing William III and Mary II as joint monarchs. The Bill effectively ensured that monarchs must operate with the consent of parliament. >> bill of rights; James II (of England); William III

Declaration of the Rights of Man and Citizen A declaration made by the French National Assembly (27 Aug 1789), proclaiming liberty of conscience, of property, and of the press, and freedom from arbitrary imprisonment. >> French Revolution [i]

decompression sickness An occupational disease of individuals who work under higher than atmospheric pressure, such as in underwater exploration; also known as **caisson disease**. If these workers return to normal atmospheric pressures too quickly, nitrogen is released as tiny bubbles, which lodge in small blood vessels throughout the body. This deprives the tissues of their normal blood supply. Permanent damage to the brain or death can follow. In less severe cases, dizziness and cramp-like pain in the muscles and joints (the *bends*) occur. >> occupational diseases

Decorated Style The form of English Gothic architecture prevalent in the late 13th-c and 14th-c, characterized by a maximum of surface decoration, usually in the form of stylized leaves and the double S-shaped curve known as an *ogee*. >> arch [i]; Gothic architecture; vault [i]

Decoration Day >> **Memorial Day**

decorative arts The design and ornamentation of objects, usually with some practical use and outside the field of 'fine art' (painting, sculpture, and architecture); nowadays more exactly called the **applied arts**. Metalwork, ceramics, glass, textiles, and woodwork have all been wrought and decorated to a degree which transcends their functional purpose. >> art; ceramics

Decroux, Etienne-Marcel [duh**kroo**] (1898–1991) French actor, responsible for the renaissance of mime in the 20th-c. He developed and taught a system of physical expression he termed *mime corporel*. >> mime

Dedication, Feast of >> **Hanukkah**

Dee, River, Welsh **Afon Dyfrdwy** River in N Wales and adjoining parts of Cheshire, England; rises in the Snowdonia region, and flows past Chester to an estuary lying W of the Wirral peninsula; length 110 km/70 mi.

Dee, John (1527–1608) Alchemist, geographer, and mathematician, born in London. He travelled widely in Europe, brought back many astronomical instruments, and earned the reputation of a sorcerer.

deed >> **covenant 1**

deep-freezing Freezing to −20°C or below in either a chest freezer or cabinet freezer. The level of ability of a freezer cabinet to maintain a sufficiently low temperature for prolonged food preservation is shown on the cabinet by a series of stars; deep-freezers will allow 3 months' storage, a level which is symbolized by four stars. >> food preservation

Deeping, (George) Warwick (1877–1950) Novelist, born in Southend, Essex. His early novels were mainly historical, and it was not until after World War 1 that he gained recognition with his bestseller, *Sorrell and Son* (1925).

Deep Space Network (DSN) A NASA tracking and telecommunications system used to operate interplanetary spacecraft. Stations are located at three widely spaced locations around the world (Goldstone, CA, USA; Canberra, Australia; Madrid, Spain) to provide a continuous communications capability in all parts of the Solar System. >> NASA; Solar System; space exploration

deer A type of hoofed mammal of families Cervidae (**true deer**, 36 species), Moschidae (**musk deer**), and Tragulidae (**mouse deer**); an artiodactyl; only true deer have antlers; true deer found worldwide except Africa and Australasia; usually found in or near woodland; male called a *stag* or *buck*, female a *hind* or *doe*, young a *fawn* or *kid* (names depend on species). >> antlers [i]; artiodactyl; chevrotain; chital; elk; fallow / musk / red / water deer; mammal [i]; muntjac; ungulate

deerhound A breed of dog, developed in Scotland from Mediterranean ancestors; tall, slim; very long legs, long tail; shaggy grey coat; head small with short soft ears; also known as the **Scottish deerhound**, **staghound**, or **buckhound**. >> dog

deerlet >> **chevrotain**

defamation The publication or communication of a false statement which tends to injure reputation or lower a person in the view of the community. In England, Wales, and the USA, it takes the form of either libel or slander; Scottish law does not distinguish between the two terms, recognizing only defamation. Both are actionable at civil law, though libel exists as a criminal offence. >> libel; slander; tort

Defence of the Realm Act A British Act introduced in 1914 at the beginning of World War 1 to give the government greater controls over the activities of its citizens. The most important control related to restrictions on press reporting and other forms of censorship. >> World War 1

defendant In law, the person who is called on to answer proceedings brought against him or her by some other person, called the **plaintiff**. In criminal cases the defendant is the accused; in civil cases, the person who is sued. The term **defender** is used in Scotland. >> court of law

Defender of the Faith (Lat *fidei defensor*) A title conferred on Henry VIII of England by Pope Leo X as a reward for the king's written opposition to the teachings of Martin Luther. It is still used by British sovereigns. >> Henry VIII; Luther

deflation A government economic policy designed to reduce inflationary pressures. Steps taken include higher interest and tax rates, and a tighter money supply. >> inflation

Defoe, Daniel [de**foh**] (1660–1731) Writer, born in London. In 1702 his satire *The Shortest Way with the Dissenters* raised Queen Anne's anger, and he was imprisoned at Newgate, where he continued his pamphleteering. He achieved lasting fame with *Robinson Crusoe* (1719–20). His other major works include *A Journal of the Plague Year*, *Moll Flanders* (both 1722), and *Roxana* (1724).

De Forest, Lee [di **for**ist] (1873–1961) Inventor, born in Council Bluffs, IA. He became a pioneer of radio, introducing the grid into the thermionic valve, and inventing the Audion and the four-electrode valve. He was widely honoured as 'the father of radio' and 'the grandfather of television'. >> radio; valve

Degas, (Hilaire Germain) Edgar [popularly **day**gah, Fr duh**gah**] (1834–1917) Artist, born in Paris. He associated with the Impressionists and took part in most of their exhibitions from 1874 to 1886. Among his best-known works are 'Dancer Lacing her Shoe' (c.1878, Paris) and 'Jockeys in the Rain' (1879, Glasgow). >> Impressionism (art)

de Gaulle, Charles (André Joseph Marie) [duh gohl] (1890–1970) French general and first president of the Fifth Republic (1958–69), born in Lille, France. With the fall of France (Jun 1940), he fled to England to raise the standard of the 'Free French', and entered Paris at the head of one of the earliest liberation forces (Aug 1944). In late 1958 he became president, and practised a high-handed yet extremely successful foreign policy, repeatedly surviving political crises by the lavish use of the referendum. He developed an independent French nuclear deterrent, signed a historic reconciliation treaty with West Germany, and blocked Britain's entry into the European Economic Community. He resigned in 1969 after the defeat of his referendum proposals for senate and regional reforms. >> France ℹ; referendum; World War 2

degaussing [dee**gows**ing] The neutralizing of an object's magnetic field using current-carrying coils to produce an opposing magnetic field of equal strength. The process is applied to ships, to protect them from magnetically activated mines. >> Gauss; magnetism

de Havilland, Sir Geoffrey [duh **ha**viland] (1882–1965) Aircraft designer, born in Haslemere, Surrey. He built his first plane in 1908 and became director of the firm bearing his name, producing many types of aircraft, including the Tiger Moth, the Mosquito, and the Vampire jet. >> aircraft ℹ

De Havilland, Olivia (Mary) (1916–) Actress, born in Tokyo. Brought up in the USA, she joined Warner Brothers (1935–42). She received Best Supporting Actress nominations for her roles in *Gone With the Wind* (1939) and *Hold Back The Dawn* (1941), and won Oscars for *To Each His Own* (1946) and *The Heiress* (1949).

dehydration Literally, 'loss of water'; but in medicine, the process of salt depletion as well as water loss. Excessive loss of salt-containing fluids (such as occurs after severe vomiting, diarrhoea, or excessive urination) particularly affects the circulation, with a rise in pulse rate and falling blood pressure. >> diabetes mellitus

Deighton, Len [**day**tn], popular name of **Leonard Cyril Deighton** (1929–) Thriller writer, born in London. A leading author of spy novels, notable titles are *The Ipcress File* (1962), *Funeral in Berlin* (1964), and the trilogy *Berlin Game* (1984), *Mexico Set* (1985), and *London Match* (1986).

Deimos [**diy**mos] One of the two natural satellites of Mars, discovered in 1877; distance from the planet 23 460 km/ 14 580 mi; diameter c.15 km/9 mi; orbital period 30 h 17 min. Like Phobos, it has a dark, cratered surface. >> Mars (astronomy); Phobos; RR964

deism [**day**izm] Belief in the existence of a supreme being who is the ground and source of reality but who does not intervene or take an active interest in the natural and historical order. It also designates a largely British 17th-c and 18th-c movement of religious thought emphasizing natural religion as opposed to revealed religion, and seeking to establish reasonable grounds for belief in the existence of God. >> theism

Dekker, Thomas (c.1570–c.1641) Playwright, born in London. His best-known works are the comedy *The Shoemaker's Holiday* (1600) and *The Honest Whore* (1604; part II, 1630). He wrote several plays in collaboration with other Elizabethan playwrights.

de Klerk, F(rederick) W(illem) [duh **klairk**] (1936–) South African statesman and president (1989–94), born in Johannesburg, South Africa. He served in National Party cabinets under P W Botha, becoming president when Botha resigned. He then set about the dismantling of apartheid, releasing Nelson Mandela and lifting the state of emergency. The culmination of the process was the signing of a new constitutional agreement with Mandela in late 1993. In the same year, he and Mandela were jointly awarded the Nobel Peace Prize. In 1994 he became vice-president in the Mandela administration, and announced his retirement from politics in August 1997. >> apartheid; Mandela; South Africa ℹ

Delacroix, (Ferdinand Victor) Eugène [duhla**krwah**] (1798–1863) Painter and a leader of the Romantic movement, born in Charenton, France. In his later work he moved away from traditional treatment in his canvases of historical and dramatic scenes, often violent or macabre in subject, such as 'Liberty Guiding the People' (1831, Louvre). >> Romanticism

de la Mare, Walter (John) [mair] (1873–1956) Writer, born in Charlton, Kent. He wrote several volumes of poetry, novels, and short stories, including the prose romance *Henry Brocken* (1904), the poetic collection *The Listeners* (1912), and his fantastic novel *Memoirs of a Midget* (1921).

Delaney, Shelagh [de**lay**nee] (1939–) Playwright, born in Salford, Greater Manchester. She left school at 16 and began writing her first and best known play, *A Taste of Honey* (1958) a year later. Later works failed to achieve equal acclaim, though she produced some notable screenplays.

de la Renta, Oscar (1932–) Fashion designer, born in Santo Domingo, Dominican Republic. He started his own company in 1965. He has a reputation for opulent, ornately trimmed clothes, particularly evening dresses, but he also designs day wear and accessories.

de la Roche, Mazo [rosh] (1885–1961) Novelist, born in Newmarket, Ontario, Canada. In 1927 she wrote *Jalna*, the first of a series of novels about the Whiteoak family. *Whiteoaks* (1929) was dramatized with considerable success.

Delaroche, (Hippolyte) Paul [duhlarosh] (1797–1856) Painter, born in Paris. A master of large historical painting, his major work was the series of murals for the Ecole des Beaux-Arts, where he became professor of painting in 1833.

de la Tour, Georges >> **La Tour, Georges de**

de la Tour, Maurice Quentin >> **La Tour, Maurice Quentin de**

Delaunay, Robert [duhloh**nay**] (1885–1941) Painter, born in Paris. He was associated with the *Blaue Reiter* (1911–2), but is principally known as the founder of Orphism. His research into colour orchestration as applied to abstract art was influential. >> *Blaue Reiter, der*; Orphism

Delaware pop (1995e) 725 000; area 5296 sq km/2045 sq mi. State in E USA; the 'First State', 'Diamond State', or 'Blue Hen State'; part of Pennsylvania until 1776; one of the original states and first to ratify the Federal Constitution, 1787; highest point, Ebright Road (135 m/ 443 ft); capital, Dover; the second smallest state; mainly an industrial state; several large corporations based in Wilmington, taking advantage of the state's taxation laws. >> Dover (USA); United States of America [i]; RR994

Delaware River River in E USA; rises in the Catskill Mts, New York, and empties into Delaware Bay; length 450 km/280 mi; navigable to Trenton. >> United States of America [i]

Delbrück, Max [del**brük**] (1906–81) Biophysicist, born in Berlin. He did much to create bacterial genetics, and to inspire early work in biophysics and molecular biology. He shared the Nobel Prize for Physiology or Medicine in 1969. >> bacteria [i]; biophysics; Bohr; molecular biology

Delft 52°01N 4°22E, pop (1995e) 91 900. Ancient city in W Netherlands, famous for linen-weaving (14th-c), pottery, and porcelain (16th-c); William the Silent assassinated here, 1584; railway; technical university (1863); birthplace of Vermeer. >> Delftware; Netherlands, The [i]; Vermeer; William I (of the Netherlands)

Delftware The Dutch and English version of faience, named after the town of Delft where it was made in large quantities in the 17th-c. Usually blue and white, its decoration is generally copied from Chinese and Japanese porcelain. >> Delft; faience; porcelain

Delhi [del**ee**], Hindi **Dilli**, formerly **Shahjahanabad** 28°38N 77°17E, pop (1995e) 9 071 000. Capital of India; second largest city in India; **Old Delhi**, enclosed within the walls built by Shah Jahan in 1638, on R Yamuna; Mughal architecture and thronged bazaars contrast with formal architecture and wide boulevards of **New Delhi** to the S, largely designed by Lutyens; New Delhi the administrative centre of India since 1912; airport; railway junction; university (1922). >> India [i]; Lutyens; Qutb Minar; Shah Jahan

Delian League [**dee**lian] The association of Greek city-states formed after the Persian Wars (478–477 BC) for the continuing defence of the Aegean area against the Persians. It was so called because the treasury of the League was initially on the island of Delos. >> Persian Wars

Delibes, (Clément Philibert) Léo [duhleeb] (1836–91) Composer, born in St Germain du Val, France. He wrote light operas, of which *Lakmé* had the greatest success, but is chiefly remembered for the ballet *Coppélia* (1870).

Delilah [de**liy**la] Biblical character, who at the instigation of the Philistines enticed Samson to reveal the secret of his great strength – his uncut hair, according to his Nazirite vow. She contrived to cut his hair to weaken him (*Judges* 16). >> Judges, Book of; Samson

DeLillo, Don (1936–) Novelist, born in New York City. His novels are highly self-aware evocations of contemporary society which defines itself through the pseudo-rituals of its subcultures, such as American football in *End Zone* (1972). Other books include *White Noise* (1984), *Mao II* (1991), and *Underworld* (1997).

delirium tremens A form of delirium which occurs following withdrawal of alcohol from alcoholics. Hallucinations often take the form of a sensation of insects crawling on the skin or visions of Lilliputian individuals or objects. It is usually associated with tremor of the hands and arms.

Delius, Frederick [**deel**ius] (1862–1934) Composer, born in Bradford, West Yorkshire. He wrote six operas, including *A Village Romeo and Juliet* (1901), and a variety of choral and orchestral works, such as *On Hearing the First Cuckoo in Spring* (1912). In 1924 he became paralysed and blind, but with the assistance of Eric Fenby (1906–97), his amanuensis from 1928, he continued to compose.

Deller, Alfred (George) (1912–79) Countertenor, born in Margate, Kent. He made many recordings of early English songs, and in 1950 formed the Deller Consort, devoted to the authentic performance of early music. >> countertenor

Del Mar, Norman (René) (1919–94) Conductor and horn player, born in London. He became principal conductor of the English Opera Group (1948–56), and conductor of the BBC Scottish Symphony Orchestra (1960–5). His son, **Jonathan Del Mar** (1951–), also became a conductor.

Delon, Alain [delõ] (1935–) Film actor, born in Paris. He became known following his success in *Purple Moon* (1960). Later films include *Rocco and His Brothers* (1960), *The Leopard* (1962), and *Swann in Love* (1984).

de Lorris, Guillaume [duh **lo**ris] >> **Guillaume de Lorris**

Delors, Jacques [duh**law(r)**] (1925–) French and European statesman, born in Paris. He joined the French Socialist Party in 1973, and served as minister of economy and finance under President Mitterrand (1981–4). He became President of the European Commission in 1985, and was elected to a second 4-year term in 1988, extended until 1995. >> European Community / Union; Mitterrand

de los Angeles, Victoria >> **Angeles, Victoria de los**

Delphi [**del**fiy], Gr **Dhelfoí**, formerly **Pytho** 38°29N 22°30E. Village and ancient site in Greece, on the slopes of Mt Parnassos; altitude 520–620 m/1706–2034 ft; renowned throughout the ancient Greek world as the sanctuary of Apollo and the seat of his oracle. >> Apollo; Greece [i]

delphinium A tall perennial, native to the N hemisphere; flowers blue, rarely pink or white, each with a conical spur and borne in long showy spikes. It contains poisonous alkaloids including delphinin. (Genus: *Delphinium*, 250 species. Family: Ranunculaceae.) >> alkaloids

Delphinus [del**fiy**nus] (Lat 'dolphin') A small N constellation. >> constellation; RR968

delta A fan-shaped body of alluvium enclosed within the bifurcating channels at the mouth of a river. It is formed when a river deposits sediment as its speed decreases, and the coastal processes of erosion are not sufficiently strong to carry the material away. Deltas may form large, fertile plains, but are subject to frequent flooding. >> Ganges, River; Mississippi, River; Nile, River; sedimentation

Deluge >> **Flood, the**

dementia A decline in intellectual capacity as a result of an alteration of brain functioning which leads to impaired social or occupational abilities. It is commonly due to cerebrovascular disease and the ageing process, in which brain cells are destroyed and brain size is markedly reduced. Features include loss of memory, alteration of personality, impaired judgment, poor impulse control, and a failure to recognize friends and relatives. >> Alzheimer's disease; brain ℹ; mental disorders

Demeter [dee**mee**ter] The Greek goddess of agriculture, especially corn, so that a basket or an ear of corn is her symbol. She is the mother of Persephone. >> Ceres (mythology); Persephone

de Meung, Jean >> **Jean de Meung**

De Mille, Agnes [duh **mil**] (1905–93) Dancer and choreographer, and writer, born in New York City. She became best known in America for the choreography of the musicals *Oklahoma!* (1943) and *Carousel* (1945).

De Mille, Cecil B(lount) [duh **mil**] (1881–1959) Film producer and director, born in Ashfield, MA. He made a reputation for box-office spectacles with such films as *The Ten Commandments* (1923, re-made in CinemaScope, 1956), and *The Greatest Show on Earth* (1952).

Demme, Jonathan (1944–) Film director, born in Long Island, NY. He directed pop videos, documentaries, and television episodes, making his cinema directorial debut with *Caged Heat* (1974). He won a Best Director Oscar for the psychological thriller *Silence of the Lambs* (1991). Later films include *Philadelphia* (1993) and *Beloved* (1998).

democracy From Greek *demos* ('people') and *kratia* ('authority'), hence 'rule by the people'; contrasted with rule by the few (**oligarchy**) or by one (**monarchy** or **tyranny**); also known as a **liberal democracy**. Since the Greeks first introduced *demokratia* in many city states in the 5th-c BC, there has been disagreement about what constitutes the essential elements of democracy. One debate concerns who should compose 'the people', and only in the 20th-c has this notion been viewed as covering the total adult citizenship. Another relates to how the people should rule, particularly in relation to the increasing size of states, which has resulted in a shift from direct democracy to systems of representation. Elections, including the right to choose among different groups of representatives offering different doctrines and party programmes, have therefore become seen as essential to democracy. >> monarchy; pluralism (politics)

Democratic Labor Party (DLP) An Australian political party, formed in 1957 from anti-communist groups which had formerly been part of the Australian Labor Party (ALP). At its height, in the late 1950s and through the 1960s, its importance lay in its ability to prevent the ALP from winning national government. >> Australian Labor Party

Democratic Party One of the two major parties in contemporary US politics. It was originally composed in the late 18th-c of those opposed to the adoption of the US Constitution. Its first successful presidential candidate was Thomas Jefferson. The party was split over slavery and secession during the Civil War (1861–5), after which it became conservative. It held a majority position in 1932, when Roosevelt introduced his 'New Deal', and added large urban areas and ethnic, racial, and religious support to its conservative Southern base. It retains the preference of the majority of Americans, but has won the Presidency on only two occasions since 1968. >> Barnburners; Copperhead; Jefferson, Thomas; Republican Party; Roosevelt, Franklin D

Democritus [de**mok**ritus] (c.460–370 BC) Greek philosopher, born in Abdera in Thrace. He travelled in the East, and was by far the most learned thinker of his time. He wrote many physical, mathematical, ethical, and musical works, but only fragments survive.

demography A branch of sociology which studies the population patterns of the past, present, and future. Demography has been very important in estimating future trends in population growth in order to calculate the pressures on global resources. >> population density; sociology

demoiselle [demwa**zel**] A crane (*Anthropoides virgo*), native to S Europe, Asia, and N Africa (migrates further S in winter); mainly white with dark chest and throat; ornamental feathers on head. (Family: Gruidae.) >> crane (ornithology)

demonology An outmoded branch of theology relating to the Devil and demons, elaborated from the later Middle Ages particularly in association with belief in witches and their power to do harm. Its most influential work was the *Malleus maleficarum* (Hammer of the Witches) by the Dominicans Kramer and Sprenger, published at Cologne in 1484. >> Devil; incubus; witchcraft

Demosthenes [de**mos**theneez] (c.383–322 BC) The greatest of the Greek orators. He came to prominence in 351 BC, when he delivered the first of a long series of passionate speeches (the 'First Philippic') advocating all-out resistance to Philip of Macedon. Swayed by his oratory, the Athenians did eventually go to war (340 BC), only to be defeated at Chaeronea (338 BC). Put on trial by the peace party of Aeschines, he fully vindicated himself in his oratorical masterpiece, 'On the Crown'. >> Aeschines; Lamian War; Philip II (of Macedon)

Denbighshire [**den**beesheer], Welsh **Sir Ddinbych** pop (1995e) 91 300; area 844 sq km / 326 sq mi. County (unitary authority from 1996) in NC Wales, UK; drained by R Clwyd; administrative centre, Ruthin; St Asaph cathedral (founded 573); international eisteddfod at Llangollen (Jul) >> Wales ℹ

dendrite >> **neurone** ℹ

dendrochronology The construction of archaeological chronologies from annual tree-ring sequences. Rings vary in width and structure from year to year, depending on the prevailing climatic conditions; overlapping patterns observed in preserved timbers can therefore be matched and linked to form an accurate and absolute chronology extending back thousands of years from the present day. >> archaeology; radiocarbon dating

Deneb >> **Cygnus**

Deneuve, Cathérine [duh**noev**], originally **Cathérine Dorléac** (1943–) Actress, born in Paris. She became well known through the unexpected popularity of the musical *Les Parapluies de Cherbourg* (1964, The Umbrellas of Cherbourg). Other films include *Belle de Jour* (1967) and *Les Voleurs* (1998).

dengue [**deng**gee] A short-lived acute feverish illness common in tropical countries, caused by a virus transmitted by mosquitoes. Characterized by headache, a brief skin rash, and enlarged lymph nodes, it usually resolves within one to two weeks. >> mosquito; virus

Deng Xiaoping [duhng syowping] or **Teng Hsiao-p'ing** (1904–97) Leader of the Chinese Communist Party, born in Sichuan province, China. In 1954 he became secretary-general of the Chinese Communist Party, but reacted strongly against the excesses of the Great Leap Forward (1958–9). When Mao Zedong launched the Cultural Revolution (1966), Deng was criticized and purged, but was restored to power in 1974. From 1978 he had taken China through a rapid course of pragmatic reforms. >> Cultural Revolution; Great Leap Forward; Mao Zedong

denier [**den**ier] A unit of weight in textiles, measuring the fineness of yarn in such materials as silk, rayon, or nylon. It is equal to the weight in grams of 9000 m of the yarn.

Materials of 15 denier would be finer than the material of 20 denier. It is now being replaced by the *tex*. >> count (textiles)

denim A popular clothing fabric made originally by filling indigo-dyed warp yarns with undyed cotton weft to give a twill structure. The indigo slowly leaches out of the fabric, causing a characteristic lightening of the blue colour. The fabric is hard-wearing, and was used for working clothes, but from the 1950s acquired a fashionable cult status. >> indigo; twill

De Niro, Robert [duh **nee**roh] (1943–) Actor and director, born in New York City. His many films include *The Godfather, Part II* (1974), *The Deer Hunter* (1978), *Raging Bull* (1980, Oscar), and *Ronin* (1998). He made his directorial debut in *A Bronx Tale* (1993).

Denis or **Denys, St** [**de**nis], Fr [duhnee] (3rd-c) Traditional apostle of France and first Bishop of Paris, who was sent from Rome about 250 to preach the Gospel to the Gauls. He was martyred at Paris under Roman Emperor Valerian (reigned 253–60). Feast day 9 October. >> apostle; Gaul

Denis, Maurice [duhnee] (1870–1943) Artist and art theorist, born in Grandville, France. One of the original group of Symbolist painters, *Les Nabis*, he helped to found the Studios of Sacred Art (1919), devoted to the revival of religious painting. >> *Nabis, Les*; Symbolists

Denmark, Dan **Danmark**, official name **Kingdom of Denmark**, Dan **Kongeriget Danmark** pop (1995e) 5 188 000; area (excluding Greenland and Faroes) 43 076 sq km/ 16 627 sq mi. Kingdom of N Europe; consists of most of the Jutland peninsula, several islands in the Baltic Sea, and some of the N Frisian Is in the North Sea; coastline 3400 km/2100 mi; capital, Copenhagen; timezone GMT +1; chief religion, Lutheranism (88%); language, Danish; unit of currency, krone of 100 øre; uniformly low-lying; no large rivers and few lakes; shoreline indented by many lagoons and fjords, largest Lim Fjord (which cut off N extremity of Denmark in 1825); cold and cloudy winters, warm and sunny summers; part of Viking kingdoms, 8th–10th-c; Danish Empire under Canute, 11th-c; joined with Sweden and Norway under one ruler, 1389; Sweden separated from the union, 16th-c, as did Norway, 1814; Schleswig-Holstein lost to Germany, 1864; N Schleswig returned after plebiscite, 1920; occupied by Germany, World War 2; Iceland independent, 1944; Greenland and Faroe Is remain dependencies, but with their own internal government; constitutional monarchy since 1849; unicameral system adopted, 1953; legislative power lies with the monarch and the Diet jointly; lack of raw materials, resulting in development of processing industries; intensive agriculture; wide range of food processing; joined European Community, 1973. >> Canute; Copenhagen; Faroe Islands; Greenland 🅘; Iceland 🅘; Kalmar Union; Vikings; RR1006 political leaders

Denning (of Whitchurch), Alfred Thompson Denning, Baron (1899–99) British judge, born in Whitchurch, Hampshire. As Master of the Rolls (1962–82) he was responsible for many, often controversial, decisions. Among his books are *The Road to Justice* (1955) and *What Next in the Law* (1982).

density The mass of a substance divided by its volume; symbol ρ, units kg/m^3. The density of water is 1000 kg/m^3. Density is measured using a hydrometer. >> Archimedes; relative density

dentistry The treatment and prevention of diseases of the mouth and teeth. Dentistry was studied at the Chinese Imperial Medical College from 620, and toothbrushes and toothpaste were known by Song times (10th–13th-c). In the West, it was first practised by barber surgeons, surgeon dentists forming a separate guild in France in the reign of Louis XIV. Several special branches of the subject

international airport

have developed. **Periodontics** is concerned with the prevention, diagnosis, and treatment of disorders of tissues that surround and support the teeth. **Orthodontics** is concerned with correcting the malposition of teeth, usually arising from faults in dental development. The provision of artificial **prosthesis** attempts to restore oral function after the loss of teeth or of tissue. **Oral surgery** is concerned with the repair of injury to the jaws by disease or by trauma. In some countries, **dental hygienists** provide services such as X-rays, scaling of teeth, and dental health education. >> caries; fluoridation of water; teeth 🅘

Denver 39°44N 104°59W, pop (1995e) 553 000. State capital in NC Colorado, USA; largest city in the state and a port on the S Platte R; founded, 1860; airport; railway; university (1864); processing, shipping, and distributing centre for a large agricultural area; professional teams, Nuggets (basketball), Broncos (football), Colorado Rockies (baseball). >> Colorado

Deodoro da Fonseca, Manuel [dayo**doo**roo da fon**say**ka] (1827–92) Brazilian general and president (1889–91), born in Alagoas province, Brazil. He headed the revolt that overthrew Emperor Pedro II, and instituted the republic. >> Brazil 🅘

deoxyribonucleic acid >> **DNA** 🅘

deoxyribose [deeoksi**riy**bohs] $C_5H_{10}O_4$. A 5-carbon sugar, particularly important for its role in the genetic material DNA. >> DNA 🅘; ribose; sugars

De Palma, Brian (1940–) Film director, born in Newark, NJ. He made his feature-length debut with *The Wedding Party* (1966), and had commercial success with *Carrie* (1976) and *The Untouchables* (1987). Later films include *Bonfire of the Vanities* (1990) and *Mission Impossible* (1996).

Dépardieu, Gérard [daypah(r)dyoe] (1948–) Actor, born in Châteauroux, France. His films include *Le Dernier Métro* (1980), *Danton* (1982), *Jean de Florette* (1986), *Cyrano de Bergerac* (1990), and *Unhook the Stars* (1997).

depilatory [de**pil**atree] A chemical used to remove unwanted hair on the skin, including alkalis, metallic sulphides, and mercaptans. They act by disrupting the chemical structure of the hair protein. >> hair

depression (economics) An economic situation where demand is slack, order-books are low, firms dispense with staff, and profits are poor or absent. A less severe form is a *recession*. >> Great Depression; recession; trade cycle; unemployment

depression (meteorology) A meteorological term for a low pressure system at high and mid-latitudes; also known as a **cyclone** at low latitudes. A depression is initiated when a wave develops on a *front* (a boundary between cold and warm air masses). Pressure falls at the crest of the wave. A *warm front* is the leading edge of the depression, followed by the *cold front*, with a warm sector between the two fronts. As the cold front travels faster than the warm front, it catches up, to produce an *occluded front*. When this happens, pressure rises and the depression loses velocity. Depressions are typically 1000–2000 km/600–1250 mi across, but are temporary features with an average lifespan of 4–7 days. >> anticyclone; atmospheric pressure; *see illustration below*

depression (psychiatry) A mental condition in which there are feelings of low mood, despondence, self-criticism, and low esteem. It may be associated with a change (up or down) in appetite for sleep, food, or sex. A wide variety of treatments can be used for this condition, including psychotherapy, drugs, and electroconvulsive therapy. >> electroconvulsive therapy; mental disorders; psychotherapy

Depression, the >> **Great Depression**

depth charge A munition used by surface warships as a means of destroying submarines, typically an explosive-packed container dropped from a warship, armed by a fuse primed to detonate when it senses the water-pressure at a predetermined depth. Nuclear depth charges with explosive radii greater than one kilometre are now in service with nuclear-equipped navies. >> submarine

de Quincey, Thomas [duh **kwin**see] (1785–1859) Writer, born in Manchester. On a visit to Bath, he met Coleridge, and through him Southey and Wordsworth; and in 1809 went to live near them in Grasmere. His *Confessions of an English Opium Eater* appeared as a serial in 1821, and brought him instant fame. >> Coleridge; Southey; Wordsworth, William

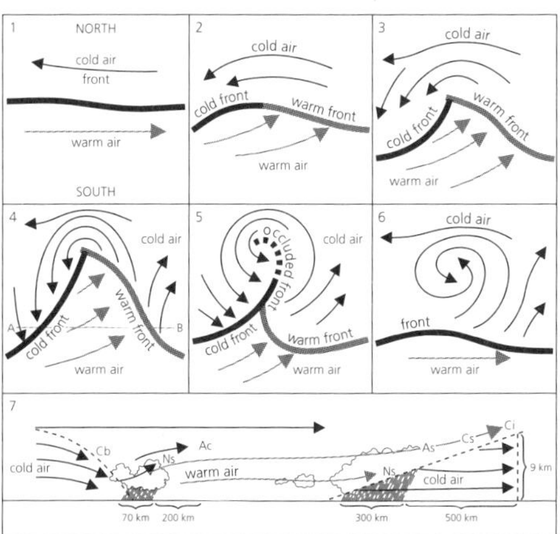

Depression – plan view of the six idealized stages in the development and final occlusion of a depression along the polar front in the Northern Hemisphere. Stage 4 shows a well developed depression system and stage 5 shows the occlusion. The cross-section is taken along the line AB in stage 4. The cloud types are: Cb - cumulonimbus; As – altostratus; Ac – altocumulus; Cs – cirrostratus; Ns – nimbostratus; Ci – cirrus.

Derain, André [duhrĩ] (1880–1954) Artist, born in Chatou, France. Best known for his Fauvist landscape pictures (1904–8), he also designed for the theatre (notably the Diaghilev ballet). >> Diaghilev: Fauvism

Derby [**dah(r)**bee] 52°55N 1°30W, pop (1995e) 233 000. City and unitary authority (from 1997) in Derbyshire, C England; chartered in 1637; railway; cathedral (1525); first silk mill (1719); porcelain centre in 18th-c (Derby ware); football league team, Derby County (Rams). >> Derbyshire; porcelain

Derby, Edward Geoffrey Smith Stanley, 14th Earl of [**dah(r)**bee] (1799–1869) British statesman and prime minister (1852, 1858–9, 1866–8), born at Knowsley Hall, Lancashire. He entered parliament as a Whig in 1828, and as colonial secretary (1833) carried the Act for the emancipation of West Indian slaves. In 1834 he joined the Conservatives, and became party leader, 1846–68. His third administration passed the Reform Bill (1867). >> Conservative Party; slave trade; Whigs

Derbyshire [**dah(r)**bisheer] pop (1995e) 959 000; area 2631 sq km/1016 sq mi. County of C England; rises to The Peak at 636 m/2086 ft; county town, Matlock; Derby a new unitary authority from 1997. >> Derby; England ℹ; Matlock

Dere Street >> **Roman roads** ℹ

Dermaptera [der**map**tera] >> **earwig**

dermatitis [derma**tiy**tis] The commonest single skin disorder; also known as **eczema**. Causes include chemical and physical irritants, hypersensitivity reactions from contact with chemicals (eg detergents, watch straps), bacteria, and ingested food and drugs. >> skin ℹ

dermatology The scientific study of the structure and function of the skin and of its diseases. It is a specialized branch of medical practice. >> dermatitis; skin ℹ

Derrida, Jacques [**de**rida] (1930–) French philosopher-linguist, born in Algeria. His critique of the referentiality of language and the objectivity of structures founded the school of criticism called *deconstruction*. The award of an honorary degree by Cambridge University in 1992 was publicly contested, prompting attacks on and defences of his work. >> structuralism

Derry (city), official name **Londonderry** (but **Derry City Council** since 1984) 55°00N 7°19W, pop (1995e) 76 800. City in Derry, NW Northern Ireland; monastery founded by St Columba, c.546; James I proclaimed the city to be part of the Corporation of London, 1613; renamed London-Derry, and settled by a Protestant colony; resisted a siege by James II for 105 days, 1689; railway; cathedral (1628–33). >> Columba, St; Derry (county); James II (of England); Protestantism

Derry (county), official name **Londonderry**, Ir **Doire** pop (1995e) 225 000; area 2067 sq km/798 sq mi. County in N Northern Ireland, bounded NW by the Republic of Ireland; hilly, with part of the Sperrin Mts rising in the S; county town, Derry. >> Derry (city); Northern Ireland ℹ

dervish A member of an Islamic mystical fraternity. Since the founding of the Qadiriya order in the 12th-c, numerous orders with lodges situated across the Muslim world have been established. One of the most famous is the Mevlani, or **whirling dervishes**. >> Sufism

DES An abbreviation of **diethylstilboestrol/diethylstilbestrol** – a synthetic oestrogen for the treatment of menopausal symptoms and prostate cancer. It is also used as the 'morning-after' pill. >> contraception; menopause; oestrogen; prostate gland

Desai, Morarji (Ranchhodji) [day**siy**] (1896–1995) Indian statesman and prime minister (1977–9), born in Gujarat. He became deputy prime minister in 1969 to lead the

Opposition Congress Party. Detained during the state of emergency (1975–7), he was then appointed leader of the newly-formed Janata Party. >> Gandhi, Indira

desalination The removal of salt from sea-water or brine to produce potable or industrially usable water, or water for ships' boilers. Distillation is the oldest process, still widely used. Membrane processes, electrodialysis, and the freezing out of ice are also used. About half of the world's desalinated water is produced in the Middle East.

Desalvo, Albert [de**sal**voh] (?–1973) Convicted US sex offender. After his arrest in late 1964 for sex attacks on women in their homes, he confessed that he was the Boston Strangler who had murdered 13 women between 1962 and 1964 in Boston, MA. He was found stabbed to death in his cell in Walpole Prison, MA.

descant A melody sung or played above another well-known one, such as a hymn tune. The term (often as **discant**) is also used for a type of mediaeval polyphony, and to distinguish the highest-pitched member of a family of instruments (eg the descant recorder). >> polyphony

Descartes, René [daykah(r)t], Lat **Renatius Cartesius** (1596–1650) Rationalist philosopher and mathematician, 'the father of modern philosophy', born in La Haye, near Tours. His aim, to refound human knowledge on a basis secure from scepticism, is expounded in his most famous work, the *Meditationes de prima philosophia* (1641, Meditations on First Philosophy). This work introduced his famous principle that one cannot doubt one's own existence as a thinking being – *cogito ergo sum* ('I think, therefore I am') – and presented the argument that mind and body are distinct substances. He virtually founded co-ordinate or analytic geometry, and made major contributions to optics. >> dualism; rationalism (philosophy); scepticism; scholasticism

desensitization Small repeated subcutaneous injections of the antigen believed to be responsible for allergic reactions in a hypersensitive individual. The antibody produced in response to the injections coats tissue cells, and blocks the access of a later dose of the offending antigen to which the individual was sensitive. >> allergy

desert An arid and empty region of the Earth, characterized by little or no vegetation, and meagre and intermittent rainfall, high evaporation rates, and low humidity and cloud cover. Low-latitude deserts such as the Sahara are hot and dry, caused by high pressure air masses which prevent precipitation. Mid-latitude deserts such as the Gobi are cold and dry, and are related to mountain barriers which seal off moist maritime winds. Polar deserts of the Arctic and Antarctic are permanently covered by snow and ice. Approximately one third of the Earth's land surface is desert. >> Antarctica [i]; Arctic; Gobi Desert; Sahara Desert; RR973

desert fox >> **fennec fox**

desert rat >> **jerboa**

Desert Rats Members of the 7th British Armoured Division, which in 1940 took as its badge the jerboa or desert rat, noted for remarkable leaps. The media applied the name generally to all British servicemen in the North Africa campaign. >> World War 2

Desert Shield / Storm >> **Gulf War 2**

de Sica, Vittorio [**see**ka] (1901–74) Actor and film director, born in Sora, Italy. He achieved international success in the neo-realist style with *Sciuscià* (1946, Shoeshine), *Ladri di biciclette* (1948, Bicycle Thieves), and *Miracolo a Milano* (1951, Miracle in Milan).

Desiderio da Settignano [dezi**de**ryoh da seti**nyah**noh] (c.1428–61) Sculptor, born in Settignano, Italy. He worked in the early Renaissance style, producing many notable portrait busts of women and children. >> Renaissance

design, argument from An argument, especially popular in the 18th-c and 19th-c, that the existence of complex organisms can be explained only by the existence of a supremely wise, powerful, beneficent God. The argument lost its appeal with the development of evolutionary theory. >> evolution; God

designer drugs Synthetic drugs, often narcotics, which are not controlled by law in the USA; they are so called because they are specifically designed by chemists to be slightly different structurally to drugs that are controlled by law (which are 'named', and thus illegal), yet still chemically so close to them that they have similar biological effects. >> ecstasy; narcotics

desk-top publishing The preparation of typeset output using a microcomputer with appropriate software for the composition of text, the creation of illustrations, the editing of structured pages, and typography. 'Publishing' in this now familiar turn of phrase is a misnomer: 'typesetting' or 'text composition' would be more appropriate. >> publishing

desman An insectivore of the mole family (2 species), native to the Pyrenees and W Asia; red-brown; long mobile snout; webbed hind feet; long tail flattened from side to side; lives in streams and pools. >> insectivore; mole (biology)

Des Moines [di**moyn**] 41°35N 93°37W, pop (1995e) 199 000. Capital of state in C Iowa, USA; developed around a fort established in 1843; city status, 1857; state capital in 1881; airport; railway; university (1881); important commercial and transportation centre in the heart of Iowa's Corn Belt. >> Iowa

Desmoulins, (Lucie Simplice) Camille (Benoist) [day-moolĩ] (1760–94) French revolutionary and journalist, born in Guise, France. An effective crowd orator, he played a dramatic part in the storming of the Bastille. He was elected to the National Convention, and voted for the death of the king. He actively attacked the Girondists, then argued for moderation, and was guillotined. >> French Revolution [i]

Desprez, Josquin >> **Josquin Desprez**

Dessalines, Jean Jacques [desa**leen**] (c.1758–1806) Emperor of Haiti (1804–06), born a slave, probably at Grande Rivière du Nord, Saint Domingue (Haiti). In the slave insurrection of 1791 he was second only to Toussaint L'Ouverture. His cruelty as emperor led to his assassination. >> Haiti [i]; Toussaint L'Ouverture

De Stijl [duh **shteel**] A group of Dutch artists and architects formed in 1917, strongly influenced by Cubism, Dutch Calvinism, and theosophy. The group advocated a new, wholly abstract aesthetic style composed solely of straight lines, primary colours, and black and white, typified by the paintings of Mondrian. The group formally ended in 1931. >> abstract art; Cubism; Mondrian; theosophy

destroyer A small fast warship designed in the late 19th-c to destroy enemy torpedo boats. It has since adopted many other roles: submarine hunting, evacuation, invasion, assault support, and convoy escort. Modern destroyers are usually guided-missile carriers. >> cruiser; warships [i]

detached retina >> **retina**

detente [day**tawnt**] An attempt to lower the tension between states as a means of reducing the possibility of war and of achieving peaceful coexistence between different social and political systems. A prominent feature of relations between the USA and USSR in the 1970s, it led to several agreements over arms (SALT) and security and co-operation (Helsinki); the concept was overtaken by events, following the break-up of the Soviet Union in 1990. >> Cold War; SALT

detention centre >> **young offender institution**

detergent A material which lowers the surface tension of water, and makes it mix better with oils and fats. Most detergents contain molecules or ions with a combination of polar (water-seeking) and non-polar (oil-seeking) parts, which serve to bind oil and water together. >> oil (earth sciences)

deterrence The concept that has developed in strategic military thinking since the 1930s, following the emergence of long-range weapons of mass destruction. It is based on the threat of effective military or economic counter-action as a means of discouraging acts of aggression. There is considerable uncertainty about the effectiveness of deterrence in different circumstances.

detonator A sensitive explosive (eg mercuric fulminate, lead azide) used in a small quantity to initiate the function of larger quantities of principal explosive. By extension, the term is used for any device containing a detonating explosive actuated by heat, percussion, friction, or electricity. >> explosives

Detroit [dee**troyt**] 42°20N 83°03W, pop (1995e) 1 080 000. Port in SE Michigan, USA; seventh largest city in the USA; founded by the French as a fur-trading outpost, 1701; surrendered to the British during the Seven Years War, 1760; handed over to the USA, 1796; much of the city rebuilt after a fire in 1805; capital of state, 1837–47; airport; railway; two universities (1877, 1933); the nation's leading manufacturer of cars and trucks; professional teams, Tigers (baseball), Pistons (basketball), Red Wings (ice hockey), Lions (football). >> Michigan

Dettori, Frankie [de**to**ree], popular name of **Lanfranco Dettori** (1970–) British jockey, born in Italy. A champion apprentice in 1990, his major wins of the decade include The Oaks (1994, 1995), St Leger (1995, 1996), and One Thousand Guineas (1998). He was champion jockey for two successive seasons (1994–5), and in 1996 was winner of all seven races on one card at Ascot.

Deucalion [dyoo**kay**lion] In Greek mythology, a son of Prometheus. When Zeus flooded the world, Deucalion and his wife Pyrrha built an 'ark' which grounded on the top of Parnassus. They restored the human race by throwing stones over their shoulders, which turned into human beings. >> Zeus

deus ex machina [**day**us eks **ma**kina] (Lat 'god from the machine') A device used mainly by classical dramatists to resolve by supernatural intervention (the god descending from above the stage) all the problems which have arisen during the course of a play.

deuterium A heavy isotope of hydrogen, in which the nucleus comprises a proton and a neutron rather than a proton alone (as for common hydrogen); symbol D or ^2H. It forms 0·015% of naturally occurring hydrogen. Water made with deuterium is called *heavy water*, and is used in some nuclear reactors. >> heavy water; hydrogen; isotopes; nuclear fusion; tritium

Deuteronomy, Book of [dyoote**ron**omee] The fifth and last book of the Pentateuch, in the Hebrew Bible/Old Testament. It was traditionally attributed to Moses, but many date it much later, c.7th-c BC. It surveys Israel's wilderness experiences, and presents an extensive code of religious laws and duties. >> Old Testament

de Valera, Eamon [deva**lay**ra] (1882–1975) Irish statesman, prime minister (1932–48, 1951–4, 1957–9), and president (1959–73), born in New York City, USA. A commandant in the 1916 rising, he was arrested and narrowly escaped the firing squad. In 1926 he became leader of Fianna Fáil, his newly-formed Republican opposition party, which won the 1932 elections. In spite of his colourful early career, his leadership was moderate, and he opposed extremism and religious intolerance. >> Fianna Fáil; Sinn Féin

devaluation A fall in the amount of foreign currency which can be obtained per unit of a country's own currency. For example, if the £ has been selling for $1·60 and falls to $1·40, it is devalued. Devaluation makes a country's exports cheaper abroad and its imports dearer at home, as long as domestic prices do not change. This tends to improve the balance of payments. Rises in import costs tend to create domestic inflation, however, so that the initial competitive advantage obtained does not last. >> balance of payments; currency; European Monetary System; exchange rates

Devanagari [devana**gah**ree] A range of alphabets used for Indian languages, consisting of a set of consonantal letter-symbols. Vowels are represented by a system of diacritics. >> alphabet ℹ

development In photography, the process by which the latent image formed by exposure to light is made visible. It generally involves reducing the exposed silver compounds in the sensitive material to black metallic silver. In colour photography, couplers may be used to form a coloured dye image at the same time. >> photography

developmental psychology A branch of psychology which examines the biological, social, and intellectual development of people from before birth throughout the life-course. Most attention has been paid to young children, in whom shifts in understanding appear more obvious. >> educational psychology; psychology

Devi, Phoolan [**de**vee], known as **Dasyu Sundari** ('Beautiful Bandit') (1957–) Bandit and folk hero, born in India. After a childhood of abuse, she was kidnapped by bandits, then joined the gang, to become one of India's most notorious criminals while attracting a national reputation among oppressed people. She surrendered in 1983 in a much publicized ceremony. Released from prison in 1994, she became a Buddhist convert, and in 1995 launched a new political party in support of the lower castes. Mala Sen's story of her life, *India's Bandit Queen* (1991) was the basis of the film *Bandit Queen* (1995).

Devil A supernatural evil agent thought to influence human behaviour, in many religious beliefs; when referring to a specific character in the Judaeo-Christian tradition, the chief of the evil spirits or fallen angels; also known as **Satan**. In religious literature the Devil appears in many different guises, human or animal, and with many different names (eg *Beelzebul*, *Belial*, *ahuras*, *jinn*). Exorcism of individuals possessed by demons is long attested in the Judaeo-Christian tradition, but cults of devil-worship (or Satanism) involving witchcraft, black magic, and the occult have persisted despite opposition throughout most of Christian history. >> Bible; demonology; Gog and Magog; hell

devil ray Any of the giant rays widespread in surface waters of tropical and warm temperate seas; pectoral fins forming large triangular wings; body width up to 6 m/20 ft; sides of head prolonged as fleshy 'horns'; tail whip-like. (Genera: *Mobula*, *Manta*. Family: Mobulidae.) >> manta ray; ray

Devil's Island >> **Salut, Iles du**

Devil's Tower 44°31N 104°57W. The first US national monument, in NE Wyoming, USA; a natural tower of volcanic rock with a flat top, 263 m/863 ft high; used as the setting for the film *Close Encounters of the Third Kind* (1977). >> Wyoming

devise >> **property**

Devlin, Bernadette >> **McAliskey, Bernadette**

devolution The delegation of authority from a country's legislature or government to a subordinate elected institution on a more limited geographical basis. Devolution is distinguished from **federalism**, where the powers of the central government and the federal bodies are set out in the constitution. Under devolution, the subordinate body receives its power from the government, which retains some right of oversight. >> federalism; home rule

Devolution, War of A conflict prompted by Louis XIV of France in pursuit of his wife's legal claims to the Spanish Netherlands. Louis's armies overran Flanders, prompting the Dutch, England, and Sweden to negotiate the Triple Alliance (1668). The war ended with a secret treaty of compromise between Louis and the Emperor Leopold (1668). >> Leopold I (Emperor); Louis XIV

Devon pop (1995e) 1 064 000; area 6711 sq km/2590 sq mi. County of SW England; rises to Dartmoor in SW and Exmoor in NE; county town, Exeter; Plymouth and Torbay new unitary authorities from 1998; naval base at Plymouth. >> Dartmoor; England [i]; Exeter; Exmoor

Devonian period A geological period of the Palaeozoic era extending from 408 to 360 million years ago. It contains the oldest widespread continental deposits in Europe (Old Red Sandstone) as well as extensive marine sediments containing fossils of armoured fish, corals, ammonites, and molluscs. >> geological time scale; Palaeozoic era; RR976

Dewar flask An insulated vessel with double walls, the inner space being made into a vacuum and silvered; heat losses by convection and radiation are thus reduced to a minimum. It was devised in 1892 by British chemist James Dewar (1842–1923) to hold gases liquefied at very low temperatures, and later developed industrial and domestic uses for maintaining liquids at constant high or low temperatures. Everyday names include **vacuum flask** and the trade name **Thermos flask**. >> insulation; vacuum

de Wet, Christiaan (Rudolf) [wet] (1854–1922) Afrikaner statesman and general, born in Smithfield district, Orange Free State. He became conspicuous in the Transvaal war of 1880–1; and in the war of 1899–1902 was the most audacious of all the Boer commanders. >> Boer Wars

Dewey, John (1859–1952) Philosopher and educator, born in Burlington, VT. A leading exponent of pragmatism, he developed a philosophy of education which stressed development of the person, understanding of the environment, and learning through experience.

Dewey decimal system A library classification system in widespread international use, devised in 1873 by US librarian Melvil Dewey (1851–1931). It recognizes 10 main classes of subject-matter, each class containing 100 numbers, with decimal subdivisions for unlimited supplementary classes. >> library science

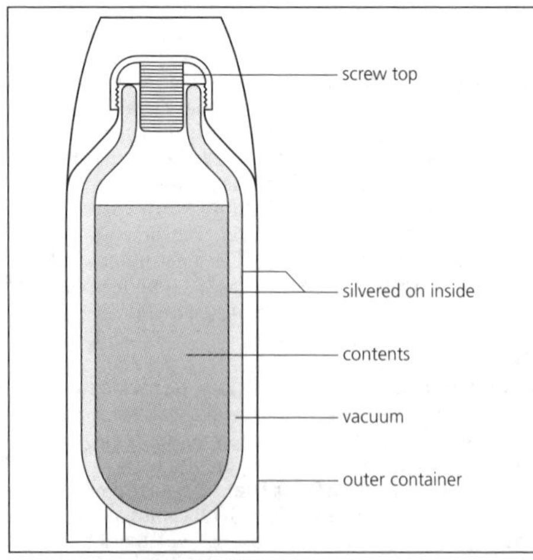

Dewar flask

dew point temperature The temperature at which a parcel of air would become saturated with water vapour if it were cooled without a change in pressure of moisture content. When moist air is cooled to below this temperature, condensation in the form of dew or hoar frost occurs. >> condensation (physics); humidity

dextrin A complex sugar, a mixture of glucose polymers obtained from starch. Its main use is to improve the palatability of starchy foods, and to reduce the osmotic load on the stomach in convalescent drinks. >> glucose; osmotic pressure; polymerization

dextrose >> **glucose** [i]

Dhaka [**dak**a], former spelling **Dacca** 23°42N 90°22E, pop (1995e) 6 608 000. Capital city of Bangladesh; capital of Mughal province of East Bengal, 1608–1704; capital of British province of East Bengal and Assam, 1905–12; major expansion since becoming capital of East Pakistan, 1947; centre of the world's greatest jute-growing region; airport; railway; two universities (1921, 1961); known as 'the city of mosques' (over 1000). >> Bangladesh [i]

dharma [**dah(r)**ma] In Hinduism, the universal law that applies to the universe, human society, and the individual. It is both a general code of ethics applicable to all, and a moral law specific to an individual's station in life. >> Buddhism; Hinduism

dhole [dohl] A member of the dog family (*Cuon alpinus*), native to S and SE Asia; red-brown, with white underneath; black tip to tail; hunts large mammals in packs; also known as **Asiatic wild dog** or **Indian wild dog**. >> Canidae

diabetes mellitus [diya**bee**teez **mel**itus] A common metabolic disorder in which there is failure of the pancreas to produce insulin in amounts needed to control sugar metabolism. As a result the blood sugar rises above normal values and spills over into the urine, causing large volumes to be produced (*polyuria*). >> hormones; insulin; pancreas

diablotin [diy**ab**lotin] >> **oilbird**

Diaghilev, Sergei Pavlovich [dee**ag**ilef] (1872–1929) Ballet impresario, born in Novgorod, Russia. His company was founded in 1909, and remained perilously in existence for 20 years, triumphantly touring Europe. Many of the great dancers, composers, and painters of his period contributed to the success of his Ballets Russes. He also encouraged several major choreographers. >> ballet; Ballets Russes

dialect >> **dialectology**

dialectic The study of the logic involved in conversational argument. As used by Hegel and Marx, dialectic is an analogous process that occurs in nature. >> dialectical materialism; logic; Marxism

dialectical materialism A central doctrine of Marxism. Its claims are that quantitative changes in matter yield qualitative changes (for example, the emergence of mind); that nature is a unity of contradictory opposites; and that the result of one opposite (thesis) clashing with another (antithesis) is a synthesis that preserves and transcends the opposites. >> dialectic; Marxism

dialectology The study of varieties of a language (**dialects**) which are regionally or socially distinctive. They are marked by having distinctive words, grammatical structures, and pronunciations. Dialects are studied by wide-ranging questionnaires which gather information about the way linguistic features are used in a geographical area. A **dialect atlas** shows dialect areas and boundaries. >> accent 1

dialysis [diy**al**isis] A process of separating dissolved substances (solutes) of different molecular weights by using the differences in their rates of diffusion across thin layers of certain materials (eg cellulose). Artificial kidney machines (**dialysers**) perform **haemodialysis**, whereby waste products (such as urea or excess salts) are removed from the patient's blood, while blood cells and protein are retained. >> kidneys

Diamond, Neil (1941–) Singer and songwriter, born in New York City. He wrote the hit 'I'm A Believer' (1966) for the Monkees, and had his first No 1 hit with 'Cracklin' Rosie' (1970). His albums include *Touching You, Touching Me* (1970), *Jonathon Livingston Seagull* (1974), and *Headed for the Future* (1986).

diamond A naturally occurring form of crystalline carbon formed at high pressures and temperatures deep in the Earth's crust; the hardest natural substance known. It is the most precious of gemstones. Major mines are near Kimberley, South Africa. **Black diamonds**, generally of poorer quality, are used for industrial purposes. >> carbon; Cullinan diamond; gemstones; Koh-i-noor

diamondback North American rattlesnake with bold diamond-shaped markings along back; also known as **diamondback rattlesnake**; the **Eastern diamondback rattlesnake** (*Crotalus adamanteus*) is the most venomous snake in North America. >> rattlesnake

diamondbird A small woodland bird native to Australia, also known as **pardalote**; short tail and bill; nests in holes. (Genus: *Pardalotus*, 5 or 8 species; experts disagree. Family: Dicaeidae.)

diamorphine >> **heroin**

Diana [diy**an**a] Roman goddess, associated with the Moon, virginity, and hunting. She was considered to be equivalent to the Greek Artemis. >> Artemis

Diana, Princess of Wales, formerly **Lady Diana (Frances) Spencer** (1961–97) Former wife of Charles, Prince of Wales, and youngest daughter of the 8th Earl Spencer, born at Sandringham, Norfolk. She became Lady Diana Spencer when her father succeeded to the earldom in 1975, and worked as a kindergarten teacher in Pimlico before marrying the Prince of Wales to great popular acclaim in 1981. They have two sons, **Prince William (Arthur Philip Louis)** (1982–) and **Prince Henry (Charles Albert David)** (1984–), known as **Prince Harry**. Seriously interested in social concerns, she became a popular public figure in her own right, and was president of Relate and many other charities. The royal couple were legally separated in 1992, and divorced in 1996. She continued to travel and work with a range of good causes, both in Britain and abroad, while receiving unprecedented worldwide media attention, with newspapers competing to report on her family situation and on her (real or imaginary) personal relationships; and it was while trying to escape the pursuit of paparazzi in Paris that she died in a car accident in August 1997. >> Charles, Prince of Wales

diaphragm (anatomy) A sheet of muscle and tendons separating the thoracic and abdominal cavities. It is the principle muscle of respiration, and is also an important muscle used in expulsive acts: coughing, vomiting, micturition, defecation, and childbirth. >> abdomen; hernia; micturition; peritoneum; respiration; thorax

diaphragm (photography) An opening, usually circular, and generally adjustable in diameter or area, which controls the amount of light passing through a lens into an optical system, such as a camera. >> camera

diarrhoea / diarrhea [diya**ree**a] The frequent passage of semi-formed or liquid motions. Acute diarrhoea usually results from inflammation of the bowel, chemical irritants in food, or infection by micro-organisms (eg dysentery). Important consequences are loss of body water, salt, and nutrients. >> dysentery

Diaspora [diy**as**pora] (Gr 'scattering', Heb *golah* or *galut* 'exile') The Jews scattered in the world outside Palestine, from either voluntary or compulsory resettlements; also known as the **Dispersion**. >> Judaism

diastole [diy**as**tolee] The interval between successive contractions of the heart. During this period, the heart chambers fill with blood flowing from the veins into the atria, and continuing into the ventricles. >> heart ℹ; systole

diastrophism [diy**as**trofizm] The deformation of large masses of the Earth's crust to form mountain ranges, ocean basins, and continents. >> orogeny; plate tectonics ℹ

diathermy [**diy**athermee] The application of heat to muscles or joints for the relief of pain. The heat is produced by means of high-frequency electric current or high-frequency electromagnetic short-wave radiation.

diatom [**diy**atm] A microscopic, single-celled green alga common in marine and freshwater habitats; possesses an often ornate, external shell (*frustule*) containing silica, and consisting of two separate valves. (Class: Bacillarophyceae.) >> green algae; silica

Diaz or **Dias, Bartolomeu** [**dee**az] (c.1450–1500) Navigator and explorer, probably born in Portugal. The first man to sail round the Cape of Good Hope (1487), he also travelled with Vasco da Gama in 1497, and with Cabral in 1500. >> Cabral; Gama, Vasco da

Díaz, (José de la Cruz) Porfirio [**dee**az] (1830–1915) President of Mexico (1876–80, 1884–1911), born in Oaxaca. Defeated in the presidential election of 1875, he seized power, and served as president for 30 years, until forced into exile. >> Mexico ℹ

diazepam >> **benzodiazepines**

diazo process >> **photocopying**

Dibdin, Michael (John) (1947–) Novelist, born in Chichester, West Sussex. In 1988 he won the Crime Writer's Award, the Gold Dagger, for *Ratking*. Later books include *Dirty Tricks* (1991), *Dark Spectre* (1995), and *Cosi Fan Tutti* (1996).

DiCaprio, Leonardo (1974–) Film actor, born in Los Angeles. He began his acting career in television at the age of 14, moved into films, and became known after his Oscar-nominated role for Best Supporting Actor in *What's Eating Gilbert Grape?* (1993). Later films include *Romeo and Juliet* (1996), *Marvin's Room*, *Titanic* (1997), *The Man in the Iron Mask* (1998), and *The Beach* (1999).

Dickens, Charles (John Huffam) (1812–70) Novelist, born in Landport, Hampshire. He took up journalism, at 22 joining a London newspaper. In 1836 his *Sketches by Boz* and *Pickwick Papers* were published; and that year he married Catherine Hogarth. They had 10 children, but were separated in 1858. Dickens worked relentlessly, producing several successful novels, which first appeared in monthly instalments, notably *Oliver Twist* (1837–9), *Nicholas Nickleby* (1838–9) and *The Old Curiosity Shop* (1840–1). His later novels include *David Copperfield* (1849–50), *Bleak House* (1852–3), *A Tale of Two Cities* (1859), *Great Expectations* (1860–1), and the unfinished *The Mystery of Edwin Drood* (1870). His novels included vigorous campaigns against some of the social abuses of the time, and influenced several reforms. They have provided the basis for many successful theatre, cinema, radio, and television adaptations.

Dickinson, Emily (Elizabeth) (1830–86) Poet, born in Amherst, MA. At the age of 23 she withdrew from all social contacts, and lived a secluded life at Amherst, writing in secret over 1000 poems. Hardly any of her work was published until after her death.

dicotyledons [diykoti**lee**dnz] One of the two major divisions of the flowering plants, often referred to simply as **dicots**; contrasted with **monocotyledons**. The seed embryo has two cotyledons, and the primary root of the seedling persists, forming a taproot. About 250 different families of dicots are currently recognized. (Subclass: Dicotyledonae.) >> cotyledons; flowering plants; monocotyledons; seed

dictator In strict terms, a single ruler who is often not elected but enjoys authority by virtue of some personal characteristic, ie an **autocrat**. In practice, a dictatorship often refers to rule by several people, unelected and authoritarian, such as a military dictatorship.

dictionary A work of reference, traditionally in the form of a book, and now often available as a computational data base, giving linguistic information about the words of a language, arranged in alphabetical order under headwords. Some dictionaries (especially those falling within the US and European – particularly French and German – traditions) add encyclopedic data, or provide special features, such as notes on usage or closely related words. The process of compiling dictionaries, and the study of the issues involved, is known as **lexicography**. >> Johnson, Samuel; Webster, Noah

Dicynodon [diy**siy**nodon] A plant-eating fossil reptile known from the late Permian period; jaws with horny plates for cutting and crushing vegetation; upper canine tusks prominent. (Order: Therapsida.) >> fossil; reptile; Therapsida

Diderot, Denis [deederoh] (1713–84) Writer and philosopher, born in Langres, France. He was the chief editor of the *Encyclopédie* (1751–65), a major work of the age of the Enlightenment. A prolific and versatile writer, he published novels, plays, satires, essays, and letters. >> Enlightenment

didgeridoo, also spelled **didjeridoo** or **didjeridu** A primitive trumpet of the Australian aborigines, made from a hollow eucalyptus branch about 120–150 cm/4–5 ft long. It is used to accompany singing and dancing. >> Aborigines; aerophone

Dido [**diy**doh] In the *Aeneid*, the daughter of the King of Tyre, who founded Carthage. Aeneas was diverted to Africa by storms, and told her his story. They fell in love, and when Aeneas deserted her she committed suicide. >> Aeneas

Didrikson, Babe, nickname of **Mildred Ella Zaharias**, *née* **Didrikson** (1914–56) Sportswoman, born in Port Arthur, TX. After an outstanding career in athletics, she became a leading golfer, and was also renowned at diving, billiards, and lacrosse. As a professional she won the US Women's Open in 1948, 1950, and 1954. >> athletics; golf

Diefenbaker, John G(eorge) [**dee**fenbayker] (1895–1979) Canadian Conservative statesman and prime minister (1957–63), born in Neustadt, Ontario. His government introduced important agricultural reforms, and extended the federal franchise to Canada's native peoples.

dielectric A non-conducting material whose molecules align or polarize under the influence of applied electric fields. Dielectrics are an essential constituent of capacitors. >> capacitance; electric dipole moment; permittivity

dielectric constant >> **permittivity**

Diemen, Antony Van >> **Tasman, Abel Janszoon**

diencephalon [diyen**se**falon] The part of the forebrain which lies deep within the cerebral hemispheres. The *thalamus* is the largest part, whose diverse functions include various motor, sensory, and emotional responses. >> brain ℹ; hypothalamus; pineal gland

Dieppe [dyep] 49°55N 1°05E, pop (1995e) 37 700. Seaport in NW France; scene of heavy fighting in World War 2; ferry links with Newhaven.

Dieri [**di**ree] Aboriginal community of the L Eyre region of South Australia. After 1860, they were drawn into European-controlled cattle stations and missions, and many now live in the cities of Adelaide and Port Augusta. >> Aborigines

Diesel, Rudolf (Christian Carl) [**dee**zl] (1858–1913) Engineer, born in Paris. Subsidized by the Krupp company, he constructed a 'rational heat motor', demonstrating the first compression-ignition engine in 1897. >> diesel engine; engine

diesel engine An internal combustion engine, working upon the diesel cycle, which ignites its fuel/air mixture by heating it to combustion point through compression. Because of this, the diesel engine is classed as a compression-ignition engine. >> Carnot cycle; Diesel; engine

diet The combination of foods which provide the necessary nutrients for the body. Often the term is used to imply a restriction of calories for slimming: strictly speaking this is a 'low-calorie' diet, just as there are low-fat diets, low-salt diets, or high-fibre diets. >> dietetics; macrobiotics; nutrients

dietetics The clinical management of a patient through dietary intervention, as practised professionally by **dietitians**. The two problems most commonly treated by dietitians are obesity and diabetes. >> diabetes mellitus; diet

diethylstilboestrol >> **DES**

Diet, Imperial The assembly of the Holy Roman Empire, mediaeval in origin, representing the separate estates of electors, princes, and free cities, and summoned at the will of the Emperor. It became increasingly little more than a permanent congress of ambassadors during the last century and a half of its existence (1663–1806). >> Holy Roman Empire; Reformation

Diet of Worms >> **Worms, Diet of**

Dietrich, Marlene [**dee**trikh], originally **Maria Magdalene von Losch** (1904–92) Film actress, born in Berlin. She became famous in a German film *Der blaue Engel* (1930, The Blue Angel), and developed a glamorous and sensual film personality in such Hollywood films as *Morocco* (1930).

differential calculus A system of mathematical rules which considers small increments of a variable x, and the corresponding changes in $f(x)$, to find the rate at which $f(x)$ is changing. The early development of calculus was associated with Isaac Newton, and independently with Gottfried Leibniz. >> Leibniz; Newton, Isaac

diffraction An interference effect, a property of waves, responsible for the spreading of waves issuing from a small aperture (eg sound waves from a public address loudspeaker). Diffraction causes the waves to 'bend round' objects, which in light produces shadows surrounded by tiny light and dark bands (**diffraction fringes**). Haloes round the Sun on misty days are caused by diffraction. >> interference; X-ray diffraction

diffusion In physics and chemistry, the movement of atoms or particles through bulk material via their random collisions. For example, atoms of a gas introduced into a volume of still air will become evenly distributed through it by diffusion. >> Brownian motion; convection; kinetic theory of gases

Digby, Sir Kenelm (1603–65) Diplomat, scientist, and writer, born in Gayhurst, Buckinghamshire. During the Civil War he was imprisoned by the parliament (1642–3), and had his estate confiscated. After the Restoration, he was chancellor to Queen Henrietta Maria until 1664. >> English Civil War; Restoration

digestion A physiological process of animals in which complex foodstuffs are broken down by enzymes into simpler components (monosaccharides, amino acids, fatty acids, and other substances) which can be used by body cells. In certain animals (eg protozoa, porifera), digestion is entirely intracellular. Many animals (eg vertebrates, arthropods) depend entirely on extracellular digestion, in which enzyme-rich fluids are secreted into the cavity of the alimentary canal. >> alimentary canal; cell; indigestion

Diggers A radical group in England formed during the Commonwealth, led by Gerrard Winstanley (1609–72), preaching and practising agrarian communism on common and waste land. The movement was suppressed and its communities dispersed by local landowners. >> Commonwealth (English history)

digital computer A programmable machine which operates using binary digital data. The basic operations carried out are simple arithmetic or logical operations, but in combination and at high speed these provide a very powerful facility. Digital computers contain (i) a *central processing unit* which controls and co-ordinates all the functions of the computer, and performs the arithmetic and logical operations; (ii) a *memory*, which holds data and program instructions; and (iii) *input/output devices*, which allow communication to and from the outside world. >> central processing unit; computer; computer memory

digitalis [dijitahlis] An extract of *Digitalis purpurea* (the foxglove) which has been used for the treatment of heart failure and oedema ('dropsy') for at least 800 years. The extract contains cardiac glycosides as active ingredients. >> foxglove; glucose; heart disease; oedema

digital recording A technique of sound recording, developed in the 1970s, in which a series of coded pulses replaces the waveform analogues of earlier methods. The advantages are that tape noise, pitch fluctuations, and distortion are virtually eliminated, as happens in the case of the compact disc and digital audiotape. Developments in the 1990s include *digital audio broadcasting*, a high-quality transmission system for radio; the *digital compact cassette*, a format for tape cassettes; and the *digital video disc* (*DVD*; originally, *digital versatile disc*), a disc similar to a compact disc, but double-sided and multi-layered, thus vastly increasing storage capacity. >> compact disc; digital techniques; NICAM; sound recording

dihydroxybutanedioic acid >> **tartaric acid**

Dijon [deezhõ], ancient **Dibio** 47°20N 5°00E, pop (1995e) 151 000. Industrial and commercial city in E France; railway; bishopric; university (1722); cathedral; historic capital of Burgundy; famous for its restaurants and its mustard; centre of wine trade. >> Burgundy

dik-dik A dwarf antelope, native to Africa; small (height, up to 40 cm/16 in); large ears, elongate nose; male with short straight horns and pronounced secretory gland in front of eye. (Genus: *Madoqua*, 3 species.) >> antelope

dikkop [dikop] >> **thick-knee**

dilatation and curettage (D and C) [dilatayshn, kyooretij] A minor gynaecological operation to investigate the cause of menstrual disorders and possible carcinoma of the uterus. A special type of scoop (*curette*) is passed through the dilated cervix into the uterine cavity. Tissue lining the cavity is removed and examined microscopically. >> menstruation; uterus [i]

dill An aromatic annual (*Anethum graveolens*), growing to 60 cm/2 ft, native to India and SW Asia; leaves feathery; flowers yellow; fruit ellipsoid, strongly compressed, dark brown with a paler wing. It is cultivated as a culinary herb. (Family: Umbelliferae.) >> herb

Dillinger, John (Herbert) [dilinjer] (1903–34) Gangster, born in Indianapolis, IN. He specialized in armed bank robberies, terrorizing Indiana and neighbouring states (1933–4). He was shot dead by FBI agents in Chicago.

Dillon, Matt (1964–) Film actor, born in Larchmont, NY. His first major film role was in Francis Ford Coppola's *The Outsiders* (1983). Later films include *Kansas* (1988), *Beautiful Girls* (1996), and *Wild Things* (1998).

DiMaggio, Joe [dimajioh], popular name of **Joseph (Paul) DiMaggio**, nicknames **Joltin' Joe** and **the Yankee Clipper** (1914–99) Baseball player, born in Martinez, CA. He spent his entire career with the New York Yankees (1936–51), holding the record for hitting safely in 56 consecutive games (1941). His second wife was the film star, Marilyn Monroe. >> baseball [i]

Dimbleby, David (1938–) Broadcaster, born in London, the son of Richard Dimbleby. Since the 1970s he has become a leading presenter and interviewer on BBC television current-affairs programmes, such as *Panorama* and *Election and Results*, and is also chairman of the BBC's *Question Time* (from 1994). >> Dimbleby, Richard

Dimbleby, Jonathan (1944–) Broadcaster, writer, and journalist, born in London, the son of Richard Dimbleby. Well known as a presenter of television current-affairs documentaries (1972–88), he regularly fronts programmes on major national events. His controversial 'official' biography of the Prince of Wales appeared in 1994. >> Dimbleby, Richard

Dimbleby, Richard (Frederick) (1913–65) Broadcaster, born in Richmond on Thames, Greater London. He became the BBC's first foreign correspondent and its first war correspondent. In the postwar era, he established himself as a magisterial TV anchorman on *Panorama*, and a commentator on major events. >> BBC; broadcasting; Dimbleby, David/Jonathan

dimer [diymer] A compound formed when two units (**monomers**), react together either by addition or by condensation. >> chemical reaction; monomer

dimethylpropane >> **pentane**

diminished responsibility A limited defence to a charge of murder which reduces the crime to one of manslaughter (England and Wales) or culpable homicide (Scotland), thereby avoiding the mandatory sentence of life imprisonment. It relates to a state of mind which substantially impairs a person's mental responsibility and which, while not amounting to insanity, borders on it. >> manslaughter; murder

diminishing returns, law of A prediction in economics that, as more capital and labour is put into a factory, the resulting increases in output will eventually start to get smaller. Ultimately the average output per unit of labour or capital will also fall.

Dinaric Alps [dinarik], Serbo-Croatian **Dinara Planina**, Ital **Alpi Dinariche** Mountain range following the Adriatic coast of Croatia and NW Albania; rises to 2522 m/8274 ft at Durmitor. >> Alps; Karst

d'Indy, (Paul Marie Théodore) Vincent [dãdee] (1851–1931) Composer, born in Paris. His works include several operas and orchestral pieces, notably *Symphonie sur un chant montagnard français* (1886, Symphony on a French Mountaineering Song). >> Franck, César

dingo An Australian subspecies of domestic dog (*Canis familiaris dingo*), descended from dogs introduced thousands of years ago with aboriginal settlers; tawny yellow; cannot bark; eats kangaroos (and now rabbits and sheep); viewed as a pest. >> Canidae; dog

Dinka E Sudanic-speaking transhumant cattle herders of the Upper Nile in the Sudan Republic. >> Sudan [i]; transhumance

dinoflagellate [diynohflajeluht] A microscopic, single-celled organism classified either as an alga (Class: Dinophyceae) or as a flagellate protozoan (Phylum: Mastigophora); characterized by two whip-like organelles (*flagella*); most species enclosed in a rigid shell (*test*) encrusted with silica. >> algae; flagellum; Protozoa; silica; systematics

dinosaur A member of a group of reptiles (Subclass: Archosauria) that dominated life on land for 140 million years from the late Triassic period until their extinction at the end of the Cretaceous period, 64 million years ago. There are over 800 species of dinosaurs, all sharing the

Dinosaurs

specialized kind of hip joint that allowed upright posture. They fall into two contrasting groups: the **reptile-hipped dinosaurs** (Order: Saurischia), and the **bird-hipped dinosaurs** (Order: Ornithischia). Many attained great size. *Diplodocus* reached a length of 28 m/90 ft but weighed only 10 tonnes, whereas *Apatosaurus* was shorter at 25 m/80 ft, but weighed 30 tonnes. These giants were slow-moving (3–4 kph/2–2½ mph), probably lived in herds and were warm-blooded. Dinosaurs laid eggs, often on a nest mound of mud, and there is evidence that some protected their young. The reason for their extinction is unknown, but a combination of climatic changes and competition from mammals in the changing conditions seems most probable. A widely promulgated theory is that the climatic changes came about as the result of a meteoritic impact. >> Ornithischia; reptile; Saurischia

Dinosaur Provincial Park A provincial park in Alberta, SW Canada; a world heritage site. In the early 20th-c the fossil remains of some 60 different species of dinosaur were discovered here. >> dinosaur ℹ

Dio Cassius [**diy**oh **ka**sius], also found as **Dion Cassius** and **Cassius Dio Cocceianus** (c.150–c.235) Roman senator and prominent man of affairs, from Bithynia in Asia Minor, who wrote a comprehensive history of Rome in Greek, extending from the foundation of the city down to his own day (229).

Diocletian [diyo**klee**shn], in full **Gaius Aurelius Valerius Diocletianus** (245–316) Roman emperor (284–305), a Dalmatian of humble birth, born in Diocles, who became the greatest of the soldier emperors of the 3rd-c. In 286 the Empire was split in two, with Diocletian retaining the East, and Maximian taking the West. Later, he divided the Empire into four. >> Nicomedia; Roman history ℹ

diode An electronic valve having two electrodes (an anode and a cathode); invented in 1904 by British physicist John Ambrose Fleming. It permits current flow in only one direction, and is thus widely used as a rectifier, changing alternating current (AC) into direct current (DC). >> Fleming, John Ambrose; light-emitting / zener diode; rectifier; triode

Diogenes of Sinope [diy**o**jeneez] (c.410–c.320 BC) Cynic philosopher, born in Sinope, Pontus. His unconventional behaviour, which became legendary in antiquity (eg looking with a lantern in daylight for an honest man), was intended to portray the ideal of a life lived according to nature. >> Antisthenes; Cynics

Diomedes [diyoh**mee**deez] or **Diomede** A Greek hero who fought in the Trojan War, even taking on the gods in battle; also a wise counsellor, the partner of Odysseus in various schemes. >> Philoctetes; Troilus

Dione [diy**oh**nee] The fourth natural satellite of Saturn, discovered in 1684; distance from the planet 377 000 km/ 234 000 mi; diameter 1120 km/700 mi; orbital period 2·737 days; heavily cratered. >> Saturn (astronomy); RR964

Dionne, Cécile, Yvonne, Annette, Emilie, and **Marie** [dee**on**] (1934–) Quintuplets successfully delivered to their French-Canadian parents, Oliva and Elzire Dionne in N Ontario, Canada. As the first documented quintuplets to survive, they soon became international celebrities. Emilie died in 1954, and Marie in 1970.

Dionysius of Halicarnassus [diyo**niy**sius] (1st-c BC) Influential Greek critic, historian and rhetorician, from Halicarnassus in Asia Minor, who lived in Rome at the time of Augustus. Much of his writing survives, including about half of his masterpiece, the *Early Roman History*. >> Roman history ℹ

Dionysius the Areopagite [diyo**niy**sius, ari**o**pagiyt] (1st-c) Greek Church leader, one of the few Athenians converted by the apostle Paul (*Acts* 17.34). Tradition makes him the first Bishop of Athens and a martyr. >> Christianity; Paul, St

Dionysius the Elder [diyo**niy**sius] (c.431–367 BC) Tyrant of Syracuse (405–367 BC) and ruler of half of Sicily. His reign was dominated by warfare with the Carthaginians. A patron of the arts, he invited Plato to his court. >> Plato

Dionysius the Younger [diyo**niy**sius] (c.397–? BC) Tyrant of Syracuse (367–357/6 BC, 347/6–344 BC), the son and successor of Dionysius the Elder. Groomed by Plato as a potential philosopher-king, he turned out to be a rake and an oppressor.

Dionysus or **Dionysos** [diyo**niy**sus] In Greek mythology, the god of wild and uncontrolled ecstasy; later, more specifically, the god of wine, associated with music and dramatic festivals. He was the son of Zeus and Semele. >> Semele; Sileni

Diophantus [diyo**fan**tus] (c.200–299) Greek mathematician, who lived at Alexandria c.275. Of his three known works, only six books of *Arithmetica*, the earliest extant treatise on algebra, have survived. >> algebra

dioptre / diopter [diy**op**ter] In optics, the power of a lens; symbol *dpt*; defined as 1 divided by focal length in metres; used mostly in optometry. >> lens; optometry

Dior, Christian [dee**aw(r)**] (1905–57) Fashion designer, born in Granville, Normandy. He founded his own Paris house in 1945, and in 1947 achieved worldwide fame with his long-skirted 'New Look'. His later designs included the 'H' line and the 'A' line.

dioxin (**tetrachlorodibenzo-*p*-**dioxin, or **TCDD**) A highly toxic contaminant of the chlorphenoxy group of herbicides whose level is currently regulated at 0·1 parts per million or less. It causes a severe form of skin eruption (*chloracne*), and in laboratory animals causes cancer and damages the fetuses of mothers exposed to it. >> Agent Orange; herbicide

diphtheria A specific infection by *Corynebacterium diphtheriae*, which usually lodges in the throat but occasionally in wounds on the skin. Formerly common, immunization has resulted in a dramatic fall in incidence. The illness is severe and potentially lethal. >> infection; Schick test

diphthong A vowel in which there is a change in auditory quality during a single syllable, as in *my*, *how*. The term is also used for a sequence of two written vowels within the same syllable, eg *fear*, *weight*. >> vowel

Diplodocus [di**plod**okus] A semi-aquatic, long necked dinosaur; body length up to 28 m/92 ft, including an extremely long, whip-like tail; plant-eating; four-legged, hindlimbs longer than forelimbs; known from the Upper Jurassic period of North America and Europe. (Order: Saurischia.) >> dinosaur [i]; Jurassic period; Saurischia

diplomatic service The body of public servants who are official representatives of their country in another country, or who provide support to them. >> civil service

Diplopoda [di**plo**poda] >> **millipede**

Dipnoi [**dip**noy] A subclass of bony fishes, comprising the lungfishes. >> bony fish; lungfish

dipper A starling-like bird, native to mountains of Eurasia and the W New World; inhabits fast-flowing streams; swims underwater using wings. (Genus: *Cinclus*, 4 species. Family: Cinclidae.) >> ouzel; starling

Diprotodon [diy**proh**todon] A heavily built, fossil marsupial known from the Pleistocene epoch of Australia; large, up to 2 m/6½ ft tall at the shoulder; front legs short; plant-eating. (Order: Diprotodonta.) >> fossil; marsupial [i]; Pleistocene epoch

Diptera [**dip**tera] >> **fly**

diptych [**dip**tik] A picture consisting of two panels, hinged like the pages of a book. Small portable devotional pictures and altarpieces sometimes took this form in the late Middle Ages. >> altarpiece

Dirac, Paul A(drien) M(aurice) [**di**rak] (1902–84) Physicist, born in Bristol. His main research was in the field of quantum mechanics, in which he applied relativity theory, and developed the theory of the spinning electron. He received the Nobel Prize for Physics in 1933. >> quantum mechanics

direct current >> **alternating current**

directed energy weapons A technology under investigation for military purposes, using energy sources such as laser beams, particle beams, plasma beams, and microwave beams, all of which travel at the speed of light. Such weapons are regarded as a vital component of the US Strategic Defense Initiative. >> laser [i]; particle beam weapons; plasma (physics); SDI

Directoire Style A French style of furniture, and women's clothes, strictly belonging to the years 1795–9, but generally used to describe the furniture fashionable between the outbreak of the French Revolution and the introduction of the Empire Style. It was a restrained Neoclassical style strongly influenced by antique Greek art. >> Directory; Empire Style; Neoclassicism (art and architecture)

Director of Public Prosecutions >> **Crown Prosecution Service**

Directory The government of the First Republic of France (1795–9), established in the Thermidorian reaction to the Reign of Terror, with five executive Directors. It was overthrown by the coup of 18 Brumaire (9–10 Nov), bringing Napoleon to power. >> French Revolution [i]; Napoleon I

dirigible A cigar-shaped, steerable, rigid-framed, fabric-covered airship. It is fitted with horizontal engines driving propellers which provide the forward thrust. >> airship; propeller

disaccharide [diy**sak**ariyd] A carbohydrate consisting of two simple sugars joined together, condensed with the elimination of water. The most abundant in nature are *sucrose* (table sugar) which combines one glucose and one fructose molecule, and *lactose*, the sugar of milk, which is a combination of glucose and galactose. Fructose, glucose, and galactose are single-unit sugars, classed as **monosaccharides**. >> carbohydrate; lactose; maltose; sucrose

disarmament Arms control which seeks to promote international security by a reduction in armed forces and/or weapons. General (ie applies to all countries) and comprehensive (ie applies to all categories of forces and weapons) disarmament was first attempted in the 1920s by the League of Nations, and by the United Nations in the 1950s, but such moves have not been successful. Disarmament is therefore limited to agreements between two or a few countries, and restricted to particular classes of weapons and troop levels. Problems arise in determining equivalences between different types of weapons held by different countries, and in verifying arms reduction treaties, especially in respect of nuclear weapons. >> chemical warfare; nuclear weapons

discant >> **descant**

discount house (UK) A financial institution which buys short-dated government stock (Treasury Bills) with money borrowed from commercial banks for very short periods. The difference between the borrowing rate and the lending rate provides the discount house with its profit. >> stocks

discount house (USA) A retail store which sells goods at a lower (**discounted**) price than is standard practice. When the use of the house is available only to members of a particular group (eg a trade union), it is a **closed-door discount house**. Such stores have also developed in other consumer countries, though not always with this label.

discus throw An athletics field event using a circular disc of wood with metal plates, weighing 2 kg/4·4 lb for men and 1 kg/2·2 lb for women. The competitor throws the discus with one hand from within the confines of a circle 2·5 m/8·2 ft in diameter, with the aim of achieving a greater distance than anyone else. The current world record for men is 74·08 m/243 ft, achieved by Jürgen Schult (1960–) of Germany in 1986 at Neubrandenburg, Germany; for women it is 76·80 m/251 ft, achieved by Gabriele Reinsch (1963–) of Germany in 1988 at Neubrandenburg, Germany. >> athletics

dish In telecommunications using microwaves, an antenna having a concave reflecting surface which acts as a secondary radiator to concentrate the signal on the main pick-up element. In television broadcasting by satellite, the main transmission dish is 2–3 m/6–10 ft in diameter, but for domestic reception 30 cm/12 in may be sufficient. >> electromagnetic radiation [i]

disinfectant A material toxic to bacteria. Phenol (carbolic acid) was one of the earliest used, but is also toxic and corrosive to humans. Phenol derivatives are, however, used in chemical toilets. >> alcohols; chlorine; phenol

disk >> **magnetic disk**

disk operating system >> **DOS**

dislocation (medicine) The displacement of a bone from its joint with another bone. Ligaments within or around the affected joint (*capsule*) binding adjacent bones together are torn or otherwise damaged. Most dislocations can be restored manually. >> bone; joint

dislocation (physics) >> **crystal defects**

Disney, Walt(er Elias) (1901–66) Artist and film producer, born in Chicago, IL. After World War 1, he set up a small studio in which he produced animated cartoons, his most famous character being Mickey Mouse (1928), for whom he provided the original voice. His first full-length coloured cartoon film was *Snow White and the Seven Dwarfs* (1937). This was followed by *Pinocchio* (1940), *Dumbo* (1941), and *Fantasia* (1940). In 1948 he began his series of coloured nature films, including *The Living Desert* (1953). He also directed several films for young people, such as *Treasure Island* (1950), and family films such as *Mary Poppins* (1964). He opened Disneyland, the first of several family amusement parks, in California in 1955, and others followed in Florida (1971), Tokyo (1983), and Paris (1992). His studios are still highly active, making feature films for cinema and television.

Dispersion >> **Diaspora**

Disraeli, Benjamin, 1st Earl of Beaconsfield [diz**ray**lee, **bek**uhnsfeeld] (1804–81) British statesman and twice prime minister (1868, 1874–80), born in London, the eldest son of an anglicized Jew, and baptized in 1817. He made his early reputation as a novelist, and is especially known for his two political novels, *Coningsby* (1844) and *Sybil* (1846). He came to prominence as a critic of Peel's free trade policies, and was Chancellor of the Exchequer in Derby's minority governments of 1852, 1858–9, and 1866–8, when he piloted the 1867 Reform Bill through the Commons. He became prime minister on Derby's resignation in 1868, but was defeated in the general election. During his second administration, Britain became half-owner of the Suez Canal (1875), and the Queen assumed the title Empress of India (1876). >> Derby, Earl; Peel; Suez Canal [i]; Tories; Victoria

Dissenters Christians who separate themselves from the established Church or general religious belief of a country. In a wider sense, it is applied to those who dissent from the very principle of an established or national Church. >> Christianity; Nonconformists

dissidents People who oppose the particular regime under which they live, often through peaceful means, and who as a result suffer discrimination and harassment from the authorities. They tend to take a moral rather than an overtly political stance in their opposition. >> Sakharov; Solzhenitsyn

distance education Teaching people, usually at home or in their place of work, by means of correspondence units, radio, cassettes, telephone, television, or microcomputer, rather than through face-to-face contact. Often a tutor may be involved to give advice or mark written work, either at a distance or through occasional meetings. >> Open University

distemper A viral disease of the dog (**canine distemper**) and ferret families, which may also spread to the seal family. It is a life-threatening disease, characterized by attacks of catarrh and severe neurological signs, such as fits. Vaccination is very effective. >> dog; ferret; virus

Distinguished Flying Cross (DFC) In the UK, a decoration instituted in 1918, awarded to officers and warrant-officers in the RAF for acts of gallantry performed on active service. The ribbon is black and white (equal diagonal stripes).

Distinguished Service Cross (DSC) In the UK, a decoration awarded to warrant officers and officers below the rank of captain in the Royal Navy for acts of gallantry or devotion to duty. The ribbon has equal stripes: black, white, black. >> Distinguished Service Order

Distinguished Service Order (DSO) A military award in the UK, founded in 1886, to recognize special service by officers of the army, navy, merchant navy, and airforce. The ribbon is red edged with blue.

distortion >> **aberrations 1** [i]

district attorney In the USA, the state or county prosecutor, who acts on information supplied by the police or a member of the public, and decides whether to initiate a prosecution; also called a **public prosecutor**, when employed by local government; an **attorney general**, when employed by the state; and a **US attorney**, when working federally. >> criminal law; prosecution

District of Columbia pop (1995e) 563 000; area 174 sq km/67 sq mi. Federal district in E USA, co-extensive with the city of Washington; established 1790–1 from land taken from Maryland and Virginia. >> Washington (DC)

dittany An aromatic herb (*Dictamnus albus*), native to Europe; flowers 4-petalled, purple or white. It gives off a highly inflammable volatile oil, which in hot conditions can ignite and burn without harming the plant; hence its alternative name, **burning bush**. (Family: Rutaceae.)

diuretics [diyu**ret**iks] Drugs which increase the production of urine, used in the treatment of fluid retention, heart failure, and high blood pressure. Certain other substances also have a diuretic effect, such as coffee. >> urine

diver A large diving bird native to N waters of the N hemisphere; plumage with fine contrasting patterns, usually black and white; also known in the USA as the **loon**. (Genus: *Gavia*, 5 species. Family: Gaviidae.)

diverticulosis A disorder of the large bowel that affects older people. Small pouches form in the lining of the bowel that penetrate the muscle coat of the gut at points of weakness. >> intestine

divertimento A light musical composition. Mozart and his contemporaries wrote divertimentos in five or more movements for an ensemble of soloists. >> Mozart

dividend An allocation of the profits of an enterprise to its shareholders. Companies may pay out all profits as dividends, retain a proportion, or pay out nothing. There is no legal obligation to pay; the distribution depends on the level of profits and the company's financial needs. Dividends are also sometimes paid when there have been no profits, but management is confident about the future, and wishes to retain the confidence of the public and shareholders. >> company; shares

divination A term applied to several traditional methods of attempting to acquire information by alleged paranormal means. The information to be interpreted is conveyed by some physical source, such as dowsing or palm reading. >> dowsing; paranormal

Divine Right of Kings The concept of the divinely-ordained authority of monarchs, widely held in the mediaeval and early modern periods. It is often associated with the absolutism of Louis XIV of France and the assertions of the Stuarts. >> absolutism; Louis XIV; Stuarts

diving Any method of descending under water. The most common form at competitive level is by jumping from an elevated board into a swimming pool. Springboard events take place from a board 3 m (9 ft 10 in) above the water; platform diving is from a rigid board 10 m (30 ft 5 in) above the water. >> scuba diving; skin-diving; RR1062

Divisional Court A court in England and Wales presided over by at least two judges from a division of the High Court. One of its functions is to hear certain appeals. >> appeal; High Court of Justice; judicial review

Divisionism In painting, a technique (sometimes called **Pointillism**) whereby small patches or spots of pure colour are placed close together so that they mix in the eye of the beholder. It was developed by some of the French Postimpressionists, notably Seurat, and designated **Neoimpressionism** by the French critic Félix Fénéon (1861–1944). >> Postimpressionism; Seurat

divorce The termination by court order of a valid marriage, the criteria for which vary greatly between countries and jurisdictions. English courts now recognize only one ground for divorce: the irretrievable breakdown of marriage. This must be supported by one of five 'facts'. The person applying for the divorce (the *petitioner*) must show that the other party (the *respondent*) has (1) committed adultery; (2) displayed unreasonable behaviour; (3) deserted the petitioner for 2 years prior to the divorce petition; (4) lived apart from the petitioner for 2 years, and consents to the divorce; or (5) lived apart for 5 years. Most US jurisdictions recognize no-fault divorce based on incompatibility, irreconcilable differences, living separate and apart for a fixed time (usually 1–3 years), or mutual consent to divorce; however, the grounds for divorce vary considerably. >> annulment; maintenance; marriage

Diwali [dee**wah**lee] The Hindu festival of lights, held in October or November (Asvina K 15) in honour of Rama, an incarnation of the god Vishnu, and Lakshmi, goddess of wealth and luck; lamps are lit and gifts exchanged. Diwali is also a Sikh and a Jain religious festival. >> Hinduism; Jainism; Sikhism; RR982

Dix, Dorothea (Lynde) (1802–87) Humanitarian, born in Hampden, ME. She was largely responsible for the emergence of the concept of mental illness in the USA, and for the establishment of mental hospitals there. In 1861 she became superintendent of women nurses for the federal government, overseeing some 2000 women who cared for the Union war-wounded.

Dixieland A style of jazz associated with the 'classic' New Orleans school, and especially with white musicians who based their music on that of the Original Dixieland Jass Band in the early 1920s. >> jazz

Djakarta >> **Jakarta**

Djem, el- [el **jem**] The world's most intact example of a Roman amphitheatre, situated in the present-day village of el-Djem in W Tunisia; a world heritage monument. It had a capacity for 35 000 people. >> amphitheatre

Djemila [**jem**ila] The former Roman garrison of Cuicul in N Algeria; a world heritage site. Founded in the late 1st-c AD, the ruins include temples, forums, thermal baths, and Christian basilicas.

Djibouti (city) [ji**boo**tee] 11°36N 43°08E, pop (1995e) 354 000. Free-port capital of Djibouti, NE Africa; built 1886–1900 in Arab style; official port of Ethiopia, 1897; airport. >> Djibouti (country) ℹ

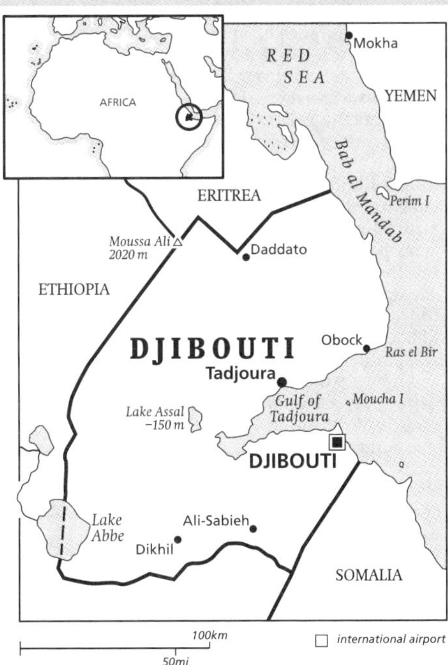

Djibouti (country) [ji**boo**tee], official name **Republic of Djibouti**, Arabic **Jumhouriya Djibouti** pop (1995e) 607 000; area 23 200 sq km/8958 sq mi. NE African republic; capital, Djibouti; timezone GMT +3; chief ethnic group, Somali (62%); chief religion, Islam (94%); official language, Arabic; unit of currency, Djibouti franc; series of plateaux dropping down from mountains to flat, low-lying, rocky desert; fertile coastal strip around the Gulf of Tadjoura; highest point, Moussa Ali, rising to 2020 m/6627 ft in the N; semi-arid climate, with hot season (May–Sep); very high temperatures on coastal plain all year round; French colonial interest in mid-19th-c, setting up French Somaliland, 1896; French Overseas Territory, following World War 2; French Territory of the Afars and the Issas, 1967; independence, 1977; new constitution, 1992; governed by a president, a legislative chamber, an executive prime minister, and a council; crop-based agriculture possible only with irrigation; livestock raising among nomadic population; some fishing on coast; economy badly affected by local wars, and by closure of Suez Canal, 1967–75; small industrial sector. >> Djibouti (city); Suez Canal ℹ; RR1006 political leaders

DNA or **deoxyribonucleic acid** The nucleic acid which occurs in combination with protein in the chromosomes, and which contains the genetic instructions. It consists of four primary nitrogenous bases (adenine, guanine, thymine, cytosine), a sugar (2-deoxy-D-ribose), and phosphoric acid, arranged in a regular structure. The skeleton of the DNA consists of two chains of alternate sugar and phosphate groups twisted round each other in the form of a double spiral, or double helix; to each sugar is attached a base; and the two chains are held together by hydrogen bonding between the bases. The sequence of bases provides in code the genetic information, which is transcribed, edited, and translated by the RNA. Each diploid human cell nucleus contains approximately 6×10^9 base pairs of DNA, totalling in length about

2 m/6·6 ft, but coiled upon itself so that it fits inside the cell nucleus of less than 10 μm in diameter. DNA replicates itself accurately during cell growth and duplication. Its structure was discovered by geneticists James Watson and Francis Crick in 1953. >> cell; chromosome ℹ; Crick; DNA profiling; genetic code ℹ; RNA; Watson, James; *see illustration*

DNA profiling A biochemical process used both to determine paternity and to identify criminals from human material (eg blood, hair, skin) left at the scene of a crime; developed in 1986 by Alec Jeffreys of Leicester University, UK. The process involves isolating DNA patterns using enzymes to break up the sample before passing an electric current through the material and exposing it to X-ray film, eventually producing an *autorad*, or DNA profile. This profile is thought to be as distinctive as fingerprints. >> DNA; forensic medicine

Dnepr, River [**dnee**per], Eng **Dnieper**, ancient **Borysthenes** River in W Russia, rising in the S Valdayskaya Vozvyshennost range; enters the Black Sea at Kherson; length, c.2200 km/1400 mi; third longest river in Europe. >> Russia ℹ

Dnepropetrovsk [duh**nye**propyetrofsk], formerly **Ekaterinoslav** (to 1926) 48°29N 35°00E, pop (1995e) 1 204 000. Port in Ukraine, on R Dnepr; founded in 1783 on the site of a Cossack village; airport; railway; university (1918); cathedral (1830–5); iron and steel centre. >> Ukraine ℹ

Dnestr, River >> **Dniester, River**

Dniester, River [**dnee**ster], also **Dnestr**, Pol **Dniestr** River in Ukraine and Moldova, rising in the Carpathian Mts; enters the Black Sea, SW of Odessa; length, 1400 km/870 mi. >> Moldova ℹ; Ukraine ℹ

Doberman(n) pinscher [**doh**berman **pin**sher] A breed of dog, developed c.1900 by a German dog-catcher, Herr Dobermann, who crossbred stray dogs, intending to produce the most vicious dog possible; subsequently crossbred with greyhounds and terriers, and now less vicious; large, lean; short brown or black and tan coat; long neck and muzzle. >> dog

dobsonfly A large, soft-bodied insect; adult wingspan up to 16 cm/6¼ in, but flight clumsy and fluttering; found near streams. (Order: Megaloptera. Family: Corydalidae, c.200 species.) >> insect ℹ

Docetism [**dos**itizm] The belief, arising in early Christianity, that the natural body of Jesus Christ was only apparent (Gr *dokeo*, 'appear, seem') and not real, thereby stressing the divinity of Christ and denying any real physical suffering on his part. >> Christology; Gnosticism

dock A perennial N temperate herb with strong roots; leaves large; flowers tiny; fruit a 3-sided nut enclosed in papery, often reddish valves. (Genus: *Rumex*, c.200 species. Family: Polygonaceae.) >> sorrel

Docklands An area of E London along the R Thames, formerly of great poverty, which attracted new housing and office developments in the 1980s. It includes the Canary Wharf tower, the tallest building in Europe. There is a new Docklands airport, and a railway connecting the area with the City.

Doctor Barnado's Homes >> **Barnardo, Thomas John**

Doctor Who A science-fiction series first broadcast on BBC television in 1963. Ten actors have portrayed the character of the Doctor: in the television series these were William Hartnell (1963–6), Patrick Troughton (1966–9), Jon Pertwee (1970–4), Tom Baker (1974–81), Peter Davison (1982–4), Colin Baker (1984–6), and Sylvester McCoy (1987–9). In addition, Peter Cushing appeared as the Doctor in two films for television (1965, 1966), Richard Hurndall appeared in a special production (1983), and Paul McGann starred in a 1996 feature film. The series has generated a worldwide cult following, its fans being known as **Whovians**.

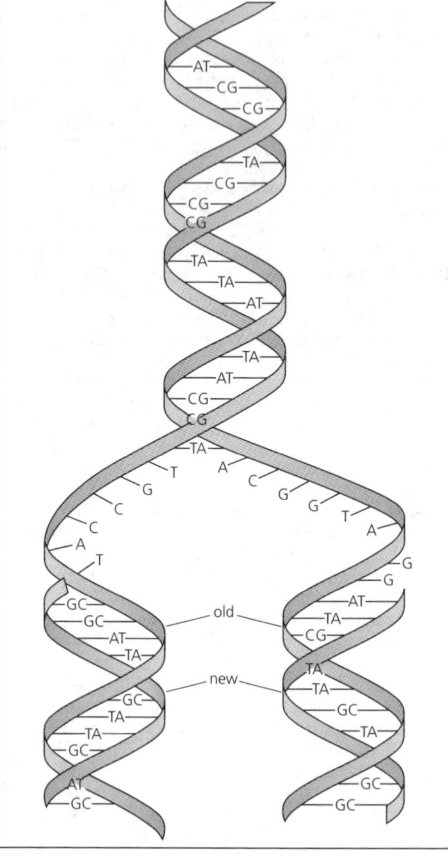

DNA replication, following Watson and Crick. The two strands of the double helix separate, and a daughter strand is laid down alongside each with a constitution determined by the base sequence of its parent strand.

dodder A parasitic annual reduced to a reddish, thread-like stem bearing clusters of tiny white or pink flowers; native to temperate and tropical regions. The germinating seed produces a short-lived root and a twining stem which moves in search of a host. A wide variety of host plants are attacked, including crop plants. (Genus: *Cuscuta*, 170 species. Family: Convolvulaceae.) >> parasitic plant

Dodecanese [dohdeka**neez**], Gr **Sporádhes** area 2000 sq km/1000 sq mi. Group of 12 main islands and several islets in the SE Aegean Sea, Greece, off SW coast of Turkey; part of Greece since 1947; chief islands include Cos, Patmos, and Rhodes; several major tourist centres. >> Cos; Patmos; Rhodes; Samos

Dodgson, Charles Lutwidge >> **Carroll, Lewis**

dodo An extinct bird related to pigeons; native to high forests in Mascarene I, E of Madagascar; turkey-like with large bill and rudimentary wings. Probable dates of extinction were during the 17th–18th-c. (Family: Raphidae, 3 species.) >> pigeon; solitaire

Dodoma [doh**doh**ma] 6°10S 35°40E, pop (1995e) 244 000. Capital of Tanzania, E Africa; altitude 1120 m/3674 ft; replaced Dar es Salaam as capital in 1974. >> Tanzania ℹ

Doenitz or **Dönitz, Karl** [**doe**nits] (1891–1980) German naval commander, born in Grünau, Germany. He planned Hitler's U-boat fleet, was made its commander in 1936, and in 1943 became commander-in-chief of the German Navy. Becoming führer on the death of Hitler, he was responsible for the final surrender to the Allies. >> submarine; World War 2

dog A carnivorous mammal (*Canis familiaris*), probably evolved from the wolf; first animal to be domesticated; c.400 modern domestic breeds, sometimes classed as *working*, *sporting*, *hound*, *terrier*, *non-sporting*, and *toy*. The name is also used for some mammals of other families (eg the *prairie dog*). The male of several mammal species is called a *dog*, the female a *bitch*, and the young a *pup*. (Family: Canidae.) >> affenpinscher; Canidae; carnivore ℹ; chihuahua; chow chow; civet; collie; dachshund; dalmatian; dhole; dingo; Doberman(n) pinscher; German shepherd; Great Dane; hound; lurcher; mastiff; Newfoundland (zoology); non-sporting dog; papillon; prairie dog; pug; puli; Pyrenean mountain dog; rottweiler; St Bernard; schipperke; Shih Tzu; spitz; sporting dog; terrier; whippet; wolf

dog daisy >> **ox-eye daisy**

Doge's Palace [dohzh] The residence of the former Doges of Venice. Parts of the structure date from the 12th-c, but the loggias and marble facade are Renaissance additions. >> Bridge of Sighs; Venice

dogfish Small bottom-living shark found from Norway to the Mediterranean; length to 75 cm/30 in, skin very rough; sold in shops as **rock eel**, **rock salmon**, or **huss**. >> shark

Dogger Bank A large sandbank forming the shallowest part of the North Sea, c.17–37 m/ 55–120 ft deep, 250 km/155 mi N of the Norfolk coast, England. >> North Sea

Dog Star >> **Sirius**

dogwood A deciduous shrub or small tree (*Cornus sanguinea*), growing to 6 m/20 ft, native to Europe, SW Asia, and North America; leaves turning purple in autumn, veins prominent; flowers small, numerous, in flat-topped clusters; petal-like bracts, white, pink, red; berries black. (Family: Cornaceae.)

Doha [**doh**ha], Arabic **ad-Dawhah** 25°25N 51°32E, pop (1995e) 238 000. Seaport capital of Qatar; reclamation of West Bay has created New Doha; airport; university. >> Qatar ℹ

Doherty, Peter (Charles) [**dok**ertee] (1940–) Immunologist, born in Brisbane, Queensland, Australia. He shared the Nobel Prize for Physiology or Medicine in 1996 for his contribution to the discovery of how the immune system recognizes virus-inflected cells – research which was first reported in 1974.

Dohnányi, Ernst von [doh**nan**yee], Hung **Ernö** (1877–1960) Composer and pianist, born in Pozsony, Hungary (now Bratislava, Czech Republic). He is best known for his piano compositions, especially *Variations on a Nursery Song*, for piano and orchestra.

Dolby system The first effective and still the most widely used noise reduction system, devised originally for professional tape recording (**Dolby A**) by Dr Ray Dolby (1933–) in the mid-1960s. He adapted the circuitry to a simpler form (**Dolby B**) widely incorporated in cassette tape players. **Dolby C** followed in the 1980s, giving noise reduction of up to 20 dB and over a wider frequency range. >> decibel; magnetic tape 1; sound recording

Dolci, Danilo [**dohl**chee] (1925–97) Social worker, born in Trieste, Italy. He qualified as an architect, but decided to fight poverty in Sicily, building schools and community centres in the poorest areas. Although not a communist, he was awarded the Lenin Peace Prize in 1956.

Doldrums Traditionally a zone of cloudy, calm conditions, with light, westerly winds associated with low atmospheric pressure. Formerly, sailing ships would often get becalmed in the Doldrums. The word has since passed into general usage to express listless despondency. >> current (oceanography); wind ℹ

Dole, Bob, popular name of **Robert Joseph Dole** (1923–) US Republican politician, born in Russell, KS. A senator for Kansas, and for several years the minority leader in the Senate, he sought the Republican nomination for the presidency in 1980 and 1988. He became majority leader in the Senate in 1994, following Republican gains in the 1994 elections, resigning in 1996 to campaign for the presidency, he was defeated by Bill Clinton. He is married to **Elizabeth Dole** (1936–), Secretary of Labor under Bush (1989–90).

dolerite [**dol**eriyt] A medium-grained basic igneous rock, dark-green in colour and composed mainly of plagioclase feldspar and pyroxene crystals. It is the common rock of dykes and sills throughout the world. >> feldspar; pyroxenes; sill

dollar ($) A unit of currency in the USA, Canada, Australia, New Zealand, and certain other countries. The US dollar is the world's most important currency. Much international trade is conducted in it, and prices of goods and commodities are often quoted in it. Also, over half the official reserves of countries are held in dollars. >> currency; Eurodollar; exchange rates

Dollfuss, Engelbert [**dol**foos] (1892–1934) Austrian statesman and chancellor (1932–4), born in Texing, Austria. In 1934 he suspended parliamentary government, drove the socialists into revolt and militarily crushed them. An attempted Nazi putsch in Vienna culminated in his assassination. >> Nazi Party; socialism

dolmen >> **chambered tomb**

Dolomites [**dol**omiyts], Ital **Alpi Dolomitiche** Alpine mountain range in NE Italy; limestone formation of jagged outlines and isolated peaks, rising to 3342 m/ 10 964 ft at Marmolada. >> Alps; Italy ℹ

dolphin A small, toothed whale. The name is usually used for species with a long slender snout and streamlined body. Species with less streamlined bodies and blunt snouts are usually called **porpoises** (especially in genera *Phocoena*, *Phocoenoides*, and *Neophocoena*); worldwide. (Family: Delphinidae, c.28 species.) >> grampus; whale ℹ

dolphinarium >> **aquarium**

dolphinfish Large, predatory, marine fish widespread in tropical and temperate seas; length up to 1·5 m/5 ft, greenish-blue above, underside silver. (Genus: *Coryphaena*. Family: Coryphaenidae.)

Domagk, Gerhard (Johannes Paul) [**doh**mak] (1895–1964) Biochemist, born in Lagow, Germany. He discovered the chemotherapeutic properties of sulphanilamide, and thus ushered in a new age in chemotherapy. In 1939, on instruction from the German government, he refused the Nobel Prize for Physiology or Medicine. >> chemotherapy; sulphonamides

Domenichino [domeni**kee**noh], originally **Domenico Zampieri** (1581–1641) Painter, born in Bologna, Italy. His masterpiece is 'The Last Communion of St Jerome' (1614) in the Vatican.

Dome of the Rock A masterpiece of Islamic architecture completed in AD 691 on Mt Moriah, Jerusalem. The shrine, which is built on an octagonal plan and surmounted by a gilded wooden cupola, encloses the holy rock where, according to tradition, Mohammed ascended to heaven and Abraham prepared to sacrifice Isaac. >> Islam; Jerusalem

Domesday Book [**doomz**day] The great survey of England S of the Ribble and Tees rivers (London and Winchester excepted), compiled in 1086 on the orders of William the Conqueror; sometimes spelled **Doomsday Book** (though the *dome* refers to houses, not to doom). Information is arranged by county and, within each county, according to tenure by major landholders; each manor is described according to value and resources. >> manor; Norman Conquest; William I (of England)

domestic fowl A bird kept worldwide for its meat or eggs, also known as the **chicken** or **hen**; domesticated over 5000 years ago. Modern breeds are grouped as **Mediterranean** or **Asian**. >> jungle fowl [i]

Domingo, Plácido [do**ming**goh] (1941–) Tenor, born in Madrid. He moved to Mexico with his family, and took his first tenor role in 1960. His vocal technique and acting ability have made him one of the world's leading lyric–dramatic tenors, notably in works by Puccini and Verdi.

Dominic, St (c.1170–1221) Founder of the Order of Friars Preachers, born in Calaruega, Old Castile. His preaching order was approved by Pope Honorius III in 1216. He was canonized in 1234. Feast day 8 August. >> Dominicans; friar

Dominica [domi**nee**ka], Fr **Dominique**, official name **Commonwealth of Dominica** pop (1995e) 83 900; area 751 sq km/290 sq mi. Island in the Windward group of the West Indies; capital, Roseau; timezone GMT −4; mainly African or mixed African–European descent; main religion, Roman Catholicism; official language, English, with French patois widely spoken; unit of currency, E Caribbean dollar; c.50 km/30 mi long and 26 km/16 mi wide, rising to 1447 m/4747 ft at Morne Diablotin; volcanic origin; central ridge, with several rivers; 67% of land area forested; climate warm and humid; visited by Columbus, 1493; colonization attempts by French and British in 18th-c; British Crown Colony, 1805; part of Federation of the West Indies, 1958–62; independence, 1978; independent republic within the Commonwealth, governed by a House of Assembly, president, prime minister, and cabinet; agricultural processing, tourism, coconut-based products: citrus fruits (notably limes); Morne Trois Pitons National Park, a world heritage site. >> Caribbean Sea; Roseau; RR1006 political leaders

Dominican Republic, Span **República Dominicana** pop (1995e) 7 994 000; area 48 442 sq km/18 699 sq mi. Republic of the West Indies; comprises E two-thirds of the island of Hispaniola, bordering W on Haiti; capital, Santo Domingo; timezone GMT −4; people mainly Spanish or mixed Spanish and African descent; state religion, Roman Catholicism; official language, Spanish; unit of currency, peso oro of 100 centavos; crossed NW–SE by Cordillera Central, with many peaks over 3000 m/10 000 ft; Pico Duarte (3175 m/10 416 ft), highest peak in the Caribbean; wide coastal plain (E); tropical maritime climate with rainy season (May–Nov); visited by Columbus, 1492; Spanish colony, 16th–17th-c; E province of Santo Domingo remained Spanish after partition of Hispaniola, 1697; taken over by Haiti on several occasions; independence in 1844, under modern name; governed by a president and a National Congress (Senate and Chamber of Deputies); economy mainly agriculture, especially sugar, cocoa; tourism expanding. >> Santo Domingo; RR1006 political leaders

Dominicans A religious order, officially *Ordo Praedicatorum* (Lat 'Order of Preachers'), abbreviated **OP**; also known as the **Friars Preachers**, **Black Friars**, or **Jacobins**. It was founded by St Dominic in 1215 in Italy to provide defenders of the Roman Catholic Faith, and is devoted mainly to preaching and teaching. >> Dominic, St; monasticism; Roman Catholicism

Dominion Day >> **Canada Day**

Domino, Fats, originally **Antoine Domino** (1928–) Singer, pianist, and composer, born in New Orleans, LA. His cheerful boogie-woogie piano style helped popularize rock-and-roll in the 1950s. His songs include 'Blueberry Hill', 'Ain't That a Shame', and 'I'm Walkin''. >> rock music

dominoes An indoor game which involves the matching of a series of rectangular blocks, with the face of each block divided into two halves, each half containing a number of spots. No two dominoes have the same markings on them. In a double-six set of dominoes, every combination between 6–6 and 0–0 is marked on the 28 dominoes. The object of the basic game is to lay out a sequence (or 'line') of dominoes, each player in turn having to put down a domino of the same value as the one left at either end of the line by a previous player.

Domitian [do**mi**shn], in full **Titus Flavius Domitianus** (51–96) Roman emperor (81–96), the younger son of Vespasian, and the last of the Flavian emperors. After the armed revolt of Saturninus (89), he unleashed a reign of terror in Rome which lasted until his own assassination. >> Roman history [i]

Don, River River in SW European Russia, rising SE of Tula; enters the Sea of Azov; length, 1958 km/1217 mi. >> Russia [i]

Donat, Robert [**doh**nat] (1905–58) Actor, born in Manchester, Greater Manchester. His many films include *The Thirty-nine Steps* (1935), *Good-bye, Mr Chips* (1939, Oscar), and *The Winslow Boy* (1948).

Donatello [dona**tel**oh], originally **Donato di Betto Bardi** (c.1386–1466) The greatest of the early Tuscan sculptors, born in Florence, Italy. He may be regarded as the founder of modern sculpture, as the first producer since classical times of statues complete and independent in themselves. Among his works are the marble statues of saints Mark and George for the exterior of Or San Michele, Florence.

Donatists [**don**atists] African Christian schismatics named after Donatus (4th-c), elected as rival to the Bishop of Carthage. The movement was rigorist and puritan, sup-

ported rebaptism, and declared invalid the sacraments celebrated by priests suspected of collaboration in times of persecution. Despite condemnation by the Catholic Church (411), it continued until the 7th–8th-c. >> heresy

Donatus, Aelius [do**nay**tus] (c.300–c.399) Latin grammarian and rhetorician, who taught at Rome AD c.360. His treatises on Latin grammar were in the Middle Ages the only textbooks used in schools, so that 'Donat' in W Europe came to mean a grammar book. >> grammar; rhetoric

Donau, River >> **Danube, River**

Doncaster, ancient **Danum** 53°32N 1°07W, urban area pop (1995e) 294 000. Town in South Yorkshire, N England; founded as a fort 1st-c AD, later an important Roman station on road from Lincoln to York; railway; railway engineering; St Leger Stakes, the oldest horse-race in England (Sep); football league team, Doncaster Rovers. >> Yorkshire, South

Donegal [doni**gawl**, **don**igol], Ir **Dún na nGall** pop (1995e) 127 000; area 4830 sq km/1865 sq mi. Scenic county in N Ireland; Slieve Snaght (N) rising to 752 m/2467 ft at Errigal; capital, Lifford; tweed manufacture, agriculture, livestock. >> Ireland (republic) ℹ; Ulster

Donegan, Lonnie, originally **Anthony Donegan** (1931–) Singer and guitarist, born in Glasgow. He had success both in Britain and the USA with such songs as 'Rock Island Line' (which launched a skiffle craze), 'Gamblin' Man', and 'Cumberland Gap', and was a widely acknowledged influence on later British guitar-based rock and pop music. >> skiffle

Donetsk [don**yetesk**], formerly **Stalino** (to 1961), **Yuzovka** (to 1924) 48°00N 37°50E, pop (1995e) 1 135 000. Industrial city in Ukraine; in the Donbas coal basin; founded, 1870; airport; railway; university (1965). >> Ukraine ℹ

Dönitz, Karl >> **Doenitz, Karl**

Donizetti, (Domenico) Gaetano (Maria) [doni**ze**tee] (1797–1848) Composer, born in Bergamo, Italy. The work which carried his fame beyond Italy was *Anna Bolena* (1830), and he had several other successes, notably *Lucia di Lammermoor* (1835).

Don Juan [hwan] A legendary figure probably derived from Spanish literature sources. He is a philanderer who has no heart, and whose career is terminated by divine intervention. This comes in the shape of a stone statue, who insists on being Juan's guest and who carries him off to Hell. Mozart's opera uses the Italian name, *Don Giovanni*. >> mythology

donkey >> **ass; mule** (zoology)

Donleavy, J(ames) P(atrick) (1926–) Writer, born in New York City, USA. His first novel, *The Ginger Man* (1955) was hailed as a comic masterpiece. Among his other works are *A Singular Man* (1963), *The Onion Eaters* (1971), and *The Wrong Information is Being Given Out at Princeton* (1997). He has been an Irish citizen since 1967.

Donne, John [duhn] (?1572–1631) Poet, born in London. Originally a Catholic, he joined the established Church, becoming Dean of St Paul's, where his sermons were extremely popular. His creative years fall into three periods. The first (1590–1601) was a time of passion and cynicism, as seen in his *Elegies* and *Songs and Sonnets*; the second is represented by his *Anniversaries* and funeral poems; and his third includes a wide range of sonnets and hymns. >> metaphysical poetry

Doohan, Mick [**doo**an], popular name of **Michael Doohan** (1965–) Motor-cyclist, born in Brisbane, Queensland, Australia. He first raced in 1984, and had achieved 46 Grand Prix wins by mid-1998. He has won five successive 500cc world championships (1994–8). >> Agostini

Doolittle, Hilda, pseudonym **H D** (1886–1961) Poet, born in Bethlehem, PA. She lived in London from 1911, and became an exponent of Imagism. Her books of poetry include *Sea Garden* (1916) and *Hymen* (1921). >> Imagism

Doomsday Book >> **Domesday Book**

dopamine [**dop**ameen] A chemical compound (*catecholamine*) widely distributed in the brain and peripheral nervous system. The degeneration of certain dopamine-containing brain cells results in Parkinsonism, and is probably also implicated in schizophrenia. >> catecholamine; Parkinson's disease; schizophrenia

doping In chemistry, adding a controlled amount of an impurity, which can radically change the properties of a substance. For example, the addition of minute quantities of aluminium or phosphorus to silicon will increase its semiconducting properties greatly. >> electrical conduction; semiconductor; silicon

Doppler effect or **shift** The change in wavelength observed when the separation between a wave source and an observer is changing; named after Austrian physicist Christian Doppler (1803–53). The wavelength increases as the source and observer move apart, and decreases as they come closer. The changing tone of passing motor vehicles represents the Doppler shift in sound waves. >> redshift; wavelength

Dorado [do**rah**doh] (Lat 'goldfish') A S constellation which includes the Large Magellanic Cloud. >> constellation; Magellanic Clouds; RR968

dorcas gazelle A gazelle (*Gazella dorcas*), native to N Africa and S Asia; light brown with white underparts; dark smudge along flank and along side of face; short backward-curving horns ringed with ridges; also known as **jebeer**. >> antelope

Dorchester, ancient **Durnovaria** 50°43N 2°26W, pop (1995e) 15 600. County town of Dorset, S England; on the R Frome; model for Casterbridge in Hardy's novels; railway; brewing. >> Dorset; Hardy, Thomas; Maiden Castle

Dordogne [daw(r)**doyn**], Fr [dawrdon], ancient **Durenius** area 9224 sq km/3597 sq mi; Department of SW France in the Aquitaine region; capital, Périgueux; popular tourist area. >> Dordogne, River

Dordogne, River Eng [daw(r)**doyn**], Fr [dawr**don**], ancient **Duranius** River in SW France, rising in the Auvergne hills; meets R Garonne to form the Gironde estuary; length 472 km/293 mi. >> France ℹ

Dordrecht [**daw(r)**drekht], also **Dordt** or **Dort** 51°48N 4°39E, pop (1995e) 114 000. River port and industrial city in W Netherlands; founded, 1008; Synod of Dort, 1618–19; railway. >> Netherlands, The ℹ

Dorians [**daw**rianz] A sub-group of Hellenic peoples, thought to have migrated into Greece around 1100 BC. Dorian settlements there included Argos, Corinth, and Sparta.

Doric order The earliest of the five main orders of classical architecture, characterized by a fluted shaft and plain capital. It is sub-divided into **Greek Doric** and **Roman Doric**, the former having no base. >> orders of architecture ℹ

dormouse A mouse-like rodent of family Gliridae (10 species); native to Africa, Europe, and C Asia; intermediate between squirrels and true mice; most resemble mice, with long bushy tails. >> mouse (zoology); rodent; squirrel

Dornier, Claude [**daw(r)n**yer] (1884–1969) Aircraft engineer, born in Kempten, Germany. In 1911 he designed the first all-metal plane. He later made seaplanes and flying-boats, and a twin-engined bomber used in World War 2. >> aircraft ℹ

Dors, Diana, originally **Diana Fluck** (1931–84) Actress, born in Swindon, Wiltshire. She made her film debut in *The Shop at Sly Corner* (1946), and became a popular sex symbol in various low-budget comedies. Later films cast her in several good character parts, as in *The Amazing Mr. Blunden* (1972).

Dorset pop (1995e) 676 000; area 2654 sq km/1024 sq mi. County of S England; bounded S by the English Channel; extensive heathlands and chalk down; county town, Dorchester; Bournemouth and Poole new unitary authorities from 1997; setting for many of Hardy's novels. >> Dorchester; England ℹ; Hardy, Thomas

Dorsey, Tommy [**daw(r)**see], popular name of **Thomas Dorsey** (1905–56) Trombonist and bandleader, born in Shenandoah, PA. His big bands were sometimes co-led by his brother **Jimmy Dorsey** (1904–57, alto saxophone, clarinet). The Dorsey Brothers Orchestra existed from 1932 to 1935, reforming again in 1953 until Tommy's death.

Dortmund [**daw(r)t**mund] 51°32N 7°28E, pop (1995e) 619 000. Industrial, mining, and commercial city in Germany; river port in the Ruhr valley, connected to the North Sea by the Dortmund–Ems Canal (272 km/169 mi); railway; university (1966). >> Germany ℹ

DOS [dos] An acronym of **Disk Operating System**, referring to the computer program – part of the operating system – which oversees the communication of data between the computer processor and its magnetic disks, as well as the management of files and programs on the disks. >> computer program; MS-DOS; operating system

dose equivalent >> **radioactivity units** ℹ

Dos Passos, John (Roderigo) (1896–1970) Novelist and war correspondent, born in Chicago, IL. His best-known work is the trilogy on US life, *U.S.A.* (1930–6).

Dostoevsky or **Dostoyevsky, Fyodor (Mikhailovich)** [dosto**yef**skee] (1821–81) Novelist, born in Moscow, the son of a surgeon. Joining revolutionary circles in St Petersburg, he was condemned to death (1849), reprieved at the last moment, and sent to hard labour in Siberia. In 1859 he returned to St Petersburg, where he wrote his masterpiece, *Prestupleniye i nakazaniye* (1866, Crime and Punishment). Other important books are *Idiot* (1868–9, The Idiot) and *Bratya Karamazovy* (1879–80, The Brothers Karamazov).

dot-matrix printer A type of impact printer, where characters are formed by the selection of sets of dots from a rectangular matrix. It is widely used with microcomputer systems, being relatively fast and inexpensive, but it can be noisy. >> computer printer

Dou or **Douw, Gerard** [dow] (1613–75) Painter, born in Leyden, The Netherlands. His 200 works include his own portrait, 'The Poulterer's Shop' (National Gallery, London) and his celebrated 'Dropsical Woman' (Louvre). >> Rembrandt

Douai Bible [**doo**ay] An early English translation of the Bible by Roman Catholic scholars. The New Testament was first published at Reims in 1582; the Old Testament in 1609. It is sometimes called the **Reims–Douai translation** (the English college at Douai having moved to Reims in 1578). >> Bible; Roman Catholicism

Douala or **Duala** [doo**a**la] 4°04N 9°43E, pop (1995e) 1 647 000. Seaport in Cameroon, W Africa; capital of German Cameroon, as Kamerunstadt, 1885–1901; present name, 1907; capital of French Cameroon, 1940–6; airport; railway; many import-export companies; centre for petroleum exploration. >> Cameroon ℹ

double bass The largest and lowest in pitch of the orchestral string instruments. There are two basic types: the first, belonging to the viol family, has sloping shoulders and a flat back; the other, belonging to the violin family, has squarer shoulders and a slightly rounded (sometimes also flat) back. Both types have four strings, tuned in fourths. The strings are often plucked, almost invariably so in jazz and dance music. >> string instrument 1 ℹ

double coconut >> **coco de mer**

double jeopardy The legal doctrine that no person can be convicted twice for the same crime, or for different crimes arising from the same set of facts unless the crimes involve substantially different wrongs. Also, no person having been acquitted of an offence can be subjected to a second trial for the same offence.

double refraction >> **birefringence**

Doublespeak Awards Mock awards made annually by the National Council of Teachers of English in the USA to those public figures who have used language that is distorted, unfactual, deceptive, evasive, or euphemistic. An example is 'collateral damage', referring to civilians killed in war.

double star A pair of stars that appear close together in our sky when viewed through a telescope. Some pairs are stars at very different distances that merely coincide from our vantage point. If the stars are close enough to be linked through their gravitational attractions, they constitute a binary star. >> binary star

double vision A weakness or paralysis of one or more of the muscles which move one or other of the eyes, resulting in a failure of the eyes to move together in parallel. As a result, light from a single object does not fall on comparable parts of the two retinae, and the object appears as two images. >> eye ℹ

Douglas 54°09N 4°29W, pop (1995e) 23 500. Seaport capital of the Isle of Man; railway; House of Keys, Manx National Museum. >> Man, Isle of

Douglas, Gawain or **Gavin** (c.1474–1522) Poet and bishop, born in Tantallon Castle, East Lothian. His works include *The Palace of Honour* (c.1501) and a translation of the *Aeneid* (finished c.1513), the first to be published in English.

Douglas, Kirk, originally **Issur Danielovitch Demsky** (1916–) Film actor, born in Amsterdam, NY. He began his screen career in 1946, his films including *Champion* (1949), *Lust for Life* (1956), and *Spartacus* (1960), and from the 1970s he also worked as a director. >> Douglas, Michael

Douglas, Michael (Kirk) (1944–) US film actor and producer, born in New Brunswick, NJ, the son of Kirk Douglas. He co-produced *One Flew Over the Cuckoo's Nest* (1975), which won five Academy Awards, and won a Best Actor Oscar for his performance in *Wall Street* (1987). Other acting roles include *Fatal Attraction* (1987) and *The Ghost and the Darkness* (1996). >> Douglas, Kirk

Douglas-Home, Sir Alec >> **Home of the Hirsel**

Doulton An English firm which began making chimney-pots and large architectural ornaments in London in the first half of the 19th-c. They later became leading art potters renowned for tiles, figures, and decorative panels in faience. >> faience; pottery

Dounreay [doon**ray**] Former nuclear research station, Caithness, Highland, N Scotland; site of world's first experimental fast-breeder nuclear reactor. >> nuclear reactor ℹ; Scotland ℹ

Douro, River [**daw**ru], Eng [**doo**roh], Span **Río Duero** [**dwe**ro], ancient **Durius** River of Spain and Portugal; rises in NC Spain, and crosses N Portugal, emptying into the Atlantic near Oporto; used extensively for irrigation and hydroelectric power; length 895 km/556 mi. >> Portugal ℹ

douroucouli [doorookoolee] A nocturnal New World monkey (*Aotus trivirgatus*); long tail, large eyes, spherical head; cannot see in colour; moves silently; the only nocturnal monkey; also known as **night monkey**, **night ape**, or **owl monkey**. >> New World monkey

dove A bird of the pigeon family. Usually the large-bodied species with rounded tails are called *pigeons*; the smaller-bodied ones with longer slender tails are called *doves*. >> pigeon; quail; turtle dove

Dover (UK), Fr **Douvres**, ancient **Dubris Portus** 51°08N 1°19E, pop (1995e) 35 600. Seaport in Kent, SE England; principal cross-Channel port, the shortest link with France (35 km/ $21\frac{3}{4}$ mi); railway; Dover Castle (13th–14th-c). >> Cinque Ports; Kent

Dover (USA) 39°10N 75°32W, pop (1995e) 30 100. Capital of state in C Delaware, USA; founded, 1683; state capital, 1777; city status, 1929; railway; university. >> Delaware

Dowding, Hugh (Caswell Tremenheere) Dowding, Baron (1882–1970) British air chief marshal of World War 2, born in Moffat, Dumfries and Galloway. As commander-in-chief of Fighter Command (1936–40), he organized the air defence of Britain, which resulted in the victorious Battle of Britain (1940). >> Britain, Battle of; World War 2

Dow Jones Index [dow] A statistic showing the state of the New York Stock Exchange, computed on working days by Dow Jones and Co. It enables a measurement to be made of changes in the price of shares of 30 leading US corporations, and is the primary indicator of share price movements in the USA. >> stock market

Dowland, John (1563–1626) Composer, lutenist, and songwriter, born possibly in Westminster. He produced several collections of music, including *Lachrimae* (1605, Tears), which contains some of the finest instrumental consort music of the period. >> lute

Down, Ir **An Dun** pop (1995e) 400 000; area 2448 sq km/ 945 sq mi. County in SE Northern Ireland; coastline indented (N–S) by Strangford Lough, Dundrum Bay, and Carlingford Lough; Mourne Mts in the S; rises to 852 m/2795 ft at Slieve Donard; county town, Downpatrick. >> Downpatrick; Northern Ireland ℹ

Downing Street A street off Whitehall in C London. Of the original terraced houses only numbers 10 (since 1735 the prime minister's official residence), 11 (used by the Chancellor of the Exchequer), and 12 (used by the party whip) remain. >> Whitehall

Downing Street declaration A joint agreement between the British and Irish governments, made in 1993, intended to provide the basis of a peace initiative in Northern Ireland. The declaration was made by British and Irish prime ministers John Major and Albert Reynolds, and recommended closer co-operation over Northern Ireland affairs, taking further the initiatives of the 1985 Anglo-Irish agreement. >> Anglo-Irish agreement; Major; Northern Ireland; Reynolds

Downpatrick, Ir **Dun Padraig** 54°20N 5°43W, pop (1995e) 10 900. County town in Down, SE Northern Ireland. St Patrick is said to have landed here in 432; reputed burial place of Saints Patrick, Columbus, and Bridget of Kildare; cathedral (1798–1812). >> Down; Patrick, St

Downs Low-lying chalk hill ranges rising in Dorset and Hampshire and extending into Surrey, Kent, and East and West Sussex, S England; North Downs rise to 294 m/964 ft at Leith Hill, South Downs to 264 m/866 ft at Butser Hill. >> England ℹ; Weald, the

downsizing A term, used by organizations employing computers extensively, which describes the process of changing from the use of very large computers centrally to the use of networks of computer workstations. These workstations are distributed around the organization, possibly as personal computers in individual offices. >> computer network; mainframe; personal computer

Down's syndrome A common congenital abnormality especially liable to affect babies born to mothers over 40 years. The head of the child is small with high cheekbones and flattened nose; the eyes are slanted, with a prominent fold over the inner part of either eye; the hands are short and broad, and there are varying degrees of mental handicap. The defect stems from a failure of one chromosome of a germ cell to split in the normal way to form a healthy ovum with 23 chromosomes. The condition is named after English physician J L H Down (1828–96), and is sometimes referred to as **mongolism**.

dowsing A technique in which a held rod, pendulum, or other indicator moves when it is brought near to a certain substance. This technique has been used to search for a wide variety of substances, including water, oil, and mineral deposits. The medical applications date from the 1920s when a French priest, the Abbé Mermet, used a pendulum for diagnosis and to select suitable herbal remedies. Many people believe that detecting the object of dowsing is a supersensory phenomenon, and that the use of an indicator is entirely incidental. >> divination; radiesthesia

Doyle, Sir Arthur Conan (1859–1930) Writer, the creator of Sherlock Holmes, born in Edinburgh. His first book, *A Study in Scarlet* (1887), introduced the super-observant, deductive Holmes, his good-natured question-raising friend, Dr Watson, and the whole apparatus of detection mythology associated with Baker Street, Holmes's fictional home. After *The Adventures of Sherlock Holmes* was serialized in the *Strand Magazine* (1891–3), the author tired of his popular creation, and tried to kill off his hero, but was compelled in 1903 to revive him.

Doyle, Roddy (1958–) Novelist, born in Dublin. His first success came with *The Commitments* (1987), the first of the internationally acclaimed Barrytown trilogy, which he completed with *The Snapper* (1990) and *The Van* (1991). He won the Booker Prize for *Paddy Clarke Ha Ha Ha* (1993).

D'Oyly Carte, Richard [**doy**lee **kah(r)t**] (1844–1901) Impresario and manager, born in London. He built the Savoy Theatre (1881) and the Royal Opera House (1887), and is best known as the first producer of the Gilbert and Sullivan operas. >> Gilbert, W S; Sullivan, Arthur

Drabble, Margaret (1939–) Novelist, born in Sheffield. Her novels include *The Radiant Way* (1987), *The Gates of Ivory* (1991), and *The Witch of Exmoor* (1996). She was the editor of the 5th edition of the *Oxford Companion to English Literature* (1985).

Draco (astronomy) [**dray**koh] (Lat 'dragon') The eighth-largest constellation, a sinuous zone of the N sky. >> constellation; RR968

Draco (law-giver) [**dray**koh] (7th-c BC) Athenian legislator. His harsh codification of the law in 621 BC has given us the word 'draconian'. With death the penalty of almost every offence, the code was so unpopular that it was largely abolished by Solon (594 BC). >> Solon

draft >> **conscription**

dragonet Any of a small family of fishes, widespread in coastal waters of tropical to warm temperate seas; includes European *Callionymus lyra* found from Norway to the Mediterranean; length up to 30 cm/1 ft, body rather flattened, pelvic fins broad, dorsal fin striped blue and yellow in male; gill openings small on top of head, eyes prominent. (Family: Callionymidae.)

dragon-fish Deep-water fish with slender snake-like body; length up to 40 cm/16 in; short head and very long mouth, bearing fang-like jaw teeth; light organs present in rows along underside of body, behind eye, and on long chin barbel that serves as lure to attract prey. (Family: Stomiatidae.)

dragonfly A large, long-bodied insect with two pairs of slender wings held horizontally at rest; large compound eyes enable adults to catch insects in flight. (Order: Odonata. Suborder: Anisoptera.) >> insect ℹ

dragon-tree An evergreen tree (*Dracaena draco*), native to the Canary Is and Madeira; short, thick branches, bearing clusters of greyish or bluish sword-shaped leaves at the tips; flowers small, greenish-white; berries orange. Red resin exuded by the trunk is known as **dragon's blood**, used in varnish. (Family: Agavaceae.) >> resin

drag racing A specialized form of motor racing which is a test of acceleration. Large-engined 'vehicles' with big rear wheels and small front ones race normally two at a time on a 400 m/440 yd straight track, from a standing start. Parachutes are fitted to the machines to help with braking. >> motor racing

Drake, Sir Francis (c.1540–96) Elizabethan seaman, born in Crowndale, Devon. In 1577 he set out with five ships for the Pacific, through the Straits of Magellan, but after his fleet was battered by storm and fire, he alone continued in the *Golden Hind*. He then struck out across the Pacific, reached the Pelew Is, and returned to England via the Cape of Good Hope in 1580. In 1585 he sailed with 25 ships against the Spanish Indies, bringing home tobacco, potatoes, and the dispirited Virginian colonists. In the battle against the Spanish Armada (1588), which raged for a week in the Channel, his seamanship and courage brought him further distinction. >> Elizabeth I; Spanish Armada

Drakensberg Mountains [**drak**nzberg], Zulu **Kwathlamba** or **Quathlamba** Mountain range in South Africa, highest peak, Thabana Ntlenyana (3482 m/11 424 ft). >> South Africa ℹ

dramatherapy The use of drama as a creative medium to help in clarifying and alleviating personal and social problems. As a practice it fuses both artistic and therapeutic skills.

draughts A popular board game played on a standard chessboard containing 64 squares of alternate colours (normally black and white); known as **checkers** in the USA. It is played by two players; each has 12 small, flat, round counters (*pieces*), one set normally being black, the other white. The pieces are lined on alternate squares on the first three rows at either side of the board. The object is to remove your opponent's pieces from the board by jumping over them onto a vacant diagonal square. >> chess; RR1051

Dravidian languages [dra**vid**ian] A group of more than 20 languages, spoken mainly in S India. The principal ones are Telugu, Tamil, Kannada, and Malayalam, which together have over 150 million speakers within the S states. >> Indo-Aryan languages

Drayton, Michael (1563–1631) Poet, born in Hartshill, Warwickshire. His best-known works are *England's Heroical Epistles* (1597) and *Poly-Olbion* (1612–22), an ambitious description of the English countryside.

Dr Barnardo's Homes >> **Barnardo, Thomas John**

dreaming >> **sleep**

Dreamtime or **The Dreaming** In the mythology of the Australian Aborigines, one of the names for the time of the Ancestors, who created the world and are still alive in the sacred places. This time continues to exist, and it may be possible to find it through dreams. >> Aborigines

dredger A vessel designed to remove spoil from the seabed in order to maintain or increase the depth in a harbour or approaches. Dredgers are also used to obtain sand and gravel from the seabed for constructional purposes.

Dred Scott decision A ruling by the US Supreme Court in 1857 which made slavery legal in all US territories. Dred Scott was a slave who had been taken by his master from Missouri (a slave state) to Illinois and Wisconsin (both free areas). After returning to Missouri, Scott sued for his freedom on the grounds that by living in a free state he had altered his status. The Missouri Supreme Court overruled a decision by a lower court which had considered Scott to be free, and was eventually supported in its view by the Supreme Court. The decision was an important element in the polarization of opinions which led to the American Civil War. >> American Civil War; slavery; Supreme Court

Dreiser, Theodore (Herman Albert) [**dry**zer] (1871–1945) Writer, born in Terre Haute, IN. His first novel *Sister Carrie* (1900), starkly realistic, was criticized for obscenity. Later works include *Jennie Gerhardt* (1911) and *An American Tragedy* (1925).

Dresden [**drez**dn] 51°02N 13°45E, pop (1995e) 512 000. City in Germany; close to the Czech frontier; former capital of Saxony; almost totally destroyed by bombing in 1945, now rebuilt; airport; railway; technical university (1828); Dresden china now manufactured in Meissen. >> Germany ℹ; Saxony

dressage [dre**sahzh**] An equestrian discipline which is a test of the horse's obedience skills, consisting of a series of movements at the walk, trot, and canter. Dressage can have its own competition or form part of a *three-day event*. >> equestrianism

Dreyer, John (Louis Emil) [**dray**er] (1852–1926) Astronomer, born in Copenhagen. He produced the standard catalogue on star clusters, nebulas, and galaxies, the *New General Catalogue* (NGC), which is still in use today. >> galaxy; nebula; star

Dreyfus, Alfred [**dray**fuhs] (1859–1935) French Jewish army officer, born in Mulhouse, France. Falsely charged with delivering defence secrets to the Germans, he was court-martialled and transported to Devil's I, French Guiana. The efforts of his wife and friends to prove him innocent provoked a vigorous response from militarists and anti-Semites. After the case was tried again (1899), he was found guilty but pardoned, and in 1906 the verdict was reversed. Proof of his innocence came when German military documents were uncovered in 1930. >> Zola

Dreyfuss, Richard [**dray**fus] (1947–) US film actor, born in New York City. He became well known following his performances in *Jaws* (1975), *Close Encounters of the Third Kind* (1977), and *The Goodbye Girl* (1977, Oscar). Later films include *Postcards from the Edge* (1990), *The American President* (1995), and *Krippendorf's Tribe* (1998).

drill A baboon (*Mandrillus leucophaeus*), native to W African forests; resembles the mandrill, but smaller, with a black face. Drills live to the N of the Sanaga R in Cameroun; mandrills live to the S. >> baboon; mandrill

Drogheda [**dro**uhduh], Ir **Droichead Átha** 53°43N 6°21W, pop (1995e) 24 500. Industrial seaport in E Ireland; Irish parliaments met here until 1494; railway; Battle of the Boyne field (1690) 6 km/3¾ mi SW. >> Boyne, Battle of the; Ireland (republic) ℹ; Louth; New Grange

dromedary A camel formerly wild in Arabia (*Camelus dromedarius*), now known only in domestication; comprises 90% of the world's camels; found in hot deserts from N Africa to SW Asia (introduced elsewhere); also known as the **Arabian camel** or **one-humped camel**. >> camel

drone The male of colonial ants, bees, and wasps, whose only function is to mate with fertile females. It plays no part in brood maintenance. (Order: Hymenoptera.) >> ant; bee; wasp

drongo A bird native to the Old World tropics; plumage usually glossy black; long forked tail; inhabits woodland. (Family: Dicruridae, 20 species.)

Dronning Maud Land >> **Queen Maud Land**

dropwort An erect perennial (*Filipendula vulgaris*), growing to 80 cm/30 in, native to Europe, W Asia, and N Africa; roots tuberous; flowers 6-petalled, cream tinged with purple, forming an irregular terminal mass. (Family: Rosaceae.) >> tuber; *see illustration on p. 265*

Drosophila [dro**sof**ila] A genus of brownish-yellow fruit flies with typically red eyes. They lay eggs near fermenting fruit, on which the larvae feed. There are c.2600 species, some of which are economically important pests of fruit. (Order: Diptera. Family: Drosophilidae.) >> fruit fly; larva; *see illustration on p. 265*

Droste-Hülshoff, Annette Elisabeth, Freiin (Baroness) **von** [**dros**tuh **hüls**hohf] (1797–1848) Poet, born near Münster, Germany, commonly regarded as Germany's greatest woman writer. Her poetry is mainly on religious themes and on the Westphalian countryside.

drug addiction or **drug dependence** A state whereby an addict habitually takes a drug, the compulsion being fuelled by a continuous need to experience the psychic effect of the particular drug or to avoid the discomfort of its absence. Frequently, addicts need to increase the dose of the drug they are taking to feel the same effect (*drug tolerance*). Addictive drugs include narcotics (eg heroin, cocaine), many types of sedative and tranquillizer, and nicotine. >> barbiturates; benzodiazepines; narcotics; nicotine

drug resistance A state in which a patient does not respond to a therapeutic drug. Bacteria may acquire resistance through gene mutation to a particular antibiotic by its overuse or misuse. Cancer cells may also acquire resistance to drugs which had previously been effective, requiring a change in the course of treatment. Similarly, insects and other pests acquire resistance to agents which previously controlled them. >> antibiotics; bacteria [i]; cancer

Druids A religious sect among the ancient Celts of pre-Christian Britain and Gaul. They acted as priests, teachers, and judges, taught the immortality of the soul and a doctrine of reincarnation, and it is also thought they offered human sacrifice. They studied ancient verse and natural philosophy, and were expert in astronomy. They were suppressed in Gaul by the Romans, and probably a little later in Britain.

drum A musical instrument consisting of a membrane of skin or plastic (rarely of other materials) stretched over a hollow resonator or frame, usually of wood or metal. Drums are normally played by striking the membrane with a stick or with the hands, and may be classified according to their shape (eg conical, cylindrical, 'hourglass', kettledrums) and whether they have a single membrane or are double-headed. >> bongos; membranophone; percussion [i]; side drum; tambourine; timpani; tom-tom

drumfish Any of a large family of marine and estuarine fishes that have the ability to produce sounds by resonating the swimbladder; also known as **croakers**. (Family: Sciaenidae.)

drumlins Small, streamlined, ice-moulded hills made of till, produced by the pressure of moving ice over glacial deposits. They often occur in groups producing a 'basket of eggs' topography. The shape indicates ice flow direction. >> glaciation; till

Drummond (of Hawthornden), William (1585–1649) Poet, born at Hawthornden, near Edinburgh. He was the first Scottish poet to write in a form of English not from Scotland. His chief collection, *Poems*, appeared in 1616.

drupe A fleshy fruit in which each of one or more seeds is enclosed by a stony layer. >> fruit; prunus; seed

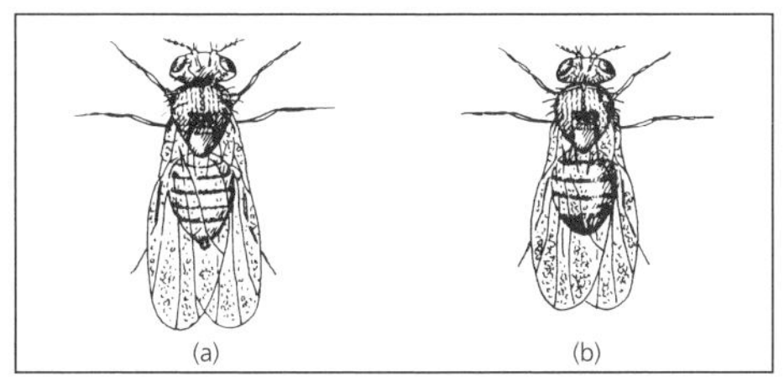

Drosophila – Female (a); male (b)

Druze [drooz] A religious faith which originated during the closing years of the Fatimid caliph al-Hakim (996–1021), whom some extremist Ismailis regarded as a manifestation of the Divinity. The Druze, who survive in parts of Jordan, Lebanon, and Syria, deviate considerably in belief and practice from the main Muslim body. They number c.500 000. >> Ismailis; Jumblat; Sharia

dryad [**dri**yad] In Greek mythology, a being originally connected with oak-trees, but more usually referring to a wood-nymph, living in or among the trees. Dryads were usually friendly, but could frighten travellers.

dry cleaning The cleaning of textiles using organic solvents rather than water. Oil and grease is dissolved by the solvent, so that solid dirt falls away easily.

Dryden, John (1631–1700) Poet, born in Aldwinkle, Northamptonshire. In 1668 he became Poet Laureate and in 1670 historiographer royal. Called to defend the king's party, he wrote a series of satires, notably *Absalom and Achitophel* (1681), which did much to turn the tide against the Whigs. To this era also belong the didactic poem *Religio laici* (1682), which argues the case for Anglicanism, and *The Hind and the Panther* (1687), marking his conversion to Catholicism.

dry ice >> **carbon; sublimation** (chemistry)

Dryopithecus [driyo**pith**ekus] A fossil ape abundant in Africa and the Mediterranean region during the Miocene epoch; about the size of a rhesus monkey; walked on all fours; brain gibbon-like; jaw projecting moderately; canine teeth prominent; includes *Proconsul*. (Superfamily: Hominoidea. Family: Pongidae.) >> ape; fossil; Miocene epoch

drypoint A method of intaglio printing whereby the metal plate is incised by direct pressure using a steel point. The greatest master was Rembrandt, who often combined drypoint with straightforward etching. >> engraving; etching; intaglio 1; Rembrandt

dry rot A serious type of timber decay caused by the fungus *Serpula lacrymans*; infected wood shows a surface growth of white filaments; common on structural timbers of buildings in damp, poorly ventilated conditions. (Subdivision: Basidiomycetes.) >> fungus

Drysdale, Russell (1912–81) Painter, born in Bognor Regis, West Sussex. His powerful scenes of the outback were a major contribution to modern art in Australia.

DTP >> **desktop publishing**

Duala >> **Douala**

dualism In philosophy, any theory which asserts the existence of two different kinds of thing. The most familiar dualism, held by Plato, Descartes, and many others, is between mind and matter. >> Descartes; monism; Plato

Dubai or **Dubayy** [doo**biy**] pop (1995e) 552 000; area 3900 sq km/1505 sq mi. Second largest of the United Arab Emirates; capital, Dubai, pop (1995e) 392 000; oil discovered in 1966. >> United Arab Emirates [i]

du Barry, Marie Jeanne Gomard de Vaubernier, comtesse (Countess), *née* **Bécu** (c.1743–93) The favourite mistress of Louis XV, born in Vaucouleurs. Her influence reigned supreme until the death of Louis in 1774. She was tried before the Revolutionary Tribunal, and guillotined. >> French Revolution [i]; Louis XV

dubbing The combination of several separate sound recordings into the final composite sound track for a motion picture or video production; sometimes known as **mixing**. The term also refers to the operation of replacing spoken dialogue of a completed sound track by its equivalent in another language, producing a **dubbed** version. >> film production

Dubček, Alexander [**dub**chek] (1921–92) Czechoslovakian statesman, born in Uhrovek, Slovakia. He rose to become first secretary in the Communist Party (1968), then introduced a series of far-reaching economic and political reforms. His liberalization policy led to the occupation of Czechoslovakia by Soviet forces (Aug 1968), and in 1969 he was replaced by Husak. In 1989, following a popular uprising, he was elected chairman of the Czechoslovak parliament. >> communism; Czechoslovakia ℹ

Dublin (city), Ir **Baile Átha Cliath**, ancient **Eblana** 53°20N 6°15W, pop (1995e) 475 000. Capital of the Irish Republic; at mouth of R Liffey; on site of Viking settlement; first Sinn Féin parliament met here, 1919; airport; railway; ferries to Liverpool and Holyhead; two universities (1591, 1908); two cathedrals; Dublin Castle, Abbey Theatre. >> Dublin (county); Ireland (republic) ℹ; Sinn Féin

Dublin (county), Ir **Baile Átha Cliath** pop (1995e) 1 018 000; area 922 sq km/356 sq mi. County in E Ireland; Wicklow Mts to the S; capital, Dublin. >> Dublin (city); Ireland (republic) ℹ

Du Bois, W(illiam) E(dward) B(urghardt) [doo **boyz**] (1868–1963) Historian, sociologist, and equal rights campaigner, born into a small black community at Great Barrington, MA. His writings explored the history and lives of African-Americans, and he helped found the National Association for the Advancement of Colored People. >> black consciousness

Dubrovnik [doo**brov**nik], Ital **Ragusa** 42°40N 18°07E, pop (1995e) 69 200. Port on the Dalmatia coast of Croatia; capital of Dalmatia; earthquake damage, 1979; badly damaged during siege by the Federal Army in the civil war, 1991; airport; car ferries to Italy and Greece; mediaeval town walls surrounding the old town, a world heritage site; cathedral. >> Croatia ℹ; Dalmatia

Dubuffet, Jean [dübüfay] (1901–85) Artist, born in Le Havre, France. He invented the concept of Art Brut, and is regarded as a forerunner of the Pop Art and Dada-like fashions of the 1960s. >> Art Brut; Dada; Pop Art

Duccio di Buoninsegna [**doo**chioh dee bwonin**sen**ya] (c.1260–c.1320) Painter, founder of the Sienese School, born in Siena, Italy. His masterpiece is the 'Maestà' for the altar of Siena cathedral (1311). >> Sienese School

Duchamp, Marcel [düshã] (1887–1968) Painter, born in Blainville, France. He was associated with several modern movements, including Cubism and Futurism, and was one of the pioneers of Dadaism. He laboured eight years on his best-known work, 'The Bride Stripped Bare by Her Bachelors, Even' (1915–23, Philadelphia). >> Cubism; Dada; Futurism

Duchovny, David (1960–) Actor, born in New York City. He achieved star success when he was given the role of Fox Mulder in the new series *The X-Files* (1993–, Golden Globe Best Actor), which has since become a cult classic. His feature film credits began with *Working Girl* (1988), and include *Beethoven* (1992) and *Kalifornia* (1993).

Duchy of Cornwall The oldest of English duchies, instituted by Edward III in 1337 to provide support for his eldest son, Edward, the Black Prince. Since 1503 the eldest son of the sovereign has inherited the dukedom; it consists of lands (totalling c.52 000 ha/130 000 acres) in Cornwall, Devon, Somerset, and S London, including the Oval cricket ground. >> Oval, the; Prince of Wales; Stannaries

Duchy of Lancaster A duchy created in 1267 by Henry III of England for his son Edmund. It was attached to the Crown in 1399 when the last Duke of Lancaster became Henry IV. The duchy lands consist of some 21 000 ha/52 000 acres of farmland and moorland, mostly in Yorkshire. It is controlled by the Chancellor of the Duchy of Lancaster, a political appointment generally held by a member of the Cabinet.

duck A smallish bird (the larger species are called **geese** or **swans**), primarily aquatic, with full webbing between the three front toes; relatively long neck; blunt flattened bill; male has penis (rare in birds). (Family: Anatidae.) >> harlequin / muscovy / perching duck; eider; gadwall; garganey; goosander; goose; merganser; shelduck; swan; teal; water fowl

duck-billed platypus A mammal native to E Australia (*Ornithorhynchus anatinus*); length, up to 75 cm/30 in; thick brown fur, soft duck-like bill, short legs with webbed feet, short flattened tail; pouch inside each cheek; male with venomous 'spur' on hind leg; also known as **platypus** or **duck-bill**. (Family: Ornithorhynchidae.) >> monotreme

duck hawk >> **peregrine falcon**

duckweed A tiny floating or submerged herb found in freshwater everywhere. It consists of a flat or convex green plant-body a few millimetres across, with a groove concealing the flowers on the margin, and roots on the underside. (Genus: *Lemna*, 15 species. Family: Lemnaceae.) >> wolfia

ductless glands >> **endocrine glands**

Dufay, Guillaume [düfay] (c.1400–74) Composer, probably born in Cambrai, France. He wrote many famous motets, such as *Nuper rosarum flores* (1436), Masses, and a large number of secular songs. >> motet

Dufourspitze [doo**foor**shpitsuh], Ital **Punta Dufour** 45°57N 7°53E. Mountain peak in Switzerland; second highest Alpine peak; height 4634 m/15 203 ft >> Alps

Dufy, Raoul [düfee] (1877–1953) Artist and designer, born in Le Havre, France. He produced many fabric designs and engraved book illustrations, and (from 1919) a series of calligraphic sketches of seascapes, regattas, and race-course scenes.

dugong [**doo**gong] A marine mammal (*Dugong dugon*), native to tropical coasts of the Old World; streamlined, with a short broad head; male with short tusks hidden beneath fleshy cheeks; front legs are flippers; hind legs absent; tail with pointed horizontal blades. (Family: Dugongidae. Order: Sirenia.) >> mammal ℹ

Duhamel, Georges [dooamel] (1884–1966) Novelist, poet, and man of letters, born in Paris. His best-known works are his novel cycles *Salavin* (1920–32) and *Chronique des Pasquier* (1933–44, The Pasquier Chronicles).

duiker [**diy**ker] A small African antelope; both sexes with arched back and short horns separated by a tuft of long hairs; two types: the **common** (**grey**, **savanna**, or **bush**) **duiker** (*Sylvicapra grimmia*), and the **forest duiker** (Genus: *Cephalophus*, 16 species). >> antelope

Duisburg [**düs**boork] 51°27N 6°42E, pop (1995e) 552 000. Industrial and commercial city in Germany; port on R Ruhr; largest inland port in Europe; badly bombed in World War 2; railway; university (1972); home of Gerhard Mercator. >> Germany ℹ; Mercator's map projection

Duisenberg, Willem (Frederik) [**dow**senberkh] (1935–) Banker and politician, born in Heerenveen, The Netherlands. He was director of The Netherlands Bank, professor of macro-economics at the University of Amsterdam, finance minister in the Den Uyl cabinet (1973–7) and director of the RABO Bank. In 1998 he was appointed first president of the European Central Bank in preference to the French candidate, on condition that he resign after four years, which is in fact against the Bank's constitution. In 1999 it was not clear whether he would do so. >> European Central Bank

Dukas, Paul (Abraham) [dükah] (1865–1935) Composer, born in Paris. His best-known work is the symphonic poem *L'Apprenti sorcier* (1897, The Sorcerer's Apprentice). He also wrote several orchestral and piano pieces.

duke In the UK, a nobleman of the highest order. A royal duke is a son of the sovereign who has been given a dukedom, such as Queen Elizabeth's son Andrew, Duke of York. >> peerage

Dukeries, the Area of NW Nottinghamshire, C England; includes Sherwood Forest and the parks of former ducal seats at Clumber, Thoresby, Welbeck, and Worksop. >> Nottinghamshire

dulcimer A type of zither, consisting of a wooden soundbox strung with a variable number of metal strings which pass over (or through) one or more bridges held in place by the pressure of the strings themselves. It is played with hammers of various types. >> chordophone; cimbalom; zither

Dulles, John Foster [**duh**lez] (1888–1959) US Republican secretary of state (1953–9), born in Washington, DC. In 1945 he advised at the Charter Conference of the UN, thereafter becoming US delegate to the General Assembly. As secretary of state, he opened a vigorous diplomacy of personal conferences with statesmen in other countries. >> United Nations

Duluth [duh**looth**] 46°47N 92°07W, pop (1995e) 90 700. Port in NE Minnesota, USA, at the W end of L Superior; established in the 1850s; airfield; railway; major lake port handling grain and iron ore. >> Minnesota; Superior, Lake

duma A political assembly in pre-revolutionary Russia. Municipal dumas (town councils) were introduced as part of local government reforms in 1870. After the 1905 revolution the State Duma, a quasi-parliamentary body, was established with limited constitutional powers. >> boyars; Revolution of 1905

Dumas, Alexandre [dümah], known as **Dumas père** ('father') (1802–70) Novelist and playwright, born in Villers-Cotterêts, France. He gained enduring success as a storyteller, his purpose being to put the history of France into novels. Among his best-known works are *Le Comte de Monte Cristo* (1844–5, The Count of Monte Cristo) and *Les Trois Mousquetaires* (1845, The Three Musketeers). His son, **Alexandre Dumas** (1824–95), often known as **Dumas** *fils*, was also a writer, whose best-known work was *La Dame aux camélias* (1848).

du Maurier, Dame Daphne [dü **moh**ryay] (1907–89) Novelist, born in London, the granddaughter of George du Maurier. She wrote several successful period romances and adventure stories, including *Jamaica Inn* (1936), *Rebecca* (1938), and *The Flight of the Falcon* (1965).

du Maurier, George (Louis Palmella Busson) [dü mohryay] (1834–96) Artist and illustrator, born in Paris. He gained a reputation as a designer and book illustrator, then joined the staff of *Punch* and became widely known as a gentle, graceful satirist of fashionable life.

Dumfries [duhm**frees**] 55°04N 3°37W, pop (1995e) 30 700. Market town and administrative centre of Dumfries and Galloway, SW Scotland; railway; Burns's House, Mausoleum. >> Burns; Dumfries and Galloway

Dumfries and Galloway pop (1995e) 148 000; area 6370 sq km/2459 sq mi. Local government council in SW Scotland; capital, Dumfries; Stranraer linked by ferry to Larne in N Ireland. >> Dumfries; Scotland ℹ

Du Mont, Allen B(alcom) [doo**mont**] (1901–65) Electronics engineer, born in New York City. In 1931 he developed cathode-ray tubes for use in oscilloscopes and television. He also invented the radio set's 'magic eye' tuning indicator. >> cathode-ray tube; thermionic valve

Dunant, (Jean) Henri [dünã] (1828–1910) Philanthropist, born in Geneva, Switzerland. He inspired the foundation of the International Red Cross, brought about the conference at Geneva (1863) from which came the Geneva Convention (1864), and in 1901 shared the first Nobel Peace Prize. >> Red Cross

Dunaway, Faye (1941–) Film actress, born in Bascom, FA. Her first starring role was in *Bonnie and Clyde* (1967). Later films include *Chinatown* (1974, Oscar nomination), *Don Juan DeMarco* (1995), *Network* (1976, Oscar), and *Fanny Hill* (1998).

Dunbar, William [duhn**bah(r)**] (c.1460–c.1520) Poet, probably born in East Lothian. He was a courtier of James IV, who gave him a pension in 1500. His poems include *Lament for the Makaris* and several satires, such as *The Dance of the Sevin Deadly Synnis*.

Dunblane [duhn**blayn**] Town near Stirling, Perthshire, Scotland, UK, the scene in March 1996 when 16 children and their teacher were killed by gunman Thomas Hamilton, who then killed himself. One of the consequences was a major national movement directed towards the banning of firearms, as well as various measures aimed at improving school security.

Duncan I >> **Macbeth**

Duncan, Isadora, originally **Angela Duncan** (1877–1927) Dancer and choreographer, born in San Francisco, CA. She was one of the pioneers of modern dance, basing her work on Greek-derived notions of beauty and harmony, but using everyday movements such as running, skipping, and walking. Her unconventional views on marriage and women's liberation gave rise to scandal. >> ballet; modern dance

Dundalk [duhn**dolk**], Ir **Dun Dealgan** 54°01N 6°25W, pop (1995e) 29 800. Capital of Louth county, NE Ireland; railway. >> Ireland (republic) ℹ; Louth

Dundee 56°28N 3°00W, pop (1995e) 169 000. Port and (since 1996) local council (Dundee City), E Scotland; royal burgh since 12th-c; airfield; railway; university (1881); Claypotts Castle (1569–88). >> Scotland ℹ

Dundee, John Graham of Claverhouse, 1st Viscount, known as **Bloody Claverse** or **Bonnie Dundee** (c.1649–89) Scottish soldier, born of a noble family. Joined by the Jacobite clans, he raised the standard for James against William and Mary, but died from a musket wound after his successful battle against Mackay at the Pass of Killiecrankie. >> Jacobites; James II (of England); William III

Dunedin [duh**nee**din] 45°52S 170°30E, pop (1995e) 113 000. City in Otago, SE South Island, New Zealand; founded by Scottish settlers, 1848; airfield; railway; university (1869). >> New Zealand ℹ

Dunfermline [dun**ferm**lin] 56°04N 3°29W, pop (1995e) 51 400. City in Fife, E Scotland; royal burgh since 1588; ancient residence of Scottish kings and the burial place of several, including Robert the Bruce; birthplace of Charles I; railway; Dunfermline Abbey and Palace (11th-c foundation). >> Bruce, Robert; Charles I (of England); Fife; Scotland ℹ

Dungeness Head [duhnj**nes**] 50°55N 0°58E. Point on the S coast of Kent, S England; nearby is Dungeness nuclear power station, with gas-cooled, graphite-moderated reactors (operational 1965), and an advanced gas-cooled reactor (1983). >> Kent; nuclear reactor ℹ

Dunkirk [duhn**kerk**], Fr **Dunkerque**, Flemish **Duinekerke** 51°02N 2°23E, pop (1995e) 73 200. Seaport in NW France; ferry connections to Dover and Harwich; during World War 2, the retreating British Expeditionary Force was rescued from the beaches near the town; railway. >> British Expeditionary Force; World War 2

Dun Laoghaire [doon**la**ee], Eng **Dunleary** [duhn**lee**ree], formerly **Kingstown** 53°17N 6°08W, pop (1995e) 55 100. Port town in Dublin county, E Ireland; dormitory town for Dublin; named Kingstown when George IV landed here in 1821; railway; ferries to Holyhead. >> Dublin (county); Holyhead; Ireland (republic) ℹ

dunlin A small wading bird (*Calidris alpina*), native to the N hemisphere; mottled brown plumage with pale underside; slender probing bill. (Family: Scolopacidae.) >> sandpiper

Dunlop, Joey, popular name of **(William) Joseph Dunlop**

(1952–) Motor-cyclist, an outstanding rider at Isle of Man TT races, born at Ballymoney, Northern Ireland. He won the Formula One TT for the sixth successive season in 1988, and was Formula One world champion 1982–6. >> motorcycle racing

Dunlop, John Boyd (1840–1921) Inventor, born in Dreghorn, North Ayrshire. In 1888 he obtained patents on the pneumatic tyre (invented 1845) for bicycles. His company, formed in 1889, became known as the Dunlop Rubber Company in 1900. >> tyre

Dunmore, Helen (1952–) British poet and novelist. Her poetry collections include *The Apple Fall* (1983) and *Secrets* (1994), and her children's novels *Going to Egypt* (1992) and *Fatal Error* (1996). In 1996 she won the inaugural Orange Prize for women fiction writers for her novel *A Spell of Winter* (1995).

Dunmow flitch A side of bacon offered as a prize to any married couple, if the husband could in honesty swear that for a year and a day he had not quarrelled with his wife, nor wished himself unmarried. Instituted at Little Dunmow, Essex, in the 13th-c or earlier, the custom has been revived in modern times.

Dunne, Finley Peter (1867–1936) Journalist and humorist, born in Chicago, IL. As 'Mr Dooley', he became widely known from 1900 as the exponent of American-Irish humorous satire on current personages and events.

dunnock A small, grey-brown, ground-feeding bird with short slender bill (*Prunella modularis*); native to Europe and W Asia (N Africa in winter); also known as **(European) hedge sparrow** or **hedge accentor**. (Family: Prunellidae.) >> accentor

Dunois, Jean d'Orléans, comte (Count) [dünwah], known as **the Bastard of Orléans** (1403–68) French general in the Hundred Years' War, born in Paris, the natural son of Louis, Duke of Orléans. He defended Orléans with a small force until its relief by Joan of Arc (1429), then inflicted several defeats on the English, forcing them out of Paris, Normandy, and Guyenne. >> Hundred Years' War; Joan of Arc

Duns Scotus, Johannes [**duhnz skoh**tus], known as **Doctor Subtilis** (Lat 'the Subtle Doctor') (c.1265–1308) Mediaeval philosopher and Franciscan theologian, probably born in Maxton, Scottish Borders. A critic of preceding scholasticism, his dialectical skill gained him his nickname; but his defence of the papacy led to his ideas being ridiculed at the Reformation (hence the word 'dunce'). >> Franciscans; scholasticism

Dunstable [**duhn**stabl] 51°53N 0°32W, pop (1995e) 49 800. Town in Bedfordshire, SC England; at the junction of the Roman Watling Street and the earlier Icknield Way; Whipsnade Zoo nearby. >> Bedfordshire

Dunstable, John [**duhn**stabl] (?–1453) The most important English composer of the 15th-c. He wrote motets, Masses, and secular songs including the three-part *O rosa bella*. >> counterpoint

Dunstan, St (c.909–88) Abbot, born near Glastonbury, Somerset. He became abbot of Glastonbury in 945. An adviser to King Edmund, he later became Bishop of Worcester (957) and of London (959), then (under King Edgar) Archbishop of Canterbury (960). Feast day 19 May. >> Christianity; Edgar

duodenal ulcer [dyoo-oh**dee**nl] An acute or persisting localized area of ulceration of the first part of the duodenum. The cause is unknown, but may be related to acid secretions of the stomach impinging on the duodenal wall. >> duodenum; ulcer

duodenum [dyoo-oh**dee**nm] A region of the alimentary canal in vertebrates, important in digestion. In humans it is the C-shaped first part of the small intestine, providing a large area for the absorption of digestive products. >> alimentary canal; duodenal ulcer; gall bladder; intestine; peptic ulcer

Du Pont [doo **pont**] Franco-American industrial family; in full, **du Pont de Nemours**. Their firm has a long history of manufacturing gunpowder, fibres, plastics, and chemicals, and played an important economic role in 19th-c Delaware.

du Pré, Jacqueline [doo **pray**] (1945–87) Cellist, born in Oxford. In 1967 she married the pianist Daniel Barenboim, with whom she gave many recitals. Her career as a player ended in 1973, when she developed multiple sclerosis.

Duralumin [dyu**ral**yumin] The trade name for an alloy of aluminium (over 90%) with copper (about 4%) and minor amounts of magnesium and manganese. It is used in the aircraft industry. >> alloy; aluminium; copper

Duras, Marguerite [düra], pseudonym of **Marguerite Donnadieu** (1914–96) Novelist, born in Gia Dinh, Vietnam. Her reputation was made by the novels she wrote in the 1950s, such as *Le Marin de Gibraltar* (1952, The Sailor from Gibraltar). She achieved a wider celebrity with the screenplay for Alain Resnais' film *Hiroshima Mon Amour* (1959, Hiroshima, My Love). >> Resnais

Durban or **Port Natal** 29°53S 31°00E, pop (1995e) 808 000. Seaport in KwaZulu Natal province, South Africa; situated on Indian Ocean coast; South Africa's third largest city; mission settlement founded here, 1834; airport; railway; university (1960). >> KwaZulu Natal; South Africa ℹ

Dürer, Albrecht [**dyoo**rer], Ger [**dü**rer] (1471–1528) Painter and engraver, born in Nuremberg, Germany. In 1497 he set up his own studio, producing many paintings, then in 1498 published his first great series of designs on wood, the illustrations of the Apocalypse. >> woodcut

Durga Puja >> **Navaratri**

Durham (UK city) [**duhr**uhm] 54°47N 1°34W, pop (1995e) 41 400. City and administrative centre of County Durham, NE England; on the R Wear; founded in the 10th-c by monks who had fled from Lindisfarne; railway; university (1832); cathedral (1093) and castle (11th-c) designated a world heritage site. >> Durham (county)

Durham (UK county) [**duhr**uhm] pop (1995e) 611 000; area 2436 sq km/ 941 sq mi. County in NE England; county town, Durham; Darlington a new unitary authority from 1997; coal-mining. >> Durham (city); England ℹ

Durkheim, Emile [**derk**hiym] (1858–1917) Sociologist, born in Epinal, France, generally regarded as one of the founders of sociology. He is perhaps best known for his concept of 'collective representations', the social power of ideas stemming from their development through the interaction of many minds. >> sociology

Durmitor [**door**mitaw(r)] 43°08N 19°01E. Highest mountain in Montenegro; in the Dinaric Alps, rising to 2522 m/8274 ft; in a national park, which is a world heritage site. >> Alps; Montenegro; Yugoslavia ℹ

Durrell, Gerald (Malcolm) [**duh**rel] (1925–95) British zoologist, traveller, writer, and broadcaster, born in Jamshedpur, India, the brother of Lawrence Durrell. His popular animal stories and reminiscences include *My Family and Other Animals* (1956) and *Birds, Beasts and Relatives* (1969). He founded a zoo and wildlife centre in Jersey. >> Durrell, Lawrence

Durrell, Lawrence (George) [**duh**rel] (1912–90) British novelist and poet, born in Darjeeling, India. He is best known for the *Alexandria Quartet* (1957–60): *Justine, Balthazar, Mountolive* and *Clea*. A series of five novels commenced in 1974 with *Monsieur*, followed by *Livia* (1978), *Constance* (1982), *Sebastian* (1983), and *Quinx* (1985). >> Durrell, Gerald

Dürrenmatt or **Duerrenmatt, Friedrich** [**dü**renmat] (1921–90) Writer, born in Konolfingen, Switzerland. His plays include *Die Ehe des Herrn Mississippi* (1952, The

Marriage of Mr Mississippi), which established his international reputation, and *Die Physiker* (1962, The Physicists).

Durrës [**doo**ruhs], formerly **Durazzo**, Turkish **Draj** 41°18N 19°28E, pop (1995e) 92 900. Seaport in W Albania, on the Adriatic Sea; founded as Epidamnos, 627 BC, and renamed Dyrrhachium, 229 BC; occupied by Italians and Austrians in World War 1, when capital of Albania, 1912–21; railway; a seaside health resort. >> Albania ℹ

durum A wheat (*Triticum durum*) with a high protein content, whose flour is used to make pasta. The flour is harder than that produced by other varieties of wheat, used in bread-making. >> pasta; semolina; wheat

Duse, Eleonora [**doo**zay] (1859–1924) Actress, born near Venice, Italy. She became the mistress of Gabriele d'Annunzio, who wrote *La Gioconda* for her. Her histrionic genius ranks 'The Duse' as one of the world's greatest actresses. >> d'Annunzio

Dushanbe [dyoo**shamb**e], formerly **Kishlak** (to 1925), **Diushambe** (to 1929), **Stalinabad** (1929–61) 38°38N 68°51E, pop (1995e) 694 000. Capital city of Tajikistan, on the R Dushanbe; airfield; railway; university (1948). >> Tajikistan ℹ

Düsseldorf [**dü**seldaw(r)f] 51°13N 6°47E, pop (1995e) 594 000. Industrial city in Germany; on the lower Rhine; city status, 1288; railway; university (1965); administrative centre of North Rhine–Westphalia province's heavy industry; birthplace of Heinrich Heine. >> Germany ℹ; Heine

Dust Bowl The semi-arid area of the US prairie states from Kansas to Texas, which suffers from dust storms. In the 1930s, after several years of overcultivation, strong winds and dry weather resulted in major dust storms and soil erosion. >> Great Plains

Dutch A member of the W Germanic family of languages, spoken by c.20 million in The Netherlands, Belgium, Suriname, and the Antilles. It is the official language of The Netherlands, and is also spoken in Belgium, where it is called **Flemish**; both dialects are officially referred to as **Nederlands**. >> Afrikaans; Germanic languages

Dutch elm disease A disease affecting all species of elm (genus: *Ulmus*) caused by the fungus *Ceratocystis ulmi*; symptoms include wilting, yellowing of foliage, and eventually death; transmitted from tree to tree by elm-bark beetle. (Order: Eurotiales.) >> elm

Dutch New Guinea >> **Irian Jaya**

Dutch Reformed Church The largest Protestant Church in Holland, stemming from the Calvinist Reformation in the 16th-c. The Dutch Reformed Church in South Africa (totally separated from the Church in Holland) was the official Church of dominant White Afrikaans-speaking nationals. >> Calvinism; Protestantism; Reformed Churches

Dutch Wars Three wars between England and the Dutch Republic (1652–4, 1664–7, 1672–4) concerned with issues of trade and the colonies. The wars brought on the decline of Dutch power, and signalled the growing predominance of the English.

Dutch West India Company The organization of Dutch merchants responsible for the settlement of New Netherland, now New York. The Company was established in 1621, and was dissolved in 1674. >> New York

Duval, Claude [düval] (1643–70) Highwayman, born in Domfront, France. He moved to England at the Restoration (1660), and pursued a successful career, gaining a popular reputation. He was hanged at Tyburn, London.

Duvalier, François [doo**val**yay], known as **Papa Doc** (1907–71) Haitian politician and president (1957–71), born in Port-au-Prince. His regime saw the creation of the civilian militia known as the Tonton Macoute. He became president for life in 1964, and was succeeded in this post by his son, **Jean-Claude Duvalier** (1951–), known as **Baby Doc**, whose regime lasted until 1986. >> Haiti ℹ

Dvořák, Antonín (Leopold) [**dvaw(r)**zhak] (1841–1904) Composer, born near Prague. His work, basically classical in structure, but with colourful Slavonic motifs, won increasing recognition, culminating in European acclaim for his *Stabat mater* (1880). In the USA he wrote his ninth symphony, the ever-popular 'From the New World'.

dwarf buffalo >> **anoa**

dwarfism A disorder of slowed growth in children, caused by many factors, such as malnutrition, rickets, and serious illness (eg congenital heart disease). True dwarfism occurs in achondroplasia, and in a number of disorders in which there is a deficiency of specific hormones. >> achondroplasia; cretinism; pituitary gland; thyroid hormone

dwarf star Strictly, any star in which the source of energy is the nuclear burning of hydrogen in its core to helium, and therefore lying on the main sequence of stellar evolution. Our Sun, 109 times the diameter of Earth, is a dwarf star. >> brown dwarf; helium; star; Sun; white dwarf

Dyak >> **Dayak**

dyeing The process of permanently changing the colour of a material. This ancient art has developed into a high-technology industry for the coloration of textiles, leather, and other goods. Dyes are usually applied by soaking the material in a solution, which is fixed onto the material by heating. >> dyestuff

dyer's rocket >> **weld**

dyestuff Strongly coloured substances, generally complex organic molecules, which are absorbed by textile materials. Indigo and cochineal are two of the best-known natural dyes. The synthetic *vat* dyes produce strong, bright colours of the highest fastness, and are often used on cotton furnishing fabrics. >> dyeing; indigo

Dyfed [**duh**vid] pop (1995e) 354 000; area 5768 sq km/ 2227 sq mi. Former county in SW Wales, UK; created in 1974, and replaced in 1996 by Cardiganshire, Carmarthenshire, and Pembrokeshire counties. >> Wales ℹ

dyke A ditch or natural watercourse. The term is also used to describe a long ridge or embankment constructed to prevent flooding, such as those in the Netherlands made to hold back the sea.

Dylan, Bob [**di**lan], pseudonym of **Robert Zimmerman** (1941–) Singer, musician, and songwriter, born in Duluth, MN. Opposition to war, the nuclear bomb, and racial and social injustice are the themes of his most famous songs, such as 'Blowin' in the Wind' and 'The Times They are a-Changin''. Later albums include *Bringing It All Back Home* (1965), *Blood on the Tracks* (1974), and *Street Legal* (1978).

dynamics In mechanics, the study of the properties of the motion of objects, and the relation of this motion to the forces causing it. >> electrodynamics; mechanics

dynamite Once a specific name, now a general term for industrial high explosives consisting of nitroglycerine absorbed on some porous or granular non-explosive substance to minimize its vulnerability to shock. >> explosives; Nobel

dyne >> **force;** RR1031

dysentery [**dis**entree] The name given to two different intestinal infections associated with diarrhoea and the passage of blood and mucus in the stool. **Bacillary dysentery** results from bacteria of the genus *Shigella*; the disease is usually mild and short-lived. **Amoebic/amebic dysentery** results from infection with the protozoan *Entamoeba histolytica*, and is more serious. >> diarrhoea; intestine; Protozoa

dyslexia Reading disability, in people with apparently adequate intellectual and perceptual abilities and adequate educational opportunities; sometimes called **alexia**. **Developmental dyslexia** is the term applied to people who have never learned to read. **Acquired dyslexia**

describes those who could once read, but who have lost this ability as a result of brain damage. There is no single theory which explains dyslexia, and the nature of the problem has been a source of some dispute; nevertheless it is common for several members of a family to exhibit similar difficulties with reading and writing. >> illiteracy; neuropsychology

dysmenorrhoea / dysmenorrhea [dismeno**ree**a] Discomfort or pain in the lower abdomen associated with menstruation. It is a common, usually mild (but sometimes very painful) complaint, which lasts 12–24 hours from the start of bleeding. >> menstruation

dyspepsia >> **indigestion**

dysphasia >> **aphasia**

dysplasia A malformation of bone, or other body tissue. It may affect any part of the body, but is particularly associated with certain conditions, such as those affecting the hip and the retina. **Hip dysplasia** is a hereditary disorder in several breeds of dog. >> bone; hip; osteology

dyspraxia >> **apraxia**

Dzaoudzi [dzoodzee] 12°47S 45°12E; pop (1995e) 9400; area 6·7 sq km/2·6 sq mi. Capital of Mayotte, on La Petite Terre I; airport. >> Mayotte

dzo >> **yak**

eagle A large-bodied bird of prey that kills its own food (smaller birds of prey – buzzards, falcons, hawks, harriers, or kites). (Family: Accipitridae, 30 species.) >> bald / sea eagle; bird of prey; buzzard; falcon; harrier (ornithology); hawk; kite (ornithology)

ear A compound organ concerned with hearing and balance, situated on the side or (in some animals) the top of the head. The **external ear** consists of the *auricle* (commonly referred to as 'the ear') and the *external auditory canal*, a tube leading down to the eardrum (*tympanic membrane*). The **middle ear** is an air-filled space, continuous with the nasopharynx via the auditory (Eustachian) tube, and contains the auditory *ossicles* (the *malleus*, *incus*, and *stapes*) and two small muscles which act to damp down sound vibrations. The **internal ear** can be divided into that concerned with hearing (the *cochlea*) and that concerned with assessing head position and its movements (the *vestibular apparatus*). >> audiology; auditory tube; deafness; Ménière's disease; sound; tinnitus; vestibular apparatus

E

Earhart, Amelia [**ay(r)**hah(r)t] (1897–1937) Aviator, born at Atchison, KS. She was the first woman to fly the Atlantic, as a passenger, and followed this by a solo flight in 1932. In 1937 she set out to fly round the world, but her plane was lost over the Pacific. >> aircraft i

earl In the UK, a member of the third most senior order of noblemen, and the most ancient title, dating from before the Norman Conquest (Danish *jarl*). The wife of an earl is a *countess*. >> peerage

Earl Marshal In the UK, the hereditary post held by the Howard Dukes of Norfolk. One of the great officers of state, the Earl Marshal is head of the College of Arms and is also responsible for organizing state ceremonies. >> heraldry i

Early English Style The form of English Gothic architecture prevalent during the 13th-c, characterized by pointed arches, rib vaults, and a greater stress on the horizontals than is found in French Gothic architecture. >> arch i; Gothic architecture; vault i

EAROM [eeay**rom**] An acronym of **Electrically Alterable Read-Only Memory**, a type of integrated circuit read-only memory, where the data can be altered electronically while the EAROM remains in circuit. >> EPROM; PROM

Earp, Wyatt (Berry Stapp) [erp] (1848–1929) Gambler, gunfighter, and lawman, born in Monmouth, IL. During his stay in Tombstone, AZ, he befriended Doc Holliday, who joined with the Earp brothers against the Clanton gang in the famous gunfight at the OK Corral (1881). Earp collaborated in the writing of his biography *Wyatt Earp, Frontier Marshal* (1931), published after his death, which portrayed him as a heroic frontiersman of the Wild West.

Earth The third planet from the Sun, having the following characteristics: mass 5·97 × 10^{24}kg; orbital period 365·26 days; radius (equatorial) 6378 km/3963 mi; obliquity 23°27'; mean density 5·52 g/cm^3; orbital eccentricity 0·017; equatorial gravity 978 cm/s^2; mean distance from the Sun 149·6 × 10^6 km/93 × 10^6 mi; rotational period 23 h 56 min 4 s. It has one large natural satellite, the Moon. There is an oxygen/nitrogen-rich atmosphere, liquid water oceans filling lowland regions between continents, and permanent water ice caps at each pole. It is unique in the Solar System in being able to support life, for which there is fossil evidence in rocks dating from 3·5 thousand million years ago; human population over 6000 million (1999). The interior of the planet is differentiated into zones: an iron/nickel-rich molten *core* (radius c.3500 km/2175 mi) an iron–magnesium silicate *Mantle* (c.85% by volume of the Earth); and a *crust* of lighter metal silicates (relatively thin, c.6 km/3½ mi thick under the oceans to c.50 km/ 30 mi under the continents). >> greenhouse effect; magnetosphere; planet; plate tectonics i; seismology; Solar System; RR971

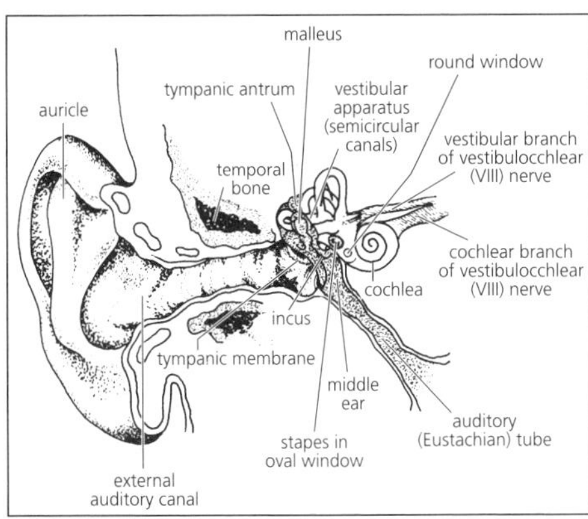

Structure of the auditory apparatus seen in a frontal section through the right side of the skull.

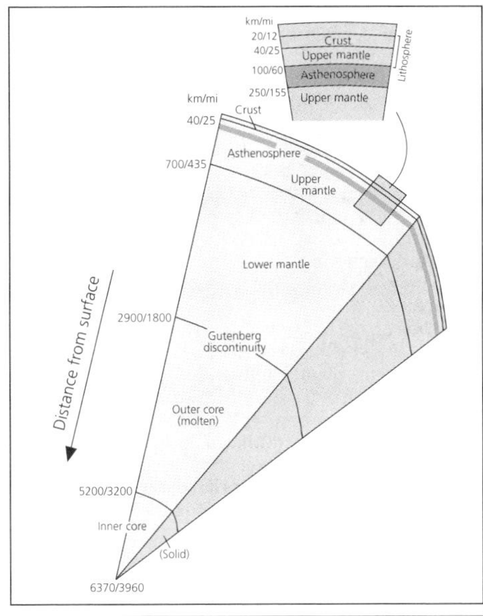

The structure of the Earth

earth pig >> **aardvark**

earthquake A series of shock waves generated at a point (*focus*) within the Earth, and caused by the movement of rocks on a fault plane releasing stored strain energy. The point on the surface of the Earth above the focus is the *epicentre*. Major earthquakes are associated with the edges of plates that make up the Earth's crust, and along mid-oceanic ridges where new crust is forming. The greatest concentration of earthquakes is in a belt around the Pacific Ocean (the 'ring of fire'), and along a zone from the Mediterranean E to the Himalayas and China. The magnitude of an earthquake is measured on the Richter scale. >> plate tectonics; Richter scale; seismology; RR974

earth sciences A general term for the study of the Earth and its atmosphere, encompassing geology and its sub-disciplines as well as oceanography, glaciology, meteorology, and the origin of the Earth and the Solar System. >> geology

earthstar A ground-living fungus with a globular fruiting body; when ripe, outer layer splits into rays, and peels back into a star-shaped structure. (Order: Lycoperdales. Genus: *Geastrum*.) >> fungus

Earth Summit The name given to the **United Nations Conference on Environment and Development (UNCED)** held in Rio de Janeiro in June 1992, at which 178 governments were represented. The aim was to find ways of minimizing the damage done to the environment by the processes associated with economic development. The *Framework Convention on Climate Change* introduced measures designed to reduce the threat of global warming. The *Convention on Biological Diversity* put forward proposals to preserve the Earth's biological diversity. *Agenda 21* was an action plan aimed at introducing sustainable development, The *Rio Declaration* included 27 principles to guide action on development and the environment. The *Forest Principles* emphasized the right of states to exploit their own forest resources while advocating general principles of sustainable forest management. A second conference (**Earth Summit II**) was held in New York in 1997, attended by 185 countries. >> biodiversity; Greenpeace; World Commission on Environment and Development

earthworm A terrestrial segmented worm found in soil, feeding mainly on decomposing organic matter; head simple, without sensory appendages; body cylindrical, length up to 4 m/13 ft. (Phylum: Annelida. Class: Oligochaeta.) >> annelid; worm

earwig A slender insect with large pincers at rear end of body, used for courtship, defence, grooming, or predation; forewings small and hard; hindwings membranous; c.1500 species, most abundant in tropics. (Order: Dermaptera.) >> insect [i]

East Bank Region in Jordan, E of the R Jordan; corresponds roughly to the former Amirate of Transjordan. >> Jordan [i]; West Bank

East End An area of London situated N of the R Thames and E of Shoreditch and Tower Bridge. The Dockland Development scheme has recently sought to bring industry and finance into the area. >> London

Easter The chief festival of the Christian Church, commemorating the resurrection of Christ after his crucifixion. Observed in the Western Churches on a Sunday between 22 March and 25 April inclusive, depending on the date of the first full moon after the spring equinox; the Orthodox Church has a different method of calculating the date. >> Christianity

Easter Island [**pas**kwa], Span **Isla de Pascua** 27°05S 109°20W; pop (1995e) 2620; area 166 sq km/64 sq mi; maximum length 24 km/15 mi; maximum width 12 km/7 mi. Chilean island 3790 km/2355 mi W of Chile; rises to 652 m/2139 ft at Terevaka; first European discovery by Dutch admiral Jacob Roggeveen on Easter Sunday 1722; islanders largely of Polynesian origin; capital, Hanga Roa; airport; famous for its *Moai* stone statues depicting the human head and trunk of local ancestors. >> Chile [i]; Polynesia

Eastern Cape One of the nine new provinces established by the South African constitution of 1994, in SE South Africa, incorporating the former Transkei and Ciskei homelands, and formerly part of Cape Provinces; capital, Bisho; pop (1996e) 5 865 000; area 170 616 sq km/65 858 sq mi; chief languages, Xhosa (85%), Afrikaans, English; second poorest province; automotive industry at Port Elizabeth; agriculture, forestry, tourism (coastal amenities and nature reserves). >> South Africa

Eastern Orthodox Church >> **Orthodox Church**

Easter Rising A rebellion of Irish nationalists in Dublin, organized by two revolutionary groups, the Irish Republican Brotherhood led by Patrick Pearse, and Sinn Féin under James Connolly (1868–1916). The rising was put down and several leaders were executed. >> nationalism; Pearse; Sinn Féin

East Germany >> **Germany** [i]

East India Company, British A British trading monopoly, established in India in 1600, which later became involved in politics, eventually wielding supreme power through a Board of Control responsible to the British parliament. During the 18th-c it received competition from other European countries, in particular France and Holland. Its monopoly was broken in 1813, and it ceased to exist as a legal entity in 1873. >> India [i]

Eastman, George (1854–1932) Inventor and philanthropist, born at Waterville, NY. In 1889 he manufactured the transparent celluloid film used by Edison and others in experiments which made possible the moving-picture industry. >> cinematography

East Sussex >> **Sussex, East**

Eastwood, Clint (1930–) Film actor and director, born in San Francisco, CA. He began acting in television Westerns, especially the *Rawhide* series (1959–65), and became an international star with three Italian-made 'spaghetti Westerns', beginning with *A Fistful of Dollars* (1964). Later films include *Unforgiven* (1992, two Oscars), *Bridges of Madison County* (1995), and *Absolute Power* (1997). He was elected mayor of Carmel-by-the-Sea, CA (1986–8).

eau de Cologne mint >> **mint**

EBCDIC code [**eb**seedik] An acronym of **Extended Binary Coded Decimal Interchange Code**, a binary code used by IBM for information exchange: 256 different characters are defined using an 8-bit code. >> ASCII code

ebonite >> **vulcanite**

ebony An evergreen or deciduous tree, native to tropical and subtropical regions; flowers solitary or in small clusters, urn-shaped with 3–5 spreading lobes, white, yellow, or reddish; fruit a berry; cultivated especially for its hard, black heartwood, and for the edible fruits. (Genus: *Diospyros*, 500 species. Family: Ebenaceae.) >> persimmon

Ebro, River [**eb**roh], ancient **Iberius** Longest river flowing entirely in Spain; rises in the Cordillera Cantabrica and flows SE to enter the Mediterranean; length, 910 km/565 mi. >> Spain [i]

Eccles, Sir John (Carew) (1903–97) Physiologist, born in Melbourne, Victoria, Australia. A specialist in neurophysiology, he shared the 1963 Nobel Prize for Physiology or Medicine for his work on the functioning of nervous impulses. >> Huxley, Andrew Fielding; nervous system

Ecclesiastes, Book of [ekleezi**as**teez] A Biblical work, specifically attributed to 'The Preacher, the son of David, King of Jerusalem', who has traditionally been identified as Solomon, although the work is more usually now dated in the post-exilic period of Israel's history. >> Old Testament; Solomon (Hebrew Bible)

Ecclesiasticus, Book of [ekleezi**as**tikus] (Lat 'the Church (Book)') Part of the Old Testament Apocrypha or Catholic deuterocanonical writings, originally attributed to a Jewish scribe c.180 BC, but later translated into Greek by his grandson; also called **The Wisdom of Jesus, the Son of Sirach**, or just **Sirach** or **Ben Sira**.

ecclesiology [ekleezi**ol**ojee] The theological study of the nature of the Christian Church. The term can also signify the science of church construction and decoration. >> Christianity

ECG >> **electrocardiography**

echidna [e**kid**na] An Australasian mammal; coat with spines; minute tail; long claws used for digging; long narrow snout and sticky tongue; eats ants and termites, or larger insects and earthworms; young develop in pouch. (Family: Tachyglossidae, 2 species.) >> monotreme

Echidna [e**kid**na] In Greek mythology, a fabulous creature, half-woman and half-snake, who was the mother of various monsters. >> Cerberus; Hydra (mythology); sphinx

echinoderm [e**kiy**noderm] A spiny-skinned marine invertebrate characterized by its typically 5-radial symmetry; body enclosed by a variety of calcareous plates, ossicles, and spines; water vascular system operates numerous tubular feet used in feeding, locomotion, and respiration. (Phylum: Echinodermata.) >> brittle star; calcium; crinoid; sea cucumber; sea urchin; starfish

Echinoidea [eki**noy**dia] >> **sea urchin**

Echiura [eki**yoo**ra] >> **spoonworm**

Echo In Greek mythology, a nymph of whom several stories are told. Either she was beloved by Pan, and was torn to pieces, only her voice surviving; or she was punished by Hera so that she could only repeat the last words of another speaker. She loved Narcissus, who rejected her, so that she wasted away to a voice. >> Hera; Narcissus; Pan

echolocation The perception of objects by means of reflected sound waves, typically high-frequency sounds. The process is used by some animals, such as bats and whales, for orientation and prey location. >> echo-sounding; sound

echo-sounding Bouncing sound waves off the sea-floor to determine the depth of water in the oceans. A device known as a *precision depth recorder* (PDR) is used to print a visual trace of the water depth and provide a picture of the sea-floor topography. >> bathymetry; echolocation; sound

Eckhart, Johannes [**ek**hah(r)t], also spelled **Eckart** or **Eckehart**, known as **Meister Eckhart** ('Master Eckhart') (c.1260–c.1327) Dominican theologian and mystic, born in Hochheim, Germany. In 1325 he was arraigned for heresy, and two years after his death his writings were condemned by Pope John XXII. >> Dominicans

eclipse 1 The passage of a planet or satellite through the shadow cast by another body. In the case of our Sun, a **solar eclipse** can occur only at new Moon, when the Moon is directly between the Earth and the Sun. A **total eclipse**, when the whole disc is obscured, lasts a maximum of 7·5 min. A **partial eclipse** of much longer duration occurs before, after, and to each side of the path of totality. Sometimes the apparent size of the lunar disc is just too small for a total eclipse, and an **annular eclipse** results, in which a bright ring of sunlight surrounds the Moon. A **lunar eclipse** occurs when the Moon passes into the shadow of the Earth, which can happen only at full moon. >> chromosphere; corona (astronomy); Moon; Sun **2** The total or partial disappearance from view of an astronomical object when it passes directly behind another object. In binary star systems it is also possible for one star to eclipse another (an *eclipsing binary star*). >> binary star; RR965, 967

ecliptic That great circle which is the projection of the Earth's orbit onto the celestial sphere, and therefore is the apparent path of the Sun across our sky. >> celestial sphere; great circle

eclogue [**ek**log] A short dramatic poem, originally with a pastoral setting and theme. Of classical derivation (notably in Theocritus and Virgil), the form was popular in the 16th–17th-c (as Spenser's *Shepheardes Calendar*, 1579). >> classicism; Theocritus; Virgil

Eco, Umberto [**ay**koh] (1929–) Semiotician, novelist, and critic, born in Allesandra, Italy. His novel *Il nome della*

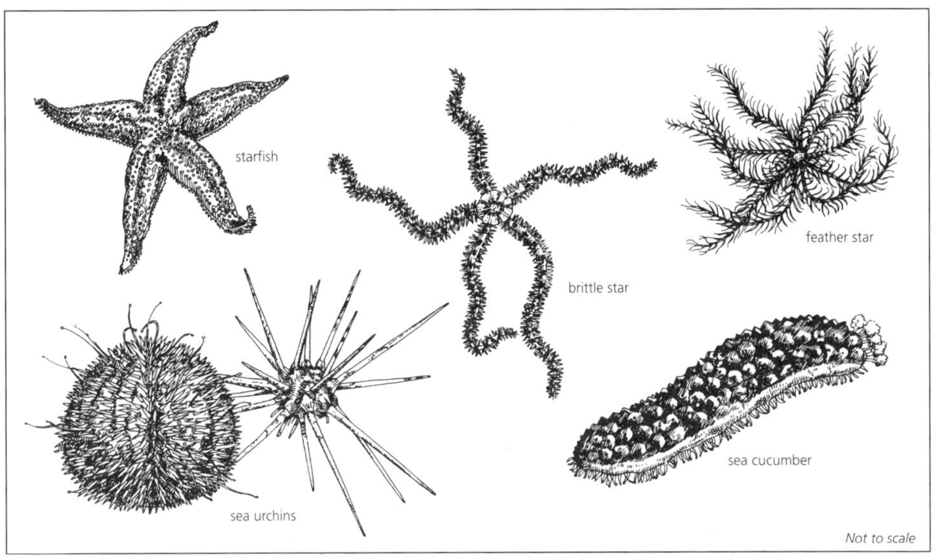

Echinoderms

rosa (1981, The Name of the Rose), an intellectual detective story, achieved instant fame, and attracted much critical attention; it was filmed in 1986. Later novels are *Foucault's Pendulum* (trans, 1988) and *L'isola del giorno prima* (1994, The Island of the Day Before). >> semiotics

ecology The study of the interaction of living organisms with their physical, biological, and chemical environment. The ecological movement of the 1960s onwards has argued that people must live within the limitations of the Earth's finite supply of resources, and that humanity is very much dependent on its environment. >> conservation (earth sciences); ecosystem; environmental studies

Economic Community of West African States (ECOWAS) An economic organization formed in 1975 by 15 W African signatories to the Treaty of Lagos: Benin, Gambia, Ghana, Guinea, Guinea-Bissau, Côte d'Ivoire (Ivory Coast), Liberia, Mali, Mauritania, Niger, Nigeria, Senegal, Sierra Leone, Togo, and Upper Volta (now Burkina Faso); Cape Verde joined in 1977.

economics The study of the allocation of scarce resources among competing ends, the creation and distribution of wealth, and national income. The first major economist was Adam Smith, and the economic theory of the classical school (*equilibrium*) dominated thinking until the 1930s. The main change in thinking at that time was the result of work by J M Keynes, whose economic theories attempted to solve the problems of depression and economic stagnation. **Microeconomics** is the study of the economic problems of firms and individuals, and the way individual elements in an economy behave. **Macroeconomics** is the study of the country as a whole, including such matters as trade, monetary policy, prices, national income, output, exchange rates, growth, and forecasting (**econometrics**). >> industry; Keynes; monetarism; Smith, Adam; social science

ecosocialism A branch of socialism of relatively recent origin which wishes to see socialist practice linked with concern for environmental and ecological matters. >> ecology; socialism

ecosystem An ecological concept which helps to explain the relationships and interactions between one or more living organisms and their physical, biological, and chemical environment (eg a pond and its associated plants, fish, insects, birds, and mammals). The study of ecosystems is commonly based on transfers of energy along a food chain. In most natural ecosystems, several food chains interact to form complex food or energy webs. >> ecology; environment; food chain; photosynthesis

ecstasy A designer drug which is supposedly mildly hallucinogenic; also called **MDMA** (methylenedioxymethamphetamine), 'E' or 'Adam'. It is reported to heighten the tactile senses of touch and skin sensations, and thereby act as an aphrodisiac. >> designer drugs; hallucinogens

ectoplasm A substance said to exude from the body of a medium during a seance, from which materializations sometimes supposedly form. It is the subject of much controversy, as some mediums were discovered to simulate such effects fraudulently. >> medium (parapsychology); seance

ECU >> **European Monetary System**

Ecuador [**ek**wadaw(r)], official name **Republic of Ecuador**, Span **República del Ecuador** pop (1995e) 11 423 000; area 270 699 sq km/104 490 sq mi. Republic in NW South America; includes the Galápagos Is 970 km/600 mi W; capital, Quito; timezone GMT −5; major ethnic groups, Amerindian (40%), mestizo (40%), white (15%); main religion, Roman Catholicism; official language, Spanish, with Quechua also spoken; unit of currency, the sucre of 100 centavos; coastal plain in the W, descending from rolling hills (N) to broad lowland basin; Andean uplands in C rising to snow-capped peaks which include Cotopaxi (5896 m/19 343 ft); forested alluvial plains in the E, dissected by rivers flowing from the Andes towards the Amazon; hot and wet equatorial climate; formerly part of Inca Empire; taken by Spanish, 1527; within Viceroyalty of New Granada; independent, 1822; joined with Panama, Colombia, and Venezuela to form Gran Colombia; left union, to become independent republic, 1830; highly unstable political history; governed by a president and a unicameral National Congress; agriculture employs c.35% of workforce. >> Andes; Galápagos Islands; Incas; Quito; RR1006 political leaders

ecumenism [e**kyoo**menizm] (Gr *oikoumene*, 'the inhabited world') A movement seeking visible unity of divided churches and denominations within Christianity. The 4th-c and 5th-c 'Ecumenical Councils' had claimed to represent the Church in the whole world. The movement encourages dialogue between churches of different denominations, joint acts of worship, and joint service in the community. >> Council of the Church; World Council of Churches

eczema >> **dermatitis**

edaphology [eeda**fol**ojee] The study of soil as a medium for growth of living organisms. The word is from Greek *edaphos* 'ground, soil'. >> soil science

Edda (Old Norse 'great-grandmother') The name of two separate collections of Old Norse literature. The **Elder Edda**, dating from the 9th-c, consists of heroic and mythological poems; the **Younger** or **Prose Edda** was written (mainly in prose) in the early 13th-c by the Icelandic poet Snorri Sturluson. >> saga; Snorri Sturluson

Eddington, Sir Arthur S(tanley) (1882–1944) Astronomer, born in Kendal, Cumbria. In 1919 his observations of star positions during a total solar eclipse gave the first direct confirmation of Einstein's general theory of relativity. He became a renowned popularizer of science, notably in *The Expanding Universe* (1933). >> astrophysics; general relativity; stellar evolution

Eddy, Mary Baker, married name **Glover** (1821–1910) Founder of the Christian Scientists (1876), born in Bow, NH. In 1866 she received severe injuries after a fall, but read about the palsied man in Matthew's Gospel, and claimed to have risen from her bed similarly healed. Thereafter she devoted herself to developing her spiritual discovery, and in 1879 organized at Boston the Church of Christ, Scientist. >> Christian Science; Congregationalism

Edelman, Gerald (Maurice) [**ay**dlman] (1929–) Biochemist, born in New York City. His research into the antibodies which form a major part of a vertebrate animal's defence against infection led to his sharing the Nobel Prize for Physiology or Medicine in 1972. >> antibodies

edelweiss [**ay**dlviys] A perennial (*Leontopodium alpinum*) growing to 20 cm/8 in, native to the mountains of SE Europe; flower-heads yellowish-white, arranged in a flat-topped cluster surrounded by pointed, spreading, star-like, woolly bracts. (Family: Compositae.) >> bract

edema >> **oedema**

Eden, Sir (Robert) Anthony, 1st Earl of Avon [**ee**dn] (1897–1977) British statesman and Conservative prime minister (1955–7), born in Windlestone, Durham. He became foreign secretary (1935), resigning in 1938 over differences with Chamberlain. Again foreign secretary (1940–5, 1951–5), he succeeded Churchill as prime minister. In 1956 he ordered British forces into the Suez Canal Zone – an action which led to his resignation. >> Churchill, Winston; Conservative Party; Suez Crisis

Eden, Garden of Biblical place associated with **Paradise**, where Adam and Eve lived prior to their sin and expulsion (*Gen* 2, 3). >> Adam and Eve

Edentata [eedn**tah**ta] (Lat 'with no teeth') An order of mammals characterized by having extra contacts between some of the bones in the spine, and by having no front teeth. >> anteater; armadillo; sloth

Ederle, Gertrude (Caroline) [**ay**derlee] (1906–) The first woman to swim the English channel, born in New York City. She won a gold medal at the 1924 Olympic Games as a member of the US 400 m relay team. On 6 August 1926 she swam the Channel from Cap Gris Nez to Kingsdown in 14 h 31 min, very nearly two hours faster than the existing men's record.

Edgar or **Eadgar** (943–75) King of Mercia and Northumbria (957) and (from 959) King of all England, the younger son of Edmund I. In c.973 he introduced a uniform currency based on new silver pennies. >> Anglo-Saxons; Edmund I

Edgar the Ætheling ('Prince') [**ath**uhling] (c.1050–1125) Anglo-Saxon prince, the grandson of Edmund Ironside. Though chosen as king after the Battle of Hastings, he was never crowned. He submitted to William the Conqueror, then rebelled and fled to Scotland (1068). He was finally reconciled with King William in 1074. >> Anglo-Saxons; Edmund Ironside; William I (of England)

Edgeworth, Maria (1767–1849) Writer, born in Blackbourton, Oxfordshire. She is best known for her children's stories, and her novels of Irish life, such as *Castle Rackrent* (1800) and *The Absentee* (1812).

Edinburgh [**ed**inbruh] 55°57N 3°13W, pop (1995e) 441 000. Capital of Scotland; port facilities at Leith; castle built by Malcolm Canmore (11th-c); charter granted by Robert Bruce, 1392; capital of Scotland, 1482; in the 1760s, New Town area designed by James Craig (1744–95), but the business centre remained in the Old Town; Nor' Loch separating old and new towns was drained and laid out as gardens (Princes Street Gardens); new local council status in 1996 (as City of Edinburgh); airport; railway; three universities (1583, 1966, 1992); cathedral (15th-c); commercial, business, legal, and cultural centre; Edinburgh Castle (oldest part, St Margaret's Chapel, 12th-c); Royal Mile from castle to Palace of Holyroodhouse; Holyrood Park, containing Arthur's Seat, extinct volcano; Scott Monument (1844), 61 m/200 ft high; Military Tattoo (Aug); International, Fringe, Jazz, and Film Festivals, and Highland Games (Aug–Sep). >> Bruce, Robert; Holyroodhouse, Palace of; Lothian; Malcolm III; Scotland ℹ; Scott, Walter

Edinburgh, Prince Philip, Duke of [**ed**inbruh] (1921–) The husband of Queen Elizabeth II of the United Kingdom, the son of Prince Andrew of Greece and Princess Alice of Battenberg, born at Corfu. He became a naturalized British subject in 1947, when he was married to the Princess Elizabeth (20 Nov). In 1956 he began the **Duke of Edinburgh Award Scheme** to foster the leisure activities of young people. >> Elizabeth II

Edison, Thomas (Alva) (1847–1931) Inventor, born at Milan, OH. He was the author of over 1000 inventions, including the printing telegraph (1871), the phonograph (1877), the electric light bulb (1879), and motion picture equipment. >> phonograph; telegraphy

Edmonton 53°34N 113°25W, pop (1995e) 655 000. Capital of Alberta province, W Canada; Fort Edmonton built by Hudson's Bay Company, 1795; destroyed by Indians, 1807, and rebuilt on new site, 1819; chosen as capital, 1905; rapid growth after discovery of oil nearby, 1947; airport; airfield; University of Alberta (1906) and Athabasca University (1972); ice hockey team, Edmonton Oilers. >> Alberta; Hudson's Bay Company

Edmund I (921–46) King of the English (from 939), the half-brother of Athelstan. He re-established control over the S Danelaw (942) and Northumbria (944), and for the remainder of his life ruled a reunited England. >> Anglo-Saxons; Athelstan; Danelaw

Edmund II, known as **Edmund Ironside** (c.980–1016) King of the English, the son of Ethelred the Unready. Chosen king by the Londoners on his father's death (Apr 1016), he defeated Canute, but was routed at Ashingdon (Oct 1016), and died soon after. >> Canute

Edmund, St, originally **Edmund Rich** (1170–1240) Clergyman and Archbishop of Canterbury, born at Abingdon, Oxfordshire. He became the spokesman of the national party against Henry III, defending Church rights. Feast day 16 November. >> Christianity; Crusades ℹ; Henry III (of England)

Edomites [**ee**domiyts] According to the Bible (*Gen* 36), the descendants of Esau who settled in the mountainous area S of the Dead Sea to the Gulf of Aqabah; in Greek, **Idumeans**. Enemies of Israel, they became a kingdom in the 8th-c BC. >> Babylonia; Bible; Esau

educational drama The use of drama within an educational system, both as a means of learning and as a subject in its own right. Often more emphasis is placed on improvization and exploration than on performance skills – on drama as process rather than on theatre as product. >> psychodrama; theatre

educational psychology A branch of psychology which applies the findings of psychology to the understanding of learning. The traditional role of the educational psychologist was often limited to one of testing children and placing 'backward' ones into special education. Today, more attention is paid to the task of assisting teachers in programmes designed to help individual children, and in advising schools about their function as organizations. >> intelligence; psychology

Edward, Lake, Zaire **Lake Rutanzige** area 4 000 sq km/1 500 sq mi. Lake in EC Africa, on the frontier between the Democratic Republic of Congo and Uganda; length, c.80 km/50 mi; width, 50 km/30 mi; altitude, 912 m/2 992 ft; European discovery by Stanley in 1889; named after the Prince of Wales (later Edward VII). >> Africa; Rift Valley; Stanley, Henry Morton

Edward I (1239–1307) King of England (1272–1307), born

in London, the elder son of Henry III and Eleanor of Provence. In the Barons' War (1264–7), he defeated Simon de Montfort at Evesham (1265), then won renown as a crusader to the Holy Land in the Eighth Crusade (1270–2). In two campaigns (1276–7, 1282–3), he annexed N and W Wales, building magnificent castles, and reasserted English claims to the overlordship of Scotland thus beginning the Scottish Wars of Independence. >> Barons' Wars; Crusades [i]; Montfort, Simon de

Edward II (1284–1327) King of England (1307–27), born in Caernarfon, Wales, the fourth son of Edward I and Eleanor of Castile. In 1301 he was created Prince of Wales, the first English heir apparent to bear the title. He was humiliated by reverses in Scotland, where he was decisively defeated at Bannockburn (1314). Throughout his reign, he mismanaged the barons, who sought to rid the country of royal favourites. He was deposed by his wife Isabella, and her lover Roger Mortimer Earl of March, and was murdered in Berkeley Castle. >> Bannockburn, Battle of; Isabella of France

Edward III, known as **Edward of Windsor** (1312–77) King of England (1327–77), born in Windsor, S England, the elder son of Edward II and Isabella of France. By banishing Queen Isabella from court, he assumed full control of the government (1330), and began to restore the monarchy's authority and prestige. He defeated the Scots at Halidon Hill (1333), and in 1337 revived his hereditary claim to the French crown, thus beginning the Hundred Years' War. He destroyed the French navy at the Battle of Sluys (1340), and won another major victory at Crécy (1346). >> Hundred Years' War

Edward IV (1442–83) King of England (1461–70, 1471–83), born in Rouen, France, the eldest son of Richard, Duke of York. He entered London in 1461, was recognized as king on Henry VI's deposition, and defeated the Lancastrians at Towton. Forced into exile by the Earl of Warwick (1470), he recovered the throne after victories at Barnet and Tewkesbury. >> Henry VI; Roses, Wars of the; Warwick, Earl of

Edward V (1470–83) King of England (Apr–Jun 1483), born in London, the son of Edward IV and Elizabeth Woodville. He and his younger brother Richard, Duke of York, were imprisoned in the Tower by their uncle Richard, Duke of Gloucester, who usurped the throne as Richard III. The two princes were never heard of again, and were most probably murdered (Aug 1483) on their uncle's orders. >> Richard III; Roses, Wars of the

Edward VI (1537–53) King of England (1547–53), born in London, the son of Henry VIII by his third queen, Jane Seymour. During his reign, power was first in the hands of his uncle, the Duke of Somerset, then of John Dudley, Duke of Northumberland. Under the Protectors the English Reformation flourished. >> Grey, Jane; Reformation

Edward VII (1841–1910) King of the United Kingdom (1901–10), born in London, the eldest son of Queen Victoria. In 1863 he married Alexandra of Denmark, by whom he had six children. As Prince of Wales, his behaviour led him into several social scandals, and the Queen excluded him from affairs of state. >> Alexandra, Queen; Victoria

Edward VIII (1894–1972) King of the United Kingdom (Jan–Dec 1936), born in Richmond, Greater London, the eldest son of George V. He abdicated in the face of opposition to his proposed marriage to Wallis Simpson, a commoner who had been twice divorced. He was then given the title of Duke of Windsor, and the marriage took place in France in 1937. His wife, the **Duchess of Windsor** (1896–1986) lived in seclusion in Paris, after her husband's death.

Edward (Antony Richard Louis), Prince (1964–) Prince of the United Kingdom, the third son of Queen Elizabeth II. After studying history at Cambridge, he joined the Royal Marines in 1986, but left the following year and began a career in the theatre, beginning as a production assistant with Andrew Lloyd Webber's Really Useful Theatre Company. In 1993 he formed his own company, Ardent Productions. >> Elizabeth II

Edward the Black Prince (1330–76) Eldest son of Edward III, born in Woodstock, Oxfordshire. In 1346, though still a boy, he fought at Crécy, and is said to have won his popular title from his black armour. He won several victories in the Hundred Years' War, including Poitiers (1356). >> Edward III; Hundred Years' War

Edward the Confessor, St (c.1003–66) King of England (1042–66), the elder son of Ethelred the Unready. Although in 1051 he probably recognized Duke William of Normandy (later William I) as his heir, on his deathbed he nominated Harold Godwinson (Harold II) to succeed, the Norman Conquest following soon after. Edward's reputation for holiness began in his lifetime, and he was canonized in 1161. Feast day 13 October. >> Ethelred (the Unready); Harold II; Norman Conquest

Edward the Elder (c.870–924) King of Wessex (899–924), the elder son of Alfred the Great. He built on his father's successes and established himself as the strongest ruler in Britain, conquering the S Danelaw (910–18), and assuming control of Mercia (918). >> Alfred; Anglo-Saxons; Danelaw; Wessex

Edward the Martyr, St (c.963–78) King of England (975–8), son of Edgar. He was murdered at Corfe, Dorset, by supporters of his stepmother, Elfrida, and canonized in 1001. Feast day 18 March. >> Edgar

Edwardes, Sir Michael (Owen) (1930–) British business executive, born in South Africa. After moving to Britain in 1966, he developed a reputation for rescuing ailing companies, and in 1977 was challenged to rescue British Leyland from commercial collapse, which he succeeded in doing over the next five years.

Edwards, Blake, originally **William Blake McEdwards** (1922–) Director and writer born in Tulsa, OK. A former actor and radio scriptwriter, he made his film directorial debut in 1955 with *Bring Your Smile Along*. He is best known for *Breakfast at Tiffanys* (1961), and his series of *Pink Panther* films (1964–78) starring Peter Sellers. Other films include *Operation Petticoat* (1959), *S.O.B.* (1981), and *Switch* (1991).

Edwards, Jonathan (1703–58) Calvinist theologian and metaphysician, born in East Windsor, CT. His works, which include *Freedom of the Will* (1754), led to the religious revival known as the 'Great Awakening'. >> Calvinism; Great Awakening

Edwin, St (584–633) King of Northumbria (616–33), brought up in North Wales. Under him, Northumbria became united, and he obtained the overlordship of all England, save Kent. He was converted to Christianity, and baptized with his nobles in 627. Feast day 12 October. >> Anglo-Saxons; Christianity

EEC >> **European Economic Community**

EEG >> **electroencephalography**

eel Any of numerous marine and freshwater fishes with an elongate cylindrical body form; median fins continuous, pelvics absent, and pectorals present or absent; adults live in fresh water, returning to sea to spawn; common European eel (*Anguilla anguilla*. Family: Anguillidae) an important food fish.

eelpout Slender-bodied fish (*Zoarces viviparous*) with broad head, long dorsal and anal fins, well-developed pectorals, abundant in European coastal waters; length up to 50 cm/20 in. (Family: Zoarcidae.)

eelworm >> **nematode**

Efate [efatee], Fr **Vaté**, Eng **Sandwich Island** 17°40S 168°23E; pop (1995e) 35 600; area 985 sq km/380 sq mi. Volcanic island, Vanuatu, SW Pacific; length, 42 km/26 mi; width, 23 km/14 mi; capital, Vila. >> Vanuatu

EFTA >> **European Free Trade Association**

egalitarianism A political philosophy which places a high value on equality among members of society, and advocates the removal of barriers to it. Egalitarianism was one of the tenets of the French Revolution, and is associated with radical and socialist politics. >> radicalism; socialism

Egbert, in Anglo-Saxon **Ecgberht** or **Ecgbryht** (?–839) King of Wessex (from 802). His successes gave him mastery over S England from Kent to Land's End, and established Wessex as the strongest Anglo-Saxon kingdom. >> Anglo-Saxons; Wessex

egg The mature female reproductive cell (*ovum*) in animals and plants; also the fertilized ovum in egg-laying animals, such as birds and insects, after it has been laid. This type of egg is covered by egg membranes, including the hard shell, which prevent it from drying out or being damaged. The eggs produced by domestic poultry (especially hens) are widely used as food. The yolk is rich in cholesterol, which has led some people for health reasons to restrict their egg intake. In 1987 an increase in food-poisoning cases due to *Salmonella* bacteria led to advice that eggs should be thoroughly cooked before being eaten. >> cholesterol; hen; reproduction; salmonella

egg-plant >> **aubergine**

eggs and bacon >> **bird's-foot trefoil**

eglantine A species of rose (*Rosa eglanteria*) with aromatic, sweet-smelling foliage; also called **sweet briar**. (Family: Rosaceae.) >> rose

Egmont, Mount, Maori **Taranaki** 39°18S 174°05E. Symmetrical volcanic peak, W North Island, New Zealand, S of New Plymouth; height, 2518 m/8261 ft. >> New Zealand ℹ

egret The name used for a number of heron species. It is not applied consistently; some species are called *egret* by some observers, and *heron* by others. >> heron

Egypt, official name **Arab Republic of Egypt**, Arabic **Jumhuriyah Misr Al-Arabiya** pop (1995e) 60 284 000; area 1 001 449 sq km/386 559 sq mi. NE African republic; capital, Cairo; timezone GMT +2; population mainly of E Hamitic origin (90%); religion, mainly Sunni Muslim, minority largely Coptic Christian; official language, Arabic; unit of currency, the gold Egyptian pound; R Nile flows N from Sudan, dammed S of Aswan, creating L Nasser; huge delta N of Cairo, 250 km/150 mi across and 160 km/100 mi N–S; narrow Eastern Desert, sparsely inhabited, between Nile and Red Sea; broad Western Desert, covering over two-thirds of the country; Sinai Peninsula (S), desert region with mountains rising to 2637 m/8651 ft at Gebel Katherîna, Egypt's highest point; 90% of population lives on Nile floodplain (c.3% of country's area); mainly desert climate, except for 80 km/50 mi-wide Mediterranean coastal fringe; very hot on coast; Neolithic cultures on R Nile from c.6000 BC; Pharaoh dynasties from c.3100 BC; Egyptian power greatest during the New Kingdom period, 1567–1085 BC; became Persian province, 6th-c BC; conquered by Alexander the Great, 4th-c BC; Ptolemaic Pharaohs ruled Egypt until 30 BC; conquered by Arabs, AD 672; Suez Canal constructed, 1869; revolt in 1879 put down by British, 1882; British protectorate, 1914; declared independent, 1922; King Farouk deposed by Nasser, 1952; Egypt declared a republic, 1953; war with Israel in 1967 resulted in loss of Sinai Peninsula; Yom Kippur War against Israel, 1973; Camp David peace conference with Israel, 1978; Israel returned disputed Taba Strip, 1989; participated in Gulf War with US-led coalition, 1991; ongoing violence from Islamic fundamentalist movements, since 1992; governed by a People's Assembly, president, prime minister, and Council; agriculture on floodplain of R Nile accounts for about a third of national income; building of Aswan High Dam extended irrigated cultivation; a major tourist area. >> Arab–Israeli Wars; Aswan; Cairo; Farouk I; Nasser; pharaoh; pyramid; Sadat; Suez Canal; RR1007 political leaders

Egyptian An extinct Afro-Asiatic language, which survives in inscriptions and papyrus manuscripts. In the 2nd-c AD, it evolved into **Coptic**, which is still used as a language of devotion by the Monophysite Christians in Egypt. >> Afro-Asiatic languages; Coptic Church; hieroglyphics ℹ

Egyptian cobra >> **asp**

Egyptian mongoose >> **ichneumon** (mammal)

Ehrenburg, Ilya Grigoryevich [**air**enberg] (1891–1967) Writer, born in Kiev, Ukraine. His novels include *Padeniye Parizha* (1941, The Fall of Paris) and *Burya* (1948, The Storm), both of which won Stalin Prizes.

Ehrlich, Paul [**air**leekh] (1854–1915) Bacteriologist, born in Strzelin, Poland. He was a pioneer in haematology, immunology, and chemotherapy, discovering a cure for syphilis. He shared the Nobel Prize for Physiology or Medicine in 1908. >> haematology; immunology

Eichmann, (Karl) Adolf [**iykh**man] (1906–62) Nazi war criminal, born in Solingen, Germany. He became a member of the SS in 1932, and organizer of anti-Semitic activities. Captured by US forces in 1945, he escaped from prison and in 1950 reached Argentina. He was traced by Israeli agents, taken to Israel in 1960, condemned, and executed. >> Nazi Party

Eid-al-Adha; Eid-al-Fitr >> **Id-al-Adha; Id-al-Fitr**

eider [**iy**der] Any of four species of sea duck native to the northern N hemisphere; also known as **eider duck**. The female lines her nest with the soft downy feathers from her breast; these are collected commercially as **eiderdown**. (Subfamily: Anatinae. Tribe: Somateriini.) >> duck

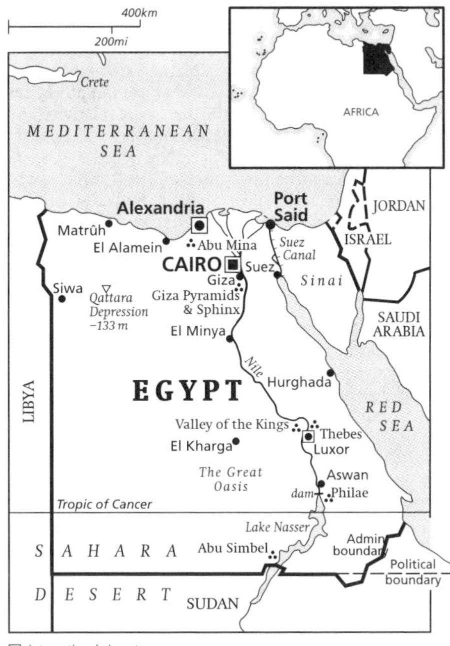

eidophor [**iy**dofaw(r)] A large-screen projection television system in which a scanning electron beam modulated by the video signal distorts the surface of an oil layer in a vacuum tube to refract the beam of light from a xenon lamp. Colour requires a triple-tube unit with the light divided by filters and recombined in projection. >> projection television

Eiffel, (Alexandre) Gustave [efel] (1832–1923) Engineer, born in Dijon, France. Apart from his most famous project, the *Eiffel Tower*, he also designed the steel framework of the Statue of Liberty, NY. >> Eiffel Tower

Eiffel Tower [**iy**fl] A famous city landmark in Paris, designed by Gustave Eiffel and erected (1887–9) in the Champs-de-Mars for the Paris Exhibition of 1889. At 300 m/984 ft high, it was the tallest building in the world until 1930. >> Eiffel, Gustave; Paris

Eiger [**iy**ger] 46°34N 8°01E. Mountain peak with three ridges in the Bernese Alps, SC Switzerland; height, 3970 m/13 025 ft; first ascent by Barrington in 1858; N face first climbed in 1938. >> Alps

Eigg [eg] Island in Highland, W Scotland; S of Skye, 11 km/7 mi from mainland (E); area 67 sq km/26 sq mi; rises to 397 m/1302 ft. >> Highland; Scotland [i]

Eight, the >> **Ashcan School**

Eightfold Path The fourth of Buddha's Four Noble Truths, prescribing the way to enlightenment. The Path involves right understanding, right aspiration, right speech, right conduct, right means of livelihood, right endeavour, right mindfulness, and right contemplation. >> Buddha; Buddhism; Four Noble Truths

Eijkman, Christiaan [**iyk**man] (1858–1930) Physician, born in Nijkerk, The Netherlands, the first to propose the concept of essential food factors, later called vitamins. He shared the Nobel Prize for Physiology or Medicine in 1929. >> vitamins [i]

Eilat or **Elat** [ay**lat**] 29°33N 34°57E, pop (1995e) 31 500. Seaport in S Israel, founded in 1949; airfield; terminus of oil pipeline from Ashkelon. >> Israel [i]

Eindhoven [**iynt**hohvn] 51°26N 5°30E, pop (1995e) 198 000. Modern industrial city in S Netherlands; airport; railway; technical university (1956); Centre of Micro-Electronics. >> Netherlands, The [i]

Einstein, Albert (1879–1955) Mathematical physicist, born in Ulm, Germany. He became world famous by his special (1905) and general (1916) theories of relativity, and was awarded the Nobel Prize for Physics in 1921. After Hitler's rise to power, he left Germany, became a US citizen and professor at the Institute of Advanced Study, Princeton, USA, and spent the remainder of his life attempting by means of his unified field theory (1950) to establish a merger between quantum theory and his general theory of relativity. He was also a champion of pacifism and liberalism. >> general relativity; mass–energy relation; Planck; special relativity [i]

Einthoven, Willem [**aynt**hohfn] (1860–1927) Dutch physiologist, born in Semarang, Indonesia. He invented the string galvanometer for measuring the elecrical rhythms of the heart (1903), introduced the term 'electrocardiogram', and was awarded the Nobel Prize for Physiology or Medicine in 1924. >> electrocardiography

Eisenhower, Dwight D(avid) [**iy**znhower], nickname **Ike** (1890–1969) US general and 34th president (1953–61), born in Denison, TX. In 1942 he commanded Allied forces for the amphibious descent on French N Africa. His talent for smooth co-ordination of the Allied staff led to his selection as Supreme Commander for the 1944 cross-channel invasion of the continental mainland. In 1952 the popularity which he had gained in Europe swept him to victory in the presidential elections, standing as a Republican, and he was re-elected in 1956. During his presidency the US government was preoccupied with foreign policy, and pursued a campaign against Communism, but was also actively involved in the civil rights movement. >> Republican Party; World War 2

Eisenstein, Sergey (Mikhaylovich) [**iy**znstiyn] (1898–1948) Film director, born in Riga, Latvia, a major influence on the development of the cinema. His films include *Potemkin* (1925), *Alexander Nevski* (1938), and *Ivan the Terrible* (1945–7).

eisteddfod [iy**stethv**od] A Welsh gathering of 12th-c origin for competitions in music and literature. The annual National Eisteddfod is held in August (entirely in Welsh) alternately in N and S Wales. >> bard; Gorsedd; Mod; Oireachtas

Ekaterinburg >> **Yekaterinburg**

El Alamein, Battle of (23 Oct–4 Nov 1942) A World War 2 battle, named after a village on Egypt's Mediterranean coast. It ended in the victory of the British Eighth Army commanded by Montgomery over Rommel's Afrika Korps.

Elam [**ee**lam] The name given in antiquity to what is now SW Iran. Its main city was Susa, and at its zenith in the 13th-c BC it ruled an empire stretching from Babylonia in the W to Persepolis in the E. >> Babylonia; Persepolis; Susa

eland [**ee**land] An African spiral-horned antelope; cattle-like, with narrow face and straight horns; the largest antelope (shoulder height, up to 1·8 m/6 ft); easily tamed; two species: the **common** (or **Cape**) **eland** (*Taurotragus oryx*) and the **giant** (or **derby**) **eland** (*Taurotragus derbianus*). >> antelope; cattle

Elara [**ee**lara] The seventh natural satellite of Jupiter, discovered in 1905; distance from the planet 11 740 000 km/ 7 295 000 mi; diameter 80 km/50 mi. >> Jupiter (astronomy); RR964

elasticity In solids, the property that a stressed material will return to its original size and shape when the stress is removed. It usually corresponds to a direct proportionality between stress and strain. >> strain; stress (physics); Young's modulus

elastic rebound theory >> **isostasy**

elastomers [ee**las**tomerz] Materials, usually synthetic, having elastic properties (ie capable of recovery from severe deformation). Examples include natural rubber and polyisoprene. >> isoprene [i]; rubber

Elat >> **Eilat**

E layer >> **Heaviside layer**

Elba, Gr **Aithalia**, Lat **Ilva** pop (1995e) 11 000; area 223 sq km/ 86 sq mi. Italian island in the Ligurian Sea, between the N Italian coast and Corsica; length 27 km/17 mi; width 18·5 km/11½ mi; chief town, Portoferraio; Napoleon lived here after his abdication (1814–15). >> Italy [i]; Napoleon I

Elbe, River [**el**buh], Czech **Labe**, ancient **Albis** River in the Czech Republic and Germany, flowing N to enter the North Sea at Cuxhaven, Germany; length 1158 km/720 mi; navigable to beyond the Czech border.

Elbert, Mount 39°05N 106°27W. Mountain in C Colorado, USA; the highest peak in the Rocky Mts (4399 m/14 432 ft). >> Colorado; Rocky Mountains

elbow The region of the upper limb between the arm and forearm; specifically, the joint between the humerus and the radius/ulna. Banging the medial side of the elbow (the 'funny bone') against a solid object may cause pain and a tingling sensation over the hand; when this happens, the ulnar nerve has been compressed between the object and the humerus. >> radius; tennis elbow; ulna

Elbrus, Mount [**el**bruhs] 43°21N 42°29E. Highest peak of the Caucasus range, S European Russia; height 5642 m/18 510 ft; highest peak in Europe. >> Caucasus Mountains

El Cid >> **Cid, El**

elder (botany) A deciduous shrub (*Sambucus nigra*), growing to 10 m/30 ft, very widespread; bark furrowed, corky; flowers creamy, in large, flat-topped clusters; berries purplish-black. The flowers and berries are used in wines and preserves, but all other parts of the plant are poisonous. (Family: Caprifoliaceae.)

elder (religion) One who by reason of age or distinction is entrusted with shared authority and leadership in a community. **1** In the ancient Biblical world, the elders of Israel exercised both religious and civil influence from the tribal period onwards; and city elders were active at a local level. In the New Testament, elders were church officials with a collective authority for general oversight of a congregation. >> Judaism **2** In Reformed Churches, an officer ordained to 'rule' along with the minister (a 'teaching' elder). Elders exercise discipline, and oversee the life of a congregation and its individual members. >> Presbyterianism; Reformed Churches

El Dorado [el do**rah**doh] Literally, 'the gilded one'; a powerful early colonial Spanish-American legend of a ruler coated in gold, believed to exist in New Granada (now Colombia); by extension, a land of fabulous wealth. >> Incas; New Granada

Eleanor of Aquitaine (c.1122–1204) Queen consort of Louis VII of France (1137–52) and of the future Henry II of England (1154–89). She was imprisoned (1174–89) for supporting the rebellion of her sons, two of whom became kings as Richard I (in 1189) and John (in 1199). >> Henry II (of England)

Eleanor of Castile [ka**steel**] (1246–90) Queen consort of Edward I of England (1254–90). She accompanied Edward to the Crusades, and is said to have saved his life by sucking the poison from a wound. The 'Eleanor Crosses' at Northampton, Geddington, and Waltham Cross are survivors of the 12 erected by Edward at the halting places of her cortège. >> Crusades ℹ; Edward I

Eleatics [eli**at**iks] A group of presocratic Greek philosophers in the 5th-c BC – Parmenides, Melissus, and Zeno – from Elea, Italy, who argued that reality is unbegotten, imperishable, atemporal, indivisible, motionless, and utterly changeless. The arguments profoundly influenced subsequent Greek philosophy. >> Parmenides; Zeno of Elea

electoral college A body made up of people who are responsible for electing a person to some office. These people can hold a particular office themselves (as in the case of the College of Cardinals who elect the Pope) or be elected from a wider electorate. The most famous college is the one that elects the president of the USA.

Electra [**elek**tra] In Greek tragedies, but not in Homer, the daughter of Agamemnon and Clytemnestra, who assisted her brother Orestes when he arrived in Argos to avenge his father, and who later married his friend Pylades. >> Agamemnon; Clytemnestra; Oedipus complex; Orestes

electrical conduction The transport of electrical charge through some substance. Only metals conduct electricity well; conduction is by means of the free electrons in the electron gas characteristic of metal structure. Ionic and covalently bound solids are insulators; but ionic solids such as salt (sodium chloride) conduct when dissolved in water, as the electrically charged ions become free to move. >> electrolysis ℹ; electron; photoconductivity; resistivity; semiconductor; superconductivity

electrical engineering A branch of engineering which studies the practical applications of electricity and electronics. It deals with the production, distribution, control, and use of electricity in all its forms, as in radio, radar, lighting, motors, power generators, and transmission systems. **Electronic engineering** developed as a subdivision of electrical engineering, and is now primarily concerned with automation, missile control systems, satellites, spacecraft, and communication systems. >> electricity; electronics; engineering; technology

electrical power The rate of transfer of energy in electrical circuits; symbol *P*, units W (watt). An electric light of power 60 W running for 1 hour consumes as much energy as a 30 W light running for 2 hours. >> electricity; energy; power

electric-arc furnace An electric furnace used particularly in steel making, where a very high temperature is generated in the 'arc' or discharge between two electrodes, the current passing through material evaporated from the electrodes. The original process was devised in 1870 by Siemens. >> Siemens; steel

electric car A motor car designed to be propelled by an electric motor. Although electric traction has been used extensively in delivery vehicles such as milk floats (UK) and in golf carts (USA), it has not been possible for the electric car to compete with the internal-combustion-engined car because of the size and weight of batteries needed. >> car ℹ; internal combustion engine

electric charge >> **charge**

electric conductance >> **resistance**

electric dipole moment Symbol *p*, units C.m (coulomb.metre), a vector quantity; for charges $+q$ and $-q$ separated by distance l (a *dipole*), the electric dipole moment is $p = ql$. >> moment ℹ; vector (mathematics)

electric eel Large freshwater fish (*Electrophorus electricus*) found in shallow streams of the Orinoco and Amazon basins; body cylindrical at front, length up to 2·4 m/8 ft; long anal fin; produces powerful electric shocks. (Family: Electrophoridae.)

electric field The region of electric influence surrounding positive or negative electric charges; symbol *E*, units V/m (volts per metre); a vector quantity. >> electricity; Gauss's law; vector (mathematics)

electric grid In the UK, the system of distributing electricity, across the country and internationally, using a network of cables to provide supplies matching peak and lesser demands with maximum economy. The largest pylons carry the primary supplies at 132 000 volts; smaller ones carry secondary supplies at 66 000 and 33 000 volts. >> current (electricity); electricity

electricity Phenomena associated with electrical charges and currents, and the study of such phenomena. Between collections of positive and negative charges there exists a potential difference. If a conducting path exists between the two charge groups, charges will flow from one to the other, constituting an electric current. Electric charge which builds up on an insulator and is thus unable to flow is termed **static electricity**. >> current (electricity); resistance

electric ray Any of a family of sluggish bottom-living marine rays, widespread in tropical to temperate seas; body disc rounded, skin smooth, tail robust; well-developed electric organs produce strong shocks to stun prey; also called **torpedo rays**. (Family: Torpedinidae.) >> ray

electric resistance >> **resistance**

electrocardiography The investigation of the electrical activity of the heart. The electric voltages produced by heartbeats can be recorded from the surface of the skin in the form of an electrocardiogram (**ECG**). Electrodes are attached to the skin of the limbs and chest, and the voltages between various pairs of electrodes are recorded. >> electricity; heart ℹ

electrochemistry The study of chemical change in a solution, resulting from the uptake of electrons from an external circuit or their supply to a circuit. Storage batteries (*accumulators*) illustrate this process, as they charge and discharge respectively. >> chemistry; electrolysis [i]

electroconvulsive therapy (ECT) A highly successful treatment for patients with severe psychiatric disorders, in which an electric current is passed through the brain of an anaesthetized patient. The technique is often used in depression and schizophrenia. >> depression (psychiatry); schizophrenia; shock therapy

electrocution Death from contact with high-voltage electric current. Electric shock induces spasm of the skeletal muscles and rapid irregular contractions of the ventricles of the heart. Electrocution is used as a method of capital punishment in some countries (eg in some US states). >> burn; heart [i]

electrodynamics The study of the motion of electric charges caused by electric and magnetic fields. >> dynamics; electrostatics; quantum electrodynamics

electroencephalography [electrohensefa**log**rafee] The investigation of the electrical activity of the brain, using electrodes applied to the scalp, and usually recorded as a tracing on paper (an electroencephalogram, or **EEG**). The EEG changes with the mental activity of the subject, and characteristic patterns of electrical activity (eg for sleep, coma, epileptic seizure) can be recognized. The *alpha rhythm* (c.10 Hz) appears with relaxation and eye closure. The *delta rhythm* (1–4 Hz) appears in deep sleep. >> brain [i]; electricity; sleep

electrolysis The splitting of a compound into simpler forms by the input of electrical energy. >> electricity

electrolyte A system, usually a solution, in which electrochemical reactions occur. It must be sufficiently conducting to allow current to pass. >> battery (electricity); electrochemistry; solution

electromagnet >> **magnet**

electromagnetic radiation Oscillating electric and magnetic fields which propagate together through empty space as a radiated wave; velocity *c*, the velocity of light. They include radio waves, light, and X-rays. >> electromagnetism; gamma rays; infrared radiation; light; microwaves; radiometry; radio waves; ultraviolet radiation; wave motion [i]; X-rays

electromagnetism Phenomena involving both electric and magnetic fields, and the study of such phenomena. The first indication of a link between electricity and magnetism was shown by Hans Christian Oersted, who demonstrated that an electrical current caused the deflection of a compass needle (1819). A unified theory of electromagnetism was first proposed by James Clerk Maxwell. >> electromagnetic radiation [i]; magnetic field [i]; Maxwell, James Clerk; Oersted

electromotive force The work done by some source in separating electrical charges to produce a potential difference capable of driving current round a circuit; often abbreviated **emf**. The unit of emf is the volt. >> electricity

electron A fundamental particle, denoted e^-, where the minus sign indicates that the charge is negative; charge of $-1{\cdot}602 \times 10^{-19}$C; mass $9{\cdot}110 \times 10^{-31}$ kg or 0·511 MeV, approximately 1/1836 that of the proton; spin $\frac{1}{2}$ fermion; stable against decay; no known size, assumed point-like; no known substructure; a carrier of negative charge in matter, including electrical currents in conductors. Electrons together with the positively charged nucleus form atoms. They were discovered by British physicist J J Thomson in 1897. >> electron gun / microscope [i]; fundamental particles; Thomson, J J

electron gun A device for producing electron beams. A heated cathode produces electrons by thermionic emission. It is an essential component of television tubes, electron microscopes, and cathode ray tubes. >> cathode; electron; electron microscope [i]; thermionics

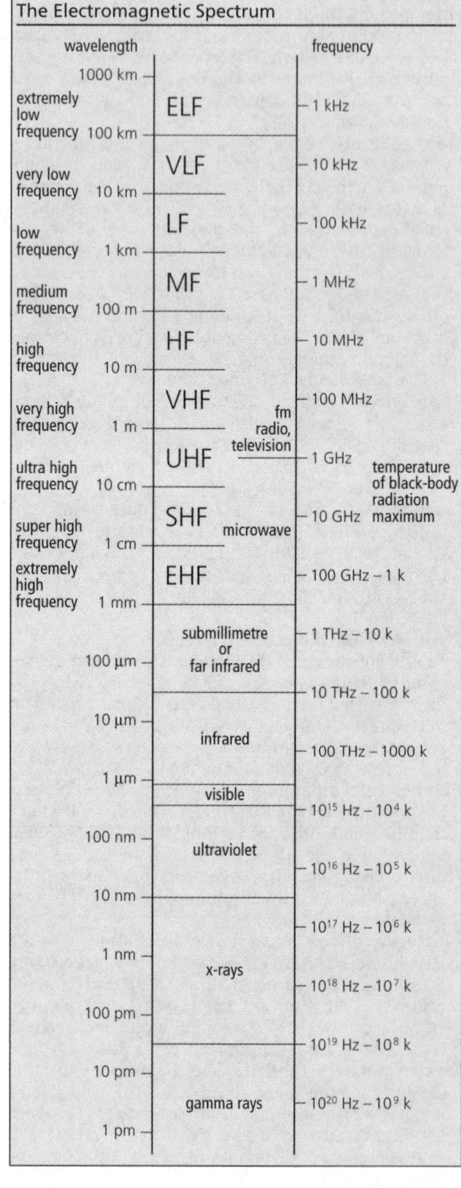

electronic data interchange (EDI) A set of standards which have been established between different computer users to enable data created by one to be sent to another in an understandable form. For example, department stores use EDI to transmit orders to suppliers.

electronic games Games programmed and controlled by a small microprocessor. Most electronic games are connected to a visual display unit and are known as **video games**. Multi-coloured visual effects and varying sounds are incorporated. The first video game appeared in the USA in the early 1970s; it was called *Pong*, and was a simple form of table tennis. >> visual display unit

electronic mail or **e-mail** The use of computer systems to transfer messages between users. Messages are usually stored centrally until acknowledged by the recipient.

electronic music Music in which the sound is generated by electronic instruments (especially synthesizers), processed by means of tape recorders heard through loudspeakers. >> Berio; Boulez; Stockhausen; electrophone; musique concrète; synthesizer

electronic photography Exposure of a single picture in a special video camera (a *still video camera*, or *SVC*), which records the image in either an analogue or digital way on a rotating 50 mm floppy magnetic disk or a solid state memory card. This has the capacity for up to 25 individual shots, which are available for immediate display on a video screen or as a paper printout within 90 seconds. >> photography; video

electronic publishing The issuing to identified users of selected, edited, textual and illustrative material taken from an electronic database. The data may be communicated on-line to the customer's computer, or transferred to a portable medium such as magnetic tape or disk or CD-ROM disk. The term is used generally to cover all publishing except print on paper. >> database

electronics The scientific study and application of the movement of electrons. Transistors facilitated the miniaturization of electronic components, as did the silicon chip and the integrated circuit. The social impact of electronics is far-reaching, including the development of television, computerized office systems, video games, personal computers, pacemakers, and spacecraft. >> computer; electron; electronic games / mail / music / photography / publishing; integrated circuit; microelectronics; optoelectronics; silicon chip; transistor

electron microscope A microscope using a beam of electrons instead of light, and magnetic or electrostatic fields as lenses. In the **transmission electron microscope** the direct passage of the beam through the specimen produces an image on a fluorescent screen. The specimen must be very thin, but the resolution is high: c.0.2–0.5 nm. In the **scanning electron microscope**, the specimen is scanned by the beam, which produces secondary electron emission, imaged on a cathode ray screen. The specimen can be thicker, and an image of some depth produced, but resolution is limited to c.10–20 nm. >> electron; electron gun; microscope; *see illustration above*

electron volt A unit of energy common in atomic, nuclear, and particle physics; symbol eV; equals the change in energy of an electron moving through a potential difference of 1 volt; 1 eV = $1{\cdot}602 \times 10^{-19}$ J (joule, SI unit); commonly used as keV (10^3 eV), MeV (10^6 eV), and GeV (10^9 eV). >> electron; joule; physics; RR1031

electrophone Any musical instrument in which the sound is generated by mechanical or electronic oscillators (eg a synthesizer) or in which acoustically generated vibrations require electrical amplification before they can be heard (eg the electric guitar). >> electronic music; guitar; musical instruments; ondes Martenot; organ; synthesizer

electroplating The depositing of a metal on another metal by electrolysis. The object to be plated is made the cathode; the metal to be deposited is derived from the anode. The plating may be intended for decoration, or to provide resistance to corrosion. >> electrolysis; metal

electro-pollution High and low frequency electromagnetic emissions (EMF) produced by such equipment as microwave ovens, computer terminals, and high voltage cables. Exposure to the EMF field may have adverse long-term effects on health and lead to such problems as headaches, impaired concentration, and stress-induced disorders. >> electromagnetism; geopathic stress

electroscope A device for detecting the presence of an electric charge and estimating its amount. The simplest form consists of two thin gold leaves which repel each other when charged, the degree of divergence indicating the amount of the charge. >> electricity

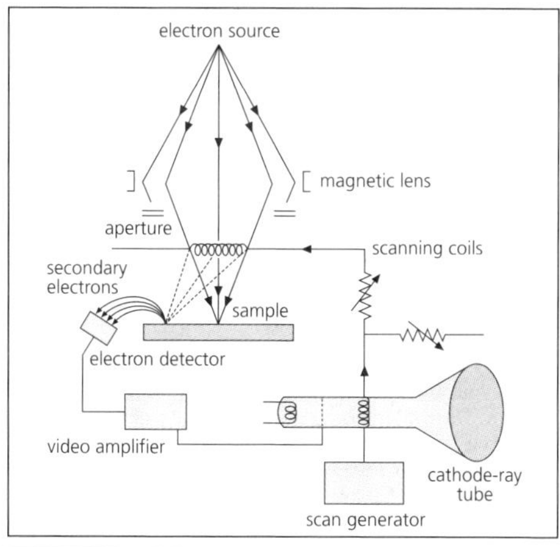

Scanning electron microscope

electrosleep >> **shock therapy**

electrostatic generator A device for producing a large electric charge, usually by the repetition of an induction process and the successive accumulation of the charge produced. Modern, very high voltage machines were initiated by the van de Graaff belt-operated generator (1929). >> electricity; van de Graaff generator

electrostatics The study of fields and potentials due to stationary electric charges. Electrostatic forces bind electrons to the nucleus in atoms. >> electricity; electrodynamics; static electricity

elegy In classical times, any poem in elegaic metre (a couplet consisting of one hexameter and one pentameter), such as those written (in Greek) by Archilochus (7th-c BC), and (in Latin) by Propertius. In modern literatures, it is a poem of mourning or lament, as in Gray's *Elegy Written in a Country Churchyard* (1751). >> metre (literature); poetry

elementary particle physics >> **particle physics**

elements >> **chemical elements**

elephant A large mammal of family Elephantidae; the only living members of order Proboscidea (many extinct forms); almost naked grey skin; massive forehead; small eyes; upper incisor teeth form 'tusks'; snout elongated as a muscular grasping 'trunk'; ears large and movable (used to radiate heat). There are two living species. The **African elephant** is the largest living land animal (height up to 3·8 m/12½ ft), with three subspecies (*Loxodonta africana*). The smaller **Asian elephant** has four subspecies (*Elephas maximus*). >> pachyderm

Elephanta Caves A group of Hindu cave-temples located on Elephanta I off the W coast of Maharashtra, India; a world heritage site. >> Hinduism; Trimurti

elephant bird An enormous bird, known from the Pleistocene and Holocene epochs; fossil remains found on Madagascar; flightless, stood up to 3 m/10 ft tall, and laid eggs more than 30 cm/1 ft long. (Family: Aepyornithidae.) >> bird [i]; Pleistocene epoch

elephantiasis [elifan**tiy**asis] A gross swelling of one or both legs, scrotum, and occasionally arms as a result of blockage of the lymphatic channels by filariasis. The condition is found only in the tropics. >> filariasis

elephant seal A huge true seal; adult male up to 6 m/20 ft long, weight 3700 kg/8150 lb; swollen pendulous snout. (Family: Phocidae, 2 species.) >> seal (marine biology)

elephant's-ear >> **begonia**

Eleusinian Mysteries [elyoo**sin**ian] The secret initiation ceremonies connected with the worship of the corn-goddess Demeter and her daughter Persephone, held annually at Eleusis near Athens in ancient times. >> mystery religions

elevator (chiefly American English) or **lift** (chiefly British English) A device which carries people or objects from one level to another in a building with several floors. The elevator car is moved through a system of cables and pulleys, which link the car to a counterweight, the power usually being generated by electricity (earlier lifting systems had used a variety of methods, such as animal, steam, and water power). The invention of the elevator fostered the development of the skyscraper in modern cities. Following the invention of a safety device by Otis in 1852, the first (steam-powered) passenger elevator was introduced in New York City in 1857. >> Otis

eleven-plus examination In the UK, a test taken by pupils towards the end of their primary education, in areas where there are selective secondary schools, to determine which school they shall attend. It declined, though did not disappear, with the spread of comprehensive schools in the 1960s and 1970s. >> comprehensive school; grammar school

Elgar, Sir Edward (1857–1934) Composer, born in Broad Heath, Hereford and Worcester. The *Enigma Variations* (1899) and the oratorio *The Dream of Gerontius* (1900) made him the leading figure of his day in English music. From 1924 he was Master of the King's Musick.

Elgin Marbles [**el**gin] Marble sculptures of the mid-5th-c BC from the Parthenon of Athens. Acquired in 1801–3 by Thomas Bruce, 7th Earl of Elgin (1766–1841), they were purchased by the government for the British Museum. In the 1980s in particular, the question of their return to Greece became a heated political issue there. >> Parthenon

El Greco >> **Greco, El**

Elijah [e**liy**ja] (9th-c BC) Hebrew prophet, whose activities are portrayed in four Bible stories (1 *Kings* 17–19, 21; 2 *Kings* 1–2). By virtue of his loyalty to God he was depicted as ascending directly into heaven. >> Kings, Book of; prophet

elint The practice of '*el*ectronic *int*elligence' gathering, in which one finds out the performance factors of hostile weapons systems by interpreting their electronic emissions. >> electronics; military intelligence

Elion, Gertrude (Belle) (1918–99) Chemist, born in New York City, USA. In 1951, working with George Hitchings (1905–98), she made and tested 6-mercaptopurine (6MP) which proved useful in cancer treatment, especially childhood leukaemia, then worked on a wide range of other drugs. She shared the Nobel Prize for Physiology or Medicine in 1988.

Eliot, George, pseudonym of **Mary Ann Evans** or **Marian Evans** (1819–80) Novelist, born at Arbury Farm, Astley, Warwickshire. She became the centre of a literary circle, one of whose members was G H Lewes, with whom she lived until his death. Her major novels were *Adam Bede* (1859), *The Mill on the Floss* (1860), *Silas Marner* (1861), *Middlemarch* (1871–2), and *Daniel Deronda* (1876).

Eliot, T(homas) S(tearns) (1888–1965) Poet, critic, and playwright, born in St Louis, MO. The enthusiastic support of Ezra Pound led to his first book of poetry, *Prufrock and Other Observations* (1917). He then published *The Waste Land* (1922) and *The Hollow Men* (1925), and edited the quarterly review, *The Criterion* from its beginning to its demise (1922–39). Later works include his major poetic achievement, *Four Quartets* (1944), and a series of plays, notably *Murder in the Cathedral* (1935). In 1948 he was awarded the Nobel Prize for Literature. >> Bloomsbury Group

Elisabethville >> **Lubumbashi**

Elisha [e**liy**sha] (second half of 9th-c BC) Hebrew prophet in succession to Elijah; his activities are portrayed in 1 *Kings* 19 and 2 *Kings* 2–9,13. He was active in Israel under several kings from Ahab to Jehoash. >> Ahab; Elijah; Kings, Books of; prophet

Elizabeth I, known as **the Virgin Queen** and later **Good Queen Bess** (1533–1603) Queen of England (1558–1603), the daughter of Henry VIII by his second wife, Anne Boleyn, born in Greenwich, London. She saw her role in Europe as a Protestant sovereign, and it is from this time that the Anglican Church was formally established. Mary, Queen of Scots, was thrown into her power (1568) and imprisoned, causing endless conspiracies among English Catholics. After the most sinister plot was discovered (1586), Elizabeth was reluctantly persuaded to execute Mary (1587), and subsequently persecuted Catholics. Philip of Spain then attacked England with his 'invincible armada' (1588), but England managed to repel the attack. A strong, cruel, and capricious woman, the 'Virgin Queen' was nevertheless popular with her subjects, as indicated by her other byname, 'Good Queen Bess'; and her reign is seen as the period when England assumed the position of a world power. >> Church of England; Mary, Queen of Scots; Spanish Armada

Elizabeth II (1926–) Queen of the United Kingdom (1952–) and head of the Commonwealth, born in London, the daughter of George VI. Formerly **Princess Elizabeth Alexandra Mary**, she was proclaimed queen on 6 February 1952, and crowned on 2 June 1953. Her husband was created Duke of Edinburgh on the eve of their wedding (20 Nov 1947), and styled Prince Philip in 1957. They have three sons, **Charles Philip Arthur George** (14 Nov 1948), **Andrew Albert Christian Edward** (19 Feb 1960), and **Edward Anthony Richard Louis** (10 Mar 1964), and a daughter, **Anne Elizabeth Alice Louise** (15 Aug 1950). >> Andrew, Duke of York; Anne, Princess; Charles, Prince; Edinburgh, Duke of; Edward, Prince

Elizabeth (Queen Mother), originally **Lady Elizabeth Bowes-Lyon** >> **George VI**

Elizabethan Style A form of early English Renaissance architecture of the period 1558–1603, characterized by symmetrical facades combined with Netherland decoration and over-sized windows. The name derives from Queen Elizabeth I of that period. A good example is Longleat, UK (c.1568 onwards). >> Elizabeth I; Jacobean Style

Elizabeth Petrovna [pe**trov**na] (1709–62) Empress (tsaritsa) of Russia (1741–62), the daughter of Peter the Great and Catherine I, born near Moscow. A war with Sweden was brought to a successful conclusion, and she took part in the War of the Austrian Succession and in the Seven Years' War. >> Austrian Succession, War of the; Seven Years' War

elk The largest of the true deer (*Alces alces*) (shoulder height, 2·4 m/8 ft); widespread in temperate N hemisphere; usually solitary; long snout; throat with loose flap of skin; antlers broad; also known in North America as **moose**. >> antlers [i]; bull (zoology); deer; elkhound; red deer

elkhound A spitz breed of dog, used in Scandinavia (especially Norway) to hunt elk; medium-sized, broad, solid body with thick grey coat; also known as **Norwegian elkhound** or **elk**. >> elk; spitz

Ellesmere Island [**el**ezmeer] Arctic island in Northwest Territories, Canada; area 196 236 sq km/75 747 sq mi; barren and mountainous; several small settlements. >> Northwest Territories

Ellice Islands >> **Tuvalu**

Ellington, Duke, popular name of **Edward Kennedy Ellington** (1899–1974) Composer, arranger, bandleader, and pianist, born in Washington, DC. He developed a unique sound for his musicians by blending instruments ingeniously into startling harmonies, as in 'Creole Love Call' (1927) and 'Mood Indigo' (1930). His creative peak is generally said to be 1939–42, with such recordings as 'Cotton Tail' and 'Take the A Train'. Later works included suites such as 'Such Sweet Thunder' (1957) and 'Gutelas Suite' (1971), film scores, ballets, and a series of 'sacred concerts' (1968–74) performed in cathedrals around the world. He led his band until a couple of months before his death from cancer, when it was taken over by his son, **Mercer Ellington** (1919–96). >> jazz

Elliott, Herb, popular name of **Herbert James Elliott** (1938–) Athlete, born in Perth, Western Australia. Winner of the gold medal in the 1500 m at the 1960 Olympics in Rome, his time of 3 min 35·6 s for that event was unbeaten for seven years. He was noted for the rigour and severity of his training schedule.

ellipse In mathematics, the locus of a point which moves so that the sum of its distances from two fixed points (or *foci*) is constant. The Cartesian equation of an ellipse can be put in the form $x^2/a^2 + y^2/b^2 = 1$. The planets move around the Sun in ellipses, and the shape is much used in art and architecture. >> conic sections ℹ; hyperbola

elliptic geometry >> **geometries, non-Euclidean**

Ellis, Alice Thomas, originally **Anna Margaret Haycraft**, née **Lindholm** (1932–) Novelist, born in Liverpool, Merseyside, NW England, UK. She studied at the Liverpool College of Art. A writer of cookery books under her original name, it was *The Sin Eater* (1977), which established her reputation as a novelist. *The 27th Kingdom* (1982) is often considered her most successful novel. Other books include *Pillars of Gold* (1992), *Cat Among the Pigeons* (1994), *Fairy Tale* (1996), and an autobiography, *A Welsh Childhood* (1990).

Ellis, (Henry) Havelock (1859–1939) Physician and writer on sex, born in Croydon, Greater London. The seven-volume *Studies in the Psychology of Sex* (1897–1928), the first detached treatment of the subject, was highly controversial at the time.

Ellis Island A small island (27.5 acres) in New York Bay, USA; named after New Jersey merchant Samuel Ellis, who owned it in the 18th-c. It served as the main immigration centre to the USA from 1892 to 1943, with c.2000 immigrants a day arriving there in the peak years of the early 20th-c. It became part of the Statue of Liberty National Monument in 1965. Sovereignty of the island changed from New York to New Jersey, following a US Supreme Court decision in 1998. >> New York City; Statue of Liberty

Ellison, Ralph (Waldo) (1914–94) Writer, born in Oklahoma City, OK. His major work was the novel, *Invisible Man* (1952), a semi-autobiographical account of a young black intellectual's search for identity. His short story *Flying Home*, was published posthumously in 1996.

elm A deciduous N temperate tree; leaves ovoid, doubly toothed, asymmetric at base; flowers tiny, appearing before leaves; seed oval, with broad papery wing. In recent years the European and N American elm populations have been largely destroyed by **Dutch elm disease**, first identified in Holland in 1967. (Genus: *Ulmus*, 45 species. Family: Ulmaceae.) >> Dutch elm disease; tree ℹ

Elmslie, George Grant (1871-1952) Scottish architect and designer. His most notable works were designed during his partnership with William Gray Purcell (1912–20), such as the Edison Building, Chicago (1912), and the Woodbury County Courthouse, Sioux City, Iowa (1915–17). He also designed furniture, metalwork, and stained glass.

El Niño [**neen**yoh] An anomalous seasonal ocean current along the coast of Peru. Under normal conditions, upwelling along the coast brings up nutrient-enriched deeper waters which result in high biological productivity. During El Niño, wind patterns along the Peruvian coast change, the upwelling is interrupted, and there is massive mortality of marine organisms. The phenomenon usually occurs around Christmas, hence the name, which is Spanish for 'the Child'. Once thought to be produced by changes in local wind conditions affecting the ocean, it is now known to be part of a much larger phenomenon related to changes in atmospheric pressure in the S Pacific, called the *southern oscillation*. The phenomenon may recur every 2–10 years, and has been blamed for such wide-ranging effects as severe storm damage along the W coast of the Americas, more frequent tropical cyclones, and severe winters in Europe and North America. Its effects were proving to be especially noticeable during 1997, with some locations experiencing dramatic climatic change (eg a major increase of rainfall on Christmas I). There is a complementary effect, known as **La Niña**, a cooling of the Pacific water, in intervening years. >> current (oceanography); Peru ℹ

elocution The study and practice of excellence in the manner and style of vocal delivery, dating from classical Greek and Roman times. Grammar, choice of vocabulary, and style are all taken into account to achieve the greatest effect in using the voice. >> oratory; rhetoric

Elohim [eloh**heem**] (Heb 'gods') A divine name for the God of Israel, the plural form here being purged of its polytheistic meaning, and used as a plural of majesty. >> God; Yahweh

El Paso [el **pa**soh] 31°45N 106°29W, pop (1995e) 568 000. City in W Texas, USA; port on the Rio Grande; founded, 1827; part transferred to Mexico in 1963; airfield; railway; university (1913). >> Texas

El Salvador, official name **Republic of El Salvador**, Span **República de El Salvador** pop (1995e) 5 811 000; area 21 476 sq km/8290 sq mi. Smallest of the Central American republics; capital, San Salvador; timezone, GMT −6; major ethnic group mestizo, (89%); chief religion, Roman Catholicism; official language, Spanish;

unit of currency, the colón of 100 centavos; two volcanic ranges run E–W; narrow coastal belt (S) rises to mountains (N), highest point, Santa Ana (2381 m/7812 ft); many volcanic lakes; earthquakes common; climate varies greatly with altitude; hot tropical on coastal lowlands; originally part of the Aztec kingdom; conquest by Spanish, 1526; independence from Spain, 1821; member of the Central American Federation until its dissolution in 1839; independent republic, 1841; war with Honduras, 1965, 1969; considerable political unrest in 1970s and 80s, with guerrilla activity directed against the US-supported government; peace plan agreed, 1991; governed by a president and National Assembly; economy largely based on agriculture; main crops coffee and cotton; sugar, maize, balsam (world's main source). >> Aztecs; San Salvador; RR1007 political leaders

Elsinore [**el**sinaw(r)], Danish **Helsingør** 56°03N 12°38E, pop (1995e) 57 100. Seaport on The Sound, NE Zealand, Denmark, opposite Helsingborg, Sweden; railway; site of Kronborg Castle, famous as the scene of Shakespeare's *Hamlet*. >> Denmark 🛈

Eluard, Paul [elwah(r)], pseudonym of **Eugène Grindal** (1895–1952) Poet, born in Saint-Denis, France. He was one of the founders of the Surrealist movement in literature. His first collection of poetry was *Capitale de la douleur* (1926, Capital of Sorrow). >> Surrealism

Elvström, Paul [**elv**stroem] (1928–) Yachtsman, born in Gentofte, Copenhagen. He is the only yachtsman to win four individual Olympic gold medals: in the Firefly class in 1948 and the Finn class in 1952, 1956, and 1960. >> sailing

Ely [**ee**lee] 52°24N 0°16E, pop (1995e) 10 400. Small city in E Cambridgeshire, EC England; on R Ouse; railway; 12th-c cathedral; Isle of Ely (higher ground surrounded by fens) the location of Hereward the Wake's defence against the Normans. >> Cambridgeshire; Hereward

Elyot, Sir Thomas, also spelled **Eliot** (c.1490–1546) Writer and diplomat, born in Wiltshire. His chief work, *The Boke Named the Gouernour* (1531), is the earliest English treatise on moral philosophy.

Elysée, Palais de l' [pale duh layleezay], Eng **Elysée Palace** Since 1873 the official residence of the French president, situated on the Rue du Faubourg Sainte-Honoré in Paris. It was built in 1718 for the Compte d'Evreux. >> Paris

Elysium [**eliz**ium] or **Elysian fields** In Greek and Roman mythology, the happy fields, often located on the borders of the Underworld, where the good remain after death in perfect happiness. >> Hades

ema >> **rhea**

e-mail >> **electronic mail**

Emancipation Proclamation A document issued by President Lincoln during the American Civil War, declaring the freedom of all slaves in areas then in arms against the US government. >> American Civil War; Lincoln, Abraham; slavery

Ember Days In the Christian Church, the Wednesday, Friday and Saturday of the weeks (Ember Weeks) following the first Sunday in Lent, Whitsunday, Holy Cross Day (14 Sep) and St Lucia's Day (13 Dec); formerly observed as special times of fasting and abstinence. >> Christianity

embezzlement The dishonest taking of money or other property entrusted to an employee on behalf of his or her employer. Many penal codes subsume this offence under theft. However, in Scots law it is distinguished from both theft and fraud. >> theft

embolism [**em**bolizm] An obstruction of a blood vessel by the accumulation and adhesion of any undissolved material (such as a blood clot) carried to the site in the bloodstream. It is usually identified according to the vessel involved (cerebral, coronary, pulmonary) or the undissolved material (air, fat). >> blood vessels 🛈; pulmonary embolism; stroke

embroidery The ornamentation of fabrics with decorative stitching – an art which dates from very early times (as shown in Egyptian tomb paintings), when the designs were sewn onto a base fabric by hand. It was highly developed in the Middle and Far East, and in India. In Europe, church vestments provided consistently sumptuous examples. While hand-embroidery survives as a craft, many of today's goods are embroidered using computer-controlled sewing machines, capable of reproducing complex multi-coloured patterns.

embryo [**em**brioh] In flowering plants, the young plant developed from an ovum and contained within the seed; in animals, the developing young, contained either within the egg membranes or inside the maternal body. >> embryology; fetus; plant; reproduction

embryology The study of the development of animals from the first division of the fertilized egg (*zygote*), through the differentiation and formation of the organ systems, to the ultimate hatching or birth of the young animal. >> biology; embryo; pregnancy 🛈

emerald A gem variety of beryl, coloured green by minor amounts of chromium oxide. The finest crystals are from Colombia. >> beryl; gemstones

Emerson, Ralph Waldo (1803–82) Poet and essayist, born in Boston, MA. His works include his prose rhapsody, *Nature* (1836), and many poems and essays, notably *The Conduct of Life* (1860). He was a transcendentalist in philosophy, a rationalist in religion, and a bold advocate of spiritual individualism.

emery A natural mixture of crystalline corundum with iron oxides, occurring as dark granules. Very hard, it is used as an abrasive. >> corundum

emigration >> **migration**

Emmy A series of annual awards presented by the American Academy of Television Arts and Sciences since 1949. It is the television equivalent of the Oscar. >> Oscar

Empedocles [em**ped**okleez] (c.490–c.430 BC) Greek philosopher and poet, born in Acragas, Sicily. In *On Nature* he introduced the doctrine of four everlasting elements, Earth, Water, Air, and Fire, which became central to Western thought for 2000 years through its adoption by Aristotle. >> Aristotle

emperor moth A large, broad-winged moth; wings grey or grey-brown with conspicuous eye-spots on forewings and hindwings. (Order: Lepidoptera. Family: Saturniidae.) >> moth

emperor penguin The largest of penguins (*Aptenodytes forsteri*), 1·2 m/4 ft tall; inhabits seas around Antarctica; single egg incubated on the male's feet for 64 days during bitter polar blizzards. >> penguin

emphysema [emfi**see**ma] A disorder of the lungs in which there is destruction of the elastic fibres that normally cause lung tissue to recoil during expiration. The condition is common in heavy cigarette-smokers in whom inhaled cigarette products activate enzymes that digest the elastic tissue. >> bronchi; lungs

Empire Day >> **Commonwealth Day**

Empire State Building An office block in Manhattan, New York City, built 1930–1. At 449 m/1472 ft high (including a 68 m/222 ft high television mast added in 1951) it was the tallest building in the world until 1970. >> New York City

Empire Style The style of decoration associated with Napoleon I's court after he became Emperor in 1804. It is massive, and heavily ornamented with classicizing motifs, particularly Egyptian sphinxes, winged lions, and caryatids. The equivalent style in Britain was **Regency**. >> classicism

empiricism A philosophical tradition which maintains that all or most significant knowledge is based on sense experience; it is usually contrasted with rationalism. Mathematical knowledge and language competence provide difficult cases for empiricism. >> Locke, John; logical positivism; rationalism (philosophy)

employers' association or **trade association** A society of companies in the same line of business, whose purpose is to discuss matters of common interest, make representations to government on industrial matters, and negotiate with trade unions. >> cartel

Empson, Sir William (1906–84) Poet and critic, born in Howden, Hull. He wrote several major critical works, notably *Seven Types of Ambiguity* (1930), and his *Collected Poems* were published in 1955.

empyema [empiy**ee**ma] An infection occurring between the two layers of the membranes which cover the lung (the *pleura*). This frequently leads to the accumulation of large amounts of infected fluid in this cavity. >> lungs

Ems, River, Dutch **Eems**, ancient **Amisia** German river, rises N of Paderborn; enters the North Sea in a 32 km/20 mi-long estuary; length 328 km/204 mi. >> Germany [i]

Ems telegram A despatch (13 Jul 1870) describing the refusal of William (Wilhelm) I of Prussia to accept French conditions over the disputed candidature to the Spanish throne. Altered and published by Bismarck, it helped achieve his aim of provoking Napoleon III of France into declaring war on Prussia. >> Bismarck; Franco-Prussian War; William I (Emperor)

emu A flightless bird native to Australia (*Dromaius novaehollandiae*); the second largest living bird (after the ostrich), 1·9 m/6¼ ft tall; runs at nearly 50 kph/30 mph; swims well; related to the cassowary. (Family: Dromaiidae.) >> cassowary

emulsifiers Chemical substances which help liquids to mix with each other, forming an emulsion. For example, oil and water, which do not normally mix, can be combined into a single phase using an emulsifier, as in margarine and mayonnaise. Emulsifying agents include algin, agar, and lecithin. >> emulsion; E-number

emulsion A suspension of one liquid in another, particularly of an oil in water. All emulsions eventually separate, 'stable' emulsions merely separating more slowly than 'unstable' ones. >> colloid; detergent

emu wren A small, brightly coloured bird native to Australia, also known as the **Australian wren** or **wren-warbler**. (Genus: *Stipiturus*, 3 species. Family: Maluridae.) >> wren

enamelling The use of brightly coloured substances similar to glass which are fired on to metalwork or ceramics as decoration. The techniques used on metalwork are champlevé, cloisonné, basse taille, and painting. Enamel decoration on ceramics is applied during a second or subsequent firing at a lower temperature on top of the main body and glaze. >> basse taille enamel; champlevé; cloisonné

Enceladus [en**sel**adus] The second natural satellite of Saturn, discovered in 1789; distance from the planet 238 000 km/148 000 mi; diameter 500 km/310 mi; orbital period 1·370 days. >> Saturn (astronomy); RR964

encephalitis [ensefa**liy**tis] A diffuse infection of the brain, caused mainly by viruses. Bacterial encephalitis is rare. The features are those of infection, plus drowsiness and a clouding of consciousness. >> brain [i]; infection; virus

encopresis >> **enuresis**

encounter group A form of group therapy in which the leader facilitates the acquisition of insight and sensitivity to others, using such techniques as bodily contact and the sharing of emotional experiences. Also known as *T*-('training') *groups*, sessions vary greatly in length and type, and can have both positive and negative effects on members. >> group therapy

encyclical, papal [en**sik**likl] Originally, a letter sent to all the churches in a particular area. The term is now restricted to official letters of instruction, usually doctrinal or pastoral in nature, issued by a pope to the whole Roman Catholic Church. >> pope; Roman Catholicism

Encyclopaedists / Encyclopedists A collective term for the distinguished editors (Diderot and d'Alembert) and contributors to the *Encyclopèdie*, a major work of social and political reference published in France (1751–76), associated with the French Enlightenment. >> Diderot; Enlightenment; Philosophes

endangered species Plant and animal species which are in danger of becoming extinct. Their classification as endangered species is made by the International Union for the Conservation of Nature and Natural Resources. The danger of extinction generally comes from habitat loss and disturbance caused by human activity, overexploitation, and in many cases pollution. >> conservation (earth sciences); Nature Reserve; wildlife refuge

Ender, Kornelia (1958–) Swimmer, born in Bitterfeld, Germany. In 1976 she became the first woman to win four gold medals (for East Germany) at one Olympic Games: the 100 m and 200 m freestyle, the 100 m butterfly, and the 4 × 100 m medley relay. >> swimming

endive An annual or biennial (*Cichorium endivia*) growing to 120 cm/4 ft, native to S Europe; flower-heads blue, in clusters of 2–5. It is widely grown as a salad plant. (Family: Compositae.)

endocrine glands [**en**dokriyn] Ductless glands, present in some invertebrates (certain molluscs, arthropods) and all vertebrates, which synthesize and secrete chemical messengers (hormones) into the blood stream, or lymph for transport to target cells. In vertebrates they collectively form a major communication system (the **endocrine system**) which with the nervous system regulates and co-ordinates body functions. Disorders of the endocrine glands are numerous, and may result in disturbances of growth and development, metabolism, and reproduction. The study of the structure, function, and disorders of the endocrine glands is **endocrinology**. >> adrenal / parathyroid / pineal / pituitary / thyroid glands; gland

endogamy and **exogamy** The broad social rules that define who are to be regarded as legitimate marriage partners in society. **Endogamy** allows marriage between members of one's own group or lineage; **exogamy** allows marriage only between members of different groups. >> marriage

endogenous opioids >> **opioid peptides**

endorphins [en**daw(r)**finz] Natural substances present throughout the body which have similar (but more controlled) effects to morphine and other narcotics. Isolated in 1975, the substances are believed to act as neurotransmitters. >> narcotics; neurotransmitter; opioid peptides

endoscopy [en**dos**kopee] The introduction of an instrument into a body aperture or duct for direct visual inspection and biopsy. It is mainly carried out today with a flexible glass fibre **endoscope**. >> biopsy; optical fibres [i]

endothelium >> **epithelium**

Endymion [en**dim**ion] In Greek mythology, a handsome shepherd of Mt Latmos, who was loved by the Moon-goddess Selene. He was also said, as King of Elis, to have founded the Olympic Games. >> Selene

energy An abstract calculable quantity associated with all physical processes and objects, whose total value is found always to be conserved; symbol E, units J (joule); one of the most important concepts in physics. It is an additive, scalar quantity, which may be transferred but never destroyed, and so provides a useful book-keeping device for the analysis of processes. It is sometimes called the capacity for doing work. The main sources of energy are fossil fuels (petroleum, coal, and natural gas), water power, and nuclear power. Solar power, wind power, and coal provide c.75% of world energy needs; natural gas c.20%; water power (hydroelectricity) c.2%; and nuclear energy c.1%. The search for new sources of energy is a continuing one, since that provided by the fossil fuels will eventually run out. >> heat; joule; kinetic energy; mass–energy relation; potential energy; power; thermodynamics; work

Enfield, Harry (1961–) British comedian, actor, and writer, known for his character-based comedy shows. *Sir Norbert Smith – a Life?* (1989) won the Silver Rose at Montreux, as did *The End of an Era* (1994). He achieved national recognition after his own BBC television series in 1991–2, following this with *Harry Enfield and Chums* (1994, 1996).

Engels, Friedrich (1820–95) Socialist philosopher, founder of 'scientific socialism', born at Barmen, Germany. He collaborated with Marx on the *Communist Manifesto* (1848). >> Marx; socialism

engine A mechanical device that transforms some of the energy of its fuel into a convenient and controllable form for use by other devices. The majority convert the motion of an oscillating piston in a cylinder to rotary motion by means of a crank linkage mechanism. The piston is made to oscillate by means of gases expanding and contracting. These gases may be created internally within the cylinder (as in **spark ignition** and **diesel engines**) or externally (as in **steam engines**). Other types of engine use the hot gases to create rotary motion direct (**gas turbine** and **Wankel engines**), while others eject their gases direct to the environment to create thrust (**jet engines**). >> alternative fuel; diesel / gas / heat / internal combustion / ion / jet / spark ignition / steam / Wankel engine; Carnot cycle; Diesel; four-stroke engine [i]; two-stroke engine; Watt

engineering The branch of technology which makes power and materials work for people. Engineers study ways of harnessing power sources, such as the use of gasoline and other fuels to power vehicles, and the conversion of water power into hydroelectricity. They also analyze and use many types of material, depending on the problem to be solved. The field as a whole was traditionally subdivided into five main branches: **civil**, **mechanical**, **mining and metallurgical**, **chemical**, and **electrical engineering**. New fields have now developed, such as aeronautical, aerospace, computer, control, marine, nuclear, and systems engineering. >> civil / control / electrical / mechanical engineering; Industrial Revolution

England, Lat **Anglia** pop (1995e) 48 903 000; area 130 357 sq km/50 318 sq mi. Largest area within the United Kingdom, forming the S part of the island of Great Britain; largely undulating lowland, rising (S) to the Mendips, Cotswolds, Chilterns, and North Downs, (N) to the N–S ridge of the Pennines, and (NW) to the Cumbria Mts; drained E by the Tyne, Tees, Humber, Ouse, and Thames Rivers and W by the Eden, Ribble, Mersey, and Severn Rivers; Lake District (NW); capital, London; linked to Europe by ferry and hovercraft, and (from 1994) by the Channel Tunnel. >> Channel Tunnel; English; English Channel / Heritage; Lake District; London; Pennines; United Kingdom [i]; RR997 counties; *see also illustration on p.287*

English A language belonging to the Germanic branch of the Indo-European family. Its unbroken literary heritage goes back to the inflecting language, Anglo-Saxon, notably in the 8th-c epic poem *Beowulf*. Standard English prose evolved from the Chancery (law-court) English of the 14th-c. Over 400 million people now speak English as a mother-tongue, and another 400 million or so use it as a second language; at least a further 500 million use it with some competence as a foreign language. English is used by over 60 countries as an official or semi-official language. It is the main world language of book and newspaper publication, of science and technology, of advertising and pop music, and of computer information storage. It is also the medium for auxiliary (restricted) languages, such as those used by international airline pilots and seafarers for intercommunication. >> Germanic languages; Old English

English Channel, Fr **La Manche**, Lat **Mare Britannicum** Arm of the Atlantic Ocean, bounded N by England and S by France; connected to North Sea by Straits of Dover (E), 34 km/21 mi wide; 565 km/350 mi long by 240 km/150 mi wide at its widest point (Lyme Bay–Golfe de St-Malo); crossings by ferry and hovercraft, one of the world's busiest shipping lanes; tunnel opened, 1994; first aeroplane crossing by Bleriot, 1909; first swum by Matthew Webb, 1875; main islands, I of Wight, Channel Is. >> Channel Islands / Tunnel; Wight, Isle of

English Civil War (1642–8) The country's greatest internal conflict, between supporters of Parliament and supporters of Charles I, caused by Parliamentary opposition to royal policies. The first major engagement took place at Edgehill in October 1642. It was a draw, but Royalist forces then threatened London, the key Parliamentary stronghold. The crucial event of 1643 was Parliament's alliance with the Scots in the Solemn League and Covenant, which led to the major Royalist defeat at Marston Moor (1644). Royalist successes in the W at Lostwithiel and Newbury (both 1643) were overtaken by major Parliamentary victories at Naseby and Langport (both 1645). The next year brought to an end the first civil war, Charles surrendering to the Scots at Newark. From June 1646 to April 1648 there was an uneasy peace and attempts at compromise. The climax came (Aug 1647) when the army presented the king with the Heads of Proposals, calling for religious toleration, and Parliamentary control of the armed forces. Charles made a secret alliance with the Scots, promising to establish Presbyterianism in England; they invaded

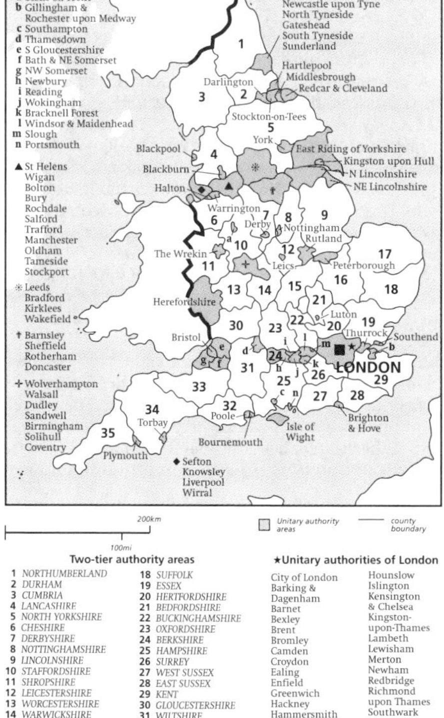

England (Apr 1648), and were repulsed only after the Battle of Preston (Aug). Bitterly fought, the second war earned Charles the epithet 'that man of blood' and, ultimately, his execution (30 Jan 1649). >> Cavaliers; Charles I (of England); Commonwealth (English history); Covenanters; Cromwell, Oliver; New Model Army

English Heritage In the UK, a body directly responsible for protecting and preserving England's collection of 12 500 designated monuments and over 300 000 'listed' buildings. The Historic Buildings and Monuments Board for Scotland, and *Cadw* (Welsh 'heritage'), have similar functions. >> Europa Nostra; National Trust

English Nature A British governmental agency, set up by the Environmental Protection Act (1990), and responsible for the conservation of England's wildlife and natural features. It continues the work of its predecessor, the Nature Conservancy Council, and works closely with the Scottish Natural Heritage and Countryside Council for Wales. >> Nature Reserve; Sites of Special Scientific Interest

English-Speaking Union A charity founded by Sir Evelyn Wrench (1882–1966) in 1918 with the purpose of 'improving understanding about people, international issues, and culture through the bond the English language provides'. Based in London, the Union also has branches in many countries.

engraving A process of printmaking by the intaglio method; also the resulting print. The term is often used less precisely to mean any process whereby a design is printed on paper. >> drypoint; etching; intaglio; line-engraving; mezzotint

enhanced radiation weapon >> **neutron bomb**

enkephalins >> **opioid peptides**

Enlightenment A European philosophical movement of the 18th-c, rooted in the 17th-c Scientific Revolution and the ideas of Locke and Newton. Its basic belief was the superiority of reason as a guide to all knowledge and human concerns; from this flowed the idea of progress and a challenging of traditional Christianity. >> Encyclopaedists; Hume, David; Locke, John; Newton, Isaac; Philosophes

Enlil The Mesopotamian god of the wind, son of Anu the sky-god, king of the gods before the creation of Marduk. >> Marduk; Mesopotamia

Enniskillen [inis**kil**in], also **Inniskilling**, Ir **Inis Ceithleann** 54°21N 7°38W, pop (1995e) 11 400. Town in Fermanagh, SW Northern Ireland; scene of a victory of William III over James II, 1689; became an important Protestant stronghold; scene of an IRA bombing at the Remembrance Day service in 1987, killing 11 people; airfield; castle ruins (15th–16th-c); cathedral (17th–18th-c). >> Fermanagh; Protestantism; William III

Ennius, Quintus [**en**ius] (c.239–169 BC) Latin epic poet and dramatist, born in Rudiae, Calabria, Italy. He introduced the hexameter into Latin; but only fragments of his many writings survive. >> epic; metre (literature)

Enoch [**ee**nok] Biblical character, son of Jared, father of Methuselah. In the Graeco-Roman era his name became attached to Jewish apocalyptic writings allegedly describing his visions (1, 2, and 3 *Enoch*). >> apocalypse; Methuselah; Pseudepigrapha

enosis [e**noh**sis] A political movement in Cyprus for union with Greece, reflecting the demands of Cypriots opposed to foreign rule, and closely associated with the leadership of the Greek Orthodox Church. Now independent, Cyprus has never achieved this union because of Turkish opposition. >> Cyprus [i]; EOKA; Grivas

Enright, D(ennis) J(oseph) (1920–) Writer, born in Leamington, Warwickshire. He has written five novels and much criticism, but is best known for his poetry. A dozen volumes since 1953 are represented in his *Collected Poems* (1987).

Ensor, James (Sydney) Ensor, Baron (1860–1949) Painter, born in Ostend, Belgium. He became known for his bizarre and fantastic images, using masks, skeletons, and other ghostly effects as symbols of the evils of society.

entablature [en**tab**lachoor] The horizontal element supported by the orders of classical architecture. It consists of an architrave, frieze, and cornice. >> orders of architecture [i]

Entebbe [en**te**bay] 0°05N 32°29E, pop (1995e) 28 100. Town in S Uganda, E Africa; on N shore of L Victoria, founded, 1893; former capital of Uganda, 1894–1962; airport; railway; scene in 1976 of a dramatic rescue by Israeli forces of Israelis whose plane had been hijacked by a group of Palestinian terrorists. >> Uganda [i]

entellus [en**tel**us] A langur native to S Asia (*Presbytis entellus*), and traditionally sacred in India; sandy brown, with a black face; long tail; also known as **entellus langur** or **hanuman monkey**. >> langur

enteric fever >> **typhoid fever**

enterprise zones Parts of a country designated by the government as areas where business start-up schemes will get favourable financial help. They are usually located in inner-city areas with high unemployment levels. Schemes of this kind are in operation in many countries.

enthalpy [**en**thalpee] An energy quantity appearing frequently in thermodynamics; symbol H, units J (joule); defined as $H = U + pV$, where U is internal energy, p is pressure, and V is volume. There is no absolute zero of enthalpy, so only changes in enthalpy can be measured. >> energy; heat; thermodynamics

entomology The branch of biology dealing with the

study of insects, the most diverse group of organisms on Earth. The development of insecticides and alternative techniques for controlling pest insects forms the basis of **applied economic entomology**. **Medical entomology** is a specialized field dealing with the study of insect carriers of numerous diseases and with the methods of controlling them. >> biology; insecticide

entresol >> **mezzanine**

entropy [**en**tropee] A thermodynamic quantity which always increases for irreversible processes, giving a direction in time for processes which might otherwise appear reversible from energy considerations alone; symbol *S*, units J/K (joules per kelvin). Entropy may be understood as a measure of disorder at a microscopic level, caused by the addition of heat to collections of atoms. The second law of thermodynamics states that for all processes entropy either is constant or increases. >> heat; thermodynamics

E-number A code number on food labels, used by food manufacturers in member states of the European Union, which identifies all materials added to the food (*E = European*). Among food additives, four categories (preservatives, colourants, anti-oxidants, and emulsifiers) each have code numbers. For example, E102 is the colourant tartrazine. >> additives; antioxidants; colouring agents; emulsifiers; food preservation

enuresis [enyu**ree**sis] A condition typified by involuntary voiding of urine. The involuntary passage of faeces is known as **encopresis**.

Enver Pasha (1881–1922) Turkish soldier and politician, born in Istanbul. A leader in the revolution of Young Turks in 1908, he later became minister of war (1914). He fled to Russia in 1918 after the Turkish surrender, and was killed in an insurrection in Turkestan. >> Young Turks

environment The conditions and influences of the place in which an organism lives. The **physical environment** describes the characteristics of a landscape (eg climate, geology) which have not been changed markedly by human impact, whereas the **geographical environment** includes the physical environment together with any human modifications (eg industrialization, urbanization). The relationship between living organisms and their environment forms part of the subject of *ecology*. Concern that large parts of the physical environment are suffering from misuse and overexploitation is central to conservation. >> conservation (earth sciences); ecology; ecosystem; environmental studies; Greens

Environmentally Sensitive Areas (ESAs) A European Community scheme introduced in 1985 to protect areas of ecological and landscape importance from drainage and loss caused by agricultural change. Examples include the Broads and the Breckland in East Anglia, UK. >> Breckland, the; Broads, the; ecology

Environmental Protection Agency A US government agency established in 1970. Its job is to determine, regulate, and enforce environmental pollution controls, such as legislation governing the use of pesticides. >> environment; pollution

environmental studies Those aspects of biology, ecology, and geography which are related to an understanding of the environment: its physical and human components. It is sometimes used synonymously with *ecology*, though environmental studies are more wide-ranging. >> biology; ecology; environment; geography

enzyme A specialized protein molecule produced by a living cell, which acts as a biological catalyst for biochemical reactions. The names of enzymes typically end in *-ase*, and they are derived from the substrates on which they act; for example, lipase is an enzyme that breaks down lipid (fat). >> amylases; catalysis; protein

Eocene epoch [**ee**ohseen] The second of the five geological epochs of the Tertiary period, lasting from 55 to 38 million years ago. It was characterized by a warmer climate and the appearance of modern flora and fauna. >> geological time scale; Tertiary period; RR976

Eohippus [eeoh**hip**us] >> ***Hyracotherium***

EOKA [ay**oh**ka] The acronym for **Ethniki Organosis Kipriakou Agonos** ('National Organization of Cypriot Struggle'), a Greek Cypriot underground movement seeking to end British rule and achieve the union of Cyprus with Greece. Founded in 1955 by Colonel George Grivas, with the support of Archbishop Makarios III, it pursued a campaign of anti-British violence. EOKA was disbanded following Makarios's acceptance of Cypriot independence (1958). In 1971–4 it was unsuccessfully resurrected as EOKA B. >> Cyprus ℹ; enosis; Grivas; Makarios III; nationalism

Eos [**ee**ohs] In Greek mythology, the goddess of the dawn, daughter of Helios, mother of Memnon. >> Memnon

Epaminondas [epami**non**das] (c.418–362 BC) Theban general and statesman, whose victory at Leuctra (371 BC) broke the military power of Sparta and made Thebes the most powerful state in Greece. >> Sparta (Greek history); Thebes

ephedrine [**ef**edrin, **ef**edreen] A drug with similar actions to adrenaline, used as a nasal decongestant. Earlier, it was also used in the treatment of asthma and low blood pressure. >> adrenaline; asthma

ephemeral An annual plant with a very short life-cycle, usually producing several generations in a single season. Many weed species are ephemeral, as are desert plants which experience very short favourable seasons. >> annual

Ephemeroptera [efeme**rop**tera] >> **mayfly**

Ephesians, Letter to the [e**fee**zhnz] New Testament writing attributed to Paul, but of disputed authorship. It sets out God's purposes in establishing the Church and uniting both Jews and Gentiles in it. >> Paul, St; Pauline Letters

Ephesus [**ef**esus], Turk **Efes** 37°5N 27°19E. Ancient city of Lydia and important Greek city-state on the W coast of Asia Minor; centre of worship of Artemis/Diana, whose temple was one of the Seven Wonders of the Ancient World; in Roman times, principal city of the province of Asia visited by St Paul. >> Artemis; Paul, St; Seven Wonders of the Ancient World

epic A heroic poem; a narrative of wars and adventures where larger-than-life characters perform deeds of great significance. The earlier epic poems, in the oral tradition, reached back into myth and legend, where men and gods moved on the same scene; among these are the Sumerian epic *Gilgamesh* (c.3000 BC), the Homeric epics *Iliad* and *Odyssey* (c.1000 BC), and the Indian *Mahabharata* (c.500 BC): also the N European epics such as the Old English *Beowulf* (8th-c) and the 13th-c German *Niebelungenlied*. The term **secondary epic** refers to works such as Virgil's *Aeneid* (30–19 BC) and Milton's *Paradise Lost* (1667), written in conscious imitation of these primary epic models. The poetic and mythological aspects are generally missing when modern works are described as 'epic'. >> Homer; literature; Milton; novel; poetry; Virgil

epicalyx An additional whorl of flower parts attached outside the sepals or calyx, which they resemble in both form and function. It is characteristic of some plants, such as members of the Rosaceae. >> flower ℹ; sepal

epicentre >> **earthquake**

Epictetus [epik**tay**tus] (c.50–c.130) Stoic philosopher, born in Hierapolis. At first a Roman slave, on being freed he devoted himself to philosophy. His *Enchiridion* is a collection of maxims dictated to a disciple. >> Stoicism

Epicurus [epi**kyoo**rus] (c.341–270 BC) Greek philosopher, founder of Epicureanism, born in Samos. He held that pleasure is the chief good, by which he meant freedom from pain and anxiety, not (as the term **epicurean** has since come to mean) one who indulges sensual pleasures without stint.

Epidaurus [epi**daw**rus] A Greek city-state situated in the E Peloponnese. It was famous in antiquity for its sanctuary to Asclepius, the god of healing, and for its magnificent open theatre, which is still used today. >> polis

epidemiology The study of the distribution and causes of disease in populations. It developed in the 19th-c, when the study of the occurrence of outbreaks in relation to the social conditions prevailing at the time led to effective measures for their control. >> medicine; screening tests

epidermis [epi**der**mis] The outermost layer of a plant or animal. In plants and many invertebrates, the epidermis is a single cell thick. In vertebrates, it is many cells thick, and in terrestrial vertebrates it is formed from dead, hardened cells. >> skin [i]

epididymis [epi**did**imis] >> **testis**

epidural anaesthesia [epi**dyoo**ral] The injection of a local anaesthetic into the epidural space located within the vertebral canal outside the dura (a membrane covering the spinal cord). It is often used in surgical procedures on the lower half of the body, and in normal or abnormal childbirth. >> anaesthetics, local; vertebral column

epiglottis A pear-shaped sheet of elastic fibrocartilage, broad above (where it lies immediately behind the tongue) and narrow below. It moves on swallowing, and partly covers the opening into the larynx. >> larynx

Epigoni [**epig**onee] In Greek mythology, the 'next generation' of heroes. After the failure of the Seven Champions to take Thebes, their sons made another expedition and succeeded. >> Diomedes; Seven against Thebes

epigram Originally, an inscription; hence, any short, pithy poem. Coleridge's definition is also an example: 'What is an epigram? A dwarfish whole,/Its body brevity, and wit its soul'. >> Martial; poetry

epigraphy [e**pig**rafee] The study of ancient inscriptions, variously inscribed on memorial stones, clay pots and tablets, marble, wood, wax, and other hard surfaces, and using a wide variety of techniques (eg carving, embossing, painting). >> hieroglyphics [i]; Ogam

epilepsy [**ep**ilepsee] A transient seizure or fit usually associated with a short-lived disturbance of consciousness. It stems from a synchronous high-voltage electrical discharge from groups of neurones in the brain. The disorder takes several forms, which include loss of consciousness with generalized convulsions (**grand mal**), short periods of loss of consciousness in which patients simply stop what they are doing and look blank ('absence' or 'drop attacks', or **petit mal**), seizures with involuntary movements of only part of the body, such as a limb (**Jacksonian epilepsy**), and short-lived sensations of smell and smacking of the lips (**temporal lobe epilepsy**). The majority of cases do not have an obvious cause. >> brain [i]; EEG

Epimetheus [epi**mee**thius] The 11th natural satellite of Saturn, discovered in 1980; distance from the planet 151 000 km/94 000 mi; diameter 140 km/90 mi. >> Saturn (astronomy); RR964

epinephrine [**epin**efrin] >> **adrenaline**

Epiphany A Christian festival (6 Jan) which commemorates the showing of the infant Jesus to the Magi (*Matt* 2), the manifestation of Jesus's divinity at his baptism (*Matt* 3), and his first miracle at Cana (*John* 2). Its eve is Twelfth Night. >> Jesus Christ; Magi

epiphyte A plant not rooted in the soil, but growing above ground level, usually on other plants. It uses such hosts for support only, and should not be confused with **parasites**, which also obtain food from their hosts. Epiphytes are especially common in tropical rainforests, where the adoption of this lifestyle allows them to grow in the light, which is otherwise shut out by the dense canopy. >> bromeliad; lichen; moss; orchid [i]

episcopacy [e**pis**kopasee] (Gr *episkopos*, 'bishop', 'superintendent') A hierarchical (as opposed to consistorial) system of Church government, with bishops occupying the dominant role and authority. In the Roman Catholic, Orthodox, and Anglican communions, those consecrated bishops are the chief ecclesiastical officers of a diocese, and have the power to ordain priests and confirm baptized members of the Church. >> Anglican Communion; bishop; Orthodox Church; Roman Catholicism

Episcopal Church, Protestant The Anglican Church in the USA, formally established in 1784 after the War of Independence. Traditionally, it has allowed more lay participation in the government of the Church than has the Church of England. >> episcopacy; Protestantism

epistemology The branch of philosophy dealing with the theory of knowledge – its sources, limits, kinds, and reliability. These central issues divide such major schools as empiricists, rationalists, and sceptics. >> empiricism; rationalism (philosophy); scepticism

epithelium [epi**theel**ium] A layer of cells lining all internal surfaces (organs, tubes, ducts) and covering the external surface of the body; the internal lining is also known as **endothelium**. Its function varies in different regions of the body (eg protection, secretion, absorption). >> cell

epoch In geology, an arbitrary unit of time used as a subdivision of a *period*. >> geological time scale; RR976

epoxy resin [i**pok**see **rez**in] A polymer formed by the condensation of epichlorohydrin and bisphenol-A. The resulting hard material is useful as an adhesive, a coating, and an embedding material for electrical components. >> polymerization; thermoset

EPROM [**ee**prom] An acronym of **electrically programmable read-only memory**, a type of integrated circuit read-only memory which can be reused by removing the chip from the computer, erasing its contents, electrically writing new data into it, and replacing it in the computer. >> EAROM; PROM

Epsom salts >> **magnesium**

Epstein, Sir Jacob [**ep**stiyn] (1880–1959) Sculptor, born in New York City. Several of his symbolic sculptures, such as 'Ecce homo' (1934), resulted in accusations of indecency and blasphemy. In the 1950s, his last two large works, 'Christ in Majesty' (in aluminium; Llandaff Cathedral) and 'St Michael and the Devil' (in bronze; Coventry Cathedral), won more immediate acclaim. >> sculpture; Symbolism

equations The statement that one mathematical expression is equal to another. Those containing only one unknown quantity are classified by the *degree* of that unknown. Equations of degree one, called **linear equations**, are of the form $ax = b$, and have the solution $x = b/a$, given $a \neq 0$. Equations of degree two, **quadratic equations**, are of the form $ax^2 + bx + c = 0$, and $a \neq 0$ have solutions $x = [-b \pm 1(b^2 - 4ac)]/2a$. Equations of degree three are called **cubic equations**. A **polynomial** equation contains the sum of multiples of powers of a variable, say x; for example $a_0x^n + a_1x^{n-1} + a_2x^{n-2}... = 0$, where $a_0 \neq 0$; n, the highest power of the unknown, is called the degree of the polynomial. >> algebra

Equator The great circle on the Earth's surface, halfway between the Poles, dividing the Earth into the N and S hemispheres; known as the **terrestrial equator**. Its own latitude is 0°, and from here latitude is measured in degrees N and degrees S. The **celestial equator** is the great

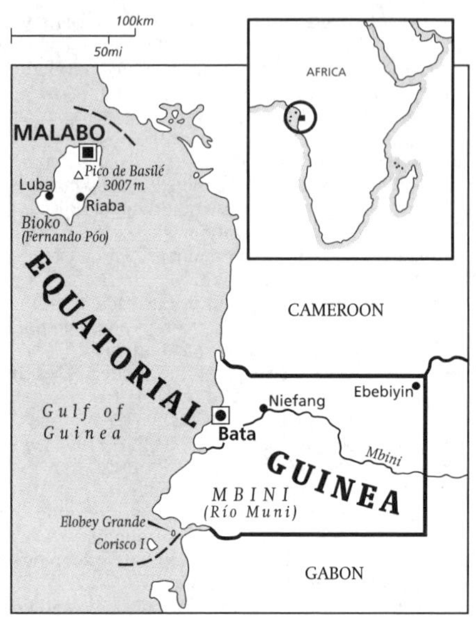

circle in the sky in the same plane as the terrestrial equator. >> Earth; great circle

Equatorial Guinea [**gi**nee], official name **Republic of Equatorial Guinea**, Span **República de Guinea Ecuatorial** pop (1995e) 472 000; mainland area 26 016 sq km/ 10 042 sq mi; total area 28 051 sq km/10 828 sq mi. Republic in WC Africa comprising a mainland area (Río Muni) and several islands in the Gulf of Guinea; capital, Malabo; timezone GMT +1; mainland population mainly Fang; chief religion, Roman Catholicism (80%); official language, Spanish; unit of currency, the CFA franc; mainland rises sharply from a narrow coast of mangrove swamps towards the heavily-forested African plateau; hot and humid equatorial climate; first visited by Europeans in 15th-c; island of Fernando Póo claimed by Portugal, 1494–1788; occupied by Britain, 1781–1843; rights to the area acquired by Spain, 1844; independence, 1968; military coup, 1975; first multi-party elections, 1993; governed by a president, prime minister, and an 80-member elected House of Representatives; economy largely based on agriculture; cocoa, coffee, timber, bananas, cassava, palm oil, sweet potatoes. >> Bioko; Malabo; RR1007 political leaders

equestrianism The skill of horsemanship. As a sport it can fall into one of four categories; **show jumping**, **dressage**, **three-day eventing** (also known as **horse trials**), and **carriage driving**. The governing body is the International Equestrian Federation. >> dressage; Pony Club; show jumping; Spanish Riding School; three-day event; RR1051

equinox 1 Either of the two points on the celestial sphere where the ecliptic intersects the celestial equator. Physically these are the points at which the Sun, in its annual motion, appears to cross the celestial equator – the **vernal equinox** as it crosses from S to N, and the **autumnal equinox** as it crosses from N to S. **2** Either of the two instants of time at which the Sun crosses the celestial equator, being about 21 March (vernal) and 23 September (autumnal). >> celestial equator / sphere

equisetum >> **horsetail**

equity (economics) The capital of a company, belonging to the shareholders. It consists of issued share capital (the money received from the sale of shares); the profits retained (traditionally known as *reserves*); share premiums (excess receipts from the sale of shares over their nominal value); and the revaluation reserve (sums resulting from the increase in the value of assets since their purchase). The shares themselves are called **equities**. >> company; shares

equity (law) A source of English and Scottish law, originally developed by the Lord Chancellor and later by the Court of Chancery. It arose from the right of litigants to petition the monarch. Trust law and equitable remedies (such as the injunction) are examples. >> Chancery Division; injunction; trust

Equuleus [e**kwool**ius] (Lat 'little horse') An insignificant N constellation, the second-smallest in the N sky. >> constellation; RR968

era The second largest of the time divisions used in geology, each being divided into a number of periods. >> geological time scale; RR976

Erasistratus [erasi**stra**tus] (c.250 BC) Greek founder of a school of medicine, born in Ceos. He studied the nature of the nervous system, and came near to discovering the circulation of the blood. >> circulation

Erasmus, Desiderius [**eraz**mus], originally **Gerrit Gerritszoon** (1466–1536) Humanist, born in Rotterdam, The Netherlands. He moved to England in 1498, becoming professor of divinity and of Greek at Cambridge. In 1519 appeared his masterpiece, *Colloquia*, an audacious handling of Church abuses. He also made the first translation of the Greek New Testament into English (1516), and edited the works of St Jerome (1519). >> humanism

Erastianism [**eras**tianizm] An understanding of the Christian Church which gives the state the right to intervene in and control Church affairs. It is associated with Thomas Erastus (1524–83), who, in 16th-c Heidelberg, had argued against Calvinists for the rights of the state in Church affairs. >> Calvinism

Erato [**e**ratoh] In Greek mythology, the Muse responsible for lyric poetry and hymns. >> Muses

Eratosthenes [era**tos**theneez] (c.276–c.194 BC) Greek astronomer and scholar, born in Cyrene. He is remembered for the first scientific calculation of the Earth's circumference. >> Earth ℹ

Erechtheum [erek**thay**um] The latest building on the Athenian Acropolis, named after the legendary king Erechtheus of Athens. It is a symmetrical, two-part Ionic marble temple, built during the Peloponnesian War (c.420–407 BC). >> Elgin Marbles; Ionic order; Parthenon

erg >> **energy; heat; work;** RR1031

ergonomics The study of work, including the design of the work situation, the analysis and training of work skills, the effects of physical and psychological environments, work-stress, errors, and accidents; also called **human engineering**. The systematic study of work developed from the early 20th-c introduction of mass production, and the use of time and motion study for job analysis and improvement. The subject has applications in such areas as factory design and the design of vehicle instruments. >> facilities management

ergot [**er**got] A fungal disease of grasses caused by *Claviceps purpurea*; forms hard black fruiting bodies (*sclerotia*) in flower-heads of infected grasses, including cereal crops. (Class: Pyrenomycetes.) >> ergotism; fungus

ergotism [**er**gotizm] A condition which results from eating bread made from rye infected with ergot. Victims develop burning sensations in the limbs, gangrene, and convulsions. Outbreaks were referred to as *St Anthony's fire*, in the belief that a visit to the tomb of this saint would bring a cure. >> alkaloids; ergot; rye

erica >> **heath**

Eridanus [**erid**anus] A long and rambling S constellation, sixth-largest in the sky. Its brightest star is Achernar. Distance: 28 parsec. >> constellation; RR968

Eridu [**ay**ridoo] The oldest of the Sumerian city-states, lying SW of Ur. Excavations of the site have revealed a continuous series of temples starting in the sixth millenium BC and ending in the third with the great ziggurat. >> Sumer; Ur; ziggurat ℹ

Erie, Lake [**ee**ree] Fourth largest of the Great Lakes, North America, on frontier between Canada and USA; 388 km/241 mi long, 48–92 km/30–57 mi wide; area 25 667 sq km/9907 sq mi; Welland Ship Canal bypasses Niagara Falls; generally closed by ice during winter months (Dec–Mar); major (US) ports include Buffalo, Cleveland, Detroit; British defeated at Battle of Lake Erie, 1813. >> Erie Canal; Great Lakes

Erie Canal [**ee**ree] An artificial waterway extending 580 km/360 mi between Albany and Buffalo, New York State. Constructed 1817–25, it provided a water route from the Hudson R to L Erie. >> Erie, Lake; New York

Erigena, John Scotus [e**ri**jena], also known as **John the Scot** (c.810–c.877) Philosopher and theologian, born in Scotia (now Ireland). His major work, *De divisione naturae* (c.865, On the Division of Nature), tried to fuse Christian and Neoplatonic doctrines and to reconcile faith and reason, but was later condemned for its pantheistic tendencies. >> Middle Ages; Neoplatonism

Erik the Red, originally **Erik Thorvaldsson** (10th-c) Norwegian sailor who explored the Greenland coast, and founded the Norse colonies there (985). His son Leif Eriksson landed in 'Vinland', often identified as America (1000). >> saga

Erinyes [e**reen**yeez] In Greek mythology, spirits of vengeance, depicted as carrying torches and covered with snakes. Their names are Alecto 'never-ceasing', Megaira 'grudger', and Tisiphone 'avenger of blood'. >> Eumenides; Orestes

Eris [**e**ris] In Greek mythology, the daughter of Night and the sister of Ares. She was present at the wedding of Peleus and Thetis and threw a golden apple 'for the fairest'; this brought Hera, Athene, and Aphrodite into contention, and was the first cause of the Trojan War. >> Paris (myth)

Eritrea [eri**tree**a], Amharic **Ertra** pop (1995e) 3 955 000; area 93 700 sq km/36 200 sq mi. State in NE Africa; capital, Asmara; timezone GMT +3; languages, Arabic, English, and several local languages, notably Tigre, Tigrinya, Danakil, Saho; chief religions, Islam (50%), Coptic Christianity (50%); unit of currency the Ethiopian birr, replaced (1997) by the nakfa; Ethiopian plateau drops to low plains; E plain includes Danakil Depression, descending to 116 m/381 ft below sea level; tropical climate, varied by altitude; annual average temperature at Asmara, 16°C, at Mitsiwa (on coast) 30°C; hot, semi-arid NE and SE lowlands receive less than 500 mm/20 in rainfall annually; severe droughts have caused widespread famine; federated as part of Ethiopia, 1952; province of Ethiopia, 1962, which led to political unrest; civil war in 1970s, with separatists making major gains; Soviet- and Cuban-backed government forces regained most areas after 1978 offensive; fall of President Mengistu (1991) led to new status as an autonomous region, with a provisional government established by the Eritrean People's Liberation Front; referendum followed by declaration of independence, 1993; transitional government for 4 years, consisting of a National Assembly, which elects the president, and a State Council; economy largely devoted to agriculture, but badly affected by drought, and heavily dependent on irrigation and foreign aid. >> Danakil Depression; Ethiopia ℹ; RR1007political leaders

ERM >> **European Monetary System**

ermine >> **stoat**

Ermine Street >> **Roman roads** ℹ

Ernst, Max(imillian) (1891–1976) Painter, born in Brühl, Germany. A founder in 1919 of the German Dada group, he later participated in the Surrealist movement in Paris. >> Dada; frottage; Surrealism

Eros (astronomy) [**ee**ros] Asteroid 433, discovered in 1898. It passed within 23 million km/14 million mi of Earth in 1975. >> asteroids

Eros (mythology) [**e**rohs], commonly [**ee**ros] In Greek mythology, the son of Aphrodite and Ares. He is first depicted on vases as a handsome athlete, then as a boy with wings and arrows, and finally, in the Hellenistic period, as a chubby baby. >> Cupid

erosion In geology, the alteration of landforms through the removal and transport of material by water, wind, glacial movement, gravity, or living organisms. Rivers are the most effective agents of erosion, forming the pattern of hills and valleys, while wave action forms the coastlines.

Erse >> **Irish**

Ershad, Hussain Muhammad [**air**shad] (1929–) Bangladeshi soldier, chief martial law administrator, and president (1983–90). Appointed army chief-of-staff in 1978, he led a bloodless military coup in 1982. He resigned in 1990, and was imprisoned (1991–7). >> Bangladesh ℹ

Erté [ertay], originally **Romain de Tirtoff** (1892-1990) Fashion designer, born in St Petersburg, Russia. He went to Paris, where he became a dress and theatrical-costume designer. He worked for the *Folies-Bergère* (1919–30), and designed the costumes for the American musical revues *The Ziegfeld Follies* and *George White's Scandals*. In the 1960s he produced lithographs and sheet-metal sculptures. His autobiography, *Things I Remember*, was published in 1976.

erysipelas [eri**si**pelas] A severe illness resulting from infection of the skin with haemolytic *Streptococcus*. Usually associated with a high fever, it is easily cured with penicillin. >> skin ℹ; *Streptococcus*

erythrocytes [**erith**rosiyts] Haemoglobin-containing blood cells, also known as **red blood cells**, present in most vertebrates. Their primary function is the transport of oxygen and carbon dioxide in the blood. They are manufactured in bone marrow. >> blood; bone marrow; haemoglobin

ESA >> **European Space Agency**

Esarhaddon [eesah(r)**ha**dn] (?–669 BC) King of Assyria (680–669 BC), son of Sennacherib and father of Assurbanipal. He is best known for his conquest of Egypt (671 BC). >> Assyria

Esau [**ee**saw] Biblical character, the elder son of Isaac. He was depicted as his father's favourite son, but was

deprived of Isaac's blessing and his birthright by his cunning brother Jacob (*Gen* 27). >> Bible; Edomites; Isaac; Jacob

Esbjerg [**ays**byer] 55°28N 8°28E, pop (1995e) 83 300. Seaport in SW Jutland, Denmark; railway; ferry link with UK and Faroe Is; base for North Sea oil and gas exploration. >> Denmark [i]

escape velocity Spacecraft velocity at which the energy of a craft is sufficient to overcome the gravitational attraction of the parent body, and will thus not return to that body. Earth escape velocity is c.11 km/s (7 mi/s) (root 2 × circular orbit velocity). >> acceleration due to gravity; low Earth orbit

Escaut, River >> **Schelde, River**

eschatology [eska**tol**ojee] The Christian doctrine concerning 'the last things' – the final consummation of God's purposes in creation, and the final destiny of individual souls or spirits and of humanity in general. The notion is sometimes represented as a present spiritual condition rather than as a future cosmic event. Some continue to adhere to the early belief in the literal 'second-coming' of Christ. >> Adventists; Christianity; millenarianism

Escherichia [esher**ik**ia] A genus of rod-shaped bacteria that occur in the intestinal tract of animals, including humans, and are common in soil and aquatic habitats. They can cause bacterial dysentery. The only species, *Escherichia coli*, has been intensively studied by microbiologists. (Kingdom: Monera. Family: Enterobacteriaceae.) >> bacteria [i]; dysentery

Escorial, El [eskori**al**] A palace-monastery built (1563–84) for Philip II in New Castile, Spain; a world heritage site. It was built by Juan Bautista de Toledo and his successor Juan de Herrara. >> Philip II (of Spain)

Esdras, Books of [**ez**dras] **1** The **First Book of Esdras**, known also as **3 Esdras** (in the Vulgate), part of the Old Testament Apocrypha; an appendix to the Catholic Bible. **2** The **Second Book of Esdras**, known also as **4 Esdras** (in the Vulgate) or **4 Ezra**, sometimes considered part of the Old Testament Apocrypha; also an appendix to the Catholic Bible. Dated probably late 1st-c; chapters 1–2 and 15–16 may be two later Christian additions, today sometimes called 5 Ezra and 6 Ezra, respectively. >> Apocrypha, Old Testament; Ezra; Pseudepigrapha

Esfahan [esfa**hahn**], ancient **Isfahan, Aspadana** 32°40N 51°38E, pop (1995e) 1 311 000. Third largest city in Iran; airport; railway; university (1950). >> Iran [i]

esker [**es**ker] A long, narrow hill of gravel and sand which may wind for long distances along a valley floor, probably formed by water flowing in tunnels underneath glaciers. >> drumlins; glaciation

Eskimo or (in Canada) **Inuit** Eskimo–Aleut-speaking peoples of North America, Russia, and Greenland, living along the N edge of the continent, from Alaskan and E Asian shores in the W to Greenland and Labrador in the E, mostly S of the Arctic Circle. They are closely related to the Aleut. An economy based on nomadic hunting and fishing has now largely given way to village settlement and seasonal employment in the wage economies of the countries where they live, mainly as labourers in the mining and oil industries. The combined populations of Eskimos and Aleuts in Russia is c.1300, with 33 000 in Alaska, 24 000 in Canada, and 43 000 in Greenland. >> Greenland [i]; Nunavut

eskimo dog >> **husky**

esophagus >> **oesophagus**

ESP >> **extrasensory perception**

esparto A tufted perennial grass (*Stipa tenacissima*), native to N Africa, and naturalized elsewhere, consisting of spikelets with long, feathery bristles in narrow panicles. The leaves are used to make paper. (Family: Gramineae.) >> grass [i]; panicle; spikelet

Esperanto The best known of the world's artificial languages, invented by Ludwig Lazarus Zamenhof in 1887, designed to overcome problems of international communication. Newspapers and journals are published in Esperanto, together with the Bible and the Koran. It is used for broadcasting, and is taught as a school subject in many countries. >> artificial language; Zamenhof

ESPRIT [**es**pree] An abbreviation for the **European Strategic Programme for Research and Development in Information Technology**, a programme of research funded by the European Commission. It aims to develop the European computer industry by supporting joint pre-competitive research projects across institutions in the member countries of the Community. >> Alvey; European Community; Framework programme

Essen 51°28N 6°59E, pop (1995e) 647 000. Industrial city in Germany; badly bombed in World War 2; bishopric; railway; headquarters of many large corporations; important centre of retail trade; Minster (9th–14th-c). >> Germany [i]; Ruhr, River

Essenes [e**seenz**] A Jewish sect renowned in antiquity for its asceticism, communistic life-style, and skill in predicting the future. >> Dead Sea Scrolls; Qumran, Community of

essential amino acids >> **amino acid** [i]

essential fatty acids >> **carboxylic acids**

essential oil A natural volatile oil produced by plants, giving a distinctive aromatic scent to the foliage. Mostly terpenoids, the oils are common in plants from hot dry habitats. >> attar; mint; oil (botany); patchouli; terpene

Essequibo, River [ese**kee**boh] Largest river in Guyana, South America; flows c.970 km/600 mi N to meet the Atlantic at a 32 km/20 mi-wide delta, W of Georgetown. >> Guyana [i]

Essex pop (1995e) 1 584 000; area 3672 sq km/1418 sq mi. County of SE England; county town, Chelmsford; Southend and Thurrock new unitary authorities from 1998. >> Chelmsford; England [i]

Essex, Robert Devereux, 2nd Earl of (1566–1601) English soldier and courtier to Elizabeth I, born in Netherwood, Hereford and Worcester. At court, he quickly rose in the favour of Elizabeth, despite his clandestine marriage in 1590 with Sir Philip Sidney's widow. He became a privy councillor (1593) and earl marshal (1597), but alienated the Queen's advisers, and there were constant quarrels with Elizabeth. His six months' lord-lieutenancy of Ireland (1599) proved a failure, and he was imprisoned. He attempted to raise the City of London, was found guilty of high treason, and beheaded. >> Elizabeth I

estate duty A tax formerly levied in the UK on the estate of a deceased person, based on the total value of the estate; small estates were exempt, and the levels of tax were varied from time to time. It has now been replaced by the **inheritance tax**. The USA has a federal **estate tax** and a related **gift tax**. >> inheritance tax; taxation

ester A compound obtained by the condensation of an alcohol with an acid. Esters are named as if they were salts, the first part being derived from the alcohol, and the second part from the acid (eg ethyl acetate from ethanol and acetic acid). >> acid; alcohols

Esther, Book of A book of the Hebrew Bible/Old Testament, telling the popular story of how Esther became the wife of the Persian king Ahasuerus (Xerxes I) and prevented the extermination of Jews. The **Additions to the Book of Esther** are several enhancements found in the Septuagint but not in the Hebrew Bible. They are part of the Old Testament Apocrypha, and appear as *Esther* 11–16 in the Catholic Bible. >> Mordecai; Old Testament; Purim; Septuagint; Xerxes I

Estonia [es**toh**nia], official name **Republic of Estonia**, Estonian **Eesti Vabariik**, Russ **Estonskaya** pop (1995e) 1 568 000; area 45 100 sq km/17 409 sq mi. Republic in E Europe, on the Baltic Sea; capital, Tallinn; timezone GMT +2; major ethnic groups, Estonian (65%), Russian (28%), Ukrainian (3%), Belorussian (2%); official language, Estonian, with Russian also spoken; religions, Evangelical Lutheran, with Orthodox minorities; currency, the kroon of 100 senti; consists of mainland area and c.800 islands, notably Saaremaa, Hiiumaa, Muhu; over 1500 lakes; 36% forested; mild climate, average annual temperatures −6°C (Jan), 17°C (Jul); average annual rainfall 650 mm/26 in; under Swedish rule from 1629; ceded to Russia, 1721; independence, 1918; proclaimed a Soviet Socialist Republic, 1940; occupied by Germany in World War 2; resurgence of nationalist movement in the 1980s; declared independence, 1991; governed by a president, prime minister, and parliament (*Riigikogu*); agricultural machinery, electric motors; grain, vegetables; timber, dairy farming, livestock, fishing. >> Baltic Sea; Soviet Union; Tallinn; RR1007 political leaders

Estremadura [ishtrema**doo**ra], Lat **Extrema Durii** ('farthest land on the Douro') area 3249 sq km/1254 sq mi. Region and former province of WC Portugal; chief town, Lisbon; popular tourist region. >> Extremadura; Portugal ℹ

estrildid finch >> **finch**

estrogens >> **oestrogens**

Esztergom [ester**gom**], Ger **Gran**, ancient **Strigonium** 47°47N 18°44E, pop (1995e) 29 400. River-port town in N Hungary; on R Danube; fortress in Roman times; capital, 10th-c; seat of primate, 1198; railway; school of forestry; birthplace of St Stephen, Hungary's first king. >> Hungary ℹ

etching A form of intaglio printing invented in the early 16th-c, whereby the design on a copper plate is bitten with acid, rather than cut directly with the engraving tool (*burin*). The greatest master of the technique was Rembrandt. >> drypoint; intaglio; Rembrandt

Eteocles [**et**iokleez] In Greek legend, the elder of Oedipus's two sons, both of whom he cursed. King of Thebes after his father's death, he refused to share power with his brother Polynices. Seven Champions attacked the city, and Eteocles was killed by Polynices. >> Oedipus; Polynices; Seven against Thebes

ethanal >> **acetaldehyde**

ethane [**ee**thayn, **e**thayn] C_2H_6, boiling point −89°C. The second member of the alkane series; an odourless gas, used for refrigeration, which forms explosive mixtures with air. >> alkanes

ethanedioic acid >> **oxalic acid**

ethanoic acid [etha**noh**ik] >> **acetic acid**

ethanol CH_3CH_2OH, boiling point 78°C, also called **ethyl alcohol**, **grain alcohol**, and simply **alcohol**. It is a colourless liquid with a characteristic odour, mainly prepared by the fermentation of sugars. An important solvent, disinfectant, and preservative, it is mainly known for its intoxicating properties in beverages. >> alcohols; sugars

ethanoyl >> **acetyl**

Ethelbert or **Æthelbert** [**eth**elbert] (c.552–616) King of Kent (560–616). In his reign Kent achieved (c.590) control over England S of the Humber, and Christianity was introduced by St Augustine (597). To him we owe the first written English laws. >> Anglo-Saxons; Augustine, St (of Canterbury)

Etheldreda or **Æthelthryth, St** [**eth**eldreeda], also known as **St Audrey** (c.630–679) Daughter of the King of East Anglia. She founded a double monastery on the Isle of Ely in 673. Feast day 23 June. >> Christianity; monasticism

Ethelred I [**e**thelred], also spelled **Æthelred** (c.830–71) King of Wessex (865–71), the elder brother of Alfred the Great. During his reign the Danes launched their main invasion of England and established their kingdom (866). He died soon after his victory over the invaders at Ashdown, in the former county of Berkshire. >> Alfred

Ethelred II [**e**thelred], known as **Ethelred the Unready**, also spelled **Æthelred** (c.968–1016) King of England (from 978), the son of Edgar. In 1013 Sweyn Forkbeard secured mastery over England, forcing Ethelred into exile in Normandy. After Sweyn's death (1014), he returned to oppose Canute, but the unity of English resistance was broken when his son, Edmund Ironside, rebelled. 'Unready' is a mistranslation of *Unraed*, which means 'ill advised'. >> Canute; Edmund Ironside; Sweyn; Vikings

Ethelred, St >> **Ailred of Rievaulx, St**

ethene >> **ethylene**

ether [**ee**ther] **1** An organic compound containing an oxygen atom bonded to two alkyl groups. The best known is **ethyl ether** (CH_3CH_2–O–CH_2CH_3), a volatile liquid, boiling point 35°C, used as an anaesthetic. >> alkyl; oxygen **2** A substance once believed to pervade all space, thought necessary as the medium of the propagation of light; also spelled **aether**. The notion is no longer required by the modern theory of light. >> light

Etherege, Sir George [**eth**erij] (1635–92) Restoration playwright, probably born in Maidenhead, S England. His plays, such as *The Comical Revenge; or, Love in a Tub* (1664), were highly popular in their day, and introduced the comedy of manners to English theatre. >> Restoration

Ethernet A model of a local area network in which the workstations of the network are linked by coaxial cable. If any network station wishes to communicate with another, it sends an addressed message along the cable; this is then recognized and picked up only by the workstation to which it is addressed. A **'thin' ethernet** uses telephone wires but transmits data more slowly than in the standard **'thick' ethernet**. >> bus; coaxial cable; local area network

ethics The branch of philosophy dealing with the concepts and principles of morality, and including such theoretical questions as the source and foundation of morality, the status and justification of moral rules, the relationship between moral and other human objectives, and the nature of responsibility. Ethics has various subfields of application, such as medical ethics and business ethics, and its meaning shades into the more everyday, descriptive sense of 'a set of standards'. >> utilitarianism

Ethiopia [eethi**oh**pia], official name **Federal Democratic Republic of Ethiopia**, formerly **Abyssinia**, Amharic **Hebretesebawit Ityopia** pop (1995e) 57 919 000; area 1 251 282 sq km/471 660 sq mi. State of NE Africa; capital, Addis Ababa; timezone GMT +3; ethnic groups include Galla (40%), Amhara and Tigray (32%); chief religions, Islam (40–5%), Ethiopian Orthodox (35–40%); official language, Amharic; unit of currency, the Ethiopian birr of 100 cents; dominated by mountainous C plateau, mean elevation 1800–2400 m/6000–8000 ft; split diagonally by the Great Rift Valley; highest point, Ras Dashan Mt (4620 m/15 157 ft); crossed E–W by Blue Nile; Danakil Depression (NE) dips to 116 m/381 ft below sea-level; tropical climate, moderated by higher altitudes; distinct wet season (Apr–Sep); hot, semi-arid NE and SE lowlands receive less than 500 mm/20 in annually; severe droughts in 1980s caused widespread famine, deaths, and resettlement, with massive amounts of foreign aid; oldest independent country in sub-Saharan Africa; the very first Christian country in Africa; Eritrea occupied by Italy, 1882; Abyssinian independence recognized by League of Nations, 1923; Italian invasion, 1935; annexation as Italian East Africa, 1936–41; Haile Selassie returned from exile, 1941; military coup, 1974; ongoing conflict with Somalia over Ogaden region; internal conflict with regional separatist Eritrean and Tigrean forces; transfer of power to People's Democratic Republic, 1987; government overthrown by separatist forces, 1991; Eritrean independence agreed after referendum, 1993; governed by a president, prime minister, Federal Council, and Council of People's Representatives; multiparty elections and new constitution, 1994; one of the world's poorest countries; over 80% of population employed in agriculture, especially subsistence farming; production severely affected by drought and civil war; distribution of foreign aid hindered by internal conflicts and poor local organization. >> Addis Ababa; Eritrea [i]; Haile Selassie; Ogaden; Tigray; RR1008 political leaders

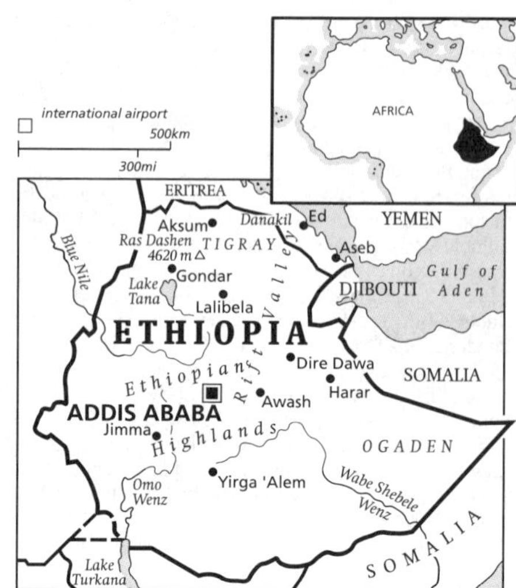

ethnicity A term which may be confused with 'race', but which refers to a shared cultural identity that has a range of distinctive behavioural and possibly linguistic features, passed on through socialization from one generation to another. Ethnic differences have been a source of political unrest, often associated with religious or clan differences. >> race

ethnography A detailed description of the culture of a particular society, based on fieldwork by ethnographers or anthropologists, using the method of participant observation. In Europe, the subject is often referred to as **ethnology**. >> anthropology; ethnomethodology

ethnolinguistics The study of the relationship between language and culture. It is concerned with all aspects of language, including its structure and usage, which have any connection with culture and society. >> ethnography; linguistics

ethnomethodology The sociological theory developed out of the work of the US sociologist Harold Garfinkel (1917–) and others in the 1960s. It studies the methods people use to accomplish successful social interaction. >> ethnography; sociology

ethnomusicology The scientific study of folk and national music, especially that of non-Western countries, in its anthropological, cultural, and social contexts. It was not until sound recording became easily available that the discipline could establish itself on a scientific basis. >> folk music; musicology

ethnoscience A branch of social/cultural anthropology which investigates folk beliefs or ideologies that correspond to such fields of Western science as medicine, astronomy, and zoology. >> anthropology; ethnography; sociology

ethology [ee**thol**ojee] The study of animal behaviour from the viewpoint of zoology and ecology. It considers the fine details of individual species behaviour in relation to properties of the natural environment to which the species has adapted (its *ecological niche*). The data are derived from direct observation and monitoring (eg by radio-tracking) of animals under natural or quasi-natural conditions. >> ecology; Lorenz; Tinbergen; zoology

ethyl [**ee**thiyl, **e**thil] C_2H_5–. A functional group derived from ethane. Adding it to a name usually indicates its substitution for hydrogen in that compound. >> ethane

ethyl alcohol >> **ethanol**

ethylene [**eth**ileen] CH_2=CH_2, IUPAC **ethene**, boiling point −104°C. A colourless gas, the first member of the alkene series. It is a very important industrial chemical, which polymerizes to **polyethylene**. >> alkenes; IUPAC

ethyne [**ee**thiyn] >> **acetylene**

Etna, Mount [**et**na], in Sicily **Mongibello** 37°45N 15°00E. Isolated volcanic mountain in E Sicily, Italy; height 3390 m/11 122 ft; Europe's largest active volcano; recent major eruptions, 1949, 1971, 1986, 1992; fertile lower slopes, growing oranges, lemons, olives, vines. >> Sicily; volcano; RR973

Eton >> **Windsor** (UK)

Etruria [e**troor**ia] The heartland of the Etruscan people, roughly corresponding to modern Tuscany. >> Etruscans

Etruscans [e**truh**sknz] A people of obscure origin who sprang to prominence in WC Italy in the 8th-c BC. Although they succumbed to the Romans politically in the 3rd-c BC, culturally their influence remained strong. Their lavishly equipped tombs show that they were particularly skilled in metal work. >> Etruria

etymology The study of the origins of the form and meaning of words and their history; a branch of historical linguistics. The **etymological fallacy** maintains that the 'real' meaning of a word is an earlier one, for example that *villain* really means 'farm labourer', because it once had this meaning. >> linguistics; semantics

Euboea [yoo**bee**a], Gr **Évvoia**, Ital **Negropon** pop (1995e) 214 000; area 3655 sq km/1411 sq mi. Second largest Greek island, in the Aegean Sea; length 144 km/89 mi; rises to 1744 m/5722 ft; capital, Chalcis. >> Aegean Sea; Chalcis; Greece ℹ

eucalyptus >> **gum tree**

eucaryote or **eukaryote** [yoo**ka**rioht] An organism in which cells have an organized nucleus, surrounded by a nuclear envelope, with paired chromosomes containing DNA that are recognizable during mitosis and meiosis. It includes all animals, plants, fungi, and many micro-organisms. >> cell; DNA ℹ; meiosis ℹ; mitosis; nucleus (biology); procaryote; Protoctista

Eucharist (Gr *eucharistia*, 'thanksgiving') For most Christian denominations, a sacrament and the central act of worship, sometimes called the **Mass** (Roman Catholic), **Holy Communion**, or **Lord's Supper** (Protestant). It is based on the example of Jesus at the Last Supper, when he identified bread and wine with his body and blood, and generally consists of the consecration of bread and wine by the priest or minister and distribution among the worshippers (*communion*). Theological interpretations vary from the literal transformation of the elements into the body and blood of Christ, to symbolism representing the real presence of Christ and a simple memorial meal. >> consubstantiation; Jesus Christ; sacrament; transubstantiation

Euclid [**yoo**klid], Gr **Eucleides** (4th–3rd-c BC) Greek mathematician who taught in Alexandria c.300 BC. His chief extant work is the 13-volume *Elements*. The approach which obeys his axioms became known as **Euclidean geometry**. >> geometries, non-Euclidean; geometry

Eudoxos of Cnidus [yoo**dok**sus, **niy**duhs] (c.408 BC–c.353 BC) Greek geometer and astronomer, born in Cnidus, Asia Minor. He established principles that laid the foundation for Euclid, then applied the subject to the study of the Moon and planets. >> Euclid; geometry

Eugene of Savoy, Prince, in full **François Eugène de Savoie Carignan** (1663–1736) Austrian general, born in Paris. He defeated the Turks on several occasions, fought against France, and while in command of the imperial army helped Marlborough at Blenheim (1704), Oudenaarde (1708), and Malplaquet (1709). >> Marlborough, Duke of; Spanish Succession, War of the

eugenics [yoo**jen**iks] The science that deals with the effects on the individual of biological and social factors. The term was coined in 1883 by Francis Galton as 'the science which deals with all influences that improve the inborn qualities'. The responsible study of eugenics was made difficult in the earlier years of this century by the propagation (eg in Germany and the USA) of political doctrines, in the name of eugenics, which were nonscientific and brutal. >> Eugenics Society

Eugenics Society [yoo**jen**iks] A society founded in London in 1907 as the Eugenics Education Society, adopting its present name in 1926. Its American counterpart changed its name in 1971 to the Society for the Study of Social Biology. It promotes research into the biological, genetic, social, and cultural factors relating to human reproduction, development, and health. >> eugenics

Eugénie, Empress >> **Napoleon III**

Euglena [yoo**glee**na] A genus of freshwater, single-celled micro-organisms with a whip-like flagellum at their front end used for swimming; usually contains chlorophyll in chloroplasts, and classified as a green alga (Class: Chlorophyceae); sometimes lacks chlorophyll, and classified as a protozoan flagellate (Phylum: Mastigophora). >> chlorophyll; chloroplast; flagellum; green algae; Protozoa

eukaryote >> **eucaryote**

Eulenspiegel, Till [**oy**lenshpeegl] A legendary 14th-c peasant prankster of Brunswick, Germany. He is celebrated in an epic poem by Gerhard Hauptmann (1928) and musically in a tone poem by Richard Strauss (1894).

Euler, Leonhard [**oy**ler] (1707–83) Mathematician, born in Basel, Switzerland. A highly prolific scholar, his many works dealt with number theory, geometry, calculus, and applications in astronomy and technology. Several important notions in mathematics are named after him. He had a prodigious memory, which enabled him to continue mathematical work and to compute complex calculations in his head, even after becoming totally blind in his 60s.

Eumenides [yoo**men**ideez] A euphemistic name given to the Erinyes after being domesticated at Athens in Aeschylus's play of the same name. The name means 'the kindly ones'. >> Aeschylus; Erinyes

Eumycota [yoo**miy**suhta] >> **fungus**

Eupen [**uh**pen] 50°38N 6°02E, pop (1995e) 17 400. Principal town in German-speaking Belgium; popular health resort and holiday centre; railway. >> Belgium ℹ

euphonium A musical instrument of the tuba family, much used in brass bands and occasionally in orchestral music. >> brass instrument ℹ; tuba

euphorbia >> **spurge**

Euphrates, River [yoo**fray**teez], Arabic **Al-Furat**, Turkish **Firat** Longest river in W Asia; length 2735 km/1700 mi; formed in EC Turkey, flows into Iraq, uniting with the Tigris to form the Shatt al-Arab, which enters the Persian Gulf; remains of several ancient cities along banks. >> Iraq ℹ

EURATOM [**yoo**ratm] Acronym for **European Atomic Energy Commission**. It was established as an independent body in 1957, but brought into the EEC in 1962. Its objectives are the promotion of peaceful uses of atomic energy. >> European Economic Community; nuclear reactor ℹ

Eureka Stockade [yu**ree**ka] In Australian history, an armed clash between goldminers and a combined police and military force at the Eureka Stockade, Ballarat, Victoria (1854). The miners had objected to the expensive mining licence imposed by the government. Public opinion swung behind the miners, and the government was forced to back down.

eurhythmics [yu**rith**miks] A system of musical training devised by Jaques-Dalcroze, designed to develop a quick response to changing rhythms by fitting bodily movements to pieces of music. >> Jaques-Dalcroze

Euripides [yu**rip**ideez] (c.480–406 BC) Greek tragic playwright, born in Athens. He wrote about 80 dramas, of which 19 survive, such as *Alcestis*, *Medea*, *Orestes*, and *Electra*.

Euro [**yoo**roh] >> **European Monetary System**

Euro, symbol € The common currency unit used in 11 countries of the European Union (Belgium, Germany, Spain, France, Ireland, Italy, Luxembourg, Netherlands, Austria, Portugal, Finland) from 1 January 1999; notes are in units of 5, 10, 20, 50, 100, 200, 500. Euro notes and coins do not enter general circulation until 2002, at which point each country has six months to phase out its old currency, replacing it with Euro notes and coins to be used throughout the Euro area ('Euroland'). In the business world, all payment and accounting systems began to use the Euro on 1 January 1999, each national currency unit being irrevocably fixed in relation to it; for example, the exchange rate with the Deutschmark was set at 1·95583. In the UK, 1 Euro was worth approximately 70p. >> European Central Bank / Monetary System / Union

Eurocurrency >> **Euromoney**

Eurodollar US dollars held in banks in Europe. Considerable sums are involved, resulting from such major concerns as the oil industry, where trade is conducted in dollars. >> dollar; Euromoney

Eurofighter The name given to the standardized air-to-air and ground-attack aircraft with which it is planned to equip the air forces of Great Britain, Spain, and The Netherlands. Plans presented in 1994 anticipate the plane being in service by 2000.

Euromoney or **Eurocurrency** Convertible currencies such as pounds sterling, French and Swiss francs, Deutschmarks, and US dollars held in banks outside the country of origin. They can be borrowed by commercial undertakings for trade. >> currency; Eurodollar

Europa (astronomy) [yu**roh**pa] The second natural satellite of Jupiter, discovered by Galileo in 1610; distance from the planet 671 000 km/417 000 mi; diameter 3140 km/1950 mi; orbital period 3·551 days. >> Galilean moons; Jupiter (astronomy); RR964

Europa (mythology) [yu**roh**pa] or **Europe** [yoo**roh**pee] In Greek mythology, the daughter of Agenor, king of Tyre, who was abducted by Zeus in the shape of a bull. Her children were Minos and Rhadamanthus. >> Zeus

Europa Nostra [yu**roh**pa **nos**tra] (Lat 'our Europe') An international federation established in 1963 for the preservation of historic sites, buildings, and monuments. It represents more than 200 organizations from 20 countries. >> English Heritage

Europe Second smallest continent, forming an extensive peninsula of the Eurasian land-mass, occupying c.7% of the Earth's surface; bounded E by Asia beyond the Ural Mts; supports over 25% of the world's population. >> European Commission / Community / Council / Economic Community / Parliament; RR971

European Atomic Energy Commission >> **EURATOM**

European Atomic Energy Community >> **European Community**

European Bank for Reconstruction and Development A bank founded in 1990 to assist the economic reconstruction of C and E Europe. It has 59 members.

European Central Bank (ECB) A bank established in Frankfurt am Main on 1 June 1998 to oversee the introduction and development of the Euro, and to set interest rates (3 per cent, at the outset). The Bank reports to the European Parliament on a yearly basis. The ECB and the national central banks together form the **European System of Central Banks** (ESCB), which govern the conduct of the single monetary policy, and whose primary objective is to maintain price stability. >> bank; Duisenberg; Euro; European Monetary Institute / System

European Coal and Steel Community (ECSC) The first European economic institution, set up in 1952. It has worked to remove customs duties and quota restrictions in coal, iron ore, and scrap, and aims to ensure that competition in these commodities is fair. >> European Economic Community

European Commission The administrative bureaucracy of the European Union. Its functions are to uphold the European ideal, propose new policy initiatives, and ensure that existing policies are implemented. It comprises 17 commissioners directly nominated by the member states; they serve a 4-year term, are each responsible for a specific area of work, and are supported by a bureaucracy employing c.15 000 people. The Commission decides by majority vote, and is collectively responsible to the European Parliament. >> European Community / Council / Parliament / Union

European Community (EC) A community of 15 Western European states initially created to achieve economic integration, but with the longer-term goal of political integration also in mind (European Union). It grew out of the European Coal and Steel Community which was established in 1952 under the Treaty of Paris by Belgium, France, Italy, Luxembourg, The Netherlands, and West Germany. In 1957, under the Treaty of Rome, the six states established the European Economic Community as what was essentially a customs union. A further nine members later joined the community. They are Denmark, Ireland, and the UK (1973), Greece (1981), Portugal and Spain (1986), and Austria, Finland, and Sweden (1995). Several other countries are seeking to become members. In 1993, the area covered by the EC became a single market, which was extended to incorporate the seven countries of the European Free Trade Association in 1994 (as the European Economic Area). Also in 1993, the EC member states concluded the process of ratifying the Maastricht Treaty, designed to strengthen the degree of co-operation within the community and to enhance political integration. The community is governed by a series of supra-national institutions: the European Council, the Council of Ministers, the European Commission, the European Parliament, the European Court of Justice, and the Court of Auditors. >> Council of Ministers; Court of Justice of the European Community; European Commission / Council / Economic Community / Monetary System / Parliament; Union

European Council The body which brings together the heads of state and/or government of the member states of the European Union. Since the mid-1960s, it has tended to take decisions on the basis of unanimity rather than majority voting. The need for agreement has resulted in severe difficulties in achieving reform, particularly in the area of agriculture. >> Council of Ministers; European Community / Union

European Court of Justice >> **Court of Justice of the European Communities**

European Currency Unit (ECU) >> **European Monetary System**

European Economic Area A trading bloc linking the European Union and the European Free Trade Association, introduced in January 1994. Its 372 million members make it the world's biggest free-trade area.

European Economic Community (EEC) An association within the European Union, established in 1958 after the Treaties of Rome (1957), often referred to as the **Common Market**. It is essentially a customs union, providing a common external tariff and a common market with the removal of barriers to trade among the members. In addition it has a number of common policies, the most important of which is the *Common Agricultural Policy*, providing for external tariffs to protect domestic agriculture and mechanisms for price support. There is also a *European Monetary System*, which regulates exchange rate movements among the member states' currencies. >> Common Agricultural Policy; customs union; EURATOM; European Commission / Community / Council / European Monetary System / Mercosur / Parliament

European Free Trade Association (EFTA) An association originally of seven W European states who were not members of the European Economic Community (EEC), intended as a counter to the EEC; it was established in 1959 under the Stockholm Convention. The members (Austria, Denmark, Norway, Portugal, Sweden, Switzerland, and the UK) agreed to eliminate over a period of time trade restrictions between them. Both the UK (1973) and Portugal (1986) left to join the EEC, but there has been a free trade agreement between the remaining EFTA countries and the European Community. Finland joined in 1985. The two groupings united as the European Economic Area in 1994. >> European Economic Community

European Monetary Institute An institution established in Frankfurt in January 1994, as a precursor to a European central bank – the second stage towards economic and monetary union. Its aims were to strengthen central bank cooperation and monetary policy co-ordination, and to prepare for the establishment of the European System of Central Banks for the conduct of a single monetary policy and the creation of a single currency. The Institute was liquidated following the establishment of the European Central Bank in 1998. >> European Central Bank

European Monetary System (EMS) A financial system set up in 1979 by member states of the European Economic Community with the immediate aim of stabilizing exchange rates and the ultimate aim of achieving Economic and Monetary Union (EMU), with a single European currency. A **European Currency Unit (ECU)** was created, but only as a unit of account; later named the **Euro**. Central banks were to consult on exchange rates, and to assist each other in stabilizing them both bilaterally and through a European Monetary Cooperation Fund. Members could join an **Exchange Rate Mechanism (ERM)**, which limited fluctuations in the exchange rates between its members. The first stage of formal EMU was established in 1990, when the Committee of Governors of the Central Banks of the EEC member states was given additional responsibilities to engage in the required preparatory work. The second stage was the replacement of this body by the European Monetary Institute (1 Jan 1994), whose activities included the introduction of a new Exchange Rate Mechanism (ERM II), adopted in mid-1997. The third stage, the adoption of the Euro by those member states which satisfied the entry conditions laid down by the EU Council, began on 1 January 1999. A new European Central Bank was set up (1 Jun 1998) to control monetary policy in the third stage. >> currency; devaluation; Euro; European Central Bank; European Economic Community; European Monetary Institute

European Parliament The representative assembly of the European Union. Despite its name, it has no legislative powers, but it does have the right to be consulted by the Council, to dismiss the Commission, and to reject or amend the Union budget. It has been directly elected since 1979. European-wide elections are held every 5 years, with seats divided as follows: Germany (99); UK, France, and Italy (87); Spain (64); The Netherlands (31); Belgium, Greece, and Portugal (25); Sweden (22); Austria (21); Denmark and Finland (16); Ireland (15); and Luxembourg (6). The administration of the Parliament lies in Luxembourg; its plenary sessions are held in Strasbourg; and its committees are in Brussels, where the Commission is based and the Councils meet. >> European Community / Union

European Recovery Program >> **Marshall, George C(atlett)**

European Space Agency (ESA) A consortium space agency of 13 European countries (Belgium, Denmark, Germany, France, Ireland, Italy, the Netherlands, Spain, Sweden, Switzerland, UK (founding nations) together with Austria and Norway, and associate member Finland) to promote space research, technology, and applications for exclusively peaceful purposes. It was created in 1975 and its headquarters is in Paris. Launches use the Ariane family of vehicles from a launch centre in Kourou, French Guiana. A major setback occurred in June 1996, when Ariane-5 exploded 40 seconds into its maiden flight. >> Giotto project; space exploration; Spacelab; Ulysses project

European Steel and Coal Community >> **European Community**

European System of Central Banks >> **European Central Bank**

European Union The political entity towards which the countries of the European Community (EC) are slowly moving, formally introduced as a designation in 1993. A milestone in this process was the *Maastricht Treaty* which includes, as its three pillars, provision for moves towards a common economic policy, a common foreign and security policy, and a common interior and justice policy. Britain is the most reticent of the 15 member-states regarding the process of union, and has opted out of the agreements to establish a common European currency and to move towards a common social policy. Negotiations to join with the Czech Republic, Estonia, Hungary, Poland, Slovenia, and Cyprus began in 1998; and admission talks started with Bulgaria, Latvia, Lithuania, Romania, and Slovakia. A single currency (the Euro) for 11 of the member states was introduced on 1 January 1999. >> Euro; European Community; Maastricht Treaty; Mercosur; RR1008 political leaders

Europort >> **Rotterdam**

Eurostar International high-speed passenger train service between London (Waterloo) and Continental Europe via the Channel Tunnel. Direct services in 1999 include Paris (and Disneyland), Brussels, Calais, and Lille, as well as Bourg St-Maurice and Moutier in the French Alps. Operated jointly by Eurostar (UK) Ltd, the French Railways (SNCF) and Belgium Railways (SNCB), it commenced operations in 1994. By 1999 there were 31 trains in the fleet, 392 m/1286 ft in length, each containing 766 passenger seats, and capable of speeds of 300 kph/186 mph. >> Channel Tunnel; railway

Eurovision Song Contest An annual contest organized by television companies throughout Europe to choose a winning pop song from among those entered by the participating countries. The first was held at Lugano, Switzerland, in 1956. >> pop music

Eurydice [yoo**ri**disee] In Greek mythology, a dryad, the wife of Orpheus. After her death, Orpheus went down to the Underworld and persuaded Hades to let her go by the power of his music. The condition was that she should follow him, and that he should not look at her until they reached the light. Not hearing her footsteps, he looked back, and she disappeared. >> dryad; Orpheus

eurypterid [yoo**rip**terid] An extinct, aquatic, water scorpion; large, up to 3 m/10 ft in length; known from the Ordovician period to the end of the Palaeozoic era. (Phylum: Arthropoda. Class: Eurypterida.) >> arthropod; Ordovician period; Palaeozoic era; scorpion

Eusebio [yoo**say**bioh], in full **Eusebio Ferreira da Silva**, nickname **the Black Pearl** (1942–) Footballer, born in Lourenço Marques, Mozambique. He made his international debut in 1961, and played for his country 77 times. At club level he played for Benfica. He retired in 1978, and was later appointed coach to Benfica. >> football [i]

Eusebius of Caesarea [yoo**see**bius] (c.264–340) Historian of the early Church, probably born in Palestine. His great work, the *Ecclesiastical History*, is a record of the chief events in the Christian Church until 324. >> Christianity

Eustachian tube [yu**stay**shn] >> **auditory tube**

eustasy [**yoo**stasee] Worldwide changes in sea level caused by the advance or recession of the polar ice caps. This has caused a gradual rise in the sea-level over the last century. >> Poles

Euston Road School A group of English painters working 1937–9 in London, including William Coldstream (1908–87), Victor Pasmore (1908–), Graham Bell (1910–43), and Claude Rogers (1909–79). They rejected abstraction and surrealism, and practised a quiet naturalism concentrating on domestic subjects. >> Pasmore

Euterpe [yooterpee] In Greek mythology, one of the Muses, usually associated with flute-playing. >> Muses

euthanasia The painless ending of life, usually as an act of mercy to relieve chronic pain or suffering. It has been advocated by pressure groups such as *Exit*, as a dignified death for the elderly who have lost the will to live. However, no country officially sanctions the practice, although in The Netherlands doctors performing euthanasia will not be prosecuted if they keep to certain guidelines. Since the 1980s, several cases of *doctor-assisted suicide* (the death of a terminally ill patient, through taking lethal drugs provided by a doctor), and associated notions such as *medicide* (*medically assisted suicide*), have been given publicity, and fuelled the medical ethical debate. During the 1990s, several US states made these practices illegal. >> hospice; Kevorkian; suicide

Evangelical Alliance A religious movement, founded in 1846 – the formal expression of an international evangelical community embracing a variety of conservative evangelical churches and independent agencies. In the USA it has been succeeded by the National Council of Churches of Christ in the United States of America. >> evangelicalism

evangelicalism Since the Reformation, a term which has been applied to the Protestant Churches because of their principles of justification through faith alone and the supreme authority accorded to scripture. It has been applied more narrowly to Protestant Churches emphasizing intense personal conversion ('born-again Christianity') and commitment in their experience of justification and biblical authority. >> Christianity; Lutheranism; Protestantism

Evangelical United Brethren Church A Christian denomination established in the USA in 1946 through the merger of the Church of the United Brethren in Christ and the Evangelical Church. In 1968 it merged with the Methodist Church to form the United Methodist Church. >> Christianity; evangelicalism; Methodism

evangelist (Gr *evangel*, 'good news') One who preaches the gospel of Jesus Christ. Although evangelizing is now understood to be the task of the whole Church, the term has been more recently applied to popular preachers at missionary rallies. >> Graham, Billy; John the Apostle, St

Evans, Sir Arthur (John) (1851–1941) Archaeologist, born in Nash Mills, Hertfordshire. Between 1899 and 1935 he excavated the city of Knossos, discovering the remains of the civilization which in 1904 he named 'Minoan', after Minos, the Cretan king of Greek legend. >> archaeology; Knossos

Evans, Dame Edith (Mary) (1888–1976) Actress, born in London. She earned a great reputation for her versatility, with many notable appearances in the plays of Shakespeare and Shaw. She continued to be active on both stage and screen into her eighties.

Evans, Sir Geraint (Llewellyn) (1922–92) Baritone, born in Pontypridd, Rhondda Cynon Taff, S Wales. He made his operatic debut at Covent Garden in 1948, and became particularly known for his comic roles. He retired from the operatic stage in 1984.

Evans, Timothy John >> **Christie, John**

Evans, Walker (1903–75) Photographer, born in St Louis, MI. His work with the writer James Agee to document the lives of the share-croppers of the Deep South, eventually published as *Let Us Now Praise Famous Men* (1941), is considered to be one of the best writer–photographer collaborations. >> Agee

evaporation The passing from a liquid phase to a gas phase; in particular, the process by which water is lost from the Earth's surface to the atmosphere as water vapour. Rates of evaporation depend on such factors as solar radiation, the temperature difference between the evaporating surface and the overlying air, humidity, and wind. >> humidity; radiation

Eve >> **Adam and Eve**

Evelyn, John [evelin, eevlin] (1620–1706) Writer, born in Wotton, Surrey. His main literary work is his *Diary*, a detailed sourcebook on life in 17th-c England.

evening primrose The name given to several very similar species of erect, robust biennials, native to North America; flowers large, broadly funnel-shaped with four narrow sepals and four overlapping yellow (sometimes red or white) petals, usually fragrant and opening at night. The oil from *Oenothera biennis* and *Oenothera lamarkiana* is claimed to be beneficial in several disorders. (Genus: *Oenothera*, 80 species. Family: Onagraceae.)

Evenki [evengkee] >> **Altaic**

event horizon >> **black hole**

Everest, Mount [evuhrest], Nepali **Sagarmatha**, Chin **Qomolangma Feng** 27°59N 95°26W. Mountain peak in the Himalayas of C Asia; height 8848 m/29 028 ft; highest mountain in the world; named after Sir George Everest (1790–1866), surveyor-general of India; summit first reached via the Southeast Ridge on 29 May 1953 by Sir Edmund Hillary and Sherpa Tenzing Norgay of Nepal in a British expedition under Col John Hunt. >> Hillary; Himalayas; Hunt, John

Everglades S Florida, USA; swampy, subtropical region, length c.160 km/100 mi, width 80–120 km/50–75 mi, area c.12 950 sq km/5000 sq mi; covers most of the Florida peninsula S of L Okeechobee; Everglades National Park in the S, a world heritage site. >> Florida; mangrove; savannah

evergreen plants Plants which retain their leaves throughout the year. They either grow in climates which have no adverse seasons or have leaves adapted to withstand cold and drought. The leaves are shed and replaced gradually, so that the plant always bears foliage. >> deciduous plants; leaf ℹ

Everly Brothers, The [eve(r)lee] American duo **Don Everly** (1937– , guitar, vocals), and **Phil Everly** (1939– , guitar, vocals). They had their first major hit with 'Bye Bye Love' (1957), and the style – close harmonies over acoustic guitars and a rock n' roll beat – became their trademark. They split up in 1973, but reformed in 1983 with a sell-out concert in London.

Evert (Lloyd), Chris(tine Marie) [evert] (1954–) Tennis player, born in Fort Lauderdale, FL. She won her first Wimbledon title in 1974 at age 19, and later won in 1976 and 1981; she also won the US singles title in 1975–80 and 1982, and several other titles. She married British tennis player John Lloyd (marriage dissolved in 1987), and in 1988 US skier Andy Mill. She retired from professional tennis in 1989 and was elected to the International Tennis Hall of Fame in 1995. >> tennis, lawn ℹ

Evesham [eevshm] 52°06N 1°56W, pop (1995e) 17 100. Town in Worcestershire, WC England; in the Vale of Evesham in a fruit- and vegetable-growing area; railway. >> England ℹ

Evita >> **Perón, Eva**

evolution Any gradual directional change; now most commonly used to refer to the cumulative changes in the characteristics of populations of organisms from generation to generation. Evolution occurs by the fixation of changes (*mutations*) in the structure of the genetic material, and the passing on of these changes from ancestor to descendant. It is well demonstrated over geological time by the sequence of organisms preserved in the fossil record. >> Darwinism; fossil; genetics; mutation

Evora [**ev**ura], ancient **Ebora** or **Liberalitas Julia** 38°33N 7°57W, pop (1995e) 38 800. Ancient walled market town in S Portugal; a world heritage site; airfield; railway; cathedral (1186), Roman Temple of Diana, old university (1551). >> Portugal ℹ

Evreux [ayvroe] 49°00N 1°08E, pop (1995e) 53 000. City in NW France; railway; cathedral (begun 11th-c).

Ewe [evay, **ay**way] A cluster of Kwa-speaking agricultural peoples of Togo, Ghana, and Benin. The coastal peoples also fish. >> Benin ℹ; Ghana ℹ; Togo ℹ

ewe >> **sheep**

Excalibur [eks**kal**iber] In Arthurian legend, the name of King Arthur's sword, which was given to him by the Lady of the Lake. As he lay dying he instructed Sir Bedivere to throw it back into the lake, where a hand drew it under. >> Arthur

exchange rates The price at which a currency may be bought in terms of a unit of another currency. Until the mid-1970s, rates were fixed from time to time; today, most are *floating* (ie the rate is determined by the ongoing supply and demand for the currency). >> devaluation; European Monetary System

excise tax A tax levied on many goods and services by governments as a way of raising revenues; often called **duty**. Best known are the duties on tobacco, alcoholic drinks, and fuel, Value Added Tax in the UK, and Sales Tax in the USA. >> taxation

executor(s) The individual(s) named in the will by a deceased person as being responsible for ensuring that his or her wishes are carried out. These duties include paying any debts from the estate, and ensuring that any balance is distributed amongst the beneficiaries according to the instructions in the will. >> probate; will

Exeter, ancient **Isca Dumnoniorum** 50°43N 3°31W, pop (1995e) 99 700. County town of Devon, SW England; on the R Exe; founded by the Romans 1st-c AD; railway; airfield; university (1955); cathedral (12th-c), Guildhall (12th-c); football league team, Exeter City (Grecians). >> Devon

existentialism A philosophical movement, closely associated with Kierkegaard, Camus, Sartre, and Heidegger. Its most salient theses are that there is no ultimate purpose to the world; that persons find themselves in a world which is vaguely hostile; that persons choose and cannot avoid choosing their characters, goals, and perspectives; and that truths about the world and our situation are revealed most clearly in moments of unfocused psychological anxiety or dread. These themes have influenced literature, psychoanalysis, and theology. >> Camus; Heidegger; Kierkegaard; Sartre

Exmoor National park in Somerset and Devon, England; area 686 sq km/265 sq mi; established in 1954; highest point, Dunkery Beacon, 520 m/1707 ft; known for its ponies; tourist area. >> Devon; Exmoor pony; Somerset

Exmoor pony The oldest British breed of horse; a small pony developed on Exmoor, Devon; height, 11·2–12·3 hands/1·2–1·3 m/3 ft 10 in–4 ft 3 in; very hardy; broad chest, deep body, stiff springy coat; brown with cream muzzle. >> Exmoor; horse ℹ

Exmouth [**eks**muhth] 50°37N 3°25W, pop (1995e) 33 900. Resort town in Devon, SW England; on the R Exe; centre for recreational sailing; railway. >> Devon

exobiology The study of extraterrestrial life; also known as **astrobiology**. Techniques include the monitoring of radio waves emitted by other star systems, and the use of space-probe experiments designed to detect life forms, or the presence of the molecules required for life to develop. >> biology; space exploration

Exodus, Book of The second book of the Pentateuch in the Hebrew Bible/Old Testament. It narrates stories about the deliverance of the Jews from slavery in Egypt, and the giving of the Law to Israel through a revelation to Moses on Mt Sinai. >> Moses; Pentateuch; Ten Commandments

exogamy >> **marriage**

exoplanet A planet orbiting a star outside the Solar System; short for **extrasolar planet**. The first such planet, orbiting 51 Pegasi, was discovered by Michael Mayor and Didier Queloz of Geneva in 1995. Others were announced in 1996 in 70 Virginis, 47 Utsaa Rajoris, and 55 Cancri, and several more have since been discovered. >> planet

exosphere The outer shell in the atmosphere (at c.400 km/250 mi) from which light gases can escape. >> atmosphere ℹ

expanding universe >> **'big bang'**

expert system A computer system which can perform at least some of the functions of the relevant human expert. Expert systems have been developed for use in areas, such as medical diagnosis, which require a large amount of organized knowledge plus deductive skills. >> artificial intelligence; knowledge-based system

Explorer 1 The first US space satellite (launched 31 Jan 1958). The simple 14-kg/31-lb spacecraft was launched on a Redstone (Jupiter C) rocket vehicle from Cape Canaveral. 'Explorer' later became the generic name of a series of relatively simple Earth orbital space physics and astronomy missions carried out by NASA. >> NASA; Van Allen radiation belts; RR970

explosives Substances capable of undergoing a rapid chemical change to produce hot gases which occupy a much greater volume, and therefore exert a sudden very high pressure. Most military and industrial explosives consist largely of nitrated carbon compounds. (The chief exception is the oldest explosive, gunpowder.) They are distinguished as **propellants** and **high explosives**. Propellants burn rapidly but smoothly, so as to exert a great but steady pressure on a projectile in the barrel of a gun. High explosives change so fast as to produce a violent and disruptive shock in adjacent material. >> detonator; gelignite; gunpowder; nitroglycerine

exposure (photography) The controlled presentation of a photosensitive surface to light in order to record an image. Exposure level is determined by the intensity of the light and the time of exposure, and must be correctly set to ensure satisfactory reproduction of tone and colour. In still cameras this is done by a suitable combination of lens aperture and shutter speed, but in motion picture and video cameras the exposure time is normally fixed, and level is set by the lens aperture. An **exposure meter** is an instrument for measuring light, giving a scale reading from which lens aperture and shutter setting may be determined. >> camera

exposure (physics) A measure of exposure to ionizing radiation, based on the amount of ionization produced in dry air by X-rays or gamma rays; symbol X, units R (röntgen). The modern notions of *absorbed dose* and *dose equivalent* are generally more useful. >> radioactivity units ℹ; X-rays

Expressionism A movement in art, architecture, and literature which aims to communicate the internal emotional realities of a situation, rather than its external 'realistic' aspect; the term was first used in Germany in 1911, but the roots of the movement can be traced to van Gogh and Gauguin in the 1880s. Traditional ideas of beauty and proportion are disregarded, so that artists can express their feelings more strongly by means of distortion, jarring colours, and exaggerated linear rhythms. The movement was also influential in literature, especially in German theatre after World War 1. >> *Blaue Reiter, der; Brücke, die*; Ensor; Fauvism; Gauguin; modern art; Munch; van Gogh

extinction The disappearance of a species from a particular habitat (*local* extinction), or the total elimination of a species worldwide. Animal species are categorized as extinct if they have not been definitely located in the wild for the past 50 years. >> species

extracellular fluid (ECF) The fluid which surrounds the cells of the body. In humans the adult volume is c.14 1/25 UK pt/30 US pt, and consists of blood plasma, the interstitial fluid of tissues, and transcellular fluids. >> plasma (physiology)

extradition The removal of a person by a state in which that person is currently located to the territory of another state where the person has been convicted of a crime, or is said to have committed a crime. Extradition treaties are normally restricted to more important crimes, but exclude political crimes.

Extranet >> **Intranet**

extrasensory perception (ESP) The apparent gaining of information about an object or event (mental or physical; past, present, or future) by means other than those currently understood by the physical sciences. Clairvoyance, telepathy, and precognition are specific types of extrasensory perception. >> clairvoyance; parapsychology; psi

extraversion >> **introversion / extraversion**

Extremadura [ekstrayma**doo**ra] or **Estremadura** [aystrayma**doo**ra] pop (1995e) 1 059 000 area 41 602 sq km/ 16 058 sq mi. Autonomous region of W Spain on the Portuguese frontier; considerable industrial development since the 1970s. >> Estremadura; Spain ℹ

extreme unction >> **anointing the sick**

extrusive rock Igneous rocks which have formed from molten magma, or volcanic fragments ejected onto the Earth's surface; also termed **volcanic rock**. They are most commonly basalt or pyroclasts. >> igneous rock; magma; pyroclastic rock

Eyck, Jan van [iyk] (c.1389–1441) Flemish painter, born (possibly) in Maaseik or Maastricht. The first master of the new realistic approach to painting in the 15th-c Netherlands, his skill is well-attested by the highly-finished 'Arnolfini Wedding Portrait' (1434, National Gallery, London).

eye A specialized receptor organ responding to light stimuli. Various forms exist, such as the stigmata of certain protozoa, the ocelli of annelids, and the compound eye of insects. In land-based vertebrates, such as humans, the eyeball is composed of two parts: the transparent *corneal* part at the front, and the opaque *scleral* part at the back. Three concentric coats form the wall of the eyeball: an outer *fibrous* coat, consisting of the cornea and sclera; a middle *vascular* coat, consisting of the choroid, ciliary body, and iris; and an inner *nervous* coat (the *retina*). The *lens* is transparent and biconvex, lying between the iris and the vitreous body; changes in its convexity alter its focal length (the greater the convexity, the shorter the focal length). Light entering the eye is refracted by the cornea, and passes through the lens, which focuses it to form an inverted image on the retina. This image is coded by the retina and sent to the visual areas of the cerebral cortex for interpretation, thus enabling the original pattern of light stimuli to be 'seen'. If the image from distant objects is focused in front of the retina, the condition is known as *myopia*, with vision being better for near objects ('short-sightedness'). If the image is focused beyond the retina, the condition is known as *hypermetropia*, with vision being better for distant objects ('long-sightedness'). Glasses using concave lenses are used to correct short sight; a convex lens is used for long sight. >> blindness; cataract; conjunctivitis; cornea; double vision; glaucoma; iris (anatomy); night blindness; ophthalmology; retina; river blindness; rods and cones; spectacles; stye; trachoma

eyespot A splash-borne disease of wheat and barley (*Pseudocercosporella herpotrichoides = Tapesia yallundae*), causing decay at the bases of growing stems. The disease is carried between seasons on crop residues, so that infection is more severe when successive susceptible crops are grown on the same field. It may be controlled by fungicidal spray or by crop rotation. (Order: Ascomycetes.) >> barley; fungus; wheat

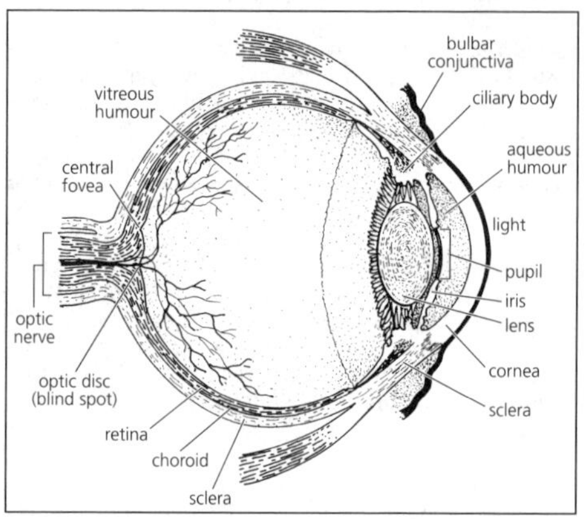

The structure of the eye

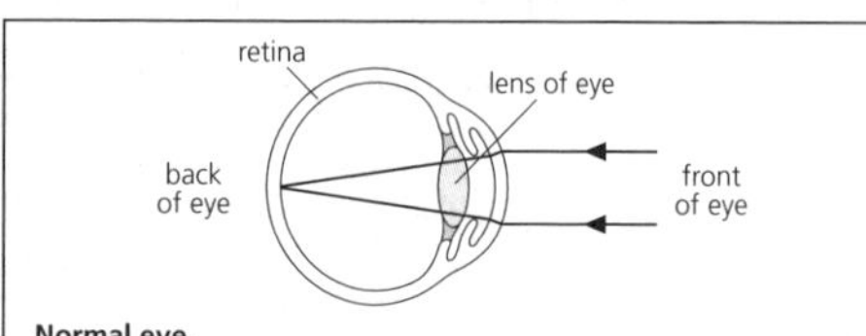

Normal eye.
The image is in focus on the retina without a correcting lens in front.

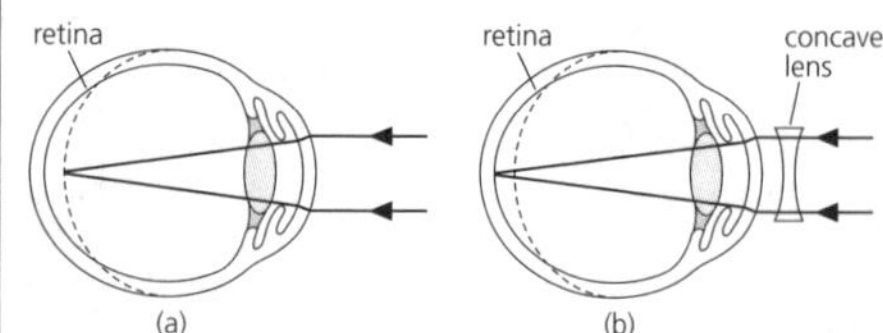

Short-sighted eye.
(a) The eye is too long and the image is not in focus on the retina.
(b) The use of a concave lens brings the image into focus.

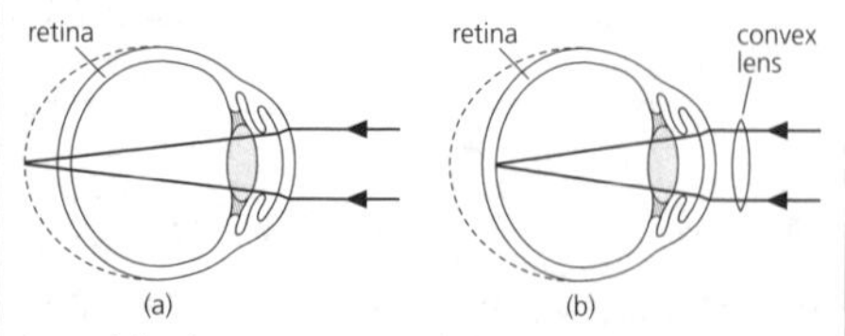

Long-sighted eye.
(a) The eye is too short and the image is not in focus on the retina.
(b) The use of a convex lens brings the image into focus.

The human eye – normal, short-sighted and long-sighted

Eyre Lakes [ayr] Dry salt lakes in NE South Australia; includes L Eyre North (145 km/90 mi long, 65 km/40 mi wide, area 7692 sq km/2969 sq mi) and L Eyre South (61 km/38 mi long, 26 km/16 mi wide, area 1191 sq km/460 sq mi); L Eyre North is the largest lake in Australia, normally a shallow pan of glistening white salt; 15 m/50 ft below mean sea-level; site of Donald Campbell's world land speed record (1964). >> Campbell, Malcolm; South Australia

Eysenck, Hans (Jurgen) [**iy**singk] (1916–97) Psychologist, born in Berlin. Much of his work was psychometric research into the normal variations of human personality and intelligence. He often held controversial views, particularly with his study of racial differences in intelligence. >> intelligence; psychometrics

Ezekiel or **Ezechiel, Book of** [ee**zee**kiel] A major prophetic work in the Hebrew Bible/Old Testament, attributed to Ezekiel, a 6th-c BC priest among the Jews exiled in Babylonian territories. The prophecies may have been the work of a later editor. >> Old Testament; prophet

Ezra the Scribe [**ez**ra] (5th–4th-c BC) Religious leader who lived in Babylon during the reign of King Artaxerxes (I or II), who reorganized the Jewish community in Jerusalem. An Old Testament book bears his name, as well as the apocryphal works of 1 and 2 Esdras (the Greek equivalent of 'Ezra'). >> Apocrypha, Old Testament; Esdras, Books of

F

Fabergé, Peter Carl [**fa**berzhay], originally **Karl Gustavovich Fabergé** (1846–1920) Goldsmith and jeweller, born in St Petersburg, Russia. He moved from the design of conventional jewellery to the creation of more elaborate and fantastic objects, notably the imperial Easter eggs commissioned by Alexander III for his tsarina in 1884.

Fabian Society A socialist group established in 1884 which took its name from the Roman general Fabius Cunctator, noted for his cautious military tactics. It adopts a gradualist approach to social reform. >> Shaw, George Bernard; socialism; Webb, Sidney and Beatrice; Wells, H G

Fabius Maximus, Quintus [**fay**bius **mak**simus], known as **Fabius Cunctator** (Lat 'the delayer') (c.260–203 BC) Roman general, statesman, and hero of the Second Punic War, whose refusal to engage Hannibal in set battle earned him his nickname. Originally a term of abuse, it became an honorific title after 216 BC, when Rome's defeat at the Battle of Cannae proved that his cautious tactics had been right. >> Punic Wars

fabliau [**fab**lioh] A short narrative poem popular in 12th–14th-c France, and also appearing in English (eg Chaucer's *Miller's Tale*). The subjects were usually bawdy, misogynist, and anti-clerical. >> Chaucer; poetry; Realism

Fabriano, Gentile da [fabri**ah**noh] (c.1370–c.1427) Painter, born in Fabriano, Italy. He painted religious subjects, notably 'The Adoration of the Magi' (1423, Florence), but few of his paintings have survived.

Fabricius, Hieronymus [fa**bree**tsius], also known as **Girolamo Fabrici** (1537–1619) Anatomist, born in Acquapendente, Italy. He made the first detailed description of the valves of the veins, the placenta, and the larynx.

fabrics >> **batik; denim; felt; tweed; twill**

Fabritius, Carel [fa**bree**tsius] (c.1624–54) Painter, born in Beemster, The Netherlands. Vermeer was much influenced by his sensitive experiments in composition and the painting of light, as in the tiny 'View of Delft' (1652, National Gallery, London). >> Vermeer

facilities management The process of efficient planning, integration, and operation of the different elements which make up a work environment. This environment may be anything from a small office to a major institution, and the facilities may include everything from day-to-day activities of catering, cleaning, and security to long-term planning considerations of office lay-out, refurbishment, and ergonomics. >> building biology; ergonomics

facsimile machine >> **fax**

factor VIII One of a series of enzymes present in the blood which controls the clotting process. Sufferers from classical haemophilia lack this factor, and are treated by intravenous administration of factor VIII that has been separated from fresh blood. This process carries the risk of transferring infections from the blood donor, such as AIDS; in the future, factor VIII may be produced using genetic engineering which will eliminate this risk. >> blood; enzyme; genetic engineering; haemophilia

factoring The purchase of goods for resale without further processing. **Debt factoring** is the purchase of debts due from a company's customers with the view to collecting them. When payment is problematical the debt will be bought at a discount. >> debt

Factory Acts Legislation passed in Britain from 1802 onwards to regulate employment in factories. The early Acts were generally concerned to limit the hours of work of women and children.

factory farming An intensive form of livestock production, usually carried out indoors with strict control over the environment and feeding regimes; also known as **battery farming**. Currently the predominant production technique for eggs, poultry meat, and pig meat, it is opposed by many environmentalists. >> environmentalism

faeces / feces [**fee**seez] Material discharged from the alimentary canal, consisting mainly of the undigested remains of ingested matter, bacteria, and water. The odour is the result of the formation of certain amines by intestinal bacteria. >> alimentary canal

Faeroe or **Faroe Islands** [**fair**oh], Danish **Færøerne** 62°00N 7°00W; pop (1995e) 47 000; area 1400 sq km/540 sq mi. Group of 22 sparsely vegetated volcanic islands in the N Atlantic between Iceland and the Shetland Is; 17 inhabited; settled by Norse, 8th-c; passed to Denmark, 1380; self-governing region of Denmark since 1948; capital, Tórshavn; largest islands, Strømø, Østerø; inhabitants speak Faroese. >> Denmark ℹ; Tórshavn

Fahd (ibn Abd al-Aziz) >> **Saud, al-**

Fahrenheit, Sir Gabriel (Daniel) [**fa**renhiyt] (1686–1736) Physicist, born in Gdańsk, Poland (formerly Danzig, Germany). He invented the alcohol thermometer in 1709, following this with a mercury thermometer in 1714. >> Fahrenheit temperature; thermometer

Fahrenheit temperature [**fa**renhiyt] A scale which takes the freezing point of water as 32°F and the boiling point as 212°F; symbol °F; introduced by German physicist Gabriel Fahrenheit. >> Fahrenheit; temperature ℹ

faience [**fiy**ahns] Earthenware decorated with an opaque glaze containing oxide of tin; the name derives from the Italian town of Faenza. English and Dutch Delftware and Italian maiolica employ exactly the same technique. >> Delftware; maiolica

fainting A brief episode of loss of consciousness, usually sudden in onset; also known as **syncope**. It is caused either by the reduction of blood supply to the brain or by changes in its electrical activity. Less commonly, low blood sugar may be responsible. >> epilepsy

Fairbanks 64°50N 147°50W, pop (1995e) 36 300. City in C Alaska; terminus of the Alaska railway and highway; founded in 1902 after the discovery of gold; university (1922). >> Alaska

Fairbanks, Douglas, (Elton), Snr, originally **Douglas Elton Ulman** (1883–1939) Film actor, born in Denver, CO. He made a speciality of swashbuckling hero parts, as in *The Three Musketeers* (1921) and *Robin Hood* (1922). His son **Douglas Fairbanks Jr** (1909–), followed in his footsteps, starring in such films as *The Prisoner of Zenda* (1937).

Fairfax (of Cameron), Thomas Fairfax, 3rd Baron (1612–71) English Parliamentary general, born in Denton, North Yorkshire. In the Civil War, he distinguished himself at Marston Moor (1644), and in 1645 was given command of the New Model Army, defeating Charles I at Naseby. >> English Civil War

fairy tales Traditional stories mainly for children, deriving from folk tales, and usually involving magic and fairies or other supernatural creatures. One of the oldest

collections is *The Arabian Nights' Entertainments* or *A Thousand and One Nights*, compiled c.1450. The first published collections of European tales were by Perrault (1697) and the Brothers Grimm (1812). These included such favourites as 'Cinderella', 'The Sleeping Beauty', and 'The Goose Girl'. >> folk tales; Grimm; nursery rhymes; Perrault

Faisalabad [**fiy**salabad], formerly **Lyallpur** (to 1979) 31°25N 73°09E, pop (1995e) 1 600 000. City in Punjab province, Pakistan; in an important cotton and wheat-growing region; railway. >> Pakistan i

faith healing The alleviation of physical and mental ailments by the prayer of a healer relying on a higher source (usually, the power of God) working in response to faith. Known in several religions, the practice is now a major feature of Christian pentecostal and charismatic movements. Critics assert that it is difficult to ascribe healing to the action of the higher source, because so little is currently understood about the effects of psychological attitudes upon the body's biochemistry. >> healing; Pentacostalism

Fajans, Kasimir [**fah**yans] (1887–1975) Physical chemist, born in Warsaw. He is best known for **Fajans's rules**, dealing with the types of bond between atoms in compounds. >> radioactivity

falabella The smallest breed of horse in the world; height, 7 hands/0·7 m/2 ft 4 in; developed by the Falabella family in Argentina; descended from a small thoroughbred and Shetland ponies. >> Shetland pony; thoroughbred

Falange [fa**lanj**], Span [fa**lan**khay] A Spanish fascist movement, founded in 1933 by José Antonio Primo de Rivera (1903–36). It was fused by Franco in 1937 with other rightist forces to form the single party of Nationalist Spain. >> fascism; Spanish Civil War

falcon Any bird of prey of the family Falconidae (c.60 species); worldwide; includes the carrion-feeding **caracara**, the **forest falcon** (large eyes, acute hearing, hunts in near-darkness), and the **true falcon** (a fast-flying predator which usually kills its prey in flight). >> bird of prey; gyrfalcon; harrier (bird); hobby; kestrel; merlin; peregrine falcon; sparrowhawk

Falcone, Giovanni [fal**koh**nay] (1939–92) Judge, born in Palermo, Sicily. In 1978 he was appointed to Palermo where he began a campaign against the Mafia, leading to the successful prosecution of 338 top members in 1987. He was killed when a bomb exploded under his car. >> Mafia

Faldo, Nick [**fal**doh], popular name of **Nicholas Alexander Faldo** (1959–) Golfer, born in Welwyn Garden City, Hertfordshire. His successes include the Professional Golfing Association championships (1978, 1980, 1981), the British Open Championship (1987, 1990, 1992), and the US Masters (1989, 1990, 1996). >> golf

Falkenlust >> **Augustusburg**

Falkland Islands, Span **Islas Malvinas** pop (1995e) 2100; area c.12 200 sq km/4700 sq mi. British Crown Colony in the S Atlantic, c.650 km/400 mi NE of the Magellan Strait; consists of East Falkland and West Falkland, separated by the Falkland Sound, with over 200 small islands; timezone GMT –4; **Falkland Islands Dependencies** (c.8 million sq km/3 million sq mi) stretch c.2400 km/1500 mi through the S Atlantic, and include South Georgia, South Sandwich Islands; population mainly of British descent; airport at Mt Pleasant near Stanley with a new runway built since the Falklands War; deeply indented coastline; hilly terrain, rising to 705 m/2313 ft at Mt Usborne (East Falkland); strong winds; narrow temperature range, 19°C (Jan), 2°C (Jul); low annual rainfall (635 mm/25 in); seen by several early navigators, including Capt John Strong in 1689–90, who named the islands; French settlement, 1764; British base established, 1765; French yielded their settlement to the Spanish, 1767; occupied in the name of the Republic of Buenos Aires, 1820; Britain asserted possession, 1833; formal annexation, 1908 and 1917; the whole area claimed since independence by Argentina; Falklands War, 1982; external affairs and defence are the responsibility of the British government, which appoints civil and military commissioners; internal affairs are governed by executive and legislative councils; chiefly agricultural economy; service industries to the continuing military presence in the islands. >> Falklands War; South Georgia; South Sandwich Islands; Stanley

Falklands War A war between Britain and Argentina, precipitated by the Argentine invasion of the Falkland Is, known to Argentinians as the **Malvinas**. Britain had ruled the islands continuously since 1833, but Argentina claimed them by inheritance from the Spanish Empire and through their proximity to her shores. When talks broke down, the Argentinian government of General Galtieri issued a warning to the British, and on 19 March merchants landed on South Georgia, ostensibly to demolish a whaling station, but they also raised the Argentine flag. On the night of 1–2 April the full-scale invasion of the Falklands began. The British immediately began to fit out a task force of almost 70 ships to retake the islands, under the command of Rear Admiral John Woodward. A 200-mile maritime exclusion zone was declared around the Falklands, and on 2 May the Argentine cruiser *General Belgrano* was sunk by the nuclear submarine *Conqueror*. South Georgia was retaken on 25 April and 5000 British troops were landed at Port San Carlos on 21 May. The British forces, under the command of Major General Jeremy Moore, took Darwin and Goose Green on 28 May, and after the recapture of the capital, Port Stanley, the Argentinians surrendered on 14 June. >> Argentina i; Falkland Islands i; Haig, Alexander; Thatcher, Margaret

Falla, Manuel de [**fal**ya] (1876–1946) Composer, born in Cadiz, Spain, whose works became known for their colourful national Spanish idiom. He is best known for his ballet, *The Three-Cornered Hat* (1919).

Fallopian tubes >> **uterine tubes**

fallout >> **radioactive fallout**

fallow deer A true deer (*Dama dama*) native to Mediterranean countries (introduced elsewhere); in summer, pale brown with white spots; in winter, grey without

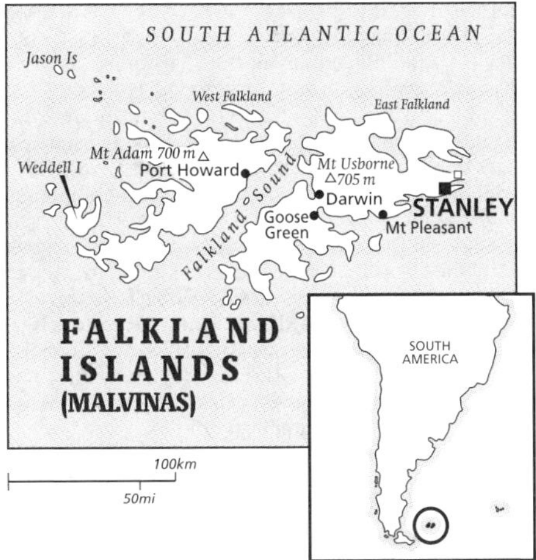

spots; antlers long, usually flattened with marginal projections. >> antlers ℹ; deer

Falwell, Jerry L [**fawl**wel] (1933–) Religious leader, born in Lynchburg, VA. In 1956, he founded Thomas Road Baptist Church, Lynchburg, VA, which became the basis of an extensive evangelical campaign. He was also responsible for founding The Moral Majority, Inc, and Liberty University. >> Baptists; evangelicalism

Famagusta [fama**goos**ta], Gr **Ammokhostos**, Turkish **Magusa** 35°07N 33°57E, pop (1995e) 20 600. Port in E Cyprus; occupies site of ancient Arsinoë, 3rd-c BC; strongly fortified by Venetians, 15th–16th-c; now under Turkish occupation; cathedral (14th-c). >> Cyprus ℹ

family of languages A set of 'daughter' languages which derive from the same 'parent' language, and which are thus genetically related. They can be represented by a *family tree*, as with the Indo-European languages, in which Celtic, Germanic, and Romance languages are all interrelated. >> comparative linguistics; Indo-European languages

family planning >> **contraception**

family therapy A type of psychiatric treatment in which the family is the therapeutic unit, and an attempt is made to change the structure and functioning of the unit as well as to improve relationships within it. The main development of this technique took place in the 1960s as a form of psychotherapy. >> psychotherapy

famine A period of food scarcity which may lead to malnutrition and death through starvation. The causes of famines are complex; they may result from natural causes, such as failure of a harvest following lack of rainfall and drought, or from combinations of political and economic circumstances such as war. Famine may also occur in a region where food is not completely scarce, but is unavailable to a sector of the population. >> Ethiopia ℹ; Irish Famine; sahel

fandango A Spanish dance in triple time, usually accompanied by guitars and castanets. It was known from c.1700 as a popular dance at roadside inns, and later became fashionable in aristocratic ballrooms.

Fanfani, Amintore [fan**fah**nee] (1908–) Italian statesman and prime minister, born in Pieve Santo Stefano, Italy. A former professor of political economics, he was prime minister on five occasions – in 1954, 1958–9, 1960–3 (twice), and 1982–3. He is a member of the Christian Democratic Party. >> Christian Democrats; Italy ℹ

Fangio, Juan Manuel [**fan**jioh] (1911–95) Racing motorist, born in Balcarce, Argentina. He first took part in European Grand Prix racing in 1949, and by 1957 had won the World Championship a record five times (1951, 1954–7). After his retirement (1958) he joined Mercedes-Benz in Argentina. >> motor racing

fantail The name used for a group of birds of uncertain affinity, native to SE Asian forests. (Genus: *Rhipidura* contains most of the c.42 species.) >> flycatcher; wagtail

fantasia An instrumental piece in which the composer's imagination is allowed free rein in one direction or another. An element of improvisation is often suggested, but some fantasias (such as Purcell's for strings) are carefully structured. >> improvisation; Purcell, Henry

Fantin-Latour, (Ignace) Henri (Jean Théodore) [fãtĩ latoor] (1836–1904) Painter, pastellist, and lithographer, born in Grenoble, France. He is best known for his flower studies and portrait groups, such as 'Hommage à Manet' (1870, Louvre). >> lithography ℹ

fanworm A sedentary marine worm that lives within a tube which it constructs; possesses a crown of tentacles or gills (*branchiae*) around its mouth, used for catching suspended food particles and for respiration; c.800 species. (Class: Polychaeta. Order: Sabellida.) >> worm

farad SI unit of capacitance; symbol *F*; defined as the capacitance of a capacitor comprising two parallel plates between which is a potential difference of one volt when the capacitor is charged with one coulomb of electricity; commonly used as μF (**microfarad**, 10^{-6} F) and pF (**picofarad**, 10^{-12} F). >> capacitance; Faraday

Faraday, Michael (1791–1867) Chemist, experimental physicist, and natural philosopher, born in Newington Butts, Surrey. His research contributed to an extremely broad area of physical science, such as the condensation of gases, the conservation of force, and studies on benzene and steel. His major work is the series of *Experimental Researches on Electricity* (1839–55), in which he reports a wide range of discoveries, notably electrolysis, and the relationship between electricity and magnetism. >> electrolysis ℹ

faraday The electrical charge on a mole ($6{\cdot}02 \times 10^{23}$) of electrons, $9{\cdot}65 \times 10^4$ coulombs. >> coulomb; Faraday; mole (physics)

Faraday cage >> **screening**

farandole [faran**dol**] A folk dance from Provence performed to music in a moderate tempo; usually played on a flute and a drum. >> Provence

farce A comic dramatic genre which focuses on both the limitations and liberties of the human body. Throughout a varied history (from Greek and Roman mimes to the Marx Brothers) it has never surrendered its anarchic purpose. Ruthless in pursuit of laughter, farce demands precision plotting and playing, bold stereotyping and mimicry, an aggressive sense of the incongruous, and a forthright recognition of the physical. Its themes never wander far from basic bodily functions. >> Labiche; Marx Brothers; Stooges, The Three; Travers

Farm Credit Administration (FCA) A system set up in the USA in the 1920s and 1930s to revive agriculture by providing adequate finance, especially mortgages. It was made independent in 1953, and is still in existence.

farming >> **dairy / factory / intensive / organic farming**

Farnaby, Giles [**fah(r)**nabee] (c.1560–1640) Composer, probably born in Truro, Cornwall. His works include madrigals and settings of the psalms, but he is best remembered for his keyboard music. >> madrigal

Farne Islands or **The Staples** A group of basaltic islets in the North Sea, 3 km/1¾ mi NE off Northumberland, NE England; St Cuthbert lived and died here; scene of heroic rescue in 1838 by Grace Darling and her father, William Darling (1795–1860), the lighthouse keeper, of survivors of the *Forfarshire*. >> Darling; North Sea

Faro [**fa**ru] 37°01N 7°56W, pop (1995e) 31 800. Industrial seaport in S Portugal; airport; railway; focal point of Algarve tourism; cathedral. >> Portugal ℹ

Faroe Islands >> **Faeroe Islands**

Faroese >> **Germanic languages; Scandinavian languages**

Farouk I [fa**rook**] (1920–65) King of Egypt (1936–52), born in Cairo. The defeat of Egypt by Israel (1948) and continuing British occupation led to increasing unrest, and General Neguib's coup (1952) forced his abdication and exile. >> Egypt ℹ

Farquhar, George [**fah(r)**ker] (c.1677–1707) Playwright, born in Londonderry, Co Londonderry. His first comedy, *Love and a Bottle* (1698), proved a success, as were several other plays, notably *The Beaux' Stratagem* (1707).

Farragut, David (Glasgow) [**fa**raguht] (1801–70) US naval commander, born near Knoxville, TN. In the Civil War he led the Union forces that captured New Orleans (1862), and took part in the siege and capture of Vicksburg (1863) and Mobile Bay (1864). >> American Civil War

Farr-Jones, Nick, popular name of **Nicholas Campbell Farr-Jones** (1962–) Rugby union player, born in Sydney, New South Wales, Australia. Captain of the Australian team (1988–90), he celebrated his 50th Test during the 1991 World Cup. >> football ℹ

Farrow, Mia (1945–) Film actress, born in Los Angeles, CA. Her film roles include *Rosemary's Baby* (1968), *The Great Gatsby* (1973), and several Woody Allen films, notably *The Purple Rose of Cairo* (1985), *Hannah and Her Sisters* (1986), and *Husbands and Wives* (1992). Earlier married to Frank Sinatra (1966–8), her relationship with Woody Allen broke up in acrimony in 1992, following her discovery of Allen's affair with their adopted teenage daughter. >> Allen, Woody

Farsi >> **Iranian languages**

farthing A small British coin, a quarter of an old (pre-decimalization) penny, its value therefore being 1/960th of £1. It was withdrawn from circulation in 1960.

Fasching [**fash**ing] or **Fastnacht** The period of merrymaking in S Germany and Austria, between Epiphany (6 Jan) and Lent. >> Munich

fasciation The abnormal, flattened growth of a single shoot, which resembles several stems fused together and often bears several inflorescences. It is common in such plants as dandelions and plantains. >> gall; inflorescence ℹ

Fasciola [fa**see**ola] >> **liver fluke**

fascism A term applied to a variety of vehemently nationalistic and authoritarian movements that reached the peak of their influence in 1930–45. The original fascist movement was founded by Mussolini in Italy (1921), and during the 1930s several such movements grew up in Europe, the most important being the German Nazi Party. The central ideas of fascism are a belief in the supremacy of the chosen national group over other races, and the need to subordinate society to the leadership of a dictator who can pursue national aggrandisement without taking account of different interests.

Fashoda [fa**shoh**da] A settlement (now called Kodok) on the upper White Nile, which was the scene of a major Anglo-French crisis in 1898. French forces withdrew following a British ultimatum.

Fasil Ghebbi [**fa**sil **ge**bee] The royal complex of Emperor Fassilides (1632–67) in Gondar, NW Ethiopia; a world heritage site. >> Ethiopia ℹ

Fassbinder, Rainer Werner [**fas**binder] (1946–82) Film director, born in Bad Wöshofen, Germany. He completed over 40 full-length films, largely politically committed criticisms of contemporary Germany, as in *Die Ehe der Maria Braun* (1979, The Marriage of Maria Braun). The most prolific writer-director-actor of the New German Cinema of the 1970s, he died at 36 as a result of alcohol and drug abuse.

Fassett, Kaffe [kayf] (1937–) Fashion designer, born in San Francisco, CA. He migrated to England in 1964, where he formed a design company producing knitting kits, needlepoint, and fabrics. His television broadcasts and books have made his colourful designs popular in Europe and the USA.

Fastnacht >> **Fasching**

fast reactor >> **nuclear reactor** ℹ

fat 1 A complex mixture of many different triglycerides, each formed when three molecules of fatty acids combine with one of glycerol. It is the major storage fuel of plants and animals. >> carboxylic acids; triglyceride **2** A white or yellowish animal tissue (*adipose tissue*) in which individual cells are swollen with the accumulation of fat forming a single globule within the cytoplasm. The stored triglycerides are an energy source for the organism. Fat acts as a packing and insulating material in many animals, but it can also act as a shock-absorber (eg under the heel). Human excess accumulation of body fat (*obesity*) arises when energy intake (diet) exceeds energy output (physical activity). >> cytoplasm; obesity

Fatah [**fa**ta] >> **PLO**

Fateh Singh, Sant [**fat**e **sing**] (1911–72) Sikh religious leader and campaigner for Sikh rights, born in the Punjab. During the 1950s he agitated for a Punjabi-speaking autonomous state, which was achieved with the creation of the Indian state of Punjab in 1966. >> Punjab (India); Sikhism

Fates >> **Moerae; Parcae**

Father Christmas >> **Santa Claus**

Father of the House (of Commons) The honorary and affectionate title given to the longest serving MP in the British parliament. In 1999, this was the former prime minister, Edward Heath. >> Commons, House of; Heath

Father's Day In some countries, a day on which fathers are honoured. In the USA and the UK, it is held on the third Sunday in June; in Australia, the first Sunday in September.

Fathers of the Church A title usually applied to the leaders of the early Christian Church, recognized as teachers of truths of the faith. The study of their writings and thought is known as *patristics*. >> Christianity; saint

Fatima (Portugal) [**fa**tima], also **Fátima** 39°37N 8°38W, pop (1995e) 7700. Pilgrimage town in C Portugal, where three peasant children claimed to have seen 'the Virgin of the Rosary' in 1917; Basilica (begun 1928, consecrated 1953). >> Portugal ℹ

Fatima (religion) c.605–33) The youngest daughter of Mohammed, and wife of the fourth Muslim caliph, Ali. From them descended the Fatimids, a radical Shiite movement, who ruled over Egypt and N Africa (909–1171), and later over Syria and Palestine. >> Mohammed; Shiites

fatty acids >> **carboxylic acids**

Faulkner or **Falkner, William (Harrison)** [**fawk**ner] (1897–1962) Writer, born in New Albany, MS. With *The Sound and the Fury* (1929) he began to experiment in literary form and style. *Sartoris* (1929) was the first in a series dealing with the social and racial problems of an imaginary Southern county, Yoknapatawpha. Other major novels include *As I Lay Dying* (1930), *Absalom, Absalom!* (1936), and *The Reivers* (1962). He was awarded the Nobel Prize for Literature in 1949.

fault In geology, a fracture in rock along which displacement has occurred due to stresses in the Earth. **Tear faults** release compressional stress by sideways displacement, the best known example being the San Andreas Fault in California. Major faults can create significant features of landscape, such as block mountains and rift valleys. >> horst; rift valley ℹ

Fauré, Gabriel (Urbain) [**foh**ray] (1845–1924) Composer, born in Pamiers, France. Though chiefly remembered for his songs, including the evergreen 'Après un rêve' (c.1865), he also wrote operas and orchestral pieces, and a much-performed *Requiem* (1887–90).

Faust [fowst] or **Faustus** [**fows**tus, **faws**tus] A legendary German scholar of the early 16th-c (derived from a historical magician of that name), who sold his soul to the devil in exchange for knowledge, magical power, and prolonged youth. His story has inspired several literary and musical works.

Fauvism [**foh**vizm] (Fr *les fauves* 'the wild beasts') A name given by a hostile critic to a group of modern painters (1898–1908) who were experimenting with vivid colours; they included Matisse, Derain, and Vlaminck. Their work was inspired by van Gogh, Gauguin, and Cézanne. >> Expressionism; Derain; Matisse; Vlaminck

Favre, Brett [fahvr] (1969–) Player of American football, born in Pass Christian, MS. He joined the Atlanta Falcons in 1991, then the Green Bay Packers as quarterback. He became only the second player to win the NFL's Most Valuable Player Award in consecutive years (1995–6), and shared the award again in 1997.

Fawcett, Dame Millicent, *née* **Garrett** (1847–1929) Women's rights campaigner, born in Aldeburgh, Suffolk. She was president of the National Union of Women's Suffrage Societies (1897–1919). >> women's liberation movement

Fawkes, Guy (1570–1606) Catholic conspirator, born in York, North Yorkshire. He served in the Spanish army in The Netherlands (1593–1604), then crossed to England at Catesby's invitation, and became a member of the Gunpowder Plot. Caught red-handed, he was tried and hanged. >> Catesby; Gunpowder Plot

fax The facsimile transmission of documents, diagrams, and photographs over a telephone network, widely available for international communication since 1986. The original is scanned by laser beam and digitally coded for transmission to the receiver, where it is printed out line by line on either thermo-sensitive paper or plain paper. >> laser

FBI >> **Federal Bureau of Investigation**

feather A structure formed from the skin of birds. It may be less than 0·5 cm/$\frac{1}{4}$ in long, or more than 1·5 m/5 ft. Birds evolved from reptiles, and feathers are modified scales. The central shaft bears many side branches (*barbs*), each barb having small side branches (*barbules*). The barbules of adjacent barbs interlock, creating the familiar flattened structure (*vane*). 'Down' feathers have flexible and sometimes branched barbs, and the barbules hold the barbs in a three-dimensional shape. Down feathers provide insulation; vaned feathers provide smooth aerodynamic surfaces. In many species feathers are important in display, and may be modified in shape and colour. >> bird [i]; reptile

February Revolution (France) The revolution in France (22–24 Feb 1848) which resulted in the abdication of King Louis Philippe, the proclamation of a republic, and the establishment of a provisional government. >> Louis Philippe; Revolutions of 1848

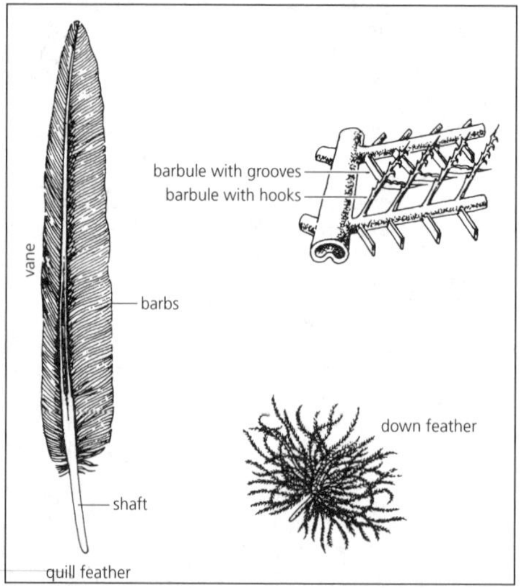

Feathers - flight feather with closeup of structure, and down feather

February Revolution (Russia) Popular demonstrations, strikes, and military mutinies in Petrograd, Russia (Feb–Mar 1917), which led to the abdication of Nicholas II and the collapse of the tsarist government.

feces >> **faeces**

Fechner, Gustav (Theodor) [**fekh**ner] (1801–87) Physicist and psychologist, born in Gross Särchen, Germany. His interest in mind-body relationships led to his book *Elemente der Psychophysik* (1860, Elements of Psychophysics), in which he developed the ideas of Ernst Heinrich Weber on the measurement of sensory thresholds, and laid the foundations for psychophysics. >> psychology; psychophysics; Weber

Fedayeen [feda**yeen**] A label commonly used to describe commandos operating under the umbrella of the Palestine Liberation Organization. The name is from the Arabic *fidai*, 'one who sacrifices oneself' (for a cause or country). >> PLO

Federal Bureau of Investigation (FBI) The US organization primarily concerned with internal security or counter-intelligence operations. It is a branch of the Department of Justice. >> police

Federal Constitutional Convention >> **Constitutional Convention**

federalism A form of territorial political organization which aims to maintain national unity while allowing for regional diversity. This is achieved by distributing different constitutional powers to national and regional governments. The key features of federalism usually are: (at least) two tiers of government enjoying their own right of existence under the constitution; separate legislative and executive powers; separate sources of revenue; an umpire (normally the supreme court) to decide upon disputes between the different levels; and a bicameral parliament which provides for representation in regional or state government. Beyond that, federalism takes a variety of forms: examples include the USA, Canada, Australia, and Germany. >> devolution

Federalist Party One of the two political parties that took shape in the USA in the 1790s. Washington (in office 1789–97) and John Adams (in office 1797–1801) were Federalist presidents, but after the 1800 election the Federalists never held the presidency, and the party slowly faded. >> Adams, John; Washington, George

Federal Reserve System (FRS) The USA Central Bank, known as 'The Fed', set up in 1913. It divides the USA into 12 districts, each with its own Federal Reserve Bank, carries out the normal duties of a central bank, and also manages cheque clearance on behalf of member banks.

Federal Theater Project A US project inaugurated in 1935 by an Act of Congress as part of the Works Projects Administration. It sought to provide employment to theatre professionals during the Depression, and 'free, adult, uncensored theatre' throughout the country. This experiment in federal sponsorship was terminated by Congress in June 1939. >> Works Projects Administration

feedback The process by which information is conveyed to the source of the original output; also, the information itself. The term comes from cybernetics, and is applied both to machines and to animal and human communication, whereby it enables the sender of a message to monitor its reception and make any necessary modification. >> biofeedback

Feininger, Lyonel (Charles Adrian) [**fiy**ninger] (1871–1956) Painter, born in New York City. After World War 1 he taught at the Bauhaus in Weimar and Dessau, and adopted a style reminiscent of Cubism. He later helped to found the New Bauhaus in Chicago. >> Bauhaus; Cubism

feldspar or **felspar** An important group of minerals constituting about half of the rocks of the Earth's crust. All are aluminosilicates containing various proportions of potassium, sodium, and calcium (and, rarely, barium). Important minerals of the group are *orthoclase* and *Microcline* (both $KAlSi_3O_8$), *albite* ($NaAlSi_3O_8$) and *anorthite* ($CaAl_2Si_2O_8$). Na,Ca feldspars are termed *plagioclase*. >> orthoclase; silicate minerals

Felidae [**fel**idee] The cat family (37 species); a family of muscular carnivores with camouflaged coloration; round head with powerful jaws, long canine teeth; sharp claws (usually retractable); cannot chew food; eats meat almost exclusively. >> caracal; carnivore ℹ; cat; cheetah; cougar; jaguar; jaguarundi; leopard; liger; lion; lynx; margay; ocelot; panther; serval; snow leopard; tiger; wild cat

feline immunodeficiency virus (FIV) A viral disease related to but quite separate from human immunodeficiency virus (HIV). It does not affect humans. A wide variety of clinical signs is seen in cats, as other organisms overcome the immune system. >> cat; HIV; virus

feline infectious enteritis (FIE) A serious, often fatal disease of cats and other Felidae; also known as **panleucopenia (FPL)**, and occasionally by the blanket term **cat flu**. It is caused by a virus of the parvovirus group. Young cats are very vulnerable, but protection by the use of a vaccine is effective. >> canine parvovirus; cat flu

Fellini, Federico [fel**ee**nee] (1920–93) Film director, born in Rimini, Italy. His highly individual films, always from his own scripts, include *La strada* (1954, The Road; foreign film Oscar winner, 1957), *Fellini's Roma* (1972) and, his most famous and controversial work, *La dolce vita* (1960, The Sweet Life; Cannes Festival prizewinner). He was presented with an Honorary Academy Award in 1993.

felony Originally, at common law, every crime which occasioned the forfeiture of land and goods, usually punishable by death. In modern times, in the USA, a felony is a crime which carries a potential punishment in a state prison of not less than one year. It corresponds roughly to an **indictable offence** in the UK, and is distinguished from a **misdemeanour**. >> indictment; misdemeanour

felspar >> **feldspar**

felt A non-woven cloth consisting of loose 'webs' of natural or synthetic fibre, or formed in fabrics by the action of moisture, heat, and repeated pressure. Felts are important industrial and domestic materials.

feminism A socio-political movement whose objective is equality of rights, status, and power for men and women. It has its roots in early 20th-c struggles for women's political emancipation (the suffragettes), but has been broadened in its political scope by the influence of radical left-wing beliefs, especially Marxism, which has led feminists to challenge both sexism and the capitalist system which is said to encourage patriarchy. >> gender; sexism; suffragettes; women's liberation movement

femur [**fee**mer] The long bone of the thigh, having a rounded head, neck, and shaft, and an expanded lower end. It is the largest and longest bone in the body. >> skeleton ℹ

fencing The art of fighting with a sword, one of the oldest sports, which can be traced back to the ancient Egyptians c.1300 BC. Modern weapons consist of the *sabre*, *foil*, and *épée*. In competitive fencing, different target areas exist for each weapon, and contestants wear electronically wired clothing to indicate successful hits. >> RR1051

Fénelon, François de Salignac de la Mothe [fayneló] (1651–1715) Roman Catholic theologian, born in Fénelon, France. His chief work, *Les Aventures de Télémaque* (1699, The Adventures of Telemachus), received the censure of Louis XIV for its political undertones. Also controversial was his *Explication des maximes des saints sur la vie intérieure* (1697, Explanation of the Sayings of the Saints on the Interior Life), which was condemned by the Pope.

Fenians [**feen**ianz] The short title of the Irish Republican Brotherhood, a nationalist organization founded in New York in 1857. The movement quickly espoused violence as a means of achieving its objective, and is best known for attacks in Manchester and London in 1867 to rescue imprisoned supporters. >> nationalism; Sinn Féin

fennec fox A small nocturnal fox (*Vulpes zerda*) native to deserts in N Africa and Kuwait; smallest member of the dog family; thick pale coat, enormous ears; also known as **desert fox**. >> Canidae; dog; fox

fennel A strong-smelling, bluish-green biennial or perennial (*Foeniculum vulgare*), growing to 2·5 m/8 ft, native to the Mediterranean region; flowers yellow; fruit ovoid, ribbed. The leaves are used as a flavouring. Certain forms are eaten raw in salads or cooked as a vegetable. (Family: Umbelliferae.) >> herb

Fens, the or **the Fen Country** Flat marshy land surrounding the Wash, in Lincolnshire, Norfolk, Suffolk, and Cambridgeshire, E England; extends 112 km/70 mi N–S and 6 km/4 mi E–W; remnant of a silted-up North Sea bay; major reclamation in 17th-c under 5th Earl of Bedford; market gardening, fruit, vegetables, grazing. >> Bedford Level; England ℹ; Wash, the

fenugreek An annual (*Trigonella foenum-graecum*) growing to 50 cm/20 in, a native of SW Asia; pea-flowers yellowish-white, solitary or in pairs; pod up to 10 cm/4 in long. Grown for fodder, its seeds are edible (used in curries), and it is also employed medicinally. (Family: Leguminosae.)

fer-de-lance [fair duh lahns] (Fr 'spearhead') A New World pit viper; powerful venom; two species: *Bothrops atrox* (**Southern fer-de-lance**) and *Bothrops asper* (**Central American fer-de-lance**); also known as **lancehead viper**. >> pit viper ℹ

Ferdinand, known as **the Catholic** (1452–1516) King of Castile, as Ferdinand V (from 1474), of Aragon and Sicily, as Ferdinand II (from 1479), and of Naples, as Ferdinand III (from 1503), born in Sos, Aragon (Spain). In 1469 he married Isabella, sister of Henry IV of Castile, and ruled jointly with her until her death. He introduced the Inquisition (1478–80), and in 1492, after the defeat of the Moors, expelled the Jews. Under him, Spain gained supremacy following the discovery of America, and by 1512 he had become monarch of all Spain. >> Holy League; Inquisition; Isabella of Castile

Ferdusi >> **Firdausi**

Ferghana [fer**gan**a] A strategic point on the ancient Silk Road from China, lying E of Samarkand. The area, now in Kyrgyzstan, is famous for its horses. >> Kyrgyzstan ℹ; Silk Road

Ferguson, Sir Alex(ander Chapman) (1941–) Football player and manager, born in Glasgow, W Scotland. A former Queens Park Rangers player, he became a manager, and had success with Aberdeen (1978–86) before taking over at Manchester United, where his achievements include the FA Cup (1990), the League and Cup double (1994, 1996), and the League/Cup/European Cup treble (1999).

Ferguson, Sarah >> **Andrew, Duke of York**

Fermanagh [fer**man**a], Ir **Fear Manach** pop (1995e) 53 600; area 1876 sq km/715 sq mi. District and county in SW Northern Ireland; rises to 667 m/2188 ft at Cuilcagh; Upper and Lower Lough Erne run SE–NW; county town, Enniskillen. >> Enniskillen; Northern Ireland ℹ

Fermat, Pierre de [fermah] (1601–65) Mathematician, born in Beaumont-de-Lomagne, France. He became a lawyer, and then turned to mathematics, making many discoveries in the properties of numbers, probabilities, and geometry. >> Fermat's last theorem; Fermat's principle

Fermat's last theorem A mathematical theorem proposed by Pierre de Fermat, which states that there are no positive integers *x*, *y*, *z*, and *n* (where *n* is greater than 2), such that $x^n + y^n = z^n$. The theorem was proved by British mathematician Andrew Wiles in 1994. >> Fermat

Fermat's principle A principle in physics: light rays travel between two points in such a way that the time taken is a minimum; stated by French mathematician Pierre de Fermat in 1657. >> Fermat

fermentation A chemical reaction in which an organic compound is broken down through the action of an enzyme. This process is typically carried out using bacteria or yeast to metabolize carbohydrates in the absence of oxygen. The two most common end-products are lactic acid and ethanol. >> anaerobe; bacteria [i]; enzyme; ethanol; lactic acid; wine; yeast; yogurt

Fermi, Enrico [**fer**mee] (1901–54) Nuclear physicist, born in Rome. In 1934 he and his colleagues in Rome split a number of nuclei by bombardment with neutrons, for which he was awarded the 1938 Nobel Prize for Physics. In the USA, he played a prominent part in developing atomic energy, and constructed the first US nuclear reactor (1942). >> fermions; nuclear physics

fermi [**fer**mee] >> RR1031

fermions Subatomic particles having half integer spin, the particles of matter; named after Italian physicist Enrico Fermi. Electrons, protons, and quarks are all fermions. >> Fermi; lepton; particle physics; spin

fern A member of a large group of spore-bearing, vascular plants related to clubmosses and horsetails. The visible plant typically has one or more large, often much-divided fronds which are characteristically coiled in a crozier shape when young, unfurling as they grow. Ferns embrace a large number of forms. A few are annuals, but most are perennials with tough rhizomes. Although more or less cosmopolitan, the majority of species are concentrated in the tropics and in the warmer, more humid parts of the world. (Class: Filicopsida or Filicinae, c.10 000 species.) >> clubmoss; horsetail; sporophyte

Fernandel [fernãdel], stage name of **Fernand Joseph Désiré Contandin** (1903–71) Film comedian, born in Marseilles, France. From 1930 he appeared in over 100 films, establishing himself internationally as the country priest of *Le Petit Monde de Don Camillo* (1953, The Little World of Don Camillo). He was renowned for his wide grin and his remarkable facial mobility.

Fernando Póo >> **Bioko**

Ferrar, Nicholas (1592–1637) Anglican clergyman and spiritual mystic, born in London. At Little Gidding in Huntingdonshire he founded a small religious community, which was broken up by the Puritans in 1647. >> Church of England

Ferrara [fay**rah**ra] 44°50N 11°38E, pop (1995e) 149 000. Ancient town in N Italy; seat of the Council of Ferrara, 1438, and of the 15th-c Renaissance court; archbishopric; railway; university (1391); cathedral (12th–14th-c). >> Italy [i]

Ferrari, Enzo [fe**rah**ree] (1898–1988) Racing-car designer, born in Modena, Italy. He became a racing driver in 1920, and in 1929 founded the company which bears his name, remaining president until 1977.

Ferraro, Geraldine A(nne) [fe**rah**roh], married name **Zacarro** (1935–) US politician, born in Newburgh, NY. She was elected as a Democrat to the US House of Representatives in 1981, and was selected in 1984 by Walter Mondale to be the first female vice-presidential candidate of a major party. In 1992 and 1998 she ran in the New York senatorial primary, but lost the nomination despite much popular support.

ferrate A compound containing iron as part of an anion. >> anion; iron

ferret A domesticated form of the European polecat (*Mustela putorius*); yellowish-white with pink eyes; sent down burrows to chase out rabbits; bred white so it is not mistaken for a rabbit. >> badger; polecat

Ferrier, Kathleen (1912–53) Contralto singer, born in Higher Walton, Lancashire. One of her greatest successes was in Mahler's *Das Lied von der Erde* (The Song of the Earth) at the first Edinburgh Festival (1947).

ferrimagnetism The magnetic property of materials (eg ferrites) for which neighbouring atomic magnetic moments are of different strengths and are aligned antiparallel. It is related to ferromagnetism, but exhibiting much weaker gross magnetic properties. >> ferrites; ferromagnetism

ferrites A class of ceramic materials composed of oxides of iron and some other metal such as copper, nickel, or manganese. Of low electrical conductivity, they are used as core material in high-frequency electrical coils, loudspeaker magnets, and video/audio tape-recorder heads. >> ceramics; ferrimagnetism; oxide

ferro-alloys Combinations of elements added to molten steel to impart various properties, such as greater corrosion resistance or strength. >> alloy; steel

ferrocene [**fe**roseen] $Fe(C_5H_5)_2$, orange solid, melting point 173°C, first prepared in 1951, in which an iron atom is symmetrically bonded to two cyclopentadienyl rings. It was the first of a series of transition metal organometallic compounds called **metallocenes**. >> metal; transition elements

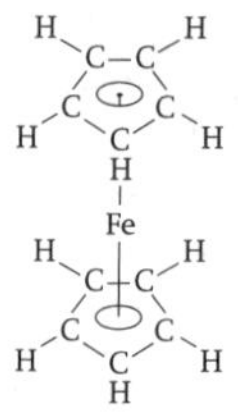

ferrocene

ferromagnetism A property of ferromagnetic substances (eg iron, nickel, cobalt, gadolinium, dysprosium, and many alloys) arising from large-scale alignment between atomic magnetic moments. An applied magnetic field intensity, supplied by a surrounding electric coil, causes a disproportionately large magnetic flux density to appear in the bulk material. A field may remain in the material even when the external field has been removed, resulting in permanent magnets. >> ferrimagnetism; magnetism

fertility drugs Drugs which treat infertility in women – usually successfully if it is due to a failure to ovulate. Early fertility drugs caused multiple pregnancies, but newer drugs such as clomiphene are not so extreme, though the incidence of twins is 10% of all successful pregnancies. >> pregnancy [i]

fertilization The union of two gametes to form a zygote, as occurs during sexual reproduction. The gametes are typically male (a sperm) and female (an egg), and both are haploid (possess a single chromosome set). Fertilization involves the fusion of the two haploid nuclei to form a diploid zygote that develops into a new individual. >> gamete; reproduction; zygote

fertilizer A substance which provides plant nutrients when added to soil. The term normally refers to inorganic chemicals containing one or more of the basic plant nutrients: nitrogen, phosphorus, or potash. It may also refer to compounds containing trace elements such as boron, cobalt, copper, iron, manganese, molybdenum, and zinc; to lime, which is used to correct acidity; or to a concentrated organic substance such as dried blood and bonemeal. >> organic farming; trace elements

Fès >> **Fez**

fescue A tufted grass with inrolled, bristle-like leaves, found almost everywhere; important as pasture grass. (Genus: *Festuca*, c.80 species. Family: Gramineae.) >> grass 🛈

Festival of Britain An event organized in 1951 to mark the centenary of the Great Exhibition held in London in 1851. The Royal Festival Hall was built for the occasion.

fetch >> **wave** (oceanography)

fetus / foetus The embryo of a mammal, especially a human, at a stage of development when all the main features of the adult form are recognizable. In humans, this stage is from 8 weeks to birth. >> embryo

feudalism In a narrow sense, the mediaeval military and political order based on reciprocal ties between lords and vassals, in which the main elements were the giving of homage and the tenure of fiefs. Polemicists apply the term to whatever appears backward or reactionary in the modern world. >> Middle Ages; vassal

Feuerbach, Ludwig (Andreas) [**foy**erbakh] (1804–72) Philosopher, born in Landshut, Germany. His most famous work was *Das Wesen des Christentums* (1841, The Essence of Christianity). His naturalistic materialism was a strong influence on Marx and Engels. >> Engels; idealism; Marx; rationalism (philosophy)

Feuillants, Club of the [foeyã] An association of moderate deputies and former members of the Jacobin Club, who aimed at establishing a constitutional monarchy in France during the first stage of the Revolution (1791). >> French Revolution 🛈; Jacobins (French history)

fever A clinical condition when the temperature of the body rises above the upper limit of normal, namely 37·7°C taken in the mouth; also known as **pyrexia**. Most fevers are due to infections, and virtually all infectious diseases cause fever. >> infection; temperature 🛈

feverfew An aromatic perennial (*Tanacetum parthenium*) growing to 60 cm/2 ft, probably native to SE Europe; flower-heads long-stalked in loose, flat-topped clusters; spreading outer florets white, inner disc florets yellow. As a medicinal herb, it is reputed to provide relief from migraines, but it has toxic side-effects. (Family: Compositae.) >> herb

Feynman, Richard (Phillips) [**fiyn**man] (1918–88) Physicist, born in New York City. He shared the Nobel Prize for Physics in 1965 for his work on quantum electrodynamics, and is also known for his visual representation of the behaviour of interacting particles, known as **Feynman diagrams**. >> electrodynamics; particle physics

Fez or **Fès** [fez] 34°05N 5°00W, pop (1995e) 599 000. City in NC Morocco; Old Fez, a world heritage site, founded in 808; New Fez founded in 1276; modern Fez (Ville Nouvelle) S of the railway; name given to a type of red felt hat worn by many Islamic followers; railway; Karaouine mosque (first built, 9th-c) became famous as a Muslim university. >> Morocco 🛈

Fianna Fáil [fi**ana foyl**] (Ir 'Militia of Ireland') An Irish political party founded in 1926 by those opposed to the 1921 Anglo-Irish Treaty. It first came to power under de Valera in 1932, and has been the governing party for most of the period since. It has consistently supported the unification of Ireland. >> de Valera

fiber >> **fibre**

Fibonacci, Leonardo [fibo**nah**chee], also known as **Leonardo Pisano** (c.1170–c.1250) Mathematician, born in Pisa, Italy, arguably the most outstanding mathematician of the Middle Ages. He popularized the modern decimal system of numerals, and made an advanced contribution to number theory. He also discovered the **Fibonacci sequence** of integers in which each number is equal to the sum of the preceding two (0,1,1,2,3,5,8...). >> number theory

fibre / fiber That part of plant carbohydrates which cannot be digested by the normal carbohydrate-digesting enzymes in the small intestine. Fibre is largely contained in the structural part of plants, ie the roots, stem, seed coat, or husk. The most abundant fibre in nature, cellulose, is made up of repeating glucose units in long single strands, making it ideal for conversion into the fabric cotton. >> bran; carbohydrate; cellulose; intestine

fibre-glass / fiber-glass A composite material for the construction of light, generally complex-curved structures, made of glass fibres embedded in a polyester or epoxy resin which can be moulded before setting; more fully described as **glass fibre reinforced plastic**. It is much used for hulls of boats, tanks for liquids, and occasionally for car bodies. In the USA, *Fibreglas* is a registered trade mark for this material. >> epoxy resin 🛈; polyesters

fibre optics >> **optical fibres** 🛈

fibres / fibers The fundamental units from which textiles are made. Natural fibres include wool, cotton, linen, jute, cashmere, and silk. Synthetic fibres are made from polymers using oil as the raw material; examples include nylons, polyesters and acrylics. >> carbon fibre; carpet; cashmere; cotton 🛈; nylon; polyesters; silk; yarn

fibrositis [fiybruh**siy**tis] An imprecise lay term referring to aching in the muscles, which may be locally tender. It is usually felt in the neck, shoulders, or back. The underlying nature of the disorder is unknown in the majority of cases. >> muscle 🛈

fibula [**fib**yoola] A long slender bone in the calf, which articulates with the foot (via the ankle joint) and the tibia. It is thought to have no weight-bearing function, but gives attachment to many of the muscles of the calf. >> foot; skeleton 🛈; tibia

Fichte, Johann Gottlieb [**fikh**tuh] (1762–1814) Philosopher, born in Rammenau, Germany. An ardent disciple of Kant, he modified the Kantian system by substituting for the 'thing-in-itself' as the absolute reality, the more subjective *Ego*, the primitive act of consciousness. In *Reden an die deutsche Nation* (1807–8, Addresses to the German Nation) he invoked a metaphysical German nationalism to resistance against Napoleon. >> Kant

Fichtelgebirge [**fikh**telgebeerguh], Czech **Smrčiny** Horseshoe-shaped mountain range in Bavaria, Germany; highest peak Schneeberg (1051 m/3448 ft). >> Bavaria; Germany 🛈

Ficino, Marsilio [fi**chee**noh] (1433–99) Philosopher, born in Figline, Italy. He was a major influence in the Renaissance revival of Platonism, which he attempted to reconcile with Christianity. >> Plato

fiddler crab A marine crab commonly found on intertidal mud flats in tropical and subtropical regions; males have a large claw used for signalling during courtship. (Class: Malacostraca. Order: Decapoda.) >> crab

FIDE [**fee**day] >> **chess**

Fidei Defensor >> **Defender of the Faith**

Field, John (1782–1837) Composer and pianist, born in Dublin. An infant prodigy, he wrote mainly for the piano (including seven concertos), and is credited with originating the nocturne. His music influenced Chopin. >> Chopin, Frédéric; nocturne

field emission The emission of electrons from a metal surface caused by the application of an intense electric field. Field emission microscopes guide electrons emitted from a sharp metal point to a screen, forming a highly magnified image of the metal's structure. >> electron; thermionics

fieldfare A thrush native to Europe and Asia (*Turdus pilaris*); found in S Greenland since 1937; brown back, mottled breast, grey head. >> redwing; thrush (bird)

Fielding, Henry (1707–54) Playwright and novelist, born at Sharpham Park, Glastonbury, Somerset. On Richardson's publication of *Pamela* (1740), he wrote his famous parody, *Joseph Andrews* (1742). Several other works followed, notably *The History of Tom Jones, A Foundling* (1749), which established his reputation as a founder of the English novel. >> novel; Richardson, Samuel

fieldmouse A mouse of genus *Apodemus* (**Old World field mice** or **wood mice**, 13 species) or of genus *Akodon* (**South American field mice** or **grass mice**, 41 species). Old World fieldmice often jump; South American fieldmice have short legs, and are less athletic. >> mouse (zoology)

Field of the Cloth of Gold, the A meeting between Henry VIII and Francis I near Calais in 1520, in which England sought to mediate in the Habsburg–Valois wars; named for the lavish pavilions of golden cloth erected by the French. >> Francis I (of France); Henry VIII

Fields, Dame Gracie, originally **Grace Stansfield** (1898–1979) Singer and variety star, born in Rochdale, Greater Manchester. With her sentimental songs and broad Lancashire humour, she won a unique place in the affections of British audiences. Her theme tune, 'Sally', she first sang in 1931.

Fields, W C, originally **William Claude Dukenfield** (1879–1946) Actor, born in Philadelphia, PA. He established his comic persona in silent films such as *Sally of the Sawdust* (1925), but his characteristic gravelly voice found its full scope with the coming of sound in the cinema during the 1930s.

Fiennes, Sir Ranulph (Twisleton-Wykeham-) [fiynz] (1944–) Explorer and expedition leader, born in Windsor, S England. He was leader of several expeditions, including the Transglobe (1979–82), tracing the Greenwich Meridian across both Poles. With Michael Stroud he completed the first unsupported crossing on foot of the Antarctic in 1993, covering 2300 km/1350 mi in 95 days.

Fiennes, Ralph (Nathaniel) [rayf fiynz] (1962–) Actor, born in Suffolk, UK. A theatre actor in the late 1980s, his film debut was in *Emily Bronte's Wuthering Heights* (1991). Later films include *Schindler's List* (1993, Golden Globe, Oscar nomination), *The Baby of Macon* (1993), and *The English Patient* (1996, Oscar nomination).

FIFA [feefa] The abbreviation of **Fédération Internationale de Football Association**, the world governing body of association football, founded in Paris in 1904. FIFA stages its World Cup tournament every four years. >> football ℹ

Fife, also sometimes called **Kingdom of Fife** pop (1995e) 351 000; area 1307 sq km/505 sq mi. Local council in E Scotland, bounded by the Firth of Tay (N), North Sea (E), and the Firth of Forth (S); Lomond Hills in the W; capital, Glenrothes. >> Glenrothes; Scotland ℹ

fife A small, high-pitched, transverse flute, with six finger-holes and (in modern and some older instruments) metal keys. Fifes have been mainly military instruments, used (like the bugle) for calls and signals, and also, in 'drum and fife' bands, for marching. >> flute; woodwind instrument ℹ

Fifteen Rebellion The name given to the first of the Jacobite rebellions against Hanoverian monarchy to restore the Catholic Stuart Kings to the British throne. The rising was begun at Braemar (Sep 1715) by the Earl of Mar, proclaiming James Edward Stuart ('the Old Pretender') as king. Jacobite forces were defeated at Preston in November, and the rebellion collapsed early in 1716. >> Jacobites; Stuart, James

fifth column A popular expression from the early days of World War 2 to describe enemy sympathizers who might provide active help to an invader. The name originally described the rebel sympathizers in Madrid in 1936 during the Spanish Civil War, when four rebel columns were advancing on the city. >> Spanish Civil War

fifth force A new force postulated by US physicist Ephraim Fischbach (1942–) and others in 1986, in addition to the four recognized fundamental forces. It is weaker than gravity, and of intermediate range. >> forces of nature ℹ

fifth-generation computers >> **computer generations**

fifty-four forty or fight A slogan used in the 1840s to advocate US seizure of British Columbia, whose N boundary is at 54°40N. The issue was resolved in 1846 by a treaty establishing the present US–Canadian border, at 49°N.

fig A member of a large genus of trees, shrubs, and climbers, mostly native to the tropics; tiny flowers borne on the inner surface of a hollow, fleshy receptacle which forms the fruit after fertilization. Many species are large evergreen trees, such as the indiarubber tree and the banyan. (Genus: *Ficus*, 800 species. Family: Moraceae.) >> banyan; indiarubber tree; peepul

figurative art Any form of visual art in which recognizable aspects of the world, especially the human figure, are represented, in however simplified, stylized, or distorted a form, in contrast to abstract or **non-figurative art**. >> abstract art; art

figurative language Language used in such a way that 'simple' meaning is elaborated and complicated by various rhetorical means. Language has been described as 'a graveyard of dead metaphors', and all forms of emphasis and parallelism, as well as imagery, may be considered 'figurative'. >> hyperbole; imagery; metaphor; poetry; rhetoric

figwort A perennial (*Scrophularia nodosa*), native to Europe and Asia; flowers with greenish, almost globose tube and five small lobes, the upper two forming a reddish-brown lip. (Family: Scrophulariaceae.)

Fiji [feejee], official name **Sovereign Democratic Republic of Fiji** pop (1995e) 775 000; land area 18 333 sq km/7076 sq mi. Melanesian group of 844 islands and islets in the SW Pacific Ocean; 1770 km/1100 mi N of Auckland, New Zealand; capital, Suva; timezone GMT +12; two main

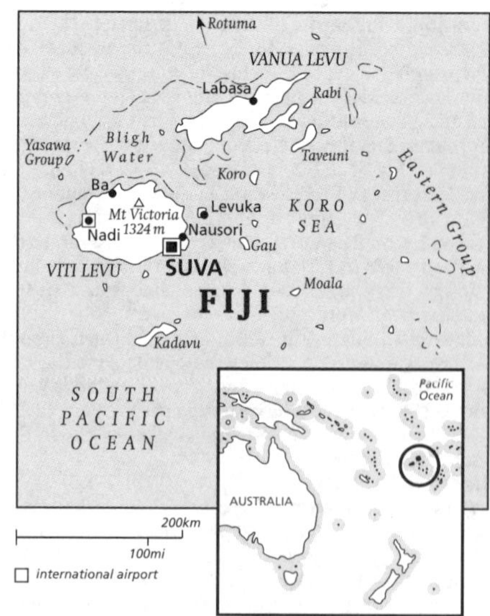

islands of Viti Levu and Vanua Levu, containing c.90% of population; chief ethnic groups, indigenous Fijians (50%) and Indian (44%); native Fijians mainly Christian (c.85% Methodist, 12% Roman Catholic); Indo-Fijians mainly Hindu (c.70%) and Muslim (25%); official language, English; unit of currency, the Fijian dollar; main archipelago located 15–22°S and 174–177°E; larger islands generally mountainous and rugged; highest peak, Tomaniivi (Mt Victoria) on Vita Levu (1324 m/4344 ft); most smaller islands consist of limestone, with little vegetation; extensive coral reef (Great Sea Reef) stretching for 500 km/300 mi along W fringe; dense tropical forest on wet, windward side (SE); mainly treeless on dry, leeward side; visited by Tasman in 1643, and by Cook in 1774; British colony, 1874; independence within the Commonwealth, 1970; 1987 election brought to power an Indian-dominated coalition, which led to military coups (May and Sep), and proclamation of a republic outside the Commonwealth; civilian government restored (Dec); new constitution upholding ethnic Melanesian political power, 1990; bicameral parliament of a nominated Senate and an elected House of Representatives; economy primarily agrarian, with sugar cane accounting for over two-thirds of export earnings; major tourist area. >> Suva; Vanua Levu; Viti Levu; RR1008 political leaders

filariasis [fila**riy**asis] A disease caused by the nematode worms *Wuchereria bancrofti* and *Brugia malayi*, once included in the genus *Filaria*. Larvae are transmitted to uninfected human beings by mosquitoes. Lymph nodes enlarge and interfere with the flow of lymph, causing gross oedema of the limbs. >> elephantiasis; nematode

filbert A species of hazel (*Corylus maxima*), native to the Balkans, and cultivated elsewhere for its edible nuts, which are completely enclosed in a leafy cup, constricted above the nut to form a neck. (Family: Corylaceae.) >> hazel; nut

filefish Deep-bodied fish common in shallow tropical and warm temperate waters; body strongly compressed, length up to 25 cm/10 in; dorsal fin spiny; scales finely toothed and rough to touch; also called **porky**. (Genus: *Stephanolepis*. Family: Balistidae.)

filibuster To hold up the passage of a bill in the US Senate, by organizing a continuous succession of long speeches in opposition. The term is also more generally applied to any attempt to delay a decision or vote by exercising the right to talk on an issue. >> guillotine; Senate

Filioque [fili**oh**kway] (Lat 'and from the Son') A dogmatic formula expressing the belief that the Holy Spirit 'proceeds' from the Son as well as from the Father. The term does not appear in the original Nicene–Constantinopolitan Creed, but was inserted by the Western Church, and insistence on its retention was a major source of tension and eventual breach between the Western (Roman Catholic) and Eastern (Orthodox) Churches in 1054. >> Nicene Creed; Orthodox Church; Roman Catholicism; Trinity

Fillmore, Millard (1800–74) US statesman and 13th President (1850–3), born in Summer Hill, NY. He was vice-president to Zachary Taylor in 1848, becoming president on his death. On the slavery question he was a supporter of 'compromise'. >> slavery

film A light-sensitive photographic emulsion on a thin flexible transparent support, originally celluloid (cellulose nitrate), but later the less inflammable cellulose triacetate. Film for still cameras is supplied in cut sheets and film packs, but more generally as short rolls in various standard widths. Motion picture film is used in long rolls, up to 300 m, in widths 16, 35, and 70 mm. >> camera

Filofax The trade name of a 'personal organizer', or portable information and filing system. Paperback-size, loose-leaf, with a flexible binder, filofaxes typically contain a diary, address book, notebook, and information sections (hence 'file of facts').

filter 1 A device for removing fine solid particles from a mixture. It usually consists of some woven or felted material (eg paper, textile), and is thus distinct from a **sieve**, which removes coarse particles with a wire mesh or perforated metal. By analogy, the term is also used for any device which separates the components of a wave system (eg sound, light, radio frequency currents). **2** In photography, a transparent material which modifies the light passing in a specified manner. It is used in front of light sources to alter colour temperature, reduce intensity, or scatter light by diffusion. >> diffusion (photography)

fin The external membranous process of an aquatic animal, such as a fish or cetacean, used for locomotion and manoeuvring; may be variously modified as suckers and claspers. The **median fins** are called *dorsal*, *anal*, and *caudal* (tail); the paired **lateral fins** are *pectorals* and *pelvics*. >> Cetacea; fish [i]

finch Any bird of the family Fringillidae; commonly kept as songbirds; bill internally modified to crush seeds. >> brambling; bullfinch; canary; chaffinch; crossbill; Darwin's finches; Fringillidae; goldfinch; greenfinch; hawfinch; linnet; quail; waxbill; weaverbird; weaver-finch; whydah

fine A financial penalty paid to the state, following conviction by a court for a criminal offence. Limits are normally set on the levels of fines inferior courts are permitted to levy, and the offender's means are generally taken into account. Failure to pay a fine without good cause can lead to imprisonment for default. >> compensation order; criminal law; sentence

Fine Gael [**feen**uh **gayl**] (Ir 'United Ireland') An Irish political party created out of the pro-Anglo-Irish Treaty (1921) wing of Sinn Féin. The first government of the Irish Free State, it has largely been in opposition since the 1930s. It supports an Irish confederation. >> Sinn Féin

finfoot A water-bird, native to Central America, S Africa, and S Asia; slender, with long pointed bill; toes with side lobes; inhabits fresh or brackish water margins; angle of wing bears a claw; also called **sungrabe**. (Family: Heliornithidae, 3 species.)

Fingal's Cave A cave situated on the coast of Staffa in the Inner Hebrides, Scotland. The cavern, which is renowned for its natural beauty, is celebrated in Mendelssohn's *Hebrides Overture*. It is 69 m/227 ft deep and of volcanic origin, being formed from huge hexagonal pillars of basalt. The name derives from the legendary Irish figure, Finn MacCool. >> basalt; Finn MacCool; Hebrides

Finger Lakes A group of long, narrow, finger-like lakes in W New York State, USA; includes (W–E) Canandaigua, Keuka, Seneca, Cayuga, Owasco, and Skaneateles lakes. >> New York

fingerprint An impression made on a surface by the pattern of ridges at the ends of fingers and thumbs. No two people have the same fingerprints, and the technique of fingerprinting has thus long been used by law enforcement agencies as a means of identification, based on the general shape of the ridge pattern, its size and position on the finger, the number of ridges in loops and whorls, and other such indicators. The formal process of fingerprinting is called **dactyloscopy**. >> DNA profiling; forensic medicine; voiceprint

finger-spelling >> **dactylology**

Finisterre, Cape [fini**stair**] (Span **Cabo**) 42°50N 9°16W. Cape at La Coruña, NW Spain; the most W point on the Spanish mainland; scene of a British naval victory against the French in 1747. >> Spain [i]

Finland, Finn **Suomi**, official name **Republic of Finland**, Finn **Suomen Tasavalta**, Swed **Republiken Finland** pop (1995e) 5 110 000; area 338 145 sq km/130 524 sq mi. Republic in N Europe; capital, Helsinki; timezone GMT +2; mainly Finns, with Swedish, Lapp, and Russian minorities; chief religion, Lutheran Christianity; first languages, Finnish (94%), Swedish (6%); unit of currency, the markka of 100 penni; a low-lying glaciated plateau, average height 150 m/500 ft; highest peak, Haltiatunturi (1328 m/4357 ft) on NW border; over 60 000 shallow lakes in SE, providing a system of inland navigation; over a third of the country N of the Arctic Circle; archipelago of Saaristomeri (SW), with over 17 000 islands; Ahvenanmaa (Åland) islands (SW); forest land covers 65% of the country, water 10%; climate ameliorated by the Baltic Sea; half annual precipitation falls as snow; sun does not go down beyond the horizon for over 70 days during summer; ruled Sweden from 1157 until ceded to Russia in 1809; Grand Duchy of the Russian tsar, 19th-c, with development of nationalist movement; independent republic, 1917; parliamentary system created, 1928; invaded by Soviets in 1939 and 1940, and lost territory to USSR after 1944; governed by a single-chamber House of Representatives and a president assisted by a Council of State; joined European Union, 1995, and the European monetary system (EMS), 1996; traditional focus on forestry and farming, with rapid economic growth since 1950s, and diversification of exports; wide use of hydroelectric power. >> Helsinki; Lapland; Saimaa; RR1008 political leaders

Finland, Gulf of Arm of the Baltic Sea (E), bounded N by Finland, S and E by Russia; c.4600 km/2900 mi long, 16–120 km/10–75 mi wide; ice cover (Dec–Mar). >> Baltic Sea

Finney, Albert (1936–) Actor, born in Salford, Greater Manchester. His definitive portrayal of the working-class rebel in *Saturday Night and Sunday Morning* (1960) established him as a star. He has received Oscar nominations for *Tom Jones* (1963), *Murder on the Orient Express* (1974), *The Dresser* (1983), and *Under the Volcano* (1984). Television work includes *A Rather English Marriage* (1998).

Finn MacCool A legendary Irish hero, the son of Cumhall, and father of Ossian (Oisin). He became leader of the Fenians, and was famous for his generosity.

fiord >> **fjord**

Fiordland [**fyaw(r)d**land] area 10 232 sq km/3949 sq mi. National park, SW South Island, New Zealand; established in 1904; a world heritage site. >> New Zealand ℹ

fir >> **silver fir**

Firdausi or **Ferd(a)usi** [fir**dow**see], pseudonym of **Abú al-Qásim Mansúr** (940–c.1020) The greatest of Persian poets, born near Tús, Khorassan. His major work was the epic poem, *Shah Náma* (1010, The Book of Kings).

fireclay Clay with high alumina content that can withstand high temperatures without excessive deformation. It is used for making firebricks and other refractory materials. >> clay; kaolin

firecrest A small bird (*Regulus ignicapillus*) native to Europe, N Africa, and Madeira; head with orange stripe and white 'eyebrows'; Europe's smallest breeding bird. (Family: Regulidae, sometimes placed in Silviidae.)

firedamp Methane found in coal mines. A mixture of methane and air is inflammable or explosive in certain proportions, and has been the cause of many pit disasters. One of the best methods of firedamp detection remains the Davy safety lamp. >> coal mining; methane; safety lamp

firefly A small, mostly nocturnal beetle; males with soft wing cases, females larva-like, often wingless; jaws hollow, used to inject digestive juices into prey; luminous organs near tip of abdomen used to produce mating signals; also known as **glowworms** and **lightning bugs**. (Order: Coleoptera. Family: Lampyridae, c.2000 species.) >> beetle

Fire of London A devastating fire which started in a baker's shop in Pudding Lane (2 Sep 1666) and lasted several days, engulfing c.160 ha/400 acres – four-fifths of the city. Casualties were low (no more than 20 died).

firethorn A thorny, evergreen shrub (*Pyracantha coccinea*) growing to c.1·5 m/5 ft, occasionally a small tree, native to S Europe; flowers numerous, 5-petalled, white, in small clusters; berries bright red. (Family: Rosaceae.)

fireworks Artificial devices, normally used for display purposes, which when ignited produce an array of coloured lights, sparks, and explosions. They contain flammable and explosive materials (eg charcoal, sulphur) which react with oxygen-yielding substances (eg nitre, chlorate of potash). The making of fireworks is called *pyrotechny*. >> Guy Fawkes Night

firmware A concept intermediate between software and hardware, used to describe devices which combine elements of each. A computer program stored in an unalterable form in an integrated circuit such as a read-only memory could be described as firmware. >> hardware; software

First, Ruth (1925–82) Radical opponent of apartheid, as activist, journalist, writer, and academic, born in Johannesburg, South Africa. In 1949 she married Joe Slovo; both were arrested and charged with treason in 1956. In 1982 she was assassinated by a parcel bomb in her office at Maputo, Mozambique. >> apartheid; Slovo

first cause >> **cosmological argument**

first fleet In Australian history, the name given to the 11 ships which left Portsmouth, England (1787) carrying the first European settlers to E Australia. The fleet carried officials, 212 marines and their families, and 579 convicts plus provisions. The fleet's captain, Arthur Phillip, decided that Botany Bay was unsuitable and proceeded north to Sydney Cove, Port Jackson, where he hoisted the British flag (26 Jan 1788). >> Australia Day; Botany Bay

first-footing >> **Hogmanay**

first-generation computers >> **computer generations**

First Nations A term used in Canada to describe Canadian aboriginal peoples. It was introduced in the 1980s as a response to French- and English-Canadian claims to be the 'two founding nations'. >> American Indians; Mercredi

First World >> **Three Worlds theory**

First World War >> **World War 1**

Firth, Colin (1960–) Actor, born in Grayshott, Hampshire. He received a BAFTA nomination for his role in the television production of *Tumbledown* (1989), and another for *Pride and Prejudice* (1995), where his brooding performance as the handsome Mr Darcy attracted unprecedented public interest. Later films include *The English Patient* (1996) and *Fever Pitch* (1997).

fiscal policy The use by government of tax and its own rate of spending to influence demand in the economy. When a government decides to lower taxes or raise public expenditure, the effect is to stimulate economic activity by increasing the demand for goods and services. In contrast, a tightening of fiscal policy is where taxes are raised or public expenditure is reduced, in order to reduce aggregate demand. >> balance of payments; inflation

Fischer, Bobby, popular name of **Robert (James) Fischer** (1943–) Chess player, born in Chicago, IL. He was world champion in 1972–5, taking the title from Boris Spassky (USSR) in a much-publicized match. He resigned his title shortly before a defence against Anatoly Karpov in 1975, and did not then compete at a major international level until 1992, when he defeated Spassky in a match which generated unprecedented levels of publicity for a chess match. >> chess

Fischer-Dieskau, Dietrich [**fish**er **dees**kow] (1925–) Baritone, born in Berlin. He is one of the foremost interpreters of German *Lieder*, particularly the song cycles of Schubert. >> *Lied*

Fischer von Erlach, Johann Bernard [**fi**sher fon **air**-lakh] (1656–1723) Architect, born in Graz, Austria. A leading exponent of the Baroque style, he designed many churches and palaces, notably the Karlskirche at Vienna, and the University Church at Salzburg. >> Baroque (art and architecture)

fish Any cold-blooded aquatic vertebrate without legs, but typically possessing paired lateral fins as well as median fins. There is a 2-chambered heart, a series of respiratory gills present throughout life in the sides of the pharynx, and a body usually bearing scales and terminating in a caudal (tail) fin. As a subgroup of the Vertebrata, the fishes are sometimes referred to collectively as *Pisces*. The *Chondrichthyes* (800 living species), containing the sharks, rays, and ratfishes, are characterized by a cartilaginous skeleton, and are commonly referred to as the **cartilaginous fishes**. By far the largest extant group are the **bony fishes** (*Osteichthyes*; 20 000 living species), exhibiting a rich diversity and found in all aquatic habitats. Although many fish have the familiar elongate shape, body form shows great variety. Body length ranges from as small as a few centimetres to over 18 m/60 ft in the massive whale shark. Many species have bright coloration, others well-developed camouflage patterns. Light organs are common in those forms living in the darkness of deep oceanic waters. >> angling; bony fish; cartilaginous fish; fin; *see illustration on p.314*

Fishbourne Roman palace near Chichester, West Sussex, discovered in 1960. Probably erected in the AD 60s for the British client-king Cogidubnus, it continued in use into the 4th-c.

fish eagle >> **osprey**

Fisher, John, St (1469–1535) Clergyman and humanist, born in Beverley, East Riding. In 1527 he pronounced against the divorce of Henry VIII, and was sent with More to the Tower. In 1535 he was made a cardinal, and soon after was tried and beheaded on Tower Hill. He was canonized in 1935; feast day 22 June. >> Henry VIII; humanism; More, Thomas

Fisher (of Lambeth), Geoffrey Fisher, Baron (1887–1972) Archbishop of Canterbury (1945–61), born in Higham-on-the-Hill, Leicestershire. In 1939 he became Bishop of London, and as Archbishop crowned Queen Elizabeth II in Westminster Abbey (1953). >> Church of England

fisher A mammal, related to the marten, native to North America; length, up to 1 m/3¼ ft; thick brown-black coat; inhabits dense forest; also known as **pekan**. (*Martes pennanti*. Family: Mustelidae.) >> marten; Mustelidae

fishing >> **angling**

fission A method of asexual reproduction by splitting into two (**binary fission**) or more (**multiple fission**) parts, each of which develops into an independent organism. The process is common among single-celled micro-organisms. >> reproduction

fitchet >> **polecat**

Fitt, Gerry, popular name of **Gerard, Baron Fitt (of Bell's Hill)** (1926–) Northern Ireland politician, born in Belfast. He founded and led the Social Democratic and Labour Party (1970–9), until he resigned the leadership to sit as an Independent Socialist. He lost his Westminster seat in 1983 when he received his peerage. >> Northern Ireland ℹ

Fitzgerald, Ella (1918–96) Singer, born in Newport News, VA. Discovered in 1934 singing in an amateur contest in Harlem, she joined Chick Webb's band and recorded several hits, notably 'A-tisket A-tasket' (1938). Her series of recordings for Verve (1955–9) in multi-volume 'songbooks' are among the treasures of American popular song. >> jazz

Fitzgerald, F(rancis) Scott (Key) (1896–1940) Novelist, born in St Paul, MN. He captured the spirit of the 1920s – 'the Jazz Age' – in *The Great Gatsby* (1925), his best-known book. His other novels include *The Beautiful and the Damned* (1922) and *Tender is the Night* (1934).

Fitzgerald, Garrett (Michael) (1926–) Irish statesman and prime minister (1981–2, 1982–7), born in Dublin. In 1969 he was elected Fine Gael member of the Irish parliament for Dublin SE, and became minister for foreign affairs (1973–7), and leader of the Fine Gael Party (1977–87). >> Fine Gael

Fitzgerald, George Francis (1851–1901) Physicist, born in Dublin. Independently of Lorentz, he concluded that a body becomes shorter as its velocity increases (the **Lorentz–Fitzgerald contraction**), a notion used by Einstein as part of his theory of special relativity. >> Lorentz; special relativity ℹ

Fitzsimmons, Bob, popular name of **Robert Prometheus Fitzsimmons** (1863–1917) Boxer, born in Helston, Cornwall. He moved to the USA in 1890, where he won the world middleweight (1891), heavyweight (1897), and light heavyweight championships (1903). >> boxing ℹ

Fiume >> **Rijeka**

Five, the A group of 19th-c Russian composers, also known as **the Mighty Handful**, who came together to promote nationalist ideals and styles in music. The group, led by Balakirev, also contained Borodin, Moussorgsky, Rimsky-

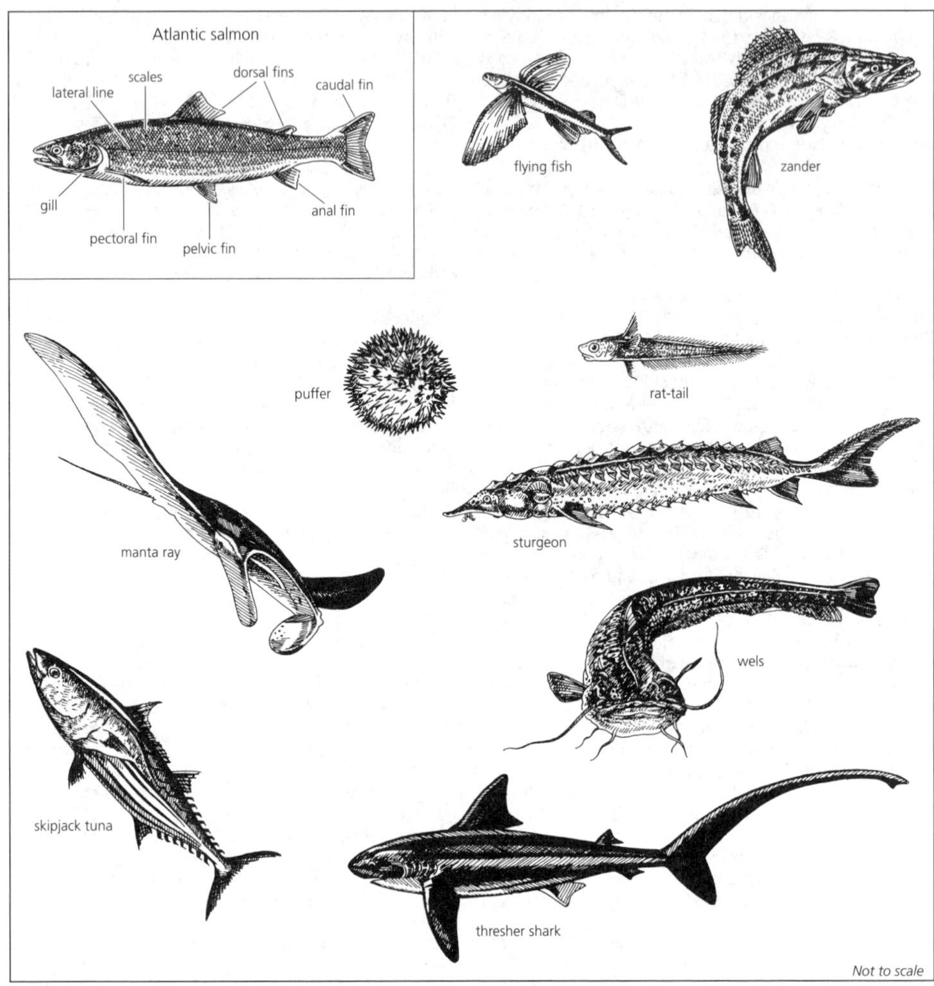

Fish

Korsakov, and César Cui (1835–1918). >> Balakirev; Borodin; Moussorgsky; Rimsky-Korsakov

Five Civilized Tribes The Muskogean-speaking nations of Indians (Chickasaws, Creeks, Choctaws, Cherokees, Seminoles) who originally inhabited the present SE USA. The Cherokees, in particular, adopted white ways, acquiring literacy in their own language and English. >> American Indians

fives A handball game played by two or four players, derived from the French game *jeu de paume* ('palm [of hand] game'). The first recorded game was at Eton School in 1825. >> handball

fjord A long, narrow, steep-sided coastal inlet extending far inland and often reaching very great depths. The best-known fjords are in Norway and E Greenland. >> glaciation

flag A species of iris (*Iris pseudacorus*) with yellow flowers 7·5–10 cm/3–4 in diameter, found in wet, swampy ground in Europe, W Asia, and N Africa. (Family: Iridaceae.) >> iris (botany)

flagellate [**fla**jiluht] A microscopic, single-celled organism that possesses 1, 2, 4, or more thread-like organelles (**flagella**), typically used for swimming. (Phylum: Mastigophora.) >> cell; flagellum; parasitology

flagellum [fla**je**lum] A thread-like structure found on some bacteria and on or in many eucaryotic organisms. Flagella usually function in locomotion, bacterial flagella rotating and eucaryotic flagella undulating as they beat. >> bacteria ℹ; eucaryote

flageolet [flajioh**let**] A simple, high-pitched, end-blown flute, made of wood, with six fingerholes; later, often fitted with metal keys and an ivory mouthpiece. It was popular during the 16th–18th-c, and did not become obsolete until about the mid-19th-c. >> flute; woodwind instrument ℹ

Flagstad, Kirsten (1895–1962) Soprano, born in Hamar, Germany. She excelled in Wagnerian roles. In 1958 she was made director of the Norwegian State Opera. >> Wagner

Flamboyant The style of French late Gothic architecture prevalent in the 15th-c, characterized by wavy flame-like tracery. It was especially common in Normandy. >> Gothic architecture; tracery ℹ

flamenco A type of Spanish song, dance, and guitar music of uncertain origin, associated particularly with Andalusia. It involves highly stylistic dance movements, the use of castanets by the dancers, and an animated technique of guitar playing. >> folk music; guitar

flamingo A large wading bird, native to South America, Africa, S Europe, and W Asia; plumage white or pink; inhabits shallow soda or brine lakes; stout, downwardly angled bill; swims well; forms immense flocks. (Family: Phoenicopteridae, 5 species.)

Flaminian Way The second of Rome's major trunk roads, constructed in 220 BC. It ran NE from Rome across the Apennines to Rimini on the Adriatic coast. >> Roman roads 🛈

Flaminius, Gaius [fla**min**ius] (?–217 BC) Roman general and statesman at the time of the Second Punic War, whose name lived on in his two most popular projects: the **Flaminian Way** and the chariot-racing arena, the **Circus Flaminius**. >> Flaminian Way; Punic Wars

Flamsteed, John (1646–1719) The first Astronomer Royal of England (1675–1719), born in Denby, Derbyshire. In 1676 he instituted reliable observations at Greenwich, near London, providing data from which Newton was later able to verify the gravitational theory. >> Newton, Isaac

Flanders, Flemish **Vlaanderen**, Fr **Flandre** Historical region of NW Belgium and NE France; autonomous in early Middle Ages; densely populated industrial area; chief towns include Bruges, Ghent; traditional textile industry; intensive farming; scene of heavy fighting in both World Wars. >> Belgium 🛈; Bruges; Ghent

flatfish Any of the bottom-dwelling mainly shallow-water fishes in which the adult body is strongly compressed laterally and asymmetrical, with both eyes on the same side of the head; nine families; important food fish. >> brill; dab; flounder; halibut; plaice; turbot

flat foot A condition affecting the normal arches of the foot. Loss of the arches strains the ligaments and muscles of the foot, and can lead to discomfort on standing. >> foot

Flathead A Salish-speaking Indian group living on L Flathead, Montana, the most easterly-based of Plateau Indian groups.

flathead Bottom-living fish of the Indo-Pacific and tropical Atlantic oceans; body slender, length up to 1 m/3¼ ft, flattened anteriorly with prominent spinose fins. (Genera: *Platycephalus, Thysanophrys*. Family: Platycephalidae.)

flat racing >> **horse racing**

flatworm A flattened, worm-like animal with a definite head but without a true body cavity (*coelom*); parasitic forms include tapeworms and flukes. (Phylum: Platyhelminthes.) >> blood fluke; fluke; tapeworm; worm

Flaubert, Gustave [flohbair] (1821–80) Novelist, born in Rouen, France. His masterpiece was *Madame Bovary* (1857), which was condemned as immoral and its author (unsuccessfully) prosecuted. *Trois contes* (1877, Three Tales) reveals his mastery of the short story.

flavouring agent Any compound when added to a food to alter its taste, the most widely used being salt and sugar. Monosodium glutamate is an example of a flavour enhancer, bringing out a 'meaty flavour'. >> monosodium glutamate; salt; sugars

flax A slender erect annual (*Linum usitatissimum*), growing to 60 cm/2 ft; flowers numerous, blue, with five spreading petals; fruit a capsule with numerous seeds. It is cultivated throughout temperate and subtropical regions for flax fibre obtained from the stems, and for linseed oil from the seeds. (Family: Linaceae.)

Flaxman, John (1755–1826) Sculptor and illustrator, born in York, North Yorkshire. He furnished the Wedgwood house with renowned pottery designs, and illustrated the *Iliad* and *Odyssey* (1793), and other works. >> Neoclassicism (art and architecture); Wedgwood, Josiah

F layer >> **Appleton layer**

flea A small, wingless insect that as an adult is a blood-feeding external parasite of warm-blooded animals (mostly mammals, but including some birds); body flattened from side to side, usually hairy; mouthparts specialized for piercing and sucking; hindlegs adapted for jumping; c.1750 species, many carriers of disease. (Order: Siphonaptera.) >> insect 🛈; larva

fleabane A leafy perennial (*Pulicaria dysenterica*) growing to 60 cm/2 ft, native to marshes in Europe, N Africa, and Asia Minor; flower-heads golden yellow, daisy-like; fruit with a parachute of hairs. Its dried leaves were formerly burned to repel insects. (Family: Compositae.)

fleawort The name applied to certain species of the genus *Senecio*. **Field fleawort** (*Senecio integrifolius*) is a variable perennial growing to 70 cm/27 in; smaller clusters of flower-heads with c.13 bright yellow outer ray florets; native to much of Europe. (Family: Compositae.)

Flecker, James Elroy (1884–1915) Poet, born in London. His best-known works are the drama *Hassan* (1922) and *The Golden Journey to Samarkand* (1913).

Flémalle, Master of >> **Campin, Robert**

Fleming, Sir Alexander (1881–1955) Bacteriologist, born near Darvel, East Ayrshire. He was the first to use anti-typhoid vaccines on human beings, pioneered the use of Salvarsan against syphilis, and discovered the antiseptic powers of lysozyme. In 1928 he discovered penicillin, for which he shared the Nobel Prize for Physiology or Medicine in 1945. >> lysozyme; penicillin

Fleming, Ian (Lancaster) (1908–64) Writer and journalist, born in London. He achieved worldwide fame and fortune as the creator of a series of spy novels, starting with *Casino Royale* (1953), built round the exploits of his amoral hero James Bond. >> Stephenson, William

Fleming, Sir John Ambrose (1849–1945) Physicist, born in Lancaster, Lancashire. He invented the thermionic valve, and was a pioneer in the application of electricity to lighting and heating on a large scale. >> thermionic valve

Fleming and Walloon The two main linguistic and cultural groups of present-day Belgium. Flemings are based in the N and W, and speak Flemish (Vlaams). The French-speaking Walloons live in the S and E. Linguistic disputes between the two groups are a major feature of Belgian politics. >> Belgium 🛈; Flanders; Wallonia

Flemish >> **Dutch**

Flemming, Walther (1843–1905) Biologist, born in Sachsenberg, Germany. In 1882 he gave the first modern account of cytology, including the process of cell division, which he named *mitosis*. >> cytology; mitosis

Fletcher, John (1579–1625) Playwright, born in Rye, East Sussex. He is best known for his collaboration with Beaumont in such works as *The Maid's Tragedy* (1611). Collaboration with Shakespeare probably resulted in *Two Noble Kinsmen* and *Henry VIII*. >> Beaumont, Francis; Shakespeare 🛈

Fleury, André-Hercule de [floeree] (1653–1743) French prelate and statesman, born in Lodève, France. He became chief minister in 1726, and also a cardinal, and effectively controlled the government of Louis XV until 1743. His moderation gave France the tranquility her tangled finances demanded, and he carried out legal and economic reforms which stimulated trade. >> Louis XIV / XV

Flinders, Matthew (1774–1814) Explorer, born in Donington, Lincolnshire. In 1795 he sailed to Australia, where he explored the SE coast, and later (1801–3)

circumnavigated the country. The Flinders R in Queensland, and the Flinders range in South Australia are named after him. >> Australia ℹ

Flinders Ranges >> **Lofty-Flinders Ranges, Mount**

flint A type of chert, occurring as grey, rounded nodules in chalk or other limestone. It breaks into sharp-edged flakes and hence was used as a Stone Age tool. >> chert

flint glass Heavy crystal glass, containing lead, highly suitable for cutting and engraving. It was first introduced c.1675, and so called because early examples were made with powdered flint instead of the more usual sand. >> glass 2 ℹ

Flintshire, Welsh **Sir y Fflint** pop (1995e) 145 300; area 437 sq km / 169 sq mi. County (unitary authority from 1996) in NE Wales, UK; administrative centre, Mold; castles at Flint, Hawarden; St Winifred's Well at Holywell; Theatre Clwyd. >> Wales ℹ

FLN The acronym for the **Front de Libération Nationale**, an organization founded in the early 1950s, which fought for Algerian independence from France under the leadership of Mohammed Ben Bella. France's inability to defeat the FLN led to the Evian conference in 1962, and complete Algerian independence. The FLN became the governing party of independent Algeria, and until 1991 was the only legal party in the country. >> Algeria ℹ; Ben Bella; OAS

floating rate >> **exchange rates**

Flodden, Battle of A victory of the English over the Scots, fought in the Scottish Borders. James IV, allied with France, invaded England in August, but was defeated by English forces under Thomas Howard, Earl of Surrey. The Scottish dead included James, and the battle ended the Scottish threat for a generation. >> James IV

Flood, the In the Bible, the story that in Noah's time God caused a widespread deluge to destroy all people because of their sin (except Noah and his family), this purge providing a new start for mankind (*Gen* 6–8) and the animal world. Similar legends are found also in other ancient near-eastern sources. >> Genesis, Book of; Gilgamesh; Noah

floppy disk or **floppy** A flexible plastic disk coated with magnetic material, used as a storage medium for microcomputers. The disks are housed in cardboard jackets and generally have a diameter of 5·25 in (13·3 cm). In use, the disks are rotated at some 300 revolutions per minute and are written to, or read from, by movable magnetic heads. 5·25 in disks can store up to 1 megabyte or more of information, the exact amount depending on the particular system. The term has also come to be used by analogy for the rigid 3·5-in/9-cm disk. >> byte; hard disk; minidisk

Flora An ancient Roman goddess of flowers and flowering plants, who appears with the Spring. She was given a temple in 238 BC, and her games were celebrated on 28 April.

Florence, Ital **Firenze** 43°47N 11°15E, pop (1995e) 410 000. Ancient city in Tuscany, Italy, on R Arno; ancient Etruscan town; cultural and intellectual centre of Italy from the Middle Ages; badly damaged by floods, 1966; archbishopric; airport; railway; university (1321); city centre a world heritage site; famed for its many religious buildings and palaces, such as the Baptistery of San Giovanni (c.1000), the Duomo (1296); Palazzo degli Uffizi (1560–74), Palazzo Pitti (15th-c and later), Ponte Vecchio (rebuilt 1345); birthplace of Dante and Macchiavelli. >> Medici; Pitti Palace; Ponte Vecchio; Tuscany; Uffizi

floret A very small or reduced flower, usually one of many aggregated together in a head which may itself resemble a single flower, as in members of the daisy family. >> daisy; flower ℹ

Florida pop (1995e) 14 355 000; area 151 934 sq km/ 58 664 sq mi. State in SE USA; the 'Sunshine State' or 'Peninsular State'; discovered and settled by the Spanish in the 16th-c; ceded to Britain in 1763, and divided into East and West Florida; given back to Spain after the War of Independence, 1783; West Florida gained by the US in the Louisiana Purchase, 1803; East Florida purchased by the US, 1819; admitted as the 27th state of the Union, 1845; seceded, 1861; slavery abolished, 1865; re-admitted to the Union, 1868; a long peninsula bounded W by the Gulf of Mexico and E by the Atlantic Ocean; C state has many lakes, notably L Okeechobee; highest point in Walton County (105 m/345 ft); S almost entirely covered by the Everglades; SE coast protected from the Atlantic by sandbars and islands, creating shallow lagoons and sandy beaches; warm sunny climate; capital, Tallahassee; many famous resorts (Palm Beach, Miami Beach); Everglades National Park, Walt Disney World entertainment park, John F Kennedy Space Center at Cape Canaveral; the nation's greatest producer of citrus fruits; the second largest producer of vegetables; large Hispanic population (especially from Cuba). >> Canaveral, Cape; Disney; Everglades; Florida Keys; Louisiana Purchase; Tallahassee; United States of America ℹ; R994

Florida Keys A series of small islands curving approx 240 km/150 mi SW around the tip of the Florida peninsula, USA; Overseas Highway (1938) runs from the mainland to Key West, 198 km/123 mi long. >> Florida

florin The name of a former British coin. Pre-decimalization this was the 2-shilling piece; post-decimalization the 'old' 10p piece, replaced in 1993. The name was earlier used for a gold coin in the reign of Edward III. >> money

Flotow, Friedrich, Freiherr von (Baron) [**floh**toh] (1812–83) Composer, born in Teutendorf, Germany. He made his reputation with several operas, notably *Martha* (1847).

flotsam, jetsam, and **lagan** [**lay**gn] Terms used in describing goods or wreckage found in the sea. **Flotsam** refers to anything found floating. **Jetsam** includes anything deliberately jettisoned from a ship. **Lagan** refers to goods on the bottom of the sea.

flounder Common European flatfish (*Platichthys flesus*) found in shallow inshore waters; upper body surface grey-brown with dark patches and orange spots, underside white; length up to 50 cm/20 in. (Family: Pleuronectidae.) >> flatfish

flour The finely ground product of a cereal seed, especially wheat, primarily used to make bread. A wheat seed consists of an outer coat (husk), with the germ (embryo), and a starchy centre (endosperm). When the seed is ground, it forms a wholemeal flour suitable for baking; if the flour is refined to increase the proportion of endosperm, white flour is produced. Wholemeal flour is richer in fibre, and an important constituent of high-fibre diets. >> cereals; fibre

flower The reproductive organ of a flowering plant (*angiosperm*) derived from a leafy shoot of limited growth in which the leaves are modified for specific roles. It typically consists of four distinct *whorls* of parts attached to a receptacle: the sepals (*calyx*), the petals (*corolla*), the stamens (*andrecium*), and the carpels or ovary (*gynecium*). Structurally, flowers can be divided into two types: **actinomorphic** or radially symmetrical, and **zygomorphic** or bilaterally symmetrical. >> carpel; epicalyx; floret; flowering plants; inflorescence ℹ; ovary; perianth; petal; pollen; receptacle; sepal; stamen

flowering plants One of the two divisions of seed plants, sometimes referred to as the **angiosperms**, the other division being the **gymnosperms**. They are characterized by having the seed enclosed in an ovary which has a specialized extension (the *stigma*) for receiving pollen. The group includes all plants in which the reproductive organ is a flower, hence the commonly used name. The flowering

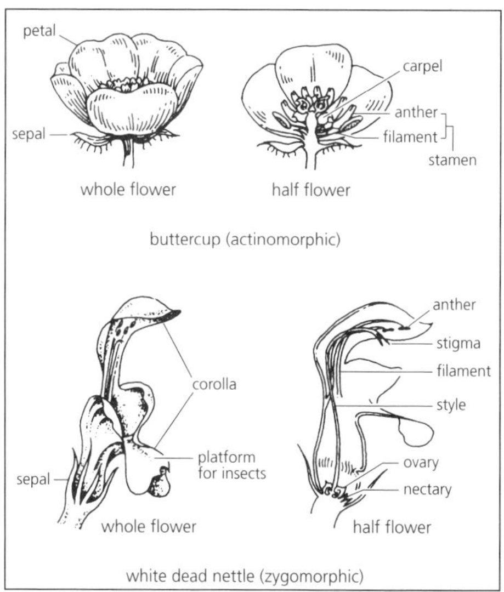

Parts of a flower

plants are divided into **monocotyledons** and **dicotyledons** on the basis of cotyledon number. They are the most common in terms of both numbers and distribution, with an estimated 250 000 species occurring in all parts of the globe. (Class: Angiospermae.) >> cotyledons; flower [i]; gymnosperms

flowering quince >> **japonica**

flows >> **stocks**

flugelhorn [**floo**glhaw(r)n] A musical instrument made of brass, somewhat like a cornet and with a similar compass, but with a slightly larger bell. It is a standard instrument in British brass bands, and is used in jazz, but is rarely found in orchestras. >> brass instrument [i]; cornet

fluid A substance which flows and is able to fill its container: a liquid, gas, or plasma. The mechanical properties of fluids are governed by the laws of fluid mechanics. >> fluidics; fluid mechanics; gas 1; liquid; plasma (physics)

fluidics The study of control and detection systems based on fluid movement. Available devices include fluid amplifiers (in which a small flow modifies a large flow), logic circuits, and switches. >> fluid mechanics; hydraulics

fluid mechanics The study of the mechanics of fluids. **Fluid statics** is concerned with the properties of fluids at rest. **Fluid dynamics** considers the properties peculiar to moving fluids. **Hydrostatics** and **hydrodynamics** are the study of stationary and moving incompressible fluids (usually liquids), respectively. **Aerodynamics** is concerned with the flow of gases, especially air. The properties of fluids include *density*, the mass per unit volume, and *compressibility*, which is high for gases but essentially zero for liquids. A fluid also exerts a *pressure* on an object immersed in it, which is the same in all directions. Objects immersed in fluid experience an upward *buoyancy* force. *Viscosity* measures a fluid's reluctance to flow, more properly its internal friction. *Flow rate* is the mass of fluid passing some point every second. >> aerodynamics [i]; fluid; fluidics; hydraulics; rheology

fluke Either of two groups of parasitic flatworms; **digenetic flukes**, typically parasites of vertebrates as adults, with complex life-cycles involving at least two hosts; **monogenetic flukes**, usually external parasites of fishes with single host life-cycles. (Phylum: Platyhelminthes. Class: Trematoda.) >> blood fluke; flatworm; parasitology

fluorescence Light produced by an object excited by means other than heating, where light emission ceases as soon as the energy source is removed. It is a type of luminescence, exploited in dyes and in the coating of fluorescent light tubes. >> fluorescent lamp; luminescence

fluorescent lamp A lamp consisting of a tube, coated inside with fluorescent material (phosphor), filled with mercury vapour, and with an electrode at each end. Light is generated by passing a current between the electrodes through the vapour, producing ultraviolet light that is converted to visible light by phosphor fluorescence. >> fluorescence; light; luminescence

fluoridation of water The production of water containing small amounts of fluorine (1 part/million), whose regular consumption greatly reduces the incidence of caries of the teeth. Water supplies in many regions contain fluorine naturally in sufficient concentrations to increase the resistance of teeth to attack. This has led the authorities to recommend the addition of fluorine to reservoirs deficient in the element. While this is done in many instances, a vociferous minority of the population who object to adding 'chemicals' to water have succeeded in preventing it from becoming universal. >> caries; fluorine; teeth [i]

fluoride A compound containing fluorine, especially one containing F^- ions. **Sodium fluoride** (NaF) is commonly added in small amounts to drinking water or dentifrice to supply fluoride ions necessary for strong dental enamel. >> CFCs; fluorine; fluorocarbons

fluorine Element 9, composed of molecules F_2, boiling point −187°C. A yellow gas, the first of the halogens, the most electronegative element, oxidation state −1 in nearly all its compounds. It is very corrosive and toxic, and occurs mainly in the mineral *fluorite* (CaF_2). >> chemical elements; fluorite; halogens; RR1036

fluorite or **fluorspar** A common mineral of calcium fluoride (CaF_2), typically blue or purple in colour, and the main source of fluorine. It is used as a flux in steel production. >> fluorine

fluorocarbons Compounds of carbon and fluorine, the simplest being CF_4, tetrafluoromethane. The C–F bond is very stable, and saturated fluorocarbons are very unreactive. >> carbon; CFCs; fluorine; ozone layer

fluorosis [floo-**roh**sis] Chronic poisoning by drinking water which contains an excessive amount of fluoride. It results in discoloration of the teeth and a disabling arthritis which chiefly affects the spine. The concentration necessary to produce fluorosis is many times that added to drinking water in reservoirs to prevent dental caries. >> fluoride

fluorspar >> **fluorite**

Flushing, Dutch **Vlissingen**, Fr **Flessingue** 51°27N 3°35E, pop (1995e) 44 800. Seaport in W Netherlands, at the mouth of the Schelde river estuary; scene of Allied landing, 1944; railway; site of a nuclear power station; 14th-c Grote Kerk. >> Netherlands, The [i]

flute Broadly speaking, a musical instrument in which a column of air is activated by the player blowing across a mouth-hole or (as in the recorder) against a sharp edge towards which the breath may be directed through a duct. The unqualified term 'flute' generally refers to the transverse concert type. This is made of wood or (more often now) of metal in three jointed sections, with 13 tone-holes, and an elaborate system of keys. >> fife; flageolet; ocarina; piccolo; recorder (music); woodwind instrument [i]

flutemouth >> **cornetfish**

flux Any substance used in metallurgical processes to promote the flow of molten metal and waste (*slag*) and to segregate unwanted impurities. Limestone fulfils this purpose in iron smelting. In soldering, rosin is often used. >> smelting; solder

fly The common name of many small flying insects. True flies have a single pair of membranous flying wings only; hindwings modified as club-shaped, balancing organs (*halteres*); mouthparts form a *proboscis* adapted for sucking, occasionally for piercing; larvae maggot-like, lacking true legs; c.150 000 species, many carriers of disease. (Order: Diptera.) >> black / bot / caddis / fruit / gad / horse / robber / sand / tsetse / warble fly; bluebottle; cranefly; Culicidae; housefly; hoverfly; insect [i]; larva; mayfly; midge; mosquito; sandfly

fly agaric [**ag**arik] A toadstool (*Amanita muscaria*) that forms a bright red fruiting body, typically with white patches on cap; common on ground under trees such as birch and pine during autumn; produces hallucinogenic poisons that can be fatal to humans if eaten. (Order: Agaricales.) >> hallucinogens; muscarine; toadstool

flycatcher A name applied to birds of three distinct groups: **New World** or **tyrant flycatchers** (Family: Tyrannidae, 375 species); **Old World flycatchers** (Family: Muscicapidae, 150 species); and **silky flycatchers** (Family: Ptilogonatidae, 4 species). All usually eat insects caught in flight. >> fantail; thrush (bird); wagtail

flying doctor service The provision of medical services to isolated communities spread over wide areas, based on the use of Air Ambulances. It is particularly well-known in the Australian interior.

Flying Dutchman A ghost ship of disastrous portent, haunting the seas around the Cape of Good Hope; its captain had sworn a blasphemous oath when he failed to round the Cape in a storm, and was condemned to sail those waters forever. The story inspired Wagner's opera *Der Fliegende Holländer* (1843). >> Wagner

flying fish Small surface-living fish with greatly enlarged pelvic and pectoral fins, and the ability to jump and glide above the water surface; *Exocoetus volitans* (length up to 30 cm/1 ft), is widespread in tropical and warm temperate seas. (Family: Exocoetidae.)

flying fox >> **bat**

flying snake A snake from SE Asia; glides between trees; launches itself into the air, then flattens the body and forms several S-shaped curves. (Genus: *Chrysopelea*, 2 species. Family: Colubridae.) >> snake

flying squirrel A squirrel with a large flap of skin between its front and hind legs; glides between trees (up to 450 m/1475 ft in one leap); 33 species in Asia and 2 species in North America. >> squirrel

Flynn, Errol (Leslie Thomson) (1909–59) Film star, born in Hobart, Tasmania. His first American film, *Captain Blood* (1935), established him as a hero of historical adventure films, and his good looks and athleticism confirmed him as the greatest Hollywood swashbuckler, in such films as *The Adventures of Robin Hood* (1938) and *The Sea Hawk* (1940). During the 1940s his off-screen reputation for drinking, drug-taking, and womanizing became legendary.

flywheel A wheel attached to the shaft of an engine, whose distribution of weight enables it to act as a smoothing device for the engine's power output. >> engine

f-number A numerical system of indicating the size of the aperture stop in a camera lens, which determines how much light is transmitted to the film and hence the control of exposure in conjunction with shutter speed. The f-number is calculated by dividing the focal length of the lens by the diameter of the clear aperture of the lens as given by the iris diaphragm. >> camera; lens

Fo, Dario [foh] (1926–) Playwright, designer, and actor, born in San Giano, Italy. His populist plays use the comic traditions of farce and slapstick, as well as surreal effects, notably in *Morte accidentale di un anarchico* (1970, Accidental Death of an Anarchist). He was awarded the Nobel Prize for Literature in 1997.

Foch, Ferdinand [fosh] (1851–1929) French marshal, born in Tarbes. He proved himself a great strategist at the Marne (1914), Ypres, and other World War 1 battles, and commanded the Allied armies in 1918. >> World War 1

foetus >> **fetus**

fog A cloud which occurs at ground level, resulting in low visibility. It forms when two air masses with differing temperatures and moisture contents mix together. **Radiation fog** develops on cold, clear nights when terrestrial radiation cools the ground surface, and lowers the temperature of the air close to the ground, causing condensation. **Advective fog** forms when warm, moist air blows over a cold ground surface, is cooled, and condensation results. >> cloud [i]; condensation (physics); dew point temperature

Föhn / Foehn wind [foen] A warm, dry wind descending on the leeward side of a mountain. As moist air rises on the windward side, it cools and loses moisture before descending and warming. It is found in the European Alps and other mountainous areas. >> wind [i]

Fokine, Michel [fo**keen**], originally **Mikhail Mikhaylovich Fokine** (1880–1942) Dancer and choreographer, born in St Petersburg, Russia. He is credited with the creation of modern ballet from the artificial, stylized mode prevalent at the turn of the century. >> choreography

Fokker, Anthony Herman Gerard (1890–1939) Aircraft engineer, born in Kediri, Java. He built his first plane in 1911, and in 1913 founded the factory at Schwerin, Germany, which made warplanes for the German air force in World War 1. >> aircraft [i]

folic acid A B vitamin found in liver and most green vegetables, required for the synthesis and functioning of red cells. A deficiency, which is rare in developed countries, leads to anaemia. >> anaemia; pregnancy [i]

Folies-Bergère [**fo**lee bair**zhair**] A music hall in Paris, opened in 1869. By the end of the 19th-c its stage was dominated by circus acts and semi-nude female performers. It remains famous for its lavish displays. >> music hall

folklore The traditional songs, tales, proverbs, legends, and beliefs of a people, embracing material culture (utensils, arts and crafts) and non-material culture (festivals, dances and rituals). A scientific study of folklore was first undertaken by Jacob Grimm. >> Grimm; mythology

folk music Music which is transmitted orally, usually with modifications from generation to generation and from place to place, so that its original form and composer are forgotten. Sound recording has greatly facilitated the collecting and transcribing of folk music in the 20th-c. >> ethnomusicology; flamenco; gospel music; monody

folk tales Traditional stories told orally and found all over the world, known – as far as one can tell – from earliest times. They fall into various categories, such as animal tales, tales involving magic, tales recounting tests, tricks, or reversals of fortune, and tales explaining the origin of customs, topographical features, or the entire cosmos. >> fairy tales; Grimm; mythology

Fomalhaut [**fo**malhoht] A bright S hemisphere star in Piscis Austrinus. Distance: 7 parsec.

Fonda, Henry (Jaynes) (1905–82) Actor, born in Grand Island, NE. His early performances, such as in *The Grapes of Wrath* (1940), established him in the role of the American folk hero, and he played many such parts over the next 30 years. His last major appearance was in *On Golden Pond* (1981, Oscar).

Fonda, Jane (1937–) Actress, born in New York City, the daughter of Henry Fonda. She married director Roger Vadim (1965–73), with whom she made *La Ronde* (1964) and *Barbarella* (1968). Later roles widened her dramatic scope, such as in *Klute* (1971, Oscar), *Coming Home* (1978, Oscar), *On Golden Pond* (1981), and *Old Gringo* (1989). She is politically active in anti-nuclear and feminist peace movements, and in the 1980s became involved with women's health and fitness activities. >> Fonda, Henry; Vadim

Fontainebleau [fõtenbloh] A magnificent 16th-c chateau built by Italian craftsmen for Francis I on the site of an earlier royal chateau-fortress at Fontainebleau in France; a world heritage site. >> chateau; Francis I (of France)

Fontana, Domenico [fon**tah**na] (1543–1607) Architect, born in Melide, Italy. He was papal architect in Rome, employed on the Lateran Palace, the Vatican Library, and St Peter's dome.

Fontanne, Lynne >> **Lunt, Alfred**

Fontenay Abbey [fõtnay] A Cistercian abbey, founded in 1119 by Bernard of Clairvaux at Fontenay in NE France; a world heritage monument. >> Clairvaux

Fonteyn, Margot [fon**tayn**], in full **Dame Margot Fonteyn de Arias**, originally **Margaret Hookham** (1919–91) Ballerina, born in Reigate, Surrey. She joined the Sadler's Wells Ballet (later the Royal Ballet) in 1934, and became one of the greatest ballerinas of the 20th-c. A new partnership with Nureyev in the 1960s extended her performing career. >> Nureyev; Royal Ballet

Foochow >> **Fuzhou**

food allergy A true allergic reaction in which there is accompanying evidence of abnormal immunological response to the food items. A reaction is set up in the body involving immunoglobulins (IgE, IgG, or IgM), which results in the release of substances (*kinins*) causing inflammation and tissue damage. >> allergy; food sensitivity

food chain The sequence of organisms on successive feeding (*trophic*) levels within an ecological community, through which energy is transferred by feeding. Energy enters the food chain mainly during photosynthesis by green plants (*primary producers*), passes to the herbivores (*primary consumers*) when they eat plants, and then to the carnivores (*secondary and tertiary consumers*) when they prey on herbivores. >> carnivore ℹ; ecology; herbivore; photosynthesis

food fortification Food to which a nutrient has been added. Many breakfast cereals are fortified with iron by the choice of the manufacturer. Margarine manufacturers are obliged to add vitamins A and D to their product. >> vitamins ℹ

food labelling The provision of identifying labels on packaged food, which must not only declare the product and manufacturer but also provide data on the product weight, the additives which have been incorporated, and nowadays a brief outline of key nutritional data. >> additives; nutrition

food poisoning An illness that arises from eating contaminated food or liquid. Most cases result from food contaminated with different species of *Salmonella*. The illness is then acute and associated with vomiting and diarrhoea. Non-bacterial food poisoning may be due to eating poisonous mushrooms and shellfish. >> botulism; salmonella; toxin

food preservation The treatment of food to maintain its quality and prevent deterioration. Drying removes the water necessary for the growth of spoilage organisms, while bacterial growth can be prevented by acidifying (pickling), salting, heating, canning, freezing, and now by irradiation. >> canning; cold storage; deep-freezing; freeze drying; lyophilization

food sensitivity A state in which, although there may be some form of intolerance to a food item, there is no evidence of any abnormal immunological reaction. The reactions may be psychological or pharmacological (eg to additives); there may be a direct irritant effect of food on the gut lining (eg spicy foods); or there may be enzyme deficiencies, in which the body is unable to process the constituents. Most food sensitivities are temporary, and can be reintroduced into the diet after a period of avoidance. >> food allergy

fool's gold >> **pyrite**

Foot, Michael (Mackintosh) (1913–) British statesman, born in Plymouth, Devon. He joined the staff of the *Tribune* in 1937, becoming editor (1948–52, 1955–60). He became a Labour MP in 1945, and was secretary of state for employment (1974–6), and deputy leader (1976–80) then leader (1980–3) of the Labour Party. He retired from the Commons in 1992. A pacifist, he has long been a supporter of the Campaign for Nuclear Disarmament. >> CND; Labour Party

foot The terminal part of the lower limb which makes contact with the ground; an instrument of support when standing, and of propulsion and restraint when walking or running. In humans there are seven tarsal bones, five metatarsals, two phalanges in the big toe, and three in the other toes. >> bunion; chilblains; chiropody; club foot; flat foot; mycetoma; nails; skeleton ℹ

foot-and-mouth disease A contagious feverish disease of artiodactyls characterized by blistering inside the mouth and in the cleft of the hooves; also known as **hoof-and-mouth disease**. In domestic stock, diagnosis would lead to the immediate destruction of the affected herd. >> artiodactyl

football A field team game, using an inflated ball, which has developed several different forms. **1 Association football** (also known as **soccer**) An 11-a-side team game played on a grass or synthetic pitch (or field) with a goal net at each end. The object is to move the ball around the field, with the feet or head, until a player is in a position to put the ball into the net and score a goal. The Football Association was formed in the UK in 1863; the Football League in 1888; and the world governing body, the Fédération Internationale de Football Association (FIFA) in 1904. The first World Cup was organized in Uruguay in 1930. **2 American football** The national winter sport in the USA, played between September and January. It is played on a rectangular field divided into 5-yd (4·6 m) segments which give the pitch a gridiron effect. The object is to score touchdowns, similar to tries in rugby, but progress has to be made upfield by a series of 'plays', and a team must make 10 yd (9·1 m) of ground within four plays, otherwise they lose possession of the ball. Teams consist of more than 40 squad members, but only 11 are allowed on to the field at any one time. The first rules were drawn up at Princeton College in 1867. The National Football League is divided into two 'leagues': the American Football Conference (AFC) and National Football Conference (NFC). The winners of the two conferences play-off each January for the Super Bowl tournament (instituted 1966–7). **3 Rugby football** A team ball game played with an oval ball on a rectangular playing area. Rugby developed from the kicking game of football in 1823, when William Webb Ellis of Rugby school picked up the ball and ran with it. The Rugby Football Union (RFU) was formed in 1871. The breakaway Northern Union was formed in 1895; and this became known as the Rugby League. **Rugby Union** was long regarded as the amateur game and **Rugby League** the professional game; but this distinction disappeared in 1995, when the amateur regulations of rugby union were repealed. There are several differences between the two games: the number of players per side differ (15 in Union, 13 in League), there are no line-outs (a method of returning the ball into play from off the field) in League, and there are differences in the way a ball is returned to play after a tackle. The object is the same, to score a try by grounding the ball in the opposing scoring area behind the goal line. Points scoring in both codes (League in brackets) is as follows: try 5 (5), conversion 2 (2), penalty 3 (2), drop goal 3 (1). **4 Australian Rules football** A handling and kicking game which is a cross between association football and rugby. It is played with 18 players per side on an oval field. The object is to score goals by kicking the ball between the opponent's goal posts. The first recorded game was played between Scotch College and Melbourne Grammar School in 1858. **5 Gaelic football** A mixture of rugby, soccer, and Australian Rules football. The first game resembling Gaelic football took place at Slane, Ireland, in 1712. Originally played with 21 players per side, it was reduced to 15 in 1913. It is played on a rectangular field. At each end is a goal which resembles a set of rugby posts with a soccer-style net attached. The object is to score points by putting the ball either into the goal net, or over the crossbar and between the uprights. **6 Canadian football** A Canadian variant of rugby football. It developed from the 1880s, adapting aspects of 'American' football, and evolving its character independently. It is different from rugby in that (like American football) the ball can be thrown forward, and it involves a 'stop-play' rather than a continuous play format. The field is 110 × 55 yds (100 m × 50 m), with 10-yd (9-m) deep end-zones. The Canadian Football League appeared in 1958 at the end of a long conflict between amateur and professional associations. It presently consists of eight teams, the best of which is annually awarded the Grey Cup. >> FIFA; Football League; rugby football; UEFA; RR1044–5, 1052, 1059; *see illustration on p.321*

Football League The oldest association football league in the world, formed after a formal meeting at the Royal Hotel, Manchester on 17 April 1888. 12 clubs became founder members. >> football 1 ℹ

foraminiferan [forami**nif**eran] An amoeba-like protozoan that secretes an external shell (*test*), typically calcareous and chambered; feeds and moves by means of protoplasmic processes (*pseudopodia*) extruded through shell openings; largely marine; includes many fossils. (Order: Foraminifera.) >> amoeba; calcium; protoplasm; Protozoa; shell

Forbidden City The Imperial Palace in Beijing, the residence of the imperial rulers of China from its construction in 1420 until the fall of the Qing dynasty in 1911. The walled and moated palace complex covers 74 ha/183 acres. >> Beijing; Qing dynasty

force An influence applied to an unrestrained object which results in a change in its motion, causing it to accelerate in some way; symbol *F*, units N (newton); a vector quantity. Force equals mass of object multiplied by acceleration (Newton's second law). >> forces of nature ℹ; Newton's laws; vector (mathematics)

forces of nature In physics, taken to mean gravitation, electromagnetism, strong nuclear force, and weak nuclear forces. Their properties are summarized in the panel. >> electromagnetism; fifth force; gravitation; strong interaction; weak interaction; *see illustration opposite*

Ford, Ford Madox, originally **Ford Hermann Hueffer** (1873–1939) Writer, born in Merton, Surrey. He is best known for his novel *The Good Soldier* (1915) and for founding the *English Review* (1908). Later works include a series of war novels, and the tetralogy *Parade's End* (1920s).

Ford, Gerald R(udolph) (1913–) US statesman and 38th president (1974–6), born in Omaha, NE. A Republican member of the House of Representatives (1949–73), on the resignation of Spiro Agnew in 1973 he was appointed vice-president, and became president when Nixon resigned because of the Watergate scandal. The full pardon he granted to Nixon made him unpopular, and he was defeated in the 1976 presidential election by Jimmy Carter. >> Nixon, Richard M; Watergate

Ford, Harrison (1942–) Actor, born in Chicago, IL. He achieved stardom in *Star Wars* (1977) and its two sequels, and also found great popularity as the archaeologist adventurer 'Indiana Jones' in a series of films beginning with *Raiders of the Lost Ark* (1981). Later films include *Witness* (1985, Oscar nomination) and *The Devil's Own* (1997).

Ford, Henry (1863–1947) Automobile engineer and manufacturer, born in Dearborn, MI. He produced his first petrol-driven motor car in 1893, and in 1899 founded a company in Detroit, designing his own cars. In 1903 he started the Ford Motor Company, pioneering the modern 'assembly line' mass-production techniques for his famous Model T (1908–9). In 1919 he was succeeded by his son **Edsel Ford** (1893–1943), and in 1945 by his grandson **Henry Ford** (1917–87). >> car ℹ

Ford, John (c.1586–c.1640) Playwright, born in Ilsington, Devon. His plays include *The Lover's Melancholy* (1629) and *'Tis Pity She's a Whore* (1633).

Ford, John, originally **Sean Aloysius O'Fearna** (1894–1973) Film director, born in Cape Elizabeth, ME. His skilful portrayal of US pioneering history reached a peak with *Stagecoach* (1939), *The Informer* (1935, Oscar), and *The Grapes of Wrath* (1940, Oscar). Later films include *How Green Was My Valley* (1941, Oscar) and *The Quiet Man* (1952, Oscar).

Ford Foundation A philanthropic foundation set up in 1936 by Henry Ford and his son, Edsel, as an international charity mainly concerned with food shortages and population control in developing nations. >> Ford, Henry

Foreign Legion The elite formation of the French Army, recruited from non-French nationals. *La Légion Etrangère* was first raised in 1831, and retains its reputation for toughness. >> army

forensic medicine The discipline which relates the practice of medicine to the law. It includes such areas as abortion, the provision of medicines, and the supply of human tissues for surgical transplantation. *Forensic pathology* includes the study of wounds self-inflicted or caused by others, and of death in which other factors than natural causes might have played a part. >> DNA profiling; medicine

Forester, C(ecil) S(cott) (1899–1966) Writer, born in Cairo. Chiefly a novelist, he also wrote biographical and travel books. He is known especially for his creation of

Forces of Nature

	gravity	electro-magnetism	weak nuclear force	strong nuclear force
Range m	infinite	infinite	10^{-18} (sub-atomic)	10^{-15} (sub-atomic)
Relative strength	6×10^{-39}	1/137	10^{-5}	1
Examples of application	orbit of Earth around Sun	force between electrical charges	radio-active β-decay	binds atomic nucleus together

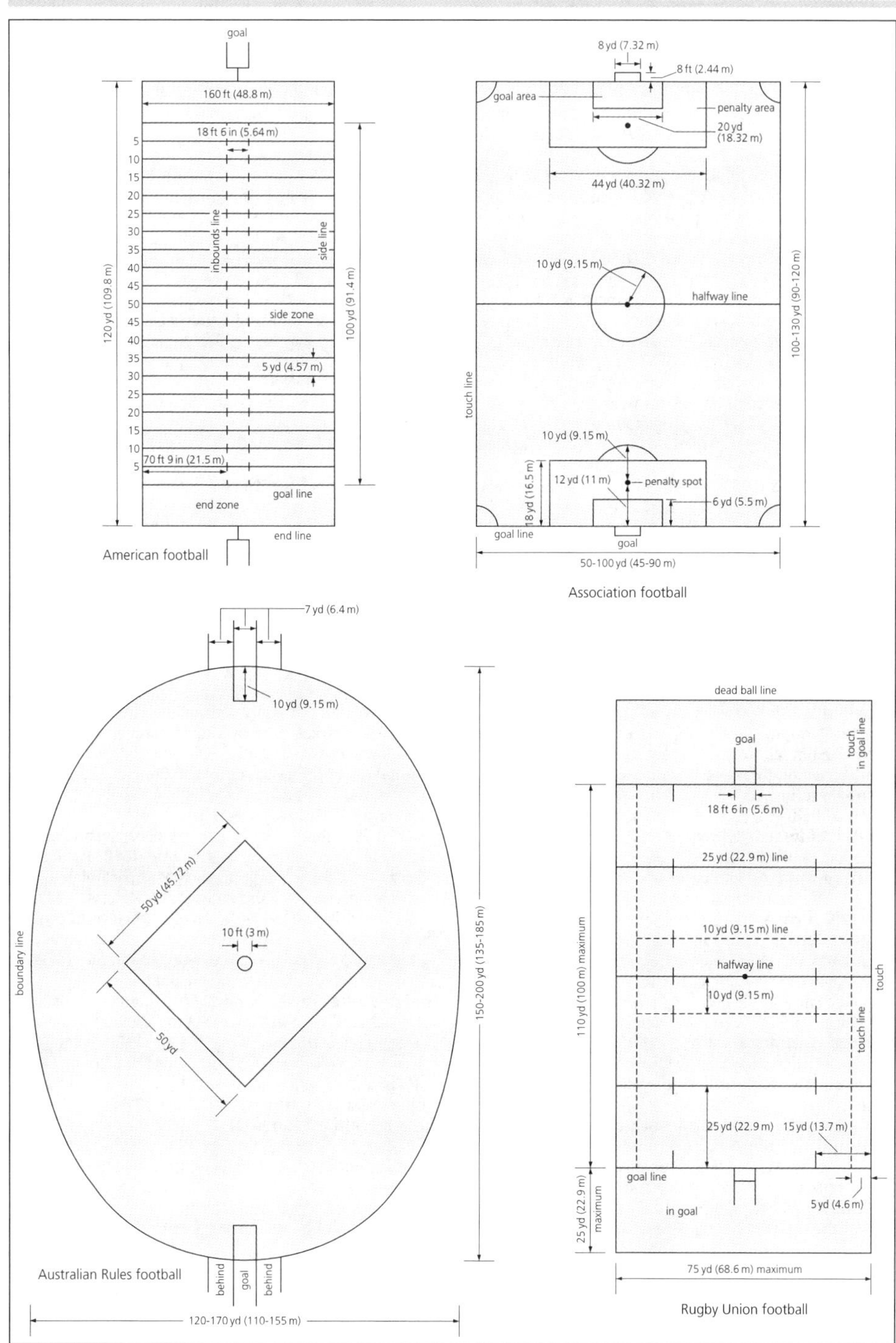

Football fields – dimensions

Captain Horatio Hornblower. Several of his works have been filmed, notably *The African Queen* (1935).

forestry The business of growing, harvesting, and marketing trees and managing the associated wildlife and recreational resources. Over 31% of the world's land area is covered by forest and woodland. Total world production of forest products reached 3·9 thousand million cubic m/5·1 thousand million cubic yd in 1990. >> agroforestry; tree ℹ

forgery The act of falsely making, reproducing, altering, or signing a document with the intention of defrauding others. It is essential to the criminal offence of forgery that the false document is to be used as if it were genuine, as in the cases of wills and bank-notes. >> counterfeiting

forget-me-not An annual or perennial, native to temperate regions; flowers tubular with five spreading lobes, often pink in bud, opening blue. (Genus: *Myosotis*, 50 species. Family: Boraginaceae.)

formaldehyde [faw(r)**mal**dehiyd] HCHO, IUPAC **methanal**, boiling point −21 °C. The simplest aldehyde, a gas with a characteristic odour, which polymerizes readily and reversibly to **paraformaldehyde** $(CH_2O)_n$. An aqueous solution, called *formalin*, is used as a disinfectant and preservative. >> aldehyde; IUPAC; methanol

Formalists A school of critics in early 20th-c Russia who believed that formal properties were of primary importance in a work of art. Roman Jakobson (1896–1982) later exported their ideas, which had considerable influence on later criticism.

Forman, Miloš (1932–) Film director, born in Caslav, Czech Republic. His tragi-comedy of insanity, *One Flew Over the Cuckoo's Nest* (1975), won five Oscars, and was successfully followed by *Hair* (1979), *Amadeus* (1983, Oscar), and *The People vs. Larry Flynt* (1996).

Formentera [formen**tay**ra] 38°43N 1°26E; pop (1995e) 4370; area 100 sq km/39 sq mi. Island in the Balearic Is, Spain; capital, San Francisco. >> Balearic Islands

formic acid HCOOH, IUPAC **methanoic acid**, boiling point 101 °C. A liquid with a pungent odour, the simplest carboxylic acid. It is a moderately strong acid; partially neutralized solutions have a pH of about 4. Formic acid is secreted by some insects, especially red ants, in the sting. It is used in textile and leather manufacture, and as an industrial solvent. >> carboxylic acids; IUPAC; pH

Fornax (Lat 'furnace') A faint S constellation. >> constellation; RR968

Forster, E(dward) M(organ) (1879–1970) Writer, born in London. His works include *Where Angels Fear to Tread* (1905), *The Longest Journey* (1907), *A Room with a View* (1908), *Howards End* (1910), and his masterpiece, *A Passage to India* (1924).

Forsyth, Bruce [**faw(r)**siyth], popular name of **Bruce Joseph Forsyth-Johnson** (1928–) Entertainer, born in Edmonton, Greater London. He trained as a dancer, but is best known as the compère or host on many UK television shows, such as *Sunday Night at the London Palladium* (1958–60) and *The Generation Game* (1971–8, 1992–4).

Forsyth, Frederick [**faw(r)**siyth] (1938–) Writer of suspense thrillers, born in Ashford, Kent. His reputation rests on three taut thrillers, *The Day of the Jackal* (1971), *The Odessa File* (1972), and *The Dogs of War* (1974).

forsythia A deciduous shrub, suckering and rooting from the tips of arching branches, native to SE Europe and E Asia; flowers yellow, with four spreading petals, in clusters appearing before leaves on last season's wood. (Genus: *Forsythia*, 7 species. Family: Oleaceae.)

Fortaleza [faw(r)ta**lay**za] 3°45S 38°35W, pop (1995e) 1 952 000. Port in NE Brazil; airfield; railway; commercial and industrial centre, especially for agriculture; two universities (1955, 1973); cathedral. >> Brazil ℹ

Fort-de-France [faw(r) duh **frãs**], formerly **Fort Royal** 14°36N 61°05W, pop (1995e) 109 000 Capital town of Martinique, Lesser Antilles, E Caribbean; airport; naval base; cathedral (1895). >> Martinique

Forth, River River in SEC Scotland; formed at Aberfoyle by the confluence of headstreams rising on Ben Lomond; flows generally E, widening into the Firth of Forth estuary; length 186 km/116 mi. >> Scotland ℹ

Fort Knox A US army post established in Kentucky in 1917, and noted as the site, since 1937, of the US Bullion Depository.

FORTRAN [**faw(r)**tran] An acronym of **FORmula TRANslation**, a widely used high-level computer programming language developed in the USA during the 1960s for mathematical, engineering, and scientific use. >> programming language

Fortuna [faw(r)**too**na] The ancient Roman goddess of Fortune. In the Middle Ages she was highly revered as a divine and moral figure, redressing human pride. Her wheel is frequently referred to, with figures seen climbing and falling off.

Fort William 56°49N 5°07W, pop (1995e) 109 000. Town in Highland, W Scotland; on E side of Loch Linnhe; airfield; railway; Inverlochy castle; Ben Nevis (SE). >> Ben Nevis; Caledonian Canal; Scotland ℹ

Fort Worth 32°45N 97°18W, pop (1995e) 493 000. City in NE Texas, USA, on the Trinity R; established as an army post, 1847; important livestock market centre; airport at Dallas–Fort Worth; airfield; railway; university (1873). >> Texas

Forty-five Rebellion The Jacobite rebellion of 1745–6 to restore the Catholic Stuart kings to the British throne. It began in July 1745 when Charles Edward Stuart ('the Young Pretender') arrived in Scotland and proclaimed his father King James III. The Jacobite forces reached as far south as Derby, but the rebellion was crushingly defeated at Culloden in 1746. >> Culloden Moor, Battle of; Jacobites; Stuart, Charles Edward

forty-niners Adventurers who swarmed to California in 1849, after the discovery of gold there the previous year. Their number may have been as high as 100 000.

forum The Roman equivalent of the Greek *agora*; originally the market-place of a town, later its civic centre. Besides shops and stalls, it contained the principal municipal buildings, such as the Council chamber and law courts. >> curia

Fosse Way >> **Roman roads** ℹ

fossil The remains of a once-living organism, usually restricted to organisms that lived prior to the last Ice Age. Fossils typically comprise the bodies or part of the organisms themselves, but also include a variety of trace fossils such as tracks and faeces. >> Ice Age; palaeontology

fossil fuel Fuels derived from the fossilized remains of plants and animals, such as peat, coal, and crude oil. >> coal; fuel; oil (earth sciences); peat

Foster, Jodie, originally **Alicia Christian Foster** (1962–) Film actress, born in New York City. Known for her child roles in such films as *Bugsy Malone* (1976), as an adult actress she received Oscars for her roles in *The Accused* (1988) and *The Silence of the Lambs* (1991). She made her directorial debut with *Little Man Tate* (1991).

Foster, Stephen (Collins) (1826–64) Songwriter, born in Pittsburgh, PA. Songs such as 'Oh! Susanna' (1848), 'Old Folks at Home' (1851), and 'Beautiful Dreamer' (1864) sold thousands of song-sheets, and became seminal works of the American songwriting tradition.

Foucault, (Jean Bernard) Léon [fookoh] (1819–68) Physicist, born in Paris. He determined the velocity of light, invented the gyroscope (1852), and improved the mirrors of reflecting telescopes (1858). >> Foucault pendulum; gyroscope; light

Foucault, Michel [fookoh] (1926–84) Philosopher, born in Poitiers, France. He sought consistently to test cultural assumptions in given historical contexts. His most important writings include *Histoire de la folie* (1961, trans Madness and Civilization) and *Les mots et les choses* (1966, trans The Order of Things).

Foucault pendulum [**foo**koh] A pendulum that is free to swing in any direction, such that the plane of swing gradually rotates as the Earth turns under it; devised by French physicist Jean Foucault in 1851. It was used as proof that the Earth spins. >> Foucault, Jean Bernard Léon

Fouché, Joseph, duc d'Otrante (Duke of Otranto) [fooshay] (1763–1829) French statesman, born in Nantes, France. He was elected to the National Convention in 1792 as a Jacobin, and in 1799 became Minister of Police, a post which he held successfully until 1815. >> French Revolution [i]; Jacobins (French history)

foul marten >> **polecat**

foumart [**foo**mah(r)t] >> polecat

founding Casting molten metal in a mould made to a high degree of precision. Mould materials are compounded of sand and clay, packed over a pattern to which the eventual casting is to conform. >> casting; metal

Fountains Abbey A Cistercian monastery founded in 1132 near Ripon, North Yorkshire, UK; a world heritage site. The abbey ruins stand in the magnificent water gardens of Studley Royal. >> abbey; Cistercians; monasticism

Fouqué, Friedrich Heinrich Karl, Baron de la Motte [**foo**kay] (1777–1843) Romantic author, born in Brandenburg, Germany. He published a long series of romances based on Norse legend and old French poetry, his masterpiece being *Undine* (1811). >> Romanticism

Fouquet, Jean [fookay] (c.1420–c.1480) Painter, born in Tours, France. His most notable illuminations are found in the *Antiquities of the Jews* of Josephus and the *Hours of Etienne Chevalier* at Chantilly.

Fouquet, Nicolas, vicomte de (Viscount of) **Melun et de Vaux, Marquis de Belle-Isle** [fookay] (1615–80) French statesman, born in Paris. Mazarin made him *procureur-général* to the parliament of Paris (1650) and Superintendent of Finance (1653). He became extremely rich, and was ambitious to succeed Mazarin, but was arrested for embezzlement (1661), and imprisoned. >> Mazarin

Four Freedoms Four basic human rights proclaimed in an annual message to Congress by President Roosevelt. They included freedom of speech and worship, and freedom from want and fear. >> Roosevelt, Franklin D

Four Horsemen of the Apocalypse Symbolic Biblical characters described in *Rev* 6 (also *Zech* 6.1–7). Each comes on a steed of different colour, symbolizing devastations associated with the world's end (black = famine; red = bloodshed, war; pale = pestilence, death), except for the white horse, which has a 'crown' and is sent 'to conquer'. >> Revelation, Book of

Fourier, (Jean Baptiste) Joseph, Baron [fooryay] (1768–1830) Mathematician, born in Auxerre, France. While working on the flow of heat he discovered the theorem which now bears his name, that any function of a variable can be expanded in a series of sines of multiples of the variable (the **Fourier series**).

Four Noble Truths The summary of the central teachings of Buddha. **1** All life involves suffering, and is inevitably sorrowful. **2** The cause of suffering and sorrow is craving or desire arising from ignorance. **3** There is escape from suffering, because craving and desire can end. **4** There is an Eightfold Path leading to the end of suffering and sorrow. >> Buddha; Buddhism; Eightfold Path

four-stroke engine An engine that works on a practical cycle with one in every four strokes of the piston being the power stroke. This is the type of engine normally used to drive motor cars. >> Carnot cycle; engine; two-stroke engine

Fourteen Points A peace programme outlined by US President Wilson to Congress in 1918. The Germans subsequently asked Wilson for an armistice agreement based on their acceptance of these points, which, with two reservations, were accepted by the Allied powers as the basis for a peace settlement. >> Atlantic Charter; Wilson, Woodrow; World War 1

Fourth of July, July Fourth, or **Independence Day** A public holiday in the USA, commemorating the adoption of the Declaration of Independence (4 Jul 1776).

Fou Ts'ong [foo tsong] (1934–) Concert pianist, born in Shanghai, China. Acclaimed as an interpreter of Mozart and Chopin, in 1958 he made his base in London, and performed extensively on the international circuit.

Fowler, H(enry) W(atson) (1858–1933) Lexicographer, born in Tonbridge, Kent. With his brother, **F(rank) G(eorge) Fowler** (1871–1918) they began a literary partnership which led to *The King's English* (1906) and the *Concise Oxford Dictionary* (1911). Henry later wrote the *Dictionary of Modern English Usage* (1926). >> dictionary; English

Fowler, William A(lfred) (1911–95) Astrophysicist, born in Pittsburgh, PA. He worked on the application of nuclear physics to all aspects of astronomy, and is considered the founder of the theory of nucleosynthesis, he was awarded the Nobel Prize for Physics in 1983. >> nucleosynthesis

Fowles, John (Robert) (1926–) Writer, born in London. His major works include *The Magus* (1966), *The French Lieutenant's Woman* (1969, filmed 1981) and *Tessera* (1993). The autobiographical *Daniel Martin* appeared in 1977.

fowl pest The name applied to two diseases of birds, **fowl plague** and **Newcastle disease**; several strains, caused by viruses; attacks nervous, digestive, and respiratory systems; often fatal.

Fox A North American Algonkin Indian group originally from N Wisconsin. They settled permanently in Iowa in 1842, retaining many traditional organizational features. >> Algonkin

Fox, Charles James (1749–1806) British statesman and foreign secretary (1782, 1783, 1806), born in London. He became secretary of state after Lord North's downfall, and in 1783 formed a coalition with him, which held office for a short period. >> North, Frederick

Fox, George (1624–91) Founder of the Quakers, born in Fenny Drayton, Leicestershire. He became a travelling preacher and a missionary, and was imprisoned on several occasions. As a writer he is remembered by his *Journal* (posthumously published), which records the birth of the Quaker movement. >> Friends, Society of

fox A small member of the dog family (21 species), worldwide except SE Asia; usually thin muzzle, large pointed ears, long bushy tail; hunts alone; renowned for its cunning; often nocturnal; lives in a den. >> Canidae; fennec fox

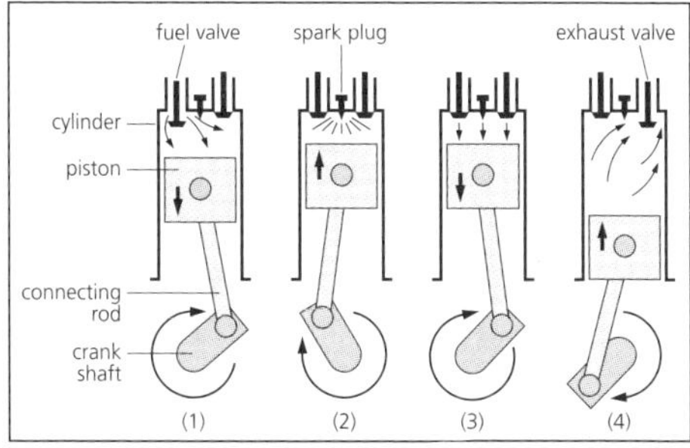

Four-stroke engine cycle. (1) Fuel and air drawn into cylinder. (2) Fuel/air mixture compressed and ignited by spark. (3) Power stroke. (4) Exhaust gases expelled.

foxglove A softly hairy biennial (*Digitalis purpurea*) growing to 150 cm/5 ft, native to Europe; tall flower-spike produced in second year; flowers all on one side of the stem, bell-shaped with five very short lobes, drooping, usually pink to purple. It is the original source of the heart drug digitalin. (Family: Scrophulariaceae.)

fox-grape >> **grapevine**

foxhound A domestic dog bred for hunting foxes; large with brown, black, and white coat; soft ears; two breeds: the **English foxhound**, and its larger descendant, the **American foxhound**. >> fox; hound

foxhunting A blood sport, which developed in the UK in the late 17th-c, and which since the early 19th-c has been regarded as the pastime of the aristocracy and the wealthy. The foxhunting season lasts from November to April. Each hunt is controlled by a *master of hounds*, and the hounds are controlled by the *huntsman*. In recent years, animal rights saboteurs have attempted to thwart hunts, and there is a movement to try to get the sport banned in the UK. >> blood sports

foxtail millet >> **millet**

fox terrier An active British terrier with a deep chest, pointed muzzle, and soft, folded ears held high; tail usually docked short when young; usually white with black and brown markings; two forms: **wire-haired** and **smooth-haired**. >> dog; Jack Russell; terrier

Foyle, Lough Inlet of the Atlantic, on the N coast of Ireland; mouth 1.5 km/0.9 mi wide; length, 24 km/15 mi; width, 16 km/10 mi. >> Ireland (island) [i]

fractals Geometrical entities characterized by basic patterns that are repeated at ever decreasing sizes. For example, trees describe an approximate fractal pattern, as the trunk divides into branches which further subdivide into smaller branches which ultimately subdivide into twigs; at each stage of division the pattern is a smaller version of the original. They were devised in 1967 by French mathematician Benoit Mandelbrot (1924–). >> chaos; geometry

fractions >> **numbers**

fracture A physical break in the continuity of a bone, most commonly the result of external force. The break takes a number of forms, from a simple transverse fracture to one in which the bone is shattered into a number of small pieces (**comminuted fracture**). Well-aligned fragments may unite while being kept in place by a simple splint. Comminuted fractures may need manipulation and the insertion of metal pins to hold the pieces together. >> bone

Framework programme A programme of research, funded by the European Commission, designed to improve the level of technical expertise and application within the European Union. It includes the ESPRIT and RACE programmes. >> ESPRIT; European Union; RACE

Frampton, Sir George James (1860–1928) Sculptor, born in London. Among his works are 'Peter Pan' in Kensington Gardens, London, and the lions at the British Museum.

franc The currency unit of many countries, notably France, Belgium, and Switzerland. The name derives from the words on a 14th-c gold coin, *Francorum rex* ('King of the Franks').

France, ancient **Gallia**, official name **Republic of France**, Fr **République Française** pop (1995e) 58 333 000, area 551 000 sq km/212 686 sq mi; overseas departments pop (1995e) 1 504 000, area 97 014 sq km/37 447 sq mi. Republic of W Europe, includes island of Corsica in the Mediterranean, and overseas departments of Guadeloupe, Martinique, French Guiana, Réunion, St-Pierre-et-Miquelon, and Mayotte; also administers overseas territories of New Caledonia, French Polynesia, Wallis and Futuna, and the Southern and Antarctic Territories; capital, Paris; timezone GMT +1; population largely of Celtic and Latin origin, with several minorities; chief religion, Roman Catholicism (90%); official language, French (also widely used as international language); unit of currency, the French franc of 100 centimes; a country of low and medium-sized hills and plateaux deeply cut by rivers; bounded S and E by large mountain ranges, notably (interior) the Armorican massif, Massif Central, Cévennes, Vosges, and Ardennes, (E) the Jura and Alps (rising to 4807 m/15 771 ft at Mont Blanc), and (S) the Pyrenees; Mediterranean climate in S, with warm, moist winters and hot dry summers; maritime type in NW; continental climate in E; Celtic-speaking Gauls dominant by 5th-c BC;

part of Roman Empire, 125 BC to 5th-c AD; invaded by several Germanic tribes, 3rd-5th-c; Franks inaugurated the Merovingian epoch, 5th-c; Carolingian peak of development, 8th-c; feudal monarchy founded by Hugh Capet, 987; Plantagenets of England acquired several territories, 12th-c; Estates General first convened by Philip the Fair (1302); lands gradually recovered in Hundred Years' War, 1337–1453, apart from Calais (regained, 1558); Capetian dynasty followed by the Valois, from 1328, and the Bourbons, from 1589; 16th-c struggle between Francis I and Emperor Charles V; Wars of Religion, 1562–98; 17th-c kings restored power of the monarchy, at its peak under Louis XIV; French Revolution, 1789; First Republic declared, 1792; French Revolutionary Wars 1793–99; First Empire, ruled by Napoleon, 1804–14; monarchy restored, 1814–48; Second Republic, 1848–52, and Second Empire, 1852–70, ruled by Louis Napoleon; Third Republic, 1870–1940; great political instability between World Wars, with several governments holding office for short periods; occupied by Germany 1940–4, with pro-German government at Vichy and Free French in London under de Gaulle; Fourth Republic, 1946–58; war with Indo-China, 1946–54; conflict in Algeria, 1954–62; Fifth Republic, 1958; governed by a president, elected every seven years, who appoints a prime minister and presides over a Council of Ministers; bicameral legislature consists of a National Assembly and a Senate; W Europe's foremost producer of agricultural products; coalfields in N France, Lorraine, and the Massif Central; hydroelectric power from the Alps; several nuclear power sites; heavy industry based around N coalfields. >> Bourbons; Capetians; Carolingians; Celts; de Gaulle; Franks; French Revolution 🛈 / Revolutionary Wars; Gaul; Hundred Years' War; Louis XIV; Merovingians; Napoleon I / III; Paris; Plantagenets; Religion, Wars of; Roman history 🛈; Valois; RR1008 political leaders

France, Anatole [frãs], pseudonym of **Jacques Anatole François Thibault** (1844–1924) Writer, born in Paris. He wrote several lively novels, which contrast with his later, satirical works notably *L'Ile des pingouins* (1908, Penguin Island). The Dreyfus case (1896) stirred him into politics as a champion of internationalism. He was awarded the Nobel Prize for Literature in 1921. >> Dreyfus

Francis I (1494–1547) King of France (1515–47), born in Cognac. The dominant feature of his reign was his rivalry with the Emperor Charles V, which led to a series of wars (1521–6, 1528–9, 1536–8, 1542–4). After establishing his military reputation against the Swiss at Marignano (1515), he later suffered a number of reverses, including his capture at Pavia (1525). >> Charles V (Emperor)

Francis II (1768–1835) Last Holy Roman Emperor (1792–1806), the first Emperor of Austria (1804–35), and King of Hungary (1792–30) and Bohemia (1792–1836), born in Florence, Italy. Defeated on several occasions by Napoleon, he made a short-lived alliance with him, but later joined with Russia and Prussia to win the Battle of Leipzig (1813). >> Napoleonic Wars

Francis of Assisi, St [a**see**zee], originally **Giovanni Bernardone** (?1181–1226) Founder of the Franciscan Order, born in Assisi, Italy. In 1205 he left his worldly life, and by 1210 had formed a brotherhood for which he drew up a rule which became the Franciscan way of life. He was canonized in 1228. He is often represented in art among animals and birds, which he called his sisters and brothers. Feast day 4 October. >> Franciscans

Francis of Sales, St [saylz], Fr [sahl] (1567–1622) Roman Catholic bishop and writer, born in Sales, France. A distinguished preacher, he became Bishop of Nicopolis (1599) and Bishop of Geneva (1602), where he helped to found a congregation of nuns of the Visitation. He was canonized in 1665; feast day 24 January. >> monasticism

Franciscans Religious orders founded by St Francis of Assisi in the early 13th-c. The first order, of **Friars Minor**, is now divided into three groups: the **Observants** (**OFM**), the **Conventuals** (**OFMConv**), and the **Capuchins** (**OFMCap**). The second order is made up of nuns, known as the **Poor Clares** (**PC**). The third order is a lay fraternity. >> Capuchins; Clare (of Assisi), St; Francis of Assisi, St

Francis Joseph I, Ger **Franz Josef I** (1830–1916) Emperor of Austria (1848–1916) and king of Hungary (1867–1916), born near Vienna. He was defeated by the Prussians in 1866, and established the Dual Monarchy of Austria–Hungary in 1867. His attack on Serbia in 1914 precipitated World War 1. >> Austria–Hungary, Dual Monarchy of

Francistown 21°11S 27°32E, pop (1995e) 64 100. Independent township in Botswana, S Africa; altitude 990 m/3248 ft; area 79 sq km/49 sq mi; industrial and commercial centre of Botswana; airfield; railway. >> Botswana 🛈

Francis Xavier, St [**zay**vier], Span **San Francisco Javier**, known as **the Apostle of the Indies** (1506–52) Roman Catholic missionary who brought Christianity to India and the Far East, born in Navarre, Spain. He became one of the first seven members of the Jesuit order (1534), and began his missionary work in Goa, India (1542). He was canonized in 1622. Feast day 3 December. >> Jesuits

Franck, César (Auguste) [frãk, sayzah(r)] (1822–90) Composer, born in Liège, Belgium. His reputation rests on a few masterpieces all written after the age of 50, the best known being a violin sonata, a string quartet, a symphony, and the *Variations symphoniques* (1885) for piano and orchestra.

Franco (Bahamonde), Francisco [**frang**koh], popular name **el Caudillo** ('the leader') (1892–1975) Spanish general and dictator (1936–75), born in El Ferrol, Galicia. He led the repression of the Asturias miners' revolt (1934), and during 1935 served as chief-of-staff. In 1936 he joined the conspiracy against the Popular Front government, becoming *generalísimo* of the rebel forces. Between 1936 and 1939 he led the Nationalists to victory, and presided over the construction of an authoritarian regime that endured until his death. During World War 2, he opted for non-belligerency rather than neutrality. During the 1950s, his anti-communism made possible a rapprochement with the Western powers. In 1969 he announced that upon his death the monarchy would return in the person of Juan Carlos, grandson of Spain's last ruling king. >> Spain 🛈; Spanish Civil War

Franco-German Treaty of Co-operation A treaty signed (Jan 1963) by President de Gaulle and Chancellor Adenauer. It made provisions for regular summit meetings, and co-operation and consultation in foreign, economic, and cultural affairs. >> Adenauer; de Gaulle

francolin A partridge native to Africa and S Asia; large bird with patches of bare skin on head and neck. (Genus: *Francolinus*, 40 species.) >> partridge; redwing

Francome, John [**frang**kuhm] (1952–) Jockey and trainer, born in Swindon, Wiltshire. In 1970–85 he rode a record 1138 winners over fences. He was seven times National Hunt champion jockey (1976, 1979, 1981–5). >> horse racing

Franco-Prussian War (1870–1) A conflict occasioned by the Hohenzollern candidature for the Spanish throne and the Ems telegram, and caused by the changing balance of power in Europe. It resulted in crushing defeats for France at Sedan and Metz, the siege of Paris, and the humiliating Treaty of Frankfurt. >> Ems telegram; Hohenzollerns; Prussia

frangipani [franji**pah**nee] A shrub or small tree (*Plumeria rubra*) growing to c.6 m/20 ft, native to tropical America; leaves oval; flowers in large clusters, very fragrant, five petals, white, yellow, or pink. The scented flowers are often placed in Buddhist temples. (Family: Apocynaceae.)

Frank, Anne (1929–45) Jewish diarist and concentration camp victim, born in Frankfurt, Germany. Her family fled from the Nazis to The Netherlands in 1933, and after the Nazi occupation hid with her family in a sealed-off office flat in Amsterdam from 1942 until they were betrayed in 1944. She died in Belsen concentration camp. The lively, moving diary she kept during her concealment was published in 1947. >> Holocaust; Nazi Party

Frankenstein A soulless creature made from parts of corpses and animated by supposed scientific means. In Mary Shelley's novel (1818), Frankenstein was the name of the monster's creator, but it has since become transferred to the monster itself. The story was made into a film in 1931 by James Whale, with Boris Karloff as the monster, and has since given rise to a whole genre of cinema films. >> science fiction; Shelley, Mary

Frankfort [**frangk**fert] 38°12N 84°52W, pop (1995e) 27 200. Capital of state in NC Kentucky, USA; founded by Daniel Boone, 1770; state capital, 1792; railway; university; trade and shipping centre for tobacco, livestock, and limestone. >> Kentucky

Frankfurt (am Main) [**frangk**foort, miyn] 50°07N 8°40E, pop (1995e) 661 000. Manufacturing and commercial city in Germany; port on R Main; most of the German emperors crowned here; international junction for rail, road, and air traffic; university (1914); headquarters of the leading German stock exchange; birthplace of Goethe; cathedral (13th–15th-c), many trade fairs. >> Germany [i]; Goethe

Frankfurt (an der Oder) [**frangk**foort, **oh**der] 52°50N 14°31E, pop (1995e) 91 900. City in Germany on R Oder; badly bombed in World War 2; railway. >> Germany [i]

frankincense An evergreen tree or shrub (*Boswellia carteri*) growing to 6 m/20 ft, native to Somaliland; flowers white, 5-petalled. Aromatic resin is obtained from cuts in the bark. (Family: Burseraceae.) >> resin

Franklin, Benjamin (1706–90) US statesman, writer, and scientist, born in Boston, MA. He set up a printing house in Philadelphia, and built a reputation as a journalist. In 1746 he began his research into electricity, proving that lightning and electricity are identical, and suggesting that buildings be protected by lightning conductors. In 1776 he was actively involved in framing the Declaration of Independence. He was US minister in Paris until 1785, then three times president of the State of Pennsylvania. After taking part in the Federal Constitutional Convention (1787), he retired from public life, and wrote an acclaimed autobiography. >> Declaration of Independence; electricity

Franklin, Sir John (1786–1847) Arctic explorer, born in Spilsby, Lincolnshire. He commanded an expedition to discover the Northwest Passage, but his ships were beleaguered by thick ice in the Victoria Strait, and he and his crew died. Their remains, and a record of the expedition, were found several years later. >> Northwest Passage

Franklin, (Stella Maria Sarah) Miles, pseudonym **Brent of Bin Bin** (1879–1954) Novelist, born in Talbingo, New South Wales, Australia. Her best-known novel, *My Brilliant Career* (1901), has been described as the first Australian novel. The annual *Miles Franklin Awards* are now among Australia's most prestigious literary prizes.

Franks Germanic peoples, originally from the lower Rhine region. Charlemagne, their greatest ruler, attempted to revive the Roman Empire in the West. They gave their name to Francia, which by the 13th-c stood for what is now France. >> Charlemagne

Franz Josef Land, Russ **Zemlya Frantsa-Iosifa** area 20 700 sq km/8 000 sq mi. Archipelago in the Arctic Ocean, NW Russia; over 160 islands of volcanic origin; declared Soviet territory in 1926; uninhabited save for a meteorological station. >> Russia [i]

Fraser, Lady Antonia, *née* **Pakenham** (1932–) British writer. She is best known for her books about important historical figures, such as *Mary Queen of Scots* (1969, James Tait Black) and *Kings and Queens of England* (1975, 1988). She married Harold Pinter in 1980. >> Pinter

Fraser, Dawn (1937–) Swimmer, born in Balmain, New South Wales, Australia. She is the only swimmer to take the same individual title at three consecutive Olympics, winning the 100 m freestyle in 1956, 1960, and 1964. She also won a gold medal in the 4 × 100 m freestyle relay in 1956. In 1964 she was banned by the Australian association for 10 years (later reduced to four) following an overexuberant party in Tokyo after winning her third Olympic title. She was elected an Independent member of the New South Wales Legislative Assembly in 1988–91. >> swimming

Fraser, (John) Malcolm (1930–) Australian statesman and Liberal prime minister (1975–83), born in Melbourne. He was minister for the army (1966–8), defence (1969–71), and education and science (1968–9, 1971–2), and became prime minister in a Liberal–National Country coalition. >> Australia; Liberal Party (Australia)

Fraser, Simon (1776–1862) Fur trader, born in Bennington, VT. He moved to Canada in 1784, worked as a clerk in the North-West Co, and was sent in 1805 to establish the first trading posts in the Rocky Mountains. In 1808 he followed the Fraser R, named after him, to its mouth. Simon Fraser University, in British Columbia, is also named after him.

Fraser River River in SW Canada, rises in the Rocky Mts, and enters the Pacific Ocean 16 km/10 mi S of Vancouver; length 1368 km/850 mi. >> Canada [i]

fraternity and sorority In the USA, associations at universities, for men and women respectively, named usually with two or three letters of the Greek alphabet (eg *Kappa Lamda*, *Sigma Chi*). They are formed mainly for social purposes; membership is by invitation, and is in some cases discriminatory. They are banned in some universities.

fraud A false statement made knowingly, recklessly, or without belief in its truth; the fact that there may have been no intention to cheat anyone is irrelevant. Any person injured by fraud may bring an action to recover damages in the tort (or delict) of deceit. Any contract induced by fraud can be rescinded or sometimes reformed at the instance of the innocent party. >> tort

Fraunhofer, Joseph von [**frown**hohfer] (1787–1826) Physicist, born in Straubing, Germany. In 1807 he founded an optical institute at Munich, where he improved prisms and telescopes, enabling him to discover the dark lines in the Sun's spectrum, since named after him.

Fray Bentos [friy **ben**tohs] 33°10S 58°20W, pop (1995e) 21 400. River port in W Uruguay, on R Uruguay; airfield; railway; ferry; former centre of meat packing and canning industry (especially corned beef), plant now closed and made into an industrial museum. >> Uruguay [i]

Frazer, Sir James George (1854–1941) Social anthropologist, classicist, and folklorist, born in Glasgow. His major work was *The Golden Bough* (1890; rewritten in 12 vols, 1911–15). >> anthropology

Frederick I (Emperor), known as **Frederick Barbarossa** ('Redbeard') (c.1123–90) Holy Roman Emperor, born of the Hohenstaufen family, who succeeded his uncle Conrad III in 1152. His reign was a continuous struggle against unruly vassals at home, the city republics of Lombardy, and the papacy. He went on several campaigns in Italy, but was severely defeated at Legnano (1176). He also led the Third Crusade against Saladin (1189). >> Crusades [i]; Hohenstaufen; Lombard League

Frederick I (of Prussia) (1657–1713) Elector of Brandenburg from 1688 (as Frederick III) and the first King of Prussia from 1701, born in Königsberg. He maintained a large court, established a standing army, and was a great patron of the arts and learning. >> Prussia

Frederick II (Emperor) (1194–1250) Holy Roman Emperor (from 1220), born in Jesi, near Ancona, the grandson of Frederick I, the last of the Hohenstaufen line. He was also King of Sicily (1198) and of Germany (1212). He devoted himself to organizing his Italian territories, but his plans were frustrated by the Lombard cities and by the popes. Embarking on the Sixth Crusade in 1228, he took possession of Jersusalem, and crowned himself king there (1229). >> Crusades ℹ; Lombard League

Frederick II (of Prussia), known as **the Great** (1712–86) King of Prussia from 1740, born in Berlin, the son of Frederick William I. He seized Silesia, and defeated the Austrians at Mollwitz (1741) and Chotusitz (1742). The second Silesian War (1744–5) left him with further territories which he retained after fighting the Seven Years' War (1756–63). In 1772 he shared in the first partition of Poland. Under him, Prussia became a leading European power. >> Austrian Succession, War of the; Prussia; Seven Years' War

Fredericksburg, Battle of In the American Civil War, a fruitless attempt by the Northern army of 113 000 to capture the town of Fredericksburg, VA, defended by a Southern army of 75 000. >> American Civil War

Frederick William, known as **the Great Elector** (1620–88) Elector of Brandenburg (1640–88), born near Berlin. He regulated the finances of the state, and reorganized the army and administrative system. He gained East Pomerania by the Treaty of Westphalia (1648), retrieving the sovereignty of Prussia from Poland (1657). His reforms laid the foundation of future Prussian greatness. >> Hohenzollerns

Frederick William III (1770–1840) King of Prussia (1797–1840), the son of Frederick William II, born in Potsdam. He was severely defeated by Napoleon at Jena and Auerstadt, but after major military reforms shared in the decisive victory of Leipzig (1813). By the Treaty of Vienna (1815) he recovered his possessions. >> Napoleonic Wars; Prussia

Fredericton 45°57N 66°40W, pop (1995e) 49 300. Capital of New Brunswick, Canada, on the St John R; originally settled by Acadians, 1731, as St Anne's Point; renamed 1785 for Prince Frederick, second son of George III; capital, 1787; airfield; railway; university (1783); cathedral (1853). >> Acadia; New Brunswick (Canada)

freefalling >> **skydiving**

Free French Frenchmen who answered General de Gaulle's appeal, broadcast from London (18 Jun 1940) to reject the impending armistice between France and Germany, and join him in fighting on. He became leader of the Free French forces. >> de Gaulle; World War 2

freehold Land or property held for use by the owner without obligation to any other owner. This is in contrast to **leasehold**, where the leaseholder has possession only for some finite period (eg 99 years), subject to payment of ground rent, reversion of the property to the ground landlord at the end of the lease, and possibly restrictions on the uses to which the property can be put. >> property

freemasonry A movement whose members (**masons**) are joined together in an association based on brotherly love, faith, and charity; the one essential qualification for membership is a belief in a supreme being. It is known for its rituals and signs of recognition that date back to ancient religions and to the practices of the mediaeval craft guild of the stonemasons (in England). During the 17th-c the masons' clubs, or *lodges*, began to be attended by gentlemen who had no connection with the trade, and the Grand Lodge of England was founded in 1717. The organization regularly comes under attack for the secrecy with which it carries out its activities.

free port An area near a port or airport where business enterprises may import materials and components free of tax or import duties, as long as the resulting finished articles are exported. The world's largest ports in this category are Hong Kong and Singapore. The UK set up six free ports in 1984, including Liverpool and Southampton. >> customs and excise

freesia A perennial (*Freesia refracta*) growing to 75 cm/30 in, producing corms, native to S Africa; flowers up to 5 cm/2 in long, goblet-shaped, creamy white, fragrant, in one-sided sprays; cultivars with orange-to-crimson or blue-to-mauve flowers. (Family: Iridaceae.)

Free State, formerly (1910–94) **Orange Free State** pop (1998e) 2 470 000; area 127 993 sq km/49 418 sq mi. One of the nine new provinces established by the South African constitution of 1994, in EC South Africa; capital, Bloemfontein (also, the judicial capital of South Africa); chief languages, Sesotho (56%), Afrikaans, Xhosa; claimed by British as the Orange River Sovereignty, 1848; independence, 1854; joined Union of South Africa as Orange Free State, 1910; a largely rural province ('the breadbasket of South Africa'); rich gold deposits. >> Bloemfontein; South Africa ℹ

Freetown 8°30N 13°17W, pop (1995e) 594 000. Seaport capital of Sierra Leone; visited by the Portuguese, 15th-c; founded in the 1790s as a foundation for freed slaves; capital of British West Africa, 1808–74; capital of Sierra Leone, 1961; airport; university (1827). >> Sierra Leone ℹ

free trade An economic doctrine that trade between countries should not be controlled in any way; there should be no tariffs or other barriers. Since the 19th-c, tariff barriers have become universal, but groups of countries may agree to lower or remove them, forming a **free-trade area**, as in the case of the EU. >> European Union; laissez-faire; tariff

free verse Verse which, while being rhythmical, observes no strict or recurrent metrical pattern. Much if not most 20th-c verse is written in free verse. Many poets (such as T S Eliot) have maintained it is more difficult to write well than formal verse. >> Eliot, T S; metre (literature); Whitman

freeze drying >> **lyophilization**

freezing >> **deep-freezing**

Frege, (Friedrich Ludwig) Gottlob [**fray**guh] (1848–1925) Mathematician and logician, born in Wismar, Germany. His *Begriffsschrift* (1879, 'Concept-script') outlined the first complete system of symbolic logic, and this was followed by his *Grundlagen der Arithmetik* (1884, The Foundations of Arithmetic), which influenced Bertrand Russell. >> Russell, Bertrand; logic

Frei (Montalva), Eduardo [fray] (1911–82) Chilean statesman and president (1964–70), born in Santiago. He became one of the leaders of the Social-Christian Falange Party in the late 1930s, and of the new Christian Democratic Party after 1957. >> Chile ℹ

Fremantle [**free**mantl] 32°07S 115°44E, pop (1995e) 25 200. Seaport city in Western Australia, at the mouth of the Swan R; founded as a penal colony, 1829; railway terminus; the Round House (1830), a former jail; a notable sailing club. >> Perth (Australia); Western Australia

French >> **Romance languages**

French, Dawn (1957–) Comedy writer and actress, born in Holyhead, Anglesey, NW Wales. She met Jennifer Saunders at drama school and formed a comedy partnership, becoming widely known with the television series *French and Saunders* (from 1987). Her own series include *Murder Most Horrid* and *The Vicar of Dibley* (International Emmy, 1998). She is married to Lenny Henry. >> Henry, Lenny; Saunders, Jennifer

French, John (Denton Pinkstone), Earl of Ypres (1852–1925) British field marshal (1913), born in Ripple, Kent. Chief of the Imperial General Staff (1911–14), he held supreme command of the British Expeditionary Force in France (1914–15), but was criticized for indecision, and resigned. >> British Expeditionary Force; World War 1

French, Marilyn (1929–) Novelist, born in New York City. She is best known for her first novel, *The Woman's Room* (1977), hailed as a pioneering feminist text for its angry study of the subjection of women. Later books include *Her Mother's Daughter* (1992) and *Our Father* (1994).

French bean >> **haricot bean**

French Guiana [gee**ah**na], Fr **La Guyane Française** pop (1995e) 120 000; area 90 909 sq km/35 091 sq mi. Overseas department of France in South America, bordering the Atlantic; capital, Cayenne; timezone GMT −3; mixed Creole, European, and Amerindian population; chief religion, Roman Catholicism; official language, French; unit of currency, the franc; low-lying near the coast; rises to 635 m/2083 ft at Mont Saint Marcel; many rocky islets along the coast, notably Devil's Island; hot and humid tropical climate; area settled by Europeans, 17th-c; territory of France, 1817; used as penal colony, 1798–1935; overseas department of France, 1946; elects two members to the French National Assembly; timber the main export, from forests covering c.80 000 sq km/ 30 000 sq mi; only 0·1% of land under cultivation. >> Cayenne; France ℹ; Salut, Iles du

French horn >> **horn**

French Polynesia [poli**nee**zhuh], formerly **French Settlements in Oceania** (to 1958), official name **Territory of French Polynesia**, Fr **Territoire de la Polynésie Française** pop (1995e) 215 000; area 3941 sq km/1521 sq mi. Island territory comprising five scattered archipelagoes in the SE Pacific Ocean, between the Cook Is (W) and the Pitcairn Is (E); capital, Papeete; timezone GMT −6; chief ethnic group, Polynesian; chief religion, Christianity (87%); official language, French and Tahitian, with local languages widely spoken; mainly volcanic, mountainous, and ringed with coral reefs; hot and humid climate (Nov–Apr); French missionary activity, 19th-c; French protectorates introduced from 1843; 'French Oceania' became an Overseas Territory, 1958; administered by a high commissioner and Council of Ministers, elected by a Territorial Assembly; economy based on agricultural smallholdings (vegetables, fruit) and plantations (coconut oil, copra); French nuclear test base. >> Marquesas Islands; Mururoa; Papeete; Society Islands; Tahiti; Tuamotu Archipelago; Tubuai Islands

French Republican calendar A calendar introduced during the French Revolution to herald the beginning of a new epoch, Year 1 dating from the declaration of the Republic (22 Sep 1792). Twelve 30-day months were introduced and divided into three 10-day weeks, eliminating Sundays. The system was abolished under Napoleon (1805). >> French Revolution ℹ; Thermidor coup

French Revolution A complex upheaval, considered a significant turning point in French history. The first major event was the summoning of the States General (spring 1789). Subsequently the National Assembly responded to public pressure, such as the storming of the Bastille (14 Jul 1789), with wide-sweeping political, social, and economic measures (1789–91), including the abolition of feudal, aristocratic, and clerical privileges, and a Declaration of the Rights of Man. Meanwhile the royal family had been removed from Versailles to Paris (Oct 1789), but after their flight to Varennes (Jun 1791) their fate was sealed. A Legislative Assembly was elected, and France was declared a republic (1792). Louis XVI and his queen, Marie Antoinette, were executed (1793). The Revolution then entered more dramatic phases, marked by political extremism and bitter rivalry between Girondins and Jacobins (the latter led by Robespierre). Though the Jacobins seized control of the Committee of Public Safety (Jul 1793) and instituted the dictatorship of the Terror, Robespierre's short-lived triumph ended with his execution (1794). The Convention suppressed the *sans-culottes* with military force before establishing the government of the Directory (1795), which was in turn overthrown by Napoleon Bonaparte in the Brumaire coup (1799). >> *ancien régime*; Bastille; Directory; French Revolutionary Wars; Girondins; Jacobins (French history); Public Safety, Committee of; Reign of Terror; Robespierre; *see illustration on p. 329*

French Revolutionary Wars A series of campaigns between France and neighbouring European states hostile to the Revolution and to French hegemony, merging ultimately into the Napoleonic Wars (1799–1815). In the War of the First Coalition (1792–7), French forces attacked the Rhine, the Netherlands, and Savoy, and later Britain, Holland, and Spain. After successfully invading the Netherlands (1794), the French broke the Coalition (1795–6), isolating Britain (1797). A Second Coalition (1798) expelled French forces from Italy and the Rhinelands, before suffering defeat by Napoleon (1799–1800). >> French Revolution ℹ; Napoleonic Wars

French Southern and Antarctic Territories, Fr **Terres Australes et Antarctiques Françaises** French overseas territory, comprising Adélie Land in Antarctica and certain islands in the S Indian Ocean; established, 1955. >> Adélie Land; Antarctica ℹ

Freneau, Philip (Morin) [fre**noh**] (1752–1832) Sailor and poet, born in New York City. He commanded a privateer in the American War of Independence, was captured by the British, and wrote *The British Prison Ship* (1781) and other patriotic poems. He founded and edited the *National Gazette* (1791–3). >> American Revolution

Freon >> **CFCs**

frequency The number of complete cycles per second for a vibrating system or other repetitive motion; symbol *f* or ν; units Hz (hertz). For wave motion, it corresponds to the number of complete waves per second. >> frequency modulation; wave motion ℹ

frequency modulation (FM) In wave motion, the altering of frequency in a systematic way, leaving amplitude unchanged. In FM radio, an electrical signal modulates the frequency of a broadcast carrier radio wave by an amount proportional to the signal amplitude. Demodulation takes place in the radio receiver to give a copy of the original signal. >> amplitude; frequency; modulation; radio waves; wave motion ℹ

fresco An ancient technique for painting on walls, perfected in the 14th–16th-c in Italy. The wall is prepared with layers of plaster, sometimes as many as four, the penultimate being marked out with the artist's design (underdrawing or *sinopia*). The final layer of lime-plaster is then laid and, while it is still wet (*fresco* means 'fresh' in Italian), the artist works on this with a water-based paint. >> Correggio; Giotto; Michelangelo; Raphael

Fresno [**frez**noh] 36°44N 119°47W, pop (1995e) 388 000. City in C California, USA; founded, 1872; city status, 1885; airfield; railway; university; centre of a wine-producing region; often called the world's raisin centre. >> California

Freud, Anna [froyd] (1895–1982) Psychoanalyst, born in Vienna, the daughter of Sigmund Freud. She emigrated with her father to London in 1938, where she became a founder of child psychoanalysis. >> psychoanalysis

Freud, Sigmund [froyd] (1856–1939) Founder of psychoanalysis, born in Freiburg, Moravia (now Příbor, Czech Republic). He studied medicine at Vienna, then special-

Events of the French Revolution 1789–1799

1789	
Mar–May	Election of deputies to the Estates General.
5 May	Opening of the Estates General.
17 Jun	Title of National Assembly adopted by the Third Estate.
Jul	The 'Great Fear'.
14 Jul	Seizing of the Bastille in Paris.
4 Aug	Abolition of the feudal regime.
26 Aug	Declaration of the Rights of Man and Citizen.
Oct	Foundation of the Club des Jacobins.
5–6 Oct	Louis XVI brought to Paris from Versailles.
19 Oct	National Assembly installed in Paris.
1790	
19–23 Jun	Abolition of hereditary nobility and titles.
Jul	Foundation of the Club des Cordeliers.
1791	
20–21 Jun	Flight of the King to Varennes.
16 Jul	Foundation of the Club des Feuillants.
13 Sep	Acceptance of the Constitution by the King.
Oct	Formation of the Legislative Assembly.
1792	
9–10 Aug	Attack on the Tuileries. Functions of the King suspended.
12 Aug	King and royal family imprisoned in the Temple.
2–6 Sep	Massacre of nobles and clergy in prisons.
21 Sep	Abolition of the monarchy.
22 Sep	Proclamation of the Republic.
1793	
17 Jan	National Convention votes for the death of the King.
21 Jan	Execution of the King.
1 Feb	Declaration of war against England and Holland.
Mar	Tribunal created in Paris (later called the Revolutionary Tribunal).
6 Apr	Creation of the Committee of Public Safety.
27 Jul	Robespierre elected to the Committee of Public Safety.
5 Sep–27 Jul 1794	Reign of Terror.
11Sep	Creation of the Revolutionary Army of Paris.
16 Oct	Trial and execution of Marie Antoinette.
24–31 Oct	Trial and execution of the Girondins.
1794	
5 Apr	Execution of the Cordeliers, including Danton.
24 Mar	Execution of the Hébertists.
8 Jun	Inaugural Feast of the Supreme Being and of Nature.
27 Jul (9 Thermidor)	Fall of Robespierre.
19 Nov	Closure of the Club des Jacobins.
1795	
21 Feb	Separation of Church and State.
31 May	Suppression of the Revolutionary Tribunal.
8 Jun	Death of Louis XVII in the Temple.
5 Oct (13 Vendémiaire)	Royalists crushed by Bonaparte.
27 Oct–4 Nov	Institution of the Directory.
1799	
9 Nov (18 Brumaire)	Abolition of the Directory.

ized in neurology, and later in psychopathology. His method of 'free association' allowed the patient to express thoughts in a state of relaxed consciousness, and included the data of childhood and dream recollections. In 1900 he published his major work, *Die Traumdeutung* (The Interpretation of Dreams), arguing that dreams are disguised manifestations of repressed sexual wishes. In 1902, he was appointed to a professorship in Vienna, out of which grew the Vienna Psychoanalytical Society (1908) and the International Psychoanalytic Association (1910). In 1933 Hitler banned psychoanalysis, and after Austria had been overrun, Freud and his family were allowed to emigrate. He settled in London, where he died. >> Freud, Anna; psychoanalysis

Frey >> **Freya**

Freya or **Freyja** [**fray**a] In Northern mythology, the goddess of love and beauty. She and her brother **Frey**, the male fertility god, were the children of Niord and Skadi.

friar A member of one of the mendicant ('begging') Christian religious orders founded in the Middle Ages. Unlike monks, they are not confined to a single monastery or abbey. >> Augustinians; Carmelites; Dominicans; Franciscans

friarbird A bird of the honeyeater family, native to N Australia and the adjacent islands of SE Asia, also known as the **leatherhead**; songbird with head partly or totally naked. (Genus: *Philemon*, 17 species. Family: Meliphagidae.) >> honeyeater

friar's balsam A resin from the stem of *Styrax benzoin* and *Styrax paralleloneurus* containing aromatic acids (benzoic and cinnamic acids), prepared in an alcoholic solution. It is used as an inhalation in the treatment of chronic bronchitis. >> resin

Fribourg [**free**boorg], Ger **Freiburg** [**friy**boork] 46°49N 7°09E, pop (1995e) 35 200. Mediaeval town in W Switzerland; founded, 1178; bishopric; railway junction; university (1889); cathedral (13th–15th-c). >> Switzerland ℹ

Frick, Henry (Clay) (1849–1919) Industrialist, born in West Overton, PA. He became chairman of the Carnegie Steel Co in 1889, reorganizing it to become the largest steel manufacturing company in the world, and in 1901 became director of United States Steel. Among his various endowments is the Frick Collection of fine art, bequeathed to New York City.

Fricker, Peter (Racine) (1920–90) Composer, born in London. He wrote several symphonies, the oratorio *The Vision of Judgment* (1957–8), and other chamber, choral, and keyboard works.

friction A force acting against the direction of motion for two objects in contact sliding across one another. Friction may be sufficient to prevent actual relative motion. It is caused by surface roughness, and by the attraction of the atoms of one surface for those of the other. >> surface physics

Friedan, Betty (Naomi) [free**dan**], *née* **Goldstein** (1921–) Feminist leader and author, born in Peoria, IL. She is best

Friarbird

known for her book *The Feminine Mystique* (1963). She was the founder and first president of the National Association for Women in 1966. >> feminism

Friedman, Milton [**freed**man] (1912–) Economist, born in New York City. Professor of economics at Chicago (1948–83), and a leading monetarist, his work includes the permanent income theory of consumption, and the role of money in determining events. He was awarded the Nobel Prize for Economics in 1976. >> monetarism

friendly society A voluntary mutual-aid organization in the UK which provides financial assistance to members in times of sickness, unemployment, or retirement. Their operations are governed by the Friendly Society Acts (1974–1984). >> insurance

Friends, Society of A Christian sect founded by George Fox and others in mid-17th-c England, and formally organized in 1667; members are popularly known as **Quakers**, possibly because of Fox's injunction 'to quake at the word of the Lord'. Belief in the 'inner light', a living contact with the divine Spirit, is the basis of its meetings for worship, where Friends gather in silence until moved by the Spirit to speak. They emphasize simplicity in all things, and are active reformers promoting tolerance, justice, and peace. >> Christianity; Fox, George

Friends of the Earth An international federation of environmental pressure groups with autonomous organizations in member countries. It conducts campaigns on topics such as safe energy, tropical rainforest destruction, and the preservation of endangered species. >> environment

frieze The middle part of an entablature on a classical building, usually decorated. It may also be the decorative band running along the upper part of an internal wall and below the cornice. >> entablature

frigate A small warship in World War 2, superior in speed and armament to a corvette, but less powerful and smaller than a destroyer. Its present role is mainly anti-submarine and general-purpose. >> warships ℹ

frigate bird A large bird, native to tropical seas; male with coloured inflatable pouch on throat. (Genus: *Fregata*, 5 species. Family: Fregatidae.)

Frigg or **Frigga** In Norse mythology, the wife of Odin, and goddess of married love (often confused with Freya). >> Odin

frilled lizard An agamid lizard (*Chlamydosaurus kingi*) native to New Guinea and N Australia; slim body; neck with large cape-like frill of brightly coloured skin; frill usually folded, but can be expanded in courtship and to deter predators. >> agamid

Friml, (Charles) Rudolf [**fri**ml] (1879–1972) Composer, born in Prague. In 1906 he settled in the USA, where he made a name as a composer of light operas, including *Rose Marie* (1924) and *The Vagabond King* (1925.).

Fringe, the Cultural events, particularly theatrical performances, presented around a Festival but not central to it. The term has thus come to be applied to theatre groups working on the margins of the establishment, or to any style of theatre not part of orthodoxy.

Fringillidae [frin**jil**idee] A family of small seed-eating birds (c.125 species); native to the Americas, Eurasia, and Africa, and introduced in Australasia; also known as **finches**. >> finch

Frisch, Karl von (1886–1982) Ethologist, born in Vienna. A key figure in the development of ethology, he is best known for his 40-year study of the honey bee, which showed that forager bees communicate information in part by the use of coded dances. In 1973 he shared the Nobel Prize for Physiology or Medicine. >> bee dancing; ethology

Frisch, Max (Rudolf) (1911–91) Playwright and novelist, born in Zürich, Switzerland. His novels include *Stiller* (1954), a satire on the Swiss way of life, and *Bluebeard* (1983). His plays, modern morality pieces, include *Andorra* (1962) and *Triptych* (1981).

Frisch, Otto Robert (1904–79) Physicist, born in Vienna. He and Meitner first described 'nuclear fission' in 1939, and in 1945 he became head of the nuclear physics division at Harwell. During World War 2 he was involved in atomic research at Los Alamos, CA, USA. >> Meitner; nuclear physics

Frisch, Ragnar (Anton Kittil) (1895–1973) Economist, born in Oslo, a pioneer of econometrics. In 1969 he shared the first Nobel Prize for Economics. >> economics

Frisian >> **Germanic languages**

Frisian Islands [**friz**eeuhn] Island chain in the North Sea, extending along the coasts of The Netherlands, Germany, and Denmark, and politically divided between these countries; includes the **North Frisian Is** (Ger **Nordfriesische Inseln**), the German **East Frisian Is** (Ger **Ostfriesische Inseln**), and the Dutch **West Frisian Is** (Dutch **Friese Eilanden**); several areas of reclaimed land. >> North Sea

fritillary (botany) [fri**til**aree] A perennial with a small scaly bulb (*Fritillaria meleagris*), native to Europe; stem growing to 50 cm/20 in; leaves grass-like, bluish; flower a broad bell 3–5 cm/1½–2 in, drooping, dull purple rarely white, with a distinctive chequered pattern. (Family: Liliaceae.)

fritillary (entomology) [fri**til**aree] A colourful, day-flying butterfly; wings typically yellow-brown with black markings; forelegs reduced, non-functional. (Order: Lepidoptera. Family: Nymphalidae.) >> butterfly

Frobisher, Sir Martin [**froh**bisher] (c.1535–94) Navigator, born in Altofts, West Yorkshire. He made several attempts to find a Northwest Passage to Cathay (1576–8), reaching Labrador and Hudson Bay. >> Drake, Francis

Froebel, Friedrich (Wilhelm August) [**froe**bl] (1782–1852) Educationist, born in Oberweissbach, Germany. In 1816 he put into practice his educational system whose aim, to help the child's mind grow naturally and spontaneously, he expounded in *Die Menschenerziehung* (1826, The Education of Man). In 1836 he opened his first kindergarten school at Blankenburg.

frog An amphibian of order Anura (3500 species), found worldwide except in the Arctic and Antarctic; short body with fewer than 10 vertebrae in the spine. The smooth wet-skinned species are called **frogs**; the rough dry-skinned species (adapted to drier habitats) are called **toads**. >> amphibian; Anura; arrow-poison / tree frog; midwife / spadefoot toad; natterjack

froghopper A small, hopping insect that feeds by sucking the sap of plants; also known as **cuckoo-spit insect** and **spittlebug**. The eggs are laid on the plants, and hatch into sedentary larvae which surround themselves with mucus-like 'cuckoo spit' that protects them against drying out and predation. (Order: Homoptera. Family: Cercopidae, c.2500 species.) >> insect ℹ; larva

frogmouth A large, nocturnal, nightjar-like bird native to Australasia (except New Zealand) and SE Asia; short but very broad bill (hence the name). (Family: Podargidae, 12 species.) >> nightjar

Froissart, Jean [frwasah(r)] (c.1333–c.1404) Historian and poet, born in Valenciennes, France. His *Chronicles*, covering European history from 1325 to 1400, were heavily influenced by his devotion to chivalric principles.

Frome [froom] 51°14N 2°20W, pop (1995e) 21 800. Town in Somerset, SW England; Anglo-Saxon origin; railway; Longleat House (1568) nearby. >> Somerset

Fromm, Erich (1900–80) Psychoanalyst, born in Frankfurt, Germany. Professor of psychiatry at New York from 1962, he was a neo-Freudian, known for his investigations into motivation. His works include *Escape from Freedom* (1941) and *The Sane Society* (1955). >> Freud, Sigmund

Frondes, the [frõd] A series of civil revolts in France during the Regency of Anne of Austria, caused by economic grievances and the excessive opportunism of central government, directed by Cardinal Mazarin. The disturbances developed into two phases: the Parlementary Fronde (1648–9), and that of the Princes (1650–3). They were crushed by royal forces under Turenne. >> Anne of Austria; Mazarin; Turenne

front A meteorological term for the sharp boundary between two parcels of air of different origin and characteristics, along which a steep horizontal temperature gradient exists. A **warm front** is the leading boundary of tropical or warm air, and a **cold front** is the leading boundary of polar or cold air. In a depression, the meeting of the cold front with the warm front results in an **occluded front**. >> cold front

Front de Libération Nationale >> **FLN**

Frontenac, Louis de Buade, comte de (Count of) [frõtenak] (1620–98) French-Canadian statesman, born in St Germain-en-Laye, France. He extended the boundaries of New France down the Mississippi, repulsed the British siege of Quebec, and broke the power of the Iroquois. >> Iroquois; Quebec (city)

front-line states An informal grouping of seven states bordering South Africa, defined by their position with respect to the apartheid system: Angola, Botswana, Mozambique, Namibia, Tanzania, Zambia, Zimbabwe. >> apartheid; South Africa ℹ

frost A meteorological condition which occurs when the air temperature is at or below the freezing point of water, causing condensation. It may cause considerable damage to plants, especially if ground frost is accompanied by air frost. >> condensation (physics)

Frost, Sir David (Paradine) (1939–) Broadcaster and businessman, born in Tenterden, Kent. He presented *That Was the Week That Was* (BBC, 1962–3), hosted many programmes in Britain and America, such as *The Frost Report* (1966–7), and interviewed world leaders in such programmes as *The Nixon Interviews* (1976–7). He was a co-founder of London Weekend Television, and also of Britain's TV-AM.

Frost, Robert (Lee) (1874–1963) Poet, born in San Francisco, CA. *A Boy's World* (1913) and *North of Boston* (1914) gave him an international reputation. *New Hampshire* (1923) won the Pulitzer Prize, as did his first *Collected Poems* in 1930 and *A Further Range* (1936).

frostbite The damage of exposed parts of the body by the direct effect of extreme cold. The fingers, nose, or feet are especially vulnerable, and the part may die and become gangrenous. >> gangrene

frottage [fro**tahzh**] A technique used by some modern artists, notably Max Ernst, whereby paper is placed over a textured surface, such as a plank of wood, and rubbed with a pencil or crayon producing an impression. >> Ernst

Froude, James Anthony [frood] (1818–94) Writer and historian, born in Dartington, Devon. A member of the Oxford Movement, his early novels were controversial, notably *The Nemesis of Faith* (1848). He then worked as an essayist and editor, and wrote his *History of England* (12 vols, 1856–69). >> Oxford Movement

fructose $C_6H_{12}0_6$. A simple sugar (a *monosaccharide*) found mainly in fruits in combination with glucose to produce the *disaccharide* sucrose (table sugar). Fructose is twice as sweet as glucose, and has been used as a sweetening agent. >> diabetes mellitus; disaccharide; glucose; sucrose

fruit Strictly, the ripened ovary and seeds of a plant, but more generally used to include any structures closely associated with these, such as a swollen receptacle. Fruits can be divided into two main groups: **dry** and **fleshy**. In the latter, the middle layer of the ovary wall becomes succulent. Further classification is based mainly on carpel or seed number, **dehiscence** (ie whether the fruit splits to release the seeds), and to a lesser extent on derivation of tissues. >> carpel; ovary; receptacle; seed

fruit fly A common name for flies of the families Drosophilidae and Tephritidae; mostly tropical. The latter contains c.4000 species of colourful flies, feeding on sap and fruit. (Order: Diptera.) >> Drosophila ℹ; fly

Frunze [**frun**zye] >> **Bishkek**

Fry, Christopher, pseudonym of **Christopher Harris** (1907–) Playwright, born in Bristol. He wrote a series of major plays in free verse, often with undertones of religion and mysticism, including *A Phoenix Too Frequent* (1946) and *The Lady's Not For Burning* (1949). His later works include *Curtmantle* (1962) and *A Yard of Sun* (1970).

Fry, Elizabeth (1780–1845) Quaker prison reformer, born in Norwich, Norfolk. After seeing the terrible conditions for women in Newgate prison, she devoted her life to prison reform at home and abroad.

Fry, Roger (Eliot) (1866–1934) Art critic, aesthetic philosopher, and painter, born in London. He is mainly remembered for his support of the Postimpressionist movement in England. He propounded an extreme formal theory of aesthetics. >> aesthetics; Postimpressionism

FT–SE Index (Financial Times–Stock Exchange Index), nickname **Footsie** A UK share index which records changes in the prices of shares of 100 leading British companies. It has been in operation since 1982, when it started with a notional value of 1000.

FT30 Index (Financial Times Index) A UK share index which records changes in the prices of shares of 30 leading British companies. It started in 1935 with a notional value of 100. >> FT–SE Index

Fu-chou >> **Fuzhou**

Fuchs, Klaus (Emil Julius) [fookhs] (1912–88) Physicist and atom spy, born in Rüsselsheim, Germany. From 1943 he worked in the USA on the atom bomb, and in 1946 became head of the theoretical physics division at Harwell, UK. In 1950 he was imprisoned for disclosing nuclear secrets to the Russians, and later worked at East Germany's nuclear research centre. >> atomic bomb

Fuchs, Sir Vivian Ernest [fookhs] (1908–) Antarctic explorer and scientist, born in the Isle of Wight, UK. As leader of the British Commonwealth Trans-Antarctic Expedition (1956–8), he made an overland crossing from Shackleton Base via the S Pole to Scott Base (3500 km/2200 mi). He was director of the British Antarctic Survey (1958–73). >> Antarctica ℹ

fuchsia [**fyoo**shuh] An evergreen or deciduous shrub, native to Central and South America and New Zealand; flowers pendulous with a long, red 4-lobed tube surrounding a purple bell with projecting stamens and style; cultivars show a wide range of flower colours. (Genus: *Fuchsia*, 100 species. Family: Onagraceae.) >> cultivar

fuel A substance capable of releasing thermal energy in chemical, electrochemical, or nuclear processes. The oldest are combustible natural fuels (such as wood and cow dung). The chief solid **fossil fuels** are fossil vegetable matter in various degrees of carbonization, such as coal, lignite, and peat. **Liquid fuels** include some vegetable oils, but are mainly petroleum products. **Gaseous fuels** mainly comprise manufactured and natural gas. Some use is made of gaseous products arising from the degradation of biological waste. **Fuel cells** operate on an electrochemical reaction which takes place between hydrogen and oxygen. **Nuclear fuels** consist of radioactive isotopes, emitting energy spontaneously by nuclear change. **Rocket fuels** operate by reaction against high speed gases emitted on combustion. >> coal; gas; nuclear reactor ℹ; petroleum

fuel injection 1 In a diesel engine, the system that injects the fuel at high pressure directly into the combustion chamber. >> diesel engine **2** In a petrol engine, a system that uses a special fuel/mixture control unit, as an alternative to a carburettor, to produce improved running and transient performance. The petrol is usually injected into the port immediately preceding the inlet valve rather than directly into the cylinder. >> carburettor; engine

Fuentes, Carlos [**fwen**tez] (1928–) Novelist and playwright, born in Mexico City. His novel *La muerte de Artemio Cruz* (1962, The Death of Artemio Cruz) established him as a major international writer. He became professor of Latin American Studies at Harvard in 1987.

Fugard, Athol (Harold Lanigan) [**foo**gah(r)d] (1932–) Playwright and theatre director, born in Middleburg, Cape Province, South Africa. His plays, set in contemporary South Africa, met with official opposition, notably *Blood Knot* (1960) and *Boesman and Lena* (1969). He has also written film scripts and a novel, *Tsotsi* (1980).

fugu [**fu**goo] A Japanese globe fish or puffer fish, eaten at special restaurants, cooked or in small slices, raw. Parts are poisonous and cause instant death. Only restaurant staff who have passed the official examination and have a special licence are allowed to prepare it.

fugue A musical composition (or part of one) in which a single theme announced by each 'voice' in turn serves to generate the whole. It usually reappears in different keys and sometimes in different guises. >> counterpoint

Fujairah, al- [al fu**jiy**ra] pop (1995e) 71 200; area 1150 sq km/444 sq mi. Member state of the United Arab Emirates; partly mountainous, with a fertile coastal plain and no desert; capital, al-Fujairah; people live mostly in scattered villages, depending on agriculture. >> United Arab Emirates [i]

Fuji, Mount [**fu**jee], or **Fujiyama**, also known as **Fuji-san** 35°23N 138°42E. Highest peak in Japan, in C Honshu; 88 km/55 mi SW of Tokyo; dormant volcano rising to 3776 m/12 388 ft; crater diameter c.600 m/2000 ft; last eruption, 1707; snow-capped (Oct–May); sacred since ancient times. >> Honshu; Japan [i]; Meiji Restoration

Fujiwara Style [fuji**wah**ra] A style of art which flourished in Japan during the late Heian period (9th–12th-c). The aristocratic Fujiwara clan built temples and pagodas, decorated in a delicate, refined manner.

Fukuoka [fu**kwo**ka], formerly **Najime** 33°39N 130°21E, pop (1995e) 1 264 000. Port in NE Kyushu, Japan; airport; railway; university (1911); institute of technology (1909). >> Kyushu

Fulani [fu**lah**nee], also called **Fulbe** or **Peul** Fula-speaking peoples dispersed across the Sahel zone of W Africa from Senegal to Cameroon. Originally pastoralists, they are today socially very diverse, and in many places are assimilated into the local culture. >> pastoralism; sahel

Fulbright, J(ames) William (1905–95) US Democratic politician, lawyer, and writer, born in Sumner, MO. As chairman of the Senate Committee on Foreign Relations, he became a major critic of the Vietnam War. He was also known for introducing the international exchange programme for scholars (*Fulbright scholarships*). >> Democratic Party; Vietnam War

Fuller, R(ichard) Buckminster (1895–1983) Inventor, designer, poet, and philosopher, born in Milton, MA. He developed the Dymaxion ('dynamic and maximum efficiency') House in 1927, and the Dymaxion streamlined, omnidirectional car in 1932. He also developed the geodesic dome. >> geodesic dome

Fuller, (Sarah) Margaret (1810–50) Writer, feminist, and revolutionary, born in Cambridgeport, MA. Her *Woman in the Nineteenth Century* (1845) is the earliest major piece of US feminist writing. >> feminism

Fuller, Roy (Broadbent) (1912–91) Writer, born in Oldham, Lancashire. His first collection, *Poems*, appeared in 1939, and his war-time experiences prompted *The Middle of a War* (1942) and *A Lost Season* (1944). His novels include *Second Curtain* (1953) and *Image of a Society* (1956). *New and Collected Poems, 1934–84* were published in 1985.

fullerenes A series of molecular allotropes of carbon, of which the best characterized are C_{60} and C_{70}; named after the designer Buckminster Fuller. First made and its structure proposed in 1985 by the astrophysicists D R Huffman (USA) and W Krätschmer (Germany), their properties are being actively investigated, such as for superconductivity. >> carbon; Fuller, Buckminster; superconductivity; *see illustration on p. 333*

Fuller's earth Fine earthy material containing montmorillonite clay; formerly used for cleansing oil and grease from wool (*fulling*), and now used for clarifying vegetable oils by absorbing impurities. >> clay

fulmar A marine tubenosed bird, native to N oceans (*Fulmarus glacialis*) or S oceans (2 species); comes to land only to breed. (Family: Procellariidae.) >> petrel; tubenose

fulminate A salt containing the ion CNO^-, also called **isocyanate**. It is an explosive; $Hg(CNO)_2$ is used as a detonator. >> explosives

Fulton, Robert (1765–1815) Engineer, born in Lancaster Co, PA. His inventions included a dredging machine and the torpedo, but he is best known for his development of the steamboat, which he made a commercial success in the USA. >> engineering

fumaric acid [fyoo**ma**rik] $C_2H_2(COOH)_2$, IUPAC **trans-butenedioic acid**, melting point 300°C (in a sealed tube). An unsaturated dicarboxylic acid, used in the manufacture of polyester resins. >> carboxylic acids; polyesters

fumitory A brittle-stemmed annual, sometimes scrambling or climbing, native to the N hemisphere and S Africa; flowers strongly zygomorphic, 2-lipped, with rounded spur. (Genus: *Fumaria*, c.50 species. Family: Fumariaceae.) >> zygomorphic flower

Funafuti [foona**foo**tee] 8°30S 179°12E, pop (1995e) 3300. Port capital of Tuvalu, SW Pacific; airfield; US military base. >> Tuvalu

Funchal [**fun**shal] 32°40N 16°55W, pop (1995e) 110 000. Capital of Madeira, on S coast of Ilha da Madeira; third largest Portuguese city; bishopric; important port and tourist resort; cathedral (1485). >> Portugal [i]

functional group A part of a molecule with characteristic reactions. Important examples include the hydroxyl group, –OH, characteristic of alcohols, and the amino group, $-NH_2$, characteristic of amines. >> aldehyde; carboxylic acids; ketone

functionalism (art and architecture) The theory, rooted in Greek philosophy, that beauty should be identified with functional efficiency. It became fashionable in the 1920s especially under Bauhaus influence. In architecture, the form of a building was to be determined by the function it was meant to fulfil – as in the famous definition of a house as a machine for living in. >> Bauhaus; International Style; rationalism (architecture)

functionalism (sociology) A theory widely accepted in social anthropology and sociology in the mid-20th-c, according to which particular social institutions, customs, and beliefs all have a part to play in maintaining a social system. The central notion is that a community or society has an enduring structure, its parts fitting together to form a single integrated system. >> anthropology; sociology; structuralism

fundamental constants A set of numerical quantities having the same fixed value for all observers. Values of these constants control all physical processes. Examples include the velocity of light, the gravitational constant,

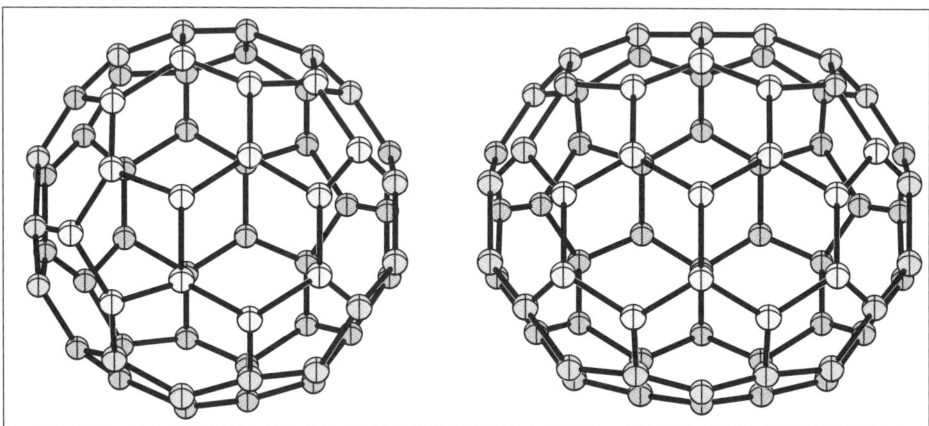

Fullerenes

and the electron charge. >> electron; gravitational constant; velocity of light

fundamental forces >> **forces of nature** ℹ

fundamentalism A theological tendency seeking to preserve what are thought to be the essential doctrines ('fundamentals') of a religion. The term was originally used of the conservative US Protestant movement in the 1920s, characterized by a literal interpretation of the Bible. Generally, it is any theological position opposed to liberalism, with important manifestations (often violent) found today in all major religions, notably Islam. >> Bible

fundamental particles Those subatomic particles that are thought to be indivisible into smaller particles. They are the **matter particles** (quarks, neutrinos, electrons, muons, and taus) and the **force particles** (gluons, photons, W and Z bosons, and gravitons). >> subatomic particles

Fundy, Bay of A bay separating the provinces of New Brunswick and Nova Scotia, E Canada. The world's greatest tidal height (16·2 m/53 ft) is used to generate electricity. >> Canada ℹ

Fünen >> **Fyn**

fungicide Any chemical (eg sulphur compounds) used to kill fungi that are harmful to plants, animals, or foodstuffs. It is particularly important in controlling rusts in cereals, blight in potatoes, and mildew in fruit. >> fungus; sulphur

fungus A primitive plant that obtains its nourishment either *saprophytically*, by secreting enzymes to dissolve insoluble organic food externally before absorption, or *parasitically*, by absorbing food from a host. True fungi belong to the division Eumycota of the kingdom Plantae, containing all fungi except the slime moulds and their allies. Fungi are sometimes classified as a separate kingdom characterized by their lack of flagella at all stages of the life-cycle; those with flagellae are transferred to the kingdom Protoctista. Many are pests of crops or are human pathogens; some are edible or produce useful by-products. >> Ascomycetes; Basidiomycetes; chanterelle; death cap; dry rot; earthstar; ergot; flagellum; fungicide; morel; mushroom; mycology; potato blight; Protoctista; rust fungus; slime mould; truffle; wet rot; yeast

funnel-web spider A predatory spider that constructs a funnel-shaped web to trap its prey. Some species are venomous. (Class: Arachnida. Order: Araneae.) >> spider

Furchgott, Robert F (1916–) Pharmacologist, born in Charleston, SC. He worked at the State University of New York Health Science Center, and shared the 1998 Nobel Prize for Physiology for his contribution to the discovery of nitric oxide as a signalling molecule in the cardiovascular system.

Furies >> **Erinyes**

furniture beetle A small, brown beetle; larvae, known as **woodworm**, are C-shaped, white and fleshy with tiny legs, which bore into dead wood as they feed; adults emerge leaving typical woodworm holes. (Order: Coleoptera. Family: Anobiidae.) >> beetle

Fürstenbund [**für**shtenbunt] A league of German Princes founded in 1785 at Frederick the Great's instigation in the last phase of his conflict with the Austrian Habsburgs. >> Frederick II (of Prussia); Habsburgs

further education A level of educational provision offered in many countries, often distinguished from **higher education**. Further education is post-school education leading, usually, to qualifications at sub-degree level, though it may not lead to any award at all but simply be taken for its own sake. Higher education takes place in institutions where most or all of the work is at degree level or above. >> vocational education

Furtwängler, (Gustav Heinrich Ernst Martin) Wilhelm [**foort**vengler] (1886–1954) Conductor, born in Berlin. He became conductor of the Gewandhaus concerts in Leipzig and of the Berlin Philharmonic, his highly subjective interpretations of the German masters arousing controversy.

furze >> **gorse**

Fuseli, Henry [**fyoo**zelee], originally **Johann Heinrich Füssli** (1741–1825) Painter and art critic, born in Zürich, Switzerland. His 200 paintings include 'The Nightmare' (1781) and two series to illustrate Shakespeare's and Milton's works, by which he is chiefly known.

fusel oil [**fyoo**zl] Organic material obtained along with ethanol in fermentation, mostly alcohols of higher molecular weight. The presence of a very small proportion of the alcohols contributes to the characteristic flavour of fermented beverages. >> ethanol; fermentation

futhark [**fuhth**ah(r)k] >> **runes** ℹ

futon [fu**ton**] A Japanese quilt, equivalent to Western eiderdowns or duvets. Most Japanese sleep on a thick futon on the tatami matting. All bedding is kept in a cupboard during the day, leaving the room free for use. >> tatami

futures In economics, a market where commodities are bought and sold for delivery at some future date. Speculators may buy futures in the hope that the price will rise, and thus be able to make a profit by selling on to others. >> equity (economics); interest

Futurism A modern art movement founded by the poet Marinetti in Milan in 1909. Futurism glorified machinery, war, speed, and the modern world generally; artists worked in a style derived from Cubism. It had petered out by c.1918. >> Cubism; Vorticism; Boccioni; Marinetti

Fuzhou, **Fu-chou**, or **Foochow** [foojoh] 26°09N 119°17E, pop (1995e) 1 504 000. City in SE China; on N bank of Min Jiang R, founded 202 BC; capital of autonomous state, 10th-c; treaty port, 1842; airfield; railway; many important pagodas and temples. >> China [i]; Opium Wars

Fyn [fün], or **Funen**, Ger **Fünen** pop (1995e) 467 000; area 3486 sq km/1346 sq mi. Danish island between S Jutland and Zealand; capital, Odense; second largest island in Denmark; agriculture ('the garden of Denmark'). >> Denmark [i]

G

gabbro A coarse-grained basic (low in silica) igneous rock composed of calcic plagioclase feldspar, pyroxene, and sometimes olivine. >> igneous rock; silica

Gable, (William) Clark (1901–60) Film actor, born in Cadiz, OH. His first leading film role was in *The Painted Desert* (1931). Growing popularity in tough but sympathetic parts soon labelled him 'the King of Hollywood', reaching its peak with his portrayal of Rhett Butler in *Gone With the Wind* (1939).

gable The section of wall which conceals the triangular end of a pitched roof. The term is generally used of Gothic architecture. A gable is steeper than its Classical equivalent – the pediment – and is often elaborately decorated. >> Gothic architecture; pediment (architecture)

Gabo, Naum [**gah**boh], originally **Naum Neemia Pevsner** (1890–1977) Sculptor, born in Bryansk, Russia. In 1920 he helped to form the group of Russian Constructivists, who had considerable influence on 20th-c architecture and design. He moved to the USA in 1946. >> Constructivism

Gabon [ga**bohn**], official name **Gabonese Republic**, Fr **République Gabonaise** pop (1995e) 1 379 000; area 267 667 sq km/103 374 sq mi. Republic of W equatorial Africa; capital, Libreville; timezone GMT +1; population comprises c.40 Bantu tribes (notably, Fang), and c.10% expatriate Africans and Europeans; chief religion, Christianity; official language, French; unit of currency, the franc CFA; on the Equator for 880 km/550 mi W–E; land rises towards the African central plateau, cut by several rivers, notably the Ogooué; typical equatorial climate, hot, wet, and humid; visited by Portuguese, 15th-c; under French control from mid-19th-c; 1849, slave ship captured by the French, the liberated slaves forming the settlement of Libreville; occupied by France, 1885; one of four territories of French West Africa, 1910; independence, 1960; new constitution, 1991; governed by a president, an appointed Council of Ministers, and a legislative National Assembly; small area of land under cultivation, but employing 65% of population; timber extraction, notably of okoumé (world's largest producer); rapid economic growth since independence, largely because of offshore oil, natural gas, and minerals. >> Libreville; RR1009 political leaders

Gabor, Dennis [ga**baw(r)**] (1900–79) Physicist, born in Budapest. Leaving Germany in 1933, he became professor of applied electron physics at Imperial College, London (1958–67). In 1971 he received the Nobel Prize for Physics for his invention of holography. >> holography

Gaborone [gabuh**roh**nay] 24°45S 25°55E, pop (1995e) 158 000. Independent township and capital of Botswana, S Africa; altitude 1000 m/3300 ft; area 97 sq km/37 sq mi; capital moved there from Mafeking, 1965; airport; university. >> Botswana ℹ

Gabriel An angel named in both the Old and New Testaments. He is said to have helped Daniel interpret visions (*Dan* 8, 9), and is also recorded as foretelling the births of John the Baptist and of Jesus (*Luke* 1). >> Annunciation

Gabriel, Peter (1950–) Singer and songwriter, born in Surrey. He co-founded the rock group Genesis, but left to pursue a solo career in 1975. A collection of his video hits was released as *CV* (1988), topping the UK music video chart. He also inaugurated the 'World of Music, Arts and Dance' (WOMAD) festival (1982).

Gabrieli, Andrea [gabri**e**lee] (c.1533–86) Composer, born in Venice. He became organist of St Mark's Church, writing madrigals, Masses, and other choral works. Several of his organ pieces foreshadow the fugue. >> fugue

Gaddafi or **Qaddafi, Colonel Muammar** [ga**da**fee] (1942–) Libyan political and military leader, born into a nomadic family. He formed the Free Officers Movement which overthrew King Idris in 1969, and became Chairman of the Revolutionary Command Council. He set about eradicating colonialism by expelling foreigners and closing down British and US bases. He also encouraged a return to the fundamental principles of Islam. A somewhat unpredictable figure, Gaddafi has openly supported violent revolutionaries in other parts of the world, has waged a war in Chad, and in the 1980s saw his territory bombed and aircraft shot down by the Americans. In 1999 he released for trial the alleged perpetrators of the bombing of the PanAm flight which crashed on Lockerbie, Scotland in 1988. >> Libya ℹ

Gaddi, Taddeo [**ga**dee] (c.1300–66) Painter, born in Florence, Italy, the godson and best pupil of Giotto. His finest work is seen in the frescoes of 'The Life of the Virgin' in the Baroncelli chapel of San Croce. >> Giotto

Gaddis, William (1922–98) Novelist, born in New York City. He worked as a freelance speech and scriptwriter before making his mark with the novel *The Recognitions* (1955). A radical satirist, he is one of America's most prominent contemporary novelists; his other works

include *JR* (1976), *Carpenter's Gothic* (1985), and *A Frolic of His Own* (1993).

gad fly A robust, biting fly; eyes usually large, often iridescent; females suck blood of cattle and horses. (Order: Diptera. Family: Tabanidae, c.2000 species.) >> fly

Gadidae [gadiday] The cod family of fishes, a large group comprising about 15 genera and 100 species of marine fish found primarily in continental shelf waters of the cool temperate N hemisphere; includes cod, burbot, haddock, ling, pollack, saithe, torsk, and whiting. >> cod

Gadsden Purchase An area in S Arizona and New Mexico bought from Mexico for $10 000 000 as a route for a transcontinental railroad. The purchase, named after US minister to Mexico James Gadsden (1788–1858), defined the present-day US/Mexican border.

gadwall A duck (*Anas strepera*) native to the N hemisphere S of 60°; male grey with black rear end; female brown; feeds at surface; eats weeds and small animals. (Family: Anatidae.) >> duck

Gaea, Gaia, or **Ge** [geea, giya, gee] In Greek mythology, 'the Earth' personified, and then the goddess of the whole Earth (not a particular piece of land). Her Roman equivalent was **Tellus**. >> Deucalion; Gigantes

Gaelic >> **Irish; Scottish Gaelic**

Gaelic football >> **football** 5 ℹ

gaffer The chief electrician in a film or television production crew, working closely with the lighting director. The charge-hand electrician working directly under the gaffer is known as the **best boy**.

Gagarin, Yuri (Alekseyevich) [gagahrin] (1934–68) Russian cosmonaut, born near Gzhatsk, Russia. He joined the Soviet Air Force in 1957, and in 1961 became the first man to travel in space, completing a circuit of the Earth in the *Vostok* spaceship satellite. After his death, Gzhatsk was renamed Gagarin. >> RR970

Gage, Thomas (1721–87) British general, born in Firle, Sussex. In 1763 he became commander-in-chief of the British forces in America. In 1775 (18 Apr) he sent a force to seize a quantity of arms at Concord; and next day the skirmish of Lexington took place which began the Revolution. >> American Revolution

Gaia hypothesis [giya] A hypothesis, first proposed by James Lovelock in 1972, which considers the Earth as an intimately linked system of physical, chemical, and biological processes, interacting in a self-regulating way to maintain the conditions necessary for life. Although named after the Greek Earth goddess, it has a scientific rather than a mystical basis. >> Earth

gaillardia [gaylah(r)dia] An annual or perennial, mostly native to North America; two species are the parents of many garden hybrids: *Gaillardia pulchella*, an annual growing to 30–60 cm/1–2 ft, yellow outer ray florets coloured crimson at the base; and *Gaillardia aristata*, a perennial growing to 70 cm/27 in with yellow and red ray florets. (Family: Compositae.)

Gainsborough, Thomas [gaynzbruh] (1727–88) Landscape and portrait painter, born in Sudbury, Suffolk. He moved to Bath in 1759, where he established himself with his portrait of Earl Nugent (1760). His best-known paintings include 'The Blue Boy' (c. 1770, San Marino), 'The Harvest Wagon' (1767, Birmingham) and 'The Watering Place' (1777, Tate, London). >> landscape painting

Gaiseric or **Genseric** [giyserik] (c.390–477) King of the Vandals and Alans (428–77), who led the Vandals in their invasion of Gaul. He captured Hippo (430) and Carthage (439), and in 455 sacked Rome.

Gaitskell, Hugh (Todd Naylor) (1906–63) British Labour politician, born in London. An MP in 1945, he was minister of fuel and power (1947) and of economic affairs (1950), and Chancellor of the Exchequer (1950–1). In 1955 he was elected Leader of the Opposition. >> Butskellism; Labour Party

galactose A simple sugar (monosaccharide), found in the sugar of milk along with glucose; otherwise, it is rare in nature. >> glucose; lactose

galago >> **bushbaby**

Galahad, Sir One of King Arthur's knights, son of Lancelot and Elaine. Distinguished for his purity, he alone was able to succeed in the adventures of the Siege Perilous and the Holy Grail. >> Arthur; Grail, Holy; Lancelot, Sir

Galápagos finches >> **Darwin's finches**

Galápagos giant tortoise The largest known tortoise (*Geochelone elephantopus*); length of shell up to 1·2 m/4 ft; native to the Galápagos Is; each island has its own subspecies, differing in shell shape. (Family: Testudinidae.) >> Galápagos Islands; tortoise; *see illustration below*

Galápagos Islands [galapagohs], Span **Archipiélago de Colón** pop (1995e) 11 100; area 7812 sq km/3015 sq mi. Ecuadorian island group on the Equator, 970 km/600 mi W of South American mainland; highest peak, Volcán Wolf (1707 m/5600 ft) on Isabela I; visited by Spanish, 1535, but no colony established; Ecuador took possession, 1832; became well known after visit of Charles Darwin, 1835; volcanic origin with some active cones; diverse vegetation and landforms, from lava deserts to tropical forests; many unique species of flora and fauna evolved independent of mainland; marine iguanas on Isla Fernandina; giant tortoises, mostly on Isabela; Galápagos National Park established in 1934; a world heritage site. >> Darwin, Charles; Ecuador ℹ

Galatians, Letter of Paul to the [galayshnz] New Testament writing, widely accepted as genuinely from the apostle Paul to the churches in some part of Galatia in C Asia Minor. >> Pauline Letters

galaxy A huge family of stars held together by the mutual gravitational attractions of one star for another. Galaxies exist in a great variety of forms, ellipticals predominating, but spirals feature prominently in popular books on account of their notable shapes. Masses range from a few million suns to 10 million million times as many. The nearest galaxies to the Milky Way are the Magellanic Clouds, some 55 000 parsec away. >> Galaxy; Magellanic Clouds; star

Galaxy The huge star family to which our Sun belongs, seen as the Milky Way. In shape it is basically a bulging flat disc, diameter 30 kiloparsec, thickness 3000 parsec at the centre, and 300 parsec elsewhere. The Sun is 8000 parsec from the nucleus. A pair of spiral arms merges from the nucleus and is superimposed on the general distribution of stars. The Galaxy as a whole rotates, faster at the centre than further out. There are around

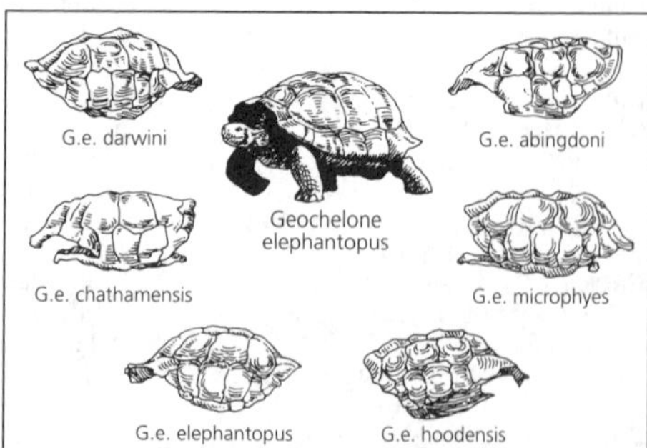

Galápagos giant tortoise, illustrating shell shape of subspecies

100 000 000 000 stars in all, and the Galaxy is 13–20 thousand million years old. >> Milky Way; star cluster

Galbraith, J(ohn) Kenneth [gol**brayth**] (1908–) Economist and diplomat, born in Iona Station, Ontario, Canada. He became professor of economics at Harvard (1949–75), and for 2 years (1961–3) was US ambassador to India. He was an advisor to Presidents Kennedy and Johnson, and is one of the major intellectual forces in American liberalism.

Galdós, Benito Pérez >> **Pérez Galdós, Benito**

Galen [**gay**len], in full **Claudius Galenus** (c.130–201) Greek physician, born in Pergamum, Mysia. He was a voluminous writer on medical and philosophical subjects, becoming the authority used by subsequent Greek and Roman medical writers. >> anatomy ℹ

galena [ga**lee**na] A lead sulphide (PbS) mineral, with very dense, dark-grey crystals. It is an important source of lead. >> lead

Galicia [ga**lee**sha] pop (1995e) 2 731 000; area 29 434 sq km/11 361 sq mi. Autonomous region of Spain in the NW corner of the Iberian peninsula extending S to the Portuguese border; a mediaeval kingdom within Castile, 11th-c; ports include Corunna and Vigo; there is a separatist political movement. >> Spain ℹ

Galilean moons The principal natural satellites of Jupiter, discovered by Galileo in 1610; Io (the innermost), Europa, Ganymede, and Callisto. They are in the same size range as the Moon, lack sensible atmospheres, and lie in near circular orbits in Jupiter's equatorial plane. >> Galileo project; Jupiter (astronomy); Voyager project ℹ; RR964

Galilee [**ga**lilee], Hebrew **Galil** N region of former Palestine and now of Israel, chiefly associated in Biblical times with the ministry of Jesus; scene of fierce fighting during the Arab invasion of Israel, 1948. >> Israel ℹ; Jesus Christ

Galilee, Sea of >> **Tiberias, Lake**

Galileo [gali**lay**oh], in full **Galileo Galilei** (1564–1642) Astronomer and mathematician, born in Pisa, Italy. He became professor of mathematics at Padua (1592–1610), where he improved the refracting telescope (1610), and was the first to use it for astronomy, discovering the satellites of Jupiter and the rings of Saturn. His realization that the ancient Aristotelian teachings about the structure of the universe were unacceptable brought severe ecclesiastical censure, and he was forced to retract before the Inquisition. By 1637 he had become totally blind. The validity of his scientific work was formally recognized by the Roman Catholic Church in 1993. >> astronomy; Copernican system

Galileo project A scientifically ambitious orbiter/atmospheric probe mission launched by space shuttle in 1989, arriving at Jupiter at the end of 1995. In October 1991 the Galileo spacecraft achieved the first successful flyby of an asteroid (Gaspra), returning close-up images and mineralogical data. >> Jupiter (astronomy); NASA

gall An abnormal outgrowth of tissue which can appear on any part of a plant, caused by insects, bacteria, fungi, nematodes, or mites. Common examples are oak-apples and the pincushion galls of roses. >> fasciation

Gall, Franz Joseph [gal] (1758–1828) Anatomist, born in Tiefenbrunn, Germany. As a physician in Vienna (1785), he evolved a theory in which a person's talents and qualities were traced to particular areas of the brain. >> phrenology

Galla or **Oromo** A cluster of Cushitic-speaking peoples of Ethiopia and N Kenya. Traditionally pastoralists, the groups in N Ethiopia are farmers, while the S Galla are still cattle herders. >> Ethiopia ℹ

Gallaudet College [**ga**luhdet] A college of higher education for the deaf, in Washington, DC. It was founded by Edward Miner Gallaudet (1837–1917) in 1857, and is financed both privately and publicly.

gall bladder A small muscular sac found near or in the liver of many vertebrates, which acts as a reservoir for the storage and concentration of bile. During digestion the gall bladder expels bile into the intestine via the biliary duct system. >> gallstones

Galle, Johann Gottfried [**gah**luh] (1812–1910) Astronomer, born in Pabsthaus, Germany. In 1846, at Berlin Observatory, he discovered the planet Neptune. >> Adams, John Couch; Leverrier; Neptune (astronomy)

galleon An elaborate, four-masted, heavily armed 16th-c warship, with a pronounced beak reminiscent of the ram on a galley, hence 'galleon'. >> ship ℹ

Galliano, John (Charles) [gali**ah**noh] (1960–) Fashion designer, born in Gibraltar. He set up a studio in London, receiving the British Fashion Council Designer of the Year Award in 1987. After moving to Paris in 1994, he again won the British Designer Award (1994, 1995), and after a period with Givenchy became designer-in-chief at Christian Dior in 1996. >> Givenchy

galliard >> **pavane**

Gallic Wars The name traditionally given to Julius Caesar's brutal campaigns (58–51 BC) against the Celtic tribes of Gaul (ancient France). They were also the occasion of his two unsuccessful invasions of Britain.

Galliformes [gali**faw(r)**meez] A worldwide order of medium-sized, mainly ground-feeding birds; also known as **gallinaceous birds**. >> curassow; domestic fowl; hoatzin; megapode; pheasant; turkey

gallinaceous birds >> **Galliformes**

gallinule [**gal**inyool] A water-bird of the rail family (c.12 species); native to the Old World and much of South America and Australia; toes often very long for walking on floating vegetation. >> moorhen; rail

Gallipoli [ga**lip**olee], Turkish **Gelibolu** Narrow peninsula in NW Turkey; between the Dardanelles (SE) and the Aegean Sea (W); length c.100 km/60 mi. >> Gallipoli campaign; Turkey ℹ

Gallipoli campaign [ga**lip**olee] A major campaign of World War 1 (1915–16). With stalemate on the Western Front, the British War Council advocated operations against the Turks to secure the Dardanelles and aid Russia. The land campaign began with amphibious assaults on the Gallipoli peninsula (Apr 1915). Australian and New Zealand forces were heavily involved. It was abandoned as a costly failure. >> Dardanelles; World War 1

gallium Ga, element 31. A metal with a remarkable liquid range (melting point 28°C, boiling point 2400°C), relatively rare and found chiefly as an impurity in ores of other elements. It is important mainly as gallium arsenide (GaAs), a compound converting electrical energy into visible light, used in light-emitting diodes. >> chemical elements; diode; metal; RR1036

gall midge A minute, delicate fly; eggs and hatching larvae often cause gall-like swellings on host plants. (Order: Diptera. Family: Cecidomyiidae, c.4000 species.) >> gall; midge

gallon >> RR1031–3

Galloway >> **Dumfries and Galloway**

gallstones Small stones in the gall bladder and its associated ducts. They are found in about 20% of individuals, but give rise to symptoms in only a small proportion of these. Most stones are composed of cholesterol with a little admixture of calcium. When they cause significant discomfort or jaundice, they are usually removed surgically. In some cases small stones may be dissolved by giving a derivative of bile salts by mouth. >> cholesterol; gall bladder

Gallup, George (Horace) (1901–84) Public opinion expert, born in Jefferson, IA. A professor of journalism, in 1935 he founded the American Institute of Public Opinion, and evolved the **Gallup polls** for testing the state of public opinion via representative samples.

gall wasp A very small wasp, each species causing a characteristic gall on its host plant, typically the oak. (Order: Hymenoptera. Family: Cynipidae, c.2000 species.) >> gall; wasp

Galsworthy, John [**golz**werthee] (1867–1933) Novelist and playwright, born in Kingston Hill, Surrey. His great sequence, *The Forsyte Saga* (1906–28), recording the life of the affluent British middle class before 1914, began a new vogue in novel writing. His plays, such as *Strife* (1909), illustrate his interest in social and ethical problems. He was awarded the Nobel Prize for Literature in 1932.

Galton, Sir Francis [**gawl**tn] (1822–1911) Scientist and explorer, born in Birmingham, West Midlands. He is best known for his studies of heredity and intelligence, such as *Hereditary Genius* (1869), which led to the field he called *eugenics*. >> eugenics

Galuppi, Baldassare [ga**loo**pee] (1706–85) Light operatic composer, born near Venice, Italy. His comic operas were extremely popular, and he also composed sacred and instrumental music. He is the subject of a well-known poem by Browning, 'A Toccata of Galuppi's'. >> Browning, Robert

Galvani, Luigi [gal**vah**nee] (1737–98) Physiologist, born in Bologna, Italy, known for his studies of the role of electrical impulses in animal tissue. The galvanometer, an instrument for measuring small electrical currents, is named after him. >> galvanizing

galvanizing The application of a zinc coating to iron or steel to protect against atmospheric corrosion. Although the term 'galvanizing' derives from Galvani, the process was not devised by him, but by Henry William Crawford in 1837. >> corrosion; Galvani; zinc

galvanometer >> **Galvani**

Galway [**gawl**way], Ir **Na Gaillimhe** pop (1995e) 179 000; area 5939 sq km/2293 sq mi. County in Connacht province, W Ireland; largest Gaelic-speaking population in Ireland; capital, Galway, pop (1995e) 50 500; port at head of Galway Bay; airfield; railway; university (1849); technical college. >> Ireland (republic) ℹ

Galway, James [**gawl**way] (1939–) Flautist, born in Belfast. He has followed a highly successful solo career, playing on a solid gold flute of great tonal range. >> flute

Gama, Vasco da [**gah**ma] (c.1469–1525) Navigator, born in Sines, Portugal. He led the expedition which discovered the route to India round the Cape of Good Hope (1497–9).

Gambetta, Leon (Michel) [gãbeta] (1838–82) French Republican statesman, born in Cahors, France. After the surrender of Napoleon III he helped to proclaim the Republic (1870), became minister of the interior, made a spectacular escape from the siege of Paris in a balloon, and for five months was dictator of France. He was briefly prime minister (1881–2). >> France ℹ; MacMahon; Napoleon III

Gambia, The, official name **Republic of the Gambia** pop (1995e) 1 053 000; area 11 295 sq km/4361 sq mi. W African republic; capital, Banjul; timezone GMT; ethnic groups include Malinke, Fula, Wolof; chief religion, Islam (95%); official language, English; unit of currency, the dalasi of 100 butut; strip of land 322 km/200 mi E–W along the R Gambia; flat country, not rising above 90 m/295 ft; tropical climate; visited by Portuguese, 1455; settled by English in 17th-c; independent British Crown Colony, 1843; independent member of Commonwealth, 1965; republic, 1970; joined Confederation of Senegambia, 1982–9; constitution provides for a president and House of Representatives; Provisional Ruling Council installed by military coup, 1994; return to civilian rule, 1997; economy chiefly agriculture, especially groundnuts; tourism. >> Banjul; Senegal ℹ; RR1009 political leaders

Gambon, Sir Michael (John) (1940–) Actor, born in Dublin. He joined the National Theatre in 1963, also working widely in repertory and with the Royal Shakespeare Company (1982–3). His television appearances include *The Singing Detective* (1986, BAFTA), and his films *Paris by Night* (1989), *Mobsters* (1992), and *Nothing Personal* (1997).

gamelan [**gam**elan] An ensemble used for traditional and ceremonial music, especially in Bali and Java. It consists mainly of tuned gongs, chimes, and other percussion instruments. >> Javanese music; percussion ℹ

gamete [**gam**eet] A specialized reproductive cell which fuses with another gamete of the opposite sex or mating type, during fertilization, to form a zygote. Gametes are typically *haploid* (possessing a single chromosome set), and the zygote is *diploid* (possessing a double set, one derived from each gamete). Gametes are usually differentiated into male and female. >> cell; chromosome ℹ; fertilization; zygote

gamete intrafallopian transfer (GIFT) A procedure undertaken to remedy infertility. Eggs are collected from the surface of the ovaries after stimulation with drugs, then introduced into the uterus together with spermatozoa, permitting natural fertilization to occur. >> pregnancy ℹ; test-tube baby

game theory The branch of mathematics that analyzes a range of problems involving decision-making, with important applications to military strategy, economics, and other applied sciences. Game theory was developed principally by French mathematician Emile Borel (1871–1956) and US mathematician Johann von Neumann (1903–57).

gametophyte The sexual (ie gamete-producing or *haploid*) generation in the life of a plant. It is the dominant part of the life-cycle in algae and bryophytes; it is the free-living but minor generation in ferns; while in flowering plants it is represented only by the pollen tube and embryo sac. >> sporophyte

gamma globulins The most abundant fraction of the antibodies in blood serum, produced by the plasma cells of B lymphocytes (derived from bone marrow); also known as **immunoglobulin G (IgG)**. Gamma globulins combine with antigens such as viruses and parasites to kill them. >> antibodies; serum

gamma rays Electromagnetic radiation of very short wavelength, less than 3×10^{-11} m; no electric charge;

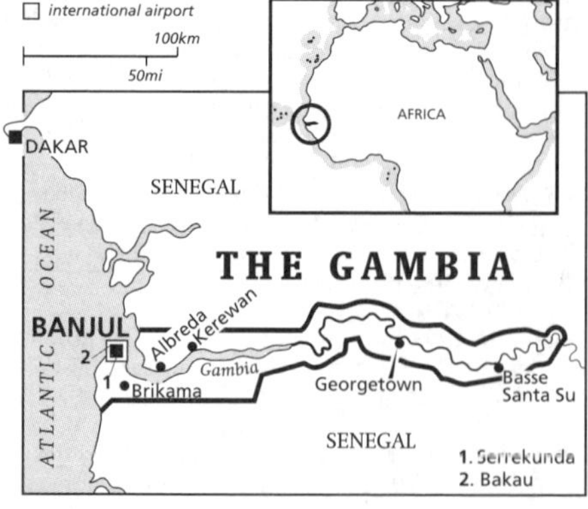

highly penetrating. Emitted in natural radioactivity, it is the result of transitions from high-energy excited states to lower-energy states in atomic nuclei. >> electromagnetic radiation ℹ

Gamow, George [gamov], originally **Georgy Antonovich Gamov** (1904–68) Physicist, born in Odessa, Ukraine. In 1948 he helped to develop the 'big bang' theory of the origin of the universe, and contributed to the analysis of the double helix model of DNA (1953). He was also a highly successful popular science writer. >> Alpher; Bethe; 'big bang'; DNA ℹ

Gand [gã] >> **Ghent**

Gandhi, (**Mohandas Karamchand**) [gandee], known as **the Mahatma** (Hindi 'of great soul') (1869–1948) Indian nationalist leader, born in Poorbandar, Kathiawar. He studied law in London, but in 1893 went to South Africa, where he spent 20 years opposing discriminatory legislation against Indians. In 1914 he returned to India, where he became leader of the Indian National Congress, advocating a policy of non-violent non-co-operation to achieve independence. Following his civil disobedience campaign (1919–22), he was jailed for conspiracy (1922–4). In 1930 he led a 320 km/200 mi march to the sea to collect salt in symbolic defiance of the government monopoly. In 1946 he negotiated with the Cabinet Mission which recommended the new constitutional structure. After independence (1947), he tried to stop the Hindu–Muslim conflict in Bengal, a policy which led to his assassination in Delhi by Nathuram Godse, a Hindu fanatic. >> Non-Co-operation Movement

Gandhi, Indira (Priyadarshini) [gandee] (1917–84) Indian stateswoman and prime minister (1966–77, 1980–4), born in Allahabad, the daughter of Jawaharlal Nehru. She became president of the Indian Congress Party (1959–60), minister of information (1964), and prime minister after the death of Shastri. She achieved a considerable reputation through her work as a leader of the developing nations, but was unable to stem sectarian violence at home. She was assassinated in New Delhi by Sikh extremists, and succeeded by her elder son, **Rajiv Gandhi**; her other son, **Sanjay Gandhi** (1946–80), was killed in an air crash. >> Gandhi, Rajiv; Indian National Congress; Shastri

Gandhi, Rajiv [gandee] (1944–91) Indian statesman and prime minister (1984–9), born in Mumbai (Bombay), India, the eldest son of Indira Gandhi. Following the death of his brother **Sanjay Gandhi** in an air crash in 1980, he was elected to his brother's parliamentary seat. After the assassination of Indira Gandhi (1984), he became prime minister, securing a record majority. He was forced to resign after his party was defeated in the 1989 election, and was assassinated 18 months later while campaigning for the Congress Party. His Italian-born widow, **Sonia**, was elected Congress president in 1998. >> Gandhi, Indira; Nehru

Ganges, River [ganjeez], Hindi **Ganga** River in N India, formed in the E Himalayas; flows W onto the Ganges Plain, then through Bihar and West Bengal; joined by the R Brahmaputra, it continues through Bangladesh as the river Padma, to form the vast Ganges–Brahmaputra delta in the Bay of Bengal; length 2510 km/1560 mi; the most sacred Hindu river. >> Hinduism; India ℹ

ganglion 1 In anatomy, an aggregation of grey (non-myelinated) nervous tissue within the nervous system, constituting the bulk of many invertebrate central nervous systems. They are often the site of communication between nerve cells. >> myelin; nervous system **2** In clinical medicine, a cyst which forms in relation to a tendon sheath, producing a painless, harmless swelling. >> cyst (medicine)

Gang of Four 1 A description given by Mao Zedong to the Shanghai-based hard-core radicals of the Cultural Revolution: Zhang Chunqiao, Yao Wenyuan, Wang Hongwen, and Jiang Qing. All were members of the politburo when they were arrested and disgraced in 1976. >> Cultural Revolution; Jiang Qing **2** In British politics, the name given to the four politicians who broke away from the Labour Party to found the Social Democratic Party in 1981: Roy Jenkins, William Rodgers, David Owen, and Shirley Williams. >> Social Democratic Party

gangrene A form of death (*necrosis*) of tissue, variably associated with bacterial infection. **Dry gangrene** refers to the death of a part of the body deprived of its blood supply, such as a foot or leg in which the supply of blood is insufficient to maintain its life. **Wet gangrene** affects internal tissues, such as the gut when deprived of its blood supply. >> gas gangrene

ganja >> **cannabis**

gannet A large marine bird closely related to the booby; native to the N Atlantic, S Africa, Australia, and New Zealand; long blue bill with no external nostrils; bare patches of blackish skin on face. (Family: Sulidae, 3 species.) >> booby

Ganymede (astronomy) [ganimeed] The third natural satellite of Jupiter, discovered by Galileo in 1610; distance from the planet 1 070 000 km/665 000 mi; diameter 5260 km/ 3270 mi; orbital period 7·155 days. The brightest of the Galilean satellites, it seems to have a large rocky core surrounded by a mantle of water and a thick crust of ice. >> Galilean moons; Jupiter (astronomy); RR964

Ganymede (mythology) [ganimeed] In Greek mythology, a beautiful boy, the son of Tros, a Trojan prince. He was carried up to Olympus, where he became the cup-bearer.

Gaoxiong [gowshyung] or **Kao-hsiung** 22°36N 120°17E, pop (1995e) 1 444 000. Special municipality and seaport in SW Taiwan; largest seaport and industrial city in Taiwan; world's largest shipbreaking centre, occupied by the Japanese, 1895–1945; airport; railway. >> Taiwan ℹ

gar Primitive slender-bodied fish confined to fresh and brackish rivers and lakes of North America; length up to 3 m/10 ft, scales rhomboidal, jaws prolonged to form a narrow snout; also called **garpikes**. (Genus: *Lepisosteus*. Family: Lepisosteidae.) >> fish ℹ

Garamba National park established in 1938 in N Democratic Republic of Congo, area 4480 sq km/1730 sq mi; noted for its unique population of white rhinoceroses; a world heritage site. >> Zaire ℹ

garbanzos >> **chick-pea**

Garbo, Greta, originally **Greta Lovisa Gustafsson** (1905–90) Film actress, born in Stockholm. She moved to the USA in 1925, where she starred in such successes as *Anna Karenina* (1935) and *Ninotchka* (1939). She retired from films in 1941, and became a US citizen in 1951, living in seclusion in New York City.

García Lorca, Federico >> **Lorca, Federico García**

García Márquez, Gabriel >> **Márquez, Gabriel García**

Gard, Pont du [põ dü gah(r)] An aqueduct built by the Romans early in the 1st-c AD to carry the water supply of the city of Nîmes in S France. It is c.275 m/900 ft long and towers 55 m/180 ft above the R Gard; a world heritage site. >> aqueduct; Nîmes

Gard, Roger Martin du >> **Martin du Gard, Roger**

Garda, Lake, ancient **Lacus Benacus** area 370 sq km/ 143 sq mi. Largest Italian lake, between Lombardy and Venetia; length 52 km/32 mi; width 5–16·5 km/3–10 mi; maximum depth 346 m/1135 ft. >> Italy ℹ

garden bunting >> **ortolan**

garden city In the UK, a planned settlement designed to provide a spacious, high-quality, living and working environment. The concept is based on 19th-c ideas of Utopian communities, and was developed by Ebenezer Howard in 1898. The first was built at Letchworth, Hertfordshire, in 1903, followed by Welwyn in 1919. The ideas were developed further in the British 'new towns' of the 1950s, and were also influential in Europe and the USA. >> green belt; Howard, Ebenezer

garden cress A slender annual (*Lepidium sativum*), single stem 20–40 cm/8–15 in; flowers small, white, cross-shaped; possibly native to W Asia. Long cultivated as a salad plant, it is the cress of mustard and cress. (Family: Cruciferae.)

gardenia An evergreen shrub or small tree, native mostly to the Old World tropics, China, and Japan; flowers white, fragrant, petals forming a tube with spreading lobes. (Genus: *Gardenia*, 250 species. Family: Rubiaceae.)

Gardiner, Stephen (c.1483–1555) Clergyman, born in Bury St Edmunds, Suffolk. He supported the royal supremacy, but opposed doctrinal reformation, and for this was imprisoned on Edward VI's accession. Released and restored by Mary in 1553, he became an arch-persecutor of Protestants. >> Edward VI; Mary I; Reformation

Gardner, Ava (Lavinnia), originally **Lucy Johnson** (1922–90) Film actress, born in Smithfield, NC. A green-eyed brunette, once voted the world's most beautiful woman, she remained a leading lady for two decades. Her films include *Mogambo* (1953), *The Barefoot Contessa* (1954), and *Night of the Iguana* (1964). She was married to Mickey Rooney, Artie Shaw, and Frank Sinatra.

Gardner, Erle Stanley (1889–1970) Crime novelist, born in Malden, MA. He is best known as the writer of the 'Perry Mason' books, later the basis of a long-running television series.

Garfield, James A(bram) (1831–81) The 20th president of the USA (Mar–Sep 1881), born in Orange, OH. He identified himself with the cause of civil service reform, thereby irritating many in his own party. He was shot at Elberon, New Jersey, by a disappointed office-seeker, Charles Guiteau.

garfish >> **needlefish**

Garfunkel, Art (1942–) Singer and actor, born in Forest Hills, NY. He teamed up with Paul Simon as a teenager, achieving major hits with 'The Sound of Silence' (1965) and *The Graduate*. The duo split up following his decision to go into acting. His films include *Catch 22* (1970), *Carnal Knowledge* (1971), and *Boxing Helena* (1993). He continued to record as a soloist, achieving a UK No 1 with 'Bright Eyes' (1979). >> Simon, Paul

garganey [**gah(r)**ganee] A small, slender duck (*Anas querquedula*), native to S Eurasia, W and NE Africa, and Indonesia; male brown with white stripe from eye to back of neck; migrates to tropics for winter. (Family: Anatidae.) >> duck

gargoyle In Gothic architecture, a stone rainwater spout carved in the form of a grotesque animal or human face, with its mouth open as if spewing the water. It is usually built so as to project well out from the parapet, thus sending the water away from the building. >> Gothic architecture

Garibaldi, Giuseppe [gari**bawl**dee] (1807–82) Italian patriot, born in Nice, France. At the outbreak of Italy's war of liberation he sailed from Genoa (May 1860) with his 'thousand' volunteers, and assisted Mazzinian rebels to free Sicily from Neapolitan control. He swiftly overran much of S Italy, and drove King Francis of Naples from his capital (Sep 1860). Thereafter he allowed the conquest of S Italy to be completed by the Sardinians under Victor Emmanuel II. >> Mazzini; Risorgimento; Thousand, Expedition of the

Garland, Judy, originally **Frances Gumm** (1922–69) Actress and singer, born in Grand Rapids, MN. She became a juvenile film star in *Broadway Melody of 1938*, followed by *The Wizard of Oz* (1939) and *Meet Me in St Louis* (1944), directed by Vincente Minelli, whom she later married. Concerts and occasional films continued with public success, but her private life was full of overwhelming difficulties, and she died in London, apparently from an overdose of sleeping pills.

garlic A perennial bulb (*Allium sativum*) up to 60 cm/2 ft; greenish-to-purple star-shaped flowers mixed with bulbils. Native to Asia, it has been cultivated in the Mediterranean region since ancient times for the strongly flavoured bulbs. (Family: Liliaceae.) >> allium

garnet A group of silicate minerals occurring mainly in metamorphic rocks. It displays a wide range of composition and colour. Some varieties are important as gemstones. >> silicate minerals

Garonne, River [ga**ron**], ancient **Garumna** Chief river of SW France, rising in the Pyrenees; meets the R Dordogne to form the Gironde estuary; length 575 km/357 mi. >> France ℹ

garpike >> **gar**

Garrett, Peter (Robert) (1953–) Popular singer and political activist, born in Sydney, New South Wales, Australia. Trained as a lawyer, since 1977 he has been lead singer with the band Midnight Oil, known for its songs dealing with issues such as Aboriginal land rights, conservation, and prison reform. He became widely known in 1984, when he stood for parliament.

Garrick, David (1717–79) Actor, theatre manager, and playwright, born in Hereford, Hereford and Worcester. For 30 years he dominated the English stage, in a wide range of parts. As joint manager of Drury Lane (1747–76) he encouraged innovations in scenery and lighting design.

garrigue [ga**reeg**] Evergreen scrubland vegetation found in areas with thin soils and a Mediterranean-type climate; also known as **garigue** or **garriga**. Low, thorny shrubs and stunted oak are characteristic.

Garrison, William Lloyd (1805–79) Abolitionist, born in Newburyport, MA. He emerged in 1830 as the foremost anti-slavery voice in the USA, founding the American Anti-Slavery Society. >> slave trade

Garter, the Most Noble Order of the (KG) The most ancient order of chivalry in Europe, founded by Edward III of England between 1344 and 1351. The emblem of the order is a gold-edged blue garter, inscribed in gold with *Honi soit qui mal y pense* (Fr 'Shamed be he who thinks evil of it'), traditionally the words spoken by Edward after he picked up the Countess of Salisbury's dropped garter.

gas 1 A state of matter in which atoms are disordered and highly mobile, moving in a random way with little interaction. Gases are characterized by low densities (typically 1/1000 of a solid), an ability to flow and to fill a container, and high compressibility. >> gas laws; phases of matter **2** A fuel which includes both **manufactured gas**, derived from solid or liquid fossil fuels, and **natural gas**, drawn from existing gaseous subterranean accumulations. Manufactured gas (or **town gas**) was made from the early 19th-c by the distillation of coal; more recently by the chemical conversion of surplus naphtha from the petroleum industry or natural solid fuels other than coal. Natural gas occurs on its own or in association with oil deposits. The main constituent of town gas is hydrogen; that of natural gas is methane. The calorific value of natural gas is about double that of town gas. >> fuel; hydrogen; methane; natural gas

Gascoigne, Paul [**gas**koyn], nickname **Gazza** (1967–) Footballer, born in Gateshead, Tyne and Wear. After Tottenham Hotspur signed him in 1988, he established

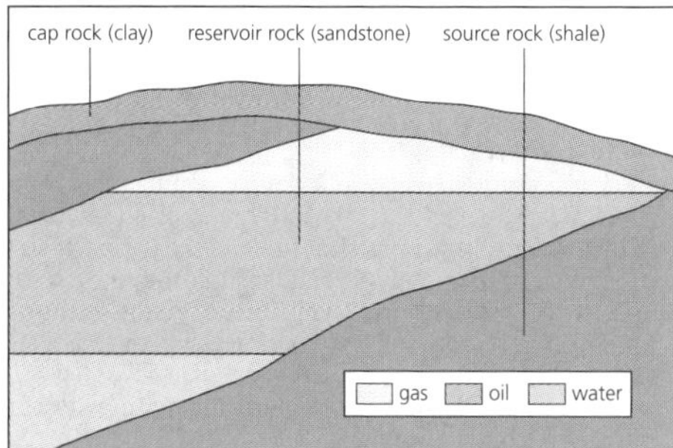

Gas 2 – reservoir formation

himself as an outstanding player and a flamboyant personality, becoming a member of the England team. During the 1991 FA Cup Final he sustained a serious knee injury which delayed his transfer to the Italian club, Lazio, eventually moving for the 1992–3 season. He received a further serious leg injury in 1994, but in 1995 signed for Rangers. In 1998 he joined Middlesbrough Football Club. >> football ℹ

Gascony [**gas**konee], Fr **Gascogne**, Lat **Vasconia** Former province in SW France; part of the Roman Empire; conquered by the Visigoths, later by the Franks, who made it a duchy; joined to Guienne, 1052; in English hands, 1154–1453. >> Aquitaine; Franks

gas-cooled reactor >> **nuclear reactor** ℹ

gas engine A specially adapted or designed internal combustion engine which uses gas as its fuel. The gas (usually methane) is stored in pressurized tanks as a liquid. >> internal combustion engine; methane

gas gangrene An infection of muscle and soft tissue by *Clostridium welchii*. The bacteria secrete a toxin that digests tissues, and causes gangrene with bubbles of gas from fermentation. >> gangrene

Gaskell, Mrs Elizabeth (Cleghorn), *née* **Stevenson** (1810–65) Writer, born in London. She did not begin to write until middle age, when she published *Mary Barton* (1848). Her other works include *Cranford* (1853) and *Wives and Daughters* (1865).

gas laws Boyle's and Charles's Laws together, interrelating pressure, volume, and temperature for a given mass of an ideal gas. These laws may be summarized in a single equation: $pV = nRT$, where p is the pressure exerted by n moles of a gas contained in a volume V at an absolute temperature T. >> Boyle; Charles' Law; gas 1

gasohol A mixture of gasoline with 5/15 % ethanol (ethyl alcohol which must be water-free), useful as a high-octane rating fuel in internal combustion engines. >> ethanol; fuel; octane number

gas oil A liquid fuel, the heavier fraction of petroleum distillation. It is used as a heating fuel and in diesel engines. >> fuel; petroleum

gasoline >> **petrol**

gastric juice A mixture of substances secreted by cells and glands within the stomach, consisting of hydrochloric acid, pepsinogen, mucus, and intrinsic factor. Excessive secretion of acid and pepsinogen may lead to the formation of **gastric ulcers**. >> pepsin; ulcer

gastritis [gas**triy**tis] Inflammation of the stomach lining. **Acute gastritis** occurs as a result of several mucosal irritants, such as alcohol and aspirin. **Chronic gastritis** occurs in older age groups, and is associated with thinning (*atrophy*) of the lining of the stomach. >> mucous membrane; stomach

gastro-enteritis [**gas**trohenteri**y**tis] Irritation and inflammation of any part of the gastro-intestinal tract, characterized by abdominal pain, vomiting, diarrhoea, and severe prostration in some cases. >> cholera; dysentery; food poisoning

gastro-intestinal tract >> **alimentary canal**

gastropod [**gas**tropod] The snails, slugs, and snail-like molluscs; body consists of a head, muscular foot, and visceral mass largely covered by a calcareous shell, usually spirally coiled; includes land and freshwater snails and slugs, as well as a great diversity of marine snails. (Phylum: Mollusca. Class: Gastropoda.) >> calcium; conch; cowrie; limpet; mollusc; sea slug; shell; slug; snail; whelk

gastrotrich [**gas**trotrik] A minute, worm-like animal found in or on bottom sediments and in association with other aquatic organisms in various habitats; body covered in a horny layer (cuticle), and may have bristles. (Phylum: Gastrotricha, c.150 species.) >> worm

gastrula [**gas**trula] The stage following the blastula in the embryonic development of animals. During this phase (**gastrulation**), cells of the embryo move into their correct position for development into the various organ systems of the adult. >> blastula; embryology

gas turbine An engine that passes the products of the combustion of its fuel/air mixture over the blades of a turbine. The turbine drives an air compressor, which in turn provides the air for the combustion process. The energy of the combustion products not taken up by the compressor can be used to provide a jet of exhaust gases, or drive another turbine. >> engine; jet engine ℹ; turbine

gas warfare >> **chemical warfare**

Gates, Bill, popular name of **William Henry Gates** (1955–) Computer engineer and entrepreneur, born in Seattle, WA. In 1977, he co-founded Microsoft to develop and produce DOS, his basic operating system for computers. When in 1981 International Business Machines (IBM) adopted DOS for its line of personal computers, his company took a giant step forward, and by age 35 he had become one of the wealthiest men in America. >> DOS; Microsoft

Gates, Horatio (1728–1806) US general, born in Maldon, Essex. He joined the British army, served in America in the Seven Years' War (1756–63), and then settled there. In the War of Independence he sided with his adoptive country, and in 1777 compelled the surrender of the British at Saratoga. In 1780 he commanded the army of the South, but was routed by Cornwallis near Camden. >> American Revolution

Gatling, Richard Jordan (1818–1903) Inventor, born in Maney's Neck, NC. He is remembered for his invention of the **Gatling gun** (1861–2), a revolving battery gun, with 10 parallel barrels, firing 1200 shots a minute. His weapon came to public notice again in 1991 when it was used as the principal weapon platform on US A10 aircraft during the Gulf War.

GATT >> **General Agreement on Tariffs and Trade**

gaucho [**gow**choh] A nomadic, fiercely independent mestizo horseman of the Argentine pampa, first appearing in the 17th-c. Gaucho skills live on among the rural population of Argentina and Uruguay. >> Argentina ℹ; pampa(s)

Gaudí (I Cornet), Antonio [gow**dee**] (1852–1926) Architect, born in Riudoms, Spain. He was the most famous exponent of Catalan *Modernisme*, one of the branches of the Art Nouveau movement, and is best known for the ornate Church of the Holy Family in Barcelona. >> Art Nouveau

Gaudier-Brzeska, Henri [**gohd**yay **bres**ka] (1891–1915) Sculptor, born in St Jean de Braye, France. A pioneering modernist who drew upon African tribal art, he rapidly developed a highly personal abstract style exemplified in both carvings and drawings. >> abstract art; London Group

Gaudron, Mary [**god**ron] (1943–) Judge, born in Moree, New South Wales, Australia. Seen as a progressive, in 1987 she became the first woman to be appointed to the High Court of Australia.

Gauguin, (Eugène Henri) Paul [gohgĩ] (1848–1903) Postimpressionist painter, born in Paris. He visited Martinique (1887), and became the leader of a group of painters at Pont Aven, Brittany (1888). From 1891 he lived mainly in Tahiti and the Marquesas Is, using local people as his subjects, and evolving his own style, *synthétisme*, reflecting his hatred of civilization and the inspiration he found in primitive peoples. >> Postimpressionism

Gaul (Lat *Gallia*) In ancient geography normally used for **Transalpine Gaul**, bounded by the Alps, the Rhine, and the Pyrenees. Julius Caesar completed the Roman conquest in 58–51 BC. With the gradual Roman withdrawal in the 5th-c, Germanic colonies became independent kingdoms. Unity was superficially achieved under Clovis and Charlemagne, and Gaul later developed into the mediaeval kingdom of France. **Cisalpine Gaul** lay S of the Alps and N of the Apennines. Conquered by the Romans in 201–191 BC, it was incorporated into Italy in 42 BC. >> Charlemagne; Franks; Roman history [i]

Gaulish >> **Celtic languages**

Gaullists Members of the French political party, the *Rassemblement pour la République* (RPR) whose programmes are based on the doctrine developed by President de Gaulle in 1958–69. Nationalistic in character, Gaullists emphasize the need for strong government, especially in relations with the European Union and foreign powers such as the USA. >> de Gaulle

Gaultier, Jean-Paul [gohtyay] (1952–) Fashion designer, born in Paris. He joined the houses of Jacques Esterel and Jean Patou before producing his own independent collection in 1976. He reached a new audience as co-host of the magazine show *Eurotrash* on British television.

Gaumont, Léon Ernest [gohmõ], Eng [**goh**mont] (1864–1946) Cinema inventor, manufacturer, and producer, born in Paris. He was responsible for the first talking pictures, demonstrated at Paris in 1910. He also introduced an early form of coloured cinematography in 1912. >> cinematography

Gaunt, John of >> **John of Gaunt**

Gauss, (Johann) Carl Friedrich [gows] (1777–1855) Mathematician, born in Brunswick, Germany. A mental prodigy, he pioneered the application of mathematics to such areas as gravitation, magnetism, and electricity. The unit of magnetic induction has been named after him. >> degaussing; Gauss's law; magnetism; number theory; RR1031

Gauss's law [gows] In electrostatics: the total electric flux through some closed surface is proportional to the total charge enclosed by that surface. The constant of proportionality is $1/\varepsilon$, where ε is permittivity. >> charge; electrostatics; Gauss; permittivity

Gauteng [khow**teng**] (Sesotho 'place of gold') One of the nine new provinces established by the South African constitution of 1994, in NC South Africa, occupying the area formerly known as the PWV (Pretoria–Witwatersrand–Vereeniging) triangle; capital, Johannesburg; pop (1996e) 7 717 000; area 18 760 sq km/7241 sq mi; chief languages, Afrikaans, Zulu, English; Pretoria is the administrative capital of South Africa; smallest province, most densely populated; commercial, financial, and industrial heartland of South Africa, containing c.70% of the labour force, and producing c.37% of GDP. >> South Africa

Gautier, Théophile [gohtyay] (1811–72) Writer and critic, born in Tarbes, France. In 1835 his celebrated novel, *Mademoiselle de Maupin*, appeared. His most important collection was *Emaux et camées* (1852, Enamels and Cameos).

gavial >> **gharial**

gavotte [ga**vot**] A French folk dance, popular also as a court dance during the 17th–18th-c, and often included in instrumental and orchestral suites of the period. It was in a moderately quick duple or quadruple metre. >> suite

Gawain or **Gawayne** [**ga**wayn] One of King Arthur's knights, the son of King Lot of Orkney, whose character varies in different accounts. In the mediaeval *Sir Gawayn and the Grene Knight*, he is a noble hero undergoing a test of faith. >> Arthur; Lancelot, Sir

Gay, John (1685–1732) Poet and playwright, born in Barnstaple, Devon. He wrote poems, pamphlets, and popular satirical *Fables*, and is best known for *The Beggar's Opera* (1728).

Gay-Lussac, Joseph Louis [gay luh**sak**] (1778–1850) Chemist and physicist, born in St Léonard, France. He made balloon ascents to study the laws of terrestrial magnetism, and to collect samples of air for analysis, which led to his major discovery, the law of volumes named after him (1808). >> Charles' Law

Gazankulu [gazang**koo**loo] pop (1995e) 1 046 000. Former national state or non-independent black homeland in Transvaal province, NE South Africa; achieved self-governing status in 1973; incorporated into Northern Province in the new constitution of 1994. >> Northern Province; South Africa [i]

Gaza Strip pop (1995e) 950 000, including c.4000 Jewish settlers; area 202 sq km/78 sq mi. A narrow strip of land bounded NW by the Mediterranean Sea; length, 50 km/30 mi; chief town, Gaza; formerly part of Egyptian Sinai, after Arab–Israeli War of 1948–9; Israeli-occupied district under military administration containing many Palestinian refugee camps, 1967–94; considerable tension in the area after the beginning of the uprising (*intifada*) in 1988; peace agreement (1993) with PLO assigned it to Palestine. >> Arab–Israeli Wars; Israel [i]

gazelle An elegant athletic antelope, native to Africa and S Asia; usually pale brown above with white underparts; when alarmed, moves by 'pronking' (or 'stotting') – a vertical leap using all four legs simultaneously. (Tribe: Antilopini, 18 species.) >> antelope; blackbuck; dorcas gazelle; gerenuk; springbok

gazelle hound >> **saluki**

Gazza >> **Gascoigne, Paul**

GCSE Abbreviation of **General Certificate of Secondary Education**, introduced in England and Wales for the first time in 1988. It merged what had previously been two separate examinations for pupils aged about 16 or older – the *General Certificate of Education* (GCE), originally aimed at about the top 20% of the ability range, and the *Certificate of Secondary Education* (CSE), which was meant for the next 40%.

Gdańsk [gdansk], formerly Ger **Danzig** 54°22N 18°38E, pop (1995e) 469 000. Industrial port in N Poland; held by Prussia, 1793–1919; free city within the Polish tariff area, 1919; Lenin shipyard the scene of much labour unrest in 1980s, in support of Solidarity; part of the *Tri-city* with Sopot and Gdynia; airport; railway; two universities (1945, 1970); maritime research institutes; largest shipyard in Poland. >> Poland [i]; Solidarity

GDP >> **gross domestic product**

gean [**gee**an] A species of cherry (*Prunus avium*) native to Europe and Asia, forming a tall tree with white flowers and dark, purplish-red, sweet or sour fruit; also called **wild** or **bird cherry**. (Family: Rosaceae.) >> cherry

gear A device used to transform one rotary motion into

another, in terms of speed and direction. The fundamental type of gear is the toothed gear wheel, which can be used in a wide variety of ways to produce the desired ratio of output rotation to input rotation. >> clutch; transmission

gecko A lizard native to warm regions worldwide; body usually flattened top to bottom; skin soft; eyes large, without movable eyelids; tongue short, often used to lick eyes; most individuals nocturnal; males are the only lizards with loud calls. (Family: Gekkonidae, 800 species.) >> lizard ℹ; tokay gecko

Geelong [jee**long**] 38°10S 144°26E, pop (1995e) 154 000. Port in S Victoria, Australia; railway; university (1974); customs house the oldest wooden building in Victoria. >> Victoria (Australia)

gegenschein [**gay**genshiyn] >> **zodiacal light**

Gehrig, (Henry) Lou(is) [**ge**rig], nickname **the Iron Horse** (1903–41) Baseball player, born in New York City. He played 2130 consecutive games for the New York Yankees between 1925 and 1939. An outstanding first-baseman, he scored 493 home runs. His final illness (amyotrophic lateral sclerosis) is widely known as 'Lou Gehrig's disease' in the USA. >> baseball ℹ

Geiger counter [**giy**ger] A device for counting atomic particles, named after German physicist Hans Geiger (1882–1945). Gas between electrodes is ionized by the passage of a particle, and so transmits a pulse to a counter. >> *illustration below*

Geisel, Ernesto [**giy**zl] (1908–96) Brazilian general and president (1974–9), born in Rio Grande do Sul. His military presidency was notable for its policy of 'decompression', which led to the restoration of democracy in 1985. >> Brazil ℹ

gel [jel] A colloidal suspension of a solid in a liquid, in which the properties of the solid predominate. An example is gelatine. >> colloid

gelatin(e) [**jel**atin] A protein formed when collagen (a fibrous protein found in animal bones, skin, and hair) is boiled in water. It is used in foods, adhesives, and photographic emulsions. >> collagens; colloid; protein

Geldof, Bob [**gel**dof], popular name of **Robert Frederick Xenon Geldof** (1954–) Rock musician and philanthropist, born in Dublin. He formed the successful rock group **Boomtown Rats** (1975–86). Moved by television pictures of widespread suffering in famine-stricken Ethiopia, he established the pop charity 'Band Aid' trust in 1984, which raised £8 million for African famine relief through the release of the record 'Do they know it's Christmas?'. Other successful 'Live Aid' charity concerts followed, and he was awarded an honorary knighthood in 1986.

gelignite A group of industrial explosives consisting of a gelatinized mixture of nitroglycerine and nitrocellulose. Inert non-explosive material promotes safety in handling. >> explosives

Gell-Mann, Murray [gel**man**] (1929–) Theoretical physicist, born in New York City. He introduced the concept of *strangeness* into the theory of elementary particles, and helped to devise the idea of quarks as constituents of all nuclei, and the idea of weak currents for understanding a type of nuclear interaction. He was awarded the Nobel Prize for Physics in 1969. >> particle physics; quark; strangeness

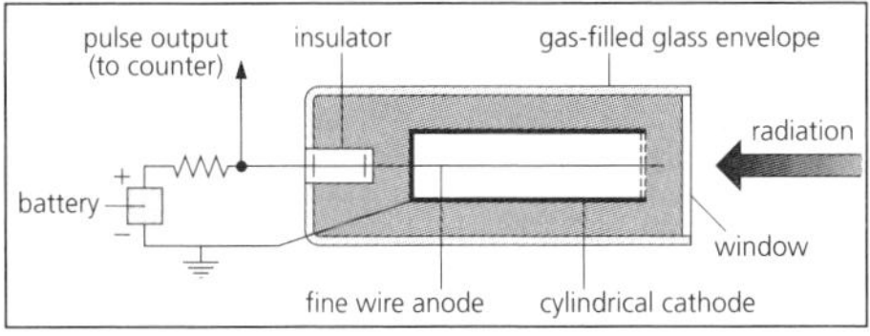

Geiger counter tube

Gemara [ge**mah**ra] (Aramaic 'completion') A commentary on the Jewish Mishnah, which together with the Mishnah constitutes the Talmud. >> Judaism; Mishnah; Talmud

Gemayel [ge**miy**el] One of the leading political families of Lebanon's Maronite Christian community. **Sheikh Pierre** (1905–84) founded the Kataeb or Phalangist Party in 1936. Originally a youth group modelled along fascist lines, its members were first elected to the Lebanese parliament in 1960. His younger son **Bashir** (1947–82), a Lebanese army officer, rose through the party and its militia during the 1975–6 civil war, and was elected President of Lebanon in 1982. Upon his assassination 20 days later he was succeeded by his elder brother **Amin** (1942–). Politically more moderate than Bashir, in his six years as president he proved unable to resolve the communal conflict stemming from the civil war. >> Lebanon ℹ

Gemini [**jem**iniy] (Lat 'twins') A conspicuous N constellation of the zodiac, with a bright pair of stars **Castor** and **Pollux**, lying between Taurus and Cancer. Castor is a double star, easily divided through a small telescope; orbital period 470 years; distance: 15 parsec. Pollux is a bright orange star, the nearest giant star to Earth; distance: 11 parsec. >> constellation; double star; star; RR968

Gemini programme [**jem**iniy] A second-generation US-crewed spacecraft programme, following Mercury and preceding Apollo, using a two-member crew. It was used to demonstrate the new capabilities of extravehicular activity, and extended astronaut endurance to a degree needed to accomplish lunar landing missions. There were 10 successful missions between March 1965 and November 1966. >> Apollo programme; Mercury programme; RR970

gemsbok >> **oryx**

gemstones A general term for precious or semi-precious stones or minerals valued for their rarity, beauty, and durability; usually cut and polished as jewels. The most highly valued are hard and transparent crystals such as diamond, ruby, emerald, and sapphire. >> beryl; chalcedony; corundum; diamond; emerald; garnet; jade; opal; pegmatite; quartz; ruby; rutile; sapphire; spinel; topaz; tourmaline; turquoise; zircon

gender The social expression of the basic physiological differences between men and women – social behaviour which is deemed to be appropriate to 'masculine' or 'feminine' roles and which is learned through primary and secondary socialization. >> sexism

gene A unit of heredity; a segment of the DNA which contains the instructions for the development of a particular inherited characteristic. >> DNA ℹ; gene therapy

genealogy The study of family history. Since the 16th-c, records of family descent have been strictly kept in many countries. A chart showing genealogical descent is a *pedigree*. In countries where wealth and position were commonly inherited, such as the UK, genealogy has been very important; but even in countries where the legal and social reasons for interest in genealogy are fewer, such as the USA and Australia, many individuals attempt to trace their 'family tree'.

General Agreement on Tariffs and Trade (GATT) An agency of the United Nations, founded in 1948 to promote international trade. GATT was based in Geneva, and had 125 members in December 1994. It successfully concluded several rounds of negotiations which greatly reduced world tariffs. It was not, however, able to stem the spread of non-tariff barriers to trade, such as voluntary export restraints. GATT was succeeded by the World

Trade Organization (WTO) in 1995. >> protectionism; tariff; United Nations; World Trade Organization

General Assembly (politics) >> **United Nations**

General Assembly (religion) The highest court, in Churches of Presbyterian order. It normally meets annually and comprises equal numbers of ministers and elders, elected by presbyteries in proportion to their size. It is presided over by a *moderator*, elected annually. >> Presbyterianism

General Medical Council (GMC) The statutory body in the UK which controls the professional standing and conduct of members of the medical profession. It is responsible for maintaining the Medical Register of those entitled to practise medicine. >> medicine

general relativity A theory of gravity deriving almost entirely from Einstein (1916). It supersedes Newton's theory of gravitation, and replaces the Newtonian notion of instantaneous action at a distance via the gravitational field with a distortion of space–time due to the presence of mass. For example, as the Earth moves round the Sun there is distortion of space–time by the Sun's greater mass. An analogy represents space–time as a rubber sheet distorted by a heavy ball representing the Sun; a smaller ball rolling by, representing a planet, will tend to fall into this depression, apparently attracted. General relativity is supported by experiments which measure the bending of starlight due to the presence of the Sun's mass, and also the precession of Mercury's orbit. >> cosmology; quantum gravity

General Strike (4–12 May 1926) A national strike in Britain, organized by the Trades Union Congress (TUC) in support of the miners' campaign to resist wage cuts. The government organized special constables and volunteers to counter its most serious effects. The TUC called off the strike, though the miners' strike continued fruitlessly for three more months. >> trade union

generation, computer >> **computer generations**

generative grammar A type of grammar, devised by US linguist Noam Chomsky in the 1950s, which explicitly defines the set of grammatical sentences in a language. Each is assigned a unique structural description, representing the grammatical knowledge (or *competence*) which a native speaker uses. In **transformational grammar**, one set of rules assigns a structure to a basal set of sentences, and another 'transforms' those structures into the forms in which they will actually occur in the language. >> Chomsky; grammar

Genesis, Book of The first book of the Hebrew Bible/Old Testament and of the Pentateuch; traditionally attributed to Moses, but considered by many modern scholars to be composed of several distinct traditions. It presents stories of the creation (Chapters 1–11), then focuses on God's dealings with the people destined to become Israel. >> Abraham; Adam and Eve; Enoch; Isaac; Jacob; Joseph; Moses; Noah; Old Testament; Pentateuch

Genet, Jean [zhuhnay] (1910–86) Writer, born in Paris. His first novel, *Notre-Dame des fleurs* (1944, Our Lady of the Flowers) created a sensation for its portrayal of the criminal world. He later turned from novels to plays, such as *Les Bonnes* (1947, The Maids) and *Les Paravents* (1961, The Screens). Sartre's book *Saint Genet* (1952) widened his fame among the French intelligentsia. >> Sartre

genet or **genette** [**jen**it] An African or European carnivore of the family Viverridae; pale with rows of dark spots and banded tail; also known as **bush cat**. (Genus: *Genetta*, 10 species.) >> carnivore [i]; civet; Viverridae [i]

gene therapy The notion that a particular gene might be inserted into the body cells of individuals who are born with a defective or absent gene. Technical difficulties have so far restricted its use. >> gene

genetic code The code in which genetic instructions are written, using an alphabet based on the four bases in DNA and RNA: *adenine*, *cytosine*, *guanine*, and *thymine* (for DNA) or *uracil* (for RNA). Each triplet of bases indicates that a particular kind of amino acid is to be synthesized (*see panel for RNA bases*). The code is non-overlapping; the triplets are read end-to-end in sequence (eg UUU = phenylalanine, UUA = leucine, CCU = proline); and there are three triplets not translated into amino acid, indicating chain termination. The code is universal and applies to all species. >> amino acid; DNA [i]; RNA

genetic counselling / counseling Advice given to prospective parents concerned at the risk of their future child suffering from a genetic disease. The procedure consists of confirmation of the diagnosis in the affected individual; calculation of the risk of occurrence of the disease from the family history and relevant clinical investigations; advice on the risk; discussion of the implications if the child should be affected; and advice on procedures by which the birth of an affected child can be avoided. >> genetics; medicine

genetic engineering The formation of new combinations of heritable material. Nucleic acid molecules, produced artificially or biologically outside the cell, are inserted into a carrier (such as a virus) so as to allow their incorporation into a host organism in which they do not naturally occur, but in which they are capable of continued propagation. Biological compounds can be produced industrially (eg human insulin, vaccines). New synthetic capabilities can be incorporated into plants (eg for nitrogen fixation). Ultimately it will be possible to excise genes responsible for hereditary disease and replace them with normal DNA sequences. The implications of genetic engineering have led to considerable public debate, and in most countries there is government control over work using recombinant DNA techniques. >> DNA [i]; gene

genetics The science of heredity. It originated with the discovery by Gregor Mendel that observable hereditary characteristics are determined by factors transmitted without change and in predictable fashion from one generation to the next. The term was coined by British biologist William Bateson in 1907. Genetics occupies a unique position, for its principles and mechanisms extend throughout almost all biology, tying together all branches that deal with individual and population variation, and giving a unifying core at all levels – the molecular structure

Genetic code: RNA triplets

1st base	2nd base: U	C	A	G	3rd base
U	Phenylalanine	Serine	Tyrosine	Cysteine	U
	Phenylalanine	Serine	Tyrosine	Cysteine	C
	Leucine	Serine	—— *	—— *	A
	Leucine	Serine	—— *	Tryptophan	G
C	Leucine	Proline	Histidine	Arginine	U
	Leucine	Proline	Histidine	Arginine	C
	Leucine	Proline	Glutamine	Arginine	A
	Leucine	Proline	Glutamine	Arginine	G
A	Isoleucine	Threonine	Asparagine	Serine	U
	Isoleucine	Threonine	Asparagine	Serine	C
	Isoleucine	Threonine	Lysine	Arginine	A
	Methionine	Threonine	Lysine	Arginine	G
G	Valine	Alanine	Aspartic acid	Glycine	U
	Valine	Alanine	Aspartic acid	Glycine	C
	Valine	Alanine	Glutamic acid	Glycine	A
	Valine	Alanine	Glutamic acid	Glycine	G

*Chain termination

of cells and tissues, the development of individuals, and the evolution of populations. >> Bateson; gene; genetic code ℹ; genetic counselling / engineering; Mendel

genette >> **genet**

Geneva [jen**ee**va], Fr **Genève**, Ger **Genf**, Ital **Ginevra** 46°13N 6°09E, pop (1995e) 173 000. City in W Switzerland, W end of L Geneva; built on the site of a Roman town; independent republic until becoming a Swiss canton in 1814; centre of the Reformation under Calvin; former seat of the League of Nations, 1920–46; capital of French-speaking Switzerland; airport; railway; university (1559); world capital of high-class watchmaking and jewellery; headquarters of over 200 international organizations; renowned for its numerous quays and its fountain, Jet d'Eau; cathedral (12th-c). >> League of Nations; Switzerland ℹ

Geneva, Lake, Fr **Lac Léman**, Ger **Genfersee**, Lat **Lacus Lemanus** area 581 sq km/224 sq mi. Lake in SW Switzerland and SE France; largest of the Alpine lakes; height, 371 m/1217 ft; maximum depth, 310 m/1017 ft; maximum width, 14 km/9 mi. >> Alps

Geneva Bible An English translation of the Bible, prepared and published in Geneva by Protestant exiles from England. It first appeared complete in 1560. >> Bible

Geneva Convention An international agreement on the conduct of warfare first framed in 1864 and ratified in 1906. It is chiefly concerned with the protection of wounded and the sanctity of the Red Cross, while prohibiting methods of war that might cause unnecessary suffering. >> international law; POW; Red Cross

Genghis Khan [**jen**gis **kahn**], also spelled **Jingis** or **Chingis Khan** ('Very Mighty Ruler'), originally **Temujin** (1162/7–1227) Mongol conqueror, born in Temujin, Mongolia. From 1211, in several campaigns, he overran the empire of N China, the Kara-Chitai empire, the empire of Kharezm, and other territories, so that by his death the Mongol empire stretched from the Black Sea to the Pacific. >> Mongols

genie >> **jinni**

Genoa [**jen**oha], Ital **Genova** 44°24N 8°56E, pop (1995e) 704 000. Largest seaport in Italy; founded as a Roman trading centre; leading Mediterranean port by 13th-c; rebuilt after World War 2; archbishopric; airport; railway; ferries; university (1471); birthplace of Columbus; Doge's Palace (13th-c), cathedral (12th–14th-c). >> Columbus, Christopher; Italy ℹ

genome [**jee**nohm] The complete genetic information about an organism. In most organisms this is contained in the DNA sequences within chromosomes, while in RNA-based viruses it is the total RNA sequence. Genome sizes have a 100 000 fold range from a few thousand base pairs in simple viruses to 10^{11} base pairs in some plants. >> DNA ℹ; genotype; human genome project; RNA

genotype The genes carried by an individual member of an organism. The interaction of gene products (RNA, protein) with each other and with the environment in which the organism develops gives rise to the **phenotype** – the characteristics that are observed. >> gene; genome

genre painting Realistic scenes from everyday life, typically on a small scale, as produced by Dutch 17th-c masters such as Steen and Vermeer. The term may be applied, however, to any period. >> Steen; Vermeer; Wilkie

Genscher, Hans-Dietrich [**gen**sher] (1927–) German statesman, born in Reideburg, Germany. In 1974 he became vice-chancellor, foreign minister, and (until 1985) Chairman of the Free Democratic Party. >> Germany ℹ; Schmidt

Genseric >> **Gaiseric**

Gent >> **Ghent**

gentian Any of several species, mostly perennials, found almost everywhere, except for Africa; many are low-growing alpines; flowers usually several cm long, funnel- or bell-shaped, with often long tubes and five spreading lobes, usually deep blue, but also white, yellow, or red. (Genus: *Gentiana*, 400 species. Family: Gentianaceae.)

Gentile da Fabriano >> **Fabriano, Gentile da**

Gentlemen at Arms, Honourable Corps of In the UK, non-combatant troops in attendance upon the sovereign. They provide an escort at coronations, state openings of parliament, receptions, royal garden parties, and during state visits.

genus [**jee**nuhs] A category in biological classification consisting of one or more closely related and morphologically similar species. The name of the genus (eg *Panthera*) and the species (eg *leo*) together form the scientific name of an organism (eg the lion, *Panthera leo*). >> systematics; taxonomy

geochemistry A branch of geology concerned with the abundances of elements and their isotopes in the Earth, and the processes that affect their distribution. It also subsumes the study of chemical processes in the evolution of the Earth and the Solar System. >> Earth ℹ; geology

geochronology The science of dating rocks or geological events in absolute terms (ie in years), usually by radiometric dating. For more recent rocks, varve counting may be applicable to Pleistocene sediments, or tree-ring dating can measure ages back to about 7000 years before the present. >> radiometric dating; varve dating

geodesic dome A structurally stable dome constructed of a grid of straight members connected to each other to form a continuous surface of small triangles. It was invented by Buckminster Fuller in the 1950s. >> Fuller, Buckminster

geodesy [jee**od**esee] A branch of science concerned with the size and shape of the Earth, its gravitational field, and the location of fixed points. Geodesic surveying, unlike plane surveying, takes into account the Earth's curvature.

Geoffrey of Monmouth (c.1100–54) Welsh chronicler, consecrated Bishop of St Asaph in 1152. His *Historia regum Britanniae* (History of the Kings of Britain), composed before 1147, introduced the stories of King Lear and Cymbeline, the prophecies of Merlin, and the legend of Arthur in the form we know. >> Arthur; Cymbeline; Lear

geography The study of the nature of the physical and human environments. It is often divided broadly into **physical geography**, which concerns the Earth's physical environment, and **human geography**, the study of people and their activities. It can be divided into a number of specialist disciplines: for example, **geomorphology**, the scientific study of the origin and development of landforms; **population geography**, concerned with the composition, distribution, growth, and migration of populations; and **resource geography**, the study of the location and exploitation of natural resources. >> biogeography; demography; ecology; geology; geomorphology; palaeogeography; phytogeography; zoogeography

geological time scale Divisions and subdivisions of geological time, based on the relative ages of rocks determined using the methods of stratigraphy. Correlations between rocks of the same age are made from a study of the sedimentary sequences and the characteristic fossils they contain. The major divisions are termed *eons* (or *aeons*) which are further subdivided into *eras*, *periods*, and *epochs*. >> geochronology; stratigraphy; RR976

geology The science of the Earth as a whole: its origin, structure, composition, processes, and history. Geology is applied to the exploration for mineral and oil deposits in the Earth. >> earth sciences; geochemistry; geological time scale; geomorphology; geophysics; mineralogy; petrology; stratigraphy; tectonics

geomagnetic field The magnetic field of the Earth which arises from the metallic core, and which may be regarded as produced by a magnetic dipole pointing towards the geomagnetic N and S Poles. Local anomalies in the magnetic field are due to variations in the nature and structure of the rocks in the crust. >> magnetic poles

geomancy [**gee**ohmansee] The study of 'earth mysteries', originally a means of divination by scattering earth on a surface and analyzing the resulting patterns. The notion now extends to studying how the Earth's own energy affects daily life. >> divination

geometric sequence A sequence in which the ratio of any one term to the next is constant; sometimes called a **geometric progression**. The terms 1,2,4,8 form a geometric sequence; 1 + 2 + 4 + 8 is a **geometric series**. >> arithmetic sequence

geometrid moth A moth, small to medium-sized, often with large and cryptically coloured wings; c.20 000 species, including many serious pests. (Order: Lepidoptera. Family: Geometridae.) >> caterpillar; moth

geometries, non-Euclidean Geometries developed by varying Euclid's fifth axiom, as stated by the British mathematician John Playfair (1748–1819), 'Through any one point there can be drawn one and only one straight line parallel to a given straight line'. Variations on this took either the form 'Through any one point can be drawn more than one straight line parallel to a given straight line' or 'Through any one point can be drawn no straight line parallel to a given straight line'. The first form was called **hyperbolic geometry**, the second **elliptic geometry**. There are other non-Euclidean geometries. >> Euclid; geometry

geometry The branch of mathematics which studies the properties of shapes and space, originally (as its name suggests) of the Earth. The Greeks from c.300 BC developed geometry on a logical basis, many of the early results being collected in Euclid's *Elements*. In the past 200 years, abstract geometries have been developed, notably by Gauss and Lobachevski. >> analytic geometry; Euclid; Gauss; geometries, non-Euclidean; Lobachevski; triangle (mathematics)

geomorphology A branch of geology (or geography) which studies and interprets landforms and the processes of erosion and deposition which form the surface of the Earth and other planets. >> erosion; geography; geology

geopathic stress [geeoh**pa**thik] A term which covers all forms of naturally occurring environmental stress, but most often applied to the adverse effects which result from electromagnetic fields and other forms of radiation, including radon gas. Environmental factors contributing to geopathic stress may include ley lines, artificial structures such as power lines, and sun spots which disturb the Earth's magnetic field. >> electropollution; ley lines

geophagy [jee**o**fajee] >> **pica**

geophysics A broad branch of geology which deals with the physical properties of Earth materials and the physical processes that determine the structure of the Earth as a whole. Major subjects include seismology, geomagnetism, and meteorology, as well as the study of large-scale processes of heat and mass transfer in the Earth and variations in the Earth's gravitational field. >> geology; geomagnetic field; meteorology; seismology

George I (1660–1727) King of Great Britain and Ireland (1714–27), born in Osnabrück, Germany, the great-grandson of James I of England. Elector of Hanover from 1698, he took relatively little part in the government of Britain, living in Hanover as much as possible.

George II (1683–1760) King of Great Britain and Ireland (1727–60), and Elector of Hanover, born at Herrenhausen, Hanover, the son of George I. In 1705 he married Caroline of Ansbach (1683–1737). In the War of the Austrian Succession, he was present at the Battle of Dettingen (1743), the last occasion on which a British sovereign commanded an army in the field. >> Austrian Succession, War of the; Walpole, Robert

George III (1738–1820) King of Great Britain and Ireland (1760–1820), Elector (1760–1815) and King (from 1815) of Hanover, born in London, who succeeded his grandfather, George II. Eager to govern as well as reign, he caused considerable friction. With Lord North he shared in the blame for the loss of the American colonies. In 1810 he suffered a recurrence of a mental derangement, and the Prince of Wales was made regent. >> American Revolution; North, Frederick

George IV (1762–1830) King of Great Britain and Hanover (1820–30), born in London, the eldest son of George III. Rebelling against a strict upbringing, he went through a marriage ceremony with a Roman Catholic, which was not recognized in English law. The marriage was later declared invalid, and in 1795 he married Princess Caroline of Brunswick, whom he tried to divorce when he was king. Her death in 1821 ended a scandal in which the people sympathized with the queen.

George V (1865–1936) King of the United Kingdom (1910–36), born in London, the second son of Edward VII. His reign saw the Union of South Africa (1910), World War 1, the Irish Free State settlement (1922), and the General Strike (1926). His consort, **Mary** (1867–1953), originally **Princess Victoria Mary Augusta Louise Olga Pauline Claudine Agnes of Teck**, was born in London, and married Prince George in 1893. She organized women's war work (1914–18), and continued with many public and philanthropic activities after the death of her husband. They had five sons and one daughter.

George VI (1895–1952) King of the United Kingdom (1936–52), born at Sandringham, Norfolk, the second son of George V. During World War 2 he continued to reside in bomb-damaged Buckingham Palace, visited all theatres of war, and delivered many broadcasts. His wife, **Elizabeth** (1900–), was born **Lady Elizabeth Angela Marguerite Bowes-Lyon** at Waldenbury, Hertfordshire. They had two children: Princess Elizabeth (later Queen Elizabeth II) and Princess Margaret. During the War she paid many visits to hospitals, civil defence centres, and women's organizations. In her later years, she continued to undertake a heavy programme of royal engagements. >> Elizabeth II; Margaret, Princess

George, St (early 4 th-c) Patron of chivalry, and guardian saint of England and Portugal. His name was early obscured by fable, such as the story of his fight with a dragon to rescue a maiden. Feast day 23 April.

George, David Lloyd >> **Lloyd-George, David**

George-Brown, Baron, originally **George (Alfred) Brown** (1914–85) British Labour politician, born in London. As secretary of state for economic affairs (1964–6), he instigated a prices and incomes policy, and later became foreign secretary (1966–8). >> Labour Party; prices and incomes policy

George Cross (GC) In the UK, a decoration bestowed on civilians for acts of great heroism or conspicuous bravery, or on members of the armed forces for actions in which purely military honours are not normally granted. It was instituted in 1940 and named after George VI.

George Medal (GM) In the UK, the second highest award which may be bestowed on civilians for acts of bravery; instituted in 1940 by George VI. The ribbon is scarlet with five narrow blue stripes.

George Town (Cayman I) 19°20N 81°23W, pop (1995e) 16 000. Capital of the Cayman Is, W Caribbean, on Grand Cayman I; airport nearby. >> Cayman Islands

George Town (Malaysia) >> **Pinang** (city)

Georgetown 6°46N 58°10W, pop (1995e) 150 000. Port capital of Guyana; founded, 1781; airport; airfield; railway; university (1963); cathedral (1887). >> Guyana [i]

Georgia (republic), official name **Republic of Georgia**, Georgian **Sakartvelos Respublika** pop (1995e) 5 481 000; area 69 700 sq km/26 900 sq mi. Republic in C and W Transcaucasia; capital, Tbilisi; timezone GMT +4; major ethnic groups, Georgian (69%), Armenian (9%), Russian (7%), Azerbaijani (5%), Ossetian (3%), Abkhazian (2%); languages, Georgian (official), Russian; religion, Georgian Church, independent of Russian Orthodox Church since 1917; currency, the lari; mountainous country, containing the Greater Caucasus (N) and Lesser Caucasus (S); highest point in the republic, Mt Shkhara (5203 m/17 070 ft); chief rivers, the Kura and Rioni; c.39% forested; Greater Caucasus borders temperate and subtropical climatic zones; average temperatures 1–3°C (Jan), 25°C (Jul) in E Transcaucasia; humid, subtropical climate with mild winters in W; Mediterranean climate in N Black Sea region; under tsarist rule from 1801; proclaimed a Soviet Socialist Republic, 1921; made a constituent republic, 1936; declaration of independence, 1991; declarations of secession by South Ossetia (1991) and of independence by Abkhazia (1992) led to military conflict; civil war, 1992; joined Commonwealth of Independent states, 1993; Abkhazia ceasefire and proposed federal status, 1994; new constitution, 1995; governed by a president, Council of Ministers, and Supreme Soviet; manganese, coal, iron and steel, oil refining, chemicals, machines, textiles, food processing, tea, tobacco, fruit; Kakhetia region famed for its orchards and wines. >> Caucasus Mountains; CIS; Transcaucasia; RR1009 political leaders

Georgia (USA) pop (1995e) 7 184 000; area 152 571 sq km/58 910 sq mi. State in SE USA; the 'Empire State of the South' or the 'Peach State'; discovered by the Spanish; settled as a British colony, 1733; named after George II; the fourth of the original 13 states (first Southern state) to ratify the Constitution, 1788; seceded from the Union, 1861; suffered much damage in the Civil War (especially during General Sherman's March to the Sea, 1864); slavery abolished 1865; last state to be re-admitted, 1870; highest point, Mt Brasstown Bald (1457 m/4780 ft); low coastal plain in the S, heavily forested; fertile Piedmont plateau, Appalachian plateau, and Blue Ridge Mts in the N; capital, Atlanta; many local paper mills in the S; leads the nation in production of pulp; major cotton textile producer; grows nearly half US crop of peanuts. >> American Civil War; Atlanta; Stone Mountain Memorial; United States of America [i]; RR994

Georgian Style English architecture of the period 1714–1830. The name is derived from the kings George I, II, III, and IV of that period. The style is characterized by a restrained use of classical elements in low relief on the exterior, and more elaborately decorated interiors.

geosynchronous Earth orbit A spacecraft orbit about the Earth's Equator, where the period of the orbit matches the Earth's day and causes the spacecraft to appear stationary at the longitude in question; orbit altitude is 36 000 km/22 500 mi. The orbit is ideally suited for communications satellites. >> launch vehicle [i]; low Earth orbit

geothermal energy Energy extracted in the form of heat from the Earth's crust, arising from a combination of the slow cooling of the Earth since its formation, and heat released from natural radioactive decay. Geologically active regions such as plate margins have higher heat flow values and result in hot springs and geysers. >> energy; geyser; hot spring

geranium The name used for two related plant genera: the **cranesbills** (Genus: *Geranium*) and the geraniums of horticulture, the **pelargoniums** (Genus: *Pelargonium*). >> cranesbill; pelargonium

Gérard, François (Pascal Simon), Baron [zhayrah(r)] (1770–1837) Painter, born in Rome. His portrait of Isabey the miniaturist (1796) and his 'Cupid and Psyche' (1798), both in the Louvre, established his reputation. He later painted several historical subjects, such as the 'Battle of Austerlitz' (1808, Versailles).

gerbil A type of mouse, native to Africa, Middle East, and C Asia; long hind legs and long furry tail; inhabits dry open country; digs burrows; one species, the **Mongolian gerbil** (*Meriones unguiculatus*) is a popular pet; also known as **jird**. (Subfamily: Gerbillinae, 81 species.) >> mouse (zoology)

Gere, Richard [geer] (1949–) Actor, born in Philadelphia, PA. After some years in theatre, he made his screen debut in 1975, and went on to star in such films as *Yanks* (1979), *American Gigolo* (1980), *Pretty Woman* (1990), *First Knight* (1995), and *Primal Fear* (1996).

gerenuk [**ge**renuk] An E African gazelle (*Litocranius walleri*); pale brown; slender, with long neck and small head; male with thick horns (usually curling forward at tips); also known as **giraffe antelope**. >> gazelle [i]

geriatrics The study of the health needs of the aged and their provision. The numbers of elderly persons have increased in recent years in most Western societies, making increasing demands on specialized health and social services, such as district nurses, home helps, meals on wheels, and health visitors. The branch of medicine which investigates the process and problems of aging is known as **gerontology**. >> medicine

Géricault, (Jean Louis André) Théodore [zhayreekoh] (1791–1824) Painter, born in Rouen, France. He painted many unorthodox and realistic scenes, notably 'The Raft of the Medusa' (1819, Louvre), as well as racing scenes and landscapes.

German, Sir Edward, originally **Edward German Jones** (1862–1936) Composer, born in Whitchurch, Shropshire. In 1901 he emerged as a light opera composer, completing Sullivan's *The Emerald Isle* after the composer's death, and writing *Merrie England* (1902). He also wrote two symphonies, orchestral suites, chamber music, and songs.

German >> **Germanic languages**

germander An annual or perennial, sometimes shrubby,

found almost everywhere; flowers greenish, pink, or purple with spreading 5-lobed lower lip, upper lip absent. (Genus: *Teucrium*, 300 species. Family: Labiatae.)

Germanic languages A branch of Indo-European comprising the **North Germanic** Scandinavian languages in N Europe, and the **West Germanic** languages English, Frisian, German, and Dutch (with its colonial variant Afrikaans in South Africa) in the W. Scandinavian inscriptions in the runic alphabet date from the 3rd-c AD. Old English and Old High German, precursors of modern English and German, are evidenced from the 8th-c, and the Scandinavian languages from the 12th-c. **East Germanic** languages are extinct, though there are manuscript remains of Gothic. >> Afrikaans; Dutch; English; family of languages; Indo-European / Scandinavian languages; Old English

Germanicus [jer**man**ikus], in full **Gaius Germanicus Caesar** (15 BC–AD 19) The son, father, and brother of Roman emperors (Tiberius, Caligula, and Claudius respectively), and heir apparent himself from AD 14. His sudden and suspicious death in Antioch marked a turning point in Tiberius's reign. >> Agrippina the Elder; Caligula; Claudius; Tiberius

germanium [jer**mayn**ium] Ge, element 32, melting point 937°C. A metalloid found in composite ores, especially with silver and zinc. It is extracted from other metals as $GeCl_4$, which boils at c.80°C. Its main use is in transistor manufacture. >> chemical elements; metalloids; transistor; RR1036

German measles A highly infectious disease of virological origin that affects older children and young adults, also called **rubella**. Although a trivial short-lived illness, its importance lies in the fact that a woman who develops the infection in the first 18 weeks of pregnancy is likely to have a child with a congenital abnormality. A vaccine to prevent the disease is now available, and is given to schoolgirls. >> measles; vaccination; virus

German shepherd A breed of large dog developed in Germany in the late 19th-c by crossing spitz breeds with local sheepdogs; thick coat; long pointed muzzle and ears; trains well; also known as **alsatian**. >> dog; sheepdog; spitz

Germany, Ger **Deutschland**, official name **Federal Republic of Germany**, Ger **Bundesrepublik Deutschland** pop (1995e) 82 235 000; area 357 868 sq km/138 136 sq mi. European state formed by the political unification of West and East Germany (3 Oct 1990); capital, Berlin; most populous state in W Europe; timezone GMT +1; population mainly Germanic, with several minorities; chief religion, Christianity, 43% Roman Catholic, 42% Lutheran; unit of currency, the deutschmark of 100 pfennig; new public holiday, Day of German Unity (3 Oct); lowland plains rise SW through C uplands and Alpine foothills to the Bavarian Alps; highest peak, the Zugspitze (2962 m/9718 ft); C uplands include the Rhenish Slate Mts, Black Forest, and Harz Mts; Rhine crosses the country S–N; complex canal system links chief rivers; oceanic influences strongest in NW; elsewhere a continental climate; ancient Germanic tribes united in 8th-c within the Frankish Empire of Charlemagne; elective monarchy after 918 under Otto I, with Holy Roman Empire divided into several hundred states; after Congress of Vienna, 1814–15, a confederation of 39 states under Austria; under Bismarck, Prussia succeeded Austria as the leading German power; union of Germany and foundation of the second Reich, 1871, with King of Prussia as hereditary German Emperor; aggressive foreign policy, eventually leading to World War 1; after German defeat, second Reich replaced by democratic Weimar Republic; political power passed to the Nazi Party in 1920s; Hitler dictator of the totalitarian Third Reich, 1933; acts of aggression led to World War 2 and a second defeat for Germany, with collapse of the German political regime; partition of Germany, 1945, with occupation of the West by the UK, USA, France, and USSR. Former **West Germany**, official name **Federal Republic of Germany** pop (1990) 62 679 035; area 249 535 sq km/96 320 sq mi, including West Berlin; established in 1949; federal system of government, built around 10 provinces (*Länder*) with considerable powers; two-chamber legislature, consisting of a Federal Diet (*Bundestag*) and Federal Council (*Bundesrat*). Former **East Germany**, official name **German Democratic Republic** pop (1990) 16 433 796; area 108 333 sq mi; administered by USSR after 1945 partition, and Soviet model of government established, 1949; anti-Soviet demonstrations put down, 1953; recognized by USSR as an independent republic, 1954; flow of refugees to West Germany continued until 1961, largely stopped by the Berlin Wall; governed by the People's Chamber, a single-chamber parliament (*Volkskammer*) which elected a Council of State, Coucil of Ministers, and National Defence Council; movement for democratic reform culminated (Nov 1989) in the opening of the Wall and other border crossings to the West, and a more open government policy; free elections (Mar 1990) paved the way for a currency union with West Germany (Jul) and full political unification (Oct). **United Germany** The 10 provinces of West Germany, joined by the five former East German provinces abolished after World War 2 (Brandenburg, Mecklenburg-West Pomerania, Saxony, Saxony-Anhalt, Thuringia), along with unified Berlin; West German electoral system adopted in East Germany; first national elections (Dec 1990); governed by a president (head of state), chancellor (head of government), and 2-chamber parliament (the *Bundesrat* and *Bundestag*); now the world's fourth greatest economy; accounts for 30% of European Union output; substantial heavy industry in NW, and wide range of manufacturing industries, especially in the W; wine in Rhine and Moselle valleys; increasing tourism, especially in the

S; much less development in the E, after the period of socialist economy; following unification, a major socio-economic division emerged between West and East, leading to demonstrations in the E provinces in 1991. >> Berlin; Bismarck; Bonn; Brandenburg; Bundestag; Charlemagne; European Union; German Art / Confederation; Hitler; Holy Roman Empire; Kohl; Mittelland Canals; Nazi Party; Pomerania; Prussia; Reich; Saxony; Thuringia; Weimar Republic; World War 2; RR1009 political leaders

germ-line therapy An attempt to insert a gene into sex cells. In contrast to somatic cell gene therapy, success in this task would alter the inheritance of genetically derived disorders in offspring. As in the case of gene therapy, the procedure remains experimental. >> gene therapy

Geronimo [je**ro**nimoh], Indian name **Goyathlay** (1829–1909) Chiricahua Apache Indian, born in Mexico. The best known of all Apaches, he forcibly resisted the internment of his people on a reservation, escaping from white control on several occasions.

gerontology >> **geriatrics**

Gershwin, George, originally **Jacob Gershvin** (1898–1937) Composer, born in New York City. In 1924 he began collaborating with his brother **Ira** (1896–1983) as lyricist, producing numerous classic songs, such as 'Lady Be Good' (1924) and 'I Got Rhythm' (1930). He also composed extended concert works including *Rhapsody in Blue* (1924), *An American in Paris* (1928), and the opera *Porgy and Bess* (1935).

Gestapo [ge**shtah**poh] An abbreviation of *Geheime Staatspolizei*, the political police of the German Third Reich, founded in 1933 by Göring. From 1936 it came under the control of Himmler, as head of the SS. >> Goering; Himmler; SS

Gethsemane [geth**sem**anee] A place outside Jerusalem near the Mt of Olives where Jesus and his disciples went to pray immediately before his betrayal and arrest (*Mark* 14.32ff); described as a 'garden' in *John* 18.1. >> Jesus Christ; Olives, Mount of

Getty, J(ean) Paul (1892–1976) Oil executive, multi-millionaire, and art collector, born in Minneapolis, MN. He entered the oil business and went on to control more than 100 companies, becoming one of the richest men in the world. He founded the J Paul Getty Museum at Malibu, CA, in 1954.

Gettysburg, Battle of (Jun–Jul 1863) A major series of engagements in the American Civil War between the army of N Virginia (Confederate) and the army of the Potomac (Union). Union victory ended any prospect of foreign recognition for the Confederacy. >> American Civil War

Gettysburg Address (19 Nov 1863) During the American Civil War, a speech given by President Lincoln at the dedication of a war cemetery in Pennsylvania on the site of the Battle of Gettysburg. >> Gettysburg, Battle of; Lincoln, Abraham

geyser [**gee**zer, **giy**zer] A natural spring which erupts intermittently, throwing up fountains of superheated water and steam from a crack deep in the Earth's crust. Geysers occur in volcanically active areas in New Zealand, Iceland, and the USA. >> geothermal energy; hot spring

Ggantija Temples [jan**tee**ja] A Copper Age temple complex on Gozo, NW Malta; a world heritage site. The two temples, built 3600–3300 BC, were excavated in 1827. >> Gozo; Three Age System

Ghana [**gah**na], official name **Republic of Ghana** pop (1995e) 17 086 000; area 238 537 sq km/92 100 sq mi. Republic of W Africa; capital, Accra; timezone GMT; c.75 tribal groups, including Akan (44%), Mossi (16%), Ewe (13%), and Ga (8%); chief religions, Christianity (43%), local beliefs (38%), Islam (12%); official language, English, with several

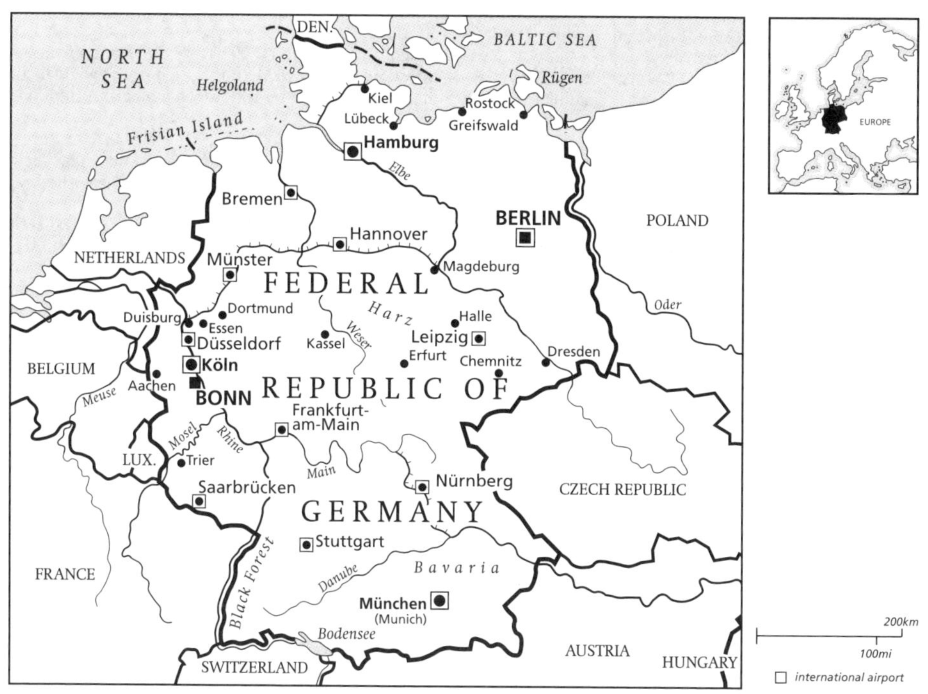

African languages spoken; unit of currency, the cedi of 100 pesewas; low-lying plains inland, leading to the Ashanti plateau (W) and R Volta basin (E), dammed to form L Volta; mountains rise (E) to 885 m/2903 ft at Afadjado; tropical climate, including a warm dry coastal belt (SE), a hot humid SW corner, and a hot dry savannah (N); visited by Europeans in 15th-c; centre of slave trade, 18th-c; modern state created by union of two former British territories, British Gold Coast (Crown Colony, 1874) and British Togoland, becoming the first British colony in Africa to achieve independence, 1957; series of military coups (1966, 1972, 1979, 1982), with the creation of a Provisional National Defence Council; new multi-party constitution, 1992; governed by a president, single-chamber parliament, and Council of State; mainly agricultural; cocoa (world's leading producer) provides two-thirds of export revenue; 40 forts and castles built along the coast from the late 15th-c onwards have been designated world heritage sites. >> Accra; Volta, River; RR1009 political leaders

gharial [**gair**ial] or **gavial** A rare S Asian crocodile-like reptile (*Gavialis gangeticus*) of family Gavialidae; length up to 6·6 m/21½ ft; very narrow snout; nostrils of male swollen as a bulbous 'pot'. >> alligator ℹ; crocodile; reptile

Ghats [gahts] Two mountain ranges in India; **Eastern Ghats** runs parallel to the Bay of Bengal, forming the E edge of the Deccan Plateau; **Western Ghats** runs parallel to the Arabian Sea, forming the W boundary of the Deccan plateau; length c.1600 km/1000 mi; highest point, Anai Mudi Peak (2695 m/8842 ft) in the Cardamon Hills. >> Deccan; India ℹ

ghee [gee] An edible fat derived from butter by removing all or most of the water. It is popular in hot climates, where the absence of water improves the keeping quality of the butter-fat. >> butter

Ghent [gent], Flemish **Gent**, Fr **Gand** 51°02N 3°42E, pop (1995e) 233 000. River port in NW Belgium, at the confluence of the Scheldt and Leie Rivers; third largest urban region in Belgium; focus of Flemish nationality; railway; university (1816); cathedral (begun 10th-c). >> Belgium ℹ

gherkin A variety of cucumber (*Cucumis sativa*) or its very small fruits. (Family: Cucurbitaceae.) >> cucumber

Ghibellines [**gib**eleenz] The pro-imperial party in Italian cities of the 13th–14th-c, favouring the involvement of the Holy Roman Emperor in Italian politics. >> Guelphs; Holy Roman Empire

Ghiberti, Lorenzo [gee**bair**tee] (1378–1455) Goldsmith, bronze-caster, and sculptor, born in Florence, Italy. In 1401 he won the competition to make a pair of bronze gates for the Baptistry of Florence Cathedral.

Ghirlandaio, Domenico [geerlan**dah**yoh], originally **Domenico di Tommaso Bigordi** (1449–94) Painter, born in Florence, Italy. His main works were frescoes, notably a series illustrating the lives of the Virgin and the Baptist in the choir of Santa Maria Novella, Florence (1490). >> fresco

Giacometti, Alberto [jiako**me**tee] (1901–66) Sculptor and painter, born in Stampa, Switzerland. He joined the Surrealists in 1930, producing many abstract constructions of a symbolic kind, arriving finally at the characteristic 'thin man' bronzes, such as 'Pointing Man' (1947, Tate, London). >> Surrealism

Giant's Causeway 55°14N 6°30W. Volcanic basalt formation on the N coast of Co Antrim, Northern Ireland; a world heritage site; according to legend, the causeway was built for giants to travel across to Scotland. >> basalt; Northern Ireland ℹ

giardiasis [jeeah(r)**diy**asis] The infestation of the intestinal tract of vertebrates with the parasite *Giardia lamblia*,

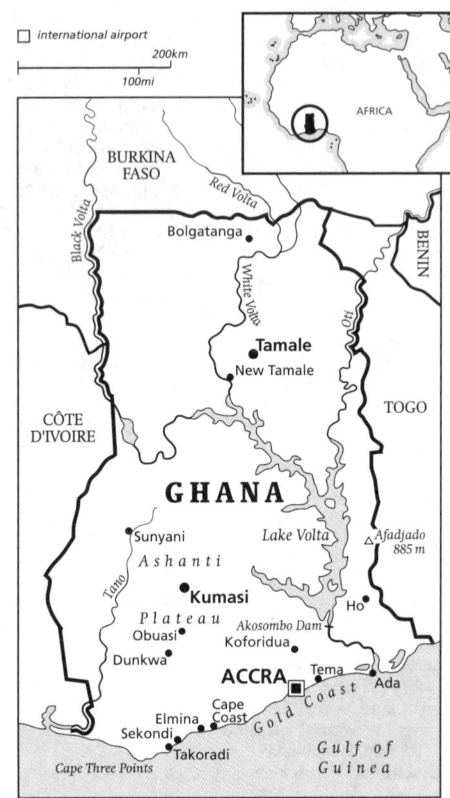

which can cause severe diarrhoea. It is one of the few infections which can be transmitted from people to animals. It is named after the French biologist Alfred Giard (1846–1908).

Gibbon, Edward (1737–94) Historian, born in Putney, Surrey. After a visit to Rome in 1764 he began his major work, *The History of the Decline and Fall of the Roman Empire* (5 vols, 1776–88).

Gibbon, Lewis Grassic, pseudonym of **James Leslie Mitchell** (1901–35) Writer, born in Auchterless, Aberdeenshire. He published the historical novels *Three Go Back* (1932) and *Spartacus* (1933) under his own name, but the trilogy *A Scots Quair* (1946) appeared under his pseudonym.

gibbon An ape native to rainforests of SE Asia; acrobatic; slender with small head; thumb small; fingers long; arms as long as body and legs together; also known as **lesser ape**. (Genus: *Hylobates*, 6 species.) >> ape; siamang

Gibbons, Grinling (1648–1721) Sculptor and woodcarver, born in Rotterdam, The Netherlands. At Chatsworth, Burghley, and other mansions he executed an immense quantity of carved fruit and flowers, cherubs' heads, and other typical Baroque embellishment. >> Baroque (art and architecture)

Gibbons, Orlando (1583–1625) Composer, born in Oxford, Oxfordshire. His compositions include services, anthems, and madrigals (notably 'The Silver Swan'), and also hymns, fantasies for viols, and music for virginals.

Gibbons, Stella (Dorothea) (1902–89) Writer, born in London. Her *Cold Comfort Farm* (1932), a light-hearted satire on melodramatic rural novels, has established itself as a classic of parody.

Gibbs, J(osiah) Willard (1839–1903) Mathematician and physicist, born in New Haven, CT. The field of chemical thermodynamics developed largely from his work, and he was a founder of physical chemistry. >> thermodynamics

Gibraltar [jib**rawl**ter], Span [kheevral**tahr**], Arabic **Jebel Tariq** 36°09N 5°21W; pop (1995e) 30 700; area 6·5 sq km/2·5 sq mi. British Crown Colony; a narrow rocky peninsula rising steeply from the low-lying coast of SW Spain at the E end of the Strait of Gibraltar; length, c.5 km/3 mi; width 1·2 km/$\frac{3}{4}$ mi, narrowing to the S; 8 km/5 mi from Algeciras; timezone GMT +1; official language, English, with Spanish widely spoken; British currency and local banknotes used; limestone massif, 'The Rock', height 426 m/1398 ft, connected to the Spanish mainland by a sandy plain; home of the Barbary apes, the only native monkeys in Europe; settled by Moors, 711; taken by Spain, 1462; ceded to Britain, 1713; Crown Colony, 1830; played a key role in Allied naval operations during both World Wars; proposal to end British rule defeated by referendum, 1967; Spanish closure of frontier, 1969–85; Spain continues to claim sovereignty; British monarch represented by a governor and House of Assembly; military base; important strategic point of control for the W Mediterranean; economy largely dependent on the presence of British forces; airport; car ferries to Tangier. >> Gibraltar, Strait of; Mediterranean Sea; Spain ℹ

Gibraltar, Strait of, Arabic **Bab al Zakak**, Lat **Fretum Herculeum** Channel connecting the Mediterranean Sea to the Atlantic Ocean; length, 60 km/37 mi; width between the Rock of Gibraltar and Cape Ceuta (the Pillars of Hercules), 24 km/15 mi; widest point, 40 km/25 mi; narrowest point, 15 km/9 mi. >> Gibraltar

Gibson, Guy (Penrose) (1918–44) British wing commander in the RAF. He led the famous 'Dambusters' raid on the Möhne and Eder Dams in 1943, an exploit for which he received the VC. >> World War 2

Gibson, Mel, originally **Columcille Gerard Gibson** (1956–) Film actor, born in Peekskill, NY. He made his film debut in Australia in 1977, and became known following his role in the action-packed *Mad Max* films (1979, 1981, 1985). Later films include *Lethal Weapon* (1987) and its sequels (1989, 1992, 1998), *Hamlet* (1990), and *Braveheart*, which he also directed (1995, Oscar Best Film).

Gibson Desert Central belt of the Western Australian Desert; area c.220 000 sq km/85 000 sq mi. >> Western Australia

Gide, André (Paul Guillaume) [zheed] (1869–1951) Writer, born in Paris. Among his best-known works are *Les Nourritures terrestres* (1897, Fruits of the Earth) and *Les Faux Monnayeurs* (1926, The Counterfeiters), as well as his *Journal*. He received the Nobel Prize for Literature in 1947.

Gideons International An international organization, which began in Wisconsin in 1898, with the aim of spreading the Christian faith by the free distribution of copies of the Bible to public places. It is named after the Biblical judge, Gideon, who led Israel against the Midianites. >> Bible; Midianites

Gielgud, Sir (Arthur) John [**geel**gud] (1904–) Actor and director, born in London. He established a reputation as Hamlet (1929), and became a leading Shakespearian actor. His film appearances include *Arthur* (1970, Oscar) and *Prospero's Books* (1991). The London *Globe* theatre was renamed after him in 1994.

Gigantes [**jiy**ganteez, gi**gan**teez] In Greek mythology, the sons of Earth and Tartaros, with snake-like legs; their name means 'the giants'. They made war on the Olympian gods, were defeated, and are buried under various volcanic islands. >> Cyclops; Titan (mythology)

Giggs, Ryan (1973–) Footballer, born in Cardiff, S Wales. He made his league debut for Manchester United in 1991, and first played for Wales later that year, becoming the youngest-ever Welsh cap. He has twice been named the Professional Football Association's Young Player of the Year (1991–2).

Gigli, Beniamino [**jeel**yee] (1890–1957) Tenor, born in Recanati, Italy. He won a worldwide reputation as a lyric-dramatic tenor of great vitality, at his best in the works of Verdi and Puccini.

gigue [zheeg] A lively dance, probably of British origin, popular during the 17th–18th-c. It became a standard movement in instrumental suites of the period. >> jig; suite

gila monster [**hee**la] An American lizard of family Helodermatidae; the only venomous lizard; length up to 600 mm/24 in; dark with yellow mottling; bead-like scales; blunt head; fat tail; two species. >> lizard ℹ

Gilbert, Cass (1859–1934) Architect, born in Zanesville, OH. He designed the first tower skyscraper, the 60-storey Woolworth Building in New York City (1912), at that time the tallest building in the world.

Gilbert, William (1544–1603) Physician and physicist, born in Colchester, Essex. He established the magnetic nature of the Earth, and was the first to use the terms 'electricity', 'electric force' and 'electric attraction'. The *gilbert*, unit of magnetomotive power, is named after him. >> electricity; magnetism

Gilbert, Sir W(illiam) S(chwenck) (1836–1911) Parodist, and librettist of the 'Gilbert and Sullivan' light operas, born in London. He wrote much humorous verse under his boyhood nickname 'Bab', collected in 1869 as the *Bab Ballads*. He is remembered for his partnership with Sir Arthur Sullivan, begun in 1871, with whom he wrote 14 popular operas, from *Trial by Jury* (1875) to *The Gondoliers* (1889). >> Sullivan, Arthur

Gilbert and George Avant-garde artists: **Gilbert Proesch** (1943–) and **George Passmore** (1944–). They made their name in the late 1960s as performance artists (the 'singing sculptures'), with faces and hands painted gold, holding their poses for hours at a time.

Gilbert of Sempringham, St (c.1083–1189) Priest, born in Sempringham, Lincolnshire. In 1131 he founded the Order of Gilbertines for monks and nuns, the only mediaeval order to originate in England. He was canonized in 1202; feast day 4 February. >> monasticism

Gilbert Islands pop (1995e) 75 600; area 264 sq km/102 sq mi. Island group of Kiribati, C Pacific Ocean; chain of 17 coral atolls spread over c.680 km/420 mi; part of the British colony of Gilbert and Ellice Is until 1977; capital, Tarawa. >> Kiribati ℹ

Gilchrist, Ellen [**gil**krist] (1935–) Writer, born in Vicksburg, MI. She has written poetry, short stories, and novels, and is known especially for her satirical treatment of the upper-class world of the southern states of the USA. Her novels include *The Annunciation* (1983) and *Net of Jewels* (1993).

gilding The ancient craft of sticking gold (or other metallic) leaf on to a surface, usually wood. Gilding flourished in the Middle Ages in manuscript illumination and panel painting, and later for picture-frames and furniture.

Giles, Bill, popular name of **William George Giles** (1939–) British weatherman, the head of the Weather Centre at the BBC since 1983. He joined the Meteorological Office in 1959, became a radio broadcaster in 1972, and moved to television in 1975. His books include *The Story of Weather* (1990).

Giles, Carl [jiylz] (1916–95) Cartoonist, born in London.

From 1937 he produced his distinctive and popular humorous drawings, first for *Reynolds News*, then (from 1943) for the *Express* newspapers.

Gilgamesh [**gil**gamesh] A Babylonian epic poem, named after its hero, the Sumerian King Gilgamesh (3rd millennium BC). It includes a story of the Flood that has striking parallels with the Biblical account. >> Babylonia; epic; Flood, the

Gill, (Arthur) Eric (Rowton) [gil] (1882–1940) Carver, engraver, and typographer, born in Brighton, East Sussex. Among his main works is 'Prospero and Ariel' (1931) at Broadcasting House, London. >> engraving; typography

Gillespie, Dizzy [gi**les**pee], popular name of **John Birks Gillespie** (1917–93) Jazz trumpeter and composer, born in Cheraw, SC. He worked in prominent swing bands (1937–44), and as a leader, often with Charlie Parker on saxophone, he developed the music called *bebop*, with dissonant harmonies and polyrhythms, a reaction to swing. >> bebop; Parker, Charlie

Gillette, King C(amp) [ji**let**] (1855–1932) Inventor of the safety razor, born in Fond du Lac, WI. He founded his razor blade company in 1903.

Gilliam, Terry [**gil**yam] (1940–) Artist and film director, born in Minneapolis, MI. Originally known for his fantasy animations in television' 'Monty Python's Flying Circus' (1969–74), he went on work in film, directing such imaginative adventures as *The Time Bandits* (1980), *The Adventures of Baron Munchausen* (1988), and *Twelve Monkeys* (1995).

gilliflower >> **stock**

Gillray, James [gil**ray**] (1757–1815) Caricaturist, born in London. He issued about 1500 caricatures of political and social subjects, notably of Napoleon, George III, and leading politicians.

Gilman, Charlotte Anna Perkins, *née* **Perkins**, earlier married name **Stetson** (1860–1935) Feminist and writer, born in Hartford, CT. Her most notable books are *Women and Economics* (1898), *The Home* (1903), and *Man-Made World* (1911). >> feminism

gilt-edged securities The name given to UK government loan stock, considered to be a safe investment. The name derives from the book in which transactions were originally recorded, which was edged in gold. >> consols; stocks

gin A spirit distilled from grain or malt, and flavoured with juniper berries. **Dutch gin** is drunk neat with beer, while **London** or **dry gin** is usually mixed with tonic.

Ginckell or **Ginkel, Godert de** [**ging**kel] (1630–1703) Dutch general, born in Utrecht. He accompanied William III to England in 1688, and fought at the Battle of the Boyne (1690). >> Boyne, Battle of the; William III

ginger A perennial native to SE Asia (*Zingiber officinale*); stem to 1 m/3¼ ft; yellow and purple flowers. The aromatic underground stem contains the essential oil *zingiberene*, used in perfumes as well as food and drink (such as ginger ale). (Family: Zingiberaceae.) >> spice

gingivitis [jinji**viy**tis] Infection of the gums by bacteria in the mouth. It causes redness and bleeding, and the gums retract from the teeth, rendering them unstable. Untreated gingivitis leads ultimately to loss of teeth. >> bacteria ℹ; dentistry

Gingrich, Newt(on Leroy) [**ging**grich] (1943–) US politician, born in Hummelstown, PA. He was elected as Republican representative for Georgia in 1979, and became Speaker of the House in 1995 with the promise of enacting a new conservative agenda. He resigned in November 1998 following the poor performance of his party in the mid-term elections.

ginkgo A deciduous gymnosperm (*Ginkgo biloba*) originally from SW China, but probably no longer existing in the wild; seed with a fleshy outgrowth covering the edible kernel; also called **maidenhair tree**. (Family: Ginkgoaceae.) >> tree ℹ

Ginola, David [zhinola] (1967–) Footballer, born in Gassin, SW France. He played for Paris St Germain, moving to the UK to join Newcastle in 1995, then Tottenham Hotspur in 1997. He had won 15 caps for France, and in 1994 was voted French Footballer of the Year, but he lost his place in the national team after France failed to qualify in the 1994 World Cup. In 1998 he highlighted the international campaign against land mines by visiting an Angolan minefield. He was player of the year (UK) in 1999.

gin rummy >> **rummy**

Ginsberg, Allen (1926–97) Poet, born in Newark, NJ. His first book, *Howl* (1957), presented the prototype poetry of the 'beat' school. His *Collected Poems* were published in 1987. >> beat generation

ginseng Either of two species of thick-rooted perennial (*Panax pseudoginseng, Panax quinquefolium*), native to North America and Asia; 5-petalled, yellowish-green flowers; round, red fruits. The powdered roots are said to have aphrodisiac as well as medicinal and rejuvenative properties. It is popular as a tonic and dietary supplement. (Family: Araliaceae.)

Giorgione [jiaw(r)ji**oh**nay], also called **Giorgio da Castelfranco**, originally **Giorgio Barbarelli** (c.1478–1510) Painter, born in Castelfranco, Italy. A great innovator, he created the small, intimate easel picture and a new treatment of figures in landscape, 'the landscape of mood'. One of his best-known works is 'The Tempest' (c.1505, Venice).

Giotto (di Bondone) [ji**ot**oh] (c.1266–1337) Painter and architect, born near Vespignano, Italy, the founder of the Florentine School of painting. His major work was the fresco cycle, 'The Lives of Christ and the Virgin', in the Arena Chapel, Padua (1305–8). In 1334 he was appointed Master of Works in Florence, designing the campanile. The fresco cycle on the life of St Francis in the Basilica of St Francis in Assisi is also attributed to him; it was severely damaged in an earthquake in 1997. >> fresco

Giotto project [ji**ot**oh] The first European interplanetary spacecraft launched in 1985 from Kourou, French Guiana, to intercept Halley's Comet. It encountered the comet successfully (13 Mar 1986) at a distance of 500 km/300 mi from the active nucleus, protected by a dust shield, and obtained TV images of the nucleus, and measurements of gases and dust. >> comet; European Space Agency

Gipsy >> **Rom**

giraffe An African ruminant mammal (*Giraffa camelopardalis*), the tallest land animal (height, 5·5 m/18 ft); extremely long legs and neck; an artiodactyl; head with 2–5 blunt 'horns'; usually pale with large angular brown blotches; also known as **camel(e)opard**. (Family: Giraffidae.) >> artiodactyl; okapi; ruminant ℹ

giraffe antelope >> **gerenuk**

Giralda [hee**ral**da] A bell tower adjacent to Seville Cathedral, in Spain. Built (1163–84) as an Islamic minaret, the tower is 93 m/305 ft high, and takes its name from the *giraldillo* or weathervane which surmounts it. >> Seville

Giraldus Cambrensis [ji**ral**dus kam**bren**sis], also known as **Gerald of Wales** or **Gerald de Barri** (c.1147–1223) Historian and clergyman, born in Manorbier Castle, Carmarthenshire. He wrote an account of Ireland's natural history and inhabitants, and in 1188 travelled through Wales to recruit soldiers for the Third Crusade, writing up his observations in the *Itinerarium Cambriae* (1191, Itinerary of Wales). >> Crusades ℹ

Giraudoux, (Hippolyte) Jean [zheerohdoo] (1882–1944) Writer and diplomat, born in Bellac, France. He is chiefly remembered for his plays, mainly fantasies based on

Greek myths and biblical lore, such as *Ondine* (1939), and *La Folle de Chaillot* (1945, The Mad Woman of Chaillot).

girl guide / scout >> **scouting**

giro [**jiy**roh] A state-operated low-cost banking system which commenced in the UK in 1968. Now called **Girobank PLC**, it is operated by the Post Office Corporation through its 20 000 post offices, carrying out the normal range of banking services.

Girondins [ji**ron**dinz], Fr [zhirõdĩ] A group of deputies in the Legislative Assembly (1791–2) and French Convention (1792–5). Sympathetic to the provinces rather than to Paris (their name derived from the Gironde region of SW France), many were executed during the Reign of Terror (1793). >> French Revolution ℹ

Girtin, Thomas [**ger**tin] (1775–1802) Landscape painter, born in London. His works were among the first to exploit watercolour as a true medium, as distinct from a tint for colouring drawings. >> landscape painting; watercolour

Gisborne [**giz**baw(r)n] 38°41S 178°02E, pop (1995e) 32 600. Port and resort town in North Island, New Zealand; site of Captain Cook's first landing, 1769; airfield; railway. >> Cook, James; New Zealand ℹ

Giscard d'Estaing, Valéry [zheeskah(r) daystĩ] (1926–) French statesman and president (1974–81), born in Koblenz, Germany. He became finance minister (1962–6), and launched his own Party (National Federation of Independent Republicans). He returned to the finance ministry in 1969, defeated Mitterrand to become president in 1974, and was then beaten by Mitterrand in 1981. >> France ℹ; Mitterrand

Gish, Lillian, originally **Lillian de Guiche** (1893–1993) Actress, born in Springfield, OH. She started in silent films as an extra under D W Griffith in 1912, and became the girl heroine in all his classics from *The Birth of a Nation* (1915) to *Orphans of the Storm* (1922). Her character roles continued into the 1970s.

Gissing, George (Robert) (1857–1903) Novelist, born in Wakefield, West Yorkshire. *Workers in the Dawn* (1880) was the first of over 20 novels largely presenting realistic portraits of poverty and misery. His best-known novel is *New Grub Street* (1891).

gittern A mediaeval musical instrument resembling a lute, but with a shorter neck. It usually had three or four courses of strings played with a plectrum. >> lute; plectrum; string instrument 2 ℹ

Giuffre, Jimmy [**joo**free], popular name of **James Peter Giuffre** (1921–) Jazz musician and composer, born in Dallas, TX. He played clarinet and saxophones with various bands during the 1940s, then specialized in the clarinet, developing a distinctive breathy tone. His compositions include several chamber and ballet pieces, and he was also active in music education.

Giulio Romano [**jool**ioh ro**mah**noh], originally **Giulio Pippi de' Giannuzzi** (c.1499–1546) Painter and architect, born in Rome. He assisted Raphael in several of his later works, and in 1524 went to Mantua, where he protected the city from floods. >> Mannerism; Raphael

Giza [**gee**za], **al-Giza**, **Gizeh**, or **al-Jizah** 30°36N 32°15E, pop (1995e) 2 447 000. Town in N Egypt; on W bank of R Nile, 5 km/3 mi SW of Cairo; railway; Sphinx, and pyramids of Khufu (Cheops), Khafra, and Mankara nearby. >> Egypt ℹ; pyramid; Seven Wonders of the Ancient World; sphinx

glaciation The coverage of the surface of the Earth by glaciers, as well as the erosive action produced by the movement of ice over the land surface. The most extensive period of recent glaciation was in the Pleistocene epoch, when polar ice caps repeatedly advanced and retreated, covering up to 30% of the Earth's surface. >> cirque; drumlins; fjord; glacier; Ice Age; moraine; Pleistocene epoch; till

glacier A body of ice originating from recrystallized snow in cirques in mountain areas and flowing slowly downslope by creep under its own weight (**alpine glaciers**). Huge glaciers on continental plateaux are termed **ice sheets**. >> cirque; glaciation

glaciology The scientific study of ice in all its forms, including its crystal structure and physical properties, as well as glaciers and ice sheets. >> glacier

gladiators In ancient Rome, heavily armed fighting men who fought duels, often to the death, in public. They were usually slaves, prisoners of war, or condemned criminals.

gladiolus A perennial with a large fibrous corm, native to Europe, Asia, and Africa; flower with a short tube and six spreading or hooded segments in a variety of colours, in one-sided spikes. (Genus: *Gladiolus*, 300 species. Family: Iridaceae.)

Gladstone, W(illiam) E(wart) (1809–98) British Liberal statesman and prime minister (1868–74, 1880–5, 1886, 1892–4), born in Liverpool. He was twice Chancellor of the Exchequer (1852–5, 1859–66), and in 1867 became leader of the Liberal Party. Frequently in office until 1894, he succeeded in carrying out a scheme of parliamentary reform which went a long way towards universal male suffrage. In his last two ministries he introduced bills for Irish Home Rule, but both were defeated. >> Liberal Party (UK)

Glamorgan >> **Mid Glamorgan; South Glamorgan; West Glamorgan**

gland A single cell or group of cells secreting specific substances (eg hormones) for use elsewhere in the body. In mammals, most glands are **exocrine**: their secretions are discharged via duct systems into the cavity of a hollow organ (eg the salivary glands), or open directly onto an outer epidermal surface (eg the sweat glands of mammals). Vertebrates and some invertebrates also possess **endocrine glands** (eg the pituitary glands in vertebrates), whose secretions are released directly into the blood stream. >> adrenal / endocrine / parathyroid / pituitary / prostate glands; glandular fever; liver; pancreas; sweat

glanders or **the glanders** A malignant disease of horses, characterized by a swelling of the glands (especially beneath the jaw) and a mucous discharge from the nostrils; fatal and contagious; may be caught by humans. >> gland; horse ℹ

glandular fever A benign but generalized and sometimes prolonged acute infectious disease due to Epstein–Barr virus (EBV), which tends to affect young people. The blood contains characteristic mononuclear cells, and the condition is technically known as **infectious mononucleosis**. There is no specific antiviral remedy. >> gland; ME syndrome; virus

glare >> **Polaroid 1**

Glaser, Donald A(rthur) [**glay**zer] (1926–) Physicist, born in Cleveland, OH. He developed the 'bubble chamber' for observing the paths of atomic particles, for which he received the Nobel Prize for Physics in 1960. >> bubble chamber

Glasgow 55°53N 4°15W, pop (1995e) 672 000. City and local council (as City of Glasgow), W Scotland; on R Clyde; largest city in Scotland; airport; railway; underground; University of Glasgow (1451); Strathclyde University (1964); Glasgow Caledonian University (1992, formerly Glasgow Polytechnic); shipyards, engineering, commerce, whisky blending and bottling, chemicals, textiles, carpets; cathedral (12th-c), Cathcart castle (15th-c), Crookston castle (15th-c), Haggs castle (1585); European City of Culture, 1990. >> Gorbals; Scotland ℹ

glasnost (Russ 'speaking aloud') A term describing the changes in attitude on the part of leaders of the Soviet Union since 1985 under Gorbachev, which brought about a greater degree of openness both within Soviet society and in its relations with foreign powers. >> Gorbachev; perestroika

Glass, Philip (1937–) Composer, born in Baltimore, MD. A proponent of minimalism in music, he attracted public notice with the first of his 12 operas, *Einstein on the Beach* (1976). Later works include *The Hydrogen Jukebox* (1990) and *Orphee* (1993). >> minimalism

glass 1 Any non-crystalline solid; one in which there is no orderly pattern, or arrangement of atoms. It is usually formed by the rapid cooling of a viscous liquid, such that the atoms have insufficient time to align into a crystal structure. >> crystals; metallic glass **2** The transparent or translucent product of the fusion of lime (calcium oxide), soda (sodium carbonate), and silica (silicon(IV) dioxide). There may be other constituents, yielding a great variety of properties. Having no sharp melting point, glass can be formed by many techniques while hot, most being variants on blowing or moulding. The best flat glass is today made by the 'float' process: molten glass flows continuously over a bed of molten tin. >> boron; flint glass; lime (chemistry); silica; *see illustration below*

glass harmonica >> **musical glasses**

glass snake A lizard native to North America, Europe, and Asia; snake-like, with no limbs; length, up to 1·3 m/4¼ ft; tail can be shed to confuse predators, and may break into several pieces; also known as **glass lizard**. (Genus: *Ophisaurus*, several species. Family: Anguidae.) >> lizard ℹ

glasswort An annual herb growing along coasts and in salt marshes more or less everywhere; fleshy, leafless jointed stems, with flowers sunk into stems; also called **marsh samphire**. It was burnt to provide soda for early glass-making. (Genus: *Salicornia*, 35 species. Family: Chenopodiaceae.)

Glauber's salt Hydrated sodium sulphate, $Na_2SO_4.10H_2O$. It is named after the German chemist Johann Rudolph Glauber (1604–70), a follower of Paracelsus. It is a mild laxative, an ingredient of many mineral waters, and was once credited with remarkable medicinal properties. >> Paracelsus

glaucoma [glaw**koh**ma] A rise in the pressure of the aqueous fluid within the eye. Acute glaucoma arises when drainage of this fluid is blocked because of infection or cataract rupture. There is sudden pain in the affected eye, variable interference with vision, and blindness may develop. >> eye ℹ

glaze In oil painting, a transparent layer of paint sometimes mixed with varnish laid over dry underpainting. In pottery it is a thin vitreous coating fused to the surface of a pot by firing. >> oil painting

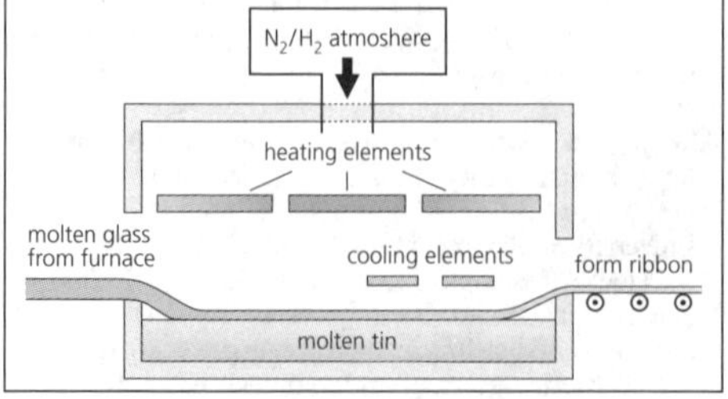

Glass – the float glass process

Glazunov, Alexander (Konstantinovich) [**glaz**unof] (1865–1936) Composer, born in St Petersburg, Russia. Among his compositions are eight symphonies, and works in every branch of music except opera.

Glendower, Owen [glen**dow**er], Welsh **Owain Glyndwr** or **Owain ap Gruffudd** (c.1354–1416) Welsh chief, born in Powys. In 1401 he rebelled against Henry IV, proclaimed himself Prince of Wales, and joined the coalition with Harry Percy Hotspur, who was defeated at the Battle of Shrewsbury (1403). >> Henry IV (of England); Percy

Glenn, John H(erschel) (1921–) Astronaut, the first American to orbit the Earth, born in Cambridge, OH. He became an astronaut in 1959, and in 1962 made a three-orbit flight in the Friendship 7 space capsule. He has been a senator from Ohio since 1975, and sought the Democratic nomination for the presidency in 1984 and 1988. He became the oldest person to travel in space when he joined the 9-day space-shuttle mission in October 1998. >> space exploration; RR970

Glennie, Evelyn (Elizabeth Ann) (1965–) Percussionist and composer, born in Ellon, Aberdeenshire. Although profoundly deaf, she studied at the Royal Academy of Music, London, winning several prizes, and made her debut recital at the Wigmore Hall in 1986. She has since received international recognition as a percussionist, playing with orchestras all over the world.

Glenrothes [glen**roth**is] 56°12N 3°11W, pop (1995e) 35 800. Administrative centre of Fife, E Scotland, designated a new town in 1948; airfield; centre for electronic research. >> Fife; Scotland ℹ

gliadin [**gliy**adin] A simple protein occurring mainly in wheat. An adverse reaction to this protein is a feature of coeliac disease. >> coeliac disease; gluten; protein

glider An aircraft that flies without the aid of mechanical propulsion. The wings may be fixed or flexible, and if the latter, the machine is known as a **hang glider**. The first piloted glider was designed in 1853 by aviator and inventor Sir George Cayley (1773–1857). >> aircraft ℹ; hang glider ℹ

Glinka, Mikhail (Ivanovich) [**gling**ka] (1804–57) Composer, born in Novospasskoye, Russia. His opera *Russlan and Ludmilla* (1842) pioneered the style of the Russian national school of composers.

Global Maritime Distress and Safety System >> **Morse code**

global warming >> **greenhouse effect**

globe artichoke A robust perennial (*Cynara scolymus*) growing to 2 m/6½ ft; leaves up to 80 cm/30 in, deeply divided; flower-heads blue, very large, surrounded by distinctive leathery, oval bracts. The soft receptacle of the young flower-heads and the fleshy bases to the bracts are eaten as a vegetable. (Family: Compositae.) >> bract; Jerusalem artichoke

Globe Theatre A theatre completed in 1599 on Bankside in London. Nearly all of Shakespeare's greatest works were performed here. A project to build a working replica of the theatre on the original site was initiated in 1970 under the direction of US actor and film producer Sam Wanamaker (1919–93), and opened in 1996. In 1989, part of the foundations of the Globe was discovered and designated a scheduled area. >> Shakespeare ℹ

globigerina [globije**riy**na] A type of amoeba-like microscopic organism commonly found in marine plankton. >> foraminiferan

globular cluster A swarm of old stars arranged characteristically as a compact sphere. It contains tens of thousands to millions of stars, formed at the same time. >> star

globulin [**glob**yulin] A simple protein folded into a globular 3-dimensional shape. It is insoluble or only sparingly soluble in water, but soluble in dilute salt solutions. >> gamma globulins; protein

glockenspiel [**glok**enshpeel] A musical instrument consisting of tuned metal bars arranged in two rows like a piano keyboard, and played with small hammers held in each hand. >> keyboard instrument; percussion ℹ

glomerulonephritis [glo**me**rulohne**friy**tis] An inflammation of the glomeruli (part of the kidneys responsible for the initial blood-filtering process) caused by foreign antigens invading the body. In young people it usually resolves in two to three weeks, but in adults may lead to persisting kidney failure. >> kidneys; oedema

Glorious Revolution or **Bloodless Revolution** The name given to the events (Dec 1688–Feb 1689) during which James II fled from England, and William III and Mary II were established by parliament as joint monarchs. The title celebrates the bloodlessness of the event, and the assertion of the constitutional importance of parliament. >> James II (of England); William III

glossolalia The practice of 'speaking in tongues' – uttering sounds whose meaning is unknown to the speaker, who is undergoing a religious experience. It is found in several Christian groups, such as Pentecostalists or charismatic Catholics, and interpreted among its practitioners as a supernatural sign of religious sincerity or conversion. >> Pentecostalism

glottis The narrow part of the larynx at the level of the vocal cords (or vocal folds), which is most directly concerned with the production of sound. >> larynx

Gloucester [**glos**ter], Lat **Glevum**, Celtic **Caer Glou** 51°53N 2°14W, district pop (1995e) 107 000. County town of Gloucestershire, SWC England; founded by Romans 1st-c AD; railway; airfield; cathedral (13th-c). >> Gloucestershire

Gloucester, Richard (Alexander Walter George), Duke of [**glos**ter] (1944–) British prince, the younger son of Henry, Duke of Gloucester (the third son of George V). In 1972 he married **Birgitte van Deurs** (1946–); they have one son, **Alexander, Earl of Ulster** (1974–) and two daughters, **Lady Davina Windsor** (1977–) and **Lady Rose Windsor** (1980–).

Gloucestershire [**glos**tersheer] pop (1995e) 548 000; area 2643 sq km/1020 sq mi. County in SWC England; features include the Cotswold Hills, Forest of Dean; drained by the R Severn; county town, Gloucester. >> Cotswold Hills; England ℹ; Gloucester

glowworm >> **firefly**

gloxinia A member of a Brazilian genus of plants with large, showy, funnel-shaped flowers in a variety of colours; related to the African violet. (Genus: *Siningia*, 20 species. Family: Gesneriaceae.) >> African violet

Glubb, Sir John Bagot, known as **Glubb Pasha** (1897–1986) British soldier, born in Preston, Lancashire. In Transjordan he organized the Arab Legion's Desert Patrol, and became Legion Commandant (1939), gaining immense prestige among the Bedouin.

glucagon [**gloo**kagon] A hormone (a polypeptide) found in vertebrates, synthesized in the pancreas. Its main action is to raise blood glucose levels by promoting the conversion of liver glycogen into glucose. >> glucose; hormones

Gluck, Christoph (Willibald) [glook] (1714–87) Composer, born in Erasbach, Bavaria. In the late 1770s, Paris was divided into those who supported Gluck's French opera style and those supporting the Italian style of Niccolo Piccinni (1728–1800) – the *Gluckists* and Piccinnists. Gluck finally conquered with his *Iphigénie en Tauride* (1779), and retired from Paris full of honour.

glucocorticoids [glookoh**kaw(r)**tikoydz] Steroid hormones synthesized and released from the adrenal cortex of vertebrates, important in carbohydrate metabolism and the resistance of the body to stress. In humans they include *cortisol* (*hydrocortisone*), *corticosterone*, and *cortisone*. >> cortisol; hormones; steroid

glucose $C_6H_{12}O_6$, also called **dextrose**. By far the most common of the six-carbon sugars, the primary product of plant photosynthesis. Starch and cellulose are both condensation polymers of glucose. >> carbon; diabetes mellitus; hyperglycemia; sugars

glue >> **adhesives**

gluon A fundamental particle that carries the strong force between quarks, and binds them together into other subatomic particles; symbol g; mass 0, charge 0, spin 1. >> fundamental particles; quark

gluten The main protein of wheat, subdivided into two other proteins, **gliadin** and **glutenin**. When mixed with water and kneaded, these proteins become aligned along one plane, imparting an elastic property to the dough. The small intestine in some people is abnormally sensitive to gliadin, a condition known as *coeliac disease*. >> coeliac disease; gliadin

glutton >> **wolverine**

glycerides [**gli**seriydz] Esters of glycerol. Glycerol forms three series of ester: mono-, di- and triglycerides. Fats are examples of triglycerides. >> ester ℹ; fat 1; glycerol

glycerine >> **glycerol**

glycerol [**gli**serol] $OHCH_2–CH(OH)–CH_2OH$, IUPAC **1,2,3-trihydroxypropane**, also known as **glycerine**, boiling point 290°C. A colourless, viscous, and sweet-tasting liquid, obtained from all vegetable and animal fats and oils by hydrolysis, and thus a by-product of soap manufacture. >> hydrolysis

glycine [**gliy**seen] $NH_2–CH_2–COOH$, IUPAC **aminoethanoic acid**, melting point 260°C. A colourless solid, freely soluble in water. It is the simplest of the amino acids, found in almost all proteins, and obtainable from them by acid hydrolysis. >> amino acid; hydrolysis

glycogen [**gliy**kojen] $(C_6H_{10}O_5)_n$. A polysaccharide found in both plant and animal tissue as an energy store. It is essentially a condensation polymer of glucose, and very similar to starch. >> glucose; polysaccharides

gnat 1 An alternative name for mosquitoes. >> Culicidae **2** A swarming gnat; a type of small, delicate fly. The males fly in dancing swarms low over water or in woodland clearings. (Order: Diptera. Family: Epididae.) >> Culicidae; fly

Gneisenau, August (Wilhelm Anton), Graf (Count) **Neithardt von** [**gniy**zuhnow] (1760–1831) Prussian general, born in Schildau, Germany. He helped to reorganize the army after its defeat by Napoleon (1807), and in the war of liberation gave distinguished service at Leipzig (1813) and Waterloo (1815). >> Napoleonic Wars

gneiss [niys] A coarse, high-grade metamorphic rock with a banded appearance due to the segregation of light- and dark-coloured minerals. >> metamorphic rock; schist

Gnosticism [**nos**tisizm] (Gr *gnosis*, 'knowledge') A system of belief which became prominent within 2nd-c Christianity. It emphasized salvation through acquiring secret revealed knowledge about cosmic origins and the true destiny of the spirit within people. Gnosticism was considered a heresy by the early Church Fathers. >> Christianity

GNP (gross national product) >> **gross domestic product**

gnu [noo] >> **wildebeest**

go The national game of Japan, first played in China c.1500 BC. It is a tactical game, played on a board divided into 324 squares (18 × 18). Each player has a supply of black or white counters. They take it in turn to fill up the board with the intention of surrounding the opponent's pieces and capturing them. >> chess

Goa [**goh**a] pop (1995e) 1 265 000; area 3496 sq km/1363 sq mi. State in W India; capital, Panaji; taken by

Portugal, 1510; occupied by India, 1961; part of Union territory of Goa, Daman and Diu until 1987; churches and convents are world heritage monuments; burial place of St Francis Xavier; >> Daman and Diu; Francis Xavier, St; India i

goat A mammal of family Bovidae; may be classified as an antelope; tail with naked undersurface; both sexes with horns; males with beard; male called a *billy*, female a *nanny*, young a *kid*; six species in genus *Capra*, including the **bezoar** and **ibex**. >> Angora goat; antelope; Bovidae; markhor; Rocky Mountain goat

goatfish >> **red mullet**

Gobbi, Tito (1915–84) Baritone, born in Bassano del Grappa, Italy. He appeared regularly with the Rome Opera from 1938, and soon made an international reputation, especially in Verdian roles such as Falstaff and Don Carlos. >> Verdi

Gobelins, Manufacture nationale des [gohbuhlĩ] A factory on the Left Bank of the R Seine in Paris. It was established in 1440 by Jean Gobelin as a dye works, and in the 17th-c a number of tapestry workshops were brought together here. >> Paris

Gobi Desert [**goh**bee] Desert in C Asia; area c.1 295 000 sq km/500 000 sq mi, extends c.1600 km/1000 mi E–W across SE Mongolia and N China; on a plateau, altitude 900–1500 m/3000–5000 ft; completely sandy in W. >> China i; desert; Mongolia i

goby [**goh**bee] Any of a large family of mostly small, elongate fishes with stout head, fleshy lips, and large eyes, abundant in coastal waters of tropical to temperate seas; length up to 25 cm/10 in, many less than 5 cm/2 in; pelvic fins joined to form single sucker-like fin. (Family: Gobiidae.) >> fish i

God Supernatural being or power, the object of worship. In some world religions (eg Christianity, Judaism, Islam) there is one God only (*monotheism*), who is transcendent, all-powerful, and related to the cosmos as creator. In other religions (eg Hinduism, Classical Greek and Roman religions, and primitive religions) many gods may be recognized (*polytheism*), with individual gods having particular properties and powers. In the Judaeo-Christian tradition, God is believed to have revealed himself in history through the life and response of the people of Israel, and, in the Christian tradition, in the life, death, and resurrection of Jesus of Nazareth, the Christ. The conviction that Jesus stood in a unique relation to God led to the development in Christian thought of the Trinitarian understanding, whereby the one God is confessed as three persons (Father, Son, and Holy Spirit) of one substance. In the mainstream Western tradition, influenced by Classical Greek philosophy as well as Christianity, God is conceived as 'being itself' or 'pure actuality' (St Thomas Aquinas), in whom there is no unactualized potentiality or becoming; as absolute, infinite, eternal, immutable, incomprehensible (ie unable to be comprehended by human thought), all-powerful (omnipotent), all-wise (omniscient), all-good (omnibenevolent), and everywhere present (omnipresent). From the time of the ancient Greeks, philosophers have tried to prove the existence of God by reason alone (ie not by divine revelation). While the philosophical consensus seems now to be that none of these arguments is coercive, discussion in the 20th-c of the matter has continued unabated. Attempts to disprove the existence of God or to show concepts of God to be incoherent have been likewise generally unpersuasive. >> deism; Islam; Jesus Christ; monotheism; pantheism; polytheism; religion; Trinity

Godard, Jean-Luc [gohdah(r)] (1930–) Film director, born in Paris. His first major film *A bout de souffle* (1960, Breathless) established him as one of the leaders of *Nouvelle Vague* cinema. His prolific output has included *Weekend* (1968), *Detective* (1984), and *Je vous salue, Marie* (1985, Hail Mary). >> Nouvelle Vague

Goddard, Robert H(utchings) (1882–1945) Physicist and rocketry pioneer, born in Worcester, MA. He elaborated the theory of rocketry, developing the first successful liquid-fuelled rocket, launched in 1926. >> rocket; Tsiolkovsky

Gödel or **Goedel, Kurt** [**goe**dl] (1906–78) Logician, born in Brno, Czech Republic. He showed in 1931 that any formal logical system adequate for number theory must contain propositions not provable in that system (**Gödel's proof**). >> logic; number theory

Godfrey of Bouillon [booeeyõ] (c.1061–1100) Duke of Lower Lorraine (1089–95), born in Baisy, Belgium. He was elected one of the principal commanders of the First Crusade, and later became its chief leader. After the capture of Jerusalem (1099) he was proclaimed king, but he refused the crown, accepting only the title Defender of the Holy Sepulchre. >> Crusades i

Godiva, Lady [go**diy**va] (11th-c) An English lady and religious benefactress, who, according to tradition, rode naked through the market-place at Coventry, in order to obtain the remission of a heavy tax imposed by her husband, Leofric, upon the townsfolk (1040).

Godolphin, Sidney Godolphin, 1st Earl of [go**dol**fin] (1645–1712) English statesman, born near Helston, Cornwall. He held various treasury positions under William III and Queen Anne, and his able management of the finances helped Marlborough in the War of the Spanish Succession (1701–13). >> Anne; William III

Godoy, Manuel de [go**thoy**] (1767–1851) Spanish court favourite and chief minister (1792–1808) under Charles IV. He achieved dictatorial power at the age of 25 through the favour of the Queen, Maria Luisa, and in 1795 assumed the title 'Prince of the Peace'. In 1796 he allied with France against England – a move which contributed to Spain losing her American Empire. >> French Revolutionary Wars

godparents In Christianity, those who act as sponsors for a child at its baptism or christening and who thereafter assume some sort of moral guardianship over the child. They are usually one or two persons of the same sex and one of the opposite. This duty is now often a simple formality; however, in S Europe and Latin America the institution is still used to create important social ties among adults. >> baptism

Godthåb or **Godthaab** [**got**hop] Eskimo **Nûk** or **Nuuk** 64°11N 51°44W, pop (1995e) 12 400. Capital and largest town of Greenland; founded, 1721; ruins of 10th-c Norse settlement nearby. >> Greenland i

Godunov, Boris (Fyodorovich) [**god**uhnof] (c.1552–1605) Tsar of Russia (1598–1605), previously Regent (from 1584) for Fyodor, the imbecile elder son of Ivan IV (the Terrible). >> Ivan IV; Time of Troubles

Godwin, also spelled **Godwine** (?–1053) Earl of Wessex, probably son of the South Saxon Wulfnoth. He became powerful under King Canute, and in 1042 helped to raise Edward the Confessor to the throne. His son Harold was for a few months Edward's successor. >> Edward the Confessor; Wessex

Godwin, Mary Wollstonecraft >> **Wollstonecraft**

Godwin, William (1756–1836) Political writer and novelist, born in Wisbech, Cambridgeshire. His major work of social philosophy was *An Enquiry Concerning Political Justice* (1793). His masterpiece was the novel, *The Adventures of Caleb Williams* (1794). He married Mary Wollstonecraft in 1797. >> Wollstonecraft

Godwin-Austen, Mount >> **K2**

godwit A large sandpiper, native to the N hemisphere but may winter in the S; bill long, very slightly upcurved. (Genus: *Limosa*, 4 species.) >> sandpiper

Goebbels or **Göbels, (Paul) Joseph** [**goe**blz] (1897–1945) Nazi politician, born in Rheydt, Germany. A bitter anti-Semite, his gift of mob oratory made him a powerful exponent of the more radical aspects of Nazi philosophy. He retained Hitler's confidence to the last, and in the Berlin bunker he and his wife committed suicide, after taking the lives of their six children. >> Hitler; Nazi Party; World War 2

Goeppert-Mayer, Maria [**goe**pert **may**er], *née* **Goepert** (1906–72) Physicist, born in Katowice, Poland. In 1948 she discovered the 'magic numbers' of subnuclear particles, and from 1950 devised a complete shell theory of nuclear structure. She shared the Nobel Prize for Physics in 1963. >> particle physics

Goering or **Göring, Hermann (Wilhelm)** [**goe**ring] (1893–1946) Nazi politico-military leader, born in Rosenheim, Germany. He founded the Gestapo, and set up the concentration camps for political, racial, and religious suspects. In 1940 he became economic dictator of Germany, and was made Marshal of the Reich, the first and only holder of the rank. In 1946 he was sentenced to death at the Nuremberg War Crimes Trial, but before his execution could take place he committed suicide. >> Hitler; Nazi Party; World War 2

Goethe, Johann Wolfgang von [**goe**tuh] (1749–1832) Poet, dramatist, and scientist, born in Frankfurt, Germany. He captured the spirit of German nationalism with his drama, *Götz von Berlichingen* (1773), following this with his novel *Die Leiden des jungen Werther* (1774, The Sorrows of Young Werther). He wrote much lyric poetry at this time, inspired by his relationships with a series of women, culminating in a profound attachment to Charlotte von Stein. Visits to Italy (1786–8, 1790) contributed to a greater preoccupation with poetical form, seen in such plays as *Iphigenie auf Tauris* (1789). In his later years he wrote *Wilhelm Meisters Lehrjahre* (1796, Wilhelm Meister's Apprentice Years), continued as *Wilhelm Meisters Wanderjahre* (1821–9, Wilhelm Meister's Journeyman Years). His masterpiece is his version of *Faust*, on which he worked for most of his life, published in two parts (1808, 1832). >> Romanticism

Gog and Magog [gog, **may**gog] Biblical names, applied in different ways to depict future foes of the people of God. *Rev* 20.8 and rabbinic literature treat Gog and Magog as paired figures representing Satan in the final conflict against God's people. In British folklore, the names are given to the survivors of a race of giants annihilated by Brutus, the founder of Britain. >> Bible; Devil; rabbi

Gogol, Nikolai (Vasilievich) [**goh**gl] (1809–52) Novelist and playwright, born in Sorochintsi, Ukraine. He became famous through two masterpieces: *Revizor* (1836, The Inspector General), a satire exposing the corruption and vanity of provincial officials, and a novel, *Myortvye dushi* (1842, Dead Souls).

Goiânia [goh**yan**ia] 16°43S 49°18W, pop (1995e) 1 158 000. City in WC Brazil; founded, 1933; railway; two universities (1959, 1960). >> Brazil ℹ

Goidelic [goy**del**ik] >> **Celtic languages**

goitre / goiter [**goy**ter] A swelling in the neck resulting from enlargement of the thyroid gland. It is often caused by iodine deficiency. >> hyperthyroidism; iodine; thyroid gland

Golan or **Golan Heights** [**goh**lan], Arabic **al-Jawlan** pop (1995e) 29 000; area 1176 sq km/454 sq mi. Israeli-occupied area of Syria administered as part of N Israel; of great strategic importance; occupied by Israel in 1967, and annexed in 1981; rises to 1204 m/3950 ft at Mt Avital. >> Arab–Israeli Wars; Israel ℹ; Syria ℹ

Gold, Thomas (1920–) Astronomer, born in Vienna. He worked with Hermann Bondi and Fred Hoyle on the steady-state theory of the origin of the universe (1948). In 1968 he suggested that pulsars are rapidly rotating neutron stars, as was later confirmed. >> Bondi; Hoyle, Fred; pulsar

gold Au, element 79, melting point 1064°C. A soft yellow metal of high density (19 g/cm^3), known from ancient times. It is rare and found uncombined in nature. Much of its value is due to its lack of reactivity, its main uses being for decoration and for monetary reserves. >> chemical elements; metal; RR1036

Goldberg, Whoopi, originally **Caryn Johnson** (1955–) Film actress, born in New York City. She achieved instant fame with her role in *The Color Purple* (1985), for which she received a Golden Globe Award. Her performance in *Ghost* (1990) won her an Oscar for best supporting actress. >> Walker

Goldblum, Jeff (1952–) Film actor, born in Pittsburgh, PA. His film debut was in 1974, and he has since become well known especially for his roles in science-fiction films, including *The Fly* (1986), *Earth Girls Are Easy* (1989), *Jurassic Park* and its sequel (1993, 1997), and *Independence Day* (1996).

Gold Coast >> **Ghana**

goldcrest A small woodland bird (*Regulus regulus*), native to Europe and Asia; head with orange or yellow stripe; also known as the **golden-crested wren**. (Family: Regulidae, sometimes placed in family Silviidae.) >> wren

Golden Bull Any document whose importance was stressed by authentication with a golden seal (Lat *bulla*). Specifically, the term is used for the edict promulgated by Emperor Charles IV in 1356 to define the German constitution.

golden calf An idolatrous image of worship, fashioned by Aaron and the Israelites at Sinai (*Ex* 32), and destroyed by Moses. >> Aaron; Moses; Sinai, Mount

Golden Fleece In Greek mythology, the object of the voyage of the *Argo*. Hermes saved Phrixus from sacrifice by placing him upon a golden ram, which bore him through the air to Colchis, where a dragon guarded the Fleece in a sacred grove. Jason obtained the fleece with Medea's help. >> Argonauts; Jason; Medea

Golden Gate Bridge A major steel suspension bridge across the Golden Gate, a channel in California, USA, connecting San Francisco Bay with the Pacific; completed in 1937; length of main span 1280 m/4200 ft. >> San Francisco

Golden Pavilion >> **Kinkakuji**

golden-rain tree >> **laburnum**

golden ratio In mathematics, a proportion obtained if a point P divides a straight line AB in such manner that $AP : PB = AB : AP$; also known as the **golden section**. It was applied to architecture by Vitruvius, and much discussed during the Renaissance. >> Vitruvius

golden retriever A breed of dog, developed in Britain in the late 19th-c; large with long golden or cream coat; solid body, strong legs, long muzzle; calm temperament; popular choice as a guide-dog for blind people. >> dog; retriever

goldenrod The name applied to several species of *Solidago*. The plant commonly grown in gardens is **Canadian golden rod** (*Solidago canadensis*), a late-flowering perennial growing to 1·5 m/5 ft, native to North America; flower-heads numerous, tiny, golden-yellow, arranged in a dense pyramidal panicle. (Genus: *Solidago*. Family: Compositae.) >> panicle

Golden Rule The name given today to the saying of Jesus about one's duty to others: 'Whatever things you wish that people would do to you, do also yourselves similarly to them' (*Matt* 7.12; *Luke* 6.31). >> Jesus Christ

Golden Temple >> **Harimandir**

goldfinch A bird native to the N hemisphere; one species in the Old World, *Carduelis carduelis*, three in the Americas; closely related to the siskin. (Genus: *Carduelis*, 4 species. Family: Fringillidae.) >> finch; siskin

goldfish Colourful carp-like freshwater fish, native to weedy rivers and lakes of Eurasia, but now very widely distributed as popular ornamental fish; body length up to 30 cm/1 ft; mouth lacking barbels. (*Carassius auratus*. Family: Cyprinidae.) >> carp

Golding, Sir William (Gerald) (1911–93) Novelist, born near Newquay, Cornwall. His first novel was *Lord of the Flies* (1954), and this was followed by *The Inheritors* (1955), *Pincher Martin* (1956), *Free Fall* (1959), and *The Spire* (1964). Later novels include *Rites of Passage* (1980, Booker Prize) and *The Paper Men* (1984). He was awarded the Nobel Prize for Literature in 1983.

Goldoni, Carlo [gol**doh**nee] (1707–93) Playwright, born in Venice, Italy. He wrote over 200 plays, including 150 comedies. Among his best-known works are *Il servitore di due padroni* (1746, the Servant of Two Masters), *Il teatro comico* (1750, The Comic Theatre), and *Il ventaglio* (1766, The Fan). >> *commedia dell'arte*; *opera buffa*

Goldsmith, Oliver (1728–74) Playwright, novelist, and poet, born in Kildare, Ireland. *The Vicar of Wakefield* (1766) secured his reputation as a novelist, *The Deserted Village* (1770) as a poet, and *She Stoops to Conquer* (1773) as a dramatist.

Goldwater, Barry M(orris) (1909–98) US politician and writer, born in Phoenix, AZ. In 1964 he became Republican nominee for the presidency, but was defeated by Lyndon Johnson. He was one of the architects of the conservative revival within the Republican Party. >> Johnson, Lyndon B; Republican Party

Goldwyn, Samuel, originally **Samuel Goldfish** (1882–1974) Film producer, born in Warsaw, Poland. He emigrated to the USA and in 1917 founded the Goldwyn Pictures Corporation, and in 1925 the Metro-Goldwyn-Mayer Company, allying himself with the United Artists from 1926. A colourful personality, many of his off-the-cuff remarks (*Goldwynisms*) have become catch phrases, such as 'include me out'.

golf A popular pastime and competitive sport, played on a course usually consisting of 18 holes. A *hole* consists of three areas: the flat starting point where the player hits the ball (the *tee*), a long stretch of mown grass (the *fairway*), and a putting *green* of smooth grass where the hole itself (10·8 cm/4¼ in) is situated. Obstacles, such as areas of sand (*bunkers*) and trees, are placed at various points. The object is to hit a small, rubber-cored ball from a starting point into the hole, which is generally 90–450 m/100–500 yd away. The winner is the player who completes a round with the lowest number of strokes. The expected number of strokes a good player would be expected to play for any given hole is referred to as the *par* for that hole. If the player holes the ball in one stroke below par, this is called a *birdie*; two strokes below is an *eagle*, one shot over par is a *bogey*; an occasional possibility is a *hole in one*. Players may carry up to 14 clubs in their golf bag, each designed for a specific purpose and shot. The ruling body of the game in Britain is the Royal and Ancient Club at St Andrews, Scotland. Major tournaments include the Open Golf Championship, the US Open, the US Professional Golfers' Association (PGA), and the US Masters. >> Masters; Royal and Ancient Golf Club of St Andrews; Ryder Cup; RR1052

golf-ball printer A high quality impact printer with a spherical print head used mainly in typewriters. The printhead is removable, allowing different typesets to be used. >> printer, computer

Golgotha >> **Calvary**

goliards Wandering scholars and clerks of the 12th–13th-c, who wrote reckless celebrations of women and wine, and satirical verses against the Church. >> satire

Goliath [go**liy**ath] Biblical character described (1 *Sam* 17) as a giant from Gath in the Philistine army who entered into single combat with the young David and was slain by a stone from David's sling, resulting in Israel's victory. >> David; Samuel, Books of

Gollancz, Sir Victor [go**langks**, go**lants**] (1893–1967) Publisher, author, and philanthropist, born in London. He founded his own firm in 1928, and after World War 2 founded the Jewish Society for Human Service, and War on Want (1951).

Gompers, Samuel [**gom**perz] (1850–1924) Labour leader, born in London. He migrated to New York City in 1863, founded the American Federation of Labor in 1886, and except for one year was its president until his death. >> American Federation of Labor

Gomułka, Władysław [go**mool**ka] (1905–82) Polish communist leader, born in Krosno, Poland. He was vice-president of the first postwar Polish government (1945–8), but his criticism of the Soviet Union led to his arrest (1951–4). He later returned to power as party first secretary (1956–71). >> communism; Poland ℹ

gomuti palm >> **sugar palm**

gonad The organ responsible for the production of reproductive cells (*germ cells* or *gametes*): in males the gonads (*testes*) produce spermatozoa, in females the gonads (*ovaries*) produce ova. In vertebrates the gonads also synthesize and secrete sex hormones. >> sex hormones; testes; uterus ℹ

Goncourt brothers [gõkoor] **Edmond de Goncourt** (1822–96) and **Jules de Goncourt** (1830–70) Novelists, born respectively at Nancy and Paris. They are especially remembered for their *Journal*, begun in 1851, a detailed record of French social and literary life which Edmond continued for 40 years. Edmond also founded in his will the Académie Goncourt to foster fiction.

Gondar >> **Fasil Ghebbi**

Gondwanaland [gond**wah**naland] The name given to the postulated S 'supercontinent' which began to break away from the single land mass Pangaea about 200 million years ago. It included Australia, Africa, Antarctica, India, and South America. >> continental drift; Laurasia

gong A percussion instrument: a circular bronze plaque, commonly suspended from a frame or bar and struck with a soft beater. The orchestral gong (or **tam-tam**) is of indefinite pitch; other, usually smaller, gongs are tuned to precise pitches. >> percussion ℹ

Góngora y Argote, Luis de [**gon**gora ee ah(r)**goh**tay] (1561–1627) Lyric poet, born in Córdoba. His reputation largely rests on his later, longer poems, such as *Solidades* and *Polifemo* (both 1613), executed in an elaborate style which came to be called **gongorism**.

gonorrhoea / gonorrhea [gonuh**ree**a] An acute infection of the genital tract acquired by sexual intercourse with a partner infected with *Neisseria gonorrhoeae*. Males suffer from a discharge from the penis, with pain on urination. Local symptoms are less obvious in females. >> urinary system; venereal disease

Gonzaga, Luigi, St [gon**zah**ga], known as **St Aloysius** (1568–91) Jesuit, born near Brescia, Italy. In a plague at Rome he devoted himself to the care of the sick, but was himself infected and died. He was canonized in 1726, and is the Italian patron saint of youth. Feast day 21 June. >> Jesuits

González, Felipe [gon**zah**lez] (1942–) Spanish statesman and prime minister (1982–96), born in Seville. He became secretary-general of the Spanish Socialist

Workers' Party in 1974, and led it to victory in the 1982 elections, forming the first left-wing administration since 1936.

Gooch, Graham (Alan) (1953–) Cricketer, born in Leytonstone, Greater London. He began his career playing for Essex. As England captain (1988–93), he led a notable victory over the West Indies in Jamaica (1989). The leading England Test run-scorer, and most-capped player, he announced his retirement in January 1995, with 8900 runs scored in 118 Tests, at an average of 42·58. >> cricket (sport) ℹ

Good Friday In the Christian Church, the Friday before Easter, commemorating the crucifixion of Jesus Christ; in many Christian denominations, a day of mourning and penance. >> Easter; Jesus Christ

Goodman, Benny, popular name of **Benjamin David Goodman**, nickname **the King of Swing** (1909–86) Clarinettist and bandleader, born in Chicago, IL. He reigned as the 'King of Swing' in the big-band era. Among his band's hit recordings were 'Let's Dance', 'Stompin' at the Savoy', and 'One O'Clock Jump'. He also featured trios and quartets with Lionel Hampton and other African-American jazz musicians. >> jazz

Goodman, John (1953–) Film actor, born in St Louis, MO. He became well known for his role as the husband Dan in the television comedy series *Roseanne* (1988–97). His major films include *King Ralph* (1991), *Barton Fink* (1991), and *The Flintstones* (1994).

Goodyear, Charles (1800–60) Inventor, born in New Haven, CT. His work led to the invention (1844) of vulcanized rubber. >> vulcanization

Goons, The Four comedians who came together after World War 2 to create the Goon Show, which revolutionized British radio comedy: **Spike Milligan**, **Peter Sellers**, **Harry Secombe**, and **Michael Bentine** (1922–). They first performed on radio together in 1951: the show, called *Crazy People*, soon became *The Goon Show*, running for nine years and winning a worldwide band of devotees. The Goons prefigured much of British comedy since the fifties, especially in their imaginative use of sound effects, their mixture of surrealism and slapstick, and their anarchic humour. >> Milligan; Secombe; Sellars

goosander A sea-duck (*Mergus merganser*) native to N areas of the N hemisphere, also known in the USA as the **common merganser**; dark head and long red bill; male with dark back. (Family: Anatidae.) >> duck

goose A term not applied precisely, but used for large birds with more terrestrial habits than the 'swans' or 'ducks' comprising the rest of the family. (Family: Anatidae.) >> barnacle / Canada goose; duck; magpie; perching duck; sheldgoose; swan; waterfowl

gooseberry A deciduous shrub (*Ribes uva-crispa*) growing to c.1 m/3¼ ft, native to Europe and N Africa; stems and branches spiny; flowers greenish, tinged purple; edible berry oval, up to 4 cm/1½ in long, green or reddish, bristly or smooth. (Family: Grossulariaceae.)

goosefish >> **anglerfish**

goosegrass An annual, sometimes overwintering; a common weed (*Galium aparine*) native to Europe and Asia; fruit a burr with two more or less equal globular halves covered in whitish bristles, dispersed by clinging or cleaving to animals; hence the alternative name **cleavers**. (Family: Rubiaceae.)

Goose Green 51°52S 59°00W, pop (1995e) 100. Settlement on East Falkland, Falkland Is. >> Falkland Islands ℹ

Goossens, Sir Eugène (1893–1962) Composer and conductor, born in London. As conductor of the Sydney Symphony Orchestra and director of the New South Wales Conservatory (1947–56), he became a major influence on Australian music.

Goossens, Léon (1897–1988) Oboist, born in Liverpool, Merseyside. He was the brother of the conductor Eugène Goossens; his sisters **Marie Goossens** (1894–1991) and **Sidonie Goossens** (1899–) became well-known harpists. >> Goossens, Eugène

gopher A name used in North America for many animals which burrow. >> souslik

goral A small goat-antelope (*Nemorhaedus goral*), native to the high mountains of E Asia; thick yellow-grey coat, pale throat; both sexes with short horns; also known as the **Himalayan chamois**. >> antelope

Gorbachev, Mikhail Sergeyevich [go(r)ba**chof**] (1931–) Soviet statesman, born in Privolnoye, Russia. He became Central Committee secretary for agriculture (1979–85); candidate member (1979–80) and full member (1980–91) of the Politburo of the Central Committee (1979–80); and, on the death of Konstantin Chernenko, general secretary of the Central Committee (1985–91). In 1988 he also became chairman of the Presidium of the Supreme Soviet (ie head of state) and in 1990 the first executive president of the USSR, with increased powers. He launched a radical programme of reform and restructuring (*perestroika*) of the Soviet economic and political system. A greater degree of civil liberty was allowed under the policy of *glasnost* ('openness' of information). In foreign and defence affairs he pursued a policy of detente and nuclear disarmament with the West. He survived an attempted coup in August 1991, but following the break-up of the USSR resigned all his offices in December of that year. >> communism; glasnost; perestroika; Soviet Union; Yeltsin

Gorbals, The A district of Glasgow, Scotland, which by the end of the 19th-c had become infamous as an area of overcrowding and deprivation. Redevelopment started in the late 1950s, and most of the old buildings were demolished in the next 20 years. >> Glasgow

Gordian knot In Phrygia, a complicated knot with which the legendary King Gordius had tied up his wagon. An oracle said that whoever succeeded in untying it would rule Asia. Alexander the Great cut it with his sword. >> Alexander the Great; Phrygia

Gordimer, Nadine (1923–) Novelist, born in Springs, South Africa. In novels such as *The Conservationist* (1974) and *A Sport of Nature* (1987), she adopts a liberal approach to problems of race and repression. She won the 1991 Nobel Prize for Literature.

Gordon, Charles George (1833–85) British general, born in Woolwich, Greater London. In 1860 he crushed the Taiping Rebellion, for which he became known as **Chinese Gordon**. In 1877 he was appointed Governor of the Sudan. He was besieged at Khartoum for 10 months by the Mahdi's troops, and was killed there two days before a relief force arrived. >> Mohammed Ahmed; Taiping Rebellion

Gordon Riots Anti-Catholic riots in London in early June 1780. They occurred after Lord George Gordon (1751–93), leader of the Protestant Association, had failed in his attempt to have clauses in the 1778 Catholic Relief Act (removing restrictions on the activities of priests) repealed. >> Catholic Emancipation

Gore, Al(bert) (1948–) US vice-president, born in Washington, DC. He studied at Harvard and Vanderbilt Universities, worked as a journalist, then became a Democratic congressman (1977–85) and senator (1985–92). He was elected vice-president to Bill Clinton in 1992. >> Clinton

Górecki, Henryk Mikolaj [go**res**kee] (1933–) Composer, born in Czernica, near Rybnik, Poland. His work, usually based on tragic themes and in very slow tempi, was virtually unknown in the West until 1993, when his *Symphony*

No. 3: Symphony of Sorrowful Songs (1973) sold over half a million copies worldwide. Later works include *Miserere* (1981).

Gorée Island [**go**ray] A small island off the Cape Verde peninsula, Senegal, formerly a major centre of slave storage before shipping to the Americas. It is now a world heritage site. >> Senegal ℹ; slave trade

Göreme [**goe**reme] Valley in Cappadocia, C Turkey; noted for its cave dwellings; a world heritage site. >> Turkey ℹ

Gorgon A terrible monster of Greek mythology. There were three Gorgons, who had snakes in their hair, ugly faces, and huge wings; their staring eyes could turn people to stone. Perseus killed Medusa (the only mortal one), and cut off her head. >> Perseus (mythology)

gorilla An ape (*Gorilla gorilla*) native to the rainforests of WC Africa; the largest primate (height, up to 1·8 m/6 ft); massive muscular body; usually walks on all fours; adult male with marked crest; black, except in old males (*silverbacks*), which have a silvery grey torso. >> ape; primate (biology)

Göring, Hermann >> **Goering, Hermann**

Gorky >> **Nizhni Novgorod**

Gorky, Arshile, originally **Vosdanig Manoog Adoian** (1905–48) Painter, born in Khorkom Vari, Turkish Armenia. He emigrated in 1920, and played a key role in the emergence of the New York school of Action painters in the 1940s. >> action painting

Gorky, Maxim, pseudonym of **Alexey Maksimovich Peshkov** (1868–1936) Novelist, born in Nizhni Novgorod, Russia. He produced several Romantic short stories, then social novels and plays, notably the drama *Na dne* (1902, The Lower Depths). An autobiographical trilogy (1915–23) contains his best writing. He was the first president of the Soviet Writers Union. His birthplace was renamed Gorky in his honour (1929–91). >> Romanticism

gorse A spiny shrub (*Ulex europaeus*) growing to 2 m/6½ ft, from Europe and NW Africa; leaves reduced to rigid needle-like spines, or small scales in mature plants; pea-flowers yellow, fragrant; also called **furze**. (Family: Leguminosae.)

Gorsedd [**gaw(r)**se<u>th</u>] A society of Welsh bards, founded in 1792 by Iolo Morganwg. It takes a major part in the organization of the National Eisteddfod, in particular the bardic ceremony. >> eisteddfod

Gorton, Sir John Grey (1911–) Australian statesman and prime minister (1968–71), born in Melbourne, Victoria, Australia. He served in the governments of Sir Robert Menzies and Harold Holt before becoming prime minister. In 1971 he resigned in favour of William McMahon, becoming deputy leader of the Liberal Party (until 1975). >> Holt; McMahon; Menzies

goshawk [**gos**-hawk] A smallish hawk with short rounded wings and a long tail (20 species). The **northern goshawk** (*Accipiter gentilis*) is found in much of the N hemisphere; other species are native to Africa, S and SE Asia, and Australia. (Family: Accipitridae.) >> bird of prey; hawk

Goshawk

Gospel Music developed in black churches of the US South from a secular musical style in the early decades of this century. It was practised both by soloists and choirs, often with instrumental accompaniment, and became known for its infectious rhythms, close harmonies, and lively presentation. Noted solo performers include Sister Rosetta Tharpe and Mahalia Jackson. The style later had a major influence on other musical styles, especially soul music. The term is also associated with the revivalist movement of the late 19th-c, and the *Gospel Hymns* (1875–94) of US evangelists Philip Paul Bliss (1838–76) and Ira David Sankey (1840–1908).

Gospels, canonical Four books of the New Testament, known as the Gospels according to Matthew, Mark, Luke, and John; called 'gospels' by the 2nd-c Church (Gr *euangelion*, 'good news'). Each portrays a perspective on the ministry and teaching of Jesus of Nazareth, concluding with an account of his arrest, crucifixion, and resurrection. >> Jesus Christ; synoptic gospels

Gothenburg [**goth**enberg], Swed **Göteborg** 57°45N 12°00E, pop (1995e) 444 000. Seaport in SW Sweden; second largest city in Sweden; founded, 1619; free port, 1921; railway; ferry services to UK, Denmark, Germany; university (1891), technical university (1829); cathedral (1633). >> Sweden ℹ

Gothic >> **black letter writing; Germanic languages**

Gothic architecture A form of architecture, usually religious, prevalent in W Europe from the 12th-c to the late 15th-c. It is characterized by a structural system comprising the pointed arch, rib vault, flying buttress, and a propensity for lofty interiors and maximum window area. >> arch ℹ; buttress ℹ; Gothic Revival; vault ℹ

Gothic novel A type of fiction, written in reaction to 18th-c rationalism, which reclaims mystery and licenses extreme emotions. Some (eg Lewis's *The Monk*, 1797) make confident forays into the unconscious, exploring sexual fears and impulses. The Gothic horror stories of the 20th-c represent a fresh development for the genre, providing the input for a new medium of expression, the horror film. >> Lewis, Matthew; rationalism (philosophy)

Gothic Revival The movement to revive Gothic architecture, prevalent during the late 18th-c and 19th-c, popular in England, France, Germany, and North America. The style was applied to a multitude of buildings including churches, railway stations, hotels, town halls, and the parliament buildings at London and Ottawa. >> Gothic architecture; Pugin

Goths Germanic peoples who moved S, possibly from the Baltic area (Gotland), dividing into two confederations, Ostrogoths and Visigoths. Displaced by the Huns, they created two kingdoms in the 5th-c out of the ruins of the Roman Empire in the W. >> Huns; Ostrogoths; Visigoths

Gotland, **Gottland**, or **Gothland** pop (1995e) 59 000; land area 3140 sq km/1212 sq mi. Island county of Sweden, in the Baltic Sea off the SE coast; colonized by Germans, 12th-c; taken by Sweden in 1280, by Denmark in 1361, and again by Sweden in 1645; capital, Visby. >> Sweden ℹ

gouache [**goo**ahsh] A type of opaque watercolour paint, also known as 'body colour', or 'poster paint' – familiar to most people from school art lessons. It was used in ancient Egypt, and widely in the Middle Ages, especially in illuminated manuscripts. >> paint; watercolour

Goujon, Jean [goozhõ] (c.1510–c.68) The foremost French sculptor of the 16th-c, probably born in Normandy. His finest work is a set of reliefs for the Fountain of the Innocents (1547–9, Louvre).

Gould, Shane (Elizabeth) (1956–) Swimmer, born in Brisbane, Queensland, Australia. She created Olympic history by being the first and only woman to win three individual gold swimming medals in world record time. She retired in 1973, at the age of 17.

Gounod, Charles (François) [**goo**noh] (1818–93) Composer, born in Paris. His major works include the comic opera, *Le Médecin malgré lui* (1858, trans The Mock Doctor), and his masterpiece, *Faust* (1859).

gourd Any of several members of the cucumber family, with hard, woody-rinded fruits of various shapes and colours. All are trailing or climbing vines with tendrils, funnel-shaped flowers, and round pear- or bottle-shaped fruits. (Family: Cucurbitaceae.) >> calabash tree; cucumber

gout A disease associated with a raised concentration of uric acid in the blood, which is deposited in the soft tissues. It predominantly affects males. >> uric acid

Gower, David (Ivon) (1957–) Cricketer, born in Tunbridge Wells, Kent. He was captain of England (1984–6, 1989), and for a while was the leading Test run-scorer, with 8231 runs in Test cricket over 117 matches. He retired in 1993, to follow a career in the media. >> cricket ℹ; Gooch

Gower, John (c.1325–1408) Mediaeval poet, a friend of Chaucer. His best-known work is the long English poem, *Confessio amantis* (c.1383), comprising over 100 stories on the theme of Christian and courtly love. >> Chaucer

Gowers, Sir Ernest (Arthur) (1880–1966) British civil servant, and author of an influential work on English usage. He wrote *Plain Words* (1948) in an attempt to maintain standards of clear English, especially in official prose. >> English

Goya (y Lucientes), Francisco (José) de [**goh**ya] (1746–1828) Artist, born in Fuendetodos, Spain. He became famous especially for his portraits, and in 1799 was made court painter to Charles IV, which led to 'The Family of Charles IV' (1800, Prado) and other works.

Goyen, Jan van [**goy**en] (1596–1656) Painter, born in Leyden, The Netherlands. He became a pioneer of realistic 'tonal' landscape, emphasizing the movement of light and shadow across wide plains and rivers under huge cloudy skies. >> landscape painting

Gozo [**goh**zoh], Maltese **Ghaudex**, ancient **Gaulus** 36°00N 14°13E; pop (1995e) 27 000 (with Comino); area 67 sq km/26 sq mi Island in the Maltese group, often called 'the Isle of Calypso'; 6 km/4 mi NW of the main island of Malta; coastline, 43 km/27 mi; chief town, Victoria. >> Malta ℹ

Gozzi, Carlo, conte (Count) [**got**zee] (1720–1806) Playwright, born in Venice, Italy. His best-known works include the comedy, *Fiaba dell' amore delle tre melarance* (1761, The Love of the Three Oranges) and *Turandot* (1762).

graben [**grah**bn] A rift valley, usually of great size, formed when a narrow block of the Earth's crust drops down between two normal faults. >> fault; horst; rift valley ℹ

Grable, Betty, originally **Ruth Elizabeth Grable** (1916–73) Actress, born in St Louis, MO. She worked as a chorus girl from the age of 13 and made her film debut in the musical *Whoopee!* (1930). She had her first major film role in *Hold 'em Jail* (1932), and became more established with *Pigskin Parade* (1936), and *Million Dollar Legs* (1939). She was adopted by American GI's during World War 2 as a pin-up girl. She went on to appear on Broadway in *Hello, Dolly* (1965).

Gracchi, (the brothers) [**gra**kee], in full **Tiberius Sempronius Gracchus** (c.168–133 BC) and **Gaius Sempronius Gracchus** (c.159–121 BC) Roman politicians who attempted to solve the major social and economic problems of their day by forcing through sweeping reforms while tribunes of the plebs (133 BC, 123–122 BC). The ruthlessness of their methods provoked a backlash which led to Tiberius being killed, and Gaius committing suicide. >> Roman history ℹ

Grace, W(illiam) G(ilbert) (1848–1915) Cricketer, born in Downend, South Gloucester. He twice captained the English team. His career in first-class cricket (1865–1908) as batsman and bowler brought 126 centuries, 54 896 runs, and 2876 wickets. >> cricket (sport) ℹ

Graces, the (Gr *Charites*) In Greek mythology, three daughters of Zeus and Hera, embodying beauty and social accomplishments. They are sometimes called **Aglaia**, **Euphrosyne**, and **Thalia**.

grackle A bird of the New World, any of 11 species of the family Icteridae (American blackbirds and orioles). The name is also used for several starlings from SE Asia and Indonesia (family: Sturnidae). >> blackbird; oriole; starling

Grade (of Elstree), Lew Grade, Baron, originally **Louis Winogradsky** (1906–98) Theatrical impresario, born near Odessa, Ukraine, the eldest of three brothers who were to dominate British showbusiness for over 40 years. He arrived in Britain in 1912, along with his younger brother Boris, who became **Bernard Delfont** (1909–94). Bernard entered theatrical management in 1941, and from 1958 to 1978 presented the annual Royal Variety Performance. Lew became managing director of ATV in 1962, and headed several large film entertainment and communications companies.

Graf, Steffi [grahf] (1969–) Tennis player, born in Brühl, Germany. She won the French Open in 1987, and took all four major titles in 1988. She won the Wimbledon title again in 1989, 1991, 1992, 1993, 1995, and 1996. >> tennis, lawn ℹ

graffito >> **sgraffito**

graft (botany) The portion of a woody plant inserted into a slot cut in the stem or rootstock of another plant, so that the vascular tissues combine and growth continues. It is successful only between closely related species. >> horticulture

graft (medicine) A tissue or organ that can be used for transplantation. An **allograft** (**homograft**) is taken from a member of the same species but one that is genetically dissimilar. An **autograft** is taken from the animal's or the patient's own body or a genetically identical individual (eg an identical twin). A **xenograft** (**heterograft**) is taken from a species different to that of the host. >> transplantation

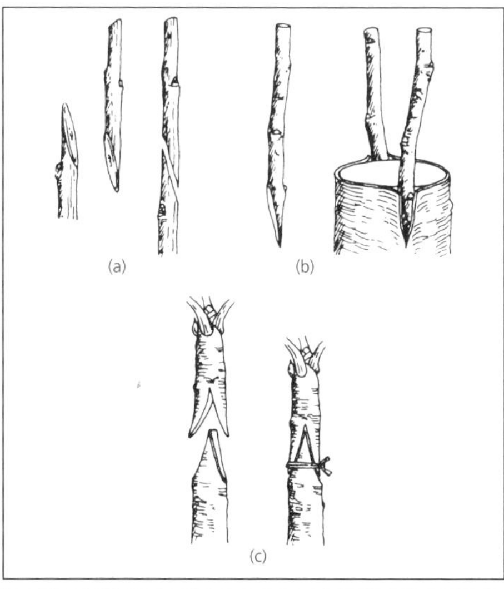

Grafts (botany) – splice (a); crown (b); saddle (c)

Graham, Billy, popular name of **William Franklin Graham, Jr** (1918–) Evangelist, born in Charlotte, NC. He was ordained a Southern Baptist minister in 1939, and quickly gained a reputation as a preacher. Since the 1950s he has conducted a series of highly organized revivalist campaigns in the USA, UK, and elsewhere. >> Baptists; evangelicalism

Graham, Martha (1894–1991) Dancer, teacher, and choreographer, born in Pittsburgh, PA. She started the Martha Graham School of Contemporary Dance in 1927, and became the most famous exponent of Expressionist modern dance in the USA. The company appeared at the Edinburgh Festival in 1996, performing reconstructions of her early works. >> choreography; Expressionism; modern dance

Grahame, Kenneth (1859–1932) Writer, born in Edinburgh. He wrote several stories for children, the best known being *The Wind in the Willows* (1908). >> Milne

Graham Land Mountainous Antarctic peninsula; rises to c.3600 m/11 800 ft at Mt Jackson. >> British Antarctic Territory

Grail, Holy or **Sangreal** In the Arthurian legends, the dish or chalice used by Christ at the Last Supper. Joseph of Arimathea brought it to Glastonbury. It appeared at Pentecost at King Arthur's table, and the knights set out to find it. >> Arthur; Jesus Christ

Grainger, Percy (Aldridge), originally **George Percy Grainger** (1882–1961) Composer and pianist, born in Melbourne, Victoria, Australia. He championed the revival of folk music, in such works as 'Molly on the Shore' and 'Shepherd's Hey' (1911), which make skilful use of traditional dance themes.

gram >> **kilogram**

grammar The study of the structure of words (also known as *morphology*), phrases, clauses, and sentences (also known as *syntax*). A **prescriptive grammar** lays down conventions of usage regarded by some sections of society as being 'correct', such as 'Never end a sentence with a preposition'. By contrast, a **descriptive grammar** describes actual usage patterns, without making value judgments about their social standing. A **comparative grammar** compares the grammatical features of languages that are genetically related, and a **universal grammar** investigates those grammatical features shared by the structure of all languages. >> generative grammar; linguistics; morphology; word class

grammar school In the UK, a selective school choosing usually the most able 15–25% of 11-year-olds on the basis of the eleven-plus examination. The oldest schools date back to mediaeval times, and were originally established to teach Latin. >> comprehensive / secondary modern school

Grammer, Kelsey (1955–) Actor, born on St Thomas, US Virgin Islands. He is best known for his role as Dr Frasier Crane, originally seen in *Cheers* (1982–93) and *Wings*, and then in *Frasier* (from 1993, 2 Emmies). His first feature film was *Down Periscope* (1996).

Grammy An annual popular music award given by the US National Academy of Recording Arts and Sciences for special achievements in the record industry. It was established in 1958.

gramophone An acoustic device for reproducing sounds, stored as acoustically generated, laterally cut grooves in the flat surface of a disc rotated on a turntable beneath a stylus. It was first demonstrated in 1888 by US inventor Emile Berliner (1851–1929). >> phonograph; sound recording

Grampian pop (1995e) 543 000; area 8704 sq km/3360 sq mi. Former region in NE Scotland; created in 1975, and replaced in 1996 by Moray and Aberdeenshire councils. >> Scotland ℹ

Grampians (Australia) Mountain range in SWC Victoria, Australia; rises to 1167 m/3829 ft at Mt William. >> Great Dividing Range

Grampians (Scotland) or **Grampian Mountains** Mountain system extending SW–NE across Scotland; rises to 1344 m/4409 ft at Ben Nevis. >> Ben Macdhui; Ben Nevis; Cairngorms; Scotland ℹ

grampus A toothed whale; correctly the **grey grampus** or **Risso's dolphin** (*Grampus griseus*), a widespread temperate and tropical deep-water species of short-nosed dolphin. (Family: Delphinidae.) >> dolphin; whale ℹ

Gramsci, Antonio [**gram**skee] (1891–1937) Political leader and theoretician, born in Ales, Sardinia, Italy. He helped to establish the separate Italian Communist Party in 1921, and in 1924 became leader of the party in parliament. In prison from 1926, his *Lettere del carcere* (1947, Letters from Prison) is now regarded as one of the most important political texts of this century. >> communism; Mussolini

Granada 37°10N 3°35W, pop (1995e) 256 000. City in Andalusia, S Spain; founded by the Moors, 8th-c; capital of the Kingdom of Granada, 1238; last Moorish stronghold in Spain, captured in 1492; archbishopric; airport; railway; university (1531); cathedral (16th-c), with tombs of Ferdinand and Isabella; Generalife Palace and the Alhambra, a world heritage site. >> Spain ℹ

granadilla Any of several species of passion flower which produce edible fruits. **Purple granadilla** (*Passiflora edulis*) has purple fruits, 5–7·5 cm/2–3 in long. (Family: Passifloraceae.) >> passion flower ℹ

Granby, John Manners, Marquess of (1721–70) British army officer, the eldest son of the Duke of Rutland. His reputation was made in the Seven Years' War (1756–63), when he led the British cavalry in a major victory over the French at Warburg (1760). >> Seven Years' War

Gran Canaria [gran ca**na**rya], Eng **Grand Canary** 28°00N 15°35W; area 1532 sq km/591 sq mi. Volcanic Atlantic island in the Canary Is; highest point, Pozo de las Nieves (1980 m/6496 ft); chief town, Las Palmas de Gran Canaria; airport. >> Canary Islands

Gran Chaco [gran **cha**koh] Lowland plain covering part of N Argentina, W Paraguay, and S Bolivia; scrub forest and grassland, with a tropical savannah climate and sparse population; cattle raising. >> Argentina ℹ; Chaco War

Grand Army of the Republic (GAR) An organization of veterans of the Union side in the American Civil War. Established in 1866, the GAR became an important force in postwar politics. >> American Civil War

Grand Banks A major fishing ground in the N Atlantic Ocean, off the coast of Newfoundland, Canada, formed by an extensive submarine plateau on the continental shelf. >> Atlantic Ocean; fog; plankton

Grand Canal, Chin **Da Yunhe** Canal in E China, length 1794 km/1115 mi, average width, 30 m/100 ft; longest artificial waterway in the world; from Beijing municipality to Hangzhou in Zhejiang province; opened in AD 610. >> canal; China ℹ

Grand Canyon Enormous gorge in NW Arizona, USA; 349 km/217 mi long; 8–25 km/5–15 mi wide from rim to rim; maximum depth c.1900 m/6250 ft; the result of large-scale erosion by the Colorado R. >> Arizona

Grand Coulee [**koo**lee] Valley in Douglas County, NE Washington, USA; the **Grand Coulee Dam** is a major gravity dam on the Columbia R, impounding L Franklin D Roosevelt; built 1933–42; height 168 m/550 ft; length 1272 m/4173 ft. >> dam

Grand Guignol [grã geen**yol**] Short sensational shows, in vogue in Paris in the late 19th-c, which depict violent crimes in a style designed to shock and titillate. Guignol was originally a puppet in the French marionette theatre.

grand mal [grã **mal**] >> **epilepsy**

Grand National The most famous steeplechase in the world, first held at Maghull near Liverpool in 1836. The race moved to its present course at Aintree in 1839. Raced over 4 mi/855 yd (7·2 km) the competitors have to negotiate 31 difficult fences. >> steeplechase 1

Grand Remonstrance The statement of Charles I of England's abuses, and of reforms made by the Long Parliament in 1640–1. >> Charles I (of England); Long Parliament

Granger, Stewart, originally **James Lablanche Stewart** (1913–93) Film actor, born in London. He assumed his professional name in the 1930s, to avoid confusion with actor James Stewart, and developed into a leading romantic star, his films including *The Man in Grey* (1943), *King Solomon's Mines* (1950), and *The Wild Geese* (1977).

granite A coarse-grained, acid (high in silica) igneous rock containing orthoclase feldspar, quartz, and mica (and/or hornblende); pale pink or grey in colour, its durability makes it an important building stone. >> feldspar; igneous rock; micas; quartz

Grant, Cary, originally **Archibald Leach** (1904–86) Actor, born in Bristol. From the late 1930s he developed in leading comedy roles, and also provided several performances for Hitchcock, such as in *Suspicion* (1941) and *North by North-West* (1959). >> Hitchcock

Grant, Duncan (James Corrow) (1885–1978) Painter, born in Rothiemurchus, Inverness, Highland. Associated with the London Group, his works were mainly landscapes, portraits, and still life.

Grant, Richard E(sterhuysen) (1957–) Actor, born in Mbabane, Swaziland. He became known following his role as the down-and-out thespian in *Withnail and I*. Later films include *The Player*. He has also published his diaries, *With Nails* (1997) and a novel, *By Design*. In 1999 he starred in BBC TV's *The Scarlet Pimpernel*.

Grant, Ulysses S(impson) (1822–85) US general and 18th president (1869–77), born in Point Pleasant, OH. He led Union forces to victory in the Civil War (1861), first in the Mississippi Valley, then in the final campaigns in Virginia, and accepted the Confederate surrender at Appomattox Court House (1865). Elected president in 1868 and 1872, he presided over the reconstruction of the South. His memoirs have been much acclaimed. >> American Civil War

Granth Sahib >> **Adi Granth**

grant-maintained school A school, established by the 1988 Education Act, which is independent of the local education authority and receives its annual grant directly from the government. In order to 'opt out' of local authority control a majority of parents must vote in favour by secret ballot. >> school

granulation >> **photosphere**

Granville-Barker, Harley (1877–1946) Actor, playwright, and director, born in London. His writing includes a famous series of prefaces to Shakespeare's plays (1927–45). >> Shakespeare ℹ

Granz, Norman (1918–) Concert impresario and record producer, born in Los Angeles, CA. He is chiefly known for his staging of the national and international tours called Jazz at the Philharmonic, and is widely recognized as the leading disseminator of jazz around the world. >> jazz

grape >> **grapevine**

grapefruit A citrus fruit (*Citrus paradisi*) 10–15 cm/4–6 in diameter, globose with thick, pale, yellow rind; some varieties may be slightly pear-shaped or have thin or pinkish rind. (Family: Rutaceae.) >> citrus

grapevine A deciduous woody climber (*Vitis vinifera*); flowers numerous, tiny, green; ripe fruits sweet, yellowish or purple, often with a waxy, white bloom. Probably native to E Asia, many varieties are now cultivated in most temperate regions, especially those with a Mediterranean climate. It is of considerable economic importance as the source of wine. Dried grapes are sold as currants, raisins, and sultanas. (Family: Vitaceae.) >> currant; wine

graph A diagram illustrating the relationship between two sets of numbers, such as the relationship between the height of a plant in centimetres and the time in days since germination. The sets of numbers may be purely algebraic; for example, described by the equation $y = x - 1$. >> equations; logarithm

graphic design A set of skills and techniques employed in the design of all printed matter. The major skills include typography, photography, illustration, and printmaking. >> typography

graphics tablet A device by which the movements of a pen over a special surface can be translated into digital input for a computer. This provides a means of converting two-dimensional information, such as maps and drawings, into computer-readable form. >> computer graphics

graphic user interface (GUI) In computing, a type of interaction between a user and the computer: the computer sends pictures to a visual display unit and the user responds by indicating which picture defines what the user wishes to do. >> visual display unit

graphite A mineral form of carbon, found in metamorphic rocks; black, soft, and greasy to the touch. It is a very good electrical conductor and dry lubricant. Mixed with clay, it is used in pencil 'leads'. >> carbon

graphology 1 The analysis of handwriting as a guide to the character and personality of the writer. It was introduced during the late 19th-c by the French abbot, Jean Hippolyte Michon (1806–81). >> chirography **2** In linguistics, the study of the writing system of a language; also the writing system itself. >> alphabet ℹ; logography; phonology; punctuation; romanization; writing systems

Grappelli, Stéphane [gra**pel**ee] (1908–97) Jazz violinist, born in Paris. He and Django Reinhardt were the principal soloists in the Quintet of the Hot Club of France (1934–9), the first European jazz band to exert an influence in the USA. >> jazz; Reinhardt, Django

Grasmere 54°28N 3°02W, pop (1995e) 1210. Scenic resort village in Cumbria, NW England; by L Grasmere; home (Dove Cottage) and burial place of Wordsworth. >> Cumbria; Wordsworth, William

grass A member of one of the largest flowering-plant families, with over 9000 species distributed worldwide. They are monocotyledons, ranging from tiny annuals to perennials over 30 m/100 ft high. A typical grass has fibrous roots and hollow, cylindrical stems which branch at the base to form a tuft. Long, narrow leaves grow singly from the nodes of the stem and have an upper part (the *blade*), and a lower part (the *sheath*), which fits around the stem like a sleeve. The junction of blade and sheath often bears a flap or ring of hairs (the *ligule*), which is diagnostically important. Grasses occur in every type of habitat, terrestrial and aquatic, including the sea, and especially in the vast, open prairies, savannah, and steppe. They are the most important economic plant group. As well as providing forage for animals in the form of grazing, hay, and silage, they include grain-bearing species (the *cereals*), which are staple foods for most of the world's population. They also provide sugar, materials for thatching, paper, mats, and even light timber. They have an important role as soil stabilizers, and are used for lawns and verges. A few are ornamentals but a number are tenacious weeds. (Family: Gramineae.) >> cereals; monocotyledons; *see illustration on p. 364*

Grass, Günter (Wilhelm) (1927–) Writer and political activist, born in Gdańsk, Poland (formerly Danzig,

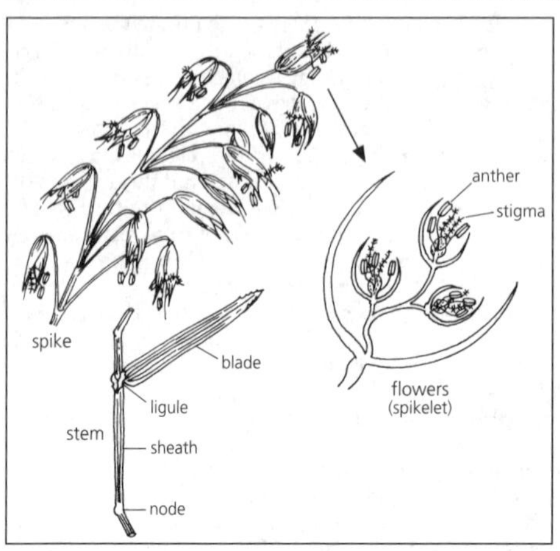

Grass – flower, stem, spike

Germany). He achieved a European reputation with his first novel, *Die Blechtrommel* (1959, The Tin Drum). Other political novels include *Hundejahre* (1963, Dog Years) and *Die Ratten* (1987, The Rats).

grasshopper A medium to large, terrestrial insect with hindlimbs adapted for jumping; forewings leathery; hindwings forming membranous fan, or reduced; many produce sound by rubbing together forewings or hindlimbs. (Order: Orthoptera.) >> insect [i]; locust

grass snake A harmless snake native to the Old World from Europe to SE Asia, and to North America; lives near water; often called **water snake** in the USA. (Genus: *Natrix*, many species. Family: Colubridae.)

Grattan, Henry (1746–1820) Irish statesman, born in Dublin. He secured Irish free trade in 1779, and legislative independence in 1782. >> Flood, Henry

Gravenhage, 's- [**skhrah**venhahguh] >> **Hague, The**

Graves, Robert (Ranke) (1895–1985) Poet and novelist, born in London. His best-known novels are *I, Claudius* and its sequel, *Claudius the God* (both 1934), which were adapted for television in 1976. His *Collected Poems* (1975) draws on more than 20 volumes.

Graves' disease >> **hyperthyroidism**

Gravettian [gra**vet**ian] A European archaeological culture of the Upper Palaeolithic Age, c.26 000–18 000 BC (sometimes referred to as the **Later Aurignacian/Later Perigordian**). It is named after the cave at La Gravette, Dordogne, SW France. >> Three Age System; Willendorf

gravitation The mutually attractive force between two objects due to their masses; expressed by Newton's law of gravitation $F = Gm_1m_2/r^2$, where F is the force between objects of mass m_1 and m_2 separated by distance r, and G is the gravitational constant. The direction of force is along a line joining the two bodies. It is the weakest of all forces, important only on a large scale. **Gravity** refers to the intensity of gravitation at the surface of the Earth or some other celestial body. >> acceleration due to gravity; escape velocity; general relativity; gravitational constant; Newton, Isaac

gravitational collapse A phenomenon which occurs when the supply of nuclear energy in the core of a star runs out, and the star cools and contracts; a prediction of general relativity. Once the star radius is less than a critical value (Schwarzschild radius, $R = 2MG/c2$, value 3 km/2 mi for the Sun), the collapse cannot be reversed by any force now known to physics. Implosion to a black hole seems inevitable. >> black hole; general relativity; gravitation; star

gravitational constant A fundamental constant, symbol G, value $6{\cdot}673 \times 10^{-11}$Nm2/kg2, which measures the strength of gravitation. >> gravitation

gravity >> **gravitation**

gravity assist The additional increment of velocity acquired by a spacecraft on passing a planet. Through accurate targeting, it can be used to speed up a spacecraft to achieve a trajectory not possible using present launch capabilities. >> gravitation

gravure A form of printing in which the image to be communicated is engraved or etched into the surface of a metal cylinder; after inking, surplus ink is removed from the surface of the cylinder, and the ink retained in the engraved cells is transferred to paper when that is brought into contact with the cylinder. >> printing [i]

Gray, Asa (1810–88) Botanist, born in Sauquoit, NY. His main works were the *Flora of North America* (1838–42), which he compiled with John Torrey, and the *Manual of the Botany of the Northern United States* (1848), often known simply as 'Gray's Manual'.

Gray, Thomas (1716–71) Poet, born in London. His masterpiece is 'Elegy Written in a Country Churchyard' (1751), set at Stoke Poges, Buckinghamshire.

gray In radioactivity, the unit of absorbed dose, ie the energy deposited in an object by radiation, divided by the mass of the object; SI unit; symbol *Gy*; 1 Gy defined as 1 J/kg. >> radioactivity units [i]

grayling Freshwater fish (*Thymallus thymallus*) widespread in clean swift rivers of N Europe; length up to 50 cm/20 in; body silvery with longitudinal violet stripes; good food fish. (Family: Thymallidae; sometimes placed in Salmonidae.) >> fish [i]

Gray's Inn >> **Inns of Court**

Graz [grahts] 47°05N 15°22E, pop (1995e) 241 000. City in SE Austria; second largest city in Austria; airport; railway; two universities (1585, 1811); cathedral (15th-c); 28 m/92 ft-high clock tower (1561); Piber Stud Farm, where Lippizaner horses bred for the Spanish Riding School in Vienna, 3·5 km/2 mi NE. >> Austria [i]

Great Australian Bight Area of the Southern Ocean off the S coast of Australia (1450 km/900 mi). >> Antarctic Ocean; Australia [i]

Great Awakening A widespread 18th-c Christian revival movement in the USA, which reached its high point in the 1740s in New England. Jonathan Edwards and George Whitefield were among its leaders. >> Christianity; Edwards, Jonathan; Whitefield, George

Great Barrier Reef Coral reef in the Coral Sea off the NE coast of Australia, 50–150 km/30–90 mi offshore and 2000 km/1200 mi long; the largest accumulation of coral known, yielding trepang, pearl-shell, and sponges. >> atoll; Australia [i]

Great Basin area 500 000 sq km/193 000 sq mi. Vast interior region in W USA, between (W) the Sierra Nevada and the Cascade Range and (E) the Wasatch Range and Colorado Plateau; rugged N–S mountain ranges; semi-arid climate; several deserts; some minerals and grazing land. >> United States of America [i]

Great Bear Lake Lake in Northwest Territories, NW Canada, on the Arctic Circle; 320 km/200 mi long; 40–177 km/25–110 mi wide; maximum depth 413 m/1356 ft; area 31 153 sq km/12 025 sq mi. >> Northwest Territories

Great Bitter Lake, Arabic **Buheiret Murrat al-Kubra** Lake on Suez Canal between Ismailiya (N) and Suez (S); Little Bitter Lake lies SE. >> Egypt [i]; Suez Canal [i]

Great Britain >> **United Kingdom** [i]

great circle A circle described on the surface of a sphere with its plane passing through the centre of the sphere. The shortest distance between any two points on a sphere lies along a great circle. >> latitude and longitude ℹ

Great Dane One of the largest breeds of dog (height, 0·75 m/2½ ft), perfected in Germany from a mastiff-like ancestor; long powerful legs; square head with deep muzzle and pendulous ears; coat short, pale brown with dark flecks. >> dog; mastiff

Great Depression The worldwide slump in output and prices, and the greatly increased levels of unemployment, which developed between 1929 and 1934. It was precipitated by the collapse of the US stock market (the 'Wall Street crash') in October 1929. >> Jarrow March; stock market

Great Divide >> **Continental Divide**

Great Dividing Range Mountain range in Queensland, New South Wales, and Victoria, Australia; extends 3600 km/2200 mi; rises to 2228 m/7310 ft at Mt Kosciusko. >> Australia ℹ

Greater Manchester >> **Manchester, Greater**

Great Exhibition An exhibition held in Hyde Park, London (May–Oct 1851), celebrating 'the Works of Industry of all Nations'. Prince Albert helped to organize the Exhibition, for which the Crystal Palace was constructed. >> Albert, Prince; Paxton

Great Indian Desert >> **Thar Desert**

Great Lakes The largest group of freshwater lakes in the world, in C North America, on the Canada–USA border; drained by the St Lawrence R; consists of Lakes Superior, Michigan (the only one entirely in the USA), Huron, Erie, Ontario; sometimes L St Clair is included; water surface c.245 300 sq km/94 700 sq mi, c.87 270 sq km/33 700 sq mi in Canada; connected by navigable straits and canals; pollution a recent problem. >> Canada ℹ; Erie / Huron / Michigan / Ontario / Superior, Lake; United States of America ℹ

Great Leap Forward A movement in China, initiated in 1958, which aimed at accelerating both industrial and agricultural progress. It planned the creation of 'communes' in a true collective system, but failed miserably. >> collective farm

Great Malvern >> **Malvern**

Great Northern War (1700–21) A war between Russia and Sweden for the mastery of the Baltic coastal region. Charles XII of Sweden defeated Peter I of Russia's army at Narva in 1700, but Peter later defeated Sweden at Poltava (1709). The war was concluded by the Treaty of Nystadt. >> Peter I

Great Plains Region of C North America; a sloping plateau, generally 650 km/400 mi wide, bordering the E base of the Rocky Mts from Alberta (Canada) to New Mexico and Texas; limited rainfall, short grass; used chiefly for stock grazing and grain growing; dry farming on unsuitable land and overpasturing led to the **Dust Bowl**, semi-arid regions where wind storms carry off large quantities of topsoil. >> United States of America ℹ

Great Red Spot The largest, best-known, and probably longest-lived 'storm' feature of Jupiter's atmosphere; a reddish oval feature in the S hemisphere, about 30 000 km/19 000 mi across. It is a region high in atmosphere exhibiting a counter-clockwise rotation lasting about 6 days. Its red colour is ascribed to chemicals (eg sulphur) in the atmosphere. >> Jupiter (astronomy)

Great Rift Valley >> **Rift Valley**

Great Salt Lake Large inland salt lake in NW Utah, USA; length 120 km/75 mi; width 80 km/50 mi; average depth 4 m/13 ft; has no outlet and fluctuates greatly in size; water is 20–7% saline; commercial salt extraction. >> Utah

Great Sandy Desert N belt of the Western Australian Desert; area c.450 000 sq km/175 000 sq mi. >> Australia ℹ

Great Slave Lake Lake in W Northwest Territories, C Canada; 480 km/300 mi long; 50–225 km/30–140 mi wide; maximum depth over 600 m/2000 ft; area 28 570 sq km/11 030 sq mi. >> Northwest Territories

Great Smoky Mountains Mountain range, part of the Appalachians, USA; rises to 2025 m/6644 ft at Clingmans Dome. >> Appalachian Mountains

Great Train Robbery >> **Biggs, Ronald**

Great Trek The movement of parties of Boers (*Voortrekkers*) which made them the masters of large tracts of the interior of S Africa. They began to leave Cape Colony in 1836 in separate trekking groups, settling in the Transvaal and Natal, and often encountering considerable native opposition. >> Afrikaners

Great Victoria Desert or **Victoria Desert** S belt of the Western Australian Desert, area c.325 000 sq km/125 000 sq mi. >> Australia ℹ

Great Wall of China (Chin *chang cheng*, 'long wall') The defensive and symbolic frontier stretching 4100 km/2550 mi across N China from the Yellow Sea to the C Asian desert; a world heritage site. The earliest connected wall was built from 221 BC to repel attacks from nomads to the N, and was improved during later dynasties. The wall is c.7·6 m/25 ft high and 3·7 m/12 ft broad, made of earth and stone with a facing of bricks. >> China ℹ; Mount Li

Great Zimbabwe Stone ruins covering an area of 25 ha/62 acres in SE Zimbabwe; a world heritage site. The site was probably occupied from the 4th-c, and the ruins date from the 8th-c onwards. The term *zimbabwe* is Bantu for 'stone houses'. >> Zimbabwe ℹ

grebe An aquatic bird, native to temperate regions or high tropical lakes worldwide; swims underwater using feet; toes lobed and slightly webbed. (Family: Podicipedidae, 22 species.) >> dabchick

Greco, El [**gre**koh] (Span 'the Greek'), nickname of **Domenikos Theotokopoulos** (1541–1614) Painter, born in Candia, Crete, Greece. He became a portrait painter whose reputation fluctuated because of the suspicion which greeted his characteristic distortions, such as his elongated, flamelike figures. His most famous painting is probably the 'Burial of Count Orgaz' (1586) in the church of San Tomé, Toledo.

Greece, ancient **Hellas**, Gr **Ellás**, official name **The Hellenic Republic**, Gr **Elliniki Dimokratia** pop (1995e) 10 513 000; area 131 957 sq km/50 935 sq mi. Republic of SE Europe, occupying the S part of the Balkan peninsula and numerous islands in the Aegean and Ionian seas; capital, Athens; timezone GMT +2; population mainly Greek (98%); chief religion, Greek Orthodox (98%); official language, Greek; unit of currency, the drachma of 100 lepta; mainland includes the Peloponnese (S), connected via the narrow Isthmus of Corinth; over 1400 islands, including Crete and Rhodes; nearly 80% of Greece is mountainous or hilly; highest point, Mt Olympus (2917 m/9570 ft); Mediterranean climate for coast and islands, with mild, rainy winters and hot, dry summers; prehistoric civilization culminated in the Minoan–Mycenean culture of Crete; Dorians invaded from the N, 12th-c BC; Greek colonies established along N and S Mediterranean and on the Black Sea; many city-states on mainland, notably Sparta and Athens; Persian invasions, 5th-c BC, repelled at Marathon, Salamis, Plataea, Mycale; Greek literature and art flourished, 5th-c BC; conflict between Sparta and Athens (Peloponnesian War) weakened the country, which was taken by the Thebans and Macedonians (4th-c BC); under Alexander the Great military expeditions penetrated Asia and Africa; Macedonian power broken by the Romans, 197 BC; part of the Eastern Byzantine Empire of Rome; ruled by Turks from 15th-c until 19th-c; national reawakening, led to independence, 1830; republic established, 1924; restored monarchy, 1935; German occupation in World War 2, followed by civil war, 1944–9; military coup, 1967; abolition of monarchy, 1969; democracy restored, 1974; governed by a prime minister, cabinet, unicameral parliament, and president; strong service sector accounts for c.55% of national income; agriculture based on cereals, cotton, tobacco, fruit, figs, raisins, wine, olive oil, vegetables; major tourist area, especially on islands; member of the European Community, 1981. >> Athens; Crete; Cyclades; Dodecanese; enosis; EOKA; Greek Orthodox Church / religion ℹ; Ionian Islands; Macedonia (Greece); Mount Athos; Olympia (Greece); Peloponnese; Persian Wars; RR1010 political leaders

Greek Orthodox Church The self-governing (*autocephalous*) Orthodox Church of Greece. After the schism of 1054, the Orthodox Church in Greece remained under the patriarch of Constantinople, but was declared independent in 1833. >> Christianity; Orthodox Church

Greek–Persian Wars >> **Persian Wars**

Greek religion The polytheistic religion of the Ancient Greeks. The gods each had a sphere of influence (eg Poseidon over the sea) or an attachment to a locality (eg Athena at Athens); often both. They are very human in their passions and spiteful jealousies; the main difference is that they do not eat human food, and they do not die. They shade into a lower group of demi-gods and heroes, whose cults centred on their tombs. >> Delphi, Oracle of; Eleusinian Mysteries; Greece ℹ; Homer; *see illustration below*

Greeley, Horace (1811–72) Editor and politician, born in Amherst, NH. He was editor of the weekly *New Yorker* in 1834, and in 1841 founded the daily New York *Tribune*. He was its leading editor until his death, and exerted a supreme influence on US opinion. >> American Civil War

Green >> **Greens**

green algae A large and diverse group of alga-like plants characterized by the photosynthetic pigments, chlorophylls *a* and *b*, which give them their green colour; found predominantly in fresh water. (Class: Chlorophyceae.) >> algae; Chlorophyta; photosynthesis

Greenaway, Kate, popular name of **Catherine Greenaway** (1846–1901) Artist and book illustrator, born in London. She became well known in the 1880s for her coloured portrayals of child life, in such works as *The Birthday Book* (1880). The **Greenaway Medal** is awarded annually for the best British children's book artist.

Greenaway, Peter (1942–) Film-maker and painter, born in London. In 1982, *The Draughtsman's Contract* won him critical acclaim, and he went on to direct a series of films preoccupied with sex, death, decay, and gamesmanship. *Prospero's Books* appeared in 1991 and *The Pillow-Book* in 1996.

□ international airport

green belt A planning measure in which areas are designated free from development to prevent urban sprawl encroaching into the countryside, and the merging of neighbouring towns. It provides open land for recreation, and protects agricultural land. >> garden city; new town

Greene, (Henry) Graham (1904–91) Writer, born in Berkhamsted, Hertfordshire. In his major novels, central religious issues emerge, especially concerning Catholicism, such as in *Brighton Rock* (1938), *The Power and the Glory* (1940), *The End of the Affair* (1951), and *A Burnt-Out Case* (1961). He also wrote plays, film scripts (notably, *The Third Man*, 1949), short stories, and essays, as well as three volumes of autobiography.

Greene, Nathanael (1742–86) US general, born in Warwick, RI. In the American Revolution, he took command of the Southern army in 1780, and though Cornwallis defeated him at Guilford Courthouse, the victory was so costly that Greene was able to recover S Carolina and Georgia, paving the way to American victory in the South. >> American Revolution

Greek religion – principal Greek gods

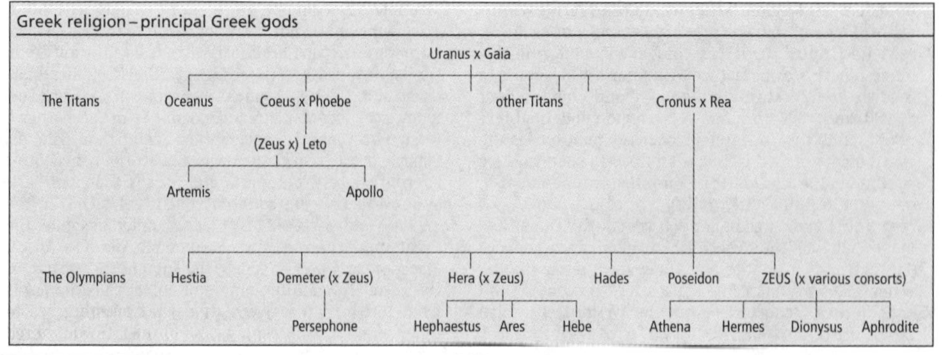

Greene, Robert (1558–92) Playwright, born in Norwich, Norfolk. His most popular work was the comedy *Friar Bacon and Friar Bungay* (c.1589), and his *Pandosto* (1588) was a source for Shakespeare's *The Winter's Tale*.

greenfinch A bird of the finch genus, *Carduelis* (4 species), native to S Europe and S Asia. (Family: Fringillidae.) >> finch; goldfinch

greenfly A soft-bodied aphid that feeds by sucking plant sap; wingless female has plump, greenish body, winged male darker; a complex life-cycle, with up to 10 generations each year produced asexually. >> aphid

Greenham Common The site of a US military base in West Berkshire, England. It was subjected to continuous picketing during most of the 1980s by the Women's Peace movement, who were opposed in particular to the siting of Cruise missiles in Britain, and in general to nuclear weaponry. The base closed down in 1992. >> Cruise missile

greenhouse effect A planetary atmosphere warming phenomenon, resulting from the absorption of infrared radiation by atmospheric constituents. Radiant energy arrives at the planetary surface mainly as visible light from the Sun, which is then re-emitted by the surface at infrared wavelengths as heat. Carbon dioxide and water vapour in the atmosphere absorb this infrared radiation and behave as a blanket, with the net effect that atmospheric temperatures rise. On Earth, the burning of fossil fuels and large-scale deforestation enhance the effect, so that there is likely to be a gradual increase in mean air temperature of several degrees, with the consequent melting of polar ice and a rise in mean sea level. (The term 'greenhouse' is misleading, since the mechanism by which glasshouses provide warming is mainly due to the inhibition of convection.) >> atmosphere ℹ; Earth ℹ; fluorocarbons; fossil fuel; ozone; radiation

Greenland, Dan **Grønland**, Eskimo **Kalâtdlit-Nunât** pop (1995e) 56 200; area 2 175 600 sq km/839 800 sq mi. Second largest island in the world (after Australia), in the N Atlantic and Arctic Oceans; capital, Nuuk (Godthåb); timezone GMT 0, −1, −4; population largely Inuit (Eskimo), with Danish admixtures; languages, Danish, Eskimo; main religions, Lutheran Christianity, Shamanism; currency, Danish krone; largely covered by an ice-cap (up to 4300 m/14 000 ft thick); coastal mountains rise to 3702 m/12 145 ft at Gunnbjørn Fjeld (SE); natural vegetation includes mosses, lichens, grasses, sedges; less than 5% inhabitable; settled by seal-hunting Eskimos from North America c.2500 BC; Norse settlers in SW, 12th–15th-c AD; explored by Frobisher and Davis, 16th-c; Danish colony, 1721; self-governing province of Denmark, 1979; elected Provincial Council sends two members to the Danish parliament; economy largely dependent on fishing from ice-free SW ports; hunting for seal and fox furs in N and E; reserves of lead, zinc, molybdenum, uranium, coal, cryolite. >> Davis, John; Denmark ℹ; Eskimo; Frobisher; Godthåb; Inuit; Peary Land

Greenland Sea area 1 205 000 sq km/465 000 sq mi. Gulf connecting the Atlantic and Arctic Oceans; cold surface current from the Arctic brings icebergs and fog. >> Arctic Ocean

Green Line 1 The dividing line between Muslim W Beirut and Christian E Beirut, Lebanon, during the 1975–6 civil war. **2** The dividing line between N (Turkish) and S (Greek) sectors of Nicosia. >> Beirut; Nicosia

green monkey >> **vervet monkey**

Green Mountain Boys A movement in the American Revolution that created the state of Vermont, from territory disputed between New York and New Hampshire. They helped capture the British fort at Ticonderoga (1775). >> Allen, Ethan; American Revolution

green paper In the UK, a document published by the government for discussion by interested parties, usually prior to formulating or changing policy. The practice first began in the late 1960s in response to calls for more consultation. >> white paper

Greenpeace An international environmental pressure group which began in Canada and the USA in 1971. It campaigns by direct action (non-violent, passive resistance) against commercial whaling and seal culling, the dumping of toxic and radioactive waste at sea, and the testing of nuclear weapons. >> environment; hazardous substances; waste disposal

green pound The special agricultural exchange rate in the EU, which ensures that currency movements are not reflected in national farm prices. The aim is that the price of each agricultural product should be the same throughout the EU. >> European Union

Greens A label applied to members of political parties and social movements which espouse ideologies having as a central tenet a concern over the damaging effect human activity is having on the environment. The first green party (the Values Party) was formed in New Zealand in 1972, to be followed in 1974 by the People Party in the UK. The most successful in parliamentary terms has been the German Green Party, which has had members of the Bundestag since 1983 and of the European Parliament since 1984. There is also a much larger green movement made up of environmental pressure groups and individuals. >> conservation; ecology; environment

greenshank A wading bird (*Tringa nebularia*), native to N Europe and N Asia; long pale green legs; long bill slightly upturned. (Family: Scolopacidae.)

Greenwich [**gren**ich], Anglo-Saxon **Grenawic** 51°28N 0°00, pop (1995e) 220 000. Borough of EC Greater London, England; site of the original Royal Greenwich Observatory; birthplace of Henry VIII, Elizabeth I, and Mary I; railway; Greenwich Hospital (1694), Royal Naval College, National Maritime Museum; clipper *Cutty Sark* and Francis Chichester's *Gypsy Moth IV* at Greenwich Pier; maritime Greenwich made a world heritage site in 1997. >> Chichester, Francis; Greenwich Mean Time; London; Millennium Dome; Royal Greenwich Observatory

Greenwich Mean Time (GMT) [**gren**ich] The basis for world time zones, set by the local time at Greenwich, near London. This is located on the Greenwich Meridian, longitude 0°, from which other time zones are calculated. It is now known as **co-ordinated universal time**. >> meridian; Royal Greenwich Observatory; standard time

Greenwich Village [**gren**ich] A district of Manhattan, New York City, which became famous during the 20th-c as the quarter of writers, intellectuals, and bohemians. It has recently developed into a more fashionable residential area. >> New York City

Greer, Germaine (1939–) Feminist, writer, and lecturer, born in Melbourne, Victoria, Australia. Her best-known book, *The Female Eunuch* (1970), portrayed marriage as a legalized form of slavery for women, and attacked the misrepresentation of female sexuality by male-dominated society. >> feminism; women's liberation movement

Gregorian calendar A calendar instituted in 1582 by Pope Gregory XIII, and now used in most of the world. Its distinguishing feature is that a century year is a leap year if, and only if, divisible by 400. This gives a year of 365·2425 days when averaged over 400 years. When introduced, a discrepancy of 10 days had built up, which was eliminated by jumping straight from 4 to 15 October in Catholic countries. Britain and its colonies (including America) switched in 1752, and also moved New Year's Day from 25 March back to 1 January. >> calendar

Gregorian chant The monophonic and (in its purest form) unaccompanied chant of the Roman Catholic liturgy. The compilation of the repertory has been credited to Pope Gregory the Great. >> chant; Gregory I; monody

Gregory I, St, known as **the Great** (c.540–604) Pope (590–604), a Father of the Church, born in Rome. There he saw some Anglo-Saxon youths in the slave market, and was seized with a longing to convert their country to Christianity. As pope, he was a great administrator, reforming all public services and ritual, and systematizing the sacred chants. He was canonized on his death; feast day 12 March. >> Anglo-Saxons; Augustine, St (of Canterbury); Gregorian chant

Gregory VII, St, originally **Hildebrand** (c.1020–85) Pope (1073–85), the great representative of the temporal claims of the mediaeval papacy, born near Soana, Italy. As pope, he worked to change the secularized condition of the Church, which led to repeated conflict with the German Emperor Henry IV. Gregory was canonized in 1606; feast day 25 May. >> antipope; pope; Roman Catholicism; simony

Gregory of Tours, St [toor], originally **Georgius Florentinus** (c.538–c.594) Frankish historian, born in Arverna (now Clermont). His *Historia Francorum* is the chief authority for the history of Gaul in the 6th-c. Feast day 17 November. >> Franks; Gaul

Grenada [gre**nay**da] pop (1995e) 91 900; area 344 sq km/133 sq mi. Most southerly of the Windward Is, E Caribbean; capital, St George's; timezone GMT –4; population mainly of African descent; chief religion, Roman Catholicism; official language, English; unit of currency, the Eastern Caribbean dollar of 100 cents; comprises the main island of Grenada (34 km/21 mi long, 19 km/12 mi wide) and the S Grenadines; Grenada volcanic in origin, with a ridge of mountains along its entire length; highest point, Mt St Catherine, rising to 843 m/2766 ft; subtropical climate; visited by Columbus, 1498, and named Concepción; settled by French, mid-17th-c; ceded to Britain, 1763; retaken by France, 1779; ceded again to Britain, 1783; British Crown Colony, 1877; independence, 1974; popular people's revolution, 1979; Prime Minister Maurice Bishop killed during further uprising, 1983; a group of Caribbean countries requested US involvement, and troops invaded the island (Oct 1983) to restore stable government; governed by a Senate, House of Representatives, prime minister, and cabinet; economy based on agriculture, notably fruit, vegetables, cocoa, nutmegs, bananas, mace; processing of agricultural products and their derivatives. >> St George's; RR1010 political leaders

grenade A munition, typically an explosive-packed container with a simple ring-pull fuse, designed for use in close-quarters fighting. It may be either thrown by hand or projected from a launcher.

Grenadines, The [**gren**adeenz] Group of 600 small islands and islets in the Windward Is, E Caribbean; administered by St Vincent (**N Grenadines**) and Grenada (**S Grenadines**); five airfields. >> Windward Islands (Caribbean)

Grenoble [gruh**nobl**], ancient **Cularo**, **Gratianopolis** 45°12N 5°42E, pop (1995e) 155 000. Ancient fortified city in E France; Mont Blanc to the NE; railway; bishopric; university (1339); cathedral 12th–13th-c; important sports and tourist centre; scene of 1964 Olympic skating championships and 1968 Winter Olympics. >> Blanc, Mont; France [i]

Grenville, Sir Richard (c.1542–91) English naval commander, a cousin of Sir Walter Raleigh. In 1585 he commanded the seven ships carrying Raleigh's first colony to Virginia. In 1591, as commander of the *Revenge*, he fought alone against a large Spanish fleet off the Azores, dying of wounds on board a Spanish ship. >> Raleigh, Walter

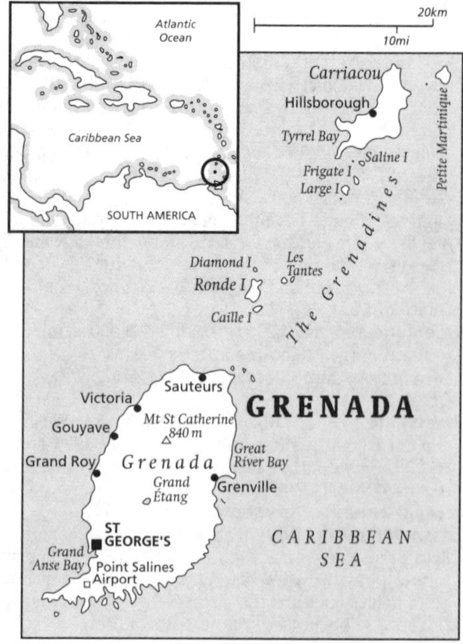

Grenville, William Wyndham Grenville, 1st Baron (1759–1834) British statesman, the son of Prime Minister George Grenville (1712–1770). He became paymaster-general (1783), home secretary (1790), and foreign secretary (1791), and in 1806–7 formed the coalition 'Government of All the Talents', which abolished the slave trade. >> slave trade

Greville, Sir Fulke, 1st Baron Brooke (1554–1628) Poet, born in Beauchamp Court, Warwickshire. He wrote several didactic poems, over 100 sonnets, and two tragedies. He was Chancellor of the Exchequer (1614–22).

Grey, Charles Grey, 2nd Earl (1764–1845) British statesman and prime minister (1830–4), born in Fallodon, Northumberland. A leading supporter of parliamentary reform, he secured the passage of the 1832 Reform Bill, and carried the Act for the abolition of slavery in the colonies. >> Reform Acts; slave trade; Whigs

Grey, Lady Jane (1537–54) Queen of England for nine days in 1553, born in Broadgate, Leicestershire, great-granddaughter of Henry VII. The Duke of Northumberland aimed to secure the succession by marrying Jane (against her wish) to his son. Three days after the death of Edward VI, she was named as his successor, but was forced to abdicate in favour of Mary, and beheaded. >> Edward VI

Grey, Zane, pseudonym of **Pearl Grey** (1875–1939) Novelist, born in Zanesville, OH. Best known of his 54 books was *Riders of the Purple Sage* (1912).

greyhound A breed of dog, now raced for sport; thin with short coat; long legs, tail, and muzzle; the **Italian greyhound** is a miniature breed developed in Italy. Greyhound racing takes place on an enclosed circular or oval track, round which dogs are lured to run by a mechanical hare. The first regular track was at Emeryville, CA, in 1919. >> dog; hound; lurcher; saluki

grey mullet Any of a large family of fish, widespread in tropical and warm temperate seas; body elongate, robust; dorsal profile rather flat; blue-grey above, sides silvery; valuable food fish in some areas. (*Chelon labrosus*. Family: Mugilidae, 4 genera.) >> fish [i]

gribble A small wood-boring crustacean that burrows into boat hulls and other submerged timber, causing extensive damage. (Class: Malacostraca. Order: Isopoda.) >> crustacean

grid reference A unique set of numbers locating any place on a map onto which a grid of numbered squares has been imposed. References in the UK are based on the National Grid. The distance eastwards (*easting*) is always given before the distance northwards (*northing*) when giving a National Grid reference. >> National Grid Reference System

Grieg, Edvard (Hagerup) [greeg] (1843–1907) Composer, born in Bergen, Norway. A strongly nationalist writer, his major works include the incidental music for Ibsen's *Peer Gynt* (1876), and the A minor piano concerto.

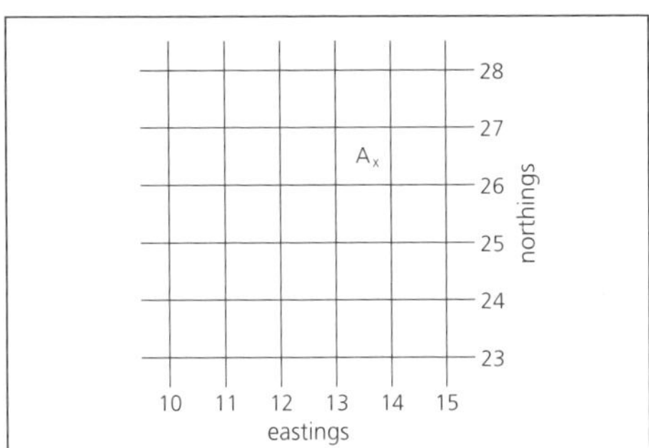

The grid reference for position A is 138264 within grid square 1326

Grierson, John [greerson] (1898–1972) Producer of documentary films, born in Kilmadock, Stirling. He made his name with *Drifters* (1929), and is regarded as the founder of the British documentary movement.

griffin or **gryphon** A fabulous beast, originating in Greek tales of the Arimaspians, who hunted the creature for its gold. It had a lion's body, and an eagle's head, wings, and claws.

Griffith, Arthur (1872–1922) Irish nationalist politician, born in Dublin. In 1905 he founded *Sinn Féin*, editing it until 1915, became an MP (1918–22), signed the peace treaty with Great Britain, and was a moderate president of the Dáil Eireann (1922). >> nationalism; Sinn Féin

Griffith, D(avid) W(ark) (1875–1948) Pioneer film director, born in Floydsfork, KY. He experimented with new techniques in photography and production, and brought out two masterpieces, *The Birth of a Nation* (1915) and *Intolerance* (1916).

Griffith, Melanie (1957–) Actress, born in New York City. She appeared in a number of films as a teenager, then after a gap of four years her adult career commenced with *Body Double* (1984). Later films include *Bonfire of the Vanities* (1990), *Reasonable Doubt* (1997), and *Lolita* (1997).

griffon An Old World vulture, native to S Europe, Africa, and S Asia; head and neck lack long feathers. (Genus: *Gyps*, 7 species.) >> vulture

Grignard, (François Auguste) Victor [greenyah(r)] (1871–1935) Organic chemist, born in Cherbourg, France. He introduced the use of organo-magnesium compounds (**Grignard reagents**), which form the basis of the most valuable class of organic synthetic reactions, for which he shared the Nobel Prize for Chemistry in 1912. >> magnesium; radical

Grigson, Sophie, popular name of **Hester Sophia Frances Grigson** (1959–) British cookery writer and broadcaster. A newspaper cookery correspondent from 1986, she became widely known through her television programmes for Channel 4, such as *Sophie's Meat Course* (1995). Among her books are *Food for Friends* and *Sophie's Table*.

Grimaldi, Joseph [grimaldee] (1779–1837) Comic actor, singer, and acrobat, born in London. From 1800 until 1828, he dominated the stage of Sadler's Wells as the figure of 'Clown' in the English harlequinade. >> harlequinade

Grimes Graves Prehistoric flint mines on the Norfolk Breckland, E England, in use c.3000–2500 BC. >> flint

Grimké sisters [grimkay] Abolitionists and feminists: **Sarah Moore Grimké** (1792–1873) and **Angelina Emily Grimké** (1805–79), born to a major slaveholding family in Charleston, SC. The sisters rejected their family's way of life, and joined the Quakers, who were officially anti-slavery. They became public figures, committed to social change. >> feminism; Garrison; slave trade

Grimm brothers Folklorists and philologists: **Jacob Ludwig Carl Grimm** (1785–1863) and **Wilhelm Carl Grimm** (1786–1859), both born in Hanau, Germany. Between 1812 and 1822 they published the three volumes known as *Grimm's Fairy Tales* (Ger *Kinder und Hausmärchen*). Jacob's *Deutsche Grammatik* (1819, Germanic Grammar, revised 1822–40) is perhaps the greatest philological work of the age; he also formulated **Grimm's Law** of sound changes. >> comparative linguistics; folklore

Grimmelshausen, Hans Jacob Christoph von [grimelshowzen] (c.1622–76) Writer, born in Gelnhausen. In later life he wrote a series of novels, the best of them on the model of the Spanish picaresque romances, such as the *Simplicissimus* series (1669–72). >> picaresque novel

Grimond (of Firth), Jo(seph) Grimond, Baron [**grim**uhnd] (1913–93) British politician, born in St Andrews, Fife. Elected leader of the Liberal Party (1956–67), he was largely responsible for the modernizing of both the Party and Liberalism, and called for a 'realignment of the left' of British politics. He was also Chancellor of the University of Kent (1970–90). >> liberalism

Grimsby, formerly **Great Grimsby** 53°35N 0°05W, pop (1995e) 90 000. Port town in North East Lincolnshire, NE England; railway; largest fishing port in England; football league team, Grimsby Town (Mariners). >> England [i]

grip The member of a camera crew in film or TV production who moves equipment and mountings. A **key grip** may also take part in associated set construction.

Griqualand [**greek**waland] Region of Eastern Cape province, South Africa; **East Griqualand** joined to Cape Colony in 1879; **West Griqualand**, including the diamond fields of Kimberley, joined in 1880. >> South Africa [i]; Transkei

grisaille [gree**ziy**] A painting executed entirely in shades of grey. This may be done for its own sake, or to look like sculpture as part of a decorative scheme. Many Renaissance painters began their pictures with a grisaille underpainting. >> engraving

Grivas, Georgeios (Theodoros) [**gree**vas] (1898–1974) Leader of EOKA, born in Trikomo, Cyprus. In 1955 he became head of the underground campaign against British rule in Cyprus, calling himself 'Dighenis' after a legendary Greek hero. In 1971 he returned secretly to Cyprus and, as leader of EOKA-B, directed a terrorist campaign for union with Greece until his death. >> Cyprus [i]; EOKA

grivet monkey >> **vervet monkey**

grizzly bear >> **brown bear**

Gromyko, Andrei Andreevich [gro**mee**koh] (1909–89) Soviet statesman and president (1985–8), born near Minsk, Belarus. As longest-serving foreign minister (1957–85), he was responsible for conducting Soviet relations with the West during the Cold War. >> Soviet Union

Groningen [**khron**ingn] 53°13N 6°35E, pop (1995e) 173 000. City in N Netherlands; bishopric; connected to its outer port, Delfzijl, by the Eems Canal; airport; railway; university (1614); large market, dealing in cattle, vegetables, fruit, and flowers. >> Netherlands, The [i]

Gropius, Walter (Adolph) [**groh**pius] (1883–1969) Architect, born in Berlin. He was appointed director of the Grand Ducal group of schools of art in Weimar, which he reorganized to form the Bauhaus, aiming at a new functional interpretation of the applied arts. When Hitler came to power, he moved to London (1934–7), and then to the USA, where he was professor of architecture at Harvard (1937–52). >> Bauhaus

grosbeak [**grohs**beek] A name applied to birds of several unrelated groups, all with a large, stout bill: the finch family Fringillidae (12–32 species); the weaver family Ploceidae (1 species); and the **cardinal grosbeaks** of the family Emberizidae (14 species). >> finch; weaverbird

Gros Morne [groh **maw(r)n**] National park on the W coast of Newfoundland, Canada, established in 1970; area 2000 sq km/775 sq mi; noted for its landscape and wildlife; a world heritage site. >> Newfoundland (Canada)

Gross, Michael [grohs], nickname **the Albatross** (1964–) Swimmer, born in Frankfurt, Germany. In 1981–7 he won a record 13 gold medals at the European Championships, and won three Olympic gold medals: the 100 m butterfly and 200 m freestyle in 1984, and the 200 m butterfly in 1988. >> swimming

gross domestic product (GDP) A measure of the wealth of a nation, calculated in any of three ways. The *output method* is the total of selling prices less the cost of bought-in materials. The *income method* is the total of wages, rents, dividends, interest, and profits. The *expenditure method* is the national expenditure on goods and services (known as 'GDP at factor cost'). The **gross national product (GNP)** is similarly calculated, but includes residents' income from economic activity overseas.

Grosseteste, Robert [**grohs**test] (c.1175–1253) Scholar, bishop, and Church reformer, born in Stradbroke, Suffolk. He undertook the reformation of abuses in the Church, which brought him into conflict both locally and with the papacy. >> Christianity; pope

Grossglockner [**grohs**glokner] 47°05N 12°44E. Mountain in the Hohe Tauern range, SC Austria; height 3797 m/12 457 ft; highest peak in Austria. >> Alps; Austria [i]

Grossmith, George [**groh**smith] (1847–1912) Comedian and entertainer, born in London. With his brother, **Weedon Grossmith** (1853–1919), he wrote *Diary of a Nobody* in *Punch* (1892). His son **George Grossmith** (1874–1935) was a well-known musical-comedy actor, songwriter, and manager of the Gaiety Theatre, London.

Grosz, George [grohs] (1893–1959) Artist, born in Berlin. While in Germany he produced a series of bitter, ironical drawings attacking German militarism and the middle classes. He fled to the USA in 1932, where he produced many oil paintings of a symbolic nature.

Grotius, Hugo [**groh**shius], also found as **Huig de Groot** (1583–1645) Jurist and theologian, born in Delft, The Netherlands. In 1625 he published his great work on international law, *De jure belli et pacis* (On the Law of War and Peace).

ground beetle An active, terrestrial beetle; adults mostly predatory, found in litter or vegetation. (Order: Coleoptera. Family: Carabidae, c.30 000 species.) >> beetle

ground elder A perennial (*Aegopodium podagraria*) native to Europe and temperate Asia; long creeping underground stems give rise to numerous leafy shoots and stems to 1 m/3¼ ft; flowers white. It is a persistent weed of gardens. Family: Umbelliferae.)

groundhog >> **woodchuck**

Groundhog Day A day (2 Feb) recognized in US popular tradition when the groundhog (or woodchuck), an American marmot, is supposed to appear from hibernation; it is said that if the groundhog sees its shadow, it goes back into hibernation for six more weeks, thereby indicating six weeks of winter weather to come.

ground ivy A creeping perennial (*Glechoma hederacea*), native to Europe and Asia; leaves rounded, bluntly toothed, in opposite pairs; flowers in pairs, 2-lipped, with long tube, violet-blue. (Family: Labiatae.)

groundnut >> **peanut**

groundsel A very variable annual (*Senecio vulgaris*) growing to 45 cm/18 in, native to Europe, Asia, and N Africa; flower-heads numerous, cylindrical, surrounded by narrow black-tipped bracts; florets yellow; fruit with a parachute of hairs. It is a common and often problematic weed. (Family: Compositae.) >> bract

grouper Large heavy-bodied fish with mottled cryptic coloration; prized as a sport fish and food fish; **Indo-Pacific grouper**, *Epinephelus lanceolatus*, may reach 3·7 m/12 ft, weight 270 kg/600 lb. (Family: Serranidae.) >> fish [i]

group therapy The interaction of several individuals on a cognitive and emotional level, as part of a therapeutic programme. It incorporates the sharing of personal experiences and feelings, with the purpose of increasing self-understanding and the treatment of psychological problems. >> encounter group

groupware Computer programs which are developed especially for the purpose of enabling groups of people either in the same or different locations to work together on a common task. A special case of groupware is the computer conference. >> computer network; video conferencing

grouse A plump, ground-dwelling bird of the family Tetraonidae (19 species); inhabits high latitudes of the N hemisphere; camouflaged coloration; short curved bill; nostrils covered by feathers; legs feathered; eats vegetation and insects. >> capercaillie; prairie chicken; ptarmigan; sandgrouse

Grove, Sir George (1820–1900) Musicologist, born in London. His major work was as editor of the *Dictionary of Music and Musicians* (1878–89). >> musicology

growth hormone (GH) A hormone (a polypeptide), secreted by the front lobe of the pituitary gland in vertebrates with jaws, which stimulates body growth; also known as **somatotrophin** or **somatotrophic hormone**. Its abnormal secretion may result in dwarfism or gigantism. >> acromegaly; hormones; peptide

growth ring >> **annual ring**

Groznyi [**groz**nee] 43°21N 45°42E, pop (1995e) 404 000. City in SE European Russia; founded as a fortress, 1818; airfield; railway; university (1972); major damage and disruption during war with Russia, 1995. >> Russia ℹ

Grünewald, Matthias [grünevalt], originally **Mathis Gothardt** (?1470–1528) Artist, architect, and engineer, probably born in Würzburg, Germany. In 1516 he completed the great Isenheim altarpiece (Colmar Museum).

grunion Slender-bodied fish (*Leuresthes tenuis*) confined to inshore waters of the Californian coast; length up to 18 cm/7 in; body with silvery side-stripe. (Family: Atherinidae.) >> fish ℹ

grunt Any of the family Haemulidae (formerly Pomadasyidae, 5 genera) of mainly tropical fishes common in shallow coastal waters and around coral reefs. They are so called because they produce audible sounds by grinding their pharyngeal teeth. >> fish ℹ

Grus [groos] (Lat 'crane') A S constellation. >> constellation; RR968

gryphon >> **griffin**

G-7 One of several economic groupings formed between states in the 1980s. G-7 consists of the seven leading industrialized countries: Canada, France, Germany, Italy, Japan, UK, and USA. Its annual meetings (the 20th in 1994) are attended by the president or prime minister of each country. The European Union and Russia were also represented at the 1994 meeting. Other groupings include G-10 (comprising 11 countries, the G-7 members plus Belgium, Netherlands, Switzerland, and Sweden) and G-24 (whose membership comes from developing countries).

guacharo >> **oilbird**

Guadalajara [gwadala**khah**ra] 20°30N 103°20W, pop (1995e) 1 807 000. City in WC Mexico; altitude 1567 m/5141 ft; founded, 1530; second largest city in Mexico; airport; railway; two universities (1792, 1935); cathedral (1561–1618), Hospicio Cabañas (a world heritage site); scene of a major industrial accident (gasline explosion) in 1992. >> Mexico ℹ

Guadalcanal [gwadalka**nal**] pop (1995e) 65 800; area 5302 sq km/2047 sq mi. Largest of the Solomon Is, SW Pacific; rises to 2477 m/8126 ft at Mt Makarakomburu; capital, Honiara; airport; scene of the first World War 2 Allied Pacific invasion northward (1942). >> Solomon Islands ℹ

Guadalquivir, River [gwadalki**veer**] (Span **Río**), ancient **Baetis**, Arabic **Vad-el-kebir** River rising in the Sierra de Cazorla, Andalusia, S Spain; enters the Atlantic at Sanlúcar de Barrameda; length, 657 km/408 mi. >> Spain ℹ

Guadalupe Hidalgo, Treaty of [gwada**loop** hi**dal**goh] (1848) The agreement that settled the Mexican War, with Mexico yielding all of Texas, Arizona, Nevada, California, and Utah, and parts of New Mexico, Colorado, and Wyoming. >> Mexican War

Guadeloupe [gwade**loop**] pop (1995e) 431 000; area 1779 sq km/687 sq mi. Overseas department of France, a group of seven islands in the C Lesser Antilles, E Caribbean; capital, Basse-Terre; largest town, Pointe-à-Pitre; timezone GMT −4; 90% black or mulatto population, with several minorities; chief religion, Roman Catholicism; official language, French; unit of currency, the French franc; main islands of Grand-Terre and Basse-Terre accommodate over 90% of the population; warm and humid climate; average annual temperature, 28°C; visited by Columbus, 1493; occupied by France, 1635; later held by Britain and Sweden; returned to France, 1816; departmental status, 1946; administrative region, 1973; Commissioner advised by a General Council and a Regional Council; economy mainly agricultural processing, especially sugar refining and rum distilling. >> Basse-Terre; Pointe-à-Pitre

Guam [gwahm] 13°N 144°E; pop (1995e) 155 000; area 541 sq km/209 sq mi. Largest and southernmost island of the Mariana Is, W Pacific Ocean, 2400 km/1500 mi E of Manila; capital, Agaña; timezone GMT +10; chief ethnic groups, Chamorro (47%), Filipino (29%) Caucasian (18%); official languages, Chamorro, English; chief religion, Roman Catholicism; length, c.48 km/30 mi long; rises to 406 m/1332 ft at Mt Lamlam; tropical maritime climate; occupied by Japan, 1941–4; unincorporated territory of the USA; elected Governor and a unicameral legislature; economy highly dependent on government activities; military installations cover 35% of the island; diversifying industrial and commercial projects; rapidly growing tourist industry. >> Agaña

guanaco [gwa**nah**koh] A wild member of the camel family (*Lama guanicoe*), native to the Andean foothills and surrounding plains; brown with white underparts and grey head; possibly ancestor of llama and alpaca. >> alpaca; Camelidae; llama

Guangzhou [kwangjoh], **Canton**, also **Kwang-chow** or **Kuang-chou** 23°08N 113°20E, pop (1995e) 4 218 000. City in S China, on Pearl R delta; founded in 200 BC; opened to foreign trade following Opium War of 1839–42; occupied by Japan, 1938–45; airport; railway; university (1958); medical college (1953); industrial and foreign trade centre in S China. >> China ℹ; Opium Wars

guanine [**gwa**neen] $C_5H_5N_5O$. One of the purine bases in DNA, normally paired with cytosine. >> DNA ℹ; purines

guano [**gwah**noh] An accumulation of animal droppings, typically of birds but also of mammals such as bats. Guano deposits are a rich source of phosphates and nitrates, and are often used as a fertilizer. >> fertilizer; nitrate; phosphate

guarana [gwa**rah**na] A woody liana (*Paullinia cupana*) with coiled tendrils, fern-like leaves and clusters of small, 5-petalled flowers; native to tropical America, cultivated in Brazil. The seeds are rich in caffeine, and it is used like cacao to produce a drink called guarana. (Family: Sapindaceae.) >> caffeine; liana

Guaraní [gwara**nee**] A Tupian-speaking South American Indian group, who lived in Brazil, Paraguay, and Argentina, practising slash-and-burn agriculture, hunting, and fishing. About a million now speak Guaraní. >> Paraguay ℹ

Guardi, Francesco [**gwah(r)**dee] (1712–93) Painter, born in Venice, Italy. He was noted for his views of Venice, full of sparkling colour, with an impressionist's eye for effects of light.

guardian A person who by right or appointment acts on behalf of another, taking care of that person's interests in full (or some cases to a limited or specified degree) as a result of the other's inability, either due to youth or (in some jurisdictions) mental incapacity. In the case of a child, the parents are normally the guardians, having full parental rights and duties, but they may arrange for the appointment of another person as guardian, in the event of their death.

Guareschi, Giovanni [gwa**res**kee] (1908–68) Writer and journalist, born in Parma, Italy. He achieved fame with his stories of the village priest, beginning with *The Little World of Don Camillo* (1950).

Guarini, (Giovanni) Battista [gwa**ree**nee] (1538–1612) Poet, born in Ferrara, Italy. His chief work was the pastoral play, *Il pastor fido* (1585, The Faithful Shepherd), which helped to establish the genre of pastoral drama.

Guarini, Guarino [gwa**ree**nee], originally **Camillo Guarini** (1642–83) Architect, philosopher, and mathematician, born in Modena, Italy. His influential *Architettura civile* (published posthumously in 1737), concerned the relationship of geometry and architecture, and he was responsible for the spread of Baroque architecture beyond Italy. >> Baroque (art and architecture)

Guarnieri [gwah(r)**nyay**ree], also found as **Giuseppe Guarneri**, known as **Giuseppe del Gesù** (1687–1745) A celebrated Italian family of violin-makers of Cremona, including **Andrea Guarnieri** (c.1626–98), his sons **Giuseppe Guarnieri** (1666–c.1740) and **Pietro Guarnieri** (1655–1720), and (most notably) Giuseppe's son **Giuseppe Guarnieri** (1698–1744). >> violin

Guatemala [gwate**mah**la], official name **Republic of Guatemala**, Span **República de Guatemala** pop (1995e) 10 557 000; area 108 889 sq km/42 031 sq mi. Northernmost of the Central American republics; capital, Guatemala City; timezone GMT −6; chief ethnic groups, Indian (41%) and mestizo; chief religion, Roman Catholicism; official language, Spanish, but several Indian languages spoken; unit of currency, the quetzal of 100 centavos; over two-thirds mountainous, with large forested areas; narrow Pacific coastal plain, rising steeply to highlands of 2500–3000 m/8000–10 000 ft; many volcanoes on S edge of highlands; humid tropical climate on lowlands and coast; rainy season (May–Oct); area subject to hurricanes and earthquakes; Mayan and Aztec civilizations before Spanish conquest, 1523–4; independence as part of the Federation of Central America, 1821; Federation dissolved, 1840; long standing claim over Belize resolved in 1991; guerrilla movement since 1960s; peace accord signed, 1996; governed by a president and a Congress of the Republic; agricultural products account for c.65% of exports, chiefly coffee, bananas, cotton, sugar; on higher ground, wheat, maize, beans; cotton, sugar cane, rice, beans on the Pacific coastal plain. >> Aztecs; Guatemala City; Mayas; RR1010 political leaders

Guatemala City or **Guatemala** [gwatuh**mah**la] 14°38N 90°22W, pop (1995e) 1 224 000. Capital city of Guatemala; founded to serve as capital, 1776; almost totally destroyed by earthquakes in 1917–18, and since rebuilt; altitude 1500 m/4920 ft; airport; railway; University of San Carlos (1680) and four other universities; cathedral (1782–1815). >> Antigua; Guatemala ℹ

Guayaquil [gwiya**keel**] 2°13S 79°54W, pop (1995e) 1 707 000. Seaport in W Ecuador; founded 1537; airport; railway; four universities (1867, 1958, 1962, 1966); banana trade (world's chief exporter). >> Ecuador ℹ

Gucci, Guccio [**goo**chee] (1881–1953) Fashion designer, born in Florence, Italy. He opened his first shop in Florence in 1920, becoming known for his leather craftsmanship and accessories. His four sons joined the firm, and in 1953 (the year he died) the first overseas shop opened in New York City. His grandson, **Maurizio** (1949–95) oversaw the resurrection of the firm in the 1980s. Following a series of legal and family disputes, the company was sold to Investcorp in 1993.

gudgeon Small bottom-dwelling freshwater fish (*Gobio gobio*) widespread in Europe; body elongate, cylindrical, length up to 20 cm/8 in; head large, mouth with pair of barbels; greenish-brown with darker patches on back, sides yellowish, underside silver. (Family: Cyprinidae.) >> fish ℹ

guelder rose [**gel**der] A deciduous shrub or small spreading tree (*Viburnum opulus*), growing to 4 m/13 ft, native to Europe and W Asia; flowers 5-petalled, white, in a cluster, outer flowers much larger than the inner; fruits berry-like, red, often persisting after the leaves have fallen. It is much grown as an ornamental under the name **snowball tree**. (Family: Caprifoliaceae.)

Guelph [gwelf] 43°34N 80°16W, pop (1995e) 93 500. Town in SE Ontario, Canada; founded, 1827; railway; university (1964); agricultural centre. >> Ontario

Guelphs The pro-papal, anti-imperial party in Italian cities in the 13th–14th-c, opposed to the power of the Holy Roman Emperors. Allied with the papacy, the Guelphs resisted the claims of potential successors, and dominated Florentine politics. >> Ghibellines; Holy Roman Empire

guenon [guh**non**] An Old World monkey native to Africa S of the Sahara; round head with beard, and 'whiskers' at side of face; slender, with long hind legs and tail. (Genus: *Cercopithecus*, c.17 species.) >> Old World / vervet monkey; talapoin

Guercino, Il [eel gwer**chee**noh], nickname of **Giovanni Francesco Barbieri** (1591–1666) Painter of the Bolognese School, born in Cento, Italy. His major work is the ceiling fresco 'Aurora' at the Villa Ludovisi in Rome for Pope Gregory XV. >> Baroque (art and architecture); fresco

guereza >> **colobus**

Guericke, Otto von [**gay**rikuh] (1602–86) Physicist, born in Magdeburg, Germany. He improved a water pump so that it would exhaust air from a container (1650), and was

□ international airport

able with this air pump to give dramatic demonstrations of pressure reduction (the **Magdeburg hemisphere**). >> electrostatics

Guernica [**gair**neeka] 43°19N 2°40W, pop (1995e) 16 200. Basque town in N Spain; German planes bombed the town in 1937, during the Spanish Civil War, an event recalled in a famous painting by Picasso (now in Madrid). >> Picasso; Spain ℹ; Spanish Civil War

Guernsey [**gern**zee] pop (1995e) 59 400; area 63 sq km/ 24 sq mi. Second largest of the Channel Is; rises to c.90 m/300 ft; airport; ferries to the UK and France; forms the Bailiwick of Guernsey with Alderney, Sark, and some smaller islands; chief town, St Peter Port. >> Channel Islands

Guevara, Che [gay**vah**ra], popular name of **Ernesto Guevara (de la Serna)** (1928–67) Revolutionary leader, born in Rosario, Argentina. He played an important part in the Cuban revolution (1956–9), after which he held government posts under Castro. He left Cuba in 1965 to become a guerrilla leader in South America, and was captured and executed in Bolivia. >> Castro

Guggenheim, Solomon R(obert) [**gu**genhiym] (1861–1949) Businessman and art collector, born in Philadelphia, PA. With the assistance of Hilla Rebay, he collected important Modernist paintings and established the Solomon R Guggenheim Foundation (1937). This was the source of funds for the Solomon R Guggenheim Museum, designed by Frank Lloyd Wright in 1959.

guided missile A weapon system which has the ability to fly towards its target under its own power. Its progress is directed either by an external source of command or by an internal computer which sends electronic guidance instructions to the missile's control surfaces. >> antiballistic / ballistic / cruise / high-speed anti-radiation / MX / Pershing / Polaris / Trident missile

guide dog A dog trained to assist the blind in finding their way, notably in urban traffic and crowded areas. The dogs are selectively bred, and include labradors, often crossed with golden retrievers, and German shepherd dogs. >> blindness

Guido d'Arezzo [**gwee**doh da**ret**zoh], also known as **Guido Aretino** (c.990–c.1050) Benedictine monk and musical theorist, probably born in Arezzo, Italy. The invention of the musical staff is ascribed to him, and he introduced the system of naming the notes of a scale with syllables. >> scale

Guildford [**gil**ferd] 51°14N 0°35W, pop (1995e) 64 700. Town in Surrey, SE England; railway; University of Surrey (1966); cathedral (completed in 1964). >> Surrey

Guildford Four [**gil**ferd] Three men and a woman who were convicted and sentenced to life imprisonment in England in 1975 for the bombing of two Guildford public houses in which seven people died, as well as for a bombing in Woolwich. The four were freed in 1989 after the Court of Appeal quashed their convictions. >> Birmingham Six; miscarriage of justice

guilds Religious and trade organizations, mediaeval in origin, but lasting into early-modern times. Trading and craft guilds controlled economic life in mediaeval towns; religious guilds flourished in cities and villages. >> Merchant Adventurers

Guilin, Kuei-lin, or **Kweilin** [gwaylin] 25°21N 110°11E, pop (1995e) 602 000. Town in S China; contains majority of China's Muslim population; badly damaged while US air base in World War 2; airfield; railway. >> China ℹ

Guillaume de Lorris [geeyohm duh **lo**ris] (c.1200–?) Poet, born in Lorris-en-Gatinais, France. He wrote the first 4000 lines of the *Roman de la Rose* (c.1235, Romance of the Rose) an allegory which was widely influential throughout mediaeval Europe. >> allegory; Jean de Meung

Guillaume de Machaut [gee**yohm** duh ma**shoh**] (c.1300–77) Poet and musician, born possibly in Reims, France. One of the creators of the harmonic art, he wrote a Mass, motets, songs, and ballads. His poetry greatly influenced Chaucer. >> Chaucer

guillemot [**gil**imot] An auk with a long pointed bill, also known as **tystie** or (in USA) **murre**. (Genera: *Uria*, 2 species, or *Cepphus*, 4 species. Family: Alcidae.) >> auk; pigeon; razorbill

Guillotin, Joseph Ignace [geeyohtĩ] (1738–1814) Physician and revolutionary, born in Saintes, France. He proposed to the Constituent Assembly, of which he was a deputy, the use of a decapitating instrument as a means of execution. This was adopted in 1791 and named after him.

guillotine A parliamentary device whereby debate on particularly contentious items of government business can be limited so that those opposing the business cannot instigate tactics designed to filibuster. It is used by all governments, usually on major pieces of legislation. >> filibuster

Guimarães [geema**rī**ysh] 41°26N 8°19W, pop (1995e) 48 000. Fortified city in N Portugal; first capital of Portugal; birthplace of Alfonso I; castle (10th-c). >> Portugal ℹ

Guinea [**gin**ee], Fr **Guinée**, formerly **French Guinea**, official name **Republic of Guinea**, Fr **République de Guinée** pop (1995e) 6 543 000; area 245 875 sq km/94 926 sq mi. W African republic; capital, Conakry; timezone GMT; ethnic groups include Fulani (40%), Malinké (25%), Susu (11%); chief religions, Islam (85%) and local beliefs (24%); official language, French, with several local languages widely spoken; unit of currency, the Guinea franc; coast characterized by mangrove forests, rising to a forested and widely cultivated narrow coastal plain; Fouta Djallon massif beyond (c.900 m/3000 ft); higher peaks near Senegal frontier include Mt Tangue (1537 m/5043 ft); savannah plains (E); forested Guinea Highlands (S); tropical climate (wet season May–Oct); cooler inland; part of Mali empire, 16th-c; French protectorate, 1849; governed with Senegal as Rivières du Sud; separate colony, 1893; constituent territory within French West Africa, 1904; overseas territory, 1946; independent republic, 1958; military coup, 1984; new constitution, 1990; Transitional Committee of National Recovery, 1991–5; governed by a president and a National Assembly; largely agricultural country; rich in minerals, with a third of the world's bauxite reserves; independence brought a fall in production as

a result of withdrawal of French expertise and investment. >> Conakry; Mali ℹ; Senegal ℹ; RR1011 political leaders

Guinea, Gulf of area 1 533 000 sq km/592 000 sq mi. Arm of the Atlantic Ocean, lying in the great bend of the W African coast; the Equator lies to the S. >> Atlantic Ocean

Guinea-Bissau [**gi**nee bi**sow**], offical name **Republic of Guinea-Bissau**, Port **Republica da Guiné-Bissau**, formerly **Portuguese Guinea** (to 1974) pop (1995e) 1 070 000; area 36 125 sq km/13 948 sq mi. Republic of W Africa, capital, Bissau; timezone GMT; chief ethnic groups, Balanta (32%), Fula (22%), Mandyako (14%), Mandingo (13%); chief religions, local beliefs (54%), Islam (38%); official language, Portuguese, with many African languages also spoken; unit of currency, CFA franc; an indented coast backed by forested coastal plains; low-lying with savannah-covered plateaux (S, E), rising to 310 m/1017 ft on the Guinea border; includes the heavily-forested Bijagos archipelago; tropical climate with a wet season (Jun–Oct); visited by Portuguese, 1446; Portuguese colony, 1879; overseas territory of Portugal, 1952; independence, 1973; military coup, 1980; new constitution, 1984; multi-party system introduced, 1991; governed by a president, prime minister, and a 100-seat National People's Assembly; military coup, 1999; economy based on agriculture, reserves of petroleum, bauxite, phosphate. >> Bissau; RR1011 political leaders

guinea corn >> **sorghum**

guinea flower >> **fritillary** (botany)

guinea fowl A sturdy, ground-dwelling bird native to Africa; plumage speckled grey; head and neck virtually naked; top of head may bear crest of feathers or horny projection (*casque*). (Family: Numididae, 7 species.)

guinea pig >> **cavy**

guineaworm A thread-like parasitic worm, a serious human parasite in Africa and India; larvae swallowed in untreated drinking water; adult worm develops in musculature of lower limbs. (Phylum: Nematoda.) >> nematode; parasitology

Guinevere [**gwin**iveer] King Arthur's queen; originally **Guanhamara** in Geoffrey of Monmouth's *History*, and there are other spellings. In later romances, much is made of her affair with Sir Lancelot (an example of courtly love). >> Arthur; Lancelot, Sir

Guinness, Sir Alec (1914–) Actor, born in London. His famous stage performances include Hamlet (1938) and Macbeth (1966). In 1958 he received an Academy Award for his part in the film *The Bridge on the River Kwai*. Later roles include Ben Kenobi in the *Star Wars* series, and Smiley in the television versions of John Le Carré's novels (1979, 1982). He was knighted in 1959 and made a Companion of Honour in 1994.

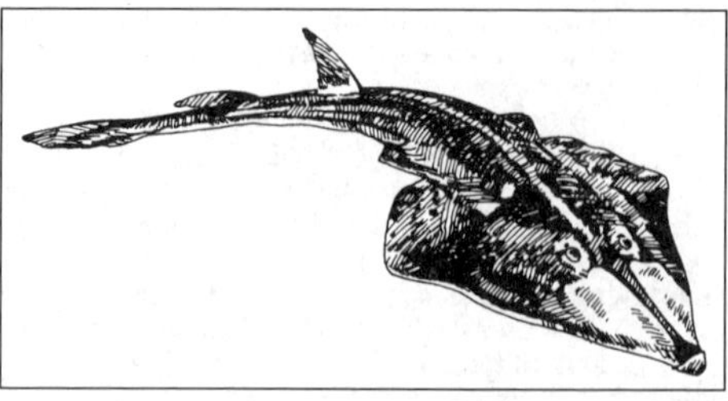

Guitar fish

Guise [geez] French ducal house of Lorraine, named after the town of Guise, whose members were prominent as staunch leaders of the Catholic Party during the 16th-c civil wars. The first duke was Claude de Lorraine (1496–1550). The line became extinct in the 17th-c.

guitar In its modern form, a musical instrument with a wooden, 'waisted' body, flat back, fretted neck, and six strings which are plucked (usually by fingers or fingernails) or strummed. Since its earliest days the guitar has been associated with folk and popular music, especially Spanish flamenco. Its elevation to the status of a recital and concerto instrument owes much to the example and influence of Segovia. The **electric guitar**, the sound of which is amplified and fed through a loudspeaker, exists in two types: the semi-acoustic, with a hollow body, and the more common type with a solid body acting not as a resonator but as an anchor for the strings, and a panel to which the electronic pickups and tone and volume controls are attached. The standard instrument has six strings, played with plectrum or fingers; the **bass guitar** has four strings, tuned one octave below the four lowest strings of the standard instrument. >> chordophone; flamenco; Hawaiian guitar; Segovia

guitar fish Bottom-dwelling, ray-like fish of families Rhinobatidae or Rhynchobatidae, in which the flattened head, broad pectoral fins, and slender body resemble the shape of a guitar or violin. >> ray; *see illustration above*

Guiyang or **Kuei-yang** [kwayyahng] 26°35N 106°40E, pop (1995e) 1 785 000. Capital of Guizhou province, S China; airfield; railway; steel, machinery, aluminium. >> China ℹ

Guizot, François (Pierre Guillaume) [geezoh] (1787–1874) Historian and statesman, born in Nîmes, France. As the king's chief adviser (1840), he promoted reactionary methods of government, and was forced to escape to London with Louis Philippe in 1848. >> Louis Philippe

Gujarat [gooja**raht**] pop (1995e) 44 568 000; area 195 984 sq km/75 650 sq mi. State in W India; independent sultanate, 1401; part of Mongol Empire, 1572; part of Bombay state, 1947; created in 1960 from the N and W Gujarati-speaking areas of Bombay state; capital, Gandhinagar; airfield; six universities; highly industrialized; scene of flood disaster in 1983, after bursting of the Fodana Dam. >> India ℹ

Gujarati [guja**rah**tee] >> **Indo-Aryan languages**

Gujranwala [guj**rahn**vala] 32°06N 74°11E, pop (1995e) 963 000. City in NE Punjab province, Pakistan; Sikh ruler Ranjit Singh born there, 1780; former Sikh capital; railway. >> Pakistan ℹ; Sikhism

gulag [**goo**lag] Acronym for **Glavnoye Upravleniye Ispravitelno-Trudovykh Lagerey** (Main Administration of Corrective Labour Camps), the Soviet Union's secret police department which administered the system of forced labour for those found guilty of crimes against the state.

Gulbenkian, Calouste (Sarkis) [gul**bengk**ian] (1869–1955) Financier, industrialist, and diplomat, born in Scutari, Turkey. A major figure in international oil negotiations for over 50 years, he left $70 000 000 and vast art collections to finance an international Gulbenkian Foundation.

Gulf, The >> **Persian Gulf**

Gulf Co-operation Council (GCC) An organization which provides for co-operation between the states surrounding the Persian Gulf. It was established in 1981 by Bahrain, Kuwait, Oman, Qatar, Saudi Arabia, and the United Arab Emirates. >> Persian Gulf

Gulf Intracoastal Waterway >> **Intracoastal Waterway**

Gulf Stream Ocean current named after the Gulf of Mexico; flows along the E coast of the USA and across the Atlantic Ocean (the N Atlantic Drift); its warm water has an important moderating effect on the climate of NW Europe. >> Mexico, Gulf of

Gulf War (1980–8) **1** (1980–88) A war between Iran and Iraq, occasioned by a dispute over the borders between the two countries, and a fear within each country of interference by the other in its internal affairs. After some border fighting in 1980, Iraqi forces advanced into Iran (22 Sep). By the time a peace was agreed (1988), following a long stalemate, the war had cost about half a million lives on both sides. Iraq accepted Iran's terms in August 1990. >> Iran ℹ; Iraq ℹ; Kurds; Persian Gulf; Shiites **2** (Jan–Feb 1991) A war caused by the invasion of Kuwait by Iraq (Aug 1990). Iraq failed to comply with a UN resolution calling on it to withdraw, which resulted in the formation of a 29-member coalition, led by the USA, launching an attack against Iraq (Operation Desert Storm) on 16 January, followed by a ground war on 24 February. Kuwait was liberated two days later, and hostilities were suspended on 28 February (a total of 43 days fighting). Iraq then accepted the US resolutions. Among notable events of the conflict were the Scud missile attacks on Israel and the defence provided by US Patriot missiles; Iraq's pumping of Kuwaiti oil into the Gulf; and the burning of Kuwaiti oil wells (all capped by November 1991). >> Hussein, Saddam; Iraq ℹ; Kuwait ℹ; Persian Gulf

gull A medium or large bird, found worldwide, usually near water; feet webbed; plumage white, grey, and black; wings long and slender; bill long, stout. (Family: Laridae, 44 species.) >> kittiwake; peewit

gullet >> **oesophagus**

gum arabic A resin which exudes from the branches of several species of *Acacia*, particularly *Acacia senegal*, a shrub or small tree native to dry areas of Africa, from Senegal to Nigeria. The gum is used as an adhesive, and in ink and confectionery manufacture. (Family: Leguminosae.) >> resin; wattle ℹ

gumbo >> **okra**

gums Dense fibrous connective tissue surrounding the base of the teeth, firmly attached to the underlying bone (the alveolar bone of the jaws). They are covered by a smooth vascular mucous membrane continuous with the lining of the lips and cheeks. >> gingivitis; teeth ℹ

gum tree A member of a genus of evergreen trees, native to and typical of Australia. Groups of species can be recognized by their characteristic bark: smooth gum trees, scaly blood-woods, fibrous stringy-barks, and hard iron-barks. They are fast-growing (the tallest reaching 97 m/318 ft), and provide useful timber and oils, including eucalyptus oil. (Genus: *Eucalyptus*, 500 species. Family: Myrtaceae.) >> tree ℹ

gun-cotton >> **nitrocellulose**

gundog >> **sporting dog**

gun-metal A form of bronze once favoured for the making of weapons. Modern gun-metal, with a composition of c.88% copper, 10% tin, and some zinc, has good anti-corrosion properties. >> bronze; corrosion

Gunn, Thom(son William) (1929–) Poet, born in Gravesend, Kent. His often erotic poems are written in an intriguing variety of regular and free forms. Volumes include *Fighting Terms* (1954), *The Passages of Joy* (1982), and *The Man With Night Sweats* (1992). He has lived in the USA since 1954.

gunnel Small slender-bodied fish found in inshore and intertidal habitats of the N Atlantic and Pacific Oceans; length up to 30 cm/1 ft; pelvic fins reduced or absent. (Family: Pholidae.) >> fish ℹ

gunpowder The oldest known explosive, a mixture of sulphur, charcoal and saltpetre (nitre, potassium nitrate). It was the principal military explosive until late in the 19th-c, and is still valuable in primers, fuses, and pyrotechnics. >> explosives

Gunpowder Plot A conspiracy by Catholic gentry, led by Robert Catesby, to blow up the English Houses of Parliament. It failed when Guy Fawkes, who placed the explosives, was arrested (5 Nov 1605). The scheme reflected Catholic desperation after the failure of previous plots to remove James I in 1603; peace with Spain in 1604, which ended the prospect of foreign support; and new sanctions against recusant Catholics, resulting in 5000 convictions in the spring of 1605. >> Catesby; Fawkes; James I (of England)

Gunwinggu An Australian Aboriginal people of W Arnhem Land. Many still live in small 'outstations' on Aboriginal land, gaining most of their subsistence by hunting and gathering, and selling bark paintings. >> Aborigines

Guomindang or **Kuomintang (KMT)** [gwohmindang] The Chinese National People's Party (or Nationalists), founded by Sun Yatsen in 1912 and later led by Jiang Jieshi. It ruled China from Nanjing, 1927–37 and 1945–9, and from Chonqing during the war with Japan, 1937–45. It retreated to Taiwan in 1949. >> Jiang Jieshi; Sun Yatsen; Taiwan ℹ

guppy Small freshwater fish (*Poecilia reticulata*) native to South and Central America but now widespread through the aquarium trade; length up to 3 cm/1¼ in; males with metallic blue-green coloration. (Family: Poecilidae.) >> fish ℹ

Gupta Empire [**gup**ta] (320–540) A decentralized state system covering most of N India. It was materially prosperous, and is known as India's 'Classical' or 'Golden' Age, when norms of Indian literature, art, architecture, and philosophy were established.

Gur Amir or **Gur Emir** [goor am**eer**] The mausoleum of Timur, Ulugh Beg, and others of the house of Timur, built in Samarkand (in present-day Uzbekistan) in the 15th-c. It was restored in 1967. >> Samarkand; Timur

gurdwara [**goord**wara] (Sanskrit, 'guru's door') A Sikh temple, or any place where the scripture is installed. >> Adi Granth; Sikhism

Gurkhas [**ger**kuhz] **1** The name of the Nepalese ruling dynasty since 1768. **2** An elite infantry unit of the British army recruited from the hill tribes of Nepal. Their characteristic weapon, the *kukri* fighting knife with its curved blade, has contributed to their fame. >> army; Nepal ℹ

gurnard [**ger**nah(r)d] Any of the bottom-living marine fishes of the family Triglidae, widespread in inshore waters of tropical to temperate seas; also called **sea**

robins; length up to 75 cm/30 in; head armoured with bony plates; pectoral fin rays used as feelers or as stilts. >> fish

guru [**goo**roo] In Hinduism, a spiritual teacher or guide who gives instruction to a disciple or pupil, who in return is required to render reverence and obedience. In Sikhism, it is identified with the inner voice of God, of which the 10 Gurus were the human vehicles. The term has developed a more general sense in recent years, referring to anyone who comes to be recognized as leader or originator of a cult or idea, not necessarily to do with religion. >> Hinduism; Sikhism

Gush Emmunim [gush emu**neem**] (Heb 'Group of those who keep the faith') An Israeli pressure group set up after the 1973 elections, dedicated to an active settlement policy in territories such as the West Bank, occupied by the Israelis after the 1967 war. >> Arab–Israeli Wars

Gustav I, originally **Gustav Eriksson Vasa** (1496–1560) King of Sweden (1523–60), founder of the Vasa dynasty. He led a peasant rising against the occupying Danes, capturing Stockholm (1523) and driving the enemy from Sweden. >> Sweden

Gustav II Adolf or **Gustavus Adolphus** (1594–1632) King of Sweden (1611–32), born in Stockholm. He recovered his Baltic provinces from Denmark, ended wars with Russia (1617) and Poland (1629), and carried out major military and economic reforms at home. In 1630 he entered the Thirty Years' War, and won several victories, notably at Breitenfeld (1631). >> Thirty Years' War

gut >> **alimentary canal**

Gutenberg, Johannes (Gensfleisch) [**goo**tnberg] (1400–68) Printer, regarded as the inventor of printing from movable type, born in Mainz, Germany. His best-known book is the 42-line Bible, often called the Gutenberg Bible (c.1455). >> printing

Guthrie, Sir (William) Tyrone (1900–71) Theatrical director, born in Tunbridge Wells, Kent. He was responsible for many fine productions of Shakespeare at the Old Vic during the 1930s, and became administrator of the Old Vic and Sadler's Wells (1939–45).

Guthrie, Woody, popular name of **Woodrow Wilson Guthrie** (1912–67) Folksinger and songwriter, born in Okemah, OK. He took to the road during the Great Depression, and wrote hundreds of songs, notably 'So Long, It's Been Good to Know You' and 'This Land Is Your Land'.

gutta percha A grey-black substance similar to rubber, but non-elastic, obtained from the latex of *Palaquium*, a genus of tropical trees related to chicle. It has been widely used in dental fillings, electrical insulation, and (especially) golf balls.(Family: Sapotaceae.) >> chicle; latex; rubber

Guy, Thomas [giy] (c.1644–1724) Philanthropist, born in London. In 1722 he founded the hospital in Southwark, London, which bears his name.

Guyana [giy**ah**na], official name **Co-operative Republic of Guyana**, formerly (to 1966) **British Guiana** pop (1995e) 750 000; area 214 969 sq km/82 978 sq mi. Republic on N coast of South America; capital, Georgetown; timezone GMT −3; population mainly East Indian (51%), black (30·5%), mixed ((11%), Amerindian (5%); chief religions, Christianity (52%), Hindu (37%), Muslim (9%); official language, English; unit of currency, the Guyana dollar of 100 cents; inland forest covers c.85% of land area; highest peak, Mt Roraima, rising to 2875 m/9432 ft in the Pakaraima Mts (W); equatorial climate in the lowlands, hot, wet, with constant high humidity; two seasons of high rainfall (May–Jul, Nov–Jan); sighted by Columbus, 1498; settled by the Dutch, late 16th-c; several areas ceded to Britain, 1814; consolidated as British Guiana; independence, 1966; republic, 1970; governed by a president and a National Assembly; high unemployment, influenced by labour unrest, low productivity, and high foreign debt; economy largely based on sugar, rice, bauxite. >> Georgetown; RR1011 political leaders

Guy Fawkes Night or **Bonfire Night** The evening of 5 November, the anniversary in the UK of the Gunpowder Plot, celebrated with fireworks and bonfires, on which are often burned effigies of Guy Fawkes known as *guys*. >> Fawkes; Gunpowder Plot

Gwalior [**gwal**iaw(r)] 26°12N 78°09E, pop (1995e) 750 000. City and former princely state in Madhya Pradesh, C India; founded, 8th-c; famous cultural centre, 15th-c; Mughal city, 15th–16th-c; taken by the British, 1780; railway; commercial centre. >> Madhya Pradesh

Gwent pop (1995e) 452 000; area 1376 sq km/531 sq mi. Former county in SE Wales, UK; created in 1974, and replaced in 1996 by Monmouthshire, Blaenau Gwent, Torfaen, and Newport counties. >> Wales

Gwyn or **Gwynne, Nell**, popular name of **Eleanor Gwyn** (c.1650–87) Mistress of Charles II of England, possibly born in London. She lived precariously as an orange girl before going on the boards at Drury Lane, where she established herself as a comedienne. >> Charles II (of England)

Gwynedd [**gwin**eth] pop (1995e) 118 000; area 3869 sq km/1494 sq mi. County in NW Wales, UK; created in 1996; formerly (1974–96) a wider area, including Anglesey, now consists only of Caernarfonshire and Merionethshire; rises to 1085 m/3560 ft at Snowdon in Snowdonia National Park; bilingual language policy; administrative centre, Caernarfon; castles at Caernarfon, Conwy, Criccieth, Harlech. >> Caernarfon; Wales

gymkhana A mixed sports meeting in a public place, especially one involving a range of horse-riding skills for young riders. They originated in India in 1860. In the USA, the term is often used for an obstacle competition for automobiles.

gymnastics A series of physical exercises now used primarily for sporting contests. Men compete on the parallel bars, pommel horse, horizontal bar, rings, horse vault, and floor exercise. Women compete on the asymmetrical bars, beam, horse vault, and floor exercise. >> RR1053

gymnosperms The commonly used name for one of the two divisions of seed plants, the other being the *flowering plants* (**angiosperms**). They are characterized by having naked seeds (ie not enclosed in an ovary). They contain both living (eg conifers) and entirely fossil groups. Early gymnosperms became the dominant vegetation during the Jurassic and Cretaceous periods. (Class: Gymnospermae.) >> Cretaceous / Jurassic period; flowering plants; seed

gymnure [**jim**nyoor] >> **moonrat**

gynaecology / gynecology [giyni**kol**ojee] The study of the functions and disorders of the female organs of reproduction. Disorders of menstruation and of fertility constitute a major part of the discipline. Liberalization of the laws relating to abortion has increased the need for specialized gynaecological care. >> cervix; ovarian follicles; uterine tubes; uterus ℹ

gynecium / gynoecium >> **carpel; flower** ℹ

Györ [dyür], Ger **Raab**, Lat **Arrabona** 47°41N 17°40E, pop (1995e) 127 000. Industrial city in NW Hungary; railway; bishopric; noted for its modern ballet company; cathedral (12th-c, rebuilt 18th-c). >> Hungary ℹ

gypsum A mineral of calcium sulphate ($CaSO_4 \cdot 2H_2O$) found in evaporite deposits as crystals (*selenite*) or fine-grained masses (*alabaster*). When partly dehydrated, it forms *plaster of Paris*, a fine, quick-setting, white powder. >> alabaster

Gypsy >> **Rom**

gypsy moth A medium-sized tussock moth; rare in Britain but a pest of fruit trees in North America; wings whitish with dark zigzag markings. (Order: Lepidoptera. Family: Lymantridae.)

gyrfalcon [**jer**fawlkn] The largest of all falcons (*Falco rusticolus*) (length 50–60 cm/20–24 in); native to Arctic regions; plumage white, grey, or dark. >> bird of prey; falcon

gyrocompass A form of gyroscope which is set to maintain a N-seeking orientation as an aid to navigation. >> compass; gyroscope

gyromagnetic ratio For spinning particles, the ratio of magnetic moment to particle spin; symbol γ, units /T/s (per tesla per second). For protons, $\gamma = 2{\cdot}675 \times 10^8$ /T/s. >> magnetic moment; spin

gyroscope An instrument consisting of a rapidly spinning wheel so mounted as to utilize the tendency of such a wheel to maintain a fixed position in space, and to resist any force which tries to change it. A free vertically spinning gyroscope remains vertical as the carrying vehicle tilts, so providing an artificial horizon. A horizontal gyroscope will maintain a certain bearing, and therefore indicate a vessel's heading as it turns. >> gyrocompass

Haakon VII [**haw**kon] (1872–1957) King of Norway (1905–57), born in Charlottenlund, Denmark. During World War 2, he carried on Norwegian resistance to Nazi occupation from England. >> Norway ℹ

Haarlem >> **Harlem**

Habakkuk or **Habacuc, Book of** [**hab**akuk] One of the 12 so-called 'minor' prophetic books of the Hebrew Bible/Old Testament, attributed to the otherwise unknown prophet Habakkuk, possibly of the late 7th-c BC. >> Old Testament; prophet

habeas corpus [**hay**bias **kaw(r)**pus] A writ requiring a person who detains another to appear in court and justify that detention. If there is no good reason for the detention, release is ordered.

Haber, Fritz [**hah**ber] (1868–1934) Chemist, born in Wrocław, Poland (formerly Breslau, Prussia). He invented the process for making ammonia from the nitrogen in the air, and was awarded the Nobel Prize for Chemistry in 1918.

H

Habsburgs One of the principal dynasties of modern Europe, pre-eminent in Germany from the mediaeval period as sovereign rulers of Austria, from which the family extended its influence to secure the title of Holy Roman Emperor (1452–1806). The zenith of Habsburg power was reached under Charles V (1500–58). His inheritance was divided between his son and brother, thus creating the **Spanish Habsburg** line, rulers of Spain until 1700, and the **Austrian Habsburgs**, whose descendants ruled in C Europe until 1918. >> Charles V (Emperor); Holy Roman Empire

hacker A computer user who communicates with other remote computers, usually via the telephone network. In recent years, the term has acquired a pejorative sense, referring to those who access remote computers without permission. >> computer

Hackman, Gene (1931–) Film actor, born in San Bernardino, CA. He earned a Best Supporting Actor Oscar nomination for his performance in *Bonnie and Clyde* (1967), an Oscar for his role in *The French Connection* (1971), and further nominations for *Mississippi Burning* (1989), and *Unforgiven* (1992). Later films include *Wyatt Earp* (1994), *Get Shorty* (1995), and *Absolute Power* (1997).

hackney horse An English breed of horse; height, 14·3–16 hands/1·5–1·6 m/4 ft 11 in–5 ft 4 in; graceful and spirited, with an emphasized strutting step; black or brown with tail held high. >> horse ℹ

haddock Bottom-living fish (*Melanogrammus aeglefinus*) widespread in cold N waters of the Atlantic; length up to c.80 cm/32 in; body dark greenish-brown on back, sides silvery grey with dark patch above pectoral fins, underside white, lateral line black; important food fish, exploited commercially throughout the N Atlantic. (Family: Gadidae.) >> fish ℹ

Hades [**hay**deez] In Greek mythology, the king of the Underworld, terrible but just; he was responsible for the seizure of Persephone. To the Greeks, Hades was always a person, never a place, but by transference the Underworld became known by that name. >> Persephone; Pluto (mythology)

Hadith [ha**deeth**] Sayings attributed to the Prophet Mohammed, prefaced by a chain of authorities through whom the tradition is said to have been transmitted. One of the chief sources of Islamic law, it is second in authority only to the Koran. >> Islam; Koran

Hadlee, Sir Richard (John) (1951–) Cricketer, born in Christchurch, New Zealand. He has scored 3124 Test runs since making his debut in 1973, in 1988 he surpassed Ian Botham's record of 383 Test wickets, and went on to a total of 431 before retiring in 1990, when he was knighted. >> Botham; cricket (sport) ℹ

Hadrian IV >> **Adrian IV**

Hadrian [**hay**drian], in full **Publius Aelius Hadrianus** (76–138) Roman emperor (117–38), successor of Trajan. He spent little of his reign at Rome, but tirelessly toured the empire, consolidating the frontiers, visiting the provinces, and promoting urban life. >> Hadrian's Wall; Trajan

Hadrian's Wall The principal N frontier of the Roman province of Britain. Built AD 122–8 on the orders of the Emperor Hadrian, it runs 117 km/73 mi from the Solway Firth to the R Tyne, the wall itself 4·5 m/15 ft high (probably with a 2 m/6 ft timber parapet), its forward defensive ditch c.8·5 m/28 ft wide and 3 m/10 ft deep. Overrun by N tribes in AD 139 and again in 367, the wall was finally abandoned c.400–410. It is now a world heritage site. >> Hadrian

hadron In particle physics, a collective term for all particles which experience strong interactions. All baryons and mesons are hadrons (eg protons and pions). >> baryon; meson

hadrosaur [**had**rosaw(r)] A duck-billed dinosaur; front of snout flattened and expanded to form duck-like bill; dentition specialized, with several rows of teeth; widely distributed during the Cretaceous period. (Order: Ornithischia.) >> Cretaceous period; dinosaur ℹ; Ornithischia

Haeckel, Ernst (Heinrich Philipp August) [**hay**kl] (1834–1919) Naturalist, born in Potsdam, Germany. One of the first to sketch the genealogical tree of animals, he strongly supported Darwin's theories of evolution. >> Darwin, Charles

haematite / hematite A mineral iron oxide (Fe_2O_3), the most important ore of iron. Powdered haematite is used as a pigment (red ochre). >> iron

haematology / hematology [heema**tol**ojee] The study of the formation and function of the cells which circulate in the bloodstream and reside in the bone marrow and lymph nodes, and of the abnormalities that cause diseases. >> blood; medicine

haemodialysis >> **dialysis**

haemoglobin / hemoglobin [heemo**glohb**in] A widely occurring red-coloured protein, found for example in some protozoa, many invertebrates, vertebrates, certain yeasts, and plants of the family Leguminosae. In vertebrates it is the oxygen-carrying pigment present in red blood cells (*erythrocytes*). >> erythrocytes; sickle cell disease; thalassaemia

haemophilia / hemophilia [heemo**fil**ia] An inherited disorder of blood coagulation, resulting from a deficiency in one of the proteins responsible for normal blood clotting. This is the antihaemophilic factor (AHF, or *factor VIII*), which is normally produced by the liver and circulates in the blood. The gene responsible is X-linked, so the condition is transmitted by the mother and reveals itself in the sons. It causes recurrent bleeding after minor trauma, mainly into joints. Bleeding can be ameliorated by giving fresh plasma which contains factor VIII, or by giving a concentrate of the factor prepared from freshly donated blood. >> AIDS; blood

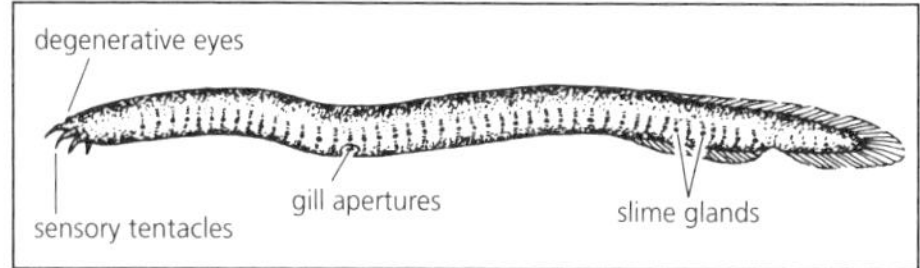

Hagfish

haemorrhage / hemorrhage [**hem**erij] Loss of blood externally or internally from any size of blood vessel. It is caused by injury to a blood vessel, or by a defect in normal blood clotting, as in haemophilia. >> blood vessels [i]; haemophilia

haemorrhoids / hemorrhoids [**hem**eroydz] A cluster of distended veins at the junction of the rectum and the anal canal, 2–3 cm/¾–1⅛ in above the opening of the anus; also known as **piles**. Usually there is no detectable cause. Haemorrhoids are very common, and can be removed surgically when large and giving discomfort; otherwise they may be treated by injections of a sclerosing solution. >> rectum

Haerbin / Haerhpin >> **Harbin**

Háfiz or **Háfez**, pseudonym of **Shams-ed-Din Mohammad** (c.1326–c.1390) Lyrical poet, born in Shiraz, Iran. A member of the mystical sect of Sufi philosophers, his short poems (*ghazals*), all on sensuous subjects, contain an esoteric signification to the initiated. >> Sufism

Haganah [ha**gah**na] The Jewish underground militia in Palestine, founded during the period of the British Mandate in the 1920s. After the declaration of the State of Israel in 1948, the Haganah became the official Israeli army. >> Israel [i]

Hagen [**hah**gn] 51°22N 7°27E, pop (1995e) 222 000. Industrial city in Germany; at junction of important traffic routes; railway. >> Germany [i]

hagfish Primitive marine fish lacking true jaws, vertebrae, paired fins, and scales; body eel-like, covered in copious slime, length up to 60 cm/2 ft; mouth slit-like surrounded by stout barbels. (Family: Myxinidae, 3 genera.)

Haggai, Book of [**hag**iy] One of the 12 'minor' prophetic books of the Hebrew Bible/Old Testament, attributed to the prophet Haggai, a contemporary of Zechariah, both of whom supported the rebuilding of the Temple in Jerusalem in c.520 BC after the return from exile. >> Old Testament; Temple, Jerusalem; Zechariah, Book of

Haggard, Sir H(enry) Rider (1856–1925) Novelist, born at Bradenham Hall, Norfolk. *King Solomon's Mines* (1885) made his work known, and was followed by *She* (1887) and several other stories.

haggis A traditional Scottish dish comprising the minced heart, liver, and lungs of a sheep, as well as suet, oatmeal, and various seasonings. The ingredients are cooked in a bag made from the *rumen* or forestomach of a sheep.

Hagia Sophia [**hah**jia soh**fee**a], or **Santa Sophia** A masterpiece of Byzantine architecture built (532–7) at Constantinople (now Istanbul). The lavishly-decorated, domed basilica was commissioned by Emperor Justinian I and designed by Anthemius of Tralles and Isidore of Miletus. >> Istanbul; Justinian

Hague, The [hayg], Dutch **Den Haag** or **'s-Gravenhage** 52°05N 4°16E, pop (1995e) 455 000. City in W Netherlands, and seat of the Dutch government; third largest city in The Netherlands; meeting-place of the States-General, 1527; centre of European diplomacy from 17th-c; Hague Convention (1907) formulated much of the law governing international warfare; headquarters of several international organizations, including the International Court of Justice; railway; noted for its furniture, pottery, and silverware. >> International Court of Justice; Netherlands, The [i]

Hague, William (Jefferson) [hayg] (1961–) British politician. Elected an MP in 1989, he acted as parliamentary private secretary to Chancellor of the Exchequer Norman Lamont (1990–3), then became under-secretary (1993–4) and minister of state for social security (1994–5), and minister for Wales (1995–7). He won the leadership of the Conservative Party following John Major's resignation in 1997.

Hague Agreement A convention of 1899 for the Pacific Settlement of International Disputes. It established a Permanent Court of Arbitration – the forerunner of the World Court. >> International Court of Justice

Hahn, Otto (1879–1968) Physical chemist, born in Frankfurt, Germany. In 1938 he bombarded uranium with neutrons to find the first chemical evidence of nuclear fission products. He was awarded the Nobel Prize for Chemistry in 1944. >> Meitner; nuclear fission

Hahnemann, (Christian Friedrich) Samuel [**hah**nuhman] (1755–1843) Physician and founder of homeopathy, born in Meissen, Germany. He experimented on the curative power of bark, but his methods caused him to be prosecuted wherever he tried to settle. >> homeopathy

Haida [**hiy**da] A Pacific Northwest Coast American Indian group in Queen Charlotte I, British Columbia, famous for their wood carvings, totem poles, and canoes. >> Tlingit

Haidar Ali [**hiy**der a**lee**], also spelled **Hyder Ali** (1722–82) Muslim ruler of Mysore, born in Budikote, Mysore, India. He waged two wars against the British, in the first of which (1767–9) he won several gains; but in 1781–2 he was defeated. >> Tippoo Sahib

Haifa or **Hefa** [**hiy**fa] 32°49N 34°59E, pop (1995e) 295 000. Industrial centre and seaport in NW Israel; third largest city in Israel; airfield; railway; university (1963); Bahai Shrine. >> Israel [i]

Haig, Alexander (Meigs) [hayg] (1924–) US army officer and statesman, born in Philadelphia, PA. A full general by 1973, he retired from the army to become White House chief-of-staff during the last days of the Nixon presidency. He served President Reagan as secretary of state in 1981–2, and sought the Republican nomination for the presidency in 1988. >> Nixon, Richard M; Reagan, Ronald; Republican Party

Haig (of Bemersyde), Douglas Haig, 1st Earl [hayg] (1861–1928) British field marshal, born in Edinburgh. In 1914 he led the 1st Army Corps in France, and in 1915 became commander of the British Expeditionary Force. He waged a costly and exhausting war of attrition, for which he was much criticized, but led the final successful offensive (Aug 1918). >> British Expeditionary Force; World War 1

haiku [**hiy**koo] A Japanese poetic miniature, consisting of three lines of 5, 7, and 5 syllables. This highly concentrated form has proved very popular outside Japan. >> metre (literature)

hail A form of precipitation comprising small balls or pieces of ice, which may reach up to 50 mm/2 in in diameter. It is generally associated with rapidly rising convection currents in low latitudes, or the passage of a cold front in temperate latitudes. >> cold front; precipitation

Haile Selassie I [**hiy**lee se**la**see], originally **Prince Ras Tafari Makonnen** (1891–1975) Emperor of Ethiopia (1930–6, 1941–74), born near Harer, Ethiopia. He led the revolution in 1916 against Lij Yasu, and became regent and heir to the throne, westernizing the institutions of his country. The disastrous famine of 1973 led to mutiny among the armed forces, and he was deposed (1974). Accusations of corruption levelled at him have not destroyed the reverence in which he is held by certain groups, notably the Rastafarians. >> Ethiopia [i]; Rastafarianism

Hailey, Arthur (1920–) Popular novelist, born in Luton, Bedfordshire. He became a naturalized Canadian in 1947. He has written many best-selling blockbusters about disasters, several of which have become successful films, such as *Airport* (1968), and *Wheels* (1971). Later novels include *The Evening News* (1990), and *Detective* (1997).

Hail Mary (Lat **Ave Maria**) A prayer to the Virgin Mary, also known as the **Angelic Salutation**, used devotionally since the 11th-c in the Roman Catholic Church. The first two parts are quotations from scripture (*Luke* 1.28, 42), the third part being added later. >> liturgy; Mary (mother of Jesus); rosary

Hailsham, Quintin (McGarel) Hogg, 2nd Viscount [**hayl**sham] (1907–) British Conservative statesman, born in London. His many posts included minister for science and technology (1959–64), and secretary of state for education and science (1964). In 1970 he was created a life peer (**Baron Hailsham of Saint Marylebone**) and became Lord Chancellor (1970–4, 1979–87). >> Conservative Party

Hainan Island [hiynan] area 34 000 sq km/13 000 sq mi. Island off S coast of China; rises to 1879 m/6165 ft at Wuzhi Shan; airport; opened to tourism and foreign trade in 1982; principal cities, Haikou, Dongfang. >> China ℹ

Haiphong [hiyfong] 20°50N 106°41E, pop (1995e) 1 617 000. Seaport in N Vietnam; founded, 1874; badly bombed in Vietnam War; third largest city in Vietnam; rail link to Kunming, China. >> Vietnam ℹ

hair A thread-like structure consisting of dead keratinized cells produced by the epidermis in mammalian skin. The covering of hair in mammals helps to maintain constant body temperature by insulating the body. >> baldness; keratin; skin ℹ

hairstreak An inconspicuous butterfly; wings typically blackish-brown, often with coloured patches; wingspan up to 40 mm/1½ in. The name is applied to several different species of the family Lycaenidae. (Order: Lepidoptera.) >> butterfly

Haiti [**hay**tee], official name **Republic of Haiti**, Fr **République d'Haiti** pop (1995e) 6 472 000; area 27 750 sq km/ 10 712 sq mi. Republic in the West Indies, occupying the W third of the island of Hispaniola; capital, Port-au-Prince; timezone GMT –5; population mainly of African descent (95%); chief religions, Roman Catholicism, voodoo; official language, French, with Creole French widely spoken; unit of currency, the gourde of 100 centimes; consists of two mountainous peninsulas (Massif du Nord (N) and Massif de la Hotte (S)), separated by a deep structural depression, the Plaine du Cul-de-Sac; highest peak, La Selle (2680 m/8793 ft); tropical maritime climate; mean monthly temperatures range from 24°C to 29°C; wet season (May–Sep); hurricanes common; Hispaniola visited by Columbus, 1492; Haiti created when W third of island ceded to France, 1697; slave rebellion followed by independence, 1804; united with Santo Domingo (Dominican Republic), 1822–44; under US occupation, 1915–34; Duvalier family had absolute power, 1957–86; after 1986 coup, new constitution provided for a bicameral assembly, led by a president and prime minister; military coup, 1992, forced President Aristide to flee the country, followed by UN and US sanctions; peaceful invasion by US forces to restore democratic government, 1994; new elections, 1995; economy based on agriculture; large plantations grow coffee, sugar, sisal. >> Duvalier; Hispaniola; Port-au-Prince; Toussaint L'Ouverture; RR1011 political leaders

Haitink, Bernard [**hiy**tingk] (1929–) Conductor, born in Amsterdam. He conducted the Amsterdam Concertgebouw Orchestra (from 1961) and the London Philharmonic (1967–79), and was appointed musical director at Glyndebourne in 1977 and at Covent Garden in 1987.

Hajj [haj] A formal pilgrimage to the holy city of Mecca during the Islamic month of Dhu-ul-Hijja. It is one of the Five Pillars of Islam. >> Islam; Mecca

hake Commercially important, edible, cod-like fish widely distributed in offshore continental shelf waters of temperate seas; length up to c.1 m/3¼ ft, head and jaws large, teeth strong; blue-grey on back, underside silvery white. (Genus: *Merluccius*. Family: Merlucciidae.) >> cod

Hakluyt, Richard [**hak**loot] (c.1552–1616) Geographer, born in Hertfordshire. He wrote widely on exploration and navigation, notably his *Principal Navigations, Voyages, and Discoveries of the English Nation* (1589). The *Hakluyt Society* was instituted in 1846.

Halakhah [**ha**lakah] The subject matter contained in the Talmudic and Rabbinic literature of Judaism dealing with the laws governing religious or civil practice in the community. It is distinguished from the **Haggadah**, which is not concerned with religious law, and includes such material as parables, fables, and prayers. >> Judaism; midrash; Talmud

Halcyone or **Alcyone** [hal**siy**onee] In Greek mythology, **1** A daughter of Aeolus, who married Ceyx, son of the Morning Star. Both were changed into sea-birds – halcyons, or kingfishers – who are fabled to calm the sea. **2** One of the Pleiades. >> Pleiades (mythology)

Hale, George Ellery (1868–1938) Astronomer, born in Chicago, IL, who discovered magnetic fields within sunspots. He initiated the construction of some of the world's largest telescopes, including the 5 m Palomar telescope.

Haleakala Crater [halayaka**la**] or **Kolekole** 20°42N 156°16W. Dormant volcano in E Maui I, Hawaii, USA; rises to 3055 m/10 023 ft; contains the largest inactive crater in the world. >> Hawaii (state); volcano

Hale-Bopp The name given to a comet discovered by amateur astronomers Alan Hale and Thomas Bopp in 1995, passing closest to the Sun in early 1997. Some 40 km in diameter, its passing produced brightness levels greater than any other comet of recent times. >> comet

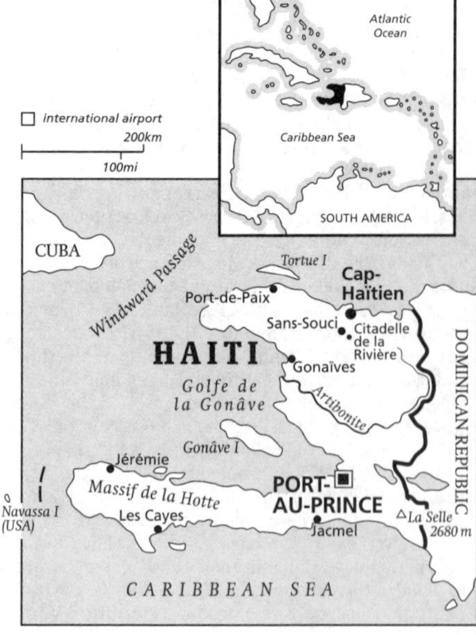

Halévy, (Jacques François) Fromental (Elié) [alayvee] (1799–1862) Composer, born in Paris. He is best known for his opera, *La Juive* (1835).

Haley, Bill, popular name of **William Haley** (1927–1981) Popular singer and musician, born in Highland Park, MI. With his group 'The Comets' he popularized rock-and-roll in the 1950s. His most famous song, 'Rock Around the Clock', was used in the film *Blackboard Jungle* (1955). >> rock music

half-life In radioactivity, the time taken for a group of atoms to decay to half their original number; symbol $T_{1/2}$, units s (second), also minutes and years. The half-life of plutonium-239 is 24 000 years; for helium-6 it is 0·8 seconds. The term also applies to the decay of excited atoms by the emission of light. >> atom; radioactivity

half-marathon >> **marathon**

halibut Largest of the Atlantic flatfishes (*Hippoglossus hippoglossus*), found on sandy and stony bottoms in cold N waters; length up to 2·5 m/8 ft; eyes on right side, mouth and teeth large; brown to greenish-brown with white underside; edible, commercially important, and prized by sea anglers. (*Hippoglossus hippoglossus*. Family: Pleuronectidae.) >> flatfish

Halicarnassus [halikah(r)**nas**us] A Greek city-state founded by the Dorians on the coast of SW Asia Minor; modern Bodrum, Turkey. It was the birth-place of Herodotos, and the site of the Tomb of Mausolus. >> Dorians; Herodotos; Mausolus, Tomb of

Halifax 44°38N 63°35W, pop (1995e) 121 000. Seaport, provincial capital of Nova Scotia, Canada; major transatlantic port and rail terminus; founded in 1749 as a British military and naval base; scene of harbour disasters, 1917, 1945; airport; four universities (1789, 1802, 1818, 1925); Citadel Hill (height 82 m/269 ft). >> Nova Scotia

Halifax, Charles Montague, 1st Earl of (1661–1715) English Whig statesman, born in Horton, Northamptonshire. He established the Bank of England (1694), and as Chancellor of the Exchequer (1694–5), introduced a new coinage. On Queen Anne's death he was made a member of the Council of Regency, and on George I's arrival (1714) became prime minister. >> Whigs

halite [**hal**iyt] The mineral form of sodium chloride (NaCl); also known as **rock salt**.

Hall, Ben(jamin) (1837–65) Bushranger, born in New South Wales, Australia. From 1862 he was increasingly involved in robbery, and became known for a series of audacious exploits. He was killed in a police ambush at the age of 28. >> bushrangers

Hall, Sir Peter (Reginald Frederick) (1930–) Theatre, opera, and film director, born in Bury St Edmunds, Suffolk. He became director of the Royal Shakespeare Company (1960–8), director of the Covent Garden Opera (1969–71), and successor to Olivier as director of the National Theatre (1973–88). He became artistic director at the Old Vic in 1997. >> Olivier; theatre

Halle or **Halle an der Saale** [**hal**uh] 51°29N 12°00E, pop (1995e) 310 000. City in EC Germany; railway; university (1694); Academy of Agricultural Science; birthplace of Handel. >> Germany ℹ; Handel

Hallé, Sir Charles [**hal**ay] (1819–95) Pianist and conductor, born in Hagen, Germany. The 1848 revolution drove him to England, and he ultimately settled in Manchester, where in 1858 he founded his famous orchestra. He was knighted in 1888.

Halley, Edmond [**hal**ee, **hawl**ee] (1656–1742) Astronomer and mathematician, born in London. From 1676 he investigated orbits in the Solar System, discovering that some comets pursue elliptical orbits. From this he successfully predicted the return of the comet named after him. >> Halley's comet

Halley's comet [**ha**lee] The most famous of all comets, first recorded by Chinese astronomers in 467 BC, a spectacular periodic comet orbiting the Sun in a retrograde direction with a period of 76 years. During its 1986 apparition, it was the subject of an intense study by an 'armada' of spacecraft. The images revealed a nucleus of irregular shape, about 16 × 8 km/10 × 5 mi. The very dark surface of the nucleus, and the presence of carbon in the comet dust indicate that there are significant quantities of organic molecules in the nucleus. >> comet; Giotto project; Halley; Sakigake and Suisei project; VEGA project

hallmarks The official marks struck on all modern and much old English, Scottish, and Irish silver and gold, and since 1975 on platinum. The metal is tested (*assayed*) for standard or quality. Hallmarks date from 1300, and each assay office had its own mark.

Hallowe'en The evening of 31 October, when spirits of the dead are supposed to return to their former homes, and witches and demons are thought to be abroad at night. This was the last day of the Celtic and Anglo-Saxon year, and many Hallowe'en customs have their origin in pagan ceremonies. In the USA, children go around demanding 'trick or treat' – if no 'treat' or present is forthcoming a 'trick' or practical joke will be played on the householder. >> All Saints' Day

Hallstatt [**hal**shtat] 47°34N 13°39E, pop (1995e) 1200. Small market town in N Austria; known for the **Hallstatt period**, the first phase of the European Iron Age (8th–4th-c BC), characterized by goods from burial tombs nearby. >> Austria ℹ; Three Age System

hallucination A sensory perception occurring without any stimulation of the sense organ. In its true form the individual is fully awake and the perception is located out of the body. Hallucinations indicate a loss of contact with reality, but they can be a normal phenomenon, such as during grief.

hallucinogens or **psychotomimetic drugs** Drugs that produce hallucinations, also called **psychedelic drugs**. Many naturally occurring hallucinogens have been used in ancient medicine and in religious ceremonies. Some are widely used (illegally) for recreational purposes. >> angel dust; LSD; magic mushrooms; mescaline

Halmahera [halma**he**ra], formerly **Djailolo** area 17 936 sq km/6923 sq mi, pop (1995e) 120 000. Largest island in the Moluccas, Indonesia; forested mountain chains, including active volcanoes; taken by the Dutch in 1683; independence, 1949. >> Moluccas

halogens [**hal**ojnz] The group of the periodic table with seven valence electrons. It comprises fluorine, chlorine,

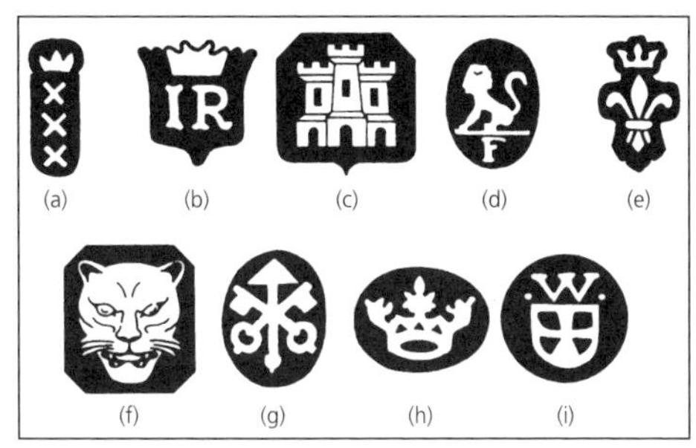

Selection of silver hallmarks - Amsterdam 18th-c (a); Jonathon Reid, Boston USA 1725–40 (b); Edinburgh (c); Florence 17th-18th-c (d); Lille 1750 (e); London (f); Rome late 17th-c (g); Stockholm 1500–1600 (h); Vienna 1570–1674 (i)

bromine, iodine, and the artificial element astatine. >> chemical elements; RR1036

Hals, Frans [hals] (c.1580–1666) Portrait and genre painter, probably born at Antwerp. Among his best-known works are 'The Laughing Cavalier' (1624, Wallace Collection, London) and 'Gypsy Girl' (c.1628–30, Louvre). >> genre painting

Hal Saflieni [hal sa**flyen**ee] A vast prehistoric rock-cut catacomb (*hypogeum*) for multiple burial in Paola, SE Malta; a world heritage site. The excavation, which was in use throughout the Copper Age, was discovered in 1902. >> Malta [i]; Three Age System

Hälsingborg >> **Helsingborg**

hamadryad (biology) [hama**driy**ad] >> **king cobra**

hamadryad (mythology) [hama**driy**ad] In Greek mythology, a tree-nymph. The hamadryad was offended or died when the tree containing her was harmed. >> dryad

hamadryas baboon [hama**driy**as] A baboon (*Papio hamadrya*) native to NE Africa and SW Arabia; silver-brown fur; naked face; long tail; sacred to ancient Egyptians; also known as **sacred baboon**. >> baboon

Hamburg [**ham**berg] 53°33N 10°00E, pop (1995e) 1 703 000; area 755 sq km/291 sq mi (including islands of Neuwerk and Scharhörn). Industrial port city in Germany; on the R Elbe, 109 km/68 mi from its mouth; largest German port; second largest city of Germany; founded by Charlemagne in the 9th-c; badly bombed in World War 2; railway; university (1919); birthplace of Brahms and Mendelssohn. >> Brahms; Charlemagne; Germany [i]; Hanseatic League; Mendelssohn

Hamersley Range Mountain range in NW Western Australia, extends for 257 km/160 mi; rises to 1244 m/4081 ft at Mt Meharry; the great iron-bearing area of Western Australia. >> Western Australia

Hamilcar [ha**mil**kah(r)], known as **Hamilcar Barca** ('Lightning') (c.270–228 BC) Carthaginian statesman and general at the time of the First Punic War, the father of Hannibal. He founded a new Carthaginian Empire in Spain, conquering most of the S and E of the peninsula. >> Hannibal; Punic Wars

Hamilton (Bermuda) 32°18N 64°48W, pop (1995e) 1140. Port, resort, and capital of Bermuda, on Great Bermuda; modern berthing and container facilities; founded 1612; capital since 1815; cathedral. >> Bermuda [i]

Hamilton (Canada) 43°15N 79°50W, pop (1995e) 338 000. City in SE Ontario, Canada, at head (W) of L Ontario; founded, 1813; site of Battle of Stoney Creek (1813); railway; McMaster University (1887); football team, Hamilton Tiger-Cats. >> Ontario

Hamilton (New Zealand) 37°46S 175°18E, pop (1995e) 154 000. City in North Island, New Zealand; airfield; railway; university (1964); noted for horse breeding and agricultural research. >> New Zealand [i]

Hamilton, Alexander (1757–1804) US statesman, born in the West Indian island of Nevis. He fought in the American Revolution, becoming Washington's aide-de-camp (1777–81), and was instrumental in the movement to establish the USA in its present political form, becoming secretary of the Treasury (1789–95). He was leader of the Federalist Party until his death. His successful effort to thwart the ambition of his rival, Aaron Burr, led to a duel in which Hamilton was killed. >> American Revolution

Hamilton, Emma, Lady, *née* **Emily Lyon** (c.1765–1815) Lord Nelson's mistress, probably born in Ness, Cheshire. In 1791 she married Sir William Hamilton (1730–1803). She first met Nelson in 1793, and bore him a daughter, Horatia (1801–81). After the death of her husband and Nelson, she became bankrupt, and fled to Calais, where she died. >> Nelson, Horatio

hamiltonian The total energy of a mechanical system; symbol *H*, units J (joule); after Irish mathematician William Hamilton (1805–65). It is equal to the sum of kinetic energy *K* and potential energy *V*. >> energy; mechanics

Hammarskjöld, Dag (Hjalmar Agne Carl) [**ham**ershohld] (1905–61) Swedish statesman, who became secretary-general of the United Nations (1953–61), born in Jönköping. At the UN, he helped to set up the Emergency Force in Sinai and Gaza (1956), and worked for conciliation in the Middle East (1957–8). He was awarded the 1961 Nobel Peace Prize. >> United Nations

hammerhead shark Large active shark of inshore tropical and temperate waters, characterized by a flattened head with broad lateral lobes; eyes and nostrils widely spaced; length up to 6 m/20 ft. (Genus: *Sphyrna*. Family: Sphyrnidae.) >> shark

Hammerstein, Oscar, II [**ham**erstiyn] (1895–1960) Librettist, born in New York City. He wrote the book and lyrics for many operettas and musical comedies. With composer Jerome Kern, he wrote *Show Boat* (1927), and with Richard Rodgers (1902–79), *Oklahoma!* (1943), *South Pacific* (1949), *The King and I* (1951), and *The Sound of Music* (1959). **Oscar Hammerstein I** was his impresario grandfather. >> Kern; musical

hammer throw An athletics field event in which the contestant throws with both hands a hammer (in fact, a metal ball with a wire handle) weighing 16 lb (7·6 kg), from within the confines of a 7 ft (2·13m) circle. The current world record is 86·74 m/284 ft 7 in, achieved by Yuriy Sedykh of Russia in 1986 at Stuttgart, Germany; for women it is 73.10 m/239 ft 8 in, achieved by Olga Kuzenkova of Russia in 1997 at Munich, Germany. >> athletics

Hammett, (Samuel) Dashiell (1894–1961) Writer, born in St Mary's Co, MD. He became the first US author of authentic 'private eye' crime stories. His best-known books are *The Maltese Falcon* (1930) and *The Thin Man* (1934).

Hammond, Dame Joan (1912–96) Soprano, born in Christchurch, New Zealand. She made her operatic debut in 1929, and became noted particularly for her Puccini roles. >> opera; Puccini

Hammurabi [hamu**rah**bee] (18th-c BC) Amorite king of Babylon (c.1792–1750 BC), best known for his Code of Laws, and for his military conquests that made Babylon the greatest power in Mesopotamia. >> Babylonia

Hampden, John (1594–1643) English parliamentarian and patriot, born in London. In 1634 he became famous for refusing to pay Charles I's imposed levy for outfitting the navy ('ship money'). He was one of the five members whose attempted seizure by Charles (1642) precipitated the Civil War. >> English Civil War

Hampi The site of the former Hindu capital of Vijayanagar, near the SW Indian village of Hampi. The city was founded in the 14th-c, and is a world heritage site. >> Hinduism

Hampshire pop (1995e) 1 607 000; area 3777 sq km/1458 sq mi. County of S England; crossed by the North Downs in the NW and W; county town, Winchester; major ports at Portsmouth, Southampton (new unitary authorities from 1997); naval bases at Portsmouth and Gosport. >> England [i]; New Forest; Winchester

Hampshire, Susan (1942–) British actress. She won Emmies for best actress in the television series *The Forsyte Saga* (1970), *The First Churchills* (1971), and *Vanity Fair* (1973). Later series include *The Grand* (1997–8). She has written about her problems with dyslexia in *Susan's Story* (1981).

Hampton Court The royal residence situated by the R Thames near London, built by Cardinal Wolsey, who occupied it until 1529. Queen Victoria declared it open to the public in 1851, and its gardens and maze are a major tourist attraction. >> Wolsey, Thomas

Hampton Institute A privately funded, co-educational college established in 1869 by Samuel Chapman (1839–93) in Hampton, VA, to provide vocational training for slaves freed after the American Civil War. It is an important centre for studies in black American history. >> American Civil War; university

hamster A small rodent of the subfamily Cricetinae (24 species); short tail, large ears; food can be stored in internal cheek pouches. One species, the **golden hamster** (*Mesocricetus auratus*), is a popular pet. >> mouse (zoology); rodent

Hamsun, Knut [**ham**soon], pseudonym of **Knut Pederson** (1859–1952) Writer, born in Lom, Norway. His best-known books are *Sult* (1888, Hunger) and *Markens grøde* (1917, The Growth of the Soil). He received the Nobel Prize for Literature in 1920.

Han Term used in China to differentiate the 93% of native Chinese population from the 7% made up of 50 ethnic minorities, including Hakka, Mongols, and Tibetans. >> China ℹ

Hancock, Lang(ley) George (1909–92) Australian mining industrialist, born in Perth, Western Australia. After discovering iron ore in several locations, he initiated the growth of Australian extractive industries. He held controversial right-wing views on politics and Aboriginal affairs, and in 1974 formed a secessionist movement in Western Australia.

Hancock, Tony, popular name of **Anthony John Hancock** (1924–68) Comedian, born in Birmingham, West Midlands. He achieved national popularity with the radio (later TV) series *Hancock's Half Hour* (1954–61). He committed suicide in Australia while attempting a television comeback.

hand The terminal part of the upper limb, used to manipulate (motor function) or assess (sensory function) the environment. It is richly endowed with sensory nerve endings and consists of a number of bony elements whose size and arrangement differs between species. In humans the bony elements are the eight carpals, the five metacarpals, the three phalanges in each finger, and the two phalanges in the thumb. >> arm; horse; nails; skeleton ℹ

handball An indoor and outdoor game first played in Germany c.1890, resembling Association football, but played with the hands. The indoor game is played with seven on each side. The outdoor game (known as **field handball**) is played on a field with 11 on each side. >> fives; football 1 ℹ; RR1053

Handel, George Frideric (1685–1759) Composer, born in Halle, Germany. In Italy (1706–10) he established a great reputation as a keyboard virtuoso and had considerable success as an operatic composer. While in London (from 1720), he developed a new form, the English oratorio, which proved to be highly popular. His most memorable work includes *Saul* (1739), *Israel in Egypt* (1739), and *Messiah* (1742). His vast output included over 40 operas, about 20 oratorios, cantatas, sacred music, and orchestral, instrumental, and vocal works. >> oratorio

Handley, Tommy, popular name of **Thomas Reginald Handley** (1892–1949) Comedian, born in Liverpool, Merseyside. In 1939 he achieved nationwide fame through his weekly programme *ITMA* (It's That Man Again), whose wit and satire helped to boost wartime morale. >> broadcasting

handwriting >> **chirography**

Handy, W(illiam) C(hristopher) (1873–1958) Composer, born in Florence, AL. He was the first to introduce the 'blues' style to printed music, his most famous work being the 'St Louis Blues' (1914). >> blues

Han dynasty Major Chinese dynasty (206 BC–AD 220), commonly divided into Early or Western Han (206 BC–AD 8), which had its capital at Changan (modern Xian), and Later or Eastern Han (25–220), with its capital at Luoyang. The Han period saw the conquest of what is now N Korea, N Vietnam, Kyrgyzstan, Uzbekistan, and Xinjiang, as well as major developments in education, science, technology, astronomy, and public health. Buddhism was introduced to China, and trade links developed with Europe via the Middle East. >> China ℹ; Xian

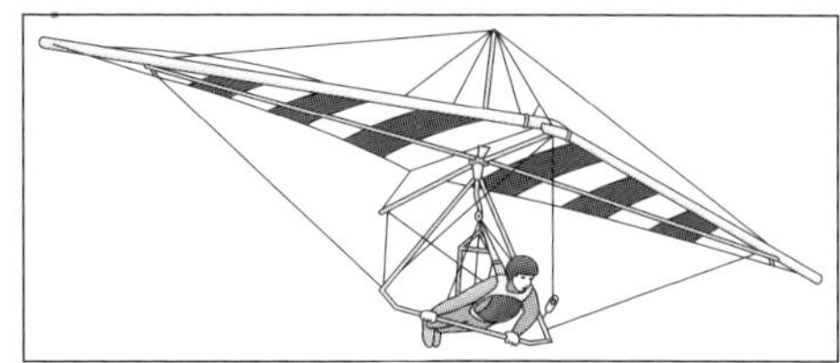

Hang glider

Hangchow >> **Hangzhou**

hang glider A person-carrying glider using a delta-shaped flexible wing, developed for NASA in the late 1950s as a gliding parachute. The pilot is suspended by a harness from the light frame holding the wing, and controls the movement of the craft by body movement. Later, engines were fitted, and the type developed into a form of ultralight aircraft called a **microlight**. Although popularized in the mid-1970s, hang gliding was pioneered in the 1890s by Otto Lilienthal in Germany. >> aircraft ℹ; glider; Lilienthal

hangul >> **red deer**

Hangzhou or **Hangchow** [hahngjoh], also **Kinsai** 30°18N 120°07E, pop (1995e) 1 582 000. City in E China; founded, 2200 BC; capital of several kingdoms and dynasties, 8th–12th-c; airfield; railway; technical university (1927); university (1959). >> China ℹ; Grand Canal

Hani, Chris [**han**ee], popular name of **Martin Thembisile Hani** (1942–93) South African political leader, born in Cofimvaba, South Africa. In 1991, he joined the ANC's National Executive Committee, and was also elected secretary-general of the South African Communist Party. He was shot dead by a white right-winger, and his murder triggered massive protests. >> African National Congress

Hanks, Tom, popular name of **Thomas J Hanks** (1957–) Film actor, born in Oakland, CA. His major films include *Sleepless in Seattle* (1993), *Apollo 13* (1995), and *Saving Private Ryan* (1998), and he received universal acclaim for his character performances in *Philadelphia Story* (1993, Oscar, Golden Globe) and *Forrest Gump* (1994, Oscar).

Hanna–Barbera [**ha**na bah(r)**be**ra] Animated cartoonists, in partnership for nearly 50 years. **William (Denby) Hanna** (1910–), born in Melrose, NM, became one of the first directors at the new MGM animation studio in 1937. He then teamed up with **Joseph (Roland) Barbera** (1911–), born in New York City, who had joined MGM as an artist. Together they created the first *Tom and Jerry* cartoons, winning seven Oscars between 1943 and 1952. They later created numerous television cartoon series using computer animation, including *The Flintstones*, *Yogi Bear*, and *Huckleberry Hound*.

Hannibal [**han**ibl] (247–182 BC) Carthaginian general and statesman, the son of Hamilcar Barca. In the Second Punic War, he left New Carthage on his famous journey (218 BC), defeated the Gauls, and crossed the Alps in fifteen days. He marched on Rome, and defeated the Romans at L Trasimene (217 BC) and at Cannae (216 BC), but was defeated by Scipio at Zama (202 BC). After several years in exile, he committed suicide to avoid Roman capture. >> Hamilcar; Punic Wars; Scipio Africanus Major

Hannover >> **Hanover**

Hanoi [ha**noy**] 21°01N 105°52E, pop (1995e) 2 242 000. Capital of Vietnam, on Red R; former capital of Vietnamese Empire, 11th–17th-c; capital of French Indo-China, 1887–1946; occupied by the Japanese in World War 2; severely damaged by bombing in Vietnam War; university (1956). >> Vietnam ℹ

Hanover, Ger **Hannover** 52°23N 9°44E, pop (1995e) 530 000. Commercial and industrial city in Germany; chartered, 1241; Elector George Louis became George I of Great Britain, 1714; badly bombed in World War 2; railway; three universities (1831, 1913, 1961). >> George I; Germany ℹ

Hanover, House of A dynasty of British monarchs, encompassing George I (1714–27), George II (1727–60), George III (1760–1820), George IV (1820–30), William IV (1830–7), and Victoria (1837–1901), though only the Georges and William are usually referred to as 'Hanoverians'.

Hansard, Luke (1752–1828) British printer. He entered the office of Hughes, printer to the House of Commons, in 1798 succeeding as sole proprietor of the business. He and his descendants printed regular parliamentary reports from 1774 to 1889, and the name is still used for these reports.

Hanseatic League A late mediaeval association of 150 N German towns, including Bremen, Hamburg, and Lübeck. It dominated trade from the Atlantic to the Baltic, and fought successful wars against neighbours between 1350 and 1450.

Hansen's disease An ancient chronic infectious disease due to *Mycobacterium leprae* that still affects 20 million people, mainly in the tropics, but is also endemic in the Middle East and S Europe; named after Norwegian bacteriologist Armauer Hansen (1841–1912), who discovered the bacillus in 1879. For centuries the disease was known as **leprosy** – a name applied to a variety of skin disorders, and still retaining (along with *leper*) strong negative emotional connations from the era when the basis of this disease was not understood; the trend in modern medical usage is to avoid this stigmatized term. The organisms show a predilection for the skin, peripheral nerves, and upper respiratory tract. >> infection

Hanson, Pauline >> **One Nation**

Hanukkah or **Chanukah** [**han**uka] An annual Jewish festival held in December (begins 25 Kislev), commemorating the rededication of the Temple at Jerusalem after the victory of Judas Maccabaeus over the Syrians in 165 BC; also known as the **Feast of Dedication** or **Feast of Lights**. >> Maccabees; RR982

Hanuman [**han**uman] The monkey-god of the Ramayana epic, who is the courageous and loyal supporter of Rama. A popular Hindu deity, he is represented as half-human and half-monkey. >> Hinduism

hanuman monkey >> **entellus**

Harald III Sigurdsson, nickname **Harald Hardrada** ('the Ruthless') (1015–66) King of Norway (1045–66). He waged war against Denmark until 1064. In 1066 he landed in England to aid Tostig against the English King Harold II, but fell at Stamford Bridge. >> Harold II

Harappa [ha**ra**pa] A prehistoric city in the Pakistani Punjab, occupied c.2300–1750 BC. Its ancient population numbered c.25 000. >> Indus Valley civilization; Mohenjo-daro

Harare [ha**rah**ray], formerly **Salisbury** (to 1982) 17°43S 31°05E, pop (1995e) 934 000. Capital and largest city of Zimbabwe; altitude, 1473 m/4833 ft; founded in 1890, and named after Lord Salisbury; airport; railway; university (1970); two cathedrals. >> Cecil, Robert; Zimbabwe

Harbin, also spelled **Haerhpin** or **Haerbin** 45°54N 126°41E, pop (1995e) 3 206 000. City in NE China; founded, 12th-c; developed as major rail junction; airfield. >> China ℹ

Harburg, E Y(ip) (1898–1981) Songwriter, born in New York City. Almost alone among his colleagues, he was politically active in civil rights groups. In his music, his convictions were realized in a quiet idealism that a better world was in the offing, as in 'April in Paris' (1932, with Vernon Duke) and his masterwork 'Somewhere Over the Rainbow' (1939, with Harold Arlen). He also wrote the clown songs for *The Wizard of Oz* (1939), and collaborated on Finian's Rainbow. >> musical

hard disk A rigid magnetic storage disk for computer data. It is generally capable of storing much more data than a similar-sized floppy disk. >> floppy / magnetic disk

Hardicanute [hah(r)dikan**oot**], also spelled **Harthacnut** (c.1018–42) King of Denmark (1035–42), and the last Danish King of England (1040–2), the only son of Canute and Emma of Normandy. His death without children led to the restoration of the Old English royal line in the person of Edward the Confessor. >> Canute; Edward the Confessor

Hardie, (James) Keir (1856–1915) British politician, born near Holytown, North Lanarkshire. He became a journalist and the first Labour candidate, entering parliament in 1892, and later served as chairman of the Labour Party (1906–8). >> Labour Party

Harding, Warren G(amaliel) (1865–1923) US statesman and 29th president (1921–3), born in Corsica, OH. Emerging as a power in the Republican Party, he won the presidency in 1920, campaigning against US membership of the League of Nations. His presidency was wracked with corruption. >> League of Nations; Republican Party

hardness A measure of a material's resistance to denting, scratching, and abrasion, related to the yield stress and tensile strength of the material. It is determined using indentation tests, which measure the size of a hole formed by a hard indenter driven into the material, as in the Vickers and Brinell tests. It is sometimes classified using the Mohs test of mineral hardness (devised by German mineralogist Friedrich Mohs in 1812), which rates talc as hardness 1 and diamond as hardness 10. >> Brinell hardness test

hardware In computing, a term used, in contrast to **software**, to include all the physical units which make up an electronic or computer system, such as keyboards, magnetic disks, circuits, and visual display units. >> firmware; software

Hardy, Oliver >> **Laurel, Stan**

Hardy, Thomas (1840–1928) Novelist and poet, born in Upper Bockhampton, Dorset. Unable to publish his poetry, he turned to the novel, and found success with *Far from the Madding Crowd* (1874). Later novels include *The Return of the Native* (1878), *The Mayor of Casterbridge* (1886), *Tess of the D'Urbervilles* (1891), and *Jude the Obscure* (1896). His main works were all tragedies, increasingly pessimistic in tone, and after *Tess* he was dubbed an atheist. He then took up poetry again, writing several volumes of sardonic lyrics, and the epic drama, *The Dynasts* (1903–8).

Hare, Sir David (1947–) Playwright and director, born in London. His politically engaged plays include *Slag* (1970) and *Plenty* (1978); *The Secret Rapture* (1988) won two awards for best play of the year. He has also written several films and television plays. Later works include *Amy's View* (1997).

Hare, William >> **Burke, William**

hare A mammal of the genus *Lepus* (11 species); also known as **jackrabbit**. There are several differences from the closely related rabbit: hares give birth to young (*leverets*) with fur, are larger, have black tips to the ears, are more solitary, and do not burrow. (Family: Leporidae. Order: Lagomorpha.) >> lagomorph; pika; rabbit

harebell A slender perennial (*Campanula rotundifolia*), native to N temperate regions; stems growing to 40 cm/15 in; flowers 5-lobed bells, blue, rarely white, drooping on slender stalks; the bluebell of Scotland. (Family: Campanulaceae.) >> bell-flower; bluebell

Hare Krishna movement [haree **krish**nah] A religious movement founded in the USA in 1965 by His Divine Grace A C Bhaktivedanta, Swami Prabhupada, as the International Society for Krishna Consciousness. It is one of the best known of the new religious movements coming from the East, largely as a result of saffron-robed people gathered in town centres chanting the Maha mantra. Devotees practise vegetarianism, do not use intoxicants, do not gamble, and are celibate apart from procreation within marriage. >> Bhagavadgita; Krishna

hare lip >> **cleft lip and palate**

Harewood, George Henry Hubert Lascelles, 7th Earl of [**hah(r)**wud] (1923–) Elder son of Princess Mary, and cousin of Queen Elizabeth II, born in Harewood, West Yorkshire. Since the 1950s he has been much involved in the direction of operatic and arts institutions, such as at Covent Garden, Edinburgh, and Leeds.

Hargreaves, James (c.1720–78) Inventor, probably born in Blackburn, Lancashire. He invented the *spinning jenny* (named after his daughter) in c.1764; and erected a spinning mill in Nottingham. >> spinning

haricot bean An annual (*Phaseolus vulgaris*) growing to 3 m/10 ft, sometimes climbing, a native of South America; pea-flowers white, yellow, or bluish, in small shortly stalked clusters; pods up to 20 cm/8 in long, containing edible ellipsoid or kidney-shaped seeds; numerous varieties are cultivated as a vegetable; also called **kidney bean** and **French bean**. (Family: Leguminosae.)

Harimandir [hariman**deer**] or **Golden Temple** The centre of the Sikh religion at Amritsar, Punjab, India. The temple dates from 1766, and houses the Granth Sahib, the holy book of the Sikhs. >> Sikhism

Harlem (The Netherlands), Dutch **Haarlem** 52°23N 4°38E, pop (1995e) 153 000. City in W Netherlands; founded, 10th-c; charter, 1245; sacked by the Spaniards (1573); railway; centre for tulip, hyacinth, and crocus bulbs. >> Netherlands, The ℹ

Harlem (USA) District in New York City, largely in N Manhattan Island, centred on 125th St; named (1658) after Haarlem, The Netherlands; a chiefly black residential area, known for its poverty and racial tension; area to the E contains a large Puerto Rican community (**Spanish Harlem**), and several other minority groups also live in the district; centre of a literary movement in the 1920s (the **Harlem Renaissance**). >> New York City ℹ

Harlem Globetrotters An American professional touring basketball team, formed in 1927. They developed a comedy routine to add to their skills, and now tour worldwide, giving exhibitions. >> basketball

Harlequin An acrobatic clown-like servant, with a costume of multi-coloured diamond-shaped patches, whose cunning and ingenuity has had a long and varied theatrical history. >> *commedia dell'arte*; harlequinade

harlequinade An English theatrical entertainment developed in the 18th-c by the actor John Rich, who specialized in the acrobatic and pantomimic portrayal of Harlequin. Scenes of this character's comic courtship of Columbine interspersed the performance of a serious play, which they served to satirize. They were the immediate precursors of the English pantomime. >> Harlequin; pantomime; Pierrot

Harley, Robert, 1st Earl of Oxford (1661–1724) British statesman, born in London. In 1710 he was made Chancellor of the Exchequer, head of the government, and (1711) Lord High Treasurer. The principal act of his administration was the Treaty of Utrecht (1713).

Harlow, Jean, originally **Harlean Carpentier**, nickname **the Blonde Bombshell** (1911–37) Film star, born in Kansas City, MO. From film performances such as *Platinum Blonde* (1931) and *Bombshell* (1933), and the scandals of her private life, she earned her nickname.

Harmattan [hah(r)ma**tan**] A hot, dry wind which blows from the Sahara desert in W Africa. Dust carried by the Harmattan may be blown across to the Caribbean. >> wind ℹ

harmonic A pitch sounded by a string or column of air vibrating at a half, a third, a quarter, etc of its length. The timbre of a voice or instrument depends on the prominence or otherwise of these harmonics (or *upper partials*) when the fundamental note is sounded. >> timbre

harmonica A musical instrument, popularly known as the **mouth organ**, in which metal 'reeds' arranged in a row are made to vibrate by the inhalation and exhalation of the player's breath. Virtuosi such as Larry Adler (1914–) and Tommy Reilly (1919–) have inspired many serious composers to write for it. >> reed instrument

harmonium A type of reed organ patented in 1842 by French instrument maker A F Debain (1809–77). The name has been widely used for reed organs in general. >> reed organ

harmony The combining of musical notes into chords, and then into sequences of chords, with emphasis on the 'vertical' component of the music rather than on the 'horizontal' fitting together of melodic strands (counterpoint). Harmony is thus generally thought of as accompanying, or 'clothing', one or more lines of melody. >> atonality; chromaticism; counterpoint; tonality

Harmsworth, Alfred (Charles William), 1st Viscount Northcliffe (1865–1922) Journalist and newspaper magnate, born near Dublin. In 1896 he revolutionized Fleet Street with his *Daily Mail*, introducing popular journalism to the UK. In 1908, he became proprietor of *The Times*. >> newspaper

Harmsworth, Harold (Sydney), 1st Viscount Rothermere (1868–1940) Newspaper magnate, born in London. He founded the Glasgow *Daily Record* and in 1915 the *Sunday Pictorial*, and after his brother's death acquired control of the *Daily Mail* and *Sunday Dispatch*. >> newspaper

harness racing A horse race in which the rider is seated in a small two-wheeled cart, known as a *sulky*. The horses either trot or *pace*, and must not gallop. Races are run on an oval dirt track measuring 400–1500 m/$\frac{1}{2}$–1 mi in circumference. >> horse racing

Harold I, nickname **Harold Harefoot** (c.1016–40) King of England (1037–40), the younger son of Canute and Ælfgifu of Northampton. Canute had intended that Hardicanute should succeed him in both Denmark and England, but in view of Hardicanute's absence in Denmark, Harold was accepted in England. >> Canute; Hardicanute

Harold II (c.1022–66) Last Anglo-Saxon king of England (1066), the second son of Earl Godwin. He defeated his brother Tostig and Harold Hardrada, King of Norway, at Stamford Bridge (Sep 1066), but Duke William of Normandy then invaded England, and defeated him near Hastings (14 Oct 1066), where he died, shot through the eye with an arrow. >> Edward the Confessor; Harold III; William I

Harold III >> **Harald III Sigurdsson**

harp A musical instrument of great antiquity existing in a wide variety of forms and sizes, its distinguishing characteristic being that its strings run in a plane perpendicular to the resonator. The modern concert harp, designed in 1810 by French pianoforte maker Sébastien Erard

(1752–1831), has a single row of 46 or 47 strings tuned to the major scale of C♭, and seven pedals by means of which any pitch may be raised by a semitone or a tone. >> string instrument 2 ℹ

Harpers Ferry Raid (1859) An attack on the Federal arsenal in Virginia, led by abolitionist John Brown, intending to launch a slave insurrection. The raiders were captured, and Brown was executed amidst great publicity. >> Brown, John; slavery

Harpies [**hah(r)**peez] In Greek mythology, fabulous monsters with women's features and bird's wings and claws. They were originally rapacious ghosts or the storm-winds. >> Argonauts

Harpocrates >> **Horus**

harpsichord A keyboard instrument in use from the 15th-c to the early 19th-c and revived in recent times, mainly for performing early music. The keys, when depressed, cause wooden *jacks*, fitted with plectrums to pluck the strings, which extend away from the keyboard and are dampened when the jacks fall into place again. >> continuo; keyboard instrument

Harrelson, Woody (1961–) Actor, born in Midland, TX. He became well known for his role as the bartender in the popular television series *Cheers* (1983–93). His feature films include *Indecent Proposal* (1993) and *The People vs. Larry Flynt* (1996, Oscar nomination). In 1996 he was arrested twice as an activist during events drawing attention to endangered forests.

harrier (mammal) A hound used for hunting hares; slightly smaller than a foxhound, with a keen sense of smell. >> foxhound; hound

harrier (ornithology) A medium-sized hawk of the worldwide genus *Circus* (10 species); wings and tail long; most nest on ground. (Family: Accipitridae.) >> falcon; hawk

Harriman, W(illiam) Averell (1891–1986) US statesman and diplomat, born in New York City. He became ambassador to the USSR (1943) and to Britain (1946), Governor of New York (1955–8), and US representative at the Vietnam peace talks in Paris (1968). He negotiated the partial nuclear test-ban treaty between the USA and USSR in 1963.

Harris S part of the Lewis with Harris island district, Western Isles, NW Scotland; area c.500 sq km/200 sq mi; tweed manufacture. >> Lewis with Harris

Harris, Sir Arthur Travers, nickname **Bomber Harris** (1892–1984) British airman, born in Cheltenham, Gloucestershire. As commander-in-chief of Bomber Command in World War 2 (1942–5) he organized mass bomber raids on industrial Germany. >> Royal Air Force

Harris, Joel Chandler (1848–1908) Writer, born in Eatonton, GA. He became known for his stories of *Uncle Remus* (1880), and several other children's books, noted for their distinctive use of Southern African-American folklore and dialect.

Harris, Paul >> **service club**

Harris, Roy, popular name of **LeRoy Ellsworth Harris** (1898–1979) Composer, born in Lincoln Co, OK. His works are ruggedly American in character and include 16 symphonies, as well as much instrumental, choral, and chamber music.

Harrisburg 40°16N 76°53W, pop (1995e) 53 800. Capital of state (since 1812) in S Pennsylvania, USA, on the Susquehanna R; scene of the Harrisburg Convention, 1788; scene of nuclear power station accident on Three Mile Island, 1979; railway; former steel industry giving way to a more diversified economy. >> Pennsylvania

Harrison, Benjamin (1833–1901) US Republican statesman and 23rd president (1889–93), born in North Bend, OH, grandson of William Henry Harrison. In 1888 he defeated Cleveland on the free trade issue, but failed to gain re-election in 1892. >> Cleveland, Grover

Harrison, George (1943–) Singer, guitarist, and songwriter, born in Liverpool, Merseyside. He played lead guitar and sang with the Beatles, and developed an interest in Indian music and Eastern religion. His solo albums include *All Things Must Pass* (1970), *Dark Horse* (1974), and *Somewhere in England* (1981). His company HandMade Films has produced feature films, including *Withnail and I* (1987). >> Beatles, The

Harrison, Sir Rex, originally **Reginald Carey Harrison** (1908–90) Actor, born in Huyton-with-Roby, Lancashire. His charming, somewhat blasé style attracted many star comedy parts, such as in *Blithe Spirit* (1945), *The Constant Husband* (1958), and *My Fair Lady* (1964, Oscar).

Harrison, Tony (1937–) Poet, born in Leeds, West Yorkshire. He became known with *The Loiners* (1970) and *Palladas* (1975). Poems on social conflict ('V'. 1985, televised 1987) and the Gulf War ('A Cold Coming', 1991) underline his commitment to public issues, confirmed in *The Gaze of the Gorgon* (1992). Later works include *The Prince's Play* (1996).

Harrison, William Henry (1773–1841) US soldier, statesman, and ninth president (1841), born in Charles City Co, VA. In the war of 1812–14 he defeated the British in the Battle of the Thames (1813). He was elected president in 1841, but died a month after his inauguration. >> Harrison, Benjamin

Harsanyi, John C (1928–) Economist, born in Budapest. He moved to the USA in 1956, joining the Haas School of Business at the University of California, Berkeley, in 1964. He shared the Nobel Prize for Economics in 1994 for his contribution to the analysis of equilibria in the theory of non-co-operative games.

Harte, Bret, pseudonym of **Francis Brett Hart** (1836–1902) Writer, born in Albany, NY. In 1868 he founded and edited the *Overland Monthly*, to which he contributed several short stories, notably those later collected in *The Luck of Roaring Camp* (1870).

hartebeest [**hah(r)**tibeest] An ox-antelope closely related to the topi; pale brown; two species: the **hartebeest** or **kongoni** (*Alcelaphus buselaphus*, 12 subspecies), and **Lichtenstein's hartebeest** (*Alcelaphus lichtensteini*). >> antelope; topi

Hartford 41°46N 72°41W, pop (1995e) 139 000. Capital of Connecticut, USA; founded by Dutch settlers, 1633; city status, 1784; railway; university; world's largest concentration of insurance companies; professional team, Whalers (ice hockey). >> Connecticut

Hartington, Lord >> Cavendish, Spencer Compton

Hartley, L(eslie) P(oles) (1895–1972) Writer, born near Peterborough, Cambridgeshire. His early short stories, such as *Night Fears* (1924), established his reputation as a master of the macabre. Later novels include *The Boat* (1950) and *The Go-Between* (1953).

Hartnell, Sir Norman (1901–78) Fashion designer and court dressmaker, born in London. His work included costumes for leading actresses, wartime 'utility' dresses, and Princess Elizabeth's wedding and coronation gowns.

haruspices [ha**rus**pikayz] In ancient Rome, the practitioners of the Etruscan system of divination, of which inspection of the entrails of sacrificial animals was the main part. Their art survived well into the Christian era. >> augury; Etruscans

Harvard University >> **Ivy League** ℹ

harvestman An extremely long-legged arthropod; body compact, carried on four pairs of long legs; female with long egg-laying tube; also called **daddy longlegs**. (Class: Arachnida. Order: Opiliones, c.4500 species.) >> arthropod

harvest-mite A small, predatory mite; tiny, red-coloured, 6-legged larvae often occur in large numbers in damp fields in autumn; feed by sucking blood of small mammals and humans; larvae known as **chiggers**. (Order: Acari. Family: Thrombidiidae.) >> mite

harvest mouse A mouse of genus *Reithrodontomys* (**American harvest mouse**, 19 species) from Central and North America; also, **Old World harvest mouse** (*Micromys minutus*) from Europe and Asia, the smallest living rodent (may weigh as little as 5 g/0·2 oz). >> mouse (zoology)

Harvey, Caroline >> **Trollope, Joanna**

Harvey, William (1578–1657) Physician, born in Folkestone, Kent, the first European to discover the circulation of the blood. His celebrated treatise, *De motu cordis et sanguinis in animalibus* (On the Motion of the Heart and Blood in Animals) was published in 1628. >> blood; Fabricius

Harwich [**ha**rich] 51°57N 1°17E, pop (1995e) 19 800. Port in Essex, SE England; railway; container freight terminal; ferries to Denmark, Germany, Holland. >> Essex

Hasdrubal [**haz**drubl] The name of several Carthaginian leaders, notably **1** Hamilcar Barca's son-in-law and successor in Spain (died 221 BC), and **2** Hannibal's younger brother, who died in battle with the Romans at the R Metaurus (207 BC). >> Hamilcar; Hannibal; Punic Wars

Hašek, Jaroslav [**ha**shek] (1883–1923) Novelist and short-story writer, born in Prague. He is best known for his novel *The Good Soldier Švejk* (1920–3), a satire on military life and bureaucracy.

Haselrig, Sir Arthur [**hay**zlrig], also spelled **Hesilrige** (?–1661) English parliamentarian, one of the five members whose attempted seizure by Charles I in 1642 precipitated the Civil War. After the Restoration, he died a prisoner in the Tower. >> Charles I (of England); English Civil War

Hashemites Arab princely family of sharifs, or descendants of the Prophet, who have ruled parts of Arabia and the Fertile Crescent in the 20th-c. They include the current royal family of Jordan. >> Hussein (ibn Talal); Jordan ℹ

hashish >> **cannabis**

Hasmoneans >> **Maccabees**

Hastings, Warren (1732–1818) British colonial administrator in India, born in Churchill, Oxfordshire. He joined the East India Company in 1750, and by 1774 was Governor-General of Bengal, making the Company's power paramount in many parts of India. On his return to England in 1784 he was charged with corruption, and after a seven-year trial, acquitted. >> East India Company, British

Hastings, Battle of (14 Oct 96) The most decisive battle fought on English soil. Norman cavalry overcame the resolute defence of the Anglo-Saxon army fighting on foot, and Harold II's death in battle cleared the way for Duke William of Normandy's coronation. >> Harold II; Norman Conquest; William I (of England)

Hatfield 51°46N 0°13W, pop (1995e) 33 600. Town in Hertfordshire, SE England; 30 km/19 mi N of London; designated a 'new town' in 1948; railway; University of Hertfordshire (1992, formerly Hatfield Polytechnic). >> Hertfordshire

Hathaway, Anne >> **Shakespeare, William** ℹ

Hathor [**hah**thaw(r)] The ancient Egyptian goddess of love, together with joyful music and dancing. She was identified by the Greeks with Aphrodite. >> Aphrodite

Hatra [**hat**ra] An ancient Parthian fortress city located between the Tigris and Euphrates rivers in N Iraq; a world heritage site. Founded in the 1st-c BC, it flourished as a trading and religious centre for four centuries. >> Parthians

Hatshepsut [hat**shep**soot] (c.1540–c.1481 BC) A queen of Egypt of the XVIIIth dynasty, the daughter of Thutmose I. She acted as Regent for Thutmose III, then had herself crowned as Pharaoh. She was represented with the regular pharaonic attributes, including a beard. >> pharaoh; Thutmose III

Hattersley, Roy (Sydney George), Baron (1932–) British statesman, born in Sheffield, South Yorkshire. He was secretary of state for prices and consumer protection (1976–9), and has since been Opposition spokesman on the environment and on home affairs, shadow Chancellor, and deputy leader of the Labour Party (1983–92). He was created a life peer in 1997. >> Labour Party

Hattusas [hatu**sas**] or **Hattusha** The ancient capital of the Hittites, now Bogazkoy in C Turkey, taken by the Hittites in the 17th-c BC, and destroyed in 1200 BC by the Sea Peoples. The ruins are a world heritage site. >> Hittites; Sea Peoples

Haughey, Charles (James) [**hokh**ee] (1925–) Irish statesman and prime minister (1979–81, 1982, 1987–92), born in Castlebar, Co Mayo. He became a Fianna Fáil MP in 1957, and held posts in justice, agriculture, and finance. After two years as minister of health and social welfare, he became premier in 1979, and defeated Garrett Fitzgerald in the 1987 elections. He was forced to resign (Jan 1992) following allegations of his involvement in a phone-tapping scandal. >> Fianna Fáil; Fitzgerald, Garrett

Hausa [**how**sa] A Chadic-speaking, predominantly Muslim people of Nigeria and Niger; the largest ethnic group in the area. They are intensive farmers, and Hausa traders are found throughout W Africa; they are also famed for their crafts. The Hausa language which has c.25 million mother-tongue speakers, is used as a lingua franca throughout N Nigeria and adjacent territories. >> Niger ℹ; Nigeria ℹ

Haussmann, Georges Eugène, Baron [**hows**man] (1809–91) Financier and town planner, born in Paris. He became prefect of the Seine (1853), improving Paris by widening streets, laying out boulevards and parks, and building bridges. >> Paris

haustorium A sucker-like organ inserted by a parasite into the cells of the host, through which food is withdrawn. It is found in fungi and parasitic flowering plants, such as dodder. >> dodder; fungus; parasitic plant

Havana [ha**va**na], Span **La Habana** 23°07N 82°25W, pop (1995e) 2 219 000. Capital city of Cuba; founded on this site, 1519; airport; railway; country's chief port on fine natural harbour; university (1721); cathedral (1704); trade in sugar, cotton, tobacco; old city centre a world heritage site. >> Cuba ℹ

Havel, Václav [**ha**vl, **vaht**slaf] (1936–) Playwright, president of Czechoslovakia (1989–92), and president of the Czech Republic (1993–), born in Prague. His work was judged subversive, and he was imprisoned in 1979 for four years, and again in 1989, but later that year was released and elected president by popular vote, following the collapse of communism. He resigned in 1992 in protest at the dissolution of Czechoslovakia, but became president of the new Czech Republic in January 1993. >> Czechoslovakia ℹ

Hawaii [ha**wah**ee] pop (1995e) 1 243 000; area 16 759 sq km/ 6471 sq mi. Pacific state of the US, a group of eight major islands (Hawaii, Kahoolawe, Kauai, Lanai, Maui, Molokai, Niihau, Oahu) and numerous islets in the C Pacific Ocean; the 'Aloha State'; reached by the Polynesians over 1000 years ago; discovered by Captain Cook in 1778, and named the Sandwich Is; monarchy overthrown, 1893; ceded itself to the USA, 1898; surprise attack by Japanese planes on the US naval base at Pearl Harbor, Oahu I (7 Dec 1941) brought the USA into World War 2; admitted to the Union as the 50th state, 1959; highest point Mauna Kea, a dormant volcano on Hawaii I (4201 m/13 783 ft), a major astronomical site; Mauna Loa (4169 m/13 678 ft) an active volcano; capital, Honolulu; defence installations at Pearl

Harbor; major tourist area. >> Cook, James; Honolulu; Mauna Kea / Loa; United States of America [i]; RR994

Hawaii [hawahee] pop (1995e) 135 000; area 10 488 sq km/ 4048 sq mi. Largest island of the US state of Hawaii; the 'orchid isle'; chief town, Hilo. >> Hawaii (state)

Hawaiian guitar A guitar with a straight body placed across the player's knees. It has metal strings which are stopped with a steel bar, instead of the fingers of the left hand, to produce the characteristic scooping (glissando) sound. Electric Hawaiian (or 'steel') guitars, sometimes free-standing, have been manufactured since the 1930s. >> guitar; string instrument 2 [i]

hawfinch A stout finch (*Coccothraustes coccothraustes*) native to Europe, Asia, and N Africa; golden-brown with black face; bill huge, strong, used for cracking tree fruits. (Family: Fringillidae.) >> finch

Haw-Haw, Lord >> **Joyce, William**

hawk A bird of prey of the family Accipitridae, the name being used especially for smaller members of the family. In the USA, the name is also used for some falcons (Family: Falconidae). >> bird of prey; buzzard; falcon; harrier (ornithology); kite (ornithology)

Hawke, Bob, popular name of **Robert (James Lee) Hawke** (1929–) Australian statesman and Labor prime minister (1983–91), born in Bordertown, South Australia. He was a skilled negotiator who won praise for his handling and settling of industrial disputes. In 1987 he became the first Labor prime minister to win a third term in office, and won a fourth term in 1990, but was defeated in a leadership contest by Paul Keating the following year. >> Australian Labor Party; Keating, Paul

Hawke (of Towton), Edward Hawke, Baron (1705–81) British admiral, born in London. His major victory was against the French at Quiberon Bay (1759), which caused the collapse of their invasion plans.

Hawking, Stephen (William) (1942–) Theoretical physicist, born in Oxford. His work has been concerned with cosmology, dealing with black holes, singularities, and the 'big bang' theory of the origin of the universe. His popular writing includes *A Brief History of Time* (1988). Since the 1960s he has suffered from a neuromotor disease, amyotrophic lateral sclerosis, causing extreme physical disability. >> 'big bang'; cosmology

Hawkins, Sir John >> **Hawkyns, Sir John**

hawk-moth A medium to large moth, typically with long, triangular wings and an elongate body, most abundant in tropics. (Order: Lepidoptera. Family: Sphingidae, c.1000 species.) >> death's-head moth; moth

Hawks, Howard (Winchester) (1896–1977) Film director, born in Goshen, IN. He had many successes over some 40 years, in such varied genres as airforce dramas (*The Dawn Patrol*, 1930), detection and crime (*The Big Sleep*, 1946), Westerns (*Rio Lobo*, 1970), and comedy (*Man's Favorite Sport?*, 1962).

Hawksmoor, Nicholas (1661–1736) Architect, born in East Drayton, Nottinghamshire. His works include the London churches, St Mary Woolnoth, St George's (Bloomsbury), and Christ Church (Spitalfields).

hawkweed A widely distributed perennial, mostly in the N hemisphere; flower-heads solitary or in loose clusters, florets usually yellow. (Genus: *Hieracium*, c.250 species. Family: Compositae.)

Hawkyns or **Hawkins, Sir John** (1532–95) British sailor, born in Plymouth. He became navy treasurer (1573), and was knighted for his services against the Armada in 1588. In 1595, with his kinsman Drake, he commanded an expedition to the Spanish Main. >> Drake, Francis; Spanish Armada

Hawn, Goldie (Jeanne) [hawn] (1945–) US actress, born in Washington, DC. She became known through her comedy roles in Rowan and Martin's *Laugh In* (1968–70), then won a best supporting actress award for her first film role in *Cactus Flower* (1969). Later films include *Private Benjamin* (1980), *First Wives Club* (1996), and the film musical *Everyone Says I Love You* (1997).

hawthorn A spiny, deciduous shrub or tree (*Crataegus monogyna*), growing to 18 m/60 ft, native to Europe; leaves deeply 3–7-lobed; flowers white, in clusters; berries (*haws*) red to maroon, flesh thin over a large stone; forms dense stock-proof hedges and attractive park or street trees; also called **quickthorn** and **may**. (Family: Rosaceae.)

Hawthorne, Nathaniel (1804–64) Novelist and short-story writer, born in Salem, MA. His first success was a collection of short stories, *Twice-Told Tales* (1837), but his best-known works are his novels, notably *The Scarlet Letter* (1850) and *The House of the Seven Gables* (1851).

Hayden, Bill, popular name of **William George Hayden** (1933–) Australian statesman, born in Brisbane, Queensland, Australia. He replaced Gough Whitlam as Labor Party leader (1977–83), then served as foreign minister in Bob Hawke's government (1983–8). He was Governor-General of Australia (1989–96). >> Australian Labor Party; Hawke, Bob; Whitlam

Haydn, Franz Joseph [**hiy**dn] (1732–1809) Composer, born in Rohrau, Austria. He entered the service of the Esterházy family as musical director in 1761, staying with them until 1790. Among his innovations were the four-movement string quartet and the 'classical' symphony. His works include 104 symphonies, about 50 concertos, 84 string quartets, 24 stage works, 12 Masses, orchestral divertimenti, keyboard sonatas, and diverse chamber, choral, instrumental, and vocal pieces.

Hayes, Helen, originally **Helen Hayes Brown** (1900–93) Actress, born in Washington, DC. Her adult stage productions brought her national popularity, and include *The Glass Menagerie* (1956) and *Long Day's Journey into Night* (1971). She also appeared in several films, notably *The Sin of Madelon Claudet* (1931, Oscar), and *Airport* (1970, Oscar). The Helen Hayes Theater in New York City was named after her.

Hayes, Rutherford B(irchard) (1822–93) US Republican statesman and 19th president (1877–81), born in Delaware, OH. Under his presidency, the country recovered commercial prosperity. His policy included reform of the civil service and the conciliation of the Southern states. >> Republican Party

hay fever A type of physical reaction affecting the eyes and nasal passages on contact with a foreign protein. The name is derived from the common cause of exposure to the pollen of grasses in the air, but the reaction is not confined to any season or to a single stimulus. Symptoms may be ameliorated by antihistamine drugs. >> allergy; anaphylaxis

haymaker >> **pika**

Haywood, William D(udley), nickname **Big Bill Haywood** (1869–1928) US labour leader, born in Salt Lake City, UT. In 1905 he helped to found the Industrial Workers of the World, which was committed to revolutionary labour politics. He was convicted of sedition in 1917, and fled from the USA in 1921, taking refuge in Russia. >> socialism; trade union

Hayworth, Rita, originally **Margarita Carmen Cansino** (1918–87) Film actress, born in New York City. She partnered both Fred Astaire and Gene Kelly in musicals of the 1940s, and found her best-known lead in *Gilda* (1946). A scandal involving her romance with Aly Khan (1949–51), whom she later married, effectively closed her Hollywood career.

hazardous substances Generally human-made substances, potentially damaging to health, which when incorrectly disposed of result in contamination and pollution of the environment. They include toxic substances, heavy metal pollutants (eg lead, mercury), and radioactive waste produced in the generation of nuclear power. >> pollution; radioactive waste; waste disposal

hazel A deciduous shrub or small tree (*Corylus avellana*), native to Europe and Asia Minor; leaves broadly oval, toothed; male catkins long, pendulous; females short, bud-like with prominent red stigmas; edible nut partially enclosed in a ragged green leafy cup. (Family: Corylaceae.)

Hazlitt, William (1778–1830) Essayist, born in Maidstone, Kent. His best-known essay collections are *Table Talk* (1821) and *The Spirit of the Age* (1825).

H-bomb >> **hydrogen bomb** ℹ

headache An aching sensation over the vault of the skull, temples, or back of the head, usually diffuse and poorly localized. The brain itself is insensitive to touch, and headaches arise from the stretching or distortion of its covering membranes, from tension arising from the muscles overlying the skull, or from vascular dilatation with increased blood supply, as occurs in generalized fevers or over-indulgence in alcohol. >> migraine

Head Start A project begun in the USA in the early 1960s to help pre-school children from a disadvantaged background prepare for schooling. The main emphasis was on language and social development, but attention was also paid to health care and parent education.

Healey (of Riddlesden), Denis (Winston) Healey, Baron (1917–) British statesman, born in Eltham, Kent. He was secretary of state for defence (1964–70), Chancellor of the Exchequer (1974–9), deputy leader (1980–3), and in 1983 was appointed shadow foreign minister, retiring in 1992. >> Labour Party

healing Any method by which an illness or injury is cured; specifically, the use of a technique which is not recognized within orthodox medicine and involves no form of physical therapy or manipulation. Techniques such as the 'laying on of hands' are seen as involving the transmission of energy from, or channelling through, a healer and into the sick person. Sometimes prayer, visualization, meditation, or other methods are used by the patient, healer, or both to help focus beneficial thoughts and energy onto the illness. >> alternative medicine; faith / psychic / pyramid healing; naturopathy

health foods An umbrella term for so-called 'whole food', additive-free food, and diet supplements such as minerals, vitamins, trace elements, essential fatty acids, and other nutrients. Many are sold simply as a supplement to diet, but some make therapeutic claims. Most health-food shops are now actively promoting alternative medicine. >> alternative medicine; diet; nutrients; vitamins ℹ

Heaney, Seamus (Justin) [**hee**nee, **shay**mus] (1939–) Poet, born on a farm in Co Londonderry. His works include *Death of a Naturalist* (1966), *Field Work* (1979), and *Station Island* (1984). He became professor of rhetoric and oratory at Harvard in 1985, and professor of poetry at Oxford in 1989. Volumes of selected poems appeared in 1980 and 1990, and his collection *The Spirit Level* in 1996. He was awarded the Nobel Prize for Literature in 1995.

Heard and McDonald Islands area 412 sq km/159 sq mi. Island group in S Indian Ocean, about 4000 km/2500 mi SW of Fremantle, Australia; an Australian external territory since 1947; made world heritage site in 1997. >> Australia ℹ

hearing >> **ear** ℹ

hearing aid A device for amplifying sound, used by persons with defective hearing. Modern aids are electronic, consisting of a microphone, amplifier, and earphone, usually compressed into a very small container to fit directly on to the ear. >> ear ℹ

Hearne, Samuel [hern] (1745–92) Explorer of N Canada, born in London. He joined the Hudson's Bay Company, and became the first European to travel overland by canoe and sled to the Arctic Ocean. >> Canada ℹ

Hearns, Thomas [hernz], nicknames **Hit Man** and **Motor City Cobra** (1958–) Boxer, born in Memphis, TN. In 1991 he became the first man to win world titles at six different weights. >> boxing

hearsay A complex rule of evidence in common-law countries which prohibits an out-of-court oral or written statement from being used in court to prove the truth of an issue. The rule is still widely followed in the USA, but has been virtually abolished in civil cases in England and Wales. It has many exceptions, generally situations in which the speaker is likely to be truthful, such as dying declarations.

Hearst, William Randolph (1863–1951) Newspaper owner, born in San Francisco, CA. He revolutionized journalism by the introduction of banner headlines, lavish illustrations, and other sensational methods. His career inspired the film *Citizen Kane* (1941).

heart A hollow muscular organ, divided into chambers (right and left *atria*, right and left *ventricles*) and enclosed within a fibrous sac (the *pericardium*) found within the thorax. It lies directly under the sternum, being protected by it and the adjacent ribs. In mammals it is separated into right and left halves concerned with pulmonary and systemic circulation respectively. The right atrium receives deoxygenated blood from the body (via the superior and inferior *venae cavae*) and from the heart itself (via the *coronary sinus*) during diastole, and conveys it to the right ventricle via the right atrioventricular opening (guarded by the *tricuspid valve*). The right ventricle expels blood into the *pulmonary trunk* (guarded by the *pulmonary valve*) and thence to the lungs. The left atrium receives blood from the lungs and conveys it to the left ventricle via the left atrioventricular opening (guarded by the *mitral valve*). The left ventricle forcibly expels blood into the *aorta* (guarded by the *aortic valve*) and thence to the rest of the body. A **heart attack** (*myocardial infarction*) occurs when part of the coronary arterial supply becomes blocked by a blood clot (*thrombus*), leading to the cessation of blood flow and death of the cardiac muscle. >> anatomy ℹ; angina; cardiac resuscitation ℹ; coronary heart disease ℹ; diastole; heart disease; pacemaker; pulmonary embolism; pulse (physiology); systole; transplantation

heartburn A burning sensation usually felt intermittently within the chest over the lower part of the breastbone. It results from regurgitation of the contents of the

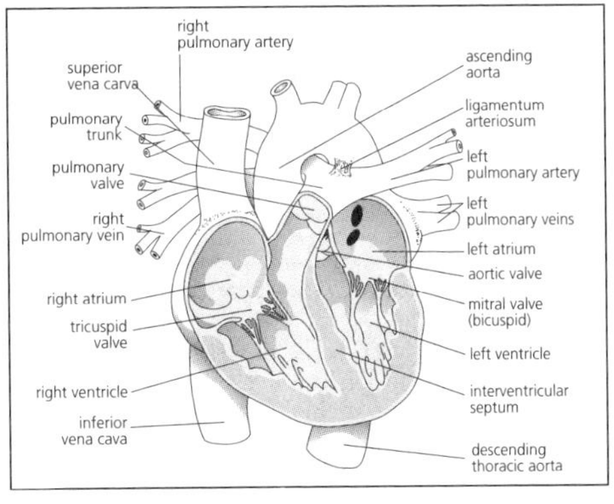

The structure of the heart

stomach into the lower part of the oesophagus, inducing a spasm. >> oesophagus

heart disease Disease of the heart and the associated blood vessels. The heart is essentially a pump. Interference with its function whatever the cause gives rise to the cardinal symptoms of shortness of breath, fluid retention (*oedema*), palpitations, chest pain, and fainting. >> angina; cardiac resuscitation ℹ; coronary heart disease ℹ; heart ℹ; hypertension; rheumatic fever

heart–lung machine An apparatus which takes over the pumping action of the heart, together with the breathing action of the lungs, so that the heart can be stopped and operated upon. The blood is filtered and kept at a suitable temperature during its passage through the machine – if necessary, for several hours. >> blood; heart ℹ; lungs

heartsease A species of violet (*Viola tricolor*), also called **wild pansy**, native to Europe. The flowers are blue, yellow, white, or a combination of these colours. (Family: Violaceae.) >> pansy; violet

heat The transfer of energy from one object to another, due solely to their difference in temperatures; symbol *Q*, units J (joule). The quantity of heat sometimes ascribed to an object or process is the total amount of energy transferred in this way. >> convection; energy; enthalpy; heat capacity; heat engine; latent heat; thermal conduction / insulation; thermodynamics

heat capacity The quantity of heat needed to produce a temperature rise of one kelvin (or 1 °C) in some material. **Specific heat capacity** *c* (also called **specific heat**), units J/(kg.K), is the heat capacity per kilogram of material. For water, c = *418 J/(kg.K)*. >> calorie ℹ; heat

heat engine The name given to a device that transforms disordered heat energy into ordered, useful, mechanical work. This is achieved by taking a working fluid at high temperature and high heat energy, and subjecting it to a thermodynamic cycle involving compression and expansion, during which time heat is expelled at a lower temperature. The differences in heat energy of the working fluid between input and output appear as work. >> Carnot cycle; engine; thermodynamics

Heath, Sir Edward (Richard George), known as **Ted Heath** (1916–) British statesman and prime minister (1970–4), born in Broadstairs, Kent. He was minister of labour (1959–60), then Lord Privy Seal (1960–3) and the chief negotiator for Britain's entry into the European Economic Community. Elected Leader of the Conservative Party in 1965, he was Leader of the Opposition until his 1970 victory. Replaced as leader by Mrs Thatcher in 1975, he has continued to play an active part in politics. He became Father of the House in 1992. He is known for his interests in yachting and music. >> Conservative Party; Thatcher, Margaret

heath A low evergreen shrub or small tree, native to Europe, Asia, N Africa, and especially S Africa; flowers often numerous, bell- or urn-shaped, pink, purple, or white. They are also called **ericas**, and are widely known as **heathers**, which is a source of possible confusion with true heather. (Genus: *Erica*, c.500 species. Family: Ericaceae.) >> heather; mycorrhiza

heather 1 A small, bushy, evergreen shrub (*Calluna vulgaris*), native to Europe, especially N and W; flowers tiny, in loose spikes, four sepals, four petals, all purple; also called **ling**. (Family: Ericaceae.) **2** >> heath

heat stroke A condition which occurs in unacclimatized individuals exposed to high environmental temperatures, in whom body temperature rises to 42–43 °C/107–108 °F or more. Treatment is by urgent cooling of the body. The condition is also known as **sunstroke**, though it may occur with or without exposure to direct sunlight. >> temperature ℹ

heaven Generally, the dwelling-place of God and the angels, and in traditional Christianity the ultimate eternal destiny of the redeemed, there to reign with Christ in glory. In modern theology, the emphasis is more on the fully-revealed presence of God, and the perfection of the divine–human relationship, than on a place. >> eschatology; God

Heavenly Twins >> **Gemini**

Heaviside layer A region of the ionosphere between c.90–120 km/55–75 mi responsible for the reflection of radio waves back to Earth; also known as the **E layer**. It was discovered in 1902 independently by Oliver Heaviside (1850–1925) in England and Arthur E Kennelly (1861–1939) in the USA (where it is also known as the **Kennelly layer**). >> Appleton layer; ionosphere; radio waves

heavy metal music A form of rock music developed from electrified blues music, with heavily amplified guitars, bass guitars, and drums, and often strident vocals. Early pioneers were Jimi Hendrix and the band Cream with Eric Clapton; classic exponents of the genre included US bands Grand Flux (Railroad), Vanilla Fudge, and Mountain, and the British Led Zeppelin, Deep Purple, and Black Sabbath. >> Clapton; Hendrix; rock music

heavy water >> **deuterium**

Hebe [**hee**bee] In Greek mythology, the goddess of youth and youthful beauty, daughter of Zeus and Hera. She became cup-bearer to the Olympians, and was married to Heracles after he was deified. >> Heracles

Hébert, Jacques René [aybair] (1757–94) French revolutionary extremist, born in Alençon, France. He played a major part in the September Massacres and the overthrow of the monarchy. After denouncing the Committee of Public Safety for its failure to help the poor, he tried to incite a popular uprising, but he and 17 of his followers (**Hébertists**) were guillotined. >> French Revolution ℹ

Hebrew A Semitic language which dates from around the 2nd millennium BC. Classical Hebrew is the written language of Judaism, and its modern variety is the official language of the state of Israel. It is spoken by c.4 million people around the world. >> Afro-Asiatic languages

Hebrews, Letter to the New Testament writing of unknown authorship and recipients. It is sometimes attributed to Paul, but this attribution was widely doubted even from early times. >> New Testament; Pauline Letters

Hebrides [**heb**rideez] Over 500 islands off the W coast of Scotland; divided into the **Inner Hebrides** (notably Skye, Rhum, Eigg, Coll, Mull, Iona, Staffa, Islay, Jura) and **Outer Hebrides** (notably Lewis with Harris, the Uists, Barra), separated by the Minch. >> Eigg; Iona; Scotland ℹ; Skye; Western Isles

Hebron, Arabic **al-Khalil**, Hebrew **Hevro** 31°32N 35°06E, pop (1995e) 117 000. City in Israeli-occupied West Bank, W Jordan; one of the oldest cities in the world, built 1730 BC; a religious centre of Islam; the home of Abraham. >> Abraham; Israel ℹ; Jordan ℹ

Hecate [**hek**atee, **hek**at] In Greek mythology, the goddess associated with witchcraft, spooks, and magic. She is worshipped with offerings at places where three roads cross, and so given three bodies in sculpture.

Hector [**hek**taw] According to Greek legend, the bravest Trojan, who led out their army to battle; the son of Priam, and married to Andromache. Achilles killed him and dragged his body behind his chariot. >> Achilles; Trojan War

Hecuba [**hek**yooba] or **Hecabe** [**hek**abee] In Greek legend, the wife of Priam, King of Troy, and mother of 18 children, including Hector and Cassandra. After the Greeks took Troy, she saw her sons and her husband killed, and was sent into slavery. >> Trojan War

hedgehog A mammal (an insectivore) native to Europe, Africa, and Asia; body covered with spines; tail short; many species dig burrows. When frightened, it can roll its body into a ball. (Family: Erinaceidae, 12 species.) >> insectivore; moonrat; tenrec

hedging >> **futures**

hedonism 1 An ethical doctrine, held by Cyrenaics, Epicureans, and most utilitarians, which maintains that the only intrinsic good is pleasure; the only intrinsic evil is pain. **2** A psychological thesis which claims that people are always motivated to seek pleasure and avoid pain. >> Cyrenaics; utilitarianism

Hegel, Georg Wilhelm Friedrich [**hay**gl] (1770–1831) Philosopher, born in Stuttgart, Germany. His major works include *Phänomenologie des Geistes* (1807, The Phenomenology of the Mind), *Wissenschaft der Logik* (1812–16, Science of Logic), and *Enzyklopädie der philosophischen Wissenschaften* (1817, trans Encyclopedia of the Philosophical Sciences), in which he set out his tripartite system of logic, philosophy of nature, and mind. His approach rejects the reality of finite and separate objects and minds in space and time, and establishes an underlying, all-embracing unity, the Absolute. The quest for greater unity and truth is achieved by the famous dialectic, positing something (*thesis*), denying it (*antithesis*), and combining the two half-truths in a *synthesis* which contains a greater portion of truth in its complexity. >> Idealism; Kant

Heidegger, Martin [**hiy**deger] (1889–1976) Philosopher, born in Messkirch, Germany. In his uncompleted main work *Sein und Zeit* (1927, Being and Time), he presents an exhaustive ontological classification of 'Being', through the synthesis of the modes of human existence. He was a key influence in Sartre's Existentialism. >> existentialism; ontology; Sartre

Heidelberg [**hiy**dlberg] 49°23N 8°41E, pop (1995e) 141 000. Industrial city in Germany; centre of German Calvinism during the 16th-c; railway; oldest university in Germany (1386); castle (1583–1610). >> Calvinism; Germany ℹ

Heifetz, Jascha [**hiy**fets] (1901–87) Violinist, born in Vilna, Lithuania. After the Revolution he settled in the USA, becoming a US citizen in 1925.

Heilong Jiang >> **Amur River**

Heine, (Christian Johann) Heinrich [**hiy**nuh] (1797–1856) Poet and essayist, born in Düsseldorf, Germany, of Jewish parentage. He established his reputation with his four-volume *Reisebilder* (1826–7, 1830–1, Pictures of Travel) and *Das Buch der Lieder* (1827, The Book of Songs). He later became leader of the cosmopolitan democratic movement, writing widely on French and German culture.

Heinz, H(enry) J(ohn) [hiynts] (1844–1919) Food manufacturer and packer, born in Pittsburgh, PA. His company was founded in 1876, introducing the famous slogan '57 varieties' 20 years later.

Heisenberg, Werner (Karl) [**hiy**znberg] (1901–76) Theoretical physicist, born in Würzburg. He helped to develop quantum mechanics, and formulated the revolutionary principle of indeterminacy in nuclear physics (1927). He received the Nobel Prize for Physics in 1932. >> quantum mechanics

Hel or **Hela** In Norse mythology, the youngest child of Loki. She was assigned by Odin to rule **Helheim** (the Underworld). >> Loki; Valhalla

Helen In Greek legend, the wife of Menelaus of Sparta, famous for her beauty; her abduction by Paris the Trojan caused the Trojan War. She was the daughter of Zeus and Leda, in mythical accounts. >> Menelaus; Trojan War

Helena, St (c.255–c.330) Mother of the Roman Emperor Constantine (the Great), born in Bithynia, Asia Minor. She early became a Christian, and in 326, according to tradition, visited Jerusalem, where she founded the basilicas on the Mount of Olives and at Bethlehem. Feast day 18 August (W), 21 May (E). >> Christianity; Constantine I (Emperor)

Helfgott, David [**helf**got] (1947–) Pianist, born in Australia. After a nervous breakdown, he developed a mood disorder which left him with a distinctive mode of playing often accompanied by vocalization. His life-story was dramatized in the film *Shine* (1995). A world tour in 1997 received a cool reception from music critics, but sell-out support and enthusiasm from the public.

helical scan A system of magnetic tape recording in which the tape is wrapped in a partial helix around a drum carrying two or more rotating heads which trace a series of tracks diagonally across its width. It enables very high frequencies to be recorded economically. >> tape recorder; videotape recorder

Helicon [**hel**ikon] The largest mountain in Boeotia. In Greek mythology, it was the sacred hill of the Muses, whose temple was to be found there. >> Boeotia; Muses; Pegasus (mythology)

helicopter A vertical take-off and landing aircraft whose lift is provided by means of a horizontal, large-diameter set of powered blades which force the air downwards and by reaction create a lifting force upwards. Forward flight is achieved by tilting the plane of the blades in the direction of flight, varying their angle to the horizontal as they rotate. >> aircraft ℹ

Heligoland, Ger **Helgoland** 54°09N 7°52E, pop (1995e) 3640. Rocky North Sea island of the North Frisian Is, Germany; area 2·1 sq km/0·8 sq mi; captured from Denmark by the UK, 1807; ceded to Germany in exchange for Zanzibar, 1890; German naval base in both World Wars. >> Frisian Islands

heliocentric system Any theory of our planetary system that has the Sun at the centre. It was proposed by Aristarchus in the 3rd-c BC, and revived with great success by Copernicus in 1543. >> Aristarchus of Samos; Copernican system

Helios [**heel**ios] In Greek mythology, the Sun-god, represented as a charioteer with four horses. In the late classical period, there was an Imperial cult of the sun, *Sol Invictus*. >> Phaethon

heliotrope A small evergreen shrub (*Heliotropium peruvianum*) 0·5–2 m/$1\frac{1}{2}$–$6\frac{1}{2}$ ft, a native of Peru; flowers small, tubular, with spreading lobes, white to lilac or violet, in terminal clusters. (Family: Boraginaceae.)

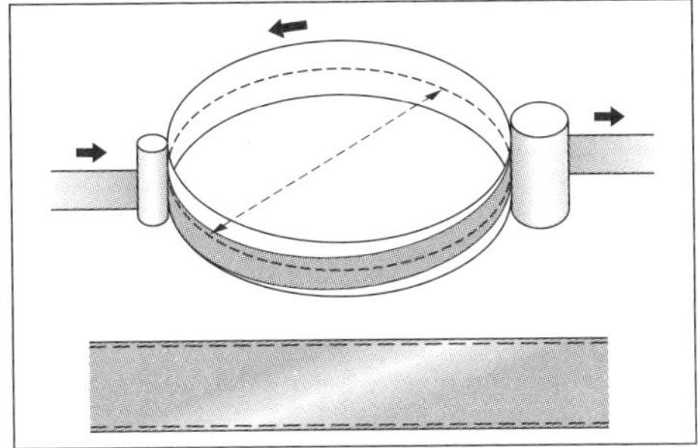

Helical scan - a continuously moving magnetic tape is wrapped around a rapidly rotating drum. The drum carries the recording heads, which trace a series of diagonal tracks.

helium He, element 2, the most inert of the chemical elements, forming no stable compounds; the lightest of the *noble* or *inert* gases. It condenses to a liquid only at −269°C (4 K). Because of its inertness and low density (less than 15% of the density of air), it is used to fill balloons. Liquid helium is used as the ultimate coolant, and was important in the discovery of superconductivity. >> chemical elements; noble gases; superfluidity; RR1036

hell In traditional Christian thought, the eternal abode and place of torment of the damned. Much contemporary Christian thought rejects the idea of vindictive punishment as incompatible with belief in a loving God. The emphasis acccordingly shifts from hell as a place of retribution to a state of being without God. >> Devil; eschatology; God

hellebore [**he**libaw(r)] A perennial with glossy divided leaves and large flowers, native to Europe and W Asia; flowers with five green, white, or pinkish-purple petaloid sepals, and up to 20 prominent 2-lipped nectar-secreting glands; highly poisonous. (Genus: *Helleborus*, 20 species. Family: Ranunculaceae.)

helleborine [**he**liborin] Either of two closely related genera of orchids. *Epipactis* (24 species), from N temperate regions and parts of the tropics, has stalked flowers in which the lower lip forms a nectar-containing cup with a tongue-like extension. *Cephalanthera* (12 species), from N temperate regions, has stalkless flowers which never open fully. (Family: Orchidaceae.) >> orchid [i]

Hellenistic Age The period from the death of Alexander the Great (323 BC) to the beginning of the Roman Empire (31 BC), during which a number of Greek or Hellenized dynasties ruled the entire area from Greece to the N of India. >> Ptolemy I Soter; Seleucids

Heller, Joseph (1923–) Novelist, born in New York City. His wartime experience forms the background for his first novel, *Catch-22* (1961), which was an immediate success; a sequel, *Closing Time*, appeared in 1994. Other novels include *Something Happened* (1974) and *Picture This* (1988). >> Catch-22

Hellespont >> **Dardanelles**

Hell's Canyon or **Grand Canyon of the Snake** Gorge on the Snake R USA; with a depth of c.2450 m/8030 ft, it is one of the deepest gorges in the world; length 65 km/40 mi. >> Snake River

Helmholtz, Hermann von (1821–94) Physiologist and physicist, born in Potsdam, Germany. The key figure in the development of science in Germany in the later 19th-c, his works are principally connected with the eye, the ear, and the nervous system. He is best known for his statement of the law of the conservation of energy.

helminthology The study of parasitic worms (**helminths**), including roundworms, flatworms, and their larval stages. >> flatworm; nematode; parasitology; worm

Helmont, Jan Baptista van (1579–1644) Chemist, born in Brussels. He invented the term *gas*, and was the first to take the melting point of ice and the boiling point of water as standards for temperature. >> chemistry

Héloïse >> **Abelard, Peter**

Helpmann, Sir Robert (Murray) (1909–86) Dancer, actor, and choreographer, born in Mount Gambier, South Australia, Australia. He was first dancer of the newly founded Sadler's Wells Ballet (1933–50), and also appeared in many films. >> ballet; Pavlova; Royal Ballet; Valois, Ninette de

Helsingborg, Swed **Hälsingborg** 56°03N 12°43E, pop (1995e) 113 000. Seaport and commercial town in SW Sweden; opposite Helsingør, Denmark; railway; ferry services to Denmark. >> Sweden [i]

Helsingfors [**hel**singfaw(r)z] >> **Helsinki**

Helsingør >> **Elsinore**

Helsinki [hel**sing**kee], Swed **Helsingfors** 60°08N 25°00E, pop (1995e) 502 000. Seaport capital of Finland; founded by Gustavus Vasa in 1550; capital, 1812; heavily bombed in World War 2; airport; railway; university (transferred from Turku, 1828); technical university (1908); cathedral (completed 1852). >> Finland [i]; Gustavus I

Helvellyn [hel**vel**in] 54°32N 3°02W. Mountain in the Lake District of Cumbria, NW England; rises to 950 m/3117 ft; Striding Edge descends to the E. >> Lake District

Helvetii [hel**way**tiee] Celtic people forced S by Germanic tribesmen in the 2nd-c BC into modern Switzerland. The official names for Switzerland derive from this source: *Helvetia* and *Confederatio Helvetica*. >> Caesar; Celts; Gaul

hem- >> **haem-**

hemichordate A bottom-living, marine invertebrate with gill slits in its pharynx similar to those of primitive vertebrates; includes the acornworms and graptolites. (Phylum: Hemichordata.)

Hemingway, Ernest (Miller) (1899–1961) Writer, born in Oak Park, IL. His major novels include *A Farewell to Arms* (1929), *For Whom the Bell Tolls* (1940), and *The Old Man and the Sea* (1952, Pulitzer). In 1954 he was awarded the Nobel Prize for Literature.

hemione >> **ass**

hemiplegia >> **paralysis**

Hemiptera [he**mip**tera] A group of insects comprising two orders, the Homoptera and the Heteroptera. >> Heteroptera; Homoptera

hemispheric specialization >> **laterality**

hemlock 1 An evergreen conifer native to North America and E Asia; branches drooping. It yields timber, Canada pitch, and tanning bark. (Genus: *Tsuga*, 15 species. Family: Pinaceae.) **2** A biennial growing to 2·5 m/8 ft, native to Europe and temperate Asia; stem hollow, furrowed, spotted with purple; flowers white; fruit ovoid; a fetid smell; all parts very poisonous; used as a poison since classical times. (*Conium maculatum*. Family: Umbelliferae.)

hemo- >> **haemo-**

hemp >> **abaca; cannabis**

hen >> **domestic fowl**

henbane An annual or biennial (*Hyoscyamus niger*), sticky-haired and fetid, native to Europe, W Asia, and N Africa; petals 5-lobed, lurid yellow and purple; poisonous. Its extracts are still used in modern medicine, mainly as sedatives. (Family: Solanaceae.)

Henderson, Fletcher (1897–1952) Pianist, arranger, and jazz bandleader, born in Cuthbert, GA. In 1924 he put together a big band, attracting the finest instrumentalists and arrangers of the time. His orchestrations helped set the standard for the swing era. >> jazz

Hendrix, Jimi, popular name of **James Marshall Hendrix** (1942–70) Rock guitarist, singer, and songwriter, born in Seattle, WA. He explored electronic tricks on his guitar at ear-splitting amplitude, to which he added stage gimmicks, playing behind his back or with his teeth. His raucous blues style influenced heavy metal bands. >> blues; rock music

Hendry, Stephen (Gordon) (1969–) Snooker player, born in Edinburgh. He became a professional in 1985, and dominated the game in the 1990s. His wins include six Embassy world championships (1990, 1992–6). In 1997–8 he won a record number of ranking events (29), but lost his No 1 world ranking position to John Higgins. >> Higgins, John

Hengist and **Horsa** Brothers, leaders of the first Anglo-Saxon settlers in Britain, said by Bede to have been invited over by Vortigern, the British king, to fight the Picts in about AD 450. >> Anglo-Saxons; Bede

Henie, Sonja [**hen**ee] (1912–69) Figure skater, born in Oslo. The winner of three Olympic gold medals (1928, 1932,

1936), she also won a record 10 individual world titles (1927–36). >> ice skating

Henley Royal Regatta Rowing races which take place annually on the R Thames at Henley-on-Thames, Oxfordshire, UK, inaugurated in 1839. It is as much an elegant social occasion for the public as a sporting one. >> rowing

Henman, Tim(othy) (1974–) Tennis player, born in Oxford, Oxfordshire. He turned professional in 1993, his achievements including the British National Championships (singles and men's doubles, 1995–6, singles 1996). He had become Britain's No 1 player by early 1997, and although he lost this position to Greg Rusedski later that year, he regained it during 1998, and reached seventh in the world rankings. >> Rusedski

henna An evergreen shrub (*Lawsonia inermis*) growing to 3 m/10 ft, native to the Old World tropics; flowers 4-petalled, white, pink, or red; fruit a 3-chambered capsule. The powdered leaves produce a red dye, used as a cosmetic for skin and hair since ancient times. (Family: Lythraceae.) >> dyestuff

Henrietta Maria (1609–69) Queen of Charles I of England, born in Paris, the youngest child of Henry IV of France. She married Charles in 1625, but her French attendants and Roman Catholic beliefs made her unpopular. In 1642, under the threat of impeachment, she fled to Holland and raised funds for the Royalist cause. >> English Civil War

Henry I (1068–1135) King of England (1100–35) and Duke of Normandy (1106–35), the youngest son of William the Conqueror. Under Henry, the Norman Empire attained the height of its power. He nominated his daughter Empress Matilda, as his heir for both England and Normandy, but after Henry's death, the crown was seized by Stephen, son of his sister, Adela. >> Angevins; Stephen; William I (of England)

Henry II (of England) (1133–89) King of England (1154–89), born in Le Mans, France, the son of Empress Matilda, Henry I's daughter and acknowledged heir, by her second husband Geoffrey of Anjou. He founded the Angevin or Plantagenet dynasty of English kings, and ruled England as part of a wider Angevin Empire. His efforts to restrict clerical independence caused conflict with his former Chancellor Thomas à Becket, Archbishop of Canterbury, which was ended only with Becket's murder (1170). He led a major expedition to Ireland (1171), which resulted in its annexation. >> Angevins; Becket

Henry II (of France) (1519–59) King of France (1547–69), born near Paris, the second son of Francis I, who became heir to the throne in 1536. He formed an alliance with Scotland, and declared war against England, which ended in 1558 with the taking of Calais. He also continued the long-standing war against the Emperor Charles V. >> Charles V (Emperor)

Henry III (of England) (1207–72) King of England (1216–72), the elder son and successor, at the age of nine, of John. His arbitrary assertion of royal rights conflicted with the principles of Magna Carta, and antagonized many nobles. Simon de Montfort and the barons rebelled, and captured the king at Lewes (1264), but were defeated at Evesham (1265). >> Barons' Wars; John; Magna Carta; Montfort, Simon de; Oxford, Provisions of

Henry III (of France) (1551–89) King of France (1574–89), born in Fontainebleau, the third son of Henry II. His reign was a period of almost incessant civil war between Huguenots and Catholics. In 1588 he engineered the assassination of the Duke of Guise, enraging the Catholic League. He joined forces with the Huguenot Henry of Navarre, and while marching on Paris was assassinated. >> Huguenots; Religion, Wars of; Valois

Henry IV (of England), originally **Henry Bolingbroke** (1366–1413) King of England (1399–1413), the first king of the House of Lancaster, the son of John of Gaunt, who was the fourth son of Edward III. He was surnamed **Bolingbroke**, from his birthplace in Lincolnshire. In 1397 he supported Richard II against the Duke of Gloucester, but was banished in 1398. On returning to England, he induced Richard to abdicate in his favour. Henry's attack on Scotland in 1400 ended in his defeat. Henry Percy (Hotspur) and his house joined with the Scots and the Welsh against him, but they were defeated at Shrewsbury (1403). >> Percy; Richard II

Henry IV (of France), originally **Henry of Navarre** (1553–1610) The first Bourbon king of France (1589–1610), born in Pau, France. He became leader of the Protestant Party, and after the massacre of St Bartholomew's Day (1572) was spared by professing himself a Catholic. In 1576 he revoked his conversion, and resumed command of the army in opposition to the Catholic League. On his accession, he became a Catholic again, thereby unifying the country, and granted Protestants liberty of conscience. >> Bourbons; Huguenots; Nantes, Edict of; Sully; Religion, Wars of

Henry V (1387–1422) King of England (1413–22), born in Monmouth, Monmouthshire, the eldest son of Henry IV. The main effort of his reign was his claim to the French crown. In 1415 he invaded France, and won the Battle of Agincourt against great odds. He was recognized as heir to the French throne and Regent of France, and married Charles VI's daughter, Catherine of Valois. >> Agincourt, Battle of; Hundred Years' War

Henry VI (1421–71) King of England (1422–61, 1470–1), born in Windsor, S England, the only child of Henry V and Catherine of Valois. Although crowned King of France in Paris in 1431, he gradually lost England's French conquests. Richard, Duke of York, seized power as Lord Protector in 1454, and defeated the king's army at St Albans (1455), the first battle of the Wars of the Roses. York's heir was proclaimed king as Edward IV after Henry's deposition (1461). In 1464 Henry returned from exile in Scotland to lead the Lancastrian cause, but was captured and imprisoned (1465–70). Richard Neville, Earl of Warwick, restored him to the throne (Oct 1470), his nominal rule ending when Edward IV returned to London (Apr 1471). After the Yorkist victory at Tewkesbury (May 1471), where his only son was killed, Henry was murdered in the Tower. >> Edward IV; Roses, Wars of the; Warwick, Earl of

Henry VII (1457–1509) King of England (1485–1509), born at Pembroke Castle, Pembrokeshire, the grandson of Owen Tudor and Catherine of Valois, the widow of Henry V. He founded the Tudor dynasty by defeating Richard III at Bosworth in 1485. His policy was to restore peace and prosperity to the country, and this was helped by his marriage of reconciliation with Elizabeth of York. Peace was concluded with France, and the marriage of his heir to Catherine of Aragon cemented an alliance with Spain. >> Bosworth Field, Battle of; Richard III; Tudors; Warbeck

Henry VIII (1491–1547) King (1509–47), born in Greenwich, Greater London, the second son of Henry VII. Soon after his accession he married Catherine of Aragon. From 1527 he determined to divorce Catherine, whose children, except for Mary, had died in infancy, and in defiance of the Roman Catholic Church was privately married to Anne Boleyn (1533). In 1534 it was enacted that his marriage to Catherine was invalid, and that the king was the sole head of the Church of England. In 1536 Catherine died, and Anne Boleyn was executed for infidelity. Henry then married Jane Seymour (c.1509–37), who died leaving a son, afterwards Edward VI. In 1540 Anne of Cleves became his fourth wife, in the hope of attaching the

Protestant interest of Germany; but dislike of her appearance caused him to divorce her speedily. He then married Catherine Howard (1540), who two years later was executed on grounds of infidelity (1542). In 1543 his last marriage was to Catherine Parr, who survived him. His later years saw further war with France and Scotland, before peace was concluded with France in 1546. >> Anne of Cleves; Boleyn; Catherine of Aragon; Church of England; Cromwell, Thomas; Fisher, St John; Howard, Catherine; More, Thomas; Parr, Catherine; Seymour, Jane; Wolsey, Thomas

Henry the Navigator (1394–1460) Portuguese prince, the third son of John I, King of Portugal, and Philippa, daughter of John of Gaunt, Duke of Lancaster. He sponsored many exploratory expeditions along the W African coast.

Henry, Joseph (1797–1878) Physicist, born in Albany, NY. He discovered electrical induction independently of Faraday, and constructed the first electromagnetic motor (1829). The unit of inductance is named after him. >> electricity; Faraday; henry

Henry, Lenny, popular name of **Lenworth George Henry** (1958–) Comedian and actor, born in Dudley, West Midlands. He joined the children's television show *Tiswas* in the 1970s, and went on to star in his own BBC television series the *Lenny Henry Show* (1984–95) and *Chef* (from 1992). He also hosts the annual BBC *Comic Relief* telethon. He is married to Dawn French. >> French, Dawn

Henry, O, pseudonym of **William Sydney Porter** (1862–1910) Writer, master of the short story, born in Greensboro, NC. His stories provide a romantic and humorous treatment of everyday life, and are noted for their use of coincidence and trick endings.

Henry, Patrick (1736–99) American revolutionary and statesman, born in Studley, VA. He was outspoken in his opposition to British policy towards the colonies, and he made the first speech in the Continental Congress (1774). >> American Revolution; Continental Congress

henry SI unit of inductance; symbol *H*; named after Joseph Henry; defined as the inductance of a closed circuit in which a current changing at the rate of 1 ampere per second produces an electromotive force (emf) of 1 volt. >> Henry, Joseph; inductance

Henry's law In chemistry, a law formulated by British chemist William Henry (1774–1836): the solubility of a gas in a liquid at any given temperature is proportional to the pressure of the gas on the liquid. >> gas 1

Henryson, Robert [**hen**rison] (c.1425–1508) Scottish mediaeval poet. His works include *The Testament of Cresseid*, and a metrical version of 13 *Morall Fabels of Esope*, often viewed as his masterpiece.

Henslowe, Philip (c.1550–1616) Theatre manager, born in Lindfield, West Sussex. In 1587 he built the Rose Theatre on the Bankside, London. His business diary (1593–1609) contains invaluable information about the stage of Shakespeare's day.

Henson, Jim, popular name of **James Maury Henson** (1936–90) Puppeteer, born in Greenville, MS. His 'Muppets' (Marionettes/puppets) achieved nationwide popularity on the children's television workshop, *Sesame Street*, from 1969, and *The Muppet Show* (1976–81), appearing also in a string of films and on a Grammy-winning album (1979). Later series included *Fraggle Rock* (from 1983) and *The Storyteller* (from 1987). >> puppetry

Henze, Hans Werner [**hen**tsuh] (1926–) Composer, born in Gütersloh, Germany. He was influenced by Schoenberg, exploring beyond the more conventional uses of the 12-tone system. His works include operas, ballets, symphonies, and chamber music.

heparin [**hep**arin] A chemical substance (a polysaccharide) found in the mast cells of the liver, lungs, and intestinal mucosa. It prevents blood clotting. >> anticoagulants; disaccharide; mast cells

hepatitis [hepa**tiy**tis] Inflammation of the liver, caused by one of several hepatic viruses. The commonest is caused by virus A (**infective hepatitis**), usually a mild febrile disorder; almost all patients recover completely within one to two months. Virus B infection (**serum hepatitis**) is much more serious, and carries a significant mortality. >> jaundice; liver; virus

Hepburn, Audrey, originally **Eda van Heemstra** (1929–93) Actress and film star, born in Brussels, Belgium. She was given the lead in the Broadway production of *Gigi* (1951), and went on to win international acclaim for *Roman Holiday* (1953, Oscar). Other popular film roles included *The Nun's Story* (1959) and *Breakfast at Tiffany's* (1961).

Hepburn, Katharine (1909–) Actress, born in Hartford, CT. From 1932 she attained international fame as a film actress, notably in *Morning Glory* (1933), *Guess Who's Coming to Dinner* (1967), *The Lion in Winter* (1968), and *On Golden Pond* (1981), all of which gained her Oscars, and *The African Queen* (1952).

Hephaestus [he**fees**tus] In Greek mythology, a god of fire, associated with volcanic sites; then of the smithy and metalwork. He was the son of Hera, who was annoyed at his lameness and threw him out of heaven. >> Vulcan (mythology)

heptane C_7H_{16}. An alkane hydrocarbon with seven carbon atoms. There are nine structural isomers, mostly in the gasoline fraction of petroleum. >> alkanes; petroleum

heptathlon A multi-event track-and-field competition, discipline for women. It consists of seven events: 100 m hurdles, shot put, high jump, 200 m, long jump, javelin, and 800 m. The world record of 7291 points was set by Jacqueline Joyner-Kersee (1962–) of the USA, at Seoul, South Korea, in 1988. >> athletics; pentathlon

Hepworth, Dame (Jocelyn) Barbara (1903–75) Sculptor, born in Wakefield, West Yorkshire. She was one of the foremost non-figurative sculptors of her time, as seen in her 'Contrapuntal Forms' (1951).

Hera [**heer**a] In Greek mythology, the daughter of Cronus and wife of Zeus. She was associated with Argos and hostile to Troy. >> Juno (mythology)

Heracles [**he**rakleez], Lat **Hercules** Greek hero, who undertook Twelve Labours for Eurystheus of Argos: (1) to kill the Nemean Lion, (2) to kill the Hydra of Lerna, (3) to capture the Hind of Ceryneia; (4) to capture the Boar of Erymanthus, (5) to clean the Stables of Augeas; (6) to shoot the Birds of Stymphalus, (7) to capture the Cretan Bull, (8) to capture the Horses of Diomedes, (9) to steal the Girdle of the Amazon, (10) to capture the oxen of the giant Geryon, (11) to fetch the Apples of the Hesperides; (12) to capture Cerberus, the guardian of Hades. >> Cerberus; Hesperides; Hydra (mythology)

Heraclitus or **Heracleitos** [hera**kliy**tus] (?–460 BC) Greek philosopher, born in Ephesus. He thought that all things are composed of opposites, constantly at strife with one another, and thus in perpetual change. Only fragments of his writings survive.

Heraklion [he**rak**lion], Gr **Iráklion**, Ital **Candia** 35°20N 25°08E, pop (1995e) 270 000. Administrative centre and capital town of Crete region (since 1971), S Greece; on N coast of Crete I; airfield; cathedral (19th-c); old city within Venetian walls (begun 1538). >> Crete

heraldry The granting and designing of pictorial devices (*arms*) originally used on the shields of knights in armour to identify them in battle. The science of describing such devices is *blazonry*. Arms are regarded as insignia of honour, and their unauthorized display is subject to legal sanction in most European countries. >> blazonry; *see illustration on p. 395*

herb A plant with a distinctive smell or taste, used to enhance the flavour and aroma of food. Herbs are usually grown in temperate climates (whereas spices are usually tropical). Some are often used for their medicinal properties, hence the speciality of the **herbalist**. >> angelica; basil; borage; celery; chamomile; chervil; costmary; dill; fennel; feverfew; herbaceous plant; horehound; lovage; marjoram; mint; mugwort; rosemary; rue; sage; spice; sweet bay; woundwort; yarrow

herbaceous plant Any non-woody plant which dies at the end of the growing season; often referred to simply as **herb**. Herbaceous perennials die back to ground level, but survive as underground organs such as bulbs or tubers, sending up new growth in the spring.

herbalism The use of herbs to prevent and cure illness; also called **herbal medicine** or **phytotherapy**. The treatment is based upon a holistic assessment of the patient, and uses whole plants, or parts of plants, rather than separating and purifying the active constituents. A computerized data bank is now available, and a pharmacopoeia has been produced by the British Herbal Medical Association. >> alternative medicine; Culpeper; herb

Herbert (of Cherbury), Edward Herbert, Baron (1583–1648) English soldier, statesman, and philosopher, born in Eyton, Shropshire, brother of George Herbert. He is regarded as the founder of English deism. His main works are *De veritate* (1624, On Truth), and *De religione Gentilium* (published 1663, On the Religion of the Gentiles). >> deism

Herbert, George (1593–1633) Clergyman and poet, born at Montgomery Castle, Powys. His verse is collected in *The Temple* (1633), and his chief prose work, *A Priest in the Temple*, was published in *Remains* (1652).

herbicide A chemical which kills weeds. **Nonselective** herbicides may be used to kill all vegetation before cultivation and planting begin. Once the crop has emerged, **selective herbicides** target the troublesome weeds only. >> agriculture

herbivore [**herb**ivaw(r)] An animal that feeds on vegetation – a label used especially of the large plant-eating mammals, such as the ungulates. Its teeth are typically adapted for grinding plants, and its gut is adapted for digesting cellulose. >> carnivore ℹ; mammal ℹ; ungulate

Herculaneum [herkyu**lay**nium] In Roman times, a prosperous town situated near Mt Vesuvius in SW Italy. It was destroyed completely in the volcanic eruption of AD 79 (now a world heritage site). >> Pompeii

Hercules [**her**kyuleez] >> **Heracles**

Hercules [**her**kyuleez] A constellation in the N sky, the fifth-largest of all, but hard to recognize because its stars are faint. >> constellation; RR968

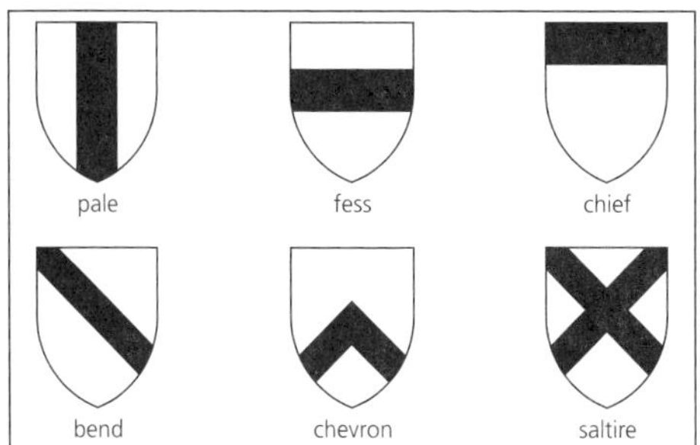

Some common heraldic devices

Herder, Johann Gottfried von (1744–1803) Critic and poet, born in Mohrungen, Germany. He wrote on folksongs, poetry, and mythology, developing a historical method best seen in his masterpiece, *Ideen zur Geschichte der Menschheit* (1784–91, Outlines of a Philosophy on the History of Man). He was a major influence on Goethe and German Romanticism. >> Goethe; Romanticism

heredity >> **genetics**

Hereford [**he**referd] 52°04N 2°43W, pop (1995e) 51 000. Administrative centre of Herefordshire (unitary authority from 1998), WC England; on the R Wye at the centre of a rich farming region; railway; cathedral (11th-c) contains the *Mappa Mundi*, a mediaeval map of the world; football league team, Hereford United. >> England ℹ

Hereford and Worcester [**he**referd, **wus**ter] pop (1995e) 705 000; area 3926 sq km/1515 sq mi. County of WC England; created 1974 from former counties of Herefordshire and Worcestershire; Herefordshire unitary authority from 1998; Malvern Hills rise SW; county town, Worcester; horticulture, especially in Vale of Evesham; cattle (Herefords). >> England ℹ; Worcester

heresy False doctrine, or the formal denial of doctrine defined as part of a particular faith. If consciously adhered to, heresy entails excommunication. Total heresy or the rejection of all faith is termed **apostasy**. >> Albigenses; Arius; Arminius; Donatists; Monophysites; Nestorians; Pelagius

Hereward, known as **Hereward the Wake** (?–c.1080) Anglo-Saxon thegn who led the last organized English resistance against the Norman invaders. He held the Isle of Ely against William the Conqueror for nearly a year (1070–1). >> Norman Conquest; thegn

Hergé [**her**zhay], Fr [airzhay], pseudonym of **Georges Rémi** (1907–83) Strip cartoonist, born in Etterbeek, Belgium. He created the *Tin-Tin* strip for the children's supplement of the newspaper *Le Vingtième Siècle*, using the pseudonym Hergé, a phonetic version of his initials, RG.

herm >> **term**

Herman, Woody, popular name of **Woodrow Charles Herman** (1913–87) Jazz musician, bandleader, singer, and composer, born in Milwaukee, WI. Playing clarinet and alto saxophone, he formed the white swing band called **the Woodchoppers** in 1936, following this with the first **Herman's Herd** in 1944. >> jazz

Hermandszoon, Jakob >> **Arminius, Jacobus**

hermaphrodite An animal or plant having both male and female reproductive organs. Species in which both sets of organs mature simultaneously often have mechanisms that prevent self-fertilization. >> reproduction

Hermaphroditus [hermafro**diy**tus] In Greek mythology, the son of Hermes and Aphrodite. The nymph Salmacis, unloved by him, prayed to be united with him; this was granted by combining them in one body. >> Aphrodite; Hermes (mythology)

hermeneutics [herme**nyoo**tiks] The theory of the interpretation and understanding of texts. Though its origins lie in ancient Greek philosophy, hermeneutics received fresh impetus in 18th-c discussions of the problems of biblical interpretation. It now includes many fields, including literary theory, the social sciences, and aesthetics.

Hermes [**her**meez] An asteroid which came within 760 000 km/475 000 mi of Earth in 1937, at that time a record. It was only a few km in diameter. >> asteroids

Hermes [**her**meez] In Greek mythology, the ambassador of the gods, the son of Zeus and Maia; depicted with herald's staff and winged sandals. He is variously associated with stones, commerce, roads, cookery, and thieving; also arts such as oratory. >> Mercury (mythology)

Hermitage A major art gallery in St Petersburg, Russia, built in the 18th–19th-c to house the art collection of the tsars, and opened to the public in 1852. After the deposition of the tsar, this became the headquarters of Kerensky's provisional government, but was stormed by the Bolsheviks (Nov 1917). It now contains over 3 million works of art, and almost 400 rooms. >> St Petersburg (Russia)

hermit crab A crab-like crustacean which uses an empty snail shell as a portable refuge covering its soft abdomen; it changes shells as it grows. (Class: Malacostraca. Order: Decapoda.) >> crab; crustacean

hernia The protrusion of tissue from its natural site through an adjacent orifice or tissue space. Examples are *inguinal*, *femoral*, and *umbilical* herniae, in which the intestine pushes its way through weak sites in the abdominal wall; the herniae emerge as externally protruding masses in the groin, over the upper thigh, and at the navel, respectively. >> abdomen; intestine

Hero of Alexandria (1st-c) Greek mathematician and inventor. He devised many machines, among them the 'aeolipile', the earliest known steam engine. He also devised the formula for expressing the area of a triangle in terms of its sides. >> triangle (mathematics)

Hero and Leander [**heer**oh, lee**an**der] A Greek legend first found in the Roman poet, Ovid. Two lovers lived on opposite sides of the Hellespont; Hero was the priestess of Aphrodite at Sestos, and Leander, who lived at Abydos, swam across each night guided by her light. When this was extinguished in a storm, he was drowned, and Hero committed suicide by throwing herself into the sea. >> Ovid

Herod [**he**rod], known as **the Great** (c.73–4 BC) King of Judea, the younger son of the Idumaean chieftain, Antipater. He owed his initial appointment as Governor of Galilee (47 BC) to Julius Caesar, and his elevation to the kingship of Judea (40 BC) to Marcus Antonius. An able administrator, he did much to develop the economic potential of his kingdom. His cruelty is reflected in the Gospel account of the Massacre of the Innocents. >> Antipater; Antonius, Marcus; Caesar

Herod Agrippa I [**he**rod a**grip**a] (10 BC–AD 44) King of Judaea (41–4), the grandson of Herod the Great. Reared at the court of the Emperor Augustus. Caligula gave him two thirds of the former kingdom of Herod the Great, while Claudius added the remaining third (41). He executed St James and imprisoned St Peter. >> Caligula; Claudius; Herod the Great

Herod Agrippa II [**he**rod a**grip**a] (c.27–c.93) King of Chalcis (49/50–53), ruler of the Ituraean principality (53–c.93), the son of Herod Agrippa I. A supporter of Rome in the Jewish War (66–70), he was rewarded for it afterwards with grants of land in Judaea. It was before him that St Paul made his defence and was found innocent. >> Herod Agrippa I; Paul, St

Herod Antipas [**he**rod **an**tipas] (?–AD 39) The son of Herod the Great and ruler (tetrarch) of Galilee and Peraea (4–39), after Herod's death. In the Christian tradition, he looms large as the capricious murderer of John the Baptist. >> Herod the Great; John the Baptist, St

Herodotos or **Herodotus** [he**rod**otus] (c.485–425 BC) Greek historian, born in Halicarnassus, Asia Minor. He travelled widely in the Middle East, collecting material for his great narrative history, which gave a record of the wars between the Greeks and the Persians. >> Persian Wars

heroin or **diamorphine** A derivative of morphine developed in 1896, and soon found to be extremely addictive. It is used to ease the severe pain that can accompany terminal illness, but even this medical use is banned in the USA. It is widely abused. >> drug addiction; morphine; narcotics

heron A wading bird related to the bittern; worldwide (mainly tropical); flies with neck retracted, not extended. (Family: Ardeidae, 64 species.) >> bittern; egret

Herophilus [he**ro**filus] (c.335–c.280 BC) Greek anatomist, born in Chalcedon. He was the first to dissect the human body, and to compare it with that of other animals.

herpes labialis >> **cold sore**

herpes simplex [**her**peez **sim**pleks] A viral infection which affects the lips, the mouth, or the genital region. Recurrent attacks are common, between which the virus lies dormant. >> virus

herpes zoster >> **shingles**

Herrick, Robert (1591–1674) Poet, born in London. His writing is mainly collected in *Hesperides* (1648), and includes such well-known lyrics as 'Cherry ripe'.

herring Surface-living marine fish (*Clupea harengus*) abundant in the N Atlantic and Arctic; body length up to 40 cm/16 in; colour deep blue on back, underside silvery white; supports important commercial fisheries, being sold fresh, smoked as kippers or bloaters, or preserved in salt or vinegar; first-year herring sold as whitebait; during the 1990s, there was increasing international concern over reduced stocks, and controversy over fishing quotas. (Family: Clupeidae.) >> whitebait

Herriot, James, pseudonym of **James Alfred Wight** (1916–95) Veterinary surgeon and writer, born in Glasgow. Beginning in the 1970s, he brought the vet's world to the notice of the public with a number of bestselling books, such as *It Shouldn't Happen to a Vet*. Feature films and television series made his work known all over the world, especially the television series *All Creatures Great and Small* (1977–80). The stories prompted a thriving tourist industry based on 'Herriot country', and transformed the public image of his profession, making veterinary medicine one of the most competitive university subjects.

Herschel, Sir William (Frederick) [**her**shl], originally **Friedrich Wilhelm Herschel** (1738–1822) Astronomer, born in Hanover, Germany. He built the largest reflecting telescopes made at the time, discovered Uranus in 1781, extensively observed double stars, and produced a notable star catalogue. >> double star; Uranus (astronomy)

Hertford [**hah(r)t**ferd] 51°48N 0°05W, pop (1995e) 23 300. County town in Hertfordshire, SE England; railway; castle (12th-c). >> Hertfordshire

Hertfordshire [**hah(r)t**ferdsheer] pop (1995e) 1 012 000; area 1634 sq km/631 sq mi. County of SE England; county town, Hertford. >> England [i]; Hertford

Hertz, Heinrich (Rudolf) (1857–1894) Physicist, born in Hamburg, Germany. His main work was on electromagnetic waves (1887), and he discovered radio waves. The unit of frequency is named after him. >> electromagnetism; Helmholtz; hertz

hertz SI unit of frequency; symbol *Hz*; named after Heinrich Hertz; defined as the number of complete cycles per second. >> frequency; Hertz

Hertzog, J(ames) B(arry) M(unnik) [**hert**zokh] (1866–1942) South African statesman and prime minister (1924–39), born in Wellington, Cape Colony, South Africa. In 1914 he founded the Nationalist Party, advocating complete South African independence. As premier, he pursued a legislative programme which destroyed the African franchise, and tightened land segregation. >> South Africa [i]

Herzl, Theodor [**her**tsl] (1860–1904) Zionist leader, born in Budapest. He was converted to Zionism, and in the pamphlet *Judenstaat* (1896, The Jewish State) called for a world council to discuss the question of a homeland for the Jews. He became the first president of the World Zionist Organization. >> Zionism

Herzog, Werner [**hert**zog], originally **Werner Stipetic** (1942–) Film director, screenwriter, and producer, born in Sachrang, Germany. He became recognized as a leading member of the New Cinema in Germany with his feature *Aguirre, der Zorn Gottes* (1973, Aguirre, Wrath of God). His general themes are metaphysical in character, often with remoteness in time or location, as in *Where the Green Ants Dream* (1984).

Heselrig, Sir Arthur >> **Haselrig, Arthur**

Heseltine, Michael (Ray Dibdin) [**hes**eltiyn] (1933–) British Conservative statesman, born in Swansea, SC Wales. He was appointed secretary of state for the environment (1979–83), and then defence secretary (1983–6). He resigned from the government in dramatic fashion by walking out of a cabinet meeting over the issue of the takeover of Westland helicopters. He stood unsuccessfully as a candidate in the leadership contest following Mrs Thatcher's resignation (1990), and under John Major became environment secretary (1990–2), President of the Board of Trade (1992–5), and deputy prime minister (1995–7). He was made a Companion of Honour in 1997. >> Conservative Party

Hesiod [**hee**siod] (fl.8th-CBC) Greek poet, born in Ascra. His *Works and Days* deals with the farmer's life; *Theogony* teaches the origin of the universe and the history of the gods.

Hesperides [hes**per**ideez] In Greek mythology, the daughters of the evening star (**Hesper**), who guard the Golden Apples together with the dragon, Ladon. >> Atalanta; Heracles

Hess, Dame Myra (1890–1965) Pianist, born in London. An immediate success on her first public appearance in 1907, during World War 2 she organized the lunchtime concerts in the National Gallery.

Hess, (Walter Richard) Rudolf (1894–1987) German politician, Hitler's deputy as Nazi Party leader, born in Alexandria, Egypt. In 1941, he flew alone to Scotland to plead the cause of a negotiated Anglo-German peace. He was held in Britain until the Nuremberg Trials (1946) when he was sentenced to life imprisonment. He remained in Spandau prison, Berlin (after 1966, as the only prisoner) until his death. >> Hitler; World War 2

Hesse [**he**suh], Ger **Hessen** pop (1995e) 5 891 000; area 21 114 sq km/8151 sq mi. A state formed in 1945 from the former Prussian province of Hesse-Nassau; wine produced along Rhine valley; capital, Wiesbaden.

Hesse, Hermann [**he**suh] (1877–1962) Novelist and poet, born in Calw, Germany. His works include *Rosshalde* (1914), *Siddhartha* (1922), *Steppenwolf* (1927), and *Das Glasperlenspiel* (1945, The Glass Bead Game). He was awarded the Nobel Prize for Literature in 1946. His psychological and mystical concerns made him something of a cult figure after his death.

Hestia [**hes**tia] Greek goddess of the hearth, the daughter of Cronus and Rhea. >> Vesta (mythology)

Heston, Charlton, originally **John Charles Carter** (1923–) Actor, born in Evanston, IL. De Mille's *The Greatest Show on Earth* (1951) and *The Ten Commandments* (1956) brought him great success, and he won an Oscar for *Ben Hur* (1959). He continued in heroic roles, his later films including *The Awakening* (1980) and *True Lies* (1994). He has also played a prominent role in US arts, theatre, and cinema organizations.

Heteroptera [hete**rop**tera] A large order of insects comprising the true bugs; body typically depressed, forewings usually leathery at base and membranous at tip; mouthparts modified for piercing and sucking; c.35 000 species, including many crop pests and disease carriers. >> bug (entomology); insect [i]

Hewish, Antony (1924–) Radio astronomer, born in Fowey, Cornwall. With his student Susan Jocelyn (Burnell) Bell (1943–), he discovered the first pulsars. He shared the Nobel Prize for Physics in 1974 with his former teacher, Sir Martin Ryle. >> pulsar; quasar; Ryle, Martin

Hewson, John (1946–) Australian politician and economist, born in Sydney, New South Wales, Australia. He became shadow minister for finance (1988–9) and shadow treasurer (1989–90), and was elected leader of the Liberal Party (1990–4). >> Liberal Party (Australia)

hexachlorophene [heksa**klo**rofeen] $C_{13}H_6Cl_6O_2$. A white powder with antiseptic properties, widely used in toilet preparations. >> antiseptic

hexadecanoic acid >> **palmitic acid**

hexadecimal coding A number notation using the number base 16. The 16 individual characters are 0–9, and A–F inclusive, representing decimal 10 to decimal 15 respectively. The notation provides a convenient means of writing binary numbers. >> binary code

hexane C_6H_{14}. An alkane hydrocarbon with six carbon atoms. There are five structural isomers. The straight-chain compound, n-hexane, $CH_3CH_2CH_2CH_2CH_2CH_3$, has boiling point 69°C. >> alkanes

hexanedioic acid >> **adipic acid**

Heyer, Georgette [**hay**er] (1902–74) Writer, born in London. Her early work includes historical novels, and fictional studies of real figures in crisis, such as William I. An outstanding authority on the Regency period, she had success with *Regency Buck* (1935) and later novels.

Heyerdahl, Thor [**hiy**erdahl] (1914–) Anthropologist, born in Larvik, Norway. In 1947 he proved, by sailing a balsa raft (the *Kon-Tiki*) from Peru to Tuamotu I in the S Pacific, that the Peruvian Indians could have settled in Polynesia. In 1970 he sailed from Morocco to the West Indies in a papyrus boat, *Ra II*, and made the journey from Iraq to Djibouti in a reed boat, the *Tigris*, in 1977–8.

Heysel stadium [**hay**zl] A football stadium in Brussels, Belgium; scene of a tragedy during the European Champions' Cup Final between Liverpool and Juventus (Turin) in 1985, when a wall and safety fence collapsed during a riot, killing 39 and injuring over 200. After that event, English football clubs were not allowed to play matches in Europe for several years – a ban which began to be lifted in 1990. >> football [i]

Heywood, Thomas (c.1574–1641) Playwright and poet, born in Lincolnshire. He shared in the composition of over 200 plays, and wrote 24 of his own, notably his domestic tragedy, *A Woman Killed with Kindness* (1607).

Hiawatha [hiya**wo**tha], Indian name **Heowenta** (16th-c) The name of a real American Indian, used by Longfellow for his hero in *The Song of Hiawatha*. The poem retells Indian legends in the manner and metre of the Finnish *Kalevala*. >> Kalevala; Longfellow

hibernation A strategy for passing the cold winter period in a torpid or resting state, found in mammals and some other animals. The animal enters a deep sleep, surviving on food reserves stored in its body during a favourable summer period. The similar strategy for surviving a hot, dry summer is known as **aestivation**.

hibiscus An annual, perennial, or shrub native to warm regions; flowers often very large and showy, 5-petalled, the stamens united into a central column. (Genus: *Hibiscus*, 300 species. Family: Malvaceae.)

hiccup / hiccough An involuntary contraction of the diaphragm causing an intake of air which is halted by spasm (closure) of the glottis, thereby producing a sharp, characteristic, inspiratory sound. Its cause is unknown, but there are many folk-remedies, such as drinking from the 'wrong side of the glass'. >> diaphragm (anatomy); glottis

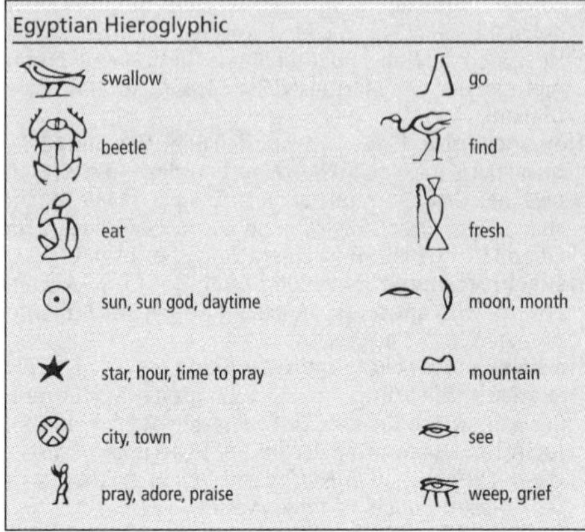

Hickock, Wild Bill >> Calamity Jane

hickory A tall deciduous tree, sometimes with shaggy bark, native to E Asia and E North America; flowers small, green, lacking petals; nut 4-valved, edible. (Genus: *Carya*, 25 species. Family: Juglandaceae.)

hidden curriculum The unwritten, informal code of conduct to which children are expected to conform in the classroom. Children are said to be rewarded not only for learning their subject curriculum but appearing to do so with enthusiasm, alertness, and deference to and respect for authority.

hieroglyphics The study of the symbols of ancient Egyptian writing; also, the symbols themselves. The characters were originally pictograms, and were named **hieroglyphs** (from the Greek 'sacred carving') because of their frequent use in religious contexts. The symbols are usually written from right to left. >> ideography; pictography ℹ

hi-fi >> high fidelity sound system

Higgins, Alex(ander Gordon), nickname **Hurricane Higgins** (1949–) Snooker player, born in Belfast. He has had a tempestuous career since becoming the youngest world champion in 1972, at age 23. He won the title for a second time in 1982. >> snooker

Higgins, John (1975–) Snooker player, born in Wishaw, Lanarkshire, Scotland. He turned professional in 1992, his wins including the German Open (1995, 1997), the British Open (1995, 1998), and the European Open (1997). His win in the Embassy World Championship (1998) gave him the No 1 ranking position (previously held by Stephen Hendry). >> Hendry

High Commissioner A person carrying out the same duties and possessing the same rank as an ambassador, representing one Commonwealth country in another Commonwealth country. >> ambassador

High Court (of Justice) A court established for England and Wales by the Judicature Acts (1873–5), principally a trial court for civil cases. It hears appeals on points of law from magistrates' courts in both civil and criminal cases, and also undertakes judicial review. In Scotland, the **High Court of Justiciary** is the supreme criminal court. >> Chancery Division; judicial review

high-definition television (HDTV) Any television system using substantially more scanning lines than the 500–600 of established broadcast standards, with improved picture quality in a wide-screen format. For example, the Japanese NHK system, Hi-Vision, uses 1125 lines at 60 fields per second (60 Hz). >> scanning ℹ; television

high energy physics >> particle physics

higher education >> further education

high fidelity sound system An assembly of sound reproduction components capable of regenerating an original musical performance to the highest attainable quality across the whole range of audible frequencies (20–20 000 Hz) and amplitudes; also known as **hi-fi**. It was a concept which emerged after World War 2, made possible by new record material (vinylite), stereophonic recording, and transistors. Digital recording, noise reduction, and the compact disc were later embellishments. >> sound recording

high jump An athletics field event in which competitors attempt to clear a bar without any aids. The height of the bar is gradually increased, and competitors are allowed three attempts to clear each new height; they are eliminated if they fail. The current world record for men is 2·45 m/8 ft $\frac{1}{2}$ in, achieved by Javier Sotomayor (Cuba) in 1993 at Salamanca, Spain; for women, it is 2·09 m/6 ft $10\frac{1}{4}$ in, achieved by Stefka Kostadinova (Bulgaria) in 1987 at Rome. >> athletics

Highland pop (1995e) 211 000; area 25 391 sq km/9804 sq mi. Council in N Scotland, includes Inner Hebrides; sparsely inhabited region of great scenic beauty; Grampian, Monadhliath, and Cairngorm Mts; rises to 1344 m/4409 ft in Ben Nevis (SW); capital, Inverness. >> Ben Nevis; Cairngorms; Caledonian Canal; Grampians; Hebrides; Inverness; Scotland ℹ

Highland Games Athletic meetings held in Scotland; the first Games were organized in 1819. A range of events takes place, in addition to specifically Scottish events such as tossing the caber. The most famous meeting is the Braemar Gathering. >> caber tossing

high-level language A computer language in which every instruction or statement is equivalent to several machine-code instructions. High-level languages, such as BASIC and PASCAL, are written using notations which are relatively easy for the user to understand. >> machine code

high school The common form of secondary school in the USA for 15–19-year-olds, following the **junior high school** phase for 11–15-year-olds. The schools are non-selective. >> secondary education

Highsmith, Patricia (1921–95) Writer, born in Fort Worth, TX. Her first novel was *Strangers on a Train* (1949, filmed 1957), but her best novels describe the criminal adventures of her psychotic hero Tom Ripley, beginning with *The Talented Mr Ripley* (1956).

high-speed anti-radiation missile (HARM) A guided missile developed initially by the US Navy after Vietnam. HARMs are equipped with a 'homing head' designed to lock onto enemy ground-based radar transmitters. >> missile, guided

high-speed photography The photographic recording of transient phenomena with very short periods of exposure. Electronic flash can be as brief as one-millionth of a second, and non-mechanical shutters (such as the polarizing Kerr cell) can operate 200 times faster. In cinematography the limit for mechanical intermittent film movement is about 600 pictures per second. >> photography

Hijra [**hij**ra], formerly also spelled **Hegira** The migration of the Prophet Mohammed from Mecca to Medina in 622. The departure marks the beginning of the Muslim era. >> Islam; Mohammed; RR982

Hilary (of Poitiers), St (c.315–c.368) Clergyman and Doctor of the Church, born in Limonum (Poitiers), France. A leading opponent of Arianism, his principal work is on the Trinity. His feast day marks the beginning of a term at Oxford and Durham universities, and English law sittings. Feast day 13 January. >> Arius; Trinity

Hildesheim [**hil**des-hiym] 52°09N 9°55E, pop (1995e)

108 000. Port in Germany; founded, 1300; railway; St Michael's Church (11th-c) and cathedral (1054–79), world heritage sites. >> Germany ℹ

Hill, Benny, popular name of **Alfred Hawthorne Hill** (1925–92) Comedian, born in Southampton, Hampshire. Named TV personality of the year in 1954, he gained national popularity with the saucy *The Benny Hill Show* (1957–66), and spent over two decades writing and performing in top-rated television specials.

Hill, Damon (Graham Devereux) (1960–) Motor-racing driver, the son of Graham Hill. He drove for Brabham in his first Grand Prix at Silverstone in 1992, and went on to win over 20 grands prix in the next four years, succeeding Nigel Mansell on the Williams team. He took third place in the world championship in 1993, was runner-up in 1994, and won in 1996. The next season he joined the TWR Arrows Yamaha team, and in 1998 drove for the Benson & Hedges Jordan Mugen Honda team. >> Hill, Graham; Mansell

Hill, Geoffrey (William) (1932–) Poet, born in Bromsgrove, Hereford and Worcester. His works include *For the Unfallen* (1959) and *The Mystery of the Charity of Charles Péguy* (1983). *New and Collected Poems 1952–1992* were published in 1994.

Hill, (Norman) Graham (1929–75) Motor-racing driver, born in London. He was world champion in 1962 (in a BRM) and in 1968 (Lotus), and won the Monaco Grand Prix five times (1963–5, 1968–9). His son, **Damon** (1960–), also went into motor-racing, succeeding Nigel Mansell on the Williams Formula One team, and winning the world championship in 1996. >> Hill, Damon; motor racing

Hill, Octavia (1838–1912) Housing reformer and founder of the National Trust, born in London. She worked among the London poor, and in 1864 commenced an influential project to improve the homes of working men in the slums.

Hill, Sir Rowland (1795–1879) Originator of penny postage, born in Kidderminster, Hereford and Worcester. In his *Post-office Reform* (1837), he advocated a low and uniform rate of postage, to be prepaid by stamps, and in 1840 a uniform penny rate was introduced.

Hillary, Sir Edmund (Percival) (1919–) Mountaineer and explorer, born in Auckland, New Zealand. As a member of Hunt's Everest expedition he reached, with Tenzing Norgay, the summit of Mt Everest in 1953. With a New Zealand party he reached the South Pole in 1958. >> Everest, Mount; Hunt, John

Hillel [**hi**lel], known as **Hillel Hazaken** (the Elder), or **Hillel Hababli** ('the Babylonian') (1st-c BC–1st-c AD) One of the most respected Jewish teachers of his time, probably born in Babylonia. Noted for his use of seven rules in expounding Scripture, his views were influential for later rabbinic Judaism. >> Judaism

Hillery, Patrick (John) (1923–) Irish politician and president of the Irish Republic (1976–90), born in Co Clare. He was previously foreign minister (1969–72) and European Commissioner for social affairs (1973–6).

Hilliard, Nicholas (1547–1619) Court goldsmith and miniaturist, born in Exeter, Devon. He founded the English school of miniature painting.

Hillsborough Football stadium in Sheffield, England. It was the scene of the worst disaster in British sporting history, when 95 Liverpool fans died and 400 people were injured at the FA Cup semi-final match between Liverpool and Nottingham Forest (15 Apr 1989). >> football ℹ

Hilton, Conrad (Nicholson) (1887–1979) Hotelier, born in San Antonio, NM. He formed the Hilton Hotels Corporation in 1946, diversifying the company in the 1950s to include car-rental and credit-card operations.

Hilton, James (1900–54) Novelist, born in Leigh, Lancashire. His books include *Lost Horizon* (1933, Hawthornden Prize), and *Goodbye Mr Chips* (1934).

Hilversum 52°14N 5°10E, pop (1995e) 86 500. City in W Netherlands; famous for its radio and television stations; fashionable residential district of Amsterdam; railway. >> Netherlands, The ℹ

Himalayas [hi**mahl**yaz, hima**lay**az] Gigantic wall of mountains in C Asia; length over 2400 km/1500 mi; three main ranges, the Outer, Middle, and Inner Himalayas, which become five ranges in Kashmir; Mt Everest rises to 8848 m/29 028 ft on the Nepal–Tibet border; other major peaks include K2 in the Karakorams (8611 m/28 251 ft), Kangchenjunga (8586 m/28 169 ft); in Hindu mythology the mountains are highly revered. >> Annapurna, Mount; Everest, Mount

Himalia [hi**mah**lia] The sixth natural satellite of Jupiter, discovered in 1904; distance from the planet 11 480 000 km/7 134 000 mi; diameter c.186 km/116 mi. >> Jupiter (astronomy); RR964

Himmler, Heinrich (1900–45) Nazi leader and chief of police, born in Munich, Germany. In 1929 he was made head of the SS (*Schutzstaffel*, 'protective force'), which he developed into a powerful party weapon, and also directed the secret police (*Gestapo*). He was captured by the Allies, and committed suicide at Lüneburg. >> Gestapo; Hitler; SS

Hindemith, Paul [**hin**duhmit] (1895–1963) Composer, born in Hanau, Germany. His works include operas, concertos, and a wide range of instrumental pieces. The modernity of his music caused it to be banned by the Nazis in 1934.

Hindenburg, Paul (Ludwig Hans Anton von Beneckendorff und) von [**hin**denberg] (1847–1934) German general and president (1925–34), born in Posnan, Poland (formerly Posen, Prussia). Recalled from retirement at the outbreak of World War 1, he won victories over the Russians (1914–15), but was forced to direct the German retreat on the Western Front (to the **Hindenburg line**). In 1933 he appointed Hitler as chancellor. >> World War 1

Hindenburg [**hin**dnberg] A famous airship, of rigid-frame construction, built by the German government in 1936, capable of carrying 72 passengers in a style matching the ocean liners of the day. After 63 successful flights, it caught fire in May 1937 while coming in to moor in New Jersey. >> airship

Hindi >> **Indo-Aryan languages**

Hindley, Myra >> **Brady, Ian**

Hinduism [**hin**duizm] The Western term for a religious tradition developed over several thousand years and intertwined with the history and social system of India. It emphasizes the right way of living (*dharma*) rather than a set of doctrines, and thus embraces diverse religious beliefs and practices. Common to most forms is the idea of reincarnation or transmigration. *Samsara* refers to the process of birth and rebirth continuing for life after life. The particular form and condition (pleasant or unpleasant) of rebirth are the result of *karma*, the law by which the consequences of actions within one life are carried over into the next. The ultimate spiritual goal of Hindus is *mohsha*, or release from the cycle of *samsara*. No specific text is regarded as uniquely authoritative. The earliest extant writings come from the Vedic period (c.1200–500 BC), and are known collectively as the Veda. Later (c.500 BC–AD 500) came the religious law books which codified the classes of society (*varna*) and the four stages of life (*ashrama*). To this were added the great epics, the Ramayana and the Mahabharata. The latter includes one of the most influential Hindu scriptures, the Bhagavadgita. Brahma, Vishnu, and Shiva are the chief gods of Hinduism, and together form a triad (the *Trimurti*). There are numerous lesser deities, including the goddesses Maya and Lakshmi. There is a great emphasis upon the performance of complex and demanding rituals under the supervision of Brahman priests and teachers. There were nearly 800 million Hindus in 1998. >> Advaita; atman; avatar; Bhagavadgita; Brahma; dharma; karma; Krishna; Lakshmi; lingam; mandala; mantra; Shiva; tantra; Trimurti; Veda; Vishnu; RR981, RR982

Hindu Kush [**hin**doo **kush**], ancient **Paropamisus** Mountain range in C Asia, an extension of the Himalayan system, covering c.800 km/500 mi; world's second highest range; rising to 7690 m/25 229 ft in Tirich Mir. >> Afghanistan ℹ

Hines, Earl (Kenneth) [hiynz], nickname **Fatha** ('Father') **Hines** (1905–83) Jazz pianist and bandleader, born in Duquesne, PA. He revolutionized jazz piano, improvising single-note lines in the treble clef and punctuating them with internal rhythms in the bass, in a style that became known as 'trumpet piano'. >> jazz

Hingis, Martina [**hing**is] (1981–) Tennis player, born in Kosice, Slovak Republic. She was brought up in Switzerland and, playing for that country, in 1997 became the youngest-ever world number one when she replaced the injured Steffi Graf. Winner of the 1996 Wimbledon doubles title, she won the singles title in 1997 at the age of 16, and won the doubles title again in 1998. >> Graf

hinny >> **mule** (zoology)

hip The outer rounded region at the side of the upper thigh. It is the joint between the head of the femur and the pelvis, possessing great strength and stability. >> femur; pelvis; skeleton ℹ

Hipparchos / Hipparchus [hi**pah(r)**kus] (2nd-c BC) Astronomer, born in Nicaea, Rhodes. He is noted for his catalogue of the positions of 1080 stars. He also found the length of the solar year (correct to 7 min).

hippeastrum [hipee**as**truhm] >> **amaryllis**

Hippocrates [hi**po**krateez] (c.460–c.377 BC) Physician, born on the Greek island of Cos. He is traditionally regarded as 'the father of medicine'. >> Hippocratic oath

Hippocratic oath An ethical code attributed to Hippocrates. Parts of it are still used in medical schools throughout the world to encourage young graduates to aspire to conduct that befits those who care for sick people. >> Hippocrates; medicine

Hippolytus [hi**pol**itus] A Greek hero, son of Theseus and Hippolyta. Theseus's new wife, Phaedra, made advances to Hippolytus, which were refused; so she falsely accused Hippolytus of rape. Theseus invoked a curse, Poseidon sent a frightening sea-monster, and Hippolytus was thrown from his chariot and killed. >> Asclepius

hippopotamus (Gr 'river horse') A mammal of family Hippopotamidae; an artiodactyl, found in two species: **hippopotamus** (*Hippopotamus amphibius*) of tropical African rivers; body large, barrel-shaped; spends day in water, emerges at night; large oblong head; four webbed toes on each foot; **pygmy hippopotamus** (*Choeropsis liberiensis*) from W Africa; inhabits swamps and forests; shoulder height, 750 mm/30 in; also known as **hippo**. >> artiodactyl

hippotigris >> **zebra**

hire purchase (UK)/ **installment credit** (US) A legal agreement to buy an article by means of small regular payments, meanwhile having use of the article. Each payment includes an element of interest as well as part of the cost of the article. >> interest

Hirohito [hiroh**hee**toh] (1901–89) Emperor of Japan (1926–89), the 124th in direct lineage, born in Tokyo. His reign was marked by rapid militarization and the aggressive wars against China (1931–2, 1937–45) and Britain and the USA (1941–5). >> Akihito; Japan ℹ; World War 2

Hiroshige, Ando [hirohsheegay] (1797–1858) Painter, born in Edo (modern Tokyo). He is celebrated for his impressive landscape colour prints.

Hiroshima [hiro**shee**ma, hi**ro**shima] 34°23N 132°27E, pop (1995e) 1 083 000. City in S Honshu I, Japan; founded as a castle, 1594; atomic bomb dropped here (6 Aug 1945), c.150 000 killed or wounded, 75% of the buildings destroyed or severely damaged; town rapidly rebuilt; airport; railway; university (1949); Peace Memorial Park. >> atomic bomb; Honshu

Hirst, Damien (1965–) Avant-garde artist, born in Bristol, SW England. He became known works which made use of dead animals, preserved in formalin, such as 'Mother and Child Divided' – four tanks contained the severed halves of a cow and calf. At the centre of debate over the nature and role of art, he became an established figure after being awarded the Turner Prize in 1995.

Hispanic American Any person resident in the USA who comes from, or whose parents came from, Spanish-speaking countries in Central and South America, including the Caribbean. They are now thought to number c.30 million, but the figures are highly inaccurate because there are many illegal immigrants. The main groups are Mexican Americans, Puerto Ricans, and Cubans.

Hispaniola [hispan**yoh**la], formerly **Santo Domingo** Second largest island of the Greater Antilles, E Caribbean; W third occupied by Haiti, remainder by the Dominican Republic; highest peak in the West Indies rises to 3175 m/10 416 ft at Pico Duarte. >> Antilles; Dominican Republic ℹ; Haiti ℹ

Hiss, Alger [**al**jer] (1904–96) US State Department official, born in Baltimore, MD. He reached high office as a State Departmnent official, then stood trial twice (1949, 1950) on a charge of perjury, having denied before a Congressional Un-American Activities Committee that he had passed secret state documents to a communist spy ring. The case roused great controversy, but he was sentenced to five years' imprisonment. Revelations from Soviet archives in 1992 seem to indicate his innocence. >> McCarthy, Joseph R

histamine [**his**tameen] A local hormone derived from the amino acid *histidine*, found in virtually all mammalian tissues, and particularly abundant in the skin, lungs, and gut. It is released by antigen–antibody reactions, and after skin damage by heat, venom, or toxins. Its actions include the dilation of blood vessels, and the stimulation of gastric acid secretion. >> amino acid; urticaria

histochemistry The chemistry of living biological tissue. It is particularly significant in the study of immune response, such as in organ transplant surgery. >> biochemistry; immunology

histology The microscopic study of the tissues of living organisms. Particular use is made of staining techniques to differentiate between cell types and between parts of cells. >> cell

histopathology The microscopic examination of diseased tissues to determine the nature of the condition. Small pieces of tissue taken at autopsy or by biopsy are subjected to a number of chemical stains which colour the cell membrane, cytoplasm, and nucleus, rendering them more easily visible. >> biopsy; cell; histology

Hitchcock, Sir Alfred (Joseph) (1899–1980) Film producer, born in London. He directed his first film in 1925, and rose to become an unexcelled master of suspense, internationally recognized for his intricate plots and novel camera techniques. His British films included *The Thirty-Nine Steps* (1935) and *The Lady Vanishes* (1938). His first US film, *Rebecca* (1940), won an Oscar. Later films included *Psycho* (1960), *The Birds* (1963), and *Frenzy* (1972).

Hitler, Adolf, popular name **der Führer** ('the Leader') (1889–1945) German dictator, born in Braunau, Upper Austria, the son of a minor customs official, originally called **Schicklgruber**. In 1919 he joined a small political party which in 1920 he renamed as the National Socialist German Workers' Party. In 1923, he attempted to overthrow the Bavarian government, but was imprisoned for nine months in Landsberg jail, during which time he produced his political testament, *Mein Kampf* (1925, My Struggle). Made chancellor in 1933, he suspended the constitution, silenced all opposition, and brought the Nazi Party to power. He created 'Greater Germany' by the Anschluss with Austria (1938), and absorbed the German-populated Sudeten region of Czechoslovakia. He then demanded from Poland the return of Danzig and free access to East Prussia, which, when Poland refused, precipitated World War 2 (3 Sep 1939). His domestic policy was one of total Nazification, enforced by the Secret State Police (*Gestapo*). He established concentration camps for political opponents and Jews, over 6 million of whom were murdered in the course of World War 2. With his early war successes, he increasingly ignored the advice of military experts, and the tide turned in 1942 after the defeats at El Alamein and Stalingrad. When Germany was invaded, he retired to his *Bunker*, an air-raid shelter under the Chancellory building in Berlin, where he went through a marriage ceremony with his mistress, Eva Braun. All available evidence suggests that Hitler and his wife committed suicide and had their bodies cremated (30 Apr 1945). >> Anschluss; Braun, Eva; Gestapo; Night of the Long Knives; SS; Stauffenberg; World War 2

Hittites A people of uncertain origin who became prominent in C Asia Minor in the first part of the second millennium BC. At their zenith (1450–1200 BC), their Empire covered most of Anatolia and parts of N Syria. >> Hattusas; Ugarit

HIV Abbreviation of **human immunodeficiency virus**; a retrovirus that can cause the breakdown of the human immune system known as *acquired immunodeficiency syndrome* (AIDS). >> AIDS; retrovirus

hives >> **urticaria**

Hizbullah or **Hizbollah** [hizbu**lah**] (Arabic 'party of God') The largest of the Shiite Islamic fundamentalist parties in Lebanon. Under Iranian sponsorship, Hizbullah's armed militia was believed to number c.5000 in 1990. The group has been associated in particular with the kidnapping of Westerners to advance its political aims, though all have subsequently been released. >> Lebanon ℹ; Shiites

Hoad, Lew(is Alan) [hohd] (1934–94) Tennis player, born in Sydney, New South Wales, Australia. With his doubles partner, Ken Rosewall, he had a meteoric rise to fame, winning the Wimbledon doubles title and a Davis Cup challenge match against the USA before he was 20 years old. He defeated Rosewall in the Wimbledon final of 1956, and won again the following year, but then turned professional. >> tennis ℹ

hoarhound >> **horehound**

hoatzin [hoh**at**sin] An unusual South American bird (*Opisthocomus hoazin*), found on wooded banks of the Amazon and Orinoco; large wings and tail; small head with untidy crest. (Family: Opisthocomidae.)

Hobart [**hoh**bah(r)t] 42°54S 147°18E, pop (1995e) 192 000. Seaport and state capital in SE Tasmania, Australia; on the Derwent R; fine natural harbour; founded as a penal colony, 1804; state capital, 1812; city status, 1842; airport; railway; University of Tasmania (1890). >> Tasmania

Hobbema, Meindert [**hob**ema], originally **Meyndert Lubbertsz(oon)** (1638–1709) Landscape painter, probably born in Amsterdam. His masterpiece, 'The Avenue, Middelharnis' (1689, National Gallery, London) greatly influenced modern landscape artists. >> landscape painting

Hobbes, Thomas (1588–1679) Political philosopher, born in Malmesbury, Wiltshire. After being introduced to Euclidean geometry, he thought to extend its method into a comprehensive science of man and society. He wrote several works on government, notably *Leviathan* (1651). >> political science

hobbits The name for the reluctant heroes, living in holes in the ground, found in the works of Tolkien. Among their number are Bilbo and Frodo Baggins. In the 1960s a cult developed, with peace-loving people sporting badges saying 'Frodo lives'. >> mythology; Tolkien

Hobbs, Jack, popular name of **Sir John Berry Hobbs** (1882–1963) Cricketer, born in Cambridge, Cambridgeshire. He played in county cricket for Surrey (1905–34) and for England (1908–30). He made 3636 runs, including 12 centuries, in test matches against Australia, and a record number of 197 centuries and 61 237 runs in first-class cricket. >> cricket (sport) ℹ

hobby A small falcon native to the Old World. (Genus: *Falco*, 4 species. Family: Falconidae.) >> falcon

hobby-horse A horse made of wood, wicker, and cloth, sometimes with a real horse's head or skull, and donned by a man in traditional rituals and dances in many parts of Europe. Hobby-horse customs are associated with fertility and general well-being, and the mock animals are probably group emblems or totems. >> folklore; morris dance; totem

Hochhuth, Rolf [**hokh**hoot] (1931–) Playwright, born in Eschwege, Germany. His play *Der Stellvertreter* (1963, The Representative), focusing on the role of the Pope in World War 2, excited controversy and introduced the fashion for 'documentary drama'.

Ho Chi-Minh [hoh chee **min**], originally **Nguyen That Thanh** (1892–1969) Statesman, prime minister (1954–5) and president (1954–69) of North Vietnam, born in Central Vietnam. He directed the successful military operations against the French (1946–54), and was a leading force in the war between North and South Vietnam during the 1960s. >> Vietnam War

Ho Chi Minh City [hoh chee **min**], formerly **Saigon** (to 1976) 10°46N 106°43E, pop (1995e) 4 270 000. Largest city in Vietnam; on R Saigon; former capital of French Indochina, 1887–1902; former capital of South Vietnam; occupied by the USA in Vietnam War; airport; chief industrial centre of Vietnam. >> Vietnam ℹ

hockey A stick-and-ball game played by two teams, each of 11 players; also known as **field hockey**, especially in the USA. The object is to move the ball around the field with the stick until a player is in a position to strike the ball into the opposing side's goal. A game lasts 70 minutes, split into two 35-minute halves. Modern hockey dates from 1875, when the English Hockey Association was formed in London. >> ice hockey; octopush; RR1053; *see illustration on p. 402*

Hockney, David (1937–) Artist, born in Bradford, West Yorkshire. Associated with the Pop Art movement from his earliest work, he has also worked in printmaking and photography, and designed sets and costumes.

Hoddinott, Alun (1929–) Composer, born in Bargoed, Caerphilly, SE Wales. He is a prolific composer of operas, symphonies, concertos, and a large corpus of choral and chamber works.

Hoddle, Glenn (1957–) Football manager and player, born in Hayes, Greater London. He made his professional debut with Tottenham Hotspur (1976), moved to AS Monaco (1986), and returned to England as player/manager of Swindon Town (1991–3), continuing this dual role

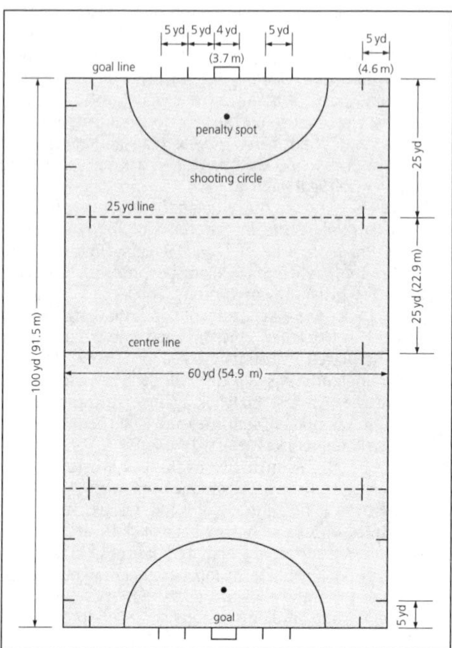

Hockey - dimensions of the field

at Chelsea (1993–6). He became England's manager in 1996, but public reaction to reported remarks about the reincarnation of people as disabled forced his resignation in 1999.

Hodgkin, Dorothy Mary, *née* **Crowfoot** (1910–94) Chemist, born in Cairo. A crystallographer, she was awarded the Nobel Prize for Chemistry in 1964 for her discoveries, by the use of X-ray techniques, of the structure of certain molecules, including penicillin, vitamin B^{12}, and insulin. >> crystallography

Hodgkin, Thomas (1798–1866) Pathologist, born in Tottenham, Greater London. He held various posts at Guy's Hospital, London, and described the glandular disease *lymphadenoma*, named after him (**Hodgkin's disease**).

Hoffman, Dustin (1937–) Actor, born in Los Angeles, CA. His first leading film role was *The Graduate* (1967), and this was followed by a number of similar 'anti-hero' roles, such as in *Midnight Cowboy* (1969) and *Marathon Man* (1976). He found wider scope in *All The President's Men* (1976), *Kramer v Kramer* (1979, Oscar), and *Rain Man* (1988, Oscar). His later films include *Outbreak* (1995), *American Buffalo* (1996), and *Mad City* (1998).

Hoffnung, Gerard (1925–59) Cartoonist and musician, born in Berlin, but raised in England. He was staff cartoonist on the London *Evening News* (1947), and later freelanced for *Punch* and other magazines. His interest in music led to his creation of the Hoffnung Music Festivals at the Royal Festival Hall. >> cartoon

Hofmannsthal, Hugo von [**hof**manztahl] (1874–1929) Poet and playwright, born in Vienna. His plays include *Electra* (1903) and the morality play *Jedermann* (1912, Everyman). He also collaborated with Richard Strauss, for whom he wrote the libretti for *Der Rosenkavalier* (1911) and other works. >> Strauss, Richard

hog >> **pig**

Hogan, Ben(jamin William), nickname **The Hawk** (1912–97) Golfer, born in Dublin, TX. In 1948 he became the first man in 26 years to win all three US major titles. He won the US Open four times before retiring in 1970. >> golf

Hogan, Paul (1941–) Comedian and actor, born in Lightning Ridge, New South Wales, Australia. He is best known for the successful films *Crocodile Dundee* and *Crocodile Dundee II*. His series of television advertisements for the Australian Tourist Board did much to promote his country, and he has become something of a national folk hero.

Hogarth, William [**hoh**gah(r)th] (1697–1764) Painter and engraver, born in London. His 'modern moral subjects' include 'A Rake's Progress' (1733–5, Sir John Soanes Museum, London), and his masterpiece, the 'Marriage à la Mode' (1743–5, Tate, London). His crowded canvases are full of revealing details and pointed subplots. >> engraving

hogfish Deep-bodied bottom-living fish, *Lachnolaimus maximus*, belonging to the wrasse family, Labridae, found in the warmer waters of the W North Atlantic; length up to 90 cm/3 ft; excellent food fish, but now scarce in some areas. >> wrasse

Hogg, James, known as **the Ettrick Shepherd** (1770–1835) Writer, born near Ettrick, Scottish Borders. He tended sheep in his youth, and became a writer of ballads which achieved some success, thanks to the patronage of Walter Scott. >> Scott, Walter

Hogg, Quintin >> **Hailsham, Viscount**

Hoggar Mountains >> **Ahaggar Mountains**

Hogmanay [**hog**manay, **hog**ma**nay**] The name in Scotland for New Year's Eve, the last day of the year. One custom associated with Hogmanay is *first-footing*, the first-foot being the first person to enter a house on New Year's Day. Traditionally the first-foot should be tall, dark-haired, and male, and should carry gifts of food, drink, and fuel.

hogweed A very variable robust biennial (*Heracleum sphondylium*), growing to 3 m/10 ft, native to N temperate regions; leaves up to 30 cm/12 in; flowers white or pinkish; also called **keck** or **cow parsnip**. The closely related **giant hogweed** (*Heracleum mantegazzianum*) is distinguished by its greater size, growing to 5 m/16 ft tall; native to SW Asia. It can cause painful skin irritations if touched in bright sunlight. (Family: Umbelliferae.)

Hohenstaufen [**hoh**enshtowfn] A German dynasty named after the castle of Staufen in Swabia. They ruled as German kings or king-emperors (1138–1254), and as kings of Sicily (1194–1266). >> Frederick I (Emperor); Frederick II (Emperor)

Hohenzollerns [**hoh**entzolernz] A German ruling dynasty of Brandenburg–Prussia (1415–1918) and Imperial Germany (1871–1918). >> Frederick I / II (of Prussia); Frederick William (of Brandenburg); Frederick William III (of Prussia); William I / II (Emperors)

Hohokam [hoh**hok**am] The prehistoric inhabitants of the S Arizona desert c.300 BC–AD 1400, ancestors of the modern Pima and Papago Indians. >> Papago

Hokan languages [**hoh**kn] A group of about 30 North American Indian languages, forming a bridge between the indigenous languages of North and South America.

Hokkaido [ho**ka**eedoh], formerly **Yezo**or **Ezo** pop (1995e) 5 753 000; area 83 513 sq km/32 236 sq mi. Northernmost and second largest island of the Japanese archipelago; 418 km/260 mi N–S, 450 km/280 mi E–W; largely mountainous, with active and inactive volcanic cones (C); rises to 2290m/7513 ft at Mt Asahi-dake; originally populated by the Ainu; capital, Sapporo. >> Ainu; Japan [i]; Sapporo

Hokusai, Katsushika [**ho**kusiy] (1760–1849) Artist and wood engraver, born in Edo (modern Tokyo). He early abandoned traditional styles of engraving for the coloured woodcut designs of the *ukiyo-e* school. He is best known for his 'Hundred Views of Mount Fuji' (1835), many of which grace Western homes in reproduction today. >> ukiyo-e

Holbein, Hans [**hol**biyn], known as **the Younger** (1497–1543) Painter, born in Augsburg, Germany, the son of **Hans Holbein the Elder** (c.1460–1524), also a painter of merit. In 1536 he became court painter to Henry VIII, his works including several portraits of eminent English people of the time, notably of Henry and his wives.

Hölderlin, (Johann Christian) Friedrich [**hoel**derlin] (1770–1843) Poet, born in Lauffen, Germany. He began to publish, with the help of Schiller, notably the philosophical novel, *Hyperion* (1797–9). >> Schiller

holding company A company which effectively controls another by owning at least half of the nominal value of its ordinary share capital or controlling the composition of its board of directors. The owned company is thereby a *subsidiary* of the holding company. >> company

Holi [**hoh**lee] A Hindu festival in honour of Krishna, occurring in February or March (Phalguna S 15), characterized by boisterous revelry, including the throwing of coloured water over people. >> Hinduism; Krishna; RR982

Holiday, Billie (Eleanora), originally **Eleanora Fagan**, nickname **Lady Day** (1915–59) Singer, born in Baltimore, MD. Her troubled life made sensational reading in her 1956 'autobiography' (actually written by William Dufty), *Lady Sings the Blues*. >> blues; jazz

Holinshed, Raphael [**hol**inshed] (?–c.1580) English chronicler, born apparently of a Cheshire family. His compilation of *The Chronicles of England, Scotland, and Ireland* (1577), was a major source for many of Shakespeare's plays. >> Shakespeare ℹ

holism A thesis which maintains that some wholes cannot be fully understood in terms of their parts; the wholes could be biological organisms, societies, art works, or networks of scientific theories.

holistic medicine An approach to medical treatment based on the theory that living creatures and the non-living environment function together as a single integrated whole (*holism*). The approach insists on the study not only of individual disease but also of the response of people to their disease, physically, psychologically, and socially. >> alternative medicine; holism

Holland >> **Netherlands, The** ℹ

Holloway, Stanley (1890–1982) Entertainer, born in London. A genial comedy actor in such Ealing film classics as *Passport to Pimlico* (1948) and *The Lavender Hill Mob* (1951), he is best known for his role of Alfred Dolittle in *My Fair Lady* on Broadway (1956–8, filmed 1964).

Hollows, Fred(erick) Cossom (1929–93) Ophthalmologist, born in Dunedin, New Zealand. Chairman of ophthalmology at Prince of Wales Hospital, Sydney, he was famed for his work on blinding eye infections among Australian Aborigines, Eritreans, and Vietnamese. In 1991 he was named Australian of the Year.

Holly, Buddy, popular name of **Charles Hardin Holley** (1936–59) Rock singer, songwriter, and guitarist, born in Lubbock, TX. His band, The Crickets, was the first to use the now standard rock-and-roll line-up of two guitars, bass, and drums. Following his death in a plane crash, he became an important cult figure. His most popular records include 'That'll Be The Day', 'Peggy Sue', and 'Oh Boy'.

holly An evergreen tree or shrub (*Ilex aquifolium*) growing to 10 m/30 ft, native to Europe; bark silvery-grey; leaves leathery, glossy above with wavy, spiny margins, prickly to the touch; flowers 4-petalled, white, followed by red berries; much-used at Christmas for decoration. (Family: Aquifoliaceae.)

hollyhock A biennial or perennial (*Althaea rosea*), native to China; stem growing to 3 m/10 ft in second year; flowers in a wide range of colours, forming a long spike. (Family: Malvaceae.)

Hollywood A suburb of Los Angeles, CA, which after 1912 developed into the centre of film production in the USA. Its studios dominated the world motion picture market from the 1920s. >> Los Angeles

HOLMES Abbreviation for **Home Office Large Major Enquiry System**, a computer system introduced in the 1980s for crime detection in the UK. >> police

Holmes, Larry, nickname **the Easton Assassin** (1949–) Boxer, born in Cuthbert, GA. He beat Ken Norton for the World Boxing Council heavyweight title in 1978, and held it until 1985, when he lost to Michael Spinks. >> boxing

Holmes, Oliver Wendell, Jr, nickname **the Great Dissenter** (1841–1935) Judge, born in Boston, MA, son of the writer, **Oliver Wendell Holmes** (1809–94). He was associate justice of the US Supreme Court (1902–32).

Holmes a Court, (Michael) Robert Hamilton [**hohmz** uh kaw(r)t] (1937–90) Entrepreneur, born in South Africa. He established the Bell Group, which in 1984 stunned the business world by bidding for BHP, Australia's largest company. His company recovered well after the 1987 stock-market crash, and he continued as one of the wealthiest people in Australia. After his death, his widow **Janet Holmes a Court** (1944–) became chair of the family company.

Holocaust The attempt by Nazi Germany to systematically destroy European Jews. Jews were herded into concentration camps, slave-labour camps, and extermination camps. By the end of the war in 1945, more than 6 million had been murdered. Other minorities were also subject to Nazi atrocities, but the major genocide was against the Jewish people. >> Babi Yar; Judaism; Nazi Party; World War 2

Holocene epoch [**hol**oseen] The most recent of the two geological epochs of the Quaternary period, from 10 000 years ago to the present time. >> geological time scale; Quaternary period; RR976

holography A method of lensless photography which gives true three-dimensional images; invented by Dennis Gabor in 1948. Modern holograms are made using laser light. The light beam is divided into two parts: one falls directly onto photographic film; the other is reflected onto the film via the object. An interference pattern forms, which is recorded on the film; and the processed film is the hologram. The image is generally viewed by illuminating the hologram using laser light. >> Gabor; interference ℹ; laser ℹ; photography

holoplankton >> **plankton**

Holothuroidea [holothuh**roy**dia] >> **sea cucumber**

Holst, Gustav (Theodore) (1874–1934) Composer, born in Cheltenham, Gloucestershire. He emerged as a major composer with the seven-movement suite *The Planets* (1914–16). Among his other major works are *The Hymn of Jesus* (1917), and his orchestral tone poem, *Egdon Heath* (1927).

Holt, Harold (Edward) (1908–67) Australian politician and prime minister (1966–7), born in Sydney, New South Wales, Australia. He joined the United Australia Party (later, the Liberal Party of Australia), becoming deputy leader in 1956, and leader and prime minister when Robert Menzies retired in 1966. He died in office. >> Liberal Party (Australia); Menzies

Holy Ghost >> **Holy Spirit**

Holyhead [holee**hed**], Welsh **Caergybi** 53°19N 4°38W, pop (1995e) 12 800. Port on Holy I, Anglesey, NW Wales, UK; railway; ferry to Dun Laoghaire and Dublin, Ireland; Holyhead Mountain 216 m/710 ft; breakwater (1845–73), 2·4 km/1½ mi long; St Cybi's Church (founded 6th-c) within 3rd-c Roman walls; Ucheldre Centre. >> Anglesey

Holy Innocents' Day A Christian festival (28 Dec) which commemorates the killing of the male children around Bethlehem by Herod (*Matt* 2). >> Herod the Great

Holy Island >> **Holyhead; Lindisfarne**

Holy League 1 (1571) An alliance of the three Catholic powers, Venice, Spain, and the Papacy, to counter Turkish supremacy in the E Mediterranean. The League's fleet commanded by Don John of Austria smashed the Turks at Lepanto (1571). >> Lepanto, Battle of **2** (1684) The union of the Empire, Poland, Venice, and the Papacy against Turkey, following the Imperial repossession of Vienna (1683). The League recovered most of Hungary for the Habsburgs, and began the reconquest of Greece (1685–7). >> Habsburgs

Holy of Holies The innermost and most sacred part of the Jewish tabernacle, and later of the Jerusalem Temple, cubic in shape, which contained the Ark of the Covenant. >> Ark of the Covenant; Tabernacle

Holy Orders >> **Orders, Holy**

Holy Roman Empire The revived mediaeval title of the Roman Empire, dating from the 9th-c, when the papacy granted the title to Charlemagne, King of the Franks. It was later bestowed upon German princely families, including the Hohenstaufens, Luxemburgs, and Habsburgs, lasting until 1806. >> Charlemagne; Frederick I (Emperor); Frederick II (Emperor); Swabian League

Holyroodhouse, Palace of [**ho**leeroodhows] The official residence in Scotland of the reigning monarch. Built in the 16th-c at Edinburgh, the palace was reconstructed in the 1670s by the architect Sir William Bruce (d.1710). >> Edinburgh

Holy Shroud or **Shroud of Turin** A relic, alleged to be the burial-sheet of Jesus Christ, known since the 14th-c, and preserved in the Cathedral at Turin since 1578. It portrays an image (clearer when shown using a photographic negative) of the front and back of a man's body, with markings that seem to correspond to the stigmata of Jesus. Radiocarbon-dating tests in 1988 indicated a late provenance for the shroud, but controversy over the methods used continued in the 1990s. The question of how the body image was produced remains open. >> Jesus Christ; radiocarbon dating

Holy Spirit A term used to denote the presence or power of God, often imbued with personal or quasi-personal characteristics; in Christian thought considered the third person of the Trinity, alongside the Father and the Son. In the New Testament, the Church is described as receiving the Spirit at Pentecost, from which time it continued to direct the Church's missionary activities. >> Christianity; Trinity

Holy Week In the Christian Church, the week before Easter, beginning on Palm Sunday. It includes Maundy Thursday and Good Friday. >> Easter; Palm Sunday

Holywell [**ho**leewel], Welsh **Treffynnon** 53°17N 3°13W, pop (1995e) 12 300. Town in Flintshire, NE Wales, UK; 'the Welsh Lourdes', place of pilgrimage since the 7th-c, where St Winefride (Gwenfrewi) was beheaded. >> Lourdes; Wales [i]

Home of the Hirsel, Baron [hyoom], formerly **Sir Alec Douglas-Home**, originally **Alexander Frederick Douglas-Home, 14th Earl of Home** (1903–95) British Conservative statesman and prime minister (1963–4), born in London. He became Commonwealth Relations secretary (1955–60) and foreign secretary (1960–3). After Macmillan's resignation, he astonished everyone by emerging as premier, renouncing his peerage and fighting a by-election. He was foreign secretary again in Edward Heath's 1970–4 government. >> Conservative Party; Heath, Edward; Macmillan, Harold

home counties Those counties which border London, and into which the city has expanded. These are Essex, Kent, Surrey, Buckinghamshire, Hertfordshire, and the former counties of Middlesex and Berkshire >> London

Home Guard A home defence militia, raised during the summer of 1940, when the German armies seemed poised to complete the conquest of W Europe by invading the UK. At first called the Local Defence Volunteers, the force was finally stood down in 1945. >> militia; World War 2

Homelands >> **apartheid; South Africa** [i]

homeopathy A practice of medicine devised by German physician Samuel Hahnemann in the early 19th-c with the principles of (1) like cures like; and (2) drug activity is enhanced by dilution. >> alternative medicine; Hahnemann

homeostasis / homoeostasis [hohmioh**stay**sis] A term initially used to describe the stability of the extracellular fluid apparent in healthy individuals. Nowadays it is often used to describe the ways in which this stability is achieved, in both humans and other animals. For example, body temperature in warm-blooded mammals is maintained by active metabolic mechanisms such as shivering, if it falls too low, or panting, if it rises too high. >> extracellular fluid; homoiothermy; physiology

Homer, Greek **Homēros** (c.8th-c BC) Greek poet to whom are attributed the great epics, the *Iliad*, the story of the siege of Troy, and the *Odyssey*, the tale of Odysseus's wanderings. Arguments have long raged over whether his works are in fact by the same hand, or have their origins in the lays of Homer and his followers (*Homeridae*). Of the true Homer, nothing is positively known.

Homer, Winslow (1836–1910) Marine and genre painter, born in Boston, MA. He painted rural and domestic scenes, but was at his best in his seascapes. >> genre painting

home rule The handing down of certain legislative powers and administrative functions, previously exercised by a higher authority, to an elected body within a geographically defined area. Since the early 1970s in the UK, for political movements such as the Scottish National Party and Irish republicans, home rule has tended to become synonymous with separatism. >> devolution; IRA; Plaid Cymru; separatism; Scottish National Party

Homestead Act (1862) A US law allowing a grant of 160 acres of public land to settlers, conditional on their staying five years, the making of improvements to the property, and the payment of fees.

homicide The killing of one human being by another. The term varies in its application among different jurisdictions. In England and Wales, for example, unlawful homicide includes the crimes of murder, manslaughter, and infanticide. In certain circumstances homicide may be lawful, such as in self-defence, but the action taken has to be reasonable in the circumstances. In both Scotland and the USA, homicide involves causing the death of another either by an act or by an intentional or negligent omission when there is a legal duty to act. Criminal homicide usually includes murder (first and second degree), manslaughter, and negligent homicide. >> infanticide; manslaughter; murder

homing overlay device Part of a US experiment to achieve a practical ballistic missile defence using space-based systems. A 'layer' of defences would be established outside the atmosphere to intercept incoming nuclear warheads. >> ballistic missile; SDI

hominid A member of the primate family Hominidae, containing humans, their immediate ancestors, and close extinct relatives. Two genera are usually recognized: *Australopithecus* and *Homo*. Anatomical amd molecular evidence indicate that the hominid and African ape lineages separated c.6–8 million years ago. The earliest definite

Homo

hominid fossils are c.5·5 million years old, although most finds are < 4 million years. >> ape; *Homo* ℹ

Homo [**hoh**moh] (Lat 'man') A genus of the family Hominidae, order Primates. *Homo* features include a medium-large brain, high brain:body ratio, bipedal gait, upright posture, opposable thumb, and adaptable hands with power and precision grip. The genus probably evolved in Africa from a species of *Australopithecus*. There are four named species, three extinct. *Homo habilis* was named in 1964 from fossil finds which some think australopithecine. It lived in E Africa (and possibly elsewhere) about 2–1·5 million years ago (mya); it had a lightly built braincase, capacity 500–700 cm^3, projecting face and jaws, relatively large front teeth, but small cheek teeth. Body size was 25–40 kg/55–88 lb with long, powerfully-muscled arms and hands, and short hindlimbs. *Homo rudolfensis* dated 1·9–1·71 mya, was probably bigger bodied than *H. habilis*, with more modern limb proportions. It had a bigger brain, capacity 750–900 cm^3, broader, flatter face and larger cheek teeth. *Homo erectus*, dated 1·8–1·6 mya, had strongly built, largely modern bodily proportions, the skull was also strongly built, with a retreating frontal, flat, thick-walled vault, capacity 800–1200 cm^3, big face and jaws, with moderate sized teeth. *Homo sapiens*, our own species, evolved from *Homo erectus* through archaic forms resembling Neanderthal man, to fully modern man, *H. sapiens sapiens*, which is first known from Africa c.100–120 000 years ago, and shortly afterwards in the Middle East. This subspecies has a relatively light build, large rounded braincase 12 000–2000 cm^3, high forehead, flat and lightly built face and jaws, slight or no brow ridges, small crowded teeth, and a definite chin. >> *Australopithecus*; CroMagnon / Java / Neanderthal / Peking Man; hominid

homoiothermy [ho**moy**ohthermee] The regulation of internal body temperature at a relatively constant level. Higher vertebrates, such as mammals and birds, are warm-blooded (**homoiothermic**), and typically have insulated body coverings to aid temperature regulation.

homology The relationship between equivalent structures and traits in living organisms, derived from the same part of the embryo but existing in different states in related organisms. The forelimb of a horse, the wing of a bird, and the human arm are all homologous structures. >> embryo

Homoptera [ho**mop**tera] A large order of insects comprising c.45 000 species, including the cicadas, plant hoppers, froghoppers, leaf hoppers, psyllids, whiteflies, aphids, scale insects, and mealybugs; hindlegs often adapted for jumping; feeding on plants, with modified mouthparts for piercing and sucking. >> insect ℹ

homosexuality A form of sexuality in which the sexual attraction is between members of the same sex. Homosexuality has been a subject of considerable political controversy in the West, especially since the formation of the Gay Liberation Movement and the onset of the AIDS virus. >> AIDS; heterosexism; lesbianism

Homs or **Hims, ancient** Emesa 34°44N 36°43E, pop (1995e) 573 000. Industrial city in WC Syria; road and rail junction; commercial centre in well-irrigated area. >> Syria ℹ

Honduras [hon**dyoo**ras], official name **Republic of Honduras**, Span **República de Honduras** pop (1995e) 5 628 000; area 112 088 sq km/43 266 sq mi. Central American republic; capital, Tegucigalpa; timezone GMT −6; population mainly of Spanish–Indian origin (90%); chief religion, Roman Catholicism; official language, Spanish; unit of currency, the lempira of 100 centavos; coastal lands (S) separated from Caribbean coastlands by mountains running NW–SE; S plateau rises to 2849 m/9347 ft at Cerro de las Minas; tropical climate in coastal areas, temperate in C and W; coastal plains average c.30°C; country devastated by hurricane Mitch in 1998; centre of Mayan culture, 4th–9th-c; settled by the Spanish, early 16th-c, and became province of Guatemala; independence from Spain, 1821; joined Federation of Central America; independence, 1838; several military coups in 1970s; since 1980, a democratic constitutional republic, governed by a president and a National Congress; dependent largely on agriculture (providing a third of national income), forestry (nearly half the land area), mining, and cattle raising. >> Tegucigalpa; Mayas; RR1011 political leaders

Honecker, Erich [**hon**eker] (1912–94) East German statesman, born in Neunkirchen, Germany. He was elected party chief in 1971, becoming head of state from 1976 to 1989, when he was dismissed as a consequence of the anti-communist revolution. Although charges were brought against him in the new united Germany, he was allowed to leave for Chile in 1993 on grounds of illness. >> Germany ℹ

Honegger, Arthur [**on**eger] (1892–1955) Composer, born in Le Havre, France. He became one of the group of Parisian composers known as *Les Six*. His dramatic oratorio *King David* established his reputation in 1921. His other works include five symphonies. >> *Six, Les*

honey A substance prepared by bees from nectar found in blossoms. Because of its palatability and its relative rarity, honey has always been a highly prized food. Its colour and flavour varies with the flora on which bees feed. >> bee; mead; sucrose

honey badger >> **ratel**

honeybee The European honeybee (*Apis mellifera*) and three other species of the genus *Apis* (Order: Hymenoptera. Family: Apidae). It is a bee that forms true perennial societies, typically consisting of one queen, several hundred drones, and 50 000 to 80 000 workers. >> bee; drone; larva

honeyeater An Australasian bird specialized to eat nectar; tongue long with brush-like tip; shows great variation in bill shape and life-style. (Family: Meliphagidae, 167 species.) >> friarbird [i]; tui

honeyguide A small brownish bird native to Africa and S or SE Asia; inhabits evergreen forest; eats insects (especially bees) and beeswax; some said to lead animals to bees' nests. (Family: Indicatoridae, c.13 species.)

honeysuckle A member of a large genus mainly comprising shrubs, with a few well-known species of woody climbers with twining stems, deciduous or evergreen; native to the N hemisphere; flowers tubular, 2-lipped, often fragrant; berries red, blue, or black. The **common honeysuckle** or **woodbine** produces sweet scent at night. (Genus: *Lonicera*, 200 species. Family: Caprifoliaceae.)

Hong Kong, Chin **Hsiang Kang** pop (1995e) 6 083 000; area 1066 sq km/412 sq mi. Special administrative region of China (from 1997), former British Crown Colony, off the coast of SE China; divided into Hong Kong Island, Kowloon, and New Territories (includes most of the colony's 235 islands); timezone GMT +8; population mainly Chinese (98%); many illegal immigrants from China and refugees from Vietnam; chief religions, Buddhism, Taoism; official languages, English, Cantonese; official currency, the Hong Kong dollar of 100 cents; subtropical climate, with hot, humid summers and cool, dry winters; ceded to Britain, 1842; New Territories leased to Britain for 99 years, 1898; occupied by the Japanese in World War 2; British Crown represented by a governor, advised by an Executive Council and a Legislative Council; Sino-British Declaration initialled, 1984, returning Hong Kong to China, 1 July 1997; designated special administrative region by China, with assurances given for continuation of economy and lifestyle for 50 years; new chief executive appointed (first incumbent, Tung Chee-hwa), with new membership of advisory councils; economy based on banking, import-export trade, tourism, shipbuilding, and a diverse range of light industry; textiles, electronic goods, watches, jewellery, cameras, footwear, toys, plastic goods; imports c.80% of its food; new international airport at Chek Lap Kok (25 km/15 mi W of Hong Kong I), opened 1998; an important freeport acting as a gateway to China for the West. >> China [i]; Kowloon; New Territories

Honiara [hohni**ah**ra] 9°28S 159°57E, pop (1995e) 40 000. Port capital of the Solomon Is, SW Pacific; airport; developed around the site of US military headquarters. >> Solomon Islands [i]

Honolulu [hono**loo**loo] 21°19N 157°52W, pop (1995e) 410 000. State capital in Hawaii, USA; noted tourist resort, with the famous beach at Waikiki; harbour entered by William Brown, an English captain, 1794; capital of the Kingdom of Hawaii, 1845; US naval base at Pearl Harbor, attacked by the Japanese (7 Dec 1941); airport; three universities; headquarters of US Pacific Fleet. >> Hawaii (state)

Honorius, Flavius [o**naw**rius] (384–423) Roman Emperor of the West (393–423). A feeble ruler, he abandoned Britain to the barbarians, and stayed in Ravenna while the Goths besieged and sacked Rome (408–10). >> Stilicho

honours list In the UK, the military and civil awards suggested by the prime minister and approved by the sovereign at New Year and on the sovereign's official birthday.

Honshu [**hon**shoo] pop (1995e) 101 140 000; area 231 119 sq km/89 212 sq mi. Largest of the four main islands of Japan; c.1290 km/800 mi long, 48–240 km/30–150 mi wide; highest peak, Mt Fuji (3776 m/12 388 ft); coastal lowlands include most of the population, and several major cities; earthquakes common; wide range of industries. >> Fuji, Mount; Japan [i]; Nagoya; Osaka; Tokyo

Honthorst, Gerrit van [**hont**haw(r)st] (1590–1656) Painter, born in Utrecht, The Netherlands. He is known for his portraits and also for his candle-lit interiors.

Hooch or **Hoogh, Pieter de** [hohkh] (c.1629–c.1684) Genre painter, born in Rotterdam, The Netherlands. His 'Courtyard of a House in Delft' (1658, National Gallery, London) is one of the best-known examples of the Dutch School of the 17th-c. >> genre painting

Hood (of Whitley), Samuel Hood, 1st Viscount (1724–1816) British admiral, born in Thorncombe, Dorset. He fought during the American Revolution, when he defeated the French in the West Indies (1782). In 1793, he directed the occupation of Toulon and the operations in the Gulf of Lyon.

Hood, Thomas (1799–1845) Poet and humorist, born in London. In his *Whims and Oddities* (1826) he showed his graphic talent in 'picture-puns', of which he seems to have been the inventor.

hoof-and-mouth disease >> **foot-and-mouth disease**

Hooke, Robert (1635–1703) Chemist and physicist, born in Freshwater, Isle of Wight. He formulated the law governing elasticity (**Hooke's law**), invented the balance spring for watches, and helped develop the telescope and microscope.

Hooker, Richard (1554–1600) Theologian, born near Exeter, Devon. His major work, on the basis of Church government, is the eight-volume *Of the Laws of Ecclesiastical Polity* (1594, 1597, 1648, 1662). It is mainly to this work that Anglican theology owes its tone and direction. >> Church of England

Hook of Holland, Dutch **Hoek van Holland** Cape in SW Netherlands; also the name of a port 27 km/17 mi W of Rotterdam; ferry links with Harwich, UK. >> Netherlands, The [i]

hookworm infestation An important cause of anaemia and ill health in tropical countries, resulting from the worms *Ancylostoma duodenale* and *Necator americanus*. The adult worm becomes hooked on to the lining of the small intestine, and sucks blood. >> anaemia; worm

hoopoe A ground-dwelling bird (*Upupa epops*) native to Africa and S Eurasia; pink body; black and white wings and tail; large crest; long curved bill. (Family: Upupidae.)

Hoover, Herbert (Clark) (1874–1964) US Republican statesman and 31st president (1929–33), born in West Branch, IA. His opposition to direct governmental assistance for the unemployed after the world slump of 1929 made him unpopular, and he was beaten by Roosevelt in 1932. >> Roosevelt, Franklin D

Hoover, J(ohn) Edgar (1895–1972) US public servant, born in Washington, DC. He became FBI director in 1924, and remained in charge until his death, campaigning against city gangster rackets in the inter-war years, and against Communist sympathizers in the post-war period. He was later criticized for abusing his position by engaging in vendettas against liberal activists. >> Federal Bureau of Investigation

Hoover Dam, formerly **Boulder Dam** (1936–47) 36°01N 114°45W. One of the world's major dams, on the Colorado

R, Arizona, USA, impounding L Mead; built 1931–6; height 221 m/726 ft; length 379 m/1244 ft; can generate 1345 megawatts of hydroelectricity; named after President Hoover. >> Colorado River (USA); dam; Hoover, Herbert

hop A perennial climber (*Humulus lupulus*) native to Europe and W Asia; stems 3–6 m/10–20 ft, twining clockwise with small hooks to aid support. Only the fruiting heads are used to flavour and preserve beer. (Family: Cannabidaceae.) >> beer; brewing

Hope, A(lec) D(erwent) (1907–) Poet and critic, born in Cooma, New South Wales, Australia. His *Collected Poems* (1972) is one of the major books of Australian verse.

Hope, Anthony, pseudonym of **Sir Anthony Hope Hawkins** (1863–1933) Writer, born in London. He is best known for his 'Ruritanian' romance, *The Prisoner of Zenda* (1894).

Hope, Bob, originally **Leslie Townes Hope** (1903–) Comedian, born near London, whose parents emigrated to the USA in 1907. In partnership with Bing Crosby and Dorothy Lamour he appeared in the highly successful *Road to...* comedies (1940–52), and in many others until the early 1970s. He was given a special Academy Award on five occasions, and he received an honorary knighthood in 1998.

Hopewell The native American culture of C USA c.100 BC–AD 400. It is notable for its geometric ceremonial earthworks and richly furnished burial mounds. >> Woodland culture

Hopi [**hoh**pee] A Shoshonean-speaking Pueblo Indian group living in Arizona, c.7000 (1990 census). They farmed corn and other crops and became famous for their basketry and pottery. >> Pueblo (Indians); Southwest Indians

Hopkins, Sir Anthony (1937–) Actor, born in Port Talbot, SC Wales. A member of the National Theatre, London, he made his film debut in 1967. His films include *The Silence of the Lambs* (1991, Oscar), *The Remains of the Day* (1994), *Amistad* (1997), and *The Mask of Zorro* (1998).

Hopkins, Gerard Manley (1844–89) Poet, born in London. He became a Catholic in 1866, joined the Jesuit order and was ordained in 1877. None of his poems was published in his lifetime. Robert Bridges published an edition in 1918, which was given a very mixed reception, largely because of Hopkins' experiments with 'sprung rhythm'; but a new edition in 1930 was widely acclaimed. His best-known poems include 'The Wreck of the *Deutschland*' and 'The Windhover'. >> Bridges, Robert

Hopkins, Harry L(loyd) (1890–1946) US administrator, born in Sioux City, IA. Under Franklin D Roosevelt he headed the 'New Deal' projects (1935–8), became secretary of commerce (1938–40), supervised the lend-lease programme (1941), and undertook several important missions to Europe during World War 2. >> Roosevelt, Franklin D

Horace, in full **Quintus Horatius Flaccus** (65–8 BC) Latin poet and satirist, born near Venusia, Italy. His earliest works were chiefly satires and lampoons, and through the influence of Virgil he came under the patronage of Maecenas. The unrivalled lyric poet of his time, he produced his greatest work, the three books of *Odes*, in 19 BC. >> Maecenas; Virgil

Horatti and Curiatii [ho**rah**tiee, kyoori**ah**tiee] An early Roman legend used to justify appeals. Under Tullus Hostilius there was war between Rome and Alba. Two groups of three brothers were selected from Rome (the Horatii) and Alba (the Curiatii) to fight, the winners to decide the battle. All were killed except one Horatius. When his sister, who was betrothed to a Curiatius, abused him, he murdered her, but was acquitted after appealing to the Roman people.

Hordern, Sir Michael (Murray) (1911–95) Actor, born in Berkhamsted, Hertfordshire. He made his professional debut in 1937. His major classical roles included King Lear (1960) and Prospero (1978), as well as several modern roles, such as in Tom Stoppard's *Jumpers* (1972) and Howard Barker's *Stripwell* (1975).

Horeb, Mount >> **Sinai, Mount**

horehound or **hoarhound** A perennial occurring in two species, native to Europe, Asia, and N Africa, both related to mint; leaves wrinkled; flowers 2-lipped, in whorls. **White horehound** (*Marrubium vulgare*) is used as a medicinal herb for cough remedies. (Family: Labiatae.) >> mint

hormones Chemical messengers synthesized and secreted in small amounts by the endocrine glands of vertebrates and some invertebrates (eg certain molluscs and arthropods), which affect the functioning of the body's cells and organs. They are usually classified chemically into *amines* (eg noradrenaline, thyroxine), *peptides* (eg oxytocin), *proteins* (eg insulin), and *steroids* (eg aldosterone, testosterone). >> amines; growth / sex hormones; peptide; protein; steroid

Hormuz, Strait of [haw(r)**mooz**] Passage linking the Persian Gulf to the Arabian Sea; 50–80 km/30–50 mi wide; a strategic route controlling ocean traffic to the oil terminals of the Gulf. >> Persian Gulf

horn A musical instrument made from metal (usually brass) tubing, with a conical bore, coiled and twisted several times and ending in a wide bell. It was traditionally associated with hunting. The tubing of the orchestral horn (or **French horn**) is about 3·6 m/12 ft in length; it has four valves and is a transposing instrument pitched in F. >> brass instrument [i]

hornbeam A deciduous tree (*Carpinus betulus*) growing to 30 m/100 ft, native to Europe and Asia Minor; flowers tiny in pendulous catkins; nutlets each with a 3-lobed wing-like bract; often called **ironwood** in the USA. (Family: Corylaceae.) >> bract

hornbill A large bird native to tropical Africa, S Asia, and Australasian islands; bill large, often brightly coloured, topped with large ornamental outgrowth; plumage black, brown, and white. (Family: Bucerotidae, 45 species.)

hornblende A common variety of the amphibole group of ferromagnesian silicate minerals; a hydrated calcium magnesium iron aluminosilicate that is dark green or black in colour. >> amphiboles; silicate minerals

Horne, Donald (Richmond) (1921–) Writer, academic, and arts administrator, born in New South Wales, Australia. His best-known book is *The Lucky Country* (1964), the title of which has become a common Australian expression. A leading member of the Australian Republican Movement, he has written *The Coming Republic* (1992). >> Australian republicanism

hornet The largest social wasp; a fierce predator, up to 35 mm/$\frac{1}{2}$ in long; yellow and black coloration. (Order: Hymenoptera. Family: Vespidae.) >> wasp

Horne-Tooke, John >> **Tooke, John Horne**

Horney, Karen, *née* **Danielsen** (1885–1952) Psychoanalyst, born near Hamburg, Germany. During the 1920s she took issue with orthodox Freudianism, particularly in relation to women's psychosexuality, and in the 1930s developed theories about the importance of sociocultural factors in human development. In 1934 she moved to New York City, where in 1941 she helped found the Association for the Advancement of Psychoanalysis. >> Freud, Sigmund; psychoanalysis

hornpipe A dance of British origin, popular in the 16th–19th-c. Although the best-known example is the 'Sailors' Hornpipe', the dance was not associated particularly with the navy.

hornwort (horned liverwort) A submerged aquatic perennial without roots; stems growing to 1 m/3$\frac{1}{4}$ ft; one flower at each node, tiny, lacking petals; fruits warty and sometimes spiny. (Genus: *Ceratophyllum*, 10 species. Family: Ceratophyllaceae.)

Horologium [horolohjium] (Lat 'clock') A faint S constellation contrived in the 1750s by French astronomer Nicolas Lacaille. >> constellation; Lacaille; RR968

Horowitz, Vladimir [horovits] (1904–89) Pianist, born in Kiev, Ukraine. He settled in the USA and became a US citizen, but in 1986 he played again in Russia.

Horrocks, Sir Brian (Gwynne) (1895–1985) British general, born in Ranikhet, India. In 1942 he commanded the 9th Armoured Division and then the 13th and 10th Corps in N Africa, and headed the 30th Corps during the Allied invasion (1944). >> Rommel; World War 2

Horsa >> **Hengist and Horsa**

horse A hoofed mammal with many domestic breeds. Modern breeds are thought to have developed from three wild ancestral types: the heavy **forest** type, and the lighter **steppe** and **plateau** types. Technically any horse up to 14·2 hands/1·5 m/58 in high at the shoulder is termed a *pony*; taller than this it is a *horse*. An *entire* (ie not castrated) male horse aged 1–4 years is called a *colt*; older than 4 years it is a *stallion*; a castrated male is a *gelding*. A female of 1–4 years is a *filly*; older than 4 years it is a *mare*. A horse less than one year old is a *foal* (*colt foal* or *filly foal*). The domestication of the horse was crucial in world history, both for agrarian and military purposes; for example, superior cavalry enabled the rapid expansion of the Huns. Fundamental, also, was the Chinese invention of the breast strap, collar harnesses (5th–6th-c AD), and stirrup (before 300). (*Equus caballus*. Order: Perissodactyla. Family: Equidae.) >> Appaloosa; ass; Cleveland bay; Clydesdale; cob; equestrianism; falabella; hackney horse; horse racing; mustang; palomino; Percheron; perissodactyl ℹ; Schleswig; shire; tarpan; thoroughbred; three-day event; zebra

horse chestnut A large, spreading, deciduous tree (*Aesculus hippocastanum*) growing to 25 m/80 ft, native to the Balkans; leaves with 5–7 leaflets, widest above the middle; flowers 4-petalled, white with yellow and pink spots, in pyramidal spikes; nuts (*conkers*) brown, shiny, two in a leathery, prickly capsule. (Family: Hippocastanaceae.)

horse fly A biting fly with large, often iridescent eyes; mouthparts form a piercing proboscis in females, inflicting painful bites. (Order: Diptera. Family: Tabanidae, c.2000 species.) >> fly

Horse Guards An elite regiment of the British Army, first raised in 1661, known as the Royal Horse Guards, whose nickname was 'the Blues'. Amalgamated in 1969 with the Royal Dragoon Guards, 'the Blues and Royals' form, with the Life Guards, the British Sovereign's *Household Cavalry*. >> army

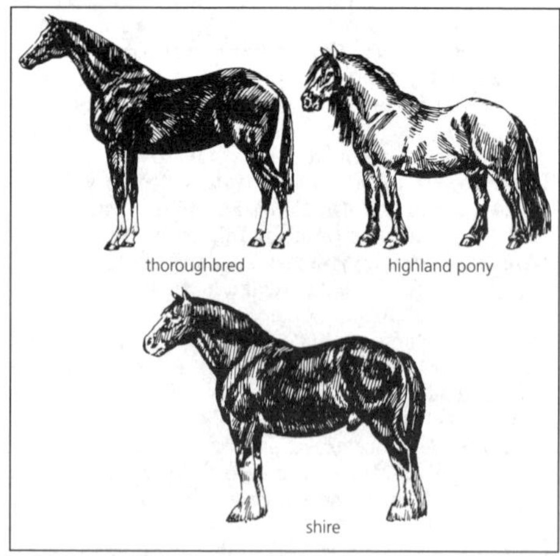

Three types of horse

Horsehead nebula A famous dark nebula in the constellation Orion, resembling the silhouette of a horse's head. >> nebula; Orion (astronomy)

Horse Latitudes Two belts of ocean calm at 30° N and S of the Equator, where conditions of high atmospheric pressure exist almost permanently. >> Doldrums; wind ℹ

horsepower Unit of power; symbol *hp*; equal to 745·7 W (watt, SI unit); almost obsolete, but still used in engineering to describe the power of machinery; equal to 1·0139 metric horsepower. >> power (physics); watt

horse racing The racing of horses against one another, each ridden by a jockey. Popularized in England in the 12th-c, most monarchs have supported the sport, which has thereby become known as 'the sport of kings'. **Flat racing** is a straightforward race on a flat surface (grass or dirt) over a predetermined distance which can be anything between 5 furlongs (1 km) and 2½ mi (4 km). **National hunt racing** involves the horses negotiating fences which can be either movable *hurdles* or fixed fences. These races (eg the Grand National) are longer than flat races, and can be anything up to 4½ mi (6·5 km) in length. Bets are usually placed on the horses likely to come first (a *win*), second (a *place*), or third (a *show*), with professional bookmaking emerging in the 19th-c (along with a host of illegal or semi-legal activities), and the Totalizator concept in the 1920s. >> harness racing; hurdling; Jockey Club; point-to-point; steeplechase 1; RR1054

horse-radish A perennial (*Armoracia rusticana*), probably native to S Europe, but long cultivated for the pungent seasoning prepared from the fleshy, cylindrical roots. (Family: Cruciferae.)

horsetail A primitive, spore-bearing perennial related to ferns and clubmosses; the only living genus of a formerly widespread group, the Sphenopsida, dominant during the Carboniferous period. All extant species are herbaceous. (Genus: *Equisetum*, 23 species. Family: Equisetaceae.) >> Carboniferous period; clubmoss; fern

horst An uplifted block of the Earth's crust, usually of great size, bounded by two normal faults. It is often elongated in shape, and may form block mountains. >> graben

Horthy (de Nagybánya), Miklós [haw(r)tee] (1868–1957) Hungarian statesman and regent (1920–44), born in Kenderes, Hungary. Minister of war in the counter-revolutionary 'White government' (1919), he opposed Bela Kun's communist regime, which he suppressed (1920). In World War 2 he supported the Axis Powers until Hungary was overrun by the Germans in 1944. >> Axis Powers; Kun

horticulture The business of growing, harvesting, and marketing fruit, vegetables, flowers, and shrubs; also practised widely as a hobby and an art form. It is usually associated with the intensive production of high-value crops, and often involves the use of irrigation in drier areas, and glass or polythene protection in cooler areas. >> landscape / market gardening

Horus [hawrus] An ancient Egyptian sky-god in the shape of a man with a hawk's head; also depicted as the child of Isis, when he is often called **Harpocrates**. >> Isis

Hosea, Book of, also spelled **Osee** [hohzeea] The first of the 12 so-called 'minor' prophetic writings of the Hebrew Bible/Old Testament; attributed to the prophet Hosea, who was active in the N kingdom of Israel c.750–725 BC. >> Old Testament; prophet

Hoskins, Bob, popular name of **Robert William Hoskins** (1942–) Actor, born in Bury St Edmunds, Suffolk. He achieved widespread public recognition with the television series *Pennies From Heaven* (1978) and as the menacing hoodlum in the film *The Long Good Friday* (1980). He acquired international stardom with his award-winning performance in *Who Framed Roger Rabbit* (1988).

hospice A type of hospital normally reserved for the treatment of the terminally ill, usually catering for specific age groups, typically children or the elderly. The term was originally used for a refuge attached to a monastery. >> euthanasia

hospital An institution in which certain kinds of illness are investigated and treated. In most developed countries today, hospitals are run as either private charities or public (state) institutions, with 'teaching hospitals' closely related to universities. Most hospitals not only cater for emergencies of all types and for those whose illnesses develop acutely and unexpectedly (the *acute hospital*), but they contain specialized departments for non-emergency work and for numerous branches of medicine. Other hospitals have become exclusively specialized, and cater for the needs of single categories of ill health, such as psychiatric, orthopaedic, maternity, paediatric, and geriatric hospitals. An additional important role is the provision of out-patient departments providing consultative services for the patients of general practitioners who are under care in their own home. In the 1990s, in the UK, hospitals were allowed to opt out of local health authority control, forming themselves into *hospital trusts* (or *NHS trusts*), the others remaining as *directly-managed units* (*DMUs*).

Hospitallers Members (priests or brother knights subject to monastic vows) of the Order of the Hospital of St John of Jerusalem, originally a purely charitable organization to care for sick pilgrims to the Holy Land. From the 12th-c they played a prominent role in the Crusades as an international religious-military order. After the loss of Acre in 1291, they transferred their headquarters to Cyprus (1292), Rhodes (1309), then Malta (1530), which they held until 1798. The Sovereign Order is now based in Rome. >> Aubusson; Crusades [i]; knight

hot-air balloon >> **balloon**

hot spring A spring of hot or warm groundwater which emerges at the Earth's surface and which often contains dissolved minerals and sulphurous gases. Very hot springs emerge as geysers, and may be used as sources of geothermal energy. >> geyser

Hotspur, Harry >> **Percy**

Hottentots >> **Khoisan**

Houdini, Harry [hoo**dee**nee], originally **Erich Weiss** (1874–1926) Magician, born in Budapest. He gained an international reputation as an escape artist, freeing himself from handcuffs, and other devices, often while imprisoned in a box under water or in mid-air.

Houdon, Jean Antoine [oodõ] (1741–1828) Classical sculptor, born in Versailles, France. His works as a portrait sculptor include busts of Diderot, Voltaire, and Napoleon.

hound A category of domestic dog; name applied to breeds developed for hunting, especially those which track by scent. >> Afghan / basset hound; beagle; bloodhound; borzoi; deerhound; dog; foxhound; greyhound; harrier (mammal); Irish wolfhound; sporting dog

housefly A small, darkish fly; females lay masses of 100–150 eggs on decaying organic matter or dung; white, worm-like maggots mature in a few days. (Order: Diptera. Family: Muscidae.) >> fly; maggot

Household Cavalry >> **Horse Guards**

housemaid's knee A painful inflammation of the liquid-filled pouch (*bursa*) in front of the knee joint, provoked by trauma or excessive kneeling. It is so called because of its former frequent occurrence as an occupational hazard. >> bursitis; knee

House of Commons >> **Commons, House of**

House of Lords >> **Lords, House of**

House of Representatives In the USA, one of the two chambers of the bicameral legislature, in which, under the constitution, all legislative power is vested. There are 435 members, and each state has at least one representative. >> bicameral system; Congress; Senate

Houses of Parliament The Palace of Westminster in London. The first palace on the site was built by King Canute in the 11th-c. The present structure was begun in 1839, and was occupied by the Commons and Lords in 1852. >> Big Ben; Commons / Lords, House of

house sparrow A small, brown and grey, ground-feeding bird (*Passer domesticus*), native to Europe, Asia, and N Africa, and introduced worldwide; also known as the **English sparrow**. (Family: Ploceidae.) >> sparrow

Housman, A(lfred) E(dward) (1859–1936) Scholar and poet, born near Bromsgrove, Worcestershire. He is best known for *A Shropshire Lad* (1896), a cycle of short, lyrical and often melancholy poems with a country setting, and *Last Poems* (1922). He saw himself chiefly as a Latinist, and devoted much of his life to an annotated edition (1903–30) of Manilius.

Houston [**hyoo**stn] 29°46N 95°22W, pop (1995e) 1 796 000. Port in SE Texas, USA; on the Houston Ship Channel (1914); fourth largest city and third busiest port in the USA; settled, 1836; capital of the Republic of Texas, 1837–9, 1842–5; two airports; railway; five universities; major oil centre with huge refineries and the largest petrochemical complex in the world; corporate headquarters of numerous energy companies; base for several space and science research firms; professional teams, Astros (baseball), Rockets (basketball), Oilers (football). >> Texas

Houston, Sam(uel) [**hyoo**stn] (1793–1863) US soldier and statesman, born in Lexington, VA. As commander-in-chief in the Texan War, he defeated the Mexicans on the San Jacinto in 1836, and achieved Texan independence. He was then elected president of the republic, and after annexation (1845) became a member of the US Senate. Houston, TX, is named after him. >> Texas

Houston, Whitney (1963–) Singer and actress, born in Newark, NJ. The album *Whitney Houston* (1985) won a Grammy award and included her first US number 1 hit single 'Saving All My Love For You'. In 1988 she broke a US chart record with seven consecutive number 1 hits. Her films include *The Bodyguard* (1992) and *The Preacher's Wife* (1996).

hovercraft >> **air cushion vehicle** [i]

hoverfly A medium to large-sized fly often found hovering over flowers; adults resemble wasps. (Order: Diptera. Family: Syrphidae, over 5000 species.) >> fly

Howard, Catherine (?–1542) Fifth wife of Henry VIII, a granddaughter of the 2nd Duke of Norfolk. She became queen in 1540. After Henry learned of her alleged premarital affairs (1541), she was accused of treason and beheaded in the Tower. >> Henry VIII

Howard, Charles, 1st Earl of Nottingham (1536–1624) English lord high admiral, a cousin of Queen Elizabeth I, who commanded the English fleet against the Spanish Armada (1588). In 1601 he quelled Essex's rising. >> Essex, Robert Devereux; Spanish Armada

Howard, Sir Ebenezer (1850–1928) Founder of the garden-city movement, born in London. His *Tomorrow* (1898) led to the laying out of Letchworth (1903) and Welwyn Garden City (1919) in Hertfordshire. >> garden city

Howard, Henry >> **Surrey, Earl of**

Howard, John (1726–90) British prison reformer, born in London. As high sheriff for Bedfordshire, he investigated the condition of prisons and prisoners. As a result, two acts were passed in 1774, one providing for fixed salaries to jailers, and the other enforcing cleanliness. >> Howard League for Penal Reform; prison

Howard, John (Winston) (1939–) Australian prime minister (1996–), born in Sydney, New South Wales, Australia. He became an MP in 1974, and went on to be deputy-leader (1983–5) then leader of the Liberal Party in Opposition (1985–9,1995–6). He became prime minister following his party's general election victory in 1996.

Howard, Leslie, originally **Leslie Howard Stainer** (1893–1943) Actor, born in London. During the 1930s he had many leading film roles, such as in *Gone with the Wind* (1939), and *The Scarlet Pimpernel* (1935). He was killed when a special mission flight from Lisbon to London was shot down.

Howard, Trevor (Wallace) (1916–88) Actor, born in Cliftonville, Kent. He sprang to stardom with *Brief Encounter* (1945), followed by *The Third Man* (1949) and *Outcast of the Islands* (1951). His versatile and often eccentric characterizations were regularly in demand for both film and television.

Howard League for Penal Reform A charity dedicated to the cause of penal reform, named after John Howard; formed by the amalgamation of the Howard Association with the Prison Reform League in 1921. >> Howard, John

Howe, Elias (1819–67) Inventor, born in Spencer, MA. He is best known for his invention (1846) of the sewing machine.

Howe (of Aberavon), (Richard Edward) Geoffrey Howe, Baron (1926–) British Conservative statesman, born in Port Talbot, SC Wales. He was Chancellor of the Exchequer (1979–1983) and foreign secretary (1983–9), and in 1989 deputy prime minister, Lord President of the Council, and Leader of the House of Commons. He resigned from the government in 1990 in opposition to Mrs Thatcher's hostility towards European monetary union. >> Conservative Party; European Monetary System; Thatcher

Howe, Richard Howe, 1st Earl (1726–99) British admiral, born in London. In the French Revolutionary Wars he defeated the French at 'the Glorious First of June' (1794). >> French Revolutionary Wars

Howe, William Howe, 5th Viscount (1729–1814) British soldier who commanded the army in North America during the American Revolution. In the American War of Independence his victories included Bunker Hill (1775), the Brandywine (1777), and the capture of New York City (1776). >> American Revolution

Howerd, Frankie, originally **Francis Alex Howard** (1922–92) Comedian and actor, born in London. He appeared regularly on television and in films, his most famous role being that of a Roman slave in *Up Pompeii* (1970–1). In the 1980s he presented several successful television series, including *Frankie Howerd on Campus* (1990).

howitzer An artillery piece in which the shell is projected at a high angle of trajectory, typically at low muzzle velocity, to fall on to its target as plunging fire. >> artillery

Hoxha, Enver, also spelled **Hodja** [**ho**ja] (1908–85) Albanian statesman, born in Gjirokastër. He founded and led the Albanian Communist Party (1941) in the fight for national independence, and became head of state, first as prime minister (1946–54), then as first secretary of the party (1954–85). >> Albania ℹ

Hoyle, Sir Fred(erick) (1915–) Astronomer, mathematician, astrophysicist, and science fiction writer, born in Bingley, West Yorkshire. He is known for his work on the origin of chemical elements, and is a leading proponent of steady state cosmology, of the notion that viruses come from outer space, and a believer in an extraterrestrial origin for life on Earth. >> steady state theory; virus

Hradčany Castle [**rad**chanee] Since 1918, the official residence of the Czech president in Prague. The Přemysl dynasty founded a stronghold on the site in the late 9th-c. This was destroyed by fire in 1303, and the present citadel, which incorporates both Gothic and Renaissance architecture, was built from 1344 onwards. The complex includes St Vitus's Cathedral and the royal palace. >> castle; Prague

Hua Guofeng [hwah gwohfeng], also spelled **Hua Kuo-feng** (1920–) Chinese statesman and prime minister (1976–80), born in Jiaocheng, Shanxi province. Under him China adopted a more pragmatic domestic and foreign policy, with emphasis on industrial and educational expansion, and closer relations with Western and Third World countries. >> China ℹ

Huang He; Huang Ho >> **Yellow River**

Huascarán [waska**ran**] area 3400 sq km/1312 sq mi. National park in W Peru; a world heritage site; part of the Andean Cordillera Occidental; it rises to 6768 m/22 204 ft. >> Peru ℹ

Hubbard, L(afayette) Ron(ald) (1911–86) Writer, founder of Dianetics® healing technology and of the Scientology® applied religious philosophy, born in Tilden, NE. During the 1930s he became a prolific writer of novels and short stories in several different genres. His most famous work, *Dianetics: the Modern Science of Mental Health* (1950), became an instant best seller, and the basic text of the Scientology movement. Later books include the science-fiction novel *Battlefield Earth* (1982) and the 10-volume *Mission Earth* series (from 1985). >> Scientology®

Hubble, Edwin (Powell) (1889–1953) Astronomer, born in Marshfield, MO. His work led to the discovery of the expanding universe, by attributing the redshifts of galaxies to velocities of recession. The **Hubble constant** is a measure of the rate at which the expansion of the universe varies with distance. >> Big Bang; redshift

Hubble Space Telescope An orbiting observatory, a joint project of the European Space Agency and NASA, launched in 1990 with a 2·4 m (94 in) aperture telescope for visible and ultraviolet observation. In the visible spectrum, it was expected to image objects more sharply than telescopes on Earth, and detect fainter sources. However, following the launch, a defect was discovered in the main optical system, which limited its performance; this was repaired in 1993, and there was a major overhaul in 1997. >> European Space Agency; NASA; telescope ℹ

huckleberry An evergreen or deciduous shrub which varies from mat-forming to erect, native to the New World; flowers urn- or bell-shaped; berries black, edible. (Genus: *Gaylussacia*, 49 species. Family: Ericaceae.)

Huddersfield 53°39N 1°47W, urban area pop (1995e) 218 000. Town in West Yorkshire, N England; on the R Colne; railway; university, 1992; woollen and worsted textiles; football league team, Huddersfield Town (Terriers). >> Yorkshire, West

Huddleston, (Ernest Urban) Trevor (1913–98) Anglican missionary, ordained in 1937. He became Bishop of Masasi, Tanzania (1960–8), Bishop Suffragan of Stepney until 1978, then Bishop of Mauritius and Archbishop of the Indian Ocean. After his retirement, he became president of the Anti-Apartheid Movement (1981–94). >> apartheid

Hudson, Henry (?–1611) English navigator, who explored the NE coast of North America. He sailed in search of a passage across the Pole (1607), reached Novaya Zemlya (1608), entered the river which was named after him (1609), and (1610) travelled through the strait and bay which now bear his name. >> Hudson Bay / River

Hudson Bay area c.1 232 250 sq km/476 000 sq mi. Inland sea in Northwest Territories, Canada; maximum length c.1600 km/1000 mi, including James Bay (S); maximum width c.1000 km/650 mi; generally ice-clogged (but open to navigation mid-July–Oct). >> Hudson; Hudson's Bay Company; Northwest Territories

Hudson River River rising in the Adirondack Mts, New York State, USA; flows 560 km/350 mi S to the Atlantic Ocean. >> Hudson; New York ℹ

Hudson River School A group of 19th-c US landscape painters, including Thomas Cole (1801–48) and Thomas Doughty (1793–1856). >> landscape painting

Hudson's Bay Company A London-based corporation which was granted a Royal Charter to trade (principally in furs) in most of N and W Canada (Rupert's Land) in 1670. It annexed its main competitor, the Northwest Company, in 1821. >> North West Company

Hué [hway] 16°28N 107°35E, pop (1995e) 290 000. Town in C Vietnam; former capital of Annam and of the Vietnamese Empire; many historical sites destroyed in Vietnam War; railway; university (1957). >> Vietnam ℹ

Hueffer, Ford Hermann >> **Ford, Ford Madox**

Huelva [**wel**va], Lat **Onuba** 37°18N 6°57W, pop (1995e) 142 000. Port in Andalusia, SW Spain; bishopric; railway. >> Andalusia; Spain ℹ

Hugh Capet >> **Capet, Hugh**

Hughes, Howard (Robard) (1905–76) Millionaire businessman, film producer and director, and aviator, born in Houston, TX. He inherited his father's oil-drilling equipment company at 18, and in 1926 began to involve himself in Hollywood, producing several films. In 1932 he began to design, build, and fly aircraft. He broke most of the world's air speed records (1935–8), then abruptly returned to film making, including *The Outlaw* (1943). He eventually became a recluse.

Hughes, Richard (Arthur Warren) (1900–76) Writer, born in Weybridge, Surrey. *The Fox in the Attic* (1961) was the first of a projected series of novels about the rise of fascism in Germany, but only one other book was completed. He also wrote several children's stories.

Hughes, Ted, popular name of **Edward (James) Hughes** (1930–98) Poet, born in Mytholmroyd, West Yorkshire. Best known for his distinctive animal poems, his first collections were *The Hawk in the Rain* (1957) and *Lupercal* (1960). He married US poet Sylvia Plath in 1956, but the marriage deteriorated, and he left her in 1962. After her suicide, he destroyed the final volume of her journal, to avoid her children seeing it – an action which brought criticism as Plath's reputation grew, and he became increasingly reclusive. He was nonetheless responsible for bringing her work before a wider public, editing her collected poems in 1981. He became poet laureate in 1984. Later works include *Rain Charm for the Duchy* (1992) and *Tales from Ovid* (1997, Whitbread). *Birthday Letters*, a series of poems about his relationship with Plath, written over 25 years, appeared unexpectedly in 1998, and won several literary prizes. >> Plath

Hughes, Thomas (1822–96) Novelist, born in Uffington, Berkshire. He is primarily remembered as the author of the public school classic, *Tom Brown's Schooldays* (1856), based on his school experiences at Rugby under the headmastership of Arnold. >> Arnold, Thomas

Hughes, William Morris (1862–1952) Australian statesman and prime minister (1915–23), born in London. He was the major proponent of conscription in World War 1, and represented Australia at the Versailles conference. He founded the United Australian Party in the early 1930s. >> Australia ℹ

HUGO [**hyoo**goh] Acronym for **Human Genome Organization**, set up in 1989 as the first international group co-ordinating activities within the human genome project. Its legal headquarters is in Geneva; its administrative headquarters is currently in London. >> human genome project

Hugo, Victor (Marie) (1802–85) Writer, born in Besançon, France. The most prolific French writer of the 19th-c, his early works include *Odes et Ballades* (1822, 1826), *Hernani* (1830), the first of the 'five-act lyrics' which compose his drama, and the novel *Notre Dame de Paris* (1831, trans The Hunchback of Notre Dame). He joined the democratic republicans; but in 1851, after the coup, he fled into exile, where he wrote several major works, notably his panoramic novel of social history, *Les Misérables* (1862). He returned to Paris in 1870, and upon his death was given a national funeral.

Huguenots [**hyoo**genohz] French Calvinist Protestants whose political rivalry with Catholics (eg the House of Guise) led to the French Wars of Religion (1562–98). Their leader, Henry of Navarre, succeeded to the throne (1589), granting them important concessions on his conversion to Catholicism (Edict of Nantes, 1598); these were later revoked by Louis XIV (1685), resulting in persecution and emigration. >> Henry IV (of France); Religion, Wars of; Saint Bartholomew's Day Massacre

Hu Jintao (1942–) Chinese politician. He became party secretary in Guizhou (1984) and Xizang (Tibet) (1988), where he pursued a hardline policy, crushing anti-Chinese demonstrations at Lhasa in 1989. A member of the Politburo standing committee in 1992, he was appointed vice-president in 1998, being seen as an eventual successor to Jiang Zemin. >> Jiang Zemin

Hull (Canada) 45°26N 75°45W, pop (1995e) 64 400. City in SW Quebec, Canada, on the Ottawa R; founded in 1801 by settlers from the USA; railway; timber. >> Ottawa; Quebec

Hull (UK), properly **Kingston-upon-Hull** 53°45N 0°20W, pop (1995e) 269 000. Seaport and unitary authority (from 1996), NE England; city status granted, 1897; a major UK container port; railway; ferry service to Rotterdam, Zeebrugge; two universities (1954, 1992); football league team, Hull City (Tigers). >> England ℹ

Hull, Clark L(eonard) (1884–1952) Psychologist, born in Akron, NY. He developed a rigorous mathematical theory of the learning process that attempted to reduce learned behaviour to a few simple axiomatic principles. Much of his work was based on reinforcement theory, as seen in *Principles of Behavior* (1943).

Hull, Cordell (1871–1955) US statesman, born in Overton, TN. He became secretary of state under Roosevelt in 1933, and attended most of the great wartime conferences. He helped to organize the United Nations, for which he received the Nobel Peace Prize in 1945. >> United Nations

Hulme, Keri (Ann Ruhi) [hyoom] (1947–) Writer, born in Otautahi, Christchurch, New Zealand. She acquired international renown when her story *The Bone People* (1984) was awarded the Booker Prize. Maori themes figure prominently in her work. >> Maori

human engineering >> **ergonomics**

human genome project An ambitious plan launched in 1985 to determine the exact sequence of all 3×10^9 base pairs in the human genome. The project is loosely co-ordinated by a number of national and international organizations, including HUGO. >> genome; HUGO; RNA

human immuno-deficiency virus >> **AIDS**

humanism Historically, a movement that arose with the Italian Renaissance, in the writings of Ficino, Pico, and later Erasmus and More. The humanists drew on classical literature and emphasized the centrality of human achievements and potential, in opposition to many of the claims of dogmatic theology and science. >> Erasmus; More, Thomas; Pico della Mirandola

human rights A concept deriving from the doctrine of natural rights, which holds that individuals, by virtue of their humanity, possess fundamental rights beyond those prescribed in law. First formally incorporated into the US Declaration of Independence (1776), most written constitutions contain a bill of rights. The UN's General Assembly adopted a Universal Declaration of Human Rights in 1948, followed in 1953 by the European Convention on Human Rights. The European Court of Human Rights was established within this framework. >> Amnesty International; civil liberties / rights

Humber, River River estuary in NE England; runs 64 km/40 mi E and SE; entrance dominated by Spurn Head; Humber Bridge, 1981. >> England 🛈; Humber Bridge

Humber Bridge Single-span suspension bridge, built (1973–81) across the R Humber, E England; length of main span 1410 m/4626 ft; total length 2220 m/7283 ft; second-longest suspension bridge (after Akashi-Kaikyo) in the world. >> Humber, River

Humberside pop (1995e) 895 000; area 3512 sq km/1356 sq mi. Former county of NE England; created in 1974 from parts of Lincolnshire and Yorkshire; replaced in 1996 by unitary authorities of East Riding of Yorkshire, Hull, North Lincolnshire, and North East Lincolnshire. >> England 🛈

Humboldt, (Friedrich Wilhelm Heinrich) Alexander, Freiherr (Baron) **von** [**hum**bohlt] (1769–1859) Naturalist and geographer, born in Berlin. His major work, *Kosmos* (1845–62), endeavours to provide a comprehensive physical picture of the universe. The ocean current off the W coast of South America is named after him.

Humboldt, (Karl) Wilhelm von [**hum**bohlt] (1767–1835) German statesman and philologist, born in Potsdam, Germany. He was the first to study Basque scientifically, and also worked on the languages of the East and of the South Sea Is. >> comparative linguistics

Hume, (George) Basil, Cardinal [hyoom] (1923–) Roman Catholic Benedictine monk and cardinal. Ordained in 1950, he became Abbot of Ampleforth in 1963, where he remained until created Archbishop of Westminster and a cardinal in 1976. >> Benedictines

Hume, David [hyoom] (1711–76) Philosopher and historian, born in Edinburgh. His major works include *A Treatise of Human Nature* (1739–40), consolidating and extending the empiricist legacy of Locke and Berkeley, the six-volume *History of England* (1746–62), and *Essays Moral and Political* (1741–2). He wrote the posthumously published *Dialogues concerning Natural Religion* in the 1750s. >> Berkeley, George; empiricism; Locke, John

Hume, John [hyoom] (1937–) Northern Ireland politician, born in Londonderry. Leader of the Social Democratic Labour Party, in 1993 he and Sinn Féin leader Gerry Adams began a series of talks, the Hume–Adams peace initiative, intended to bring about an end to violence in Northern Ireland. He shared the 1998 Nobel Peace Prize with David Trimble for his efforts to find a peaceful solution to the conflict. >> Adams, Gerry; Trimble

humidity The amount of water vapour in a sample of air, usually expressed as relative or absolute humidity. **Absolute humidity** is the total mass of water in a given volume of air, expressed in grams per cubic centimetre. Warmer air is able to hold more water vapour than cold air. >> hygrometer

hummingbird A small bird restricted to the New World; often brightly coloured; feeds on nectar from plants; fast wing-beat and modification of wing structure allows hovering. (Family: Trochilidae, 320 species.) >> thornbill

humpback whale A baleen whale of the rorqual family (*Megaptera novaeangliae*), found worldwide; dark back and pale undersurface; wide tail and very long slender flippers; jaws and flippers with many rough knobs; have complex 'songs' unique to each population. >> baleen 🛈; rorqual; whale 🛈

humped cattle >> **zebu**

Humperdinck, Engelbert (1854–1921) Composer, born in Siegburg, Germany. He composed several operas, one of which, *Hänsel und Gretel* (1893), was highly successful.

Humphrey, Doris (1895–1958) Dancer, choreographer, and teacher, born in Oak Park, IL. She wrote the key text on dance composition in modern dance, *The Art of Making Dances* (1959). >> choreography

Humphrey, Hubert H(oratio) (1911–78) US Democratic statesman, born in Wallace, SD. He built up a strong reputation as a liberal, but, as vice-president from 1964 under Johnson, alienated many of his supporters by defending the policy of continuing the war in Vietnam. He narrowly lost the 1968 election to Nixon. >> Johnson, Lyndon B; Nixon, Richard M; Vietnam War

Humphries, (John) Barry (1934–) Comic performer and satirical writer, born in Melbourne, Victoria, Australia. He created the Barry McKenzie comic strip in *Private Eye* (1964–73), and wrote and appeared in *The Adventures of Barry McKenzie* (1972). He is best known for his characters **Sir Les Patterson** and 'housewife megastar' **Dame Edna Everage**, who have frequently appeared on television and in film.

humus Decomposed organic matter, usually present in the topsoil layers. It improves soil structure, making cultivation easier, and gives the soil a characteristically dark colour. >> soil

hundred An old subdivision of a shire, sometimes containing about 100 hides (c.12 000 acres), which had its own court, and formed a unit of local administration in the government of England from at least the 10th-c to the 19th-c.

Hundred Days (Mar–Jun 1815) The period between Napoleon I's escape from Elba and his defeat at the Battle of Waterloo, during which he returned to Paris and tried to reconstitute the Empire. >> Napoleon I; Waterloo, Battle of

Hundred Years' War A series of wars between England and France dated by convention 1337–1453. When Edward III claimed the French throne, from 1340 styling himself 'king of England and France', traditional rivalries exploded into a dynastic struggle. In 1417 the English turned from raiding to territorial conquest, a task ultimately beyond their resources. Eviction from Guyenne (1453) reduced England's French territories to Calais (lost 1558) and the Channel Is. >> Agincourt, Battle of; Angevins; Edward III

Hungarian uprising (Oct–Nov 1956) National insurgency in Budapest following the denunciation of Stalin at the 20th Soviet Communist Party Congress. When the new prime minister, Imre Nagy, announced plans for Hungary's withdrawal from the Warsaw Pact, Soviet troops and tanks crushed the uprising, and Nagy was executed. >> Nagy; Stalin; Warsaw Pact

Hungary, Hung **Magyarország**, official name **Republic of Hungary**, Hung **Magyar Köztársaság** pop (1995e) 10 220 000; area 93 035 sq km/35 912 sq mi. Republic in the Danube basin, C Europe; capital, Budapest; timezone GMT +1; population mainly Magyar (92%), with several minorities; chief religions, Roman Catholic (67%), Calvinist (20%); official language, Magyar; unit of currency, the forint of 100 fillér; drained by the R Danube (flows N–S) and its tributaries; crossed (W) by a low spur of the Alps, highest peak, Kékestetö (1014 m/3327 ft); landlocked position gives a continental type of climate, with a marked difference between summer and winter; kingdom formed under St Stephen I, 11th-c; conquered by Turks, 1526; part of Habsburg Empire, 17th-c; Austria and Hungary reconstituted as a dual monarchy, 1867; republic, 1918; communist revolt led by Béla Kun, 1919; monarchical constitution restored, 1920; new republic with communist government, 1949; uprising crushed by Soviet forces, 1956; collapse of Communist rule, followed by multi-party elections, 1990; governed by a president, prime minister, and National Assembly; large-scale nationalization as part of the centralized planning strategy of the new republic, 1946–9; greater independence to individual factories and farms, from 1968. >> Budapest; Habsburgs; Hungarian uprising; Kun; RR1011 political leaders

Huns An Asiatic people who in 375 overran the Gothic tribes of S Russia, and precipitated the great Germanic migration into the Roman Empire. United under Attila, they laid waste parts of Gaul and Italy (451–2), but were then forced to retreat. >> Attila; Gaul: Goths; Vandals

Hunt, Henry, known as **Orator Hunt** (1773–1835) Radical agitator, born in Upavon, Wiltshire. He was a well-to-do farmer who in 1800 became a staunch radical, and spent his life advocating the repeal of the Corn Laws and parliamentary reform. >> Corn Laws

Hunt, (William) Holman (1827–1910) Painter, born in London. He helped to inaugurate the Pre-Raphaelite Brotherhood. His works in this vein included, notably, 'The Light of the World' (1854, Oxford). >> Pre-Raphaelite Brotherhood

Hunt (of Llanfair Waterdine), (Henry Cecil) John Hunt, Baron (1910–98) Mountaineer, born in Marlborough, Wiltshire. In 1953 he led the first successful expedition to Mt Everest, and in 1958 led the British party in the British–Soviet Caucasian mountaineering expedition. >> Everest, Mt; Hillary

Hunt, (James Henry) Leigh (1784–1859) Poet and essayist, born in Southgate, Greater London. From 1808 he edited with his brother *The Examiner*, which became a focus of Liberal opinion. His *Autobiography* (1850) is a valuable picture of the times.

hunter–gatherers Populations living entirely, or almost so, by hunting animals and gathering food. In 10 000 BC the entire world population consisted of hunters and gatherers; today they are fewer than 0·001%, including the Pygmies in Africa and Australian Aborigines. >> Aborigines; Pygmies

Huntingdon 52°20N 01°12W, pop (1995e) 21 100, with Godmanchester. Town in Cambridgeshire, EC England; on Great Ouse R; railway; birthplace of Oliver Cromwell. >> Cambridgeshire; Cromwell, Oliver

Huntingdon, Selina Hastings, Countess of, *née* **Shirley** (1707–91) Methodist leader, born in Staunton Harold, Leicestershire. Joining the Methodists in 1739, she made Whitefield her chaplain, and assumed a leadership among his followers, who became known as 'the Countess of Huntingdon's Connexion'. >> Methodism; Whitefield, George

Huntingdonshire Former county of EC England; part of Cambridgeshire since 1974. >> Cambridgeshire

Huntington's chorea [ko**ree**a] An inherited disorder of the brain, in which slowly developing dementia is associated with uncontrolled jerking or slow writhing movements. It is named after US physician George Sumner Huntington (1850–1916). >> chorea

Huntsville 34°44N 86°35W, pop (1995e) 169 000. Town in N Alabama, USA; railway; university; major US space research centre. >> Alabama

Hunyady, János [**hoon**yodi] (c.1387–1456) Hungarian statesman and warrior. His life was one unbroken crusade against the Turks, whom he defeated in several campaigns, notably in the storming of Belgrade (1456).

Hurd, Douglas (Richard) [herd] (1930–) British statesman, born in Marlborough, Wiltshire. A Conservative MP from 1974, he became Northern Ireland secretary (1984), home secretary (1985), and foreign secretary (1989–95). He stood unsuccessfully as a candidate in the leadership contest following Mrs Thatcher's resignation (Nov 1990), remaining foreign secretary under John Major. He was made a Companion of Honour in 1996. >> Conservative Party; Thatcher

hurdling 1 An athletics event which involves foot racing while clearing obstacles (**hurdles**) en route. Race distances are 100 m and 400 m for women, 110 m and 400 m for men. The height of a hurdle varies according to the type of race: $2\frac{3}{4}$ ft (84 cm) for the 100 m; 3 ft (91·4 cm) for the 400 m; and $3\frac{1}{2}$ ft (106·7 cm) for the 110 m. Hurdles are also included in the steeplechase. **2** A form of horse race in which the horses have to clear hurdles. It is not as testing as the steeplechase. >> steeplechase

hurdy-gurdy A mechanically bowed string instrument known since mediaeval times. The player turns a handle which causes a wooden wheel to rotate and to sound a number of accompanimental drone strings. Melodies are played on a simple keyboard, operated by the other hand. >> string instrument 1 [i]

hurling or **hurley** An Irish 15-a-side team field game played with curved sticks and a ball. The object is to hit the ball with the stick into your opponents' goal: under the crossbar scores 3 points; above the crossbar but between the posts scores 1 point. It has been played since 1800 BC. >> RR1054

Huron [**hyoo**ron] Iroquoian-speaking North American Indians, who settled in large towns and farming villages in Quebec and Ontario in the 16th-c. Defeated by the Iroquois in 1648–50, they were finally driven by whites to Oklahoma.

Huron, Lake [**hyoo**ron] Second largest of the Great Lakes, North America, on the US–Canadian frontier; 330 km/ 205 mi long; 294 km/183 mi wide; area 59 570 sq km/ 22 994 sq mi, 60% in Canada; empties into L Erie (E) via the St Clair R, L St Clair, and the Detroit R; generally icebound in winter months (Dec–Apr). >> Great Lakes

hurricane An intense, often devastating, tropical storm which occurs as a vortex spiralling around a low pressure system. Wind speeds are very high (above 34 m/s/75 mph), but the centre (*eye*) of the storm is characterized by calm weather. Hurricanes usually develop between July and October, and move in a W or NW direction (SW in the S hemisphere), losing energy as they reach land. They are also known as **typhoons** in the western N Pacific and **cyclones** in the Bay of Bengal. Each year they are named in alphabetical sequence as they occur (excluding rare letters, such as Q and X), to avoid confusion when more than one storm is being followed at the same time. Different sets of names are used in the central Pacific, eastern Pacific, and the Atlantic Basin. In the Atlantic, for example, the names are English, Spanish, and French, and occur in a six-year cycle. Originally female names were used, but male names were introduced for the first time in 1978. Names are sometimes retired, if their storms are exceptionally damaging (such as David in 1979 and Bob in 1991). >> Beaufort Scale; RR975

Hurt, John (1940–) Actor, born in Chesterfield, Derbyshire. He won BAFTA awards for *Midnight Express* (1978) and *The Elephant Man* (1980); other films include *Alien* (1978), *Nineteen Eighty Four* (1984), and *Rob Roy* (1995).

Hurt, William (1950–) Actor, born in Washington, DC. He won a Best Actor Oscar for *Kiss of The Spiderwoman* (1985), and Oscar nominations for *Children Of A Lesser God* (1986) and *Broadcast News* (1987). Later films include *Jane Eyre* (1996) and *Michael* (1996).

husky A domestic dog, one of several spitz breeds traditionally used in the Arctic as a beast of burden (especially to pull sledges); also known as **eskimo dog**. >> Alaskan malamute; spitz

Huss or **Hus, John** (c.1369–1415) Bohemian religious reformer, born in Husinec, Czech Republic. After writing his main work, *De ecclesia* (1413, On the Church), he was called before a General Council at Constance, and burned after refusing to recant. The anger of his followers in Bohemia led to the Hussite Wars. >> Hussites; Reformation

hussars Light cavalry, regiments of which were formed in many national armies from the late 18th-c onwards. They were modelled on an idealized 'Hungarian' style of horseman-warrior, with an exotic uniform and an elaborate fur helmet.

Hussein (ibn Talal) [hu**sayn**] (1935–99) King of Jordan (1952–99), born in Amman. He steered a middle course in the face of the political upheavals inside and outside his country, favouring the Western powers, and pacifying Arab nationalism. After increasingly frequent raids by the PLO into Israel from Jordan, he ordered the Jordanian army to move against them, and after a short civil war (1970), the PLO leadership fled abroad. His decision to cut links with the West Bank (1988) prompted the PLO to establish a government in exile. In the 1990s he became prominent as a peace-maker in the Middle East, several times taking a public role in the talks between Israel and the Palestinians. He was married four times; his second wife, Toni Gardiner, was an Englishwoman, by whom he had an heir, Abdullah, in 1962. >> Jordan ℹ; PLO

Hussein, Saddam [hu**sayn**], also spelled **Sadam Husain** (1937–) President of Iraq (1979–), born in Takrit. He played a prominent part in the 1968 revolution and on the retirement of al-Bakr, became sole president. His attack on Iran in 1980, to gain control of the Strait of Hormuz, led to a war of attrition which ended in 1988. He invaded Kuwait in 1990, but was forced to withdraw when he was defeated by a coalition of Arab and Western forces in Operation Desert Storm (1991). Iraq has since suffered international isolation and economic sanctions. >> Gulf War; Iraq ℹ

Husserl, Edmund (Gustav Albrecht) [**hu**serl] (1859–1938) Philosopher, founder of the school of phenomenology, born in Prossnitz, Czech Republic. His chief work was the two-volume *Logische Untersuchungen* (1900–1, Logical Investigations) defending the view of philosophy as an *a priori* discipline. >> phenomenology

Hussites Followers of John Huss, who in the early 15th-c constituted a movement for the reform of the Church in Bohemia (Czech Republic). They anticipated many aspects of the 16th-c Reformation. >> Huss; Reformation

Huston, John (Marcellus) [**hyoos**tn] (1906–87) US film director, born in Nevada, MO. His films include *The Maltese Falcon* (1941), *The African Queen* (1951), *Moby Dick* (1956), and the musical, *Annie* (1982).

Hutton, James (1726–97) Geologist, born in Edinburgh. His book *A Theory of the Earth* (1795) forms the basis of modern geology. >> geology

Hutton, Len, popular name of **Sir Leonard Hutton** (1916–90) Cricketer, born in Fulneck, West Yorkshire. He was the inspiration of England after World War 2, and skipper of the team which regained the Ashes in 1953. Playing for England against Australia at the Oval in 1938, he scored a world record 364 runs. During his first-class career (1934–60) he scored 40 140 runs (average 55·51), including 129 centuries. >> Ashes, the; cricket (sport)

Hutu and Tutsi Bantu-speaking peoples of the republics of Burundi and Rwanda, EC Africa, speaking the same language and having a common culture. The Hutu, mostly peasant farmers, comprise more than 80% of the total population in both countries. They were subjugated by the Tutsi, warrior–pastoralists of Nilo-Hamitic stock, who migrated S in the 14th–15th-c. The Tutsi dominated Rwanda until 1961, when Belgian colonial rulers helped the Hutu to seize power and form the first independent government, and 10 000 Tutsi were killed. In Burundi, the Hutu led an unsuccessful revolt against the Tutsi in 1971, in which over 100 000 Hutu were massacred by the army, and 120 000 fled to Tanzania. In 1994, following the shooting down of an aircraft carrying President Habyarimana, Hutu militias sought revenge on the Tutsi minority. About a million people were killed in subsequent months. Following successes by the Tutsi-led Rwanda Patriotic Front, over the next year some 2 million refugees (mainly Hutu) fled to neighbouring countries. Conflict was continuing in 1999, against a backdrop of international concern. >> Burundi ℹ; pastoralism; Rwanda ℹ

Huxley, Aldous (Leonard) (1894–1963) Novelist and essayist, born in Godalming, Surrey. His reputation was made with his satirical novels *Crome Yellow* (1921) and *Antic Hay* (1923). Later novels include *Point Counter Point* (1928) and his best-known work, *Brave New World* (1932).

Huxley, Sir Andrew Fielding (1917–) Physiologist, born in London. He helped to provide a physico-chemical explanation for nerve transmission, and outlined a theory of muscular contraction. He shared the Nobel Prize for Physiology or Medicine in 1963. >> Eccles; muscle ℹ; neurone ℹ

Huxley, Sir Julian (Sorell) (1887–1975) Biologist, born in London. He applied his scientific knowledge to political and social problems, formulating a pragmatic ethical theory based on the principle of natural selection. He was the first director-general of UNESCO (1946–8), the grandson of T H Huxley. >> Huxley, T H; natural selection

Huxley, T(homas) H(enry) (1825–95) Biologist, born in Ealing, Greater London. He became the foremost expounder of Darwinism, to which he added an anthropological perspective in *Man's Place in Nature* (1863). He also wrote essays on theology and philosophy from the viewpoint of an 'agnostic', a term he introduced. >> agnosticism; Darwinism

Huygens, Christiaan [**hoy**genz] (1629–95) Physicist and astronomer, born in The Hague, The Netherlands. In 1655 he discovered the ring and fourth satellite of Saturn, and in 1657 made the first pendulum clock. In optics he propounded the wave theory of light, and discovered polarization. >> light

Huysmans, Joris Karl [**hoys**mahnz] (1848–1907) Novelist of Dutch origin, born in Paris. His best-known works are *À rebours* (1884, Against the Grain), a study of aesthetic decadence, and the controversial *Là-bas* (1891, Down There), which dealt with devil-worship.

hyacinth A bulb native to the Mediterranean region and Africa; flowers bell-shaped, held horizontally or drooping in spikes. (Genus: *Hyacinthus*, 30 species. Family: Liliaceae.)

Hyades [**hiy**adeez] A bright open cluster of stars c.46 parsec distant. It makes a V-shaped group for the bull's face in Taurus. >> open cluster; Taurus

hyaena >> **hyena**

hybrid An individual animal or plant resulting from cross-breeding between genetically dissimilar parents. It is typically used for the offspring of mating between parents of different species or subspecies, such as the mule (produced by crossbreeding an ass and a horse). >> genetics

Hyde, Douglas, Ir **Dubhighlas de Hide** (1860–1949) Writer, philologist, and first president of Ireland (1938–45), born in Frenchpark, Co Roscommon. He was founder and first president (1893–1915) of the Gaelic League, and professor of Irish in the National University (1909–32).

Hyde Park A royal park covering 255 ha/630 acres in C London. It was first opened to the public during the reign of James I. >> London

Hyderabad (India) [**hiy**drabad] 17°22N 78°26E, pop (1995e) 3 253 000. Capital of Andhra Pradesh, S India; founded in 1589 as capital of the Kingdom of Golconda; joined with India, 1948; Muslim stronghold in S India; airfield; railway; four universities (1918, 1964, 1972, 1974); commercial centre. >> Andhra Pradesh

Hyderabad (Pakistan) [**hiy**drabad], also **Haidarabad** 25°23N 68°24E, pop (1995e) 1 171 000. City in Sind province, SE Pakistan; on the R Indus; provincial capital from 1768 until captured by the British in 1843; airfield; railway; university (1947). >> Pakistan [i]

Hyder Ali >> **Haidar Ali**

Hydra (astronomy) [**hiy**dra] (Lat 'sea serpent') The largest and longest constellation in the sky, extending from the celestial equator into the S hemisphere, but with no particularly bright stars. >> constellation; RR968

Hydra (biology) [**hiy**dra] A genus of solitary, freshwater coelenterates; stalk-like body attached at the base; apical mouth surrounded by tentacles; typical green colour derived from green algal cells contained in body. (Phylum: Cnidaria. Class: Hydrozoa.) >> algae; coelenterate

Hydra (Greece) [**hiy**dra], Gr **Ídhra** pop (1995e) 3890; area 50 sq km/ 20 sq mi. Island in the Aegean Sea, Greece, off the E coast of the Peloponnese; chief town, Hydra; tourism. >> Aegean Sea; Greece [i]

Hydra (mythology) [**hiy**dra] In Greek mythology, a many-headed monster, the child of Typhon and Echnida, whose heads regrew when struck off. It was killed by Heracles. >> Heracles

hydrangea [hiy**draynj**a] An evergreen or deciduous shrub, or a climber with aerial roots, native to Asia, and North/South America; **lacecaps** have heads with large, sterile flowers surrounding the fertile ones; **hortensias** or **mop-heads** have heads composed entirely of large, sterile flowers. Both forms produce blue flowers on acid soils, pink on alkaline soils. (Genus: *Hydrangea*, 80 species. Family: Hydrangaceae.)

hydrate A compound containing water, usually one in which the water is present as 'water of crystallization', such as in gypsum ($CaSO_4.2H_2O$), a hydrate of calcium sulphate. >> water

hydraulics The study of systems using liquids, whether stationary or moving, for the transmission of force; often, water or oil is the transmitting fluid. Any machine which uses, controls, or conserves a liquid makes use of the principles of hydraulics. The applications include such fields as irrigation, domestic water supply, hydroelectric power, and the design of dams, canals, and pipes. Most motor vehicles have hydraulic braking systems. >> fluidics; fluid mechanics

hydrobiology The branch of biology dealing with the study of life in aquatic habitats, especially those in freshwater. Its core is formed by the study of planktonic plants and animals. >> biology; plankton

hydrocarbons Compounds containing only carbon and hydrogen. Many hundreds of such compounds are known, and most occur in coal, petroleum, or natural gas. There are two main subdivisions: **aliphatic hydrocarbons**, of which methane (CH_4) is the simplest, and **aromatic hydrocarbons**, based on benzene. >> carbon; hydrogen

hydrocephalus [hiydroh**se**faluhs] The abnormal accumulation of cerebrospinal fluid within the ventricular system inside the brain. It causes distension of the brain and, in infants, enlargement of the skull. >> brain [i]; cerebrospinal fluid

hydrochloric acid An aqueous solution of hydrogen chloride (HCl), a strong acid, fully dissociated into H^+ and Cl^- ions. Gastric juice in the human stomach is 2% hydrochloric acid. >> acid; chlorides; hydrogen

hydrocortisone >> **corticosteroids; cortisol**

hydrocyanic acid [hiydrohsiy**an**ik] Hydrogen cyanide (HCN), or its aqueous solution; also known as **prussic acid**. Pure hydrogen cyanide is an exceedingly poisonous liquid, boiling at 26°C, and having an odour of almonds. >> acid; cyanide; hydrogen; pH

hydrodynamics >> **fluid mechanics**

hydroelectric power (HEP) Electricity generated using the potential energy of water. It is a renewable energy source with considerable potential worldwide, although it accounts for only a small proportion of the world's energy needs. The world's largest HEP scheme is at Itaipu on the Parana R. >> alternative energy; electricity; Itaipu Dam

hydrofluoric acid Hydrogen fluoride (HF), or its aqueous solution. Although extremely corrosive, it is only a moderately strong acid, partially neutralized solutions having a pH of about 3. >> acid; fluoride; hydrogen; pH

hydrofoil A vessel able to raise itself clear of the water on attaining a certain speed. Foils are fitted at a depth greater than the draft of the hull. Successful trials were first held in Italy in 1906, but 50 years elapsed before the Italians put it to commercial use. Speeds of around 40 knots are common in commercial service. >> hovercraft [i]; jetfoil

hydrogen H, element 1, the lightest of the chemical elements, the commonest isotope having only one proton and one electron in an atom. Its stable form is a gas with diatomic molecules (H_2). Although it makes up more than 90% of the atoms in the universe, it is much less common on Earth, and mainly occurs combined with oxygen in water and with carbon in hydrocarbons. >> chemical elements; hydrogenation; RR1036

hydrogenation The addition of hydrogen to a compound, also often called **reduction**. It occurs, for example, in the conversion of ethylene to ethane, important in the saturation of fats and in petroleum refining. >> hydrogen

hydrogen bomb The popular name (often shortened to **H-bomb**) for thermonuclear weapons which achieve their destructive effects through the intense release of heat and blast produced when the nuclei of hydrogen isotope materials used in the construction of the weapon are fused together in a nuclear reaction. The reaction is triggered by the detonation of an atomic bomb used as the weapon's core. The hydrogen bomb was first developed in the USA at Los Alamos laboratories. The first successful test was at Enewetak Atoll in November 1952. >> nuclear fission / fusion / weapons; *see illustration on p. 416*

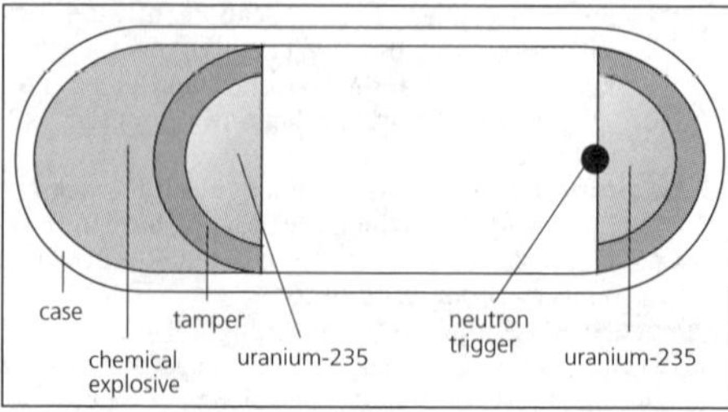

Atomic bomb, gun barrel design. Chemical explosives drive together two portions of uranium to produce a single portion of mass greater than the critical mass. Tamper reflects neutrons back into the uranium. An alternative design relies on compressing fissionable material, using a surrounding jacket of explosives.

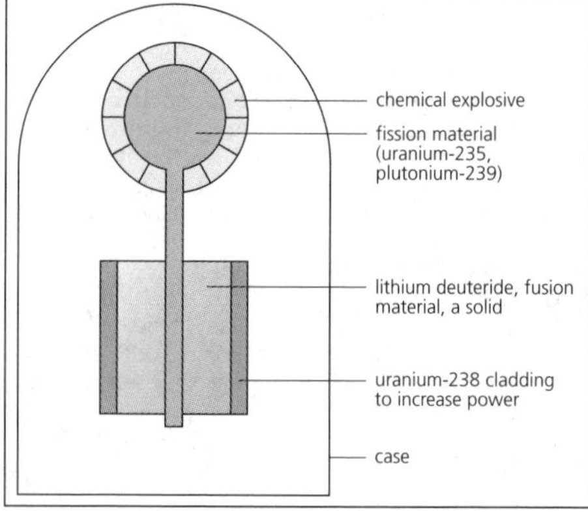

Schematic diagram of a hydrogen bomb. The top portion is a fission (atomic) bomb, used to initiate the lower fusion section.

hydrography The science of charting the water-covered areas of the Earth, including the determination of water area, coastline, and depth, as well as the flow characteristics of rivers, lakes, and seas.

hydrology The science concerned with the occurrence and distribution of water on or near the Earth's surface, in oceans and in the atmosphere, particularly in relation to the interaction of water with the environment and fresh water as a resource. **Applied hydrology** covers topics such as irrigation schemes, dam design, drainage, flood control, and hydroelectric power.

hydrolysis [hiy**drol**isis] The splitting of a molecule by the action of water. The technique is applied, for example, in the conversion of an ester into an alcohol and an acid (eg fats into fatty acids and glycerol). >> ester; molecule; water

hydrophobia >> **rabies**

hydroponics The growing of plants in nutrient solutions, without soil. The method is especially used in the production of high-quality tomatoes and cucumbers, under glass.

hydrostatics >> **fluid mechanics**

hydrotherapy >> **hyperthermia**

hydroxide The ion OH^- or a compound containing it. The only metal hydroxides soluble in water are those of the alkali metals and, to a lesser extent, calcium, strontium, and barium. >> alkali

hydroxybenzene >> **phenol**

hydroxybutanedioic acid >> **malic acid**

hydroxypropanoic acid >> **lactic acid**

Hydrozoa [hiydro**zoh**a] A class of mainly marine coelenterates in which the life-cycle involves alternation between attached polyp and planktonic medusa phases. (Phylum: Cnidaria.) >> coelenterate; coral; medusa; polyp (marine biology)

Hydrus [**hiy**drus] (Lat 'water snake') An inconspicuous constellation of the S hemisphere. >> constellation; Hydra (astronomy); RR968

hyena or **hyaena** [hiy**ee**na] A nocturnal carnivorous mammal; stocky, dog-like, with short back legs; large head with strong jaws; inhabits plains in SW Asia and Africa. (Family: Hyaenidae, 3 species.) >> aardwolf; carnivore ℹ; dog

Hygeia [hiy**gee**a] In Greek mythology, a minor deity, the daughter of Asclepius; the name is a personification of the word for 'health'. >> Asclepius

hygrometer [hiy**grom**eter] A meteorological instrument used for measuring the relative humidity of the air. A **hygrograph** gives a continuous record of relative humidity. >> humidity

Hyksos [**hik**sos] The so-called 'shepherd kings' of ancient Egypt, who founded the XVth dynasty there c.1670 BC. They were originally desert nomads from Palestine.

Hymen [**hiy**men] In ancient Greece and Rome, the god of marriage. He is depicted as a youth with a torch.

Hymenoptera [hiymen**op**tera] A diverse order of insects containing about 130 000 species, including the sawflies, horntails, wasps, bees, and ants; adults typically with two pairs of membranous wings; mouthparts adapted for chewing, or sucking nectar; social organization exhibited by many species. >> insect ℹ

hymn A song of praise to God, usually with a non-Biblical text in verses. It is sung congregationally with accompaniment on the organ or other instruments. >> chorale; liturgy; Psalms, Book of

Hypatia [hiypa**tee**a] (c.375–415) Greek philosopher, daughter of Theon, an astronomer and mathematician of Alexandria. Associated by many Christians with paganism, she was murdered by a fanatical mob. >> Neoplatonism

hyperactivity The combination of overactive, poorly controlled behaviour with inattention and lack of concentration for a particular task. This condition is most frequently seen in children. >> attention

hyperbola In mathematics, the locus of a point which moves so that the difference of its distances from two fixed points (*foci*) is constant. Some of the comets move in hyperbolae, and the curve is much used in architecture. >> conic sections ℹ; geometry

hyperbole Exaggeration, used often for comic or rhetorical effect, as throughout the writings of Rabelais, or in the mouth of Shakespeare's Falstaff. It is the staple of the tabloid press, and also of ordinary conversation ('I'm dying for a drink'). >> figurative language

Hyperboreans In Greek mythology, an unvisited people of fabled virtue and prosperity, living in the land 'beyond the North Wind'.

hypercube An arrangement of computers in the form of a cube. Communications links between the computers enable them to carry out tasks in parallel. >> computer; parallel processing

hyperglycemia / hyperglycaemia [hiypergliy**seem**ia] A level of blood sugar above the upper limit of the normal range (>160 mg/100 ml). >> diabetes mellitus

Hyperion (astronomy) [hiy**peer**ion] The seventh natural satellite of Saturn, discovered in 1848; distance from the planet 1 481 000 km/920 000 mi; diameter 400 km/250 mi; orbital period 21·277 days. >> Saturn (astronomy); RR964

Hyperion (mythology) [hiy**peer**ion] In Greek mythology, a Titan, son of Uranus and Gaia, and father of Eos (the Dawn), Helios (the Sun), and Selene (the Moon); later identified with the Sun. >> Helios

hypermedia A form of document which can be held on a computer, consisting of elements of text, audio and video sequences, and computer programs, linked together in such a way that users can move from one element to another and back again. When these operations are carried out within a database consisting solely of texts, the domain is known as **hypertext**.

hypermetropia >> **eye** 🛈

Hyperrealism >> **Photorealism**

hypersensitivity >> **allergy**

hypertension A condition in which both systolic and diastolic blood pressure (BP) rise above normal levels. All levels of BP above normal damage blood vessels; the greater the increase, the greater the damage. In the majority of cases the cause of high BP is unknown. >> blood pressure

hypertext >> **hypermedia**

hyperthermia The use of artificial fever for the treatment of disease. The fever can be induced by heat, hydrotherapy (water-treatment, in the form of steam or hot bath immersion), diathermy, and the injection of foreign protein. Since fever is one of the body's natural reactions to the presence of infection or other disease, it is reasoned that a high body temperature may have beneficial effects. >> diathermy; fever; temperature

hyperthyroidism Oversecretion of thyroid hormones, leading to an increase in the body's metabolic rate; also known as **Graves disease** after Irish physician Robert James Graves (1796–1853). Symptoms include a warm skin with tremor of the hands, weight loss, a rapid heart rate with palpitations, and protrusion of the eyes. >> goitre; thyroid hormone

hypnosis A temporary trance-like state induced by suggestion, in which a variety of phenomena (eg increased suggestibility and alterations in memory) can be induced in response to verbal or other stimuli. A hypnotic trance is not in any way related to sleep, but there is a constriction of responses by the hypnotized subject. The technique was first used by Mesmer in France, and the term *hypnosis* was coined by the British surgeon James Braid (1795–1860). >> Mesmer

hypnotics Drugs that promote drowsiness and sleep. They include benzodiazepines and barbiturates. >> barbiturates; benzodiazepines; sedative

hypo Popular name for sodium thiosulphate, incorrectly known as 'hyposulphite'. It is used as a fixing solution in photographic processing. >> photography

hypoglycemia / hypoglycaemia [hiypohgliy**seem**ia] A level of blood sugar below the lower limit of normal (60 mg/100 ml), causing weakness, sweating, faintness, and ultimately mental confusion. It is often due to an overdose of insulin in diabetic patients. >> diabetes mellitus; insulin

hypophysis [hiy**po**fisis] >> **pituitary gland**

hypothalamus [hiypoh**thal**amus] A region of the vertebrate brain, situated below the thalamus, which has an important regulatory role regarding the internal environment (eg water balance, body temperature in mammals). It is also involved in the control of emotions by the limbic system. >> brain 🛈; diencephalon; homeostasis

hypothermia [hiypoh**ther**mia] The presence of a deep body temperature of 35°C or less, measured clinically by a rectal thermometer. It occurs after immersion in cold water; in old age after exposure to low environmental temperatures; and following periods of prolonged unconsciousness or immobilization. >> temperature 🛈

hypothyroidism [hiypoh**thiy**roydizm] Reduced function of the thyroid gland, with a fall in the secretion of thyroid hormones. Body metabolism falls, and patients develop an increased dislike of cold weather; physical and mental activity slows down. >> thyroid hormone

Hyracotherium [hiyrako**thee**rium] The first fossil horse, known from the early Eocene epoch of North America, Europe, and Asia; four hoofed toes on forelimbs, three on hind limbs; formerly known as *Eohippus*. (Family: Equidae.) >> Eocene epoch; fossil; horse 🛈

hyrax [**hiy**raks] A mammal, native to Africa and Arabia; superficially resembles a large guinea pig, with pointed muzzle and round ears; the only members of the order Hyracoidea; also known as **daman**, **dassie**, **rock rabbit**, or (in Bible) **cony**. (Family: Procaviidae, 11 species.) >> cavy; mammal 🛈

Hyrcanus I, John [heer**kay**nus] (2nd-c BC) High priest of Israel and perhaps also a king subject to Syrian control (c.134–104 BC); the son of the high priest Simon, and in the line of Hasmonean priestly rulers. >> Maccabees

hyssop [**his**op] A small, shrubby perennial (*Hyssopus officinalis*) growing up to 60 cm/2 ft, native to S Europe and W Asia; flowers 2-lipped, violet-blue, in whorls forming long, loose 1-sided spikes; originally cultivated as a medicinal herb. (Family: Labiatae.) >> herb

hysterectomy [histe**rek**tomee] The surgical removal of the uterus. This operation is indicated in cases of malignant tumours of the uterus, in benign growths when these have become large, and when excessive menstrual bleeding is severe and not controlled by hormone treatment. >> uterus 🛈

hysteria In its most general sense, a colloquial and derogatory term, used especially for histrionic behaviour. More specifically, it is used in psychiatry to describe a personality profile or a neurotic illness. It may also describe a symptom in which there is a physical manifestation without an organic cause. >> neurosis

Hyssop

I

iamb [**iy**am] A metrical foot consisting of one unstressed and one stressed syllable, as in the word 'release'. It is the most common measure in English verse. >> metre (literature)

Iapetus (astronomy) [iy**a**pitus] The eighth natural satellite of Saturn, discovered in 1671; distance from the planet 3 560 000 km/ 2 212 000 mi; diameter 1460 km/910 mi; orbital period 79·331 days. >> Saturn (astronomy); RR964

Iapetus (mythology) [iy**api**tus] In Greek mythology, one of the Titans, the father of Prometheus, Epimetheus, Atlas, and Menoetius. >> Titan

Ibadan [iba**dan**] 7°23N 3°56E, pop (1995e) 1 378 000. City in Nigeria; founded in the 1830s; British control, 1896; airfield; railway; regarded as the intellectual centre of the country; university (1948). >> Nigeria ℹ

Ibáñez, Vicente Blasco >> **Blasco Ibáñez, Vicente**

Ibárruri (Gómez), Dolores [ee**ba**-ruree], known as **la Pasionaria** ('The Passionflower') (1895–1989) Spanish politician and orator, born in Gallarta. With the outbreak of the Civil War (1936), she became the Republic's most emotional and effective propagandist. After the war, until 1977, she took refuge in the USSR, becoming president of the Spanish Communist Party in exile. >> Spanish Civil War

Iberian Peninsula [iy**beer**ian] area c.593 000 sq km/ 229 000 sq mi. The region of Europe SW of the Pyrenees, including Portugal and Spain; Iberia is an ancient name for Spain. >> Portugal ℹ; Spain ℹ

Iberians A group of iron-age peoples inhabiting the S and E periphery of present-day Spain, and extending N into present-day France as far as the Rhône valley. >> Three Age System

ibex A wild goat with high sweeping curved horns; horns round in cross-section and ringed with ridges; two species: **ibex** (*Capra ibex*) from the mountains of Europe, N Africa, and S Asia; **Spanish ibex** (*Capra pyrenaica*) from the Pyrenees. >> goat

Ibibio [ibi**bee**oh] A cluster of Kwa-speaking peoples of SE Nigeria. Agriculturalists, they are also renowned for their wood-carvings. >> Nigeria ℹ

ibis A wading bird native to tropical and warm temperate regions; long curved bill; face naked. (Family: Threskiornithidae, c.23 species.)

Ibiza [i**bee**tha] or **Iviza** [ee**vee**tha], ancient **Ebusus** pop (1995e) 70 600; area 572 sq km/221 sq mi. Third largest island in the Balearic Is; a major tourist island; capital, Ibiza, pop (1995e) 25 500, founded by the Carthaginians, 645 BC. >> Balearic Islands

IBM >> **International Business Machines**

Ibo >> **Igbo**

Ibsen, Henrik (Johan) (1828–1906) Playright and poet, born in Skien, Norway. His international reputation began with *Brand* and *Peer Gynt* (1866–7). He regarded his historical drama, *Kejser og Galilaeer* (1873, Emperor and Galilean) as his masterpiece, but his fame rests more on the social plays which followed, notably *Et Dukkehjem* (1879, A Doll's House) and *Gengangere* (1881, Ghosts). In his last phase he turned more to Symbolism, as in *Vildanden* (1884, The Wild Duck), *Rosmersholm* (1886), and *Bygmester Solness* (1892, trans The Master-Builder). The realism of *Hedda Gabler* (1890) was a solitary escape from Symbolism.

Icaria [i**ka**ria], Gr **Ikaría** area 255 sq km/98 sq mi. Greek island in the Aegean Sea; named after the legendary Icarus; Ayios Kyrikos is a popular resort. >> Aegean Sea; Greece ℹ; Icarus (mythology)

Icarus (astronomy) [**ik**arus] Asteroid no.1566, discovered in 1949, diameter 1·5 km/0·9 mi. It has an orbital period of 1·12 years and occasionally passes close to Earth. >> asteroids

Icarus (mythology) [**ik**arus, **iyk**arus] In Greek mythology, the son of Daedalus. His father made him wings to escape from Crete, but he flew too near the Sun; the wax holding the wings melted; and he fell into the Aegean at a point now known as the Icarian Sea. >> Daedalus

ICBM >> **intercontinental ballistic missile**

ice The common solid form of water, stable below 0°C. Unlike most solids, it is less dense than its liquid, because the strong hydrogen bonds formed hold the molecules in a relatively open network. >> water

Ice Age A period of time in the Earth's history when ice sheets and glaciers advanced from polar regions to cover areas previously of temperate climate. Several ice ages are known, the most recent ('the Ice Age') being from c.1 million years ago and lasting until c.10 000 years ago. >> glaciation

iceberg A floating mass of ice, detached from ice sheets or glaciers, drifting on ocean currents for up to several years and for many hundreds of kilometres before melting. With only a fraction of their mass above water level they are a danger to shipping, particularly in the N Atlantic. >> glacier

icebreaker A vessel designed to clear waterways of ice by propelling itself onto the surface of the ice, breaking it with the weight of the fore part of its hull, which is specially shaped and strengthened for this purpose. Icebreakers are commonly employed in Russia, the Baltic, and Canada. >> ship ℹ

ice hockey A sport played on ice between two teams of six players all wearing ice skates and protective clothing. It is a fast game, played with sticks and a small, circular, rubber puck, on a rink 56–61 m/184–200 ft long and 26–30 m/ 85–98 ft wide. The aim is to hit the puck into your opponent's goal. It is thought to have been first played in Canada in the 1850s. The governing body is the International Ice Hockey Federation, founded in 1908. >> hockey ℹ; RR1055; *see illustration on p. 419*

Iceland, Icelandic **Ísland**, official name **Republic of Iceland**, Icelandic **Lýdhveldidh Ísland** pop (1995e) 268 000; area 103 000 sq km/40 000 sq mi. Island state lying between the N Atlantic and Arctic Oceans, 900 km/550 mi W of Norway; capital, Reykjavík; timezone GMT; chief religion, Lutheran Protestantism (95%); official language, Icelandic; major ethnic group, Icelandic (96%); unit of currency, the króna of 100 aurar; several active volcanoes; famous for its geysers; many towns heated by subterranean hot water; heavily indented coastline with many long fjords; high ridges rise to 2119 m/6952 ft at Hvannadalshnjúkur (SE); several large snowfields and glaciers; average daily temperatures, minimum −2°C (Jan), maximum 14°C (Jul–Aug); settled by the Norse, 9th-c; world's oldest parliament, the *Althing*, 10th-c; union with Norway, 1262; union with Denmark, 1380; independent kingdom in personal union with Denmark, 1918; independent republic, 1944; extension of the fishing limit around Iceland in 1958 and 1975 precipitated the 'Cod War' disputes with the UK; governed by a parliament,

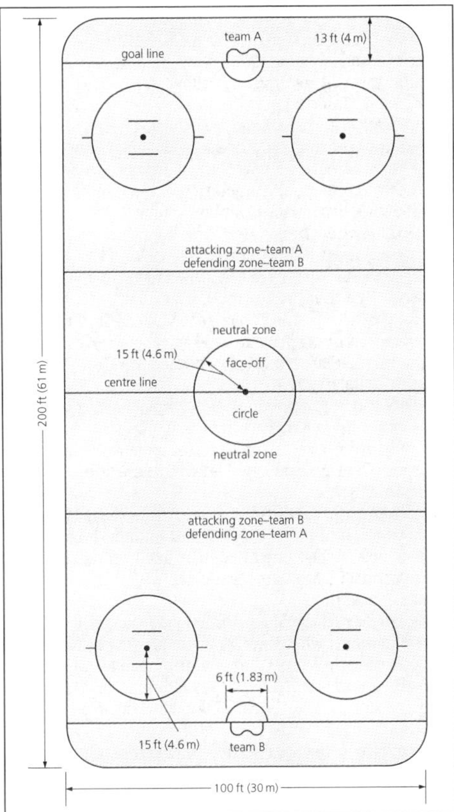

Ice hockey

president, prime minister, and cabinet; economy based on inshore and deep-water fishing (three-quarters of the national income). >> Reykjavík; Surtsey Island; Thingvellir; RR1012 political leaders

Icelandic >> **Germanic / Scandinavian languages**

Iceland spar >> **calcite**

Iceni [**ikay**nee] An ancient British tribe occupying what is now Norfolk and NW Suffolk. They rebelled in AD 47 and again in 60, when their queen, Boadicea, led them and other tribes in a major revolt against Rome. >> Boadicea

ice skating 1 Figure skating, artistic dancing on ice. Competitions are held for individual, pairs, and ice dancing. **2 Speed skating**, in which one competitor races against another on an oval ice track over distances of 500–10 000 m (550–11 000 yd). >> RR1055

I-ching [ee ching] >> **Book of Changes**

ichneumon (insect) [ik**nyoo**mn] A slender, parasitic wasp; females often have elongate egg-laying tube; larvae feed on other insects as parasites. (Order: Hymenoptera. Family: Ichneumonidae.) >> wasp

ichneumon (mammal) [ik**nyoo**mn] The largest living mongoose (*Herpestes ichneumon*) (length, 1 m/3¼ ft), native to Africa and the Middle East; also known as **Egyptian mongoose** or **Pharaoh's rat**. >> mongoose; Viverridae ℹ

ichthyosaur [**ik**thiosaw(r)] An aquatic reptile with streamlined body for fast swimming; tail typically large, paddle-like; known mainly from the Jurassic period. (Subclass: Ichthyopterygia.) >> Jurassic period; reptile

Icknield Way [**ik**neeld] A Neolithic track linking Salisbury Plain in SE England to the E coast. The Romans gravelled it and used it as a secondary road. >> Roman roads ℹ; Salisbury Plain

Ickx, Jacky [iks] (1945–) Motor-racing driver, born in Brussels. He was world champion in 1982–3 (both Porsche), and won the Le Mans 24-hour race a record six times. >> motor racing

icon (art and religion) (Gr *eikon*, 'image') A representation of Christ, the Virgin Mary, angels, saints, or even events of sacred history, used since the 5th-c for veneration and an aid to devotion, particularly in the Greek and Russian Orthodox Churches. They are typically in Byzantine style, flat, and painted in oils on wood, often with an elaborately decorated gold or silver cover. >> iconoclasm; Orthodox Church

icon (computing) In computing, a small image or symbol used in graphic displays to represent an item such as a program or disk drive. Commands can be given to the computer using a mouse to point at an icon, thereby selecting the task related to the icon that needs to be performed. >> mouse (computing)

iconoclasm [iy**kon**oklazm] (Gr 'image breaking') The extreme rejection of the veneration of images. The practice was supported by the pope and the Roman emperor in the 8th-c, and again by certain Reformers in the 16th-c. >> icon (art/religion); Reformation

iconography The branch of art history which, faced with a picture, or any kind of image, takes as its central question: who or what is represented? Originally concerned with the identification of portraits, it now covers the whole science of subject-matter and symbolism.

Ictinos or **Ictinus** [ik**tiy**nus] (5th-c BC) Greek architect, who shares with Callicrates the glory of designing the Parthenon at Athens (447–438 BC). >> Bassae; Parthenon

Idaho [**iy**da-hoh] pop (1995e) 1 164 000; area 216 422 sq km/83 564 sq mi. State in NW USA; the 'Gem State'; first European exploration by Lewis and Clark, 1805; held jointly by Britain and the USA until 1846; Territory of Idaho established, 1863; admitted to the Union as the 43rd state, 1890; bounded N by Canada (British Columbia); highest point Borah Peak (3860 m/12 664 ft); largely rugged, mountainous country, with nearly half the state (mostly N) under national forest; Snake R Plain is one of the largest irrigated areas in the USA; capital, Boise; mainly an agricultural state; contains one of the deepest gorges in the world (Hell's Canyon). >> Boise; Hell's Canyon; Lewis, Meriwether; United States of America 🅘; RR994

Id al-Adha [eed al **adh**a] The Muslim 'Feast of Sacrifice', celebrating the faith of Abraham, who was willing to sacrifice his son at Allah's request. >> Abraham; Allah; RR982

Id al-Fitr [eed al **fee**ter] A Muslim festival, the 'Feast of Breaking Fast', occurring on the first day after Ramadan. >> Ramadan; RR982

ide >> **orfe**

idealism In philosophy, the theory that the material world is in some sense created by the mind and does not exist independently of it; the only things which really exist are minds and their contents. Physical objects are collections of ideas that exist only in so far as they are perceived by finite, human minds or by the infinite mind, God. >> materialism

ideography [idi**og**rafee] The study of writing systems which use symbols called **ideographs** or **ideograms** – a development from primitive picture writing, found in early systems of the Far and Middle East. An ideograph represents an abstract concept to which its shape bears no clear relationship; for example, a hand might represent friendship. Most of the symbols come to represent words, and are thus more precisely referred to as *logographs*. >> hieroglyphics 🅘; pictography 🅘

idiolect [**id**iohlekt] The total linguistic system of an individual, in a given language, at any specific time. Different preferences in usage, grammar, vocabulary, and pronunciation serve to keep idiolects apart. >> dialectology

idiophone Any musical instrument whose sound proceeds from the body of the instrument itself, without the action of vibrating strings, membranes, loudspeakers, or columns of air. >> bell; carillon; castanets; Jew's harp; maracas; musical glasses; musical instruments; percussion 🅘; saw, musical; tuning fork

Idomeneus [iy**dom**enyus] The leader of the Cretans who assisted the Greeks at Troy. Being caught in a storm at sea, he vowed to sacrifice the first thing he met on his safe return. This was his own son; and after carrying out the sacrifice he was driven into exile. >> Homer; Trojan War

Idumeans >> **Edomites**

Ife [**ee**fay] A ceremonial and trading centre in SW Nigeria, occupied from the 11th-c AD, from which the Yoruba dispersed to found their kingdoms. The related Benin tradition may also derive from Ife. >> Benin 🅘; Yoruba

Igbo or **Ibo** [**ee**boh] An agricultural people of E Nigeria; their language is a member of the Kwa branch of the Niger–Congo family. They established the short-lived state of Biafra (1960–70). >> Biafra; Niger–Congo languages; Nigeria 🅘

Ignarro, Louis J (1941–) Pharmacologist, born in New York City. He worked at the University of California, Los Angeles (from 1985), and shared the 1998 Nobel Prize for Physiology or Medicine for his contribution to the discovery of nitric oxide as a signalling molecule in the cardiovascular system.

Ignatius (of Antioch), St [ig**nay**shus] (c.35–c.107) One of the apostolic Fathers, reputedly a disciple of St John, the second Bishop of Antioch. According to Eusebius, he died a martyr in Rome. Feast day 17 October. >> apostle; Christianity

Ignatius de Loyola, St >> **Loyola, Ignatius of, St**

igneous rock Rocks that have formed by crystallization of magma originating within or below the Earth's crust. *Plutonic* rocks form deep in the Earth and are coarse-grained (eg granite); *volcanic* rocks form on the Earth's surface and are fine-grained (eg basalt); and *hypabyssal* rocks form at relatively shallow depths (eg dolerite). >> basalt; dolerite; granite; magma

ignis fatuus [**ig**nis **fa**tyoouhs] Flickering lights sometimes seen at night in marshy areas, and thought to be due to the spontaneous combustion of marsh gas (methane) generated by decaying vegetation. It is commonly termed **will-o'-the-wisp** or **Jack-o'-lantern**. >> methane

Iguaçu [igwa**soo**] National park on both sides of the border between Argentina and Brazil; area 1950 sq km/750 sq mi; 82 m/269 ft-high Iguaçu Falls; a world heritage site.

iguana [ig**wah**na] A lizard, native to the New World, Madagascar, Fiji, and Tonga; often has crest of tooth-like projections along back; tongue thick and fleshy. (Family: Iguanidae, 650 species.) >> anole; basilisk (biology); chuckwalla; lizard 🅘

Iguanodon [ig**wah**nodon] A heavily built two-legged dinosaur; up to 8 m/26 ft in length; plant-eating; known mainly from the Lower Cretaceous period of Europe. (Order: Ornithischia.) >> Cretaceous period; dinosaur 🅘; Ornithischia

Ijsselmeer or **Ysselmeer** [**es**elmair] area 1240 sq km/480 sq mi. Shallow lake in NW Netherlands, formed from the S part of the Zuider Zee inlet by the construction of the Afsluitdijk Sea Dam (1932).

Ikaría >> **Icaria**

ikebana [eekay**bah**na] The formal Japanese style of flower arrangement, which selects a few blooms or leaves and places them in a very careful relationship to one another.

Illinois [ili**noy**] pop (1995e) 11 937 000; area 145 928 sq km/56 345 sq mi. State in NC USA; the 'Prairie State'; 21st state admitted to the Union, 1818; explored by Jolliet and Marquette in 1673 and settled by the French; included in French Louisiana, it was ceded to the British in 1763 and by the British to the USA in 1783; capital, Springfield; mostly flat prairie producing maize, soybeans, wheat; chief cities include Chicago; highest point, Charles Mound (376 m/1234 ft); diverse manufacturing centred on the Chicago area. >> Chicago; Springfield (Illinois); United States of America 🅘; RR994

illiteracy >> **literacy**

illuminance In photometry, the incident luminous flux per unit area, ie the amount of visible light available to provide illumination per square metre; symbol *E*, units lx (lux); also called **illumination**. >> light; photometry 🅘

Illyria [**il**iria] In antiquity, the E seaboard of the Adriatic and its mountainous hinterland. It was roughly the equivalent of the W half of former Yugoslavia and NW Albania.

ilmenite [**il**meniyt] A black oxide mineral, iron titanate ($FeTiO_3$), found in basic igneous rocks and beach sand deposits. It is the major ore of titanium. >> titanium

Ilyushin, Sergey Vladimirovich [il**yoo**shin] (1894–1977) Aircraft designer, born in Dilialevo, Russia. His designs include the Il-4 long-range bomber, which was important in World War 2. Afterwards his passenger aeroplanes became the basic Soviet carriers. >> aircraft 🅘

imagery Figurative language; the illustration and emphasis of an idea by analogies and parallels of different kinds, to make it more concrete and objective. Images may be explicit in the form of a simile ('As cold as any stone') or implicit in the form of a metaphor ('You blocks, you stones, you worse than senseless things'). Imagery is often thought of as mainly visual, but images often invoke the other senses and may operate even on an abstract level. >> figurative language; Imagism; metaphor; Symbolism

imaginary number >> **numbers**

Imagism An early 20th-c poetic movement which sought to return (and confine) poetry to its essential ingredient, the image, which 'presents an intellectual and emotional complex in an instant of time' (Ezra Pound). It has been widely influential. >> imagery; poetry; Pound

imam [**imahm**] **1** A religious leader and teacher of a Sunni Muslim community, who leads worship in the mosque. **2** A title given to the founders or great leaders of Muslim communities or schools. **3** A charismatic leader among Shiite Muslims, who believe that in every generation there is an imam who is an infallible source of spiritual and secular guidance. The line of imams ended in the 9th-c, and since then the ayatollahs serve as the collective caretakers of the office until the return of the expected imam. >> ayatollah; Shiites; Sunnis

IMAX [**iy**maks] A large-screen cinematograph system, developed in Canada in 1968. Film is projected on a screen typically 18–23 m/60–75 ft wide and 14–18 m/45–60 ft high, and viewed by an audience seated comparatively close so that the picture fills their field of vision. OMNIMAX was a further development in 1972, using wide-angle lenses for projection on a domed screen c.23 m/75 ft in diameter. >> cinematography

Imhotep [im**hoh**tep] (fl.27th-c BC) Egyptian physician and adviser to King Zoser (3rd dynasty). He was later worshipped as the life-giving son of Ptah, god of Memphis. The Greeks identified him with Asclepius. >> Asclepius; Saqqarah

Immaculate Conception The belief that the Virgin Mary from the moment of her conception was free from sin. It was promulgated as a dogma of the Roman Catholic Church by Pope Pius IX in 1854. >> Mary (Mother of Jesus); Roman Catholicism

immigration >> **migration 1**

immortelle The name applied to various species of the daisy family (Compositae), cultivated for the papery flower-heads which retain their colour and are often used dried in flower arrangements.

immunity In medicine, the ability to resist the development of a disease-causing organism. It varies from individuals who are extremely vulnerable to a specific infection to those who are resistant to it. Naturally occurring or **innate immunity** protects individuals who have not had previous contact with a particular infection. **Acquired immunity** is provoked by the presence of the infecting agent in the tissue. There are two specific reactions within the body. The first is the production of antibodies which circulate in the blood; the second is **cell-mediated immunity**, in which sensitized cells in the tissue react directly with the foreign agent and destroy it. >> antibodies; immunization; interferons

immunity, diplomatic A provision of the Vienna Convention on Diplomatic Relations (1961), an international treaty, which states that diplomatic agents will have immunity from all criminal jurisdiction of the receiving state and immunity from certain civil jurisdiction. The ambassador may waive immunity.

immunization The artificial introduction into the body (*inoculation*) of antigens which are themselves harmless, derived from micro-organisms capable of causing specific disease, in order to provoke the production of protective antibodies. It is widely carried out for poliomyelitis, tuberculosis, measles, and mumps. >> antibodies; immunity; vaccination

immunoglobulin >> **antibodies**

immunology Originally the study of the biological responses of a living organism to its invasion by bacteria, viruses, or parasites, and its defence against these. It now also includes the study of the body's reaction to foreign substances, particularly proteins, such as those in transplanted organs. >> auto-immune diseases; immunity; inflammation

immunosuppression The controlled suppression of the immune response of the body to the presence of foreign protein. This occurs in a number of special clinical conditions, such as organ transplantation, and in the treatment of certain malignant tumours and auto-immune disorders. Several groups of drugs can be used; its major disadvantage is that it renders patients vulnerable to infections. >> immunity; immunology

impact printer A printer which relies on the character being pressed onto the paper via an inked ribbon. Examples include dot matrix, daisy-wheel, golfball, and line printers. >> computer printer

impala [im**pah**la] An African grazing antelope (*Aepyceros melampus*); golden brown, paler on underside; dark stripe each side of tail; male with lyre-shaped horns ringed with ridges. >> antelope

impatiens [im**pay**shienz] A member of a large genus of annuals and perennials, native to Europe, Asia, most of Africa, and North America; translucent, watery stems; flowers hanging horizontally from a slender stalk, showy; fruit a capsule exploding audibly and scattering seeds. Hybrids between *Impatiens holstii* and *Impatiens sultanii*, with mostly red, pink, or white flowers, are popular ornamentals known as **busy Lizzie**. (Genus: *Impatiens*, 500–600 species. Family: Balsaminaceae.) >> balsam

impeachment A legal process for removing undesirable persons from public office. Originating in mediaeval England, it was revived in the 17th-c during the conflict between the monarch and parliament. Impeachment is a cumbersome method because of the problem of defining unacceptable behaviour and crimes. The move to impeach US President Nixon did, however, force his resignation. >> Clinton, Bill; Nixon, Richard M

impedance In alternating current circuits, a measure of the restriction of current flow (in much the same way as resistance is used for direct current circuits); defined as voltage divided by current; symbol Z, units Ω (ohm). >> alternating current; reactance; resistance

Imperial Conferences >> **Colonial and Imperial Conferences**

imperialism The extension of the power of the state through the acquisition, normally by force, of other territories, which are then subject to rule by the **imperial power**. The main era of imperialism was the 1880s to 1914, when many European powers sought to gain territories in Africa and Asia. The term is now often applied to any attempts by developed countries to interfere in underdeveloped countries. There is also increasing interest in the idea of *neocolonialism*, where certain countries are subjugated by the economic power of developed countries, rather than through direct rule. >> colony; indirect rule

Imperial War Museum The Museum of British and Commonwealth military operations since 1914, founded in London as a memorial to those who died in World War 1.

impetigo [impe**tiy**goh] A superficial infection of the skin common in children, usually due to *Staphylococcus aureus*. Infection affects the face, hands, and knees. >> skin [i]; *staphylococcus*

impotence Inability in males to engage in sexual intercourse because of failure to achieve an erection. A minority of cases of impotence are from organic diseases, and physiological problems (such as insufficient bloodlow or the side-effects of medication) may also be factors. More commonly a number of psychological causes are responsible, such as the strength of the sexual drive, and marital, family, and social relationships. >> penis [i]

Impressionism A modern art movement which started in France in the 1860s; the name, coined by a hostile critic, was taken from Claude Monet's picture, 'Impression: sunrise' (1872). The Impressionists rejected the dark tones of 19th-c studio painting, set up their easels out-of-doors, and tried to capture the brilliant effects of sunlight on water, trees and fields, and pretty girls. >> landscape painting; Postimpressionism; Monet; Pissarro; Renoir, Pierre Auguste; Sisley

imprinting The process whereby animals rapidly learn the appearance, sound, or smell of significant individual members of their own species (eg parent) or important subcategories (eg suitable mates) through being exposed to them, often during a restricted period of life. >> ethology

improvisation The performance of music without following a predetermined score; an important constituent of music for many centuries. In the classical concerto, for example, the cadenza provided a major formal context for brilliant soloistic improvisation. The art of improvising on a given theme has survived mainly in organ lofts and in jazz, where both individual and ensemble improvisations have always played an important role. >> blues; cadenza; jazz

Imran Khan, in full **Ahmad Khan Niazi Imran** (1952–) Cricketer, born in Lahore, Pakistan. A fast bowler and astute captain, he inspired Pakistan's rise to prominence in world cricket. After leading Pakistan to the 1992 World Cup, he retired with a score of 3807 runs and 362 wickets in Test matches. He married in 1995, and has since been developing a career in politics. >> cricket [i]

incandescent lamp A lamp which produces visible light from a heated source or filament. Examples include arc lamps, gas lights, and filament electric light bulbs. >> electricity; light

Incarnation (Lat 'the putting on of flesh') In Christianity, the union between the divine and human natures in the one Jesus Christ; the 'Word' of God becoming 'flesh' (*John* 1.14). The term is also appropriate to other religions (eg Hinduism) in which a life-spirit is given a material form. >> Jesus Christ

Incas or **Inka** Originally a small group of Quechua-speaking Indians living in the C Andean highlands; during the 15th-c, one of the world's major civilizations, and the largest Precolumbian state in the New World, with an estimated population of 5–10 million. In the 11th-c, they established their capital at Cuzco, the Sacred City of the Sun, where they built huge stone temples and fortresses, and covered their buildings in sheets of gold. During the 15th-c, they brought together much of the Andean area, stretching along the entire W length of South America. In 1523, Spanish invaders under Pizarro captured the emperor Atahualpa, whom they later murdered, and by the 1570s Indian power was totally destroyed. >> Atahualpa; Pizarro; Quechua

Ince, Paul (1967–) Footballer, born in Ilford, E Greater London. A midfielder, he played for West Ham, Manchester United, and Inter Milan, signing for Liverpool in 1997. By mid-1998 he had won 39 caps playing for England.

incendiary bomb A bomb which causes its destructive effects by burning fiercely and igniting the structures on which it lands. It was used with great effect by both sides during World War 2. >> bomb

incense A mixture of gums and spices which gives off a fragrant odour when burnt. It is widely used in many religious rites, and its smoke is often regarded as symbolic of prayer. >> religion

incest Sexual relations with close kin. In Western society, it refers to sex in the nuclear family other than between man and wife, but the precise specification of when a relationship is too close to allow sexual relations varies between cultures.

Inch'ŏn [in**chon**], also **Jinsen** or **Chemulpo** 37°30N 126°38E, pop (1995e) 1 901 000. City in W Korea; on the coast of the Yellow Sea; scene of battle between Japanese and Russian navies, 1904; UN forces landed there during Korean War, 1950; major port for Seoul, to which it is linked by subway; university (1954). >> Korea [i]; Seoul

incomes policy >> **prices and incomes policy**

income tax A major source of government revenue, levied on personal incomes. Income below some lower limit is usually exempt, and the tax rate levied on further slices of income varies, at rates fixed from time to time in the budget. There may also be a range of special tax allowances, such as for charitable covenants. >> budget; PAYE; taxation

incubus [**ing**kyubus] A malevolent male spirit supposed in mediaeval superstition to have intercourse with women in their sleep. Witches and demons were the offspring of such unions. The equivalent female spirit was a **succubus**. >> succubus

Independence Day >> **Fourth of July**

Independence Hall A building in Independence National Historical Park, Philadelphia, PA, where the Declaration of Independence was proclaimed (1776); a world heritage site. The Liberty Bell, rung at the proclamation, is kept here. >> Declaration of Independence

Independent Labour Party (ILP) A British political party, socialist in aim, formed in 1893 with the objective of sending working men to parliament. Many of its leaders played a major part in founding the Labour Party in 1906, to which it was affiliated until 1932. In 1975, the ILP returned to the Labour Party as a publishing body and pressure group. >> Labour Party

independent schools Schools in the UK which are not dependent on either the government or local authorities for their income, but derive it principally from the fees paid by parents. >> maintained school; public school

index >> **indexing**

index / indices A notation which simplifies the writing of products, eg $2 \times 2 \times 2 \times 2$ is written 2^4, where 4 is the index (or *exponent*); it can be extended to give meaning to fractional, negative, and other indices. >> indexing

index fund An investment fund where shares are bought in all the companies listed in the main stock exchange index, then held. In this way the portfolio of shares will always equal movements in the stock market. >> Dow Jones Index; FT–SE Index; stock market

indexing The compiling of systematic guides to the location of words, names, and concepts in books and other publications. An index consists of a list of entries, each of which comprises a heading, together with any qualifying phrase and/or subheading(s), and at least one page reference or cross-reference ('see...'). Several procedures are available, such as 'letter-by-letter' indexing (in which *seabird* would appear before *sea horse*) and 'word-by-word' indexing (in which *sea horse* would appear before *seabird*). >> library science

Index Librorum Prohibitorum [**in**deks lib**raw**rum prohhibi**taw**rum] (Lat 'index of forbidden books') A list of books which members of the Roman Catholic Church were forbidden to read. It originated with the Gelasian Decree (496), and was frequently revised, but in 1966 it was decided to publish no further editions. >> Roman Catholicism

index-linking Adjusting the price of goods, the interest on investments, or the level of salaries and wages, upwards or downwards in proportion to rises or falls in the retail price index. The strategy is popular in times of high inflation. >> inflation; retail price index

India, Hindi **Bharat**, official name **Republic of India** pop (1995e) 944 157 000; area 3 166 829 sq km/1 222 396 sq mi. Federal republic in S Asia, divided into 25 states and seven union territories; capital, New Delhi; timezone GMT +5½; chief ethnic groups, 72% Indo-Aryan, 25% Dravidian; chief religion, Hinduism (80%); official languages, Hindi, English, and 16 others; unit of currency, the Indian rupee of 100 paise; Asia's second largest state; folded mountain ridges and valleys in N, highest peaks over 7000 m/23 000 ft; C river plains of the Ganges, Yamuna, Ghaghari, and Brahmaputra to the S; control measures needed to prevent flooding; Thar Desert NW of Rajasthan, bordered by semi-desert areas; Deccan Plateau in the S peninsula, with hills and wide valleys, bounded by the Western and Eastern Ghats; coastal plains, important areas of rice cultivation; climate dominated by the Asiatic monsoon; rains come from the SW (Jun–Oct); rainfall decreases E–W on the N plains, with desert conditions in extreme W; tropical in S even in cool season; cyclones and storms on SE coast (especially Oct–Dec); Indus civilization emerged c.2500 BC, destroyed in 1500 BC by the Aryans, who developed the Brahmanic caste system; Mauryan Emperor Asoka unified most of India, and established Buddhism as the state religion, 3rd-c BC; spread of Hinduism, 2nd-c BC; Muslim influences during 7th–8th-c, with sultanate established at Delhi; Muslim Empire founded 1175; Mughal Empire established by Babur, 1526, extended by Akbar and Aurangzeb; Portuguese, French, Dutch, and British footholds in India, 18th-c; conflict between France and Britain, 1746–63; development of British interests represented by the East India Company; British power established after the Indian Mutiny crushed, 1857; movement for independence, late 19th-c; Government of India Act (1919) allowed election of Indian ministers to share power with appointed British governors; further Act (1935) allowed election of independent provincial governments; passive resistance campaigns of Gandhi from 1920s; independence granted, 1947, on condition that a Muslim state be established (Pakistan); Indian states later reorganized on a linguistic basis; Pakistan–India war over disputed territory in Kashmir and Jammu, 1948; federal democratic republic within the Commonwealth, 1950; Hindu–Muslim hostility, notably in 1978, and further India–Pakistan conflict in 1965 and 1971; separatist movements continue, especially relating to Sikh interests in the Punjab; suppression of militant Sikh movement in 1984 led to assassination of Indira Gandhi; Rajiv Gandhi assassinated, 1991; each of the 25 states administered by a governor appointed by the president; each state has an Assembly; national government consists of a president, a prime minister, a Council of States, and a House of the People; over two-thirds of the labour force employed in agriculture; floods and drought cause major problems; considerable increase in industrial production since independence. >> caste; Delhi; East India Company, British; Gandhi; Gandhi, Indira; Hinduism; Indian dance / Mutiny / National Congress; Mughal Empire; Pakistan [i]; Punjab (India); Sikhism; RR1012 political leaders

Indiana [indi**a**na] pop (1995e) 5 841 000; area 93 716 sq km/ 36 185 sq mi. State in E USA, S of L Michigan; the 'Hoosier State'; 19th state to join the Union, 1816; visited by La Salle in 1679 and 1681; occupied by the French, who ceded the state to the British in 1763; scene of many major Indian battles; hilly in the S, fertile plains in the C, and flat glaciated land in the N; capital, Indianapolis; grain, soybeans, pigs, cattle; bituminous coal, limestone, steel and iron, chemicals, motor vehicles, electrical goods. >> Indianapolis; La Salle; United States of America [i]; RR994

Indianapolis [indian**a**polis] 39°46N 86°09W, pop (1995e) 771 000. Capital of state in C Indiana, USA, on the White R; founded, 1820; state capital, 1825; airport; railway;

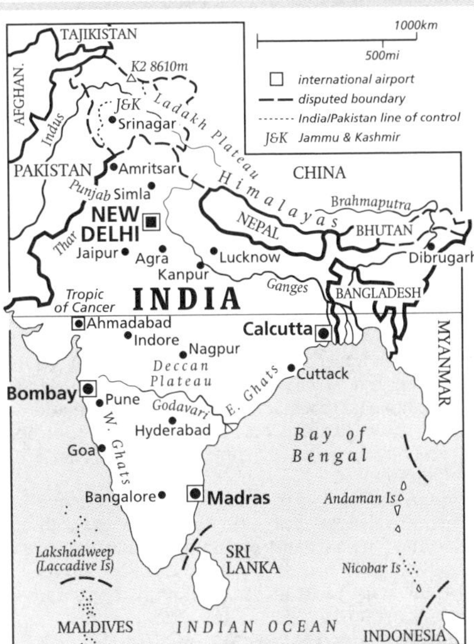

university (1855); professional teams, Indiana Pacers (basketball), Colts (football); Motor Speedway (where the world-famous 'Indianapolis 500' motor race is held). >> Indiana

Indian dance An ancient dance tradition based on Hindu thought, but showing Arab and Mughal influences. Classical dance forms are of religious or court origin, while folk forms are social and based in village life. Religious or mythical themes rely on the poetic language of codified hand gestures and facial expressions. They are accompanied by traditional instruments such as the tabla and sitar, and by voices, often in rhythmic counterpoint to the dance. >> Hinduism

Indian languages >> **Devanagari; Dravidian languages; Indo-Aryan languages**

Indian Mutiny (1857–9) A serious uprising against British rule, triggered off by the belief among Indian troops in British service that new cartridges had been greased with animal fat – something which would have been abhorrent to both Hindus and Muslims. The mutiny at Meerut (10 May 1857) spread throughout N India; Delhi quickly fell; and Kanpur and Lucknow garrisons were beseiged. The British finally regained full control in mid-1858. >> India [i]

Indian National Congress A broad-based political organization, founded in 1885, which spearheaded the nationalist movement for independence. It has been the dominant political party in India since 1947. >> Non-Co-operation Movement; Quit India Movement

Indian Ocean, ancient **Erythræan Sea** area 73 426 000 sq km/ 28 350 000 sq mi. Third largest ocean in the world; width c.6400 km/4000 mi at the Equator; maximum depth of 7125 m/23 375 ft in the Java Trench; linked to the Mediterranean by the Suez Canal.

Indian Territory Land set aside in the USA as a 'permanent' home for native Americans removed from the area E of the Mississippi R between 1825 and 1840. Originally it included most of Oklahoma and parts of Kansas and Arkansas, but by the end of the 19th-c most of it had been opened to whites. >> Five Civilized Tribes

indiarubber tree An evergreen tree (*Ficus elastica*) with elliptical, leathery, very glossy leaves, native to India and SE Asia. A source of rubber, young specimens are sold as house-plants under the name **rubber plants**. (Family: Moraceae.) >> rubber

indictment [in**diyt**ment] A document specifying the particulars of an offence of which a person is accused. **Indictable offences** in England and Wales are those triable before a judge (or sheriff in Scotland) and jury, such as murder. However, some less serious indictable offences, such as theft, may be tried on a summary basis in a lower court or without a jury. The Fifth Amendment to the US constitution guarantees the right to indictment by a Grand Jury for 'capital or infamous crimes'. >> Crown Court; jury; justice of the peace

indigestion Upper abdominal pain or discomfort related to eating; also known as **dyspepsia**. It is an extremely common complaint that may be precipitated by overeating, or by particular foods such as spices, fried foods, or beer. The condition is usually relieved by taking antacids. >> digestion

indigo A dye obtained from a species of *Indigofera*, particularly anil (*Indigofera anil*), a tropical American shrub, and *Indigo tinctoria*, a shrubby perennial growing to 2·5 m/8 ft; pea-flowers red, in short clusters. It is now mainly used to dye the warp yarns of denim. (Family: Leguminosae.) >> anil; dyestuff

indigo bird / finch >> **whydah**

indirect rule A form of colonial rule especially characteristic of British rule in Africa during the interwar years, involving the use of existing political structures, leaders and local organs of authority. It was adopted on grounds of its cheapness and to allow for independent cultural development, but was increasingly criticized for its failure to introduce a modernizing role into colonial administration, and was gradually given up after 1945. >> imperialism

Indo-Aryan languages The easternmost branch of the Indo-European languages, comprising some 500 languages spoken in N and C India. Its subgroupings are exemplified by Panjabi (or Punjabi, c.73 million) in the NW; Gujarati (c.43 million) and Marathi (c.65 million) in the W and SW; Hindi and Urdu (together, 240 million) in the mid-N; and Bengali and Assamese (together, c.93 million) in the E. (Figures are for first-language speakers.) >> Indo-European languages; Romani; Sanskrit

Indo-European languages The family of languages which developed in Europe and S Asia, and which gave the modern languages of W Europe (eg the Germanic, Romance, and Celtic languages) as well as many in the Baltic states, Russia and N India. The parent language of the family has been labelled **Proto-Indo-European** (PIE); there is no documentary evidence for it, but it is thought to have been spoken before 3000 BC. >> Celtic / Germanic / Indo-Aryan / Iranian / Romance / Slavic languages; comparative linguistics; family of languages [i]; Sanskrit

Indo-Iranian languages The E branch of the Indo-European family of languages. It comprises the Iranian and Indo-Aryan subgroups. >> Indo-Aryan / Indo-European / Iranian languages

Indonesia [indoh**nee**zha], official name **Republic of Indonesia**, Bahasa Indonesia **Republik Indonesia**, formerly **Netherlands Indies, Dutch East Indies, Netherlands East Indies, United States of Indonesia** pop (1995e) 194 956 000; area 1 906 240 sq km/735 809 sq mi. Republic of SE Asia, comprising the world's largest island group; five main islands, Sumatra, Java, Kalimantan (two-thirds of Borneo I), Sulawesi, Irian Jaya (W half of New Guinea I); capital, Jakarta; timezones GMT +7 to +9; chief ethnic groups, Javanese, Sundanese, Madurese, Malays; chief religion, Islam (90%); official language, Bahasa Indonesia, with English, Dutch, and Javanese widely spoken; unit of currency, the rupiah; 13 677 islands and islets, of which c.6000 are inhabited; hot and humid equatorial climate; dry season (Jun–Sep), rainy season (Dec–Mar); average temperature of 27°C on island coasts, falling inland and with altitude; settled in early times by Hindus and Buddhists whose power lasted until the 14th-c; Islam introduced, 14th–15th-c; Portuguese settlers, early 16th-c; Dutch East India Company established, 1602; Japanese occupation in World War 2; independence proclaimed, 1945, under Sukarno; federal system replaced by unified control, 1950; military coup, 1966; governed by a president, elected for a 5-year term, a 500-member House of People's representatives, and a 1000-member People's Consultative Assembly; separatist movements in Irian Jaya and East Timor; United Nations refuses to recognize Indonesian sovereignty in East Timor; mainly agrarian economy, notably rice; oil, natural gas, and petroleum products from Borneo and Sumatra account for nearly 60% of national income; small manufacturing industry; widespread forest fires, caused severe pollution throughout the region, 1997. >> Bali; Borneo; Irian Jaya; Jakarta; Java (country); Kalimantan; Komodo; Moluccas; Nias; Sulawesi; Sumatra; Sunda Islands; Timor; RR1012 political leaders; *see illustration on p. 425*

Indo-Pacific languages A hypothesized group of languages, centred on Papua New Guinea. There seem to be about 3·5 million speakers, but little is known of the languages, and many tribes have not been contacted. The grouping is highly speculative, linking the Papuan languages (themselves genetically diverse) with Andamanese and the extinct languages of Tasmania.

Indra In Hinduism, the Vedic king of the gods, to whom many of the prayers of the Rig Veda are addressed. >> Hinduism; Veda

indri or **indris** A leaping lemur (*Indri indri*), the largest living primitive primate (body length, 70 cm/27½ in); very short tail; dark with white legs and hindquarters; fluffy round ears; has a very loud, far-reaching cry. >> lemur; prosimian

Indricotherium [indriko**theer**ium] The largest land mammal that ever lived; known from the Oligocene epoch of C Asia; a gigantic, hornless rhinoceros standing 5·4 m/18 ft at the shoulder. (Order: Perissodactyla.) >> mammal [i]; Oligocene epoch; rhinoceros

inductance A measure of a coil's ability to produce a voltage in another coil (**mutual inductance**, *M*) or in itself (**self inductance**, *L*) via changing magnetic fields; units H (henry). It is equal to the ratio of electromotive force produced to rate of change of current. >> electromotive force

induction (logic) An inference from particular, observed instances to a general law or conclusion. The premisses of a sound induction may give good reason for believing the conclusion ('The Sun has always risen in the past, therefore it will rise tomorrow') but do not logically entail the conclusion. >> confirmation; logic; premiss

induction (obstetrics) The initiation of childbirth by artificial means. A common technique is the injection of the hormone oxytocin, which causes contractions of the uterus. >> hormones; obstetrics

indulgences In Roman Catholicism, grants of remission of sin to the living, following repentance and forgiveness; also, to the dead in purgatory. Abuses in the Middle Ages, leading to the 'buying and selling' of places in heaven, finally occasioned Martin Luther's '95 Theses', which launched the Reformation. Little reference is made to them today. >> Luther; purgatory; Reformation; Roman Catholicism

Indurain, Miguel [**in**duhran] (1964–) Racing cyclist, born in Villava, Spain. In 1991 he won the first of five successive Tours de France races (1991–5) becoming the first to achieve this distinction, and in 1996 won an Olympic Gold in the time trial. He retired in 1997.

Indus (Lat 'Indian') An inconspicuous constellation of the S hemisphere. >> constellation; RR968

Indus, River, Sanskrit **Sindhu** River of Asia, the longest of the Himalayan rivers (3000 km/1900 mi); rises in Xizang region (Tibet); flows into Pakistan; enters the Arabian Sea in a level, muddy delta. >> India ℹ; Indus Valley Civilization; Pakistan ℹ

indusium >> **sorus**

industrial action The activities of trade unions, or groups of workers or employers, to bring pressure on the others when negotiations and/or arbitration have failed to settle industrial disputes. Action by workers can include go-slows or 'working to rule', overtime bans, or strike action; action by employers may involve lockouts. >> picketing; strike (economics); trade union

industrial disease >> **occupational diseases**

industrial espionage The illicit acquisition of information about a company's activities. Such information may concern formulae, designs, personnel, or business plans. Methods include theft of documents, telephone tapping, and computer hacking.

industrial relations The dealings and relationships between the management and the workforce of a business, particularly one where trade unions are present and collective bargaining is normal; also known as **labour** or **employee relations**. The main topics covered include pay, hours and conditions of work, holidays, security of employment, and disciplinary and grievance procedures. >> ACAS; industrial action; trade union

Industrial Revolution A term usually associated with the accelerated pace of economic change, the associated technical and mechanical innovations, and the emergence of mass markets for manufactured goods, beginning in Britain in the last quarter of the 18th-c with the mechanization of the cotton and woollen industries of Lancashire, C Scotland, and the West Riding of Yorkshire. The mechanization of heavier industries (iron and steel) was slower, but sustained the Industrial Revolution in its second phase from c.1830. >> engine; industry; spinning; steel

industrial textiles Textiles used for industrial purposes, as found in the manufacture of conveyor belts, filter cloths, geotextiles, and ropes. Some 30% of all textile products are categorized as industrial.

industry A group of business enterprises which produce or supply goods or services. **Primary industries** are those based on the use of the earth for cultivation (eg agriculture, forestry, fishing) or the extraction of raw materials (eg mining, quarrying). **Secondary industries** (or **manufacturing industries**) are those which process raw materials into consumer products and components; they are often divided into **heavy industries**, involving the large-scale use of plant, machinery, personnel, and output (eg iron and steel, machinery) and **light industries**, involving production on a much smaller scale (eg electronics, food processing). **Tertiary industries** (or **service industries**) are those which do not produce goods, but provide support for other areas of the economy (eg banking, law) or are concerned with quality of life (eg tourism, entertainment). >> economics; Industrial Revolution

Indus Valley Civilization The earliest known S Asian civilization, flourishing c.2300–1750 BC around the R Indus in Pakistan. Over 100 sites have been identified with important urban centres at Mohenjo-daro and Harappa (Pakistan), and Kalibangan and Lothal (W India). >> Harappa; Mohenjo-daro

inertia The reluctance of a massive object to change its motion. Inherent to mass, it is present in the absence of gravity. Newton's first law is sometimes called the **law of inertia**. >> mass; moment of inertia; Newton's laws

inertial guidance An automatic navigation system used in guided missiles, aeroplanes, and submarines, which depends on the tendency of an object to continue in a straight line (*inertia*). Any changes in the direction and magnitude of motion of the vehicle are sensed and corrected automatically. >> inertia

infallibility In the Roman Catholic Church, the claim that statements on matters of faith or morals, made by a pope speaking *ex cathedra* (Lat 'from the throne'), or by a General Council if confirmed by the pope, are guaranteed the assistance of the Holy Spirit (ie free from error). The claim is rejected by Protestants. >> Council of the Church; Holy Spirit; pope; Roman Catholicism

Infante / Infanta [in**fan**tay, in**fan**ta] In Spain and Portugal, the title given to the sons and daughters of the sovereign.

infanticide In England and Wales, a term used for the crime committed where a mother causes the death of her child.

The child must be under 1 year old, and the mother must have been disturbed in her mind as a result of the stress of the birth. In the USA, the offence is usually subsumed under the general homicide statute, and in Scotland it is usually tried as culpable homicide. >> homicide

infantile paralysis >> **poliomyelitis**

infant school A UK school taking children from the age of 5 up to 7 or 8. In areas with middle schools, such schools are sometimes known as **first schools**. >> middle school; primary education

infection The invasion of the body by micro-organisms that are capable of multiplying there and producing illness. An infection begins by the entry of an organism at a specific site, such as the skin or respiratory passage. This is followed by a short interval in which the person feels well (the *incubation period*), then by dispersion of the organism throughout the body, usually with the predominant involvement of one or more specific tissues, as in cystitis (the bladder) or pneumonia (the lungs). >> communicable disease; micro-organism

inference In logic, a sequence of steps leading from a set of premisses to a conclusion. Rules of inference are rules for the construction of good and valid arguments. >> induction (logic); logic; premiss

inferiority complex A fundamental sense of inadequacy and insecurity out of proportion to real circumstances. An example may be short individuals who have a driven need to assert themselves in social situations to overcome their sensitivity about their height. >> narcissism

infertility The inability of a male or female to have children. Estimates of people who have subnormal levels of fertility amount to c.10% of couples, with a wide range of causes affecting both partners. In the female, factors include failure of ovulation, obstruction of the uterine (Fallopian) tubes, or abnormalities in the uterus. In the male, factors include the absence or inadequate production of sperm. >> artificial insemination; gamete intrafallopian transfer; test-tube baby; uterine tubes

infinity In mathematics, a number greater than any other number. The symbol ∞ was first used for infinity by the English mathematician John Wallis (1616–1703). >> Cantor; set

inflammation A defensive reaction of the body's tissues to invasion by pathogenic micro-organisms, or to the presence of a foreign body or other injury. Certain types of white blood cells and monocytes are attracted to the site, and these engulf and digest micro-organisms and tissue debris. The reaction is accompanied by local swelling and pain. >> blood; immunity; infection

inflation An economic situation of widespread and persistent increases in prices and wages. Common measures of inflation are the retail price index, which covers a wide range of consumer goods, and the gross domestic product deflator, an index of all goods prices. Economists differ over the cause of inflation: the main models blame excess demands and excessive pay rises in the money supply. Cost inflation, in which each price or wage rate rises because others have risen, or are expected to rise, does not explain how inflation starts, but does explain why it is so persistent once it has started. Governments have often tried to cure inflation, frequently incurring unemployment in the process, without much success. >> deflation; index-linking; monetarism; prices and incomes policy; retail price index

inflorescence The arrangement of more than one flower on the stem, together with any associated structures. The type of inflorescence is often significant in recognizing plant families. In **cymose inflorescences** the *meristem* of the main axis differentiates into a flower with new growth coming from a lateral branch (*monochasia*) or branches (*dichasia*) which in turn are terminated by a flower. In **racemose** [**ra**simohz] **inflorescences**, the main axis continues to grow, flowers being formed below the tip. >> flower ℹ; meristem

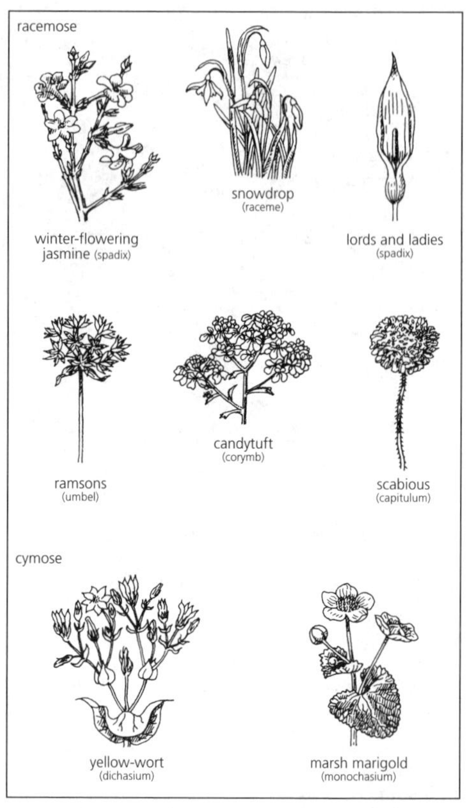

Types of inflorescence

influenza or **flu** A viral infection which causes an acute respiratory illness associated with headache, fever, and muscle pain. Vaccination is difficult, because the virus develops different strains with varying antigenic properties. The name is derived from *influentia coeli*, a mediaeval name for the disease, thought to be due to the influence of the sky. >> respiration; virus

information superhighway >> **Internet**

information technology A term commonly used to cover the range of technologies relevant to the transfer of information, in particular to computers, digital electronics, and telecommunications. Developments during the 1970s and 1980s, such as satellite and optical-based communication methods, have been responsible for enormous scientific and commercial growth in this area. >> computer; electronics; telecommunications; very large scale integration

information theory The mathematical theory of information, deriving from the work of the US mathematicians Claude E Shannon and Warren Weaver, in particular *The Mathematical Theory of Communication* (1949), and from the theory of probability. It is concerned with defining and measuring the amount of information in a message, with the encoding and decoding of information, and with the transmission capacity of a channel of communication. >> communication theory; computer science

infrared astronomy The study of celestial objects by their radiation in the wavelength range 1000 nm–1 mm. Many objects emit most of their radiation in the infrared waveband. This type of astronomy has increased in importance with the availability of two-dimensional detector arrays. >> astronomy; infrared radiation

infrared photography Photography which uses wavelengths beyond visible red light. Black-and-white film has medical and forensic application. Multilayer colour film including an infrared sensitive emulsion gives a false colour rendering in which natural vegetation appears red or magenta; this is used in aerial surveying. >> photography

infrared radiation Electromagnetic radiation of a wavelength a little longer than light, between 10^{-3} m and $7{\cdot}8 \times 10^{-7}$ m; discovered by William Herschel in 1800. Emitted by oscillating and rotating molecules and atoms, and invisible to the naked eye, it is perceived by us as 'radiant heat'. Infrared detectors are used in night and smoke vision systems (for fire fighting), intruder alarms, weather forecasting, and missile guidance systems. >> electromagnetic radiation ℹ; Herschel; infrared astronomy / photography; radiometry ℹ

infrasound Sound having a frequency of less than 20 Hz. Such waves cannot be heard by humans, but may be felt. Infrasonic waves are produced by explosions and by an unsteady airflow past an object. >> sound

infrastructure The network of factors which enables a country's economy or an industrial operation to function effectively. They include such matters as transport, power, communication systems, housing, and education.

Inge, William Ralph [ing], known as **the Gloomy Dean** (1860–1954) Clergyman, born at Crayke, North Yorkshire. He was Dean of St Paul's (1911–34), earning his byname from the pessimism displayed in his sermons and newspaper articles. >> Christianity; theology

Ingham, Sir Bernard [**ing**am] (1932–) Journalist, born in Hebden Bridge, West Yorkshire. A government press adviser (1976) and under-secretary in the Department of Energy (1978–9), he became nationally known after his appointment as chief press secretary to prime minister Margaret Thatcher (1979–90). >> Thatcher

Ingres, Jean Auguste Dominique [ĩgruh] (1780–1867) Painter, born in Montauban, France. He was the leading exponent of the Classical tradition in France, and is especially known for his nudes, including 'Baigneuse' (1808, Louvre) and 'La Source' (completed 1856, Musée d'Orsay). >> classicism

inheritance tax A UK tax started in 1986 which replaced capital transfer tax. It is levied on the value of a deceased person's 'estate', and includes property, land, investments, and other valuable assets. In the USA, such taxes are collected by the individual states. >> taxation

Initial Teaching Alphabet >> **i.t.a.**

injection The administration by a syringe of a drug or other pharmacological preparation in solution or suspension through a needle inserted into the skin (*intradermal*), underneath the skin (*subcutaneous*), into the muscle tissue (*intramuscular*), or into a vein (*intravenous*). >> immunization; vaccination

injection engine >> **fuel injection**

injection moulding A process used in the manufacture of plastics. Raw plastic, usually in granular form, is heated until soft enough to squeeze through a nozzle into a mould of the shape of the desired article. This type of manufacture is highly automated. >> plastics

injunction A court order in equity instructing a defendant to refrain from committing some act or, less commonly (but found for example in the USA), to carry out some act; the term **interdict** forbidding a particular act is used in Scots law. It is a remedy; for example, a prohibitory injunction might be granted to stop a continuing nuisance. >> equity (law)

ink A substance, usually coloured, used for writing, drawing, or printing; known in China before 1100 BC. At its simplest, it is a solution of a pigment or dye in a liquid (eg soot in water). >> quill

Inka >> **Incas**

Inkatha [in**kah**ta] A Zulu-based political organization, founded in South Africa in 1928, and now led by Chief Buthelezi; in full, **Inkatha yeNkululeku yeSizwe**. *Inkatha* refers to the woven headring worn by the Zulu to support loads; *yeNkululeku yeSizwe* means 'freedom for the nation'. Its disagreement with the politics of the African National Congress and its fear that the ANC was being priviledged in constitutional talks has led to violent conflict between members of the two organizations, despite efforts for reconciliation between Buthelezi and Mandela. >> African National Congress; Buthelezi; Mandela

ink-jet printer A type of fast and relatively quiet printer which produces characters or graphics by squirting very fine jets of rapid-drying ink onto paper. >> computer printer

INLA >> **Irish National Liberation Army**

inlaying A method of decorating furniture and other wooden objects by cutting away part of the surface of the solid material, and replacing it with a thin sheet of wood in another contrasting colour.

Inner Mongolia, Chin **Nei Mongol** pop (1995e) 23 001 000; area 450 000 sq km/173 700 sq mi. Autonomous region in N China; two-thirds grasslands, remainder desert; capital, Hohhot. >> China ℹ; Mongolia ℹ

Inner Temple >> **Inns of Court**

Innis, (Emile Alfredo) Roy (1934–) Civil rights activist, born in St Croix, US Virgin Isles. He joined the Congress of Racial Equality (CORE) in 1963, advocating black separatism and community school boards, and became CORE national president in 1968. >> civil rights; Congress of Racial Equality

Innocent III, originally **Lotario de' Conti di Segni** (1160–1216) Pope (1198–1216), born in Agnagni, Italy. His pontificate is regarded as the high point of the temporal and spiritual supremacy of the Roman see. He proclaimed the Fourth Crusade (1202–4) to recover the Holy Places. He excommunicated King John for refusing to recognize Stephen Langton as Archbishop of Canterbury. >> John; Langton; pope

Innocents' Day >> **Holy Innocents' Day**

Innsbruck [**inz**bruk] 47°17N 11°25E, pop (1995e) 119 000. City in W Austria; in the valley of the R Inn, surrounded by mountains; a mediaeval old town, with narrow and irregular streets and tall houses in late Gothic style; popular winter skiing centre; 1964 and 1976 Winter Olympic Games held here; university (1914–23); cathedral (1717–22). >> Austria ℹ

Inns of Court Voluntary unincorporated societies having the exclusive right to confer the rank of barrister in England, Wales, and Northern Ireland. For England and Wales, four Inns have existed in London since the 14th-c: the Inner Temple, the Middle Temple, Lincoln's Inn, and Gray's Inn. >> barrister; Temple

inoculation >> **immunization**

Inönü, Ismet [inoe**nü**], originally **Mustafa Ismet** (1884–1973) Turkish soldier, prime minister (1923–37, 1961–5), and president (1938–50), born at Izmir, Turkey. As the first premier of the new republic, he introduced many political reforms, and was elected president in 1938 on Atatürk's death. >> Atatürk

inorganic chemistry That branch of chemistry which deals with the structures, properties, and reactions of the elements and compounds of elements other than carbon. >> chemistry; organic chemistry

inositol A component of phytic acid in cereal and other vegetable foods. Some species (eg mice) require inositol for growth; humans do not, though large amounts are present in the body, especially in the brain.

input–output analysis In economics, an analysis which shows how materials and goods flow between industries, and where additional value is created. It assists economists in understanding how different sectors of the economy are interrelated. >> Leontief

Inquisition A tribunal for the prosecution of heresy, originally of the mediaeval Christian Church, introduced by Pope Gregory IX (13th-c). The activities of the inquisitors were later characterized by extremes of torture and punishment, notoriously in the case of the **Spanish Inquisition**. >> heresy

INRI The first letters of the Latin wording of the inscription placed on Jesus's cross at Pilate's command (*John* 19.19–20): *Iesus Nazarenus, Rex Iudaeorum* ('Jesus of Nazareth, the king of the Jews'). >> crucifixion; Jesus Christ; Pilate

insect An arthropod belonging to the largest and most diverse class of living organisms, the Insecta; c.1 million recognized species, grouped into 28 orders; head typically bears a pair of feelers (*antennae*) and a pair of compound eyes; each of three thoracic segments bears a pair of legs, the last two also typically bear a pair of wings each. >> Arachnida; Hemiptera; Heteroptera; Homoptera; Hymenoptera; Lepidoptera; Neuroptera; Orthoptera; Phasmida; Protura; *see illustration on p. 429*

insecticide A substance which kills insects. Most commonly these are synthetic organic compounds, applied as sprays by farmers. There is current concern about these substances entering the food chain and having a detrimental impact on wildlife, and perhaps on humans. >> DDT; food chain

insectivore The most primitive of placental mammals, native to Africa, Europe, Asia, and North America; small with narrow pointed snout; eats insects and other invertebrates. (Order: Insectivora, 345 species.) >> hedgehog; mammal [i]; mole (biology); shrew; tenrec

insectivorous plant >> **carnivorous plant**

insider dealing (UK) or **insider trading** (US) A business situation where an individual takes advantage of information about a company before it is made public, in order to make a profit (or avoid a loss) by dealing in the company's stocks or shares. It is illegal in most countries. >> shares; stocks

insolation The amount of solar radiation (both diffuse and direct) which reaches the Earth. Insolation varies with latitude and season: it is consistently high at the Equator, and high at the Poles during the polar summer, but zero in winter. >> albedo; solar constant; radiation

insomnia Unsatisfactory sleep, whether in quantity or in quality. It may be a component of a variety of physical or mental disorders. There may be difficulty in either initiating or maintaining sleep, a preoccupation about sleep, and interference with social and occupational functioning. >> sleep; sleep-walking

installment credit >> **hire purchase**

instinct An unlearned tendency to behave in a particular way. Instinctive behaviours are those actions or reactions to specific stimuli, shown in similar form by all normally developed members of a species (or sex or age-group thereof), no specific life experience being necessary for their emergence.

insulation >> **thermal insulation**

insulator A material or covering which prevents or reduces the transmission of electricity, heat, or sound. All electrical devices are insulated for protection from the passage of electricity. Thermal insulators keep things hot, cold, or maintain an even temperature. Sound insulators act as mufflers. >> thermal insulation

insulin [**in**syulin] A protein of vertebrates, secreted by B-cells of the islets of Langerhans (in the pancreas) in response to increases in blood glucose concentration (eg after a meal). Its main action is to lower blood glucose concentration by accelerating its uptake by most tissues (except the brain), and promoting its conversion into glycogen and fat. >> diabetes mellitus; glucose; hypoglycemia; pancreas

insurance A system of guarding an individual or institution against the possibility of an event occurring which will cause some harm – usually financial. The insured pays a fee (the *premium*) to an insurance company. The size of the premium (calculated by actuaries) depends on the size of the risk at stake, the number of premiums to be received, and the risk (or chance) of the event occurring. There are four main classes of insurance: marine, fire, life, and accident. >> actuary; life / national insurance; Lloyds

intaglio [in**tah**lioh] **1** A technique of printmaking. The design is incised into a metal plate, ink is forced into the cut lines and wiped off the rest of the surface; damp paper is laid on top; and both plate and paper are rolled through a press. >> engraving; etching; relief printing **2** A type of engraved gem in which the design is cut into the stone, instead of standing up in relief as in a *cameo*. >> cameo

integers >> **numbers**

integrated circuit A single chip of semiconductor, such as silicon, in which a large number of individual electronic components are assembled. Integrated circuits are smaller, lighter, and faster than conventional circuits. They use less power, are cheaper, and last longer. The circuit is usually made from pure silicon, doped with impurities – the type of impurity determining the job of that part of the chip: transistors, diodes, or resistors. >> microchip; microelectronics; semiconductor; silicon

integrated optics The study of minute optical devices linked by light guides into single units containing several components. Currently experimental, it may offer improved information-handling capacity, low weight, and high protection against interference, compared to conventional electronic chips. >> optoelectronics; silicon chip

Integrated Services Digital Network (ISDN) A service provided by the Posts, Telegraph and Telephones Authorities, which allows voice and data communications to be effected on the same line. This enables voice messaging to be carried out in the same way as data transmission. Facilities are available also for transmitting television pictures of medium quality. >> codec; public switched telephone network

intelligence The ability to respond adaptively to novel situations. Psychologists attempt to measure this ability by constructing tests which appear related to intelligence, and extensively using these tests on a target population, so enabling them to assess the mental age of any individual. **IQ** (**intelligence quotient**) equals mental age divided by actual (chronological) age. >> mental handicap

intelligence service A state agency which gathers information regarded as important to state security concerning foreign threats. In democratic countries it is usually kept separate from internal security agencies, whereas in such countries as the former USSR the KGB was responsible both for external espionage and internal counter-intelligence. In the USA and UK, the CIA and MI6 respectively are examples of the former, while the FBI and

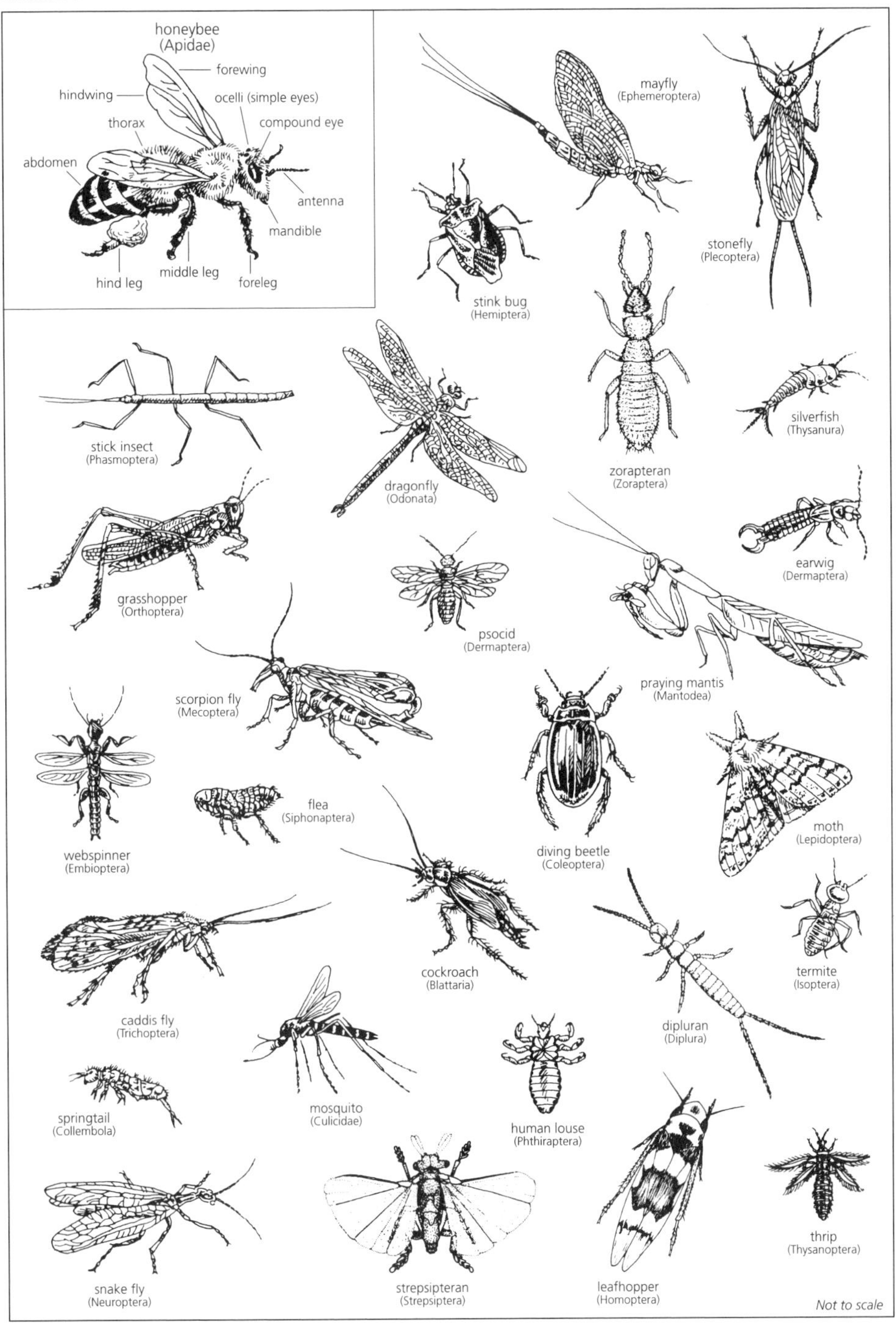

Insects - representatives of each order, with inset of a typical insect (honeybee)

MI5 are examples of the latter. The extent to which the UK government has been concerned to suppress all information relating to MI5 operations was apparent in the lengthy court battle in Australia and the UK to prevent publication, or reporting in the media, of the book *Spycatcher*. This was written by Peter Wright, a former intelligence officer, who alleged misconduct and 'misuse' of the law by MI5, in particular as it related to a 'plot' to destabilize the Wilson government of the 1970s. In 1991 the first woman to head MI5 was appointed (Stella Rimington). This was also the first time that the name of the head of the service was made public. Following the end of the Cold War the emphasis has changed to economic intelligence and the fight against domestic terrorism. >> Central Intelligence Agency; Federal Bureau of Investigation; military intelligence

intelligent building A building in which all areas of the building have been linked by cable capable of providing voice, video, and data communications. These communications could be used, for example, to provide continuous monitoring of the building, to ensure that the temperature, lighting, and environment always obey preset parameters. >> computer network

intensive care The continuous monitoring of several vital bodily functions in very seriously ill patients or in premature infants. The variables most commonly assessed are systemic arterial blood pressure, heart output, central venous blood pressure, pulmonary artery blood pressure, blood oxygen, carbon dioxide, sugar and acidity, the electrical activity of the heart, pulse and respiratory rate, and body temperature.

intensive farming Farming with relatively high input levels, especially of fertilizers, sprays, and pharmaceuticals. It produces higher yields per hectare, which may compensate for limited farm size and allow the small farmer to make an acceptable income. >> factory farming

interactive video A closed-circuit recorded video system in which the display responds to the instructions of the viewer. Applications range from simple press-button or touch-screen question-and-answer interactions to complex branched learning programmes. >> closed circuit television

intercellular fluid >> **interstitial fluid**

intercontinental ballistic missile (ICBM) A very large, long-range nuclear-armed missile developed by the USA and the former Soviet Union from the late 1950s onwards. ICBMs are based in silos spread out over a wide land mass. >> ballistic missile; MIRV

interest The amount of money charged by a person or institution that lends a sum to a borrower. The sum lent, on which interest is calculated, is known as the *principal*. The **interest rate** is the percentage payable; for example, an 8% interest rate on £100 gives the lender £8 interest at the end of a year. In **simple interest**, the interest gained in a given year is paid to the lender, so that the principal available does not change from year to year. In **compound interest**, the interest gained in a given year is not paid to the lender, but is added to the principal, which thereby increases year by year. >> hire purchase

interest group >> **pressure group**

interference In physics, the result of two or more waves of similar frequency passing through the same point simultaneously. An interference pattern is determined by the relative phases of the constituent waves. Interference is a property of all types of waves, including light. It is exploited in interferometers, including certain telescopes, compact disc players, phased-array radar, and holography. >> diffraction; interferometer; phase; wave motion ℹ

interferometer A device which relies on monitoring the interference pattern formed by combining two wave beams, usually light, derived from a single source. The technique is used in the study of gas flow, in wind tunnels, and in plasma physics. >> interference ℹ

interferons A class of protein molecules produced by body cells that are part of the body's defences against infection, notably by viruses. They appear to inhibit the multiplication of viruses within cells, and to stimulate the immune system to combat infection. Their use in medical practice remains uncertain. >> immunity; virus

Intergovernmental Panel on Climatic Change A panel established by the World Meteorological Organization and the UN Environment Programme in 1988 to assess the scientific information relating to climatic change, such as emissions of greenhouse gases and ensuing alterations to the Earth's climate. Comprised of more than 400 scientists from 25 countries, the panel first reported in 1990. >> greenhouse effect

intermezzo An instrumental piece, especially for piano, in a lyrical style and in no prescribed form. Earlier it was used for short, comic interludes performed on stage between the acts of a serious opera.

internal combustion engine An engine (such as a diesel or petrol engine) which burns its fuel/air mixture within the engine as part of its operating cycle. This cycle may be *two stroke* (one power stroke for every two strokes of the piston) or *four stroke* (one power stroke for every four strokes of the piston). >> carburettor; diesel / gas / Wankel engine; motorcycle

internal energy In thermodynamics, the difference between the heat supplied to a system and the work done by that system on its surroundings; symbol *U*, units J (joule). >> enthalpy; heat; thermodynamics

International An abbreviation of **International Working Men's Association**, the name given to attempts to establish international co-operative organizations of socialist, communist, and revolutionary groups. The **First International** was created in 1864 with Marx playing a significant role in its development. The **Second International** was formed in Paris in 1889, and still survives as a forum for reformist socialist parties. The **Third International** (Comintern) was founded by Lenin, and represented communist parties until abolished in 1943. There was a brief attempt in the 1930s by Trotsky to launch a **Fourth International**. >> Comintern; communism; Lenin; Marx; Trotsky

International Amateur Athletic Federation (IAAF) The supreme governing body which controls athletics worldwide. Founded in Stockholm in 1912, it is responsible for ratifying world records. By 1999 there were 209 member federations. >> athletics

International Atomic Energy Agency (IAEA) An international agency, founded in 1957, which promotes research and development into the peaceful uses of nuclear energy, and oversees a system of safeguards and controls governing the misuse of nuclear materials for military purposes. It is based in Vienna, and by early 1999 had 128 members. >> nuclear physics / reactor ℹ

International Baccalaureate An award taken by 18-year-old school leavers, and accepted in most countries as a qualification for entry to higher education. It is particularly popular in international schools or with students whose parents have to work abroad. >> tertiary education

International Bank for Reconstruction and Development (IBRD) A bank, generally known as the **World Bank**, founded in 1945, to help raise standards of living in the developing countries. It is affiliated to the United Nations, and based in Washington, DC. >> bank; Bretton Woods Conference; International Development Association; United Nations

International Brigades In the Spanish Civil War (1936–9), foreign volunteer forces recruited by the Comintern and by individual communist parties to assist the Spanish Republic. They played a particularly important role in the defence of Madrid (1936–7). >> Comintern; Spanish Civil War

International Bureau for American Republics >> **Pan-American Union**

International Business Machines Inc (IBM) A US computer manufacturing and sales company, for many years the most successful in the world. Although initially concerned with mainframe computers, it launched the IBM personal computer in 1983. Their machines, now including other personal computers of the same design (**IBM compatible** computers), occupy c.85% of the personal computer market. >> computer; personal computer

International Campaign to Ban Landmines (ICBL) A campaign, launched in 1991, with the aim of banning antipersonnel landmines. There are thought to be over 100 million such mines scattered over large areas on several continents. The campaign is coordinated by a steering committee of 16 organizations, and brings together over 1,300 non-governmental organizations in over 75 countries. The campaign and its coordinator, Jody Williams, shared the Nobel Peace Prize in 1997. A treaty signed by 133 countries, and ratified by 58, to ban the use, production, stockpiling, and transfer of landmines, became international law in March 1999. >> Williams, Jody

International Confederation of Free Trade Unions (ICFTU) An association of trade union federations from countries in W Europe, USA, and the British Commonwealth, located in Brussels, and founded in 1949. Its aim is collaboration between free and democratic trade unions throughout the world. In 1999 it represented 206 trade unions in 141 countries and territories. >> trade union; World Federation of Trade Unions

International Court of Justice A court established by the United Nations for the purpose of hearing international law disputes; known widely as the 'World Court'. The court sits at The Hague, The Netherlands. >> Hague Agreement; international law; United Nations

International Development Association (IDA) An organization affiliated to, but distinct from, the International Bank for Reconstruction and Development, based in Washington, DC. It was set up in 1960 to provide help to the world's 50 poorest countries by giving them aid on very easy terms.

International Gothic A style of art which flourished in W Europe c.1375–c.1425, characterized by jewel-like colour, graceful shapes, and realistically-observed details.

International Labour Organization An autonomous agency associated with the League of Nations, founded in 1919, which became a specialized agency of the United Nations in 1946. It is concerned with industrial relations and the pay, employment, and working conditions of workers. >> League of Nations; United Nations

international law The law that governs relationships between nation states. It is based principally on custom; there is no worldwide international legislature, and thus the enforcement of international law may pose problems. Although there is an International Court, it may only adjudicate with the consent of the parties. >> immunity, diplomatic; International Court of Justice; law; sea, law of the

International Monetary Fund (IMF) A financial agency affiliated to the United Nations, and located in Washington, DC. Formed in 1945, its functions include promoting international monetary co-operation and assisting states in need. It had 182 members at the beginning of 1999. >> Bretton Woods Conference

international monetary system A financial system which enables international trade to function effectively. Until 1914, the pound sterling was the currency in which most world trade was conducted. By 1945, the US dollar had taken over the role. The EU nations are now moving towards a linked currency system. Some countries have convertible currencies, in that they can be bought and sold freely and exchanged for one another. >> Bretton Woods Conference; European Monetary System

International Olympic Committee (IOC) The multi-sport organizational body responsible for the summer and winter Olympics, formed in 1894. Member countries of the IOC are allowed two delegates on the organization's ruling body. >> Olympic Games

International Packet Switching Service (IPSS) A service provided by the Posts, Telegraph and Telephones Authorities which allows a computer to send a packet of data to another computer anywhere in the world, without a physical wire communication being established between the two. The sender is charged only for the number of packets and their destination, and not for the length of time that the sender and receiver are linked together. >> packet switching; public switched telephone network

International Standard Book Numbering (ISBN) A system of 10-digit numbers allocated to books on publication. Internationally adopted in 1971, each book has its own number printed on the reverse of the title page and on the back cover.

International Style **1** A term sometimes used by art historians to refer to the more or less homogeneous Gothic style which flourished throughout Europe c.1400. >> International Gothic **2** A term first used in the USA to describe a new style of architecture developed in the 1920s, principally in Europe; also known as the **Modern Movement**. It is characterized by geometric shapes, an absence of decoration, white rendered walls, flat roofs, large expanses of glass, and asymmetrical compositions. >> Bauhaus; *De Stijl*; Postmodernism; prefabrication

International Telecommunication Union (ITU) An agency of the United Nations, which since 1947 has promoted worldwide co-operation in all aspects of telecommunications, such as the regulation of radio frequencies. >> broadcasting; United Nations

International UN Agencies >> **United Nations;** RR993

International Union of Pure and Applied Chemistry >> **IUPAC**

International Working Men's Association >> **International**

International Youth Hostel Association An organization found in some 50 countries which provides simple, low-cost accommodation for those wishing to travel. In many youth hostels the guests cook their own meals and help with the cleaning.

Internet An association of computer networks with common standards which enable messages to be sent from any host on one network to any host on any other. It developed in the 1970s as an experimental network designed to support military research, and steadily grew to include federal, regional, campus, and other users. It is now the world's largest computer network, with over 100 million hosts connected by 2000, providing an increasing range of services and enabling unprecedented numbers of people to be in touch with each other through electronic mail, discussion groups, and the provision of digital 'pages' on every conceivable topic. The **World Wide Web** is an Internet facility designed for multimedia use, in which individuals or organizations make available 'pages' of information to other users anywhere in the world, generally at no cost, but in the case of certain commercial operations (such as an encyclopedia) through subscription. Some commentators have likened the Internet to an amalgam of television, telephone, and conventional publishing, and the term **cyberspace** has been coined to capture the notion of a world of information present or possible in digital form (the **information superhighway**). During the 1990s, alongside claims that the Internet provides fresh opportunities for self-publishing, creativity, and freedom of speech, there has been increasing concern about the safeguarding of rights of privacy and intellectual property, the application of existing laws to the Internet (in such domains as pornography and libel), the extent to which the content of some of the new 'virtual communities' can or should be regulated, and the impact that the growing numbers of Internet communities ('cyburbia') will have on individuals and on society as a whole. The potential of the Internet is also currently limited by relatively slow data-transmission speeds, and by the problems of information management and retrieval posed by the existence of such a vast amount of information. >> computer network; electronic mail; International Packet Switching Service; Intranet

interplanetary matter Material in the Solar System other than the planets and their satellites. It includes streams of charged particles from the solar wind, dust, meteorites, and comets. >> dark matter; Solar System

Interpol [**in**terpol] Originally the telegraphic address, adopted in 1946, of the **International Criminal Police Organization** (earlier, **Commission**), initiated by Prince Albert I of Monaco in 1914. The address became widely used as a name, and was formally incorporated into the organization's title in 1956 as **ICPO–Interpol**. It is an international organization which exists to promote international co-operation in law enforcement. Member states are linked by a secure messaging system, and have direct access to specially designed international law enforcement databases. Interpol manages and stores information on behalf of its members, and provides criminal analysis services. A key factor in international co-operation is understanding the different legal frameworks within which national police forces work; Interpol works to promote harmonization in this area, and offers model legislation on such topics as extradition. Based in Lyon, France, it had 177 members in 1999. >> police

intersection >> **set**

interstitial fluid [inter**sti**shl] That part of the extracellular fluid which lies outside the vascular system and surrounds the tissue cells of animals; also known as **tissue fluid** and **intercellular fluid**. >> extracellular fluid; plasma (physiology)

intestacy The situation where a person dies without a valid will. In the case of a **partial intestacy**, the will does not provide for the disposal of the entire estate. >> property

intestine A tube of muscular membrane extending from the pyloric opening of the stomach to the anus, generally divided into the **small intestine** (*duodenum*, *jejunum*, and *ileum*), the **large intestine** (*caecum*, *appendix*, and the *ascending*, *transverse*, *descending*, and *sigmoid colon*), and the **rectum**. The length of the small intestine is c.6 m/20 ft and of the large intestine c.1 m/5 ft, but there is considerable variation. >> alimentary canal; colitis; diverticulitis; dysentery; hernia; rectum

Intifada [inti**fah**da] A Palestinian uprising which erupted in 1987 in the Gaza Strip and quickly spread to the West Bank. The uprising reflected frustrations with two decades of Israeli military occupation, the expansion of Israeli settlement in the Occupied Territories, and the failure of the PLO and the Arab states to change the status quo. The armed response from Israeli forces, combined with Palestinian anti-collaboration violence, claimed nearly 1000 Palestinian lives. However, the Intifada is credited with breaking the political deadlock. The term is now widely used to mean any mass uprising against oppressive rule. >> Gaza Strip; Israel ℹ; PLO; West Bank

Intolerable Acts (1774) The American name for laws passed by parliament to punish Massachusetts for the Boston Tea Party (1773). >> Boston Tea Party

intonaco >> **fresco**

intonation The melody of an utterance, brought about by the distinctive use of pitch patterns in sentences. It has several functions, notably the marking of grammatical structure (eg statements with a falling pitch, and questions with a rising pitch), and the expression of speaker attitudes. >> prosody

intoxilyzer >> **breathalyzer**

intracellular fluid The fluid contained within cells. In humans the total adult volume is about 28 l/49 UK pt/59 US pt. Its principal components (apart from water) are potassium ions, organic phosphates, and proteins. >> extracellular fluid; interstitial fluid

Intracoastal Waterway A shipping route extending 5000 km/3100 mi along the E coast of the USA from Massachusetts to Florida (the **Atlantic Intracoastal Waterway**) and from Florida to Texas (the **Gulf Intracoastal Waterway**). It consists of natural water routes, such as bays and rivers, linked by canals.

Intranet The use of Internet technology to provide an organization with an internal communications network. A development of the mid-1990s, such networks can either be linked to the global Internet, or be completely isolated from it. An Intranet system which permits links to selected outside organizations is an *Extranet*. >> Internet

intra-ocular lens implantation A perspex lens introduced into the front chamber of the eye following surgical removal of a cataract. >> eye ℹ; lens

intra-uterine device >> **contraception**

Intrepid >> **Stephenson, William**

introversion / extraversion Psychological terms formerly used as two categories of personality (**introvert** or **extravert**). The distinction is now considered to be a dimension with high levels of extraversion and introversion at the extremes. Strongly extraverted individuals are sociable, excitement-seeking, and carefree. They are often aggressive, may lose their temper quickly, and be unreliable. Strongly introverted individuals are quiet, reserved, and have few friends. They dislike excitement, are reliable, serious-minded, and like a well-ordered life.

intrusive rock Igneous rock formed by the emplacement and crystallization of magma formed at depth into higher levels of the Earth's crust. Igneous intrusions form a variety of rock masses. >> dyke (geology); sill

Inuit >> **Eskimo**

Invalides, Hôtel des [ohtel dayzăva**leed**] A hospital for the care of old and disabled soldiers, founded in Paris by Louis XIV and built in 1671–6. The main building, which is now mainly given over to a museum, was designed by Libéral Bruant (c.1635–97). The courtyard is the location of Napoleon's tomb. >> Paris

Invar [in**vah(r)**] An alloy containing 65% iron with 35% nickel. It has very low thermal expansion, and hence is used in surveying rods and pendulum bars. >> alloy; iron; nickel

Inverness 57°27N 4°15W, pop (1995e) 43 100. Capital of Highland, NE Scotland; at mouth of R Ness; airfield; railway; NE terminus of the Caledonian Canal. >> Caledonian Canal; Highland; Scotland ℹ

inversion temperature >> **Joule–Thompson effect**

invertebrate A multicellular animal that lacks a vertebral column. It includes the vast majority (over 97%) of all animal species. >> vertebral column

invert sugar >> **sucrose** ℹ

investment A term used in economics in two different, though related, senses: the acquisition of financial assets with a view to income or capital gains; and the creation of productive assets, which may be 'fixed investment' (ie buildings and equipment) or stocks and work in progress. In ordinary speech the term is even more widely used: people 'invest' in works of art and antiques, and even in football pools. >> interest; investment bank / company

investment bank A US bank handling new share issues, often in a syndicate with others. It is similar in function to the British merchant bank. >> bank; investment; merchant bank

investment company or **investment trust** A company which holds a portfolio of shares in a range of other companies, aimed at obtaining a reasonable dividend yield, growth, and with less risk (ie a *balanced portfolio*). >> investment; unit trust

invisibles The export and import of services; opposed to goods, which are known as **visibles**. Invisible exports include tourism, shipping, air freight, banking, insurance, and other financial services.

in vitro fertilization >> **test-tube baby**

Io (astronomy) [**iy**oh] The first natural satellite of Jupiter, discovered by Galileo in 1610; distance from the planet 422 000 km/ 262 000 mi; diameter 3630 km/2260 mi; orbital period 1·769 days. >> Galilean moons; Jupiter (astronomy); RR964

Io (mythology) [**iy**oh] In Greek mythology, the daughter of Inachos of Argos. She was beloved by Zeus, who turned her into a heifer to save her from Hera's jealousy. >> Argus 1

iodine I, element 53, melting point 114°C. A violet solid with a sharp odour; a halogen, not found free in nature, but as an impurity in sodium nitrate deposits, and concentrated in kelp and other seaweeds. An essential element in biological systems, lack of it causes goitre in humans. It is used in medicine as an antiseptic. >> chemical elements; goitre; halogens; RR1036

iodoform [iy**oh**dofaw(r)m] CHI_3, triiodomethane, melting point 119°C. A yellow solid with a peculiar odour, used as a mild antiseptic.

ion An atom which has lost one or more electrons (a *positive* ion) or which has gained one or more electrons (a *negative* ion). Atoms with a net positive charge are called **cations**; those with a net negative charge, **anions**. The type and magnitude of a charge is indicated by a superscript sign; for example, the positively charged sodium ion is identified as Na^+, and the negatively charged chloride ion as Cl^-. The formation of ions is called **ionization**. Ions are present in all animal and plant cells, where they are involved in many important and diverse roles, including the activation of enzymes, osmotic balance, and nerve impulse conduction. >> action potential; atom; electrolysis ℹ; electron; ionizer

Iona [iy**oh**na] A remote island off Mull, W Scotland, the site of a monastery established in AD 563 by the Irish missionary St Columba to convert the inhabitants of N Britain to Christianity. In c.1200 a Benedictine abbey was founded on the site. >> Benedictines; Columba, St; Lindisfarne

Ionesco, Eugène [yo**nes**koh] (1912–94) Playwright, born in Slatina, Romania. He became a prolific writer of one-act plays which came to be seen as typical examples of the Theatre of the Absurd, such as *Rhinoceros* (1959). After 1970, his writing was mainly non-theatrical, including essays, children's stories, and a novel. >> absurdism

Ionia [iy**oh**nia] In antiquity, the C part of the W coast of Asia Minor. It was the birthplace of Greek philosophy and science. >> Ephesus; Miletus

Ionian Islands [iy**oh**nian], Gr **Iníoi Nísoi**or **Eptánisos** pop (1995e) 196 000; area 2307 sq km/890 sq mi. Region and island group of W Greece; a chain of about 40 islands, including Corfu; under British control, 1815–64. >> Cephalonia; Corfu; Greece ℹ; Zacynthus

Ionian Sea [iy**oh**nian] Part of the Mediterranean Sea, lying W of the Greek islands and S of Italy. >> Mediterranean Sea

ionic >> **chemical bond**

Ionic order [iy**on**ik] One of the five main orders of classical architecture, displaying slim, usually fluted shafts, and spiral scrolls known as *volutes* on the capitals. It originated in Ionia in the 6th-c BC. >> orders of architecture ℹ

ionization >> **ion**

ionizer [**iy**oniyzer] An electrical apparatus which generates a negative electrical charge that is taken up by airborne particles, including smoke and dust; these are then attracted to earth, thus clearing the air. The electrical activity from appliances such as heaters, computers, and televisions tend to destroy negative charges, leaving the atmosphere with a relative positive charge which is thought to contribute to respiratory problems, headaches, allergies, and depression. >> ion

ionosphere The region of the Earth's upper atmosphere from c.50–500 km/30–300 mi in height where short-wave radiation from the Sun is absorbed and partly ionizes the gas molecules or atoms, removing their outer electrons and leaving them positively charged. The ionized layers reflect short-wavelength radio waves, and so make long-distance radio communication possible. >> atmosphere ℹ; aurora; ion; radio waves; thermosphere

ion plating Coating a metal surface by exposing it to ions of a metal, generated by discharge or thermionically. The ions are directed to the metal by making it the cathode in a low pressure discharge circuit. The process is able to coat intricate surfaces uniformly and firmly. >> ion; metal

Ios [**ee**os] 36°43N 25°17E; area 108 sq km/42 sq mi. Island of the Cyclades, Greece, in the Aegean Sea. Homer is said to have died here. >> Cyclades

Iowa [**iy**ohwa] pop (1995e) 2 865 000; area 145 747 sq km/ 56 275 sq mi. State in NC USA; the 'Hawkeye State'; 29th state admitted to the Union, 1846; became part of USA with the Louisiana Purchase, 1803; became a state, 1846; capital moved from Iowa City to Des Moines, 1857; highest point is Ocheyedan Mound (511 m/1677 ft); almost entirely prairie-land (95%) with rich soil; chief crops corn and soybeans; leads the nation in corn and pig production; industry dominated by food processing and machinery manufacture. >> Des Moines; Louisiana Purchase; United States of America ℹ; RR994

ipecacuanha [ipikakyoo**ah**na] A perennial (*Cephaelis ipecacuanha*) with roots thickened to resemble a string of beads, native to Brazil; flowers small, white, in heads. The roots provide a drug used to induce vomiting and to treat dysentery. (Family: Rubiaceae.)

Iphigeneia [iyfije**niy**a] According to Greek legend, the daughter of Agamemnon and Clytemnestra. She was about to be sacrificed at Aulis as the fleet could not sail to Troy, because the winds were against it. At the last moment she was saved by Artemis. >> Agamemnon; Clytemnestra; Trojan War

Ipswich, Anglo-Saxon **Gipeswic** 52°04N 1°10E, pop (1995e) 108 000. Port and county town in Suffolk, E England; at the head of the R Orwell estuary; a major wool port in the 16th-c; railway; home of Thomas Gainsborough; football league team, Ipswich Town. >> Gainsborough; Suffolk

IQ >> **intelligence**

Iqbal, Sir Mohammed [**ik**bal] (1875–1938) Poet and philosopher, born in Sialkot, Pakistan (formerly, India). He achieved fame through his mystical and nationalistic poetry. His efforts to establish a separate Muslim state contributed to the formation of Pakistan. >> Pakistan ℹ

Iquique [ee**kee**kay] 20°13S 70°09W, pop (1995e) 162 000. Free port in N Chile; founded in 16th-c; partly destroyed by earthquake, 1877; airfield; railway. >> Chile ℹ

Iquitos [ee**kee**tohs] 3°51S 73°13W, pop (1995e) 287 000. City in NE Peru; on W bank of the Amazon, 3700 km/ 2300 mi from its mouth; limit of navigation for ocean vessels; access only by air and river; chief town of Peru's jungle region; university (1962). >> Peru ℹ

IRA Abbreviation of **Irish Republican Army**, an anti-British paramilitary guerrilla force established in 1919 by Irish nationalists to combat British forces in Ireland. It was suppressed by the Irish government in the 1922 rising, and remained largely inactive until the late 1960s. In 1969, a major split in its ranks led to the formation of the **Provisional IRA** alongside the **Official IRA**, and a serious schism between the two sides in the early 1970s. The Official IRA generally supported political action to achieve Irish unity. The Provisionals became the dominant republican force, responsible for shootings and bombings in the N of Ireland, Britain, and W Europe. The organization announced a ceasefire (1 Sep 1994), but this was withdrawn (9 Feb 1996) following dissatisfaction with political progress, and a new campaign began, with bombs causing severe damage in Docklands, London, and Manchester, UK. The ceasefire was resumed (20 July 1997), but IRA opposition to the decommissioning of arms continued to hinder the peace process. >> McGuinness; Sinn Féin

Iran [**iran**], formerly **Persia** (to 1935), official name **Islamic Republic of Iran**, Arabic **Jumhuri-e-Eslami-e-Iran** pop (1995e) 65 127 000; area 1 648 000 sq km/ 636 128 sq mi. Republic in SW Asia; capital, Tehran; timezone GMT +3½; major ethnic groups, Persian (63%), Turkic (18%); chief religion, Islam (93% Shiite, 5% Sunni); official language, Farsi, with several minority languages; unit of currency, the rial; largely composed of a vast arid C plateau, average elevation 1200 m/4000 ft; bounded N by the Elburz Mts, rising to 5670 m/18 602 ft at Mt Damavand; Zagros Mts in W and S; mainly a desert climate; hot and humid on Persian Gulf; frequent earthquakes; an early centre of civilization, dynasties including the Achaemenids and Sassanids; ruled by Arabs, Turks, and Mongols until the Safavid dynasty, 16th–18th-c, and the Qajar dynasty, 19th–20th-c; military coup, 1921, with independence under Reza Shah Pahlavi, 1925; protests against his son Mohammed Reza Shah's regime in 1970s led to revolution, 1978; exile of Shah and proclamation of Islamic Republic under Ayatollah Khomeini, 1979; occupation of US embassy in Tehran, 1979–81; Gulf War following invasion by Iraq, 1980–8; US trade sanctions introduced, 1995; governed by a president who appoints other ministers, and a Consultative Assembly; the Faqih is the appointed religious leader with authority to protect the constitution; world's fourth largest oil producer, but production severely disrupted by the 1978 revolution and Gulf War; a third of the population involved in agriculture and forestry. >> Gulf War 1; Iran-Contra scandal; Iranian Revolution; Islam; Khomeini; Pahlavi; Persian Empire; Tehran; RR1012 political leaders

over 60 million people. >> Indo-Iranian languages; Zoroastrianism

Iran–Contra scandal or **Irangate** The popular nickname for a political scandal in 1986 that grew out of the Reagan administration's efforts to obtain the release of US captives held in the Middle East by the covert supply of arms to the government of Iran. In an additional complication, officials (notably, Colonel Oliver North) tried to use the proceeds of arms sales to Iran as a means of financing support for the anti-government *Contra* rebels in Nicaragua, without the knowledge of the president. >> Iran ℹ; Reagan; Watergate

Irangate >> **Iran–Contra scandal**

Iranian languages A branch of the E Indo-European language family, spoken in the region of present-day Iran and Afghanistan. Modern Iranian languages, of which Persian (Farsi) is one of the major examples, are spoken by over 60 million people. >> Indo-Iranian languages; Zoroastrianism

Iranian Revolution A revolution in Iran (1978-9), the consequence of widespread discontent at rapid socio-economic change and the authoritarian rule of the shah. It took the exiled religious scholar Ayatollah Khomeini as its figurehead, and ended with the exile of the shah and the establishment of the Islamic Republic. >> Bani-Sadr; Iran ℹ; Khomeini; Pahlavi

Iran-Iraq War >> **Gulf War 1**

Iraq [**irak**], official name **Republic of Iraq**, Arabic **al-Jumhuriya al-Iraquia** pop (1995e) 20 645 000; area 434 925 sq km/167 881 sq mi. Republic in SW Asia; capital, Baghdad; timezone GMT +3; major ethnic groups 79% Arab, 16% Kurd (largely in NE); chief religion, Islam; official language, Arabic; unit of currency, the dinar; largely comprises the vast alluvial tract of the Tigris–Euphrates lowland (ancient Mesopotamia); rivers join to form the navigable Shatt al-Arab; mountains (NE) rise to over 3000 m/9800 ft; desert in other areas; mainly arid climate; summers very hot and dry; winters often cold; part of the Ottoman Empire from 16th-c until World War 1; captured by British forces, 1916; British-mandated territory, 1921; independence under Hashemite dynasty, 1932; monarchy replaced by military rule, 1958; since 1960s, Kurdish nationalists in NE fighting to establish a separate state; invasion of Iran, 1980, led to the Iran–Iraq War, lasting until 1988; invasion and annexation of Kuwait, Aug 1990; UN sanctions led to the 1991 Gulf War (Jan–Feb), and Iraqi withdrawal; UN imposed a no-fly zone over S Iraq to protect the Shiites, and a security zone in N Iraq to protect Kurdish refugees, 1992; ongoing confrontation with UN (1997–8) over access of weapons inspectors to sensitive sites, leading to US/UK air-strikes (Operation Desert Fox) in December 1998; a democratic socialist republic, governed by Revolutionary Command Council, which elects a president; Kurdish regional assembly has limited powers of legislation; world's sec-

ond largest producer of oil, but production severely disrupted during both wars, with several oil installations destroyed; 1991 war caused major damage to several cities, industrial plants, and infrastructure; rich archaeological remains, especially along the Euphrates valley. >> Baghdad; Gulf War; Hussein; Islam; Kurds; RR1012 political leaders

Ireland (island) Lat **Hibernia** Island on W fringe of Europe, separated from Great Britain by the Irish Sea; maximum length 486 km/302 mi, maximum width 275 km/171 mi; since 1921, divided politically into the independent 26 counties of the **Republic of Ireland** (area 70 282 sq km/ 27 129 sq mi; pop (1995e) 3 499 000), and **Northern Ireland**, part of the UK, containing six of the nine counties of the ancient province of Ulster (area 14 120 sq km/5450 sq mi; pop (1995e) 1 631 000); known poetically as **Erin**, the name is also in widespread use for the Republic of Ireland. >> Ireland (republic) ℹ; Northern Ireland ℹ

Ireland (republic), Ir **Eire** [**ay**ruh], official name also **Republic of Ireland** pop (1995e) 3 499 000; area 70 282 sq km/ 27 129 sq mi. Republic occupying S, C, and NW Ireland, divided into 26 counties grouped into the four provinces of Ulster, Munster, Leinster, and Connacht; bounded NE by Northern Ireland, part of the UK; capital, Dublin; timezone GMT; population largely Celtic; main religion, Roman Catholic (92%); official languages, Irish Gaelic and English; main Gaelic-speaking area (W) known as the *Gaeltacht*; unit of currency, the Irish pound (*punt*); mountainous landscapes in W and SW, creating a landscape of ridges and valleys; lowlands in the E; mild and equable climate; rainfall heaviest in W; occupied by Goidelic-speaking Celts during the Iron Age; high kingship established AD c.200, capital at Tara (Meath); conversion to Christianity by St Patrick, 5th-c; SE attacked by Vikings, c.800; Henry II of England declared himself lord of Ireland, 1171, but English influence restricted to area round Dublin (the Pale); Henry VIII took the title 'King of Ireland', 1542; Catholic rebellion suppressed by Oliver Cromwell, 1649–50, during English Civil War; supporters of deposed Catholic King James II defeated by William III at the Battle of the Boyne, 1690; struggle for Irish freedom developed in 18th–19th-c, including such revolutionary movements as Wolfe Tone's United Irishmen, 1796–8, and later Young Ireland, 1848, and the Fenians, 1866–7; Act of Union, 1801; Catholic Relief Act (1829), enabling Catholics to sit in parliament; Land Acts (1870–1903), attacking Irish poverty; 1846 famine, reduced population by over 2 million; two Home Rule Bills introduced by Gladstone (1886, 1893); third Home Rule Bill passed in 1914, but never came into effect because of World War 1; armed rebellion, 1916; republic proclaimed by Sinn Féin, 1919; partition proposed by Britain, 1920; treaty signed, 1921, giving dominion status, subject to right of Northern Ireland to opt out; this right exercised, and frontier agreed, 1925; renamed Eire, 1937; left Commonwealth, 1949; Anglo-Irish Agreement signed, 1985; a president (head of state) elected for seven years; National Parliament (*Oireachtas*) includes a House of Representatives (*Dáil Eireann*) and a Senate (*Seanad Eireann*); a prime minister (*taoiseach*) is head of government; two-thirds covered by improved agricultural land, with much of the remainder used for rough grazing of sheep and cattle; mainly mixed pastoral farming with some arable cropping; forestry developed since 1950s; fishing; recent growth in light industry; major tourist area; several peat-fired power stations; member of the European Community in 1973. >> Anglo-Irish Agreement; Dublin (city); Fenians; Gladstone; Grattan; Ireland ℹ (island); Irish; Irish Famine; Land League; Northern Ireland; O'Connell; Parnell; Patrick, St; Sinn Féin; Tone; Young Ireland; RR1012 political leaders

Ireland, John (Nicholson) (1879–1962) Composer, born at Bowdon, Cheshire. He established his reputation with his Second Violin Sonata (1917), and between the wars was a prominent member of the English musical renaissance.

Irenaeus, St [ire**nay**us] (c.130–c.200) One of the Christian Fathers of the Greek Church, probably born near Smyrna. He is chiefly known for his opposition to Gnosticism, and for his attempts to prevent a rupture between Eastern and Western Churches over the computing of Easter. Feast day 28 June (W), 23 August (E). >> Easter; Gnosticism

Irene [iy**ree**nee] In Greek mythology, a personification of 'peace'; one of the Horae, or 'seasons'.

Ireton, Henry [**iy(r)**tn] (1611–51) English soldier, born in Attenborough, Nottinghamshire. Cromwell's son-in-law from 1646, he was one of the most implacable enemies of the king, and signed the warrant for his execution. >> English Civil War

Irgun (Zvai Leumi) [ir**gun**zviy **loo**mee] (Heb 'National Military Organization') A Jewish commando group in Palestine, founded in 1937, whose aim was the establishment of the State of Israel by any means. Led by Menachem Begin, it was the nucleus for the Herut Party in Israel. >> Begin; Israel ⓘ

Irian Jaya [irian **jiy**ah], Eng **West Irian**, formerly **Dutch New Guinea** pop (1995e) 1 794 000; area 421 981 sq km/ 162 885 sq mi. Province of Indonesia, comprising the W half of New Guinea and adjacent islands; rises to 5029 m/16 499 ft at Jaya Peak; part of Indonesia, 1963; ongoing separatist guerrilla movement; capital, Jayapura. >> Indonesia ⓘ

iridology [iri**dol**ojee] The detailed study of the visible parts of the eye, especially the iris, which is used as a diagnostic aid in conjunction with other forms of therapy. Iridologists claim that, since the nervous system comes to the body surface in the eyes, so the condition of all parts of the body is reflected in the eye's appearance. >> alternative medicine; eye ⓘ; iris (anatomy)

iridosmine >> **osmiridium**

iris (anatomy) The coloured part of the vertebrate eye, an opaque diaphragm extending in front of the lens and having a circular opening (the *pupil*). The contraction of these muscle fibres alters pupil size and so regulates the amount of light entering the eye. Bright light decreases and dim light increases pupil size. >> eye ⓘ; iridology

iris (botany) A perennial, sometimes evergreen, native to N temperate regions; flowers large, showy, the parts in threes and structurally complex, often in a combination of colours; fruit a capsule, sometimes with brightly coloured seeds. (Genus: *Iris*, 300 species. Family: Iridaceae.) >> flag (botany); orris

Iris In Greek mythology, the goddess of the rainbow, which seems to reach from Earth to heaven. She therefore became the messenger of the gods.

Irish The Celtic language spoken in Ireland; also known as **Erse**. Designated the first official language of the Republic of Ireland, there are over a million speakers, and an active literary tradition. Most speakers of Irish as a mother-tongue come from the W fringes of the country, which have been designated as an area of protection for the language, the *Gaeltacht*. >> Celtic languages

Irish Famine The widespread starvation of Irish peasantry which followed the effects of potato blight in 1845–7, and the consequent destruction of the crop. Because of starvation and emigration, the population of Ireland fell by almost 25% between 1845 and 1851. >> potato

Irish National Liberation Army (INLA) The military wing of the Irish Republican Socialist Party, a small paramilitary group which committed few terrorist attacks, but was noted for the ruthless nature of those it did carry out. It was responsible for the killing of the Conservative MP Airey Neave (1979). It announced a ceasefire in August 1998. >> IRA; Irish Republican Socialist Party

Irish Republican Army >> **IRA**

Irish Republican Socialist Party A political party formed in 1974 largely as a breakaway group from the official Sinn Féin. It was involved in a feud with the Official IRA in the 1970s, and subsequently moved closer to the Provisional Sinn Féin. >> IRA; McAliskey; Sinn Féin

Irish Sea area 103 600 sq km/39 990 sq mi. Arm of the Atlantic Ocean between Ireland and Great Britain; 210 km/130 mi long by 225 km/140 mi at its widest point. >> Atlantic Ocean

Irish setter A breed of dog, developed in Ireland, with a glossy red-brown coat; hair forming fringes on tail, underside, and backs of legs; also known as **red setter**. >> dog; setter

Irish terrier An active medium-sized terrier with a coarse reddish-tan coat; ears soft, held high; tip of muzzle with a surrounding brush of longer hair; tail docked, but left longer than in most terriers. >> dog; terrier

Irish wolfhound The tallest domestic breed of dog (shoulder height, 80 cm/30½ in); very old breed, used for hunting by the Celts; long (usually grey) coat; soft ears. >> hound

Irkutsk [ir**kutsk**] 52°18N 104°15E, pop (1995e) 645 000. Capital city in S Siberian Russia; founded as a fortress, 1661; airport; on the Trans-Siberian Railway; university (1918); one of the largest economic centres of E Siberia. >> Russia ⓘ; Trans-Siberian Railway

iron Fe (from Lat *ferrum*), element 26, a metal with density of 7·8 g/cm^3, melting point 1535°C. It is the fourth most common element in the Earth's crust, not found uncombined except in some meteorites. Learning to recover (*smelt*) it from its ores (mainly the oxide Fe_2O_3) was a major step in human civilization. Most iron is used as metal, usually alloyed with some quantities of other elements, especially carbon and silicon. Steel is iron alloyed with other metals, mainly vanadium, chromium, manganese, and nickel. It is an essential element in biology, particularly as part of haemoglobin. >> blast furnace ⓘ; chemical elements; corrosion; RR1036

Iron Age >> **Three Age System**

Ironbridge A historic industrial town in the Severn R gorge, Shropshire, the birthplace of England's Industrial Revolution. In 1778–9 Europe's first iron bridge was cast and erected here; 196 ft (59·8 m) long, its centre span 100 ft (30·5 m). Ironbridge Gorge is a world heritage site. >> Industrial Revolution; Williamsburg

ironclad A 19th-c term for warships which were either protected by iron plates or built entirely of iron, and more recently of steel. The first ironclad was the French frigate *La Gloire* of 1859. >> warships ⓘ

Iron Cross A military decoration (an iron cross edged with silver) instituted in Prussia in 1813, reinstated in 1870 for the Franco-Prussian War and as a German medal in 1914 and 1939 for the two World Wars. The ribbon is black, white, and gold.

iron curtain A term used to describe the separation of certain E European countries from the rest of Europe by the political and military domination of the Soviet Union. First used in 1943, the term became widely known after Churchill used it in a speech in 1946. >> Churchill, Winston; Soviet Union

iron lung >> **respirator**

Irons, Jeremy (John) [**iy**onz] (1948–) Actor, born in Cowes, Isle of Wight. He became well known after his role in *The French Lieutenant's Woman* (1981) and the television series *Brideshead Revisited* (1981). Later films include *Reversal of Fortune* (1990, Oscar), *Carrington* (1995), and *The Man in the Iron Mask* (1998).

Ironside, William Edmund Ironside, Baron (1880–1959) British field marshal, born in Ironside, Aberdeenshire. He was Chief of the Imperial General Staff at the outbreak of World War 2, and placed in command of the home defence forces (1940). The 'Ironsides', fast light-armoured vehicles, were named after him. >> civil defence; World War 2

Iroquois [**ir**okwoy] A North American Indian people concentrated in the Great Lakes area. They speak Iroquoian languages of the Hokan-Siouan family, c.49 000 (1990 census). >> Iroquois Confederacy

Iroquois Confederacy [**ir**okwoy] A confederation of Iroquois groups during the 17th–18th-c in upper New York State: the Mohawk, Oneida, Onondaga, Cayuga, and Seneca, later joined by the Tuscarora; also known as the **Iroquois League** or the 'Six Nations'. The League broke up during the American Revolution. >> Iroquois

irradiance >> **radiometry** ⓘ

irrational numbers >> **numbers**

Irrawaddy, River >> **Ayeyarwady, River**

irrigation The application of water to soil and crops. In dry areas water may be applied by flooding or through inter-row channels. More general application techniques include rain guns, sprinklers, and, more expensively, drip lines, which provide water to plants and trees on an individual basis. >> desert

Irtysh, River [ir**tish**] Chief tributary of the R Ob in Kazakhstan and Russia; rises in N China; length, 4248 km/ 2640 mi. >> Ob, River

Irvine (of Lairg), Alexander Andrew Mackay Irvine, Baron (1940–) British judge. He was called to the bar in 1967, and became a QC (1978) and a deputy judge in the High Court (1987). Appointed shadow Lord Chancellor (1992–7), he became Lord Chancellor in 1997. He was made a life peer in 1987.

Irving, Sir Henry, originally **John Henry Brodribb** (1838–1905) Actor and theatre manager, born in Keinton-Mandeville, Somerset. He gained a reputation as the greatest English actor of his time, and in 1878 began a theatrical partnership with Ellen Terry which lasted until 1902. >> Terry

Irving, John (1942–) Novelist, born in Exeter, NH. He made his name with *The World According To Garp* (1978, filmed 1982). Later books include *The Hotel New Hampshire* (1981) and *A Prayer for Owen Meany* (1989).

Irving, Washington, pseudonym **Geoffrey Crayon** (1783–1859) Man of letters, born in New York City. Under his pseudonym he wrote *The Sketch Book* (1819–20), a miscellany containing such items as 'Rip Van Winkle' and 'The Legend of Sleepy Hollow'.

Isaac [**iy**zak] Biblical character, son of Abraham by Sarah, through whose line of descent God's promises to Abraham were seen to continue. He was nearly sacrificed by Abraham at God's command (*Gen* 22). >> Abraham; Bible; Esau; Jacob

Isabella I, also known as **Isabella the Catholic** (1451–1504) Queen of Castile (1474–1504), born in Madrigal de las Altas Torres, the daughter of John II, King of Castile and León. In 1469 she married Ferdinand V of Aragon, with whom she ruled jointly from 1479. During her reign, the Inquisition was introduced (1478) and the Jews expelled (1492). She sponsored the voyage of Columbus to the New World. >> Columbus, Christopher; Ferdinand the Catholic; Inquisition

Isabella of France (1292–1358) Daughter of Philip IV of France, who in 1308 married Edward II of England at Boulogne. She became the mistress of Roger Mortimer, with whom she overthrew and murdered the king (1327). >> Edward II; Mortimer

Isaiah [iy**ziy**a], Heb **Jeshaiah** (8th-c BC) The first in order of the major Old Testament prophets, son of Amoz. A citizen of Jerusalem, he began to prophesy c.747 BC. >> Isaiah, Book of; prophet

Isaiah or **Isaias, Book of** [iy**ziy**a] A major prophetic work in the Hebrew Bible/Old Testament, ostensibly from the prophet Isaiah, active in Judah and Jerusalem in the latter half of the 8th-c BC. Many scholars doubt the unity of the contents. >> Isaiah; Old Testament

ISBN >> **International Standard Book Numbering**

ischaemic / ischemic heart disease >> **coronary heart disease** ⓘ

Isherwood, Christopher (William Bradshaw) (1904–86) Novelist, born in Disley, Cheshire. His best-known works, *Mr Norris Changes Trains* (1935) and *Goodbye to Berlin* (1939), were based on his experiences (1930–3) as an English tutor in Berlin, and later inspired *Cabaret* (musical, 1966; film, 1972). In collaboration with Auden, a school friend, he wrote three prose-verse plays with political overtones, and also *Journey to a War* (1939). In 1939 he emigrated to California to work as a scriptwriter, and where he also developed an interest in Hinduism. >> Auden

Ishiguro, Kazuo [ishi**goo**roh] (1954–) Novelist, born in Japan. His third novel, *The Remains of the Day* (1989, filmed 1993), won the Booker Prize and established his reputation. Later books include *The Unconsoled* (1995).

Ishmael [**ish**mayel] Biblical character, the son of Abraham by Hagar, his wife's maid; expelled into the desert with his mother Hagar from Abraham's household after the birth of Isaac. He is considered the ancestor of the Bedouin tribes of the Palestinian deserts (the Ishmaelites). >> Abraham; Bible

Ishtar [**ish**tah(r)] Originally a Mesopotamian mother-goddess of love and war; also known as **Astarte**; later the goddess of love, identified with the planet Venus. >> Mesopotamia; Tammuz

Isidore of Seville, St [**iz**idaw(r), se**vil**] (c.560–636) Ecclesiastic, encyclopedist, and historian, born either in Seville or Carthagena, Spain. A voluminous writer, his most influential work was the encyclopedia, *Etymologies*. He was canonized in 1598; feast day 4 April.

isinglass [**iy**zingglahs] A pure gelatin found in fish. Its particular use is in the clarification of fermented beverages. The name is also applied to a form of mica, with similar appearance. >> gelatin; micas

Isis [**iy**sis] Ancient Egyptian goddess, wife of Osiris and mother of Horus, sometimes portrayed with horns and the Sun's disc. In Hellenistic and Roman times, she was a central figure in mystery religions. >> Osiris

Islam [iz**lahm**] The Arabic word for 'submission' to the will of God (Allah), the name of the religion originating in Arabia during the 7th-c through the Prophet Mohammed. Followers of Islam are known as Muslims, or Moslems, and their religion embraces every aspect of life. They believe that individuals, societies, and governments should all be obedient to the will of God as it is set forth in the Koran, which they regard as the Word of God revealed to his Messenger, Mohammed. There are five essential religious duties known as the **Pillars of Islam**. (1) The *shahada* (profession of faith) is the sincere recitation of the twofold creed: 'There is no god but God' and 'Mohammed is the Messenger of God'. (2) The *salat* (formal prayer) must be performed at five points in the day (varying with time of sunrise and sunset) while facing towards the holy city of Mecca. (3) Alms-giving through the payment of *zakat* ('purification') is the duty of sharing one's wealth out of gratitude for God's favour, according to the uses laid down in the Koran. (4) There is a duty to fast (*saum*) during the month of Ramadan. (5) The *Hajj* or pilgrimage to Mecca is to be performed if at all possible at least once during one's lifetime. *Sharia* is the sacred law of Islam, and applies to all aspects of life, not just religious practices. There is an annual cycle of festivals, including the Feast of the Sacrifice (*Id al-Adha*), commemorating Abraham's willingness to sacrifice Isaac, which comes at the end of the Hajj pilgrimage, and the *Id al-Fitr*, marking the end of the month of fasting in Ramadan. There are two basic groups within Islam. *Sunni Muslims* are in the majority, and they believe that correct religious guidance derives from the practice or *sunna* of the Prophet. They recognize the first four caliphs as Mohammed's legitimate successors. The *Shiites* comprise the largest minority group, and they believe that correct religious guidance obtains from members of the family of the Prophet, on which basis they recognize only the line of Ali, the fourth caliph and nephew and son-in-law of Mohammed as the Prophet's legitimate successors. There are a number of sub-sects of Islam, and in 1999 there were over 1150 million Muslims throughout the world. >> Allah; ayatollah; Black Muslims; dervish; Druze; Hajj; Hijra; imam; jihad; Kaba; Koran; Mahdi; Mecca; Mohammed; mullah; Muslim Brotherhood; Shiites: Sunnis; Wahhabis; RR981, 982

Islamabad [is**lam**abad] 33°40N 73°08E, pop (1995e) 296 000. Capital city of Pakistan, on the R Jhelum; a modern planned city, built since 1961; two universities (1965, 1974); centre of agricultural region. >> Pakistan ℹ

Islamic law >> **Sharia**

Isle of Man >> **Man, Isle of**

Isle of Wight >> **Wight, Isle of**

Ismailis [izmay**ee**leez] Adherents of a secret Islamic sect, one of the main branches of the Shiites; also known as the **Seveners**. It developed from an underground movement (c.9th-c), reaching political power in Egypt and N Africa in the 10th–12th-c. >> Aga Khan; Islam; Shiites

Ismailiya or **Ismailia** [izmiy**lee**a] 30°36N 32°15E, pop (1995e) 246 000. City in NE Egypt; on W bank of Suez Canal; founded in 1863; railway; market gardening in irrigated area. >> Suez Canal

Ismail Pasha [isma**eel**] (1830–95) Khedive of Egypt, born in Cairo, the second son of Ibrahim Pasha. His massive development programme included the building of the Suez Canal, which was opened in splendour in 1869. >> Egypt ℹ; Suez Canal

isobar 1 In meteorology, a line on a weather map joining places of equal barometric pressure. The closer the lines are together, the stronger the pressure gradient force, and therefore the stronger the winds. >> atmospheric pressure; bar **2** In thermodynamics, a line of constant pressure on a graph, depicting the relationship between volume and temperature. >> thermodynamics

Isocrates [iys**o**krateez] (436–338 BC) Greek orator and prose writer, born in Athens. He became an influential teacher of oratory (c.390 BC), and presented rhetoric as an essential foundation of education. >> rhetoric

isocynate >> **fulminate**

isohyet [iysoh**hiy**et] A line on a weather map joining places receiving equal amounts of rainfall. >> isoline; rainfall

isolationism A foreign policy strategy of withdrawing from international affairs as long as the country's interests are not affected. It was practised most notably by the USA, which kept out of the League of Nations and World War 2 until attacked by the Japanese. >> Monroe Doctrine

isoline [**iy**sohliyn] A line on a map which joins places of equal value; also known as an **isopleth**. For example, on a temperature map, places recording the same temperature are joined by an isotherm. >> isobar; isohyet; isotherm; map

isomers [**iy**sohmerz] Substances having the same molecular formula but with the atoms connected differently. >> molecule

isometrics [iysoh**met**riks] A form of physical exercise in which muscles are contracted, but not allowed to move the associated joints. Muscles are used in this way when exerting force on a closed door or fixed bar. >> muscle ℹ

isopentane >> **pentane**

isopleth >> **isoline**

Isopoda [iys**op**oda] A diverse order of crustaceans characterized by a flattened body and seven similar pairs of thoracic legs; typically bottom-living in aquatic habitats, some (the woodlice), are highly successful in terrestrial habitats. (Class: Malacostraca.) >> crustacean; woodlouse

isoprene [**iy**sohpreen] C_5H_8, IUPAC 2-methylbuta-1,3-diene, boiling point 34°C. A liquid, used in the production of synthetic rubber, it is also the basic unit from which terpene molecules are constructed. >> rubber; terpene

isopropyl >> **propyl**

Isoptera [iys**op**tera] >> **termite**

ISO speed rating The sensitivity to light of photographic material expressed on a numerical scale defined by the International Standards Organization (ISO). It replaces both the former systems established by the American Standards Association (ASA) and a Deutsche Industrie Norm (DIN). A film speed is expressed in the form ISO 200/24°, the first set of digits referring to an arithmetical film speed, the second to a logarithmic system.

isotherm 1 In meteorology, a line on a weather map joining places of equal temperature. >> isoline; temperature ℹ **2** In thermodynamics, a line of constant temperature on a graph, depicting the relationship between volume and pressure. >> thermodynamics

isotopes Species of the same element that are chemically identical, having the same proton number, but of different atomic masses due to a differing number of neutrons in the nucleus. All elements have isotopes. >> chemical elements; radioisotope

Israel, Heb **Yisrael**, official name **State of Israel**, Heb **Medinat Yisrael** pop (1995e) 5 843 000, excluding E Jerusalem and Israeli settlers in occupied territories; area within the boundaries defined by 1949 armistice agreements, 20 770 sq km/8017 sq mi. State in the Middle East; capital, Jerusalem; timezone GMT +2; population mainly Jewish (83%), Arab (11%); chief religions, Judaism (85%), Islam (11%), Christianity and others (4%); official languages, Hebrew, Arabic; unit of currency, the new Israeli shekel; extends 420 km/261 mi N–S; width varies from 20 km/12 mi to 116 km/72 mi; mountainous interior, rising to 1208 m/3963 ft at Mt Meron; mountains in Galilee and Samaria, dropping E to below sea-level in the Jordan–Red Sea rift valley; R Jordan forms part of E border; Negev desert (S) occupies c.60% of the country's area; typically Mediterranean climate in N and C, with hot, dry summers and warm, wet winters; Zionist movement founded by Theodor Herzl, end of 19th-c; thousands of Jews returned to Palestine, then part of the Ottoman Empire; Britain given League of Nations mandate to govern Palestine and establish Jewish national home there, 1922; British evacuated Palestine, and Israel proclaimed independence, 1948; invasion by Arab nations, resulting in armistice, 1949; Six-Day War, 1967, brought Israeli control of the Gaza Strip, Sinai Peninsula as far as the Suez Canal, West Bank of the R Jordan including the E sector of Jerusalem, and the Golan Heights in Syria; Camp David conference between Egypt and Israel, 1978; Israeli withdrawal from Sinai, 1979; invasion of Lebanon, forcing the PLO to leave Beirut, 1982–5; renewed tension since 1988, with uprising of Arabs in occupied territories (the *intifada*); missile attacks by Iraq in Gulf War, 1991; peace agreement with PLO, and planned recognition of Palestine, 1993; withdrawal from Gaza and Jericho, 1994; conflict with Jordan formally ended, 1994; assassination of Yitzhak Rabin, 1995; accord on partial Israeli withdrawal from West Bank population centres, 1995; a parliamentary democracy with a prime minister and cabinet, and a unicameral parliament (*Knesset*); president elected for a

maximum of two 5-year terms; over 90% of exports are industrial products; major tourist area, primarily to the religious centres; a world leader in agro-technology, with areas of intensive cultivation; major irrigation schemes, including the 'National Water Carrier' project to transfer water from L Tiberias in the N to the Negev desert in the S; the *kibbutz* system produces c.40% of food output, but in recent years has turned increasingly towards industry. >> Arab–Israeli Wars; East Bank; Galilee; Gaza Strip; Golan; Hebrew; Jerusalem; Jordan, River; Judaism; Judea; Negev; Palestine; Tel Aviv–Yafo; Tiberias, Lake; West Bank; RR1013 political leaders

Israel, tribes of In the Bible, a confederacy of 12 tribes generally traced to Jacob's 12 sons – six by Leah (Reuben, Simeon, Levi, Judah, Issachar, Zebulun), two by Rachel (Joseph, Benjamin), two by Rachel's maid Bilhah (Dan, Naphtali), and two by Leah's maid Zilpah (Gad, Asher). During the settlement of Canaan and the Transjordan, the tribes were allocated portions of land (*Josh* 13–19); but the Levites, a priestly class, had no allocation and possibly were never a 'tribe' as such, and Joseph's 'tribe' was actually two tribes, traced to his two sons Ephraim and Manasseh (*Gen* 48). The number of tribes was thereby maintained as 'twelve'. >> Bible; Jacob; Ten Lost Tribes of Israel

issuing house A merchant bank which specializes in the issue of shares and bonds on the stock market. >> merchant bank

Istanbul [istan**bul**], or **Stamboul**, formerly **Byzantium** (c.660 BC–AD 330), **Constantinople** (330–1930) 41°02N 28°57E, pop (1995e) 7 280 000. Capital city in NW Turkey, on both sides of the Bosporus; seaport of Turkey; founded and renamed by Constantine I in AD 330 on the site of ancient Byzantium, becoming the new capital of the Roman Empire; remains of ancient Constantinople are a world heritage site; see of the patriarch of the Greek Orthodox Church and of the Armenian Church; airport; railway; five universities (1453, 1773, 1863, 1883, 1911); suspension bridge (first in 1973) links European and Asian sections; Topkapi Palace (15th-c), Hagia Sophia Basilica (6th-c). >> Bosporus Bridge; Constantine I (Emperor); Hagia Sophia; Turkey i

Istria [**ee**stria], Serbo-Croatian **Istra** area 3160 sq km/ 1220 sq mi. Peninsula at the N end of the Adriatic Sea, Yugoslavia; occupied by Croats, Slovenes, and Italians; formerly part of Italy; ceded to Yugoslavia, 1947 (apart from Trieste); chief town, Pula. >> Trieste; Yugoslavia i

i.t.a. Abbreviation of **Initial Teaching Alphabet**, devised in 1959 by UK educationist Sir (Isaac) James Pitman (1901–85), to assist children in the early stages of reading. It is a lower-case system of 44 symbols in which each symbol represents a phoneme, giving a closer correlation between symbol and sound than in traditional English orthography, which it was to supplement. Its popularity has declined since the 1970s. >> alphabet i; graphology; phoneme

Itaipu Dam [**ee**tiypoo] A major earth- and rock-fill gravity buttress dam on the R Paraná at the Brazil–Paraguay frontier; completed in 1985; height 189 m/620 ft. It has the capacity to generate 12 600 megawatts of hydroelectricity, and is claimed to be the largest hydroelectric complex in the world. >> dam; Paraná, River

Italian >> **Romance languages**

Italic languages The early languages spoken in the area of modern Italy. The major language of the group was *Latin*, the language of Rome, evidenced in inscriptions from the 6th-c BC; it is used now only in formulaic contexts of religion, and in public (usually governmental) declamations. The modern Romance languages ultimately belong to the Italic family. >> Romance languages

italic script A sloping style of handwriting introduced by Aldus Manutius of Venice in c.1500, which was later introduced into printing. Today, it has a wide range of functions, including the identification of foreign words, book titles, and emphatic utterance. >> Aldus Manutius; typography

Italy, Ital **Italia**, official name **Italian Republic**, Ital **Repubblica Italiana** pop (1995e) 57 333 000; area 301 252 sq km/116 314 sq mi. Republic of S Europe, comprising the boot-shaped peninsula extending S into the Mediterranean Sea, as well as Sicily, Sardinia, and some smaller islands; capital, Rome; timezone GMT +1; chief religion, Roman Catholicism; official language, Italian, with German also spoken in the Trentino-Alto Adige, French in Valle d'Aosta, and Slovene in Trieste–Gorizia; unit of currency, the lira; Italian peninsula extends c.800 km/500 mi SE from the Lombardy plains; Apennines rise to peaks above 2900 m/9000 ft; Alps (N) form an arc from Nice to Fiume; broad, fertile Lombardo-Venetian plain in basin of R Po; several lakes at foot of the Alps, including Maggiore, Como, and Garda; flat and marshy on Adriatic coast (N); on the Riviera (W), coastal mountains descend steeply to the Ligurian Sea; island of Sicily separated from the mainland by the 4 km/2½ mi-wide Strait of Messina; includes the volcanic cone of Mt Etna (3390 m/11 122 ft); Sardinia rises to 1835 m/6020 ft at Monti del Gennargentu; great climatic variation with relief and latitude; hot and sunny summers, short and cold winters; higher areas of peninsular Italy are cold, wet, often snowy; coastal regions have a typical Mediterranean climate; Adriatic coast colder than the W coast, and receives less rainfall; long hours of sunshine in extreme S during summer; in pre-Roman times, inhabited by the Etruscans (N), Latins (C), and Greeks (S); most regions part of the Roman Empire by 3rd-c BC; invaded by barbarian tribes in 4th-c AD, last Roman emperor deposed in 476; later ruled by the Lombards and by the Franks under Charlemagne, who was crowned Emperor of the Romans in 800; part of the Holy Roman Empire under Otto the Great, 962; conflict between popes and emperors throughout Middle Ages; dispute between Guelphs and Ghibellines, 12th-c; divided among five powers, 14th–15th-c (Kingdom of Naples, Duchy of Milan, republics of Florence and Venice, the papacy); major contribution to European culture through the Renaissance; numerous republics set up after French Revolution; Napoleon crowned Emperor of Italy, 1804; 19th-c upsurge of liberalism and nationalism (*Risorgimento*); unification achieved by 1870 under Victor Emmanuel II of Sardinia, aided by Cavour and Garibaldi; fought alongside Allies in World War 1; Fascist movement brought Mussolini to power, 1922; conquest of Abyssinia, 1935–6, and Albania, 1939; alliance with Hitler in World War 2 led to the end of the Italian Empire; a democratic republic since 1946, when the monarchy was abolished; parliament consists of a Chamber of Deputies and a Senate; a president appoints a prime minister; continued political instability, with over 50 governments in power since the formation of the republic; industry largely concentrated in the N; poorer agricultural region in the S; Po valley a major agricultural region. >> Apennines; Cavour; Garibaldi; Ghibellines; Guelphs; Mussolini; Po, River; Roman history 🛈; Rome; Sardinia; Sicily; RR1013 political leaders

itch An irritating sensation in the upper surface of the skin. It may become a distressing complaint, also known as **pruritus**, which may be localized to one area (eg lice, scabies) or generalized, in which case the skin may appear normal. >> jaundice; scabies; skin 🛈

Ito, Hirobumi [**ee**toh] (1841–1909) Japanese statesman and premier (1885–8, 1892–6, 1898, 1900–1), born in Choshu province. He drafted the Meiji constitution (1889), and played a major role in building up the modern state. >> Meiji Restoration

Itúrbide, Agustín de [ee**toor**bi<u>th</u>ay] (1783–1824) Mexican general, born in Morelia. He became prominent in the movement for Mexican independence, and made himself emperor as Agustín I (1822–3). He was forced to abdicate, and was executed.

IUD >> **contraception**

IUPAC [**yoo**pak] Acronym for **International Union of Pure and Applied Chemistry**, best known as the more-or-less acknowledged authority on chemical nomenclature. Its system attempts to provide clear rules for naming compounds unambiguously.

Iuppiter >> **Jupiter** (mythology)

Ivan III, known as **the Great** (1440-1505) Grand Prince of Moscow (1462–1505), born in Moscow. He succeeded in ending his city's subjection to the Tartars, and in 1472 assumed the title of 'Sovereign of all Russia'.

Ivan IV, known as **the Terrible** (1530–84) Grand prince of Moscow (1533–84), born near Moscow, the first to assume the title of 'tsar' (Lat *Caesar*). In 1564 the treachery of one of his counsellors led him to embark on a reign of terror, directed principally at the feudal aristocracy. He nonetheless did much for Russian culture and commerce. >> boyars

Ivanovo [ee**vahn**ovo], formerly **Ivanovo-Voznesensk** (1871–1932) 57°00N 41°00E, pop (1995e) 487 000. City in C European Russia; on R Uvod; founded, 1871; railway; historic centre of Russia's cotton-milling. >> Russia

Ives, Charles E(dward) (1874–1954) US composer, born at Danbury, CT. His compositions are firmly based in the American tradition, and include four symphonies, chamber music, and many songs.

Iviza >> **Ibiza**

Ivor Novello Awards A British award given annually since 1956 for the best popular song, musically and lyrically. >> Novello

Ivory, James (Francis) (1928–) Film director and writer, born in Berkeley, CA. With Ismail Merchant he formed Merchant-Ivory Productions in 1961, achieving international success with *Shakespeare Wallah* (1965), which he wrote with Ruth Jhabvala. He went on to direct a series of films based on major works in English literature, such as *The Bostonians* (1984) and *Howard's End* (1992). >> Jhabvala; Merchant

ivory Pieces of walrus and elephant tusk, regarded as precious material by many societies throughout the world. Carved ivory ornaments, jewellery and religious objects were produced in China from about the 15th-c BC. Modern concern for wildlife conservation has now strictly curtailed its supply. >> elephant; walrus

Ivory Coast >> **Côte d'Ivoire** ℹ

ivy An evergreen woody climber (*Hedera helix*), growing to 30 m/100 ft, native to Europe and W Asia; adhesive aerial roots; flowers greenish-yellow, 5-petalled; fruits berry-like, black, ribbed, poisonous. (Family: Araliaceae.)

Ivy League A group of long-established and prestigious colleges in NE USA. The league was formally established in 1956 to oversee inter-collegiate sports. >> university

Ivy League

institution	founded
Harvard University, Cambridge, Massachusetts	1636
Yale University, New Haven, Connecticut	1701
University of Pennsylvania, Philadelphia, Pennsylvania	1740
Princeton University, Princeton, New Jersey	1746
Columbia University, New York City, New York	1754
Brown University, Providence, Rhode Island	1764
Dartmouth College, Hanover, New Hampshire	1769
Cornell University, Ithaca, New York	1865

Iwo Jima [eewoh **jee**ma] area c.21 sq km/8 sq mi. The most important and largest of the Volcano Is; in the W Pacific Ocean, 1222 km/759 mi S of Tokyo; 8 km/5 mi long; maximum width 4 km/2½ mi; scene of major battle of World War 2 (1944–5); returned to Japan, 1968.

Ixion [ik**see**on] In Greek mythology, a king of Thessaly, the first murderer; also the father of the Centaurs. He was bound to a wheel of fire, usually located in the underworld. >> centaur

iz(z)ard [**iz**ah(r)d] >> **goat**

Izhevsk [**izhefsk**], formerly **Ustinov** (1985–7) 56°49N 53°11E, pop (1995e) 700 000. Capital city of Udmurtia, Russia; founded, 1760; renamed in honour of Soviet armaments politician, Dmitri Fedorovich Ustinov (1908–84); airfield; railway; university; cultural and educational centre. >> Russia ℹ

Izmir [eez**meer**], formerly **Smyrna** 38°25N 27°10E, pop (1995e) 1 959 000. Port and third largest city in Turkey; severely damaged by earthquakes, 1928, 1939; airfield; railway; two universities (1955, 1982). >> Turkey ℹ

Izzard, Eddie [**iz**ah(r)d] (1962–) British comedian, born in Aden, Yemen. His family moved to the UK, where he worked in street theatre and comedy clubs before devising a theatre act as a stand-up comic. He became nationally known through live videos of his major shows at the Ambassadors (1993) and the Albery (1995) in London.

jabiru [**jab**iroo] A name used for several species of stork; especially *Jabiru mycteria* of Central and South America. >> stork

Jabneh [**jab**ne], or **Jamnia** An ancient city on the coastal plain S of modern Tel Aviv. Famous Jewish scholars gathered there to lay the foundations for the Mishnah. >> Judaism; Mishnah

jacamar [**jak**amah(r)] A bird native to the New World tropics; long bill and tail; iridescent plumage; nests on ground in burrow. (Family: Galbulidae, 15 species.)

jacana [**jak**ana] A bird native to the tropics worldwide; inhabits freshwater lakes and ponds; toes extremely long; walks on floating vegetation; also known as **lily-trotter** or **lotus bird**. (Family: Jacanidae, 8 species.)

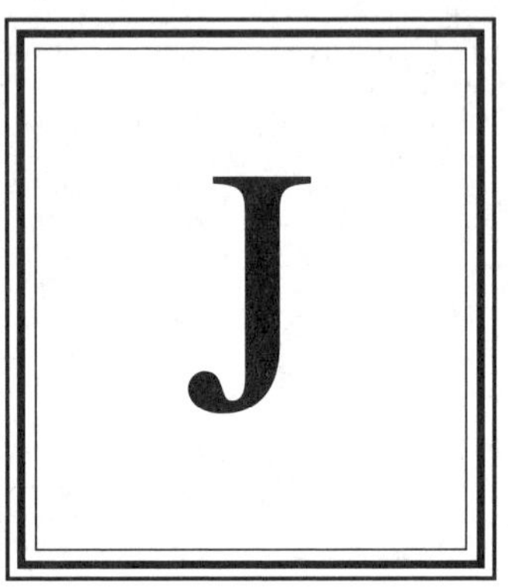

jacaranda A small deciduous tree (*Jacaranda mimosifolia*) growing to 12 m/40 ft; flowers drooping, funnel-shaped, blue. Native to Argentina, it has been widely planted in warm regions as an ornamental and street tree. (Family: Bignoniaceae.)

jacinth [**ja**sinth] A rare red, orange, or yellow gemstone variety of the mineral zircon. >> zircon

Jack the Ripper Unidentified English murderer who, between August and November 1888, murdered and mutilated five prostitutes in the East End of London. The murderer was never discovered, but speculation about the murderer's identity was still continuing in the 1990s.

jackal A member of the dog family, resembling a large fox in appearance and habits; three African species; also, the **golden jackal** (*Canis aureus*) from N Africa to SE Asia. (Family: Canidae.) >> aardwolf; Canidae; fox

jackass >> **kookaburra**

jackdaw Either of two species of bird of the genus *Corvus*: the omnivorous jackdaw (*Corvus monedula*) from N Africa, Europe, and W Asia; and the insect-eating **daurian jackdaw** (*Corvus dauuricus*) from E Asia. Both nest in holes.

Jacklin, Tony, popular name of **Anthony Jacklin** (1944–) Golfer, born at Scunthorpe, North Lincolnshire. He won the 1969 Open at Royal Lytham, and in 1970 won the US Open at Hazeltine (the first British winner for 50 years). He was appointed captain of the European Ryder Cup team in 1983.

jackrabbit >> **hare**

Jack Russell A small terrier, developed in Britain by Rev John Russell (1795–1883); sent into foxes' burrows. >> fox terrier

Jackson 32°18N 90°12W, pop (1995e) 204 000. Capital of state in C Mississippi, USA, on the Pearl R; established as a trading post, 1792; state capital, 1822; named after President Andrew Jackson; much of the city destroyed by Sherman's forces during the Civil War, 1863; airfield; railway; university; many civil rights demonstrations in the 1960s. >> American Civil War; Jackson, Andrew; Mississippi

Jackson, Andrew, nickname **Old Hickory** (1767–1845) US statesman and seventh president (1829–37), born at Waxhaw, SC. In the war of 1812 against Britain, he was given command of the South, and became famous for his defence of New Orleans (1815). His election as president was the result of a campaign in which he gained the support of the mass of voters – a new development in US politics which came to be called 'Jacksonian democracy'. >> War of 1812

Jackson, Betty (1940–) Fashion designer, born in Backup, Lancashire. She became chief designer with Quorum (1975–81), and is now design director of Betty Jackson Ltd. In 1985 she was British Designer of the Year and won the British Fashion Council award.

Jackson, Glenda (1936–) Actress and politician, born in Birkenhead, Merseyside. She became a leading member of the Royal Shakespeare Company before appearing in films in 1967, winning two Oscars for *Women in Love* (1969) and *A Touch of Class* (1973). Later films include *Beyond Therapy* (1985) and *Business as Usual* (1986). She became a Labour MP in 1992.

Jackson, Helen (Maria) Hunt, *née* **Fiske** (1830–85) Writer and campaigner for American Indian rights, born in Amherst, MA. Her foremost works were the non-fiction *A Century of Dishonor* (1881) and the novel *Ramona* (1884). >> civil rights

Jackson, Jesse (Louis) (1941–) Clergyman and politician, born in Greenville, NC. An active participant in the civil rights movement, in 1984 and 1988 he sought the Democratic nomination for the presidency, the first African-American to mount a serious candidacy for the office. >> civil rights; Democratic Party

Jackson, Mahalia (1911–72) Gospel singer, born in New Orleans, LA. The daughter of a clergyman, her strong religious background and the influence of contemporary blues music were unmistakeably evident in her singing style. Two notably successful records were 'Move On Up a Little Higher' and 'Silent Night'.

Jackson, Michael (1958–) Pop singer, born in Gary, IN. With his brothers in the pop group The Jacksons, he knew stardom from the age of 11, and sang on four consecutive Number One hits. His first major solo album was *Off The Wall* (1979), and he consolidated his career with *Thriller* (1982), which sold over 35 million copies, and *HIStory* (1995). He developed a reclusive lifestyle in adulthood, though continuing to tour widely. Worldwide publicity surrounded him in 1993, when allegations about his sexual life caused the cancellation of an international tour on health grounds. He married Lisa Marie Presley in 1994, but they divorced in 1996. Later that year he married Debbie Rowe; their son, Prince Michael, was born in 1997.

Jackson, Thomas Jonathan, nickname **Stonewall Jackson** (1824–63) Confederate general in the American Civil war, born in Clarksburg, WV. During the Civil War, he commanded a brigade at Bull Run, where his firm stand gained him his byname, and showed tactical superiority in the campaign of the Shenandoah valley (1862). He was accidentally killed by his own troops. >> American Civil War

Jacob Biblical character, son of Isaac, patriarch of the nation Israel. He supplanted his elder brother Esau, obtaining his father Isaac's special blessing and thus being seen as the inheritor of God's promises. He fathered 12 sons, to whom Jewish tradition traces the 12 tribes of Israel. >> Bible; Esau; Isaac; Israel, tribes of

Jacobean Style A form of English Renaissance architecture from the period 1603–25. The name derives from King James I of that period. The style is characterized by large windows and a symmetry of facades.

Jacobi, Sir Derek (George) [ja**kohbee**] (1938–) Actor, born in London. He made his professional theatrical debut in 1961, and worked with both the National Theatre and the Royal Shakespeare Company. His roles include *I, Claudius* (1977) and *Cadfael* for television, and the films *Dead Again* (1991) and *Hamlet* (1996); but his main work continues to be in the theatre. In 1995–7 he was associate director of the Chichester Festival Theatre.

Jacobins >> **Dominicans**

Jacobins [**jak**obinz] A radical political group in the French Revolution, based at the premises of the Dominican or 'Jacobin' fathers in Paris (1789). It became the instrument of the Reign of Terror (1793–4), the name being associated thereafter with left-wing extremism. >> French Revolution ℹ

Jacobites Those who supported the claim of the Catholic James II, and his successors, to the British throne. The Jacobites launched two rebellions, in 1715 and 1745, against the Protestant Hanoverian succession. >> Fifteen Rebellion; Forty-five Rebellion; James II (of England)

Jacobson, Dan (1929–) Novelist and short-story writer, born in South Africa, who moved to Britain in 1958. He began writing in the 1950s, with *The Trap* (1955), later novels including *The Beginners* (1966), *Her Story* (1987), and *The God-Fearer* (1993).

Jacopo della Quercia [ya**koh**poh dela **kwair**chia] (c.1374–1438) Sculptor, born in Siena, Italy. His greatest works include the city's fountain (the 'Fonte Gaia', executed 1414–19) and the reliefs on the portal of San Petronia, Bologna. >> Sienese School

Jacopone da Todi >> **Todi, Jacopone da**

Jacquard, Joseph Marie [zhakah(r)] (1752–1834) Silk-weaver, born in Lyon, France. His invention (1801–8) of the Jacquard loom enabled an ordinary workman to produce highly intricate weaving patterns. >> weaving

Jacquerie [**zhak**uhree] (1358) A serious peasant rebellion in NE France, noted for its savagery. Started by mercenaries following the English victory at Poitiers (1356), it ended when the insurgents were massacred.

jade A semi-precious stone, either of two distinct mineral species: the relatively rare *jadeite* (a green pyroxene) which is often translucent, and *nephrite* (a variety of amphibole) which has a waxy lustre. Commonly green or white in colour, it is often used in ornamental carvings. >> amphiboles; gemstones; pyroxenes

jaeger >> **skua**

Jaffa >> **Tel Aviv-Yafo**

Jagger, Mick >> **Rolling Stones**

Jagiellons [yag**yel**onz] The ruling dynasty of Poland-Lithuania, Bohemia, and Hungary, which dominated EC Europe from the Baltic to the Danube in the 15th–16th-c. It was founded when Jagiello, Grand Duke of Lithuania, became King of Poland (1386–1434).

jaguar A big cat (*Panthera onca*), found from S USA to N Argentina; coat with rings of dark blotches surrounding dark spots; some individuals almost black. >> Felidae

jaguarundi or **jaguarondi** [jagwa**run**dee] A member of the cat family (*Felis yagouaroundi*), found from S USA to Paraguay; short legs; long body; grey or reddish-brown. >> Felidae

Jainism [**jiyn**izm] An indigenous religion of India which regards Vardhamana Mahavira (599–527 BC), said to be the last Tirthankara, as its founder. Jains believe that salvation consists in conquering material existence through adherence to a strict ascetic discipline, thus freeing the 'soul' from the working of karma for eternal all-knowing bliss. Liberation requires detachment from worldly existence, an essential part of which is the practice of *Ahimsa*, non-injury to living beings. They numbered nearly 5 million in 1999. >> Ahimsa; karma; Tirthankara

Jaipur [**jiy**poor] 26°53N 75°50E, pop (1995e) 1 575 000. Capital of Rajasthan state, NW India; founded, 1727; railway; university (1947); known as the 'pink city' since 1875, when Sawai Ram Singh had all the buildings of the bazaar painted pink. >> Rajasthan

Jakarta or **Djakarta** [ja**kah(r)**ta], formerly **Batavia** 6°08S 106°45E, pop (1995e) 9 367 000. Seaport capital of Indonesia; on NW coast of Java; largest Indonesian city; developed as a trading post, 15th-c; headquarters of Dutch East India Company, 17th-c; capital, 1949; airport; railway; 11 universities (1950–60). >> Indonesia ℹ

Jakobson, Roman (Osipovich) [**yah**kobson] (1896–1982) Linguist, born in Moscow. The founder of the Moscow Linguistic Circle (which generated Russian formalism), he moved in 1920 to Czechoslovakia (starting the Prague Linguistic Circle), and finally in 1941 to the USA. >> Formalists; linguistics; structuralism

Jamaica pop (1995e) 2 519 000; area 10 957 sq km/4 229 sq mi. Island in the Caribbean Sea; capital, Kingston; timezone GMT −5; chief ethnic groups, African (76%), Afro-European (15%); chief religion, Christianity; official language, English, with Jamaican Creole widely spoken; unit of currency, the Jamaican dollar of 100 cents; third largest island in the Caribbean; maximum length, 234 km/145 mi; width, 35–82 km/22–51 mi; mountainous and rugged, particularly in the E, where the Blue Mts rise to 2256 m/7401 ft; humid and tropical climate at sea-level, more temperate at higher altitudes; visited by Columbus in 1494; settled by Spanish, 1509; West African slave labour imported for work on sugar plantations from 1640; British occupation, 1655; self-government, 1944; independence, 1962; a governor-general appoints a prime minister and cabinet; bicameral parliament consists of a House of Representatives and a Senate; plantation agriculture still employs about a third of the workforce; major producer of bauxite. >> Kingston (Jamaica); RR1013 political leaders

James I (1566–1625) The first Stuart king of England (1603–25), also King of Scotland (1567–1625) as **James VI**, born in Edinburgh Castle, the son of Mary, Queen of Scots, and Henry, Lord Darnley. When he began to govern for himself, he ruled through his favourites, which caused a rebellion, and a period of imprisonment. On Elizabeth's death, he ascended the English throne as great-grandson of James IV's English wife, Margaret. At first well received, his favouritism again brought him unpopularity. >> Authorized Version of the Bible

James II (1633–1701) King of England and Ireland (1685–8), also King of Scotland, as **James VII**, born in London, the second son of Charles I. After he became a convert to

Catholicism, several unsuccessful attempts were made to exclude him from the succession. His actions in favour of Catholicism raised general indignation, and William, Prince of Orange, was formally asked to invade (1688). James escaped to France, where he was warmly received by Louis XIV. He made an ineffectual attempt to regain his throne in Ireland, which ended in the Battle of the Boyne (1690). >> Popish Plot; Stuart, James; William III

James IV (1473–1513) King of Scots (1488–1513), the eldest son of James III. In 1503 he married Margaret Tudor, the eldest daughter of Henry VII – an alliance which led ultimately to the union of the crowns. However, he adhered to the French alliance when Henry VIII joined the League against France, and invaded England. He was killed at the Battle of Flodden, Northumberland. >> Henry VII / VIII; Scotland i

James, St, also known as **St James the Just** (1st-c) Listed with Joseph, Simon, and Judas (*Matt* 13.55) as a 'brother' of Jesus of Nazareth, and identified as the foremost leader of the Christian community in Jerusalem (*Gal* 1.19, 2.9; *Acts* 15.13). Feast day 1 May. >> Jesus Christ

James, St, also known as **St James the Less** (1st-c) One of the 12 apostles. He may be the James whose mother Mary is referred to at the crucifixion of Jesus. Feast day 3 May. >> apostle; crucifixion

James, St, also known as **St James the Great** (1st-c) One of Jesus's 12 apostles, often listed with John (his brother) and Peter as part of an inner group closest to Jesus. According to *Acts* 12.2, he was martyred under Herod Agrippa I (c.44). Feast day 25 July. >> apostle

James, Clive (Vivian Leopold) (1939–) Writer, satirist, broadcaster, and critic, born in Sydney, New South Wales, Australia. His television programmes have been a combination of chat, humour, and commentary, and include *Saturday Night Clive*, as well as a series of 'documentaries' set in cities around the world.

James, Harry (Hagg) (1916–83) Jazz trumpeter and bandleader, born in Albany, GA. He played with Benny Goodman before forming and leading his own band in 1938, and enjoyed success through the 1940s and 1950s. >> Goodman; jazz

James, Henry (1843–1916) Novelist, born in New York City. His work as a novelist falls into three periods. In the first, he is mainly concerned with the impact of American life on the older European civilization, as in *Roderick Hudson* (1875), *Portrait of a Lady* (1881), and *The Bostonians* (1886). From 1869 he made his home in England, chiefly in London and in Rye, Sussex. His second period is devoted to purely English subjects, such as *The Tragic Muse* (1890) and *The Spoils of Poynton* (1897). He reverted to Anglo-American attitudes in his last period, which includes *The Wings of a Dove* (1902) and his masterpiece, *The Ambassadors* (1903). The acknowledged master of the psychological novel, he was a major influence on 20th-c writing.

James, Jesse (Woodson) (1847–82) Wild West outlaw, born in Centerville, MO. He and his brother **Frank James** (1843–1915) led numerous bank, train, and stagecoach robberies before Jesse was murdered for a reward by Robert Ford, a gang member.

James, P D, pseudonym of **Phyllis Dorothy White, Baroness James of Holland Park** (1920–) Detective-story writer, born in Oxford, Oxfordshire. Her novels include *Shroud for a Nightingale* (1971), *Original sin* (1994), and *A Certain Justice* (1997). The futuristic novel *The Children of Men* (1992) represents a new departure.

James, William (1842–1910) Psychologist and philosopher, born in New York City, the brother of the novelist Henry James. His books include *The Principles of Psychology* (1890) and *The Varieties of Religious Experience* (1902). He helped found the American Society for Psychical Research. >> James, Henry; parapsychology

Jameson Raid An expedition against the South African Republic (Dec 1895–Jan 1896), to help topple the government of President Kruger. Leander Starr Jameson (1853–1917), administrator for the South Africa Company at Fort Salisbury, led a detachment of British South Africa Police into the Transvaal, but they were easily defeated. The German kaiser, Wilhelm II, sent a telegram of congratulation to Kruger, and the incident caused a major government crisis in Britain as well as precipitating the resignation of Cecil Rhodes as Cape premier and contributing to the tensions that led to the Boer War. >> Kruger; South Africa i

Jamestown (St Helena) 15°56S 5°44W, pop (1995e) 1400. Seaport capital and only town on the British island of St Helena in the S Atlantic; passenger and cargo services. >> St Helena

Jamestown (USA) A deserted town, 24 km/15 mi inland from Chesapeake Bay, Virginia, USA, the site of the first successful British settlement in America. It was founded in 1607 by 105 settlers as James Fort.

Jammu-Kashmir [**jam**oo kash**meer**] pop (1995e) 8 355 000; area 101 283 sq km/39 095 sq mi. State in the extreme N of India; part of the Mughal Empire, 1586; Afghan rule, 1786; annexed to the Sikh Punjab, 1819; Kashmir asked for agreements with both India and Pakistan at independence, 1947; attacked by Pakistan, and acceded to India; further hostilities, 1965, 1972; summer capital, Srinagar; winter capital, Jammu; governed by a Legislative Council and Legislative Assembly; manufacturing industry largely in Jammu; horticulture widespread in Kashmir. >> India i; Pakistan i

Jamnia >> **Jabneh**

Janáček, Leoš [**ya**nachek] (1854–1928) Composer, born in Hukvaldy, Czech Republic. Devoted to the Czech folksong tradition, he wrote several operas, a Mass, instrumental chamber pieces, and song cycles.

Jane, Frederick Thomas (1865–1916) Naval author, journalist, and artist, born in Upottery, Devon. He founded and edited *Jane's Fighting Ships* (1898) and *All the World's Aircraft* (1909), the annuals by which his name is best known. >> warships i

JANET >> **Joint Academic Network**

janissaries [**jan**isareez] An elite force of Turkish soldiers established in the 14th-c. Throughout their history they mutinied several times, and were finally suppressed.

Jan Mayen [yahn **miy**en], formerly Eng **Hudson's Tutches** area 380 sq km/147 sq mi. Norwegian volcanic island in the Arctic Ocean; length 53 km/33 mi; highest point, Beerenberg (2277 m/7470 ft); discovered by Henry Hudson in 1608; annexed to Norway, 1929; radio and meteorological stations. >> Norway i

Jansen, Cornelius (Otto) [**jan**sen], Dutch [**yahn**sen] (1585–1638) Roman Catholic theologian, founder of the reform movement known as **Jansenism**, born in Acquoi, the Netherlands. His 4-volume work, *Augustinus* (published 1640) sought to prove that the teaching of St Augustine on grace, free will, and predestination was opposed to the teaching of the Jesuit schools. The book was condemned by Pope Urban VIII in 1642, but the controversy raged in France for nearly a century, when a large number of Jansenists emigrated to the Netherlands. >> Roman Catholicism

Jansky, Karl (Guthe) [**yan**skee] (1905–50) Radio engineer, born in Norman, OK. His fundamental discovery (1932) was of radio waves from outer space, which allowed the development of radio astronomy during the 1950s. >> radio astronomy

Januarius, St [janyu**ah**rius], Ital **San Gennaro** (?–c.305) Christian martyr, whose body is preserved in Naples

Cathedral, with two phials supposed to contain his blood. The solid matter in the phials is said to liquefy on his feast day, and at several other times during the year. Feast day 19 September. >> Christianity

Janus (astronomy) [**jay**nuhs] The 10th natural satellite of Saturn, discovered in 1966; distance from the planet 151 000 km/ 94 000 mi; diameter 200 km/120 mi. >> Saturn (astronomy); RR964

Janus (mythology) [**jay**nuhs] An ancient Roman divinity who guards the 'gate' or the door. He became the god of beginnings, and is the god of the first month (January). He is always depicted in art with two faces, one at the back of the head.

Japan, Jap **Nippon** or **Nihon** pop (1995e) 124 641 000; area 377 728 sq km/145 803 sq mi. Island state comprising four large islands (Hokkaido, Honshu, Kyushu, Shikoku) and several small islands off the E coast of Asia; capital, Tokyo; timezone GMT +9; population over 99% Japanese; chief religions, Shinto, Buddhism; official language, Japanese; unit of currency, the yen; islands consist mainly of steep mountains with many volcanoes; Hokkaido (N) central range runs N–S, rising to over 2000 m/6500 ft, falling to coastal uplands and plains; Honshu, the largest island, comprises parallel arcs of mountains bounded by narrow coastal plains; includes Mt Fuji (3776 m/ 12 388 ft); heavily populated Kanto plain in E; Shikoku and Kyushu (SW) consist of clusters of low cones and rolling hills, mostly 1000–2000 m/3000–6000 ft; Ryukyu chain of volcanic islands to the S, largest Okinawa; frequent earthquakes, notably in Kanto (1923), Kobe (1995); oceanic climate, influenced by the Asian monsoon; heavy winter rainfall on W coasts of N Honshu and in Hokkaido; short, warm summers in N, and severe winters, with heavy snow; variable winter weather throughout Japan, especially in N and W; typhoons in summer and early autumn; mild and almost subtropical winters in S Honshu, Shikoku, and Kyushu; summer heat often oppressive, especially in cities; developed into small states by 4th-c; culture strongly influenced by China, 7th–9th-c; ruled by feudal shoguns for many centuries; little contact with the West until the Meiji Restoration, 1868; successful wars with China, 1894–5, and Russia, 1904–5; Korea annexed, 1910; occupied Manchuria, 1931–2; entered Pacific War with surprise attack on the US fleet at Pearl Harbor, Hawaii, 1941; occupied British and Dutch possessions in SE Asia, 1941–2; pushed back during 1943–5; atomic bombs on Hiroshima and Nagasaki, 1945; strong economic growth since 1960s; a constitutional monarchy with an emperor in symbolic role, and a prime minister and cabinet; bicameral Diet (*Kokkai*), with a House of Representatives and a House of Councillors; limited natural resources, with less than 20% of the land under cultivation; intensive crop production (principally of rice); major industrial developments since 1960s especially in computing, electronics, and vehicles. >> Ainu; Fuji, Mount; Hokkaido; Honshu; Japanese; Kyushu; Meiji Restoration; Shikoku; Shogun; Tokyo; World War 2; RR1013 political leaders

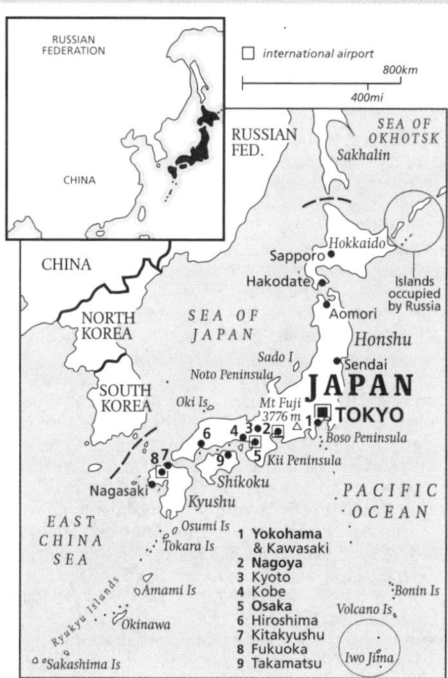

Japan, Sea of area 978 000 sq km/378 000 sq mi. Arm of the Pacific Ocean, bounded by S and N Korea (SW), Russia (N and W), and the islands of Japan (E and S). >> Pacific Ocean

Japanese The language of Japan, spoken by c.122 million in Japan, and a further 2 million elsewhere, mainly in the USA and Brazil. It has written records from the 8th-c in Chinese characters (*kanji*), still used in one of the Japanese writing systems. >> ideography; kanji; syllabary

Japanese tosa >> **mastiff**

japanning A European substitution for Oriental lacquer, produced with layers of copal varnish. Japanned tinwares were produced commercially in Britain in the late 18th-c. >> lacquer

Japheth [**jay**feth] Biblical character, one of the sons of Noah who survived the Flood, the brother of Shem and Ham. He is portrayed as the ancestor of peoples in the area of Asia Minor and the Aegean (*Gen* 10). >> Bible; Flood, the; Noah

Japonaiserie A term used for the imitation of Japanese motifs, patterns, and compositions by European artists from the mid-19th-c to the early 20th-c. >> chinoiserie

japonica [ja**pon**ika] A deciduous, sometimes spiny shrub (*Chaenomeles speciosa*), native to E Asia; flowers 5-petalled, bowl-shaped, usually scarlet, produced on old wood; also known as **flowering quince** or **Japanese quince**. (Family: Rosaceae.)

Jaques-Dalcroze, Emile [zhak dal**krohz**] (1865–1950) Music teacher and composer, born in Vienna, Austria. He originated eurhythmics, a method of expressing the rhythmical aspects of music by physical movement. >> eurhythmics

Jardine, Douglas (Robert) [**jah(r)**din] (1900–58) Cricketer, born in Mumbai (Bombay), India. He was captain of England during the controversial 'bodyline' tour of Australia (1932–3), where he employed Harold Larwood to bowl extremely fast at the batsman's body, the first use of intimidatory bowling in the game. The event almost caused England and Australia to sever diplomatic relations. >> cricket (sport) [i]

Jarrow March (Oct 1936) A march to London by unemployed workers in the Co Durham shipbuilding and mining town, to put the unemployed case. It alerted the more prosperous South and Midlands to the problems of depressed areas. >> Great Depression

Jarry, Alfred [zharee] (1873–1907) Writer, born in Laval, France. His satirical play, *Ubu-Roi*, was first written when he was 15; later rewritten, it was produced in 1896. He wrote short stories, poems, and other plays in a Surrealist style, inventing a logic of the absurd which he called *pataphysique*. >> Surrealism

Jaruzelski, General Wojciech (Witold) [yaru**zel**skee] (1923–) Polish general, prime minister (1981–5), head of state (1985–9), and president (1989–90), born near Lublin, Poland. As premier, in 1981, in an attempt to ease the country's economic problems and to counteract the increasing influence of *Solidarity*, he declared a state of martial law, which was lifted in 1982. >> Poland [i]; Solidarity

jasmine A slender shrub or woody climber, sometimes evergreen; flowers tubular with spreading lobes; fruit a berry. **Winter jasmine** (*Jasminum nudiflorum*), an evergreen shrub native to China, has bright yellow flowers in winter. **Summer jasmine** (*Jasminum officinale*), a deciduous climber native to Asia, has fragrant white flowers in summer. (Genus: *Jasminum*, 300 species. Family: Oleaceae.)

Jason [**jay**sn] In Greek legend, the son of Aeson, King of Iolcos. He was sent on the quest of the Golden Fleece, leading the Argonauts to Colchis; there he obtained the fleece with Medea's assistance. >> Argonauts; Golden Fleece; Medea

Jason, David (1940–) Actor, born in Edmonton, Greater London. Best known as a television actor, his many series include *Open All Hours* (1976, 1981–5), *Only Fools and Horses* (several series), and *The Darling Buds of May* (1990–3). He received BAFTAs for Best Actor (1988) and Best Light Entertainment Performer (1990).

jasper A red variety of chalcedony. >> chalcedony

Jaspers, Karl (Theodor) [**yas**perz] (1883–1969) Philosopher, born in Oldenburg, Germany. His main work is the three-volume *Philosophie* (1932), a systematic exposition of existential philosophy. With the advent of Nazism, he had his work banned, but stayed in Germany, and for his uncompromising stand was awarded the Goethe Prize in 1947. >> existentialism

Jataka [**jah**taka] Stories of the Buddha's previous births, contained in the Buddhist Sutra literature. >> Buddha; Buddhism

jaundice A condition in which there is a rise in the amount of bile pigments (bilirubin and biliverdin) in the blood. These stain the skin and other tissues, including the whites of the eyes, a greenish-yellow colour. Jaundice arises as a result of excessive breakdown of the blood pigment, haemoglobin, severe liver disease, or obstruction in the bile duct, such as a gallstone. >> hepatitis; liver; phototherapy

Jaurès, (Auguste Marie Joseph) Jean [zhohres] (1859–1914) Socialist leader, writer, and orator, born in Castres, France. The main figure in the founding of the French Socialist Party, he was assassinated in Paris. >> socialism

Java (computing) Trade-name of a programming language devised to create machine-independent networking applications; the name derives from Java coffee, whose strong, rich properties were thought by its devisers to be just as applicable to their new language. It has proved to be of special value to designers of pages of the World Wide Web, where special effects on the page can be created by embedding the name of a short program (*applet*) which downloads and runs when the page is accessed. >> programming language

Java (country) [**jah**va], Indonesian **Jawa** pop (1995e) 119 550 000; area 132 187 sq km/51 024 sq mi. Island of Indonesia, in the Greater Sunda group; one of the most densely populated islands in the world; major cities include Jakarta, Bandung, Surabaya; mountainous, rising to 3371 m/ 11 059 ft at Gunung Sumbung; covered with dense rainforest; noted for its batik method of cloth decoration. >> batik; Indonesia [i]; Jakarta; Javanese

Java Man The first known fossil of *Homo erectus*, found in Java in 1891 by the Dutch anatomist Eugène Dubois (1858–1940). It was long known by the name he gave it: *Pithecanthropus erectus*. Subsequent discoveries show specimens to date from ?0·8–0·3 million years ago. >> *Homo* [i]

Javanese The largest ethnic group of Java, Indonesia. Their language (Javanese), a member of the Austronesian family, has a literary tradition dating from the 8th-c. The people are Muslim with some Hindu traditions. >> Indo-Pacific languages; Java (country)

Java Sea Area 430 000 sq km/165 000 sq mi. Sea of SE Asia, bounded N by Borneo, S by Java, and W by Sumatra.

javelin throw An athletics field event of throwing a spear-like javelin. The men's javelin is 2·6–2·7 m/8·6–8·10 ft in length, and weighs 800 g/1 lb 12 oz; the women's javelin is 2·2–2·3 m/7 ft 3 in in length, and weighs at least 600 g/1·5 lb. The current world record for men is 98·48 m/323 ft, achieved by Jan Zelezny (1966–) of the Czech Republic in 1996 at Jenna, Germany; for women it is 80·00 m/262 ft 5½ in, achieved by Petra Meier-Felke (1959–) of Germany, in 1988 at Potsdam, Germany. >> athletics

jaw The upper and lower bones surrounding the mouth, which contain the teeth. The upper jaw (**maxilla**) is usually firmly fixed to the face, while the lower jaw (**mandible**) moves against it. >> mouth; teeth [i]

jay A name used for many birds, usually of the crow family (Corvidae, 42 species), especially the **common jay** (*Garrulus glandiarus*) from N areas of the Old World. >> crow

Jay, John (1745–1829) US statesman and jurist, born in New York City. He became secretary for foreign affairs (1784–9), Chief Justice of the Supreme Court (1789–95), and Governor of New York (1795–1801). He is especially remembered for the American–British treaty of 1794, which has been given his name.

Jayawardene, Junius Richard [jaya**wah(r)**denay] (1906–96) Sri Lankan statesman and president (1978–89), born in Colombo. He became minister of finance (1947–53), Opposition leader (1970–7), prime minister (1977–8), and finally president. >> Sri Lanka [i]

jazz A type of music developed from ragtime and blues in the S states of the USA during the second decade of the 20th-c, originating among black musicians. Prominent features of the earliest New Orleans jazz included *syncopation* (strongly accented rhythms which conflict with the basic pulse of the music), collective *improvisation*, and the exploitation of unusual timbres and extreme ranges in an ensemble which consisted typically of clarinet, trumpet (or cornet), trombone, piano, double bass (played pizzicato), guitar, and drums. >> bebop; blues; Dixieland; improvisation; ragtime; rhythm and blues; salsa; third stream

jazz dance North American form of vernacular dancing performed to the rhythms of jazz. It is a popular dance style, used in musical shows on Broadway and in the UK (eg *Cats*).

Jean de Meung [zhã duh mõe], or **Jean Clopinel** (c.1250–1305) Poet, born in Meung-sur-Loire, France. His great work is the lengthy continuation (18 000 lines) of the *Roman de la Rose*.

Jeans, Sir James (Hopwood) [jeenz] (1877–1946) Astrophysicist and popularizer of science, born in Ormskirk, Lancashire. He made important contributions to the theory of gases, quantum theory, and stellar evolution, and became widely known for his popular exposition of physical and astronomical theories. >> gas 1; quantum field theory

jebeer >> **dorcas gazelle**

Jedda or **Jeddah** 21°29N 39°16E, pop (1995e) 1 947 000. Seaport in WC Saudi Arabia; on the E shore of the Red Sea; Saudi Arabia's commercial capital and largest port; airport; university (1967). >> Saudi Arabia [i]

jeep The name given to a general purpose (GP) light vehicle developed in World War 2 for the United States Army. It became renowned for its exceptional sturdiness and capability for operating on rough terrain, because of its high clearance and four-wheel drive. Its design led to the manufacture of such types as the Range Rover. >> car ℹ

Jefferson, Thomas (1743–1826) US statesman and third president (1801–9), born in Shadwell, VA. He took a prominent part in the first Continental Congress (1774), and drafted the Declaration of Independence (1776). Events of his administration included the Louisiana Purchase (1803) and the prohibition of the slave trade. >> Louisiana Purchase

Jefferson City 38°34N 92°10W, pop (1995e) 36 800. Capital of state in C Missouri, USA, on the Missouri R; city status, 1839; railway; university (1866). >> Missouri

Jeffreys (of Wem), George Jeffreys, Baron, known as **Judge Jeffreys** (1648–89) Judge, born in Acton, Wrexham. His journey to the West Country to try the followers of Monmouth earned the name of *the Bloody Assizes* for its severity. He was Lord Chancellor (1685–8), but on James II's flight was imprisoned in the Tower, where he died. >> Bloody Assizes; James II (of England); Monmouth, James; Popish Plot

Jeffries, John (1744–1819) Balloonist and physician, born in Boston, MA. He settled in England, and in 1785 made the first balloon crossing of the English channel with Jean Pierre Blanchard (1753–1809).

Jehovah [je**hoh**va] Term used since the 11th-c as a form of the Hebrew name for Israel's God, **Yahweh**. It is formed from a combination of the Latinized consonants of the Hebrew word *YHWH* with the vowels of the Hebrew word *Adonai* ('Master, Lord'). >> Yahweh

Jehovah's Witnesses A millenarian movement organized in the USA in 1884 under Charles Taze Russell (1852–1916). They believe in the imminent second coming of Christ, and refuse to obey any law which they see as a contradiction of the law of God – refusing, for example, to take oaths, enter military service, or receive blood transfusions. They numbered 5.9 million in 1998. >> millenarianism

Jellicoe, John Rushworth Jellicoe, 1st Earl [**je**likoh] (1859–1935) British admiral, born in Southampton, Hampshire. Commander-in-chief at the outbreak of World War 1, his main engagement was the Battle of Jutland (1916). He later organized defences against German submarines. >> World War 1

jellyfish A typically bell-shaped, marine coelenterate with a ring of marginal tentacles and a central mouth on the undersurface; body displays a 4-part radial symmetry. (Phylum: Cnidaria. Class: Scyphozoa.) >> coelenterate; medusa

Jenkins (of Hillhead), Roy (Harris) Jenkins, Baron (1920–) British statesman, born in Abersychan, Torfaen, SE Wales. His posts include minister of aviation (1964–5), home secretary (1965–7, 1974–6), and Chancellor of the Exchequer (1967–70). He resigned as an MP in 1976 to take up the presidency of the European Commission (1977–81). He co-founded the Social Democratic Party (1981), and became its first leader, standing down after the 1983 election in favour of David Owen. Defeated in the 1987 election, he was given a life peerage and also became Chancellor of Oxford University. >> Labour Party; Owen, David; Social Democratic Party

Jenkins' Ear, War of A war between Britain and Spain starting in 1739, and soon merging into the wider War of the Austrian Succession (1740–8). The name derives from Captain Robert Jenkins, who claimed to have had an ear cut off by Spanish coastguards in the Caribbean. >> Austrian Succession, War of the

Jenner, Edward (1749–1823) Physician, born in Berkeley, Gloucestershire. In 1796 he inoculated a child with cowpox, then two months later with smallpox, and the child failed to develop the disease. This led to the widespread use of vaccination. >> smallpox; vaccination

Jennings, Pat(rick) (1945–) Footballer, born in Newry, Co Down. A goalkeeper, he played for Watford, Tottenham Hotspur, and Arsenal, making 747 League appearances. He is Britain's most capped footballer, playing for Northern Ireland 119 times. He retired in 1986. >> football ℹ

jerboa A mouse-like rodent; moves by jumping; hind legs at least four times as long as front legs; ears large; long tail, with long hairs at tip; does not drink; also known as **desert rat**. (Family: Dipodidae, 31 species.) >> rodent

Jeremiah or **Jeremias, Book of** [jere**miy**a] A major prophetic work of the Hebrew Bible/Old Testament, attributed to the prophet Jeremiah, who was active in Judah c.627–587 BC. The work is notable for its record of the prophet's inner struggles, persecution, and despair. >> Lamentations of Jeremiah; Old Testament

Jeremais >> **Jeremiah, Book of**

Jerez (de la Frontera) [he**reth**], also **Xeres** 36°41N 6°07W, pop (1995e) 184 000. Picturesque town in Andalusia, S Spain, giving its name to *sherry*; airport; noted centre for sherry, wine, and brandy. >> Andalusia; sherry; Spain ℹ

Jericho [**je**rikoh], Arabic **Eriha**, Heb **Yeriho** 31°51N 35°27E, pop (1995e) c.25 000. Oasis town in Israeli-occupied West Bank, W Jordan; focus of the state of Palestine (area 62 sq km/24 sq mi), following Israeli–PLO peace agreement, 1993); 95% Sunni Muslim, 5% Christian; farming, tourism; site of the world's earliest known town, continuously occupied c.9000–1850 BC; scene of famous siege during the Israelite conquest of Canaan, when it is said that the walls fell down at the shout of the army under Joshua. >> Israel ℹ; West Bank

Jerome, St [je**rohm**], originally **Eusebius Hieronymus** (c.342–420) Christian ascetic and scholar, born in Stridon, Croatia. He made the first translation of the Bible from Hebrew into Latin (the *Vulgate*). Feast day 30 September. >> Bible; Christianity

Jerome, Jerome K(lapka) [je**rohm**] (1859–1927) Humorous writer, novelist, and playwright, born in Walsall, Staffordshire. His *Three Men in a Boat* (1889) established itself as a humorous classic.

Jersey pop (1995e) 87 200; area 116 sq km/45 sq mi. Largest of the Channel Is, lying W of Normandy; chief languages, English with some Norman-French; airport; ferries to UK and France; capital, St Helier; noted for its dairy farming (Jersey cattle) and potatoes; tourism; Jersey Zoological

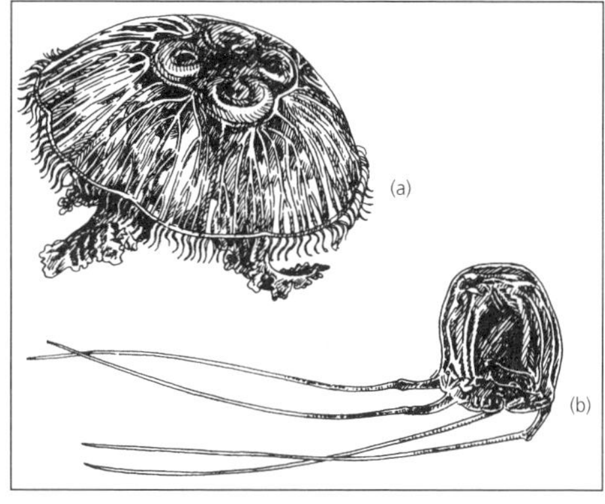

Jellyfish - *Aurelia* (common jellyfish) (a); boxjelly (b)

Park founded by Gerald Durrell in 1959. >> Channel Islands ℹ

Jerusalem, Hebrew **Yerushalayim** 31°47N 35°15E, pop (1995e) 629 000. Capital city of Israel; a holy city of Christians, Jews, and Muslims; old city is a world heritage site, surrounded by a fortified wall and divided into four quarters (Armenian, Muslim, Christian, Jewish); ancient holy city, frequently referred to in Biblical sources; part of Roman Empire (1st-c BC); under Muslim rule until conquered by Crusaders, and Kingdom of Jerusalem established, 1099; retaken by Saladin, 1187; ruled by Ayyubids and Mamluks from Cairo until conquered by the Ottomans in 1516 (ruled until 1917); capital of Palestine, 1922–48; divided between Israel and Jordan by 1949 armistice; declared capital of Israel, 1950, but lacks international recognition; E Jerusalem annexed after Six-Day War, 1967; airfield; railway; Hebrew University (1925); 12th-c Cathedral of St James, Temple Mount, El Aqsa Mosque (705–15), Dome of the Rock (685–705), Western Wall, Church of the Holy Sepulchre (1099), Garden of Gethsemane, Mount of Olives. >> Dome of the Rock; Gethsemane; Israel ℹ; Olives, Mount of; Temple, Jerusalem; Western Wall

Jerusalem artichoke A large perennial growing to 2·8 m/9·2 ft (*Helianthus tuberosus*), a native of North America; numerous underground shoots with potato-like tubers; flower-heads yellow; cultivated for its edible tubers. (Family: Compositae.) >> globe artichoke; tuber

Jespersen, (Jens) Otto (Harry) [**yes**persen] (1860–1943) Philologist, born in Randers, Denmark. He wrote several major works on grammar, and contributed to the development of phonetics and linguistics. He also invented an international language, 'Novial'. >> linguistics

Jesuits A religious order, the **Society of Jesus (SJ)**, founded in 1534 by Ignatius de Loyola. A non-contemplative order, it demands strict obedience, compliance with Ignatius's Spiritual Exercises, and special loyalty to the pope. Jesuits have been leading apologists for the Roman Catholic Church. >> Loyola, Ignatius de, St; pope; Roman Catholicism

Jesus Christ (c.6 /5 BC–AD c.30 /33) The central figure of the Christian faith, whose nature as 'Son of God' and whose redemptive work are traditionally considered fundamental beliefs for adherents of Christianity. 'Christ' became attached to the name 'Jesus' in Christian circles in view of the conviction that he was the Jewish Messiah ('Christ'). Jesus of Nazareth is described as the son of Mary and Joseph, and is credited with a miraculous conception by the Spirit of God. He was apparently born in Bethlehem c.6–5 BC (before the death of Herod the Great in 4 BC), but began his ministry in Nazareth. After having been baptized by John the Baptist in the Jordan, he gathered a group of 12 apostles, and began his public ministry. The main records of his ministry are the New Testament Gospels, which show him proclaiming the coming of the kingdom of God, and in particular the acceptance of the oppressed and the poor into the kingdom. He was mainly active in the villages and country of Galilee, where he performed many healings, exorcisms, and other miracles. The duration of his ministry is uncertain, but was probably a 3-year period. He was executed by crucifixion under the order of Pontius Pilate, the Roman procurator, perhaps because of the unrest Jesus's activities were causing. The date of death is uncertain, but is usually considered to be in 30 or 33. Accounts of his resurrection from the dead and later events are preserved in the Gospels, Pauline writings, and Acts of the Apostles. >> Christianity; crucifixion; Gospels, canonical; John the Baptist, St; Mary (mother of Jesus); Pilate

jet A resinous, hard, black variety of lignite, formed from wood buried on the sea floor. It is often polished, and used in jewellery. >> coal

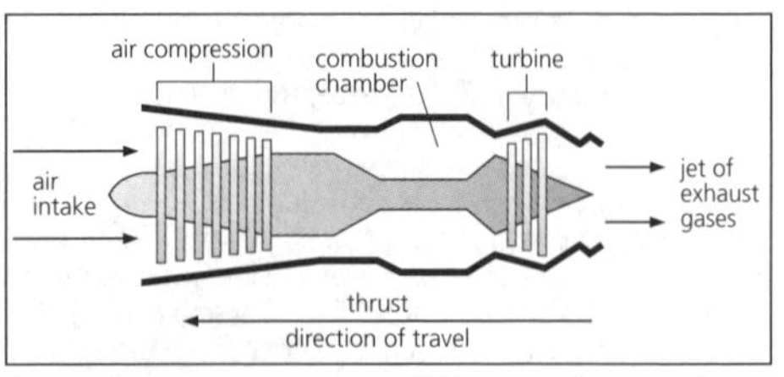

Jet engine

jet engine An engine that accelerates a fluid into its surrounding environment to form a fast-moving jet. The reaction felt by the engine to this expulsion is the *thrust force*, which acts in the opposite direction to the jet. This reactive thrust force is the propulsion force of the engine. >> gas turbine; ramjet

jetfoil A hydrofoil with a waterjet form of propulsion. Water is sucked in from the sea and expelled at great pressure through the after foils. >> hydrofoil

jet lag Unpleasant mental and bodily sensations associated with fatigue, inability to concentrate, and impaired judgment, induced by rapid air travel through several time-zones. The condition usually subsides within a few days and appears to be related to a disturbance in biological circadian rhythms. >> biological rhythm

jew's harp A simple musical instrument held between the player's lips and teeth. A flexible metal tongue is set in motion with the hand, and the pitch and timbre of its vibrations are controlled by the mouth. >> idiophone

Jhabvala, Ruth [jab**vah**la], *née* **Prawer** (1927–) Writer, born in Cologne, Germany. Significant novels include *To Whom She Will Marry* (1955), *The Householder* (1960), and *Heat and Dust* (1975, Booker). Among her notable screenplays are *Shakespeare Wallah* (1965) and *A Room with a View* (1986, Oscar). >> Ivory; Merchant

Jhelum, River [**jay**luhm] River in Asia, the most westerly of the five rivers of the Punjab, Pakistan; rises in the Himalayas, meets the R Chenab SW of Jhang Maghiana; length 725 km/450 mi. >> Pakistan ℹ

Jiang Jieshi [jiang jieshee], or **Chiang Kai-shek** [chang kiy shek] (1887–1975) Leader of the Chinese government and the Guomindang (Nationalist Party) in mainland China (1925–49), then in Taiwan. Born in Zhejiang, in 1918 he joined the separatist revolutionary government of Sun Yixian (Sun Yatsen), and in 1925 launched an expedition against the Beijing government, entering Beijing in 1928. Defeated by communist forces in the civil war, he retreated to Taiwan (1949) where, under US military protection, he maintained unyielding hostility to the new People's Republic. His son, **Jiang Jingguo** (Chiang Ching-kuo, 1918–), became prime minister in 1971 and president in 1978. >> communism; Guomindang; Sun Yixian; Taiwan ℹ

Jiang Jingguo [jiang jinggwoh] >> **Jiang Jieshi**

Jiang Qing [jiang ching], also spelled **Chiang Ch'ing** (1914–91) Third wife of Mao Zedong, born in Zhucheng, Shandong Province, China. An actress in Shanghai, she met Mao Zedong, and became his wife in 1939. Active in revolutionary propaganda, she attacked alleged bourgeois penetration of the arts, and was a leader of the Cultural Revolution (1965–9). After Mao's death (1976) she was arrested with three others, and sentenced to death, though the sentence was later commuted. >> Cultural Revolution; Gang of Four; Mao Zedong

Jiang Zemin (1926–) Chinese president (1993–), born in Yangzhou, Jiangsu Province, China. A cautious reformer, loyal to the party, he was inducted into the Politburo in 1987, and became party leader (1989) and chairman of the Central Military Commission (1990).

Jiddah >> **Jedda**

jig A dance of Great Britain and Ireland, the **Irish jig** involving rapid footwork, a rigidly-held body and vigorous leaps. Several different types are recorded. Jig music is usually in 6/8 time, with some varieties (the **hop** or **slip jig**) in 9/8 time. >> gigue

jihad [jee**had**] (Arabic 'struggle') The term used in Islam for 'holy war'. According to the Koran, Muslims have a duty to oppose those who reject Islam, by armed struggle if necessary, and jihad has been invoked to justify both the expansion and defence of Islam. >> Islam; Koran; Mecca

Jilong [jee**lung**], also **Keelung** or **Chi-lung**, formerly Span **Santissima Trinidad** 25°06N 121°34E, pop (1995e) 368 000. Second largest seaport in Taiwan; occupied by the Spanish and Dutch, 17th-c; destroyed by earthquake, 1867; occupied by the Japanese, 1895–1945; naval base. >> Taiwan ℹ

Jim Crow Laws A nickname for US state laws passed after the end of slavery to keep black people in a segregated subordinate condition. They were abolished in the mid-20th-c. >> civil rights

Jiménez, Juan Ramón [hi**may**neth] (1881–1958) Lyric poet, born in Moguer, Spain. He made his birthplace famous by his delightful story of the young poet and his donkey, *Platero y yo* (1914, Platero and I), one of the classics of modern Spanish literature. He was awarded the Nobel Prize for Literature in 1956.

jimson weed >> **thorn apple**

Ji'nan [jeenahn], **Tsinan**, or **Chi-nan**, nickname **City of Springs** 36°41N 117°00E, pop (1995e) 2 577 000. Capital of Shandong province, E China; founded in 8th-c BC; commercial centre in the Tang dynasty, 618–907; airfield; railway. >> China ℹ

Jinja [**jin**ja] 0°27N 33°14E, pop (1995e) 62 600. Second largest city in Uganda; on the N shore of L Victoria; airfield; railway. >> Uganda ℹ

Jinnah, Muhammad Ali [**ji**na] (1876–1948) Indian Muslim politician, born in Karachi, India (now Pakistan). His advocacy of a separate state for Muslims led to the creation of Pakistan in 1947, and he became its first governor-general. >> Pakistan ℹ

jinni (plural **jinn**), or **genie** In Arab mythology a supernatural creature that could take human or animal form and then interfered, often vengefully, in human affairs. They are frequently mentioned in the Koran and in the collection of oriental tales called *The Arabian Nights*. >> Koran

jird >> **gerbil**

Joachim of Fiore or **Joachim of Floris** [**joh**akim] (c.1135–1202) Mystic, born in Calabria. Abbot of the Cistercian monastery of Corazzo, he is known for his mystical interpretation of history, recognizing three ages of increasing spirituality. >> Bible; Cistercians

Joad, C(yril) E(dwin) M(itchinson) [johd] (1891–1953) Writer and controversialist, born in Durham. He wrote 47 highly personal books, notably *Guide to Philosophy* (1936), and was a fashionable atheist until his last work, *Recovery of Belief* (1952). He is also remembered for his BBC Brains Trust intervention, 'It all depends what you mean by ...'.

Joan, Pope (9th-c) Fictitious personage long believed to have been, as John VII, pope (855–58). One legend claims she was born at Mainz, and elected pope while in male disguise. Her reign is said to have ended abruptly when she died on giving birth to a child during a papal procession. >> pope

Joan of Arc, St, Fr **Jeanne d'Arc**, known as **the Maid of Orléans** (c.1412–31) French patriot and martyr, born into a peasant family in Domrémy. At the age of 13 she heard saints' voices bidding her rescue France from English domination. Clad in a suit of white armour and flying her own standard, she entered Orleans (1429), forced the English to retire, and took the Dauphin to be crowned Charles VII at Rheims. Later captured and sold to the English, she was put on trial (1431) for heresy and sorcery, and burned. She was canonized in 1920. Feast day 30 May. >> Hundred Years' War

Job, Book of [johb] A major book of the wisdom literature of the Hebrew Bible/Old Testament, probably drawing on old popular traditions. Job persists in his struggles until presented with the inscrutable majesty of God directly. >> Old Testament; wisdom literature

Jocasta [joh**kas**ta] In Greek legend, the wife of King Laius of Thebes and mother of Oedipus, later unwittingly becoming the wife of her son; she is called **Epikaste** in Homer. She killed herself when she discovered her incest. >> Oedipus

Jockey Club The controlling body for horse racing in Britain, founded c.1750 at the Star and Garter Coffee House, Pall Mall, London. In 1968 the Jockey Club and National Hunt Committee amalgamated. >> horse racing

Jodl, Alfred [**yoh**dl] (1890–1946) German general, born in Aachen, Germany. He became the planning genius of the German High Command and Hitler's chief adviser. He was found guilty of war crimes at Nuremburg (1946) and executed. >> Hitler; World War 2

Jodrell Bank 53°13N 2°21W. Observatory station in Cheshire, NWC England; leading radio astronomy centre. >> observatory

Joel, Billy (1949–) Singer, songwriter, and pianist, born in Long Island, NY. He earned a gold disk with the album *Piano Man* (1974); later albums include *Stormfront* (1989) and *River of Dreams* (1993).

Joel, Book of One of the 12 so-called 'minor' prophetic writings of the Hebrew Bible/Old Testament, attributed to Joel, of whom nothing is known, but who is today usually assigned to the post-exilic period (c.400–350 BC). >> Old Testament; prophet

Joffre, Joseph Jacques Césaire [zhofruh] (1852–1931) French general, born in Rivesaltes. As French chief-of-staff (1914) and commander-in-chief (1915), he carried out a policy of attrition against the German invaders of France. >> World War 1

Johanan ben Zakkai, Rabban [**yoh**hanan ben **za**kiy] (1st-c) Prominent Jewish teacher and leader of the reformulation of Judaism after the fall of Jerusalem (AD 70), who helped to found rabbinic Judaism. >> Judaism; rabbi

Johannesburg [joh**han**izberg], Afrikaans [yoh**han**uhsberkh], abbreviated **Jo'burg** 26°10S 28°02E, pop (1995e) 1 725 000 (metropolitan area). Largest city in South Africa, and capital of Gauteng province; altitude 1665 m/5462 ft; founded in 1886 after the discovery of gold in the Witwatersrand; airport; railway; two universities (1922, 1966). >> Gauteng; South Africa ℹ; Soweto; Witwatersrand

John, also known as **John Lackland** (1167–1216) King of England (1199–1216), the youngest son of Henry II, born in Oxford, Oxfordshire. He tried to seize the crown during Richard I's captivity in Germany (1193–4), but was forgiven and nominated successor by Richard, who thus set aside the rights of Arthur, the son of John's elder brother Geoffrey. After Arthur was murdered on John's orders (1203), Philip II of France marched against him and conquered all but a portion of Aquitaine (1204–5). In 1206 John refused to receive Stephen Langton as Archbishop of Canterbury, and in 1208 his kingdom was placed under papal interdict. He was then excommunicated (1209), and finally conceded (1213). His oppressive government led to demands for constitutional reform. The barons met the king at Runnymede, and forced him to grant the Great Charter (Magna Carta) (Jun 1215). His repudiation of the Charter precipitated the first Barons' War (1215–17). >> Barons' War; Langton, Stephen; Magna Carta; Richard I

John, St, also known as **John, son of Zebedee** and **John the Evangelist** (1st-c) One of the 12 apostles, son of Zebedee, and the younger brother of James; one of the inner circle of disciples who were with Jesus at the Transfiguration and Gethsemane. He spent his closing years at Ephesus, after having written the Apocalypse, the Gospel, and the three Epistles which bear his name (though his authorship has been disputed). Feast day 27 December.

John XXIII, originally **Angelo Giuseppe Roncalli** (1881–1963) Pope (1958–63), born in Sotto il Monte, Italy. He convened the Second Vatican Council (1962–5) to renew the religious life of the Church, with the aim of eventual unity of all Christians. >> pope; Vatican Councils

John, Augustus (Edwin) (1878–1961) Painter, born in Tenby, Pembrokeshire. His favourite themes were gipsies, fishing folk, and naturally regal women, as in 'Lyric Fantasy' (1913), and he painted portraits of several political and artistic contemporary figures.

John, Sir Elton (Hercules), originally **Reginald Kenneth Dwight** (1947–) Rock singer and pianist, born in Pinner, Greater London. He was one of the top pop stars of the 1970s, known for such songs as 'Rocket Man' and 'Goodbye Yellow Brick Road', and for his clownish garb that included huge glasses, sequinned and fringed jump suits, and ermine boots. His recording of 'Candle in the Wind '97', sung at the funeral of Princess Diana, became the largest-selling single in history within a month of its release. >> pop music

John of Austria, Don, Span **Don Juan** (1547–78) Spanish soldier, the illegitimate son of the Emperor Charles V, born in Regensburg, Germany. He defeated the Moors in Granada (1570) and the Turks at Lepanto (1571). >> Lepanto, Battle of

John of Damascus, St, also called **St John Damascene** (c.675–c.749) Theologian and hymn writer of the Eastern Church, born in Damascus. He defended the use of images in church worship during the iconoclastic controversy. Feast day 4 December. >> iconoclasm

John of Gaunt (1340–99) Duke of Lancaster, the fourth son of Edward III, born in Ghent, Belgium. He became highly influential as a peacemaker during the troubled reign of Richard II. On his second wife's death (1394) he married his mistress, Catherine Swynford, by whom he had three sons; from the eldest descended Henry VII. >> Richard II

John of Leyden (1509–36) Anabaptist leader, born in Leyden, The Netherlands. He went to Münster, became head of the movement, and set up a 'kingdom of Zion', with polygamy and community of goods. In 1535 the city was taken, and John and his accomplices were executed. >> Anabaptists; Zion

John of the Cross, St, originally **Juan de Yepes y Álvarez** (1542–91) Christian mystic, the founder with St Teresa of the Discalced Carmelites, born in Fontiveros, Spain. Imprisoned at Toledo (1577), he wrote a number of poems, such as *Canto espiritual* (The Spiritual Canticle), highly regarded in Spanish mystical literature. He was canonized in 1726; feast day 14 December. >> Carmelites; Teresa of Ávila, St

John the Baptist, St (1st-c) Prophetic and ascetic figure referred to in the New Testament Gospels, the son of a priest named Zechariah; roughly contemporary with Jesus of Nazareth. Seen as a forerunner of Christ, he baptized Jesus and others at the R Jordan. He was executed by Herod Antipas. Feast day 24 June.

John Birch Society A moderately sized, extreme right-wing pressure group in the USA which promotes conservative ideas and policies, and is strongly patriotic and anti-communist. Founded in 1958, the name derives from a US missionary and intelligence officer, killed by Chinese communists on 25 August 1945, who was seen by the Society as the first hero of the Cold War. >> Cold War; Republican Party; right wing

John Bull A personification of the typical Englishman, or of England itself, first depicted in *The History of John Bull* by Arbuthnot. In many political cartoons of the 18th-c and 19th-c, he is drawn as a short stocky figure, often wearing a waistcoat showing the British flag. >> Arbuthnot

John Henry The hero of an American ballad, who pits himself against a steam drill, and succeeds in crushing more rock than the machine, but dies from the effort.

John o'Groats [jonuh**grohts**] Locality in NE Highland, NE Scotland; 'from Land's End to John o' Groats', a common phrase for the length of Britain (970 km/603 mi apart); named after Dutchman John de Groot, who settled in Scotland in the 16th-c. >> Land's End; Scotland ℹ

John Paul I, originally **Albino Luciani** (1912–78) Pope (Aug–Sep 1978), born in Forno di Canale, Italy. The first pope to use a double name (from his two immediate predecessors, John XXIII and Paul VI), he died after only 33 days in office, the shortest pontificate of modern times. >> pope

John Paul II, originally **Karol Jozef Wojtyła** (1920–) Pope (1978–), born in Wadowice, Poland, the first non-Italian pope in 450 years. Ordained in 1946, he was created cardinal in 1967. His pontificate has seen many foreign visits, in which he has preached to huge audiences. In 1981 he survived an assassination attempt, when he was shot in St Peter's Square by a Turkish national, Mehmet Ali Agca, the motives for which have remained unclear. A champion of economic justice and an outspoken defender of the Church in Communist countries, he has been uncompromising on moral issues. >> pope

Johns, Jasper (1930–) Painter, born in Augusta, GA. Attracted by the Dadaist ideas of Marcel Duchamp, he chose to paint flags, targets, maps, and other pre-existing images in a style deliberately clumsy and banal. He was one of the founders of Pop Art. >> action painting; Dada; Duchamp; Pop Art

Johns, W(illiam) E(arl) (1893–1968) Writer, born in Hertford, Hertfordshire. He served in the Royal Flying Corps and RAF, and after 1930 edited *Popular Flying*, where he first wrote his stories featuring Captain James Bigglesworth ('Biggles'). He went on to write over 70 novels.

Johnson, Amy (1903–41) Aviator, born in Hull. She flew solo from England to Australia (1930), to Japan via Siberia (1931), and to Cape Town (1932), making new records in each case. >> aircraft ℹ

Johnson, Andrew (1808–75) US statesman and 17th president (1865–9), born in Raleigh, NC. Made vice-president in 1865, on Lincoln's assassination (1865) he became president. A Democrat, his conciliatory policies were opposed by Congress; he vetoed the congressional measures, was impeached, and acquitted. >> American Civil War; Democratic Party; Lincoln, Abraham

Johnson, Dame Celia (1908–82) Actress, born in Richmond, Greater London. Well established on the stage, she is best remembered on film for her performance in *Brief Encounter* (1945).

Johnson, James Weldon (1871–1938) Writer and diplomat, born in Jacksonville, FL. He became secretary of the National Association for the Advancement of Colored

People (1916–30), and from 1930 was professor of creative literature at Fisk University.

Johnson, Lyndon B(aines), also known as **LBJ** (1908–73) US statesman and 36th president (1963–9), born in Stonewall, TX. Vice-president in 1960, he was made president after Kennedy's assassination, and was returned to the post in 1964 with a huge majority. His administration passed the Civil Rights Act (1964) and the Voting Rights Act (1965), which helped the position of African-Americans in US society. The escalation of the war in Vietnam led to unpopularity, and he retired in 1969. >> civil rights; Kennedy, John F; Vietnam War

Johnson, Magic, popular name of **Earvin Johnson** (1959–) Basketball player; born in Lansing, MI. He played 12 years as a guard for the Los Angeles Lakers (1980–91), was named to the All-NBA (National Basketball Association) team nine times (1983–91), and was voted the league's Most Valuable Player three times (1987, 1990, 1991). He retired from the NBA in 1992 when he tested positive for the HIV virus, but returned to play for the Lakers in 1996. His autobiography was called, simply, *Magic* (1983). >> basketball

Johnson, Pamela Hansford (1912–81) Writer, born in London. Best known for her portrayal of her native post-war London, her books include *An Avenue of Stone* (1947), *A Bonfire* (1981), and several works of nonfiction, such as *On Iniquity* (1967). In 1950 she married the novelist C P Snow. >> Snow, C P

Johnson, Samuel, known as **Dr Johnson** (1709–84) Lexicographer, critic, and poet, born in Lichfield, Staffordshire. From 1747 he worked for eight years on his *Dictionary of the English Language*, started the moralistic periodical, *The Rambler* (1750), and wrote his prose tale of Abyssinia, *Rasselas* (1759). In 1762 he was given a crown pension, which enabled him to figure as arbiter of letters and social personality, notably in The Literary Club, of which he was a founder member (1764). In 1773 he went with Boswell on a tour of Scotland. His chief later work is *Lives of the Poets* (1779–81). His reputation as man and conversationalist outweighs his literary reputation. >> Boswell; dictionary

Johnson, Virginia E >> **Masters and Johnson**

Johor or **Johore** [jo**haw(r)**] pop (1995e) 2 372 000; area 18 985 sq km/7328 sq mi. State in S Peninsular Malaysia, occupying the entire S tip of the peninsula; capital, Johor Baharu. >> Malaysia ℹ

joint The region of contact between bones of the body. **Fibrous joints** allow almost no movement, because the two bones are held firmly together by fibrous tissue. These include the joints between the skull bones, and between the roots of the teeth and the alveolar bone. **Cartilaginous joints** unite two bones by a continuous plate of cartilage, such as those between the bodies of the vertebrae. **Synovial joints** are specialized to allow free movement, and constitute the majority of permanent joints with the limbs. >> arthritis; bone; dislocation (medicine); osteoarthritis; skeleton ℹ; sprain; synovitis; vertebral column

Joint Academic Network (JANET) A computer network provided in the UK to link computer centres in higher education and research establishments, providing electronic mail, file transfer, and the ability for a user at one computer centre to log into the facilities at another. Gateways are provided to other networks. >> computer network

Joint European Torus (JET) A research facility in nuclear fusion comprising a large doughnut-shaped experimental fusion reactor, which became operational in 1983 at Abingdon, Oxfordshire, UK. It stands c.9 m/30 ft high, and weighs c.3000 tonnes. >> nuclear fusion; tokamak

Joinville, Jean, sieur de (Lord of) [zhwĩveel] (c.1224–1317) Historian, born in Joinville, France. He took part in the Crusade of Louis IX (1248–54), in which the army was defeated, and he and Louis were imprisoned at Acre, and ransomed. He later wrote up these events in his *Histoire de Saint Louis* (completed by 1309). >> Crusades ℹ; Louis IX

Joliot-Curie, Irène [zholioh kyooree], *née* **Curie** (1897–1956) Physical chemist, the daughter of Pierre and Marie Curie, born in Paris. In 1934 she and her husband **Frédéric** (1900–58) succeeded in producing radioactive elements artificially, for which they received the 1935 Nobel Prize for Chemistry. >> Curie, Marie; radioactivity

Jolson, Al [**johl**son], originally **Asa Yoelson** (1886–1950) Actor and singer, born in Srednike, Russia, and raised in Washington and New York. His sentimental songs, such as 'Mammy', 'Sonny Boy', and 'Swanee', delivered on one knee, arms outstretched, brought tears to the eyes of vaudeville audiences in the 1920s. >> vaudeville

Jonah or **Jonas, Book of** One of the 12 so-called 'minor' prophetic writings of the Hebrew Bible/Old Testament. It emphasizes Israel's role in addressing the heathen nations. >> Old Testament; prophet

Jonas >> **Jonah, Book of**

Jonathan (c.11th-c BC) Biblical character, the son and heir of Saul (the first King of Israel) and loyal friend of David. He was killed in the battle of Gilboa against the Philistines. >> David; Old Testament; Saul

Jones, Bobby, popular name of **Robert (Tyre) Jones** (1902–71) Golfer, born in Atlanta, GA. He won the (British) Open three times (1926–7, 1930) and the US Open four times (1923, 1926, 1929–30). In 1930 he took the Amateur and Open titles of both countries. >> golf

Jones, Daniel (1881–1967) Phonetician, born in London. He compiled the *English Pronouncing Dictionary* (1917), and produced several influential textbooks. His 'cardinal vowels' act as a reference system for the description of the vowels of real languages. >> phonetics

Jones, (Alfred) Ernest (1879–1958) Psychoanalyst, born in Llwchwy, S Wales. A lifelong disciple and friend of Freud, he introduced psychoanalysis to the UK and USA, founding the British Psychoanalytical Society in 1913. >> Freud, Sigmund; psychiatry

Jones, Henry, pseudonym **Cavendish** (1831–99) Writer on whist and other games, born in London. The author of manuals on several games, he is mainly remembered for his codification of the rules of whist (1862). >> whist

Jones, Inigo (1573–1652) The first of the great English architects, born in London. He studied landscape painting in Italy, and from Venice introduced the Palladian style into England. His designs include the Queen's House at Greenwich (1635) and the Banqueting House in Whitehall (1622), both in London. >> stage

Jones, Jack, popular name of **James (Larkin) Jones** (1913–93) Trade unionist, born in Liverpool, Merseyside. He was general secretary of the Transport and General Workers Union (1969–78), favouring the decentralization of trade-union power to the local branch. >> trade union

Jones, John Paul, originally **John Paul** (1747–92) American naval officer, born in Kirkbean, Dumfries and Galloway. He joined the navy at the outbreak of the War of Independence, and performed a number of daring exploits off the British coast, capturing and sinking several ships. >> American Revolution

Jones, Mary Harris, known as **Mother Jones** (1830–1930) US labour agitator, born in Co Cork, Ireland. She devoted herself to the cause of labour, travelling to areas of labour strife, especially in the coal industry.

Jones, Tom, originally **Thomas Jones Woodward** (1940–) Singer, born in Pontypridd, S Wales. He became known following his hit single, 'It's Not Unusual' (1965). His version of 'Green Green Grass of Home' (1966) was his biggest selling single, other hits including 'What's New Pussycat?' (1965), 'Delilah' (1968), and 'She's a Lady' (1971).

Jones, Sir William (1746–94) Orientalist, born in London. He devoted himself to Sanskrit, whose startling resemblance to Latin and Greek he pointed out in 1787. >> family of languages 🛈; Sanskrit

Jongkind, Johan Barthold [**yong**kint] (1819–91) Painter, born in Lattrop, The Netherlands. He exhibited with the Barbizon painters, and was an important precursor of Impressionism. >> Barbizon School; Impressionism (art)

Jönköping [yoen**koe**ping] 57°45N 14°10E, pop (1995e) 115 000. Industrial town in S Sweden; charter, 1284; railway; focus point for agriculture and forestry. >> Sweden 🛈

Jonson, Ben(jamin) (1572–1637) Playwright, born in London. He joined Henslowe's company, where he killed a fellow player in a duel. His *Every Man in His Humour*, with Shakespeare in the cast, was performed in 1598. His four chief plays are *Volpone* (1606), *The Silent Woman* (1609), *The Alchemist* (1610), and *Bartholomew Fair* (1614), and he also wrote several masques. A major influence on 17th-c poets (known as 'the tribe of Ben'), he was appointed poet laureate in 1617.

Joplin, Scott (1868–1917) Composer and pianist, born in Texarkana, AR. His 'Maple Leaf Rag' (1899) made ragtime music a national craze, and was the first of his several popular rags. Ragtime experienced a revival in the 1970s, and Joplin's music (especially 'The Entertainer') became more widely known. >> ragtime

Jordaens, Jakob [**yaw**dahns] (1593–1678) Painter, born in Antwerp, Belgium. He painted several altarpieces, and became known for his scenes of merry peasant life, such as 'The King Drinks' (1638, Brussels). >> altarpiece

Jordan, official name **Hashemite Kingdom of Jordan**, Arabic **Al-Mamlaka al-Urduniya al-Hashemiyah** pop (1995e) 4 565 000; area 96 188 sq km/37 129 sq mi (including 6644 sq km/2565 sq mi in the West Bank). Kingdom in the Middle East; capital, Amman; timezone GMT +2; population mainly of Arab descent; chief religion, Islam (Sunni, 95%), with Christian and other minorities; official language, Arabic; unit of currency, the Jordanian dinar; divided N–S by Red Sea–Jordan rift valley, much lying below sea-level, lowest point −400 m/−1312 ft at the Dead Sea; highest point, Mt Ram (1754 m/5754 ft); c.90% of Jordan is desert, annual rainfall below 200 mm/8 in; summers uniformly hot and sunny; typically Mediterranean climate elsewhere, with hot, dry summers and cool, wet winters; part of Roman Empire; Arab control, 7th-c; centre of Crusader activity, 11th–12th-c; part of Turkish Empire from 16th-c until during World War 1; area divided into Palestine (W of R Jordan) and Transjordan (E of R Jordan), administered by Britain; Transjordan independence, 1946; British mandate over Palestine ended, 1948; Israel control of West Bank after Six-Day War, 1967; civil war, following attempts by Jordanian army to expel Palestinian guerrillas from West Bank, 1970–1; claims to the West Bank ceded to the Palestine Liberation Organization, 1974; links with the West Bank cut, 1988, prompting the PLO to establish a government in exile; conflict with Israel formerly ended, 1994; a monarchy, in which the king is head of state and of government; parliament consists of a Senate and House of Representatives; oil, phosphate (world's third largest exporter), light manufacturing; major investment in Jordan valley agricultural development. >> Amman; Arab–Israeli Wars; East Bank; PLO; West Bank; RR1013 political leaders

Jordan, River River in the Middle East; rises in the Anti-Lebanon mountains; flows over 320 km/200 mi S through L Tiberias and El Ghor to the Dead Sea; S half separates the East Bank of Jordan from the Israeli-occupied West Bank; many biblical associations, especially with the life of Jesus. >> Israel 🛈; Jesus Christ; Jordan 🛈

Jordan, Dorothea, *née* **Bland** (1762–1816) Actress, born near Waterford, Ireland. For nearly 30 years she kept her hold on the public mainly in comic tomboy roles. In 1790 commenced her connection with the Duke of Clarence, afterwards William IV, which endured until 1811, and by whom she had 10 of her 15 children. >> William IV

Jordan, Michael (Jeffrey), nickname **Air Jordan** (1963–) Basketball player, born in New York City. He played with the Chicago Bulls from 1984, holds the record for most points in an NBA play-off game (63), and was a member of the USA Olympic gold medal-winning team in 1984 and 1992. He announced his retirement in 1993, turned to baseball, but rejoined the Bulls in 1995, and in 1996 took the NBA scoring title for the eighth time to break Wilt Chamberlain's record, and won it again in 1997. In 1998 he won his sixth NBA title with the Chicago Bulls. He retired in 1999. >> basketball

Joseph, St (1st-c BC) Husband of the Virgin Mary, a carpenter in Nazareth, who last appears in the Gospel history when Jesus is 12 years old. Feast day 19 March. >> Jesus Christ

Joseph Biblical character and subject of many stories in *Gen* 37–50; the 11th son of Jacob, but the first by his wife Rachel. He is depicted as Jacob's favourite son (marked by the gift of a multicoloured coat) who was sold into slavery by his jealous brothers, yet who by prudence and wisdom rose to high office in Pharaoh's court. Eventually he is reconciled with his brothers. >> Israel, tribes of; Jacob; Old Testament

Joseph (of Portsoken), Keith (Sinjohn) Joseph, Baron (1918–94) British Conservative statesman, born in London. A former secretary of state for social services (1970–4) and industry (1979–81), he then held the education and science portfolio (1981–6). >> Conservative Party; Thatcher

Joseph, Père, known as **l'Eminence grise** ('Grey Eminence'),

Golan Heights and West Bank occupied by Israel since 1967

originally **François Joseph le Clerc du Tremblay** (1577–1638) French diplomat and mystic, born in Paris. He became Cardinal Richelieu's secretary in 1611. His nickname derives from his contact with Richelieu (the 'Red Eminence'), for whom he went on several important diplomatic missions. >> Richelieu

Joseph of Arimathea, St [arima**thee**a] (1st-c) A rich Israelite, a secret disciple of Jesus, and a councillor in Jerusalem. He went to Pontius Pilate and begged the body of Jesus, burying it in his own rock-hewn tomb. According to tradition, he brought the Holy Grail to England. Feast day 17 March (W), 31 July (E). >> Grail, Holy; Jesus Christ; Pilate

Joséphine de Beauharnais, *née* **Marie Josèphe Rose Tascher de la Pagerie** (1763–1814) First wife of Napoleon Bonaparte, and French empress, born in Trois-Ilets, Martinique. She married Napoleon in 1796, accompanied him on his Italian campaign, and in Paris attracted round her the most brilliant society of France. The marriage, being childless, was dissolved in 1809. >> Napoleon I

Josephson, Brian (David) (1940–) Physicist, born in Cardiff. In 1962 he deduced the existence of **Josephson effects** used in certain superconducting devices. He shared the Nobel Prize for Physics in 1973. >> superconductivity

Josephson constant The international standard of voltage measurement; symbol K_J, defined as $2e/h$, where e is the electron charge and h is Planck's constant; based on the Josephson effect (discovered by Brian Josephson). >> Josephson; volt

Josephus, Flavius [joh**see**fus], originally **Joseph ben Matthias** (c.37–?) Jewish historian and soldier, born in Jerusalem. In Rome he produced several writings on Jewish history and religion, including *History of the Jewish War* (75–9) and *Antiquities of the Jews* (93).

Joshua or **Josue, Book of** A book of the Hebrew Bible/Old Testament named after its main hero, Joshua (originally Hoshea, but renamed by Moses). It continues the stories of the Pentateuch, beginning with the death of Moses. >> Old Testament; Pentateuch

Josiah [joh**siy**a] (7th-c BC) Biblical character, King of Judah (c.639–609 BC). He is credited with destroying pagan cults and attempting to centralize worship in Jerusalem and the Temple. >> Old Testament

Jospin, Lionel [zhospĩ] (1937–) Prime minister of France (1997–), born in Meudon, France. Elected to the National Assembly in 1981, he became first secretary of the Socialist Party (1981–8), then held posts in education (1988–92) and foreign affairs (1992–7), before being elected prime minister.

Josquin des Prez or **Prés** [zhoskĩ day **pray**] (c.1440–1521) Composer, probably born in Condé, France, possibly a pupil of Ockeghem. One of the greatest masters of Renaissance polyphony, he left about 20 Masses and numerous motets. >> Ockeghem; polyphony

Jotunheimen [**yoh**toonhiymn] or **Jotunheim** Highest mountain range in Europe, SC Norway; rises to 2470 m/8104 ft at Glittertind.

Joule, James (Prescott) [jool] (1818–89) Physicist, born in Salford, Greater Manchester. He showed that heat is a form of energy, established the mechanical equivalent of heat, and formulated the absolute scale of temperature. >> energy; joule; Joule–Thomson effect

joule [jool] SI unit of energy, work done, and quantity of heat; symbol J; named after James Joule; defined as the work done by a force of one newton applied over a distance of 1 metre in the direction of the force. >> calorie ℹ; energy; heat; Joule; work

Joule–Thomson effect The change in temperature of a gas when passed through a nozzle and allowed to expand; named after James Joule and William Thomson (Lord Kelvin). For a gas already at low temperature, the expansion produces further cooling. For a gas above a certain temperature, the effect causes warming. >> cryogenics; gas 1; Joule; Kelvin

Jovian [**joh**vian], in full **Flavius Claudius Jovianus** (c.331–64) Roman emperor (363–4), appointed by the army in Mesopotamia on Julian's death in battle. He was immediately forced to make a humiliating peace with Shapur II, ceding great tracts of Roman territory to Sassanian Persia. >> Julian; Shapur II

Joyce, James (Augustine Aloysius) (1882–1941) Writer, born in Dublin. His early work includes short stories, *Dubliners* (1914), and *A Portrait of the Artist as a Young Man* (1914–5). His best-known book, *Ulysses*, appeared in Paris in 1922, but was banned in the UK and USA until 1936. *Work in Progress* began to appear in 1927, and finally emerged as *Finnegans Wake* (1939). His work revolutionized the novel form, partly through the abandonment of ordinary plot for *stream of consciousness*, but more fundamentally through his unprecedented exploration of language. >> stream of consciousness

Joyce, William, nickname **Lord Haw Haw** (1906–46) British traitor, born in New York City. Throughout World War 2, he broadcast from Radio Hamburg propaganda against Britain, gaining his nickname from his upper-class drawl. He was captured by the British, tried, and executed in London. >> World War 2

joystick A computer peripheral, similar to a mouse, which controls the movement of a cursor on a visual display terminal. Like the joystick of an aeroplane, it can indicate movement in any direction. >> mouse (computing)

Juan Carlos I [hwan **kah(r)**los] (1938–) King of Spain (1975–), born in Rome, the grandson of Spain's last ruling monarch, Alfonso XIII (1886–1941). In 1962 he married **Princess Sophia of Greece** (1938–), and they have three children. In 1969 Franco named him as his successor, and he was proclaimed king on Franco's death in 1975. He presided over Spain's democratization, helping to defeat a military coup (1981). >> Franco; Spain ℹ

Juan Fernández Islands [**hwan** fer**nan**dez] Group of three Chilean islands in the Pacific Ocean, 640 km/398 mi W of mainland; total area 181 sq km/70 sq mi; Alexander Selkirk shipwrecked on Robinson Crusoe (1704–9) (basis of Defoe novel, *Robinson Crusoe*). >> Chile ℹ

Juárez, Benito Pablo [**hwah**res] (1806–72) Mexican national hero and president (1861–72), born in San Pablo Guelatao, Mexico. During the civil war of 1857–60, he assumed the presidency, and was elected to that office on the Liberal victory (1861). He successfully resisted the French invasion under Maximilian. >> Maximilian, Ferdinand Joseph; Mexico ℹ

Jubilees, Book of An account purporting to be an extended revelation to Moses during his 40 days on Mt Sinai, a book of the Old Testament Pseudepigrapha, perhaps from the mid-2nd-c BC. It has also been called the *Little Genesis* or the *Testament of Moses*. >> Moses; Pseudepigrapha

Judah, Kingdom of [**joo**da] An ancient Jewish state established when the united monarchy split into the kingdoms of Judah (in the S) and Israel (in the N) in the late 10th-c BC. Jerusalem was in the kingdom of Judah. >> Israel, tribes of; Old Testament

Judaism The religion of the Jews, central to which is the belief in one God, the transcendent creator of the world who delivered the Israelites out of their bondage in Egypt, revealed his law (*Torah*) to them, and chose them to be a light to all humankind. The Hebrew Bible is the primary source of Judaism. Next in importance is the *Talmud*, which consists of the *Mishnah* (the codification of the oral Torah) and a collection of extensive early rabbinical commentary. Various later commentaries and the standard code of Jewish law and ritual (*Halakhah*) produced in the late Middle Ages have been important in shaping Jewish practice and thought. The family is the basic unit of Jewish ritual. The Sabbath, which begins at sunset on Friday and ends at sunset on Saturday, is the central religious observance. The synagogue is the centre for community worship and study. Its main feature is the 'ark' containing the hand-written scrolls of the Pentateuch. The rabbi is primarily a teacher and spiritual guide. There is an annual cycle of religious festivals and days of fasting. The first of these is Rosh Hashanah, New Year's Day; the holiest day in the Jewish year is Yom Kippur, the Day of Atonement. Other annual festivals include Hanukkah and Pesach, the family festival of Passover. Today most Jews are the descendants of either the *Ashkenazim* or the *Sephardim*, each with their marked cultural differences. There are also several religious branches of Judaism. *Orthodox* Judaism (19th-c) seeks to preserve traditional Judaism. *Reform* Judaism (19th-c) represents an attempt to interpret Judaism in the light of modern scholarship and knowledge – a process carried further by *Liberal* Judaism. *Conservative* Judaism attempts to modify orthodoxy through an emphasis on the positive historical elements of Jewish tradition. In 1998 there were nearly 15 million Jews. >> Amidah; Ark of the Covenant; Ashkenazim; Bar Mitzvah; Bible; covenant 2; Gemara; Halakhah; Hanukkah; Holocaust; Israel ℹ; Kabbalah; Kaddish; Kiddush; menorah; Messiah; midrash; Mishnah; Passover; patriarch; Pentateuch; rabbi; Reform Judaism; sabbath; Sephardim; Shema; Star of David; synagogue; Talmud; tefellin; Temple, Jerusalem; Torah; Tosefta; Yom Kippur; Zionism; RR981, 982

Judas Iscariot [is**ka**ryot] (1st-c) One of the 12 apostles of Jesus. He is the one who betrayed Jesus for 30 pieces of silver by helping to arrange for his arrest at Gethsemane by the Jewish authorities (*Mark* 14.43–6). >> apostle; Jesus Christ

Judas tree A deciduous tree (*Cercis siliquastrum*) growing to 10 m/30 ft, native to the Mediterranean region; pea-flowers pink, usually appearing before the leaves; pods up to 10 cm/4 in long. By tradition, this is the tree from which Judas Iscariot hanged himself. (Family: Leguminosae.) >> Judas Iscariot

Jude, St or **Thaddeus** (1st-c) One of the 12 apostles, probably the Judas who was one of the 'brethren of the Lord', the brother of James. A New Testament letter is named after him, but the authorship of the work is disputed. Feast day 28 October (W), 19 June or 21 August (E). >> apostle

Judea [joo**dee**a] Roman–Greek name for S Palestine, area now occupied by SW Israel and W Jordan; chief town, Jerusalem; since 1967, West Bank and E Jerusalem occupied by Israel. >> Israel ℹ; Jordan ℹ; West Bank

judge A public officer with authority to adjudicate in both civil and criminal disputes; in some jurisdictions (eg the USA) this authority is limited to a single branch of law. In the UK, judges are appointed by the Crown on the advice of the prime minister, in the case of the Court of Appeal and House of Lords; and on the advice of the Lord Chancellor, in the case of High Court and circuit judges. Judges are usually appointed from the ranks of experienced barristers. In the USA, state and local judges are often appointed subject to election or confirmation by the public after a fixed time. Federal judges are appointed for life. >> circuit; Court of Appeal; High Court of Justice; recorder

Judges, Book of A book of the Hebrew Bible/Old Testament, with 'judges' referring to the tribal heroes (such as Deborah, Gideon, and Samson) whose acts of leadership are described. Its stories probably underwent editing at several stages of Israel's history. >> Old Testament

judicial review In England and Wales, a legal means of obtaining remedies in the High Court against inferior courts, tribunals, and administrative bodies. A similar procedure is available in other jurisdictions. >> High Court of Justice

Judith, Book of Book of the Old Testament Apocrypha, possibly dating from the Maccabean period (mid-2nd-c BC). It tells the story of how Judith saved the city of Bethulia from siege by the Assyrian army. >> Apocrypha, Old Testament; Maccabees

judo An unarmed combat sport, developed in Japan, and useful in self-defence. Contestants wear a *judogi* (loose fitting suit) and compete on a mat to break their falls. They are graded in their abilty from 5th to 1st *Kyu*, and then 1st *Dan* to the highest, 12th *Dan*. Different coloured belts indicate a fighter's grade. >> martial arts

Jugendstil >> **Art Nouveau**

Juggernaut [**juhg**ernawt] (Sanskrit 'protector of the world') A Hindu deity equated with Vishnu. His temple is at Puri in E India, and is noted for its annual festival. The modern English sense of a massive, irresistible force (and its application to a large, heavy vehicle) is related to the belief that devotees of the god threw themselves beneath the wheels of the cart bearing his image during the festival procession. >> Hinduism; Vishnu

Jugoslavia >> **Yugoslavia** ℹ

jugular veins Blood vessels draining the structures of the head and neck. The **internal jugular vein** returns blood from the brain, face, and much of the neck (particularly the deeper structures). The **external jugular vein** returns blood from the scalp and superficial aspects of the neck. >> neck

Jugurtha [jug**oor**tha] (c.160–104 BC) King of Numidia (118–105 BC), after whom the Jugurthine War (112–104 BC) is named. His surrender to Marius's deputy, Sulla, ended the war, but was the starting point of the deadly feud between Marius and Sulla which plunged Rome into civil war 20 years later. >> Marius; Numidia; Sulla

Juilliard School [**joo**liah(r)d] Music conservatory at Lincoln Center, New York City. Founded in 1905 as the Institute of Musical Art, it is now named after US financier Augustus D Juilliard, following a bequest made upon his death in 1919.

jujitsu The Japanese art of offence and self-defence without weapons, used by the Samurai. Jujitsu forms the basis of many modern forms of other combat sports, such as judo, aikido, and karate. >> martial arts; samurai

jujube [**joo**joob] A deciduous shrub (*Ziziphus jujuba*) growing to 9 m/30 ft, native to the E Mediterranean region; characteristic zig-zag stem and paired spines, one hooked, one straight; flowers yellow; olive-like edible fruits black. (Family: Rhamnaceae.) >> lotus

Julia The name of numerous ladies of the Julian family (*gens*), notably: **1** the wife of Marius and aunt of Julius Caesar; **2** the daughter of Augustus by his first wife Scribonia (39 BC–AD 14), banished for adultery in 2 BC; **3** the daughter of **2** and Agrippa (c.19 BC–AD 28). >> Herod Agripipa I; Marius

Julian, in full **Flavius Claudius Julianus**, known as **Julian the Apostate** (332–63) Roman emperor (361–3), the son of a half-brother of Constantine the Great. He publicly proclaimed himself a pagan, and initiated a vigorous policy of reviving the old pagan cults.

Julian or **Juliana of Norwich** (c.1342–1413) English mystic who probably lived in isolation outside St Julian's Church, Norwich. Her work, *Sixteen Revelations of Divine Love*, has been a lasting influence on theologians stressing the power of the love of God. >> mysticism

Juliana, in full **Juliana Louise Emma Marie Wilhelmina** (1909–) Queen of the Netherlands (1948–80), born in The Hague. On the German invasion of Holland (1940), she escaped to Britain and later resided in Canada. She later became Queen on the abdication of her mother, Wilhelmina, and herself abdicated in favour of her eldest daughter, Beatrix. >> Beatrix; Bernhard Leopold

Julian calendar A calendar established in 46 BC by Julius Caesar, further modified in AD 8, when leap years were correctly implemented, then used in Catholic Europe until 1582, when it was replaced by the Gregorian calendar. Caesar inserted an extra 67 days into 43 BC, and decreed a year of 365 days, with an extra day every fourth year. >> Caesar; Gregorian calendar

Julian date The number of days that have elapsed since 1200 GMT on 1 January 4713 BC, giving a calendar independent of month and year used for analyzing periodic phenomena, epecially in astromony. The Julian day beginning at noon on 1 January 2000 is 2 451 544. Devised in 1582 by Joseph Justus Scaliger (1540–1609), it has no connection with the Julian calendar. >> calendar

July Days (2–5 Jul 1917) Anti-government demonstrations in Petrograd marking a decisive stage in the Russian Revolution. Lenin judged the time for a proletarian-socialist revolution to be premature, and urged restraint. >> Lenin; Russian Revolution

July Revolution (1830) A three-day revolt in Paris which ended the Bourbon Restoration, forcing the abdication of the reactionary Charles X (r.1824–30). It resulted in the establishment of a more liberal regime under Louis Philippe. >> Bourbons; Louis Philippe

Jumblat, Kemal (1919–77) Lebanese Socialist statesman and hereditary Druze chieftain, born in the Chouf Mts, Lebanon. He founded the Progressive Socialist Party in 1949. Following his assassination in an ambush, his son **Walid Jumblat** became leader of the Druze. >> Druze; Lebanon [i]; socialism

Jumna, River >> **Yamuna, River**

jumping bean A seed of *Sebastiania pringlei*, a Mexican shrub of the spurge family Euphorbiaceae. It provides food for the larva of the small moth *Carpocapsa solitaris*, which occupies the seed. Warmth intensifies movement of the larva, causing the 'bean' to jump or jerk erratically. >> moth; spurge

Juneau [**joo**noh] 58°18N 134°25W, pop (1995e) 31 500. Seaport capital of state in SE Alaska, USA; developed as a gold-rush town after 1880; airport; trade centre, with an ice-free harbour. >> Alaska

June War >> **Arab–Israeli Wars**

Jung, Carl (Gustav) [yung] (1875–1961) Psychiatrist, born in Kesswil, Switzerland. He met Freud in Vienna in 1907, became his leading collaborator, and was president of the International Psychoanalytic Association (1911–14). Increasingly critical of Freud's approach, his *Wandlungen und Symbole der Libido* (1911–12, trans The Psychology of the Unconscious) caused a break in 1913. He then developed his own theories, which he called 'analytical psychology', that included a description of psychological types ('extraversion/introversion'); the exploration of the 'collective unconscious'; and the concept of the psyche as a 'self-regulating system' expressing itself in the process of 'individuation'. >> Freud, Sigmund; psychoanalysis

Jungfrau [**yung**frow] 46°33N 7°58E. Mountain peak in the Bernese Alps, SC Switzerland; height 4158 m/13 642 ft. >> Alps

jungle fowl A pheasant native to E India and SE Asia; inhabits forest and scrub; ancestral to the domestic fowl. (Genus: *Gallus*, 4 species.) >> domestic fowl; pheasant

Juninho [zhoo**nee**nyo], popular name of **Osvaldo Giroldo Jr** (1973–) Footballer, born in Brazil. A midfielder, he joined Middlesbrough in 1995 from São Paulo, moving to Atletico Madrid in 1997. He was Footballer of the Year in 1994, and scored on his international debut for Brazil in 1995. A broken leg kept him out of the game for several months in early 1998.

junior high school >> **high school**

juniper An evergreen coniferous tree or shrub native to most of the N hemisphere; leaves needle- or scale-like, in some species on the same tree; cones fleshy, berry-like. The foliage yields an oil used in perfume, and the berries are used to flavour gin. (Genus: *Juniperus*, 60 species. Family: Cupressaceae.) >> conifer; red cedar 2

Junkers [**yung**kerz] Prussian aristocrats whose power rested on their large estates, and on their traditional role as army officers and civil servants. Their position came increasingly under threat in late 19th-c Germany, but they jealously safeguarded their privileges and power. >> Prussia

Juno (astronomy) The third asteroid to be discovered, in 1804. Its diameter is 247 km/153 mi. >> asteroids

Juno (mythology) In Roman mythology, the supreme goddess, and the wife of Jupiter. She was later identified with Hera. >> Hera (mythology); Jupiter (mythology)

Jupiter (astronomy) The fifth planet from the Sun, and the innermost of the giant outer planets. In recent years it has been observed in close-up by Pioneer 10 and 11 spacecraft and by Voyagers 1 and 2. Its basic characteristics are: mass $1{\cdot}901 \times 10^{27}$ kg; equatorial radius 71 400 km/44 400 mi; polar radius 66 750 km/41 476 mi; mean density 1·33 g/cm^3; rotational period 9 h 55 min 41 s; orbital period 11·9 years; inclination of equator to orbit 3·1°; mean distance from the Sun 5·203 AU. It is made primarily of hydrogen (82%) and helium (17%). The face of the planet is covered by clouds, organized into bands, called *belts* and *zones*. Zones are light, and cold (−130°C) because they are high in the atmosphere; belts are darker and warmer clouds (−40°C) at a lower elevation; and a third, warmer level of clouds has also been observed (20°C). The uppermost clouds are inferred to be solid ammonia, the middle clouds ammonium hydrosulphide, and the lowest clouds water. The rotation period at the poles is 5 min longer than that at the equator – a differential which contributes to the formation of a richly coloured banded structure in the cloudy atmosphere. Complex currents and vortices are observed within the bands, including a long-lived atmospheric storm called the *Great Red Spot*. The Jovian moons number at least 16. A dark ring of dust around the planet was discovered by Voyager. >> Galilean moons; Pioneer programme; planet; Shoemaker–Levy 9; Solar System; Voyager project [i]; RR964

Jungle fowl

Jupiter (mythology) or **Iuppiter** The chief Roman god, equivalent to Greek Zeus, originally a sky-god with the attributes of thunder and the thunderbolt. >> Zeus

Jura Mountains [joora] Limestone mountain range in E France and W Switzerland, forming a plateau 250 km/ 155 mi long by 50 km/31 mi wide; highest point in France, Crêt de la Neige (1718 m/5636 ft). >> France ℹ; Switzerland ℹ

Jurassic period [jurasik] A geological period of the Mesozoic era extending from c.213 to 144 million years ago; characterized by large reptiles on land, sea, and air, with shallow seas rich in marine life (eg ammonites), and the appearance of the first birds; mammals still primitive. >> geological time scale; Mesozoic era; RR976

jurisprudence The science or philosophy of law. It has some claim to be regarded as a science of law, in that it seeks to ascertain regularities in human behaviour: judicial behaviourists claim good success rates in predicting the outcome of legal decision-making. >> law

jury A group of persons of varying numbers who decide, on the basis of evidence, matters of fact in criminal or civil cases. They are usually 12 in number, although in Scotland 15 jurors sit in criminal trials. In the USA certain juries also have a role in deciding whether a person should be prosecuted for a particular crime; these juries, known as **Grand Juries**, have up to 23 people sitting on them. In England and Wales jurors are chosen from the electoral roll, and must be aged between 18 and 65. In the USA great effort is taken to ensure that jurors are selected randomly from the general population. In England and Wales a majority verdict (10 to 2) is now permitted, and many US states allow majority verdicts; in Scotland, jurors have in addition to guilty or not guilty, a third verdict of not proven; all that is required is a simple majority of 8 to 7. Certain people are ineligible for jury service (eg members of the Judiciary, the clergy, and the mentally ill) or may be excused (eg MPs, doctors), or disqualified (eg if previously convicted of certain types of offence). Many countries including Italy, France, and Germany have abandoned the institution altogether.

Jussieu [zhüsyoe] The name of a family of French botanists, notably **Bernard de Jussieu** (c.1699–1777), who created the botanical garden at Trianon for Louis XV, and adopted a system which has become the basis of modern natural botanical classification. >> botany

justice of the peace (JP) A judicial appointment, also known as a **magistrate**. Their principal function is to preside in the *magistrates' courts*, administering immediate (or *summary*) justice in the majority of cases, and committing the most serious cases for further trial elsewhere. A legally qualified clerk advises on the law. When trying cases, a JP in Scotland may sit alone, but in England and Wales sits with at least one other colleague. In the USA, JPs are usually elected but sometimes appointed. Magistrates now receive basic training, but no salary. American JPs also have an important role in the performing of marriages. >> stipendiary magistrate; summary trial

Justin (Martyr), St (c.100–c.165) One of the Fathers of the Church, born in Sichem, Samaria. He founded a school of Christian philosophy at Rome, where he is said to have been martyred. Feast day 1 June. >> Fathers of the Church

Justinian [justinian], in full **Flavius Petrus Sabbatius Justinianus** (c.482–565) Roman emperor (527–65), the protégé of his uncle, the Byzantine Emperor, Justin (r.518–27). Through his generals, Belisarius and Narses, he recovered N Africa, Spain, and Italy, and carried out a major codification of the Roman law (the **Justinian Code**), begun in 529.

jute An annual (*Corchorus capsularis*) growing to 3·5 m/ $11\frac{1}{2}$ ft, native to S Asia; flowers yellow. The stems are used in hessian and sacking. (Family: Tiliaceae.)

Jutes A Germanic people whose original homeland was the N part of the Danish peninsula (Jutland). They participated in the 5th-c Germanic invasions of Britain and settled in Kent and the Isle of Wight. >> Anglo-Saxons

Juvenal, in full **Decimus Junius Juvenalis** (c.55–c.130) Roman lawyer and satirist, born in Aquinum, Italy. His 16 verse satires (c.100–128) deal with a wide range of subjects, notably the corruption and immorality of the times.

juvenile court A court specifically concerned with the interests of children and young persons, where the emphasis is on rehabilitation and treatment rather than punishment. Some juvenile courts deal both with those children who have committed offences and with those who are believed to be in need of care and protection as a result of acts committed against them, while others deal solely with young offenders. >> youth court

juvenilia The very early works of writers who later become well-known. Jane Austen's *Minor Works* (published 1932) contain extensive entertaining examples. >> Austen

K

Kaba, Kaaba, or **Kabah** [**ka**ba] The most sacred site in Islam, situated within the precincts of the Great Mosque at Mecca, Saudi Arabia. It is a small cube-shaped building, unadorned except for the sacred Black Stone, a meteorite, set into the E corner of its walls. The stone, or *qibla*, is the focus-point to which Muslims turn when they pray. >> Islam; Mecca

Kabbalah [ka**bah**la] (Heb 'tradition') Jewish religious teachings originally transmitted orally, predominantly mystic in nature, and ostensibly consisting of secret doctrines. Adherents aimed to discover mysteries hidden in the Jewish Scriptures using special methods of interpretation. >> Judaism

Kabuki [ka**boo**kee] Originally a city entertainment in Japan, particularly popular from 1650 to 1850, designed to last from dawn to dusk. Modern performances present selected acts or highlights from the traditional repertoire. >> bunraku; Noh

Kabul [**kah**bul] 34°30N 69°10E, pop (1995e) 1 979 000. Capital city of Afghanistan; in a high mountain valley, commanding the approaches to the Khyber Pass; capital of Mughal Empire, 1504–1738; modern state capital in 1773; university (1931); airport. >> Afghanistan ℹ

Kabyle [ka**beel**] A Berber people of Algeria. They speak Kabyle, an Afro-Asiatic language, and are predominantly Muslims. >> Algeria ℹ; Berber

Kádár, János [**kah**da(r)] (1912–89) Hungarian statesman, premier (1956–8, 1961–5) and first secretary (1956–88), born in Kapoly, Hungary. When the anti-Soviet uprising broke out in 1956, he was a member of the 'national' government of Imre Nagy, but then formed a puppet government which repressed the uprising. >> communism; Hungarian uprising; Nagy; Stalin

Kaddish [ka**deesh**] (Aramaic 'holy') An ancient Jewish congregation prayer, mostly in Aramaic, which marks the closing parts of daily public worship, praising the name of God and seeking the coming of the kingdom of God. >> Judaism

Kafka, Franz [**kaf**ka] (1883–1924) Novelist, born in Prague. His three unfinished novels were published posthumously: *Der Prozess* (1925, The Trial), *Das Schloss* (1926, The Castle), and *Amerika* (1927). He has influenced many authors with his vision of society (often called 'Kafkaesque') as a pointless, rational organization, with tortuous bureaucratic and totalitarian procedures, into which the bewildered individual has strayed.

Kaieteur Falls [**kiy**uhtoor] Waterfall in C Guyana, on the R Potaro; nearly five times the height of Niagara, with a sheer drop of 226 m/742 ft. >> Guyana ℹ

Kaikoura Ranges [kiy**koh**ra] Mountain ranges in NE South Island, New Zealand; length 40 km/25 mi; highest peak, Mt Tapuaenuku (2885 m/9465 ft). >> New Zealand ℹ

Kairouan [kayr**wan**] 35°42N 10°01E, pop (1995e) 88 000. City in NE Tunisia; founded in 671; capital of the Aglabite dynasty, 9th-c; an important Muslim holy city. >> Islam; Tunisia ℹ

Kaiser [**kiy**zer] The title assumed (Dec 1870) by the Prussian king, William (Wilhelm) I, following the unification of Germany and the creation of the German Empire. It was used until 1918. >> William I / II (Emperors)

Kaiser, Georg [**kiy**zer] (1878–1945) Playwright, born in Magdeburg, Germany. His plays established him as a leader of the Expressionist movement, such as *Von Morgens bis Mitternachts* (1916, From Morn to Midnight), *Gas I* (1918), and *Gas II* (1920). >> Expressionism

kakapo [**kah**kapoh] A flightless, ground-dwelling parrot (*Strigops habroptilus*), native to New Zealand, also known as an **owl parrot**; face with owl-like array of radiating feathers; nocturnal; seriously endangered. (Family: Psittacidae.) >> parrot

kakee >> **persimmon**

Kakopetria [kakoh**pet**ria] 34°59N 32°54E. Summer resort town in Cyprus; tomb of Archbishop Makarios III. >> Cyprus ℹ; Makarios III

kala-azar [kahla a**zah(r)**] >> **leishmaniasis**

Kalahari [kala**hah**ree] Desert region of Africa, in SW Botswana, SE Namibia and N Cape Province, South Africa; area c.260 000 sq km/100 000 sq mi; elevation generally 850–1000 m/2800–3280 ft; annual average rainfall over whole area, 150–500 mm/6–20 in; sparsely inhabited by nomads. >> Botswana ℹ; Khoisan; Namibia ℹ

kale A very hardy mutant of cabbage (*Brassica oleracea*, variety *acephala*) with dense heads of plain or curled, green or purple leaves; widely grown as a vegetable and fodder crop. The leaves are sometimes called *borecole*. (Family: Cruciferae.) >> cabbage

Kalevala [**kah**levahla] The name given to a compilation of Finnish legends, published by Elias Lönnrot in 1835, and now regarded as the Finnish national epic. The poem is in a trochaic metre, imitated by Longfellow in *Hiawatha*.

Kalgoorlie [kal**goor**lee], or **Kalgoorlie–Boulder** 30°49S 121°29E, pop (1995e) 26 400. Gold-mining town in Western Australia; gold discovered here, 1887–8; 60% of Australia's gold mined in the suburb of Boulder; airfield; railway; Flying Doctor centre. >> Western Australia

Kali [**kah**lee] The Hindu goddess of destruction, who is also represented as the Great Mother, the giver of life. She is the consort of Shiva. >> Hinduism; Shiva

Kalidaša [kali**dah**sa] (c.5th-c) Indian poet and dramatist, best known through his drama *Abhijnana-Sakuntala* (The Recognition of Sakuntala).

Kalimantan [kali**man**tan] pop (1995e) 8 710 000. Group of four provinces in the Indonesian part of Borneo: **Kalimantan Berat**, **West Kalimantan**, or **West Borneo**, pop (1995e) 3 541 000, area 146 760 sq km/56 649 sq mi, capital, Pontianak; **Kalimantan Selatan**, **South Kalimantan**, or **South Borneo**, pop (1995e) 2 840 000, area 37 660 sq km/14 537 sq mi, capital, Banjarmasin; **Kalimantan Tengah**, **Central Kalimantan**, or **Central Borneo**, pop (1995e) 433 000, area 152 600 sq km/58 904 sq mi, capital, Palangkaraya; **Kalimantan Timur**, **East Kalimantan**, or **East Borneo**, pop (1995e) 2 052 000, area 202 440 sq km/78 142 sq mi, capital, Samarinda; an active guerrilla separatist movement. >> Borneo; Indonesia ℹ

Kalinin, Mikhail Ivanovich [ka**lee**nin] (1875–1946) Soviet statesman, born in Tver, Russia. He was formal head of state after the 1917 Revolution and during the years of Stalin's dictatorship (1919–46). >> Stalin

Kalmar or **Calmar** 56°39N 16°20E, pop (1995e) 58 100. City in SE Sweden; railway; castle (11th-c). >> Kalmar Union; Sweden ℹ

Kalmar Union The dynastic union of Denmark, Norway, and Sweden achieved at Kalmar, Sweden, where in 1397 Eric of Pomerania was crowned king of all three kingdoms.

In 1523 Sweden broke away from the Union, but Norway was united with Denmark until 1814.

Kama [**kah**ma] The Hindu god of love; also, one of the four ends of life in Hindu tradition. In this view, the pursuit of love or pleasure is necessary for life, but should be regulated by considerations of dharma. >> dharma; Hinduism

Kamchatka [kam**chat**ka] area 270 033 sq km/104 233 sq mi. Large peninsula in E Siberian Russia, separating the Sea of Okhotsk (W) from the Bering Sea (E); extends c.1200 km/750 mi S; width, 130–480 km/80–300 mi. >> Russia ℹ

kamikaze [**kam**ikahzee] (Jap 'divine wind') A term identifying the volunteer suicide pilots of the Japanese Imperial Navy, who guided their explosive-packed aircraft onto enemy ships in World War 2. They emerged in the last year of the Pacific War, when 1465 pilots died in the battle for Okinawa, destroying 26 US warships and damaging 164. Other kamikaze tactics (eg using boats and submarines) were also employed. >> World War 2

Kampala [kam**pah**la] 0°19N 32°35E, pop (1995e) 648 000. Capital of Uganda; founded, late 19th-c; capital, 1963; airport at Entebbe; railway; Makerere University (1922); two cathedrals. >> Uganda ℹ

Kampuchea >> **Cambodia** ℹ

kana >> **syllabary**

Kananga [ka**nang**ga], formerly **Luluabourg** (to 1966) 5°53S 22°26E, pop (1995e) 402 000. City in WC Democratic Republic of Congo, on R Lulua; scene of a mutiny by Congo Free State troops, 1895; airfield; railway. >> Zaire ℹ

Kanarese >> **Kannada**

Kanchenjunga >> **Kangchenjunga**

Kandahar [kanda**hah(r)**] 31°36N 65°47E, pop (1995e) 341 000. City in S Afghanistan; capital of Afghanistan, 1748–73; airfield; agricultural market. >> Afghanistan ℹ

Kandinsky, Wasily [kan**din**skee] or **Vasily Vasilyevich** (1866–1944) Russian painter, born in Moscow. In Russia (1914–21) he founded the Russian Academy and in 1922 was in charge of the Weimar Bauhaus. He was a leader of the *Blaue Reiter* group. >> Bauhaus; *Blaue Reiter, der*

Kandy [**kan**dee], known as **City of the Five Hills** 7°17N 80°40E, pop (1995e) 110 000. City in Sri Lanka; royal city until 1815; commercial centre for tea-growing area; focal point of the Buddhist Sinhalese culture; Dalada Maligawa (Temple of the Tooth). >> Buddha; Sri Lanka; Temple of the Tooth

kangaroo A marsupial, usually with long hind legs used for hopping, short front legs, and a long stiff tail; young (a *joey*) develops in a pouch on the mother's abdomen; large species tend to be called *kangaroos*, smaller species *wallabies*. (Family: Macropodidae, 50 species.) >> marsupial ℹ; tree kangaroo

kangaroo rat A squirrel-like rodent, native to North America; hind legs longer than front legs; long tail with long hairs at tip; moves by hopping. (Genus: *Dipodomys*, 22 species. Family: Heteromyidae.) >> rodent; squirrel

Kangchenjunga or **Kanchenjunga, Mount** [kanchen**jung**ga], Tibetan **Gangchhendzönga**, Nepali **Kumbhkaran Lungur** 27°42N 88°09E. Mountain in the Himalayan range; third highest mountain in the world; five peaks, the highest at 8586 m/28 169 ft; scaled by the Charles Evans British Expedition in 1955. >> Himalayas

Kang de >> **Puyi**

KaNgwane [kahng**gwah**nay] Former national state or non-independent black homeland in Natal province, South Africa; self-governing status, 1971; incorporated into KwaZulu Natal following the South African constitution of 1994. >> KwaZulu Natal; South Africa ℹ

kanji [**kan**jee] A character in Chinese writing, as used in Japan. Kanji are slightly simpler than the Chinese originals, and are pronounced differently.

Kankan [kan**kan**] 10°22N 9°11W, pop (1995e) 117 000. Town in E Guinea; second largest town in Guinea; railway terminus; commercial and transportation centre. >> Guinea ℹ

Kannada [**kan**ada] A Dravidian language of S India; also known as **Kanarese**, spoken mainly in the state of Karnataka. It has about 25 million speakers, and has written records from the 5th-c. >> Dravidian languages

Kano [**kah**noh] 12°00N 8°31E, pop (1995e) 745 000. City in N Nigeria; ancient Hausa settlement; modern city founded in the 19th-c; city walls nearly 18 km/11 mi long; airport; railway; university (1975). >> Nigeria ℹ

Kanpur [**kahn**poor], formerly **Cawnpore** 26°35N 80°20E, pop (1995e) 2 120 000. City in Uttar Pradesh, N India; on R Ganges; ceded to the British, 1801; entire British garrison massacred during the Indian Mutiny, 1857; airfield; railway; university (1966); major trade and industrial centre. >> Uttar Pradesh

Kansas [**kan**zas] pop (1995e) 2 591 000; area 213 089 sq km/82 277 sq mi. State in C USA; the 'Sunflower State'; part of the Louisiana Purchase, 1803; 34th state admitted to the Union (as a free state), 1861; highest point, Mt Sunflower (1227 m/4025 ft); land rises steadily from prairies (E) to semi-arid high plains (W); suffered severe land erosion in the 1930s (part of the Dust Bowl); capital, Topeka; nation's leading wheat producer; major cattle state. >> Louisiana Purchase; Topeka; United States of America ℹ; RR994

Kansas City (Kansas) [**kan**zas] 39°07N 94°38W, pop (1995e) 157 000. River-port city in E Kansas, USA; port at the junction of the Kansas and Missouri Rivers, adjacent to Kansas City, Missouri; settled by Wyandotte Indians, 1843; sold to the US government, 1855; railway; market for surrounding agricultural region. >> Kansas

Kansas City (Missouri) [**kan**zas] 39°06N 94°35W, pop (1995e) 451 000. River-port city in W Missouri, USA; on the S bank of the Missouri R, adjacent to its sister city, Kansas City, Kansas; established, 1838; city status, 1853; present name, 1889; airport; railway; university (1929); nation's leading winter-wheat market; jazz centre in the 1930s–40s; professional teams (representing the two Kansas Cities), Royals (baseball), Chiefs (football). >> Missouri

Kant, Immanuel [kant] (1724–1804) Philosopher, born in Königsberg, Germany. His main work is the *Kritik der reinen Vernunft* (1781, Critique of Pure Reason), in which he provided a response to the empiricism of Hume. He also wrote critiques of ethics and aesthetics. His thought exerted great influence on subsequent philosophy. >> Hume, David; idealism

Kanto earthquake The worst Japanese earthquake of modern times, occurring in E Japan in 1923. Old Tokyo and Yokohama were destroyed. >> RR974

Kanuri [ka**nu**ree] A Nilo-Saharan-speaking people of Bornu, NE Nigeria, and SE Niger. Muslim since the 11th-c, they have a highly stratified social organization. >> Niger ℹ; Nigeria ℹ

kaolin [**kay**olin] A pure clay composed chiefly of the mineral *kaolinite*, a hydrous aluminium silicate; also known as **china clay**. It is used in the manufacture of fine porcelain, and as a filler in paper making and paints. >> clay; fireclay

Kapil Dev, Nihanj (1959–) Cricketer, born in Chandigarh, India. An all-rounder, he led India to victory in the 1983 World Cup, and became the youngest player (at 24 years 68 days) to perform a Test double of 2000 runs and 200 wickets. In 1994 he broke Sir Richard Hadlee's record of 431 Test wickets by taking 432 wickets in his 130th Test match. >> cricket (sport) ℹ

kapok tree [**kay**pok] One of various members of the baobab family, with fruits containing seeds embedded in cotton-like fibres, used as filling for cushions, etc. (Family: Bombacaceae.) >> baobab

Kapoor, Anish [ka**poor**] (1954–) Artist and sculptor, born in Bombay, India, moving to London in 1973. He has exhibited at major venues around the world, and his awards include the Premio Duemila Venice Biennale (1990) and the Turner Prize (1991).

Karachi [ka**rah**chee] 24°51N 67°02E, pop (1995e) 7 518 000. Provincial capital of Sind province, SE Pakistan; Pakistan's principal seaport; founded, 18th-c; under British rule from 1843; former capital, 1947–59; airport; railway; university (1951). >> Pakistan ℹ

Karageorge, Turk **Karadjordje** ('Black George'), also **Czerny George**, nickname of **George Petrović** (1766–1817) Leader of the Serbians in their struggle for independence, born in Viševac, Serbia. He led a revolt against Turkey, and in 1808 was recognized as Prince of Serbia by the Sultan. When Turkey regained control of Serbia (1813) he was exiled, and on his return was murdered.

Karajan, Herbert von [**ka**ra-yan] (1908–89) Conductor, born in Salzburg, Austria. In 1955 he was made principal conductor of the Berlin Philharmonic, with which he was mainly associated until his resignation in 1989.

karakul [**ka**rakl] A breed of sheep native to Asia; also known as **caracul**. The name is also used for the skin of a young lamb of this breed, and for cloth which resembles this fur. >> sheep

Kara-Kum [kara **koom**], Russ **Peski Karakumy** area c.300 000 sq km/120 000 sq mi. Extensive desert in Turkmenistan, E of the Caspian Sea (W). >> Turkmenistan ℹ

Karamanlis, Konstantinos [karaman**lees**], also spelled **Caramanlis** (1907–98) Greek statesman, prime minister (1955–63, 1974–80), and president (1980–5, 1990–5), born in Próti, Greece. During his administration, Greece signed a Treaty of Alliance with Cyprus and Turkey. As premier in 1974, he supervised the restoration of civilian rule. >> Greece ℹ

karat >> **carat**

karate [ka**rah**tay] A martial art of unarmed combat, dating from the 17th-c, which was developed in Japan in the present century. The aim is to be in total control of the muscular power of the body, so that it can be used with great force and accuracy at any instant. In fighting an opponent, blows do not actually make physical contact. Levels of prowess are symbolized by coloured belts. >> martial arts; RR1056

Karelia [ka**reel**ia], Russ **Karelskaya** pop (1995e) 808 000; area 172 400 sq km/66 560 sq mi. Constituent republic of Russia; in mediaeval times, an independent state with strong Finnish associations; under Swedish domination, 17th-c; annexed by Russia, 1721; constituted as a Soviet Socialist Republic, 1923; heavily forested. >> Russia ℹ

Karen Sino-Tibetan-speaking, ethnically-diverse groups of S Myanmar. Sometimes divided into White Karen and Red Karen, they have united in common opposition to Burmese control. >> Myanmar ℹ; Sino-Tibetan languages

Kariba Dam A major concrete arch dam on the Zambezi R at the Zambia–Zimbabwe border, impounding L Kariba; completed in 1959; height 128 m/420 ft; length 579 m/1900 ft. >> dam; Zambezi, River

Karloff, Boris, originally **William Henry Pratt** (1887–1969) Film star, born in London. After several silent films he made his name as the monster in *Frankenstein* (1931), and spent his career mostly in popular horror films.

Karlovy Vary [**kah(r)**lovee **va**ree], Ger **Karlsbad** 50°14N 12°53E, pop (1995e) 60 200. Town in Czech Republic; airport; railway; famous health resort with hot alkaline springs. >> Czech Republic ℹ

Karlsbad >> **Karlovy Vary**

Karlsruhe [**kah(r)lz**roouh] 49°03N 8°23E, pop (1995e) 284 000. City in Germany; port on R Rhine; former capital of Baden; railway; university (1825); palace (1752–85). >> Germany ℹ

karma [**kah(r)**ma] (Sanskrit 'action' or 'work') In Indian tradition, the principle that a person's actions have consequences meriting reward or punishment. Karma is the moral law of cause and effect by which the sum of a person's actions are carried foward from one life to the next. >> Hinduism

Karnataka [**kah(r)**nataka], formerly **Mysore** pop (1995e) 48 500 000; area 191 773 sq km/74 024 sq mi. State in SW India; formed as Mysore in 1956, bringing the Kannada-speaking population of five states together; renamed Karnataka, 1973; bicameral legislature comprises a Legislative Council and a Legislative Assembly; capital, Bangalore. >> Bangalore; India ℹ; Kannada

Karoo [ka**roo**] Dry steppe country in South Africa, from the Orange R down to the Cape. >> South Africa ℹ

Kárpathos [**kah(r)**pathos], Ital **Scarpanto**, ancient **Carpathus** pop (1995e) 4940; area 301 sq km/116 sq mi. Mountainous island of the Dodecanese group, E Greece; length 48 km/30 mi; rises to 1216 m/3989 ft; capital, Pigadhia. >> Dodecanese; Greece ℹ

Karpov, Anatoly Yevgenyevich [**kah(r)**pof] (1951–) Chess player and world champion (1975–85), born in Zlatoust, Russia. He became world champion by default after Bobby Fischer refused to defend his title (1975), and successfully defended the title until losing to Kasparov in a controversial match (1985). He defeated Jan Timman of Belgium in an official world championship match in 1993. >> Fischer, Bobby; Kasparov

Karski, Jan, original surname **Kozielecki** (1914–) Polish resistance hero, born in Lodz, Poland. During World War 2, he gathered evidence of Nazi atrocities against Polish Jews, and was the first to present documented proof of Hitler's extermination policy to Allied leaders in Britain and the USA. After discovery by German intelligence, he emigrated to the USA in 1942. He was made an honorary citizen of Israel in 1994.

Karst, Slovenian **Kras**, Ital **Carso** Barren, stony limestone plateau in the Dinaric Alps of SW Slovenia; notable caves at Postojna; the name has come to be used in geography to describe limestone topography of this kind. >> Dinaric Alps

karting Motor racing of small four-wheeled vehicles, usually with single-cylinder and two-stroke engines. They are raced in categories dependent on engine size. >> motor racing

karyology [kari**o**lojee] The branch of cytology dealing with the study of nuclei inside cells, especially with the structure of chromosomes. >> chromosome ℹ; cytology

Kasdan, Lawrence (1949–) Film director, born in Miami Beach, FA. He gained a co-writer credit on *The Empire Strikes Back* (1980) before becoming a director with *Body Heat* (1981). Later films include *The Accidental Tourist* (1989), *Grand Canyon* (1991) and *Wyatt Earp* (1996).

Kashmir >> **Jammu-Kashmir**

Kasparov, Gary (Kimovich) [kas**pah**rof] (1963–) Chess player, born in Baku, Azerbaijan. When he beat Anatoly Karpov for the world title (Nov 1985) he became the youngest world champion, at the age of 22 years 210 days. He is now the highest-ranked active player, with a rating of 2812 (in March 1999). Long-term friction between him and the international chess organization, FIDE, resulted in his establishing the Grandmasters' Association in 1987, and arranging a World Championship match in 1993 without FIDE involvement, in which he defeated Nigel Short of Britain. In 1996 he competed against Deep Blue, the world's best chess-playing computer, winning four of the six games, but was decisively beaten in a rematch the following year. >> chess

Kassel or **Cassel** 51°19N 9°32E, pop (1995e) 201 000. Cultural, economic, and administrative centre in Germany; on the R Fulda; an important traffic junction; badly bombed in World War 2; railway; university (1971). >> Germany [i]

Kästner, Erich [**kest**ner] (1899–1974) Writer, born in Dresden, Germany. He is best known for his children's books, which include *Emil und die Detektive* (1928, Emil and the Detectives).

Katanga [ka**tang**ga] The southernmost province of Democratic Republic of Congo, rich in minerals. In 1960, when the Congo (Zaire) achieved independence, Katanga (known as Shaba, 1971–97) attempted to secede under the leadership of Moise Tshombe (1919–69). The unitary state was later recreated under the military leadership of President Mobutu (1930–). >> Lumumba; Zaire [i]

Kathmandu or **Katmandu** [katman**doo**], formerly **Kantipur** 27°42N 85°19E, pop (1995e) 522 000. Capital of Nepal; altitude 1373 m/4504 ft; built in its present form, 723; Gurkha capital, 1768; British seat of administration, 18th-c; university (1959); commercial centre, religious centre, tourism; the Vale of Kathmandu is a world heritage site. >> Nepal [i]

Katowice [kato**veet**se], Ger **Kattowitz** 50°15N 18°59E, pop (1995e) 370 000. City in S Poland; centre of the Upper Silesian Industrial Region; airport; railway; two universities (1945, 1968); cathedral. >> Poland [i]

katydid [**kay**tidid] A large, grasshopper-like insect in which sound communication is well-developed. (Order: Orthoptera. Family: Tettigoniidae, c.5000 species.) >> grasshopper

Katyn massacre [ka**tin**] A massacre of 14 000 Polish army officers in May 1940 in the Katyn forest near Smolensk, Belarus. Their mass graves were discovered by German occupying forces in 1943. In 1989 the Soviet–Polish historical commission reported that the crime was most probably committed by the Soviet security service (NKVD). >> World War 2

Kauai [**kow**iy], formerly **Kaieiewaho** pop (1995e) 57 400; area 1692 sq km/653 sq mi. Island of the US state of Hawaii; chief town, Lihue. >> Hawaii (state)

Kaufman, George S(imon) [**kowf**man] (1889–1961) Playwright, born in Pittsburgh, PA. His Broadway hits include *You Can't Take It with You* (1936, Pulitzer) and *The Man Who Came to Dinner* (1939). >> Broadway

Kaufman, Philip [**kawf**man] (1936–) Film director and screenwriter, born in Chicago, IL. His major films include *Invasion of the Body Snatchers* (1978), *The Unbearable Lightness of Being* (1988), and *China: The Wild East* (1995). He also wrote the stories for *The Outlaw Josey Wales* (1975) and *Raiders of the Lost Ark* (1981).

Kaunas [**kow**nas], formerly **Kovno** (to 1917) 54°52N 23°55E, pop (1995e) 440 000. Ancient town and river port in Lithuania; on the R Neman; capital of independent Lithuania, 1918; airfield; railway; castle (13th–17th-c). >> Lithuania [i]

Kaunda, Kenneth (David) [ka**oon**da] (1924–) Zambian statesman and president (1964–91), born in Lubwa. He founded the Zambian African National Congress (1958), played a leading part in his country's independence negotiations, and became the country's first president. After a failed military coup in 1990, he agreed to multiparty elections in 1991, but lost the presidency. In 1997 he was put under house arrest following a failed coup attempt, though he denied any involvement. >> Zambia [i]

Kaunitz(-Rietberg), Wenzel Anton, Fürst von (Prince of) [**kow**nits **reet**berg] (1711–94) Austrian statesman and chancellor (1753–92), born in Vienna. As chancellor, he instigated the Diplomatic Revolution, and directed Austrian politics for almost 40 years under Maria Theresa and Joseph II. >> Maria Theresa

kauri pine An evergreen conifer, native to SE Asia and Australasia. It is the source of an important resin as well as timber. One species, *Agathis australis*, is an important forest tree in New Zealand. (Genus: *Agathis*, 20 species. Family: Araucariaceae.) >> conifer; resin

kava A Polynesian beverage made by fermenting chewed or grated, peeled roots of *Piper methysticum*, a relative of black pepper. The drink is narcotic and sedative as well as intoxicating. >> narcotics; pepper 1

Kawasaki [kawa**sa**kee] 35°32N 139°41E, pop (1995e) 1 180 000. Port city in E Honshu, Japan; railway. >> Honshu

Kay, John >> **Arkwright, Sir Richard**

kayak [**kiy**ak] A small double-ended craft of Eskimo design, similar to a canoe, but enclosed except for a very small cockpit. It is usually propelled with a double-ended paddle. >> canoe

Kaye, Danny, originally **David Daniel Kaminski** (1913–87) Stage, radio, and film actor, born in New York City. *Wonder Man* (1944) made his reputation as a film comedian. Later films include *The Secret Life of Walter Mitty* (1946), *The Inspector General* (1950), and *Hans Christian Andersen* (1952). He received an Honorary Oscar in 1955.

Kazakh or **Kazak** [ka**zak**] A Turkic-speaking Mongoloid people of Kazakhstan and adjacent areas in China. Traditionally nomadic pastoralists, they are now on collective cattle farms, though many are still nomadic. >> Kazakhstan; nomadism; pastoralism

Kazakhstan [kazak**stahn**], official name **Republic of Kazakhstan**, Kazakh **Qazaqstan Respublikasï**, Russ **Kazakhskaya** pop (1995e) 17 155 000; area 2 717 300 sq km/1 048 878 sq mi. Republic in S Asia; capital, Astana (from 1998), formerly Almaty (Alma-Ata); timezone GMT +5/6; major ethnic groups, Kazakh (40%), Russian (37%), German (6%), Ukrainian (5%); languages, Kazakh (official), Russian, German; religions, Sunni Muslim, Russian Orthodox, Protestant; currency, the tenge; steppeland (N) gives way to desert (S); lowest elevation near the E shore of the Caspian Sea (132 m/433 ft below sea-level); mountain ranges in the E and SE; chief rivers, the Irtysh, Syr-Darya, Ural, Emba, Ili; continental climate, with hot summers and extreme winters; wide range of temperatures, −17°C in N/C and −3°C in S (Jan), 20°C in N and 29°C in S (Jul); strong, dry winds common in N; became a constituent republic of the Soviet Union, 1936; declared independence, 1991; new constitution, 1995; governed by a president, prime minister, 40-member Senate and 67-member Assembly; coal, iron ore, bauxite, copper, nickel, oil; oil refining, metallurgy, heavy engineering, chemicals, leatherwork, footwear, food processing; cotton, fruit, grain, sheep. >> Astana; Commonwealth of Independent States [i]; Kazakh; Soviet Union; RR1014 political leaders; *see illustration on p.461*

Kazan [ka**zan**] 55°45N 49°10E, pop (1995e) 1 116 000. River-port city in E European Russia; founded, 13th-c; airport; railway; university (1804); cathedral (19th-c); important industrial and cultural centre of the Volga. >> Russia [i]

Kazan, Elia [ka**zan**], originally **Elia Kazanjoglous** (1909–) Stage and film director, born in Istanbul. He began as a film director in 1944, and won Oscars for *Gentleman's Agreement* (1948) and *On the Waterfront* (1954). He co-founded the Actors' Studio in 1947. A lifetime achievement award at the 1999 Oscars ceremony was given a mixed response, with opponents recalling that Kazan had given the names of communists in the film industry to the Un-American Activities Committee in the 1950s. >> Actors' Studio

Kazantzakis, Nikos [kazan**za**kis] (1883–1957) Writer, born in Heraklion, Crete, Greece. He is best known for the novel *Vios kai politia tou Alexi Zormpa* (1946, trans Zorba

the Greek, filmed 1964) and the long autobiographical poem, *Odissa* (1938, The Odyssey, a Modern Sequel).

kazoo or **bazouka** A child's musical instrument, consisting of a short metal tube flattened at one end, with a hole in the top covered by a disc of membrane. This imparts a buzzing edge to the tone when the player sings or hums into the flattened end. >> membranophone

Kean, Edmund (c.1789–1833) Actor, born in London. A highly successful tragic actor, his irregularities lost him public approval, his reputation being ruined when he was successfully sued for adultery in 1825. >> theatre

Keating, Paul (John) (1944–) Australian statesman and prime minister (1991–6), born in Sydney, New South Wales, Australia. As treasurer (1983–91), he was the main architect of the government's economic policies. Elected leader by the Labor Party in 1991, he retired from parliament following the election defeat of 1996. He declined the award of Companion to the Order of Australia in 1997 – the first living former prime minister not to accept.

Keating, Tom (1918–84) Artist and forger, born in London. A self-confessed 'art imitator', he claimed to have produced some 2000 fakes in 25 years. His activity came to light in 1976. He was arrested, but charges were dropped when his health declined.

Keaton, Buster, popular name of **Joseph Francis Keaton** (1895–1966) Film comedian, born in Piqua, KS. Renowned for his 'deadpan' expression, he starred in and directed such classics as *The Navigator* (1924) and *The General* (1926). He received a special Academy Award in 1959.

Keaton, Diane [**kee**ton] (1946–) Film actress, born in Los Angeles, CA. She became known through her roles in several of Woody Allen's films, such as *Annie Hall* (1977, Oscar), *Manhattan* (1979), and *Manhatten Murder Mystery* (1993). Other films include *Reds* (1981) and *Baby Boom* (1987). >> Allen, Woody

Keaton, Michael (1951–) Actor, born in Caraopolis, PA. His breakthrough came with the film *Mr Mom* (1983), and five years later, after *Beetlejuice* (1988) and *Clean and Sober* (1988), he was named Best Actor by national film critics. Other films include *Batman* (1989), *Batman Returns* (1992), and *Multiplicity* (1996).

Keats, John (1795–1821) Poet, born in London. His first book of poems (1817) was fiercely criticized, but he was nonetheless able to produce *Lamia and Other Poems* (1820), a landmark in English poetry, which contains his major odes. Seriously ill with tuberculosis, he died in Rome. >> Romanticism

Keble, John [**kee**bl] (1792–1866) Anglican churchman and poet, born in Fairford, Gloucestershire. His sermon on 'National Apostasy' (1833) began the *Oxford Movement*, encouraging a return to High Church ideals. Keble College, Oxford, was erected in his memory. >> Oxford Movement

keck >> **cow parsley; hogweed**

Kedah [kay**dah**] pop (1995e) 1 591 000; area 9425 sq km/ 3638 sq mi. State in NW Peninsular Malaysia; governed by Thailand from early 19th-c until 1909, when it came under British rule; capital, Alor Setar. >> Malaysia ℹ

Keeler, Christine >> **Profumo, John**

Keeling Islands >> **Cocos Islands**

Keelung >> **Jilong**

keeshond [**kays**hond] A small, sturdy spitz breed of dog from The Netherlands; grey with dark tinges; head dark with pale rings around eyes; coat very thick, especially around neck; tail tightly curled. >> spitz

kefir [**ke**feer] A fermented milk originating in the Caucasus. Traditionally made from camel's milk, it is now made from cow's milk. >> milk

Keflavik [**kef**lavik, kyepla**veek**] 64°01N 22°35W, pop (1995e) 7900. Fishing port in SW Iceland; important trade centre since the 16th-c; airport. >> Iceland ℹ

Keillor, Garrison [**kee**ler], pseudonym of **Gary Edward Keillor** (1942–) Humorous writer and radio performer, born in Anoka, MN. In 1974 he began to host the live radio show, 'A Prairie Home Companion', delivering a weekly monologue set in the quiet, fictional mid-western town of Lake Wobegon. His books include the best-selling *Lake Wobegon Days* (1985) and *We Are Still Married* (1989).

Keitel, Wilhelm [**kiy**tl] (1882–1946) German field marshal, born in Helmscherode, Germany. He was made chief of the Supreme Command of the Armed Forces (1938), and in 1945 was one of the German signatories of surrender in Berlin. He was convicted of war crimes at Nuremberg, and executed. >> World War 2

Kelantan [ke**lan**tan] pop (1995e) 1 375 000; area 14 796 sq km/5711 sq mi. State in NE Peninsular Malaysia; governed by Thailand from early 19th-c until 1909, when it came under British rule; capital, Kota Baharu. >> Malaysia [i]

Keldysh, Mstislav (Vsevoldvich) (1911–78) Mathematician and space programme leader, born in Riga. He was a leading figure in the development of the theory of rocketry and in the emergence of the USSR in space exploration. >> Soviet space programme

Keller, Helen (Adams) (1880–1968) Writer and educator, born in Tuscumbia, AL. She lost her sight and hearing after an illness at 19 months, but was educated by **Anne Mansfield Sullivan** (later Mrs Macy), who taught her to speak, read, and write. She became distinguished as a lecturer and writer.

Kellogg–Briand Pact A proposal made in 1927 by French foreign minister Aristide Briand (1862–1932) to US secretary of state Frank B Kellogg (1856–1937) that the two countries should sign a pact renouncing war as an instrument of national policy. In 1928 the pact was signed by 65 states (the **Pact of Paris**).

Kells >> **Ceanannus Mór**

Kelly, Gene, popular name of **Eugene Curran Kelly** (1912–96) Actor, dancer, and film director, born in Pittsburgh, PA. His stage success in *Pal Joey* led to a Hollywood debut in *For Me and My Gal* (1942), followed by a long series of musicals, such as *An American in Paris* (1951), and *Singin' in the Rain* (1952). In 1951 he received a special Academy Award for his versatility.

Kelly, Grace >> **Rainier III**

Kelly, Ned, popular name of **Edward Kelly** (1855–80) Outlaw, born in Beveridge, Victoria, Australia. He was a horse-thief who (from 1878) became a bushranger in Victoria and New South Wales, working with a gang whose daring robberies received widespread publicity. His trademark was his home-made armour. He was hanged at Melbourne. >> bushrangers

Kelman, James (1946–) Novelist and short-story writer, born in Glasgow, Scotland. He published his first novel, *The Busconductor Hines*, in 1984. Regarded as one of the major talents in contemporary Scottish fiction, he won the Booker Prize in 1994 for *How Late It Was, How Late*.

keloid [**kee**loyd] The overgrowth of scar tissue (fibroblasts and collagen) in response to a surgical or accidental wound of the skin. It appears as a raised, warm, reddened, tender lump along the line of the wound. >> skin [i]

kelp A large brown seaweed common in lower inter-tidal and subtidal zones in colder seas. (Division: Phaeophyceae. Order: Laminariales.) >> seaweed

kelpie A breed of dog developed in Australia as a sheepdog; medium size with thick, coarse coat and bushy tail; muzzle pointed; ears erect; also called **Australian kelpie**. >> sheepdog

Kelvin (of Largs), William Thomson, 1st Baron (1824–1907) Mathematician and physicist, born in Belfast. He carried out fundamental research into thermodynamics, helping to develop the law of the conservation of energy, and the absolute temperature scale (now given in kelvin). He also presented the dynamical theory of heat, and developed notions in electricity and magnetism, and hydrodynamics. >> kelvin; thermodynamics

kelvin Base SI unit of thermodynamic temperature; symbol *K*; defined as the fraction 1/273·16 of the thermodynamic temperature of the triple point of water; named after Lord Kelvin; always written K, not °K. >> Kelvin; phases of matter [i]; temperature [i]; thermodynamics; RR1033

Kemble The name of a famous British acting family of the 18th-c. The founding member was **Roger** (1721–1802), a travelling manager. His granddaughter, **Frances Ann**, known as **Fanny** (1809–93), became one of the leading actresses of the 19th-c. >> Siddons

Kempe, Margery [kemp], *née* **Brunham** (c.1373–c.1440) English religious mystic, wife of a burgess of Lynn. She wrote a spiritual autobiography, *The Book of Margery Kempe* (c.1432–6). >> mysticism

Kempe, Rudolf [**kem**puh] (1910–76) Conductor, born near Dresden, Germany. He appeared frequently at Covent Garden, London, and was principal conductor of the Royal Philharmonic Orchestra (1961–75).

Kempe, William [kemp] (c.1550–c.1603) English comic actor, a leading member of Shakespeare's company in the last decade of the 16th-c. In 1600 he performed a 9-day morris dance from London to Norwich.

Kempis, Thomas à [**kem**pis], originally **Thomas Hemerken** (1379–1471) Religious writer, so called from his birthplace, Kempen, Germany. An Augustinian monk, his many writings include the influential devotional work *Imitatio Christi* (c.1415–24, The Imitation of Christ). >> Christianity

Kenai bear >> **brown bear**

kendo The Japanese martial art of sword fighting, now practised with *shiani*, or bamboo swords. **Kendokas** (participants) wear traditional dress of the Samurai period, including face-masks and aprons. >> martial arts; samurai

Kendrew, Sir John (Cowdery) (1917–97) Biochemist, born in Oxford, Oxfordshire. For his discovery of the structure of myoglobin, he shared the Nobel Prize for Chemistry in 1962. >> blood

Keneally, Thomas (Michael) [ke**nee**lee] (1935–) Novelist, born in Sydney, New South Wales, Australia. His novels are frequently historical, and include *Schindler's Ark* (1982, Booker Prize; filmed in 1993 as *Schindler's List*), the story of an industrialist who saved the lives of Polish Jews during the early 1940s. *Our Republic* (1993) expresses his passionate support for the Australian republican cause.

Kennedy, Edward M(oore) (1932–) US politician, born in Brookline, MA, brother of John F and Robert F Kennedy. In 1969 he became the youngest-ever majority whip in the US Senate, but his involvement the same year in a car accident at Chappaquiddick, in which a woman companion (Mary Jo Kopechne) was drowned, dogged his subsequent political career, and caused his withdrawal as a presidential candidate in 1979. >> Democratic Party

Kennedy, Jackie >> **Onassis, Jacqueline Kennedy**

Kennedy, John F(itzgerald), also known as **JFK** (1917–63) US statesman and 35th president (1961–3), born in Brookline, MA, the son of Joseph P Kennedy. He was the first Catholic, and the youngest person, to be elected president. His 'New Frontier' in social legislation involved a federal desegregation policy in education, and civil rights reform. He displayed firmness and moderation in foreign policy, in 1962 inducing Russia to withdraw its missiles from Cuba, and achieving a partial nuclear test-ban treaty with Russia in 1963. On 22 November, he was assassinated by rifle fire while being driven in an open car through Dallas, TX. The alleged assassin, **Lee Oswald**, was himself shot two days later during a jail transfer. >> Bay of Pigs; civil rights; Onassis, Jacqueline; Oswald, Lee Harvey

Kennedy, Joseph P(atrick) (1888–1969) US businessman and diplomat, born in Boston, MA. The grandson of an Irish Catholic immigrant, he became a multimillionaire in the 1920s. In 1914 he married **Rose Fitzgerald**, and had nine children, including four sons, at whose political disposal he placed his fortune. The eldest, **Joseph Patrick** (1915–44), was killed in a flying accident while on naval service in World War 2. The others achieved international political fame. >> Kennedy, Edward M / John F / Robert F

Kennedy, Nigel (Paul), professional name (from 1997) **Kennedy** (1956–) British violinist. He made his debut as a concert soloist in 1977, and has since played with many of the world's major orchestras. His recording of Vivaldi's *Four Seasons* held the No 1 spot in the UK Classical Chart for over a year (1989–90).

Kennedy, Robert F(rancis) (1925–68) US politician, born in Brookline, MA, brother of John F and Edward M Kennedy. An efficient manager of his brother John's presidential campaign, he became an energetic attorney general (1961–4), notable in his dealings with civil rights problems. After winning the 1968 Californian Democratic presidential primary election, he was shot, and died the following day. His assassin, Sirhan Bishara Sirhan, a 24-year-old Jordanian-born immigrant, was sentenced to the gas chamber in 1969, but was not executed.

Kennedy Space Center, John F US space centre situated on Merrit I and Cape Canaveral (known as Cape Kennedy 1963–73) off the E coast of Florida. It is the principal launch site for the US space exploration programme conducted by NASA. >> NASA

kennel cough An infection of the upper respiratory tract in dogs, resulting in a characteristic, harsh, non-productive cough. Bacteria (*Bordetella bronchiseptica*) and various viruses are the main agents involved. The disease is highly infectious, and evidence of up-to-date vaccination is usually required by boarding establishments before accepting dogs at risk. >> dog

Kenneth I, known as **Kenneth MacAlpin** (?–858) King of the Scots of Dal Riata (from 841) and King of the Picts (from c.843). He combined the territories of both peoples in a united kingdom of Scotia (Scotland N of the Forth–Clyde line). >> Picts

Kensington and Chelsea 51°30N 0°12W, pop (1995e) 152 000. Borough of C Greater London, UK; N of R Thames; Kensington granted the designation 'Royal Borough' by Edward VII in 1901; railway; Kensington Palace, Kensington Gardens, Victoria and Albert Museum, Science Museum, British Museum (Natural History). >> London

Kent pop (1995e) 1 543 000; area 3731 sq km/1440 sq mi. County in SE England; rises to 251 m/823 ft in the North Downs; The Weald in the SW; high chalk cliffs, especially at Dover; county town, Maidstone; principal cross-Channel ports, Dover, Folkestone, Ramsgate, Sheerness; Medway a unitary authority from 1998; known for its fruit and hops ('the Garden of England'). >> England [i]; Maidstone

Kent, Edward (George Nicholas Paul Patrick), Duke of (1935–) British prince, the eldest son of Duke George Edward Alexander Edmund (1902–42), who was the fourth son of King George V and Queen Mary. He was commissioned in the army in 1955, and in 1961 married **Katharine Worsley**. They have three children: **George Philip Nicholas, the Earl of St Andrews** (1962–), **Helen Marina Lucy, Lady Helen Windsor** (1964–), and **Nicholas Charles Edward Jonathan, Lord Nicholas Windsor** (1970–). George married **Sylvana Tomaselli** (1957–) and they have one son, **Edward, Lord Downpatrick** (1988–). Lady Helen Windsor married Timothy Taylor to become Lady Helen Taylor; they have two sons, **Columbus George Donald Taylor** (1994–) and **Cassius Edward Taylor** (1996–). >> Alexandra, Princess; Kent, Prince Michael of

Kent, Prince Michael of (1942–) British prince, the younger brother of Edward, Duke of Kent. He married in 1978 **Baroness Marie-Christine von Reibniz**, and their children are **Frederick Michael George David Louis, Lord Frederick Windsor** (1979–) and **Gabriella Marina Alexandra Ophelia, Lady Gabriella Windsor** (1981–). >> Kent, Edward, Duke of

Kent, William (1685–1748) Painter, landscape gardener, and architect, born in Bridlington, East Riding. The principal exponent of the Palladian style of architecture in England, his best-known work is the Horse Guards block in Whitehall. >> Palladianism

Kentucky pop (1995e) 3 864 000; area 104 658 sq km/ 40 410 sq mi. State in EC USA; the 'Bluegrass State'; part of the territory ceded by the French, 1763; explored by Daniel Boone from 1769; first permanent British settlement at Boonesborough, 1775; originally part of Virginia; admitted to the Union as the 15th state, 1792; highest point, Mt Black (1263 m/4144 ft); C plain known as Bluegrass country; capital, Frankfort; famous for the distilling of bourbon whiskey (still the country's leading producer), and for its thoroughbred racehorses; nation's leading coal producer. >> Boone; Frankfort; Mammoth Cave; United States of America [i]; RR994

Kentucky and Virginia Resolutions (1798) Declarations by two state legislatures that the Alien and Sedition laws violated the US Constitution. They were written by Thomas Jefferson (Kentucky) and James Madison (Virginia). >> Alien and Sedition Acts; Jefferson; Madison, James

Kenya [**ken**ya], formerly [**keen**ya], official name **Republic of Kenya** pop (1995e) 29 520 000; area 564 162 sq km/ 217 766 sq mi. Republic of E Africa; capital, Nairobi; timezone GMT +3; ethnic groups include Kikuyu (18%), Luhya (12%), Luo (11%); chief religions, Christianity (66%), local beliefs (26%); official languages, English and Swahili, with many tribal languages spoken; unit of currency, the Kenya shilling; crossed by the Equator; SW plateau rises to 600–3000 m/2000–10 000 ft, includes Mt Kenya (5200 m/17 058 ft); Great Rift Valley (W) runs N–S; dry, arid semi-desert in the N, generally under 600 m/2000 ft; tropical climate on coast, with high temperatures and humidity; Mombasa, average annual rainfall 1200 mm/ 47 in, average daily temperatures 27–31°C; very early fossil hominids found in the region by anthropologists; coast settled by Arabs, 7th-c; Portuguese control, 16th–17th-c; British control as East African Protectorate, 1895; British colony, 1920; independence movement led to the Mau Mau rebellion, 1952–60; independence, 1963; first leader, Jomo Kenyatta; governed by a president with a unicameral National Assembly; international pressure from aid donors led to multi-party elections, 1992, and gave President Arap Moi a fourth term of office; result condemned by opposition parties; agriculture accounts for a third of national income; national parks and game reserves attract large numbers of tourists. >> Kenyatta; Leakey; Mau Mau; Nairobi; Rift Valley; RR1014 political leaders; *see illustration on p. 464*

Kenya, Mount 0°10S 37°18E. Extinct volcano cone in C Kenya; second highest mountain in Africa; highest peak, Batian (5199 m/17 057 ft). >> Kenya [i]

Kenyatta, Jomo [ken**ya**ta], originally **Kamau Ngengi** (c.1889–1978) Kenyan statesman and president (1964–78), born in Mitumi, Kenya. Charged in 1952 with leading the Mau Mau terrorist organization (a charge he denied), he was exiled. In 1960, while still in detention, he was elected president of the new Kenya African National Union Party, became prime minister in 1963, then president. >> Kenya [i]; Mau Mau

Kenzo, in full **Kenzo Takada** (1940–) Fashion designer, born in Kyoto, Japan. He creates clothes with both Oriental and Western influences, and is a trend-setter in the field of knitwear.

Kepler, Johannes (1571–1630) Astronomer, born in Weil-der-Stadt, Germany. He showed that planetary motions were far simpler than had been imagined. >> Brahe;

Kepler's laws of planetary motion

Kepler's laws of planetary motion Fundamental laws deduced by Kepler from Tycho Brahe's data. (1) Each planet travels an elliptical orbit with the Sun at one focus. (2) For a given planet radius, the vector to the Sun sweeps equal areas in equal times. (3) For any two planets, the squares of the periods are proportional to the cubes of the distances from the Sun. >> Brahe; Kepler; vector (mathematics)

Kerala [**ke**rala] pop (1995e) 31 426 000; area 39 000 sq km/ 15 000 sq mi. State in S India, capital, Trivandrum; governed by a unicameral legislature; created out of the former state of Travancore–Cochin under the 1956 States Reorganization Act. >> India ℹ; Trivandrum

keratin [**ke**ratin] A tough, fibrous protein synthesized by the outer layer of the skin (*epidermis*) of vertebrates. It is the major component of hair, nails, claws, horns, feathers, scales, and the dead outer layers of cells of skin. >> protein

keratosis [kera**toh**sis] Small dark scaly lesions on exposed parts of the skin, commonly found in individuals over 60 years of age and in younger white-skinned residents in sunny climates. >> melanoma

Kerensky, Alexander Fyodorovich [ke**ren**skee] (1881–1970) Russian socialist, born in Simbirsk, Russia. He took a leading part in the 1917 Revolution, becoming premier in the provisional government. Deposed by the Bolsheviks, he fled to France. >> Russian Revolution

Kerkuane Carthaginian town in N Tunisia, founded in the 5th-c BC and abandoned c.140 BC after the destruction of Carthage; a world heritage site. >> Carthage

Kermode, Sir (John) Frank [ker**mohd**] (1919–) Literary critic, born in the Isle of Man. His works include *Romantic Image* (1957) and *Forms of Attention* (1985).

Kern, Jerome (David) (1885–1945) Songwriter, born in New York City. He wrote a string of successful Broadway shows, notably *Show Boat* (1928, book and lyrics by Hammerstein). >> Hammerstein

kerosene or **paraffin** A petroleum distillation product, with larger molecules and consequently less volatility than the fraction used for gasoline (petrol). It is now an important source of domestic heating, and is the main fuel for jet engines. >> alkanes; fuel

Kerouac, Jack [**ke**rooak], popular name of **Jean Louis Kerouac** (1922–69) Writer, born in Lowell, MA. He is best known for *On the Road* (1957), a spontaneous work expressing the youthful discontent of the 'beat generation'. Later works in this vein, all autobiographical in character, include *The Subterraneans* (1958) and *Big Sur* (1962). >> beat generation

Kerr, John [kair] (1824–1907) Physicist, born in Ardrossan, North Ayrshire. He carried out valuable research on polarized light in magnetic and electric fields, and the **Kerr effects** which result.

Kerr, Sir John (Robert) [kair] (1914–91) Lawyer and administrator, born in Sydney, New South Wales, Australia. As Governor-General of Australia (1974–7) he made Australian constitutional history when he resolved a political impasse by exercising the regal 'reserve powers', sacking the elected prime minister, Gough Whitlam, and asking leader of the Liberal opposition, Malcolm Fraser, to form a caretaker government and call a general election. >> Fraser, Malcolm; Whitlam

Kerry, Ir **Chiarraighe** pop (1995e) 121 000; area 4701 sq km/ 1815 sq mi. County in Munster province, SW Ireland; capital, Tralee; includes Killarney and Listowel. >> Killarney; Ireland (republic) ℹ; Munster; Tralee

Kesey, Ken (Elton) [**kee**zee] (1935–) Writer, born in La Junta, CO. His best-known work is *One Flew Over the Cuckoo's Nest* (1962; filmed, 1975). The novel *Sailor Song* appeared in 1993.

Kesselring, Albert [**kes**lring] (1885–1960) German air commander in World War 2, born in Markstedt, Germany. He led the Luftwaffe attacks on France and on Britain, and in 1943 was made commander-in-chief in Italy. He was released from a sentence of life imprisonment in 1952. >> World War 2

kestrel A falcon of the worldwide genus *Falco* (13 species), especially *Falco tinnunculus*; inhabits open country; catches prey on ground after hovering. (Family: Falconidae.) >> bird of prey; falcon

ketch A two-masted fore-and-aft-rigged sailing vessel. The shorter (after-) mast, called the *mizzen*, is placed in position forward of the rudder post. By contrast, in a **yawl**, this mast is placed aft of the rudder post. >> yacht ℹ

ketones [**kee**tohnz] IUPAC **alkanones**. Organic compound containing a carbonyl (C=O) group bonded to two other carbon atoms. The simplest example is acetone (CH_3COCH_3).

Kettering, Charles F(ranklin) (1876–1958) Engineer, born in Loudonville, OH. He invented the electric starter motor for cars, discovered the cause of 'knocking' in car engines,

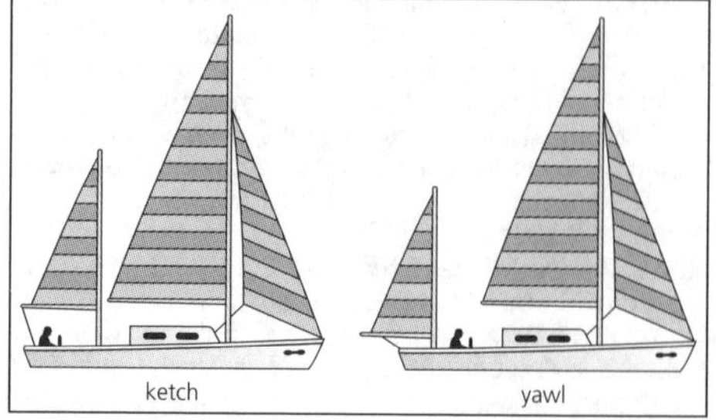

and invented the refrigerant known as Freon™. >> CFCs; knocking

kettledrum >> **timpani**

Kevorkian, Jack [kuh**vaw(r)**kian], media nickname **Dr Death** (1928–) Physician, born in Pontiac, MI. An advocate of euthanasia, he has been charged with murder and assisting suicide, but found not guilty. In 1998 he became internationally known when a video showing the death of one of his clients was shown on national television, a strategy he had chosen to bring the public debate on euthanasia to a head. He was again charged, and found guilty of second-degree murder, receiving a prison sentence of 10–25 years. >> euthanasia

Kew Gardens The Royal Botanical Gardens at Kew, Surrey, England. The gardens, inherited by George III from his mother, were given to the nation in 1841 and occupy 120 ha/300 acres. >> botanical garden

key >> **tonality**

keyboard instrument A musical instrument in which the different pitches are controlled by means of a keyboard, ie a succession of levers arranged in two rows. The front row produces the notes of the diatonic C major scale, the rear the pitches in between; played in order from left to right, they produce an ascending 12-note chromatic scale. The term **keyboards** is also often used as a collective term for all the electronic keyboard instruments (electric pianos, electronic organs, and synthesizers) in a pop group. >> accordion; aerophone; celesta; chordophone; clavichord; electrophone; glockenspiel; harpsichord; ondes Martenot; organ; piano; spinet; synthesizer; virginals

key grip >> **grip**

Keynes (of Tilton), John Maynard Keynes, Baron [kaynz] (1883–1946) Economist, born in Cambridge, Cambridgeshire. In both World Wars he was an adviser to the Treasury. The unemployment crises inspired his two great works, *A Treatise on Money* (1930) and the revolutionary *General Theory of Employment, Interest and Money* (1936). >> Keynesian

Keynesian [**kayn**zian] A follower of the economic concepts propounded by economist J M Keynes in the 1930s. The 'Keynesian revolution' changed the view of how economies should be managed, arguing that economies could be in equilibrium at less than full employment. Unless demand in the economy is stimulated, growth and therefore full employment are not possible. Keynesian theories were subject to critical appraisal in the 1960s and 1970s by Monetarists. >> Chicago School (economics); Keynes; monetarism; Neo-Keynesianism

Keystone A US film production company of silent films (1912–19), founded by Mack Sennett. It specialized in knockabout comedy shorts, especially those featuring the **Keystone Kops** troupe.

KGB Abbreviation of **Komitet Gosudarstvennoy Bezopasnosti** ('Committee for State Security'), after 1953 one of the Soviet Union's two secret police organizations with joint responsibility for internal and external order and security. It underwent radical reform, following glasnost and the failure of the 1991 coup in the USSR, and is now known as the Ministry of State Security. >> glasnost; intelligence service; police; Soviet Union

Khama, Sir Seretse [**kah**ma] (1921–80) African statesman and president of Botswana (1966–80), born in Serowe, Bechuanaland (now Botwsana). He was the first prime minister of Bechuanaland in 1965, and first president of Botswana. >> Botswana ℹ

Khamsin [**kam**sin] A hot, dry dust-laden SE wind which blows from desert areas in N Africa and Arabia. The word means '50', as it regularly blows for a 50-day period. >> Sirocco; wind

Khan, Mohammad Ayub (1907–74) Pakistani soldier and president (1958–69), born in Abbottabad. He became president after a bloodless coup, and introduced a system of Basic Democracies. Following widespread civil disorder, he resigned in 1969, and martial law was re-established. >> Pakistan ℹ

Kharkov [**khah(r)**kof], Ukrainian **Kharkiv** 50°00N 36°15E, pop (1995e) 1 645 000. City in Ukraine; founded as a fortress, 1655–6; badly damaged in World War 2; airport; railway junction; Donets Basin coalfield nearby; university (1805); two cathedrals (1689, 1821–41). >> Ukraine ℹ

Khartoum [kah(r)**toom**] or **El Khartûm** 15°33N 32°35E, pop (1995e) 673 000. Capital of Sudan; founded, 1820s; garrison town in 19th-c; scene of the British defeat by the Mahdi, 1885; city regained by Lord Kitchener, 1898; major communications and trade centre; regarded as the economic link between the Arab countries (N) and the African countries (S); airport; railway; university (1955); three cathedrals. >> Gordon, Charles George; Kitchener; Mahdi; Sudan ℹ

khat [kaht] A shrub (*Catha edulis*) growing in E Asia and the SW part of the Arabian peninsula, whose leaves are chewed for their stimulant effect. The active principle is *cathinone*. >> betel-nut

Khatchaturian, Aram [kacha**too**ryan] (1903–78) Composer, born in Tiflis, Georgia. His compositions include three symphonies, concertos, ballets, instrumental music, and film scores.

khedive [ke**deev**] An ancient Persian title acquired from the Ottoman Sultan by the autonomous Viceroy of Egypt, Ismail, in 1867. It was used until Egypt became a British protectorate (1914). >> Ismail Pasha

Khmer [kmair] An Austro-Asiatic language, spoken by over 7 million people; also known as **Cambodian**. Inscriptions date from the 6th–7th-c. >> Austro-Asiatic languages

Khmer Empire [kmair] An empire in SE Asia, founded in the 6th-c, with its capital at Angkor Thom from 802 onwards. Angkor was abandoned in 1431, and the Khmer Empire had collapsed by 1460. >> Angkor Thom

Khmer Rouge [kmair **roozh**] A Cambodian communist guerrilla force. It gained control in 1975 and, led by Pol Pot, set about a drastic transformation of 'Democratic Kampuchea', involving mass forced evacuation from the towns to the countryside, the creation of agricultural co-operatives, and the execution of thousands of 'bourgeois elements'. More than 90% of Cambodia's traditional artists, performers, and scholars were murdered. In 1979, Vietnam invaded, and the Khmer Rouge withdrew to Thai border region. They mounted a fresh offensive following Vietnamese withdrawal in 1989. The Paris Conference on Cambodia brought about a ceasefire (1991) and an international peace plan launched by the UN, which led to elections in 1993. However, the Khmer Rouge refused to take part in the elections or to become part of the new political system, and tension remained, with continued fighting between government troops and guerrillas. The organization was banned in 1994. >> Cambodia ℹ; Pol Pot

Khoisan [**koy**san] A collective term for the San (Bushmen) and Khoi (Hottentot) peoples of S Africa. They live mainly in the Kalahari Desert of Botswana and in Namibia.

Khomeini, Ayatollah Ruhollah [ho**may**nee] (1900–89) Iranian religious and political leader, born in Khomeyn, Iran. A Shiite Muslim opposed to the pro-Western regime of Shah Mohammed Reza Pahlavi, he was exiled in 1964. He returned to Iran amid great popular acclaim in 1979 after the collapse of the Shah's government, and became virtual head of state. Under his leadership, Iran underwent a turbulent 'Islamic Revolution' in which a return was made to the strict observance of Muslim principles and traditions. >> Iran ℹ; Islam; Pahlavi

Khrushchev, Nikita Sergeyevich [khrush**chof**, **khrush**chof] (1894–1971) Soviet statesman, first secretary of the Soviet Communist Party (1953–64), and prime minister (1958–64), born in Kalinovka, Ukraine. He became First Secretary soon after the death of Stalin, and three years later denounced Stalinism. Among the events of his administration were the Poznan riots and Hungarian uprising (1956), and the failed attempt to install missiles in Cuba (1962). He was replaced by Brezhnev and Kosygin, and went into retirement. >> Brezhnev; Cuban missile crisis; Hungarian uprising; Kosygin; Stalin

Khyber Pass [**kiy**ber] A defile through the Safed Koh mountain range on the frontier between Pakistan and Afghanistan. It is 45 km/28 mi long, and reaches heights of 1280 m/3518 ft.

kiang [ki**ang**] >> **ass**

kibbutz, plural **kibbutzim** A Jewish co-operative settlement in Israel which was self-supporting in terms of food supplies and many other goods. Kibbutzim spread in the 1950s as part of Israeli attempts at self-sufficiency. One of their distinctive features was the collective responsibility members took for child-rearing. Since c.1970, however, the movement to include children within the nuclear family has grown, and is now the norm. >> Israel ℹ

Kidd, William, known as **Captain Kidd** (c.1645–1701) Privateer and pirate, probably born in Greenock, Inverclyde. In 1696 he was commissioned to suppress piracy, but turned pirate himself. He was hanged in London.

Kiddush [ki**dush**] (Heb 'sanctification') A prayer usually recited by the head of the family over a cup of wine at the start of a meal in the home on the eve of a Sabbath or festival. It is sometimes used also in synagogues to consecrate the Sabbath or a festival. >> Judaism; Sabbath

kidney bean >> **haricot bean**

kidney machine >> **dialysis**

kidneys The urine-producing organs of vertebrates. In humans the symmetrical, bean-shaped kidneys are situated in the upper rear part of the abdominal wall, one each side of the vertebral column. Each kidney weighs about 130 g/4·6 oz, and consists of approximately 1 million *nephrons* (the functional units) and supporting tissue. >> anatomy ℹ; dialysis; glomerulonephritis; pyelonephritis; transplantation; uraemia

Kiel [keel] 54°02N 10°08E, pop (1995e) 251 000. Port city in Germany; Kiel Canal (1877–95), 98 km/61 mi between North Sea and Baltic Sea; badly bombed in World War 2; railway; ferry service to Scandinavia; naval base; university (1665); castle (13th-c). >> Germany ℹ

Kielder Water [**keel**der] Reservoir in Northumberland, NE England; one of the largest artificial lakes in Europe, supplying water to the industrial NE; built 1974–82 by damming R North Tyne. >> England ℹ; Tyne, River

Kierkegaard, Søren (Aabye) [**keer**kuhgah(r)d] (1813–55) Philosopher and religious thinker, born in Copenhagen. He is regarded as one of the founders of existentialism. In *Afsluttende uvidenskabelig Efterskrift* (1846, Concluding Unscientific Postscript), he attacked all philosophical system building. >> existentialism; Hegel

Kiesinger, Kurt Georg [**kee**singer] (1904–88) West German Conservative statesman and chancellor (1966–9), born in Ebingen, Germany. Long a supporter of Adenauer's plans for European unity, he formed with Brandt a government combining the Christian Democratic Union and the Social Democrats, until in 1969 he was succeeded as chancellor by Brandt. >> Adenauer; Brandt, Willy; Germany ℹ

Kiev [kee-ef], Ukrainian **Kiyiv**, also **Kiyev** 50°28N 30°29E, pop (1995e) 2 667 000. Capital city of Ukraine, on R Dnepr; founded, 6th–7th-c; capital of mediaeval Kievan Russia, 9th-c; capital of Ukraine, 1934; besieged and occupied by Germany in World War 2; airport; railway; major industrial, cultural, and scientific centre; university (1834); cathedral (1037). >> Ukraine ℹ

Kikuyu [ki**koo**yoo] A Bantu-speaking agricultural people of the C highlands of Kenya, and the country's largest ethnic group. After Kenya's independence (1963) they provided many of the country's political leaders. >> Kenya ℹ; Kenyatta; Mau Mau

Kildare [kil**dair**], Ir **Cill Dara** pop (1995e) 122 000; area 1694 sq km/654 sq mi. County in Leinster province, E Ireland; low-lying C plain known as the Curragh; capital, Naas; national stud at Tully, racecourse at the Curragh. >> Ireland (republic) ℹ; Leinster; Naas

Kilimanjaro [kiliman**jah**roh] (Chagga 'glitttering mountain") 3°02S 37°20E. Mountain on the frontier between Tanzania and Kenya, E Africa; height 5895 m/19 340 ft; highest point on the African continent; first climbed in 1889. >> Kenya, Mount; Tanzania ℹ

Kilkenny [kil**ken**ee], Ir **Cill Choinnigh** pop (1995e) 73 100; area 2062 sq km/796 sq mi. County in Leinster province, SE Ireland; fertile county watered by R Nore; Slieve Ardagh Hills rise W; capital, Kilkenny, pop (1995e) 17 500. >> Ireland (republic) ℹ; Leinster

Killarney [ki**lah(r)**nee] Ir **Cill Airne** 52°03N 9°30W, pop (1995e) 9900. Resort town in Kerry county, Munster, SW Ireland; centre of scenic lakeland area; railway. >> Ireland (republic) ℹ; Kerry

killer whale A toothed whale (*Orcinus orca*), found worldwide in cool coastal waters; length, 9–10 m/30–33 ft; black with white underparts; white patches on head; dorsal fin narrow and vertical. (Family: Delphinidae.) >> grampus; whale ℹ

Killy, Jean-Claude [keelee] (1943–) Alpine skier, born in Val d'Isère, France. He won all three alpine skiing titles at the 1968 Olympics, and was combined world champion in 1966 and 1968. >> skiing

kilobyte >> **byte**

kilocalorie >> **calorie** ℹ

kilogram Base SI unit of mass; symbol *kg*; defined as equal to the international prototype of the kilogram, a platinum–iridium bar kept at the International Bureau of Weights and Measures; commonly used as **gram** (g, 1/1000 kg) and tonne (*t*, 1000 kg); 1 kg = 2·205 pounds. >> mass

kilohm >> **ohm**

kilometre >> **metre** (physics)

kiloparsec >> **parsec**

kiloton A measure of explosive power; symbol *kT*; one kiloton equivalent to the explosive power of 1000 tons of TNT; used to describe the destructive power of nuclear weapons; one **megaton**, MT, equals 1000 kT. >> explosives; TNT ℹ

kilowatt >> **watt**

kilowatt-hour The total energy consumed by a device of power 1 kilowatt operating for 1 hour; symbol *kWh*; equal to $3·6 \times 10^6$ J (joule, SI unit); standard unit for the electricity supply industry. >> electricity; watt

Kilvert, (Robert) Francis (1840–79) Clergyman, born near Chippenham, Wiltshire. His *Diary* (1870–9), discovered in 1937, is an important historical document of his period, describing his daily life.

Kimberley 28°45S 24°46E, pop (1995e) 183 000. City in Northern Cape province, South Africa; major diamond-mining centre since its foundation, 1871; under siege in the Boer War, 1899–1900; airfield; railway; two cathedrals. >> Kimberley, Siege of; Northern Cape; South Africa ℹ

Kimberley, Siege of (1899–1900) One of the three sieges of the second Boer War, in which Boer forces attempted to pen up their British opponents. The town was relieved by General French. >> Boer Wars; French, John; Kimberley

Kim Il-sung [kim il**sung**], originally **Kim Song-ju** (1912–94) North Korean soldier, statesman, prime minister (1948–72),

Kimono

and president (1972–94), born near Pyongyang, North Korea. He founded the Korean People's Revolutionary Army in 1932, proclaimed the Republic in 1948, and became effective head of state. He established a unique personality cult wedded to an isolationist, Stalinist political-economic system, and named his son, **Kim Jong-Il** (1942–), as his successor. >> Korea, North ℹ

kimono [ki**moh**noh] Japanese traditional costume, today mostly worn for special occasions, such as weddings and the tea ceremony, or informally. Plain colours are for men; bright for girls and young women. The *obi* (waist sash) for women is frequently of an expensive material.

kinaesthesis / kinesthesis [kinuhs**thee**sis] Perceived sensations of position and movement of body and limbs, and of the force exerted by muscles. *Proprioception* also includes information about posture and movement not consciously perceived, as well as the senses of balance, rotation, and linear acceleration. >> ear ℹ; muscle

kindergarten A nursery school for children under the age at which they must legally attend school. In many countries the kindergarten is organized on informal lines, with the emphasis on social development as well as on preparation for formal schooling. >> nursery school; preschool education

kinematics >> **dynamics**

kine pox >> **cow pox**

kinescoping [**kin**eeskohping] A US term for the recording of a television or video programme on cinematograph film. >> telerecording

kinesiology [kiyneezi**ol**ojee] A system of diagnosis and treatment which uses assessment of a patient's muscle responses to manual pressure to detect and locate blockage and imbalance of energy flow; developed by US chiropracter George Goodheart. Diagnosis is based on the belief that each group of muscles is related to other distant parts of the body, and generally follows the principles of traditional Chinese medicine. >> acupuncture; alternative medicine; traditional Chinese medicine

kinetic To do with motion; in chemistry, to do with the speed of reactions. Mixtures which reach equilibrium quickly are called *labile*; those which react slowly *inert*.

kinetic art A term applied to certain types of modern art, especially sculptures, which move. Examples include the hanging mobiles of the US sculptor Alexander Calder (1898–1976), all the parts of which revolve separately to create changing patterns in space. >> mobile

kinetic energy Energy associated with an object's motion; a scalar quantity; symbol K, units J (joule). For an object of mass m moving with velocity v, kinetic energy $K = Mv^2/2$. >> energy; work

kinetic energy weapons Weapons which achieve their destructive effect by the sheer force of their impact; distinguished from those which do damage by blast and heat (**chemical energy** or **explosive weapons**) on arrival at the target. An arrow fired from a bow or a bullet fired from a gun is a kinetic energy weapon. >> kinetic energy; rail gun

kinetic theory of gases A classical theory of gases in which a gas is assumed to comprise large numbers of identical particles which undergo elastic collisions and obey Newtonian mechanics. >> diffusion (science)

King, Billie Jean, *née* **Moffat** (1943–) Tennis player, born in Long Beach, CA. Between 1961 and 1979 she won a record 20 Wimbledon titles, including the singles in 1966–8, 1972–3, and 1975. She also won 13 US titles (including four singles), four French titles (one singles), and two Australian titles (one singles). In 1987 she was elected to the International Tennis Hall of Fame. >> tennis, lawn ℹ

King, Cecil (Harmsworth) (1901–87) Newspaper proprietor, born in Totteridge, Hertfordshire. He became chairman of Daily Mirror Newspapers Ltd and Sunday Pictorial Newspapers Ltd (1951–63), and chairman of the International Publishing Corporation and Reed Paper Group (1963–8).

King, Larry, originally **Lawrence Harvey Zeiger** (1933–) Talk-show host, born in New York City. He joined CNN in 1985, taking *Larry King Live* to the top of the ratings by 1992, widely watched for its commentary and debate on contemporary events.

King, Martin Luther, Jr (1929–68) Clergyman, born in Atlanta, GA. A leader of the black Civil Rights movement, in 1964 he received the Kennedy Peace Prize and the Nobel Peace Prize. His greatest successes came in challenging the segregation laws of the South. He was assassinated in Memphis, TN, by **James Earl Ray**. A national holiday in King's honour has been recognized in many states since 1986. >> civil rights

King, Stephen (Edwin) (1947–) Novelist, born in Portland, ME. He achieved success with his first novel, *Carrie* (1974), and became known for his vivid treatment of horrific and supernatural themes, later books (many of which have been filmed) including *The Shining* (1976), *It* (1986), and *Bag of Bones* (1998).

King, W(illiam) L(yon) Mackenzie (1874–1950) Canadian Liberal statesman and prime minister (1921–6, 1926–30, 1935–48), born in Berlin (modern Kitchener), Ontario, Canada. His view that the dominions should be autonomous communities within the British E mpire resulted in the Statute of Westminster (1931). >> Canada ℹ

King Charles spaniel A breed of dog developed in Britain; a small active spaniel with short legs and long ears; also known as the **Cavalier King Charles spaniel**. >> dog; spaniel

king cobra The world's largest venomous snake (*Ophiophagus hannah*), native to India and SE Asia; (length, up to 5·5 m/18 ft): also known as **hamadryad**. >> cobra

kingcup A perennial (*Caltha palustris*) growing in wet marshy places throughout the N hemisphere; leaves glossy, kidney-shaped; flowers cup-shaped, golden-yellow, up to 5 cm/2 in across; also called **marsh marigold**. (Family: Ranunculaceae.)

kingdom The highest category into which organisms are classified. Modern systems recognize five kingdoms: *Monera* (comprising the procaryotes such as bacteria and blue-green algae), *Protoctista* (comprising the eucaryotic protozoans and some flagellated algae and fungi), *Fungi* (the eucaryotic fungi that lack flagella at all stages of their life-cycle), *Plantae* (plants), and *Animalia* (animals). >> animal; eucaryote; flagellum; fungus; plant; procaryote; Protoctista; Protozoa; taxonomy

kingfisher A bird found almost worldwide (especially Old World tropics); short-tailed, with large head; bill usually long, straight; bright blue-green back. (Family: Alcedinidae, c.85 species.) >> kookaburra

King James Bible >> **Authorized Version of the Bible**

Kingman, Sir John (Frank Charles) (1939–) British academic. He chaired the Committee of Inquiry into the Teaching of the English Language (1987–8), which produced the *Kingman Report*, a major influence on changing practices in English language teaching in British schools in the 1990s.

Kings, Books of A pair of books of the Hebrew Bible/Old Testament, a compilation of stories about the kings and prophets of Judah and Israel from the enthronement of Solomon to the fall of the kingdom of Israel in c.721 BC, and the final collapse of Judah and Jerusalem in c.587/6 BC. >> Old Testament

king's evil >> **scrofula**

Kingsley, Ben (1943–) Actor, born in Snainton, North Yorkshire. He joined the Royal Shakespeare Company (1970–80, 1985–6), and achieved fame for his title role in the film *Gandhi* (1980, Oscar). Other films include *Schindler's List* (1993), and *Twelfth Night* (1996). Notable stage performances include the 1997 production of *Waiting for Godot* at the Old Vic, London.

Kingsley, Charles (1819–75) Writer, born in Holne vicarage, Dartmoor, Devon. A 'Christian Socialist', his social novels, such as *Alton Locke* (1850), had great influence at the time. His best-known works are *Westward Ho!* (1855), *Hereward the Wake* (1866), and his children's book, *The Water Babies* (1863).

Kingston (Canada) 44°14N 76°30W, pop (1995e) 60 100. City in SE Ontario, Canada; founded, 1784; Canadian naval base in War of 1812; capital of United Canada, 1841–4; railway; Royal Military College (1876); Queen's University (1841). >> Canada ℹ; Ontario

Kingston (Jamaica) 17°58N 76°48W, pop (1995e) 670 000. Capital city of Jamaica; founded, 1693; capital, 1870; airport; railway; Institute of Jamaica (1879); University of the West Indies (1948). >> Jamaica ℹ

Kingston-upon-Hull >> **Hull**

Kingston-upon-Thames [temz] 51°25N 0°17W, pop (1995e) 139 000. Borough of SW Greater London, on R Thames; said to have been the coronation place of Anglo-Saxon kings; railway; Kingston University (1992, formerly Polytechnic). >> London ℹ

Kingstown 13°12N 61°14W, pop (1995e) 20 700. Capital and main port of St Vincent, Windward Is; airfield; cathedral. >> St Vincent

King William's War (1689–97) The first of the great wars between France and England for the control of North America. Known in Europe as the **War of the League of Augsburg**, it was settled by the Treaty of Ryswick (1697). >> Augsburg, League of

kinkajou [**king**kajoo] A nocturnal mammal (*Potos flavus*) native to Central and South America; superficially monkey-like, with a round head, small rounded ears, short face, large eyes, and long clasping tail; also known as **honey bear** or **potto**. (Family: Procyonidae.) >> mammal ℹ; monkey ℹ

Kinkakuji [kinkakujee] or **Golden Pavilion** A three-tiered gilded pavilion built in 1394 by Ashikaga Yoshimitsu (1358–1408) at Kyoto, Japan. The present building dates from 1955; it is a faithful reconstruction of the original which was burnt down. >> Kyoto

Kinnock, Neil (Gordon) (1942–) British Labour politician, born in Tredegar, Blaenau Gwent, SE Wales. He became an MP in 1970, and was chief Opposition spokesman on education (1979–83). A skilful orator, he was elected party leader in 1983, and resigned after the 1992 general election. He became a European Commissioner (with responsibility for transport) in 1994. >> Labour Party

kinnor A musical instrument of the ancient Hebrews – a type of lyre plucked with the fingers or a plectrum. >> lyre; string instrument 2 ℹ

Kinsey, Alfred (Charles) (1894–1956) Zoologist and social scientist, born in Hoboken, NJ. He is best known for his controversial studies *Sexual Behavior in the Human Male* (1948) and *Sexual Behavior in the Human Female* (1953). >> social science

Kinshasa [kin**sha**sa], formerly Belgian **Léopoldville** (to 1964) 4°18S 15°18E, pop (1995e) 3 671 000. River-port capital of Democratic Republic of Congo; on the R Congo opposite Brazzaville; founded by Stanley, 1887; capital of Belgian colony, 1926; airport; railway; university (1954). >> Stanley, Henry Morton; Zaire ℹ

Kinski, Klaus, originally **Nikolaus Gunther Nakszynski** (1926–91) Film actor, born in Zoppot, Poland. He played minor parts in spaghetti Westerns, then became known for his leading roles in the films of Werner Herzog, such as *Aguirre, the Wrath of God* (1972) and *Fitzcarraldo* (1982). He was also acclaimed for his role in *Nosferatu, the Vampyre* (1979).

Kintyre [kin**tiy(r)**] Peninsula in Argyll and Bute, SWC Scotland; runs S to the **Mull of Kintyre** from a narrow isthmus; 64 km/40 mi long; average width 13 km/8 mi. >> Scotland ℹ

Kipling, (Joseph) Rudyard (1865–1936) Writer, born in Mumbai (Bombay), India. His verse collections *Barrack Room Ballads* (1892) and *The Seven Seas* (1896) were highly successful, as were the two *Jungle Books* (1894–5), which have become classic animal stories, *Kim* (1901), and the *Just So Stories* (1902). He was awarded the Nobel Prize for Literature in 1907.

Kirchhoff, Gustav (Robert) [**keerkh**hohf] (1824–87) Physicist, born in Königsberg, Germany. He investigated electrical networks, heat, and optics, and with Robert Wilhelm Bunsen (1811–99) developed the technique of spectroscopy, with which they discovered caesium and rubidium. >> spectroscopy

Kirchner, Ernst Ludwig [**keerkh**ner] (1880–1938) Artist, born in Aschaffenburg, Germany. He became the leading spirit in the formation of the Expressionist group, *die Brücke* (1905–13). Many of his works were confiscated by the Nazis in 1937. >> *Brücke, die*; Expressionism

Kirghizia >> **Kyrgyzstan**

Kiribati, [**kir**ibas], formerly **Gilbert Islands**, official name **Republic of Kiribati** pop (1995e) 79 700; total land area 717 sq km/277 sq mi. Group of 33 low-lying coral islands scattered over c.3 000 000 sq km/1 200 000 sq mi of the C Pacific Ocean; comprises the Gilbert Group, Phoenix Is, and 8 of the 11 Line Is; capital, Bairiki on Tarawa; timezone GMT –12; population chiefly Micronesian; chief religion, Christianity; main languages, Gilbertese and English; unit of currency, the Australian dollar; islands seldom rise to more than 4 m/13 ft, usually consisting of a reef enclosing a lagoon; maritime equatorial climate in C islands, tropical further N and S; periodic drought in some islands; Gilbert and Ellice Is proclaimed a British protectorate, 1892; annexed, 1915; Ellice Is severed links with Gilbert Is to form separate dependency of Tuvalu, 1975; Gilbert independence as Kiribati, 1979; a sovereign and democratic republic, with a president and an elected

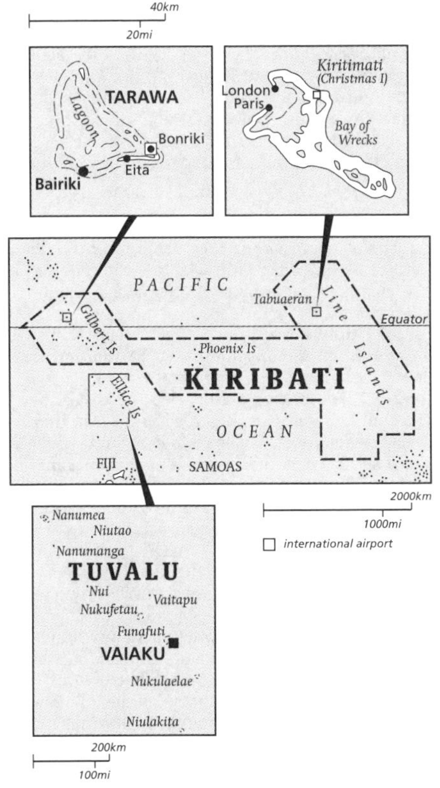

House of Assembly; phosphates, copra, coconuts, bananas, pandanus, breadfruit, papaya, sea fishing. >> Kiritimati; Pacific Ocean; Tuvalu; RR1014 political leaders

Kiritimati [krismas], Eng **Christmas Island** 2°00N 157°30W; pop (1995e) 2840; area 390 sq km/150 sq mi. Largest atoll in the world, one of the Line Is, Kiribati; visited by Captain Cook, 1777; annexed by the British, 1888; used as an air base; nuclear testing site in late 1950s. >> Cook, James; Kiribati ℹ

Kirkpatrick, Jeane (Duane Jordan) (1926–) US stateswoman and academic, born in Duncan, OK. She became Georgetown University's professor of government in 1978, and was appointed permanent representative to the UN by President Reagan (1981–5).

Kirkwall 58°59N 2°58W, pop (1995e) 6700. Port capital of Orkney, N Scotland; on island of Mainland; airport; cathedral (1137–1200). >> Orkney; Scotland ℹ

Kirov, Sergey Mironovich [**ki**rof] (1886–1934) Russian revolutionary and politician, born in Urzhun, Russia. He played an active part in the October Revolution and Civil War, and in 1934 became a secretary of the Central Committee. He was assassinated at his Leningrad headquarters, possibly at the instigation of Stalin, and his death served as the pretext for a widespread campaign of reprisals. >> October Revolution; Stalin

Kisangani [keesan**gah**nee], formerly **Stanleyville** (to 1966) 0°33N 25°14E, pop (1995e) 371 000. City in NC Democratic Republic of Congo; on the R Congo; founded by Stanley, 1882; airport; university (1963). >> Zaire ℹ

Kissinger, Henry (Alfred) [**ki**sinjer] (1923–) US secretary of state (1973–6) and academic, born in Fürth, Germany. He became President Nixon's adviser on national security affairs in 1969, was the main American figure in the negotiations to end the Vietnam War (for which he shared the 1973 Nobel Peace Prize), and became secretary of state under Nixon and Ford. His 'shuttle diplomacy' was aimed at bringing about peace between Israel and the Arab states. He published *Diplomacy* (1994). >> Arab–Israeli Wars; Ford, Gerald R; Nixon, Richard M; Vietnam War

Kistna, River >> **Krishna, River**

kit A small violin, usually with four strings and a narrow body, in use from the 16th-c to the 19th-c, especially by dancing masters. >> string instrument 1 ℹ; violin

Kita-Kyushu [**kee**ta **kyu**shoo] 33°52N 130°49E, pop (1995) 1 034 000. City in N Kyushu, Japan; airport; railway; Japan's leading centre for chemicals and heavy industry. >> Kyushu

kit-cat portrait A life-size half-length portrait painted on a canvas 36 × 28 in (c.90 × 70 cm). The term derives from Kneller's series of portraits painted c.1700–17 of the members of the Kit-Cat Club in London (now in the National Portrait Gallery). >> Kneller

Kitchener (of Khartoum and of Broome), (Horatio) Herbert Kitchener, 1st Earl (1850–1916) British field marshal, born near Ballylongford, Co Kerry, Ireland. By the final rout of the Khalifa at Omdurman (1898), he won back the Sudan for Egypt. Commander-in-chief in South Africa (1900–2), he brought the Boer War to an end. He then became commander-in-chief in India (1902–9), and secretary for war (1914), when he organized manpower on a vast scale ('Kitchener armies'). >> Boer Wars; World War 1

kite (ornithology) A hawk of the subfamily Milvinae (**true kites**) or Elaninae (**white-tailed kites**), found worldwide; the most varied and diverse group of hawks. (Family: Accipitridae, c.27 species.) >> hawk

kite (recreation) A frame covered with a light fabric or paper, flown on a long string. It was first documented in China (AD 549) in relation to military communications. They are popular as a leisure activity, and have practical applications in meteorology and surveying.

kithara A musical instrument of classical antiquity, resembling a lyre. The strings were plucked with a plectrum. >> lyre; string instrument 2 ℹ

Kitt, Eartha (Mae) (c.1928–) Entertainer and singer, born in North, SC. Her vocal vibrancy, fiery personality, and cat-like singing voice made her a top international cabaret attraction and recording artiste. She received the Golden Rose of Montreux for *Kaskade* (1962), and was appropriately cast as Catwoman in the television series *Batman* (1966).

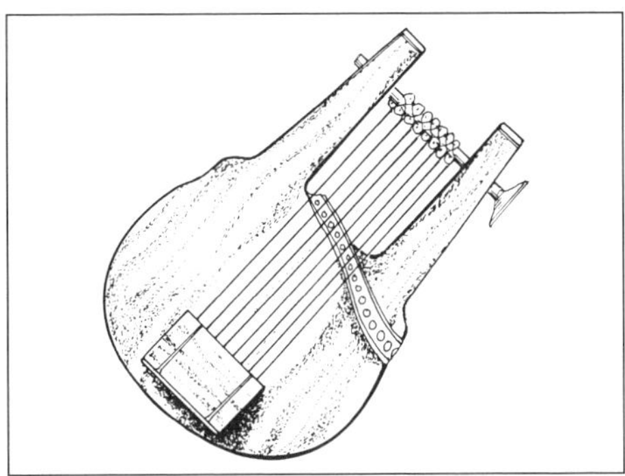

Kithara

kittiwake Either of two species of marine bird of the genus *Rissa*: the **black-legged kittiwake** (*Rissa tridactyla*) from N areas of the N oceans; and the **red-legged kittiwake** (*Rissa brevirostris*) from the Bering Sea. (Family: Laridae.) >> gull

Kitwe [**keet**way] 12°48S 28°14E, pop (1995e) 573 000. Modern mining city in Copperbelt province, Zambia; Zambia's second largest town; railway. >> Copperbelt; Zambia ℹ

Kitzbühel [**kitz**büel] 47°27N 12°23E, pop (1995e) 8500. Winter sports resort in C Austria; railway; health resort, tourism, casino. >> Alps

Kivu, Lake [**kee**voo] area 4750 sq km/1800 sq mi. Lake in EC Africa; length, c.95 km/60 mi; width, 50 km/30 mi; altitude, 1460 m/4790 ft. >> Rift Valley

Kiwanis International >> **service club**

kiwi A flightless nocturnal bird; native to New Zealand; small eyes; acute sense of smell (rare in birds); long curved bill with nostrils at tip; strong legs. (Genus: *Apteryx*, 3 species. Family: Apterygidae.)

kiwi fruit A woody climber (*Actinidia chinensis*), native to China, and also called **Chinese gooseberry**, but cultivated in New Zealand, hence the better-known name; flowers creamy, 6-petalled; fruit oblong-oval, furry with reddish-green hairs, flesh green, sweet, surrounding black seeds. (Family: Actinidiaceae.) >> climbing plant

Kjölen Mountains [**kyoe**luhn] or **Kolen Mountains** Mountain range along the boundary between NE Norway and NW Sweden; rises to 2111 m/6926 ft at Kebnekaise. >> Sweden ℹ

Klaproth, Martin Heinrich [**klap**roht] (1743–1817) Chemist, born in Wernigerode, Germany. He devised new analytical methods, and discovered zirconium, uranium, strontium, and titanium. >> chemical elements

Klee, Paul [klay] (1879–1940) Artist, born in Münchenbuchsee, Switzerland. A member of the *Blaue Reiter* group (1911–12), he taught at the Bauhaus (1920–32). His early work consists of bright watercolours, but after 1919 he worked in oils, producing small-scale, mainly abstract pictures, as in his 'Twittering Machine' (1922, New York). >> abstract art; Bauhaus; *Blaue Reiter, der*

Klein, Calvin (Richard) [kliyn] (1942–) Fashion designer, born in New York City. He became known for the simple but sophisticated style of his clothes, including 'designer jeans'.

Klein, Melanie [kliyn] (1882–1960) Austrian child psychoanalyst. A student of Sigmund Freud, she was the first to use the content and style of children's play to understand their mental processes. >> Freud, Sigmund

Kleist, (Bernd) Heinrich (Wilhelm) von [kliyst] (1777–1811) Playwright and poet, born in Frankfurt an der Oder, Germany. His best plays are still popular, notably *Prinz Friedrich von Homburg* (1821). His novellas, such as *Michael Kohlhaas* (1810–11), also became well known.

Klemperer, Otto (1885–1973) German conductor, born in Wrocław, Poland (formerly Breslau, Prussia). In his later years, he concentrated mainly on the German classical composers, and was particularly known for his interpretation of Beethoven. He also composed six symphonies, a Mass, and Lieder. >> *Lied*

Klimt, Gustav (1862–1918) Painter, born in Vienna, the leading master of the Vienna *Sezession*. His murals for the University of Vienna (1900–3) used a Symbolist style which caused great controversy. >> *Sezession*; Symbolists

Kline, Kevin [kliyn] (1947–) Film actor, born in St Louis, MO. Though known for his dramatic abilities, it was his comic role in *A Fish Called Wanda* (1988) that earned him an Oscar as Best Supporting Actor. Later films include *Chaplin* (1992), *Looking for Richard* (1996), and *Fierce Creatures* (1997).

Klinger, Friedrich Maximilian von (1752–1831) Playwright and romance writer, born in Frankfurt, Germany. The *Sturm-und-Drang* school was named after one of his tragedies. >> *Sturm und Drang*

Klippel, Robert Edward (1920–) Sculptor, born in Sydney, New South Wales, Australia. His sculptures are intricate and complex, often made of metal 'found objects' welded together (hence the name 'junk sculpture'), though he does also work with wood, plaster, and bronze.

Klitzing constant A constant which forms the international standard of resistance measurement; symbol R_K, defined as h/e^2, where h is Planck's constant and e is the electron charge; named after Klaus von Klitzing (1943–).

Klondike gold rush A flood of prospectors (largely US) when gold was discovered in Canada Yukon Territory in 1896. The rush lasted for five years. >> Yukon

Klopstock, Friedrich Gottlieb (1724–1803) Poet, born in Quedlinburg, Germany. Regarded in his own time as a great religious poet, he helped to inaugurate the golden age of German literature, especially by his lyrics and odes.

Klosters [**kloh**sterz] 46°54N 9°54E, pop (1995e) 3800. Alpine winter skiing resort in E Switzerland; comprises the villages of Platz, Dörfli, and Brücke. >> Alps

Kluane National park in SW Yukon territory, Canada; established in 1972; along with the Wrangell–St Elias park, forms the world's largest nature reserve; a world heritage site. >> Yukon

klystron A device for amplifying microwave beams. It is used in particle accelerators and radar, and may also be used as a producer of microwaves. >> microwaves

knapweed The name for many species of *Centaurea*, mostly perennials; hard rounded flower-heads surrounded by many closely overlapping bracts; florets purple or yellow. (Genus: *Centaurea*. Family: Compositae.)

knee Commonly used to refer to the region around the knee-cap (*patella*); more specifically, in anatomy, the largest joint in the human body, being the articulation between the femur and the tibia. It allows a wide range of movement. >> femur; housemaid's knee; joint; skeleton ℹ; tibia

Kneller, Sir Godfrey [**kne**ler], originally **Gottfried Kniller** (1646–1723) Portrait painter, born in Lübeck, Germany. His best-known works are his 48 portraits of members of the Whig 'Kit-Cat Club' (1700–17, National Portrait Gallery, London), and of nine sovereigns. >> kit-cat portrait

Knesset [**kne**set] The Israeli parliament. Its term of office is four years, and the country's president is elected by the Knesset for five years. >> Israel ℹ

Knievel, Evel [**knee**vel, **ee**vel], professional name of **Robert Craig Knievel** (1938–) Motorcycle stunt performer, born in Butte, MT. He began carrying out motorcycle stunts as a teenager, eventually forming Evel Knievel's Motorcycle Devils in 1965, becoming known for his spectacular and dangerous performances. He later managed the stunt career of his son, **Robbie Knievel**.

Knight, Dame Laura *née* **Johnson** (1877–1970) Artist, born in Long Eaton, Derbyshire. She produced a long series of oil paintings of the ballet, the circus and gypsy life, in a lively and forceful style.

knight In the UK, a title of honour granted as a reward for services, permitting the use of *Sir* with one's name; originally (in the Middle Ages) men who formed an elite cavalry. The ideal of knighthood involved the maintenance of personal honour, religious devotion, and loyalty to one's lord. >> (Orders of) Bath / British Empire / Companions of Honour / Garter / St Michael and St George / Thistle; Hospitallers; knight bachelor; Templars

knight bachelor (KB) In the UK, the lowest, but most ancient, form of knighthood, originating in the reign of Henry III. A KB is not a member of any order of chivalry. >> knight

Knights Hospitallers / of Jerusalem / of Malta / of Rhodes >> **Hospitallers**

Knights Templars >> **Templars**

knitting An ancient craft used for making fabric by linking together loops of yarn using two, three, or four hand-held needles. The first knitting machine was invented in England by William Lee (c.1550–c.1610). The manufacture of knitted fabrics in tubular form is known as *circular knitting*; such fabrics are often used in underwear and sportswear. >> yarn

knocking An audible shuddering sound produced by an engine, because of the uneven burning of its air/fuel mixture. To overcome the problem, antiknocking fuels are used. >> antiknock; diesel engine

Knossos [**kno**sos] An Aegean Bronze Age town at Kephala, NC Crete, flourishing c.1900–1400 BC, and covering c.50 ha/125 acres. Its Minoan palace was discovered in 1899, and later partly reconstructed by Sir Arthur Evans. >> Evans, Arthur; Minoan civilization

knot Either of two species of sandpiper; the widespread **knot** or **red knot** (*Calidris canutus*); and the **eastern knot** or **great knot** (*Calidris tenuirostris*) from E regions of the Old World. >> sandpiper

knotgrass A spreading annual (*Polygonum aviculare*), a widespread weed; each node of the stem enclosed in a silvery sheath; leaves small, elliptical, with small pink or white flowers. (Family: Polygonaceae.)

knowledge-based system A computer system which operates on knowledge, organized as a set of rules, rather than on data. It is used to mirror human decision-making processes, such as medical diagnosis or actuarial assessments. >> expert system

Know-Nothing movement (1856) The popular name for the anti-immigrant American Party in 19th-c USA. It was so called from the response members were instructed to give to questioning: 'I know nothing'.

Knox, John (c.1513–72) Protestant reformer, born near Haddington, East Lothian. A Catholic priest, he was influenced by George Wishart to work for the Lutheran reformation. After Wishart was burned (1546), Knox joined the reformers defending the castle of St Andrews, and became a minister. He was kept a prisoner until 1549, then became a chaplain to Edward VI. On Mary's accession (1553), he fled to Geneva, where he was much influenced by Calvin. After returning to Scotland he founded the Church of Scotland (1560). >> Calvin; Church of Scotland; Reformation; Wishart

Knox, Ronald (Arbuthnott) (1888–1957) Theologian and essayist, born in Birmingham, West Midlands. A convert to Catholicism, he wrote an influential translation of the Bible, and several works of apologetics, as well as detective novels. >> apologetics; Bible

Knox-Johnston, Robin, popular name of **Sir William Robert Patrick Knox-Johnston** (1939–) British yachtsman, the first person to circumnavigate the world non-stop and single-handed, 14 June 1968–22 April 1969. He is also holder of the British Sailing Trans Atlantic Record (1986: 10 days, 14 hours, 9 mins), and he co-skippered *Enza* achieving the world's fastest circumnavigation under sail (1994: 74 days, 22 hours, 17 mins, 22 secs).

koala [koh**ah**la] E Australian marsupial (*Phascolarctos cinereus*); thick soft grey or grey-brown fur with white chest; round head with small eyes, erect fluffy ears, large dark nose pad; also known (incorrectly) as a **koala bear**. (Family: Phascolarctidae.) >> marsupial [i]

koatimundi >> **coati**

Kobe [**koh**bay] 34°40N 135°12E, pop (1995e) 1 485 000. Port in C Honshu, Japan; Japan's international leading commercial port; railway; 15 universities; badly damaged by earthquake, January 1995. >> Honshu

Koblenz >> **Coblenz**

Koch, (Heinrich Hermann) Robert [kokh, **roh**bert] (1843–1910) Bacteriologist, born in Klausthal, Germany. He discovered the tuberculosis bacillus (1882), and later the cholera bacillus (1883), and received the Nobel Prize for Physiology or Medicine in 1905. >> cholera; tuberculosis

Köchel, Ludwig Ritter von [**koe**khel] (1800–77) Musicologist, born in Stein, Austria. He is known as the compiler of the catalogue of Mozart's works, which he arranged in chronological order, giving them the numbers (K1, etc) commonly used to identify them today. >> Mozart

Kodály, Zoltán [**koh**diy] (1882–1967) Composer, born in Kecskemét, Hungary. Among his best-known works are the *Háry János* suite (1926) and several choral compositions, especially his *Psalmus Hungaricus* (1923) and *Te Deum* (1936). >> Bartók

Kodiak Island 57°20N 153°40W, pop (1995e) 15 700. Island in the Gulf of Alaska, USA; 160 km/100 mi long; scene of the first settlement in Alaska (by the Russians, 1784); till 1804 the centre for Russian interests in the USA; home of the Kodiak brown bear (grizzly), the largest living carnivore. >> Alaska

Koechlin, Pat >> **Smythe, Pat**

Koestler, Arthur [**kest**ler] (1905–83) Writer and journalist, born in Budapest. His masterpiece is the political novel *Darkness at Noon* (1940). His nonfiction books and essays deal with politics, scientific creativity, and parapsychology, notably *The Act of Creation* (1964). He became a British citizen in 1948. He and his wife were active members of the Voluntary Euthanasia Society, and, after he developed a terminal illness, they committed suicide. >> euthanasia; parapsychology

Kofun [**koh**fuhn] The burial-mounds characteristic of early historic Japan, which have given their name to the archaeological period AD c.300–700. >> Nara

Koheleth >> **Ecclesiastes, Book of**

Koh-i-noor [koh**ee**noor] (Persian 'mountain of light') A famous Indian diamond with a history dating back to the 14th-c. It was presented to Queen Victoria in 1850, and is now among the British crown jewels. >> crown jewels; diamond

Kohl, Helmut (1930–) German statesman and chancellor (1982–98), born in Ludwigshafen-am-Rhein. After the collapse of the Schmidt coalition in 1982, he was installed as interim chancellor, and in the elections of 1983 formed a government which adopted a central course between political extremes. He presided over the unification of Germany in 1990. >> Christian Democrats; Germany [i]; Schmidt

kohlrabi [**kohl**rabee] A variety of cabbage (*Brassica oleracea*, variety *caulorapa*) with a very short, swollen, green or purple stem. It is eaten as a vegetable. (Family: Crucifereae.) >> cabbage

Kohn, Walter [kohn] (1923–) Chemist, born in Vienna. He became the founding director of the Institute of Theoretical Physics at the University of California, Santa Barbara. He shared the 1998 Nobel Prize for Chemistry for his contribution to studies of the properties of molecules and the chemical processes in which they are involved – specifically, for his development of the density-functional theory.

Kok, Willem, known as **Wim Kok** (1938–) Trade Union official, politician, and Dutch prime minister (1994–), born in Bergambacht, The Netherlands. After holding various posts in the Netherlands Association of Trade

Unions, he became chairman of the Federation of Dutch Trade Unions in 1981. In 1985 he entered parliament, representing the PvdA (Partij van de Arbeid) from 1986. He served as finance minister and vice premier (1989–94) before becoming prime minister.

Kokoschka, Oskar [ko**kosh**ka] (1886–1980) Artist, born in Pöchlarn, Austria. He travelled widely, and painted many Expressionist landscapes in Europe. >> Expressionism

kola or **cola** An evergreen tree native to tropical Africa. The woody fruits contain glossy nuts high in caffeine, which is released when the nuts are chewed. (Genus: *Cola*, 125 species. Family: Sterculiaceae.) >> caffeine

Kola Peninsula [**ko**la], Russ **Kol'skiy Poluostrov** Peninsula in NW European Russia, forming the NE extension of Scandinavia; length, 400 km/250 mi; width, 240 km/150 mi. >> Russia [i]

Kolbe, St Maximilian (Maria) [**kol**buh] (1894–1941) Franciscan priest, born near Łódź, Poland. He was arrested by the Gestapo in 1941, and imprisoned in Auschwitz, where he gave his life in exchange for one of the condemned prisoners, Franciszek Gajowniczek. He was canonized in 1982. Feast day 14 August.

Kolchak, Alexander Vasilevich (1874–1920) Russian admiral and leader of counter-revolutionary (White) forces during the Russian Civil War, born in the Crimea. He established an anti-Bolshevik government in Siberia, and proclaimed himself 'Supreme Ruler' of Russia. He was captured and shot by Red Army forces in Irkutsk. >> Russian Civil War; White Russians

Kolekole >> **Haleakala Crater**

Kolen Mountains >> **Kjölen Mountains**

Köln >> **Cologne**

Kolyma, River [koli**ma**] River in E Russia, rising in the Khrebet Cherskogo; enters the E Siberian Sea; length, 2513 km/1562 mi. >> Russia [i]

Komodo [ko**moh**doh] 8°35S 119°30E. Small island in Indonesia; part of the Lesser Sunda Is. >> Komodo dragon [i]

Komodo dragon A rare SE Asian monitor lizard (*Varanus komodoensis*), native to the islands of Komodo, Flores, Pintja, and Padar (Indonesia); the world's largest lizard (length, up to 3 m/10 ft); occasionally attacks and kills people; also known as **Komodo lizard** or **ora**. >> Komodo

Kompong Som or **Kampong Saom** 10°38N 103°30E. Seaport in S Cambodia; a new city, completed in 1960; chief deepwater port and commercial centre of Cambodia; airfield; railway. >> Cambodia [i]

Komsomol [**kom**somol] The All-Union Leninist Communist League of Youth, founded in 1918, incorporating almost all persons between the ages of 14 and 28. It served as a recruiting ground for party membership during the communist years, and disbanded in 1991. >> Communist Party of the Soviet Union

kongoni >> **hartebeest**

Konstanz >> **Constance**

Kon Tiki [kon **tee**kee] A balsa-wood raft built in 1947 by Thor Heyerdahl. He and five others sailed 6000 km/3800 mi from South America to Polynesia in the 13·7 m/45 ft-long raft to prove his theories on the migration of early man. >> Heyerdahl

Komodo dragon

Konya [**kon**ya], ancient **Iconium** 37°51N 32°30E, pop (1995e) 572 000. Holy city in SC Turkey; visited by St Paul; order of the Whirling Dervishes founded here by Islamic mystical poet, Jalal al-Din Rumi, known as Mevlana ('our lord'); airfield; railway; trade centre of a rich agricultural region. >> dervish; Paul, St; Turkey [i]

kookaburra Either of two species of bird of the kingfisher family: the **laughing kookaburra** or **laughing jackass** (*Dacelo novaeguinae*) from Australia; and the **blue-winged kookaburra** or **howling jackass** (*Dacelo leachii*) from Australia and New Guinea. They inhabit dry forest and savannah, and have loud laugh-like cries. (Family: Alcedinidae.) >> kingfisher

Kópavogur [**kop**avogur] 64°06N 21°56W, pop (1995e) 17 100. Second largest town in Iceland; developed since 1945 to house people working in Reykjavík. >> Iceland [i]; Reykjavík

kopje >> **tor**

Koran or **Qu'ran** [ko**rahn**] The sacred book of Islam. It is held to be the direct word of God, revealed piecemeal to the Prophet Mohammed as a message for all humanity. >> Islam; Mohammed

Korda, Sir Alexander, originally **Sándor Laszlo Korda** (1893–1956) Film producer, born in Puszta, Hungary. His many films as producer include *The Private Life of Henry VIII* (1932), which he also directed, *The Third Man* (1949), and *Richard III* (1956).

Kordestan >> **Kurdistan**

Korea or **South Korea**, official name **Republic of Korea**, Korean **Tae Han Minguk** pop (1995e) 44 853 000; area 98 913 sq km/38 180 sq mi. Republic of E Asia occupying the S half of the Korean peninsula; separated from North Korea by a demilitarized zone at 38°N; capital, Seoul; timezone GMT +9; population mainly Korean, with a small Chinese minority; chief religions Confucianism, Shamanism, Christianity, Buddhism; official language, Korean; unit of currency, the won; an official observer at the United Nations, not holding UN membership; Taebaek Sanmaek range runs N–S along the E coast; descends to broad, undulating coastal lowlands; c.3000 islands off the W and S coasts; largest is Cheju do, which contains Korea's highest peak, 1950 m/6398 ft; extreme continental climate, with cold winters and hot summers; ruled by the ancient Choson dynasty until 1st-c BC; split into three rival kingdoms, united in 668 by the Silla dynasty; succeeded by the Koryo dynasty, 935; Yi dynasty, 1392–1910; independence recognized by China, 1895; annexation by Japan, 1910; entered by Russia (from N) and USA (from S) to enforce the Japanese surrender, dividing the country at the 38th parallel; North Korean forces invaded, 1950; UN forces assisted South Korea in stopping the advance, 1950–3; military coup, 1961; assassination of Park Chung Hee, 1979; non-aggression pact signed with N Korea, 1991; governed by a president, a State Council, and a National Assembly; light consumer goods, with a shift towards heavy industries; one of the world's largest deposits of tungsten; only a fifth of Korea suitable for cultivation; hosted the Olympic Games in 1988. >> Korean; Korean War; Seoul; RR1014 political leaders; *see illustration on p. 473*

Korea, North, official name **Democratic People's Republic of Korea**, Korean **Choson Minjujuui In'min Konghwaguk** pop (1995e) 23 518 000; area 122 098 sq km/47 130 sq mi. Socialist state in East Asia, in the N half of the Korean peninsula; separated from South Korea to the S by a demilitarized zone of 1262 sq km/487 sq mi; capital, Pyongyang; timezone GMT +9; major ethnic group, Korean;

traditional religions, Buddhism and Confucianism, but religious activities now minimal; official language, Korean; unit of currency, the won of 100 chon; on a high plateau occupying the N part of a mountainous peninsula which projects SE from China; many areas rise to over 2000 m/7000 ft; temperate climate, with warm summers and severely cold winters; Korean Peninsula conquered by Chinese, 1392; formally annexed by Japan, 1910; N area occupied by Soviet troops, meeting US troops from the S along latitude 38°N; Korean War, 1950–3; demilitarized zone established, 1953; reunification talks, 1980, broken off by North Korea; non-aggression agreement signed with S Korea in 1991; death of Kim Il Sung, 1994; governed by a president and a Supreme People's Assembly; traditionally agricultural population on low coastal zones in the E and W; extensive destruction during the Korean War, but rapid recovery with Soviet and Chinese aid; c.48% of workforce employed in agriculture, generally on large-scale collective farms. >> Korean; Korean War; Pyongyang; RR1014 political leaders

Korean A language of uncertain origin, showing resemblances to the Altaic family and to Japanese. It is spoken by over 50 million people in N and S Korea, China, Japan, and Russia. >> Altaic

Korean War (1950–3) A war between Communist and non-Communist forces in Korea, which had been partitioned along the 38th parallel in 1945 after Japan's defeat. The Communist North invaded the South in 1950, and a United Nations force intervened, driving the invaders back to the Chinese frontier. China then entered the war, and together with the N Koreans occupied Seoul. The UN forces counter-attacked, and by 1953, when an armistice was signed, had retaken all territory S of the 38th parallel. >> Korea ℹ; Korea, North ℹ; MacArthur, Douglas; United Nations

Koresh, David [**ko**resh] (1960–93) Cult leader, born in Texas, USA. He was the charismatic leader of a heavily armed group of Branch Davidians (a sect which had split away from the Seventh Day Adventist Church in 1959) who were put under siege by federal agents at a ranch in Mount Carmel, Waco, TX, in 1993. The siege ended after a devastating fire in which Koresh and many of his followers were killed.

Kórinthos >> **Corinth**

Kornberg, Arthur (1918–) Biochemist, born in New York City. In 1959 he shared the Nobel Prize for Physiology or Medicine for showing how DNA molecules are duplicated in bacterial cells, and replicating this process in the test-tube. >> DNA ℹ

Korolyov, Sergey (Pavlovich) [**ko**rolyof], also spelled **Korolev** (1907–66) Rocketry pioneer, aerospace engineer, and space programme leader, born in Zhitomir, Ukraine. He developed the first Soviet intercontinental ballistic missile, and was leader of the Soviet space programme. >> Soviet space programme

Koror [**koh**raw(r)] 7°21N 134°31E, pop (1995) 11 100. Capital town of Belau, W Pacific Ocean, on Koror I; airport on neighbouring island of Babeldoab. >> Belau

Kós >> **Cos**

Kosciusko, Mount [koseeuhs**koh**] 36°28S 148°17E. Highest mountain in Australia (2228 m/7310 ft); in the Snowy Mts of the Australian Alps, New South Wales. >> Australia ℹ

Kościuszko or **Kościusko, Thaddeusz (Andrzej) Bonawentura** [kosh**choosh**koh] (1746–1817) Polish general and patriot, born near Slonim, Lithuania. In 1776 he volunteered to serve in the American Revolution, and fought in several campaigns, returning to Poland in 1784. His defeat of the Russians at Raclawice was followed by a rising in Warsaw; he established a provisional government, but was defeated at Maciejowice (1794) and taken prisoner until 1796.

kosher Food fulfilling the requirements of Jewish Law, including the manner of preparation. In orthodox Judaism, only certain animals, which must be ritually slaughtered, may be eaten. >> Judaism

Košice [**ko**shitsuh], Ger **Kaschau**, Hung **Kassa** 48°43N 21°14E, pop (1995e) 240 000. Industrial city in Slovak Republic; on R Hornád; formerly part of Hungary;

airport; railway; technical university (1952); cathedral (13th-c). >> Slovak Republic [i]

Kosovo [**kos**uhvuh], Serbo-Croat, Albanian **Kosova** pop (1995e) 1 978 000; area 10 887 sq km/4200 sq mi. Province of S Serbia; capital, Pristina; 90% of population Albanian (Kosovars, mostly Muslim); agricultural region; central part of Serbian kingdom, 11th–14th-c; under Ottoman rule, 14th-c–1912; annexed by Serbia, 1912; incorporated into Kingdom of Serbs, Croats, and Slovenes, 1918 (Yugoslavia from 1929); part of Greater Albania under Italian occupation, 1941–3; autonomous province of Serbia to 1989; declared independence in 1990, with president and parliament elected in 1992, but implementation disallowed by Serbian authorities; conflict between Serbia and ethnic Albanian armed resistance movement (Kosovo Liberation Army) since late 1997; NATO observers introduced, 1998; focus of international concern in early 1999, following escalation of conflict, with fresh reports of war crimes and violations of human rights; failure of peace talks at Rambouillet Chateau near Paris (Feb); increase of Serbian incursions into Kosovo (Mar), with displacement of Kosovar Albanians; onset of NATO air-strikes campaign (Operation Allied Force) against targets in Yugoslavia (Mar); massive escalation in numbers of refugees forced to leave Kosovo, with over a million displaced by mid-April, burning of Albanian villages, and reports of widespread atrocities; further build-up of NATO forces in the region (May); ongoing international diplomatic efforts, resulting (Jun) in the entry of a NATO peace-keeping force (KFOR), the withdrawal of Serb troops, and the first return of refugees. >> Milosevic; Serbia

Kosrae [**koz**ray], formerly **Kusaie** pop (1995e) 7700; area 100 sq km/40 sq mi. Island group, one of the Federated States of Micronesia, W Pacific; capital, Lelu; airport on Kosrae I. >> Micronesia, Federated States of

Kossoff, David (1919–) British actor, writer, and illustrator. He became known for his portrayal of Jewish characters, and for his short stories based on Jewish traditions and culture. He is also well known for his Bible storytelling programmes on radio and television.

Kossuth, Lajos [**ko**sooth, **lo**yosh], also Hung [koshut] (1802–94) Hungarian statesman, a leader of the 1848 Hungarian Revolution, born in Monok, Hungary. He was appointed provisional governor of Hungary (1849), but internal dissensions led to his resignation, and he fled to Turkey, and then to England. >> Hungary [i]; Revolutions of 1848

Kosygin, Alexey Nikolayevich [ko**see**gin] (1904–80) Russian statesman and premier (1964–80), born in St Petersburg, Russia. First deputy prime minister (with Mikoyan) from 1960, he succeeded Khrushchev as chairman of the Council of Ministers. He resigned in 1980 because of ill health. >> communism; Khrushchev; Mikoyan

koto A Japanese zither, about 1·85 cm/6 ft long, with 13 silk strings stretched across movable bridges which allow a variety of tunings. It is placed on the floor; the player sits cross-legged or kneels before it, and plucks the strings using plectra. >> plectrum; string instrument 2 [i]; zither

Kotor [**kot**uh(r)] A region of both natural and culturo-historical interest, located on the Montenegrin coast; a world heritage site. >> Montenegro

Kotzebue, August (Friedrich Ferdinand) von [**kotze**-byoo] (1761–1819) Playwright, born in Weimar, Germany. He wrote about 200 poetic dramas, notably *Menschenhass und Reue* (1789–90, trans The Stranger), as well as tales, satires, and historical works. He was assassinated at Mannheim as an alleged spy.

Koulouri >> **Salamis** (Greece)

koumiss or **kumiss** A fermented drink obtained from ass's or mare's milk. Originally made by nomadic peoples of C Asia, it has been used both as medicine and beverage. >> milk

Koussevitsky, Serge [koose**vit**skee], originally **Sergei Alexandrovich Koussevitsky** (1874–1951) Conductor, born in Vishni-Volochok, Russia. He was conductor of the Boston Symphony Orchestra (1924–49), and established a Music Foundation which commissioned works from several major composers.

Kowloon [kow**loon**], also **Jiulong** area 11 sq km/4 sq mi. Peninsula and region of Hong Kong; railway link to Guangzhou (Canton); site of Hong Kong's airport. >> Hong Kong [i]

Kozhikode [**koh**zhuhkohd], formerly **Calicut** 11°15N 75°43E, pop (1995e) 867 000. Port city in Kerala, SW India; trade centre since the 14th-c; railway; university (1968); gave its name to calico cotton. >> Kerala

Krafft-Ebing, Richard, Freiherr von (Baron) [kraft **eb**ing] (1840–1902) Psychiatrist, born in Mannheim, Germany. A specialist in nervous diseases, he was an early investigator of sexual disorders. >> psychiatry

krait [kriyt] A venomous Asian snake of genus *Bungarus* (several species); related to the cobra, but smaller and lacks a 'hood'; causes many deaths each year in India. >> sea snake; snake

Krajina [**kra**jina] Serbian enclave in SW Croatia; proclaimed autonomy as Serbian Autonomous Region (SAR), 1990; administrative base, Knin; unilaterally declared status as republic, 1991. >> Bosnia and Herzegovina [i]; Croatia [i]

Krakatoa [kraka**toh**a] Volcanic island in the Sunda Strait between Java and Sumatra. Active for the last million years, it erupted catastrophically in 1883. Several tsunamis were generated, causing the deaths of 36 000 people in the coastal areas of Java and Sumatra. >> Indonesia [i]; tsunami; volcano

Kraków or **Cracow** [kra**kuf**], Ger **Krakau**, ancient **Cracovia** 50°04N 19°57E, pop (1995e) 757 000. Industrial city in S Poland, on R Vistula; third largest city in Poland; capital, 1305–1609; airport; railway; includes Nowa Huta industrial centre; Jagiellonian University (1364); technical university (1945); cathedral (14th-c), royal castle; Market Square (14th-c), a world heritage site. >> Poland [i]

Kramer, Dame Leonie (Judith) [**kray**mer] (1924–) Academic, writer, and administrator, born in Melbourne, Victoria, Australia. Chancellor of Sydney University (1991), she is a prominent member of the group 'Australians for Constitutional Monarchy', founded in 1992 in response to growing republican sentiment.

Krasnoyarsk [krasno**yah(r)sk**] 56°08N 93°00E, pop (1995e) 932 000. Fast-growing river-port capital in W Siberian Russia, on the R Yenisey; founded as a fortress, 1628; airport; on the Trans-Siberian Railway; university (1969). >> Russia [i]

Kray brothers Convicted British murderers, twin brothers who ran a criminal Mafia-style operation in the East End of London in the 1960s: **Ronald Kray** (1933–95) and **Reginald Kray** (1933–). Following a series of increasingly violent activities, they were tried at the Old Bailey in 1969, and sentenced to life imprisonment of not less than 30 years.

Krebs, Sir Hans (Adolf) (1900–81) Physiologist, born in Hildesheim, Germany. He shared the Nobel Prize for Physiology or Medicine in 1953 for his work on the nature of metabolic processes. >> Krebs cycle

Krebs cycle A sequence of biochemical reactions in biological systems which results in the release of large amounts of energy; named after Hans Adolf Krebs, and also called the **citric acid cycle**. >> Krebs; metabolism

Kreisler, Fritz [**kriys**ler] (1875–1962) Violinist, born in

Vienna. He became internationally known as a violinist, and also composed violin pieces, a string quartet, and an operetta, *Apple Blossoms* (1919), which was a Broadway success.

Kremlin The mediaeval citadel of a Russian town, generally used with reference to the Kremlin at Moscow, which was originally constructed of wood in the 12th-c, subsequently rebuilt in brick in the 14th-c, and later embellished so that its palaces and cathedrals reflect a variety of architectural styles. It was the residence of the tsars until 1712, and in 1918 became the political and administrative headquarters of the USSR. >> Moscow

Kreutzer, Rodolphe [**kroy**tzer] (1766–1831) Violinist, born in Versailles, France. From 1784 until 1810 he was one of the leading concert violinists in Europe. He became friendly with Beethoven, who dedicated a sonata to him. >> Beethoven; violin

krill A typically oceanic, shrimp-like crustacean, length up to 50 mm/2 in; often migrates to surface, massing into vast aggregations that form the main food source of baleen whales. (Class: Malacostraca. Order: Euphausiacea.) >> crustacean; shrimp; whale i

Krishna [**krish**na] According to Hindu tradition, the eighth incarnation, in human form, of the deity Vishnu. A great hero and ruler, the Mahabharata tells the story of his adventures. Disguised as a charioteer in an eve-of-battle dialogue with Arjuna, he delivers the great moral discourse of the Bhagavadgita. >> Bhagavadgita; Hare Krishna movement; Hinduism; Vishnu

Krishna or **Kistna, River** [**krish**na] River in S India; rises in the Western Ghats; enters the Bay of Bengal; length 1300 km/800 mi; its source is sacred to Hindus. >> Hinduism; India i

Krishna Menon, V(engalil) K(rishnan) [**krish**na **me**non] (1896–1974) Indian politician and diplomat, born in Kozhikode (formerly Calicut), Malabar. He was India's first high commissioner in London (1947), and the leader of the Indian delegation to the United Nations (1952). >> India i

Krishnamurti, Jiddu [krishna**moor**tee] (1895–1986) Theosophist, born in Madras. He was educated in England by Annie Besant, who in 1925 proclaimed him the Messiah. Later he rejected this persona, and travelled the world advocating a way of life unconditioned by the narrowness of nationality, race, and religion. >> Besant, Annie; theosophy

Kristiansen, Ingrid, *née* **Christensen** (1956–) Athlete, born in Trondheim, Norway. A former cross-country skiing champion, and now an outstanding long-distance runner, she is the only person to hold world best times for the 5000 m, 10 000 m, and marathon, which she achieved in 1985–6. She was the world cross-country champion in 1988. >> athletics; marathon

Kristianstad [krist**yan**stad] 56°02N 14°10E, pop (1995e) 74 200. Seaport in S Sweden, on R Helge; founded by Denmark, 1614; ceded to Sweden, 1658; taken by the Danes, 1676–8. >> Sweden i

Kropotkin, Pyotr Alexeyevich, Knyaz (Prince) [kro**pot**kin] (1842–1921) Geographer and anarchist, born in Moscow. In 1872 he associated himself with the extremist section of the International, and was imprisoned (1874–6, 1883–6). Settling in England, he wrote on anarchism, social justice, and many other topics. He returned to Russia in 1917. >> anarchism; International

Kroto, Harold [**kroh**toh] (1939–) Chemist, born in Wisbech, Cambridgeshire. He shared the Nobel Prize for Chemistry in 1996 for his contribution to the discovery of fullerenes (1985).

Kru A Kwa-speaking people of Liberia and Côte d'Ivoire. The largest settlement is now in Monrovia. >> Côte d'Ivoire i; Liberia i

Kruger, Paul [**kroo**ger], in full **Stephanus Johannes Paulus Kruger**, nickname **Oom** ('Uncle') **Paul** (1825–1904) Afrikaner statesman and president (1883–1902) of the South African Republic, born in Colesberg, South Africa. He became leader of the independence movement when Britain annexed Transvaal (1877). During the second Boer War (1899–1902), he came to Europe to seek (in vain) alliances against Britain, making his headquarters at Utrecht. >> Boer Wars

Krugerrand A gold coin of the Republic of South Africa, 1 ounce in weight, named after the Boer statesman Paul Kruger (the *rand* being the unit of South African currency). They are bought for investment, and are not part of the everyday currency of South Africa. >> Kruger

Krupp, Gustav, originally **Gustav von Bohlen und Halbach** (1870–1950) Industrialist, born in The Hague. A Prussian diplomat who married **Bertha Krupp** (1886–1957), heiress to the Krupp industrial empire, a special imperial edict allowed him to adopt his wife's surname. During World War 1, his firm manufactured the long-range gun for the shelling of Paris, nicknamed 'Big Bertha'. He later gave financial support to Hitler, and connived in secret rearmament. After World War 2, the Krupp empire was split up by the Allies. >> Hitler

krypton Kr, element 36, the fourth of the noble gases. It liquefies at −150°C, and makes up about 0·0001% of the atmosphere. >> chemical elements; noble gases; RR1036

K2 or **Mount Godwin-Austen** 35°53N 76°30E. Second highest mountain in the world and highest in the Karakoram range, NE Pakistan; height 8611 m/28 250 ft; named for English topographer Henry Godwin-Austen; the second peak to be measured in this range (hence, K2). >> Himalayas

Kuala Lumpur [**kwah**la **lum**poor] 3°08N 101°42E, pop (1995e) 1 388 000. Capital of Malaysia; large Chinese and Indian population; former capital of Selangor; capital of Federated Malay States, 1895; designated a Federal Territory, 1974; airport; railway; university (1962); technical university (1954); commercial centre; Petronas Twin Towers (1996), in 1998 tallest building in the world (451.9 m/1483 ft). >> Malaysia i; Petronas Twin Towers

Kubitschek (de Oliveira), Juscelino [**kub**shek] (1902–76) Brazilian statesman and president (1956–61), born in Diamantina, Minas Gerais, Brazil. His government sponsored rapid economic growth and the dramatic building of a new capital, Brasília. >> Brazil i

Kublai Khan [**koo**bliy kahn] (1214–94) First emperor (1279–94) of the Yuan dynasty in China, the grandson of Genghis Khan. He was acclaimed Great Khan in 1260, with suzerainty from the Pacific to the Black Sea. The splendour of his court was legendary. >> Genghis Khan; Polo, Marco

Kubrick, Stanley [**koo**brik] (1928–99) Screen writer, film producer, and director, born in New York City. His films include *Spartacus* (1960), *Lolita* (1962), *Dr Strangelove* (1964), *2001: A Space Odyssey* (1965), *A Clockwork Orange* (1971), and *The Shining* (1980).

Kudelka, James [ku**del**ka] (1955–) Ballet dancer, choreographer, and director, born in Newmarket, Ontario, Canada. He joined the National Ballet of Canada, then Les Grands Ballets Canadiens in Montreal. Artist in residence at the National Ballet of Canada from 1992, he took over as director in 1996.

Kudrow, Lisa [**kud**roh] (1963–) Actor, born in Encino, CA. She became known for her role as Ursula in *Mad About You* (1992–), then achieved a major success as Phoebe Buffay (Ursula's 'twin sister') in the acclaimed television series *Friends* (1994–). Her feature films include *Mother* (1996) and *Romy and Michelle's High School Reunion* (1997).

Kuei-yang >> **Guiyang**

Kuhn, Thomas (Samuel) [koon] (1922–96) Philosopher

and historian of science, born in Cincinnati, OH. His book *The Structure of Scientific Revolutions* (1962) challenged the idea of cumulative, unidirectional scientific progress. His theory of 'paradigms', as sets of related concepts which compete for acceptance in times of rapid scientific change or revolution, has been influential in many fields of enquiry. >> philosophy of science

Kuiper, Gerard (Peter) [**kiy**per] (1905–73) Astronomer, born in Harencarspel, The Netherlands. He pioneered the spectroscopy of planetary atmospheres, and laid the groundwork for early exploration missions of the space age.

Ku Klux Klan The name of successive terrorist organizations in the USA, thought to derive from Greek *kyklos* 'circle'. The first was founded after the Civil War (1861–5): the members, disguised in robes and hoods, terrorized blacks and their sympathizers in the South. It faded after Federal measures were passed against it, but was re-established in a stronger form after World War 1, attacking Catholics, foreigners, Jews, and organized labour, as well as blacks. It was revived again by the fear of communism in the 1950s, then by opposition to the civil rights movements in the 1960s, but strong measures from the federal government (under President Johnson) imposed some control. The organization is still sporadically active in various parts of the USA. >> Johnson, Lyndon B; terrorism

kulaks The most progressive stratum of the late 19th-c and early 20th-c Russian peasantry. They developed after the emancipation of the serfs, and engaged in capitalist farming and entrepreneurial activities. During the collectivization of agriculture in the 1930s, Stalin 'liquidated' the kulaks as a class. >> capitalism; Stalin

kulan [**koo**lan] >> **ass**

Kulturkampf [kul**toor**kampf] In the German Empire, a 'cultural conflict' between the Prussian state and the Roman Catholic Church. It was inspired by Bismarck's suspicion of Catholics' extra-German loyalties. Most intense during 1870–8, it effectively ended by 1886. >> Bismarck; Roman Catholicism

Kumasi [koo**mah**see], known as **Garden City**, **City of the Golden Stool** 6°45N 1°35W, pop (1995e) 486 000. Second largest city in Ghana; centre of the Ashanti kingdom since the 17th-c; airfield; railway; university (1951); large market centre for cocoa-growing region. >> Ashanti; Ghana ℹ

kumquat or **cumquat** [**kuhm**kwot] A spiny evergreen shrub closely resembling citrus, native to E and SE Asia; fruits look and taste like tiny oranges, and are often candied. (Genus: *Fortunella*, 6 species. Family: Rutaceae.) >> citrus

Kun, Béla (1886–c.1939) Hungarian Communist leader, born in Szilágycseh, Hungary. In 1919 he set up a Soviet republic in Hungary, but his policy of nationalization alienated much of the population, and his regime was overthrown. >> Hungary ℹ; Stalin

Kundera, Milan [**kun**daira] (1929–) Novelist, born in Brno, Czech Republic. In 1975 he fled to Paris, where he has lived ever since. He came to prominence in the West with *Kniha smichu a zapomneni* (1979, The Book of Laughter and Forgetting). *Nesnesitelna lehkost byti* (The Unbearable Lightness of Being) appeared in 1984, and was filmed in 1987.

Küng, Hans (1928–) Roman Catholic theologian, born in Sursee, Switzerland. A professor at Tübingen from 1960, his questioning of received interpretations of Catholic doctrine and Christianity aroused controversy, and the Vatican withdrew his licence to teach as a Catholic theologian in 1979.

kung fu A form of Chinese unarmed combat dating from the 6th-c, when it was practised at the Shaolin Temple. The best known form is **wing chun**, popularized by the actor Bruce Lee (1940/41–73) in several films. >> martial arts

Kunlun Shan [kunlun shahn] or **K'un-lun Shan** Mountain range in W China; length 2500 km/1500 mi; rises to 7723 m/25 338 ft at Muztag peak. >> China ℹ

Kunming or **K'un-ming** 25°04N 102°41E, pop (1995e) 1 728 000. City in S China, on Yunnan plateau; altitude 1894 m/6214 ft; major market and transport centre from 279 BC; spring-like weather and scenery ('City of Eternal Spring'); airfield; railway; university (1934); agricultural university. >> China ℹ

Kuomintang >> **Guomindang**

Kurchatov, Igor (Vasilevich) [**koor**chatof] (1903–60) Physicist, born in Sim, Russia. He was the leading figure in the building of Russia's first atomic (1949) and thermonuclear (1953) bombs. >> atomic bomb

Kurdistan or **Kordestan** [koordi**stahn**] pop (1995e) 1 244 000; area 24 998 sq km/9649 sq mi. Province in NW Iran, bounded W by Iraq; capital, Sanandaj; inhabited by Kurds, who also occupy parts of NE Iraq, SE Turkey, and NE Syria; in 1920 a Kurdish autonomous state was agreed at the Treaty of Sèvres, but the terms were never carried out; new Kurdish Council formed after elections, 1992, not recognized by central government. >> Iran ℹ; Kurds

Kurds A W Iranian-speaking ethnic group settled in neighbouring mountainous areas of Turkey, Iraq, Iran, Syria, and the former Soviet Union, an area which they themselves call **Kurdistan**, and numbering over 20 million. They are currently the world's largest ethnic group without its own state. They have been Sunni Muslims since the 7th-c AD. They are politically oppressed in Turkey, and have suffered religious persecution in Iran. In Iraq, their failure to achieve autonomous status for Kurdistan has resulted in hostilities between Kurds and government forces. Following the Gulf War (1991), there was an Iraq offensive against Kurdish rebels. Many sought refuge in Turkey and Iran, while troops tried to maintain safe havens in Iraq. There were elections to a Kurdistan National Assembly in 1992, but the future of the indepedent Kurdish state proposed in N Iraq remained unclear. In Turkey, an armed separatist movement, the Kurdistan Workers' Party (PKK), has been active since the mid-1980s. Its leader, Abdullah Ocalan, was captured in Kenya (Feb 1999) and imprisoned in Turkey, triggering widespread international protests by Kurdish supporters. >> Kurdistan; Sunnis

Kurgan culture The semi-nomadic population of the S Russian steppes in the fourth millennium BC, characterized archaeologically by burials sprinkled with red ochre beneath a barrow mound or *kurgan*.

Kuril Islands [ku**reel**], Russ **Kurilskiye Ostrova** area 15 600 sq km/6000 sq mi. Archipelago off the N Japanese coast; extends c.1200 km/750 mi from the tip of Kamchatka Peninsula to the NE coast of Hokkaido I, Japan; over 50 islands, actively volcanic, with hot springs; visited in 1634 by the Dutch; divided between Russia and Japan, 18th-c; all ceded to Japan, 1875; occupied by Soviet troops, 1945; part of the USSR, 1947; claimed by Japan. >> Russia ℹ

Kurosawa, Akira [kuroh**sah**wa] (1910–98) Film director, born in Tokyo. He was renowned for his adaptation of the techniques of the Noh theatre to film-making, in such films as *Rashomon* (1951), which won the Venice Film Festival prize, and *The Seven Samurai* (1954). Also characteristic were his literary adaptations, such as *The Lower Depths* (1957, from Dostoyevsky) and *Ran* (1985, from *King Lear*). >> Noh

kuru [**ku**roo] A form of prion disease endemic to the Fore peoples of Papua New Guinea in the early part of the 20th century. It is a chronic disease, involving progressive neurological symptoms and brain degeneration, which affects mainly women and children. A feature of the brain pathology is the presence of **kuru plaques** formed from prion protein amyloid fibres. Kuru was thought to be transmitted by cannibalistic funerary rites, and changes in these practices have led to a marked reduction in the disease incidence. >> amyl; bovine spongiform encephalopathy; central nervous system; Creutzfeldt-Jacob disease; prion disease

Kurzweil, Raymond C [**kertz**viyl] (1948–) Computer scientist, a pioneer of reading technology, born in New York City. In the 1970s he led the development of the first device capable of carrying out automatic optical character recognition, and followed this with several other machines. In 1982 he founded Kurwzeil Music Systems and Kurzweil Applied Intelligence (dealing in automatic speech recognition), and in 1996 became founder-chairman of Kurzweil Educational Systems.

Kush An independent kingdom on the Nile which emerged from the Egyptian province of Nubia in the 11th-c BC. In the 8th-c BC Kush conquered Egypt, and established the XXVth dynasty which ruled until the Assyrian conquest in 671–666 BC.

Kutab Minar >> **Qutb Minar**

Kutch, Rann of [kuch], also spelled **Kachch**, or **Cutch** area 9000 sq km/3474 sq mi. Region of salt marsh in the Indian state of Gujarat and Sind province, Pakistan; once a shallow arm of the Arabian Sea; scene of Indo-Pakistani fighting in 1965. >> Gujarat; Sind

Kutuzov, Mikhail Ilarionovich, Knyaz (Prince) [ku**too**zof] (1745–1813) Russian field marshal, born in St Petersburg, Russia. In 1812, he fought Napoleon obstinately at Borodino, and obtained a major victory over Davout and Ney at Smolensk. >> Napoleonic Wars

Kuwait [koo**wayt**], official name **State of Kuwait**, Arabic **Dowlat al-Kuwait** pop (1995e) 1 019 000; area 17 818 sq km/ 6878 sq mi. Independent state at head of Persian Gulf; capital, Kuwait City; timezone GMT +3; major ethnic group, Kuwaiti (41%); chief religion, Islam (85%); official language, Arabic; unit of currency, the dinar; consists of mainland and nine offshore islands; terrain flat or gently undulating, rising SW to 271 m/889 ft; low ridges in NE generally stony with sparse vegetation; hot and dry climate, average annual rainfall 111 mm/4 in; summer temperatures very high, often above 45°C (Jul–Aug); humidity often over 90%; sandstorms common all year; port founded in the 18th-c; Britain responsible for Kuwait's foreign affairs, 1899; British protectorate, 1914; independence, 1961; invasion and annexation by Iraq (Aug 1990), leading to Gulf War (Jan–Feb 1991), with severe damage to Kuwait City and infrastructure; Kuwaiti government-in-exile in Saudi Arabia (until March 1991); large refugee emigration; major postwar problems, including burning of Kuwaiti oil wells by Iraq and pollution of Gulf Waters by oil; emir is head of state, governing through an appointed prime minister and Council of Ministers; oil discovered, 1938, and before the Gulf War provided 95% of government revenue; active programme of economic diversification; agriculture gradually expanding; economy badly damaged by the Gulf War. >> Gulf War 2; Kuwait City; RR1014 political leaders

Kuwait City, Arabic **al-Kuwayt**, formerly **Qurein** 29°20N 48°00E, pop (1995e) 38 100. Capital city of Kuwait, on S shore of Kuwait Bay; developed in the late 1940s after discovery of oil; suburban port of Shuwaikh, SW; airport; university (1966); severely damaged during Gulf War (1991). >> Kuwait ℹ

Kuybyshev [**koo**ibishef] >> **Samara**

Kuznets Basin [kuz**nets**] Basin of the Tom R in Russia; a major industrial zone, with rich deposits of coal and iron ore. >> Russia ℹ

Kuznetsov, Alexander Vasilievich [kuz**net**sof] (1929–79) Writer, born in Kiev. He is best known for *Babi Yar* (1966), a novel about the massacre of Ukrainian Jews by the German SS in 1941. He defected to England in 1969, changing his name to **A Anatoli**. >> Babi Yar

Kwakiutl [kwaki**oo**tl] A N Pacific Coast American Indian group living on the coast of British Columbia as fishermen and traders. They were famed for their woodwork, frequently painted in bright colours, and for their elaborate dances and ceremonies, including the potlatch. >> Northwest Coast Indians

KwaNdebele [kwahndebe**be**lay] Former national state or non-independent black homeland in Transvaal province, NE South Africa; self-governing status, 1981; incorporated into Mpumalanga following the South African constitution of 1994. >> apartheid; Mpumalanga; South Africa ℹ

Kwang-chow >> **Guangzhou**

kwashiorkor [kwashi**aw(r)**ker] A nutritional disorder of young children, stemming from an inadequate intake of protein in the diet. In Africa, it frequently begins after weaning. >> protein

KwaZulu Natal [kwah**zoo**loo na**tahl**] pop (1996e) 7 672 000; area, 91 481 sq km/35 312 sq mi. One of the nine new provinces established by the South African constitution of 1994, in E South Africa, on the Indian Ocean; comprises former areas of Natal and KwaZulu; Natal, annexed to Cape Colony, 1844; separate colony, 1856; joined Union of South Africa, 1910; KwaZulu, former national state or non-independent black homeland; self-governing status, 1971; provincial status, 1994; capital, to be decided between Ulundi or Pietermaritzburg; Durban, business port and second largest city in South Africa; chief languages, Zulu (80%), English, Afrikaans; 'the garden province'. >> South Africa ℹ

Kyd, Thomas (1558–94) Playwright, born in London. His tragedies early brought him reputation, especially *The Spanish Tragedy* (c.1592), and he has been credited with a share in several plays.

Kyoto [**kyoh**toh] 35°02N 135°45E, pop (1995e) 1 476 000. City in C Honshu, Japan; founded, 8th-c; capital of Japan, 794–1868; railway; 22 universities, including university of industrial arts and textiles (1949); over 2000 temples and shrines; Nijo-jo Castle (1603), containing the Imperial Palace; Kinkakuji, the Golden Pavilion (1394). >> Honshu; Kinkakuji; Nijo-jo Castle

Kyrgyzstan [keergiz**stahn**], official name **Republic of Kyrgyzstan**, also spelled **Kirgizstan**, Kyrgyz **Kyrgyz Respublikasy**, Russ **Kirgiziya** pop (1995e) 4 694 000; area 198 500 sq km/76 621 sq mi. Republic in NE Middle Asia; capital, Bishkek (formerly Frunze); timezone GMT +5; major ethnic groups, Kyrgyz (52%), Russian (21%); chief religion, Sunni Muslim; official languages, Russian, Kyrgyz; currency, the som; largely occupied by the Tien Shan Mts; highest point within the republic at Pik Pobedy (7439 m/24 406 ft); chief river, the Naryn; typical desert climate in N, W, and SE; hot, dry summers in valleys; mean annual temperature −18°C (Jan), 28°C (Jul); under the Mongols from 1685; incorporated into the Russian Empire, 1876; part of an independent Turkestan republic, 1917–24; Kara-Kyrgyz Autonomous Province established, 1924; became an autonomous republic, 1926; proclaimed a constituent republic of the Soviet Union, 1936; independence in 1991; governed by a president, prime minister, Legislative Assembly, and Assembly of People's Representatives; metallurgy, machines, coal, natural gas, textiles, food processing, gold; wheat, cotton, tobacco, animal husbandry. >> Commonwealth of Independent States ℹ; Soviet Union; RR1014 political leaders

Kyushu [**kyu**shoo] pop (1995e) 13 462 000; area 42 084 sq km/16 244 sq mi. Island region in Japan; southernmost and most densely populated of the four main islands; rising to 1935 m/6348 ft at Mt Miyanoura-dake; subtropical climate; heavily forested apart from the NW; major industrial towns include Fukuoka, Kagoshima, Nagasaki. >> Japan ℹ

Kyzyl-Kum [**ki**zil **kum**], Russ **Peski Kyzylkum** area 300 000 sq km/115 000 sq mi. Extensive desert in Kazakhstan and Uzbekistan; extends SE from the Aral Sea; rises to 922 m/3025 ft in the C. >> Kazakhstan ℹ; Uzbekistan ℹ

La (in place name) >> *also under initial letter of the following word*

Laban, Rudolf von [**lay**bn] (1879–1958) Dancer, choreographer, and dance theoretician, born in Pozsony (now Bratislava, Slovak Republic). As the leader of the C European dance movement he was instrumental in the development of modern dance as a theatre form. He also developed an influential notation system (**Labanotation**). >> choreography; dance notation

Labiche, Eugène [labeesh] (1815–88) Playwright, born in Paris. He wrote over 100 comedies, farces, and vaudevilles, such as *Le Chapeau de paille d'Italie* (1851, The Italian Straw Hat).

labile [**lay**biyl] >> **kinetic**

Labor Day >> **Labour Day**

labor union >> **trade union**

Labour / Labor Day A day of celebration, public demonstrations, and parades by trade unions and labour organizations, held in many countries on 1 May, or the first Monday in May; in the USA, Canada, and Bermuda it is the first Monday in September, and in New Zealand the fourth Monday of October.

Labour Party A British socialist/social democratic political party, originally formed in 1900 as the Labour Representation Committee to represent trade unions and socialist societies. Twenty-six MPs were elected in 1906, and the name changed to the Labour Party. The first minority Labour government was elected in 1924. The first majority Labour government (1945–51) established the welfare state and carried out a significant nationalization programme. Since then Labour have been in office 1964–70, 1974–9, and 1997–. The leader and deputy leader are elected annually when in opposition by an electoral college composed of trade unions, constituency parties, and the Parliamentary Labour Party. In the 1990s, the Party developed a policy of combining traditional socialist values with a concern to respond to the new ideals and aspirations of the individual (**New Labour**). >> New Labour; social democracy; socialism

labour / labor relations >> **industrial relations**

Labrador area 285 000 sq km/110 000 sq mi. Mainland part of Newfoundland, Canada; mainly a barren plateau, part of Canadian Shield; many lakes; interior region awarded to Newfoundland, 1927, disputed by Quebec. >> Newfoundland

Labrador retriever A breed of dog, developed in Britain from imported Newfoundland dogs and local breeds; large, with muscular legs and body; long tail and muzzle; short, pendulous ears; thick fawn or black (occasionally brown) coat; also known as **labrador**. >> dog; retriever

Labrador Sea Arm of the Atlantic Ocean between Newfoundland and Greenland; cold SE-flowing Labrador Current brings icebergs. >> Atlantic Ocean

La Bruyère, Jean de [brooyair] (1645–96) Writer, born in Paris. His major work is the satirical *Caractères de Théophraste* (1688, Characters of Theophrastus), which gained him a host of implacable enemies as well as an immense reputation. >> Theophrastus

laburnum A deciduous tree (*Laburnum anagyroides*) growing to 7 m/23 ft, native to S and C Europe; pea-flowers yellow, numerous, in pendent leafy clusters; pods up to 6 cm/2½ in long, hairy when young; seeds black; also called **golden rain** or **golden chain**. All parts but especially the seeds are extremely poisonous. (Family: Leguminosae.)

Lacaille, Nicolas Louis de [lakiy] (1713–62) Astronomer, born in Rumigny, France. He travelled to South Africa (1750–5) to draw up the first reliable catalogue of S hemisphere stars, and named 14 new constellations. >> constellation; star

Laccadive Islands >> **Lakshadweep Islands**

lace An ornamental fabric in which a large number of separate threads are twisted together into a decorative network, such as for the edges of items of clothing or furnishing. Hand-made lace is still widely produced, but machines have been used for making lace since 1808.

L

lacecap >> **hydrangea**

Lacerta [la**ser**ta] (Lat 'lizard') A smallish, faint N constellation. It includes the object BL Lacertae, the prototype of a class of quasar-like objects. >> constellation; quasar; RR968

lacewing A medium to large insect possessing two pairs of similar, membranous wings, each with a lacework of veins; adults and larvae predatory, with simple, biting mouthparts. (Order: Neuroptera.) >> insect [i]

Lachesis >> **Moerae**

Lachlan River [**lak**lan] River in New South Wales, Australia; rises in the Great Dividing Range, N of Canberra; flows 1484 km/922 mi to join the Murrumbidgee R. >> New South Wales

lac insect A bug that lives in clusters on twigs of trees; females legless, with reduced antennae; body enclosed in a protective shell of resinous secretion from which shellac is made. (Order: Homoptera. Family: Kerridae.) >> shellac

Laclos, Pierre (Ambroise François) Choderlos de [la**kloh**] (1741–1803) Soldier, novelist, and politician, born in Amiens, France. He is remembered for his masterpiece, *Les Liaisons dangereuses* (1782, Dangerous Liaisons), a novel in letter form. It has been successfully adapted for the theatre and in several films.

lacquer A hard waterproof substance made from the resin of the lacquer tree. A very ancient Chinese invention, it can be coloured, polished, carved, and used to decorate wooden vessels and furniture. >> lacquer tree

lacquer tree A deciduous tree (*Rhus vernicifera*) growing to c.9 m/30 ft, native to China and Japan; flowers tiny, 5-petalled, yellowish, in drooping clusters; also called **varnish tree**. A resin obtained from cuts in the stem is a major constituent of Chinese and Japanese lacquer. (Family: Anacardiaceae.) >> resin

Lacroix, Christian [lakrwah] (1951–) Fashion designer, born in Arles, France. In 1981 he joined Jean Patou, which showed his first collection in 1982. In 1987 he opened the House of Lacroix in Paris, making his name with ornate and frivolous clothes.

lacrosse A stick-and-ball field game derived from a North American Indian game, so called because French settlers thought the stick resembled a bishop's crozier (*crosse*). It is a team game usually played with 10 on each side on a pitch measuring 100–110 m/110–120 yd by 55–75 m/60–85 yd. The object is to score goals by throwing the ball into the goal using the lacrosse stick, or *crosse*. The crosse is at least 0·9 m/3 ft in length with a triangular net attached to the end in which to catch the ball. >> RR1056

lactation The process of suckling a newborn infant. During pregnancy, milk-producing glands in the breasts proliferate, and hormones from the front pituitary stimulate the secretion of milk, which is further augmented when the infant suckles. >> pituitary gland

lactic acid CH_3–CH(OH)–COOH, IUPAC **2-hydroxypropanoic acid**. An acid which takes its name from milk, where it is formed on souring. It is an important stage in the breakdown of carbohydrates during respiration. >> IUPAC

lactose $C_{12}H_{22}O_{11}$. A sugar occurring in the milk of all mammals. It is a disaccharide, a combination of glucose and galactose, and only slightly sweet-tasting. >> disaccharide

ladies' fingers >> **okra**

Ladoga, Lake, Russ **Ozero Ladozhskoye**, Finnish **Laatokka** area 17 700 sq km/6800 sq mi. Largest lake in Europe, in European Russia, close to the Finnish border; length, 219 km/136 mi; maximum depth, 230 m/755 ft. >> Russia ℹ

ladybird A rounded, convex beetle usually red, black, or yellow with a pattern of spots or lines; adults and larvae feed mostly on aphids and other plant pests; also known as a **ladybug**. (Order: Coleoptera. Family: Coccinellidae.) >> aphid; beetle

ladybug >> **ladybird**

Lady chapel A chapel dedicated to the Virgin Mary. It is usually built behind the main altar, and forms an extension to the main building. >> Mary (mother of Jesus)

Lady Day >> **Annunciation**

Ladysmith, Siege of (1899–1900) A siege of the second Boer War in which Boer forces attempted to pen up their British opponents. General Sir Redvers Buller (1839–1908) succeeded in raising the siege on 28 February 1900. >> Boer Wars

laetrile [**lay**triyl] The trade name of the drug *Amygdalin* (bitter almond), which can be extracted from some fruit stones (eg apricot). Formerly known as vitamin B_{17}, it was recommended as a cancer cure. It was never recognized as effective by orthodox medical opinion, and was banned from use as being potentially dangerous. >> cancer; cyanide; vitamins ℹ

Lafayette, Marie Joseph (Paul Yves Roch Gilbert Motier), marquis de [lafiyet] (1757–1834) French soldier and politician, born in Chavagniac, France. He fought in America against the British during the War of Independence (1777–9, 1780–2), and in the National Assembly of 1789 presented a draft of a declaration of the Rights of Man. Hated by the Jacobins for his moderation, he defected to Austria, returning to France during the Consulate. He later became a radical leader of the Opposition (1825–30). >> Jacobins (French history)

La Fayette, Marie Madeleine (Pioche de la Vergne), comtesse de (Countess of) [lafiyet], known as **Madame de La Fayette** (1634–93) Novelist and reformer of French romance writing, born in Paris. Her major novel is *La Princesse de Clèves* (1678), a vivid picture of the court life of her day.

La Fontaine, Jean de [fon**ten**] (1621–95) Poet, born in Château-Thierry, France. His major work is the collection of over 200 verse stories, *Fables choisies mises en vers* (1668, Selected Fables in Verse), in translation usually called 'La Fontaine's Fables'.

lager >> **beer**

Lagerfeld, Karl [**lah**gervelt] (1939–) Fashion designer, born in Hamburg, Germany. He was design director at Chanel, and updated the Chanel look. Known for his high quality ready-to-wear clothing, he showed the first collection under his own label in 1984.

Lagerkvist, Pär (Fabian) [**lah**gerkvist] (1891–1974) Writer, born in Växjö, Sweden. His works include *Bödeln* (1934, The Hangman), *Dvärgen* (1944, The Dwarf), and *Barabbas* (1951). He received the Nobel Prize for Literature in 1951.

Lagerlöf, Selma (Ottiliana Lovisa) [**lah**gerloef] (1858–1940) Novelist, born in Mårbacka, Sweden. Her fairy tales and romances earned her the 1909 Nobel Prize for Literature – the first woman to receive the distinction.

lagomorph [**lag**oma(r)wf] An order of mammals comprising rabbits, hares, and pikas; virtually worldwide; long soft fur, long ears, short tails, fully furred feet, slit-like nostrils which can be closed. (Order: Lagomorpha, 58 species.) >> hare; pika; rabbit

Lagos [**lay**gos] 6°27N 3°28E, pop (1995e) 1 434 000. Chief port of Nigeria, settled c.1700; occupied by the British, 1851; colony of Lagos, 1862; part of the S Nigeria protectorate, 1906; capital of Nigeria, 1960–82; airport; university (1962); tanker terminal. >> Nigeria ℹ

Lagrange, Joseph Louis, comte de l'Empire (Count of the Empire) [la**grãzh**], originally **Giuseppe Luigi Lagrangia** (1736–1813) Mathematician and astronomer, born in Turin, Italy. In 1766 he became director of the Berlin Academy, where he worked on number theory, mechanics, the Solar System, and algebraic equations. His major work was the *Mécanique analytique* (1788, Analytical Mechanics). >> Lagrangian; Lagrangian points; mechanics

lagrangian [la**gron**jian] The difference between kinetic energy K and potential energy V; symbol L, units J (joule); $L = K - V$. It is the fundamental expression of the properties of a mechanical system. >> Lagrange

lagrangian points [la**gron**jian] Five points in the plane of revolution of two bodies where gravitational forces balance so as to allow a small third body to remain in equilibrium. For example, the Trojan asteroids are found in stable orbits at L-4 and L-5 points, forming an equilateral triangle with the Sun and Jupiter. >> gravity; Lagrange

La Guardia, Fiorello H(enry) [la **gah(r)d**ia] (1882–1947) US politician and lawyer, born in New York City, where he spent most of his career. A popular mayor (1933–45), he initiated housing and labour safeguards schemes. One of the city airports is named after him.

Lahore [la**haw(r)**] 31°34N 74°22E, pop (1995e) 4 304 000. Second largest city in Pakistan; taken in 1849 by the British, who made it the capital of Punjab; railway; two universities (1882, 1961); trade and communications centre; considered the cultural capital of Pakistan. >> Pakistan ℹ

laissez-faire [laysay **fair**] (Fr 'leave alone to do') An economic doctrine advocating that commerce and trade should be permitted to operate free of controls of any kind. It was a popular view in the mid-19th-c.

lake A body of water surrounded by land, and lying in a hollow which may be caused by Earth movement, glaciation, volcanic craters, or the collapse of the roof of limestone caves. Saltwater lakes may be parts of seas or oceans cut off by Earth movement, or formed in areas of low rainfall where mineral salts can accumulate due to evaporation. >> RR971

Lake District Part of Cumbria, NW England; area of c.1800 sq km/700 sq mi noted for its scenery; a system of glaciated valleys and ribbon lakes; lakes include Windermere, Derwent Water, Ullswater, Bassenthwaite, Thirlmere, Buttermere, and Coniston Water; mountains include Scafell, Skiddaw, Helvellyn. >> Coniston Water; Helvellyn; Lake poets; Scafell; Skiddaw; Ullswater; Windermere, Lake

lake dwellings >> **Swiss lake dwellings**

Lakeland terrier A medium-sized terrier developed in the English Lake District to hunt foxes; coarse coat, very thick on the legs, forehead, and muzzle. >> dog; terrier

Lake Placid 44°18N 74°01W, pop (1995e) 2530. Resort in N New York State, USA; in the Adirondack Mts; scene of Winter Olympic events (1932, 1980). >> New York (state)

Lake poets A phrase used for the poets who took up

residence in the English Lake district in the early 19th-c. Wordsworth and Coleridge were the best known. >> Coleridge; Wordsworth, William

Laker, Sir Freddie, popular name of **Sir Frederick Alfred Laker** (1922–) Business entrepreneur, born in Kent. In 1966 he headed the successful Laker Airways Ltd, but was severely set back by the failure of the 'Skytrain' project (1982).

Laker, Jim, popular name of **James Charles Laker** (1922–86) Cricketer, born in Saltaire, Yorkshire. He made test cricket history at Old Trafford in 1956 when he took 19 Australian wickets for 90 runs. During his career (1946–64) he took 1944 wickets. >> cricket [i] (sport)

Lakshadweep Islands [**lahk**shadweep], formerly **Laccadive Islands** (to 1973) pop (1995e) 55 900; area 32 sq km/12 sq mi. Union territory of India, comprising 10 inhabited and 17 uninhabited coral islands in the Arabian Sea 300 km/190 mi off the Malabar Coast of Kerala; ruled by British, 1792; ceded to India, 1956; population mainly Muslim. >> India [i]

Lakshmi [**lak**shmee] The Hindu goddess of prosperity and good fortune, the consort of Vishnu, sometimes called 'the lotus-goddess'. She is associated with Diwali, the autumn festival of lights. >> Diwali; Hinduism; Vishnu

Lalique, René [la**leek**] (1860–1945) Jeweller and glassware designer, born in Ay, France. His glass designs, decorated with relief figures, animals, and flowers, were an important contribution to the Art Nouveau and Art Deco movements. >> Art Deco; Art Nouveau

Lamaism [**lah**maizm] The religion of Tibet, a form of Mahayana Buddhism, dating from the 8th-c. The Dalai Lama is the traditional spiritual and temporal ruler of Tibet. Upon the death of a reigning Lama, a search is conducted to find an infant who is his reincarnation. >> Buddhism; Dalai Lama

Lamarck, Jean Baptiste (Pierre Antoine) de Monet, Chevalier de [la**mah(r)k**] (1744–1829) Naturalist and pre-Darwinian evolutionist, born in Bazentin, France. His major work was the *Histoire des animaux sans vertèbres* (1815–22, Natural History of Invertebrate Animals). >> evolution

Lamartine, Alphonse (Marie Louis) de [lamah(r)**teen**] (1790–1869) Poet, statesman, and historian, born in Mâcon, France. His best-known work was his first volume of lyrical poems, *Méditations poétiques* (1820, Poetic Meditations). He was a member of the provisional government in the 1848 Revolution.

Lamb, Charles, pseudonym **Elia** (1775–1834) Essayist, born in London. He achieved a success through the joint publication with his sister of *Tales from Shakespeare* (1807). His best-known works are the essays he wrote under the pen name of **Elia**.

lamb >> **sheep**

Lambert, Constant (1905–51) Composer, conductor, and critic, born in London. His best-known composition is the choral work in jazz idiom, *The Rio Grande* (1927).

Lambert, Johann Heinrich (1728–77) Mathematician, born in Mülhausen, Germany. He first showed how to measure scientifically the intensity of light (1760). The unit of light intensity is named after him.

Lambert, John (1619–84) English general, born in Calton, Yorkshire. In the English Civil War, he commanded the cavalry at Marston Moor (1644). He headed the cabal which overthrew Richard Cromwell (1659), and at the Restoration was imprisoned (1661) until his death. >> English Civil War

Lambeth Conferences Gatherings of bishops of the Anglican Communion throughout the world for consultations, but without legislative powers. The first conference was held in 1867 at Lambeth Palace, the London house of the Archbishop of Canterbury. It is normally convened every 10 years. >> Anglican Communion

lamellibranch [la**mel**ibrangk] >> **bivalve**

Lamentations (of Jeremiah) A book of the Hebrew Bible/Old Testament, probably dated shortly after the Babylonian conquest of Jerusalem (c.587/586 BC), attributed in tradition to the prophet Jeremiah. It consists of five poems lamenting the destruction of Jerusalem. >> Old Testament

Lamian War [**lay**mian] (323–322 BC) The unsuccessful revolt of the Greek states from Macedon after the death of Alexander the Great. >> Macedon

Laminaria [lamin**air**ia] >> **kelp**

Lammas [**lam**as] In the UK, a former church festival (1 Aug); the name means 'loaf-mass', the festival originally being held in thanksgiving for the harvest, with the consecration of loaves made of flour from the newly harvested wheat.

lammergeier [**lam**ergiyer] An Old World vulture (*Gypaetus barbatus*), native to S Europe, Africa, India, and Tibet; also known as the **bearded vulture**; grey back; reddish head and underparts; white chest; dark 'beard' of stiff feathers. (Family: Accipitridae.) >> vulture

Lamont (of Lerwick), Norman Lamont, Baron [la**mont**] (1942–) British politician, born in Lerwick, Shetland Is. He was appointed financial secretary to the Treasury in 1986, and in 1990 managed John Major's successful campaign for the Conservative Party leadership and was rewarded with the post of Chancellor of the Exchequer. Following his replacement in the 1993 Cabinet reshuffle, he launched an attack on Major's policies. He was given a life peerage in 1998. >> Major

Lampedusa, Giuseppe Tomasi, duca di (Duke of) **Palma** [lampe**doo**za] (1896–1957) Writer, born in Palermo, Sicily. His only complete work, *Il gattopardo* (The Leopard), was published in 1958.

lamprey Primitive jawless fish (*Petromyzon marinus*) found in marine and adjacent fresh waters of the N Atlantic; length up to 90 cm/36 in; mouth sucker-like with rasping teeth; may be a serious pest to local fisheries. (Family: Petromyzonidae.)

lamp shell An unsegmented, marine invertebrate possessing a bivalve shell and a long stalk; feeds using an array of tentacles around the mouth; contains c.350 living species; over 12 000 fossil species described. (Phylum: Brachiopoda.) >> bivalve

LAN >> **local area network**

Lancashire pop (1995e) 1 426 000; area 3063 sq km/1182 sq mi. County of NW England; county town, Preston; Blackpool and Blackburn unitary authorities from 1998; ports at Heysham, Fleetwood; world centre for cotton manufacture in 19th-c. >> England [i]; Lancaster

Lancaster (UK) 54°03N 2°48W, pop (1995e) 50 300. Town in Lancashire, NW England; on R Lune; chartered, 1193; city status, 1937; university (1964); railway; 12th-c castle, on site of Roman fort. >> Lancashire

Lancaster (USA) >> **Lincoln** (USA)

Lancaster, Burt, popular name of **Stephen Burton Lancaster** (1913–94) Film actor, born in New York City. Cast early on in a succession of tough-guy roles, he increasingly found opportunities to show his dramatic abilities, notably in *From Here to Eternity* (1953), *Elmer Gantry* (1960, Oscar), and *Birdman of Alcatraz* (1962). Later films include *Local Hero* (1983) and *Field of Dreams* (1989).

Lancaster, Sir Osbert (1908–86) Cartoonist and writer, born in London. He began drawing cartoons for the *Daily Express* in 1939, creating Maudie Littlehampton and other characters.

Lancaster, Duchy of >> **Duchy of Lancaster**

Lancaster, House of The younger branch of the

Plantagenet dynasty, founded by Edmund 'Crouchback', the younger son of Henry III and first earl of Lancaster (1267–96), whence came three kings of England: Henry IV (1399–1413); Henry V (1413–22); and Henry VI (1422–61, 1470–1). >> Plantagenets; Roses, Wars of the

lancehead viper >> **fer-de-lance**

lancelet >> **amphioxus**

Lancelot, Sir or **Launcelot du Lac** The most famous of King Arthur's knights, though a relatively late addition to the legend. He was the courtly lover of Guinevere, and the father of Galahad by Elaine. >> Arthur

lancet A sharp pointed arch in a building, mainly used in Early English architecture of the 13th-c. It may also refer to a tall and narrow pointed-arch window of the same period. >> Early English Style

Lanchow >> **Lanzhou**

Land, Edwin (Herbert) (1909–91) Inventor and physicist, born in Bridgeport, CT. His 'Land Polaroid' camera (1947) was a system of instant photography, with developing agents incorporated in the film itself. >> Polaroid

Landers, Ann, pseudonym of **Esther Pauline Friedman** (1918–) Journalist, born in Sioux City, IA. In 1955 she inherited her job as a Chicago-based advice columnist from a previous 'Ann Landers', creating an international institution, and has since won many public service awards for her open discussions of medical issues.

Land League An association formed in Ireland in 1879 by Michael Davitt to agitate for greater tenant rights, in particular the '3 Fs': *fair rents*; *fixity of tenure* while rents were paid; and *freedom* for tenants to sell rights of occupancy. Gladstone conceded the essence of these demands in the 1881 Land Act.

Landor, Walter Savage (1775–1864) Writer, born in Warwick, Warwickshire. He wrote poems, plays, and essays, but is mainly remembered for his prose dialogues, *Imaginary Conversations* (1824–9).

Landowska, Wanda (Louise) [lan**dof**ska] (1877–1959) Pianist, harpsichordist, and musical scholar, born in Warsaw. In 1927 she established in Paris her Ecole de Musique Ancienne, where she gave specialized training in the performance of old works. >> harpsichord

landrace A type of domestic pig; long, pale body with large pendulous ears; bred mainly for bacon; three varieties. >> pig

landrail >> **corncrake**

land registration A legal procedure in which ownership of land (*title*) is officially registered. In England and Wales, this is with the **Land Registry**, though registration is not yet compulsory in all areas. Registration simplifies the procedure whereby land is transferred from vendor to purchaser. In the USA, all states have recording systems for instruments affecting the title to land. >> conveyance

landscape gardening The art of laying out gardens and estates for aesthetic or spiritual effect. A variety of techniques are used, including terracing, the use of artificial mounds, still and running water, walls, and trees. In 18th-c Europe, formal landscaping (as in the work of Le Nôtre, who made heavy use of symmetry, topiary, and artificial ornament) gave way to an artfully informal naturalism, seen particularly in the work of Kent, Repton, and Capability Brown. >> Brown, Lancelot; Kent, William; Le Nôtre; Repton

landscape painting The representation of natural history in art. The depiction of unified landscape for its own sake, frequently with a moral dimension, dates only from the 16th-c in Europe, though 600 years earlier in China. >> Barbizon / Danube / Hudson River School; seascape painting

Landseer, Sir Edwin (Henry) (1802–73) Artist, born in London. Dogs and deer were his main subjects, and several of his pictures are located in the highlands of Scotland. His paintings include 'Monarch of the Glen' (1851), and his most famous sculptures are the bronze lions in Trafalgar Square (1867).

Land's End, ancient **Bolerium** 50°03N 5°44W. A granite headland in Cornwall, SW England; the W extremity of England. >> Cornwall; John o'Groats

Lane, Sir Allen, originally **Allen Lane Williams** (1902–70) Publisher and pioneer of paperback books, born in Bristol. In 1935 he formed Penguin Books Ltd, a revolutionary step in the publishing trade.

Lang, Fritz (1890–1976) Film director, born in Vienna. His films include *Metropolis* (1926) and, after moving to the USA, *Fury* (1936) and *The Big Heat* (1953).

Langdon, Harry (Philmore) (1884–1944) Film comedian, born in Council Bluffs, IA. He appeared in several popular feature films, notably *Tramp Tramp Tramp* (1926), *The Strong Man* (1926), and *Long Pants* (1927), and is remembered for his character as a baby-faced innocent, bemused by the wider world.

Lange, David (Russell) [**long**ee] (1942–) New Zealand statesman and prime minister (1984–9), born in Auckland, New Zealand. A lawyer by profession, he became leader of the Labour Party in 1983, and prime minister in the fourth Labour government. >> New Zealand ℹ

Langland, William, also spelled **Langley** (c.1332–c.1400) Poet, probably born in Ledbury, Hereford and Worcester. He is credited with the authorship of the great mediaeval alliterative poem on the theme of spiritual pilgrimage, *Piers Plowman*.

Langley, Samuel Pierpont (1834–1906) Astronomer and aeronautics pioneer, born in Roxbury, MA. He invented the bolometer for measuring the Sun's radiant heat, and was the first to build a heavier-than-air flying machine – a steam-powered model aircraft.

Langmuir, Irving [**lang**myoor] (1881–1957) Physical chemist, born in New York City. He received the Nobel Prize for Chemistry in 1932 for his work on solid and liquid surfaces. His many inventions include the gas-filled tungsten lamp and atomic hydrogen welding. >> tungsten

Langobards >> **Lombards**

Langton, Stephen (c.1150–1228) Theologian, born (possibly) in Lincolnshire. He studied at the University of Paris. He became a cardinal in 1206, and Archbishop of Canterbury in 1207. He sided warmly with the barons against King John, and his name is the first of the subscribing witnesses of Magna Carta. >> Magna Carta

Langtry, Lillie, popular name of **Emilie Charlotte Langtry**, *née* **Le Breton**, nickname **the Jersey Lily** (1853–1929) Actress, born in Jersey, Channel Is. One of the most noted beauties of her time, she made her first important stage appearance in 1881, and managed the Imperial Theatre. She was also known for her close friendship with Edward VII.

language **1** A species-specific communicative ability, restricted to humans, which involves the use of sounds, grammar, and vocabulary, according to a system of rules. Though other animals can communicate vocally and by gesture, they are restricted to a particular set of messages, genetically given, which cannot be creatively varied. >> linguistics **2** An individual manifestation of **1**, found within a particular community. The designation of 'language' status is dependent on a wide variety of social, linguistic, and political considerations, and as a result, estimates of the number of living languages in the world (usually ranging between 5000 and 7000) are uncertain. >> language laboratory

language laboratory A room made up of banks of booths, each one containing a cassette recorder for a student's use, connected to a central console. At the console, a language instructor monitors the performance of students as they listen to taped exercises and record their responses to them. Its great advantage is that the students are able to advance at their own pace. Modern laboratories are now often equipped with video recorders and various kinds of computational aids. >> language

Languedoc [lãguh**dok**] Former province in S France; name derived from the local variety of language, *langue d'oc* (Provençal); centre of wine production. >> France ℹ

langur [lang**goor**] An Old World monkey, native to S and SE Asia; prominent dark 'eyebrows'; slender hand with short thumb; long tail; inhabits forests; two genera: **langur** or **leaf monkey** (*Presbytis*, 15 species) and **snub-nosed langur** (*Pygathrix*, 4 species). >> entellus; Old World monkey

Lanier, Sidney [la**neer**] (1842–81) Poet, born in Macon, GA. Among his writings are a novel and several works of criticism, but he is best remembered for his poems, which broke away from traditional metrical techniques. >> metre (literature)

lanolin [**lan**olin] A waxy material occurring naturally in wool. It is a mixture of esters of cholesterol with stearic, palmitic, and oleic acids. It forms strong emulsions with water, and is used in toilet preparations and ointments. >> emulsion (chemistry); ester

Lansbury, George (1859–1940) British politician, born near Lowestoft, Suffolk. Active as a radical, he founded and edited the *Daily Herald* (1912–22), and became leader of the Labour Party (1931–5). >> Labour Party; socialism

L'Anse aux Meadows [**lahn**see **med**ohz] An isolated Norse settlement of nine turf-built houses in Newfoundland, Canada, discovered in 1961. Built AD c.970–1000, the settlement proves that the Vikings reached North America in pre-Columbian times. It is a world heritage site. >> Vikings; Vínland

Lansing 42°44N 84°33W, pop (1995e) 132 000. Capital of state in SC Michigan, USA, on the Grand R; railway; car and truck manufacturing centre. >> Michigan

lanternfish Any of the small deep-sea fishes of family Myctophidae (6 genera), widely abundant in the world's oceans; length up to 15 cm/6 in; head blunt, eyes large, body with numerous light organs in characteristic patterns.

lanthanides [**lan**thaniydz] or **rare earth elements** Elements with atomic numbers from 58–72 inclusive. They have very similar chemistry, mainly forming compounds in which they show oxidation state +3. >> actinides; chemical elements; RR1036

Lanza, Mario, originally **Alfredo Arnold Cocozza** (1921–59) Tenor, born in Philadelphia, PA. Discovered while working in the family's grocery business, he went on to Hollywood to appear in several musicals. His most famous role was in *The Great Caruso* (1951).

Lanzhou [lahnjoh], **Lan-chou**, or **Lanchow** 36°01N 103°19E, pop (1995e) 1 734 000. Capital of Gansu province, NC China, on the upper Yellow R; airfield; railway; university (1946); centre for China's atomic energy industry since 1960. >> China ℹ

Laoighis, Laois [**lay**ish], or **Leix** [layks], formerly **Queen's County** pop (1995e) 51 900; area 1720 sq km/664 sq mi. County in Leinster province, SC Ireland; capital, Portlaoighise. >> Ireland (republic) ℹ; Portlaoighise

Laos [lows], official name **Lao People's Democratic Republic**, Lao **Sathalanalat Paxathipatai Paxaxôn Lao** pop (1995e) 4 791 000; area 236 800 sq km/91 405 sq mi. Republic in SE Asia; capital, Vientiane; timezone GMT +7; E area largely depopulated by war; ethnic groups include 60% Laotian, 35% hill tribes; chief religions, Buddhism, animism; official language, Lao; unit of currency, the kip of 100 at; landlocked country on the IndoChinese Peninsula; dense jungle and rugged mountains (E), rising to 2751 m/9025 ft; Mekong R flows NW–SE; monsoonal climate (heaviest, May–Sep); average annual temperatures in Vientiane, 14–34°C; visited by Europeans, 17th-c; dominated by Thailand in 19th-c; formed French Indo-Chinese Union with Cambodia and Vietnam, 1887; French protectorate, 1893; occupied by Japanese in World War 2; independence from France, 1949; civil war, 1953–75, between the Lao government, supported by the USA, and the communist-led Patriotic Front (*Pathet Lao*), supported by North Vietnam; monarchy abolished and communist republic established, 1975; Supreme People's Assembly elected, 1989; new constitution, 1991; governed by a president, prime minister, and 99-member National Assembly; agricultural economy suffered severely in the civil war. >> Vientiane; RR1014 political leaders

Laozi [lautsee], also spelled **Lao-tzu** or **Lao-tse** ('Old Master') (?6th-c BC) A sage and recluse, the reputed founder of Taoism, probably a legendary figure. The *Tao Te Ching* or the *Lao Tzu*, the most venerated of the three classical texts of Taoism, is attributed to him, though it dates from much later. >> Taoism

La Paz [la **pas**] 16°30S 68°10W, pop (1995e) 1 131 000. Capital of Bolivia, altitude 3636 m/11 929 ft; founded by Spanish, 1548; airport; railway; university (1830); cathedral. >> Bolivia ℹ; Sucre

lapis lazuli [lapis **laz**yuliy, **laz**yulee] A deep-blue ornamental stone, principally lazurite (a silicate of sodium and aluminium), found in metamorphosed limestones. >> silicate minerals

Laplace, Pierre Simon, Marquis de [laplas], also known as **Comte de** (Count of) **Laplace** (1749–1827) Mathematician and astronomer, born in Beaumont-en-Auge, France. His 5-volume *Mécanique céleste* (1799–1825, Celestial Mechanics) is a landmark in applied mathematics.

Lapland, Swed **Lappland**, Finn **Lapin Lääni** pop (1995e) 205 000, area 98 938 sq km/38 190 sq mi. Province of N Finland, mainly within Arctic Circle; largely tundra (N),

forest (S), and mountains (W); occupies c.30% of total area of Finland; provincial capital, Rovaniemi. The area generally called Lapland also includes large parts of Norway, Sweden, and Russia. >> Finland 🅘; Lapp; Rovaniemi; tundra

La Plata [la **plah**ta] 34°52S 57°55W, pop (1995e) 573 000. Port on the R Plate, SW of Buenos Aires; founded in 1882; three universities (1884, 1965, 1968); named **Eva Perón** (1946–55); railway; main outlet for produce from the pampas. >> Argentina 🅘; Plate, River

Lapp A people living in the sparsely populated N areas of Finland, Sweden, Norway, and Russia, with more than half in Norway. Most are fishermen, while others farm, breed reindeer, are foresters, and work in factories. >> Lapland

laptop computer A small lightweight computer, usually powered by internal batteries, which can easily be carried around and used comfortably on the user's lap. They became generally available in the mid-1980s. >> computer; notebook; plasma screen

lapwing A plover, especially the **common lapwing** (*Vanellus vanellus*); inhabits grassland, cultivation, water edges, and swamps. (Genus: *Vanellus*, 10 species. Family: Charadriidae.) >> peewit; plover

Lara, Brian (1969–) Cricketer, born in Cantaro, Trinidad, West Indies. He came to prominence in the 1994 season, when he broke several cricketing records, including a world record Test innings of 375 for the West Indies against England. He became the world's first batsman to score over 500 runs in one innings in first-class cricket.

larch A deciduous conifer native to colder parts of the N hemisphere; long shoots rough-textured with persistent bases of fallen leaves; short shoots with tufts of needles; widely planted for timber. (Genus: *Larix*, 10–12 species. Family: Pinaceae.) >> conifer

lard A fat produced from pigs, widely used in cooking and baking, and also in the preparation of certain perfumes and ointments. **Lard oil** is used as a lubricant and in soap manufacture.

Lardner, Ring(gold Wilmer) (1885–1933) Writer, born in Niles, MI. He wrote prolifically in a variety of forms: novels, plays, satirical verse (*Bib Ballads*, 1915), and an autobiography, *The Story of a Wonder Man* (1927), but is mainly appreciated for his short stories.

lark A small, dull-coloured songbird, found mainly in the Old World, especially Africa; nests on ground. (Family: Alaudidae, 75 species.) >> magpie; meadowlark; mudlark; skylark

Larkin, Philip (Arthur) (1922–85) Poet and novelist, born in Coventry, West Midlands. His collections of poems include *The Less Deceived* (1955) and *High Windows* (1974). He also edited the *Oxford Book of Twentieth Century English Verse* (1973).

larkspur An annual native to the N hemisphere; related to delphiniums; flowers blue, pink, or white, borne in short spikes. (Genus: *Consolida*, 40 species. Family: Ranunculaceae.) >> delphinium

Larnaca [**lah(r)**naka], Gr **Larnax**, Turkish **Larnaka**, **Iskele** 34°55N 33°36E, pop (1995e) 66 100. Port in S Cyprus; airport; old Turkish fort (1625), now a museum. >> Cyprus 🅘

La Rochefoucauld, François, duc de (Duke of) [la rosh-fookoh] (1613–80) Writer, born in Paris. He was an active member of the opposition to Cardinal Richelieu, and fought in the Fronde revolts (1648–53). His major works were written while in retirement: *Mémoires* (1664) and the epigrammatic collection commonly known as the *Maximes* (1665, Maxims). >> Frondes; Richelieu

Larousse, Pierre (Athanase) [la**roos**] (1817–75) Lexicographer and encyclopedist, born in Toucy, France. He wrote several grammars, dictionaries, and other text-books, notably his *Grand dictionnaire universel du XIXe siècle* (15 vols, 1865–76). >> dictionary

larva A general term for a stage in an animal's development between hatching and the attainment of the adult form, or maturity. Larval stages are often typical of the group, such as the caterpillar larva of butterflies.

laryngitis [larin**jiy**tis] Acute or chronic inflammation of the larynx, with swelling of the vocal cords. It often accompanies infection elsewhere in the respiratory tract. >> larynx

larynx That part of the air passage lying in humans between the trachea (below) and the laryngopharynx (above), situated in the middle of the front of the neck; also called the 'voice box', because it contains the *vocal cords*. It consists of a framework of cartilages joined together by a number of ligaments and moves upwards on swallowing. The prominent hard projection in the front of the neck, especially in males (the *Adam's apple*), is part of the thyroid cartilage. >> cartilage; glottis; laryngitis; trachea; vocal cords

La Salle, René Robert Cavelier, sieur de (Lord of) [la **sal**] (1643–87) Explorer, born in Rouen, France. He settled in Canada in 1666, and descended the Ohio and Mississippi to the sea (1682), naming the area Louisiana (after Louis XIV of France). >> Louisiana

La Scala [la **skah**la], or **Teatro Alla Scala** (Ital 'theatre at the stairway') The world's most famous opera house, built (1776–8) on the site of the Church of Santa Maria della Scala in Milan, Italy.

Las Casas, Bartolomé de [las **kah**sas], known as **the Apostle of the Indians** (1474–1566) Missionary priest, born in Seville, Spain. He sailed in the third voyage of Columbus (1502) to Hispaniola, and travelled to Cuba (1513). His desire to protect the natives from slavery led him to visit the Spanish court on several occasions. >> Columbus, Christopher; slave trade

Lascaux [las**koh**] A small, richly-decorated Palaeolithic cave of c.15 000 BC near Montignac, Dordogne, SW France, renowned for its naturalistic mural paintings and engravings of animals. It was closed in 1963, when humidity changes threatened the paintings, and a replica was opened nearby. >> Magdalenian; Palaeolithic art

laser A device which produces light, infrared, or ultraviolet radiation with special properties, using a system of excited atoms; the name is an acronym of *light amplification by the stimulated emission of radiation*. The first laser was built in 1960 by physicist Theodore Maiman. Laser action depends on the choice of special atomic systems for which an energy supply is able to raise large numbers of atoms to excited states, ready to emit photons when stimulated. Mirrors at either end of the laser reflect light end-to-end inside the laser to maintain its action. At one end, the mirror is partially transparent, allowing a portion of the light to escape to produce a laser beam. Laser light is monochromatic (all one colour), coherent (in step), produced as a beam which does not spread, and travels large distances undiminished in intensity. The many uses of lasers include supermarket bar code scanners, welding, surveying, phototherapy in medicine, eye surgery, hologram production, compact disc systems, and directed energy weapons. >> chemical laser; laser printer; semiconductor laser; *see illustration on p. 485*

laser printer A type of printer which uses a small laser to generate characters. It generally operates using xerographic principles, and is capable of producing very high quality typescript and graphics. >> laser 🅘; xerography 🅘

laser typesetter A form of typesetting used by printers in which the characters are drawn by a computer-controlled laser onto a bromide film. The bromide film is then used

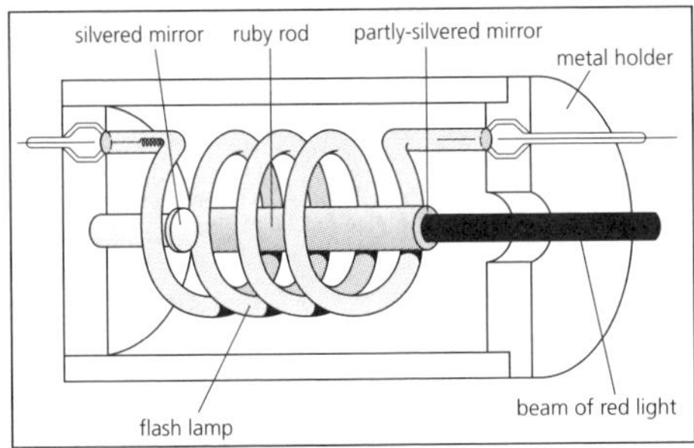

Section through a ruby laser

to etch a lithographic plate from which the required documents are printed. >> laser ℹ; lithography ℹ

Laski, Harold J(oseph) (1893–1950) Political scientist and socialist, born in Manchester. The development of his political philosophy, a modified Marxism, can be seen in his many books, such as *Authority in the Modern State* (1919). >> Marx; socialism

Laski, Marghanita (1915–88) Writer and critic, born in Manchester, the niece of Harold Laski. Her first novel, *Love on the Supertax*, appeared in 1944. She wrote extensively for newspapers and reviews, and published a number of critical works. >> Laski, Harold

Las Palmas (de Gran Canaria) [**pal**mas] pop (1995e) 756 000; area 4072 sq km/1572 sq mi. Spanish province in the Canary Is, comprising the islands of Gran Canaria, Lanzarote, and Fuerteventura; capital, Las Palmas (de Gran Canaria), pop (1995e) 345 000, resort and seaport (Puerto de la Luz); airport; cathedral. >> Canary Islands

Lassa fever An infectious disease caused by a virus confined at the present time to sub-Saharan W Africa. It is associated with pharyngitis, muscle pain, and high fever, and carries a high mortality. >> virus

Lassus, Orlandus, also known as **Orlando di Lasso** (c.1532–94) Composer, born in Mons, Belgium. He wrote several Masses, motets, and psalms, and also a large number of madrigals and songs in French and German.

Last Supper In the New Testament Gospels, the last meal of Jesus with his disciples on the eve of his arrest and crucifixion. It is considered significant for Jesus's words over the bread and cup of wine, where he declares 'This is my body' and 'This is my blood' (*Mark* 14.22–4). The event is commemorated in the sacrament of Holy Communion. >> Eucharist; Jesus Christ

Las Vegas [las **vay**gas] (Span 'the meadows') 36°10N 115°09W, pop (1995e) 331 000. Largest city in Nevada, USA; settled by Mormons, 1855–7; city status, 1911; airport; railway; university (1957); noted for its gaming casinos and 24-hour entertainment. >> Mormons; Nevada

La Tène [la **ten**] A prehistoric site on the shores of L Neuchâtel, Switzerland, excavated from 1858. Its name is commonly used to describe the later European Iron Age that succeeded Hallstatt culture c.500 BC. >> Maiden Castle; Three Age System

latent heat Heat absorbed or released when a substance undergoes a change of state at a constant temperature, such as solid to liquid (*latent heat of fusion*) or liquid to gas (*latent heat of vaporization*); symbol *L*, units J (joule). >> heat

laterality or **lateralization** A characteristic of the human brain, in which the left and right cerebral hemispheres are specialized for different functions; also known as **hemispheric specialization**. In the majority of people, the left hemisphere is specialized for language functions, and the right for the perception of complex patterns, both visual (eg faces) and tactile. >> brain ℹ

Lateran Church of St John The oldest of the four patriarchal basilicas of Rome, the episcopal seat of the pope as Bishop of Rome. The present building dates from the 16th-c. >> pope

Lateran Councils A series of councils of the Church held at the Lateran Palace, Rome, between the 7th-c and the 18th-c. The Fourth or Great Council (1215) defined the doctrine of the Eucharist (*transubstantiation*). >> Council of the Church; Eucharist

Lateran Treaty (1929) An agreement between the Italian fascist state and the papacy, ending a church-state conflict dating from 1870. Italy recognized the sovereignty of Vatican City, and Catholicism as the country's only religion; the papacy recognized the Italian state, and accepted the loss of other papal territories as irreversible. >> Papal States; pope

laterite Tropical soil in which seasonal fluctuations of groundwater have concentrated aluminium and iron oxide, forming a thick, hard, reddish layer. It is often used as roadstone. >> soil

latex A milky fluid found in special cells or ducts (*lactifers*) and present in many different plants. It is usually white, but can be colourless, yellow, orange, or red, and contains various substances in solution or suspension, such as starch and rubber. >> alkaloids; chicle; gutta percha; papaw; poppy; rubber; spurge; starch; sugars

lathe A common machine tool used to shape workpieces of various materials. The tools for boring, threading, cutting, or facing the workpiece are brought into contact with it either manually or under machine control. >> machine tools

Latimer, Hugh (c.1485–1555) Protestant reformer and martyr, born in Thurcaston, Leicestershire. He was one of the divines who examined the lawfulness of Henry's marriage, and declared on the king's side; but he opposed the Six Articles of Henry VIII, for which he was imprisoned in 1536, 1546, and 1553. He was tried for heresy under Mary and burned at Oxford. >> Protestantism; Reformation

Latin >> **Italic / Romance languages**

Latin America The 18 Spanish-speaking republics of the Americas, plus Portuguese-speaking Brazil (the largest Latin-American country) and French-speaking Haiti.

latitude and longitude Two dimensions used in mapping. The **latitude** of a point on the Earth's surface is the angular distance, N or S from the Equator (at latitude 0°); the Poles are at latitude 90°; lines (*parallels*) of latitude are parallel circles running E–W joining points of equal latitude. Important lines of latitude are the Tropic of Cancer (23·5° N), Tropic of Capricorn (23·5° S), the Arctic Circle (66·5° N), and the Antarctic Circle (66·5° S). Lines (*meridians*) of **longitude** are great circles running N–S and meeting at the Poles; the longitude is measured as an angular distance from the Greenwich meridian defined as 0° up to 180° E or W. >> cartography; Earth ℹ; great circle; *see illustration on p. 486*

Latium [**lay**shium] In antiquity, the area SE of Rome between the Apennine Mts and the sea. Densely populated in early Roman times, by the imperial period it had become the recreation area of the Roman rich, who filled it with luxurious villas.

La Tour, Georges de (1593–1652) Artist, born in Vic-sur-Seille, France. Only 14 of his paintings have been found, the best known being candle-lit religious scenes, such as 'St Jerome' and 'St Joseph' (Louvre).

La Tour, Maurice Quentin de [la**toor**], also spelled **Latour** (1704–88) Pastellist and portrait painter, born in St Quentin, France. His portraits include those of Louis XV, Madame de Pompadour, Voltaire, and Rousseau.

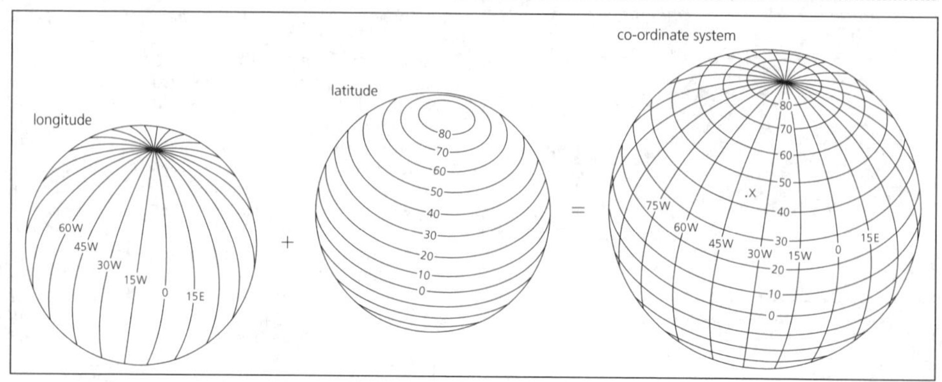

Lines of longitude and latitude give a co-ordinate system that permits the location and identification of all points on the Earth's surface (measured in degrees °, minutes′, and seconds″). The point x would have the following co-ordinate locations: 44°10′10″N, 39°25′40″W.

Latrobe, Benjamin (Henry) [la**trohb**] (1764–1820) Architect and civil engineer, born in Fulneck, West Yorkshire. He emigrated to the USA in 1795, where he introduced the Greek Revival style and was surveyor of public buildings in Washington, DC (1803–17). His most notable work is the Basilica of the Assumption of the Blessed Virgin Mary, Baltimore (begun 1805). >> Fulton

Latter-Day Saints (LDS) >> **Mormons**

Latvia, official name **Republic of Latvia**, Latvian **Latviya**, Russ **Latviskaya** pop (1995e) 2 620 000; area 64 600 sq km/ 24 900 sq mi. Republic in NE Europe; capital, Riga; timezone GMT +2; major ethnic groups, Latvian (52%), Russian (34%), Belorussian (5%), Ukrainian (4%), Polish (2%), Lithuanian (1%); religions, predominantly Evangelical Lutheran, with Orthodox and Roman Catholic minorities; official language, Latvian; unit of currency, the lats; flat, glaciated region; highest point, C Vidzeme (Livonia), elevation 312 m/1024 ft; NW coast indented by the Gulf of Riga; chief river, the Daugava; over 40% forested; mild climate, with high humidity; summers cool and rainy; average mean temperature −2°C (Jan), 17°C (Jul); average annual rainfall 700–800 mm/28–31 in; incorporated into Russia, 1721; independent state, 1918; proclaimed a Soviet Socialist Republic by the Soviet Union, 1940; occupied by Germany in World War 2; re-emergence of nationalist movement in the 1980s; declared independence, 1991; governed by a president, prime minister, and 100-member parliament (*Saeima*); machines, metalworking, instruments, electrical engineering, electronics, chemicals, furniture, knitwear, food processing, fishing; cattle, pigs, oats, barley, rye, potatoes, flax; well-developed national folklore, particularly in the 1860s when the Latvian theatre was founded in Riga (1868). >> Soviet Union; RR1015 political leaders

Latynina, Larisa Semyonovna [la**tee**nina] (1934–) Gymnast, born in Kherson, Ukraine. In 1956 and 1964 she collected 18 Olympic medals, a record for any sport, winning nine golds. >> gymnastics

Laud, William [lawd] (1573–1645) Archbishop of Canterbury, born in Reading, S England. He became a Privy Councillor (1626), Bishop of London (1628), and Archbishop of Canterbury (1633). With Strafford and Charles I, he worked for absolutism in Church and state. In Scotland, his attempt (1635–7) to anglicize the Church led to the Bishops' Wars. In 1640 the Long Parliament impeached him, and he was executed. >> Bishops' Wars; Long Parliament; Strafford

Lauda, Niki [**low**da], popular name of **Nikolas Andreas Lauda** (1949–) Motor-racing driver, born in Vienna. He was three times world champion, in 1975, 1977 (both Ferrari), and 1984 (Marlboro–McLaren), despite a horrific crash in 1976. He finally retired in 1985 after 25 career wins, and became the proprietor of Lauda-Air. >> motor racing

laudanum [**law**danum] A preparation of opium introduced by Paracelsus in the early 16th-c. Addiction to laudanum was socially acceptable until the early 19th-c. >> opium; Paracelsus

Lauder, Estée [**lawd**er], *née* **Mentzer** (c.1910–) Businesswoman, born in New York City. She co-founded Estée Lauder Inc with her husband **Joseph Lauder** in 1946, and had great success with the fragrance 'Youth Dew' in the 1950s.

Lauder, Sir Harry (MacLennan) [**lawd**er] (1870–1950) Singer, born in Edinburgh. Originally a music hall comedian, he made his name as a singer of Scots songs, many of which he wrote himself, such as 'Roamin' in the Gloamin'. >> music hall

Lauderdale, John Maitland, Duke of [**lawd**erdayl] (1616–82) Scottish statesman, born in Lethington, East Lothian. He was taken prisoner at Worcester (1651), and imprisoned. At the Restoration (1660) he became Scottish secretary of state. A privy councillor, he was a member of the Cabal, advisers to Charles II. >> Cabal; English Civil War; Restoration

laughing gas >> **nitrous oxide**

laughing jackass / kookaburra >> **kookaburra**

Laughlin, Robert B (1950–) Physicist, born in Vesalia, CA. He graduated from MIT in 1979, joining Stanford University, and shared the 1998 Nobel Prize for Physics for his contribution to the discovery of a new form of quantum fluid with fractionally charged excitations.

Laughton, Charles [**law**tn] (1899–1962) Actor, born in Scarborough, North Yorkshire. He began to act in films in 1932, and portrayed a wide range of memorable roles, such as Henry VIII in *The Private Life of Henry VIII* (1932, Oscar) and Captain Bligh in *Mutiny on the Bounty* (1935).

Launceston [**lon**sestn] 41°25S 147°07E, pop (1995e) 70 000 (Greater Launceston). Second largest city in Tasmania, Australia; airfield; railway. >> Tasmania

launch vehicle A rocket-propelled vehicle used to carry aloft spacecraft from the Earth's surface, generally consisting of several 'stages' which separate sequentially as fuel in each is consumed. The thrust is provided by the controlled explosive burning of liquid fuels (eg kerosene and oxygen, hydrogen and oxygen) or solid propellants (typically a synthetic rubber fuel mixed with an oxidized powder). >> spacecraft; space shuttle [i]; *see illustration below*

Laurasia The name given to the N 'supercontinent' comprising present-day North America, Europe, and Asia, excluding India, which began to break away from the

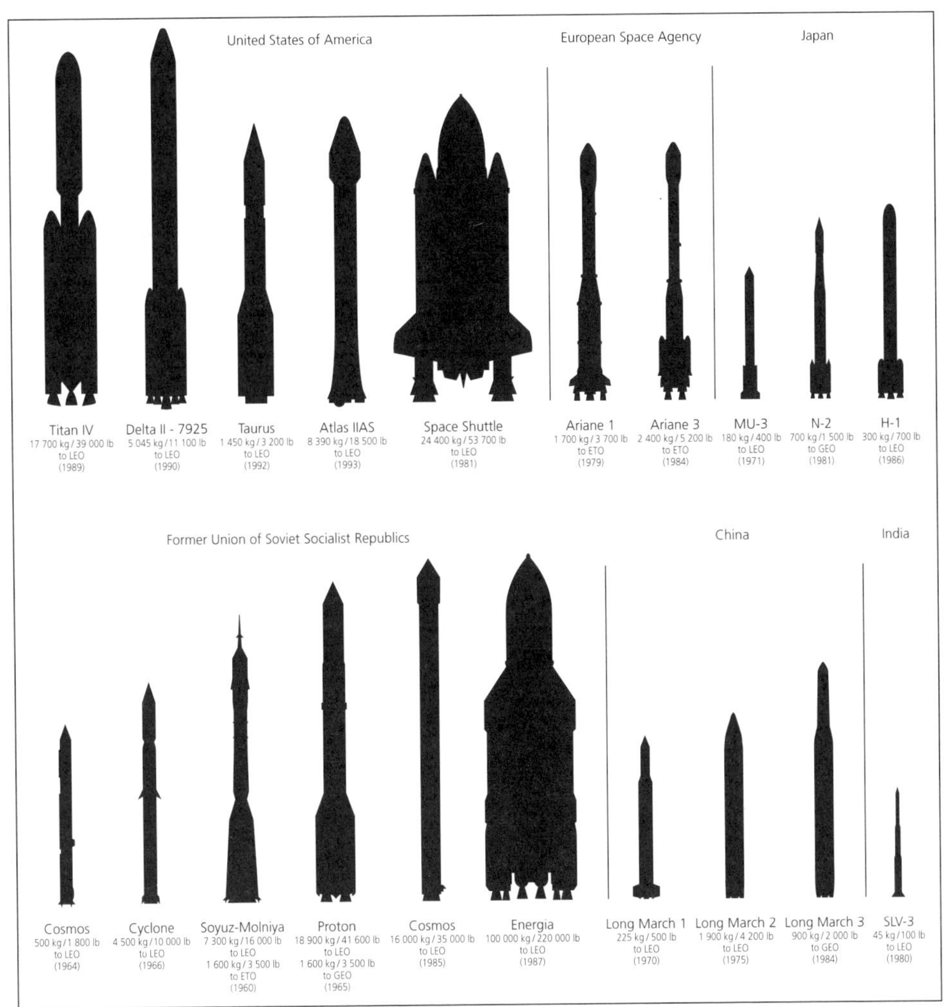

International space launchers - a selection of major launch vehicles as of 1993. The data refer to lift capacity (given in kg/lb, in most cases to the nearest hundred) and year of launch. LEO Low Earth Orbit (c.200 km/125 mi). GEO Geosynchronous Earth Orbit (36 000 km/22 000 mi). ETO Elliptical Transfer Orbit (intermediate between LEO and GEO).

single land mass Pangaea about 200 million years ago. >> continental drift; Gondwanaland

laurel A name applied to various unrelated trees and shrubs which have glossy, leathery, evergreen leaves, but mainly to members of the large family Lauraceae, in which the tissues contain numerous oil cavities and are aromatic. >> sweet bay

Laurel and Hardy Comedians who formed the first Hollywood film comedy team. The 'thin one', **Stan Laurel** (1890–1965), originally **Arthur Stanley Jefferson**, was born in Ulverston, Lancashire, England. He went to the USA in 1910, and worked in silent films from 1917. The 'fat one', **Oliver Hardy** (1892–1957), born near Atlanta, GA, joined a troupe of minstrels before drifting into the film industry. They came together in 1926. They made many full-length feature films, but their best efforts are generally thought to be their early (1927–31) shorts.

Lauren, Ralph [**lo**ren], originally **Ralph Lifschitz** (1939–) Fashion designer, born in New York City. He is famous for his American styles, such as 'prairie look' and 'frontier fashions'.

Laurentian Shield >> **Canadian Shield**

Laurier, Sir Wilfrid [**lo**ryay] (1841–1919) Canadian statesman and prime minister (1896–1911), born in St Lin, Quebec, Canada. Leader of the Liberal Party (1887–1919), he was the first French-Canadian to be prime minister of Canada. >> Canada i

laurustinus [loruh**stiy**nuhs] A dense evergreen shrub or small tree (*Viburnum tinus*), growing to 7 m/23 ft, native to S Europe; flowers 5-petalled, white, in clusters; fruit berry-like, dark, metallic blue. (Family: Caprifoliaceae.)

Lausanne [loh**zan**] 46°32N 6°39E, pop (1995e) 128 000. Tourist resort and convention centre in W Switzerland; seat of the Federal Supreme Court; on N shore of L Geneva; railway junction; university (1891); seat of the International Olympic Committee; cathedral (1275). >> Switzerland i

lava Hot molten rock erupted onto the Earth's surface from a volcano. On solidification it forms volcanic igneous rocks such as rhyolite, andesite, or basalt. >> igneous rock; magma; volcano

Laval, Pierre (1883–1945) French statesman and prime minister (1931–2, 1935–6), born in Châteldon, France. In the Vichy government he was Pétain's deputy (1940), then his rival. As prime minister (1942–4), he openly collaborated with the Germans. After the war he was executed in Paris. >> Pétain; Vichy

lavallier >> **microphone** i

La Vallière, Louise-Françoise de La Baume le Blanc, duchesse de (Duchess of) [la val**yair**] (1644–1710) Mistress of Louis XIV of France (1661–7), born in Tours. She bore the king four children, and remained at court reluctantly after Mme de Montespan superseded her (1667). >> Louis XIV

lavender A small aromatic shrub, native mainly to Mediterranean regions and Atlantic islands, typical of dry scrub; flowers 2-lipped, lavender or mauve, in dense spikes. (Genus: *Lavandula*, 28 species. Family: Labiatae.)

Laver, Rod(ney George) [**lay**ver], nickname **the Rockhampton Rocket** (1938–) Tennis player, born in Rockhampton, Queensland, Australia. The first person to achieve the Grand Slam twice (1962, 1969), he won four singles titles at Wimbledon (1961–2, 1968–9). >> tennis, lawn i

Lavoisier, Antoine Laurent [lavwazyay] (1743–94) Chemist, born in Paris, regarded as the founder of modern chemistry. In 1788 he showed that air is a mixture of gases which he called oxygen and nitrogen, thus disproving the earlier theory of phlogiston. His major work is the *Traité élémentaire de chimie* (1789). He also devised the modern method of naming chemical compounds. Politically a liberal, and despite his many reforms, he was guillotined in Paris on a contrived charge of counter-revolutionary activity. >> chemical elements; phlogiston theory

Law, (Andrew) Bonar [**law**, **bo**ner] (1858–1923) British statesman and prime minister (1922–3), born in New Brunswick, Canada. In 1911 he succeeded Balfour as Unionist leader. He acted as colonial secretary (1915–16), Chancellor of the Exchequer (1916–18), and Lord Privy Seal (1919), before serving for a short time as premier. >> Balfour

Law, William (1686–1761) Clergyman, born in Kingscliffe, Northamptonshire. He wrote several treatises on Christian ethics and mysticism, notably the *Serious Call to a Devout and Holy Life* (1729), which influenced the Wesleys. >> Wesley, John

law Specifically, a rule of conduct laid down by a controlling authority; generally, the whole body of such rules, recognized and enforced by society in the courts. In common law systems, the courts are particularly influential in developing the law, through the accretion of case decisions. In states with a written constitution, such as the USA, the Supreme Court may have the power to declare particular laws unconstitutional. >> civil / international law; jurisprudence; Law Commission; sea, law of the; Supreme Court

Law Commission Body established by the Law Commissions Act (1965) for England and Wales and for Scotland, appointed by the Lord Chancellor from the judiciary and from practising and academic lawyers. Its function is to examine the law with a view to reform and codification. >> law; Lord Chancellor

Lawler, Ray(mond Evenor) (1921–) Playwright and actor, born in Melbourne, Australia. He achieved international fame with his play about the outback, *Summer of the Seventeenth Doll* (1955), in which he took the leading role.

Lawrence D(avid) H(erbert Richard) (1885–1930) Poet and novelist, born in Eastwood, Nottinghamshire. He achieved fame with *Sons and Lovers* (1913), but was prosecuted for obscenity after publishing *The Rainbow* (1915). He left England in 1919, living in Italy, Australia, the USA, and Mexico, and returning to Italy for health reasons in 1921. Other major novels include *Women in Love* (1921), *The Plumed Serpent* (1926), and *Lady Chatterley's Lover* (1928). He also wrote many short stories, short novels, and travel books. His letters are an important part of his output.

Lawrence, Ernest (Orlando) (1901–58) Physicist, born in Canton, SD. He constructed the first cyclotron for the production of high-energy atomic particles, and was awarded the Nobel Prize for Physics in 1939. >> cyclotron

Lawrence, T(homas) E(dward), known as **Lawrence of Arabia** (1888–1935) British soldier and writer, born in Tremadoc, Gwynedd. In 1916 he was appointed the British liaison officer to the Arab Revolt, and was present at the taking of Aqaba in 1917 and of Damascus in 1918. His account of the Arab Revolt, *Seven Pillars of Wisdom*, became one of the classics of war literature, and his exploits received so much publicity that he became a legendary figure. >> World War 1

Law Society The professional body for solicitors in England and Wales; a separate Law Society exists for Scotland. It has disciplinary powers relating to solicitors' conduct, and prescribes the rules governing their admission to practice. >> solicitor

Lawson, Henry (1867–1922) Poet, born in Grenfell, New South Wales, Australia. His bush ballads and stories, published by *The Bulletin* from 1888, were immensely popular, and many now see him as the national poet. He was given a state funeral when he died. >> Lawson, Louisa

Lawson, Louisa (1848–1920) Suffragist and social reformer, born in Mudgee, New South Wales, Australia. In 1888 she founded *Dawn*, Australia's first feminist journal, which elevated women's affairs and promoted women's suffrage. >> Lawson, Henry

Lawson (of Blaby), Nigel, Baron (1932–) British Conservative statesman, born in London. Elected to parliament in 1974, he became financial secretary to the Treasury (1979–81), energy secretary (1981–3), and Chancellor of the Exchequer (1983–9). >> Conservative Party

laxative A drug which causes emptying of the bowels; also known as a **purgative**. Examples include castor oil and diphenylmethane. >> castor-oil plant

Laxness, Halldór (Guðjónsson Kiljan) (1902–98) Writer, born in Reykjavík. His works include *Salka Valka* (1934), a story of Icelandic fishing folk, and the epic *Sjálfstaet folk* (1934–5, Independent People). He was awarded the Nobel Prize for Literature in 1955.

Layamon [**lay**amon] (13th-c) English priest and poet, who lived at Areley Kings, on the R Severn, Hereford and Worcester. He wrote one of the first poems in Middle English, recounting the history of England from the arrival of a legendary Trojan, Brutus, down to the 7th-c AD.

Lazarists A religious order, founded in France at the priory of St Lazare, Paris, in 1625 by St Vincent de Paul; properly known as the **Congregation of the Mission** (**CM**); also called the **Vincentians**. >> Vincent de Paul, St

L-dopa or **levodopa** A drug used very effectively in the treatment of Parkinson's disease. It reduces symptoms in more than two-thirds of patients. >> Parkinson's disease

Leach, Bernard (Howell) (1887–1979) Studio potter, born in Hong Kong. He studied in Japan (1911–19), then established a pottery at St Ives, Cornwall, where he made earthenware and stoneware. He played a crucial role in promoting handmade pottery which could be appreciated as art. >> pottery; stoneware

Leach, Johnny, popular name of **John Leach** (1922–) Table tennis player, born in Romford, Essex. He won the world singles title in 1949 and 1951, and represented his country 152 times. >> table tennis

Leacock, Stephen (Butler) (1869–1944) Economist and humorist, born in Swanmore, Hampshire, UK. His family emigrated to Canada when he was six. His popular short stories, essays, and parodies include *Literary Lapses* (1910) and *Nonsense Novels* (1911).

lead Pb (from Lat *plumbum*) element 82, a soft, dense (11·5 g/cm^3) metal, melting point 328°C. Its main natural source is the sulphide (PbS). Its good corrosion resistance and easy workability led to its early use in plumbing and for corrosive liquids containers, with considerable toxic results, as it is slowly oxidized in the presence of air and water. >> chemical elements; metal; RR1036

leaf The main photosynthetic organ of green plants, divided into a blade (*lamina*) and a stalk (*petiole*). The lamina is usually broad and thin, to present maximum surface area to sunlight and allow easy diffusion of gases and water vapour to and from the leaf. It is composed of several distinct layers of tissues: the *epidermis* protects the inner tissues – the *palisade layer*, which is the primary site of photosynthesis, and the *spongy mesophyll*, which has large air spaces and is the primary site of gas exchange. A network of vascular tissues, the *veins*, transports water and sap to and from the leaf. The epidermis secretes a waxy cuticle, mostly impervious to water and gases which enter and leave via pores (*stomata*) concentrated in the lower surface of the leaf. Leaves range from a few mm to 20 m/65 ft in length, exhibit a great variety of shapes, and may be entire, toothed, lobed, or completely divided into separate *leaflets*. Leaves may also have specialized functions, such as water-storage in succulents, traps in carnivorous plants, and tendrils in climbers. >> bract; cotyledons; palmate; photosynthesis; pinnate

leaf beetle A robust, often brightly coloured beetle; most are surface feeders on plant leaves. (Order: Coleoptera. Family: Chrysomelidae, c.35 000 species.) >> beetle; Colorado beetle

leaf hopper A small, hopping insect that feeds by sucking sap or cell contents of plants; causes damage by direct feeding, by toxic secretions, and by transmitting viral diseases. (Order: Homoptera. Family: Cicadellidae, c.20 000 species.) >> insect [i]; virus

League of Nations An international organization whose constitution was drafted at the Paris Peace Conference in 1919. The main aims were to preserve international peace and security by the prevention or speedy settlement of disputes and the promotion of disarmament. It became increasingly ineffective in the later 1930s, and after World War 2 transferred its functions to the United Nations. >> Paris Peace Conference; United Nations

League of Rights An Australian populist right-wing organization, founded in 1960 by Eric Butler (1916–). The League, which operates on the fringe of conservative politics, supports God, the Queen, the Commonwealth of Nations, apartheid, and private enterprise.

Leakey, L(ouis) S(eymour) B(azett) [**lee**kee] (1903–72) Anthropologist, born in Kabete, Kenya. His great discoveries took place in E Africa, where in 1959 he and his wife **Mary Leakey** (1913–96, *née* Nicol) unearthed the skull of

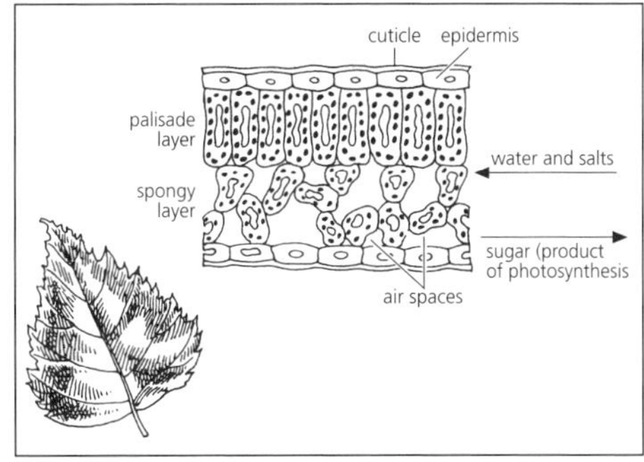

Leaf with cross section to show vascular structure

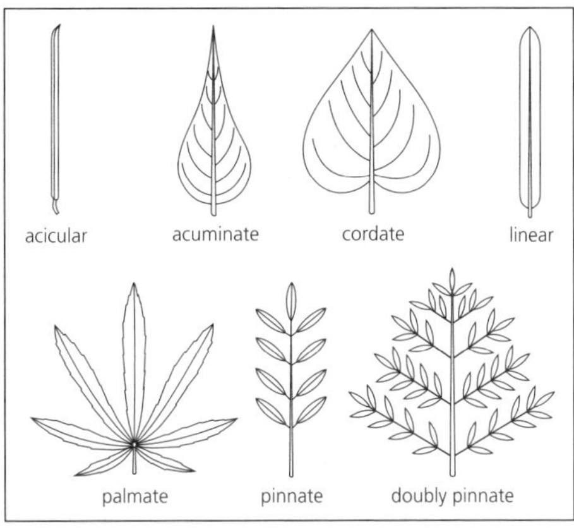

Leaf types

Zinjanthropus. In 1964 they found the remains of *Homo habilis* and in 1967 of *Kenyapithecus africanus*. Their son, **Richard Leakey** (1944–), has continued to make further important finds in the area. >> *Homo* ℹ; *Zinjanthropus*

Lean, Sir David (1908–91) Film director, born in Croydon, Greater London. In the 1950s he produced three great epics: *The Bridge Over the River Kwai* (1957), *Lawrence of Arabia* (1962), and *Doctor Zhivago* (1965). Later films were *Ryan's Daughter* (1970) and *A Passage to India* (1984). In 1990, he became the first non-American to receive a life achievement award from the American Film Institute.

Leander >> **Hero and Leander**

Leaning Tower, Ital **Torre Pendente** Marble building in Pisa, N Italy, 54 m/177 ft high, begun in 1173, completed in 1372. The ground beneath the tower began to sink after three stories had been built, and the tower is now c.6·5 m/18 ft out of line. It is currently closed to visitors. >> Pisa

leap year In the Gregorian calendar, a year of 366 days, with a day added to the month of February. Any year whose date is a number exactly divisible by four is a leap year, except years ending in 00, which must be divisible by 400 to be accounted leap years. The extra day is added every 4 years to allow for the difference between a year of 365 days and the actual time it takes the Earth to circle the Sun (approximately 365¼ days). >> Julian calendar

Lear A legendary king of Britain, first recorded in Geoffrey of Monmouth, though his name resembles that of the Celtic god of the sea. Leicester is named after him.

Lear, Edward (1812–88) Artist and writer, born in London. He is remembered for his illustrated books of travels, and for his books of nonsense verse, beginning with *A Book of Nonsense* (1846). >> limerick

lease A legal arrangement, also known as a **tenancy**, whereby the **lessor** (or landlord) grants the **lessee** (or tenant) the right to occupy land for a defined period of time. >> land registration; property

leaseback An economic operation where a business sells an asset (such as property), the buyer renting (ie leasing) the asset back to the business. The firm continues to have use of the asset, but also has cash from the proceeds of the sale which it can use in other ways. >> lease

leasehold >> **freehold**

leather Animal skin rendered durable and resistant to wear and degeneration by tanning. The cleaned skin is soaked in solutions which contain tannins (tannic acids widely distributed in nature) or chrome salts. The properties of leather are due to its fibrous and porous structure, and to its resistance to deterioration on repeated wetting and drying. >> tannins

leatherback turtle A sea-turtle (*Dermochelys coriacea*), worldwide in warm seas; the largest turtle (length, over 1·5 m/5 ft); no shell (adult has only small bony plates embedded in leathery skin); long front limbs (over 2·5 m/8 ft tip to tip); no claws; also known as **leathery turtle**. (Family: Dermochelyidae.) >> turtle (biology)

leatherhead >> **friarbird** ℹ

leatherjacket >> **cranefly**

Leavis, F(rank) R(aymond) [**lee**vis] (1895–1978) Critic, born in Cambridge, Cambridgeshire. He edited the journal *Scrutiny* (1932–53), and wrote several major critical works, such as *The Great Tradition* (1948) and *The Common Pursuit* (1952). Throughout his work (much of it shared with his wife Q D Leavis, 1906–81) he stresses the moral value of literary study.

Lebanon, Fr **Liban**, official name **Republic of Lebanon**, Arabic **Al-Jumhouriya al-Lubnaniya** pop (1995e) 2 919 000; area 10 452 sq km/4034 sq mi. Republic on the E coast of the Mediterranean Sea, SW Asia; capital, Beirut; timezone GMT +2; population mainly Arab (93%), with several minorities; chief religions, Christianity and Islam; official language, Arabic; unit of currency, the Lebanese pound; narrow coastal plain rises gradually E to the Lebanon Mts, peaks including Qornet es Saouda (3087 m/10 128 ft); arid E slopes fall abruptly to the fertile El Beqaa plateau, average elevation 1000 m/3300 ft; Anti-Lebanon range in the E; Mediterranean climate, varying with altitude, with hot, dry summers and warm, moist winters; part of the Ottoman Empire from 16th-c; after the massacre of (Catholic) Maronites by Druzes in 1860, Mt Lebanon was granted a special autonomous status by the Ottomans; Greater Lebanon, based on this area, created in 1920 under French mandate; Muslim coastal regions incorporated, despite great opposition; constitutional republic, 1926; independence, 1943; Palestinian resistance units established in Lebanon by late 1960s, despite government opposition; several militia groups developed in the mid-1970s; outbreak of civil war, 1975; Israel invaded S Lebanon, 1978, 1982; siege of Palestinian and Syrian forces in Beirut led to the withdrawal of Palestinian forces, 1982; unilateral withdrawal of Israeli forces brought clashes between the Druze (backed by Syria) and Christian Lebanese militia; ceasefire announced in late 1982, but broken many times; Syrian troops entered Beirut in 1988 in an attempt to restore order; timetable for militia disarmament introduced, 1991; Western hostages released, 1991; continuing conflict between Hizbullah and Israel in S Lebanon, mid-1990s; constitution provides for a Council of Ministers, president (a Maronite Christian), prime minister (a Sunni Muslim), cabinet, and parliament, equally divided between Christians and Muslims; commercial and financial centre of the Middle East, until the civil war, which severely damaged economic infrastructure and reduced industrial and agricultural production; tourism virtually collapsed, but began to revive in the mid-1990s. >> Arab–Israeli Wars; Beirut; Druze; Hizbullah; Islam; Israel ℹ; PLO; Shiites; Sunnis; Syria ℹ; RR1015 political leaders; *see illustration on p. 491*

Lebed, Alexander (Ivanovich) [**lje**bed] (1950–) General and politician, born in Novocherkassk, Russia. He served in Afghanistan (1981–2) and the Causacus (1988–90), and became Commander of the 14th Army in Moldova in 1992. After retiring from the army in 1995, he entered politics, coming to international attention during the 1996 presidential elections. He then gave his support to Yeltsin, was appointed National Security Advisor, and acted as chief negotiator in the Chechen conflict. After what many observers saw as a power struggle within the Kremlin, Yeltsin dismissed him. He then formed the Russian Popular Republican Party, and announced the continuation of his presidential aspirations. >> Yeltsin

LeBlanc, Matt (1967–) Actor, born in Newton, MA. He played a range of television roles before achieving success as Joey Tribbiani in the acclaimed series *Friends* (1994–). Roles in feature films include *Lookin' Italian* (1994), *Ed* (1996), and *Lost in Space* (1997).

Lebowa [le**boh**a] pop (1995e) 3 002 000. Former national state or non-independent black homeland in NE South Africa; self-governing status, 1972; incorporated into Northern Province in the South African constitution of 1994. >> apartheid; Northern Province; South Africa ℹ

Le Brun, Charles [luh **brõe**] (1619–90) Historical painter, born in Paris. He helped to found the Academy of Painting and Sculpture in 1648, and was employed by Louis XIV in the decoration of Versailles (1668–83).

Le Carré, John [luh **ka**ray], pseudonym of **David John Moore Cornwell** (1931–) Novelist, born in Poole, Dorset. His first published novel, *Call for the Dead* (1961) introduced his 'anti-hero' George Smiley, who appears in most

of his stories. Among his successes are *Tinker, Tailor, Soldier, Spy* (1974) and *The Perfect Spy* (1986). Many of his novels have been successfully filmed or televised.

lecithin [**les**uhthin] >> **choline**

Leconte de Lisle, Charles Marie René [luh**kõt** duh **leel**] (1818–94) Poet, born in Saint-Paul, Réunion. He exercised a profound influence on all the younger poets, heading the school called *Parnassiens*. His poetry was published in four major collections between 1858 and 1895.

Le Corbusier [luh kaw(r)**büs**yay], pseudonym of **Charles Edouard Jeanneret** (1887–1965) Architect and city planner, born in La Chaux-de-Fonds, Switzerland. He published, with Amédée Ozenfant (1886–1966), the Purist manifesto, and developed a theory of the interrelation between modern machine forms and architectural techniques. His first building, based on the technique of the *Modulor* (a system using units whose proportions were those of the human figure), was the *Unité d'habitation* ('Living unit'), Marseille (1945–50). His city planning designs include those proposed for Algiers (1932–42), several other cities, and realized at Chandigarh in India (1951). >> architecture

LED >> **light-emitting diode**

Leda (astronomy) [**lee**da] The 13th natural satellite of Jupiter, discovered in 1974; distance from the planet 11 100 000 km/ 6 900 000 mi; diameter 16 km/10 mi. >> Jupiter (astronomy); RR964

Leda (mythology) [**lee**da] In Greek mythology, the wife of Tyndareus, and mother, either by him or Zeus, of Castor and Pollux, Helen, and Clytemnestra. A frequent subject in art is Zeus courting Leda in the form of a swan. >> Castor and Pollux; Clytemnestra; Helen

LED printer A form of computer printer, similar to a xerographic printer, where the ionization of the drum is carried out using a row of light-emitting diodes (LEDs) rather than a laser beam. >> printer

Lee, Ann, known as **Mother Ann** (1736–84) Religious mystic, born in Manchester. In 1758 she joined the 'Shaking Quakers', or 'Shakers', who saw in her the second coming of Christ. She emigrated with her followers to the USA in 1774, founding the parent Shaker settlement. >> Shakers

Lee, Christopher (1922–) Film actor, born in London. His gaunt appearance and sinister image led to acclaimed performances in *Dracula* (1958) and its sequels, as well as in other horror movies. Later films include *The Three Musketeers* and its sequel (1973, 1989) and *The Stupids* (1996).

Lee, David M (1931–) Physicist, born in Rye, NY. He worked at Cornell University, where he contributed to the discovery of the superfluidity of helium-3. He shared the Nobel Prize for Physics in 1996.

Lee, (Nelle) Harper (1926–) Novelist, born in Monroeville, AL. Her first and only novel, *To Kill a Mockingbird* (1960, filmed 1962), a story of racial prejudice set in a Southern town, received a Pulitzer Prize.

Lee (of Ashridge), Jennie Lee, Baroness (1904–88) British socialist stateswoman, born in Lochgelly, Fife. She became the youngest elected woman MP (1929–31), and married Aneurin Bevan in 1934. Re-elected to parliament in 1945, as minister for the arts (1967–70) she established the Open University. >> Bevan; socialism

Lee, Laurie (1914–97) Writer, born in Slad, Gloucestershire. He was best known for his autobiographical stories of childhood and country life, *Cider With Rosie* (1959), *As I Walked Out One Midsummer Morning* (1969), and *I Can't Stay Long* (1975). *A Moment of War* (1991), recalls his experiences during the Spanish Civil War.

Lee, Robert E(dward) (1807–70) Confederate general, born in Stratford, VA. He was in charge of the defences at Richmond, and defeated Federal forces in the Seven Days' Battles (1862). His strategy in opposing General Pope, his invasion of Maryland and Pennsylvania, and other achievements are central to the history of the Civil War. In 1865, he surrendered his army to General Grant at Appomattox Courthouse, VA. >> American Civil War

Lee, Spike, popular name of **Shelton Jackson Lee** (1957–) Film-maker, born in Atlanta, GA. *She's Gotta Have It* (1986) established him internationally. Later films, centred around African-American culture, include *School Daze* (1988), *Do the Right Thing* (1989), *Mo' Better Blues* (1990), and *Get on the Bus* (1996).

leech A specialized ringed worm related to the earthworms; body highly contractile, usually with a sucker at each end; many are blood-feeders on vertebrate hosts. One species was used in early medicine for 'bleeding' patients suffering from various illnesses. (Phylum: Annelida. Subclass: Hirudinea.) >> earthworm; worm

leechee >> **litchi**

Leeds 53°50N 1°35W, urban area pop (1995e) 766 000. City in West Yorkshire, N England; in the 18th-c an important centre of cloth manufacture; universities (1904, 1992); major industrial and cultural centre; railway (important early freight and passenger centre); Town Hall (1858), Kirkstall Abbey (1147); Leeds Music Festival (every 3 years, Apr); International Pianoforte Competition (every 3 years, Sep); football league team, Leeds United (Peacocks). >> Yorkshire, West

leek A perennial with strap-shaped, sheathing leaves in two rows, and white flowers sometimes mixed with bulbils. It is now cultivated as a vegetable (*Allium porrum*). (Family: Liliaceae.) >> allium

Leeuwarden [**lay**vah(r)dn], Frisian **Liouwert** 53°12N 5°48E, pop (1995e) 88 200. City in N Netherlands, on the R Ee; railway; economic and cultural capital of Friesland; cattle market; Grote Kerk (13th–16th-c). >> Netherlands, The ℹ

Leeuwenhoek, Antonie van [**lay**venhook] (1632–1723) Scientist, born in Delft, The Netherlands. He became a renowned microscopist, the first to observe bacteria, protozoa, spermatozoa, and features of the blood. >> microscope

Leeward Islands (Caribbean), Span **Islas de Sotavento** Island group of the Lesser Antilles in the Caribbean Sea; from the Virgin Is (N) to Dominica (S); sheltered from the NE prevailing winds. >> Antilles; West Indies Federation

Leeward Islands (French Polynesia), Fr **Iles sous le Vent** pop (1995e) 26 900; area 507 sq km/196 sq mi. Island group of the Society Is, French Polynesia; chief town, Uturoa (Raiatea). >> Society Islands

Le Fanu, (Joseph) Sheridan [**lef**uhnyoo] (1814–73) Writer and journalist, born in Dublin. His novels include *The House by the Churchyard* (1863) and *Uncle Silas* (1864). He also wrote short stories, mainly of the supernatural.

Lefkosia >> **Nicosia**

Left Bank The S bank of the R Seine in Paris, an area occupied by numerous educational establishments, including the University of Paris and the Ecole des Beaux Arts. It is noted as a haunt of writers and intellectuals. >> Paris, University of

leg A term commonly used to refer to the whole of the lower limb, primarily used for support and movement; more precisely, in anatomy, the region between the knee and ankle joints. The bones are the *femur* in the thigh, the *tibia* and *fibula* in the leg, and the *tarsals*, *metatarsals*, and *phalanges* in the foot. >> femur; fibula; foot; skeleton [i]

legacy >> **property**

Legal Aid A scheme which provides those with limited financial means with advice and assistance from solicitors, barristers or advocates, and aids with representation at civil and criminal trials and certain tribunals. In the UK, civil legal aid is administered by the Law Society; help is means-tested, and a contribution may be required. A person seeking criminal aid applies to the court, when the offence carries a possible penalty of 6 months or more, and may be granted if the person's financial circumstances requires it, and if, in the case of summary offences, the interest of justice is served. In serious offences, Legal Aid is granted by the relevant Legal Aid Board, once granted no contribution from the applicant is required. In the USA, there is a constitutional right in criminal cases to be represented by a lawyer appointed by the court, where someone has insufficient means to pay privately. The Legal Services Corporation provides financial assistance for legal help in non-criminal proceedings for those unable to afford such help. Similar schemes exist in many other countries. >> civil law; Law Society; Lord Chancellor

Léger, Fernand [layzhay] (1881–1955) Painter, born in Argentan, France. He helped to form the Cubist movement, but later developed his own 'aesthetic of the machine', as in 'Contrast of Forms' (1913, Philadelphia). >> Cubism

Leghorn >> **Livorno**

leghorn A small breed of domestic fowl; named after Legorno (now Livorno) in Italy. >> domestic fowl

legion The principal unit of the Roman army. It was made up of 10 cohorts, each one of which was divided into six centuries. >> century

Légion d'Honneur [layzhõ donoe(r)] (Legion of Honour) In France, a reward for civil and military service created by Napoleon I in 1802. The five grades are chevalier, officer, commander, grand officer, and grand cross.

legionnaire's disease A serious form of pneumonia caused by the bacterium *Legionella pneumophilia*. The organisms are transmitted by water droplets from shower heads, humidifiers, and cooling towers. It is so named because the first outbreak affected members of the American Legion in Philadelphia. >> legionella; pneumonia

Legion of Mary An organization founded in Ireland in 1921 to enable lay members of the Roman Catholic Church to engage in apostolic (missionary and charitable) work. It was inspired by writings devoted to the Virgin Mary by St Louis Marie Grignon de Montfort (1673–1716). >> Mary (mother of Jesus)

legitimacy The legal status of a child at birth. A child is legitimate if born when its parents are validly married to each other, and the child is the biological issue of the couple, though most US jurisdictions presume legitimacy where the child is born to a married woman living with her husband who is not impotent. A person born illegitimate may be legitimized by the subsequent marriage of his or her parents.

legume A dry, 1-many-seeded fruit of the pea family (*Leguminosae*). When ripe it splits into two valves, each bearing alternate seeds. Many kinds are eaten as vegetables. >> fruit; pea [i]; vegetable

Lehár, Franz [luh**hah(r)**] (1870–1948) Composer, born in Komárom, Hungary. His works include two violin concertos, but he is best known for his operettas, which include *The Merry Widow* (1905) and *The Count of Luxembourg* (1909).

Le Havre [luh **hahvr**], formerly **Le Havre-de-Grace** 49°30N 0°06E, pop (1995e) 202 000. Commercial seaport in NW France; Allied base in World War 1; largely rebuilt since heavy damage in World War 2; chief French port for transatlantic passenger liners; ferry service to UK. >> Napoleon I

Lehmann, Lilli [**lay**man] (1848–1929) Soprano, born in Würzburg, Germany. She took part in the first performance of Wagner's *Ring* cycle (1876) at Bayreuth. >> Wagner

Lehmann, Lotte [**lay**man] (1888–1976) Soprano, born in Perleberg, Germany. She was noted particularly for her performances in operas by Richard Strauss, including two premieres. >> Strauss, Richard

Leibniz, Gottfried Wilhelm [**liyb**nits] (1646–1716) Philosopher and mathematician, born in Leipzig, Germany. He visited London in 1673, becoming involved in a controversy over whether he or Newton was the inventor of the infinitesimal calculus. His great influence, especially upon Russell, was primarily as a mathematician and as a pioneer of modern symbolic logic. >> calculus; rationalism (philosophy); Russell, Bertrand

Leicester [**les**ter], Lat **Ratae Coritanorum** 52°38N 1°05W, pop (1995e) 287 000. City and county town of Leicestershire, C England; unitary authority from 1997; an important royal residence in mediaeval times; charter granted by Elizabeth I, 1589; two universities (1957, 1992); railway; many Roman remains; cathedral (14th-c); football league team, Leicester City. >> Lear; Leicestershire

Leicester, Robert Dudley, Earl of [**les**ter], also known as **Baron Denbigh** and **Sir Robert Dudley** (c.1532–88) English nobleman, the favourite and possibly the lover of Elizabeth I. He continued to receive favour in spite of his unpopularity at court and two secret marriages, and was appointed in 1588 to command the forces against the Spanish Armada. >> Elizabeth I; Spanish Armada

Leicester (of Holkham), Thomas William Coke, Earl of [**les**ter, **holk**am] (1752–1842) Agriculturalist, the 'father of experimental farms', born in London. People visited his estate from all over the world, and special meetings were held at sheep-clipping time – called 'Coke's Clippings' – the last of which took place in 1821.

Leicestershire [**les**tersheer] pop (1995e) 927 000; area 2553 sq km/985 sq mi. County of C England; Leicester and Rutland new unitary authorities from 1997; administrative centre, Leicester. >> England [i]; Leicester

Leiden >> **Leyden**

Leif Eriksson [layv **e**rikson] (fl.1000) Icelandic explorer, the son of Eric the Red, the first European to reach

America. c.1000 he discovered land which he named Vinland after the vines he found growing there.

Leigh, Mike [lee] (1943–) Playwright and theatre director, born in Salford, Greater Manchester. He has scripted a distinctive genre based on actors' improvizations around given themes. His most successful work for the theatre has had a second life on film, as in *Bleak Moments* (1970), and on television, as in *Abigail's Party* (1977). Later films include *Secrets and Lies* (1996), and *Career Girls* (1997).

Leigh, Vivien [lee], originally **Vivian Hartley** (1913–67) Actress, born in Darjeeling, India. She was put under contract by Alexander Korda, playing in *Fire Over England* (1937) against Laurence Olivier, whom she subsequently married (1940–60). Her star role of Scarlett O'Hara in *Gone With the Wind* (1939) brought her an Oscar, as did her role in *A Streetcar Named Desire* (1951).

Leinster [**len**ster] pop (1995e) 1 847 000; area 19 633 sq km/7578 sq mi. Province in E Ireland; capital, Dublin. >> Ireland (republic) 🛈

Leipzig [**liyp**zig], ancient **Lipsia** 51°20N 12°23E, pop (1995e) 528 000. City in SE Germany; airport; railway; Karl Marx University (1409); college of technology; centre for commerce, education, and music (associations with Bach and Mendelssohn). >> Germany 🛈

Leipzig, Battle of [**liyp**zig] (1813) The overwhelming defeat of Napoleon's forces by the armies of the Fourth Coalition, also called the **Battle of the Nations**. He was heavily outnumbered by the Allied force of Austrians, Prussians, Russians, and Swedes. >> Napoleonic Wars

leishmaniasis [leeshma**niy**asis] A group of conditions caused by the protozoan *Leishmania*, conveyed by sandflies, occurring on the Mediterranean shores, Africa, and S Asia; also known as **kala-azar**. The *skin form* of the disease occurs as pimples which enlarge and ulcerate. The *visceral form* affects the liver, spleen, and lymph nodes. >> Protozoa

Leitrim [**lee**trim], Ir **Liathdroma** pop (1995e) 23 400; area 1526 sq km/589 sq mi. County in Connacht province, Ireland; capital, Carrick-on-Shannon. >> Connacht; Ireland (republic) 🛈

Lely, Sir Peter [**lee**lee], originally **Pieter van der Faes** (1618–80) Painter, born in Soest, The Netherlands. Court painter to Charles II, his 13 Greenwich portraits of English admirals (1666–7) are among his best works.

Lemaître, Georges (Henri) [luhmaytruh] (1894–1966) Astronomer, born in Charleroi, Belgium. His most important paper led to the concept of the 'big bang' theory of the universe. >> 'big bang'; cosmology

Léman, Lac >> **Geneva, Lake**

Le Mans [luh **mã**], ancient **Oppidum Suindinum** 48°00N 0°10E, pop (1995e) 150 000. Commercial city in NW France; ancient capital of Maine; fortified by the Romans, 3rd–4th-c; railway junction; cathedral (11th–15th-c); annual 24-hour motor race (Jun). >> motor racing

Lemieux, Mario [luhmyoe] (1965–) Ice hockey player, born in Montreal, Canada. He joined the Pittsburgh Penguins in 1984. In 1993, after nine seasons, he was the fifth all-time goal scorer. >> ice hockey 🛈

lemma >> **theorem**

lemming A mouse-like rodent of the tribe Lemmini (9 species); large powerful head, long fur, short tail. The **Norway lemming** (*Lemmus lemmus*) undergoes a population 'explosion' every 3–4 years. When this happens there is a mass migration. The direction of migration appears random, and sometimes groups reaching large bodies of water will swim offshore and drown in large numbers. There is no basis for the popular belief that lemmings march suicidally into the sea. >> mouse (zoology); rodent

Lemnos [**leem**nos], Gr **Límnos** pop (1995e) 16 700; area 476 sq km/184 sq mi. Greek island in the N Aegean Sea, off the NW coast of Turkey; length 40 km/25 mi; rises to 430 m/1411 ft; airfield; capital, Kastron. >> Greece 🛈

lemon A citrus fruit (*Citrus limoni*) 6–12·5 cm/$2\frac{1}{2}$–$4\frac{3}{4}$ in diameter; ovoid, with thick, bright yellow rind and sour pulp. (Family: Rutaceae.) >> citrus; lime (botany) 2

lemon sole Common European flatfish (*Microstomus kitt*) found in shelf waters from N Norway to the Bay of Biscay; body oval, length up to 65 cm/26 in; mouth small; brown with a mosaic of yellow and green patches; valuable food fish. (Family: Pleuronectidae.) >> flatfish

lemur [**lee**mer] A primitive primate from Madagascar; large eyes and pointed snout; most species with long tail; 27 species in three families: **lemur** (*Lemuridae*), **mouse** (or **dwarf**) **lemur** (*Cheirogaleidae*), and **leaping lemur** (*Indriidae*). >> colugo; indri; prosimian

Le Nain [nã] A family of French painters: three brothers, **Antoine** (c.1588–1648), **Louis** (c.1593–1648), and **Mathieu** (c.1607–77). All were born in Laon and were foundation members of the Académie in 1648. Louis is considered the best, with his large genre-scenes of peasant life. >> genre painting

Lena, River [**lyen**a] River in Siberian Russia; rises in the Baykalskiy Khrebet, enters the Laptev Sea; length, 4400 km/2700 mi. >> Russia 🛈

Lenclos, Ninon de [lãkloh], popular name of **Anne de Lenclos** (1620–1705) Courtesan of good family, born in Paris. Her lovers included several leading members of the aristocracy, as well as political and literary figures.

Lendl, Ivan [**len**dl] (1960–) Tennis player, born in Ostrava, Czech Republic. He became a US citizen in 1992. He dominated male tennis in the 1980s, winning the singles title at the US Open (1985–7), French Open (1984, 1986–7), and Australian Open (1989), and becoming the Masters champion (1986–7). He won 94 singles titles, but failed to win at Wimbledon. He was forced to retire in December 1994 because of a spinal condition. >> tennis, lawn 🛈

Lend-Lease Agreement The means by which the USA lent or leased war supplies and arms to Britain and other countries during World War 2. Up to the end of August 1945, the UK received about £5000 million worth of materials. >> World War 2

L'Enfant, Pierre Charles [lãfã] (1754–1825) Architect and city planner, born in Paris. He moved to America in 1977, where he fought the British in the Revolutionary War. At Washington's invitation, in 1791 he submitted a plan for the new federal capital in the District of Columbia, which became an influential model of urban planning. >> Washington (DC)

Lenin, Peak, Russ **Lenina, Pik**, formerly **Mt Kaufmann** 39°21N 73°01E. Highest peak in the Alayskiy Khrebet, and second highest in Russia; height, 7134 m/23 405 ft; first climbed in 1928.

Lenin, Vladimir Ilyich, originally **Vladimir Ilyich Ulyanov** (1870–1924) Marxist revolutionary and politician, born in Simbirsk, Russia. From 1897 to 1900 he was exiled to Siberia for participating in underground revolutionary activities. At the Second Congress of the Russian Social Democratic Labour Party (1903) he caused the split between the Bolshevik and Menshevik factions. In October he led the Bolshevik revolution and became head of the first Soviet government. At the end of the ensuing Civil War (1918–21) he introduced the New Economic Policy, which his critics in the Party saw as a 'compromise with capitalism' and a retreat from strictly Socialist planning. His birthplace was renamed Ulyanovsk in his honour (1924–91). >> Bolsheviks; Lenin Mausoleum; Russian Revolution

Leningrad >> **St Petersburg**

Leninism >> **Marxism-Leninism**

Lenin Mausoleum Burial vault, designed by Aleksey V

Shchusev and built in 1930 in Red Square, Moscow, where Lenin's embalmed body may be viewed by the public. >> Lenin; Red Square

Lennon, John (1940–80) Pop star, composer, songwriter, and recording artist, born in Liverpool, Merseyside. He was the Beatles rhythm guitarist, keyboard player, and vocalist, and a partner in the Lennon–McCartney song-writing team. He married Japanese artist Yoko Ono (1933–) – his second marriage – in 1969. Together they invented a form of peace protest by staying in bed while being filmed and interviewed, and the single recorded under the name of The Plastic Ono Band, 'Give Peace a Chance' (1969), became the 'national anthem' for pacifists. On the birth of his son, Sean (1975–), he retired from music to become a house-husband. He was shot and killed by an obsessed schizophrenic, Mark Chapman, but continues to be revered by new generations of fans. His son Julian (1963–) has had some success as a singer/musician. >> Beatles; McCartney

Leno, Dan [**lee**noh], originally **George Galvin** (1860–1904) Comedian, born in London. He appeared for many years in the annual pantomime at Drury Lane. >> pantomime

Le Nôtre, André [luh **nohtr**] (1613–1700) The creator of French landscape gardening, born in Paris. He designed the gardens at Versailles, and laid out St James's Park in London. >> landscape gardening

lens A transparent optical element comprising two refracting surfaces, at least one of which is curved; parallel light rays passing through the lens may converge (and focus at a point) or diverge, depending on the lens shape. Lenses are characterized by their *focal length* (the distance at which the image of a distant object is most sharply defined) and their *aperture* or *f-number* (the light transmission). >> aberrations 1 🛈; camera

Lent In the Christian Church, the weeks before Easter, observed as a period of prayer and penance in commemoration of Christ's 40-day fast in the wilderness; in the Western Churches, Lent begins on Ash Wednesday; in the Eastern Churches, it begins eight weeks before Easter. >> Ash Wednesday; Carnival; Easter

lenticel A small pore in a stem or root, with a similar role to that of stomata in leaves, allowing the passage of gases to and from tissues.

lentil An annual growing to c.40 cm/15 in (*Lens culinaris*); pea-flowers white, veined with lilac, borne 1–3 on a long stalk; pods rectangular with 1–2 disc-shaped seeds. The seeds (lentils) are rich in protein. (Family: Leguminosae.) >> protein; vegetable

Lenya, Lotte [**layn**ya], originally **Karoline Wilhelmine Blamauer** (1900–81) Singer, born in Vienna. She married Kurt Weill in 1926, and made an international reputation as Jenny in Weill's *Die Dreigroschenoper* (1928, The Threepenny Opera). >> Weill

Leo III, known as **Leo the Isaurian** (c.680–741) Byzantine Emperor (717–41), born in Syria. In 726 he prohibited the use of images in public worship, which led to more than a century of controversy. >> iconoclasm

Leo I, St, known as **the Great** (c.390–461) Pope (440–61), and one of the most eminent of the Latin Fathers. He summoned the Council of Chalcedon in 451. Feast day 10 November (W), 18 February (E). >> Fathers of the Church; pope

Leo III, St (c.750–816) Pope (795–816), born in Rome. He crowned Charlemagne Emperor of the West (800), thus initiating the Holy Roman Empire. He was canonized in 1673. Feast day 12 June. >> Charlemagne; Holy Roman Empire; pope

Leo X, originally **Giovanni de' Medici** (1475–1521) Pope (1513–21), born in Florence, Italy. His vast project to rebuild St Peter's, and his permitting the preaching of an indulgence in order to raise funds, provoked the Reformation. >> indulgences; pope; Reformation

Leo (Lat 'lion') A N constellation of the Zodiac, lying between Cancer and Virgo. **Leo Minor** ('little lion') is a hard-to-see constellation N of Leo. >> constellation; RR968

León (Mexico) [lay**on**] 21°06N 101°41W, pop (1995e) 968 000 Town in SC Mexico; altitude, 1804 m/5919 ft; railway; commercial centre. >> Mexico 🛈

León (Spain) [lay**on**] 42°38N 5°34W, pop (1995e) 145 000. City in NW Spain; bishopric; capital of a mediaeval kingdom; railway; cathedral (13th–14th-c). >> Spain 🛈

Leonard, 'Sugar' Ray (1956–) US boxer, born in Wilmington, DE. He fought 12 world title fights, and became WBC world welterweight champion in 1977, adding the WBA light middleweight champion in 1981. He is the only boxer to have been world champion at five weights. >> boxing 🛈

Leonardo da Vinci [leeo**nah(r)**doh da **veen**chee] (1452–1519) Painter, sculptor, architect, and engineer, born in Vinci, Rome. In 1482 he settled in Milan, where he painted his 'Last Supper' (1498) on the refectory wall of Santa Maria delle Grazie. In 1500 he entered the service of Cesare Borgia in Florence as architect and engineer, and with Michelangelo decorated the Sala del Consiglio in the Palazzo della Signoria with historical compositions. About 1504 he completed his most celebrated easel picture, 'Mona Lisa' (Louvre). His notebooks contain original remarks on most of the sciences, including biology, physiology, hydrodynamics, and aeronautics. >> Borgia, Cesare; Michelangelo

Leoncavallo, Ruggero [leeonka**va**loh] (1857–1919) Opera composer, born in Naples, Italy. He wrote a number of operas, of which only *I Pagliacci* (1892) achieved lasting success.

Leonidas [lee**on**idas] (?–480 BC) King of Sparta (c.491–480 BC), hero of the Persian Wars. He perished at Thermopylae, fighting to check the Persian advance into C Greece. >> Persian Wars; Thermopylae

Leonids [**lee**uhnidz] A meteor shower due around 17 November each year that is spectacular at 33-year intervals. The last major sighting was 1966. >> meteor

Leontief, Wassily [lay**on**tyef, **va**silee] (1906–99) Economist, born in St Petersburg, Russia. In 1973 he was awarded the Nobel Prize for Economics for developing the input-output method of economic analysis used for planning and forecasting. >> economics

leopard A member of the cat family (*Panthera pardus*), found from Siberia to Africa; solitary; reddish- or yellowish-brown with small empty rings of dark blotches; black individuals (**black panthers**) sometimes found in dense forests. >> Felidae

Leopardi, Giacomo [layoh**pah(r)**dee] (1798–1837) Poet and scholar, born in Recanati, Italy. He was a gifted, congenitally handicapped child whose afflicted life was lived in hopeless despondency and unrequited love. Among his most noted works are those collected under the title *I canti* (1831).

Leopold I (Emperor) (1640–1705) Holy Roman Emperor (1658–1705), born in Vienna. Committed throughout his long reign to the defence of the power and unity of the House of Habsburg, he faced constant external threats from the Ottoman Turks and the King of France, in addition to the hostility of the Hungarian nobility. >> Habsburgs

Leopold I (of Belgium) (1790–1865) First king of the Belgians (1831–65), born in Coburg, Germany, son of Francis, Duke of Saxe-Coburg and uncle of Queen Victoria. He was an influential force in European diplomacy prior to Bismarck's ascendancy. >> Belgium 🛈; Bismarck

Leopold II (1835–1909) King of the Belgians (1865–1909), born in Brussels, the son of Leopold I. In 1885 he became King of the Congo Free State, which was annexed to Belgium in 1908. >> Belgium ℹ; Congo ℹ

Leopold III (1901–83) King of the Belgians (1934–51), born in Brussels. He ordered the capitulation of the Belgian army to the Germans (1940), thus opening the way to Dunkirk. >> World War 2

Léopoldville >> **Kinshasa**

Lepanto, Battle of [le**pan**toh] (1571) The defeat of the Turkish navy in the Gulf of Corinth, ending the Turks' long-standing domination of the E Mediterranean. It was inflicted by the Christian forces of Spain and the Italian states in coalition. >> John of Austria

Le Pen, Jean-Marie [luh **pen**] (1928–) French politician. He formed the National Front in 1972, and this party, with its extreme right-wing policies, emerged as a new 'fifth force' in French politics in the 1986 Assembly elections. A controversial figure and noted demagogue, he unsuccessfully contested the presidency in 1988. >> right wing

Lepenski Vir [le**pen**skee **veer**] A small prehistoric settlement on the banks of the R Danube in the Iron Gates Gorge, Yugoslavia, dating from c.6500–5500 BC. It includes the earliest monumental sculpture in Europe.

Lepidoptera [lepi**dop**tera] A large order of insects comprising the 165 000 species of butterflies and moths; adults have two pairs of membranous wings covered with scales; forewings and hindwings coupled together; mouthparts typically modified as a slender sucking proboscis. >> butterfly; insect ℹ; moth

Lepidus, Marcus Aemilius [**le**pidus] (?–13 /12 BC) Roman statesman of the civil war era (49–31 BC), who first rose to prominence under Caesar, becoming his deputy at Rome. He reached the high point of his career in 43 BC, when he formed the Second Triumvirate with Antonius and Octavian. >> Caesar; triumvirate

leprechaun [**lep**rekawn] A fairy of Irish folklore, traditionally a tiny old man occupying himself with cobbling, and the possessor of a crock of gold whose whereabouts he could be persuaded to reveal by threats of violence.

leprosy >> **Hansen's disease**

Leptis Magna or **Lepcis Magna** 32°59N 14°15E. An ancient seaport of N Libya, the site of spectacular Roman remains; now a world heritage site. It was founded by the Phoenicians as a trading post perhaps as early as the 7th-c BC. >> Libya ℹ; Phoenicia

lepton In particle physics, a collective term for all those particles of half integer spin (ie fermions) not affected by strong interactions. The leptons are electrons, muons, and taus, and their respective neutrinos. >> particle physics

Lepus [**lee**pus] (Lat 'hare') A constellation in the S sky, easy to see S of Orion. >> constellation; Orion (astronomy); RR968

Lermontov, Mikhail Yuryevich [**ler**montof] (1814–41) Writer, born in Moscow. He is best known for his novel *Geroy nashego vremeni* (1840, A Hero of Our Time).

Leroux, Gaston (Louis Alfred) [leroo] (1868–1927) Writer, born in Paris. His first novel, *The Seeking of the Morning Treasures* (trans, 1903) was followed by a series of detective stories. His best-known work, *The Phantom of the Opera* (1911), attracted little attention in its early days, but became a hit following a Lon Chaney film in 1924.

Lerwick [**ler**wik] 60°09N 1°09W, pop (1995e) 8000. Capital of Shetland, N Scotland; airfield; ferry terminus; Fort Charlotte (1665). >> Scotland ℹ; Shetland

Lesage, Alain René [luh**sahzh**], also spelled **Le Sage** (1668–1747) Novelist and playwright, born in Sarzeau, France. He is best known for his picaresque 4-volume novel *Histoire de Gil Blas de Santillane* (1715–35, The Adventures of Gil Blas of Santillane). >> picaresque novel

Le Saux, Graeme [luh **soh**] (1968–) Footballer, born in Jersey, Channel Is. A left back defender, he played in Jersey, then joined Chelsea, later moving to Blackburn Rovers, and returning to Chelsea in 1997. He joined England in 1995, and though an injury kept him out of the team for a while, he had won 25 caps by mid-1998.

lesbianism A sexual attraction and expression between women, which may or may not involve the complete exclusion of men as potential sexual partners. As with male homosexuality, lesbianism has become increasingly politicized in the latter part of the 20th-c. >> homosexuality

Lesbos, Gr **Lesvos** or **Mitilini** pop (1995e) 106 000; area 1630 sq km/629 sq mi. Greek island in the E Aegean Sea; third largest island of Greece; length 61 km/38 mi; hilly, rising to 969 m/3179 ft; in classical times, a centre of Greek lyric poetry; chief town, Mitilini. >> Greece ℹ

Lescot, Pierre [leskoh] (c.1515–78) Renaissance architect, born in Paris. His masterpiece was the Louvre, one wing of which he completely rebuilt. >> Louvre

Lesotho [le**soo**too], official name **Kingdom of Lesotho** pop (1995e) 2 017 000; area 30 355 sq km/11 720 sq mi. S African kingdom completely bounded by South Africa; capital, Maseru; timezone GMT +2; population mainly Bantu (Basotho); chief religion, Christianity (90%); official languages, Sesotho, English; unit of currency, the loti (maloti); Drakensberg Mts in NE and E, highest peak Thabana-Ntlenyana (3482 m/11 424 ft); serious soil erosion, especially in W; main rivers, the Orange and the Caledon; mild and dry winters; warm summer season (Oct–Apr); originally inhabited by hunting and gathering bushmen; Bantu arrived, 16th-c, and Basotho nation established; incorporated in Orange Free State, 1854; under British protection as Basutoland, 1869; independence, 1960; Kingdom of Lesotho, 1966; a hereditary monarchy, with the king assisted by a Military Council and a Council of Ministers; Moshoeshoe II forced into exile, 1990, replaced by his son; new constitution and elections (first since 1970) to restore civilian rule, 1993; bicameral legislature consists of a Senate and National Assembly; Moshoeshoe returned to the throne (1994), but

died in a car accident, 1996; status of the monarchy a continuing issue; economy based on intensive agriculture and male contract labour working in South Africa; Highlands Water Scheme begun in 1988; to be completed by 2020. >> Maseru; South Africa [i]; RR1015 political leaders

less developed countries (LDCs) The majority of the world's countries, typically characterized by poverty, low levels of nutrition, health, and literacy, poorly developed industry, transport, and communications, and the export of agricultural products and minerals. The notion includes a very wide variety. Many countries, while still on average underdeveloped, have growing industrial sectors. The most backward LDCs, however, especially in Africa, continue to be poor. >> International Bank for Reconstruction and Development; Three Worlds theory

Lesseps, Ferdinand (Marie), vicomte de (Viscount of) [**les**eeps] (1805–94) Engineer, born in Versailles, France. In 1854 he began to plan the Suez Canal, finally built 1859–69. In 1881 work began on his scheme for a Panama Canal. >> Suez Canal

Lessing, Doris (May), *née* **Tayler** (1919–) Writer, born in Kermanshah, Iran. She was brought up in Southern Rhodesia, the setting for her first novel, *The Grass is Singing* (1950). Her later works include the five-book sequence *The Children of Violence*; *The Golden Notebook* (1962), her best-known novel; and *The Good Terrorist* (1985).

Lessing, Gotthold Ephraim (1729–81) Writer and man of letters, born in Kamenz, Germany. *Laokoon* (1766) is a critical treatise defining the limits of poetry and the plastic arts. *Minna von Barnhelm* (1767) is the first German comedy on the grand scale.

Lethe [**lee**thee] In the Greek and Roman Underworld, the name of a slow-moving river. When the souls of the dead drank from it, they forgot their lives on Earth.

Letterman, David (1947–) Television talk-show host, born in Indianapolis, IN. He became well-known following guest-host appearances on the Johnny Carson Show in 1979–80, hosted a late-night show for MBC from 1982, then in 1993 joined CBS as host of 'Late Night with David Letterman'.

letter of credit A document issued by a bank or other body in which the issuer undertakes to substitute its financial strength for that of the beneficiary, when presented with a draft (bill of exchange) or other demand for payment along with other specified documents. They are especially used abroad, as a means of paying for foreign goods.

letterpress A form of printing in which the image to be communicated is placed on a relief surface of metal or wood, and transferred as an inked impression to the printing foundation, usually paper. To be read correctly on the paper, the printing image has to be reversed from left to right. In the last 25 years, letterpress has been largely superseded by offset lithography. >> printing [i]

lettuce An annual or perennial, very widespread but mostly N temperate; leaves often with prickly margins; flower-heads small, often in clusters, yellow or blue. It is an important salad plant, its numerous cultivars being divided into two main groups: *cos*, with upright heads of crisp oblong leaves, and the round-headed *cabbage* types, with broadly rounded leaves. (Genus: *Lactuca*, 100 species. Family: Compositae.)

leucocytes [**lyoo**kohsiyts] Blood cells without respiratory pigments, also known as **white blood cells**, whose function is to combat injury and bacterial, parasitic, and viral infection. In vertebrates the major types are *granulocytes*, sometimes called *polymorphs* (neutrophils, eosinophils, basophils) and *agranulocytes* (lymphocytes, monocytes). >> blood; lymphocyte

leucotomy >> **psychosurgery**

leukaemia / leukemia [l(y)oo**kee**mia] A group of malignant disorders of the white cells of the blood which tend to be progressive and fatal. The cause is unknown, but leukaemias are associated with exposure to ionizing radiation, cytotoxic drugs, and benzene in industry. The occurrence of the disease in clusters has suggested an infective cause. Treatment usually necessitates biopsy of the bone marrow, where many white cells are manufactured. >> biopsy; blood

Leuven [**loe**ven], Fr **Louvain**, Ger **Lowen** 50°53N 4°42E, pop (1995e) 86 500. University town in Belgium; centre of cloth trade in Middle Ages; largely destroyed in World War 1; Catholic University (1425), reorganized into French- and Flemish-speaking divisions since 1970; railway. >> Belgium [i]

Levant, The [le**vant**] A general name formerly given to the E shores of the Mediterranean Sea, from W Greece to Egypt. The **Levant States** were Syria and Lebanon, during the period of their French mandate, 1920–41. >> Lebanon [i]; mandates; Syria [i]

Le Vau or **Levau, Louis** [luh **voh**] (1612–70) Architect, born in Paris. His design of Vaux-le-Vicomte (1657–61), in which he collaborated with the landscape gardener Le Nôtre and the painter Le Brun, was a milestone in French architecture. The team went on to work at Versailles (from 1661), where Le Vau designed the garden facade. >> Baroque (art and architecture); Le Brun; Le Nôtre; Versailles

Levellers A radical political movement during the English Civil War and the Commonwealth. It called for the extension of manhood franchise to all but the poorest, religious toleration, and the abolition of the monarchy and the House of Lords. >> Commonwealth (English history); English Civil War

Leverhulme (of the Western Isles), William Hesketh Lever, 1st Viscount [**lee**verhyoom], also known as **Baron Leverhulme of Bolton-Le-Moors** (1851–1925) Soap manufacturer, born in Bolton, Lancashire. In 1884 he began to turn a small soap works into a national business, and developed Port Sunlight as a model industrial village.

Leverrier, Urbain Jean Joseph [luh**ve**ryay] (1811–77) Astronomer, born in St Lô, France. Interested in planetary motions, he correctly predicted the existence of Neptune in 1846. >> Adams, John Couch; Neptune (astronomy)

Levesque, Rene [luh**vek**] (1922–87) Canadian politician and premier of Quebec (1976–85), born in Campbellton, New Brunswick, Canada. Elected to the Quebec National Assembly as a Liberal in 1960, in 1968 he founded the separatist *Parti Québecois*. >> *Parti Québecois*; Quebec

Levi, Primo [**lay**vee] (1919–87) Writer, born in Turin, Italy. All of his novels are attempts to understand the nature of

The letterpress process – ink is carried on the surface of the image in raised relief

Nazi barbarity and the variety of responses to it. They include *Se questo è un Uomo* (1947, If this is a Man) and its sequel, *La tregua* (1963, The Truce). >> Nazi Party

Leviathan [le**viy**athan] A rare Hebrew loan-word of uncertain derivation, apparently used to refer to a kind of sea or river monster. It may have been a mythical supernatural figure, perhaps symbolic of chaos or evil.

Levinson, Barry (1942–) Film director and producer, born in Baltimore, MD. His directorial debut, *Diner* (1982), earned him an Oscar nomination for Best Screenplay. Other films include *Good Morning Vietnam* (1987) and *Rain Man* (1988, Oscar). He later produced *Donnie Brasco* (1997), and produced/directed *Sphere* (1997) and *Wag the Dog* (1998).

levirate A marriage custom or law which expects a widow to marry a brother (either real or a close relative classified as such) of her deceased husband. A **sororate** is a custom whereby a man has the right to marry his wife's sister, though this normally applies only if the wife is childless or dies young.

Lévi-Strauss, Claude [**lay**vee **strows**] (1908–) Social anthropologist, born in Brussels. A major influence on contemporary anthropology, his four-volume study *Mythologiques* (1964–72) studied the systematic ordering behind codes of expression in different cultures. >> anthropology; structuralism

Levites [**lee**viyts] Descendants of the Biblical character Levi (one of Jacob's sons), who apparently formed a class of auxiliary ministers dedicated to the care of the Tabernacle and eventually the Jerusalem Temple (*Num* 3.5–10). >> Leviticus, Book of; Zadokites

Leviticus, Book of [le**vit**ikus] A book of the Hebrew Bible/Old Testament, the third book of the Pentateuch, the English title referring to the priestly traditions of the Levites. It was probably compiled from earlier materials during the exile. >> Levites; Pentateuch

levodopa >> **L-dopa**

Lewinsky, Monica [luh**win**skee] (1973–) Former White House intern, born in San Francisco, CA. She joined the White House in 1995, then moved to the Pentagon. She became internationally known in January 1998 during the official investigation into claims of sexual harrassment made by Paula Jones against President Clinton (a claim later dismissed and settled). It was alleged that Lewinsky had had an 18-month sexual relationship with the president, and that he had persuaded her to deny the affair in her deposition to lawyers acting for Jones, and then subsequently denied the affair himself, while under oath. The enquiry was fuelled by a series of covert tape recordings of conversations betwen Lewinsky and the president made by her friend Linda Tripp (1950–), a former White House aide. Lewinsky continued to maintain a high national profile into 1999, following Clinton's acquittal. >> Clinton, Bill; Starr

Lewis, (Frederick) Carl(ton) (1961–) Athlete, born in Birmingham, AL. He won four gold medals at the 1984 Olympic Games, two at the 1988 Olympics, two more at the 1992 Olympics, and another at the 1996 Olympics . >> athletics

Lewis, C Day >> **Day-Lewis, C**

Lewis, C(live) S(taples) (1898–1963) Mediaevalist and Christian apologist, born in Belfast. His best-known book is *The Screwtape Letters* (1942), one of several works which expound issues of Christian belief and practice. He is also known for his children's stories of the land of Narnia, beginning with *The Lion, the Witch, and the Wardrobe* (1950).

Lewis, Edward B (1918–) Developmental biologist, born in Wilkes-Barre, PA. He shared the Nobel Prize for Physiology or Medicine in 1995 for his research into how genes control early development of the human embryo. Using the fruit fly, he investigated how genes could control development of body segments into specialized organs.

Lewis, Jerry Lee (1935–) Rock singer, country singer, and pianist, born in Ferriday, LA. His 1957 recordings 'Whole Lotta Shakin' and 'Great Balls of Fire' became classics of rock, copied by successive generations of musicians. >> rock music

Lewis, John L(lewellyn) (1880–1969) Labour leader, born near Lucas, IA. President of the United Mine Workers (1920–60), he was active in creating the Congress of Industrial Organizations in 1935, and served as its president until 1940. >> trade union

Lewis, Meriwether (1774–1809) Explorer, born in Charlottesville, VA. With William Clark he was joint leader of the first overland transcontinental expedition to the Pacific coast and back (1804–6). >> Clark, William

Lewis, M(atthew) G(regory), nickname **Monk Lewis** (1775–1818) Novelist, born in London. His best-known work is the Gothic novel *The Monk* (1795). >> Gothic novel

Lewis, (Harry) Sinclair (1885–1951) Novelist, born in Sauk Center, MN. *Main Street* (1920) was the first of a series of best-selling novels satirizing the materialism and intolerance of American small-town life. Other works include *Babbitt* (1922), *Elmer Gantry* (1927), and *Dodsworth* (1929). He received the 1930 Nobel Prize for Literature.

Lewis, (Percy) Wyndham [**wind**am] (1882–1957) Artist, writer, and critic, born in Nova Scotia, Canada. With Ezra Pound he founded *Blast*, the magazine of the Vorticist school. His writings include the satirical novel *The Apes of God* (1930) and the multi-volume *The Human Age* (1955–6), as well as literary criticism and autobiographical books. >> Pound; Vorticism

Lewis and Clark Expedition >> **Clark, William; Lewis, Meriwether**

Lewis with Harris area 2134 sq km/824 sq mi. Island in the Western Isles, NW Scotland; largest and northernmost of the Hebrides; Lewis (N) linked to Harris (S) by a narrow isthmus. >> Hebrides

lexicography >> **dictionary**

Lexington 42°27N 71°14W, pop (1995e) 29 200. Town in NE Massachusetts, USA; flashpoint of the American War of Independence. >> American Revolution; Revere

Leyden [**liy**dn], Dutch **Leiden** 52°09N 4°30E, pop (1995e) 115 000. University city in W Netherlands; charter, 1266; famous for its weaving, 14th-c; besieged for a year by the Spaniards, 1573; as a reward for their bravery the citizens were given Holland's first university, 1575; birthplace of several painters, notably Rembrandt. >> Netherlands, The [i]; Rembrandt

Leyden jar [**liy**dn] The earliest device for storing electric charge, named after the University of Leyden, where it was invented in 1746. A glass jar was coated inside and outside with metal foils, which were connected by a rod passing the insulating stopper. >> capacitance; electricity

ley lines [lay] Visible lines that connect ancient sites and features (eg burial mounds, standing stones) across the countryside. They have been interpreted as ancient trading tracks, as 'energy lines' which can be detected by dowsing, and as 'spirit lines' which begin and end in cemeteries. >> divination; dowsing

Lhasa [**lah**sa], Chin **Lasa**, known as **The Forbidden City** 29°41N 91°10E, pop (1995e) 150 000. Capital of Tibet (Xizang), SW China; altitude 3600 m/11 800 ft; airfield; ancient centre of Tibetan Buddhism, with many temples and holy sites; closed to foreigners in 19th-c; Chinese occupation, 1951; many monks have fled (including the Dalai Lama), especially after uprising in 1959. >> Buddhism; China [i]; Dalai Lama; Tibet

liane [li**ahn**], or **liana** [li**ah**na] A woody climber growing from the ground to the top of the tree canopy, where it branches out and produces flowers. >> climbing plant

Libby, Willard (Frank) (1908–80) Chemist, born in Grand Valley, CO. He received the Nobel Prize for Chemistry in 1960 for his part in the invention of the carbon-14 method of dating. >> radiocarbon dating

libel A defamatory statement published in permanent form. In many jurisdictions this is extended to include broadcast by wireless telegraphy (radio, television), and words spoken during the public performance of a play; also, the libel need not involve words – a sculpture or painting may be libellous. The expression is not used in this sense in Scottish law, being subsumed under defamation. In the USA, defamation on radio and television is usually classified as slander. >> defamation; slander

Liberace [libuh**rah**chee], also known as **Walter Busterkeys**, originally **Wladziu Valentino Liberace** (1919–87) Entertainer, born in Milwaukee, WI. His television series, *The Liberace Show* (1952–7), won him an Emmy as Best Male Personality. His enduring career rested on his live performances and a flamboyant life style, full of piano-shaped swimming pools, glittering candelabra, and sartorial excess.

Liberal Democrats >> **Liberal Party (UK); Social Democratic Party**

liberalism A political philosophy developed largely in the 18th–19th-c associated with the rise of the new middle classes, challenging the traditional monarchical, aristocratic, or religious views of the state. Classical liberalism argues for limited government, and the values traditionally espoused are those of freedom – of the individual, religion, trade and economics (expressed in terms of *laissez faire*), and politics. In the 20th-c, liberalism in most countries has been overtaken by socialism as the major radical challenge to conservative parties, and has come to occupy a position in the centre ground, finding it difficult to establish a firm electoral base. >> laissez-faire; Liberal Party (UK)

Liberal Party (Australia) Australia's largest conservative political party, formed by R G Menzies in 1944 from existing conservative groups. Under Menzies (prime minister, 1949–66), the party followed policies of economic growth and conservative pragmatism, espousing private enterprise. It is the main alternative to the Australian Labor Party, achieving success under John Howard in 1996. >> Australian Labor Party; Menzies

Liberal Party (Canada) A Canadian national and provincial political organization that grew out of 19th-c reformism. At the federal level, it regained power in the general election of 1993. >> Chrétien; King, W L Mackenzie; Laurier; Progressive Conservative Party; Trudeau

Liberal Party (UK) A British political party, originating in the mid 19th-c, whose electoral appeal was to the new middle classes and working-class elite of skilled artisans. The Liberals and Conservatives were the two major parties until 1922, since when it has become a centrist minority party. After the formation of the Social Democratic Party (SDP) in 1980, the Liberal Party entered into an electoral 'Alliance', and in 1987 voted to merge with the SDP, subsequently forming the **Social and Liberal Democratic Party**, from 1988 known as the **Liberal Democrats**. >> liberalism; Social Democratic Party

liberation theology A style of theology originating in Latin America in the 1960s. Accepting a Marxist analysis of society, it stresses the role and mission of the Church to the poor and oppressed in society, of which Christ is understood as liberator. Its sympathy for revolutionary movements led to clashes with established secular and religious authorities. >> Jesus Christ; Marxism; theology

Liberia [liy**beer**ia], official name **Republic of Liberia** pop (1995e) 3 029 000; area 113 370 sq km/42 989 sq mi. Republic in W Africa; capital, Monrovia; timezone GMT; population mainly indigenous tribes (95%), remainder being repatriated slaves from the USA (Americo-Liberians); chief religions, local beliefs; official language, English, with many local languages spoken; unit of currency, the Liberian dollar; low coastal belt with lagoons, beaches, and mangrove marshes; land rises inland to mountains, reaching 1752 m/5748 ft at Mt Nimba; equatorial climate, with high temperatures and abundant rainfall; high humidity during rainy season (Apr–Sep), especially on coast; mapped by the Portuguese, 15th-c; created as a result of the activities of several US philanthropic societies, wishing to establish a homeland for former slaves; founded in 1822; constituted as the Free and Independent Republic of Liberia, 1847; military coup and assassination of president, 1980, established a People's Redemption Council, with a chairman and a cabinet; new constitution, 1986, with an elected Senate and House of Representatives; civil war, followed by arrival of West African peacekeeping force, 1990; UN-sponsored peace agreement, 1993, provided for a 6-member Council of State and 35-member Transitional National Assembly; peace accord signed, 1995; elections held, 1997; economy based on minerals, especially iron ore; two-thirds of the population rely on subsistence agriculture; largest merchant fleet in the world, including the registration of many foreign ships. >> Monrovia; slave trade; RR1015 political leaders

Liberty, Statue of The representation of a woman holding aloft a torch, which stands at the entrance to New York harbour; a world heritage site. It was designed by the French sculptor Bartholdi, and assembled in 1886. The statue is 40 m/152 ft high. >> Bartholdi

Liberty Bell >> **Independence Hall**

Libra [**lee**bra] (Lat 'scales') An inconspicuous S constellation zodiac, lying between Virgo and Scorpius. >> constellation; zodiac [i]; RR968

librarianship >> **library science**

Library of Congress The US depository and largest

library in the world, founded in 1800 in Washington, DC. Its functions include the provision of reference materials for the US Congress. >> Washington (DC)

library program A computer program which carries out a specific function and which can be incorporated into another program doing a more sophisticated task. For example, a library program to print a current debit can be incorporated into a program to print a credit-card customer's statement. >> computer program

library science The study of all aspects of library functions. It covers such topics as selection and acquisition policy, classification systems, and cataloguing, as well as bibliography and administration. As a discipline in its own right, library science, or **librarianship**, is a late 19th-c development.

Libreville [leebruh**veel**] 0°30N 9°25E, pop (1992e) 400 000. Capital of Gabon, W Africa; founded in 1849 as a refuge for slaves freed by the French; occupied by the British and Free French, 1940; airport; railway; university (1970); cathedral; first Central African Games, 1976. >> Gabon ℹ

Librium >> **benzodiazepines**

Libya, official name **Socialist People's Libyan Arab Jamahiriya** pop (1995e) 4 848 000; area 1 758 610 sq km/ 678 823 sq mi. N African state; capital, Tripoli; timezone GMT +1; major ethnic groups, Berber and Arab (97%); chief religion, Islam (mainly Sunni); official language, Arabic; unit of currency, the Libyan dinar of 1000 dirhams; mainly low-lying Saharan desert or semi-desert; land rises (S) to over 2000 m/6500 ft in the Tibesti massif; highest point, Pic Bette (2286 m/7500 ft); Mediterranean climate on coast; controlled at various times by Phoenicians, Carthaginians, Greeks, Vandals, and Byzantines; Arab conquest in 7th-c; Turkish rule from 16th-c until Italians gained control in 1911; named Libya by the Italians, 1934; heavy fighting during World War 2, followed by British and French control; independent Kingdom of Libya, 1951; military coup established a republic under Muammar Gaddafi, 1969, led by a Revolutionary Command Council; foreign military installations closed down in early 1970s; relations with other countries strained by controversial activities, including alleged organization of international terrorism; diplomatic relations severed by UK after the killing of a policewoman in London, 1984; Tripoli and Benghazi bombed by US Air Force in response to alleged terrorist activity, 1986; two Libyan fighter planes shot down by aircraft operating with US Navy off N African coast, 1989; alleged base of terrorist operation which caused the Lockerbie air disaster (1988); suspects extradicted to stand trial in The Netherlands (Mar 1999), followed by suspension of international sanctions; a socialist state, governed by a chief-of-state, a General People's Committee, and a General People's Congress; once a relatively poor country, with an agricultural economy based on barley, olives, fruit, dates, almonds, tobacco; economy transformed by discovery of oil and natural gas, 1959. >> Gaddafi; Islam; Lockerbie; Sahara Desert; Tripoli (Libya); RR1015 political leaders

lice >> **louse**

lichen [**liy**kn, **li**chn] A type of composite organism formed as an association between a fungus and an alga or blue-green bacterium. The body may be encrusting, scale-like, leafy, or even shrubby, according to species. The fungal partner typically belongs to the Ascomycetes. >> algae; blue-green bacteria; fungus

Lichtenstein, Roy [**likh**tenstiyn] (1923–97) Painter, born in New York City. From the early 1960s he produced many of the best-known images of American Pop Art, especially frames from comic books complete with speech balloons, enlarged onto canvases and painted in primary colours. >> Pop Art

licorice >> **liquorice**

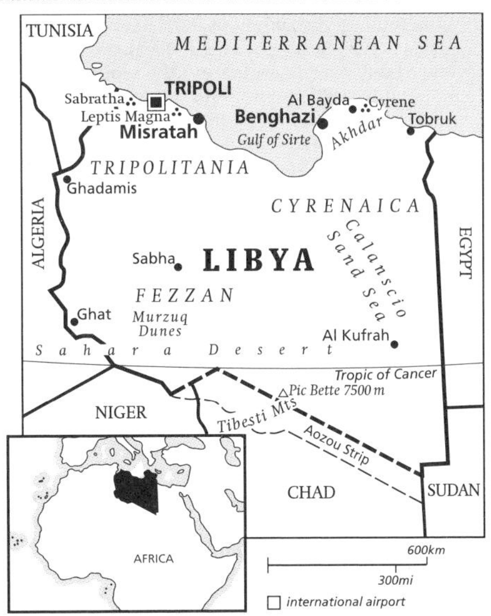

Lie, Trygve (Halvdan) [lee, **trig**vuh] (1896–1968) Lawyer, the first secretary-general of the United Nations, born in Oslo. Elected secretary-general in 1946, he resigned in 1952 over Soviet opposition to his policy of intervention in the Korean War. >> United Nations

Liechtenstein [**likh**tnshtiyn], official name **Principality of Liechtenstein**, Ger **Fürstentum Liechtenstein** pop (1995e) 31 000; area 160 sq km/62 sq mi. Independent Alpine principality in C Europe; fourth smallest country in the world; land boundary 76 km/47 mi; capital, Vaduz; timezone GMT +1; chief religion, Roman Catholicism (87%); official language, German; unit of currency, the Swiss franc; bounded W by the R Rhine; mean altitude, 450 m/1475 ft; forested mountains rise to 2599 m/8527 ft in the Grauspitz; average high temperature in summer, 20–28°C; average annual rainfall, 1050–1200 mm/ 41–47 in; formed in 1719; part of Holy Roman Empire until 1806; a constitutional monarchy ruled by the hereditary princes of the House of Liechtenstein; governed by a prime minister, four councillors, and a unicameral parliament; industrial sector developing since 1950s, export-based, centred on specialized and high-tech production; joined European Free Trade Association in 1991. >> Vaduz; RR1015 political leaders

Lied [leet] plural **Lieder** A song with German words. It generally refers to the solo songs with piano of the great German Romantic composers. >> Brahms; Schubert; Schumann, Robert

lie detector An instrument supposed to indicate whether a person to which it is applied is responding truthfully to questions; also known as a **polygraph**. Involuntary physiological reactions detected by electrodes attached to the subject's skin indicate stresses. Its validity is not universally acknowledged nor accepted judicially.

Liège [lyezh], Flemish **Luik**, Ger **Lüttich** 50°38N 5°35E, pop (1995e) 198 000. River port in E Belgium, at confluence of Ourthe and Meuse rivers; bishopric; fifth largest city in Belgium; railway; centre of former coal-mining area; university (1817); cathedral. >> Belgium ℹ

lifeboat A vessel designed specifically for saving life at sea; also, a craft carried by seagoing vessels to save the lives of personnel in the event of abandoning ship. Lionel Lukin is believed to have been the first to build a lifeboat, in

1786, basing it at Bamburgh Head, Northumberland, UK. The first mechanically powered lifeboat was launched, equipped with a steam engine, in 1890. Several countries now run lifeboat services; some are government controlled, and others are voluntary. >> Royal National Lifeboat Institution (RNLI)

life insurance Insurance designed to provide protection against financial hardship for dependents following the death of the insured person; also (especially in the UK) called **life assurance**. *Whole life policies* run for the whole of a person's life, accumulating a cash value which is paid when the policy matures (or is surrendered), but which is less than the policy's face value. *Endowment policies* run for a specified period of time, and pay the full face value when the policy matures. *Term policies* run for a specified number of years, but when the policy expires there is no cash sum remaining. Policies may be for a fixed money amount or are *with profits*, where the amount payable is related to the profits the life company has been able to make by investing the premium. >> annuity; insurance

Liffey, River [**li**fee] River in E Ireland, rising in N Wicklow county; flows through Dublin to the Irish Sea; length 80 km/50 mi. >> Dublin (city); Ireland (republic) ℹ

ligament A tough band of tissue connecting bones (eg across joints) or supporting internal organs (eg peritoneal ligaments). Ligaments act to prevent mechanical disruption at joints, and as sensory organs for the perception of movement and joint position. >> bone; joint

ligand [**lig**and] A molecule or ion bonded to another. It is most often used to describe species bonded to the central metal ion in a co-ordination compound.

liger [**liy**ger] A member of the cat family, resulting from the mating of a male lion with a female tiger. The offspring produced when a male tiger mates with a female lion is called a **tigon**. >> Felidae

Ligeti, György (Sándor) [lige**t**ee] (1923–) Composer, born in Dicsöszent-Márton, Hungary. He has developed an experimental approach to composition, as seen in his first large orchestral work, *Apparitions* (1958–9), and in *Aventures* (1962).

light The visible portion of the electromagnetic spectrum, corresponding to electromagnetic waves ranging in wavelength from approximately $3{\cdot}9 \times 10^{-7}$ m (violet) to $7{\cdot}8 \times 10^{-7}$ m (red) (corresponding frequencies $7{\cdot}7 \times 10^{14}$ Hz and $3{\cdot}8 \times 10^{14}$ Hz, respectively). Different wavelengths of light are perceived by humans as different colours. *White light* is composed of light of different wavelengths (colours), as may be seen by dispersing the beam through a prism. Light of a single colour is called *monochromatic*, as in the laser. Light as an electromagnetic wave was deduced by James Clerk Maxwell: light can also be viewed as composed of particles (*photons*) of definite energy. The modern description of light is as particles whose behaviour is governed by wave principles according to the rules of quantum theory. In geometrical optics (eg lens systems), light is thought of as rays, travelling in straight lines, causing shadows for opaque objects. >> electromagnetic radiation ℹ; fluorescence; laser ℹ; luminescence; optics ℹ; photometry ℹ; photon; quantum mechanics; stroboscope; velocity of light

light-emitting diode (LED) A tiny semiconductor diode which emits light when an electric current is passed through it. It is used in electronic calculator displays and digital watch read-outs.

lightning A visible electric discharge in the form of a flash of light which results from charge separation in a thundercloud. The reflection of lightning on surrounding clouds, in which the illumination is diffused, is known as **sheet lightning**. >> lightning conductor

lightning bug >> **firefly**

lightning conductor A means of protecting buildings and tall structures from lightning strikes; also called a **lightning rod**. It consists of a metal rod or strip, usually made of copper, placed at the highest point of a building. The lower end of the rod is connected to earth by a low-resistance cable. >> lightning

lightpen A computer input device used in conjunction with a visual display unit (VDU). The pen is held against the screen of the VDU, and its position can be used to generate or to alter information on the screen. >> input device

Lights, Feast of >> **Hanukkah**

light year The distance travelled through empty space in 1 tropical year by any electromagnetic radiation: $9{\cdot}4607 \times 10^{12}$ km/$5{\cdot}8788 \times 10^{12}$ mi. It is not usually used by astronomers, who prefer the parsec. >> light; parsec; tropical year

lignite >> **coal**

lignum vitae [**lig**num **viy**tee] An evergreen tree (*Guaiacum officinale*) growing to c.10 m/30 ft, native to W Indies; bark pale, smooth; flowers blue, 5-petalled. It is a source of durable timber. (Family: Zygophyllaceae.)

Ligurian Sea [liy**gyu**rian] Arm of the Mediterranean Sea, bounded N and E by NW Italy and S by Corsica and Elba. >> Mediterranean Sea

lilac A deciduous shrub or small tree (*Syringa vulgaris*), native to the Balkans; growing to 3–7 m/10–23 ft, flowers lilac or white, fragrant; fruit a pointed capsule. (Family: Oleaceae.)

Lilburne, John (c.1614–57) English revolutionary, born near London, who became a leading figure in the Levellers during the English Civil War. He was repeatedly imprisoned for his pamphlets. >> English Civil War; Levellers

Lilienthal, Otto [**leel**yentahl] (1849–96) Aeronautical inventor, born in Anklam, Germany. He studied bird flight in order to build heavier-than-air flying machines resembling the birdman designs of Leonardo da Vinci. >> aeronautics; Leonardo da Vinci

Lilith [**lil**ith] In Jewish legend, the first wife of Adam; or, more generally, a demon woman. >> Adam and Eve

Lille [leel], formerly Flemish **Lisle** or **Ryssel**, ancient **Insula** 50°38N 3°03E, pop (1995e) 177 000. Industrial and commercial city in N France; badly damaged in both World Wars; road and rail junction; part of the main industrial centre of N France; university (1560); cathedral (begun, 1854), 16th-c citadel. >> France ℹ

Lillie, Beatrice (Gladys) (1898–1989) Revue singer, born in Toronto, Ontario, Canada. She became renowned from 1914 in music hall and the new vogue of 'intimate revue'. Her film appearances include *Thoroughly Modern Millie* (1967).

Lilongwe [lee**long**gway] 13°58N 33°49E, pop (1995e) 295 000. Capital of Malawi, SE Africa; altitude 1100 m/3600 ft; capital since 1975; airport; railway. >> Malawi ℹ

lily A perennial with a bulb formed from swollen, overlapping, scale-like leaves, native to N temperate regions; flowers with six segments, large, terminal, often hanging; mostly white, yellow to red, purple, and often spotted; stamens long, protruding. (Genus: *Lilium*, 80 species. Family: Liliaceae.); *see illustration on p. 501*

lily-of-the-valley A perennial growing to 20 cm/8 in (*Convallaria majalis*), native to Europe and Asia; flowers drooping, globular bells with six short lobes, white, fragrant; berries red; cultivated for ornament, and as a source of perfume. (Family: Liliaceae.)

lily-trotter >> **jacana**

Lima [**lee**ma] 12°06S 77°03W, pop (1995e) 7 051 000. Federal capital of Peru; founded by Pizarro, 1535; chief city of Spanish South America until independence;

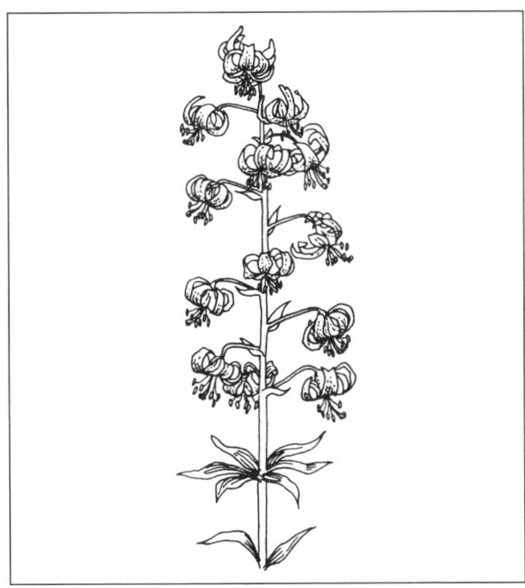

Lily - *Lilium martagon* (Turk's cap lily)

devastated by earthquake, 1746; airport; railway; 10 universities; cathedral (16th-c). >> Peru ℹ; Pizarro

Limassol [**lim**asol], Gr **Lemesos**, Turkish **Limasol** 34°41N 33°02E, pop (1995e) 143 000. Port in S Cyprus; airfield; wine-making, export of fruit and vegetables; castle (14th-c). >> Cyprus ℹ

limbo In mediaeval Christian theology, the abode of souls excluded from the full blessedness of the divine vision, but not condemned to any other punishment. They included unbaptized infants and Old Testament prophets. >> Christianity; purgatory

lime (botany) **1** A deciduous N temperate tree; flowers fragrant, white, 5-petalled, in pendulous clusters; fruits rounded, the whole cluster with a wing-like bract which aids in dispersal; also called **liden**. (Genus: *Tilia*, 50 species. Family: Tiliaceae.) >> basswood **2** A citrus fruit resembling lemon, but smaller and more globose. *Citrus limetta*, the sweet lime, is possibly a mutant of lemon. (Family: Rutaceae.) >> citrus; lemon

lime (chemistry) mainly calcium oxide or hydroxide, produced by heating limestone above 800°C, expelling carbon dioxide. The dry product is called **quicklime**; the addition of water converts the oxide to hydroxide or 'slaked' lime. >> calcium; limestone

Limerick, Ir **Luimneach** pop (1995e) 161 000; area 2686 sq km/1037 sq mi. County in Munster province, SW Ireland; capital, Limerick, pop (1995e) 74 900 founded, 1197; scene of major sieges by Cromwell and William III; railway; two cathedrals (12th-c, 19th-c). >> Ireland (republic) ℹ

limerick 'The limerick, it would appear, / Is a verse form we owe Edward Lear: / Two long and two short / Lines rhymed, as was taught, / And a fifth just to bring up the rear'. Lear, in fact, popularized the form, which is known from the early 19th-c. It is especially used with the opening: 'There was a ...' (young man from Dundee, young lady of Cheam, etc). >> Lear, Edward

limestone A sedimentary rock consisting mainly of carbonates, primarily calcite (calcium carbonate, $CaCO_3$) or dolomite ($CaMg(CO_3)_2$), with detrital sand or clay as impurities. Most limestones are organically formed from the secretions, shells, or skeletons of plants and animals such as corals and molluscs. Inorganic limestones are formed by precipitation from water containing dissolved carbonates. Limestone is of economic importance as a building material, and as a source of lime and cement. >> calcite; carbonates; Karst; oolite; stalactites and stalagmites; travertine

limner A painter of portraits 'in little', ie in miniature. Nicholas Hilliard's treatise *The Art of Limning* (c.1600) describes the highly specialized techniques required. >> Holbein; miniature painting

Limoges [lee**mohzh**]es, ancient **Augustoritum Lemovicensium**, later **Lemovic** 45°50N 1°15E, pop (1995e) 138 000. Ancient town in C France; Gallic tribal capital, destroyed 5th-c; sacked by the English, 1370; road and rail junction; famed for manufacture of enamels and porcelain since 18th-c; university (1808); meteorological observatory; cathedral (begun, 1273). >> porcelain

Limousin or **Limosin, Léonard** [limoozĩ] (c.1505–77) Painter in enamel, born in Limoges, France. He was appointed head of the royal factory at Limoges by Francis I. >> Francis I

limpet A primitive snail with a simple, flattened, conical shell; lives attached to rocks by its muscular foot; found in the inter-tidal zone or shallow seas. (Class: Gastropoda. Order: Archaeogastropoda.) >> snail

Limpopo, River [lim**poh**poh], also **Crocodile River** River in SE Africa; length c.1600 km/1000 mi; rises in the S Transvaal and flows into the Indian Ocean.

Linacre, Thomas (c.1460–1524) Humanist and physician, born in Canterbury, Kent. He was king's physician to Henry VII and Henry VIII, and founded the Royal College of Physicians. >> Renaissance

Lin Biao or **Lin Piao** [lin byow] (1907–71) A leader of the Chinese Communist Party, born in Hupeh province, China. He became minister of defence in 1959, and in 1968 replaced the disgraced Liu Shaqi as heir apparent to Mao Zedong. After differences with Mao and an abortive coup, he was killed in a plane crash in Mongolia, apparently while fleeing to the USSR. >> Mao Zedong

Lincoln (UK) [**ling**kn] 53°14N 0°33W, pop (1995e) 88 200. County town of Lincolnshire, EC England; centre of the wool trade in the Middle Ages; railway; parts of 3rd-c Roman wall remain; Lincoln Castle; cathedral (1073); football league team, Lincoln City (Imps). >> Lincolnshire

Lincoln (USA) [**ling**kn], formerly **Lancaster** (to 1867) 40°49N 96°41W, pop (1995e) 201 000. Capital of state in SE Nebraska, USA; state capital in 1867, when it was renamed after President Lincoln; railway; two universities (1867, 1887); trade in grain and livestock. >> Lincoln, Abraham; Nebraska

Lincoln, Abraham (1809–65) US Republican statesman and 16th president (1861–5), born near Hodgenville, KY. He was elected president on a platform of hostility to slavery's expansion. When the Civil War began (1861), he defined the issue in terms of national integrity, a theme he restated in the Gettysburg Address of 1863, and in the same year proclaimed freedom for all slaves in areas of rebellion. On 14 April 1865 he was shot at Ford's Theatre, Washington, by an actor, John Wilkes Booth, and died next morning. >> American Civil War; Booth, John Wilkes

Lincoln Center for the Performing Arts A group of theatres, recital halls, etc erected to the W of Broadway, New York City. The complex was completed in 1969. >> New York City

Lincoln Memorial A monument in Washington, DC, dedicated in 1922 to President Abraham Lincoln. The building, designed on the plan of a Greek temple by Henry Bacon (1866–1924), houses the statue of Lincoln (6 m/19 ft high) by Daniel Chester French (1850–1931). >> Lincoln, Abraham

Lincolnshire [**ling**knsheer] pop (1995e) 615 000; area 5915 sq km/2284 sq mi. Flat agricultural county in EC England; county town, Lincoln; Fens drained in 17th-c. >> England [i]; Fens; Lincoln (UK)

Lincoln's Inn >> **Inns of Court**

Lind, Jenny, originally **Johanna Maria Lind**, known as **the Swedish Nightingale** (1820–87) Soprano, born in Stockholm. She made her debut in Stockholm in 1838, and attained great popularity everywhere. After 1856 she lived in England.

Lindbergh, Charles A(ugustus) [**lind**berg] (1902–74) Aviator, born in Detroit, MI. He made the first solo non-stop transatlantic flight (New York–Paris, 1927), in the monoplane *The Spirit of St Louis*. His young son was kidnapped and murdered in 1932, the most publicized crime of the 1930s.

Lindemann, Frederick Alexander >> **Cherwell, Viscount**

linden >> **lime** (botany) **1**

Lindisfarne [**lin**disfah(r)n] area 10 sq km/3¾ sq mi. An island off the NE coast of England, renowned for its monastery founded from Iona by St Aidan in AD 634; also known as **Holy Island**. The Lindisfarne Gospels were illuminated here, probably in the 690s, by Eadfrith (Bishop, 698–721). The island is accessible from the mainland at low water by a causeway. >> Aidan, St; Cuthbert, St; Iona; Vikings

Lindow Man >> **bog burials**

Lindrum, Walter (1898–1960) Billiards player, born in Kalgoorlie, Western Australia. In 1932 he set the current world break record of 4137 while playing Joe Davis. >> billiards; Davis, Joe

Linear A A system of writing found throughout Minoan Crete. It was used mainly by administrators in the compilation of inventories. >> Linear B; Minoan civilization

Linear B A system of writing found on clay tablets at Mycenaean palace sites. Deciphered in the 1950s by Michael Ventris, it is (unlike Linear A) an early form of Greek. >> Linear A; Mycenaean civilization

line-engraving A method of intaglio printing, the metal plate being cut with a *burin*. The technique originated in 15th-c Germany. >> intaglio

Lineker, Gary (Winston) [**lin**eker] (1960–) Footballer, journalist, and broadcaster, born in Leicester, Leicestershire. He played for Leicester City, Everton, Barcelona, Tottenham Hotspur, and Grampus 8, Nagoya, Japan. He made his England debut in 1984 (captain 1990–2), playing in the 1986 and 1990 World Cups, and winning Player of the Year awards in 1986 and 1992. Retiring in 1994, he became a presenter of sports programmes for the BBC, and a familiar figure on television commercials.

linen Yarn and fabrics made from flax fibres, probably the earliest textile made from plants. Linen fabrics and yarns are fine, strong, and lustrous, but are less used today because of their poor easy-care properties. >> flax

line printer A type of printer, usually associated with larger computer systems, which prints a complete line of information at a time. It is very fast, especially when compared with printers that print one character at a time. >> computer printer

ling (botany) >> **heather** 1

ling (fish) Slender-bodied fish (*Molva molva*) of the cod family, abundant in offshore waters of the NE Atlantic from Norway to Biscay; length up to 2 m/6½ ft; mottled brownish-green on back. (Family: Gadidae.) >> cod

lingam [**ling**gam] The principal symbolic representation of the Hindu deity Shiva, a phallic-shaped emblem. The female equivalent is the **yoni**, the shaped image of the female genitalia. >> Hinduism; Shiva

lingua franca [**ling**gwa **frang**ka] An auxiliary language used for routine and often restricted purposes by people who speak different native languages. English and French are frequently used for this purpose in many parts of the world. >> auxiliary language

linguistic philosophy A movement within 20th-c English-language analytic philosophy, associated particularly with the later work of Wittgenstein and with Ryle and Austin. The main methodological assumption is that traditional philosophical problems arise from a misuse of language. >> Ryle, Gilbert; Wittgenstein

linguistics The scientific study of language. The discipline is concerned with such matters as providing systematic descriptions of languages, investigating the properties of language structures as communicative systems, exploring the possibility that there are universals of language structure, and accounting for the historical development of linguistic systems. It began with the publication of Ferdinand de Saussure's *Cours de Linguistique Générale* (1916, Course in General Linguistics), which introduced the distinction between *diachronic* (historical) linguistics, and *synchronic* (descriptive) linguistics, and laid the foundation for the era of **structural linguistics**, which dominated the first half of the 20th-c. The major development in the second half of the 20th-c has been the emergence of generative grammar, originally proposed by linguist Noam Chomsky in *Syntactic Structures* (1957), and since elaborated in a wide range of works. >> comparative / neuro- / psycho- / socio- / statistical / text-linguistics; Chomsky; dialectology; grammar; phonetics; phonology; pragmatics; semantics; Saussure; stylistics

Linklater, Eric (Robert) (1899–1974) Novelist, born in Dounby, Orkney. While in the USA (1928–30) he wrote *Poet's Pub* (1929), the first of a series of satirical novels which include *Juan in America* (1931) and *Private Angelo* (1946).

Linnaeus, Carolus [lin**ay**us], Swed **Carl von Linné** (1707–78) Botanist, the founder of modern taxonomy, born in Råshult, Sweden. Two of his books, *Species plantarum* (1753) and *Systema naturae* (10th edition, 1758–9), are the official starting-point for the current system of binomial Latin names for plants and animals. In many other books he described schemes of classification, grouping plants and animals into genera, classes, and orders. >> binomial nomenclature; botany; taxonomy; zoology

linnet Any of three species of finch of the genus *Carduelis*, especially the **Eurasian linnet** (*Carduelis cannabina*); native to Europe, N Africa, and W Asia. (Family: Fringillidae.) >> finch

Linz [lints] 48°18N 14°18E, pop (1995e) 210 000. Industrial town in N Austria; on R Danube, centre of a rich agricultural region; extensive port installations; third largest city in Austria; University of Social and Economic Sciences (1966); many historical buildings, including early 16th-c castle. >> Austria [i]

lion A member of the cat family (*Panthera leo*), native to Africa and NW India; brown; male with mane of long dark hair; inhabits grassland and open woodland; often territorial; lives in 'prides' averaging 15 individuals; the only cat that hunts in groups. >> Felidae; liger

Lions Clubs, International Association of >> **service club**

Lipchitz, Jacques [**lip**shitz], originally **Chaim Jacob Lipchitz** (1891–1973) Sculptor, born in Druskininkai, Lithuania. An exponent of Cubism, in the 1930s he developed a more dynamic style which he applied to bronze figure and animal compositions. >> Cubism

Lipizzaner [lipit**sah**ner] A breed of horse, developed at Lipizza in Austria in the 16th-c from the Andalusian horse; height, 15–16 hands/1·5–1·6 m/5 ft–5 ft 4 in; grey or pale brown. >> Spanish Riding School

Li Po [lee poh], also found as **Li Bo** and **Li T'ai Po** (c.700–762) Poet, born in Szechwan Province, China. A Taoist, interested in nature, mountains, and alchemy, he wrote over 1000 imaginative and rhapsodic free-style poems. Many were about drinking, such as 'Wine Song'.

Lippershey, Hans or **Jan** [**lip**ershay], also spelled **Lippersheim** (c.1570–1619) Dutch lens grinder, born in Wesel, Germany. He has been called the inventor of the telescope, but this is unproven. Certainly, in 1608 he offered the government of The Netherlands what we would now call a refracting telescope, and shortly afterwards others, such as Galileo, constructed similar devices. >> Galileo; telescope [i]

Lippi, Filippino [**li**pee] (c.1458–1504) Painter, born in Prato, near Florence, Italy, the son of Filippo Lippi. He completed c.1484 the frescoes in the Brancacci Chapel in the Carmine, Florence, left unfinished by Masaccio. >> fresco; Lippi, Fra Filippo; Masaccio

Lippi, Fra Filippo [**li**pee], known as **Lippo** (c.1406–69) Religious painter, born in Florence. Italy. His greatest work was on the choir walls of Prato cathedral, begun in 1452. His later works are deeply religious and include a series of 'Nativities'.

Lippmann, Walter (1889–1974) Journalist, born in New York City. A special writer for the *Herald Tribune*, his daily columns became internationally famous, and he won many awards, including the Pulitzer Prize for International Reporting (1962).

liqueur A spirit, usually distilled from grain, mixed with syrup, and with the addition of fruits, herbs, or spices to infuse a strong aroma and taste. Liqueurs have a high alcohol content, and are usually drunk in small quantities after a meal. Examples include Cointreau, Bénédictine, and Chartreuse (France), Tia Maria (Jamaica), and Drambuie (Scotland).

liquid A dense form of matter which is able to flow but unable to transmit twisting forces; density typically a few per cent less than the corresponding solid. It is virtually incompressible; the atoms are constantly changing position in a random way. >> boiling point; fluid mechanics; liquid crystals; phases of matter [i]

liquidation >> **bankruptcy**

liquid crystals Organic materials, crystalline in the solid state, which form a partially ordered state (the **liquid crystal state**) upon melting, and become true liquids only after the temperature is raised further. Their optical transparency can be reduced by applying electric fields, a property extensively exploited in displays for watches, calculators, and other electronic devices. >> crystals; liquid

liquidity In business and banking, actual money, or assets that are easily convertible into money. **Liquid assets** are cash, short-term investments, and debtors (ie amounts due from customers).

liquorice or **licorice** A perennial growing to 1 m/3¼ ft (*Glycyrrhiza glabra*), native to SE Europe and W Asia; pea-flowers whitish-violet. Its roots are a source of liquorice, used medicinally and as a confectionery ingredient. (Family: Leguminosae.)

Lisbon, Port **Lisboa**, ancient **Olisipo** or **Felicitas Julia** 38°42N 9°10W, pop (1995e) 675 000. Seaport and capital of Portugal, on N bank of R Tagus; settlement in Roman Empire; occupied by Moors, 8th-c; Portuguese capital, 1256; devastated by earthquake, 1755; Chiado shopping district of old town destroyed by fire, 1988; archbishopric; airport; railway; university (1911); 16th-c Tower of Belém and Jerônimos Monastery, a world heritage site; cathedral (1150). >> Belém Monastery; Portugal [i]

Lisdoonvarna [lishdoon**vah(r)**na] 53°02N 9°17W, pop (1995e) 835. Spa town in Clare county, Munster, W Ireland; leading sulphur-spring health centre; Lisdoonvarna fair (Oct). >> Clare; Ireland (republic) [i]

LISP [lisp] Acronym for **LISt Processing**, a high-level computer programming language designed for use with non-numeric data. It is widely used in artificial intelligence applications. >> artificial intelligence; programming language

Lissitsky, El(iezer) [li**sit**skee], also spelled **Lissitzky** (1890–1941) Painter, born in Smolensk, Russia. He painted in a totally abstract style, based on arrangements of simple lines, planes, and cubes, and became a leading Constructivist. >> abstract art; Constructivism; Suprematism

Lister (of Lyme Regis), Joseph Lister, Baron (1827–1912) Surgeon, born in Upton, Essex. His great work was the introduction (1865) of the use of antisepsis, which revolutionized modern surgery.

Listeria [lis**teer**ia] A genus of typically rod-shaped bacteria, motile by means of flagella and exhibiting a tumbling motion. It grows best in the presence of small quantities of oxygen; some strains cause food poisoning. >> bacteria [i]; flagellum

Liszt, Franz (1811–86) Composer and pianist, born in Raiding, Hungary. From 1835 to 1839 he lived with the Comtesse d'Agoult, by whom he had three children. He gave concerts throughout Europe, and in 1847 met Princess Carolyne zu Sayn-Wittgenstein with whom he lived until his death. His works include 12 symphonic poems, Masses, two symphonies, and a large number of piano pieces.

litany A form of prayer used in public or private worship. Supplications or invocations are made by the priest or minister, to which the congregation replies with a fixed formula.

litchi, litchee, leechee, or **lychee** [**liy**chee] An evergreen tree (*Litchi chinensis*) native to China; flowers white, starry; edible fruit 2·5–4 cm/1–1½ in long, ovoid with thin, horny, red-brown rind enclosing a single seed surrounded by sweet, white pulp. (Family: Sapindaceae.)

literacy The ability to read and write in a language. Discussion of the problem of **illiteracy**, both within a country and on a world scale, is complicated by the difficulty of measuring the extent of the problem in individuals. Defining even minimal levels is difficult, especially today, with increasing demands being made on people to be literate in a wider range of contexts. Current world estimates suggest that c.900 million adults are illiterate to a greater or lesser extent. National literacy campaigns in several countries have raised public awareness, and standards are slowly rising. >> dyslexia; oracy

literary agent A person who sells the various rights in a book to publishers and other potential purchasers (eg film companies) on behalf of the author, and represents the author in negotiations. The agent retains a percentage of the author's earnings as commission.

litharge [**li**thah(r)j] Lead(II) oxide (PbO); a bright yellow pigment used in paints. >> lead; oxide

lithium Li, element 3, melting point 181 °C. The lightest of the alkali metals; not common, but found widely in several minerals. Its compounds are used in organic synthesis; its salts have found application as anti-depressants in psychiatry. >> alkali; anti-depressants; chemical elements; RR1036

lithography A method of printing, invented by Aloys Senefelder in 1796, based on the principle that grease (ie ink) and water do not mix. A flat surface is treated so that the image area alone will attract ink. Ink and water are then applied to the surface; ink adheres to the image area and water to the non-image area. Paper is then brought into contact with the printing surface. In **offset lithography**, the image to be printed is created photographically

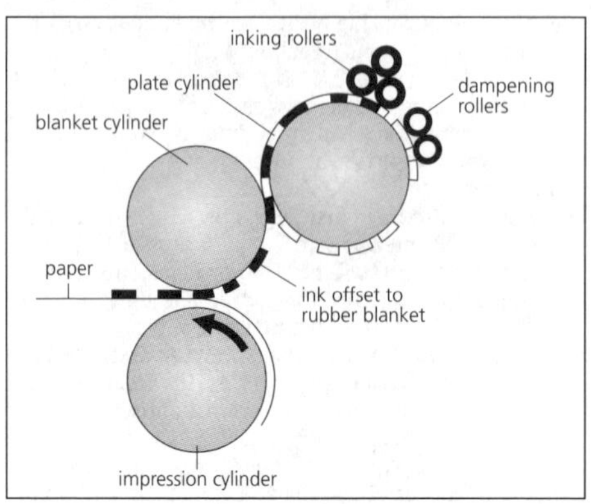

Lithography – An offset litho press

and the printing plate is wrapped round a cylinder. When the plate cylinder has been inked and dampened, the image is transferred ('offset') to a rubber 'blanket' cylinder and then transferred again to the printing substrate (normally paper, but also metal and plastic). >> printing ℹ; Senefelder

lithosphere Part of the Earth, consisting of the crust and the solid outermost layer of the upper mantle, extending to a depth of around 100 km/60 mi. >> Earth ℹ

Lithuania, official name **Republic of Lithuania**, Lithuanian **Lietuvos Respublika** pop (1995e) 3 775 000; area 65 200 sq km/25 167 sq mi. Republic in NE Europe, on the Baltic Sea; capital, Vilnius; timezone GMT +2; major ethnic groups, Lithuanian (80%), Russian (9%), Polish (7%), Belorussian (2%); religions, Roman Catholic, with small minority of Evangelical Lutherans and Reformists; official language, Lithuanian; currency, the litas of 100 centai; glaciated plains cover much of the area; central lowlands with gentle hills in W and higher terrain in SE; highest point, Jouzapine in the Asmenos Hills, 294 m/964 ft; 25% forested; some 3000 small lakes, mostly in E and SE; chief river, the Nemunas; continental climate, affected by maritime weather of W Europe and continental E; average annual temperatures −5°C (Jan), 16°C (Jul); average annual rainfall 630 mm/25 in; united with Poland, 1385–1795 (officially 1569); intensive russification led to revolts in 1905 and 1917; occupied by Germany in both World Wars; proclaimed a republic, 1918; annexed by the USSR, 1940; growth of nationalist movement in the 1980s; declared independence in 1990, but not recognized until 1991; governed by a president, prime minister, and single-chamber parliament (*Seimas*); electronics, electrical engineering, computer hardware, instruments, machine tools, shipbuilding, synthetic fibres, fertilizers, plastics, food processing, oil refining; cattle, pigs, poultry, grain, potatoes, vegetables. >> Soviet Union; RR1015 political leaders

litmus A complex vegetable dye traditionally used as a pH indicator. It is red in acid solutions and blue in alkaline ones. >> pH

litre Unit of volume; symbol *l*. The litre is no longer considered to be a precisely defined unit of volume. Officially the term may be used as a name for the cubic decimetre, but should not be used for high accuracy measurements. The precise unit of volume is the cubic metre, approximately 1000 litres. >> RR1031–3

Little Bighorn, Battle of the, also known as **Custer's Last Stand** (25 Jun 1876) The engagement between US cavalry, under Lieutenant-Colonel Custer, and the Sioux and Cheyenne, under Sitting Bull and Crazy Horse. The Indians destroyed Custer's force. >> Cheyenne (Indians); Custer; Sioux; Sitting Bull

Little Richard, popular name of **Richard Wayne Penniman** (1932–) Rock-and-roll singer and pianist, born in Macon, GA. 'Tutti Frutti' (1955) brought him international popularity. Most of his recordings from 1958 to 1964 were of Gospel songs, but in the mid-1960s he made a comeback with 'Whole Lot Of Shaking Goin' On', 'Lawdy Miss Clawdy', and his album *The Rill Thing*. >> rock music

Little Rock 34°45N 92°16W, pop (1995e) 185 000. City in C Arkansas, USA; largest city in the state, and a port on the Arkansas R; settled, 1821; railway; university; in 1957 Federal troops were sent to the city to enforce a 1954 US Supreme Court ruling against segregation in schools. >> Arkansas; civil rights

Littlewood, (Maudie) Joan (1914–) Theatre director, born in London. She pioneered work in left-wing, popular theatre, forming the Theatre Workshop in 1945. After settling at the Theatre Royal Stratford East in 1953, her productions included *The Hostage* (1958) and *Oh! What A Lovely War* (1963). >> Theatre Workshop

liturgy (Gr *leitourgia*, 'duty, service') The formal corporate worship of God by a Church. It includes words, music, actions, and symbolic aids, and in Christian form is derived from Jewish ritual.

Liupanshui or **Liu-p'an-shui** [lioopahnshway] 25°45N 104°40E, pop (1995e) 1 977 000. City in Guizhou province, S China; railway. >> China ℹ

Liu Shaoqi [lyoo showchee], also spelled **Liu Shao-ch'i** (1898–1969) Leading figure in the Chinese Communist revolution, born in Hunan, China. In 1943 he became Party secretary, and succeeded Mao Zedong in 1959. After the Cultural Revolution (1966), the extreme left made Liu their principal target, and in 1968 he was stripped of all his posts. >> Cultural Revolution; Mao Zedong

Live Aid >> **Geldof, Bob**

liver In vertebrates, a large, unpaired gland with digestive functions, situated in the upper part of the left-hand side of the abdominal cavity under cover of the ribs. It secretes bile, facilitates the digestion and absorption of fats, and deals with the newly absorbed products of digestion. It also manufactures the anticoagulant heparin and other plasma proteins, stores glycogen, fat, iron, copper, and

the vitamins A, D, E, and K, detoxifies harmful substances, and destroys red blood cells. >> anatomy [i]; cirrhosis; digestion; hepatitis; jaundice

liver fluke A leaf-like, parasitic flatworm (*Fasciola hepatica*), with a mouth sucker on its cone-shaped front end; can be a serious pest of domesticated animals. (Phylum: Platyhelminthes. Class: Trematoda.) >> flatworm; parasitology

Liverpool 53°25N 2°55W, pop (1995e) 473 000. Seaport in Merseyside, NW England; on the right bank of the R Mersey estuary; founded in the 10th-c, became a borough in 1207 and a city in 1880; importance enhanced in the 18th-c by the slave trade and the Lancashire cotton industry; major world trading centre and the UK's most important seaport for Atlantic trade; railway; container terminal (1972); linked to Birkenhead under the R Mersey by road and rail tunnels (1934, 1971); airport; universities (1903, 1992); Catholic cathedral, modern design by Frederick Gibberd on earlier classical foundation by Edward Lutyens (consecrated 1967); Anglican cathedral, designed by Giles Gilbert Scott (begun 1904, completed 1980); Royal Liver Building (landmark at Pier Head), St George's Hall, Albert Dock redevelopment, Maritime Museum, Tate in the North (1987), Walker Art Gallery; Royal Liverpool Philharmonic Orchestra; home of the Beatles (museum, 1984), and many other pop groups; football league teams, Liverpool (Reds) and Everton (Toffeemen); International Garden Festival held here in 1984; Grand National steeplechase at Aintree (Apr). >> Beatles, The; Mersey, River; Merseyside

Liverpool, Robert Banks Jenkinson, 2nd Earl of (1770–1828) British statesman and Tory prime minister (1812–27), born in London. He became foreign secretary (1801–4), home secretary (1804–6, 1807–9), and secretary for war and the colonies (1809–12). As premier, he oversaw the final years of the Napoleonic Wars and the War of 1812–14 with the USA. >> Napoleonic Wars; Tories

Liverpool poets A group of poets writing out of Liverpool, beginning in the 1960s. The best known are Adrian Henri (1932–), Roger McGough (1937–), and Brian Patten (1946–).

liverwort A small, spore-bearing, non-vascular plant of the Class Hepaticae, closely related to mosses and hornworts. They are divided into two types: **thalloid** liverworts have a flattened, often lobed or branched body (the *thallus*); **foliose** or leafy liverworts have slender, creeping stems with three rows of leaves, of which usually only two develop fully. They are found almost everywhere, but are restricted to damp, shady habitats. >> bryophyte; gametophyte; hornwort; moss; rhizoid; spore; sporophyte

livery companies In the UK, charitable and professional associations in the City of London, which have developed from the craft and trade guilds of the Middle Ages. The 12 'great' companies (nominated in 1514) are the mercers, grocers, drapers, fishmongers, goldsmiths, merchant taylors, skinners, haberdashers, salters, ironmongers, vintners, and clothworkers. >> London

Livia Drusilla (58 BC–AD 29) Augustus's wife (39 BC–AD 14) and key backroom figure in the early days of the Roman Empire. The mother of Tiberius by her first husband, Tiberius Claudius Nero, she plotted strenuously to ensure his succession. >> Augustus; Roman history [i]; Tiberius

Livingstone, David (1813–73) Missionary and traveller, born in Blantyre, South Lanarkshire. He worked for several years in Bechuanaland, then travelled N (1852–6), discovering L Ngami and the Victoria Falls (1855). He led an expedition to the Zambezi (1858–63), and discovered L Shirwa and L Nyasa. He later disappeared while searching for the sources of the Nile, and was found in 1871 by Stanley, sent to look for him by the *New York Herald*. >> Nile, River; Stanley

Living Theater / Theatre A theatre begun by Judith Malina (1926–) and Julian Beck (1925–85) in 1947 as an Off-Broadway venture. Its main feature was a conscious refusal to separate the art of theatre from the art of living. >> Broadway; theatre

Livius >> **Livy**

Livorno [lee**vaw(r)**noh], Eng **Leghorn** 43°33N 10°18E, pop (1995e) 184 000. Port in W Tuscany, Italy; railway; ferries to Corsica; cathedral (17th-c). >> Tuscany

Livy [**li**vee], in full **Titus Livius** (c.59 BC–AD 17) Roman historian, born in Patavium, Italy. His history of Rome, from its foundation to the death of Drusus (9 BC), comprised 142 books, of which 35 have survived.

lizard A reptile, found worldwide except in the coldest regions. Some have no obvious limbs and resemble snakes; but most differ from snakes in having eyelids and an obvious ear opening. (Suborder: Sauria or Lacertilia. Order: Squamata, c.3750 species.) >> agamid; chameleon; gecko; gila monster; glass snake; reptile; skink; slowworm; snake

Lizard Point 49°56N 5°13W. Promontory in Cornwall, SW England; the most S point on the UK mainland, near Lizard Town. >> Cornwall

Ljubljana [lyoobl**yah**na], Ital **Lubiana**, ancient **Emona** 46°00N 14°30E, pop (1995e) 292 000. Capital of Slovenia; founded, 34 BC; capital of the former Kingdom of Illyria, 1816–49; badly damaged by earthquake, 1895; ceded to Yugoslavia, 1918; airport; railway; university (1595); education and convention centre; cathedral. >> Slovenia [i]

llama A member of the camel family (*Lama glama*), found in the C Andes; domesticated c.4500 years ago; used mainly as a beast of burden; long flat-backed body with long erect neck and long ears; dense coat. >> Camelidae

Llanfairpwllgwyngyll [hlanviyrpulh**gwin**gihl], in full **Llanfairpwllgwyngyllgogerychwyrndrobwllllantysiliogogogoch** ('St Mary's Church in the hollow of the white hazel near a rapid whirlpool and the Church of St Tysilio by the red cave') 53°13N 4°12W. Village in Anglesey, NW

Lizards - flying lizard (a); tuatara (b)

Wales, UK; gained notoriety through the extension of its name (to 58 letters) by a poetic cobbler in the 18th-c; first Women's Institute in Britain founded here, 1915. >> Menai Straits; Anglesey

Llangefni [hlan**gev**nee] 53°16N 4°18W, pop (1995e) 4710. Town in Anglesey, NW Wales, UK; administrative centre for the island; Oriel Môn. >> Anglesey

Llangollen [hlan**go**lhen] 52°58N 3°10W, pop (1995e) 3150. Town in Denbighshire, NE Wales, UK; on the R Dee; site of annual international musical eisteddfod since 1947. >> Denbighshire; eisteddfod

Llano Estacado [**lah**noh esta**kah**doh] ('staked plain') Area 78 000 sq km/30 000 sq mi. Vast semi-arid S portion of the Great Plains, in E New Mexico and W Texas, USA. >> Great Plains

llanos [**lyah**nos] The savannah grasslands of the plains and plateaux of the Orinoco region (Colombia, Venezuela), N South America, traditionally an important livestock farming area. >> savannah

Llewellyn, Richard [hloo**el**in], pseudonym of **Richard Dafydd Vivian Llewellyn Lloyd** (1907–83) Writer, born in St David's, Pembrokeshire. He became a best-selling novelist with *How Green Was My Valley* (1939).

Lleyn Peninsula [hleen] Peninsula in Gwynedd, NW Wales, UK; chief towns, Pwllheli, Porthmadog. >> Gwynedd

Llosa, Mario Vargas [**hoh**sa] (1936–) Novelist, born in Arequipa, Peru. His novels include *Pantaleon y las visitidores* (1973, Captain Pantoja and the Special Service), *Aunt Julia and the Scriptwriter* (1977), and *A Fish in the Water* (1994). *The War at the End of the World* (1985) is one of several works whose political impact led to Llosa being proposed as president of Peru.

Lloyd, Harold (Clayton) (1893–1971) Film comedian, born in Burchard, NE. He made hundreds of short, silent comedies, adopting from 1917 his character of the unassuming 'nice guy' in horn-rimmed glasses and a straw hat. He received an honorary Academy Award in 1952.

Lloyd, Marie, originally **Matilda Alice Victoria Wood** (1870–1922) Music-hall entertainer, born in London. Among her most famous songs were 'Oh, Mr Porter' and 'My Old Man Said Follow the Van'.

Lloyd-George (of Dwyfor), David Lloyd George, 1st Earl (1863–1945) British Liberal statesman and prime minister (1916–22), born in Manchester, of Welsh parentage. He was President of the Board of Trade (1905–8), Chancellor of the Exchequer (1908–15), minister of munitions (1915), secretary for war (1916), and superseded Asquith as coalition prime minister, carrying on a forceful war policy. He negotiated with Sinn Féin, and conceded the Irish Free State (1921) – a measure which brought his downfall. >> Asquith; Liberal Party (UK)

Lloyd's An international market for insurance, based in London. It originated in Edward Lloyd's coffee house in Tower Street in the City of London, from 1688. All kinds of insurance are now handled worldwide. The members (*underwriters*) of Lloyd's are organized into syndicates, and risks are spread among the members of the syndicate so that no single individual (or 'name') carries too large a risk personally. There is, however, no limit to a member's liability, and large losses made by some syndicates in 1990 and 1991 have given rise to controversy concerning the management of Lloyds, and limited liability has been proposed. *Lloyd's Shipping Index* gives daily information about the worldwide movements of over 20 000 merchant vessels. >> insurance; Lloyd's Register of Shipping; Lutine Bell

Lloyd's Register of Shipping A publication which catalogues information about the construction and characteristics of individual vessels, to help insurance underwriters. 'A1 at Lloyd's' refers to the top grade of the classification made by the Register, indicating that the vessel is in first-class order. >> insurance; Lloyd's

Lloyd-Webber, Andrew Lloyd Webber, Baron (1948–) Composer, born in London. He met Tim Rice in 1965, and together they wrote a 'pop oratorio' *Joseph and the Amazing Technicolour Dreamcoat* (1968) which was extended and staged in 1972. Their greatest success was the 'rock opera' *Jesus Christ Superstar* (staged 1971, filmed 1973). His later musicals include *Evita* (1978), *Cats* (1981), *Starlight Express* (1983), *The Phantom of the Opera* (1986), and *Sunset Boulevard* (1993). >> Lloyd-Webber, Julian

Lloyd Webber, Julian (1951–) Cellist, born in London, the brother of Andrew Lloyd Webber. He made his UK debut in 1972, and has since performed with all the major British orchestras, appeared internationally, and made many recordings. >> Lloyd-Webber, Andrew

Llull or **Lull, Ramón** [lul], Eng **Raymond Lully**, known as **the Enlightened Doctor** (c.1235–1315) Franciscan theologian and philosopher, born in Palma, Majorca. His major work is the *Ars magna* (The Great Art), condemned in 1376 for its attempt to link faith and reason, but later viewed more sympathetically. His followers, known as **Lullists**, combined religious mysticism with alchemy. >> Franciscans; mysticism

Llywelyn [hloo**el**in] The name of two Welsh princes. **Llywelyn ap Iorwerth** or **Llywelyn the Great** (?–1240) successfully maintained his independence against King John and Henry III, and gained recognition of Welsh rights in the Magna Carta (1215). **Llywelyn ap Gruffydd** (?–1282) helped the English barons against Henry III, and opposed Edward I, who forced his submission. >> Edward I; Henry III (of England); John; Magna Carta

loach Slender-bodied freshwater fish of the family Cobitidae (7 genera), found in rivers and lakes throughout Europe and Asia; length commonly less than 10 cm/4 in; mouth fringed with barbels.

Lobachevsky, Nikolay Ivanovich [loba**chef**skee] (1792–1856) Mathematician, born in Nizhni Novgorod, Russia. In 1829 he published the first geometry on non-Euclidean principles. >> geometries, non-Euclidean

lobefish Any of the mainly fossil bony fishes belonging to the Sarcopterygii, but including also the extant lungfishes (Dipnoi) and the coelacanth (Crossopterygii). >> bony fish

lobelia [loh**beel**ia] A member of a large and very diverse genus, ranging from small annuals to shaggy, columnar perennials reaching several metres high; found almost everywhere, but mostly tropical and subtropical, especially in the New World; flowers usually red, blue, or violet, with five fused petals forming a curved, 2-lipped tube. (Genus: *Lobelia*, 200–300 species. Family: Campanulaceae.)

lobotomy >> **psychosurgery**

lobster A large marine crustacean with a well-developed abdomen and the front pair of legs modified as pincers (*chelipeds*), one for crushing and one for cutting; length up to 60 cm/2 ft; edible, caught commercially using pots or wickerwork traps (creels). (Class: Malacostraca. Order: Decapoda.) >> crustacean

local area network (LAN) A system which allows communication between computers situated within a well-defined geographical area, and which does not use the public telephone system. By contrast, a **wide area network** or **long distance network** allows computer communication over a large geographical area, generally using the telephone system. >> acoustic coupler; electronic mail; packet switching

local education authority (LEA) A regional government organization responsible for education in its area. In the UK, this is usually a city or county council. The elected members of the LEA are local politicians; professional officers are responsible for the day-to-day running of the education system in their area.

local government A set of political institutions constitutionally subordinate to the national, provincial, or federal government, with delegated authority to perform certain functions within territorially defined parts of the state. Some of the services most commonly provided by local government include education, public transport, roads, social services, housing, leisure and recreation, public health, and water. >> borough

Locarno Pact [lo**kah(r)**noh] An agreement reached in 1925 at an international conference held at Locarno, Italy, guaranteeing post-1919 frontiers between France, Belgium, and Germany, and the demilitarization of the Rhineland. The treaty was signed by France, Germany, and Belgium, and guaranteed by Britain and Italy.

Lochner, Stefan [**lokh**ner] (c.1400–1451) Painter, born in Meersburg, Germany. He became the principal master of the Cologne School, marking the transition from the Gothic style to Naturalism. >> Naturalism

Loch Ness Monster >> **Ness, Loch**

lock A means of altering the height of a canal waterway while allowing the passage of boats. A **pound lock** has a chamber which can be filled and emptied of water by opening and closing paddles, to bring the level to the upper or the lower height. The lower gates are usually double, pointing upstream so as to be pressed together by the water. >> canal

Locke, John (1632–1704) Philosopher, born in Wrington, Somerset. His major work, the *Essay Concerning Human Understanding* (1690), accepted the possibility of rational demonstration of moral principles and the existence of God, but its denial of innate ideas, and its demonstration that 'all knowledge is founded on and ultimately derives itself from sense...or sensation', was the real starting point of British empiricism. >> empiricism

Lockerbie 55°07N 3°22W, pop (1995e) 3010. A town in Dumfries and Galloway, SW Scotland, the scene of Britain's worst air disaster, when a Pan Am Boeing 747 flying from Frankfurt to New York via London crashed on 21 December 1988, killing 270, including several townspeople. The explosive device which led to the disaster was thought to have been taken on board at Frankfurt. Efforts to extradite suspected Libyan terrorists to stand trial were finally successful in early 1999, the trial taking place at a Scottish court at Camp Zeist in The Netherlands.

lockjaw >> **tetanus**

Lockwood, Margaret (1916-90) English actress, born in Karachi, Pakistan (formerly India). She made her film debut in *Lorna Doone* (1935), and starred in the Alfred Hitchcock film *The Lady Vanishes* (1938). In the late 1940s she was Britain's most popular leading lady, appearing regularly in theatre productions.

locomotive The vehicle that provides the tractive force to haul trucks and carriages on a railway. The world's first locomotive was built by Richard Trevithick in 1801, and although many famous locomotives (such as 'Puffing Billy' and 'Locomotion') were used on railways to haul coal after that time, it was not until 1829 that the 'Rocket' won the Rainhill trials and inaugurated the full-time carriage of passengers. By the mid-19th-c, the steam locomotive had developed into a form which did not change substantially thereafter. During the 20th-c the steam locomotive has been progressively displaced as the main type of locomotive by diesel, diesel-electric, and electric motive power. New types of propulsion are currently under test, such as the use of linear electric motors for propulsion coupled with magnetic levitation. >> diesel / internal combustion engine; railway; Stephenson, George; Trevithick; *see illustration on p.508*

locust Any of several species of grasshoppers, with a 2-phase life cycle. At low population density they are solitary in behaviour, but at high density they become gregarious, swarming and migrating, often causing massive destruction of vegetation. (Order: Orthoptera. Family: Acrididae.) >> grasshopper

locust tree >> **carob**

lodestone >> **magnetite**

Lodge, David (John) (1935–) Novelist and critic, born in Dulwich, Greater London. His novels include *Changing Places* (1975), *Nice Work* (1988), *Paradise News* (1991), and *Therapy* (1995).

Lodge, Henry Cabot (1850–1924) US Republican senator, historian, and biographer, born in Boston, MA. He prevented the USA joining the League of Nations in 1920. His grandson, **Henry Cabot Lodge Jr**, (1902–85) was US representative at the United Nations (1953–60) and participated in the Vietnam peace talks in 1969. >> League of Nations

Lodge, Thomas (c.1558–1625) Playwright, romance writer, and poet, born in London. His best-known work is the pastoral romance, *Rosalynde* (1590), which was the source of Shakespeare's *As You Like It*. >> pastoral

Łódź [wudzh, lodz] 51°49N 19°28E, pop (1995e) 858 000. Industrial city in C Poland; second largest city in Poland; charter, 500; development since 1820 through the textile industry; railway; two universities (1945). >> Poland [i]

loerie >> **turaco**

Loesser, Frank (Henry) [**ler**ser] (1910–69) Songwriter and composer, born in New York City. He achieved international fame with the music and lyrics for *Guys and Dolls* (1950). Later musicals included *The Most Happy Fella* (1956) and *How to Succeed in Business Without Really Trying* (1961).

Loess Region [**loh**is] NC Chinese highlands; area 400 000 sq km/150 400 sq mi; altitude 800–2000 m/2600–6500 ft; covered with a layer of wind-blown loamy deposit (*loess*); site of China's oldest anthropoid remains (700 000 years ago) and principal Palaeolithic to Neolithic sites; location of first historical Chinese dynasty (16th-c BC), and the power-centres of all later dynasties until 12th-c AD. >> China [i]; soil

Loewe, Frederick [loh] (1904–88) Composer, born in Berlin. He went to the USA in 1924, and worked as a composer on a number of Broadway musicals, in collaboration with Alan Jay Lerner (1918–86), including *My Fair Lady* (1956).

Lofoten Islands [loh**foh**tn] area 1425 sq km/550 sq mi. Mountainous island group in the Norwegian Sea, off the NW coast of Norway. >> Norway [i]

Lofty-Flinders Ranges, Mount Mountain ranges in South Australia state, Australia; extending 800 km/500 mi; Mt Lofty Ranges in the S, comparatively low, rising to Mt Lofty (727 m/2385 ft); Flinders Ranges in the N rising to St Mary Peak (1166 m/3825 ft); tourist area. >> South Australia

Logan, Mount 60°34N 140°24W. Highest mountain in Canada, and second highest in North America; rises to 5950 m/19 521 ft in the St Elias Mts, SW Yukon territory. >> Canada [i]

loganberry An accidental hybrid between raspberry and blackberry which arose in the garden of Judge Logan of California, after whom it was named. The fruits, which resemble raspberries, are much larger and more tart than either parent. (Family: Rosaceae.)

logarithm The power n to which a number a must be raised to equal another number b, ie 'the logarithm to the base a of b': $a^n = b \Rightarrow \log_a b = n$; for example, since $10^2 = 100$, $\log_{10}100 = 2$. Logarithms were used extensively as calculating aids before the advent of computers. >> base (mathematics); Napier, John

loggia [**loh**jia] A gallery in a building, behind an open

Stephenson's 'Planet', supplied to the Liverpool and Manchester Railway in 1830.

New York Central and Hudson River Rail Road No 999, which achieved a world record of 181 kph/112.5 mph in 1893.

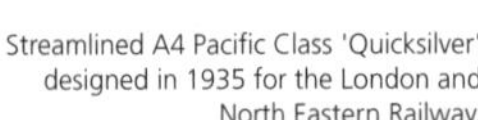

Streamlined A4 Pacific Class 'Quicksilver' designed in 1935 for the London and North Eastern Railway.

British Rail high-speed train, which in 1973 achieved the world record for diesel-powered locomotives of 230 kph/142 mph.

Japanese 'Bullet' train, operating on the *Shinkansen* lines, with a top speed of 240 kph/149 mph.

French TGV (train à grande vitesse). These electric-powered locomotives are capable of speeds up to 300 kph/186 mph.

Locomotives

arcade or colonnade, and facing onto a garden, street, or square. It is sometimes a separate structure. >> colonnade

logic The formal, systematic study of the principles of valid inference and correct reasoning. **Deductive logic** is the study of inferences that are valid (or invalid) in virtue of their structure, not their content. 'If A then B; A; therefore B' is valid whatever the value of A and B; and any inference with that structure is valid. There are two main parts of elemental deductive logic. **Propositional logic** deals with the inferences involving simple sentences in the indicative mood joined by such connectives as *not* (negation), *and* (conjunction), *or* (disjunction), and *if...then* (conditional). **Predicate logic** deals with sentences in the indicative mood involving such quantifying terms as *some*, *all*, and *no*. Thus, 'All cats are mammals, and no mammals are worms; therefore no cats are worms' is a (valid) inference in predicate logic. The investigation of deductive inference has also been extended beyond propositional and predicate logic to include: **modal logic**, which treats the notion of necessity and possibility; **epistemic logic**, the logic of knowledge and belief; **many-valued logic**, which allows some sentences to be assigned a designation other than true or false; **tense logic**, which analyses inferences involving such temporal notions as past, present, and future; and **deontic logic** which deals with imperatives, practical reasoning, and expressions of obligation. **Inductive logic** is the study of inferences which are not deductively valid, but are such that the premisses, if true, would increase the likelihood of the truth of the conclusion, and this leads naturally to probability theory and statistics. Aristotle wrote the first systematic treatises on logic; Boole and others evolved a rigorous mathematical logic in the 19th-c >> Boole; Frege; induction (logic); inference; Russell, Bertrand; Tarski; Whitehead

logical positivism A philosophical movement beginning with the Vienna Circle in the 1920s and 1930s under the leadership of Moritz Schlick and Rudolf Carnap, and associated in Britian with A J Ayer. Most of metaphysics, ethics, and religious discourse was said to be literally meaningless, since its propositions could not be verified by observation and experiment nor by logical deduction. >> Ayer; Carnap; Schlick; verificationism; Vienna Circle

logography The study of writing systems in which the symbols (**logographs** or **logograms**) represent whole words, or, in some cases, components of words. A few logographs are found in European languages, such as & ('and'), and £ ('pound'); but Chinese and Japanese are the most famous examples of a logographic writing system. >> ideography; pictography ℹ

Lohengrin [**loh**engrin] In Germanic legend, the son of Parsifal. He leaves the temple of the Grail and is carried to Antwerp in a boat drawn by swans. There he saves Princess Elsa of Brabant, and is about to marry her; but she asks forbidden questions about his origin, and he is forced to leave her. >> Perceval, Sir

Loire, River [lwah(r)], ancient **Liger** River in E France, rising in the Massif Central; empties into the Bay of Biscay; length 1020 km/634 mi; valley known for its vineyards. >> France ℹ

Loki [**loh**kee] A mischievous Norse god; originally a Giant, he was later accepted into the company of the gods. Although he plays tricks on them, he is also able to save them from danger by his cleverness. >> Hel

Lollards A derisive term applied to the followers of the English theologian John Wycliffe (14th-c). The movement, responsible for the translation of the Bible into the vernacular, was suppressed. >> Bible; Wycliffe

Lombard, Peter, known as **Magister Sententiarum** ('Master of Sentences') (c.1100–60) Theologian, born near Novara, Italy. His work was the standard textbook of Catholic theology down to the Reformation. >> Roman Catholicism

Lombard League A coalition of N Italian cities, established in 1167 to assert their independence as communes (city-republics) against the German emperor, Frederick I Barbarossa. >> Frederick I (Emperor)

Lombardo, Pietro [lom**bah(r)**doh] (c.1435–1515) Sculptor and architect, born in Carona, Italy. He ran the most important workshop in Venice, specializing in tomb sculpture. The Church of Santa Maria dei Miracoli (1481–9) was his design. >> Venetian School

Lombards A Germanic people settled in Hungary – their name deriving from the long beards (*langobardi*) they traditionally wore – who invaded N Italy in AD 568 under their king, Alboin. Their kingdom was annexed by Charlemagne in 774. >> Charlemagne

Lombardy [**lom**bah(r)dee], Ital **Lombardia** pop (1995e) 8 976 000; area 23 835 sq km/9200 sq mi. Region of N Italy; capital, Milan; highly developed industrial and agricultural region in the S; tourism important in the mountains. >> Italy ℹ; Lombards

Lomé [**loh**may] 6°10N 1°21E, pop (1995e) 501 000. Seaport capital of Togo; important market centre, noted for its marble, gold, and silver crafts; airport; railway junction; university (1965). >> Togo ℹ

Lomé Convention A series of conventions governing the European Union's trading relationship with 70 (as of 1999) developing countries in Africa, the Caribbean, and the Pacific (the 'ACP countries'). The first convention was signed in 1975, with follow-up conventions every five years (1979, 1984). The 1989 convention was for a 10-year period, and a renewal was expected in 1999.

Lomond, Loch [**loh**mond] Largest lake in Scotland; area 70 sq km/27 sq mi; 34 km/21 mi long; narrow in the N, opening out to 8 km/5 mi in the S; up to 190 m/625 ft deep; major tourist area. >> Scotland ℹ

Lomu, Jonah [**loh**moo] (1975–) Rugby union player, born in Mangere, New Zealand, of Tongan parents. Selected for the New Zealand All Blacks in 1994, he became internationally known as a member of the World Cup squad, his massive physique (1.95 m/6 ft 5 in; 119 kg/266 lb) making him an awesome opponent. A kidney disorder kept him out of the game for over a year, but he returned to international rugby at the end of 1997.

London, Lat **Londinium** (in the 4th-c, **Augusta**) 51°30N 0°10W, pop (1995e) 7 007 000 (Greater London), 3240 (City of London). Capital city of England and the UK; on the R Thames in SE England; **Greater London** consists of 32 boroughs and the City of London, area 1579 sq km/610 sq mi; from 1st–5th-c, a Roman town (AD c.43), situated where the Thames narrowed to its lowest convenient crossing; sacked by Boadicea, c.61; later surrounded by a defensive wall, fragments of which remain (c.350); received charter privileges, 1067; mayoralty established, 1191; major building programmes in Middle Ages; extended W, especially in 16th-c; Great Plague (1665), Great Fire (1666), followed by major reconstruction; in 17th-c developed into a major trade centre; severe damage especially to City and East End in World War 2 (the Blitz), with much subsequent rebuilding; administered by London County Council, 1888–1963, and by the Greater London Council until 1986, its functions then transferring to the boroughs and other bodies; **City of London**, occupying site of the old mediaeval city N of the Thames, is the financial and business centre; **City of Westminster** is the administrative and judicial centre, including the Houses of Parliament, Buckingham Palace, and government departments; the **West End** is the main shopping and entertainment centre, around Oxford Street, Piccadilly, and Regent Street; extensive dockland, much now scheduled for redevelopment; headquarters of Port of London Authority; extensive underground system (known as 'the Tube'); main airports at Heathrow (W) and Gatwick (S), also at London City, Luton (N), and Stansted (E); markets (Billingsgate, Smithfield; Nine Elms at Vauxhall, replacing Covent Garden, now a tourist centre); parks (Battersea / Hyde / Regent's / St James's Parks, Kensington Gardens); zoological gardens at Regent's Park; leading cultural centre, with many theatres, museums (British / London / Natural History / Science / Victoria and Albert), galleries (National / National Portrait / Tate Galleries, Courtauld Institute), concert halls (Albert /

Queen Elizabeth / Royal Festival / Wigmore Halls, Barbican Centre), churches and cathedrals (Saint Paul's / Westminster Cathedrals; Westminster Abbey and St Margaret's Church, a world heritage site); London University (from 1836); polytechnics gained University status in 1992; football league teams, Arsenal (Gunners), Charlton Athletic (Valiants), Chelsea (Blues), Crystal Palace (Eagles), Fulham (Cottagers), Leyton Orient ('O's'), Millwall (Lions), Queens Park Rangers ('R's'), Tottenham Hotspur (Spurs), Watford (Hornets), West Ham United (Hammers), Wimbledon (Dons). >> Big Ben; Billingsgate Market; British Museum; Buckingham Palace; Covent Garden; Downing Street; East End; Hampton Court; Houses of Parliament; Hyde Park; Imperial War Museum; Inns of Court; London Bridge / Festival Ballet / Museum / University; Mayfair; Monument, the; National Gallery; National Portrait Gallery; Natural History Museum; Old Bailey; Oval, the; Royal Opera House; St James's Palace; St Paul's Cathedral; Science Museum; Smithfield; Tate Gallery; Temple; Temple Bar; Tower Bridge; Tower of London; Victoria and Albert Museum; Wembley Stadium; Westminster Abbey; Whitehall

London, Jack, pseudonym of **John Griffith Chaney** (1876–1916) Novelist, born in San Francisco, CA. His books include *The Call of the Wild* (1903), *Sea-Wolf* (1904), and *The Iron Heel* (1907).

London Bridge A bridge over the R Thames linking Southwark with the City of London. The 1831 5-arch bridge was dismantled and sold to Lake Havasu City, AZ, in 1968. It was replaced by a concrete structure. >> London

Londonderry >> **Derry**

London Festival Ballet A company which emerged from Markova and Dolin's groups of Ballets Russes dancers in 1950. It offers regular London seasons and extensive tours. >> ballet; Markova

London Group A society of British artists founded in 1913 by Nash, Epstein, Fry, and others. It held regular exhibitions for half a century. >> Epstein; Fry, Roger Eliot; Nash, Paul

London Missionary Society (LMS) Formed in London in 1795 by evangelical Protestants to undertake missionary work in the Pacific islands. It later operated in other parts of the world, including Africa. >> evangelicalism

London Museum A museum at London Wall in the City of London, created from the former London and Guildhall museums and opened in 1975. >> London

London University A federation of colleges, medical schools, and research institutions established as a university in London in 1836. >> London; *see panel above*

London University

College	Founded
Wye College (Ashford) (controlled by London University since 1900)	1447
Royal Veterinary College	1791
Birkbeck College	1823
University College London	1826
King's College London (merged with Queen Elizabeth College and Chelsea College 1985)	1829
School of Pharmacy	1842
Goldsmith's College (controlled by London University since 1904)	1891
London School of Economics and Political Science	1895
Institute of Education (controlled by London University since 1932; school of London University since 1987)	1902
Imperial College of Science, Technology and Medicine	1907
School of Oriental and African Studies	1916
Royal Holloway and Bedford New College (Egham) (founded through merger of Bedford College and Royal Holloway College)	1985
Queen Mary and Westfield College (founded through merger of Queen Mary College and Westfield College)	1989

Long, Huey (Pierce), nickname **Kingfish** (1893–1935) US Democratic politician, born near Winnfield, LA. After 1930 he was both Governor of Louisiana and a US senator. He enjoyed virtually total control of his state until his assassination by Carl Weiss.

Long Beach 33°47N 118°11W, pop (1995e) 470 000. City in SW California, USA; developed rapidly after the discovery of oil, 1921; railway; university (1949); location for the British cruise liner *Queen Mary*, now a museum-hotel-convention centre. >> California

longbow An English bow with a shaft of yew-wood 1·5 m/5 ft long, which could shoot an arrow capable of penetrating plate armour at 400 yd (365 m). It dominated the battlefield for 200 years from 1300, proving decisive at the Battles of Crécy, Poitiers, and Agincourt. >> crossbow

Longchamp >> **Bois de Boulogne**

long-distance network >> **local area network**

Longfellow, Henry Wadsworth (1807–82) Poet, born in Portland, ME. *Voices of the Night* (1839), his first book of verse, made a favourable impression, and this was followed by several other works, notably *Evangeline* (1847), and *The Song of Hiawatha* (1855).

Longford, Ir **Longphort** pop (1995e) 30 100; area 1044 sq km/403 sq mi. County in NW Leinster province, C Ireland; capital, Longford, pop (1995e) 6800. >> Ireland ℹ

Longinus, Dionysius [lonjiynus] (c.213–73) Greek Neoplatonic rhetorician and philosopher. He is the supposed author of the treatise on excellence in literature, *On the Sublime*, which influenced many Neoclassical writers. >> Neoclassicism (art and architecture); Neoplatonism; rhetoric

Long Island area 3600 sq km/1400 sq mi, length 190 km/118 mi. Island in SE New York State, USA, bounded N by Long Island Sound; separated from the Bronx and Manhattan by the East River, and from Staten I by the Narrows; settled by the Dutch in 1623, and by the English, c.1640; site of the Battle of Long Island (1776) in the US War of Independence, when British forces under Howe defeated American forces under Washington. >> American Revolution; New York (state)

longitude >> **latitude and longitude** ℹ

long jump An athletics field event in which the competitors leap for distance into a sandpit after running up to a take-off board. It is sometimes called the **running broad jump**. The current world record for men is 8·95 m/29 ft 4¼ in, achieved by Mike Powell (USA) in 1991 at Tokyo; and for women is 7·52 m/24 ft 8¼ in, achieved by Galina Chistyakova (USSR) in 1988 at St Petersburg, Russia. >> athletics; triple jump

Longman, Thomas (1699–1755) Publisher, born in Bristol. He bought a bookselling business in Paternoster Row, London, in 1724, and was the founder of the British publishing house that still bears his name.

Long March The epic of Chinese communist revolutionary history. In 1934 the Red Army was blockaded in SE China by Jiang Jieshi's forces. In October, Mao Zedong, Zhu De, and Lin Biao broke out with 100 000 troops to lead a 13 000 km/8000 mi evacuation westwards then north. The march ended in Shaanxi, N China, the following October. The Long March established Mao's supremacy in the party. >> Mao Zedong

Long Parliament An English parliament called (Nov 1640) by Charles I after his defeat by the Scots in the second Bishops' War. It was legally in being 1640–60, but did not meet continuously. It attacked prerogative rights and alleged abuses of power by the king and his ministers. Moderates were eliminated in Pride's Purge (Dec 1648), and the remaining Rump was dismissed by Cromwell in 1653. >> Bishops' Wars; Pride, Thomas; Rump Parliament

long-range navigation system >> **loran**

longship A vessel used by the Vikings in their voyages of exploration, plunder, and conquest. The largest were 45 m/150 ft in length, very strong, and propelled by both oars and sail. >> ship ℹ; Vikings

long-sightedness >> **eye** ℹ

Lonsdale Belt In boxing, a championship belt awarded to a fighter who wins a British title fight. It is named after the 5th Earl of Lonsdale, who presented the first belt to the National Sporting Club in 1909. >> boxing ℹ

loofah An annual climbing vine with tendrils (*Luffa cylindrica*), native to the tropics; flowers yellow, funnel-shaped; fruit marrow-like, up to 30 cm/12 in long, roughly cylindrical. The sponge-like item used in bathrooms is the fibrous vascular tissue of the fruit left when the soft parts are removed. (Family: Cucurbitaceae.)

look-and-say A method of teaching reading through whole-word recognition. The aim is to teach words as meaningful entities, rather than as sequences of phonic syllables. >> phonics

loon >> **diver**

Lope de Vega >> **Vega, Lope de**

loquat [**loh**kwat] A small evergreen tree (*Eriobotrya japonica*) with very hairy twigs, native to China; leaves coarse, reddish, hairy beneath; flowers white, fragrant, in terminal clusters; fruits 3–6 cm/$1\frac{1}{4}$–$2\frac{1}{2}$ in, round, yellowish-orange, flesh sweet and edible. (Family: Rosaceae.)

loran Acronym for **long-range navigation system**. Radio pulses emitted at fixed intervals by pairs of transmitters define a grid pattern, over a very large area. The timing of the reception of these paired pulses by an aircraft or ship indicates its position on the network. >> radio

Lorca, Federico García [**law(r)**ka, gah(r)**see**a] (1899–1936) Poet, born in Fuente Vaqueros, Spain. His best-known works are his gypsy songs, *Canciones* (1927, Songs) and *Romancero Gitano* (1928, 1935, The Gypsy Ballads). He also wrote several successful plays. He was assassinated in the Spanish Civil War at Granada.

Lord Chancellor The head of the judiciary of England and Wales, a member of the cabinet, and the Speaker of the House of Lords. He appoints, and may dismiss, magistrates and circuit judges. >> Lords, House of

Lord Chief Justice The president or head of the Queen's Bench Division of the High Court in England and Wales, and of the Criminal Division of the Court of Appeal. >> Court of Appeal; High Court of Justice

Lord Howe Island 31°33S 159°04E, pop (1995e) 535. Volcanic island in the Pacific Ocean, 702 km/436 mi NE of Sydney; part of New South Wales; area 16·6 sq km/6·4 sq mi; rises to 866 m/2841 ft; discovered, 1788; a world heritage site. >> New South Wales

Lord-Lieutenant [left**en**ant] In the UK, the sovereign's permanent representative in a county or county borough of England, Wales, or Northern Ireland, or in a part of one of the Scottish regions. The lordly prefix is by custom only, and the office is now primarily one of honour.

Lords, House of The non-elected house of the UK legislature. Its membership (currently c.1200) includes hereditary peers and life peers; also the two archbishops and certain bishops of the Church of England. Its functions are mainly deliberative, its authority being based on the expertise of its membership. It also constitutes the most senior court in the UK. >> Lord Chancellor; parliament; woolsack

lords-and-ladies A perennial native to Europe and N Africa (*Arum maculatum*), with glossy dark-green arrow-head-shaped leaves and poisonous scarlet berries; also called **cuckoo-pint**. (Family: Araceae.) >> arrowroot

Lord's Cricket Ground A cricket ground founded by Thomas Lord (1755–1832) in 1814 in NW London. It is the home of the Marylebone Cricket Club (MCC) and the Middlesex County Cricket Club, and the recognized home of cricket. >> Ashes; cricket (sport) ℹ

Lord's Prayer A popular prayer of Christian worship, derived from *Matt* 6.9–13 and (in different form) *Luke* 11.2–4; also known as the **Pater Noster** ('Our Father'). It is a model for how Jesus's followers are to pray. >> Jesus Christ

Lorelei [**lo**reliy] The name of a precipitous rock on the Rhine, dangerous to boatmen and celebrated for its echo. The story of the siren of the rock whose songs lure sailors to their death originates in Heine's poem *Die Lorelei* (1827). >> Rhine, River

Loren, Sophia [lo**ren**], originally **Sofia Scicolone** (1934–) Film actress, born in Rome. She became the protégée, and later the wife, of the producer Carlo Ponti (1912–), and gained the lead in *The Pride and the Passion* (1957). Her performance under the direction of De Sica in *La Ciociara* (1961, Two Women) won her an Oscar.

Lorentz, Hendrik Antoon [**loh**rents] (1853–1928) Theoretical physicist, born in Arnhem, The Netherlands. He shared the Nobel Prize for Physics in 1902 for his theory of electromagnetic radiation, which prepared the way for Einstein's theory of relativity. >> electromagnetism; special relativity ℹ

Lorenz, Konrad (Zacharias) [**loh**rents] (1903–89) Zoologist, a founder of the science of ethology, born in Vienna. His work in the late 1930s favoured the investigation of animal behaviour in the wild. He shared the Nobel Prize for Physiology or Medicine in 1973. >> ethology

Lorenzetti, Ambrogio [loren**ze**tee] (c.1280–c.1348) Artist, born in Siena, Italy. He is best known for his allegorical frescoes in the Palazzo Pubblico at Siena. His brother, **Pietro** (c.1280–c.1348), also belonged to the Sienese School. >> fresco; Sienese School

Lorenzo [lo**ren**zoh], known as **il Monaco** ('the Monk'), originally **Piero di Giovanni** (c.1370–c.1425) Painter, born in Siena, Italy. His major work is the 'Coronation of the Virgin' (1413, Florence). >> Sienese School

lorikeet >> **lory**

loris A primitive primate, native to forests in S and SE Asia; no tail; pale face with dark rings around large eyes; three species. (Family: Lorisidae.) >> prosimian

Lorrain, Claude >> **Claude Lorrain**

Lorraine [lo**ren**], Ger **Lothringen** pop (1995e) 2 376 000; area 23 547 sq km/9089 sq mi. Region and former province of NE France, duchy since the 10th-c; part of France, 1766; ceded to Germany as part of Alsace-Lorraine, 1871; returned to France after World War 1; chief towns, Metz, Nancy. >> Alsace

Lorraine, Cross of [lo**rayn**] A cross with two horizontal crosspieces. The symbol of Joan of Arc, it was adopted by the Free French forces leader (Charles de Gaulle) in 1940.

Lorris, Guillaume de >> **Guillaume de Lorris**

lory [**law**ree] A parrot of the subfamily Loriinae (c.60 species), found from SE Asia to Australia; tongue has brush-like tip. Smaller species are called **lorikeets**. (Family: Psittacidae.) >> parrot

Los Alamos [los **al**amos] 35°52N 106°19W, pop (1995e) 12 700. Community in N New Mexico, USA; a nuclear research centre since 1943; the first nuclear weapons were developed here during World War 2. >> atomic bomb; New Mexico

Los Angeles 34°04N 118°15W, pop (1995e) 3 818 000. Seaport in California, USA; founded by the Spanish, 1781; originally called **Nuestra Señora Reina de Los Angeles**; captured from Mexico by the US Navy, 1846; established, 1850; second largest US city; three airports; railway; five universities; harbour on San Pedro Bay, 40 km/25 mi S of city centre; major industrial and research centre; high density of road traffic; smog a major problem; professional teams, Dodgers (baseball), Clippers, Lakers (basketball), Raiders, Rams (football), Kings (ice hockey); district of Hollywood a major centre of the US film and television industry; Hollywood Bowl; Universal Film Studios; Disneyland; scene of summer Olympic Games, 1984. >> California; Hollywood; Watts Towers

Losey, Joseph (Walton) [**loh**see] (1909–84) Film director, born in La Crosse, WI. His films include *The Servant* (1963) and *The Go-Between* (1971), as well as the quite untypical *Modesty Blaise* (1966).

Lossiemouth [**los**eemowth] 57°43N 3°18W, pop (1995e) 7700. Port town in Moray, NE Scotland; air force base nearby; birthplace of Ramsay MacDonald. >> MacDonald, Ramsay; Scotland [i]

Lot Biblical character, portrayed in Genesis as the nephew of Abraham. Stories describe his rescue from the wickedness of Sodom by Abraham and two angels. Lot's wife is described as looking back during this escape and being turned into 'a pillar of salt'. >> Abraham; Old Testament

Lothian [**loh**thian] pop (1995e) 748 00; area 1755 sq km/ 677 sq mi. Former region in E Scotland (1975–96); replaced in 1996 by North Lanarkshire, Falkirk, West Lothian, Midlothian, East Lothian, and City of Edinburgh councils. >> Scotland [i]

Lots, Feast of >> **Purim**

lottery A way of raising money through the sale of chances (tickets) and the use of a random procedure to decide the prize-winners. Very large numbers of people take part, producing a correspondingly large sum of money which (after deduction of taxes and organizational expenses) is available for prizes. Many countries now organize state lotteries, which provide an attractive extra source of government income, as well as offering a promise of vast wealth for a few. They have also been used to finance major projects, such as roads, buildings, and universities, as well as projects to do with the arts, the environment, and all forms of charity. Famous lotteries include those of Italy, Ireland (the Irish Hospitals' Sweepstake), and Australia (where a lottery helped finance the Sydney Opera House). Britain's national lottery began in 1994. >> premium bond

lotus A name given to three different plants. The sacred lotus of Egypt (*Nymphaea lotus*) is a species of waterlily. The sacred lotus of India and China (*Nelumbium nuciferum*), traditionally associated with the Buddha, has circular leaves with the stalks attached in the centre of the blade, and pink and white flowers. The lotus of classical times (*Ziziphus lotus*) is a type of jujube from the Mediterranean region. >> jujube; waterlily

lotus bird >> **jacana**

Lotus 123 A popular computer package to enable the user to work on a spreadsheet. It is a registered trade mark of Lotus Development Corporation. >> computer package; spreadsheet

Louangphrabang or **Luang Prabang** [lu**ang**pra**bang**] 19°53N 102°10E, pop (1995e) 59 800. Town in W Laos; former capital, 1946–75; centre of agricultural region. >> Laos [i]

loudspeaker or **speaker** A device which converts electrical energy into sound waves. The loudspeaker is fed a current having frequencies and amplitudes proportionate to some original sound waves. It reconverts these signals, radiating a new set of sound waves which reproduce at a listener's ears as nearly as possible the acoustic experience of the original performance. The majority of loudspeakers use the electromagnetic principle. An alternating signal current passes through one or more voice coils set in powerful permanent magnetic fields. The alternating magnetic fields which result cause the coils (and the diaphragm or cone to which each one is fixed) to move to and fro in vibration, and it is this mechanical vibration that regenerates the sound waves. >> electromagnetism; microphone [i]; sound recording

Louis IX, St (1214–70) King of France (1226–70), born in Poissy, France. He led the Seventh Crusade (1248), but was defeated in Egypt, and ransomed. He embarked on a new Crusade in 1270, and died of plague at Tunis. He was canonized in 1297; feast day 25 August. >> Crusades [i]

Louis XIV, known as **le Roi soleil** ('the Sun King') (1638–1715) King of France (1643–1715), born in St Germain-en-Laye, the son of Louis XIII. During his minority (1643–51) France was ruled by his mother, Anne of Austria, and her Chief Minister, Cardinal Mazarin. In 1660 Louis married the Infanta Maria Theresa, elder daughter of Philip IV of Spain, through whom he was later to claim the Spanish succession for his second grandson. His obsession with France's greatness led him into aggressive foreign and commercial policies, particularly against the Dutch. His patronage of the Catholic Stuarts also led to the hostility of England after 1689, but his major political rivals were the Austrian Habsburgs, particularly Leopold I. His attempt to create a Franco–Spanish Bourbon bloc led to the formation of the Grand Alliance of England, the United Provinces, and the Habsburg Empire, and resulted in the War of the Spanish Succession (1701–13). His determination to preserve the unity of the French state and the independence of the French Church led him into conflict with the Jansenists, the Huguenots, and the papacy, with damaging repercussions. His long reign nonetheless marked the cultural ascendancy of France within Europe, symbolized by the Palace of Versailles. >> Bourbons; Dutch Wars; Frondes; Leopold I (Emperor); Maintenon; Mazarin; Spanish Succession, War of the

Louis XV, known as **Louis le Bien-Aimé** ('Louis the Well-Beloved') (1710–74) King of France (1715–74), born in Versailles, France, the great-grandson of Louis XIV. His reign coincided with the great age of decorative art in the Rococo mode (dubbed the Louis XV style). Until he came of age (1723) he was guided by the regent, Philippe d'Orléans, and then by the Duc de Bourbon. In 1726 Bourbon was replaced by the king's former tutor, the elderly Fleury, who skilfully steered the French state until his death (1744). Thereafter Louis allowed the govern-

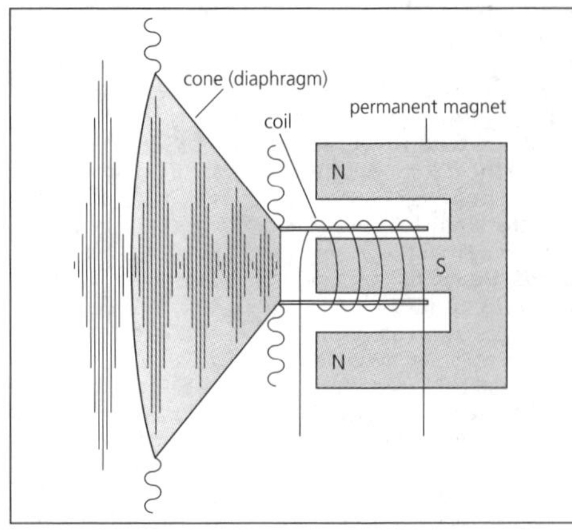

A moving coil loudspeaker

ment to drift into the hands of ministerial factions, while indulging in secret diplomatic activity through his own network of agents – a system which brought confusion to French foreign policy. France was drawn into a trio of continental wars which culminated in the loss of the French colonies in America and India (1763). >> Austrian Succession, War of the; du Barry; Fleury; Pompadour; Rococo; Seven Years' War

Louis XVI (1754–93) King of France (1774–93), born in Versailles, France, the grandson of Louis XV. He was married in 1770 to the Archduchess Marie Antoinette, daughter of the Habsburg Empress Maria Theresa, to strengthen the Franco-Austrian alliance. He failed to give consistent support to ministers who tried to reform the outmoded financial and social structures of the country, such as Turgot (1774–6) and Necker (1776–81). To avert a crisis, he agreed in 1789 to summon the States General. However, encouraged by the queen, he resisted demands from the National Assembly for sweeping reforms, and in October was brought with his family from Versailles to Paris as hostages to the revolutionary movement. Their attempted flight to Varennes (Jun 1791) branded them as traitors. In August an insurrection suspended Louis's constitutional position, and in September the monarchy was abolished. He was tried for conspiracy and guillotined in Paris. >> French Revolution ℹ; Marie Antoinette; Necker; Turgot

Louis (Charles) XVII (1785–95) Titular King of France (1793–5), born in Versailles, France the second son of Louis XVI and heir to the throne from June 1789. After the execution of his father (Jan 1793) he remained in the Temple prison in Paris until his death. >> French Revolution ℹ

Louis XVIII, originally **Louis Stanislas Xavier, comte de** (Count of) **Provence** (1755–1824) King of France in name from 1795 and in fact from 1814, born in Versailles, France, the younger brother of Louis XVI. He fled from Paris in June 1791, finally taking refuge in England, becoming the focal point for the Royalist cause. His restoration was interrupted by Napoleon's return from Elba, but after Waterloo (1815) he again regained his throne. >> French Revolution ℹ; Napoleon I

Louis, Joe [**loo**is], popular name of **Joseph Louis Barrow**, nickname **the Brown Bomber** (1914–81) Boxer, born in Lafayette, AL. He beat James J Braddock (1905–74) for the world heavyweight title in 1937, and held the title for a record 12 years, making a record 25 defences. >> boxing ℹ

Louisiade Archipelago [looeezi**ahd**] pop (1995e) 22 300; area 1550 sq km/600 sq mi. Mountainous island group in Papua New Guinea, SE of New Guinea; named in 1768 after Louis XIV of France. >> Papua New Guinea

Louisiana [loozee**a**na] pop (1995e) 4 389 000; area 123 673 sq km/47 752 sq mi. State in S USA; the 'Pelican State'; named after Louis XIV of France, claimed for France by La Salle, 1682; most of the E region ceded to Spain in 1763, then to the USA in 1783; W region acquired by the USA in the Louisiana Purchase, 1803; admitted to the Union as the 18th state, 1812; seceded from the Union, 1861; re-admitted, 1868; Mississippi large delta area in the S; highest point Mt Driskill (162 m/532 ft); capital, Baton Rouge; over half the land area forested, supporting a major lumber and paper industry; highly productive in agriculture; a major source of pelts, especially muskrat; second only to Texas in oil and natural gas production (mainly offshore); leads the nation in salt and sulphur production; world famous for the jazz music which grew up in and around New Orleans; special population groups of Creoles (French descent) and Cajuns (descendants of French Acadians driven from Canada by the British in the 18th-c). >> Baton Rouge; La Salle; Louisiana Purchase; New Orleans; United States of America ℹ; RR994

Louisiana Purchase (1803) The sale by France to the USA of an area between the Mississippi R and the Rocky Mts for $15 000 000. The purchase gave the USA full control of the Mississippi Valley. >> Louisiana

Louis Napoleon >> **Napoleon III**

Louis-Philippe [fi**leep**], known as **the Citizen King** (1773–1850) King of the French (1830–48), born in Paris, the eldest son of the Duke of Orléans, Philippe Egalité. At the Revolution he entered the National Guard, and with his father renounced his titles to demonstrate his progressive sympathies. He lived in exile from 1793 to 1814. In 1830 he was elected lieutenant-general of the kingdom, and after the July Revolution was given the title of King of the French. Political corruption and economic depression caused discontent, and he abdicated at the onset of the 1848 revolution. >> Bourbons; French Revolution ℹ; Revolutions of 1848

Louisville [**loo**eevil] 38°15N 85°46W, pop (1995e) 282 000. City in NW Kentucky, USA; port at the Falls of the Ohio R; settled, 1778; named after Louis XVI of France; city status, 1828; largest city in the state; university (1798); a major horse breeding centre; important shipping point for coal. >> Kentucky

Lourdes [loordz], Fr [loord] 43°06N 0°00W, pop (1995e) 17 100. Town and important site of Roman Catholic pilgrimage in Hautes-Pyrénées department, S France; Bernadette Soubirous was led by a vision of the Virgin Mary to the springs at the Grotte de Massabielle in 1858; since then, the scene of many reputed miraculous cures. >> Bernadette, St; Mary (mother of Jesus)

lourie >> **turaco**

louse A secondarily wingless insect, parasitic on warm-blooded vertebrates. **Sucking lice** (Order: Anoplura) suck blood of mammals; length up to 6 mm/¼ in; bodies flattened, legs with claws for attaching to host; c.300 species. They include two varieties of human louse: **head lice** (*Pediculus humanus capitis*) and **body lice** (*Pediculus humanus humanus*), both transmitted by direct contact; lay eggs (*nits*) on hair and clothing. **Biting lice** (Order: Mallophaga) live mostly on birds; c.2700 species. >> booklouse; insect ℹ; psyllid

Louth [lowth], Ir **Lughbhaidh** pop (1995e) 90 000; area 821 sq km/317 sq mi. County in NE Leinster province, Ireland; capital, Dundalk. >> Dundalk; Ireland (republic) ℹ

Louvain [loo**vĩ**] >> **Leuven**

L'Ouverture, Toussaint >> **Toussaint L'Ouverture**

Louvois, François Michel le Tellier, marquis de [loovwah] (1641–91) French statesman and secretary of state for war under Louis XIV, born in Paris. He was recognized as a brilliant administrator and the king's most influential minister in the years 1683–91. >> Louis XIV

Louvre [loovr] The national museum of art in Paris, and one of the finest art collections in the world. It was built for Francis I in 1546. >> Francis I

lovage A strong-smelling perennial (*Levisticum officinale*) growing to 2·5 m/8 ft, native to Iran; flowers small, greenish-yellow; fruit ellipsoid with narrowly winged ribs. (Family: Umbelliferae.) >> herb

love apple >> **tomato**

lovebird A small parrot native to Africa and Madagascar; female sometimes larger than male; a popular cagebird. They preen one another, hence the name. (Genus: *Agapornis*, nine species. Family: Psittacidae.) >> parrot; *see illustration on p. 514*

Lovecraft, H(oward) P(hillips) (1890–1937) Short-story writer, born in Providence, RI. His reputation as a skilful practitioner of the tale of horror is almost entirely posthumous, based on *The Outsider and Others* (1939).

love-in-a-mist An annual native to Europe and W Asia

Lovebird

(*Nigella damascena*); finely divided, feathery leaves and bracts; large, pale blue flowers; a globular, papery capsule. (Family: Ranunculaceae.)

Lovelace, Richard (1618–57) Cavalier poet, probably born in Woolwich, Greater London. In 1642 he wrote 'To Althea, from Prison' ('Stone walls do not a prison make...'), and in 1649 published his best-known work, *Lucasta*. >> Cavaliers

Lovell, Sir (Alfred Charles) Bernard (1913–) Astronomer, born in Oldham Common, Gloucestershire. Director of the Nuffield Radio Astronomy Laboratories at Jodrell Bank, he is distinguished for his pioneering work in radio telescope design, space research, and the physics of radio sources. >> radio astronomy

Low, Sir David (Alexander Cecil) (1891–1963) Political cartoonist, born in Dunedin, New Zealand. In 1927 he joined the *Evening Standard*, for which he drew some of his most successful cartoons, including the notable Colonel Blimp.

lowan >> **mallee fowl**

Low Countries A term used to refer to The Netherlands and Belgium. It derives its name from the low-lying coastal plain of both countries.

low Earth orbit (LEO) A spacecraft orbit about the Earth typically used for manned missions and for Earth remote-sensing missions; the minimum altitude above the surface is c.200 km/125 mi to minimize drag effects of the Earth's atmosphere. Typical orbital periods are c.100 min; circular velocity c.7·8 km/s (4·9 mi/s). >> escape velocity; geosynchronous Earth orbit

Lowell, Amy (1874–1925) Imagist poet, born in Brookline, MA. She produced volumes of free verse which she named 'unrhymed cadence' and what she called 'polyphonic prose', as in *Sword Blades and Poppy Seed* (1914). >> Imagism

Lowell, Percival (1855–1916) Astronomer, born in Boston, MA. He is somewhat notorious for his observations alleging canals on Mars, but he correctly predicted the existence of Pluto. >> Tombaugh

Lowell, Robert (Traill Spence), Jr (1917–77) Poet, born in Boston, MA. He is especially known for his poems on painfully autobiographical subjects, giving rise to the style of 'confessional' poetry, as in *Notebook* (1969), *History* (1973), and *Day by Day* (1977). >> confessional poetry

Lowestoft [**loh**istoft] 52°29N 1°45E, pop (1995e) 65 100. Port town and resort in Suffolk, E England; railway; known for its fishing industry. >> Suffolk

Lowry, L(aurence) S(tephen) [**low**ree] (1887–1976) Artist, born in Manchester. From the 1920s he produced many pictures of the Lancashire industrial scene, mainly in brilliant whites and greys, peopled with scurrying stick-like men and women.

Lowry, (Clarence) Malcolm [**low**ree] (1909–57) Novelist, born in New Brighton, Merseyside. His reputation is based on *Under the Volcano* (1947), a novel set in Mexico, where he lived 1936–7.

Loy, Myrna [loy] (1905–93) Film actress, born in Helena, MT. She made her debut in *Pretty Ladies* (1925), went on to play a series of exotic female roles, then developed a bright and witty persona in such films as *The Great Ziegfeld* (1936) and *Too Hot to Handle* (1938). Known as the 'Queen of Hollywood', she continued to appear in films until the early 1980s, and received an honorary Oscar in 1991.

Loyalists Refugees from the 13 British American colonies who fled to Britain, New Brunswick, Nova Scotia, Prince Edward Island, and Canada (1783) as a result of the American War of Independence (1765–88). >> American Revolution

Loyalty Islands, Fr **Iles Loyauté** pop (1995e) 20 300; area 1981 sq km/765 sq mi. Group of coral islands in the SW Pacific Ocean; dependency of the Territory of New Caledonia; capital, We (Lifu I). >> New Caledonia

Loyola, Ignatius of, St [loy**oh**la], originally **Iñigo López de Recalde** (1491 or 1495–1556) Theologian, born in his ancestral castle of Loyola in Guipúzcoa, Spain. In 1534 he founded with six associates the Society of Jesus. The author of the influential *Spiritual Exercises*, he was canonized in 1622; feast day 31 July. >> Jesuits

LSD or **lysergic acid diethylamide** A hallucinogen which was a popular drug of abuse in the 1960s and early 1970s, taken as 'microdots' and known as 'California sunshine', 'white lightning', 'purple haze', or simply 'acid'. The cult of LSD-taking was promoted by Dr Timothy Leary (1920–96), who was dismissed from his post as clinical psychologist at Harvard in 1963. >> hallucinogens

Luanda [**lwan**da], formerly also **Loanda**, Port **São Paulo de Loanda** 8°50S 13°15E, pop (1995e) 2 130 000. Seaport capital of Angola; founded in 1575; the centre of Portuguese administration from 1627; a major slave trading centre with Brazil in 17th–18th-c; airport; railway; university (1962); cathedral. >> Angola ℹ

Luang Prabang >> **Louangphrabang**

Luba-Lunda Kingdoms A succession of African states occupying territory in what is now Democratic Republic of Congo. They were powerful in the 17th–18th-c, involved in slave and ivory trading. >> slave trade; Zaire ℹ

Lübeck [**lü**bek] 53°52N 10°40E, pop (1995e) 222 000. Commercial and manufacturing seaport in NE Germany; major city in the Hanseatic League; railway; birthplace of Thomas Mann; cathedral (1173); noted for its red wine trade and its marzipan; the Hanseatic City is a world heritage site. >> Germany ℹ; Hanseatic League; Mann

Lubitsch, Ernst [**loo**bich] (1892–1947) Film director, born in Berlin. He established himself as the creator of witty sophisticated light comedies, such as *The Love Parade* (1929) and *Ninotchka* (1939). He received a Special Academy Award in 1947.

Lublin [lub**leen**] 51°18N 22°31E, pop (1995e) 356 000. City in E Poland; a castle town, gaining urban status in 1317; railway; university (1918); cathedral (16th-c). >> Lublin, Union of; Poland ℹ

Lublin, Union of [lub**yeen**] (1569) An Act uniting Poland and the Grand Duchy of Lithuania. The Union completed the formal unification of the two states begun in the 14th-c. >> Jagiellions; Lublin

Lubumbashi [lubum**ba**shee], formerly **Elisabethville** (to 1966) 11°40S 27°28E, pop (1995e) 750 000. City in SE Democratic Republic of Congo; founded, 1910; airport; railway; university (1955); copper mining and smelting; cathedral. >> Zaire ℹ

Lucan [**loo**kn], in full **Marcus Annaeus Lucanus** (39–65) Roman poet, born in Córdoba, Spain. In 62 he published the first three books of his epic *Pharsalia* on the civil war between Pompey and Caesar. After Nero forbade him to write poetry, he joined a conspiracy against him, but was betrayed and compelled to commit suicide. >> Nero

Lucan, Richard John Bingham, 7th Earl of [**loo**kn], known as **Lord Lucan** (1934–?) British aristocrat, and alleged murderer. He disappeared in 1974, when police found the body of the Lucan family's nanny, Sandra Rivett. The police failed to trace him, and in 1975 a coroner's jury charged him with the murder. Speculation about his whereabouts continues to this day.

Lucas, Robert E, Jr (1939–) Economist, born in Yakima, WA. He won the Nobel Prize for Economics in 1995 for developing and applying the hypothesis of rational expectations in macroeconomic analysis. He is known for his 'Lucas critique' (1976), showing that shifts in economic policy often produce a completely different outcome if people adapt their expectations to new policy stances.

Lucas van Leyden [**lay**dn], or **Lucas Jacobsz** (1494–1533) Painter and engraver, born in Leyden, The Netherlands. His masterpiece is the triptych, 'The Last Judgment' (1526, Leyden). >> engraving

Luce, Clare Boothe, *née* **Boothe** (1903–87) Playwright, born in New York City. She wrote several successful plays, such as *The Women* (1936) and *Kiss the Boys Goodbye* (1938). She later became US ambassador to Italy (1953–7).

Luce, Henry R(obinson) (1898–1967) Magazine publisher and editor, born in Shandong province, China, to a missionary family. He co-founded and edited *Time* (1923), which aimed to present news in narrative style, and later founded *Fortune* (1930) and *Life* (1936).

Lucerne [loo**sern**], Ger **Luzern** 47°03N 8°18E, pop (1995e) 61 500. Resort city in C Switzerland, on W shore of L Lucerne; railway junction; lake steamers; cathedral (17th-c). >> Switzerland ℹ

Lucerne, Lake, Ger **Vierwaldstätter See** area 114 sq km/44 sq mi. Fourth largest of the Swiss lakes; length 38 km/24 mi; maximum depth 214 m/702 ft. >> Lucerne; Switzerland ℹ

lucerne A bushy perennial (*Medicago sativa*, subspecies *sativa*) growing to 90 cm/3 ft; leaves with three leaflets, broadest and toothed towards the tip; pea-flowers purple or blue; fruit a spiral pod with 1½–3 coils; also called **alfalfa**. (Family: Leguminosae.)

Lucian [**loo**shan] (c.117–c.180) Greek rhetorician, born in Samosata, Syria. He devoted himself to philosophy, and produced a new form of literature – humorous dialogue. His satires include *Dialogues of the Gods* and *Dialogues of the Dead*. >> rhetoric

Lucid, Shannon [**loo**sid] (1943–) US astronaut and biochemist, who in 1996 set a new record for the longest US space mission (188 days) in orbit aboard the *Mir* space station. She became the first woman to be awarded the Congressional Space Medal of Honor.

Lucifer >> **Devil**

Lucknow [**luhk**now] 26°50N 81°00E, pop (1995e) 1 723 000. Capital of Uttar Pradesh, NC India; capital of the Kingdom of Oudh, 1775–1856; capital of the United Provinces, 1877; British garrison besieged for five months during the Indian Mutiny, 1857; airfield; railway; university (1921). >> Indian Mutiny; Uttar Pradesh

Lucretia [loo**kree**sha] (6th-c BC) According to Roman legend, the wife of Collatinus. She was raped by Sextus, son of Tarquinius Superbus; after telling her story, she committed suicide. >> Tarquinius Superbus

Lucretius [loo**kree**shus], in full **Titus Lucretius Carus** (1st-c BC) Latin poet and philosopher. His major work is the 6-volume hexameter poem *De rerum natura* (On the Nature of Things).

Lucullus, Lucius Licinius [loo**ku**lus] (c.110–57 BC) Roman politician and general, famous for his victories over Mithridates VI, and also for his enormous wealth and patronage of the arts. >> Mithridates VI Eupator

Luddites The name given to groups of workers who in 1811–12 destroyed newly introduced textile machinery in the North of England, because they feared that many jobs would be lost; known as 'the Luds', after their leader, Ned Ludd. The term has since been used to describe any resistance to technological innovation.

Ludendorff, Erich von [**lu**dendaw(r)f] (1865–1937) General, born near Poznan, Poland. He became chief-of-staff under Hindenburg, defeated the Russians at Tannenberg (1914), and conducted the 1918 offensives on the Western front. In 1923 he was a leader in the unsuccessful Hitler putsch at Munich. >> Hindenburg, Paul von; World War 1

Luderitz [**lü**derits], formerly **Angra Pequena** 26°38S 15°10E, pop (1995e) 10 100. Seaport in SW Namibia; Diaz landed here in 1486; first German settlement in SW Africa, 1883; railway. >> Diaz, Bartolomeu; Namibia ℹ

Ludlow 52°22N 2°43W, pop (1995e) 8400. Historic market town in Shropshire, WC England; developed in the 12th-c around a Norman fortress; Ludlow Castle (11th-c). >> Shropshire

Ludwigshafen (am Rhein) [**lud**viks-hahvn] 49°29N 8°27E, pop (1995e) 167 000. Commercial and manufacturing river port in Germany; on W bank of the R Rhine. >> Germany ℹ

Luftwaffe [**luft**vahfuh] (Ger 'air-weapon') The correct name for the German Air Force, re-established in 1935 under Göring, in contravention of the Treaty of Versailles. Dominant in the years of German victory in World War 2, the Luftwaffe had all but ceased to exist by 1945. The Federal Republic of Germany's air force, also known as the Luftwaffe, was re-established in 1956. >> Britain, Battle of; Göring

Lugano [loo**gah**noh] 46°01N 8°57E, pop (1995e) 26 800. Resort town in S Switzerland, on N shore of L Lugano; on road and rail route over the St Gotthard Pass; third largest financial centre in Switzerland; cathedral (13th-c). >> Switzerland ℹ

Lugansk [lu**gansk**], formerly **Voroshilovgrad** (1970–91) 48°35N 39°20E, pop (1995e) 506 000. City in E Ukraine; founded, 1795; airfield; railway; iron and steel. >> Ukraine ℹ

lugeing [**loozh**ing] Travelling across ice on a toboggan sled, usually made of wood with metal runners. The rider sits upright or lies back, as opposed to lying on the stomach in tobogganing. The luge is approximately 1·5 m/5 ft in length, and is steered by the feet and a hand rope. >> bobsledding

lugworm A large annelid worm that burrows in soft inshore or estuarine sediments; breathes using external gills along body; widely used as fishing bait. (Class: Polychaeta. Order: Capitellida.) >> annelid

Luik [loyk] >> **Liège**

Lukács, Georg or **György** [**loo**kach] (1885–1971) Marxist philosopher and critic, born in Budapest. He was a prolific writer on literature and aesthetics, as in his early work *Die Theorie des Romans* (1916, The Theory of the Novel). >> Socialist Realism

Luke, St (1st-c) New Testament evangelist, a Gentile Christian. He is first named as author of the third Gospel in the 2nd-c, and tradition has ever since ascribed to him both that work and the Acts of the Apostles. Feast day 18 October. >> Acts of the Apostles

Lull, Ramón >> **Llull, Ramón**

Lully, Jean Baptiste [**loo**lee], originally **Giovanni Battista Lulli** (1632–87) Composer, born in Florence, Italy. He composed many operas, in which he made the ballet an essential part, and also wrote church music, dance music, and pastorals.

Lully, Raymond >> Llull, Ramón

Luluabourg >> Kananga

lumbago [luhm**bay**goh] An imprecise term used to indicate pain or discomfort in the back over the lumbar region, without identifying or defining a specific cause. >> vertebral column

lumbar puncture The introduction of a needle between the vertebrae in the lower back (the *lumbar* region) into the narrow space lying between the inner two layers of membranes surrounding the spinal cord and its nerve roots. Its purpose is to obtain a sample of cerebrospinal fluid for examination in the diagnosis of infections or bleeding. >> cerebrospinal fluid; vertebral column

Lumbini [lum**bee**nee] Town and centre of pilgrimage in the W Terai of Nepal; the birthplace of Buddha; world heritage site. >> Buddha; Nepal ℹ

lumen [**loo**min] SI unit of luminous flux; symbol *lm*; defined as the luminous flux emitted from a light source of intensity 1 candela into a solid angle of 1 steradian. >> photometry ℹ

Lumière, Auguste (Marie Louis) [lüm**yair**] (1862–1954) Inventor of photographic equipment, along with his brother, **Louis Jean** (1864–1948), both born in Besançon, France. In 1893 they developed a cine camera, the *cinématographe*, and showed the first motion pictures using film projection in 1895. >> cinematography ℹ

luminescence The emission of light from a substance for reasons other than heating. **Photoluminescence** corresponds to a bombardment with light, exploited in zinc sulphide-based paints, which continue to glow after the external light source is removed. **Bioluminescence** is observed in fireflies, resulting from chemical reactions. Solids which luminesce are called *phosphors*. >> bioluminescence; fluorescence; light; phosphorescence

luminosity The intrinsic or absolute amount of energy radiated per second from a celestial object. Stars vary greatly in their observed luminosities, from 1 million times more to 1 thousand million times less than the Sun. In astronomy, luminosity is measured in *magnitudes*. >> magnitude; star

luminous flux The total flow of visible light available for illumination from some source, taking into account the source's ability to generate visible light; symbol Φ, unit *lm* (lumen). >> light; lumen; photometry ℹ

luminous intensity The flow of visible light capable of causing illumination, emitted from a source per unit solid angle; symbol *I*, unit cd (candela). It is independent of distance from source. A related quantity is **luminance**, formerly called **brightness**, symbol *L*, units cd/m^2, the luminous intensity per square metre. >> light; photometry ℹ

lumpsucker Heavy-bodied fish (*Cyclopterus lumpus*) widespread in the N Atlantic and Arctic Oceans; length up to 60 cm/2 ft; body rounded, bearing rows of spiny plates and with a large underside sucker. (Family: Cyclopteridae.)

Lumumba, Patrice (Hemery) [lu**mum**ba] (1925–61) Congolese statesman, born in Katako Kombé, Congo. He became the leader of the Congolese national movement, and premier when the Congo became an independent republic in 1960 (now Zaire). He was deposed after four months, and soon after assassinated. >> Congo ℹ

Luna programme A highly successful evolutionary series of Soviet lunar missions carried out between 1959 and 1976. Luna 2 (1959) was the first spacecraft to impact the Moon; Luna 3 (1959) acquired the first pictures of the lunar far side; Luna 9 (1966) achieved the first soft landing, and returned the first TV pictures from the surface. >> Moon; Soviet space programme; RR970

Lunar Orbiter programme A series of US spacecraft used to survey the Moon at high resolution from a lunar orbit, prior to the crewed Apollo landings. Launched 1966–7, and equipped only with cameras, it provided the database for a selection of Apollo landing sites. >> Apollo programme; Moon

Lund 55°42N 13°10E, pop (1995e) 92 100. Ancient city in SW Sweden; bishopric; railway; university (1666); technical institute (1961); cathedral (1080). >> Sweden ℹ

Lunda >> Luba-Lunda Kingdoms

Lundy Island [**luhn**dee] Island in the Bristol Channel, off the NW coast of Devon, SW England; two lighthouses; area 9·6 sq km/3·7 sq mi; National Trust area, since 1969. >> Bristol Channel

Lüneburger Heide [**lün**eberguh **hiy**duh] ('Luneburg Heath') A region of moorland and forest lying between the R Aller and R Elbe in W Germany, where Field Marshal Montgomery accepted the capitulation of the German Army (4 May 1945). >> Montgomery, Bernard Law

lungfish Any of a small group of freshwater fishes with a pair of lungs on the underside of the gut, connected to the oesophagus; gills much reduced; includes the African (Family: Protopteridae), Australian (Family: Ceratodontidae), and South American lungfish (Family: Lepidosirenidae). >> lungs

lungs The organs of respiration, where the exchange of oxygen and carbon dioxide between the blood and air takes place. They are present in terrestrial vertebrates (reptiles, birds, mammals) and some fish (eg lungfish). In humans the paired lungs lie within the *pleural cavities* of the thorax. Each lung is highly elastic, and is divided into a number of lobes, each of which is further subdivided; each lobe receives a *bronchus* (*bronchiole* when the lobules become small) and blood vessels. The subdivisions continue until the respiratory bronchioles divide into a cluster of *alveoli*, where gaseous exchange occurs. At rest, the volume of air passing in and out of the lungs at each breath is about 500 ml: this can increase eight-fold during extreme exertion. >> anatomy ℹ; emphysema; empyema; pleurisy; pneumoconiosis; pneumonia; pneumothorax; respiration; trachea; tuberculosis

Lunt, Alfred (1892–1977) and **Fontanne, Lynne**, originally **Lillie Louise Fontanne** (1887–1983) Acting partnership, born in Milwaukee, WI, and Woodford, Essex, respectively. They were married in 1922, and from 1924 became a popular husband-and-wife team, known especially for their performances in Noel Coward's plays, such as *Design for Living* (1933). Broadway's Lunt–Fontanne Theatre, opened in 1958, was named in the couple's honour, and in 1964 they received the US Medal of Freedom. >> Coward; Terry, Ellen

Luo [**loo**oh] A Nilotic-speaking people of W Kenya. Mainly farmers and fishers, they are the second largest ethnic group in Kenya. >> Kenya ℹ

Luoyang or **Loyang** [lwohyahng] 34°47N 112°26E, pop (1995e) 1 289 000. City in NC China; capital of ancient China during the E Zhou dynasty, 770–256 BC; railway; Baimasi Temple (founded AD 75); Longmen Caves, with c.100 000 images and statues of Buddha (5th–7th-c). >> China ℹ

Lupercalia [looper**kay**lia] An ancient festival of purification and fertility. It was held every year in ancient Rome (on 15 Feb) at a cave on the Palatine Hill called the Lupercal.

lupin A member of a large group of annual and perennial herbs or shrubs, native to America and the Mediterranean region; pea-flowers in long, terminal, often showy spikes, blue, pink, yellow, or white; pods splitting open explosively to release the seeds. (Genus: *Lupinus*, 200 species. Family: Leguminosae.)

Lupus [**loo**pus] (Lat 'wolf') A small S constellation next to Centaurus, known since Greek times. >> constellation; RR968

lupus erythematosus >> **systemic lupus erythematosus**

lupus vulgaris [**loo**pus vul**gah**ris] Tuberculosis of the skin, now rare in countries in which pulmonary tuberculosis is well controlled. It causes ulceration and scarring of the skin of the face or neck. >> tuberculosis

lurcher A cross-bred dog formerly kept by poachers for catching rabbits and hares; usually a cross between a greyhound and a collie. >> collie; dog; greyhound

Lusaka [loo**sa**ka] 15°26S 28°20E, pop (1995e) 1 041 000. Capital of Zambia; replaced Livingstone as capital of former N Rhodesia, 1935; capital of Zambia, 1964; airport; railway; university (1965); cathedral (1957). >> Zambia ℹ

Lusitania [loosi**tay**nia] A Cunard passenger liner of 31 000 tonnes gross, sunk in the Irish Sea in 1915 by a German U-boat, with great loss of life. The Germans claimed she was carrying armaments, but this was officially denied by the British.

Lusophone Community, formally the Comunidad dos Paises de Língua Portuguesa An organization to facilitate social, cultural, and economic co-operation among Portuguese-speaking countries: Angola, Brazil, Cape Verde, Guinea-Bissau, Mozambique, Portugal, and São Tomé and Principe. It was formally created in 1996.

lute A European stringed instrument in use from the Middle Ages to the 18th-c, and revived in modern times for performing early music. It has a large pear-shaped body, a wide neck, and is plucked with the right hand. >> chitarrone; pipa; sitar; string instrument 2 ℹ; theorbo; ud

Luther, Martin (1483–1546) Religious reformer, born in Eisleben, Germany. During a visit to Rome in 1510–11, he was angered by the sale of indulgences. In 1517 he drew up 95 theses on indulgences, which he nailed on the church door at Wittenberg, and publicly burned the papal bull issued against him. He was summoned to appear before the Diet at Worms, and was put under the ban of the Empire. In 1525 he married a former nun, Katharina von Bora. The drawing up of the Augsburg Confession marks the culmination of the German Reformation (1530). His translation of the Bible became a landmark of German literature. >> Augsburg Confession; indulgences; Lutheranism; Reformation

Lutheranism Churches derived from the Reformation of Martin Luther, and the doctrine which they share. The doctrine emphasizes justification by faith alone, the importance of scripture, and the priesthood of all believers. Three sacraments are recognized: baptism, Eucharist, and penance. The Lutheran World Federation, a free association of Lutheran Churches, was founded in 1947. >> Luther; Protestantism; sacrament

Luthuli or **Lutuli, Albert (John Mvumbi)** [lu**too**lee] (c.1899–1967) Resistance leader, born in Zimbabwe (formerly Rhodesia). He became president-general of the African National Congress, and dedicated himself to a campaign of nonviolent resistance, for which he was awarded the Nobel Peace Prize in 1960.

Lutine Bell [**loo**teen] A bell formerly rung at Lloyd's of London insurers' offices to announce the loss of a ship or other news of great importance to the underwriters. The bell belonged to a vessel (HMS *Lutine*), carrying gold bullion, which foundered off the Dutch coast in 1799. Nowadays it is rung mainly on ceremonial occasions. >> insurance; Lloyd's

Luton [**loo**tn] 51°53N 0°25W, pop (1995e) 182 000. Industrial town and unitary authority (from 1997) in Bedfordshire, SC England; railway; airport; football league team, Luton Town (Hatters). >> Bedfordshire

Lutosławski, Witold [lootoh**slav**skee] (1913–94) Composer, born in Warsaw. His works include the *Variations on a Theme of Paganini* (1941) for two pianos, three symphonies, concertos, songs, and chamber music.

Lutuli, Albert John >> **Luthuli, Albert John**

Lutyens, Sir Edwin Landseer [**lut**yenz] (1869–1944) Architect, born in London. His best-known projects are the Cenotaph in Whitehall, London (1919–20), and the laying out of New Delhi, India (1912–30).

lux SI unit of illuminance; symbol *lx*; defined as 1 lumen of luminous flux incident on 1 square metre. >> photometry ℹ

Luxembourg (city) [**luhk**smberg] 49°37N 6°08E, pop (1995e) 78 500. Capital of Luxembourg; also site of the Court of Justice of the European Communities, the General Secretariat of the European Parliament, and other bodies; airport; railway. >> European Parliament; Luxembourg (country) ℹ

Luxembourg or **Luxemburg** (country) [**luhk**smberg], official name **Grand Duchy of Luxembourg**, Fr **Grande-Duché de Luxembourg**, Ger **Grossherzogtum Luxemburg**, Letzeburgish **Grousherzogdem Lëtzebuerg** pop (1995e) 402 000; area 2586 sq km/998 sq mi. Independent, constitutional monarchy in NW Europe; capital, Luxembourg; timezone GMT +1; a quarter of the population is foreign; chief religion, Roman Catholicism (97%); languages, French (official), Letzeburgish, German; unit of currency, the Luxemburgish franc, linked to the Belgian franc; divided into the two natural regions of Ösling (N), wooded, hilly land, average height 450 m/ 1475 ft, and Gutland, flatter, average height 250 m/ 820 ft; made a Grand Duchy by the Congress of Vienna, 1815; granted political autonomy, 1838; recognized as a neutral independent state, 1867; occupied by Germany in both World Wars; joined Benelux economic union, 1948; neutrality abandoned on joining NATO, 1949; a hereditary monarchy with the Grand Duke as head of state; parliament has a Chamber of Deputies and a State Council; head of government is the prime minister; important international

centre. >> Benelux; Luxembourg (city); RR1016 political leaders

Luxembourg, Palais du [pale dü lüksãboorg] Since 1958, the seat of the French Senate in Paris. The palace was built in 1613–14 by Salomon de Brosse (1565–1626). >> Paris

Luxemburg, Rosa (1871–1919) German revolutionary, born in Poland. With the German politician, Karl Liebknecht (1871–1919), she formed the Spartacus League, which later became the German Communist Party. She was murdered during the Spartacus revolt in Berlin.

Luxor [**luhk**saw(r)], Arabic **al-Uqsor**, or **al-Uqsur** 25°41N 32°24E, pop (1995e) 176 000. Winter resort town in EC Egypt; known as Thebes to the Greeks; numerous tombs of pharaohs in Valley of the Kings. >> Egypt [i]; pharaoh

Lu Xun [loo shün], also spelled **Lu-hsün** or **Lu-hsin** (1881–1936) Writer, born in Shaoxing, China. His short story, *Diary of a Madman* (1918), was an immediate success, as was his 1921 book, *The True Story of Ah Q.*

Luzon [loo**zon**] pop (1995e) 32 558 000; area 108 130 sq km/ 41 738 sq mi. Largest island of the Philippines; Cordillera Central rises to 2929 m/9609 ft in the NW at Mt Puog; occupied by Japanese in World War 2; chief city, Manila. >> Manila; Philippines [i]

Lvov [li**vof**], Pol **Lwow**, Ger **Lemberg**, Ukrainian **Lwiw** 49°50N 24°00E, pop (1995e) 802 000. City in Ukraine; founded, 1256; part of Poland (1340–1772), then given to Austria; ceded to Poland after World War 1; ceded to USSR, 1939; airfield; railway junction; centre for Ukrainian culture; university (1661); cathedral. >> Ukraine [i]

Lyallpur >> **Faisalabad**

lycanthropy [liy**kan**thropee] In popular belief, the assumption by humans of the shapes of other animals, typically the most dangerous beast of the area. In Europe and N Asia it is usually a wolf or bear.

Lyceum [liy**see**um] The school of philosophy founded by Aristotle in 335 BC, in a gymnasium just to the E of the city walls of Athens. It rivalled the Academy of Plato as a research centre in the ancient world. >> Aristotle; Plato; Strato; Theophrastus

lychee >> **litchi**

Lycurgus [liy**ker**gus] The name of various Greeks, including, in mythology, **1** The King of Thrace who opposed Dionysus and was blinded, **2** The founder of the Spartan constitution, with its military caste-system. >> Sparta (Greek history)

Lydgate, John [**lid**gayt] (c.1370–c.1451) Poet, born in Lidgate, Suffolk. His major works are the narrative poems *The Troy Book*, *The Siege of Thebes*, and the *Fall of Princes*.

Lydia [**li**deeuh] In antiquity, the area of W Asia Minor lying inland of Ionia. Its capital was Sardis. At the height of its power in the 7th-c and 6th-c BC, it was the centre of an empire which stretched from the Aegean to C Turkey. >> Ionia

Lyly, John [**li**lee] (c.1554–1606) Writer, born in the Weald of Kent. He is remembered for the style of his writing, as seen in his two-part prose romance *Euphues* (1578, 1580), which led to the term *euphuism* for artificial and extremely elegant language.

lymph A clear, colourless tissue fluid comprising protein, water, and other substances derived from blood, and conveyed in an independent system of thin-walled vessels. It contains lymphocytes for destroying infective organisms. >> blood; lymphocyte; scrofula

lymphocyte [**lim**fohsiyt] A type of white blood cell (*leucocyte*), present in blood and lymph vessels and in spleen and lymph nodes. Lymphocytes are classified as bone-marrow-derived B lymphocytes (*B cells*) and thymus-derived T lymphocytes (*T cells*). They have an essential role in the production of antibodies. >> AIDS; antibodies; leucocytes; lymph

Lynch, Jack, popular name of **John Lynch** (1917–) Irish statesman and Fianna Fáil prime minister (1966–73, 1977–9), born in Cork. He held ministerial posts in education (1957–9), industry and commerce (1959–65), and finance (1965–6), before becoming prime minister. A strong supporter of the Catholic minority in Ulster, he drew criticism from both Ulster and mainland Britain. >> Fianna Fáil; Northern Ireland [i]

Lynx A very faint N constellation near to Ursa Major. >> constellation; Ursa Major; RR968

lynx A nocturnal member of the cat family, native to the northern N Hemisphere; plain brown or with dark spots; very short tail; tips of ears tufted; cheeks with long 'whiskers'; two species: **lynx** (*Felis lynx*), and the rare **Spanish lynx** (*Felis pardina.*) >> bobcat; Felidae

Lyon [leeõ], Eng also **Lyons**, ancient **Lugdunum** 45°46N 4°50E, pop (1995e) 428 000. Manufacturing and commercial city in SC France; at confluence of Rhône and Saône Rivers; third largest city in France; Roman capital of Gaul; airport; road and rail junction; metro; archbishopric; two universities (1875, 1896); cathedral (12th–15th-c); leading centre of French textile industry, particularly silk production; international exhibition hall (Eurexpo). >> France [i]

Lyons, Sir John (1932–) Linguist, born in Manchester. A specialist in semantics and linguistic theory, his major publications include *Semantics* (1977), *Language, Meaning and Context* (1980), and *Linguistic Semantics* (1995). >> linguistics; semantics

Lyons, Joseph Aloysius (1879–1939) Australian statesman and prime minister (1932–9), born in Stanley, Tasmania. In 1931 he founded the United Australian Party, and became prime minister until his death. >> Australia [i]

lyophilization or **freeze drying** The process for the removal of solvent or adherent water from materials (eg blood plasma, foodstuffs, beverage bases) while in a frozen condition. >> food preservation

Lyra [**liy**ra] ('harp') A small but obvious N constellation. It includes the fifth-brightest star, Vega, as well as the prototype variable RR Lyrae, and the Ring nebula. >> constellation; Polaris; variable star; RR968

lyre A musical instrument of great antiquity, with a resonator, two arms, and a crossbar. Gut strings, from 3 to 12 in number, were stretched from the front of the resonator to the crossbar, and plucked with a plectrum. >> crwth; kinnor; kithara [i]; string instrument 2 [i]

lyrebird Either of two species of a shy, ground-feeding, Australian bird of the genus *Menura*; long legs; flies poorly but runs well; tail of male shaped like lyre; spectacular display and song. (Family: Menuridae.)

Lysenko, Trofim Denisovich [li**seng**koh] (1898–1976) Biologist and plant physiologist, born in Karlovka, Ukraine. Using political affiliation rather than scientific recognition for advancement, he became director of the Academy of Agricultural Sciences (1938–56, 1958–62) and in 1948 declared the accepted Mendelian theory erroneous, banishing many outstanding Soviet scientists. >> genetics; Mendel

Lysithea [liysi**thee**a] The 10th natural satellite of Jupiter, discovered in 1938; distance from the planet 11 720 000 km/ 7 283 000 mi; diameter 40 km/25 mi. >> Jupiter (astronomy); RR964

lysosome [**liy**sosohm] A membrane-bound sac which contains numerous enzymes capable of digesting a wide variety of substrates. They are involved in the digestion of food and in the destruction of bacteria in white blood cells. >> blood; digestion; enzyme

lysozyme [**liy**sohziym] An enzyme present in tears, saliva, sweat, milk, and nasal and gastric secretions; also known as *muramidase*. It destroys bacterial cell walls by digesting their polysaccharide component. >> disaccharide; enzyme

Lytham St Anne's [**lith**am] 53°45N 3°01W, pop (1995e) 43 100. Resort town in Lancashire, NW England; railway; championship golf course. >> Lancashire

Lyttelton, Humphrey [**li**tltuhn] (1921–) Jazz trumpeter and bandleader, born in Windsor, S England. He formed a band in 1948, and later became the leading figure in the British revival of traditional jazz. His group expanded to an octet, and presented a range of more modern jazz styles. >> jazz

Lytton (of Knebworth), Edward George Earle Bulwer-Lytton, Baron [**li**tn] (1803–73) Writer and statesman, born in London. He wrote many popular novels, especially on historical themes, such as *The Last Days of Pompeii* (1834) and *Harold* (1843), as well as plays and essays.

Maasai >> **Masai**

Maastricht [mah**strikht**], ancient **Traiectum ad Mosam** or **Traiectum Tungorum** 50°51N 5°42E, pop (1995e) 121 000. City in S Netherlands, on the R Maas; commercial hub of an area extending well into Belgium; railway junction; noted for its vegetable and butter markets; location of conference on European union, 1991. >> Maastricht Treaty; Netherlands, The ℹ

Maastricht Treaty [mah**strikht**, **mah**strikht] An agreement reached in 1991 at Maastricht, The Netherlands, during a meeting of the heads of state and government of the European Community. It was the conclusion of a series of inter-governmental conferences on European political union and economic/monetary union which had been taking place since December 1990. The summit agreed a treaty framework for European union, incorporating political and economic agreements and setting a timetable for their implementation, and providing for new security/defence co-operation. The treaty required ratification by the 12 national governments: rejection by Denmark necessitated a revision of the ratification timetable, but by the end of 1992 all countries except Denmark and the UK had ratified, and these did so in mid-1993. >> European Union; Maastricht

M

Maazel, Lorin (Varencove) [mah**zel**] (1930–) Conductor, born in Neuilly, France. He has directed orchestras in Berlin, Cleveland, OH, and Vienna, and was conductor of the Pittsburgh Symphony Orchestra (1986–96).

Mabinogion, The [mabi**nog**ion] The name widely given to a collection of 12 mediaeval Welsh stories, first translated by English diarist Charlotte Guest (1812–95), and published in three volumes (1838–49). It includes the tales of Branwen, Culhwch and Olwen, Geraint and Enid, Llud and Llefelys, Manawydan, Math, Owain, Peredur, Pwyll, Taliesin, the Dream of Macsen Wledig, and the Dream of Rhonabwy. >> Welsh literature

Mabo, Eddie Koiki [**mah**boh] (1940–92) Traditional leader of the Meriam people of Murray I in Torres Strait, Australia. In 1982, with four other Meriam people, he began legal proceedings against the Queensland government, seeking recognition of their traditional ownership of the island and its surrounding seas. In 1992 the High Court of Australia held that Australian common law recognizes a form of native title, making it a landmark case.

McAdam, John Loudon (1756–1836) Road builder, born in Ayr, South Ayrshire. His *Macadam surfaces* used crushed stone bound with gravel, and raised the carriageway to improve drainage. He was made surveyor (1816) to the Bristol Turnpike Trust, and later made surveyor-general of metropolitan roads.

macadamia nut [maka**day**mia] An evergreen tree (*Macadamia integrifolia*) growing to c.20 m/65 ft, native to NE Australia; flowers in long, drooping spikes, with four creamy segments; fruits green, splitting to reveal round, edible nut. (Family: Proteaceae.)

McAleese, Mary [maka**lees**] (1951–) President of Ireland (1997–), born in Belfast. A professor of criminal law, in the 1980s she became known as a campaigner for many social causes. She was the first woman and Catholic pro-vice-chancellor at Queen's University, Belfast, in 1994. Despite her northern background, she became the presidential successor to Mary Robinson in the 1997 election. >> Robinson, Mary

McAliskey, Bernadette (Josephine) [muhka**lis**kee], *née* **Devlin** (1947–) Northern Ireland political activist, brought up in Dungannon, Co Tyrone, Ireland. She became the youngest MP in the House of Commons since William Pitt, when elected as an Independent Unity candidate in 1969. Arrested while leading Catholic rioters in the Bogside, she was sentenced to nine months' imprisonment. In 1971 she lost Catholic support when she gave birth to an illegitimate child, and was defeated in the general election. >> IRA; Northern Ireland ℹ

Macao [ma**kow**], Chin **Aomen**, Port **Macáu** pop (1995e) 470 000; area 16 sq km/6 sq mi. Overseas province of Portugal; a flat, maritime tropical peninsula in SE China and the nearby islands of Taipa and Colôane; on the Pearl R delta; airport; capital, Nome de Deus de Macau; population largely Chinese (99%); chief religions, Buddhism, Roman Catholicism; official languages Portuguese, Chinese (Cantonese generally spoken); unit of currency, the pataca of 100 avos; a Chinese territory under Portuguese administration; due to return to Chinese rule in 1999 (20 Dec); governor appointed by Portugal. >> China ℹ; Portugal ℹ

macaque [ma**kahk**] An Old World monkey, native to S and SE Asia (18 species) and NW Africa (*Barbary ape*); legs and arms of equal length; tail often short; buttocks with naked patches. (Genus: *Macaca*, 19 species.) >> barbary ape; Old World monkey; rhesus monkey

macaroni >> **pasta**

MacArthur, Douglas (1880–1964) US general, born in Little Rock, AR. In 1941 he became commanding general of the US armed forces in the Far East, and from Australia directed the recapture of the SW Pacific (1942–5). In 1950 he led the UN forces in the Korean War. >> Korean War; World War 2

Macassar >> **Makassar Strait; Ujung Padang**

Macaulay, Dame (Emilie) Rose (1881–1958) Novelist, essayist, and poet, born in Rugby, Warwickshire. She won a considerable reputation as a social satirist, with such novels as *Dangerous Ages* (1921). Her best-known novel is *The Towers of Trebizond* (1956).

Macaulay (of Rothley), Thomas Babington Macaulay, Baron [muh**kaw**lee] (1800–59) Essayist and historian, born in Rothley Temple, Leicestershire. He became an MP (1830), established his powers as an orator in the Reform Bill debates, and became secretary of war (1839–41). He wrote the highly popular *Lays of Ancient Rome* (1842). His major work, the *History of England from the Accession of James II*, was published between 1848 and 1861, the fifth volume unfinished.

macaw A large parrot native to the Caribbean, and to Central and tropical South America; nests in holes. (Genera: *Ara*, *Anodorhynchus*, *Cyanopsitta*, c.16 species.) >> parrot

Macbeth (c.1005–57) King of Scots (1040–57), the legend of whose life was the basis of Shakespeare's play. The *mormaer* (provincial ruler) of Moray, he became king after slaying Duncan I in battle near Elgin. He was defeated and killed by Duncan's son, Malcolm Canmore. >> Malcolm III

McBride, Willie John, popular name of **William John McBride** (1940–) Rugby union player, born in Toomebridge, Co Antrim. A lock forward, he made a record 17 appearances for the British Lions, and played for Ireland 63 times. >> football 3

MacBride principles A code of conduct for Northern Ireland advocated by Irish statesman Sean MacBride (1904–88), and adopted in 1976, recommending that local firms should aim for balanced community representation in their staff recruitment. The code was created as part of a policy of creating jobs for the Catholic minority in Northern Ireland, and was initially focused on US companies which had branches in the region.

Maccabees [**mak**abeez] An important Jewish family, and those of its party (also known as the **Hasmoneans**) who initially resisted the influences of Greek culture on Israel during Syrian rule over Palestine. **Judas Maccabeus** (or **ben Mattathias**) led a revolt in 168 BC, which was continued by his sons, resulting eventually in semi-independence from Syrian control. >> Maccabees, Books of the

Maccabees or **Machabees, Books of the** [**mak**abeez] Four writings, the first two being part of the Old Testament Apocrypha and the last two being assigned to the Old Testament Pseudepigrapha. >> Apocrypha, Old Testament; Maccabees; Pseudepigrapha

McCarthy, Joseph R(aymond) (1909–57) US Republican politician and inquisitor, born in Grand Chute, WI. His unsubstantiated accusations that Communists had infiltrated the State Department led to his becoming chairman in 1953 of the powerful Permanent Subcommittee on Investigations. The anti-Communist witchhunt which ensued became known as **McCarthyism**. >> communism; Un-American Activities Committee

McCarthy, Mary (Therese) (1912–89) Writer and critic, born in Seattle, WA. Her novels include *The Company She Keeps* (1942), *The Group* (1963), and *Cannibals and Missionaries* (1979).

McCartney, Sir Paul [muh**kah(r)t**nee] (1942–) Pop star, composer, songwriter, guitarist, and recording artist, born in Liverpool, Merseyside. The Beatles' bass guitarist, vocalist, and member of the Lennon–McCartney songwriting team, he made his debut as a soloist with the album *McCartney* (1970), heralding the break-up of the group. In 1971 he formed the band Wings with his wife, **Linda** (1942–98, *née* Eastman). 'Mull of Kintyre' (1977) became the biggest selling UK single (2·5 million). He created and starred in the film *Give my Regards to Broad Street* (1984), and with Carl Davis wrote the *Liverpool Oratorio* (1991). >> Beatles, The; Lennon

McClellan, George B(rinton) (1826–85) US Union general in the Civil War, born in Philadelphia, PA. His Virginian campaign ended disastrously at Richmond (1862), and though he forced Lee to retreat at Antietam, he failed to follow up his advantage, and was recalled. >> American Civil War

McClure, Sir Robert (John le Mesurier) [muh**kloor**] (1807–73) Explorer, born in Wexford, Ireland. He commanded a ship in Franklin's 1850 Artic expedition that penetrated E to the coast of Banks Land, where he was icebound for nearly two years. Rescued by another ship which had travelled from the W, he thus became the first person to accomplish the Northwest Passage. >> Franklin, John; Northwest Passage

McCormack, John (Francis) (1884–1945) Tenor, born in Athlone, Ireland. He made his London debut in 1907, and sang at Covent Garden, appearing also in oratorio and as a *Lieder* singer. He later turned to popular sentimental songs.

McCormick, Cyrus (Hall) (1809–84) Inventor of the reaper, born in Rockbridge County, VA. He manufactured more than six million harvesting machines during his lifetime. >> combine harvester 🛈

McCullers, (Lula) Carson, *née* **Smith** (1917–67) Writer, born in Columbus, GA. She is known for her realistic, tragic, and often symbolic novels, notably *The Heart is a Lonely Hunter* (1940) and *The Member of the Wedding* (1946, filmed 1952).

McCullough, Colleen [muh**kuh**luh] (1937–) Novelist, born in Wellington, New South Wales, Australia. Her books include *The Thorn Birds* (1977), which sold 20 million copies, *The First Man in Rome* (1990), and *The Grass Crown* (1991).

MacDiarmid, Hugh [muhk**der**mid], pseudonym of **Christopher Murray Grieve** (1892–1978) Poet, born in Langholm, Dumfries and Galloway. A founder-member of the Scottish National Party, he established himself as the leader of a vigorous Scottish Renaissance with *A Drunk Man Looks at the Thistle* (1926).

Macdonald, Flora (1722–90) Scottish heroine, born in South Uist, Western Isles. After the rebellion of 1745, she conducted the Young Pretender, Charles Edward Stuart, disguised as 'Betty Burke', to safety in Skye. For this she was imprisoned in the Tower of London, but released in 1747.

Macdonald, Sir John A(lexander) (1815–91) Canadian statesman and prime minister (1857–8, 1864, 1867–73, 1878–91), born in Glasgow. He was instrumental in bringing about the confederation of Canada, and in 1867 formed the first government of the new Dominion. >> Canada 🛈

MacDonald, (James) Ramsay (1866–1937) British statesman and prime minister (1924, 1929–31, 1931–5), born at Lossiemouth, Moray. He became an MP in 1906, and was prime minister and foreign secretary of the first British Labour government. He met the financial crisis of 1931 by forming a largely Conservative 'National' government. >> Labour Party

McDonald, Trevor (1939–) Television journalist and newscaster, born in Trinidad. He became a reporter for ITN in 1973, then a sports correspondent (1978), diplomatic correspondent (1980), and diplomatic editor (1987). He became nationally known after he joined ITN's *News at Ten* (1990–9).

MacDonnell Ranges Mountain ranges in Northern Territory, C Australia; extend 320 km/200 mi W from Alice Springs; rising to 1524 m/5000 ft at Mt Liebig. >> Northern Territory

mace A spice obtained by grinding up the red, net-like aril which surrounds the seed of the nutmeg tree (*Myristica fragrans*). It is poisonous if consumed in large quantities. >> nutmeg; spice

Macedon [**ma**sedon] In antiquity, the territory to the N of Greece abutting on to the NW corner of the Aegean. Philip II (359–336 BC) transformed it into the most powerful state in Greece. It became a Roman province in 146 BC. >> Lamian War

Macedonia (Greece) [mase**doh**nia], Gr **Makedhonia** pop (1995e) 2 263 000; area 34 177 sq km/13 192 sq mi. N region of Greece; capital, Thessaloniki; mountainous, with fertile plains. >> Greece 🛈; Mount Athos

Macedonia (republic) [mase**doh**nia], Serbo-Croatian **Makedonija**, also called **Former Yugoslav Republic of Macedonia (FYROM)** pop (1994) 1 937 000; area 25 713 sq km/9925 sq mi. Republic in the Balkans, SE Europe; capital, Skopje; timezone GMT +2; chief ethnic groups, Macedonian Slav (66%), Albanian (23%), with Turk, Serb, and other minorities (minority totals disputed as underestimates by Albanians and Serbs); religions, Macedonian Orthodox Christian (autocephalous), Muslim; language, Macedonian, status as language or dialect is a political issue with Greece; currency, the denar; landlocked, mountainous region; divided from Greek Macedonia by the Kožuf and Nidže ranges; highest point, Korab

(2764 m/9068 ft); chief rivers, the Struma and Vardar; continental climate; average annual temperatures 0°C (Jan), 24°C (Jul); often heavy winter snowfalls; average annual rainfall 500 mm/20 in; part of Macedonian, Roman, and Byzantine empires; settled by Slavs, 6th-c; conquered by Bulgars, 7th-c, and by Serbia, 14th-c; incorporated into Serbia after the Balkan Wars; united in what later became Yugoslavia, 1918, but continuing demands for autonomy; occupied by Bulgaria, 1941–4; declaration of independence as the Republic of Macedonia, 1991, opposed by central government; 1991 constitution defined Macedonia as a state based on citizenship, not ethnicity; further attempt to rename the country, to gain international recognition, as Republic of Macedonia (Skopje), 1992; ongoing opposition by Greece to the use of the name Macedonia; governed by a president, prime minister, and an Assembly; largely agricultural economy; mining of minerals, iron ore, lead, zinc, nickel; steel, chemicals, textiles. >> Skopje; Yugoslavia 🅸; RR1016 political leaders

McEnroe, John (Patrick) [**ma**kenroh] (1959–) Lawn tennis player, born in Wiesbaden, Germany. He won the Wimbledon title three times (1981, 1983–4), the US singles four times (1979–81, 1984), and was World Championship Tennis champion in 1979, 1981, and 1983–4. His outbursts on court were the source of much adverse publicity. >> tennis, lawn 🅸

Macgillycuddy's Reeks [mak**gil**ikuhdeez **reeks**] Mountain range in Kerry county, Munster, SW Ireland, rising to 1041 m/3415 ft at Carrantuohill, highest peak in Ireland. >> Ireland (republic) 🅸

McGonagall, William [muh**gon**agl] (1830–1902) Doggerel poet, born in Edinburgh, the son of an Irish weaver. He gave readings in public houses, published broadsheets of topical verse, and in Edinburgh was lionized by the legal and student fraternity.

McGovern, George S(tanley) [muh**guh**vern] (1922–) US Democratic politician, born in Avon, SD. He sought the Democratic presidential nomination in 1968, and opposed Nixon in the 1972 presidential election, but was defeated. He tried again for the presidential nomination in 1984, but withdrew. >> Democratic Party; Nixon, Richard M

McGuffey, William (Holmes) [muh**guh**fee] (1800–73) Educator, born near Claysville, PA. He compiled the famous *McGuffey Readers*, six elementary schoolbooks (1836–57) that sold 122 million copies and became standard texts for generations of 19th-c US children.

McGuinness, Martin [muh**gi**nis] (1950–) Sinn Féin politician, born in Londonderry, Northern Ireland. A militant supporter of the IRA, who served two jail sentences in the Irish Republic, he developed a major role as a political strategist during the Northern Ireland peace process in the 1990s. He became an MP, though he does not attend at Westminster, and Sinn Féin's senior minister in the Stormont Assembly. >> Adams, Gerry; IRA; Sinn Féin

Mach, Ernst [mahk] (1838–1916) Physicist and philosopher, born in Turas, Austria. He influenced aeronautical design and the science of projectiles. His writings also greatly influenced Einstein and laid the foundations of logical positivism. >> logical positivism; Mach number

Machabees >> **Maccabees, Books of the**

Machaut, Guillaume de >> **Guillaume de Machaut**

Machel, Samora Moïsés [ma**shel**] (1933–86) The leader of the guerrilla campaign (FRELIMO) against Portuguese rule in Mozambique, and first president (1975–86). Although a Marxist, he established warm relations with Western governments, and attempted an accommodation with the South African regime. >> Mozambique 🅸

Machiavelli, Niccolò (di Bernardo dei) [makia**vel**ee] (1469–1527) Italian statesman and political theorist, born in Florence, Italy. His masterpiece is *Il Principe* (1532, The Prince), whose main theme is that all means may be used in order to maintain authority. It was condemned by the pope, and its viewpoint gave rise to the adjective **machiavellian**.

machine An assembly of connected parts arranged to transmit or modify force to perform useful work. All machines are based on six types: (1) lever; (2) wheel and axle; (3) pulley; (4) inclined plane; (5) wedge; and (6) screw. >> tools

machine code The fundamental instructions which can

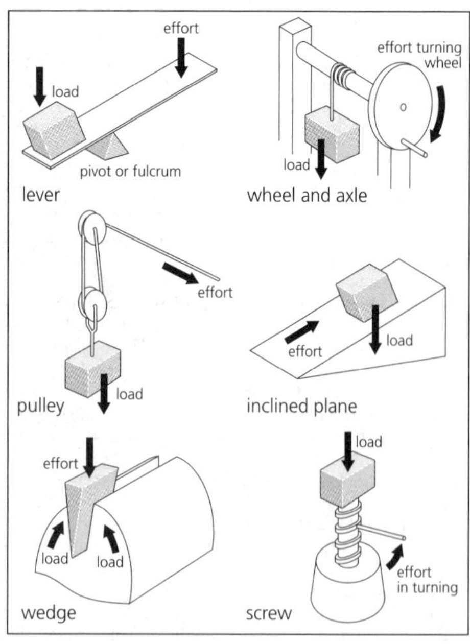

Machine – six types

be directly understood and acted on by a computer, written in a hexadecimal system. >> assembly language; hexadecimal coding; high-level language

machine-gun A gun firing a rifle calibre bullet with an automated ammunition feed and firing cycle, allowing sustained automatic fire. In 1883 inventor Hiram Maxim hit on the principle of using the force of recoil to eject the spent cartridge, chamber a new one, close the breech block, and fire. >> Bren gun; Browning automatic rifle; Maxim; submachine-gun

machine tools A variety of powered machines used in industry to work and shape components made of metal or other material. They include lathes, planes, saws, and milling machines. Finer tolerances and greater repeatability of product is possible with machine tools than with hand tools. >> lathe

Mach number [mak] Unit of velocity; symbol *Ma*; defined as the ratio of velocity of an object to that of sound in some medium, usually air; an aircraft travelling at Ma 1 has velocity 331·5 m/s, the velocity of sound in air. >> Mach; sound; velocity

Machu Picchu [**ma**choo **pee**choo] 13°07S 72°34W. Ruined Inca city in SC Peru; a world heritage site; on the saddle of a high mountain; discovered in 1911 by US explorer Hiram Bingham. >> Incas; Peru ℹ

Macintosh A model of personal computer known particularly for its use of windows and icons to communicate with the user. It is very popular among users involved in aspects of graphic design work. Macintosh is a trade mark of Apple Computer Inc of California. >> icon (computing); personal computer; windows

Macintosh, Charles (1766–1843) Manufacturing chemist, born in Glasgow, who in 1823 patented a method of waterproofing fabric, to which he gave his name. The technique involved the use of rubber dissolved in a naphtha solution to cement two pieces of cloth. >> fabrics; naphtha; rubber

McKay, Heather [muh**kiy**], *née* **Blundell** (1941–) Squash player, born in Queanbeyan, New South Wales, Australia. She won the British Open in 16 successive years (1962–77), 14 Australian titles (1960–73), and was World Champion in 1976 and 1979. >> squash rackets

Macke, August [**mah**kuh] (1887–1914) Expressionist painter, born in Meschede, Germany. Profoundly influenced by Matisse, he and Franz Marc founded the *Blaue Reiter* group. >> *Blaue Reiter, der*; Expressionism; Marc; Matisse

Mackenzie, Sir (Edward Montague) Compton (1883–1972) Writer, born in West Hartlepool, Co Durham. He wrote a large number of novels, notably *Sinister Street* (1913–14) and *Whisky Galore* (1947).

Mackenzie, William Lyon (1795–1861) Canadian politician, born in Dundee. In 1837 he published a declaration of Canadian independence, and headed a band of reform-minded insurgents, but was forced to flee to the USA. He returned to Canada in 1849, becoming a journalist and a member of the Legislative Assembly (1850–8). >> Canada ℹ

Mackenzie Range Mountain range in Northwest Territories, NW Canada; extends c.800 km/497 mi SE–NW; rises to 2972 m/9750 ft at Keele Peak; named after Scottish explorer Sir Alexander Mackenzie (1755?–1820). >> Canada ℹ; Rocky Mountains

Mackenzie River River in Northwest Territories, NW Canada; issues from the Great Slave Lake; enters the Beaufort Sea; length 4241 km/2635 mi. >> Northwest Territories

mackerel Surface-living fish (*Scomber scombrus*) widespread and locally abundant in the N Atlantic; length up to 60 cm/2 ft; body slender, rounded in section, tail deeply forked, small finlets between dorsal and anal fins; bright blue or green with dark blue or black bars, underside silvery white; important food fish. (Family: Scombridae.)

Mackerras, Sir (Alan) Charles (MacLaurin) [muh**ke**ras] (1925–) Conductor, born in Schenectady, NY. He has been musical director of the Sadler's Wells (later English National) Opera (1970–9), of the Sydney Symphony Orchestra, and the Welsh National Opera (1987–92). He was principal guest conductor, Scottish Chamber Orchestra (1992–5), and with the Czech Philharmonic from 1996.

Mckillop, Mary Helen [muh**kil**op], known as **Mother Mary of the Cross** (1842–1909) Religious, born in Fitzroy, Queensland, Australia. With Father Tenison-Woods she founded in 1866 the Society of the Sisters of St Joseph of the Sacred Heart in Penola, South Australia. Her beatification was approved in 1993.

McKinley, William (1843–1901) US Republican statesman and 25th president (1897–1901), born in Niles, OH. In his first term, the war with Spain (1898) took place, with the conquest of Cuba and the Philippines. He was shot by an anarchist at Buffalo. >> Republican Party

McKinley, Mount 63°04N 151°00W. Mountain in SC Alaska, USA; highest peak in North America; consists of two peaks (6194 m/20 321 ft, 5934 m/19 468 ft). >> Alaska; McKinley, William

Mackintosh, Charles Rennie (1868–1928) Architect and designer, born in Glasgow. He became a leader of the *Glasgow Style*, a movement related to Art Nouveau. As well as interiors and furniture, his designs include the Glasgow School of Art (1896–1909). >> Art Nouveau

McLaughlin, Audrey (1936–) Canadian politician, born in Dutton, Ontario, Canada. She has been an MP for the Yukon Territory since 1987, and leader of the federal New Democratic Party since 1989.

Maclean, Alistair [muh**klayn**] (1922–87) Writer, born in Glasgow. His first novel *HMS Ulysses* (1955) became an immediate best-seller. Later books included *The Guns of Navarone* (1957) and *Where Eagles Dare* (1967).

Maclean, Donald (Duart) [muh**klayn**] (1913–83) British traitor, born in London. He joined the diplomatic service in 1934, and from 1944 acted as a Soviet agent. In 1951 he disappeared with Burgess to the USSR. >> Burgess, Guy

Macleish, Archibald [muh**kleesh**] (1892–1982) Poet, born in Glencoe, IL. He won Pulitzer Prizes for *Conquistador* (1932), *Collected Poems 1917–52* (1953), and his social drama in modern verse, *J.B.* (1959). He was assistant secretary of state (1944–5).

Macleod, Iain (Norman) [muh**klowd**] (1913–70) British Conservative statesman, born in Skipton, North Yorkshire. He became minister of health (1952–5), minister of labour (1955–9), secretary of state for the Colonies (1959–61), and chairman of the Conservative Party (1961–3). He died in office as Chancellor of the Exchequer. >> Conservative Party

Macleod, J(ohn) J(ames) R(ickard) [muh**klowd**] (1876–1935) British physiologist, born in Clunie, Perth and Kinross. In 1922 he was a member of the group who discovered insulin, for which he shared the 1923 Nobel Prize for Physiology or Medicine. >> Banting; insulin

McLuhan, (Herbert) Marshall [muh**kloo**an] (1911–80) Writer, critic, and cultural theorist, born in Edmonton, Alberta, Canada. He held controversial views on the effect of the communication media on the development of civilization, claiming that it is the media, not the ideas which they disseminate, that influence society. His books include *The Gutenberg Galaxy* (1962), *Understanding Media* (1964), and *The Medium is the Message* (with Q Fiore, 1967). >> mass media; semiotics

Macmahon, Marie Edme Patrice Maurice de, duc de (Duke of) **Magenta** [makmahon] (1808–93) Marshal and second president of the Third Republic, born in Sully,

France, descended from an Irish Jacobite family. He suppressed the Commune (1871), and succeeded Thiers as president (1873). Failing to assume dictatorial powers, he resigned in 1879, thus ensuring the supremacy of parliament. >> Commune of Paris; Thiers

McMahon, Sir William [muhk**mahn**] (1908–88) Australian statesman and prime minister (1971–2), born in Sydney, New South Wales, Australia. He took over the premiership when John Gorton lost a vote of confidence in 1971, and continued to lead his party until 1977. >> Gorton; Liberal Party (Australia)

McManaman, Steve [muhk**ma**naman] (1972–) Footballer, born in Liverpool, Merseyside. A midfielder, he served an apprenticeship at Liverpool, then joined the club, moving to Real Madrid in 1999. By mid-1998 he had won 22 caps playing for England.

Macmillan, (Maurice) Harold, 1st Earl of Stockton (1894–1986) British Conservative statesman and prime minister (1957–63), born in London. He was minister of housing (1951–4) and defence (1954–5), foreign secretary (1955), Chancellor of the Exchequer (1955–7), and succeeded Eden as premier. He gained unexpected popularity with his infectious enthusiasm, effective domestic policy ('most of our people have never had it so good'), and resolute foreign policy. >> Conservative Party; Eden

Macmillan, Sir Kenneth (1929–92) Ballet dancer, choreographer, and ballet company director. He became artistic director of the Royal Ballet in 1970, and its principal choreographer in 1977. >> Royal Ballet

McNaghten rules [muhk**nawt**n] A legal set of principles which state when a defendant who is believed to be insane should not be convicted of a crime or offence. The rules were developed subsequent to the 19th-c murder trial of Daniel McNaghten, a case in which insanity was proved. >> murder

McNamara, Robert S(trange) (1916–) US Democratic politician and businessman, born in San Francisco, CA In 1961 he joined the Kennedy administration as secretary of defense, being particularly involved in the Vietnam War. In 1968 he resigned to become president of the World Bank (until 1981). >> Democratic Party; Kennedy, John F; Vietnam War

MacNeice, Louis [muhk**nees**] (1907–63) Writer, born in Belfast. Closely associated with the British left-wing poets of the 1930s, his books include *Autumn Journal* (1939) and *The Burning Perch* (1963). >> Auden

Mâcon [ma**kõ**], ancient **Matisco** 46°19N 4°50E, pop (1995e) 39 700. Manufacturing city in C France, on the R Saône; episcopal see from the 6th-c until the Revolution; road and rail junction; commercial centre of major wine area; remains of 12th-c cathedral.

McPherson, Aimée Semple, *née* **Kennedy** (1890–1944) Religious leader, born near Ingersoll, Ontario, Canada. She founded the Church of the Foursquare Gospel and flourished as an evangelist, preaching a simple gospel of personal salvation. >> evangelicalism

Macquarie, Lachlan [muhk**kwo**ree] (1761–1824) Soldier and colonial administrator, born on the I of Ulva, Argyll and Bute. He became Governor of New South Wales in 1810 after the deposition of Bligh. Known as 'the father of Australia' he has given his name to the Lachlan and Macquarie rivers, and to Macquarie I. >> Bligh; New South Wales

Macquarie Island 54°30N 158°56W, area 123 sq km/ 47 sq mi. Island lying 1345 km/835 mi SW of Tasmania, Australia; rises to 425 m/1400 ft; nature reserve (1933); made world heritage site, 1997. >> Macquarie; Tasmania

McQueen, (Terence) Steve(n) (1930–80) Actor, born in Slater, MO, who gained a reputation as a tough unconventional rebel, both on and off the screen. Typical of his successes were *The Magnificent Seven* (1960), *Bullitt* (1968), and *An Enemy of the People* (1977).

macramé [ma**krah**mee] A type of coarse lace produced by knotting and plaiting, which enjoyed a widespread revival in the mid-19th-c. It was used to make decorative fringed borders for costumes as well as furnishings. >> lace

Macready, William Charles [muh**kree**dee] (1793–1873) Actor and theatre manager, born in London. He was the leading English actor of his day, notable for his Shakespearian roles. He became manager of Covent Garden in 1837, and of Drury Lane in 1841.

macrobiotics A 'perfect diet', influenced by Zen Buddhist philosophy at the turn of the century, thought to improve health and prolong life. All foods are seen as either *yin* (eg fruit) or *yang* (eg bread), and a strict balance of intake is prescribed. >> diet; yin and yang

macroeconomics >> **economics**

macronutrients >> **nutrients**

macro-photography or **photomacrography** The photography of small objects or details using normal or special purpose camera lenses, in contrast to **photomicrography**, which uses two-stage magnification by objective and eyepiece lenses. >> photomicrograph

McVeigh, Timothy (James) [muhk**vay**] (1968–) Convicted bomber, born in Pendleton, NY. He joined the army in 1988, took part in Operation Desert Storm, and was discharged in 1991. He became internationally known when he was charged with the bombing of the Alfred P Murrah US government building in Oklahoma City in 1995, in which 168 people died. At his trial in 1997, a Denver jury found him guilty of conspiracy and murder, and he was sentenced to death, though a series of appeals was expected. Two other conspirators, Terry Nichols (1955–) and Michael Fortier (1969–), were also later convicted.

Madagascar [mada**gas**ker], official name **Republic of Madagascar**, Malagasy **Repoblikan'i Madagasikara** pop (1995e) 13 456 000; area 587 041 sq km/226 658 sq mi. Island republic in the Indian Ocean; world's fourth largest island; length (N–S) 1600 km/980 mi; capital, Antananarivo; timezone GMT +3; population mainly Malagasy tribes; chief religions, Christianity (51%), local beliefs (47%); national language, Malagasy, with French widely used; dissected N–S by a ridge of mountains rising to 2876 m/9436 ft at Maromokotra; average annual rainfall 1000–1500 mm/40–60 in, higher in tropical coastal region; settled by Indonesians, 1st-c AD and by African traders, 8th-c; visited by Portuguese, 16th-c; French established trading posts, late 18th-c; claimed as a protectorate, 1885; autonomous overseas French territory (Malagasy Republic), 1958; independence, 1960; became Madagascar, 1977; new multi-party constitution, 1992; governed by a president and a National People's Assembly; chiefly agricultural economy. >> Antananarivo; RR1016 political leaders; *see illustration on p. 525*

Madara Rider An 8th-c bas-relief, carved out of the sheer cliff face in the village of Madara, E Bulgaria; a world heritage monument. The near life-size sculpture depicts a man on horseback trampling a lion beneath his horse's hooves. >> bas-relief; Bulgaria ℹ

Madariaga (y Rojo), Salvador de [ma<u>th</u>ari**ah**ga] (1886–1978) Spanish diplomat and writer, born in La Coruña, Spain. An opponent of the Franco regime, he was in exile 1936–76. He was the author of many historical works, especially on Spain and Spanish-America. >> Franco; Spain ℹ

mad cow disease >> **bovine spongiform encephalopathy**

madder An evergreen perennial (*Rubia tinctoria*), native to the Mediterranean; stems trailing or scrambling by means of small downwardly directed hooks; flowers small, yellow, 5-petalled; berries reddish-brown. The roots produce the dye alizarin. (Family: Rubiaceae.) >> dyestuff

Madeira (Islands) [ma**deera**], Port **Arquipélago da Madeira** 32°45N 17°00W, pop (1995e) 260 000; area 796 sq km/307 sq mi. Main island in an archipelago off the coast of N Africa, 980 km/610 mi SW of Lisbon; name often given to the group as a whole; occupied by the Portuguese, 15th-c; capital, Funchal; highest point, Pico Ruivo de Santana (1862 m/6111 ft); sugar cane, fruit, farming, fishing, wine, embroidery, crafts, tourism. >> Funchal; Portugal ℹ

Madeira, River [ma**day**ra] River in NW Brazil, the longest tributary of the Amazon; length with its headstream, the Mamoré, over 3200 km/2000 mi. >> Amazon, River; Brazil ℹ

Maderna, Bruno [ma**dair**na] (1920–73) Composer and conductor, born in Venice, Italy. In 1954 he became involved with electronic music, founding with Berio the Studio di Fonologia Musicale of Italian Radio. >> Berio; electronic music

Madhya Pradesh [**ma**dya pra**daysh**] pop (1995e) 71 588 000; area 442 841 sq km/170 937 sq mi. Largest state in India; ruled by the Gonds, 16th–17th-c, and Marathas, 18th-c; occupied by the British, 1820; called Central Provinces and Berar, 1903–50; formed under the States Reorganization Act, 1956; capital, Bhopal. >> Bhopal; India ℹ

Madison 43°04N 89°24W, pop (1995e) 202 000. Capital of state in S Wisconsin, USA; state capital, 1836; city status, 1856; airfield; railway; university (1836); trading and manufacturing centre in agricultural region. >> Wisconsin

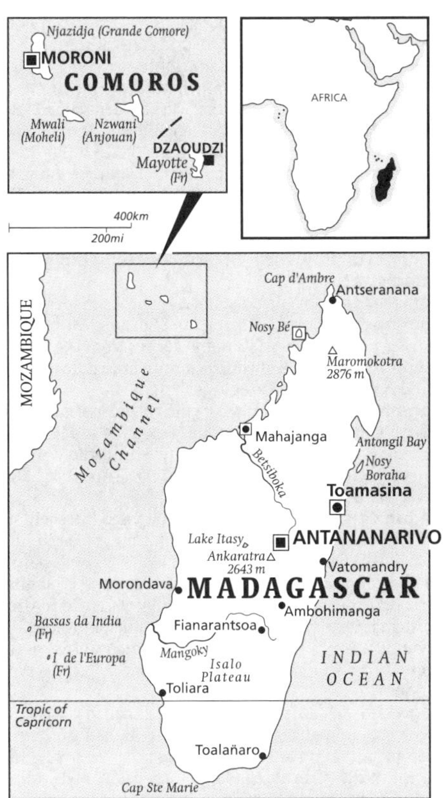

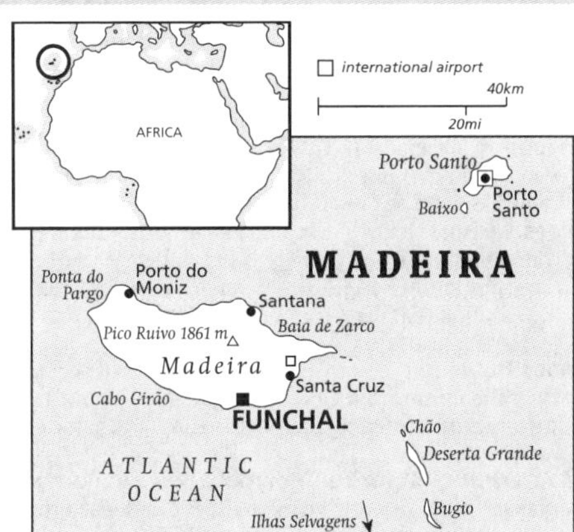

Madison, James (1751–1836) US statesman and fourth president (1809–17), born in Port Conway, VA. He played a major role in the Constitutional Convention of 1787, and became secretary of state under Jefferson. His period in office saw the European wars, and conflict with Britain (1812). >> Constitutional Convention; War of 1812

Madison Avenue A street in Manhattan, New York City, extending N to the R Harlem from Madison Square. With its glittering skyscrapers and expensive boutiques, it is seen as the centre of the advertising industry. >> New York City

Madonna, in full **Madonna Louise Ciccone** (1958–) Pop singer, born in Rochester, MI. Her first album, *Madonna* (1983), included five US hit singles. Later albums included *Like A Virgin* (1984), *True Blue*, and *You Can Dance* (1987). She has also acted in films, including *Desperately Seeking Susan* (1985) and *Shanghai Surprise* (1986). Her defiant and raunchy stage appearances were being reinforced in several media in the early 1990s, with the publication of a controversial collection of erotic photographs of herself in *Sex* (1992), alongside the album, *Erotica*. Later films include *Body of Evidence* (1993) and *Evita* (1996).

Madras [ma**dras**], official name **Chennai** (November 1996). 13°08N 80°19E, pop (1995e) 5 803 000. Capital of Tamil Nadu, SE India; fourth largest city in India, and chief port of Tamil Nadu; founded by the British, 17th-c; airport; railway; university (1857); St Mary's Church (1680), thought to be the oldest Anglican church in Asia. >> Tamil Nadu

Madrid [ma**drid**] 40°25N 3°45W, pop (1995e) 2 933 000. Capital of Spain; altitude, 655 m/2149 ft, the highest capital city in Europe; archbishopric; airport; railway; metro; two universities (1508, 1968); site of a Moorish fortress until 11th-c; under siege for nearly three years in the Civil War; capital (replacing Valladolid), 1561; El Escorial, a world heritage site; Royal Palace (18th-c), Prado Museum, El Retiro Park. >> Prado; Spain ℹ; Spanish Civil War

madrigal A polyphonic song, usually secular and without instrumental accompaniment. It was cultivated especially in Italy during the 16th-c, and is characterized by a mixture of contrapuntal and chordal style and by serious, Petrarchan, and usually amorous verses. >> polyphony; Byrd, William; Gabrieli, Andrea; Gibbons, Orlando; Lassus; Monteverdi; Palestrina; Petrarch

Madura foot >> **mycetoma**

Madurai [madu**riy**] 9°55N 78°10E, pop (1995e) 1 030 000. City in Tamil Nadu, S India; capital of the Pandyan kingdom and the Nayak dynasty; occupied by the British, 1801; airfield; railway; university (1966); large Dravidian temple complex (14th–17th-c). >> Tamil Nadu

Maecenas, Gaius (Cilnius) [miy**see**nas] (?–8 BC) Roman politician who played a key role in the rise to power of Augustus. He was a patron of the arts, encouraging such poets as Horace and Virgil. >> Augustus; Horace; Virgil

maenads [**mee**nads] In Greek mythology, 'mad women', who followed Dionysus (Bacchus) on his journeys; also known as **Bacchae** or **Bacchantes**.

Maes, Nicholas [mays] (1634–93) Painter, born in Dordrecht, The Netherlands. He specialized in small genre subjects, especially kitchen scenes (eg 'Woman Scraping Parsnips', 1655, National Gallery, London), and old women praying. >> genre painting

Maes Howe [mayz **how**] A chambered tomb of the early 3rd millennium BC on Orkney, N Scotland. It is outstanding for its construction and preservation. >> chambered tomb

Maeterlinck, Maurice (Polydore Marie Bernard) [**may**terlingk], also known as **comte** (Count) **Maeterlinck** (1862–1949) Writer, born in Ghent, Belgium. He became a disciple of the Symbolist movement, and in 1889 produced his first volume of poetry, *Les Serres chaudes* (trans Hot House Blooms). His plays include *Pelléas et Mélisande* (1892), on which Debussy based his opera. He was awarded the Nobel Prize for Literature in 1911. >> Symbolism

Mafeking, Siege of (1899–1900) The most celebrated siege of the second Boer War. Colonel Robert Baden-Powell and a detachment of British troops were besieged by the Boers from October 1899 until May 1900. The news of their relief aroused public hysteria in Britain. >> Baden-Powell; Boer Wars

Mafia (Ital 'swank') A powerful criminal organization, originating as a secret society in 13th-c Italy. It developed (along with its modern name) in the 19th-c, and from Italy moved to the USA, where it became known as *Cosa Nostra* ('Our Affair'). There have been many attempts to suppress the Mafia, but its system of family loyalty and code of silence makes progress difficult. A widespread protest against the Mafia spread in Italy during 1993, following the murder of several senior people involved in anti-Mafia law enforcement, and a number of public figures were accused of corruption and forced to resign.

Magdalenian [magda**leen**ian] The last Upper Palaeolithic archaeological culture of W Europe, named after the cave of La Madeleine, Dordogne, SW France, excavated in 1863. Many sites dated c.17 000–12 000 BC are known, notably the painted caves of Lascaux and Altamira. >> Altamira; Lascaux; Palaeolithic art; Three Age System

Magdeburg [**mahk**deboorg] 52°08N 11°36E, pop (1995e) 289 000. River-port city in C Germany; on R Elbe; former capital of Saxony, and important mediaeval trading town; badly bombed in World War 2; railway; college of medicine; college of technology (1953); cathedral (13th–16th-c). >> Germany ℹ; Saxony

Magellan, Ferdinand [ma**je**lan] (c.1480–1521) Navigator, born near Villa Real, Portugal. He sailed from Seville (1519) around the foot of South America to reach the ocean which he named the Pacific (1520). He was killed in the Philippines, but his ships continued back to Spain (1522), thus completing the first circumnavigation of the world. The Strait of Magellan is named after him.

Magellanic Clouds Two dwarf galaxies, satellites of the Milky Way, visible as cloudy patches in the S night sky, first recorded by Magellan in 1519, 52 and 58 kiloparsec away, and each containing a few thousand million stars. >> galaxy; Magellan; Milky Way

Magellan project A US space mission which mapped Venus at sub-kilometre resolution using side-looking radar from a Venus orbit. A single spacecraft was launched in 1989, and images were returned to Earth in the latter half of 1990. >> Venus (astronomy)

Magen David >> **Star of David**

Maggiore, Lake (Ital **Lago**) [ma**jaw**ray], ancient **Verbanus Lacus** area 212 sq km/82 sq mi. Second largest of the N Italian lakes; N end in the Swiss canton of Ticino; length 65 km/40 mi; width 3–5 km/1¾–3 mi; maximum depth 372 m/1220 ft. >> Italy ℹ

maggot The grub-like larval stage of many true flies. (Order: Diptera.) >> fly; larva

Maghreb [**mag**reb], Eng **Maghrib** area c.9 million sq km/ 3·5 million sq mi. Area of NW Africa including the countries of Morocco, Algeria, and Tunisia; largely occupied by the Kabyle, Shluh, and Tuareg. In Arabic, it refers to Morocco only. >> Africa

Magi [**may**jiy] **1** Members of the priestly clan of the Persians. Classical Greek and Roman writers used the term in a derogatory sense to refer to sorcerers and 'quacks'. **2** A group of unspecified number guided by a mysterious star (*Matt* 2.1–12), who came from 'the East' and presented gifts to the infant Jesus in Bethlehem. Origen (3rd-c AD) suggested they were three because of the three gifts of gold, frankincense, and myrrh. Later Christian tradition named them as Caspar, Melchior, and Balthazar. >> Jesus Christ

magic Beliefs and practices which promise a power to intervene in natural processes, but which have no scientific basis. Two common principles of magical belief are that 'like affects like' – that a cloud of smoke rising to the sky will bring rain, for example; and that 'part affects whole' – so that by burning a person's hair-cuttings, for instance, that person will be damaged.

magic mushroom A mushroom, chiefly the British liberty-cap mushroom *Psilocybe semilanceata*, which contains the hallucinogen *psilocybin*. Its use is cultish among young people, who take it as an infusion, adding it to boiling water. >> hallucinogens; mushroom

Maginot Line [**ma**zhinoh] French defensive fortifications stretching from Longwy to the Swiss border, named after André Maginot (1877–1932), French minister of defence (1924–31). The line was constructed (1929–34) to act as protection against German invasion, but Belgium refused to extend it along her frontier with Germany. The German attack of 1940 through the Low Countries largely bypassed it. >> World War 2

magistrate >> **justice of the peace; stipendiary magistrate**

Maglemosian [maglem**oh**zian] A N European Mesolithic culture extending from Britain to S Scandinavia and NW Russia c.8000–5600 BC; its name derives from the Danish *Magle Mose* ('Great Bog') on Zeeland, where notable early finds were made. >> Three Age System

magma Molten rock, formed by the partial melting of the Earth's mantle. Under certain geological conditions it may migrate upwards and solidify within the crust, or may reach the surface, where it is erupted as lava. >> igneous rock; lava

Magna Carta The 'Great Charter', imposed by rebellious barons on King John of England at Runnymede in June 1215, designed to prohibit arbitary royal acts by declaring a body of defined law and custom which the king must respect in dealing with all his free subjects. It was the first systematic attempt to distinguish between kingship and tyranny, and was of fundamental importance to the constitutional development of England. >> Barons' War; John

magnesia Magnesium oxide (MgO), also called **periclase**; a white solid, melting point 2850°C, obtained from heating magnesium carbonate, used as a heat-resisting material. **Milk of magnesia** is a suspension of hydrated magnesia used as a laxative. >> magnesium

magnesium Mg, element 12, melting point 649°C. A silvery metal, always found combined in nature, but mainly as the carbonate in magnesite ($MgCO_3$) and dolomite ($CaMg(CO_3)_2$). It is used in alloys for its lightness (density 1·7 g/cm^3), and for flares and flash bulbs because of the bright white light produced by its reaction with oxygen. Hydrated magnesium sulphate is known as *Epsom salts*. >> chemical elements; magnesia; RR1036

magnet A source of magnetic field; always with two poles, named N (north) and S (south), since no isolated single pole exists; like poles repel; opposite poles attract. A permanent magnet is usually made from a ferromagnetic material which at some time has been exposed to a magnetic field. An **electromagnet** is some suitable core material around which is wrapped a current-carrying coil. >> ferromagnetism; magnetism

magnetic disk A disk coated with magnetizable material on one or both sides. Magnetic disks are an important type of computer storage medium. Data is written to or read from a set of concentric tracks on the disk by magnetic read/write heads. Two general classes exist: the so-called *hard* disks made of rigid material, and *floppy* disks made of flexible plastic. Disks may be removable from the disk drive or non-removable. >> Bernoulli disk; floppy disk; hard disk; magnetic tape 2; minidisk

magnetic field A region of magnetic influence around a magnet, moving charge, or current-carrying wire; denoted by B, the magnetic flux density, units T (tesla), and by H, the magnetic field strength, units A/m (amps per metre) >> magnetism

magnetic flux The flow of magnetic influence from the N to S poles of a magnet, or around a current-carrying wire; symbol Φ, units Wb (weber). It is the product of magnetic flux density B (sometimes called 'magnetic field') and area. >> magnetic field 🛈; magnetism

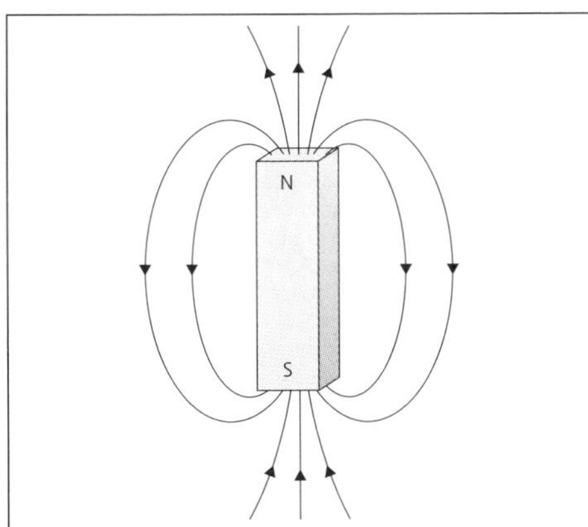

A permanent bar magnet showing lines of magnetic field; N and S denote north and south poles respectively

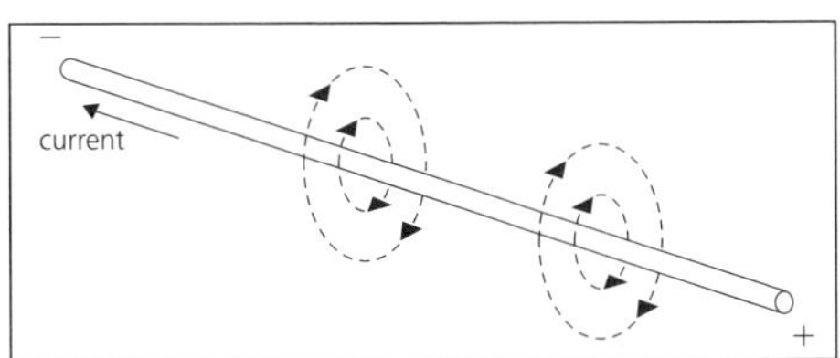

Lines of magnetic field circulate around current-carrying wires

magnetic moment A property of magnets, currents circulating in loops, and spinning charged particles that dictates the strength of the turning force exerted on the system by a magnetic field, B; symbol μ, units A.m^2 (amp.metre-squared) or J/T (joules per tesla); a vector quantity; also called the **magnetic dipole moment**. Turning force (torque), Γ is $\Gamma = \mu B \sin\theta$, where θ is the angle between μ and B directions. >> magnetization; magnon 🛈; moment 🛈; torque 🛈

magnetic poles The two points on the Earth's surface to which a compass needle points. The N and S magnetic poles have geographical co-ordinates 78·5°N 69°W and 78·5°S 111°E, and move very slowly with time. >> geomagnetic field

magnetic storm A disturbance in the Earth's magnetic field causing global disruption of radio signals and the occurrence of auroras. They are caused by the interaction of charged solar particles with the Earth's magnetic field. >> aurora; geomagnetic field

magnetic susceptibility The ratio of magnetization M to magnetic field strength H; symbol κ, expressed as a pure number. It expresses the dependence of a magnetic field in a material on an external field which results only from current in the magnetizing coils. >> magnetism; magnetization

magnetic tape 1 A clear plastic film coated with crystalline magnetic particles embedded in varnish, first demonstrated as an effective sound recording and reproducing medium in the 1930s. It has now been extended to video recording, and data storage for computers. Professional recording practice of the 1980s employed multiple-track open-reel tape, storing the sounds in digital form, while domestic use came to be dominated by the compact cassette introduced first by Philips in 1964. >> Dolby system; sound recording; tape recorder; videotape **2** A storage medium used on larger computers, the most common being 2400 ft (c.750 m) reels of 0.5 in (12.7 mm)-wide tape. In recent years, smaller format magnetic cartridge tape systems have been used as archiving ('back-up') systems for microcomputers, especially those employing Winchester disks. All magnetic-tape systems are relatively slow, compared to magnetic disks, since the access time required to obtain a particular piece of information depends on its position on the tape. >> computer; magnetic disk

magnetic vector potential A vector quantity whose rate of change with distance is related to magnetic field in a complex way; symbol A, units Wb/m (webers per metre). Electric current is the source for A, as electric charge is for electrostatic potential. >> magnetic field 🛈

magnetism Phenomena associated with magnetic fields and magnetic materials, and the study of such phenomena. All magnetic effects ultimately stem from moving electric charges, and all materials have magnetic properties. >> electromagnetism; ferromagnetism; magnet; magnetic field 🛈 / flux / moment / susceptibility / vector potential; magnetization

magnetite or **lodestone** An iron oxide mineral (Fe_3O_4) with a very strong natural magnetism. It is a valuable ore of iron. >> iron; spinel

magnetization Magnetic moment per unit volume, resulting from the individual magnetic moments contributed by molecules of the material; symbol M, units A/m (amps per metre); expresses how much a material is magnetized. >> magnetic moment; magnetism

magneto A simple machine which generates alternating current, using the principle that a current is generated when a conductor moves through a magnetic field. It is used with combustion engines to provide the power for the sparking plugs. >> electricity; magnetism

magnetosphere The region surrounding Solar System bodies having magnetic fields, in which the field is confined under the influence of the streaming solar wind. It is a teardrop-shaped region whose size and shape are constantly readjusting to the variations of the solar wind. >> aurora; solar wind; Van Allen radiation belts

magnetron A device for generating microwaves. It comprises an evacuated chamber with a central cathode surrounded by a circular anode. Electrons expelled from the cathode circle it under the influence of electric and magnetic fields. Microwave production results from resonances between the moving electrons and cavities in the anode. It is today widely used in microwave ovens. >> anode; cathode; microwaves

magnification A measure of an optical system's power to reduce or enlarge an image. It is approximately equal to the ratio of size of image to size of object. >> lens; optics

Magnitogorsk [mag**nyi**togaw(r)sk], formerly **Magnitnaya** 53°28N 59°06E, pop (1995e) 449 000. Industrial town in SW Siberian Russia, on the R Ural; built, 1929–31; airfield; railway; one of the largest centres of the metallurgical industry. >> Russia

magnitude A measure of the brightness of a celestial object. The brightest stars visible to the human eye are said to be 'first magnitude' and the dimmest as 'sixth magnitude'; equal magnitude steps are in logarithmic progression. The **apparent magnitude** of a star is its brightness measured at the Earth, which depends on distance and luminosity. More useful physically is **absolute magnitude**; this is the observed apparent magnitude converted to what the object would have at an (arbitrary) distance of 10 parsec. >> Hipparchos; luminosity; star

magnolia A deciduous or evergreen shrub or tree native to E North America and E Asia; leaves often glossy; flowers generally large, cup-shaped, with several whorls of white or pink segments. (Genus: *Magnolia*, 80 species. Family: Magnoliaceae.)

magnon In magnetic materials, oscillation in the relative orientations of atomic spins, which correspond to magnetization waves. >> magnetism

Magnusson, Magnus (1929–) British writer and broadcaster. He is chiefly known for presenting a wide range of radio and television programmes, notably the annual series of *Mastermind* (1972–97). His books include *Vikings!* (1980) and *Treasures of Scotland* (1981).

Magog >> **Gog and Magog**

magot [ma**goh**] >> **Barbary ape**

magpie A bird of the crow family (13 species); especially the **black-billed magpie** (*Pica pica*). The name is also used for black-and-white birds in several other families. >> crow

Magritte, René (François Ghislain) [ma**greet**] (1898–1967) Painter, born in Lessines, Belgium. He was a leading member of the Belgian Surrealist group in the 1920s, and in the 1960s was acclaimed in the USA as an early innovator of Pop Art. >> Pop Art; Surrealism

Magyar A Uralic language spoken as a national language by c.11 million people in Hungary, and by a further 3 million in the surrounding areas. >> Uralic languages

Magnon – 1 Spin vectors on a lines of adjacent atoms in magnetic material 2 The same line of atoms viewed from above. A wave can be associated with these spins

Mahabalipuram monuments [ma**hah**balipuram] A collection of Hindu temples at Mahabalipuram in Tamil Nadu, S India; a world heritage site. They date from the 7th–8th-c, and are noted for their rich carvings. >> Hinduism; Tamil Nadu

Mahabharata [maha**bhah**rata] The sacred book of the Hindus, its 110 000 couplets making it the longest epic in the world. Dating back to the first millennium BC, it was orally transmitted and not printed until the 19th-c. >> Hinduism; Ramayana

Maharashtra [mahah**rash**tra] pop (1995e) 85 240 000; area 307 762 sq km/118 796 sq mi. State in W India; ruled by the Muslims, 14th–17th-c; British control, early 19th-c; became a state in 1960; capital, Bombay; governed by a Legislative Council and Legislative Assembly; industry largely in Mumbai, Poona, and Thana. >> Bombay; India

Maharishi [maha**ri**shee] (Sanskrit, 'great sage') The Hindu title for a guru or spiritual leader. In the West, the teaching of Transcendental Meditation by the Maharishi Mahesh Yogi is well known. >> guru; Transcendental Meditation

Mahayana [maha**yah**na] (Sanskrit, 'greater vehicle') The form of Buddhism commonly practised in China, Tibet, Mongolia, Nepal, Korea, and Japan. It dates from about the 1st-c, when it arose as a development within Buddhism in N India. >> bodhisattva; Buddhism

Mahdi [**mah**dee] (Arabic, 'divinely guided one') The name given by Sunni Muslims to those who periodically revitalize the Muslim community. Sunnis look forward to a time before the Last Day when a Mahdi will appear and establish a reign of justice on Earth. >> Islam; Mohammed Ahmed; Sunnis

Mahé [**mah**-hay] 4°41S 55°30E; pop (1995e) 69 400; area 153 sq km/59 sq mi. Main island of the Seychelles, Indian Ocean; Victoria, capital of the Seychelles, on the NW coast; airport. >> Seychelles

mah-jong or **mah-jongg** A Chinese game, usually played by four people using 144 small tiles divided into three suits and four sets of honour tiles. The aim is to collect sequences of tiles, in the manner of rummy card games. The name means 'sparrow', a bird of mythical great intelligence, which appears on one of the tiles. >> rummy

Mahler, Gustav (1860–1911) Composer, born in Kalist, Czech Republic. His mature works consist entirely of songs and nine large-scale symphonies, with a tenth left unfinished. He is best known for the song-symphony *Das Lied von der Erde* (1908–9, The Song of the Earth).

mahogany An evergreen tree (*Swietenia mahagoni*) native to Central America and the Caribbean Is; flowers 5-petalled, yellowish, in loose clusters. It is one of several timbers commercially called mahogany, a reddish wood of high quality, heavy, hard, and easily worked. (Family: Meliaceae.) >> tree

Mahomet >> **Mohammed**

Mahratta >> **Maratha**

Maiden Castle A spectacular Iron Age hillfort near Dorchester, Dorset, UK, with multiple earthwork ramparts and ditches. The existing defences date to c.150 BC, their complex entrances remodelled c.70 BC. >> Three Age System

Maidstone 51°17N 0°32E, pop (1995e) 92 300. County town in Kent, SE England; on the R Medway; railway; birthplace of William Hazlitt. >> Hazlitt; Kent

Maier, Ulrike [**miy**er] (1965–94) Skier, born in Austria. She won the world Supergiant slalom skiing championship twice before her fatal accident during a practice run at Garmisch-Partenkirchen. She was the first women skier to be killed in a World Cup race.

Mailer, Norman [**may**ler] (1923–) Writer, born in Long Branch, NJ. His best-known novels are *The Naked and the Dead* (1948), a panoramic World War 2 novel, and *American Dream* (1964). Identified with many of the US liberal protest movements, his political studies include *The Armies of the Night* (1968, Pulitzer).

Maillol, Aristide (Joseph Bonaventure) [ma**yol**] (1861–1944) Sculptor, born in Banyuls-sur-Mer, France. He is particularly known for his representations of the nude female figure in a style of monumental simplicity and classical serenity.

mailmerge A word-processing facility which allows inserts to be placed in a standard document. It is widely used for the bulk mailing of circulars in letter form, as it gives these the semblance of having been individually produced. >> word processor

Maiman, Theodore H(arold) [**miy**man] (1927–) Physicist, born in Los Angeles, CA. After working on the maser, by 1960 he devised the first working laser. >> laser ℹ; maser; Schawlow

Maimonides, Moses [miy**mon**ideez], originally **Moses ben Maimon** (1138–1204) Jewish philosopher, born in Córdoba, Spain. A major influence on Jewish thought, he wrote an important commentary on the Mishna, and a philosophical work arguing for the reconciliation of Greek philosophy and religion. >> Mishnah

Mainbocher [**mayn**boshay], originally **Main Rousseau Bocher** (c.1890–1976) Fashion designer, born in Chicago, IL. He started his couture house in Paris in 1930, one of his creations being Mrs Wallis Simpson's wedding dress. He opened a salon in New York City in 1940, which continued until 1971. >> Edward VIII

Maine pop (1995e) 1 245 000; area 86 153 sq km/33 265 sq mi. New England state in the NE corner of the USA; the 'Pine Tree State' or 'Lumber State'; explored by the Cabots in the 1490s; settled first by the French in 1604, and by the English in 1607; separated from Massachusetts in 1820, when admitted to the Union as 23rd state; crossed by the Appalachian Mts which rise to 1605 at Mt Katahdin; dotted with over 1600 lakes; N 80% forested; capital, Augusta; largest town, Portland; S coastal strip mainly arable; main industries agriculture, forestry, fishing. >> Augusta (Maine); United States of America ℹ; RR994

mainframe computer A somewhat dated term still used to refer to very large capacity computers, and to distinguish them from the smaller computers now widely available. However, the distinction between mainframe and other computers is not always clear. >> microcomputer

maintained school In the UK, a school which receives its money from a local education authority. It is often known popularly as a 'state school', though this term is inappropriate in a country where the state does not run schools. >> independent schools; public school

maintenance A term used in England and Wales for money payments paid by one marriage partner to help support the other during or following legal separation or divorce. The payments are often referred to as *alimony*, but terminology varies (eg it is *aliment* or *periodical allowance* in Scotland). >> divorce

Maintenon, Françoise d'Aubigné, Marquise de (Marchioness of) [mĩtenõ], (1635–1719) Second wife of Louis XIV of France, born in Niort, France. In 1652 she married the crippled poet, Paul Scarron, and on his death was reduced to poverty. In 1669 she took charge of the king's two sons by Mme de Montespan. After the queen's death (1683) Louis married her secretly. She was accused of having great influence over him, especially over the persecution of Protestants. >> Louis XIV; Montespan; Scarron

Mainz [miynts], Fr **Mayence** 50°00N 8°16E, pop (1995e) 186 000. Old Roman city in Germany; on left bank of R Rhine; important traffic junction and commercial centre; railway; centre of the Rhine wine trade; Gutenberg set up his printing press here; university (1477); cathedral (mostly 11th–13th-c). >> Germany ℹ; Gutenberg

maiolica [ma**yol**ika], also (19th-c) spelled **majolica** Tin-glazed earthenware produced in Italy since before 1250. In the Renaissance period the decoration was often similar to the work of contemporary Italian painters. >> Majorca; Renaissance

maize The only cereal (*Zea mays*) native to the New World, originally tropical and developed as a major food crop by the Indians of Central America; also called **sweet corn** and **Indian corn**. It is a robust annual, its heads eaten ripe or unripe as a vegetable. The grains and foliage are used for animal fodder, and it also yields flour, starch, syrup, alcohol, and paper. (Family: Gramineae.) >> cereals

majlis [**maj**les] (Arabic 'council') Any of a number of political institutions in the Middle East, ranging from parliaments to advisory councils for rulers.

Major, John (1943–) British statesman and prime minister (1990–7), born in London. He became an MP in 1976, and rose to become chief secretary to the Treasury. He was unexpectedly made foreign secretary in Margaret Thatcher's Cabinet reshuffle in 1989, and soon after replaced Nigel Lawson as Chancellor of the Exchequer. He won the leadership contest following Mrs Thatcher's resignation, and became prime minister in November 1990. He resigned as leader of the Conservative party after they lost the 1997 general election, and was made a Companion of Honour in 1998. >> Conservative Party; Lawson; Thatcher

Majorca [ma**yaw(r)**ka], Span **Mallorca**, ancient **Balearis Major** pop (1995e) 299 000; area 3640 sq km/1400 sq mi. Largest island in the Balearics, W Mediterranean; chief town, Palma; Sierra del Alfabia rises to 1445 m/4741 ft; taken in 1229 by James I of Aragón; in the Middle Ages, famous for its porcelain (maiolica); popular tourist resort. >> Balearic Islands; Palma; Spain ℹ

majuscule [**ma**juhskyool] A form of writing in which the letters are of uniform height, as if contained within a pair of horizontal lines. Usually called CAPITAL letters, the Greek and Roman alphabets were originally written in this way. It is contrasted with the later system known as **minuscule**, in which parts of some letters extend above and below the horizontal lines ('small letters'), such as *h*, *g*. >> graphology

Makale >> **Mekele**

Makarios III [ma**ka**ryos], originally **Mihail Khristodoulou Mouskos** (1913–77) Archbishop and primate of the Orthodox Church of Cyprus, and president of Cyprus (1960–74, 1974–77), born in Ano Panciyia. He reorganized the *enosis* (union) movement, was arrested in 1956, but returned to a tumultuous welcome in 1959 to become chief Greek-Cypriot Minister in the new Greek–Turkish provisional government. >> Cyprus ℹ; Enosis

Makassar >> **Ujung Padang**

Malabo [**mal**aboh], formerly **Clarencetown** or **Port Clarence**, and **Santa Isabel** 3°45N 8°50E, pop (1995e) 12 400. Seaport capital of Equatorial Guinea, W Africa; on island of Bioko, Gulf of Guinea; founded by British in 1827; airfield. >> Bioko; Equatorial Guinea ℹ

malabsorption The failure of intestinal absorption of nutrients taken as food. In general, this results in diarrhoea, abdominal pain and distension, loss of weight, anaemia, and features of specific vitamin deficiencies. The most important cause in the UK is coeliac disease. >> coeliac disease; Crohn's disease; intestine

Malacca or **Melaka** [ma**la**ka] pop (1995e) 657 000; area

1657 sq km/640 sq mi. State in SW Peninsular Malaysia; one of the former Straits Settlements; capital, Malacca, pop (1995e) 123 000; centre of a great trading empire since the 15th-c; held at various times by the Portuguese, Dutch, and British; large Chinese population. >> Malaysia [i]

Malacca, Strait of [muhlakuh] Channel between the Malaysia Peninsula and the Indonesian island of Sumatra; 800 km/500 mi long by 50–320 km/30–200 mi wide; links the Andaman Sea to the S China Sea.

Malachi or **Malachias, Book of** [malakhiy] The last of the 12 so-called 'minor' prophetic writings of the Hebrew Bible/Old Testament; probably anonymous, since *Malachi* in Hebrew means 'my messenger'; usually dated c.510–460 BC. >> Old Testament; prophet

malachite [malakiyt] A hydrated copper carbonate mineral ($Cu_2CO_3(OH)_2$) found in weathered copper ore deposits. It is bright green in colour. >> copper

Málaga [malaga], ancient **Malaca** 36°43N 4°23W, pop (1995e) 516 000. Port in Andalusia, S Spain; founded by the Phoenicians, 12th-c BC; part of Spain, 1487; bishopric; airport; railway; car ferries to Casablanca, Tangier, Genoa; university (1972); Moorish Alcazaba, cathedral (16th–18th-c); birthplace of Picasso. >> Andalusia; Picasso; Spain [i]

Malagasy [malagasee] The peoples of the island of Madagascar, comprising about 50 ethnic groups; Malagasy languages are Austronesian. The traditional economy is based on agriculture. >> Madagascar [i]

Malamud, Bernard [malamuhd] (1914–86) Novelist and short-story writer, born in New York City. His novels include *The Natural* (1952), *The Fixer* (1966), and *Dublin's Lives* (1979).

malamute [malamyoot] >> **Alaskan malamute**

Malan, Daniel (François) [malan] (1874–1959) South African statesman and prime minister (1948–54), born in Riebeek West, South Africa. In 1939 he founded with Hertzog the reunited Nationalist Party, and in 1948 became premier and minister for external affairs, introducing the apartheid policy. >> apartheid; Hertzog

malaria A disease caused by infection with one of four species of *Plasmodium* transmitted by the bite of infected mosquitoes (*Anopheles*). The disease is endemic or sporadic through most of the tropics and subtropics. Several effective drugs are available for treatment. >> Anopheles; blackwater fever; mosquito; spleen

Malawi [malahwee], official name **Republic of Malawi** pop (1995e) 10 753 000; area 118 484 sq km/44 747 sq mi. SE African republic; capital, Lilongwe; timezone GMT +2; population largely Bantu; chief religions, Protestantism (55%), Roman Catholicism (20%), Islam (20%); official languages, English, Chichewa; unit of currency, the kwacha of 100 tambala; crossed N–S by the Great Rift Valley, containing Africa's third largest lake, L Nyasa (L Malawi); Shire highlands (S) rise to nearly 3000 at Mt Mulanje; tropical climate in S, with high year-round temperatures, 28–37°C; average annual rainfall, 740 mm/30 in; more moderate temperatures in C; visited by the Portuguese, 17th-c; European contact established by David Livingstone, 1859; Scottish church missions in the area; claimed as the British Protectorate of Nyasaland, 1891; British colony, 1907; in the 1950s joined with N and S Rhodesia to form the Federation of Rhodesia and Nyasaland; independence, 1964; republic, 1966; new constitution, 1993; governed by a president and a National Assembly, all elected for 5 years; economy based on agriculture, which employs 90% of the population. >> Banda; Lilongwe; Livingstone, David; RR1016 political leaders

Malawi, Lake >> **Nyasa, Lake**

Malay (langauge) The language of the Malay Peninsula, which has provided the modern standard language, **Bahasa Indonesia**, known as **Bahasa Malaysia** in Malaysia. A pidginized form, **Bazaar Malay**, has been a lingua franca in the region for centuries. A further variety, **Baba Malay**, is used by Chinese communities in Malaysia. >> Malay (people)

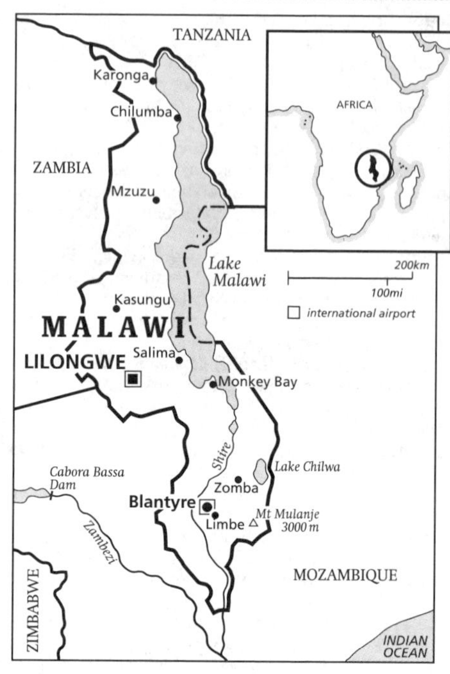

Malay (people) A cluster of Malay-speaking (Austronesian) peoples of the Malay Peninsula and neighbouring territory, including parts of Borneo and Sumatra. Hindu Indian influence on their culture is strong. >> Austronesian languages; Malay (language)

Malayalam [malayahlam] The Dravidian language associated with the S Indian state of Kerala. It has c.34 million speakers. >> Dravidian languages; Kerala

Malaysia [malayzha] pop (1995e) 20 000 000; area 329 749 sq km/127 283 sq mi. Independent federation of states in SE Asia, comprising 11 states and a federal territory in Peninsular Malaysia, and the E states of Sabah and Sarawak on the island of Borneo; capital, Kuala Lumpur; timezone GMT +8; ethnic groups include Malay (59%), Chinese (32%), Indian (9%); official language, Bahasa Malaysia (Malay), but Chinese, English, and Tamil also spoken; unit of currency, the Malaysian ringgit; mountain chain of granite and limestone running N–S, rising to Mt Tahan (2189 m/7182 ft); peninsula length 700 km/435 mi, width up to 320 km/200 mi; mostly tropical rainforest and mangrove swamp; Mt Kinabalu on Sabah, Malaysia's highest peak, 4094 m/13 432 ft; tropical climate strongly influenced by monsoon winds; high humidity; part of Srivijaya Empire, 9th–14th-c; Hindu and Muslim influences, 14th–15th-c; Portugal, the Netherlands, and Britain vied for control from the 16th-c; Singapore, Malacca, and Penang formally incorporated into the British Colony of the Straits Settlements, 1826; British protection extended over Perak, Selangor, Negeri Sembilan, and Pahang, constituted into the Federated Malay States, 1895; protection treaties with several other states (Unfederated Malay States), 1885–1930; occupied by Japanese in World War 2; Federation of Malaya, 1948; independence, 1957; constitutional monarchy of

Malaysia, 1963; Singapore withdrew from the Federation, 1965; governed by a bicameral federal parliament; head of state is a monarch elected for 5 years by his fellow sultans; advised by a prime minister and cabinet; discovery of tin in the late 19th-c brought European investment; rubber trees introduced from Brazil; minerals include iron ore, bauxite, oil, natural gas. >> Johor; Kedah; Kelantan; Kuala Lumpur; Malacca; Negeri Sembilan; Pahang; Perak; Perlis; Pinang (state); Sabah; Sarawak; Selangor; Singapore [i]; Terengganu; RR1016 political leaders

Malcolm III, nickname **Malcolm Canmore** ('Big Head') (c.1031–93) King of Scots (1058–93), the son of Duncan I. He conquered S Scotland, but did not become king until he had defeated and killed Macbeth (1057). He launched five invasions of England. >> Macbeth

Malcolm, George (John) (1917–97) Harpsichordist and conductor, born in London. He was Master of the Music at Westminster Cathedral (1947–59), since when he has earned a wide reputation as a harpsichord soloist. >> harpsichord

Malcolm X, originally **Malcolm Little** (1925–65) Political leader, born in Omaha, NE. He entered the Nation of Islam (Black Muslims) and became a leading spokesman for its separatist policies, but left the organization in 1964. Since his assassination in Harlem he has become a symbol of urban black resistance and anger. >> Black Muslims

Maldives [**mol**diyvz], formerly **Maldive Islands**, official name **Republic of Maldives**, Dhivehi **Dhivehi Jumhuriya** pop (1995e) 251 000; land area 300 sq km/116 sq mi. Island archipelago in the Indian Ocean; 670 km/416 mi SW of Sri Lanka; capital, Malé; timezone GMT +5; population mostly of Aryan origin; official religion, Islam (Sunni); official language, Dhivehi, but English widely spoken; unit of currency, the Maldivian rupee (*rufiyaa*) of 100 laaris; small and low-lying islands, with sandy beaches fringed with coconut palms; average annual rainfall, 2100 mm/83 in; average daily temperature, 22°C; former dependency of Ceylon; British protectorate, 1887–1965; independence, 1968; governed by a president, a ministers' *Majlis* (cabinet), and a citizens' *Majlis*; agriculture, fishing, shipping, tourism. >> Indian Ocean; Islam; Malé; RR1016 political leaders

Malé [**ma**lee], Dhivehi **Daviyani** 4°00N 73°28E, pop (1995e) 64 800; area 2 sq km/0·77 sq mi. Chief atoll and capital of the Maldives; airport. >> Maldives

Malebranche, Nicolas [malbrãsh] (1638–1715) Philosopher, born in Paris. His major work is *De la recherche de la vérité* (1674, Search after Truth), which defends many of Descartes' views. >> Descartes

maleic acid [ma**lay**ik] $C_4H_4O_8$, IUPAC *cis*-**butenedioic acid**, melting point 139°C. A geometrical isomer of fumaric acid, but with a much lower melting point. >> acid; fumaric acid; IUPAC

Malenkov, Georgiy Maksimilianovich [**mal**yenkof] (1902–88) Soviet statesman and premier (1953–5), born in Orenburg, Russia. He was involved in the purges of the 1930s under Stalin, and succeeded Stalin as Party first secretary and premier. He was replaced by Khrushchev. >> communism; Stalin

Malesherbes, Chrétien (Guillaume de Lamoignon) de [malzairb] (1721–94) French statesman, born in Paris. At Louis XVI's accession (1774) he was made secretary of state for the royal household, instituting prison and legal reforms, but resigned in 1776. Despite his reforming zeal, he was mistrusted as an aristocrat during the Revolution, and was guillotined. >> French Revolution [i]; Louis XVI

Malevich, Kazimir (Severinovich) [ma**lay**evich] (1878–1935) Painter, born in Kiev, Ukraine. With Mondrian he was one of the earliest pioneers of pure abstraction, founding the Suprematist movement. >> abstract art; Suprematism

Mali [**mah**lee], official name **Republic of Mali**, Fr **République de Mali** pop (1995e) 10 173 000; area 1 240 192 sq km/478 841 sq mi. Republic in W Africa; capital, Bamako; timezone GMT; chief ethnic groups, Mande tribes; chief religion, Islam (90%); official language, French, with local languages widely spoken; unit of currency, the Mali franc; landlocked country on the fringe of the Sahara; lower part of the Hoggar massif (N); arid plains 300–500 m/1000–1600 ft; mainly savannah land in the S; main rivers the Niger, Bani, and Sénégal; featureless desert land (N) with little rainfall; a Sahelian transition zone over a third of the country, with a 3-month rainy season; mediaeval state controlling the trade routes between savannah and Sahara, reaching its peak in the 14th-c;

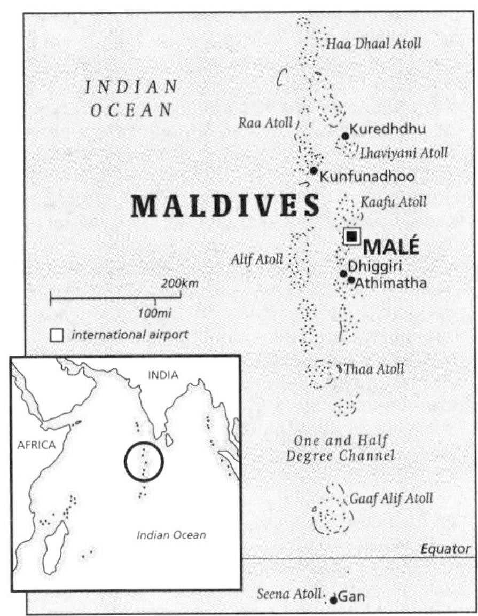

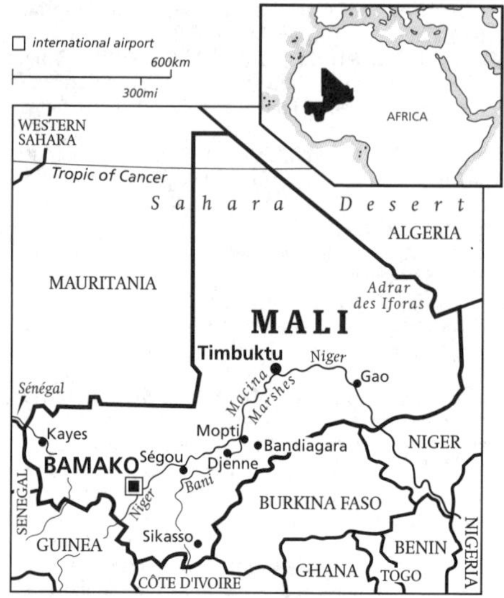

governed by France, 1881–95; territory of French Sudan (part of French West Africa) until 1959; partnership with Senegal as the Federation of Mali, 1959; separate independence, 1960; military regime, 1968; further coup, 1991, led to new constitution, 1992; governed by a president, prime minister, and National Assembly; economy mainly subsistence agriculture; crops severely affected by drought conditions. >> Bamako; sahel; Songhai; RR1016 political leaders

malic acid HOOC–CH_2–CH(OH)–COOH, IUPAC **2-hydroxybutanedioic acid**, melting point 100°C. An acid found in unripe fruit, especially apples. >> acid; IUPAC

Malinke [ma**ling**kay] or **Mandingo** A cluster of autonomous Mande-speaking agricultural peoples of Mali, Guinea, Senegal, and neighbouring areas. >> Mande

Malinowski, Bronislaw (Kasper) [mali**nof**skee] (1884–1942) Anthropologist, born in Kraków, Poland. He was the pioneer of 'participant observation' as a method of fieldwork (notably, in the Trobriand Is), and a major proponent of functionalism in anthropology. >> anthropology

Malipiero, (Gian) Francesco [mali**pyay**roh] (1882–1973) Composer, born in Venice, Italy. He wrote symphonic, operatic, vocal, and chamber music, and edited Monteverdi and Vivaldi.

mallard A dabbling duck (*Anas platyrhynchos*) found near water throughout the N hemisphere; blue patch on wing; male with green head and thin white neck ring; the ancestor of nearly all domestic ducks. (Family: Anatidae.)

Mallarmé, Stéphane [malah(r)**may**] (1842–98) Symbolist poet, born in Paris. A leader of the Symbolist school, his works include *Hérodiade* (1864), and *L'Après-midi d'un faune* (1865, published 1876), which inspired Debussy's prelude. >> Debussy; Symbolism

Malle, Louis [mal] (1932–95) Film director, born in Thumeries, France. The success of his second film *Les Amants* (1958, The Lovers) brought recognition, and he received critical acclaim for such works as *Calcutta* (1969), *Le Souffle au coeur* (1971, Dearest Love), *Au Revoir Les Enfants* (1987, Goodbye, Children), and *Damage* (1993).

mallee [**ma**lee] A scrubland vegetation zone in the semi-arid parts of SE and SW Australia. Dwarf eucalyptus shrubs dominate, growing to 2 m/6 ft in height. >> gum tree

mallee fowl A megapode bird (*Leipoa ocellata*) native to Australia; brown with white spots on wings; inhabits dry scrubland; also known as **lowan**. (Family: Megapodiidae.) >> mallee; megapode

mallow N temperate annual and perennial herb; flowers with petals, rose, purple, or white, often with dark veins; stamens numerous, united into a central column; fruit a flat whorl of 1-seeded segments. (Genus: *Malva*, 40 species. Family: Malvaceae.)

Malmö [**mal**moe] 55°35N 13°00E, pop (1995e) 241 000. Fortified seaport in SW Sweden; third largest city in Sweden; under Danish rule until 1658; railway. >> Sweden ℹ

malnutrition A deficiency of protein or of one or more of the other essential ingredients of a diet. Undernutrition occurs when insufficient food energy is taken and, when prolonged, may lead to profound weight loss. The insufficiency may involve one or several vitamin deficiencies. >> kwashiorkor; pellagra; protein; rickets; scurvy; vitamins ℹ

Malory, Sir Thomas (?–1471) English writer, known for his work, *Le Morte d'Arthur* (The Death of Arthur). From Caxton's preface, we are told that Malory was a knight, and that he finished his work in the ninth year of the reign of Edward IV (1461–70). >> Arthur; Caxton

Malouf, David [ma**loof**] (1934–) Novelist, born in Brisbane, Queensland, Australia. His books include *An Imaginary Life* (1978), *The Great World* (1991, Miles Franklin Award), *Remembering Babylon* (1993), and *Conversations at Curlow Creek* (1997).

Malraux, André (Georges) [mal**roh**] (1901–76) French statesman and novelist, born in Paris. Minister of cultural affairs (1960–9), he is known for his novels, notably *La Condition humaine* (1933, Man's Fate; Prix Goncourt) and *L'Espoir* (1937, Man's Hope).

Malta, official name **Republic of Malta**, Maltese **Repubblika ta' Malta**, ancient **Melita** pop (1995e) 370 000; area 316 sq km/122 sq mi. Archipelago in the C Mediterranean Sea, comprising the islands of Malta (246 sq km/95 sq mi), Gozo (67 sq km/26 sq mi), and Comino (2·7 sq km/1 sq mi), with some uninhabited islets; 93 km/58 mi S of Sicily; capital, Valletta; timezone GMT +1; population, European; chief religion, Roman Catholic Apostolic; languages, English and Maltese; unit of currency, the Maltese lira of 100 cents; highest point, 252 m/830 ft; well-indented coastline; dry summers and mild winters; average annual rainfall c.400 mm/16 in; average daily winter temperature, 13°C; controlled at various times by Phoenicia, Greece, Carthage, and Rome; conquered by Arabs, 9th-c; given to the Knights Hospitallers, 1530; British Crown Colony, 1815; important strategic base in both World Wars; for its resistance to heavy air attacks, the island was awarded the George Cross in 1942; achieved independence, 1964; republic, 1974; governed by a president, prime minister, cabinet, and House of Representatives; airport; tourism and ship repair are the major industries; naval dockyards now converted to commercial use; developing as a transshipment centre for the Mediterranean. >> Comino; Gozo; Maltese (language); Valletta; RR1016 political leaders; *see illustration on p. 533*

Maltese (language) A language spoken by 300 000 people on the island of Malta, related to the W dialects of Arabic. It is the only variety of Arabic written in the Roman alphabet. >> Arabic; Malta ℹ

Maltese (zoology) A small toy spaniel developed in Italy (name probably derived from the Sicilian town of Melita); colour uniform; hair straight, coat very long and thick, reaching ground; legs short, hidden by coat. >> spaniel

Malthus, Thomas Robert (1766–1834) Economist, born near Dorking, Surrey. His *Essay on the Principle of Population*

(1798) argued that the population has a natural tendency to increase faster than the means of subsistence, and that efforts should be made to cut the birth rate, either by self-restraint or birth control – a view which later was widely misrepresented under the name of **Malthusianism**.

maltose [**mawl**tohs] $C_{12}H_{22}O_{11}$. A condensation dimer of two molecules of glucose which are produced when it is hydrolysed; also known as **malt sugar**. It is derived from the limited hydrolysis of starch. >> dimer; glucose; hydrolysis; starch

malt sugar >> **maltose**

Malvern [**mawl**vern] or **Great Malvern** 52°07N 2°19W, pop (1995e) 31 400. Town in Hereford and Worcester, WC England; popular health resort in the Malvern Hills; railway; Elgar lived and is buried here. >> Elgar; Hereford and Worcester

Malvinas [mal**vee**nas] >> **Falkland Islands**

mamba A venomous African snake of the family Elapidae; strong venom; two species: the **black mamba** (*Dendroaspis polylepis*), correctly the **black-mouthed mamba**, with body dark brown or grey, never black; and the **green mamba** (Dendroaspis angusticeps). >> snake

Mamet, David (Alan) [**ma**met] (1947–) Playwright and film director, born in Chicago, IL. His works include the plays *American Buffalo* (1976) and *Speed the Plow* (1987), the screenplays *The Postman Always Rings Twice* (1981) and *The Untouchables* (1986), the films (as director) *House of Games* (1986) and *Homicide* (1991), and the novel *The Village* (1994). He received the Pulitzer Prize for Drama in 1984.

Mamluks or **Mamelukes** Slave soldiers who constituted the army of the Ayyubid sultanate established in Egypt by Saladin in the 1170s. Their commanders (*amirs*) created a professional army of high quality. They continued to rule in Egypt until their massacre by Mohammed Ali in 1811. >> Ottoman Empire; Saladin

mammal An animal characterized by having mammary glands in the female, along with several other features, such as a covering of hair (very sparse in some mammals). Mammals are divided into **placental mammals**, in which the young develop in a womb (the *uterus*) and are born in an advanced stage of development; **marsupials**, in which the young are born in a very early stage and develop outside the mother's body, usually in a pouch; and **monotremes** (or **egg-laying mammals**), in which the young hatch from an egg outside the body of the mother. (Class: Mammalia, c.4000 species.) >> animal; Bovidae; Camelidae; deer; insectivore; mammary gland; marsupial ℹ; monotreme; Mustelidae; *see illustration on p.534*

mammary gland In female mammals, a gland responsible for the production and release of milk to feed their young. They are located on the surface of the chest or abdomen, and may be concentrated into an udder. >> gland

mammoth A specialized elephant originating in Africa, which spread in the early Pleistocene epoch through Eurasia and North America. The **woolly mammoth** was abundant in tundra regions, and had long hair and a thick fat layer for insulation. It died out c.12 000 years ago. (Order: Proboscidea.) >> elephant; Pleistocene epoch; tundra

Mammoth Cave A system of subterranean passages and caverns created by limestone erosion and extending over 480 km/300 mi in W Kentucky. The area is a world heritage site. >> Kentucky

mammoth tree A massive evergreen conifer (*Sequoiadendron giganteum*) confined to the W slopes of the Sierra Nevada Mts, California; also called **giant redwood**, **California big tree**, or **wellingtonia**. Age estimates range from 400–4000 years. (Family: Taxodiaceae.) >> conifer

Man, Isle of pop (1995e) 73 800; area 572 sq km/221 sq mi. British island in the Irish Sea; rises to 620 m/2034 ft at Snaefell; capital, Douglas; ruled by the Welsh, 6th–9th-c, then by the Scandinavians, Scots, and English; purchased by the British Government between 1765 and 1828, and now a crown possession (not part of the UK); the island has its own parliament, the bicameral Court of Tynwald, which consists of the elected House of Keys and the Legislative Council; acts of the British parliament do not generally apply to Man; Manx survived as an everyday language until the 19th-c; airport; ferries; used as a tax haven; annual Tourist Trophy motorcycle races. >> Celtic languages; Douglas; United Kingdom ℹ

Managua [ma**nag**wa] 12°06N 86°18W, pop (1995e) 1 240 000. Commercial centre and capital city of Nicaragua; badly damaged by earthquake in 1931 and 1972, and by civil war in the late 1970s; airport; railway; university (1961). >> Nicaragua ℹ

manakin A small bird native to C and tropical South America; short bill, wings, and (usually) tail; toes partially joined; noted for its complex display. (Family: Pipridae, c.53 species.)

Manama [ma**na**ma], Arabic **al-Manamah** 26°12N 50°38E, pop (1995e) 160 000. Seaport capital of Bahrain, a free trade port. >> Bahrain ℹ

Manasseh, Prayer of [ma**na**se] Short, eloquent writing of the Old Testament Pseudepigrapha, ostensibly the work of Manasseh, a wicked king of Judah (c.687–642 BC), expressing his personal confession of sin and petition for pardon. Most scholars date the work from the 2nd-c BC to the 1st-c AD. >> Pseudepigrapha

manatee [mana**tee**] An aquatic mammal, found from Brazil to SE USA, and in W Africa; large rounded body; short head with square muzzle; front legs are flippers; no hind legs; tail ends in a flat horizontal disc. (Order: Sirenia. Family: Trichechidae, 3 species.) >> mammal ℹ

Manaus or **Manáos** [ma**nã**os] 3°06S 60°00W, pop (1995e) 1 212 000. River-port city in N Brazil, on the N bank of the R Negro; the collecting point for produce of a vast area; founded, 1660; free zone established, 1967; airfield; university (1965); Teatro Amazonas opera house (1896, rebuilt 1929 and 1974). >> Amazon, River; Brazil ℹ

Manchester, Lat **Mancunium** 53°30N 2°15W, pop (1995e) 423 000. Metropolitan district in Greater Manchester urban area, NW England, on the R Irwell; Roman town: focal point of English cotton industry during the

Mammals

Industrial Revolution; became a city in 1853; railway; airport; connected to the Irish Sea by the 57 km/35 mi Manchester Ship Canal (1894); UK's second largest commercial centre; cultural centre for NW; Hallé Orchestra; three universities (1880, 1824, 1992): cathedral (15th-c): Free Trade Hall (1843); football league teams, Manchester

City (Blues), Manchester United (Reds). >> Industrial Revolution; Manchester, Greater; Manchester Ship Canal

Manchester, Greater pop (1995e) 2 581 000; area 1287 sq km/497 sq mi. Metropolitan county of NW England, consisting of 10 boroughs; metropolitan council abolished in 1986; county town, Manchester. >> Manchester

Manchester Ship Canal An artificial waterway in the UK linking Manchester with the Mersey estuary. The canal, which is 57 km/35 mi long, was opened in 1894. >> canal; Manchester

Manchukuo or **Manzhouguo** [manchookwoh] A Japanese puppet-state established in 1932 in Manchuria. Puyi, the last Qing emperor, was its nominal head. The regime ended with the defeat of Japan in 1945. >> Manchuria; Puyi; Sino–Japanese Wars 2

Manchuria A region of NE China; mountainous area, sparsely populated by nomadic tribes; Manchus overthrew Ming dynasty to become the last Chinese emperors (Qing dynasty); vast natural resources of timber and minerals; Russian military control, 1900; captured by Japan, 1931, and part of puppet state of Manchukuo; Russian control re-asserted, 1945; Chinese sovereignty recognized, 1950, but border area with Russia a continuing focus of political tension. >> China i; Manchukuo; Manchus; Puyi; Qing dynasty

Manchus A nomadic people of Jürchen stock in Manchuria who ruled all China from 1644 to 1912 under the Qing dynasty. There are now about 2·5 million Manchu people in China. >> Manchuria; Qing dynasty

Mancini, Henry [man**see**nee], popular name of **Enrico Mancini** (1924–94) Composer, born in Cleveland, OH. His Oscar-winning compositions include the songs 'Moon River' (1961) and 'Days of Wine and Roses' (1962), and the film scores for *Breakfast at Tiffany's* (1961) and *Victor/Victoria* (1982). He composed more than 80 film scores, including the theme for the *Pink Panther* films, and won 20 Grammy Awards.

mandala [**man**dala] Circular designs in Hindu and Buddhist religious art, representing the universe or other aspects of their beliefs. They are used as a focus and aid to concentration in worship and meditation. >> Buddhism; Hinduism

Mandalay [manda**lay**] 21°57N 96°04E, pop (1995e) 677 000. River-port city in C Myanmar; on R Ayeyarwady; airfield; railway; university (1964); commercial centre, tourism; Kuthodaw Pagoda. >> Myanmar i

Mandarin >> **Chinese**

mandarin A citrus fruit (*Citrus reticulata*) with yellow to deep orange-red fruits, very like small oranges but with thin, loose rind. Its species include satsumas and tangerines. (Family: Rutaceae.) >> citrus; orange; satsuma; tangerine

mandates A system under which former territories of the German and Ottoman Empires were administered by the victorious powers of World War 1 under supervision by the League of Nations. Britain and France acquired mandates in the Middle East and Africa, while Belgium acquired Rwanda-Urundi, South Africa acquired South-West Africa, and Australia and New Zealand acquired New Guinea and Western Samoa. >> League of Nations

Mande [**man**day] A cluster of Mande-speaking agricultural peoples of W Sudan, Sierra Leone, Liberia, and Côte d'Ivoire. They include the Bambara, Dyula, Malinke, Mende, and Soninke. >> Malinke

Mandela, Nelson (Rolihlahla) [man**de**la] (1918–) South African statesman and president (1994–), born in Transkei, South Africa. He was a lawyer in Johannesburg, then joined the African National Congress in 1944. For the next 20 years he directed a campaign of defiance against the South African government, and in 1964 was sentenced to life imprisonment. The 1980s saw a co-ordinated international campaign for his release, finally successful in 1990. He was elected president of the African National Congress in 1991, and was closely involved in constitutional negotiations with President de Klerk which led to South Africa's first all-race elections in 1994. In 1993 he shared the Nobel Peace Prize with de Klerk for their work towards dismantling apartheid, and in 1995 was awarded the Order of Merit. He retired from active politics at the 1999 general election. >> African National Congress; apartheid; Mandela, Winnie; racism; South Africa i

Mandela, Winnie [man**de**la], also **Madikizela-Mandela**, popular name of **Nomzano Zaniewe Winifred Mandela** (1934–) Former wife of Nelson Mandela, born in Bizana, South Africa. She married Mandela in 1958, and was subsequently banned, restricted, detained, and jailed a number of times. In 1990, after her husband was released from prison, she took an increasingly prominent role in the African National Congress (ANC), until her conviction on charges of kidnapping and assault. In 1992, the Mandelas divorced. She continued to operate as a militant figure under ANC colours, making a political comeback in late 1993, and given a role in the 1994 government as deputy minister for arts, culture, science, and technology (dismissed in 1995). She figured prominently in the proceedings of the Truth and Reconciliation Commission in 1997. >> Mandela, Nelson

Mandelbrot, Benoit (1924–) Mathematician, born in Warsaw. A central figure in the development of fractals, his book *The Fractal Geometry of Nature* (1982) was important in demonstrating the potential application of fractals to natural phenomena. His name is applied to a particular set of complex numbers which generate one type of fractal (the *Mandelbrot set*), whose visually attractive properties have captured public interest since the 1980s. >> fractals

Mandelson, Peter [**man**delson] (1954–) Politician, born in London. He became an MP in 1992, and in 1996 worked exclusively on the Labour Party election campaign. In the 1997 government he became a Minister without Portfolio – an influential member of the cabinet, responsible for assisting the prime minister in policy matters, and in 1998 was appointed president of the Board of Trade and secretary of state for trade and industry. He was forced to resign in December of that year following criticism of his actions in not declaring a loan from Treasury minister Geoffrey Robinson which had enabled him to make a private house purchase in 1996.

Mandelstam, Osip [**man**duhlstam] (1891–1938) Poet, born in Warsaw. His early poems led to arrest (1934) by the Soviet authorities, and his death was reported from Siberia in 1938. His collected works were published in three volumes (1964–71).

Mandeville, Jehan de or **Sir John** [**man**devil] (14th-c) The name assigned to the compiler of a famous book of travels, published apparently in 1366, and translated from the French into many languages.

Mandingo >> **Malinke**

mandolin A plucked string instrument, about 60 cm/2 ft long, developed in the 18th-c. It has a pear-shaped body somewhat like a lute's, a fretted fingerboard, and a pegbox set back at an angle. There are four pairs of steel strings, played with a plectrum. >> plectrum; string instrument 2 i

mandrake A thick-rooted perennial (*Mandragora officinalis*) native to Europe; leaves in a rosette; flowers blue; berries yellow to orange. Once widely regarded for its medicinal and narcotic properties, it has been the subject of many superstitions. (Family: Solanaceae.) >> narcotics

mandrill A baboon (*Mandrillus sphinx*) native to W African forests; stocky with short limbs and thick coat; tail minute; buttocks red-blue; naked face with scarlet muzzle and bright blue, ridged cheeks (especially in male). >> baboon; drill

Manet, Edouard [manay] (1832–83) Painter, born in Paris. His 'Déjeuner sur l'herbe' (1863, Luncheon on the Grass) was rejected by the Salon, and although the equally provocative 'Olympia' was accepted in 1865, the Salon remained hostile to him. He exhibited in the *Salon des Refusés*, and helped to form the group out of which the Impressionist movement arose. >> Impressionism (art); Salon

mangabey [**mang**gabee] An Old World monkey, native to tropical Africa; slender with long tail, long coat; pronounced whiskers on sides of face. (Genus: *Cercocebus*, 4 species.) >> Old World monkey

manganese Mn, element 25, melting point 1244°C. A transition metal, density about 7·4 g/cm^3, always found combined in nature, but mainly as the dioxide, MnO_2. It is mainly used in alloy steels. Potassium permanganate is a convenient and strong oxidizing agent in aqueous solution. >> alloy; chemical elements; metal; oxidation; RR1036

mange [maynzh] A contagious skin disease of domestic animals. It results from infestation with several types of mites which burrow into the skin, causing itching and irritation. >> itch; mite; skin ℹ

mangel-wurzel >> **beet**

mangetout [mãzh **too**] >> **pea** ℹ

mango An evergreen tree (*Mangifera indica*) growing to 18 m/60 ft, native to SE Asia; flowers tiny, white, with 4–5 petals; fleshy fruit 7–10 cm/2¾–4 in, oval to kidney-shaped, yellow flushed with red. It is grown for the sweet-tasting, edible fruit. (Family: Anacardiaceae.)

mangrove Any of several unrelated tropical or subtropical trees, all sharing similar structure and biology, growing on coastal and estuarine mud-flats. All possess either aerial roots or *pneumatophores*, special breathing roots which help aerate the root system in swampy ground. (Main genera: *Rhizophora*, 7 species, and *Brugeria*, 6 species. Family: Rhizophoraceae. Also *Avicennia*, 14 species. Family: Avicenniaceae.)

Manhattan pop (1995e) 1 515 000, area 72 sq km/28 sq mi. An island forming one of the five boroughs of the City of New York, New York State, E USA; settled by the Dutch as part of New Netherlands in 1626; taken by the British in 1664; major financial and commercial centre based around Wall Street and the World Trade Center; headquarters of the United Nations; Broadway, Empire State Building, Greenwich Village; six universities; named after a local tribe of Indians. >> New York City

Manhattan project The codename for the most secret scientific operation of World War 2, the development of the atomic bomb, undertaken in the USA from 1942. The first atomic weapon was detonated at Alamogordo, New Mexico (16 Jul 1945). >> atomic bomb

Manichaeism [mani**kee**izm] or **Manichaeanism** A religious sect founded by the prophet Manes (or Mani) (c.216–76), who began teaching in Persia in 240. His teaching was based on a primaeval conflict between the realms of light and darkness. The purpose of religion is to release the particles of light imprisoned in matter, and Buddha, the Prophets, Jesus, and finally Manes have been sent to help in this task. The Zoroastrians executed Manes, but the sect survived in the West until the 10th-c. >> Zoroastrianism

Manila [ma**nil**a] 14°36N 120°59E, pop (1995e) 1 783 000. Capital of the Philippines on Luzon I; founded, 1571; taken by the USA during the Spanish–American War, 1898; badly damaged in World War 2; airport; railway; several universities (earliest, 1611). >> Philippines ℹ

Manila hemp >> **abaca**

manioc >> **cassava**

Manipur [**man**ipoor] pop (1995e) 1 977 000; area 22 356 sq km/8629 sq mi. State in NE India; British rule in 1891; administered from the state of Assam until 1947, when it became a union territory; became a state in 1972; capital, Imphal; governed by a Legislative Assembly. >> India ℹ

Manitoba [mani**toh**ba] pop (1995e) 1 159 000; area 649 950 sq km/ 250 945 sq mi. Province in C Canada; known as the 'land of 100 000 lakes', the result of glaciation; land rises in W and S to 832 m/2730 ft at Mt Baldy; capital, Winnipeg; trading rights given to Hudson's Bay Company, 1670; French claims ceded to the British under the Treaty of Paris, 1763; settlement on the Red R from 1812; joined the confederation, 1870, provoking insurrection under Riel; major development of area after railway reached Winnipeg in the 1880s; governed by a lieutenant-governor and a Legislative Assembly; cereals (especially wheat), livestock, vegetables, fishing, timber, hydroelectric power, mining, tourism. >> Canada ℹ; Métis; Red River Rebellion; Riel; Winnipeg

manitou [**man**itoo] A term used by the Algonkin Indians of the E Woodlands of North America to designate the supernatural world and to identify any manifestation of it. >> Algonkin

Manizales [mani**sal**ays] 5°03N 75°32W, pop (1995e) 297 000. City in C Colombia; altitude 2153 m/7064 ft; founded, 1848; railway; centre of coffee area; university (1950); cathedral (unfinished). >> Colombia ℹ

Mankowitz, (Cyril) Wolf [**mang**kohvits] (1924–98) Writer, playwright, and antique dealer, born in London. His fiction includes the novel *A Kid for Two Farthings* (1953), the play *The Bespoke Overcoat* (1954), the films *The Millionairess* (1960) and *Casino Royale* (1967), and the musicals *Expresso Bongo* (1958–9), *Pickwick* (1963), and *Stand and Deliver!* (1972).

Mann, Thomas (1875–1955) Novelist, born in Lübeck, Germany. His works include *Buddenbrooks* (1901), *Der Tod in Venedig* (1913, Death in Venice; filmed, 1971), and *Der Zauberberg* (1924, The Magic Mountain), for which he won the Nobel Prize for Literature in 1929. His best-known work was a modern version of the mediaeval legend, *Doktor Faustus* (1947).

manna The name of several edible plant products, some of which have been proposed as the biblical food dropped from heaven during the Israelites' flight from Egypt. Lichen (*Lecanora esculenta*) from Asia Minor, the source of lichen bread and manna jelly, curls into balls when dry and blows in the wind. >> lichen; Old Testament

Mannerism A form of art and architecture prevalent in France, Spain, and especially Italy during the 16th-c, characterized by overcrowded detail, and an irrational manipulation of classical elements, for playful or startling effect. In art, leading Mannerists included Giulio Romano, Pontormo, and Parmigiano, whose pictures are painted with jewel-like colours, and sculptors such as Cellini. >> Cellini; Giulio Romano; Parmigiano; Pontormo; *trompe l'oeil*

Mannheim [**man**hiym] 49°30N 8°28E, pop (1995e) 320 000. Commercial and manufacturing river port in Germany; on right bank of R Rhine; one of the largest inland harbours in Europe; seat of the Electors Palatine, 18th-c, when it became a cultural centre; badly bombed in World War 2; railway; university (1907); castle. >> Germany ℹ

mannikin A small seed-eating bird, native to Africa S of

Sahara, India, and SE Asia; inhabits forest, open country, and cultivation. (Genus: *Lonchura*, 23 species. Family: Estrildidae.)

Manning, Henry Edward, Cardinal (1808–92) Roman Catholic cardinal, born in Totteridge, Hertfordshire. At the Council of 1870, he was a zealous supporter of the infallibility dogma; and, named cardinal in 1875, he continued as a leader of the Ultramontanes. >> infallibility; Ultramontanism

manometer A device for measuring pressure exerted by or within a fluid (gas or liquid). It usually refers to various U-tube methods, pressure being shown by the difference in the height of the fluid (such as mercury) in the two arms of the tube, one arm being connected to the fluid whose pressure is being measured.

manor A basic feature of English society from the 11th-c to the 15th-c. The 'typical' manor used to be regarded as an agricultural estate coincident with the village, and comprising the lord's estate (demesne) or home farm, attached villein tenements providing labour services on the demesne, and free tenements owing rents. In reality, there was a pronounced lack of uniformity. Manors, which might be concentrated or dispersed, frequently cut across villages; some consisted solely or largely of demesne; others contained only peasant tenements; and labour dues varied widely. >> Domesday Book; feudalism; villein

Mansard or **Mansart, François** [mãsah(r)] (1598–1666) Architect, born in Paris. He brought a simplified adaptation of the Baroque style into use in France, and made fashionable the high-pitched type of roof which bears his name. >> Baroque (art and architecture)

Mansell, Nigel [**man**sl] (1954–) Motor-racing driver, born in Birmingham, West Midlands. He entered Formula 1 racing in 1980, retiring in 1992 after winning the driver's championship with eight wins. He joined the Haas–Newman Indy car-racing team in the USA, becoming Indy car champion in 1993, his first year, briefly returned to Formula 1 in 1995, driving for McLaren, then retired. >> Indianapolis; motor racing

Mansfield, Katherine, pseudonym of **Kathleen Mansfield Murry**, *née* **Beauchamp** (1888–1923) Short-story writer, born in Wellington, New Zealand. She married John Middleton Murry in 1918. Her chief works are *Bliss* (1920), *The Garden Party* (1922), and *Something Childish* (1924). >> Murry, John Middleton

manslaughter An English legal term for a form of unlawful homicide, covering a wide spectrum of culpability, including behaving recklessly or negligently but without an intention to kill; known as *culpable homicide* in Scottish law. Mitigating factors, such as provocation, may reduce an offence from murder to manslaughter (often called **voluntary manslaughter** in the USA). Grossly negligent behaviour or omission, in certain circumstances, which results in unintended death may also constitute the offence (often called **involuntary manslaughter** in the USA). There is a separate statutory offence of causing death by reckless driving; this is often called *vehicular homicide* in the USA. >> homicide; murder

Manson, Charles (1934–) Cult leader, born in Cincinnati, OH. Members of his cult conducted a series of grisly murders in California in 1969, including that of actress Sharon Tate. He and his accomplices were spared the death penalty due to a Supreme Court ruling against capital punishment. >> Polanski

manta ray Largest of the devil rays, exceeding 6 m/20 ft in width and 1300 kg/2800 lb in weight; mouth broad, situated across front of head. (Genus: *Manta*. Family: Mobulidae.) >> devil ray

Mantegna, Andrea [man**ten**ya] (c.1431–1506) Painter, born near Vicenza. In 1460 he settled in Mantua, where his major works included nine tempera pictures representing the 'Triumph of Caesar' (1482–92). He was also an engraver, architect, sculptor, and poet. >> tempera

mantis A medium to large insect that has a well-camouflaged body and a mobile head with large eyes; waits motionless for insect prey to approach before striking out with its grasping, spiny forelegs; in some species, the female eats the male head-first during copulation. (Order: Mantodea, c.1800 species.) >> insect [i]; praying mantis

Mantle, Mickey (Charles) (1931–95) Baseball player, born in Spavinaw, OK. The American League's Most Valuable Player in 1956, he once hit a home run measured at a record 177 m/565 ft. >> baseball [i]

Mantoux test [man**too**] Intradermal injection of an extract prepared from tuberculosis bacilli. The skin reaction measures the immune response to tuberculosis. When positive, the patient is known to suffer from or to have suffered from tuberculosis. It is named after French physician Charles Mantoux (1877–1947). >> immunity; injection; tuberculosis

mantra [**man**truh] In Hindu ritual, the belief that the repetition of a special phrase or word in meditation and devotion helps to concentrate the mind and aids in the development of spiritual power. >> Hinduism

Mantua [**man**tyua], Ital **Mantova** 45°10N 10°47E, pop (1995e) 61 700. City in Lombardy, N Italy, on R Mincio; founded in Etruscan times; railway; ringed by ancient walls and bastions; cathedral (10th–18th-c). >> Italy [i]; Lombardy

Manu [ma**noo**] In Hindu mythology, the forefather of the human race, to whom the Manu Smirti ('Lawbook of Manu') is attributed. >> Hinduism

manure Organic material which is used to fertilize land. It usually consists of livestock excrement, generally mixed with straw or other litter used in the animals' living quarters. >> humus; soil

Manuzio, Aldo >> **Aldus Manutius**

Manx cat A breed of domestic cat, native to the Isle of Man; a British short-haired type; thick double-layered coat; no tail; also known as a **rumpy**. >> cat

Manzoni, Alessandro [mant**soh**nee] (1785–1873) Novelist and poet, born in Milan, Italy. He published his first poems in 1806, and spent the next few years writing sacred lyrics and a treatise on the religious basis of morality. The work which gave him European fame is his historical novel, *I promessi sposi* (1825–7, The Betrothed). He was a strong advocate of a united Italy, and became a senator of the kingdom in 1860. Verdi composed his *Requiem* in Manzoni's honour.

Maoism Specifically, the thought of Mao Zedong (Tse-tung), and more broadly a revolutionary ideology based on Marxism–Leninism adapted to Chinese conditions. Maoism shifted the focus of revolutionary struggle from the urban workers or proletariat to the countryside and the peasantry. There were three main elements: strict Leninist principles of organization, Chinese tradition, and armed struggle as a form of revolutionary activity. Since his death, his use of the masses for political purposes, his economic reforms, and his conception of political power have been increasingly criticized inside and outside China as seriously misguided and too rigid. >> Mao Zedong; Marxism-Leninism

Maori [**mow**ree] Polynesian people who were the original inhabitants of New Zealand. The first of them arrived, probably from the Marquesas Is, about AD 800, and by 1800 numbered over 100 000. In the 19th-c they came to be outnumbered and dominated by European (*pakeha*) settlers. By 1896 their population had shrunk to 42 200.

There has been some improvement in the 20th-c. Numbers have risen (279 000 in 1981), and since the 1970s they have become politically more assertive. The Maori language has been officially encouraged, and they have obtained the return of some of their land. >> Anglo-Maori Wars; Polynesia

Mao Zedong [mow dzuhdoong], also spelled **Mao Tse-tung** (1893–1976) Leader and leading theorist of the Chinese communist revolution, born in Hunan province, the son of a farmer. He took a leading part in the May Fourth Movement (1919), then became a Marxist and a founding member of the Chinese Communist Party (1921). After the break with the Nationalists in 1927, he evolved the guerrilla tactics of the 'people's war', and in 1934 led the Communist forces on the Long March to Shanxi. He increased the political and military power of his party, ousted the regime of Jiang Jieshi from the Chinese mainland, and proclaimed the new People's Republic of China (1949) with Mao as both Chairman of the Chinese Communist Party and President of the Republic. In 1958 he launched his Great Leap Forward in rural and agricultural development, and in 1965 the Cultural Revolution. After his death, a strong reaction set in against 'cult of personality' and the excessive collectivism which had emerged, but his anti-Stalinist emphasis on rural industry and on local initiative was retained by his successors. >> communism; Cultural Revolution; Great Leap Forward; Long March; Maoism; May Fourth Movement

map The graphic representation of spatial information about a place on a plane surface through the use of symbols and signs. Maps are generally produced for specific purposes (eg *topographical* maps show relief and terrain features; *thematic* maps illustrate particular features, such as maps of population density). >> cartography; isoline; map projection [i]; surveying; topography

maple A member of a large genus of deciduous trees, native to N temperate regions; leaves variable in shape but typically palmately lobed with 3–13 toothed lobes; flowers in clusters, small, greenish, purple, or red; characteristic fruit of two winged seeds fused at base, eventually splitting apart, the wings acting as propellers. Many species produce striking autumn colours, especially reds and purples. Maple syrup is obtained from the sap of the **sugar maple** (*Acer saccharum*). (Genus: *Acer*, 200 species. Family: Aceraceae.) >> palmate

Mappa Mundi [**map**a **mun**dee] (Lat 'map of the world') A celebrated 13th-c map of the world, owned by Hereford Cathedral, Hereford, UK. The map is on vellum, measuring 163 × 137 cm/64 × 54 in, and shows the world as a round plate, with Jerusalem centrally located. In 1988 there was a public outcry over proposed plans to sell the map, to help raise funds for the Cathedral. The proposal was subsequently withdrawn, following assistance given by the National Heritage Memorial Fund. >> Hereford

map projection The method of portraying the spherical surface of the Earth on a flat surface. Because a sphere is three-dimensional in form, and a map two-dimensional, there is inevitably some distortion: the representation of distance (true scale), direction (true bearing), area, and shape cannot be shown correctly together on the same map. Consequently different map projections have been developed. The greatest distortions occur when a large area, such as the whole of the Earth's surface, is being mapped. >> Mercator's projection

Maputo [ma**poo**toh], formerly **Lourenço Marques** (to 1976) 25°58S 32°32E, pop (1995e) 1 181 000. Seaport capital of Mozambique, visited by the Portuguese, 1502; capital of Portuguese East Africa, 1907; airport; railway; university (1962); an outlet for several SE African countries. >> Mozambique [i]

Maquis [ma**kee**] The local name given to the dense scrub in Corsica; name adopted in German-occupied France by the resistance groups. >> World War 2

marabou A large stork (*Leptoptilos crumeniferus*) native to Africa S of Sahara; also known as the **marabou stork**; head and neck naked; nests in trees. (Family: Ciconiidae.) >> adjutant; stork

Maracaibo [mara**kiy**boh] 10°44N 71°37W, pop (1995e) 1 346 000. Second largest city in Venezuela, on NW shore of L Maracaibo; airport; two universities (1891, 1973); oil production and processing. >> Venezuela [i]

Maracaibo, Lake [mara**kiy**boh] (Span **Lago de**) area 13 000 sq km/5000 sq mi. Lake in NW Venezuela; length, c.210 km/130 mi; contains one of the world's greatest oilfields. >> Venezuela [i]

maracas [muh**ra**kuhs] A pair of rattles, originally gourds filled with dried seeds, used as a rhythm instrument in Latin American and occasionally Western orchestral music. >> idiophone

Maradona, Diego [mara**do**na] (1960–) Footballer, born in Lanus, Argentina. In June 1982 he became the world's most expensive footballer when he joined Barcelona for £5 million. He captained Argentina to their second World Cup in 1986, only for his career to founder amid accusations of drug-taking. Following a 15-month ban, he returned by popular demand, though without a club, to the World Cup side as captain in 1994, but was again suspended from the team following a positive drug test. He signed for Santos in 1995 and announced his retirement in 1997. >> football [i]

maral >> **red deer**

Marat, Jean Paul [mara] (1743–93) French revolutionary politician, born in Boudry, Switzerland. Elected to the National Convention, he became a leader of the Mountain, and advocated radical reforms. He was fatally stabbed in his bath by a Girondin supporter, Charlotte Corday; thereafter he was hailed as a martyr. >> Corday; French Revolution [i]; Girondins; Mountain, the

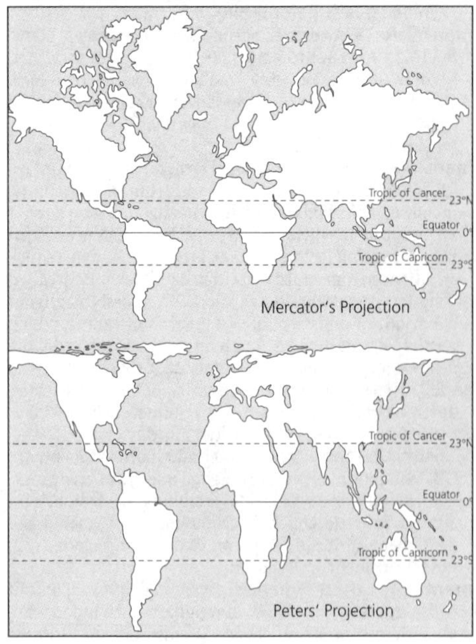

Map projections

Maratha or **Mahratta** [ma**rah**ta] A Marathi-speaking people of Maharashtra, W India. Historically they are famed as warriors and for promoting Hinduism. >> Hinduism; Maharashtra

marathon A long-distance running race, normally on open roads, over the distance 42 km 195 m/26 mi 385 yd. The race was introduced at the first modern Olympic Games in 1896 to commemorate the run of the Greek courier (according to legend, Pheidippides) who ran the c.39 km/24 mi from Marathon to Athens in 490 BC with the news of a Greek victory over the Persian army. The current marathon distance was first used at the 1908 London Olympics. The distance was standardized in 1924. It is now a popular event for the non-competitive enthusiast, with many thousands competing in the annual marathons in London, Boston, and New York City. It was supplemented in the 1980s by the **half-marathon**, run over the distance 21 km/13 mi 192½ yd. >> Marathon, Battle of

Marathon, Battle of (490 BC) The decisive Athenian victory over the Persians on the E coast of Attica, which brought the First Persian War to an end. >> marathon; Persian Wars

Marbella [mah(r)**bay**a] 36°30N 4°57W, pop (1995e) 77 400. Port and resort on the Costa del Sol, Andalusia, S Spain. >> Costa del Sol; Spain ℹ

marble A metamorphic rock formed by the recrystallization of limestone and dolomite. It is white when pure, but its impurities give it a distinctive coloration. >> limestone; metamorphic rock

Marburg [**mah(r)**boorg] 50°49N 8°36E, pop (1995e) 75 400. City in Germany; on the R Lahn; railway; university (1527); castle (15th–16th-c). >> Germany ℹ

Marc, Franz (1880–1916) Artist, born in Munich, Germany. He helped to found the *Blaue Reiter* group in 1911. Most of his paintings were of animals (eg 'Tower of the Blue Horses', 1911, Minneapolis) portrayed in forceful colours. >> *Blaue Reiter, der*

marcasite [**mah(r)**kaseet] An iron sulphide mineral (FeS_2). It is found in sedimentary rocks, and also associated with major ore deposits of the Mississippi Valley. >> sedimentary rock

Marceau, Marcel [mah(r)**soh**] (1923–) Mime artist, born in Strasbourg, France. His white-faced character, Bip, became famous from his appearances on stage and television throughout the world. Since 1978 he has been head of the *Ecole de Mimodrame Marcel Marceau*. >> mime

Marches, the, Ital **Marche** pop (1995e) 1 453 000; area 9693 sq km/3741 sq mi. The area of EC Italy between the Apennines and the Adriatic Sea, centred on Ancona. Except for the narrow coastal plain, it is mostly mountainous.

marchioness >> **marquess**

March to the Sea >> **Sherman, William Tecumseh**

Marciano, Rocky [mah(r)si**ah**noh], originally **Rocco Francis Marchegiano**, nickname **the Rock from Brockton** (1923–69) Heavyweight boxing champion, born in Brockton, MA. He made his name by defeating the former world champion, Joe Louis, in 1951. When he retired in 1956 he was undefeated as world champion. >> boxing ℹ; Louis, Joe

Marconi, Guglielmo [mah(r)**koh**nee] (1874–1937) Inventor, born in Bologna. He pioneered wireless telegraphy in Italy and England, sending signals across the Atlantic in 1901, and shared the Nobel Prize for Physics in 1909. >> telegraphy

Marco Polo >> **Polo, Marco**

Marco Polo's sheep >> **argali**

Marcos, Ferdinand (Edralin) [**mah(r)**kos] (1917–89) Philippines statesman and president (1965–86), born in Ilocos Norte, Philippines. His regime as president was marked by increasing repression and political murders (notably, the assassination of Benigno Aquino in 1983). He was overthrown in 1986 by a popular front led by Corazon Aquino. He went into exile in Hawaii, where he and his wife, **Imelda**, fought against demands from US courts investigating charges of financial mismanagement and corruption. His body was returned for burial in 1993, and soon afterwards Imelda was convicted of corruption and sentenced to 18 years imprisonment. She was released on bail, appealed against her sentence, and was acquitted in 1998. Still commanding a great deal of popular support, she was re-elected to congress for Leyte province in 1996. >> Aquino; Philippines ℹ

Marcus Aurelius Antoninus >> **Aurelius**

Marcuse, Herbert [mah(r)**koo**zuh] (1898–1979) Marxist philosopher, born in Berlin. An influential figure of the Frankfurt School, his books include *Reason and Revolution* (1941) and *Eros and Civilization* (1955). >> Marx

Mar del Plata [**mah(r)** thel **pla**ta] 38°00S 57°30W, pop (1995e) 438 000. Port in E Argentina; founded in 1874; one of the prime holiday resorts of South America; railway; airfield; two universities (1958, 1962). >> Argentina ℹ

Mardi Gras [**mah(r)**dee **grah**] The French name (literally 'fat Tuesday') for Shrove Tuesday, the day before the beginning of Lent; Mardi Gras carnivals, beginning some time before Shrove Tuesday, are held in many places. >> Carnival; Lent; Shrove Tuesday

Marduk [**mah(r)**duk] Originally the patron deity of the city of Babylon. He later became the supreme god of Babylonia. >> Babylon

Marfan's syndrome [**mah(r)**fan] An inherited disease of connective tissue in which arms and legs grow to abnormal lengths; also known as **arachnodactyly**. It is named after French paediatrician Bernard Jean Antoinin Marfan (1858–1942).

Margaret (of Scotland), St (c.1046–93) Scottish queen, born in Hungary, sister of Edgar the Atheling. She married the Scottish king, Malcolm Canmore, and did much to assimilate the old Celtic Church to the rest of Christendom. She was canonized in 1250. Feast day 16 November or 19 June. >> Christianity; Edgar the Atheling; Malcolm III

Margaret (Rose), Princess (1930–) British princess, second daughter of George VI and sister of Queen Elizabeth II, born in Glamis Castle, Angus. In 1960 she married **Antony Armstrong-Jones** (divorced, 1978), who was created Viscount Linley and Earl of Snowdon in 1961. The former title devolved upon their son, **David Albert Charles** (1961–), who married Serena Alleyne Stanhope in 1993. They also have a daughter, **Sarah Frances Elizabeth** (1964–), who married Daniel Chatto in 1994, and they have a son **Samuel David Benedict Chatto** (1996–). >> Snowdon, Earl of

Margaret of Anjou [ãzhoo] (1430–82) Queen Consort of Henry VI of England from 1445, born in Lorraine, France, the daughter of René of Anjou. During the Wars of the Roses, she was a leading Lancastrian. Defeated at Tewkesbury (1471), she was imprisoned in the Tower for four years, until ransomed by Louis XI. >> Henry VI; Roses, Wars of the

Margaret Tudor (1489–1541) Queen of Scotland, born in London, the eldest daughter of Henry VII. She became the wife of James IV of Scotland (1503) and the mother of James V, for whom she acted as regent. >> Tudors

margarine A butter-substitute that does not contain dairy fat, usually made from vegetable oils and skimmed milk, and supplemented with vitamins A and D. The degree of hydrogenation of the original oil determines how much remains of the original polyunsaturates. >> hydrogenation; polyunsaturated fatty acids; vitamins ℹ

margay [**mah(r)**gay] A rare member of the cat family (*Felis wiedii*), found from N Mexico to N Argentina; pale with ring-like dark spots; rear feet adapted for climbing. >> Felidae

marguerite [mah(r)ge**reet**] >> **ox-eye daisy**

Mari [**mah**ree] The most important city on the middle Euphrates in the third and second millennia BC until its destruction c.1759 BC by the Babylonians. It was the centre of a vast trading network in NW Mesopotamia. >> Babylonia; Mesopotamia

maria [ma**riy**a] (singular **mare** [**mah**ray]) Dark regions mainly on the nearside of the Moon. They are flat plains of basalt formed 3–3·9 thousand million years ago. Dense concentrations of material beneath the maria are known as *mascons*. >> basalt; Moon

Mariana Islands, in full **Commonwealth of the Northern Mariana Islands** pop (1995e) 51 000; area 471 sq km/ 182 sq mi. Group of 14 islands in the NW Pacific, c.2400 km/ 1500 mi E of the Philippines; capital, Saipan; mainly volcanic; held by the USA under UN mandate after World War 2, 1947–78; separate status, 1975; self-governing commonwealth of the USA, 1978–90; trusteeship ended 1990. >> United States Trust Territory of the Pacific Islands

Marianas Trench An oceanic trench off the I of Guam and the N Marianas Is, Pacific Ocean. Its deepest point, Challenger Deep, 11 040 m/36 220 ft, is the Earth's maximum ocean depth. >> Pacific Ocean

Maria Theresa (1717–80) Archduchess of Austria, Queen of Hungary and Bohemia (1740–80), born in Vienna, the daughter of Emperor Charles VI. Her Habsburg claim led to the War of the Austrian Succession. In 1741 she received the Hungarian crown, and in 1745 her husband was elected Holy Roman Emperor. Military conflict was renewed in the Seven Years' War, and by 1763 she was finally forced to recognize the status quo of 1756. >> Austrian Succession, War of the; Habsburgs; Seven Years' War

mariculture The cultivation of marine fish, shellfish, and algae; distinguished from **aquaculture**, which includes both freshwater and saltwater organisms. Practices vary from raising fish, shellfish, and algae in protected enclosures to releasing salmon from hatcheries in the hope of catching them years later when they return to the same waters to spawn.

Marie Antoinette (Josèphe Jeanne) (1755–93) Queen of France, born in Vienna, the daughter of Maria Theresa and Francis I, and sister of Leopold II. She was married to the Dauphin, afterwards Louis XVI (1770), to strengthen the Franco-Austrian alliance, and exerted a growing influence over him. She aroused criticism by her extravagance and opposition to reform, and helped to alienate the monarchy from the people. After the king's execution, she was arraigned before the Tribunal and guillotined. >> French Revolution [i]; Louis XVI

Marie Celeste An American 103-ft brigantine, found abandoned in the mid-Atlantic in 1872. She had left New York for Genoa, and was encountered by an English ship 400 miles off the Portuguese coast. There were plenty of supplies on board, as well as the crew's personal possessions, but the ship's lifeboat was missing, as were several navigational papers and instruments, suggesting that everyone had left anticipating some danger, and had been unable to return. Several speculative accounts of the mystery were propounded, and the event continues to intrigue over a century later. The ship continued in service, despite its reputation, sinking off Haiti in 1885.

Marie de France (12th-c) Poet, born in Normandy, France. She spent much of her life in England, where she wrote several verse narratives based on Celtic stories.

Marie de Médicis [maydeesees], Ital **Maria de' Medici** [**may**dichee] (1573–1642) Queen Consort of Henry IV of France, born in Florence, Italy. After her husband's death (1610) she acted as regent for her son (later Louis XIII), but her capricious behaviour led to her confinement in Blois when Louis assumed royal power (1617). Further intrigues led to her exile in 1630. >> Medici

Marie Louise (1791–1847) Empress of France, born in Vienna, the daughter of Francis I of Austria. She married Napoleon in 1810 (after his divorce from Joséphine), and in 1811 bore him a son, who was created King of Rome and who became Napoleon II. >> Napoleon I

marigold A name applied to several different species of the daisy family, Compositae. >> African / pot marigold

marijuana or **marihuana** >> **cannabis**

marimba In modern orchestras and pop groups, a percussion instrument resembling a xylophone, but with a lower compass and played with soft beaters. >> percussion [i]; xylophone

Mariner programme A series of spacecraft launched by NASA to begin the exploration of the inner and outer Solar System. The programme included the first planetary flyby (Mariner 2, Venus, Dec 1962), the first mission to Mercury (Mariner 10, Mar 1974, Sep 1974, and Mar 1975), and the first detailed observations of Jovian, Saturnian, and Uranian systems (Mariner *Jupiter-Saturn* – renamed *Voyager* – 1979–86). >> NASA; Solar System; RR970

Marines Soldiers, under naval command, who nevertheless are equipped and organized to make war on land. Marines have been used as combat forces in their own right, specializing in such operations as commando raiding and amphibious assault. >> Royal Marines

Marinetti, Filippo (Tommaso) Emilio [mari**ne**tee] (1876–1944) Italian writer, born in Alexandria, Egypt. He published the manifesto for Futurism in 1909, his ideas influencing several painters and sculptors. >> Futurism

Marini, Marino [ma**ree**nee] (1901–80) Sculptor, born in Pistoia, Italy. He worked mainly in bronze in a traditional figurative style, his favourite subjects including horses and riders, portraits, and dancers. >> bronze

Marino, Dan [ma**ree**noh] (1961–) Player of American football, born in Pittsburgh, PA. An outstanding quarterback with the Miami Dolphins, in the 1984 season he gained 5084 yards passing to create a National Football League record. >> football [i]

marionettes >> **puppetry**

Maritain, Jacques [mareetĩ] (1882–1973) Catholic philosopher and diplomat, born in Paris. His philosophical writings include *Les degrés du savoir* (1932, The Degrees of Knowledge), but he is best known outside France for his many writings on art, politics, and history. >> Aquinas; Bergson

Maritime Trust A national organization in the UK to restore, maintain, and display ships of historic or technical importance. It was set up in 1969, on the initiative of Prince Philip.

Mariupol [mari**up**ol], formerly **Zhdanov** 47°05N 37°34E, pop (1995e) 528 000. Seaport in Ukraine, at the mouth of R Kalmius; founded, 1779; airfield; railway; noted mud-bath resort. >> Ukraine [i]

Marius, Gaius (c.157–86 BC) Roman general and politician, born in Arpinum. Famous for his victories over Jugurtha (105 BC), the Teutones (102 BC), and the Cimbri (101 BC), it was by his army reforms that he made his greatest impact on the state. His final years were dominated by his rivalry with Sulla. >> Cinna; Jugurtha; Sulla

Marivaux, Pierre (Carlet de Chamblain de) [mareevoh] (1688–1763) Playwright, born in Paris. He wrote many comedies on romantic themes, such as *Le Jeu de l'amour et du hasard* (1730, The Game of Love and Chance). His affected style, full of witty plays on words, came to be known as 'Marivaudage'.

marjoram [**mah(r)**joram] A somewhat bushy perennial (*Origanum vulgare*), native to Europe, the Mediterranean, and Asia; flowers small, 2-lipped, white or purplish-pink, in dense spikes. It is cultivated as a culinary herb, often under the name **oregano**. (Family: Labiatae.) >> herb

Mark, Gospel according to The second book of the New Testament canon, the shortest of the four gospels; anonymous, but traditionally attributed to John Mark. It places relatively greater emphasis on Jesus's miracle-working, opposers, and death. The Gospel begins abruptly, and may have ended equally abruptly, since the disputed stories of the resurrection appearances in *Mark* 16.9–20 are likely to be a late addition.

Mark, St, also called **John Mark** (fl.1st-c) Described in the New Testament as 'John whose surname was Mark' (*Acts* 12.12, 25), and a helper of the apostles Barnabas and Paul during their first missionary journey. He is often considered the Mark who is accredited in 2nd-c traditions with the writing of the second Gospel. Feast day 25 April. >> Barnabas; Paul, St

Mark Antony >> **Antonius, Marcus**

Markarian galaxy >> **galaxy**

market economy An economic system where prices, wages, and what is made and sold are determined by market forces of supply and demand, with no state interference. The contrast is with a *command economy*, where the state takes all economic decisions. >> free trade; laissez-faire

market gardening The intensive production of horticultural crops on smallholdings, especially fruit and vegetables for local markets. It may incorporate pick-your-own enterprises, where labour is scarce. >> horticulture; intensive farming

marketing The management of a business with the customer in mind. It aims to identify a market where a potential exists for profitable business, and to take the necessary steps to satisfy that market by careful planning of the 'marketing mix' or the 'Four Ps': product, price, place, and promotion (including advertising). >> marketing board; telemarketing

marketing board A statutory body which has the power to control some aspect(s) of production, processing, or marketing for a specific commodity. Most frequently used for agricultural commodities, it is particularly common in North America. >> agriculture

markhor [**mah(r)**kaw(r)] A wild goat (*Capra falconeri*) native to the mountains of S Asia; the largest goat; long horns extremely thick, close (or joined) at base, with sharp spiral ridge around outside. >> goat

Markievicz, Constance (Georgine), Countess [mah(r)-**kyay**vich], *née* **Gore-Booth** (1868–1927) Irish nationalist, born in London, married to the Polish **Count Casimir Markievicz**. She fought in the Easter Rising (1916), and was sentenced to death but reprieved. Elected the first British woman MP in 1918, she did not take her seat. >> Easter Rising; nationalism

Markova, Dame Alicia [mah(r)**koh**va], originally **Lilian Alicia Marks** (1910–) Ballerina, born in London. She danced with the Diaghilev company 1925–9, and became well known for her appearances with Sadler's Wells (later, the Royal Ballet) and the London Festival Ballet. >> ballet

Markov chain In mathematics, a chain of events in which the probability of moving from one state to another depends on the existing state. The notion is named after the Soviet mathematician Andrei Andreevich Markov (1856–1922).

Markowitz, Harry M [**mah(r)**kovits] (1927–) Economist, born in Chicago, IL. He shared the 1990 Nobel Prize for Economics for developing the theory of the rational behaviour involved in portfolio selection under uncertainty. >> Miller, Merton; portfolio theory

Marks (of Broughton), Simon Marks, Baron (1888–1964) Businessman, born in Leeds, West Yorkshire. In 1907 he inherited the 60 Marks and Spencer 'penny bazaars', which his father Michael had built up from 1884. In collaboration with Israel (later Lord) Sieff (1899–1972), his brother-in-law, he developed Marks and Spencer into a major retail chain, the 'St Michael' brand label becoming a guarantee of high quality at a reasonable price.

marl Carbonate-rich clay deposits formed by the weathering of impure limestones. >> clay; limestone

Marlborough, John Churchill, 1st Duke of [**mah(r)l**bruh] (1650–1722) English general, born in Ashe, Devon. In 1678 he married Sarah Jennings (1660–1744), a close friend and attendant of Princess Anne, through whom he obtained advancement. He commanded the British forces in the War of the Spanish Succession, winning several great victories – Donauwörth and Blenheim (1704), Ramillies (1706), Oudenaarde and the capture of Lille (1708) – for which he was richly rewarded with Blenheim Palace and a dukedom. Forced by political interests to align himself with the Whig war party (1708), his influence waned with theirs after 1710. He was dismissed on charges of embezzling, and left England until the accession of George I (1714), when he was restored to his former offices. >> Anne; Blenheim Palace; Spanish Succession, War of the; Whigs

Marley, Bob, popular name of **Robert Nesta Marley** (1945–81) Singer, guitarist, and composer of reggae music, born near Kingston, Jamaica. With his band, **the Wailers**, he popularized reggae in the 1970s. He was a disciple of Rastafarianism. >> Rastafarianism; reggae

marlin Any of several large, fast-swimming, highly agile billfishes widespread in warm seas; length up to 4·5 m/14¾ ft; highly prized as sport fish. (Genera: *Makaira*, *Tetrapturus*. Family: Istiophoridae.)

Marlowe, Christopher (1564–93) Playwright, born in Canterbury, Kent. He was the most significant of Shakespeare's predecessors in English drama. His *Tamburlaine the Great* (c.1587) shows his discovery of the strength and variety of blank verse, and this was followed by *The Jew of Malta* (c.1590), *The Tragical History of Dr Faustus* (c.1592), partly written by others, and *Edward II* (c.1592). He led an irregular life, and was fatally stabbed at Deptford in a tavern brawl.

Marmara [**mah(r)**mara] or **Marmora, Sea of**, Turkish **Marmara Denizi**, ancient **Propontis** area 11 474 sq km/4429 sq mi. Sea in NW Turkey, between Europe (N) and Asia (S); connected (E) with the Black Sea through the Bosporus and (W) with the Aegean Sea through the Dardanelles; length, c.200 km/125 mi. >> Bosporus; Dardanelles; Istanbul; Turkey [i]

Marmes Man Prehistoric human remains found in 1965 on R J Marmes's ranch in Washington, USA. About 11 000 years old, they rank as early evidence for the peopling of North America from E Asia. >> *Homo* [i]

marmoset [**mah(r)**moset] A monkey-like primate, native to South America; thick fur, long tail; thumb not opposable; nails long, curved, pointed. (Family: Callitrichidae, 17 species.) >> monkey [i]; tamarin; titi

marmot [**mah(r)**mot] A large, ground-dwelling squirrel native to Europe, Asia, and North America; length, c.750 mm/30 in; lives in burrows; hibernates for up to 9 months. (Genus: *Marmota*, 11 species.) >> squirrel; woodchuck

Marne, Battle of the (1914) A battle early in World War 1, in which General Joffre's French armies and the British

Expeditionary Force halted German forces which had crossed the Marne, thus ending German hopes of a swift victory. >> British Expeditionary Force; Joffre; World War 1

Marne, River, ancient **Matrona** River in C France rising in the Langres Plateau; meets the R Seine near Paris; length 525 km/326 mi; scene of two major battles in World War 1 (1914, 1918). >> World War 1

Maronite Church A Christian community originating in Syria in the 7th-c, claiming origin from St Maro (d.407). Condemned for its Monothelite beliefs in 680, the Church survived in Syria and elsewhere, and since 1182 has been in communion with the Roman Catholic Church. >> Monothelites

Marprelate Tracts Seven pamphlets covertly published in London, 1587–9. The pseudonymous author, 'Martin Marprelate', satirized the Elizabethan Church and bishops, and favoured a Presbyterian system. The Tracts led to statutes against dissenting sects and sedition (1593). >> Presbyterianism

Marquesas Islands [mah(r)**kay**saz], Fr **Iles Marquises** pop (1995e) 8600; area 1189 sq km/459 sq mi. Mountainous, wooded volcanic island group of French Polynesia, 1184 km/736 mi NE of Tahiti; includes Nuku Hiva (where Herman Melville lived), and Hiva Oa (where Gauguin painted); acquired by France, 1842; chief settlement, Taiohae (Hiva Oa). >> French Polynesia; Gauguin; Melville

marquess or **marquis** In the UK, a nobleman holding a title in the second rank of the peerage. The word (from Latin *Marchio*) originally denoted a commander of a march, or frontier area. The wife of a marquess is a **marchioness**. >> peerage

marquetry Veneers (thin sheets of highly polished woods of different colours) applied to furniture in ornamental patterns. A popular technique throughout W Europe in the later 17th–18th-c, the finest examples were by French cabinetmakers of the reigns of Louis XIV, XV, and XVI. **Parquetry** is marquetry arranged in geometrical patterns, popular in England in the second half of the 17th-c.

Márquez, Gabriel García [**mah(r)**kez] (1928–) Novelist, born in Aracataca, Colombia. His best-known work is *Cien años de soledad* (1967, One Hundred Years of Solitude). He received the Nobel Prize for Literature in 1982.

marquis >> **marquess**

Marrakesh or **Marrakech** [mara**kesh**] 31°49N 8°00W, pop (1995e) 587 000. Second largest city in Morocco; one of Morocco's four imperial cities, founded in 1062; airport; railway; university; Medina, a world heritage site. >> Morocco ℹ

marram grass A tough perennial (*Amophila arenaria*) with creeping rhizomes, native to coasts of W Europe; leaf-blades inrolled, panicles spike-like. It is often planted on dunes as a sand-binder. (Family: Gramineae.) >> grass ℹ

marriage In anthropology, the legitimate long-term mating arrangement institutionalized in a community. If a union is called marriage, this implies that husband and wife have recognized claims over their partners; and it renders the children born of such a union legitimate heirs to both parents. Marriage also creates relationships of affinity between a person and his or her spouse's relatives. In many parts of the world a man may legitimately marry more than one wife (*polygyny*), but it is very unusual for a woman to be permitted more than one husband (*polyandry*). >> divorce; endogamy and exogamy; levirate; polygamy

marrow >> **bone marrow**

marrow A trailing or climbing vine (*Cucurbita pepo*) native to America, long cultivated as a vegetable; flowers yellow, 12·5 cm/5 in diameter, funnel-shaped; fruit up to 90 cm/3 ft or more long, cylindrical, oval, or round; rind green or yellow, with thick flesh surrounding numerous seeds. (Family: Cucurbitaceae.) >> courgette; squash (botany); vegetable

Marryat, Frederick (1792–1848) Naval officer and novelist, born in London. He wrote a series of novels on sea life, notably *Peter Simple* (1833) and *Mr Midshipman Easy* (1836). He later wrote stories for children, notably *The Children of the New Forest* (1847).

Mars (astronomy) The fourth planet from the Sun; the outermost of the terrestrial-type planets, with an eccentric orbit at a mean distance of 1·52 AU, and a diameter about half that of Earth. Its basic planetary characteristics are: mass $6{\cdot}42 \times 10^{23}$ kg; mean density 3·93 g/cm^3; equatorial gravity 372 cm/s^2; day (sidereal) 24 h 37 min 22 s; year 687 days; obliquity 25°11′; orbital eccentricity 0·093. A characteristically red planet, it has been the subject of popular interest as a possible abode of life. There are two small natural satellites, Phobos and Deimos. Modern understanding dates back to the first spacecraft flyby of the planet in 1965 (NASA's Mariner 4), and continues witht he Pathfinder series of probes, beginning in 1997. It is a dry, cold planet with a thin, 95% carbon dioxide atmosphere. The atmospheric circulation is marked by annual episodes of violent dust-storm activity. There is a complex surface of cratered uplands, lowland plains, and massive volcanic regions. A variety of channel-like features (the 'canals') are observed. Viking lander soil analysis revealed no organic material, and indicates that the soil/atmospheric chemistry destroys organics. >> Deimos; Mariner / Mars programme; Phobos; planet; Solar System; Viking project; volcano; RR964

Mars (mythology) The Roman god of war, second only to Jupiter. The month of March is named after him.

Marseille [mah(r)**say**], also Eng **Marseilles**, ancient **Massilia** 43°18N 5°23E, pop (1995e) 825 000. Second largest city in France and leading port of the Mediterranean; founded c.600 BC by Greeks; Old Port (Vieux Port) on a rocky peninsula; airport; railway; metro; archbishopric; university; two cathedrals (11th–12th-c, 1852–93). >> France ℹ

Marsh, Dame Ngaio (Edith) [**niy**oh] (1899–1982) Detective-story writer, born in Christchurch, New Zealand. Her novels and short stories, featuring Superintendent Roderick Alleyn of Scotland Yard, include *Vintage Murder* (1937), and *Black as he's Painted* (1974).

Marshall, George C(atlett) (1880–1959) US general and statesman, born in Uniontown, PA. He became secretary of state (1947–9) and originated the Marshall Aid plan for the postwar reconstruction of Europe. He was awarded the Nobel Peace Prize in 1953.

Marshall, John (1755–1835) Jurist, born in Germantown, VA, the foremost chief justice in the history of the US Supreme Court. He established the American doctrine of the judicial review of federal and state legislation.

Marshall, Thurgood (1908–93) Judge, born in Baltimore, MD. He served as solicitor general of the United States (1965–7), before becoming the first African-American justice of the US Supreme Court (1967–91).

Marshall Islands pop (1995e) 56 600; area c.180 sq km/70 sq mi. Republic in the C Pacific Ocean; capital, Dalap-Uliga-Darrit (on Majuro Atoll); archipelago c.925 km/800 mi in length; two parallel chains of coral atolls; GMT +12: Micronesian population, chiefly Christian, speaking English and Marshallese; explored by the Spanish, 1529; US nuclear weapon tests held on Bikini and Enewetak atolls, 1946–62; Trust Territory, 1947–78; self-governing republic, 1979; compact of free association with the USA, 1982; trusteeship ended, 1990; governed by a president, elected by a parliament; tropical agriculture. >> United States Trust Territory of the Pacific Islands; RR1016 political leaders

marsh gas >> **methane**

marsh marigold >> **kingcup**

Mars Observer project A US Mars orbiter spacecraft launched in September 1992. Contact with the spacecraft was lost in August 1993, just before the scheduled Mars orbit insertion. A replacement mission was being planned for launch in 1996. >> Mars (astronomy); Mars programme; NASA

Mars programme A Soviet series of robotic Mars exploration projects (1962–74), including flybys, orbiters, and hard-landers. It was less successful than other Soviet planetary missions. The Soviets resumed Mars exploration in 1988. Two more missions in the series are planned. >> Mars (astronomy); Soviet space programme

Marston, John (1576–1634) Playwright, born in Wardington, Oxfordshire. His plays include *The Malcontent* (1604), and *Eastward Ho!* (1605), a satirical comedy written in conjunction with Chapman and Jonson. >> Chapman; Jonson

Marston Moor, Battle of (1644) A major conflict in the English Civil War, in which parliamentary forces under Oliver Cromwell defeated royalist forces led by Prince Rupert. The defeat led to the virtual collapse of Charles I's cause in the N. >> English Civil War

marsupial A mammal, native to Australasia and the New World; young often develop in a pouch which opens forwards (climbing species) or backwards (burrowing species). (Order: Marsupialia, 266 species.) >> bandicoot; dasyure; kangaroo; koala; mammal [i]; numbat; opossum; phalanger; possum; Tasmanian devil; thylacine [i]; wombat [i]; yapok

Martello towers [mah(r)**tel**oh] Small circular forts with thick walls. Many were erected on the S and SE coast of England in the early 19th-c to provide observation posts and defence against a projected French invasion. The name comes from Cape Mortella, Corsica, where such a tower was captured by a British Fleet in 1794.

marten A mammal of genus *Martes* (7 species), native to Europe, Asia, and North America; solid body with sharp nose and long bushy tail. (Family: Mustelidae.) >> Mustelidae; sable

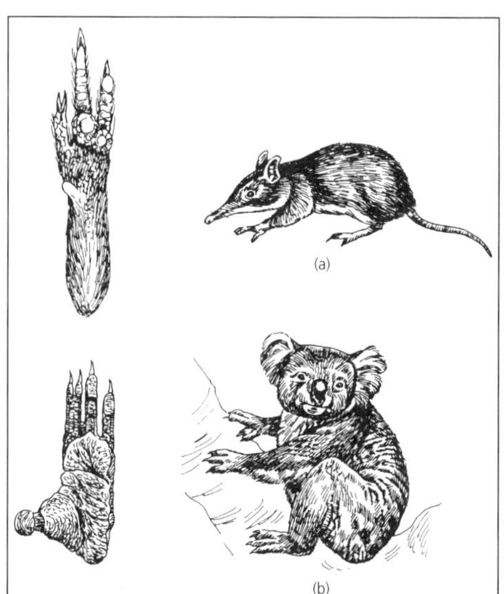

Marsupials – bandicoot (a) and koala (b), showing feet adapted as grooming combs.

Martha's Vineyard Island in the Atlantic off the SE coast of Massachusetts, USA; area 280 sq km/108 sq mi; chief town, Edgartown; summer resort; so called because the first English settlers found an abundance of wild grapes growing here. >> Massachusetts

Martial, in full **Marcus Valerius Martialis** (c.40–c.104) Latin poet and epigrammatist, born in Spain. He is remembered for his 12 books of epigrams, mainly satirical comments on contemporary events and society. >> epigram

martial arts Styles of armed or unarmed combat developed in the East. In modern times most of these arts have developed into popular sports in the West. >> aikido; judo; jujitsu; karate; kendo; kung fu; ninjutsu; taekwondo; tai chi chuan

martial law The imposition of military rule on the civilian population, either by the leader of an occupying army, or by a territory's own government. In the latter case, it most commonly occurs after there has been a military coup or during a period of colonial rule.

martin A bird of the swallow family. Those with short tails are usually called 'martins', those with long tails 'swallows'. The names are not applied consistently. (Family: Hirundinidae 23 species.) >> swallow

Martin, St (c.316–c.400) Patron saint of France, born in Sabaria, Pannonia. He founded the first monastery near Poitiers c.360, and in 371–2 was made Bishop of Tours. Feast day 11 (W) or 12 November (E). >> monasticism

Martin, Steve (1945–) Film actor, born in Waco, TX. He made his film debut in *The Absent Minded Waiter* (1977), which received an Oscar nomination for best short film. Later films include *All Of Me* (1984), *Father of the Bride* and its sequel (1991, 1995), and *Sergeant Bilko* (1996).

Martín de Porres, St [**poh**res] (1579–1639) South American saint, who spent his entire life in the Dominican Order in Lima, Peru, ministering to the sick and poor. He was canonized in 1962. Feast day 3 November. >> Dominicans

Martin du Gard, Roger [mah(r)tĩ dü gah(r)] (1881–1958) Novelist, born in Neuilly, France. He is known for his 8-novel series *Les Thibault* (1922–40), dealing with family life during the first decades of the present century. He was awarded the Nobel Prize for Literature in 1937.

Martini, Simone [mah(r)**tee**nee] (c.1284–1344) Painter, born in Siena, Italy. The most important artist of the 14th-c Sienese School, his work is notable for its grace of line and use of colour, as in his 'Annunciation' (Uffizi). >> Sienese School

Martinique [mah(r)ti**neek**] pop (1995e) 385 000; area 1079 sq km/416 sq mi. Island in the Windward group of the Lesser Antilles, E Caribbean; capital, Fort-de-France; timezone GMT –4; population mainly of African or mixed descent; chief religion, Roman Catholicism; official language, French, with creole widely spoken; unit of currency, the French franc; length, 61 km/38 mi; width, 24 km/15 mi; highest point, Mt Pelée (1397 m/4583 ft); tropical climate with high humidity; visited by Columbus, 1502; French colony, 1635; overseas department of France, 1946; administered by a commissioner-general and a Regional Council; economy based largely on agriculture. >> Fort-de-France; Pelée, Mount; Windward Islands

Martin Luther King Day In the USA, the third Monday in January; a federal public holiday in honour of the civil rights leader, commemorated in about half of the US states. The date of the celebration varies from state to state. >> King, Martin Luther

Martinmas In the UK, the feast of St Martin (11 Nov), a day on which traditionally rents were paid, servants hired, and livestock slaughtered for winter salting.

Martinů, Bohuslav [**mah(r)**tinoo] (1890–1959) Composer, born in Polička, Czech Republic. A prolific composer, his music includes symphonies, concertos, ballets (notably *Ishtar*), and operas.

Marvell, Andrew [**mah(r)**vl] (1621–78) Poet, born in Winestead, Hull. He is remembered for his pastoral and garden poems, notably 'To His Coy Mistress'. >> metaphysical poetry; pastoral

Marx, Karl (Heinrich) (1818–83) Founder of modern international communism, born in Trier, Germany, the son of a Jewish lawyer. With Engels as his closest collaborator, he reorganized the Communist League, and in 1848 finalized the *Communist Manifesto*, which attacked the state as the instrument of oppression, and religion and culture as ideologies of the capitalist class. In 1849 he settled in London, where he wrote the first volume of his major work, *Das Kapital* (1867). He died in London, with this work unfinished. >> communism; Engels; Feuerbach; Hegel; Marxism; Marxism–Leninism

Marx Brothers Family of film comedians, born in New York City, comprising **Julius** (1895–1977), or **Groucho**; **Leonard** (1891–1961), or **Chico**; **Arthur** (1893–1961), or **Harpo**; and **Herbert** (1901–79), or **Zeppo**. Another brother, **Milton** (?1897–1977), known as **Gummo**, left the act early on. Their main reputation was made in a series of films, such as *Animal Crackers* and *Monkey Business* (both 1932). Zeppo retired from films in 1935. Each had a well-defined stencil: Groucho with his wisecracks; Chico, the pianist with his own technique; and Harpo, the dumb clown and harp maestro. The team broke up in 1949.

Marxism The body of social and political thought informed by the writings of Karl Marx. Much of his writing, especially *Das Kapital*, was concerned with the economic dynamics of capitalist societies, seeing the state as an instrument of class rule supporting private capital and suppressing the masses. This situation would eventually lead to revolution, whereby the working class would seize the state and establish a dictatorship of the proletariat, and class differences would disappear (socialism). This classless society would eventually lead to the withering away of the state, producing a communist society. It is generally recognized that Marx's writings regarding the transformation to socialism and the nature of socialism lacked detail. In consequence, Marxism has adopted a wide range of interpretations. >> Marx; Marxism–Leninism; Neo-Marxism

Marxism–Leninism A distinct variant of Marxism formulated by Lenin, who prior to the Bolshevik revolution argued for direct rule by workers and peasants, and advocated direct democracy through the soviets (councils). Leninist principles of a revolutionary vanguard have become the central tenet of all communist parties. Lenin modified Marx's theory of historical materialism, contending that revolutionary opportunities should be seized when they arose, and not when the social and economic conditions of capitalist crisis leading to proletarian revolution existed. >> Lenin; Maoism; Marxism; Russian Revolution

Mary, also known as **Our Lady** or **the Blessed Virgin Mary** (?–c.63) Mother of Jesus Christ; also entitled **Our Lady** or **the Blessed Virgin Mary**. In the New Testament she is most prominent in the stories of Jesus's birth (Matthew and Luke), and only occasionally appears in Jesus's ministry. According to the Acts of the Apostles, she remained in Jerusalem during the early years of the Church, and a tradition places her tomb there. The belief that her body was taken up into heaven is celebrated in the festival of the Assumption, defined as Roman Catholic dogma in 1950. Her Immaculate Conception has been a dogma since 1854. Belief in the apparitions of the Virgin at Lourdes, Fatima, and in several other places attracts many thousands of pilgrims each year. In Roman Catholic and Orthodox Christianity, she holds a special place as an intermediary between humankind and God. >> Assumption; Hail Mary; Immaculate Conception; Jesus Christ; Orthodox Church; Roman Catholicism; rosary

Mary I, Tudor (1516–58) Queen of England and Ireland (1553–8), born in Greenwich, Greater London, the daughter of Henry VIII by his first wife, Catherine of Aragon. A devout Catholic, on her accession she repealed anti-Catholic legislation, revived Catholic practices, and aimed to cement a Catholic union with Philip II of Spain. These aspirations provoked Wyatt's rebellion, followed by the execution of Jane Grey and the imprisonment of Mary's half-sister, Elizabeth. Her persecution of some 300 Protestants earned her the name of 'Bloody Mary' in Protestant hagiography. Calais was lost to the French in the year of her death. >> Grey, Lady Jane; Philip II (of Spain)

Mary II >> **William III**

Mary, Queen of Scots (1542–87) Queen of Scotland (1542–67) and Queen Consort of France (1559–60), born at Linlithgow Palace, West Lothian, daughter of James V of Scotland by his second wife, Mary of Guise. In 1565 she married her cousin, Henry Stewart, Lord Darnley, a grandson of Margaret Tudor, but was soon alienated from him. The murder of Rizzio, her Italian secretary, by Darnley and a group of Protestant nobles in her presence (1566) confirmed her insecurity. The birth of a son, the future James VI, failed to bring a reconciliation. Darnley was mysteriously killed in an explosion at Kirk o' Field (1567); the chief suspect was the Earl of Bothwell, who underwent a mock trial and was acquitted. Mary's involvement is unclear, but she consented to marry Bothwell. The Protestant nobles rose against her; she surrendered at Carberry Hill, and was compelled to abdicate. Placing herself under the protection of Queen Elizabeth, she found herself instead a prisoner for life. Her presence in England gave rise to countless plots to depose Elizabeth and restore Catholicism. Finally, after the Babington conspiracy (1586) she was brought to trial for treason, and executed. >> Babington; Bothwell; Darnley; Elizabeth I; Rizzio

Mary of Teck, in full **Victoria Mary Augusta Louise Olga Pauline Claudine Agnes** >> **George V**

Maryland pop (1995e) 5 105 000 area 27 090 sq km/ 10 460 sq mi. State in E USA; the 'Old Line' or 'Free State'; first settlement, 1634, at St Mary's (state capital until 1694); seventh of the original 13 states to ratify the Constitution, 1788; gave up territory for the establishment of the District of Columbia; abolished slavery, 1864; Chesapeake Bay stretches N through the state, almost splitting it in two; highest point Mt Backbone (1024 m/ 3360 ft); capital, Annapolis; major city, Baltimore (85% of the population live in this area); Eastern Shore noted for its scenic beauty. >> Annapolis; Baltimore; District of Columbia; United States of America [i]; RR994

Mary Magdalene, St [**mag**dalen] (1st-c) New Testament character; *Magdalene* possibly means 'of Magdala', in Galilee. *Luke* 8.2 reports that Jesus exorcized seven evil spirits from her; thereafter she appears only in the narratives of Jesus's passion and resurrection. Feast day 22 July. >> Jesus Christ; New Testament

Mary Rose A warship built in 1511 for Henry VIII and rebuilt in 1536. In 1545, while in action against the French off Portsmouth, she capsized and sank with the loss of most of her crew. Her remains were salvaged in 1982 in a complex and much-publicized operation, and are now exhibited at Portsmouth. >> Wasa

Masaccio [ma**sa**chio], originally **Tommaso de Giovanni di Simone Guidi** (1401–28) Painter, born in San Giovanni Valdarno, Italy. A pioneer of Renaissance painting, he worked in Florence, where he executed frescoes in collaboration with Masolino. >> fresco; Masolino

Masada [ma**sah**da] or **Mezada** A Roman hilltop fortress established 37–31 BC by the Palestinian ruler Herod in barren mountains W of the Dead Sea; within Israel since 1947. Seized by zealots during the First Jewish Revolt in AD 66–70, it was taken by the Roman army in 73 after a lengthy siege which culminated in the mass suicide of all 400 defenders. >> Herod the Great; Judaism; Roman history ℹ

Masai or **Maasai** [ma**siy**] A people of the Rift Valley area of Kenya and Tanzania, speaking a Nilotic language. They are nomadic and semi-nomadic cattle herders. >> nomadism

Masaryk, Tomáš (Garrigue) [masa**rik**] (1850–1937) First president of the Czech Republic (1918–35), born in Hodonin, Czech Republic. While in exile during World War 1 he organized the Czech independence movement. >> Czechoslovakia ℹ

Mascagni, Pietro [mas**kan**yee] (1863–1945) Composer, born in Livorno, Italy. He is best known for his one-act opera, *Cavalleria Rusticana* (1890).

Mascarene Islands [mazka**reen**], Fr **Archipel des Mascareignes** Island group in the Indian Ocean, 700–800 km/ 450–500 mi E of Madagascar; named after the 16th-c Portuguese navigator, Mascarenhas. >> Mauritius ℹ; Réunion; Rodrigues Island

mascon >> **maria**

Masefield, John (1878–1967) Poet and novelist, born in Ledbury, Hereford and Worcester. His sea poetry includes *Salt Water Ballads* (1902), and his narrative poetry *Reynard the Fox* (1919). He also wrote novels, plays, and works for children, such as *The Box of Delights* (1935). He became poet laureate in 1930.

maser A device which produces microwaves from excited atoms or molecules, devised in 1954 by US physicist Charles Townes and others; the name is an acronym of *microwave amplification by the stimulated emission of radiation*. Masers employ the same physical principles as lasers, but produce lower frequency radiation. They are used as sensitive low-noise amplifiers for radar and satellite communications. >> laser ℹ; microwaves; Townes

Maseru [ma**see**roo] 29°19S 27°29E, pop (1995e) 136 000. Capital of Lesotho; on the R Caledon; altitude 1506 m/ 4941 ft; founded, 1869; airport; railway terminus; university (1964). >> Lesotho ℹ

Mashhad [mash**had**] or **Meshed** 36°16N 59°34E, pop (1995e) 1 916 000. Second largest city in Iran; industrial and trade centre; airport; railway; university (1956). >> Iran ℹ

masochism >> **sadomasochism**

Masolino (da Panicale) [masoh**lee**noh], originally **Tommaso di Cristoforo Fini** (1383–c.1447) Artist, born in Panicale, Italy. A distinguished early Renaissance painter, he collaborated with Masaccio in the Brancacci chapel. >> fresco; Masaccio

Mason, James (1909–84) Actor, born in Huddersfield, West Yorkshire. He was nominated for an Oscar for *A Star Is Born* (1954), *Georgy Girl* (1966), and *The Verdict* (1982). Other respected performances from more than 100 films include *Lolita* (1962) and *The Shooting Party* (1984).

Mason–Dixon Line The border between Maryland and Pennsylvania, drawn in 1763–7 by British astronomer Charles Mason (1730–87) and Jeremiah Dixon (1733–79). It is regarded as the boundary between 'the North' and 'the South'.

Masoretes or **Massoretes** [**mas**ohreets] (Heb 'transmitters of tradition') Jewish scholars who preserved traditions regarding the text of the Hebrew Bible, especially creating a system of vowel signs to reflect the pronunciation of the Hebrew consonantal text in the 9th–10th-c (the Masoretic Text). >> Hebrew; Old Testament

masque An aristocratic celebration composed of poetry, song, dance, and (usually) elaborate mechanical scenery, unified by a theme or emblematic story. The Royal masques of Tudor and Stuart England are best known for the collaboration of Ben Jonson and Inigo Jones. >> Jones, Inigo; Jonson

mass An intrinsic property of all matter and energy, the source of gravitational field; symbol *m*, units kg (kilogram). It is perceived as an object's weight (the downward-acting force due to gravity) or its inertia (its reluctance to change its motion). The mass of an object increases with its velocity, according to special relativity. >> density; gravitation; inertia; mass–energy relation; mechanics; weight

Mass (Lat *missa*, from *missio* 'dismissal') The sacrament of the Eucharist (Holy Communion) in the Roman Catholic Church and some other churches. Masses perform different functions in the life of the Church, eg a Requiem Mass for the dead, a Nuptial Mass for a marriage. >> Eucharist; Jesus Christ; Roman Catholicism; sacrament

Massachusetts pop (1995e) 6 062 000; area 21 455 sq km/ 8284 sq mi. New England state in NE USA; the 'Bay State' or 'Old Colony'; third most densely populated state; one of the original states of the Union, sixth to ratify the Constitution; Pilgrim Fathers settled at Plymouth in 1620; colony of Massachusetts founded 1629; first shots of the War of Independence fired at Lexington in 1775; rises from an indented coastline to a stony, upland interior and gentle, rolling hills to the W; highest point Mt Greylock (1049 m/3442 ft); capital, Boston. >> American Revolution; Boston; Pilgrims; United States of America ℹ; RR994

Massawa [ma**sah**wa] or **Mitsiwa** 15°37N 39°28E, pop (1995e) 49 300. Seaport in Eritrea; occupied by Italy, 1885; capital of Italian Eritrea until 1897; largely rebuilt after earthquake in 1921; railway; commercial centre; naval base. >> Eritrea; Ethiopia ℹ

Masséna, André [masayna] (1758–1817) Leading French general of the Revolutionary and Napoleonic Wars, born in Nice. He distinguished himself in Napoleon's Italian campaign (1796–7), and defeated the Russians at Zürich (1799). He was forced to retreat in the Iberian Peninsula by Wellington's forces. >> French Revolutionary Wars; Napoleonic Wars

mass–energy relation A relationship in physics, stated by Einstein, expressed as $E = mc^2$, where E is energy, c is the velocity of light, and m is mass, as measured for a moving object. It corresponds to the statement that all energy has mass. >> Einstein; energy; mass; special relativity ℹ; velocity of light

Massenet, Jules (Emile Frédéric) [**ma**senay] (1842–1912) Composer, born in Montaud, France. His operas include *Don César de Bazan* (1872) and *Manon* (1884), and he also wrote oratorios, orchestral suites, music for piano, and songs.

Massey, Raymond (Hart) (1896–1983) Actor, born in Toronto, Ontario, Canada. He is best known for his role as Dr Gillespie in the long-running *Dr Kildare* series during the 1960s.

Massif Central [maseef sõtral] Area of ancient rocks in SEC France, occupying about a sixth of the country; generally over 300 m/1000 ft; highest peak, Puy de Sancy in the Monts Dore (1885 m/6184 ft). >> France ℹ

Massine, Léonide [ma**seen**], originally **Leonid Fyodorovich Miassin** (1896–1979) Dancer and choreographer, born in Moscow. He was principal dancer and choreographer with Diaghilev (1914–21, 1925–8) and the Ballet Russes de Monte Carlo (1938–43). >> Ballets Russes

Massinger, Philip (1583–1640) Playwright, born near Salisbury, Wiltshire. Much of his work is a collaboration with others, particularly Fletcher. His comedies include *A New Way to Pay Old Debts* (1633). >> Fletcher

mass media >> **media**

mass number >> **nucleon number**

mass spectrometer A machine for measuring the proportions and masses of the atomic species in some sample; invented in 1919 by British scientist Francis Aston (1877–1945). Ions formed from a gaseous sample are passed through a magnetic field, where they are deflected by an amount depending on their mass. >> ion; particle physics

Massys or **Matsys, Quentin** [ma**sees**] (c.1466–c.1530) Painter, born in Louvain, Belgium. His pictures are mostly religious, with decided touches of realism. His many portraits include the notable 'Erasmus'.

mast cells Cells with granules containing histamine, heparin, and other chemicals. Tissue injury and infection causes the release of the granular contents, resulting in inflammatory and allergic responses. >> antibodies; heparin; histamine; leucocytes; urticaria

mastectomy >> **breast cancer**

master An artistic status achieved within the mediaeval guild system. Artists and craftsmen followed several years' apprenticeship before becoming 'masters', through production of a 'masterpiece'. The term **Old Master** is used loosely to refer to any major painter from Giotto to Cézanne, regarded as a model of traditional excellence.

Masters The popular name for the **US Masters** golf tournament, played every April over four rounds of the course at Augusta, GA, USA. An invitational event, only the world's top players take part. The first Masters was in 1934. >> golf

Masters, Edgar Lee (1869–1950) Writer, born in Garnett, KS. He is mainly remembered for his satirical *Spoon River Anthology* (1915), epitaphs in free verse dealing with the lives of people in the Midwest.

Masters and Johnson Human sexuality researchers and authors: **William H(owell) Masters** (1915–), born in Cleveland, OH, and **Virginia E(shelman) Johnson** (1925–), born in Springfield, MO. In 1964 they established the Reproductive Biology Research Foundation, where the study of sexual intercourse was carried out using volunteer subjects under laboratory conditions. *Human Sexual Response* (1966), became an international best-seller. They married in 1971 and divorced in 1991.

mastic An evergreen shrub, sometimes a small tree (*Pistacia lentiscus*) growing to 8 m/26 ft, native to the Mediterranean region; flowers tiny, in dense heads; fruits round, red becoming black, very aromatic. The mastic resin is used both in medicine and as a varnish sealant. (Family: Anacardiaceae.) >> resin

mastiff A large domestic dog; originally any large dog, but now restricted to three breeds: the **Old English mastiff** (short pale coat, long legs and tail, heavy head with short pendulous ears, deep muzzle and jowls), the rare **Tibetan mastiff**, and the **Japanese tosa**. >> bull-mastiff; bull terrier; dog; Great Dane

mastodon A browsing, elephant-like mammal found in woodland savannahs during the Miocene epoch, almost worldwide in distribution; became extinct in the Pleistocene epoch. (Order: Proboscidea.) >> elephant; mammal ℹ; Miocene / Pleistocene epoch

mastoid process The large bony prominence behind the ear. It is part of the temporal bone, and contains air cells (**mastoid air cells**) which communicate with the middle ear cavity. >> ear ℹ; skull

Mastroianni, Marcello [mastroy**ah**nee] (1924–96) Film actor, born in Fontana Liri, Italy. His major films included

Matamata

La dolce vita (1959, The Sweet Life) and *Otto e Mezzo* (1963, $8\frac{1}{2}$). He received Oscar nominations for *Divorzio all'Italiano* (1962, Divorce, Italian Style), *Una giornata particolare* (1977, A Special Day), and *Oci ciornie* (1987, Dark Eyes).

Matabeleland [mata**bee**leeland] Region of W and S Zimbabwe; named after the Matabele Bantu; acquired by the British South Africa Company, 1889; part of Southern Rhodesia, 1923; chief town, Bulawayo. >> Bulawayo; Zimbabwe ℹ

Mata Hari [**mah**ta **hah**ree], (Malay 'sun'), pseudonym of **Margaretha Geertruide MacLeod**, *née* **Zelle** (1876–1917) Courtesan and spy, born in Leeuwarden, The Netherlands. She became a dancer in Paris and adopted her stage name. Found guilty of espionage for the Germans during World War 1, she was shot in Paris.

matamata [mata**ma**ta] A side-necked turtle from South America; large head shaped like an arrowhead; shell with a jagged irregular surface. (*Chelus fimbriatus*. Family: Chelidae.) >> Chelonia ℹ

materialism The philosophical view that everything is composed exclusively of physical constituents located in space and time. Materialists thus deny the independent existence of minds, mental states, spirit, or abstract entities such as universals and numbers. >> dialectical materialism; idealism

materials science The study of the engineering properties of materials, as dictated by their microscopic structure. It has been responsible for the development of several new materials, such as conducting rubber, metallic glasses, and the fibreglass and carbon fibre composites used in sports equipment. >> rheology; solid-state physics

mathematical logic The application of mathematical rigour and symbolic techniques to the study of logic – for example, the development of formal languages and axiom systems for constructing logical proofs. >> Frege; logic; mathematics

mathematics A systematic body of knowledge built on certain axioms and assumptions, principally relating to numbers and spatial relationships. Abstract ideas in mathematics may be classified as **pure mathematics**, and their applications as **applied mathematics**; but many abstract ideas (eg set theory) have had practical applications (eg electrical networks) and many practical problems (eg the fair distribution of lottery prizes) have stimulated abstract ideas (the concept of a random number). >> algebra; arithmetic; differential calculus; games, theory of; geometry; new mathematics; number theory; statistics; topology; trigonometry; Archimedes; Cantor; Descartes; Euclid; Fermat; Gauss; Leibniz; Lobachevski; Newton, Isaac; Pascal; Pythagoras; Thales

Mather, Cotton [**ma**ther] (1663–1728) Colonial minister, born in Boston, MA. He reported on American botany, and was one of the earliest New England historians. His reputation suffered because of his involvement in the

Salem witchcraft trials of 1692. >> Puritanism; Salem (Massachusetts)

Matisse, Henri (Emile Benoît) [ma**tees**] (1869–1954) Painter, born in Le Cateau, France. The leader of the *Fauves*, his most characteristic paintings display a bold use of brilliant areas of primary colour, organized within a rhythmic two-dimensional design. >> Fauvism

Matlock 53°08N 1°32W; pop (1995e) 14 400. County town in Derbyshire, C England; railway; formerly a spa town. >> Derbyshire

Mato Grosso [**ma**toh **gro**soh], formerly **Matto Grosso** pop (1995e) 2 198 000; area 881 000 sq km/340 000 sq mi. State in CW Brazil; half the area under forest; capital, Cuiabá. >> Brazil ℹ

matrilineal descent A descent system in which family or clan membership, inheritance, and succession is traced through the mother's daughters. One of the most famous examples was found on the Trobriand Is, New Guinea.

Matsys, Quentin >> **Massys, Quentin**

matter The substances of which everything in the universe is composed. At one level, this is taken to mean atoms bound together into bulk matter. At the ultimate level, matter means the spin $\frac{1}{2}$ particles such as electrons and quarks, bound together by spin 1 force particles such as photons and gluons. >> phases of matter ℹ; particle physics

Matterhorn, Fr **Mont Cervin**, Ital **Monte Cervino** 45°59N 7°39E. Mountain peak in Switzerland, in the Pennine Alps; height, 4478 m/14 691 ft; first climbed by British mountaineer Edward Whymper in 1865. >> Alps

Matthau, Walter [**ma**tow], originally **Walter Matuschanskavasky** (1920–) US film actor, born in New York City. The son of Russian-Jewish immigrants, he began working in Yiddish theatre, then gained recognition on Broadway. His films include *The Odd Couple* (1968), *Hello Dolly* (1969), *Cactus Flower* (1969), and *The Odd Couple II (1998).*

Matthew, St (1st-c) One of the 12 apostles, a tax gatherer before becoming a disciple of Jesus. According to tradition he was the author of the first Gospel, a missionary to the Hebrews, and suffered martyrdom. Feast day 22 July >> Jesus Christ

Matthew Paris (c.1200–59) Chronicler and Benedictine monk. *Chronica Majora* gives the fullest available account of events in England between 1236 and 1259. >> Benedictines

Matthews, Sir Stanley (1915–) Footballer, born in Hanley, Staffordshire. He played for Stoke City and Blackpool, and 54 times for England. He was twice Footballer of the Year (1948, 1963), and the inaugural winner of the European Footballer of the Year award in 1956. >> football ℹ

Matthias I, known as **Matthew Corvinus**, Hung **Mátyás Corvin** (c.1443–90) King of Hungary (1458–90), born in Kolozsvár (Cluj-Napoca), Hungary, the second son of János Hunyady. He drove back the Turks, and considerably extended his territory, capturing Vienna in 1485. He greatly encouraged arts and industry, and reformed finances and justice. >> Hunyady

Matthias, William (James) (1934–92) Composer, born in Whitland, Pembrokeshire. His works include an opera *The Servants* (1980), two symphonies, several concertos, and the anthem written for the wedding ceremony of the Prince and Princess of Wales (1981).

Maudling, Reginald (1917–79) British Conservative statesman, born in London. His posts included minister of supply (1955–7), paymaster-general (1957–9), President of the Board of Trade (1959–61), colonial secretary (1961–2), and Chancellor of the Exchequer (1962–4). He resigned as home secretary in 1972, implicated in the bankruptcy proceedings of architect John Poulson. >> Conservative Party; Heath

Maugham, W(illiam) Somerset [mawm] (1874–1965) Writer, born in Paris. He published his successful first novel, the lurid *Liza of Lambeth*, in 1897. Later works include the novels *Of Human Bondage* (1915), and the plays *The Moon and Sixpence* (1919), *Cakes and Ale* (1930), and *The Razor's Edge* (1945). He is best known for his short stories, several of which were filmed, such as *Quartet* (1949).

Maui [**mow**ee] pop (1995e) 113 000; area 1885 sq km/728 sq mi. Second largest island of the US state of Hawaii; chief town, Wailuku; rises to 3055 m/10 023 ft at Haleakala. >> Hawaii (state)

Mau Mau A secret society which led a revolt of the Kikuyu people of Kenya in the 1950s. British troops were deployed in its suppression, but the cost convinced Britain that decolonization was imperative. >> Kikuyu

Mauna Kea [**mow**na **kay**a] 19°50N 155°28W. Dormant volcano in NC Hawaii, USA; rises to 4201 m/13 783 ft; several large telescopes at the summit. >> Hawaii (state); volcano

Mauna Loa [**mow**na **loh**a] 19°28N 155°35W. Active volcano in C Hawaii, USA; rises to 4169 m/13 678 ft; last erupted 1987. >> Hawaii (state); volcano

Maundy Thursday [**mawn**dee] The Thursday before Easter, so called from Latin *mandatum*, 'commandment', the first word of the anthem traditionally sung on that day; in memory of Christ's washing his disciples' feet (*John* 13.4–10). In Britain, special money (**Maundy money**) is given by the sovereign to the same number of elderly poor people as there are years in the sovereign's age.

Maupassant, (Henri René Albert) Guy de [mohpasã] (1850–93) Novelist and short-story writer, born near Dieppe, France. He joined the Naturalist group led by Zola. His first success, *Boule de suif* (1880, Ball of Fat), was followed by a decade in which he wrote c.300 short stories, as well as such novels as *Une Vie* (1883, trans A Woman's Life) and *Bel-Ami* (1885). >> Naturalism; Zola

Maupertuis, Pierre Louis Moreau de [mohpertwee] (1698–1759) Astronomer and mathematician, born in St Malo, France. He is best known for his 'principle of least action' in explaining the paths of moving bodies.

Mauriac, François [mohriak] (1885–1970) Novelist, born in Bordeaux, France. He is regarded as the leading French Catholic novelist of the 20th-c, dealing with the themes of temptation, sin, and redemption. His main works include the novels *Le Baiser au lépreux* (1922, The Kiss to the Leper) and *Thérèse Desqueyroux* (1927), and his play *Asmodée* (1938). He received the 1952 Nobel Prize for Literature. >> Roman Catholicism

Maurice, Prinz van Oranje, Graaf van Nassau (Prince of Orange, Count of Nassau) (1567–1625) Stadtholder of the United Provinces of the Netherlands, born in Dilenburg, the son of William the Silent. He became captain-general of the armies of the United Provinces during their War of Independence from Spain. He checked the Spanish advance, and by his steady offensive (1590–1606) liberated the N provinces of the Netherlands. >> William I (of the Netherlands); United Provinces of the Netherlands

Maurists [**maw**rists] A French Benedictine congregation of St Maur, founded in the early 17th-c. Suspected of being influenced by Jansenism, they were eventually dissolved in 1818. >> Benedictines; Jansen; monasticism

Mauritania [mori**tay**nia], Fr **Mauritanie**, Arabic **Muritaniyah**, official name **Islamic Republic of Mauritania**, Fr **République Islamique de Mauritanie** pop (1995e) 2 295 000; area 1 029 920 sq km/397 549 sq mi. Republic in NW Africa; capital, Nouakchott; timezone GMT; chief ethnic groups, Moor (30%), black (30%), mixed (40%); official religion, Islam; official language, Arabic, with French and local languages also spoken; unit of currency, the

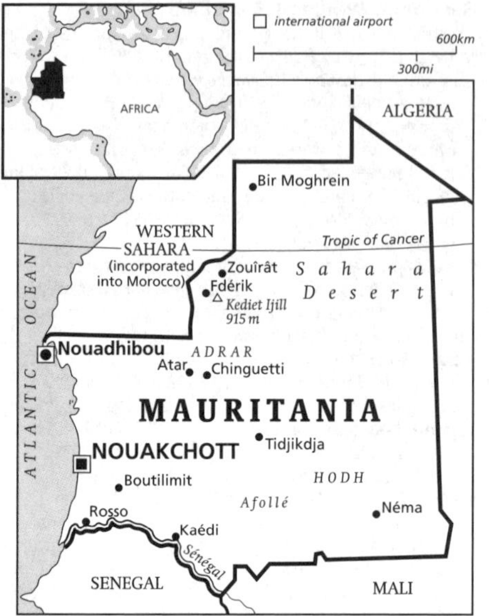

ouguiya of 5 khoums; Saharan zone in N two-thirds of the country; coastal zone, with minimal rainfall; Sahelian zone, with savannah grasslands; Sénégal R zone, the chief agricultural region; highest point, Kediet Ijill (915 m/ 3002 ft) in the NW; visited by Portuguese, 15th-c; French protectorate within French West Africa, 1903; French colony, 1920; independence, 1960; military coup, 1979; became a republic, 1992; governed by a president, National Assembly, and Senate; 80% of population rely on subsistence agriculture; crop success constantly under threat from drought; mining based on vast iron ore reserves, also copper and gypsum. >> Nouakchott; Sahara Desert; sahel; Western Sahara; RR1016 political leaders

Mauritius [mo**ri**shuhs] pop (1995e) 1 141 000 (excluding Rodrigues I); area 1865 sq km/720 sq mi. Republic in the Indian Ocean, an island c.800 km/500 mi E of Madagascar; includes the dependencies of Rodrigues I, Agalega Is, and Cargados Carajos Is (St Brandon Is); sovereignty of Tromelin I in dispute between France and Mauritius; 61 km/38 mi long by 47 km/29 mi wide; capital, Port Louis; timezone GMT +4; over two-thirds of the population are Indo-Mauritians; chief religions, Hinduism (over 50%), Christianity (30%), Islam (17%); official languages, English, with French and Creole widely spoken; unit of currency, the Mauritius rupee of 100 cents; volcanic island, highest peak, Piton de la Petite Rivière Noire (826 m/2710 ft); surrounded by coral reefs enclosing lagoons and sandy beaches; tropical-maritime climate, mean temperatures at sea-level 26°C (Nov–Apr), 22°C (May–Oct); visited by the Portuguese and Dutch, 16th-c; settled by the French, 1722; ceded to Britain, 1814; governed jointly with Seychelles as a single colony until 1903; independent sovereign state within the Commonwealth, 1968–92; became a republic, with governor-general named as president, 1992; prime minister presides over a cabinet, responsible to the Legislative Assembly; sugarcane industry employs over a quarter of the workforce. >> Port Louis; Rodrigues Island; Seychelles [i]; RR1016 political leaders

Maurois, André [mohrwah], pseudonym of **Emile Herzog** (1885–1967) Writer and biographer, born in Elbeuf, France. His many works include studies of Shelley (1923), Disraeli (1927), Voltaire (1935), and Proust (1949).

mausoleum >> **Gur Amir; Lenin Mausoleum; Mount Li; Taj Mahal**

Mausolus, Tomb of [**mow**zolus] A huge, ornate tomb built at Halicarnassus in SW Asia Minor around 350 BC by Mausolus's widow, Queen Artemisia II of Caria (reigned c.353–350 BC). >> Seven Wonders of the Ancient World

Maxim, Sir Hiram (Stevens) (1840–1916) Inventor, born in Sangersville, ME. He is best known for the invention of the first fully automatic machine-gun (1883). >> machine-gun

Maximilian, Ferdinand Joseph (1832–67) Emperor of Mexico (1864–7), born in Vienna, the younger brother of Emperor Francis Joseph I. In 1863, he accepted the offer of the crown of Mexico, supported by France; but when Napoleon III withdrew his troops, he refused to abdicate, and was executed. >> Juárez; Mexico [i]; Napoleon III

maxwell >> **RR1031**

Maxwell, James C(lerk) (1831–79) Physicist, born in Edinburgh. In 1873 he published his great *Treatise on Electricity and Magnetism*, which treats mathematically Faraday's theory of electrical and magnetic forces. His greatest work was his theory of electromagnetic radiation, which established him as the leading theoretical physicist of the century. >> electromagnetism; Maxwell–Boltzmann distribution

Maxwell, (Ian) Robert, originally **Ludvik Hoch** (1923–91) Publisher and politician, born in Slatinske Dòly, Czech Republic. He founded the Pergamon Press, became a Labour MP (1964–70), and had many business interests. Following his death in suspicious circumstances, it transpired that he had secretly siphoned large sums of money from two of his companies and from employee pension funds to preserve his financial empire.

Maxwell–Boltzmann distribution A description of the distribution of energy among the atoms or molecules of a (perfect) gas; made by British physicist James Clerk Maxwell and Austrian physicist Ludwig Boltzmann in 1868. >> Boltzmann; kinetic theory of gases; Maxwell, James Clerk

Maxwell Davies, Sir Peter >> **Davies, Sir Peter Maxwell**

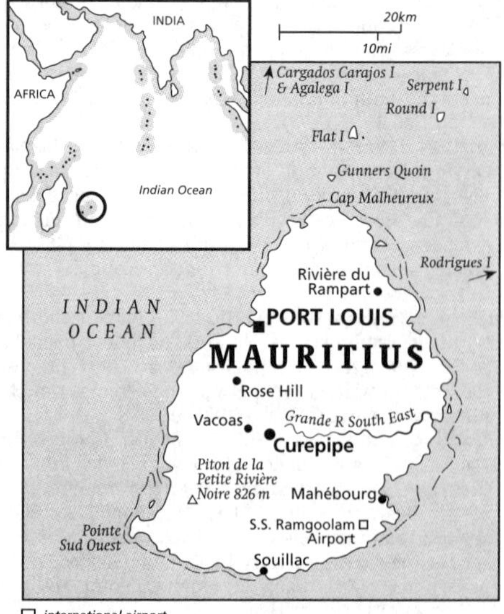

may >> **hawthorn**

Mayakovsky, Vladimir (Vladimirovich) [miya**kof**skee] (1893–1930) Poet, born in Bagdadi, Georgia. Regarded as the leader of the Futurist school, during the Russian Revolution (1917) he emerged as the propaganda mouthpiece of the Bolsheviks. >> Futurism; Russian Revolution

Mayas [**miy**az] The best-known civilization of the classic period of Middle America (AD 250–900). They developed astronomy, calendrical systems, hieroglyphic writing, and ceremonial architecture, including pyramid temples. Maya civilization started to decline c.900.

maybug >> **cockchafer**

Mayer, Louis B(urt) [**may**er], originally **Eliezer Mayer** (1885–1957) Film mogul, born in Minsk, Belarus. His family emigrated to the USA, where in 1924 he became vice-president of Metro-Goldwyn-Mayer. He was in charge of the studios for more than 25 years.

Mayfair A district in London where throughout the 17th-c a fair was held in May. It became a fashionable residential area in the late 19th-c and early 20th-c, but is now largely given over to offices. >> London

Mayflower A three-masted carrack in which the Pilgrims sailed from Plymouth to North America in 1620. The ship was only 27·5 m/90 ft in length, and the voyage took 66 days. Her 100 passengers, Puritan refugees from religious intolerance, became 101 by the end of the journey (there were two births and one death during the passage). >> carrack; Plymouth (UK)

mayfly A winged insect with a short adult life. Mayflies live as aquatic larvae for up to four years, then emerge as non-feeding, flying adults that survive only 2–72 hours. (Order: Ephemeroptera, c.2000 species.) >> insect ℹ

May Fourth Movement A student demonstration in Beijing on 4 May 1919 which crystallized the aspirations of those who struggled for a new China. Originally a protest against the Japanese takeover of Germany's rights in Shandong, the movement spread nationwide. >> China ℹ

mayhem A common-law crime involving the intentional disfigurement of another person. The disfigurement has to be of a permanent, though not necessarily disabling character, such as cutting off an ear or a finger. >> assault

Mayo [**may**oh], Ir **Mhuigheo** pop (1995e) 110 000; area 5398 sq km/2084 sq mi. County in Connacht province, W Ireland; capital, Castlebar; Knock, scene of apparition of Virgin Mary in 1879, major place of pilgrimage, served by new airport; Croagh Patrick, Ireland's holy mountain, scene of annual pilgrimage (Jul). >> Castlebar; Ireland (republic) ℹ; Mary (mother of Jesus)

Mayo, Charles Horace [**may**oh] (1865–1939) Surgeon, born in Rochester, MN. With his father and brother he organized the Mayo Clinic within what is now St Mary's Hospital, Rochester. The family were pioneers in the practice of group medicine.

mayor The political head of a town or city government. The name is used in a vast range of political systems, but the role and status of mayors vary considerably. In some cases the mayor can have significant executive powers, while in others the role is largely a ceremonial one.

Mayotte [ma**yot**], Eng **Mahore** pop (1995e) 117 000; area 374 sq km/144 sq mi. Small island group of volcanic origin, in the Mozambique Channel, W Indian Ocean; administered by France; two main islands; Grande Terre (area 360 sq km/140 sq mi), rising to 660 m/2165 ft at Mt Benara; La Petite Terre or Ilot de Pamandzi (area 14 sq km/5 sq mi); capital, Dzaoudzi; chief languages, French, Mahorian; French colony, 1843–1914; attached with the Comoros Is to Madagascar; overseas territory of France; airport. >> Comoros; Dzaoudzi; France ℹ

maypole Traditionally, a tall pole decorated with vegetation and ribbons on the first of May, and the focus of festivities on that day to welcome Spring and ensure fertility. From the later 19th-c a shorter pole was substituted, around which children perform a plaited-ribbon dance. >> traditional dance

Mays, Willie (Howard), nickname **the Say Hey Kid** (1931–) Baseball player, born in Westfield, AL. An outstanding batter, centerfielder, and baserunner with the San Francisco Giants and New York Mets (1951–73), he was the leading all-round player of the era. >> baseball ℹ

Mazarin, Jules [mazarĩ], known as **Cardinal Mazarin**, originally **Giulio Raimondo Mazzarino** (1602–61) Neapolitan clergyman, diplomat, and statesman, born in Pescine, Italy. Through the influence of Richelieu he was elevated to cardinal, succeeding his mentor as first minister in 1642. Blamed by many for the civil disturbances of the Frondes, he twice fled the kingdom. He concluded the Peace of Westphalia (1648), and negotiated the Treaty of the Pyrenees (1659), ending the prolonged Franco-Spanish conflict. >> Frondes; Richelieu

Mazatlán [masat**lan**] 23°11N 106°25W, pop (1995e) 347 000. Seaport in W Mexico; airfield; railway; largest Mexican port on the Pacific; main industrial and commercial centre in the W. >> Mexico ℹ

mazurka A quick Polish dance in triple metre, with a strong accent on the second or third beat. Chopin wrote numerous examples for piano solos. >> Chopin, Frédéric

Mazzini, Giuseppe [mat**see**nee] (1805–72) Patriot and republican, born in Genoa, Italy. He founded the Young Italy Association (1833), and in 1848 collaborated with Garibaldi in attempting to keep the patriot struggle alive in the Alps. During the events of 1859–60 he and his supporters worked strenuously but vainly to make the new Italy a republic. >> Garibaldi; Italy ℹ; Risorgimento

Mbabane [mba**ba**nay] 26°18S 31°06E, pop (1995e) 48 700. Capital of Swaziland; capital, 1902; administrative and commercial centre; iron ore; casino. >> Swaziland ℹ

MBE >> **British Empire, Order of the**

Mbeki, Thabo (Mvuyelwa) [**mbe**kee] (1942–) Leader of the African National Congress (ANC), born in Idutywa, South Africa. Elected to the National Executive Committee of the ANC in 1975, he became one of its most influential leaders. After the organization was unbanned in 1990, he returned to South Africa, and played a major role in the negotiations for a new political dispensation. He was made first deputy president in the new administration (1994), and in 1997 succeeded Mandela as president of the ANC. >> African National Congress

Mc surnames >> **Mac**

MCC Abbreviation of **Marylebone Cricket Club**, whose headquarters are at Lord's Cricket Ground, N London. It was founded in 1787 by a group of noblemen, and retained responsibility for the making of cricket laws until 1969. >> cricket (sport) ℹ; Lord's Cricket Ground

mead An alcoholic beverage derived from fermented honey. It was widely drunk in Anglo-Saxon England, and was known as *hydromel* by the Romans. >> honey

Mead, Margaret (1901–78) Anthropologist, born in Philadelphia, PA. Her books include *Coming of Age in Samoa* (1928) and *New Lives for Old* (1956). Increasingly she became a freelance media heavyweight, particularly well known for her views on educational and social issues. >> anthropology

Meade, Richard (John Hannay) (1938–) Equestrian rider, born in Chepstow, Monmouthshire. One of Britain's most successful Olympians, he won three gold medals – the three-day event team golds in 1968 and 1972, and the individual title in 1972 (on Laurieston). >> equestrianism

meadow grass A perennial grass (*Poa pratensis*) with creeping, rooting stems forming rather stiff tufts; variable and widespread throughout the temperate N hemisphere.

It is important as a pasture grass. (Family: Gramineae.) >> grass

meadowlark A bird native to the New World; plumage streaked and mottled on back; nests on ground. (Genus: *Sturnella*, 5 species. Family: Icteridae.) >> lark

mealybug A scale insect that infests all parts of its host plants; adult female flattened, males enclosed in cocoon-like sac; distributed worldwide. (Order: Homoptera. Family: Pseudococcidae, c.1100 species). >> scale insect

mean In mathematics, the sum of *n* scores, divided by *n*; colloquially called the 'average'. The **arithmetic mean** is obtained by adding a set of scores and dividing the total by the number of scores; for example, the arithmetic mean of the scores 6, 2, 8, 4 is 5 ($6 + 2 + 8 + 4 = 20$; $20 \div 4 = 5$). The **geometric mean** of *n* scores is the *n*th root of the product of those scores; for example, the geometric mean of 2, 9, 12 is 6, since $2 \times 9 \times 12 = 216$, and $\sqrt[3]{216} = 6$. >> median; mode (mathematics); statistics

mean free path The average distance travelled by some atom or molecule before colliding with another, typically about 60 nm in gases; symbol *l*, units m (metre). >> atom; kinetic theory of gases

mean life In atomic, nuclear, and particle physics, the average time taken for an excited atom to lose energy or for a particle to decay; symbol τ, units s (second). >> half-life

means test A method of assessing an individual or family's eligibility for some kind of financial assistance, used by government agencies and local authorities. The 'means' refers to a person's income and other sources of money. Aid is given on a sliding scale, and above a certain level no help is given.

measles A widespread viral childhood disease spread by airborne infected droplets. It begins with catarrhal symptoms, followed by the development of a generalized blotchy red rash. >> German measles; virus

meat The edible muscle of animals, the most common forms including beef, pork, bacon, lamb, and poultry. The flesh of many other species is also eaten as meat, including the horse, buffalo, camel, dog, deer, rabbit, and monkey. >> vegetarianism

Meath [meeth], Ir **na Midhe** pop (1995e) 105 000; area 2339 sq km/903 sq mi. County in Leinster province, E Ireland; former kingdom; capital, Trim. >> Ireland (republic)

Mecca [**me**ka], Arabic **Makkah**, ancient **Macoraba** 21°30N 39°54E, pop (1995e) 859 000. Islamic holy city in WC Saudi Arabia; birthplace of Mohammed; chief shrine of Muslim pilgrimage; city closed to non-Muslims; al-Harram Mosque with the Kaba and sacred Black Stone. >> Islam; Kaba; Mohammed; Saudi Arabia

mechanical engineering The branch of engineering concerned with the design, construction, and operation of machines of all types. Mechanical engineers design, operate, and test engines that produce power from steam, petrol, nuclear energy, and other sources, and a wide range of associated equipment. >> engineering; machine

mechanics The study of the motion of objects as a result of the forces acting on them. Motion in a straight line is called *linear* or *rectilinear* motion, and is described using mass *m*, velocity *v*, acceleration *a*, momentum *p*, and force *F*; *rotational* motion is described using moment of inertia *I*, angular velocity v, angular acceleration α, angular momentum *L*, and torque X. **Quantum mechanics** governs objects the size of atoms (10^{-10} m) or less. **Classical mechanics** corresponds to all other aspects of mechanics, and includes **Newtonian mechanics**, **celestial mechanics** (the motion of stars and planets), general relativity, **fluid mechanics**, and **relativistic mechanics** (for objects moving at high velocity). >> fluid mechanics; general relativity; quantum mechanics; statistical mechanics

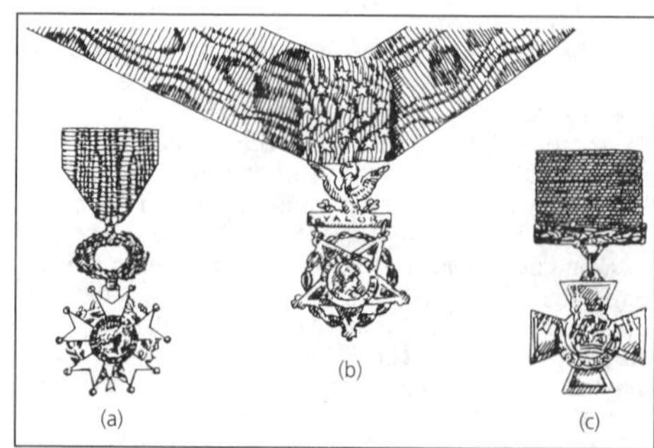

Medals – Legion of Honour, France (a); Medal of Honor, USA (b); Victoria Cross, UK (c)

Mecklenburg Declaration of Independence (1775) Resolutions adopted in Mecklenburg County, N Carolina, during the American Revolution, denying all British authority. >> American Revolution

medal A piece of metal, often in the form of a coin or cross, bearing a device or inscription, struck or cast in commemoration of an event or as a reward for merit. Medals may be awarded for personal bravery, for participation in an event or battle, or for sports.

Medal of Honor (MH, MOH) In the USA, the highest decoration awarded for heroism, instituted in 1861; it is worn on a blue ribbon decorated with white stars.

Medawar, Sir Peter (Brian) [**me**dawah(r)] (1915–87) Zoologist, born in Rio de Janeiro, Brazil. He shared the 1960 Nobel Prize for Physiology or Medicine for his discovery of acquired immunological tolerance. He is also well known for his general books on the nature of science. >> immunology

Medea [me**dee**a] In Greek mythology, a witch, the daughter of Aeetes, the King of Colchis, who assisted Jason in obtaining the Golden Fleece. When deserted by Jason at Corinth, she fled in her aerial chariot after killing her children. >> Golden Fleece; Jason

Medellín [mede**yeen**] 6°15N 75°36W, pop (1995e) 1 521 000. City in NW Colombia, and leading industrial centre; airport; railway; five universities; cathedral. >> Colombia

Medes [meedz] An ancient people living to the SW of the Caspian Sea. They were at their peak in the 7th-c and 6th-c BC.

media A collective term for television, radio, cinema, and the press. The media are nowadays often discussed as a single entity, because of their combined importance as providers of entertainment and information, their presumed power to mould public opinion and set standards, the growth of cross-ownership among the various sectors, and their often parasitic interest in each other's personalities and problems. >> broadcasting

median In mathematics, the middle score, when the scores are arranged in order of size; for example, the scores 1, 5, 3, 7, 2 are re-arranged 1, 2, 3, 5, 7, and the middle score is 3. >> mean; mode

Medicaid and **Medicare** Two US schemes to provide health care, introduced by the federal government in 1965. **Medicaid** is operated by state governments, and provides financial assistance to low-income persons. **Medicare** is for persons over the age of 65. Similar schemes operate in several other countries, such as Australia. >> medicine

Medici [**may**deechee], Fr **Médicis** A banking family which virtually ruled Florence from 1434 to 1494, though without holding formal office. They were overthrown by the republic in 1494, but restored to power in 1512, and from 1537 became hereditary dukes of Florence. >> Catherine de' Medici; Leo X; Marie de Médicis

medicine The science and practice of preventing, alleviating, and curing human illness. Although the study of anatomy grew rapidly from the time of Aristotle and the Alexandrian medical school in 300 BC, physiology and ideas of organ function remained rudimentary. Chinese medicine is documented from 600 BC, and the first Chinese medical treatise was 1st-c BC. The major contribution of Greek medicine was in the field of medical ethics, and the Hippocratic code of conduct is still invoked today. Roman medicine was pre-eminent in public health, with its emphasis on clean water, sewage disposal, and public baths. Arabian medicine made significant contributions to chemistry and drugs, and set up the first organized medical school in Salerno (c.900). In Padua, Vesalius corrected the anatomical misconceptions of Galen. The major medical discovery of the 17th-c was the circulation of the blood; 100 years later, oxygen and its relationship to blood. The value of post-mortem studies was demonstrated by Morgagni in Padua. New methods of examination were introduced, notably the stethoscope (by Laënnec) and percussion of the chest. Jenner showed the benefit of vaccination to prevent smallpox. The germ theory of disease dominated the 19th-c, and Pasteur virtually created the science of bacteriology, from which Lister was inspired to develop the concept of antisepsis. Progress in the 20th-c has been unparalleled, being distinguished by the growth in modern technology and the development of rigorous experimental testing. Developments were stimulated rather than hindered by World Wars 1 and 2, in such areas as rehabilitation after injury, blood transfusion, anaesthesia, and chemotherapy, including the development of antibiotics and vitamins and the discovery of insulin and cortisone. New concepts have included genetic disease, the baleful effects of some lifestyles and environmental pollution, vaccination for the majority of infectious diseases, artificial organ and life-support systems, organ transplantation, and the science of immunology. >> alternative / community / forensic / preventive medicine; epidemiology; geriatrics; gynaecology; haematology; neurology; nursing; obstetrics; oncology; ophthalmology; orthopaedics; paediatrics; pathology; perinatology; serology; surgery; Jenner; Lister, Joseph; Morgagni; Pasteur

medick An annual and perennial, native to Europe, W Asia, and N Africa; pea-flowers small, mostly yellow; fruit usually a spirally coiled pod, often spiny. (Genus: *Medicago*, 100 species. Family: Leguminosae.)

Medina [me**dee**na], Arabic **Madinah, Al** 24°35N 39°52E, pop (1995e) 695 000. Islamic holy city in Saudi Arabia; contains the tomb of Mohammed; important pilgrimage trade; city closed to non-Muslims; airfield; Islamic university (1961); centre of a large date-growing oasis. >> Mohammed; Saudi Arabia ℹ

meditation Devout and continuous reflection on a particular religious theme, practised in many religions and serving a variety of aims, such as deepening spiritual insight, or achieving union with the divine will. >> religion

Mediterranean Sea, ancient **Mediterraneum** or **Mare Internum** area 2 516 000 sq km/971 000 sq mi. World's largest inland sea, lying between Africa, Asia, and Europe; connected with the Atlantic by the Straits of Gibraltar; includes the Ligurian, Adriatic, Aegean, Ionian, and Tyrrhenian Seas; length, 3860 km/2400 mi; maximum width, 1610 km/1000 mi; maximum depth, 4405 m/14 452 ft; 'Mediterranean climate' of hot, dry summers and mild winters with rainstorms; seaboard highly favoured as holiday and health resort; maritime highway since ancient times, connecting Europe with the E; Suez Canal (1869) increased its importance; pollution a major problem. >> Suez Canal

medium Especially in spiritualism, a person through whom spirits of the dead are claimed to demonstrate their presence by means of spoken or written messages (via **mental mediums**), or apparently paranormal physical effects (via **physical mediums**). >> ectoplasm; materialism; seance; spiritualism

Medjugorje [medyoo**gor**ye] 43°20N 17°49E. Village in Bosnia and Herzegovina; since 1981, claimed to be the scene of regular appearances by the Virgin Mary to a group of local children; now a major site of pilgrimage, but since 1990 number of pilgrims much reduced by civil war. >> Bosnia and Herzegovina ℹ; Mary (mother of Jesus)

medlar A small deciduous tree or shrub (*Mespilus germanica*), growing to 6 m/20 ft, native to SE Europe; flowers solitary, white; fruit brown, becoming soft and edible when over-ripe. (Family: Rosaceae.)

Médoc [maydok] District in Gironde department, SW France; famous for its clarets, notably at Haut-Médoc. >> France ℹ; wine

medulla oblongata [me**duh**la oblong**gah**ta] The lower part of the brain stem, continuous with the pons above and with the spinal cord below. It contains the 'vital centres' concerned with the reflex control of the cardiovascular and respiratory systems. It also helps to govern swallowing, sneezing, coughing, and vomiting. >> brain stem

medusa [me**dyoo**za] The free-swimming phase in the life-cycle of a coelenterate. The body is typically discoid or bell-shaped, with marginal tentacles and a centrally located mouth on the underside. >> coelenterate; jellyfish; polyp (marine biology)

Medusa [me**dyoo**za] In Greek mythology, the name of one of the Gorgons, whose head is portrayed with staring eyes and snakes for hair. >> Gorgon; Perseus (mythology)

Medway Towns Urban area in Kent, SE England; includes Gillingham and Rochester (merging as Medway unitary authority, 1998), Chatham, and Strood on the R Medway, E of London. >> Kent

Mee, Arthur (1875–1943) Journalist, editor, and writer, born in Stapleford, Nottinghamshire. He is most widely known for his *Children's Encyclopaedia* (1908).

Meech Lake Accord A Canadian constitutional package, put together by the government of Brian Mulroney in 1987 at a conference at Meech L, N of Ottawa. It proposed a fresh federal structure for Canada, giving the provinces more authority, and recognized Quebec as a 'distinct society'. The Accord died after it failed to receive the support of all 10 Provinces and First Nations leaders in 1990. >> Canada ℹ; Charlottetown Accord; First Nations; Mulroney

Meegeren, Han van >> **van Meegeren, Han**

meerschaum [**meer**shuhm] or **epiolite** A hydrated magnesium silicate mineral, which forms fine, fibrous masses like white clay and is easily carved. It is used for pipe bowls. >> silicate minerals

megabyte >> **byte**

megalith (Gr *mega*, 'large' + *lithos*, 'stone') In European prehistory, a monument built of large, roughly-dressed stone slabs; sometimes called a **cromlech**. Most are of Neolithic date. >> chambered tomb; menhir; stone circles; Three Age System

Megaloptera [mega**lop**tera] >> **alderfly; dobsonfly**

megaparsec >> **parsec**

megapode An Australasian ground-living bird; sturdy body with large legs and feet; also known as **mound bird**, **mound builder**, or **incubator bird**. (Family: Megapodiidae, 12 species.) >> jungle fowl ℹ

Megatherium [mega**theer**ium] The largest ground sloth, found in Central and South America during the Pleistocene epoch; a two-legged grazer; forelimbs large, hindlimbs short but massive. (Order: Xenarthra.) >> Pleistocene epoch; sloth

megaton >> **kiloton**

megavitamin therapy A form of nutritional therapy based on the work of Linus Pauling, who believed that very large doses of vitamin C could cure or prevent the common cold by having a direct anti-viral effect and also by enhancing the effect of the immune system. Large doses of various vitamins have been used to treat patients with a wide variety of disorders, such as schizophrenia and depression, on the assumption that these problems may be the result of vitamin deficiency. However, some vitamins taken in excessive amounts may cause toxic effects. >> cold; nutrients; Pauling; vitamins ℹ

megawatt >> **watt**

Megiddo [**meg**idoh] In antiquity, an important town in N Palestine controlling the main route from Egypt to Syria. Among its most impressive remains are the 9th-c stables of the Israelite kings.

megohm >> **ohm**

Mehta, Ved (Parkash) [**may**ta] (1934–) Writer, born in Lahore, India. Blind from the age of four, he went to the USA when he was 15. He has had a distinguished career as a journalist, contributing chiefly to *The New Yorker*. *Continents of Exile* is an acclaimed series of autobiographical books (1972–89).

Mehta, Zubin [**may**ta] (1936–) Conductor, born in Mumbai (Bombay), India. His posts as conductor or musical director have included the Los Angeles Philharmonic (1962–78) and the New York Philharmonic (1978–91), and he is now the musical director of the Israel Philharmonic Orchestra.

Meiji Restoration (1868) [**may**jee] An important point in Japanese history, when the last Shogun was overthrown in a short civil war, and the position of the emperor (Meiji, the title of Mutsuhito, who ruled until 1912) was restored to symbolic importance. >> Mutsuhito; Shogun

Meiji Tenno >> **Mutsuhito**

meiosis [miy**oh**sis] One of the principal mechanisms of nuclear division in living organisms, resulting in the formation of gametes (in animals) or sexual spores (in plants). A diploid nucleus (ie one possessing a double set of chromosomes) undergoes two successive divisions. The phases of meiosis are *leptotene* (the appearance of chromosomes as threads in the nucleus), *zygotene* (the pairing of chromosomes to form bivalents), *pachytene* (the separation of bivalents), and *diplotene* (the moving apart of chromosomes). >> cell; chromosome ℹ; gamete; mitosis; nucleus (biology)

Meir, Golda [may**eer**], originally **Goldie Myerson**, *née* **Mabovitch** (1898–1978) Israeli stateswoman and prime minister (1969–74), born in Kiev. As prime minister, her efforts for peace in the Middle East were halted by the fourth Arab–Israeli War (1973). >> Arab–Israeli Wars; Israel ℹ

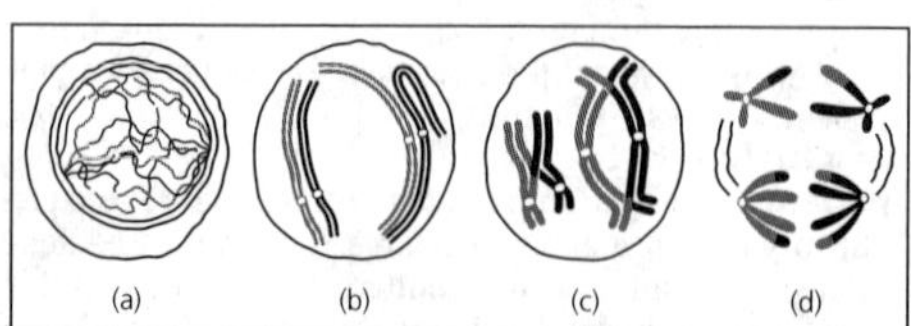

Four stages in meiosis – leptotene (a); zygotene (b); pachytene (c); diplotene (d)

Meissen porcelain [**miy**sn] Porcelain made at Meissen, near Dresden; the first factory in Europe to make true hard-paste porcelain. The secret was discovered in 1708 by Johann Friedrich Böttger (1682–1719). >> porcelain

Meissonier, (Jean Louis) Ernest [maysonyay] (1815–91) Painter, born in Lyon, France. His works were largely of military and historical scenes, including several of the Napoleonic era.

Meistersinger [**miy**sterzinger] Members of German guilds of the 14th–16th-c devoted to the encouragement of poetry and music in strict traditional forms. Their activities form the basis for Wagner's opera *Die Meistersinger von Nürnberg* (1868). >> Minnesinger; Wagner

Meitner, Lise [**miyt**ner] (1878–1968) Physicist, born in Vienna. In 1917 she shared with Hahn the discovery of the radioactive element protactinium, and became known for her work in nuclear physics. With her nephew O R Frisch she devised the idea of nuclear fission in late 1938. >> Frisch, Otto Robert; Hahn; nuclear physics

Mekele or **Makale** [ma**kal**ay] 13°32N 39°33E, pop (1995e) 84 900. Capital of Tigray region, NE Ethiopia; airport; major refugee centre during the severe drought of 1983. >> Ethiopia ℹ; Tigray

Meknès [mek**nes**] 33°53N 5°37W, pop (1995e) 427 000. City in N Morocco; one of Morocco's four imperial cities, founded in the 12th-c; capital until 1728; railway. >> Morocco ℹ

Mekong River [**mee**kong], Chin **Lancang Jiang** River in Indo-China, SE Asia; rises on the Tibet Plateau, China; delta on the South China Sea; length c.4000 km/2500 mi.

Melaka >> **Malacca**

Melanchthon, Philipp [me**langk**thon], originally **Philipp Schwartzerd** (1497–1560) Religious reformer, born in Bretten, Germany; his *Loci Communes* (1521) is the first great Protestant work on dogmatic theology, and the Augsburg Confession (1530) was composed by him. >> Augsburg Confession; Luther; Reformation

Melanesia One of the three broad geographical–cultural areas of the Pacific. It includes the islands of New Guinea, the Solomons, Vanuatu, and New Caledonia. The peoples of Melanesia typically have dark skin, kinky hair, large jaws, and a high incidence of blood group B. >> Micronesia; Oceania; Polynesia

melanins [**mel**aninz] Dark brown pigments which in different concentrations give coloration (shades of yellow and brown) to the eyes, skin, hair, feathers, and scales of many vertebrates. In humans they help protect the skin against the damaging effects of sunlight. >> albinism; birthmark; melanoma; skin ℹ

melanoma [mela**noh**ma] A pigmented tumour due to overgrowth of melanin-producing cells in the basal cell layer of the skin. A proportion become malignant, and spread to other parts of the body. >> keratosis; melanins

Melba, Dame Nellie, professional name of **Helen Armstrong**, *née* **Mitchell** (1861–1931) Prima donna, born in Melbourne, Australia; her professional name derives from the city. Her coloratura soprano voice won her worldwide fame. 'Peach Melba' and 'Melba toast' were named after her.

Melbourne 37°45S 144°58E, pop (1995e) 3 195 000. Port and state capital in Victoria, Australia; on the Yarra R; founded in 1835, named after the British prime minister, Lord Melbourne; state capital, 1851; capital of Australia when federal parliament sat here, 1901–27; two airports; railway; underground; Australia's biggest cargo port; five universities (1855, 1958, 1964, 1991, 1992); two cathedrals;

Flemington racecourse (holds the Melbourne Cup horse race); site of 1956 summer Olympic Games. >> Victoria (Australia)

Melbourne, William Lamb, 2nd Viscount (1779–1848) British statesman and Whig prime minister (1834, 1835–41), born in London. He formed a close relationship with the young Queen Victoria, but took little part in public affairs after his election defeat in 1841. His wife (1785–1828) wrote novels as **Lady Caroline Lamb**, and was notorious for her 9-months' devotion to Lord Byron. >> Grey, Charles; Victoria; Whigs

Melchett, Baron >> **Mond, Ludwig**

Melchites [**mel**khiyts] Christians who follow the Byzantine rite, and who belong to the Patriarchates of Alexandria, Antioch, and Jerusalem. During the 5th-c, they supported the Byzantine emperor in his opposition to the Monophysites. >> Monophysites; Orthodox Church

Méliès, Georges [maylyes] (1861–1938) Illusionist and film maker, born in Paris. He was a pioneer in trick cinematography to present magical effects.

Melilla [may**lee**lya], ancient **Russadir** 35°21N 2°57W, pop (1995e) 61 600. Free port and modern commercial city on N coast of Morocco; with Ceuta, forms a region of Spain; founded as a port by the Phoenicians; free port since 1863; re-occupied by Spain in 1926; airport; car ferries to Málaga. >> Ceuta; Spain ℹ

melilot [**mel**ilot] Typically an annual or biennial, native to Europe, Asia, and N Africa; pea-flowers small, yellow or white. It is used for fodder, and also for flavouring cheeses. (Genus: *Melilotus*, 20 species. Family: Leguminosae.)

Mellon, Andrew W(illiam) (1855–1937) Financier, philanthropist, and politician, born in Pittsburgh, PA. As secretary of the Treasury in 1921 he made controversial fiscal reforms. He endowed the National Gallery of Art in Washington, DC.

melodrama A theatrical genre which became a mass entertainment in Europe and the USA throughout the 19th-c. It is a style which emphasizes the depiction of story, the creation of suspense, and the use of sensational episodes.

melody A basic constituent of music, being a succession of pitches arranged in some intelligible order. Between c.1675 and 1925, melodic inspiration (a gift for composing 'good tunes') became more and more highly prized as the token of a composer's originality. Since then, many composers have sought to express their musical personalities in other ways, through the use of texture, rhythm, etc. >> harmony; music; rhythm

melon A trailing or climbing vine (*Cucumis melo*) with tendrils, probably native to Africa; flowers yellow, funnel-shaped; fruit up to 25 cm/10 in long, round or ovoid; rind green or yellow, leathery; edible flesh thick, sweet, surrounding numerous seeds. (Family: Cucurbitaceae.)

Melos [**mee**los], Gr **Mílos** area 151 sq km/58 sq mi. Southwesternmost island of the Cyclades, Greece; main town, Plaka. >> Cyclades

Melpomene [mel**pom**inee] The Greek Muse of tragedy. >> Muses

meltdown A catastrophic event in a nuclear reactor. The temperature of the reacting core rises to a point at which the fuel rods melt, and radioactive material may be released into the environment. >> Chernobyl; nuclear reactor ℹ; radioactivity

melting point The temperature at which a solid becomes liquid. If heat is applied to a solid, its temperature rises until the melting point is reached, when heat energy is then absorbed to form liquid from the solid. >> phases of matter ℹ

Melville, Herman (1819–91) Novelist, born in New York City. His journeys on a whaling ship were the subject matter of his first novels, *Typee* (1846) and *Omoo* (1847), and his masterpiece *Moby-Dick* (1851). After 1857 he wrote only some poetry, leaving his long story, *Billy Budd, Foretopman* in manuscript.

membranophone Any musical instrument in which the sound is generated by the vibrations of a stretched membrane. The most important are the various kinds of drum. >> drum; kazoo; musical instruments; percussion ℹ; tambourine

Memlinc or **Memling, Hans** [**mem**ling] (c.1435–1494) Religious painter, born in Seligenstadt, Belgium. His works include the triptych of the 'Madonna Enthroned' at Chatsworth (1468). He was also an original and creative portrait painter.

Memnon [**mem**non] In Greek mythology, a prince from Ethiopia, the son of Eos and Tithonus, who was killed at Troy by Achilles. >> Achilles

Memorial Day A national holiday in the USA, held on the last Monday in May in honour of American war dead; originally instituted as **Decoration Day** in 1868 in honour of soldiers killed in the American Civil War.

Memphis (Egypt) An important town in ancient Egypt on the W bank of the Nile. The capital of Lower Egypt under the pharaohs, it declined in importance under the Ptolemies. >> pharaoh; Ptolemy I Soter; Saqqarah ℹ

Memphis (USA) [**mem**fis] 35°08N 90°03W, pop (1995e) 658 000. Port in SW Tennessee, USA, on the Mississippi R; largest city in the state; site of military fort, 1797; city established, 1819; captured by Union forces during the Civil War (battle of Memphis, 1862); airfield; railway; two universities (1848, 1912); Martin Luther King Jr assassinated here (1968); Graceland, home of Elvis Presley; Beale Street, regarded as the birthplace of the blues. >> American Civil War; blues; King, Martin Luther; Presley; Tennessee

Menai Straits [**men**iy] Channel separating Anglesey from the mainland of NW Wales, UK; length 24 km/15 mi; width varies from 175 m/575 ft to 3·2 km/2 mi; crossed by the Menai Suspension Bridge, built by Telford (1819–26), length 176 m/580 ft, and the Britannia railway/road bridge (1980), rebuilt after fire in 1970 seriously damaged the original tubular railway bridge of Robert Stephenson (1846–9). >> Stephenson, Robert; Telford, Thomas; Anglesey

Menander [me**nan**der] (c.343–291 BC) Greek comic dramatist, born in Athens. Only a few fragments of his work were known until 1906, and in 1957 the complete text of the comedy *Dyskolos* (The Bad-Tempered Man) was found in Geneva.

Menchik-Stevenson, Vera (Francevna), *née* **Menchik** (1906–44) Chess player, born in Moscow. Recognized as the finest of all female chess players, she held the world title from 1927 (the first champion) to 1944. >> chess

Mencius [**men**shius], Latin name **Meng-tzu** (Master Meng) (c.371–c.289 BC) Philosopher and sage, born in Shantung, China, who founded a school modelled on that of Confucius. After his death his disciples collected his sayings and published them as the *Book of Meng-tzu*. >> Confucius

Mencken, H(enry) L(ouis) (1880–1956) Philologist, editor, and satirist, born and educated in Baltimore, MD. He greatly influenced the US literary scene in the 1920s. His major work, *The American Language*, was published in 1918, and in 1924 he founded the *American Mercury*, editing it until 1933. >> English

Mendel, Gregor (Johann) (1822–84) Botanist, born in Heinzendorf, Austria. Abbot of the Augustinian monastery in Brno, he pursued research into plant breeding, and eventually established his 'laws' governing the nature of inheritance, which became the basis of modern genetics. Recognition came many years after his death. >> genetics

Mendeleyev, Dmitri Ivanovich [mendel**ay**ef] (1834–1907) Chemist, born in Tobolsk, Russia. He devised the periodic classification (or table) by which he predicted the existence of several elements which were subsequently discovered. Element 101 (*mendelevium*) is named after him. >> periodic table

Mendelssohn(-Bartholdy), (Jakob Ludwig) Felix [**men**dlsuhn] (1809–47) Composer, born in Hamburg, Germany, the grandson of Moses Mendelssohn, and the son of a Hamburg banker who added the name Bartholdy. Among his early successes as a composer was the *Midsummer Night's Dream* overture (1826). A tour of Scotland in the summer inspired him with the *Hebrides* Overture and the *Scottish Symphony*. Other major works include his oratorios *St Paul* (1836) and *Elijah* (1846).

Mendelssohn, Moses [**men**delsuhn] (1729–86) Philosopher and biblical scholar, born in Dessau, Germany. A zealous defender of enlightened monotheism, he was an apostle of deism. >> deism

Mendès-France, Pierre [**men**dez **frãs**] (1907–82) French statesman and prime minister (1954–5), born in Paris. As prime minister, he ended the war in Indo-China, but his government was defeated on its N African policy. >> France [i]

Mendicant Orders (Lat *mendicare*, 'to beg') Religious Orders in which friars were not permitted to hold property, either personally or in common. >> Augustinians; Carmelites; Dominicans; Franciscans; monasticism; Orders, Holy

Mendip Hills Hill range in SW England; extending 37 km/23 mi; rises to 326 m/1069 ft at Blackdown. >> Cheddar; England [i]

Mendoza [men**thoh**sa] 32°48S 68°52W, pop (1995e) 127 000. City in W Argentina; altitude 756 m/2480 ft; belonged to Chile until 1776; destroyed by fire and earthquake in 1861; airport; railway; four universities (1939, 1959, 1960, 1968); centre of a large, irrigated agricultural area, dealing mainly in wine. >> Argentina [i]

Menelaus [meni**lay**us] In Greek legend, the younger brother of Agamemnon. He was King of Sparta, and married to Helen. >> Agamemnon; Helen; Proteus; Trojan War

menhir [**men**eer] (Welsh *maen*, 'stone' + *hir*, 'long') In European prehistory, a single standing stone or megalith. >> megalith

Ménière's disease [**men**yair, muh**nyair**] Paroxysmal attacks of vertigo, usually abrupt in onset, accompanied by tinnitus and progressive deafness, and sometimes associated with nausea. It is a disorder of the inner ear of unknown cause, affecting mainly middle-aged and elderly persons. It is named after French physician Prosper Ménière (1799–1862). >> deafness; ear [i]; tinnitus

meningitis [menin**jiy**tis] An infection of the membranes (pia and arachnoid) covering the brain. **Viral meningitis** is usually short-lived and harmless; **bacterial meningitis** is more serious and may cause death. The onset is usually sudden, with headache, fever, stiffness of the neck on flexion, and dislike of the light. >> brain [i]; lumbar puncture

meniscus [muh**nis**kuhs] >> **surface tension** [i]

Mennonites [**men**oniyts] Dutch and Swiss Anabaptists who later called themselves Mennonites after one of their Dutch leaders, Menno Simons (1496–1559). Most of their 1 million adherents live in the USA. >> Anabaptists

Menon, Krishna >> **Krishna Menon**

menopause Strictly defined as the cessation of menstruation, but more commonly used to refer to the period of time (up to eight years beforehand) when the menstrual cycle becomes less regular; also known as **climacteric**. The complete cessation of menstruation usually occurs between 45 and 50 years. It is often accompanied by physical and psychogenic disturbances. >> menstruation; oestrogens

menorah [me**noh**ra] A candelabrum of seven branches, with three curving upwards on each side of a central shaft. It is an ancient symbol of Judaism, and the official symbol of the modern State of Israel. >> Judaism

menorrhagia [meno**ray**jia] Excessive menstrual bleeding. It commonly results from local abnormalities of the uterus, but also arises from disorders of the hormones controlling normal menstruation. >> menstruation

Menotti, Gian Carlo [me**not**ee] (1911–) Composer, born in Cadegliano, Italy. His operas *The Consul* (1950) and *The Saint of Bleecker Street* (1954) both won Pulitzer Prizes. *Amahl and the Night Visitors* (1951) was a successful television opera.

Mensa (Lat 'table') An inconspicuous constellation in the S sky. It was named by Lacaille after Table Mountain, Cape Province, South Africa, where he had an observatory. >> constellation; Lacaille; RR968

Mensa International An organization of people whose members are admitted only after they 'have established by some standard intelligence test, that their intelligence is higher than 98% of the population'. Founded in England in 1945, branches now exist in over 60 countries. >> intelligence

Mensheviks [**men**sheviks] (Russ 'minority-ites') Members of the moderate faction of the Marxist Russian Social Democratic Labour Party, which split with Lenin's Bolsheviks in 1903. The Mensheviks opposed Lenin's policies on party organization and his revolutionary tactics. >> Bolsheviks; Lenin; Russian Revolution

menstruation A periodic discharge from the vagina of blood, mucus, and debris from the disintegrating mucous membrane of the uterus, in response to hormone changes when the ovum is not fertilized. It lasts 3–5 days. In women of child-bearing age (13–50 years), it occurs at approximately 4-week intervals. The first menstrual period in life is known as *menarche*, the last as *menopause*. >> amenorrhea; dysmenorrhea; menopause; menorrhagia; ovarian follicle

mental disorders A group of conditions with psychological or behavioural manifestations which may be accompanied by impaired functioning. Examples include anxiety, dementia, drug addictions, eating disorders, schizophrenia, and sleep disorders. >> anorexia nervosa; bulimia nervosa; dementia; mental handicap; neurosis; paranoia; psychiatry; psychosis; schizophrenia

mental handicap A condition in which people have an intelligence quotient of less than 70, with deficits in their ability to live independently, evidenced before age 18. Four types are generally recognized: **mild** (IQ 50–70), **moderate** (IQ 35–49), **severe** (IQ 20–34), and **profound** (IQ <20). The cause is unknown in c.75% of cases. >> intelligence

menthol $C_{10}H_{20}O$, a terpene alcohol, melting point 43°C. A waxy solid, the main constituent of oil of peppermint, it is used as a flavouring, a mild antiseptic, a decongestant, and a local anaesthetic. >> alcohols; camphor; terpene

menu A set of options presented to the user by a computer program. A program which communicates with the user solely by providing choices from interlinked menus is said to be **menu-driven**. >> computer program

Menuhin, Yehudi Menuhin, Baron [**men**yooin] (1916–99) Violinist, born in New York City. At the age of seven he appeared as a soloist, and won international renown as a virtuoso violinist. In 1962 he founded a school for musically gifted children near London. He took British nationality in 1985. His sister **Hephzibah** (1920–81) was a gifted pianist. >> violin

Menzies, Sir Robert Gordon [**men**zees] (1894–1978) Australian statesman and prime minister (1939–41, 1949–66), born in Jeparit, Victoria, Australia. His first term as premier was as head of the United Australia Party, his second as head of the Liberal Party, which he formed in 1944. >> Liberal Party (Australia)

Mercalli intensity scale [mer**kal**ee] A scale of 12 points, devised by Italian seismologist Giuseppe Mercalli (1850–1914), for measuring the intensity of an earthquake. The scale is based on the damage done, rather than on the total energy released, and so varies from place to place. It has been superseded by the Richter scale. >> Richter scale; RR974

Mercator's map projection [mer**kay**ter] A map projection devised in 1569 by Flemish cartographer Gerardus Mercator (1512–94), which was the first of real use for navigation purposes. It is based on parallels equal in length to that of the Equator. As a result, a line of constant bearing appears as a straight line rather than the curved line on a globe. The major distortion is that area is exaggerated at high latitudes. >> map projection ⓘ; meridian

Mercer, David (1928–80) Playwright, born in Wakefield, West Yorkshire. His plays include *Ride a Cock Horse* (1965) and *Cousin Vladimir* (1978). He has also written screenplays (eg *Morgan*, 1965; *Family Life*, 1972) and many TV plays.

mercerizing The chemical treatment of cotton with strong alkalis, to make it stronger, lustrous, and more silk-like. The process was devised in 1844 by British chemist John Mercer (1791–1866). >> alkali; cotton ⓘ

Merchant, Ismail, originally **Ismail Noormohamed Abdul Rehman** (1936–) Film producer, born in Mumbai (Bombay), India. In 1961 he collaborated with James Ivory in setting up a film company, Merchant-Ivory Productions. Their films include *Shakespeare Wallah* (1965), the Oscar-nominated *A Room With A View* (1985), *The Remains of the Day* (1993), and *Surviving Picasso* (1996). >> Ivory

Merchant Adventurers Local guilds exporting woollen cloth from 14th-c London. Formed in 1407, they increasingly dominated trade at the expense of smaller ports; from 1496, their headquarters were in Antwerp. >> guilds

merchant bank A UK bank specializing in trading and company financial matters; similar to a US *investment bank*. The term is traditionally used to describe members of the Accepting Houses Committee, dealing primarily with bills of exchange. >> accepting house; bank; investment bank; issuing house

Merchant Navy The commercial ships of a nation, a term first used by King George V in a speech in 1922. The mercantile marine was classed as an armed service throughout World War 2. In 1939 there were over 9000 ships in Britain's Merchant Navy, but by the 1990s the number had dwindled to under 2000. >> navy

Mercia A kingdom of the Anglo-Saxon heptarchy, with its main centres at Tamworth, Lichfield, and Repton. Mercian supremacy reached its height under Offa, but by the early 10th-c Mercia had been brought under the direct rule of Wessex. >> Anglo-Saxons; Offa; Wessex

Merckx, Eddy [merks], nickname **the Cannibal** (1945–) Cyclist, born in Woluwe St Pierre, Belgium. He won the *Tour de France* a record-equalling five times (1969–72, 1974), the Tour of Italy five times, and all the major classics. He retired in 1978. >> cycling

Mercosur Span, **Mercosul** (Portuguese) ('Southern Common Market') A common market agreement, signed in 1991 between Argentina, Brazil, Paraguay, and Uruguay, which aimed to introduce free movement of goods and services; inaugurated on 1 January 1995. Its secretariat is in Montevideo, Uruguay. Chile and Bolivia joined as associate members in 1996. It is the world's fourth largest free trade grouping, with over 200 million people. >> APEC; European Union; LAFTA

Mercouri, Melina [mer**koor**ee], originally **Anna Amalia Mercouri** (1923–94) Film actress, born in Athens. She started in films in 1955, and found international fame in 1960 with *Never on Sunday*. Always politically involved, she was exiled from Greece (1967–74), returned to be elected to parliament in 1977, and became minister of culture from 1981.

Mercredi, Ovide [**mair**kredee] (1946–) Canadian aboriginal affairs activist, born in Grand Rapids, Manitoba, Canada. A Cree Indian, he became a lawyer, and was made National Chief of the Assembly of First Nations in 1991. His book, *In the Rapids: Navigating the Future of First Nations* appeared in 1993. >> First Nations

Mercury (astronomy) The innermost planet of the Solar System; an airless, lunar-like body with the following characteristics: mass $3·30 \times 10^{26}$ g; radius 2439 km/1516 mi; mean density 5·4 g/cm^3; rotational period 58·65 days; orbital period 88 days; obliquity ~0°; orbital eccentricity 0·206; mean distance from the Sun $57·9 \times 10^6$ km/$36·0 \times 10^6$ mi. The equatorial surface temperatures reach 430°C, while on the night side temperatures may drop to −180°C. It has a weak magnetic field (c.1% of Earth's), and a very tenuous sodium atmosphere. One hemisphere of the surface was mapped by Mariner 10 (1974–5), the other is still unknown. It has an apparently lunar-like crust, shaped by asteroidal bombardment and episodes of volcanic flooding. >> Mariner programme; planet; Solar System

mercury (chemistry) Hg (from Lat *hydrargyrum*), element 80, melting point −39°C, boiling point 357°C. Silver in colour, unique among metals by being a liquid at normal temperatures; also known as **quicksilver**. A relatively unreactive metal, it is found free in nature, but is much more common as the sulphide (HgS), called *vermilion* when used as a pigment. It is used in both temperature- and pressure-measuring equipment. The vapour and soluble salts are toxic and cumulative. >> chemical elements; metal; RR1036

Mercury (mythology) or **Mercurius** A Roman god, principally of trading, who was identifed with Hermes, and inherited his mythology. >> Hermes (mythology)

Mercury programme The first US crewed spaceflight programme, the precursor to the Gemini and Apollo programmes, using a one-man crew. The first suborbital flight (5 May 1961) was piloted by Alan Shepard; the first orbital flight (20 Feb 1962) by John Glenn. The spacecraft demonstrated a life-support system and the basic elements of recovery.

Meredith, George (1828–1909) Writer, born in Portsmouth, Hampshire. He achieved popularity with *The Egoist* (1879) and *Diana of the Crossways* (1885). His main poetic work is *Modern Love* (1862).

merganser [mer**gan**ser] A sea duck native to the N hemisphere and SE Brazil; slender serrated bill; also known as **saw-bill**. (Genus: *Mergus*, 5 species. Subfamily: Anatinae. Tribe: Mergini.) >> duck

merger A business arrangement in which two companies bring together their operations and form a single company. The share capital of the two companies is replaced by an issue of shares in the new company, shareholders of the old companies receiving new shares on a formula basis. >> Monopolies Commission

meridian At any location, the great circle on the Earth at right angles to the Equator passing from N to S Poles. All celestial objects reach their highest point in the sky here, and the Sun is on the meridian at local noon. >> latitude and longitude ⓘ

Mérimée, Prosper [mayreemay] (1803–70) Writer, born in

Paris. His novels include *Colomba* (1841) and *Carmen* (1843), the source of Bizet's opera. >> Bizet

merino A breed of sheep, originating in Spain, which produce a heavy thick white fleece of very high quality. Australia is by far the largest producer of merino wool.

Merionethshire >> **Gwynedd**

meristem A region of growth or potential growth in a plant, such as the tips of shoots and roots, or buds.

Merleau-Ponty, Maurice [mairloh põtee] (1908–61) Philosopher, born in Rochefort-sur-mer, France. His books include *La Structure du comportement* (1942, The Structure of Behaviour) and *Phénoménologie de la perception* (1945, The Phenomenology of Perception). >> phenomenology

merlin A small falcon native to the N hemisphere (*Falco columbarius*); lacks white cheeks of other falcons; also known as **pigeon hawk**. (Family: Falconidae.) >> falcon

Merlin In the Arthurian legends, a good wizard or sage whose magic was used to help King Arthur. He was the son of an incubus and a mortal woman, and therefore indestructible; but he was finally entrapped by Vivien, the Lady of the Lake, and bound under a rock for ever. He was famous for his prophecies. >> Arthur

Meroe >> **Kush**

meroplankton >> **plankton**

Merovingians [merohvinjianz] The original Frankish royal family, named after the half-legendary Merovech or Meroveus (the 'sea-fighter'). Clovis was the first Merovingian king to control large parts of Gaul. >> Franks

Mersey, River [merzee] River in NW England; formed at junction of Goyt and Tame Rivers; flows 112 km/70 mi W into the Irish Sea at Liverpool Bay. >> England [i]

Merseyside pop (1995e) 1 433 000; area 652 sq km/252 sq mi. County of NW England created in 1974 from parts of Lancashire and Cheshire; metropolitan council abolished in 1986; chief town, Liverpool. >> England [i]; Liverpool; Mersey, River

Merthyr Tydfil [merther tidvil], Welsh **Merthyr Tudful** pop (1995e) 59 500; area 111 sq km / 43 sq mi. County (unitary authority from 1996) in S Wales, UK; administrative centre, Merthyr Tydfil. >> Wales [i]

Merton, Robert C (1944–) Economist, born in New York City. He worked at MIT, joining Harvard Business School in 1988. He shared the 1997 Nobel Prize for Economics for his contribution to a new method of determining the value of derivatives.

mesa [maysa] An area of high, flat land (tableland) with steep escarpments formed by the remnants of horizontal resistant rocks, and underlain by softer rock. >> butte

Mesa Verde [maysa verday] (Sp 'green table') An area of precipitous canyons and wooded volcanic mesa in SW Colorado, USA; a world heritage site. It is renowned for its Anasazi Indian cliff-dwellings.

mescal >> **century plant**

mescal button >> **peyote**

mescaline [meskalin, -leen] A hallucinogenic drug from the Mexican cactus *Lophophora williamsi*, also known as *Anhalonium lewinii*. It was widely used during the 'psychedelic era' of the 1960s. >> cactus [i]; hallucinogens

Meshed >> **Mashhad**

Mesmer, Franz Anton [mezmer] (1734–1815) Physician and founder of mesmerism, born near Constance, Germany. He claimed that there exists a power, which he called 'magnetism', that could be used to cure diseases. In 1778 he went to Paris, where he created a sensation; but in 1785 a learned commission reported unfavourably, and he retired into obscurity in Switzerland. >> hypnosis

Mesoamerica or **Middle America** The area covered by Central America and Mexico together. Because Mexico is geographically a part of North America, this term is often used to identify features of cultural or historical importance which both regions share. >> Chichén Itzá; Monte Albán; Teotihuacán

Mesolithic >> **Three Age System**

meson [meezon] In particle physics, a collective term for strongly interacting subatomic particles having integer spin, each comprising a quark–antiquark pair. Mesons, especially pi-mesons (pions), are responsible for holding together protons and neutrons in atomic nuclei. >> boson; particle physics; pion

Mesopotamia [mesopotaymia] Literally, 'the land between the rivers'; the name in antiquity for the area between the Tigris and Euphrates. **Lower Mesopotamia** was the home of the Sumerian and Babylonian civilizations; **Upper Mesopotamia** was the home of the Assyrians. The world's first urban civilization emerged here during the fourth millennium BC; the Mesopotamian Empire was established c.2300 BC. >> Assyria; Babylonia; Eridu; Sumer; Ur; Uruk

Mesosaurus A lightly built, aquatic reptile known from the late Carboniferous to the early Permian periods in South America and S Africa; up to 1 m/3¼ ft long. (Class: Anapsida. Order: Mesosauria.) >> Carboniferous / Permian period; reptile

mesosphere A region of the atmosphere from c.50–80 km/30–50 mi, between the stratosphere below and the thermosphere above. It is characterized by rapidly falling temperature with height, from around 0°C to −100°C. >> atmosphere [i]

Mesozoa [mezozoha] A small phylum of multicellular animals found as internal parasites of marine invertebrates such as cephalopod molluscs. >> Cephalopoda [i]; parasitology; phylum

Mesozoic era [mezozohik] A major division of geological time extending from c.250 to 65 million years ago; subdivided into the Triassic, Jurassic, and Cretaceous periods. It was the age of the giant reptiles and the beginning of mammalian life. >> Cretaceous / Jurassic / Triassic period; geological time scale; RR976

Messager, André (Charles Prosper) [mesazhay] (1853–1929) Composer and conductor, born in Montluçon, France. He wrote several operettas and three ballets, notably *Les Deux pigeons* (1886, The Two Pigeons).

Messerschmitt, Willy [mesershmit], popular name of **Wilhelm Messerschmitt** (1898–1978) Aviation designer and production chief, born in Frankfurt, Germany. During World War 2 he supplied the Luftwaffe with its foremost types of combat aircraft. >> aircraft [i]

Messiaen, Olivier (Eugène Prosper Charles) [mesiã] (1908–92) Composer and organist, born in Avignon, France. His music, which has evolved new methods of pitch organization and intricate mathematical rhythmic systems, is motivated by religious mysticism and a keen interest in birdsong.

Messiah [mesiya] (Heb 'anointed one') In Jewish writings from c.2nd-c BC onwards, one who would help deliver Israel from its enemies, aid in its restoration, and establish a worldwide kingdom. In Christian thought, the role is interpreted as fulfilled in Jesus of Nazareth. >> Christianity; Jesus Christ; Judaism

Messier, Charles [mesyay] (1730–1817) Astronomer, born in Badonviller, France. He is mainly remembered for the Messier Catalog of 103 star clusters, nebulae, and galaxies. >> astronomy

Messina, Strait of, ancient **Fretum Siculum** Channel between Sicily and the Italian mainland; minimum width (N) 5 km/3 mi; length 35 km/22 mi. >> Italy [i]; Sicily

ME syndrome An abbreviation for **myalgic encephalomyelitis syndrome**, a condition following certain viral infections which cause self-limited feverish illnesses. It is characterized by weakness, diffuse muscle pains, depression, and headaches, which persist for several months and which ultimately resolve.

metabolism The complete range of biochemical processes taking place within living organisms. It comprises those processes which produce complex substances from simpler components, with a consequent use of energy (**anabolism**), and those which break down complex food molecules, thus liberating energy (**catabolism**). In nutrition, it refers to an efficient way of burning food calories to give the body the energy it needs for its various functions. **Basal metabolism** is the minimum energy expenditure needed to maintain all the vital functions of the body – the energy expended during sleep, or while the body is resting. >> biochemistry; nutrition

metal An element whose solid phase is characterized by high thermal and electrical conductivities. Pure metals are all lustrous, opaque, cold to the touch, and more or less malleable. Most elements are metals, and metallic properties increase from lighter to heavier elements in each group of the periodic table and from right to left in each row. >> chemical elements; metallurgy; RR1036

metal fatigue A weakness which develops in a metal structure that has been subjected to many repeated stresses, even though they may be intermittent. As a result, the structure may fail under a load which it could initially have sustained without fracture. >> metal

metallic glass Metal in an amorphous condition (ie the atoms of the metal have no regular or crystalline arrangement); first produced in 1960 by US materials scientist William Klement (1937–). Metallic glasses are useful for transformer cores, and for forming very strong components such as gears. >> glass i

metallocene >> **ferrocene**

metallography The study of the structure of metals, usually implying the use of microscopy or X-ray diffraction. Various kinds of structure can be observed, arising from grain, crystalline structure, and the inclusion of impurities. >> metallurgy; microscope; X-ray diffraction

metalloids Elements midway between being metals and non-metals. They make a diagonal band across the periodic table, and are generally considered to include boron, silicon, germanium, arsenic, antimony, tellurium, and polonium. >> chemical elements; metal; RR1036

metallurgy The technique and science of extracting metals from their ores, converting them into useful forms, and establishing the conditions for their fabrication. The changes undergone by metals are now important aspects of metallurgy, as are the physics and chemistry of corrosion prevention. >> corrosion; metallography; ore

metamorphic rock Rock formed by the alteration of pre-existing rock by intense heat and/or pressure, and often accompanied by the action of hot fluids in the Earth's crust. Slates, schists, and gneisses are metamorphic rocks. >> gneiss; orogeny; schist; slate

metamorphosis In biology, an abrupt structural change, as seen in the marked changes during the development of an organism, especially the transformation from larva to adult, or from one larval stage to the next. >> biology; larva

metaphor (Gr 'carrying from one place to another') A figurative device in language where something is referred to, implicitly, in terms of something else: the Moon is a goddess, life a dark wood, the world a stage. An explicit comparison ('Life, like a dome of many-coloured glass') is a *simile*. >> figurative language; imagery

metaphysical poetry A term applied to some English poetry of the late 16th-c and early 17th-c, on account of its use of unusual and sometimes difficult ideas in relation to emotional states. Dr Johnson referred to the way in which in this poetry 'heterogeneous ideas are yoked by violence together'. >> Cowley; Crashaw; Donne; Herbert, George; Marvell; Vaughan

metaphysics A traditional branch of philosophy which deals at the most general level with the nature of existence – what it is, what sorts of things exist, of what categories, and in what structure. The origin of the term is a reference to the text Aristotle wrote 'after the Physics'. >> Aristotle; ontology

Metastasio, Pietro [meta**stah**zioh], originally **Pietro Armando Dominico Trapassi** (1698–1782) Poet, born in Rome. He wrote the libretti for 27 operas, including Mozart's *Clemenza di Tito*, and in 1729 became court poet at Vienna.

metastasis [me**ta**stasis] The occurrence of tumour tissue in organs distant from the site of the primary tumour. It is characteristic of malignant tumours, where malignant cells are transported by way of the bloodstream or lymphatics. >> cancer

metazoan [meta**zoh**an] A multicellular animal with its body organized into specialized tissues and organs; a member of the subkingdom Eumetazoa. >> kingdom

meteor A piece of matter (dust, sand, grit) which gives off a streak of light seen when it burns up in the Earth's atmosphere; popularly known as a *shooting star*. A **meteor shower** can be seen when the Earth passes through a trail of dust left by a comet in interplanetary space. >> cosmic dust; meteorite; Perseids

Meteor Crater or **Barringer Crater** An impact crater 1·3 km/0·8 mi across near Flagstaff, AZ; estimated age 20 000 years. It is believed to be the result of the impact of a meteorite c.10 m/11 yd across. >> meteorite; Tunguska event

meteorite A lump of interplanetary debris that survives a high-speed passage through the atmosphere and hits the ground. Meteorites mostly derive from asteroids, with a few from the Moon and possibly even from Mars. The types are stony, iron, and stony-iron; some have intriguing inclusions of organic material. A meteorite is known as a **meteoroid** while travelling in space. >> asteroids; meteor; Meteor Crater

meteoroid >> **meteorite**

meteorology The scientific study of global atmospheric processes: the receipt of solar radiation, evaporation, evapotranspiration, and precipitation, and the determination of, and changes in, atmospheric pressure (and, therefore, wind). Meteorology is generally concerned with the short-term processes (ie hours and days rather than months and seasons) operating in the troposphere and mesosphere. >> atmosphere i; climate; weather; wind i

methanal >> **formaldehyde**

methane [**mee**thayn, **me**thayn] CH_4. The simplest of the alkane or paraffin hydrocarbons. Formed by the anaerobic decomposition of organic matter, it is the main constituent of natural gas, and was originally called **marsh gas**. >> gas 2 i; hydrocarbons

methanogen >> **Archaebacteria**

methanoic acid >> **formic acid**

methanol [**meth**anol] CH_3OH, also called **methyl** or **wood alcohol**, boiling point 65°C. A colourless, poisonous liquid, now synthesized from hydrogen and carbon monoxide. It is an important starting chemical in synthesis, a solvent, and a denaturing agent for ethyl alcohol. >> methylated spirits

Method, the Both a style of acting and a system of training for the working actor, developed in the USA by Lee Strasberg. The method stresses inner motivation and psychological truth. A well-known exponent of this style is Marlon Brando. >> Actors' Studio; Strasberg

Methodism A Christian denomination founded in 1739 by John Wesley as an evangelical movement within the Church of England, becoming a separate body in 1795. The movement spread rapidly as he travelled the country on horseback and sent other evangelical leaders to the American colonies. The principal doctrines of the Church are laid down in Wesley's sermons, his notes on the New Testament, and his Articles of Religion. In 1998 there were c.34 million Methodists worldwide. >> Church of England; evangelicalism; Wesley, John

Methodius, St >> **Cyril and Methodius, Saints**

Methuselah [mi**thoo**zela] The eighth and longest-lived of the Hebrew patriarchs, who lived before the Flood. His supposed 969 years makes him the paragon of longevity. >> patriarch 1

methyl alcohol >> **methanol**

methylated spirits Ethyl alcohol with additives to make it poisonous and unpalatable, and hence unsuitable for beverage use; also called **denatured alcohol**. Its major ingredients are methanol, pyridine, and benzene. >> ethanol

methylbenzene >> **toluene**

methylbutane >> **pentane**

Metis (astronomy) [**mee**tis] A tiny natural satellite of Jupiter, discovered in 1979; distance from the planet 128 000 km/79 000 mi; diameter 40 km/25 mi.>> RR964

Métis [**may**tee] The mixed blood offspring of French-Canadian and native Indian marriages. They were the descendants of the *coureurs de bois*, the French fur traders who ranged throughout the interior of America from the 1660s.

metre (UK) **/ meter** (US) (literature) (Gr *metron* 'measure') The recurrence of a rhythmic pattern in poetry, within the line and over larger units (*stanzas*). Different languages measure different things to establish metre. In the classical languages, it is length (or 'quantity'); in Chinese, it is pitch; in Germanic languages, stress. Some English metre works by stress count, some by counting both stressed and unstressed syllables (as in the traditional iamb, dactyl, etc). >> blank verse; iamb; poetry; verse

metre (UK) **/ meter** (US) (physics) Base SI unit of length; symbol *m*; defined as the length of the path travelled by light in a vacuum during an interval of 1/299 792 458 of a second; commonly used as **kilometre** (*km*, 1000 m), **centimetre** (*cm*, 1/100 m) and **millimetre** (*mm*, 1/1000 m). >> units (scientific)

metronome A device for indicating and determining the tempo of a musical work. The type in common use, patented in 1815 by Johann Nepomuk Maelzel (1770–1838), works like a pendulum clock; its rate of swing, and therefore of 'tick', is controlled by an adjustable weight on the upper extension of a pendulum arm.

Metternich, Klemens (Wenzel Nepomuk Lothar), Fürst von (Prince of) [**met**ernikh] (1773–1859) Austrian statesman, born in Coblenz, Germany. He took a prominent part in the Congress of Vienna (1814), and between 1815 and 1848 was the most powerful influence for conservatism in Europe, contributing much to the tension that produced the upheaval of 1848. >> Vienna, Congress of; Revolutions of 1848

Metz [mets], ancient **Divodurum Mediomatricum** 49°08N 6°10E, pop (1995e) 123 000. Fortified town in NE France; on R Moselle; strategic focus of crossroads; residence of Merovingian kings, 6th-c; later, part of Holy Roman Empire; taken by France, 1552; part of Germany from 1871 until after World War 1; scene of major German defence in 1944 invasion; World War 1 military cemetery nearby; airport; bishopric; university (1971); Gothic cathedral (1250–1380); trade in coal, metals, wine. >> Merovingians; World War 2

Meung, Jean de >> **Jean de Meung**

Meuse, River [moez], Dutch **Maas**, ancient **Mosa** River in NE France, Belgium, and The Netherlands, rising on the Langres Plateau, NE France; enters the North Sea in the Rhine delta; length 950 km/590 mi. >> Belgium [i]; France [i]; Netherlands, The [i]

Mexican War (1846–8) A war between Mexico and the USA, which began in territory disputed between Texas (annexed by the USA but claimed by Mexico) and Mexico. US troops invaded Mexico and forced a capitulation in which Mexico ceded most of the present-day SW United States. >> Guadalupe Hidalgo, Treaty of; Wilmot Proviso

Mexico, Span **México** or **Méjico**, official name **United Mexican States**, Span **Estados Unidos Mexicanos** pop (1995e) 89 872 000; area 1 978 800 sq km/763 817 sq mi. Federal republic in S North America; capital, Mexico City; timezones GMT −8 to −6; chief ethnic groups, Mestizo (60%), Amerindian (30%); chief religion, Roman Catholicism (80%); official language, Spanish; unit of currency, the peso of 100 centavos; narrow coastal plains; land rises steeply to a C plateau, c.2400 m/7800 ft; volcanic peaks to the S, notably Citlaltépetl (5699 m/18 697 ft); limestone lowlands of the Yucatán peninsula stretch into the Gulf of Mexico (SE); region subject to earthquakes; great climatic variation between coastlands and mountains; desert or semi-desert conditions in NW; typically tropical climate on E coast; generally wetter on S coast; considerable temperature variations in N, cold in winter, hot in summer; centre of Indian civilizations for over 2500 years; Gulf Coast Olmecs based at La Venta, Zapotecs at Monte Albán at Oaxaca, Mixtecs at Mitla, Toltecs at Tula, Maya in the Yucatán, Aztecs at Tenochtitlán; Spanish arrival, 1516; Viceroyalty of New Spain established; struggle for independence, 1810–21; federal republic, 1824; lost territory to the USA in 1836 and after the Mexican War, 1846–8; civil war, 1858–61; occupation of Mexico City by French forces in 1863–7; revolution, 1910–17; revolt in S state of Chiapas by Zapatista National Liberation Army, 1994; governed by a president and bicameral Congress, consisting of a Senate and Chamber of Deputies; wide range of mineral exports; major discoveries of oil and natural gas in the 1970s (now world's fourth largest producer); fluorite

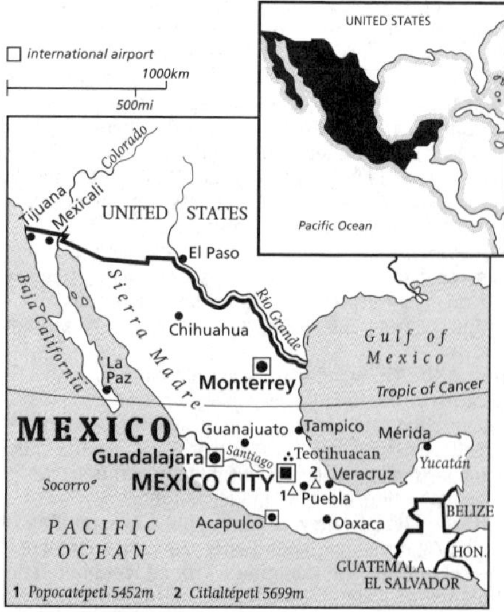

and graphite (world's leading producer); large petrochemical industry; important trading relationship with USA, especially after free-trade-area agreement in 1993; major economic crisis (Dec 1994), followed by package of loan guarantees from the USA (Feb 1995). >> Aztecs; Cortés; Mayas; Mexican War; Mexico City; Olmecs; Toltecs; Zapotecs; RR1016 political leaders

Mexico, Gulf of area 1 543 000 sq km/596 000 sq mi. Gulf on the SE coast of North America; deepest point, Sigsbee Deep (3878 m/12 723 ft); oil and natural gas resources on continental shelves.

Mexico City, Span **Ciudad de México** 19°25N 99°10W, pop (1995e) 10 536 000. Federal district and capital of Mexico; in C Mexico, altitude 2200 m/7200 ft, area 50 sq km/20 sq mi; largest city in the world; built on the site of the Aztec capital, Tenochtitlán; city centre a world heritage site; airport; railway; seven universities; cathedral (16th–19th-c), National Palace (1692); location of 1968 summer Olympic Games; major earthquake (1985) killed c.20 000. >> Mexico ℹ

Meyerbeer, Giacomo [**miy**erbayer], originally **Jakob Liebmann Meyer Beer** (1791–1864) Operatic composer, born in Berlin. His operas include *Robert le Diable* (1831) and *Les Huguenots* (1836).

mezzanine [**mez**aneen] An intermediate floor in a building, placed between two main (usually lower) storeys; also known as an **entresol**.

Mezzogiorno [metzoh**jaw(r)**noh] pop (1995e) 20 485 000. Geographical region comprising regions of S Italy and the islands of Sicily and Sardinia; a largely agricultural area; name ('midday') refers to the heat of the region; devastated by earthquake (1980). >> Italy ℹ

mezzotint [**met**zohtint] A technique of engraving which gives tonal rather than linear effects. Invented c.1640, it was rendered obsolete by photography in the 19th-c. >> engraving

Miami [miy**am**ee] 25°47N 80°11W, pop (1995e) 398 000. Port city in SE Florida, USA; settled around a military post in the 1830s; since 1945, one of the country's most famous and popular resorts; airport; railway; major tourist industry with extensive recreational facilities; hub of a large agricultural region; large numbers of immigrants (nearly half the metropolitan population is Hispanic); professional teams, Dolphins (football), Heat (basketball), Marlins (baseball). >> Florida; Miami Beach

Miami Beach 25°47N 80°08W, pop (1995e) 103 000. Town in SE Florida, USA, on an island across Biscayne Bay from Miami; area developed in 1920s; railway; connected to Miami by four causeways; popular year-round resort, famous for its 'gold coast' hotel strip. >> Florida; Miami

Miao [myow] A Sino-Tibetan-speaking mountain people of SE Asia and S China, constituting many different groups. Population more than 4 million, mostly in China. >> Sino-Tibetan languages

Micah, Book of [**miy**ka] or **Micheas, Book of** One of the 12 so-called 'minor' prophetic books of the Hebrew Bible/Old Testament, attributed to the prophet Micah of Moresheth-gath, a contemporary of Isaiah in Judah and active in the late 8th-c BC. Some parts may be of later date (6th–5th-c BC). >> Isaiah; Old Testament; prophet

micas [**miy**kaz] An important group of common rock-forming minerals characterized by a layer structure which gives the crystals a platy form and a perfect basal cleavage. Important members are *muscovite* (white mica), a light, silvery-coloured potassium aluminium silicate, and *biotite*, which is dark brown, and contains additional iron and magnesium. >> silicate minerals

Michael (angel) An angel described as the guardian of Israel (*Dan* 10, 12). He appears as a great patron, intercessor, and warrior in later Jewish non-canonical works. >> Michaelmas

Michael (of Romania) (1921–) King of Romania (1927–30, 1940–7), born in Sinaia, Romania, the son of Carol II (1893–1953). He first came to the throne on the death of his grandfather, his father having renounced his own claims in 1925. In 1930 he was supplanted by his father Carol (r. 1930–40), then returned to the throne when the Germans gained control of Romania. In 1944 he helped to overthrow the dictatorship of Antonescu, but was later compelled to abdicate (1947), and has since lived in exile near Geneva. >> Romania ℹ

Michael, George, originally **Yorgos Kyriatou Panayiotou** (1963–) Singer and songwriter, born in Finchley, Greater London. A partner with **Andrew Ridgeley** (1963–) of the band Wham!, he released his debut solo single 'Careless Whisper' in 1985, which reached number 1 in the UK charts. His debut solo album, *Faith*, stayed in the US charts for over a year.

Michaelmas [**mi**klmas] In the Christian Church, the feast of St Michael and All Angels (29 Sep); a quarter-day in England and Wales. >> Michael (angel); quarter-day

Michaelmas daisy [**mi**klmas] A member of a large group of perennial cultivars of aster, mostly derived from the North American *Aster novi-belgii*; flower-heads daisy-like; spreading outer florets blue, pink, red, or white; inner disc florets yellow. (Genus: *Aster*. Family: Compositae.) >> aster

Micheas [mi**kay**as] >> **Micah, Book of**

Michelangelo [miykl**an**jeloh], in full **Michelangelo di Lodovico Buonarroti Simoni** (1475–1564) Sculptor, painter, and poet, born in Caprese, Italy. His 'Cupid' was bought by Cardinal San Giorgio, who summoned him to Rome (1496). In Florence he sculpted the marble 'David', and the 'Pietà' in the cathedral. In 1503 Julius II summoned him back to Rome, where he was commissioned to design the pope's tomb, and decorated the ceiling of the Sistine Chapel with paintings (1508–12). His last pictorial achievement was 'The Last Judgment' (1537), and the next year he was appointed architect of St Peter's, to which he devoted himself until his death.

Michelin, André [**mich**elin], Fr [meeshlĩ] (1853–1931) Tyre manufacturer, born in Paris. He and his younger brother **Edouard** (1859–1940) were the first to use demountable pneumatic tyres on motor cars. They also initiated the production of high-quality road maps and guide books. >> tyre

Michelson, A(lbert) A(braham) [**mik**elsn] (1852–1931) Physicist, born in Strzelno, Poland. He is chiefly remembered for his experiment with US chemist **Edward Williams Morley** (1838–1923) to determine ether drift, the negative result of which set Einstein on the road to the theory of relativity. He was the first US scientist to receive a Nobel Prize (1907). >> ether 2; special relativity ℹ

Michigan [**mish**igan] pop (1995e) 9 654 000; area 151 579 sq km/58 527 sq mi. State in NC USA; the 'Great Lake State' or the 'Wolverine State'; 26th state admitted to the Union, 1837; settled by the French, 1668; ceded to the British, 1763; handed over to the USA in 1783 and became part of Indiana Territory; Territory of Michigan established, 1805; 99 909 sq km/38 565 sq mi of the Great Lakes lie within the state boundary; highest point Mt Curwood (604 m/1982 ft); capital, Lansing; major tourist area; the S part of the state is highly industrialized; motor vehicles and parts, iron and steel (second in the country for iron ore production); corn and dairy products. >> Detroit; Great Lakes; Lansing; United States of America ℹ; RR994

Michigan, Lake Third largest of the Great Lakes (area 58 020 sq km/22 400 sq mi) and the only one lying entirely within the USA; 494 km/307 mi long; maximum width 190 km/118 mi; maximum depth 281 m/922 ft;

linked in the NE with L Huron via the Strait of Mackinac. >> Great Lakes

Michiko >> **Akihito**

Mickiewicz, Adam (Bernard) [mits**kyay**vich] (1798–1855) National poet of Poland, born near Novogrodek, Lithuania. His masterpiece is the epic *Pan Tadeusz* (1834, Thaddeus). In 1853 he went to Italy to organize the Polish legion.

microbe >> **micro-organism**

microchip A tiny wafer of semiconductor material, such as silicon, processed to form an integrated circuit. Using large-scale integration (LSI) or very large scale integration (VLSI), up to 100 000 transistors can be built into the chip. When memory and logic circuits are built in, it becomes known as a **microprocessor**. >> integrated circuit; semiconductor; silicon

microcomputer A computer based on a single chip microprocessor plus necessary memory and input and output devices. The term (often abbreviated to **micro**) was first applied to the small desktop computers which first appeared in the 1970s. >> microchip

microeconomics >> **economics**

microelectronics A branch of electronics concerned with producing and using microcircuits – miniaturized electronic circuits consisting of tiny transistors, integrated circuits, and other electronic components often contained in one microchip. Microelectronic circuiting is used in computers, inertial guidance systems, and spacecraft. >> electronics; integrated circuit; microchip

microfarad >> **farad**

microfilm Black-and-white photographic material of extremely fine grain and high resolution for document copying on a greatly reduced scale. Microfilms are usually read by enlarged projection. >> photocopying

microfloppy disk >> **minidisk**

microgravity A state of free-fall weightlessness experienced in spacecraft. Gravitational effects of the spacecraft itself make it difficult to obtain less than one-millionth Earth gravity for experimentation. There are limited opportunities for microgravity experiments in the small space stations presently available. >> space station

microlight >> **hang glider** ℹ

micrometre >> **micron**

micron Unit of length; symbol μ; defined as one micrometre or 10^{-6} m; commonly used in biological sciences. >> metre

Micronesia A collection of island groups in the N Pacific. Included are the Marianas, Carolines, Marshalls, Kiribati (Gilbert Is), and Nauru. Most are of atoll formation, and very small. The people are outwardly distinguishable from Melanesians and Polynesians, and analysis of their blood typing suggests that they are a distinctive racial grouping. >> atoll; Melanesia; Polynesia

Micronesia, Federated States of pop (1995e) 119 000; land area 700 sq km/270 sq mi. Federal republic in W Pacific Ocean, consisting of four states (Yap, Chuuk (Truk), Ponape (Pohnpei), Kosrae) formerly belonging to the US Trust Territory of the Pacific Is; comprises all the Caroline Is except Belau; capital, Palikir (on Ponape); timezone GMT +11; major ethnic groups, Trukese (41%), Ponapeian (26%); chief religion, Christianity; chief languages, English (official), with several local languages spoken; currency, the US dollar; islands vary from high mountainous terrain to low coral atolls; tropical climate, with occasional typhoons; heavy rainfall all year; settled by Spanish seafarers, 1565; formally annexed by Spain, 1874; sold to Germany, 1899; control mandated to Japan by League of Nations, 1920; American navy took control at end of World War 2, 1945; part of UN Trust Territory of the Pacific, 1947; compact of free association with the USA, 1982; trusteeship ended, 1990; independence, 1991, with USA continuing to control in defence and foreign relations; governed by a president and a National Congress; agricultural economy, especially tropical fruits, coconuts, vegetables. >> Kosrae; Ponape; Truk; Yap; RR1008 political leaders

micronutrients >> **nutrients**

micro-organism An organism of microscopic size, typically not visible to the unaided eye; also referred to as a **microbe**. >> algae; bacteria ℹ; fungus; lichen; Protoctista; viroid; virus; yeast

microphone A device that converts acoustic waves in air to electrical signals for transmission, recording, and reproduction. First developed by Bell and Edison in 1876–7 for telephony, microphones are widely employed in telecommunications, sound recording, and hearing aids. In all types, impinging sound waves cause corresponding oscillations of a diaphragm. These movements in their turn vary a resistance (**carbon microphones**, as in telephone receivers), capacitance (**condenser microphones**), electromagnetic field (**dynamic** and **coil microphones**), or the shape of a piezo-electric crystal (**crystal microphones**), each producing a variation in electrical output. A **lavallier** [la**val**yay] is a small personal microphone worn by the speaker on a neck-cord or coat lapel, allowing freedom of movement. >> Bell, Alexander Graham; Edison; loudspeaker ℹ; piezo-electric effect; sound recording; telephone

microprocessor >> **microchip; microcomputer**

microscope An optical instrument for producing enlarged images of minute objects. The compound microscope, in which a second lens further magnifies the image produced by a primary lens, was invented in the Netherlands in the late 16th-c. The effectiveness of compound light microscopes is limited by the resolving power of the lens; magnifications can be achieved up to a maximum of 1 000. Electron microscopes allow magnifications of over 50 000. >> electron microscope ℹ

Microscopium (Lat 'microscope') A small, faint S constellation, introduced in the 18th-c. >> constellation; RR968

Microsoft A computer company which came into prominence with the design and supply of the operating system

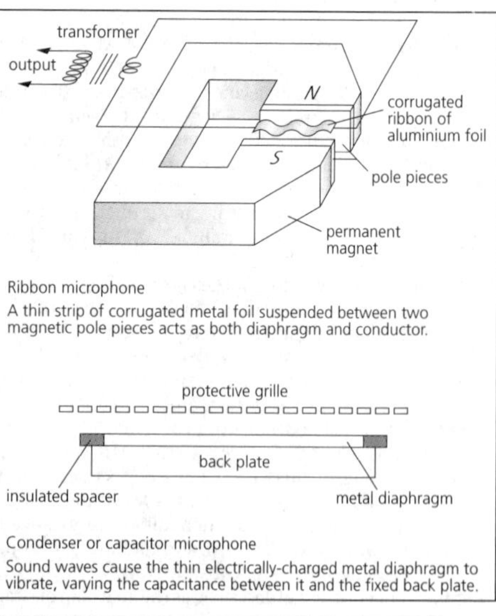

Ribbon microphone

A thin strip of corrugated metal foil suspended between two magnetic pole pieces acts as both diaphragm and conductor.

Condenser or capacitor microphone

Sound waves cause the thin electrically-charged metal diaphragm to vibrate, varying the capacitance between it and the fixed back plate.

Two types of microphone

(MS-DOS) for the IBM personal computer. The system is supported by spreadsheet and word-processing packages and more recently by the windows application software. >> DOS; Gates, Bill; International Business Machines; MS-DOS; windows

microteaching A technique used in the training of teachers which involves the trainee practising a specific teaching skill (such as questioning or explaining) for a short time with a small group of children, receiving feedback such as a tutor's comments, a written appraisal, or seeing a videotape of the mini-lesson.

microtone A musical interval smaller than a semitone. Microtones are indigenous to some musical cultures, especially in the East, and they occur naturally in the harmonic series. >> scale ℹ

microwave background radiation >> **cosmic background radiation**

microwave oven An oven, first constructed in 1947, which uses microwave radiation to heat food. The radiation penetrates inside food, where it is absorbed primarily by water molecules, causing heat to spread through the food. This penetration effect makes heating much faster than in conventional ovens. >> microwaves

microwaves Electromagnetic radiation of wavelength between 1 mm and 10 cm, less than radio waves and more than infrared. They are produced by klystrons and magnetrons, and used in radar, communications, and microwave ovens. >> electromagnetic radiation ℹ; klystron; magnetron; microwave background radiation; microwave oven

micturition >> **urine**

Midas [**miy**das] A legendary King of Phrygia. As a reward for helping the satyr, Silenus, Dionysus gave Midas a wish, and he asked that anything he touched should turn to gold. However, this caused so many difficulties (eg in eating) that he asked to be released; he was told to bathe in the River Pactolus, which thereafter had golden sands. >> Dionysus

Middle Ages The period of European history between the collapse of the Roman Empire in the West and the Renaissance (c.500–c.1500); sometimes, however, the term is restricted in its use to the four or five centuries after the year 1000, characterized by such features as the emergence of national states and the spiritual attainments of the Church in what was above all an age of faith. >> Crusades ℹ; Dark Ages; feudalism; serfdom

Middle America A geographical region encompassing Mexico, Central America, and the West Indies; includes the Gulf of Mexico and the Caribbean.

Middle East A loosely defined geographical region encompassing the largely Arab States to the E of the Mediterranean, together with Cyprus, Turkey, and the countries of North Africa. The region conventionally includes the countries of Syria, Lebanon, Israel, Jordan, Egypt, Iraq, Iran, Kuwait, Saudi Arabia, Bahrain, Qatar, Oman, United Arab Emirates, Yemen, Sudan, Libya, Tunisia, Algeria, and Morocco.

Middlesbrough [**mid**lzbruh] 54°35N 1°14W, pop (1995e) 147 000. Port town and (from 1996) unitary authority, NE England; on the R Tees estuary; developed around the iron industry in the 19th-c; railway; university, 1992. >> England ℹ; Tees, River

middle school A type of school in the UK for children aged 8–12 or 9–13. The former are regarded as primary, the latter as secondary schools. >> primary education; secondary education

Middlesex Former county of England, which lost its official identity after local government reorganization in 1965. Most of its area was subsumed under Greater London, with some districts transferred to Surrey and Hertfordshire. The name continues to be used by many local organizations. >> England ℹ

Middle Temple >> **Inns of Court**

Middleton, Thomas (c.1570–1627) Playwright, born in London. His works include the satirical *A Game at Chess* (1624), and the tragedy *Women Beware Women* (?1621). He also collaborated in many plays, such as *The Changeling* (1622), with William Rowley (c.1585–c.1642).

Middle West or **Midwest** The region of the USA comprising the states between the Great Lakes and the upper Mississippi R valley: Illinois, Indiana, Iowa, Kansas, Minnesota, Missouri, Nebraska, Ohio, and Wisconsin. >> corn belt

Midgard [**mid**gah(r)d] Middle Earth, the land in which human beings live, according to Norse mythology.

midge A small, delicate fly that gathers in vast swarms at dusk near standing water; adults gnat-like but non-biting, as mouthparts are poorly developed. (Order: Diptera. Family: Chironomidae, c.5000 species.) >> fly; gall midge

midget >> **dwarfism**

Mid Glamorgan pop (1995e) 546 000; area 1018 sq km/ 393 sq mi. Former county in S Wales, UK; created in 1974, and replaced in 1996 by Merthyr Tydfil, Caerphilly, Bridgend, and Rhondda Cynon Taff counties. >> Wales ℹ

Midianites [**mid**ianiyts] An ancient semi-nomadic people dwelling in the desert area of the Transjordan. They are portrayed as enticing the Israelites into idolatry, but are overcome by Gideon (*Jud* 6–8).

Midland Canal >> **Mittelland Canal**

Midler, Bette [bet] (1945–) Comedienne and actress, born in Honolulu, HI. She developed a popular nightclub act with outrageously bawdy comic routines, and in 1974 received a Tony Award for a record-breaking Broadway show. Her performance in the film *The Rose* (1979) earned her an Oscar nomination. Later films include *Big Business* (1988), *The First Wives Club* (1996), and *That Old Feeling* (1997).

midnight sun A phenomenon during the summer period within the Arctic and Antarctic circles, when the Sun remains continuously above the horizon. There is an equal period in winter when the Sun does not rise at all. >> solstice

midrash [**mid**rash] In general terms, teaching linked to a running exposition of scriptural texts, especially found in rabbinic literature. The term can also apply to the genre of rabbinic writings which consist of such interpretations. >> Judaism

midsummer The summer solstice or 'longest day', which falls in the northern hemisphere on 21 or 22 June, depending on the locality. **Midsummer Day**, a quarter-day in England and Wales, is 24 June. It is preceded by **Midsummer Night**, when supernatural beings are said to roam abroad. >> quarter-day; solstice

Midway Islands 28°15N 177°25W; pop (1995e) 450; area 3 sq km/1 sq mi. Circular atoll enclosing two small islands in the C Pacific Ocean 1850 km/1150 mi NW of Oahu, Hawaii; annexed by USA, 1867; submarine cable station since 1905; military airbase since 1941; Allied air victory in the Battle of Midway (1942) was a turning point in World War 2. >> Pacific Ocean

midwife toad A European frog of the family Discoglossidae; lives away from water; mates on dry land; male wraps eggs around his legs and carries them until they hatch, then puts tadpoles in water. >> frog

Mies van der Rohe, Ludwig [**mees** van duh **roh**uh], also spelled **Miës**, originally **Ludwig Mies** (1886–1969) Architect and designer, born in Aachen, Germany. His designs include the German Pavilion for the Barcelona Exhibition (1929) and the Seagram Building, New York (1956–9). He was director of the Bauhaus at Dessau and Berlin (1930–3), and moved to Chicago in 1938. >> Bauhaus

mifepristone >> **contraception**

migraine A recurrent, usually one-sided headache, often accompanied by vomiting and a disturbance of vision. It tends to occur in young people, lasts a few hours, and lessens in severity and frequency with age. It is believed to arise from the constriction of arterioles within the brain followed by their dilatation. >> headache

migration 1 In anthropology and sociology, a movement of population within or between countries. Migration within countries has been preponderantly towards urban centres, seen by migrants as attractive alternatives to rural overpopulation and its associated deprivation. International migration (*emigration*) may be a response to other factors, such as political threats against minority groups or warfare. >> demography **2** In biology, the movement of organisms or their dispersal stages (seeds, spores, or larvae) from one area to another; usually the periodic two-way movements that take place over relatively long distances and along well-defined routes. >> ethology

Mihailović, Dragoljub [mi**hiyl**ohvich], nickname **Drazha** (1893–1946) Serbian soldier, born in Ivanjica, Serbia. He remained in Yugoslavia in 1941 after the German occupation, forming groups (*Chetniks*) to wage guerrilla warfare. He was executed in Belgrade by the Tito government for collaboration. >> Chetniks; Tito; World War 2

Mikonos or **Mykonos** [**mee**konos] pop (1995e) 5700; area 85 sq km/33 sq mi. Island of the Cyclades, Greece; airfield; several noted resorts. >> Cyclades; Greece ℹ

Mikoyan, Anastas Ivanovich [miko**yan**] (1895–1978) Soviet statesman, born in Sanain, Armenia. He supported Stalin against Trotsky, and in 1926 became minister of trade, doing much to improve Soviet standards of living. >> Stalin; Trotsky

Milan, Ital **Milano** 45°28N 9°12E, pop (1995e) 1 438 000. Commercial city in Lombardy, N Italy, on R Olna; Gallic town, taken by the Romans in 222 BC; later the chief city of the Western Roman Empire; from 12th-c, ruled by the dukes of Milan; Duchy of Milan held by Spain, 16th-c; ceded to Austria, 1713; capital of Kingdom of Italy, 1797–1814; held by Austria, 1815–60; two airports; railway junction; underground; two universities (1920, 1923); Santa Maria delle Grazie (15th-c, with Leonardo da Vinci's 'Last Supper' on the wall of the adjoining monastery), a world heritage site; cathedral (14th-c), Palazzo dell'Ambrosiana (1603–9), La Scala opera house (1775–8). >> Italy ℹ; La Scala; Leonardo da Vinci

mildew Any fungal disease of a plant in which the thread-like fungal strands are visible on the leaves of the host plant as pale or white patches. >> fungus

Milesians [miy**lee**zhnz] A group of Presocratic philosopher-scientists who came from Miletus in Ionia and were active in the 6th-c BC. Thales, Anaximander, and Anaximenes are usually regarded as the first Greek philosophers, in the sense that they offered rational rather than supernatural accounts of cosmology. >> Anaximander; Anaximenes; Miletus; Presocratics; Thales

Miletus [miy**lee**tus] A prosperous Greek city-state in Ionia on the W coast of Asia Minor. It was the birthplace of the Milesians. >> Ionia; Milesians; Naukratis; Thales

milfoil >> **yarrow**

Milhaud, Darius [**mee**oh] (1892–1974) Composer, born in Aix-en-Provence, France. For a time he was a member of *Les Six*. He was a prolific composer, writing several operas, ballets, and symphonies, and orchestral, choral, and chamber works. >> *Six, Les*

Militant Tendency A British political group which came to prominence in the 1980s. (*Militant* is a newspaper published originally by Labour Party members espousing Marxist positions). Its supporters infiltrated a number of local Labour Parties and the Young Socialists (its youth wing). Fearing the adverse electoral publicity resulting from Militant activities, the Labour Party moved to expel members of Militant on the grounds that they were members of a separate political party. After this, Militant's influence in the Party declined. >> Trotskyism

Military Cross (MC) A military award in the UK, instituted in 1914, awarded to captains, lieutenants, and warrant officers in the Army for acts of gallantry or devotion to duty. The ribbon has equal stripes: white, purple, white. >> Distinguished Service Order

military intelligence The collection and evaluation of information relevant to military decision making. Intelligence can be gathered by many means, such as listening to enemy electronic emissions (electronic intelligence, or *elint*), monitoring signals traffic (*Sigint*), the use of surveillance satellites, and traditional espionage techniques. National agencies which collate information at a strategic level include the US Defense Intelligence Agency (DIA) and the British Secret Intelligence Service (SIS). The practice of resisting and frustrating hostile attempts to gain military, political, or scientific intelligence is known as **counter-intelligence**. >> elint; intelligence service; RECONSAT

military science The theoretical study of warfare and of the strategic, tactical, and logistic principles behind it. It is concerned with such unchanging principles as the primacy of the objective, concentration of force, economy of force, surprise, and manoeuvre. >> blitzkrieg; Clausewitz; strategic studies

militia A military force raised (usually in times of emergency) for national defence, separate from the regular army. These national forces are raised by government decree, and can thus be distinguished from guerrilla forces. >> Home Guard; national guard

milk A white or whitish liquid secreted by the mammary glands of female mammals to nourish their young. The milk of many species has been consumed by humans from earliest times, especially cow's milk, with goat's, ewe's, and buffalo milk also making a significant contribution in various parts of the world. Milk is about 88% water, 4·8% lactose, 3·2% protein, and 3·9% fat. *Cream* is the yellowish surface layer of fat which forms when milk is allowed to stand. This may be removed, leaving water emulsion and **skimmed milk**. Low-fat milk, which is increasing in popularity, is produced by partially removing the fat (by 50% – **semi-skimmed milk**). >> butter; cheese; kefir; koumiss; pasteurization; UHT milk; yoghurt

milk of magnesia A suspension of magnesium hydroxide ($Mg(OH)_2$) used as an antacid to sooth an acid stomach. It can also be used as a mild laxative. >> hydroxide; laxative; magnesium

milkwort A perennial herb or small shrub, found almost everywhere; flowers in spikes, five sepals, two inner large, often brightly coloured, enclosing three petals fused with eight stamens to form a tube. (Genus: *Polygala*, 500–600 species. Family: Polygalaceae.)

Milky Way A diffuse band of light across the sky, resulting from the combined light of thousands of millions of faint stars in our Galaxy. Strictly it means the belt of light seen in the night sky, but the term is used freely, as the name of the Galaxy to which our Sun belongs. >> Galaxy

Mill, John Stuart (1806–73) Philosopher and social reformer, born in London. He was educated by his father, Scottish philosopher James Mill (1773–1836), and became an MP in 1865, supporting women's suffrage and liberalism. His major writings include *Principles of Political*

Economy (1848), *On Liberty* (1859), and his most widely known work, *Utilitarianism* (1863). >> utilitarianism

Millais, Sir John Everett [milay] (1829–96) Painter, born in Southampton, Hampshire. He became a founder of the Pre-Raphaelite Brotherhood, his works in this style including the controversial 'Christ in the House of His Parents' (1850, Tate, London). He later became well known for his woodcut illustrations for magazines. >> Pre-Raphaelite Brotherhood; woodcut

Millay, Edna St Vincent [mi**lay**] (1892–1950) Poet, born in Rockland, ME. She received the Pulitzer Prize with *The Harp-Weaver* (1923).

millenarianism [milin**air**eeuhnizm] The belief held by some Christians that there will be a thousand-year (millennium) reign of the saints, either before or immediately after the return of Christ. The belief is usually based on an interpretation of *Rev* 20. 1–7. In recent decades, the term has been used more broadly by social scientists, referring to any religious group looking forward to a sudden and early transformation of the world. >> Adventists; apocalypse; cargo cult; Plymouth Brethren

Millennium Dome The centrepiece of the UK's millennial celebrations, opening on 31 December 1999, designed by the Richard Rogers Partnership, and built in Greenwich, at an estimated cost (in 1998) of £758 million: diameter 320 m/1050 ft, height 50 m/164 ft, circumference 1 km/0.62 mi, floor space 8 hectares/20 acres. Its contents include thematic areas devoted to the mind, the body (including the world's largest representation of the human form), spiritual belief, workplace skilling, the nature of learning, the financial world, relaxation and imagination, leisure and play, community, the environment, planet Earth, and the nature of British identity today.

Miller, Arthur (1915–) Playwright, born in New York City. His major works include *All My Sons* (1947), *Death of a Salesman* (1949, Pulitzer), *The Crucible* (1953), *A View from the Bridge* (1955), and *Playing for Time* (1981). In 1956 he received considerable publicity from his marriage to Marilyn Monroe (divorced 1961), and an appearance before the Un-American Activities Committee for alleged communist sympathies.

Miller, (Alton) Glenn (1904–44) Bandleader and trombonist, born in Clarinda, IA. In 1938 he enjoyed phenomenal success with his 'sweet' ensemble sound, fox-trot rhythms, and well-drilled showmanship. During 1939–42, his hit records included 'Moonlight Serenade' (his theme song), 'Little Brown Jug', and 'In the Mood'. He joined the US Air Force in 1942, and assembled a large orchestra which he took to England, but was killed while travelling in an aircraft lost without trace over the English Channel.

Miller, Henry (Valentine) (1891–1980) Writer, born in New York City. His early books, *Tropic of Cancer* (1934) and *Tropic of Capricorn* (1938), published in Paris, were originally banned in Britain and the USA for their sexual explicitness. Later work includes the series *Sexus* (1945), *Plexus* (1949), and *Nexus* (1960).

Miller, Jonathan (Wolfe) (1934–) Actor and director, born in London. He qualified as a doctor, and his career has combined medical research with contributions to stage and television. He came to public attention as part of the *Beyond the Fringe* team (1961–4), and has since directed for several theatres, including the National Theatre, English National Opera, and the Old Vic. He is also known for his television work, notably the BBC series *The Body in Question* (1977) and *States of Mind* (1982).

Miller, Keith (Ross) (1919–) Cricketer, born in Melbourne, Victoria, Australia. In the great Don Bradman Test side of 1948, he established himself as the world's leading all-rounder of the time. During his career he scored 2598 runs in 55 Test matches, including seven centuries, and took 170 wickets. >> Bradman; cricket ℹ

Miller, Merton (1923–) Economist, born in Boston, MA. In 1990 he shared the Nobel Prize for Economics for his contributions in applying economic theory to the field of corporate finance. >> economics; Markowitz

miller's thumb >> **bullhead**

Millet, Jean François [meeay] (1814–75) Painter, born in Gruchy, France. After the 1848 Revolution he settled at Barbizon. His paintings of rustic life included 'Sower' (1850) and 'The Gleaners' (1857). >> Barbizon School

millet A small-grained, rather inferior cereal from the tropics and warm temperate regions, grown in poor areas or as emergency crops mainly for animal feed and bird seed. (*Panicum miliaceum*. Family: Gramineae.) >> cereals

millibar >> **bar** (physics)

Milligan, Spike, popular name of **Terence Alan Milligan** (1918–) Humorist, born in Ahmadnagar, India. He became known through co-writing and performing in *The Goon Show* (1951–9). His unique perspective on the world, allied to an irrepressible sense of the ridiculous, has been a major influence on British humour. >> Goons, the

Millikan, Robert (Andrews) (1868–1953) Physicist, born in Morrison, IL. His oil drop experiment demonstrated that electric charge always occurs in multiples of a fixed electron charge, and measured the value of this charge. He was awarded the 1923 Nobel Prize for Physics. >> charge; electron

millilitre >> **litre**

milllimetre >> **metre** (physics)

millipede A long-bodied, terrestrial arthropod; typically with double body segments, each bearing two pairs of walking legs. (Class: Diplopoda, c.10 000 species.) >> arthropod

Mills, Sir John (Lewis Ernest Watts) (1908–) Actor, born in Felixstowe, Suffolk. Much in demand for typically English roles, his character parts were often outstanding, as in *Great Expectations* (1946) and *The History of Mr Polly* (1949). Later roles were in *Ryan's Daughter* (1978, Oscar), *Gandhi* (1982), and *Deadly Advice* (1994). He is the father of actresses **Juliet** (1941–) and **Hayley** (1946–).

Milne, A(lan) A(lexander) (1882–1956) Writer, born in London. In 1924 he achieved world fame with his book of children's verse, *When We Were Very Young*, written for his own son, Christopher Robin; further classics include *Winnie-the-Pooh* (1926) and *The House at Pooh Corner* (1928).

Milo of Croton [**miy**loh, **mee**loh] (6th-c BC) Greek athlete, from Crotona in Magna Graecia. He was twelve times victor for wrestling at the Olympic and Pythian games, and commanded the army which defeated the Sybarites (511 BC).

Milosevic, Slobodan [mi**lo**suhvich] (1941–) President of Serbia (1990–) and Yugoslavia (1997–), born in Pozarevac, Serbia. He studied law at Belgrade University, then began a career in management and banking before entering politics. He is the founder and president of the socialist party of Serbia. He became the focus of world attention during the Kosovo crisis and NATO confrontation in early 1999. >> Kosovo; Yugoslavia ℹ

Miłosz, Czeslaw [**mee**wosh, **chezh**wof] (1911–) Poet, born in Szetejnie, Lithuania. His books include *Hymn of the Pearl* (1981) and *Hymn of the Earth* (1986) (trans titles). A selection of his wartime essays, *Legends of Modernity* (trans title), appeared in 1996. He was awarded the Nobel Prize for Literature in 1980.

Milstein, César [**mil**stiyn] (1927–) Molecular biologist, born in Bahía Blanca, Argentina. His main research has been into the production of monoclonal antibodies. He shared the Nobel Prize for Physiology or Medicine in 1984. >> antibodies

Miltiades, the Younger [mil**tiy**adeez] (c.550–489 BC) Athenian general, statesman, and the chief architect of the Greek victory at Marathon. >> Marathon, Battle of

Milton, John (1608–74) Poet, born in London. His early works include *L'Allegro* and *Il Penseroso* (1632), *Comus* (1633), and *Lycidas* (1637). Becoming involved in the Civil War with revolutionary ardour, he wrote very little poetry for the next 20 years. Instead, he published a series of controversial pamphlets, and became official apologist for the Commonwealth. Blind from 1652, after the Restoration he devoted himself wholly to poetry. The theme of his epic sacred masterpiece, *Paradise Lost*, had been in his mind since 1641. He began to write it in 1658, and it was completed in 1665. It was followed by *Paradise Regained* and *Samson Agonistes* (both 1671). He is widely esteemed as a poet second only to Shakespeare. >> English Civil War

Milton Keynes [keenz] 52°03N 0°42W, pop (1995e) 186 000. Industrial new town (since 1967) and unitary authority (from 1997) in Buckinghamshire, SC England; designed on a grid pattern; Open University (1969); railway. >> Buckinghamshire

Milwaukee [mil**waw**kee] 43°02N 87°55W, pop (1995e) 666 000. City in SE Wisconsin, USA, on the W shore of L Michigan; largest city in the state; settled by German immigrants in the mid-19th-c; airfield; railway; two universities (1857, 1908); leading manufacturer of diesel and petrol engines; home of several breweries; professional teams, Brewers (baseball), Bucks (basketball). >> Wisconsin

Mimas [**miy**mas] A natural satellite of Saturn, discovered in 1789; distance to the planet 186 000 km/116 000 mi; diameter 390 km/240 mi; orbital period 0·942 days. >> Saturn (astronomy); RR964

mime In terms of ancient theatre, both a short dramatic sketch and a professional entertainer. In 20th-c theatre, it signifies the art of silent corporeal expression as espoused by Etienne Decroux and popularized by Marcel Marceau. >> Decroux; Marceau; pantomime

mimosa >> **wattle** 🛈

mimulus An annual or perennial, found almost everywhere, many from North America; flowers usually yellow with red blotches. (Genus: *Mimulus*, 100 species. Family: Scrophulariaceae.) >> musk

Minas Gerais [**mee**nas zhe**riys**] pop (1995e) 17 131 000; area 587 172 sq km/226 648 sq mi. State in SE Brazil; accounts for half of Brazil's mineral production (iron ore, gold, diamonds); capital, Belo Horizonte. >> Belo Horizonte; Brazil 🛈; Ouro Prêto

mind An entity usually contrasted with the body or matter, as the mental is with the physical, but variously understood in the history of thought. In its broadest sense (included in or conflated with the meaning of *soul*) it is taken to be the distinction between the animate and the inanimate; in a narrower sense it is taken to be the distinguishing feature of *persons*, and related to self-consciousness and identity. It has posed problems of definition and explanation for philosophers, psychologists, and cognitive scientists, who from their different standpoints have tried to relate it to the brain and to behaviour and have considered analogies with computer software. >> behaviourism; cognitive science

Mindanao [minda**nah**oh] pop (1995e) 14 838 000; area 99 040 sq km/38 229 sq mi. Island in the S Philippines; mountainous, rising to 2954 m/9691 ft at Mt Apo; chief towns, Davao, Zamboanga; Islamic secessionist movement since mid-1970s; Autonomous Region of Muslim Mindanao created, 1989; peace agreement, 1996. >> Davao; Philippines 🛈; Zamboanga

Mindelo [meen**day**loo] 16°54N 25°00W, pop (1995e) 39 200. City and chief port (Porto Grande) of Cape Verde; important refuelling point for transatlantic ships. >> Cape Verde 🛈

Mindoro [min**doh**roh] pop (1995e) 912 000; area 9732 sq km/3756 sq mi. Island of the Philippines; rises to 2585 m/8481 ft at Mt Halcon; chief town, Calapan. >> Philippines 🛈

Mindszenty, József, Cardinal [mind**sen**tee], (1892–1975) Roman Catholic clergyman, born in Mindszent, Hungary. Primate of Hungary (1945), he became internationally known in 1948 when charged with treason by the Communist government in Budapest, and imprisoned (1949–55). He was then granted asylum in the US legation at Budapest (1956–71). >> Roman Catholicism

mine An explosive munition concealed in a fixed place, which achieves its destructive effects when the target moves onto or comes near it. Mines may be planted at sea or 'sown' on land, shallowly buried underground.

mineralogy The study of the chemical composition, physical properties, and occurrence of minerals. Major aspects of the subject include identification, classification and systematics, crystallography, and mineral associations in rocks and ore deposits. >> minerals

mineral oil A term used to distinguish lubricating oils of mineral origin from those of vegetable or animal origin. It is widely used for machinery. >> oil (earth sciences)

minerals Naturally occurring substances, generally inorganic and crystalline, with a homogeneous structure and a chemical composition defined within specified limits; classified by chemical composition and crystal structure. They are the constituents of rocks in the Earth. >> gemstones; mineralogy; ore; silicate minerals

mineral waters Naturally occurring groundwaters rich in dissolved minerals derived from the rocks through which they flow. They are associated with medicinal properties, and may be used for bathing or drinking water.

Minerva [mi**ner**va] The Roman goddess of handicrafts, identified with Athena. >> Athena

minesweeper A small vessel designed or adapted to cut the moorings of mines, thus allowing them to float to the surface where they are destroyed by gunfire. >> mine; warships 🛈

Ming dynasty (1368–1644) Major Chinese dynasty, established by Hongwu (r.1368–98) and consolidated by Yongle (r.1403–24). Its capital was shifted from Nanjing to Beijing in 1421. The period is known for its philosophical, historical, and literary writing, its porcelain, lacquer, and cloisonné, its opulent life style, and its developments in manufacturing and medicine. >> China 🛈

miniature painting A term sometimes used for the small pictures in illuminated manuscripts, and (more often, and properly) for the 'portraits in little' that were so popular in Elizabethan England. >> limner

minicomputer >> **mainframe computer**

minidisk A very compact magnetic disk storage medium for microcomputers, sometimes known as a **microfloppy disk**. There are presently at least four different sizes varying from about 2·75 in to 4 in (c.7–10 cm) in diameter. Unlike floppy disks, minidisks are enclosed in a rigid jacket. >> floppy disk

minilab A device for the rapid production of colour prints. The film is developed in an automated machine and the negatives placed in an automatic printer/processor using a long roll of colour paper. The exposure paper is processed immediately, and dry finished prints emerge. Results are available in an hour or less. >> colour negative; processing

Minimal Art A modern art movement that has flourished since the 1950s, mainly in the USA. Typical are the monochrome canvases of US painter Ad Reinhardt (1913–67), and the prefabricated firebricks of US sculptor Carl André (1935–). In all cases the art content may be described as minimal. >> *De Stijl*; modern art; Suprematism

minimalism In music, a style of composition, increasingly prominent since the 1960s, which abjures the complexities of many earlier 20th-c techniques in favour of simple harmonic and melodic units repeated many times, usually with phased modifications and superimpositions, in an unchanging, 'mechanical' metre. The term is shared with several other art forms (eg painting, theatre) which make use of their medium in a reduced or simplified way. >> Glass; Minimal Art

minimum lending rate (MLR) Formerly the minimum rate of interest at which the Bank of England would lend to discount houses. It superseded the bank rate in 1973, and was itself superseded in 1981 by the *bank base rate*. >> bank base rate

mining The extraction of useful mineral substances from the Earth. In surface, strip, and open-cast mining, the soil is stripped away, and the ore, coal, clay, or mineral is dug directly. At greater depths the deposits are approached by horizontal tunnels dug from vertical shafts (*drifts*). >> coal mining

mink A mammal of genus *Mustela*; thick dark brown coat important to the fur trade (other colours produced by captive breeding); two living species: most important commercially is the **American mink** from North America; also, the **European mink**. (Family: Mustelidae.) >> Mustelidae

Minneapolis [mineeapolis] 44°59N 93°16W, pop (1995e) 391 000. Largest city in Minnesota, USA; port on the Mississippi R to the W of its twin city, St Paul; part of Fort Snelling military reservation, 1819; later developed as a centre of the timber and flour milling industries; city status, 1867; airport; railway; university (1851); centre for enormous grain and cattle area; financial capital of the upper Midwest; professional teams, Minnesota Twins (baseball), Minnesota Vikings (football), Minnesota North Stars (ice hockey), Minnesota Timberwolves (basketball). >> Minnesota; St Paul

Minnelli, Liza (May) [minelee] (1946–) Singer and actress, born in Los Angeles, CA, the daughter of Vincente Minnelli (1910–86) and Judy Garland. She was the youngest-ever actress to win a Tony Award, for *Flora, the Red Menace* (1965). She won an Oscar for *Cabaret* (1972), and later appeared in *New York, New York* (1977) and with Dudley Moore in the *Arthur* films. >> Garland, Judy; Moore, Dudley

Minnesinger [minuhzinger] Aristocratic German minstrels who performed songs of courtly love in the 12th–14th-c. >> *Meistersinger*; Walther von der Vogelweide

Minnesota [minisohta] (Siouan 'watery cloud') pop (1995e) 4 642 000; area 218 593 sq km/84 402 sq mi. State in N USA, the 'North Star State' or the 'Gopher State'; 32nd state admitted to the Union, 1858; permanently settled after the establishment of Fort Snelling, 1820; area became Minnesota Territory in 1849; settled by many Scandinavians in the 1880s; over 11 000 lakes scattered throughout the state; highest point Mt Eagle (701 m/2300 ft); glaciated terrain in the N; capital, St Paul; major tourist area; prairies in the S and W; agriculture the leading industry; nation's second biggest producer of dairy products, hay, oats, rye, turkeys. >> Louisiana Purchase; Minneapolis; St Paul; United States of America [i]; RR994

minnow Small freshwater fish (*Phoxinus phoxinus*) widely distributed in lakes and streams of N Europe and Asia; length up to 13 cm/5 in; body slender, cylindrical, mouth small; variable greenish-brown above, underside yellowish. (Family: *Cyprinidae*.)

Minoan civilization [minohan] The brilliant Bronze Age culture which flourished in the Aegean area in the third and second millennia BC, reaching its zenith around the middle of the second millennium (1700–1450 BC). Its most impressive remains come from Crete, at Knossos, Phaestus, Mallia, and Zakron. The civilization came abruptly to an end c.1450 BC. The cause is unknown. >> Knossos; Mycenaean civilization

Minogue, Kylie [minohg] (1968–) Singer and actress, born in Melbourne, Victoria, Australia. She achieved fame around the world for her role in the television soap opera, *Neighbours*. In 1987 she began a successful recording career, and her 1988 single 'I Should Be So Lucky', had huge sales.

minor In the UK, a person who has not yet reached the age of 18; in Scots law, a distinction is drawn between *pupils* (up to age 12 for girls, 14 for boys) and *minors* (from those ages to age 18); in the USA, the age of majority varies across jurisdictions and according to different purposes. Minors cannot validly enter certain contracts, such as a contract for a loan. >> adoption; guardian

Minorca [minaw(r)ka], Span **Menorca**, ancient **Balearis Minor** pop (1995e) 62 500; area 700 sq km/270 sq mi. Second largest island in the Balearics, W Mediterranean, NE of Majorca; length, 47 km/29 mi; breadth, 10–19 km/6–12 mi; low-lying, rising to 357 m/1171 ft at Monte Toro; airport at Mahón, the island capital. >> Balearic Islands

minor planet >> **asteroids**

Minos [miynos] A legendary King of Crete (or several kings). In Greek mythology, he was the son of Zeus and Europa. In the Underworld he became a judge of the dead. >> Ariadne; Daedalus; Minotaur; Pasiphae; Theseus

Minotaur [miynotaw(r)] The son of Pasiphae and a bull from the sea, half bull and half human; the name means Minos's bull. It was kept in a labyrinth, and killed by Theseus with the help of Ariadne. >> Daedalus; Pasiphae; Theseus

Minsk 53°51N 27°30E, pop (1995e) 1 661 000. Capital city of Belarus, on the R Svisloch; one of the oldest towns in the state, c.11th-c; under Lithuanian and Polish rule; part of Russia, 1793; badly damaged in World War 2; airport; railway junction; university (1921); cathedral (17th-c). >> Belarus [i]

Mint >> **Royal Mint**

mint A perennial native to temperate regions, especially in the N hemisphere; whorls of small pale pink to purplish flowers. Its characteristic pungent scent is due to the presence of essential oils containing menthol. Mints are grown for their culinary value as herbs and flavourings. Many have distinctive odours, including peppermint (*Mentha × piperita*) and spearmint (*Mentha spicata*). (Genus: *Mentha*, 25 species. Family: Labiatae.) >> catmint; essential oil; herb; horehound; pennyroyal

Mintoff, Dom(inic) (1916–) Maltese Labour statesman and prime minister (1955–8, 1971–84), born at Cospicua, Malta. As premier, his demands for independence and accompanying political agitation led to the suspension of Malta's constitution (1959). He resigned in 1958 to lead the Malta Liberation Movement, and followed a policy of moving away from British influence. >> Malta [i]

Minton ceramics One of the principal British potteries of the 19th–20th-c, founded in 1796 by Thomas Minton (1765–1826). They produced pottery and porcelain, making large quantities of willow pattern. >> porcelain; pottery; willow pattern

minuet A French dance in triple metre and moderate tempo, popular among the European aristocracy in the 17th–18th-c. It became a standard movement in the symphony. >> scherzo; symphony

minuscule [minuhskyool] >> **majuscule**

Minutemen Militiamen, particularly in New England, who were prepared to take up arms at very short notice. They were important in the first months of the US War of Independence. >> Bunker Hill, Battle of

Miocene epoch [miyoseen] A geological epoch of the Tertiary period, from c.24 to 5 million years ago. It was characterized by great mountain-building episodes, which formed the Alps and Himalayas, and the development of most modern mammalian groups. >> geological time scale; Tertiary period; RR976

MIPS [mips] Acronym for **millions of instructions per second**. It is a measure of the speed at which computers can operate.

Mira [**miy**ra] (Lat 'the Wonderful') A star (*omicron Ceti*) in the constellation Cetus. It is a red giant, varying on a cycle of 331 days from 10th magnitude (minimum) to third magnitude (maximum). It is the prototype for **Mira variables** – variable stars with long periods of months or more. >> Cetus; magnitude; red giant; variable star

Mirabeau, Honoré Gabriel Riqueti, comte de (Count of) [meeraboh] (1749–91) French revolutionary politician and orator, born in Bignon, France. His political acumen made him a force in the National Assembly, while his eloquence endeared him to the people. He advocated a constitutional monarchy on the English model, but his views were rejected by the revolutionaries. >> French Revolution ℹ

miracle play >> **mystery play**

mirage An optical illusion caused by the refraction of light through thin surface layers of air with different temperature and hence density, causing objects near the horizon to become distorted. It appears as a floating and shimmering image on the horizon, particularly in deserts, on very hot days. >> light; refraction

Miranda A natural satellite of Uranus, discovered in 1948; distance from the planet 130 000 km/81 000 mi; diameter 480 km/300 mi. Its very complex surface, observed by Voyager 1 in 1986, suggests a history of almost total destruction and subsequent re-accretion. >> Uranus; Voyager project ℹ; RR964

Miranda warning >> **right to silence**

Miró, Joán [mee**roh**, hwan] (1893–1983) Artist, born in Barcelona, Spain. A founder of Surrealism, his paintings are predominantly abstract, and his humorous fantasy makes play with a restricted range of pure colours and dancing shapes, as in 'Catalan Landscape' (1923–4, New York). >> abstract art; Surrealism

Mirren, Helen (1945–) Actress, born in London. She appeared in a wide range of classical theatre roles, and won the Best Actress award at Cannes for *Cal* (1984). Later films include *The Madness of King George* (1994) and *Some Mother's Son* (1997). Her role as Jane Tennison in the television series *Prime Suspect* (from 1991) made her a household name in the UK.

Mirrlees, James(Alexander) (1914–96) Economist, born in Minnigaff, Dumfries and Galloway, Scotland. He shared the Nobel Prize for Economics in 1996 for his work in analyzing the consequences of incomplete financial information

mirror A smooth surface which reflects large amounts of light, usually made of glass with a highly reflective metal deposit on the front or back, or of highly polished metal. Large astronomical mirrors can be over 5 m/16 ft across, but mirrors of all sizes are used in optical instruments. Half-silvered mirrors are used as one-way mirrors between a well-lit and a dim room. >> aberrations ℹ; optics ℹ; telescope ℹ

Mir (Peace) **space station** A Soviet space station (launched Feb 1986) which evolved from Salyut, having more power (solar panels) and more docking ports (five) than previous spacecraft, allowing for the build-up of a modular station. It is used for long-duration spaceflight experience, and for biomedical, science, and applications experiments. The station was repaired in 1997, after an unmanned cargo ship collided with one of its modules, and was scheduled for termination in mid-1999. >> Salyut space station; space station

MIRV [merv] Acronym for **Multiple, Independently-targeted Re-entry Vehicle**, a nuclear-armed warhead, numbers of which may be incorporated in the front end of a large ballistic missile to be dispensed over a target area. >> ballistic missile; Trident missile

miscarriage >> **abortion**

miscarriage of justice A criminal case where an injustice has or may have been committed, either in the preparation of the case or at trial, resulting in an innocent person being convicted or an 'unsafe and unsatisfactory' verdict of guilt being returned. There can be several reasons for such a miscarriage, including non-disclosure of evidence, inappropriate questioning, or the giving of partisan evidence by prosecution scientists. >> Birmingham Six; Christie, John; Guildford Four

misdemeanour / misdemeanor At common law, any offence other than treason or a felony; in most US jurisdictions, a criminal offence other than a felony, with a punishment of a fine or less than one year in a local prison. The felony/misdemeanour distinction in the UK was abolished by the Criminal Law Act of 1967. >> felony; indictment; summary trial; treason

Mishima, Yukio, pseudonym of **Hiraoka Kimitake** (1925–70) Writer, born in Tokyo. His great tetralogy, *Hojo no umi* (1965–70, Sea of Fertility), spanned Japanese life and events in the 20th-c. He became expert in the martial arts, and in 1968 founded the Shield Society, dedicated to the revival of *Bushido*. He committed ritual suicide in protest against modern Japanese decadence.

Mishnah [**mish**nuh], (Heb 'repetition', referring to the practice of learning by repetition) An important written collection of rabbinic laws, supplementary to the legislation in Jewish Scriptures. Its general arrangement can be traced to Rabbi Akiva (AD c.120), its final editing to Rabbi Judah the Prince (AD c.200). >> Akiva ben Joseph; Judaism; Torah

Miskolc [**meesh**kolts] 48°07N 20°50E, pop (1995e) 194 000. Second largest city in Hungary; airfield; railway; technical university of heavy industry (1870); castle of Diósgyör. >> Hungary ℹ

Missal The liturgical book of the Roman Catholic Church, containing liturgies for the celebration of Mass throughout the year. It includes all the prayers, Biblical readings, ceremonial, and singing directions. >> liturgy; Mass; Roman Catholicism

missile >> **guided missile**

Mississippi pop (1995e) 2 676 000; area 123 510 sq km/ 47 689 sq mi. State in S USA, the 'Magnolia State'; held by France, Britain, and Spain in turn, becoming part of the USA in 1795; the 20th state to join the Union, 1817; seceded, 1861; re-admitted in 1870; highest black population of any state (35%); highest point Mt Woodall (246 m/807 ft); much of the S state covered in pine woods; fertile coastal plain; capital, Jackson; major cotton-producing area between Mississippi and Yazoo Rivers; petroleum, natural gas (over a third of the land given over to oil and gas development); fisheries prominent along the Gulf coast; the lowest per capita income in the USA; a centre of the civil rights movement in the 1960s. >> civil rights; Jackson (MS); United States of America ℹ; RR994

Mississippian period >> **Carboniferous period**

Mississippi River River in C USA; rises in N Minnesota; enters the Gulf of Mexico in SE Louisiana, near New Orleans; length 1884 km/2348 mi; the second longest river in the USA, after the Missouri; when the Missouri is considered part of the main stream, length from the Red Rock–Jefferson R is 6019 km/3740 mi; several artificial levees on the banks of the lower river help to cope with flooding; delta swampland dissected by numerous distributaries (*bayous*); navigable as far as Minneapolis;

steamboat era in the 19th-c. >> Missouri River; United States of America [i]

Missouri [mizooree] pop (1995e) 5 309 000; area 180 508 sq km/69 697 sq mi. State in C USA, the 'Show Me State'; became part of USA with the Louisiana Purchase, 1803; a territory in 1812; admitted as the 24th state in 1821 under the Missouri Compromise; Ozark Plateau in the SW; highest point Mt Taum Sauk (540 m/1772 ft); split into two parts by the Missouri R; to the N, open prairie-land with corn and livestock, particularly hogs and cattle; to the S, foothills and the Ozarks, much of which is forested; capital, Jefferson City; more farms than any other state except Texas; mines yield over 90% of the nation's lead; starting point for the pioneering advance W across the continent. >> Jefferson City; Louisiana Purchase; Missouri Compromise; United States of America [i]; RR994

Missouri Compromise (1820) An agreement to admit Missouri, with slavery, and Maine (separated from Massachusetts), without it, to statehood simultaneously, in order to preserve a sectional balance in the US Senate. >> Missouri; slave trade

Missouri River Second longest river in the USA, and chief tributary of the Mississippi; formed in SW Montana; joins the Mississippi just N of St Louis; length 3725 km/2315 mi (with longest headstream, 4125 km/2563 mi); navigation (as far as Fort Benton) is dangerous. >> Mississippi River; United States of America [i]

Mistinguett [meestĩget], originally **Jeanne Marie Bourgeois** (1875–1956) Dancer and actress, born in Enghien-les-Bains, France. She was the most popular French music-hall artiste for 30 years, reaching the height of success with Maurice Chevalier at the Folies Bergère. >> Chevalier; music hall

Misti, Volcán El or **El Misti** [**mees**tee] 16°18S 71°24W. Dormant volcano in S Peru, in the Andean Cordillera Occidental; height, 5843 m/19 170 ft; last eruption, 1600; observatory near its summit. >> Peru [i]; volcano

mistletoe A hemiparasitic evergreen shrub (*Viscum album*) native to Europe, N Africa, and Asia; stem growing to 1 m/3¼ ft, branches regularly forked; flowers small, in tight clusters of 3–5, greenish-yellow, males and females on separate plants; berries white. The plant, venerated by the druids, was widely held to cure sterility and counteract poisons. Nowadays it is used as a Christmas decoration. (Family: Loranthaceae.) >> parasitic plants

Mistral A strong, cool wind common in S France. It originates in the Massif Central, and blows down the Rhône Valley. >> wind [i]

Mistral, Frédéric [meestral] (1830–1914) Poet, born in Maillane, France. He became a founder of the Provençal renaissance movement (the *Félibrige* school) and received the Nobel Prize for Literature in 1904.

Mistral, Gabriela [mee**stral**], pseudonym of **Lucila Godoy de Alcayaga** (1889–1957) Writer, educationalist, and diplomat, born in Vicuña, Chile. Her works include *Sonetos de la muerte* (1914, Sonnets of Death) and *Desolación* (1922, Desolation). She was awarded the Nobel Prize for Literature in 1945.

Mitchell, George (John) (1934–) US lawyer and politician, born in Waterville, ME. Appointed senator for Maine in 1980, he achieved national prominence for his interrogation of Oliver North during the Iran-Contra investigation, and was elected Senate majority leader in 1989. He retired from the Senate in 1995, but became internationally known as the mediator in charge of the talks leading to the Good Friday agreement in April 1998. >> Iran–Contra scandal; Northern Ireland

Mitchell, Joni, *née* **Roberta Joan Anderson** (1943–) Singer and songwriter, born in McLeod, Alberta, Canada. She moved to the USA in the mid-1960s, and in 1968 recorded her first album, *Joni Mitchell*. Many of her songs, notably 'Both Sides Now', have been recorded by other singers. >> pop music

Mitchell, Margaret (1900–49) Novelist, born in Atlanta, GA. Her only novel, *Gone with the Wind* (1936), sold over 25 million copies, was translated into 30 languages, and filmed (1939).

Mitchell, R(eginald) J(oseph) (1895–1937) Aircraft designer. He designed seaplanes for the Schneider trophy races (1922–31) and later the Spitfire, whose triumph he did not live to see. >> aircraft [i]; seaplane

Mitchum, Robert (1917–97) Film actor, born in Bridgeport, CT. A prolific leading man particularly associated with the post-war film noir thriller, his laconic, heavy-lidded manner disguised a potent screen presence. His major films included *Night of the Hunter* (1955), *The Sundowners* (1960), and *Farewell My Lovely* (1975).

mite A small, short-bodied arthropod with head and abdomen fused into a compact body; typically with four pairs of walking legs; mouthparts include a pair of fangs; c.30 000 described species. (Class: Arachnida. Order: Acari.) >> arthropod; harvest-mite; tick

Mitford, Nancy (Freeman) (1904–73) Writer, born in London. She established a reputation with such witty novels as *The Pursuit of Love* (1945) and *Love in a Cold Climate* (1949). In *Noblesse Oblige* (1956), she popularized the 'U' (upper-class) and 'non-U' classification of linguistic usage. >> U and non-U

Mithr or **Mithras** A god worshipped in the early Roman Empire, of Persian origin, and identified with the sun. The cult was predominantly military, and restricted to males. The main story was of his fight with the bull, which he conquers and sacrifices.

Mithridates VI (Eupator) [mithri**dah**teez], also spelled **Mithradates**, known as **the Great** (?–63 BC) King of Pontus (c.115–63 BC), a hellenized ruler in the Black Sea area, whose attempts to expand his empire led to a series of wars (the **Mithridatic Wars**) with Rome (88–66 BC). He was defeated by Sulla (c.86 BC), Lucullus (72–71 BC), and Pompey (66 BC), and later took his own life. >> Lucullus; Pompey the Great; Sulla

Mitla [**meet**la] 16°54N 96°16W. Ancient city in C Oaxaca, S Mexico; former centre of the Zapotec civilization. >> Mexico [i]; Zapotecs

mitochondrion [miytoh**kon**drion] A typically oval-shaped structure, often about 2 μm long, found in large numbers in eucaryotic cells. It functions as a major site for metabolic activities that release energy by breaking down food molecules. >> eucaryote; metabolism

mitosis [miy**toh**sis] The normal process of nuclear division and separation that takes place in a dividing cell, producing two daughter cells, each containing a nucleus with the same complement of chromosomes as the mother cell. >> cell; chromosome [i]; meiosis [i]

mitre / miter (Gr *mitra*, 'turban') The liturgical headwear of a bishop of the Western Christian Church. It takes the form of a shield-shaped, high, stiff hat, representing the 'helmet of salvation'. >> bishop; vestments [i]

MIT school In linguistics, a label applied to the group of US linguists associated with the Massachusetts Institute of Technology (MIT), who have developed the concept of generative grammar, under the influence of Noam Chomsky. >> Chomsky; generative grammar

Mitsiwa >> **Massawa**

Mittelland Canal [**mit**eland] (Ger 'Midland Canal') A system of German canals and rivers linking the Dortmund–Ems Canal with Magdeburg. The waterway was completed in the late 1930s. It is 325 km/202 mi in length. >> canal

Mitterrand, François (Maurice Marie) [meetuhrã]

(1916–96) French statesman and socialist president (1981–95), born in Jarnac, France. For many years a stubborn opponent of de Gaulle, he became secretary of the Socialist Party in 1971. Following his victory in 1981, he embarked on a programme of nationalization and job creation in an attempt to combat stagnation and unemployment. He was re-elected president in 1988, but defeated by Jacques Chirac in 1995. >> de Gaulle; socialism

mix; mixing >> **dubbing**

mixed-ability groups >> **streaming**

mixed economy >> **market economy**

Mnemosyne [neemozinee] In Greek mythology, a Titan, daughter of Earth and Heaven, and mother of all the Muses. The name means 'Memory'. >> Muses

Mo, Timothy (Peter) [moh] (1950–) Novelist, born in Hong Kong. He attracted attention with his first novel, *The Monkey King* (1978), set in Hong Kong. Later books include *The Redundancy of Courage* (1991) and *Brownout on Breadfruit Boulevard* (1995).

moa An extinct bird native to New Zealand; a large ratite (up to 3 m/10 ft high) with long neck and legs, no wings; slow-moving. (Family: Dinornithidae, c.12 species.) >> Ratitae

Moabites [mohabytes] An ancient Semitic people who in Old Testament times inhabited the area to the SE of the Dead Sea. They were believed to be descended from Lot. >> Lot; Semites

Moabite Stone [mohabiyt] An inscribed basalt slab, discovered in 1868, which describes the successful revolt of Mesha, king of Moab, against the Israelites in the 7th-c BC. >> Old Testament

Mobile [mohbeel] 30°41N 88°03W, pop (1995e) 208 000. Port in SW Alabama, USA; settled by the French, 1711; ceded to the British, 1763; city status, 1819; scene of a Federal victory at the naval battle of Mobile Bay, 1864; railway; university (1963). >> Alabama

mobile A name first applied by Marcel Duchamp to the hanging wire-and-metal sculptures of Alexander Calder. They have been widely imitated. >> Calder; Duchamp; kinetic art

mobile communications A system which provides a simple, convenient means of communication for people who wish to keep in touch when travelling. The first system was a ship-borne radio. In modern times the term also refers to personal communication systems such as CB radio, radio paging, and car and pocket phones which use cellular radio. Cellular radio employs local radio transmitters, covering small areas (*cells*), which receive and transmit calls in association with the telecommunications network. >> citizens' band radio; pager; pocket phone; telecommunications

Möbius strip [moebius] In topology, a one-sided surface bounded by a single continuous line; devised by German mathematician August Ferdinand Möbius (1790–1868). Take a long, thin rectangle *ABCD*, and join *A* to *B*, and *C* to *D*. This forms a cylinder, with two surfaces, an inside and an outside. Now take a similar rectangle *ABCD*, and join *A* to *C*, *B* to *D*. Starting at any point *P* on the surface now formed, we can draw a continuous line over the surface to reach the point at the 'other' side of *P*. >> topology

Mobutu, Sese Seko [mobootoo], originally Joseph Désiré Mobutu (1930–97) Zairean soldier and president (1965–97), born in Lisala, Democratic Republic of Congo (formerly Zaire, and earlier, Belgian Congo). A sergeant-major in the Belgian colonial *force publique*, he came to power in a military coup in 1960. He was forced to stand down May 1997 following an uprising led by Laurent Kabila. >> Zaire i

Mobutu Sese Seko, Lake >> **Albert, Lake**

mockingbird A bird native to the New World; thrush-like with sharp, slightly curved bill and long tail; sings well; excellent mimic; also known as mocking-thrush. (Family: Mimidae, 16 species.) >> thrush (bird)

mock orange A deciduous, temperate shrub, mainly from E Asia; flowers fragrant, usually white, bowl-shaped, with four petals and numerous stamens; fruit a capsule. It is named for the resemblance of its flowers to those of the orange, but in horticulture it is sometimes called syringa, the botanical name for lilac. (Genus: *Philadelphus*, 75 species. Family: Hydrangaceae.) >> lilac

Mod The annual autumn musical and literary festival of Gaelic-speaking Scotland organized by An Comunn Gaidhealach (the Gaelic language society) on the model of the Welsh eisteddfod; first held in Oban in 1892. >> eisteddfod; Gaelic

mode In mathematics, the commonest of a set of scores; for example, the mode of 1, 2, 3, 4, 4, 5 is 4. >> mean; median

modello [modeloh] A small, but complete and detailed painting or drawing made to show to a patron before embarking on the full-size work. Superb oil *modelli* exist by Rubens and Tiepolo. >> Rubens; Tiepolo

modem [mohdem] Acronym for **MOdulator/DEModulator**, a device which converts digital information from computers into electrical signals that can be transmitted over telephone lines and vice versa. >> acoustic coupler; telegraphy

moderator A person who presides over Presbyterian Church courts, such as the kirk session, presbytery, synod, or General Assembly. In Reformed Churches generally, the term is applied to the chairman of official Church gatherings. >> Presbyterianism; Reformed Churches

modern art A term used widely but imprecisely to refer to all the 'progressive' movements in 19th–20th-c art. Towards the end of the 19th-c a number of artists, including Cézanne, Gauguin, van Gogh, Ensor, and Munch, challenged in various ways the traditional approach to painting based on such notions as naturalistic figure-drawing and Renaissance perspective. Their innovations inspired the younger generation around 1904–5. Picasso and Braque developed Cubism (1906–8), the most widely influential of all modern movements. The *Blaue Reiter* group in Munich pushed further away from imitation (1912–14), and a purely abstract art emerged in the hands of Kandinsky and Klee. In Moscow in 1917 Malevich

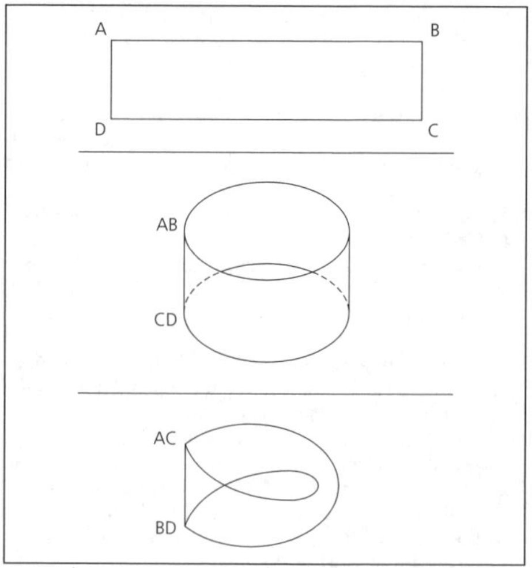

Möbius strip

developed a totally abstract art which he called 'Suprematism'. By 1916 a nihilist reaction known as 'Dadaism' was already emerging in Zürich; it attacked all artistic values, but itself contributed to the ideas of the early Surrealists, who launched their first manifesto in Paris in 1924. >> abstract art; Armory Show; *Blaue Reiter, der*; *Brücke, die*; Cubism; Dada; Expressionism; Fauvism; Futurism; Postimpressionism; Suprematism; Surrealism; Braque; Kandinsky; Kirchner; Klee; Matisse; Picasso; Rouault

modern dance A theatre form of dance which flowered 1910–45 and continues today, rejecting the established form of dance, ballet. Greek myths, psychological states, political comment, the mechanization of life, and alienation have been common themes. Isadora Duncan and Ruth St Denis are often credited with originating the modern movement in the first two decades of this century, the former in returning to natural movements, the latter in using exotic Far Eastern influences. Later, Martha Graham and Doris Humphrey emerged as major figures. In Germany in the 1970s–80s, Pina Bausch's dramatic theatrical works continued the modern, expressionist movement. >> Bausch; dance notation; Duncan, Isadora; Graham, Martha; postmodern dance

Modernism A generic term which refers to experimental methods in different art forms in the earlier part of the 20th-c. These experiments were stimulated by a sharpened sense of the arbitrariness of existing artistic conventions, and doubts about the human place and purpose in the world. Dada, Surrealism, and various anti-genres are all manifestations of Modernism. >> Braque; Dada; Eliot, T S; Joyce, James; Picasso; Schoenberg; Surrealism; Webern

Modern Movement >> **Bauhaus; International Style** 2

Modigliani, Amedeo [mohdeel**yah**nee] (1884–1920) Painter and sculptor of the modern school of Paris, born in Livorno, Italy. In 1918, his first one-man show included some very frank nudes, and the exhibition was closed for indecency. He received recognition only after his death.

Modigliani, Franco [mohdeel**yah**nee] (1918–) US economist, born in Rome. He was awarded the Nobel Prize for Economics in 1985 for his work on personal saving and on corporate finance. >> economics

modulation The imposition of regular changes on some background, usually a beam of particles or radiation, and often as a means of conveying information via the beam. A broadcast signal is used to modulate the electron beam inside a television set to reproduce the picture. >> amplitude modulation; frequency modulation

module A unit measure of proportion in architecture used to regulate all the parts of a building. In classical architecture, this meant the diameter of the column at the base of the shaft. Since World War 2, it is particularly used as the common unit of measure that co-ordinates the sizes of all the components in a standardized or *modular* building, so that they may be fitted together with maximum ease and flexibility. >> orders of architecture [i]; prefabrication

modulus >> **shear / Young's modulus**

Moerae or **Moirai** [**moy**ree, **moy**riy] In Greek mythology, the fates; a trio of goddesses who control human destiny and sometimes overrule the gods. **Lachesis** [**la**kesis] ('the distributor') allots the destinies of human beings; **Clotho** [**kloh**thoh] ('the spinner') spins the thread of life; and **Atropos** [**a**tropos] ('the inflexible') cuts it.

Mogadishu [moga**di**shoo], Somali **Muqdisho**, Ital **Mogadiscio** 2°02N 45°21E, pop (1995e) 525 000. Seaport capital of Somalia; founded, 10th-c; taken by the Sultan of Zanzibar, 1871; sold to Italy, becoming capital of Italian Somaliland, 1905; occupied by British forces in World War 2; airport; university (1954); mosques (13th-c), cathedral (1928). >> Somalia [i]

Mogadon >> **benzodiazepines**

Mogollon [moguh**yohn**] A prehistoric culture of the American SW AD c.300–1350, artistically notable for its vigorous ceramics, extending from S Arizona and New Mexico to the Chihuahuan and Sonoran deserts of Mexico. >> Anasazi; Zuni

Mogul >> **Mughal**

mohair >> **Angora goat**

Mohammed or **Mahomet** (Western forms of Arabic **Muhammad**) (c.570–c.632) Prophet of Islam, born in Mecca, the son of Abdallah, a poor merchant. Orphaned at six, he was cared for first by his grandfather, then by his uncle, and earned his living by tending sheep. At 25 he led the caravans of a rich widow, whom he later married. When he was 40, Gabriel appeared to him on Mt Hira, near Mecca, and commanded him in the name of God to preach the true religion. Four years later he was told to come forward publicly as a preacher. The basis of his teaching was the Koran, which had been revealed to him by God. At first dismissing him as a poet, the Meccans finally rose against him and his followers. He sought refuge at Medina in 622 (the date of the Mohammedan Era, the *Hijra* or *Hegira*), and assumed the position of highest judge and ruler of the city. He then engaged in war against the enemies of Islam. In 630 he took Mecca, where he was recognized as chief and prophet, and thus secured the new religion in Arabia. In 632 he undertook his last pilgrimage to Mecca, and there on Mt Arafat fixed the ceremonies of the pilgrimage (*Hajj*). He fell ill after his return, and died at the house of the favourite of his nine wives, Aïshah, the daughter of Abu Bakr. >> Islam; Koran

Mohammed II or **Mehmet II**, known as **the Conqueror** (1432–81) Ottoman sultan (1451–81), born in Adrianople. He took Constantinople in 1453, thus extinguishing the Byzantine Empire, and conquered Greece. >> Byzantine Empire; Hospitallers

Mohammed Ahmed, known as **the Mahdi** (1844–85) Rebel leader, born in Dongola, Sudan. A rebel against Egyptian rule in the E Sudan, he defeated Hicks Pasha and an Egyptian army. In 1885 his forces took Khartoum, resulting in the death of General Gordon. >> Gordon, Charles George; Mahdi

Mohawk [**moh**hawk] An Iroquoian-speaking North American Indian group, living around L Champlain. A member of the Iroquois League, they were defeated by US troops in 1777, and crossed into Canada, settling in Ontario. >> Iroquois Confederacy

Mohenjo-daro [mo**hen**joh **da**roh] A prehistoric walled city on the R Indus, in Sind, Pakistan; a world heritage site. Occupied c.2300–1750 BC, it covered 100 ha/250 acres and held an ancient population of c.30–40 000. >> Indus Valley Civilization

Moholy-Nagy, László [**moh**hoy **nodj**] (1895–1946) Artist, born in Bàcsborsod, Hungary. He was an abstract painter, experimental photographer, theatrical designer, and pioneer constructivist, using translucent and transparent plastic materials. He founded in 1937 the New Bauhaus in Chicago. >> abstract art; Bauhaus; Constructivism

Mohorovičić discontinuity [mohho**roh**vichich] (or **Moho**) The zone separating the Earth's crust from the mantle, lying at c.6 km/3·5 mi below the ocean floor but up to 70 km/45 mi below the surface of the continents. It is named after its discoverer, Croatian geophysicist Andrija Mohorovičić (1857–1936). >> Earth [i]; seismology

Mohs scale >> **hardness**

Moi, Daniel Arap [moy] (1924–) Kenyan politician and president (1978–), born in Rift Valley Province. He served as a minister from 1961, and became vice-president under Kenyatta in 1967. Despite an increasingly autocratic rule during the 1980s, he won multi-party elections in 1992. >> Kenya ℹ

Mojave or **Mohave Desert** [moh**hah**vee] Desert in S California, USA, part of the Great Basin; area c.65 000 sq km/25 000 sq mi; annual rainfall c.120 mm/4·7 in. >> desert; Great Basin

molasses A brownish syrup, obtained as a by-product of the sugar-beet or sugar-cane industry; it is what remains once the sugar has been refined. It is widely used as an animal feed supplement, and in the production of rum and treacle. >> rum

Mold, Welsh **Yr Wyddgrug** 53°10N 3°08W, pop (1995e) 9400. Administrative centre of Flintshire, NE Wales, UK; on the R Alyn; railway; Theatre Clwyd. >> Flintshire

Moldavia and Wallachia [mol**day**via, wo**lay**kia] Two independent Balkan principalities formed in the 14th-c: Moldavia in NE Romania; Wallachia in S Romania. In the 16th-c they were incorporated into the Ottoman Empire, but they gained autonomy by the Treaty of Adrianople (1829). In 1862 they merged to form the unitary Principality of Romania; Russian Moldavia became a Soviet Socialist Republic in 1940, and declared independence as the Republic of Moldova in 1991. >> Moldova; Ottoman Empire; Romania ℹ

Moldova [mol**doh**va], official name **Republic of Moldova**, formerly (to 1990) **Moldavian SSR**, Russ **Moldavskaya** pop (1995e) 4 367 000; area 33 700 sq km/13 008 sq mi. Republic in E Europe; capital, Kishinev; major ethnic groups, Moldovan (64%), Ukrainian (14%), Russian (13%), Gagauzi (4%), Jewish (2%); religions, Christian (mainly Russian Orthodox, with some Baptist and Roman Catholic); languages, Moldovan (official), with some Ukrainian also spoken; currency, the leu; landlocked area consisting of hilly plains, reaching a height of 429 m/1409 ft at Mt Balaneshty (C); level plain of Beltsy Steppe and uplands (N); chief rivers, the Dnestr and Prut; warm, moderately continental climate; long dry periods in S; average annual temperatures −5°C (N) and −3°C (S) (Jan), 20°C (N) and 23°C (S) (Jul); average annual rainfall 450–550 mm/18–22 in; proclaimed a Soviet Socialist Republic, 1940; under German occupation, 1941–4; declaration of independence, 1991; new constitution, 1994; autonomous status granted to the regions of Gagauzia and Transdniestr, 1994; governed by a president, prime minister, and 104-member parliament; wine, tobacco, food-canning, machines, electrical engineering, instruments, knitwear, textiles, fruit. >> Commonwealth of Independent States ℹ; RR1016 political leaders

mole (biology) A mammal native to lowlands in Europe, Asia, and North America; an insectivore; dark with minute eyes, short tail; enlarged forelimbs used for digging. (Family: Talpidae, 27 species.) >> desman; insectivore

mole (medicine) Usually a small flat congenital lesion in the skin resulting from the proliferation of small blood vessels and containing scattered pigment cells (*birthmarks*). Occasionally these are more extensive and form raised patches (*plaques*). >> birthmark; skin ℹ

mole (physics) Base SI unit of amount of substance; symbol *mol*; defined as the amount of substance of a system which contains as many elementary entities as there are atoms in 0·012 kg of carbon-12.

molecular biology The study of the structure and function of the large organic molecules associated with living organisms, especially the nucleic acids (DNA and RNA) and proteins. >> biology; molecule; nucleic acids; protein

molecule A finite group of two or more atoms, which is the smallest unit of a substance having the properties of that substance. Molecular compounds include water, most organic compounds, globular proteins, and viruses. Non-molecular compounds include metals, ionic compounds, and diamond. >> atom; chemical bond

Molière [molyair], pseudonym of **Jean Baptiste Poquelin** (1622–73) Playwright, born in Paris. From the publication of *Les Précieuses ridicules* (1659, The Affected Young Ladies) no year passed without at least one major dramatic achievement, such as *Tartuffe* (1664), *Le Misanthrope* (1666, The Misanthropist), and *Le Bourgeois gentilhomme* (1670).

Molina, Luis de [moh**lee**na] (1535–1600) Jesuit theologian, born in Cuenca, Spain. His main work was *Concordia liberi arbitrii cum gratiae donis* (1588, The Harmony of Free Will with Gifts of Grace), which presented the view (later known as **Molinism**) that predestination to eternal happiness or punishment depends on God's foreknowledge of the free determination of human will. >> Jesuits; theology

mollusc [**mol**uhsk] An unsegmented invertebrate animal, typically with an underside muscular foot and a mantle above, covered by calcareous scales or a solid calcareous shell. A posterior cavity contains gills for respiration. Visceral organs are typically protected by a shell secreted by the mantle. There are c.80 000 species. (Phylum: Mollusca.) >> ammonite; bivalve; calcium; clam; limpet; octopus; oyster; slug; snail; squid

molly Small, colourful, freshwater fish (*Poecilia sphenops*) found in Central America; length up to 12 cm/4¾ in; greenish-brown above, rows of orange spots along sides, dorsal fin with orange and black markings. (Family: Poeciliidae.)

Molly Maguires A secret organization of (primarily Irish) miners, involved in industrial disputes in Pennsylvania during the 1870s. The prosecution of their leaders led to hangings and imprisonments, which crushed the group.

Molnár, Ferenc [**mohl**nah(r), **fe**rents] (1878–1952) Writer, born in Budapest. He is best known for his novel *A Pál utcai fiúk* (1907, The Paul Street Boys), and his plays *Az ördög* (1907, The Devil) and *Liliom* (1909).

Moloch [**moh**lok] In the Bible, a god of the Canaanites and other peoples, in whose cult children were sacrificed by fire. The name is used for any excessive and cruel religion.

moloch [**moh**lok] An agamid lizard (*Moloch horridus*) native to W Australia; entire body covered with large thorn-like spines; also known as **thorny devil** or **horny devil**. >> agamid

Molokai [molo**kiy**] area 670 sq km/260 sq mi. Island of the US state of Hawaii; Kalaupapa leper settlement (pop 130) on the N coast. >> Hawaii (state)

Molotov, Vyacheslav Mikhailovich [**mo**lotof], originally **Vyacheslav Mikhailovich Skriabin** (1890–1986) Russian statesman and premier (1930–41), born in Kukaida, Russia. He was Stalin's chief adviser at Teheran and Yalta, and was present at the founding of the United Nations (1945). After World War 2, he emerged as the uncompromising champion of world Sovietism; his *nyet* ('no') at meetings of the UN became a byword, and fostered the Cold War. >> Khrushchev; Stalin; United Nations

Moltke, Helmuth (Karl Bernhard), Graf von (Count of) [**molt**kuh] (1800–91) Prussian field marshal, born in Parchim, Germany. His reorganization of the Prussian army led to the successful wars with Denmark (1863–4), Austria (1866), and France (1870–1). >> Prussia

Moluccas [mo**luh**kas], Indonesian **Maluku**, or **Spice Islands** pop (1990) 2 029 000; area 74 505 sq km/ 28 759 sq mi. Island group and province of Indonesia; includes c.1000 islands, notably Halmahera, Seram, Buru; mostly volcanic and mountainous; visited by the Portuguese, 1512; under Dutch rule, early 17th-c; secession movement in the S Moluccas followed Indonesian independence (1949), still continuing in The Netherlands; capital, Ambon. >> Indonesia ℹ

molybdenum [mo**lib**denum] Mo, element 42, density 10·2 g/cm^3, melting point 2610°C. A grey metal, occurring most commonly as the disulphide, MoS_2. It is an ingredient of several steel alloys. >> alloy; chemical elements; metal; RR1036

Molyneux, Edward (Henry) [**mol**inyoo] (1891–1974) Fashion designer, born in London. He was famous for the elegant simplicity of his tailored suits with pleated skirts, and for his evening wear.

Mombasa [mom**ba**sa] 4°04S 39°40E, pop (1995e) 645 000. Kenya's main port; capital of British East Africa Protectorate, 1888–1907; used as a British naval base in World War 2; airport; railway terminus. >> Kenya ℹ

moment In physics, a general term referring to a system's ability to rotate under the application of an external force. The moment of force in mechanics is called *torque*. >> torque ℹ

moment of inertia In mechanics, the notion that, for a rotating object, the turning force required to make the object turn faster depends on how the object's mass is distributed about the axis of rotation; symbol I, units kg.m^2. For a uniform disc of radius r and mass m spinning horizontally about its centre, $I = mr^2/2$. >> mass; mechanics

momentum The product of mass and velocity; symbol p, units kg.m/s; a vector quantity. 'Force equals the rate of change of momentum with time' is the proper statement of Newton's second law. For a closed system on which no forces act, momentum is conserved – an essential principle in physics. >> angular momentum; mechanics; velocity

Mommsen, (Christian Matthias) Theodor (1817–1903) Historian, born in Garding, Germany. His greatest work is his *Römische Geschichte* (3 vols, History of Rome, 1854–5), in which he applied the new historical method of critical examination of sources. He was awarded the Nobel Prize for Literature in 1902.

Mon An agricultural people of Burma and Thailand, thought to have come originally from W China, establishing a kingdom in Burma in about the 9th-c. They speak an Austro-Asiatic language, also known as **Tailang**. >> Austro-Asiatic languages; Myanmar ℹ; Thailand ℹ

Monaco [**mon**akoh], official name **Principality of Monaco** pop (1995e) 30 600; area 1·9 sq km/$\frac{3}{4}$ sq mi. Constitutional monarchy on the Mediterranean Riviera, close to the Italian frontier with France; capital, Monaco; timezone GMT +1; population 58% French; unit of currency, the French franc; nearest airport at Nice; heliport at Fontvieille; warm, dry summers and mild winters; under protection of France since the 17th-c, apart from a period under Sardinia, 1815–61; governed by a hereditary prince as head of state, a minister of state, heading a Council of Government, and a National Council. >> France ℹ; Monte Carlo; RR1017 political leaders

Monaghan [**mon**aghan], Ir **Mhuineachain** pop (1995e) 50 800; area 1290 sq km/498 sq mi. County in Ulster province, Ireland; capital, Monaghan pop (1995e) 6200. >> Ireland (republic) ℹ

monarchy A political system in which a single person is a political ruler, whose position normally rests on the basis of divine authority, backed by tradition. In Europe, the democratic revolutions of the 18th–20th-c saw an end to what was until then the most widely known form of government. A number of countries, however, maintained **constitutional monarchies**, where the sovereign acts on the advice of government ministers who govern on his or her behalf. >> republic

monasticism A form of religious life found in both Christianity and Buddhism, emphasizing the perfection of the individual either through a solitary ascetic existence or more often through life in a consecrated community. Members of such communities are known as **monks**. In Christianity the most significant early monastic legislation was the rule of Benedict (480–543), which became a standard in Western Christianity. In the 13th-c several new orders emerged, known as *friars* or *mendicant orders*, which combined monastic life with missionary preaching to those outside. >> Augustinians; Benedictines; Capuchins; Carmelites; Carthusians; Cistercians; Dominicans; Franciscans; Maurists; Mendicant Orders; nun; Passionists; Premonstratensians; Taizé

monazite [**mon**aziyt] A phosphate mineral containing rare-earth metals (*lanthanides*) such as lanthanum, cerium, yttrium, and thorium, and important as the major source of these metals. >> lanthanides; phosphates

Monck, George >> **Monk, George**

Mond, Ludwig (1839–1909) Chemist and industrialist, born in Kassel, Germany. He perfected a sulphur recovery process, founded an alkali works, and devised a process for the extraction of nickel. His son, **Alfred Moritz Mond, Baron Melchett** (1868–1930), helped to form Imperial Chemical Industries (ICI). >> nickel; Solvay process; sulphur

Mondale, Walter F(rederick) (1928–) US Democratic politician, born in Ceylon, MN. He served under President Carter as vice-president (1977–81), and obtained the Democratic nomination in 1984, but lost to Reagan. He became US ambassador to Japan in 1993. >> Carter, Jimmy; Democratic Party; Reagan

Mondrian, Piet [**mon**drian], originally **Pieter Cornelis Mondriaan** (1872–1944) Artist, born in Amersfoort, The Netherlands. He founded, with Theo van Doesburg, (1883–1931) the *De Stijl* movement in architecture and painting. His rectilinear abstracts in black, white, and primary colours have had considerable influence, and he is considered the leader of Neoplasticism. >> *De Stijl*; Neoplasticism

Monet, Claude [monay] (1840–1926) Impressionist painter, born in Paris. He exhibited at the first Impressionist exhibition in 1874; one of his works, 'Impression: soleil levant' (Impression: Sunrise, 1872, Paris), gave the name to the movement. >> Impressionism (art)

monetarism An economic policy based on the control of a country's money supply. It assumes that the quantity of money in an economy determines its economic activity, and particularly its rate of inflation. If the money supply is allowed to rise too quickly, prices will rise, resulting in inflation. To curb inflationary pressures, governments therefore need to reduce the supply of money and raise interest rates. This view was a major influence on British and US economic policy in the 1980s.

Monetary Compensation Amount >> **green pound**

money A generally acceptable and convenient medium of exchange, in order to avoid the problems of barter; also a representation of value and a means of storing value. It is usually in the form of coins or notes, but it can be any generally accepted object. The first bank notes issued in Europe were by the Bank of Stockholm in 1661. Money is now increasingly not in tangible form, but consists of balances in accounts at banks, exchange being by means of cheques, credit-cards or charge-cards, and by *credit-transfer*, where one account is reduced (debited) and another increased (credited) by the same amount electronically. Many definitions of money are in use. In the UK, for example, the narrow definition, M0, refers to the stock of notes and coins in circulation, banks' till money, and bankers' balances at the Bank of England. Also in use are M1, M2, M3, and other measures, each containing additional items. >> credit card

money spider A small, dark-coloured spider that constructs a sheet-like web on vegetation; very abundant in N hemisphere. The name is derived from the folk belief that a spider on one's clothes was a sign of good luck or money coming. (Order: Araneae. Family: Liniphiidae.) >> spider

Monge, Gaspard, comte de (Count of) **Péluse** [mõzh] (1746–1818) Mathematician, physicist, and inventor of descriptive geometry, born in Beaune, France. In 1795 he published his treatise on the application of geometry to the arts of construction. >> geometry

Mongo A cluster of Bantu-speaking peoples of forested regions of C Democratic Republic of Congo, organized into many small chiefdoms. >> hunter-gatherers; Zaire ℹ

Mongol >> **Altaic**

Mongolia, Mongolian **Mongol Uls**, formerly **Mongolian People's Republic** (1924–92) pop (1995e) 2 302 000; area 604 800 sq km/1 566 500 sq mi. Republic of EC Asia; capital, Ulaanbaatar; timezone GMT +7 (W), +8 (C), +9 (E); chief ethnic group, Mongol (80%); chief religion traditionally Tibetan Buddhism; official language, Khalkha Mongol; unit of currency, the tugrik of 100 möngö; landlocked mountainous country; highest point, Tavan-Bogdo-Uli, 4373 m/14 347 ft; lower SE section runs into the Gobi Desert; lowland plains mainly arid grasslands; continental climate, with hard and long-lasting frosts in winter; arid desert conditions prevail in the S; originally the homeland of nomadic tribes, which united under Ghengis Khan in the 13th-c to become part of the great Mongol Empire; assimilated into China, and divided into Inner and Outer Mongolia; Outer Mongolia declared itself an independent monarchy, 1911; Mongolian People's Republic formed in 1924, not recognized by China until 1946; new consitution, 1992; governed by a president, prime minister, and single-chamber parliament (*Great Hural*); traditionally a pastoral nomadic economy; series of 5-year plans aiming for an agricultural-industrial economy; 70% of agricultural production derived from cattle raising. >> Genghis Khan; Gobi Desert; Mongols; Ulaanbaatar; RR1017 political leaders

mongolism >> **Down's syndrome**

Mongoloid >> **race**

Mongols Mongolian and S Siberian tribes who created the largest empire in world history (including C Asia, China, Korea, Russia, and Persia), of key importance in the process of cultural diffusion. United under Genghis Khan in 1206, they conquered China under his grandson Kublai, who ruled as first emperor of the Yuan dynasty (1271–1368). >> Genghis Khan; Kublai Khan; Mongolia

mongoose A carnivorous mammal, native to S and SE Asia and Africa; adept at killing snakes and rats. (Family: Viverridae, 36 species.) >> carnivore ℹ; Viverridae ℹ

monism In philosophy, the metaphysical doctrine either that only one thing really exists in the universe; or that there is only one *kind* of thing, as in materialism (matter) and idealism (mind). >> idealism; materialism; metaphysics

monitorial system A concept of early 19th-c British education, developed by British educationalists Andrew Bell (1753–1832) and Joseph Lancaster (1778–1838), to train young school leavers to act as teachers' assistants or 'monitors'.

monk >> **monasticism**

Monk or **Monck, George, 1st Duke of Albemarle** (1608–70) General, born in Great Potheridge, Devon. He joined the Commonwealth cause and served successfully in Ireland, Scotland, and in the first Dutch War (1652–4). Fearing a return to Civil War, he was instrumental in bringing about the restoration of Charles II. >> Dutch Wars; English Civil War

Monk, Thelonious (Sphere) (1917–82) Composer and pianist, born in Rocky Mount, NC. Although once called the 'High Priest of Bebop', and credited with helping to create the jazz style of the 1940s, his idiosyncratic melodies stood apart from the main currents of the day. >> jazz

monkey A primate of the group Anthropoidea; two subgroups: the **Platyrrhine** or **flat-nosed monkeys** from the New World (includes New World monkeys and marmosets), and the **Catarrhine** or **downward-nosed monkeys** from the Old World. >> Anthropoidea; marmoset; New World monkey; Old World monkey; primate; *see illustration on p. 573*

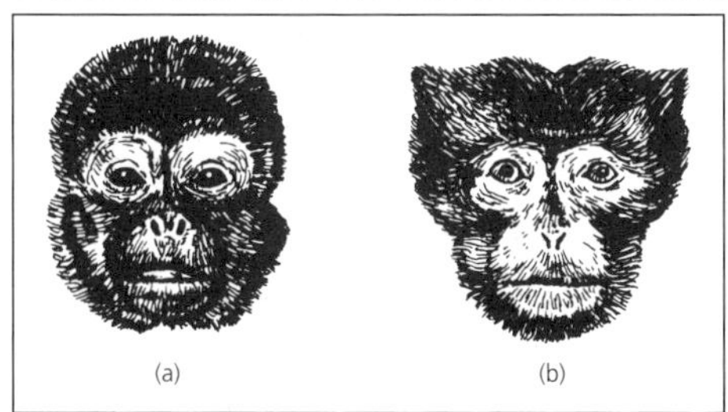

Monkeys – New World (a) and Old World (b)

monkey nut >> **peanut**

monkey-puzzle An evergreen conifer (*Araucaria araucana*) native to Chile and Argentina; branches in open whorls, covered with hard, sharp-pointed, triangular, overlapping leaves; also known as **Chile pine**. (Family: Araucariaceae.) >> araucaria; conifer

monkfish Largest of the angelsharks (*Squatina squatina*) common in the E North Atlantic and Mediterranean; length up to 1·8 m/6 ft; head flattened, mouth anterior, gill openings lateral, pectoral fins very broad, tail slender; also called **angelfish**. (Family: Squatinidae.) >> angelfish

monkshood A perennial (*Aconitum napellus*) with blackish, tuberous roots, native to Europe and NW Asia; flowers mauve, with a cowl-shaped helmet or hood; also called **aconite**. It is used as a narcotic and painkiller, but is highly poisonous. (Family: Ranunculaceae.) >> narcotics

Monmouth, James Scott, Duke of (1649–85) Illegitimate son of Charles II of England, born in Rotterdam, The Netherlands. He had substantial popular support, and as a Protestant became a focus of opposition to James II. In 1685 he landed at Lyme Regis, and asserted his right to the crown. He was defeated at the Battle of Sedgemoor, and beheaded in London. >> Charles II (of England); James II (of England); Rye House Plot

Monmouth, Battle of (1778) An engagement in New Jersey between British and American troops during the US War of Independence. It was notable for Washington's suspension of General Charles Lee (1731–82) from command. >> American Revolution

Monmouthshire [**mon**muhthsheer], Welsh **Sir Fynwy** pop (1995e) 84 200; area 851 sq km/328 sq mi. County (unitary authority from 1996) in SE Wales, UK; drained by R Wye and R Usk; Brecon Beacons in NW; administrative centre, Cwmbran; tourism, especially in Wye Valley; castles at Abergavenny, Caldicott, Chepstow, Monmouth, Raglan, Usk; Tintern Abbey (12th-c). >> Brecon Beacons; Wales [i]

Monoceros [mo**no**seros] (Gr 'unicorn') A constellation in the Milky Way, next to Orion, containing several clusters and nebulae. >> constellation; Orion; RR968

monoclonal antibody [**mon**ohklohnal **an**tibodee] A pure antibody produced in bulk by artificial means, used in medicine for treating diseases (eg some cancers) and in scientific research. It is produced from animals which have been immunized with particular antigens. >> antibodies; cell; lymphocyte

monocotyledons [monohkoti**lee**dnz] One of two major divisions of the flowering plants, often referred to simply as **monocots**; contrasting with *dicotyledons* (*dicots*). The seed embryo has only one cotyledon, and the primary root of the seedling soon withers, leaving only a fibrous root system. Monocots form a much smaller group than dicots, with about 60 families currently recognized, although some (eg grasses, palms, orchids, lilies) are among the largest families of flowering plants. (Subclass: Monocotyledonae.) >> dicotyledons; flowering plants

Monod, Jacques (Lucien) [monoh] (1910–76) Biochemist, born in Paris. He shared the Nobel Prize for Physiology or Medicine in 1965 for his work on the mechanisms governing the activity of genes. >> biochemistry; gene

monody In music, a single vocal or instrumental line, in contrast to polyphony. The term is often applied to the continuo-accompanied solo vocal music of the early 17th-c. >> continuo; Gregorian chant; plainchant; polyphony

monomer [**mon**omer] A simple molecule which can add to or condense with itself to form a *polymer*. An amino acid is a monomer of a protein; ethylene (CH_2=CH_2) is the monomer of polyethylene $(-CH_2-CH_2-)_n$. >> polymerization

mononucleosis, infectious >> **glandular fever**

Monophysites [mo**no**fisiyts] (Gr 'one nature') Adherents to the doctrine that Christ did not have two natures after his Incarnation – one human and one divine – but rather had only one nature, which was effectively divine since the divine apparently dominated the human. The view was condemned by the Council of Chalcedon (451). >> Christology; Monothelites

Monopolies Commission or **Monopolies and Mergers Commission** A UK government body set up in 1948 as the *Monopolies and Restrictive Practices Commission*. It has wide powers to investigate activities which may be against the public interest, particularly with respect to mergers, takeovers, and monopoly situations. >> merger; monopoly

monopoly A business situation where there is only one supplier of a good or service. This is unusual except where there is only one possible source of supply (**natural monopoly**) or the state excludes competition (eg in postal services). In economics, the term refers to a lack of competition. >> Monopolies Commission

monorail A railway using a single rail for the support of the train. The rail may be above or below the train, and the train may be stabilized if necessary by guide wheels and gyroscopes. Considerable research has gone into investigating non-wheeled methods of support, such as using air cushions and magnetic levitation. Monorails are used almost exclusively for public transport, notably in Tokyo and Seattle. >> gyroscope; railway

monosaccharide [mono**sa**kariyd] A simple sugar, the monomer of a polysaccharide, formed from it by condensation polymerization. >> polysaccharides; sugars

monosodium glutamate (MSG) A flavouring agent used to enhance the meat flavour of many processed foods containing meat or meat extracts. It is commonly associated with the 'Chinese Restaurant Syndrome', an array of symptoms associated with eating a Chinese meal in which excess MSG has been used. >> flavouring agent

monotheism The belief that only one God exists. It developed within the Jewish faith, and remains a feature of Judaism, Christianity, and Islam. It is opposed to both polytheism and pantheism. >> God; pantheism; polytheism

Monothelites [mo**no**theliyts] A Christian group who believed that in the person of Jesus Christ there was only one will, not two (one human, one divine). They were condemned at the Council of Constantinople in 680. >> Maronite Church; Monophysites

monotreme [**mo**nohtreem] An egg-laying mammal; lays soft-shelled eggs which hatch after 10 days; suckles young for 3–6 months; no teeth as adults. (Order: Monotremata, 3 species.) >> duck-billed platypus; echidna; mammal [i]

Monroe, James (1758–1831) US statesman and fifth president (1817–25), born in Westmoreland Co, VA. His most popular acts as president were the recognition of the Spanish-American republics and the promulgation of the *Monroe Doctrine*. >> Monroe Doctrine

Monroe, Marilyn, stage name of **Norma Jean Mortenson** or **Baker** (1926–62) Film star, born in Los Angeles, CA. After a childhood spent largely in foster homes, she became a photographer's model in 1946, and came to star in many successful films as a sexy 'dumb blonde'. She studied at Strasberg's Actors' Studio and went on to win acclaim in *Bus Stop* (1956). Divorced from her third husband, Arthur Miller, in 1961, she died in 1962 from an overdose of sleeping pills, and has since become a symbol of Hollywood's exploitation of beauty and youth. >> DiMaggio; Miller, Arthur; Strasberg

Monroe Doctrine A major statement of American foreign policy, proclaimed in 1823, attributed to President James Monroe, but written by secretary of state John Quincy Adams. It announced (1) the existence of a separate political system in the Western hemisphere, (2) US hostility to attempts to extend European influence, and (3) non-interference with existing European colonies or in European affairs. >> Adams, John Quincy; Monroe, James

Monrovia [mon**roh**via] 6°20N 10°46W, pop (1995e) 595 000. Seaport capital of Liberia, W Africa; founded by the American Colonization Society, 1822; original name Christopolis, changed to Monrovia after the US president; airport; railway terminus; university (1862); Firestone rubber plantation and processing centre nearby. >> Liberia [i]

Mons [mõs], Eng [monz], Flemish **Bergen** 50°28N 3°58E, pop (1995e) 93 300. Commercial and cultural city in S Belgium; built on site of one of Caesar's camps; often a battlefield, notably in World War 1 (Aug 1914); railway; university (1965); cathedral. >> Belgium [i]

Monsarrat, Nicholas (John Turney) [**mon**sarat] (1910–79) Novelist, born in Liverpool, Merseyside. During World War 2 he served in the navy, and then wrote his best-selling novel *The Cruel Sea* (1951), which was filmed.

monsoon climates Climates characterized by distinct wet and dry seasons, resulting from the seasonal migration of the intertropical convergence zone and changes in wind direction; they are found in tropical areas, especially Asia. Much of the agriculture of Asia is dependent on the monsoon, but the timing of its arrival is variable, and if it is late there is generally less rainfall.

monstera [mon**steer**a] A tall climber or liane (*Monstera deliciosa*) native to tropical America; leaves heart-shaped, developing deep notches and sometimes holes as tissue between veins ceases to grow; also called **Swiss cheese plant**. It is a popular house plant. (Family: Araceae.) >> liane

monstrance A liturgical vessel, usually of gold or silver frame with a glass window, used to display the Eucharistic host or consecrated bread. It enables the host to be venerated by worshippers. >> Eucharist; liturgy

montage [mon**tahzh**] **1** In art, a technique whereby illustrations or photographs are cut from papers or magazines, arranged in new ways, and mounted. A development of collage, it was used by the Dadaists and Surrealists. >> collage; Dada; Surrealism **2** In film editing, a sequence containing a series of rapidly changing images, often superimposed to convey a visually dramatic effect.

Montagu, Lady Mary Wortley [**mon**tagyoo], *née* **Pierrepont** (1689–1762) Writer, born in London, who gained a brilliant reputation among literary figures. While in Constantinople with her husband, she wrote her entertaining *Letters* describing Eastern life.

Montaigne, Michel (Eyquem) de [mõ**ten**] (1533–92) Essayist, born at the Château de Montaigne, Périgord, France. He is remembered for his *Essais* on the ideas and personalities of the time, which introduced a new literary genre, and provided a major contribution to literary history.

Montale, Eugenio [mon**tah**lay] (1896–1981) Poet, born in Genoa, Italy. He was the leading poet of the modern Italian *hermetic* school, his primary concern being with language and symbolic meaning. He received the 1975 Nobel Prize for Literature.

Montana [mon**tan**a] pop (1995e) 863 000; area 380 834 sq km/147 046 sq mi. State in NW USA; the 'Treasure State'; most of the state acquired by the Louisiana Purchase, 1803; border with Canada settled by the Oregon Treaty, 1846; became the Territory of Montana, 1864; gold rush after 1858 discoveries; ranchers moved into the area in 1866, taking over Indian land; six Indian reservations now in the state; 41st state to join the Union, 1889; fourth largest US state; crossed by the Missouri and Yellowstone Rivers; highest point Granite Peak (3901 m/12 798 ft); the Great Plains (E) largely occupied by vast wheat fields and livestock farms; W dominated by the Rocky Mts, covered in dense pine forests; capital, Helena; tourism a major state industry; copper, silver, gold, zinc, lead, manganese in the mountainous W; petroleum, natural gas, large coalmines in the E. >> Louisiana Purchase; United States of America [i]; RR994

Montana, Joe [mon**tan**a], popular name of **Joseph C Montana, Jr** (1956–) Player of American football, born in New Eagle, PA. He joined the San Francisco 49ers in 1979, and led them to victories in four Super Bowls (1982, 1985, 1989, 1990). The League's most valuable player in 1989, he joined the Kansas City Chiefs 1993–5, before retiring. >> football [i]

Montand, Yves [mõtã, eev], originally **Ivo Livi** (1921–91) Actor-singer, born in Monsummano Alto, Italy. His films include *Le Salaire de La peur* (1953, The Wages of Fear), *Let's Make Love* (1960), and Z (1968). In the 1980s he became a distinguished elder statesman of the French film industry.

Montanism [**mon**tanizm] A popular Christian movement whose name derives from Montanus of Phrygia (AD c.170). Its ecstatic prophecies and literal expectation of the imminent end of the age won a wide following of churches in Asia Minor, though its austere ethical and spiritual ideals were opposed by the Catholic Church. >> Christianity

Mont Blanc [mõ **blã**] Highest alpine massif of SE France, SW Switzerland, and NW Italy; 25 peaks over 4000 m/13 000 ft; highest peak, Mont Blanc (4807 m/15 771 ft); frontiers of France, Switzerland, and Italy meet at Mt Dolent (3823 m/12 542 ft); road tunnel (12 km/7½ mi long) connects France and Italy; tunnel closed by fire which killed over 40 people, March 1999; first climbed in 1786 by J Balmat and M G Paccard; chief resort, Chamonix. >> Alps

montbretia [mon**bree**sha] A perennial (*Crocosmia* × *crocosmiiflora*) growing to 90 cm/3 ft; flowers orange, funnel-shaped, in one-sided sprays. (Family: Iridaceae.)

Montcalm (de Saint Véran), Louis Joseph de Montcalm-Grozon, marquis de [mõkalm] (1712–59) French general, born in Condiac, France. He took command of the French troops in Canada (1756), and defended Quebec, where he died in the battle against General Wolfe. >> Seven Years' War; Wolfe, James

Monte Albán [**mon**tay al**ban**] The ancient capital of the Zapotecs of S Mexico; a world heritage site. In use c.400 BC–AD 800, it occupied an area of 40 sq km/15 sq mi at its peak (c.200–700), with a population of c.20 000. >> Zapotecs

Monte Carlo [**mon**tay **kah(r)**loh] 43°46N 7°23E. Resort town in Monaco; famous Casino, providing c.4% of national revenue, built in 1878; annual car rally, world championship Grand Prix motor race. >> Monaco

Montefiore, Sir Moses (Haim) [monte**fyoh**ray] (1784–1885) Philanthropist, born in Livorno, Italy. From 1829 he was prominent in the struggle for the rights of Jews, making several journeys throughout Europe on their behalf. >> Zionism

Montego Bay [mon**tee**goh], locally **Mobay** 18°27N 77°56W, pop (1995e) 86 800. Free port and principal tourist centre of Jamaica; airport; railway. >> Jamaica ℹ

Montenegro [monte**nee**groh], Serbo-Croatian **Crna Gora** pop (1995e) 623 000; area 13 812 sq km/5331 sq mi. Republic in federation of Yugoslavia (along with Serbia); mountainous region; independent monarchy until 1918; became constituent republic of Yugoslavia, 1946; in favour of maintenance of Yugoslavia as a federation, 1991; capital, Titograd; focus of NATO air-strikes, along with Serbia, in Kosovo crisis of early 1999. >> Serbia; Titograd; Yugoslavia ℹ

Montespan, Françoise Athenaïs de Rochechouart, marquise de (Marchioness of) [mõtespã] (1641–1707) Mistress of Louis XIV, born in Tonnay-Charente, France, the daughter of the Duc de Mortemart. She became the king's mistress in c.1667, and after her marriage was annulled (1674) was given official recognition of her position. She bore the king seven children. >> Louis XIV

Montesquieu, Charles Louis de Secondat, Baron de la Brède et de [mõteskyoe] (1689–1755) Philosopher and jurist, born near Bordeaux, France. His best-known work is the comparative study of legal and political issues, *De l'esprit des lois* (1748, The Spirit of Laws), which was a major influence on 18th-c Europe.

Montessori, Maria [monte**saw**ree] (1870–1952) Physician and educationalist, born in Rome. She opened her first 'children's house' in 1907, developing a system of education for children of three to six, based on freedom of movement, considerable choice for pupils, and specially-designed activities and equipment. **Montessori schools** were also developed for older children.

Monteverdi, Claudio [montay**vair**dee] (1567–1643) Composer, born in Cremona, Italy. His works include eight books of madrigals, operas, and (his greatest contribution to church music) the Mass and Vespers of the Virgin (1610), which contained tone colours and harmonies well in advance of their time. >> madrigal

Montevideo [montevi**day**oh] 34°55S 56°10W, pop (1995e) 1 328 000. Capital of Uruguay, on the R Plate; founded, 1726; capital, 1830; airport; railway; university (1849); cathedral (1790–1804); German battleship *Graf Spee* scuttled offshore during the Battle of the River Plate (1939). >> Plate, River; Uruguay ℹ

Montez, Lola [mon**tez**], originally **Marie Dolores Eliza Rosanna Gilbert** (1818–61) Dancer and adventurer, born in Limerick, Ireland. She became a dancer in London, and while in Munich (1846) gained influence over the eccentric artist-king, Ludwig I (1786–1868), who created her Countess of Landsfeld. >> Revolutions of 1848

Montezuma II [monte**zoo**ma] (1466–1520) Mexican emperor (1502–20), warrior and legislator, who died at Tenochtitlán during the Spanish conquest. >> Cortés

Montfort, Simon de, Earl of Leicester (c.1208–1265) English statesman and soldier, born in Montfort, France. In 1238 he married Henry III's youngest sister, Eleanor. He was leader of the barons in their opposition to the king, defeated him at Lewes (1264), and became virtual ruler of England. The barons soon grew dissatisfied with his rule, and the king's army defeated him at Evesham, where he was killed. >> Barons' Wars; Henry III (of England)

Montgolfier brothers [mõgolfyay] Aeronautical inventors: **Joseph Michel Montgolfier** (1740–1810) and **Jacques Etienne Montgolfier** (1745–99), born in Annonay, France. They constructed a balloon which in 1783 achieved a flight of 9 km/5½ mi over Paris. >> balloon

Montgomery 32°23N 86°19W, pop (1995e) 199 000. Capital of state in C Alabama, USA, on the Alabama R; state capital, 1847; Confederate States of America formed here, 1861; occupied by Federal troops, 1865; railway; university (1874); important market centre for farming produce; scene of 1955 bus boycott by blacks protesting against segregation. >> Alabama; American Civil War; civil rights

Montgomery (of Alamein), Bernard Law Montgomery, 1st Viscount (1887–1976) British field marshal, born in London. He gained renown as arguably the best British field commander since Wellington, establishing a remarkable rapport with his troops. He commanded the 8th Army in N Africa, defeated Rommel at El Alamein (1942), played a key role in the invasion of Sicily and Italy (1943), and was appointed commander-in-chief, ground forces, for the Allied invasion of Normandy (1944). In 1945, the German forces surrendered to him on Lüneberg Heath. >> D-Day; El Alamein, Battle of; Normandy Campaign; World War 2

month The time for the Moon to orbit the Earth, relative to a reference point. The Moon orbits the Earth in 27·32 days (relative to the stars), passing through the familiar cycle of lunar phases. The lunar month of 29·53 days is the interval between successive new Moons. Twelve lunar months is less than one solar year, so the calendar months are arbitrarily longer than lunar months.

Montherlant, Henri (Marie Joseph Millon) de [mõtairlã] (1896–1972) Writer, born in Paris. His major work is a 4-novel cycle, beginning with *Les jeunes filles* and *Pitié pour les femmes* (1936, trans Pity for Women).

Montoneros [monto**nair**os] Argentine urban guerrillas claiming allegiance to Peronism and (from 1970) staging terrorist actions against the military regime then in power. Repudiated by Perón himself (1974), they renewed their attacks on the regime installed in 1976, meeting with severe repression. >> Peronism

Montpelier [mont**peel**yer] 44°16N 72°35W, pop (1995e) 8500. Capital of Vermont, USA; on the Winooski R; settled, 1780; state capital, 1805; railway; Vermont College (1834). >> Vermont

Montpellier [mõpelyay] 43°37N 3°52E, pop (1995e) 214 000. Industrial and commercial city in S France; founded around a Benedictine abbey, 8th-c; airport; railway; bishopric; university (1289); cathedral (1364); Jardin des Plantes, France's first botanical garden (1593).

Montreal [montree**awl**], Fr **Montréal** [mõrayal] 45°30N 73°36W, pop (1995e) 1 080 000. River-port city in Quebec, Canada; on Montreal I, on the St Lawrence R (ice-free May–Nov); largest city in Canada, and second largest French-speaking city in the world; first visited by Cartier, 1535; fort, 1611; developed as a fur-trading centre; surrendered to British, 1760; capital of Canada, 1844–9; British garrison withdrawn, 1870; two airports; railway; metro; four universities (1821, 1876, 1969, 1974); two cathedrals; major commercial centre; professional teams, Montreal Expos (baseball), Montreal Canadiens (ice hockey); location of 1967 World's Fair (Expo) and 1976 Olympic Games. >> Cartier; Quebec (province)

Montreux [mõ**troe**] 46°27N 6°55E, pop (1995e) 20 000. Winter sports centre and resort town in SW Switzerland; at E end of L Geneva; railway; casino; Golden Rose Television Festival (spring), International Jazz Festival (Jun–Jul). >> Switzerland ℹ

Montrose, James Graham, 1st Marquess of (1612–50) Scottish general. He led the Royalist army to victory at Tippermuir (1644), but after the Royalist defeat at Naseby (1645), his remaining force was defeated at Philiphaugh. He fled to Europe, returning to Scotland after Charles's execution, but was defeated at Invercharron (1650) and hanged in Edinburgh. >> English Civil War

Mont-Saint-Michel [mõ sĩ mi**shel**] A rocky isle off the coast of Normandy, NW France, famous for its Gothic abbey; a world heritage site. A Benedictine settlement was first established here in the 8th-c. >> Benedictines; Normandy

Montserrat [montsuh**rat**], also **Emerald Isle** pop (pre-1997 disaster) 11 000, (post-1997) c.4 000; area 106 sq km/ 41 sq mi. Volcanic island in the Leeward Is, E Caribbean; British overseas territory; capital, Plymouth; timezone GMT -4; population of mixed African and European descent; chief religion, Christianity; official language, English; unit of currency, the East Caribbean dollar; length, 18 km/11 mi; maximum width, 11 km/7 mi; mountainous, heavily forested; seven active volcanoes; tropical climate, with low humidity; visited by Columbus, 1493; colonized by English and Irish settlers, 1632; plantation economy based on slave labour; British Crown Colony, 1871; joined Federation of the West Indies, 1958–62; British sovereign represented by a governor, with an Executive Council and a Legislative Council; tourism the mainstay of the economy, accounting for 25% of national income; island severely damaged by hurricane Hugo in 1989; most of the island, including the capital, destroyed by eruption of Soufriere Hills volcano, June 1997, followed by gradual resettlement of the population. >> Leeward Islands (Caribbean); Plymouth (Montserrat)

Monty Python, in full **Monty Python's Flying Circus** An anarchic satirical series, shown on BBC television between 1969 and 1974, starring Graham Chapman (1941–89), John Cleese, Eric Idle, Terry Jones, and Michael Palin. The series changed the face of British television humour, with its inspired lunacy, surreal comedy, and animated graphics (by Terry Gilliam), and generated a cult following which was eventually international. The troupe later collaborated on such films as *The Life of Brian* (1979) and *The Meaning of Life* (1983). >> Cleese; Palin; satire

Monument, the A Doric column in C London, surmounted by a representation of a flame-encircled globe, designed by Wren and erected (1671–7) to commemorate the Fire of London. The structure is 61.5 m/202 ft high. >> Doric order; Fire of London; London [i]; Wren, Christopher

Moody, Dwight L(yman) (1837–99) Leading independent US evangelist, born in Northfield, MA. In 1870 he was joined by **Ira David Sankey** (1840–1908), who accompanied his preaching with singing and organ playing. >> evangelicalism

Moog synthesizer >> **synthesizer**

Moon The Earth's only natural satellite, lacking any atmosphere; about a quarter the size of the Earth, and treated as one of the family of terrestrial planets. It has the following characteristics: mass $0{\cdot}073 \times 10^{27}$ g; radius (equatorial) 1738 km/1080 mi; mean density 3·34 g/cm^3; equatorial gravity 162 cm/s; rotational period 27·3 days; orbital period 27·3 days; average distance from Earth 384 400 km/238 850 mi. The equality of rotational and orbital rates is due to tidal despinning of the Moon into a stable synchronous period, so that the same hemisphere of the Moon always faces the Earth. The brighter surface regions (*highlands*) represent the original lunar crustal material shaped by saturation bombardment of meteoritic material. The dark surface regions (*mare* regions), located mainly on the side observable from Earth, represent basaltic (volcanic) flooding of basins created by major asteroidal impacts. The popular current theory for the creation of the Moon involves the impact of a Mars-sized object with the Earth, and the accretion of the Moon in Earth orbit from debris torn from the Earth's mantle. >> Apollo / Luna / Lunar Orbiter / Ranger / Surveyor programme; Earth [i]; RR966–7

moonfish Large, midwater fish (*Lampris guttatus*) widespread in tropical and temperate seas; length up to 1·5 m/5 ft; body deep, compressed, fins well-developed, protruding mouth, lacking teeth; colour very characteristic, deep blue on back spotted with white, underside silver, fins deep red; also called **opah**. (Family: Lampridae.)

Moonies A derisive name applied to members of the religious movement founded in 1954 by Korean evangelist Sun Myung Moon (1920–). Known as the **Unification Church** (in full, the Holy Spirit Association for the Unification of World Christianity), the organization was founded in 1954 in South Korea, and moved to Tarrytown, NY, in the 1970s. Mass marriages are one of the movement's more public activities. The missionary activities of the Church have attracted a great deal of criticism, especially from parents who believe that their children have been brainwashed. The organization's financial affairs have also been the subject of investigation, and in 1982 Moon was fined and sentenced to 18 months imprisonment for US tax evasion. He has continued to live chiefly in the USA, where he owns several companies, but has encountered increasing opposition to his movement there, and also in several countries where he has tried to expand, especially in C and S America. In the late 1990s he was developing a centre at Jardim, W Brazil, as a new 'garden of Eden'. >> evangelicalism; religion; sect

moonrat A SE Asian insectivorous mammal; resembles closely related hedgehogs, but lacks spines and has a longer tail; several species reputed to be the most evil-smelling animals; also known as **hairy hedgehog** or **gymnure**. (Family: Erinaceidae, 5 species.) >> hedgehog; insectivore

moonstone A semi-precious gemstone variety of the mineral potassium feldspar. It has a pale opalescent lustre because of its fine-scale oriented microstructure, which diffracts light. >> feldspar

Moore, Archie, originally **Archibald Lee Wright**, nickname **the Mongoose** (1913 /16–98) Boxer, born in Benoit, MI. His actual date of birth is uncertain, but he was still the oldest man to hold a world title when he beat Joey Maxim (1922–) for the light-heavyweight title in 1952 at the age of 39 (or 36). >> boxing [i]

Moore, Bobby, popular name of **Robert Frederick Chelsea Moore** (1941–93) Footballer, born in London. He had a long career with West Ham United (1958–74) and Fulham (1974–7), and was capped a record 108 times, 90 of them as captain. He led the victorious England side in the 1966 World Cup. >> football [i]

Moore, Brian (1921–99) Writer, born in Belfast. His first novel, *Judith Hearne*, appeared in 1955; later works include *The Doctor's Wife* (1976) and *Black Robe* (1985), both short-listed for the Booker Prize, and *The Statement (1995).*

Moore, Demi, originally **Demetria Guynes** (1962–) Film actress, born in Roswell, NM. She became well known following her role in *Ghost* (1990), later films including *Indecent Proposal* (1992), *Striptease* (1996), and *G.I. Jane* (1997).

Moore, Dudley (Stuart John) (1935–) British actor, comedian, and composer. He was one of the successful *Beyond the Fringe* team (1960–4), and joined Peter Cook for the TV series *Not only... but also* (1964–70). He went on to star in several films including *10* (1979), *Arthur* (1981), and *Crazy People* (1990). An accomplished musician, he has performed with his own jazz piano trio, and composed for several films and plays. >> Cook, Peter

Moore, G(eorge) E(dward) (1873–1958) Philosopher, born in London. His major ethical work was *Principia Ethica* (1903), in which he argued against the naturalistic fallacy, and he was also editor (1921–47) of *Mind*. He was a leading influence on the Bloomsbury group. >> Bloomsbury group; naturalistic fallacy

Moore, Henry (Spencer) (1898–1986) Sculptor, born in Castleford, West Yorkshire. He produced mainly figures and groups in a semi-abstract style based on the organic forms and rhythms found in landscape and natural rocks. His interest lay in the spatial quality of sculpture, an effect he achieved by the piercing of his figures. His major works include 'Madonna and Child' (1943–4) in St Matthew's Church, Northampton. >> abstract art

Moore, Sir John (1761–1809) British general, born in Glasgow. He is remembered for his command of the British army in Spain (1808–9), where he was forced to retreat to Coruña. There he was mortally wounded (as recounted in the poem by Charles Wolfe). >> Peninsular War; Wolfe, Charles

Moore, Marianne (Craig) (1887–1972) Poet, born in St Louis, MO. Her *Collected Poems* appeared in 1951, and *Complete Poems* in 1967.

Moore, Patrick (Alfred Caldwell) (1923–) British amateur astronomer, writer, broadcaster, and musician. He is best known as the enthusiastic and knowledgeable presenter of the long-running BBC television programme *The Sky at Night* (1957–). He has published over 60 books, and is an accomplished xylophone player and composer.

Moore, Roger (George) (1927–) Film star, born in London. On television he won stardom as the action-man hero of such series as *Ivanhoe* (1958), and *The Saint* (1962–9). He brought a lightweight insouciance to the role of James Bond in seven films between *Live and Let Die* (1973) and *A View to a Kill* (1985).

Moores, Sir John (1896–1993) Businessman, born in Eccles, Greater Manchester. He founded Littlewoods football pools in 1923, established a mail-order business in Britain in 1932, and opened the first store in the Littlewoods chain in 1937. Liverpool John Moores University is named after him.

moorhen Either of two species of rail of genus *Gallinula*, especially the **moorhen**, **common gallinule**, or **Florida gallinule** (*Gallinula chloropus*), found worldwide; also the **lesser** or **little moorhen** (*Gallinula angulata*), found in sub-Saharan Africa. >> gallinule; rail

Moors Muslims from N Africa who conquered the Iberian Peninsula in the 8th-c AD. The Hispanic Christian kingdoms fought Wars of Reconquest, which by the mid-13th-c eliminated the Moors from all but the small S kingdom of Granada (conquered in 1492).

Moors Murderers >> **Brady, Ian**

moose >> **elk**

moped [**moh**ped] A small, lightweight motorcycle fitted with pedals, and capable of being pedalled if necessary. It was established as a means of personal transport before World War 2, but it was not until after the War that its economy made it attractive. This economy was achieved by lightness of design and the application of the two-stroke engine. >> motorcycle

moraine A sedimentary deposit of poorly sorted rock and detritus transported by glaciers and ice-sheets. Different classes of moraine correspond to the different zones of glaciers where deposition occurs (eg terminal moraines, lateral moraines). >> glaciation; till

morality play A play which dramatizes a moral argument, presenting the opposition between good and evil, often with characters who personify abstractions. It was popular in England in the late mediaeval and early Tudor period. Unlike the mystery play, it was not tied to religious festivals, and was performed by professional actors. >> allegory; mystery play

Moral Majority A US political action committee founded in 1979 which has played a leading part in the revival of the New Right. It is associated with Christian fundamentalists who in the 1980s came to play a prominent role in US politics. >> New Right

Moral Rearmament A movement founded by Frank Buchman in 1938 to deepen the spirituality and morality of Christians. It succeeded the 'Oxford Group Movement' (founded 1921), and expanded its goals to include political and social concerns. >> Buchman; Christianity

moral theology A theological discipline concerned with ethical questions considered from a specifically Christian perspective. In Roman Catholic teaching, it deals traditionally with God as the goal of human life, and provides instruction on spirituality and the means of grace. It has become increasingly ecumenical, and concerned with issues such as peace, justice, and bioethics. >> Christianity; ecumenism; ethics; theology

Morar, Loch [**mo**rer] Loch in W Highland, W Scotland; 19 km/12 mi long; deepest loch in Britain (310 m/1017 ft). >> Highland; Scotland ℹ

Moravia [mo**ray**via], Czech **Morava**, Ger **Mähren** Historic province of the Czech Republic; chief towns include Brno, Ostrava, Olomouc; early mediaeval kingdom (Great Moravia), 9th-c; part of Bohemia, 1029; under Habsburg rule from early 16th-c; province of Czechoslovakia, 1918; united with Silesia, 1927–49; political status under discussion, 1991. >> Czech Republic ℹ

Moravia, Alberto [mo**ray**via], pseudonym of **Alberto Pincherle** (1907–90) Novelist and short-story writer, born in Rome. His first novel was a major success, *Gli indifferenti* (1929, trans The Time of Indifference), portraying in a fatalistic way the preoccupation with sex and money of bourgeois Roman society. Later works include *Racconti romani* (1954, Roman Tales).

Moravian Brethren A Protestant body descended from an association of Brethren formed in Bohemia in 1457, and driven out in 1722 by persecution. In 1734 the Moravian Church was established in North America, where most members live today. >> Protestantism

Moray, James Stuart, Earl of [**muh**ree] (1531–70) Regent of Scotland (1567–70), the natural son of James V of Scotland, and half-brother of Mary, Queen of Scots. He acted as Mary's chief adviser (1560), but opposed her marriage to Darnley. He became regent for Mary's baby son when she abdicated (1567), and defeated her army at Langside (1568). He was killed at Linlithgow by one of Mary's supporters. >> Mary, Queen of Scots

Morceli, Noureddine [maw(r)se**lee**] (1970–) French athlete, born in Tenes, Algeria. World champion over 1500 m in 1991 – the youngest ever – he repeated his success in 1993 and 1995. He held the world record in 1995 for 1500 m, the mile, 2000 m and 3000 m, and in 1996 was Olympic 1500 m champion.

Mordecai [**maw(r)**dekiy] (c.5th-c BC) Biblical hero, described in the Book of Esther as a Jew in exile in Persia who gained the favour of King Xerxes, and used his influence to protect Jews from an edict issued against them. The event is commemorated by the annual Jewish feast of Purim. >> Esther, Book of

More, Henry [moor] (1614–87) Philosopher and poet, born in Grantham, Lincolnshire. He was a leading member of the Cambridge Platonists. His works include the *Divine Dialogues* (1668). >> Cambridge Platonists

More, Sir Thomas [moor], also **St Thomas More** (1478–1535) English statesman and scholar, born in London. On the fall of Wolsey (1529), he was appointed Lord Chancellor, but resigned in 1532 following his opposition to Henry's break with the Roman Catholic Church. On refusing to recognize Henry as head of the English Church, he was imprisoned and beheaded. A leading humanist scholar, as revealed in his Latin *Utopia* (1516) and many other works, he was canonized in 1935. Feast day 22 June. >> Henry VIII; Reformation; Wolsey

Morecambe, Eric, originally **Eric Bartholomew** (1926–84) Comedian, born in Morecambe, Lancashire. He teamed up in 1943 with fellow entertainer, **Ernie Wise** (originally

Ernest Wiseman) (1925–99), eventually becoming Britain's leading comedy double-act.

morel [m**o**rel] An edible fungus (*Morchella esculenta*); fruiting body consists of a pale stalk (*stipe*) and brownish, egg-shaped head with a pitted or ridged surface. (Subdivision: Ascomycetes. Order: Pezizales.) >> fungus

Morgagni, Giovanni Battista [maw(r)**gan**yee] (1682–1771) Physician and pathologist, born in Forli, Italy. He correlated pathological lesions with symptoms in over 700 cases, and is traditionally considered to be the 'father of morbid anatomy'. >> anatomy ℹ; pathology

Morgan, Sir Henry (c.1635–88) Welsh buccaneer, born in Llanrumney, S Wales. He led many raids against the Spanish and Dutch in the West Indies and Central America. His most famous exploit was the sacking of Porto Bello and Panama (1671). He later became Deputy Governor of Jamaica. >> buccaneers

Morgan, J(ohn) P(ierpont) (1837–1913) Financier and philanthropist, born in Hartford, CT. In 1895 he founded the international banking firm of J P Morgan and Co, providing US government finance, and developing interests in steel, railroads, and shipping.

Morgan, Thomas Hunt (1866–1945) Geneticist, born in Lexington, VA. He proved that Mendel's 'genetic factors' are the chromosomes, and showed the link between genes and chromosomes. He received the Nobel Prize for Physiology or Medicine in 1933. >> chromosome ℹ; genetics; Mendel

Morgan le Fay In Arthurian legend, an enchantress, 'Morgan the Fairy', King Arthur's sister, and generally hostile towards him. >> Arthur

Morisot, Berthe (Marie Pauline) [morisoh] (1841–95) Painter, born in Bourges, France. She was the leading female exponent of Impressionism. >> Impressionism (art)

Morley, Edward Williams >> **Michelson, A A**

Morley, Robert (1908–92) Actor and writer, born in Semley, Wiltshire. In his film career, from 1938, he played many individual character parts, including the title role in *The Trials of Oscar Wilde* (1960).

Mormons [**maw**muhnz] A religious movement based on the visionary experiences of Joseph Smith, who organized it as the 'Church of Jesus Christ of Latter-Day Saints' in 1830 at Fayette, NY. Smith claimed to have been led to the Book of Mormon, inscribed on golden plates and buried 1000 years before in a hill near Palmyra, NY. It teaches Christ's future establishment of the New Jerusalem in America. Subjected to persecution, the Mormons moved W, and Brigham Young finally led most of them to the valley of the Great Salt Lake, Utah (1847). There were c.10 million worldwide in 1998. >> Smith, Joseph; Young, Brigham

morning-after pill >> **contraception; DES**

morning glory An annual (*Ipomoea tricolor*) growing to 3 m/10 ft, native to tropical America; climbing by means of twining stems; flowers up to 12·5 cm/5 in diameter, funnel-shaped, blue with yellow throat, sometimes purple or red. (Family: Convolvulaceae.)

morning sickness Nausea and vomiting during the first three months of pregnancy, which affects c.50% of women. It tends to subside thereafter, and is believed to result from associated hormonal changes. >> pregnancy ℹ

Moro, Aldo [m**o**roh] (1916–78) Italian statesman and prime minister (1963–4, 1964–6, 1966–8, 1974–6, 1976), born in Maglie, Italy. Red Brigade left-wing terrorists kidnapped him in Rome in 1978, and subsequently murdered him. >> Red Brigades

Morocco [muh**ro**koh], official name **The Kingdom of Morocco**, Arabic **al-Mamlakah al-Maghribiyah** pop (1995e) 28 010 000; area 409 200 sq km/157 951 sq mi. N African kingdom; capital, Rabat; timezone GMT; population almost all of Arab-Berber origin; religion, Islam; official language, Arabic, with French also important; unit of currency, the dirham of 100 francs; dominated by a series of folded mountain ranges, rising in the Haut Atlas (S) to 4165 at Mt Toubkal; broad coastal plain; Mediterranean climate on N coast; average annual rainfall 400–800 mm/15–30 in, decreasing towards the Sahara, which is virtually rainless; N coast occupied by Phoenicians, Carthaginians, and Romans since 12th-c BC; invasion by Arabs, 7th-c AD; European interest in the region in 19th-c; Treaty of Fez, 1912, established Spanish Morocco (capital, Tétouan) and French Morocco (capital, Rabat); international zone of Tangier created, 1923; protectorates gained independence, 1956; former Spanish Sahara (Western Sahara) under joint control of Spain, Morocco, and Mauritania, 1975; became responsibility of Morocco, 1979; a 'constitutional' monarchy, with the king presides over an appointed cabinet, which is led by a prime minister; unicameral Chamber of Representatives; over half the population engaged in agriculture; largest known reserves of phosphate; tourism centred on the four imperial cities and the warm Atlantic resorts. >> Tangier; Western Sahara; RR1017 political leaders

Moroni [mo**roh**nee] 11°40S 43°16E, pop (1995e) 24 000. Capital of Comoros; airport; pilgrimage centre at Chiouanda. >> Comoros

Morpeth 55°10N 1°41W, pop (1995e) 15 000. County town of Northumberland, on the R Wansbeck; railway; remains of Morpeth Castle (14th-c). >> Northumberland

Morpheus [**maw(r)**fyoos] In Roman mythology, one of the sons of Somnus ('sleep') who sends or impersonates images of people in the dreamer's mind.

morphine A drug derived from opium, used to ease severe pain. Because of its addictive potential, its use is controlled. In overdoses it causes death by suppressing respiration. >> drug addiction; opium

morphology (biology) The form and structure of an individual organism, with special emphasis on its external features. >> anatomy ℹ

morphology (linguistics) The study of **morphemes**, the smallest indivisible units of meaning in the structure of a word (eg *anti-lock-ing*, *horse-s*). It recognizes such notions as roots, inflections, and affixes. >> grammar

Morris, Desmond (John) (1928–) British popular writer on zoology. His study of human behaviour in *The Naked Ape* (1967) was a best-seller, and was followed by many television programmes on animal and social behaviour. His other books include *Manwatching* (1977) and *Illustrated Babywatching* (1995).

Morris, Robert (1931–) Sculptor and mixed media artist, born in Kansas City, MO. He moved to San Francisco in 1950, becoming active as a painter and in improvisatory theatre. He settled in New York City in 1961, specializing in minimalist works, earthwork projects, and scatter pieces.

Morris, Robert L(yle) (1942–) Psychologist, born in Canonsburg, PA. In 1985 he was appointed the first Koestler professor of parapsychology at the University of Edinburgh. >> parapsychology

Morris, William (1834–96) Craftsman and poet, born near London. He associated with the Pre-Raphaelite Brotherhood, then specialized in the revival of handicrafts and the art of house decoration and furnishing. He organized the Socialist League, and in 1890 set up the Kelmscott Press, issuing his own works and reprints of classics. >> Arts and Crafts Movement; Pre-Raphaelite Brotherhood

morris dance A form of traditional dance found in England. Its distinctive features are stamping and hopping performed by files of performers usually dressed in white and always carrying some prop – a stick, handkerchief, or garland.

Morrison (of Lambeth), Herbert Stanley Morrison, Baron (1888–1965) British Labour statesman, born in London. He was minister of transport (1929–31), minister of supply (1940), and home secretary (1940–5). He served in the War Cabinet from 1942, and became a powerful postwar figure, acting as deputy prime minister (1945–51). >> Labour Party

Morrison, Toni, *née* **Chloe Anthony Wofford** (1931–) Novelist, born in Lorain, OH. Her early titles include *The Bluest Eye* (1970) and *Song of Solomon* (1977). Two later novels, *Tar Baby* (1981) and *Beloved* (Pulitzer, 1988), confirmed her as a leading novelist of her generation, and she received the Nobel Prize for Literature in 1993.

Morrison, Van, popular name of **George Ivan Morrison** (1945–) Singer, musician, and songwriter, born in Belfast. His first solo hit was 'Brown-Eyed Girl' (1967) and a year later he released the highly acclaimed, surreal album *Astral Weeks*. Other successes of that period included 'Caravan' (1970). He continued to record into the 1990s, with such albums as *The Healing Game* (1996).

Morse, Samuel F(inley) B(reese) (1791–1872) Artist and inventor, born in Charlestown, MA. He developed the magnetic telegraph (1832–5), which along with the **Morse code** (1838) brought him honours and rewards after the opening of the first telegraph line between Washington and Baltimore (1844). >> Morse code; telegraphy

Morse code A binary code for the transmission of verbal messages, devised during the 1830s by Samuel Morse. Each letter of the alphabet, numeral, and punctuation mark was assigned a distinctive combination of (short) dots and (long) dashes. Modern telegraphy has made greater use of the more economical **Baudot code**, devised in 1874 by French engineer Jean Maurice Emile Baudot (1845–1903). In 1988, the International Maritime Organization (the United Nations body on shipping safety) agreed to introduce from 1993 the **Global Maritime Distress and Safety System**, which uses satellite technology. >> Morse

mortar (building) Any one of many mixtures of lime and sand or (modern) cement and sand with water, which provide a bond between bricks, masonry, or tiles. >> cement

mortar (military) A weapon, used typically by infantry forces, which projects a small bomb at a high trajectory to fall on enemy forces at short range. >> bomb

mortar and pestle A device known in various forms since ancient times for grinding granular material into powder. The **mortar** is a shallow bowl of abrasive stone. The **pestle** is a conical piece of the same material with a rounded end, with which the material to be ground is forced against the bowl.

mortgage [**maw**gij] An arrangement whereby a lender (the **mortgagee**) lends money to a borrower (the **mortgagor**), the loan being secured on the mortgagor's land. Mortgages have played a significant role in permitting the spread of home ownership. >> property

Mortimer, Sir John (Clifford) (1923–) Playwright and novelist, born in London. He came to prominence as a dramatist with his one-act play *The Dock Brief* (1957). Television plays and stories about the disreputable barrister Horace Rumpole began in 1978.

Morton, H(enry) V(ollam) (1892–1979) Travel writer and journalist, born in Birmingham, West Midlands. The author of many informally written travel books, he is best known for *In Search of London* (1951), and others in the *In Search of...* series.

Morton, James Douglas, 4th Earl of (c.1516–81) Regent of Scotland (1572–8) for James VI. He was made Lord High Chancellor by Mary Stuart (1563); yet he was involved in the murders of Rizzio (1566) and Darnley (1567), and helped to overthrow the queen. He succeeded Moray as regent, but his high-handed treatment of the nobles and clergy caused his downfall (1581), and he was executed at Edinburgh. >> Darnley; Mary, Queen of Scots; Moray; Rizzio

Morton, Jelly Roll, popular name of **Ferdinand Joseph La Menthe Morton** (1885–1941) Jazz composer, bandleader, and pianist, born in Gulfport, LA. His unaccompanied piano solos made best sellers of such tunes as 'King Porter Stomp' and 'Jelly Roll Blues', and he made powerful orchestral arrangements for his band, **The Red Hot Peppers**. >> jazz

Morton, John Cameron (Andrieu Bingham Michael), pseudonym **Beachcomber** (1893–1979) British writer and journalist. He was best known for his regular humorous column in the *Daily Express* under the name of **Beachcomber**.

mosaic The technique of making decorative designs or pictures by arranging small pieces of coloured glass, marble, or ceramic in a bed of cement. It was much used by the Romans for pavements, by the early Christians and Byzantines for murals in churches, and also by Islamic artists.

Mosaic Law >> **Torah**

Mosasaurus [**moh**sasawrus] A very large, marine lizard abundant in Cretaceous seas around N Europe and America; swimming mainly by movements of tail; paddle-like limbs used for steering; head long, teeth long and sharp. (Order: Squamata.) >> Cretaceous period; lizard [i]

moschatel [moska**tel**] A perennial (*Adoxa moschatellina*) native to the N hemisphere, 5–10 cm/2–4 in high; flowers greenish-yellow, forming an almost square head, each face formed by a 5-petalled flower (hence the alternative name, **town hall clock**) plus a 4-petalled flower at the top. (Family: Adoxaceae.) >> *see illustration on p.580*

Moscow, Russ **Moskva** 55°45N 37°42E, pop (1995e) 9 057 000. Capital and largest city of Russia, on the R Moskva; known from the 12th-c; capital of the principality of Muscovy, 13th-c; invaded by Napoleon, 1812; capital

Moschatel – plant and flower head

of the Russian SFSR, 1918; capital of the USSR, 1922; airport; railway; underground; universities (1755, 1960); Academy of Sciences; Moscow Art Theatre, Bolshoi Theatre of Opera and Ballet, Moscow State Circus; Kremlin (1300); Uspenski (Assumption) Cathedral (1475–9), Cathedral of the Archangel (1333, rebuilt 1505–9), Blagoveshchenski (Annunciation) Cathedral, St Basil's Cathedral (16th-c); Red Square; Lenin Mausoleum; scene of the 1980 Olympic Games. >> Bolshoi Ballet; Kremlin; Lenin Mausoleum; Red Square; Russia [i]; St Basil's Cathedral; Tretyakov Gallery

Moselle, River [moh**zel**], Ger **Mosel**, ancient **Mosella** River in Germany, Luxembourg, and NE France; rises in the French Vosges; flows N and NE to enter the R Rhine at Coblenz; length 514 km/319 mi; a major wine area. >> Germany [i]

Moses [**moh**ziz] (c.13th-c BC) Major character of Israelite history, portrayed in the Book of Exodus as the leader of the deliverance of Hebrew slaves from Egypt and the recipient of the divine revelation at Mt Sinai. Stories about his early life depict his escape from death as an infant, his upbringing in the Egyptian court, and his prediction of a series of miraculous plagues to persuade the Pharaoh to release the Hebrews. Traditions then describe Moses' leadership of the Israelites during their 40 years of wilderness wanderings. He was traditionally considered the author of the five books of the Law, but this is doubted by modern scholars. >> Aaron; Exodus, Book of; Judaism; Passover; Pentateuch; Sinai, Mount; Torah

Moses, Ed(win Corley) (1955–) Athlete, born in Dayton, OH. The world's most successful hurdler over 400 m, he was the world champion in 1983, and Olympic champion in 1976 and 1984. >> athletics

Moses, Grandma, popular name of **Anna Mary Robertson Moses** (1860–1961) Artist, born in Greenwich, NY. She began to paint childhood country scenes at about the age of 75, when arthritis made it difficult for her to sew, and achieved great popular success throughout the USA.

Moslem >> **Islam**

Mosley, Nicholas [**mohz**lee], **Baron Ravensdale** (1923–) Writer, born in London. He published his first novel, *Spaces of the Dark* in 1951. Later novels include *The Rainbearers* (1955), *Accident* (1966, filmed 1967), *Hopeful Monsters* (1990, Whitbread Prize), and *Children of Darkness and Light* (1996).

Mosley, Sir Oswald (Ernald) [**mohz**lee] (1896–1980) Politician, born in London. In 1932 he founded the British Union of Fascists, remembered for its anti-Semitic violence in the East End of London and its support for Hitler. Detained under the Defence Regulations during World War 2, he founded another racialist party, the Union Movement, in 1948. >> fascism; Hitler

mosquito, also known as **gnat** A small, slender fly with a piercing proboscis; eggs laid in water; blood-feeding females act as intermediate hosts of malaria, yellow fever, filariasis, dengue, and other disease organisms; distributed worldwide. (Order: Diptera. Family: Culicidae, c.3000 species.) >> Aedes; Culicidae; fly; insect [i]; malaria

Mosquito Coast Undeveloped lowland area in E Honduras and E Nicaragua, Central America, following the Caribbean coast in a 65 km/40 mi-wide strip of tropical forest, lagoons, and swamp; controlled by the British, 1665–1860. >> Caribbean Sea

Moss, Stirling (1929–) Motor-racing driver, born in London. He won many major races in the 1950s, but never won a world title, though he was runner-up twice. A bad crash at Goodwood in 1962 ended his career. >> motor racing

moss A small, spore-bearing, non-vascular plant of the class Musci, related to liverworts and hornworts. Mat- or cushion-forming mosses are found almost everywhere, most often in damp, shady places. However, some species are better able to withstand drying out, and a few even inhabit very dry places such as walls. >> hornwort; liverwort

Mosul [moh**sool**] 36°21N 43°08E, pop (1995e) 762 000. City in NW Iraq, on W bank of R Tigris; chief town of N Mesopotamia, 8th–13th-c; airfield; railway; university (1967); agricultural market centre. >> Iraq [i]; Mesopotamia

motet A sacred musical work, originating in the 13th-c and cultivated during the Renaissance as an unaccompanied polyphonic piece, reaching its highest point of development in the works of such composers as Palestrina and Byrd. After 1600, motets often included instrumental accompaniment, but the term continued to distinguish sacred works in Latin from others (cantatas and anthems) in the vernacular. >> polyphony; Byrd, William; Palestrina

moth An insect belonging to the order Lepidoptera, which comprises the butterflies and moths. Moths are distinguished from butterflies by being active mostly at night, by folding their wings flat over the body when at rest, and by having complex comb-like tips to their antennae; but there are exceptions. >> cactus / death's-head / emperor / geometrid / gypsy / hawk- / noctuid / puss / pyralid / saturnalid / tiger / tineid moth; butterfly; corn borer; silkworm

mother-in-law's-tongue A perennial (*Sansevieria trifasciata*) native to W Africa; leaves to 1 m/3¼ ft, stiff, erect, sword-shaped, fleshy, dark green with pale bands; flowers greenish white; berries orange. It is a widely grown house plant, also called **sansevieria** and **snake plant**, from the patterning on its leaves. (Family: Agavaceae.)

Mother Lode The gold-mining region in the W foothills of the Sierra Nevada, California, USA. It was the centre of the Californian gold rush.

Mother's Day A day set apart in honour of mothers: in the UK, Mothering Sunday, the fourth Sunday of Lent; in Australia, Canada, and the USA, the second Sunday in May.

Motherwell 55°48N 4°00W, pop (1995e) 29 300. Administrative centre of North Lanarkshire, C Scotland; railway; engineering. >> Scotland ℹ

Motion, Andrew (1952–) Poet, biographer, and novelist, born in London. Professor of creative writing at the University of East Anglia (1995–), his works include *A Writer's Life* (1994, Whitbread) and seven volumes of poetry (as of 1999). He was appointed poet laureate in 1999. >> RR1042

moto-cross A specialist form of motorcycle racing over a circuit of rough terrain, and taking advantage of natural hazards such as streams and hills. The first moto-cross was held at Camberley, Surrey, UK, in 1924. The sport is also often known as **scrambling**. >> motorcycle racing

motorcycle A two-wheeled vehicle designed to carry a rider and frequently a passenger for transport and pleasure, using a two- or four-stroke internal combustion engine to drive the rear wheel, with steering being accomplished by the rider turning the front wheel. A sidecar was often fitted to provide extra passenger accommodation. They developed in the mid-1890s. >> moped; motorcycle racing / trials

motorcycle racing The racing of motorcycles, first organized by the Automobile Club de France in 1906, from Paris to Nantes and back. The most famous races are held on the roads of the Isle of Man each June, and are known as the *TT (Tourist Trophy)* races; first held in 1907. Races are held for each of the following engine-size categories: 80 cc, 125 cc, 250 cc, 500 cc, and sidecar. Other forms of motorcycle racing include speedway moto-cross (scrambling), and motorcycle trials riding. >> moto-cross; motorcycle; motorcycle trials; speedway; RR1057

motorcycle trials One of the oldest forms of motorcycle competition. Trials riding is a severe test of the machine's durability, held over tough predetermined courses of normally 50–60 km/30–40 mi. >> motorcycle racing

motor insurance A system by which motorists pay premiums, often annual, to an insurance company, which will then pay costs arising from accident, damage, or theft. In many countries there is a legal requirement to have *third party* insurance before using public roads; this covers damage and injury except to the insured and to the insured's own vehicle and passengers. *Comprehensive* insurance is needed in order to cover damage and injury in these other cases. >> car; insurance

motor neurone disease A rare disorder of the central nervous system in which the nerve cells responsible for muscular movement slowly degenerate. Affected persons have progressive difficulty in speaking and moving the limbs. The cause is unknown. >> central nervous system

motor racing The racing of finely tuned motor cars, which can either be purpose-built or modified production vehicles. The most popular form of motor racing is Formula One grand prix racing for high-powered purpose-built cars which can average well over 240 kph/150 mph. A season-long world championship (Mar–Nov), involves usually 16 races at different venues worldwide. Other popular forms include Formula 3000, Formula Three, rallying, sports car, Indy car racing in the USA, Formula Ford, hill climbing, and production car races. The first race was in 1894, from Paris to Rouen; the first grand prix was the French, in 1906. Current famous races include the Le Mans 24-hour endurance race, the Monte Carlo Rally, and the Indianapolis 500. >> drag racing; karting; rally; stock-car racing; RR1057

Motown A black-owned record company, founded in 1959 by Berry Gordy (1929–) in Detroit, MI ('Motortown'). Early Motown hits by Smokey Robinson and the Miracles were followed by dozens more rhythm-and-blues and soul classics in the 1960s, recorded by the Supremes, the Jackson Five, the Temptations, and others. >> Jackson, Michael; rhythm and blues; soul (music); Wonder

Mott, Lucretia, *née* **Coffin** (1793–1880) Abolitionist and feminist, born in Nantucket, MA. A Quaker, she became involved in anti-slavery agitation in the 1830s, helping to organize the American Anti-Slavery Society (1833) and the Anti-Slavery Convention of American Women (1837). >> slave trade; women's liberation movement

motte and bailey An earth and timber fortification of Norman date. It consisted of an artificial mound or *motte* surrounded by a ditch, a separately defended outer court or *bailey* adjoining to one side. >> Normans

mould Any fungus, particularly one with an abundant, woolly mycelium of thread-like strands, often with visible spore-bearing structures. >> fungus

moulting The shedding of an external covering, such as the periodic loss of hair by mammals and feathers by birds. Feather shedding in birds is usually gradual and does not affect flight, but in some birds (eg ducks) all flight feathers are shed simultaneously, and the bird is temporarily flightless. >> feather ℹ; hair

mound bird / builder >> **megapode**

Mountain, the A group of Jacobin extremist deputies in the French Convention, led by Robespierre, so-called because they sat high up at the back of the Assembly where they overlooked their political opponents, the Girondins, and the uncommitted majority who were known collectively as 'the Plain'. >> Jacobins (French history); Plain, the; Robespierre

mountain ash >> **rowan**

mountain avens [**a**vinz] A dwarf, creeping, evergreen shrub to 8 cm/3 in (*Dryas octopetala*) native to arctic regions and high mountains; flowers 7–10-petalled, white, heliotropic; fruits with feathery plume. (Family: Rosaceae.) >> avens; tropism

mountain beaver A squirrel-like rodent (*Aplodontia rufa*) native to the Pacific coast of North America; not a true beaver; the most primitive living rodent; stocky with a minute hairy tail; also known as **sewellel**, **boomer**, or **whistler**. (Family: Aplodontidae.) >> beaver; rodent

mountaineering The skill of climbing a mountain aided by ropes and other accessories, such as crampons. The most popular form in the UK is **rock climbing**; **snow and ice climbing** is practised on the higher peaks of the world. All the world's highest peaks have now been conquered, and present-day mountaineering expeditions aim to climb previously untried routes.

mountain laurel An evergreen shrub or small tree (*Kalmia latifolia*) native to North America; flowers saucer-shaped, 5-lobed, white, pink, or red; also called **calico bush**. (Family: Ericaceae.)

Mount Athos, Gr **Agíon Oros** pop (1995e) 1590; area 336 sq km/130 sq mi. Autonomous administration in Macedonia region, Greece; Mt Athos, rising to 1956 m/6417 ft, is the 'Holy Mountain' of the Greek Church, associated with the monastic order of St Basil since the 9th-c; declared a theocratic republic in 1927. >> Greece ℹ; Greek Orthodox Church

Mountbatten (of Burma), Louis (Francis Albert Victor Nicholas) Mountbatten, 1st Earl (1900–79) British admiral of the fleet and statesman, born in Windsor, S England, younger son of Prince Louis of Battenberg and Princess Victoria of Hesse, granddaughter of Queen Victoria. In World War 2 he became chief of Combined Operations Command (1942), and played a key role in preparations for D-Day. In 1943 he was appointed supreme commander, SE Asia, where he defeated the Japanese offensive into India (1944), worked closely with Slim to reconquer Burma (1945), and received the Japanese surrender at Singapore. In 1947 he became last Viceroy of

India. He was assassinated by Irish terrorists near his summer home, Classiebawn Castle, Co Sligo. >> Combined Operations Command; D-Day; Slim; World War 2

Mountbatten, Prince Philip >> **Edinburgh, Duke of**

Mounties The popular name of the **Royal Canadian Mounted Police**, the federal police force of Canada. The organization was founded in 1873, and until 1920 was known as the North West Mounted Police. The red jacket and broad-brimmed hat worn by its officers are features of their distinctive uniform.

Mount Li The burial place of Qin Shihuangdi, the first Emperor of China (259–210 BC); a world heritage site. It is renowned for the discovery in 1974 of a life-size army of c.7500 painted terracotta figures deployed in military formation in chambers underground. >> Qin dynasty; terracotta; *see illustration below*

Mount of Olives >> **Olives, Mount of**

Mount Palomar Observatory An observatory on Palomar mountain near San Diego, CA, the site of the 5 m/200 in Hale reflector telescope (1948), which has made numerous contributions to observational astronomy and cosmology. The first Palomar Optical Sky Survey in the 1950s is a primary database used by all observatories. >> observatory; telescope 🛈

Mount Sinai >> **Sinai, Mount**

Mount Vernon The family home of George Washington on the Potomac R in Virginia. Washington and his wife, Martha, are buried there. >> Washington, George

Mourne Mountains [mawn] Mountain range in SE Northern Ireland; length 24 km/15 mi; rises to 852 m/2795 ft at Slieve Donard. >> Northern Ireland 🛈

mouse (computing) A computer input device which can be moved around on a flat surface causing a cursor to move around the computer screen in response. It can be used to choose options pointed to on the screen. >> input device

mouse (zoology) A name used for many small unrelated species in the rodent family, found worldwide, especially for members of genus *Mus* (36 species throughout Old World); **house mouse** (*Mus musculus*), from Asia, has dispersed globally in association with humans. (Family: Muridae.) >> dormouse; fieldmouse; gerbil; hamster; harvest mouse; lemming; rat; rodent; vole

mousebird >> **coly**

Moussorgsky, Modest (Petrovich) [mu**saw(r)g**skee], also spelled **Mussorgsky** or **Musorgsky** (1839–81) Composer, born in Karevo, Russia. A member of the Glinka-inspired nationalist group in St Petersburg, his masterpiece is the opera *Boris Godunov* (1874). His piano suite *Pictures from an Exhibition* (1874) has also kept a firm place in the concert repertoire. >> Glinka

Mousterian [moo**steer**ian] A European archaeological culture of the Middle Palaeolithic Age (c.70 000–40 000 BC), named after the cave at Le Moustier, Dordogne, SW France. Its stone tools are probably the work of Neanderthal peoples. >> Neanderthal Man; Three Age System

mouth The first part of the gastro-intestinal tract; in mammals one of its characteristic features is the movable muscular lips and cheeks, which are intimately related to chewing, and in humans to speech. >> alimentary canal; cleft lip and palate; cold sore; teeth 🛈; tongue

mouth organ >> **harmonica**

mouth-to-mouth respiration >> **artificial respiration** 🛈

movement In music, a self-contained section of a longer work, such as a concerto or symphony. It may be linked to the movement that precedes or follows it, with which it is usually contrasted in tempo or key (often both). >> concerto; sonata; symphony

movies >> **cinematography**

Movietone The trade name for one of the first sound-on-film recording and reproducing systems, launched by Fox in 1927. It was used initially for newsreels, and subsequently for all their feature film production.

Moynihan, Daniel P(atrick) (1927–) Academic and politician, born in Tulsa, OK. He served in the administrations of Presidents Johnson and Nixon, acquiring notoriety as the author of *The Negro Family: The Case for National Action* (1965). In 1976, he won a Democratic seat in the US Senate, from which he intends to retire in 2000. >> Johnson, Lyndon B; Nixon, Richard M

Mozambique [mohzam**beek**], official name (from 1991) **Republic of Mozambique**, Port **República de Moçambique** pop (1995e) 18 138 000; area 799 380 sq km/308 641 sq mi. SE African republic; capital, Maputo; timezone GMT +2; chief ethnic groups, the Makua-Lomwe (37%), Shona (10%), Thonga (23%); chief religions, local beliefs (60%), Christianity (30%); official language, Portuguese; unit of

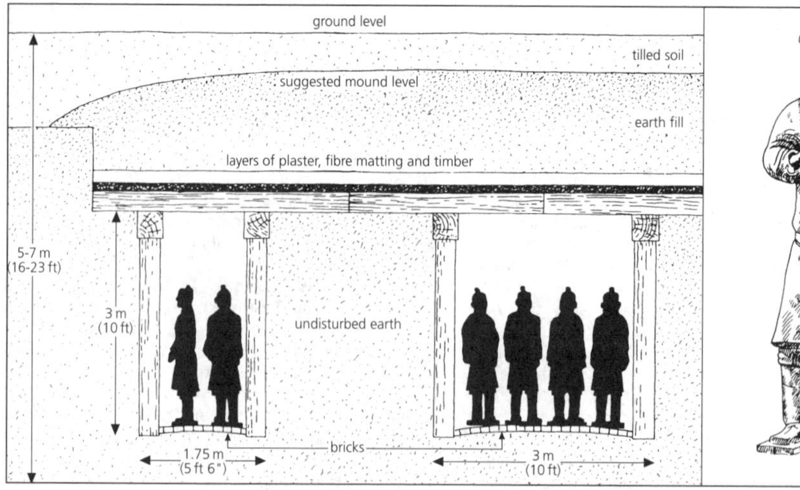

Mount Li

currency, the escudo of 100 centavos; main rivers, the Zambezi and Limpopo, providing irrigation and hydroelectricity; savannah plateau inland, mean elevation 800–1000 m/2600–4000 ft; highest peak, Mt Binga, 2436 m/7992 ft; tropical coastal lowland climate; originally inhabited by Bantu peoples from the N, 1st–4th-c AD; coast settled by Arab traders; visited by Portuguese explorers by the late 15th-c; part of Portuguese India since 1751; Mozambique Portuguese East Africa, late 19th-c; overseas province of Portugal, 1951; independence movement formed in 1962, the Frente de Libertação de Moçambique (FRELIMO), with armed resistance to colonial rule; independence, 1975; continuing civil war, with first peace talks in 1990; socialist one-party state, 1975–90; new constitution, 1990; peace accord, 1992; multi-party elections, 1994; governed by a president, prime minister, and Assembly of the Republic; badly affected by drought (1981–4), internal strife, and a lack of foreign exchange; 85% of the population involved with agriculture. >> Maputo; Zambezi, River; RR1017 political leaders

Mozart, Wolfgang Amadeus [**moht**sah(r)t] (1756–91) Composer, born in Salzburg, Austria. A child prodigy, he made his first professional tour (as a pianist) through Europe when he was six. After some years in Salzburg as *Konzertmeister* to the archbishop, he resigned (1781) and settled in Vienna. His operas *The Marriage of Figaro* (1786) and *Don Giovanni* (1787) made it impossible for the court still to overlook the composer, and he was appointed court composer to Joseph II in 1787. He wrote over 600 compositions (indexed by Köchel), including 41 symphonies, and many concertos, string quartets, and sonatas. >> Köchel

Mpumalanga [mpuma**lang**ga] (Swati 'land of the rising sun') One of the nine new provinces established by the South African constitution of 1994, in NE South Africa, situated largely on high plateau grasslands; formerly constituted part of Transvaal; capital, Nelspruit, pop (1996e) 2 646 000; area 81 816 sq km/31 581 sq mi; chief languages, Siswati (40%), Zulu (28%), Afrikaans; game reserves, including Kruger National park. >> South Africa; Transvaal

MS-DOS An operating system developed by Microsoft for the IBM personal computer; it is a registered trade mark. This system has contributed largely to the success of the IBM product. >> DOS; operating system; personal computer

Mubarak, (Mohammed) Hosni (Said) [mu**ba**rak] (1928–) Egyptian statesman and president (1981–), born in al-Minufiyah, Egypt. Vice-president under Sadat (1975), he continued the same domestic and international policies, including firm treatment of Muslim extremists, and the peace process with Israel. >> Egypt ℹ; Sadat

mucous membrane [**myoo**kuhs] A sheet of fibrous tissue that lines every cavity or canal of the body which opens to the exterior (eg the alimentary tracts). It provides a barrier between the cells that form the body and the external environment. >> purpura

mudhopper Very distinctive fish (*Periophthalmus koelreuteri* and *Periophthalmodon schlosseri*) widespread in the Indo-Pacific; locally common on mud flats, living much of the time out of water; length 15–25 cm/6–10 in; eyes raised on top of head; paired fins used as props and for locomotion across the mud; also called **mudskipper**. (Family: Gobiidae.)

mudlark Either of two species of bird of the genus *Grallina*, also known as **mudnester** or **mudnest builder**: the black-and-white **magpie lark** (*Grallina cyanoleuca*), from open woodland in Australia; and the **torrent lark** (*Grallina bruijni*), from mountain streams in New Guinea. (Family: Grallinidae.) >> lark

mudpuppy A salamander from North America (*Fecturus maculosus*); spends entire life in water; brown-grey with feathery gills; limbs with four toes; deep narrow tail. (Family: Proteidae.) >> salamander ℹ

mudskipper >> **mudhopper**

muesli [**myooz**lee] A popular breakfast cereal now available in a wide variety of mixtures, which include cereals, nuts, and fruits. These mixtures have been developed from the raw food diet of Dr Max Birchner-Brenner (1867–1939). >> cereals

muezzin [moo**ez**in] In Islam, an official of the mosque who issues the call to prayer to the faithful. The name means 'announcer'. >> Islam

mufti In Islamic religion, a man trained in the *Sharia*, or Muslim divine law, and who can give legal opinions (*fatwa*) on questions. >> Islam

Mufulira [muful**eer**a] 12°30S 28°12E, pop (1995e) 245 000. Mining city in Zambia; world's second largest underground copper mine nearby; railway. >> Copperbelt; Zambia ℹ

Mugabe, Robert (Gabriel) [mu**gah**bay] (1924–) Zimbabwean statesman, first prime minister (1980–), and president (1987–), born in Kutama, Zimbabwe. In 1963 he co-founded the Zimbabwe African National Union (ZANU). After a 10-year detention in Rhodesia (1964–74), he spent five years in Mozambique preparing for independence (1980). Though he formerly espoused a pragmatic Marxism, and declared his intention of turning Zimbabwe into a one-party state, multi-party elections were held in 1990 (which he won), and his party dropped all references to 'Marxism-Leninism' and 'scientific socialism' from its constitution in 1991. >> Zimbabwe ℹ

Mughal or **Mogul Empire** An important Indian Muslim state (1526–1857), founded by Babur (1526–30). Akbar (1556–1605), defeated the Afghan challenge at Panipat (1556) and extended the empire to include territory between Afghanistan and Deccan. Akbar was succeeded by Jehangir (1605–27) and Shah Jehan (1627–58). Its last great emperor was Aurangzeb (1658–1707), who extended the limits of the empire further south. The empire disintegrated under Maratha and British pressure. Its last emperor was exiled by the British after the 1857 uprising. >> Akbar the Great; Indian Mutiny

mugwort An aromatic perennial growing to 120 cm/4 ft, native to many temperate areas; leaves dark green above, silvery with woolly hairs below; flower-heads reddish-brown, crowded on long leafy stems. The young leaves are used as a condiment for goose, duck, and pork. (Genus *Artemisia*. Family: Compositae.) >> herb

Muhammad >> **Mohammed**

Muharram [mu**ha**ram] The first month of the Muslim year; also used as the name of a religious celebration culminating in Ashura. >> Mohammed; Shiites; RR981

Muir, Edwin [myoor] (1887–1959) Poet, born in Deerness, Orkney. His poems appeared in eight slim volumes, dating from 1925, notably in *The Voyage* (1946) and *The Labyrinth* (1949).

Mujahideen [moojaha**deen**] ('holy warriors') Muslim guerrillas who resisted the Soviet occupation of Afghanistan after the invasion (Dec 1979). After the Soviet withdrawal in 1989, they experienced much internal dissent over their role in the country's future. The term is also used more generally than in relation to the Afghan conflict, referring to any Muslim whose armed struggle can be said to be in the interest of the faith. >> Afghanistan [i]; Islam

mujtahid [mooj**tah**hid] A religious scholar who exercises personal interpretation of the *Sharia* or Muslim divine law. Shiism allows such interpretations, while Sunnism has usually refused them. >> Sharia; Shiites; Sunnis

Mukden >> **Shenyang**

mulberry A deciduous tree, of oriental origin, but long cultivated; male and female flowers in separate catkin-like spikes; individual fruits juicy, coalescing so that the whole spike forms the 'berry'. (Genus: *Morus*, 10 species. Family: Moraceae.)

Muldoon, Sir Robert (David) [muhl**doon**] (1921–92) New Zealand statesman and prime minister (1975–84), born in Auckland, New Zealand. After 5 years as minister of finance, he became party leader in 1974. >> New Zealand [i]

mule (textiles) A spinning frame invented by Samuel Crompton in 1779, which fully mechanized the hand spinning process. It was regarded as a hybrid of two previous inventions, hence its name. >> Crompton, Samuel; Industrial Revolution; spinning

mule (zoology) An animal produced from the mating of a male donkey with a female horse. If a male horse mates with a female donkey the result is a **hinny**. Both are usually sterile. >> donkey; horse [i]

Mulhouse [muhl**ooz**], Ger **Mulhausen** 47°45N 7°21E, pop (1995e) 112 000. Industrial and commercial river port in NE France; second largest town in Alsace; imperial free city from 1308; allied with the Swiss, 1515–1648; independent republic until 1798, then voted to become French; under German rule in 1871, reverting to France in 1918; railway; university. >> Alsace

mullah [**mu**la] (Arabic, 'master') In Islam, a scholar, teacher, or man of religious piety and learning. It is also a title of respect given to those performing duties related to Islamic Law. >> Islam; Sharia

mullein [**mu**luhn] Typically a biennial or perennial, often very hairy, with a tall, erect stem, native to Europe and Asia; flowers in long dense spikes, 5-petalled, yellow, pink, purple, or white. (Genus: *Verbascum*, 360 species. Family: Scrophulariaceae.)

mullet >> **grey mullet; red mullet**

Mulliken, Robert (Sanderson) (1896–1986) Chemist and physicist, born in Newburyport, MA. He was awarded the 1966 Nobel Chemistry Prize for his work on chemical bonds and the electronic structure of molecules. >> chemical bond; molecule

Mullingar [muhlin**gah(r)**], Ir **Muileann Cearr** 53°32N 7°20W, pop (1995e) 11 800. Market town and capital of Westmeath county, E Ireland; railway; cathedral. >> Ireland (republic) [i]; Westmeath

Mulready, William [muhl**ree**dee] (1786–1863) Painter, born in Ennis, Co Clare. He specialized in genre paintings, becoming best known for his rural scenes, such as 'Interior of an English Cottage' (1828). >> genre painting

Mulroney, (Martin) Brian (1939–) Canadian politician and prime minister (1984–93), born in Baie Comeau, Quebec, Canada. He became leader of the Progressive Conservative Party in 1983, won a landslide election victory in 1984, and was re-elected in 1988, but forced to resign in 1993. >> Canada [i]; Charlottetown / Meech Lake Accord

Multan [mul**tan**] 30°10N 71°36E, pop (1995e) 1 075 000. City in Punjab province, Pakistan; ruled by the emperors of Delhi 1526–1779, and by the Afghans until 1818; under British rule, 1849; airfield; railway. >> Pakistan [i]

multilateralism In economics, a system where a group of countries negotiate trade and payments arrangements, rather than dealing bilaterally. In trade, multilateralism is summed up by the 'most favoured nation' clause, whereby imports from any member country are to be treated no less favourably than those from any other member. In payments, multilateral settlement means that a country need only be concerned to balance its payments with other countries in total, and need not keep its payments in bilateral balance. >> free trade; General Agreement on Tariffs and Trade

multimedia (computing) The tools and techniques used in computing to allow computer programs to handle sound, picture, and video components. In a multimedia system one could use the computer to select extracts from a piece of music which could then be broadcast with a full video picture of the orchestra and hi-fi sound, or could be broadcast in sound only with the video displaying the score. >> computer program

multimedia (projection) Audio-visual presentation from groups of slide projectors programmed to show a complex sequence of images on a very wide screen with accompanying sound from tape recording. >> audio-visual aids; slide

multiple sclerosis A disease associated with loss of the normal coating of neurones (*myelin*) in the brain and spinal cord, which affects about 1 in 2000 people. One theory of its cause is that the process is auto-immune. Clinical features include weakness of the limbs, double vision, vertigo, and inability to co-ordinate movements (*ataxia*), all of which can be transient but recurrent, and slowly become more severe. >> auto-immune diseases; neurone [i]

multiple star Three or more stars gravitationally bound in complex orbits. The star complex Alpha Centauri is an example of such a system. >> Centaurus; star

multiplexer A device in data communications which enables the inputs from a number of communication lines to be concentrated and fed down a single line.

Mumbai >> **Bombay**

Mumford, Lewis (1895–1990) Sociologist and writer, born in Flushing, NY. He wrote on architecture and urbanization in such works as *The Story of Utopias* (1922) and *The City in History* (1961), stressing the unhappy effects of technology on society. >> sociology

mummers English traditional actors providing entertainment at seasonal festivals. In the 18th-c the mummers' Christmas play evolved, based on a legend of St George, with a duel between champions ending in the death of one of them and his revival by a doctor.

mumps A viral, feverish infection spread by droplets, especially common among children and young adults. A characteristic feature is pain and swelling of one or both parotid glands near the angle of the jaw. >> gland; virus

Munch, Edvard [mungk] (1863–1944) Painter, born in Löten, Norway. He was obsessed by subjects such as death and love, which he illustrated in an Expressionist Symbolic style, using bright colours and a tortuously curved design, as in 'The Scream' (1893, Oslo). >> Expressionism; Symbolism

Münchhausen, (Karl Friedrich Hieronymus), Freiherr von (Baron) [**munch**howzen] (1720–97) Soldier, born in Bodenwerder, Germany. He served in Russian campaigns against the Turks, and became proverbial as the narrator of ridiculously exaggerated exploits. >> Münchhausen's syndrome

Münchhausen's syndrome [**münsh**howzn] In medicine, individuals who wander the country and present themselves at different hospitals with different but spurious physical complaints, many of which need investigation to establish their false nature. >> Münchhausen

Muncie [**muhn**see] 40°12N 85°23W, pop (1995e) 74 800. City in E Indiana, USA, on W fork of the White R; settled, 1824; city status, 1865; railway; university (1918); represented as the 'average American town' in the 1929 sociological study *Middletown* by R & H Lynd. >> Indiana

Munda An Austroasiatic-speaking people settled in hilly and forested regions of E and C India. >> Austro-Asiatic languages

Munich [**myoo**nikh], Ger **München** 48°08N 11°35E, pop (1995e) 1 270 000. Capital of Bavaria province, Germany, on the R Isar; founded, 1158; capital of Bavaria, from 1506; badly bombed in World War 2; railway; university (1471); technical university (1868); cathedral (15th-c), Nymphenburg Palace (17th-c); Oktoberfest (beer festival); site of summer Olympic Games (1972). >> Bavaria; Germany [i]; Pinakothek, Alte

Munich Agreement An agreement signed (29 Sep 1938) at a conference in Munich by the British prime minister Chamberlain, the French prime minister Daladier, Mussolini, and Hitler. It ceded the Sudeten area of Czechoslovakia to Germany. >> Chamberlain, Neville; Daladier; Hitler; Mussolini

Munich Putsch The abortive attempt by Hitler to overthrow the state government of Bavaria in 1923, as a prelude to the establishment of the Nazi regime in Germany. Hitler was tried for treason, and sentenced to five years' imprisonment. >> Hitler; Nazi Party

Munnings, Sir Alfred (1878–1959) Painter, born in Suffolk. A specialist in the painting of horses and sporting pictures, he was well known for his forthright criticism of modern art.

Munro, H(ector) H(ugh) [muhn**roh**], pseudonym **Saki** (1870–1916) Writer, born in Akyab, Myanmar. He is best known for his humorous and macabre short stories, such as *Reginald* (1904) and *The Chronicles of Clovis* (1911). He was killed on the Western front in World War 1.

Munsell Color System A system for measuring and naming colours, devised by US painter Albert H Munsell (?–1918). The Munsell Book of Colour contains 1200 samples grouped according to hue, saturation, and brilliance.

Munster [**muhn**ster] pop (1995e) 1 002 000; area 24 127 sq km/9313 sq mi. Province in S Ireland; comprises the counties of Clare, Cork, Kerry, Limerick, Tipperary, and Waterford; a former kingdom. >> Ireland (republic) [i]

Münster [**mun**ster] 51°58N 7°37E, pop (1995e) 268 000. City in Germany; on the R Aa; member of the Hanseatic League; capital of former province of Westphalia; bishopric; railway; university (1780); cathedral (1225–65). >> Germany [i]; Hanseatic League

muntjac or **muntjak** A true deer, native to India and SE Asia; face with 'V'-shaped ridge; arms of 'V' continued as freely projecting bony columns; projecting canine teeth; call resembles a dog barking; also known as **barking deer** or **rib-faced deer**. (Genus: *Muntiacus*, 5 species.) >> deer

Müntzer, Thomas [**münt**ser], also spelled **Münzer** or **Monczer** (c.1489–1525) Anabaptist preacher, born in Stolberg, Germany. In 1525 he was elected pastor of the Anabaptists of Mühlhausen, where his communistic ideas soon aroused the whole country. A leader of the Peasants' Revolt (1524–5), he was executed at Mühlhausen. >> Anabaptists; Peasants' Revolt

muon A fundamental particle, produced in weak radioactive decays of pions; symbol μ; mass 106 MeV; charge −1; spin $\frac{1}{2}$. It behaves like a heavy electron, but decays to an electron and neutrinos. >> fundamental particles; lepton; pion

Murad, Ferid (1936–) Pharmacologist, born in Whiting, IN. He worked at Virginia, Stanford, and (from 1988) Northwestern universities, and shared the 1998 Nobel Prize for Physiology or Medicine for his contribution to the discovery of nitric oxide as a signalling molecule in the cardiovascular system.

mural A painting or carving on a wall. Murals, representing human and animal motifs as well as pure pattern, have existed since prehistoric times. A great deal survives from the Ancient Near East: the Egyptians, for instance, used distemper or gouache for decorating their tombs, while the Babylonians and Assyrians made extensive use of stone low-relief sculpture. Roman wall decoration is seen from the excavations at Pompeii, Herculaneum, and Stabiae (2nd-c BC–AD 79). Mosaic was much favoured during the Byzantine period in Italy, fresco during the later Middle Ages and Renaissance. >> fresco; mosaic; relief sculpture

muramidase >> **lysozyme**

Murasaki, Shikibu [mura**sah**kee] (978–c.1031) Court lady and writer, born in Kyoto, Japan. She wrote the saga *Genji Monagatari* (The Tale of Genji), a classic of Japanese literature, and considered to be the world's earliest novel.

Murat, Joachim [mürah] (1767–1815) French marshal and king of Naples (1808–15), born in La Bastide-Fortunière, France. He married Napoleon's sister, Caroline, after helping him become First Consul. After failing to gain the Spanish crown (1808), he was proclaimed King of the Two Sicilies. He fought at Leipzig, but concluded a treaty with the Austrians, hoping to save his kingdom. On Napoleon's return from Elba, he recommenced war against Austria, but was defeated, and executed. >> Napoleonic Wars

Murcia, Eng [**mer**sha], Span [**moor**thya] pop (1995e) 1 041 000; area 11 313 sq km/4367 sq mi. Region and province of SE Spain; thinly populated, except in the river valleys; capital, Murcia, pop (1995e) 321 000; former capital of Moorish kingdom; airport; railway; university (1915); cathedral (14th-c). >> Spain [i]

murder Unlawful homicide other than manslaughter, infanticide (where separately recognized), or causing death by reckless driving. In England and Wales, a person can be convicted of murder only where the crime was committed with malice aforethought. In many US jurisdictions (and also in Scotland), the notion of 'malice aforethought' is not relevant: murder is the intentional killing of another without justification, excuse, or mitigating circumstances, or in the perpetration of a felony (US). In the UK, the sentence on conviction is life imprisonment, but several countries provide for capital punishment. >> capital punishment; infanticide; manslaughter

Murdoch, Dame (Jean) Iris (1919–99) Novelist and philosopher, born in Dublin. Her books include *Under the Net* (1954), *The Sea, The Sea* (1978, Booker), *The Philosopher's Pupil* (1983), and *Jackson's Dilemma* (1995). She also wrote plays and several philosophical and critical studies.

Murdoch, Lachlan (Keith) (1971–) Media executive, born in London, the son of Rupert Murdoch. In 1995 he became publisher of *The Australian* newspaper, and by 1997 was executive chairman of News Limited. One of a trio of possible heirs to Rupert, Lachlan is the only sibling with a seat on News Corporation's board. >> Murdoch, Rupert

Murdoch, (Keith) Rupert (1931–) Media proprietor, born in Melbourne, Victoria, Australia. He built a substantial newspaper and magazine publishing empire in Australia, the USA, Hong Kong, and the UK, including the *Sun*, the *News of the World*, and *The Times* and its related publications in Britain. He also has major business interests in other media industries, especially television, films, and publishing.

Murdock, William (1754–1839) Engineer and inventor of coal gas for lighting, born near East Ayrshire, Strathclyde. His distillation of coal to make coal gas began at Redruth in 1792.

Murillo, Bartolomé Esteban [moo**reel**yoh] (1618–82) Painter, born in Seville, Spain. His pictures naturally fall into two groups: scenes from low society, mostly executed early in his life, and religious works.

Murmansk [**moor**mansk], formerly **Romanov-na-Murmane** (to 1917) 68°59N 33°08E, pop (1995e) 477 000. Seaport in Russia; founded, 1916; most important Russian fishing port (ice-free); airfield; railway. >> Russia ℹ

Murphy, Eddie, popular name of **Edward Reagan Murphy** (1961–) Comic actor, born in New York City. His films include *Trading Places* (1983), *Beverly Hills Cop* (1984, and its sequel, 1987), and *Dr Dolittle* (1998), and he made his directorial debut with *Harlem Nights* (1989).

Murray, (George) Gilbert (Aimé) (1866–1957) Classical scholar, writer, and lifelong Liberal, born in Sydney, New South Wales, Australia. His work as a classical historian and translator of Greek dramatists brought him acclaim as the leading Greek scholar of his time.

Murray, Sir James (Augustus Henry) (1837–1915) Philologist and lexicographer, born in Denholm, Scottish Borders. His major project was the editing of the New English Dictionary, begun in 1879. He edited about half the work himself, and created the organization for its completion (in 1928). >> dictionary

Murray, Len, popular name of **Baron Lionel Murray of Telford** (1922–) Trade unionist, born in Shropshire. He became general secretary of the Trades Union Congress (1973–84), and was made a life peer in 1985. >> trade union

Murray River Longest river in Australia; rises in the Australian Alps; length 2570 km/1600 mi; enters the Southern Ocean SE of Adelaide; receives the Darling R 640 km/400 mi from its mouth (the Murray-Darling is 3750 km/2330 mi long); used extensively for irrigation and hydroelectric power. >> Australia ℹ

Murrow, Ed(ward Egbert) R(oscoe) (1908–65) Broadcasting journalist, born in Greensboro, NC. He made his name as a radio journalist during the Battle of Britain and the Blitz. In 1946 he was appointed CBS vice-president and director of public affairs.

Murrumbidgee River [muhruhm**bi**jee] River in New South Wales, Australia; rises in the Snowy Mts; flows 1759 km/1093 mi to join the Murray R on the Victoria border. >> Murray River

Murry, John Middleton (1889–1957) Writer and critic, born in London. His poetry, essays, and criticism had a strong influence on the young intellectuals of the 1920s. He was the husband of Katherine Mansfield. >> Mansfield, Katherine

Mururoa [muru**roh**a] 139°00W 22°00S, pop (1995e) 3230. Remote atoll in French Polynesia, used by France as a nuclear testing site. >> French Polynesia

Musca (Lat fly) A small S constellation near Crux. >> constellation; Crux; RR968

muscarine [**muhs**karin, -reen] A substance isolated from the poisonous mushroom *Amanita muscaria*. In W Europe, extracts were used as fly-killing agents (the common name for the mushroom is *fly agaric*). >> fly agaric; mushroom

Muscat [**muhs**kat], Arabic **Masqat** 27°37N 58°36E, pop (1995e) 360 000. Seaport capital of Oman; occupied by the Portuguese, 1508–1650; airport; residence of the Sultan. >> Oman ℹ

muscle A contractile tissue consisting of fibres bound together by connective tissue and specialized to convert chemical energy into mechanical energy for movement. **Skeletal muscle** is generally attached to bone and, being under central nervous control, is principally concerned with voluntary movement. **Smooth muscle** is present mainly in the walls of hollow structures (eg the gut, uterus, blood vessels, ducts). **Cardiac muscle** is present only in the heart, where it is in continuous rhythmical contraction. >> anatomy ℹ; fibrositis; heart ℹ; isometrics; muscular dystrophy; myasthenia gravis; paralysis; rheumatism

muscovite >> **micas**

muscovy duck A large duck (*Cairina moschata*) native to Central and tropical South America; wild male black/green with white patches on wing; dark bare skin on face. Domestic breeds are grey, white, or speckled, with a scarlet skin patch. (Family: Anatidae.) >> duck

muscular dystrophy A genetically determined group of disorders in which muscles undergo progressive degener-

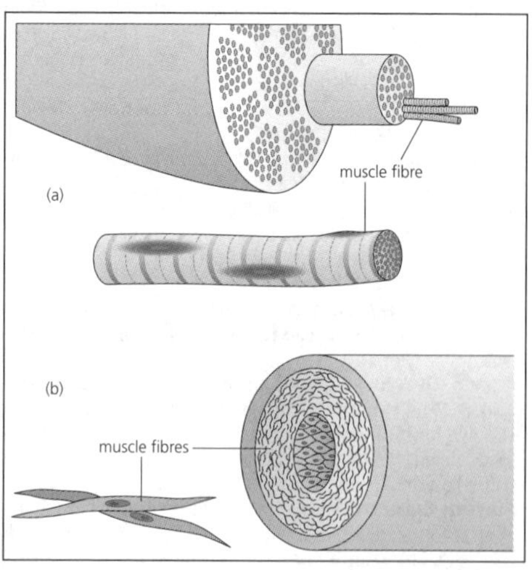

Muscle – Section through skeletal muscle (a) and smooth muscle – a blood vessel (b), with detail of muscle fibres

ation and increase of fibrous tissue (*fibrosis*). The condition appears early in life, and causes symmetrical weakness and wasting of groups of muscles. >> muscle ℹ

Musée d'Orsay [müzay daw(r)**say**] A museum in Paris, developed on the site of the former railway station and hotel, the Gare d'Orsay, and incorporating several of its architectural features. Originally designed by French architect Victor Laloux (1850–1937), the building was converted into a museum in 1984–5. It contains a wide range of artistic works produced chiefly between 1848 and 1914. >> Paris ℹ

Muses In Homer, the nine daughters of Zeus and Mnemosyne, who inspire the bard: **Calliope**, epic poetry; **Clio**, history; **Erato**, lyric poetry, hymns; **Euterpe**, flute; **Melpomene**, tragedy; **Polyhymnia**, acting, music, dance; **Terpsichore**, lyric poetry, dance; **Thalia**, comedy; **Urania**, astronomy.

Museveni, Yoweri Kaguta [moose**vay**nee] (1945–) Ugandan statesman and president (1986–). He became head of the Front for National Salvation against Idi Amin (1971–9). As president, he has been responsible for the reconstruction of the country after its civil war. >> Amin; Uganda ℹ

Musgrave Ranges [**muhz**grayv] Mountain ranges in South Australia; extend 80 km/50 mi; rise to 1440 m/4724 ft at Mt Woodroffe. >> South Australia

mushroom The cultivated mushroom (*Agaricus bisporus*); fruiting body comprises a short white stalk (*stipe*) and rounded cap with brownish gills on the underside; also used as a general name for any similar-shaped fungus. (Subdivision: Basidiomycetes. Order: Agaricales.) >> Basidiomycetes; fungus

Musial, Stan(ley Frank) [**myoo**zial], nickname **Stan the Man** (1920–) Baseball player, born in Donora, PA. He topped the National League's batting list seven times (1943–57) and retired in 1962 with a National League record of 3630 hits to his credit. >> baseball ℹ

music An orderly succession of sounds of definite pitch, whose constituents are melody, harmony, and rhythm. Almost as fundamental to a perception of the nature of music, however, is *articulation*, which embraces not only the phrasing, dynamics, etc that breathe life into a musical performance, but also the composer's creative use of silence. Virtually all musical structures entail a degree of audible repetition, even if this cannot always be fully grasped at a first hearing. Music is therefore a kind of aural patterning rather than aural painting – abstract rather than representational. This is not to deny its capacity to elicit a strong emotional response, but the essential nature of music is possibly closer to mathematics than to any of its sister arts. >> chamber / classical / electronic / folk / gospel / pop / programme / rock music; Baroque (music); conducting; harmony; jazz; melody; musical instruments; musicology; musique concrète; Neoclassicism (music); opera; polyphony; Romanticism; rhythm; tonality

musical A distinctive genre of musical theatre, where a strong story is fused with a musical score and professional choreography, found in both theatre and cinema. Feature films with spectacular show-business song-and-dance themes followed rapidly on the introduction of sound-film.

musical glasses An instrument, also known as the **glass harmonica**, consisting of glass vessels of various sizes and pitches which were struck or stroked to produce musical, bell-like sounds. Various types were popular in the 18th-c. >> idiophone

musical instruments Devices for producing musical sounds, among the oldest cultural artefacts known. The instruments of the modern symphony orchestra are commonly divided into four types: *woodwind*, *brass*, *percussion*, and *strings*. Another classification is according to the method of playing them: whether they are bowed, blown, struck, plucked, strummed, or (as with keyboard instruments) touched. The classification now generally regarded as standard was devised by musicologists Erich von Hornbostel (1877–1935) and Kurt Sachs (1881–1959), and published in 1914. They divided instruments into four main classes according to the physical characteristics of the sound source (ie the vibrating agent): *aerophones* (in which the sound is generated by air), *chordophones* (by one or more strings), *idiophones* (by the body of the instrument itself), and *membranophones* (by a stretched membrane). To these a fifth class has since been added: *electrophones*, in which the sound is produced by electromagnets, oscillators, or other non-acoustic devices. >> aerophone; chordophone; electrophone; idiophone; membranophone; music; orchestra; percussion ℹ; transposing instrument; brass / reed / string / woodwind instrument ℹ

music hall Mass entertainment of the Victorian era which developed in the music rooms of London taverns. Itinerant performers perfected short turns with stage business and comic songs to suit their individual style. >> Folies-Bergère

musicology The scientific and scholarly study of music, including the recovery and evaluation of source material, the study of music's historical context, and the analysis of particular works and repertories. Modern musicologists need to command many specialized skills, including a knowledge of palaeography, paper-types, watermarks, and rastrology (the study of how music staves are drawn). >> ethnomusicology; music; palaeography

Musil, Robert (Elder von) [**moo**sil] (1880–1942) Novelist, born in Klagenfurt, Austria. His masterpiece is a very long, unfinished novel *Der Mann ohne Eigenschaften* (The Man without Qualities), written between 1930 and 1942.

musique concrète [müzeek kõ**kret**] Music composed of 'natural' (ie non-electronic but not necessarily musical) sounds, which are then mixed and manipulated on tape and heard through loudspeakers. The technique originated with French composer Pierre Schaeffer (1910–) in the 1940s. >> electronic music

musk A species of mimulus (*Mimulus moschatus*) with yellow flowers, native to North America from British Columbia to the California region. It was formerly cultivated for its scent, but the plants are nowadays scentless. (Family: Scrophulariaceae.) >> mimulus

musk deer A deer native to wet mountain forests in E Asia; kangaroo-like head has no antlers; male with gland on abdomen, producing a pungent oily jelly (*musk*), used in perfumes to make the scent longer-lasting. (Genus: *Moschus*, 3 species. Family: Moschidae.) >> deer

muskeg The poorly drained sphagnum moss peat-bog and marshland found in the tundra and taiga areas of N Canada. It is underlain by permafrost. >> permafrost; taiga; tundra

muskellunge [**muhs**keluhnj] Largest of the pike fishes (*Esox masquinongy*) in the Great Lakes of North America and associated rivers; length up to 2·4 m/8 ft. (Family: Esocidae.) >> pike

musket A heavy firearm, the most important infantry weapon from the late 17th-c to the mid-19th-c. Smooth-bored and muzzle-loading, the musket required a high degree of training to operate. >> arquebus

Muskie, Edmund S(ixtus) (1914–96) US lawyer and statesman, born in Rumford, ME. Secretary of state under President Carter, he was Democratic candidate for the vice-presidency in 1968. >> Carter, Jimmy; Democratic Party

musk ox A large goat-antelope (*Ovibos moschatus*) native to the Arctic tundra of North America; very thick long shaggy dark-brown coat; head large, with flat horns meeting in mid-line. >> antelope

muskrat A large nocturnal water rat (*Ondatra zibethicus*) native to North America; thick fur exploited commercially; has a musky smell; also known as **musquash**. >> water rat

Muslim >> **Islam**

Muslim Brotherhood An Islamic movement, founded in Egypt in 1928 by an Egyptian schoolteacher, Hasan al-Banna. Its original goal was the reform of Islamic society by eliminating Western influences and other decadent accretions. >> Islam; Sunnis

musquash >> **muskrat**

mussel A sedentary bivalve mollusc found in estuaries and shallow seas, attached to a substrate by means of tough filaments; commonly used for human consumption. (Class: Pelecypoda. Order: Mytiloida.) >> bivalve; mollusc

Musset, (Louis Charles) Alfred de [müsay] (1810–57) Poet and playwright, born in Paris. In 1833 he met the novelist George Sand, and there began the stormy love affair which coloured much of his work after that date, notably in his autobiographical novel *La Confession d'un enfant du siècle* (1835, The Confession of a Child of the Age). >> Sand

Mussolini, Benito (Amilcare Andrea), known as **il Duce** ('the Leader') (1883–1945) Prime minister of Italy (1922–43) and dictator, born in Predappio, Romagna. In 1919 he helped found the *Fasci di Combattimento* as a would-be revolutionary force, and in 1922 became prime minister, his success symbolized by the March on Rome (Oct 1922). His rule saw the replacement of parliamentarism by a totalitarian system; the establishment of the Vatican state (1929); the annexation of Abyssinia (1935–6) and Albania (1939); and the formation of the Axis with Germany. His declaration of war on Britain and France was followed by a series of defeats in Africa and the Balkans. Following the Allied invasion of Sicily (1943), he was overthrown and arrested (Jul 1943). Rescued from imprisonment by German paratroopers, he was placed in charge of the puppet Italian Social Republic, but in 1945 he was captured by the Italian Resistance and shot. >> Axis Powers; fascism; totalitarianism; World War 2

Mussorgsky, Modest >> **Moussorgsky, Modest**

mustang A breed of horse, developed naturally in North America as a wild horse; descended from Spanish horses introduced by the Conquistadors; height, 14–15 hands/ 1·4–1·5 m/4 ft 8in–5 ft. >> horse 🅘

Mustapha Kemel Atatürk >> **Atatürk, Mustapha Kemal**

mustard An erect annual growing to 1 m/3¼ ft; yellow, cross-shaped flowers. Commercial mustard is produced from ground seeds of two of the species. (Family: Cruciferae.) >> brassica

mustard gas A light-yellow, oily liquid which becomes a gas above 14°C, acting as a powerful vesicant (producer of blisters) that attacks the human skin, eyes, and lungs. It was used as a poison gas at Ypres by the Germans in July 1917. Chemically, it is 2,2′-dichlorodiethylsulphide, $(Cl–CH_2–CH_2)_2S$, boiling point 216°C. >> chemical warfare; poison gas

Muste, A(braham) J(ohn), originally **Abraham Johannes Muste**, known as **A J** (1885–1967) Labour leader and pacifist, born in Zierikzee, The Netherlands. His family moved to the USA in 1891, where he became a minister. As director of Brookwood Labor College (1921–33), he helped train labour activists ('Musteites'). A mystical experience brought him back to Christian pacifism, and during the 1950s he was active in civil rights and world peace movements. Sometimes called 'America's Gandhi', he was a leading influence on 20th-c social movements in the USA.

Mustelidae [muhs**tel**idee] A family of carnivorous mammals (67 species), found worldwide except in Australasia and Madagascar; usually with long thin body, short legs, long tail. >> badger; carnivore 🅘; fisher; mammal 🅘; marten; mink; otter; polecat; skunk; stoat; weasel; wolverine

mutation An abrupt change in the genetic characteristics of an organism. In **chromosomal** mutations there is a deletion, breakage, or rearrangement of chromosome material. In **molecular** mutations there is a physico-chemical change in the DNA sequence. >> chromosome 🅘; DNA 🅘

Mutsuhito [mutsu**hee**toh]], **Meiji Tenno** (1852–1912) Emperor of Japan who became the symbol of Japan's modernization. He is commemorated by the Meiji Shrine in Tokyo. >> Ito; Meiji Restoration

muttonbird The alternative name of the **short-tailed shearwater** (*Puffinus tenuirostris*) from S Australia and the Pacific, or the **sooty shearwater** (*Puffinus griseus*) from New Zealand. >> petrel; shearwater

mutual fund >> **open-ended investment company**

Muzorewa, Abel (Tendekayi) [muzo**ray**wa] (1925–) Zimbabwean politician and clergyman, born in Umtali, Zimbabwe. In 1971 he became president of the African National Council, and prime minister of 'Zimbabwe Rhodesia' in 1979. After independence his party was defeated by the Patriotic Front of Mugabe and Nkomo. >> Mugabe; Nkomo; Zimbabwe 🅘

MX missile An abbreviation used for **Missile Experimental**, the codename of a US third-generation land-based intercontinental ballistic missile. It was eventually deployed as the 'Peacekeeper' missile from 1987 onwards in land-based silos in the US Mid-west. >> missile, guided

Myanmar [**myan**mah(r)], formerly (to 1989) **Burma**, official name **Union of Myanmar**, Burmese **Pyidaungzu Myanma Naingngandaw** pop (1995e) 46 398 000; area 678 576 sq km/261 930 sq mi. Republic in SE Asia; capital, Yangon (Rangoon); timezone GMT +6½; main ethnic group, Burman (72%); main religion, Theravada Buddhism (85%); official language, Burmese, with several minority languages; unit of currency, the kyat of 100 pyas; rimmed in the N, E, and W by mountains rising (N) to Hkakabo Razi (5881 m/19 294 ft); principal rivers, Ayeyarwady, Thanlwin, Sittang; tropical monsoon climate; coastal and higher mountains of E and N have heavy annual rainfall, 2500–5000 mm/100–200 in; first unified in 11th-c by King Anawrahta; invasion by Kubla Khan, 1287; second dynasty established, 1486, but plagued by internal disunity and wars with Siam from 16th-c; new dynasty under King Alaungpaya, 1752; annexed to British India following Anglo-Burmese wars (1824–86); separated from India, 1937; occupied by Japanese in World War 2; independence as Union of Burma under prime minister U Nu, 1948; military coup under U Ne Win, 1962; single-party socialist republic, 1974; People's Assembly elects a State Council, which elects a president, prime minister, and Council of Ministers; army coup, 1988, leading to formation of a State Law and Order Restoration Council, headed by a chairman; replaced by a State Peace and Development Council, 1997; Aung San Sun Kyi (Nobel Peace Prize, 1991), main opposition leader, placed under house arrest in 1989, released in 1995; constitutional conference ongoing since 1992; largely dependent on agriculture and forestry. >> Buddhism; Ayeyarwady River; monsoon climates; Yangon; RR1017 political leaders; *see illustration on p. 589*

myasthenia gravis [miyas**thee**nia **grah**vis] A condition characterized by the inability to sustain a contraction of voluntary (*somatic*) muscles. The muscles become rapidly fatigued, but recover temporarily after a period of rest. >> muscle i

Mycenae [miy**see**nee] A fortified town in the Argolid, associated in Greek tradition with Agamemnon, the conqueror of Troy. It has extensive Bronze Age remains. >> Agamemnon; Mycenaean civilization

Mycenaean / Mycenean civilization [miyse**nee**an] A brilliant Bronze Age culture which flourished in Greece and the Aegean in the second millennium, reaching its high point in Greece in the 13th-c BC. >> Minoan civilization; Mycenae; Tiryns

mycetoma [miyse**toh**ma] A painless swelling arising from a specific fungal infection (*Eumycetes* or *Actinomycetes*). It often enters the body through the skin with a thorn, so the lesion occurs commonly in the feet or legs; it is also known as **Madura foot**. >> fungus

mycology [miy**kol**ojee] The identification, description, and classification of the great diversity of fungi. Fungi are usually identifiable only when they are fruiting, as their vegetative bodies consist of a mass of filamentous threads (*hyphae*), and are similar in appearance in the majority of species. >> fungus

Mycoplasma The smallest, self-replicating micro-organisms, usually 150–300 nm in diameter. A distinct nucleus is lacking, as are cell walls. There are c.60 species, all except one being parasitic on vertebrates, plants, and insects. (Kingdom: Monera. Class: Mollicutes.) >> micro-organism; spiroplasm

mycorrhiza [miyko**riy**za] A common symbiotic association formed between a fungus and the roots of a plant. Mycorrhizal systems have enhanced absorption abilities, and infected plants compete better than non-infected ones, while the fungus benefits from nutrients supplied by the plant. >> fungus; parasitic plant; symbiosis

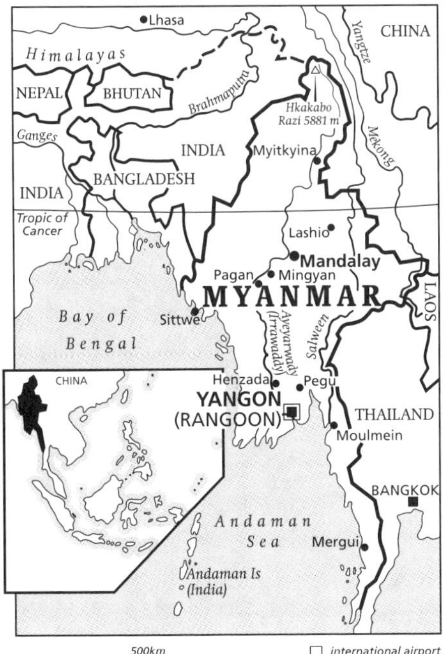

myelin [**miy**elin] A soft, white substance (a complex of protein lipids) forming a multilayered insulating sheath around the large-diameter axons of vertebrate and crustacean neurones. This increases the speed of conduction of the action potential along the axon. >> neurone i; neuropathology

myeloma [miye**loh**ma] The excessive proliferation of antibody-producing plasma cells (derived from B-lymphocytes). These cells infiltrate the bone marrow, and may lead to tender local tumours in the skeleton. >> plasma (physiology)

Myers, F(rederic) W(illiam) H(enry) (1843–1901) Psychical researcher, born in Keswick, Cumbria. In 1882 he helped found the Society for Psychical Research. >> parapsychology

Mykonos >> **Mikonos**

My Lai incident [mee liy] The massacre of several hundred unarmed inhabitants of the S Vietnamese village of My Lai by US troops during the Vietnam War (Mar 1968), an incident exposed by *Life* magazine photos in 1969. The officer responsible, Lieutenant Calley, was court-martialled in 1970–1. >> Vietnam War

mynah / myna A bird of the starling family (13 species), native to India and SE Asia; good imitator of sounds and speech. >> starling

myocardial infarction [miyoh**kah(r)**dial] The death of muscle cells of the heart, occurring when the demand for oxygen by the cardiac muscles outstrips supply. The cardinal symptom is pain over the chest, which unlike that of angina persists for several hours. It may cause little bodily disturbance beyond a few days of tiredness, but it may lead to heart failure, cardiac irregularities, and cardiac arrest. >> angina; coronary heart disease i

Myolodon [miy**o**lodon] The last of the ground sloths, surviving in Patagonia until recent times, now extinct. (Order: Xenarthra.) >> sloth

myopia >> **eye** i

Myrdal, (Karl) Gunnar [**mer**dal] (1898–1987) Economist, politician, and international civil servant, born in Gustafs Dalecarlia, Sweden. He shared the Nobel Prize for Economics in 1974, principally for his work on the application of economic theory to Third World countries. >> Three Worlds Theory

Myriapoda [miri**ap**oda] A diverse group of terrestrial arthropods containing the millipedes (Class: Diplopoda), centipedes (Class: Chilopoda), and two small classes, Symphyla and Pauropoda. All have a segmented trunk that is not differentiated into thorax and abdomen. >> arthropod; centipede; millipede

Myrmidons [**mer**midnz] In Greek legend, a band of warriors from Thessaly who went to the Trojan War with Achilles. >> Achilles

Myron [**miy**ron] (fl.c.480–440 BC) Sculptor, born in Eleutherae, Greece. He worked in bronze, and is known for the celebrated 'Discobolos' (Discus Thrower).

myrrh 1 A spiny, deciduous shrub, native to Africa and W Asia. Several species exude the aromatic resin myrrh used in incense and perfume. (Genus: *Commiphora*, 185 species. Family: Burseraceae.) >> resin **2** >> sweet cicely

myrtle An evergreen shrub of the family Myrtaceae, found mainly in South America, but also in other warm locations; common myrtle grows to over 5 m/16 ft; leaves thick, oil-bearing; solitary white flowers, c.1·8 cm/0·7 in long; purple-black berries; oil formerly used as an antiseptic. (Genus: *Myrtus*, c.16 species.) >> evergreen plants

Mysore [miy**saw(r)**] 12°17N 76°41E, pop (1995e) 520 000. City in Karnataka state, SW India; formerly the dynastic capital of Mysore state; founded, 16th-c; railway; university (1916); known as 'the garden city of India' because of its wide streets and numerous parks. >> Karnataka

mystery play A mediaeval play based upon a Biblical

episode. Cycles of plays (notably, those of York and Wakefield) tell a continuous story, often portraying the Christian vision from the Creation to the Day of Judgment. These plays, and the later **miracle plays** on the Virgin and saints' lives, represent an important phase in the evolution of secular drama from religious ritual. >> morality play

mystery religions Religious cults of the Graeco-Roman world, full admission to which was restricted to those who had gone through certain secret initiation rites or mysteries. The most famous were those of Demeter at Eleusis in Greece. >> Eleusinian mysteries

mysticism The spiritual quest in any religion for the most direct experience of God. Characteristically, mysticism concentrates on prayer, meditation, contemplation, and fasting, so as to produce the attitude necessary for what is believed to be a direct encounter with God. Notable Christian mystics include such diverse figures as St Augustine, St Francis of Assisi, and St Teresa of Ávila. >> God; meditation; religion

mythology The traditional stories of a people, often orally transmitted. The subject-matter of myths is either the gods and their relations with human or other beings, or complex explanations of physical phenomena. Until recently *mythology* meant Greek mythology, distinct in its concentration on stories of heroes and heroines. Recent scholarship has found unexpected parallels in myths from widely different sources, showing their function in determining social behaviour. >> allegory; folklore

myxoedema / myxedema [miksuh**dee**ma] The deposition of a substance (*mucopolysaccharide*) under the skin, which causes thickening, swelling, and pallor of the face, and a characteristic facial appearance. >> hypothyroidism; polysaccharides; thyroid hormone

myxomatosis [miksoma**toh**sis] A contagious viral disease of rabbits, characterized by the presence of jelly-like tumours (*myxomata*); devastated wild rabbit populations in Europe in the 1950s. >> rabbit; virus

Naas [nays], Ir **Nás na Riogh** 53°13N 6°39W, pop (1995e) 11 100. Market town and capital of Kildare county, Ireland; former capital of the kings of Leinster; noted horse-racing area. >> Ireland (republic) ⓘ; Kildare

Nabis, Les [nabee] A small group of artists working in Paris c.1890– c.1900 under the influence of Gauguin. >> Bonnard; Denis; Gauguin; Vuillard

Nablus [na**bloos**] 32°13N 35°16E, pop (1995e) 104 000. Town in Israeli-occupied West Bank, NW Jordan; market centre for an agricultural region; Great Mosque (rebuilt, 1167, as Crusader church). >> Israel ⓘ; Jordan ⓘ

N

Nabokov, Vladimir [na**boh**kof] (1899–1977) Writer, born in St Petersburg, Russia. A considerable Russian author, he established himself also as a novelist in English, notably with his controversial book *Lolita* (1955), dealing with the desire of a middle-aged intellectual for a 12-year-old girl.

Nader, Ralph [**nay**der] (1934–) Lawyer and consumer activist, born in Winsted, CT. His best-seller about the automobile industry, *Unsafe at Any Speed* (1965), led to the passage of improved car safety regulations in 1966. He became head of the Public Citizen Foundation in 1980.

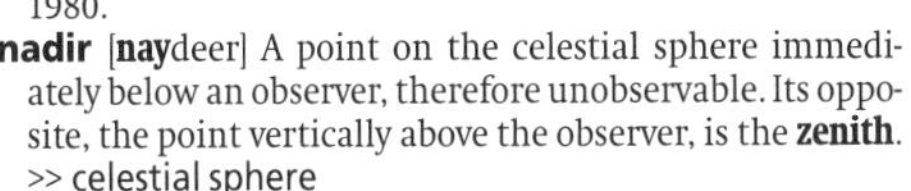

nadir [**nay**deer] A point on the celestial sphere immediately below an observer, therefore unobservable. Its opposite, the point vertically above the observer, is the **zenith**. >> celestial sphere

Naevius, Gnaeus [**nee**vius] (c.264–c.194 BC) Poet and playwright, probably born in Campania. Fragments of an epic on the Punic War, *De bello Punico*, are extant.

naevus >> **birthmark**

Nagaland [**nah**galand] pop (1995e) 1 316 000; area 16 527 sq km/6379 sq mi. State in NE India; administrative centre, Kohima; governed by a State Assembly; former territory of Assam; became a state in 1961; strong movement for independence among Naga tribesmen. >> India ⓘ

Nagarjuna [na**gah(r)**juna] (c.150–c.250) Indian Buddhist monk-philosopher. He was the founder of the Madhyamika or Middle Path school of Buddhism. >> Buddhism

Nagasaki [naga**sa**kee] 32°45N 129°52E, pop (1995e) 450 000. City in W Kyushu, Japan; visited by the Portuguese, 1545; centre for Jesuit missionaries from 16th-c; target for the second atomic bomb of World War 2 (9 Aug 1945), destroying over a third of the city; airport; railway; university (1949); Peace Park. >> Kyushu

Nagorno-Karabakh [na**gaw(r)**noh kara**bakh**], Russ **Nagorno-Karabakhskaya** area 11 400 sq km/4400 sq mi. Autonomous region in Azerbaijan, established in 1923 after the reversal of a decision to unite the region with Armenia; administrative centre, Stepanakert; in Karabakhsky and Murovdag ranges of the Caucasus; majority of population Armenian, leading to claims by Armenia for its incorporation into that republic; opposed by Azerbaijan and former Soviet Union, leading to military conflict from 1988 onwards; ceasefire agreement signed, 1994. >> Armenia ⓘ; Azerbaijan ⓘ

Nagoya [na**goy**a] 35°08N 136°53E, pop (1995e) 2 133 000. Port in C Honshu, Japan; founded as a castle, 17th-c; fourth largest city of Japan; heavily bombed in World War 2; airport; railway; two universities (1939, 1950); Nagoya Castle (rebuilt, 1959), Atsuta Shrine (c.1st-c). >> Honshu

Nagpur [**nahg**poor] 21°08N 79°10E, pop (1995e) 1 756 000. City in Maharashtra, WC India; founded, 18th-c; former capital of Berar and Madhya Pradesh states; airfield; railway; university (1923). >> Maharashtra

Nagy, Imre [noj, **im**ray] (1895–1958) Hungarian statesman and prime minister (1953–5), born in Kaposvar, Hungary. When Soviet forces began to put down the 1956 revolution, he was displaced by the Soviet puppet János Kádár, and executed. >> Hungarian uprising

Nahum, Book of [**nay**hum] One of the 12 so-called 'minor' prophetic writings of the Hebrew Bible/Old Testament, attributed to a prophet named Nahum, about whom little else is known. >> Old Testament; prophet

naiad [**niy**ad] In Greek mythology, a nymph who inhabits springs, rivers, and lakes. >> nymph

Naidoo, Jay (Jayaseelan) [**niy**doo] (1954–) South African labour leader and opponent of apartheid, born in Durban, South Africa. When the Congress of South African Trade Unions (COSATU) was founded in 1985, he was elected general secretary. From 1990 he was active in the negotiations for a new political dispensation in South Africa. >> apartheid; trade union

nails Rectangular plates of horny tissue found on the back of the end bones (*terminal phalanges*) of each digit. They grow at c.1 mm/0.04 in per week, faster in summer than in winter. >> foot; hand

Naipaul, Sir V(idiadhar) S(urajprasad) [niy**pawl**] (1932–) Novelist, born in Chaguanas, Trinidad. He has lived in England since 1950. A sequence of comic novels set in Trinidad concluded with *A House for Mr Biswas* (1961). Later novels include *The Enigma of Arrival* (1987) and *A Way in the World* (1994).

Nairobi [niy**roh**bee] 1°17S 36°50E, pop (1995e) 1 697 000. Capital of Kenya; largest city in E Africa; airport; railway; centre of communications and commerce; university (1956); cathedral (1963). >> Kenya ⓘ

Nakasone, Yasuhiro [naka**soh**nay] (1918–) Japanese statesman, and prime minister (1982–8), born in Takasaki, E Japan. As premier, he supported the renewal of the US–Japan Security Treaty, and maintained close relations with US President Reagan. >> Japan ⓘ; Reagan

Namaqualand [na**ma**kaland], Afrikaans [na**mak**walant] Region in S Namibia and W South Africa; N and S of the Orange R; European presence since 1665; indigenous peoples known as Namaquas or Nama. >> Namibia ⓘ

Namatjira, Albert [namat**jeer**a] (1902–59) Artist, born in Hermannsberg Lutheran mission, near Alice Springs, Northern Territory, Australia. A member of the Aranda Aboriginal people, he achieved wide fame for his European-influenced watercolour landscapes. >> Aranda

Namen [**na**men] >> **Namur**

Namib Desert [**na**mib] Desert in W Namibia; length, c.1300 km/800 mi; width, 50–160 km/30–100 mi. >> Namibia ⓘ

Namibia [na**mib**ia], formerly **Southwest Africa** (to 1968), earlier **German South-West Africa** pop (1995e) 2 156 000; area 824 292 sq km/318 261 sq mi. Republic in SW Africa; capital, Windhoek; timezone GMT +2; population mainly African (85%), chiefly Ovawambo; religion, Christianity (90%) official language, English; unit of currency, the Namibian dollar; desert along the Atlantic Ocean coast; inland plateau, mean elevation 1500 m/5000 ft; highest

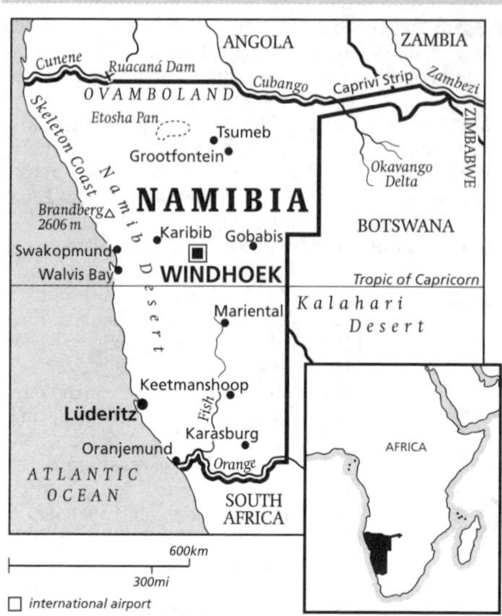

point, Brandberg (2606 m/8550 ft); Kalahari Desert to the E and S; average annual rainfall at Windhoek, 360 mm/ 14 in; average maximum daily temperature, 20–30°C; British and Dutch missionaries from late 18th-c; German protectorate, 1884; mandated to South Africa by the League of Nations, 1920; UN assumed direct responsibility in 1966, changing name to Namibia in 1968, and recognizing the Southwest Africa People's Organization (SWAPO); South Africa continued to administer the area as Southwest Africa; SWAPO commenced guerrilla activities in 1966; bases established in S Angola, involving Cuban troops, in 1970s; interim administration installed by South Africa, 1985; full independence, 1990; governed by a president, prime minister, and cabinet, and an elected National Assembly; agriculture employs c.60% of the population; indigenous subsistence farming in the N; major world producer of diamonds and uranium. >> Kalahari; Namib Desert; South Africa ℹ; Southwest Africa People's Organization; Windhoek; RR1017 political leaders

Namier, Sir Lewis (Bernstein) [**nay**myer], originally **Ludwik Bernstein Niemirowski** (1888–1960) Historian, born near Warsaw. He created a school of history in which the emphasis was on detailed analysis of events and institutions, particularly parliamentary elections.

Namur [namür], Eng [na**moor**], Flemish **Namen** 50°28N 4°52E, pop (1995e) 105 000. City in Belgium, at confluence of Sambre and Meuse Rivers; conquered by the Germans in 1914 and 1940; railway; university (1831); cathedral (1751–67). >> Belgium ℹ

Nanak [**na**nak], known as **Guru Nanak** (1469–1539) Founder of Sikhism, born near Lahore, present-day Pakistan. A Hindu by birth and belief, he fell under Muslim influence, and denounced many Hindu practices as idolatrous. His doctrine, set out later in the Adi Granth, sought a fusion of Brahmanism and Islam on the grounds that both were monotheistic. >> Adi Granth; Brahmanism; Hinduism; Islam; Sikhism

Nana Sahib [**na**na **sah**heeb], originally **Brahmin Dundhu Panth** (c.1820–c.1859) Indian rebel, who became known as the leader of the Indian Mutiny in 1857. After the collapse of the rebellion he escaped into Nepal. >> Indian Mutiny

Nanchang or **Nan-ch'ang** [nan**chang**] 28°38N 115°56E, pop (1995e) 1 468 000. Industrial city in SE China; founded 201 BC; centre of abortive uprising (1927) led by pro-communist Guomindang officers; airfield; railway; university; distribution centre for kaolin clay. >> China ℹ

Nancy [nãsee] 48°42N 6°12E, pop (1995e) 102 000. Manufacturing city in NE France, on R Meurthe; former capital of Lorraine; part of France, 1766; road and rail junction; university (1572); cathedral (1703–42); noted for its 18th-c Baroque architecture, a world heritage site. >> Lorraine

nandu >> **rhea**

Nanjing [nahnjing] or **Nanking** 32°03N 118°47E, pop (1995e) 2 872 000. City in SE China, on the Yangtze R; founded, 900 BC; capital of China 220–589, 907–79, 1356–68; centre of Taiping Rebellion (1850–64); river port and trade centre; open port after the Opium War (1842); airfield; railway; university (1902). >> China ℹ; Opium Wars; Taiping Rebellion

Nanking >> **Nanjing**

Nanning or **Nan-ning** 22°50N 108°06E, pop (1995e) 1 248 000. City in S China; founded during the Yuan dynasty; closed to foreigners until 1977; airfield; railway; agricultural trade. >> China ℹ; Yuan dynasty

Nansen, Fridtjof [**frit**yof] (1861–1930) Explorer, scientist, and statesman, born near Oslo. His greatest scheme was to reach the N Pole by letting his specially built ship, the *Fram*, get frozen into the ice N of Siberia and drift towards Greenland. In this way he reached in 1895 the highest latitude till then attained, 86°14N. In 1922 he was awarded the Nobel Peace Prize for Russian relief work. >> Poles

Nantes [nãt], Breton **Naoned**, ancient **Condivincum**, later **Namnetes** 47°12N 1°33W, pop (1995e) 252 000. Manufacturing and commercial seaport in W France; at head of Loire estuary; seventh largest city in France; France's leading port in 18th-c; major bomb damage in World War 2; railway; university (1962); Gothic cathedral; birthplace of Jules Verne. >> Nantes, Edict of; Verne

Nantes, Edict of [nãt] (1598) A law promulgated by Henry IV of France granting religious and civil liberties to his Huguenot subjects at the end of the Wars of Religion. It was revoked by Louis XIV in 1685. >> Huguenots; Religion, Wars of

Nantucket (Algonquian 'narrow-tidal-river-at') pop (1995e) 6100. Island in the Atlantic off the SE coast of Massachusetts, USA; area 122 sq km/47 sq mi; formerly an important whaling centre; now a summer resort. >> Massachusetts

napalm [**nay**pahm] A munition (usually air-launched in canisters by aircraft) containing petroleum gel which uses flame for its destructive effects. It is an aluminium soap of naphthenic and palmitic acids (which give the substance its name). >> gel

naphtha [**naf**tha] A mixture of hydrocarbons obtained either from coal tar or from petroleum, used mainly as a solvent. It has a boiling range of about 100–180°C. >> hydrocarbons

naphthalene [**naf**thaleen] $C_{10}H_8$, melting point 80°C. A white, waxy solid, containing two fused benzene rings; obtained from the distillation of coal tar. Important as a starting material in the synthesis of dyestuffs and plastics, it is familiar as the main ingredient of mothballs. >> benzene ℹ

Napier [**nay**pyer] 39°29S 176°58E, pop (1995e) 54 400. Seaport in North Island, New Zealand; largely destroyed by earthquake in 1931; airfield; railway; centre of a rich farming area. >> New Zealand ℹ

Napier, John [**nay**pyer] (1550–1617) Mathematician, the inventor of logarithms, born near Edinburgh. He also devised a calculating machine, using a set of rods called **Napier's bones**. >> logarithm

Naples, Ital **Napoli**, Lat **Neapolis** 40°50N 14°15E, pop (1995e) 1 211 000. Seaport in SW Italy; founded c.600 BC; capital of Napoleon's Parthenopean Republic, 1799, and of the Sicilian kingdom, 1806; joined Kingdom of Italy, 1860; severely damaged in World War 2, and by earthquakes, 1980; archbishopric; airport; railway; university (1224); cathedral (13th–15th-c). >> Italy [i]; Pompeii

Napoleon I, Fr **Napoléon Bonaparte**, Ital **Napoleone Buonaparte** (1769–1821) French general, consul, and emperor (1804–15), born in Ajaccio, Corsica. He commanded the artillery at the siege of Toulon (1793), and in 1796 married Joséphine, widow of the Vicomte de Beauharnais. In Italy, he defeated the Piedmontese and Austrians, and made several gains through the Treaty of Campo Formio (1797). Intending to break British trade by conquering Egypt, he captured Malta (1798), and entered Cairo; but after the French fleet was destroyed by Nelson at the Battle of the Nile in 1798 (also known as The Battle of Aboukir Bay), he returned to France (1799). The *coup d'état* of 18th Brumaire followed (9 Nov 1799) in which Napoleon assumed power as First Consul, instituting a military dictatorship. He then routed the Austrians at Marengo (1800), and consolidated French domination by the Concordat with Rome and the Peace of Amiens with Britain (1802). Elected consul for life, he assumed the hereditary title of emperor in 1804. War with Britain was renewed, and extended to Russia and Austria. Forced by Britain's naval supremacy at Trafalgar (1805) to abandon the notion of invasion, he attacked the Austrians and Russians, gaining victories at Ulm and Austerlitz (1805). Prussia was defeated at Jena and Auerstadt (1806), and Russia at Friedland (1807). After the Peace of Tilsit, he became the arbiter of Europe. He then tried to cripple Britain with the Continental System, and sent armies into Portugal and Spain, which resulted in the unsuccessful Peninsular War (1808–14). In 1809, wanting an heir, he divorced Joséphine, who was childless, and married the Archduchess Marie Louise of Austria, a son being born in 1811. Believing that Russia was planning an alliance with Britain, he invaded, defeating the Russians at Borodino (1812), before entering Moscow, but he was forced to retreat. In 1813 his victories over the allied armies continued at Lützen, Bautzen, and Dresden, but he was routed at Leipzig, and France was invaded. Forced to abdicate, he was given the sovereignty of Elba (1814). The unpopularity of the Bourbons motivated him to return to France in 1815. He regained power for a period known as the Hundred Days, but was defeated at Waterloo. He fled to Paris, abdicated, and was banished to St Helena, where he died. >> Continental System; French Revolution [i]; Hundred Days; Joséphine; Napoleonic Wars; Peninsular War; Waterloo, Battle of

Napoleon II, in full **François Charles Joseph Bonaparte** (1811–32) Son of Napoleon I by the Empress Marie Louise, born in Paris. Styled King of Rome at his birth, after his father's abdication he was brought up in Austria, though allowed no active political role. >> Napoleon I

Napoleon III, until 1852 **Louis Napoleon**, originally **Charles Louis Napoleon Bonaparte** (1808–73) President of the Second French Republic (1848–52) and emperor of the French (1852–70), born in Paris, the third son of Louis Bonaparte (the brother of Napoleon I) and Hortense Beauharnais. He made two abortive attempts on the French throne (1836, 1840), for which he was imprisoned, but after the 1848 Revolution he was elected president, and assumed the title of emperor. His reign coincided with the Crimean War (1854–6), the expeditions to China (1857–60), the annexation (1860) of Savoy and Nice, and the ill-starred intervention in Mexico (1861–7). He unwisely declared war on Prussia in 1870 and suffered humiliating defeat. He went into exile in England, living in Kent until his death. >> Franco-Prussian War; Revolutions of 1848

Napoleonic Wars (1800–15) The continuation of the Revolutionary Wars, fought to preserve French hegemony in Europe. The wars began with Napoleon's destruction of the Second Coalition (1800). After a peaceful interlude (1802–3) Britain resumed hostilities, prompting Napoleon to prepare for invasion, and encouraging the formation of a Third Coalition (1805–7). While Britain retained naval superiority (1805), Napoleon established territorial domination, resulting in the invasions of Spain (1808) and Russia (1812). Gradually the French were overwhelmed by the Fourth Coalition (1813–14); the Hundred Days' epilogue ended with Waterloo (1815). >> Continental System; Hundred Days; Leipzig / Trafalgar / Waterloo, Battles of; Napoleon I; Peninsular War; Vienna, Congress of

Nara [**nah**ra] 34°41N 135°49E, pop (1995e) 355 000. City in S Honshu, Japan; first urban capital of Japan, 710; centre of Japanese Buddhism; railway; women's university (1908); Daibutsu-den (Great Buddha Hall) in Todaiji (East Great Temple, founded 743), housing bronze statue of Buddha (22 m/72 ft tall). >> Buddhism; Honshu

Narayan, R(asipuram) K(irshnaswamy) [na**riy**an] (1906–) Novelist and short-story writer, born in Madras, India. His novels include *Swami and Friends* (1935), *Mr Sampath* (1949), *The World of Nagaraj* (1990), and *The Grandmother's Tale* (1993).

Narayanganj [na**ra**yangganj] 23°36N 90°28E, pop (1995e) 516 000. City in SE Bangladesh, on R Meghna; river port for Dhaka; collection centre for jute, hides, and skins; major industrial region. >> Bangladesh [i]; Dhaka

narcissism A condition of self-infatuation. It may manifest as exhibitionism, indifference to criticism, and fantasies of unlimited sexual prowess, intelligence, or attractiveness. >> inferiority complex; Narcissus

narcissus [nah(r)**sis**uhs] A bulb native to Europe, the Mediterranean region, and W Asia; flowers solitary or several on a long stalk, central trumpet or cup (the *corona*), surrounded by six spreading perianth segments, white, yellow, or pink. Horticulturally a division is made into *daffodils*, with the corona equalling or longer than the perianth, and *narcissi*, with the corona shorter than the perianth. (Genus: *Narcissus*, 60 species. Family: Amaryllidaceae.) >> daffodil; perianth

Narcissus [nah(r)**sis**us] In Greek mythology, a beautiful youth who fell in love with his reflection in a pool; he pined away and was changed into a flower. >> Echo

narcolepsy An extreme tendency towards excessive sleepiness often associated with cataplexy, in which sleep onset is accompanied by dreaming. Sleep paralysis and hallucinations are accompanying features. >> sleep

narcotics Drugs related to morphine which, in the literal sense, induce *narcosis* or stupor. In common parlance the term has been adopted to include all addictive drugs. >> analgesics; cannabis; cocaine; drug addiction; heroin; laudanum; morphine; opium

Narmada [**nah(r)**mada] or **Narbada, River** River of India, rising in the Maikala range; enters the Gulf of Cambay; length 1245 km/774 mi; a sacred river to Hindus. >> Hinduism; India [i]

Narnia [**nah(r)**nia] A mythical country, the scene of a sequence of novels by C S Lewis, beginning with *The Lion, The Witch, and The Wardrobe* (1950). >> Lewis, C S

Narses [**nah(r)**seez] (c.478–573) Famous general of the Emperor Justinian, born in Armenia. He reasserted Byzantine control over Rome and Italy by his victories over the Ostrogoths (550–4). >> Justinian

Narvik [**nah(r)**vik] 68°26N 17°25E, pop (1995e) 19 000.

Seaport in N Norway; airfield; ice-free harbour; occupied by Germany, 1940; scene of World War 2 naval battles. >> Norway ℹ

narwhal [**nah(r)**wuhl] A small, toothed whale (*Monodon monoceros*) native to the Arctic seas; mottled brown; no dorsal fin; two teeth (at front of upper jaw); in male, left tooth grows forwards forming a long straight tusk. (Family: Monodontidae.) >> whale ℹ

NASA (National Aeronautics and Space Administration) An independent agency of the US Government responsible for the civil space programme, established in 1958 by President Eisenhower, with its headquarters in Washington DC. Individual projects are implemented at different field centres: *Ames Research Center* (Mountain View, CA) for aeronautics; *Goddard Space Flight Center* (Greenbelt, MD) for astronomy and Earth sciences; *Jet Propulsion Laboratory* (Pasadena, CA) for Solar System exploration; *Johnson Space Center* (Houston, TX) for manned missions; *Kennedy Space Center* (Cape Canaveral, FL) for launch operations; *Langley Research Center* (Norfolk, VA) for aeronautics; *Lewis Research Center* (Cleveland, OH) for space technologies; and *Marshall Space Flight Center* (Huntsville, AL) for launch vehicles and space science. >> space exploration

Naseby, Battle of [**nayz**bee] (14 Jun 1645) A major conflict of the English Civil War in the E Midlands. The Royalist forces of Charles I were defeated by Parliament's New Model Army led by Fairfax. >> English Civil War

Nash, John (1752–1835) Architect and city planner, born in London. He designed Regent's Park and Marble Arch, recreated Buckingham Palace, and laid out Trafalgar Square and St James's Park. >> London

Nash, John F (1928–) Economist, born in Bluefield, WV. He shared the Nobel Prize for Economics in 1994 for his contribution to the analysis of equilibria in the theory of non-co-operative games.

Nash, (Frederic) Ogden (1902–71) Humorous writer, born in Rye, NY. His subject matter was the everyday life of middle-class America, which he described in a witty and acute manner in such books as *Hard Lines* (1931) and *Marriage Lines* (1964).

Nash, Paul (1899–1946) Painter, born in London. He won renown as a landscape painter, and also as a war artist, with such pictures as 'Battle of Britain' and 'Totes Meer' (1940–1, Tate, London).

Nash, Richard, nickname **Beau Nash** (1674–1762) Dandy, born in Swansea, SC Wales. In 1705 he became master of ceremonies at Bath, which he transformed into a leading fashionable centre. >> Bath

Nashe or **Nash, Thomas** (1567–1601) Playwright and satirist, born in Lowestoft, Suffolk. He plunged into the Martin Marprelate controversy, attacking the Puritans in *Pierce Penilesse* (1592). Other works include the satirical masque, *Summer's Last Will and Testament* (1592), and the picaresque tale, *The Unfortunate Traveller* (1594). >> Marprelate Tracts; picaresque novel

Nashville–Davidson, commonly **Nashville**, nickname **Music City, USA** 36°10N 86°47W, pop (1995e) 526 000. Capital of state in N Tennessee, USA; port on the Cumberland R; settled as Nashborough, 1799; renamed Nashville, 1784; state capital, 1843; merged with Davidson, 1963; airfield; railway; three universities (1867, 1872, 1909); famed for its music industry (country and western); Country Music Hall of Fame. >> country and western; Natchez Trace; Tennessee

Nasik [**nah**sik] 20°02N 75°30E, pop (1995e) 782 000. City in WC India; a holy place of Hindu pilgrimage. >> Hinduism

Nassau (Bahamas) [**na**saw] 25°05N 77°20W, pop (1995e) 13 500. Capital of the Bahamas on New Providence I; airport; a popular winter tourist resort. >> Bahamas ℹ; New Providence

Nassau (European history) [**na**sow] A Burgundian noble family, who rose as servants of the Habsburgs, then rebelled against their authority in the Low Countries. William of Orange (1533–84), and his brother Louis (1538–74), Count of Nassau, supported and led the Dutch Revolt (1566–1648). >> Habsburgs

Nasser, Gamal Abdel (1918–70) Egyptian statesman, prime minister (1954–6), and president (1956–70), born in Alexandria. Dissatisfied with the corruption of the Farouk regime, he was involved in the military coup of 1952. As president, he nationalized the Suez Canal, which prompted Britain and France, in collaboration with Israel, to seek his forcible overthrow. In 1958 he created a federation with Syria (the United Arab Republic), but Syria withdrew in 1961. >> Egypt; Farouk I

Nasser, Lake, Arabic **Buheiret en-Naser** Lake in S Egypt; length 500 km/310 mi; area c.5000 sq km/1930 sq mi; created after building the Aswan High Dam (1971). >> Aswan; Egypt ℹ; Nasser

nasturtium [na**ster**shuhm] An annual or perennial, trailing or climbing by twining leaf-stalks, native to Mexico and temperate South America; flowers large, roughly trumpet-shaped with five petals and a backward-projecting spur, in shades of yellow, orange, and scarlet. (Genus: *Tropaeolum*, 90 species. Family: Balsaminaceae.)

Natal (Brazil) [na**tahl**] 5°46S 35°15W, pop (1995e) 653 000. Port in NE Brazil; airfield; railway; university (1958); cathedral; 16th-c fort. >> Brazil ℹ

Natal (South Africa) >> **KwaZulu Natal**

Natchez Trace A road built by the US Army in the early 19th-c to link Nashville, TN, with the then pioneer outpost of Natchez in Mississippi, 725 km/450 mi distant. >> Nashville–Davidson

Nation, Carry (Amelia), *née* **Moore** (1846–1911) Temperance agitator, born in Garrard Co, KY. A large, powerful woman of volcanic emotions, she went on hymn-singing, saloon-smashing expeditions with a hatchet in many US cities, attacking what she considered to be illegal drinking places.

National Academy of Design The main official academy of art in the USA. Founded in 1826, it still exists as an exhibiting society for more traditionally-minded artists.

national accounts A set of accounts showing how much a nation has produced and consumed during some period, normally a year. This will include the composition of goods and services produced, by sector; the division of expenditures between consumption, investment, government, imports, and exports; and the division of incomes between wages, profits, rents, interest, taxes, and transfer payments. >> gross domestic product

National Aeronautics and Space Administration >> **NASA**

National Association for the Advancement of Colored People (NAACP) A group which aims to extend awareness among the country's African-American population of their political rights. It was founded in the USA in 1909. >> civil rights

National Audubon Society [**aw**duhbon] A US private conservation organization named after the US artist and naturalist, John James Audubon. It manages more than 60 wildlife sanctuaries in the USA. >> Audubon; conservation (earth sciences)

National Council of the Churches of Christ in the USA An association of Protestant, Eastern Orthodox, and National Catholic Churches formed in 1950 in the USA. It is committed to the principle of manifesting the oneness of the Church of Christ. >> Christianity

national curriculum A curriculum for all the schools in a country. Some countries (eg France) have had one for many years; some (eg the USA) do not have one at all. England and Wales introduced one in 1988, consisting of three 'core' subjects (English, maths, science), and seven 'foundation' subjects (art, geography, history, music, physical education, technology, and, in secondary schools only, a modern language). Some variation in practice is allowed (eg to take account of the status of Welsh in Wales). >> core curriculum

national debt >> **national accounts**

National Economic Development Council (NEDC), nickname **Neddy** A UK forum set up in 1962 where government, industry, and unions could meet to discuss economic affairs. Many 'little Neddies' were created, relating to specific industries. NEDC was closed in 1992. >> quango

National Front (NF) A strongly nationalist political party in Britain which centres its political programme on opposition to immigration, and calls for the repatriation of ethnic minorities even if they were born in the UK. The party was created in 1960. Its political appeal declined with the election of a Conservative government in 1979. Many of the Front's leaders are avowedly racist and anti-semitic. >> neofascism

National Gallery An art gallery in London housing the largest collection of paintings in Britain. It was opened in 1824, and moved to its present premises in Trafalgar Square in 1838. >> London

National Gallery of Art A gallery endowed by Andrew W Mellon and opened in Washington, DC in 1941. It is a branch of the Smithsonian Institution. >> Smithsonian Institution

National Gallery of Australia An art gallery on the shores of L Burley Griffin in Canberra, opened in 1982. It houses a permanent collection showing the history of Australian art, including Aboriginal art, and has several other collections. >> Aboriginal art; Canberra

National Geographic Society In the USA, a scientific and educational organization, founded in 1888. It publishes a monthly journal, *National Geographic*. >> geography

National Grid Reference System A unique grid reference for mapping purposes for any part of the UK. The country has been divided by the Ordnance Survey into a number of grid squares, 100 × 100 km (62.1 mi), each with its own identifying letters. Each square is further subdivided into numbered 1 km (0.62 mi) squares. >> grid reference; northing; Ordnance Survey of Great Britain

national guard A militia or reserve military force. The US National Guard is organized on a state-by-state basis, its members voluntarily enlisting for military training and for service in aiding the civil power when called upon by the state governor. >> militia

National Health Service (NHS) A system of health care established in the UK in 1948. It is largely a free service available to the whole population, funded out of general taxation, and the largest single employer of labour in the UK. >> hospital; medicine

National Heritage Memorial Fund A fund set up in 1980 as a memorial to those who have died in service for the UK. It is used to help acquire and preserve land, buildings, and objects of outstanding scenic, historic, architectural, artistic, and scientific interest. >> conservation (earth sciences)

National Hockey League The pre-eminent association of professional ice hockey teams in Canada and the USA. Established in 1917 at Montreal, it was originally composed of four teams from Ontario and Quebec, and later expanded to include larger numbers of teams from American cities. A championship series is played annually for the Stanley Cup. >> ice hockey [i]

national hunt racing >> **horse racing**

national insurance A system whereby the state insures all its residents against illness, disability, unemployment, and old age. In the UK, for example, a National Insurance Scheme is funded by compulsory contributions on all workers above a low exemption limit and their employers. The contributions cover only a small part of the total cost of the scheme, the remainder coming from central government revenues. >> insurance; social security

nationalism A political doctrine which views the nation as the principal unit of political organization. A primary aim of nationalists, therefore, is to secure the right to belong to an independent state based on a particular national grouping. With the exception of anti-colonial movements, nationalism is based around a conservative, and sometimes romantic political philosophy that emphasizes the nation's past. >> Plaid Cymru; Scottish National Party; separatism

nationalization Taking into public ownership an entire industry, normally a public utility. The main reasons for nationalization are that an industry is crucial to the economy and in need of government direction, has suffered a period of decline which needs to be reversed, or is important to national defence. There is also the view, based on a socialist ideology, that public ownership is desirable to prevent the concentration of economic power in private hands. >> privatization; socialism

National Lottery >> **lottery**

National Park According to the United Nations, an area of educational and scientific importance for habitat and wildlife, of great beauty, and of recreational value, but which has suffered little human impact, so remaining a relative wilderness. It should also be protected from resource development and be relatively unpopulated. National parks date back to 19th-c USA, where the first was established around the Yellowstone R, WY, in 1872. >> Countryside Commission; wildlife refuge

National Party (Australia) The third largest party in Australia since 1920, originally named the **Country Party**. It is conservative in social matters, generally favours policies of free trade and low tariffs, and supports government public expenditure. Since 1923 it has been in coalition with the Conservative Party. >> Liberal Party (Australia)

National Physical Laboratory A state laboratory established in 1900 at Teddington, near London, to research and develop industrial and scientific standards of measurement.

National Portrait Gallery A gallery of portraits of distinguished people in British history. Opened in London in 1859, it was moved to its present position adjoining the National Gallery in 1895. >> National Gallery

national product >> **gross domestic product**

National Radio Astronomy Observatory The principal radio astronomy observatory of the USA, with headquarters at Charlottesville, VA. In 1988 its 91 m/300 ft dish, used at Green Bank since 1963, collapsed from metal fatigue. Plans were rapidly made to replace it with a new 100 m dish, due to begin operations in 1999. >> observatory; radio astronomy

National Road A road built in the early 19th-c from Cumberland, MD, to Vandalia, IL, and eventually to St Louis, MO. It played an important role in the expansion of the West.

National Security Adviser A member of staff who is responsible for advising the US president on security matters. He is regarded as a senior figure in the White House.

National Security Council A body created by Congress in 1947 to advise the US president on the integration of domestic, foreign, and military policies relating to national security. It is composed of the president, vice-president, secretary of state, secretary of defense, and director of the Office of Emergency Planning. >> Congress

national service >> **conscription**

National Socialism >> **Nazi Party**

National Socialist German Worker's Party >> **Nazi Party**

National Society for the Prevention of Cruelty to Children (NSPCC) A child welfare society, founded in 1884. It has over 200 inspectors in England, Wales, and Northern Ireland who investigate reports of cruelty to, or neglect of, children. >> child abuse

national theatre A theatre which is endowed by the state and is usually situated in the national capital. In Britain, a National Theatre was not inaugurated until 1962, and since 1976 has occupied its own building on the South Bank. >> Olivier, Laurence

National Trust In the UK, a charity founded in 1895 with the full name 'The National Trust for Places of Historic Interest and Natural Beauty'. Its membership stands at over 1 million, making it the largest and most influential conservation body in Britain. >> conservation (earth sciences); English Heritage

Nation of Islam >> **Black Muslims**

Nations, Battle of the >> **Leipzig, Battle of**

Nativity, the The story of the miraculous birth of Jesus of Nazareth to Mary. The year of Jesus's birth is usually fixed at c.6 BC. The festival of Christmas has been celebrated since the 4th–5th-c on 25 December throughout most of Christendom. >> Christmas; Jesus Christ

NATO [**nay**toh] Acronym for **North Atlantic Treaty Organization**. An organization established by a treaty signed in 1949 by Belgium, Canada, Denmark, France, Iceland, Italy, Luxembourg, The Netherlands, Norway, Portugal, the UK, and the USA; Greece and Turkey acceded in 1952, West Germany in 1955, and Spain in 1982. Poland, the Czech Republic, and Hungary joined in 1999. NATO was established as a military alliance to defend W Europe against Soviet aggression. Its institutions include a Council, an International Secretariat, and the Supreme Headquarters Allied Powers, Europe (SHAPE). After the 1989 changes in E Europe, a NATO summit in London (1990) began the process of redefining NATO's military and political goals, and in 1997 NATO and Russia signed a Founding Act on Mutual Relations, allowing for NATO's eastward expansion. In March 1999, NATO authorized air-strikes in Yugoslavia, in response to Serbian measures against the ethnic Albanian population in Kosovo. >> Kosovo

natterjack A European true toad (*Bufo calamita*); rough green skin with thin yellow line along spine; the loudest European toad (croak may be heard 2 km/$1\frac{1}{4}$ mi away). >> frog

Natufian [na**too**fian] A Mesolithic culture of SW Syria, Lebanon, and Palestine (c.12 800–10 500 BC), named after the Palestinian site, Wadi en-Natuf. >> Three Age System

natural childbirth Successful labour entirely without or with minimal use of drugs or outside assistance. It is facilitated by a full awareness of the nature of childbirth, developing psychological attitudes which reduce anxiety and fear, and increase pain tolerance. >> pregnancy [i]

natural gas Gas which occurs in subterranean accumulations, often in association with petroleum deposits. It mainly consists of simple hydrocarbons, mostly methane, with some propane. It is one of the most widely used and versatile of fuels, and a source of other chemicals. When used as a gas supply, it is adulterated with other gases to give it an odour. >> gas 2 [i]; methane; petroleum

Natural History Museum The popular name for the British Museum (Natural History), housed since 1881 in S Kensington, London. >> British Museum

Naturalism A term used in art criticism for the faithful copying of nature, with no attempt to 'improve' or idealize the subject; used in this sense in 1672 by Giovanni Pietro Bellori (1615–96) to characterize the work of Caravaggio and his followers. It later became used to describe the incorporation of scientific method into art, especially literature. >> Caravaggio; Realism

naturalistic fallacy A term in ethics, coined by G E Moore: the mistake of thinking that goodness is some natural or empirical property of things, such as their capacity to produce pleasure; more generally, the alleged mistake of inferring normative conclusions from factual premises – an 'ought' from an 'is'. >> Moore, G E

natural selection The complex process by which environmental factors determine the differential reproduction of genetically different organisms. It is viewed as the force which directs the course of evolution by preserving those traits best adapted to survive. >> evolution

Nature Conservancy Council >> **English Nature**

Nature Reserve A protected area for the conservation and management of wildlife and habitat. In the UK these range from National Nature Reserves, in the care of English Nature, to reserves managed by the National Trust, local authorities, and county naturalist trusts. >> conservation (earth sciences); endangered species; English Nature; wildlife refuge

naturopathy [natyu**rop**athee] A holistic approach to health care which aims to create favourable conditions in which the body's own natural powers of healing will eliminate any illness and then continue to maintain health. The symptoms of an illness are seen as part of the healing process, so these are not suppressed; instead, the body is encouraged to correct its own disturbed equilibrium. >> alternative medicine; healing

Naughtie, (Alexander) James [**nokh**tee] (1951–) Journalist and broadcaster, born in Scotland. He became presenter of the BBC's *The World At One* (1988–94), and joined *Today* in 1994. He has also presented several documentary series, such as *The Thin Blue Line* (1993).

Naukratis [**naw**kratis] A Greek town in the Delta of Egypt, established by the Milesians c.675 BC. It was the commercial centre of the Greeks in Egypt until the foundation of Alexandria (c.331 BC). >> Miletus

Nauru [na**oo**roo], official name **Republic of Nauru** 0°32S 166°56E; pop (1995e) 9900; area 21.3 sq km/8.2 sq mi; circumference 20 km/12 mi. Small isolated island in the WC Pacific Ocean, 4000 km/2500 mi NE of Sydney, Australia; government offices in Yaren district (no capital city as such); timezone GMT +12; several small scattered settlements; half population Nauruans, remainder mixed; religion, mostly Protestant; language, Nauruan, with English widely understood; Australian currency used; ground rises from sandy beaches to give fertile coastal belt, c.100–300 m/300–1000 ft wide, the only cultivable soil; central plateau inland, highest point 65 m/213 ft, mainly phosphate-bearing rocks; tropical climate; under German administration from the 1880s until 1914; after 1919, League of Nations mandate, administered by Australia; self-government, 1966; full independence, 1968; unicameral parliament elects a president, who appoints a cabinet; economy based on phosphate mining, but reserves now very limited; tax haven. >> mandates; Pacific Ocean; RR1017 political leaders

Nausicaa [nawsi**kay**a] In Homer's *Odyssey*, the daughter of King Alcinous. She welcomed Odysseus when he landed in Phaeacia. >> Odysseus

nautilus [**naw**tilus] A primitive cephalopod mollusc with an external spiral shell; numerous tentacles present around mouth; four gills; eyes like a pinhole camera in design, without lenses; only a single living genus known. (Class: Cephalopoda. Subclass: Nautiloidea.) >> Cephalopoda ℹ; mollusc; shell

Navajo or **Navaho** [**na**vahoh] Athapascan-speaking North American Southwest Indians, the second largest Indian group in the USA, numbering c.219 00 (1990 census). They settled in 1888 on a reservation in Arizona (presently 15 million acres). >> Southwest Indians

Navaratri [nava**rah**tree] A Hindu festival held in the autumn (Asvina S 1–10) in honour of the goddess Durga, and also commemorating the victory of Rama over Ravana, the Demon King; also known as **Durga Puja** [**door**guh **poo**juh]. >> Hinduism; RR982

Navarre [na**vah(r)**], Span **Navarra** pop (1995e) 520 000; area 10 421 sq km/4022 sq mi. Region and former kingdom of N Spain; united with Castile, 1515; capital, Pamplona. >> Pamplona; Spain ℹ

nave The W part of a church open to the laity, as opposed to the chancel or choir; more specifically, the middle section of the W limb between the side aisles. >> chancel; church ℹ

navel >> **umbilical cord**

Navigation Acts Protective legislation in Britain passed between 1650 and 1696, designed to increase England's share of overseas carrying trade. The laws stated that all imports to England had to be in English ships or in those of the country of origin. They were not repealed until 1849. >> American Revolution; free trade

Navratilova, Martina [navrati**loh**va] (1956–) Tennis player, born in Prague. The winner of a record-equalling nine singles titles at Wimbledon (1978–9, 1982–7, 1990), she won 167 singles titles (including 18 Grand Slam events) and 165 doubles titles with her partner Pam Shriver (including 37 Grand Slam events), becoming the most prolific winner in women's tennis. In 1994 she retired from competitive singles tennis. She has become known as a spokeswoman on several social issues, notably gay rights, animal rights, and ecology, as well as on issues to do with the status of women and young players in tennis. She became a US citizen in 1981. >> tennis, lawn ℹ

navy The branch of the armed forces whose main function is the projection of military power at and by sea. The role of naval forces is manifold, primarily the protection of lines of communication for the safe transport of troops and supplies (and its converse, denying the enemy the freedom of the seas). In the two World Wars, naval power was of critical importance, with the added dimensions of submarine, amphibious, and carrier warfare. >> Marines; Royal Australian Navy; Royal Navy; warships ℹ

Naxos [**nak**sos] pop (1995e) 15 000; area 428 sq km/165 sq mi. Largest island of the Cyclades, Greece, in the S Aegean Sea; length 35 km/22 mi; width 26 km/16 mi; rises to 1002 m/3287 ft; chief town, Naxos. >> Cyclades; Greece ℹ

Nazareth, Hebrew **Nazerat** 32°41N 35°16E, pop (1995e) 64 300. Town in N Israel; mainly Christian population; home of Jesus for most of his life; Church of the Annunciation. >> Israel ℹ; Jesus Christ

Nazca [**nas**ka] A pre-Columbian culture located along the S Peruvian coast, and flourishing between c.200 BC and AD 500. It was noted for its distinctive style of pottery and large-scale 'lines' (best seen from the air) on the desert surface.

Naze, the, Norwegian **Lindesnes** 57°59N 7°03E. Cape on the S extremity of Norway, projecting into the North Sea at the entrance to the Skagerrak. >> Norway ℹ

Nazi Party A German political party which originated as the German Worker's Party, founded in 1919 to protest against the German surrender of 1918, and renamed the *Nationalsozialistische Deutsche Arbeiterpartei* (National Socialist German Worker's Party, or Nazi Party) in 1920. Adolf Hitler became the party's leader the following year. Its ideology was extremely nationalist, imperialist, and racist, maintaining that the world was divided into a hierarchy of races: Aryans, of whom Germans were the purest example, were the supreme culture-bearing race, while the Jews were the lowest. In 1933 Hitler was appointed chancellor in a coalition government, a position from which he, aided by the party, was able to build up a personal dictatorship, through legal measures, terror, and propaganda. Once in power, the Nazis ruthlessly crushed opposition, and in the late 1930s invaded Austria and the Sudetenland, which according to the ideology was necessary for obtaining land for the 'master race'. During World War 2, their actions included slave labour, plunder, and mass extermination. Nazism as a political ideology is now viewed very much as the expression of extreme inhumanity and fanatical nationalism. >> fascism; Hitler

Ndebele [nduh**bee**lee] or **Matabele** A Bantu-speaking people of SW Zimbabwe and N South Africa. In the 1890s they resisted white pioneers' encroachment on their land, but were ruthlessly suppressed.

N'djamena [nja**mee**na], formerly **Fort Lamy** 12°10N 14°59E, pop (1995e) 700 000. Capital of Chad, NC Africa; founded by French, 1900; bombed by Italians, 1942; airport; university (1971). >> Chad ℹ

Ndola [n**doh**la] 13°00S 28°39E, pop (1995e) 466 000. Capital of Copperbelt province, C Zambia; airport; railway; technical college; commercial centre of a major mining area. >> Copperbelt; Zambia ℹ

Neagh, Lough [lokh **nay**] area 396 sq km/153 sq mi. Large lake in C Northern Ireland; length, 29 km/18 mi; width, 18 km/11 mi; largest lake in the British Isles. >> Northern Ireland ℹ

Neanderthal Man [nee**an**dertahl] *Homo sapiens neanderthalensis*. A distinctive form of archaic *Homo sapiens*, with a long, flat, braincase (capacity 1200–1800 cm), a retreating frontal, heavy brow ridge, and projecting face with a large nose; fully upright with a stocky, muscular body build (height 1.55–1.8 m/5 ft 1 in–5 ft 10 in). Fossil evidence indicates Neanderthal characters evolved slowly from about 0.5 million years ago, but the full set of features only occur after c.0.1 million years ago in Europe, S Russia, and S W Asia. In W Europe they disappeared c.33 000 years ago with the arrival of anatomically modern humans (*H. sapiens sapiens*); in SW Asia the two subspecies coexisted for c.60 000 years. >> *Homo* ℹ

neap tide An especially small tidal range occurring twice monthly, produced by the tidal forces of the Sun and Moon acting in opposition. They occur when the Moon is in its first and third quarters. >> tide

near-death experience (NDE) A striking experience sometimes reported by those who have recovered from being close to death. It generally includes an out-of-the-body experience in which one travels through a dark void or tunnel towards a bright light, and then may encounter religious figures or deceased loved ones. It is often accompanied by strong feelings of peacefulness. >> out-of-the-body experience

nearsightedness >> **eye** ℹ

Neath and Port Talbot, Welsh **Castell-Nedd a Phort Talbot** pop (1995e) 140 100; area 442 sq km / 171 sq mi. County (unitary authority from 1996) in SC Wales, UK; drained by R Neath and R Avan; administrative centre, Port Talbot, known for its steelworks; castle, abbey and Roman fort at Neath. >> Wales ℹ

Nebraska [ne**bras**ka] pop (1995e) 1 649 000; area 200 342 sq km/77 355 sq mi. State in C USA; the 'Cornhusker State'; part of the Louisiana Purchase, 1803; became a territory in 1854; the 37th state admitted to the Union, 1867; capital, Lincoln; highest point Johnson Township

(1654 m/5426 ft); E region undulating fertile farmland, growing corn; further W, on the Great Plains, grass cover helping to stabilize eroded land; agriculture dominates the economy; cattle (second largest producer in the country), corn, hogs, wheat, sorghum. >> Lincoln (USA); Louisiana Purchase; United States of America ℹ; RR994

Nebuchadnezzar II [nebookad**ne**zer], also spelled **Nebuchadrezzar** (c.630–562 BC) King of Babylon (605–562 BC). Under him, Babylonian civilization reached its height, and its empire extended as far as the Mediterranean. In the West, he is remembered chiefly for his deportation of the Jews to Babylonia (586 BC). >> Babylonia; Babylonian Exile

nebula A cloud of gas and dust in space, appearing either light or dark. Examples include Crab nebula, Horsehead nebula, and Orion nebula. >> Crab nebula; Horsehead nebula; Orion

neck That part of the body which connects the head and the thorax as well as the upper limbs to the trunk. It contains the continuations of many structures: the vertebral column, alimentary and respiratory tracts, blood vessels and their branches, lymph nodes and lymphatic vessels, groups of muscles, and several cranial and cervical nerves. >> anatomy ℹ; jugular veins; larynx; trachea; vagus; vertebral column

Necker, Jacques (1732–1804) Statesman and financier, born in Geneva, Switzerland. As director-general of finances in France, he attempted reforms, but was dismissed (1781). Recalled to deal with the impending financial crisis (1788), he summoned the States General, but his proposals aroused royal opposition, and he was again dismissed. >> Louis XVI

nectar A sugary fluid secreted by specialized glands (*nectaries*) usually found in flowers, and used to attract insect pollinators.

nectarine A smooth-skinned variety of peach. (*Prunus persica*, variety *nectarina*. Family: Rosaceae.) >> peach

Neddy >> **National Economic Development Council**

Nederlands >> **Dutch**

needlefish Slender-bodied fish with very long jaws forming a narrow bill; widespread in tropical and warm temperate seas; length up to 1.2 m/4 ft; also called **garfish**. (Family: Belonidae.)

Ne'eman, Yuval (1925–) Physicist and politician, born in Tel Aviv, Israel. He became a member of the Israeli Knesset in 1981, and has held ministerial posts in the areas of science and development. In physics he has worked on the role of symmetry in particle physics, and co-authored the influential book *The Eight-Fold Way* with Murray Gell-Mann. >> Gell-Mann; particle physics

Neer, Aernout or **Aert van der** (1603/4–77) Painter, born in Amsterdam. He specialized in wintry river scenes, the emphasis almost always on the effect of the Moon peering through ragged clouds. >> landscape painting

Neeson, Liam (1952–) Film actor, born in Ballymena, Northern Ireland. He received an Oscar nomination for his role as Schindler in *Schindler's List* (1993), and went on to play the title roles in *Rob Roy* (1995) and *Michael Collins* (1996).

Nefertiti [nefer**tee**tee] (14th-c BC) Egyptian queen, the consort of Akhenaton. She is immortalized in the sculptured head found at Amarna in 1912, now in the Berlin museum. >> Akhenaton

negative An image in which the tonal scale of the original scene is inverted, light areas being reproduced as dark and vice versa. In a **colour negative** the hues of the original are also represented in their complementary colours. >> film; photography

Negeri Sembilan [neg**ree** sembi**lahn**] pop (1995e) 815 000; area 6643 sq km/2564 sq mi. State in SW Peninsular Malaysia; capital, Seremban. >> Malaysia ℹ

Negev [ne**gev**] Area 12 200 sq km/4700 sq mi. Hilly desert region of S Israel; hilly in the S, reaching 1935 m/6348 ft at Har Ramon; increasing kibbutz settlement. >> Israel ℹ; kibbutz

negligence A tort (or delict, in Scotland) applicable to a very wide range of situations. To succeed in negligence, the plaintiff must prove that the defendant owed him or her a duty of care; that the duty was breached in this instance; and that the breach caused damage to the plaintiff (known as *actual* or *proximate cause* in the USA). Road accidents are a common source of negligence claims. >> tort

Negro, River [**neg**roh] (Port **Rio**) Important N tributary of the Amazon, N Brazil; rises in SE Colombia; length c.2250 km/1400 mi. >> Amazon, River; Brazil ℹ

Nehemiah, Book of [neehe**miy**a] A book of the Hebrew Bible/Old Testament, named after a Jewish official of the King of Persia, who apparently led a return to Judea by Jewish exiles. >> Old Testament

Nehru, Jawaharlal [**nair**oo], known as **Pandit** ('Teacher') **Nehru** (1889–1964) Indian statesman and prime minister (1947–64), born in Allahabad, India. Imprisoned several times by the British, in 1929 he was elected president of the Indian National Congress. As India's first prime minister, he introduced a policy of industrialization, reorganized the states on a linguistic basis, and brought the dispute with Pakistan over Kashmir to a peaceful solution. >> Gandhi; Indian National Congress; Pakistan ℹ

nekton Swimming marine organisms, capable of locomotion at speeds greater than those of ocean currents; distinct from plankton, which are drifters. Nekton range in size from tiny fish to giant sperm whales. >> plankton

Nelson, Horatio (1758–1805) British admiral, born in Burnham Thorpe, Norfolk. In 1794 he commanded the naval brigade at the reduction of Bastia and Calvi where he lost the sight of his right eye, and in an action at Santa Cruz had his right arm amputated. In 1798 he followed the French fleet to Egypt, destroying it at Aboukir Bay. On his return to Naples, he fell in love with Emma, Lady Hamilton, and began a liaison with her which lasted until his death. In 1805 he gained his greatest victory, against the combined French and Spanish fleet at Trafalgar. During the battle he was mortally wounded on his flagship, HMS *Victory*. >> Aboukir Bay, Battle of; Hamilton, Emma; Napoleonic Wars; Trafalgar, Battle of

Nelson, Willie (1933–) Country singer, songwriter, and guitarist, born in Abbott, TX. After writing and recording many country-music hits in the 1960s, he later gained a wider audience with such albums as *Shotgun Willie* (1972) and *Stardust* (1978). >> country and western

nematode An unsegmented worm, typically circular in section; body covered with cuticle; head end with terminal mouth, surrounded by lips and three rings of sense organs; c.12 000 species described; also known as **eelworms**, **roundworms**, or **pinworms**. (Phylum: Nematoda.) >> ascaris; filariasis; worm

Nemertea [ne**mer**tia] >> **ribbon worm**

nemesia [ne**mee**zha] An annual (*Nemesia strumosa*) growing to 60 cm/2 ft, native to S Africa; flowers with 2-lobed upper lip and large, spreading 3-lobed lower lip, in a range of colours. (Family: Scrophulariaceae.)

Nemesis [**nem**esis] In Greek mythology, the goddess of retribution. She primarily represents the penalty the gods exact for human folly, excessive pride, or too much good fortune.

Nemirovich-Danchenko, Vladimir (Ivanovich) [ne**mi**rohvich dan**cheng**koh] (1858–1943) Theatre director, writer, and teacher, born in Ozurgety. Co-founder with Stanislavsky of the Moscow Art Theatre, he became sole director.

Nenets A Uralic-speaking ethnic group living in N Russia, originally known as **Samoyed** or **Yurak**. Formerly nomadic, they are now settled in villages. >> Uralic languages

Nennius (fl.769) Writer, from Wales, the reputed author of *Historia Britonum*. The book gives the mythical account of the origins of the Britons, the Roman occupation, and the settlement of the Saxons, and closes with King Arthur's 12 victories. >> Arthur

Neoclassicism (art and architecture) A classical revival affecting all the visual arts, including architecture and the decorative arts, which flourished from c.1750 onwards, lasting well into the 19th-c. A reaction against the decorous excesses of Baroque and Rococo, it began in Rome, but spread throughout W Europe and North America. In painting, the style reached its peak in the works of David, eg 'Oath of the Horatii' (1784, Louvre). Buildings are usually characterized by pure geometric form, restrained decoration, unbroken contours, an overall severe appearance, and sometimes monumental proportions. >> classicism; David, Jacques Louis; Rococo

Neoclassicism (music) A 20th-c music movement which sought to restore the ideals, and to some extent the style and vocabulary, of the 18th-c classical period. It is associated particularly with Stravinsky's middle-period works (c.1920–30). >> classical music; Stravinsky

Neoexpressionism A vague term sometimes used for all forms of abstract art which are regarded as conveying strong emotions, or which seem to have been produced by the artist in a heightened emotional state. Examples include Kandinsky's work after c.1920, or US Action Painting. >> abstract art; action painting; Kandinsky

neofascism Fascist ideas and movements that have continued after the demise of the inter-war fascist dictatorships. Neofascism in W Europe has been especially opposed to immigration from former colonial and Mediterranean countries, and has used this as a major campaigning platform. >> fascism

Neoimpressionism >> **Divisionism**

Neo-Keynesianism or **new Keynesianism** [**kaynz**ianizm] A term introduced in 1982, related to the economic theories of J M Keynes, but modified to apply to the economic situation of the time. It recognizes three government economic targets: growth, balance of payments equilibrium, and adequate investment. These aims can be met by tax policy, exchange rates, and interest rates. >> Keynesian

Neolithic >> **Three Age System**

neologism [nee**ol**ojizm] A term referring to any newly coined word, usually identifying a new concept. In the 1980s, English neologisms included *stagflation*, *yuppie*, *glitz*, *pocketphone*, and *user-friendly*.

Neo-Marxism The doctrines of Marxists who draw upon Marx's early writings, which had a more utopian emphasis than his later works concerned with economics and historical materialism. A key feature is its self-critical approach, which accepts the need for a review of theory, rather than a rigid acceptance of dogma. >> Marxism

neon Ne, element 10. The second noble gas, forming c.0.002% of the atmosphere, and obtained by the fractional distillation of liquid air. It is used mainly in gas discharge tubes and gas lasers, where it emits a characteristic red glow. >> chemical elements; noble gases; RR1036

neopentane >> **pentane**

neoplasm >> **tumour**

Neoplasticism A term invented c.1917 by Mondrian to describe his own particularly severe form of abstract art. He permitted only primary colours, black, white, and grey, and restricted his shapes to squares or rectangles defined by vertical and horizontal lines. >> *De Stijl*; Mondrian

Neoplatonism A school of philosophy founded by Plotinus (205–270), lasting into the 7th-c, which attempted to combine doctrines of Plato, Aristotle, and the Pythagoreans. >> Plotinus

Nepal [ne**pawl**, nay**pal**], official name **Kingdom of Nepal**, Nepali **Nepal Adhirajya** pop (1995e) 20 827 000; area 145 391 sq km/56 121 sq mi. Independent kingdom lying along the S slopes of the Himalayas, C Asia; capital, Kathmandu; timezone GMT +5¾; chief religion, Hinduism (86%), the only official Hindu kingdom in the world; official language, Nepali; unit of currency, the Nepalese rupee; landlocked, length E–W 880 km/547 mi, width 144–240 km/90–150 mi N–S; high fertile valleys in the 'hill country' at 1300 m/4300 ft, notably the Vale of Kathmandu (a world heritage site); dominated by the glaciated peaks of the Himalayas, highest Mt Everest, 8848 m/29 028 ft; climate varies from subtropical lowland, with hot, humid summers and mild winters, to an alpine climate over 3300 m/10 800 ft, where peaks are permanently snow-covered; originally a group of independent hill states, united in the 18th-c; constitutional monarchy ruled by a hereditary king; period of unrest, 1990, was followed by a reduction of the king's powers, a new constitution, and fresh elections, 1991; king now rules with a Council of Ministers; a bicameral parliament consists of an elected House of Representatives and a National Council; agriculture employs 90% of the people; hydroelectric power developing; tourism becoming increasingly important. >> Gurkhas; Himalayas; Kathmandu; RR1017 political leaders

nephanalysis (Gr *nephos* 'cloud') A meteorological term for the study of clouds, in particular the amount and frequency of different cloud forms. >> cloud ℹ

nephrite >> **jade**

nephritis >> **glomerulonephritis**

nephrons >> **kidneys**

Neptune (astronomy) The eighth planet from the Sun, the outermost of the four 'gas giant' planets; discovered in 1846 as a result of a prediction by Leverrier to explain anomalies in the observed orbit of Uranus; encountered by Voyager 2 (24 Aug 1989); at least eight moons; mass 17·2 times that of Earth; radius 24 750 km/15 400 mi; mean density 1·7 g/cm³; rotational period 0·67 days; orbital period 164·8 years; inclination of equator 29·6°; eccentricity

of orbit 0·010; mean distance from Sun 30·06 AU. It is an apparent twin of Uranus internally, composed of hydrogen and helium, but with much more carbon, nitrogen, and oxygen than Jupiter and Saturn. Its bluish-green coloration is produced by methane in the upper atmosphere. There are two main rings (53 000 km/33 000 mi and 63 000 km/ 40 000 mi from Neptune's centre) and one diffuse inner ring. >> Nereid; planet; Solar System; Triton (astronomy); Voyager project ℹ

Neptune (mythology) The Roman water-god. He was later identified with Poseidon, whose characteristics and mythology he acquired. >> Poseidon

Nereid [**nee**reeid] A natural satellite of Neptune, discovered in 1949; distance from the planet 5 510 000 km/ 3 424 000 mi; diameter c.300 km/190 mi, but estimates vary greatly. >> Neptune (astronomy); RR964

nereid [**nee**reeid] In Greek mythology, a sea-nymph, one of the 50 or (in some accounts) 100 daughters of Nereus and Doris. They lived with their father in the depths of the sea. >> Nereus

Nereus [**nee**ryoos] In Greek mythology, a sea-god, the wise old man of the sea who always tells the truth. Heracles had to wrestle with him to find the location of the Golden Apples. >> Heracles

Nergal [**ner**gahl] The Mesopotamian god of the Underworld; at first, a solar deity capable of killing enormous numbers of people in the heat of noon-day. >> Mesopotamia

Neri, St Philip [**nair**ee] (1515–95) Founder of the Oratory, born in Florence, Italy. In 1551 he became a priest, and gathered around him a following of disciples which in 1563 became the Congregation of the Oratory. He was canonized in 1622; feast day 26 May. >> Oratorians

Nero [**nee**roh], in full **Nero Claudius Caesar**, originally **Lucius Domitius Ahenobarbus** (37–68) Emperor of Rome (54–68), the son of Gnaeus Domitius Ahenobarbus and the younger Agrippina, daughter of Germanicus. His mother engineered his adoption by the Emperor Claudius, her fourth husband. Initially his reign was good, thanks to his three main advisers: his mother, the philosopher Seneca, and the Praetorian Prefect Burrus. But after her murder (59), and their fall from favour, Nero neglected affairs of state, and corruption set in. He was blamed for the Great Fire of Rome (64), despite assiduous attempts to make scapegoats of the Christians. He was toppled from power by the army, and forced to commit suicide. >> Agrippina (the Younger); Claudius; Poppaea Sabina

Neruda, Pablo (Neftali Reyes) [ne**roo**tha] (1904–73) Poet and diplomat, born in Parral, Chile. He made his name with *Veinte poemas de amor ya una canción desesperada* (1924, Twenty Love Poems and a Song of Despair). His other works include *Residencia en la tierra* (1925–31, Residence on Earth) and *Canto General* (1950, General Song). He received the Nobel Prize for Literature in 1971.

nerve (cell) >> **neurone** ℹ

nerve gas An agent of chemical warfare, whose deadly effects are achieved by attacking the human body's central nervous system. Paralysis and death come within seconds of absorption. >> chemical warfare

Nervi, Pier Luigi [**nair**vee] (1891–1979) Architect, born in Sondrio, Italy. He achieved an international reputation by his designs for the Olympic Games in Rome (1960). He also designed San Francisco Cathedral (1970).

nervous system That part of the body concerned with controlling and integrating the activity of its various parts. It is composed of nerves (*neurones*) and supporting cells. The transfer of information between nerve cells (at *synapses*) is usually by the release of small quantities of *transmitter substances*. In all activities involving the nervous system, there are three components involved: a *receptive* or *sensory* component, an integrative component and an *effector* or *motor* component. In higher animals the integrative component has undergone the greatest development, and forms the major part of the nervous system. In mammals the nervous system is divided into **central** and **peripheral** parts, both parts working together as a functioning unit: the central part comprises the brain and spinal cord, while the peripheral part comprises the remainder. >> brain ℹ; central nervous system; neuralgia; neurology; neurone ℹ; neuropathology; neurophysiology; neurotoxins; neurotransmitter; paralysis; peripheral nervous system; prion disease; synapse

Nesbit, E(dith), maiden name and pseudonym of **Mrs Hubert Bland** (1858–1924) Writer, born in London. She is best remembered for her children's stories, such as *The Wouldbegoods* (1901) and *The Railway Children* (1906).

Nesselrode, Karl (Robert) Vasilyevich, Graf (Count) [nesel**roh**duh] (1780–1862) Russian diplomat, born in Lisbon, Portugal. He became foreign minister in 1822, and dominated Russian foreign policy for 30 years.

Ness, Loch Loch in Highland, N Scotland; 38 km/24 mi long; average width 2 km/1¼ mi; maximum depth 230 m/ 755 ft; part of the Caledonian Canal; said to be inhabited by a 12–15 m/40–50 ft-long 'monster'; no clear results from scientific investigations. >> Caledonian Canal; Highland; Scotland ℹ

nest A domicile or home constructed, typically by birds, for the purpose of containing and protecting eggs and young. Young birds that remain in the nest for a prolonged period after hatching are known as *nidicolous*; those that leave soon after hatching are known as *nidifugous*. >> bird ℹ

Nestor [**nes**taw(r)] A senior Greek leader in the Trojan War, the son of Neleus. In the *Iliad*, Homer portrays him as a long-winded sage, whose advice is often not taken. >> Trojan War

Nestorians Followers of Nestorius, Bishop of Constantinople (died c.451), who is alleged to have taught the doctrine, later declared heretical, of two persons (one human, one divine) as well as two natures in the incarnate Christ. >> Christology; heresy

Netanyahu, Benjamin [netan**ya**hoo], nicknamed in Israel **Bibi** (1949–) Israeli prime minister (1996–), born in Tel Aviv, Israel. He was elected to the Israeli parliament in 1988, becoming leader of the Likud Party in 1993. A hardliner on security issues, he campaigned on a platform of peace with security, and defeated Shimon Peres by a narrow margin in the 1996 elections. >> Peres

netball A women's seven-a-side court game, invented in the USA in 1891 and developed from basketball. The court is 100 ft (30·5 m) long and 50 ft (15.25 m) wide. The object is to score goals by throwing the ball through the opponent's net, which is attached to a circular hoop suspended on a post 10 ft (3·05 m) high. >> basketball; RR1057

Netherlands, The or **Holland**, Dutch **Nederland**, official name **Kingdom of the Netherlands**, Dutch **Koninkrijk der Nederlanden** pop (1995e) 15 449 000; area 33 929 sq km/ 13 097 sq mi. Maritime kingdom of NW Europe; also includes the islands of the Netherlands Antilles; European coastline 451 km/280 mi; capital, Amsterdam; seat of government, The Hague; largest city, Rotterdam; timezone GMT +1; population mainly of Germanic descent; chief religions, Roman Catholicism (32%), Dutch Reformed Church (15%); official language, Dutch; unit of currency, the gulden (guilder) of 100 cents; generally low and flat, except SE; much of the coastal area lies below sea-level, protected by coastal dunes and artificial dykes; cool, temperate, maritime climate; part of Roman Empire, to 4th-c AD; part of Frankish Empire by 8th-c; incorporated into the Holy Roman Empire; lands passed

to Philip II, who succeeded to Spain and the Netherlands, 1555; Revolt of the Netherlands against Spanish Habsburg rule 1566; attempts to stamp out Protestantism led to rebellion, 1572; seven N provinces united against Spain, 1579; United Provinces independent, 1609; overrun by the French, 1795–1813, who established the Batavian Republic; united with Belgium as the Kingdom of the United Netherlands until 1830, when Belgium withdrew; neutral in World War 1; occupied by Germany, World War 2, with strong Dutch resistance; joined with Belgium and Luxembourg to form the Benelux economic union, 1948; a parliamentary democracy under a constitutional monarchy; government led by a prime minister and a bicameral States-General; Rotterdam and the newly-constructed Europort are major European ports of transshipment, handling goods for member countries of the European Union; Amsterdam a world diamond centre; highly intensive agriculture and horticulture (especially bulbs); world's largest exporter of dairy produce. >> Amsterdam; Benelux; Dutch; Dutch Reformed Church / Wars; Hague, The; Netherlands Antilles / East Indies; Philip II (of Spain); Revolt of the Netherlands; United Provinces of the Netherlands; RR1017 political leaders

Netherlands, Austrian and Spanish Ten provinces in the S of the Low Countries, predominantly Catholic, and united to Spain through Emperor Charles V. They were ceded to the Austrian Habsburgs by the Treaty of Utrecht (1713), and achieved independence from Austria (1794) in the French Revolutionary Wars. >> Charles V (Emperor); Habsburgs; United Provinces of the Netherlands

Netherlands Antilles [an**til**eez], Dutch **Nederlandse Antillen** pop (1995e) 192 000; area 993 sq km/383 sq mi. Islands in the Caribbean Sea, comprising the Southern group (Leeward Is) of Curaçao, Aruba, and Bonaire, 60–110 km/37–68 mi N of the Venezuelan coast, and the Northern group (Windward Is) of St Maarten, St Eustatius, and Saba; an autonomous region of The Netherlands; capital, Willemstad; timezone GMT –4; 85% of the population of mixed African descent; official language, Dutch, with English and Papiamento widely spoken; unit of currency, the Antillian guilder; tropical maritime climate; visited by Columbus, initially claimed for Spain; occupied by Dutch settlers, 17th-c; sovereign of The Netherlands is head of state, represented by a governor, a Council of Ministers, and a unicameral legislature; economy based on refining of crude oil imported from Venezuela; aim of industrial diversification, especially tourism. >> Aruba; Bonaire; Curaçao; Willemstad

Netherlands East Indies The name applied to Indonesia until 1945, when Dr Sukarno declared independence. The Dutch recognized Indonesia's independence in 1948. >> Indonesia ℹ; Sukarno

nettle >> **dead-nettle; stinging nettle**

nettle rash >> **urticaria**

network >> **local area network**

Neuchâtel [noesha**tel**], Ger **Neuenburg** 44°60N 6°56E, pop (1995e) 34 100. Town in W Switzerland, on W shore of L Neuchâtel; railway; university (1909); research centre for the Swiss watch industry. >> Switzerland ℹ

Neuchâtel, Lake [noesha**tel**], (Fr **Lac de**) area 218 sq km/84 sq mi. Largest lake to lie wholly within Switzerland; major wine-growing area. >> Neuchâtel; Switzerland ℹ

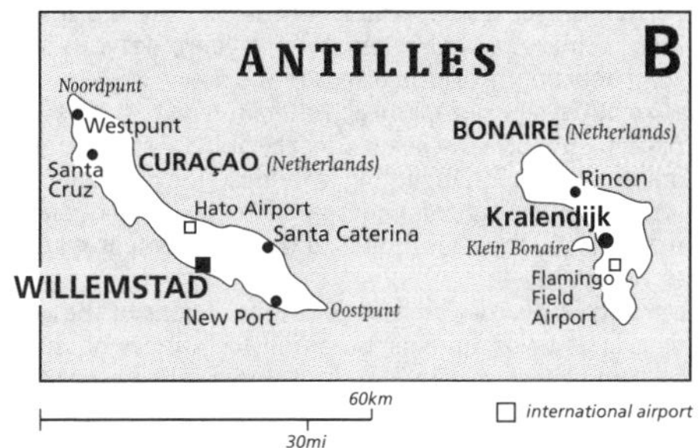

Neumann, (Johann) Balthasar [**noy**man] (1687–1753) Architect, born in Eger, Germany. He designed many outstanding examples of the Baroque style, notably Würzburg Palace and Schloss Bruchsal. >> Baroque (art and architecture)

Neumann, John Von [**noy**man] >> **Von Neumann, John**

neuralgia [nyoo**ral**jia] Pain arising from a sensory nerve, and felt over the surface of the body supplied by the affected nerve. In the most common type, **trigeminal neuralgia**, the cause is unknown. Pain, usually severe and paroxysmal, is felt over the forehead, face, or jaw supplied by one or more of the branches of the trigeminal (Vth cranial) nerve. >> nervous system

neural network An arrangement of computers linked together in a way which attempts to mimic the activity of the brain. The individual computers undertake specific tasks and relate the outcome of those tasks to other computers in the network. >> artifical intelligence; computer network

Neurath, Otto [**noy**raht] (1882–1945) Philosopher and social theorist, born in Vienna. A member of the influential Vienna Circle of logical positivists, he wrote on sociology, education, and social policy. >> logical positivism; Vienna Circle

neuritis >> **neuropathy**

neuroanatomy >> **anatomy** [i]

neurolinguistic programming (NLP) A system of training which aims to develop the ability to communicate, to achieve rapid learning, to improve behaviour patterns, and to change destructive habits in oneself and others. The system is based on the work of the psychotherapists Milton Erickson, Fritz Perls, and Virginia Satir. >> psychotherapy

neurolinguistics The study of the neurological basis of language use: in particular, how the brain controls the processes of speech and comprehension. >> brain [i]; linguistics; neurology

neurology The branch of medicine which deals with the study of physical diseases of the central nervous system (the brain and spinal cord) and its peripheral nerves. >> medicine; nervous system; neuropathology

neurone / neuron [**nyoo**rohn, -ron] The functional unit of the nervous systems of animals; also known as a **nerve cell**. Neurones process and transmit information to target tissues, usually through the mediation of chemicals (*neurotransmitters*). Vertebrate neurones typically consist of a cell body (with a well-developed nucleus surrounded by a mass of cytoplasm), an *axon* (with terminal branches specialized to carry information to target tissues), and *dendrites* (receiving information from axon terminals of other neurones). Most invertebrate neurones lack dendrites. >> nervous system; neurotransmitter; synapse

neuropathology The study of the disease processes which affect the nervous system. These include diseases of the brain, degenerative disorders such as Parkinsonism and prion disease, neuropathies, and demyelinating disorders such as multiple sclerosis. >> myelin; nervous system; neuropathy; prion disease

neuropathy [nyoo**rop**athee] A term which covers all pathological processes that affect peripheral somatic and autonomic nerves, including inflammation of the nerves (*neuritis*). When there is widespread involvement of many nerve fibres, the condition is known as **polyneuropathy**. >> nervous system

neurophysiology The study of the functions of the nervous systems of animals. Common techniques of study are the electrical stimulation of nerve cells using electrodes, and techniques borrowed from other disciplines (eg autoradiography). >> nervous system

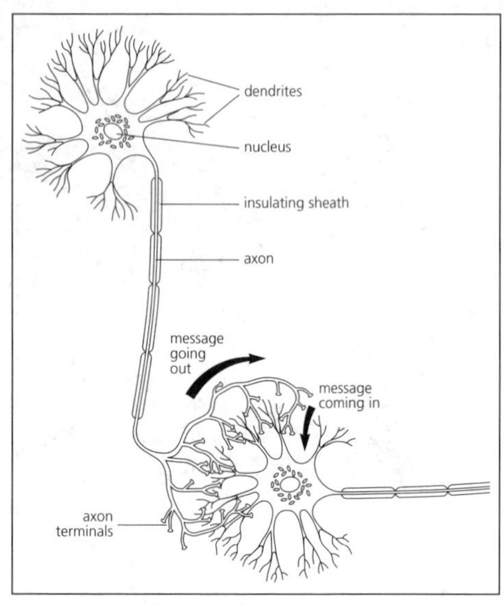

Vertebrate neurones

neuropsychology The study of psychological phenomena in the light of what is known about brain organization and function. Neuropsychologists are often concerned with brain damage, the aim being to identify disabilities, discover methods of rehabilitation, and use this information to make inferences about the normal mind and brain. >> agnosia; amnesia; aphasia; brain [i]; dyslexia; psychology

Neuroptera [nyoo**rop**tera] An order of primitive winged insects, including the snakeflies, lacewings, and antlions; typically two pairs of similar wings with lace-like veins; mouthparts of a simple, biting type. >> antlion; insect [i]; lacewing; larva

neurosis A mental illness often associated with high levels of anxiety and representing exaggerated and/or unconscious ways of dealing with conflicts. The condition is enduring, and reality remains intact. Examples include obsessive-compulsive disorders and phobic disorders. >> phobia; psychosis

neurotoxins Naturally occurring or synthetic substances which specifically or predominantly affect the nervous system. Examples are aconitum (from aconite), and toxins of bacterial origin such as tetanus. >> botulism; nerve gas; nervous system

neurotransmitter A chemical substance (eg acetylcholine, noradrenaline) released as a messenger from nerves. It enables the transmission of a nervous impulse across the narrow gap (*synapse*) between a nerve ending and a muscle, gland, or another nerve. >> acetylcholine; nervous system

neutralization In acid–base reactions, the mixing of chemically equivalent amounts of acid and base to give a solution near pH 7. >> acid; base (chemistry); pH

neutrino A fundamental particle; symbol ν; mass not known exactly, but small, possibly zero; charge 0; spin $\frac{1}{2}$, with spin direction always opposing the direction of motion; senses only gravitational and weak nuclear forces; produced in weak radioactive decays; three species known, corresponding to the electron, muon, and tau. >> fundamental particles

neutron A component particle of the atomic nucleus; symbol *n*; mass 1.675×10^{-27}kg (939.6 MeV), charge 0, spin $\frac{1}{2}$; held in the nucleus by strong nuclear force. Free neutrons decay to protons, electrons, and antineutrinos. >> neutron bomb / star; quark

neutron bomb More precisely an **enhanced radiation (ER) weapon**, a nuclear munition small enough to be used on the battlefield, fired as an artillery shell or short-range missile warhead, which on detonation produces radiation effects rather than blast and heat. The destructive effect is therefore aimed against living things rather than vehicles and buildings. >> bomb; neutron; radiation

neutron star A star that has collapsed so far under gravity that it consists almost entirely of neutrons. Stars of more than 1·5 solar masses shrink until pressure between the neutrons balances the inward pull of gravity. They are observed as pulsars. >> gravity; neutron; pulsar; supernova

Nevada [ne**vah**da] pop (1995e) 1 539 000; area 286 341 sq km/110 561 sq mi. State in W USA; the 'Sage Brush State', 'Battle Born State', or 'Silver State'; part ceded by Mexico to the USA in the Treaty of Guadalupe Hidalgo, 1848; separate territory, 1861; joined the Union as the 36th state, 1864; highest point Boundary Peak (4006 m/ 13 143 ft); mainly within the Great Basin, a large arid desert interspersed with barren mountain ranges; capital, Carson City; the driest of all the states; mostly unpopulated and uncultivated, with a few oases of irrigation; Hoover Dam creates L Mead; mining (mercury, barite, and several other minerals); a major gold supplier; oil discovered, 1954; agriculture not highly developed; tourism, notably Death Valley National Monument (partly in Nevada), and the gambling resorts of Las Vegas and Reno (gaming taxes a primary source of state revenue); very rapid population growth (50% increase between 1980 and 1990). >> Carson City; Great Basin; Guadalupe Hidalgo, Treaty of; Las Vegas; Reno; United States of America [i]; RR994

Nevado (mountain) >> *under accompanying name*

Never Never Land Area of Northern Territory, Australia, SE of Darwin; featured in Mrs Aeneas Gunn's book, *We of the Never Never* (1908).

nevus >> **birthmark**

New Age A period of time recognized as our Solar System passes through one sign of the Zodiac to the next. It takes c.2000 years to travel through each star sign, each of which constitutes an 'age'. The Piscean age (represented by water) started with the beginning of the Roman Empire, and we are now entering the new age of Aquarius (an air sign). In the early 1990s, various groups of people united chiefly by their unattached lifestyle came to be called 'new age travellers' by the UK media. >> Zodiac

New Amsterdam >> **New York City**

Newark (UK) [**nyoo**ah(r)k], properly **Newark-on-Trent** 53°05N 0°49W, pop (1995e) 33 100. Town in Nottinghamshire, C England; railway; Newark Castle place of King John's death. >> John; Nottinghamshire

Newark (USA) [**nyoo**erk], locally [**noo**erk] 40°44N 74°10W, pop (1995e) 280 000. Largest city in NE New Jersey, USA; port on Newark Bay; an important road, rail, and air centre; settled by Puritans from Connecticut, 1666; city status, 1836; airport; railway; university (1934); cathedral; insurance and financial centre; linked to New York City by underground rail. >> New Jersey; Puritanism

Newbery, John (1713–67) Publisher and bookseller, born in Berkshire. He was the first to publish books specifically for children, and was part-author of some of the best of them, notably *Goody Two-Shoes*. Since 1922 the **Newbery Medal** has been awarded annually for the best American children's book.

New Britain, formerly **Neu-Pommern** pop (1995e) 285 000; area 37 800 sq km/14 600 sq mi. Largest island of the Bismarck Archipelago, Papua New Guinea; length, 480 km/298 mi; width, 80 km/50 mi; capital, Rabaul. >> Bismarck Archipelago

New Brunswick pop (1995e) 768 000; area 73 440 sq km/ 28 355 sq mi. Province in E Canada; capital, Fredericton; forested, rocky land, generally low-lying, rising in the NW; several rivers and lakes; first settled by French fur traders; 'Acadia' ceded to Britain by the Treaty of Utrecht, 1713; many United Empire Loyalist immigrants, and separation from Nova Scotia, 1783; joined confederation, 1867; governed by a lieutenant-governor and Legislative Assembly. >> American Revolution; Canada [i]; Fredericton

New Caledonia, Fr **Nouvelle Calédonie** pop (1995e) 186 000; area 18 575 sq km/7170 sq mi. Territory in the SW Pacific Ocean, 1100 km/680 mi E of Australia, comprising New Caledonia, Loyalty Is, Isle des Pins, Isle Bélep, and the uninhabited Chesterfield and Huon Is; capital, Nouméa; timezone GMT +11; chief ethnic groups, Melanesians (43%), Europeans (37%); chief religion, Roman Catholicism; official language, French, with English widely spoken; unit of currency, the French Pacific franc; long, narrow main island, 400 km/250 mi in length; rises to 1639 m/5377 ft at Mt Panie; C mountain chain; mild Mediterranean-type climate; warm and humid; visited by Captain Cook, 1774; annexed by France as a penal settlement, 1853; French Overseas Territory, 1946; governed by a high commissioner and Territorial Council; serious disturbances in the mid-1980s when indigenous Melanesians began their struggle for independence; decision to stay part of France after referendum of voters, 1987; agreement (1998) provides for referendum on independence within 15–20 years, and gradual transfer of powers; nickel (world's third largest producer). >> Cook, James; France [i]; Nouméa

Newcastle (Australia) [**nyoo**kahsl] 32°55S 151°46E, pop (1995e) 452 000. City in New South Wales, Australia, on the E coast; founded as a penal settlement, 1804; scene of Australia's biggest earthquake (1989); airfield; railway; university (1965). >> New South Wales

Newcastle (UK) [**nyoo**kahsl], locally [nyoo**kasl**], in full **Newcastle upon Tyne**, Lat **Pons Aelii** 54°59N 1°35W, pop (1995e) 293 000. Administrative centre of Tyne and Wear, NE England; on R Tyne; cultural, commercial, and administrative centre for the NE of England; founded 11th-c; city status 1882; railway; underground; ferries to N Europe; two universities (1963, 1992); two cathedrals (15th-c, 1844); 12th-c castle keep; football league team, Newcastle United (Magpies). >> Tyne and Wear

Newcastle, Duke of >> **Pelham, Thomas**

Newcastle disease >> **fowl pest**

Newcomen, Thomas [**nyoo**kuhmen] (1663–1729) Inventor, born in Dartmouth, Devon. By 1698 he had invented the atmospheric steam engine, and from 1712 it was being used for pumping water out of mines. >> steam engine

New Criticism A critical theory which concentrates on the text itself, the 'words on the page', to the exclusion of extrinsic information. It was developed by such critics as Cleanth Brooks (1906–) and John Crowe Ransom (1888–1974) in the USA in the 1930s and 1940s, and in its turn provided a basis for the technique of *practical criticism*. >> Formalists

New Deal The administration and policies of US President Roosevelt, who pledged a 'new deal' for the country during the campaign of 1932. He embarked on active state economic involvement to combat the Great Depression. Historians often distinguish the **first New Deal** (1933–4), concerned primarily with restarting and stabilizing the economy, from the **second New Deal** (1935–9), aimed at social reform. >> Roosevelt, Franklin D

New Delhi >> **Delhi**

New Democratic Party (NDP) A Canadian political party which succeeded the Co-operative Commonwealth Federation as Canada's social democratic political party in 1961. Formally supported by the Canadian Labour Congress, the NDP has formed provincial governments in several provinces, but never risen above third party status nationally. >> Canada [i]

New English Bible An English translation of the Bible from the original languages undertaken by an interdenominational committee of scholars under the auspices of the University Presses of Cambridge and Oxford since 1948. The first edition of the New Testament was completed in 1961, and the first complete Bible was produced in 1970. It was substantially revised in 1989 under the title of the **Revised English Bible**. >> Bible

New Forest An area of heath, woodland, and marsh covering c.37 300 ha/92 200 acres of S Hampshire, England; a popular tourist area. William the Conqueror appropriated the area for his new 'forest' (royal hunting land) in 1079. It is now administered by 10 Verderers. >> Hampshire; New Forest pony

New Forest pony A breed of horse, developed naturally in the New Forest, Hampshire, England; classed as two types: **Type A** (height, 12–13.2 hands/1.2–1.4 m/4 ft–4 ft 6 in) and the more solid **Type B** (height, 13.2–14.2 hands/1.4–1.5 m/4 ft 6 in–4 ft 10 in). >> horse [i]

Newfoundland (Canada) [**nyoo**fnland] pop (1995e) 603 000; area 405 720 sq km/156 648 sq mi. Province in E Canada, consisting of the island of Newfoundland and the coast of Labrador, separated by the Strait of Belle Isle; capital, St John's; a roughly triangular island, rising to 814 m/ 2671 ft (W); mainly a rolling plateau with low hills; Vikings visited Labrador AD c.1000; coastline explored by Cabot, 1497; British sovereignty declared, 1583 (Britain's first colony); self-governing colony, 1855; voted to unite with Canada, 1949; governed by a lieutenant-governor and a House of Assembly. >> Cabot, John; Canada [i]; Labrador; St John's

Newfoundland (zoology) [**nyoo**fnland] A breed of dog, developed in Newfoundland; large, very thick-set, with an enormous heavy head; broad deep muzzle and small ears and eyes; very thick, black, double-layered, water-resistant coat; webbed feet. >> dog

New France North American colonies claimed by France from the 16th-c, including Canada, Acadia, and Louisiana. Canada and Acadia were lost to the British incrementally up to 1763; Louisiana was sold to the USA in 1803. >> Acadia; Louisiana Purchase

New Frontier The administration and policies of US President Kennedy (1961–3). It was characterized by a high international profile and a liberal domestic stance. >> Kennedy, John F

Newgate From the 13th-c to 1902, the main prison of the City of London, whence many convicted criminals were taken to Tyburn for hanging. >> London

New General Catalogue (NGC) An astronomical catalogue published in 1888 by J L E Dreyer, Armagh Observatory, Northern Ireland, listing 7840 nebulae, galaxies, and clusters. >> astronomy; Dreyer

New Granada, Span **Nueva Granada** The official name in the Spanish-American Empire for the area now covered by the Republic of Colombia. >> Colombia [i]

New Grange A megalithic passage grave of c.3200 BC in the Boyne R valley, Ireland. The ornament of the kerb, passage, and chamber is among Europe's finest prehistoric art. >> chambered tomb; megalith

New Guard In Australian history, an extreme right-wing organization formed in New South Wales in 1932. Its principal achievement was the disruption of the official opening of Sydney Harbour Bridge (1932). The Guard was defunct by 1935.

New Hampshire pop (1995e) 1 114 000; area 24 032 sq km/9279 sq mi. State in NE USA; the 'Granite State'; explored by Champlain and Pring, 1603–5; ninth of the original 13 states to ratify the Federal Constitution; forested mountains in the N (White Mts), highest point Mt Washington (1917 m/6289 ft); S largely devoted to arable farming and grazing; capital, Concord; chief agricultural products dairy and greenhouse products, maple syrup, hay, apples, eggs; diverse manufacturing industries. >> Champlain; Concord (New Hampshire); United States of America [i]; RR994

New Haven, formerly **Quinnipiac** (to 1640) 41°18N 72°55W, pop (1995e) 130 000. Port town in S Connecticut, USA; on Long Island Sound; founded by Puritans, 1638; joint capital of state with Hartford, 1701–1875; railway; Yale University (1701); diverse industrial development. >> Connecticut; Puritanism

New Hebrides >> **Vanuatu**

New Ireland, formerly **Neu-Mecklenburg** pop (1995e) 96 100; area 8647 sq km/3338 sq mi. Second largest island in the Bismarck Archipelago, Papua New Guinea; length, 480 km/298 mi; average width, 24 km/15 mi; capital, Kavieng. >> Bismarck Archipelago

New Jersey pop (1995e) 7 878 000; area 20 168 sq km/7787 sq mi. State in E USA; the 'Garden State'; one of the original states of the Union, third to ratify the Federal Constitution; colonized after the explorations of Verrazano (1524) and Hudson (1609); Appalachian Highlands fall down through Piedmont Plateau to low coastal plains, broken by ridges of the Palisades; highest peak Mt High Point (550 m/1804 ft); 40% of the land forested, mostly in the SE; capital, Trenton; NE highly industrialized and densely populated; the rest mainly arable and grazing; a major industrial and commercial area; many tourist centres. >> Hudson, Henry; Trenton; United States of America [i]; RR994

New Jerusalem, Church of the A religious sect based on the teachings of the Swedish scientist and seer, Emanuel Swedenborg. Through visionary experiences he saw that a first dispensation of the Christian Church had ended and a new one was beginning, the 'New Jerusalem'. His first church was organized in London in 1783. >> Swedenborg

New Labour A movement in the UK Labour Party which accepts a policy of combining traditional socialist values with a concern to respond to the new ideals and aspirations of the individual. It is associated with the approach of Tony Blair, especially in his concern to develop a 'stakeholder economy', where each member of society has an interest in the state's economic progress. It involved a rethinking of several traditional principles, such as the rewriting of Clause Four of the Labour Party constitution, which had affirmed the commitment to common ownership of industry and services. Those who do not share these views are sometimes referred to as 'Old Labour'. >> Blair; Labour Party

New Left A Neo-Marxist movement which espoused a more libertarian form of socialism compared to orthodox Marxism. The movement had some influence in the 1960s, particularly in student politics and in opposition to the Vietnam War, but it never became an effectively organized political force. >> Neo-Marxism; New Right

Newman, John Henry, Cardinal (1801–90) Theologian, born in London. He became a vigorous member of the

Oxford Movement, composing a number of its tracts. A convert to Catholicism in 1845, he joined the Oratorians, later publishing his spiritual autobiography, *Apologia pro vita sua* (1864). A moderate in the controversies of the Vatican Council, he was made a cardinal in 1879. >> Oratorians; Oxford Movement; Roman Catholicism

Newman, Paul (Leonard) (1925–) Film actor, born in Cleveland, OH. His good looks and rugged individualism have brought continued success in a wide range of parts, as in *Cool Hand Luke* (1967), *Butch Cassidy and the Sundance Kid* (1969), and *The Sting* (1973). In addition to winning several Oscars, he was given an Honorary Academy Award in 1986.

Newman, Randy (1944–) Singer and songwriter, born in Los Angeles, CA. He established himself as a major songwriter, with something of a cult following, before his debut vocal album *Randy Newman* (1968). Later albums included *Sail Away* (1972) and *Little Criminals* (1978).

new mathematics A term used to denote mathematical topics introduced into the school curriculum later than other more traditional activities, and which are thus usually less familiar to parents and the general public. The actual mathematics is not in itself 'new'. >> mathematics

New Mexico pop (1995e) 1 685 000; area 314 914 sq km/121 593 sq mi. State in SW USA; the 'Land of Enchantment'; first explored by the Spanish in the early 1500s; first white settlement at Santa Fe, 1609; governed by Mexico from 1821; ceded to the USA in the Treaty of Guadalupe Hidalgo, 1848; organized as a territory (1850), including Arizona and part of Colorado; admitted to the Union as the 47th state, 1912; over a third of the population Hispanic; highest point Wheeler Peak (4011 m/13 160 ft); mainly broad deserts, forested mountain wildernesses, and towering barren peaks; forests mainly in the SW and N; mostly semi-arid plain with little rainfall; capital, Santa Fe; farming in the well-irrigated valley of the Rio Grande; nation's chief producer of uranium, potash, perlite; tourism important (warm, dry climate and striking scenery); several military establishments and atomic energy centres; Los Alamos atomic research centre built, 1943; first atomic bomb explosion at White Sands, 1945; several mountain Indian reservations. >> Guadalupe Hidalgo, Treaty of; Santa Fe; United States of America ℹ; RR994

New Model Army An English army established by Parliament (1645) to strengthen its forces in the Civil War against the Royalists. The county and regional armies of Essex, Manchester, and Waller were merged into a successful national force. >> English Civil War

New Netherland A Dutch colony in the valley of the Hudson R. The first settlement was Fort Orange (Albany), founded in 1617, Nieuw Amsterdam followed in 1624; it was conquered by the English and named New York in 1664. >> New York

New Orleans [**aw(r)**leenz] 29°58N 90°04W, pop (1995e) 517 000. City in SE Louisiana, USA; 'Crescent City', located on a bend in the Mississippi; founded by the French, 1718; capital of French Louisiana, 1722; ceded to Spain, 1763; passed to the US in the Louisiana Purchase 1803; French influence still evident today; prospered in the 19th-c as a market for slaves and cotton; gained a lasting reputation for glamour and wild living; industrial growth in the 20th-c after the discovery of oil and natural gas in the region; New Orleans musicians contributed to the early development of jazz, late 19th-c; airport; railway; five universities; cathedral; oil and petrochemical industries; shipbuilding yards; professional team, Saints (football); French Quarter; Mardi Gras (Feb–Mar). >> jazz; Louisiana

Newport (Isle of Wight) 50°42N 1°18W, pop (1995e) 21 600. River port, market town, and administrative centre of Isle of Wight, S England; on the R Medina; Parkhurst prison nearby; 12th-c Carisbrooke Castle. >> Wight, Isle of

Newport (USA) 41°29N 71°19W, pop (1995e) 28 400. Port in SE Rhode Island, USA; settled, 1639; city status, 1853; haven for religious groups; railway; several US Navy establishments; Newport Jazz Festival, 1954–71; yachting (including America's Cup races). >> Rhode Island

Newport (Wales), Welsh **Casnewydd** pop (1995e) 137 400; area 191 sq km/74 sq mi. County (unitary authority from 1996) in SE Wales, UK; administrative centre, Newport, on R Usk; steel, aluminium, electronics, chemicals, market gardening; Roman fort at Caerleon. >> Wales ℹ

New Providence pop (1995e) 186 000; area 207 sq km/80 sq mi. Island in the NC Bahamas; length 32 km/20 mi; capital, Nassau; airport; popular tourist resort. >> Bahamas ℹ; Nassau (Bahamas)

New Right A wide-ranging ideological movement associated with the revival of conservatism in the 1970s and 1980s, particularly in the UK and USA. It is strongly in favour of state withdrawal from ownership, and a free-enterprise system. There is also a strong moral conservatism – an emphasis on respect for authority, combined with a strong expression of patriotism and support for the idea of the family. In the USA it has been associated with the emergence of Christian fundamentalism. >> conservatism; fundamentalism; Moral Majority

New River Gorge Bridge Longest single arch steel span bridge in the world, on the New River N of Fayetteville, West Virginia; length 923 m/3030 ft; arch span 518 m/1700 ft; height 267 m/876 ft; completed in 1977. >> bridge

New Ross, Ir **Baila Nua** 52°24N 6°56W, pop (1995e) 6000. Mediaeval town and river port in Wexford county, SE Ireland; home of the Kennedy family in Dunganstown, 8 km/5 mi S. >> Ireland (republic) ℹ; Kennedy, John F; Wexford (county)

news agency An organization providing a general or specialized news service. Agencies range from large, publicly-quoted companies (eg Reuters) and state-owned concerns (eg TASS) to small private operations. >> Agence France Press; Associated Press; Reuter; TASS; Xinhua

New Siberian Islands, Russ **Novosibirskiye Ostrova** area 28 250 sq km/10 900 sq mi. Uninhabited archipelago in the Arctic Ocean; rises to 374 m/1227 ft. >> Russia ℹ

New South Wales pop (1995e) 6 060 000; area 801 428 sq km/309 400 sq mi. State in SE Australia; first British colony, named by Captain Cook, who landed at Botany Bay, 1770; first settlement at Sydney, 1788; coastal lowlands give way to tablelands, formed by the Great Dividing Range (highest point Mt Kosciusko, 2228 m/7310 ft); fertile irrigated plains further W comprise two-thirds of the state; capital, Sydney; the most populous and most heavily industrialized state in Australia. >> Australia ℹ; Cook, James; Sydney

New Spain, Span **Nueva España** The formal title of the Spanish viceroyalty covering the area of modern Mexico. >> Mexico ℹ

newspaper A regularly published account of recent events. Modern newspapers are printed, usually by offset lithography, on large sheets, folded once and inserted one within another, and published at daily, weekly, or (occasionally) monthly frequencies. The modern newspaper can be traced back to the British publications, the *Corante* (1621) and *Weekly Newes* (1622). The first daily paper was the *Daily Courant* (1702), and the first true evening paper the *Courier* (1792). Technical developments include mechanized metal typesetting, photoengraved illustrations, phototypesetting, offset lithography, and facsimile transmission of text and pictures. The revolution in news gathering and editorial preparation has equalled the technical advances. In the mid-1990s, c.18 000 newspapers were being published around the world, with over 200 million newspapers printed daily. >> news agency; printing [i]

New Style date The dating system which followed the adoption of the Gregorian calendar by Great Britain and its American colonies (14 Sep 1752); previous dates are referred to as **Old Style** dates. The new system eliminated 11 days to get in step with Europe, and moved the day on which the count of years changes from the Feast of the Annunciation (25 Mar) back to 1 January. >> Gregorian calendar

New Sweden A Swedish colony, founded at Fort Christina (Wilmington) on the Delaware R in 1633, with Dutch investment and involvement. It was absorbed by New Netherland in 1655. >> New Netherland

newt An amphibian of order Urodela; breeds in water; young (called the *eft* stage) live on land for 1–7 years. (Family: Salamandridae.) >> amphibian; salamander [i]

New Territories area 950 sq km/367 sq mi. Region of Hong Kong; includes part of the mainland and over 200 islands. >> Hong Kong

New Testament Along with the Old Testament, the sacred literature of Christianity. It is called 'New Testament' because its writings are believed to represent a new covenant of God with his people, centred on the person and work of Jesus Christ, as distinct from the old covenant with Israel which is described in the 'Old Testament'. The 27 New Testament writings were originally composed in Greek, mainly in the 1st-c AD, unlike the Old Testament writings which are primarily in Hebrew and from earlier centuries. >> Acts of the Apostles; Apocrypha, New Testament; Bible; Gospels, canonical; Hebrews, Letter to the; Pauline Letters; Revelation, Book of

Newton, Sir Isaac (1642–1727) Physicist and mathematician, born in Woolsthorpe, Lincolnshire. In 1665–6 the fall of an apple is said to have suggested the train of thought that led to the law of gravitation. He studied the nature of light, and devised the first reflecting telescope. His *Philosophiae naturalis principia mathematica* (1687, Mathematical Principles of Natural Philosophy) established him as the greatest of all physical scientists. He was appointed master of the Mint from 1699 till the end of his life, and he also sat in parliament on two occasions. During his life he was involved in many controversies, notably with Leibniz over the question of priority in the discovery of calculus. >> gravitation; Leibniz; light; Newton's laws; optics [i]; telescope [i]

newton SI unit of force; symbol *N*; named after Isaac Newton; defined as the force which causes an acceleration of 1 m/s^2 for an object of mass 1 kg. >> force; Newton, Isaac

Newton's laws The basic expression of Newtonian mechanics; formulated in 1687 by Isaac Newton. *First law*: the velocity of an object does not change unless a force acts on it. *Second law*: a force F applied to an object of mass m causes an acceleration a according to $F = ma$. *Third law*: every action has an equal and opposite reaction. >> force; inertia; mass; momentum

new town A British solution to problems of city growth: a planned, self-contained settlement designed to relieve urban congestion. Dating from the 1946 New Towns Act, 14 were designated between 1947 and 1950, and seven more since then. Examples include Cumbernauld, Cwmbran, Harlow, and Milton Keynes. >> garden city; green belt

new universities Universities built to accommodate the expanding numbers entering higher education in Britain during the postwar period: Keele (1949); Sussex (1961); Essex (1961); York (1963); Lancaster (1964); East Anglia (1964); Kent (1965); Warwick (1965); Stirling (1967); Open (1969). The term has also come to be applied to polytechnics in Britain which acquired university status in 1992. >> polytechnic; red-brick universities

New Wave >> **Nouvelle Vague**

New World monkey A monkey inhabiting Central and South America; nostrils wide apart and opening to the side (unlike Old World monkeys); some species with prehensile (grasping) tails. (Family: Cebidae, 32 species.) >> capuchin; douroucouli; monkey [i]; saki; spider monkey; squirrel monkey; titi; woolly monkey

New Year's Day The first day of the year (1 Jan) in countries using the Gregorian calendar. Communities using other calendars celebrate New Year on other dates: the Jewish New Year, for example, is Rosh Hashanah (1 Tishri), which falls in September or October. >> Gregorian calendar; RR981

New York pop (1995e) 18 317 000; area 127 185 sq km/ 49 108 sq mi. State in NE USA; the 'Empire State'; second most populous state; one of the original states of the Union, 11th to ratify the Federal Constitution; explored by Hudson and Champlain, 1609; Dutch established posts near Albany, 1614, settled Manhattan, 1626; New Netherlands taken by the British, 1664; Adirondack Mts rise in the N, Catskill Mts in the S; highest point, Mt Marcy (1629 m/5344 ft); state contains 11 334 sq km/4375 sq mi of the Great Lakes; extensive woodland and forest in the NE, elsewhere a mixture of cropland, pasture, and woodland; capital, Albany; New York City the chief ethnically mixed centre of population in the USA. >> Albany (USA); Champlain; Erie Canal; Hudson, Henry; New York City; United States of America [i]; RR994

New York City or **New York** 40°43N 74°00W, pop (1995e) 7 455 000. Largest city in the USA and largest port, at the mouth of the Hudson R; with 1200 km/750 mi of waterfront; trading post established in 1624 by Henry Hudson; colonized by the Dutch and named New Amsterdam 1625; captured by the British in 1664 and named New York after the king's brother, the Duke of York; Washington inaugurated here as first US president; rapid commercial and industrial growth after the opening of the Erie Canal, 1825; divided into five boroughs – Bronx (Bronx Co), Brooklyn (Kings Co), Manhattan (New York Co), Queens (Queens Co), Staten Island (Richmond Co); eight universities; railway; two airports; major world financial centre, with Stock Exchange in Wall Street; professional teams, Mets, Yankees (baseball), Knickerbockers (basketball), Giants, Jets (football), Islanders, Rangers (ice hockey); the country's centre for fashion, arts, and entertainment, with many museums and galleries; Central Park. >> Broadway; Brooklyn Bridge; Empire State Building; Greenwich Village; Liberty, Statue of; Lincoln Center for the Performing Arts; Madison Avenue; New York (state); Rockefeller Center; Times Square; Tin Pan Alley; United Nations; Verrazano-Narrows Bridge; Wall Street; World Trade Center

New Zealand, Maori **Aotearoa** pop (1995e) 3 560 000; area 268 812 sq km/103 761 sq mi. Independent state in the Pacific Ocean SW of Australia; consists of two principal islands (North and South) separated by the Cook Strait, and several minor islands; total length, 1770 km/1100 mi; capital, Wellington; timezone GMT +12; chief ethnic groups, European (74%), Maori (10%); chief religion, Christianity (59%); official languages, English, Maori; unit of currency, the New Zealand dollar of 100 cents; North Island mountainous in the centre, with many hot springs; peaks rise to 2797 m/9176 ft at Mt Ruapehu; South Island mountainous for its whole length, rising in the Southern Alps to 3764 m/12 349 ft at Mt Cook; landslide in 1991 lowered its summit by 11 m to 3753 m/ 12 313 ft; largest area of level lowland is the Canterbury Plain, South Island; highly changeable weather, with all

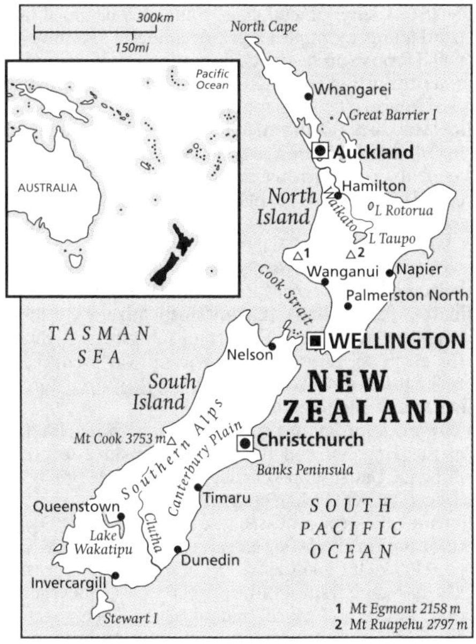

months moderately wet; almost subtropical in N and on E coast, with mild winters and warm, humid summers; settled by Maoris from SE Asia before 1350; first European sighting by Abel Tasman in 1642, named Staten Landt; later known as Nieuw Zeeland, after the Dutch province; sighted by Captain Cook, 1767; first settlement, 1792; dependency of New South Wales until 1840; annexed by Britain 1840; outbreaks of war between immigrants and Maoris, 1860–70; Dominion of New Zealand, 1907; independent within the Commonwealth, 1947; governed by a prime minister, cabinet, and House of Representatives; economy based on farming, especially sheep and cattle; one of the world's major exporters of dairy produce; third largest exporter of wool; substantial coal and natural gas reserves; 80% of electricity supplied by hydroelectric power; tourism a growing sector. >> Cook, James; Maori; Tasman; Wellington; RR1018 political leaders

Ney, Michel, duc d' (Duke of) **Elchingen** [nay] (1769–1815) French marshal, born in Saarlouis, France. He distinguished himself at Jena (1806), Eylau, and Friedland (1807), and commanded the third corps of the Grand Army in the Russian campaign (1813), for which he received the title of Prince of Moskowa. He accepted the Bourbon restoration, but deserted to Napoleon, and led the centre at Waterloo. He was condemned for high treason, and shot in Paris. >> Napoleonic Wars; Waterloo, Battle of

Ngorongoro Crater [ng**goh**rong**goh**roh] Crater in N Tanzania, in the Rift Valley; its rim is at an altitude of c.2100 m/6900 ft, and its floor lies c.600 m/2000 ft below this level; area, c.260 sq km/100 sq mi; centre of a conservation region, and a world heritage site. >> Olduvai Gorge; Rift Valley; Tanzania ℹ

Nguni [**ngoo**nee] A cluster of Bantu-speaking peoples of S Africa. The main groups today include the Zulu, Swazi, and Xhosa of South Africa and Swaziland; the Ndebele of Zimbabwe; and the Ngoni of Zambia, Malawi, and Tanzania. >> Ndebele; Swazi; Xhosa; Zulu

nhandu >> **rhea**

niacin >> **nicotinic acid**

Niagara Falls Two waterfalls in W New York, USA and S Ontario, Canada; between L Erie and L Ontario, on the international border; American Falls 55.5 m/182 ft high, 328 m/1076 ft wide; Canadian Falls, known as Horseshoe Falls, 54 m/177 ft high, 640 m/2100 ft wide; world-famous tourist attraction since early 19th-c; twin resort towns of Niagara Falls in New York (visited by Louis Hennepin 1678) and Ontario; scene of many daredevil exploits, such as the tightrope crossing by Blondin (1859). >> New York (state); Ontario

Niamey [neea**may**] 13°32N 2°05E, pop (1995e) 495 000. River-port capital of Niger; airport; railway terminus; university (1971). >> Niger ℹ

Niarchos, Stavros (Spyros) [**nyah(r)**kos] (1909–96) Shipowner, born in Athens. He became the controller of one of the largest independent fleets in the world, pioneering the construction of supertankers.

Nias [**nee**as] Island in the Indian Ocean, 125 km/78 mi off the W coast of Sumatra, Indonesia; 240 km/159 mi long by 80 km/50 mi wide; airfield; chief town, Gunungsitoli. >> Indonesia ℹ

Nibelungen [**nee**belungen] In mediaeval German legends, a race of dwarfs who live in Norway and possess a famous treasure. The *Nibelungenlied* recounts how Siegfried obtained the treasure and his later misfortunes. >> Wagner

Nicaea, Council of [niy**see**a] **1** (325) The first ecumenical Council of the Church, called by Emperor Constantine to settle the doctrinal dispute between the Arians and the Orthodox on the person of Christ. >> Arius **2** (787) A Council of the Church called to deal with the question of the veneration of images. >> iconoclasm

NICAM An acronym for **near instantaneously companded** [i.e. compressed and expanded] **audio multiplex**, a digital system used in television transmissions which provides high-quality stereophonic sound. First used by the BBC in 1986, it is now found in several other countries. A decoder attached to a television set enables the viewer to receive stereo sound along with any television programme which has recorded it. >> digital recording

Nicaragua [nikar**ag**wa], official name **Republic of Nicaragua**, Span **República de Nicaragua** pop (1995e) 4 553 000; area 148 000 sq km/57 128 sq mi. Largest of the Central American republics; capital, Managua; timezone GMT −6; population mainly of mixed Indian, Spanish, and African descent; chief religion, Roman Catholicism; official language, Spanish; unit of currency, the córdoba oro of 100 centavos; mountainous W half, with volcanic ranges rising to over 2000 m/6500 ft (NW); two large lakes, Lago de Nicaragua and Lago de Managua, behind the coastal mountain range; rolling uplands and forested plains to the E; tropical climate, average annual temperatures 15–35°C according to altitude; rainy season (May–Nov) when humidity is high; country devastated by hurricane Mitch in 1998; colonized by Spaniards, early 16th-c; independence from Spain, 1821; left the Federation of Central America, 1838; dictatorship under Anastasio Somoza, 1938; Sandinista National Liberation Front seized power, 1979, and established a socialist junta; former supporters of the Somoza government (the contras), based in Honduras and supported by the USA, carried out guerrilla activities against the junta from 1979; ceasefire and disarmament agreed, 1990; governed by a president and a national Constituent Assembly; agriculture accounts for over two-thirds of total exports. >> Managua; Somoza; RR1018 political leaders; *see illustration on p. 608*

Nice [nees], Ital **Nizza**, ancient **Nicaea** 43°42N 7°14E, pop (1995e) 353 000. Fashionable coastal resort in SE France;

fifth largest city in France; airport; railway; university (1965); cathedral (1650); leading tourist centre; palm-lined Promenade des Anglais. >> Mediterranean Sea

Nicene Creed [**niy**seen] An expanded formal statement of Christian belief, based on the creed of the first Council of Nicaea (325). It is still publicly recited in Eucharistic liturgies. >> Christianity; Eucharist; Nicaea, Council of

Nichiren Buddhism [nichi**ren**] A sect founded by the Japanese Buddhist reformer Nichiren (1222–82); sometimes called the **Lotus** sect, because of his claim that the Lotus Sutra contained the ultimate truth. >> Buddhism

Nicholas II (1868–1918) The last tsar of Russia (1895–1917), born near St Petersburg, Russia. He took command of the Russian armies against the Central Powers in 1915. Forced to abdicate at the Revolution, he was shot with his family at Yekaterinburg. >> Russian Revolution

Nicholas, St (4th-c) Bishop of Myra, Lucia, and patron saint of Russia. He is the patron of youth, merchants, sailors, travellers, and thieves. His identification with Father Christmas began in Europe, and spread to America, where the name was altered to *Santa Claus*. The tradition of exchanging gifts on Christmas Day derives from a legend of his benevolence. Feast day 6 December >> Christmas

Nicholas or **Nicolaus of Cusa** [**kyoo**za] (1401–64) Cardinal and philosopher, born in Cusa, Germany. A Renaissance scientist in advance of his time, he wrote on astronomy, mathematics, philosophy, and biology. >> Renaissance

Nicholson, Ben (1894–1982) Artist, born in Denham, Buckinghamshire. Although he produced several purely geometrical paintings and reliefs, he generally used as a starting point conventional still-life objects. His second wife was Barbara Hepworth. >> abstract art; Hepworth

Nicholson, Jack (1937–) Film actor, born in Neptune, NJ. He has created a versatile range of antiheroes, winning Oscars for *One Flew over the Cuckoo's Nest* (1975), *Terms of Endearment* (1984), and *As Good As It Gets* (1997). Other notable performances have included *The Shining* (1980), *The Witches of Eastwick* (1986), and *Batman* (1989).

nickel Ni, element 28, density 8 g/cm^3, melting point 1450°C. A silvery metal, most commonly obtained from pentlandite, a complex sulphide of nickel and iron. The metal forms a protective oxide coating, is used in coinage and cutlery, and is an ingredient of many stainless steels. >> chemical elements; metal; RR1036

Nicklaus, Jack (William) [**nik**lows] (1940–) Golfer, born in Columbus, OH. He has won all the world's major tournaments: the (British) Open (1966, 1970, 1978), the US Open (1962, 1967, 1972, 1980), the US Professional Golfers Association tournament a record-equalling five times (1963, 1971, 1973, 1975, 1980), and the US Masters a record six times (1963, 1965–6, 1972, 1975, 1986). >> golf

Nicobar Islands >> **Andaman and Nicobar Islands**

Nicolai, (Carl) Otto (Ehrenfried) [**ni**koliy] (1810–49) Composer and conductor, born in Königsberg, Germany. His opera *The Merry Wives of Windsor* was produced in Berlin just before his death.

Nicolaus >> **Nicholas of Cusa**

Nicomedia [niykoh**mee**dia] In antiquity, the capital first of the kingdom and then of the Roman province of Bithynia. Under Emperor Diocletian (AD 284–316), it was the capital of the E half of the Roman Empire.

Nicosia [niko**see**a], proposed new name **Lefkosia** (1995), Gr **Levkosia**, Turkish **Lefkosa**, ancient **Ledra** 35°11N 33°23E, pop (1995e) 181 000. Capital city of Republic of Cyprus; on R Pedias; capital since 12th-c; 'Green Line' divides the city into northern (Turkish) and southern (Greek) sectors; agricultural trade centre; old city surrounded by Venetian-built walls (late 16th-c); technical institute (1968); cathedral. >> Cyprus [i]

nicotine $C_{10}H_{14}N_2$. An alkaloid derived from pyridine, found in the leaves of the tobacco plant. It is a poisonous and addictive material, usually indulged in for its relaxing properties. >> alkaloids; drug addiction; pyridine; smoking; tobacco

nicotinic acid A B vitamin found usually in plants and animals, important in the production of energy inside cells. It generally exists in the form of **nicotinamide**. In cereals, nicotinic acid is present as **niacytin**. >> vitamins [i]

Niebuhr, Barthold Georg [**nee**boor] (1776–1831) Historian, born in Copenhagen. His main work, the *Römische Geschichte* (1811–32, History of Rome), marked him out as a founder of the 19th-c school of German historical scholarship. >> Stein, Baron von

Nielsen, Carl (August) [**neel**sen] (1865–1931) Composer, born in Nørre-Lyndelse, Denmark. He is particularly known for his six symphonies, and he also wrote concertos, choral and chamber music, the operas *Saul and David* (1902) and *Masquerade* (1906), and a huge organ work, *Commotio* (1931).

Niemöller, (Friedrich Gustav Emil) Martin [**nee**moeler] (1892–1984) Lutheran pastor, born in Lippstadt, Germany. He publicly opposed the Nazi regime, and was placed in concentration camps until 1945. He was then responsible for the 'Declaration of Guilt' by the German Churches for not opposing Hitler more strenuously. >> Lutheranism; Nazi Party

Niepce, (Joseph) Nicéphore [nyeps] (1765–1833) Chemist, born in Chalon-sur-Saône, France. He succeeded in producing a permanent photographic image on metal (1822), said to be the world's first. >> photography

Nietzsche, Friedrich (Wilhelm) [**nee**chuh] (1844–1900) Philosopher and critic, born in Röcken, Germany. He determined to give his age new values, Schopenhauer's 'will to power' serving as the basic principle. His major work, *Also sprach Zarathustra* (1883–5, Thus Spake Zarathustra) develops the idea of the 'overman'. Much of his esoteric doctrine appealed to the Nazis, and he was a major influence on existentialism. >> existentialism; Schopenhauer

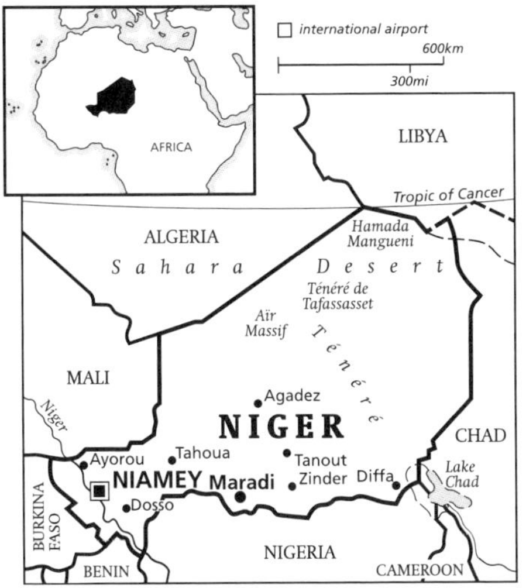

Niger [**niy**jer], official name **Republic of Niger**, Fr **République du Niger** pop (1995e) 9 050 000; area 1 267 000 sq km/ 489 191 sq mi. Republic in W Africa; capital, Niamey; timezone GMT +1; chief ethnic group, Hausa (54%); chief religion, Islam; official language, French, with Hausa and Djerma widely spoken; unit of currency, the franc CFA; on S fringe of the Sahara Desert, on a high plateau; water in quantity found only in the SW (R Niger) and SE (L Chad); one of the hottest countries of the world; occupied by the French, 1883–99; territory within French West Africa, 1904; independence, 1960; military coup, 1974; new constitution, 1992; governed by a president, prime minister, and 83-member National Assembly; economy dominated by agriculture and mining; production badly affected by severe drought conditions in the 1970s. >> Hausa; Niamey; Sahara Desert; sahel; RR1018 political leaders

Niger, River [**niy**jer] River in W Africa; length c.4100 km/ 2550 mi; third longest river in Africa; rises 280 km/175 mi from the Atlantic coast; enters the Gulf of Guinea through a wide delta; first explored by Mungo Park, 1795–6. >> Africa; Park, Mungo

Niger–Congo languages The largest language family in Africa, with 1000 languages spread over almost the entire continent S of the Sahara. It is usually divided into six subgroups of languages: Adamawa-Eastern, Benue–Congo, Kwa, Mande, Voltaic, and West Atlantic. Among the important Niger–Congo languages are Igbo, Swahili, Wolof, Yoruba, and Zulu. The largest group is the Benue–Congo, which comprises c.700 languages; of these, c.500 belong to the *Bantu* group.

Nigeria, official name **Federal Republic of Nigeria** pop (1995e) 96 171 000; area 923 768 sq km/356 574 sq mi. Republic in W Africa; capital, Abuja; timezone GMT +1; over 250 tribal groups, notably the Hausa and Fulani (N), Yoruba (S), and Ibo (E); chief religions, Islam (c.50%), Christianity (34%); official language, English, with Hausa, Yoruba, Edo, and Ibo widely used; unit of currency, the naira of 100 kobos; undulating area of tropical rainforest and oil palm bush behind a coastal strip; open woodland and savannah further N; edge of the Sahara Desert (far N); numerous rivers, notably the Niger and Benue; Gotel Mts on SE frontier, highest point, Mt Vogel (2024 m/6640 ft); Ibadan (SE), average daily maximum temperature 31°C, average annual rainfall 1120 mm/ 44 in; centre of the Nok culture, 500 BC–AD 200; several African kingdoms in Middle Ages (eg Hausa, Yoruba); Muslim immigrants, 15th–16th-c; British colony at Lagos, 1861; protectorates of N and S Nigeria, 1900; amalgamated as the Colony and Protectorate of Nigeria, 1914; federation, 1954; independence, 1960; federal republic, 1963; military coup, 1966; E area formed Republic of Biafra, 1967; civil war, and surrender of Biafra, 1970; military coups 1983 and 1985; major civil and religious unrest, 1992; elections to a bicameral parliament held, then annulled, 1993; military coup, 1993; new constitution and return to civilian rule, 1999; oil provides c.90% of exports; half the population still engaged in agriculture; world's largest supplier of columbite. >> Abuja; Biafra; Lagos; Niger, River; RR1018 political leaders

night blindness Reduced ability to adapt to the dark and to see in dim light, resulting from lack of vitamin A (retinol). This vitamin is an essential component of rhodopsin, upon which colour vision in the retina depends. >> eye ℹ; vitamins ℹ

Nightingale, Florence, known as **the Lady of the Lamp** (1820–1910) Hospital reformer, born in Florence, Italy. After the Battle of Alma (1854) she led a party of 38 nurses to organize a nursing department at Scutari, where she soon had 10 000 under her care. She was later involved in army sanitary reform, the improvement of nursing, and public health in India. >> Crimean War

nightingale Either of two species of thrush of the genus *Luscinia*, native to Europe, Asia, and N Africa; mid-brown with paler breast; male renowned for its song; often sings at night. (Family: Turdidae.) >> thrush (bird)

nightjar A nocturnal bird of the widespread family Caprimulgidae (c.70 species); mottled brown with short bill. >> frogmouth; oilbird

Night of the Long Knives The event which took place in Germany (29–30 Jun 1934) when the SS, on Hitler's orders, murdered Röhm and some 150 other leaders of the Sturmabteilung (SA 'storm troopers'). It has been estimated that up to 1000 of Hitler's political rivals were killed. >> Brownshirts; Hitler; Röhm, Ernst

nightshade >> **deadly nightshade; woody nightshade**

nihilism (Lat, literally 'nothing-ism') A term invented by Turgenev in connection with his character, the revolutionary Bazarov, in *Fathers and Sons*, and later applied to other members of the Russian radical intelligentsia. It popularly denotes the disillusioned rejection of conventional moral values and institutions. >> Turgenev

Niigata [**nee**gata] 37°58N 139°02E, pop (1995e) 485 000. Port in N Honshu, Japan; airport; railway; three universities. >> Honshu

Nijinska, Bronislava [ni**zhin**ska] (1891–1972) Ballet dancer and choreographer, born in Minsk, Belarus, the sister of Vaslav Nijinsky. She danced with the Diaghilev company in Paris and London (1909–14), then joined Diaghilev in 1921 as principal choreographer. After 1938 she lived and worked mainly in the USA. >> ballet; choreography; Diaghilev; Nijinsky

Nijinsky, Vaslav [ni**zhin**skee] (1890–1950) Dancer, born in Kiev, Ukraine, brother of Bronislava Nijinska. Diaghilev encouraged his choreography, which foreshadowed the development of modern ballet. In 1913, his *Le sacre du printemps* (The Rite of Spring) was regarded as outrageous in its subversion of ballet and its use of Stravinsky's rhythmically complex score. >> ballet; choreography; Diaghilev

Nijmegen or **Nimeguen** [**niy**muhkhn, **niy**maygn], Ger **Nimwegen**, ancient **Noviomagus** 51°50N 5°52E, pop (1995e) 149 000. City in E Netherlands; on the R Waal, Roman fort, AD 69; former residence of the Carlovingian kings; member of the Hanseatic League; railway; university (1923). >> Hanseatic League; Netherlands, The ℹ

Nijo-jo Castle [nijohjoh] A stronghold built in 1603 in Kyoto, Japan, by Tokugawa Ieyasu. The complex is set in fine landscaped gardens and surrounded by a moat. >> castle; Kyoto

Nike [**niy**kee, **nee**kay] The Greek goddess of Victory, either in war or in an athletic contest. She is the frequent subject of sculpture, often shown as a winged figure. The Roman equivalent was Victoria.

Nile, Battle of the >> **Aboukir Bay, Battle of**

Nile, River [niyl], Arabic **Nahr en-Nil** River in E and NE Africa; longest river in the world; length from its most remote headstream (Luvironza R), 6695 km/4160 mi; Victoria Nile flows N through L Kyoga into NE end of L Albert; Albert Nile flows N through NW Uganda, becoming known as the White Nile at the Sudanese frontier; joined by the Blue Nile at Khartoum, to become the Nile proper, c.3000 km/1900 mi from its delta on the Mediterranean Sea; opens out into a broad delta N of Cairo, 250 km/155 mi E–W and 160 km/100 mi N–S; flows through two mouths (Rosetta and Damietta), both c.240 km/150 mi long; Egypt's population and cultivated land almost entirely along the floodplain; European discovery of Blue Nile's source made by James Bruce, 1768–73. >> Albert / Blue / Victoria / White Nile; Aswan; Bruce, James; Egypt ℹ; Speke

nilgai [**nil**giy] An Indian spiral-horned antelope (*Boselaphus tragocamelus*), the largest Indian antelope; male bluish with short slightly curved horns, tuft of dark hairs on throat; female brown without horns; also known as **blue bull** or **bluebuck**. >> antelope

Nilgiri Hills [**neel**giree] Hills linking the Eastern Ghats with the Western Ghats, Tamil Nadu state, S India; highest point, Doda Betta (2636 m/8648 ft). >> Ghats

nimbostratus clouds [**nim**bohstratuhs] Dark-grey, rain-producing clouds of the stratus family. They are found at relatively low layers of the atmosphere, c.1000–3000 m/3000–9000 ft. Cloud symbol: Ns. >> cloud ℹ; nimbus clouds; stratus clouds

nimbus Another word for the halo, circular or square, which surrounds the heads of sacred persons in much religious art. It is common in Roman art, and was taken over by the early Christians.

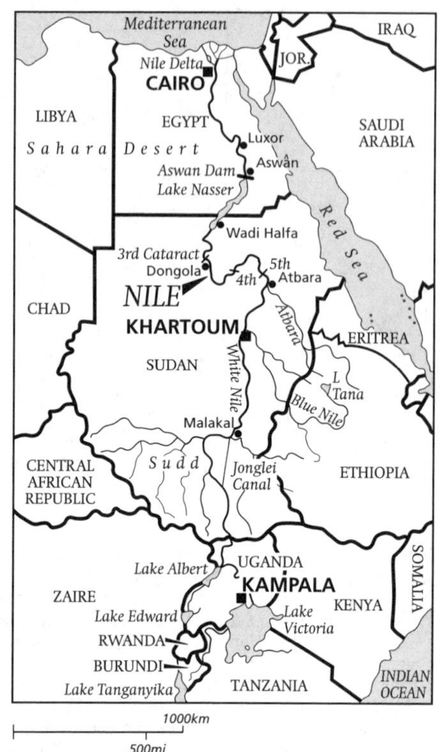

nimbus clouds Clouds which produce rain or snow. For example, cumulonimbus clouds form from convectional cooling and are associated with thunderstorms, while nimbostratus clouds give more or less continuous rain. >> cloud ℹ

Nîmes [neem], ancient **Nismes** or **Nemausus** 43°50N 4°23E, pop (1995e) 132 000. Ancient town in S France; principal city of Roman Gaul; Protestant stronghold in 16th-c; airport; railway; bishopric; cathedral (11th-c); centre of silk industry (cloth 'de Nîmes', name later contracted to 'denim'); Roman buildings and monuments. >> Gard, Pont du; Gaul

Nimitz, Chester W(illiam) [**nim**its] (1885–1966) US admiral, born in Fredericksburg, TX. In World War 2 he commanded the US Pacific Fleet, his conduct of naval operations being a major factor in the defeat of Japan. >> World War 2

Nimoy, Leonard [**ni**moy] (1931–) Actor, director, and producer, born in Boston, MA. He came to be identified with the half-Vulcan/half-human character of Spock in the *Star Trek* series (1966–9). When the series was reprised as feature films (1979–91), he produced the third and fourth instalments, and scripted the fourth. His work as a director includes *Three Men and a Baby* (1987) and *Holy Matrimony* (1994).

Nimrod In the Table of Nations (*Gen* 10), purportedly the son of Cush and great-grandson of Noah. He was a legendary warrior and hunter, allegedly one of the first to rule over a great empire after the Flood. >> Flood, the

Nin, Anaïs [neen, **an**aees] (1903–77) Novelist and short-story writer, born in Neuilly, France. Her early work includes novels and short stories, but her reputation as an artist and seminal figure in the new feminism of the 1970s rests on her *Journals* (1966–83). >> feminism

ninety-five theses A series of points of academic debate with the pope, posted by Martin Luther on the church door at Wittenberg in 1517. They attacked many practices of the Church, including indulgences and papal powers. This act is generally regarded as initiating the Protestant Reformation. >> indulgences; Luther; Reformation

Nineveh [**nin**evuh] One of the most important cities of ancient Assyria, located E of the Tigris, and the site of royal residences from c.11th-c BC. It was at its height in the 8th–7th-c BC under Sennacherib, but fell in 612 BC to the Medes and Persians. >> Assyria

Ningbo or **Ning-po** [ningboh] 29°54N 121°33E, pop (1995e) 1 225 000. Port city in E China; traditional outlet for silk and porcelain; designated a special economic zone; railway. >> China ℹ

ninjutsu An armed Japanese martial art, whose origins are obscure because of the secrecy surrounding the *Ninja*, who were assassins. In the 1980s it became popular as a cult in the cinema and video world. >> martial arts

Niño, El >> **El Niño**

Niobe [**niy**ohbee] In Greek mythology, the daughter of Tantalus and the wife of Amphion. She had twelve children (or more) and said she was better than any mother, including Leto. This provoked Leto's children, Apollo and Artemis, who killed her children, and turned the weeping Niobe into a weeping rock on Mt Sipylos.

Nirvana [neer**vah**na] In Buddhism, the attainment of supreme bliss, tranquillity, and purity, when the fires of desire are extinguished. >> Buddhism

Niš or **Nish** [neesh], ancient **Naisus** 43°20N 21°54E, pop (1995e) 178 000. Industrial town in SEC Serbia, on R Nišava; occupied by Bulgaria until 1918; airfield; railway; university (1965). >> Serbia; Yugoslavia ℹ

nit An egg laid by a louse of the order Phthiraptera, especially used of eggs of the human head and body lice. >> louse

Niterói [neete**roy**] 22°54S 43°06W, pop (1995e) 522 000. Port in SE Brazil, opposite Rio de Janeiro; founded 1573; former state capital; connected to Rio by a bridge, length 14 km/9 mi; railway; university (1960). >> Brazil ℹ; Rio de Janeiro

nitinol An elastic type of metal wire containing nickel and titanium.

nitrate A salt of nitric acid, containing the NO_3^- ion. Potassium and sodium nitrates occur in nature (*saltpetre* or *Chile saltpetre*), and are used in food preservation, fertilizers, and explosives. >> nitric acid; nitrite; nitro-; salt

nitre [**niy**ter] >> **potassium**

nitric acid HNO_3, melting point −42°C. A strong, oxidizing acid, made commercially by the oxidation of ammonia. It is important in the manufacture of agricultural chemicals and explosives. >> acid; ammonia

nitrite A salt of nitrous acid (HNO_2), containing the ion NO_2^-. Nitrites are the most effective means of reducing the growth of the bacteria causing botulism. >> botulism; nitrate; nitro-; salt

nitro- The name for the group $-NO_2$, isomeric with the nitrite group, but bonded through nitrogen. Most organic nitro-compounds are explosive, such as trinitrotoluene (TNT). >> explosives; nitrite; nitroglycerine

nitrocellulose A chemical compound formed by the action of nitric acid on cellulose; first made in 1845. Its explosive properties proved unmanageable until it was turned into the form known as **gun-cotton**. Some forms of cellulose nitrate, less explosive but still highly inflammable, were for many years used in plastics and as a film base. >> cellulose; explosives; nitroglycerine

nitrogen N, element 7, boiling point −196°C. In the form of diatomic molecules (N_2), it is the most abundant gas in the atmosphere, of which it makes up 78%. Conversion of nitrogen to water-soluble forms, such as ammonia and nitrates, is called **nitrogen fixation**. This can be carried out by soil bacteria, and industrially by the Haber process. The main uses of its compounds are in agricultural fertilizers and in explosives. >> chemical elements; gas 1; nitrogen cycle ℹ; RR1036

nitrogen cycle The dynamic system of changes in the nature of nitrogen-containing compounds circulating between the atmosphere, the soil, and living organisms. It includes the fixation of gaseous molecular nitrogen into nitrogenous compounds by micro-organisms, lightning, or other processes; the oxidation of ammonia to nitrite and nitrite to nitrate by aerobic organisms (*nitrification*); the decomposition of organic matter by putrefaction; and the eventual release of gaseous nitrogen by the reduction of nitrates and nitrites, typically by anaerobic micro-organisms (*denitrification*). >> aerobe; nitrogen; *see illustration on p. 612*

nitroglycerine An explosive liquid made by the action of nitric acid (mixed with sulphuric acid) on glycerol. At first considered impossibly dangerous, from 1867 Nobel made its use more general by mixing it with moderators. It is a constituent of several mixed explosives (eg gelignite). >> explosives; glycerol; nitric acid; Nobel

nitrous oxide Boiling point −88°C. Dinitrogen oxide, N_2O, isoelectronic with carbon dioxide; also called **laughing gas**. It has a slightly sweet odour, and is used as a general anaesthetic for short periods, especially in dentistry. >> anaesthetics, general; nitrogen; oxide

Niue [**nyoo**ay] 19°02S 169°55W; pop (1995e) 2100; area 259 sq km/100 sq mi. Coral island in the S Pacific Ocean, 2140 km/1330 mi NE of New Zealand; main settlement, Alofi; timezone GMT +12; chief religion, Christianity; official language, English; New Zealand currency used; mainly coral, with a flat, rolling interior and porous soils; highest point, 70 m/230 ft; subtropical and damp climate; visited by Captain Cook, 1774; European missionaries in mid-19th-c; British protectorate, 1900; annexed to New Zealand, 1901; since 1974, internal self-government in free association with New Zealand, which still maintains responsibility for defence and foreign affairs; governed by a Legislative Assembly, headed by a premier; mainly agricultural economy. >> Cook, James; New Zealand ℹ; Pacific Ocean

Niven, David, popular name of **James David Graham Nevins** (1909–83) Film actor, born in Kirriemuir, Angus. He became established in urbane romantic roles with an English style, his films including *Around the World in 80 Days* (1956), *Separate Tables* (1958, Oscar), *The Guns of Navarone* (1961), and *55 Days at Peking* (1963).

Nixon, Richard M(ilhous) (1913–94) US statesman and 37th president (1969–74), born in Yorba Linda, CA. He lost the 1960 election to Kennedy, but won in 1968, and was re-elected in 1972. He resigned in 1974 under the threat of impeachment after several leading members of his government had been found guilty of involvement in the Watergate affair, but was given a full pardon by President Ford. >> Republican Party; Watergate

Nizhni Novgorod [**nizh**nee **nov**gorod], formerly **Gorky** (1929–91) 56°20N 44°00E, pop (1995e) 1 452 000. River-port in E European Russia; founded as a frontier post, 1221; famous for its annual trade fairs (1817–1930); earlier name in honour of Maxim Gorky; airport; railway; university (1918). >> Russia ℹ

Nkomo, Joshua (Mqabuko Nyongolo) [**nkoh**moh] (1917–) Zimbabwean statesman, born in Semokwe, Zimbabwe. President of the Zimbabwe African People's Union (ZAPU), in 1976 he formed the Popular Front with

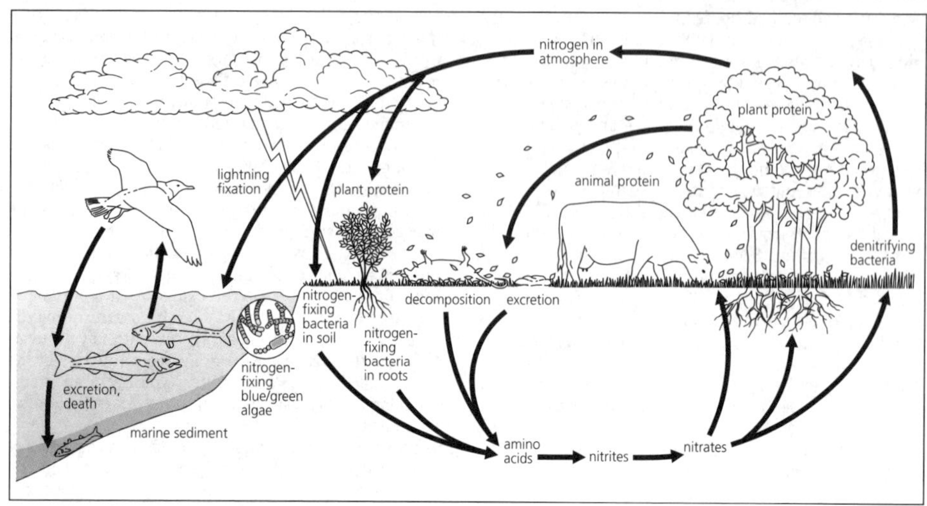

Nitrogen cycle

Robert Mugabe to press for black majority rule in an independent Zimbabwe, and was given a Cabinet post in the Mugabe government in 1980. However, tension between his party and Mugabe's led to his dismissal in 1982. >> Mugabe; Zimbabwe i

Nkrumah, Kwame [**nkroo**ma] (1909–72) Ghanaian statesman, prime minister (1957–60), and president (1960–6), born in Nkroful, Ghana. Called the 'Gandhi of Africa', he was a significant leader both of the movement against white domination and of Pan-African feeling. Economic reforms led to political opposition and the formation of a one-party state in 1964. His regime was overthrown by a military coup during his absence in China. >> Ghana i

Noah [**noh**uh] Biblical character, depicted as the son of Lamech; a 'righteous man' who was given divine instruction to build an ark in which he, his immediate family, and a selection of animals were saved from a widespread flood over the Earth (*Gen* 6–9). Noah's sons (Japheth, Ham, and Shem) are depicted as the ancestors of all the nations on Earth. >> Flood, the; Genesis, Book of; Gilgamesh

Nobel, Alfred Bernhard [noh**bel**] (1833–96) Inventor and manufacturer, born in Stockholm. He discovered how to make a safe and manageable explosive (dynamite). >> explosives; Nobel Prizes

Nobel Prizes [noh**bel**] Prizes awarded each year from the income of a trust fund established by the will of Alfred Nobel to those who, in the opinion of the judges, have contributed most in the fields of physics, chemistry, physiology or medicine, literature, and peace. The first prizes were awarded in 1901. A sixth prize, for economics, was established by the Swedish National Bank in 1968, and awarded for the first time in 1969. >> Nobel; RR1041

Nobile, Umberto [**noh**bilay] (1885–1978) Engineer and aviator, born in Lauro. He built the airships *Norge* and *Italia*, but was wrecked in *Italia* when returning from the North Pole (1928). >> airship; Amundsen

noble gases The final or zeroth group of the periodic table; also called the **rare** or **inert gases**. They are all gases at normal temperatures, and were called 'noble' because they were long thought to form no chemical compounds. >> argon; gas 1; helium; krypton; neon; radon; xenon

noble metals Metals which are intrinsically unreactive and not readily subject to corrosion. Gold, silver, and the 'platinum metals' are the best examples. Metals such as aluminium and chromium, whose corrosion resistance is due to an adhering coat of oxide, are called *passive*. >> corrosion; metal

Noctiluca [nokti**loo**ka] An unusually large, single-celled marine organism; a dinoflagellate, moving by means of whip-like flagella; bioluminescent, producing flashes of light when disturbed. (Class: Dinophyceae.) >> flagellum

noctilucent cloud Very high altitude (80 km/50 mi) dusty clouds visible as a rippled or veiled structure after sunset from about May to August in the N hemisphere. They consist of water ice frozen onto a dust core. >> cloud i

noctuid moth [**nok**tyooid] Any of a large family, the Noctuidae, of typically drab, nocturnal moths (Order: Lepidoptera); c.21 000 species, many of which cause serious damage to crops; also known as the **owlet moth**. >> moth

nocturne A piece of music, usually in a meditative, languid style. The title has been used for piano pieces by John Field (its inventor), Chopin, and Fauré, and for orchestral pieces by Mendelssohn and Debussy. >> Field, John

noddy >> **tern**

Noel-Baker (of the City of Derby), Philip (John) Noel-Baker, Baron (1889–1982) British Labour statesman, born in London. He was secretary of state for air (1946–7), and of Commonwealth Relations (1947–50), and minister of fuel and power (1950–1). He was awarded the Nobel Peace Prize in 1959. >> Labour Party

Noether, (Amalie) Emmy [**noe**ter] (1882–1935) Mathematician, born in Erlangen, Germany. She emigrated to the USA in 1933. One of the leading figures in the development of abstract algebra, the theory of **Noetherian rings** has been an important subject of later research. >> algebra

Noh Classical theatre of Japan in which imitation, gesture, dance, mask-work, costume, song, and music are fused in a concise stage art. Five schools of Noh exist, and most of the plays they perform were written before 1600. >> Japan i

Nolan, Sir Sidney (Robert) (1917–92) Painter, born in Melbourne, Victoria, Australia. He made his name with a series of 'Ned Kelly' paintings, begun in 1946, following this with an 'explorer' series. He was also a theatrical designer and book illustrator. >> Kelly, Ned

Nolde, Emil [**nol**duh], pseudonym of **Emil Hansen** (1867–1956) Artist, born in Nolde. He was one of the most important Expressionist painters, his powerful style being summed up by the phrase 'blood and soil'. >> *Brücke, die*; Expressionism

Nollekens, Joseph [**nol**ekenz] (1737–1823) Neoclassical sculptor, born in London. He executed likenesses of most of his famous contemporaries, such as Goldsmith, Johnson, Fox, Pitt, and George III. >> Neoclassicism (art and architecture)

nomadism A way of life characterized by moving from one place to another, with no fixed residence. Most nomadic people (eg the Bedouin, the Kirghiz) are either hunter-gatherers or pastoralists. Some are described as **semi-nomadic** (eg the Fulani), as they remain settled in one area for a span of time and cultivate crops. As various governments have restricted movements of people, nomadism has declined in recent decades. >> Bedouin; hunter-gatherers; pastoralism

nominalism In metaphysics, the view that only individual things exist in the full sense. Universals and properties (eg 'redness') have no independent reality, but are just names. >> metaphysics

non-aligned movement A movement of states which espoused the position of not taking sides in the major division within world politics between the USA and USSR. A number of recently de-colonized countries have favoured non-alignment as a mark of their independence. A formal Non-Aligned Movement, begun in 1961, holds regular conferences; there were 113 members in the mid-1990s.

Nonconformists Originally, those Protestants in England and Wales in the 17th-c who dissented from the principles of the Church of England. It now generally refers to Christians who refuse to conform to the doctrine and practice of an established or national Church. >> Christianity; Dissenters

Non-Co-operation Movement An unsuccessful nationalist campaign (1919–22) led by Gandhi and Congress to force the British to grant Indian independence. The movement involved the boycott of Government institutions and foreign goods, and was abandoned when the protest became violent. >> Gandhi

non-Euclidian geometries >> **geometries, non-Euclidian**

nonjurors Those who refused to swear an oath of loyalty to William III and Mary II in 1689, since to do so would infringe the divine right of monarchical succession. Most were clerics, who were then deprived of their offices. >> William III

Nono, Luigi [**noh**noh] (1924–90) Composer, born in Venice, Italy. He was a leading composer of electronic, aleatory, and serial music. >> electronic music; serialism

Non-Proliferation Treaty (NPT) A treaty signed in 1968 by the USA, Soviet Union, UK, and an open-ended list of over 100 other countries. It seeks to limit the spread of nuclear weapons, and for states to pursue only peaceful uses of nuclear energy. >> nuclear weapons

non-renewable resources Resources (ie objects of material or economic use to society, such as minerals, timber, and fish) which have evolved or formed over such long time periods that their exploitation is not sustainable. Examples include fossil fuel deposits (coal, oil, gas) and mineral deposits (iron, gold). >> fossil fuel; recycling; renewable resources

nonsense verse Verse which is written in defiance of sense and logic to satisfy the ear and the spirit rather than the intelligence. Edward Lear (1812–88) wrote famous examples, as did Lewis Carroll in the two *Alice* books. >> Carroll; Lear, Edward

non-sporting dog A category of domestic dog; name used for breeds bred as pets/companions (except very small such breeds, which are called **toy dogs**); includes dogs formerly bred for sport (eg bulldog, some poodles); sometimes includes **working dogs** (eg collies). >> bulldog; collie; dog; Pekinese; Pomeranian; poodle; sporting dog

non-verbal communication (NVC) Those forms of interpersonal communication beyond the spoken or written word; often referred to as body language. The messages communicated may be deliberate (eg winking or bowing), or unintentional (eg blushing or shivering).

Noonuccal, Oodgeroo [nu**nuh**kl, **u**juhroo], originally **Kath(leen Jean Mary) Walker** (1920–93) Poet and Aboriginal rights activist, born in Brisbane, Queensland, Australia. She was the first Aboriginal writer to be published in English, with her collection of poems *We are Going* (1964). >> Aborigines

Nootka An American Indian group of the Northwest Pacific Coast. They were famous as whalers, and became wealthy during the late 18th-c through the fur trade. >> Northwest Coast Indians

Norbertines >> **Premonstratensians**

Nordenskjöld, Nils (Adolf Erik), Baron [**naw(r)**denshoel] (1832–1901) Arctic navigator, born in Helsinki. He accomplished (1878–9) the navigation of the Northeast Passage, from the Atlantic to the Pacific along the N coast of Asia. >> Northeast Passage

Nördliche Kalkalpen [**nerd**likhuh kal**kal**pen] Mountain range of the E Alps in C Austria, rising to 2995 m/9826 ft at Hoher Dachstein. >> Alps

Norfolk (UK) [**naw(r)**fuhk] pop (1995e) 774 000; area 5368 sq km/2073 sq mi. County in E England; low-lying, with fens in W; Norfolk Broads in E; county town, Norwich; offshore natural gas; Sandringham royal residence, Shrine of Our Lady of Walsingham. >> Norwich

Norfolk (USA) [**naw**fuhk] 36°51N 76°17W, pop (1995e) 282 000. Seaport and independent city, SE Virginia, USA, on the Elizabeth R; settled, 1682; city status, 1845; centre of fighting in the American Revolution and the Civil War; largest city in the state; airfield; railway; Norfolk State College (1935); headquarters of the US Atlantic Fleet, largest naval base in the world. >> Virginia

Norfolk Island [**naw(r)**fuhk] 29°04S 167°57E; pop (1995e) 2110; area 35 sq km/13 sq mi; length 8 km/5 mi. Fertile, hilly island in the W Pacific Ocean, 1 488 km/925 mi NE of Sydney, Australia; a British penal settlement in 1788–1806 and 1826–55; an Australian external territory since 1913; English and Tahitian spoken. >> Australia [i]; Pacific Ocean

Noriega, Manuel (Antonio) [nori**ay**ga] (1939–) Panamanian soldier and politician, born in Panama City. He became the ruling force behind the Panamanian presidents (1983–9). Alleging his involvement in drug trafficking, the US authorities ordered his arrest in 1989: 13 000 US troops invaded Panama to support the 12 000 already there. He surrendered in January 1990, and was taken to the USA for trial. Found guilty in 1992, he was sentenced to 40 years imprisonment.

Norma (Lat 'level') A small, faint S hemisphere constellation. >> constellation; RR968

Norman, Barry (Leslie) (1933–) British writer and television film critic. In 1973 he joined BBC television as host of *Film '73*, then wrote and presented the show (1973–81, 1983–97) until joining Sky television in 1998. Other work includes the series *The Hollywood Greats* (1977–9, 1984–5) and *Talking Pictures* (1988).

Norman, Greg(ory John), nickname **the Great White**

Shark (1955–) Golfer, born in Mount Isa, Queensland, Australia. Rated the world's top player in 1986, he has won the Australian Open (1980, 1985, 1987), the (British) Open (1986, 1993), and the World Match Play Championship (1986). >> golf

Norman, Jessye (1945–) Soprano, born in Augusta, GA. She made her operatic debut in *Tannhaüser* at Berlin in 1969, and in *Aïda* at both La Scala and Covent Garden in 1972. She has since toured widely at music festivals and concerts.

Norman Conquest A fundamental watershed in English political and social history. It not only began the rule of a dynasty of Norman kings (1066–1154), but entailed the virtual replacement of the Anglo-Saxon nobility by Normans, Bretons, and Flemings, many of whom retained lands in N France. >> Angevins; Domesday Book; Hastings, Battle of; William I (of England)

Normandy, Fr **Normandie** Former duchy and province in NW France; leading state in Middle Ages; William Duke of Normandy conquered England in 1066; focus of English–French dispute in 12th–14th-c, until became part of France in 1449; scene of Allied invasion, 1944. >> Normandy Campaign; William I

Normandy Campaign (1944) A World War 2 campaign which began on D-Day (6 Jun 1944). Allied forces under the command of General Eisenhower began the liberation of W Europe from Germany by landing on the Normandy coast. Heavy fighting ensued for three weeks before Allied troops captured Cherbourg (27 Jun). >> D-Day; Eisenhower; World War 2

Normans By the early 11th-c, a name (derived from 'Northmen', ie Vikings) applied to all the people inhabiting Normandy, a duchy (and later province) in N France. They completed the conquest and aristocratic colonization of England and a large part of Wales, established a kingdom in S Italy and Sicily, and founded the Norman principality of Antioch. >> Norman Conquest; Rollo

norm-referenced test A test which compares candidates with each other, usually spreading marks over a normal distribution, with most in the middle and few at each extreme. Most conventional tests which give percentages of A to E grades are of this kind.

Norns In Norse mythology, the equivalent of the Fates, three sisters who sit under the tree Yggdrasil and spin the web of Destiny. Their names are Urd (who knows the past), Verlandi (the present), and Skuld (the future). >> Odin; Parcae

North, Frederick, 8th Baron North (1732–92) British statesman and prime minister (1770–82), born in London. He was widely criticized both for failing to avert the Declaration of Independence by the North American colonies (1776) and for failing to defeat them in the subsequent war (1776–83). >> American Revolution

North, Oliver (1943–) US soldier, born in San Antonio, TX. Appointed a deputy-director of the National Security Council by President Reagan in 1981, he played a key role in a series of controversial military and security actions. Implicated in the Irangate scandal, he was forced to resign in 1986. >> Iran–Contra scandal

North, Sir Thomas (?1535–?1601) English translator, born in London. He is known for his translation of Plutarch's *Lives of the noble Grecians and Romans* (1579), which Shakespeare used in many of his plays. >> Plutarch; Shakespeare ℹ

North America Third largest continent, extending 9600 km/6000 mi from 70°30N to 15°N; area c.24 million sq km/9¼ million sq mi; separated from Asia by the Bering Strait; includes Canada, USA, and Mexico; numerous islands, including Baffin I, Newfoundland, and the West Indies; ranges include the Rocky Mts, Alaska Range (including Mt McKinley, highest point), and Appalachian Mts; major lake system, the Great Lakes; major rivers include the Mississippi, Missouri, Rio Grande, and St Lawrence. >> Canada ℹ; Mexico ℹ; United States of America ℹ

North American Free Trade Agreement (NAFTA) An association of the USA, Canada, and Mexico, established in 1992 to create a free-trade area covering all of North America, eliminating over a period of time customs duties and other restrictions; Chile likely to join in due course. Finally ratified in late 1993, the bloc is now the second largest free-trade area in the world, with c.360 million customers. >> free trade; Free Trade Agreement

Northampton 52°14N 0°54W, pop (1995e) 190 000. County town in Northamptonshire, C England; on R Nene; originally a Saxon town; destroyed by fire in 1675; designated a 'new town' in 1968; railway; football league team, Northampton Town (Cobblers). >> new town; Northamptonshire

Northamptonshire pop (1995e) 601 000; area 2367 sq km/914 sq mi. Agricultural county in C England; county town, Northampton. >> England ℹ; Northampton

North Atlantic Treaty Organization >> **NATO**

North Carolina pop (1995e) 7 176 000; area 136 407 sq km/52 669 sq mi. State in SE USA; the 'Tar Heel State' or 'Old North State'; unsuccessful settlement on Roanoke I in the 1580s; part of the Carolina grant given by Charles II, 1663; named North Carolina, 1691; a royal province, 1729; location of Mecklenburg Declaration of Independence (1775); twelfth of the original 13 states to ratify the Constitution, 1789; withdrew from the Union, 1861; slavery abolished, 1865; re-admitted to the Union, 1868; highest point Mt Mitchell (2037 m/6683 ft); chain of coastal islands with constantly shifting sand dunes, enclosing several lagoons; low land gives way to the rolling hills of the Piedmont; fast-flowing rivers provide hydroelectric power for manufacturing industries; in the W the Blue Ridge and Great Smoky Mts; capital, Raleigh; major tourist area; provides 40% of all US tobacco; industrial growth greatest of any Southern state since World War 2. >> Raleigh (North Carolina); United States of America ℹ; RR994

Northcliffe, Lord >> **Harmsworth, Alfred**

North Dakota [da**koh**ta] pop (1995e) 631 000; area 183 111 sq km/70 702 sq mi. State in NC USA; 'Sioux State', 'Flickertail State'; became part of USA in the Louisiana Purchase, 1803; included in Dakota Territory, 1861; separated from South Dakota to become the 39th state admitted to the Union, 1889; sparsely populated; highest point, White Butte (1069 m/3507 ft); semi-arid conditions in the W; E region a flat, fertile plain, covered almost entirely by crops, chiefly spring wheat, barley, sunflowers, and flaxseed (nation's leading producer of all these crops); capital, Bismarck; major cattle state; oil (NW) and lignite coal (W); several Indian reservations. >> Bismarck (USA); Louisiana Purchase; United States of America ℹ; RR994

North Downs Way Long-distance footpath in S England; length 227 km/141 mi; follows the crest of the North Downs from Farnham to Dover. >> Downs

Northeast Passage A shipping route through the S Arctic Ocean along the N coast of Europe and Asia, connecting the Atlantic and Pacific Oceans. It was not successfully travelled until 1878–9.

Northern Cape One of the nine new provinces established by the South African constitution of 1994, in W South Africa; formerly part of Cape Provinces; largely semi-arid; NW frontier with Namibia formed by the Orange R; largest province, smallest population; pop (1996e) 746 000; area 363 389 sq km/140 268 sq mi; capital, Kimberley; chief languages, Afrikaans (65%),

Setswana (22%), Xhosa; Kalahari-Gemsbok National Park. >> Cape Provinces; South Africa

Northern Ireland, also **Ulster** pop (1995e) 1 648 000; area 14 120 sq km/5450 sq mi (including 663 sq km/256 sq mi of inland water). Constituent division of the United Kingdom of Great Britain and Northern Ireland; occupies the NE part of Ireland, centred on Lough Neagh; Mourne Mts in the SE; capital, Belfast; timezone GMT; chief religions, Roman Catholicism (28%), Presbyterianism (23%), Church of Ireland (19%); separate parliament established in 1920, with a 52-member House of Commons and a 26-member Senate; Protestant majority in the population, generally supporting political union with Great Britain; many of the Roman Catholic minority look for union with the Republic of Ireland; violent conflict between the communities broke out in 1969, leading to the establishment of a British army peace-keeping force; sectarian murders and bombings continued both within and outside the province; as a result of the disturbances, parliament was abolished in 1972; powers are now vested in the UK Secretary of State for Northern Ireland; formation of a 78-member Assembly, 1973; replaced by a Constitutional Convention, 1975; Assembly re-formed in 1982, but Nationalist members did not take their seats; under the 1985 Anglo-Irish agreement, the Republic of Ireland was given a consultative role in the government of Northern Ireland; all Northern Ireland MPs in the British parliament resigned in protest, 1986; the agreement continued to attract controversy in subsequent years; fresh talks between the main parties and the Irish government, 1992; IRA and loyalist ceasefires, 1994; joint Irish/British Framework Document (1995), aimed at providing a basis for all-party talks; proposals include new political bodies with province-wide executive responsibilities (notably, a unicameral Assembly elected by proportional representation), new North-South institutions, and enhanced East-West structures; IRA call off ceasefire (Feb 1996), and commence new campaign, with bombings on UK mainland (notably London and Manchester); start of all-party talks (but with Sinn Féin excluded), 1996; Good Friday agreement, 1998, proposed (i) 108-member Northern Ireland Assembly elected by proportional representation, run by a 12-member executive committee; (ii) North-South Ministerial Council; (iii) amendment to Ireland's constitution on Irish claims to Northern Ireland; (iv) replacement of UK Government of Ireland Act; (v) Council of the Isles, including members from north and south, and from Scottish and Welsh assemblies; (vi) the whole to be put to the people in a referendum (ratified in May 1998). >> Anglo-Irish Agreement; Belfast; Downing Street declaration; INLA; IRA; Ireland (republic) ℹ; Stormont; RR998

northern lights >> **aurora**

Northern Province One of the nine new provinces established by the South African constitution of 1994, in N South Africa; Limpopo R to the N; formerly part of Transvaal, and includes former homelands of Lebowa and Gazankulu; capital, Pietersburg; pop (1996e) 4 128 000; area 119 606 sq km/46 168 sq mi; chief language, Pedi (56%), Shangaan (22%), Venda; largely bushveld, with some mountains and forests; lowest per capita income in the country. >> South Africa; Transvaal

Northern Territory pop (1995e) 186 000; area 1 346 200 sq km/520 000 sq mi. One of the two mainland territories of Australia, covering about a sixth of the continent; part of New South Wales, 1824; annexed by South Australia, 1863; transferred to Federal Government control, 1911; achieved self-government, 1978; mainly within the tropics; land rises S to the Macdonnell Ranges, reaching 1524 m/5000 ft at Mt Liebig; good pasture land in the

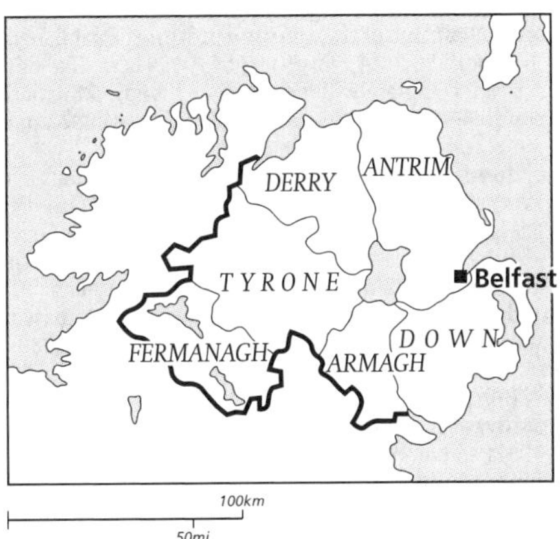

N (Barkly Tableland), largely flat and arid in the S (Simpson Desert); Ayers Rock in Uluru national park; capital and chief port, Darwin; many Aboriginal settlements. >> Aborigines; Australia ℹ; Ayers Rock; Darwin

Northern War >> **Great Northern War**

North German Confederation The state system and constitutional arrangement created in 1866 by Bismarck, chancellor of Prussia, following the Prussian defeat of Austria and the dissolution of the German Confederation. It was dissolved with the creation of the German Empire in 1871. >> Bismarck; Prussia

northing A grid line which runs W to E on a map, but which is numbered northwards. It is related to the **easting**, a grid line which runs N to S, and which is numbered eastwards. The northing number associated with a place is always given after the number of the easting when citing a grid reference. >> grid reference; National Grid Reference System

North Island >> **New Zealand**

North Korea >> **Korea, North** ℹ

North Pole >> **Poles**

North Sea area 520 000 sq km/201 000 sq mi. Arm of the Atlantic Ocean between continent of Europe (E) and UK (W), from Shetland Is (N) to Straits of Dover (S); length c.950 km/600 mi; maximum width 650 km/400 mi; generally shallow, lying on wide continental shelf, with banks running across from Yorkshire coast (eg Dogger

Bank); important fishing grounds; extensive offshore oil and gas exploitation; some land reclamation in the Dutch polder area. >> Atlantic Ocean; North Sea Oil

North Sea oil Oil and gas deposits in the sedimentary rocks below the North Sea, first discovered in 1969 in Norwegian waters (the Ekofisk field) and in 1975 in the UK sector. Reserves are estimated at 12 thousand million barrels. >> North Sea; oil (earth sciences)

Northumberland pop (1995e) 309 000; area 5032 sq km/1943 sq mi. County in NE England; Pennines in the W; rises in the N to 755 m/2 477 ft at The Cheviot; Holy I and the Farne Is lie off the coast; Kielder Water (artificial lake, 1982); county town, Morpeth; many Roman remains, especially Hadrian's Wall; castles at Alnwick and Bamburgh. >> England ℹ; Morpeth

Northumberland, Dukes of >> **Percy**

Northumbria The largest kingdom of the Anglo-Saxon heptarchy. In the 7th-c it established a broad dominance in Britain both N and S of the Humber, while in the 8th-c the Northumbrian monasteries gained a European-wide reputation for sanctity and learning. The kingdom came to an end in 876. >> Anglo-Saxons; Edwin, St

North West One of the nine new provinces established by the South African constitution of 1994, in NW South Africa; completely land-locked; capital Mmabatho; pop (1996e) 3 043 000; area 118 710 sq km/45 822 sq mi; resort complex at Sun City. >> South Africa

Northwest Coast Indians North American Indians living along the Pacific coastline from Alaska to NW California. They consisted of a number of different groups, who were wealthy, hierarchical, and had highly developed artistic traditions. >> Haida; Kwakiutl; Nootka; Tlingit

North West Company A trading partnership based in Montreal and Fort William, Canada, from the 1780s to 1821. It merged into the Hudson's Bay Company in 1821. >> Hudson's Bay Company

Northwest Frontier pop (1995e) 16 293 000; area 74 521 sq km/28 765 sq mi. Federal province in Pakistan; bounded W and S by Afghanistan and N by India; linked to Afghanistan by the Khyber Pass; inhabited mainly by the Pathans, renowned for their warlike character; capital, Peshawar. >> Khyber Pass; Pakistan ℹ; Peshawar

Northwest Ordinance >> **Ordinance of 1787**

Northwest Passage A route through the S Arctic Ocean, N Canada, and along the N coast of Alaska. From the 16th-c attempts were made to find it, but not until 1903–6 was it first traversed by Amundsen. >> Amundsen; Franklin, John; Frobisher

Northwest Territories pop (1995e) 61 200; area 3 426 320 sq km/1 322 902 sq mi. Canadian territory consisting of the Arctic islands, the islands in Hudson and Ungava Bays, and the land N of 60°N, between Hudson Bay and the Yukon territory; sparsely populated, two-thirds Athapaskan-speaking peoples and Inuit; capital, Yellowknife (since 1967); formerly called Rupert's Land and North West Territory; entered Canadian federation, 1870; governed by a commissioner and a Legislative Assembly; Nunavut established in the E, 1999. >> Canada ℹ; Hudson's Bay Company; Nunavut; Yellowknife

North York Moors National park chiefly in North Yorkshire, England; area 1432 sq km/553 sq mi; established in 1952. >> Yorkshire, North

North Yorkshire >> **Yorkshire, North**

Norway, Norwegian **Norge**, official name **Kingdom of Norway**, Norwegian **Kongeriket Norge** pop (1995e) 4 345 000; area 323 895 sq km/125 023 sq mi. NW European kingdom, occupying the W part of the Scandinavian peninsula; capital, Oslo; timezone GMT +1; most of the population of Nordic descent; Lapp minority in far N; chief religion, Evangelical-Lutheran (95%); official language, Norwegian, in the varieties of Bokmål and Nynorsk; unit of currency, the krone of 100 øre; a mountainous country; Kjölen Mts form the N part of the boundary with Sweden; Jotunheimen range in SC Norway; much of the interior over 1500 m/5000 ft; numerous lakes, the largest being L Mjøsa (368 sq km/142 sq mi); irregular coastline with many small islands and long deep fjords; Arctic winter climate in the interior highlands, with snow, strong winds, and severe frosts; comparatively mild conditions on coast; rainfall heavy on W coast; a united kingdom achieved by St Olaf in the 11th-c, whose successor, Cnut, brought Norway under Danish rule; united with Sweden and Denmark, 1389; annexed by Sweden as a reward for assistance against Napoleon, 1814; growing nationalism resulted in independence, 1905; declared neutrality in both World Wars, but occupied by Germany 1940–5; a limited, hereditary monarchy; government led by a prime minister; parliament comprises an upper house and a lower house; economy based on the extraction and processing of raw materials, using plentiful hydroelectric power; oil and natural gas from North Sea fields; less than 3% of the land is under cultivation; area covered with productive forests was 21% in 1985. >> Canute; Lapland; Oslo; Vikings; RR1018 political leaders

Norway spruce The most common species of spruce (*Picea abies*) native to Europe and planted on a vast commercial scale. It is a source of timber, pitch, spruce beer, and, in Britain, Christmas trees. (Family: Pinaceae.) >> spruce

Norwegian >> **Scandinavian languages**

Norwegian Sea area 1 383 000 sq km/534 000 sq mi. N Atlantic sea bounded by NW coast of Norway and E coast of Iceland; generally ice-free. >> Atlantic Ocean

Nor-wester >> **Föhn / Foehn wind**

Norwich [**no**rich] 52°38N 1°18E, pop (1995e) 129 000. County town in Norfolk, E England; provincial centre for

the largely agricultural East Anglia; major textile centre in 16th-17th-c; railway; University of East Anglia (1964); cathedral (1096); football league team, Norwich City (Canaries). >> Norfolk (UK)

Norwich School A group of provincial English landscape painters, in oil and watercolour, working in Norwich 1803–34. >> Cotman; Crome; landscape painting

nose The protrusion from the front of the face above the mouth and below the eyes. Part of the respiratory tract, it consists of an external part (with a skeleton of bone and cartilage) and an inner cavity. The functions of the nasal cavity are olfaction (smell) and changing the nature of the inspired air. The rich vascular network also warms the air. Because of this network, the nose has a tendency to bleed profusely if it is hit. >> respiration; sinus

Nostradamus [nostra**dah**mus], Latin name of **Michel de Notredame** (1503–66) Astrologer, born in St Rémy, France. He became a doctor of medicine in 1529, and set himself up as a prophet c.1547. His *Centuries* of predictions in rhymed quatrains (1555–8), expressed generally in obscure and enigmatical terms, brought him a great reputation.

notebook A very compact form of personal computer which can be accommodated inside a briefcase. Even so, most notebooks offer the same facilities as a desk-top personal computer. >> laptop / personal computer; plasma screen

nothosaur [**no**thosaw(r)] A long-necked, marine reptile; flourished during the Triassic period, but extinct by the early Jurassic period; limbs well adapted for swimming. (Order: Sauropterygia. Suborder: Nothosauria.) >> Jurassic period; reptile; Triassic period

notochord [**noh**tohkaw(r)d] A rod-like structure which extends almost the entire length of the body in larvae and some adult chordates. It lies behind the gut but below the nerve cord, providing flexible support for the body. It is replaced by the vertebral column in most vertebrates. >> Chordata; vertebral column

Notre Dame (de Paris) [**no**truh **dam** duh pa**ree**] An early Gothic cathedral on the Ile de la Cité in Paris. It was commissioned by Maurice de Sully, Bishop of Paris, in 1159 and constructed over a period of two centuries (1163–1345). >> cathedral; Paris

Nottingham, Anglo-Saxon **Snotingaham** or **Notingeham** 52°58N 1°10W, pop (1995e) 288 000. City and (from 1998) unitary authority in Nottinghamshire, C England; on the R Trent; founded by the Danes; became a city in 1897; Civil War started here in 1642; railway; two universities (1948, 1992); castle (17th-c); football league teams, Nottingham Forest (Reds), Nottingham County (Magpies). >> Nottinghamshire

Nottinghamshire pop (1995e) 1 041 000; area 2164 sq km/836 sq mi. County in the R Trent basin of C England; Pennines in W, remains of Sherwood Forest in SW; county town, Nottingham (unitary authority from 1998). >> Dukeries, the; England ℹ; Nottingham; Robin Hood

Notungulata [notuhngyoo**lah**ta] A large order of extinct, South American, plant-eating mammals, known from the late Palaeocene to the Pleistocene epochs. >> herbivore; mammal ℹ; Palaeocene / Pleistocene epoch

Nouadhibou [nooadee**boo**], Fr **Port Etienne** 20°54N 17°00W, pop (1995e) 72 100. Mauritania's main seaport; linked by rail to the iron ore mines near Zouîrât; airport. >> Mauritania ℹ

Nouakchott [**nwak**shot] 18°09N 15°58W, pop (1995e) 481 000. Capital of Mauritania; founded on an important caravan route, 1960; airport. >> Mauritania ℹ

Nouméa [noo**may**a], formerly **Port de France** 22°16S 166°26E, pop (1995e) 73 400. Seaport capital of New Caledonia; capital, 1854; US air base in World War 2; airport; cathedral. >> New Caledonia

nouveau roman [noovoh rohmã] (Fr 'new novel') A type of novel written (and theorized) by French novelists of the 1950s in reaction against established fictional forms. >> Realism; Robbe-Grillet; Sarraute

nouvelle cuisine [noovel kwi**zeen**] A movement away from the elaborate food of classical cuisine to a simpler, more natural presentation. The approach began in the 1970s, and was given emphasis by the French chef Michel Guérard (1933–). The first consideration is the quality of the fresh produce, with the aim of achieving lightness by using less fat and no flour in sauces.

nouvelle vague [noovel vahg] (Fr 'new wave') The 'New Wave' group of young French film directors of the late 1950s and 1960s, who wished to discard many of the conventional formulae of the current cinema. They used the freedom of lightweight hand-held cameras outside the studio, with unconventional editing and sound.

nova In a binary star system near the end of its life, the phenomenon where one star becomes a giant, and its atmosphere spills over to its companion, a white dwarf. A nuclear explosion is triggered on the white dwarf, whose luminosity increases up to 10 000 times for a few months. >> binary star; white dwarf

Novak, Kim, originally **Marilyn Pauline Novak** (1933–) Film actress, born in Chicago, IL. She became a leading box-office attraction of the 1950s – perhaps the last of the 'sex goddesses' produced by the Hollywood star system. Her films include *The Man With The Golden Arm* (1955), *Pal Joey* (1957), *Vertigo* (1958), and *The Mirror Crack'd* (1980).

Novalis [noh**va**lis], pseudonym of **Friedrich Leopold von Hardenberg** (1772–1801) Romantic poet, born in Oberwiederstedt, Germany. Known as the 'prophet of Romanticism', he is best known for his *Geistliche Lieder* (1799, Sacred Songs) and *Hymnen an die Nacht* (1800, Hymns to the Night). >> Romanticism

Nova Scotia [**noh**va **skoh**sha] pop (1995e) 995 000; area 55 490 sq km/21 424 sq mi. Province in SE Canada; includes Cape Breton I to the NE, connected by causeway; capital, Halifax; deeply indented coastline, low hill ranges, many lakes and small rivers; probably first visited by Vikings and European fishermen; settled by the French as Acadia, 1604–5; mainland assigned to Britain in the Treaty of Utrecht, 1713, Cape Breton I remaining French until seized in 1758; many United Empire Loyalists settled here after the American Revolution; Cape Breton I a separate province from 1784, re-incorporated into Nova Scotia, 1820; joined the Canadian federation, 1867; governed by a lieutenant-governor and a House of Assembly. >> Acadia; American Revolution; Canada ℹ; Cape Breton Island; Halifax

Novaya Zemlya [**no**vaya zim**lya**] area 81 279 sq km/31 374 sq mi. Archipelago in the Arctic Ocean, between the Barents Sea (W) and Kara Sea (E), NW Russia; two large islands separated by a narrow strait; length, 960 km/596 mi; rises to heights above 1000 m/3000 ft; some settlement on W coast; formerly used for thermonuclear testing. >> Russia ℹ; Ural Mountains

novel A work of fiction, most often in prose. The term (literally meaning 'new' or 'news') came into general use in the 18th-c to describe that form of fiction which centred on the life of an individual, as in *Robinson Crusoe* and *Tom Jones*. The novel quickly became the dominant literary form in the West; and such writers as Dickens and George Eliot, Balzac and Zola, Dostoevsky and Tolstoy, helped create the moral and imaginative climate of their age. In the 20th-c the novel has been developed by (among others) Joyce, Proust, Virginia Woolf, and Nabokov. >> epic; Gothic novel; novella; short story

novella (Ital 'tale', 'news') Originally a short story, as in Boccaccio's *Decameron*. The term is now used to define (if somewhat precariously) a prose fiction which is longer than a short story but shorter than a novel. >> novel; short story

Novello, Ivor [noveloh], originally **David Ivor Davies** (1893–1951) Actor, composer, songwriter, and playwright, born in Cardiff. His most successful works were the 'Ruritanian' musical plays such as *The Dancing Years* (1939) and *King's Rhapsody* (1949).

Novgorod [nofgorod] 58°30N 31°20E, pop (1995e) 236 000. City in NW European Russia; on R Volkhov; one of the oldest cities in Russia, known in the 9th-c; badly damaged in World War 2; railway; centre of an important agricultural area; cathedral (1045–50). >> Russia ℹ

Novi Sad [novee sahd], Ger **Neusatz** 45°15N 19°51E, pop (1995e) 181 000. Commercial and industrial city in N Serbia; on R Danube; railway; university (1960); Petrovaradin castle; cathedral. >> Serbia; Yugoslavia ℹ

Novosibirsk [novosyibyeersk], formerly **Novonikolaevsk** (1903–25) 55°00N 83°05E, pop (1995e) 1 462 000. River port in S Siberian Russia, on the R Ob; founded, 1893; on the Trans-Siberian Railway; university (1959); leading economic centre of Siberia; Kuznetsk Basin coal and iron deposits nearby. >> Russia ℹ

NTSC (National Television Systems Commission), responsible for the coding system for colour television introduced in the USA in 1954. It has since then generally adopted throughout the Americas and Japan for all 525-line 60 Hz transmission. >> colour television ℹ; PAL; SECAM

Nu, U [noo] ('uncle'), originally **Thakin Nu** (1907–95) Burmese statesman and prime minister (1948–56, 1957–8, 1960–2), born in Wakema, Myanmar (Burma). The first prime minister of the independent Burmese Republic, he was overthrown by a military coup in 1962, and imprisoned, but released in 1966. >> Myanmar ℹ

Nubian Desert [nyoobian] area c.400 000 sq km/ 155 000 sq mi. Desert in NE Sudan; a sandstone plateau between the Red Sea and the R Nile. >> Sudan ℹ

Nubian monuments [nyoobian] A group of world heritage monuments around L Nasser in Ethiopia, many of which were rescued from flooding during the construction of Aswan High Dam. They include the 13th-c BC temples of Ramses II at Abu Simbel. >> Abu Simbel; Aswan

nuclear disarmament A political movement which emerged soon after the advent of nuclear weapons, demanding their control and eventual abolition. Although the US and Soviet governments had some success in reaching arms limitation treaties, such as the Intermediate range Nuclear Forces (INF) agreement (1987), mass political movements such as the British Campaign for Nuclear Disarmament (CND) have continued to attract support. >> Non-Proliferation Treaty; Nuclear Test-Ban Treaty; nuclear weapons

nuclear fission The splitting of a heavy atomic nucleus into two approximately equal portions, with the emission of free neutrons and energy; discovered by Italian physicist Enrico Fermi in 1934. Fission in uranium and plutonium forms the basic mechanism of nuclear power and atomic bombs. >> atomic bomb; chain reaction; Fermi; nuclear physics

nuclear fusion The fusing together of two lightweight atomic nuclei, typically isotopes of hydrogen or lithium, having a total rest mass which exceeds that of the products. The mass difference is made up by energy released in the process. Such fusions are possible in the high-temperature environments of the Sun and nuclear explosions. Fusion reactors attempt to reproduce such conditions in a controlled way. The chief experimental fusion reactors are the Joint European Torus (JET) in the UK, the Tokamak Fusion Test Reactor at Princeton, USA and JT60 near Tokyo in Japan. In 1991, JET scientists achieved a breakthrough, combining hydrogen and tritium to produce over a million watts of energy in a reaction which was sustainable for two minutes. >> cold fusion; deuterium; hydrogen bomb ℹ; Joint European Torus; nuclear physics; tritium

nuclear magnetic resonance (NMR) An analytic technique, important in chemistry, which relies on magnetic resonance involving protons. It is an important imaging technique in medicine, complementary to X-ray imaging, known as **magnetic resonance imaging (MRI)**. >> proton

nuclear physics The study of the properties and composition of the atomic nucleus. Early nuclear physics experiments include the study of natural radioactivity, and the demonstration of the existence of the nucleus in 1911. The nucleus is probed using X-rays, neutrons, mesons, and electrons. The applications of nuclear physics include nuclear power, nuclear weapons, and radioisotopes in medicine. >> nuclear fission / fusion; nucleus (physics); radioactivity

nuclear power >> **nuclear fission / fusion / reactor** ℹ

nuclear reactor A device for producing a continuous supply of heat energy from controlled radioactivity. Certain radioactive atomic nuclei, on being struck by neutrons, generate additional neutrons. This is self-sustaining if the speed of the neutrons is not too great. A nuclear reactor therefore has (i) a 'fuel', which may be uranium 235 or 238, or plutonium 239; (ii) a moderator, to control the speed and number of neutrons; and (iii) a heat exchange system, to utilize the heat generated (generally by operating the steam-driven turbines of a conventional electric power station). A **boiling water reactor** uses the cooling water itself as the source of steam for the turbines. In a **pressurized water reactor**, the coolant is water under such pressure that it reaches a high temperature without evaporation, and is used to heat boiler water via a heat exchanger. A **gas-cooled reactor** uses carbon dioxide or some other gas as a coolant, heating turbine water via a heat exchanger. A **fast reactor** has no moderator, and generally uses liquid sodium as a coolant. A **breeder reactor** uses uranium 238 enriched with plutonium 239; it produces more Pu 239, and is the type of reactor used to generate material for atomic weapons. >> containment building; meltdown; nucleonics; plutonium; radioactivity; uranium

Nuclear Test-Ban Treaty A 1963 treaty prohibiting the testing of nuclear weapons on or above the surface of the Earth, originally put forward by the USA, USSR, and UK. The impact of the treaty was somewhat diminished by its boycott by two nuclear nations, France and China. All five nations signed a comprehensive Test Ban Treaty in 1996. >> nuclear disarmament / weapons

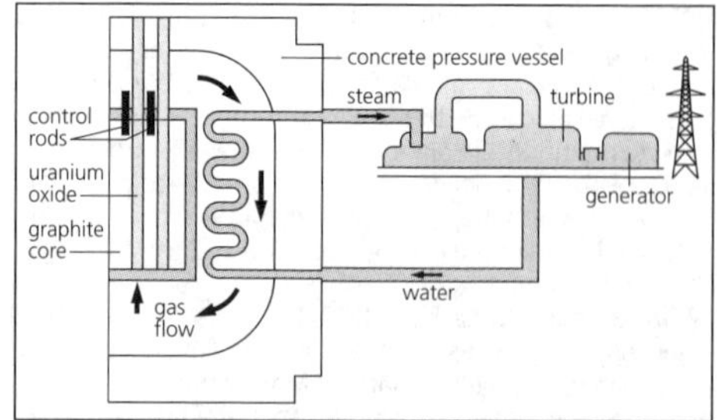

Nuclear reactor – Advanced Gas-cooled Reactor (AGR): section through an electricity-generating power station

nuclear weapons Weapons of mass destruction employing the energy-liberating nuclear phenomena of fission or fusion for their effects. According to their size and the means of delivery, they may be classified as **tactical short-range weapons** for use against enemy battlefield forces; **theatre medium-range weapons** for use against deep military targets; and **strategic long-range weapons** for use against enemy cities and command centres. >> atomic bomb; hydrogen bomb [i]; kiloton; missile, guided; nuclear disarmament

nucleic acids Large molecules which store genetic information, produced by living cells, and composed of a chain of nucleotides. Two forms are found: deoxyribonucleic acid (DNA) and ribonucleic acid (RNA), which may be either single- or double-stranded. >> cell; DNA [i]; molecule; nucleotide; RNA

nucleonics The technology associated with nuclear reactors and their functioning. It entails the study of the techniques of assembling the radioactive material, the transfer of heat energy to boilers and turbines for the production of electricity, and the installation of all these units in structures which will be safe. It is also concerned with the design and use of instruments which monitor and control radioactivity, as well as with the disposal of radioactive waste material. >> nuclear reactor [i]

nucleon number The total number of protons plus neutrons in an atomic nucleus; symbol *A*; also called the **mass number**. This total differs for different isotopes, and so is useful for labelling them. >> proton number

nucleosynthesis The creation of chemical elements by nuclear reactions in stars and other cosmic explosions. Hydrogen burning in stars, and nuclear explosions at the end of a star's life, have formed all other elements by transmutation. >> chemical elements; helium; hydrogen

nucleotide A portion of a nucleic acid consisting of a purine or pyrimidine base, a sugar molecule, and a phosphate group bonded together. There are four principal nucleotides in DNA. >> DNA [i]; purines; pyrimidines

nucleus (astronomy) **1** The central core of a comet, about 1–10 km/ $\frac{1}{2}$–6 mi across, consisting of icy substances and dust. >> comet **2** The central part of a galaxy or quasar, possibly the seat of unusually energetic activity within the galaxy. >> galaxy; quasar

nucleus (biology) The chromosome-containing structure found in most non-dividing eucaryotic cells; delimited from the surrounding cytoplasm by a double membrane; typically ovoid or spherical, sometimes irregularly shaped. >> cell; chromosome [i]; cytoplasm; eucaryote

nucleus (physics) The core of an atom, comprising various numbers of protons and neutrons, making up c.99.975% of an atom's mass. The number of protons equals the total positive charge of the nucleus, and equals the number of electrons in a complete atom. The nuclear components are bound together by strong nuclear force. The nucleus diameter is approximately 10^{-14} m. >> atom; nuclear physics

Nudibranchia [nyoodi**brang**kia] >> **sea slug**

Nuesslein-Volhard, Christiane [**nüs**liyn **fol**haht] (1942–) Developmental biologist, born in Magdeburg, Germany. She shared the Nobel Prize for Physiology or Medicine in 1995 for her research into how genes control early development of the human embryo. Using the fruit fly, her contribution, in collaboration with Wieschaus, was to identify a number of genes which determine the body plan and formation of body segments.

Nuffield, William Richard Morris, 1st Viscount (1877–1963) Motor magnate and philanthropist, born in Worcester, Hereford and Worcester. He became the first British manufacturer to develop the mass production of cheap (Morris) cars. In 1943 he established the Nuffield Foundation for medical, scientific, and social research.

Nuffield Radio Astronomy Laboratories An institution at Jodrell Bank, Cheshire, UK, founded in 1945, operated by the University of Manchester. It contains the first fully steerable radio telescope (76 m/250 ft), completed in 1957, now called the Lovell telescope. >> radio astronomy; telescope [i]

Nujoma, Sam Daniel [nu**joh**ma] (1929–) Namibian nationalist leader, and first president of independent Namibia (1990–), born in Ongandjern, Namibia. He founded the South-West Africa People's Organization (SWAPO), and led the Namibian armed struggle against South Africa from 1966. He returned from exile in 1989 to win the presidential election. >> Namibia [i]

Nuku'alofa [**noo**kualohfah] 21°09S 175°14W, pop (1995e) 22 500. Port and capital town of Tonga, S Pacific; on Tongatapu I; university; royal palace (1867). >> Tonga [i]

Nullarbor Plain [**nuhl**abaw] Vast plateau in SW South Australia and S Western Australia; extends for 480 km/ 300 mi; maximum height 305 m/1000 ft; crossed by the Trans-Australian Railway, the world's longest straight stretch of railway (478 km/297 mi). >> Australia [i]

numbat An Australian marsupial (*Myrmecobius fasciatus*); narrow pointed head with horizontal black line through eye; hindquarters with grey and white hoops; long bushy grey tail; female without a pouch; eats termites; also known as **banded anteater** or **marsupial anteater**. (Family: Myrmecobiidae.) >> marsupial [i]

numbers A concept used initially in counting, to compare the sizes of groups of objects. **Natural numbers** (or *cardinal numbers*) are the numbers used in counting, 1,2,3,4,5.... These are always *whole numbers*. The set of *integers* comprises all the natural numbers (the *positive integers*), *zero*, and the *negative numbers*...−3,−2,−1. The **rational numbers** are all the numbers that can be expressed in the form m/n, where m and n are two integers, positive or negative. Rational numbers include *proper fractions* (those whose numerator is less than their denominator, eg $\frac{3}{8}$) and *improper fractions* (those whose numerator is greater than their denominator, eg $\frac{8}{3}$). **Mixed numbers** are the sum of an integer and a proper fraction, eg $2\frac{1}{2}$. *Decimal fractions* are those with denominator a power of 10, written as 0·3, 0·345, etc. **Irrational numbers** are all real numbers that are not rational. Some can be expressed as the roots of algebraic equations with rational coefficients, eg $\sqrt{3}$ is a root of $x^2 = 3$. Those that cannot be so expressed are called **transcendental numbers**, eg π, e, e^2. **Real numbers** are all numbers that do not contain an **imaginary number** (a square root of a negative number). The positive square root of −1 is denoted by i (occasionally *j*). **Complex numbers** have a real and an imaginary part, eg 3 + 4*i*. >> amicable numbers; numeral; perfect numbers

Numbers, Book of A book of the Hebrew Bible/Old Testament, the fourth book of the Pentateuch; called 'Numbers' in Greek tradition because of the census of the tribes recorded in the first chapters. It describes the wanderings of Israel after the Exodus. >> Moses; Old Testament; Pentateuch

number theory The abstract study of the relationship between numbers, by which is meant positive rational numbers. An example of an early problem is one solved by Diophantus: 'Find three numbers such that their sum is a perfect square, and the sum of any two is a perfect square' (41, 80, 320). In the 17th-c Fermat proved many results in number theory. >> Diophantus; Fermat's last theorem; numbers; prime number

numeral In mathematics, the symbol used to represent a number. The commonest system of numerals today is the Hindu–Arabic, possibly invented by the Hindus and brought to Europe by the Arabs. This uses the symbols 0, 1, 2, 3,...9 and the idea of place-value to represent each whole number. Other systems of numerals include the Roman and the Greek. >> numbers; Roman numerals

numerology The mystical study of numbers, derived mainly from Hindu and Arabic teaching, but also from Jewish and Chinese traditions. Each number has a size, quality, vibration, and mystical value, and the study of their symbolism can be used as a method of divination. >> yin and yang

Numidia [nyu**midi**a] The Roman name for the region in N Africa to the W and S of Carthage. It roughly corresponds to modern Algeria.

numismatics The study and collecting of coins, notes, and other similar objects, such as medals. The first known coins were issued by the Lydians of Anatolia in the 7th-c BC. Coin collectors worldwide were brought together in 1936, when the International Numismatics Foundation was set up.

nun A member of a religious order of women living under vows of poverty, chastity, and obedience. The term includes women living in enclosed convents, as well as sisters devoted to service of the sick or poor. >> monasticism; Orders, Holy; Ursulines

Nunavut (Inuktitut, 'Our land') A semi-autonomous Inuit (Eskimo) territory (c.2 000 000 sq km/775 000 sq mi) in E Northwest Territories, Canada, stretching from Manitoba to the North Pole; capital, Iqaluit. Its creation was agreed in 1991 following negotiations between the federal government of Canada and Inuit leaders, and it was officially created on 1 April 1999. >> Northwest Territories

Nunn, Trevor (Robert) (1940–   ) Stage director, born in Ipswich, Suffolk. He became the Royal Shakespeare Company's artistic director (1968–87), and also directed the musicals *Cats* (1981), *Starlight Express* (1984), and *Aspects of Love* (1989). He was appointed director of the Royal National Theatre from 1997. >> National Theatre; Royal Shakespeare Company

Nuremberg [**nyoo**remberg], Ger **Nurnberg** 49°27N 11°05E, pop (1995e) 511 000. Commercial and manufacturing city in Germany; on the R Pegnitz; second largest city in Bavaria; scene of Mastersingers' contests during the Renaissance; annual meeting place of Nazi Party after 1933; badly bombed in World War 2; scene of German war criminal trials (1945–6); railway; birthplace of Albrecht Dürer; Imperial Castle (12th–16th-c). >> Bavaria; Dürer; Germany [i]; Nazi Party; Nuremberg Laws / Trials

Nuremberg Laws [**nyoo**remberg] Two racial laws promulgated in Nuremberg in 1935 during a Nazi Party rally. The first deprived of German citizenship those not of 'German or related blood', the second made marriage or extra-marital relations illegal between Germans and Jews. >> Nazi Party

Nuremberg Trials [**nyoo**remberg] Proceedings held by the Allies at Nuremberg after World War 2 to try Nazi war criminals. An International Military Tribunal sat from November 1945 until October 1946. Twenty-one Nazis were tried in person. >> Goering; Hess, Rudolf; Nazi Party; Ribbentrop

Nureyev, Rudolf (Hametovich) [**noor**ayef] (1938–93) Ballet dancer, born in Irkutsk, Russia. While touring with the Kirov Ballet in 1961, he obtained political asylum in Paris. He made his debut at Covent Garden with the Royal Ballet in 1962, and became Fonteyn's regular partner, his virtuosity making him one of the greatest male dancers of the 1960s. He became ballet director of the Paris Opera in 1983. >> Fonteyn; Royal Ballet

Nurmi, Paavo (Johannes) [**noor**mee] (1897–1973) Athlete, born in Turku, Finland. He won nine gold medals at three Olympic Games (1920–8), and set 22 world records at distances ranging from 1500–20 000 m. >> athletics

Nürnberg >> **Nuremberg**

nursery rhymes Traditional rhymes, essentially adult-inspired, passed on from parent to child as nursery entertainment. Most date from no earlier than the 18th-c; the earliest printed collection appeared in 1744. A major collection of nursery rhymes and children's books, made by Iona Opie (1923–   ) and Peter Opie (1918–82), is housed in the Bodleian Library, Oxford.

nursery school A school for children under the age at which schooling becomes compulsory. The teachers are usually trained, by comparison with *playgroups*, which make greater use of volunteer helpers. >> preschool education

nursing The branch of medicine which provides care for the sick and injured, and assumes responsibility for the patients' physical, social, and spiritual needs that encourage recovery. Nurses comprise the largest single group of health workers. They do not have the authority to prescribe specific medical or surgical remedies or drugs, but assist doctors and surgeons in carrying out treatment, and help to monitor its effects. >> medicine; Nightingale; St John ambulance brigade

nut A dry, non-splitting fruit with a woody shell, often seated in a cup-like structure and containing several seeds, only one of which develops fully. In non-specialist use, the term is often applied to any woody fruit or seed. >> Brazil nut; hazel; walnut

nutcracker Either of two species of crow of the genus *Nucifraga*: the **nutcracker** (*Nucifraga caryocatactes*) of Europe and Asia; and **Clark's nutcracker** (*Nucifraga columbiana*) of W North America. (Family: Corvidae.) >> crow

nuthatch A small bird of the family Sittidae (c.23 species), inhabiting rocks or woodland in the N hemisphere; short tail, sharp straight bill; eats insects (sometimes nuts).

nutmeg An evergreen tree (*Myristica fragrans*) growing to 9 m/30 ft, native to the Moluccas, Indonesia; flowers waxy, yellow, 3-lobed bells; fruit fleshy, pear-shaped, containing a single, large seed (the nutmeg) surrounded by a red outgrowth from which mace is made. Both spices contain a narcotic, and are poisonous in large quantities. (Family: Myristicaceae.) >> mace; narcotics

nutria >> **coypu**

nutrients All components of foods and all diet supplements. **Macronutrients** are energy proteins, carbohydrates, and fats; **micronutrients** are minerals, vitamins, and various chemical substances present in tiny quantities (the *trace elements*).

nutrition The scientific study of all aspects of what organisms eat. It involves the analysis of what people eat, the psychology of why they eat, what happens to food in the body, and how the balance of food affects health. An expert in nutrition is known as a **nutritionist**. >> nutritional medicine

nutritional medicine The study of the interaction of nutritional factors within the human body to find ways of treating disease and maintaining health. It includes the study of the properties of the nutrients themselves, and the physiology of digestion, absorption, and biochemical utilization. >> medicine; nutrition

nyala An African spiral-horned antelope; greyish-brown with thin vertical white lines; two species: **nyala** (*Tragelaphus angasi*), found in SE Africa; and **mountain nyala** (*Tragelaphus buxtoni*), from high forest in Ethiopia. >> antelope

Nyasa [ni**a**sa] or **Malawi, Lake**, Mozambique **Niassa** area 28 500 sq km/11 000 sq mi. Lake in SEC Africa; third largest lake in Africa, in the S section of the Great Rift Valley; altitude, 437 m/1434 ft; sometimes known as the 'Calendar Lake' because it is 365 miles long and 52 miles across, at its widest point; a world heritage site. >> Rift Valley

Nyerere, Julius (Kambarage) [nye**rair**ay] (1922–) Tanzanian statesman and president (1962–85), born in Butiama, Tanzania. He was premier when Tanganyika was granted internal self-government (1961), and president on independence (1962). In 1964 he negotiated the union of Tanganyika and Zanzibar, as Tanzania. >> Tanzania i

nylon A generic term for the most widely-produced type of synthetic fibre, used commercially since 1938. It is a polyamide whose lightness and elasticity make it available for use both in fibre and solid form. It is also an extremely strong and hard-wearing material. Its uses are therefore varied, including ropes, tyre cords, engineering components, furnishings, and apparel. >> polyamides

Nyman, Michael [**niy**man] (1944–) Pianist and composer, born in London. He formed the Michael Nyman Band in 1977, for which he composed several works characterized by highly charged, stylized, rhythmical chord progressions, in which his own piano playing is a driving force. His compositions include scores for the films of Peter Greenaway, and for the films *Carrington* and *The Piano*, and a piano concerto (1994). >> Greenaway, Peter

nymph In Greek mythology, one of the 'young women', nature-spirits, who live in streams (*naiads*), trees (*hamadryads*), the sea (*nereids*), as well as rocks and mountains. They are long-lived but not immortal. >> dryad; hamadryad (mythology); naiad; nereid

nymphalid butterfly A butterfly of the family Nymphalidae; typically colourful, with long hair-like scales; c.8200 species, including admirals, emperors, fritillaries, and tortoiseshell butterflies. (Order: Lepidoptera.) >> butterfly

nymphomania >> **satyriasis**

O

Oahu [oh**ah**hoo] pop (1995e) 938 000; area 1526 sq km/589 sq mi. Third largest island of the US state of Hawaii; chief town, Honolulu; naval base at Pearl Harbor. >> Hawaii (state); Honolulu

oak A member of a large genus of often massive and long-lived trees and also small shrubs, native to the N hemisphere; leaves deciduous or evergreen; flowers tiny, 4–7-lobed; fruit an acorn seated in a scaly cup. It is a traditional source of excellent timber, and also of cork and bark for tanning. (Genus: *Quercus*, 450 species. Family: Fagaceae.) >> acorn; tree ℹ

Oakland 37°49N 122°16W, pop (1995e) 408 000. Port in W California, USA, on the E shore of San Francisco Bay; founded, 1850; two airports; railway; observatory; professional teams, A's (baseball), Golden State Warriors (basketball). >> California

Oakley, Annie, popular name of **Phoebe Anne Oakley Moses** (1860–1926) Sharpshooter and Wild West performer, born near Woodland, OH. She won fame in Buffalo Bill's Wild West Show, but her career ended when she was injured in a train crash in 1901. >> Cody

OAS 1 Abbreviation of **Organisation de l'Armée Secrète** ('Secret Army Organization'), the clandestine organization of French Algerians, active (1960–2) in resisting Algerian independence. It caused considerable violence until thrown into rapid decline by Algerian independence (Jul 1962).>> Algeria ℹ; FLN **2** >> Organization of American States

Oasis British pop group, formed in 1992 with five members, all but one from Manchester, UK: **Liam Gallagher** (1972– , vocals), **Noel Gallagher** (1967– , lead guitar, backing vocals, songwriter), **Paul 'Bonehead' Arthurs** (1965– , rhythm guitar), **Paul 'Guigsy' McGuigan** (1971– , bass guitar), and **Tony McCarroll** (drums), replaced in 1995 by **Alan White** (1972– , born in London). Their first single, 'Supersonic' (1994), became an immediate number 1 hit. Their first album, *Definitely Maybe* (1994) was the fastest selling debut album in British pop history, later albums including *What's The Story (Morning Glory)* (1995) and *Be Here Now* (1997). The group rose to become the leading band of the 1990s, touring widely, the flamboyant personal lives of the Gallagher brothers attracting the kind of media attention that had not been since the Beatles (with whom – along with God – they readily compared themselves).

Oates, Lawrence (Edward Grace) (1880–1912) Explorer, born in London. In 1910 he joined Scott's Antarctic Expedition, and was one of the party of five to reach the S Pole in 1912. Lamed by severe frostbite, and convinced that his condition would fatally handicap his companions' prospect of survival, he walked out into the blizzard, sacrificing his life. >> Scott, R F

Oates, Titus (1649–1705) English conspirator and perjurer, born in Oakham, Leicestershire. In 1677 he fabricated a 'Popish Plot', supposedly directed at the life of Charles II. When the plot was made public, he became the hero of the day; but two years later he was found guilty of perjury, and imprisoned. He was freed at the Revolution of 1688. >> Charles II (of England); Popish Plot

oath A solemn expression from a person giving evidence in court or making a sworn written statement. The traditional wording is 'I swear by Almighty God that the evidence which I shall give shall be the truth, the whole truth, and nothing but the truth'. Alternatively, it is possible to *affirm*, that is to solemnly promise to tell the truth. Other traditional or religious practices may be recognized. >> court of law; perjury

oats A cereal (*Avena sativa*), probably native to the Mediterranean basin, and cultivated in temperate regions, especially in the N hemisphere, tolerating a wide climatic range, and growing where other cereals fail. It is an important human and animal food, though less so in recent times. (Family: Gramineae.) >> cereals; grass ℹ

Ob, River [op] Chief river of the W Siberian Lowlands, C Russia; enters the Kara Sea; length, 3650 km/2268 mi; with the R Irtysh, its chief tributary, length 5570 km/3461 mi, the world's fourth longest river; frozen for 5–6 months of the year. >> Russia ℹ

Obadiah, Book of [ohba**diy**a] One of the 12 so-called 'minor' prophetic writings of the Hebrew Bible/Old Testament; named after the otherwise unknown prophet, whose name means 'Servant of God'; sometimes called **Book of Abdias**. The work may have originated soon after the fall of Jerusalem in 587/6 BC. >> Edomites; Old Testament; prophet

Obelia [oh**beel**ia] A genus of marine invertebrate animals; hydroids, living in colonies, commonly found growing on seaweeds in the inter-tidal zone on shores. (Phylum: Cnidaria. Class: Hydrozoa.) >> Hydrozoa

obelisk A tall pillar, usually made of granite, square in section, tapering upwards, and ending in a small pyramid. Well-known examples are Cleopatra's Needles (c.1475 BC), one of which is now located on the Victoria Embankment, London, the other in Central Park, New York City.

Oberammergau Passion Play [ohber**am**ergow] A dramatization every 10 years of the Passion of Christ, performed by villagers of Oberammergau in Bavaria, Germany. It is performed in fulfilment of a vow made in 1663, when the village was saved from plague. >> Jesus Christ

Oberon (astronomy) [**oh**beron] The outermost satellite of Uranus, discovered in 1787 by Herschel; distance from the planet 583 500 km/362 600 mi; diameter 1500 km/950 mi. >> Herschel; Uranus (astronomy); RR964

Oberon (mythology) [**oh**beron] In European literature, the name of the king of the fairies, as in Shakespeare's *A Midsummer Night's Dream* and Wieland's *Oberon*. >> Titania

obesity [oh**bee**zitee] An excessive amount of body fat, with the affected person being overweight; the most common nutritional disease in affluent societies. It arises because of an imbalance of energy intake over expenditure, but many factors (eg endocrine, genetic) influence its development. >> fat 2

obo [**oh**boh] A term derived from 'oil/bulk ore', a vessel designed to carry oil and bulk ore either together or separately. This is a relatively new class of vessel, first built in the mid-1960s. By the early 1990s total obo tonnage was 20 million gross tonnes. >> ship ℹ

oboe A musical instrument made of wood in three jointed sections, opening to a small bell; it is fitted with a double reed. It first appeared in recognizable form in the mid-17th-c and was widely used in the 18th-c. In the orchestra it is normally the oboe that sets the pitch for the other instruments. >> cor anglais; reed instrument; woodwind instrument ℹ

Obote, (Apollo) Milton [o**boh**tay] (1924–) Ugandan nationalist leader, prime minister (1962–6) and president (1967–71, 1981–5), born in Lango, Uganda. He ruled Uganda both before and after the dictatorship of Idi Amin. He was deposed in 1985, and fled into exile in Zambia. >> Amin; Uganda ℹ

O'Brien, Edna (1932–) Novelist, born in Tuamgraney, Co Clare, Ireland. Her novels include *The Country Girls* (1960), *House of Splendid Isolation* (1994), and *Down by the River* (1996). Her short stories are also highly regarded; the best from several collections appear in *The Fanatic Heart* (1985).

O'Brien, Flann, pseudonym of **Brian O'Nolan**, also known as **Myles na Gopaleen** (1911–66) Writer, born in Strabane, Co Tyrone, Ireland. As 'Myles na Gopaleen' he made regular satirical contributions to the *Irish Times*. His novels include *At Swim-Two-Birds* (1939), *The Hard Life* (1960), and *The Dalkey Archive* (1964).

observatory The instruments and associated buildings for conducting astronomical research of any kind. This broad definition includes the structures of native proto-astronomers, such as the builders of Stonehenge and Meso-American pyramids, the great mountain observatories of professionals in Hawaii, Australia, and Chile, the backyard shed of the keen amateur, and satellites carrying telescopes far above the atmosphere. Modern optical observatories are situated on mountain-tops to get above cloud and light pollution, with oceanic islands being particularly satisfactory. >> Arecibo / Mauna Kea / Mount Palomar / National Radio Astronomy / Royal Greenwich Observatory; Royal Observatory, Edinburgh; astronomy; Nuffield Radio Astronomy Laboratories; telescope ℹ

obstetrics [ob**stet**riks] The medical and surgical care of pregnancy and childbirth. It involves the prenatal care and assessment of the woman's ability to undergo labour, the assessment of the size and health of the fetus in the womb, the detection of diseases related to pregnancy, the diagnosis of the position of the fetus in the uterus, and the conduct of the delivery. Also important are the control of pain and the diagnosis and treatment of complications. >> caesarian section; pregnancy ℹ

ocarina [oka**reen**a] A simple, egg-shaped musical instrument belonging to the flute family, with a protruding mouthpiece, six fingerholes, and two thumbholes. It is made from terracotta. >> flute; terracotta; woodwind instrument ℹ

O'Casey, Sean, originally **John Casey** (1880–1964) Playwright, born in Dublin. His early plays, such as *Juno and the Paycock* (1924), were written for the Abbey Theatre. He was awarded the Hawthornden Prize in 1926. His later work includes *Cock-a-doodle Dandy* (1949) and *The Bishop's Bonfire* (1955). >> Abbey Theatre

occultism Activities purporting to achieve communication with the supernatural. The term includes magic, divination, certain types of spiritualism, and witchcraft. >> magic; spiritualism; tarot

occupational diseases Diseases which arise in the course of employment; also known as **industrial disease**, in the context of industrial work. For example, many chemicals and dyes induce dermatitis. Inhalation of industrial products affects the lungs, and may lead to pneumoconiosis or asbestosis. Ionizing radiation may cause leukaemia. Compressed-air workers suffer damage to their ears and fingers, and welders may damage their eyes. Such events have led to the development of *industrial medicine*. >> community medicine; decompression sickness; pneumoconiosis; silicosis

occupational therapy The treatment of physical and psychiatric conditions through specific activities in order to help people reach their maximum level of function and independence. Activities include opportunities for amateur dramatics, and access to vocationally orientated workshops.

oceanarium >> **aquarium**

Oceania [ohshi**ah**nia], also **Oceanica** A general name applied to the isles of the Pacific Ocean, including Polynesia, Melanesia, Micronesia, Australasia, and sometimes the Malaysian islands. >> Pacific Ocean

oceanic ridges Giant undersea mountain ranges, rising above the surrounding sea floor 1–4 km/$\frac{1}{2}$–2$\frac{1}{2}$ mi, which wind their way around the globe for over 80 000 km/50 000 mi and cover 35% of the sea floor. The Mid-Atlantic Ridge is the best-known ridge system. Large areas of the sea floor which rise more than several hundred metres above the level of the ocean basin floor are **oceanic rises**.

Oceanides [oh**see**anideez] In Greek mythology, the innumerable nymphs who inhabit the ocean and other watery places. They are the daughters of Oceanus and Tethys. >> Oceanus

oceanography The study of the oceans, also referred to as **oceanology**. **Geological oceanography** deals with the structure and origin of the ocean floor, and the processes which operate along the shoreline. **Chemical oceanography** deals with the chemical properties of seawater, and the reactions which take place in the ocean. **Physical oceanography** covers the physical processes in the ocean, including ocean currents, waves, tides, and the interaction between the atmosphere and the ocean. **Biological oceanography** deals with marine organisms and their relationship with their environment. >> biology; chemistry; geology; physics

Oceanus [oh**see**anus] In Greek mythology, a Titan, the son of Uranus and Gaia. He is a benign god who personifies the stream of Ocean which was assumed to surround the world. >> Titan

ocelot [**os**elot] A rare member of the cat family (*Felis pardalis*), found from S USA to N Argentina; pale with dark spots and lines; sometimes reared as pets; also known as **painted leopard** or **tigrillo**. >> Felidae

ochre Earth consisting of a mixture of hydrated iron oxides and clay, light yellow to brown in colour. It is ground to a powder and used as a pigment.

Ockham, William of >> **William of Ockham**

O'Connell, Daniel, known as **the Liberator** (1775–1847) Irish Catholic political leader, born near Cahirciveen, Co Kerry, Ireland. In 1823 he formed the Catholic Association, which successfully fought elections against the landlords. His election as MP for Co Clare precipitated a crisis in Wellington's government, which eventually granted Catholic Emancipation (1829), enabling him to take his seat in the Commons. >> Catholic Emancipation

O'Connor, Feargus Edward (1794–1855) Chartist leader, born in Connorville, Co Cork, Ireland. His Leeds *Northern Star* (1837) became the most influential Chartist newspaper. He attempted, without great success, to unify the Chartist movement via the National Charter Association (1842). >> Chartism

O'Connor, Sandra Day, *née* **Day** (1930–) Jurist, born in El Paso, TX. In 1981 President Reagan named her as the first woman justice of the US Supreme Court. >> Reagan; Republican Party

octadecanoic acid >> **stearic acid**

octane number The measure of ability of a fuel to resist knocking (premature ignition) in the cylinder of an internal combustion engine. >> cetane number; knocking

Octans (Lat 'octant') An inconspicuous S constellation. >> constellation; RR968

October Revolution (1917) The overthrow of the Russian provisional government by Bolshevik-led armed workers (Red Guards), soldiers, and sailors (25–26 Oct 1917). The members of the provisional government were replaced by the Soviet of People's Commissars, chaired by Lenin – the first Soviet government. >> Bolsheviks; Lenin

October War >> **Arab–Israeli Wars**

octopus A carnivorous marine mollusc with a short, sac-like body and eight arms largely connected by webbing; reaches 5.4 m/18 ft in length, and with a maximum outstretched arm-span of nearly 9 m/30 ft; when alarmed, may eject a cloud of ink. (Class: Cephalopoda. Order: Octopoda.) >> Cephalopoda [i]; mollusc

octopush A form of hockey played underwater, first introduced in South Africa in the 1960s. Teams consist of six players who use miniature hockey sticks and a puck replacing the ball. >> hockey [i]

ode (Gr 'song') A lyric poem, usually of some length and formal complexity. Pindar in Greek, Horace in Latin, and Keats in English were notable practitioners. >> Horace; Keats; Pindar

Odense [**oh**densuh] 55°24N 10°25E, pop (1995e) 179 000. Port and chief town on Fyn I, Denmark; third largest city of Denmark; railway; university (1964); birthplace of Hans Andersen. >> Andersen; Denmark [i]

Oder, River [**oh**der], Czech, Polish **Odra**, ancient **Viadua** River in C Europe rising in E Sudetes Mts of Czech Republic; enters the Baltic Sea; length 854 km/531 mi; canal links to W and E Europe. >> Poland [i]

Oder–Neisse Line [**oh**der **niy**suh] The Polish–German border, drawn by the Allies (1944–5), and involving the transfer to Poland of large areas of pre-war Germany. >> Germany [i]; Poland [i]

Odessa [oh**de**sa] 46°30N 30°46E, pop (1995e) 1 129 000. Seaport in Ukraine, on NW shore of the Black Sea; centre of the battleship *Potemkin* mutiny in the 1905 Revolution; naval base; leading Black Sea port; large health resorts nearby; railway; university (1865); cathedral (1855–69). >> Revolution of 1905; Ukraine [i]

Odets, Clifford [oh**dets**] (1906–63) Playwright and actor, born in Philadelphia, PA. A leading author of the 1930s, his works include *Waiting for Lefty* (1935) and *Golden Boy* (1937).

Odette, popular name of **Odette Hallowes**, formerly **Churchill** (to 1955) and **Sansom** (to 1946), née **Brailly** (1912–95) French wartime resistance heroine, born in Amiens, France. Brought up in France, she married an Englishman in 1931 and moved to London. Sent to France as an agent, she was arrested by the Germans in 1943, and sent to Ravensbruck concentration camp. Her wartime exploits were retold in a successful film, *Odette* (1950), starring Anna Neagle.

Odin [**oh**din] In Norse mythology, the All-Father, the god of poetry and the dead; also known as **Woden** (English) or **Wotan** (German). He gave one eye to the Giant Mimir in exchange for wisdom.

Odo [**oh**doh] (c.1036–97) Bishop of Bayeux (1049–97) and Earl of Kent, the half-brother of William the Conqueror. He may have commissioned the Bayeux tapestry. >> Bayeux Tapestry; William I (of England)

Odoacer [ohdoh**ay**ser], also found as **Odovacar** (?–493) Germanic warrior who destroyed the W Roman Empire, and became the first barbarian king of Italy (476–93). He was challenged and overthrown by the Ostrogothic King Theodoric (489–93). >> Roman history [i]; Theodoric

Odonata [**oh**donata] >> **damselfly; dragonfly**

Odysseus [o**dis**yoos] A Greek hero, known in Latin as **Ulixes**, from which **Ulysses** is derived. The son of Laertes, King of Ithaca, he took part in the Trojan War. He took ten years to return from Troy, encountering many romantic adventures, described in Homer's *Odyssey*. >> Homer; Trojan War

Oe, Kenzaburo [**oh**ay] (1935–) Novelist and short-story writer, born in Shikoku, Japan. His major books include *A Personal Matter* (1964, trans 1968), *The Silent Cry* (1967, trans 1974, Tanizaki Prize), and *A Healing Family* (trans 1996). He received the Nobel Prize for Literature in 1994.

oedema / edema [uh**dee**ma] The generalized accumulation of excess amounts of body fluids (water and salts) within and around the tissues of the body. In the majority of cases it is caused by heart, kidney, or liver failure.

Oedipus [**ee**dipus] In Greek legend, a Theban hero of whom it was foretold that he would kill his father and marry his mother. He fled from his adoptive parents when an oracle revealed his destiny, but on the way to Thebes he killed his father Laius by chance, was made the new ruler of the city and married its queen, Jocasta. When all was revealed, he blinded himself. >> Jocasta; Oedipus complex; sphinx

Oedipus complex [**ee**dipus] A psychoanalytic term describing the erotic feelings of a son for his mother, and an associated sense of competitiveness towards the father. The female equivalent is the **Electra complex**. Both terms were coined by Freud. >> Freud, Sigmund; Oedipus

Oersted, Hans Christian [**oe(r)**sted] (1777–1851) Physicist, born in Rudkøbing, Denmark. In 1820 he discovered the magnetic effect of an electric current. The unit of magnetic field strength is named after him. >> electromagnetism; RR1031

oesophagus / esophagus [ee**sof**aguhs] A long, muscular tube passing from the lower part of the pharynx through the thorax to the stomach; also known as the **gullet**. In adult humans it is c.24 cm/9.5 in long. >> pharynx; stomach

oestrogens / estrogens [**ee**strojenz] Steroid sex hormones (eg *oestradiol*, *oestriol*, *oestrone*) produced in the ovary, placenta, testis, and adrenal cortex. They are responsible for the development of female secondary sexual characteristics in humans. They are also used in oral contraceptives and in the treatment of certain cancers (eg of the prostate). >> androgens; contraception; puberty; steroid

oestrus / estrus [**ee**struhs] The period of maximum sexual receptivity, or heat, in female mammals. It is usually also the time of release of the egg from the ovary. >> ovarian follicle; ovary

Offa (?–796) King of Mercia (757–96). He was the greatest Anglo-Saxon ruler in the 8th-c, treated as an equal by Charlemagne. His reign represents an important but flawed attempt to unify England, with the Mercian supremacy collapsing soon after his death. >> Anglo-Saxons; Mercia; Offa's Dyke

offal All the organs of slaughtered animals other than muscles and bones. Several of these organs (such as the liver and kidneys) are eaten; others (such as the gut) are discarded.

Offaly [**of**alee], Ir **Ua bhFailghe** pop (1995e) 58 100; area 1997 sq km/771 sq mi. County in C Ireland; Slieve Bloom Mts rise in the SW; capital, Tullamore; large tracts of peat used as fuel for power stations. >> Ireland (republic) [i]; Tullamore

Offa's Dyke An interrupted linear earthwork 130 km/80 mi long linking the R Dee near Prestatyn, N Wales, with the Severn Estuary at Chepstow. Erected in the late 8th-c AD by Offa, King of Mercia, to define the W boundary of his kingdom, it marks the traditional boundary between England and Wales. >> Anglo-Saxons; Offa

Off-Broadway >> **Broadway**

Offenbach, Jacques [**of**enbahkh], originally **Jacob Eberst** (1819–80) Composer, born in Cologne, Germany. He composed many light, lively operettas, such as *Orphée aux enfers* (1858, Orpheus in the Underworld). He also produced one grand opera, *Les contes d'Hoffmann* (Tales of Hoffmann), which was not produced until 1881. >> opera buffa

Office, Divine or **Holy** In the pre-Reformation Western Church and in the Roman Catholic Church, prayers which must be said by priests and religious every day, originally at fixed hours. >> Breviary

Office of Management and Budget The office which the US president uses to control the financial operations of government, created in 1970 out of the Bureau of the Budget. It is an important political arm of the presidency. >> Reagan

offset lithography >> **lithography** ℹ

O'Flaherty, Liam (1897–1984) Writer, born in the Aran Is, Co Galway, Ireland. His novels include *The Informer* (1926), which was a great popular success, *The Assassin* (1928), and *Land* (1946).

Ogaden [oga**den**] Geographical area in SE Ethiopia; dry plateau; part of Abyssinia, 1890; part of Italian East Africa, 1936–41; largely inhabited by Somali-speaking nomads; area claimed by Somalia in 1960s; Somali invasion in 1977 repulsed by Ethiopian forces; fighting continued throughout the 1980s. >> Ethiopia ℹ; Somalia ℹ

Ogam or **Ogham** [**og**am] A writing system used from around the 4th-c AD for writing Irish and Pictish. The alphabet has 20 letters composed of sets of parallel straight lines, cut to and across the vertical corners of stone monuments. >> alphabet ℹ

Ogden, C(harles) K(ay) (1889–1957) Linguistic reformer, born in Fleetwood, Lancashire. In the 1920s he conceived the idea of Basic English, a simplified form of English with only 850 words, to provide a practical means of international communication. >> English; Richards, I A

Ogdon, John (Andrew Howard) (1937–89) Pianist, born in Mansfield Woodhouse, Nottinghamshire. In 1962 he was joint prizewinner in the Tchaikovsky Competition in Moscow. Illness forced him to give up playing for several years.

Ogham >> **Ogam**

Ogilvy, Mrs Angus >> **Alexandra, Princess**

O'Hara, John (Henry) (1905–70) Novelist and short-story writer, born in Pottsville, PA. Several of his novels were made into successful films, such as *Butterfield 8* (1935; film, 1960) and *Ten North Frederik* (1955; film, 1958). *Pal Joey* (1940) was adapted into a celebrated musical comedy.

O. Henry >> **Henry, O.**

O'Higgins, Bernardo, known as **the Liberator of Chile** (1778–1842) Chilean revolutionary, born in Chillán, Chile. The son of an Irish-born Governor of Chile, he played the major role in the Chilean struggle for independence. He became the first leader of the new Chilean state in 1817, but was deposed in 1823. >> Chile ℹ

Ohio [oh**hi**yoh] pop (1995e) 11 193 000; area 107 040 sq km/41 330 sq mi. State in E USA; the 'Buckeye State'; visited by La Salle in 1669; 17th state to join the Union, 1803; part of the Allegheny plateau; capital, Columbus; grain, livestock, coal (E and SE Appalachian coalfield); major industrial centre. >> Columbus; La Salle; United States of America ℹ; RR994

Ohio River River in EC USA; formed at Pittsburgh; flows to join the Mississippi at Cairo, IL; length 2101 km/1306 mi (including the Allegheny). >> United States of America ℹ

Ohlin, Bertil (Gotthard) (1899–1979) Economist and politician, born in Klippan, Sweden. He is best known for the **Heckscher–Ohlin theorem**, which states that countries will export goods that are produced with their relatively abundant factors of production, and import those goods produced with their scarce factors. He shared the 1977 Nobel Prize for Economics. >> Meade, James Edward

Ohm, Georg Simon (1787–1854) Physicist, born in Erlangen, Bavaria. His main discoveries were in the field of electricity. >> ohm; Ohm's law

ohm SI unit of electrical resistance; symbol Ω; a resistance of 1 ohm exists between two points of a conductor if a potential difference of 1 volt causes a current of 1 amp to flow between them; named after Georg Ohm; commonly used as **kilohms** (kΩ, 10^3 ohms) and **megohms** (MΩ, 10^6 ohms); resistance is measured using an **ohmmeter**. >> electricity; Ohm; resistance

ohmmeter >> **ohm**

Ohm's law In electrical circuits, the result that potential difference U and current I satisfy $U = IR$ for resistance R; for alternating current circuits, $U = IZ$, where Z is impedance; stated by Georg Ohm in 1827. >> electricity; impedance; Ohm; resistance

Ohrid [**okh**rid], Ital **Ohrida** 41°06N 20°49E, pop (1995e) 67 000. Town in the SW of the Former Yugoslav Republic of Macedonia; on the shores of L Ohrid; airfield; tourism; old town, a world heritage site; cathedral; castle. >> Macedonia, Former Yugoslav Republic of ℹ

oil (botany) A fluid secreted by special glands in many plants, often forming food reserves in fruits and seeds such as olives, palms, rape, and flax. Volatile *essential oils* are produced by aromatic plants, especially in dry regions. *Edible oils* are obtained from many plants, including soy beans, maize, olives, sunflowers, coconut, and rapeseed. >> essential oil; palm oil

oil (earth sciences) A fossil fuel that is chemically a complex mixture of hydrocarbons, formed from organic remains by the action of heat and pressure over millions of years; known as *natural* or *crude* oil. It occurs together with natural gas and solid hydrocarbons (collectively termed *petroleum*) as well as water. When refined it is used as a primary fuel for industry, with great economic importance. >> hydrocarbons; North Sea Oil; petroleum

oilbird A nightjar-like bird (*Steatornis caripensis*) native to N South America and Trinidad; uses echolocation; also known as the **guacharo** or **diablotin**. Its fledglings are very fat, and were formerly boiled to extract oil, used for cooking. (Family: Steatornithidae.) >> nightjar

oil painting A method of painting which employs drying oils (such as linseed oil) in the medium. In use since Roman times, the technique was perfected and adapted to painting pictures in the 15th-c. >> painting

oil palm A tree (*Elaeis guineensis*) reaching 15 m/50 ft, native to tropical Africa; leaves 4.5 m/15 ft, feathery. The numerous oval, orange fruits are rendered down for oil. (Family: Palmae.) >> palm

Oireachtas [**er**akhtas] An annual Irish gathering organized, on the lines of the Welsh eisteddfod, by the Gaelic League; first held in 1898. >> eisteddfod

Oistrakh, David (Fyodorovitch) [**oy**strak] (1908–74) Violinist, born in Odessa, Ukraine. He made several concert tours in Europe and the USA, and was awarded the Stalin (1945) and Lenin (1960) Prizes.

Ojibwa [oh**jib**wa] An Algonkin North American Indian group originally concentrated around L Superior and L Huron; called **Chippewa** by the Europeans; c.104 000 (1990 census).

Ojos del Salado, Cerro [**oh**khohs thel sa**la**thoh] 27°05S 68°35W. Andean peak rising to 6908 m/22 664 ft on the Argentina–Chile border; second highest peak in the W hemisphere, after Aconcagua; world's highest active volcano. >> Andes

okapi [oh**kah**pee] A mammal of the giraffe family (*Okapia johnstoni*) native to Democratic Republic of Congo; reddish-brown with long neck, large ears, and extremely long tongue; face and lower legs pale; upper legs and hindquarters with thin horizontal stripes; male with two blunt 'horns'. >> giraffe

Okavango, River [ohka**vang**goh] Third largest river in S Africa; rises in C Angola; length 1600 km/1000 mi.

Okayama [ohka**ya**ma] 34°40N 133°54E, pop (1995e) 604 000. Port in SW Honshu, Japan; railway; university (1949); dominated by the 'Castle of the Crow' (16th-c). >> Honshu

Okeechobee, Lake [ohkee**choh**bee] Lake in SC Florida, USA; largest lake in S USA; area 815 sq km/315 sq mi. >> Florida

O'Keeffe, Georgia (1887–1986) Painter, born in Sun Prairie, WI. As early as 1915 she pioneered abstract art in America (eg 'Blue and Green Music', 1919) but later moved towards a more figurative style. >> abstract art

Okefenokee Swamp [ohkefe**noh**kee] (Muskogean 'water-shaking') Area of swamp land in SE Georgia and NE Florida, USA; important wildlife refuge. >> Florida; Georgia

Okinawa [ohki**na**wa] pop (1995e) 1 265 000; area 2263 sq km/874 sq mi. Region of Japan comprising the S part of the Ryukyu group; island of Okinawa is the largest in the group (area 1176 sq km/454 sq mi); taken by the USA in World War 2; returned to Japan, 1972; capital, Naha. >> Japan i

Oklahoma [ohkla**hoh**ma] (Muskogean 'red people') pop (1995e) 3 313 000; area 181 083 sq km/69 919 sq mi. State in SW USA; the 'Sooner State'; mostly acquired by the USA in the Louisiana Purchase, 1803; Indians forced to move here in the 1830s (Indian Territory); Indians then lost the W region to whites (Oklahoma Territory, 1890); merged Indian and Oklahoma territories admitted into the Union as the 46th state, 1907; Ouachita Mts in the SE; Wichita Mts in the SW; highest point, Black Mesa (1516 m/4974 ft); in the W, high prairies part of the Great Plains; capital, Oklahoma City; major agricultural products livestock and wheat; large oil reserves and associated petroleum industry. >> Louisiana Purchase; Oklahoma City; United States of America i; RR994

Oklahoma City 35°30N 97°30W, pop (1995e) 468 000. State capital in C Oklahoma, USA, on the N Canadian R; settled around a railway station, 1889; state capital, 1910; developed rapidly after oil discovered, 1928; largest city in the state; airport; railway; university (1911); terrorist bomb destroyed federal office block, April 1995; oil production; processing centre for livestock, grain, cotton. >> Oklahoma

okra [**ohk**ra, **ok**ra] A vegetable crop (*Hibiscus esculentis*), originating in tropical Africa, and producing cylindrical edible fruits up to 20 cm/8 in long which are eaten immature, either cooked or fresh; also known as **ladies' fingers** or **gumbo**. The crop is widely cultivated in the tropics and sub-tropics. (Family: Malvaceae.) >> vegetable

Okri, Ben [**ok**ree] (1959–) Novelist and short-story writer, born in Minna, Nigeria. His first books were the autobiographical novels *Flowers and Shadows* (1980) and *The Landscapes Within* (1981). Later works include the novels *The Famished Road* (1991, Booker Prize) and *A Way of Being Free* (1997).

Olah, George A [**ol**a] (1927–) Chemist, born in Budapest. He left Hungary in 1956 for Canada, then the USA. He received the 1994 Nobel Prize for Chemistry for the study of hydrocarbons, and of new ways to use them, identifying an intermediate stage of short-lived compounds ('carbocations') in organic chemical reactions.

Öland [**oe**land] pop (1995e) 26 100; area 1344 sq km/519 sq mi. Elongated Swedish island in the Baltic Sea, off the SE coast of Sweden; length, 136 km/84 mi; largest island in Sweden; chief town, Borgholm; castle (12th–13th-c). >> Sweden i

Olav V [**oh**laf] (1903–91) King of Norway (1957–91), born near Sandringham, Norfolk, the only child of Haakon VII and Maud, daughter of Edward VII. In 1929 he married **Princess Martha** (1901–54) of Sweden, and had two daughters and a son, **Harald** (1937–), King of Norway (1991–). >> World War 2

Old Bailey A street in the City of London, and, by association, the Central Criminal Court located there. The present building dates from 1907; the bronze statue of Justice surmounting its dome is a notable London landmark. >> Crown Court; London

Oldcastle, Sir John, nickname **Good Lord Cobham** (c.1378–1417) Lollard leader and knight of England. An intimate of Henry V when Prince of Wales, he was convicted on charges of heresy in 1413. He conspired with other Lollards to take control of London, but was caught and executed. Shakespeare's Falstaff is based partly on him. >> Henry V; Lollards

Old Catholics A group of Churches separated at various times from the Roman Catholic Church, including the Church of Utrecht (separated 1724), and German, Austrian, and Swiss Catholics who refused to accept papal infallibility (1870); also some former Poles and Croats in North America. >> infallibility; Roman Catholicism

Old Church Slavonic >> **Slavic languages**

Old Comedy Athenian comic theatre of the 5th-c BC. The only complete plays extant are by Aristophanes. >> Aristophanes

Oldenburg, Claes (Thure) (1929–) Sculptor, born in Stockholm. He blends Surrealism and Pop Art, especially in his giant models of everyday objects made of canvas stuffed with foam rubber and painted in bright colours. >> Pop Art; Surrealism

Old English The language of the Anglo-Saxons in England, in the period before the Norman Conquest; also known as **Anglo-Saxon**. Glosses to Latin texts survive from the 8th-c; the epic poem *Beowulf* (composed in the 8th-c) is preserved in an 11th-c manuscript. Anglo-Saxon was written in an Irish form of the Latin alphabet, introduced by monks. >> Anglo-Saxons; English; Germanic languages

Old English sheepdog A breed of dog, developed in Britain in the 18th-c to protect cattle; long, untidy coat, often hiding ears and eyes; usually white with large dark patches; short tail. >> dog; sheepdog

Oldfield, Bruce (1950–) Fashion designer, born in London. He showed his first collection in London in 1975. His designs include evening dresses for royalty and screen stars, and ready-to-wear clothes.

Old High German >> **Germanic languages**

Oldman, Gary (1959–) Film actor, born in London. He became known following his portrayal of punk rocker Sid Vicious in the film *Sid and Nancy* (1986). Later films include Prick up Your Ears (1987), *Bram Stoker's Dracula* (1992), *Immortal Beloved* (1994), and *The Fifth Element* (1997).

Old Masters >> **master**

Old Persian >> **Iranian languages**

Old Style date >> **New Style date**

Old Testament The sacred literature of Judaism, in which the corpus of writings is known simply as the Jewish Scriptures or Hebrew Bible, or even sometimes the Torah; it was also adopted by Christians as part of their sacred writings, and they began to call it the 'Old Testament' as distinct from the Christian writings that constitute the 'New Testament'. The canon of the Jewish religious community, which was fixed AD c.100, was arranged into three parts – the **Law**, the **Prophets**, and the **Writings** – although the precise arrangement and divisions of the books have varied through the centuries. The Law consists of the five books of the Pentateuch (Genesis, Exodus, Leviticus, Numbers, Deuteronomy). The Prophets have been divided since about the 8th-c AD into the *former* and *latter* prophets: the former prophets consist of the narratives (presumed written by prophets) found in Joshua, Judges, Samuel, and Kings, and the latter prophets consist of

Isaiah, Jeremiah, Ezekiel, and the Book of the Twelve Prophets (Hosea, Joel, Amos, Obadiah, Jonah, Micah, Nahum, Habakkuk, Zephaniah, Haggai, Zechariah, Malachi). The Writings contain all remaining works: Psalms, Proverbs, Job, Song of Songs, Ruth, Lamentations, Ecclesiastes, Esther, Daniel, Ezra-Nehemiah, and Chronicles. >> Apocrypha, Old Testament; Bible; Christianity; Judaism; New Testament; Pentateuch; Pseudepigrapha

Olduvai Gorge [**ol**duviy] 2°58S 35°22E. A gorge within the Ngorongoro conservation area of the Rift Valley, N Tanzania. It is of great archaeological importance as the source of some of the oldest known 'human' remains. >> *Homo* ℹ; Leakey; Ngorongoro Crater; Tanzania ℹ

Old World monkey A monkey of family Cercopithecidae (76 species); nostrils close together and opening downwards or forwards (unlike New World monkeys); tails never grasping, sometimes short; buttocks may have naked patches of skin. >> baboon; colobus; guenon; langur; macaque; mangabey; monkey ℹ; New World monkey; proboscis monkey; talapoin

oleander [oli**an**der] An evergreen shrub (*Nerium oleander*) growing to 5 m/16 ft, native to the Mediterranean region; leaves leathery; flowers tubular with five spreading lobes, pink or white. All parts are poisonous. (Family: Apocynaceae.)

oleaster [oli**as**ter] A deciduous, sometimes thorny, shrub or tree (*Elaeagnus angustifolia*) growing to 13 m/42 ft, native to W Asia; leaves dull green above, covered with minute silvery scales beneath; flowers tubular with four spreading lobes, silver outside, yellow inside, fragrant; berries silvery-yellow. (Family: Eleagnaceae.)

olefin(e)s [**oh**luhfinz] >> **alkenes**

Oléron, Ile d' [eel dolayrõ], ancient **Uliarus** Wooded fertile island in E Bay of Biscay, W France; France's second largest off-shore island (after Corsica); 3 km/1¾ mi from mainland; area 157 sq km/68 sq mi; length 30 km/19 mi; linked by modern toll-bridge. >> Biscay, Bay of

oligarchy In ancient Greece, the term applied to city-states such as Corinth and Thebes, where political power was in the hands of a minority of its male citizens. They contrasted with democracies such as Athens and Argos, where power was held by the majority. >> polis

Oligocene epoch [o**lig**oseen] A geological epoch of the Tertiary period from c.37 to 25 million years ago, and characterized by colder climate, the general retreat of the seas, and the evolution of many modern mammals. >> geological time scale; Tertiary period; RR976

oligomer [o**lig**omer] A small polymer, generally consisting of three to ten monomer units; examples include oligopeptides and oligosaccharides. >> carbohydrate; peptide

oligopoly [oli**go**polee] An economic situation where an industry is dominated by a few suppliers. In economic theory, it constitutes one type of imperfect competition. >> monopoly

Olivares, Gaspar de Guzman y Pimental, conde-duque de (Count-Duke of) [oli**vah**rez] (1587–1645) Spanish statesman, favourite and chief minister of Philip IV (1623–43), born in Rome. He took Spain into renewed conflict with the United Provinces and challenged France over the Mantuan Succession (1628–31) and in the Thirty Years' War (1635–48). After Spanish defeats, he was dismissed in 1643, and died in exile. >> Thirty Years' War

olive A long-lived evergreen tree (*Olea europaea*) native to the Mediterranean region, growing to 15 m/50 ft; trunk silvery, gnarled with numerous cavities; leaves leathery, dark green above, pale beneath; flowers small, white, four petals; fruit succulent, oily, green, ripening over one year to black. The cultivated olive (variety *europaea*) has been grown since early times as an important source of olive oil. (Family: Oleaceae.)

Oliver, King, popular name of **Joseph Oliver** (1885–1938) Cornettist, composer, and bandleader, born in Abend, LA. He moved to Chicago, where in 1922 he formed his Creole Jazz Band, and is remembered for his discovery of Louis Armstrong. His compositions, such as 'Dippermouth Blues' and 'Dr Jazz', have become part of the standard traditional repertoire. >> Armstrong, Louis; jazz

Olives, Mount of or **Mount Olivet** [**ol**ivet] A rocky outcrop overlooking the Old City of Jerusalem across the Kidron Valley, a traditional Jewish burial ground. It is the supposed location of the ascension of the risen Jesus. >> Jerusalem; Jesus Christ

Olivier (of Brighton), Laurence (Kerr) Olivier, Baron (1907–89) Actor, producer, and director, born in Dorking, Surrey. He played all the great Shakespearean roles, while his versatility was underlined by his virtuoso display in *The Entertainer* (1957) as a broken-down low comedian. His films include *Henry V*, *Hamlet*, and *Richard III*. Divorced from his first wife, **Jill Esmond** in 1940, in the same year he married English actress **Vivien Leigh** (1913–67), whose film career included the role of Scarlett O'Hara in *Gone With the Wind*. They were divorced in 1960, and in 1961 he married English actress **Joan Plowright** (1929–). In 1962 he became director of the Chichester Theatre Festival and (1963–73) of the National Theatre. After 1974 he appeared chiefly in films and on television, notably in *Brideshead Revisited* (1982) and *King Lear* (1983). >> National Theatre

olivine [**ol**iviyn] A silicate mineral ranging in composition from Fe_2SiO_4 (*fayalite*) to Mg_2SiO_4 (*forsterite*); glassy, hard, and typically olive-green in colour. Its gem quality crystals are termed *peridot*. >> silicate minerals

Olmecs Members of a highly elaborate Middle American Indian culture on the Mexican Gulf Coast, at its height 1200–600 BC. The Olmecs influenced the rise and development of the other great civilizations of Middle America. They were probably the first people in the area to devise glyph writing and the 260-day Mesoamerican calendar. >> hieroglyphics ℹ

Olmsted, Frederick (Law) (1822–1903) Landscape architect, born in Hartford, CT. He was architect-in-chief of the improvement scheme for Central Park, New York City, and later designed other important public park schemes, including the grounds surrounding Washington, DC, and the campus at Berkeley, CA.

Olympia (Greece), Gr **Olímbia** 37°38N 21°39E. Village and national sanctuary in S Greece, on R Alfios; chief sanctuary of Zeus, from c.1000 BC; site of the Panhellenic religious festival held every 4 years from 776 BC; railway; major excavations in 19th-c; Temple of Zeus (5th-c BC). >> Greece ℹ; Pythian Games; Zeus, statue of

Olympia (USA) 47°03N 122°53W, pop (1995e) 38 700. Seaport capital of Washington State, USA; at the S end of Puget Sound; founded at the end of the Oregon Trail, 1850; capital of Washington Territory, 1853; railway. >> Oregon Trail; Washington (state)

Olympians In Greek mythology, a collective name for the major gods and goddesses, who were thought to live on Mt Olympus. >> Olympus, Mount (Greece)

Olympic Games A sports gathering held every 4 years by athletes from all over the world, each celebration taking place at a different venue. They evolved from the ancient Greek games, held at Olympia, which go back at least to the 8th-c BC. They were banned in AD 393 by the Christian Emperor Theodosius I, probably because of their pagan practices, and were revived in 1896 by French educator Pierre de Fredi, Baron de Coubertin (1863–1937), with Athens as the first venue. Today, more than 6000 competitors from around 100 nations compete at each games.

Since 1924 a separate Winter Olympic Games has been staged, and held in the same year as the Summer Games, until 1992, when it was decided to stage it midway between the Summer Games. >> RR1043

Olympus, Mount (Cyprus) [o**lim**puhs] 34°56N 32°52E. Mountain in the Troödos range of C Cyprus, rising to 1951 m/6401 ft; highest peak on the island. >> Cyprus ℹ

Olympus, Mount (Greece) [o**lim**pus], Gr **Olimbos** Range of mountains between Macedonia and Thessalia regions, N Greece; highest point, Mitikas (2917 m/9570 ft); traditionally the abode of the dynasty of gods headed by Zeus. >> Greece ℹ; Zeus

Om [om, ohm] A mystical and sacred monosyllable in Hindu tradition, the sound of which was believed to have a divine power. It was used at the beginning and end of prayers, as a mantra for meditation, and as an invocation itself. >> Hinduism; Upanishads

Omagh [oh**mah**], Ir **An Omaigh** 54°36N 7°18W, pop (1995e) 17 900. County town of Tyrone, WC Northern Ireland, on R Strule; inside the 19th-c Catholic parish church is the Black Bell of Drumragh (9th-c); town centre badly damaged by bomb-attack (Aug 1998), which killed 29, the worst incident of the Northern Ireland troubles since the 1960s. >> Tyrone

Omaha (Indians) [**oh**maha] A Siouan-speaking North American Plains Indian group, originally from the Atlantic seaboard. They now live on reservations in Nebraska. >> Plains Indians

Omaha (Nebraska) [**oh**maha] 41°17N 96°01W, pop (1995e) 351 000. City in E Nebraska, USA; a port on the Missouri R; fur-trading post, 1812; city status, 1867; largest city in the state; airport; railway; two universities (1878, 1908); major livestock market and meat-processing centre; centre for medical research; air force base. >> Nebraska

Oman [oh**man**], formerly **Muscat and Oman**, official name **Sultanate of Oman** pop (1995e) 1 845 000; area 300 000 sq km/115 800 sq mi. Independent state in the extreme SE corner of the Arabian peninsula; capital, Muscat; timezone GMT +4; population mainly Arabic; chief religion, Ibadhi Muslim; official language, Arabic; unit of currency, the Omani rial; the tip of the Musandam peninsula in the Strait of Hormuz is separated from the rest of the country by an 80 km/50 mi strip belonging to the United Arab Emirates; several peaks in the Jabal Akhdar over 3000 m/10 000 ft; vast sand desert in NE; desert climate with much local variation; hot and humid coast (Apr–Oct); relatively temperate in mountains; light monsoon rains in S (Jun–Sep); dominant maritime power of the W Indian Ocean in 16th-c; separatist tribal revolt, 1964, led to a police coup that installed the present sultan in 1970; independent state ruled by a sultan who is both head of state and premier, and who appoints a Cabinet and Consultative Council; oil discovered in 1964, now provides over 90% of government revenue; natural gas an important source of industrial power; attempts made to diversify the economy; c.70% of the population relies on agriculture. >> Muscat; RR1018 political leaders

Oman, Gulf of NW arm of the Indian Ocean, lying between Oman and Iran; linked to the Persian Gulf by the Strait of Hormuz, and (SE) to the Arabian Sea; 480 km/300 mi long. >> Hormuz, Strait of; Indian Ocean

Omar or **Umar** [**oh**mah(r)] (c.581–644) The second caliph (634–44), the father of one of Mohammed's wives, who succeeded Abu-Bakr. He was assassinated at Medina by a slave. >> Abu-Bakr; Mohammed

Omar Khayyám [ka**yam**], also spelled **Umar Khayyám** (c.1050–c.1122) Astronomer-poet, born in Nishapur, Persia. He was known to the Western world as a mathematician, until in 1859 Edward FitzGerald published a translation of his *Rubáiyát* ('Quatrains'). The original work is now regarded as an anthology of which little or nothing may be by Omar.

ombudsman [**om**budzman] An official who investigates complaints regarding administrative action by governments – so-called 'mal-administration'. The findings do not have the force of law, and are put in the form of reports from which it is hoped remedial action will result. The first such institution was created in Sweden at the beginning of the 19th-c, and today most countries have followed the lead. >> Parliamentary Commissioner for Administration

Omdurman [**om**doorman] 15°37N 32°29E, pop (1995e) 719 000. Major suburb of Khartoum, C Sudan; military headquarters of Mohammed Ahmed (the Mahdi), 1884; captured by the British under Kitchener, 1898; university (1961). >> Kitchener; Mohammed Ahmed; Sudan ℹ

OMNIMAX >> **IMAX**

omnivore Any animal, or human, whose diet includes both the flesh of animals and vegetable material; there may be specialized teeth to deal with the varied foodstuffs. >> carnivore ℹ; herbivore

Omsk 55°00N 73°22E, pop (1995e) 1 179 000. River port in W Siberian Russia; at the confluence of the Irtysh and Om Rivers; founded as a fortress, 1716; airport; on the Trans-Siberian Railway; university (1974). >> Russia ℹ; Trans-Siberian Railway

onager [**on**ajer] >> **ass**

Onassis, Aristotle (Socrates) [oh**na**sis] (1906–75) Greek millionaire shipowner, born in Smyrna, Turkey. He built up one of the world's largest independent fleets, and became a pioneer in the construction of supertankers. In 1968 he married **Jacqueline Bouvier Kennedy**. >> Onassis, Jacqueline Kennedy

Onassis, Jacqueline Kennedy, *née* **Jacqueline Lee Bouvier**, popularly known as **Jackie Kennedy** (1929–94) US first lady (1961–3), born in Southampton, NY. She married John F Kennedy in 1953. Her stoic behaviour after Kennedy's death enhanced her standing with the public, but she stunned the world when in 1968 she married the

Greek millionaire shipping magnate, Aristotle Onassis. After Onassis's death (1975), she worked in publishing. >> Kennedy, John F; Onassis, Aristotle

oncology [ong**kol**ojee] The branch of medicine concerned with the nature and origin of tumours, including the study of their natural history and response to treatment by drugs, surgery, or ionizing radiation (radioactive substances or X-rays). >> cancer; medicine

Ondaatje, Michael [on**da**chee] (1943–) Poet, novelist, and editor, born in Colombo, Sri Lanka. He moved to Canada in 1962, becoming a university lecturer. His novel *The English Patient* was co-winner of the Booker Prize in 1992 (filmed 1996, Oscar).

ondes Martenot [**õd mah(r)**tenoh] An electronic musical instrument invented in 1928 by Maurice Martenot; the name derives from Fr *ondes* '[musical] waves'. A keyboard, capable of producing a vibrato, is played by the right hand; the left operates the controls for timbre and dynamics. >> electrophone; keyboard instrument

O'Neal, (Patrick) Ryan (1941–) Film actor, born in Los Angeles, CA. He became well known as Rodney Harrison in the television series *Peyton Place*, a character he played for nearly five years. His films include *Love Story* (1970), *Paper Moon* (1973), *Faithful* (1996), and *Hacks* (1997).

Onega, Lake [on**yeg**a], Russ **Ozero Onezhskoye** area 9720 sq km/3752 sq mi. Second largest lake in Europe, NW European Russia; length, 250 km/155 mi; maximum depth, 120 m/394 ft; numerous islands (N). >> Russia ℹ

Oneida [oh**niy**da] An Iroquoian-speaking North American Indian agricultural group, the smallest tribe of the Iroquois League, originally based in C New York State. >> Iroquois Confederacy

O'Neill, Eugene (Gladstone) (1888–1953) Playwright, born in New York City. He joined the Provincetown Players in 1915, for whom *Beyond the Horizon* (1920, Pulitzer) was written. His best-known works are *Desire Under the Elms* (1924), *The Iceman Cometh* (1946), and *Long Day's Journey into Night* (1957, Pulitzer). He was the first US dramatist to receive the Nobel Prize for Literature, in 1936. >> Provincetown Players

O'Neill (of the Maine), Terence (Marne) O'Neill, Baron (1914–90) Northern Ireland statesman and prime minister (1963–9), born in Co Antrim, Northern Ireland. A member of the Northern Ireland parliament (1946–70), he became minister for home affairs (1956) and finance (1956–63), and then prime minister. He was a supporter of closer cross-border links with the Republic. >> Northern Ireland ℹ

One Nation Australian political party, formed in 1997 by Pauline Hanson, an Australian businesswoman elected as an independent MP in 1996. It advocates curbs on Asian immigration, the removal of Aboriginal welfare programmes, and a protectionist economic policy. It received strong support in the 1998 Queensland state elections, but increasing nationwide condemnation of its policies brought a major setback in the 1998 federal elections, with Hanson losing her Queensland seat. >> Australia ℹ

onion Any of several species of the genus *Allium*, probably originating in Asia, and all grown as vegetables. The ordinary onion (*Allium cepa*) has solitary, globular, or flask-shaped bulbs, often of great size, and inflated stalks bearing white flowers. **Spanish onion** is a variety with white-skinned bulbs; the **shallot** a variety with clusters of small, oval bulbs. (Family: Liliaceae). >> allium

on-line processing The use of computers to undertake tasks where transactions are initiated and data entered from terminals located in the users' offices. Common examples are the booking of airline tickets, holidays, hotels, and car hire, and transactions in building societies and some banks. >> batch processing; data processing

Ono, Yoko >> **Lennon, John**

onomastics [onoh**mas**tiks] The study of the history, development, and geographical distribution of proper names. All categories of names are included, such as people's first names and surnames, place names, home names, and the names of boats, trains, and pets. >> semantics

onomatopoeia [onomato**pee**a] (Gr 'name-making') The imitation of a natural (or mechanical) sound in language. This may be found in single words (*screech, babble, tick-tock*) or in longer units. It is especially heard in poetry.

Ontario pop (1995e) 10 704 000; area 1 068 580 sq km/412 578 sq mi. Province in SE Canada; capital, Toronto; rocky Canadian Shield in N, with clay belt suitable for farming; many lakes; N area sparsely populated, densely wooded; most populated and second largest province; widely explored by French fur traders and missionaries, 17th-c; British territory, 1763; many United Empire Loyalist immigrants after the American War of Independence; constituted as Upper Canada, 1791; separatist rebellion, 1837–8; joined to Lower Canada, 1840; modern province established at time of confederation, 1867; governed by a lieutenant-governor and a 125-member legislature. >> American Revolution; Canada ℹ; Ottawa; Toronto

Ontario, Lake Smallest of the Great Lakes, North America, on US–Canadian border; length 311 km/193 mi; breadth 85 km/53 mi; maximum depth 244 m/800 ft; area 19 011 sq km/7338 sq mi, just over half in Canada; connected (SW) with L Erie via the Niagara R and the Welland Ship Canal; outlet, the St Lawrence R (NE); never ice-bound. >> Great Lakes; St Lawrence River; Welland Ship Canal

ontological argument One of the traditional arguments for the existence of God, first developed by Anselm. God is defined as the being than which nothing greater can be conceived; something which exists must be greater than something which does not; therefore God must exist. >> Anselm, St; God

ontology A central part of metaphysics: the theory of what sorts of things really exist. A materialist will argue that matter is the only fundamental existent, in terms of which everything else must be explained. >> metaphysics

Onychophora [oni**kof**ora] A sub-phylum of primitive arthropods, comprising the velvet worms; sometimes classified as a separate phylum. >> *Peripatus*; velvet worm

onyx >> **agate**

oolite [**oh**uhliyt] A limestone composed of *ooliths*, ie rounded grains made of concentric layers of radiating fibres of carbonate, usually aragonite or calcite. Coarser oolites (> 3 mm/$\frac{1}{8}$ in diameter) are termed *pisolites*. >> calcite; limestone

Oort cloud [aw(r)t] A hypothesized source of the long-period comets; a spherical 'halo' about the Sun at a distance of c.50 000 AU; named after Dutch astronomer Jan Hendrik Oort (1900–92), who first noted the clustering of aphelia of new comets in this region. >> astronomical unit; comet; periapsis; Solar System

Oostende [oh**sten**duh] >> **Ostend**

opah [**oh**pa] >> **moonfish**

opal A natural form of amorphous (non-crystalline) silica (SiO_2). It is usually white, but gems have a characteristic play of rainbow colours. >> gemstones; silica

Op Art An abbreviation for **Optical Art**, a modern art movement of the 1960s which exploits the illusionistic effects of abstract spiral or wavy patterns, stripes, spots, etc. Hungarian-born French painter Victor Vasarely (1908–97)

and British painter Bridget Riley (1931–) were leading exponents. >> abstract / modern art

OPEC (Organization of Petroleum Exporting Countries) [**oh**pek] An international economic organization set up in 1960 with its headquarters in Vienna, originally consisting of 13 oil-producing countries (now 11). The founder members were Iran, Iraq, Kuwait, Saudi Arabia, and Venezuela; and they were later joined by Algeria, Ecuador (withdrew, 1992), Gabon (withdrew, 1996), Indonesia, Libya, Nigeria, Qatar, and the United Arab Emirates (formerly Abu Dhabi). Its purpose is to co-ordinate the petroleum policy of members to protect their interests. >> cartel; petroleum

open-cast mining >> **mining**

open-ended investment company An investment company which pools the funds of its shareholders, and invests in a diversified portfolio of stocks and shares. Such a company contrasts with a **closed-end investment company**, which has a fixed amount of share capital. >> investment company; unit trust

open-hearth process A steel-making process devised in 1860 by William Siemens (1823–83) and first successfully operated in 1864 by Pierre Emile Martin (1824–1915). The molten pig iron from which the steel is to be made is not in direct contact with the fuel providing the heat, but only with the hot flames from combustion which play on a shallow hearth containing pig-iron, scrap, and a flux. >> iron; Siemens; steel

open plan An arrangement of rooms in a building in which the internal doors and walls have been reduced to a minimum, or even omitted altogether. It is particularly associated with the International Style architecture of the 1920s and 1930s, and with offices and private housing after World War 2.

open shop >> **closed shop**

open systems interconnection (OSI) An international standard for the definition of connections between computers, which allows computers of different makes and architectures to communicate with each other for the transfer of data. The organization committed to the establishment of software and standards to enable computers to fulfil these requirements is the **Open Software Foundation (OSF)**. >> Unix

Open University An institution of higher education which enables students to study for a degree without attendance. Courses are usually based on a credit system, and the student graduates when sufficient credits have been amassed. The teaching is frequently carried out through correspondence units and broadcast or taped supporting programmes. >> credits; School of the Air

opera A stage work in which music plays a continuous or substantial role. The genre originated in China from the 10th-c, and in Europe at Florence c.1600. In Italy, opera, whether serious or comic, has usually been sung throughout; elsewhere other types have developed which alternate songs with spoken dialogue (*semi-opera* in England, *opéra comique* in France, *Singspiel* in Germany). Wagner's music dramas aimed at a *Gesamtkunstwerk* which united the arts of music, poetry, gesture, and painting. >> aria; La Scala; *opera buffa*; *opéra comique*; *opera seria*; operetta; overture; recitative; Royal Opera House; semi-opera; *Singspiel*; Sydney Opera House; Wagner; zarzuela

opera buffa Italian comic opera, especially of the 18th-c, with dialogue in recitative. Mozart's *Le nozze di Figaro* (1786, The Marriage of Figaro) is an outstanding example of the genre. >> opera; Mozart; recitative

opéra comique French opera, with spoken dialogue, originally comic but later including such dramatic operas as Bizet's *Carmen* (1875). >> Bizet; opera

opera seria Italian serious opera of the 18th-c and early 19th-c, exhibiting a rigid separation of aria and recitative. It reached its highest point of development in Mozart's *Idomeneo* (1781) and *La clemenza di Tito* (1791). >> aria; opera; recitative

operating system A computer program which supervises the running of all other programs on a computer. Common microprocessor operating systems are CP/M and MS DOS. >> DOS

operetta Light opera, with spoken dialogue and usually dancing, exemplified in the stage works of Offenbach, Strauss, and Sullivan. >> opera; Offenbach; Strauss, Johann (the Younger); Sullivan, Arthur

Ophir [**oh**fer] A land of unknown location, mentioned in the Bible as famous for its resources of gold; it is variously placed in Arabia, India, or E Africa. >> Bible

Ophiuchus [of**yoo**kus] (Gr 'serpent bearer') A large constellation on the celestial equator. >> constellation; RR968

ophthalmia [op-, of**thal**mia] Inflammation of the conjunctival membrane covering the eye in the newborn, or arising in one eye as a consequence of injury to the other eye. >> conjunctivitis; eye [i]

ophthalmology [op-, ofthal**mol**ojee] The branch of medical practice concerned with disorders and diseases of the eyes. It includes general or systemic diseases that may affect the eye, and their medical or surgical treatment. >> eye [i]; medicine

Ophuls or **Opüls, Max** [**o**püls], originally **Max Oppenheimer** (1902–57) Film director, born in Saarbrücken, Germany. His major films include *La Ronde* (1950, The Round) and *Lola Montez* (1955).

Opie, John [**oh**pee] (1716–1807) Portrait and historical painter, born near St Agnes, Cornwall. His portraits interested his teacher John Wolcot (1738–1819), by whom he was taken to London to become the 'Cornish Wonder', producing such works as 'The Murder of Rizzio' (1787).

opinion poll The taking of opinions from a sample of the electorate regarding their voting intentions, their views of political leaders, and wider political attitudes. They are also used to assess consumer preferences. Polls originated in the USA in the 1930s, and today are commonplace both at and between elections.

opioid peptides [**oh**pioyd **pep**tiydz] A family of chemical substances (peptides), including *enkephalins*, *endorphins*, and *dynorphins*, which are found in the brain, spinal cord, pituitary gland, gastro-intestinal tract, and adrenal medulla; also known as **endogenous opioids**. In the brain and spinal cord they appear to be involved in pain perception. >> endorphins; pain; peptide

Opitz (von Boberfeld), Martin (1597–1639) Poet, born in Bunzlau, Germany. He wrote in a scholarly style which influenced German poetry for 200 years, and introduced Renaissance poetic thinking into Germany.

opium The dried extract of the unripe seed capsules of the opium poppy, *Papaver somniferum*, which contains several narcotic alkaloids, including morphine. It was used by many ancient cultures for its properties of relieving pain, inducing sleep, and promoting psychological effects of peace and well-being. >> alkaloids; narcotics; Opium Wars

Opium Wars Two wars (1839–42, 1856–60) between China and the Western powers, especially Britain, fought over the question of commercial rights in China. When the Chinese attempted to stop opium imports (1839), a British force besieged Guangzhou (Canton), and imposed the Treaty of Nanjing (Nanking) in 1842. This opened Guangzhou, Nanjing, Shanghai, Fuzhou (Foochow), and Xiamen (Amoy) to Western trade. The Second Opium War, or **Arrow War**, began when Chinese boarded a Hong Kong ship (*The Arrow*), flying a British flag but suspected of piracy (1856). British troops occupied Guangzhou, and an Anglo-French army marched on Beijing. The Treaties of

Tianjin (Tientsin) in 1858 opened 10 more ports and legalized the opium traffic. These treaties established a strong Western influence in China, and helped stir up nationalist sentiments which led to the 1911 revolution. >> China ℹ; Guangzhou; Nanjing

Oporto [o**paw(r)**toh], Port **Porto** 41°08N 8°40W, pop (1995e) 309 000. City in N Portugal, on R Douro; second largest city in Portugal; bishopric; railway; university (1911); cathedral (12th-c). >> Portugal ℹ

opossum [**opo**sm] A marsupial of family Didelphidae (75 species), native to the New World; hind foot with opposable 'thumb', and lacking the 'comb' of many Australian marsupials; New World marsupials called opossums; Australian marsupials of similar appearance called **possums**. >> marsupial ℹ; possum

Oppenheimer, J(ulius) Robert [**o**penhiymer] (1904–67) Nuclear physicist, born in New York City. He became director of the atom bomb project at Los Alamos (1943–5). Opposing the hydrogen bomb project, in 1953 he was suspended from secret nuclear research as a security risk, but was awarded the Enrico Fermi prize in 1963. >> atomic bomb; hydrogen bomb ℹ

opposition (astronomy) The moment when a planet is opposite the Sun, as observed in our sky. It crosses the meridian at local midnight, which is therefore the best time for observing. >> planet; meridian; Sun

opposition (politics) The right of parties and political movements not holding government office to criticize the government and seek to replace it by offering alternative policies. In democratic systems the **Opposition** normally consists of those parties which oppose the government through parliamentary channels, their activities being recognized in electoral procedures. >> parliament

Ops The Roman goddess of plenty, the consort of Saturn, identified with Rhea. >> Rhea (mythology)

optical character reader (OCR) A machine which can read standard texts into a computer using a combination of optical and computer techniques. >> character recognition

optical fibres Fibres of transparent optical material, usually glass, for transmitting images or data. Each fibre consists of a core and an outer cladding of lower refractive index: light travels through the core and is contained within it by refraction. In telecommunications, optical fibres transmit data very long distances (up to 50 km/30 mi at one stretch). The technique is also used in medicine for viewing inaccessible parts of the body (*endoscopy*). >> endoscopy; light; telecommunications

optics The study of light and of instruments using light. Modern optical developments include optical fibres and their use in communications, optical logic elements and potentially optical computers, spatial filtering (eg allowing the removal of unwanted horizontal lines from photographs), the mass production of plastic lenses with complicated curved surfaces, lasers, and holography. >> holography; integrated optics; laser ℹ; lens; light; magnification; microscope; mirror; optical fibres ℹ; telescope ℹ; *see illustration on p. 632*

opting out >> **grant-maintained school**

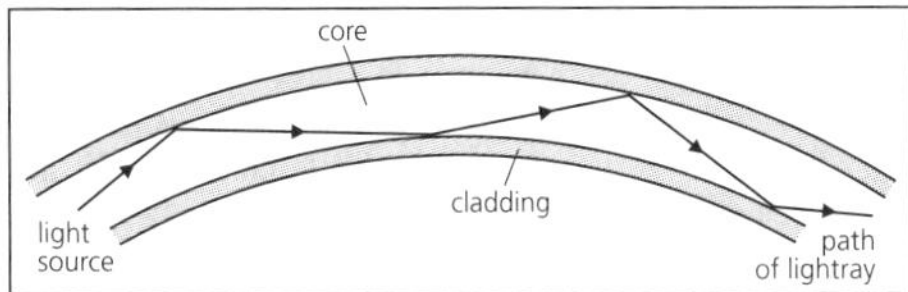

Section through optical fibre

options market A market in which traders can buy the right to buy or sell shares or commodities at a pre-agreed 'exercise price' at some future date or within some future period. Options markets exist only for a few widely traded shares and commodities. >> shares; stocks

optoelectronics The study of the production and control of light by electronic devices, such as semiconductor lasers, liquid crystals, and light-emitting diodes. It provides the technology for electronic displays in watches and calculators. >> electronics; integrated optics; liquid crystals; optical fibres ℹ

optometry [op**tom**etree] The assessment of the function of the eye, with special reference to errors of refraction, and the provision of appropriate corrective lenses and spectacles. It also now includes the specialized examination of the eye to diagnose a wide range of defects. These assessments are carried out by *optometrists*. >> eye ℹ

opuntia [o**puhn**sha] A large genus of cacti with stems made up of flattened, spiny, pear-shaped segments; native to the Americas, but widely introduced elsewhere. (Genus: *Opuntia*, 250 species. Family: Cactaceae.) >> cactus ℹ; prickly pear

Opus Dei [**oh**pus **day**ee] (Lat 'work of God') The title of a Roman Catholic society, founded in 1928, to promote the exercise of Christian virtues by individuals in secular society. In some countries and at certain periods (eg Spain in the mid-20th-c) it acquired a measure of political power. >> Roman Catholicism

ora >> **Komodo dragon** ℹ

orache [**o**rich] A member of a genus of annuals or perennials, found almost everywhere, some forming small shrubs; the whole plant often mealy white; flowers tiny, green. (Genus: *Atriplex*, 200 species. Family: Chenopodiaceae.)

oracle Divine prophetic declarations about unknown or future events, or the places (such as Delphi) or inspired individuals (such as the Sibyls) through which such communications occur. In ancient Greek stories, these revelations were usually given in response to questions put to the gods. >> Delphi; prophet; Sibyl

Oracle The teletext system operated by the UK Independent Broadcasting Association as a commercial service since 1981. The name is an acronym of *Optional Reception of Announcements by Coded Line Electronics*. In 1993 it was renamed *Teletext on 3*. >> Ceefax; teletext

oracle bones Inscribed shoulder blades of pig, ox, and sheep (later tortoise shells) used for divination by the Shang monarchs of N China, 16th–11th-c BC. The patterns of cracks made by hot brands applied to the bones were read as guidance from royal ancestors.

oracy The ability to express oneself coherently and to listen with good comprehension. The fostering of these skills has come to be seen as an important goal of childhood education, alongside the traditional focus on reading and writing. >> literacy

oral contraceptives >> **contraception**

oral history The means of discovering information about the past by interviewing subjects. The technique has been increasingly used since the 1970s to augment the written record, especially in areas where 'orthodox' sources are deficient or unobtainable.

oral surgery >> **dentistry**

Oran [o**rahn**] or **Wahran** 35°45N 0°38W, pop (1995e) 770 000. Seaport in N Algeria; founded 8th-c; first ruled by Arabs, then Spaniards (1509–1708), Turks (1708–32), and French (1831–1962); airport; railway; university (1965); fortress (16th-c). >> Algeria ℹ

Orange [o**rãzh**] 44°08N 4°48E, pop (1995e) 29 000. Town in SE France, on the R Rhône; developed around a group of Roman monuments, now a world heritage site. >> France ℹ

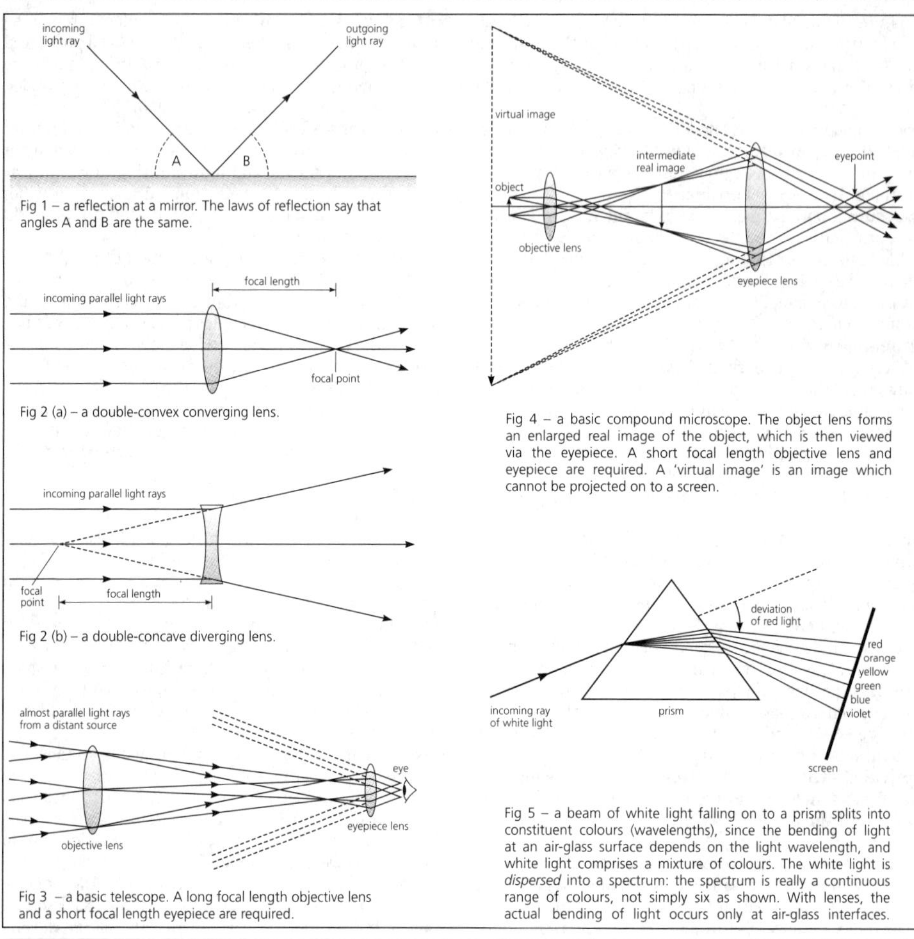

Fig 1 – a reflection at a mirror. The laws of reflection say that angles A and B are the same.

Fig 2 (a) – a double-convex converging lens.

Fig 2 (b) – a double-concave diverging lens.

Fig 3 – a basic telescope. A long focal length objective lens and a short focal length eyepiece are required.

Fig 4 – a basic compound microscope. The object lens forms an enlarged real image of the object, which is then viewed via the eyepiece. A short focal length objective lens and eyepiece are required. A 'virtual image' is an image which cannot be projected on to a screen.

Fig 5 – a beam of white light falling on to a prism splits into constituent colours (wavelengths), since the bending of light at an air-glass surface depends on the light wavelength, and white light comprises a mixture of colours. The white light is *dispersed* into a spectrum: the spectrum is really a continuous range of colours, not simply six as shown. With lenses, the actual bending of light occurs only at air-glass interfaces.

Optics

Orange, Princes of >> **William I** (of the Netherlands); **William III**

orange A citrus fruit 7–10 cm/$2\frac{3}{4}$–4 in diameter, globular with thick, often rough rind. The familiar edible fruit is the **sweet orange** (*Citrus sinensis*). **Bergamot orange** (*Citrus bergamia*) is grown as a source of bergamot oil. (Genus: *Citrus*. Family: Rutaceae.) >> citrus; mandarin

Orange Free State >> **Free State**

Orange Order An association that developed from the Orange Society, which had been formed in 1795 to counteract growing Catholic influence in Ireland. The name was taken from the Protestant Dutch dynasty represented by William III. Organized in 'Lodges', it has operated as organized Protestantism in Northern Ireland since partition. >> Protestantism; William III

Orange River, Afrikaans **Oranjerivier** River in Lesotho, South Africa, and Namibia; rises in the Drakensberg Mts in NE Lesotho; enters the Atlantic Ocean; length 2100 km/1300 mi; dammed in several places as part of the **Orange River Project** (begun 1963) to provide irrigation and power. >> Lesotho i; Namibia i

orang-utan An ape (*Pongo pygmaeus*) native to forests of Sumatra and Borneo; height, 1.5 m/5 ft; sparse covering of long shaggy red-brown hair; armspan up to 2.25 m/ $7\frac{1}{2}$ ft; adult male with large naked fatty folds around face. >> ape

Oratorians 1 A community of priests, followers of St Philip of Neri (16th-c), living together without vows, and devoted to prayer, preaching, and attractive services of worship. >> Neri **2** Priests of the French Oratory, or **Oratory of Jesus Christ**, founded in 1611 and re-established in 1852. This community is noted for educating priests and furthering popular devotion.

oratorio A non-liturgical, quasi-dramatic sacred work, usually for solo voices, chorus, and orchestra. It takes its name from the Italian 'prayer-hall' in which the earliest oratorios were performed in the mid-17th-c. Examples include Handel's oratorios, originally performed in the London theatres, Haydn's *The Creation* (1798), and works by Mendelssohn and Elgar. >> Elgar; Handel; Haydn; Mendelssohn

oratory The art and practice of public speaking. Effective oratory requires that the choice of language, its style, and mode of delivery should be appropriate for a given audience, location, and occasion. Its major forms (legal, political, ceremonial) can be traced back to earliest times, notably to the Greek orators of the 4th-c BC (eg Demosthenes), and the Roman orators of the 1st-c BC (eg Cicero).

In modern times, oratory continues to be effectively practised, as can be seen in the speeches of Hitler, Churchill, John F Kennedy, and Martin Luther King Jr, and the radio or television debates and 'fireside chats' used by leading politicians. >> Cicero; Demosthenes; rhetoric

orbit In astronomy, the path followed by any celestial object or satellite moving through a gravitational field. A **geostationary orbit** is one followed by a satellite above the Equator at 35 900 km/22 300 mi, where it keeps in exact step with the Earth's rotation and is thus always in the same part of the sky. >> gravitation; satellite

Orcagna [aw(r)**kan**ya], originally **Andrea de Cione** (c.1308–c.1368) Painter, sculptor, and architect, born in Florence, Italy. His greatest paintings are frescoes, an altarpiece in Santa Maria Novella, Florence, and 'Coronation of the Virgin' (National Gallery, London). >> altarpiece; fresco

orchestra Originally the name for the semi-circular space in front of a stage, later extended to the body of instrumentalists that performed there; today, a regular constituted body of string players, with additional woodwind, brass, and percussion as required. The advent of the concerto in the late 17th-c stimulated the formation of four-part string orchestras, and by the end of the 18th-c the standard orchestra for the symphonies of Haydn and Mozart included also pairs of flutes, oboes, bassoons, horns, trumpets, timpani, and (sometimes) clarinets. The modern symphony orchestra consists of about 100 players. >> musical instruments; promenade concert

orchid A monocotyledonous plant belonging to the family Orchidaceae, one of the largest and most advanced flowering-plant families, containing some 17 000 species. Orchids are found in virtually all parts of the world except Antarctica, but are especially abundant in the tropics. They are best known for their complex, often spectacular and exotic flowers, and for their highly developed pollination mechanisms. They exert a strong fascination for many people, and numerous species are now commonly cultivated, with whole societies devoted to their study and care. >> cattleya; cymbidium; helleborine; twayblade; vanilla

Orczy, Emma, Baroness [**awt**see, **awk**see] (1865–1947) Writer, born in Tarna-Eörs, Hungary. *The Scarlet Pimpernel* (1905) was her first success, followed by many popular adventure romances.

Orchids

Order in Council In British government, legislation made by the Monarch in Council allowed by act of parliament, but which does not need to be ratified by parliament. In practice the decisions are taken by government ministers, not by the monarch. >> parliament

Order of Merit (OM) In the UK, a decoration for those who have provided pre-eminent service to the country. Instituted by Edward VII in 1902 and limited to 24 members, it comprises a military and a civil class. The ribbon is blue and scarlet.

Orders, Holy Grades of ministry in Orthodox, Roman Catholic, and Anglican Churches. **Major Orders** consist of ordained ministers, bishops, priests, and deacons (and, in the Western Church, subdeacons). **Minor Orders** include, in the Western Church, lectors, porters, exorcists, acolytes; in the Eastern Church, subdeacons. Major Orders constitute the hierarchy of the Church, to be distinguished from the laity. A distinction is also drawn between **First Orders** (fully professed men), **Second Orders** (fully professed women), and **Third Orders** (those affiliated usually to one of the Mendicant Orders). >> bishop; deacon; Mendicant Orders; priest; Tertiaries

orders of architecture The arrangement of the parts of a column and an entablature in classical architecture according to one of five accepted principles, or orders: Tuscan, Doric, Ionic, Corinthian, Composite. Originally developed by the ancient Greeks, the earliest surviving codification is by the 1st-c Roman Vitruvius. >> Composite / Corinthian / Doric / Ionic / Tuscan order; column; entablature; frieze; *see illustration on p.634*

Ordinance of 1787 An Act of the American Continental Congress establishing procedures by which newly-settled Western territories could enter the American union on the basis of full political equality with the original states. >> Continental Congress

Ordnance Datum (OD) The mean sea level in the UK, used as a fixed reference from which the elevations of all points in the country are surveyed. The equivalent in the USA is the **Sea Level Datum**. >> surveying

Ordnance Survey of Great Britain The survey and mapping agency established by the 1841 Ordnance Survey Act, although founded initially in 1791 as the Trigonometrical Survey. Maps were originally produced at a scale of 1 in to the mi. The basic scales are 1: 1250 (1 cm to 1250 cm or 1 in to 1250 in, ie 50 in to the mi), 1: 2500 (or c.50 in to the mi), and 1: 10 000, which supersedes the 1: 10 350 (c.6 in to the mi). >> National Grid reference system

Ordovician period [aw(r)do**vish**ian] The second of the geological periods of the Palaeozoic era, extending from c.505 to 438 million years ago. All animal life was restricted to the sea; numerous invertebrates flourished, and the first vertebrates appeared (jawless fish). >> geological time scale; Palaeozoic era; RR976

ore A mineral deposit from which metallic and non-metallic constituents can be extracted. Ores may be formed directly from crystallizing magma, precipitated from hydrothermal fluids associated with igneous activity, or concentrated in alluvial deposits after weathering. >> magma; minerals

oregano [ori**gah**noh, o**reg**anoh] >> **marjoram**

Oregon [**o**riguhn] pop (1995e) 3 192 000; area 251 409 sq km/ 97 073 sq mi. State in NW USA; the 'Beaver State'; established as a fur-trading post, 1811; occupied by both Britain and the USA, 1818–46, when the international boundary was settled on the 49th parallel; became a territory, 1848; joined the Union as the 33rd state, 1859; population grew

The five orders of architecture

after 1842 with settlers following the Oregon Trail; split by the Cascade Range; fertile Willamette R valley in the W, with the Coast Ranges beyond; High Desert in the E, a semi-arid plateau used for ranching and wheat-growing; highest point, Mt Hood (3424 m/11 234 ft); about half the area forested; capital, Salem; produces over a quarter of the USA's softwood and plywood; major tourist region; Crater Lake National Park in the SW. >> Oregon boundary dispute; Oregon Trail; Salem (Oregon); United States of America [i]; RR994

Oregon boundary dispute A disagreement between the British and US governments over the frontier between respective possessions on the W coast of North America. The Oregon Treaty (1846) settled on the 49th parallel, dipping S at Juan de Fuca Strait to maintain British claims to Vancouver Island. >> Oregon

Oregon Trail The main route for emigration to the far W of the USA in the 1840s. The trail began at Independence, Missouri, crossed the Rockies at South Pass in Wyoming, and terminated at the mouth of the Columbia R. >> Oregon

Orestes [**ores**teez] In Greek legend, the son of Agamemnon and Clytemnestra. After his father's murder he went into exile, but returned to kill Aegisthus and his mother, for which he was pursued by the Erinyes. >> Aegisthus; Agamemnon; Erinyes

orfe [aw(r)f] Freshwater fish (*Leuciscus idus*) widespread in lowland rivers and lakes of E Europe and C Russia; length up to 40 cm/16 in; greenish-brown on back, sides silver, underside white; also known as **ide**. (Family: Cyprinidae.)

Orff, Carl (1895–1982) Composer, born in Munich, Germany. He is best known for his operatic setting of a 13th-c poem, *Carmina Burana* (1937); later works include *Oedipus* (1959) and *Prometheus* (1966).

organ The name of various types of musical instruments, but without further qualification referring to an instrument in which air from a windchest, fed by bellows, is released under pressure into metal or wooden pipes of various lengths and bores by the action of keys operated by the player's fingers or feet. The ranks of pipes are brought into action by means of drawknobs (or *stops*). The **cinema organ**, with its distinctive 'voicing' and its special effects (train hooter, telephone bell, etc) was developed in the early 20th-c, especially by the Wurlitzer Company in the USA, to accompany silent films and to play popular medleys during intervals. In **electronic organs**, an invention of the 1920s, the pipes are replaced by other means of tone production, such as electromagnets and oscillators. >> aerophone; barrel organ; calliope; electrophone; keyboard instrument; reed organ

organic chemistry That part of chemistry which deals specifically with the structures and reactions of the compounds of carbon. These compounds are much more numerous than those of the other elements. >> carbon; chemistry

organic farming Farming without synthetic chemical fertilizers, sprays, or pharmaceuticals. Fertility is maintained through the addition of animal manures and composts, and through rotations which include nitrogen-fixing plants such as clover. In some countries there is a premium market for certified organic produce. >> fertilizer

Organisation de l'Armée Secrète >> **OAS**

Organisation Européene pour la Recherche Nucléaire (CERN) (European Organization for Nuclear Research) The principal European centre for research in particle physics, supported by most European countries; located in Geneva; founded in 1954, and originally called the **Conseil Européene pour la Recherche Nucléaire**. >> particle physics

Organization for Economic Co-operation and Development (OECD) An international organization set up in 1961 to assist member states to develop economic and social policies aimed at high sustained economic growth with financial stability. In early 1999 it had 29 members. It is located in Paris.

Organization for International Economic Co-operation >> **COMECON**

Organization for Security and Co-operation in Europe (OSCE), formerly known as **Conference on Security and Co-operation in Europe (CSCE)** A political grouping first established in 1975 and which came to prominence after the European political revolution of 1989–90. It embraces Europe, USA, and Canada, and had 54 member states in 1999 (with Albania the only European non-participant). Its secretariat opened in Prague in 1991.

Organization of African Unity (OAU) An organization founded in 1963 by representatives of 32 African governments meeting in Addis Ababa, which dedicated itself to the eradication of all forms of colonialism in Africa. Less active in recent years, it had 52 members in 1999.

Organization of American States (OAS) A regional agency established in 1948 for the purpose of co-ordinating the work of a variety of inter-American agencies, recognized within the terms of the United Nations Charter. The vast majority of states within the Americas are members (34 in 1999). >> Pan-American Union; United Nations

Organization of Arab Petroleum Exporting Countries (OAPEC) An organization formed under the umbrella of the Organization of Petroleum Exporting Countries (OPEC) in 1968 by Saudi Arabia, Kuwait, and Libya, with its headquarters in Kuwait. By 1972 all the Arab oil producers had joined. >> OPEC

Organization of Central American States An agency established in 1951 by Costa Rica, El Salvador, Guatemala, Honduras, and Nicaragua (Panama refused to join) to promote economic, social, and cultural co-operation. In 1965 this was extended to include political and educational co-operation.

Organization of Petroleum Exporting >> **OPEC**

Organization of the Islamic Conference An organization of sovereign Muslim states, formed in 1971, with the aims of promoting Islamic solidarity, safeguarding Muslim holy places, and promoting the rights of all Muslim peoples. It had 54 members in 1999. >> Abdul Rahman

oribi [**o**ribee] A dwarf antelope (*Ourebia ourebi*) native to Africa S of the Sahara; pale brown with tufts of long hairs on the knees; males with short spike-like horns. >> antelope

orienteering A form of cross-country running with the aid of a map and compass. The sport was devised by Swedish youth leader Ernst Killander in 1918, and based on military training techniques. Popular in the Nordic countries, it developed as an international sport in the 1960s. >> RR1057

origami [ori**gah**mee] The art of making models of animals or other objects by folding sheets of paper into shapes with the minimum use of scissors or other implements. It originated in the 10th-c in Japan, where it is widely practised.

Origen [**o**rijen] (c.185–c.254) Christian Biblical scholar and theologian of Alexandria, Egypt, who became head of the catechetical school in Alexandria. His views on the unity of God and the salvation of the devil were condemned by Church Councils in the 5th–6th-c.

Original Dixieland Jass Band The first band to make a jazz record. It consisted of Nick LaRocca (1889–1961), cornet; Eddie Edwards (1891–1963), trombone and violin; Larry Shields (1893–1953), clarinet; Henry Ragas (1890–1919), piano; and Tony Sbarbaro (1897–1969), drums; all were born in New Orleans, LA. Their recordings in 1917 launched jazz as an international phenomenon. They also established *jazz* as its name: a rival club owner castigated them as players of 'jass music', meaning it was suitable only for brothels, and they impudently added the word to their band name. >> jazz

original sin The traditional Christian doctrine that, by virtue of the Fall, every human being inherits a 'flawed' or 'tainted' nature in need of regeneration and with a disposition to sinful conduct. >> Christianity; sin

oriole A bird of the Old World family Oriolidae (**Old World orioles**, 28 species) or the New World family Icteridae (**American orioles**, c.90 species). >> blackbird; bobolink; grackle; redwing

Orion (astronomy) [o**riy**on] Perhaps the most conspicuous of all constellations, although only 26th in size. Equatorial, and thus visible in both hemispheres, with bright stars Rigel and Betelgeuse (1st magnitude) poised above brilliant Sirius in Canis Major. The **Orion nebula** is found in the 'sword' of Orion. It is the nearest and brightest emission nebula, 500 parsec away. >> Betelgeuse; constellation; Rigel; Sirius; RR968

Orion (mythology) [o**riy**on] In Greek mythology, a gigantic hunter, beloved by Eos and killed by Artemis. He was changed into a constellation. >> Artemis; Eos

Orissa [o**ri**sa] pop (1995e) 34 110 000; area 155 782 sq km/60 132 sq mi. State in E India; ceded to the Marathas, 1751; taken by the British, 1803; subdivision of Bengal until 1912, when province of Bihar and Orissa created; separate province, 1936; became a state, 1950; capital, Bhubaneswar; governed by a Legislative Assembly. >> India [i]

Orkney [**aw(r)k**nee] pop (1995e) 20 200; area 976 sq km/377 sq mi. Group of islands off NE Scotland; 15 main islands (especially Mainland, South Ronaldsay, Sanday, Westray, Hoy); capital, Kirkwall, on Mainland; Norse dependency from 9th-c; annexed by Scotland from Norway and Denmark, 1472; fishing, farming, weaving; North Sea oil terminal on Flotta; oil service bases on Mainland and Hoy; Neolithic village at Skara Brae; isolated stack (height 137 m/449 ft), Old Man of Hoy (NW of Hoy); Scapa Flow, sea area within the islands, used in World Wars 1 and 2 as a major naval anchorage; German Fleet surrendered there in 1918. >> Scotland [i]; Skara Brae

Orlando 28°33N 81°23W, pop (1995e) 183 000. City in C Florida, USA; settled c.1844; airfield; railway; tourism, aerospace, and electronic industries; Walt Disney World. >> Disney; Florida

Orleans [aw(r)**lee**anz], Fr **Orléans**, ancient **Aurelianum** 47°54N 1°52E, pop (1995e) 108 000. Ancient town in C France; on R Loire; associated with Joan of Arc, 'The Maid of Orleans', who raised the English siege here in 1429; road and rail junction; bishopric; centre of fruit and

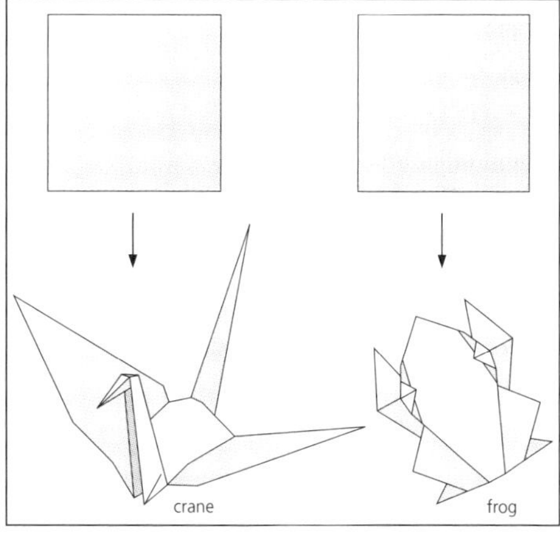

Origami figures – the crane is usually the first one taught

vegetable region; university (1309); cathedral (13th–16th-c). >> Hundred Years' War; Joan of Arc

Orléans, Charles, duc d' (Duke of) [aw(r)layã] (1391–1465) Poet, born in Paris. In 1406 he married his cousin Isabella, widow of Richard II of England. He commanded at Agincourt (1415), was taken prisoner, and carried to England, where he lived for 25 years, composing courtly poetry in French and English. >> Agincourt, Battle of

Orléans, Louis Philippe Joseph, duc d' (Duke of) [aw(r)layã], known as **Philippe Egalité** ('equality') (1747–93) French Bourbon prince, born in Saint-Cloud, the cousin of King Louis XVI and father of Louis Philippe. At the Revolution he supported the Third Estate, and in 1792 renounced his title of nobility for his popular name. At the Convention he voted for the king's death but was arrested after the defection of his eldest son to the Austrians (1793), and guillotined. >> French Revolution [i]

Orléans, House of The junior branch of the Valois and Bourbon dynasties in France. >> Bourbons; Louis Philippe; Orléans, Louis Philippe Joseph; Valois

Ormandy, Eugene [**aw(r)**mandee], originally **Jenö Ormandy** (1899–1985) Conductor, born in Budapest. He conducted the Minneapolis Symphony Orchestra (1931–6) and the Philadelphia Orchestra (1936–80).

ormer >> **abalone**

ormolu or **ormulu** A gilded metal alloy of copper, zinc, and tin used in France since the 17th-c for candelabra, clocks, and other decorative luxury objects. >> alloy

Ornithischia [aw(r)ni**thisk**ia] The bird-hipped dinosaurs, characterized by the backward-pointing pubis bone in the pelvic girdle, similar to that of birds. They comprise exclusively plant-eating groups. >> ankylosaur; Ceratopsia; dinosaur [i]; hadrosaur; Iguanodon; *Protoceratops*; *Stegosaurus*; *Triceratops*

Ornitholestes [aw(r)nitho**les**teez] >> ***Coelurus***

ornithology The study of birds. It includes observations on the evolutionary relationships of the different groups, the distribution of species and populations, ecology, conservation, migration, behaviour of individuals, birdsong, anatomy, physiology, biochemistry, and genetics. >> bird [i]

orogeny [o**ro**jenee] A period of mountain-building involving intense deformation and subsequent uplift of rocks when crustal plates collide. The plate boundaries define an **orogenic belt** which forms a fold-mountain chain. Examples include the Himalayas, which resulted from the collision of the Indian and Asian continental plates. >> igneous rock; intrusive rock; plate tectonics [i]

Oromo >> **Galla**

Orozco, José Clemente [o**ros**koh] (1883–1949) Painter, born in Zapotlán, Mexico. He was one of the greatest mural painters of the 20th-c, decorating public buildings in Mexico and the USA, in a powerful realistic style, verging on caricature, which acted as a vehicle for his revolutionary socialist ideas.

Orpheus [**aw(r)**fyoos] A legendary Greek poet from Thrace, able to charm beasts and even stones with the music of his lyre. In this way he obtained the release of his wife Eurydice from Hades. >> Eurydice; Hades

Orphism A modern art movement which flourished c.1912, experimenting with pure colour in ways that heralded abstract painting. The leading exponent was Delaunay. >> Delaunay; modern art

orris A white-flowered species of iris (*Iris germanica*, variety *florentina*), with fleshy rhizomes which provide **orris root**, used in perfumery. (Family: Iridaceae.) >> iris; rhizome

Ortega y Gasset, José [aw(r)**tay**ga ee ga**set**] (1883–1955) Philosopher and existentialist humanist, born in Madrid. His critical writings on modern authors made him an influential figure, and his *La rebelión de las masas* (1930, The Revolt of the Masses) foreshadowed the Civil War. >> existentialism

Ortelius [aw(r)**teel**ius], Lat name of **Abraham Ortels** (1527–98) Cartographer, born in Antwerp. His *Theatrum Orbis Terrarum* (1570, Epitome of the Theatre of the World) was the first great atlas. >> cartography; engraving

orthoclase [**aw(r)**thoklayz] A form of the mineral potassium feldspar; usually pink and a primary constituent of granite. >> feldspar; granite

orthodontics >> **dentistry**

Orthodox Church or **Eastern Orthodox Church** A communion of self-governing Churches recognizing the honorary primacy of the Patriarch of Constantinople. It includes the patriarchates of Alexandria, Antioch, Constantinople, and Jerusalem, and the Churches of Russia, Bulgaria, Cyprus, Serbia, Georgia, Romania, Greece, Poland, Albania, and the Czech and Slovak Republics. >> Greek Orthodox Church; patriarch; Russian Orthodox Church

orthopaedics / orthopedics [aw(r)tho**pee**diks] The branch of surgery concerned with injuries and disorders affecting the skeleton. It includes the treatment of fractures and dislocations, the correction of deformities of posture, and the surgical replacement of damaged joints by artificial prostheses. >> bone; dislocation (medicine); fracture (medicine); skeleton [i]; vertebral column

Orthoptera [aw(r)**thop**tera] An order of medium-to-large insects found in all terrestrial habitats; hindlegs usually modified for jumping; many produce sound by rubbing their limbs or wings (*stridulation*). >> cricket (entomology); grasshopper; katydid; locust

ortolan [**aw(r)**tohlan] A bunting found from Europe to Mongolia (*Emberiza hortulana*) (winters in N Africa); also known as the **ortolan bunting** or **garden bunting**. >> bunting

Orton, Joe, popular name of **John Kingsley Orton** (1933–67) Playwright, born in Leicester, Leicestershire. He is known for his erotic and anarchic farces, among them *Loot* (1964) and *What the Butler Saw* (1967). He was murdered by his male lover in London. *The Orton Diaries* contain startling revelations. >> absurdism

Orwell, George, pseudonym of **Eric Arthur Blair** (1903–50) Novelist and essayist, born in Motihari, Bengal, India. He developed his own brand of socialism in *The Road to Wigan Pier* (1937) and many essays. He is best known for his satire of totalitarian ideology in *Animal Farm* (1945), and for the prophetic novel *1984* (1949). >> socialism

oryx [**o**riks] A grazing antelope with very long slender horns; pale with striking white and dark markings on face and underparts; three species in genus *Oryx*, two from Africa, one from the Middle East. >> antelope

Osaka [oh**sa**ka], formerly **Naniwa** 34°40N 135°30E, pop (1995e) 2 646 000. Port city in S Honshu, Japan; developed around a castle, built 16th-c; city almost completely destroyed in World War 2; now third largest city in Japan; airport; railway; subway; several universities; part of the Osaka–Kobe industrial area. >> Honshu; Kobe

Osborne, John (James) (1929–94) Playwright and actor, born in London. *Look Back in Anger* (1956) and *The Entertainer* (1957), established him as the leading younger exponent of British social drama. The 'hero' of the first, Jimmy Porter, became the prototype 'Angry Young Man'. >> Angry Young Men

Oscar The familiar name for the statuettes awarded annually by the American Academy of Motion Picture Arts and Sciences for outstanding performances and creative and technical achievement in films shown during the preceding year. There are many accounts of the origin of the name, all speculative: in one account, it arose when a secretary at the Academy said that the figure reminded her of her Uncle Oscar. >> RR1042

oscillation A repetitive periodic change. Electrical currents in radio receivers oscillate, for example. Mechanical oscillations, such as those in a building caused by passing traffic, are usually called **vibrations**. >> damping; oscillator; periodic motion

oscillator A circuit for converting direct current (DC) into alternating current (AC), of a required frequency. Part of the output is returned via a feedback circuit to the input. >> electricity; oscillation; superheterodyne

Osee >> **Hosea, Book of**

O'Shane, Pat(ricia) June (1941–) Magistrate, born in Mossman, Queensland, Australia. In 1978 she was the first person of Aboriginal descent to be called to the bar. She has made a number of progressive, well-publicized decisions concerning women and Aboriginal people. >> Aborigines

Osheroff, Douglas D [**osh**erhof] (1945–) Physicist, born in Aberdeen, WA. He studied at Cornell University, working under Lee and Richardson as part of the team which in 1972 discovered the superfluidity of helium-3. He shared the Nobel Prize for Physics in 1996.

osier A species of willow forming a shrub or small tree (*Salix viminalis*), growing to 3–5 m/10–16 ft; native to Europe and Asia; often grown as a source of *withies* – long pliant stems used, for example, in basketwork. >> willow

Osiris [oh**siy**ris] Ancient Egyptian god, the husband of Isis. He became king of the Underworld, and was seen as the judge of the soul after death. >> Isis

Oslo [**oz**loh], formerly **Christiania** or **Kristiania** 59°55N 10°45E, pop (1995e) 474 000. Capital city of Norway; founded, 11th-c; under the influence of the Hanseatic League, 14th-c; destroyed by fire, 1624; rebuilt by Christian IV and renamed Christiania; capital, 1905; renamed Oslo, 1925; bishopric; airports; railway; largest port in Norway, the base of a large merchant shipping fleet; university (1811); cathedral (17th-c), royal palace (1825–48), castle (13th-c). >> Hanseatic League; Norway ℹ

osmiridium [ozmi**rid**ium] A naturally occurring alloy of osmium and iridium in which the iridium content is less than 35%; *iridosmine* has osmium greater than 35%. It occurs with platinum ores. >> alloy; platinum

osmosis >> **osmotic pressure**

osmotic pressure [oz**mo**tik] The pressure that must be exerted on a solution containing a given concentration of solute separated from a sample of the pure solvent by a membrane which prevents the solvent's passage. Exerting a pressure greater than the osmotic pressure causes the solvent to pass from the solution to the solvent; this 'reverse osmosis' is a method of purifying water. Osmosis is an important process in living organisms, especially aquatic organisms. >> solution

Osnabrück [**ohz**nabrük] 52°17N 8°03E, pop (1995e) 168 000. Manufacturing city in Germany; badly bombed in World War 2; railway; bishopric; university (1973); cathedral (13th-c). >> Germany ℹ

osprey A large bird of prey (*Pandion haliaetus*), inhabiting sea coasts or inland waters worldwide; also known as **fish hawk** or **fish eagle**; dives on fish, grasping them in its talons. (Family: Pandionidae.) >> bird of prey

Ossa, Mount 41°54S 146°01E. Highest mountain in Tasmania (1617 m/5305 ft). >> Tasmania

Ossian or **Oisín** Legendary Irish poet and warrior, the son of the 3rd-c hero Fingal or Fionn MacCumhail. The Scottish poet **James Macpherson** (1736–96) professed to have collected and translated his works, though it was later shown that the poems were largely of his own devising. >> Romanticism

Ostade, Adriaen van [os**tah**duh] (1610–85) Painter and engraver, born in Haarlem, The Netherlands. His subjects are taken mostly from everyday peasant life. His brother, **Isaak** (1621–49), treated similar subjects, but excelled at winter scenes and landscapes.

Ostend, Flemish **Oostende**, Fr **Ostende** 51°13N 2°55E, pop (1995e) 69 400. Seaport in W Belgium; principal ferry port for UK (Dover and Folkestone); largest seaside resort in Belgium; headquarters of the Belgian fishing fleet; railway. >> Belgium ℹ

osteoarthritis A common disease of joints of both humans and other animals; also known as **osteoarthrosis**. Over 80% of those over middle age are affected. The condition is a primary degeneration and disintegration of the articular cartilage, which tends to affect the weight-bearing joints such as the hips; but no joint is immune. The cause is unknown, though wear and tear is often invoked. >> arthritis; bone; joint

osteology The scientific study of bone and bones. It is used in anthropology for species identification and carbon dating, in clinical medicine for the assessment of development in the individual, and in forensic medicine for the reconstruction and sexing of victims. >> bone

osteomalacia [ostiohma**lay**sha] A metabolic disorder of bone caused by a lack of vitamin D. In children and adolescents, normal growth is retarded, and the condition is called *rickets*. >> bone; rickets; vitamins ℹ

osteomyelitis [ostiohmiye**liy**tis] Infection within bone. It arises either as a result of blood-borne infection (eg tuberculosis) or, less commonly, following direct injury. >> bone

osteopathy [osti**op**athee] A system of treatment originally based on the belief that abnormalities in the skeletal system are responsible for a wide range of diseases by interfering with the blood supply to the region affected. Osteopaths use such techniques as massage and manipulation, stretch various joints, and apply high-velocity thrusts. >> alternative medicine; bone; chiropractic; skeleton ℹ

osteoporosis [ostiohpo**roh**sis] Thinning and weakening of bones because of a loss of calcium from their substance. There is a characteristic stooping posture. It tends to occur in elderly women, and appears to be related to a reduction in the level of sex hormones. >> bone; calcium; Cushing's disease

Ostia [**os**tia] The ancient town situated at the mouth of the Tiber in W Italy. It was Rome's main naval base during the Punic Wars. >> Punic Wars

Ostpolitik [ostpoli**teek**] The policy initiated in West Germany in the 1960s to normalize relations with communist countries which recognized the German Democratic Republic and to reduce hostility between

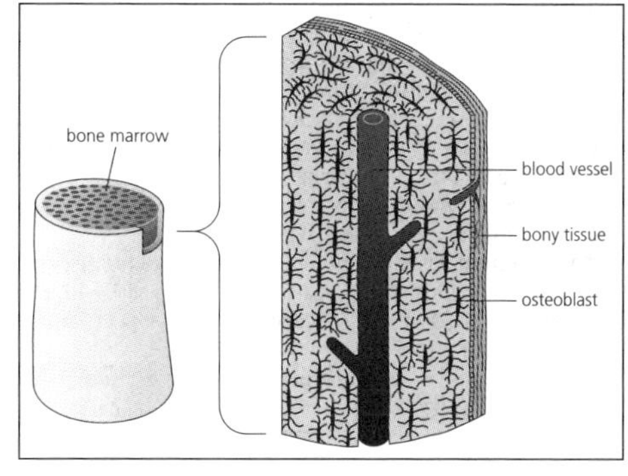

Osteology – section through a long bone

West Germany and its Eastern neighbours. Largely masterminded by Willy Brandt, the policy can be viewed as a forerunner of detente. >> Brandt, Willy; detente

ostracism In ancient Athens, the means whereby unpopular citizens could be banished for up to 10 years without loss of property or citizenship.

ostracod A small, short-bodied crustacean with a hinged bivalve shell that completely encloses the body; legs typically adapted for walking over substrate; over 10 000 fossil species and 5700 living species. (Class: Ostracoda.) >> bivalve; crustacean

Ostrava [**os**trava] 49°50N 18°13E, pop (1995e) 333 000. Industrial city in Czech Republic; airport; railway. >> Czech Republic ℹ

ostrich The largest living bird (*Struthio camelus*) (height up to 2.75 m/9 ft); unable to fly; fastest animal on two legs (c.70 kph/45 mph); largest egg of any living bird; inhabits dry areas of Africa. (Family: Struthionidae.)

Ostrogoths A Germanic people, forming one of the two great Gothic tribes, who entered Italy in 489 and established a kingdom under Theodoric. The kingdom collapsed in the mid-6th-c, but was revived by the Lombards. >> Goths; Lombards; Theodoric

Oswald, St (c.605–642) Anglo-Saxon King of Northumbria (633–41). He established Christianity in Northumbria with St Aidan's help. Feast day 5 August. >> Aidan, St; Anglo-Saxons

Oswald, Lee Harvey (1939–1963) The alleged killer of President Kennedy, born in New Orleans, LA. Two days after the assassination, he was killed at Dallas by nightclub owner Jack Ruby (1911–67), before he could stand trial. The Warren Commission held him to be responsible for the assassination, although the belief that he was part of a conspiracy still persists. >> Kennedy, John F

Oswega / Oswega tea [os**wee**guh] >> **bergamot 1**

Otaka, Tadaaki [**oh**taka] (1947–) Japanese conductor. He made his professional debut in 1971, and went on to become conductor of the Tokyo Philharmonic Orchestra (1971–91, laureate 1991–), and principal conductor of the BBC National Orchestra of Wales (1987–95, laureate 1996–) and the Kioi Sinfonietta, Tokyo (1995–).

Otis, Elisha (Graves) [**oh**tis] (1811–61) Inventor, born in Halifax, VT. In 1852, he designed and installed the first lift to incorporate an automatic brake, thus paving the way for the development of the skyscraper.

O'Toole, Peter (Seamus) (1932–) Actor, born in Connemara, Co Galway, Ireland. His performance in *Lawrence of Arabia* (1962) made him an international film star. Nominated seven times for an Oscar, his other films include *The Last Emperor* (1987), and *Fairytale: A True Story* (1997).

Ottawa 45°25N 75°43W, pop (1995e) 333 000. Capital of Canada, in E Ontario on the Ottawa R; founded as Bytown, 1826; present name, 1854; capital of United Provinces, 1858; national capital, 1867; two-thirds English-speaking, one-third French; airport; railway; two universities (1848, 1942); Peace Tower in parliament buildings, 88 m/289 ft high; Eternal Flame on Parliament Hill, lit 1967; professional teams, Ottawa Senators (ice hockey), Ottawa Rough Riders (football). >> Canada ℹ; Ontario

Ottawa River, Fr **Rivière des Outaouais** Canadian river, the largest tributary of the St Lawrence; rises in the Canadian Shield; length 1270 km/780 mi. >> Canada ℹ; St Lawrence River

otter A mammal of family Mustelidae; streamlined, with a flattened muzzle; brown with paler underparts; tail thick at base; feet usually webbed; inhabits streams and lakes; 12 species in genera *Lutra* (**river otters**), *Aonyx* (**clawless otters**), and *Pteronura* (the **giant otter**). >> Mustelidae

otto >> **attar**

Otto, Nikolaus (August) (1832–91) Engineer, born near Schlangenbad, Germany. In 1876 he invented the four-stroke internal combustion engine, the sequence of operation of which is named the **Otto cycle** after him. >> internal combustion engine

Ottoman Empire A Muslim empire founded c.1300 by Sultan Osman I (1259–1326), and originating in Asia Minor. Ottoman forces entered Europe in 1345, conquered Constantinople in 1453, and by 1520 controlled most of SE Europe, including part of Hungary, the Middle East, and N Africa. Following the 'golden age' of Sulaiman the Magnificent, the empire began a protracted decline. It joined the Central Powers in 1914, and collapsed with their defeat in 1918. >> Islam; Sulaiman I; Turkey ℹ; Young Turks

Otway, Thomas (1652–85) Playwright, born in Trotton, West Sussex. His best-known works are the tragedies *The Orphan* (1680) and *Venice Preserved, or a Plot Discovered* (1682).

Ouagadougou [waga**doo**goo] 12°20N 1°40W, pop (1995e) 639 000. Capital of Burkina Faso, W Africa; part of the Ivory Coast until 1947; capital of Mossi empire from 15th-c; captured by French, 1896; airfield; terminus of railway line from Abidjan (Nigeria); university (1969); cathedral. >> Burkina Faso ℹ

Oudenaarde [**oo**denah(r)d], Fr **Audenarde** 50°50N 3°37E, pop (1995e) 27 300. Town in W Belgium; site of defeat of French by Marlborough and Prince Eugene (1708); railway; traditional centre for carpet-weaving and tapestries. >> Belgium ℹ

Ouija board [**wee**ja, **wee**jee] A board bearing letters, words, and numbers, upon which an indicator such as an upturned glass is placed. Several people rest their fingers on the indicator, which then moves without their conscious volition across the board. It can then purportedly spell out messages which provide information about events or situations unknown to the people present. The word originates from the French and German words for *yes* (*oui* and *ja*).

Oulu [**ow**loo], Swed **Uleåborg** 65°00N 25°26E, pop (1995e) 103 000. Seaport in W Finland, established, 1605; destroyed by fire, 1822; airfield; railway; university (1958). >> Finland ℹ

ounce >> **snow leopard**

Our Lady >> **Mary** (mother of Jesus)

Ouro Prêto [**oh**roh **pray**toh], formerly **Vila Rica** Town founded in 1711 in Minas Gerais, the mining area of NE Brazil; a world heritage site; centre of gold and diamond trading during the colonial era, with wealth reflected in its architecture. >> Minas Gerais

Ouse, River [ooz] **1** River in East Sussex, S England; length 48 km/30 mi; enters the English Channel at Newhaven. **2** River in Yorkshire, NE England; length 96 km/60 mi; enters the R Trent where it becomes the Humber estuary. **3** River in Northamptonshire, C England; length 256 km/159 mi; enters the Wash; also known as the **Great Ouse**. **4** Tributary of the Great Ouse river; length 38 km/24 mi; also known as the **Little Ouse**. >> England ℹ

ousel >> **ouzel**

out-of-the-body experience (OOBE or **OBE)** An experience in which people have the sensation that their consciousness exists in a separate location from their body. The experience often feels as real to them as normal everyday life reality.

ouzel or **ousel** A thrush (*Turdus torquatus*) native to Europe, N Africa, and SW Asia; dark with pale wings and white crescent on breast; also known as the **ring ouzel**. >> thrush (bird)

ouzo [**oo**zoh] A traditional Greek spirit flavoured with aniseed, and usually drunk with water. >> spirits

Oval, the One of the largest cricket grounds in England, located at Kennington, S London. It is the headquarters of Surrey County Cricket Club. >> cricket (sport) ℹ; London

Ovamboland [oh**vam**bohland] Region in N Namibia; chief indigenous peoples, the Ovambo. >> Angola ℹ; Namibia ℹ

ovarian follicle A structure within the mammalian ovary, part of which may develop into a mature ovum to be released at ovulation; also known as **Graafian follicle**, named after the Dutch physiologist, Reinier de Graaf (1641–73). >> menstruation; ovary; pregnancy ℹ; uterine tubes

ovary The reproductive organ in a female animal in which the eggs are produced, and which may also produce hormones. Ovaries are typically paired, and release their eggs down *oviducts* or uterine tubes. In plants the term refers to the hollow base of the carpel, containing the ovules. >> carpel; ovarian follicle; uterine tubes

Overland Telegraph A telegraph line crossing Australia and linking it with the outside world; opened in 1872. The line covered 3175 km/1972 mi between Port Augusta (South Australia) to Darwin (Northern Territory). >> telegraphy

over-the-counter drugs (OTCs) Those drugs which may be purchased directly from a pharmacy without a prescription, such as aspirin. Some problems arise with OTCs, such as their inappropriate use (eg an overdose) and their dangerous interactions with some prescription drugs. >> pharmacy

over-the-counter (OTC) trading Trading in stocks and shares other than via the stock exchange. Over-the-counter shares are issued by companies too small for Stock Exchange listing; they are often considered to be a very risky investment. >> shares; stocks

overture An orchestral prelude to an opera or other work, or (since the early 19th-c) an independent, usually descriptive, concert piece of similar length. >> opera; programme music

Ovett, Steve [oh**vet**], popular name of **Steven Michael James Ovett** (1955–) Athlete, born in Brighton, East Sussex. Gold medallist in the 800 m at the 1980 Olympics, he also won a bronze in the 1500 m. He broke the world record at 1500 m (three times), at one mile (twice) and at two miles.

Ovid [**o**vid], in full **Publius Ovidius Naso** (43 BC–AD 17) Latin poet, born in Sulmo, Italy. His major poems are the three-book *Ars Amatoria* (Art of Love) and the 15-book *Metamorphoses*, a collection of stories in which a transformation (metamorphosis) plays some part.

Oviedo [ov**yay**thoh] 43°25N 5°50W, pop (1995e) 196 000. City in NW Spain; former capital of Asturias; bishopric; airport; railway; university (1608); cathedral (14th-c). >> Asturias; Spain ℹ

Ovimbundu [ovim**bun**doo] A Bantu-speaking agricultural people of the Benguela Highlands of Angola, comprising some 20 indigenous chiefdoms. >> Angola ℹ

ovo-lacto vegetarians >> **vegetarianism**

ovulation >> **ovarian follicle**

ovule The female sex-cell of seed plants which, after fertilization, forms the seed. In gymnosperms the ovules lie exposed on the scales of the female cone; in flowering plants they are enclosed within an ovary. >> flowering plants; gymnosperms; ovary

ovum >> **egg**

Owen, Alun (Davies) (1926–94) Playwright, born in Liverpool, Merseyside. A prolific writer for television and radio, his works include *The Rough and Ready Lot* (1958), *Progress to the Park* (1959), and a musical collaboration with Lionel Bart, *Maggie May* (1964).

Owen (of the City of Plymouth), David (Anthony Llewellyn), Baron (1938–) British politician, born in Plymouth, Devon. He was secretary for health (1974–6), and foreign secretary in the Labour government (1977–9). One of the so-called 'Gang of Four' who formed the Social Democratic Party (SDP) in 1981, he became its leader in 1983. In 1988, after the SDP voted to accept merger, Owen led the smaller section of the party to an independent existence. Retiring from the commons in 1992, he became (with Cyrus Vance) a UN peace envoy in war-torn former Yugoslavia. He was made a Companion of Honour in 1994. >> Social Democratic Party; Vance–Owen plan

Owen, Michael (1979–) Footballer, born in Chester, Cheshire. A centreforward, he joined Liverpool in 1996, and rapidly established a reputation, becoming FA Young Player of the Year in 1997–8. By mid-1998 he had won five caps for England, becoming its youngest member and scorer, and was a member of the 1998 World Cup team.

Owen, Robert (1771–1858) Social reformer, born in Newtown, Powys. In 1800 he became manager and part owner of the New Lanark cotton mills, Lanarkshire, where he set up a social welfare programme, and established a 'model community'.

Owen, Wilfred (1893–1918) Poet, born in Oswestry, Shropshire. His poems, expressing a horror of the cruelty and waste of war, were edited by his friend Siegfried Sassoon in 1920. He himself was killed in action on the Western Front. >> Sassoon

Owens, Jesse (James Cleveland) (1913–80) Athlete, born in Danville, AL. Within 45 min on 25 May 1935 at Ann Arbor, MI, he set five world records (100 yd, long jump, 220 yd, 220 yd hurdles, 200 m hurdles). His long jump record stood for 25 years. >> athletics

owl A predatory nocturnal bird, found worldwide; large head and broad flat face; forwardly directed eyes; acute sight and hearing. There are two families: **typical owls** (Strigidae, c.120 species) and **barn owls**, **grass owls**, and **bay owls** (Tytonidae, 11 species). Tytonidae differ in having smaller eyes, long slender legs, a serrated middle claw, and a heart-shaped face. (Order: Strigiformes.) >> barn / tawny owl; bird of prey

ox A ruminant mammal of genus *Bos* (5 species); an artiodactyl. The name is used especially for the domestic bullock used as a draught animal. >> artiodactyl; aurochs; bull; cattle; ruminant ℹ; yak

oxalic acid [oks**al**ik] IUPAC **ethanedioic acid**, HOOC–COOH, colourless crystals; melting point of the dihydrate is 101 °C. It occurs in many plants, especially rhubarb, and is poisonous. >> acid; crystals

oxalis A perennial, sometimes an annual, found almost everywhere; leaves clover-like with three (sometimes more) leaflets; flowers 5-petalled, funnel-shaped; fruits with catapult mechanism for dispersing seeds. (Genus: *Oxalis*, 800 species. Family: Oxalidaceae.)

Oxenstierna or **Oxenstern, Axel Gustafsson, Greve** (Count) [**oks**ensherna, **oks**enstern] (1583–1654) Swedish statesman, born near Uppsala, Sweden. From 1612 he served as chancellor, and during most of the minority of Queen Christina he was effective ruler of the country (1636–44). He brought the Thirty Years' War to a successful conclusion at the Peace of Westphalia (1648). >> Thirty Years' War

ox-eye daisy A variable clump-forming perennial (*Leucanthemum vulgare*), growing to 1 m/40 in, native to Europe; flower-heads up to 5 cm/2 in or more across, long-stalked, solitary; spreading outer florets white, inner disc florets yellow; also called **marguerite** and **dog** or **moon daisy**. It was formerly used as a medicinal herb. (Family: Compositae.)

OXFAM A British charity based in Oxford, dedicated to alleviating poverty and distress throughout the world; an abbreviated form of **Oxford Committee for Famine Relief**. Founded in 1942, most of its funds provide long-term development aid to Third World countries. >> Three Worlds Theory

Oxford, Lat **Oxonia** 51°46N 1°15W, pop (1995e) 114 000. County town of Oxfordshire, SC England; on Thames and Cherwell Rivers; university (12th-c); Oxford Brookes University, 1992; Royalist headquarters in Civil War; airfield; railway; industry located in the suburb of Cowley (notably vehicles); cathedral (12th-c); football league team, Oxford United ('U's'). >> Oxford University [i]; Oxfordshire

Oxford, Provisions of (1258) A baronial programme imposing constitutional limitations on the English crown. Henry III had to share power with a council of barons, parliaments, and other officers. In 1261 the pope absolved Henry from his oath to observe the Provisions. >> Barons' War; Henry III (of England)

Oxford Movement A movement within the Church of England, beginning in 1833 at Oxford, which sought the revival of high doctrine and ceremonial; also known as **Tractarianism**. Initiated by 'tracts' written by Keble, Newman, and Pusey, it led to Anglo-Catholicism and ritualism. >> Anglo-Catholicism; Church of England; Keble; Newman, John Henry; Pusey

Oxfordshire pop (1995e) 607 000; area 2608 sq km/1007 sq mi. County in the S Midlands of England; county town, Oxford. >> England [i]; Oxford; Thames, River

Oxford University The oldest university in Britain, having its origins in informal groups of masters and students gathered in Oxford in the 12th-c. Prestigious university institutions include the Bodleian Library, the Ashmolean Museum, and the Oxford University Press (founded in 1585). >> Ashmolean Museum; Bodleian Library; Oxford

oxidation The loss of electrons, always accompanied by reduction, the gain of the same electrons. Chemical reactions in which electrons are transferred from one atom to another are called **oxidation–reduction** or **redox** reactions. Elements in compounds are conveniently given an **oxidation state** or **oxidation number** which relates to their redox properties. This is expressed using Roman numerals, as in manganese(VII) or Mn^{VII}. >> electron; reduction

oxides >> **oxygen**

oxlip A perennial with a rosette of crinkled leaves, with drooping flowers at the tip of a common stalk. The true oxlip (*Primula elatior*), from C and N Europe, has pale yellow flowers all hanging on one side of the stalk. (Family: Primulaceae.)

oxopropanoic acid >> **pyruvic acid**

Oxus, River >> **Amudarya, River**

oxyacetylene welding A technique much used in cutting metal and in joining two pieces of metal by melting them together at the point of contact (*welding*). The temperature obtained by burning acetylene with oxygen is the highest obtainable by any gas–oxygen flame (over 3200 °C).

oxygen O, element 8, boiling point −183 °C. By far the commonest element in the Earth's crust, of which it makes up nearly 50%; in various combined forms it also constitutes 21% of the atmosphere as diatomic molecules (O_2). All higher forms of life depend on oxygen. The element boils at 13 °C higher than nitrogen, and is isolated by the fractional distillation of air. Oxygen occurs widely in organic and inorganic compounds (**oxides**), mainly showing oxidation state −2. >> chemical elements; nitrogen; oxygen cycle; ozone; RR1036

oxygen cycle The dynamic system of changes in the nature of oxygen-containing compounds circulating between the atmosphere, the soil, and living organisms. The main biological phase involves the use of gaseous oxygen during respiration in animals and plants, with the consequent production of water and carbon dioxide, and the use of these products by green plants during photosynthesis, resulting in the liberation of gaseous oxygen. >> nitrogen cycle [i]; oxygen; photosynthesis

oyster Bivalve mollusc with unequal valves, the left valve typically being cemented to a hard substrate; often cultivated for human consumption (in oyster farms), regarded as a delicacy; some species used for the production of pearls. (Class: Pelecypoda. Order: Ostreoida.) >> bivalve; mollusc

oystercatcher A large plover-like bird; black or black-and-white; long reddish bill and legs; eats invertebrates, especially bivalve shellfish; also known as the **sea pie**. (Genus: *Haematopus*, 4 species. Family: Haematopodidae.) >> plover

Oz, Amos (1939–) Novelist, born in Jerusalem. His novels describe the tensions of life in modern Israel, and include *Ma'kom aher* (1966, Elsewhere, Perhaps) and *Po y-sham be-Erets Yisre'el bis-setary* (1982, In the Land of Israel).

ozalid process >> **photocopying**

Ozark Mountains [**oh**zahk] (Fr *aux arks*, 'at the arks') Highlands in SC USA; area c.129 500 sq km/50 000 sq mi, altitude generally 300–360 m/1000–1200 ft. >> United States of America [i]

ozone A form of oxygen having molecules O_3. It is formed by the action of ultraviolet radiation on ordinary oxygen, and is a gas, boiling point −112°C. >> CFCs; oxygen; ozone layer

ozone layer The part of the stratosphere at a height of c.22 km/14 mi in which the gas ozone (O_3) is most concentrated. It is produced by the action of ultraviolet light from the Sun on oxygen (O_2) in the air. The ozone layer shields the Earth from the harmful effects of solar ultraviolet radiation, but can be decomposed by complex chemical reactions, notably involving chlorofluorocarbons (CFCs). International concern over the appearance of a 'hole' in the ozone layer over the Antarctic in the 1980s led to a movement for the withdrawal of CFC-producing devices. In 1987 the Montreal Protocol was signed by around 40 countries to limit their use, with the intention that by 1999 worldwide consumption of CFCs should be 50% of 1986 levels. In 1989, the European Community meeting in Brussels agreed to cut CFC consumption by 85% as soon as possible, and altogether by the end of the century. Reports that short-lived holes have been observed above the Arctic have led to renewed efforts in Europe to reach agreement on an accelerated reduction in CFC consumption. The Antarctica hole was estimated to be 28 million sq km in 1998 (an increase of 5% compared with 1996). >> atmosphere [i]; CFCs; fluorocarbons; greenhouse effect; ozone

Oxford University

College	Founded	College	Founded
University College	1249	Pembroke	1624
Balliol	1263	Worcester	1714
Merton	1264	St Catherine's	1868
St Edmund Hall	1278	Keble	1870
Exeter	1314	Hertford	1874
Oriel	1326	Lady Margaret Hall	1878
Queen's	1340	Somerville	1879
New College	1379	St Hugh's	1886
Lincoln	1427	St Hilda's[1]	1893
All Souls	1438	St Peter's	1929
Magdalen	1458	Nuffield[2]	1937
Brasenose	1509	St Antony's[2]	1950
Corpus Christi	1517	St Anne's	1952
Christ Church	1546	Linacre[2]	1962
Trinity	1554	Wolfson[2]	1965
St John's	1555	St Cross[2]	1965
Jesus	1571	Green[2]	1979
Wadham	1612	Rewley House[3]	1990

[1]Women's colleges [2]Graduate colleges
[3]Continuing and part-time education college

paca [**pa**ka] A cavy-like rodent native to Central and South America. (Genus: *Cuniculus*, 2 species. Family: Dasyproctidae.) >> cavy; rodent

pacemaker A cell or object that determines the rhythm at which certain events occur. In vertebrates, pacemaker cells are present in the heart and in the longitudinal muscle of the stomach and ureter. In patients with heart block, artificial pacemakers (usually battery-operated and implanted under the skin) stimulate the heart electrically to maintain higher rates of cardiac contraction. >> heart [i]

Pachelbel, Johann [**pa**khelbel] (c.1653–1706) Composer and organist, born in Nuremberg, Germany whose works profoundly influenced J S Bach. His best-known composition is the *Canon in D Major*. >> Bach, Johann Sebastian

P

pachinko [pa**ching**koh] The Japanese game of pinball, the word coming from the sound of a steel ball running round a pinball machine. It is Japan's most popular relaxation. >> yakuza

pachyderm [**pak**iderm] A mammal of the (now obsolete) group Pachydermata ('with thick skin'). The name was used for those ungulates which do not 'chew the cud', especially the elephants, but also other perissodactyls. >> perissodactyl [i]; ungulate

Pacific Community, formerly **South Pacific Commission** (to 1997) An organization set up in 1947 by Western states then exercising colonial rule in the S Pacific. The purpose was to advance the economic and social interests of the peoples under their control within a framework of regional co-operation. The S Pacific nations also joined, from the 1960s, as they became independent.

Pacific Islands >> **United States Trust Territory of the Pacific Islands**

Pacific Ocean area c.181 300 000 sq km/70 000 000 sq mi. Ocean extending from the Arctic to the Antarctic, between North and South America (E) and Asia and Oceania (W); covers a third of the Earth and almost half the total water surface area; S part sometimes known as the South Sea; rim of volcanoes ('Pacific Ring of Fire'), deep open trenches, and active continental margins; greatest known depth, Challenger Deep in the Marianas Trench, 11 040 m/36 220 ft; ocean floor largely a deep sea-plain, average depth 4300 m/14 100 ft; many islands, either volcanic (eg Hawaii) or coral, mainly in the E section. >> plate tectonics [i]

pacifism The doctrine of opposition to all wars, including civil wars. Its most obvious feature is the personal commitment to non-participation in wars, except possibly in a non-combatant role. Pacifists also advocate efforts to maintain peace and support disarmament. >> nuclear disarmament

Pacino, Al(berto) [pa**chee**noh] (1940–) Film actor, born in New York City. His first main role came as Michael in *The Godfather* (1972), which he followed with acclaimed performances in *Serpico* (1973) and *The Godfather, Part II* and *III* (1974, 1990). Later films include *Scent of a Woman* (1992, Oscar), *The Devil's Advocate* (1997).

packet switching A service provided by Posts, Telegraph and Telephones Authorities which allows one computer to send a message to a second computer in the form of a set of packets which are transmitted over specially dedicated telephone lines. Packets from different subscribers are all sent down the same line in sequence. This removes the need for the telephone line to be dedicated to the two computers for the whole of the time that they are communicating and is, therefore, much cheaper for the users than a continuous link would be. >> International Packet Switching Service; public switched telephone network

Pact of Paris >> **Kellogg–Briand Pact**

Padang [pa**dang**] 1°00S 100°21E, pop (1995e) 805 000. Main seaport on the W coast of Sumatra, Indonesia; third largest city in Sumatra; airfield; railway; university (1956). >> Sumatra

Padania [pa**da**nia] Area in N Italy declared to be an independent republic by the secessionist Northern League (led by Umberto Bossi) in 1996. It comprises over a third of the country, including all the land around the R Po, and extending to the S of Florence, from coast to coast. The declaration received widespread publicity, but limited support, and was condemned by the Italian government >> Italy [i]

paddlefish Archaic sturgeon-like freshwater fish of family Polyodontidae, with only two living representatives; head produced into a long snout; known as fossils from the Eocene and Upper Cretaceous periods. >> Cretaceous period; Eocene epoch; sturgeon

Paderewski, Ignacy (Jan) [paduh**ref**skee] (1860–1941) Pianist, composer, and patriot, born in Kurylowka, Poland. In 1919 he served briefly as the first premier of Poland and was elected president of Poland's provisional parliament in 1940. >> Poland [i]

Padua [**pad**yooa] Ital **Padova**, ancient **Patavium** 45°24N 11°53E, pop (1991e) 218 000. City in NE Italy; on the R Bacchiglione; railway junction; 16th-c university; tomb of St Antony of Padua, a pilgrimage site; cathedral (16th-c); botanical garden (Orto Botanico) a world heritage site. >> Antony of Padua, St; Italy [i]

paediatrics / pediatrics [peedi**at**riks] The medical care of infants and children, and the study of the diseases which affect them. It encompasses the care of the newborn child, including problems such as failure to breathe, jaundice, failure to thrive, congenital malformations, and special care units. >> medicine

paedophilia / pedophilia A sexual interest in children (of either sex). Active interference is illegal, and there is often long-term psychological trauma experienced by the child.

Paestum [**pee**stum] An ancient Greek town in SW Italy in the region of Naples, founded c.600 BC by Sybaris. It was renowned for its Doric temples.

Páez, José Antonio [pa**ez**] (1790–1873) Venezuelan general and president (1831–5, 1839–43, 1861–3), born in Aragua, Venezuela. He commanded forces of *llaneros* ('cowboys') in the war of independence as principal lieutenant of Simón Bolívar, and became president after the break-up

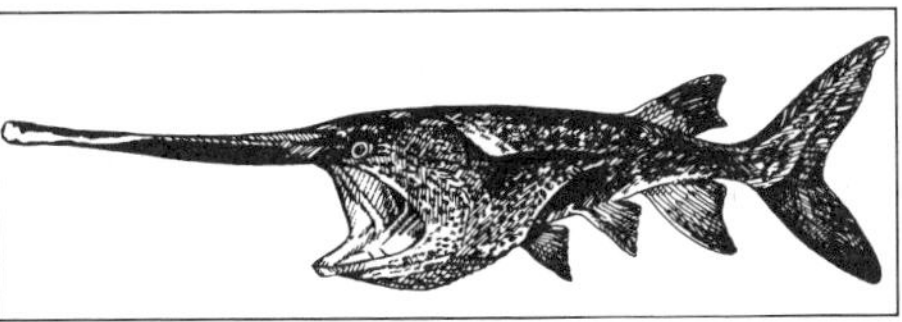

Paddlefish

of Gran Colombia. >> Bolívar; Spanish–American Wars of Independence; Venezuela 🛈

Paganini, Niccolo [paga**nee**nee] (1782–1840) Violin virtuoso, born in Genoa, Italy. He revolutionized violin technique, his innovations including the use of stopped harmonics. His compositions include six violin concertos.

Page, Sir Frederick Handley (1885–1962) Pioneer aircraft designer and engineer, born in Cheltenham, Gloucestershire. In 1909 he founded the firm of aeronautical engineers which bears his name. His Hampden and Halifax bombers were used in World War 2. >> aircraft 🛈

Pagemaker A desk-top publishing package in which page composition, including full graphics, is the principal objective. >> desk-top publishing

pager A small radio receiver used in one-way communication to alert an individual or deliver a short message; not normally used with voice transmission. It works within a small area using one low-power transmitter, or over larger areas using multiple transmitters. >> mobile communications; radio

Paget's disease [**pa**jet] A chronic disorder of the adult skeleton, of unknown origin, in which normal bone growth and replacement is disturbed; named after English surgeon James Paget (1814–99), and also known as **osteitis deformans**. >> bone; skeleton 🛈

pagoda [pa**goh**da] A Buddhist reliquary cairn or mound (*stupa*), modified by Chinese architectural principles, found throughout E Asia. It is a multi-storied tower, with each storey having a roof of glazed tiles. >> Buddhism; stupa

Pahang [pa**hang**] pop (1995e) 1 188 000; area 35 965 sq km/ 13 882 sq mi. State in E Peninsular Malaysia; formerly part of the kingdom of Malacca; capital, Kuantan. >> Malaysia 🛈

Pahlavi, Mohammad Reza [**pah**lavee] (1919–80) Shah of Persia, born in Tehran, Iran, who succeeded on the abdication of his father, Reza Shah, in 1941. His reign was marked by social reforms, but protest at western-style 'decadence' grew among the religious fundamentalists, and he was forced to leave Iran in 1979. >> Iran 🛈; Khomeini

pain An unpleasant sensation – in the simplest case, the stimulation of nerve endings by a strong stimulus, such as heat, pressure, or tissue damage. Pain receptors are located over most of the body surface and at many internal sites. When stimulated, they initiate reflex responses within the spinal cord, and convey information to the brain. The degree of pain is determined not only by the intensity of the stimulus, but also by psychological factors which can increase or decrease the release of pain-killing peptides (endorphins and enkephalins) within the brain and spinal cord. >> analgesics; nervous system; opioid peptides

Paine, Thomas (1737–1809) Radical political writer, born in Thetford, Norfolk. In 1774 he sailed for Philadelphia, where his pamphlet *Common Sense* (1776) argued for complete independence. In 1787 he returned to England, and wrote *The Rights of Man* (1791–2), in support of the French Revolution. Arraigned for treason, he fled to Paris, where he wrote *The Age of Reason*, in favour of deism. >> deism; French Revolution 🛈; radicalism

paint A colouring substance consisting of two basic elements, pigment and medium. Pigments have been derived from earths (eg yellow ochre), minerals (eg malachite), and dyes (organic and, since the mid-19th-c, synthetic). These are reduced to powder, and dispersed in whatever medium (eg oil) the artist is using. >> acrylic painting; bitumen; fresco; glaze; gouache; oil painting; painting; palette; tempera; watercolour

painted lady A medium-sized butterfly; wings brick-red with black patches, and white patches on point of forewings. (Order: Lepidoptera. Family: Nymphalidae.) >> butterfly

painting An art which originated in prehistoric times; but the modern sense of the word, the skilful arrangement of colours on a surface to create an independent work, has been current only since the Renaissance. >> action / genre / landscape / seascape painting; art; paint; still life

Paisley, Rev Ian (Richard Kyle) [**payz**lee] (1926–) Militant Protestant clergyman and politician, born in Armagh, Northern Ireland. He founded the Protestant Unionist Party, and since 1974 has been the Democratic Unionist MP for North Antrim. A rousing orator, he is fiercely opposed to the IRA, Roman Catholicism, and the unification of Ireland. >> IRA; Presbyterianism

Paiute [piy**oot**] Two separate Numic-speaking American Indian groups, traditionally hunter-gatherers, divided into the S Paiute (Utah, Arizona, Nevada, California) and the N Paiute (California, Nevada, Oregon) c.11 000 (1990 census).

Pakistan, official name **Islamic Republic of Pakistan** pop (1995e) 141 783 000; area 803 943 sq km/310 322 sq mi. State in S Asia; capital, Islamabad; timezone GMT +5; chief ethnic groups, Punjabi, Sindhi, Pathan, Baluchi; population includes nearly five million refugees from Afghanistan; chief religion, Islam (97%); official language, Urdu, with English and several local languages spoken; unit of currency, the Pakistan rupee of 100 paisas; largely centred on the alluvial floodplain of the R Indus; bounded N and W by mountains rising to 8611 m/ 28 250 ft at K2; climate dominated by the Asiatic monsoon; temperatures at Islamabad, maximum 40°C (Jun), minimum 2°C (Jan); remains of Indus valley civilization over 4000 years ago; Muslim rule under the Mughal Empire, 1526–1761; British rule over most areas, 1840s; separated from India to form a separate state for the Muslim minority, 1947; consisted of **West Pakistan** (Baluchistan, North-West Frontier, West Punjab, Sind) and **East Pakistan** (East Bengal), physically separated by

1610 km/1000 mi; occupied Jammu and Kashmir, 1949 (disputed territory with India, and the cause of wars in 1965 and 1971); proclaimed an Islamic republic, 1956; differences between E and W Pakistan developed into civil war, 1971; E Pakistan became an independent state (Bangladesh); military coup in 1977; military coup by General Zia ul-Haq in 1977, with execution of former prime minister Bhutto in 1979; new constitution (1985) strengthened Zia's powers; Benazir Bhutto elected prime minister, 1988, deposed 1990, re-elected 1993; deposed 1996; ethnic (Muslim/Sindh) violence, especially in Karachi, 1994, and ongoing; governed by an elected president, prime minister, and bicameral federal parliament; agriculture employs 55% of the labour force; extensive irrigation network; cotton production important, supporting major spinning, weaving, and processing industries. >> Bangladesh ℹ; Bhutto; India ℹ; Indus Valley Civilization; Islam; Islamabad; Mughal Empire; Zia-Ul-Haq; p.0000 political leaders

PAL [pal] Acronym for **Phase Alternating Line**, the coding system for colour television developed in Germany and the UK from 1965, and widely adopted for 625-line 50 Hz transmission in Europe and many other parts of the world. >> colour television ℹ; NTSC; SECAM

pala [**pah**la] An altarpiece consisting of a single large picture, instead of several small ones; also known as a **pala d'altare**. The type first appeared in Florence c.1430. >> altarpiece

Palach, Jan [**pa**lakh] (1948–69) Czech philosophy student, who as a protest against the invasion of Czechoslovakia by Warsaw Pact forces (1968) burnt himself to death in Wenceslas Square, Prague.

Palaeocene / Paleocene epoch [**pal**iohseen] The first of the geological epochs of the Tertiary period, from c.66 to 55 million years ago. The vast majority of dinosaurs had disappeared, and mammals suddenly diversified. >> geological time scale; Tertiary period; RR976

palaeography / paleography The study of the styles of handwriting used by scribes in ancient and mediaeval times. The aim is to establish the provenance or authenticity of specific texts, by relating the hand of a particular scribe, in a particular document, to the styles prevailing in the relevant historical period. >> chirography

Palaeolithic / Paleolithic >> **Three Age System**

Palaeolithic / Paleolithic art The art of the Old Stone Age, created c.30 000 years ago, the oldest known. Preserved in limestone caves in France and Spain are impressive murals representing hunting scenes. Small sculptures were also made. >> Altamira; Lascaux; Three Age System

palaeontology / paleontology The study of fossils; especially, the reconstruction of the organism from its fossil remains and the study of the processes of fossilization. >> fossil

Palaeozoic / Paleozoic era [paleeoh**zoh**ik] A major division of geological time extending from c.590 to 250 million years ago; subdivided into the Cambrian, Ordovician, and Silurian periods (the **Early Palaeozoic** era), and the Devonian, Carboniferous, and Permian periods (the **Late Palaeozoic** era). >> geological time scale; RR976

palantype [**pal**antiyp] The UK trade name of a shorthand typewriter known by the trade name **stenotype** in the USA. Using a silent keyboard, the operator produces on bands of paper a phonetic version of ongoing utterances. The output is later transcribed to produce a normal typescript. >> shorthand ℹ

palate A structure forming the roof of the mouth and the floor of the nasal cavity. It is divided into the **hard palate**, towards the front (formed by bone) and the mobile fibromuscular **soft palate**, towards the back (which is continuous with the hard palate). The soft palate hangs downwards into the pharynx (separating its nasal and oral parts), and consists mainly of muscle attached to a fibrous base. It may be tensed and raised to close off the nasopharynx, as in swallowing or when producing certain sounds. >> cleft lip and palate; mouth; pharynx

Palatinate, the A German Rhenish principality; capital, Heidelberg. It was elevated to an imperial Electorate in 1356, and became the leading Protestant German state and head of the Protestant Union (1608). In the 18th-c it lost significance, and was finally absorbed into the German Reich (1871). >> Heidelberg; Protestantism; Reich

Palau >> **Belau**

Palawan [pa**lah**wan], formerly **Paragua** (1902–5) pop (1995e) 425 000; area 11 780 sq km/4547 sq mi. Island of the W Philippines; rises in the S to 2054 m/6739 ft at Mt Mantalingajan; chief town, Puerto Princesa. >> Philippines ℹ

Pale The 'land of peace' where English rule prevailed in late mediaeval Ireland. It was defined as the four counties of Dublin, Kildare, Louth, and Meath in 1464, but the Act of 1495 showed a smaller area. >> Ireland (island) ℹ

Palembang [pa**lem**bang] 2°59S 104°45E, pop (1995e) 1 072 000. River-port city on S Sumatra I, Indonesia; former capital of the Srivijaya Empire (7th–12th-c); airfield; university (1960). >> Sumatra

Palenque [pa**leng**kway] A Mayan city of AD 600–800 on the slopes of the Chiapas Mts, S Mexico, celebrated for its beauty and distinctive architecture: a world heritage site. >> Mayas

Paleo-, paleo- >> **Palaeo-, palaeo-**

Palermo [pa**ler**moh] 38°08N 13°23E, pop (1995e) 737 000. Port on N coast of Sicily, Italy; founded by Phoenicians, 7th–8th-c BC; archbishopric; airport; railway; ferries; university (1777); cathedral (12th-c). >> Sicily

Palestine A country in the Middle East whose boundaries have been transformed by political considerations across the 20th-c. Following the break-up of the Ottoman Empire in the settlement after World War 1, Palestine was created as a British mandate. In 1947 Britain relinquished control to the UN, which imposed a two-state solution, one Jewish and one Arab, with Jerusalem under international control. The 1948 Arab–Israeli War left Israel in possession of 77% of the mandated territory; and as Jordan annexed the West Bank (including East Jerusalem) and Egypt administered the small Gaza Strip, Palestine effectively disappeared from the map. Israel occupied East Jerusalem, the West Bank, and the Gaza Strip in the June 1967 War, since which time these regions have been collectively referred to as the **Occupied Territories**. In 1988, Jordan severed its ties to the West Bank in deference to the PLO's claim to be the legitimate representative of the Palestinian people, and the PLO then proclaimed the State of Palestine. In 1993, a historic peace agreement was signed between the PLO and Israel, which provided for an Israeli withdrawal from the Gaza Strip and the West Bank town of Jericho. These two areas would be under full Palestinian authority, and a degree of self-rule would be allowed in the rest of the West Bank. An accord on partial Israeli withdrawal from the West Bank population centres was agreed in 1995, followed by some redeployment of Israeli troops in Hebron. A period of stalemate was broken by the US-brokered Wye agreement (Oct 1998), by which Israel would redeploy its forces from further West Bank areas, and the Palestinians would strengthen anti-terrorist measures and cancel anti-Israel provisions in their national charter. >> Gaza Strip; Israel ℹ; Jericho; Jordan ℹ; PLO; West Bank

Palestine Liberation Organization >> **PLO**

Palestrina, Giovanni Pierluigi da [pale**stree**na] (c.1525–94) Composer, born in Palestrina, Italy. The most distinguished composer of the Renaissance, he composed over 100 Masses, motets, hymns, and other church pieces.

palette In art, a term with two main senses: **1** A flat wooden plate on which painters arrange their colours. **2** The range of colours used by an artist. By extension, this sense has come to be used in computing, referring to the range of colours available using computer graphics. >> computer graphics; paint

Palgrave, Francis Turner [**pal**grayv] (1824–97) Poet and critic, born in Great Yarmouth, Norfolk. He is best known as the editor of *Golden Treasury of Songs and Lyrical Poetry* (1861), which influenced poetic taste for many years.

Palin, Michael (Edward) [**pay**lin] (1943–) British scriptwriter and actor. He joined the team in *Monty Python's Flying Circus* (1969–74), co-wrote and acted in the Monty Python films, and won a BAFTA Award for his role in *A Fish Called Wanda* (1988). He went on to present a popular series of travel documentaries for BBC-TV, beginning with *Around the World in Eighty Days* (1989), and another around the Pacific rim (*Full Circle*, 1997). >> Monty Python

palindrome A word or phrase which reads the same backwards as forwards, such as 'madam' and 'Draw, o coward!'.

Palladianism [pa**lay**dianizm] An architectural style of the 17th-c and 18th-c derived from the Renaissance buildings and writing of the Italian architect, Andrea Palladio (1508–80), and characterized by the use of symmetrical planning and the application of Roman architectural forms. Especially popular in England, it was first used by Inigo Jones for the Banqueting House, London (1619–22). >> Jones, Inigo

Pallas The second asteroid to be found (1802), 590 km/ 370 mi across. >> asteroids

palm A woody plant found throughout the tropics, typical of oceanic islands, with a few species reaching warm temperate regions. Palms are monocotyledons. Most species are trees, achieving their full diameter as seedlings, subsequent growth increasing only their height. Leaves are mostly fan- or feather-shaped, with numerous, pleated segments, and can reach 20 m/65 ft in length. The fruits are 1-seeded berries, dry, fleshy or fibrous, oily rather than starchy, often brightly coloured, and showing a great size range. Palms are of immense economic importance, especially in the tropics, where they provide a range of basic products, including vegetables, starch, fruits and nuts, timber, fibre, sugar, alcohol, and wax. (Family: Palmae.) >> monocotyledons; palm oil; tree ℹ

Palma (de Mallorca) [**pal**ma] 39°35N 2°39E, pop (1995e) 299 000. Seaport and chief city of Majorca I, Balearic Is; bishopric; airport; university (1967); castle (14th-c), cathedral (13th–16th-c). >> Majorca

palmate In botany, the shape of a leaf in which four or more leaflets arise from the same point, and spread like the fingers of a hand. >> leaf ℹ

Palmer, Arnold (Daniel) (1929–) Golfer, born in Latrobe, PA. His wins include the (British) Open (1961–2), the US Open (1960), and the US Masters (1958, 1960, 1962, 1964).

Palmerston (of Palmerston), Henry John Temple, 3rd Viscount (1784–1865) British statesman and Liberal prime minister (1855–8, 1859–65), born in Broadlands, Hampshire. He served as secretary of war (1809–28), and was three times foreign secretary (1830–4, 1835–41, 1846–51). His robust defences of British interests abroad secured him the name of 'Firebrand Palmerston'. A more comfortable nickname was **Pam**, and his frequently xenophobic foreign policy won him substantial popular support in Britain. He is associated with 'Gunboat Diplomacy', whereby Britain employed, or threatened to employ, its unchallengeable naval supremacy to resolve overseas differences in its favour. As premier in 1855, he vigorously prosecuted the Crimean War with Russia. >> Crimean War; Liberal Party (UK)

Palmerston >> **Darwin** (Australia)

Palmerston North 40°20S 175°39E, pop (1995e) 73 500. City in North Island, New Zealand; airfield; railway; university (1926); agricultural research centre. >> New Zealand ℹ

palmitic acid [pal**mi**tik] $C_{15}H_{31}COOH$, IUPAC **hexadecanoic acid**, a saturated fatty acid, melting point 63°C. It is obtained from many animal and plant sources, especially milk and palm oil (from which the name is derived). >> carboxylic acids; IUPAC; napalm; soap

palm oil A major edible oil, obtained from the fruit of several types of palm tree. It is widely used for the manufacture of margarine, as well as in soap, candles, and lubricating grease. >> palm

Palm Springs 33°50N 116°33W, pop (1995e) 44 000. Resort city in S California, USA; founded, 1876; developed as a luxurious desert resort in the early 1930s; airfield; hot springs. >> California

Palm Sunday In the Christian Church, the Sunday before Easter, commemorating the entry of Jesus into Jerusalem, when the crowd spread palm branches in front of him. >> Easter; Jesus Christ

Palmyra (Pacific Ocean) [pal**miy**ra] 5°52N 162°05W. Uninhabited atoll enclosing 50 small islets in the Pacific Ocean 1600 km/ 1000 mi S of Honolulu; annexed by USA, 1912; site for nuclear waste disposal since 1986. >> Pacific Ocean

Palmyra (Roman history) [pal**miy**ra] In Roman times, a flourishing oasis town controlling the trade routes between N Syria and Babylonia. At the height of its power in the 3rd-c AD, it briefly ruled the E half of the Empire. >> Petra

palomino [palo**mee**noh] A horse with a distinctive type of colouring, found in various breeds; pale golden brown with white mane and tail; also known as **California sorrel**. >> horse ℹ

Palouse >> **Appaloosa**

palynology [payli**nol**ojee] The analysis of pollen grains preserved in sediments and soils to reconstruct variations in vegetation over time. >> archaeology; pollen ℹ

pampa(s) The extensive grassland (prairie) region of Argentina and Uruguay around the R Plate estuary. It is a major centre for cattle ranching. >> prairie; steppe

Pamplona [pam**ploh**na], Lat **Pampeluna** or **Pompaelo** 42°48N 1°38W, pop (1995) 181 000. City in N Spain; on R Arga; archbishopric; capital of the Kingdom of Navarre, 10th-c; airport; railway; university (1952); cathedral (14th–15th-c); Fiesta of San Fermin (Jul), with bull-running in the streets. >> Navarre; Spain ℹ

Pan (astronomy) The 18th natural satellite of Saturn, discovered in 1990 from photographs taken nine years earlier by the Voyager 2 space probe; distance from the centre of Saturn 133 600 km/83 000 mi; diameter 20 km/12 mi; orbital period 0·58 days. >> Saturn; RR964

Pan (mythology) A Greek god, the 'nourisher' of flocks and herds, depicted with goat-like ears, horns, and legs. His pan-pipe is made of reeds. >> Selene; Syrinx

Pan-Africanist Congress (PAC) A black political party in South Africa which broke away from the African National Congress in 1958 under the leadership of Robert Sobukwe (1924–78). It pursued a distinctly black and radical policy, its campaign of resistance leading to the Sharpeville massacre. It was one of the political parties unbanned by President de Klerk. >> African National Congress; de Klerk; Sharpeville massacre

Panama, Span **Panamá**, official name **Republic of Panama**, Span **República de Panamá** pop (1995e) 2 669 000; area 77 082 sq km/29 753 sq mi. Republic occupying the SE end of the isthmus of Central America; capital, Panama

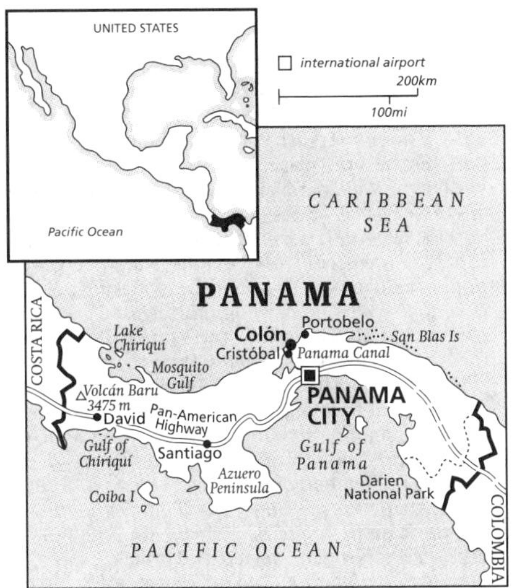

City; timezone GMT –5; chief ethnic groups, mixed Spanish–Indian (70%), West Indian (14%); chief religion, Roman Catholicism; official language, Spanish; unit of currency, the balboa of 100 cents; mostly mountainous; Serranía de Tabasará (W) rises to over 2000 m/6500 ft; Azuero peninsula in the S; lake-studded lowland cuts across the isthmus; dense tropical forests on the Caribbean coast; tropical climate; visited by Columbus, 1502; under Spanish colonial rule until 1821; joined the Republic of Greater Colombia; separation from Colombia after a US-inspired revolution, 1903; assumed sovereignty of the 8 km/5 mi-wide Canal, previously administered by the USA, 1979; National Guard strongman Manuel Noriega ousted by US military invasion, 1989, in part to end official drug trafficking; governed by a president and Legislative Assembly; Canal revenue accounts for four-fifths of the country's wealth; great increase in banking sector since 1970. >> Colombia ℹ; Noriega; Panama Canal; Panama City; RR1019 political leaders

Panama Canal A canal bisecting the Isthmus of Panama and linking the Atlantic and Pacific Oceans. It is 82 km/51 mi long, and 150 m/490 ft wide in most places; built by the US Corps of Engineers (1904–14). Panama has guaranteed the neutrality of the waterway when it takes over operational control of the canal in 2000. >> Panama ℹ

Panama City, Span **Panamá** 8°57N 79°30W, pop (1995e) 663 000. Capital city of Panama; founded, 1673; airport; railway; two universities (1935, 1965); on the Pan-American Highway; historic district and Salón Bolivar, a world heritage site. >> Panama ℹ

Pan-American Games A multi-sport competition for athletes from North, South, and Central American nations. First held at Buenos Aires, Argentina, in 1951, they now take place every four years.

Pan-American Highway A network of designated roads extending 27 000 km/17 000 mi across the Americas from Alaska to Chile.

Pan-American Union An organization founded in 1890 to foster political and economic co-operation among American states, and to draw North and South America closer together; first called the **International Bureau for American Republics**. In 1948 it became part of the wider Organization of American States. >> Organization of American States

Pancake Day >> **Shrove Tuesday**

Panchen Lama [**pan**chen **lah**ma] A spiritual leader and teacher in Tibetan Buddhism, second in importance to the Dalai Lama, and said to be the reincarnation of the Buddha Amitabha. >> Dalai Lama; Lamaism

pancreas [**pang**krias] A soft gland made up of small lobes associated with the alimentary canal of vertebrates with jaws. In humans it is c.12–15 cm/4.5–6 in long. One part produces an alkaline mixture of digestive enzymes (the **pancreatic juices**); another (the islets of Langerhans) synthesizes hormones involved in carbohydrate metabolism. >> alimentary canal; diabetes mellitus; gland

panda A mammal of the family Ailuropodidae; inhabits bamboo forests in mountains; two species: **giant panda** (*Ailuropoda melanoleuca*) from China; bear-like with large round head; white with black legs, shoulders, chest, ears, and area around eyes; also the **red panda**, **lesser panda**, or **cat bear** (*Ailurus fulgens*) found from S China to N Myanmar; red-brown with black underparts and tail tip; dark rings around tail; white markings on face. >> mammal ℹ

Pandit, Vijaya Lakshmi, *née* **Swarup Kumari Nehru** (1900–90) Indian politician and diplomat, born in Allahabad India, the sister of Nehru. In 1953, she became the first woman president of the UN General Assembly, and Indian High Commissioner in London (1954–61). >> Nehru

Pandora [pan**daw**ra] In Greek mythology, the first woman, adorned by the gods with special qualities. Zeus gave her a box from which all the evils which plague mankind came out; only Hope was left in the bottom of the box. >> Prometheus

panegyric [pane**ji**rik] A speech, poem, or song of praise addressed to an individual, group, or institution. An example is Mark Antony's oration on Caesar in Shakespeare's *Julius Caesar*.

Pangaea [pan**jee**a] The name given to the hypothesized 'supercontinent' comprising Gondwanaland and Laurasia which made up the Earth's continental crust before the Jurassic period. >> continental drift; Gondwanaland; Jurassic period; Laurasia

pangamic acid A component of many seeds, whose chemical name is n-di-isopropyl-glucuronate. Although it is promoted as a vitamin (B_{15}), it serves no known nutritional function. >> vitamins ℹ

pangolin [pang**goh**lin] A mammal native to Africa and S and SE Asia; pointed head with small eyes; long broad tail; long tongue and no teeth; eats ants and termites; covered in large overlapping horny plates; the only member of the order Pholidota; also known as **scaly anteater**. (Genus: *Manis*, 7 species.) >> anteater

Panhandle Any territory comprising a narrow strip of land running out from a large area in the shape of a pan handle; in the USA, applied to areas in (1) NW Texas, (2) NW Oklahoma, (3) N Idaho, (4) NE West Virginia, (5) N West Virginia, (6) SE Alaska, (7) Nebraska, and (8) an extension of the Golden Gate Park in San Francisco. >> United States of America ℹ

panicle A branched, racemose type of inflorescence. The term is often used for any complexly-branched inflorescence. >> inflorescence ℹ

Paninari [pani**nah**ree] An Italian youth cult of the 1980s named from the sandwich bars where its members gathered. They wore expensive 'designer' clothes presenting a tough militaristic image.

Panjabi >> **Indo-Aryan languages**

Pankhurst, Emmeline, *née* **Goulden** (1857–1928) Suffragette, born in Manchester. In 1905 she organized the Women's Social and Political Union, and fought for women's suffrage by violent means, on several occasions being arrested and going on hunger strike. >> women's liberation movement

panpipes A musical instrument made of various lengths of hollowed cane or wood joined together in a row. The player blows across the top to sound a different pitch from each pipe. >> woodwind instrument ℹ

pansy Any of several species or varieties of violet, in which the flat, 5-petalled flowers are held in a vertical plane and often resemble a face. The cultivated pansy has large flowers with overlapping petals in a wide range of colours. (Genus: *Viola*. Family: Violaceae.) >> heartsease; violet

pantheism The belief that God and the universe are ultimately identical. It is a characteristic feature of Hinduism and certain schools of Buddhism. >> Buddhism; God; Hinduism

pantheon A temple in Rome dedicated to all the gods, begun by Agrippa in 27 BC and rebuilt by Hadrian (AD 100–125), and now S Maria Rotonda. The name is more generally used for any burial place or Temple of Fame.

panther A member of the cat family, but not a distinct species. The name is used for the black form of the leopard (especially in the combination **black panther**) or as an alternative name for the cougar. >> cougar; Felidae; leopard

pantomime A theatrical term used to describe the silent dramatization of a story through gesture and movement, often by a single performer. Also, a Christmas play, loosely connected to a fairy-tale or nursery-rhyme, developed in Victorian and Edwardian Britain. >> harlequinade; mime

pantothenic acid A B vitamin which acts as a co-factor in several enzyme reactions. It is found widely in nature. >> enzyme; vitamins ℹ

Panzer (Ger 'armour') A term used in the German armed forces, applied particularly to armoured fighting vehicles. The Panzer divisions (essentially tank forces) were the most important component of the German army during World War 2. >> armoured fighting vehicle

papacy >> **pope**

Papa Doc >> **Duvalier, François**

Papago [**pa**pagoh] A Uto-Aztecan-speaking group of North American Indians, originally semi-nomadic wild food gatherers. They live chiefly on reservations in Arizona.

Papal States The 'States of the Church', straddling rural, mountainous areas of C Italy, comprising territories received by treaties and donations in the Middle Ages. They were annexed by Italy in 1870, but the papacy refused to recognize their loss until the Lateran Treaty (1929), which established the Vatican papal state. >> Lateran Treaty; pope

papaw [pa**paw**] A small, unbranched tree (*Carica papaya*) growing to 6 m/20 ft, with very soft wood and copious latex; a crown of long-stalked leaves up to 75 cm/30 in wide; flowers yellow; fruit up to 30 cm/12 in long, oval, yellow; also called **papaya** and **pawpaw**. It is widely cultivated throughout the tropics for its juicy but bland fruits. (Family: Caricaceae.) >> latex

papaya >> **papaw**

Papeete [papay**ay**tay] 17°32S 149°34W, pop (1995e) 91 500. Capital and chief port of French Polynesia, on NW coast of Tahiti; airport. >> French Polynesia; Tahiti

Papen, Franz von [**pa**pen] (1879–1969) German politician, born in Werl, Germany. He was Hitler's vice-chancellor (1933–4), and ambassador to Austria (1936–8) and Turkey (1939–44). Taken prisoner in 1945, he was acquitted at the Nuremberg Trials. >> Hitler; Nuremberg Trials

paper Material in sheet form used for a wide range of functions, notably writing, drawing, printing, and packaging. Invented in China in AD 105, it was originally produced from pulped rags or plant fibres. From the 19th-c, wood pulp and cellulose have largely been used in its manufacture, but plant fibres (eg esparto grass) and rags continue to be used, and the recycling of waste paper is increasingly practised on ecological grounds. The world uses some 200 million tons of paper each year. >> ink; parchment; pen; pencil; printing ℹ; *see illustration below*

paper-bark birch A species of birch with peeling white bark (*Betula papyrifolia*), which is used to make canoes. It is native to North America. (Family: Betulaceae.) >> birch

paper nautilus [**naw**tilus] An octopus-like marine mollusc (*Argonauta*); female c.30 cm/12 in long, male only 1 cm/0.4 in long; widely distributed in tropical and subtropical seas. (Class: Cephalopoda.) >> mollusc; octopus

Paphos [**pa**fos] 34°45N 32°23E, pop (1995e) 30 600. Resort town in SW Cyprus; capital of Cyprus during Roman times; old city founded probably in Mycenaean period, a world heritage site; 7th-c Byzantine castle. >> Cyprus ℹ; Mycenae

papilionid butterfly [pa**pil**yonid] A butterfly of the family Papilionidae; medium to very large, and often brightly coloured; c.550 species. (Order: Lepidoptera.) >> butterfly

papilloma [papi**loh**ma] Localized overgrowths of cells of the surface of tissues such as the skin, intestinal lining, or bladder.

papillon [**pa**pilon] A toy breed of dog developed in France several centuries ago; small with long fine coat; ears with fringes of hair, resembling a butterfly's wings. >> dog

Pappus of Alexandria (4th-c) Greek mathematician, whose eight-book *Synagoge* (Collection) is extant in an incomplete form.

paprika >> **pepper** 1

Papua New Guinea, official name **Independent State of Papua New Guinea** pop (1995e) 4 093 000; area 462 840 sq km/178 656 sq mi. Island group in the SW Pacific Ocean, 160 km/100 mi NE of Australia, comprising the E half of the island of New Guinea, the Bismarck and Louisiade Archipelagos, the Trobriand and

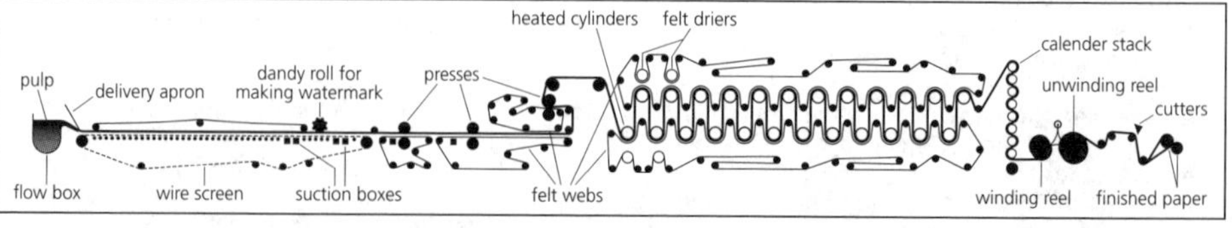

The Fourdrinier paper-making machine, invented by French engineer Henry Fourdrinier (1766–1854) and his brother, Sealy, and introduced into England in 1803. The fibres are first separated and soaked to produce paper pulp, which is then filtered to make a fibre sheet. Most of the water is removed by pressing and suction. The sheet is carried by an endless reel of felt around a long series of steam-heated cylinders, which dry out the remaining water. The dry sheet then passes through a set of smoothing rollers (calenders), which provide the finished quality. Further processes, such as glazing or sizing, can be applied for special purposes.

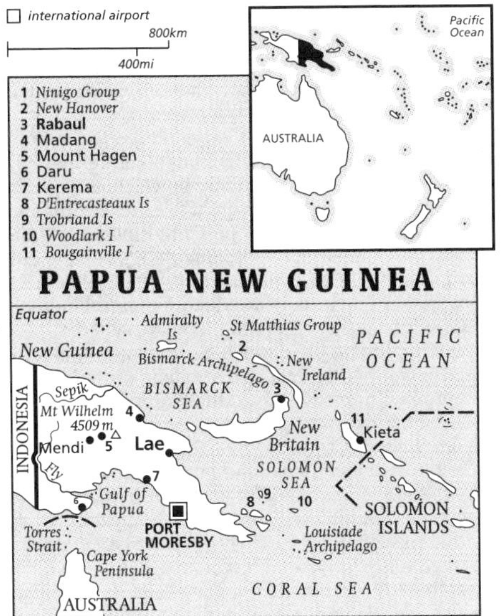

D'Entrecasteaux Is, and other off-lying groups; capital, Port Moresby; timezone GMT +10; chief ethnic group, Melanesian; chief religions, Christianity, magico-religious beliefs; official languages, Tok Pisin, English, Hiri Motu, with c.750 other languages spoken; complex system of mountains, highest point, Mt Wilhelm (4509 m/ 14 793 ft); mainly covered with tropical rainforest; typically monsoonal climate, with temperatures and humidity constantly high; British protectorate in SE New Guinea, 1884; some of the islands under German protectorate, 1884; German New Guinea in NE, 1899; German colony annexed by Australia in World War 1; Australia mandated to govern both British and German areas, 1920; combined in 1949 as the United Nations Trust Territory of Papua and New Guinea; independence within the Commonwealth, 1975; a governor-general represents the British Crown; governed by a prime minister and cabinet, with a unicameral national parliament; over two-thirds of the workforce engaged in farming, fishing, forestry. >> Bismarck Archipelago; Bougainville; mandates; Port Moresby; RR1019 political leaders

papyrus [pa**piy**ruhs] An aquatic perennial (*Cyperus papyrus*) native to N Africa; stems growing to 4 m/13 ft; leaves grass-like; flowers tiny, yellowish. The ancients made paper by pressing wet strips of the pithy stems side by side. (Family: Cyperaceae.) >> paper

parable A metaphor in narrative form with the purpose not so much of imparting propositional truths or general moral lessons as challenging the perspective of the hearer. In the Bible, parables are frequently used by Jesus in his preaching about the kingdom of God. >> metaphor; New Testament

parabola In mathematics, the locus of a point whose distance from a fixed point (the *focus*) is equal to its distance from a fixed line (the *directrix*). It is one of the classical conic sections. >> conic sections [i]; hyperbola

Paracelsus [para**sel**sus], originally **Philippus Aureolus Theophrastus Bombastus von Hohenheim** (1493–1541) Alchemist and physician, born in Einsiedeln, Switzerland. He travelled widely and acquired great fame as a medical practitioner, introducing laudanum, sulphur, lead, and mercury into Western therapeutics.

paracetamol [para**see**tamol] A mild painkiller commonly used for headache, menstrual pain, etc. It will also reduce body temperature during fever. >> analgesics

parachuting The act of jumping out of an aircraft and eventually landing with the aid of a parachute. French aeronaut André-Jacques Garnerin (1769–1823) made the first recorded descent over Paris in October 1797, when he was released from a balloon. >> skydiving

paradox In logic, a contradictory or implausible conclusion which seems to follow by valid argument from true premisses. 'This sentence is false' appears to be true if false, and false if true. Such paradoxes played an important role in the work of Russell and Frege on the foundations of mathematical logic. >> Frege; logic; Russell, Bertrand

paraffin >> **kerosene**

paraffin wax Solid hydrocarbon wax, originally produced from shale c.1850, but now made from petroleum. It is used for candles, waterproofing, textile conditioning, polishes, and ointments. >> petroleum; wax

Paraguay [**pa**ragwiy], official name **Republic of Paraguay**, Span **República del Paraguay** pop (1995e) 4 896 000; area 406 750 sq km/157 000 sq mi. Landlocked country in C South America; capital, Asunción; timezone GMT –4; population mainly mixed Spanish–Guaraní (95%); chief religion, Roman Catholicism (97%); official language, Spanish, but Guaraní also spoken; unit of currency, the guaraní of 100 centimos; divided into two regions by the R Paraguay; Gran Chaco in the W, mostly cattle country or scrub forest; more fertile land in the E; Paraná Plateau at 300–600 m/1000–2000 ft, mainly wet, treeless savannah; tropical NW, with hot summers and warm winters; temperate SE; originally inhabited by Guaraní Indians; arrival of the Spanish, 1537; arrival of Jesuit missionaries, 1609; independence from Spain, 1811; War of the Triple Alliance against Brazil, Argentina, and Uruguay, 1864–70; Chaco War with Bolivia, 1932–5; civil war, 1947; General Alfredo Stroessner seized power in 1954, forced to stand down following a coup in 1989; new constitution, 1992; governed by a president, Senate, and Chamber of Deputies; agriculture employs 40% of the labour force. >> Asunción; Chaco War; Gran Chaco; Guaraní;

Paraguay, River; Stroessner; Triple Alliance, War of the; RR1019 political leaders

Paraguayan War >> **Triple Alliance, War of the**

Paraguay, River [para**gwiy**] (Span **Río**), Port **Rio Paraguai** River in C South America; a chief tributary of the R Paraná; rises in Brazil; length 2300 km/1450 mi. >> Paraná, River

parakeet The name used for some small parrots with long pointed tails (c.37 species). >> parrot; swift

paraldehyde [pa**ral**dehiyd] $(C_2H_4O_3)_3$. An oligomer containing three molecules of acetaldehyde; a liquid boiling at 128°C. >> acetaldehyde; polymerization

Paralipomenon [parali**pom**enon] >> **Chronicles, Books of**

parallax In astronomy, an apparent displacement in the position of any celestial object caused by a change in the position of the observer; specifically, a change because of the motion of the Earth through space.

parallel distributed processing >> **connectionism**

parallel processing The use of two or more processors simultaneously to carry out a single computing task, each processor being assigned a particular part of the task at any given time. This differs from conventional computing, where the whole task is carried out sequentially by one processor. The approach promises greatly increased computing speeds for certain types of task. >> hypercube; Transputer

Paralympics ('beside the Olympics') The equivalent of the Olympic Games for disabled people, inaugurated in 1960, and held every four years where possible in the same city or country as the Olympic Games. The major events of the Summer games include archery, basketball, boccia, cycling, fencing, judo, power/weight lifting, shooting, soccer, swimming, table tennis, tennis, and volleyball; Winter games have been held since 1976. >> British Sports Association for the Disabled; International Sports Organization for the Disabled; Olympic Games; RR1043

paralysis Loss of movement resulting from interference with the nerve supply to a muscle or muscles. It may arise from destruction of the motor nerve cells in the brain (eg *hemiplegia*, in which muscles on one side of the body are affected) or in the spinal cord (eg infantile paralysis). *Paraplegia* refers to the loss of muscle power affecting both lower limbs. In *quadriplegia* all four limbs are affected. >> brain ℹ; muscle ℹ; nervous system

Paramaribo [parama**ree**boh] 5°54N 55°14W, pop (1995e) 252 000. Federal capital and chief port of Suriname; capital of British Suriname, 1651; under Dutch rule, 1814–1975; airport; university (1968); cathedral (19th-c). >> Suriname ℹ

Paramecium [para**mees**ium] A genus of single-celled micro-organisms, ovoid in shape, length up to 0.33 mm/0.013 in; cells contain two types of nucleus; hair-like processes (*cilia*) arranged uniformly over cell surface; common in aquatic habitats. (Phylum: Ciliophora.) >> cell; nucleus (biology)

Paraná, River [para**na**] (Span **Río**), in Brazil **Alto Parana** Major river of South America; rises in SE C Brazil and joins the R Uruguay after 3300 km/2000 mi to form the R Plate estuary on the Atlantic. >> Itaipu Dam; Paraguay, River; Plate, River

parana pine >> **araucaria**

paranoia An excessive tendency to suspiciousness and sensitivity to being rebuffed. Paranoid individuals may presume by merely seeing a police car, for example, that there is an elaborate plot to put them in jail, and that the plot has been directed by an unknown authority. >> mental disorders

paranormal Beyond the bounds of what can be explained in terms of currently held scientific knowledge. The use of the term allows for the possibility that new discoveries in physics may account for events which are now classified as paranormal. This is in contrast with the term *supernatural*, which implies a non-physical explanation for events. >> parapsychology; poltergeist

paraplegia >> **paralysis**

parapsychology The scientific study of certain aspects of the paranormal, primarily those in which an organism appears (i) to receive information from its environment through some means not presently understood (also known as **extrasensory perception** or ESP), or (ii) to exert an influence on its environment through some means not presently understood (also known as **psychokinesis** or **PK**). >> extrasensory perception; psi; Rhine, J B

parasitic plant A plant which obtains some or all of its food and/or shelter from another plant. Many fungi and some plants have adopted this lifestyle. Among flowering plants total parasites include broomrapes, rafflesias, and dodders. A much larger group are the semi-parasitic plants, which possess green leaves and are able to manufacture at least some nutrients, but which supplement their food supply from a host. They are termed **hemiparasites**, and include mistletoe and eyebrights. >> broomrape; dodder; mistletoe; mycorrhiza; rafflesia; saprophyte

parasitology [parasi**tol**ojee] The study of organisms which live on and at the expense of another living creature (the *host*) and of their interactions. >> arthropods; Protozoa; worm

parasympathetic nervous system >> **autonomic nervous system**

parathyroid glands In humans a set of glands, usually four in number, closely associated with the back of the thyroid gland. Their removal in mammals causes death within a few days. >> thyroid gland

paratyphoid fever A generalized infection by a species of *Salmonella*. It is related to but less serious than that responsible for typhoid fever. >> typhoid fever

Parcae [**pah(r)**see, **pah(r)**kiy] The fates. The name originally referred to a Roman birth-goddess. She was later trebled, and identified with the Moerae. >> Moerae

parchment A prepared but untanned animal skin, usually of a sheep, goat, or calf, developed by the Greeks c.2nd-c BC as a medium of writing. In mediaeval Europe parchment was used for manuscripts and later for printed books. A high quality, fine-grained parchment is known as *vellum*. >> paper ℹ

parchment-bark >> **pittosporum**

pardalote >> **diamondbird**

Pareto, Vilfredo [pa**ray**toh] (1848–1923) Economist and sociologist, born in Paris. His *Trattato di sociologica generale* (1916, trans The Mind and Society), with its theory of governing elites, anticipated some of the principles of fascism. >> fascism; sociology

Paricutín [pareekoo**teen**] 19°29N 102°17W. Active volcano in WC Mexico; height 2774 m/9101 ft. >> Mexico ℹ; volcano

Paris (France), ancient **Lutetia** 48°50N 2°20E, pop (1995e) 2 218 000. Capital of France, on R Seine; originally a Roman settlement; capital of Frankish kingdom, 6th-c; established as capital, 987; R Seine spanned here by 30 bridges, oldest the Pont Neuf (1578–1604); tourist river boats ('bateaux mouches'); bounded by Bois de Boulogne (W), Bois de Vincennes (E); divided into 20 arrondissements; 'Left Bank' (formerly associated with the aristocracy, later with writers and artists) and 'Right Bank' (formerly associated with the middle class); headquarters of many international organizations (notably UNESCO); airports at Orly (S), Charles de Gaulle (Roissy), and Le Bourget (NE); métro; Sorbonne University (12th-c); one of the world's main tourist centres; world centre of high fashion and production of luxury goods; wide range of heavy and light industry in suburbs; *Right Bank*: Arc de Triomphe, Champs Elysées, Place de la Concorde, Centre Pompidou (1977), Louvre, Montmartre, L'Opéra (1861–75), Tuileries gardens; *Left Bank*: Eiffel Tower (1889), Hôtel des Invalides, Palais du Luxembourg, Musée d'Orsay, Notre Dame Cathedral (1163), Montparnasse and Latin Quarter; Euro Disney Theme Park. >> Arc de Triomphe; Bois de Boulogne; Centre Beaubourg; Eiffel Tower; Elysée, Palais de l'; Folies-Bergère; France ℹ; Gobelins; Haussmann; Invalides, Hôtel des; Left Bank; Louvre; Luxembourg, Palais du; Musée d'Orsay; Notre Dame; Paris, University of; Quai d'Orsay; Tuileries; Versailles

Paris (mythology) In Greek mythology, a prince of Troy, the son of Priam and Hecuba; also called **Alexander**. Called upon to decide which of Hera, Aphrodite and Athene was the fairest and should be awarded Eris's golden apple ('the judgment of Paris'), he chose Aphrodite, who had offered him Helen, the most beautiful woman in the world, as an inducement. He then abducted Helen, and so caused the Trojan War. >> Eris; Helen; Trojan War

Paris, Matthew >> **Matthew Paris**

Paris, Treaty of 1 (1761–3) The peace settlement ending the Seven Years' War (1756–63), signed by Britain, France, and Spain. British gains from France included Canada, and America E of the Mississippi, and led to British colonial supremacy. >> Seven Years' War **2** (1814–15) Successive peace settlements involving France and the victorious coalition of Britain, Austria, Prussia, Russia, Sweden, and Portugal, restoring the Bourbon monarchy to France in place of the Napoleonic Empire, before and after the Hundred Days (1815). >> Napoleonic Wars **3** (1951) >> European Coal and Steel Community

Paris, University of A university founded c.1170 on the left bank of the R Seine in Paris. In the 14th-c it was pre-eminent among European universities. As a result of student demands for educational reform in 1968, the university was re-organized into 13 independent faculties, known as *Universités de Paris I à XIII*. >> Paris; university

parish council The smallest unit of local elective government in the UK, dating from the 16th-c and originally based on an area covered by one church. It is not normally elected along party political lines, but has close links with the local community. >> local government

Paris Peace Conference 1 (1919–20) A meeting of 32 'allied and associated powers' who met in Paris to draw up a peace settlement after World War 1.>> Versailles, Treaty of; World War 1 **2** (1946) A meeting of the five members of the Council of Foreign Ministers (UK, France, USA, Russia, China) and 16 other nations involved in the war against the Axis Powers. It drew up peace treaties with Bulgaria, Finland, Hungary, Romania, and Italy. >> Axis Powers; World War 2

parity (economics) (A term used when central banks undertake to limit fluctuations in exchange rate; abbreviated as **par**; the **par rate** is that around which the margin of fluctuation is measured. A security stands at par if its market price is equal to its face value.

parity (physics) In quantum mechanics, a quantity which monitors the behaviour of a system under change from left- to right-handed co-ordinates; symbol *P*. >> quantum numbers

parity check A simple means of detecting errors in transmitted binary data. Each byte contains a **parity bit** which is set to indicate whether the byte contains an odd or even number of 1s. This bit is then checked on reception to ensure that it is consistent. This system will not detect all errors, and more complex systems are now in general use. >> bit; byte

Park, Mungo (1771–1806) Explorer, born in Fowlshiels, Scottish Borders. In 1795–6 he made a journey along the Niger R, and was killed during a second journey a decade later.

Parker, Alan (1944–) Film director, born in London. He made his feature-length cinema debut with *Bugsy Malone* (1976). Later films include *Midnight Express* (1978), *Fame* (1979), *The Commitments* (1991), and *Evita* (1996).

Parker, Charlie, popular name of **Charles (Christopher) Parker**, nickname **Bird** or **Yardbird** (1920–55) Jazz alto saxophonist, born in Kansas City, KS. In New York, he joined Dizzy Gillespie and other musicians in expanding the harmonic basis for jazz. The new music, called *bebop*, developed an adventuresome young audience at the end of World War 2. >> bebop

Parker, Matthew (1504–75) The second Protestant Archbishop of Canterbury, born in Norwich, Norfolk. Deprived of his preferments by Queen Mary, he was made Archbishop of Canterbury by Elizabeth I (1559). He was in charge of the formulation of the Thirty-nine Articles (1562). >> Church of England; Thirty-nine Articles

Parkes, Sir Henry (1815–96) Australian statesman, born in Stoneleigh, Warwickshire, UK. Five times premier of New South Wales, in 1891 he helped draft a constitution for a federated Australia. >> Australia ℹ

Parkinson, C(yril) Northcote (1909–93) Writer, historian, and political scientist, born in Barnard Castle, Co Durham. He is especially known for his serio-comic tilt at bureaucratic malpractices in *Parkinson's Law: the Pursuit of Progress* (1958). **Parkinson's Law** – that work expands to fill the time available for its completion, and subordinates multiply at a fixed rate, regardless of the amount of work produced – has passed into the language.

Parkinson's disease A disorder of the central nervous system in which the neurones of the basal ganglia are specifically affected; also known as **paralysis agitans**, and named after British physician James Parkinson (1755–1824). These neurones secrete dopamine as their neurotransmitter, and its lack affects the ability to control muscle movement and tone. >> central nervous system; dopamine

parliament The general term in most English-speaking countries for the national legislative body, normally elected by popular vote. Its role is to pass legislation and keep a check on the activities of the government or executive. In the UK, parliament is constituted by the House of Lords and the elected House of Commons. Proposed laws must go through a defined procedure in both Houses and receive the royal assent, before becoming statutes. >> bicameral system; Commons / Lords, House of; unicameral system

Parliamentary Commissioner for Administration The British ombudsman for central administration, established in 1967, who examines complaints of maladministration. The commissioner works closely with a House of Commons select committee. >> ombudsman; select committee

Parma [**pah(r)**ma] 44°48N 10°19E, pop (1995e) 182 000. City in N Italy; on R Parma; major cultural centre in Middle Ages; railway; university (13th-c); cathedral (12th-c). >> Italy ℹ

Parmenides [pah(r)**men**ideez] (c.515–c.445 BC) Greek philosopher, a native of the Greek settlement of Elea in S Italy, and founder of the Eleatic school. >> Eleatics; Presocratics

Parmigianino [pah(r)mijia**nee**noh], also called **Parmigiano**, originally **Girolamo Francesco Maria Mazzola** (1503–40) Painter of the Lombard School, born in Parma, Italy. At Bologna he painted his famous Madonna altarpiece for the nuns of St Margaret. >> altarpiece; Mannerism

Parnell, Charles Stewart [pah(r)**nel**] (1846–91) Irish politician, born in Avondale, Co Wicklow, Ireland. In 1879 he was elected president of the Irish National Land

League, and in 1886 allied with the Liberals in support of Gladstone's Home Rule Bill. He remained an influential figure until 1890, when he was cited as co-respondent with Katherine O'Shea in a divorce case, and was forced to retire. >> Gladstone; nationalism

parole A conditional release given to a prisoner who still has part of a sentence left to serve. In the UK, for example, prisoners may be considered for parole after one-third of the sentence or after a fixed period (of either 1 year or 6 months), has been completed. Release is conditional, and those paroled are supervised by a probation officer. In the USA, a parole board considers release, based on extensive guidelines, usually after a fixed portion of the sentence has been served. >> sentence

Paros [**pay**ros] area 195 sq km/75 sq mi; pop (1995e) 8300. Third largest island of the Cyclades, Greece; chief town, Parikia; famous for its marble and churches. >> Cyclades; Greece ℹ

Parque Nacional de Los Glaciares [glas**ya**rays] Andean national park in Patagonia, Argentina; area 4459 sq km/ 1721 sq mi; established in 1937; a world heritage site. >> Argentina ℹ

parquetry >> **marquetry**

Parr, Catherine (1512–48) Sixth (and surviving) wife of Henry VIII, the daughter of Sir Thomas Parr of Kendal. As queen (1543), she persuaded Henry to restore the succession to his daughters. Very soon after Henry's death (1547) she married a former suitor, Lord Thomas Seymour of Sudeley, and died in childbirth the following year. >> Henry VIII

parrot A colourful bird, native to warm regions worldwide; bill large, hooked; good at mimicking human voice. (Family: Psittacidae, c.330 species.) >> budgerigar; cockatiel; cockatoo; kakapo; lory; lovebird ℹ; macaw; parakeet

parrot disease >> **psittacosis**

parrotfish Colourful fish belonging to the family Scaridae (4 genera), in which jaw teeth are fused into a parrot-like beak; body compressed, length 20–100 cm/8–40 in.

Parry, Sir (Charles) Hubert (Hastings) (1848–1918) Composer, born in Bournemouth, Hampshire. He wrote oratorios, symphonies, and many other works, but is best known for his unison chorus 'Jerusalem' (1916), sung at the end of each season of Promenade Concerts in London.

Parry, Joseph (1841–1903) Musician, born in Merthyr Tydfil, S Wales. He composed oratorios, operas, and songs, and became one of the leading hymn-writers in the Welsh tradition.

parsec (**pc**) A unit of length, used for distances beyond the Solar System. The term is a contraction of **parallax second**, and is the distance at which the astronomical unit (AU) subtends one second of arc; it equals 206 265 AU, $3{\cdot}086 \times 10^{13}$ km/$1{\cdot}918 \times 10^{13}$ mi, 3·26 light years. The larger units **kiloparsec** (kpc) and **megaparsec** (Mpc) for 1000 and 1 000 000 pc respectively are also widely used. >> astronomical unit

Parseeism [**pah(r)**seeizm] The religion of the descendants of the ancient Zoroastrians, who fled Persia after its conquest and settled in India in the 8th-c. They live mainly in the region round Bombay, and preach a rule of life conforming to the purity of Ahura Mazda. >> Ahura Mazda; Zoroastrianism

Parsifal >> **Perceval, Sir**

parsing The analyzing and labelling of the grammatical components of a sentence, according to their function within some grammatical framework, such as 'subject', 'verb', and 'object'. Introduced in schools during the 19th-c, parsing fell into disfavour during the 1950s because of its uninspiring techniques. During the 1980s a move to re-introduce some form of parsing, as an antidote to the perceived widespread ignorance of grammar, received increasing support. >> grammar

parsley A biennial or perennial (*Petroselinum crispum*), growing to 75 cm/30 in, but usually smaller; leaves triangular, shining, divided into wedge-shaped segments; flowers yellowish, petals notched; fruit ovoid. It is widely cultivated as a flavouring. (Family: Umbelliferae.) >> cow parsley

parsnip A biennial growing to 1.5 m/5 ft, but usually smaller, native to Europe and W Asia; flowers yellow; fruit ellipsoid, broadly winged. It is grown commercially for the sweet, fleshy tap-roots, which are eaten as a vegetable and used as fodder for livestock. (*Pastinaca sativa*. Family: Umbelliferae.)

parson bird >> **tui**

Parsons, Talcott [**tawl**cot] (1902–79) Sociologist, born in Colorado Springs, CO. He became one of the most prominent US sociologists, developing a functionalist analysis of social systems. >> functionalism; sociology

parthenocarpy >> **fruit**

parthenogenesis [pah(r)thenoh**jen**esis] The development of an individual from an egg without fertilization by a male gamete (*sperm*). Eggs that develop parthenogenetically are usually diploid (possessing two chromosome sets) and genetically identical with the mother. >> fertilization; gamete; water flea

Parthenon The principal building of the Athenian Acropolis, a Doric temple of Pentelic marble dedicated to Athena *Parthenos* ('the Maiden'); a world heritage site. Built 447–433 BC to the plans of Ictinus and Callicrates under the supervision of Phidias, in 1687 it was reduced to a shell by an explosion while housing a powder magazine during the Turkish–Venetian war. >> Acropolis; Athena; Doric order; Elgin marbles; Erechtheum; Phidias

Parthians The inheritors of the E territories of the Seleucids, from the 3rd-c BC ruling an empire that stretched from the Euphrates to the Indus. They were Rome's main rivals for power in the east. >> Hatra

particle accelerators Machines for accelerating charged subatomic particles, usually electrons or protons, to high velocity. The basic configurations are straight (linear accelerators) or circular (synchrotrons). In the latter, magnetic fields control the beam path. Both use radiofrequency electric fields to provide acceleration. >> cyclotron; klystron; linear accelerator; particle physics; synchrotron ℹ

particle beam weapons The use of high-energy subatomic particles, generated in nuclear accelerators and turned into a directable beam, as a practical weapon. One of the goals of late 20th-c military research is to prove the technology of this approach, which would be used, for example, to shoot down missiles in space. >> directed energy weapons

particle detectors Devices for detecting and identifying subatomic particles in particle physics experiments. They are designed to measure total energy, charge to mass ratio, velocity, position, and time. >> bubble chamber; cloud chamber; particle physics; scintillation counter

particle physics The study of the fundamental components of matter and the forces between them; also called **high energy physics** or **elementary particle physics**. Most particle physics experiments involve the use of large particle accelerators, necessary to force particles close enough together to produce interactions. All theories in particle physics are quantum theories, in which symmetry is of central importance. Atoms are viewed as comprising a central nucleus surrounded by electrons, the nucleus being composed of protons and neutrons. These protons, neutrons, the particles from which they are made, and other related objects are the entities studied in particle physics. Subatomic particles thought to be indivisible into smaller particles are known as *fundamental particles*: these are the matter particles (quarks, neutrinos, electrons, muons, and taus) and the force particles (gluons, photons, W and Z bosons, and gravitons). The important forces acting between these particles are the electromagnetic, strong nuclear, and weak nuclear forces. During the 1950s, studies revealed other particles of various masses, some exhibiting unusual or 'strange' behaviour. A new quantum number called *strangeness*, conserved in strong but not in weak interactions, was invented to explain these results. Other quantum numbers have subsequently been introduced to account for observed particle interactions. Current research focuses on resolving difficulties in existing theories, constructing unified theories of strong, weak, and electromagnetic forces, and incorporating gravity to give a complete theory of the physical universe. >> nuclear physics; particle accelerators; particle detectors; quantum electrodynamics / gravity; strong interaction; subatomic particles; weak interaction

Parti Québecois (PQ) [kaybekwah] A separatist political party in Canada, established in 1968. Led by René Lévesque until 1985, the *péquistes* formed the government in Quebec in 1976, and were elected for a second term in 1981. >> Charlottetown / Meech Lake Accord; Lévesque; Quebec

partita [pah(r)**tee**ta] In music of the Baroque period, **1** one of a set of instrumental variations (*partite*); **2** a set of instrumental dances. >> suite; variations

partnership A form of business organization where the owners share all the profits – or take all the losses – according to some predetermined formula. There are usually not more than 20 partners, though larger partnerships do exist.

Partridge, Eric (Honeywood) (1894–1979) Lexicographer, born near Gisborne, New Zealand. He became a freelance author and lexicographer, specializing in studies of style, slang, and colloquial language, such as his *Usage and Abusage* (1947).

partridge A drab, plump, short-tailed bird of the pheasant family; found from Europe to SE Asia, and in Africa. (Family: Phasianidae, 84 species.) >> francolin; pheasant; tinamou

par value >> **parity** (economics)

Pasargadae [pa**sah(r)**gadiy] The site in S Iran chosen by Cyrus the Great in 546 BC to be the capital of the new Achaemenid empire. >> Achaemenids; Cyrus II

Pascal, Blaise [pas**kal**] (1623–62) Mathematician, physicist, theologian, and man-of-letters, born in Clermont-Ferrand, France. In 1647 he invented a calculating machine, and later the barometer, the hydraulic press, and the syringe. He defended Jansenism against the Jesuits in *Lettres provinciales* (1656–7). Fragments jotted down for a case book of Christian truths were discovered after his death, and published as the *Pensées* (1669, Thoughts).

PASCAL A high-level computer programming language, named after the French mathematician, Blaise Pascal, which was developed from ALGOL in the late 1960s. >> Pascal; programming language

pascal SI unit of pressure; symbol *Pa*; named after French mathematician Blaise Pascal; defined as the pressure due to a force of 1 newton acting on an area of 1 square metre. >> Pascal; pressure

Pascua, Isla de >> **Easter Island**

Pashtun or **Pathan** [pa**tahn**] A cluster of Pashto-speaking agricultural and herding people of NW Pakistan and SE Afghanistan. They are the most numerous group in Afghanistan, numbering 6.2 million; 6.7 million live in Pakistan.

Pasiphae (astronomy) [pa**sif**ayee] The eighth natural satellite of Jupiter, discovered in 1908; distance from the planet 23 500 000 km/ 14 603 000 mi; diameter 50 km/30 mi. >> Jupiter (astronomy); RR964

Pasiphae (mythology) [pa**sif**ayee] In Greek mythology, the daughter of Helios, and wife of Minos, King of Crete. She loved a bull sent by Poseidon, and became the mother of the Minotaur. >> Minotaur

Pasmore, (Edwin John) Victor (1908–98) Artist, born in Chelsham, Surrey. One of the founders of the Euston Road School (1937), he developed a highly abstract style, in which colour is often primarily used to suggest relief. >> abstract art; Euston Road School

Pasolini, Pier Paolo [pasoh**lee**nee] (1922–75) Film director, born in Bologna, Italy. He became known for such films as *Il Vangelo secondo Matteo* (1964, The Gospel According to St Matthew) and *The Canterbury Tales* (1972).

passacaglia [pasa**kahl**ya] A musical structure in which a continuously repeated bass line or harmonic progression provides the basis for a set of uninterrupted variations. >> variations

Passchendaele, Battle of [**pash**endayl] (1917) The third battle of Ypres during World War 1; a British offensive notable for appallingly muddy conditions, minimal gains, and British casualties of at least 300 000. In the final action, Canadians captured the village of Passchendaele, NE of Ypres. >> World War 1; Ypres, Battles of

passerine Any bird of the worldwide order Passeriformes ('perching birds'); includes the **songbirds** (Suborder: Oscines); comprises more than half the living species of birds; four toes, one pointing backwards and opposing the others; wing has 9–10 primary feathers; tail usually with 12 main feathers. >> songbird

passion flower A member of a large genus of climbers with twining tendrils, native to America, a few to Asia and Australia; flowers large, showy, with five coloured sepals alternating with five petals, said to symbolize the crucifixion, with the inner corona of filaments representing the crown of thorns, and the styles the cross and nails; yellow or purple edible berry (known as **passion fruit** or **granadilla**), up to 10 cm/4 in long. (Genus: *Passiflora*, 500 species. Family: Passifloraceae.) >> crucifixion; granadilla; sepal; style (botany)

passion fruit >> **passion flower** ℹ

Passionists A religious order, founded in Italy in 1720 by St Paul of the Cross; properly known as the **Congregation of the Barefooted Clerics of the Most Holy Cross and**

Passion flower

Passion of our Lord Jesus Christ. Their declared objective is to maintain the memory of Christ's sufferings and death. >> Jesus Christ; monasticism

passive smoking Inhalation by non-smokers of tobacco smoke introduced into the atmosphere by smokers. Evidence suggests that this gives rise to a small increase (c.10%) in the probability of developing carcinoma of the lung. >> cancer; smoking

Passover An annual Jewish festival, occurring in March or April (15–22 Nisan), commemorating the exodus of the Israelites from Egypt; named from God's passing over the houses of the Israelites when he killed the first-born children of the Egyptians (*Ex* 13); also known as **Pesach** [**pay**sakh]. >> Judaism; RR982

pasta A mixture of water, wheat flour (hard), and occasionally egg, originating in Italy. The dough is extruded through dies of various shapes, and dried to provide a wide variety of types (eg canneloni, spaghetti, lasagne, macaroni, and ravioli). >> durum; semolina

pastel Powdered pigment mixed with a little gum or resin and shaped into sticks like crayons. The artist works directly onto the paper. >> paint

Pasternak, Boris (Leonidovich) [**pas**ternak] (1890–1960) Lyric poet, novelist, and translator, born in Moscow. His major work, *Dr Zhivago*, caused a political furore, and was banned in the USSR, but was an international success after its publication in Italy in 1957. Expelled by the Soviet Writers' Union in 1958, he was compelled to refuse the Nobel Prize for Literature.

Pasteur, Louis [**paster**] (1822–95) Chemist and microbiologist, born in Dôle, France. He established that putrefaction and fermentation were caused by micro-organisms, and in 1881 showed that sheep and cows 'vaccinated' with the attenuated bacilli of anthrax received protection against the disease. >> pasteurization

pasteurization A mild heat treatment used to kill micro-organisms in milk. The process heats the milk at 63–66°C for 30 minutes or 72°C for 15 seconds. It was discovered by the French chemist, Louis Pasteur. >> milk; Pasteur; UHT milk

pastoral (Lat 'pertaining to shepherds') A poem or other work expressing love of and longing for an idealized rural existence. Deriving from Theocritus, the pastoral mode has been much imitated and adapted. >> eclogue; Theocritus

pastoralism A way of life characterized by keeping herds of animals, such as cattle, sheep, camels, reindeer, goats, and llamas. It is common in dry, mountainous, or severely cold climates not suitable for agriculture. Many pastoralists are nomadic, and some have become important long-distance traders. >> nomadism

pastoral staff A crook-shaped stick carried by bishops; otherwise called a **crozier**. It represents the rod of correction and the crook of care. >> bishop

Patagonia [pata**goh**nia] area 489 541 sq km/188 963 sq mi. Region of S Argentina; a semi-arid tableland rising in terraces from the Atlantic coast to the base of the Andes; many immigrants in 19th-c, especially from Wales. >> Argentina i

Patan [**pa**tan], also **Lalitpur** 27°40N 85°20E, pop (1995e) 218 000. City in C Nepal, 5 km/3 mi SE of Kathmandu; founded, 7th-c; capital of the Nepali kingdom, 17th-c; captured by the Gurkhas, 1768; known as the 'city of artists'. >> Nepal i

patchouli A shrubby aromatic perennial (*Pogostemon cablin*) growing to 1 m/3¼ ft or more, native to the tropics and subtropics of SE Asia; flowers white, tubular, 2-lipped, in whorls. It yields an aromatic essential oil used in perfumery. (Family: Labiatae.) >> essential oil

paten [**pa**tn] A circular metal plate, often of silver or gold, on which bread is placed at the celebration of the Eucharist. >> Eucharist

patent A formal document which gives inventors the exclusive right for a period of years to exploit the product or process they have created, either by operating it themselves or by licensing others to use it. Patents have the disadvantage of restricting the diffusion of new techniques, but the merit of increasing the incentive to spend on research and development.

Pater, Walter (Horatio) [**pay**ter] (1839–94) Critic and essayist, born in London. He became known with his *Studies in the History of the Renaissance* (1873), and exercised considerable influence on the aesthetic movements of his time. >> aesthetics

Pater Noster [**pah**ter **nos**ter] >> **Lord's Prayer**

Paterson, A(ndrew) B(arton), nickname **Banjo Paterson** (1864–1941) Journalist and poet, born in Narrambia, New South Wales, Australia. He wrote several books of light verse, but is best known as the author of 'Waltzing Matilda'.

Pathan >> **Pashtun**

Pathé, Charles [**pa**thay], Fr [patay] (1863–1957) Film pioneer, born in Paris. In 1896 he founded Société Pathé Frères with his brothers, which by 1912 had become one of the largest film production organizations in the world. They introduced the newsreel in 1909.

pathology The scientific study of disease in humans and other living organisms. It includes the detection of micro-organisms and of chromosome and enzyme defects, the microscopic study of cells and tissues, and microchemical analyses. >> biopsy; medicine

Patmore, Coventry (Kersey Dighton) (1823–96) Poet, born in Woodford, Essex. His major work, *The Angel in the House* (1854–62), was followed by his conversion to Catholicism. Thereafter he wrote mainly on mystical or religious themes.

Patmos area 34 sq km/13 sq mi; pop (1995e) 2650. Island of the Dodecanese, Greece; chief town, Hora; St John the apostle lived here for 2 years. >> Dodecanese; Greece i; John the Apostle, St

Patna [**pat**na] 25°37N 85°12E, pop (1995e) 993 000. Winter capital of Bihar, E India; on S bank of R Ganges; French trading post, 1732; university (1917); major rice-growing region; noted for its handicrafts. >> Bihar

Paton, Alan (Stewart) [**pay**tn] (1903–88) Writer and educator, born in Pietermaritzburg, South Africa. From his deep concern with the racial problem in South Africa sprang several novels, notably *Cry, the Beloved Country* (1948) and *Too Late the Phalarope* (1953).

patriarch 1 The head of a family or tribe. In Biblical literature, usually applied either to the 10 purported ancestors of the human race prior to the Flood, or more commonly to Abraham, Isaac, Jacob, and Jacob's 12 sons. >> Bible; Flood, the; Israel, tribes of **2** An ecclesiastical title used since about the 6th-c for the bishops of the five important ecclesiastical centres of the early Christian Church: Alexandria, Antioch, Constantinople, Jerusalem, and Rome. >> bishop; Christianity

patricians In ancient Rome, the members of a select number of aristocratic clans or *gentes*, such as the Julii. The precise origins of this elite are obscure and still much debated. >> plebeians

Patrick, St (c.385–461) Apostle of Ireland, born (perhaps) in S Wales. Ordained a bishop at 45, he became a missionary to Ireland (432), and fixed his see at Armagh (454). Feast day 17 March.

patristics >> **Fathers of the Church**

Patten, Chris(topher Francis) (1944–) British politician, born in London. He became minister for overseas development (1986), secretary of state for the environment (1989), and party chairman (1991). Credited with master-minding the Tory victory in the 1992 election, he lost his own seat and was appointed Governor of Hong Kong (1992–7). He was made a European Commissioner in 1999.

pattern recognition >> **character recognition**

Patton, George S(mith) (1885–1945) US general, born in San Gabriel, CA. He played a key role in the Allied invasion of French N Africa (1942), led the US 7th Army in its assault on Sicily (1943), commanded the 3rd Army in the invasion of France, and contained the German counter-offensive in the Ardennes (1944). >> World War 2

Pau [poh] 43°19N 0°25W, pop (1995e) 86 500. City in SW France; on right bank of R Gave de Pau; former capital of Béarn province, 1464; health resort, winter sports centre; road and rail junction; castle (12th–15th-c).

Paul, St, originally **Saul of Tarsus** (?10–65/67 AD) Apostle to the Gentiles and important theologian of the early Christian Church, born of Jewish parents at Tarsus, Cilicia. A persecutor of Christians, on his way to Damascus (c.34–35) he was converted to Christianity by a vision of Christ, and began to preach the Christian message. His missionary journeys included visits to Asia Minor and through Galatia and Phrygia to Macedonia and Achaia, where in Corinth he was especially successful. An extensive mission was also undertaken in Ephesus. On his return to Jerusalem, he was apparently imprisoned for 2 years, transferred to Rome, and according to later tradition was executed by Nero (c.64). Thirteen New Testament letters are traditionally attributed to him. Feast day 29 June. >> Acts of the Apostles; Christianity; Pauline Letters

Paul VI, originally **Giovanni Battista Montini** (1897–1978) Pope (1963–78), born in Concesio, Italy. He travelled more widely than any previous pope, and initiated important advances in the move towards Christian unity. >> ecumenism

Pauli, Wolfgang [**pow**lee] (1900–58) Theoretical physicist, born in Vienna. In 1925 he formulated the 'exclusion principle' in atomic physics (that no two electrons, or other fermions, may occupy exactly the same quantum state), and in 1931 postulated the existence of an electrically neutral particle (the neutrino). He was awarded the 1945 Nobel Prize for Physics. >> nuclear physics

Paulin, Tom [**paw**lin] (1949–) Poet, born in Leeds, West Yorkshire. His books include *A Sense of Justice* (1977) and *Seize the Fire* (1990), and he edited the Faber books of political (1986) and vernacular verse (1990). He is also known in the UK as a contributor to television discussion programmes on the arts.

Pauline Letters or **Pauline Epistles** A set of New Testament writings ascribed to the apostle Paul, usually numbering 13. Modern scholars are confident of Paul's authorship in only seven cases (Romans, 1 and 2 Corinthians, Galatians, Philippians, 1 Thessalonians, and Philemon), and debate the authenticity of 2 Thessalonians, Colossians, Ephesians, and the Pastoral Letters. >> New Testament; Paul, St

Pauling, Linus (Carl) [**paw**ling] (1901–94) Chemist, born in Portland, OR. He applied quantum theory to chemistry, and was awarded the Nobel Prize for Chemistry in 1954 for his contributions to the theory of valency. He became a controversial figure from 1955 as the leading scientific critic of US nuclear deterrent policy. Awarded the Nobel Peace Prize in 1962, he was the first person to have received two full Nobel Prizes. >> valency

pavane [pa**van**] A stately dance of the 16th–17th-c, probably of Italian origin. It was often linked to a livelier dance, generally in triple time, known as a *galliard* (from Fr 'merry').

Pavarotti, Luciano [pava**ro**tee] (1935–) Tenor, born in Modena, Italy. He won the international competition at the Teatro Reggio Emilia in 1961, and made his operatic debut there the same year. He made his US debut in 1968, and is internationally known as a concert performer.

Pavese, Cesare [pa**vay**zay] (1908–50) Writer, born in Cuneo, Italy. He is best known for his novel *La luna e i falò* (1950, The Moon and the Bonfires). His work exerted a strong influence on later Italian fiction and film making.

Pavia [pa**vee**a], ancient **Ticinum** 45°12N 9°09E, pop (1995e) 86 300. City in N Italy, on R Ticino; railway; university (1361); cathedral (begun 1487). >> Italy ℹ

Pavlov, Ivan Petrovich [**pav**lov] (1849–1936) Physiologist, born in Ryazan, Russia. From 1902 he studied what later became known as Pavlovian or classical conditioning in animals. A major influence on the development of behaviourism in psychology, he was awarded the Nobel Prize for Physiology or Medicine in 1904. >> behaviourism; conditioning; psychology

Pavlova, Anna [**pav**lova] (1881–1931) Ballerina, born in St Petersburg, Russia. In 1909 she travelled to Paris with the Ballets Russes, and after 1913 danced with her own company in reduced versions of the classics in many parts of the world. >> Ballets Russes

Pavo [**pah**voh] (Lat 'peacock') A constellation in the S hemisphere. >> constellation; RR968

pawnbroking A system of money-lending in which an article, usually personal property, is deposited with an agent (the **pawnbroker**) as security for the loan. The article can be redeemed within a given time on repayment of the loan plus interest. Articles unredeemed at the end of the period become the property of the pawnbroker.

pawpaw >> **papaw**

Paxman, Jeremy (Dickson) (1950–) British television presenter and journalist. He joined the BBC 1 *Tonight* team in 1977, and worked on several other programmes before joining BBC 2's *Newsnight* (1989), on which he developed a reputation as a tough but fair interviewer. He became presenter of *University Challenge* in 1994, and took over Radio 4's *Start the Week* in 1998.

Paxton, Sir Joseph (1801–65) Gardener and architect, born near Woburn, Bedfordshire. He designed a building for the Great Exhibition of 1851 (nicknamed the 'Crystal Palace'), which he re-erected in Sydenham (destroyed by fire in 1936). >> landscape gardening

PAYE An abbreviation of **pay as you earn**, a UK taxation system whereby income tax is deducted from a worker's pay by an employer before handing over the wage. The amount to be collected is determined by reference to each person's *tax code*, calculated at the start of each fiscal year. Several other countries have a payroll deduction plan of this kind. >> income tax

Payton, Walter (1954–) Player of American football, born in Columbia, MS. In his career with the Chicago Bears (1975–88), he rushed for 16 726 yards, a National Football League record. >> football ℹ

pay TV The non-broadcast distribution of video entertainment to a restricted audience of subscribers who pay for the programmes viewed. The programmes are received either by individual cable connection or by scrambled microwave or satellite transmission requiring a rented decoder. >> television

Paz, La >> **La Paz**

Paz, Octavio (1914–98) Poet, born in Mexico City. He was a writer of great energy and versatility, with 30 volumes from 1933; his *Collected Poems* (1957–87), in Spanish and English, were published in 1988. He received the Nobel Prize for Literature in 1990.

Paz Estenssoro, Victor [**pahs** esten**saw**roh] (1907–) Bolivian revolutionary and politician, born in Tarija, Bolivia. Following the 1952 Revolution he served as president (1952–6, 1960–4). Ousted by a military coup, he later served again as president (1985–9). >> Bolivia ℹ

PC >> **personal computer**

PCBs Abbreviation of **polychlorobiphenyls**, usually a mixture of compounds in which chlorine is substituted for many of the hydrogen atoms in biphenyl, $C_{12}H_{10}$, a molecule in which two phenyl groups are joined to one another. Their stability makes them excellent flame retardants and electrical insulators, but their eventual degradation products are toxic. >> phenyl

PCP >> **angel dust**

pea A botanical term used as a suffix, referring to several plants of the family Leguminosae, but especially to members of the genus *Pisum*. The best-known species are **sweet pea** (*Lathyrus odoratus*) and **garden pea** (*Pisum sativum*), a climbing annual growing to 2 m/6½ ft, native to S Europe and N Africa; flowers up to 3.5 cm/1½ in long, white, pink or purplish, in small clusters of 1–3; pods up to 12 cm/4¾ in long, oblong, containing up to 10 seeds. It has been cultivated since prehistoric times for the edible seeds (*peas*) eaten as a vegetable, fresh, dried, frozen, or canned. Many cultivars are also widely grown, including the smaller-seeded *petit pois*, and also *mangetout*, where the whole pod is consumed. >> *illustration below*

Peace Corps An agency of volunteers funded by the US government, established in 1961. Volunteers numbered more than 10 000 in 52 countries in 1966, but in the 1980s the corps was asked to leave some countries hostile to US policies. >> Voluntary Service Overseas

Peace River River in W Canada, rising in British Columbia as the Finlay R; enters the Slave R; length 1923 km/ 1195 mi to the head of Finlay R. >> Canada ℹ

peace studies Educational courses designed to explore the role of the military in society, international strategic relationships, and those conditions that most promote peace and human welfare in society. >> military science

peach A small deciduous tree (*Prunus persica*), growing to 6 m/20 ft; flowers pink, rarely white, appearing before leaves; fruit globular, velvety 4–8 cm/1½–3 in, yellow flushed red with thick sweet flesh, stone grooved. (Family: Rosaceae.) >> nectarine; prunus

Peacock, Thomas Love (1785–1866) Novelist, born in Weymouth, Dorset. His satirical romances include *Headlong Hall* (1816), *Melincourt* (1817), and *Nightmare Abbey* (1818). In each case a company of humorists meet in a country house, and the satire arises from their conversation rather than from character or plot.

peacock Either of two species of pheasant (Genus: *Pavo*) from the forests of India and SE Asia: especially the **Indian peafowl** (*Pavo cristatus*); alternatively known as **peafowl**; the female sometimes called **peahen**. The peacock is known for its resplendent train (extending to some 1.5 m/5 ft), in which each feather ends with a brightly coloured, ring-shaped feature (the 'eye'). The peacock displays his tail by raising it above and behind his head. Males are mainly blue-green or green-bronze; females are green or brown, and lack a train. The birds are known for their ill temper. >> pheasant

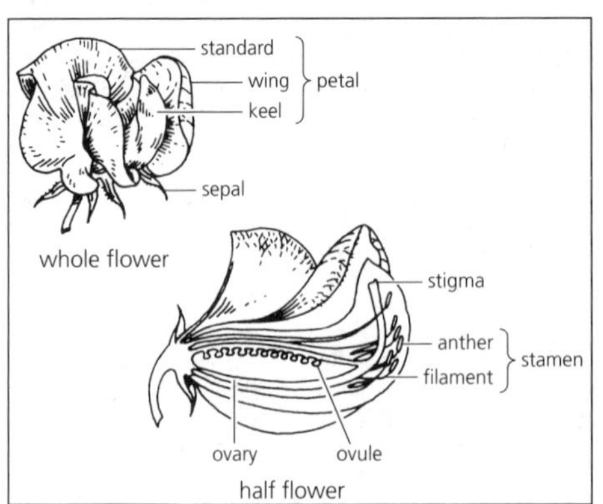

Pea flower

peafowl >> **peacock**

Peak District National park in NC England; area 1404 sq km/542 sq mi; established in 1951; mainly in Derbyshire; limestone caves, notably at Peak Cavern, near Castleton; highest point, Kinder Scout, 727 m/2088 ft. >> Derbyshire

Peake, Mervyn (Laurence) (1911–68) Writer and artist, born in Kuling, China. He is best known for his Gothic fantasy trilogy of novels: *Titus Groan* (1946), *Gormenghast* (1950), and *Titus Alone* (1959), and his novel *Mr Pye* (1953). >> Gothic novel

peanut An annual (*Arachis hypogaea*), growing to 50 cm/ 20 in, native to South America; pea-flowers yellow; also called **groundnut** or **monkey nut**. It is widely grown for the edible seeds (*peanuts*), used in confectionery and as a source of peanut oil. (Family: Leguminosae.)

pear A deciduous, usually thorny tree or shrub, native to Europe and Asia; flowers white or pinkish, in flat-topped clusters; fruit round or top-shaped as well as pear-shaped. (Genus: *Pyrus*, 30 species. Family: Rosaceae.) >> tree ℹ

Pearce, Stuart (1962–) Footballer, born in London. A left back, he played for Coventry City before moving to Nottingham Forest (1985–97), where he also acted for a time as player/manager, and Newcastle United (1997–). By mid-1998 he had won 76 caps for England (including several as captain from 1992).

pearlfish Elongate and very slender fish widespread in tropical and warm temperate seas, living inside sea cucumbers, sea urchins, and other marine invertebrates; length up to 30 cm/12 in. (Family: Carapidae, 2 genera.)

Pearl Harbor US deep-water naval base on the island of Oahu in the US Pacific Ocean state of Hawaii, adjacent to Honolulu, established in 1908. The bombing of the base by the Japanese (7 Dec 1941), brought the USA into World War 2. >> Hawaii (state); World War 2

pearlite A type of steel formed by an intimate intergrowth of iron with iron carbide. It has a lustrous sheen. >> iron; steel

Pearl River >> **Zhu Jiang**

Pears, Sir Peter (Neville Luard) [peerz] (1910–86) Tenor, born in Farnham, Surrey. In 1946 he helped Britten found the English Opera Group, and was co-founder with him of the Aldeburgh Festival (1948). >> Britten

Pearse, Patrick (or **Pádraic**) **Henry** [peers] (1879–1916) Writer, educationist, and nationalist, born in Dublin. He commanded the insurgents in the Easter Rising of 1916, and was proclaimed president of the provisional government. After the revolt had been quelled, he was court-martialled and shot. >> Easter Rising

Pearson, Lester B(owles) (1897–1972) Canadian statesman and prime minister (1963–8), born in Newtonbrook, Ontario, Canada. Secretary of state for external affairs (1948–57), his efforts to resolve the Suez Crisis were rewarded with the Nobel Peace Prize in 1957. >> Suez Crisis

Peary, Robert (Edwin) [peeree] (1856–1920) Admiral and explorer, born in Cresson Springs, PA. He made eight Arctic voyages to the Greenland coast, in 1891–2 arriving on the E coast by crossing the ice. In 1909 he led the first expedition to the North Pole. >> North Pole

Peary Land Region of N Greenland on the Arctic Ocean, forming a mountainous peninsula; not covered by ice; explored by Peary in 1892 and 1900. >> Greenland [i]; Peary

Peasants' Revolt An English popular rising of June 1381, among townsmen as well as peasants, based in Essex, Kent, and London. Precipitated by the three oppressive poll taxes of 1377–81, it was quickly suppressed. >> poll tax; Tyler, Wat

Peasants' War (1524–5) Probably the largest peasant uprising in European history, raging through Germany. It was denounced by Luther, and suppressed by the princes.

peat The partially decomposed remains of plants which accumulate and are preserved in waterlogged conditions in areas of cool, humid climate. It is the first stage in the formation of coal, and is widely used as a form of fuel (eg in Ireland and Russia). >> coal

pecan A deciduous tree (*Carya pecan*) growing to 45 m/150 ft, native to E North America; flowers small, green, lacking petals; nut 4–5 cm/1½–2 in, roughly oblong, reddish-brown, edible. (Family: Juglandaceae.)

peccary [**pek**aree] A mammal native to forest and dry scrubland in Central and South America; a New World equivalent of the Old World pig, but smaller, with three toes on each hind foot; tusks grow downwards. (Family: Tayassuidae, 3 species.) >> artiodactyl; pig

Peck, (Eldred) Gregory (1916–) Film star, born in La Jolla, CA. He received an Oscar for his portrayal of a liberal Southern lawyer in *To Kill a Mockingbird* (1962). Among his other films are *Spellbound* (1945), *Twelve O'Clock High* (1949), and *The Omen* (1976).

Peckinpah, Sam [**pe**kinpah] (1925–84) US film director, born in Fresno, CA. He portrayed a harshly realistic view of the lawless US West, accentuating the inherent violence, as in *Major Dundee* (1965) and *The Wild Bunch* (1969).

Pecos River [**pay**kohs] River in S USA; rises in the Sangre de Cristo Mts; flows S to join the Rio Grande; length 1490 km/925 mi. >> United States of America [i]

Pécs [paych], Ger **Fünfkirchen**, Lat **Sopianae** 46°05N 18°15E, pop (1995e) 168 000. Industrial city in S Hungary; bishopric; university (1367, refounded 1922), university of medicine (1923); centre of a noted wine-producing area. >> Hungary [i]

pectin A complex molecule (a homopolysaccharide) especially rich in galacturonic acid. It functions as a cement-like material in plant cell walls, and is abundant in fruits such as apples. >> galactose; molecule; polysaccharides

pediatrics >> **paediatrics**

pediment In classical architecture, a triangular section of wall above the entablature and enclosed by the sloping cornices, ie a low-pitched gable. >> cornice; entablature; frieze

pedology The study of soil as a natural phenomenon. It embraces soil mapping, the study of soil formation and development, and the subdisciplines of soil chemistry, soil physics, and soil microbiology. >> soil science

pedometer A device for counting the number of paces taken by the wearer. It usually consists of a free pendulum, operating a ratchet, which moves a toothed wheel one tooth per pace; this is then connected to a dial counter.

pedophilia >> **paedophilia**

Pedra Furada [**ped**ra fu**rah**da] Rock shelter in Piaui region, Brazil, the earliest human settlement yet known in the Americas. It suggests that early modern humans reached the New World more than 30 000 years ago, around the time they arrived in Europe and Australia, and much earlier than previously thought. >> American Indians; radiocarbon dating

Peel, Sir Robert (1788–1850) British statesman and prime minister (1834–5, 1841–6), born near Bury, Lancashire. As home secretary (1822–7, 1828–30), he carried through the Catholic Emancipation Act (1829) and reorganized the London police force (whose members became known as 'Peelers' or 'Bobbies'). As prime minister, his decision to phase out agricultural protection by repealing the Corn Laws (1846) split his party, and precipitated his resignation. >> Corn Laws; police

Peele, George (c.1558–96) Playwright, born in London. His best-known works are the pastoral *The Arraignment of Paris* (1584) and the historical play *Edward I* (1593).

peepul A species of strangler fig (*Ficus religiosa*) native to SE Asia, and regarded as sacred in India; also called **pipal** or **bo-tree**. (Family: Moraceae.) >> fig

peerage In the UK, holders of the title of duke, marquess, earl, viscount, or baron, who make up, in that order of precedence, the titled nobility. Their privileges have been reduced; the two main ones remaining are their right to sit in the House of Lords, and their exemption from jury service.

peewit An alternative name for the lapwing (*Vanellus vanellus*); also known as **pewit**. It was formerly an alternative name for the **black-headed gull** (*Larus ridibundus*). >> gull; lapwing

Pegasus (astronomy) (Lat 'winged horse') The seventh largest constellation, conspicuous in the N hemisphere >> constellation; RR968

Pegasus (mythology) In Greek mythology, a winged horse, which sprang from the body of the Medusa after her death. Bellerophon caught it with Athene's assistance.

pegmatite [**peg**matiyt] Very coarse-grained igneous rocks with varied and sometimes exotic mineralogy due to concentrations of the rarer elements. They are the source of many gem-quality and uncommon minerals. >> gemstones; igneous rock

Pei, I(eoh) M(eng) [pay] (1917–) Architect, born in Canton, China. He emigrated to the USA in 1935. His principal projects include Mile High Center, Denver, the 60-storey John Hancock Tower, Boston, and the glass pyramids at the Louvre, Paris.

Peierls, Sir Rudolph (Ernest) [piylz] (1907–95) Theoretical physicist, born in Berlin. He applied quantum theory to solids and to magnetic effects, and then turned to nuclear physics, working on the atomic bomb project throughout World War 2. >> atomic bomb; nuclear fission

Peirce, Charles Sanders [peers] (1839–1914) Philosopher and logician, born in Cambridge, MA. He is known for his contributions to pragmatism, including the development of a pragmatic theory of meaning; and he also worked on mathematical logic. His theory of meaning helped establish the new field of semiotics. >> semiotics

pekan >> **fisher**

Pekinese or **Pekingese** A toy breed of dog, developed in China 2000 years ago; long body with short legs; tail curved over back; long, pendulous ears; flat face, muzzle virtually non-existent; coat very long, fine; also known as **peke**. >> dog

Peking >> **Beijing**

Pelagianism >> **Pelagius**

Pelagius [pe**lay**jius] (c.360–c.420) A British or Irish monk, who settled in Rome c.400. His view that salvation can be achieved by the exercise of human powers (**Pelagianism**) was condemned as heretical by Councils in 416 and 418. >> Christianity; heresy

pelargonium An annual or perennial, native mainly to S Africa; flowers in a range of colours in clusters. They include the so-called 'geraniums' of horticulture. (Genus: *Pelargonium*, 250 species. Family: Geraniaceae.) >> cranesbill

Pelasgians [pe**laz**gianz] The name given by the Greeks to the indigenous, pre-Greek peoples of the Aegean region.

Pelau >> **Belau**

Pelé [**pe**lay], popular name of **Edson Arantes do Nascimento** (1940–) Footballer, born in Três Corações. Widely held to be the best player in the game's history, he played in Brazil's winning team in the 1958, 1962, and 1970 World Cup finals. His first-class career was spent at Santos (1955–74) and with the New York Cosmos (1975–7), scoring 1281 goals. He is a national hero in Brazil. He was appointed a sports minister in the Brazilian cabinet in 1994. >> football ℹ

Pelecypoda [pele**sip**oda] >> **bivalve**

Pelée, Mount [pe**lay**], Fr **Montagne Pelée** 14°18N 61°10W. Active volcano on Martinique I, E Caribbean; height, 1397 m/4583 ft; erupted in 1902 killing over 26 000 people in the town of St Pierre. >> Martinique; volcano

Peleus [**peel**yoos] In Greek mythology, the King of Phythia in Thessaly, who had to capture Thetis, a nereid, before he could marry her. He was the father of Achilles. >> Achilles; Eris; Thetis

Pelham, Henry [**pel**am] >> **Pelham (-Holles), Thomas**

Pelham (-Holles), Thomas, 1st Duke of Newcastle [**pel**am] (1693–1768) British statesman and prime minister (1754–6, 1757–62). A Whig and a supporter of Walpole, in 1724 he became secretary of state, and held the office for 30 years. He succeeded his brother, **Henry Pelham** (c.1696–1754) as premier, and was extremely influential during the reigns of George I and II. >> George I / II (of Great Britain); Walpole, Robert; Whigs

pelican A large aquatic bird from warm regions worldwide; bill long, with lower part sack-like; eats fish and crustaceans. (Genus: *Pelecanus*, 8 species. Family: Pelecanidae.) >> bird ℹ

pellagra [pe**lay**gra] A nutritional disease which results from a deficiency of niacin (a vitamin of the B group). It occurs in Africa or as a result of malabsorption of food. >> vitamins ℹ

Pelopidas [**pel**opidas] (c.410–364 BC) Theban general and statesman who, with Epaminondas, established the short-lived Theban hegemony over Greece in the 360s BC. He played a prominent part in the Theban victory over Sparta at Leuctra (371 BC). >> Epaminondas; Sparta (Greek history); Thebes

Peloponnese [pelopo**neez**], Gr **Pelopónnisos** pop (1995e) 1 103 000; area 21 379 sq km/8252 sq mi. Peninsular region of Greece, the most southerly part of the Greek mainland, to which it is linked by the Isthmus of Corinth; a popular holiday region. >> Greece ℹ

Peloponnesian War [pelopo**nee**shan] (431–404 BC) The war waged throughout the Greek world on land and sea by the Spartans and their allies. The underlying cause was Athenian imperialism. Following Persian intervention on the side of the Spartans, the Athenians were defeated. >> Pericles; Sparta (Greek history); Thirty Tyrants

pelota [pe**loh**ta] The generic name for various hand, glove, racket, or bat-and-ball court games which all developed from the French *jeu de paume* ('palm [of hand] game'). It is one of the world's fastest games.

pelvis **1** The region of the trunk that lies below the abdomen. It contains part of the gastro-intestinal tract, part of the urinary system, and some of the genital organs.>> abdomen **2** A ring of bone which serves to transmit forces from the lower limbs to the trunk. It consists of the two hip bones, the sacrum, and the coccyx. >> coccyx; hip; pyelonephritis; sacrum; skeleton ℹ

pelycosaur [pe**lik**osaw(r)] A carnivorous fossil reptile known from the Carboniferous to the late Permian periods, mostly in North America; skull mammal-like; typically with expanded sail along back. (Subclass: Synapsida. Order: Pelycosauria.) >> Carboniferous period; Permian period; reptile

Pemba pop (1995e) 320 000; area 981 sq km/379 sq mi. Island region of Tanzania, in the Indian Ocean; capital, Chake Chake; cloves (world's largest producer). >> Tanzania ℹ

Pembrokeshire, Welsh **Sir Penfro** pop (1995e) 113 600; area 1590 sq km/614 sq mi. County (unitary authority from 1996) in SW Wales, UK; administrative centre, Haverfordwest; ferries to Ireland (Rosslare) from Fishguard; Caldy I priory and monastery; castles at Pembroke, Cilgerran, Carew; St David's Cathedral. >> Wales ℹ

PEN Initials standing for 'poets, playwrights, editors, essayists, novelists', an international association, founded by C A Dawson Scott in 1921, to promote understanding between writers, and to defend freedom of expression.

penance (Lat *poena*, 'punishment') Both the inner turning to God in sorrow for sin, and the outward discipline of the Church in order to reinforce repentance by prayer, confession, fasting, and good works. In the Orthodox and Roman Catholic Churches, penance is a sacrament. >> confession; sacrament

Penang [pe**nang**], also **Pulau Pinang** pop (1995e) 1 286 000; area 1044 sq km/403 sq mi. State in NW Malaysia; first British settlement in Malaya; capital, Pinang (formerly George Town). >> Pinang (city); Malaysia ℹ

Penates [pen**ay**teez, pen**ah**teez] In Roman religion, the guardians of the storeroom; 'Lares and Penates' were the household gods.

pencil In art, originally a brush, a meaning still found in the 18th-c. Drawing sticks of graphite encased in wood were in use by the 17th-c, but modern hard and soft pencils, in which the graphite is mixed with clay and fired in a kiln, were first devised in France c.1790 by French inventor Nicholas-Jacques Conté (1755–1805). The hardness of a pencil depends on the amount of clay used along with the graphite, and is indicated by a hardness rating, such as 8B (very soft) to 10H (very hard). >> graphite; silverpoint

Penda (c.575–655) King of Mercia (c.632–55). He established mastery over the English Midlands, and was frequently at war with the kings of Northumbria. >> Anglo-Saxons; Mercia; Northumbria

Penderecki, Krzysztof [pen**dres**kee] (1933–) Composer, born in Debica, Poland. His works include *Threnody for the Victims of Hiroshima* (1960), the opera *The Devils of Loudon* (1969), and a St Luke Passion.

Pendleton, Don(ald Eugene) (1927–95) Author, born in Little Rock, AR. He is best known for his series of 38 'Executioner' novels, starring Mack Bolan. Launched in 1969 with *War Against the Mafia*, the series led to the emergence of a new genre of 'action/adventure' writing in the 1970s, especially popular in North America.

pendulum In its simplest form, a weight, suspended by a wire or rod from a firm support, and allowed to swing freely to and fro under the influence of gravity. The swing period does not depend on the weight of the bob nor on the size of the swing (for small swings), which is why pendulums are used in clocks. >> Foucault pendulum; periodic motion

Penelope In Greek legend, the wife of Odysseus, who faithfully waited 20 years for his return from Troy. She tricked her suitors by weaving a shroud for Odysseus' father (which had to be finished before she could marry), and undoing her work every night. >> Odysseus

Penghu Qundao [punghoo] or **P'eng-hu Ch'ün-tao**, Span, Port **Pescadores** pop (1995e) 98 200; area 127 sq km/49 sq mi. Island archipelago of Taiwan; 85% of the population lives on the largest island, Penghu. >> Taiwan ℹ

penguin A flightless seabird, native to S hemisphere;

wings modified as flippers. (Family: Spheniscidae, 18 species.) >> bird ℹ; emperor penguin; fairy penguin

penicillin An antibiotic produced by the mould *Penicillium*. In 1928, Fleming first noted its activity against the bacterium *Staphylococcus* when his culture plate accidentally became contaminated with the mould. Several types are now used, such as ampicillin and benzylpenicillin (penicillin G). >> antibiotics; Fleming, Alexander

Peninsular Campaign (1862) In the American Civil War, an extended attempt by the Union army under General McClellan to take Richmond, Virginia (the Southern capital), by moving up the peninsula between the James and York Rivers. The effort failed, but Confederate troops were unable to drive the Northerners off the peninsula. >> American Civil War; Seven Days' Battles

Peninsular War (1808–14) The prolonged struggle for the Iberian peninsula between the occupying French and a British army under Wellington (formerly Wellesley), supported by Portuguese forces. British troops repulsed Masséna's Lisbon offensive (1810–11) and advanced to liberate Spain. Wellington's army then invaded SW France (1813–14). >> Masséna; Napoleonic Wars; Wellington, Duke of

penis A part of the male urogenital system composed mainly of erectile tissue and traversed by the *urethra*. The skin over the body of the penis is thin, delicate, freely mobile, and largely free from hairs. Towards the base of the glans penis it forms a free fold (the *foreskin*) which overlaps the glans to a variable extent (the foreskin is surgically removed in circumcision so that the glans is always visible). The size of the penis varies with the amount of blood present within the erectile tissue. >> circumcision; gonorrhoea; semen; syphilis; testis; urinary system; venereal disease

Penn, William (1644–1718) Quaker leader and founder of Pennsylvania, born in London. He was imprisoned for his writings (1668), and while in the Tower wrote the most popular of his books, *No Cross, no Crown*. In 1681 he obtained a grant of land in North America, which he called Pennsylvania in honour of his father. He sailed in 1682, and governed the colony for two years. >> Friends, Society of; Pennsylvania

Penney, William (George) Penney, Baron (1909–91) Physicist, born in Gibraltar. Director of the Atomic Weapons Research Establishment at Aldermaston, Berkshire (1953–9), he was the key figure in the UK's success in producing its own atomic (1952) and hydrogen bombs (1957). >> atomic bomb

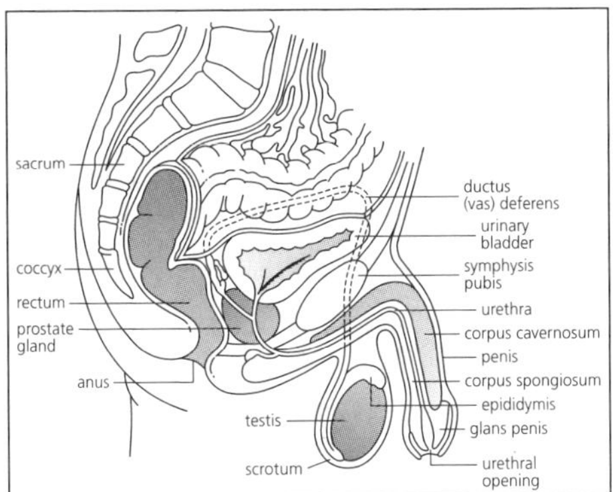

Penis – Main male organs of reproduction and surrounding structures

Pennines or **Pennine Chain**, nickname **the backbone of England** Mountain range in N England; extends S from Northumberland to Derbyshire; fold of carboniferous limestone and overlying millstone grit, worn into high moorland and fell; rises to 893 m/2930 ft at Cross Fell; **Pennine Way** footpath extends 402 km/250 mi from Derbyshire to the Scottish Borders. >> England ℹ

Pennsylvania [pensil**vay**nia] pop (1995e) 12 200 000; area 117 343 sq km/45 308 sq mi. State in E USA; the 'Keystone State'; one of the original states of the Union, second to ratify the Federal Constitution; first settled by the Swedish, 1643; taken by the Dutch, and then by the British in 1664; region given by King Charles II to William Penn, 1681; scene of many battles in the American Revolution and Civil War; capital, Harrisburg; major industrial state, noted for its coal mining. >> American Civil War; American Revolution; Harrisburg; Penn; United States of America ℹ; RR994

Pennsylvanian period >> **Carboniferous period**

pennyroyal A species of mint (*Mentha pulegium*) native to Europe and the Mediterranean, and also found in N America, with pale green leaves, mauve flowers, and strong, slightly peppermint, scent. It is used for soups and stuffings. As a mildly spicy tea, it is sometimes recommended for its physiological effects or as a herbal remedy. However, its oils contain pulegone, which is extremely toxic, and in some circumstances (eg when used in an attempt to induce abortion) it has proved lethal. (Family: Labiatae.) >> mint

pension A payment made to an individual who has retired from work, on a weekly or monthly basis, related to the wage or salary being earned before retirement. **Company pension schemes** operate by receiving contributions from employees and employers; the funds are invested, and the pensions are paid from the proceeds of the investment. In the UK, a **state pension scheme** (SERPS, or State Earnings Related Pension Scheme) is available for individuals without a company pension. The state also pays a basic old-age pension (introduced 1909). >> annuity

Pentagon The central offices of the US military forces and the Defense Department, in Arlington, VA. The complex was built in 1941–3, and covers 10 ha/29 acres. It is composed of five 5-storey, pentagonal buildings. >> Arlington

pentane C_5H_{12}, an alkane hydrocarbon with five carbon atoms. There are three structural isomers: **n-pentane**, $CH_3CH_2CH_2CH_2CH_3$ (boiling point 36°C); **isopentane** (IUPAC **methylbutane**), $CH_3CH_2CH(CH_3)CH_3$ (boiling point 28°C); and **neopentane** (IUPAC **dimethylpropane**), $CH_3C(CH_3)_2CH_3$ (boiling point 10°C). >> alkanes; hydrocarbons; IUPAC

Pentateuch [**pen**tatyook] The five Books of Moses in the Hebrew Bible/Old Testament, comprising Genesis, Exodus, Leviticus, Numbers, and Deuteronomy; also called the *Torah*. The works are now believed by modern scholars to be composed of several strands of traditions from various periods. Together they trace Israel's origins from the earliest times. >> Moses; Old Testament

pentathlon A five-event track-and-field discipline for women, seldom contested, having been replaced in 1981 by the seven-event heptathlon. The events were the 100 m hurdles, shot put, high jump, long jump, and 800 m. The **modern pentathlon** is a five-sport competition based on miltary training. The events are cross-country riding on horseback, epée fencing, pistol shooting, swimming, and cross-country running. >> heptathlon; RR1057

pentatonic scale A musical scale with five notes in the octave, most commonly equivalent to the first, second, third, fifth, and sixth degrees of the major scale. >> scale ℹ

Pentecost [**pen**tekost] **1** The Jewish feast of Shabuoth. >> Shabuoth **2** A festival day in the Christian calendar, some 50 days after the death and resurrection of Jesus, commemorating the event when the Holy Spirit was said to have come upon Jesus's apostles in Jerusalem, enabling them to 'speak in other tongues' to those present. >> Christianity; Holy Spirit; Pentecostalism; Whitsunday

Pentecostal Churches >> **Pentecostalism**

Pentecostalism [penti**kos**talizm] A modern Christian renewal movement inspired by the descent of the Holy Spirit experienced by the Apostles at the first Christian Pentecost, and marked by speaking in tongues, prophecy, and healing. Pentecostal churches are characterized by a literal interpretation of the Bible, informal worship during which there is enthusiastic singing and spontaneous exclamations of praise, and the exercise of the gifts of the Holy Spirit. There are over 22 million Pentecostals worldwide. >> charismatic movement; Christianity; faith healing; Holy Spirit; Pentecost

pentyl >> **amyl**

penumbra 1 An area of partial shadow on the Earth during a total eclipse of the Sun. In this zone, observers see a partial eclipse only. >> eclipse **2** The lighter periphery of a sunspot, surrounding the umbra. >> sunspot

Penzance [pen**zans**] 50°07N 5°33W, pop (1995e) 20 900. Town in Cornwall, SW England; chief resort town of 'the Cornish Riviera'; railway; ferry and helicopter services to Scilly Is. >> Cornwall

Penzias, Arno (Allan) [**pen**zias] (1933–) Astrophysicist, born in Munich, Germany. His research detected residual radiation from the 'big bang' at the origin of the universe. He shared the Nobel Prize for Physics with Robert W(oodrow) Wilson (1936–) in 1978. >> 'big bang'; cosmology

peony A perennial herb or shrub, native to Europe (especially Greece), Asia, and W North America; flowers large, showy, ranging in colour from white or yellow to pink or red, up to 15 cm/6 in across, with 5–10 petals and numerous stamens. (Genus: *Paeonia*, 33 species. Family: Paeoniaceae.)

People's Liberation Army >> **Red Army** (China)

Pepin III, known as **Pepin the Short** (c.714–68) King of the Franks (751–68), the founder of the Frankish dynasty of the Carolingians, the father of Charlemagne. He was chosen king after the deposition of Childeric, the last of the Merovingians. >> Carolingians; Charlemagne; Franks

pepper 1 An annual native to the New World tropics. It has white flowers and large, fleshy, edible berries in a variety of shapes and colours. Its hot, spicy flavour is due to the chemical *capsaicin*. Used whole or ground into powder, peppers include paprika, chillies, cayenne pepper, and red pepper; the familiar green peppers are simply unripe red peppers. (Genus: *Capsicum*, 50 species. Family: Solanaceae.) **2** A tropical shrub or climber (*Piper nigrum*) with long, slender spikes of minute flowers and small hard fruits. The dried, unripe fruits are called *black peppercorns*. Removal of the outer layer yields *white peppercorns*. Both are used whole or ground as spice or condiment. (Family: Piperaceae.) >> spice

pepperidge >> **tupelo**

peppermint >> **mint**

pepsin A digestive enzyme, present in the gastric juice of vertebrates, which breaks down dietary protein into polypeptides of various sizes. It is active only in the acid environment of the stomach. >> digestion; enzyme; peptide

peptic ulcer The erosion and ulceration of a small part of the lining of either the stomach or the duodenum. >> duodenum; stomach; ulcer

peptide A molecule obtained by the partial hydrolysis of proteins, a short chain (oligomer) of amino acids. Longer polymers (generally 50 or more amino acids) are called **polypeptides** or proteins. >> amino acid; hydrolysis; oligomer; protein

Pepys, Samuel [peeps] (1633–1703) Naval administrator and diarist, born in London. His diary runs from 1 January 1660 to 31 May 1669 – a detailed personal record and a vivid picture of contemporary life. It was written in cipher, and not decoded until 1825. >> Restoration

Perak [**pe**rak] pop (1995e) 2 502 000; area 21 005 sq km/ 8108 sq mi. State in W Peninsular Malaysia; capital, Ipoh; one of the wealthiest states in Malaysia since the discovery of tin in the 1840s. >> Malaysia [i]

Perceval, Sir, or **Parsifal** In the Arthurian legends, a knight who went in quest of the Holy Grail. >> Arthur; Grail, Holy

Perceval, Spencer (1762–1812) British statesman, and prime minister (1809–12), born in London. He was shot while entering the House of Commons by a bankrupt Liverpool broker, John Bellingham. >> Tories

perch Name used for many of the freshwater fish in the families Percidae and Centropomidae; deep-bodied, length up to 50 cm/20 in; green and brown with dark vertical bands.

Percheron [**per**shuhron] A heavy breed of horse, developed in France; height, 15·2–17 hands/1·6–1·7 m/5 ft 2 in–5 ft 5 in; black or grey; deep, solid body with strong neck and short, very muscular legs; the most popular heavy draught horse worldwide. >> horse [i]

perching duck A duck of the tribe Cairinini (8 species), including the genera *Aix*, *Nettapus*, *Callonetta*, *Cairina*, *Chenonetta*, and *Sarkidiornis*. They nest in holes or (**muscovy duck**) in hollows. The tribe also includes four species of geese, called **perching geese**. >> duck; goose; mandarin duck; muscovy duck; teal

percussion A category of musical instruments, essentially idiophones and membranophones, which are played by being struck or shaken. >> celesta; cymbals; glockenspiel; gong; idiophone; marimba; membranophone; musical instruments; side drum; steel band; timpano; triangle (music); tubular bells; vibraphone; wood block; xylophone

Percy A noble N England family, whose founder, **William de Percy** (c.1030–96), travelled to England with the Conqueror. The most famous member of the family was **Henry** (1364–1403), the famous 'Hotspur', who fell fighting against Henry IV at Shrewsbury. >> Henry IV (of England)

peregrine falcon A fast, agile falcon (*Falco peregrinus*), found virtually worldwide; dives vertically on prey, or chases in flight; also known as **duck hawk**. >> falcon

perennial A plant which lives for at least several years. **Herbaceous perennials** die back to ground level each year, surviving as underground organs such as bulbs or rhizomes. **Woody perennials** retain their aerial stems, which put out further growth each year. >> annual; biennial; bulb; herbaceous plants; rhizome

Peres, Shimon [**pe**rez], originally **Shimon Perski** (1923–) Israeli statesman and prime minister (1984–6, 1995–6), born in Wolozyn, Poland. He entered into a unique power-sharing agreement with the leader of the Consolidation Party (Likud), Yitzhak Shamir, becoming prime minister for two years, when Shamir took over. Peres was replaced as Labour Party leader by Itzhak Rabin in 1992, and shared the Nobel Peace Prize with him in 1994. >> Rabin; Shamir

perestroika [pere**stroy**ka] The process of 'reconstructing' Soviet society through a programme of reforms initiated from 1985 by General Secretary Gorbachev. The reforms were directed at relaxing state controls over the economy, eliminating corruption from the state bureaucracy, and democratizing the Soviet communist party. >> glasnost; Gorbachev

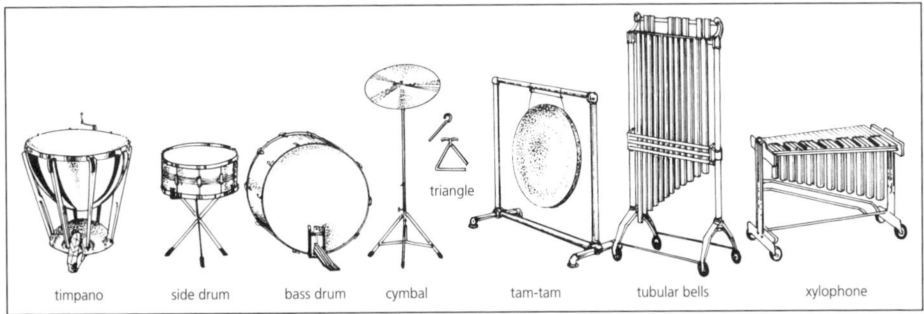

Percussion instruments (to scale)

Pérez de Cuellar, Javier [**pe**rez duh **kway**ah(r)] (1920–) Peruvian diplomat, born in Lima. He became a representative to the United Nations in 1971, and served as secretary-general (1982–91). He played a prominent role in the Falklands Crisis, and in the negotiations for the release of the hostages from Lebanon in 1991. >> United Nations

Pérez Galdós, Benito [**pe**rez gal**dos**] (1843–1920) Writer, born in Las Palmas, Canary Islands. He is regarded as Spain's greatest novelist after Cervantes. His series of 46 short novels, *Episodios nacionales* (1873–1912), gives a vivid picture of 19th-c Spain from the viewpoint of the people. >> Cervantes

perfect numbers In mathematics, a number where the sum of its divisors is equal to the number itself. Thus the divisors of 6 are 1, 2, 3, and 1 + 2 + 3 = 6; the divisors of 28 are 1, 2, 4, 7, 14, and their sum is 28; the next perfect number is 496. In Euclid's *Elements* a formula is given for finding perfect numbers: if $2^n - 1$ is prime, then $2^{n-1}(2^n - 1)$ is a perfect number. >> Euclid; numbers

Pergamum (Asia Minor) [**per**gamum] or **Pergamon** An ancient city in NW Asia Minor, which in Hellenistic times was the capital of the Attalids. Under their patronage it became a major centre of art and learning. >> Bergama

Pergamum (Berlin) A branch of the Staatliche (state) museum in Berlin, housing one of the world's finest collections of Greek, Roman, and Eastern art and antiquities. >> Berlin

Pergolesi, Giovanni Battista [pergo**lay**zee] (1710–36) Composer, born in Jesi, Italy. His comic intermezzo *La serva padrona* (1732) influenced the development of *opera buffa*. He wrote much church music, notably his great *Stabat Mater*. >> *opera buffa*

peri [**pee**ree] In Persian mythology, the generic name given to a good fairy or genie.

perianth The two outer whorls of floral parts (sepals and petals) taken together. When the whorls are not clearly distinguishable, the individual parts are referred to as **perianth segments**. >> flowering plants; sepal

periapsis The closest point of approach of an orbiting body (planet, comet, spacecraft, etc) to the primary body; contrasted with **apoapsis**, the furthest point. For orbits about the Sun, **perihelion** is the point of closest approach; **aphelion** the furthest distance. For orbits about the Earth, the closest point is **perigee**; the furthest distance **apogee**.

periclase >> **magnesia**

Pericles [**pe**rikleez] (c.495–429 BC) General and statesman of the aristocratic Alcmaeonid family, who presided over the 'Golden Age' of Athens, and was virtually its uncrowned king (443–429 BC). His unremitting hostility to Sparta brought about the Peloponnesian War (431–404 BC). >> Alcmaeonids; Peloponnesian War; Sparta (Greek history)

peridot >> **olivine**

peridotite [peri**doh**tiyt] A coarse-grained igneous rock rich in the mineral olivine together with pyroxene and other ferromagnesian minerals. It is thought to be a major constituent of the Earth's mantle. >> igneous rock; olivine; pyroxenes

perigee >> **periapsis**

Périgord [payreegaw(r)] Part of the former province of Guyenne, SW France; chief town, Périgueux; Palaeolithic (Perigordian) caves. >> Three Age System

perihelion >> **periapsis**

perinatology The study of disorders of the newborn that occur in the perinatal period, ie in the period shortly before birth and during the first four weeks of life. It includes the care of such disorders as distressed breathing, bleeding, and birth injuries. >> obstetrics

period >> **geological time scale**

period >> **menstruation**

periodic motion Any motion which repeats itself in a regular way, such as the swing of a pendulum, a weight bouncing on a spring, or wave motion. >> mechanics; oscillation; pendulum; wave motion [i]

periodic table The method of listing the chemical elements in terms of increasing atomic number, so that the rows represent increasing occupancy of an electron subshell, and the columns represent equivalent numbers of valency electrons. The first version was devised by Mendeleyev in 1869. >> chemical elements; Mendeleyev; RR1036

periodontics >> **dentistry**

Peripatus [pe**rip**atus] A genus of velvet worm typically found in humid forest litter; body segmented, length up to 150 mm/6 in; head with a pair of antennae and jaws. (Phylum: Arthropoda. Subphylum: Onychophora.) >> velvet worm

peripheral nervous system (PNS) That part of the nervous system arranged into a large number of nerves, which connects the central nervous system with other tissues of the body. It is divided into an **autonomic** part, involved in voluntary (automatic) responses, and a **somatic** part, comprising in humans the 12 pairs of *cranial nerves* and some 31 pairs of *spinal nerves*, which are involved in voluntary acts and in monitoring the external and (in part) the internal environments of the body. >> autonomic nervous system; nervous system

periscope An optical instrument for viewing an object concealed from view by a barrier. The basic principle is the use of two mirrors, parallel but separated by some distance: light from the object being observed reaches the first mirror, is reflected downwards, then reflected again at the second mirror, its whole path being somewhat in the form of a Z. >> mirror

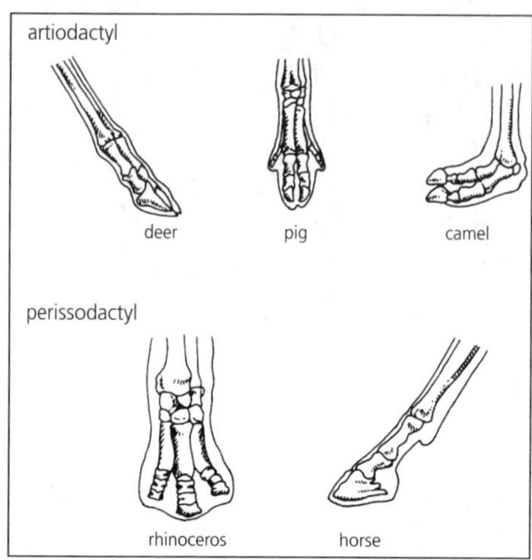

Perissodactyl and artiodactyl hooves

perissodactyl [perisoh**dak**til] ('odd-toed ungulate') A hoofed mammal of order Perissodactyla (16 species); foot with one or three functional toes (the first absent on all feet, the fifth absent on hindfeet). >> artiodactyl; horse i; mammal i; rhinoceros; tapir; ungulate

peristyle [**pe**ristiyl] A series of columns surrounding an open court, temple, or other building. It is particularly used in classical architecture, such as the Lincoln Memorial, Washington, DC (dedicated, 1922).

peritoneum [perito**nee**um] The fluid-secreting lining of the abdominal cavity and part of the pelvic cavity. Inflammation of the peritoneum caused by infection or by irritant substances is known as **peritonitis**. >> abdomen; pelvis

periwinkle (botany) An evergreen, creeping shrub, native to Europe, W Asia, and N Africa; flowers white, mauve, or blue-purple, tubular with five flat, asymmetric lobes; widely known as **myrtle** in the USA. (Genus: *Vinca*, 5 species. Family: Apocynaceae.)

periwinkle (marine biology) A marine snail commonly found in the inter-tidal zone on shores; aperture closed off by a horny plate on the foot. (Class: Gastropoda. Order: Mesogastropoda.)

perjury A crime committed by a person who, when giving evidence in a court under oath (or having affirmed or declared), wilfully makes a false statement. The crime is essentially one of disregarding the oath: someone who makes several false statements during a single case may be convicted of only a single perjury. >> court of law; oath

Perkins, Anthony (1932–92) Actor, born in New York City. After several early films, he achieved international fame as the maniacal Norman Bates in Hitchcock's *Psycho* (1960), with its three sequels (1983, 1986, 1990). >> Hitchcock

Perkins, Charles (Nelson) (1936–) Bureaucrat and activist, born in Australia of Arunta and European descent. He was a leader of the Aboriginal movement in the 1960s, his 'freedom rides' bringing injustice to Aboriginal people to public attention. He later became chairman of the Aboriginal Development Commission (1981–4) and head of the Department of Aboriginal Affairs (1984–9). >> Aborigines

Perkins, Kieren (John) (1973–) Swimmer, born in Brisbane, Queensland, Australia. He set four world records in the year leading up to the 1992 Barcelona Olympics, where he won the 1500m freestyle final, breaking the world record in the process. He won a gold medal for the same race at the Olympic Games in 1996.

Perl, Martin (Lewis) (1927–) Physicist, born in Brooklyn, NY. His study of elementary particles led to his detection of the tau lepton – a short-lived, heavy-weight cousin of the electron, and one of the fundamental building blocks of matter. He shared the Nobel Prize for Physics in 1995.

Perlis [per**lis**] pop (1995e) 211 000; area 818 sq km/316 sq mi. State in NW Peninsular Malaysia; smallest state in Malaysia; Langkawi Is lie offshore; capital, Kangar. >> Malaysia i

Perm, formerly **Molotov** (1940–57) 58°01N 56°10E, pop (1995e) 1 109 000. Industrial city in NE European Russia, on R Kama; founded, 1723; airfield; railway; university (1916). >> Russia i

permafrost Perennially frozen ground in low temperature regions of the Earth. It is underlain at depth by unfrozen ground, and also overlain by an active surface layer which thaws in summer and refreezes in the autumn.

permalloy An alloy of iron and nickel, which is easily magnetized and demagnetized. >> alloy; iron; nickel

permeability The ratio of magnetic flux density B in some material to the applied magnetic field strength H; symbol μ, units H/m (henrys per metre); $B = \mu H$. >> magnetism

Permian period A geological period of the Upper Palaeozoic era, extending from c.286 to 250 million years ago. It was marked by the extinction of many groups of marine invertebrate animals and the diversification of reptiles. >> geological time scale; Palaeozoic era; RR976

permittivity A measure of the degree to which molecules of some material polarize (align) under the influence of an electric field; symbol ε, units F/m (farad per metre). >> electricity

permutational art A form of modern art in which certain features of the work are subject to change. Such changes may be predetermined by the artist (as in computer graphics) or left to chance. >> modern art

Perón, (Maria) Eva (Duarte de) [pe**ron**], known as **Evita** (1919–52) The second wife of Argentine President Juan Perón, born in Los Toldos, Argentina. An actress before her marriage in 1945, she became a powerful political influence and a mainstay of the Perón government. The successful musical *Evita* (1979) was based on her life. >> Perón, Juan

Perón, Isabelita [pe**ron**], popular name of **Maria Estela Perón** *née* **Martínez Cartas** (1931–) President of Argentina (1974–6), born in La Rioja province, Argentina. A dancer who became the third wife of Juan Perón (1961), she was made vice-president when he returned to Argentina in 1973. She took over the presidency at his death in 1974, but after a military coup in 1976 she was imprisoned for five years. On her release, she settled in Madrid. >> Perón, Juan

Perón, Juan (Domingo) [pe**ron**] (1895–1974) Argentinian soldier and president (1946–55, 1973–4), born in Lobos. He took a leading part in the army coup of 1943, gaining widespread support through his social reforms. Deposed and exiled in 1955, he returned in triumph in 1973, and won an overwhelming electoral victory, but died the following year. >> Argentina i; Perón, Eva / Isabelita; Peronism

Peronism [**pe**ronizm] A heterogeneous Argentine political movement formed in 1945–6 to support Juan Domingo Perón and his government. The movement later underwent division, but it survived Perón's death (1974), and made a good showing in the congressional elections of 1986. Its ideology is an amalgam of nationalism and social democracy, strongly coloured by loyalty to the memory of Perón. >> Argentina [i]; Perón, Juan

Perot, (Henry) Ross [pe**roh**] (1930–) Businessman and politician, born in Texarkana, TX. He founded the Electronic Data Systems Corporation Inc, Dallas, in 1962, and was its chairman and chief executive (1982–6). He became internationally known when he stood as an independent candidate in the 1992 and 1996 US presidential elections. >> Bush, George; Clinton, Bill

peroxide A compound containing the ion O_2^{2-} or the group –O–O–. **Hydrogen peroxide** (H_2O_2) is an important oxidizing agent and bleach.

Perpignan [**per**peenyã] 42°42N 2°53E, pop (1995e) 109 000. Market town and resort in S France; settled in Roman times; capital of former province of Roussillon; chartered, 1197; scene of Church Council, 1408; united to France, 1659; road and rail junction; university (14th-c); cathedral (14th–17th-c).

Perrault, Charles [peroh] (1628–1703) Writer, born in Paris. He is best known for his eight fairy tales, the *Contes de ma mère l'oye* (1697, trans Tales of Mother Goose), which included 'The Sleeping Beauty' and 'Red Riding Hood'.

Perry, Fred(erick John) (1909–95) Tennis and table tennis player, born in Stockport, Greater Manchester. He won the world table tennis title in 1929, the men's lawn tennis singles title at Wimbledon in 1934–6, and was the first man to win all four major titles.

Perry, Matthew (1969–) Actor, born in Williamstown, MA. He became known for his role as Chandler Bing in the acclaimed television series *Friends* (1994–). Roles in feature films include *Fools Rush In* (1997) and *Edwards and Hunt: The First American Road Trip* (1997).

perry An alcoholic beverage made from fermenting pears. It is produced commercially in the UK, Germany, and France, and is very popular in the UK. >> cider; tannins

Perseids [per**see**idz] A major meteor shower visible for a week or so before and after peaking on 12 August each year, the date on which the Earth crosses the orbit. >> meteor; RR965

Persephone [per**sef**onee] In Greek mythology, the daughter of Demeter and Zeus, originally called Kore ('maiden'); known as **Proserpine** in Latin. Hades abducted her and made her queen of the Underworld. >> Demeter

Persepolis [per**sep**olis] The site in the mountains of Iran of the palaces and graves of the Achaemenid rulers of Persia; a world heritage site. It was sacked by Alexander the Great in 331 BC. >> Achaemenids; Persian Empire

Perseus (astronomy) [**per**syoos] A N hemisphere constellation, in the Milky Way. It includes a double cluster of stars visible to the naked eye. >> Algol; constellation; Milky Way; RR968

Perseus (mythology) [**per**syoos] In Greek mythology, the son of Zeus and Danae. He killed the Gorgon, and used its head to rescue Andromeda and save his mother. >> Andromeda; Gorgon

Pershing, John J(oseph), nickname **Black Jack** (1860–1948) US general, born in Laclede, MO. In 1917 he commanded the American Expeditionary Force in Europe, and after the war became chief-of-staff (1921–4). >> World War 1

Pershing missile A medium-range, land-based missile with a nuclear warhead, deployed by the US Army in West Germany from 1983 onwards. >> missile, guided

Persia >> **Iran** [i]

Persian >> **Iranian languages**

Persian cat A type of long-haired domestic cat; round head and short face; many breeds. The name is still used in the USA for breeds which in Britain are called *long-hairs* (eg *blue Persian* = *blue long-hair*). >> cat

Persian Empire An empire created by the Achaemenids in the second half of the 6th-c BC, extending from NW India to the E Mediterranean. It was overthrown by Alexander the Great in the 330s BC. >> Achaemenids; Persian Wars

Persian Gulf also **The Gulf**, **Arabian Gulf** Lat **Sinus Persicus** area 238 800 sq km/92 200 sq mi. Arm of the Arabian Sea, connected to it via the Gulf of Oman and the Strait of Hormuz; bounded N by Iran, NW by Iraq and Kuwait, W by Saudi Arabia and Qatar, and S by the United Arab Emirates; length 885 km/550 mi; maximum width 322 km/200 mi; average depth 100 m/325 ft; important source of oil; scene of great tension during the Iran–Iraq War and the Gulf War; suffered major oil pollution during the Gulf War (Feb 1991). >> Arabian Sea; Gulf War

Persian Wars The name given to the two punitive expeditions launched by the Persian kings, Darius I and Xerxes, against Greece in 490 and 480–479 BC. The first ended in catastrophe for the Persians at Marathon; the second ended in the twin defeats for the Persians at Plataea and Mycale. >> Marathon, Battle of; Plataea; Salamis; Thermopylae

persimmon [per**sim**on] Any of several species of ebony, widely cultivated for their fleshy berries, which are edible but very astringent until fully ripe; also called **date plums**. (Family: Ebonaceae.) >> ebony

personal computer (PC) A term used to describe microcomputers in general, and also used by the firm of IBM in its range of microcomputers. >> microcomputer

perspective In art, any method whereby the illusion of depth is achieved on a flat surface. Most methods are based on the fact that objects appear smaller in proportion to their distance from the beholder, and that receding parallel lines appear to meet on the horizon at what is called the *vanishing point*. The Greeks developed scientific perspective as a by-product of their interest in optics and geometry perspective. >> Piero della Francesca

Perspex The proprietary name for a flat sheet form of polymethylmethacrylate resin, of notably high transparency. >> resin

perspiration >> **sweat**

Perth (Australia) 31°58S 115°49E, pop (1995e) 1 209 000. State capital of Western Australia, near the mouth of the Swan R; the commercial, cultural, and transportation centre on the W coast; founded, 1829; city status, 1856; rapid development after the discovery of gold, 1897; fifth largest city in Australia; airport; railway; four universities (1911, 1975, 1987, 1990); two cathedrals; scene of the Commonwealth and Empire Games, 1962. >> Western Australia

Perth (Scotland) 56°24N 3°28W, pop (1995e) 42 500. Administrative centre of Perth and Kinross council, E Scotland; on R Tay; scene of assassination of James I, 1437; railway; castle. >> Scotland [i]

perturbation In astronomy, any small deviation in the equilibrium motion of a celestial object caused by a change in the gravitational field acting on it. Perturbations in the orbit of Uranus led directly to the discovery of Neptune in 1846. >> Neptune (astronomy)

perturbation theory A mathematical technique frequently used to obtain approximate solutions to equations describing physical systems that are too complicated to solve exactly. The problem is rewritten in two portions: one which can be solved exactly, and a smaller part (the **perturbation**) which allows the calculation of corrections to the first answer. >> equations

pertussis >> **whooping cough**

Peru, official name **Republic of Peru**, Span **República del Peru** pop (1995e) 23 407 000; area 1 284 640 sq km/495 871 sq mi. Republic on the W coast of South America; capital, Lima; timezone GMT –5; major ethnic groups, Quecha (47%), Mestizo (32%); chief religion, Roman Catholicism; official languages, Spanish and Quechua; unit of currency, the new sol of 100 céntimos; arid plains

and foothills on the coast, with areas of desert and fertile river valleys; C sierra, average altitude 3000 m/10 000 ft, contains 50% of the population; forested Andes and Amazon basin (E), with major rivers flowing to the Amazon; mild temperatures all year on coast; arid desert in the S; typically wet, tropical climate in Amazon basin; highly developed Inca civilization; arrival of Spanish, 1531; Viceroyalty of Peru established; independence declared, 1821; frequent border disputes in 19th-c (eg War of the Pacific, 1879–83), continuing with Ecuador in recent decades, notably in 1981, 1995; several military coups; terrorist activities by Maoist guerrillas, especially Sendero Luminoso; new constitution, 1993; governed by a president and a Congress; one of the world's leading producers of silver, zinc, lead, copper, gold, iron ore; 80% of Peru's oil extracted from the Amazon forest. >> Incas; Lima; Sendero Luminoso; RR1019 political leaders

Perugia [pay**roo**jia] 43°07N 12°23E, pop (1995e) 146 000. Town in Umbria, Italy; founded by Etruscans; taken by Romans, 295 BC; archbishopric; railway; university (1276); cathedral (15th-c). >> Umbria

Perugino [peru**jee**noh] (Ital 'the Perugian'), originally **Pietro di Cristoforo Vannucci** (c.1450–1523) Italian painter, born in Città della Pieve, Italy. He painted several frescoes in the Sistine Chapel at Rome, notably 'Christ Giving the Keys to Peter' (1481–2). >> fresco

Pesach >> **Passover**

Peshawar [pe**shah**wa(r)] 34°01N 71°40E, pop (1995e) 817 000. Capital of North-West Frontier province, Pakistan; city of the Pathan people; under Sikh rule, early 19th-c; occupied by the British, 1849; airfield; railway; university (1950); major trade centre on the Afghan frontier. >> Khyber Pass; Pakistan 🄸

Pestalozzi, Johann Heinrich [pesta**lot**see] (1746–1827) Educationalist, a pioneer of mass education for poor children, born in Zürich, Switzerland. His method sees the process of education as a gradual unfolding, prompted by observation, of the child's innate faculties. *Pestalozzi International Children's Villages* have been established at Trogen, Switzerland (1946) and Sedlescombe, Surrey, UK (1958).

pesticide Any substance used to kill insects, rodents, weeds, fungi, or other living things which are harmful to plants, animals, or foodstuffs. >> fungicide; herbicide; insecticide

Pétain, (Henri) Philippe (Omer) [paytĩ] (1856–1951) French soldier and statesman, born in Cauchy-à-la-Tour, France. When France collapsed in 1940, he negotiated the armistice with Germany and Italy, and became chief-of-state, establishing his government at Vichy. After the liberation, he was tried in the French courts for collaboration with Germany, his death sentence for treason being commuted to life imprisonment. His role remains controversial, and some still regard him as a patriot rather than a traitor. >> Vichy; World War 2

petal One of the second whorl of flower parts, collectively termed the *corolla*. It is usually large and brightly coloured to attract pollinators. >> flower 🄸

Peter I, known as **the Great** (1672–1725) Tsar of Russia (1682–1721) and emperor (1721–5), born in Moscow. He embarked on a series of sweeping military, fiscal, administrative, educational, cultural, and ecclesiastical reforms, many of them based on W European models. He fought major wars with the Ottoman Empire, Persia, and in particular Sweden, which Russia defeated in the Great Northern War (1700–21). This victory established Russia as a major European power, and gained a maritime exit on the Baltic coast, where Peter founded his new capital, St Petersburg (1703). >> Great Northern War; Romanovs

Peter, St, originally **Simon** or **Simeon bar Jona** ('son of Jona') (1st-c) One of the 12 apostles of Jesus, a fisherman living in Capernaum, who was renamed by Jesus as **Cephas** or Peter (meaning 'rock') in view of his leadership among the disciples. Immediately after Jesus's ascension, Peter appears as the leader of the Christian community in Jerusalem. Tradition says that he was executed with his head downward in Rome (c.64), and he is regarded by the Roman Catholic Church as the first Bishop of Rome. Two New Testament letters bear his name, but the authenticity of both is often disputed. Feast day 29 June. >> apostle; Jesus Christ

Peter the Hermit (c.1050–c.1115) Monk, a preacher of the first Crusade, born in Amiens, France. He led the second army, which reached Asia Minor, but was defeated by the Turks at Nicaea. He then accompanied the fifth army in 1096, which reached Jerusalem. >> Crusades 🄸

Peter and Paul Fortress A stronghold founded in 1703 by Peter the Great on a small island in the Neva R delta, and around which the city of St Petersburg sprang up. It has been a museum since 1922. >> St Petersburg (Russia)

Peter Lombard >> **Lombard, Peter**

Peterloo Massacre (1819) The name given to the forcible break-up of a mass meeting about parliamentary reform held at St Peter's Fields, Manchester. The Manchester Yeomanry charged into the crowd, killing eleven people. 'Peterloo' was a pun on the Waterloo victory of 1815. >> Reform Acts

Peterson, Oscar (Emmanuel) (1925–) Jazz pianist, born in Montreal, Quebec, Canada. In 1949 he became an international star when he joined a concert tour called 'Jazz at the Philharmonic' in New York. He is especially known for his extraordinary keyboard facility, and has recorded as a soloist and accompanist more than any other musician.

Petipa, Marius [peteepa] (1818–1910) Dancer, ballet master, and choreographer, born in Marseille, France. He went to St Petersburg in 1847 to join the Imperial Ballet, and as ballet master created 46 original ballets, the most famous being *The Sleeping Beauty* (1890) and *Swan Lake* (1895). >> ballet

Petit, Roland [puh**tee**] (1924–) Choreographer and dancer, born in Paris. In 1948 he founded Ballets de Paris de Roland Petit, and in 1972 the Ballet de Marseille. >> ballet

petit mal [pe**tee mal**] >> **epilepsy**

petit pois [pe**tee pwah**] >> **pea** ℹ

Petra [**pe**tra], Arabic **Wadi Musa** 30°20N 35°26E. Ancient rock-cut city in SW Jordan; capital of the Nabataean Arabs until their conquest by Rome in the early 2nd-c AD; a world heritage site. >> Jordan ℹ; Palmyra (Roman history)

Petrarch [**pe**trah(r)k], in full **Francesco Petrarca** (1304–74) Poet and scholar, born in Arezzo, Italy. In 1327 at Avignon he first saw Laura, who inspired him with a passion which has become proverbial for its constancy and purity. The earliest of the great Renaissance humanists, he wrote widely on the classics, but he is best known for the series of love poems addressed to Laura, the *Canzoniere*. His writing proved to be a major influence on many authors, notably Chaucer. >> Chaucer; humanism

petrel A seabird of the order Procellariiformes (tubenoses): small species called *petrels*; larger species called *albatrosses*. They include fulmars, prions, shearwaters, gadfly petrels (all from the family Procellariidae), storm petrels (*Hydrobatidae*), and diving petrels (*Pelecanoididae*). >> albatross; fulmar; muttonbird; shearwater; tubenose

Petrie, Sir (William Matthew) Flinders [**pee**tree] (1853–1942) Archaeologist and Egyptologist, born in Charlton, Kent. He surveyed Stonehenge (1874–7), but turned from 1881 entirely to Egyptology, beginning by surveying the pyramids and temples of Giza, and excavating the mounds of Tanis and Naucratis. >> archaeology

petrified forest The results of a fossilizing process in which wood is gradually replaced by silica, through the infiltration of mineral-rich water. The fine structural detail may be perfectly preserved during the process, as in the Petrified Forest National Park in Arizona, USA. >> silica

petrochemicals Organic chemicals made from products of the petroleum industry or from natural gas. Simple chemical reactions on distillates provide materials for conversion to plastics, fibres, detergents, etc. >> natural gas; petroleum

petrogenesis; petrography >> **petrology**

petrol (UK) or **gasoline** (US) A liquid fuel for use in those internal combustion engines in which the fuel–air mixture is ignited by a spark. It consists of a mixture of many volatile hydrocarbons derived from petroleum. It normally contains additives such as lead compounds (to improve performance) or rust inhibitors. In the 1980s, environmental concern led to a rapid increase in the use of unleaded petrol, but criticisms of reduced performance led to the development of a *superunleaded* petrol, with the addition of benzene and other compounds. Debate continues over the environmental impact of these additives. >> alternative fuel; benzene; catalytic converter; internal combustion engine; petroleum

petroleum Crude oil, probably of biological origin, occurring as accumulations under impervious rock. Normally liquid, it ranges from being light and mobile to very viscous, and is often associated with gas or water. Its main constituents are a variety of hydrocarbons. >> hydrocarbons; oil; petrol

petrology The study of rocks: their composition, mineralogy, mode of occurrence, and origin. **Petrography** is concerned with the textural and mineralogical description of rocks, often studied by optical microscopy of thin slices, while **petrogenesis** is concerned with their origin. >> rock

Petronas Twin Towers At the beginning of 1999, the tallest building in the world (each tower is 451.9 m/ 1483 ft), completed in Kuala Lumpur in 1996. It has 88 storeys, and was designed by Cesar Pelli and Associates. >> Kuala Lumpur

petunia A bushy, free-flowering annual (*Petunia* × *hybrida*) native to South America, with large, funnel-shaped flowers. It is a popular garden plant grown for its brightly coloured, often striped flowers. (Family: Solanaceae.)

Peul >> **Fulani**

Pevsner, Antoine (1886–1962) Sculptor, born in Oryol, Russia. In Moscow he helped to form the Suprematist group, but in 1920 broke away to issue the *Realist Manifesto* with his brother, Naum Gabo. Exiled from Russia, he migrated to Paris. >> Constructivism; Gabo; Suprematism

Pevsner, Sir Nikolaus (Bernhard Leon) (1902–83) Art historian, born in Leipzig, Germany, an authority on English architecture. His best-known works are *An Outline of European Architecture* (1942), and the 50-volume Penguin series, *The Buildings of England* (1951–74).

pewit >> **peewit**

pewter A grey alloy consisting mainly of tin with other constituents, such as antimony. It is traditionally used in candlesticks, drinking vessels, and other utensils. >> alloy; antimony; tin

peyote or **peyot** [pay**oh**tee] A small cactus (*Lophophora williamsii*) native to Mexico and Texas; also called **mescal button**. It was used by American Indians to produce a drug containing the hallucinogen *mescalin*, used in religious rites. (Family: Cactaceae.) >> cactus ℹ; hallucinogens

Pfeiffer, Michelle [**fiy**fer] (1958–) Film actress, born in Santa Ana, CA. She played several film and television roles before gaining recognition in *The Witches of Eastwick* (1987) and *Dangerous Liaisons* (1988). Other films include *Frankie and Johnny* (1991), *Batman Returns* (1992), *Up Close and Personal* (1996), and *The Deep End of the Ocean* (1998).

pH A measure of the acidity of a solution; it is approximately the negative of the common logarithm of the concentration of hydrogen ions in a solution. It varies between 0 (strongly acidic) and 14 (strongly basic). A neutral solution has pH = 7. >> acid; base (chemistry); litmus

Phaeophyceae [feeoh**fiy**see-ee] The class of seaweeds comprising the brown algae; also known as the Phaeophyta. >> brown algae; seaweed

Phaethon [**fay**ithohn] or **Phaeton** [**fay**iton, **fay**ton] In Greek mythology, the son of Helios the sun-god and Clymene. He asked to drive the chariot of the Sun, but swung it too near the Earth, so Zeus destroyed him with a thunderbolt.

phagocyte [**fag**osiyt] Any cell which engulfs and usually digests particles, micro-organisms (bacteria), or harmful cells. Many unicellular animals are phagocytic. In most multicellular animals, phagocytes fulfil a protective and cleansing role. >> bacteria ℹ; blood

phalanger [fa**lan**jer] An Australasian nocturnal marsupial; thick fur, small ears, large forward-facing eyes, long grasping tail; inhabits trees; also known as **cuscus**. (Genus: *Phalanger*, 10 species. Family: Phalangeridae.) >> marsupial ℹ

phalarope [**fal**erohp] A sandpiper of the genus *Phalaropus* (3 species); widespread; breeds in N hemisphere, winters in S tropics; adapted for swimming. >> sandpiper

Phanerozoic time [fanero**zoh**ik] A geological term used to describe the period of c.590 million years from the end of the Precambrian era to the present. >> geological time scale; Precambrian era; RR976

pharaoh The title applied to the god-kings of ancient Egypt from the New Kingdom (c.1500 BC) onwards. Pharaohs were the chief mediators between their mortal subjects and the gods, and after death were believed to become gods themselves. Best known are Tutankhamun (c.1352 BC), Rameses II (the pharaoh of the Exodus), and Rameses III (the conqueror of the Sea Peoples). >> Abu Simbel; Egyptian history, Ancient [i]; Sea Peoples

Pharisees [**fa**riseez] An influential minority group within Palestinian Judaism before AD 70, mainly consisting of laymen. They were noted for their punctilious observance of written and oral laws regarding ritual purity, cleansings, and food laws. In the New Testament Gospels, they are often portrayed as the opponents of Jesus. >> Jesus Christ; Judaism; Sadducees

pharmacology A branch of medical science which studies the actions, uses, and undesirable side-effects of drugs. The first descriptions of remedies from plant sources were made by the ancient Greeks and Chinese. Dioscorides' *De materia medica* (AD c.60) was the first basic Western pharmacopoeia. The subject became a scientific discipline in the 19th-c. >> pharmacopoeia; psychopharmacology; toxicology

pharmacopoeia [fah(r)mako**pee**a] A book of standards for drugs, advising on identity, purity, and identification. In most countries there is an official pharmacopoeia, and any dispensed drug must comply with its standards. >> pharmacology

pharmacy Originally the science of preparing, compounding, and dispensing medicines. Since more potent drugs have become available (mid-1940s), the scope of pharmacy has become increasingly concerned with more clinical functions, such as the checking of doses and drug interactions. >> apothecary; pharmacology; prescription

Pharos of Alexandria [**fair**os] A marble watch tower and lighthouse on the island of Pharos in the harbour of Alexandria, built by Ptolemy II (285–246 BC). It was the first of its kind. >> Seven Wonders of the Ancient World

pharyngitis [farin**jiy**tis] A sore throat; one of the commonest medical complaints, usually the result of bacterial or viral infection of the lining tissues of the pharynx. >> pharynx

pharynx A space formed by mucose membrane-covered muscle situated behind and communicating with the nose, mouth, and larynx. The upper areas contain accumulations of lymphoid tissue (the tonsils) which, it is thought, help to guard against airborn infection. >> adenoids; larynx; pharyngitis; respiration

phase In wave motion, the fraction of a wave cycle completed by a time variable, where one complete cycle corresponds to 2π radians; alternatively, an argument of a function describing a wave. The phase difference, ϕ radians, represents the degree to which one wave leads or lags behind another; for $\phi = 0$ or 2π, the waves are in phase; for $\phi = \pi$, the waves are antiphase. >> coherence; phases of matter [i]; wave (physics) [i]

phases of matter The three possible states of matter: solid, liquid, and gas. The phase of a particular substance depends on temperature and pressure. A change from one phase to another, as in boiling or melting, is called a **phase transition**. >> gas 1; liquid; solid

Phasmida [**faz**mida] An order of large insects with either elongate bodies and limbs (stick insects) or flattened, leaf-like bodies and limbs (leaf insects); length up to 30 cm/1 ft; c.2500 species, all of which are foliage feeders, mostly tropical or subtropical in distribution. >> insect [i]

pheasant A large, plump, ground-feeding bird, native to Africa (1 species) and Asia; short wings and fast, low flight; male brightly coloured with long tail; many species bred for sport. (Family: Phasianidae, 48 species.) >> francolin; jungle fowl [i]; partridge; peacock; quail; tragopan

phenanthrene [**fen**anthreen] $C_{14}H_{10}$, melting point 101 °C. A crystalline solid, an aromatic hydrocarbon containing three fused benzene rings. It occurs in coal tar, and is suspected of being carcinogenic. >> hydrocarbons

phencyclidine >> **angel dust**

phenobarbitone >> **barbiturates**

phenol [**fee**nol, **fe**nohl] C_6H_5OH, IUPAC **hydroxybenzene**, also called **carbolic acid**, used as an antiseptic where its corrosive properties are not a problem. A major constituent of coal tar, it is also synthesized in large quantities, as it has applications in the manufacture of fibres, resins, dyes, drugs, and explosives. >> corrosion; IUPAC

phenology [fe**nol**ojee] The branch of biology which studies the timing of natural phenomena. Examples include seasonal variations in vegetation, and their relationship with weather and climate. >> biology

phenomenalism In philosophy, the theory that statements about physical objects are in the end equivalent to statements about factual or possible perceptual experiences. >> Berkeley, George; Hume, David

phenomenology A philosophical movement begun by Husserl, in its broadest sense it is a descriptive philosophy of experience. Its central method is to describe carefully one's conscious processes, concentrating on subjective experiences and suspending all beliefs and assumptions about their 'external' existence and causation. The result is supposed to be a non-empirical, intuitive enquiry into the real essences or meanings that are common to different minds. >> Heidegger; Husserl; Sartre

phenothiazines [feenoh**thiy**azeenz] A class of drugs introduced in the 1950s and used in the treatment of psychiatric disorders such as schizophrenia and mania. >> psychiatry; schizophrenia

phenyl [**fee**niyl, **fe**nil] C_6H_5-. A group derived by the removal of one hydrogen atom from a benzene ring. >> benzene; ring

phenylamine >> **aniline**

phenylketonuria [fenilkeeto**nyoo**ria] A genetically determined defect in the metabolism of phenylalanine (an amino acid contained in protein). Phenylalanine accumulates in the body, and may cause mental deficiency. >> amino acid

phenylmethanal >> **benzaldehyde**

phenylmethyl >> **benzyl**

pheromone [**fe**romohn] A chemical substance secreted to the outside by an animal, which has a specific effect on

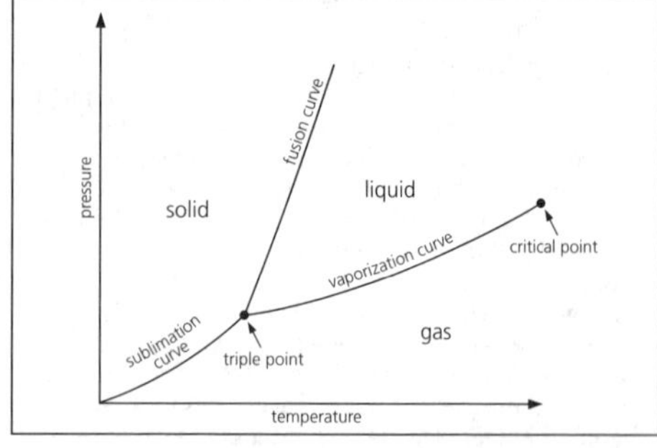

Phase – A typical phase diagram showing the phases of a substance of various temperatures and pressures. A substance melts from solid to liquid, for example, at temperatures and pressures defined by the fusion curve. The *triple point* is the only temperature and pressure where all three phases coexist. Liquid and gas phases are distinct only for temperature and pressures less than the critical point; at temperatures higher than this critical temperature, gas cannot be liquified.

another member of the same species, such as mating or aggression. Pheromones are common in insects, and are also found in rodents and monkeys.

Phidias [**fiy**dias] (5th-c BC) Sculptor, born in Athens. He constructed the Propylaea and the Parthenon, carving the gold and ivory Athena there and the Zeus at Olympia. >> Parthenon

Philadelphia 39°57N 75°10W, pop (1995e) 1 628 000. Major deep-water port in SE Pennsylvania, USA, at the confluence of the Schuylkill and Delaware Rivers; noted centre for culture, education, and medical research; fifth largest city in the USA; first settled by Swedes in the 1640s; birthplace of the nation, where the Declaration of Independence was signed, 1776; Constitutional Convention met here, 1787; US capital, 1790–1800; heavily involved in the anti-slavery movement and the Civil War; airport; railway; four universities (1740, 1851, 1884, 1891); service economy supplanting the dwindling manufacturing industry; naval dockyard; professional teams, Phillies (baseball), 76ers (basketball), Eagles (football), Flyers (ice hockey); Liberty Bell (Independence Hall). >> American Revolution; Independence Hall; Penn; Pennsylvania

philadelphus [fila**del**fuhs] >> **mock orange**

philately The collecting of stamps, one of the world's most popular hobbies, particularly with schoolchildren. The first stamp-collector is thought to have been John Tomlynson, who started collecting on 7 May 1840, the day after the issue of the world's first postage stamp, the penny black.

Philby, Kim, popular name of **Harold Adrian Russell Philby** (1912–88) Double agent, born in Ambala, India. Already recruited as a Soviet agent, he was employed by the British Secret Intelligence Service (MI6), from 1944–6 as head of anti-communist counter-espionage. In 1963 he disappeared to Russia, where he was granted citizenship. >> Burgess, Guy

Philemon and Baucis [fiy**lee**mon, **baw**sis] An old couple, man and wife, who were the only ones to entertain the Greek gods Zeus and Hermes when they visited the Earth. They were made priest and priestess, and allowed to die at the same time, when they were changed into trees. >> Hermes (mythology); Zeus

Philemon, Letter to [fiy**lee**mon] The shortest of Paul's letters, usually accepted as genuinely from the apostle to an individual Christian named Philemon. It probably dates from the late 50s or the early 60s AD. >> Paul, St

Philip II (of Macedon) (382–336 BC) King of Macedon (359–336 BC), the father of Alexander the Great. He created a powerful unified state at home (359–353 BC), then made himself master of the whole of independent Greece, with his decisive victory at Chaeronea (338 BC). >> Alexander the Great; Macedon

Philip II (of Spain) (1527–98) King of Spain (1556–98) and Portugal (as Philip I, 1580–98), born in Valladolid, Spain. Following the death of his first wife, Maria of Portugal, he married Mary I (1554), becoming joint sovereign of England. Before Mary's death (1558) he had inherited the Habsburg possessions in Italy, the Netherlands, Spain, and the New World. To seal the end of Valois–Habsburg conflict, he married Elizabeth of France (1559). As the champion of the Counter-Reformation, he sought to crush Protestantism, first in the Low Countries (from 1568), then in England and France, but his Armada (1588) was destroyed, and he was unable to subdue the Netherlands. >> Counter-Reformation; Habsburgs; Mary I; Revolt of the Netherlands; Spain ℹ; Spanish Armada; Valois

Philip III, known as **Philip the Good** (1396–1467) Duke of Burgundy (1419–67), born in Dijon, France. He created one of the most powerful states in later mediaeval Europe, and was a committed crusader against the Ottoman Turks. >> crusades ℹ

Philip V (1683–1746) First Bourbon king of Spain (1700–46), born in Versailles, France, the grandson of Louis XIV and Maria Theresa. He gained the throne at the Peace of Utrecht (1713), but lost the Spanish Netherlands and Italian lands. >> Bourbons

Philip VI (1293–1350) First Valois king of France (1328–50). His right to the throne was denied by Edward III of England, leading to the Hundred Years' War with England. In 1346 Edward III defeated Philip at Crécy. >> Edward III; Hundred Years' War; Valois

Philip, St (1st-c) One of the disciples of Jesus, listed among the 12. Traditions suggest he was martyred on a cross. Feast day 3 May (W) or 14 November (E). >> apostle; Jesus Christ

Philip, Prince >> **Edinburgh, Duke of**

Philippi, Battle of [fi**lip**iy] (42 BC) The decisive battle in N Greece in which Antony and Octavian (later the Emperor Augustus) defeated Brutus and Cassius, and thus avenged the murder of Julius Caesar. >> Antonius, Marcus

Philippians, Letter to the [fi**lip**ianz] New Testament writing, widely accepted as genuinely from the apostle Paul to a Christian community that he had founded earlier at Philippi in Macedonia. >> Paul, St

philippic A denunciation in speech or writing, direct and often abusive. The term derives from Demosthenes' orations (c.350 BC) attacking Philip of Macedon. >> Demosthenes; panegyric

Philippines [**fil**ipeenz], official name **Republic of the Philippines**, Pilipino **Republika ng Pilipinas** pop (1995e) 67 900 000; area 299 679 sq km/115 676 sq mi. Republic consisting of an archipelago of more than 7100 islands and islets, NE of Borneo; major islands, Luzon, Mindanao, Samar, Palawan, Mindoro, Panay, Negros, Cebu, Leyte, Masbate, Bohol; capital, Manila; timezone GMT +8; chief ethnic group, Filipino, with several minorities; chief reli-

gion, Roman Catholicism; official language, Pilipino, with English and many local languages also spoken; unit of currency, the peso of 100 centavos; largely mountainous, with N–S ridges rising to over 2500 m/8000 ft; forests cover half the land area; lowlands have a warm and humid tropical climate throughout the year, average 27°C; claimed for Spain by Magellan, 1521; ceded to the USA after the Spanish–American War, 1898; became a self-governing Commonwealth, 1935; occupied by the Japanese in World War 2; independence, 1946; communist guerrilla activity in N; Muslim separatist movement in S (Mindanao); martial law following political unrest, 1972–81; exiled political leader Benigno Aquino assassinated on returning to Manila in 1983; coup in 1985 ended the 20-year rule of President Ferdinand Marcos; new constitution, 1987; attempted coup, 1989, with continuing political unrest; presidential elections, 1992; Mindanao peace agreement, 1996; governed by a president, Senate, and House of Representatives; farming employs nearly half the workforce. >> Aquino; Luzon; Magellan; Manila; Marcos; Mindanao; Mindoro; Palawan; Spanish–American War; Visayan Islands; RR1019 political leaders

Philistines The ancient warlike inhabitants of the coastal area of the SE Mediterranean between present-day Jaffa and Egypt. They were constantly at odds with the Israelites of the hinterland. >> David; Samson

Phillips, Mark, Captain >> **Anne, Princess**

Phillips, William D (1948–) Physicist, born in Wilkes-Barre, PA. He graduated in 1976 from MIT, joining the National Institute of Standards and Technology in Gaithersburg, MD. In 1997 he shared the Nobel Prize for Physics for his contribution to the development of methods to cool and trap atoms with laser light.

Philoctetes [filok**tee**teez] A Greek hero, the son of Poeas, who inherited the bow of Heracles and its poisoned arrows. It was prophesied that only with the arrows of Heracles could Troy be taken. He entered the battle, killing Paris. >> Heracles; Trojan War

philodendron [filo**den**dron] An evergreen plant native to warm regions of the New World; many species are popular house plants. (Genus: *Philodendron*, 275 species. Family: Araceae.)

Philo Judaeus [**fiy**loh ju**day**us] (c.20 BC–c.AD 40) Hellenistic Jewish philosopher, born in Alexandria. His work brought together Greek philosophy and the Hebrew scriptures. >> Judaism; Old Testament

Philomela and Procne [filuh**mee**la, **prok**nee], or **Philomel, Progne** In Greek mythology, the daughters of Pandion, King of Athens. Procne married Tereus, King of Thrace, who raped Philomela and removed her tongue; but she was able to tell Procne by a message in her embroidery.

Philosophes [filo**zof**] The leaders of the French Enlightenment – political commentators, writers, and propagandists. Their great collective work was the *Encyclopédie*. >> Diderot; Encyclopaedists; Enlightenment; Montesquieu; Voltaire

philosophy Literally the love of wisdom, a subject which deals with some of the most general questions about the universe and our place in it. Philosophy differs from science, in that its questions cannot be answered empirically, by observation or experiment; and from religion, in that its purpose is entirely intellectual, and allows no role for faith or revelation. Philosophy tends to proceed by an informal but rigorous process of conceptual analysis and reasoning. The major branches are *metaphysics*, the inquiry into the most general features, relations, and processes of reality; *epistemology*, the investigation of the possibility, types, and sources of knowledge; *ethics*, the study of the types, sources, and justification of moral values and principles; and *logic*, the analysis of correct and incorrect reasoning. Philosophical issues can arise concerning other areas of inquiry, for example, in art, law, religion, and science. >> Aristotle; Augustine, St (of Hippo); Descartes; epistemology; ethics; Leibniz; Locke, John; logic; metaphysics; Plato; Presocratics

philosophy of science A branch of philosophy, often approached through the history of science, which studies the nature of scientific theories, explanations, and descriptions, and relates them to general philosophical issues in epistemology, logic, or metaphysics. >> philosophy

Phiz >> **Browne, Hablot Knight**

phlebitis [fle**biy**tis] Inflammation of a vein, commonly associated with varicose veins, or following thrombosis of the blood within veins, when it is referred to as **thrombophlebitis**. The veins of the leg are commonly affected. >> thrombosis; varicose veins; vein

phloem [**floh**em] Tissue which transports sap from the leaves to other parts of a plant. It is either located in the vascular bundles or forms the inner bark of woody plants. >> xylem

phlogiston theory [flo**jis**tn] A theory, popular in the 18th-c, whereby a material undergoing combustion was held to lose a substance (*phlogiston*) to the atmosphere. The theory became increasingly untenable as it became clear that the products of combustion always weigh more than the material burnt.

phlox A mat-forming or erect annual or perennial, almost exclusively native to North America and Mexico; flowers tubular with five notched lobes, often white, pink, or blue, sometimes fragrant, in dense terminal heads. (Genus: *Phlox*, 67 species. Family: Polemoniaceae.)

Phnom Penh [(p)nom **pen**] 11°35N 104°55E, pop (1995e) 997 000. River-port capital of Cambodia, at the confluence of Mekong R and Tonlé Sap (lake); founded by the Khmers, 1371; capital, 1434; under Japanese occupation in World War 2; railway; several universities; current population uncertain, because of continuing refugee problem. >> Cambodia [i]

phobia A reaction of extreme fear to an object or situation not ordinarily considered dangerous. Avoidance behaviour may occur. The major forms of phobia are **simple phobia** (in which people are afraid of a specific object or situation) and **social phobia** (in which they are concerned about their behaviour in front of others). >> neurosis

Phobos [**foh**bos] The larger of the two natural satellites of Mars, discovered in 1877; distance from the planet 938 000 km/583 000 mi; diameter 27 km/17 mi; orbital period 7 h 39 min. Spacecraft achieved a rendezvous with Phobos in April 1989. >> Deimos; Mars (astronomy); Mars programme; Viking project; RR964

Phocis [**foh**kis] The region in C Greece to the W of Boeotia, in which Delphi was situated. >> Delphi

Phoebe (astronomy) [**fee**bee] The ninth natural satellite of Saturn, discovered in 1898; distance from the planet 12 950 000 km/ 8 047 000 mi; diameter 220 km/137 mi; orbital period 550·5 days. >> Saturn (astronomy); RR964

Phoebe (mythology) [**fee**bee] In Greek mythology, a Titaness, identified with the Moon. Later she was confused with Artemis. >> Artemis

Phoenicia [fuh**nee**sha] The narrow strip in the E Mediterranean between the mountains of Lebanon and the sea, where the cities of Arad, Byblos, Sidon, and Tyre were located. It derived its name from the Phoenicians, who dominanted the area from the end of the second millennium BC. From here came their most important contribution to Western culture – the alphabet. >> alphabet [i]; Byblos

Phoenix (USA) [**fee**niks] 33°27N 112°04W, pop (1995e) 1 039 000. State capital in SC Arizona, USA, on the Salt R; largest city in the state; settled, 1870; state capital, 1889; airport; railway; hub of the rich Salt River Valley; important centre for data-processing and electronics research; popular winter and health resort; professional teams, Suns (basketball), Cardinals (football). >> Arizona

Phoenix (astronomy) [**fee**niks] A S hemisphere constellation. >> constellation; RR968

phoenix / phenix [**fee**niks] A legendary bird, which lives a long time. It kills itself on a funeral pyre, but is then reborn from the ashes. The idea of resurrection appealed to Christian allegorists.

Phoenix, River (1970–93) Film actor, born in Madras, OR. He made his film debut in *Explorers* (1985), and received a Best Actor Oscar nomination for his role in *Running on Empty* (1988). Later films included *Indiana Jones and the Last Crusade* (1989) and *Love You To Death* (1990). His early death was due to a drugs overdose.

Phoenix Park murders The murder in Dublin on 6 May 1882 of the recently appointed chief secretary for Ireland, Lord Frederick Cavendish (1836–82), and his under-secretary, Thomas Henry Burke (1829–82), by a terrorist nationalist group called 'The Invincibles'. Five of the murderers were arrested and hanged. >> nationalism

phoneme The smallest unit in the sound system of a language, capable of signalling a difference of meaning between words. For example, the English words *pail* and *tail* are distinguished by the initial consonant phonemes /p/ and /t/. The number of phonemes in a language varies greatly, from less than a dozen to well over 80. >> phonetics; phonology

phonetics The study of the range of sounds which can be produced by the human vocal organs. *Articulatory phonetics* studies the movements of the vocal organs (such as the tongue, lips, and larynx); *acoustic phonetics*, the physical properties of the sound waves produced in speech; and *auditory phonetics*, the way in which the listener uses ear and brain to decode sound waves. >> linguistics; phonology

phonics A general method of teaching children to read by recognizing the relationship between individual letters and sounds. It builds up the pronunciation of new words by saying them sound by sound, as with the one-to-one correspondences between *cat* and [k-a-t]. >> look-and-say

phonograph The first practical device for recording and reproducing sounds stored as grooves cut in cylinders, mainly of wax, rotated beneath a stylus by hand or clockwork. Demonstrated by Edison in 1877, it came to be widely applied in home musical entertainment during the next half-century. >> Edison, Thomas Alva; gramophone; sound recording

phonology The study of the sound system of a language, and of the general properties of sound systems. Phonologists study the way the sound segments (or **phonemes**) are organized in languages, and also the patterns of pitch, loudness, and other voice qualities. >> linguistics; phoneme; phonetics

phosphates Salts of phosphoric acid. Phosphates occur in various minerals, especially apatite, and are mined for use as fertilizers. >> phosphoric acid; superphosphates

phospholipid A special category of fats, the main component of all biological membranes. Phospholipids also store arachidonic acid.

phosphor >> **luminescence**

phosphorescence Light produced by an object excited by a means other than heat, where the light emission continues after the energy source has been removed; a type of luminescence. An example is the long after-glow on a television screen, after the television has been switched off. >> light; luminescence

phosphoric acid H_3PO_4. A tribasic acid, with three series of salts. Dehydration gives phosphorus pentoxide (P_2O_5), an excellent drying agent. >> acid; phosphate

phosphorus P, element 15, the second element of the nitrogen group. It is not found free in nature, but may be prepared both as a very reactive, molecular, white form (P_4), melting point 44°C, and as a variety of less reactive, high-melting polymeric solids with colours ranging from red to black. It is found in many minerals, particularly apatite, mainly as calcium phosphate. Phosphorus is essential to life, being required for DNA and RNA. Industrial uses include matches and agricultural fertilizers. >> chemical elements; DNA ℹ; nitrogen; polymerization; RR1036

photino >> **supersymmetry**

photocell >> **photoelectric cell**

photochemistry The study of chemical reactions brought about by the absorption of visible and ultraviolet light, and of those reactions that produce light. The decomposition or dissociation of molecules by exposure to light is known as **photolysis**. >> light

photoconductivity The increase in conductivity of a material (usually a semiconductor, such as silicon) resulting from the exposure to light. The effect is exploited in light-sensitive detectors and switches, and in television cameras. >> electrical conduction; light

photocopying The photographic reproduction of written, printed, or graphic work. In **xerography** an image of the original is focused on to a photosensitive surface (a selenium plate or cylinder), which converts light into electric charge. This electrostatic image attracts charged ink powder, and the image is then permanently fixed by heating. The **ozalid process** (also called the **diazo process**) uses paper coated with diazonium compounds. This is exposed to ultraviolet light through a transparent original. Only the diazo in the shadows of the original is developed by ammonia vapour to give a positive print. >> xerography ℹ

photoelectric cell, also known as **photocell** A device sensitive to light which responds to radiation with an electrical effect. It is generally based on a semiconductor (eg selenium, germanium). They are used in light meters (eg in photography), light detectors (eg in burglar alarms), and spacecraft power supplies. >> electricity; semiconductor

photogrammetry The use of photographic records to determine precise measurements. It is principally applied in map-making by aerial survey, but is also used for medical, forensic, and architectural purposes. >> aerial photography

photography The recording and reproduction of images on light-sensitive materials by chemical processes. In 1816 Nicéphore Niepce in France tried to record the optical image formed in a camera obscura, and in 1822 succeeded in obtaining a photographic copy of an engraving superimposed on glass. By 1839 Daguerre had established a reliable process. About the same time in England, Fox Talbot discovered the process of developing and fixing the exposed image as a negative and making a positive print. Scott Archer (1813–57) in 1851 invented the collodion 'wet plate', and dry plates coated with sensitized emulsion were produced commercially in the mid-1870s, followed by celluloid-based film from 1889. >> aerial / colour / electronic / high-speed / stereoscopic / time-lapse photography; camera; Niepce; Talbot

photoluminescence >> **luminescence**

photolysis >> **photochemistry**

photomacrography >> **macro-photography**

photometry The measurement of light and its rate of flow. Photometric quantities (see table) are measured using **photometers**. The technique is important in photography and lighting design. >> illuminance; light; luminous flux / intensity; *see table on p. 668*

photomicrograph A photograph of an object as observed through a microscope. Optical means can provide magnifications up to about × 2000. For an electron microscope,

Photometry

Photometric Quantities	Symbols	Units	Corresponding Radiometric Quantities
luminous flux	Φ	lumen (lm)	radiant power
luminous intensity	I	candela (cd)	radiant intensity
luminance	L	cd/m^2	radiance
illuminance	E	lux (lx)	irradiance

magnifications of $\times 10^6$ or more can be achieved. >> macrophotography; microscope

photo-montage An assembly of selected images achieved either by physically mounting cut-out portions of prints on a backing, or by combination printing from several separate negatives in succession. It is widely used in the preparation of advertising display material. >> photography

photon The quantum or particle of light. Light and all other electromagnetic radiation comprises a stream of photons, each of which has energy $E = h\nu$, where h is Planck's constant and ν is frequency. Photons have no (rest) mass and are spin 1. In quantum theory they transmit electromagnetic force. >> light; quantum mechanics

Photorealism A style of modern painting, also called *Hyperrealism* or *Superrealism*. Pictures are meticulously painted in a style of extreme naturalism like a sharply-focused coloured photograph. >> modern art; naturalism

photosphere The visible surface of the Sun or a star. About 500 km/300 mi thick, it is the zone from which the light we see actually comes. The temperature is c.6000 K. >> Sun

photosynthesis The complex process in which light energy is used to convert water and carbon dioxide into simple carbohydrates. Light-absorbing pigments, notably chlorophyll, are essential to the process, which can be carried out only by green plants and photosynthetic bacteria. >> carbohydrate; carbon; chlorophyll; light

phototherapy Body exposure to cool blue light (420–480 nm), free of ultraviolet light. It is used in the treatment of jaundice occurring in the newborn. >> jaundice; light

phototypesetter A machine for composing type and creating an image of the composed type on film or paper, ready for exposure to a plate for printing. The individual characters may be stored in the machine either as images on film, or digitally within the machine's computer memory. >> printing ℹ

photovoltaic effect The production of electrical current by light falling on some material, usually a semiconductor. The effect is the basic mechanism of solar cells. >> electromotive force; semiconductor; solar cell

phrenology [fre**nol**ojee] The analysis of mind and character by the study of the shape and contours of the skull. It is based on the erroneous belief that this reflects the degree of development of the underlying regions of the brain. It was popular in Europe during the early 19th-c. >> brain ℹ; skull

Phrygia [**fri**jia] The name of the kingdom in antiquity with which the legendary Midas is associated. At its widest extent around the beginning of the first millennium, it consisted of the C plateau of Asia Minor and its W flank.

phylloxera [filok**seer**a] A dwarf, aphid-like insect that can kill grape vines. (Order: Homoptera. Family: Phylloxeridae.) >> aphid; insect ℹ

phylogeny [fiy**lo**jenee] The relationships between groups of animals as determined by their evolutionary history. Groups are linked together on the basis of the recency of common ancestry. >> evolution

phylum [**fiy**luhm] In animal classification, one of the major groupings, forming the principal category below *kingdom*, and comprising classes and lower categories. Phyla represent the major types of animals. >> kingdom; systematics; taxonomy

physalis [**fis**alis] A soft-leaved annual or perennial; found almost everywhere; salver-shaped, 5-petalled flowers. (Genus: *Physalis*, 100 species. Family: Solanaceae.)

physical chemistry The study of the dependence of physical properties on chemical composition, and of the physical changes accompanying chemical reactions. >> chemistry; physics

physics The study of matter and forces, at the most basic level. Physics as a discernible discipline began during the Renaissance, with Copernicus' model of planetary motion and Galileo's mechanics. Astronomy and mechanics continued to dominate the field, with the work of Newton, Kepler, and others. Newton's theories dominated physics for two centuries, and was in part responsible for a philosophy that attempted to explain all phenomena in terms of mechanics. The physicists' view of the world has changed dramatically due to two major developments in the early part of the 20th-c. The first was Einstein's theory of special relativity; the second was the development of quantum theory and atomic theory, made possible by work in thermodynamics, electromagnetism, and the new radiations. It has led to modern solid state physics, as well as atomic, nuclear, and particle physics. >> astrophysics; particle / solid state / surface physics; mechanics; special relativity ℹ; thermodynamics; Copernicus; Einstein; Galileo; Kepler; Newton, Isaac

physiology An experimental science concerned with the study of the functions of living things. It includes studies of the processes that go on in cells (eg photosynthesis); of how tissues or organs work; and of how living things respond to their environment. >> biology

physiotherapy The application of physical treatment to restore the function of muscles and joints after injury, surgery, or disease. Treatment varies widely, but includes active and passive exercises, massage, and the application of heat by infrared and short-wave diathermy. >> diathermy; muscle ℹ

phytic acid A store of phosphorus present in most cereals and legumes; also called *inositol hexaphosphate*. This acid can bind such minerals as calcium, iron, and zinc, and reduce their bio-availability. >> inositol; phosphorus

phytogeography The study of the factors responsible for the past and present distribution of plants on the Earth's surface. It is part of the larger discipline of biogeography. >> biogeography

phytoplankton >> **plankton**

phytosaur [**fiy**tosaw(r)] An extinct reptile with a crocodile-like body; teeth inserted in sockets (*thecodontic*); known from the late Triassic period of North America, Europe, and Asia. (Subclass: Archosauria.) >> reptile; Triassic period

phytotherapy >> **herbalism**

pi (π) [piy] In mathematics, the ratio of a circle's circumference to its diameter (3·14159...). Archimedes proved that $223/71 < \pi < 22/7$, ie $3{\cdot}1408 < \pi < 3{\cdot}14285$. It is now known to over ten million decimal places. >> Archimedes; circle

Piacenza [pya**chen**tsa], ancient **Placentia** 45°03N 9°41E, pop (1995e) 112 000. City in N Italy, on R Po; railway; cathedral (12th–13th-c); well-preserved circuit of 16th-c walls. >> Italy ℹ

Piaf, Edith [**pee**af], popular name of **Edith Giovanna Gassion** (1915–63) Singer, born in Paris. Known as *Piaf* (Parisian argot 'little sparrow'), she is mainly remembered for her songs, such as 'Non, je ne regrette rien'.

Piaget, Jean [**pyah**zhay] (1896–1980) Psychologist, born in Neuchâtel, Switzerland. He is best known for his research on the development of cognitive functions in children, in such pioneering studies as *La Naissance de l'intelligence chez l'enfant* (1948, The Origins of Intelligence in Children). >> cognitive psychology

piano The most important domestic and recital instrument for over 200 years, first made by Cristofori in Florence in the last years of the 17th-c. The main difference between its mechanism and that of the earlier clavichord is that the hammers (tipped with felt) rebound after they have struck the string, and this made possible the dynamic contrasts from which the instrument derived its full name (**pianoforte** = quiet/loud). The modern piano is fitted with a mechanism operated by two pedals: the left ('soft') pedal makes the tone quieter; the other sustains it after the keys have been released. >> clavichord; Cristofori; keyboard instrument; player piano

pianola A trade name for a type of player piano manufactured by the Aeolian Corporation in the USA. >> player piano

piapiac [peea**pee**ak] A crow native to C Africa (*Ptilostomus afer*); black with thick black bill and very long tail. (Family: Corvidae.) >> crow

pica [**piy**ka] The consumption of non-food items, including in particular the consumption of soil, known as *geophagia* or *geophagy*. Among humans, geophagy is especially common in W Africa.

Picabia, Francis [pi**kah**bia] (1879–1953) Artist, born in Paris. He was one of the most anarchistic of modern artists, involved in Cubism, Dadaism, and Surrealism. His anti-art productions, often portraying senseless machinery, include many of the cover designs for the American magazine *291*, which he edited. >> Cubism; Dada; Surrealism

Picardy [**pik**a(r)dee], Fr **Picardie** pop (1995e) 1 865 000; area 19 399 sq km/7488 sq mi. Region and former province of N France; flat landscape, crossed by several rivers (eg Somme, Oise) and canals; scene of heavy fighting during World War 1. >> World War 1

picaresque novel (Sp *picaro* 'rogue') A novel which dealt originally with the comic misfortunes of a low-life character; now applied more loosely to the adventures of any character living on his or her wits, and often on the road.

Picasso, Pablo [pi**kas**oh] (1881–1973) Artist, born in Málaga, Spain. He was the dominating figure of early 20th-c art. His 'blue period' (1902–4), a series of striking studies of the poor, gave way to the gay, life-affirming 'pink period' (1904–6), full of harlequins, acrobats, and the incidents of circus life. He then turned to brown, and began to work in sculpture. His break with tradition came with 'Les Demoiselles d'Avignon' (1906–7, New York), the first exemplar of analytical Cubism, a movement which he developed with Braque (1909–14). His major creation is 'Guernica' (1937, Madrid), expressing in synthetic Cubism his horror of the bombing of this Basque town during the Civil War. >> Braque; Cubism

Piccard, Auguste (Antoine) [peekah(r)] (1884–1962) Physicist, born in Basel, Switzerland. In 1932 he ascended in a balloon 16 940 m/55 563 ft into the stratosphere, and in 1948, explored the ocean depths off W Africa in a bathyscaphe of his own design. His twin brother, **Jean (Felix) Piccard** (1884–1963) also made pioneer balloon ascents. >> bathyscaphe

piccolo A small transverse flute pitched one octave higher than the standard instrument. >> flute; transposing instrument; woodwind instrument ℹ

Pichincha [pee**cheen**cha] 0°10S 78°35W. Andean volcano in NC Ecuador; rises to 4794 m/15 728 ft; last eruption, 1981; site of decisive battle (1822) in fight for independence. >> Andes

Pickering, William H(ayward) (1910–) Rocket scientist, born in Wellington, New Zealand. As director of the Jet Propulsion Laboratory in the USA (1954–76), he oversaw the first orbit of the Earth by a US satellite (1958), the first US soft landings on the Moon, and the first missions to Mars (Mariner IX), Venus, and Mercury (Mariner X). >> NASA; space exploration

picketing The action by a trade union in an industrial dispute to try to persuade fellow-workers and others not to go to work, or do business with the company involved in the dispute. Pickets stand outside the gates of the factory or offices, and lobby all who would go in. Trade union legislation in the UK now limits picketing to the place where the picket actually works, and requires that it be carried out peacefully. Picketing was formerly illegal in the USA, but is now allowed under a variety of state regulations. >> industrial action

Pickford, Mary, originally **Gladys Mary Smith** (1893–1979) Actress, born in Toronto, Ontario, Canada. She made her first film in 1913, and quickly gained the title of 'America's sweetheart', playing an innocent heroine in many silent films. She founded United Artists Film Corporation in 1919.

Pico della Mirandola, Giovanni, comte (Count) [**pee**koh, mi**ran**dola] (1463–94) Renaissance philosopher, born in Mirandola, Italy. He wrote Latin epistles and elegies, a series of Italian sonnets, and a major study of free will. >> Renaissance

Pico de Orizaba >> **Citlaltépetl**

picofarad >> **farad**

picric acid $C_6H_2(NO_2)_3OH$, 2,4,6-trinitrophenol, melting point 122°C. A yellow solid, made by nitrating phenol. A weak acid, it is a yellow dye and an explosive. >> phenol; TNT

pictography The study of writing systems, which make use of symbols called **pictographs** or **pictograms** – direct, stylized representations of objects in the real world, drawn in outline. Pictographic writing is the oldest form of writing known, and occurs very widely throughout the world; the earliest discovered in Egypt is dated to c.3000 BC. >> graphology; hieroglyphics ℹ; ideography

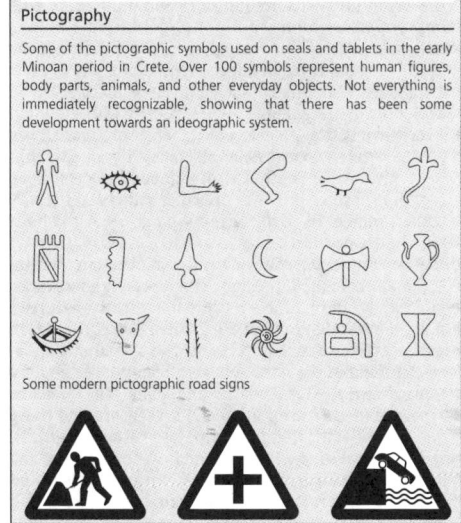

Pictography

Some of the pictographic symbols used on seals and tablets in the early Minoan period in Crete. Over 100 symbols represent human figures, body parts, animals, and other everyday objects. Not everything is immediately recognizable, showing that there has been some development towards an ideographic system.

Some modern pictographic road signs

Pictor (Lat 'easel') A small, inconspicuous S constellation, near the Large Magellanic Cloud. >> constellation; Magellanic Clouds; RR968

Picts (Lat *picti* 'painted people') A general term coined by the Romans in the 3rd-c for their barbarian enemies in Britain N of the Antonine Wall. The name derives from the local custom of body tattooing. >> Antonine Wall; Kenneth I

piculet >> **woodpecker**

pidgin A language with a highly simplified grammar and vocabulary, the native language of no one, which develops when people who lack a common language attempt to communicate. Pidgins flourish in areas of trade contact. Some have developed into important systems of communication, such as Tok Pisin in Papua New Guinea. >> creole

Piedmont [**peed**mont], Ital **Piemonte** pop (1995e) 4 356 000; area 25 400 sq km/9800 sq mi. Region of N Italy; centre of Italian unification in 19th-c; capital, Turin. >> Italy ℹ

Pied Piper of Hamelin In German legend a 13th-c piper who charmed Hamelin's rats out of the city with his pipe-music. He was refused his fee, and in revenge lured all the children away from the city.

Pierce, Franklin (1804–69) US statesman and 14th President (1853–7), born in Hillsboro, NH. As president he tried unsuccessfully to bridge the widening chasm between the South and the North. >> American Civil War

Piero della Francesca [**pyay**roh, fran**chays**ka] (c.1420–92) Painter, born in Borgo San Sepolcro, Italy. He is known especially for his series of frescoes, 'The Legend of the True Cross' (1452–66), at the church of San Francesco in Arezzo. >> fresco; perspective

Piero di Cosimo [**pyair**oh di **kohz**imoh], originally **Piero di Lorenzo** (c.1462–c.1521) Painter, born in Florence, Italy. His later work is largely devoted to mythological scenes, such as 'Death of Procris' (c.1500, National Gallery, London).

Pierre [pyayr] 44°22N 100°21W, pop (1995e) 13 600. Capital of state in C South Dakota, USA, on the Missouri R; founded as a railway terminus, 1880; state capital, 1889; centre of a grain and dairy region. >> South Dakota

Pierrot Originally **Pedrolino**, a servant role in the *commedia dell' arte*. Pierrot gained his white face and white floppy costume on the French stage. His childlike manner and his pathos, dumb and solitary, was the creation of the great 19th-c pantomimist Deburau. >> *commedia dell' arte*; pantomime

pietà [peeuh**ta**] (Ital 'pity') In art, the representation of the dead Christ mourned by angels, apostles, or holy women. A famous example is Michelangelo's marble 'Pietà' (c.1500) in St Peter's, Rome. >> Jesus Christ; Michelangelo

Pietermaritzburg [peeter**ma**ritzberg] or **Maritzburg** 30°33S 30°24E, pop (1995e) 250 000. City in KwaZulu Natal province, E South Africa; founded by Boers, 1838; capital of former province of Natal; railway; university (1910); centre of rich farming area. >> Afrikaners; KwaZulu Natal

Pietism [**piy**etizm] Originally, a movement within Lutheranism in the 17th-c and 18th-c stressing good works, Bible study, and holiness in Christian life. It was a reaction against rigid Protestant dogmatism. >> Lutheranism

piezo-electric effect [piy**eet**zoh] The appearance of an electric field in some material as a result of the application of stress, as in quartz and bone. The effect is exploited in gas cooker lighters, load sensors, and transducers. >> electric field; stress (physics); transducer

pig A mammal native to woodland in Europe, S Asia, and Africa; an artiodactyl; stout body with short legs and coarse hair; short thin tail; face in front of ears and small eyes very long; snout muscular, flattened, disc-like; male called *boar*, female called *sow*, young called *piglets*; also known as **hog** or **swine**. (Family: Suidae, 9 species.) >> artiodactyl; babirusa; landrace; warthog; wild boar

pigeon A bird of the widespread family Columbidae (c.255 species); plump with round bill; many domestic breeds. >> dove; petrel; wood pigeon

Piggott, Lester (Keith) (1935–) Jockey, born in Wantage, Oxfordshire. During his career he rode 4349 winners in Britain (1948–85), and was champion jockey 11 times. After retiring, he took up training at Newmarket, but was imprisoned (1987–8) for tax offences. He resumed his career as a jockey in 1990 and retired in 1995.

pig-iron The product of the blast furnace. The molten iron is run into channels which have moulds led off them, fancifully likened to pigs in a litter. This cast-iron has a high proportion of carbon (c.4%) which has to be reduced to under 1% to form steel. >> blast furnace ℹ; steel

pigweed >> **amaranth**

pika [**pee**ka, **piy**ka] A mammal of order Lagomorpha, native to C and NE Asia and W North America; resembles a small rabbit, with short legs, short rounded ears, and minute tail; also known as **cony**. (Family: Ochotonidae, 14 species.) >> hyrax; lagomorph

pike Any of the large predatory freshwater fish of the family Esocidae; distinguished by an elongate body with dorsal and anal fins set close to the tail; snout pointed, jaws large; length up to 1.5 m/5 ft; mottled greenish-brown.

pikeperch >> **zander**

piket >> **skunk**

pilaster [pi**las**ter] A rectangular pillar that projects only slightly from the wall of a building. In classical architecture it is usually designed according to one of the five orders. >> orders of architecture ℹ

Pilate, Pontius [**pon**shus], Lat **Pontius Pilatus** (1st-c) Roman appointed by Tiberius in AD c.26 as prefect of Judea, having charge of the state and the occupying military forces. Although based in Caesarea, he also resided in Jerusalem, and is known for his order to execute Jesus of Nazareth at the prompting of the Jewish authorities. >> Annas; Jesus Christ

pilchard Small herring-like surface-living fish (*Sardina pilchardus*) widespread in the E North Atlantic and Mediterranean; length up to 25 cm/10 in; greenish-blue above, underside silver; important commercial fish, usually canned for marketing; also called **sardine**. (Family: Clupeidae.) >> herring

piles >> **haemorrhoids**

Pilgrimage of Grace (Oct 1536–Jan 1537) A major Tudor rebellion in N England directed against the policies and ministers of Henry VIII. It was led by Lord Thomas Darcy (1467–1537), Robert Aske (?–1537), and 'pilgrims' carrying banners of the Five Wounds of Christ. The leaders and over 200 others were executed. >> Henry VIII

Pilgrims or **Pilgrim Fathers** The 102 English religious dissenters who left to establish Plymouth Colony in America in 1620, after crossing the Atlantic aboard the *Mayflower*. They originally came from Lincolnshire. >> *Mayflower*

Pilgrim's Way A long-distance footpath in Surrey and Kent, S England, opened in 1972. Its name derives from the popular belief that it was used by mediaeval pilgrims travelling from Winchester to Canterbury.

pill >> **contraception**

Pillars of Hercules The ancient mythological name for the promontories flanking the Strait of Gibraltar: the Rock of Gibraltar and Cueta, N Africa. >> Mediterranean Sea

pillars of Islam >> **Islam**

pilotfish Marine fish (*Naucrates ductor*) which derives its name from the behaviour of juveniles that swim alongside ships or larger fish such as sharks; length up to

60 cm/2 ft; greyish-blue on back with banding on sides. (Family: Carangidae.)

pilotis [pi**lo**tee, pilo**teez**] Posts or columns used on the ground floor of a building to raise most of the main body to first-floor level, leaving unenclosed space below. They are particularly associated with the work of Le Corbusier. >> Le Corbusier

pilot whale A toothed whale of family Delphinidae; black with bulbous overhanging snout; two species. >> whale ℹ

Pilsen >> **Plzeň**

Piłsudski, Józef (Klemens) [pil**sud**skee] (1867–1935) Polish marshal and statesman, born near Vilna, Poland. He declared Poland's independence in 1918, and served as president until 1922. He returned to power in 1926 by means of a military coup, and established a dictatorship. >> Poland ℹ; socialism

Piltdown Man A supposed early fossil man found in 1912 near Piltdown, Sussex, England; named *Eoanthropus* ('Dawn Man'). Later study proved the find a forgery. >> *Homo* ℹ

pimento >> **allspice**

pi-meson >> **pion**

pimpernel A sprawling annual weed (*Anagallis arvensis*); flowers on long slender stalks, five petals. Scarlet and blue pimpernels are different coloured forms of the same plant. (Family: Primulaceae)

PIN [pin] Acronym for **Personal Identification Number**; a unique number allocated to the users of computer-based equipment which allows the identity of each user to be established. It is often used in modern banking systems.

Pinakothek, Alte [**al**tuh pee**na**kohtek] A museum founded in 1836 in Munich, Germany, housing one of the finest collections of German, Dutch, Flemish, and Spanish paintings. The adjacent **Neue** [**noy**uh] **Pinakothek** was established in 1853. >> Munich

Pinang [pi**nang**], or **Penang**, formerly **George Town** 5°26N 100°16E, pop (1995e) 343 000. Capital of Pinang state, W Peninsular Malaysia; named after King George III of Great Britain; Malaysia's chief port; railway. >> Malaysia ℹ; Pinang (state)

pinchbeck An alloy of copper and zinc, but with less zinc than in brass. It is named after London watchmaker Christopher Pinchbeck (1670–1732) who used it to simulate gold. >> alloy; brass; copper; zinc

Pinckney, Charles (Cotesworth) (1746–1825) US statesman, born in Charleston, SC. He was Washington's aide-de-camp at Brandywine and Germantown, and a member of the convention that framed the US constitution (1787). >> American Revolution

Pincus, Gregory (Goodwin) (1903–67) Biologist, born in Woodbine, NJ. His research led to the development of the contraceptive pill. >> contraception

Pindar (c.522–c.440 BC) The chief lyric poet of Greece, born near Thebes. He became famous as a composer of odes for people in all parts of the Greek world. Only his *Epinikia* (Triumphal Odes) have survived entire. >> ode

Pindus Mountains, Gr **Píndhos Oros** Mountain range in WC and NW Greece; length c.500 km/310 mi; highest peak, Smolikas (2633 m/8638 ft). >> Greece ℹ

pine A member of a large genus of evergreen conifers widespread throughout the N hemisphere. The leaves are of three kinds: (1) seedling leaves, narrow, toothed; (2) adult scale leaves, borne on long shoots but soon falling; (3) adult needle leaves in bundles of 2, 3, or 5, according to species, borne on short shoots in the axils of the scale leaves. The cones are woody, at least two years old when ripe. Pines are of great commercial importance, and are planted on a vast scale. The timber is resistant to decay because of a high content of resin, rich in oil of turpentine. (Genus: *Pinus*, 70–100 species. Family: Pinaceae.) >> conifer; resin; tree ℹ

pineal gland [**pin**ial] A small gland of vertebrates situated above the third ventricle of the brain. It synthesizes the hormone *melatonin*, and has an important role in determining seasonal breeding patterns in some mammals. >> biological rhythm; seasonal affective disorder

Pinero, Sir Arthur (Wing) [pi**nair**oh] (1855–1934) Playwright, born in London. He wrote several farces, but is best known for his social dramas, notably *The Second Mrs Tanqueray* (1893).

pink An annual, biennial, or perennial herb, native to the temperate N hemisphere; flowers with five petals, pink, also red or white, often scented. The genus includes the well-known carnations and sweet williams of horticulture. (Genus: *Dianthus*, 300 species. Family: Caryophyllaceae.) >> carnation; sweet william

Pinkerton, Allan (1819–84) Detective, born in Glasgow. He founded the Pinkerton National Detective Agency in 1850, and headed a Federal intelligence network during the Civil War.

pinnate The shape of a leaf divided into several lobes or leaflets arranged in two opposite rows along the stalk. In **bi-pinnate** leaves, the leaflets are themselves pinnate. >> leaf ℹ

Pinochet (Ugarte), Augusto [**pee**nohshay] (1915–) Chilean dictator, born in Valparaíso, Chile. He led the military coup overthrowing the Allende government (1973), and in 1980 enacted a constitution giving himself an eight-year presidential term (1981–9). He stood down as president in 1990 following the democratic election of Patricio Aylwin. In October 1998 he became the centre of international attention when he was arrested in London, following a request from Spain for his extradition to stand trial for 'crimes of genocide and terrorism'. in which some of the victims had been Spanish nationals. The arrest caused tension between UK and Chile, and civil unrest in Chile between Pinochet supporters and opponents. At the beginning of 1999, Pinochet remained under house arrest in the UK, pending the outcome of legal procedures. >> Allende; Chile ℹ

pinochle [**pee**nuhkl] A card game derived from *bézique*. Two packs of 24 cards are used, all cards from 2–8 having been discarded. The object is to win tricks, and to score points according to the cards won. >> bézique

pint >> **litre**

pintail A dabbling duck of the genus *Anas* (3 species): two are native to South America and the Caribbean; one to the N hemisphere (*Anas acuta*). The male has long central tail feathers.

Pinter, Harold (1930–) Playwright, born in London. His first major play, *The Birthday Party* (1958), was badly received, but was revived after the success of *The Caretaker* (1960). Later plays include *The Homecoming* (1965), and *No Man's Land* (1975), and he has written many television and film scripts. His work is highly regarded for the way it uses the unspoken meaning behind inconsequential everyday talk to induce an atmosphere of menace. A major new play, *Moonlight*, was produced in 1993, and *Ashes to Ashes* appeared in 1996.

Pintupi A people of Australia's Western Desert. Most now live in or around the communities of YaiYai, Docker River, and Haast's Bluff. Pintupi artists were influential early members of the art school which developed at Papunya in the 1970s. >> Aborigines

pinworm >> **nematode**

pin-yin >> **Chinese**

pion [**piy**on] A strongly interacting subatomic particle of the meson family; symbol π; spin zero; also called a **pi-meson**. Charged pions decay to muons and neutrinos; neutral pions decay to gamma rays. Discovered in 1947, pions are carriers of strong nuclear force. >> meson; particle physics

Pioneer programme A series of relatively simple spin-stabilized spacecraft launched by the USA 1958–78. Pioneers 10 and 11 (launched in 1972 and 1973) achieved the first flybys of Jupiter and of Saturn. Pioneer 12 was the first US Venus orbiter, and Pioneer 13 explored Venus's atmosphere (1978). >> NASA; RR970

pipa A Chinese lute with a pear-shaped body, short neck, fretted soundboard, and four silk strings plucked with the fingernails. >> lute; string instrument 2 ℹ

pipal >> **peepul**

pipefish Distinctive fish with a very slender segmented body, small mouth on a tubular snout, and delicate fins; with seahorses and seadragons comprises the family Syngnathidae (11 genera); length up to 60 cm/2 ft, typically much smaller. >> fish ℹ

Piper, John (1903–92) Artist, born in Epsom, Surrey. He is known for his pictures of war damage, and his topographical pictures, notably the watercolours of 'Windsor Castle' commissioned by the Queen in 1941–2. He also created the stained-glass design in Coventry Cathedral. >> abstract art

Piper Alpha An oil-drilling platform in the North Sea, off the coast of Scotland, which was destroyed by an explosion in July 1988. The disaster killed 167.

pipes of Pan >> **panpipes**

pipistrelle [pi**pi**strel] A bat of family Vespertilionidae; genus *Pipistrellus* (46 species), found worldwide except South America. >> bat

pipit A wagtail of the worldwide genus *Anthus* (34 dull-coloured species), or the more colourful African genera *Tmetothylacus* (1 species) and *Macronyx* (8 species, the 'long-claws'). >> wagtail

Piquet, Nelson [**pee**kay], originally **Nelson Souto Maior** (1952–) Motor-racing driver, born in Rio de Janeiro, Brazil. He was world champion in 1981, 1983 (both Brabham), and 1987 (Williams). He won 23 grand prix between 1978 and a serious accident in 1991. >> motor racing

Piraeus [piy**ree**us], Gr **Piraiéus** 37°57N 23°42E, pop (1995e) 208 000. Major port in Greece; 8 km/5 mi SW of Athens; rail terminus; ferries to the Greek islands. >> Athens; Greece ℹ

Pirandello, Luigi [piran**del**oh] (1867–1936) Writer, born in Girgenti, Sicily, Italy. He became a leading exponent of the 'grotesque' school of contemporary drama. Among his plays are *Six Characters in Search of an Author* (1921). In 1934 he was awarded the Nobel Prize for Literature.

Piranesi, Giambattista [pira**nay**zee], or **Giovanni Battista** (1720–78) Architect and copper-engraver of Roman antiquities, born in Venice, Italy. He developed original techniques of etching, and was a major influence on Neoclassicism. >> etching; Neoclassicism (art and architecture)

piranha [pi**rah**na] Any of several voracious predatory freshwater fishes widespread in rivers of South America; length up to 60 cm/2 ft; strong jaws and sharp interlocking teeth; extremely aggressive flesh-eating fish, often feeding in large shoals. >> fish ℹ

Pire, Dominique (Georges) [peer] (1910–69) Dominican priest and educator, born in Dinant, Belgium. He was awarded the 1958 Nobel Peace Prize for his scheme of 'European villages' for elderly refugees and destitute children. >> Dominicans

Pisa [**pee**za] 43°43N 10°24E, pop (1995e) 108 000. City in Tuscany, W Italy, on the R Arno; archbishopric; airport; railway; university (1338); birthplace of Galileo; cathedral (11th–12th-c); campanile (the 'Leaning Tower', 1173–1372); Piazza del Duomo is a world heritage site. >> Galileo; Italy ℹ

Pisanello, Antonio [peesa**ne**loh], originally **Antonio Pisano** (c.1395–1455) Medallist and painter, born in Pisa, Italy. Little of his painting survives, but numerous drawings attest to his mastery of the International Gothic style. >> International Gothic

Pisano, Andrea [pee**sah**noh], also known as **Andrea da Pontedera** (c.1270–1349) Sculptor, born in Pontedera, Italy. He settled in Florence, where he completed the earliest bronze doors of the baptistery (1336).

Pisano, Nicola [pee**sah**noh] (c.1225–78/84) Sculptor, probably born in Apulia, Italy. His works include the pulpit of the baptistery at Pisa (1260) and the pulpit of Siena cathedral (1268).

Pisces [**piy**seez] (Lat 'fishes') A large N constellation of the zodiac which lacks bright stars, and so is hard to identify. It lies between Aquarius and Aries. >> constellation; zodiac ℹ; RR968

Piscis Austrinus [**piy**sis os**triy**nus] (Lat 'southern fish') A small S hemisphere constellation, which includes the first magnitude star Fomalhaut. >> constellation; RR968

Pisistratus [piy**sis**tratus], also spelled **Peisistratos** (c.600–527 BC) Tyrant of Athens (561–c.556 BC, 546–527 BC). A patron of the arts, he invited the leading Greek poets of the day to settle in Athens, where he set about fostering a sense of national unity by instituting or expanding great religious and cultural festivals. >> tyrant

Pissarro, Camille [peesaroh] (1830–1903) Impressionist artist, born in St Thomas, Danish West Indies. He was the leader of the original Impressionists, and the only one to exhibit at all eight of the Group exhibitions in Paris (1874–86). >> Impressionism (art)

pistachio [pi**stah**shioh] A small deciduous tree (*Pistachio vera*) growing to 6 m/20 ft, native to W Asia; flowers greenish, in long, loose heads; fruit 2–2.5 cm/¾–1 in, red-brown, nut-like. It is widely cultivated for its edible seeds, used in confectionery. (Family: Anacardiaceae.)

pistil >> **carpel**

pistol A hand-held firearm first developed from 'hand-cannons' in the 14th-c. The application of the revolver principle in the 1830s made the pistol a multi-shot weapon, followed by the development of 'automatic' weapons c.1900 (such as the Luger and Browning). >> revolver

pit bull terrier >> **bull terrier**

Pitcairn Islands pop (1995e) 56; area 27 sq km/10 sq mi. Volcanic island group in the SE Pacific Ocean; comprises Pitcairn I (4.5 sq km/1.7 sq mi) and the uninhabited islands of Ducie, Henderson, and Oeno; chief settlement, Adamstown; timezone GMT +9; chief religion, Seventh Day Adventism; official language, English; New Zealand currency in use; Pitcairn I rises to 335 m/1099 ft; equable climate; visited by the British, 1767; occupied by nine mutineers from HMS *Bounty*, 1790; overpopulation led to emigration to Norfolk I in 1856, some returning in 1864; transferred to Fiji, 1952; now a British Crown Colony, governed by the High Commissioner in New Zealand. >> *Bounty* Mutiny; Norfolk Island; Pacific Ocean

pitch (acoustics) An aspect of auditory sensation which makes listeners judge a sound as relatively 'high' or 'low'. The pitch at which a musical note sounds, and to which instruments are tuned, is a' = 440 Hz, adopted in 1955.

pitch (chemistry) The black, semi-solid residue left after the distillation of tar, used in bitumen and road-surfacing. It contains a complex mixture of hydrocarbons and resins. >> tar

pitchblende or **uraninite** Uranium oxide (UO_2), the chief ore of uranium; hard, very dense, and radioactive. >> uranium

pitcher plant Any of the members of three separate families of carnivorous plants, in which the leaves are modified to form lidded pitcher traps containing water and enzymes. Insect prey drown in the fluid-filled base, and are digested by the plant. The Sarraceniaceae are native to E North America, California, and tropical South America; the Nepenthaceae are native to the tropics of SE Asia, Australia, and Madagascar; the Cephalotaceae contain a single species, the **flycatcher plant** (*Cephalotus follicularis*), native to W Australia. >> carnivorous plant; enzyme

Piteşti [pee**tesht**] 44°51N 24°51E, pop (1995e) 162 000. City in Romania, on R Argeş; railway junction. >> Romania ℹ

Pithecanthropus [pithe**kan**thropus] A name formerly used for the fossil ape-man, *Homo erectus*, which includes Java Man and Peking Man. >> *Homo* ℹ

Pitjantjatjara The principal Aboriginal language of Australia's Western Desert, spoken by several thousand people. An active literacy programme has resulted in it becoming one of the most widely-used written Aboriginal languages. >> Aborigines

Pitman, Sir Isaac (1813–97) Inventor of a shorthand system, born in Trowbridge, Wiltshire. He was also interested in the development of spelling reform. In 1842 he brought out the *Phonetic Journal*. >> shorthand ℹ; spelling reform

Pitney, Gene (1941–) Singer and songwriter, born in Hartford, CT. His hits as a writer include 'Rubber Ball' and 'Hello Mary Lou' (both 1961). Among his hits as a singer were '24 Hours From Tulsa' (1963) and 'Something's Gotten Hold Of My Heart' (1967).

Pitot tube [**pee**toh] An instrument for measuring the velocity of a flowing fluid; named after French engineer Henri Pitot (1695–1771). The pressure observed by an attached manometer is a function of velocity. >> anemometer ℹ; manometer

Pitt, William, 1st Earl of Chatham, also known as **Pitt the Elder** (1708–78) British statesman and orator, born in London. He led the young 'Patriot' Whigs, and in 1756 became nominally secretary of state, but virtually premier. The king's enmity led him to resign in 1757, but public demand caused his recall. He was again compelled to resign when his Cabinet refused to declare war with Spain (1761). He formed a new ministry in 1766, but ill health contributed to his resignation in 1768. His second son, William, was twice prime minister. >> Pitt (the Younger); Seven Years' War; Whigs

Pitt, William, also known as **Pitt the Younger** (1759–1806) British statesman and prime minister (1783–1801, 1804–6), born in Hayes, Kent, the second son of the Earl of Chatham (William Pitt, the Elder). His first ministry lasted for 18 years, during which he carried through important reforms, his policy being influenced by the political economy of Adam Smith. He negotiated coalitions against France (1793, 1798), and after the Irish rebellion of 1798, proposed a legislative union which would be followed by Catholic emancipation. The union was effected in 1800, but Pitt resigned office rather than contest George III's hostility to emancipation. >> George III; Napoleonic Wars; Smith, Adam

Pitti Palace [**pi**tee] A palace in Florence, Italy, designed by Brunelleschi in the 15th-c, originally the residence of the Grand Dukes of Tuscany. The palace now houses museums of silverware and of modern art, and the Palatine Gallery. >> Brunelleschi; Florence

pittosporum [pi**tos**porum] An evergreen shrub or small tree, mostly native to Australasia but also to parts of Africa and Asia; flowers 5-petalled, purple, white, or greenish-yellow, and often fragrant; also called **parchment-bark**. (Genus: *Pittosporum*, 150 species. Family: Pittosporaceae.)

Pittsburgh 40°26N 80°01W, pop (1995e) 408 000. City in W Pennsylvania, USA; Fort Duquesne built here by the French; taken by the British and renamed Fort Pitt, 1758; city status, 1816; airport; railway; three universities (1787, 1878, 1900); city's traditional steel industry largely replaced by service industries; third largest US corporate headquarters; professional teams, Pirates (baseball), Steelers (football), Penguins (ice hockey). >> Pennsylvania

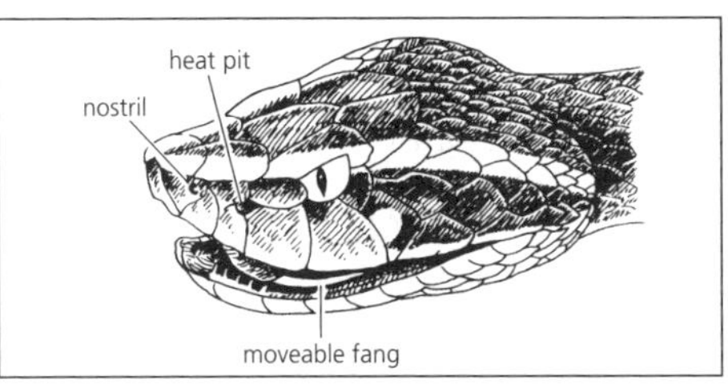

Pit viper

pituitary gland [pit**yoo**itree] A vertebrate endocrine gland situated within the skull; also known as the **hypophysis**. It acts mainly by controlling the activities of all the other endocrine glands. >> acromegaly; dwarfism; endocrine glands; lactation

pit viper A viper of the subfamily Crotalinae (142 species), sometimes treated as a separate family (Crotalidae, with the remaining vipers called *true vipers*); front of face with small heat-sensitive pit on each side. >> bushmaster; copperhead; cottonmouth; fer-de-lance; viper ℹ

Pius V, St, originally **Michele Ghislieri** (1504–72) Pope (1566–72), born near Alessandria, Italy. He implemented the decrees of the Council of Trent (1545–63), excommunicated Queen Elizabeth I (1570), and organized the expedition against the Turks (1571). He was canonized in 1712. Feast day 30 April. >> Lepanto, Battle of; Trent, Council of

Pius IX, known as **Pio Nono**, originally **Giovanni Maria Mastai-Ferretti** (1792–1878) Pope (1846–78), born in Senigallia, Papal States. He decreed the dogma of the Immaculate Conception in 1854, and called the Vatican Council (1869–79), which proclaimed papal infallibility. His pontificate is the longest in papal history. >> Immaculate Conception; infallibility; pope

Pius XI, originally **Ambrogio Damiano Achille Ratti** (1857–1939) Pope (1922–39), born in Desio, Italy. He signed the Lateran Treaty (1929), which brought into existence the Vatican State. >> pope; Vatican City

Pius XII, originally **Eugenio Maria Giuseppe Giovanni Pacelli** (1876–1958) Pope (1939–58), born in Rome. During World War 2 the Vatican did much humanitarian work, notably for prisoners of war and refugees; but there has been continuing controversy over his attitude to the treatment of the Jews in Nazi Germany, critics arguing that he could have used his influence with Catholic Germany to prevent the massacres, others that any attempt to do so would have proved futile and might have worsened the situation. >> Nazi Party; pope

pixel From *pic*ture *el*ement, the smallest resolved unit of a video image which has specific luminance and colour. Its proportions are determined by the number of lines making up the scanning raster and the resolution along each line. >> television

Pizarro, Francisco [pee**thah**roh] (c.1478–1541) Conquistador, born in Trujillo, Spain. In 1526 he and Almagro sailed for Peru, and in 1531 began the conquest of the Incas. Dissensions between Pizarro and Almagro led to the latter's execution. In revenge, Almagro's followers assassinated Pizarro at Lima. >> Almagro; Incas

PK >> **psychokinesis**

placebo [pla**see**boh] An inactive substance given as a drug to a patient, who may benefit from the belief that the drug is active. Because patients can improve under this illusion, in most countries new drugs are tested for clinical efficacy in trials where a placebo is given to one group.

placenta (anatomy) [pla**sen**ta] An organ which develops in the uterus of all pregnant mammals, except monetremes. It is attached to the uterus of the mother, and connected to the fetus by the umbilical cord. It secretes a number of hormones essential for pregnancy. >> chorionic villus sampling; hormones; umbilical cord; uterus ℹ

placenta (botany) [pla**sen**ta] Tissue to which the ovules or spores of plants are attached. The arrangement of ovules is termed **placentation**, and is an important diagnostic character in many plants. >> ovule; spore

Placid, Lake >> **Lake Placid**

Placodermi [**plak**odermee] An extinct class of primitive, jawed fishes known primarily from the Devonian period; large head covered by shield composed of bony plates; body heavily armoured. >> Devonian period; fish ℹ

plagioclase [**play**jioklayz] >> **feldspar**

plague The most notorious epidemic disease of all time, caused by infection with *Yersinia* (formerly *Pasteurella*) *pestis*, carried by fleas that infest rodents and squirrels which then bite humans. The features are those of a severe infection with the development of 'buboes', ie swollen, acutely inflamed lymph nodes; hence the name **bubonic plague**. In the 14th-c, outbreaks of plague (*black death*) killed half the population of Europe. >> lymph

plaice Common European flatfish (*Pleuronectes platessa*) widespread in continental shelf waters from N Norway to the Mediterranean; length up to 90 cm/3 ft; both eyes on right side; upper surface brown with orange spots, underside white; important food fish. (Family: Pleuronectidae.) >> flatfish

Plaid Cymru [pliyd **kuhm**ree] The Welsh National Party, founded in 1925, with the aim of achieving independence for Wales. It finds support mainly in the N of the country. >> nationalism

Plain, the, known as the *Marais* The majority of deputies in the French Revolutionary Convention, politically uncommitted to a particular faction, although broadly aligned with the Girondins. >> French Revolution ℹ; Girondins; Mountain, the

plainchant The unaccompanied, single-strand music to which the Mass and other parts of the Roman liturgy were sung (and to some extent still are). It is notated, without precise indications of rhythm, on a four-line staff. >> chant; Gregorian chant; liturgy; monody

Plains Indians North American Indian groups who lived on the Great Plains between the Mississippi R and the Rocky Mts in the USA and Canada. Most were nomadic or semi-nomadic buffalo hunters living together in small bands. White settlers finally destroyed their power, placing the surviving Indians in reservations. >> American Indians; Cheyenne (Indians); Comanche; Crow; nomadism; Omaha; Sioux

plainsong >> **plainchant**

plaintiff >> **defendant**

Planck, Max (Karl Ernst Ludwig) (1858–1947) Theoretical physicist, born in Kiel, Germany. His work on the second law of thermodynamics and blackbody radiation led him to abandon classical Newtonian principles and introduce the quantum theory (1900), for which he was awarded the Nobel Prize for Physics in 1918. >> Planck's constant; quantum field theory

Planck's constant A fundamental constant appearing in all equations of quantum theory; symbol h, value $6{\cdot}626 \times 10^{-34}$ J.s (joule.second); introduced by Max Planck in 1900. It relates the energy E of a quantum of light to its frequency ν by $E = h\nu$. >> fundamental constants; Planck

plane In mathematics, a surface such that if any two points in that surface are joined by a straight line, all the points on the straight line lie on the surface. The equation of a general plane in rectangular Cartesian co-ordinates is $ax + by + cz + d = 0$.

planet A nonluminous body gravitationally bound to the Sun or a star, and rotating in orbit in a prograde direction (ie counter-clockwise, viewed from N). The theory of planetary formation suggests that they condense from material left over during primary star formation. They should therefore be common, but they are extremely hard to detect (the first extrasolar planet, 52 Pegasi B, was detected in 1995, with others discovered in 1996). In the Solar System there are nine major planets and innumerable minor planets, or *asteroids*. The major planets comprise the *inner*, terrestrial planets (Mercury, Venus, Earth, Mars), and the giant gaseous *outer* planets (Jupiter, Saturn, Uranus, Neptune), together with unique, distant Pluto. All except Mercury and Venus have associated moons or, for the outer planets, systems of moons. All are believed to have been formed about 4.6 thousand million years ago. Jupiter is by far the most massive planet, containing over two-thirds of the material in the Solar System apart from the Sun. Many searches have been made for a tenth planet in our Solar System; if it exists, it is small and very remote. >> asteroids; Earth ℹ; exoplanet; Jupiter / Mars / Mercury / Neptune / Pluto / Saturn / Uranus / Venus (astronomy); Moon; Solar System; RR964

planetarium A special building with a dome in which a projector produces an impression of the stars in the night sky. A famous example is the London Planetarium.

planetary nebula A shell of glowing gas surrounding an evolved star, from which it was ejected. There is no connection with planets: the name derived from the visual similarity between the disc of such a nebula and the disc of a planet.

plane tree A tall, long-lived deciduous tree, native to S Europe, Asia, and especially North America; distinctive flaking bark, revealing large creamy or pink patches. (Genus: *Platanus*, 10 species. Family: Platanaceae.)

planimeter A mathematical instrument for measuring the area enclosed by an irregular curve. A pointer moved around the perimeter is connected by lever arms to an integrating mechanism.

plankton Organisms without effective means of locomotion; drifters. They have been subdivided into plant (**phytoplankton**) and animal (**zooplankton**) types. Most are microscopic in size. >> hydrobiology; nekton

planographic printing >> **printing** ℹ

plant An organism which typically uses sunlight as an energy source via photosynthetic pathways involving the green pigment chlorophyll (Kingdom: Plantae). Plants are mostly non-motile and lack obvious excretory and nervous systems, and sensory organs. They are eucaryotic, and typically possess cell walls composed largely of cellulose. >> botany; carnivorous / climbing / herbaceous / parasitic / pitcher / vascular plant; cell; chlorophyll; eucaryote; kingdom; photosynthesis

Plantagenets The name of the royal dynasty in England from Henry II to Richard II (1154–1399), then continued by two rival houses of younger lines, Lancaster and York, until 1485. The dynasty was so called because, allegedly, Henry II's father Geoffrey, Count of Anjou, sported a sprig of broom (Old Fr, *plante genêt*) in his cap. >> Edward I / II / III; Henry III (of England); John; Richard I

plantain 1 Typically an annual or perennial, sometimes a shrub, often a weed; very widespread; a rosette of narrow, strongly veined leaves; flowers tiny, with four brownish or green petals, packed into a dense, erect spike. (Genus: *Plantago*, 265 species. Family: Plantaginaceae.) **2** >> banana

Plantation of Ireland The colonization and conquest of Ireland, begun in 1556 and continued to 1660. The incomers were at first mainly English, but Scottish settlers moved to Ulster in 1608–11. The policy led to rebellions by the native Irish and the Anglo-Irish aristocracy, and the eventual conquest of Ireland under Cromwell, in which possibly two-thirds of the Irish died. >> Cromwell, Oliver

plant hopper A small, hopping insect that feeds by sucking sap or cell contents of plants; species include pests of economically important crops, such as rice and sugar cane. (Order: Homoptera. Family: Delphacidae, c.1300 species.) >> insect ℹ

plasma (physics) A fourth state of matter comprising a fluid of ions and free electrons, formed for example by the extreme heating of a gas, and characterized by powerful electrical forces between the particles. Plasma properties are studied in **plasma physics**. The main interest is the creation of controlled nuclear fusion, with the ultimate aim of power generation. >> electron; ion; magnetosphere; nuclear fusion; tokamak

plasma (physiology) [**plaz**ma] The fluid portion of whole blood, in which the blood cells are suspended. It transports nutrients, waste products, and chemicals involved in the clotting process, as well as hormones and drugs, to their target cells. >> myeloma; plasmapheresis

plasmapheresis [plazma**fe**resis] or **plasma exchange** The circulation of whole blood outside the body, during which centrifugal force separates the cells and plasma, which is replaced by fresh plasma or plasma albumin. The purpose is to remove a damaging plasma component such as an abnormal antibody. >> blood; myasthenia gravis; plasma (physiology)

plasma screen A form of display screen used with computers in which the screen can be made very flat. It is therefore suitable for notebook and laptop computers. >> laptop computer; notebook

Plasmodium [plaz**moh**dium] A genus of parasitic protozoans containing the micro-organisms that cause malaria in humans; life-cycle involves stages in an intermediate host, the mosquito, and stages in the blood or other organs of a final vertebrate host. (Phylum: Apicomplexa. Class: Sporozoa.) >> malaria; mosquito; parasitology; Protozoa

Plassey, Battle of [**pla**see] (1757) A decisive British victory under Clive over Siraj ud Daula, Nawab of Bengal, India. The victory was an important step in the British acquisition of Bengal. >> Clive

plaster >> **gypsum**

plastics Originally any soft, formable material; now commonly used for synthetic organic resins which can be softened by heating, and then shaped or cast. Some (called *thermoset*, eg phenol-formaldehyde resin) are then resistant to softening on further heating; others (called *thermoplastic*, eg polyethylene and polystyrene) may be repeatedly softened. Plastics may be designed with almost any desired property, ranging from great heat stability to rapid natural decomposition in soil, and from good electrical insulators to conductors. >> resin

plastic surgery The grafting of skin and subcutaneous tissue from a healthy site on the body to one that has suffered damage from disease, trauma, or burns. It also includes surgical operations undertaken for cosmetic purposes, such as face-lifting, reshaping noses, and removing unsightly fat. >> surgery

Plataea [pla**tee**a] **1** A Greek city-state in Boeotia, which shared with Athens the honour of defeating the Persians at Marathon. **2** The site in 479 BC of a decisive Greek victory over the Persians. >> Boeotia; Marathon; Persian Wars

Plate, River, Span **Río de la Plata** A wide, shallow estuary of the Paraná and Uruguay Rivers on the E coast of South America, between Argentina (S and W shore) and Uruguay (N shore); area 35 000 sq km/13 510 sq mi; length 320 km/200 mi; width 220 km/140 mi at its mouth and 45 km/28 mi at Buenos Aires; scene of a naval engagement (Dec 1939) between three out-gunned British cruisers and the formidable German pocket-battleship *Graf Spee* (**Battle of the River Plate**); the *Graf Spee* inexplicably disengaged, and was trapped in the neutral port of Montevideo, to be scuttled a few days later. >> Paraná, River; Uruguay, River

Plateau Indians North American Indian groups who lived on the plateau between the Rocky Mts and the Cascade Range. Most groups lived in camps during the summer, hunting and fishing; during the severe winters, they sheltered in villages located along the rivers. During the 19th-c European settlers fought with the Indians over land, forcing the survivors into reservations. >> American Indians; Chinook; Salish

platelets Small disc-like structures (2–4 μ in diameter) found in the blood of all mammals, produced in bone marrow. They contain factors important in the arrest of bleeding and in wound healing. >> bone marrow

plate tectonics A model of the structure and dynamics of the Earth's crust, developed in the 1960s to explain such observations as continental drift, mid-ocean ridges, the distribution of earthquakes, and volcanic activity. The theory proposes that the Earth's lithosphere is made up of a number of relatively thin, rigid plates which may include both continental and ocean crust and which move relative to one another. Plate boundaries are defined by major earthquake zones and belts of volcanic activity. Plate collisions result in the formation of mountain belts such as the Alps and Himalayas. >> continental drift; Earth ℹ; earthquake; lithosphere; orogeny; *see illustration p. 676*

platform tennis A variation of paddle tennis, a cross between lawn tennis and squash. It is a popular outdoor winter sport in the USA. >> squash rackets; tennis, lawn ℹ

Plath, Sylvia (1932–63) Poet, born in Boston, MA. She married Ted Hughes in 1956. Her first collection *The Colossus* appeared in 1960, and a novel *The Bell Jar* in 1963, shortly before she committed suicide in London. Her *Collected Poems*, edited by Hughes, appeared in 1981. >> Hughes, Ted

platinum Pt, element 78, density 21.5 g/cm^3, melting point 1772°C. A precious metal, which occurs occasionally uncombined but more importantly as a sulphide. Similar to gold in its unreactivity, it is used for jewellery and for laboratory vessels. >> chemical elements; hydrogenation; metal; platinum metals; RR1036

platinum metals A series of elements which occur together in nature, and have similar properties: ruthenium (Ru), rhodium (Rh), palladium (Pd), osmium (Os), iridium (Ir), and platinum (Pt). >> chemical elements; RR1036

Plato (c.428–347 BC) Greek philosopher, probably born in Athens of an aristocratic family. He became a disciple of Socrates, who appears in most of Plato's 35 dialogues, then before 368 BC founded his own Academy at Athens. In the *early* dialogues, the main interlocutor is Socrates, and the main interest is the definition of moral concepts (eg courage in *Laches*). In the *middle* dialogues, Plato increasingly outlines his own doctrines (eg the theory of forms in the *Republic*). The *later* dialogues express his rigorous self-criticism (eg the *Sophist*). Taken as a whole, his philosophy has been so enormously influential that the whole subsequent Western tradition was described by Whitehead as a series of 'footnotes to Plato'. >> Aristotle; Neoplatonism; Platonism; Socrates; Sophists

Platonic solids In mathematics, solids whose faces are congruent regular polygons. There are five such solids: the *tetrahedron* (four faces, each an equilateral triangle);

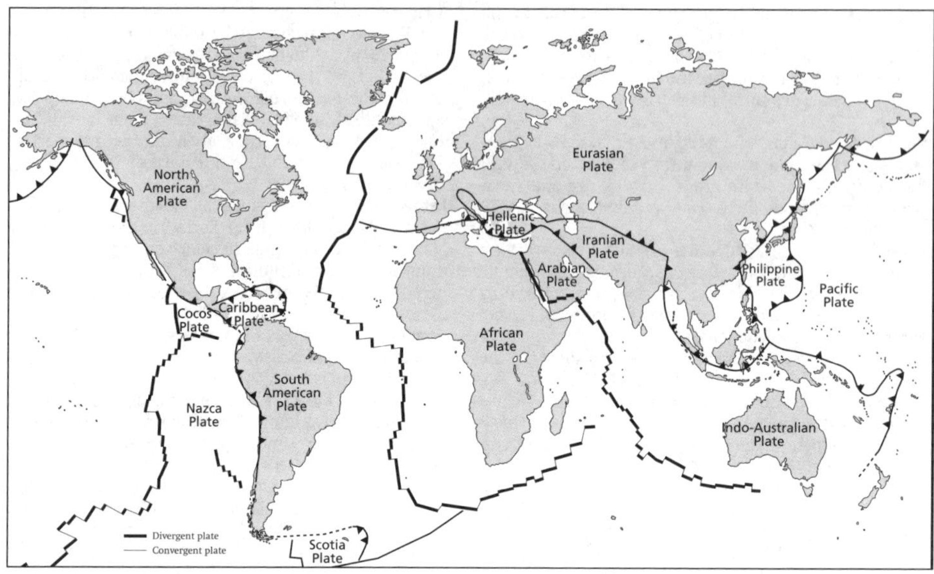

Plate tectonics – major lithospheric plates

the *cube* (six faces, each a square); the *octahedron* (eight faces, each a pentagon); the *dodecahedron* (12 faces, each a hexagon); and the *icosahedron* (20 faces, each an equilateral triangle). All five were described by Plato. >> Plato; polygon

Platt, David (Andrew) (1966–) Footballer, born in Chadderton, Greater Manchester. A midfielder, he played for Crewe Alexandra, Aston Villa, Bari, Juventus, Sampdoria, and Arsenal, and won 62 caps for England (captain, 1994–6). Retiring as a player in 1998, he became coach of Sampdoria, but left after seven weeks.

Platyhelminthes [plateе**hel**minths] A phylum of flattened, worm-like animals comprising parasitic groups, such as the tapeworms (Class: Cestoda) and flukes (Class: Trematoda), and free-living groups, such as the planarians (Class: Tricladida). >> fluke; parasitology; systematics; tapeworm; worm

platypus >> **duck-billed platypus**

Plautus, Titus Maccius [**plaw**tus] (c.250–184 BC) Comic playwright, born in Sarsina, Italy. About 130 plays have been attributed to him, but many are thought to be the work of earlier playwrights which he revised. Varro limited the genuine comedies to 21, and these 'Varronian comedies' are the ones which have survived. >> Varro

Player, Gary (Jim) (1935–) Golfer, born in Johannesburg, South Africa, whose major wins span four decades (1950s–1980s). His successes include the (British) Open (1959, 1968, 1974), the US Open (1965), and the US Masters (1961, 1974, 1978).

player piano A mechanism attached to a piano (or a piano fitted with such a mechanism) in which a perforated roll passes over a brass 'tracker bar' and causes those keys to be depressed to which the perforations correspond. The mechanism is driven by suction generated by pedals operated by the player's feet. >> keyboard instrument; piano; pianola

playing cards Small rectangular cards used for playing card games. A standard pack contains 52 cards divided into four *suits*; hearts, clubs, diamonds, and spades. Each suit is subdivided into 13 cards numbered as follows: ace, 2–10, and the court (or picture) cards, jack, queen, and king. Most packs also contain two cards known as jokers, which can be given any value, but they are used in very few games. The earliest playing cards were used in China in the 10th-c. The pack was standardized at 52 in the 15th-c. >> baccarat; bézique; blackjack; bridge (recreation); canasta; chemin de fer; cribbage; pinochle; poker; pontoon; rummy; tarot; whist

plea bargaining A controversial administrative device of resolving criminal cases, in which the defendant pleads guilty to a lesser offence or one carrying a lighter punishment, with the consent of the court and the prosecution, in order to conserve resources by moving cases through the system more quickly. It is controversial, because there is concern that the innocent might plead guilty to secure lesser sentences, to avoid long trials, or under pressure from their lawyers; conversely, when cases are disposed of without a complete disclosure of all the facts, defendants may escape with lighter sentences. >> criminal law

Pleasence, Sir Donald [**ple**zuhns] (1919–95) Actor, born in Worksop, Nottinghamshire. He scored a huge success as the malevolent tramp, Davies, in Harold Pinter's *The Caretaker* (1960), and appeared in many films, often as a villain, such as *Dr Crippen* (1962) and *Cul-de-Sac* (1966).

plebeians [ple**bee**anz] or **plebs** In early Rome, citizens other than the patricians, who were the ruling elite. By the late Republic, some plebeian clans (such as the Claudians) had come to be part of the ruling aristocracy. >> patricians

plebiscite >> **referendum**

Plecoptera [ple**kop**tera] >> **stonefly**

plectrum A short length of metal, tortoise-shell, ivory, plastic, or other material worn on the fingers or held between them, to pluck a string instrument such as the guitar and mandolin. >> string instrument 2 ℹ

Pléiade, La [play**ad**] (Fr 'the Pleiades') A group of French poets of the 16th-c who sought to emancipate the French language (and literature) from mediaevalism by introducing Greek and Latin models. The best known were Ronsard and du Bellay (1522–60). >> Ronsard

Pleiades (astronomy) [**plee**adeez, **pliy**adeez] An open cluster of stars in Taurus, familiarly known as the **Seven Sisters**. Distance: 125 parsec. >> Taurus

Pleiades (mythology) [**pliy**adeez] In Greek mythology, the seven daughters of Atlas and Pleione: Maia, Taygete, Elektra, Alkyone, Asterope, Kelaino, and Merope. >> Orion (mythology)

Pleistocene epoch [**pliy**stoseen] The earlier of the two geological epochs of the Quaternary period, from 2 million years ago to 10 000 years ago; termed the *Ice Age* in the N hemisphere. It was marked by the evolution of man and familiar mammalian life. >> geological time scale; glaciation; Ice Age; Quaternary period; RR976

Plekhanov, Georgiy Valentinovich [ple**kah**nof] (1856–1918) Marxist philosopher, historian, and journalist, 'the father of Russian Marxism', born in Gundalovka, Russia. He was a major intellectual influence on the young Lenin, but denounced the October Revolution. >> Lenin; Marxism; October Revolution

plesiosaur [**ples**iosaw(r)] A marine reptile known from the Mesozoic era; body broad and compact, with large limbs developed as paddles; neck typically long, head small with a long snout bearing sharp teeth. (Order: Sauropterygia.) >> Mesozoic era; pliosaur; reptile

pleurisy [**ploo**rizee] Inflammation of membranes in the chest cavity (*pleura*) by micro-organisms, especially bacteria or viruses. It induces sharp pain on one or other side of the chest, aggravated by breathing. >> empyema; lungs

Plimsoll, Samuel (1824–98) Social reformer, 'the sailors' friend', born in Bristol. He caused the Merchant Shipping Act (1876) to be passed. Every owner was ordered to mark upon the side of a ship a circular disc (the **Plimsoll line**), with a horizontal line drawn through its centre, down to which the vessel might be loaded.

Pliny (the Elder), in full **Gaius Plinius Secundus** (23–79) Roman scholar, born in Novum Comum (Como), Gaul. He wrote a 37-volume encyclopedia, the *Historia Naturalis* (77, Natural History), his only work to survive.

Pliny (the Younger), in full **Gaius Plinius Caecilius Secundus** (c.62–c.114) Roman writer and administrator, born in Novum Comum (Como), Gaul, who became the adopted son of Pliny the Elder. He was the master of the epistolary style, his many letters providing an insight into the life of the upper class in the 1st-c.

Pliocene epoch [**pliy**oseen] The last of the geological epochs of the Tertiary period, from 5 to 2 million years ago and immediately preceding the Pleistocene epoch. >> geological time scale; Tertiary period; RR976

pliosaur [**pliy**osaw(r)] A powerfully built plesiosaur known from Mesozoic seas; short neck and enormous head. (Order: Sauropterygia.) >> Mesozoic era; plesiosaur

PLO (Palestine Liberation Organization) An umbrella organization for the diverse factions seeking the creation of a Palestinian state in part or the whole of British Mandated Palestine. **Fatah**, the Movement for the Liberation of Palestine, founded by Yasser Arafat, is the largest of the groups. After its withdrawal from Beirut during the Israeli siege of 1982, the PLO was based in Tunis. Since 1988 it has called for a two-state solution to the Palestinian–Israeli dispute, and in 1993 signed an agreement with Israel formally recognizing the state of Palestine. >> Arafat; Fatah; Palestine

Ploieşti [plo**yesht**] 44°57N 26°01E, pop (1995e) 248 000. City in SC Romania; railway; major centre for the petroleum industry. >> Romania ℹ

Plotinus [plo**tiy**nus] (c.205–70) Philosopher, the founder of Neoplatonism, probably born in Lycopolis in Egypt. His 54 works were edited by his pupil, Porphyry, who arranged them in six groups of nine books, or *Enneads*. >> Neoplatonism; Plato; Porphyry

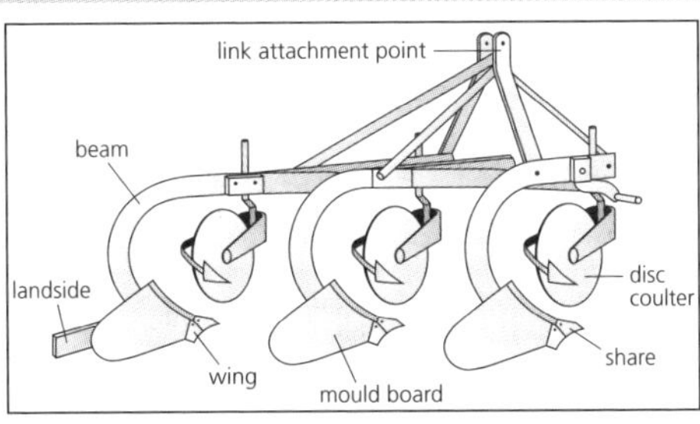

Plough – A three-furrow mounted plough, showing the three ploughing bodies attached to a steel frame. Each body consists of a *coulter*, which cuts a vertical slice, and a *share*, which makes a horizontal cut underneath; the slice is then turned by the *mould board*. The lateral accuracy and stability of each body is maintained by a *landslide*.

Plough, the A familiar pattern of seven bright stars within Ursa Major; also called the **Big Dipper** (chiefly US) and **Charles's Wain**. The two stars furthest from the handle (the Pointers) point almost directly to Polaris, the North Star. >> Polaris; Ursa Major

plough An implement used for turning over the soil into ridges and furrows, so that surface vegetation is buried and seed-bed preparation can begin. Modern ploughs are made of steel and are tractor-drawn. >> stump-jump plough; tractor

Plovdiv [**plov**dif], formerly **Philippopoli**, Lat **Evmolpia**, Thracian **Pulpudeva** 42°08N 24°25E, pop (1995e) 361 000. City in C Bulgaria; on the R Maritsa; airport; railway; second largest city in Bulgaria; Roman amphitheatre. >> Bulgaria ℹ

plover A small to medium-sized bird, found worldwide; short tail, long legs; bill straight, same length as head; includes lapwings and dotterels. (Family: Charadriidae, 63 species.) >> lapwing; oystercatcher; thick-knee; wrybill

Plowright, Joan >> **Olivier, Laurence**

plum Any of various species of the genus *Prunus*. The widely grown plum of orchards (*Prunus domestica*) is a small deciduous tree or shrub; ovoid yellow, red, purplish, or black fruit; sweet flesh enclosing a large stone. (Family: Rosaceae.) >> blackthorn; bullace; damson; prunus

pluralism Any metaphysical theory which is committed to the ultimate existence of two or more kinds of things. For example, mind–body dualists, such as Descartes, are pluralists. >> Descartes; dualism; metaphysics; monism

Plutarch [**ploo**tah(r)k], Gr **Ploutarchos** (c.46–c.120) Historian, biographer, and philosopher, born in Chaeronea, Boeotia, Greece. His extant writings comprise a series of essays on ethical, political, religious, and other topics, and several historical works, notably *Bioi paralleloi* (Parallel Lives), a gallery of 46 portraits of the great characters of preceding ages. North's translation of this work into English (1579) was the source of Shakespeare's Roman plays. >> North, Thomas

Pluto (astronomy) The ninth and most distant planet from the Sun, smaller than our Moon, discovered in 1930 by Clyde Tombaugh after an extensive search. It is accompanied by a large moon, Charon, discovered in 1978. The two objects may be escaped satellites of Neptune. Pluto's known characteristics are: mass 0·002 of Earth; radius 1150 km/715 mi; mean density 2·0 g/cm^3; inclination of equator 120°; rotational period 6·387 days; orbital period 248·5 years; eccentricity of orbit 0·248; mean distance from the Sun 39·53 AU. There is a thin atmosphere of methane gas. >> Charon (astronomy); planet; Solar System; Tombaugh

Pluto (mythology) In Greek mythology, originally the god of wealth, **Plutos**. The name later became a synonym for Hades. >> Hades

plutonium Pu, element 94, essentially a synthetic element, density 19.8 g/cm^3, melting point 641 °C. First prepared by a neutron bombardment of uranium, its most stable isotope (^{238}Pu) has a half-life of nearly 25 000 years. It is mainly important as a fissile nuclear fuel. >> chemical elements; nuclear reactor [i]; uranium; RR1036

Plymouth (Montserrat) [**plim**uhth] 16°44N 62°14W, pop (1995e) 3540. Port capital of Montserrat, E Caribbean. >> Montserrat

Plymouth (UK) [**plim**uhth] 50°23N 4°10W, pop (1995e) 263 000. Seaport and (from 1998) unitary authority in Devon, SW England; at the confluence of the Tamar and Plym Rivers; Pilgrim Fathers set out from here in the *Mayflower*, 1620; severe bombing in World War 2; major base for the Royal Navy; ferry links to Santander, Roscoff, and St Malo; railway; airfield; university, 1992; Plymouth Hoe, where Drake is said to have finished his game of bowls before leaving to fight the Spanish Armada; Eddystone Lighthouse 22 km/ 14 mi offshore; football league team, Plymouth Argyle (Pilgrims). >> Devon; Drake; Pilgrims; Spanish Armada

Plymouth (USA) [**plim**uhth] 41°57N 70°40W, pop (1995e) 46 000. Town in SE Massachusetts, USA; first permanent European settlement in New England, founded by Pilgrims in 1620; railway; 'living history' community at Plimouth Plantation. >> Massachusetts; Pilgrims

Plymouth Brethren A religious sect founded by a group of Christian evangelicals in 1829 in Dublin, Ireland. It spread to England, where in 1832 a meeting was established at Plymouth, Devon. Millenarian in outlook, the sect is characterized by a simplicity of belief, practice, and style of life based on the New Testament. >> Christianity; evangelicalism; millenarianism

Plynlimon Fawr [plin**li**mon **vowr**] 52°28N 3°47W. Mountain rising to 752 m/2467 ft on the Cardiganshire–Powys border, C Wales, UK. >> Wales [i]

Plzeň [**puhl**zen], Ger **Pilsen** 49°40N 13°10E, pop (1995e) 176 000. Industrial city in Czech Republic; railway. >> Czech Republic [i]

pneumococcus [nyoomoh**kok**us] A common name for the bacterium *Streptococcus pneumoniae*, one of the causative agents of pneumonia. (Kingdom: Monera. Family: Streptococcaceae.) >> bacteria [i]; *Streptococcus*

pneumoconiosis [nyoomohkon**yoh**sis] A lung disease caused by the inhalation of air containing dust particles. A common industrial disorder, it occurs among coal and other miners and sand-blasters. >> lungs; occupational disease

pneumonia [nyoo**moh**nia] Inflammation of the lungs from infection by bacteria or viruses. In contrast to bronchitis, the infection involves the terminal alveolar saccules deep in the lungs, where oxygen exchange normally takes place. It is usually an acute illness of sudden onset, often with shortness of breath and pleurisy. >> bronchitis; lungs; pleurisy

pneumothorax [nyoomoh**thaw**raks] The occurrence of air between the two layers of pleura surrounding each lung (the *pleural space*). This separates the two layers and, depending on the amount, impairs ventilation. >> lungs

Po, River [poh], ancient **Padus**, Gr **Eridanos** River in N Italy, rising in the Cottian Alps; enters the Adriatic Sea; length 652 km/405 mi; longest river in Italy; its valley is the most fertile agricultural region in the country. >> Italy [i]

Pocahontas [pohka**hon**tas], personal name **Matoaka** (1595–1617) American-Indian princess, the daughter of an Indian chief, Powhatan, who twice saved the life of Captain John Smith, leader of a group of colonists who settled in Chesapeake Bay in 1607. She embraced Christianity, was baptised Rebecca, married an Englishman, John Rolfe (1585–1622), and went to England with him in 1616.

pochard [**poh**cherd] A duck of the worldwide tribe, Aythyini (15 species), comprising the diving-duck genera *Aythya* and *Netta*. It nests on the ground. >> white-eye

pocket borough British parliamentary boroughs, especially before the First Reform Act (1832), which were directly controlled by one landed proprietor. >> parliament; Reform Acts; rotten borough

pocket phone A portable telephone handset, used with a cellular radio or other mobile communication system, small enough to fit into the pocket. It enables users to make direct-dial telephone calls wherever they are. >> mobile communications; telephone

Podgorica [pod**go**ritsa], formerly **Titograd** (1946–92) 42°28N 19°17E, pop (1995e) 119 000. Capital of Montenegro on R Morava; badly damaged in World War 2; originally named after Marshal Tito; airfield; railway; university (1973). >> Montenegro; Tito; Yugoslavia [i]

podiatry [po**diy**atree] >> **chiropody**

Poe, Edgar Allan (1809–49) Poet and story writer, born in Boston, MA. He became known with *Tales of the Grotesque and Arabesque* (1840), and several short stories, notably 'The Murders in the Rue Morgue' (1841), the first detective story. His weird and fantastic stories, dwelling by choice on the horrible, were both original and influential. His poem 'The Raven' (1845) won immediate fame. >> Gothic novel

poetic licence The poet's practice of taking liberty with known facts in the interests of telling a more interesting or more effective story. The historical Hotspur was 20 years older than Prince Henry; in *Henry IV*, for dramatic purposes, Shakespeare makes them the same age. >> figurative language; Realism

Poet Laureate A poet appointed by the British sovereign with the duty (no longer obligatory) of writing verse upon significant royal and national occasions. The first was John Dryden, who held office 1668–88. The post is now also recognized in the USA.

poetry (Gr *poiein* 'to make') Originally, any creative literary work; the term is still so defined in Shelley's *Defence of Poetry* (1821). With the development and diversification of literary forms, 'poetry' came to be used for metrical composition in any mode, as distinct from writing in prose. But the weakening of such distinctions (with the prose poem and the poetic novel) has meant that a strict separation is not maintainable. The theory and practice of poetry, concerning itself with such fundamental questions as what poetry is, what it does, and how it should be written, is known as **poetics**. >> concrete / confessional / metaphysical / skaldic poetry; Cavalier / Lake / Liverpool poets; metre (literature)

Pohnpei >> **Ponape**

poikilotherm [poy**kil**ohtherm] An animal that has no internal mechanism for regulating body temperature, so that it fluctuates with changes in ambient temperatures. It is often termed *cold-blooded*, but body temperatures may be maintained at a high level as a result of activity, or by behaviour patterns such as basking. >> temperature [i]

Poincaré, (Jules) Henri [pwīkaray] (1854–1912) Mathematician, born in Nancy, France. He created the theory of automorphic functions, using new ideas from group theory, non-Euclidean geometry, and complex function theory. In a 1889 paper he originated the theory of chaos, and contributed many of the basic ideas to such fields as topology, triangulation, and homology. >> chaos

Poincaré, Raymond (Nicolas Landry) [pwīkaray] (1860–1934) French statesman, prime minister (1912–13,

1922–4, 1926–9), and president (1913–20), born in Bar-le-Duc, France. His national union ministry averted ruin in 1926. >> France 🛈

poinsettia [poyn**set**ia] A deciduous shrub native to Mexico (*Euphorbia pulcherrima*). The flower is in fact a specialized inflorescence (*cyathium*) with large vermilion bracts resembling petals. (Family: Euphorbiaceae.) >> bract; inflorescence 🛈; spurge

Pointe-à-Pitre [pwĩt a **pee**truh] 16°14N 61°32W, pop (1995e) 99 100. Seaport and capital town of Guadeloupe, on SW coast of island of Grande-Terre; airport. >> Guadeloupe

Pointe-Noire [pwĩt **nwah(r)**] 4°48S 11°53E, pop (1995e) 498 000. Seaport in SW Congo, W Africa; W terminus of railway from Brazzaville; airfield; centre of Congo's oil industry. >> Congo 🛈

pointer A sporting dog belonging to one of several breeds developed to detect game; stands rigidly, like a statue, with the muzzle pointing towards the prey animal. >> setter; sporting dog

Pointers >> **Plough, the**

Pointillism >> **Divisionism**

point-to-point An event featuring horse races for amateur riders over a cross-country course, normally on farmland. Original courses went from one point to another, hence the name, but are now often over circular or oval courses with a mixture of artificial and natural fences. >> horse racing

poise [pwahz] Unit of (dynamic) viscosity; symbol *P*; a viscosity of 1 poise equals a pressure of 0.1 Pa (pascal) applied for 1 second; named after French physician Jean-Louis-Marie Poiseuille (1799–1869). >> viscosity; RR1031

poison-arrow frog >> **arrow-poison frog**

poison gas Chemical munitions fired in artillery shells or released from containers which spread toxic or disabling gases onto the battlefield. Such gases (used in World War 1) included mustard, phosgene, and chlorine. >> chemical warfare

poison ivy A shrub or woody vine, native to North America (*Rhus toxicodendron*); leaves with three leaflets, sometimes resembling oak leaves, hence the alternative name, **poison oak**, regarded as a separate species by some authorities; flowers white. All parts produce a resin containing the chemical urushinol, which is poisonous to the touch, causing severe dermatitis. (Family: Anacardiaceae.) >> dermatitis; resin; sumac

poison oak >> **poison ivy**

Poisson, Siméon Denis [pwasõ] (1781–1840) Mathematician, born in Pithiviers, France. He is known for his research into celestial mechanics, electromagnetism, and also probability, where he established the law governing the distribution of large numbers (the **Poisson distribution**). >> statistics

Poitier, Sidney [**pwa**tyay] (1924–) Actor and director, born in Miami, FL. His films include *Lilies of the Field* (1963, Oscar), *In the Heat of the Night* (1967), and *One Man One vote* (1997). He has also directed a number of lowbrow comedies, such as *Stir Crazy* (1980) and *Ghost Dad* (1990).

Poitiers [**pwat**yay] 46°35N 0°20E, pop (1995e) 85 000. Market town in W France; Roman settlement; former capital of Poitou; site of French defeat by English, 1356; road and railway junction; bishopric; university (1431); 4th-c Baptistry (France's oldest Christian building), cathedral (12th–13th-c). >> France 🛈; Poitou

Poitou [pwatoo] Former province in W France; chief town, Poitiers; held by England until 1369. >> Poitiers

poker A gambling card game for two to eight players which started in the USA in the 19th-c. The object is to get (or convince your opponents that you have) a better hand than theirs. There are several varieties. >> playing cards

Pokhara Valley [**poh**kara] Valley in Nepal, C Asia; town of Pokhara at an altitude of 913 m/2995 ft; road and air flights from Kathmandu. >> Himalayas; Nepal 🛈

Poland, Polish **Polska**, official name **The Republic of Poland** pop (1995e) 39 003 000; area 312 683 sq km/120 695 sq mi. Republic in C Europe; coastline 491 km/305 mi; capital, Warsaw; timezone GMT +1; population mainly Polish, of W Slavic descent; chief religion, Roman Catholicism (94%); official language, Polish; unit of currency, the zloty of 100 groszy; mostly part of the great European plain, with the Carpathian and Sudetes Mts (S) rising in the High Tatra to 2500 m/8200 ft at Mt Rysy; richest coal basin in Europe in the W (Silesia); flat Baltic coastal area; main rivers, the Vistula and Oder; forests cover a fifth of the land; continental climate, with severe winters and hot summers; emergence as a powerful Slavic group, 11th-c; united with Lithuania, 1569; divided between Prussia, Russia, and Austria, 1772, 1793, 1795; semi-independent state after Congress of Vienna, 1815; incorporated into the Russian Empire; independent Polish state after World War 1; partition between Germany and the USSR, 1939; invasion by Germany, 1939; major resistance movement, and a government in exile during World War 2; People's Democracy established under Soviet influence, 1944; rise of independent trade union, Solidarity, in 1980; state of martial law imposed, 1981–3; loss of support for communist government and major success for Solidarity in 1989 elections; constitution amended in 1989 to provide for a 2-chamber legislature; nearly 50% of the land under cultivation; major producer of coal. >> Jagiellons; Solidarity; Walesa; Warsaw; RR1020 political leaders

Polanski, Roman [po**lan**skee] (1933–) Film director, scriptwriter, and actor, born in Paris of Polish parents. He made his first Hollywood film *Rosemary's Baby* in 1968, exploring the nature of evil and personal corruption. After the murder of his wife in the Manson killings in 1969, he went through a troubled period and left the USA

under a cloud. Later productions include *Frantic* (1988), and *Bitter Moon* (1992).

Polanyi, Michael [po**lan**yee] (1891–1976) Physical chemist and social philosopher, born in Budapest. He did notable work on reaction kinetics and crystal structure, and wrote much on the freedom of scientific thought, philosophy of science, and social science.

polar bear A bear native to the Arctic ice pack and surrounding seas (*Thalarctos maritimus*); white with long neck and small head; swims well. >> bear

Polar Circle >> **Arctic Circle**

Polaris [po**lah**ris] The brightest star in the constellation Ursa Minor, currently lying (by chance) within 1° of the N celestial pole; also called the **Pole Star**. This star was much used for simple navigation. >> Poles

Polaris missile [poh**lah**ris] A first-generation US submarine-launched ballistic missile under development from the mid-1950s. It is no longer operational with the US Navy, but a modified version will continue with the Royal Navy's four Polaris-equipped submarines, until replaced by the Trident system. >> ballistic missile; Trident missile

polarity therapy A form of therapy devised by Randolph Stone (1890–1983), who taught that the body has five energy centres corresponding to the five elements (earth, water, fire, air, and ether), and that most illnesses are caused by a blockage in the flow of energy between these centres. >> alternative medicine

polarization A property of (transverse) waves in which wave oscillations occur in a direction which is either constant or varies in a well-defined way. Illustration (a) shows a wave moving in *x* direction along a rope, polarized in the *y* direction, and Illustration (b) in the *z* direction. These are both linear polarizations, since each portion of rope moves up and down in straight lines. Polarization in electromagnetic radiation (including light) is dictated by the electric part of the wave. Skylight, reflected light, and scattered light are all (partially) polarized. >> birefringence

Polaroid 1 A trade name for doubly refracting material; developed by US physicist Edwin Land in 1938. A plastic sheet is strained so as to align its molecules, thus making it refract light preferentially, ie linearly polarized in one direction, otherwise it is absorbed. It is familiar in sun-glasses to reduce the glare from light polarized on reflection. >> polarization 🄸; refraction **2** The trade name of an instant photography system developed by Land for black-and-white (1948) and colour (1963). The film is processed with viscous chemical reacting substances applied in the camera immediately after exposure. >> Land; photography

polder [**pol**der] A Dutch term for a flat area of land reclaimed from the sea or a river flood-plain, and protected from flooding by dykes (eg the partial reclamation of the Zuider Zee in The Netherlands). >> IJsselmeer

Pole, Reginald, Cardinal (1500–58) Roman Catholic archbishop, born at Stourton Castle, Staffordshire. He opposed Henry VIII on divorce, lost all his preferments, and went to Italy, where he was made a cardinal (1536). In the reign of the Catholic Queen Mary, he returned to England as papal legate, became one of her most powerful advisers, returned the country to Rome, and became Archbishop of Canterbury. >> Henry VIII; Mary I; Reformation

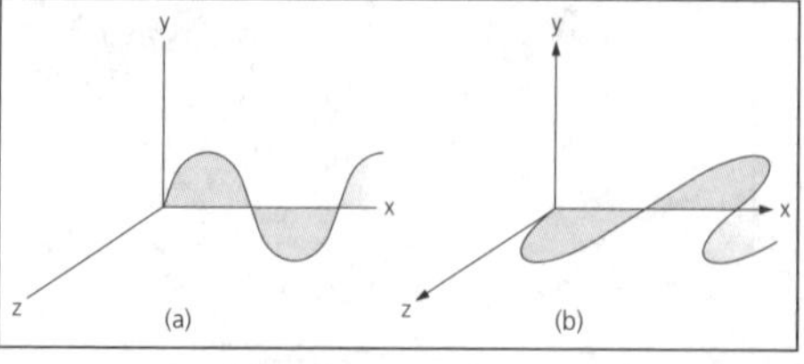

Polarization

pole >> **magnetic poles; Poles**

polecat A mammal of family Mustelidae; resembles a large weasel (length, 60 cm/24 in); dark with pale marks on face and ear tips. (Genus: *Mustela*, 2 species.) >> ferret; Mustelidae; skunk; weasel; zorilla

Poles The two diametrically opposite points at which the Earth's axis cuts the Earth's surface; known as the **geographical poles**. The North Pole is covered by the Arctic Ocean, and the South Pole by the land mass of Antarctica. The **magnetic poles** are the positions towards which the needle of a magnetic compass will point. The South Pole was first reached by Amundsen on 14 December 1911, a month before the British team, led by Scott, which arrived on 17 January 1912; the North Pole was first reached by Robert E Peary on 6 April 1909. >> Amundsen; Earth 🄸; magnetic poles; Peary; Scott, Robert

Pole Star >> **Polaris**

pole vault An athletics field event; a jumping contest for height using a fibreglass pole for leverage to clear a bar. The current indoor world record for men is 6.15 m/20 ft 2 in, achieved by Sergey Bubka (Ukraine) in 1993; for women, it is 4.55 m/14 ft 7 in, achieved by Emma George (Australia) in 1998. >> athletics

Poliakoff, Stephen [**pol**yakof] (1952–) Playwright and film director, born in London. He made his debut as a playwright in 1974 with *Clever Soldiers*; later works include *Breaking the Silence* (1984), *Playing with Trains* (1989), and *Blinded by the Sun* (1996). He wrote and directed the film *Close My Eyes* (1991) and the television play *Shooting the Past* (1999).

police The group of persons responsible for and concerned with the enforcement of law and maintenance of civil order. The police receive their authority from the legislature and act in the public interest. In addition to national forces, there are a number of specialized police forces concerned with the security and protection of particular areas, such as military establishments or railway stations. >> CID; Crown Prosecution Service; Federal Bureau of Investigation; HOLMES; Interpol; KGB; Mounties; Peel; procurator fiscal; Scotland Yard; sheriff; Special Branch; Sûreté

policy unit A small group of officials in a government department, or other public agency, whose role is to supply information, advice, and analysis to policy-makers, normally politicians.

Polignac, Auguste Jules Armand Marie, prince de [poleenyak] (1780–1847) French statesman, born in Versailles, France. He became in 1829 head of the last Bourbon ministry, which promulgated the St Cloud Ordinances that cost Charles X his throne (1830). >> July Revolution

poliomyelitis [**poh**liohmiye**liy**tis] An infection by a virus that predominantly affects the motor neurone cells in the spinal cord; also known as **infantile paralysis** or simply **polio**. The features are those of an infectious disease which, in some cases, is followed by widespread muscle paralysis. A vaccine taken by mouth is effective. >> Sabin; Salk; spinal cord; virus

polis [**pol**is, **pol**ays] (plural **poleis**) Conventionally translated 'city-state', the principal political and economic unit of classical Greece (eg Athens, Corinth, Thebes, Sparta). Always self-governing, they were usually economically self-sufficient as well. >> Corinth; oligarchy; Sparta (Greek history); Thebes

Polish >> **Slavic languages**

Polish Corridor An area of formerly German territory granted to Poland by the Treaty of Versailles (1919). It divided E Prussia from the rest of Germany, and its recovery was one of Hitler's aspirations during the late 1930s. >> Hitler; Poland ℹ

Politburo [**pol**itbyooroh] The Political Bureau of the Central Committee of the Communist Party of the Soviet Union; at various times, known as the **Presidium**. It was the highest organ of the party. Elected by the Central Committee, there were 12 members plus seven candidate members who had no votes, but in practice membership was decided by the politburo itself under the General Secretary, who presided over it. >> Communist Party of the Soviet Union

political action committee A non-party organization in the USA, which contributes money to candidates for public office. The committees are created by various organized interests, such as unions, trade associations, and groups with strong political beliefs.

political correctness A pejorative term for the view which demands that all instances of real or perceived linguistic discrimination against social groups should be eradicated. The movement, espoused especially by US political liberals, has focused on those aspects of language which seem to preserve demeaning attitudes towards disadvantaged or oppressed groups, such as the use of *black* with negative overtones (as in the idiom *be in my black books*). The most sensitive domains are to do with race (racism), gender (sexism), sexual affinity, ecology, and (physical or mental) personal development. The view was at first supported by many concerned with the rights of minorities, but by attracting extremists it has attracted increasing antagonism and ridicule (eg people who are less than beautiful might be described as 'aesthetically challenged'). The inflexible condemnation of 'incorrect' vocabulary has itself been condemned for its intolerance, reminding some of the 'thought police' of futuristic novels. >> racism; sexism

political economy The name given to economics in the late 18th-c and early 19th-c. The term has not been much used in the present century, reflecting the fact that the scope of economics is today much wider, dealing with many more issues than national economic affairs and the role of government. >> economics

political philosophy The philosophical study both of the concepts, values, and arguments used in political science and of the substantive issues involved in the exercise and distribution of political power. It addresses such issues as the nature of the state, the relations between Church and state, individual rights, democracy, and law and freedom. >> political science

political science The academic discipline which describes and analyses the operations of government, the state, and other political organizations, and any other factors which influence their behaviour, such as economics. A major concern is to establish how power is exercised, and by whom, in resolving conflict within society. **Political theory** (of which **political philosophy** is a subbranch) has two principal concerns: the clarification of values in order to demonstrate the purpose of political activity, and thereby the way in which society 'ought' to proceed (eg in allocating resources); and the testing of theories drawn from empirical research.

politics >> **political science**

Polk, James K(nox) (1795–1849) US statesman and 11th president (1845–9), born in Mecklenburg Co, NC. During his presidency, Texas was admitted to the Union (1845), and after the Mexican War (1846–7) the USA acquired California and New Mexico. >> Mexican War

polka A quick dance of Bohemian origin, in duple metre, with an accent on the second beat. It was a favourite 19th-c ballroom dance.

poll >> **opinion poll**

pollack Cod-like fish (*Pollachius pollachius*) found in inshore waters of the N Atlantic from Norway to the Mediterranean; length up to 1.3 m/4¼ ft; lower jaw protrudes beyond upper; greenish-brown on back, sides pale yellow, underside white. (Family: Gadidae.) >> cod

Pollack, Sydney (1934–) Film director and producer, born in South Bend, IN. He made his debut as a feature film director with *Slender Thread* (1965). Later films include *They Shoot Horses Don't They?* (1969), *Tootsie* (1982), *Out of Africa* (1985, 2 Oscars), and *Sabrina* (1995).

pollen The male sex-cells of seed plants, produced in large numbers in the anthers of flowering plants and the pollen-sacs of gymnosperms. Wind-borne pollen is smooth and light; that carried by insects is often heavier and sticky. The outer coat of the grain is very resistant to decay, and fossilized pollen can be used to investigate the vegetation of prehistoric times. >> flowering plants; gymnosperms; stigma

pollen analysis >> **palynology**

pollock >> **saithe**

Pollock, (Paul) Jackson (1912–56) Artist, born in Cody, WY. He was the leading exponent of action painting in the USA. His art developed from Surrealism to abstract art and the first drip paintings of 1947. >> action painting; Surrealism

poll tax >> **community charge**

pollution The direct or indirect introduction of a harmful substance into the environment. Different categories include air pollution (eg acid rain), freshwater pollution (eg discharge of chemical effluent from industry into rivers), marine pollution (eg oil spills from tankers), noise pollution (eg from aircraft), land pollution (eg the burial of toxic waste), and visual pollution (eg the intrusion of industry into an area of scenic beauty). >> acid rain ℹ; hazardous substances; radioactive waste; waste disposal

Pollux >> **Gemini**

Polo, Marco (1254–1324) Merchant and traveller, born in Venice. He is commonly believed to have given Europe the first eye-witness account of Chinese civilization. His *Il milione* (The Million, trans The Travels of Marco Polo) claimed that his father and uncle, having visited Kublai Khan (1260–9), took him on their second visit (1271–5). He stayed in China until 1292 in Kublai Khan's service, becoming Governor of Yangzhou, before returning home. His account, printed in 1477, helped incite the voyages of Western discovery; but the historicity of his account has been questioned. >> Kublai Khan

polo A stick-and-ball game played on horseback by teams of four. The playing area measures 300 yd/274 m by 160 yd/146 m making it the largest of all ball games. The object is to strike the ball with a hand-held mallet into the opposing goal, which measures 8 yd/7.3 m wide by 10 ft/3 m high. Each game is divided into 7-minute periods known as *chukkers*. >> water polo; RR1058

polonaise A Polish dance in a moderate triple metre. Chopin wrote some famous examples for piano, but the dance itself dates from the 16th-c or earlier. >> Chopin, Frédéric

Pol Pot [pol **pot**], also called **Saloth Sar** (1926–98) Cambodian politician, born in Kompong Thom Province. He became leader of the Khmer Rouge guerrillas, defeating Lon Nol's military government in 1976. As prime minister, he set up a totalitarian regime which caused the death, imprisonment, or exile of millions. Overthrown in 1979, he withdrew to the mountains to lead the Khmer Rouge forces. After a show trial in Cambodia in 1997, he was condemned to life imprisonment. >> Cambodia ℹ; Khmer Rouge

Poltava [pol**tah**va] 49°35N 34°35E, pop (1995e) 324 000. Industrial city in Ukraine, on R Vorskla; known since the 7th-c; site of Swedish defeat by Peter the Great, 1709; railway; cathedral (1689–1709). >> Ukraine [i]

poltergeist Unusual apparently paranormal physical disturbances, such as movement and/or breakage of objects, which seem to depend upon the presence of a particular living person. This individual is often referred to as the 'agent' or 'focus'. >> paranormal; psychokinesis

polyamides Large molecules formed by the condensation polymerization of diamines with dicarboxylic acids. These complementary molecules give the same type of amide linkage as that found in natural protein fibres, such as silk and wool. >> amides; polymerization

polyanthus [poli**an**thuhs] A garden hybrid (*Primula* × *polyanthus*) derived mainly from the primrose and the cowslip, with the large flowers of the former, borne in heads like the latter. (Family: Primulaceae.) >> cowslip; primrose

Polybius [po**li**bius] (c.200–c.120 BC) Greek politician, diplomat, and historian from Megalopolis in the Peloponnese, who wrote of the rise of Rome to world-power status (264–146 BC). Only five of the original 40 books survive.

polycarbamates >> **polyurethanes**

Polycarp, St (c.69–c.155) Greek Bishop of Smyrna, who bridges the little-known period between the age of his master, the apostle John, and that of his own disciple Irenaeus. His only extant writing is the *Epistle to the Philippians*. Feast day 23 February. >> Irenaeus, St; John, St

polychlorobiphenyls >> **PCBs**

Polyclitus or **Polycleitos** [poli**kliy**tus] (5th-c BC) Greek sculptor from Samos, a contemporary of Phidias, known for his statues of athletes. One of his greatest works is the bronze 'Doryphorus' (Spear Bearer, Naples). >> Phidias

Polycrates [po**li**krateez] (6th-c BC) Tyrant of Samos (540–522 BC), who turned Samos into a major naval power, and made her the cultural centre of the E Aegean. >> tyrant

polyesters Large molecules formed by the condensation polymerization of dialcohols with dicarboxylic acids. Synthetic fibres include Terylene (ICI) and Dacron (Du Pont): they impart crease-resistant and easy-care properties to domestic textiles. Their high strength, abrasion resistance, and chemical inertness are also exploited industrially. >> ester; polymerization

polyethylene A family of thermoplastics of a waxy nature, made by subjecting ethene (ethylene) to high pressures at moderate temperatures; commonly known as **polythene**. Valuable as an insulator, it is easy to work into vessels with high chemical resistance. >> ethylene; thermoplastic

polygamy A form of marriage where a person has more than one spouse at the same time. The concept includes *polygyny*, the most common, where a man has more than one wife, and *polyandry*, where a woman has more than one husband. >> marriage

polygon In mathematics, a plane figure whose boundaries are segments of straight lines. A **regular polygon** has sides equal in length, and all the interior angles at the vertices are equal. There is an infinite number of regular figures. >> geometry; plane; polyhedron

polyhedron In mathematics, a solid completely bounded by plane surfaces. There are only five regular polyhedra, those bounded by congruent regular polygons. Polyhedra are of great importance in crystallography and mineralogy. >> plane; Platonic solids; polygon

Polyhymnia [pole**ehim**nia, po**lim**nia] In Greek mythology, one of the Muses, associated with dancing or mime. >> Muses

polymerization The forming of a large molecule, a **polymer**, by the combination of smaller ones (*monomers*). Combinations of two molecules are called **dimers**; of three, **trimers**. Small polymers (usually of three to ten monomers) are known as **oligomers**. Polymers may contain anything from 100 to over 10 000 monomer residues. >> polyamides; polyesters; polysaccharides; protein; resin

polymethylmethacrylate >> **Perspex**

Polynesia A large triangular area in the EC Pacific extending from Hawaii in the N to New Zealand in the S and to Easter I in the E. It includes Tuvalu (Ellice Is), Tokelau, Samoa, Tonga, Cook Is, Marquesas, and Society Is (Tahiti). Polynesians are typically of medium height, stocky build, with light-to-medium skin colour, and little body hair; there is a high rate of blood group N, a low rate of B, and an absence of Rh-negative. >> Melanesia; Micronesia; Oceania

polyneuropathy >> **neuropathy**

Polynices or **Polyneices** [poli**niy**seez] A Greek hero, the second son of Oedipus, who led the Seven against Thebes. >> Eteocles; Seven against Thebes

polynomial An algebraic expression containing several terms added to or subtracted from each other, eg $a + 2b - 3c$. >> algebra; equations

polyp (marine biology) The individual, soft-bodied, sedentary form of a coelenterate; body consists of a cylindrical trunk with an apical mouth surrounded by tentacles. (Phylum: Cnidaria.) >> coelenterate; medusa

polyp (medicine) A small tumour growing from the lining surface of an organ, such as the large intestine, nose, or larynx. It may need surgical removal. >> tumour

polypeptide >> **peptide**

Polyphemus [poli**fee**mus] In Greek mythology, one of the Cyclopes, who imprisoned Odysseus and some of his companions in his cave. They blinded his one eye, and told Polyphemus that 'No one' had hurt him. As a result, when he called on the other Cyclopes for help, and they asked who had attacked him, they did not understand his answer. >> Cyclops

polyphony [po**lif**onee] Music in more than one part. In general usage the term implies counterpoint, rather than simple chordal texture (homophony). One might thus talk of 'Renaissance polyphony' with reference to the Masses, motets, and madrigals of the 16th-c, but not of 'Romantic polyphony' with reference to 19th-c music. >> counterpoint; melody; monody

polypody [po**li**podee] A perennial fern with creeping rhizomes, found almost everywhere; often epiphytic; fronds solitary, deeply lobed, or divided. (Genus: *Polypodium*, 75 species. Family: Polypodiaceae.) >> epiphyte; fern; rhizome

polypropylene A thermoplastic made by passing propene (propylene) over a phosphoric acid catalyst at a moderately high temperature, or by passing propene into heptane with a catalyst. It is useful as a moulding material. >> thermoplastic

polysaccharides [polee**sa**kariydz] Large carbohydrate molecules resulting from the condensation polymerization of sugars. Common polysaccharides include starch and cellulose, both polymers of glucose. >> carbohydrate; disaccharide; sugars

polystyrene >> **styrene**

polytechnic An institution of higher education devoted to the teaching of many subjects. What distinguishes it from a university is that more of its courses have a strong vocational bias, often involving actual work experience during the course. However, it is not exclusively devoted to vocational work, and may offer liberal studies as well. Research is also undertaken, especially in conjunction with industry. In Britain, polytechnics were given university status in 1992. >> university; vocational education

polytetrafluorethylene (PTFE) A thermosetting plastic polymer with important surface-modifying properties. PTFE has a low coefficient of friction which makes it valuable in non-lubricated bearings, ski-surfaces, etc. Its anti-stick properties make it useful in cooking utensils. >> plastics; polymerization; thermoset

polytheism The belief in or worship of many gods, characteristic not only of primitive religions but also of the religions of classical Greece and Rome. >> animism; monotheism; pantheism

polythene >> **polyethylene**

polyunsaturated fatty acids Dietary fats largely comprised of glycerol combined with three fatty acids, the whole molecule being a *triglyceride*. Fatty acids can be **saturated**, **mono-unsaturated**, or **polyunsaturated**, depending on the number of carbon-to-carbon bonds which are not fully saturated with hydrogen atoms. An adequate intake of these fats can contribute to the maintenance of acceptable levels of blood cholesterol. All marine oils, and most vegetable oils (but not palm and coconut oils) are polyunsaturated fats. The main such fat in nature is linoleic acid, an essential component of the human diet (one of the **essential fatty acids**). >> carboxylic acids; cholesterol; prostaglandins

polyurethanes [poli**yoo**rethaynz] or **polycarbamates** Large molecules formed from the addition polymerization of butane-1,4-diol and hexane-1,6-di-isocyanate, which give lightweight, flexible or rigid foams. They are widely used in coatings and adhesives, and the flexible form is found in swimsuits and corsets. >> fulminate

polyuria >> **diabetes mellitus**

polyvinylacetate [poliviynil**as**etayt] A polymer of vinyl acetate monomer ($CH_2COO.CH{=}CH_2$) used in adhesives, plasticizers, and concrete additives. >> polymerization; vinyl

polyvinylchloride (PVC) [poliviynil**klaw**riyd] A family of polymers of vinyl chloride ($CH_2 = CHCl$). It is generally mixed with additives or fillers to give materials useful for their limited flexibility, such as floor coverings, luggage, furnishing, and electric wire coating. >> polymerization; vinyl

pomegranate A deciduous, sometimes spiny, shrub or tree (*Punica granatum*) growing to 9 m/30 ft, native to SW Asia; fruit 5–8 cm/2–3 in, globose with yellow or reddish, leathery skin; seeds numerous, each embedded in translucent, purplish, juicy and sweet flesh. (Family: Punicaceae.)

Pomerania [pome**ray**nia], Ger **Pommern**, Polish **Pomorze** Region of NC Europe along the Baltic Sea from Stralsund (Germany) to the R Vistula in Poland; a disputed territory, 17th–18th-c; divided among Germany, Poland, and the free city of Danzig, 1919–39; divided between East Germany and Poland, 1945. >> Germany [i]; Poland [i]

Pomeranian A toy breed of dog developed from spitz breeds in Britain during the 19th-c; thick double-layered coat; tail curled only at tip, carried across the back. >> dog; non-sporting dog; spitz

Pomona [po**moh**na] Roman goddess of fruit-trees and their fruit, especially apples and pears.

Pompadour, Jeanne Antoinette Poisson, marquise de (Marchioness of) [**pom**padoor], known as **Madame de Pompadour** (1721–64) Mistress of Louis XV, born in Paris. A woman of remarkable grace, beauty, and wit, she assumed the entire control of public affairs, and for 20 years swayed state policy, appointing her own favourites. She was a lavish patroness of architecture, the arts, and literature. >> Louis XV

pompano [**pom**panoh] Any of several large deep-bodied marine fish which with jacks and scads comprise the family Carangidae (11 genera); head with steep profile, tail deeply forked; widespread in open oceanic waters, especially warm seas.

Pompeii [pom**pay**ee], Ital **Pompei** [**pom**pay] 40°45N 14°27E, pop (1995e) 24 000. Ruined ancient city in SW Italy, at the S foot of Vesuvius, 20 km/12 mi SE of Naples; world heritage site; an important port and agricultural, wine, and perfume centre in Roman times; damaged by a violent earthquake in AD 63; great eruption of Vesuvius in AD 79 covered the whole city with a layer of ashes and pumice-stone 6–7 m/20–23 ft deep; systematic excavation since 18th-c with many buildings well-preserved by the volcanic ash; two-fifths of the city still remains buried; modern town lies to the E. >> Herculaneum; Vesuvius

Pompey [**pom**pee], in full **Gnaeus Pompeius Magnus**, known as **Pompey the Great** (106–48 BC) Roman politician and general of the late Republic, whose military talents led to his victories over the Marians (83–82 BC), Sertorius (77 BC), Spartacus (71 BC), the pirates (67 BC), and Mithridates VI (66 BC). Consistently outmanoeuvred in the 50s BC by Julius Caesar, he was finally defeated by him in the Battle of Pharsalus (48 BC), and was assassinated in Egypt shortly after. >> Caesar; Marius; Spartacus; triumvirate

Pompidou, Georges (Jean Raymond) [põpeedoo] (1911–74) French statesman, prime minister (1962, 1962–6, 1966–7, 1967–8), and president (1969–74), born in Montboudif, France. He helped to draft the constitution for the Fifth Republic (1958), and negotiated a settlement in Algeria (1961) and in the student-worker revolt of 1968. >> de Gaulle; France [i]

Pompidou Centre >> **Centre Beaubourg**

Ponape or **Pohnpei** [**pon**pay] pop (1995e) 35 300; area 345 sq km/133 sq mi. One of the Federated States of Micronesia, W Pacific; comprises the island of Ponape (303 sq km/117 sq mi) and eight outlying atolls; capital, Kolonia. >> Micronesia, Federated States of

Ponce de León, Juan [**pon**thay thay lay**on**] (1460–1521) Explorer, born in San Servas, Spain. He was a member of Columbus's second expedition (1493), explored Puerto Rico (1510), and was the first European to discover Florida (1513).

Pondicherry [**pon**dicheree] pop (1995e) 874 000; area 492 sq km/190 sq mi. Union territory in S India; founded, 1674, the chief French settlement in India; transferred to India, 1954; union territory, 1962; capital, Pondicherry; governed by a Council of Ministers responsible to a Legislative Assembly. >> India [i]

pond skater An aquatic bug which lives and moves over water surface, supported by surface tension. (Order: Heteroptera. Family: Gerridae, c.400 species.) >> bug (entomology)

pondweed An aquatic perennial, native to freshwater habitats everywhere; submerged leaves translucent; floating leaves, if present, opaque, green. (Genus: *Potamogeton*, 100 species. Family: Potamogetonaceae.)

Ponta Delgada [põta del**gah**da] 37°29N 25°40W, pop (1991) 21 091. Largest town in the Azores, on S coast of São Miguel I. >> Azores

Pontedera, Andrea da >> **Pisano, Andrea**

Ponte Vecchio [**pon**tay **vek**yoh] A bridge across the R Arno at Florence, completed in 1345 by Taddeo Galli. The lower walkway is lined with jewellers' shops above which an upper corridor, built by Vasari, links the Pitti Palace with the Uffizi. >> Florence; Pitti Palace; Uffizi; Vasari

Pontiac's Conspiracy or **Rebellion** (1763) An unsuccessful attempt by American Indians of the Ohio and Great Lakes country to drive whites out of the area W of Niagara. It was led by Pontiac (c.1720–69), chief of the Ottawa tribe.

pontoon A popular card game which is a variation of

blackjack. The object is to try to obtain a total of 21 with your cards, and is thus also known as *vingt-et-un* (Fr '21'). >> blackjack

pontoon bridge A floating bridge supported by pontoons. The structure may be temporary, as for military usage, or permanent, where deep water and adverse ground conditions make piers expensive. Typically the pontoons consist of flat bottomed boats, hollow metal cylinders, or concrete rafts.

Pontormo, Jacopo da [pon**taw(r)**moh], originally **Jacopo Carrucci** (1494–1557) Painter, born in Pontormo, Italy. His masterpiece is the 'Deposition' (c.1525), a chapel altarpiece in Santa Felicità, Florence. >> fresco

Pontypridd [ponti**prith**] 51°37N 3°22W, pop (1995e) 32 000. Valley town in Rhondda Cynon Taff, S Wales, UK; on the R Taff; railway; Glamorgan University (1992, formerly Polytechnic of Wales). >> Royal Mint; Wales ℹ

pony >> **Dartmoor / Exmoor / New Forest / Shetland pony; horse** ℹ

Pony Club A worldwide organization with the aim of establishing good horsemanship among children through championships and rallies. It was established in 1929. >> equestrianism

pony express A rapid mail service from St Joseph, MO, to San Francisco, CA, using relays of riders and horses. Established in 1860, the service was withdrawn after the completion of the first transcontinental telegraph line a year later. >> telegraphy

poodle A French breed of dog, developed originally for hunting; three sizes: *standard* (taller than 38 cm/15 in), *miniature*, and *toy* (less than 28 cm/11 in); narrow head with pendulous ears; thick coat often clipped for ornamental effect. >> non-sporting dog

pool An American table game played in many forms. It uses 16 balls, and a cue similar to that used in snooker. The most popular form is the variation known as **8-ball pool**. The object is to sink all balls of a certain design, and then finally the black ball (the No. 8 ball, hence the name). >> billiards; snooker

Poona or **Pune** 18°34N 73°58E, pop (1995e) 1 688 000. City in Maharashtra state, W India; former capital of the Marathas; under British rule, 1818; important colonial centre; airfield; railway; university (1949). >> Maharashtra

Poopó, Lake [pohoh**poh**] (Span **Lago**) Lake in W Bolivia; length 97 km/60 mi; width 32–48 km/20–30 mi; c.2.5 m/8.2 ft deep. >> Bolivia ℹ

Poor Clares >> **Franciscans**

Poor Laws Legislation in Britain originally formulated in 1598 and 1601, whereby relief of poverty was the responsibility of individual parishes. As the population grew and rates rose at the end of the 18th-c, the poor laws were increasingly criticized. The Poor Law Amendment Act of 1834 radically changed the system. >> Speenhamland system; workhouse

Pop Art A modern art form based on the commonplace and ephemeral aspects of 20th-c urban life, such as soup cans, comics, movies, and advertising. Leading contributors in the 1960s include Jasper Johns (1930–), Andy Warhol (1926–87), and Roy Lichtenstein (1923–97). >> Surrealism

Popayán [popa**yan**] 2°27N 76°22W, pop (1995e) 157 000. Historic city in SW Colombia; founded, 1536; serious earthquake, 1983; cathedral; university (1827). >> Colombia ℹ

Pope, Alexander (1688–1744) Poet, born in London. He became well known as a satirical poet, and a master of the heroic couplet. His major works include *The Rape of the Lock* (1712), *The Dunciad* (1728, continued 1742), the *Epistle to Doctor Arbuthnot* (1735), the philosophical *Essay on Man* (1733–4), and a series of satires imitating the epistles of Horace (1733–8). >> Horace

pope (Lat *papa*, Gk *papas*, 'father') The title of the Bishop of Rome as head or Supreme Pontiff of the Roman Catholic Church. He is elected by a conclave of the College of Cardinals, his authority deriving from the belief that he represents Christ in direct descendancy from the Apostle Peter, said to be the first Bishop of Rome. The claim to infallibility was formalized at the First Vatican Council in 1870. >> antipope; apostle; Cardinals, College of; conclave; infallibility; Roman Catholicism; Vatican Councils; RR1029–30

Popish Plot An apocryphal Jesuit conspiracy in 1678 to assassinate Charles II of England, slaughter Protestants, and place James, Duke of York, on the throne. It was created by opportunist rogues Titus Oates (1649–1705) and Israel Tonge (1621–80). >> Oates, Titus

poplar A deciduous, N temperate tree; flowers tiny, in pendulous catkins appearing before leaves; seeds with cottony white hairs, which give rise to the American name **cottonwood**. (Genus: *Populus*, 35 species. Family: Salicaceae.) >> aspen; tree ℹ

Pople, John A (1925–) Chemist, born in Burnham-on-Sea, Somerset. He graduated from Cambridge in mathematics in 1951, and taught at Northwestern University, IL. He shared the 1998 Nobel Prize for Chemistry for his contribution to methods that can be used for theoretical studies of the properties of molecules and the chemical processes in which they are involved – specifically, for his development of computational methods in quantum chemistry.

pop music Popular commercial music, with its audience mainly among the young, current since the late 1950s. Inaugurated by rock and roll, it has since diversified to include elements from a diverse range of musical sources, including soul, reggae, country and western, and various ethnic styles. Pop music is generally played, presented, and marketed for a teenage audience, with success measured in terms of the various pop charts (particularly in the UK the Music Week/Gallup/BBC chart, and in the USA the Billboard chart), which list records in order of sales attained. >> Beatles, The; country and western; gospel music; pop group; punk rock; reggae; rhythm and blues; rock music; salsa; soul (music)

Popocatépetl [popohka**tay**petl] 19°01N 98°38W. Dormant volcano in C Mexico, height 5452 m/17 887 ft; last eruption, 1702. >> Mexico ℹ; volcano

Poppaea Sabina [po**pay**a sa**bee**na] (?–65) Roman society beauty and voluptuary who before her marriage to the Emperor Nero (62) had been the wife of his playboy friend, the future Emperor Otho. >> Nero

Popper, Sir Karl (Raimund) (1902–94) Philosopher, born in Vienna. His major contributions to scientific methodology include *Die Logik der Forschung* (1934, The Logic of Scientific Discovery). He left Vienna during Hitler's rise to power, later becoming professor of logic and scientific method at London (1949–69).

poppy The name given to many members of the family Papaveraceae. All produce latex, are often brightly coloured, and have flowers with two sepals and four overlapping petals. Red poppies, which grew wild in the fields of Flanders, are used in November as a symbol of remembrance of those who died in the two World Wars. >> corn poppy; latex

Popski's Private Army A British fighting unit in World War 2. It was raised in October 1942 by Lt-Col Vladimir Peniakoff (1897–1951), known as 'Popski', and engaged in intelligence-gathering and hit-and-run attacks behind enemy lines in N Africa and Italy. >> World War 2

population density A measure of the number of people living within a standard unit of area, useful for comparative purposes. For example, the population density of The Netherlands (1983) was 422.4 per sq km/1094 per sq mi,

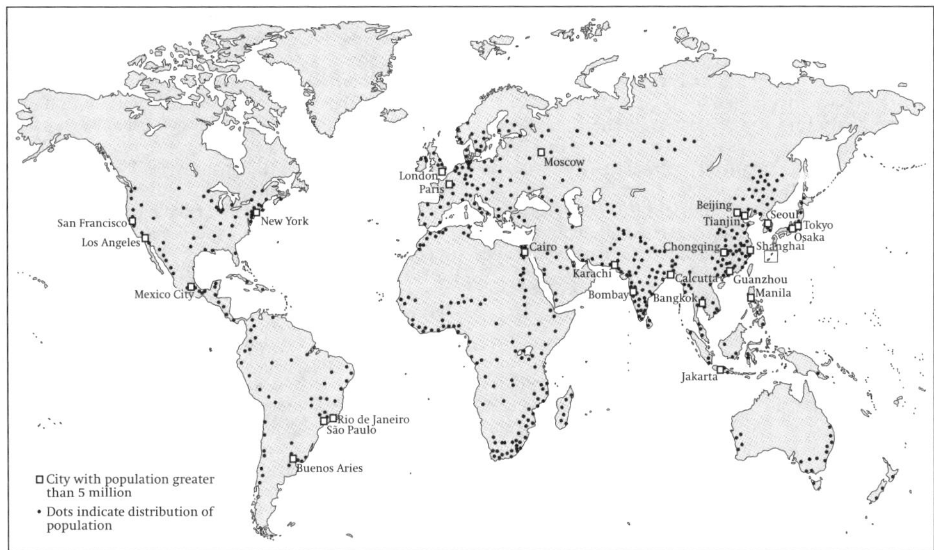

World population density map

and for Australia (1984) 2 per sq km/5.2 per sq mi. These measurements take no account of the area of habitable land, and density is often calculated to relate population to cultivable land or some other economic indicator.

porcelain A hard, vitreous, translucent material, contrasting with thicker, more porous pottery. Porcelain was first manufactured by the Chinese in the Tang dynasty (7th–10th-c). The first European attempts to make it were at the Medici factory in Florence in the 1570s, but real success was only achieved at Meissen in the early 18th-c. >> Limoges; Meissen / Sèvres porcelain; Minton ceramics; pottery

porcupine A cavy-like rodent; some hairs modified as long sharp spines; 22 species in two families: ground-dwelling family Hystricidae (**Old World porcupines**) from Africa and S Asia, and tree-climbing family Erithizontidae (**New World porcupines**), widespread in the New World. >> cavy; rodent

porcupine-fish Large bottom-living fish (*Diodon hystrix*) widespread in shallow waters of tropical seas; length up to 90 cm/3 ft; body covered with long sharp spines; inflates body as a defence to become almost spherical with spines erect. (Family: Diodontidae.)

porgy >> **sea bream**

Porifera [po**rif**era] >> **sponge**

porky >> **filefish**

pornography The presentation of erotic behaviour intended to cause sexual arousal, typically using film, graphic, or written media. It is widely considered to be a demeaning representation of sexuality and the body. Most authorities distinguish between 'soft' and illegal 'hard core' pornography, but many, especially feminists, argue that the 'softer' version should be banned as well. Pornography is now a major industry; difficulties of definition and changing social attitudes have led to problems of control and law enforcement.

porosity A mechanical property of solids, a measure of their ability to allow the passage of a fluid. The narrow channels that make a material porous allow it to absorb fluid via capillarity, as a sponge absorbs water. >> capillarity

porphyria [paw(r)**fi**ria] A group of inherited disorders involving the excess production of the chemical substances known as *porphyrins*. They cause a wide range of abnormalities, including pigmentation of the skin, abdominal pain, and mental confusion. It entered the British royal family, and was most acutely displayed in the supposed 'madness' of George III. It is sometimes called 'the royal malady', not because of its royal connections, but due to the production of purple urine. >> skin [i]

Porphyry [**paw(r)**fuhree] (c.233–304) Neoplatonist philosopher, born in Tyre or Batanea. His most influential work was the *Isagoge*, a commentary on Aristotle's *Categories*, widely used in the Middle Ages. >> Neoplatonism; Plotinus

porpoise >> **dolphin**

Porres, St Martín de >> **Martín de Porres, St**

Porsche, Ferdinand [paw(r)shuh] (1875–1951) Automobile designer, born in Hafersdorf, Germany. In 1934 he designed a revolutionary type of cheap car with the engine in the rear, to which the Nazis gave the name *Volkswagen* ('people's car'). The Porsche sports car was introduced in 1950. >> car [i]

port A sweet, fortified wine, first produced in the upper Douro valley, N Portugal. The wine used to be transported down the fast-flowing river to Oporto (hence the name), but is today taken by road. >> fermentation; wine

Port Augusta 32°30S 137°27E, pop (1995e) 15 400. Town in South Australia; airfield; railway; base for the flying doctor service. >> flying doctor service; South Australia

Port-au-Prince [paw(r)t oh **prīs**] 18°33N 72°20W, pop (1995e) 799 000. Seaport capital of Haiti; on the W coast of Hispaniola I; railway; archbishopric; university (1944); cathedral (18th-c). >> Haiti [i]

Port Elizabeth 33°58S 25°36E, pop (1995e) 794 000 (metropolitan area). Seaport in Eastern Cape province, South Africa, on the Indian Ocean; Fort Frederick, 1799; founded, 1820; airfield; railway; university (1964). >> South Africa [i]

Porter, Cole (1892–1964) Songwriter, born in Peru, IN. He ranked high in the golden period of American popular song, with such pieces as 'Night and Day' (1932) and 'Don't Fence Me In' (1944), and such musical comedies as *Kiss Me Kate* (1948) and *Can-Can* (1953). >> musical

Porter, Sir George (1920–) Physical chemist, born in Stainforth, North Yorkshire. He studied very fast reactions in gases, using a combination of electronic and spectroscopic techniques, and was awarded the Nobel Prize for Chemistry in 1967. >> gas 1; spectroscopy

Porter, Katherine Anne (1890–1980) Short-story writer and novelist, born in Indian Creek, TX. Apart from short stories, she is best known for a long allegorical novel, *The Ship of Fools* (1962).

Porter, Peter (Neville Frederick) (1929–) Poet, born in Brisbane, Queensland, Australia. He emigrated to England in 1951. His *Collected Poems* appeared in 1983, and *Dragons in their Pleasant Palaces* in 1997.

porter >> **beer** ℹ

portfolio theory The analysis of how investors allocate their wealth between the various types of asset available. It assumes that all would prefer the best available return for any given degree of risk, and the lowest degree of risk for any expected rate of return. Different investors choose between expected profits and safety differently, to suit their own wealth and temperament. >> investment 1

Port Harcourt [**hah(r)**kert] 4°43N 7°05E, pop (1995e) 395 000. Nigeria's second largest port; on R Bonny; established in 1912; airport; railway link to the Enugu coalfields; university (1975). >> Nigeria ℹ

portico [**paw(r)**tikoh] A colonnaded and roofed space attached to a building and forming an entrance way. It is usually classical in style, with detached or attached columns and a pediment above. >> colonnade; column; pediment

Portillo, Michael (Denzil Xavier) [paw(r)**ti**loh] (1953–) British Conservative statesman. He became an MP in 1984 and was appointed minister of state for transport (1988–90) and the environment (1990–2), chief secretary for the Treasury (1992–4), secretary of state for employment (1994–5), and defence secretary (1995–7). He lost his seat in the 1997 general election.

Portland (Maine) 43°39N 70°16W, pop (1995e) 65 300. Business capital and chief port of Maine, USA; established, 1632; city status, 1832; state capital, 1820–32; railway; Westbrook Junior College (1831); birthplace of Longfellow. >> Longfellow; Maine

Portland (Oregon) 45°32N 122°37W, pop (1995e) 491 000. Freshwater port in NW Oregon, USA, on the Willamette R; largest city in the state; laid out, 1845; airport; railway; university (1901); professional team, Trail Blazers (basketball). >> Oregon

Portland, Isle of Rocky peninsula on Dorset coast, S England; connected to the mainland by a shingle ridge (Chesil Beach); area 12 sq km/4.6 sq mi; naval base at Portland Harbour; Portland Stone (limestone); Portland Castle built by Henry VIII (1520). >> Dorset

Portland, Duke of >> **Bentinck, William Henry Cavendish**

Portland Cement >> **cement**

Portlaoighise [paw(r)t**lay**ish] or **Port Laoise**, formerly **Maryborough** 53°02N 7°17W, pop (1995e) 8300. Capital of Laoighis county, Leinster, Ireland; railway. >> Ireland (republic) ℹ; Laoighis

Port Louis [**loo**is] 20°18S 57°31E, pop (1995e) 150 000. Seaport capital of Mauritius; established, 1735; university (1965); two cathedrals; handles almost all of the trade of Mauritius. >> Mauritius ℹ

Port Moresby [**maw(r)z**bee] 9°30S 147°07E, pop (1995e) 215 000. Seaport capital of Papua New Guinea; Allied base in World War 2; airport; university (1965). >> Papua New Guinea ℹ

Port Natal >> **Durban**

Port of Spain 10°38N 61°31W, pop (1995e) 52 400. Seaport capital of Trinidad and Tobago, NW coast of Trinidad; capital of Trinidad, 1783; airport; principal commercial centre in the E Caribbean; two cathedrals. >> Trinidad and Tobago ℹ

Porton Down A research centre established by the Ministry of Defence in Wiltshire, S England, for the investigation of biological and chemical warfare. >> chemical warfare

Porto Novo 6°30N 2°47E, pop (1995e) 293 000. Seaport capital of Benin, W Africa; settled by the Portuguese, centre for slave and tobacco trading; though the official capital, there is little political and economic activity, this taking place in Cotonou; railway. >> Benin ℹ; Cotonou

Portree 57°24N 6°12W, pop (1995e) 1950. Port in Highland region, NW Scotland; largest town on Skye. >> Highland; Scotland ℹ; Skye

Port Royal [roy**al**] A French religious and intellectual community occupying the former convent of Port-Royal-des-Champs, near Paris. It was associated with the Jansenist movement, and founded by the Abbé de Saint-Cyran (1637). The community was dispersed in 1665. >> Augustine, St (of Hippo)

Portrush, Ir **Port Rois** 55°12N 6°40W, pop (1995e) 5700. Town in Antrim, NE Northern Ireland, on the N coast; railway; tourist centre for the Giant's Causeway. >> Antrim (county); Giant's Causeway

Port Said [sa**eed**], Arabic **Bur Said** 31°17N 32°18E, pop (1995e) 506 000. Seaport in NE Egypt; on Mediterranean coast at N end of Suez Canal; founded, 1859. >> Egypt ℹ; Suez Canal

Port San Carlos 51°30S 58°59W. Settlement on the W coast of East Falkland, Falkland Is; British Task Force landed near here in May 1982, during the Falklands War. >> Falkland Islands

Portsmouth (UK) 50°48N 1°05W, pop (1995e) 191 000. Seaport city and (from 1997) unitary authority in Hampshire, S England; on Portsea I; major naval base; railway; university, 1992; ferries to the Channel Is, France, and the I of Wight; birthplace of Charles Dickens; Nelson's flagship HMS *Victory*; Tudor warship, *Mary Rose*; Royal Navy Museum; Southsea Castle; football league team, Portsmouth (Pompey). >> Dickens; Hampshire; Nelson, Horatio

Portsmouth (Virginia) 36°50N 76°18W, pop (1995e) 112 000. Port city, SE Virginia, USA, on the Elizabeth R; founded, 1752; evacuated and burned by Union troops during the Civil War, 1861, then retaken, 1862; part of a US naval complex; railway. >> American Civil War; American Revolution; Virginia

Port Sudan [soo**dan**] 19°38N 37°07E, pop (1995e) 281 000. Sudan's main port; founded, 1906; airfield; railway; handles most of the country's trade. >> Sudan ℹ

Port Talbot >> **Neath and Port Talbot**

Portugal, official name **Republic of Portugal**, Port **República Portuguesa**, ancient **Lusitania** pop (1995e) 9 793 000; area 91 630 sq km/35 370 sq mi. Country in SW Europe on the W side of the Iberian peninsula; includes the autonomous regions of the Azores and Madeira; capital, Lisbon; timezone GMT; unit of currency, the escudo of 100 centavos; Macao still administered by Portugal; chief mountain range, the Serra da Estrêla (N), rising to 1991 m/6532 ft; four main rivers (Douro, Minho, Tagus, Guadiana), all beginning in Spain; basically a maritime climate; most rainfall in winter; became a kingdom under Alfonso Henriques, 1140; major period of world exploration and beginning of Portuguese Empire, 15th-c; under Spanish domination, 1580–1640; invaded by the French, 1807; monarchy overthrown and republic established, 1910; dictatorship of Dr Salazar, 1932–68; military coup in 1974, followed by 10 years of political unrest under 15 governments; governed by a president, a prime minister and Council of Ministers, and a unicameral

Assembly; several labour-intensive areas in the economy, such as textiles, leather, wood products, cork, ceramics; large forests of pine, oak, cork-oak, eucalyptus, and chestnut covering about 20% of the country; tourism, especially in the S; joined the European Community in 1985. >> Azores; European Community; Macao; Madeira; Peninsular War; Salazar; RR1020 political leaders

Portuguese >> **Romance languages**

Portuguese man-of-war A jellyfish-like coelenterate which floats at the ocean surface, held up by a gas-filled float; lives as a colony; long stinging tentacles hang down from the float; can inflict painful stings on swimmers. (Phylum: Cnidaria. Order: Siphonophora.) >> coelenterate; jellyfish ℹ

Porvoo [**paw(r)**voh], Swed **Borgå** 60°24N 25°40E, pop (1995e) 20 700. Picturesque town in SE Finland; established, 1346; bishopric; boat service to Helsinki; home of national poet, Johan Runeberg; cathedral (15th-c). >> Finland ℹ; Runeberg

Poseidon [po**siy**dn] In Greek mythology, the brother of Zeus, god of water and the sea, depicted with a trident in his hand. He is responsible for earthquakes and similar destructive forces. >> Amphitrite; Neptune (mythology)

positivism In philosophy, the position that all genuine knowledge is derived from and validated by science. Developed from the British empiricist tradition, it was first explicitly formulated in the 19th-c, and taken up by those optimistic about the benefits of scientific progress for humanity and who were hostile to theology and metaphysics. >> logical positivism

positron The antiparticle partner to the electron; symbol e^+; mass and spin same as electron, but charge +1; discovered in 1932 by US physicist Carl Anderson (1905–91) and British physicist Patrick Blackett (1897–1974), by observing tracks left in cloud chambers by cosmic rays. >> antiparticles

possum An Australian marsupial of family Burramyidae (**pygmy possum**, 7 species), family Pseudocheiridae (**ringtail possum**, 16 species), family Phalangeridae (**scaly-tailed possum** plus 3 species of **brushtail possum**), or family Petauridae (**Leadbetter's possum** plus 2 species of **striped possum**). The name is commonly used for **opossum** in the USA. >> marsupial ℹ; opossum

postal service The collection, sorting, and delivery of mail. National postal services have existed since the early 19th-c, using a network of post offices and post boxes for the collection of letters, cards, parcels, and other missives. In some countries, private operators now provide competition for the former monopoly state suppliers. Post offices may also offer a range of additional counter services, such as savings accounts and telegrams. >> Hill, Rowland; philately

post and lintel / lintol A form of architectural construction consisting of vertical, loadbearing posts supporting horizontal lintels to create openings. It is typified by Greek architecture. The technique is also known as **trabeated** construction. >>

Postimpressionism An imprecise term coined by the art critic Roger Fry c.1910 to cover the more progressive forms of French painting since c.1880. The painters included van Gogh, Gauguin, Cézanne, and Matisse. >> Fry, Roger; Impressionism (art); modern art

postmodern dance A late 1960s form of dance based on ordinary movement rather than stylized techniques. It has links with Eastern movement forms and martial arts. >> modern dance

Postmodernism A term used in architecture to describe a style or concept that supersedes 20th-c modernism and the International Style in particular. It is generally applied to buildings which draw upon an eclectic range of stylistic precedents, especially classical. In recent years the term has been increasingly used to identify a basic rejection of previously widely-held architectural beliefs, and has also emerged in relation to such fields as literature and cinema. >> International Style 2

post office >> **postal service**

postpartum haemorrhage / hemorrhage Bleeding in the mother in excess of 500 ml (c.1 pt) occurring in the first 24 hours after the birth of the baby. It has many causes. >> haemorrhage; uterus ℹ

post-production The completion stages of a film after shooting up to the first public showing. The picture is finally edited to the director's satisfaction, and the original negative cut to conform; music and sound effects are

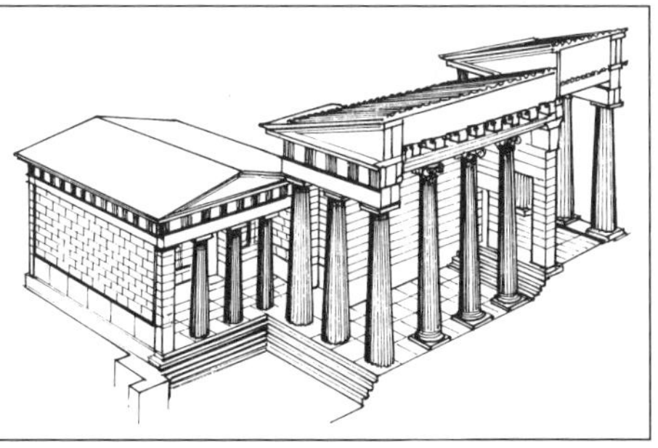

An example of post and lintel construction – Propylaea, Athens, 437–432 BC (restored)

recorded and mixed with the actors' dialogue in dubbing the final track. Corresponding stages are followed for a video production.

PostScript A computer language which has been developed to provide a uniform means of describing pages of text and/or graphics. It is widely used in desk-top publishing. >> desk-top publishing

post-traumatic stress A prolonged response to an event outside the range of normal human experience, such as wartime involvement. Features include nightmares, flashback experiences, and a sense of numbness.

potash Potassium oxide, K_2O. The term is generally used for any potassium compounds used as fertilizers whose potassium content is reported in terms of the equivalent amount of K_2O, or about 1·2 times the percentage by weight of potassium. >> fertilizer; potassium

potassium K (Lat *kalium*), element 19, melting point 63°C. One of the most reactive metals, and the third of the alkali metal group. It is not found free in nature, but obtained chiefly from mineral deposits of the chloride (KCl) and the nitrate (KNO_3, also known as *nitre* or *saltpetre*). Its compounds are important mainly as agricultural chemicals and explosives. >> alkali; chemical elements; metal; nitrate; RR1036

potassium–argon dating A radiometric method for dating rocks more than 100 000 years old. It uses the fact that radioactive isotope potassium-40 decays with a known half-life to yield argon-40, and hence the amount of each isotope in a rock can be used to determine its age. >> argon; potassium; radiometric dating

potato A well-known tuber-producing plant and staple crop throughout temperate regions of the world; an erect to somewhat sprawling perennial. The tubers vary greatly in size, shape, colour, and taste. The skins can be white, yellow to brown, pink, red, or purplish-black, and the flesh white to yellow, pink, or purple. The 'eyes' on a potato are dormant buds, which in favourable conditions give rise to new stems. There are thousands of varieties, all regarded as belonging to a single species, *Solanum tuberosum*. The potato is native to South America, and probably first arrived in Spain c.1565, and separately in England towards the end of the 16th-c (though not, as legend would have it, brought by Sir Walter Raleigh). Potatoes are susceptible to a number of diseases, including viruses and potato blight. Production of higher-yielding and disease-resistant strains is a priority for crop breeders. (Family: Solanaceae.) >> potato blight; tuber

potato blight A widespread disease of potato and related plants caused by the fungus *Phytophthora infestans*, especially in wet weather. A severe outbreak in Ireland in the 1840s caused the great Irish potato famine. (Class: Oomycetes. Order: Peronosporales.) >> fungus; potato

Potemkin, Grigoriy Alexandrovich [pot**yom**kin] (1739–91) Russian field marshal, born near Smolensk, Russia. He entered the Russian army, attracted the notice of Catherine II, and became her intimate favourite, heavily influencing Russian foreign policy. There is some reason to believe they were secretly married. >> Catherine II

potential A scalar quantity associated with a force whose rate of change with distance is proportional to the strength of that force; symbol *V*. In a gravitational field, it is the potential energy of an object of mass 1 kg; in an electric field it is the potential energy of a charge of 1 C. >> potential difference / energy; potentiometer

potential difference A quantity in physics, often called **voltage**; symbol *U*, units V (volt). A potential difference is said to exist between two points if work must be done against an electric field to carry a charge from one point to the other. The potential difference between the terminals of a battery indicates the battery's ability to drive current around a circuit. >> electricity; electromotive force; electron volt; potential

potential energy The energy stored by an object by virtue of its position in the region of influence of some force; symbol *V*, units J (joule). For example, work done in compressing a spring is stored as elastic potential energy in the spring. >> energy; potential

potentilla A member of a large genus of annuals or perennials, sometimes creeping, rarely small shrubs, native to N temperate regions; **cinquefoils** with 5-petalled flowers, and **tormentils** with 4-petalled flowers. (Genus: *Potentilla*, 500 species. Family: Rosaceae.) >> tormentil

potentiometer An instrument for the accurate measurement or control of electrical potential. Potentiometers are used in electronic circuits, especially as volume controls in transistor radios. >> electricity; potential; transistor

potholing >> **speleology**

pot marigold An annual to perennial (*Calendula officinalis*), growing to 70 cm/27 in; slightly sticky to the touch; flower-heads solitary, up to 7 cm/2¾ in across; outer ray florets orange or yellow; fruit boat-shaped. (Family: Compositae.)

Potomac River [po**toh**mak] River in West Virginia, Virginia, and Maryland, USA; rises in the Allegheny Mts; flows through Washington, DC, into Chesapeake Bay; length 460 km/286 mi. >> United States of America ℹ

Potosí [potoh**see**] 19°34S 65°45W, pop (1995e) 124 000. City in SW Bolivia; altitude 4070 m/13 353 ft; founded by Spanish in 1545; major silver-mining town in 17th–18th-c; airfield; railway; chief industrial centre of Bolivia; university (1892); cathedral; nearby mint (Casa Real de Moneda), founded 1542, rebuilt 1759, now a museum and world heritage site. >> Bolivia ℹ

Potsdam 52°23N 13°04E, pop (1995e) 145 000. City in Germany; on R Havel; former residence of German emperors and Prussian kings; badly bombed in World War 2; railway; Academy of Political Science and Law; Central Meteorological Centre; Sans Souci palace and park (1745–7). >> Germany ℹ; Potsdam Conference; Sans Souci

Potsdam Conference A conference which met during the final stages of World War 2 (17 Jul–2 Aug 1945). Churchill (and later Attlee), Stalin, and Truman met to discuss the post-war settlement in Europe. It was agreed that Poland's W frontier should run along the Oder–Neisse line, and the decision was made to divide Germany into four occupation zones. >> Oder–Neisse line; World War 2

Potter, (Helen) Beatrix (1866–1943) Writer, born in London. She wrote many books for children, which she illustrated herself, creating such popular characters as Peter Rabbit (1900) and Benjamin Bunny (1904).

Potter, Dennis (Christopher George) (1935–94) Playwright, born in Coleford, Gloucestershire. His first success was *Vote, Vote, Vote for Nigel Barton* (1965). Later works include *Pennies from Heaven* (1978), *Blue Remembered Hills* (1979, BAFTA), *Cream in my Coffee* (1982, Prix Italia), and *Lipstick on Your Collar* (1993). He completed *Karaoke* and *Cold Lazarus* just before his death.

Potter, Paul (1625–54) Painter and etcher, born in Enkhuizen, The Netherlands. His best pictures are small pastoral scenes with animal figures, but he also painted large pictures, notably the life-size 'Young Bull' (1647, The Hague). >> etching

Potter, Stephen (Meredith) (1900–69) British writer and radio producer. He is best known for his humorous studies of the art of demoralizing the opposition, such as *Gamesmanship* (1947), *Lifemanship* (1950), and *One-Upmanship* (1952).

Potteries, The NW Midlands urban area in the upper Trent valley of Staffordshire, C England; extends c.14 km/9 mi (NW–SE) by 5 km/3 mi (W–E); railway; since the 18th-c, the heart of the English china and earthenware industry. >> pottery; Stoke-on-Trent

pottery Vessels made out of fired clay, produced by mankind since the earliest civilizations. They can be hand-built, moulded, or in more sophisticated societies thrown on a wheel. Pottery tends to be soft and rather porous, and is therefore normally protected by a **glaze**, which also gives a shiny decorative appearance. >> clay; Delftware; Doulton; faience; maiolica; porcelain; Spode; stoneware; Toby jug; Wedgwood, Josiah

potto A primitive primate (*Perodicticus potto*) native to Africa; resembles the slow loris, but has a dark face and short tail; four spines on back of neck. (Family: Lorisidae.) The name **golden potto** is used for the related angwantibo. >> angwantibo; kinkajou; loris; prosimian

Poulenc, Francis [poolãk] (1899–1963) Composer, born in Paris. He became a member of *Les Six*, and was prominent in the reaction against Impressionism. He is best known for his considerable output of songs, such as *Fêtes galantes* (1943). >> *Six, Les*

Pound, Ezra (Loomis) (1885–1972) Poet, born in Hailey, ID. He was an experimental poet, whom T S Eliot regarded as the motivating force behind modern poetry. His main work is *The Cantos*, a loosely-knit series of poems, which he began during World War 1, and which were published in many instalments, 1930–59. >> Eliot, T S; Modernism

pound (economics) The unit of currency of the UK (the **pound sterling**), and certain other countries. The symbol £ is derived from letter *L* for *libra*, a measure of weight. It was formerly divided into 20 shillings and 240 pence; but since decimalization in 1971 it is divided into 100 pence (*new pence*). >> currency

pound (physics) >> **kilogram**

poundal >> **RR1031**

Poussin, Nicolas [poosĩ] (1594–1665) Painter, born near Les Andelys, France. The greatest exponent of French classicism, deeply influenced by Raphael and the Antique, his masterpieces include two sets of the 'Seven Sacraments'. >> classicism

poverty trap An anomaly in a social welfare and taxation system which occurs when individuals, previously unemployed and claiming various social benefits, obtain work, and find that they are taxed, so ending up with less net income than before. >> income tax

POW Abbreviation of **prisoner-of-war**, whose treatment was first codified by International Treaty at the Hague Conference of 1899. This stated that POWs must be humanely treated, and not obliged to divulge military information other than name, rank, and number. >> Geneva convention

powder metallurgy Making metal shapes by compressing powdered metal into a finished or near-finished shape. First used for tungsten lamp filaments, it is now used for such products as tungsten carbide cutting tools and self-lubricating bearings. >> metallic glass; sintering

Powell, Anthony (Dymoke) (1905–) Novelist, born in London. After World War 2, he wrote a major series of satirical social novels, *A Dance to the Music of Time* (1951–75; televised, 1997) – 12 volumes covering 50 years of British upper-middle-class life and attitudes.

Powell, Colin (Luther) (1937–) US army officer, born in New York City. The first black officer to rise to full general, he was appointed President Reagan's National Security Advisor in 1987, and Chairman of the Joint Chiefs of Staff in 1989. He had overall responsibility for the US military operation against Iraq in 1990–1. >> Gulf War 2

Powell, (John) Enoch (1912–98) British Conservative statesman, born in Birmingham, West Midlands. His outspoken attitude on the issues of non-white immigration and racial integration came to national attention in 1968, and as a consequence he was dismissed from the shadow Cabinet. He was elected as an Ulster Unionist MP in October 1974, losing his seat in 1987. >> Conservative Party

Powell, Michael (1905–90) Film director, scriptwriter, and producer, born near Canterbury, Kent. With Emeric Pressburger (1902–88) he formed The Archers company in 1942, and for more than 10 years made a series of unusual and original features, such as *Black Narcissus* (1947) and *The Tales of Hoffman* (1951).

Powell, Robert (1944–) Actor, born in Salford, Lancashire. He became widely known through his role in *Jesus of Nazareth* (1977), later films including *Frankenstein* (1984), and *The Mystery of Edwin Drood* (1993). His television work includes *The Detectives* (1989) and *The First Circle* (1991).

power The rate of change of work with time; symbol *P*, units W (watt). To lift an object some distance into the air requires a fixed amount of work, but to do the job more quickly requires more power. >> electrical power; work

powerboat racing The racing of boats fitted with high-powered and finely-tuned engines. A boat was first fitted with a petrol engine in 1865, by Frenchman Jean Joseph Lenoir (1822–1900). The first race was c.1900. >> RR1058

Powhatan Confederacy [powuh**tan**] A group of North American Algonkin Indian tribes inhabiting the Tidewater region of Virginia at the time of the first white contact; named after chief Powhatan. Initially receptive, the Indians grew suspicious of the newcomers, and in 1622 and 1644 launched massive (but unsuccessful) attacks on them. >> Algonkin

Powys [**pow**is] pop (1995e) 122 000; area 5077 sq km/ 1960 sq mi. Mountainous county in E Wales, UK; created in 1974, and status reaffirmed in 1996; Lake Vyrnwy (reservoir); administrative centre, Llandrindod Wells; Brecon Beacons National Park. >> Brecon Beacons; Wales ℹ

Powys, John Cowper [**pow**is] (1872–1964) Writer and critic, born in Shirley, Derbyshire. He is best known for his long novels on West Country and historical themes, such as *A Glastonbury Romance* (1932) and *Owen Glendower* (1940). His brothers **Llewelyn** (1884–1939) and **T(heodore) F(rancis)** (1875–1953) were also writers.

Poznań [**poz**nan], Ger **Posen** 52°25N 16°53E, pop (1995e) 595 000. City in W Poland, on R Warta; capital of Poland until 13th-c; bishopric; airfield; railway; noted for its choirs and the Polish Theatre of Dance; two universities (1918, 1919); castle (13th-c), cathedral (18th-c, largely rebuilt). >> Poland ℹ

Prado [**prah**doh] The Spanish national museum in Madrid, housing the world's finest collection of Spanish art. The gallery was opened to the public in 1819.

Praesepe [priy**see**pee] >> **Cancer**

Praetorian Guard [pri**taw**rian] An elite corps in imperial Rome – effectively, the emperor's bodyguard. Their real influence dates from the 20s AD, when they were concentrated in a single barracks in Rome itself.

Praetorius, Michael [pri**taw**rius] (1571–1621) Composer, born in Creuzburg, Germany. As well as being one of the most prolific composers of his time (especially of church music), he wrote an important treatise *Syntagma musicum* (1614–20).

praetors [**pree**terz] In ancient Rome, the chief law officers of the state, elected annually, second only to the consuls in importance. The office could not be held before the age of 33.

pragmatics In linguistics, the study of the way context influences the use and understanding of language, particularly in interactive situations such as in addressing, being polite, or being persuasive. This includes the study of speech acts; for example, *I promise*, used in appropriate circumstances, *is* to promise.

Prague, Czech **Praha** 50°05N 14°25E, pop (1995e) 1 219 000. Industrial and commercial capital of Czech Republic, on R Vltava; important trading centre since 10th-c; capital of newly-created Czechoslovakia, 1918; occupied by Warsaw Pact troops, 1968; historical centre declared a conservation area, 1971; archbishopric; airport; railway; metro; Charles University (1348); technical university (1707); Hradčany Castle, two cathedrals. >> Czech Republic [i]; Hradčany Castle

Praia [**prah**ya] 14°53N 23°30W, pop (1995e) 40 200. Port and capital of the Republic of Cape Verde; airport; naval shipyard. >> Cape Verde [i]

prairie The extensive grassland and treeless region of N USA and Canada. Its fertile soils encouraged ploughing and cultivation, and the prairies are now a major arable area. Cattle ranching is also important. >> pampa(s); steppe

prairie chicken A grouse native to C USA (*Tympanuchus cupido*); upright tail; long upright feathers on head; inflatable orange neck sacs; inhabits prairie. >> grouse

prairie dog A North American squirrel; length, up to 45 cm/18 in, with short tail; digs extensive burrow systems. (Genus: *Cynomys*, 5 species.) >> squirrel

prairie schooner A type of wagon used by emigrants making the journey W across the USA in the 19th-c, with cloth covers stretched over hoops. They were commonly known as **covered wagons**, and also as **Conestoga wagons**, from the place in Pennsylvania where they were originally manufactured.

prairie wolf >> **coyote**

Prasad, Rajendra [pra**sad**] (1884–1963) Indian statesman and president (1950–62), born in Zeradei, Bihar, India. He was president of the Indian National Congress on several occasions between 1934 and 1948, and became India's first president in 1950. >> Gandhi (M K); Indian National Congress

Pratchett, Terry (1948–) Author, born in Beaconsfield, Buckinghamshire. He is best known for his series of fantasy novels, Discworld, which began in 1983 with *The Colour of Magic* and which had reached a 23rd novel, *Carpe Jugulum* in 1998. Other works include the 'Truckers' trilogy (called the 'Bromeliad' trilogy in the USA), and a series of Johnny Maxwell novels.

pratincole [**prat**ingkohl] A bird of the Old World family Glareolidae, subfamily Glareolinae (8 species); long wings, short tail; short black bill with reddish base; short legs (*Glareolus*, 7 species) or long legs (*Stiltia*). >> courser

Prairie dog

prawn A general name for many shrimp-like crustaceans. *Prawn* and *shrimp* are interchangeable common names, with usage varying according to local tradition. (Class: Malacostraca. Order: Decapoda.) >> crustacean; shrimp

Praxiteles [prak**sit**eleez] (4th-c BC) Sculptor, a citizen of Athens. His works have almost all perished, but several of his statues are known from Roman copies.

praying mantis A large, green mantis which lies motionless in wait for its prey, holding its grasping forelegs in an attitude suggestive of prayer; found in Europe. (Order: Mantodea. Family: Mantidae.) >> insect [i]; mantis

Precambrian era A geological time before the Phanerozoic, from the formation of the Earth (c.4600 million years ago) to c.590 million years ago; subdivided into the Archean and the Proterozoic eons. >> geological time scale; RR976

precedent 1 A doctrine of law, present in most legal systems, whereby an earlier court's decision or judgment on the same point of law involving similar facts is followed by another court at a later date. Precedent is sometimes referred to as 'judge-made law', as opposed to statute law; but precedent can be overruled by statute, and where any conflict exists the statute takes precedence. >> common law; court of law; statute **2** A copy of a legal document, such as a will or a deed, which is used or adapted as a model or style for drafting other documents. >> will

precession In rotational mechanics, the progressive change in orientation of the axis of rotation. For example, a child's spinning top spins about its own axis, but also wobbles or precesses about the vertical. The Earth precesses in a complicated way. >> gyroscope; mechanics

precious stones >> **gemstones**

precipitate Insoluble material formed during a chemical reaction in solution. Examples include the deposition of scale in a kettle and the formation of soap scum by hard water. >> chemical reaction

precipitation A climatic term covering rainfall, drizzle, snow, sleet, hail, and dew. As rising air cools, it condenses around dust particles to form water droplets and clouds. If the droplet grows to a critical size, it will fall as precipitation; the type reaching the ground depends on the air temperature between the cloud and the ground. >> cloud [i]; condensation (physics); fog; hail; rainfall; rime; sleet; snow; thunderstorm

predestination In Christian theology, the doctrine that the ultimate salvation or damnation of each human individual has been ordained beforehand. It was first fully articulated by Augustine during his controversy with the Pelagians. The Protestant Reformers Luther and Calvin defended the doctrine, though in varying degrees. Jakob Arminius (1560–1609) rejected the Calvinist view of predestination, and argued that the divine sovereignty was compatible with human free will. >> Arminianism; Augustine, St (of Hippo); Calvinism; free will; Lutheranism; Pelagius

pre-eclampsia [pree-e**klamp**sia] A potentially serious, abnormal condition of late pregnancy, in which blood pressure rises to above 140/90 mmHg, protein appears in the urine, and there is swelling of the limbs; also known as **pregnancy hypertension**. It is an uncommon condition, of unknown cause. >> blood pressure; eclampsia; pregnancy [i]

prefabrication In architecture, the manufacture of parts or the whole of a building in a factory or other place away from the construction site. First considered in earnest during the 1920s, it was subsequently put into practice on a wide scale during the post-war years. Since the 1960s, the practice has been increasingly referred to as **systems building**.

Length of Pregnancy in some Mammals

Animal	Gestation period*	Animal	Gestation period*
camel	406	kangaroo	40
cat	62	lion	108
cow	280	mink	50
chimpanzee	237	monkey, rhesus	164
dog	62	mouse	21
dolphin	276	opossum	13
elephant, African	640	orangutan	245–275
ferret	42	pig	113
fox	52	rabbit	32
giraffe	395–425	rat	21
goat	151	reindeer	215–245
guinea pig	68	seal, northern fur	350
hamster	16	sheep	148
hedgehog	35–40	skunk	62
horse	337	squirrel, grey	44
human	266	tiger	105–109
hyena	110	whale	365

*average number of days

preference shares Shares issued by a company, without voting rights, which carry a fixed rate of dividend (or interest). The holders have a prior claim on the profits of the company over ordinary shareholders. >> shares

pregnancy A physiological process in which female, live-bearing mammals nurture their developing young within the uterus; also known as **gestation**. It begins when the fertilized ovum embeds itself in the uterine wall (*implantation*), and ends with the birth of the offspring (*parturition*). The duration of pregnancy is species-specific: smaller animals with large litters generally have short gestation periods (eg hamsters, 16 days). >> eclampsia; superovulation syndrome; test-tube baby; uterus ℹ

prelude A piece of instrumental music which precedes a longer work, or is coupled with another of comparable length, especially a fugue. Until the 17th-c, independent preludes were often written, or improvised, to test an instrument's tuning. >> fugue; suite

premenstrual syndrome / tension (PMS, PMT) A condition in which a variety of symptoms occur in relation to menstruation which interfere with normal life. It is of variable duration, has components that are both physical (eg abdominal pain, sleep disturbance) and mental (eg irritability, depression), and does not usually commence at the very beginning of puberty. The causes are unknown. >> menstruation

premier >> **prime minister**

Premier Division The name of the English football league first division, comprising the top 22 English sides, established as a separate organization in the 1992–3 season. The three lower divisions (2, 3, and 4) were renamed 1, 2, and 3, respectively. >> football ℹ

Preminger, Otto [**pre**minjer] (1906–86) Film director and producer, born in Vienna. He emigrated to the USA in 1935, and after some years of directing on the Broadway stage, made *Laura* (1944), often considered his best film. Later films included *Porgy and Bess* (1959), *Exodus* (1960), and *The Human Factor* (1979).

premiss A sentence which is explicitly assumed in an argument. In *Paris is larger than London; therefore London is smaller than Paris*, 'Paris is larger than London' is the only premiss. >> inference

premium bond A UK government security, introduced in 1956, and issued in numbered units of one pound. The accumulated interest on bonds sold is distributed through a lottery in the form of weekly and monthly tax-free cash prizes. Winning numbers are selected by a computer known as ERNIE (Electronic Random Number Indicator Equipment). >> bond; lottery

Premonstratensians [preemonstra**ten**sianz] A religious order founded by St Norbert at Prémontré, France, in 1120; also known as the **Norbertines** or **White Canons**. They are noted for parish education and mission work. >> monasticism

preparatory school In the UK, an independent fee-paying school for children up to the age when they might move to a public school, or to a maintained secondary school if parents no longer wish to pay fees. It usually caters for pupils up to the age of 13. In the USA, a preparatory school is one which prepares students for college, equivalent to the British public school. >> public school; secondary education

Pre-Raphaelite Brotherhood (PRB) A group of artists formed in London in 1848 with the aim of revolutionizing early Victorian art; their preference was for the styles of the 15th-c (ie pre-Raphael). PRB pictures are recognizable by their bright colours, hard-edged forms, shallow picture-space, and meticulous attention to detail. >> Hunt, William Holman; Millais; Raphael; Rossetti, Dante Gabriel

presbyopia >> **eye** ℹ

presbyter >> **elder** (religion)

Presbyterianism The conciliar form of Church government of the Reformed Churches, deriving from the 16th-c Reformation led by John Calvin in Geneva and John Knox in Scotland. Government is by courts at local congregational (eg kirk session), regional (presbytery), and national (General Assembly) levels. *Elders* (ordained laymen) as well as ministers play a leading part in all courts. >> Calvin; elder (religion); General Assembly (religion); Knox, John; presbytery 3; Reformed Churches

presbytery 1 The E part of the chancel of a church, behind the choir. >> church ℹ **2** The traditional name for the dwelling-house of priests in the Roman Catholic Church. >> Roman Catholicism **3** In Presbyterianism, a church court composed of equal numbers of elders and ministers, presided over by a moderator, and overseeing a geographical grouping of congregations. >> moderator; Presbyterianism

preschool education The provision of education for children under the statutory school age. This can either be in nursery or kindergarten, where there will usually be trained personnel, or in playgroups, where parent volunteers work with playgroup leaders. >> kindergarten; nursery school

Prescott, John (Leslie) (1938–) British politician, born in Prestatyn, Denbighshire. He was elected to the European Parliament in 1975, and became leader of the Labour group (1976–9). He became deputy prime minister and secretary of state for the Environment and Transport, with extra responsibilities for regional policy in the 1997 Labour government.

prescription An order for drugs written by a physician to a pharmacist, who will supply the correct medicine to the patient. Until the 1940s prescriptions were written entirely in Latin. >> pharmacy

president The name used by a head of state who is not appointed on a hereditary basis. Some presidents perform a largely formal and ceremonial role, ensuring that a government is formed (eg Ireland). Others share constitutionally in governing with the prime minister, cabinet, and legislature (eg France). Yet others effectively act as head of the government (eg the USA). >> prime minister

Presidential Medal of Freedom The highest American award for civilians in peacetime, given for contributions to the interests of the USA, or to world peace, or for cultural achievements.

Presidium >> **Politburo**

Presley, Elvis (Aron) (1935–77) Rock singer, born in Tupelo, MS. In 1953 he recorded some sides for Sun

Records in Memphis, TN, then in 1956 'Heartbreak Hotel' sold millions of copies. His performances, featuring much hip-wriggling and sexual innuendo, incited hysteria in teenagers. He made 45 records that sold in the millions, including 'Hound Dog', 'Love Me Tender', and 'Jailhouse Rock'. His Hollywood films such as *Loving You* (1957), *King Creole* (1958), and *GI Blues* (1960) became enormous moneymakers. He died at Graceland, his Memphis mansion, which is now a souvenir shrine for his many fans. >> pop music; rock music

Presocratics The first Greek (and therefore Western) philosophers, who came 'before Socrates' in the 6th-c and 5th-c BC. They sought natural rather than mythological explanations for phenomena. >> Anaxagoras; Anaximander; Anaximenes; Democritus; Empedocles; Heraclitus; Parmenides; Socrates

Pressburg >> **Bratislava**

pressure Force per unit area; symbol *p*, units Pa (pascal). It is measured using barometers or pressure gauges. >> atmospheric pressure; bar (physics); barometer; force; pressure gauge; sound; torr

pressure gauge A gauge which measures pressure in enclosed vessels and containers, such as boilers and pipes. Inside the gauge is a *Bourdon tube*, which is normally hook-shaped. When the pressure inside exceeds that outside, the tube straightens. This movement is transferred to move a pointer around a calibrated dial. >> pressure

pressure group A voluntary organization formed to articulate a particular political interest or cause; also called an **interest group**, and in the USA known as **lobbyists**. It differs from a political party in that it does not seek political office.

pressurized water reactor >> **nuclear reactor** ℹ

PRESTEL An interactive computer-based information system provided over the telephone network in the UK by British Telecom. It provides access to a wide variety of information sources. >> viewdata

Prester John A mythical Christian priest-king of a vast empire in C Asia. The story almost certainly related to the Christian kingdom of Ethiopia, which had been cut off by the Islamic conquest of Egypt. >> Ethiopia ℹ

Preston 53°46N 2°42W, pop (1995e) 131 000. County town of Lancashire, NW England; part of Central Lancashire New Town; on the R Ribble; site of Royalist defeat in the Civil War (1648); 18th-c centre of the cotton industry; railway; university (1994); football league team, Preston North End (Lillywhites). >> English Civil War; Lancashire

Prestonpans [prestn**panz**] 55°57N 3°00W, pop (1995e) 8000. Town in East Lothian, E Scotland; railway; site of Scottish victory over the English (1745). >> Scotland ℹ

Prestwick 55°30N 3°12W, pop (1995e) 13 600. Town in South Ayrshire, SW Scotland; airport (the official international gateway for Scotland); railway. >> Scotland ℹ

Pretoria [pri**taw**ria] 25°45S 28°12E, pop (1995e) 576 000 (metropolitan area). Administrative capital of South Africa, and alternative capital of Gauteng province; altitude 1369 m/4491 ft; founded, 1855; capital of South African Republic, 1881; railway; two universities (1873, 1908). >> Gauteng; Johannesburg; South Africa ℹ

Pretorius, Andries (Wilhelmus Jacobus) [pre**taw**rius] (1799–1853) Afrikaner leader, born in Graaff-Reinet, South Africa. He joined the Great Trek of 1836 into Natal, where he was chosen commandant-general, and later trekked again across the Vaal. Pretoria was named after him. >> Great Trek

Pretorius, Marthinus (Wessel) [pre**taw**rius] (1819–1901) Afrikaner soldier and statesman, born in Graaff-Reinet, South Africa, the son of Andries Pretorius. He was elected president of the South African Republic (1857–71) and of the Orange Free State (1859–63).

preventive medicine A branch of medical practice concerned with the prevention of disease. This is achieved by measures that (1) control the environment, such as clean air legislation, (2) ensure a clean and suitable food and water supply, (3) promote mass medication (eg schemes of immunization), (4) organize programmes for the eradication of disease (eg smallpox, diphtheria), and (5) promote safer lifestyles largely by education (eg the promotion of condoms to reduce the possibility of AIDS). >> medicine; vaccination

Previn, André (George) [**pre**vin] (1929–) Conductor and composer, born in Berlin. He spent some years as a jazz pianist, and became musical director of symphony orchestras at Houston, (1967–9), London (1968–79), and Pittsburgh, (1976–86). He has composed musicals, film scores, and orchestral works, and done a great deal to bring classical music to the attention of a wide public.

Prévost, (Antoine François), l'Abbé [prayvoh] (1697–1763) Novelist, born in Hesdin, France. He is best known for *Manon Lescaut* (1731), originally published as the final part of a seven-volume novel.

Priam [**pri**yam] In Greek legend, the King of Troy. He was son of Laomedon, and husband of Hecuba, and is presented in the *Iliad* as an old man. At the sack of Troy, he was killed by Neoptolemus. >> Hector; Trojan War

Pribilof Islands [**prib**ilof] Group of four islands in the Bering Sea, Alaska, USA; two inhabited (St Paul, St George); area 168 sq km/65 sq mi; centre of seal fur trade. >> Alaska

Price, (Mary Violet) Leontyne (1927–) Soprano, born in Laurel, MS. A notable Bess (1952–4) in Gershwin's *Porgy and Bess*, she was the first black opera singer on television, in *Tosca* for NBC (1955). >> Barber

Price, Nick, popular name of **Nicholas Raymond Leige Price** (1957–) Golfer, born in Durban, South Africa. His family moved to Zimbabwe, where he turned professional in 1977. His wins include the PGA World Series (1983), the United States PGA Championship (1992, 1994), and the (British) Open (1994).

Price, Vincent (Leonard) (1911–93) Actor and writer, born in St Louis, MO. Known for his distinctive, low-pitched, creaky, atmospheric voice, and his quizzical, mock-serious facial expressions, he went on to star in a series of acclaimed Gothic horror movies, such as *The Pit and the Pendulum* (1961) and *The Abominable Dr Phibes* (1971).

price index >> **retail price index**

prices and incomes policy An attempt by government to control inflation by acting directly on prices and wages, either by persuasion or by law. This contrasts with the view that inflation should be controlled by monetary or fiscal policies to influence demand, or supply-side measures to improve productivity. The correct structure of prices and wages is controversial, and the government's power to control prices and wages is uneven. It is impossible for governments to avoid prices and incomes policy entirely, as they are themselves major purchasers of goods and employers of labour. Efforts at prices and incomes policy have been sporadic, in the UK in the 1960s and 1970s, and in France in the early 1980s. >> stop–go policy

prickly heat A common generalized skin disorder in tropical countries that may also affect local areas of skin in temperate climates. Obstruction to the ducts of sweat glands results in a crop of small red pimples associated with itching. >> skin ℹ; sweat

prickly pear A species of opuntia (*Opuntia vulgaris*) often cultivated for its reddish, juicy, edible fruits. (Family: Cactaceae.) >> opuntia

Pride, Sir Thomas (?–1658) English parliamentarian during the Civil War, born (possibly) near Glastonbury. When the House of Commons betrayed a disposition to effect a settlement with Charles I, he was appointed by the army (1648) to expel its Presbyterian Royalist members (**Pride's Purge**). >> Charles I (of England); English Civil War

priest The person authorized to sacrifice. In Christianity, the term derives from the Old Testament sacrificial system. Now, mainly in Roman Catholic and Orthodox usage, it refers to an ordained officer authorized to administer the sacraments, in particular the Eucharist (the sacrifice of the Mass). >> Eucharist; Mass; Old Testament; Orders, Holy; sacrament

Priestley, J(ohn) B(oynton) (1894–1984) Writer, born in Bradford, West Yorkshire. In 1929 his novel *The Good Companions* (1929) gained him wide popularity. He established his reputation as a playwright with *Dangerous Corner* (1932), *Time and the Conways* (1937), and other plays on space-time themes, as well as popular comedies, such as *Laburnum Grove* (1933). His wife, **Jacquetta Hawkes** (1910–96), was an archaeologist and writer.

Priestley, Joseph (1733–1804) Chemist and clergyman, born in Fieldhead, West Yorkshire. He is best known for his research into the chemistry of gases, and his discovery of oxygen. His controversial views on religion and political theory (he was a supporter of the French Revolution) led him in 1794 to leave in fear of his life for America, where he was well received.

primary In politics, an election to choose the candidates for an election to public office. It differs from other forms of candidate selection in that the primary election is not organized by political parties, but by the government authority for which the election is to be held. The procedure is commonly associated with the USA.

primary education The first phase of statutory education, usually covering the years from 5 or 6 up to 11 or 12. In most countries, the emphasis is on the coverage of a wide range of subjects and themes usually taught by the class teacher. There is also emphasis on social and personal development, and on 'learning by doing'. >> pre-school education; secondary education

primate (biology) A mammal of the order Primates (c.180 species); most inhabit tropical forests; both eyes face forwards; hands and (usually) feet with grasping 'opposable thumb', used for climbing; cerebral hemispheres of brain well developed. Living species are usually placed in two suborders: the Strepsirhini (**prosimians**) and the Haplorhini (**tarsiers** and **Anthropoidea**). >> Anthropoidea; ape; mammal [i]; marmoset; monkey [i]; prosimian; tarsier

primate (religion) The most senior bishop of a given area; for example, in the Church of England the Archbishop of Canterbury is primate of All England. >> bishop; Church of England

prime minister The leader of and usually head of a government; also known as a **premier**. In general, prime ministers have to work through collective decision-making in a *cabinet*, although they can enjoy certain separate powers. In electoral systems, they are usually the leader of the largest party or coalition in parliament. >> cabinet

prime number In mathematics, a positive integer greater than 1 that has no divisors other than 1 and itself. Number theorists have tried to devise functions $f(n)$ which produce only prime numbers for positive integer values of n, but so far all have failed. >> number theory

prime rate The US bank base lending rate, at which the bank will lend to its best ('prime') customers. This rate applies to only 50 or so large US corporations, all others paying higher rates. >> bank base rate; minimum lending rate

Primo de Rivera (y Orbaneja), Miguel [**pree**moh t͟he ri**ve**ra] (1870–1930) Spanish general, born in Jerez de la Frontera, Spain. In 1923 he led a military coup, inaugurating a dictatorship which lasted until 1930. His son, **José Antonio Primo de Rivera** (1903–36) founded the Spanish Fascist Party, *Falange Española* in 1933, and was executed by the Republicans in 1936. >> fascism; Spanish Civil War

primrose A stemless perennial (*Primula vulgaris*) native to Europe, W Asia, and N Africa; flowers long-stalked with spreading, pale yellow, rarely pink petals. (Family: Primulaceae.) >> oxlip; polyanthus; sepal

Prince, stage name by which **Prince Roger Nelson** is most widely known (1958–) Pop-singer and composer, born in Minneapolis, MN. Named after the Prince Roger Trio, a jazz band in which his father was a pianist, he began singing as a teenager, and released *For You* in 1978. International success followed the release of *1999* (1982), the film and album *Purple Rain* (1984), and *Batman* (1989). He changed his name to the unpronounceable glyph 0(+> in 1993, and has since adopted the designation of **The Artist (formerly known as Prince)**. >> pop music

Prince Edward Island pop (1995e) 138 000; area 5660 sq km/2185 sq mi. Province in E Canada; island in the Gulf of St Lawrence; rises to 142 m/466 ft; capital, Charlottetown; visited by Cartier, 1534; French claim as Île St Jean; settled by Acadians; captured by British, 1758; annexed to Nova Scotia, 1763; separate province, 1769; modern name, after Queen Victoria's father, 1798; joined Canada, 1873; governed by a lieutenant-governor and Legislative Assembly. >> Canada [i]; Cartier; Charlottetown

Prince of Wales In the UK, the title conferred (by custom, not law) on the sovereign's eldest son. Wales was ruled by a succession of independent princes from the 5th-c; the first to be acknowledged by an English king was Llewelyn ap Gruffudd (r. 1246–82) in 1267. Tradition holds that after the death of Llewelyn in battle (against the English), Edward I presented his own infant son to the Welsh people at Caernarfon Castle as their prince. The title has been used since that time. >> Charles, Prince of Wales

Princess Royal A title sometimes bestowed on the eldest, or only, daughter of a sovereign. George V's daughter Mary was Princess Royal until her death in 1965; the title was conferred by the Queen on Princess Anne in 1987.

Princeton 40°21N 74°40W, pop (1995e) 12 200. Borough in WC New Jersey, USA, on the Millstone R; founded by Quakers, 1696; scene of a British defeat by George Washington, 1777; a noted centre for education and research; university (1746); Institute for Advanced Study. >> Ivy League [i]; New Jersey

printed circuit A technique which replaces individual wiring between components in electronic circuits. It is made by depositing a network of thin, metallic connections on to a board, the electronic components usually being soldered to pins on the other side of the board. Printed circuit boards can be mass-produced, and their use enables circuit assembly to be easily automated. >> electronics; integrated circuit

printer >> **computer printer**

printing A set of techniques for placing an image on a foundation in a controlled sequence of identical copies; the foundation is generally paper, and the colouring agent is generally ink. The techniques include *relief*, *planographic* (surface), and *intaglio* (recess) printing. The principal forms of relief printing are *letterpress* and *flexography*; those of planographic printing, *lithography* and the obsolescent *collotype*. Intaglio printing is typified by *gravure*, but most of the techniques used by artists in printmaking (engraving, drypoint, mezzotint, and etching) also fall into this category. Printing probably originated in 6th-c China (a text survives from 594), and newspaper was first printed c.860. Printing with metal plates developed in the 11th-c; movable metal type c.1050. The first European block printing dates from 1375. Gutenberg began printing

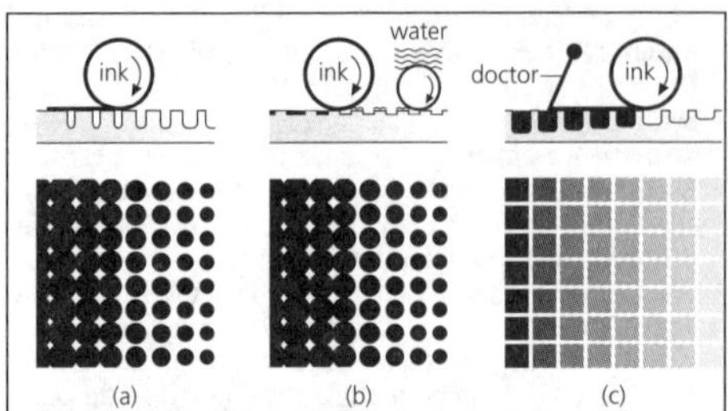

Three methods of printing. (a) The relief or letterpress process with dots of varying size. (b) The surface, lithographic, or planographic process, with the same kind of dot system as (a). (c) The recess or intaglio process, with rectangular prints varying in intensity but not in size.

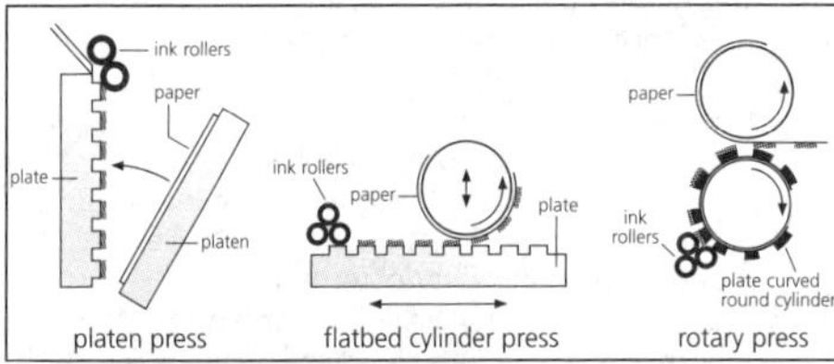

Three kinds of letterpress printing press

in 1436, and Caxton in 1475. The oldest form of printing, letterpress, depends upon pressure for the satisfactory transfer of ink to paper. Later design improvements included the 'Dutch' press developed in Amsterdam and introduced into N America in 1639. The wooden handpress was superseded in 1795 by the first all-metal press, the Stanhope. The 19th and 20th-c saw the development of increasingly elaborate mechanical presses. Offset lithography developed at the beginning of the 20th-c, and came into widespread use. Techniques of typesetting can now create the typographic image direct, either on film or on paper, thus cutting out the need for typesetters to set and store metal type. >> gravure; letterpress [i]; lithography [i]; phototypesetter; screen-process printing

prion disease [**pri**yon] A new category of diseases whose defining feature is an abnormal folding of a cellular protein; an abbreviation derived from **proteinaceous infectious particles**. Mutations, insertions, and other variations in the prion protein gene (chromosome 20 in humans) cause the disease or modify its progression. Genetic changes result in the abnormal folding of the prion protein, and result in a chronic condition characterized by neuronal damage, degeneration in the central nervous system, and resistance to the process of breaking down proteins. This molecular pathology uniquely produces a genetically inherited disease that is also potentially transmissible to any species possessing a prion gene. Symptoms of prion disease include difficulties with balance, walking, and speech, electroencephalographic changes, and dementia. It is a rare disorder in humans, and is more common in some species of animals (notably, cows and sheep). The possibility of inter-species transmission between cattle with BSE and humans through eating contaminated foodstuffs gave rise to major public health anxieties in the UK in the early 1990s. >> bovine spongiform encephalopathy; central nervous system; Creutzfeldt-Jacob disease; kuru; protein; scrapie; species

Prior, Matthew (1664–1721) Diplomat and poet, born in Wimborne, Dorset. He is best known for his light occasional verse, collected as *Poems on Several Occasions* (1709).

Priscian [**pri**shian], Lat **Priscianus** (6th-c) Latin grammarian, born in Caesarea. His 18-volume *Institutiones grammaticae* (Grammatical Foundations) was highly regarded in the Middle Ages. >> grammar; Italic languages

prism In mathematics, a solid geometrical figure: its section is a rectilineal figure, with parallel edges. In optics, it is a transparent object used to produce or study the refraction and dispersion of light. >> geometry; refraction

prison That part of the penal system where criminals are held in custody for varying lengths of time determined by the courts as punishment for offences. Prisons developed rapidly from the early 19th-c; before then, banishment and corporal or capital punishment were the main ways of dealing with offenders. Conditions in the earliest municipal prisons were usually atrocious, and were improved only through the work of penal reformers such as Elizabeth Fry. Problems of overcrowding still dog many prisons today. >> Fry, Elizabeth; Howard, John

Priština [**preesh**tina] 42°39N 21°10E, pop (1995e) 213 000. Chief city of Kosovo region, Yugoslavia; former capital of Serbia; airfield; railway; university (1976); population decimated by forced removal of ethnic Albanians (Mar–Apr 1999); severely damaged in the ensuing Yugoslavia/NATO conflict. >> Serbia; Yugoslavia [i]

Pritchett, Sir V(ictor) S(awdon) (1900–97) Writer and critic, born in Ipswich, Suffolk. He became known for his critical works, such as *The Living Novel* (1946), short stories (2 vols, 1982, 1983), and travel books.

private enterprise An economic system where individuals may engage in a business venture using their own resources and without needing state approval, as long as the venture does not contravene existing laws. It contrasts with **public enterprise**, where the activity is carried out by a state-owned or -controlled organization.

privateering >> **buccaneers**

privatization The return to private ownership of organizations which are owned at present by the state. The government issues shares in the company to be privatized, and offers them for sale to the public. Several cases took place in Britain in the 1980s, including British Telecom and British Gas. >> nationalization; shares

privet A mostly temperate, evergreen or deciduous shrub or small tree; leaves leathery; flowers tubular with four spreading lobes, creamy, fragrant; berries black or purple, poisonous. Several species are used for garden hedges. (Genus: *Ligustrum*, c.40 species. Family: Oleaceae.)

Privy Council A body which advises the British monarch, appointed by the crown. In previous times, particularly the Tudor period, it was a highly influential group; today its role is largely formal. Its membership is over 300. >> Order in Council

Prix de l'Arc de Triomphe [**pree** duh **lahk** duh **tree**õf] The richest horse race in Europe, held at the end of the season over 2400 m/2625 yd at Longchamp, near Paris, on the first Sunday in October. First run in 1920, it is the leading race in Europe for horses at least three years old.

Prizren [**preez**ren] 42°12N 20°43E, pop (1995e) 139 000. Town in SW Serbia; on R Prizrenska Bistrica; built on the site of a Roman town (Theranda); important mediaeval trade centre; part of Albania, 1941–4; railway. >> Serbia; Yugoslavia [i]

probability theory The mathematical study of relative probabilities in processes involving uncertainty, for example tossing a coin or rolling dice. The foundations of the subject were laid by Pascal and Fermat in the 17th-c. >> decision theory; Fermat; Pascal; statistics

probate The official proving of a will. The executor of the will applies to the court for a certificate confirming the validity of the will and the authority of the executor to administer the estate of the deceased. The term is not used in all jurisdictions (eg in Scotland). >> will (law)

probation A method of dealing with offenders where, instead of a sentence of imprisonment, a court may order the offender to be supervised for a fixed period by a **probation officer**. Offenders must agree to be placed on probation after the obligations under the order are explained to them. >> community service order

proboscis monkey [pro**bo**sis] An Old World monkey (*Nasalis larvatus*) native to Borneo; pale with darker 'cap' on head, and dark back; long tail; protruding nose, which in adult males becomes bulbous and pendulous. >> langur; Old World monkey

procaryote or **prokaryote** [proh**ka**rioht] An organism that lacks an organized nucleus separated from the surrounding cytoplasm by a nuclear membrane. They are predominantly single-celled micro-organisms, such as the bacteria and blue-green algae, or infectious agents of cells, such as the viruses. >> bacteria ℹ; eucaryote; nucleus (biology); virus

Proclus [**proh**klus] (c.412–85) Greek Neoplatonist philosopher, born in Constantinople. The last head of Plato's Academy, his approach combined the Roman, Syrian, and Alexandrian schools of thought in Greek philosophy into one theological metaphysic. >> Neoplatonism

Proconsul >> ***Dryopithecus***

Procop(ius) >> **Prokop**

Procopius [pro**koh**pius] (c.499–565) Byzantine historian, born in Caesarea, Palestine. He accompanied Belisarius on his campaigns against the Persians, the Vandals in Africa, and the Ostrogoths in Italy. His principal works are histories of the wars, and of the court of Justinian. >> Belisarius; Justinian

Procrustes [proh**kruhs**teez] In the legend of Theseus, a robber, living in Attica, who made travellers lie on his bed, and either cut or lengthened them to fit it; his name means 'the stretcher'. Theseus gave him the same treatment, and killed him.

procurator fiscal A public offical in Scotland who is responsible for pursuing the prosecution of crimes and offences in the sheriff court and the district court. The 'fiscal' is also responsible for reporting serious crimes to the Crown Office, which may merit prosecution in the High Court, as well as for investigating all cases of sudden, accidental, or suspicious deaths. >> coroner; criminal law; prosecution; sheriff

producer In the motion picture industry, the person who brings the initial concept to practical reality, organizing budgetary control, choosing the director, and holding the balance between the director and other important members of the production team. Producers are also concerned with distribution for the international market, and exploitation on television and video. In major television organizations, one producer is often in charge of a series of programmes, working with several different directors or presenters. In radio broadcasting, the producer has a dual role, being also the person who actually controls the making of the programmes (the province of the *director*, in other media).

productivity The ratio of output to input in an industrial context. It usually refers to the quantity of goods or commodities produced in relation to the number of employees engaged in the operation (**labour productivity**). **Total productivity** includes the input of capital also. The notion is important in wage negotiations: **productivity bargaining** balances a proposed increase in wages with an anticipated rise in productivity. >> time and motion study

profit The difference for a company between its sales revenue and the costs attributable to those sales. Profit may be calculated before or after deducting interest payments, and before or after deducting taxation charges. The surplus may be paid out to shareholders as a dividend, or retained by the business (as *reserves*) to finance capital expenditure. **Profit sharing** is a scheme whereby a percentage of the profits of a company is given to staff in the form of an additional bonus payment. **Profitability** is the measurement of how effectively a company has used the resources available to it. There are also many **non-profit-making** companies, where a surplus is ploughed back into the company, or (as in the case of charities) used for charitable purposes. >> company; dividend; equity (economics); satisficing

Profumo, John (Dennis) [pro**fyoo**moh] (1915–) British Conservative statesman. Secretary of state for war in 1960, he resigned in 1963 after deceiving the House of Commons about the nature of his relationship with Miss Christine Keeler, who was at the time also involved with a Russian diplomat. He later became chairman (1982–5) then president of Toynbee Hall, London.

progesterone [proh**jes**terohn] A steroid present in both sexes of all vertebrates. In female mammals it acts to prepare the uterus for implantation of the embryo, inhibits ovulation during pregnancy, and prepares the breasts for lactation. >> gonad; hormones; pregnancy ℹ; steroid

program; programmer >> **computer program**

programmed learning A form of learning developed in the 1960s, based on the behaviourist learning theories of US psychologist B F Skinner. He stressed the need for short frames of information to be given, followed by an active response and the immediate reinforcement of correct answers. Programmed-learning principles have been influential in the development of microcomputer software and the interactive video disc. >> behaviourism; Skinner, B F; video disc

programme music Music which paints a scene or tells a story. Among early examples are the violin concertos by Vivaldi called *The Four Seasons*, but it was in the 19th-c, with the increased resources of the symphony orchestra, that composers most effectively gave musical expression to literary and other extra-musical ideas, notably in the concert overture and the symphonic poem. >> overture; symphonic poem; Vivaldi

programming language An artificial language which allows people to instruct computers to carry out specific tasks. Many programming languages have been developed; among the relatively common high-level languages are ADA, APL, ALGOL, BASIC, COBOL, CORAL, FORTH, FORTRAN, LISP, PASCAL, and PROLOG (*see separate entries*). >> assembly language; computer program; high-level language; Java (computing)

Progressive Conservative (PC) Party A Canadian political party, mainly active at the federal level, but with branches in most provinces and territories. It originated in C Canada in the 1850s, though with roots going back to 18th-c Toryism. The PCs have formed the government nationally five times since the 1940s, but were resoundingly defeated in the general election in 1993. >> Campbell, Kim; Canada ℹ; Mulroney; Tories

progressive education A term used to denote teaching which places greater emphasis on the wishes of the child. It usually involves greater freedom of choice, activity, and movement than traditional forms of teaching.

Progress spacecraft An uncrewed version of the Soviet Soyuz crewed spacecraft, modified as a resupply vehicle for the Salyut and Mir space stations. After unloading, the spacecraft is separated and removed from orbit to burn up in the atmosphere. >> Soviet space programme; Soyuz spacecraft; space station

Prohibition (1920–33) An attempt to stop the sale of all alcoholic drinks in the USA, authorized by the 18th amendment to the Constitution (1919) and the Volstead Act (1920). Prohibition met great resistance, and generated a large bootlegging industry. It was ended in 1933.

projection television A television system in which images are projected through special wide-aperture lenses on a large external screen, usually using three high-brightness cathode ray tubes in the component colours red, green, and blue. The limited brightness output limits the width of an external high-reflection screen to c.4 m/13 ft. >> eidophor; television; xenon

projective tests In psychology, a number of somewhat contentious procedures for assessing personality. Their use involves the presentation of ambiguous or unstructured material onto which the testee is assumed to project his/her personality. The most famous is the Rorschach Psychodiagnostic Technique, which requires subjects to describe what they see in 10 bilaterally symmetrical inkblots. >> personality; Rorschach

projector An apparatus for presenting an enlarged image on a screen from a transparency such as a photographic slide or film. In a motion picture projector, each frame is held stationary at an illuminated aperture for a brief period, and then advanced by an intermittent sprocket or reciprocating claw, the light being cut off by a rotating shutter during the movement. The sound track on the film is reproduced at a separate sound head where the film is moved continuously at constant speed. >> cinematography

prokaryote >> **procaryote**

Prokofiev, Sergey Sergeyevitch [prohk**of**ief] (1891–1953) Composer, born in Sontsovka, Ukraine. His works have a vast range, including seven symphonies, nine concertos, ballets, operas, suites, cantatas, sonatas, and songs, and his most popular work, *Peter and the Wolf* (1936).

Prokop or **Procop(ius)** [**proh**kop, pro**koh**pius], known as **the Bald** or **the Great** (c.1380–1434) Bohemian Hussite leader, a follower of Žiška, and on his death, the leader of the Taborites. He repeatedly defeated German armies, but fell in battle at Lipany, Hungary. >> Hussites; Žiška

prolactin [proh**lak**tin] A hormone secreted by the front part of the pituitary gland which initiates lactation in mammals and stimulates the production of progesterone. >> hormones; lactation; pituitary gland

prolapsed intervertebral disc A condition which arises when the nucleus of the disc situated between the bodies of the vertebrae is forced outwards through the surrounding joint capsule; commonly known as a **slipped disc**. It is caused by an excessive load being placed on the joints between the bodies of the spinal vertebrae, such as in heavy or awkward lifting, and is followed by back pain or sciatica. >> vertebral column

proletariat In radical and socialist philosophy, a term coined to denote the **working class**, ie those who live by their labour and do not own property. *Lumpenproletariat* was coined by Marx to refer to those in big cities from whom class identification could not be expected. >> Marxism

pro-life movement Organized opposition to the legality of induced abortion, and to laboratory experiments on human embryos. There are a number of national organizations and pressure groups, such as Operation Rescue in the USA, the Society for the Protection of the Unborn Child (SPUC), and LIFE. Active support comes from members of several religions, notably Roman Catholics, but also Muslims and Jews. >> abortion

PROLOG A high-level programming language based on mathematical logic, widely used in artificial intelligence applications. PROLOG has, to some extent, replaced LISP. >> LISP; programming language

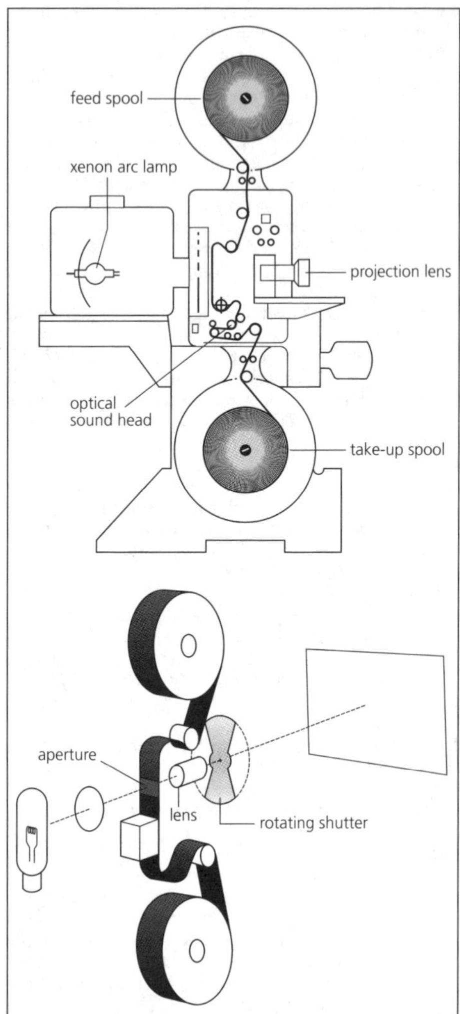

Cine projector principle – each successive frame of the film is momentarily held stationary while its image is projected on the screen; a rotating shutter obscures the beam during the movement to the next frame.

PROM [**pee**rom] An acronym of **programmable read-only memory**, a special type of integrated circuit read-only memory (ROM) into which the user can write data after manufacture. Once written, the data cannot be altered. >> EAROM; EPROM; ROM

promenade concert A musical performance, especially by an orchestra, during which some at least of the audience are offered floor space, without seats, at reduced prices. The London 'proms' were started at the Queen's Hall by Sir Henry Wood in 1895; they transferred to the Royal Albert Hall in 1941. >> orchestra; Wood, Henry

Prometheus [proh**mee**thyoos] In Greek mythology, a Titan; his name means 'the foreseeing'. He stole fire from heaven to help mankind, whom Zeus wished to destroy, and was punished by being chained to a rock in the

Caucasus; every day an eagle fed on his liver, which grew again in the night. Heracles shot the eagle and set Prometheus free. >> Heracles; Zeus

promissory note A signed document containing a written promise to undertake to pay a sum of money on or by a specific date. The document is legally binding and is signed, for example, when a bank customer takes out a loan.

prongbuck >> **pronghorn**

pronghorn A North American antelope (*Antilocapra americana*); male called **prongbuck**; pale brown with prominent eyes; male horns with frontal 'prong' and backward-curving tips. >> antelope

proof spirit >> **alcohol strength**

propane C_3H_8, boiling point −42°C. The third in the alkane series of hydrocarbons; a gas obtained from petroleum and natural gas, used as a fuel and a refrigerant. >> alkanes; gas 2 [i]; propyl

propanone >> **acetone**

propeller A device used principally by ships and aeroplanes to transform the rotational energy of an engine into directed thrust. To accomplish this, the propeller is fitted with blades radiating from a central hub, each blade being of aerofoil cross section. As the propeller rotates, the water or air is accelerated backwards, producing a reactive force in the forward direction. >> aerodynamics [i]; aeroplane; propfan; ship [i]

Propertius, Sextus [pro**per**shius] (c.48–c.15 BC) Latin elegiac poet, probably born in Asisium (Assisi), Italy. The central figure of his inspiration was his mistress, to whom he devoted the first of his four surviving books, *Cynthia*. >> elegy

property Something owned or possessed – a notion whose precise definition varies greatly between different jurisdictions. In Anglo-US law, **real property** includes lands and buildings; other kinds of property are known as **personal property**. **Chattels** are movable goods, classed as personal property. A gift of personal property made by will is a **legacy**; a gift of real property made by will is a **devise**. **Intellectual property** is a general term covering intangible rights in the product of intellectual effort. It includes copyright in published work, and patents granted to protect new inventions. >> copyright; lease

propfan An aircraft propeller designed for a turbo-engine, enabling large amounts of power to be delivered by increasing the number and area of the blades in comparison with a conventional aircraft propeller. >> propeller; turbine

prophet One who is inspired to reveal a message from a divine being; an important figure in many religious traditions, sometimes a lone figure opposing the established cult or social order (eg Jeremiah, Amos, and Hosea in the Old Testament). Their messages usually address a specific situation or problem. >> God; New Testament; Old Testament; oracle

proportional representation Any system of voting designed to ensure that the representation of voters is in proportion to their numbers. In the *list system* the number of candidates on a party's list who are elected depends on the proportion of votes they receive in national elections. In the *single transferable vote*, votes are cast in multi-member constituencies and an ordered preference for all the candidates can be expressed on the ballot paper, votes being transferred from one candidate to another to enable them to gain the necessary quota to be elected. Most W European countries (but not the UK) use proportional representation. The case against it is that it produces unstable coalitions, and breaks the bond between MPs and their constituencies.

proprioception >> **kinaesthesis**

propyl [**proh**piyl, -pil] $CH_3CH_2CH_2$–. A group derived from propane. **Isopropyl** is the isomeric $(CH_3)_2CH$–. Propyl and isopropyl alcohols (propan-1-ol and propan-2-ol) are both used as solvents and as substitutes for ethanol in non-beverage applications. >> ethanol; propane

propylaeum or **propylaea** [prohpi**lee**um, prohpi**lee**a] An important entrance gateway or vestibule. It is usually in front of a sacred building, as on the Acropolis, Athens (437–432 BC). >> Acropolis

proscenium An arch and opening of a stage wall separating the auditorium of a theatre from the acting and scenic area. Its development, linked to a concept of theatrical illusion, dominated Western drama until the early 20th-c, becoming a 'fourth wall' through which the audience, sitting in darkness, could see and eavesdrop.

prosecution The initiation and pursuance of criminal proceedings against an individual in a criminal court. Common law systems are *accusatorial*, with the burden of proof normally resting with the prosecution to prove the offence beyond reasonable doubt. Civil law systems, such as France and Germany, are *inquisitorial*, whereby the prosecutor presents the case to court, but it is the responsibility of the judge to investigate the facts of the case and if necessary to call and question witnesses. >> civil law; common law; criminal law; Crown Prosecution Service; district attorney; procurator fiscal

Proserpine >> **Persephone**

prosimian A primate of the suborder Strepsirhini (40 species); wet nose with slit-like nostrils; tip of nose, between nostrils, with an obvious vertical groove; also known as **primitive primate**. >> aye-aye; indri; lemur; loris; potto

prosody The pitch, loudness, tempo, and rhythm of speech. A particular application of prosodic study is in relation to poetry, where it provides a means of analyzing the rhythmical properties of lines (*metrics*), as part of the study of versification. >> intonation; metre (literature)

Prost, Alain [prost], nickname **the Professor** (1955–) Motor-racing driver, born in St Chamond, France. The first Frenchman to win the world title, he won in 1985–6 (both for Marlboro-McLaren), was runner-up in 1983–4 and 1988, and won again in 1989 (for Maclaren–Honda) and 1993, when he announced his retirement. His 699.5 championship points is a world record. >> motor racing

prostaglandins [prosta**glan**dins] A family of unsaturated fatty acids produced by virtually every tissue of the body in response to particular stimuli. Their physiological role is unclear, but they are implicated in platelet function, the natural prevention of ulcers, and the causes of inflammation. >> carboxylic acids

prostate gland A partly muscular, partly glandular, accessory male sex organ in mammals, lying within the pelvis below the bladder, encircling part of the urethra. During sexual arousal it contributes an alkaline fluid to semen, accounting for approximately one-third of its volume. After age 50 the gland may atrophy; however, an excessive increase in the size of the side and middle lobes may also occur, compressing the urethra, and adversely affecting the functioning of the kidneys. Treatment involves the removal of part or all of the gland. >> semen; urinary system

prosthesis [pros**thee**sis] An artificial substitute for a part of the body. Examples include a mechanical arm or leg, artificial dentures, and tooth implants. >> dentistry

Protagoras [proh**tag**oras] (c.490–421 BC) Greek philosopher, born in Abdera, Greece. He taught a system of practical wisdom based on the doctrine that 'man is the measure of all things'. >> Sophists

protea [**proh**tia] A shrub or small tree, native to tropical and especially S Africa, where they are very diverse. The spectacular 'flowers' are actually inflorescences containing numerous small true flowers in the centre, surrounded by petal-like bracts. (Genus: *Protea*, 130 species. Family: Proteaceae.) >> bract; inflorescence 🅘

protectionism A government policy of protecting domestic industries against foreign competition. Devices used include tariffs, quotas on imports, subsidies for domestic firms, and preference in state purchasing. Protection is supposed to be checked by international treaties. >> General Agreement on Tariffs and Trade; quotas, import; tariff

Protectorate A regime established by the Instrument of Government, the work of army conservatives, England's only written constitution. The Lord Protectors, Oliver Cromwell (ruled 1653–8) and his son Richard (ruled 1658–9), issued ordinances and controlled the armed forces, subject to the advice of a Council of State and with Parliament as legislative partner. It failed to win support, and its collapse led to the Restoration. >> Commonwealth (English history); Restoration

protectorate A territory over which the protecting state enjoys power and jurisdiction short of full sovereignty; not formally annexed, it can come about by treaty, grant, or usage. The commonest types were the 19th–20th-c colonial protectorates, such as Botswana, all of which have now achieved independence. >> Protectorate

protein One of the three essential types of energy foods. It is a natural condensation polymer of amino acids occurring mainly as structural tissue in animals but also as enzymes in both animals and plants. Nearly all proteins are derived from 20 amino acids. >> amino acid; carbohydrate; fat; prion disease

Proterozoic eon The later of the two geological eons into which the Precambrian era is divided; the period of time from 2500 million years ago until the beginning of the Cambrian period 590 million years ago. >> Archaean eon; geological time scale; Precambrian era; RR976

Protestantism The generic term for expressions of Christian faith originating from the 16th-c Reformation as a protest against Roman Catholicism. Common characteristics include the authority of scripture, justification by faith alone, and the priesthood of all believers. There were over 400 million Protestants in 1999. >> Anabaptists; Baptists; Calvinism; Church of Scotland; Congregationalism; Dutch Reformed Church; Episcopal Church, Protestant; Lutheranism; Nonconformists; Presbyterianism; Reformation; Unitarians

Proteus [**proh**tyoos] A genus of typically rod-shaped bacteria that move by means of flagella. They are found primarily in the intestines and faeces of humans and other animals. (Kingdom: Monera. Family: Enterobacteriaceae.) >> bacteria 🅘; intestine

Proteus [**proh**tyoos] In Greek mythology, a sea god, associated with seals, and a shape-changer; he will give answers to questions after a wrestling match.

protista >> **Protoctista**

Protoceratops [prohtoh**se**ratops] A primitive ceratopsian dinosaur, known from the Upper Cretaceous period of E Asia; rear frill on skull well developed; teeth for shearing. (Order: Ornithischia.) >> Ceratopsia; Cretaceous period; dinosaur 🅘

protochordate [prohtoh**kaw(r)**dayt] An informal name for any of the chordates (phylum: Chordata) that lack a vertebral column. >> amphioxus; Chordata; tunicate

Protoctista [prohtok**tis**ta] A kingdom of relatively simple, eucaryotic organisms, comprising the single-celled protozoans and those algae and fungi that possess flagellated spores. They vary greatly in size, from the smallest micro-organisms (eg. *Chlorella*) to the giant kelps. The smallest members of this kingdom, generally composed of a single cell, or only a few cells, are known as **protists**, in some classifications. >> algae; *Chlorella*; eucaryote; flagellum; fungus; kelp; kingdom; Protozoa

Proto-Indo-European >> **Indo-European languages**

proton A component particle of the atomic nucleus; symbol *p*; mass 1.673×10^{-27} kg (938.3 MeV), charge +1, spin $\frac{1}{2}$. It is held in the nucleus by strong nuclear force. >> nucleus (physics); proton number; quark

proton number The number of protons in an atomic nucleus, equal to the number of electrons in an atom; symbol Z; also called **atomic number**. Each element has a unique proton number. >> atom; nucleon number; proton

protoplasm The complex, translucent substance that makes up every living cell. In eucaryotes, protoplasm is divisible into *nucleoplasm* (the protoplasm in the nucleus) and *cytoplasm* (the protoplasm in the rest of the cell). >> cell; cytoplasm; eucaryote

Protozoa A diverse group of unicellular micro-organisms found free-living, as consumers of organic matter, in all kinds of habitats, and as parasites or associates of other organisms; typically possess a single nucleus, sometimes two or more; usually reproduce by splitting in two (binary fission). >> amoeba; cell; parasitology; radiolaria; Sarcodina

Protura [pro**tyoo**ra] An order of small, primitively wingless insects that lack eyes and antennae; use forelegs as feelers; possess three pairs of rudimentary limbs on abdominal segments; c.120 species. >> insect 🅘

Proudhon, Pierre Joseph [proodõ] (1809–65) Socialist and political theorist, born in Besançon, France. His first important book, *Qu'est-ce que la propriété?* (1840, What is Property?), affirmed the bold paradox 'property is theft', because it involves the exploitation of the labour of others. His greatest work was the *Système des contradictions économiques* (1846, System of Economic Contradictions). >> socialism

Proulx, E(dna) Annie [proo] (1935–) Novelist, born in Norwich, CT. In 1988 her collected stories were published as *Heart Songs and Other Stories*. She turned to novel writing with *Postcards* (1992), and won the Pulitzer Prize for her second book, *The Shipping News* (1994). Later works include *Accordion Crimes* (1996).

Proust, Marcel [proost] (1871–1922) Novelist, born in Auteuil, France. In 1912 he produced the first part of his 13-volume masterpiece, *A la recherche du temps perdu* (trans Remembrance of Things Past). The second volume won the Prix Goncourt in 1919. His massive novel, exploring the power of the memory and the unconscious, as well as the nature of writing itself, has been profoundly influential.

Provence [pro**vãs**], Lat **Provincia** Former province in SE France; part of France, 1481; distinctive Romance dialect; tourism (especially on Riviera). >> France 🅘

Proverbs, Book of A book of the Hebrew Bible/Old Testament, attributed in the opening title to Solomon, but probably consisting of collected wisdom traditions from several centuries. >> Old Testament; Solomon (Hebrew Bible)

Providence 41°49N 71°24W, pop (1995e) 162 000. Capital of Rhode Island, USA; port at the head of Providence R; established, 1636; city status, 1832; an early haven for religious dissenters; airport; railway; Brown University (1764); popular sailing resort. >> Dissenters; Rhode Island

Provincetown Players A US theatre group (1915–29) remembered for the work of its leading playwright Eugene O'Neill and designer Robert Edmond Jones. >> O'Neill, Eugene

Provisional IRA >> **IRA**

Provisional Sinn Féin >> **Sinn Féin**

Provisions of Oxford >> **Oxford, Provisions of**

Proxima Centauri [**prok**sima sen**taw**ree] >> **Centaurus**

Prudhoe Bay [**proo**doh] Bay on N coast of Alaska, USA, on the Beaufort Sea; pipeline links Arctic oil fields with Valdez on the Gulf of Alaska. >> Alaska

Prud'hon, Pierre Paul [prüdõ] (1758–1823) Painter, born in Cluny, France. Patronized by the empresses of Napoleon, he was made court painter, and among his best work is a portrait of Joséphine. >> Napoleon I

prunus A tree or shrub of a large temperate genus containing many well-known ornamentals and orchard fruits; fruit a single stony seed surrounded by a fleshy outer layer. (Genus: *Prunus*, 400 species. Family: Rosaceae.) >> almond; apricot; blackthorn; cherry; drupe; peach; plum

Prusiner, Stanley B (1942–) Neurologist, born in the USA. He graduated from the University of Pennsylvania in 1968, then worked at the University of California, Berkeley and San Francisco. He shared the 1998 Nobel Prize for Physiology or Medicine for his discovery of prions. >> prion disease

Prussia A N European state, originally centred in the E Baltic region as a duchy owing suzerainty to Poland. The kingdom of Prussia was founded in 1701; under Frederick William I (1713–40) and Frederick II ('the Great') (1740–86) it acquired W Prussia and Silesia, and gained considerable territory in W Germany at the Congress of Vienna (1815). During the 19th-c it emerged as the most powerful German state, and ultimately the focus of German unification. Within the German Empire (1871–1918) and the Weimar Republic (1919–33), it retained considerable autonomy and influence. As a legal entity, Prussia ceased to exist with the post-1945 division of Germany. >> Austro-Prussian War; Franco-Prussian War; Frederick William; Frederick William III; North German Confederation; Zollverein

prussic acid >> **cyanide; hydrocyanic acid**

Prynne, William [prin] (1600–69) Puritan pamphleteer, born in Swanswick, Somerset. In 1633 appeared his *Histrio-Mastix: the Players Scourge*, which contained an apparent attack on the queen, for which he was imprisoned. Released in 1640 by the Long Parliament, he prosecuted Laud (1644), and became an MP (1648). After Cromwell's death he returned to parliament as a Royalist, for which he was made Keeper of the Tower Records. >> Laud; Long Parliament; Protectorate; Puritanism

Psalms, Book of A book of the Hebrew Bible/Old Testament; also known as the **Psalter**. It consists of 150 hymns or poems of various types, representing material from several centuries. It was the most important type of mediaeval illustrated book. >> Old Testament

Psalter >> **Psalms, Book of**

psephology [se**fol**ojee] The study of elections and voting. It is popularly associated with the analysis of voting figures and the forecasting of outcomes, but covers all aspects of elections and electoral systems.

Pseudepigrapha [syoode**pig**rafa] An ancient Jewish (and sometimes Christian) body of literature which is not part of the Jewish Scriptures or of major Christian versions of the Old Testament or of the Apocrypha, but which is similar to the Old Testament in character. It spans roughly the period 200 BC–AD 200, and includes apocalypses (eg 1 Enoch, 4 Ezra), testaments (eg Testaments of the 12 Patriarchs), wisdom literature, prayers, and psalms (eg Prayer of Manasseh, Psalms of Solomon), and additions to Old Testament stories (eg Life of Adam and Eve). >> Apocrypha, Old Testament; Jubilees, Book of; Maccabees, Books of the; Manasseh, Prayer of; Old Testament; Solomon, Psalms of

pseudopodium [syoodoh**poh**dium] A lobe-like protrusion, usually temporary, of the cell body of amoeboid cells, brought about by cytoplasmic streaming. Pseudopodia function as a means of locomotion, and also as a way of feeding (by engulfing food particles). >> amoeba; cell; cytoplasm

psi [psiy, siy] A parapsychological term for certain paranormal processes, embracing both extrasensory perception and psychokinesis. This letter of the Greek alphabet was felt to be most appropriate to stand for things considered as psychic. >> extrasensory perception

psittacosis [(p)sita**koh**sis] A systemic infection associated with pneumonia, caused by a micro-organism (*Chlamydia*) contracted from infected birds; also known as **parrot disease**. >> chlamydia; pneumonia

psoriasis [(p)so**riy**asis] A common persisting or recurring skin disorder, in which small red scaly patches form in the superficial layers of the skin, particularly affecting the elbows, knees, scalp, and nails. The cause is unknown. >> skin ℹ

Psyche [**siy**kee] In Greek mythology, 'the soul', usually represented by a butterfly. In the story told by Apuleius, she was beloved by Cupid. >> Cupid

psychedelic drugs >> **hallucinogens**

psychiatry A branch of medicine concerned with the study, diagnosis, prevention, and treatment of mental and emotional disorders. Within psychiatry, there is a range of sub-specialties including **child psychiatry**, **forensic psychiatry** (the study and treatment of patients who have broken the law), and **psychotherapy**. The range of conditions treated by psychiatrists is wide, and includes patients suffering from psychoses (in which there is a loss of contact with reality), neuroses (in which anxiety is a major component), eating disorders, mental retardation, and sleep disorders. >> Adler; autism; behaviour therapy; Freud, Sigmund; hallucination; Jung; mental disorders; neurosis; Pavlov; psychoanalysis; psychosis

psychical research >> **parapsychology**

psychic healing A form of therapy in which the healer uses a patient's aura to diagnose the problem or illness that has brought about the consultation, and then transmits to the patient the energy that is needed for healing. In **psychic surgery**, healers work upon a patient by moving their hands over the diseased parts. >> aura; healing

psychoanalysis The theory and clinical practice of a form of psychology which emphasizes unconscious aspects of the mental life of an individual. The treatment, pioneered by Freud, is a form of therapy which attempts to eliminate conflict by altering the personality in a positive way. The study of dreams was used as a way of understanding people's deeper emotions. >> Adler; Freud, Sigmund; Jung; unconscious

psychokinesis (PK) One of the two major categories of allegedly paranormal phenomena (the other being extrasensory perception). It is defined as the influencing by a living agent of a physical system or object by means other than those currently understood by the physical sciences. The phenomenon was earlier referred to as **telekinesis**. >> extrasensory perception; parapsychology; psi

psycholinguistics The study of the psychology of language. Psycholinguists are variously concerned with first and second language acquisition, language production and comprehension, and linguistic deficits such as aphasia and dyslexia. >> linguistics; psychology

psychology The science of mental life – a succinct definition used by US psychologist William James in 1890. Modern psychology began with the great advances in science and medicine of the 19th-c, including work on comparative studies of behaviour, human abilities, the functions of the nervous system, 'irrational' behaviour, intelligence, and the nature of learning. Contemporary psychology has seen a revival of interest in cognitive processes, with new interpretations using concepts from communication theory and computer systems. The application of psychological methods pervades many aspects of everyday life, such as the investigation of opinions and prejudices, the design of work and leisure environments, personnel management, counselling, and therapy. >> clinical / developmental / educational psychology; neuropsychology; phrenology; psychoanalaysis; psychometrics; psychophysics; Binet; Darwin, Charles; Freud; Helmholtz; Pavlov; Skinner

psychometrics A branch of psychology concerned with the measurement of psychological characteristics, especially intelligence, abilities, personality, and mood states. >> psychology

psychopathology A term used in psychiatry and clinical psychology, referring to any form of mental illness or aberration. >> psychiatry

psychopharmacology The science of the mechanisms, uses, and side-effects of drugs that modify psychological function and behaviour. >> pharmacology

psychophysics Methods originated by Gustav Fechner in 1860 as an attempt to quantify, as psychophysical laws, the relationships between physical stimulation and sensations. Measures of *sensitivity* describe the constraints on perception provided by the sensory apparatus. *Scaling* methods assess the magnitude of the effect of different amounts of stimulation. >> Fechner

psychosis A psychiatric term with a variety of uses. It is most clearly used when referring to psychiatric illnesses in which there is a loss of contact with reality, in the form of delusions or hallucinations. It is also used with reference to two main groups of psychiatric illnesses: **organic psychoses** are caused by diseases affecting the brain; **functional psychoses** do not have a known physical cause. >> hallucination; neurosis; psychiatry

psychosomatic disorder A set of real physical symptoms (eg headaches, high blood pressure) which have been caused, maintained, or exacerbated by emotional factors; also called a **psychophysiological disorder**. >> psychiatry

psychosurgery A procedure in which there is surgery on a brain regarded as histologically normal, with the intention of influencing the course of a behaviour disorder. The intention is to create a lesion in the brain to remove pathological thoughts and feelings with the preservation of normal functions. These procedures were initially referred to as **lobotomy** in the USA and **leucotomy** in Europe. >> mental disorders

psychotherapy The treatment of emotional problems by a trained therapist, with the object of removing or modifying maladaptive feelings or behaviours and the promotion of what is referred to as 'personal growth and development'. There are various styles of treatment, including individual psychotherapy, marital counselling, family psychotherapy, and group psychotherapy. >> family therapy; group therapy

psychotomimetic drugs >> **hallucinogens**

psyllid [**sil**id] A jumping plant louse; feeds by sucking sap; distributed worldwide. (Order: Homoptera. Family: Psyllidae, c.1300 species.) >> gall; louse

Ptah [tah, ptah] An early Egyptian god associated with Memphis, and represented in human shape. Originally the creator of the world, he is later the god of craftsmanship.

ptarmigan [**tah(r)**migan] A grouse of the N hemisphere, inhabiting the high-altitude Alpine zone and tundra; plumage mottled grey in summer, white in winter, with thickly feathered feet and toes acting as snowshoes. (Genus: *Lagopus*, 3 species.) >> grouse

Pteranodon [te**ran**odon] A huge pterosaur from the late Cretaceous period of North America; wingspan up to 7 m/23 ft; long toothless beak counterbalanced by a bony crest arising at neck joint; tail reduced to short stump. (Order: Pterosauria.) >> Cretaceous period; pterosaur

Pteraspis [te**ras**pis] A fossil jawless vertebrate; known from the late Ordovician to the Devonian periods; body eel-like, without paired fins. (Class: Pteraspidimorphi.) >> Devonian period; Ordovician period

pteridophyte [**te**ridohfiyt] Any spore-bearing vascular plant, in some classifications forming the division Pteridophyta. >> clubmoss; fern; horsetail; spore; whisk fern

pterodactyl [tero**dak**til] >> **pterosaur**

pterosaur [**ter**osaw(r)] An extinct, flying reptile known from the late Triassic to the end of the Cretaceous period; ranged in size from sparrow-like to a wingspan of 15 m/50 ft; narrow, leathery wings supported by elongated fourth finger; formerly known as **pterodactyls**. (Subclass: Archosauria. Order: Pterosauria.) >> Cretaceous period; *Pteranodon*; reptile; Triassic period

Ptolemaic system [tole**may**ik] The planetary system described in the 2nd-c AD by Claudius Ptolemaeus of Alexandria. It is Earth-centred, with the planets moving in circular orbits. It was widely used as the definitive description of the Solar System until overthrown by Copernicus in 1543. >> Copernican system; Ptolemy; Solar System

Ptolemy I Soter ('Saviour') [**tol**emee] (c.366–c.283 BC) Macedonian general, in the army of Alexander the Great, who became ruler of Egypt after Alexander's death (323 BC). In 304 BC he adopted the royal title, and thus founded the Ptolemaic dynasty. In 285 BC, he was succeeded by his son, **Ptolemy II Philadelphus**, the greatest of the Ptolemaic kings. Alexandria (with its royally founded museum and library) became the chief centre for learning in the Mediterranean world. >> Cleopatra; Pharos of Alexandria

Ptolemy [**tol**emee], in full **Claudius Ptolemaeus** [tole**may**us] (fl.127–145) Greek astronomer and geographer, who worked in the great library in Alexandria. His book *Almagest* is the most important compendium of astronomy produced until the 16th-c. >> Ptolemaic system

puberty The period of change from childhood to adulthood, characterized by the attainment of sexual maturity and full reproductive capacity. It begins earlier in girls (about age 11) than in boys (about age 13), and lasts between 3 and 5 years. In both sexes there is an accelerated growth of the body and the development of secondary sexual characteristics: the development of breasts, appearance of pubic hair, and onset of menstruation in girls; the appearance of pubic and facial hair, enlargement of the penis, and deepening of the voice in boys. >> hormones

public debt The total amount of government borrowings, both short-term, such as treasury bills, and long-term bonds; also known as the **government debt** or the **national debt**. >> national accounts

public prosecutor >> **district attorney**

Public Record Office (PRO) The British national depository of government papers, selected archives, and legal documents to be permanently preserved – for example, the Magna Carta, Domesday Book, and Shakespeare's will. Established in 1838, it is now housed in Kew, Surrey.

Public Safety, Committee of A French Revolutionary political body, set up in the war crisis (Apr 1793) to organize defence against internal and external enemies. Its members came to exercise dictatorial powers during the Reign of Terror. >> French Revolution ℹ

public school In England, a fee-paying school for pupils of secondary age, often over 11 for girls and over 13 for boys; famous examples include Charterhouse, Eton, Harrow, Rugby, and Westminster. In the USA, it is the exact opposite: a school run by public authorities where fees are not paid. >> independent schools; maintained school

public sector borrowing requirement (PSBR) The amount of money a government needs to raise in a fiscal year by borrowing. The need arises from tax revenues and other income being less than the total expenditure budgeted by the various government departments. Reducing the PSBR has been seen in the UK as important in restricting the growth of the money supply, and thus for the control of inflation. >> inflation

public switched telephone network (PSTN) The conventional telephone network provided by the Posts, Telegraph and Telephones Authorities for normal voice communication. It is of particular interest to computer specialists since, by using modems, data communication between computers can be effected over a public telephone line. The line is in use, and has to be paid for, for the whole of the time of transmission. >> packet switching

Puccini, Giacomo (Antonio Domenico Michele Secondo Maria) [pu**chee**nee] (1858–1924) Operatic composer, born in Lucca, Italy. His first great success was *Manon Lescaut* (1893), but this was eclipsed by *La Bohème* (1896), *Tosca* (1900), and *Madama Butterfly* (1904). His last opera, *Turandot*, was left unfinished at his death.

Pucelle, Jean [püsel] or **Pucello, Johan** (c.1300–c.1355) French painter. He ran an important workshop in Paris from the 1320s onwards, specializing in illuminated manuscripts.

Pucello, Johan >> **Pucelle, Jean**

puddling process **1** A process for converting pig iron (high carbon) into wrought iron (very low carbon) by melting it in a small furnace in which it is worked to remove carbon (by exposure to oxidation by air) and the slag. >> wrought iron **2** The agitation of a concrete mix to promote settling and uniformity of texture.

Pudovkin, Vsevoled (Illarianovich) [pu**dof**kin] (1893–1953) Film director and writer, born in Penza. His films include the silent classics *Mat* (1926, Mother), *Konets Sankt-Peterburga* (1927, The End of St Petersburg) and *Potomok Chingis-Khan* (1928, trans Storm Over Asia).

Puebla [**pway**bla] or **Heróica Puebla de Zaragoza** 19°03N 98°10W, pop (1995e) 1 170 000. City in SC Mexico; altitude 2150 m/7054 ft; damaged by earthquake, 1973; railway; two universities (1937, 1940); famous for its glazed tiles which cover the domes of many of its 60 churches; cathedral (17th-c); historic centre now a world heritage site. >> Mexico ℹ

Pueblo [**pweb**loh] North American Indians of SW USA, living in settlements called *pueblos* in multi-storied, permanent houses made of clay. Culturally and linguistically diverse, they include the Hopi and Zuni. >> cliff dwellings; Hopi; Southwest Indians; Zuni

puerperal fever [pyoo**er**peral] Any fever arising in the period immediately following childbirth. It was formerly a serious complication of childbearing. >> obstetrics

Puerto Rico [**pwair**toh **ree**koh], formerly **Porto Rico** (to 1932), official name **Commonwealth of Puerto Rico** pop (1995e) 3 683 000; area 8897 sq km/3434 sq mi. Easternmost island of the Greater Antilles; capital, San Juan; timezone GMT −4; population mostly of European descent; chief religion, Roman Catholicism; official language, Spanish, with English widely spoken; unit of currency, the US dollar; almost rectangular in shape; length, 153 km/95 mi; width, 58 km/36 mi; crossed W–E by mountains, rising to 1338 m/4389 ft at Cerro de Punta; islands of Vieques and Culebra also belong to Puerto Rico; average annual temperature, 25°C; high humidity; originally occupied by Carib and Arawak Indians; visited by Columbus, 1493; remained a Spanish colony until ceded to the USA, 1898; high levels of emigration to the USA, 1940s–50s; became a semi-autonomous Commonwealth in association with the USA, 1952; executive power is exercised by a governor; a bicameral legislative assembly consists of a Senate and House of Representatives; manufacturing is the most important sector of the economy. >> Antilles; San Juan; United States of America ℹ; *see illustration below*

puff adder A viper which inhabits grassland; two species: the **puff adder** (*Bitis arietans*) from Africa and the Middle East; length, up to 2 m/6½ ft; very thick mottled brown body; puffs up the body with air when alarmed; the **dwarf puff adder** (*Bitis peringueyi*) from SW Africa; length, 30 cm/12 in. >> adder; viper ℹ

puffball A globular, often spherical fruiting body of certain fungi (the Gasteromycetes); spores released when the wall of the puffball ruptures. (Subdivision: Basidiomycetes. Order: Lycoperdales.) >> Basidiomycetes; fungus

puffer Any of several stout-bodied marine and freshwater fish which can inflate the body with air or water to become almost spherical; widespread in shallow warm seas; some organs and tissue extremely poisonous. (Family: Tetraodontidae, 7 genera.) >> fish ℹ

puffin Any of four species of auk of the genus *Fratercula* (2 species), *Cerorhinca* (1 species), or *Lunda* (1 species); bill large, deep, multicoloured; nests in burrows or rock crevices. *Cerorhinca* is nocturnal. >> auk

pug A toy breed of dog developed in China; similar origins to the Pekinese, but with a short coat; now taller and heavier than the Pekinese, but face still flat, and tail carried over back. >> dog; Pekinese

Pugachev, Yemelyan Ivanovich [**pu**gachef], also spelled **Pugachov** (1726–75) Russian Don Cossack, pretender to the Russian throne and leader of a mass rebellion against Catherine II (1773–5), proclaiming himself to be Peter III, Catherine's murdered husband. Pugachev's name later became a byword for the spirit of peasant revolution in Russia. He was captured in 1774 and executed. >> Catherine; Cossacks

Pugachov >> **Pugachev**

Pugin, Augustus (Welby Northmore) [**pyoo**jin] (1812–52) Architect, born in London. He designed a large part of the decoration and sculpture for the new Houses of Parliament (begun 1840), and did much to revive Gothic architecture in England. >> Gothic Revival; Houses of Parliament

Pugwash Conference A series of conferences first held in Pugwash, Nova Scotia, in 1957, which brought together scientists concerned about the impact on humanity of nuclear weapons. It owed much to the initiative of

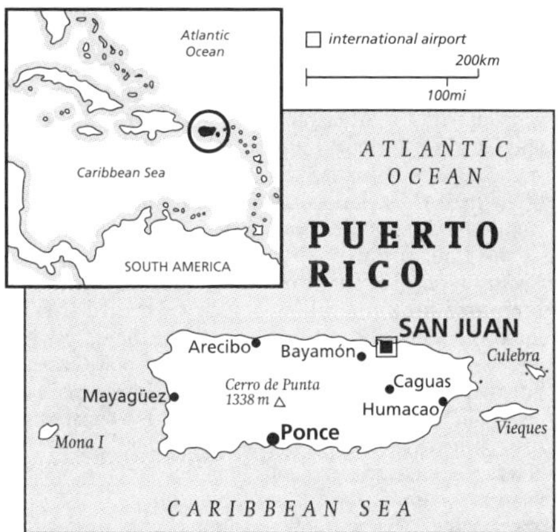

Bertrand Russell, and along with its president, Joseph Rotblat, it received the Nobel Peace Prize in 1995. >> Rotblat; Russell, Bertrand

Pula [**poo**la], Ital **Pola**, Lat **Pietas Iulia** 44°52N 13°52E, pop (1995e) 59 800. Seaport and resort town in W Croatia, on the Adriatic coast; built on the site of a former Roman colony; airport; railway; car ferries to Italy; Roman amphitheatre, temple; cathedral; castle (17th-c). >> Croatia; Yugoslavia ℹ

puli [**poo**lee] A medium-sized breed of dog developed in Hungary for hunting and as a sheepdog; ears pendulous; tail curls over back; coat thick and long, often reaching the ground. >> dog

Pulitzer, Joseph [**poo**litser] (1847–1911) Newspaper proprietor, born in Makó, Hungary. In his will he established annual **Pulitzer Prizes** in the fields of literature, drama, history, music, and journalism. >> RR1042

pulley A simple machine: a wheel with a grooved rim in which a rope can run. This changes the direction of force applied to the rope, and so can be used to raise heavy weights by pulling downwards. >> machine ℹ

Pullman, George (Mortimer) (1831–97) Inventor, born in Brocton, NY. In 1859 he made his first sleeping-cars on trains, and also introduced dining-cars.

pulmonary embolism The passage of a blood clot (*thrombus*) into the arteries to the lungs. It may lodge in the main pulmonary artery and cause sudden death. >> embolism

pulsar A cosmic source of rapid and regular bursts of radio waves. Pulsars are collapsed neutron stars, having a mass similar to the Sun, but a diameter of only 10 km/6 mi or so. >> neutron star

pulse (botany) A general name applied to peas, beans, and lentils, the edible ripe seeds of several plants of the pea family. (Family: Leguminosae.) >> bean; lentil; pea ℹ; protein

pulse (physiology) A pressure wave generated by the ejection of blood from the left ventricle into the vascular system. The number of pulsations per minute reflects heart rate, which in humans is between 70 and 90 at rest. >> blood; circulation

puma >> **cougar**

pumice A very light and porous igneous rock, usually granitic in chemical composition, formed by solidifying the froth caused by vigorous degassing of volatile substances from a lava during eruption. It is used as an abrasive. >> granite; lava

pump A machine for moving a fluid or gas from one place to another; commonly used to move fluids, often water, through pipes. *Pressure pumps* are used to blow up tyres, footballs, and other containers. *Evacuation pumps* suck air from sealed containers to make a partial vacuum. >> machine ℹ

pumpkin A trailing or climbing vine (*Cucurbita maxima*) native to America; flowers 12.5 cm/5 in diameter, funnel-shaped; fruit usually globular, often reaching great size and weight; rind and flesh orange, rather fibrous, surrounding numerous seeds; cultivated as a vegetable. It is often used to make Hallowe'en lanterns by placing a candle in the hollowed out centre, and carving a face in the rind, through which the light shines. (Family: Cucurbitaceae.) >> squash (botany); vegetable

Punch and Judy A glove-puppet show – named after the man and wife who are its central characters – which developed in Britain from the marionette plays based on Pulcinella, the impudent hunchback of the *commedia dell' arte*. Punch, operated by the right hand, is a constant figure, while the challenges of the left hand introduce character after character to be defeated by Punch's anarchic vigour. >> *commedia dell' arte*; puppetry

punctuation The part of a language's writing system which provides clues to the way a text is organized. Early writing systems made little or no use of punctuation. Some conventions organize the text into grammatical or semantic units, such as paragraphs and words (spaces), sentences, clauses and phrases (full-stop, comma, colon, semi-colon). Other conventions carry meaning of their own: the question mark identifies a sentence type, while the apostrophe marks possession (*John's*) and contractions (*I'm, must've*). >> graphology

Pune >> **Poona**

Punic Wars [**pyoo**nik] The three wars fought and won in the 3rd-c and 2nd-c BC by Rome against the Phoenician (Punic) city, Carthage. The first (264–241 BC) resulted in Rome's acquisition of her first overseas province, Sicily, hitherto a Carthaginian territory. The second (218–201 BC) saw Carthage surrender to Rome all her remaining overseas possessions. The third (149–146 BC) ended in the capture and total destruction of Carthage itself.

Punjab (India) [**pun**jahb] pop (1995e) 21 855 000; area 50 362 sq km/19 440 sq mi. State in NW India, bounded W and NW by Pakistan; capital (jointly with Haryana), Chandigarh; population c.60% Sikh in Indian Punjab, mainly Muslim in Pakistani Punjab; part of the Mughal Empire until end of 18th-c; annexed by the British after the Sikh Wars (1846, 1849); autonomous province, 1937; partitioned between India and Pakistan into East and West Punjab on the basis of religion, 1947; Indian state renamed Punjab, reformed as a Punjabi-speaking state, 1956 and 1966; governed by a Legislative Assembly; Alkai Dai Party campaigns for Sikh autonomy. >> India ℹ; Punjab (Pakistan); Sikh Wars

Punjab (Pakistan) [**pun**jahb] pop (1995e) 69 622 000; area 205 334 sq km/79 259 sq mi. Province in Pakistan, bounded E and S by India; chiefly Muslim population; capital, Lahore. >> Pakistan ℹ; Punjab (India)

Punjabi >> **Indo-Aryan languages**

punk rock A type of anarchistic rock music, originating in the late 1970s with such groups as Generation X and The Sex Pistols. Their very loudly amplified performances were characterized by the public use of swear words, outrageous behaviour, and clothes and hairstyles which sought to challenge establishment values. >> pop music; rock music

Punt, land of In antiquity, the area to the S of Egypt near the mouth of the Red Sea. From the third millennium BC, it was the source for the Egyptians of incense, myrrh, gold, and ivory.

Punta Arenas [**pun**ta a**ray**nas] 53°09S 70°52W, pop (1995e) 133 000. Most southerly city in Chile, on the Straits of Magellan; airfield; sheep-farming trade, exporting wool, skins, and frozen meat. >> Chile ℹ

pupa The life-cycle stage of an insect during which the larval form is reorganized to produce the definitive adult form. It is commonly an inactive stage, enclosed in a hard shell (*chrysalis*) or silken covering (*cocoon*). >> insect ℹ

pupil >> **eye** ℹ

puppetry The art and craft of manipulating inanimate figures for performance. There are three major means of manipulation: from above, by strings, as with **marionettes**; from below, behind or beside, by inserting a hand into the puppet, as with **glove puppets**; and from below or behind, by supports activating the head, body, and limbs, as with **rod-puppets**. In the UK, puppetry is often seen only as a children's show, but in many cultures it is appreciated as a major art form, sometimes with a religious significance. >> bunraku; Punch and Judy; shadow puppets

Puppis [**pup**is] (Lat 'ship's stern') A S constellation, partly in the Milky Way, which includes many notable star clusters. >> constellation; Milky Way; RR968

Purcell, Henry [persel], earlier [persel] (1659–95) Composer, born in London. Though his harpsichord pieces and his trio-sonatas for violins and continuo have retained their popularity, he is best known for his vocal and choral works. He also wrote an opera, *Dido and Aeneas* (1689). Of his many songs, 'Nymphs and Shepherds' is probably the best known.

purchase tax An excise tax levied on consumer goods, and added to the price paid by the customer; the rate varies with the type of goods. In the UK it was replaced by value-added tax in 1973. >> excise tax; taxation; VAT

purgative >> **laxative**

purgatory In Roman Catholic and some Orthodox teaching, the place and state in which the souls of the dead suffer for their sins before being admitted to heaven. >> heaven; Orthodox Church; Roman Catholicism

Purim [**pyu**rim, pu**reem**] The Jewish Feast of Lots, celebrated on 14 or 15 Adar (about 1 Mar), commemorating the deliverance of the Jews from a plot to have them massacred, as related in the Book of Esther. >> Esther, Book of; Judaism

purines [**pyoo**reenz] A group of organic bases, the most important of which are adenine and guanine, part of the nucleotide chains of DNA and RNA. >> DNA [i]; RNA

Puritanism The belief that further reformation was required in the Church of England under Elizabeth I and the Stuarts. It arose in the 1560s out of dissatisfaction with the 'popish elements', such as surplices, which had been retained by the Elizabethan religious settlement. It included the separatist churches that left England for Holland and America from 1590 to 1640, and several 'presbyterian', 'independent', and more radical groups. >> Church of England; Nonconformists; Restoration

Purkinje, Johannes (Evangelista) [**poor**kinyay] (1787–1869) Histologist and physiologist, born in Libochovice, Czech Republic. An early user of the improved compound microscope, he discovered a number of microscopic anatomical structures, some of which are named after him. >> anatomy [i]; microscope

Purple Heart In the USA, a decoration instituted in 1782 as an award for gallantry; it was revived in 1932, since when it has been awarded for wounds received in action. The ribbon is purple with white edges.

purpura [**per**pyoora] A condition in which there is spontaneous bleeding into the skin or mucous membranes, giving rise to small scattered areas of bruising. >> blood; mucous membrane; skin [i]

purslane A name applied to several different plants. **Common purslane** (*Portulacca oleracea*), a weed very widespread in warm regions, is a fleshy-leaved annual with yellow, 4–6-petalled flowers. The related **pink purslane** (*Claytonia sibirica*), native to W North America, is an annual or perennial with long-stalked leaves and white or pink 5-petalled flowers. (Family: Portulaccaceae.)

pus Yellow liquid often formed after localized inflammation, such as an abscess, or on the surface of a wound, caused by certain bacteria (known as *pyogenic* bacteria). >> abscess; inflammation

Pusan or **Busan** [poo**sahn**] 5°05N 129°02E, pop (1995e) 3 971 000. Seaport and second largest city in Korea; airport; railway; international ferry; hydrofoil; two universities (1946–7); UN Memorial Cemetery from the Korean War. >> Korea [i]

Pusey, E(dward) B(ouverie) [**pyoo**zee] (1800–82) Theologian, born in Pusey, Oxfordshire. He joined Newman in the Oxford Movement (1833), contributing several tracts, notably those on baptism and the Eucharist. >> Newman, John Henry; Oxford Movement; theology

Pushkin, Alexander Sergeyevich [**push**kin] (1799–1837) Poet, born in Moscow. Hailed in Russia as its greatest poet, his first success was the romantic poem *Ruslan and Lyudmila* (1820), followed by the verse novel *Eugene Onegin* (1828), the historical tragedy *Boris Godunov* (1831), and several other large-scale works.

Puttnam, David (Terence), Lord (1941–) Film-maker, born in London. Following his first feature film *S.W.A.L.K* (1969), he became known for such successful productions as *Bugsy Malone* (1976) and *Chariots of Fire* (1981, four Oscars). In 1986 he became chief executive of Columbia Pictures, but returned to Britain after a year. Later films include *Memphis Belle* (1990), *Being Human* (1994), and *Le Confessional* (1995). He received a life peerage in 1997.

putty A cement made of fine, powdered chalk or white lead, mixed with linseed oil, which hardens on being exposed to air. It is used for filling wood, and for fixing glass in frames. **Putty powder** is a fine, tin oxide powder used for polishing glass and granite. >> cement

Puvis de Chavannes, Pierre (Cécile) [püvee duh sha**van**] (1824–98) Painter, born in Lyon, France. He is best known for his murals on public buildings, notably the life of St Geneviève in the Panthéon, Paris.

Puyi, Pu Yi, or **P'u-i** [pooyee], personal name of the **Xuantong** Emperor (1906–67) Last emperor of China (1908–12) and the first of Manchukuo (1934–5), born in Beijing. Known in the West as Henry Puyi, in 1932 he was called from private life by the Japanese to be provincial dictator of Manchukuo, under the name of **Kangde**. Taken prisoner by the Russians in 1945, he was tried in China as a war criminal (1950), pardoned (1959), and became a private citizen. The story of his life was made into a successful film, *The Last Emperor*, in 1988. >> Manchukuo

PVC >> **polyvinylchloride**

Pycnogonida [piknuh**gon**ida] >> **sea spider**

pyelitis >> **pyelonephritis**

pyelonephritis [piyelohne**friy**tis] A bacterial inflammation of the pelvis, the kidney, and surrounding kidney tissue, usually associated with infection in the lower urinary tract, such as the bladder. It causes an acute infection accompanied by high fever and back pain; persisting or recurrent infection may lead to renal failure. >> kidneys; pelvis; urinary system

Pygmalion [pig**may**lion] In Greek mythology, a king of Cyprus, who made a statue of a beautiful woman. He prayed to Aphrodite, and the sculptured figure came to life. >> Shaw, George Bernard

Pygmies A small-statured people living in C Africa (averaging 1.50 m/4.9 ft in height). The best known are the forest-dwelling Mbuti of Democratic Republic of Congo and the Twa of the Great Lakes savannahs.

Pym, Barbara (Mary Crampton) (1913–80) Novelist, born in Oswestry, Shropshire. She is best known for her series of satirical novels on English middle-class society, including *Excellent Women* (1952) and *Quartet in Autumn* (1977).

Pym, John [pim] (1584–1643) English politician, born in Brymore, Somerset. In 1641 he took a leading part in the impeachment of Strafford, and helped to draw up the Grand Remonstrance. >> English Civil War; Grand Remonstrance; Strafford

Pynchon, Thomas [**pin**chon] (1937–) Novelist, born in Glen Cove, NY. His books include *V* (1963), *The Crying of Lot 49* (1966), and *Gravity's Rainbow* (1973).

Pyongyang [pyuhng**yang**], Jap **Heijo** 39°00N 125°47E, pop (1995e) 2 716 000. Capital of North Korea; Korea's oldest city, founded allegedly in 1122 BC; capital of Choson kingdom, 300–200 BC; colony of China, 108 BC; capital of North Korea since 1948; rebuilt after the Korean War; airport; railway; university (1946). >> Korea, North [i]

pyorrhoea / pyorrhea [piyo**ree**a] >> **dentistry**

pyracantha >> **firethorn**

pyralid moth [**pi**ralid] A moth of the family Pyralidae;

adults often slender with long hindlimbs; c.20 000 species, many pests of crops and dried vegetable products. (Order: Lepidoptera.) >> moth

pyramid An architectural structure on a triangular, square, or polygonal base, with triangular sides meeting in a single point. In Egyptian architecture, it is a sepulchral stone monument with a square base. The phrase **the Pyramids** usually refers to the Fourth Dynasty pyramids of the Giza plateau on the SW outskirts of modern Cairo. The Great Pyramid of Cheops (c. 2589–2566 BC) is 146 m/480 ft high, 230 m/755 ft square, and 2 352 000 cu m/27 688 000 cu ft in volume, made up of 2.5 million limestone blocks each of 2.5 tonnes. >> Ship of Cheops; sphinx

pyramid healing A form of healing which uses the electromagnetic energy thought to be mystically concentrated within the dimensions of a pyramid. The height of the Great Pyramids is the radius of a circle whose circumference is the same as the circumference of the square base. >> healing; pyramid

Pyramus and Thisbe [**pi**ramus, **thiz**bee] Two lovers, kept apart by their parents, who conversed through a crack in the wall between their houses, and agreed to meet at Ninus's tomb outside the city of Babylon. Finding Thisbe's blood-stained cloak, Pyramus thought she had been killed by a lion, and committed suicide. When she found him, Thisbe killed herself on his sword.

Pyrenean mountain dog A breed of dog developed in the Pyrenees several centuries ago to protect sheep; large powerful body with heavy head; thick, usually pale-coloured, coat. >> dog

Pyrenees [pire**neez**], Fr **Pyrénées**, Span **Pirineos** Mountain range extending W–E from the Bay of Biscay to the Mediterranean Sea, separating the Iberian Peninsula from the rest of Europe; stretches 450 km/280 mi along the French–Spanish frontier; includes Andorra; highest point, Pic de Aneto (3404 m/11 168 ft); Gouffre de la Pierre St Martin, one of the deepest caves in the world. >> Andorra [i]; Europe

Pyrenees, Treaty of the (1659) A treaty between France and Spain ending the hostilities of the Thirty Years' War. It marked the end of Spanish military and political dominance in W Europe. >> Thirty Years' War

pyrethrum [piy**ree**thruhm] A perennial, growing to 45 cm/18 in (*Tanacetum cinerariifolium*), native to parts of the Balkan peninsula, but extensively cultivated, especially in E Africa and South America; flower-heads solitary, daisy-like, spreading outer florets white. An insecticide is prepared from the extracts of the powdered and dried flower-heads. (Family: Compositae.) >> insecticide

Pyrex® A trade name for a borosilicate glass with a high silica content, some boron, and some aluminium. It has high mechanical strength, resistance to strong alkalis and acids, and a low coefficient of thermal expansion. These properties favour its extensive domestic use. >> borax; glass [i]

pyrexia >> **fever**

pyridine [**pi**rideen] C_5H_5N, boiling point 115°C. An organic base with a vile odour. It occurs in a fraction of coal tar, and is carcinogenic. >> base (chemistry); tar

pyridoxine A B vitamin (B_6) which acts as a co-enzyme involved in the metabolism of amino acids. Although a deficiency is rare, B_6 is frequently used as a vitamin supplement for the treatment of mild depression, although its efficacy is disputed. >> amino acid; enzyme; vitamins [i]

pyrimidines [pi**rim**ideenz] A group of organic bases, the most important of which are cytosine, thymine, and uracil, part of the nucleotide chains of DNA and RNA. >> DNA [i]; RNA

pyrite A metallic yellow iron sulphide (FeS_2) mineral, common and widespread; also termed 'fool's gold' because of its colour. It is used as a source of sulphur and in the manufacture of sulphuric acid. >> gold; marcasite; sulphur

pyroclastic rock A general name given to rocks formed from fragments of lava ejected from a volcano into the atmosphere.

pyrolysis The decomposition of a substance by heating in the absence of oxygen. The most important example is the pyrolysis or 'cracking' of petroleum, by which alkanes are converted into shorter alkanes and alkenes, eg propane may be converted to ethene and methane. >> alkanes; petroleum

pyrometer A type of thermometer for measuring high temperatures. In the optical pyrometer, the heat colour of the hot object is compared to that of a heated filament through which a controlled current is passed. >> thermometer

pyrope [**piy**rohp] >> **garnet**

pyroxenes [**piy**rokseenz] A large group of silicate minerals including many important rock-forming minerals; important members of the group are enstatite, diopside, augite, pigeonite, and jadeite. >> silicate minerals

Pyrrho [**pi**roh] (c.360–c.270 BC) Philosopher, born in Elis, Greece. He established the philosophical tradition later called *scepticism*. He recommended that since we know nothing we should 'suspend judgment' and thus achieve 'an imperturbable peace of mind'. >> scepticism

Pyrrhus [**pi**rus] (c.318–272 BC) King of Epirus (modern Albania) (307–303 BC, 297–272 BC), an ambitious ruler whose aim was to revive the empire of his second cousin, Alexander the Great. Unsuccessful in this goal (283 BC), he came into conflict with Rome. Though he won two battles against her (280–279 BC), his losses, particularly at Asculum (279 BC), were so great that they gave rise to the phrase 'Pyrrhic victory'. >> Alexander the Great

pyruvic acid [piy**roo**vik] CH_3–CO–COOH, IUPAC **2-oxo-propanoic acid**. The non-chiral oxidation product of lactic acid. >> chirality; lactic acid

Pythagoras [piy**thag**oras] (6th-c BC) Philosopher and mathematician, born in Samos, Greece. About 530 BC he established a religious community in S Italy. Pythagoreanism was a way of life, of moral abstinence and purification; its teaching included the doctrine of the transmigration of souls between successive bodies. The school is best known for its studies of the relations between numbers. >> Pythagoras's theorem

Pythagoras's theorem [piy**thag**oras] A mathematical proposition advanced by Pythagoras, that in any right-angled triangle, the square on the hypotenuse is equal to the sum of the squares on the other two sides. The converse of the theorem is also true: in any triangle in which the square on the longest side is equal to the sum of the squares on the other two sides, the angle opposite the longest side is a right angle. >> geometry; Pythagoras; triangle (mathematics)

Pythian Games [**pith**ian] In ancient Greece, one of the main Pan-Hellenic festivals, held every four years in the sanctuary of Apollo Pythios at Delphi. 'Pythios' or 'python slayer' was the name under which Apollo was worshipped there. >> Delphi; Olympia (Greece)

Pythias >> **Damon and Pythias**

python A snake of family Pythonidae (27 species), sometimes included in the boa family; native to Africa, S and SE Asia, Australasia, and (a single species) Central America; a constrictor; eye with vertical slit-like pupil; females lay eggs and often incubate these until they hatch. >> boa; constrictor

pyx A small metal box used in the Roman Catholic Church for carrying the Blessed Sacrament to the sick; also a larger receptacle for exposing the host or consecrated bread. >> Eucharist; Roman Catholicism

Pyxis [**pik**sis] (Lat 'compass') >> **Vela**

Q

Qaddafi, Muammar >> **Gaddafi, Muammar**

Qatar [**ka**tah], official name **State of Qatar**, Arabic **Dawlat al-Qatar** pop (1995e) 597 000; area 11 437 sq km/4415 sq mi. Low-lying state on the E coast of the Arabian Peninsula, comprising the Qatar Peninsula and numerous small offshore islands; capital, Doha; timezone GMT +3; population 40% Arab, 18% Pakistani, 18% Indian; chief religion, Islam; official language, Arabic; unit of currency, the riyal; the peninsula, 160 km/100 mi and 55–80 km/34–50 mi wide, slopes gently from the Dukhan Heights (98 m/321 ft) to the E shore; barren terrain, mainly sand and gravel; desert climate; high humidity; British protectorate after Turkish withdrawal, 1916; independence, 1971; a hereditary monarchy, with an emir who is both head of state and prime minister; Council of Ministers assisted by a Consultative Council; economy based on oil; offshore gas reserves thought to be an eighth of known world reserves. >> Doha; RR1020 political leaders;

Qin dynasty or **Ch'in dynasty** [chin] (221–206 BC) The first dynasty to rule over a united China, founded by Qin Shihuangdi. Its achievements included the standardization of Chinese script, weights, and measures, and the construction of the Great Wall. >> China ⓘ; Great Wall of China

Qingdao, **Tsingtao**, or **Ch'ing-tao** [chingdow] 36°04N 120°22E, pop (1995e) 2 253 000. Resort seaport city in E China, on the Yellow Sea; occupied by Japan in World War 1; airfield; railway. >> China ⓘ

Qing dynasty [ching] (1644–1912) The last imperial Chinese dynasty. They took the appellation Manchu in 1635, and the dynastic title Qing in 1636. Building a power base in Manchuria, Mongolia, and Korea, they subsequently extended supremacy over all China. The dynasty was overthrown by revolutionaries in 1911. >> Boxer Rising; China ⓘ; Manchus; Taiping Rebellion

Qinghai–Tibet Plateau >> **Tibet Plateau**

Qinhuangdao or **Ch'in-huang-tao** [chinhwahngdow] 39°55N 119°37E, pop (1995e) 559 000. Port in N China; designated a special economic zone in 1985; linked by pipeline to the Daqing oil field; railway. >> China ⓘ

Qin Shihuangdi [**chin** shihwang**dee**], also spelled **Ch'in Shih Huang-ti** (259–210 BC) First true emperor of China, who forcibly unified much of modern China following the decline of the Zhou dynasty. He consolidated N defences into a Great Wall, and drove the Huns from S of the Yellow R. He conquered the S, built canals and roads, divided China into 36 military prefectures, destroyed feudalism, and disarmed nobles. He was buried in a starry mausoleum with c.7500 life-size terracotta guards. >> China ⓘ; Huns; Mount Li; Zhou dynasty

Qoheleth [koh**hel**eth] >> **Ecclesiastes, Book of**

Qom [koom] 34°39N 50°57E, pop (1995e) 721 000. Industrial town in Iran; on R Anarbar; road and rail junction; gas pipeline; pilgrimage centre for Shiite Muslims; shrine of Fatima. >> Iraq ⓘ; Islam

Quadragesima [kwodra**je**sima] In the Western Christian Church, the first Sunday in Lent, so called from its being approximately 40 days before Easter (Lat *quadragesimus*, 'fortieth'). >> Lent

quadratic equations >> **equations**

quadrature The position of a planet or the Moon when the angular distance from the Sun, as measured from the Earth, is 90°. >> Moon; planet

quadrille A popular 19th-c dance, performed to music (often arranged from contemporary tunes) in a lively duple time.

quadriplegia >> **paralysis**

quadrivium (Lat 'the place where four roads meet') The four scientific disciplines of astronomy, geometry, arithmetic, and music, which together with the *trivium* of grammar, rhetoric, and logic constituted the university curriculum of the seven liberal arts in the Middle Ages. >> scholasticism

quadrophonic sound A system attempting greater authenticity in reproducing concert-hall musical performances by the use of four signal channels and four loudspeakers placed in a square around the listener. Unconvincing results, additional equipment costs, and no single industry standard restricted this to being an episode of the 1970s. >> loudspeaker ⓘ; sound recording

Quadruple Alliance **1** (1718) A treaty signed by Britain, France, and the Habsburg emperor, to which the Dutch were expected to accede, to ensure the principle of collective security in W Europe. **2** (1815) A treaty signed initially by Austria, Prussia, Russia, and Britain, and acceded to by France in 1818, confirming the 1815 Paris and Vienna provisions for 20 years.

quaestors [**kwee**sterz] Junior, annually elected, financial officers at Rome. The quaestorship was the lowest rank in the hierarchy of offices, the *cursus honorum*, and could not be held before the age of 25. >> Senate, Roman

quagga [**kwa**ga] An extinct zebra native to S Africa (*Equus*

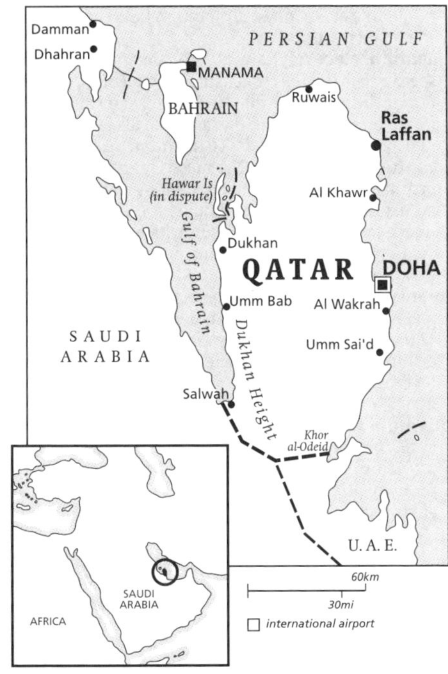

quagga); stripes only on head and shoulders; brown body, white legs and tail; last individual died in 1883. >> zebra

Quaid, Dennis [kwayd] (1954–) Film actor, born in Houston, TX. His films include *Innerspace* (1987), *Postcards from The Edge* (1990), and *The Parent Trap* (1998). His television work includes the highly rated *Bill* and its sequel (1981, 1983).

Quai d'Orsay [kay daw(r)say] The embankment on the left bank of the R Seine in Paris, and by association the French Foreign Ministry located there. >> Paris

quail A small, short-tailed bird of the pheasant family Phasianidae; native to the New World (29 species) and the Old World (10 species). The name is also used for several other species. >> pheasant

Quakers >> **Friends, Society of**

quango A shortened form of the term **quasi-non-governmental organization**, a type of organization which became common in the USA, being established by the private sector but largely or entirely financed by the federal government. In the UK the term has been applied to non-departmental bodies that are neither part of a central government department nor part of local government, such as the Monopolies Commission. Many are merely advisory bodies.

Quant, Mary [kwont] (1934–) Fashion designer, born in London. Her clothes were particularly fashionable in the 1960s, when the geometric simplicity of her designs, especially the miniskirt, and the originality of her colours became a feature of the 'swinging Britain' era.

quantity theory of money An economic theory stating that money supply (M) and its velocity of circulation (V) – how fast it changes hands – is more or less equal to the aggregate of prices (P) and the quantity of goods etc (Q) available. So, $MV = PQ$. >> monetarism

quantum chromodynamics A widely accepted theory of strong nuclear force in which quarks are bound together by gluons; proposed in 1973; also known as **QCD**. Quarks interact because of a 'colour' quantity on each in a way analogous to the interaction between charged particles. >> gluon; particle physics; quantum field theory; quark; strong interaction

quantum electrodynamics A modern theory of high-speed (relativistic) electromagnetic interactions, developed during the 1940s; also called **QED**. Charged subatomic particles interact via photons, the quantum of electromagnetic radiation. >> electrodynamics; quantum field theory

quantum field theory The most sophisticated form of quantum theory, in which all matter and force particles are expressed as sums over simple waves. It is essential for understanding the processes in which particles are created or destroyed. >> quantum mechanics; relativistic quantum mechanics

quantum gravity Gravitation acting at submicroscopic length scales where quantum effects are important. Theories of quantum gravity seek to combine features of quantum mechanics and general relativity, but no consistent theory has yet been developed. >> general relativity; quantum mechanics

quantum mechanics A system of mechanics applicable at distances of atomic dimensions, 10^{-10} m or less, and providing for the description of atoms, molecules, and all phenomena that depend on properties of matter at the atomic level. The basic concept derives from the work of Max Planck, who proposed that light is composed of photons – minute packets (*quanta*) of light. The development of quantum mechanics applicable to particles moving at high speed is known as **relativistic quantum mechanics**. A further development of quantum theory, incorporating the creation and destruction of particles, took place during the 1940s and is called **quantum field theory**. The wave-like nature of electrons and other particles is expressed by wavefunctions, the most fundamental way of describing either simple particles or other more complicated quantum systems. Particles such as electrons are no longer considered as point-like objects, but are spread out in a way governed by wavefunctions. Quantum mechanics necessarily means dealing with a probabilistic description of nature, and thus contrasts with classical mechanics, in which the precise properties of every object are in principle calculable. >> Planck; quantum field theory / gravity / numbers; relativistic quantum mechanics; spin

quantum numbers Simple numbers or vectors that specify the state of a quantum system and the results of observations performed on that system. Subatomic particles and atomic states are classified by quantum numbers. >> quantum mechanics

quarantine A period during which people or animals suspected of carrying a contagious disease are kept in isolation. Originally quarantine was an attempt to prevent the spread of plague in the 14th-c: ships arriving at port were kept offshore for 40 days. Later the principle was applied to many infectious diseases, and the time shortened to relate to the incubation period of the particular infection. The practice is still applied to dogs and other animals imported from overseas to the UK, as a defence against the spread of rabies; a 6-month period is normal. >> rabies

quark A fundamental component of matter; symbol q. Though there is experimental support for quarks, none has been observed directly. It is thought that six quark types exist, identified by 'flavours': *up*, *down*, *strange*, *charm*, *top*, and *bottom*. Each flavour quark carries one of three possible 'colours'. Quarks have spin $\frac{1}{2}$, mass uncertain, and have charges of $\pm\frac{1}{3}$ or $\pm\frac{2}{3}$. According to current theory, subatomic particles composed of quarks are bound together by gluons. >> gluon; particle physics

Quark XPress A desk-top publishing package which offers facilities for both text and graphic manipulation. >> desk-top publishing

Quarles, Francis [kwaw(r)lz] (1592–1644) Religious poet, born near Romford, Essex. His best-known work is the emblem book (a series of symbolic pictures with verse commentary), *Emblems* (1635), and a prose book of aphorisms, *Enchyridion* (1640).

quarter-day Any of the four days in the year (i.e. one every quarter-year) on which rents and similar charges are traditionally paid; in England and Wales, the quarter-days are Lady Day (25 Mar), Midsummer Day (24 Jun), Michaelmas (29 Sep) and Christmas Day (25 Dec); Scottish quarter-days are Candlemas (2 Feb), Whitsunday (15 May), Lammas (1 Aug) and Martinmas (11 Nov). They are different in the USA (1 Jan, 1 Apr, 1 Jul, 1 Oct). >> equinox; solstice

quartz The crystalline form of silicon dioxide (SiO_2), one of the most common minerals in the Earth's crust. The clear crystals are known as *rock crystal*, but it is commonly white and translucent. Semi-precious varieties (eg amethyst) may be coloured. It is very important industrially because of its piezo-electric properties. >> chalcedony; piezo-electric effect; silicate minerals

quartzite A rock produced by the recrystallization of sandstone by metamorphism, and consisting of interlocking crystals of quartz (**metaquartzite**). It is also a sandstone with purely siliceous cement (**orthoquartzite**). >> quartz; sandstone; silica

quasar [**kway**zah(r)] A distant, compact object far beyond our Galaxy, which looks starlike on a photograph, but has a redshift characteristic of an extremely remote object. The word is a contraction of **quasi-stellar object**. The distinctive features of quasars are an extremely compact structure and high redshift corresponding to velocities approaching the speed of light. They are the most distant and luminous objects in the universe. >> black hole; redshift

Quasimodo, Salvatore [kwazee**moh**doh] (1901–68) Poet, born in Syracuse, Sicily, Italy. His early work was Symbolist in character, as in *Ed é subito sera* (1942, And Suddenly it's Evening), and he became a leader of the *hermetic* poets. After World War 2 his poetry dealt largely with social issues.

quassia [**kwo**shia] A shrub or small tree (*Quassia amara*) native to tropical America; flowers tubular, red. The bitter wood containing the chemical *quassiin* is used medicinally to counter dysentery. (Family: Simaroubaceae.)

Quaternary period [kwa**ter**naree] A geological period of the Cenozoic era extending from 2 million years ago to the present day; subdivided into the Pleistocene and Holocene epochs. It is characterized by extensive glaciations in the N Hemisphere and the emergence of mankind. >> Cenozoic era; geological time scale; glaciation; RR976

quaternions In algebra, a set of four ordered real numbers subject to certain laws of composition. Developed by William Hamilton (1803–65), they provide an example of a non-commutative algebra, as multiplication is not commutative. >> algebra; numbers

Quayle, (James) Dan(forth) [kwayl] (1947–) US politician, born in Indianapolis, IN. He worked as a lawyer, journalist, and public official, becoming a Republican member of Congress (1977–81) and Senate (1981–8). He was elected vice-president under George Bush in 1988. >> Bush, George

Quebec (city) [kwe**bek**], Fr **Québec** [kaybek] 46°50N 71°15W, pop (1995e) 178 000. Capital of Quebec province, Canada, on the St Lawrence R; built on Cape Diamond, cliff rising 100 m/328 ft; 92% French-speaking; French colony founded, 1608; capital of New France, 1663; captured by the British under Wolfe, 1759; ceded to Britain, 1763; capital of Lower Canada (1791) and Quebec (1867); airport; railway; two universities (1852, 1968); professional team (ice hockey), Quebec Nordiques; Citadel fortress (a world heritage site). >> Abraham, Plains of; Cartier; Quebec (province); Wolfe, James

Quebec (province) [kwe**bek**], Fr **Québec** [kaybek] pop (1995e) 7 319 000; area 1 540 680 sq km/594 856 sq mi. Largest province in Canada; capital, Quebec; Canadian Shield in N four-fifths, a rolling plateau dotted with lakes; rises to 1588 m/5210 ft at Mont d'Iberville; S part intensely cultivated; most population in St Lawrence valley; claimed for France by Cartier, 1534; province of New France, 1608; captured by British, 1629; restored to France, 1632; transferred to Britain by Treaty of Paris, 1763; constituted as Lower Canada, 1791; province of Quebec, 1867, with English and French as official languages; strong separatist movement emerged in 1960s, but 1980 referendum decided against sovereignty-association, and a further referendum was narrowly defeated in 1995; governed by a lieutenant-governor and Legislative Assembly. >> Canada i; Cartier; Quebec (city)

Quechua [**kech**wa] A South American Indian language of the Andean-Equatorial group. The official language of the Incas, it is now spoken by 8 million from Colombia to Chile, and is widely used as a lingua franca. >> Incas; lingua franca

Queen, Ellery The pseudonym of two US writers of crime fiction, **Frederic Dannay** (1905–82) and his cousin **Manfred B Lee** (1905–71), both born in New York City. They wrote many popular books, using 'Ellery Queen' both as their pseudonym and as the name of their detective. They also used the pseudonym **Barnaby Ross** as the author of their other detective, Drury Lane.

Queen Anne's lace >> **cow parsley**

Queen Anne Style The architecture, furniture, and silver designed during the reign of Queen Anne (1702–14), notable for carefully calculated proportions and a lack of applied ornament. The style was revived in English architecture in the last third of the 19th-c, characterized by mullioned windows, handsome brickwork, and imposingly grouped chimneys. >> Anne

Queen Anne's War (1702–1713) The second of the four intercolonial wars waged by Britain and France for control of colonial North America, known in Europe as the **War of the Spanish Succession**. Settled by the Treaty of Utrecht (1713), the war resulted in British control of Newfoundland, Acadia, and Hudson Bay. >> Spanish Succession, War of the

Queen Charlotte Islands, Haida **G'waii** pop (1995e) 5600; area 9790 sq km/3779 sq mi. Archipelago of c.150 islands off the W coast of British Columbia, W Canada; extend over c.100 km/60 mi. >> Canada i

Queen Elizabeth Islands area over 390 000 sq km/150 000 sq mi. Northernmost islands of the Canadian Arctic Archipelago, situated N of latitude 74°N; named in 1953. >> Canada i

Queen Maud Land, Norwegian **Dronning Maud Land** Main part of Norwegian Antarctic Territory (between 20°W and 45°W and S of 60°S), extending to the S Pole; claimed by Norway in 1939. >> Antarctica i

Queens pop (1995e) 1 987 000; area 283 sq km/109 sq mi. Borough of New York City, USA; connected to Manhattan by the Queensboro Bridge; contains the two New York airports. >> Long Island; New York City

Queen's Award In the UK, an award given annually on the Queen's birthday (21 Apr). Established in 1965, there are now two separate awards, one for export achievement, and the other for technological achievement.

Queensberry, Sir John Sholto Douglas, 8th Marquess of (1844–1900) British aristocrat, a keen patron of boxing, who supervised the formulation in 1867 of new rules to govern that sport, since known as the **Queensberry Rules**. >> boxing i

Queen's Counsel (QC) A senior member of the English or Scottish Bar, when the monarch is a queen; the equivalent term under a king is **King's Counsel (KC)**. A practising barrister of 10 years' standing may apply to become a Queen's Counsel (or 'take silk' – a reference to the gowns worn by such counsel). >> barrister; Inns of Court

Queensland pop (1995e) 3 148 000; area 1 727 200 sq km/666 900 sq mi. Second largest state in Australia; established as a penal colony, 1824; open to free settlers, 1842; part of New South Wales until 1859; Cape York Peninsula in the N; the Great Dividing Range runs N–S, separating a fertile coastal strip to the E from dry plains to the W; tropical climate in the N; most population in the SE; capital, Brisbane; provides 22% of Australia's agricultural production, with sugar the main export crop; Great Barrier Reef runs parallel to the Pacific coast; major resort areas with fine surfing beaches. >> Australia i; Brisbane; Great Barrier Reef

Queneau, Raymond [kenoh] (1903–76) Novelist and poet, born in Le Havre, France. The best of his poetry is contained in *Les Ziaux* (1943) and *Si tu t'imagines* (1952, If you suppose). His novels include *Zazie dans le métro* (1959, Zazie in the Metro, filmed 1960).

Quercia, Jacopo della >> **Jacopo della Quercia**

Querétaro [ke**ray**taroh] 20°38N 100°23W, pop (1995e) 504 000. City in C Mexico; altitude, 1865 m/6119 ft; important in the 1810 independence rising; railway; university (1618). >> Mexico i

Quesnay, François [kenay] (1694–1774) Physician and economist, born in Mérey, France, known for his essays in political economy. He became a leader of the *Economistes*, also called the Physiocratic School.

Quetta [**kwe**ta] 30°15N 67°01E, pop (1995e) 419 000. Capital of Baluchistan province, W Pakistan; altitude 1650 m/5500 ft; strategic location between Afghanistan and the Lower Indus valley; acquired by the British, 1876; badly damaged by earthquake, 1935; airfield; railway; centre of a fruit-growing area. >> Pakistan ⓘ

quetzal A Central American bird (*Pharomachrus mocinno*), inhabiting mountain forests; male with red underparts, green head and back, and very long trailing tail; also known as the **resplendent quetzal** or **resplendent trogon**. Revered by the Mayans and Aztecs, it is the national bird of Guatemala. >> trogon

Quetzalcoatl [ketzlkoh**atl**] The feathered serpent god of the pre-Columbian Aztec and Mayan cultures of Central America. He is represented variously as a culture hero, as a deity and creator, and as the Aztec high priest. He is associated with the invention of the calendar and the re-creation of human life. >> Aztecs; Mayas

Quezon City [**kay**son] 14°39N 121°01E, pop (1995e) 1 858 000. Residential city in the Philippines; on Luzon I; former capital, 1948–76; university (1908). >> Philippines ⓘ

quicklime >> **calcium**

quicksilver >> **mercury**

quickthorn >> **hawthorn**

quill A pen made from the tapered stem of a bird's feather, especially the outer wing feathers of geese. Quills were the chief writing implement from the 6th-c AD until the advent of steel pens in the mid-19th-c. >> pen

Quiller-Couch, Sir Arthur [**kwil**er **kooch**], pseudonym **Q** (1863–1944) Man of letters, born in Bodmin, Cornwall. He edited the *Oxford Book of English Verse* (1900) and other anthologies, and published several volumes of essays and criticism. He also wrote poems, short stories, and humorous novels of Cornwall and the sea, often under his pseudonym.

quillwort A spore-bearing vascular plant related to clubmosses, mostly aquatic pteridophytes distributed throughout the world. (Genus: *Isoetes*, 75 species. Family: Isoetaceae.) >> clubmoss; pteridophyte; selaginella; spore

Quimper [kĩpair] or **Quimper Corentin** 48°00N 4°09W, pop (1995e) 64 400. Manufacturing and commercial town in NW France; on estuary of R Odet; railway; pottery (Quimper or Brittany ware) since 16th-c; cathedral (13th-c).

quince A deciduous shrub or small tree (*Cydonia oblonga*) reaching 1.5–7.5m/5–25 ft, native to Asia; flowers pale pink, bowl-shaped, resembling apple blossom; fruit apple- or pear-shaped, fragrant but hard when ripe, mainly used in preserves. (Family: Rosaceae.) >> japonica

Quine, Willard Van Orman [kwiyn] (1908–) Philosopher and logician, born in Akron, OH. His books include *The Logic of Sequences* (1990), and *From Stimulus to Science* (1995). >> logic

quinine A drug used in the prevention of malaria, and sometimes in its treatment. It is present in the bark of various *Cinchona* trees native to the Andes, but it is also cultivated in Sri Lanka, India, and Java. >> malaria; quinoline

Quinnipiac >> **New Haven**

quinoline [**kwin**olin] C_9H_7N, boiling point 238°C. An organic base, related to pyridine. Both it and the isomeric **isoquinoline** are oily liquids, constituents of coal-tar. Quinine and other alkaloids are derivatives of quinoline. >> alkaloids; base (chemistry); pyridine

quinone $C_6H_4O_2$. One of two isomers derived from benzene (*benzoquinones*) or derivatives of these. They are highly coloured, and a quinone group is often a chromophore of a dyestuff. >> benzene; chromophore; isomers

Quinquagesima [kwinkwa**je**sima] In the Western Christian Church, the Sunday before Lent, so called from its being 50 days before Easter, counting inclusively (Lat *quinquagesimus*, 'fiftieth'). >> Lent

quinsy [**kwin**zee] The formation of an abscess in and around the tonsils. It is a complication of severe tonsillitis resulting from a bacterial infection. >> abscess; tonsils

Quintero, Serafin Alvarez >> **Alvarez Quintero, Serafin**

quipu [**kee**poo] An accounting system of knotted cords developed by the Peruvian Incas and others. The system was a complex one, with strings and knots of various lengths, shapes, and colours. >> Incas

Quirk, (Charles) Randolph, Baron (1920–) Grammarian and writer on the English language, born in the Isle of Man. Major grammars in which he was involved are *A Grammar of Contemporary English* (1972) and *A Comprehensive Grammar of the English Language* (1985).

Quisling, Vidkun (Abraham Lauritz Jonsson) [**kwiz**ling] (1887–1945) Diplomat and fascist leader, born in Fyresdal, Norway. He founded the *Nasjonal Samling* ('National Unity') in imitation of the German National Socialist Party (1933), and became puppet prime minister in occupied Norway. Executed in 1945, his name has since become synonymous with 'traitor'. >> fascism; World War 2

Quit India Movement A campaign launched (Aug 1942) by the Indian National Congress calling for immediate independence from Britain. Gandhi and other Congress leaders were arrested, and the movement quickly suppressed. >> Gandhi

Quito [**kee**toh] 0°14S 78°30W, pop (1995e) 1 246 000. Capital of Ecuador; altitude 2850 m/9350 ft; former Inca capital (old city designated a world heritage site); captured by Spanish, 1534; airport; railway; three universities (1769, 1869, 1946); cathedral. >> Ecuador ⓘ

Qumran, community of [kum**ran**] An exclusive Jewish sect, located near the NW corner of the Dead Sea. They were destroyed during the Jewish revolt of AD 66–70, but many of their writings were discovered in 1947 as part of the Dead Sea Scrolls. >> Dead Sea Scrolls; Judaism

quoits An outdoor game demanding great accuracy, which involves the throwing of a metal ring at a peg. It has been a popular sport in England since the middle of the 14th-c.

quotas, import A means of restricting imports of a commodity or product by limiting the quantity that can be imported in a particular period. The aim is to protect domestic industry and preserve foreign currency reserves. >> protectionism

Qu'ran >> **Koran**

Qutb Minar or **Kutab Minar** [kutb mi**nah(r)**] A famous city landmark in Delhi, India. Built in 1199 as a Muslim tower of victory, the Qutb Minar is 72.5 m/263 ft high. >> Delhi

QwaQwa [**kwa**kwa] Former national state or non-independent black homeland in South Africa; self-governing status, 1974; incorporated into KwaZulu Natal following the new South African constitution of 1994. >> KwaZulu Natal; South Africa ⓘ

Rabat (Malta) [ra**bat**] 35°53N 14°25E, pop (1995e) 13 500. Town in SWC Malta; St Paul lived in a cave here after shipwreck, AD 60. >> Malta

Rabat (Morocco) [ra**bat**] 34°02N 6°51W, pop (1995e) 694 000. Capital of Morocco, one of Morocco's four imperial cities; founded, 12th-c; French colonialists established a Residency-General, 1912; airport; railway; university (1957); fortress (14th-c). >> Morocco

rabbi (Heb 'my lord', or 'my master/teacher') In Judaism after AD 70, a title for accredited Jewish teachers or sages; prior to 70, used less technically as a form of respectful address. The teachings of these early sages are preserved in the Mishnah, the Talmud, and many other forms of rabbinic literature. Today rabbis also have pastoral functions and a role in worship, much like ministers of other faiths. >> Judaism; Mishnah; synagogue

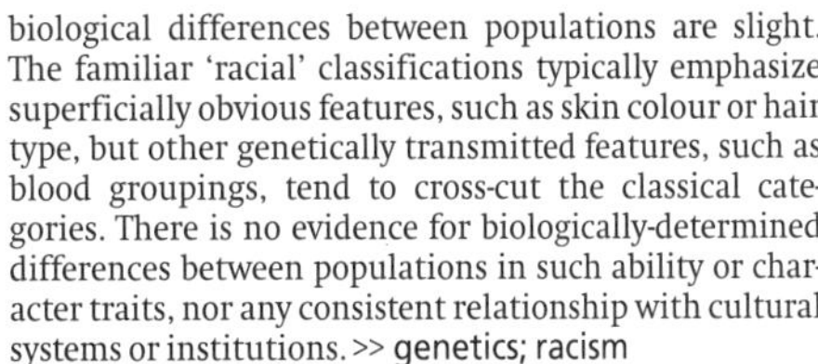

rabbit A mammal of the order Lagomorpha, family Leporidae (23 species); differs from the closely related **hare** in several respects (different skull features, smaller, gives birth to naked young, lives in groups, burrows to produce complex warrens, lacks black ear tips); also called **con(e)y** – a name often used for rabbit skin. >> chinchilla rabbit; cottontail; hare; hyrax; myxomatosis; pika

rabbitfish >> **chimaera**

Rabelais, François [ra**b**elay], pseudonym (an anagram of his name) **Alcofribas Nasier** (?1494–?1553) Satirist, physician, and humanist, born in or near Chinon, France. He is remembered for his comic and satirical *Pantagruel* (1532) and *Gargantua* (1534), published under his pseudonym, though condemned by the Church. >> humanism

rabies [**ray**beez] A virus infection that affects a wide range of animals, such as dogs, cats, foxes, skunks, and vampire bats; also known as **hydrophobia**. It is transmitted to humans by bites and licks on skin abrasions or intact mucous membranes. The central nervous system and salivary glands are predominantly affected, leading to delusions and hallucinations. The alternative name stems from the violent contractions of the diaphragm and inspiratory muscles induced by drinking. Death is almost invariable. >> virus

Rabin, Itzhak [ra**been**] (1922–95) Israeli soldier, statesman, and prime minister (1974–7, 1992–5), born in Jerusalem. He was appointed chief-of-staff in 1964, heading the armed forces during the Six-Day War (1967). He became Labour Party leader and prime minister, resigning in 1977 when involved in a scandal over accounts he kept in the USA. He later served as defence minister (1984–90), and became prime minister again in 1992. He shared the Nobel Peace Prize in 1994. He was assassinated by a right-wing Israeli law student.

raccoon A mammal of genus *Procyon* (7 species), native to North and Central America; grey with dark bands around tail; face pale with black band across eyes. (Family: Procyonidae.) >> coati

race A biologically distinctive major division of a species, in which the differences between recognized races exceed the variation within them. While useful in describing variation in many plants and animals, where race is often equated with subspecies, the concept has little or no value for describing human biological diversity. In the past 500 years, contacts between all human groups have been intensive; gene pools are in constant flux; and the biological differences between populations are slight. The familiar 'racial' classifications typically emphasize superficially obvious features, such as skin colour or hair type, but other genetically transmitted features, such as blood groupings, tend to cross-cut the classical categories. There is no evidence for biologically-determined differences between populations in such ability or character traits, nor any consistent relationship with cultural systems or institutions. >> genetics; racism

RACE [rays] Acronym for **Research in Advanced Communications in Europe**, a European special programme of research in telecommunications particularly related to data communications. >> Framework programme

racehorse >> **thoroughbred**

raceme >> **inflorescence**

Rachmaninov, Sergey Vasilyevich [rakh**ma**ninof], also spelled **Rachmaninoff** and **Rakhmaninov** (1873–1943) Composer and pianist, born in Nizhni Novgorod. He wrote operas, orchestral works, and songs, but is best known for his piano music, which includes four concertos, the popular *Prelude in C Sharp Minor*, and his last major work, the *Rhapsody on a Theme of Paganini* (1934) for piano and orchestra.

racial discrimination Treating someone in a particular way because of their race or ethnicity. The term is usually understood to mean negative discrimination, that is, treating people in a way which will disadvantage them relative to other social groups. >> race; racism

Racine, Jean (Baptiste) [ra**seen**] (1639–99) Dramatic poet, born in La Ferté-Milon, France. His major verse tragedies include *Andromaque* (1667), *Britannicus* (1669), *Bérénice* (1679), *Bajazet* (1672), and *Phèdre* (1677). He later wrote two religious plays on Old Testament subjects, *Esther* (1689) and *Athalie* (1691).

racism An ideology that claims to explain an alleged inferiority of certain racial or ethnic groups in terms of their biological or physical characteristics. Racist beliefs have been used to justify genocide and the maintenance of systems of inequality (such as apartheid). >> racial discrimination

rackets (UK) / **racquets** (US) A racket-and-ball game played on a walled court by two or four players. Thought to have originated in the Middle Ages, it is regarded as the forerunner of many modern games. >> real tennis; RR1058

Rackham, Arthur [**rak**am] (1867–1939) Artist, born in London. A watercolourist and book illustrator, he was well known for his typically Romantic and grotesque pictures in books of fairy tales, such as *Peter Pan* (1906).

racoon >> **raccoon**

rad In radioactivity, an old unit for absorbed dose; symbol rad; 1 rad is equivalent to 0.01 J/kg, or 0.01 y (gray, SI unit); an abbreviation of **radiation**. >> gray; radioactivity units

radar Acronym for **radio detection and ranging**, a system developed in the 1930s whereby the position and distance of objects can be determined by measuring the time taken for radio waves to be reflected and returned. It is used in navigation, air control, fire control, storm detection, and by motorway police. >> radio

radar astronomy The use of pulses of radio waves to detect the distances and map the surfaces of objects in the Solar System. It has been applied with great success to Venus. >> astronomy; Solar System

Radcliffe, Ann, *née* **Ward** (1764–1823) Novelist, born in London. She became well known for her Gothic novels, notably *The Romance of the Forest* (1791), *The Mysteries of Udolpho* (1794), and *The Italian* (1797). >> Gothic novel

Radhakrishnan, Sir Sarvepalli [rahda**krish**nan] (1888–1975) Indian philosopher, statesman, and president (1962–7), born in Tiruttani, Madras, India. He was professor of Eastern religions and ethics at Oxford (1936–52), before becoming vice-president of India (1952–62), and president. >> India [i]

radian SI unit for measuring angles in a plane: symbol *rad*; 1 radian is the angle subtended at the centre of a circle by an arc along the circumference equal in length to the circle's radius; thus π radians = 180°.

radiance; radiant intensity / power >> **radiometry** [i]

radiation A general term for the processes by which energy is lost from a source without physical contact. It refers to various radioactive and electromagnetic emissions. >> electromagnetic radiation [i]; radiation sickness; radioactivity

radiation sickness A common complication of the application of radiotherapy to parts of the body in the course of treatment for malignant tumours. Weakness, nausea, and vomiting are common, both during and after treatment. The skin may become abnormally red in patches (*erythema*). >> radiotherapy; tumour

radical An unstable molecule containing unpaired electrons (eg CH_3, methyl). The term is also used as a synonym for 'group' in the sense of 'part of a molecule'. >> molecule

radicalism Any set of ideas, of either left or right, which argues for more substantial social and political change than is supported in the political mainstream. What is radical is a matter of judgment, and so the term is very widely applied.

radiesthesia [raydies**thee**zha] The use of dowsing as a method of diagnosing disease and selecting a suitable treatment, usually in the form of a herbal or homeopathic remedy. One method uses a pendulum: diagnosis is made by comparing the response of the pendulum to that observed with reference samples taken in various disease states. >> dowsing

radio The transmission of sound signals through space by means of radio-frequency electromagnetic waves. In 1888 the German physicist Heinrich Hertz produced and detected radio waves. Guglielmo Marconi constructed a device to translate radio waves into electrical signals, and in 1901 transmitted signals across the Atlantic Ocean. Radio broadcasting became routinely available during the 1920s, when such institutions as the BBC came into being. >> BBC; broadcasting; citizens' band (CB) radio; electromagnetic radiation [i]; Hertz; loudspeaker [i]; Marconi; microphone [i]; radio astronomy / beacon / galaxy / waves; telegraphy

radioactive dating >> **radiocarbon dating**

radioactive fallout The radioactive substances produced by a nuclear explosion, carried away from the site by winds, and deposited (either from dry air as particles, or dissolved in rain) causing contamination. Fallout from the Chernobyl accident in 1986 included caesium-134, caesium-137, iodine-131, plutonium-239, and strontium-90. >> Chernobyl; nuclear reactor [i]; radioactivity

radioactive tracer A radioactive isotope of an element substituted specifically in a compound in order to 'tag' it. Much has been learned about the mechanisms of reactions in this way, as the reactant supplying a specific atom to a product can be identified. >> radioactivity

radioactive waste A byproduct of the many processes involved in the generation of nuclear power. *Low-level* and *intermediate-level* waste is generally buried in pits. *High-level* waste is generally stored in stainless steel tanks, and continually cooled. One possibility for storage is vitrification (solidification in glass), to reduce the volume of waste. Proposals exist for the burial of high-level waste either under the seabed or deep underground on land. The production and storage of radioactive waste is a major international environmental issue. >> Greenpeace; hazardous substances; nuclear reactor [i]; waste disposal

radioactivity The spontaneous decay of atomic nuclei, resulting in the emission of particles and energy; discovered by Antoine Henri Becquerel in 1896. The possible emissions are alpha particles, beta particles, and gamma rays. Radioactivity is detected and measured using Geiger counters. >> alpha decay; Becquerel; beta decay; gamma rays; half-life; Geiger counter [i]; radioactivity units [i]; radioisotope

radioactivity units The activity of a radioactive source expressed in **becquerels** *Bq*, where 1 Bq is one decay per second. The **gray**, *Gy*, measures the energy deposited in some object by the radiation: the *absorbed dose*. Different types of radiation cause different degrees of biological damage; for example, 1 Gy of alpha radiation causes 20 times as much damage as 1 Gy of beta radiation. This potential for causing harm is expressed as *dose equivalent*, units **sievert**, *Sv*, which is the product of absorbed dose in Gy and a *relative biological effectiveness* (RBE) factor. Radiation limits for working places and the environment are expressed in Sv. >> becquerel; exposure (physics); gray; radioactivity; sievert

radio astronomy The exploration of the universe by detecting radio emission from celestial objects. The frequency range is very great, from 10 mHz to 300 gHz. A variety of antennas are used, from single dishes to elaborate networks of telescopes. >> astronomy; radio waves

radio beacon A fixed radio transmitting station, sending out a coded signal characteristic of that station. This helps aircraft pilots and ships' captains to navigate safely, especially in bad weather conditions. >> direction finder; radio

radiobiology The branch of biology concerned with the effects of radioactive materials on living organisms, and with the use of radioactive tracers to study metabolic processes. >> biology; metabolism; radioactivity

radiocarbon dating A radiometric method for measuring the decay of the radioactive isotope carbon-14 in organic material up to 80 000 years old, developed in 1948–9 by Willard Libby. Living animals and plants take in carbon, which contains some radioactive carbon-14. When the organism dies, it stops taking in carbon, and as the carbon-14 decays, its proportion to the total amount of carbon decreases in a way which is directly related to the time elapsed since death. >> carbon; dendrochronology; Libby; radioactivity

radiochemistry The production and use of radioisotopes to study chemical compounds and their reactions. An example is the synthesis of compounds incorporating

Radioactivity Units

Name	Definition	Unit	Old unit
activity	rate of disintegrations	Bq	Ci (curie)
absorbed dose	energy deposited in object, divided by mass of object	Gy	rad
dose equivalent	absorbed dose x RBE	Sv	rem

RBE	Radiation
20	alpha
10	neutron
1	beta, gamma, X-ray

radioactive atoms in specific sites, to see whether those atoms are present in a product of a subsequent chemical reaction. >> chemistry

radio galaxy A galaxy which is an intense source of cosmic radio waves. In such objects, an active galactic nucleus (almost certainly a black hole) is producing immense quantities of electrons travelling at almost the speed of light. When these encounter a magnetic field, they spiral around the field lines, emitting synchrotron radiation as radio waves. >> black hole; galaxy; quasar

radiogram A single device capable of both receiving radio broadcasts and playing gramophone records. It was developed during the 1930s, and incorporated a record player which made use of the radio's amplifier and speaker. >> radio; record player

radiography Producing a photographic image (actually a shadow-image) of a structure which is penetrated by X-rays, gamma-rays, or electrons. The first radiograph was made by Röntgen in 1895, and the technique is now highly developed for medical diagnosis and for non-destructive industrial testing. >> gamma rays; Röntgen; X-rays

radio-immunoassay A method using radioactively labelled material corresponding to a substance to be measured, together with a specific antibody to the substance. The degree of binding of the antibody to the labelled substance can be used to calculate the amount of substance present in a biological fluid, such as blood. >> radioactivity

radioisotope An isotope which spontaneously undergoes radioactive decay. It may be naturally occurring or artificially produced. All isotopes of all elements with an atomic number above 83 are radioisotopes. >> isotopes; radiocarbon dating; RR1036

Radiolaria [raydiohl**lair**ia] An informal grouping of marine single-celled organisms (protozoans). They have a typically spherical cell body, with an elaborate skeleton consisting of radiating spikes of silica. (Class: Actinopoda.) >> Protozoa

radiometric dating A method for determining the absolute age of a rock by measuring the amount of radioactive element present and comparing it to the amount of stable element into which it decays. >> potassium–argon / radiocarbon / rubidium–strontium / uranium–lead dating; radioactivity

radiometry The measurement of radiated electromagnetic energy, especially infrared; see table for symbols and units. *Radiant power* is the total power from a source; *radiant intensity* is radiant power per unit solid angle, and is used to describe sources that do not radiate uniformly in all directions; *radiance* is radiant intensity per unit area; *irradiance* is total power per unit area. >> electromagnetic radiation ℹ; photometry ℹ

radiosonde (radiosounding) balloon [**ray**diohsond] A package of instruments sent up with a weather balloon to measure pressure, temperature, and humidity as the balloon rises to high altitudes (20 000 m/65 000 ft). Information is transmitted back to ground-receiving stations by radio signals. A **rawindsonde** (radar wind sounding) balloon is a version of radiosonde which also measures wind speed and direction. >> weather

radio telescope >> **telescope** ℹ

radiotherapy The use of radiation (especially X-rays) to treat disease, especially malignant tumours, which are more sensitive to certain kinds of radiation than are normal tissues. Radioactive materials can also be used (eg a tiny pellet), implanted directly into the tumour to give a carefully calculated total dose. The technique has proved particularly successful in the treatment of cancer. >> cancer; tumour; X-rays

Radiometry

Radiometric quantity	Symbol	Units
radiant power	Φ	W
radiant intensity	I	W/sr
radiance	L	W/sr.m²
irradiance	E	W/m²

radio waves Electromagnetic radiation of wavelength greater than about 10 cm. It is produced by oscillating electric currents in antennas, and travels at the velocity of light. >> amplitude modulation; frequency modulation; radio

radish An annual or biennial (*Raphanus sativus*) with a tuberous root, irregularly lobed leaves, and cross-shaped, white to purplish flowers. Its origin is unknown, but it has been used as a vegetable since Ancient Egyptian times. (Family: Cruciferae.) >> tuber; vegetable

radium Ra, element 88, melting point 700°C. A metal, with all its isotopes radioactive. The most stable isotope, ^{226}Ra, has a half-life of only 1620 years, and occurs in uranium ores as a product of radioactive decay. It is a source of α-particles, and combined with beryllium, a neutron source. Radium salts exhibit fluorescence. >> chemical elements; neutron; uranium; RR1036

radius >> **arm**

radon Rn, element 86, boiling point −62°C. The heaviest of the noble gases. It has several isotopes: that with the longest half-life (4 days) is ^{222}Rn, formed with radium. It is continuously liberated to the atmosphere by natural radioactive decay; its primary use is in radiotherapy. >> chemical elements; noble gases; radium; xenon; RR1036

Raeburn, Sir Henry [**ray**bern] (1756–1823) Portrait painter, born near Edinburgh. He painted the leading members of Edinburgh society in a typically bold, strongly-shadowed style.

Raeder, Erich [**ray**der] (1876–1960) German grand admiral, born in Wandsbek, Germany. In 1928 he was made commander-in-chief of the navy, and in 1943 head of an anti-invasion force. At the Nuremberg Trials (1946), he was sentenced to life imprisonment, but released in 1955. >> World War 2

RAF >> **Royal Air Force**

raffia palm A tree growing to 7.5 m/25 ft, native to Africa; leaves 18 m/60 ft, feathery. The surface of the young leaflets is stripped to provide raffia fibre. (Genus: *Raffia*, 30 species. Family: Palmae.) >> palm

Raffles, Sir (Thomas) Stamford (1781–1826) Colonial administrator, born at sea, off Port Morant, Jamaica. He became Lieutenant-Governor of Java (1811–16), and as Lieutenant-Governor of Benkoelen (1818–23) established a settlement at Singapore (1819). A famous Singapore hotel carries his name.

rafflesia The best-known member of an entirely parasitic family of flowering plants from the tropics and subtropics. Native to Malaysia, it parasitizes woody vines and has enormous flowers. The flowers of *Rafflesia arnoldii* are the largest in the world, reaching 1m/3¼ ft in diameter. They are typical carrion flowers, the whole structure being coloured to resemble rotting meat, and producing a strong putrid smell which attracts flies to pollinate them. (Genus: *Rafflesia*, 12 species. Family: Rafflesiaceae.) >> parasitic plant

Rafsanjani, Ali Akbar Hashemi [rafsan**jah**nee] (1934–) Iranian president (1989–97), born in Rafsanjan, Iran. After the 1979 revolution, he helped to found the ruling Islamic Republican Party, and in 1980 he was chosen as Speaker of the Majlis (Lower House). He was the most influential figure in Iran after Khomeini, and succeeded him as president. >> Iran ℹ; Khomeini

raga In Indian music, the equivalent of the Western 'mode', but with broader connotations of melodic contour, performance style, ornamentation, etc. >> scale ℹ

Raglan (of Raglan), Lord Fitzroy James Henry Somerset, Baron (1788–1855) British general, born at Badminton, Gloucestershire. In 1854 he led an ill-prepared force against the Russians in the Crimea, his ambiguous order leading to the Charge of the Light Brigade (1854) at Balaclava. His name was given to the **raglan sleeve**, which came into use in the 1850s. >> Crimean War

Ragnarok [**rag**narok] In Norse mythology, the final battle between the gods and the monstrous forces hostile to them. Though gods and monsters die, a new world will arise.

ragtime A type of syncopated US music popular from c.1890 to c.1920, when it yielded to (and influenced) the new jazz style. 'Rags' were composed mainly for piano, and ragtime was popularized by Scott Joplin and other pianist–composers. It had a revival in the 1970s. >> jazz; Joplin

ragwort A robust biennial or perennial (*Senecio jacobaea*), growing to 1.5 m/5 ft, native to Europe and W Asia; flower-heads numerous, bright golden yellow and daisy-like, in dense flat-topped clusters. It is poisonous to livestock if eaten in quantity. (Family: Compositae.)

Rahman, Shaikh Mujibur [**rah**man] (1920–75) First prime minister (1972–5) and president (1975) of Bangladesh, born in Tongipara, Bangladesh (formerly East Bengal). In 1966 he was arrested and imprisoned for two years for provoking separatism. In 1970 he launched a non-co-operation campaign which escalated into civil war and the creation of Bangladesh. He was overthrown and killed in a coup in Dacca. >> Bangladesh [i]; Pakistan [i]

Rahner, Karl (1904–84) Leading Roman Catholic theologian, born in Freiburg, Germany. In his voluminous writings (such as his multivolume *Theological Investigations*), he uses insights from existentialism while remaining true to the tradition of Aquinas. He played a major role as consultant at the Second Vatican Council (1962–6). >> Aquinas; existentialism

Raikes, Robert [rayks] (1735–1811) Philanthropist, born in Gloucester, Gloucestershire. He pioneered the Sunday School movement in 1780.

rail A bird of the worldwide family Rallidae (c.130 species), possibly the most widespread group of terrestrial birds; large legs, short rounded wings, and short tails. >> coot; corncrake; crake; gallinule; jacana; moorhen

rail gun 1 A heavy artillery piece mounted on a railway carriage. **2** A proposed component of the Strategic Defense Initiative, a land-based, short-range system for the last-ditch defence of individual land targets. It uses electrical energy to accelerate kinetic energy munitions to very high velocities. >> kinetic energy weapons; SDI

railway The general name given in the UK to a transport system that has as its central feature the operation of a locomotive hauling passenger carriages or freight trucks on specially mounted tracks or rails, called the **permanent way**. The geographical area covered by the rails forms a **rail network**, and the operation of all trains on the network together with their scheduling, control, and engineering support services form a **railway system**. North American usage retains the historical name of **railroad** to describe the above definition of railway, and uses the term **railway** to describe the permanent way, ie the rails, their fixings, and associated engineering. The world's first railway, the Stockton and Darlington, was opened in 1825, and was used mainly for the carriage of coal and other goods, and some passengers, employing both steam locomotives and horses for traction. It was not until 1830, and the opening of the Liverpool and Manchester Railway, that a full passenger-carrying railway, solely dependent on steam locomotives, became operational. The 'Best Friend of Charleston' pulled the first train on US soil in 1830, and by 1869 it was possible to cross the USA by rail. >> Canadian Pacific Railway; Eurostar; locomotive [i]; Shinkansen; underground

rainbow An arc of light comprising the spectral colours, formed when the Sun's rays are refracted and internally reflected by raindrops acting as prisms or lenses. It is visible when the Sun is behind the observer and the rain is in front. >> spectrum

Rainbow Snake In Australian aboriginal religion, the great fertility spirit, both male and female, creator and destroyer; known as **Julunggul**. It is associated with streams and waterholes, from which it emerges in the creation-story and leaves special markings on the ground. >> Aborigines

Raine, Craig (Anthony) (1944–) Poet, born in Shildon, Co Durham. Poetry editor at Faber and Faber (1981–91), his books include *The Onion, Memory* (1978), *Selected Poetry* (1992), and *Clay: Whereabouts Unknown* (1996).

rainfall A type of precipitation in which water droplets reach the ground in liquid state. When water droplets are small, rain may be called *drizzle*. In temperate and humid regions, rainfall may form the major contribution to annual precipitation totals. >> acid rain; precipitation; rain gauge; sleet

rainforest The vegetation type found in wet equatorial regions and other areas of high precipitation. Tropical rainforests are characterized by a great diversity of plant and animal species, a closed canopy layer which allows little light to reach the forest floor, and rapid nutrient cycling within the forest. Many of the trees have considerable commercial value, and large areas are being cleared. Deforestation is also occurring to create new agricultural areas (cattle ranching) and industry (mining). The United Nations Food and Agricultural Organization estimates that c.100 000 sq km/c.40 000 sq mi are cleared each year. This rate of disappearance is alarming many conservationists, because of the extinction of unique plant and animal species. Tropical rainforests also play an important role in the global climate system, which could also be disrupted by clearance. >> selva; tropics

rain gauge A meteorological instrument used to measure the amount of rainfall for a given period. It is commonly in the form of a bucket, with an opening of known size, which funnels rain into a measuring cylinder below. >> rainfall

Rainier, Mount [**rayn**yer] 46°51N 121°46W. Dormant volcano in WC Washington, USA; height 4395 m/14 419 ft; highest point in the Cascade Range; the largest single-peak glacier system in the USA. >> Washington (state)

Rainier III [raynyay], in full **Rainier Louis Henri Maxence Bertrand de Grimaldi** (1923–) Prince of Monaco (1949–), born in Monaco. In 1956 he married **Grace (Patricia) Kelly** (1929–82), a US film actress, whose successful career included *High Noon* (1952), *Rear Window* (1954), and *High Society* (1956), before she retired on her marriage. There are two daughters, **Princess Caroline Louise Marguerite** (1957–) and **Princess Stephanie Marie Elisabeth** (1965–), and a son, **Prince Albert Alexandre Louis Pierre** (1958–). Princess Grace died after a car accident in 1982. >> Monaco

Rais or Raiz, Baron >> **Retz, Baron**

raisins Black or white grapes, dried naturally or artificially. They have a high sugar content, and are used widely in cake- and bun-making to impart sweetness. >> grapevine

Rajasthan [**rah**jastahn] pop (1995e) 47 498 000; area 342 214 sq km/132 095 sq mi. State in NW India, formed in 1948; capital, Jaipur; governed by a Legislative Assembly; Thar desert in the W. >> India [i]; Jaipur

Rakhmaninov, Sergei >> **Rachmaninov**

Raleigh [**rah**lee] 35°46N 78°38W, pop (1995e) 225 000. Capital of state in EC North Carolina, USA; established, 1788; named after Sir Walter Raleigh; airfield; railway; two universities (1865, 1887). >> North Carolina; Raleigh, Sir Walter

Raleigh, Sir Walter [**raw**lee, **ra**lee], also spelled **Ralegh** (1552–1618) Courtier, navigator, and writer, born in Hayes Barton, Devon. He became prime favourite of Queen Elizabeth, and in 1584 sent the first of three expeditions to America. After the arrival of the Earl of Essex at court, he lost influence. He took little part in the intrigues at the close of Elizabeth's reign, but his enemies turned James I against him, and he was imprisoned (1603). While in the Tower, he wrote his *History of the World* (1614), and several other works. Released in 1616, he made an expedition to the Orinoco in search of a gold-mine, which was a failure, and led to his execution. >> Elizabeth I; James I (of England)

rally A form of motor racing which demands skill and endurance from driver and navigator. Rallies are raced over several days (sometimes weeks) using modified production cars. Famous rallies include the Monte Carlo Rally, the RAC Lombard Rally, and the Safari Rally. >> motor racing

ram >> **sheep**

RAM [ram] Acronym for **random access memory** (sometimes **read-and-write memory**), a type of computer memory, usually integrated circuits, which can be read from and written to. RAM is used in all computers; data contained in RAM is lost when the electrical power is removed. >> computer memory; ROM

Ramadan [rama**dahn**] The ninth month of the Muslim year, observed as a month of fasting during which Muslims abstain from eating and drinking between sunrise and sunset; the Ramadan fast is one of the five 'pillars', or basic duties, of Islam. >> Id-al-Fitr; Islam; RR982

Ramadan War >> **Arab–Israeli Wars**

Ramakrishna [rama**krish**na], originally **Gadadhar Chatterjee** (1836–86) Hindu religious teacher, born in Hooghly, Bengal, India. He formed a religious order which bore his name, and established its headquarters in Calcutta. His most noteworthy disciple was Swami Vivekananda. >> Vivekananda

Raman, Sir Chandrasekhara (Venkata) [**rah**man] (1888–1970) Physicist, born in Trichinopoly, India. In 1930 he was awarded the Nobel Prize for Physics for his discoveries relating to the scattering of light. >> optics ℹ

Ramaphosa, Cyril (Matamela) [rama**poh**za] (1952–) South African politician and trade unionist, born in Johannesburg, South Africa. He played a prominent part in the protest politics of the 1980s, and in 1991 became the secretary-general of the African National Congress, resigning in 1996. >> African National Congress; trade union

Ramapithecus [rama**pith**ekus] A fossil ape, known from the Miocene epoch of E Europe, Asia, and E Africa; ground-dwelling, walked on all fours; jaws robust; canine teeth low as in early hominids. (Family: Pongidae.) >> ape; Miocene epoch

Ramayana [rama**yah**na] One of the two great Sanskrit epics of ancient India, which tells the story of Rama, his wife Sita, and the evil forces ranged against them. Though ascribed to the sage Valmiki, it derives from oral tradition. Its 24 000 couplets make it one-quarter the length of the *Mahabharata*. >> epic; Hinduism; Mahabharata

Rambert, Dame Marie [**rom**bair], originally **Cyvia Rambam** (1888–1982) Ballet dancer and teacher, born in Warsaw. In 1913 she worked with Diaghilev's Ballets Russes. In 1935 she formed the Ballet Rambert, and remained closely associated with it through its change to a modern dance company in the 1960s. >> Ballets Russes; modern dance

Ramblers' Association A British federation of local rambling clubs, established in 1935. It campaigns for access to open countryside, defends outstanding landscape and rights-of-way, and is one of the main advocates of long-distance footpaths.

Rameau, Jean Philippe [ramoh] (1683–1764) Composer, born in Dijon, France. His *Traité de l'harmonie* (1722, Treatise on Harmony) is a work of fundamental importance in the history of musical style. He wrote many operas, as well as ballets, harpsichord pieces, and vocal music.

Rameses or **Ramses II** [**ram**zeez], known as **the Great** (13th-c BC) King of Egypt (1304–1237 BC), whose long and prosperous reign marks the last great peak of Egyptian power. He has left innumerable monuments, among them the great sandstone temples at Abu Simbel. >> Abu Simbel

Rameses or **Ramses III** [**ram**(e)seez] (12th-c BC) King of Egypt (1198–1166 BC), famous primarily for his great victory over the Sea Peoples. Tradition identifies him with the pharaoh who oppressed the Hebrews of the Exodus. >> Exodus, Book of; Sea Peoples

ramjet A type of jet engine in which fast-moving air is slowed down by a diffuser, which produces a corresponding increase in the air's pressure. This high-pressure air then has fuel injected into it, and the mixture is continuously burned. The resulting hot gases are ejected rearwards in the form of a jet of gas. This method of jet propulsion is practical up to speeds of eight times the speed of sound. >> jet engine ℹ; scramjet

Ramos-Horta, José [**ra**mos **haw(r)**ta] (1950–) East Timorese activist. A former guerilla member of the independence movement in East Timor, he withdrew to Australia following the 1975 Indonesian invasion, becoming East Timor's international spokesman, and has since sought international support for a peaceful solution. He shared the Nobel Prize for Peace in 1996.

Ramsay, Allan (c.1685–1758) Poet, born in Leadhills, South Lanarkshire. His works include the pastoral comedy, *The Gentle Shepherd* (1725), and an edited collection of Scots poetry, *The Evergreen* (1724).

Ramses >> **Rameses**

Ramsey (of Canterbury), (Arthur) Michael Ramsey, Baron (1904–88) Archbishop of Canterbury (1961–74), born in Cambridge, Cambridgeshire. He was Bishop of Durham (1952–6) and Archbishop of York (1956–61). As Archbishop of Canterbury he worked for Church unity, making a historic visit to Pope Paul VI in the Vatican in 1966. >> Paul VI

Ramsgate 51°20N 1°25E, pop (1995e) 38 300. Port town in Kent, SE England; railway; hovercraft service to France; yachting, fishing, tourism; Celtic cross marks the spot where St Augustine is supposed to have landed in 597. >> Augustine, St (of Canterbury); Cinque Ports; Kent

Ramus, Petrus [ramü], Lat name of **Pierre de la Ramée** (1515–72) Humanist, born in Cuts, France. His attempts to reform the science of logic excited much hostility among the Aristotelians, and his *Dialectic* (1543) was suppressed. He later became a Protestant (c.1561), and was murdered in the massacre of St Bartholomew's Day. >> St Bartholomew's Day Massacre

rancidity The reaction of atmospheric oxygen with fats, which reduces vitamin A and E levels in foods. Antioxidants are commonly added to foods to prevent the development of rancidity. >> antioxidants; vitamins ℹ

Rand >> **Witwatersrand**

Randolph, A(sa) Philip (1889–1979) Labour leader and civil rights activist, born in Crescent City, FL. He built the first successful black trade union, the Brotherhood of

Sleeping Car Porters (1925). The founder of the Negro American Labor Council in 1960, he directed the civil rights march on Washington in 1963. >> civil rights

Randstad Urban conurbation of settlements in NW Netherlands, forming a horse-shoe shape around a central agricultural zone; contains most of the Dutch population; chief cities, Amsterdam, Rotterdam, Utrecht, The Hague. >> Netherlands, The [i]

Ranger programme The first US series of lunar spacecraft missions, designed to study the surface characteristics of the Moon prior to the Apollo manned landings. The spacecraft were targeted to impact the Moon after telemetering images of increasingly high resolution. The first successful mission was Ranger 7 (Aug 1964). >> Moon

Rangoon >> **Yangon**

Ranjit Singh [**ran**jit sing], known as **the Lion of the Punjab** (1780–1839) Sikh ruler, born in Budrukhan, India. Succeeding his father as ruler of Lahore, he fought to unite all the Sikh provinces, and became the most powerful ruler in India. >> Sikhism

Rank (of Sutton Scotney), J(oseph) Arthur Rank, Baron (1888–1972) Film magnate, born in Hull. He became chairman of many film companies, and did much to promote the British film industry.

Rankine temperature >> **temperature** [i]

Ransome, Arthur (Mitchell) (1884–1967) Writer, born in Leeds, West Yorkshire. He wrote critical and travel books before making his name with books for young readers, notably *Swallows and Amazons* (1931).

ransoms A perennial growing to 45 cm/18 in (*Allium ursinum*), native to Europe and Asia; narrow bulb consisting of a single leaf base, 2–3 broadly elliptical leaves, and white, star-shaped flowers; smells strongly of garlic. (Family: Liliaceae). >> allium

Rantzen, Esther (Louise) (1940–   ) Television presenter and producer, born in Berkhamsted, Hertfordshire. During 1973–94 she produced and presented *That's Life*, a populist consumer programme. In 1988 she received the Richard Dimbleby Award for her contributions to factual television. Since 1995 she has presented the talk-show *Esther*.

rape (botany) A biennial herb (*Brassica rapus*, variety *arvensis*) growing to 1 m/3¼ ft; bluish-green leaves; yellow, cross-shaped flowers. It is grown for fodder and, increasingly, as a source of rape-oil, obtained from crushed seeds, and rape-seed cake, made from the residue. (Family: Cruciferae.) >> brassica; herb

rape (law) The crime committed when a male forces a woman to have sexual intercourse without her freely given consent. The maximum sentence is life imprisonment. The law now recognizes rape by a husband against his wife, and in some US jurisdictions against a man. **Statutory rape** occurs when a man takes sexual advantage of someone deemed unable to understand the nature of sexual intercourse, such as a severely mentally-handicapped person or someone below the age of consent.

Raphael [**raf**ael], in full **Raffaello Sanzio** (1483–1520) Painter, born in Urbino, Italy. In Florence he completed several sweet Madonnas, as well as such works as 'The Holy Family' (Madrid). In 1508 he went to Rome, where he produced his greatest works, including the frescoes in the papal apartments of the Vatican, and the cartoons for the tapestries of the Sistine Chapel. In 1514 he succeeded Bramante as architect of St Peter's. >> Bramante

rap music A musical style which started in the streets of New York with inner-city high-school students chanting crude incantations over rock records customized by reversing the turntable and distorting the amplification. In 1983, 'It's Like That' by Run-D.M.C., a trio of schoolmates from the borough of Queens, sold 500 000 copies, heralding the music conquest of the suburbs. The main effect comes from a tortuous backbeat. The lyrics went unnoticed until increasingly flagrant advocacy of drug use, promiscuity, authority-bashing, and rioting led to bans and legal threats. >> rock music

rare earths >> **lanthanides**

rare gases >> **noble gases**

Ras al-Khaimah [**ras** al **khiy**ma] pop (1995e) 110 000; area 1690 sq km/652 sq mi. Northernmost of the United Arab Emirates; capital, Ras al-Khaimah; offshore oil production began in 1984. >> United Arab Emirates [i]

Rasmussen, Knud (Johan Victor) [**raz**musen] (1879–1933) Explorer and ethnologist, born in Jacobshavn, Greenland. From 1902 he directed several expeditions to Greenland, in 1910 established Thule base on Cape York, and in 1921–4 crossed by dog-sledge from Greenland to the Bering Strait. >> Greenland [i]

raspberry A deciduous shrub (*Rubus idaeus*) growing to c.2 m/6½ ft, native to Europe and Asia; straight, slender prickles; woody, biennial stems from buds on the roots; flowers 5-petalled, white; red berry. It is cultivated for fruit. (Family: Rosaceae.)

Raspe, Rudolf Erich >> **Münchhausen, Baron von**

Rasputin, Grigoriy [ras**pyoo**tin] (?1871–1916) Peasant and self-styled religious 'elder', born in Pokrovskoye, Russia. He gained the confidence of the emperor (Nicholas II) and empress by his ability to control through hypnosis the bleeding of the haemophiliac heir to the throne. A notorious lecher and drunkard, his political influence led to his murder by a clique of aristocrats. >> Nicholas II

Ras Shamra texts [rahs **shahm**ra] Some 350 texts, inscribed on tablets, found 1928–60 on the site of ancient Ugarit in NW Syria, many written in a previously unknown cuneiform script now described as 'Ugaritic', and others in Babylonian. >> cuneiform [i]

Rastafarianism A religious movement from the West Indies, followed by about a million people. It largely derives from the thought of Jamaican political activist Marcus Garvey (1887–1940), who advocated a return to Africa as a means of solving the problems of black oppression. When Haile Selassie was crowned Emperor of Ethiopia in 1930, he came to be viewed as the Messiah, with Ethiopia seen as the promised land. Rastafarians follow strict taboos governing what they may eat (eg no pork, milk, coffee); ganja (marijuana) is held to be a sacrament; they usually wear their hair in long dreadlocks; and they cultivate a distinctive form of speech. >> black consciousness; Haile Selassie I

rat A mouse-like rodent of family Muridae; name used generally for many unrelated species in this family, especially for members of genus *Rattus* (c.80 species throughout the Old World). It can spread human diseases (bubonic plague was spread by fleas of the black rat). >> rodent; water rat

ratel A badger-like mammal (*Mellivora capensis*) native to Africa and S Asia, dark brown with top of head and centre

Ratel

of back pale yellowish-grey; fearless, with very tough skin; eats small animals, carrion, and vegetation; follows honeyguides to beehives and takes the honey; also known as **honey badger**. (Family: Mustelidae.) >> badger; honeyguide; Mustelidae

rates The system of local taxation in use in the UK up to 1990 (for England and Wales; up to 1989 for Scotland). The **rateable value** of properties was decided by public valuers, and the rate per pound was set by the local authority. Because rates were paid only by occupiers of property, this system was regarded as unfair, since other residents had votes for the bodies determining the level of rates, but did not pay for the cost of the policies. Rates were therefore replaced by the community charge, though rating valuations stayed as the basis for charges by water companies. However, after much opposition, in 1993 there was a return to the system of basing local taxation on property values. >> community charge; taxation

ratfish >> **chimaera**

Rathenau, Walther [**raht**enow] (1867–1922) German statesman and industrialist, born in Berlin. He organized German war industries during World War 1, and later dealt with reparations. His attempts to negotiate with the Allies, and the fact that he was Jewish, made him extremely unpopular in nationalist circles, and he was murdered. >> reparations; World War 1

Rather, Dan [**ra**ther] (1931–) Television news presenter and writer, born in Wharton TX. He became a television journalist, then White House correspondent and London bureau chief (1963–74). His national profile grew as co-editor of *60 Minutes* (1975–81), and he went on to become anchor of *CBS Evening News* (from 1981).

Rathlin Island area 14 sq km/5½ sq mi. Island in N Antrim, N Northern Ireland; length, 8 km/5 mi; up to 5 km/3 mi wide; rises to 137 m/449 ft; St Columba founded a church here, 6th-c. >> Antrim (county); Columba, St

rationalism (architecture) A 20th-c conception of architecture which pursues the most logical possible solution to every aspect of building. It is particularly associated with the work of most of the Bauhaus and International Style architects of the 1920s and 1930s. >> Bauhaus; functionalism (art and architecture); International Style

rationalism (philosophy) In philosophy, the tradition represented by the 17th-c figures Descartes, Leibniz, and Spinoza who believed that the general nature of the world could be established by reason alone, through *a priori* knowledge independent of sense-experience; it is usually contrasted with *empiricism*. In a popular sense, the term expresses a commitment to reason as opposed to faith, convention, or emotion, and is therefore contrasted with *irrationalism*. >> empiricism

rational number >> **numbers**

Ratitae [ra**tiy**tee] (Lat *ratis* 'raft') An obsolete term for flightless running birds, such as the ostrich and emu (which are still referred to as **ratites**). The breastbone in these birds has lost its keel and become flat (or 'raft-like'). >> bird ℹ

rattan palm [ra**tan**] A member of a large genus of tropical climbing palms with slender, extremely long stems up to 180 m/500 ft. The stems are stripped to make rattan canes, widely used for furniture, baskets, and other items; also the very strong malacca cane used for walking sticks. (Genus: *Calamus*, 375 species. Family: Palmae.) >> palm

Rattigan, Sir Terence (Mervyn) (1911–77) Playwright, born in London. His plays include *French Without Tears* (1936), *The Winslow Boy* (1946), *The Browning Version* (1948), and *Ross* (1960).

Rattle, Sir Simon (Denis) (1955–) Conductor, born in Liverpool, Merseyside. After winning the International Conductors' Competition in 1974, he worked with orchestras in Bournemouth, Liverpool, and the BBC. He became widely acclaimed as the principal conductor of the City of Birmingham Symphony Orchestra (1991–98). Since 1981 he has been principal guest conductor of the Los Angeles Philharmonic.

rattlesnake A New World pit viper of genus *Crotalus* (28 species); tail with a segmented rattle (except in the **Santa Catalina rattlesnake**, *Crotalus catalinensis*); rattle made from modified scales (one segment added at each moult, but old segments are lost); venom attacks blood cells. >> diamondback; pit viper ℹ; sidewinder ℹ

Rauschenberg, Robert [**rowsh**enberg] (1925–) Artist, born in Port Arthur, TX. He is one of the most aggressive US modernists, whose collages and 'combines' incorporate a variety of rubbish (eg rusty metal, old tyres, stuffed birds). >> Dada; Pop Art; readymade

Ravel, Maurice [ra**vel**] (1875–1937) Composer, born in Ciboure, France. His works include *Pavane pour une infante défunte* (1899, Pavane for a Dead Princess), *Rapsodie espagnole* (1908), the 'choreographic poem' *La Valse* (1920), and *Boléro* (1928), intended as a miniature ballet.

raven A large crow, especially the **great raven** (*Corvus corax*) of the N hemisphere; omnivorous; territorial; does not nest in colonies. (Genus: *Corvus*, 9 species.) >> crow

Ravenna [ra**ven**a] 44°25N 12°12E, pop (1995e) 143 000. Town in NE Italy; capital of W Roman Empire in AD 402, and of later Ostrogothic and Byzantine rulers; archbishopric; railway; cathedral (18th-c). >> Italy ℹ

Ravi [**rah**vee] **River**, ancient **Hydraotes** River in NW India and Pakistan; one of the five rivers of the Punjab; rises in the SE Pir Panjal range; joins the R Chenab; length 765 km/475 mi. >> Punjab (India, Pakistan)

Rawalpindi [rahwal**pin**dee] 33°40N 73°08E, pop (1995e) 1 171 000. City in Punjab province, Pakistan; strategically important location controlling routes to Kashmir; occupied by the British, 1849; interim capital, 1959–69; airfield; railway; military and commercial centre. >> Pakistan ℹ

rawindsonde [**ray**winsond] >> **radiosonde balloon**

Rawsthorne, Alan (1905–71) Composer, born in Haslingden, Lancashire. He wrote a wide range of works, including three symphonies, eight concertos, choral and chamber music, and several film scores.

ray Any of the numerous small to large bottom-dwelling cartilaginous fishes in families Anacanthobatidae, Pseudorajidae, Rajidae (skates and rays), Gymnuridae (butterfly ray), Rhinopteridae, Mobulidae (devil rays), Torpedinidae (electric rays), and Myliobatidae (eagle rays); front part of the body strongly flattened with broad pectoral fins; mouth and gill openings on the underside. >> cartilaginous fish; devil / electric ray; sawfish; skate; stingray

Ray, John (1627–1705) Naturalist, born in Black Notley, Essex. His classification of plants, with its emphasis on the species as the basic unit, was a foundation of modern taxonomy. >> taxonomy

Ray, Man, originally **Emanuel Rudnitsky** (1890–1976) Painter, sculptor, photographer and film-maker, born in Philadelphia, PA. He became a major figure in the development of Modernism, founding the New York Dadaist movement. He became interested in films, and during the 1930s produced many photographs and 'rayographs' (photographic montages). >> Dada; Modernism

Ray, Satyajit [riy] (1921–92) Film director, born and educated in Calcutta, India. India's leading film maker, his films include the trilogy *Pather Panchali* (1954, On the Road), *Aparajito* (1956, The Unvanquished), *Apur Sansar* (1959, The World of Apu), and *An Enemy of the People* (1989). He received an Academy Lifetime Achievement Award in 1991.

Rayleigh scattering The scattering of light by objects which are small compared to the wavelength of light; described by British physicist Lord Rayleigh (1842–1919). The Rayleigh scattering of sunlight by air molecules makes the sky appear blue, since blue light is scattered more than other frequencies. >> light

rayon A textile fibre formed from cellulose (a constituent of wood pulp), first produced late in the 19th-c. Improvements in manufacturing methods have made modern rayon fibres important as domestic and industrial materials. >> viscose

Razi >> **Rhazes**

razorbill An auk native to the N Atlantic (*Alca torda*); black bill, with vertical white stripe near tip. >> auk

razor shell A burrowing marine bivalve with two similar elongate shell valves; shell closed by two muscles. (Class: Pelecypoda. Order: Veneroida.) >> bivalve; shell

Re [ray] or **Ra** [rah] In Egyptian religion, the ancient Sun-god of Heliopolis. He is depicted as a falcon with the Sun's disc on his head. >> Amun

reactance In alternating current circuits containing inductors and capacitors, the factor which determines the phase relationship between current and voltage; symbol *X*, units Ω (ohms). >> alternating current; capacitance; inductance

reactive armour A form of protection for military vehicles such as tanks against the kind of 'hollow-charge' warhead typically used in infantry-fired antitank missiles; also known as **Chobham armour**. Reactive armour itself detonates locally, neutralizing the attacking weapon's effects.

Read, Sir Herbert (1893–1968) Poet and art critic, born near Kirby Moorside, North Yorkshire. He became known as a poet and a writer on aesthetics in such works as *The Meaning of Art* (1931). >> aesthetics

Reading [**red**ing] 51°28N 0°59W, pop (1995e) 140 000. Unitary authority (from 1998) and former county town of Berkshire, S England, on the R Thames; unitary authority from 1998; railway; university (1926); rapidly developing commercial centre; 12th-c Benedictine abbey, burial place of Henry I; football league team, Reading (Royals). >> Henry I (of England)

readymade In modern art, any object not made by the artist but chosen by him or her and exhibited as a 'work of art'. Thus Duchamp exhibited a bottle-rack in 1914 and (most notoriously) a urinal, which he entitled 'Fountain' in 1917. >> Dada; Duchamp; modern art

Reagan, Ronald (Wilson) [**ray**gn] (1911–) US Republican statesman and 40th president, born in Tampico, IL. He went to Hollywood in 1937 and made over 50 films, beginning with *Love Is On the Air* (1937). He became Governor of California in 1966, stood unsuccessfully for the Republican presidential nomination in 1968 and 1976, but in 1980 defeated Jimmy Carter, and won a second term in 1984, defeating Walter Mondale. He introduced a major programme of economic change, took a strong anti-communist stand, especially in the Middle East and Central America, and introduced the Strategic Defense Initiative. In 1981 he was wounded in an assassination attempt. During his second term, he reached a major arms-reduction accord with Soviet leader Gorbachev. >> Carter, Jimmy; Gorbachev; Mondale; Republican Party; SDI

Realism (art and literature) In art criticism, a term (especially with a capital R) referring to the deliberate choice of ugly or unidealized subject-matter, sometimes to make a social or political point. Realism with a small 'r' is often used rather vaguely as the opposite of 'abstract'. More generally, in literature and art, the term refers to the advocacy of verisimilitude, as encountered in the Realist movement of mid-19th-c France, which flourished (as Naturalism) in the revolutionary scientific confidence of that era. >> Ashcan School; Naturalism; Socialist Realism; social realism

realism (philosophy) **1** The theory supporting the common-sense view that the world and its contents do not depend for their existence on the fact that some mind (whether human or divine) is aware of them. It is opposed to *idealism* and *phenomenalism*. **2** The theory held by Plato and others that universals (eg 'redness') or abstract entities (eg numbers) have a real existence outside the mind and apart from their instances. It is opposed to *nominalism*. >> nominalism; verificationism

real numbers >> **numbers**

real tennis An indoor racket-and-ball game played on a walled court, similar to rackets, but containing specifically designed hazards. A minority sport, it is also known as 'royal' or 'court' tennis. >> rackets; RR1058

real-time computing A notion which applies to those computing systems where near-simultaneous response to input data is a necessary requirement; examples include air-traffic control, point-of-sale terminals, and vehicle control. >> time-sharing (computing)

Reardon, Ray(mond) [**reer**dn] (1932–) Snooker player, born in Tredegar, Blaenau Gwent, SE Wales. The first of the great snooker players of the modern era, he was dominant in the 1970s, being world professional champion six times (1970, 1973–6, 1978). >> snooker

reasoning Mental activity in which the reasoner moves from given information to a novel conclusion, in a series of steps that the reasoner can justify. Reasoning may be **deductive**, arriving at a conclusion from a set of premises (eg proving a theorem in mathematics), or **inductive**, when we try to create a new generalization based on available evidence. >> psychology

Réaumur, René Antoine Ferchault de [rayohmür] (1683–1757) Polymath, born in La Rochelle, France. His thermometer (with spirit instead of mercury) has 80 degrees between the freezing and boiling points. >> temperature ℹ

Rebecca Riots A popular protest movement by Welsh peasants and agricultural labourers in W Wales in the late 1830s and early 1840s. The rioters took their text from *Genesis* 24:60: 'And they blessed Rebecca and said unto her, let thy seed possess the gates of those which hate thee'. Each band of rioters had a Rebecca for a leader – often a man disguised as a woman.

rebirthing A form of psychotherapy based on the idea that traumatic experiences at birth may result in negative thoughts and attitudes in later life. Regression back to birth and reliving the experience may allow these attitudes to be corrected. **Water rebirthing** for example, involves being submerged in a bath of water. >> psychotherapy

Rebuck, Gail (Ruth) [**ree**buhk], married name **Gould** (1952–) Publisher, born in London. Appointed publishing director at Century Publishing in 1982, she stayed with the company when it became Century Hutchinson (1985) and also when this was taken over by Random House (1989), and in 1991 became chair and chief executive of Random House UK.

rebus [**ree**buhs] The enigmatic representation in visual form of the sounds of a name or word. As a form of visual pun, rebuses are often used to puzzle or amuse, such as a drawing of a ray-gun (='Reagan'), or the letters CU (='see you'). They are an ancient means of communication, being found in early forms of picture-writing. >> pictography ℹ

Récamier, (Jeanne Françoise) Julie (Adélaide) [ruhkamyay], *née* **Bernard** (1777–1849) Hostess, born in

Lyon, France. Her salon became a fashionable meeting-place, especially for former Royalists and those opposed to Napoleon. >> Napoleon I

receptacle In flowering plants, the area at the tip of the flower-stalk to which the floral parts are attached. Usually convex, it may become swollen or expanded to enclose the carpels, and play an important role in fruit formation. >> carpel; flower ℹ; fruit

receptors In physiology, specialized sites, usually within the cell membrane, which have evolved to bind and mediate the effects of neurotransmitters and hormones, but which also mediate the effects of many substances foreign to the body (such as drugs); also known as **binding sites**. >> cell

recession An economic situation where demand is sluggish, output is not rising, and unemployment is on the increase. Not as severe a downturn as a depression, it is usually identified when gross domestic product declines for two successive quarters. >> depression (economics); gross domestic product; reflation

Recife [re**see**fay] 8°06S 34°53W, pop (1995e) 1 496 000. Port in NE Brazil, at the mouth of the R Capibaribe; most important commercial and industrial city in the NE; airport; two universities (1951, 1954); Forte do Brum (1629). >> Brazil ℹ

recitative A type of musical declamation which allows the words to be delivered naturally and quickly, and is therefore indispensable in those types of all-sung opera, oratorio, and cantata in which dialogue and narrative are interrupted by long or numerous arias. >> aria; opera buffa / seria

RECONSAT An abbreviation of *recon*naissance *sat*ellite, a military space system placed into Earth orbit. It is equipped with sensors capable of recording objects (such as military units) and activities on the ground, and relaying that information to Earth stations for analysis. >> spacecraft

Reconstruction The period after the American Civil War when the South was occupied by Northern troops, while major changes went forward in its way of life. These included the destruction of slavery and the attempted integration of the freed black people. Resistance to it among white southerners resulted in the founding of the Ku Klux Klan in 1866. >> American Civil War; Jim Crow Laws; Ku Klux Klan

recorder (law) In the legal system of England and Wales, a part-time judge. Those appointed are barristers or solicitors. Recorders sit mainly in the Crown Court. >> Crown Court; judge

recorder (music) A type of end-blown duct flute in two or three jointed sections, with seven fingerholes and a thumbhole. It is made of wood or (in recent times) plastic in various sizes, the most common being the **descant** and the **treble**. It has been revived in the 20th-c as a school instrument and for playing early music. >> flute; woodwind instrument ℹ

recording >> **sound recording**

record player The successor to the gramophone. It was essentially a turntable, pick-up, and arm which reproduced the music or other sounds recorded on discs (gramophone records), usually through its own amplifier and speaker. >> gramophone; pick-up; sound recording

rectifier A device that changes alternating current (AC), which continuously reverses direction, into direct current (DC), by allowing it to flow in one direction only. Most electronic equipment needs direct current. >> electricity

rectilinear motion >> **mechanics**

rector In the Church of England, the parish priest receiving full tithe rents; in other Anglican churches, generally a parish priest; in Roman Catholicism, the priest in charge of a religious house, college, or school; in some countries (eg Scotland), the senior officer of a university, elected by students. >> priest

rectum That part of the gastro-intestinal tract between the sigmoid colon and the anal canal. When gastro-intestinal contents enter the rectum, the individual has the urge to defaecate. >> alimentary canal; anus; colon; haemorrhoids; peritoneum

recycling Putting waste substances back into productive use. It is a means of reducing the demand on non-renewable resources, and of preventing problems of pollution and waste disposal. Examples include the pulping of waste paper to make recycled paper, the existence of bottle banks to collect used glass, and the smelting of metals from scrap. >> conservation (earth sciences); non-renewable resources; waste disposal

red admiral A large butterfly found widely in the N hemisphere; upperside of wings black with scarlet bands and patches of white and blue. (Order: Lepidoptera. Family: Nymphalidae.) >> butterfly

Red Army (China) Communist army built up by Zhu De at Mao Zedong's Jiangxi soviet after 1927. It was distinguished by more egalitarian command, disciplined treatment of civilians, the dissemination of political ideas, and the use of guerrilla tactics. In the civil war after 1945, it defeated the Nationalist forces, having been reorganized as the **People's Liberation Army (PLA)** in 1946. It now numbers three million troops, and is a significant political as well as military force. >> Cultural Revolution; Mao Zedong; Zhu De

Red Army (USSR) The Red Army of Workers and Peasants (*RKKA, Rabochekrest'yanshi Krasny*), the official name of the army of the Soviet Union (1918–45).

red-brick universities Those English universities founded in the late 19th-c or first half of the 20th-c in the provincial cities: Manchester (1880; new charter 1903), Liverpool (1903; affiliated to Manchester, 1884–1903), Leeds (1904; affiliated to Manchester, 1887–1904), Birmingham (1900), Sheffield (1905), Bristol (1909), Reading (1926), Southampton (1952, University College 1902), Exeter (1955, University College, 1922), and Leicester (1957, University College 1918). >> new universities; university

Red Brigades, Ital **Brigate Rosse** A left-wing Italian terrorist group which began operating in 1974 as a response to the failure of the New Left, involved in bombings and killings. Its activities were largely directed at the kidnapping and killing of Italian judges, politicians, and businessmen, such as the former Italian premier Aldo Moro in 1978. >> terrorism

red cedar 1 A species of *arbor vitae* (*Thuja plicata*), native to North America, which yields red timber. (Family: Cupressaceae.) >> arbor vitae **2** The commercial name for timber from the American species of juniper, *Juniperus virginiana*, often used for pencils. >> juniper

Red Crescent >> **Red Cross**

Red Cross An international agency founded by the Geneva Convention (1864) to assist those wounded or captured in war. All branches use the symbol of the red cross on a white ground, except Muslim branches, which use the red crescent, Israel, which uses a red Star of David, and Iran, which uses a red lion and sun. >> Dunant, Henri; Geneva Convention

red currant A species of currant (*Ribes rubrum*) native to W Europe. It produces edible red berries on old wood. The **white currant** is merely a white-berried form. (Family: Grossulariaceae.) >> currant

red deer A true deer (*Cervus elephas*) widespread in the temperate N hemisphere (introduced in Australia and New Zealand); also known as the **Bactrian deer**, **Yarkand deer**,

maral, **shou**, **hangul**, or (in North America) **wapiti** or **elk**. Each antler usually has five tines (the *Swedish* form); if each has six, the stag is a *Royal*; if each has seven, it is a *Wilson*. >> antlers ℹ; deer

Redford, (Charles) Robert (1937–) Actor and director, born in Santa Barbara, CA. His films include *Butch Cassidy and the Sundance Kid* (1969), *The Sting* (1973), and *Up Close and Personal* (1996). As a director, his films include *Ordinary People* (1980, Oscar) and *The Horse Whisperer* (1998).

red giant A cool red star, 10–100 times the radius of the Sun, but of similar mass. It develops in a late stage of stellar evolution, after the main sequence. Hydrogen in the core is exhausted, and the outer layers expand. >> hydrogen

Redgrave, Sir Michael (Scudamore) (1908–85) Actor, born in Bristol. His notable stage performances included Richard II (1951), Prospero (1952), and Antony (1953), and he also had a distinguished film career, starting with Hitchcock's *The Lady Vanishes* (1938). He married the actress **Rachel Kempson** (1910–) in 1935, and their three children are all actors; **Vanessa**, **Corin** (1939–), and **Lynn** (1944–). >> Redgrave, Vanessa

Redgrave, Vanessa (1937–) Actress, born in London, the daughter of Michael Redgrave. Her films include *Morgan, a Suitable Case for Treatment* (1966), *Julia* (1977, Oscar), and *Mrs Dalloway* (1998). She is well known for her active support of left-wing causes.

Red Guards Young radical Maoist activists (mostly students) who spread the 1966 Cultural Revolution across China, destroying whatever was 'old', and rebelling against all 'reactionary' authority. >> Cultural Revolution; Mao Zedong

red-hot poker A perennial native to S Africa (*Kniphofia uvaria*); flowers tubular, downward-angled, red, turning orange then yellow with age, in dense, poker-shaped spikes on stems up to 2 m/6½ ft high. (Family: Liliaceae.)

red mullet Colourful marine fish widespread in tropical and warm temperate seas; mouth with pair of large chin barbels; also called **goatfish**. (Family: Mullidae, 3 genera.)

Red River (China), Chin **Yuan Jiang**, Vietnamese **Song Hong** River rising in C Yunnan province, China; flows into the Gulf of Tongking in a large delta; length, c.800 km/500 mi. >> Vietnam ℹ

Red River (USA) River in S USA; rises in N Texas in the Llano Estacado; flows S to the Gulf of Mexico; length 1966 km/1222 mi. >> United States of America ℹ

Red River Colony A British colony founded by the Earl of Selkirk in Rupert's Land (Manitoba) on the Assiniboine and Red Rivers in 1812. It was the focus of ethnic, racial, and commercial rivalries. >> Métis; Red River Rebellion

Red River Rebellion A movement for self-determination in 1869–70 by the resident Métis population of Red River Colony, Canada (now Manitoba), led by Louis Riel. Canada agreed to the terms of the rebels (in the Manitoba Act, 1870). >> Métis; Red River Colony; Riel

red salmon >> **sockeye**

Red Sea, ancient **Sinus Arabicus** area c.453 000 sq km/175 000 sq mi. NW arm of the Indian Ocean, between the Arabian Peninsula and Egypt, Sudan, and Ethiopia; connected to the Mediterranean Sea by the Suez Canal; divided into the Gulfs of Suez and Aqaba by the Sinai Peninsula (NW); a narrow sea, up to 360 km/225 mi wide, 2335 km/1450 mi long; name probably derives from reddish seaweed found here; major trade route. >> Indian Ocean; Suez Canal

red setter >> **Irish setter**

redshift The displacement of features in the spectra of astronomical objects, particularly galaxies and quasars, towards the longer wavelengths. This is generally interpreted as a result of the Doppler effect resulting from the expansion of the universe. >> Doppler effect; spectrum; universe

Red Spot, Great >> **Jupiter** (astronomy)

Red Square The central square of Moscow. Its Russian name (*Krasnaya Ploshchad*) derives from the Old Slavonic *krasny* ('beautiful' or 'red'). The translation of 'red' has become established only in the 20th-c. >> Kremlin; Lenin Mausoleum; Moscow

red squirrel A small tree-dwelling squirrel; coat reddish-brown; four species: the **European red squirrel** (*Sciurus vulgaris*) from Europe and Asia, and the **North American red squirrels** or **chickarees** of genus *Tamiasciurus*. >> squirrel

reduction A chemical process involving the gain of electrons, always accompanied by oxidation, the loss of electrons. It often involves the gain of hydrogen or the loss of oxygen by a compound. >> hydrogenation; oxidation

redundancy Dismissal of employees whose work is no longer needed. This may occur through a fall in the demand for their products, or through technical progress leading to automation of production. If the need for labour falls slowly, adjustment may be possible through natural wastage, ie not replacing those who leave. If demand falls quickly, redundancies occur. Employers often prefer to offer sufficiently favourable terms to induce voluntary redundancy, to preserve the morale of their remaining workforce; where this fails, compulsory redundancies may occur. >> productivity; unemployment

redwing A thrush native to Europe, Asia, and N Africa (*Turdus iliacus*); speckled breast, red sides, and cream 'eyebrow'; migrates S in autumn, often with fieldfares. >> oriole; thrush (bird)

redwood >> **coast redwood**

Redwood, John (1951–) British politician, born in Dover, Kent. Elected a Conservative MP in 1987, he became secretary of state for Wales (1993–5). He was a strong but ultimately unsuccessful contender for leadership of his party, following Major's resignation in 1997.

reed A tall grass found (*Phragmites australis*) almost everywhere; stout, erect stems 2–3 m/6–10 ft high. It forms vast beds in swamps or shallow water, and is used for good-quality thatch. (Family: Gramineae.) >> grass ℹ

Reed, Sir Carol (1906–76) Film director, born in London. He produced or directed several major films, such as *Kipps* (1941), *The Fallen Idol* (1948), and *Oliver!* (1968, 2 Oscars), but is best known for *The Third Man* (1949).

reedbuck An African grazing antelope of genus *Redunca*; pale brown with white underparts; male with horns curving forward at tip; female without horns; three species. >> antelope

reed instrument Any woodwind instrument whose sound is produced by a stream of air causing a 'reed' (which may be of cane, metal, or plastic) to vibrate. The reed may be single (as in the clarinet) or double (as in the oboe); it may vibrate freely (as in the harmonica and the crumhorn) or be controlled by the player's lips (as in all orchestral reed instruments). >> aerophone; basset-horn; bassoon; clarinet; cor anglais; crumhorn; harmonica; oboe; reed organ; sarrusophone; woodwind instrument ℹ

reedmace An aquatic perennial (*Typha latifolia*), more or less cosmopolitan; stems robust, growing to 2·5 m/8 ft leaves grass-like; also called **cat's-tail**, **false bulrush** and, erroneously, **bulrush**. It often forms extensive reed-swamps. (Family: Typhaceae.) >> bulrush

reed organ A musical instrument in which reeds, brought into play by means of one or more keyboards, are made to vibrate freely by air under pressure from bellows. Reed organs were at one time popular as domestic instruments and also in small churches. >> accordion; concertina; harmonium; organ; reed instrument

reef >> atoll

reefer A vessel designed to carry refrigerated cargoes in specially cooled and insulated compartments. Modern cargoes include carcases of beef, dairy produce, and most kinds of fruit. >> ship ℹ

reeve >> ruff

Reeve, Christopher (1952–) Film actor, born in New York City. He had various stage and television roles before becoming universally known as the star of *Superman* and its sequels (1978, 1980, 1983, 1991). In 1994 he became wheel-chair bound following an accident.

Reeves, Keanu [kee**ah**noo] (1965–) Film actor, born in Beirut, Lebanon. *Bill and Ted's Excellent Adventure* (1989), and its sequel (1991) brought him international recognition. Later films include *Much Ado About Nothing* (1993), *Little Buddha* (1994), and *Feeling Minnesota* (1996).

referendum A device of direct democracy whereby the electorate can pronounce, usually for or against, on some measure put before it by government; also known as a **plebiscite**. Most commonly referenda are held on constitutional changes, rather than on government policy.

reflation In economics, government action designed to stimulate an economy which is in a period of recession. Strategies include increasing government expenditure, lowering taxes, and reducing interest rates. >> recession

reflectance >> reflection

reflecting telescope >> telescope ℹ

reflection In physics, the bouncing off from a suitable surface of a beam of light, sound, or other wave at an angle equal to that of the incident beam. **Reflectance** is the measured ratio of incident intensity to reflected intensity. >> mirror; refractive index

reflex A rapid, involuntary, and stereotyped action made by an animal in response to a particular stimulus involving the central nervous system. An example is the rapid withdrawal of the hand after touching a very hot surface.

reflex camera A camera in which an image of the scene being photographed is shown on the viewfinder screen by way of a mirror. In **single-lens reflex** (**SLR**) types, the mirror is at 45° behind the camera lens and is automatically swung out of the way immediately before exposure. The **twin-lens reflex** has two matched lenses coupled for focusing. >> camera

reflexology An ancient system of diagnosis and treatment, dating from c.3000 BC, based on the belief that an image of the entire body, including the internal organs, is represented on the surface of the foot. Palpation of the feet locates sites of blocked energy flow, and treatment is given by pressure and massage to disperse the blockages and stimulate the internal organs. >> alternative medicine; traditional Chinese medicine

Reform Acts Legislation in Britain which altered parliamentary constituencies and increased the size of the electorate. The main Acts were: **1832** (known as the **Great Reform Act**), which gave the vote to almost all members of the middle classes, and introduced a uniform £10 franchise in the borough; **1867**, which gave the vote to all settled tenants in the boroughs, thus creating a substantial working-class franchise for the first time; **1884**, which extended a similar franchise to rural and mining areas; **1885**, which aimed to create parliamentary constituencies of broadly equal size; **1918**, which created a universal male suffrage and gave the vote to women of 30 years and over; **1928**, which gave the vote to all adult women; and **1969**, which lowered the minimum voting age from 21 years to 18. >> pocket borough; rotten borough

Reformation The Protestant reform movements in the Christian Church, inspired by and derived from Martin Luther, John Calvin, and others in 16th-c Europe. Various factors are common to all reforms: a Biblical revival and translation of the Word of God into the vernacular; an improvement in the intellectual and moral standards of the clergy; emphasis on the sovereignty of God; and insistence that faith and scriptures are at the centre of the Christian message. In Germany, Luther's 'ninety-five theses' (1517) questioned the authority of the Church and led to his excommunication. The Lutheran Church then spread rapidly, in Switzerland under Zwingli and later under Calvin, neither of whom allowed any form of worship or devotion not explicitly warranted by scripture. In England, Henry VIII declared that the king was the supreme head of the English Church, and appropriated Church property; in 1549 the Book of Common Prayer, embodying Reformation doctrine, was published, and under Elizabeth I a strong anti-papal stance was taken. In Scotland, under the influence of Calvin and the leadership of John Knox, the Presbyterian Church of Scotland was established in 1560, and remains the national Church. >> Book of Common Prayer; Calvin, John; Christianity; Church of England; Church of Scotland; Henry VIII; Knox, John; Luther; ninety-five theses; Protestantism; Reformed Churches

Reformation, Catholic >> Counter-Reformation

Reformed Churches Churches deriving from Calvin's Reformation in 16th-c Geneva, adopting a conciliar or presbyterian form of Church government. They are now worldwide in extent. >> Calvin, John; Presbyterianism; Reformed Church in America

Reformed Church in America A Christian denomination established in 1628 with the organization of the Collegiate Church for the early Dutch Reformed settlers. It adopted its current name in 1867. >> Protestantism; Reformed Churches

Reform Judaism A movement beginning in early 19th-c Germany for the reform of Jewish worship, ritual, and beliefs in the light of modern scholarship and knowledge. >> Judaism

Reform Party A Canadian political party, established to articulate discontent in the W of the country. It captured the third largest number of seats in the 1993 general election, almost all from Alberta and British Columbia. >> Canada ℹ

refracting telescope >> telescope ℹ

refraction A change in the direction of a wave as it passes from one medium to another in which the wave velocity is different, for example a sound wave passing from hot to cold air. It is expressed by Snell's law, $\sin \theta_A / \sin \theta_B$ = constant. Light passing into a substance of higher refractive index is bent towards normal. The distortion of partially submerged objects, rainbows, and mirages are all caused by the refraction of light. >> birefringence; refractive index

refractive index A measurement of the ratio of velocity of light (or other electromagnetic wave) in a vacuum to that in matter; symbol n; always greater than 1; n(air) = 1.0003, n(water) = 1.33, so the velocity of light in water is about 75% of that in air.

refractories Materials which are neither deformed nor chemically changed by exposure to high temperatures. This makes them suitable for containers, structural materials, and components, particularly in metallurgical operations, such as furnace linings. Naturally occurring refractories include silica, fireclay, and alumina. Synthetic refractories include the high-melting carbides and nitrides used in nuclear power plant. >> alumina; carbide; fireclay; silica

refrigerator An insulated enclosed space, with a cooling mechanism to reduce its temperature, which preserves foodstuffs for short periods. The earlier *ice-house* used ice as a coolant, but from c.1875 mechanical means were introduced, compressing a coolant outside to allow it to expand inside and thus absorb heat. From c.1910 domestic models were available, now running at 4°C. A colder-running version (at c.–20°C) is the *deep freeze*, which can store food for some months. >> cold storage; deep-freezing; food preservation

Regency Style An elegant Neoclassical style current in England for about the first quarter of the 19th-c. Like the Empire Style in France, it made bold use of Greek motifs and Egyptian devices. >> Empire Style; Neoclassicism (art and architecture)

Regensburg [**ray**gnzboorg], Fr **Ratisbon**, ancient **Castra Regina** 49°01N 12°07E, pop (1995e) 126 000. Commercial city in Germany; at confluence of R Regen and R Danube; Imperial Diets held here, 1663–1806; bishopric; railway; river harbour; university (1962); cathedral (13th–16th-c). >> Diet; Germany [i]

regent The person appointed to act for the monarch if he/she is incapacitated, unavailable, or under 18. In the UK, it is customary for the next heir to the throne to be regent.

reggae [**reg**ay] A type of popular music, of Jamaican origin but drawing on Afro-American traditions and influenced by rock. Among prominent reggae artists are Bob Marley and the Wailers. >> Marley; pop music

Reggio di Calabria [**rej**ioh dee ka**lab**ria] 38°06N 15°39E, pop (1995e) 183 000. Seaport in S Italy; founded by Greek colonists, 8th-c BC; archbishopric; airfield; railway; ferry to Sicily. >> Calabria

Reggio nell'Emilia [**rej**ioh nelay**meel**ia] 44°42N 10°37E, pop (1995e) 136 000. City in N Italy; founded by the Romans; railway; cathedral (13th-c). >> Italy [i]

Regina [re**jiy**na] 50°30N 104°38W, pop (1995e) 179 000. Capital of Saskatchewan province, SC Canada; founded, 1882 as capital of Northwest Territories; named in honour of Queen Victoria; capital, 1905; centre of grain, potash, and oil industries; airport; railway; university (1917); professional team, Saskatchewan Rough Riders (football). >> Diefenbaker; Saskatchewan

Regiomontanus [rejiohmon**tay**nus], Lat name of **Johannes Müller** (1436–76) Mathematician and astronomer, born in Königsberg (Lat *Mons Regius*, hence his pseudonym), Germany. He established the study of algebra and trigonometry in Germany.

regolith The layer of fine, powdery material on the Moon produced by the repeated impact of meteorites. It is up to 25 m/80 ft thick. >> meteorite; Moon

regression One of many defence mechanisms in which the individual returns to behaviour more suitable to an earlier age. This can be a component of a psychotherapy process and can also occur in physical illness. >> psychotherapy

Regulus, Marcus Atilius [**reg**yulus] (3rd-c BC) Roman general and statesman of the First Punic War, whose heroic death at the hands of the Carthaginians earned him legendary status. >> Punic Wars

Reich [riykh] The term used to describe the German Empire. The Holy Roman Empire was regarded as the **First Reich**, and unified Germany after 1870 was referred to as the **Second Reich** (**Kaiserreich**). After 1933, the enlarged Germany envisaged in Hitler's plans was known as the **Third Reich**. >> Hitler; Holy Roman Empire; Kaiser

Reich, Wilhelm [riykh] (1897–1957) Psychoanalyst, born in Dobrzcynica, Austria. He broke from the Freudian school, developing a theory in which neuroses resulted from repressed, undissipated feelings or sexual energy. He emigrated to the USA in 1939, and established the pseudo-scientific 'Orgone' Institute, but died in gaol after being prosecuted for promoting a fraudulent treatment. During the sexual revolution of the 1960s, he was a cult figure in the USA. >> Freud, Sigmund; psychoanalysis

Reichenbach, Hans [**riykh**enbakh] (1891–1953) Philosopher of science, born in Hamburg, Germany. An early associate of the logical positivists, he made important technical contributions to probability theory and the philosophy of science in such works as *Philosophie der Raum-Zeit-Lehre* (1927–8, Philosophy of Space and Time), and *The Rise of Scientific Philosophy* (1951). >> logical positivism

Reichstag fire [**riykh**stag] The deliberate burning down of Germany's parliament building (27 Feb 1933), shortly after the Nazi accession to power. A deranged Dutch ex-communist, van der Lubbe, was accused of arson and executed. The new Nazi government used the situation to ban and suppress the German Communist Party. >> Nazi Party

Reign of Terror (1793–4) The extreme phase of the French Revolution, characterized by the systematic execution of political opponents of the Jacobins and supposed sympathizers of the Counter-Revolution. 40 000 people are thought to have been killed in Paris and the provinces. >> French Revolution [i]; Jacobins (French history)

Reims >> **Rheims**

reincarnation The belief that, following death, some aspect of the self or soul can be reborn in a new body (human or animal), a process which may be repeated many times. This belief is fundamental to many Eastern religions, such as Hinduism and Buddhism. >> Buddhism; Hinduism

reindeer A true deer (*Rangifer tarandus*) native to high latitudes of the N hemisphere; the only deer in which females have antlers; long coat of hollow hairs; hooves broad; also known as **caribou** ('shoveller'). >> antlers [i]; deer

Reiner, Rob [**riy**ner] (1945–) Film actor, director, and producer, born in New York City. He became known for his role in *All in the Family* (1971–8, 2 Emmies), later roles including *Sleepless in Seattle* (1993) and *The First Wives Club* (1996). He has produced and directed several films, notably *When Harry Met Sally* (1989) and *Ghosts of Mississippi* (1996).

Reines, Frederick (1918–98) Physicist, born in Paterson, NJ. For his discovery of the free neutrino, one of the basic particles of the universe, he shared the Nobel Prize for Physics in 1995.

Reinhardt, Django [**riyn**hah(r)t], popular name of **Jean Baptiste Reinhardt** (1910–53) Jazz guitarist, born in Liverchies, Belgium. He played in the Quintet of the Hot Club of France with Stephane Grapelli, and became the first European jazz musician to influence the music. >> Grapelli; jazz

Reith (of Stonehaven), John (Charles Walsham) Reith, Baron [reeth] (1889–1971) British statesman and engineer, born in Stonehaven, Aberdeenshire. He became the first general manager of the BBC in 1922 and its director-general (1927–38). The BBC inaugurated the *Reith Lectures* in 1948 in honour of his influence on broadcasting. >> BBC

relational database A form of organizing data in a computer in which each entity is stored separately as a table, and the relationships between entities are stored as another table. In the database for the present encyclopedia, for example, the individual entries are stored in one file, and the relationships between entries (such as the indexing of the words in the entries, which controls the alphabetical order) are stored separately.

relative atomic mass The mass of atoms, expressed in atomic mass units u, eg carbon-12 is 12.0000 u by definition, nitrogen-14 is 14.0031 u; symbol A_r; formerly called **atomic weight**. >> periodic table; RR1036

relative density Density measured relative to some standard, typically water at 20°C; symbol *d*, expressed as a pure number; measured using hydrometers; formerly called **specific gravity**. For example, for alcohol, density $\rho = 789\ kg/m^3$, $d = 0.791$. >> alcohols; density (physics); proof spirit

relativistic quantum mechanics Quantum mechanics consistent with special relativity, and thus applicable to fast-moving systems; originally developed by British physicist Paul Dirac in 1928. >> Dirac; quantum mechanics

relativity >> **general relativity; special relativity** ℹ

relay An electrical or solid-state device, operated by changes in input, which is used to control or operate other devices connected to the output. They have a range of applications in telephone exchanges, switches, and automation systems. >> electricity; solid-state device

relics Material remains (eg bones, skin) of, or objects which have been in contact with, a saint or person worthy of special religious attention. In many religions they are objects of veneration.

relief printing A print, made from a block (usually wood or lino) which has been cut away in those parts intended to be left white; the method contrasts with intaglio or surface prints. The ink adheres to the raised (relief) parts only. >> intaglio; printing ℹ; woodcut

relief sculpture A type of sculpture in which the forms are raised above the background, but not shaped fully. In **low relief** (or **bas-relief**) the design is hardly raised above the surface, as on a coin, while in **high relief** the forms may be almost free-standing. >> bas-relief; sculpture

religion A concept which encompasses varied sets of traditions, practices, and ideas. Some religions involve the belief in and worship of a god or gods, but this is not true of all. Christianity, Islam, and Judaism are theistic religions, while Buddhism does not require a belief in gods, and where it does occur, the gods are not considered important. There are theories of religion which construe it as wholly a human phenomenon, without any supernatural or transcendent origin and point of reference, while others argue that some such reference is the essence of the matter. Boundary disputes exist; for example, debate continues as to whether Confucianism is properly to be considered a religion; and some writers argue that Marxism is in important respects a religion. >> Baha'i; Buddhism; Christianity; cult; fundamentalism; God; Hinduism; Islam; Jainism; Judaism; Lamaism; millenarianism; Pentecostalism; sect; Shinto; Sikhism; Taoism; theology; voodoo; Zoroastrianism

Religion, Wars of (1562–98) A series of religious and political conflicts in France, caused by the growth of Calvinism, noble factionalism, and weak royal government. Civil wars were encouraged by Philip II of Spain's support of the Catholic Guise faction and by Elizabeth I's aid to the Huguenots. They ended when Henry of Navarre returned to Catholicism and crushed the Guise Catholic League (1589–98). >> Catherine de' Medici; Guise; Huguenots

rem In radioactivity, an old measure of dose equivalent; symbol rem; equal to absorbed dose in rad multiplied by relative biological effectiveness, 1 rem = 0.01 Sv (sievert, SI unit); an abbreviation of **röntgen equivalent in man**. >> radioactivity units ℹ; sievert

Remarque, Erich Maria [ruh**mah(r)k**] (1898–1970) Novelist, born in Osnabrück, Germany. His first novel, *Im Westen nichts Neues* (1929, trans All Quiet on the Western Front), was an immediate success, and was filmed in 1930.

Rembrandt (Harmenszoon van Rijn) [**rem**brant] (1606–69) Painter, born in Leyden, The Netherlands. His early works include religious and historical scenes, unusual in Protestant Holland. He settled in Amsterdam (1631), where he ran a large studio and took numerous pupils. 'The Anatomy Lesson of Dr Nicolaes Tulp' (1632, The Hague) assured his reputation as a portrait painter. In 1634 he married Saskia van Ulenburgh (1613–42), and in the year of her death produced his masterpiece, 'The Night Watch' (Amsterdam). His extravagance, especially as a collector, led to bankruptcy in 1656. His preserved works number over 650 oil paintings, 2000 drawings and studies, and 300 etchings.

Remembrance Sunday In the UK, the Sunday nearest 11 November, on which are commemorated those who died in the two world wars; formerly Armistice Day. A two-minute silence is observed at 11 am. >> Veterans' Day

Remington, Eliphalet (1793–1861) US firearms manufacturer and inventor, born in Suffield, CT. He pioneered several improvements in small arms manufacture, including the first successful cast steel rifle barrel in the USA.

Remington, Frederic (Sackrider) (1861–1909) Painter, sculptor, and illustrator, born in Canton, NY. He became a painter of the American West, illustrating Geronimo's Apache campaign (1882) and the Indian Wars of 1890–1. He also wrote and illustrated several books on his adventures.

Remonstrants Christians adhering to the Calvinistic doctrine of Jacobus Arminius (17th-c Holland), whose followers were also known as **Arminians**. They were named after the 'Remonstrance', a statement of Arminian teaching dating from 1610. >> Arminius; Calvinism

remora [**rem**uhra] Slender-bodied fish (*Remora remora*) widespread in warm seas; large sucking disc on head, with which it attaches firmly to other fish, especially sharks; length up to 45 cm/18 in; also called **shark-sucker**. (Family: Echeneidae.) >> fish ℹ

remote sensing A method of measuring the characteristics of an object without touching it. The term is usually applied to images of the Earth taken by satellites, and to cameras in aircraft which can be used to map different phenomena. >> weather satellite

Renaissance From the French for 'rebirth', referring to the revival of classical literature and artistic styles at various times in European history. Such renaissances occurred in the 8th-c and 9th-c, in the 12th-c, and from the 14th-c to the 16th-c. The first, or **Carolingian Renaissance**, centred upon the recovery of classical Latin texts in cathedral schools; the second, or **Twelfth-century Renaissance**, was marked by the foundation of universities and the rediscovery of Aristotle's ethical and philosophical works; and the third (usually called **the Renaissance**) was distinguished for the development of naturalistic works of art, the study of ancient Greek authors, above all Plato, and the critical study of Christian texts. This third revival is often said to mark the beginnings of modern times. >> Charlemagne; classicism; Plato

Rendell (of Babergh), Ruth Rendell, Baroness [**ren**dl], originally **Ruth Barbara Grasemann**, occasional pseudonym **Barbara Vine** (1930–) Detective-story writer, born in London. Her detective stories featuring Chief Inspector Wexford (eg *Simisola*, 1994), and mystery thrillers (eg *A Judgement in Stone*, 1977) have formed the basis of a successful TV series, *The Ruth Rendell Mysteries*.

renewable resources Resources with a yield which is sustainable and which may be used without danger of exhaustion, such as solar power, wind energy, and hydroelectric power. Some renewable resources (eg crops, timber, fish) are sustainable in the long term only through careful management. >> alternative energy; non-renewable resources

Renfrew (of Kaimsthorn), (Andrew) Colin Renfrew, Baron (1937–) Archaeologist, born in Stockton-on-Tees, Durham. Since 1981 he has been professor of archaeology at Cambridge. He has contributed to several pioneering archaeological programmes on BBC television, notably in the *Chronicle* series. >> archaeology

Reni, Guido [**ray**nee] (1575–1642) Baroque painter, born near Bologna, Italy. The fresco painted for the Borghese garden house in Rome, 'Aurora and the Hours' (1613–14), is usually regarded as his masterpiece. >> Baroque (art and architecture); fresco

Renner, Karl (1870–1950) Austrian statesman, chancellor (1918–20, 1945), and president (1945–50). born in Unter-Tannowitz, Austria. He became the first chancellor of the Austrian Republic, and first president of the new republic. >> Austria [i]

Rennes [ren], Breton **Roazon**, ancient **Condate** 48°07N 1°41W, pop (1995e) 204 000. Industrial and commercial city in NW France; capital of Brittany, 10th-c, and now its economic and cultural centre; largely rebuilt after major fire, 1720; badly bombed in World War 2; airport; road and rail junction; archbishopric; university (1461); cathedral (largely rebuilt, 19th-c). >> Brittany

rennet An extract from the stomach of most young animals, but particularly the calf and the lamb, which contains the enzyme *rennin*. It causes the main milk protein *casein* to precipitate, thus allowing the milk to clot. It is sometimes used in recipes and the manufacture of cheese. >> casein; milk

Rennie, John (1761–1821) Civil engineer, born in Phantassie, East Lothian. He became famous as a bridge-builder, constructing several bridges over the R Thames. He also designed London docks. >> civil engineering

Reno [**ree**noh] 39°31N 119°48W, pop (1995e) 171 000. City in W Nevada, USA, on the Truckee R; settled, 1859; airport; university (1874); noted for its casinos. >> Nevada

Renoir, Jean [renwah(r)] (1894–1979) Film director, born in Paris, the son of Pierre Auguste Renoir. His major works include his antiwar masterpiece, *La Grande Illusion* (1937, Grand Illusion) and *La Règle du jeu* (1939, The Rules of the Game). He received an honorary Academy Award in 1975. >> Renoir, Pierre Auguste

Renoir, Pierre Auguste [ruhn**wah**] (1841–1919) Impressionist artist, born in Limoges, France. In 1874–9 and 1882 he exhibited with the Impressionists. His picture of sunlight filtering through leaves – 'Le Moulin de la Galette' (1876, Louvre) – epitomizes his colourful, happy art. >> Impressionism (art)

reparations Payments imposed on the powers defeated in war to cover the costs incurred by the victors. For example, they were levied by the Allies on Germany at the end of World War 1. >> World War 1

Representatives, House of >> **House of Representatives**

reproduction The act or process of producing offspring; one of the essential properties of a living organism. Reproduction in its simplest form is an asexual process involving the division of an organism into two or more parts by fission, budding, spore formation, or vegetative propagation. Sexual reproduction involves the formation of specialized gametes (such as sperm and egg) by meiosis, and the fusion of a pair of gametes to form a zygote. >> biology; gamete; meiosis [i]

reptile An animal of the class Reptilia (6547 species), which evolved from primitive amphibians; most live on land; breathe with lungs, not gills; dry waterproof skin with horny scales (not separated, like those of a fish, but folds of skin); classified in four orders: Squamata (lizards and snakes), Chelonia (Testudinata or Testudines – tortoises and turtles), Crocodylia (or Loricata – crocodiles, alligators, etc), and Rhyncocephalia (the tuatara); many extinct species, including dinosaurs, pterodactyls, plesiosaurs, and ichthyosaurs. >> alligator [i]; amphibian; Chelonia [i]; crocodile; dinosaur [i]; lizard [i]; mammal [i]; palaeontology; snake; tortoise; tuatara; turtle (biology)

Repton, Humphrey (1752–1818) Landscape gardener, born in Bury St Edmunds, Suffolk. He completed the change from the formal gardens of the early 18th-c to the 'picturesque' types favoured later. >> landscape gardening

republic A form of state and government where, unlike a monarchy (which is hereditary), the head of state and leader of the government are periodically appointed under the constitution. It thus covers most modern states. Republics now vary considerably in form, ranging from liberal democratic states to personal dictatorships. >> monarchy

Republican Party One of the two main parties in US politics, created in 1854 out of the anti-slavery movement that preceded the Civil War. It found almost immediate success when Lincoln was elected president in 1860, and held the presidency except for four terms until Roosevelt in 1933. Since then there has been a period of split party control, with the Republicans often winning the presidency, and the Democrats holding the majority in Congress. Traditionally supported by voters with high income, education, and social status, its largest support is in NE industrial and W farming areas. It is identified with big business rather than unions, and with white Anglo-Saxons rather than ethnic minorities. In the 1980s, it became rather more conservative in outlook. >> Democratic Party; mugwump

requiem [**re**kwee-em] (Lat 'rest') In the Roman Catholic Church, a Mass for the dead. In addition to its liturgical use, it has become a musical form; composers who have written requiems include Mozart, Fauré, and Britten. >> liturgy; Mass

reredos [**reer**edos] >> **altarpiece**

resale price maintenance (RPM) The action of manufacturers in fixing the prices at which their products may be resold by retailers. RPM was stopped in the UK by the Restrictive Trade Practices Act (1956) and the Retail Prices Act (1964), except for a few special cases, such as the Net Book Agreement. Manufacturers can now set only a 'recommended' resale price. >> cartel

reserves Gold and convertible currency held by countries as a result of receiving payment for exports. Falling reserves occur as a result of imports being greater than exports. In banking, the term refers to the notes and coins banks must hold in case of a sudden demand (a 'run on the bank'). In accountancy, it refers to the profits which have been ploughed back into a company. >> balance of payments; equity (economics)

resin A natural or synthetic polymer which softens on heating. The term is loosely used to include any polymer, as in 'ion-exchange resins'. >> polymerization; rosin; shellac

resistance A measure of the potential difference U needed to produce direct current I in an electrical circuit component; symbol R, units Ω (ohm); $R = U/I$ by definition. It measures a component's ability to restrict current flow. I/R is called conductance. >> electrical conduction / power; impedance; Ohm's law; potential difference; resistivity; resistor

Resistencia [reseestensia] 27°28S 58°59W, pop (1995e) 229 000. Agricultural, commercial, and industrial capital of Chaco province, N Argentina; on the R Barranqueras; founded as Jesuit mission, mid-18th-c; airport; railway. >> Argentina [i]

resistivity The electrical resistance of a metre cube of material, constant for a given material at a specific temperature; symbol ρ, units Ω.m (ohm.metre). 1/ρ is conductivity. >> electrical conduction; resistance

resistor A component in an electrical circuit designed to introduce a known resistance to the flow of current. Resistance changes with temperature rise, increasing in metals, and falling in semiconductors. >> resistance; semiconductor

Resnais, Alain [ruhnay] (1922–) Film director, born in Vannes, France. His first feature film was *Hiroshima mon amour* (1959, Hiroshima my Love), and this was followed by the controversial *L'Année dernière à Marienbad* (1961, Last Year at Marienbad), hailed as a surrealistic and dreamlike masterpiece by some, as a confused and tedious failure by others.

Respighi, Ottorino [res**pee**gee] (1879–1936) Composer, born in Bologna, Italy. His works include nine operas, the symphonic poems, *Fontane di Roma* (1916, Fountains of Rome) and *Pini di Roma* (1924, Pines of Rome), and the ballet *La Boutique fantasque*, produced by Diaghilev in 1919. >> Diaghilev

respiration A physiological term with a range of related meanings: (1) the act of breathing, whereby terrestrial animals move air in and out of their lungs, and aquatic animals pump water through their gills; (2) the uptake of oxygen from and the release of carbon dioxide to the environment; and (3) the metabolic processes by which organisms derive energy from foodstuffs by utilizing oxygen (**aerobic respiration**) or without the involvement of oxygen (**anaerobic respiration**); often referred to as **tissue** or **cell respiration**. >> artificial respiration ℹ; lungs; respirator

respirator A mechanical method of delivering oxygen to and removing carbon dioxide from a patient who is suffering from severe respiratory failure. It expands the lungs intermittently through a tube introduced into the trachea. >> respiration

Restoration The return of Charles II to England (Jun 1660) at the request of the Convention Parliament, following the collapse of the Protectorate regime. Parliament took the lead in passing the Clarendon Code (1661–5) outlawing dissent from the Book of Common Prayer (1662). >> Protectorate

resurrection A form of re-animation of a person after death, the belief in which can be traced to late Biblical Judaism and early Christianity. Christian faith affirms the resurrection of Jesus Christ in particular, signifying God's vindication of Jesus. >> Christianity; eschatology; Jesus Christ; Judaism; reincarnation

retable >> **altarpiece**

retail price index (RPI) A means of calculating the general trend of prices of goods and services; popularly known as **the cost of living index**. It is used as the main indicator of inflation, and is calculated each month by identifying the prices that an average household will have paid for a basket of goods and services. >> index-linking

Reticulum [re**tik**yulum] (Lat 'net') A small S constellation near the Large Magellanic Cloud. >> constellation; Magellanic Clouds; RR968

retina The innermost lining of the vertebrate eyeball, which transmits information about the visual world to the brain. It consists of an outer pigmented layer and an inner (cerebral) layer of photosensitive cells (*rods* and *cones*) and neurones. The cerebral layer radiates out from the *optic disc* (the region where the nerve fibres leave the eyeball to form the optic nerve) to the periphery. The optic disc is nonpigmented and insensitive to light, and is known as the *blind spot*. Light focused by the lens forms an inverted image on the retina. This stimulates the rods and cones to generate impulses which are transmitted via the optic nerve to the visual areas of the cortex. >> eye ℹ

retinol The active form of vitamin A. In the diet, retinol is found in margarine, oily fish, and dairy fats. It acts to maintain the integrity of skin and lung and is also involved in the synthesis of visual purple, which determines our ability to adapt vision to darkness. Retinol can be synthesized from dietary carotene found in carrots and green leafy vegetables – hence the belief that carrots help eyesight. >> vitamins ℹ

retriever A sporting dog belonging to one of several breeds developed to assist hunters. When game has been shot, the retriever is sent to the point where it fell to collect it and bring it to the hunter. >> golden retriever; griffon (mammal); Labrador retriever; sporting dog

retrovirus A virus c.100 nm in diameter, with an outer envelope enclosing the core. The genetic information is stored in a molecule of single-stranded ribonucleic acid. (Family: Retroviridae.) >> RNA; virus

Returned Services League In Australia, an organization recruited from men and women with military service overseas. Its functions are social (welfare care and clubs) and political: it forms a major pressure group, with direct access to the Cabinet.

Retz (Jean François Paul de Gondi), Cardinal de (1614–79) Prelate, born in Montmirail, France. He plotted against Mazarin, and exploited the Parlementary Fronde (1648) to further his own interests and the power of the Church. In his last years he wrote his *Mémoires*, a classic in 17th-c French literature. >> Frondes, the; Louis XIV; Mazarin

Réunion [rayoon**yon**], formally **Bourbon** pop (1995e) 654 000; area 2512 sq km/970 sq mi. Island in the Mascarenes archipelago, Indian Ocean; capital, St Denis; timezone GMT +4; established as a French penal colony, 1638; overseas department, 1946; part of an administrative region, 1973; governed by a commissioner, a General Council, and a Regional Council. >> Mascarene Islands; St Denis (Réunion)

Reuter, Paul Julius, Freiherr (Baron) **von** [**roy**ter], originally **Israel Beer Josaphat** (1816–99) Founder of the first news agency, born in Kassel, Germany. He developed the idea of a telegraphic news service, and in 1851 moved his headquarters to London. >> news agency; telegraphy

revelation Generally, the disclosure of what was previously unknown, usually by divine or preternatural means. In religion, it is used to refer to disclosures by God or the divine as distinguished from that attained by the human processes of observation and reason. >> Bible; God; Koran

Revelation, Book of or **the Apocalypse of St John** The last book in the New Testament, whose author is named as 'John', an exile on the island of Patmos (1.9), although scholars differ about his precise identity. Chapters 4–22 consist of symbolic visions about future tribulations and judgments marking the End times and the return of Christ. >> apocalypse; eschatology; New Testament

Revere, Paul [re**veer**] (1735–1818) US patriot, born in Boston, MA. On 18 April 1775, the night before Lexington and Concord, he started for Concord, where arms were secreted. He was turned back by a British patrol, and his mission was completed by Dr Samuel Prescott. It was Revere, however, whom the poet Longfellow immortalized for the 'midnight ride'. >> American Revolution

Revised English Bible >> **New English Bible**

revisionism A doctrinal deviation from the ideological stance of a communist party or state; also, the critical re-assessment of Marxist theories. In general, the term has polemical overtones, and is applied to those thought to have broken with Marxist–Leninist orthodoxy. >> communism

Revolt of the Netherlands (1568–1648) Uprisings and wars against Spanish Habsburg rule by 17 provinces in the Low Countries, also called the **War of Independence**, the **Eighty Years' War**, and the **Dutch Revolt**. The rebels were led by William of Orange and his Protestant naval force of 'sea beggars' (*Watergeuzen*). Independence was recognized by Spain in 1648. >> Blood, Council of; Charles V (Emperor); Habsburgs; William I (of the Netherlands)

Revolution of 1905 A series of nationwide strikes, demonstrations, and mutinies in Russia, sparked off by the massacre of peacefully demonstrating workers by soldiers in St Petersburg on *Bloody Sunday* (9 Jan 1905). Faced with continuing popular unrest, Nicholas II was forced to make concessions. >> Nicholas II; Russian Revolution

Revolutions of 1848 A succession of popular uprisings in various W and C European countries during 1848–9. In France the abdication of Louis Philippe was followed by the Second Republic; liberal constitutions were granted in Austria and in many German states; Britain experienced Chartism. The revolutions collapsed from internal weakness or military suppression, and aroused reaction. >> Chartism; Louis Philippe

revolver A single-barrelled pistol with a revolving breech containing chambers for cartridges (usually six), which automatically brings a new cartridge into alignment for firing after each shot. The first practical example was produced by Samuel Colt in 1835. >> Colt, Samuel; pistol

rex A domestic cat with an unusually thin curly coat; a *foreign short-haired* variety; three forms: **Cornish**, **Devon**, and **German**. The name is also used for a rabbit with a short outer coat. >> cat; rabbit

Reykjavík [**rayk**yaveek] 64°09N 21°58W, pop (1995e) 103 000. Capital and chief port of Iceland; founded, 874; chartered, 1786; seat of Danish administration, 1801; capital, 1918; seat of Icelandic parliament; Lutheran bishopric; airport; university (1911); heating system uses nearby hot springs. >> Iceland [i]

Reynaud, Paul [raynoh] (1878–1966) French statesman, born in Barcelonnette, France. He was premier for a short time during the fall of France in 1940, and was imprisoned by the Germans during World War 2.

Reynolds, Albert (1933–) Irish statesman and prime minister (1992–4), born in Roosky, Co Roscommon, Ireland. He held several ministerial offices from 1979, and became prime minister in the 1992 elections, but his party (Fianna Fáil) lost its majority, forcing the formation of a coalition with the Labour Party in 1993. He lost the support of the Labour Party in November 1994, and was forced to resign.

Reynolds, Sir Joshua [**re**nuhldz] (1723–92) Portrait painter, born in Plympton, Devon. His works include 'Dr Samuel Johnson' (c.1756, National Portrait Gallery, London) and 'Sarah Siddons as the Tragic Muse' (1784, San Marino, CA). He produced over 2000 works, from which 700 engravings have been executed. >> engraving

Reza Pahlavi, Mohammed >> **Pahlavi, Mohammed Reza**

Rhadamanthus or **Rhadamanthys** [rada**man**thus] In Greek mythology, a Cretan, son of Zeus and Europa. He did not die but was taken to Elysium, where he became the just judge of the dead.

Rhaetian [**ree**shn] >> **Romance languages**

rhapsody A piece of music in which the composer allows his imagination to range more or less freely over some theme, story, or idea, without regard for any prescribed structure. Liszt's Hungarian Rhapsodies are examples of what is essentially a Romantic genre. >> Liszt; Romanticism

Rhätikon [**ray**tikon] Mountain range of the E or Rhaetian Alps, rising to 2965 m/9728 ft at Schesaplana. >> Alps

Rhazes or **Razi** [**ray**zeez, **ray**zee], in full **Abu Bakr Muhammad ibn Zakariya ar-Razi** (10th-c) Persian physician and alchemist, who lived in Baghdad. His encyclopedia had considerable influence on medical science in the Middle Ages.

rhea [**ree**a] A South American ratite, resembling the ostrich, but smaller (up to 1.5 m/5 ft), duller plumage, and larger wings; can swim; also known as the **ema**, **nandu (nhandu)**, or **American ostrich**. (Family: Rheidae, 2 species.) >> ostrich; Ratitae

Rhea (astronomy) [**ree**a] The fifth natural satellite of Saturn, discovered in 1672; distance from the planet 527 000 km/ 327 000 mi. It is the second largest moon in its system, diameter 1530 km/950 mi; orbital period 4.518 days. >> Saturn (astronomy); RR964

Rhea or **Rheia** (mythology) [**ree**a] In Greek mythology, a Titan, sister and wife of Cronus. She was the mother of Zeus and other Olympian gods. >> Cronus; Zeus

Rhee, Syngman (1875–1965) Korean statesman, born near Kaesong, Korea. After the unsuccessful rising of 1919, he became president of the exiled Korean Provisional Government. On Japan's surrender (1945) he returned to become the first elected president of South Korea (1948). >> Korea, South [i]

Rheims [reemz], Fr **Reims** [rĩs], ancient **Durocortorum**, later **Remi** 49°15N 4°02E, pop (1995e) 186 000. Historic town in NE France; on right bank of R Vesle; port on Aisne–Marne Canal; bishopric since 4th-c, now an archbishopric; former coronation site of French kings; extensive damage in World War 1; scene of German surrender, 1945; road and rail junction; major wine-producing centre (especially champagne); university (1967); Gothic cathedral (13th-c).

Rhenish Slate Mountains, Ger **Rheinisches Schiefergebirge** Extensive plateau of Germany, dissected by the Rhine and its tributaries; highest peak, the Grosser Feldberg (879 m/2884 ft). >> Germany [i]; Rhine, River

rheology [ree**ol**ojee] The study of the deformation and flow of materials subjected to force. It includes the viscosity of liquids and gases, strain and shear due to stresses in solids, and plastic deformation in metals. >> tribology; viscosity

rhesus factor A series of closely related but distinct antigens (*agglutinogens*) usually present in the plasma membranes of human red blood cells. Individuals with the factor are **Rh+**; those without are **Rh−**. An Rh− woman carrying her first Rh+ child may produce anti-Rh antibodies after the birth. During the next pregnancy, these antibodies may cross the placenta, and if the fetus is Rh+ they may cause *haemolytic disease of the newborn*. The ratio of Rh+ to Rh− differs between ethnic populations. >> antibodies; blood; genetics

rhesus monkey A macaque (*Macaca mulatta*) native to S Asia from Afghanistan to Indochina; stocky; sandy-brown; used widely for medical research; also known as **rhesus macaque**. >> macaque

rhetoric The spoken and written language of persuasion. In the classical and mediaeval world, it was a formal branch of learning concerned with the techniques and devices required to persuade or convince an audience. Aristotle, Cicero, and Quintilian developed theories of successful speech-making. Subsequently it came to signify elaborate and pompous language, which is nonetheless empty and insincere. In recent years, there has been a renewed interest in presenting a message in the most effective way. >> Aristotle; Cicero; oratory; Quintilian; semiotics

rheumatic fever A common disease especially of children and adolescents in Asia and Africa, arising from an immunological reaction to preceding infection with cer-

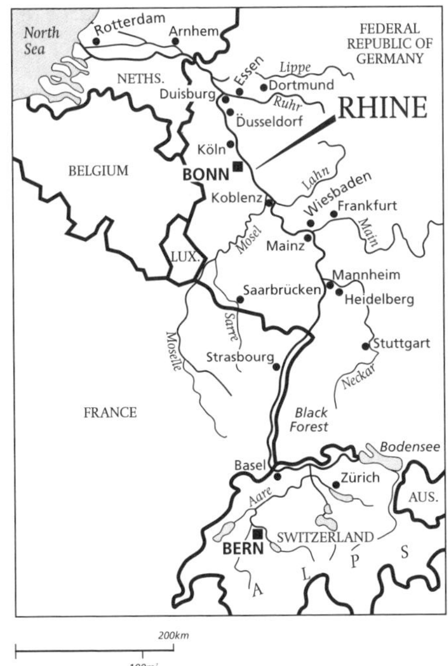

tain strains of *Streptococcus*. Serious rheumatic heart disease can produce incompetence of the valves of the heart. >> chorea; heart ℹ; *Streptococcus*

rheumatism A non-specific name given to aches and pains in muscles, particularly in the shoulders and back, and common in older people. >> arthritis; muscle ℹ

Rhine, River, Ger **Rhein**, Dutch **Run**, Fr **Rhin**, ancient **Rhenus** River in C and W Europe, rising in SE Switzerland; divides into two major branches in The Netherlands, the Lek and Waal, before entering the North Sea; length, 1320 km/820 mi; widely connected by canals to other rivers.

Rhine, J(oseph) B(anks) (1895–1980) Psychologist, a pioneer of parapsychology, born in Juniáta, PA. His experiments involving packs of specially designed cards established the phenomenon of extrasensory perception on a statistical basis. >> parapsychology

rhinoceros The second largest land animal (after the elephant), native to S and SE Asia and Africa; a perissodactyl mammal of the family Rhinocerotidae; skin tough, usually with few hairs; long head with small eyes placed well forward; nose with 'horn(s)' made from fibrous outgrowths of the skin; five species: also known as **rhino**. >> perissodactyl ℹ; woolly rhinoceros

rhizoid A uni- or multicellular thread-like structure found in algae, mosses, liverworts, and ferns. Rhizoids anchor the plant to the substrate and absorb water, but unlike true roots are not differentiated into separate tissues. >> algae; fern; liverwort; moss; root (botany)

rhizome A horizontally growing underground stem. It is either slender and fast-growing, allowing the plant to spread vegetatively, or fleshy and acting as a food store. >> stem (botany)

Rhizopoda [riy**zo**poda] A large group of protozoans distinguished on the basis of their types of pseudopodia; includes the amoebae and foraminiferans. >> amoeba; Protozoa

Rhode Island pop (1995e) 1 008 000; area 3139 sq km/ 1212 sq mi. New England state in NE USA; 'Little Rhody' or the 'Ocean State'; smallest US state, but the second most densely populated; one of the original states, 13th to ratify the Federal Constitution; gave protection to Quakers in 1657 and to Jews from the Netherlands in 1658; rises from the Narragansett Basin in the E to flat and rolling uplands in the W; highest point, Jerimoth Hill (247 m/810 ft); capital, Providence. >> Providence; United States of America ℹ; RR994

Rhodes, Gr **Ródhos**, Ital **Rodi** pop (1995e) 93 500; area 1398 sq km/540 sq mi. Largest island of the Dodecanese, Greece; length 72 km/45 mi; maximum width 35 km/ 22 mi; fourth largest Greek island; ridge of hills rise to 1215 m/3986 ft; originally settled by Mycenean Greeks, 1400 BC; Knights of the Order of St John settled here, 1309–1522; held by Italy, 1912–47; capital, Rhodes, pop (1995e) 44 700; airfield; Temple of Aphrodite (3rd-c BC). >> Dodecanese; Knights Hospitallers; Seven Wonders of the Ancient World

Rhodes, Cecil (John) (1853–1902) British colonial statesman, born in Bishop's Stortford, Hertfordshire. He secured the charter for the British South Africa Company (1889), whose territory was later to be named after him as Rhodesia. In 1890 he became prime minister of Cape Colony, but was forced to resign in 1896. He was a conspicuous figure during the Boer War of 1899–1902, when he organized the defences of Kimberley. His will founded scholarships at Oxford for Americans, Germans, and colonials (*Rhodes scholars*). >> Boer Wars; Jameson raid; Zimbabwe ℹ

Rhodes, Wilfred (1877–1973) Cricketer, born in Kirkheaton, West Yorkshire. He played for Yorkshire and England, and during his career (1898–1930) took a world record 4187 wickets and scored 39 722 runs. He performed the 'double' of 1000 runs and 100 wickets 16 times. >> cricket (sport) ℹ

Rhodes, Zandra (1940–) Fashion designer, born in Chatham, Kent. She showed her first collection in 1969, and is noted for her distinctive, exotic designs in floating chiffons and silks.

Rhodesia >> **Zimbabwe** ℹ

rhododendron An evergreen shrub or small tree, native to N temperate regions but found only on acid soils; flowers in clusters at tips of main branches, funnel or bell-shaped; 5–10 petals and stamens. Several hundred cultivars are known, with flowers varying greatly in size and colour. (Genus: *Rhododendron*, c.1200 species. Family: Ericaceae.) >> cultivar

Rhodope Mountains [**ro**dopee], Bulgarian **Rhodopi** Range of mountains stretching NW–SE in SW Bulgaria and NE Greece, rising to 2925 m/9596 ft at Musala; length 290 km/180 mi. >> Bulgaria ℹ

Rhondda, Cynon, Taff [**ron**tha, **kuh**non, taf] pop (1995e) 239 000; area 424 sq km / 164 sq mi. County (unitary authority from 1996) in S Wales, UK; administrative centre, Cardiff; former major coal mining area; Royal Mint at Llantrisant. >> Royal Mint; Wales ℹ

Rhône, River River in C and SW Europe, rising in S Switzerland, and flowing to its delta on the Mediterranean; length, 812 km/504 mi; joined at Lyon by its largest tributary, the Saône. >> France ℹ

rhubarb A long-lived perennial herb (*Rheum rhaponticum*), related to dock, and native to Siberia; basal leaves large, heart-shaped, wavy, with edible green or red stalks; flowers small, white, 6-petalled; leaves can be poisonous. (Family: Polygonaceae).

Rhyl [ril] 53°19N 3°29W, pop (1995e) 24 200. Seaside resort town in Denbighshire, NE Wales, UK; railway; funfair, promenade. >> Wales ℹ

rhyme The repetition of the same or a similar syllable, for rhetorical effect, typically at the end of a poetic line. There is a limitless variety of rhyme schemes. 20th-c poets have explored half-rhyme, as in Wilfred Owen's 'Strange Meeting', where *friend/frowned* and *killed/cold* are rhymes. >> sonnet

rhyolite [**riy**oliyt] A silica-rich volcanic igneous rock with a composition approximately equivalent to granite. It is fine-grained or glassy. >> igneous rock; pumice

Rhys, Jean [rees], pseudonym of **Gwen Williams** (1894–1979) Novelist, born in Roseau, Dominica. Her best-known novel is *Wide Sargasso Sea* (1966), a 'prequel' to Charlotte Bronte's *Jane Eyre*.

rhythm A pattern marked by the regular recurrence of elements, found in speech, music, dance, and other forms of behaviour, and more generally in the cyclical changes of nature. In speech, rhythm is most noticeable in the metrical patterns of poetry. In music, it is the constituent that has to do with metre, note-lengths, and accent rather than with pitch. Music is said to be 'strongly rhythmic' when the basic pulse is firmly emphasized or when a rhythmic pattern is insistently repeated; but rhythmic subtlety in music depends more on the play between an established pulse and the melodic or harmonic accents that disturb it, or between one rhythmic pattern and another (**cross-rhythm**). >> eurhythmics; music; rhythm and blues

rhythm and blues A type of popular music dating from the 1940s and 1950s which combined melodic and textual features of the blues with the rhythm section of a pop group (electric guitars, keyboards, and drum set). It was an important forerunner of rock and roll, and was itself superseded by soul. >> blues; jazz; pop music; soul (music)

rhythm method >> **contraception**

Rialto Bridge [ree**al**toh] A bridge spanning the Grand Canal in Venice. It was built in 1588–92 by Antonio da Ponte. >> Venice

rib A curved, twisted strip of bone passing around the thorax from the vertebral column to articulate indirectly with the sternum. There are twelve pairs in humans, of which the eleventh and twelfth are not attached at the front (**floating ribs**). They provide protection for the lungs, heart, and great vessels. >> bone; respiration; skeleton [i]; sternum; thorax

Ribbentrop, Joachim von [**rib**entrop] (1893–1946) German statesman, born in Wesel, Germany. He became ambassador to Britain (1936) and foreign minister (1938–45). Captured in 1945, he was executed at Nuremberg. >> World War 2

Ribble, River River rising in the Pennine Hills of North Yorkshire, N England; flows 120 km/75 mi to meet the Irish Sea in a broad estuary. >> England [i]

ribbon worm An unsegmented, bilaterally symmetrical worm found mainly on or in shallow marine sediments, occasionally in fresh water; may reach lengths of over 20 m/65 ft. (Phylum: Nemertea.) >> worm

Ribera, José or **Jusepe de** [ree**ve**ra], known as **Lo Spagnoletto** ('the Little Spaniard') (1588–1656) Painter and etcher, born in Játiva, Spain. He is noted for the often gruesome realism with which he treated religious and mythological subjects, such as the martyrdom of the saints.

riboflavin A B vitamin (B_2), an essential active component (*co-enzyme*) involved in energy transfers in cells, found especially in green vegetables, milk, eggs, liver, and yeast. >> vitamins [i]

ribonucleic acid >> **RNA**

ribose [**riy**bohs] $C_5H_{10}O_5$. A pentose or 5-carbon sugar, occurring in the structure of ribonucleic acids (RNA). >> deoxyribose; RNA

Ricardo, David [ri**kah(r)**doh] (1772–1823) Political economist, born in London. In 1817 appeared the work on which his reputation chiefly rests, *Principles of Political Economy and Taxation*.

Ricci, Nina, originally **Maria Nielli** (1883–1970) Fashion designer, born in Turin, Italy. She joined Raffin in 1908, and stayed with him for 20 years, eventually becoming his partner. She showed her first collection in 1932, and her fragrances in 1941, and developed a wide range of further products in cosmetics, furs, and fashion accessories.

Ricci, Sebastiano [**ree**chee] (1659–1734) Painter, born in Belluno, Italy. He worked throughout Europe, becoming one of the leading decorative painters of his day.

Riccio, David >> **Rizzio**

Rice, Tim, popular name of **Sir Timothy Miles Bindon Rice** (1944–) Lyricist, writer, and broadcaster, born in Buckinghamshire. He is best known for writing the lyrics for *Joseph and the Amazing Technicolour Dreamcoat* (1968), *Jesus Christ Superstar* (1971), and *Evita* (1978). Later works include the lyrics for *Chess* (1984), *Starmania* (1991), and *Beauty and the Beast* (1997). >> Lloyd Webber

rice An important cereal grass (*Oryza sativa*), with open panicles, drooping with numerous grains. The premier food plant of Asia, It is cultivated in flooded paddy fields, with many varieties adapted to different water-levels. Recent breeding programmes have produced successful, high-yielding, semi-dwarf varieties. (Family: Gramineae.) >> cereals; grass [i]; panicle

Richard I, known as **Richard Coeur de Lion** or **Richard the Lionheart** (1157–99) King of England (1189–99), born in Oxford, the third son of Henry II and Eleanor of Aquitaine. Of his 10-year reign, he spent only five months in England, devoting himself to crusading, and defending the Angevin lands in France. He took Messina (1190), Cyprus, and Acre (1191) during the Third Crusade, and advanced to within sight of Jerusalem. On the return journey, he was arrested at Vienna (1192), and remained a prisoner of the German Emperor Henry VI until he agreed to be ransomed (1194). He was killed while besieging the castle of Châlus, Aquitaine. >> Angevins; Crusades [i]; Walter, Hubert

Richard II (1367–1400) King of England (1377–99), born in Bordeaux, France, the younger son of Edward the Black Prince. He succeeded his grandfather, Edward III, at the age of 10. He displayed great bravery in confronting the rebels during the Peasants' Revolt (1381); but already parliament was concerned about his favourites, and the reign was dominated by the struggle between Richard's desire to act independently, and the magnates' concern to curb his power. He exiled several lords, including Henry Bolingbroke (later Henry IV). Having failed to restrain the king by constitutional means, the magnates resolved to unseat him from the throne. Bolingbroke invaded England unopposed, and Richard was deposed in his favour (Sep 1399). He died in Pontefract Castle, Yorkshire, possibly of starvation. >> Henry IV (of England); John of Gaunt; Peasants' Revolt

Richard III (1452–85) King of England (1483–5), born in Fotheringhay Castle, Northamptonshire, the youngest son of Richard, Duke of York. He was created Duke of Gloucester by his brother, Edward IV, in 1461. When Edward died (1483) and was succeeded by his under-age son, Edward V, Richard acted first as protector; but within three months, he had himself proclaimed and crowned as the rightful king. Young Edward and his brother were probably murdered in the Tower on Richard's orders (though not all historians agree). His rival, Henry Tudor (later Henry VII), confronted him in battle at Bosworth Field, where Richard was killed. Though ruthless, he was not the absolute monster Tudor historians portrayed him to be. Nor is there proof he was a hunchback. >> Bosworth Field, Battle of; Edward IV / V; Henry VII

Richard, Cliff, popular name of **Sir Harry Roger Webb** (1940–) Pop-singer, born in Lucknow, India. He moved to England at the age of eight, and formed his own band in 1958. Originally called The Drifters, the group changed its name to The Shadows, and after the success of 'Living Doll' (1959) it was hailed as Britain's answer to American rock. He made a series of family musical films during the 1960s, including *The Young Ones* (1961) and *Summer Holiday* (1962), and played the leading role in the musical *Heathcliff* (1996). Following his conversion to Christianity, his clean-cut image damaged his reputation with rock fans, but he has nevertheless become a British entertainment institution.

Richards, Frank, pseudonym of **Charles (Harold St John) Hamilton** (1875–1961) Children's writer, born in London. He wrote for boys' papers, particularly for *Gem* (1906–39) and *Magnet* (1908–40), and became known as the author of the 'Tom Merry', 'Billy Bunter', and other school-story series.

Richards, Sir Gordon (1904–86) Jockey and trainer, born in Oakengates, Shropshire. Between 1921 and 1954 he rode a record 4870 winners in Britain, and was champion jockey a record 26 times between 1925 and 1953.

Richards, I(vor) A(rmstrong) (1893–1979) Literary critic and scholar, born in Sandbach, Cheshire. He pioneered the detailed critical study of literary texts in the 20th-c. With C K Ogden he wrote *The Meaning of Meaning* (1923), followed by the influential *Principles of Literary Criticism* (1924). >> Ogden, C K

Richards, Viv, popular name of **Isaac Vivian Alexander Richards** (1952–) Cricket player, born in Antigua. In 1976 he scored a record 1710 Test runs in one calendar year. He captained the West Indies (1985–91), and scored 8540 runs in 121 Test matches, including 24 centuries. >> cricket (sport) ℹ

Richardson, Miranda (1958–) Actress, born in Southport, Lancashire. Her films include *Empire of The Sun* (1987), *Damage* (1992, BAFTA for Best Supporting Actress), *Tom and Viv* (1994), and *The Apostle* (1997). She also appeared as Queen Elizabeth in the television comedy series *Blackadder* (1990).

Richardson, Sir Ralph (David) (1902–83) Actor, born in Cheltenham, Gloucestershire. His association with the Old Vic company commenced in 1930, and he was asked to lead its postwar revival. His films included *The Fallen Idol* (1948) and *Doctor Zhivago* (1965).

Richardson, Robert C (1937–) Physicist, born in Washington, DC. At Cornell he contributed to the discovery of the superfluidity of helium-3, and shared the Nobel Prize for Physics in 1996.

Richardson, Samuel (1689–1761) Novelist, born in Mackworth, Derbyshire. His novels include *Pamela* (1740), *Clarissa* (1748), published in seven volumes, and *Sir Charles Grandison* (1754). In using the epistolary method, he helped to develop the dramatic scope of the novel, then little regarded as a literary form. >> novel

Richelieu, Armand Jean du Plessis, Cardinal, duc de (Duke of) [**reesh**lyoe] (1585–1642) French statesman and first minister of France (1624–42), born in Richelieu, near Chinon, France. A protégé of the queen mother, Marie de' Medicis, he became minister of state (1624), and as chief minister was the effective ruler of France. His principal achievement was to check Habsburg power, ultimately by sending armies into the Spanish Netherlands, Alsace, Lorraine, and Roussillon. >> Habsburgs

Richler, Mordecai (1931–) Writer, born in Montreal, Quebec, Canada. His best-known novel is *The Apprenticeship of Duddy Kravitz* (1959), which was later filmed, although *St Urbain's Horseman* (1971) is a more ambitious work. He has also written a memoir, *This Year in Jerusalem* (1994).

Richmond (UK), properly **Richmond-upon-Thames [temz]** 51°28N 0°19W, pop (1995e) 167 000. Borough of SW Greater London, England; on the R Thames; railway; Hampton Court Palace, Royal Botanic Gardens (Kew Gardens). >> London

Richmond (USA) 37°33N 77°27W, pop (1995e) 219 798. Port and capital of state in E Virginia, USA, on the James R; trading post (Fort Charles), 1645; state capital, 1779; Confederate capital during the Civil War; captured by Union forces, 1865; airfield; railway; three universities (1804, 1832, 1865); corporate headquarters centre. >> American Civil War; Virginia

Richter, Hans (1843–1916) Conductor, born in Raab, Hungary. He was an authority on the music of Wagner, with whom he was closely associated in the Bayreuth festivals. >> Wagner

Richter, Johann Paul (Friedrich), pseudonym **Jean Paul** (1763–1825) Novelist and humorist, born in Wunsiedel, Germany. He produced a wide range of works, achieving success with such romances as *Die unsichtbare Loge* (1793, The Invisible Lodge), *Hesperus* (1795), and the four-volume *Titan* (1800–3).

Richter, Sviatoslav (Teofilovich) (1915–97) Pianist, born in Zhitomir, Ukraine. Winner of the Stalin Prize in 1949, he made extensive concert tours, and had been associated with the music festivals at Aldeburgh and Spoleto.

Richter scale A logarithmic scale, devised in 1935 by US geophysicist Charles Richter (1900–85), for representing the energy released by earthquakes. A figure of two or less is barely perceptible, while eight or more is a major earthquake. >> earthquake; RR974

Richthofen, Ferdinand (Paul Wilhelm), Baron von [**rikht**hohfn] (1833–1905) Geographer, geologist, and traveller, born in Karlsruhe, Germany. His research helped to develop the field of geomorphology. >> geomorphology

ricin [**riy**sin, **ri**sin] An extremely toxic protein present in the castor bean (*Ricinus sanguineui*) of the family Euphorbiaceae). It has been proposed as a chemical warfare agent. >> castor-oil plant; toxin

rickets A disorder of infants and growing children resulting from a deficiency of vitamin D. There is a failure to calcify the growing ends of long bones, swelling, and enlargement of the ends of the ribs in front of the chest. >> osteomalacia; vitamins ℹ

Rickettsia [ri**ket**sia] A genus of typically rod-shaped micro-organisms with bacteria-like cell walls. Rickettsias multiply inside or in close association with cells of animal hosts. They include the causative agents of trench fever and other human diseases. (Kingdom: Monera. Family: Rickettsiaceae.) >> bacteria ℹ; micro-organism

Rickman, Alan (1946–) British actor. He played a wide range of theatre roles during the 1980s, then became known for his film work, including *Truly, Madly, Deeply* (1991), *Robin Hood, Prince of Thieves* (1991, BAFTA Best Supporting Actor), *Sense and Sensibility* (1996), and *Rasputin* (1996, Emmy).

riddle An utterance, often cast in a traditional form, whose intention is to mystify or mislead; a linguistic guessing game. In Europe, riddles tend to be short questions, generally restricted to children's games and conversation. In ancient Greece, they had a serious purpose, being used by judges, oracles, and others to test a person's wisdom.

Ridgeway A long-distance footpath in England running 137 km/85 mi from Beacon Hill, Buckinghamshire, to Overton Hill, Wiltshire.

Ridgway, Matthew B(unker) (1895–1993) US soldier, born in Fort Monroe, VA. He commanded the 82nd

Airborne Division in Sicily (1943) and Normandy (1944), the 18th Airborne Corps in the North West Europe campaign (1944–5), and the US 8th Army in UN operations in Korea (1950). >> World War 2

Riding for the Disabled The organized riding of horses and ponies to enrich the lives of seriously disabled people, especially children. People with Down's syndrome, cerebral palsy, spina bifida, and other such disabilities are taught to ride suitable mounts under careful supervision.

riding the marches A Scottish ritual, also called **common riding**, the equivalent of English *beating the bounds*. It is performed on horseback, chiefly in the towns of S Scotland. >> beating the bounds

Ridley, Nicholas (c.1500–1555) Protestant martyr, born near Haltwhistle, Northumberland. An ardent reformer, he became Bishop of London (1550), and helped Cranmer prepare the Thirty-nine Articles. On the death of Edward VI he espoused the cause of Lady Jane Grey, and was executed at Oxford. >> Cranmer, Thomas; Grey, Jane; Reformation; Thirty-nine Articles

Rie, Dame Lucie [ree] (1902–95) Studio potter, born in Vienna. In the 1940s and 1950s she made ceramic buttons and tableware, but later concentrated on stoneware or porcelain bowls and vases with a variety of textured and coloured glazes. >> porcelain; stoneware

Riefenstahl, Leni [**ree**fenshtahl], popular name of **Berta Helene Amalie Riefenstahl** (1902–) Film-maker, born in Berlin. Her films include *Triumph des Willens* (1935, Triumph of the Will), a compelling record of a Nazi rally at Nuremberg, and *Olympia* (1938), an epic documentary of the Berlin Olympic Games.

Riel, Louis [ree-**el**] (1844–85) Canadian political leader, born in Red River Settlement, Rupert's Land. He headed the Red River Rebellion in 1869–70, and became president of the provisional government. Following a second uprising (1885) in what is now Saskatchewan, he was arrested and executed. >> Métis; Red River Rebellion

Riemann, (Georg Friedrich) Bernhard [**ree**man] (1826–66) Mathematician, born in Breselenz, Germany. His early work was on the theory of functions, but he is best remembered for his development of non-Euclidian geometry. >> geometries, non-Euclidian

Rienzi, Cola di [rien**zee**], also spelled **Rienzo** (1313–54) Italian patriot, born in Rome. In 1347 he incited the citizens to rise against the rule of the nobles, but was killed in a reaction against him. >> Italy ℹ

Rif or **Riff** A cluster of Berber agricultural and herding groups of NE Morocco. Famed as warriors, in the 1920s they defeated the Spanish, but were eventually conquered by combined French and Spanish forces.

Rifkind, Sir Malcolm (Leslie) (1946–) British Conservative statesman, born in Edinburgh. Elected an MP in 1974, he became secretary of state for Scotland (1986–90), transport (1990–2), defence (1992–5), and foreign secretary (1995–7). He lost his seat in the 1997 general election, the year he received a knighthood.

rifle A type of firearm developed into a practical weapon in the mid-19th-c in which the barrel of the gun is internally grooved in a spiral form. The bullet is spun as it passes down the bore, the spin stabilizing it in flight and thus increasing its accuracy. Today's military **assault rifles** are lightweight, fully automatic weapons with great range and accuracy. >> bayonet

rift valley An elongated trough in the Earth's crust bounded by normal faults; also termed a **graben**. It is a region of tension in the Earth's crust arising from crustal plates moving apart. >> plate tectonics ℹ; Rift Valley; *see illustration below*

Rift Valley or **Great Rift Valley** Major geological feature running from the Middle East S to SE Africa; from Syria to Mozambique; contains the Sea of Galilee, Dead Sea, Gulf of Aqaba, and Red Sea; W branch (also known as the Albertine Rift), along the edge of the Congo basin, includes lakes Albert, Edward, Kivu, and Tanganyika. >> Africa; rift valley ℹ

Riga [**ree**ga] 56°53N 24°08E, pop (1995e) 889 000. Seaport capital of Latvia; on the R Daugava; trading station, 1201; member of the Hanseatic League, 1282; capital of independent Latvia, 1918–40, and from 1991; occupied by Germany in World War 2; airport; railway; military base; cultural centre and seaside resort; university (1919); castle (1330), cathedral (13th-c, rebuilt 16th-c); historic centre, a world heritage site. >> Latvia ℹ

Rigel [**riy**juhl] A supergiant in Orion, the seventh brightest star in our sky, and also one of the most luminous of all stars. Distance: 320 parsec. >> luminosity; Orion (astronomy); supergiant

Rigg, Dame Diana (1938–) Actress, born in Doncaster, S Yorkshire. She played Emma Peel in the popular *The Avengers* television series, then joined the National Theatre (1972). Among her films are *Evil Under the Sun* (1982) and *A Good Man in Africa* (1994), and her television work includes *Mother Love* (1990, BAFTA). She received a Tony award for *Medea* (1994).

rig(ging) >> **sailing rig** ℹ

rightsizing A strategy for organizing the use of mainframe, mini, and personal computers in an organization, in such a way that data is held on the type of computer and at the location for which it is most suited. >> computer; downsizing; mainframe; minicomputer; personal computer

right to silence In most legal jurisdictions, a right which protects criminal suspects from answering questions put to them by the relevant authority. In the UK, police are required to *caution* suspects about their right to silence and right to legal advice. In the USA, police are required to give all suspects a *Miranda warning*, based on the United States Supreme Court case *Miranda v. Arizona* (1966), in which the court held that prosecutors may not use incriminating statements of suspects unless strict procedural safeguards are followed to guarantee the suspect's awareness of the constitutional right to remain silent and to have an attorney.

right wing One end of the political continuum, originally

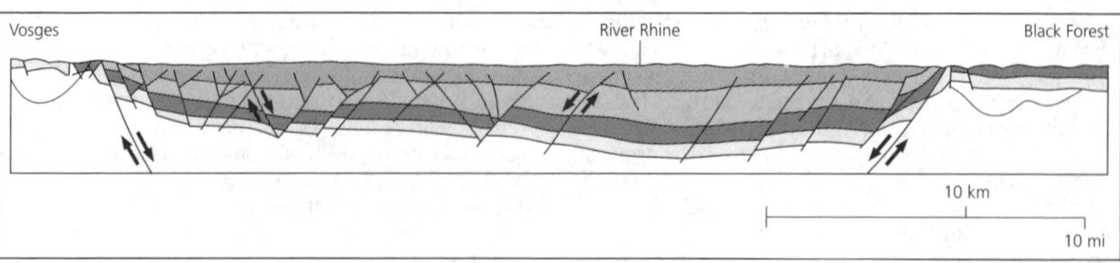

Rift valley – Rhine graben

identifying those who supported the institutions of the monarchy during the French Revolution. In the 19th-c the term was applied to those who were conservative in their view, supporting authority, the state, tradition, property, patriotism, and institutions such as the Church and family. In the 20th-c, the right has also developed a radical, non-conservative side. >> conservatism; New Right

rigidity >> **shear modulus**

rigor mortis [**ri**ger **maw(r)**tis] A temporary stiffening of the body after death because of the depletion of adenosine triphosphate and phosphoryl creatinine within skeletal muscle fibres. It usually begins 3 hours after death and is completed by 12 hours. The effects persist for 3–4 days, after which flaccidity returns.

Rijeka [ri**ye**ka], Ital **Fiume** 45°20N 14°27E, pop (1995e) 172 000. Seaport town in W Croatia, on R Rečina; Croatia's largest port; former Roman base (Tarsatica); occupied by the Slavs, 7th-c; naval base of the Austro-Hungarian Empire until 1918; ceded to Italy, 1924; ceded to Yugoslavia, 1947; airfield; railway; ferries; university (1973); castle, cathedral. >> Croatia ℹ

Rijksmuseum [**riyks**moozayum] ('state museum') The national art gallery in Amsterdam, The Netherlands. The present building was designed by Petrus Cuypers and erected in 1877–85.

Rila Mountain [**ree**la], Bulgarian **Rila Planina** Mountain in W Bulgaria; highest range in the Balkan peninsula, rising to 2925 m/9596 ft at Musala. >> Rhodope Mountains

Riley, Bridget (1931–) Artist, born in London. She is a leading practitioner of Op Art (eg 'Fall' 1963, Tate, London). She was made a Companion of Honour in 1998. >> Op Art

Rilke, Rainer Maria [**ril**kuh] (1875–1926) Lyric poet, born in Prague. Among his major works are *Die Sonnette an Orpheus* (Sonnets to Orpheus) and *Duineser Elegien* (Duino Elegies), both written in 1923.

rille [ril] A straight or winding valley, with a U-shaped cross-section, found in the lunar maria. Rilles mark places where molten lava has flowed in the past. >> lava; maria

Rimbaud, (Jean Nicolas) Arthur [**rī**boh] (1854–91) Poet, born in Charleville, France. His most popular work is *Le Bateau ivre* (1871, The Drunken Boat). In 1871 Verlaine invited him to Paris, where they led together a life of ill repute. Before the relationship ended (1873), Rimbaud wrote *Les Illuminations* (1872), which show him to be a precursor of Symbolism. >> Symbolism; Verlaine

rime A form of precipitation in which surfaces are coated in opaque ice. It forms when ice accretes on objects through the freezing, on impact, of supercooled water droplets. >> frost; precipitation

Rimington, Stella >> **intelligence service**

Rimsky-Korsakov, Nikolai (Andreyevich) [**rim**skee **kaw(r)**sakof] (1844–1908) Composer, born in Tikhvin, Russia. In 1887–8 he produced his three great orchestral masterpieces – *Capriccio Espagnol*, *Easter Festival*, and *Scheherazade*. Ever conscious of his bygone technical shortcomings, he rewrote almost all his early work. >> Balakirev

rinderpest [**rin**derpest] An infectious disease of ruminant mammals; also known as **cattle plague**. It is characterized by blood in the faeces, fever, and swelling of the mucous membranes. >> ruminant ℹ

ring In chemistry, a closed group of atoms. For carbon compounds, rings of five or six atoms are the most stable.

Ring nebula >> **Lyra**

ring of fire A belt of major earthquake and volcanic activity around the Pacific Ocean, defining the boundary between crustal plates. >> earthquake; plate tectonics ℹ; volcano

ringworm A common skin disease resulting from a fungal infection of the outer layers of the skin. It usually affects the scalp, groin, and the clefts of the toes. >> athlete's foot; fungus

Rinzai Zen >> **Zen Buddhism**

Rio de Janeiro [**ree**oh duh zha**neer**oh], known as **Rio** 22°53S 43°17W, pop (1995e) 6 574 000. Port city in SE Brazil; Pão de Açucar (Sugar Loaf Mountain) rises to 396 m/1299 ft; discovered, 1502; first settled by the French, 1555; taken by the Portuguese, 1567; seat of the Viceroy, 1763; capital of Brazil, 1834–1960; trade in coffee, sugar, iron ore; major international tourist centre, with famous beaches at Copacabana, Ipanema, Leblon; airport; two airfields; railway; metro; three universities (1920, 1940, 1950); many colonial and 19th-c buildings; figure of Christ on the highest peak, Corcovado (690 m/2264 ft); world-famous Carnival, on the days preceding Lent. >> Brazil ℹ

Rio Grande [**ree**oh **grand**, **gran**day] **Río Bravo**, **Río Bravo del Norte**. River in SW USA and N Mexico; rises in the Rocky Mts, SW Colorado; enters the Gulf of Mexico; length 3033 km/1885 mi. >> Mexico ℹ; United States of America ℹ

Rioja [ree**okh**a] pop (1995e) 264 000; area 5034 sq km/1943 sq mi. Region of N Spain; major wine-producing area; capital, Logroño. >> Spain ℹ

Río Muni [**ree**oh **moo**nee] area 26 016 sq km/10 042 sq mi. Mainland territory of Equatorial Guinea, WC Africa; chief town, Bata. >> Equatorial Guinea ℹ

Riot Act Legislation in Britain concerned to preserve public order, first passed in 1714. When 12 or more people were unlawfully assembled and refused to disperse, they were, after the reading of a section of this Act by a person in authority, immediately considered felons having committed a serious crime.

Ripon [ripn] 54°08N 1°31W, pop (1995e) 13 600. Town in North Yorkshire, N England; reckoned to be England's second oldest town; racecourse; cathedral. >> Colchester; Fountains Abbey; Yorkshire, North

risk analysis A technique used in insurance and in business which attempts to calculate the effect of the 'worst possible' outcome of a venture. Risk analysis looks at all possible outcomes, assigning probabilities to each so that all the options are quantified. >> actuary

Risorgimento [rizaw(r)zhi**men**toh] (It 'resurgence', 're-birth') The 19th-c movement by which Italy achieved unity and nationhood. It began with the 1830 revolutions and, after failure in 1848–9, reached fruition under the leadership of Piedmont/Sardinia (1859–70). In 1859–61 the Austrians were expelled from Lombardy, and the C Italian duchies, the Papal States, and Naples/Sicily united with Sardinia to form the Kingdom of Italy. >> Cavour; Garibaldi; Mazzini; Thousand, Expedition of the

river A body of flowing water restricted to a relatively narrow channel by banks. It typically originates as a stream in high ground, and moves downhill, eroding a channel which grows as tributaries join the flow, and often carving out major valleys. In its middle stages the river flows more slowly, and meanders begin to form; while in its mature stages deposition of sediment and the formation of broad flood-plains and deltas is characteristic. >> hydrology; valley; RR972; *see illustration on p. 730*

Rivera, Diego [ri**vay**ra] (1886–1957) Painter, born in Guanajuato, Mexico. In 1921 he began a series of murals in public buildings depicting the life and history of the Mexican people. His art is a blend of folk art and revolutionary propaganda.

river blindness An infection caused by the filaria *Onchocerca volvulus*; also known as **onchocerciasis**. Eye involvement causes itching, inflammation, glaucoma, and blindness. >> eye ℹ; filariasis; glaucoma

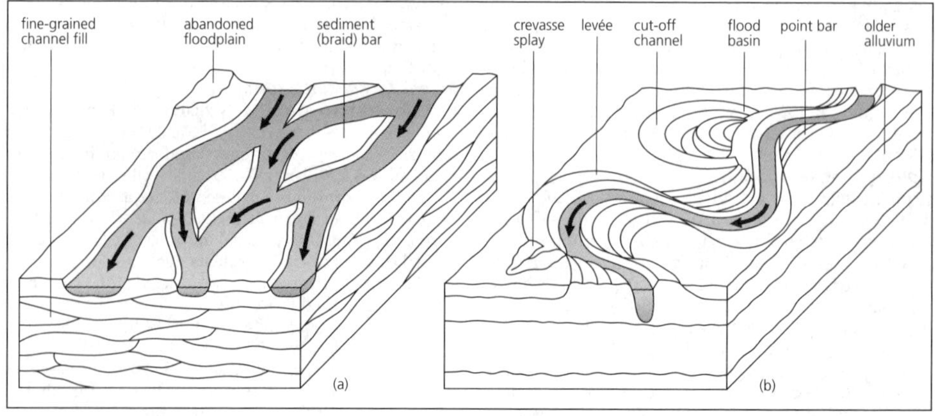

Sections of river channels showing a braided river (a) with cross-stratified gravels and sand, and a meandering river (b) with levées.

Rivers, Joan, professional name of **Joan Alexandra Molinsky** (1933–) Comedienne and writer, born in Larchmont, NY. The regular guest host of *The Tonight Show* (1983–6), she went on to host *The Late Show* (1986–7) and her own daytime talk show in 1989. She has also worked as a film director and recording artist, and her books include *Bouncing Back* (1997).

Riviera The Mediterranean coast between Toulon, France, and La Spezia, Italy. It is a narrow coastal strip bordered by the Alps to the N, and includes many holiday resorts.

Riyadh [ri**yad**], Arabic **Ar Riyad** 24°41N 46°42E, pop (1995e) 2 602 000. Capital city of Saudi Arabia; formerly a walled city; airport; railway; communications centre; three universities (1950, 1957, 1984); over 1000 mosques. >> Saudi Arabia [i]

Rizzio, David [**rit**sioh], also spelled **Riccio** (?1533–1566) Courtier and musician, born in Pancalieri, Italy. He entered the service of Mary, Queen of Scots in 1561, and was made her French secretary in 1564. He negotiated her marriage with Darnley (1565), who became jealous of his influence, and plotted his death. >> Darnley; Mary, Queen of Scots

RNA or **ribonucleic acid** A nucleic acid found throughout the cell, distinguished from DNA by the substitution of the pyrimidine base, uracil, for thymine. **Nuclear RNA** is formed as a complementary strand to a section of DNA base sequences. The intron sequences are then excised to give mature **messenger RNA**, which passes through the nuclear membrane to the ribosomes in the cytoplasm. **Transfer RNA** collects the free amino acids in the cytoplasm, and transports them to the ribosomes, where they are laid down in the sequence dictated by the messenger RNA. >> amino acid; cell; DNA [i]

Roach, Hal, popular name of **Harald Eugene Roach** (1892–92) Film producer, born in Elmira, NY. In 1914 he formed a production company to make short silent comedies, whose players included Harold Lloyd and Will Hays, and after 1928 continued with sound. In 1984 he was given a Special Academy Award for his achievements.

roach Freshwater fish (*Rutilus rutilus*) found in rivers and lakes of Europe; body moderately deep, length up to 45 cm/18 in; greenish-brown on back, sides silver, pelvic and anal fins red. (Family: Cyprinidae.) >> fish [i]

roadrunner A ground-dwelling cuckoo, native to SW USA and Central America; long tail and legs; head with short crest. (Genus: *Geococcyx*, 2 species.) >> cuckoo

Road Town 18°26N 64°32W, pop (1992e) 3000. Seaport and capital of the British Virgin Is, E Caribbean. >> Virgin Islands, British

Roanoke [**roh**anohk] 37°16N 79°56W, pop (1995e) 104 000. City in SW Virginia, USA, on the Roanoke R; settled, 1740; airfield; railway. >> Virginia

Roaring Forties >> **westerlies**

Robbe-Grillet, Alain [rob **gree**yay] (1922–) Novelist, born in Brest, France. After his first novel, *Les Gommes* (1953, The Erasers), he emerged as the leader of the *nouveau roman* group, contributing to the form such novels as *La Jalousie* (1959, Jealousy). He has also written film scenarios, notably *L'Année dernière à Marienbad* (1961, Last Year at Marienbad). >> *nouveau roman*

robber fly An active, predatory fly commonly found in open sunny habitats; forelegs robust, armed with strong bristles for gripping insect prey caught in flight. (Order: Diptera. Family: Asilidae, c.5000 species.) >> fly

robbery The taking of personal property from the person or immediate presence of another against his or her will through the use of violence or intimidation. A threat of violence is sufficient. >> theft

Robbia, Luca della (c.1400–82) Sculptor, born in Florence, Italy. He executed ten panels of figures for the cathedral there (1431–40), and later made a bronze door with ten panels of figures in relief for its sacristy (1448–67). He is also known for his figures in terracotta. >> terracotta

Robbins, Jerome (1918–98) Dancer, choreographer, and director, born in New York City. His collaboration with Leonard Bernstein resulted in his most famous musical, *West Side Story* (1957). >> Bernstein, Leonard; choreography

Robbins (of Clare Market), Lionel Charles Robbins, Baron (1898–1984) Economist and educationist, born in Sipson, Greater London. Professor of economics at the London School of Economics (1929–61), he chaired the **Robbins Committee** on the expansion of higher education in the UK (1961–4). >> higher education

Robbins, Tim (1958–) Film actor, director, and writer, born in West Govina, CA. He wrote, directed, and composed the songs for the critically acclaimed *Bob Roberts* (1992). His films include (as actor) *The Shawshank Redemption* (1994) and *The Moviegoer* (1998) and (as producer, director, and writer) *Dead Man Walking* (1995).

Robert I >> **Bruce, Robert**

Robert II (1316–90) King of Scots (1371–90), the son of

Walter, hereditary steward of Scotland. He founded the Stuart royal dynasty. >> Stuarts

Robert, Duke of Normandy >> **Henry I** (of England)

Roberts (of Kandahar, Pretoria, and Waterford), Frederick Sleigh Roberts, 1st Earl (1832–1914) British field marshal, born in Cawnpore, India. He served as supreme commander in South Africa during the Boer War, relieving Kimberley (1900). >> Boer Wars; Kimberley, Siege of

Roberts, Julia (1967–) US film actress, born in Smyrna, GA. She made her screen debut in 1988, and became well known following *Steel Magnolias* (1989) and *Pretty Woman* (1990). Later films include *Hook* (1991), *The Pelican Brief* (1993), and *Stepmom* (1998).

Roberts, Tom (1856–1931) Painter, born in Dorchester, Dorset. His best work, which deals with pioneering life in the bush, was produced in Australia in the late 1880s and 1890s.

Robertson, George (Islay MacNeill) (1946–) British statesman, born in Dunoon, Argyll, and Bute, Scotland. He was elected an MP in 1978, rising to be spokesman on Scotland in the shadow cabinet (1993–7). He became defence secretary in the 1997 Labour government.

Robeson, Paul (Bustill) [**roh**bsn] (1898–1976) Singer and actor, born in Princeton, NJ. He appeared in works ranging from *Show Boat* to *Othello*, gave song recitals, notably of Negro spirituals, and appeared in numerous films. In the 1950s, his left-wing views caused him to leave the USA for Europe (1958–63), and he retired after his return.

Robespierre, Maximilien François Marie Isidore de [rohbspyair] (1758–94) French revolutionary leader, born in Arras. He became a prominent member of the Jacobin Club, and emerged in the National Assembly as a popular radical, known as 'the Incorruptible'. In 1793 he became a member of the Committee of Public Safety and for three months dominated the country, introducing the Reign of Terror and the cult of the Supreme Being. But as his ruthless exercise of power increased, his popularity waned. He was guillotined on the orders of the Revolutionary Tribunal. >> French Revolution ℹ; Jacobins (French history)

Robey, Sir George [**roh**bee], originally **George Edward Wade** (1869–1954) Comedian, born in Herne Hill, Kent. Dubbed 'the Prime Minister of Mirth', he was famous for his bowler hat, black coat, hooked stick, and thickly painted eyebrows.

robin A bird of the thrush family Turdidae (44 species), usually with a red breast; especially the Eurasian/N African robin (*Erithacus rubecula*); traditionally seen as a symbol of Christmas. >> thrush (bird)

Robin Goodfellow In English 16th-c and 17th-c popular belief, a mischievous fairy, also called **Puck** or **Hobgoblin**. His characteristic activities are listed in *A Midsummer Night's Dream* (2.i).

Robin Hood A legendary 13th-c outlaw, known for his archery, who lived in Sherwood Forest in the English N Midlands, celebrated in ballads dating from the 14th-c. He protected the poor, and outwitted, robbed, or killed the wealthy and officials, notably the Sheriff of Nottingham. >> Peasants' Revolt

Robinson, Edward G, originally **Emanuel Goldenberg** (1893–1973) Film actor, born in Bucharest, Romania. He became famous as the gangster Rico in *Little Caesar* (1930), a typecasting which dogged him for many years. He was posthumously awarded a special Academy Award in 1973. >> McCarthy, Joseph R

Robinson, Edwin Arlington (1869–1935) Poet, born in Head Tide, ME. He received Pulitzer Prizes for his *Collected Poems* (1922), *The Man Who Died Twice* (1924), and *Tristram* (1927).

Robinson, (William) Heath (1872–1944) Artist, cartoonist, and book illustrator, born in London. His fame rests mainly on his humorous drawings satirizing the machine age, displaying 'Heath Robinson' contraptions of absurd and complicated design but with highly practical and simple aims, such as the raising of one's hat.

Robinson, Joan V(iolet), *née* **Maurice** (1903–83) Economist, born in Camberley, Surrey. She was one of the most influential economic theorists of her time, and a leader of the Cambridge School, which developed macro-economic theories of growth and distribution, based on the work of Keynes. >> Keynes; economics

Robinson, Jackie, popular name of **Jack Roosevelt Robinson** (1919–72) The first black player to play major league baseball, born in Cairo, GA. He became a star infielder and outfielder for the Brooklyn Dodgers (1947–56), and led them to six National League pennants and one World Series, in 1955. >> baseball ℹ

Robinson, Mary, *née* **Bourke** (1944–) Irish politician and president (1990–7), born in Ballina, Mayo, Ireland. She left the Labour Party in protest against the Anglo-Irish Agreement (1985), then returned to run for President of Ireland. Against all the odds she defeated Brian Lenihan of the Fianna Fáil Party to take office as Ireland's first woman president. In 1997 she became the UN High Commisioner for Human Rights. >> Anglo-Irish Agreement; Ireland (republic) ℹ

Robinson, Sugar Ray, originally **Walker Smith** (1920–89) Professional boxer, born in Detroit, MI. He turned professional in 1940, and was never knocked out in 201 contests. He held the world welterweight title (1946–51) and the world middleweight title (1950–1). >> boxing ℹ

roble beech A tree similar to the beech, and replacing that genus in the S hemisphere; also called **southern beech**. It differs chiefly by having nuts in threes, enclosed in a spiny or scaly case. (Genus: *Nothofagus*, 35 species. Family: Fagaceae.) >> beech

robotics (cybernetics) The application of automatic machines (*robots*) to perform tasks traditionally done by humans. Robots are widely used in industry to perform simple repetitive tasks accurately and without tiring, and to work in environments which are dangerous to human operators. They can also be used as sensors, equipped for artificial vision, touch, and temperature sensing. If the robots are in human form, they are called *androids*. >> automation

robotics (dance) >> **street dance**

Rob Roy (Gaelic 'Red Robert'), nickname of **Robert MacGregor** or **Campbell** (1671–1734) Outlaw, born in Buchanan, Stirling, Scotland. After his lands were seized by the Duke of Montrose, he gathered his clansmen and became a brigand. His career gave rise to many stories about his brave exploits. His life was romanticized in the novel by Sir Walter Scott.

Robson, Dame Flora (McKenzie) (1902–84) Actress, born in South Shields, Durham. She became famous for her historical roles in plays and films, such as Queen Elizabeth in *Fire over England* (1931).

Rochas, Marcel [rosha] (1902–55) Fashion designer, born in Paris. He set up a couture house in Paris in 1925, launching his first fragrances in 1931, and the sheepskin jacket in 1942. The couture house closed upon his death in 1955, but his wife Hélène took over the perfume department until she left the company in 1989.

Rochdale 53°38N 2°09W, pop (1995e) 97 500. Town in Greater Manchester, NW England; railway; textiles (especially cotton); Co-operative Society founded here in 1844; football league team, Rochdale. >> Manchester, Greater

Rochester (UK), ancient **Durobrivae** 51°24N 0°30E, pop (1995e) 25 200. Town in Kent, SE England; railway; cathedral (12th-c); castle (11th-c). >> Kent

Rochester (NY, USA) 43°10N 77°37W, pop (1995e) 236 000. City in W New York, USA; port on Genesee R; first settled, 1811; city status, 1834; airfield; railway; university (1850). >> New York (state)

rock A naturally occurring material which comprises the solid Earth. Rocks are an assemblage of minerals, and are classified according to origin. >> igneous / metamorphic / sedimentary rock; petrology

rock ape >> **Barbary ape**

rock art >> **Palaeolithic / Paleolithic art**

Rockefeller, John D(avison) [rokuhfeler] (1839–1937) Industrialist and philanthropist, born in Richford, NY. In 1875 he founded with his brother **William Rockefeller** (1841–1922) the Standard Oil Company, securing control of the US oil trade. He gave over $500 million in aid of medical research, universities, and churches, and established in 1913 the **Rockefeller Foundation** 'to promote the wellbeing of mankind'. His son, **John D Rockefeller, Jr** (1847–1960) built the Rockefeller Center in New York City. His third son, **Nelson A(ldrich) Rockefeller** (1908–79), became Republican Governor of New York State (1958–73), and was vice-president (1974–7) under President Ford. >> Ford, Gerald R; Republican Party

Rockefeller Center A complex of 14 skyscrapers commissioned by John D Rockefeller Jr (1874–1960) and built (1931–40) in Manhattan, New York City. The centre includes the Radio City Music Hall. >> New York City; Rockefeller

rocket A self-propelling device in which the fuel substances needed to produce the propulsion are carried internally. The term most commonly refers to space vehicles, although it can also apply to distress rockets and fireworks. In addition, rockets are used to power missiles, and for supersonic and assisted-take-off aeroplane propulsion. **Solid fuel rockets** commonly use a mixture of nitrocellulose and nitroglycerin as the fuel source. The more efficient **liquid fuel rockets** use kerosene (fuel) and liquid oxygen (oxidant). >> launch vehicle 🅘; oxygen

Rockhampton 23°22S 150°32E, pop (1995e) 62 800. City in Queensland, Australia, on the Fitzroy R; railway; university (1992); centre of Australia's largest beef-producing area. >> Queensland

Rockingham, Charles Watson Wentworth, 2nd Marquess of (1730–82) British statesman and prime minister (1765–6, 1782). He repealed the Stamp Act, affecting the American colonies, and opposed Britain's war against the colonists. He died soon after taking office in 1782. >> American Revolution; Stamp Act

rock music A type of popular music, originally called **rock and roll**, which spread throughout the USA and Europe in the 1950s. It began as a basically simple musical style, dominated by a strong dance beat and by the use of the electric guitar. It developed out of country and western, and more particularly from rhythm and blues – a style which previously had been played almost exclusively by US black artists. The term 'rock and roll' was popularized by Cleveland disc jockey Alan Freed. The music gained widespread popularity during the late 1950s, when major artists included Bill Haley, Elvis Presley, and Chuck Berry. Primarily aimed at and enjoyed by a young audience, it became an important symbol of teenage rebellion. Since then, rock music has diversified into a distinct series of subgenres – such as **hard rock** in the late 1960s and early 1970s and **punk rock** in the late 1970s – most of which have been characterized not only by musical differences but by their own associated features in dress, lifestyle, and (since the 1980s) video publicity. >> Beatles, The; Berry; country and western; Dylan; Haley; Hendrix; pop music; Presley; punk rock; rhythm and blues; Rolling Stones, The

rockrose A small evergreen shrub, mostly native to the Mediterranean region and parts of Asia; flowers 5-petalled, white, yellow, or red. (Genus: *Helianthemum*, 100 species. Family: Cistaceae.)

rock salt >> **halite**

Rocky Mountain goat A wild goat (*Oreamnos americanus*) native to the mountains of North America; thick shaggy white coat and short backward-curved horns; also known as **mountain goat**, **goat antelope**, or **antelope goat**. >> goat

Rocky Mountains or **Rockies** Major mountain system of W North America, extending from C New Mexico generally NNW through the USA, into W Canada and N Alaska and reaching the Bering Strait N of the Arctic Circle; about 4800 km/3000 mi long; forms the continental divide, separating the Pacific drainage from the Atlantic and Arctic; highest point in the USA Mt Elbert (4399 m/14 432 ft), in Canada Mt Robson (3954 m/12 972 ft) important source of mineral wealth; several national parks. >> North America

Rocky Mountain sheep >> **bighorn**

Rococo [ro**koh**koh] (Fr *rocaille*, 'rock-work') In art history, the period following the late Baroque in European art and design. It flourished especially in France and S Germany c.1700–50, until superseded by the Neoclassical taste spreading from Rome. Rococo sought effects of charm and delicacy on a small scale – surface effects rather than bold masses. It was therefore most successful as a style of interior decoration. >> Baroque (art and architecture); Watteau

Roddenberry, Gene, popular name of **Eugene Wesley Roddenberry** (1921–91) Writer, and film and television producer, born in El Paso, TX. A former pilot and policeman, he became a full-time writer in the 1950s. He is best known as the creator and producer of *Star Trek*, and the originator of the phrase 'Beam me up, Scottie'. >> *Star Trek*

Roddick, Anita (Lucia) (1943–) Retail entrepreneur, born in Brighton, East Sussex. In 1976 she opened a small shop in Brighton selling beauty products made from natural products, not tested on animals, and supplied in refillable containers. Her growing commitment to ecology and the Third World brought great success to the Body Shop chain in the 1980s. >> ecology

rodent A mammal of worldwide order Rodentia (3 suborders, 30 families, 1702 species); 40% of all living mammal species are rodents; chisel-like upper and lower incisor teeth grow continuously, kept short by gnawing. >> beaver; cavy; hamster; jerboa; kangaroo rat; mouse; porcupine; squirrel

rodeo A US sport, consisting mainly of competitive riding and a range of skills which derive from cowboy ranching practices. The events include bronco riding, with and without saddle, bull riding, steer wrestling, calf roping, and team roping.

Rodgers, Richard >> **Hammerstein, Oscar**

Rodin, (René François) Auguste [rohdĩ] (1840–1917) Sculptor, born in Paris. The great 'La Porte de l'enfer' (The Gate of Hell) was commissioned for the Musée des Arts Décoratifs in 1880. Among his other works is 'Le Penseur' (1904, The Thinker), in front of the Panthéon in Paris.

Rodrigues Island [roh**dree**gez] 19°45S 63°20E, pop (1995e) 39 900. Island in the Indian Ocean; part of the Mascarene Is; a dependency of Mauritius; rises to 396 m/1299 ft at Mt Limon; chief town, Port Mathurin. >> Mauritius 🅘

rods and cones Photoreceptor cells of the vertebrate retina, so called because of their shapes. Rods are sensitive to dim light (*scotopic*) and function at twilight. Cones are sensitive to bright light (*photopic*) and function in daylight. >> colour vision; eye 🅘; retina

Roentgen, Wilhelm Konrad von >> **Röntgen**

Rogation Days In the Christian Church, the three days before Ascension Day, once observed with fasting, processions, and prayers to God for a successful harvest (**rogations**, Lat *rogare*, 'to ask').

Rogers, Carl R(ansom) (1902–87) Psychotherapist, born in Oak Park, IL. His book *Client-centered Therapy* (1951) developed the notion of open therapy sessions and encounter groups in which patients talk out their problems under the supervision of a passive therapist. >> encounter group; group therapy; psychotherapy

Rogers, Ginger >> **Astaire, Fred**

Roget, Peter Mark [**ro**zhay] (1779–1869) Scholar and physician, born in London. He is best known for his *Thesaurus of English Words and Phrases* (1852).

Röhm, Ernst [roem], also spelled **Roehm** (1887–1934) German soldier, politician and Nazi leader, born in Munich, Germany. The organizer and commander of the stormtroopers ('Brownshirts'), his plans to increase the power of this force led to his execution on Hitler's orders. >> Night of the Long Knives

Rolfe, Frederick William (Serafino Austin Lewis Mary), pseudonym **Baron Corvo** (1860–1913) Novelist, historian, and essayist, born in London. He converted to Roman Catholicism, but failed in his efforts to join the priesthood. His best-known novel is *Hadrian the Seventh* (1904).

Rolland, Romain [rolã] (1866–1944) Writer, born in Clamecy, France. He published several biographies and a 10-volume novel, *Jean-Christophe* (1904–12), and in 1915 was awarded the Nobel Prize for Literature.

roller A crow-like bird of the widespread Old World family Coraciidae (11 species); usually blue and brown; somersaults in flight when displaying (hence its name). >> crow

roller skating A pastime first seen in Liège, Belgium, in 1760. The modern four-wheeled skate was introduced by the US inventor James L Plymton in 1863. Competitions exist as for ice skating: individual, pairs, dancing, and speed skating. Blade-type skates are now replacing the corner-wheel model. >> ice skating; RR1058

Rolling Stones, The Rock group, with members **Mick Jagger** (1943–) vocals, **Keith Richards** (1943–) guitar, **Bill Wyman** (1941–) bass, **Charlie Watts** (1942–) drums, **Ron Wood** (1947–) guitar, former member **Brian Jones** (1944–69) guitar, one of the most successful popular music groups to emerge in the 1960s. They first performed together in 1962. Among their hits were 'Satisfaction' and 'Jumpin' Jack Flash'. >> rock music

Rollo, originally **Hrolf** (c.860–c.932) Viking leader who secured from Charles III of France in 911 a large district on condition of being baptized and becoming Charles's vassal. This grant was the nucleus of the duchy of Normandy. >> Normans; Vikings

Rolls, C(harles) S(tewart) (1877–1910) Motorist and aeronaut, born in London. From 1895 he experimented with the earliest motor cars, and combined with Henry Royce for their production. >> car [i]; Rolls-Royce; Royce, Henry

Rolls-Royce A major British firm of car engine and aero-engine manufacturers, founded in 1906. In the 1970s the firm was split into two separate companies, following financial problems caused by the high cost of aero-engine research and development. >> Rolls; Royce, Henry

ROM [rom] Acronym of **read-only memory**, a type of computer memory which can only be read from; the data is fixed during the manufacture of the chip. ROM is used where the data does not have to be altered. >> EAROM; EPROM; PROM; RAM

Rom A travelling people whose origins lie in the subcontinent of India, now concentrated in S Europe, but found throughout the world; popularly called **Gypsies**, but not by the people themselves. 'Traveller' is generally the preferred term in Britain. There are an estimated 9–12 million Rom today, worldwide. >> Romani

Romains, Jules [romĩ], pseudonym of **Louis Farigoule** (1885–1972) Writer, born in Saint-Julien-Chapteuil, France. His poems *La Vie unanime* (1908) brought about the Unanimist school, devoted to a belief in universal brotherhood and group consciousness. His best-known works are the comedy *Knock, ou le triomphe de la médecine* (1923, Dr Knock, or the triumph of medicine) and the 27-volume cycle of novels, *Les Hommes de bonne volonté* (1932–46, Men of Good Will).

Roman Catholicism The doctrine, worship, and life of the Roman Catholic Church. A direct line of succession is claimed from the earliest Christian communities, centring on the city of Rome, where St Peter (claimed as the first bishop of Rome) was martyred. The Church was the only effective agency of civilization in Europe, and after the 11th-c schism with the Byzantine or Eastern Church, it was the dominant force in the Western world, the Holy Roman Empire. The Protestant Reformation of the 16th-c inspired revival, the most dramatic reforms being enacted by the two Vatican Councils of the 19th-c and 20th-c. The Second Vatican Council (1962–5) signalled a new era, with a new ecumenical spirit pervading the Church. Great emphasis was placed on the Church as the 'people of God', with the laity being given a much more active part in liturgy. Doctrine is declared by the pope, or by a General Council with the approval of the pope, and is summarized in the Nicene Creed. Scripture and the tradition of the Church are both accepted as authoritative. Principal doctrines are similar to those of mainstream Protestant and Orthdox Churches – God as Trinity, creation, redemption, the person and work of Jesus Christ, and the place of the Holy Spirit – the chief doctrinal differences being the role of the Church in salvation, and its sacramental theology. Ancient traditional practices such as the veneration of the Virgin Mary and the Saints, or the Stations of the Cross, are still regarded as valuable aids to devotion. >> Aquinas; Bible; Council of the Church; Mary (mother of Jesus); Mass; Peter, St; pope; Reformation, Catholic; sacrament; Stations of the Cross; Trinity; Vatican Councils

Romance languages The languages which developed from the 'vulgar' or spoken form of Latin used throughout the Roman Empire. The major ones are Italian, French, Spanish, Portuguese, and Romanian, all of which are official languages in their respective states. There are also several other varieties, such as Sardinian, Rhaetian (dialectal variants in N Italy and Switzerland), and Catalan, used mainly in NE Spain. Over 700 million people now speak a Romance language or a creole based on one. French is spoken by c.72 million as a mother-tongue, and is used as a second language by a further 200 million; Spanish is spoken by over 270 million; Portuguese by c.175 million; and Italian by c.63 million. >> creole; Indo-European languages

Roman Curia (Lat *curia*, 'court') An organization in the Vatican (Rome) which administers the affairs of the Roman Catholic Church under the authority of the pope. It is comprised of congregations (administrative), tribunals (judicial), and offices (ministerial). >> Roman Catholicism; Vatican City

Roman history The Monarchy (753–509 BC). Founded, according to tradition, in 753 BC, Rome was initially ruled by kings, of whom Romulus was the first and Tarquinius Superbus the seventh and last. **The Republic** (509–31 BC). Brought into being with the overthrow of the monarchy, the Republican system of government was designed to

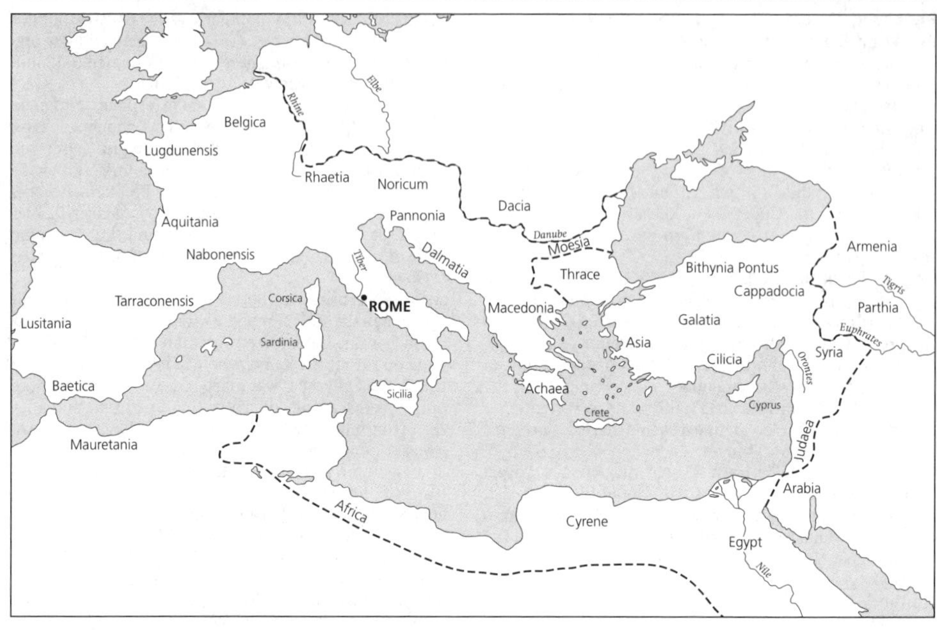

The Roman Empire in the 1st century AD

prevent a tyrant ever ruling Rome again. Executive power was entrusted to two annually elected officials (*consuls*); their advisory council, the Senate, provided the necessary elements of experience and continuity. The system brought stability, and Rome grew rapidly from a small city-state into an empire. The Republic perished at Actium after decades of civil war. **The Empire** (31 BC–AD 476 in the W, AD 1453 in the E). The Roman Empire was the creation of one man, Augustus. Pretending that he had restored the Republic, in reality he and his successors were absolute monarchs. Abroad, the expansionism of Republican days was abandoned, and territorial limits were set – the Rhine and Danube in Europe, the Euphrates in Asia. Subsequent modifications were few; Britain (43), Dacia, and Arabia (both annexed by Trajan in 106) were the only significant later additions. The Rhine–Danube frontier was the hardest to hold, and in the 5th-c, hordes of tribesmen (eg Huns, Vandals, Ostrogoths) poured into the W provinces carrying all before them. The last emperor, Romulus Augustulus, was deposed in 476. The E provinces proved more resilient; here the barbarian challenge was contained for another thousand years, until the E capital Constantinople fell to the Ottoman Turks in 1453. >> Actium, Battle of; Augustus (Octavian); consul 1; Gallic Wars; Punic Wars; Roman roads; Senate, Roman; *see illustration above and on p.735*

Romani The language of the Gypsies, of Indo-Aryan origin, earlier spelled **Romany**. There are now many dialects, which have taken on features of the languages with which they have come into contact in various parts of the world. >> Gypsy; Indo-Aryan languages; Rom

Romania, **Roumania**, or **Rumania**, official name **Republic of Romania**, Romanian **Republica România** pop (1995e) 23 033 000; area 237 500 sq km/91 675 sq mi. Republic in SE Europe; capital, Bucharest; timezone GMT +2; population mainly Romanian (89%), with Hungarian and Romani minorities; chief religion, Eastern Orthodox Christianity (80%); official language, Romanian, with French widely spoken; unit of currency, the leu of 100 bani; Carpathian Mts form the heart of the country; highest peak, Negoiul (2548 m/8359 ft); crossed by many rivers; c.3500 glacial ponds, lakes, and coastal lagoons; over a quarter of the land forested; continental climate, with cold, snowy winters and warm summers; mildest area in winter along the Black Sea coast; formed from the unification of Moldavia and Wallachia, 1862; monarchy created, 1866; Transylvania, Bessarabia, and Bucovina united with Romania, 1918; support given to Germany in World War 2; occupied by Soviet forces, 1944; monarchy abolished and People's Republic declared, 1947; Socialist Republic declared, 1965; increasingly independent of the USSR from the 1960s; leading political force was the Romanian Communist Party, led by dictator Nicolae Ceauşescu; violent repression of protest sparked a popular uprising and the overthrow of the Ceauşescu regime, 1989; new constitution, 1991, provided for an elected president and prime minister, a Chamber of Deputies and a Senate; since World War 2, a gradual change from an agricultural to an industrial economy; state owns nearly 37% of farm land, mainly organized as collectives and state farms. >> Bucharest; Carpathian Mountains; Ceauşescu; Moldavia and Wallachia; Transylvania; RR1020 political leaders; *see illustration on p. 735*

Romanian >> **Romance languages**

romanization The use of the Roman alphabet to replace a language's writing system constructed on a different principle. This procedure has been very common in language planning, especially in countries where the native script is non-alphabetic in character, as in Chinese logographic writing. >> alphabet [i]; logography

Roman numerals The Roman symbols for numbers, which have a fixed value, and do not use the concept of place-value. The symbols generally used are I = 1, V = 5, X = 10, L = 50, C = 100, D = 500, and M = 1000. A symbol may be repeated up to three times (eg XVIII = 18). >> numeral

Romanovs [**roh**manofs] The second (and last) Russian royal dynasty (1613–1917). The first Romanov tsar (Mikhail) was elected in 1613. The Romanovs ruled as absolute autocrats, allowing no constitutional or legal checks on their political power. The dynasty ended with the execution of Nicholas II in 1918. >> Alexander I; Catherine II; Nicholas II; Peter I; Russian Revolution

Roman roads A network of usually straight roads radiating from ancient Rome. Built primarily for military purposes, the roads also served an important commercial function. The Appian Way, built in the 3rd-c BC and linking Rome with present-day Capua, was the first great Roman road.

Romans, Letter to the A New Testament book, written by the apostle Paul in c.55–8, which presents his understanding of salvation for both Gentiles and Jews, and warns against libertine and legalistic interpretations of the Christian message. >> New Testament; Paul, St

Romanticism A large-scale movement of the mind in the late 18th/early 19th-c, which affected the whole of human understanding and experience. Romanticism placed the individual at the centre of his/her own world, and permitted the free expression of feeling and emotion. Writers associated with Romanticism are, in England, Wordsworth, Coleridge, Blake, Keats, Shelley, and Byron; in Germany, Goethe and Schiller; in France, Rousseau and Hugo. Artists included Turner, Constable, and Goya. In music, the period saw the growth of the modern symphony orchestra, and a general expansion of the inherited genres of opera, symphony, concerto, etc, in which composers could express a response to literature and the other arts. The works of the major Romantic composers (eg Beethoven, Mahler, Wagner) form the staple repertory of modern concert halls and opera houses.

Romany >> Rom; Romani

Romberg, Sigmund (1887–1951) Composer of operettas born in Nagykanizsa, Hungary. He settled in the USA 1909. Of more than 70 works, his most famous *Blossom Time* (1921), *The Student Prince* (1924), *The Deser* (1926), and *The New Moon* (1928). >> operetta

Rome, Ital **Roma** 41°53N 12°30E, pop (1995e) 2 Capital city of Italy; on the R Tiber; on the left bank are the Seven Hills of Rome – the Capitoline (50 m/165 ft), Quirinal (52 m/172 ft), Viminal (56 m/185 ft), Esquiline (53 m/175 ft), Palatine (51 m/168 ft), Aventine (46 m/152 ft), and Caelian (50 m/165 ft) – on which the ancient city was built during the 8th-c BC; centre of the Roman Empire; sacked by Germanic tribes, 5th-c; ecclesiastical centre from 6th-c; Vatican City on W bank; capital of unified Italy, 1871; two airports; railway; metro; university (1303); important centre of fashion and film; headquarters of many cultural and research institutions; centre of Rome is a world heritage site; Palazzo Venezia (15th-c), Forum Romanum (AD 113), Colosseum (from AD 75), Pantheon (27 BC), Trevi Fountain (1762); numerous churches, notably St Peter's (in the Vatican), St John Lateran (Rome's cathedral). >> Capitoline Hill; Italy ℹ; Lateran Treaty; Roman history ℹ; St Peter's Basilica; Sistine Chapel; Terme; Vatican City

Rome, Treaties of >> **EURATOM; European Community**

Rommel, Erwin (Johannes Eugen) (1891–1944) German field marshal, born in Heidenheim, Germany. He led a Panzer division during the 1940 invasion of France, then commanded the Afrika Korps, where he achieved major successes, but was eventually driven into retreat. He condoned the plot against Hitler's life, and after its discovery committed suicide. >> El Alamein, Battle of; World War 2

Romney, George [**rom**nee, **ruhm**nee] (1734–1802) Painter, born in Dalton-in-Furness, Lancashire. His reputation rivalled that of Reynolds, his many pictures of Lady Hamilton being particularly well known. >> Reynolds, Joshua

Romulus and Remus [**rom**yulus, **ree**mus] In Roman legend, the twin sons of Mars and the Vestal Virgin Rhea

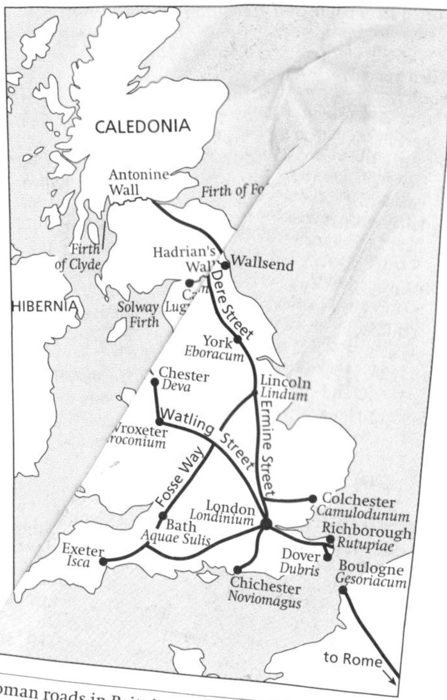

ief Roman roads in Britain

Silvia. They were thrown into the Tiber, which carried them to the Palatine, where they were suckled by a she-wolf. In building the wall of Rome, Remus was killed by Romulus. Having founded Rome, Romulus was later carried off in a thunderstorm. >> Roman history 🛈

Romulus Augustulus [**rom**yulus aw**guhs**tyulus] (5th-c AD) The last Roman emperor of the West, deposed by Odoacer in 476. >> Odoacer; Roman history 🛈

Ronaldo (Luiz Nazario de Lima) [ro**nal**doh], nickname **Ro-Ro** (1976–) Footballer, born in Bento Ribero, Brazil. A forward, he played for Cruzeiro, Brazil, then PSV Eindhoven and Barcelona, moving to Inter Milan in 1997. He has been twice International Footballer of the Year (1996, 1997) and European Player of the Year (1997, 1998). By mid-1998 he had won 40 caps playing for Brazil.

Ronay, Egon [**ro**nay, **ee**gon] (1920–) Gastronome and writer, born in Hungary. He emigrated to England in 1946 and opened his own restaurant in London (1952–5). He founded his first annual guide, *Egon Ronay's Guide to Hotels and Restaurants*, in 1956.

roncey >> **cob**

rondo A musical structure in which restatements of the initial theme are separated by contrasting episodes, eg on the pattern A–B–A–C–A–B–A, perhaps with an introduction and a coda.

Ronsard, Pierre de [rõsah(r)] (1524–85) Renaissance poet, born in La Possonière, France. A leader of the *Pléiade* group, his early works include *Odes* (1550) and *Amours* (1552), and he later wrote reflections on the state of the country. >> Pléiade, La

Röntgen, Wilhelm Konrad von [**roent**guhn], also spelled **Roentgen** (1845–1923) Physicist, born in Lennep, Germany. In 1895 he discovered the electromagnetic rays which he called X-rays, for which he was awarded the first Nobel Prize for Physics in 1901. >> rad; rem; X-rays

röntgen or **roentgen** [**ront**guhn, -juhn] The unit of exposure to ionizing radiation; symbol *R*; named after Wilhelm Röntgen. >> radiation; Röntgen

Röntgen rays >> **X-rays**

rook A crow (*Corvus frugilegus*) native to Europe, Asia, and N Africa; black with pale bare patch on face; forms dense nesting colonies in trees (*rookeries*). >> crow

Roon, Albrecht (Theodor Emil), Graf (Count) **von** (1803–79) Prussian army officer, born near Kolberg, Poland. He became [illegible]ar minister (1859–73), and effectively reorganized the [illegible]my, which helped make possible Prussian victories in [illegible] wars of the 1860s and 1870s. >> Austro–Prussian Wa[illegible]anco–Prussian War

Rooney, Mickey, origin[illegible] **Joe Yule, Jr** (1920–) Film actor, born in New York [illegible] He became known for his child roles in the Mickey [illegible] later [illegible]ire (1927–33) and Andy Hardy (1937–8) series, *Babes in* [illegible] including *Boy's Town* (1938, Special Oscar), *Breakfast at Tiffany's* [illegible]939), *Summer Holiday* (1948), and including once to [illegible]). He was married eight times, He returned to the stage in 197[illegible]ress Ava Gardner. *Babes*, and won an Emmy for hi[illegible]e musical *Sugar* (1982). He wrote and acted in *The* [illegible]on role in *Bill* [illegible]*f O B Taggart* (1995).

Roosevelt, (Anna) Eleanor [ro[illegible] **rooz**velt] (1884–1962) US first lady, the wife of Fr[illegible] Roosevelt and the niece of Theodore Roosevelt. [illegible] activist, she had a strong part in shapin[illegible]endent her husband's New Deal administration. [illegible]ies of owhood she was a major figure in Democra[illegible] wid-tics. >> New Deal; Roosevelt, Franklin D [illegible]li-

Roosevelt, Franklin D(elano) [**rohz**uhvelt] nickname **FDR** (1882–1945) US Democratic state[illegible] 32nd president (1933–45), born in Hyde Park, N[illegible] the economic crisis with his *New Deal* for nationa[illegible]ery (1933), and became the only president to be re-elected three times. He strove in vain to ward off war, and was brought in by Japan's action at Pearl Harbor (1941). He met with Churchill and Stalin at Teheran (1943) and Yalta (1945). >> New Deal; World War 2

Roosevelt, Theodore [**rohz**uhvelt, **rooz**velt], known as **Teddy Roosevelt** (1858–1919) US statesman and 26th president (1901–9), born in New York City. Elected Republican vice-president in 1900, he became president on the death (by assassination) of McKinley, and was re-elected in 1904. An 'expansionist', he insisted on a strong navy, and introduced a *Square Deal* policy for social reform. >> McKinley, William; Republican Party; Square Deal

Root, Elihu (1845–1937) US statesman, born in Clinton, NY. He was awarded the Nobel Peace Prize in 1912 for his promotion of international arbitration.

root The part of a plant's axis which usually lies underground, absorbing water and nutrients, and anchoring the plant in the soil; also commonly serving as a storage organ. It develops either by repeated branching to form a mass of fibrous **lateral roots** or by forming a central **tap-root** with relatively few laterals. Roots can be modified in various ways to add to their functions. **Pneumatophores** are specialized breathing roots developed in swampy, oxygen-poor ground. Roots which develop above ground are called **aerial roots**; they grow from stems or leaves, and absorb moisture direct from the atmosphere. Other types of aerial root include **buttress** or **prop roots**, which help support the stem or trunk, and **climbing** and **adhesive** roots, which help to elevate the plant. >> epiphyte; mycorrhiza; photosynthesis; rhizoid; stem (botany); symbiosis

root The basic element of a word, to which affixes can be added to give derived forms. For example, from the root *kind*, we may derive *un-kind*, *kind-ly*, *kind-ness*, etc. A root to which other elements have been added, so that the form can serve as the basis for inflections, is known as a **stem**.

rope A length of thick fibre used to secure objects together. The fibres are twisted or plaited for added strength, and can be natural (eg hemp, sisal, flax, jute, cotton) or synthetic (eg nylon, polyester). Wire ropes are also used as cables on suspension bridges. >> fibres

Roraima, Mount [ro**riy**ma] 5°12N 60°43W. Highest peak (2875 m/9432 ft) in the Guiana Highlands; a giant table mountain, total area 67 sq km/26 sq mi.

ro-ro [**roh**roh] A term derived from 'roll on, roll off', a vessel designed to permit vehicles to drive on and off the ship under their own power. >> ship 🛈

rorqual [**raw(r)**kwal] A baleen whale of worldwide family Balaenopteridae (6 species); longitudinal furrows on throat; small dorsal fin near tail; comprises **blue**, **sei**, **fin**, **minke**, **Bryde's**, and **humpback** whales. >> whale 🛈

Rorschach, Hermann [**raw(r)**shahkh] (1884–1922) Psychiatrist and neurologist, born in Zürich, Switzerland. He devised a diagnostic procedure for mental disorders based upon the patients' interpretation of a series of standardized ink blots (the **Rorschach test**). >> psychiatry

Rosa, Salvator [**roh**za] (1615–73) Painter, born near Naples, Italy. He owes his reputation mainly to his landscapes of wild and savage scenes.

Rosario [ro**sa**rioh] 33°00S 60°40W, pop (1995e) 1 140 000. Third largest city in Argentina; on the R Paraná; Argentina's largest inland port, founded in 1725; airport; railway; university (1968); cathedral; distribution outlet for local agricultural provinces; racecourse. >> Argentina 🛈

rosary A form of religious meditation, in which a sequence of prayers is recited using a string of beads or a knotted cord, each bead or knot representing one prayer in the sequence. In Christianity, it most commonly refers to the

Rosary of the Blessed Virgin Mary, which probably dates from the 13th-c. >> Mary (mother of Jesus)

Roscius [**rosh**ius], in full **Quintus Roscius Gallus** (c.134–62 BC) Roman comic actor, a slave by birth. He became the greatest comic actor in Rome, and was freed from slavery by the dictator, Sulla. >> Sulla

Roscommon, Ir **Ros Comáin** pop (1995e) 51 500; area 2463 sq km/951 sq mi. County in Connacht province, WC Ireland; capital, Roscommon, pop (1995e) 1400; 13th-c abbey and castle. >> Ireland (republic) ℹ

rose A member of a genus of shrubs or scrambling perennials, nearly all native to the N hemisphere. They are semi-evergreen, many retaining at least some leaves throughout the winter. The flowers of wild species are 5-petalled, flat or shallowly dish-shaped, white or yellow to red or purple, and often fragrant. Cultivated forms show a greater range of colours. The orange, red, or black fruit (*hip* or *hep*) is attractive to birds and animals, and a rich source of vitamin C. Prized for centuries for their beauty and as a source of perfume, roses are probably the world's most widely cultivated ornamental plants. They are very hardy, tolerate most growing conditions, and provide a profusion of forms and colours. Several distinct types have been developed by horticulturists, and there are now over 20 000 named cultivars. The rose has been extensively used as both a decorative and a heraldic symbol, for example by the Royal Houses of York and Lancaster, and is the national emblem of England. (Genus: *Rosa*, 250 species. Family: Rosaceae.) >> attar; cultivar

Rose, Pete(r Edward) (1942–) Baseball player, born in Cincinnati, OH. In his career (1963–86), spent mainly with the Cincinnati Reds, he had a record 4256 base hits. He was banned from baseball in 1989 after an investigation into alleged gambling offences. >> baseball ℹ

Roseanne, popular name of **Roseanne Barr** (1952–) Actor and producer, born in Salt Lake City, UT. After hosting a number of television specials and series, she became known for her realistic, unglamorized sitcom *Roseanne* (1988–97). Her film credits include *She-Devil* (1989) and *Blue in the Face* (1995).

Roseau [ro**zoh**], formerly **Charlotte Town** 15°18N 61°23W, pop (1995e) 16 100. Seaport and capital town of Dominica, Windward Is; cathedral (1841); trade in tropical fruit and vegetables. >> Dominica

Rosebery, Archibald Philip Primrose, 5th Earl of (1847–1929) British statesman and Liberal prime minister (1894–5), born in London. He became foreign secretary (1886, 1892–4) under Gladstone, whom he succeeded as premier. He was noted for his racehorse stables, and in his later years as a biographer of British statesmen. >> Gladstone; Liberal Party (UK)

rosemary A dense, aromatic, evergreen shrub (*Rosmarinus officialis*), growing to 2 m/6½ ft, native to the Mediterranean; flowers pale blue; widely cultivated for ornament and as a culinary herb. (Family: Labiatae.) >> herb

Rosenberg [**roh**zenberg] Alleged spies: **Julius Rosenberg** (1918–53) and **Ethel Rosenberg** (1915–53), husband and wife, both born in New York City. They joined the Communist Party, and were part of a transatlantic spy ring uncovered after the trial of Klaus Fuchs in Britain. They became the first US civilians to be executed for espionage. They had many supporters who claimed that the couple were the victims of the witch-hunt atmosphere of the early 1950s. >> Fuchs, Klaus

Roses, Wars of the (1455–85) A series of civil wars in England, which started during the weak monarchy of Henry VI; named from the emblems of the two rival branches of the House of Plantagenet, York (white rose) and Lancaster (red rose) – a symbolism which was propagated by the Tudor dynasty (1485–1603), which united the

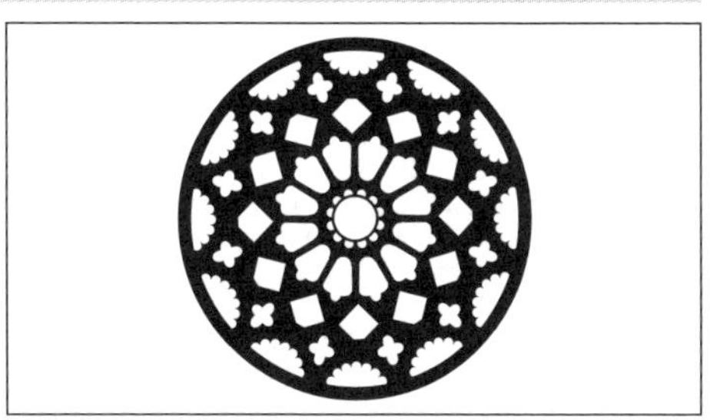

Rose or wheel window – Chartres cathedral

two roses. The wars began when Richard, Duke of York, claimed the protectorship of the crown after the king's mental breakdown (1453–4), and ended with Henry Tudor's defeat of Richard III at Bosworth (1485). >> Henry VI; Henry VII; Plantagenets; Richard III

Rose Theatre A London playhouse built c.1587 by Philip Henslowe on land he had leased on the S bank of the Thames. Rebuilt in 1592, the Rose was where Marlowe's plays were first performed, as well as some of the early plays of Shakespeare. The foundations were discovered in 1989. >> Globe Theatre; Henslowe; Marlowe; Shakespeare ℹ

Rosetta Stone A black basalt slab with a trilingual inscription in Greek and Egyptian hieroglyphic and demotic, found in 1799 on the Rosetta branch of the R Nile; now in the British Museum. It allowed hieroglyphs to be deciphered for the first time. >> Champollion; hieroglyphics ℹ

rose window A round window with mullions or tracery radiating outwards from the centre, filled with stained or painted glass. Commonly associated with Gothic architecture, it is also known as a **wheel window**. >> Gothic architecture; tracery ℹ

rosewood A high-quality wood scented like roses, because of the presence of aromatic gum. It is obtained from various trees of the genus *Dalbergia*, native to the tropics and subtropics. (Family: Leguminosae.)

Rosh Hashanah [rosh ha**shah**na, hasha**nah**] The Jewish New Year (1 Tishri), which falls in September or October. >> Judaism

Rosicrucianism [rohzi**kroo**shnizm] An esoteric movement which spread across Europe in the early 17th-c. In 1614–15 two pamphlets appeared in Germany and were attributed to Christian Rosenkreutz (1378–1484), who claimed to possess occult powers. He founded the Order of the Rosy Cross, and the pamphlets invited men of learning to join. No trace of the Order has been found, but many occult organizations claim Rosicrucian origins. >> occultism

rosin A resin obtained as the residue from the distillation of turpentine, melting point c.120°C; also called **colophony**. It is used as a flux in soldering. >> resin; turpentine tree

Roskilde [**rohs**kilduh] 55°39N 12°07E, pop (1995e) 50 000. Port and ancient town in Zealand, Denmark; capital of Denmark, 10th-c–1443; Peace of Roskilde, 1658; railway; university (1970); cathedral (12th-c); museum, including 1000-year-old Viking longboats. >> Denmark ℹ

Ross, Sir James Clark (1800–62) Polar explorer, born in London. He discovered the N magnetic pole in 1831, then commanded an expedition to the Antarctic seas (1839–43), where Ross Barrier, Sea, and Island are named after him. >> Antarctica ℹ

Ross Dependency Land area 413 500 sq km/159 600 sq mi; permanent shelf ice area 337 000 sq km/ 130 000 sq mi.

Antarctic territory administered by New Zealand (since 1923), including all the land between 160°E and 150°W and S of 60°S; no permanent inhabitants. >> Antarctica ℹ

Rossellini, Roberto [rose**lee**nee] (1906–77) Film director, born in Rome. His films include *Roma, città aperta* (1945, Rome, Open City), made with hidden cameras in a style which came to be known as 'neo-Realism', *Paisà* (1946, Paisan) and *Il generale della Rovere* (1959, General della Rovere).

Rossetti, Christina (Georgina) [ro**ze**tee] (1830–94) Poet, born in London, the sister of Dante Gabriel Rossetti. A devout Anglican, and influenced by the Oxford Movement, she wrote mainly religious poetry. >> Oxford Movement; Rossetti, Dante Gabriel

Rossetti, Dante Gabriel [ro**ze**tee] (1828–82) Poet and painter, born in London. He trained at the Royal Academy in London, and c.1850 helped to form the Pre-Raphaelite Brotherhood. His early work was on religious themes, such as 'The Annunciation' (1850, Tate); his later manner became more secular, and more ornate in style. >> Pre-Raphaelite Brotherhood

Rossini, Gioacchino (Antonio) [ro**see**nee] (1792–1868) Composer, born in Pesaro, Italy. Among his early successes were *Tancredi* (1813) and *L'Italiana in Algeri* (1813, The Italian Girl in Algiers), and in 1816 he produced his masterpiece, *Il Barbiere di Siviglia* (The Barber of Seville). His overtures have continued to be highly popular items in concert programmes.

Rosslare [ros**lair**], Ir **Ros Láir** 52°17N 6°23W, pop (1995e) 840. Port town in Wexford county, SE Ireland; ferry links with Fishguard and Milford Haven. >> Wexford

Ross Sea Extension of the Pacific Ocean in Antarctica; McMurdo Sound (W) generally ice-free in late summer, an important base point for exploration; main islands, Roosevelt (E) and Ross (W). >> Antarctica ℹ

Rostand, Edmond [rostã] (1868–1918) Poet and playwright, born in Marseille, France. He achieved international fame with *Cyrano de Bergerac* (1897), the story of the nobleman with the enormous nose.

Rostock or **Rostock-Warnemünde** 54°04N 12°09E, pop (1995e) 258 000. Industrial port in N Germany; on the Baltic Sea; founded, 12th-c; former Hanseatic League port; badly bombed in World War 2, rebuilt in the 1950s; university (1419); 15th-c town hall. >> Germany ℹ; Hanseatic League

Rostov-na-Donu [ro**stof** na do**noo**], Eng **Rostov-on-Don** 47°15N 39°45E, pop (1995e) 1 036 000. Port in SE European Russia; on R Don; major grain-exporting centre in the 19th-c; airport; railway; university (1917). >> Russia ℹ

Rostropovich, Mstislav Leopoldovich [rostro**poh**vich] (1927–) Cellist and conductor, born in Baku, Azerbaijan. In 1975, while in the USA, he and his wife decided not to return to the USSR; he then became musical director and conductor of the National Symphony Orchestra, Washington (1977–94).

Rotary International >> **service club**

Rotblat, Joseph (1908–) Physicist and anti-nuclear activist, born in Warsaw. He moved to the UK in 1939, and after the war devoted himself to the peaceful application of nuclear physics. He helped to found the annual series of conferences on arms control in Pugwash, Nova Scotia, in 1957 (the Pugwash Conferences), acting first as secretary-general (1957–73) and later as president (from 1988). He received the Nobel Peace Prize, along with the Conferences, in 1995. >> Pugwash Conference

Roth, Henry (1906–95) Novelist, born in Tysmienica, Austria-Hungary. He moved to New York in 1907. His only novel, *Call It Sleep* (1934), is a classic treatment of Jewish immigrant life and childhood.

Roth, Philip (Milton) (1933–) Novelist, born in Newark, NJ. His books include *Letting Go* (1962), *Portnoy's Complaint* (1969), and *American Pastoral* (1997).

Rotherham [ro<u>th</u>eram] 53°26N 1°20W, pop (1995e) 124 000. Town in South Yorkshire, N England; on the R Don; railway. >> Yorkshire, South

Rothermere, Viscount >> **Harmsworth, Harold Sydney**

Rothko, Mark, originally **Marcus Rothkowitz** (1903–70) Painter, born in Dvinsk, Russia. During the 1940s he was influenced by Surrealism, but by the early 1950s he had evolved a distinctive form of Abstract Expressionism. >> action painting; Surrealism

Rothschild, Meyer (Amschel), Eng [**roths**chiyld], Ger [**roht**shilt] (1743–1812) Financier, born in Frankfurt, Germany. He began as a moneylender, and became the financial adviser of the Landgrave of Hesse. His five sons continued his firm, establishing branches in other countries, and negotiated many of the great government loans of the 19th-c. >> Napoleonic Wars

rotifer [**roh**tifer] A microscopic aquatic animal with an unsegmented body; swims by means of a ring of beating hair-like structures that resembles a spinning wheel; group contains c.1800 species; also known as **wheel animalcules**. (Phylum: Rotifera.)

Rotorua [rohto**roo**a] 38°07S 176°17E, pop (1995e) 55 700. Health resort in North Island, New Zealand; in a region of thermal springs, geysers, and boiling mud. >> New Zealand ℹ

rotten borough The name given to certain British parliamentary boroughs before the Great Reform Act of 1832, which had few voters and were usually controlled by a landowner or by the Crown. Examples were Gatton, Dunwich, and Old Sarum. >> pocket borough; Reform Acts

Rotterdam 51°55N 4°30E, pop (1995e) 602 000. Industrial city and chief port of The Netherlands; at the junction of the R Rotte with the Nieuwe Maas, 24 km/15 mi from the North Sea; major commercial centre of NW Europe since the 14th-c; Europort harbour area inaugurated, 1966; city centre almost completely destroyed by German bombing, 1940; railway; underground; university (1973); shipbuilding (largest shipyard in Europe); petrochemicals (largest plant on the Continent of Europe); birthplace of Erasmus; philharmonic orchestra. >> Erasmus; Netherlands, The ℹ

rottweiler [**rot**viyler] A German breed of dog, developed around the Alpine town of Rottweil to protect cattle; agile, with heavy muscular body and neck; powerful muzzle and short soft ears; short black and tan coat; tail docked short; popular guard dogs; attracted adverse publicity in the late 1980s, following reports of fatal attacks on children. >> dog

Rouault, Georges (Henri) [roo-oh] (1871–1958) Painter and engraver, born in Paris. He was apprenticed to a stained-glass designer in 1885, and retained the art's glowing colours, outlined with black, in his paintings of clowns, prostitutes, and Biblical characters. >> Fauvism

Roubaix [roobay] 50°42N 3°10E, pop (1995e) 101 000; Industrial town in NW France; chartered in 1469; centre of N France textile industry.

Roubillac, Louis François [roobeeyak], also spelled **Roubiliac** (1702–1762) Sculptor, born in Lyon, France. His statue of Handel for Vauxhall Gardens (1738) first made him popular, and he completed statues of Newton, Shakespeare and others.

Rouen [rooã], Lat **Rotomagus** 49°27N 1°04E, pop (1995e) 106 000. River-port in NW France; on right bank of R Seine; fifth largest port in France; former capital of Upper Normandy; scene of trial and burning of Joan of Arc, 1431; badly damaged in World War 2, but reconstructed largely as a Ville Musée (museum town); road and rail junction;

university (1967); birthplace of Flaubert; restored Gothic cathedral (13th–16th-c); Gros Horloge (clock tower). >> Flaubert; Joan of Arc

Rouget de Lisle, Claude Joseph [roozhay duh **leel**] (1760–1836) French army officer, born in Lons-le-Saunier, France. He wrote and composed the *Marseillaise* when stationed in 1792 at Strasbourg.

Rough Riders The nickname for the First US Volunteer Cavalry Regiment, commanded during the Spanish-American War (1898) by Colonel Leonard Wood (1860–1927) and Lieutenant-Colonel Theodore Roosevelt. >> Roosevelt, Theodore; Spanish–American War

roulette A casino game played with a spinning wheel and ball. The wheel is divided into 37 segments numbered 0–36, but not in numerical order. All numbers are alternately either red or black except the 0. Punters bet, before and during the spin of the wheel, on the landing place of the ball after the wheel has stopped spinning. Bets can also be placed as to whether the winning number will be odd or even, or red or black. >> casino

Roumania >> **Romania** ℹ

rouncy >> **cob**

rounders An outdoor bat-and-ball game from which baseball probably derived. Each team consists of nine players, and the object, after hitting the ball, is to run around the outside of three posts before reaching the fourth and thus scoring a rounder. >> baseball ℹ

Roundheads >> **Cavaliers**

roundworm infestation A condition in which roundworms (*nematodes*) live within the body of their hosts, many without causing disease. >> filariasis; hookworm infestation; nematode; river blindness; toxocariasis

Rous, (Francis) Peyton [rows] (1879–1970) Pathologist, born in Baltimore, MD. The **Rous chicken sarcoma**, which he discovered in 1911, remains the best-known example (as well as the first) of a cancer produced by a virus. In 1966 he shared the Nobel Prize for Physiology or Medicine. >> cancer; virus

Rousseau, Henri Julien Félix [roosoh], known as **le Douanier** ('the Customs Officer') (1844–1910) Primitive painter, born in Laval, France. He produced painstaking portraits, exotic imaginary landscapes, and dreams, such as 'Sleeping Gypsy' (1897, New York). >> Salon

Rousseau, Jean-Jacques [roosoh] (1712–78) Political philosopher, educationist, and essayist, born in Geneva, Switzerland. His *Discourse sur l'origine et les fondements de l'inégalité parmi les hommes* (1755, Discourse on the Origin and Foundations of Inequality Amongst Men) emphasized the natural goodness of human beings, and the corrupting influences of institutionalized life. His masterpiece, *Du contrat social* (1762, The Social Contract), had a great influence on French revolutionary thought, introducing the slogan 'Liberty, Equality, Fraternity'. The same year he published his major work on education, *Emile*, in novel form. In England he wrote most of his *Confessions* (published posthumously, 1782).

Rousseau, (Pierre Etienne) Théodore [roosoh] (1812–67) Landscape painter, born in Paris. During the 1840s he settled at Barbizon, where he worked with a group of other painters, becoming leader of the Barbizon School. >> Barbizon School

Roux, (Pierre Paul) Emile [roo] (1853–1933) Bacteriologist, born in Confolens, France. In 1894 he helped to discover diphtheria antitoxin, and he also worked on rabies and anthrax. >> diphtheria

Rovaniemi [rovan**yay**mee] 66°29N 25°40E, pop (1995e) 34 500. City in Finland; established, 1929; airfield; railway; centre for timber trade; largely destroyed by fire, 1944–5, and rebuilt by Alvar Aalto. >> Aalto; Lapland

Rovno [**rov**no], Polish **Rowne**, Ger **Rowno** 50°39N 26°10E, pop (1995e) 243 000. City in Ukraine, on R Uste; formerly in Poland; railway. >> Ukraine ℹ

rowan [**roh**an] A slender deciduous tree (*Sorbus aucuparia*), growing to 20 m/65 ft, native to Europe; flowers creamy, in large clusters; berries red, rarely yellow; also called **mountain ash**. (Family: Rosaceae.)

Rowe, Nicholas [roh] (1674–1718) Poet and playwright, born in Little Barford, Bedfordshire. Three of his plays became very popular: *Tamerlane* (1702), *The Fair Penitent* (1703), and *Jane Shore* (1714). In 1715 he was appointed poet laureate.

rowing A sport or pastime in which a boat is propelled by oars as opposed to mechanical means. If there is only one rower with two oars it is known as **sculling**. Rowing involves two or more people, each rower having one oar. Famous races include the Oxford and Cambridge Boat Race (began 1829), and the Diamond Sculls and Grand Challenge Cup, both contested at the Henley Royal Regatta every year. >> Boat Race; Henley Royal Regatta; RR1059

Rowland, Tiny, originally **Rowland W Furhop** (1917–98) Financier, born in India. He joined Lonrho (the London and Rhodesian Mining and Land Company) in 1961, and became its chief executive and managing director. In 1983 he became chairman of *The Observer* newspaper, which he sold to *The Guardian* in 1993. He stepped down from Lonrho in 1994, following a bitter battle for control of the company with German property tycoon Dieter Bock.

Rowlandson, Thomas (1756–1827) Caricaturist, born in London. Some of his best-known works are his illustrations to the 'Dr Syntax' series (1812–21) and 'The English Dance of Death' (1815–16).

Rowley, Thomas [**roh**lee] >> **Chatterton, Thomas**

Royal Academy of Arts A British academy founded in 1768 under royal patronage, with the aim of holding annual exhibitions (which are still held). Its premises are at Burlington House, London.

Royal Academy of Dramatic Art (RADA) A London theatre school founded in 1904 by Beerbohm Tree, and granted its Royal Charter in 1920. It is located in Chenies Street. Major refurbishment of its Malet Street premises began in 1997. >> Tree

Royal Academy of Music A London conservatory founded in 1822, opened in 1823, and granted its royal charter in 1830. It moved to its present location in Marylebone in 1912.

Royal Air Force (RAF) Britain's air force, established in 1918. Today the RAF comprises three Commands: Strike, Support, and RAF Germany. >> Britain, Battle of

Royal and Ancient Golf Club of St Andrews (R & A) The ruling body of the game of golf in the eyes of most countries (the USA being a notable exception). The R & A was formed in 1754 and adopted its present name in 1834. >> golf

royal assent A legal stage through which a bill has to pass in the UK before it becomes law. The monarch's approval is a formality; it has never been withheld in modern times. >> parliament

Royal Australian Air Force (RAAF) Australia's air force, established in 1921. It saw service in all theatres of World War 2.

Royal Australian Navy (RAN) Australia's Navy, established in 1911. Based on the British Royal Navy, it had an early success in 1914 in sinking the German raider *Emden*, and saw action in the Atlantic, Mediterranean, and the Pacific. >> navy

Royal Ballet Britain's national ballet company, the inspiration of Dame Ninette de Valois. It gave its first performances in 1931, became Sadler's Wells Ballet and, in

1936, the Royal Ballet. Its famous dancers have included Margot Fonteyn, Alicia Markova, and Anthony Dowell. >> ballet; Valois, Ninette de

Royal British Legion An organization for all ex-servicemen and women, and serving members of HM Forces. Formed in 1921, its aim is to provide social and welfare services for its members and to perpetuate the memory of those who died in the service of their country. It provides poppies for the Remembrance (or Poppy Day) Appeal each November. >> American Legion; Remembrance Sunday

Royal Canadian Mounted Police >> **Mounties; police**

Royal College of Music A London conservatory founded by royal charter in 1883. It moved to its present location in Prince Consort Road in 1894.

Royal Commission In the UK, a body appointed by the sovereign on the prime minister's recommendation to investigate and report on the operation of laws which it is proposed to change. It may also deal with social, educational, or other matters about which the government wishes to make general, long-term policy decisions.

Royal Family, British >> **Anne, Princess; Charles, Prince; Edinburgh, Duke of; Edward, Prince; Elizabeth II; Gloucester, Duke of; Kent, Duke of; Margaret, Princess; Spencer, Lady Diana; York, Duke of**

royal garden parties In the UK, four summer gatherings held in June/July by the Queen, three in the grounds of Buckingham Palace, and the other at the Palace of Holyroodhouse, Edinburgh. Up to 10 000 people are invited to each party.

Royal Greenwich Observatory An observatory founded by Charles II of England in 1675. Its role in the preparation of calendars and time-keeping was of major importance until the mid-20th-c. Its transit circle has been used since 1851 for the accurate measurement of time; and in 1884 it was agreed to take the axis of this telescope as the prime meridian of longitude. Its headquarters moved to Cambridge in 1990. >> Greenwich Mean Time; observatory ℹ

Royal Horticultural Society A society founded in the UK in 1804. An experimental garden is maintained at Wisley, Surrey; shows and competitions, notably the Chelsea Flower Show, are held annually. >> horticulture

Royal Institution In the UK, a learned scientific society founded in 1799 by the physicist, Count Rumford. Lectures are still given at its headquarters in Albemarle Street, London, notably the Christmas lectures for young people. >> Rumford, Benjamin Thompson

royal jelly A highly nutritious substance produced by the salivary glands of the worker bees to nourish the queen bee and those larvae that are destined to become queens. There are many anecdotal reports of its beneficial effects on humans. It is usually taken in the form of a rather expensive dietary supplement, but it has also been incorporated into some cosmetic products, where it is claimed to have a rejuvenating action on the skin. >> bee; larva

Royal Marines (RM) Britain's Marine force, which can trace its origin to the Lord High Admiral's Regiment first raised in 1664. The first RM Commando units were raised in 1942. >> Marines

Royal Mint The British government department responsible for manufacturing metal coins. The London mint probably dates from AD 825. It is now situated in Llantrisant, S Wales.

Royal National Lifeboat Institution (RNLI) In the UK, a rescue organization manned by volunteers and financed by voluntary contributions, founded in 1824. The modern RNLI operates over 200 lifeboat stations and maintains over 250 active vessels. >> lifeboat

Royal Navy (RN) The naval branch of the British armed forces. Originating in the time of Henry VIII, it reached its peak at the end of World War 2, when it had more than 500 warships. It has been responsible for the operation of Britain's nuclear deterrent since 1969. >> navy; nuclear weapons; warships ℹ

Royal Observatory, Edinburgh An observatory at Edinburgh, Scotland, UK, founded in 1822. It is responsible for operating the UK telescopes at the Mauna Kea Observatory. >> Mauna Kea Observatory; observatory ℹ

Royal Opera House The home of the Royal Ballet and the Royal Opera in Bow Street, London. The present building, by Edward Middleton Barry (1830–80), opened in 1858. >> Covent Garden

Royal Shakespeare Company An English theatre company based in Stratford-upon-Avon and London. It was developed out of the Shakespeare Memorial Theatre by Peter Hall between 1960 and 1968. >> Hall, Peter

Royal Society (RS) In the UK, a prestigious scientific institution – the oldest in the world to have enjoyed continuous existence. Its inaugural meeting was held in London in 1660 and the Society was granted a royal charter in 1662. >> Newton, Isaac

Royal Society for Nature Conservation, also known as **The Wildlife Trusts** A British conservation society which co-ordinates the work of county naturalist trusts and urban wildlife groups. It was founded in 1912, and now manages over 2000 reserves (1997). >> conservation (earth sciences); Nature Reserve

Royal Society for the Prevention of Cruelty to Animals >> **RSPCA**

Royal Society for the Protection of Birds >> **RSPB**

Royal Victorian Order An order of knighthood instituted in 1896 by Queen Victoria, designed to reward distinguished service to the sovereign. The motto is 'Victoria' and the ribbon blue with red and white edges.

Royce, Sir (Frederick) Henry (1863–1933) Engineer, born in Alwalton, Cambridgeshire. He made his first car in 1904, and his meeting with C S Rolls in that year led to the formation (1906) of Rolls-Royce, Ltd. >> car ℹ; Rolls

RSPB In the UK, an abbreviation of **Royal Society for the Protection of Birds**. It is now one of the major conservation bodies, owning over 100 nature reserves. >> bird ℹ

RSPCA In the UK, an abbreviation of **Royal Society for the Prevention of Cruelty to Animals**, the main animal welfare society, founded in 1824. In the USA there are several animal societies. The oldest is the American Society for the Prevention of Cruelty to Animals (1866), but the Animal Protection Society of America (1968) has a larger membership.

Ruapehu, Mount [rooa**pay**hoo] 39°18S 175°40E. Active volcano and highest peak on North Island, New Zealand; rises to 2797 m/9176 ft; last eruption, 1995–6. >> New Zealand ℹ

rubber A resilient, elastic substance obtained from a variety of unrelated, latex-producing, tropical trees. Raw rubber, or **caoutchouc**, is obtained from the milky latex exuded by the trees as a response to injury. The latex is collected by making a series of spiral cuts halfway around the circumference of the trunk, allowing the fluid to collect in cups. It is is congealed using acid, pressed, and sometimes smoked, before undergoing manufacture into final products. Initially, rubber was collected solely from wild trees in Brazil, but from c.1900 they were introduced as plantation trees to other tropical countries, notably Malaysia, which has become the world's largest producer. **Synthetic rubbers**, made by the polymerization of isoprene or substituted butadienes, exceed natural rubber in the quantity used. >> indiarubber tree; isoprene; latex; polymerization; vulcanization

rubber plant / tree >> **indiarubber tree; rubber**
Rubbia, Carlo (1934–) Physicist, born in Gorizia, Italy. From 1960 he headed the team at CERN (the European Organisation for Nuclear Research) in Geneva using the proton–antiproton collider. He shared the Nobel Prize for Physics in 1984 for work leading to the discovery of the W and Z sub-atomic particles. >> W / Z particle
Rubbra, Edmund (1901–86) Composer, born in Northampton, Northamptonshire. He wrote 11 symphonies, chamber, choral and orchestral music, songs, and solo instrumental works. >> polyphony
rubella >> **German measles**
Rubens, (Peter Paul) [**roo**benz] (1577–1640) Painter, born in Siegen, Germany. In 1608 he settled in Antwerp, becoming court painter to the Archduke Albert. His triptych 'The Descent from the Cross' (1611–14) in Antwerp Cathedral is one of his early masterpieces. In 1622 he was invited to France by Marie de Médicis, for whom he painted 21 large subjects on her life and regency (Louvre). In 1628 he was sent on a diplomatic mission to Spain, and there executed some 40 works. The following year he became envoy to Charles I of England, where his paintings included 'Peace and War' (National Gallery, London). >> Charles I (of England); Marie de Médicis
rubidium–strontium dating A method of radiometric dating for rocks more than 10 million years old. It uses the fact that the radioactive isotope rubidium-87 decays with a known half-life to yield strontium-87, and hence the amount of each isotope in a rock or mineral can be used to determine its age. >> radiometric dating
Rubik's Cube A mathematical puzzle named after its inventor, Hungarian architect Ernö Rubik (1944–). A coloured cube is divided into 26 small incomplete cubes, each of which will pivot. There are c.$4{\cdot}3 \times 10^{22}$ combinations, but only one possible way of getting all six sides to form a different colour. It became a world craze in the late 1970s.
Rubin, Robert E [**roo**bin] (1938–) US statesman, born in New York City. He became a lawyer, then joined the White House as assistant to the president for economic policy (1993–5). He became secretary of the Treasury in 1995, and was reappointed to this post in 1997.
Rubinstein, Artur [**roo**binstiyn] (1887–1982) Pianist, born in Łódź, Poland. After World War 2 he lived in the USA, making frequent extensive concert tours.
Rubinstein, Helena [**roo**binstiyn] (1870–1965) Beautician and business executive, born in Cracow, Poland. She moved in the 1890s to Australia, where she opened the country's first beauty salon in Melbourne (1902). In 1915 she emigrated to New York City and launched an international business empire. Her success was spiced by a 50-year feud with arch-rival Elizabeth Arden. >> Arden, Elizabeth; Lauder, Estée
Ruby, Jack L, originally **Jacob Rubenstein** (1911–67) Assassin, born in Chicago, IL. Two days after the assassination of President John F Kennedy, he shot and killed Lee Harvey Oswald, the alleged assassin of the president. He was sentenced to death in 1964, but died while awaiting a second trial. >> Kennedy, John F; Oswald, Lee Harvey
ruby A gem variety of corundum, coloured deep crimson to pale red by the presence of minor impurities of chromium. >> chromium; corundum
rudbeckia A biennial or perennial, native to North America; large flower-heads, characterized by the conical receptacle in the centre, giving rise to the alternative name of **coneflower**; outer ray florets red, yellow, or orange. (Genus: *Rudbeckia*, 15 species. Family: Compositae.)
rudd Freshwater fish (*Scardinius erythrophthalmus*) widespread in European rivers and lakes; length up to 40 cm/16 in; greenish-brown on back, sides yellow, fins reddish. (Family: Cyprinidae.) >> fish ℹ
Rudolf I (1218–91) German king (1273–91), the founder of the Habsburg sovereign and imperial dynasty, born in Schloss Limburg, Germany. Chosen king by the electors, he was recognized by the pope in 1274. >> Habsburgs
Rudolf, Lake >> **Turkana, Lake**
rue A small aromatic evergreen shrub (*Ruta graveolens*) with acrid scent and taste, native to the Balkans; leaves bluish-green; flowers with 4–5 rather dirty yellow petals curved up at the tips. It is cultivated as a culinary and medicinal herb. (Family: Rutaceae.) >> herb
ruff A sandpiper (*Philomachus pugnax*) native to Europe, Asia, and Africa; breeding male with naked face and large ruff of feathers around neck. >> sandpiper
Rugby 52°23N 1°15W, pop (1995e) 60 100. Town in Warwickshire, C England; on R Avon; famous boys' public school (1567); railway. >> Arnold, Thomas; Warwickshire
rugby football >> **football 3**
Ruhr, River [roor] River in Germany; rises N of Winterberg; flows W to the R Rhine at Duisburg; length 213 km/132 mi; its valley is an important mining and industrial area; cities include Essen, Bochum, Dortmund. >> Germany ℹ
Ruïsdael, Jacob van >> **Ruysdael, Jacob van**
Ruiz, Nevado del [roo**ees**] 4°53N 75°22W. Active Andean volcanic peak in WC Colombia; rises to 5399 m/17 713 ft; erupted in 1985, with loss of many lives. >> Andes; Colombia ℹ
rum A spirit distilled either from sugar cane, freshly crushed, or from the fermentation of molasses, a by-product of the West Indian sugar-cane industry. The British navy gave rum a special status by providing a daily tot to all serving sailors. >> molasses
Rumania >> **Romania** ℹ
rumba A dance of Cuban origin which became popular as a ballroom dance in the 1930s. Its distinctive rhythm, often played on maracas or bongos, is the *tresillo*, a bar of eight quavers/eighth-notes divided 3 + 3 + 2. >> bongos; maracas
Rumford, Count >> **Royal Institution**
ruminant A mammal of suborder Ruminantia, comprising the *traguloids* (chevrotains) and *pecorans* (other deer, giraffes, and Bovidae), and suborder Tylopoda (the camel family); an artiodactyl; many-chambered stomach breaks down coarse plant material; camels and chevrotains have three chambers; pecorans have four; regurgitates mouthfuls (*cud*), chews them thoroughly, then reswallows; also known as a **cud-chewer**. >> artiodactyl; Bovidae; Camelidae; chevrotain; deer; giraffe; mammal ℹ
rummy A large family of domestic card games. In one popular version, each player has seven cards, and the object is to form them into two hands, one of three cards and one of four (or one hand of seven) by taking and discarding cards from the pack. The hand obtained must be three (or four) cards of the same denomination, or a sequence of three (or four) cards of the same suit. A variation popular

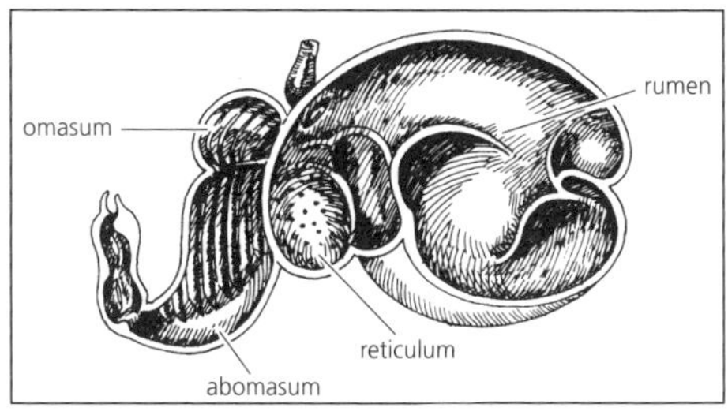

Ruminant – the four chambers of the pecoran stomach

in the USA is **gin rummy**, in which hands (of three or four) are laid face upwards, and can be added to by players in certain circumstances during the game. Points are deducted according to which cards are left in the hand when one of the players wins the game by disposing of all his or her cards.

Rump Parliament The members of the British Long Parliament who were left after Pride's Purge of 'presbyterian' elements (1648), numbering about 60. It abolished the monarchy and the House of Lords. When it fell out with the army, Cromwell dismissed it (1653). It was recalled in 1659, and dissolved itself in 1660. >> Long Parliament; Pride, Thomas

Rum Rebellion In Australian history, an uprising in Sydney which deposed the governor of New South Wales, Captain William Bligh (1808). It occurred because of personal antagonisms, and Bligh's attempt to end the use of rum as a currency. >> Bligh

Runcie (of Cuddesdon), Robert (Alexander Kennedy) Runcie, Baron [**ruhn**see] (1921–) British Anglican churchman, born in Crosby, Lancashire. He was Bishop of St Albans for 10 years before becoming Archbishop of Canterbury (1980–91). He presided at the Lambeth Conference in 1987. >> Church of England; Lambeth Conferences

Rundstedt, (Karl Rudolf) Gerd von [**rund**shtet] (1875–1953) German field marshal, born in Aschersleben, Germany. In 1939 he directed the attacks on Poland and France. Checked in the Ukraine in 1941, he was relieved of his command, but in 1942 was given a new command in France. He was recalled after the success of the 1944 Allied invasion, but returned to direct the Ardennes offensive. >> World War 2

Runeberg, Johan Ludvig [**roon**uhberg] (1804–77) Finnish poet, writing in Swedish, born in Jakobstad, Finland. His major work is the verse romance based on Scandinavian legend, *King Fjala* (1844). One of his poems became Finland's national anthem.

runes The letters of the earliest Teutonic alphabet; widely known as the *futhark*, from the names of its first six symbols (*f*, *u*, *th*, *a*, *r*, *k*). Used mainly by the Scandinavians and the Anglo-Saxons, it comprised 24 basic symbols, though there was considerable regional variation both in the overall number of symbols and the symbol shapes used. Runes are preserved in c.4000 inscriptions and a few manuscripts, dating from the 3rd-c AD. >> Anglo-Saxons

runner bean A twining perennial (*Phaseolus coccineus*) growing to 5 m/16 ft, native to tropical America; peaflowers scarlet or less commonly white, in stalked clusters; pods up to 40 cm/16 in long, containing large red, kidney-shaped seeds. It is a common garden vegetable. (Family: Leguminosae.)

running >> **athletics; cross-country running**

Runnymede A meadow on the S bank of the R Thames, Surrey, SE England; here, or on Magna Carta Island in the river, King John signed the Magna Carta in 1215. >> Magna Carta; Surrey

ᚠ	f	ᚷ	g	ᛇ	ï	ᛖ	e
ᚢ	u	ᚹ	w	ᛈ	p	ᛗ	m
ᚦ	þ	ᚻ	h	ᛉ	x	ᛚ	l
ᚩ	o	ᚾ	n	ᛋ	s	ᛝ	ng
ᚱ	r	ᛁ	i	ᛏ	t	ᛟ	œ
ᚳ	k	ᛄ	j	ᛒ	b	ᛞ	d

A version of the runic alphabet found in Britain

Runyon, (Alfred) Damon (1884–1946) Writer, born in Manhattan, KS. He is best known for his short stories about underworld New York life. His collection *Guys and Dolls* (1931) was adapted for a musical revue (1950) and film (1955).

Rupert, Prince, also known as **Rupert of the Rhine** (1619–82) Royalist commander in the English Civil War, born in Prague, the third son of the Elector Palatine Frederick V and Elizabeth, daughter of James I of England. A notable cavalry leader, he won several victories, but was defeated at Marston Moor (1644) and dismissed by Charles I. Banished by parliament, he led the small Royalist fleet until it was routed by Blake (1650). >> Blake, Robert; Charles I (of England); English Civil War

rupture >> **hernia**

Rusedski, Greg [ru**zet**skee] (1973–) Tennis player, born in Montreal, Quebec, Canada. He became a British subject in 1995. A left-handed player, known for his very fast serves, he moved ahead of Tim Henman to become British No 1 in 1997, but finished ninth in the world listings, two places behind Henman, at the end of the 1998 season.

rush A densely tufted annual or evergreen perennial; typically found in cold and wet places; flowers with six segments, brownish, in dense heads. (Genus: *Juncus*, 300 species. Family: Juncaceae.)

Rush, Geoffrey (1951–) Actor, born in Toowoomba, Queensland, Australia. Known as a theatre actor in Australia, he received international recognition for his role as David Helfgott in the 1996 film *Shine* (awards include Oscar, Golden Globe, BAFTA).

Rush, Ian (1961–) Footballer, born in St Asaph, Denbighshire. He played for Liverpool (1981–6), scoring 110 goals in 182 league matches, then played for Juventus, returning to Liverpool in 1988, joined Leeds United in 1996, and then moved to Newcastle United (1997–8). He has been a regular member of the Welsh international team since 1980. >> football ℹ

Rushdie, (Ahmad) Salman (1947–) Writer, born in Mumbai (Bombay), India, of Muslim parents. He became widely known after the publication of his second novel, *Midnight's Children* (1981, Booker, James Tait Black). *The Satanic Verses* (1988) caused worldwide controversy because of its treatment of Islam from a secular point of view, and in 1989 he was forced to go into hiding because of a sentence of death passed on him by Ayatollah Khomeini of Iran (officially lifted in 1998). Later books include the novels *The Moor's Last Sigh* (1995, Whitbread) and *The Ground Beneath Her Feet* (1999). >> Khomeini

Rushmore, Mount 43°53N 103°28W. Mountain in W South Dakota, USA, in the Black Hills; a national memorial; height 1943 m/6375 ft; famous for the gigantic sculptures of four past US presidents (Washington, Jefferson, Roosevelt, Lincoln); each head 18 m/60 ft high; constructed 1927–41 under the direction of Gutzon Borglum. >> Borglum; South Dakota

Rusk, (David) Dean (1909–94) US statesman, secretary of state 1961–9, born in Cherokee Co, GA. As secretary of state under Kennedy, he played a major role in the Cuban crisis of 1962. He retained the post under the Johnson administration. >> Johnson, Lyndon B; Kennedy, John F

Ruska, Ernst (1906–88) Physicist, born in Heidelberg, Germany. For his development of the electron microscope, he was awarded the 1986 Nobel Prize for Physics. >> electron microscope ℹ

Ruskin, John (1819–1900) Writer and art critic, born in London. His critical works, such as *Modern Painters*

(1843–60) and *The Stones of Venice* (1851–3) made him the critic of the day, and his social criticism gave him the status of a moral guide or prophet. >> Gothic revival

Russell, Bertrand (Arthur William) Russell, 3rd Earl (1872–1970) Philosopher and mathematician, born in Trelleck, Monmouthshire. His major works were *Principles of Mathematics* (1903), and (with A N Whitehead) *Principia mathematica* (1910–13). In 1907 he offered himself as a Liberal candidate, but was turned down for his 'freethinking'. In 1918 his pacifism led to his serving 6 months in prison. Later works included *An Enquiry into Meaning and Truth* (1940) and *Human Knowledge* (1948). After 1949 he became a champion of nuclear disarmament. The single most important influence on 20th-c analytic philosophy, he was awarded the 1950 Nobel Prize for Literature. >> logic; Moore, G E; Whitehead

Russell, Henry Norris (1877–1957) Astronomer, born in Oyster Bay, NY. Independently of Ejnar Hertzsprung (1873–1967), he discovered the relationship between stellar absolute magnitude and spectral type.

Russell, Jack, popular name of **John Russell** (1795–1883) 'Sporting parson', born in Dartmouth, Devon. He became curate of Swymbridge near Barnstaple (1832–80), and master of foxhounds. The **Jack Russell terrier** was named after him.

Russell, (Ernestine) Jane (Geraldine) (1921–) Film actress, born in Bemidji, MN. Known for her striking looks, she became one of the leading Hollywood sex symbols of the 1950s, her major films including *Paleface* (1948) and *Gentlemen Prefer Blondes* (1953).

Russell (of Kingston Russell), John Russell, 1st Earl, known as **Lord John Russell** (1792–1878) British statesman and Whig-Liberal prime minister (1846–52, 1865–6), born in London. He became prime minister after the Conservative Party split over the repeal of the Corn Laws (1846). In Aberdeen's coalition of 1852 he was foreign secretary, but lost popularity over alleged incompetent management of the Crimean War, and retired in 1855 (though recalled as foreign secretary in 1859 and as premier after Palmerston's death). >> Aberdeen, Earl of; Crimean War; Palmerston, Viscount; Whigs

Russell, Ken, popular name of **Henry Kenneth Alfred Russell** (1927–) Film director, born in Southampton. He produced experimental studies of Debussy, Isadora Duncan, Delius, and Richard Strauss, which gradually abandoned naturalism. His feature films include *Women in Love* (1969), *The Devils* (1971), *The Rainbow* (1989), and *Lady Chatterley's Lover* (1993).

Russell, William, Lord (1639–83) English Whig politician. A leading member of the movement to exclude James II from the succession, he was arrested with others for participation in the Rye House Plot (1683), and beheaded in London. >> Rye House Plot; Shaftesbury, Earl; Whigs

Russell, Willy, popular name of **William Martin Russell** (1947–) Playwright, born in Whiston, Lancashire. Among his best-known plays are *Educating Rita* (1979), *Blood Brothers* (1983), and *Shirley Valentine* (1986).

Russia, official name **Russian Federation**, formerly (1917–91) the **Russian SFSR (Soviet Federal Socialist Republic)**, Russ **Rossiyskaya** pop (1995e) 149 899 000; area 17 075 400 sq km/6 591 100 sq mi. Republic occupying much of E Europe and N Asia; c.75% of the area of the former USSR and over 50% of its population; capital, Moscow; timezones GMT +2 to +12; major ethnic groups, Russian (82%), Tatar (3%), Ukrainian (3%), and c.100 other ethnic groups; religions, Christian (Russian Orthodox, 25%), Muslim; languages, Russian (official), and c.100 other languages; currency, the rouble; vast plains dominate the W half; Ural Mts separate the E European Plain (W) from the W Siberian Lowlands (E), highest peak, Narodnaya (1894 m/6214 ft); E European Plain in the W, largely below 300 m/1000 ft, dissected by several major rivers, notably the S-flowing Dnepr, Don, Volga; Caucasus Mts form a bridge between the Black Sea (W) and the Caspian Sea (E), and between Europe (N) and Asia (S); E of the R Yenisey lies the C Siberian Plateau; in SW Siberia the Altay range rises to 5000 m/16 000 ft; over 20 000 lakes, the largest being the Caspian Sea, L Taymyr, L Baikal; several different climatic regions, from polar (N) to subtropical (S); average temperature at Moscow −9.4°C (Jan), 18.3°C (Jul); average annual rainfall, 630 mm/24.8 in; conditions drier in extreme SE, with mild winters along Black Sea coasts (the 'Russian Riviera'); continental climate in Siberia, with very cold and prolonged winters, and short, often warm summers; settled by many ethnic groups, including the nomadic Slavs, Turks, and Bulgars, 3rd–7th-c; conquered by Mongols 1236; Moscow established as centre of political power in the N, 14th–15th-c; under Catherine II (the Great) Russia became a great power, extending territory S and W; February 1917 Revolution ended the monarchy, followed in October by Bolshevik seizure of political power; 5-year Civil War followed between revolutionary (Red) and counter-revolutionary (White) forces; socialist republic formed within the new Soviet Union, 1922; independence in 1991, following the break-up of the Soviet Union; new constitution, 1993; war in Chechnya, 1994–6; governed by a president, prime minister, and Federal Assembly, consisting of a State *Duma* and a Federation Council. oil, natural gas, coal, peat, gold, copper, platinum, zinc, tin, lead; metallurgy, machines, ships, vehicles, chemicals, textiles, timber; wheat, fruit, vegetables, sugar beet. >> Caspian Sea; Chechnya; Commonwealth of Independent States ℹ; communism; Gorbachev; Lenin; Moscow; Siberia; Soviet Union; Stalin; Ural Mountains; Yeltsin; RR1020 political leaders; *see illustration on p.744*

Russian >> **Slavic languages**

Russian blue A breed of domestic cat; *foreign short-haired* variety; thick blue-grey coat, each hair often with a silver tip; large thin ears and green eyes; also known as an **Archangel cat**. >> cat

Russian Civil War (1918–22) A war which took place in Russia following the October 1917 Revolution. Anti-Bolshevik forces (Whites) led by tsarist generals mounted a series of military and political campaigns against the new Soviet regime. They were opposed by the Soviet Red Army, created by Trotsky, which successfully fought back against the Whites between 1918 and 1922. >> Bolsheviks; Russian Revolution; Trotsky; White Russians

Russian Orthodox Church A Church originating from missionary activity of the see of Constantinople of the Orthodox Church, with a community organized at Kiev in the 9th-c. The contemporary Russian Church retains fidelity in doctrine and liturgy to its Orthodox inheritance, but is also developing its national character. >> Christianity; Orthodox Church

Russian Revolution (1917) The revolution which overthrew the Russian imperialist regime and set up the first communist state. Mass demonstrations of revolutionary workers and soldiers in Petrograd led to the abdication of Nicholas II in February 1917. There followed a period of power-sharing between a provisional government and the Petrograd Soviet, known as 'dual power'. Lenin's Bolsheviks refused to collaborate, and in October led an insurgency of armed workers, soldiers, and sailors, seizing political power and establishing the first Soviet government. >> Bolsheviks; Mensheviks; April Theses; February Revolution (Russia); July Days; October Revolution

Russian Space Agency An agency established in 1992 to

administer the civilian and commercial space programme of the Russian Federation. It is based on the principal assets and ongoing projects of the former Soviet space programme, most of which were carried out within Russian territory. Earlier the Soviet space programme had been a dominant element in the exploration of space since the launch of Sputnik in 1957. Military and civilian programmes were administered by a complex organization whose characteristic secrecy increasingly diminished in the 1980s as the programme took on an international emphasis. Three principal launch sites (cosmodromes) are Biakonur (or Tyuratam), Plesetsk, and Kaputstin Yar, which in the past have launched about 100 spacecraft per year. The mission control facility is located in Kaliningrad (near Moscow). >> Mars programme; Mir space station; space exploration

Russian wolfhound >> **borzoi**

Russo–Finnish War (1939–40) A war between the USSR and Finland during the winter of 1939–40 (the **Winter War**). Soviet forces invaded Finland to secure Finnish territory from which to defend Leningrad against German attack. Finland was forced to cede territory to the Soviet Union. >> World War 2

Russo–Japanese War (1904–5) A war between the Russian Empire and Japan over rival territorial claims and imperial ambitions in N China. The war ended in Japanese victory with the Treaty of Portsmouth (1905).

Russo–Turkish Wars A series of wars between the Russian and Ottoman Empires from the 17th-c to the 19th-c, principally for domination of the Black Sea and adjacent regions. Many areas gained their independence or were incorporated into the Russian Empire. >> Ottoman Empire

rust The product of corrosion, especially of iron-containing materials. It consists mainly of iron(III) oxide (Fe_2O_3) or hydrated forms. >> corrosion

rust fungus A parasitic fungus that occurs as a thread-like network (*mycelium*) between cells of the host plant; includes the genus *Puccinia*, containing over 4000 species. (Subdivision: Basidiomycetes. Order: Uredinales.) >> Basidiomycetes; fungus; parasitology

Rutanzige, Lake >> **Edward, Lake**

Ruth, Book of A book of the Hebrew Bible/Old Testament, usually dated c.5th–4th-c BC, presenting a popular story ostensibly set in the time of Israel's tribal judges. Ruth became the mother of Obed, grandfather of David. >> David; Old Testament

Ruth, Babe, popular name of **George Herman Ruth**, nicknames **the Babe**, **the Bambino**, **the Sultan of Swat** (1895–1948) Baseball player, born in Baltimore, MD. He joined the New York Yankees in 1920, and when he retired in 1935 had scored 714 home runs, a figure not bettered until 1974. *The Babe Ruth Story* was filmed in 1984; *The Babe* in 1991. >> baseball [i]

Rutherford (of Nelson), Ernest Rutherford, 1st Baron (1871–1937) Physicist, a pioneer of subatomic physics, born near Nelson, New Zealand. With Frederick Soddy he proposed that radioactivity results from the disintegration of atoms (1903), and later he developed the modern conception of the atom. He received the Nobel Prize for Chemistry in 1908. >> atom; radioactivity; Soddy

Rutherford, Dame Margaret (1892–1972) Theatre and film actress, born in London. She gained fame as a character actress and comedienne, played Agatha Christie's 'Miss Marple' in a series of films from 1962, and won an Oscar for her role in *The VIPs* in 1964.

Ruthwell Cross A runic stone cross at Ruthwell, near Dumfries, S Scotland, dating from the 7th-c. It is carved with scenes from the New Testament and stands 5 m/18 ft high. >> runes [i]

rutile [**roo**tiyl, -teel] A titanium dioxide (TiO_2) mineral, usually red-brown to black due to impurities of iron oxide, widespread in igneous and metamorphic rocks and in veins with quartz. It is a source of titanium and is also used as a gemstone. >> gemstones; titanium

Rutland County in the UK, known as the smallest in England, incorporated into Leicestershire in 1974, then made a unitary authority in 1997. It has given its name to a reservoir, Rutland Water. >> Leicestershire

Ruysdael, Jacob van [**roys**dahl], also spelled **Ruïsdael** (c.1628–82) Landscape painter, born in Haarlem, The Netherlands. His best works are country landscapes, and he also excelled in cloud effects, particularly in his seascapes. >> landscape painting

Ruyter, Michiel Adriaanszoon de [**roy**ter] (1607–76)

Dutch admiral, born in Vlissingen, The Netherlands. He gave distinguished service in the three Anglo-Dutch Wars (1652–4, 1665–7, 1672–8), winning notable victories in the Four Days' Battle off Dunkirk (1666) and a daring raid up the Rivers Medway and Thames (1667), in which much of the English fleet was destroyed. In the third war, his victories prevented a seaborne invasion of the United Provinces, but he was mortally wounded in a battle against the French off Sicily. >> Dutch Wars

Rwanda [roo**an**da], official name **Republic of Rwanda** pop (1995e) 8 430 000; area 26 338 sq km/10 169 sq mi. Landlocked republic in C Africa; capital, Kigali; timezone GMT +2; chief ethnic groups, Hutu (84%), Tutsi (14%); chief religions, Roman Catholicism (45%), local beliefs (25%); official languages, French, Kinyarwanda, and English, with Kiswahili widely used in commerce; unit of currency, the Rwanda franc; at a relatively high altitude, highest point Karisimbi (4507 m/14 787 ft); a highland tropical climate; in the 16th-c the Tutsi tribe moved into the country and took over from the Hutu, forming a monarchy; German protectorate, 1899; mandated with Burundi to Belgium as the Territory of Ruanda-Urundi, 1919; United Nations Trust Territory administered by Belgium, after World War 2; unrest in 1959 led to a Hutu revolt and the overthrow of Tutsi rule; independence, 1962; military coup, 1973; return to civilian rule, 1980; rebellion launched by (mainly Tutsi) Rwandan Patriotic Front, 1990; new constitution, 1991, provides for a multi-party democracy governed by a National Development Council, a president, and a Council of Ministers; peace accord with rebels, 1993; death of President Habyarimana in an air crash brought unprecedented outbreak of inter-ethnic violence, 1994; major refugee problem in neighbouring countries, 1995; ethnic conflict continuing; governed by a president, prime minister, and Transitional National Assembly; elections scheduled for 1999; largely agricultural economy, but severely disrupted by civil war. >> Burundi [i]; Hutu and Tutsi; mandates; RR1020 political leaders

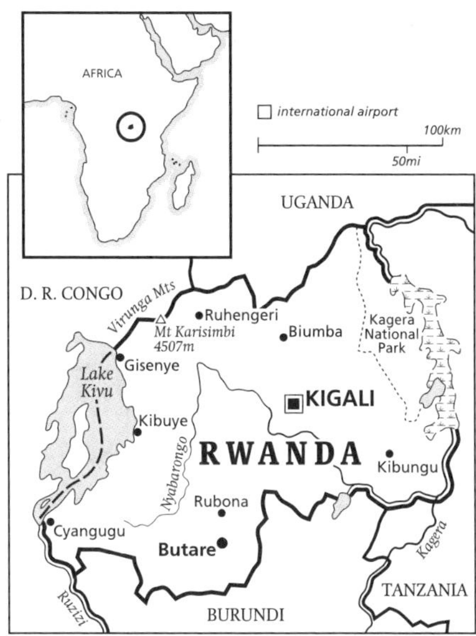

Ryan, Meg (1963–) Film actress, born in Fairfield, CT. She became well known after *When Harry Met Sally* (1989), later films including *Sleepless in Seattle* (1993), *French Kiss* (1995), which she also co-produced, and *City of Angels* (1998).

Ryan, (Lynn) Nolan (1947–) Baseball player, born in Refugio, TX. He is regarded as one of the fastest pitchers ever seen in major league baseball. He retired in 1993 with more strikeouts (5714) than any player in baseball history. >> baseball [i]

Ryazan [rya**zan**] 54°37N 39°43E, pop (1995e) 532 000. City in W Russia; on R Oka; founded, 1095; railway. >> Russia [i]

Ryder (of Warsaw), Sue Ryder, Baroness >> **Cheshire, (Geoffrey) Leonard**

Ryder, Winona [wi**noh**na] (1971–) Film actress, born in Winona, MI. Her films include *Beetlejuice* (1988), *Edward Scissorhands* (1990), and *Mermaids* (1990). She received a Best Supporting Actress Oscar nomination for *The Age of Innocence* (1993), and a Best Actress nomination for her role as Jo in *Little Women* (1995).

Ryder Cup A golf tournament played every 2 years between professional male golfers from the USA and Europe. First played at Worcester, MA, in 1927, the Cup was donated by English businessman Samuel Ryder (1859–1936). >> golf

rye A cereal (*Secale cereale*) resembling barley, but with longer, narrower ears. It succeeds on poor soils, and is cultivated mainly in cold regions such as North America and E Europe. It is used to make black bread, crispbreads, alcohol, and straw for hats and thatching. (Family: Gramineae.) >> barley; cereals

Rye House Plot An alleged plot by Whigs (1683) to murder Charles II of England and James, Duke of York, at Rye House near Hoddesdon, Hertfordshire. The conspirators were betrayed and captured; two of them, Algernon Sidney and William, Lord Russell, were executed. >> Charles II (of England); Sidney, Algernon

Rykov, Alexey Ivanovich [**ree**kof] (1881–1938) Russian revolutionary and politician, born in Saratov, Russia. He helped organize the October Revolution in Petrograd (1917) and was appointed People's Commissar for Internal Affairs in the first Soviet government. In 1928 after opposing Stalin's economic policies, he was arrested and shot. >> October Revolution; Stalin

Ryle, Gilbert (1900–76) Philosopher, born in Brighton, East Sussex. He is best known for his book *The Concept of Mind* (1949), which argued against the mind/body dualism ('the ghost in the machine') proposed by Descartes. >> Descartes; dualism; linguistic philosophy

Ryle, Sir Martin (1918–84) Radio astronomer, born in Brighton, East Sussex, the nephew of Gilbert Ryle. His development of interferometers enabled him to survey the most distant radio sources, and his work paved the way for renewed support of the 'big bang' theory. He was appointed Astronomer Royal in 1972, and shared the Nobel Prize for Physics in 1974. >> Hoyle, Fred; interferometer; radio astronomy

Ryukyu Islands [**ryuk**yoo], Jap **Nansei-shoto**, also called **Luchu Islands** pop (1995e) 1 260 000; area 2255 sq km/871 sq mi. Archipelago of over 50 islands SW of Kyushu, Japan, extending in a long chain for c.650 km/400 mi towards Taiwan; chief island Okinawa; became part of Japan, 1879; under US control, 1945; islands gradually returned to Japan in 1953, 1972. >> Japan [i]; Okinawa

Saar, River [zah(r)], Fr **Sarre** River in France and Germany; rises in the Vosges; enters the R Moselle; length 240 km/ 150 mi; its valley is a noted wine area. >> Vosges Mountains

Saarbrücken [**zah(r)**brükn], Fr **Sarrebruck** 49°15N 6°58E, pop (1995e) 198 000. City in Germany; on the R Saar; economic and cultural centre of Saarland; railway; university (1948); noted for its trade fairs. >> Germany ℹ

Saarinen, Eero (1910–61) Architect, born in Kirkkonummi, Finland. His designs for Expressionist modern buildings include the Trans-World Airlines Kennedy Terminal, New York City (1956–62). >> Expressionism

Saatchi & Saatchi [**sah**chee] Advertisers: **Charles Saatchi** (1943–) and **Maurice Saatchi** (1946–), both born in Iraq. They immigrated to England in 1947, set up an advertising agency in 1970, and were engaged by the Conservative Party in 1978 to create election posters and slogans. They became the world's largest agency, but suffered badly in the stock market crash at the end of the decade. In 1995, following a controversial share option package, chairman Maurice Saatchi left the company, and set up a new agency. >> advertising

S

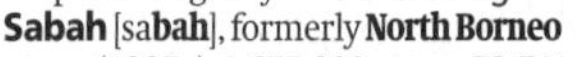

Sabah [sa**bah**], formerly **North Borneo** pop (1995e) 1 655 000; area 73 711 sq km/ 28 452 sq mi. State in E Malaysia, on the N tip of Borneo; highest peak, Mt Kinabalu, 4094 m/13 432 ft; British protectorate, 1882; member of the Federation of Malaysia, 1963; capital, Kota Kinabalu. >> Borneo; Malaysia ℹ

Sabbath or **Shabbat** (Heb 'cessation', 'rest') The seventh day of the week, which in Jewish belief is designated a day of rest and cessation from labour, beginning just before sunset on Fridays. >> Judaism; rabbi

Sabin, A(lbert) B(ruce) [**say**bin] (1906–93) Microbiologist, born in Białystok, Poland. He is best known for his research into a live virus as a polio vaccine, which has replaced the Salk vaccine, as it gives longer-lasting immunity, and is capable of being given orally. >> poliomyelitis; Salk; vaccination; virus

Sabines [**sab**iynz] A people of ancient Italy, inhabiting the mountainous country NE of Rome. Often at war with the Romans, they were ultimately absorbed by them.

sable An Asian marten (*Martes zibellina*) with a thick and silky winter coat valuable to the fur trade. The fur of the **American pine marten** (*Martes americana*) is known as *American sable* or *Hudson Bay sable*. >> marten

Sabra and Chatila Palestinian refugee camps on the outskirts of Beirut, Lebanon, developed in the 1950s and 1960s. They were the scene of a massacre of Palestinians by Christian Phalangists in 1983. >> Beirut

Sabratha Phoenician colony founded in the 8th-c BC on the NW coast of present-day Libya; the ruins are a world heritage site. >> Phoenicia

sabretooth A fossil cat, often referred to as **sabretooth tiger**, but not closely related to the tiger; upper canine teeth enlarged, sabre-like; became extinct in the late Pleistocene epoch. (Genus: *Smilodon*. Family: Felidae.) >> cat; fossil; Pleistocene epoch

saccharin [**sak**arin] $C_7H_5NO_3S$, melting point 229°C. A white solid which has more than 400 times the sweetening power of sucrose. It is used as an artificial sweetener. >> sucrose

Sacco and Vanzetti [**sa**koh, van**ze**tee] **Nicola Sacco** (1891–1927) and **Bartolomeo Vanzetti** (1888–1927) Italian immigrants to the USA, executed for murders which they were said to have committed during a payroll robbery in 1920. There was considerable protest about the justice of the verdict, as it was widely felt that they had been convicted for their anarchist beliefs.

Sachs, Hans [zahkhs] (1494–1576) Poet and playwright, born in Nuremberg, Germany. He headed the Meistersingers of Nuremberg in 1554, and in that role was idealized in Wagner's opera. >> Wagner

sackbut >> **trombone**

Sacks, Oliver (Wolf) (1933–) Neurologist, born in London. In New York City, he worked with patients who had contracted a form of sleeping sickness, and became known following his account of the brief cure they experienced after receiving treatment with L-dopa, *Awakenings* (1973; filmed, 1990). His insights into unusual syndromes, along with an appealing literary style, resulted in a series of best-selling books, such as *The Man who Mistook his Wife for a Hat* (1986) and *The Island of the Colorblind* (1998).

Sackville, Thomas, 1st Earl of Dorset (1536–1608) Poet and statesman, born in Buckhurst, Sussex. He collaborated with Thomas Norton (1532–84) in the tragedy *Gorboduc* (1561), the first English play in blank verse. >> blank verse

Sackville-West, Vita, popular name of **Victoria Mary Sackville-West** (1892–1962) Poet and novelist, born in Knole, Kent. Her best-known novels are *The Edwardians* (1930) and *All Passion Spent* (1931). In 1913 she married diplomat and critic **Harold (George) Nicolson** (1886–1968). Her intimate relationship with Virginia Woolf occasioned the latter's *Orlando* (1928).

sacrament A Christian rite understood as an outward and visible sign of an internal and spiritual grace. Orthodox and Roman Catholic Churches recognize seven sacraments: baptism, confirmation, the Eucharist (Mass), penance, extreme unction, holy orders (ordination), and matrimony. Protestant Churches recognize only baptism and the Eucharist (Communion) as sacraments. >> anointing the sick; baptism; confirmation (religion); Eucharist; penance

Sacramento 38°35N 121°29W, pop (1995e) 405 000. Capital of state, C California, USA, on the E bank of the Sacramento R; settled, 1839; state capital, 1854; airport; railway; university (1947); professional team, Kings (basketball). >> California

Sacramento River Longest river in California, USA; rises in the Klamath Mts; flows 615 km/382 mi S to Suisin Bay; joins with the San Joaquin to form the Central Valley Project for flood-control, irrigation, and hydroelectricity. >> California

sacrum A triangular-shaped bone at the lower end of the vertebral column, formed by fusion of the five sacral vertebrae. It gives attachment to the muscles of the back. >> pelvis; skeleton ℹ; vertebral column

Sadat, (Mohammed) Anwar el- [sa**dat**] (1918–81) Egyptian statesman and president (1970–81), born in the Tala district. He sought settlement of the conflict with Israel, meeting the Israeli premier in Jerusalem (1977) and at Camp David, USA (1978), in which year he and Begin were jointly awarded the Nobel Peace Prize. Following criticism by hard-line Muslims, he was assassinated in Cairo by extremists. >> Begin; Islam

Saddam Hussein >> **Hussein, Saddam**

saddle-bill stork >> **jabiru**

Sadducees [**sad**yuseez] A major party within Judaism (c.2nd-c BC–AD 70), the name probably deriving from the priest Zadok, whose descendants held priestly office from Solomon's times. They were mainly aristocrats, associated with the Jerusalem priesthood. >> Judaism; Pharisees; Solomon (Hebrew Bible); Zadokites

Sade, Marquis de [sahd], popular name of **Donatien Alphonse François, comte** (Count) **de Sade** (1740–1814) Writer, born in Paris. Condemned to death at Aix for his cruelty and sexual practices, he escaped, but was later imprisoned at Vincennes (1777) and in the Bastille (1784), where he wrote *Les 120 Journées de Sodome* (c.1784, The 120 Days of Sodom). His name has provided the language with the word **sadism**. >> sadomasochism

Sadler's Wells >> **Royal Ballet**

sadomasochism Sexual behaviour in which gratification is based on the infliction (**sadism**) or receipt (**masochism**) of pain or humiliation; often abbreviated as **SM**.

Safavids [sa**fah**weedz] A Persian dynasty (1501–1736) which laid down the foundations of the modern Iranian state. It made Shiism the official religion, and saw a flowering of the arts. >> Shiites

safety lamp A device used by miners to detect explosive methane gas in mines (*firedamp*), invented in 1815 by Sir Humphry Davy. Any methane present would cause a change in the appearance of the flame, but a double layer of wire gauze surrounding it prevented the gas igniting. >> Davy; firedamp; methane [i]

safflower An annual growing to 1 m/3¼ ft (*Carthamus tinctorius*); flower-heads thistle-like, up to 3 cm/1¼ in across, the florets bright red-orange; probably native to W Asia. Formerly a dye plant, it is now grown mainly for the seeds, which yield a useful oil. (Family: Compositae.) >> dyestuff

saffron An autumn-flowering species of crocus (*Crocus sativus*), native to S Europe and Asia, with lilac flowers. It is a source of saffron, used as a food dye and as flavouring. (Family: Iridaceae.) >> crocus

Safire, William [**sa**fiyr] (1929–) Journalist, born in New York City. A former public relations writer, he became a Washington-based columnist for the *New York Times* in 1973. He won the Pulitzer Prize for commentary in 1978, and went on to become a national figure known for his weekly column devoted to language matters.

saga (Old Norse 'saying') A mediaeval Icelandic or Scandinavian prose narrative, transcribed from oral tradition after 1100, and later composed in writing. The term is also more generally used of any extended narrative, in fact or fiction.

Sagan, Carl (Edward) [**say**gn] (1934–96) Astronomer and writer, born in New York City. He worked on planetary atmospheres and surfaces, the origin of life on Earth, and the possibility of extraterrestrial life, and did much to popularize astronomy and other aspects of science. >> astronomy

Sagan, Françoise [sagã], pseudonym of **Françoise Quoirez** (1935–) Novelist, born in Paris. At 18 she wrote the best-selling *Bonjour tristesse* (1954, Good Morning, Sadness). *Aimez-vous Brahms?* (Do You Like Brahms?) appeared in 1959.

sage An aromatic shrub (*Salvia officinalis*) growing to 0.5 m/1½ ft, native to S Europe; flowers purplish, 2-lipped, the upper lip hooded. It is widely cultivated as a culinary and medicinal herb. (Family: Labiatae.) >> herb; salvia

sagebrush The name applied to certain North American species of *Artemisia*, including **big sagebrush** (*Artemisia tridentata*), a much-branched aromatic shrub growing to 3 m/10 ft; flower-heads small, greenish, and inconspicuous; also called **sagebush**. (Genus: *Artemisia*. Family: Compositae.)

sagebush >> **sagebrush**

Sagitta [**sa**jita] (Lat 'arrow') The third-smallest constellation, lying in the Milky Way near Cygnus. >> constellation; Cygnus; Milky Way; RR968

Sagittarius [saji**tair**ius] (Lat 'archer') A S constellation of the zodiac, lying between Scorpius and Capricornus. >> constellation; zodiac [i]; RR968

sago palm A small tree with large feathery leaves, native to SE Asia and the Pacific. Its trunk provides sago, a primary source of carbohydrate in the tropics. (Genus: *Metroxylon*, 15 species. Family: Palmae.) >> palm

saguaro [sa**gwah**roh] The largest of the cacti (*Carnegiea gigantea*), slow-growing, reaching 21 m/70 ft, with a thick stem, candelabra-like branches, and white flowers; found only in Arizona, S California, and Mexico. (Family: Cactaceae.) >> cactus [i]

Sagunto [sa**goon**toh], Arabic **Murviedro** (to 1877), ancient **Saguntum** 39°42N 0°18W, pop (1995e) 55 900. Town in E Spain; on R Palancia; Roman theatre, fortress. >> Spain [i]

Sahara Desert (Arabic 'wilderness') Desert in N Africa; the largest desert in the world, area 7.7 million sq km/3 million sq mi; average width, 1440 km/895 mi across N Africa from the Atlantic to the Libyan Desert, in which it continues unbroken to the Nile, and beyond that in the Nubian Desert to the Red Sea; areas of drift sand, rock, or gravel and pebbles; scattered outlets of surface water at oases, where agriculture is possible; generally void of vegetation; climate arid since the glacial epoch, when the region was relatively humid with a park savannah vegetation; camel caravans follow routes marked by oases; oil exploration near the Algeria–Libya frontier; phosphates in Morocco and Western Sahara; first crossed by Europeans in the 1820s. >> desert

sahel [sa**hel**] A vegetation zone intermediate between desert and savannah conditions where rainfall is irregular and unpredictable. The vegetation is a transitional scrubland. The name is most commonly applied to the area S of the Sahara (**the Sahel**), which frequently suffers from drought and famine. >> Sahara Desert; savannah

saiga [**say**ga] A goat-antelope native to Asia (*Saiga tatarica*); thick pale brown coat; eyes protruding; nose grotesquely swollen with large downward-facing nostrils at tip; male with short yellow horns; inhabits cold steppelands. >> antelope

Saigon >> **Ho Chi Minh City**

Sailer, Toni (Anton) [**ziy**ler] (1935–) Alpine skier, born in Kitzbühel, Austria. In 1956, he became the first man to win all three Olympic skiing titles (downhill, slalom,

Head of saiga

giant slalom), and was the world combined champion in 1956 and 1958. >> skiing

sailfish Large agile billfish (*Istiophorus platypterus*) widely distributed in open ocean surface waters; length up to 3.5 m/11½ ft; blue-grey above, underside silver; long tall dorsal fin. (Family: Istiophoridae.) >> fish ℹ

sailing A term used to describe the sport or pastime of travelling over water in a suitable craft, especially one with sails. As a pastime, most use is made of small single- or double-sailed dinghies; but large ocean-going yachts may be 25 m/80 ft or more in length. Several classes of racing yacht are recognized in Olympic and major international competitions. >> Admiral's Cup; America's Cup; RR1065

sailing rig >> *see panel below*

Saimaa [**siy**mah] Lake system extending over the Finnish Lake Plateau, SE Finland; total area 4400 sq km/1700 sq mi; fifth largest lake system in Europe. >> Finland ℹ

sainfoin [**san**foyn] A perennial growing to 80 cm/30 in (*Onobrychis viciifolia*), possibly native to C Europe; pea-flowers bright pink veined with purple; pods 1-seeded; widely cultivated for fodder. (Family: Leguminosae.)

saint In Roman Catholic and Orthodox teaching, a man or woman recognized as being in heaven because of their special qualities. Veneration of saints (often martyrs) began in the 2nd-c, and individual saints were eventually looked to for intercession and devotion. An elaborate procedure is required before canonization may proceed. >> canonization; Orthodox Church; Roman Catholicism

St Albans [**awl**bnz], Lat **Verulamium** 51°46N 0°21W, pop (1995e) 78 300. Town in Hertfordshire, England; on R Ver; named after the first Christian martyr to be executed in Britain; royal charter, 1553; city status (1887); railway; cathedral (1115, founded as Benedictine abbey, 793); Roman theatre. >> Hertfordshire

St Andrews 56°20N 2°48W, pop (1995e) 15 200. Town in Fife, E Scotland; university (oldest in Scotland, founded 1412); remains of castle (1200) and cathedral (12th–13th-c); St Andrews Royal and Ancient Golf Club; British Amateur Golf Championships (Jun). >> Fife; Scotland ℹ

St Anthony's fire >> **ergotism**

St Anton am Arlberg 47°08N 9°52E, pop (1995e) 2390. Winter sports resort in the Lechtal Alps (Arlberg massif), W Austria; major skiing centre. >> Alps

St Bartholomew's Day Massacre (24 Aug 1572) The slaughter of French Huguenots in Paris, ordered by King Charles IX and connived at by the Queen Mother, Catherine de' Medici, to coincide with celebrations for the marriage of Marguerite de Valois and Henry of Navarre (18 Aug). >> Catherine de' Medici; Huguenots

St Basil's Cathedral Part of the Historical Museum in Moscow. It was built (1555–61) as the Cathedral of the Intercession of the Virgin. The present title was adopted after 1588, when a chapel was added to house the remains of the ascetic Basil the Blessed. >> Moscow

St Bernard The heaviest breed of dog (up to 100 kg/220 lb), developed at the Hospice of St Bernard in Switzerland to track people lost in the mountain snow; orange-brown and white; large with broad head, deep muzzle, pendulous ears; also known as **Great St Bernard**. >> dog

St Bernard's Passes Two transalpine frontier passes: the **Great St Bernard**, which crosses the Pennine Alps between Martigny in Switzerland and Aosta in Italy, and the **Little St Bernard**, which crosses the Graian Alps between Aosta and Bourg St Maurice in France. St Bernard of Menthon founded hospices in both passes in the 10th-c. >> Alps; Bernard of Menthon, St

St Catharines 43°10N 79°15W, pop (1995e) 137 000. Town in SE Ontario, S Canada; founded, 1784; at entrance to Welland Ship Canal; railway; university (1964); heart of Canada's fruit belt and major wine-growing region. >> Ontario

St Christopher-Nevis >> **St Kitts-Nevis**

St Croix [saynt **kroy**], formerly **Santa Cruz** pop (1995e) 53 300; area 218 sq km/84 sq mi. Largest of the three main US Virgin Is, Caribbean; main towns, Christiansted (former capital of the Danish West Indies) and Frederiksted. >> Virgin Islands, United States

St-Cyr, Ecole de [ay**kol** duh sĩ **seer**] A French military academy founded by Napoleon at Fontainebleau but transferred to St-Cyr in 1808. The school was moved to Coetquidan in Brittany after World War 2, but retained the name of its former home. >> Napoleon I

St David's, Welsh **Tyddewi** 51°54N 5°16W, pop (1995e) 1840. Village in Pembrokeshire, SW Wales; episcopal seat; 12th-c cathedral honours the 6th-c Welsh patron saint, Dewi (David); mediaeval place of pilgrimage. >> Wales ℹ

St-Denis (France) [sĩ duh**nee**] 48°56N 2°21E, pop (1995e) 93 600. Modern industrial town and railway centre in NC France; N suburb of Paris; 12th-c Gothic Basilica of St-Denis, with tombs of several French monarchs. >> Paris

Sailing Rig

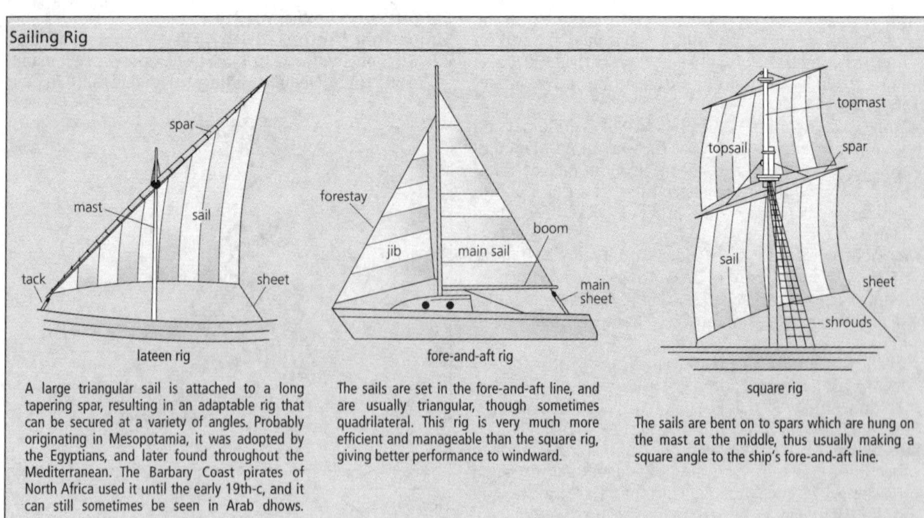

lateen rig

A large triangular sail is attached to a long tapering spar, resulting in an adaptable rig that can be secured at a variety of angles. Probably originating in Mesopotamia, it was adopted by the Egyptians, and later found throughout the Mediterranean. The Barbary Coast pirates of North Africa used it until the early 19th-c, and it can still sometimes be seen in Arab dhows.

fore-and-aft rig

The sails are set in the fore-and-aft line, and are usually triangular, though sometimes quadrilateral. This rig is very much more efficient and manageable than the square rig, giving better performance to windward.

square rig

The sails are bent on to spars which are hung on the mast at the middle, thus usually making a square angle to the ship's fore-and-aft line.

St-Denis (Réunion) [sī duh**nee**] 20°52S 55°27E, pop (1995e) 133 000. Capital of Réunion, on the N coast; airport. >> Réunion

Saint Denis, Ruth, originally **Ruth Dennis** (1879–1968) Dancer, choreographer, and teacher, born in Newark, NJ. With Ted Shawn she started the Denishawn school and company, a training ground for modern dancers. >> choreography; modern dance

Sainte-Beuve, Charles Augustin [sīt boev] (1804–69) Literary critic, born in Boulogne, France. He produced several volumes of poetry, critical articles on French literature, and several books of 'portraits' of literary contemporaries. His speeches in favour of liberty of thought earned him great popularity.

St Elias, Mount [e**li**yas] 60°17N 140°55W. Mountain in St Elias Mts, on the Yukon–Alaska border, USA; rises to 5489 m/18 008 ft; second highest peak in the USA. >> United States of America ℹ

St Elmo's fire A blue-green-coloured electrical discharge which occurs during thunderstorm weather around the masts of ships, weather-vanes, and aircraft wing tips.

St-Etienne [sītay**tyen**] 45°27N 4°22E, pop (1995e) 205 000. Manufacturing town in SW France; railway; university; school of mining (1816); centre of metallurgical industry since 16th-c. >> France ℹ

Saint-Exupéry, Antoine (Marie Roger) de [sīt egzüpay**ree**] (1900–44) Airman and writer, born in Lyon, France. His philosophy of 'heroic action' is found in such novels as *Vol de nuit* (1931, Night Flight). He is also known for his popular children's fable for adults, *Le Petit Prince* (1943, The Little Prince).

St Gallen [sankt **gal**en], Fr **St Gall** [sī **gal**] 47°25N 9°23E, pop (1995e) 76 000. Ancient abbey town in NE Switzerland; developed around the abbey founded by St Gall, 7th-c; a world heritage site; university; cathedral (18th-c). >> Switzerland ℹ

St George's 12°03N 61°45W, pop (1995e) 8100. Port and capital town of Grenada, on SW coast; founded, 1650; airport. >> Grenada ℹ

St George's Channel Stretch of sea between the SE of Ireland (W) and Wales (E), connecting the Atlantic Ocean with the Irish Sea; narrowest between Carnsore Point (Ireland) and St David's Head (Wales), 74 km/46 mi across.

St Gotthard Pass [**got**ah(r)d] 46°34N 8°31E. Mountain pass and tunnel (road and rail, 15 km/10 mi) between Andermatt and Airolo, in the Lepontine Alps, SC Switzerland; height, 2108 m/6916 ft; pass open between June and October; St Gotthard Hospice (14th-c). >> Alps

St Helena [he**lee**na] 15°58S 5°43W; pop (1995e) 6800; area 122 sq km/47 sq mi. Volcanic island in the S Atlantic; a British territory, 1920 km/1200 mi from the SW coast of Africa; highest point, Diana's Peak (823 m/2700 ft); discovered by the Portuguese on St Helena's feast day, 1502; annexed by the Dutch, 1633; annexed by the East India Company, 1659; Napoleon exiled here, 1815–21; Ascension and Tristan da Cunha made dependencies, 1922; port and capital, Jamestown; economy heavily subsidised by UK. >> Ascension Island; Jamestown (St Helena); Napoleon I; Tristan da Cunha

St Helens 53°28N 2°44W, pop (1995e) 109 000. Industrial town in Merseyside, NW England; railway. >> Merseyside

St Helens, Mount 46°12N 122°12W. Volcano in SW Washington, USA, in the Cascade Range; rises to 2549 m/8363 ft; major eruption in 1980. >> volcano; Washington (state)

St Ives 50°12N 5°29W, pop (1995e) 10 700. Resort town in Cornwall, SW England; railway. >> Cornwall

St James's Palace Until the mid-19th-c, one of the principal royal palaces in London. Only parts of the original Tudor palace built for Henry VIII remain. >> Tudors

Saint John (Canada) 45°16N 66°03W, pop (1995e) 79 600. Seaport in S New Brunswick, Canada, at mouth of St John R; harbour ice-free all year; French fort, 1631–5; taken by British, 1758; largely destroyed by fire, 1877; airfield; railway. >> New Brunswick (Canada)

Saint John (US Virgin Is) pop (1995e) 2870; area 52 sq km/20 sq mi. Smallest of the three main US Virgin Is, Caribbean. >> Virgin Islands, United States

St John Ambulance Brigade A worldwide charitable organization that provides medical and nursing help to the aged, sick, and injured. It derives its inspiration from the Hospitallers, a military and religious order founded in the 11th-c (the Knights of Saint John of Jerusalem). >> Hospitallers; nursing

Saint John's 47°34N 52°41W, pop (1995e) 102 000. Port and provincial capital of Newfoundland, E Canada; Cabot landed here, 1497; British possession, 1583; held by the French, taken by the British, 1762; airport; railway; university (1925); two cathedrals. >> Newfoundland (Canada)

St John's wort An annual or perennial, sometimes a shrub, native throughout temperate regions and tropical mountains; flowers often large and showy, yellow, 5-petalled with numerous stamens; fruit a capsule or berry. (Genus: *Hypericum*, 400 species. Family: Guttifereae.)

Saint-Just, Louis (Antoine Léon Florelle) de [sī zhüst] (1767–94) French revolutionary, born in Decize, France. He was elected to the National Convention (1792), became a devoted follower of Robespierre and was made president of the Convention (1794). He was guillotined with Robespierre in the Thermidorian Reaction. >> French Revolution ℹ; Robespierre

St Kilda 57°49S 8°34E. A group of small volcanic islands in the Atlantic Ocean, 100 km/62 mi W of Scotland; abandoned in 1930, having been inhabited for 2000 years; major bird colonies; a world heritage site. >> Atlantic Ocean

St Kitts-Nevis, official name **Federation of St Kitts and Nevis**, with **Christopher** a former alternative for **Kitts** pop (1995e) 42 800, with c.10,000 on Nevis; area 269 sq km/104 sq mi. Independent state in the N Leeward Is, E Caribbean; comprises the islands of St Christopher (St Kitts), and Nevis; capital, Basseterre; timezone GMT −4; population mainly of African descent; chief religion, Christianity; official language, English; unit of currency, the East Caribbean dollar; St Kitts, length 37 km/23 mi, area 168 sq km/65 sq mi, mountain range rises to 1156 m/3793 ft at Mt Liamuiga; Nevis, 3 km/1¾ mi SE, area 93 sq km/36 sq mi, dominated by a C peak rising to 985 m/3232 ft; warm climate, average annual temperature 26°C, average annual rainfall 1375 mm/54 in; low humidity; St Kitts the first British colony in the West Indies, 1623; control disputed between France and Britain, 17th–18th-c; ceded to Britain, 1783; St Kitts and Nevis united in 1882, along with Anguilla; state in association with the UK, 1967; separation of Anguilla, 1980; independence, 1983; British monarch is represented by a governor-general; governed by a prime minister and two legislative chambers; referendum on Nevis I secession failed to achieve two-thirds majority, 1998; sugar, electronic goods, tourism. >> Anguilla; Basseterre; Charlestown; Leeward Islands (Caribbean); RR1021 political leaders

Saint-Laurent, Yves (Henri Donat Mathieu) [sī lohrã] (1936–) Fashion designer, born in Oran, Algeria. In 1962 he opened his own house, and launched the first of his 160 Rive Gauche boutiques in 1966, selling ready-to-wear clothes, a trend which many other designers were to follow.

St Lawrence River, Fr **St Laurent** A principal river of North America, in E Canada, the chief outlet for the Great Lakes; issues from NE end of L Ontario and flows NE to the

Gulf of St Lawrence; forms part of border between Canada and USA; total length 1197 km/744 mi; increases gradually in width to c.145 km/90 mi; formerly navigable for ocean-going vessels only as far as Montreal; St Lawrence Seaway (1955–9) between L Ontario and Montreal now allows passage to Great Lakes; often partly unnavigable in winter months. >> Canada [i]; Great Lakes

Saint Leger, Barry [**se**linjer, saynt **le**jer] (1737–89) British army colonel. He fought in the American Revolution, and founded horse-racing stables at Doncaster in 1776. The **St Leger** race was named for him in 1778.

St-Lô [sĩ **loh**], ancient **Briovera**, later **Laudus** 49°07N 1°05W, pop (1995e) 23 500. Market town in NW France; fortified by Charlemagne; almost completely destroyed in World War 2, but mediaeval part of town largely preserved; railway. >> Charlemagne

St-Louis [sĩ loo**ee**] 16°01N 16°30W, pop (1995e) 117 000. Seaport in Senegal; built in 1658 as a French trading company fort, and prospered with the slave trade; capital of French West Africa, 1895–1902; airfield; railway terminal. >> Senegal [i]

St Louis [saynt **loo**is] 38°37N 90°12W, pop (1995e) 412 000. City and port in E Missouri, USA, on the Mississippi R; settled by the French, 1764; under Spanish control, 1770–1800; ceded to the USA, 1804; city status, 1822; largest city in the state; busiest inland port on the Mississippi; a major land transport hub; railway; three universities (1818, 1853, 1960); professional teams, Cardinals (baseball), Blues (ice hockey); Gateway Arch, 192 m/630 ft high. >> Missouri

St Lucia [**loo**sha] pop (1995e) 140 000; area 616 sq km/238 sq mi. Second largest of the Windward Is, E Caribbean; capital, Castries; timezone GMT −4; population mainly of African descent (90%); chief religion, Roman Catholicism; official language, English, with French patois widely spoken; unit of currency, the Eastern Caribbean dollar; length, 43 km/27 mi; maximum width, 23 km/14 mi; mountainous centre, rising to 950 m/3117 ft at Mt Gimie; tropical climate; reputedly visited by Columbus, 1502; disputed ownership between Britain and France, 17th–18th-c; British Crown Colony, 1814; independence, 1979; British monarch represented by a governor-general; House of Assembly and Senate; tourism the fastest-growing sector of the economy. >> Castries; Windward Islands (Caribbean); RR1021 political leaders

St-Malo [sĩ **mah**loh] 48°39N 2°00W, pop (1995e) 50 800. Old port in W France; at mouth of R Rance; badly damaged in World War 2; birthplace of Chateaubriand. >> Chateaubriand

St Mark's Cathedral, Ital **San Marco** A church constructed in 1063–71 on the site of a 9th-c shrine which housed the relics of St Mark, in Venice. It became a cathedral in 1807. >> Mark, St; Venice

St Michael and St George, Most Distinguished Order of In the UK, an order of chivalry for those who have rendered distinguished service abroad. There are three classes: Knights and Dames Grand Cross (GCMG), Knights and Dames Commanders (KCMG/DCMG), and Companions (CMG). The motto is *Auspicium melioris aevi* (Lat 'a pledge of better times').

St Moritz [**mo**rits], Ger **Sankt Moritz**, Fr **Saint** [sĩ] **Moritz**, Romansch **San Murezzan** 46°30N 9°51E, pop (1995e) 5600. Resort town in SE Switzerland; altitude 1853 m/6079 ft; railway; spa; winter sports resort, home of the 1928 and 1948 Winter Olympics; Cresta Run (bobsledding). >> Switzerland [i]

St-Nazaire [sĩ na**zair**] 47°17N 2°12W, pop (1995e) 68 100. Seaport and industrial town in W France; on right bank of R Loire; major debarkation port for American Expeditionary Force in World War 1; German submarine base in World War 2, in which the town was largely destroyed. >> Nantes

St Paul 44°57N 93°06W, pop (1995e) 289 000. Capital of state in SE Minnesota, USA; a port on the Mississippi River E of its twin city Minneapolis; founded, 1838; capital of Minnesota Territory, 1849; city status, 1854; state capital, 1858; railway; university (1854); major industrial and commercial centre for a vast agricultural region. >> Minneapolis; Minnesota

saintpaulia >> **African violet**

St Paul's Cathedral A Baroque cathedral on Ludgate Hill, London, built by Wren to replace the mediaeval cathedral destroyed by the Fire of London in 1666. It is surmounted by a central lantern dome which still dominates the C London skyline. >> Fire of London; Wren, Christopher

St Peter's Basilica The largest Christian church, started in 1506 in Rome on the site of the 4th-c basilica built by Emperor Constantine. The present building was designed by Bramante on a Greek cross plan, but in 1605 Maderna was instructed to extend the nave, thereby changing the plan to that of a Latin cross. The immense dome, designed by Michelangelo and completed by Giacomo della Porta and Domenico Fontana, has a diameter of 42 m/137 ft. >> Bramante; Constantine I (Emperor); Michelangelo; Raphael

St Petersburg, Russ **Sankt Peterburg**, formerly **Petrograd** (1914–24), **Leningrad** (1924–91) 59°55N 30°25E, pop (1995e) 5 070 000. Port in NW European Russia; on the R Neva, at the head of the Gulf of Finland; largest Russian Baltic port (frozen, Jan–Apr) and second largest Russian city; former capital of the Russian Empire, 1712–1918; founded by Peter the Great, 1703; scene of a major siege by Germany in World War 2, 1941–4; airport; railway junction; university (1819); Academy of Sciences (1726); Winter Palace (1754–62, rebuilt 1839), St Isaac Cathedral (19th-c), Kazan Cathedral (1801–11), Fortress of Peter and Paul (1703), St Nicholas Navy Cathedral (1753–62). >> Hermitage; Peter and Paul Fortress; Russia [i]

St Pierre et Miquelon [sĩ **pyair** ay meek**lõ**] pop (1995e) 6600; area 240 sq km/93 sq mi. Two islands comprising a French overseas department, S of Newfoundland; main town, St Pierre; settled by Breton and Basque fishermen, 16th–17th-c; disputed between UK and France, 19th-c; confirmed as French territory, 1946. >> France [i]

St-Quentin [sĩ kãtĩ] 49°51N 3°17E, pop (1995e) 64 000. Industrial town in N France, on R Somme; railway; centre of woollen industry in Middle Ages; surrounded by battlefields throughout World War 1; 12th–15th-c basilica.

Saint-Saëns, (Charles) Camille [sĩ sãs] (1835–1921) Composer and music critic, born in Paris. His works include five symphonies; 13 operas; symphonic poems; piano, violin, and cello concertos; the popular *Carnaval des animaux* (1886, Carnival of the Animals); and church music, including his *Messe solennelle* (1855).

Saint-Simon, Claude Henri de Rouvroy, comte de (Count of) [sĩ seemõ] (1760–1825) Social reformer, the founder of French socialism, born in Paris. His writing was a reaction against the savagery of the revolutionary period, and proclaimed a brotherhood of man in which science and technology would become a new spiritual authority. >> socialism

Saint-Simon, Louis de Rouvroy, duc de (Duke of) [sĩ seemõ] (1675–1755) Writer, born in Paris. He joined the court of Louis XIV, and from the 1690s kept a journal, published as his *Mémoires* (1752), giving impressions and descriptions of court life up to 1723. >> Louis XIV

St Swithin's Day >> **Swithin, St**

St Thomas pop (1995e) 50 800; area 72 sq km/28 sq mi. One of the three main US Virgin Is, Caribbean; length, 21 km/13 mi; rises to 474 m/1555 ft at Crown Mt; capital,

Charlotte Amalie; airport. >> Virgin Islands, United States

St-Tropez [sĩ trohpay] 43°16N 6°39E, pop (1995e) 6000. Fashionable resort on the Mediterranean coast, SE France; former small fishing port now frequented by yachtsmen, artists, and tourists. >> Riviera

St Valentine's Day (14 Feb) A day on which special greetings cards (**valentine cards** or **valentines**) are sent, usually anonymously, to a person or people to whom one feels attracted. The saint ostensibly commemorated on this day was an obscure 3rd-c Roman priest, and none of the traditions connected with 14 February have anything to do with him. There is a traditional English belief that birds choose their mates on this day.

St Vincent, official name **Saint Vincent and the Grenadines** pop (1995e) 120 000; land area 390 sq km/150 sq mi. Island group of the Windward Is, E Caribbean; capital, Kingstown; timezone GMT −4; population mainly of African descent; chief religion, Protestantism; official language, English; unit of currency, the East Caribbean dollar; comprises the island of St Vincent (length, 29 km/18 mi; width, 16 km/10 mi) and the N Grenadine Is; St Vincent volcanic in origin; highest peak Soufrière, active volcano (1234 m/4048 ft), most recent eruption 1979; tropical climate; visited by Columbus, 1498; British control, 1763; part of West Indies Federation, 1958–62; independence, 1979; British sovereign represented by a governor-general; a prime minister leads a House of Assembly; economy based on agriculture; world's largest producer of arrowroot. >> Grenadines, The; Kingstown; West Indies Federation; Windward Islands (Caribbean); RR1021 political leaders

St Vincent, Cape, Port **Cabo de São Vicente** 37°01N 8°59W. Rocky headland 60 m/200 ft above sea-level on the Atlantic coast, Portugal; SW extremity of Portugal; in the 12th-c a ship bearing the body of St Vincent came ashore here; scene of a British naval victory over the Spanish fleet in 1797. >> Portugal ℹ

St Vitus' dance >> **chorea**

Saipan [siypan] pop (1995e) 41 500; area 122 sq km/47 sq mi. Largest of the N Mariana Is, W Pacific; length 23 km/14 mi; airport. >> Mariana Islands

saithe [sayth] Commercially important codfish (*Pollachius virens*) widely distributed in inshore waters of the N Atlantic; length up to 1.2 m/4 ft; dark green on back, sides and underside silvery grey; also called **coalfish**, **coley**, or **pollock**. (Family: Gadidae.) >> cod

Saka Era [sahka] An era of dating in India calculated from AD 78. It has been used alongside Gregorian dates by the Indian Government since 1957. >> RR981

Sakai [sakaee] 34°35N 135°28E, pop (1995e) 817 000. City in SC Honshu, Japan; formerly an important port. >> Honshu

saké [sakay] A Japanese rice wine, brewed in Japan for centuries, and very popular in winter. It is generally warmed in small bottles and drunk from small cups. >> rice

Sakhalin [sakaleen], Jap **Karafuto** area 74 066 sq km/28 589 sq mi. Island in the Sea of Okhotsk, E Russia; length, 942 km/585 mi; maximum width, 160 km/100 mi; first Russian visit, 1644; colonized by the Japanese, 18th-c; ceded to Russia in exchange for the Kuril Is, 1875; Japan gained control of S area, 1905; ceded to the USSR, 1945; severe climate; largely forested. >> Russia ℹ

Sakharov, Andrey [sakarof] (1921–89) Physicist, born in Moscow. He is credited with a critical role in developing the Soviet hydrogen bomb. In 1958 he opposed nuclear weapon tests, thereafter supporting East–West co-operation and human rights, and in 1975 was awarded the Nobel Peace Prize. Exiled to Nizhni Novgorod (formerly Gorky) in 1980 as a leading dissident, he lived under poor conditions until restored to favour in 1986. >> Bonner; civil rights

Sakhmet or **Sekmet** [sakmet] An ancient Egyptian goddess of Memphis, depicted with the head of a lioness; her name means 'powerful'. She is associated with savage cruelty.

saki [sakee] A New World monkey; coat long, especially around face; tail long; broad mouth turns downwards at sides. (Genus: *Pithecia*, 4 species.) >> New World monkey

Saki >> **Munro, H H**

Sakigake and Suisei project [sakeegakay, sooisay] The first Japanese interplanetary spacecraft, launched to intercept Halley's comet. *Sakigake* ('forerunner') was launched (Jan 1985) as a test spacecraft for *Suisei* ('comet', launched Aug 1985). They made highly successful encounters (11 and 8 Mar 1986 respectively). >> Halley's comet

Saladin [saladin], in full **Salah ed-din Yussuf ibn Ayub** (1137–93) Sultan of Egypt and Syria, the leader of the Muslims against the crusaders in Palestine, born in Tekrit, Mesopotamia. He defeated the Christians in 1187, recapturing almost all their fortified places in Syria, but a further crusade captured Acre in 1191, and he was defeated. >> Crusades ℹ; Islam

Salamanca [salamangka], ancient **Helmantica** or **Salmantica** 40°58N 5°39W, pop (1995e) 164 000. City in W Spain; on R Tormes; scene of British victory over the French in the Peninsular War, 1812; bishopric; railway; university (1218), a leading centre of learning until the end of the 16th-c; old and new cathedrals. >> Peninsular War; Spain ℹ; Unamuno

salamander An amphibian widespread in the temperate N hemisphere and tropical South America; slim body with long tail. (Order: Urodela, 358 species.) >> amphibian; axolotl; mudpuppy; newt; olm; siren

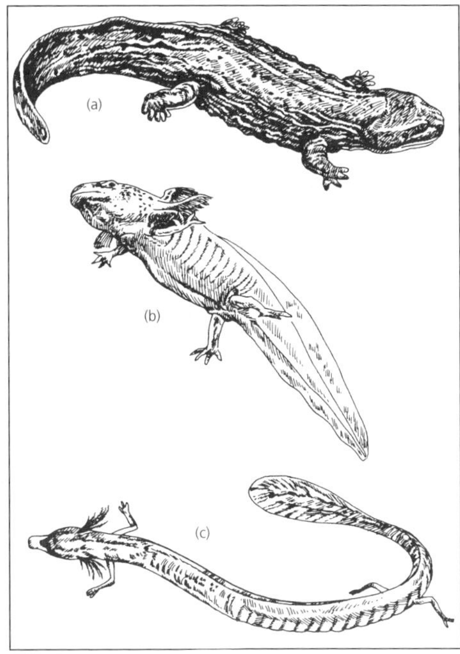

Salamanders – hellbender (a), axolotl (b) and olm (c)

Salamis (Cyprus) [**sal**amis] The principal city of prehistoric and classical Cyprus, founded c.1075 BC. It flourished particularly during the 8th–4th-c BC, but was destroyed by earthquake in AD 332–42. >> Cyprus ℹ

Salamis (Greece) [**sal**amis] or **Koulouri** 37°58N 23°30E, pop (1995e) 21 700. Town in Greece, on the W coast of Salamis I; to the E, scene of a decisive Greek naval victory over the Persians, 480 BC. >> Greece ℹ; Persian Wars

sal ammoniac [sal a**moh**niak] >> **ammonium**

Salazar, António de Oliviera [sala**zah(r)**] (1889–1970) Portuguese dictator (1932–68), born near Coimbra, Portugal. As premier, in 1932 he introduced a new, authoritarian regime, the *Estado Novo* ('New State'). He was also minister of war (1936–44) and of foreign affairs (1936–47) during the delicate period of the Spanish Civil War. >> Spanish Civil War

Salem (Massachusetts) [**say**lem] 42°31N 70°53W, pop (1995e) 38 400. Residential suburb of Boston on Massachusetts Bay; settled, 1626; 20 people executed as witches here, 1692; railway; birthplace of Nathaniel Hawthorne. >> Hawthorne; Massachusetts

Salem (Oregon) [**say**lem] 44°56N 123°02W, pop (1995e) 121 000. State capital in NW Oregon, USA; on the Willamette R; founded by Methodist missionaries, 1841; capital of Oregon Territory, 1851; state capital, 1859; railway; university (1842). >> Oregon

Salerno [sa**lair**noh] 40°40N 14°46E, pop (1995e) 163 000. Industrial town in Campania, Italy; founded by the Romans, 197 BC; one of the earliest universities in Europe; scene of major World War 2 fighting, after Allied landing, 1943; archbishopric; railway; new university (1970); cathedral (11th-c). >> Italy ℹ

Sales, Francis of >> **Francis of Sales, St**

sales tax A tax levied on goods sold, usually a percentage of the price. It is levied in the USA by most states, at differing rates, and on most products. >> purchase tax; taxation; VAT

Salford [**sawl**ferd] 53°30N 2°16W, pop (1995e) 90 900. City in Greater Manchester, NW England; on the R Irwell and Manchester Ship Canal; chartered in 1230; designated a city in 1926; railway; docks for Manchester; university (1967); cathedral (1848). >> Manchester, Greater

Salians >> **Franks**

salicylic acid [sali**sil**ik] A drug first prepared from an extract of meadowsweet (*Spirea ulmaria* – hence the word *aspirin*), and in 1838 from an extract of willow bark; its salt, *sodium salicylate*, was first used therapeutically in 1875. It was superseded in 1899 by the more potent *acetylsalicylic acid* (aspirin). >> aspirin; willow

Salieri, Antonio [sal**yay**ree] (1750–1825) Composer, born in Verona, Italy. He wrote over 40 operas, an oratorio, and Masses, and became a famous rival of Mozart.

Salinger, J(erome) D(avid) [**sal**injer] (1919–) Writer, born in New York City. His fame rests on the novel *The Catcher in the Rye* (1951); other books include *Franny and Zooey* (1961) and, after a long period of silence, *Hapworth 16, 1924* (1997).

salinity The saltiness of seawater, ie the total amount of dissolved substances in seawater, usually reported in parts per thousand (‰), grams of solute per kilogram of sea water. The average salinity of ocean water is about 35‰. >> salt

Salisbury (Rhodesia) [**sawlz**bree] >> **Harare**

Salisbury (UK) [**sawlz**bree], sometimes called **New Sarum** 51°05N 1°48W, pop (1995e) 41 200. City in Wiltshire, S England; Old Sarum (3 km/1¾ mi N), Iron Age hill fort, later the centre of settlement, but abandoned when New Sarum was founded in 1220 (though continued to return two members to parliament until the passing of the Reform Bill, 1832); railway; 13th-c cathedral, with the highest spire in Britain, contains one of four copies of the Magna Carta. >> Magna Carta; Wiltshire

Salisbury, Marquess of [**sawlz**bree] >> **Cecil, Robert**

Salisbury Plain [**sawlz**bree] A chalk plateau of open downs in Wiltshire, S England, rising to an average of 140 m/450 ft and covering some 77 700 ha/192 000 acres. Much of the area is now either under cultivation or used for army training, but it remains remarkable for a number of prehistoric sites, particularly Stonehenge. >> Stonehenge

Salish [**say**lish] North American Indian groups, part of the Plateau Indian culture, who originally settled between the Rocky Mts and the Cascade Mts. Today they are mostly settled on small reservations, working as farmers and labourers. >> Plateau Indians

saliva A secretory product of insect and terrestrial vertebrate salivary glands. In the latter it is a clear, often sticky solution of salts and proteins. It includes *mucin*, which binds food together and lubricates the throat to facilitate swallowing.

Salk, Jonas E(dward) [sawlk] (1914–95) Virologist, discoverer in 1953 of the first vaccine against poliomyelitis, born in New York City. In 1953–4 he prepared inactivated poliomyelitis vaccine, given by injections, which (after some controversy) was successfully tested. >> poliomyelitis; Sabin; vaccination

sallow Any of several species of willow with broad, greyish leaves, and catkins (the 'pussy willows' of hedgerows) appearing before the leaves. (Family: Salicaceae.) >> willow

salmon Large anadromous (ascending rivers to breed) fish (*Salmo salar*), widespread and locally common in the N Atlantic (**Atlantic salmon**) and in NW North America (**Pacific salmon**); length up to 1.5 m/5 ft; greatly prized as game fish; with the trouts and charrs, comprise the very important family Salmonidae. >> fish ℹ; sockeye

salmonella [salmo**nel**a] A genus of rod-shaped, typically motile bacteria that are disease-causing agents of the human intestine. The genus includes the causative agents of typhoid and paratyphoid fever, as well as bacterial dysentery and food poisoning. (Kingdom: Monera. Family: Enterobacteriaceae.) >> bacteria ℹ; food poisoning; typhoid fever

Salome [sa**loh**mee] (1st-c) The traditional name of the daughter of Herodias. She danced before Herod Antipas, and was offered a reward. At her mother's instigation, she was given the head of John the Baptist. >> Herod Antipas; John the Baptist, St

Salon [salõ] In France, an exhibition of art by members of the French Royal Academy, originating in 1667 and held then in the *Salon d'Apollon* of the Louvre Palace, Paris. In the 19th-c the selection jury refused to hang many of the Impressionist and Postimpressionist painters, whose work was then shown (1863 and 1883) in the **Salon des Refusés**. The **Salon des Indépendents** is an annual art exhibition first held in Paris in 1884. In recent years, the term has come to be applied to other kinds of exhibition, such as the book-fair, **Salon du Livre**. >> Impressionism (art)

Salonica or **Salonika** [sa**lon**ika], Gr **Thessaloníki** 40°38N 22°58E, pop (1995e) 1 001 000. Seaport and second largest city of Greece; founded, 315 BC; capital of Roman Macedonia, 148 BC; held by Turkey, 1430–1912; base for Allied operations in World War 1; airport; railway; two universities (1925, 1957); 5th-c and 9th-c basilicas. >> Greece ℹ

Salote Tupou III [sa**loh**tay] (1900–65) Queen of Tonga, remembered in Britain for her colourful and engaging presence during her visit for the coronation of Elizabeth II (1953). >> Tonga

salp >> **tunicate**

salsa A type of popular music of Cuban origin, taken to the E USA in the 1940s and 1950s, since when it has both merged with jazz and absorbed other influences, while retaining its distinctive rhythm.

salsify A plant, usually biennial (*Tragopogon porrifolius*), growing to 125 cm/50 in, native to the Mediterranean region; flower-heads violet-purple; fruit with a large feathery parachute of hairs. It is widely grown for its edible fleshy root. (Family: Compositae.)

SALT [sawlt] Acronym for **Strategic Arms Limitation Talks**, held between the USA and USSR. There were two rounds of talks. The first began in Helsinki in 1969, designed to place a numerical limit on intercontinental nuclear weapons. An agreement (SALT 1) was reached in 1974. After this there was a hardening of attitudes in the West against the intentions of the USSR, partly because of its refusal to allow on-site verification. In consequence, SALT 2 (1979) was not ratified by the US Senate, and it was withdrawn. Both sides have, however, kept to the limitations set. With the end of the Cold War, the USA and Russia moved to reduce rather than merely limit nuclear weapons and the focus shifted to the Strategic Arms Reduction Talks (START).

salt An ionic compound derivable in principle from the reaction of an acid with a base. Most salts are solids at normal temperatures, and dissolve in water. Common salt is sodium chloride (NaCl). >> acid; base (chemistry); salinity

Salta [**sal**ta] 24°46S 65°28W, pop (1995e) 391 000. City in NW Argentina; on the R Arias; altitude 1190 m/3904 ft; founded, 1582; airport; railway; site of battle in which Spanish royalists were defeated (1813); university (1967); commercial and trade centre for extensive agricultural and mining area; cathedral. >> Argentina ℹ

Saltillo [sal**tee**yoh] 25°30N 101°00W, pop (1995e) 489 000. Resort city in N Mexico; altitude 1609 m/5279 ft; founded, 1575; railway; university (1867, refounded 1957); cathedral (18th-c). >> Mexico ℹ

Salt Lake City 40°45N 111°53W, pop (1995e) 182 000. State capital in N Utah, USA; on the Jordan R, near the S end of the Great Salt Lake; settled by Mormons, 1847; world centre of the Mormon Church (60% of the population are Mormons); railway; university (1850); processing centre for irrigated agricultural region; professional team, Jazz (basketball). >> Mormons; Utah

saltpetre >> **potassium**

saltwort A prickly, much-branched annual (*Salsola kali*), native to the N hemisphere; stems red-striped; flowers tiny, green. It is salt-tolerant, growing on sandy shores. (Family: Chenopodiaceae.)

saluki [sa**loo**kee] The fastest breed of dog, developed in Arabia to hunt in the desert with Bedouin; oldest of the greyhound group; also known as **Arabian hound** or **gazelle hound**. >> greyhound

Salut, Iles du [eel dü sa**lü**] Island archipelago c.13 km/ 8 mi off the coast of French Guiana, NE South America; includes Ile du Diable (Devil's I); housed notorious French penal colonies from 1898 until 1940s. >> French Guiana ℹ

Salvador, El >> **El Salvador** ℹ

Salvador [salva**daw(r)**], also known as **Bahia** 12°58S 38°29W, pop (1995e) 2 230 000. Port capital of Bahia state, NE Brazil; founded, 1549; capital of Brazil until 1763; airfield; railway; university (1946); older parts of the upper city are a national monument and world heritage site. >> Bahia; Brazil ℹ

salvage Compensation paid to someone (the **salvor**) who saves maritime property (a ship or its cargo) from loss or damage. The service must be rendered at sea or in tidal waters. A salvor may claim an award in the courts, where he or she has acted voluntarily. Salvage may also be the subject of prior agreement between the salvor and the property owner. >> Admiralty Court

Salvation Army A non-sectarian Christian organization founded in the East End of London by William Booth in 1865, dedicated to minister to the poor and needy. It retains a military-style structure and evangelical atmosphere, and its members, both men and women, wear distinctive uniform. It is now established in over 80 countries. >> Booth, William; Christianity; evangelicalism

salvia A member of a large genus of tropical and temperate annual or perennial herbs and shrubs; flowers 2-lipped, the upper often hooded. Popular garden plants include the scarlet-flowered annual *Salvia splendens*. (Genus: *Salvia*, 700 species. Family: Labiatae.) >> sage

sal volatile [sal vo**lat**ilee] >> **ammonium**

Salween, River >> **Thanlwin, River**

Salyut (Salute) **space station** [sal**yoot**] The first-generation Soviet space station, capable of docking with the Soyuz crew ferry and Progress resupply vehicle; it provides 100 m^3/3500 cu ft of living space for up to five cosmonauts. Two versions have been flown – the first in 1971, the last (Salyut 7) in 1982. The station's orbit eventually decays, with the vehicle re-entering the atmosphere and burning up. >> Soviet space programme; Soyuz spacecraft

Salzburg [**zahlts**boorg] 47°25N 13°03E, pop (1995e) 149 000. City in C Austria; on the R Salzach; railway; university (re-opened 1962); archbishopric; cathedral (1614–28); fortress of Hohensalzburg (1077) dominates the town; birthplace of Mozart, a fame reflected in the Mozarteum (musical academy) and the Mozart Festival (Jan). >> Austria ℹ; Mozart

Salzkammergut [**zalts**kamergut] E Alpine region in C Austria; popular tourist area with many lakes; name originally applied to a salt-mining area around Bad Ischl. >> Austria ℹ

Samara [sa**mah**ra], formerly (1935–91) **Kuybyshev** 53°10N 50°10E, pop (1995e) 1 268 000. River-port city in EC European Russia; on the R Volga; founded as a fortress, 1586; Soviet government transferred here in World War 2, 1941–3; airport; railway; university (1969). >> Russia ℹ

Samaria [sa**mair**ia] The site in C Palestine of the ancient capital of the N kingdom of the Hebrews, Israel. Destroyed by the Assyrians c.722 BC, Herod the Great rebuilt and enlarged it in the 20s BC. It is now in the Israeli-occupied West Bank. >> Assyria

Samaritans 1 A sect of Jewish origin, living in Samaria, who were in tension with the Jews of Judea well into New Testament times. A small remnant survives today. >> Judaism **2** A group founded in London in 1953 by an Anglican priest, Chad Varah (1911–), providing a telephone counselling service to support those who are depressed or contemplating suicide. It is named after the 'Good Samaritan' in the parable of Jesus. A free, confidential, and anonymous service is offered for 24 hours a day.

Samarkand [samah(r)**kand**] 39°40N 66°57E, pop (1995e) 404 000. City in Uzbekistan; a major industrial, scientific, and cultural centre; Abbasid capital, 9th–10th-c; ruled by the Uzbeks, 16th–19th-c; airfield; railway; university (1933). >> Silk Road; Uzbekistan ℹ

samba A Brazilian dance which existed in various rural and urban forms, always accompanied by singing, before it was taken up as a ballroom dance in the 1930s.

samizdat [samiz**dat**] (Russian *sam*, 'self' + *izdatelstvo*, 'publishing') Privately circulated editions of book-length and shorter texts not authorized for publication in the former USSR. The publishing of such work abroad was known as **tamizdat** (Russian *tam*, 'there').

Samoa [sa**moh**a], formerly (to 1997) **Western Samoa**, official name **The Independent State of Samoa** pop (1995e)

193 000; area 2842 sq km/1097 sq mi. Territory in the SW Pacific Ocean, 2600 km/1600 mi NE of Auckland, New Zealand; four islands inhabited (Upolu, Savai'i, Apolima, Manono); capital, Apia; timezone GMT −11; chief ethnic group, Polynesian; chief religion, Christianity; official languages, Samoan, English; unit of currency, the tala of 100 sene; formed from ranges of extinct volcanoes, rising to 1829 on Savai'i; thick tropical vegetation; several coral reefs along coast; tropical climate; visited by the Dutch, 1722; 1899 commission divided Samoa between Germany (which acquired Western Samoa) and the USA (which acquired Tutuila and adjacent small islands, now known as American Samoa); New Zealand granted a League of Nations mandate for Samoa, 1919; UN Trust Territory under New Zealand, 1946; independence, 1962; governed by a chief as head of state, a prime minister, and a Legislative Assembly; largely agricultural subsistence economy; tourism increasing. >> American Samoa; Apia; mandates; Trust Territory; RR1021 political leaders

Samos [**say**mos] pop (1995e) 42 900; area 476 sq km/184 sq mi. Wooded island in the E Aegean Sea, Greece; rises to 1440 m/4724 ft in the W; birthplace of Pythagoras. >> Greece ℹ; Pythagoras

Samothrace [**sam**ohthrays], Gr **Samothráki** pop (1995e) 4170; area 178 sq km/69 sq mi. Greek island in the NE Aegean Sea; rises to 1600 m/5249 ft. >> Aegean Sea; Greece ℹ

Samoyed (people) >> **Nenets**

Samoyed (zoology) [**sam**oyed] An active spitz breed of dog, developed in Siberia; medium-sized with an extremely thick coat of straight pale hairs; tail carried over back only when alert, loosely curled. >> dog; spitz

samphire A fleshy, much-branched perennial (*Crithmum maritimum*), growing to 30 cm/12 in, native to coastal areas of Europe, the Mediterranean, and the Black Sea; flowers yellowish. The fleshy leaves are sometimes made into a pickle. (Family: Umbelliferae.)

Sampras, Pete (1971–) Tennis player, born in Washington, DC. He turned professional in 1988, and went on to become the youngest men's champion in the 1990 US Open, which he subsequently won in 1993, 1995, and 1996. His wins include the Association of Tennis Professionals Tour World Championship in 1991, 1994, and 1996–7, and Wimbledon in 1993–5 and 1997–8, and he reached No 1 in the world rankings in five successive years (1993–8).

Samson (c.11th-c BC?) A legendary hero of the tribe of Dan, purportedly the last of Israel's tribal leaders ('judges') prior to Samuel. Stories tell of his great strength, and his fatal infatuation with Delilah. When she cut his hair, breaking his Nazirite vow, he lost his strength, and was held by the Philistines until his hair grew back and he pulled down their temple upon them. >> Delilah; Judges, Book of

Samuel (Heb probably 'name of God') (11th-c BC) In the Hebrew Bible/Old Testament, the last of the judges and first of the prophets. He presided over Saul's election as the first king of Israel, but finally anointed David as Saul's successor, rather than Saul's own son, Jonathan. >> David; Jonathan; prophet; Samuel, Books of; Saul

Samuel, Books of Two books of the Old Testament; also called **1** and **2 Kings**, in some Catholic versions. They are probably a compilation from several, partially-overlapping sources. >> Kings, Books of; Old Testament; Samuel

samurai [**sa**muriy] Japanese warrior-gentry. An elaborate military feudal system: knights (*samurai*) held land from lords (*daimyo*) for military service. They were expected to display such virtues as loyalty, self-sacrifice, and valour, and to avoid dishonour by ritual suicide. They became involved in administration under the Tokugawas (17th–19th-c). Shinto bushido developed from samurai ethics under the later Tokugawas, influencing the Japanese army's officer class pre-1945. >> Tokugawa

San >> **Khoisan**

Sana [sa**nah**] 15°27N 44°12E, pop (1995e) 548 000. Political capital of Republic of Yemen; former capital of North Yemen; altitude 2170 m/7119 ft; walled city, a world heritage site; university (1970). >> Yemen ℹ

San Andreas Fault A major fault in the Earth's crust running for about 950 km/600 mi through NW California to the Colorado Desert. It marks the boundary between the Pacific and American crustal plates, which are slipping past each other at an average rate of 1 cm/$\frac{3}{8}$ in a year. Sudden movements can cause earthquakes, the most notable of which devastated San Francisco in 1906. Serious movement also occurred in 1989, 1993, and 1994. >> earthquake; fault

San Antonio 29°25N 98°30W, pop (1995e) 988 000. City in SC Texas, USA, on the San Antonio R; tenth largest city in the USA; settled by the Spanish, 1718; captured by the Texans in the Texas Revolution, 1835; scene of the Mexican attack on the Alamo, 1836; airport; railway; two universities (1852, 1869); military aviation centre; industrial, trade, and financial centre for a large agricultural area; professional team, Spurs (basketball); the Alamo, Tower of the Americas (229 m/750 ft high). >> Alamo; Texas

sanction In international law, penalties imposed by one state against another. *Retorsion* is a lawful act designed to injure another state, such as the withdrawal of economic aid. *Reprisals* are acts ordinarily illegal, but which are made lawful on account of a prior unlawful act committed by the other state. >> international law

Sand, George [sã, zhaw(r)zh], pseudonym of **(Amandine) Aurore (Lucile) Dudevant**, *née* **Dupin** (1804–76) Writer, born in Paris. The companion of several poets, artists, philosophers, and politicians, she wrote over 100 books, the most successful being those describing rustic life, such as *François le champi* (1848).

sand Grains of rock and mineral with sizes between 63 μm and 2 mm (0.0025–0.079 in), formed by the physical weathering of rocks, and composed of resistant minerals (usually quartz) not destroyed during weathering. Many shorelines consist of sandy beaches. >> quartz; silica

sandalwood A hemiparasitic tree (*Santalum album*) native to SE Asia. A fragrant timber is obtained from the white outer wood, used for carvings, incense, and joss sticks. Sandal oil is made from the yellow heartwood, and the roots are used for perfume and soap. (Family: Santalaceae.) >> parasitic plant

Sandburg, Carl (1878–1967) Poet, born in Galesburg, IL. His books include *Cornhuskers* (1918) and *Good Morning, America* (1928). Interested in folksongs, he published a collection in *The American Songbag* (1927), and also wrote a vast *Life of Abraham Lincoln* (6 vols, 1926, 1939).

sanderling A pale sandpiper (*Calidris alba*) native to the N hemisphere; inhabits tundra and (in winter) coasts. >> sandpiper; *see illustration on p. 755*

sandfly A small, hairy fly commonly found in moist, shady habitats; may act as carriers of diseases, such as leishmaniasis. (Order: Diptera. Families: Psychodidae and Phlebotamidae.) >> fly; leishmaniasis

sandgrouse A bird native to Africa, Asia, and S Europe; resembles a plump pigeon. (Family: Pteroclididae, 16 species.) >> grouse; pigeon

sand hopper A semiterrestrial crustacean, with a flattened body, capable of vigorous jumping; also known as a **beach flea**. (Class: Malacostraca. Order: Amphipoda.) >> crustacean

San Diego [san dee**ay**goh] 32°43N 117°09W, pop (1995e) 1 217 000. Seaport in SW California; sixth largest city in the USA; naval and marine base; airport; railway; four universities; cultural, convention, and research centre; professional teams, Padres (baseball), Chargers (football); San Diego de Alcalá mission. >> California

Sandino, Augusto César [san**dee**noh] (1895–1934) Nicaraguan revolutionary, born in Niquinohomo (or La Victoria), Nicaragua. He led guerrilla resistance to US occupation forces after 1926, and was later murdered near Managua. The Nicaraguan revolutionaries of 1979 (later known as **Sandinistas**) took him as their principal hero. >> Nicaragua ℹ

Sandjak of Novi Pazar, Serbo-Croat **Sandžak**, Turkish **Sancak** Historical province of the Ottoman Empire, comprising 8000 sq km/3000 sq mi on both sides of border between Serbia and Montenegro. By 1992 it was a potential flashpoint in the wars of Yugoslav succession, with more than half of its 400 000 population composed of Slav Muslims. >> Montenegro; Serbia; Yugoslavia ℹ

Sandown 50°39N 1°09W, pop (1995e) 17 000 (with Shanklin). Town in Isle of Wight, S England; home of the poet Swinburne; railway. >> Swinburne; Wight, Isle of

sandpiper A wading bird, widespread, mostly native to the N hemisphere, migrating to the S during the N winter; long legs and bill. (Family: Scolopacidae, c.86 species.) >> curlew; dunlin; godwit; knot; phalarope; ruff; sanderling ℹ; snipe; woodcock

sandstone A sedimentary rock composed of grains of sand (usually quartz) cemented together by a matrix, usually silica or calcium carbonate. It is quarried as a building stone. >> sand; sedimentary rock

Sandwich, John Montagu, 4th Earl of (1718–92) British politician, remembered as the inventor of **sandwiches**, which he devised in order to eat while playing around the clock at a gaming-table. He was First Lord of the Admiralty under both Henry Pelham and Lord North (1748–51, 1771–82). >> North, Frederick; Pelham, Baron

Sandwich Island >> **Efate**

San Francisco 37°47N 122°25W, pop (1995e) 793 000. City in W California, USA; connected to Marin county (N) by the Golden Gate Bridge, one of the longest single-span suspension bridges in the world (1280 m/4200 ft, excluding the approaches); mission and pueblo founded by the Spanish, 1776 (named Yerba Buena); Mexican control, 1821; taken by the US Navy, 1846; renamed San Francisco, 1848; terminus of the first transcontinental railway, 1869; devastated by earthquake and fire, 1906; several areas seriously damaged by earthquake, 1989; tram (cable-car); railway; airport; four universities; financial and insurance centre of W coast; major tourist, cultural, and convention centre; professional teams, Giants (baseball), 49ers (football); largest Chinatown in the USA; Fisherman's Wharf, Nob Hill mansions; Alcatraz I in San Francisco Bay, site of a Federal prison (1934–63). >> California; Golden Gate Bridge

Sanderling

Sangay [san**giy**] 2°00S 78°20W. Active Andean volcano, EC Ecuador; rises to 5230 m/17 159 ft. >> Andes

Sanger, Frederick (1918–) Biochemist, born in Rendcombe, Gloucestershire. He revealed the full sequence of the 51 amino acids in insulin, for which he was awarded the Nobel Prize for Chemistry in 1958. He then worked on the problems of the nucleic acids, and devised new methods to elucidate molecular structures for these also. His Nobel Prize for Chemistry in 1980 made him the first to receive two such awards. >> amino acid; DNA ℹ; genetics; insulin

Sanger, Margaret (Louise), *née* **Higgins** (1883–1966) Social reformer and founder of the birth control movement, born in Corning, NY. She started the first US birth-control clinic in New York City in 1916, but was charged with creating a 'public nuisance', and imprisoned for 30 days. After a world tour, she founded the American Birth Control League in 1921. >> contraception

Sanhedrin [san**hed**rin] (Gr 'council', also called by Josephus the *gerousia*, Gr 'senate') A Jewish council of elders meeting in Jerusalem, which during the Graeco-Roman period acquired internal administrative and judicial functions over Palestinian Jews, despite foreign domination. >> Judaism

sanicle A perennial (*Sanicula europaea*) growing to 60 cm/2 ft, native to woods in Europe, Asia, and Africa; flowers white or pink; fruit thickly covered with hooked bristles. (Family: Umbelliferae.)

San Joaquin River [san wa**keen**] River in C California, USA; rises in the Sierra Nevada; joins the Sacramento R; 510 km/317 mi long. >> California

San José [san hoh**zay**] 9°59N 84°04W, pop (1995e) 325 000. Capital city of Costa Rica; altitude 1150 m/3773 ft; founded, 1737; capital, 1823; airport; railway; university (1940); cathedral. >> Costa Rica ℹ

San Jose [san hoh**zay**] 37°10N 121°53W, pop (1995e) 857 000. City in W California, USA; first city in the state, 1777; state capital, 1849–51; railway; university. >> California

San Juan [san **hwan**] 18°29N 66°08W, pop (1995e) 458 000. Seaport capital of Puerto Rico; founded, 1510; airport; two universities (1912, 1950); El Morro (1591, old Spanish fortress), cathedral (16th-c). >> Puerto Rico ℹ

Sankara [**sangk**ara, **shangk**ara] (?700–?750) Hindu philosopher and theologian, born in Kerala, India. The most famous exponent of Advaita (the Vedanta school of Hindu philosophy), he is the source of the main currents of modern Hindu thought. >> Hinduism

Sankey, Ira David >> **Moody, Dwight Lyman**

Sankt Gallen >> **St Gallen / St Moritz** (*under* **Saint**)

San Luis Potosí [san loo**ees** poto**see**] 22°10N 101°00W, pop (1995e) 583 000. City in NC Mexico; altitude 1877 m/6158 ft; founded as a Franciscan mission; railway; university (1826); cathedral. >> Juárez; Mexico ℹ

San Marino [san ma**ree**noh], official name **Most Serene Republic of San Marino**, Ital **Serenissima Repubblica di San Marino** pop (1995e) 24 500; area 61 sq km/23 sq mi. Landlocked republic in C Italy; the world's smallest republic; land boundaries, 34 km/21 mi; capital, San Marino, pop (1995e) 2450; timezone GMT +1; chief religion, Roman Catholicism; official language, Italian; units of currency, the Italian lira and San Marino lira; ruggedly mountainous, centred on the limestone ridges of Monte Titano (793 m/2602 ft); temperate climate, with cool winters and warm summers; founded by a 4th-c Christian saint as a refuge against religious persecution; treaty of friendship with the Kingdom of Italy, preserving independence, 1862; governed by an elected unicameral parliament and a Congress of State; two members selected to serve as co-chiefs of state (captains regent) every six months; a secretary of state acts as head of government; over 50% of national income from tourism; >> RR1021 political leaders

San Martín, José de [san mah(r)**teen**] (1778–1850) South American patriot, born in Yapeyú, Argentina. He played a major role in winning independence from Spain for Argentina, Chile, and Peru, defeating the Spanish at Chacubuco (1817) and Maipó (1818), and became Protector of Peru (1821–2). >> Spanish–American Wars of Independence

San Miguel de Tucumán or **Tucumán** [san mee**gel** thay tuku**man**] pop (1995e) 529 000. City in NW Argentina; on the R Salí; founded, 1565; site of defeat of Spanish royalists in 1812; airport; railway; two universities (1914, 1965); cathedral. >> Argentina ℹ

San Salvador [san salva**daw(r)**] 13°40N 89°18W, pop (1995e) 550 000. Capital city of El Salvador, on the R Acelhuate; altitude, 680 m/2230 ft; founded, 1525; destroyed by earthquake, 1854; capital, 1839; railway; cathedral. >> El Salvador ℹ

San Salvador de Jujuy or **Jujuy** [san salva**thor** thay khoo**khoo**ee] 24°10S 65°48W, pop (1995e) 130 000. Resort city in N Argentina; on the R Grande de Jujuy; founded, 1561; airport; railway; cathedral (18th-c). >> Argentina ℹ

sans-culottes [sã kü**lot**] (Fr, literally 'without breeches') The French name for the mass of the working populace in French towns at the time of the Revolution, but more specifically applied to small-time Parisian shopkeepers, craftsmen, wage-earners, and unemployed who were politically active. >> French Revolution ℹ

San Sebastián, Span [san sayvas**tyan**], Basque **Donostia** 43°17N 1°58W, pop (1995e) 171 000. Fortified Basque seaport and fashionable resort in N Spain; on R Urumea; bishopric; airport; railway. >> Spain ℹ

sansevieria [sansi**veer**ia] >> **mother-in-law's-tongue**

Sanskrit The name given to the early forms of Indo-Aryan, at c.1000 BC, in which the sacred Hindu texts known as the Vedas were written. Their grammatical form and pronunciation have been scrupulously preserved as a matter of religious observance. >> Indo-Aryan languages; Veda

Sansovino, Jacopo [sanso**vee**noh], originally **Jacopo Tatti** (1486–1570) Sculptor and architect, born in Florence, Italy. He was responsible for bringing the High Renaissance style from Florence to Venice. From 1529 he was chief architect in Venice, where he is noted for several buildings, notably the Library of St Mark (1537–54). >> Renaissance architecture

Sans Souci [sã soo**see**] A Rococo palace built (1745–7) at Potsdam, Germany, for Frederick II of Prussia. It has been preserved in its original state, and houses several picture galleries. >> Potsdam; Rococo

Santa Ana 14°00N 79°31W, pop (1995e) 266 000. City in NW El Salvador; second largest city in the country; railway; on the Pan-American Highway; cathedral. >> El Salvador ℹ

Santa Anna, Antonio López de (1797–1876) Mexican soldier, president (1833–6), and dictator (1839, 1841–5), born in Jalapa, Mexico. Following the Texas revolt (1836), he defeated Texan forces at the Alamo, but was then routed at San Jacinto R. He returned to power on two occasions (1846, 1853). >> Mexican War; Mexico ℹ; Texas

Santa Barbara 34°25N 119°42W, pop (1995e) 93 700. Resort in SW California, USA; founded, 1782; railway; university (1891); Santa Barbara Mission (established 1786). >> California

Santa Claus A name derived from *Sinte Klaas*, a Dutch dialect form of St Nicholas, the patron saint of children, on whose feast day (6 Dec) presents were traditionally given to children; also known as **Father Christmas**. The English of New York took over from the Dutch the name and the present-giving custom, now transferred to Christmas Day. Countries vary greatly in the way they act out these traditions. >> Christmas

Santa Cruz or **Santa Cruz de la Sierra** 17°45S 63°14W, pop (1995e) 617 000. City in E Bolivia; country's second largest city; founded in 1561 by Spanish; airport; railway; university (1880); cathedral. >> Bolivia ℹ

Santa Cruz de Tenerife [**san**ta **krooth** thay tene**ree**fay] 28°28N 16°15W, pop (1995e) 191 000. Seaport in Canary Is, on N coast of Tenerife I; airport. >> Canary Islands

Santa Fe (Argentina) [santa **fay**] 31°38S 60°43W, pop (1995e) 464 000. River-port city in NE C Argentina; at the mouth of the R Salado; founded, 1573; airfield; railway; two universities (1919, 1959). >> Argentina ℹ

Santa Fe (USA) [santa **fay**] 35°41N 105°57W, pop (1995e) 62 900. State capital in NC New Mexico, USA; founded by the Spanish, 1609; after Mexican independence, 1821, centre of trade with the USA; occupied by US troops, 1846; territorial capital, 1851; railway; noted for Indian wares; cathedral. >> New Mexico

Santa Marta [**san**ta **mah(r)**ta] 11°18N 74°10W, pop (1995e) 184 000. Caribbean port in N Colombia; at mouth of R Manzanares; founded, 1525; Bolívar died here (1830); airport; railway; leading seaside resort. >> Bolívar; Colombia ℹ

Santander [santan**dair**] 43°27N 3°51W, pop (1995e) 191 000. Seaport and resort in N Spain; bishopric; airport; railway; car ferries to Plymouth, Gijón; university (1972); cathedral (13th-c). >> Spain ℹ

Santander, Francisco de Paula [santan**dair**] (1792–1840) Colombian statesman, born in Rosario de Cúccuta, Colombia. He acted as vice-president of Grancolombia (1821–7) during Bolívar's campaigns, and was president of New Granada (modern Colombia) in 1832–7. >> Colombia ℹ; Spanish–American Wars of Independence

Santarém (Brazil) [santa**rem**] 2°26S 54°41W, pop (1995e) 264 000. River-port in N Brazil, at the junction of the Tapajós and Amazon Rivers; founded, 1661; third largest town on the Amazon; airfield. >> Amazon, River; Brazil ℹ

Santarém (Portugal) [santa**rã**], ancient **Scalabis** or **Praesidium Julium** 39°12N 8°42W, pop (1995e) 23 600. Walled town in C Portugal; railway. >> Portugal ℹ

Santa Rosa de Copán >> **Copán**

Santa Sophia >> **Hagia Sophia**

Santayana, George [santa**yah**na], originally **Jorge Augustín Nicolás Ruiz de Santayana** (1863–1952) Philosopher, poet, and novelist, born in Madrid. He became known as a philosopher and stylist, in such works as *The Life of Reason* (5 vols, 1905–6), *Realms of Being* (4 vols, 1927–40), and his novel *The Last Puritan* (1935).

Santer, Jacques [sã**tair**] (1937–) European statesman, born in Wasserbillig, Luxembourg. He studied law, entered politics in 1966, and went on to serve three successive terms as prime minister of Luxembourg (1984–95). In 1975 he became a member of the European Parliament, and in 1995 was elected president of the European Commission.

Santiago [san**tyah**goh], **Gran Santiago**, or **Santiago de Chile** 33°27S 70°38W, pop (1995e) 5 695 000. Capital of Chile, crossed E–W by R Mapocho; founded, 1541; capital, 1818; often damaged by floods, fires, and earthquakes; airport; railway; three universities (1738, 1888, 1947); cathedral; Avenida O'Higgins (the Alameda) stretches for more than 3 km/1¾ mi; Santa Lucía Hill, site of first fort. >> Chile ℹ

Santiago (de los Caballeros) [san**tyah**goh] 19°30N 70°42W, pop (1995e) 524 000. City in Dominican Republic; second largest city in country; airfield; most important trading centre in N; scene of decisive battle of Dominican struggle for independence, 1844; cathedral, fort. >> Dominican Republic ℹ

Santiago de Compostela [santyahgoh thay kompostayla], ancient **Campus Stellae**, Eng **Compostella** 42°52N 8°37W, pop (1995e) 88 200. City in Galicia, NW Spain, on R Sar; former capital of the Kingdom of Galicia; world-famous place of pilgrimage in the Middle Ages (shrine of St James); airport; railway; university (1501); old town is a world heritage site; cathedral (11th–12th-c). >> Galicia; Spain ℹ

Santiago de Cuba [santyahgoh thay kooba] 20°00N 75°49W, pop (1995e) 425 000. Cuba's second largest city; founded, 1514; formerly capital of the republic; scene of Castro's 1953 revolution; rail terminus; university (1947); cathedral (1528); San Pedro de la Roca Castle, a world heritage site. >> Castro; Cuba ℹ

Santiago del Estero [santyahgoh thel estayroh] 27°48S 64°15W, pop (1995e) 211 000. City in N Argentina; on the R Dulce; oldest Argentinian town, founded in 1553; university; railway; airfield; agricultural trade and lumbering centre; cathedral. >> Argentina ℹ

Santo Domingo, formerly (1936–61) **Ciudad Trujillo** 19°30N 70°42W, pop (1995e) 2 509 000. City in S Dominican Republic, on R Ozama; founded, 1496; airport; harbour; highway junction; university (1538); cathedral (1514–40), castle (1514). >> Dominican Republic ℹ

Santorini [santoreenee], Gr **Santorin**, ancient **Thera** or **Thíra** pop (1992e) 7400; area 75 sq km/29 sq mi. An island in the S Cyclades. The last great eruption of its volcano (c.1470 BC) has been held responsible (probably mistakenly) for the rapid decline of Minoan civilization. >> Cyclades; Greece ℹ; Minoan civilization; RR973

Santos [santohs] 23°56S 46°22W, pop (1995e) 530 000. Port in SE Brazil; founded in 1534; the most important Brazilian port; major industrial area around the oil refinery and hydroelectric plant at Cubatão; railway. >> Brazil ℹ

São Francisco, River [sõw franseeskoh] (Port **Río**) River in E Brazil; rises in the Serra de Canastra; enters the Atlantic; length 2900 km/1800 mi. >> Brazil ℹ

Saône, River [sohn], ancient **Arar** River in E France rising in the Mts Faucilles (Vosges); meets the R Rhône at Lyon; length 480 km/298 mi. >> France ℹ

São Paulo [sõw powloh] 23°33S 46°39W, pop (1995e) 12 108 000. City in SE Brazil, on the R Tietê; founded by Jesuits, 1554; airport; airfield; railway; three universities (1934, 1952, 1970); cathedral; leading commercial and industrial centre in South America; fastest-growing South American city. >> Brazil ℹ

São Tomé and Príncipe [sõw tomay, preensipe], Port **São Tomé e Príncipe**, official name **Democratic Republic of São Tomé and Príncipe** pop (1995e) 135 000; area 1001 sq km/387 sq mi. Equatorial island republic in the Gulf of Guinea, off the coast of W Africa; comprises São Tomé, Príncipe, and several smaller islands; capital, São Tomé; timezone GMT; official language, Portuguese; unit of currency, the dobra; volcanic islands, heavily forested; São Tomé lies c.440 km/275 mi off the coast of N Gabon, area 845 sq km/326 sq mi, greatest height 2024 m/6640 ft; Príncipe lies c.200 km/124 mi off Gabon; tropical climate; visited by the Portuguese, 1469–72; Portuguese colony, 1522; resistance to Portuguese rule from 1953; independence, 1975; new constitution, 1990; governed by a president, prime minister, and National People's Assembly; economy based on agriculture, employing c.70% of the population; restructuring of the economy announced in 1985, with greater involvement in management, commerce, banking, and tourism. >> Gabon ℹ; Portugal ℹ; RR1021 political leaders

sapi-utan or **sapi-outan** >> **anoa**

sapodilla plum >> **chicle**

Sapor II >> **Shapur II**

Sapper, pseudonym of **Herman Cyril McNeile** (1888–1937) Novelist, born in Bodmin, Cornwall. He achieved fame as the creator of 'Bulldog' Drummond, the aggressively patriotic hero of a series of thrillers written between 1920 and 1937, of which *The Final Count* (1926) is a typical example.

sapphire A gem variety of corundum, coloured by the addition of minor amounts of impurity. It occurs in a variety of colours (except red, when it is termed *ruby*), but blue is the most valuable. >> corundum; gemstones; ruby

Sappho [safoh] (c.610–c.580 BC) Greek poet, born in Lesbos. The most celebrated female poet of antiquity, she wrote lyrics unsurpassed for depth of feeling, passion, and grace. Only two of her odes are extant in full. >> ode

Sapporo [sapohroh] 43°05N 141°21E, pop (1995e) 1 707 000. City in WC Hokkaido, Japan; founded, 1871; railway; subway; university (1876); Snow Festival (Jan–Feb); scene of 1972 Winter Olympics. >> Hokkaido

saprophyte [saprohfiyt] A plant which feeds on the products of decay. It includes many fungi. A few flowering plants are saprophytic; they have reduced leaves, lack chlorophyll, and form symbiotic associations with mycorrhizal fungi. >> chlorophyll; fungus; mycorrhiza; symbiosis

Saqqarah [sakara] The large necropolis of Memphis in Egypt, where several pharaohs and many noble Egyptians were buried. The most famous surviving monument is the stepped pyramid of Zozer (c.2630 BC), designed by Imhotep. >> Memphis (ancient Egypt); pyramid

sarabande A 16th-c dance of Spanish or Latin-American origin in triple time. In a different form and slower tempo it became a standard movement of the Baroque suite. >> Baroque (music); suite

Saragossa [saragosa], Span **Zaragoza**, ancient **Salduba** 41°39N 0°53W, pop (1995e) 591 000. Industrial city in NEC Spain; on R Ebro; scene of a long siege against the French in the Peninsular War, 1808–9; archbishopric; airport; railway; university (1553); two cathedrals. >> Spain ℹ

Sarah or **Sarai** (Heb 'princess') Biblical character, wife and half-sister of Abraham, who is portrayed as having accompanied him from Ur to Canaan. Long barren, she is said to have eventually given birth to Isaac in her old age as God promised. >> Abraham; Isaac; Old Testament

Sarajevo [sarayayvoh] 43°52N 18°26E, pop (1995e) 426 000. Capital of Bosnia and Herzegovina; on R Miljacka; governed by Austria, 1878–1918; scene of the assassination of Archduke Francis Ferdinand and his wife (28 Jun 1914); under siege and badly damaged in civil war, 1992–3; airport; railway; university (1946); educational and cultural centre; site of 1984 Winter Olympic Games; two cathedrals. >> Bosnia and Herzegovina ℹ; World War 1

Saramago, José [saramahgoh] (1922–) Writer, born in Azinhaga, Portugal. A former technician, journalist and translator, since 1979 he has worked as a writer, his major

The step pyramid at Saqqarah

works including *O Evangelho Segundo Jesus Christo* (1991, The Gospel According to Jesus Christ) and *Todos os Nomes* (1997, All the Names). He was awarded the Nobel Prize for Literature in 1998.

Sarandon, Susan [**sa**randon], originally **Susan Abigail Tomalin** (1946–) Film actress, born in New York City. She began her screen career in 1970, and became well known after her role in *The Rocky Horror Picture Show* (1975). Later films include *The Witches of Eastwick* (1987), *Thelma and Louise* (1991), *Dead Man Walking* (1995, Oscar), and *Stepmom* (1998).

Saransk [sa**ransk**] 54°12N 45°10E, pop (1995e) 323 000. City in C European Russia, on R Insar; founded as a fortress, 1641; railway; university (1957). >> Russia ℹ

Saratoga, Battle of [sara**toh**ga] (Oct 1777) One of the most important engagements of the US War of Independence. Actually fought near modern Schuylerville, New York, the battle brought the defeat of a large British army under John Burgoyne by American troops under Horatio Gates. >> American Revolution; Burgoyne; Gates

Saratov [sa**rat**of] 51°30N 45°55E, pop (1995e) 919 000. River port in E European Russia, on R Volga; founded as a fortress, 1590; airport; railway; university (1909); cathedral (1689–95). >> Russia ℹ

Sarawak [sa**rah**wak] pop (1995e) 1 879 000; area 124 449 sq km/48 037 sq mi. State in E Malaysia, on NW coast of Borneo; narrow coastal strip, and highly mountainous forested interior; highest peak, Mt Murud (2423 m/7949 ft); given by the Sultan of Brunei to James Brooke, the 'white raja' in 1841, and governed by the Brooke family until World War 2; British protectorate, 1888; Crown Colony, 1946; capital, Kuching. >> Borneo; Malaysia ℹ

Sarcodina [sah(r)ko**diy**na] A subphylum of protozoans, all of which possess some kind of pseudopodia; cell body typically naked, sometimes with a shell; reproduces by splitting in two (binary fission). >> phylum; Protozoa; pseudopodium; systematics

sarcoma [sah(r)**koh**ma] A malignant tumour in connective tissue, bone, or muscle. Sarcomas are much less common than **carcinomas**, which arise from the lining tissues of the skin and internal organs. >> cancer

Sardanapalus [sah(r)da**nap**alus] (7th-c BC) Legendary Assyrian king, notorious for his effeminacy and sensual lifestyle. He probably represents an amalgam of at least three Assyrian rulers, one of them being Assurbanipal. >> Assyria

sardine >> **pilchard**

Sardinia, Ital **Sardegna** pop (1995e) 1 652 000; area 24 000 sq km/9300 sq mi. Region and island of Italy; settled by Phoenicians; formed part of Kingdom of Sardinia, 18th-c; capital and chief port, Cagliari; length 272 km/169 mi; width 144 km/89 mi; largely hilly, rising to 1835 m/6020 ft in the Monti del Gennargentu; mineral-bearing SW; fertile alluvial plain of Campidano. >> Cagliari; Corsica; Italy ℹ; Sardinia, Kingdom of

Sardinia, Kingdom of An Italian kingdom created 1718–20 through the Duchy of Savoy's acquisition of Sardinia, in compensation for the loss of Sicily. In 1861, Victor Emmanuel II of Sardinia became the first King of Italy. >> Risorgimento

Sardinian >> **Romance languages**

Sardis [**sah(r)**dis] The capital of Lydia and the political centre of Asia Minor in the pre-Hellenistic period. It was a flourishing city in Roman imperial times. >> Lydia

sardonyx [**sah(r)**doniks] A white and brown variety of onyx. >> agate

Sardou, Victorien [sah(r)**doo**] (1831–1908) Playwright, born in Paris. His plays include *Les Pattes de monde* (1860, trans A Scrap of Paper), *La Tosca* (1887), and over 60 others.

Sargasso Sea [sah(r)**gas**oh] Sluggish area of the Atlantic Ocean, between the Azores and the West Indies within the 'Horse Latitudes'; a still sea, allowing great biological activity; abundance of surface gulfweed. >> Atlantic Ocean; Horse Latitudes

Sargent, John Singer [**sah(r)**jnt] (1856–1925) Painter, born in Florence, Italy. Most of his work was done in England, where he became the most fashionable portrait painter of his age.

Sargent, Sir (Harold) Malcolm (Watts) [**sah(r)**jnt] (1895–1967) Conductor, born in Ashford, Kent. He conducted the Royal Choral Society from 1928, the Liverpool Philharmonic Orchestra (1942–8), and the BBC Symphony Orchestra (1950–7). From 1948 he was in charge of the London Promenade Concerts.

Sark, Fr **Sercq** pop (1995e) 632; area 4 sq km/$1\frac{1}{2}$ sq mi. Smallest of the four main Channel Islands, lying between Guernsey and France; consists of Great and Little Sark, connected by an isthmus; separate parliament (the Chief Pleas); Seigneurie of Sark established by Elizabeth I; ruler known as the Seigneur (male) or Dame (female); no cars allowed on the island. >> Channel Islands ℹ

Sarmatia [sah(r)**may**sha] In Roman times, the area to the N of the Black Sea and the middle and lower Danube occupied by the Sarmatians, a nomadic people closely related to the Scythians. >> Scythians

saros [**say**ros] The natural cycle over which sequences of lunar and solar eclipses repeat themselves. The period is 6585.32 days (c.18 years): over this cycle the Earth, Sun, and Moon return to the same relative positions.

Saroyan, William [sa**roy**an] (1908–81) Writer, born in Fresno, CA. His first work, *The Daring Young Man on the Flying Trapeze* (1934), a volume of short stories, was followed by a number of highly original novels, such as *The Human Comedy* (1943), and plays, such as *The Time of Your Life* (1939).

Sarraute, Nathalie [sa**roht**], *née* **Nathalie Ilyanova Tcherniak** (1902–) Writer, born in Ivanovo, Russia. A leading exponent of the *nouveau roman*, her books include *Tropismes* (1939, Tropisms), *Portrait d'un inconnu* (1947, Portrait of a Man Unknown), and *Entre la vie et la mort* (1968, Between Life and Death). Later works include *ICI* (1995). >> *nouveau roman*

sarrusophone [sa**rooz**ofohn] A musical instrument made of brass in various sizes, with a double reed. It was designed by a French bandmaster, W Sarrus, in 1856 as a substitute for oboes and bassoons in military bands, but enjoyed only brief success. >> reed instrument

sarsaparilla [saspa**ril**a] A climbing, prickly perennial, native to tropical and subtropical regions; flowers greenish or yellowish; berries red or black. The berries are used to make a type of soft drink, and the dried roots yield a drug used to treat rheumatism. (Genus: *Smilax*, 350 species. Family: Smilacaceae.)

Sarto, Andrea del [**sah(r)**toh], originally **Andrea d'Agnolo**, or **Andrea Vannucchi** (1486–1531) Painter, born in Florence, the son of a tailor (*sarto*, 'tailor'). Many of his most celebrated pictures are in Florence. >> fresco

Sartre, Jean-Paul [sahtr] (1905–80) Existentialist philosopher and writer, born in Paris. His novels include the trilogy, *Les Chemins de la liberté* (1945–9, The Roads to Freedom), and he also wrote a large number of plays, such as *Huis clos* (1944, trans In Camera/No Exit). His philosophy is presented in *L'Etre et le néant* (1943, Being and Nothingness). In 1964 he was awarded (but declined) the Nobel Prize for Literature. In the later 1960s he became heavily involved in opposition to US policies in Vietnam. >> de Beauvoir, Simone; existentialism

SAS Abbreviation of **Special Air Service**, a British army unit specializing in clandestine and anti-terrorist operations.

First formed in 1941 as a special commando unit to parachute behind enemy lines, the SAS (motto 'Who Dares Wins') was revived as a regular unit of the British Army in 1952 for special operations.

sashimi [sa**shee**mee] Japanese sliced raw fish, considered a delicacy, and served in many special restaurants. Slices of raw fish on small portions of boiled seasoned rice are called *sushi*. >> fugu

Saskatchewan [sa**ska**chuan] pop (1995e) 1 050 000; area 652 380 sq km/251 883 sq mi. Province in W Canada; capital, Regina; fertile plain in S two-thirds; rises to 1392 m/4567 ft in the Cypress Hills (SW); many lakes; Hudson's Bay Company land, acquired by Canada in 1869 to become part of Northwest Territories; land disputes led to North West-Rebellion, 1885; province of Canada, 1905; governed by a Lieutenant-Governor and an elected Legislative Assembly; wheat (about two-thirds of Canada's production), potash (largest fields in the world). >> Canada [i]; Hudson's Bay Company; Regina

Saskatchewan River [sa**ska**chuan] River in S Canada; rises in the Rocky Mts; flows E into L Winnipeg; length 1300 km/800 mi. >> Canada [i]

Saskatoon [saska**toon**] 52°10N 106°40W, pop (1995e) 197 000. Town in Canada, on the S Saskatchewan R; settled in 1882 as a temperance colony; airfield; railway; university (1907); centre of large grain-growing area. >> Saskatchewan

Sasquatch >> **Bigfoot**

sassafras [**sa**safras] A name applied to several different plants. True sassafras (*Sassafras albidum*), is a large shrub or tree, growing to 30 m/100 ft, native to E North America; aromatic foliage; inconspicuous greenish flowers; blue-grey, berry-like fruits. **Oil of sassafras**, chiefly a flavouring, is distilled from the bark, twigs, and roots. (Family: Lauraceae.)

Sassanids [sa**sa**nidz] The aggressive Persian dynasty that overthrew the Parthian Empire in AD 224. They were driven from Mesopotamia by the Arabs in AD 636. >> Parthians; Persian Empire

Sassoon, Siegfried (Lorraine) [sa**soon**] (1886–1967) Poet and novelist, born in Brenchley, Kent. World War 1, in which he served, gave him a hatred of war, fiercely expressed in his *Counterattack* (1918) and *Satirical Poems* (1926). His later poetry was increasingly devotional, and he became a Catholic in 1957.

SAT 1 In the United States an abbreviation for **Scholastic Aptitude Test**, a general examination of verbal and mathematical skills not related to specific course work, taken in the USA by high-school pupils wishing to attend university. **2** In England and Wales the term is an abbreviation for **Standard Assessment Task**, a test administered to children at the ages 7, 11, 14, and 16 to discover what level of the national curriculum they have reached.

Satan >> **Devil**

Satanism The worship of Satan or other figures of demonology. It may include the perversion of religious rituals (eg the black Mass), the practice of witchcraft, and other practices associated with the occult. >> Devil; occultism; witchcraft

satellite 1 A spacecraft orbiting the Earth or some other heavenly body. The first artificial satellite was Sputnik 1, launched by the USSR on 4 October 1957, and there are now more than 3000 satellites orbiting the Earth for remote sensing, military surveillance, communications, and space astronomy. >> satellite television; spacecraft **2** The moons of the planets in our Solar System. Jupiter and Saturn have extensive systems. >> Solar System

satellite television Television transmission using super-high-frequency beam linkage by way of an artificial satellite followed in its elliptical terrestrial orbit; commenced in 1962 with Telstar. Shortly after, satellites in fixed geostationary orbit above the Equator were introduced, providing continuous communication without tracking. In direct broadcasting from satellite (DBS), programmes are relayed at sufficient power to serve domestic TV receivers within a specific territory, known as the 'footprint', using small individual dish antennae of 60 cm/23 in diameter or less. >> dish; satellite; television

sati or **suttee** [sa**tee**] A custom which led Indian widows to burn themselves alive on husbands' funeral pyres. It was prohibited during Mughal times, and suppressed by the British in 1828.

Satie, Erik (Alfred Leslie) [satee] (1866–1925) Composer and pianist, born in Honfleur, France. He wrote ballets, lyric dramas, and whimsical pieces in violent revolt against musical orthodoxy.

satinwood A deciduous tree (*Chloroxylon swietenia*) growing to 25 m/80 ft, native to S India and Sri Lanka; leaves to 60 cm/2 ft; flowers 5-petalled, creamy-white, in clusters. It provides very hard, heavy, yellow wood, valued for its satin-like lustre. (Family: Flindersiaceae.)

satisficing [**sat**isfiysing] In economics, an alternative theory to the view that human activities can be seen as choosing between known alternatives with the aim of maximizing something, usually profits for firms. Satisficing argues that uncertainty makes maximizing very difficult. Instead, activities proceed by trial and error. Any policy, such as price cutting, is continued as long as it produces results which are up to some acceptable level. If the results fall below this level, trial and error starts again. This theory owes much to the US economist H A Simon (1916–). >> profit

satsuma [sat**soo**ma] A citrus fruit (*Citrus reticulata*); a variety of mandarin with an easily detachable rind. (Family: Rutaceae.) >> citrus; mandarin

saturated In chemistry, a term describing a hydrocarbon containing no multiple bonds. The name derives from the fact that these compounds contain the maximum amount of hydrogen for their carbon content. Alkanes are saturated hydrocarbons; alkenes and alkynes are **unsaturated**. >> hydrocarbons

saturated fatty acids >> **polyunsaturated fatty acids**

Saturn (astronomy) The sixth planet from the Sun, notable for its ring system – first seen by Galileo in 1610, and first identified by Huygens in 1656. It has 18 known moons, the largest of which is Titan, which alone has an atmosphere. Its main characteristics are: mass 5.69×10^{26} kg; mean density 0.69 g/cm^3; equatorial radius 60 000 km/37 000 mi; polar radius 53 500 km/33 300 mi; rotational period 10 h 14 m; orbital period 29.5 years; inclination of equator 27°; mean distance from the Sun 9.54 AU. Like Jupiter, it is a hydrogen/helium planet with a presumed innermost core of rocky composition and several Earth masses, an outer core of metallic hydrogen and helium, a liquid mantle of hydrogen/helium, and an atmosphere about 1000 km/600 mi deep. It is believed to have several cloud layers: solid ammonia (the highest), ammonium hydrosulphide, water ice, and water/ammonia. The rings were observed by Voyager to have particle-size distribution ranging up to several metres. Their infrared signature suggests that they are made of water ice – possibly created by break-up of a moon whose orbit decayed inside the limit where tidal flexing exceeded the moon's material strength. >> Dione; Enceladus; Galileo; Huygens; Hyperion; Iapetus; Jupiter (astronomy); Mimas; Phoebe (astronomy); planet; Rhea; Solar System; Tethys; Titan; Voyager project [i]; RR964

Saturn (mythology) or **Saturnus** A Roman god. At his festival

(**Saturnalia**, 17 Dec) slaves had temporary liberty, and presents were exchanged.

saturniid moth [saterneeid] A moth of the family Saturniidae; large, with wingspan up to 30 cm/12 in; conspicuous eyespots and banded markings present on wings; c.1300 species, including the *atlas* and *emperor moths*. (Order: Lepidoptera.) >> emperor moth; moth

satyr In Greek mythology, a minor deity associated with Dionysus; usually depicted with goat-like ears, tail, and legs. Rural, wild and lustful, the satyrs were said to be the brothers of the nymphs. >> Dionysus; nymph; satyriasis

satyriasis [satiriyasis] Pathological exaggerated sexual drive or excitement in a male. The corresponding drive in females is known as **nymphomania**. >> psychoanalysis

Saud, al- [sowd] Royal family and founders of the Kingdom of Saudi Arabia. **Abdul Aziz ibn Saud** (1880–1953), also known as **Ibn Saud**, came out of exile in Kuwait to consolidate his family's rule over most of the Arabian peninsula in the 1920s and, naming the country after his family, declared himself king of Saudi Arabia in 1932. **Faisal ibn Abd al-Aziz** (reigned 1964–75) led the kingdom to prominence by the strategic use of its oil power. The current ruler of Saudi Arabia is **Fahd ibn al-Aziz** (reigned 1982–), whose reign has suffered from economic recession and regional insecurity, notably the two Gulf Wars. >> OPEC; Saudi Arabia [i]; Wahhabis

Saudi Arabia [sowdee araybia], official name **Kingdom of Saudi Arabia**, Arabic **Al-Mamlaka al-Arabiya as-Saudiya** pop (1995e) 17 124 000; area 2 331 000 sq km/899 766 sq mi. Arabic kingdom comprising about four-fifths of the Arabian Peninsula; capital, Riyadh; timezone GMT +3; population mainly Arab (90%); chief religion, Islam; official language, Arabic; unit of currency, the riyal; Red Sea coastal plain bounded E by mountains; highlands in SW contain Jebel Abha, Saudi Arabia's highest peak (3133 m/10 279 ft); interior comprises two extensive areas of sand desert, the Nafud (N) and the Great Sandy Desert (S); some large oases; hot and dry climate; day temperatures may rise to 50°C in the interior; night frosts common in N and highlands; Red Sea coast hot and humid; sparse mean annual rainfall, c.10 mm/0·4 in; famed as the birthplace of Islam, a centre of pilgrimage to the holy cities of Mecca, Medina, and Jedda; modern state founded by Abd al-Aziz Ibn Saud who by 1932 united the four tribal provinces of Hejaz (NW), Asir (SW), Najd (C), and al-Hasa (E); governed as an absolute monarchy based on Islamic law and Arab Bedouin tradition; a king is head of state and prime minister, assisted by a Consultative Council; oil discovered in the 1930s; now the world's leading oil exporter; reserves account for about a quarter of the world's known supply; rapidly developing construction industry; large areas opened up for cultivation in 1980s. >> Islam; Jedda; Mecca; Medina; Riyadh; RR1021 political leaders

sauerkraut [sowerkrowt] A popular German food, produced by layering alternately shredded white cabbage and salt in a wooden box. Air is expelled by placing a weight on top. The cabbage salt layers are left for 3–4 weeks to ferment. >> cabbage

Saul [sawl] (11th-c BC) In the Hebrew bible, the first king to be elected by the Israelites. He became jealous of David, his son-in-law, and was ultimately at feud with the priestly class. Saul fell in battle with the Philistines on Mt Gilboa. >> David; Old Testament; Samuel

Saul of Tarsus >> **Paul, St**

Sault Sainte Marie [soo saynt maree], Fr [soh sĩt maree] 46°32N 84°20W, pop (1995e) 86 500. Town in SW Ontario, Canada, on N shore of St Mary's R; opposite Sault Ste Marie, Michigan; fort, 1751, taken by the British, 1762; Soo canals link L Superior and L Huron (177 m/581 ft); airport; railway. >> Great Lakes; Ontario

Saunders, Jennifer (1958–) British comedy writer and actress. She teamed up with Dawn French in a comedy act, making a breakthrough into television with 'The Comic Strip Presents ...' (1990), and several series of 'French and Saunders'. She became internationally known following the success, as writer and actress, of her comedy series *Absolutely Fabulous* (1993–5; Emmy, 1993).

Saurischia [sawriskia] The reptile-hipped dinosaurs; characterized by a forward-pointing pubis bone in the pelvic girdle, as in modern reptiles. They comprise the Theropoda, including the two-legged flesh-eaters such as *Tyrannosaurus*; and the giant plant-eating forms belonging to the Sauropodomorpha, including *Diplodocus*. >> *Allosaurus*; *Coelurus*; dinosaur [i]; *Diplodocus*; *Tyrannosaurus rex*

saury [sawree] Agile, slender-bodied fish, widespread and locally common in temperate ocean surface waters; head pointed or forming a narrow beak; body length up to 45 cm/18 in. (Family: Scomberosocidae, 2 genera, 4 species.)

sausage A cylindrical portion of minced meat, usually blended with breadcrumbs and herbs, and enclosed in an edible casing. Originally, the casing came from prepared animal intestine; today it is made from edible carbohydrate polymers. >> meat

sausage dog >> **dachshund**

Saussure, Ferdinand de [sohsür] (1857–1913) Linguist, born in Geneva, Switzerland, often described as the founder of modern linguistics. *Cours de linguistique générale* (1916, Course in General Linguistics) was compiled from the lecture notes of his students after his death. His focus on language as an 'underlying system' inspired a great deal of later semiology and structuralism. >> linguistics; structuralism

Savannah 32°05N 81°06W, pop (1995e) 153 000. City in E Georgia, USA; port near the mouth of the Savannah R; founded, 1733; during the War of Independence, held by the British, 1778–82; captured by Sherman during the Civil War, 1864; airfield; railway; city's historic district designated a national historic landmark. >> American Revolution / Civil War; Georgia

savannah The grassland region of the tropics and subtropics, located between areas of tropical rainforest and desert. The length of the arid season prevents widespread tree growth; the scattered trees which do exist, such as acacia and baobab, are adapted to reduced precipitation levels. >> sahel; tropics

Save the Children Fund In the UK, the largest international children's charity, founded in 1919, and having as its president the Princess Royal. It is concerned with the rescue of children from disaster and the longer-term welfare of children in need. Together with the US **Save the Children Federation**, it is a member of the **International Save the Children Alliance**.

Savile, Jimmy [**sa**vil], popular name of **Sir James Wilson Vincent Savile** (1926–) Television and radio personality, born in Leeds, West Yorkshire. A former miner, he achieved fame as a disc jockey. He has used his nationwide prominence and popularity to raise huge sums of money for deserving causes.

savings and loan associations >> **building society**

Savonarola, Girolamo [savona**roh**la] (1452–98) Religious and political reformer, born in Ferrara, Italy. His eloquent preaching began to point towards a political revolution as the means of restoring religion and morality. When a republic was established in Florence (1494), he was its guiding spirit, fostering a Christian commonwealth. Accused of heresy, he was burned in Florence. >> humanism

savory Either of two related species of culinary herbs. **Summer savory** (*Satureja hortensis*) is a slender, bushy annual native to the Mediterranean. **Winter savory** (*Satureja montana*) is a woody perennial native to S Europe. (Genus: *Satureja*. Family: Labiatae.) >> herb

Savoy, House of Rulers of the duchy of Savoy, a trans-alpine area in present-day Switzerland and France, from the 11th-c to the 19th-c. Its heyday in European politics was from the mid-14th-c to the mid-15th-c.

saw, musical A common handsaw used as a musical instrument by pressing it towards the thigh and drawing a violin bow across the straight edge. The pitch is controlled by the curve of the blade. >> idiophone

saw-bill >> **merganser**

Sawchuk, Terry, popular name of **Terrance (Gordon) Sawchuck** (1929–70) Ice hockey player, born in Winnipeg, Manitoba, Canada. One of the game's greatest goalminders, he appeared in 971 games 1950–70, a record for a goalminder. >> ice hockey

sawfish A very large and distinctive ray, with a greatly prolonged snout, armed on each side with a regular row of strong blunt teeth; widespread in tropical seas; length up to 7.5 m/25 ft. (Family: Pristidae, 1 genus.) >> ray

sawfly A wasp-like insect which lacks a constricted waist; egg-laying tube large, saw-like, and used for depositing eggs deep into plant tissues. (Order: Hymenoptera. Suborder: Symphyta.) >> insect [i]; wasp

Saxe, (Hermann) Maurice, comte de (Count of), usually called **Marshal de Saxe** (1696–1750) Marshal of France, born in Goslar, Germany, the illegitimate son of Augustus II, King of Poland. In the War of the Austrian Succession (1740–8) he invaded Bohemia, taking Prague by storm, and later won victories at Fontenoy (1745), Raucoux (1746), and Lauffeld (1747). >> Austrian Succession, War of the

Saxe-Coburg-Gotha [**saks koh**berg **go**tha] The name of the British royal family, 1901–17. King Edward VII inherited it from his father, Prince Albert, the second son of the Duke of Saxe-Coburg-Gotha. The obviously Germanic name was abandoned during World War 1. >> Edward VII

saxhorn A musical instrument, made from brass tubing, resembling a small tuba, with the mouthpiece set at right angles and an upright bell. It was patented in 1843 by French instrument-maker Adolphe Sax (1814–94), and manufactured in various sizes. >> brass instrument [i]; tuba

saxifrage [**sak**sifrij] A member of a large, varied genus of annuals or perennials, native to N temperate regions and South America, mainly in arctic or alpine regions; flowers usually 5-petalled, white, yellow, through pink to purple; fruit a capsule. (Genus: *Saxifraga*, 370 species. Family: Saxifragaceae.)

Saxo Grammaticus (Lat 'the Scholar') (c.1140–1206) Chronicler, born in Zealand. He wrote the *Gesta Danorum*, a Latin history of the Danes, in 16 books.

Saxons A Germanic people from the N German plain. With the Angles, they formed the bulk of the invaders who conquered and colonized most of what became England. They were especially prominent in Essex, Sussex, and Wessex. >> Anglo-Saxons; Wessex

Saxony A German ducal and electoral state which experienced many changes of fortune. Prominent from the 9th–11th-c, and again in the 16th–17th-c, it was finally merged in the North German Confederation (1866) and the German Reich (1871). >> Germany; Protestantism; Reich

saxophone A single-reed musical instrument, made of metal with a wide conical bore. It was patented in 1846 by French instrument-maker Adolphe Sax (1814–94), and made in a variety of sizes and pitches, the most frequently used being the alto and tenor instruments. These are usually joined by the soprano and baritone instruments to form the saxophone quartet; bass and contrabass sizes are also in use. >> reed instrument; woodwind instrument [i]

Sayers, Dorothy L(eigh) (1893–1957) Writer, born in Oxford, Oxfordshire. She became a celebrated writer of detective stories, introducing her hero Lord Peter Wimsey in various accurately observed milieux – such as advertising in *Murder Must Advertise* (1933) or bell-ringing in *The Nine Tailors* (1934).

SBS Abbreviation of **Special Boat Service**, the naval arm of British Military Special Forces responsible for all non-conventional maritime operations. It provided the blueprint for the formation of the American SEALS (Sea, Air, Land teams). >> SAS

scabies [**skay**beez] A harmless common itchy skin infestation with the itch-mite (*Sarcoptes scabei*), which burrows below the skin surface. >> itch; mite; *Streptococcus*

scabious A perennial growing to 70 cm/27 in (*Scabiosa columbaria*), native to Europe, W Asia, and N Africa; flowers bluish-lilac, with five unequal petals, in heads 1.5–3.5 cm/$\frac{1}{2}$–1$\frac{1}{2}$ in across. (Family: Dipsacaceae.)

Scafell Pike [skaw**fel**], also spelled **Scawfell** 54°28N 3°12W. Mountain in Lake District of Cumbria, NW England; highest peak in England, 977 m/3205 ft. >> Lake District

scalar In mathematics, a physical quantity which can be represented by a real number, having magnitude but not direction, such as mass, time, and temperature. >> numbers; vector (mathematics)

scald >> **burn**

scale In music, the notes forming the basic vocabulary of a melodic or harmonic system, arranged in a succession of upward or downward steps. Some of the more important scales in Western music are shown here, in each case with middle C as the starting note (*tonic*). >> microtone; pentatonic scale; serialism; tonality; tone 1; *see illustration on p. 762*

scale insect A plant-sucking bug; wingless adult females usually protected by a scale-like wax covering secreted over the body; males non-feeding, with one pair of wings;

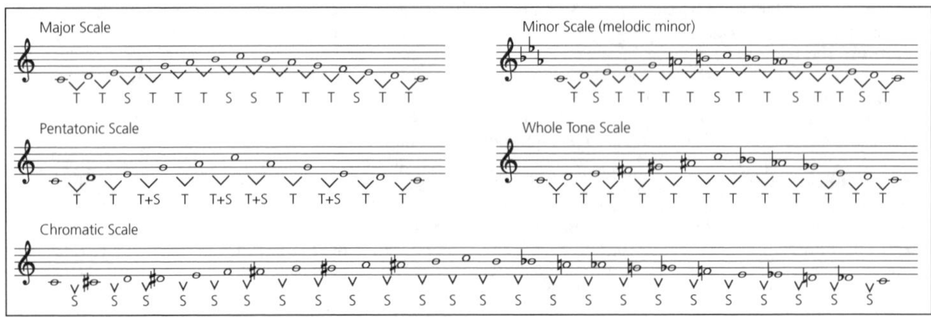

Musical scales – T = tone, S = semitone

c.4000 species, including many pests. (Order: Homoptera. Family: Coccidae.) >> bug (entomology)

Scalfaro, Oscar (Luigi) [skal**fah**roh] (1918–) Italian politician and president (1992–), born in Novara, Piedmont, Italy. He was a leader of the Azione Cattolica (Catholic Action) movement, a member of the Constituent Assembly (1946), then a deputy. He served as minister for transport (1966–8, 1972), education (1972–3), and the interior (1983–7), before becoming president.

Scaliger, Julius Caesar [**skal**ijer], originally **Benedetto Bordone** (1484–1558) Italian humanist scholar, born in Riva, Italy. His third son, **Joseph Justus Scaliger** (1540–1609), became one of the most erudite scholars of his day, best known for his *Opus de emendatione temporum* (1583), a study of earlier methods of calculating time. >> humanism; Renaissance

scallop A marine bivalve mollusc with unequal shell valves; lives unattached to a substrate, and is able to swim by clapping its valves together; fished commercially for human consumption. (Class: Pelecypoda. Order: Ostreoida.) >> bivalve; mollusc

scampi The Italian culinary term for large Gulf shrimps or Dublin Bay prawns, usually fried in batter. >> prawn

Scandinavian languages The languages of the N Germanic branch of Indo-European, including Norwegian (c.5 million in Norway and the USA), Swedish (c.9 million in Sweden, Finland, and the USA), Danish (c.5 million in Denmark, Germany, and the USA), Icelandic (c.0·25 million in Iceland and the USA), and Faroese (c.40 000 in the Faroe Is). These languages are mutually intelligible to varying degrees. >> Germanic languages

scanning The exploration of a picture area along a systematic series of lines, providing information in sequential form. For TV broadcasting, two sets of interlaced alternate scanning lines are employed, giving a total picture coverage of 525 lines 30 times a second for American NTSC and 625 lines 25 times a second for European PAL. Optical scanning at a much slower rate is also employed for the transmission of facsimile documents and pictures over land lines. >> television

Scapa Flow The area of open water in the Orkney Is, Scotland, surrounded by the islands of Mainland, Hoy, Flotta, S Ronaldsay, and Burray. It was a British naval base in World Wars 1 and 2. In 1919 the German naval fleet was scuttled there.

scapula A triangular bone on each side of the body over the upper part of the back (second to seventh ribs). With the clavicle it forms the *pectoral girdle*. It moves in conjunction with the shoulder joint to increase the total range of movement of the upper limb. >> bone; clavicle; skeleton [i]

Scarborough [**skah(r)**bruh] 54°17N 0°24W, pop (1995e) 40 500. Coastal resort town in North Yorkshire, N England; England's oldest spa town; railway; castle (12th-c); football league team, Scarborough. >> Yorkshire, North

Scardino, Marjorie (Morris) [skah(r)**dee**noh] (1947–) Businesswoman, born in Texas. She trained as a lawyer, later becoming president of the Economist Newspaper Group in New York (1985–92), and its chief executive in London (1992–6). She joined the Pearson group as its chief executive in 1997, and was named businesswoman of the year in 1998.

Scarfe, Gerald (1936–) Cartoonist, born in London. His cartoons are based on extreme distortion in the tradition of Gillray (eg Mick Jagger's lips are drawn larger than the rest of his face). >> Asher; Gillray

Scargill, Arthur (1938–) Trade unionist, born in Leeds, West Yorkshire. He became president of the National Union of Mineworkers in 1982, and is primarily known for his strong defence of British miners through a socialist politics that has often brought his union into conflict with government. This was most notable during the miners' strike of 1984–5, and again in 1990 as a result of British Coal's plans to close most deep-mine collieries. >> socialism; trade union

Scarlatti, (Pietro) Alessandro (Gaspare) [skah(r)**la**tee] (1660–1725) Composer, born in Palermo, Sicily, Italy. He reputedly wrote over 100 operas, of which 40 survive complete, including *Tigrane* (1715). He also wrote 10 Masses, c.700 cantatas, and oratorios, motets, and madrigals.

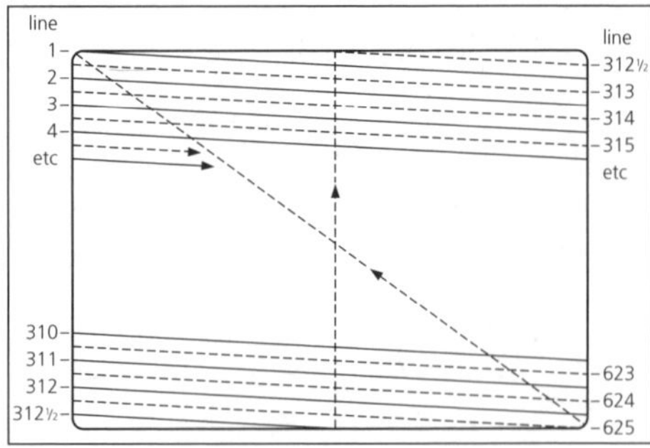

Interlaced scanning – in the system, 312½ lines (shown solid) are scanned from top to bottom in $\frac{1}{50}$ sec. The interlacing lines (shown broken) are scanned in the next $\frac{1}{50}$ sec to give a complete 625 lines scan every $\frac{1}{25}$ sec.

Scarlatti, (Giuseppe) Domenico [skah(r)**la**tee] (1685–1757) Composer, born in Naples, Italy, the son of Alessandro Scarlatti. He was a skilled harpsichordist, and is mainly remembered for the 555 sonatas written for this instrument. >> harpsichord; Scarlatti, Alessandro; sonata

scarlet fever An acute infectious disease of children caused by haemolytic streptococci, usually in the pharynx and tonsils. A sore throat is followed by a generalized red skin rash. It responds rapidly to antibiotics. >> ear [i]; *Streptococcus*

scarlet pimpernel >> **pimpernel**

Scarron, Paul [skarõ] (1610–60) Writer, born in Paris. He is best known for his realistic novel, *Le Roman comique* (1651–7, The Comic Novel). In 1652 he married Françoise d'Aubigné (later, Madame de Maintenon). >> Maintenon, Madame de

scattering In physics, the redirection of a beam of light or sound, or a stream of particles resulting from a collision. Scattering experiments are an important source of information in atomic, nuclear, particle, and solid state physics. >> spectroscopy; X-ray diffraction

Scawfell >> **Scafell Pike**

scepticism / skepticism A philosophical tradition which casts doubt on the possibility of human knowledge, either in general or in some particular sphere. Pyrrho is usually credited as the founder, and from 280–80 BC it was the official philosophy of the Academy. >> Pyrrho

Schaffhausen [shaf**how**zn], Fr **Schaffhouse** 47°42N 8°38E, pop (1995e) 35 400. Industrial town in NE Switzerland; on the R Rhine; well-preserved mediaeval town; railway; Minster (1087–1150). >> Switzerland [i]

Scharnhorst, Gerhard Johann David von [**shah(r)n**haw(r)st] (1755–1813) Prussian general and military reformer, born in Bordenau, Germany. He worked with Gneisenau to reform the Prussian army after its defeat by Napoleon. He was fatally wounded fighting the French at Lützen. >> Gneisenau; Prussia

Schawlow, Arthur (Leonard) [**show**loh] (1921–99) Physicist, born in Mount Vernon, NY. With his brother-in-law Charles Townes he devised the laser, although the first working model was made by Maiman in 1960. He shared the Nobel Prize for Physics in 1981. >> laser [i]; Maiman; Townes

Scheel, Walter [shayl] (1919–) West German statesman and president (1974–9), born in Solingen, Germany. He was minister for economic co-operation (1961–6) and foreign minister (1969–74), and in 1970 negotiated treaties with the USSR and Poland. >> Germany [i]

scheelite [**sheel**iyt] A mineral calcium tungstate ($CaWO_4$) occurring in hydrothermal veins and pegmatites. It is an important ore of tungsten. >> tungsten; wolframite

Schelde or **Scheldt, River** [**skel**duh, skelt], Fr **Escaut** River rising in N France; meets the North Sea through two estuaries (East and West Schelde) in The Netherlands; length 435 km/270 mi.

Schelling, Friedrich (Wilhelm Joseph) von [**shel**ing] (1775–1854) Philosopher, born in Leonberg, Germany. His early work culminated in his *System des transzendentalen Idealismus* (1800, System of Transcendental Idealism). >> idealism

scherzo [**skairt**soh] A lively musical piece, though not necessarily a 'joke', as the Italian name suggests. Haydn and Beethoven established it as an alternative to the minuet in the classical symphony and sonata. >> Beethoven; Haydn; minuet

Schiaparelli, Elsa [skyapa**rel**ee] (1896–1973) Fashion designer, born in Rome. Her designs were inventive and sensational, and she was noted for her use of colour, including 'shocking pink', and her original use of traditional fabrics.

Schiaparelli, Giovanni (Virginio) [skyapa**rel**ee] (1835–1910) Astronomer, born in Savigliano, Italy. He discovered the asteroid Hesperia, and termed vague linear features on Mars as 'canali' (1877). >> asteroids; Lowell, Percival; Mars (astronomy)

Schick Test A test of the susceptibility to diphtheria, in which a small amount of diphtheria toxin is injected into the skin. It is named after the Austrian paediatrician, Bela Schick (1877–1967). >> diphtheria

Schiele, Egon [**shee**luh] (1890–1918) Painter, born in Tulln, Austria. He developed a powerful form of Expressionism in which figures, often naked and emaciated, fill the canvas with awkward, anguished gestures. >> Expressionism; Sezession

Schiller, (Johann Christoph) Friedrich (von) [**shil**er] (1759–1805) Playwright, poet, and historian, born in Marbach, Germany. His works include the poem *An die Freude* (Ode to Joy), later set to music by Beethoven in his choral symphony. His last decade was highly productive, including the dramatic trilogy, *Wallenstein* (1796–9), held to be the greatest German historical drama, *Maria Stuart* (1800), and *Wilhelm Tell* (1804). >> *Sturm und Drang*

Schinkel, Karl Friedrich [**shing**kl] (1781–1841) Architect, born in Neuruppin, Germany. He designed a wide range of buildings, in classical style, and introduced new streets and squares in Berlin.

schipperke [**ship**erkee] A breed of dog, developed in Belgium, originally used as a watchdog on barges; small, lively; erect pointed ears, pointed muzzle, no tail; thick, usually black, coat; also known as **little boatman**, **little captain**, or **little corporal**. >> dog

schist [shist] A medium-grade regional metamorphic rock characterized by a foliated texture, resulting from the alignment of layers of mica minerals. >> metamorphic rock; micas

schistosomiasis [skistoso**miy**asis] A common cause of illness in tropical countries, resulting from infestation with *Schistosoma*, a fluke; also known as **bilharziasis**. The flukes pass through the blood circulation, where they cause disease of the lungs, bladder, liver, and large bowel. >> blood fluke

schizophrenia A major psychiatric disorder characterized by an alteration of thinking and perception, including a loss of contact with reality. In addition there may be a basic change in personality, a loss of normal emotional responsiveness, and considerable withdrawal. The causes are not fully understood, but there is a major genetic component. Management includes drug treatment, skilful counselling, and rehabilitation. >> catatonia; psychosis

Schlegel, August Wilhelm von [**shlay**gl] (1767–1845) Poet and critic, born in Hanover, Germany. He is famous for his translations of Shakespeare and other authors, and for founding Sanskrit studies in Germany. His brother, **Karl Wilhelm Friedrich Schlegel** (1772–1829), also born at Hanover, became the greatest critic produced by the German Romantics, writing widely on comparative literature and philology. >> Romanticism

Schleiermacher, Friedrich (Ernst Daniel) [**shliy**ermahkher] (1768–1834) Theologian and philosopher, born in Wrocław, Poland (formerly Breslau, Prussia). He was a leader of the movement which led to the union in 1817 of the Lutheran and Reformed Churches in Prussia, and is widely held to be the founder of modern Protestant theology. >> Lutheranism; Protestantism; Reformed Churches

Schlesinger, Arthur M(eier), Jr [**shlez**injer] (1917–) Historian, born in Columbus, OH. He became special assistant to President Kennedy (1961–3). His publications include *The Age of Jackson* (1945) and *A Thousand Days: John F Kennedy in the White House* (1965), both Pulitzer prizewinners. >> Kennedy, John F

Schlesinger, John [**shlez**injer] (1926–) Actor and director, born in London. His early films, of contemporary social realism, were *A Kind of Loving* (1962) and *Billy Liar* (1963). Later films display a considerable range, as seen in *Midnight Cowboy* (1969), *Marathon Man* (1976), *Honky Tonk Freeway* (1980), *Madame Sousatka* (1989), and *Cold Comfort Farm* (1996).

Schleswig [**shlez**vig] A breed of heavy horse, developed in Germany; height, 15.2–16 hands/1.5–1.6 m/5 ft 2 in–5 ft 4 in; usually pale brown with yellow mane; short powerful legs; also known as **Schleswig heavy draught**. >> horse ℹ

Schleswig-Holstein [**shlez**vig **hol**shtiyn] pop (1995e) 2 700 000; area 15 721 sq km/6068 sq mi. Northernmost province of Germany; includes the North Frisian Is; capital, Kiel; coast includes an extensive swimming and sailing resort area; focus of a dispute between Denmark and Prussia in the 19th-c, leading to annexation by Prussia, 1866. >> Frisian Islands; Germany ℹ; Prussia

Schlick, Moritz [shlik] (1882–1936) Philosopher, born in Berlin. One of the leaders of the 'Vienna Circle' of logical positivists, he was shot down on the steps of the university by a deranged student. >> logical positivism; Vienna Circle

Schlieffen, Alfred, Graf von (Count of) [**shlee**fn] (1833–1913) Prussian field marshal, born in Berlin. He advocated the plan which bears his name (1895), on which German tactics were unsuccessfully based in World War 1. He envisaged a German breakthrough in Belgium and the rapid defeat of France by a movement through Holland. >> World War 1

Schliemann, Heinrich [**shlee**man] (1822–90) Archaeologist, born in Neubukow, Germany. He hoped to find the site of the Homeric poems by excavating the tell at Hisarlik in Asia Minor, the traditional site of Troy. From 1871 he discovered nine superimposed city sites, one containing a considerable treasure (found 1873) which he over-hastily identified as Priam's. >> Homer; tell; Troy

Schmidt, Helmut (Heinrich Waldemar) [shmit] (1918–) West German statesman and chancellor (1974–82), born in Hamburg, Germany. He was minister of defence (1969–72) and of finance (1972–4), and succeeded Brandt as chancellor in 1974, describing his aim as the 'political unification of Europe in partnership with the United States'. >> Brandt, Willy; Germany ℹ

schnauzer [**shnowt**ser] A German breed of dog; terrier-like with thick wiry coat; marked eyebrows, moustache, and beard; top of head flat, with short pendulous ears. >> dog; terrier

Schneider Trophy [**shniy**der] A flying trophy for seaplanes presented by French armaments magnate Jacques Schneider in 1913. After being won outright by Great Britain in 1931 the contest ceased, but the races were revived in the 1980s. >> seaplane

Schnitzler, Arthur [**shnits**ler] (1862–1931) Playwright and novelist, born in Vienna. His highly psychological, often strongly erotic works include his one-act play cycles *Anatol* (1893) and *Reigen* (1900, filmed as *La Ronde*, 1950).

Schoenberg, Arnold [**shoen**berg], also spelled **Schönberg** (1874–1951) Composer, born in Vienna. His *Chamber Symphony* caused a riot at its first performance in 1907 through its abandonment of the traditional concept of tonality. He became known for his concept of '12-note' or 'serial' music, used in most of his later works. >> atonality; serialism

scholastic aptitude test >> **SAT**

scholasticism The Catholic philosophical tradition dominant in the mediaeval universities of the 12th–14th-c in Western Europe. It is characterized by its use of philosophy in the service of theology, and its use of ancient authorities such as Aristotle and St Augustine. >> Aquinas; Augustine, St (of Hippo); dialectic

Scholes, Myron S (1941–) US economist. He graduated from MIT in 1970, and went on to join Harvard Univesity. He shared the 1997 Nobel Prize in Economics for his contribution to a new method of determining the value of derivatives.

Schönberg, Arnold >> **Schoenberg, Arnold**

Schönbrunn Palace [**shoen**brun] A Baroque palace in Vienna, designed (1696–1730) by Fischer von Erlach for Emperor Leopold I, and converted for Maria Theresa's use in the 1740s. >> Fischer von Erlach; Maria Theresa; Vienna

School of the Air A two-way radio educational service for Australian children living in isolated areas; begun in South Australia in 1951 to supplement correspondence teaching and reduce feelings of isolation. >> Open University

schooner A sailing vessel with more than one mast, each fore-and-aft-rigged. The masts are usually of equal height, but when two-masted the forward one is often shorter. >> ship ℹ

Schopenhauer, Arthur [**shoh**penhower] (1788–1860) Philosopher, born in Gdańsk, Poland (formerly Danzig, Germany). His chief work, *Die Welt als Wille und Vorstellung* (1819, The World as Will and Idea), emphasizes the central role of human will as the creative, primary factor in understanding.

Schreiner, Olive (Emilie Albertina) [shriy**ner**], pseudonym **Ralph Iron** (1855–1920) Writer, born in Wittebergen, South Africa. *The Story of an African Farm* (1883) was the first sustained, imaginative work to come from Africa. In her later work she became a passionate propagandist for women's rights, pro-Boer loyalty, and pacifism.

Schröder, Gerhard [**shroe**der] (1944–) German statesman and chancellor (1998–), born in Mossenberg, Germany. He qualified as a lawyer, and entered parliament as a social democrat in 1980. He became minister president of Lower Saxony in 1990, and defeated Helmut Kohl to become chancellor in 1998. >> Kohl

Schrödinger, Erwin [**shroe**dinger] (1887–1961) Physicist, born in Vienna. He originated the study of wave mechanics as part of the quantum theory with his celebrated wave equation, for which he shared the Nobel Prize for Physics in 1933. >> Dirac; quantum field theory; wave motion ℹ

Schubert, Franz (Peter) [**shoo**bert] (1797–1828) Composer, born in Vienna. His major works include the 'Trout' piano quintet (1819), his C major symphony (1825), and his B minor symphony (1822), known as the 'Unfinished'; but he is particularly remembered as the greatest exponent of German songs (*Lieder*), which number c.600. He also wrote a great deal of choral and chamber music. >> *Lied*

Schumacher, Michael [**shoo**maker] (1969–) Motor-racing driver, born in Hürth-Hermuhlheim, Germany. He made his Formula One debut with Jordan in 1990, then joined Benetton, with whom he became world champion in 1994 and 1995. He joined Ferrari in 1996, and achieved second place in the 1997 championship, but lost this position following an enquiry into a driving incident.

Schuman, Robert [**shoo**man] (1886–1963) French statesman and prime minister (1947–8), born in Luxembourg. As foreign minister (1948–52) he proposed the **Schuman plan** (1950) for pooling the coal and steel resources of W Europe. >> European Economic Community

Schumann, Clara (Josephine) [**shoo**man], *née* **Wieck** (1819–96) Pianist and composer, born in Leipzig, Germany. Her compositions include chamber music, songs, and many piano works, including a concerto. She married Robert Schumann in 1840. >> Schumann, Robert

Schumann, Elisabeth [**shoo**man] (1885–1952) Operatic soprano and *Lieder* singer, born in Merseburg, Germany. She made her debut in Hamburg in 1909, and in 1919 was engaged by Richard Strauss for the Vienna State Opera, later specializing in *Lieder*. >> *Lied*; Strauss, Richard

Schumann, Robert (Alexander) [**shoo**man] (1810–56) Composer, born in Zwickau, Germany. He produced a large number of compositions, until 1840 almost all for the piano. He then married Clara Wieck, and under her influence began to write orchestral works, notably his A minor piano concerto (1845) and four symphonies. He also wrote chamber music and a large number of songs (*Lieder*). >> *Lied*; Schumann, Clara

Schuschnigg, Kurt von [**shush**nik] (1897–1977) Austrian statesman and chancellor (1934–8), born in Riva, Italy (formerly Austria-Hungary). His attempt to prevent Hitler occupying Austria led to his imprisonment until 1945. He then lived in the USA. >> Austria ℹ; World War 2

Schwann, Theodor [shvahn] (1810–82) Physiologist, born in Neuss, Germany. He discovered the enzyme pepsin, investigated muscle contraction, and extended the cell theory from plants to animal tissues. >> cell; pepsin

Schwarzenberg, Felix (Ludwig Johann Friedrich) [**shvah(r)ts**enberg] (1800–52) Austrian statesman, born in Krummau, Austria. During the 1848 Revolution, he was made prime minister, and created a centralized, absolutist, imperial state. His bold initiatives temporarily restored Habsburg domination of European affairs. >> Habsburgs; Prussia; Revolutions of 1848

Schwarzenegger, Arnold [**shwaw(r)ts**eneger] (1947–) US film actor, born near Graz, Austria. He won several body-building titles, and in the 1980s became the leading figure in muscular action films, beginning with *Conan the Barbarian* (1982), which became increasingly technological and violent with *The Terminator* (1984) and *Total Recall* (1990). A more humane side emerged in such films as *Twins* (1988) and *Junior* (1994).

Schwarzkopf, (Olga Maria) Elisabeth (Friederike) [**shvah(r)ts**kopf] (1915–) Soprano, born in Janotschin, Poland. She made her debut at Berlin in 1938, first specializing in coloratura roles and later appearing more as a lyric soprano, especially in recitals of *Lieder*. >> coloratura; *Lied*

Schwarzkopf, H Norman [**shvah(r)ts**kopf], nickname **Stormin' Norman** (1934–) US army officer, born in Trenton, NJ. He commanded US and allied forces against Iraq during 'Operation Desert Storm' in 1991, then retired from the army. >> Gulf War 2

Schwarzschild, Karl [**shvah(r)ts**shild] (1873–1916) Theoretical astrophysicist, born in Frankfurt, Germany. He computed exact solutions of Einstein's field equations in general relativity. The **Schwarzschild radius** is the critical radius at which an object becomes a black hole if collapsed or compressed indefinitely. >> black hole; general relativity; gravitational collapse

Schweitzer, Albert [**shviyts**er] (1875–1965) Medical missionary, theologian, musician, and philosopher, born in Kaysersberg, Germany. In 1896 he made his famous decision that he would live for science and art until he was 30, and then devote his life to serving humanity. His religious writing includes *Von Reimarus zu Wrede* (1906, trans The Quest of the Historical Jesus), and major works on St Paul. True to his vow, despite his international reputation in music and theology, he began to study medicine in 1905, and after qualifying (1913) set up a hospital to fight leprosy and sleeping sickness at Lambaréné, French Equatorial Africa, where he remained for the rest of his life. He was awarded the Nobel Peace Prize in 1952. >> Hansen's disease; Paul, St; theology; trypanosomiasis

Schwerin [**shvay**reen] 53°37N 11°22E, pop (1995e) 132 000. City in N Germany; former capital of Mecklenburg state; railway; cathedral (13th-c). >> Germany ℹ

Schwimmer, David [**shwim**er] (1966–) Actor and director, born in New York City. He played several small roles in television series, eventually becoming known for his role as Ross Geller in the acclaimed television series *Friends* (1994–). Roles in feature films include *Crossing the Bridge* (1992) and *The Pallbearer* (1996).

Schwitters, Kurt [**shvi**terz] (1887–1948) Artist, born in Hanover, Germany. He joined the Dadaists, developing a form of collage (*merz*) using such everyday detritus as broken glass, tram tickets, and scraps of paper picked up in the street. >> collage; Dada

Schwyz [shveets] 47°02N 8°39E, pop (1995e) 13 200. Town in C Switzerland; the town and canton gave their name to the whole country; railway. >> Switzerland ℹ

sciatica [siy**at**ika] Pain in the distribution of the sciatic nerve (ie over the buttocks and the back of the leg as far as the foot). It is commonly due to pressure on the lumbosacral nerve roots of the sciatic nerve. >> nervous system; prolapsed intervertebral disc

science fiction Fiction that focuses on the technical possibilities and human effects of scientific advance. The first novelist to explore this theme systematically was Jules Verne, with four novels (1863–73) including *20 000 Leagues under the Sea* (1870). H G Wells's novels include *The Time Machine* (1895) and *The First Men in the Moon* (1901). Major authors, such as Ray Bradbury (eg *Fahrenheit 451*, 1954), Arthur C Clarke (eg *Childhood's End*, 1954), and Isaac Asimov (eg *Foundation Trilogy*, 1957–63), did not emerge until after World War 2. >> Asimov; Ballard; Bradbury, Ray; Verne; Vonnegut; Wells, H G

Science Museum A museum in S Kensington, London, housing the most important British collection of scientific and technological exhibits.

science park A concentration of scientific and high technology industries and businesses on one site. The term includes research parks established by universities to promote academic and business links in science, and technology parks designed for the commercial exploitation of high technology. Science parks began in the USA in the 1930s.

Scientology® (Latin, *scio* 'know' + Greek *logos* 'study') An applied religious philosophy and non-denominational religion, founded in the USA by L Ron Hubbard in 1952. The Church of Scientology was formed by Scientologists in 1954. It holds man to be an intrinsically spiritual being of unlimited ability and beneficence, its goal the achievement of complete certainty of one's spiritual existence and relationship to the Supreme Being. A central technique is **Dianetics**® (Greek *dia* 'through' + *nous* 'soul'), a spiritual healing technology aimed at the improvement of mental ability and the alleviation of psychosomatic ills. >> Hubbard

Scilly, Isles of [**sil**ee] pop (1995e) 1950; area 16 sq km/ 6 sq mi. A group of c.140 islands and islets W of Land's End, Cornwall, SW England; administered by Duchy of Cornwall; includes the five inhabited islands of St Mary's (chief town, Hugh Town), St Martin's, Tresco, St Agnes, Bryher. >> Cornwall

scintillation counter A device for detecting the passage of charged particles, using materials such as sodium iodide, or special plastics which emit light (**scintillate**) when charged particles pass through them. The technique is an important means of timing the passage of particles in particle physics experiments. >> particle detectors

Scipio Africanus [**skip**ioh], in full **Publius Cornelius Scipio Africanus**, also called **Scipio Africanus Major** (236–c.183 BC) Roman general of the Second Punic War. His victory at Ilipa (206 BC) forced the Carthaginians out of Spain, and his defeat of Hannibal at Zama (202 BC) broke the power of Carthage altogether. >> Hannibal; Punic Wars

Scipio Aemilianus [**ski**pioh aymili**ah**nus], in full **Scipio Aemilianus Publius Cornelius**, also called **Scipio Africanus Minor** (185–129 BC) Roman statesman, general, and orator, the adopted grandson of Scipio Africanus Major. He was famous primarily for the sack of Carthage in the Third Punic War (146 BC), the destruction of Numantia (133 BC), and his patronage of the arts. >> Punic Wars

scirocco >> **Sirocco**

scissorbill >> **skimmer**

scoliosis [skoli**oh**sis] >> **vertebral column**

scorpion A terrestrial arthropod; body typically elongate, up to 18 cm/7 in long, including a long tail bearing a conspicuous terminal sting; c.1200 species, mostly tropical in distribution. (Class: Arachnida. Order: Scorpiones.) >> Arachnida; arthropod

scorpionfish Robust, bottom-living, marine fish with well-developed fin and body spines, frequently armed with venom glands; widespread in tropical to cool temperate seas; length up to 40 cm/16 in. (Family: Scorpaenidae, 11 genera.)

Scorpius (Lat 'scorpion') Constellation in the S sky; often wrongly called **Scorpio**. It is a constellation of the zodiac, lying between Libra and Sagittarius. The brightest star is Antares. Distance: 130 parsec. >> constellation; zodiac i; RR968

Scorsese, Martin [**skaw(r)**sayzee] (1942–) Film director, born in Flushing, Long Island, NY. His many films include *Taxi Driver* (1976), *New York, New York* (1977), *Raging Bull* (1980), *GoodFellas* (1990), *The Age of Innocence* (1993), and *Kundun* (1998). >> De Niro

Scotch whisky A spirit distilled from malted barley, either **single malt**, the product of one distillery, or **blended** whiskies. Grain whisky, distilled from barley and maize in continuous stills, is now used as the base for much of the blended whisky. >> barley; maize; spirits; whisky

Scotland pop (1995e) 5 127 000; area 78 742 sq km/30 394 sq mi (water 1603 sq km/619 sq mi). Northern constituent part of the United Kingdom, comprising all mainland N of the border (from Solway to Berwick) and the island groups of Outer and Inner Hebrides, Orkney, and Shetland; local government reorganization (1996) established 32 single-tier councils; maximum length 441 km/274 mi, maximum width 248 km/154 mi; capital, Edinburgh; other chief towns, Glasgow, Dundee, Aberdeen; Scottish Gaelic known or used by c.80 000; divided into Southern Uplands (rising to 843 m/2766 ft at the Merrick), Central Lowlands (most densely populated area), and Northern Highlands (divided by the fault line following the Great Glen, and rising to 1344 m/4409 ft at Ben Nevis); W coast heavily indented; several wide estuaries on E coast, primarily Firths of Forth, Tay, and Moray; many freshwater lochs in the interior, largest Loch Lomond (70 sq km/27 sq mi) and deepest Loch Morar (310 m/1020 ft); Roman attempts to limit incursions of N tribes marked by Antonine Wall and Hadrian's Wall; beginnings of unification, 9th-c; wars between England and Scotland in Middle Ages; Scottish independence declared by Robert Bruce, recognized 1328; Stuart succession, 14th-c; crowns of Scotland and England united in 1603; parliaments united under Act of Union in 1707; unsuccessful Jacobite rebellions, 1715, 1745; devolution proposal rejected in 1979; successful 1997 vote for devolved Scottish parliament in 2000; since 1974, divided into 12 regions and 53 districts; industries mainly in C region, based on local coal, but all heavy industry declined through the 1980s, with closure of many pits; oil services on E coast; tourism especially in Highlands. >> Andrew, St; Bruce, Robert; Edinburgh; Gaelic; Kenneth I; Scottish National Party / reels; Stuarts; thistle; Union, Acts of; RR998

Scotland Yard, officially **New Scotland Yard** The headquarters of the Metropolitan Police at Westminster in London. Its name derives from its original site by Great Scotland Yard. >> police

Scott, George C(ampbell) (1927–) Film actor, born in Wise, VA. Early roles including *The Hustler* (1961) and *Dr Strangelove* (1963). He won an Oscar for *Patton* (1969), but refused to accept it (the first actor to do so), and also refused the Emmy he won for *The Price* (1970). Later films include *Dick Tracy* (1989) and *Country Justice* (1997).

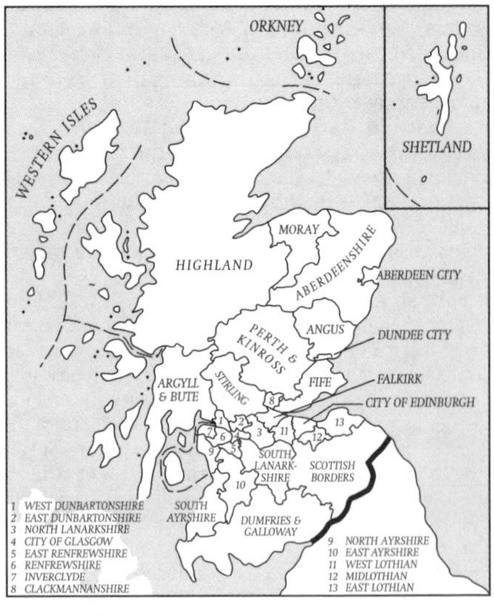

Scott, Sir George Gilbert (1811–78) Architect, born in Gawcott, Buckinghamshire. He became the leading practical architect of the British Gothic revival, as seen in the Albert Memorial (1862–3), St Pancras Station and Hotel in London (1865), and Glasgow University (1865). >> Gothic Revival

Scott, Paul (Mark) (1920–78) Novelist, born in London. His reputation is based on four novels collectively known as the *Raj Quartet* (1966–74), in which he gave an exhaustive account of the British withdrawal from India.

Scott, Sir Peter (Markham) (1909–89) Artist, ornithologist, and broadcaster, born in London. He began to exhibit his paintings of bird scenes in 1933, and after 1945 led several ornithological expeditions. His writing and television programmes helped to popularize natural history. >> ornithology

Scott, R(obert) F(alcon) (1868–1912) Antarctic explorer, born near Devonport, Devon. In 1910 he led an expedition to the South Pole (17 Jan 1912), only to discover that the Norwegian expedition under Amundsen had beaten them by a month. All members of his party died. >> Amundsen; Antarctica ℹ; Oates, Lawrence

Scott, Ronnie (1927–96) Jazz saxophonist and night club owner, born in London. In 1959 he opened a jazz club in London's Soho district, which became an international landmark. >> jazz

Scott, Sir Walter (1771–1832) Novelist and poet, born in Edinburgh. His narrative poems made him the most popular author of the day. His historical novels fall into three groups: those set in the background of Scottish history, from *Waverley* (1814) to *A Legend of Montrose* (1819); a group which takes up themes from the Middle Ages and Reformation times, from *Ivanhoe* (1819) to *The Talisman* (1825); and his remaining books, from *Woodstock* (1826) until his death. His last years were spent in immense labours for his publishers, much of it hack editorial work, in an attempt to recover from bankruptcy following the collapse of his publishing ventures in 1826. His journal is an important record of this period of his life.

Scottish Borders pop (1995e) 105 000; area 4672 sq km/1803 sq mi. Council in SE Scotland, formerly the region of **Borders**; crossed E–W by Southern Uplands; capital, Newtown St Boswells, near Melrose. >> Scotland ℹ

Scottish National Heritage A British governmental agency, set up by the 1991 National Heritage (Scotland) Act, which came into effect in 1992. The Act merged into a single body the Nature Conservancy Council for Scotland, set up in 1991, with the Countryside Commission for Scotland.

Scottish National Party (SNP) A political party formed in 1928 as the National Party of Scotland, which merged with the Scottish Party in 1933. Its principal policy aim is independence for Scotland from the UK. >> home rule; nationalism; Scotland ℹ

Scottish reels A form of stepping dance performed to music in 4/4 time and showing French aristocratic connections. The feet are in balletic positions with the weight on the balls of the feet. Men's costume is the kilt; women wear dresses with a tartan sash. >> Scotland ℹ

Scottish terrier A breed of dog; long body with very short legs; short erect tail; long head, with eyebrows, moustache, and beard; short erect ears; coat black, thick and wiry, almost reaching the ground; also known as **Scottie**. The coarser-haired form is called the **Aberdeen terrier**. >> dog; terrier

Scottish universities >> *panel*

scouting The practice of teaching the young to become good citizens and leaders, based on the principles laid down by Robert Baden-Powell, founder of the Boy Scout movement in 1908. The Scout Association operates in over 100 nations, and has over 14 million members, classified into *Beaver Scouts* (aged 6–8), *Cub Scouts* (aged 8–11), *Scouts* (11–16), and *Venture Scouts* (16–29). Their motto is 'Be prepared'. The corresponding association for girls, known as *Girl Scouts* or *Girl Guides*, was founded in 1910 by Baden-Powell and his sister, Agnes. In the UK, its four classes of membership are *Rainbow Guides* (aged 5–7), *Brownie Guides* (aged 7–10), *Guides* (10–16), and *Ranger Guides* (14–20); in the USA, the groups are *Brownies* (7–8), *Juniors* (9–11), *Cadettes* (12–14), and *Seniors* (15–17). There are around 7 million Guides throughout the world. >> Baden-Powell

scrambling >> **moto-cross**

scrambling circuit A circuit or device used to protect the security of voice, data, or video signals in communication systems. The original signal is coded by the scrambler before transmission, and reconstituted into its original form at the receiver.

scramjet A special ramjet designed for operation at very high speeds (c.6–25 times the speed of sound) where the performance of a conventional ramjet becomes impracticable. The gases flowing through the engine's combustion chamber move at supersonic rather than subsonic speed. >> jet engine ℹ; ramjet

scrapie [**skray**pee] A progressive degenerative disease of the central nervous system of sheep and goats worldwide. There are two forms of the disease: in one, there is uncontrollable itching, the animal scraping itself against objects (hence the name); in the other, there is drowsiness, trembling of the head and neck, and paralysis of the legs. The animals usually die within six months of the first symptoms appearing. >> bovine spongiform encephalopathy; virus

scree Loose, angular fragments of rock debris, formed by the action of rain and frost, which accumulate on hill slopes; also termed **talus**.

screen The surface on which an image is displayed, reflective for front projection, translucent for back projection. In the cinema theatre, the screen is perforated with a pattern of small holes so that sound from loudspeakers behind is not seriously attenuated.

screening A system which prevents the pick-up or transmission of stray electrical signals; also known as **shielding**. Grids in the front of microwave ovens shield users from harmful microwaves. Conducting enclosures and meshes shield electrical signals. >> electricity; magnetic field ℹ; microwaves

screening tests Investigations that are carried out on apparently well persons in order to identify unrecognized disease. *Prescriptive* screening is carried out solely for the benefit of the individual, to detect disease at an early stage in its development, as in blood pressure measurement and chest radiography. >> epidemiology; radiography

Scottish Universities

Institution	Founded	Chartered
St Andrews	1411	1413
Glasgow	1451	1453
Aberdeen	1494	1496
Edinburgh	1582	1582
Strathclyde	1796 (as a college)	1964
Heriot Watt	1821 (as a college)	1966
Dundee	1881 (as a college)	1967
Stirling	1967	1967
Paisley	1897 (as a college)	1992
Robert Gordon	1903 (as a college)	1992
Caledonia	1875 (as a college)	1993
Napier	1964 (as a college)	1993

screen-process printing A form of printing in which ink is forced through the mesh of a screen (originally – but less frequently today – made of silk). It is used for a wide range of commercial printed work in which large areas of solid colour are required, such as posters and showcards, and in the decoration of fabrics. >> printing [i]

screw pine A member of a large genus of evergreen trees and shrubs, native to Old World tropics, superficially resembling palms; fruit pineapple-shaped, starchy, in some species edible like breadfruit. (Genus: *Pandanus*, 600 species. Family: Pandanaceae.) >> breadfruit

Scriabin, Alexander Nikolayevich [**skryah**byin] (1872–1915) Composer and pianist, born in Moscow. His compositions include three symphonies, two tone poems, and 10 sonatas.

scribe In general, a writer of documents or copyist; more specifically, in post-exilic and pre-rabbinic Judaism, a class of experts on the Jewish law (the *sopherim*). >> Judaism; rabbi

Scribner, Charles, originally **Charles Scrivener** (1821–71) Publisher, born in New York City. In 1846 he co-founded the New York publishing firm bearing his name, *Scribner's Magazine*, dating from 1887.

scrofula [**skro**fyula] Tuberculosis of the lymph nodes of the neck, with abscess formation and ulceration of the overlying skin. Now a rare condition, it was formerly known as 'the King's evil', because of the popular belief that the sovereign's touch would cure it. >> lymph; tuberculosis

scrotum The pouch which in most male mammals holds the testes. It is necessary for normal germ cell production because the temperature of the deeper part of the body is high enough to damage the developing germ cells. >> testis

scuba diving A form of underwater swimming with the aid of a self-contained underwater breathing apparatus (abbreviated as *scuba*), or *aqualung*. The first such device was developed by Jacques Yves Cousteau and Emil Gagnan in 1943. >> Cousteau; skin-diving

sculling >> **rowing**

sculpin >> **bullhead**

Sculptor A small, faint S constellation, but including several galaxies. >> constellation; galaxy; RR968

sculpture Traditionally, modelling in a soft material such as clay or wax, the result sometimes being cast in metal, or carving from some hard material such as stone or wood. In the 20th-c much work joins together prefabricated pieces, a technique known as *assemblage*. Early Greek bronzes were cast from wooden models, using the 'lost wax' process, but most Renaissance and modern bronzes are cast from clay originals. An alternative process involves firing the clay model in a kiln, to produce a terracotta. Since the Renaissance the preference has been for displaying the natural surface of the material used. Marble, the most prestigious stone, has normally been given a high polish. >> assemblage; bronze; cire perdue; mobile; relief sculpture

scumbling A technique in painting whereby one colour is dragged or rubbed across another to give a rich, rough texture. The effect depends upon allowing the underneath layer to show through in irregular patches. >> glaze

scurvy A nutritional disorder which results from a lack of vitamin C. Bleeding occurs into the skin, around teeth and bones, and into the joints. >> vitamins [i]

scurvy-grass A N temperate annual or perennial; flowers white, cross-shaped. The sharp-tasting leaves, rich in vitamin C, were used by 17th-c sailors to combat scurvy. (Genus: *Cochlearia*, 25 species. Family: Cruciferae.) >> scurvy; vitamins [i]

Scutari, Lake [skut**ah**ree], Albanian **Ligen i Shkodrës**, Serbo-Croatian **Skadarsko Jezero**, ancient **Lacus Labeatis** Lake in SW Yugoslavia and NW Albania; area 370 sq km/143 sq mi. >> Albania [i]; Yugoslavia [i]

Scutum (Lat 'shield') A small S constellation in the Milky Way. >> constellation; Milky Way; RR968

Scylla [**si**la] In Greek mythology, a sea-monster usually located in the Straits of Messina opposite to Charybdis. Originally a woman, she was changed into a snake with six heads. >> Charybdis

Scyphozoa [skiyfo**zoh**a] A class of jellyfish with gastric tentacles derived from the stomach wall and 4-radial body symmetry. (Phylum: Cnidaria.) >> jellyfish [i]

Scythians [**si**thianz] In Graeco-Roman times a nomadic people of the Russian steppes who migrated to the area N of the Black Sea in the 8th-c BC, displacing the Cimmerians. >> nomadism

SDI Abbreviation of **Strategic Defense Initiative**, the controversial proposal first made by President Reagan in 1983 (dubbed by the press 'Star Wars') that the US should develop the technologies for a defensive layered 'shield' of weapons based primarily in space, able to shoot down incoming ballistic missiles. >> homing overlay device; particle beam weapons

SDP >> **Social Democratic Party**

sea A part of an ocean which is generally shallower and defined by somewhat loosely drawn boundaries related to the surrounding landmasses. Large inland lakes may also be called seas, such as the Caspian Sea and the Dead Sea.

sea, law of the A branch of international law, which divides the sea into three zones. *Internal waters* include ports, rivers, lakes, and canals. *Territorial waters* include the width of sea adjacent to a coastal state, which legally belongs to that state. The width has traditionally been 5 km/3 mi, generally measured from the low water line, although many states now claim a greater width. Foreign ships have a right of innocent passage through territorial waters. Outside the territorial waters are the *high seas*, which may be used freely by all shipping. Many states claim exclusive economic zones extending beyond territorial waters; for example, exclusive fishery rights extending for 320 km/200 mi are now claimed by most coastal states. >> international law

sea anemone [a**nem**onee] A typically solitary, marine coelenterate with a cylindrical body attached at its base to a substrate, and bearing a circle of tentacles at the top around its mouth; c.800 species known. (Phylum: Cnidaria. Order: Actiniaria.) >> coelenterate

sea bass Large fish (*Cynoscion nobilis*) found in inshore waters along the Pacific coast of North America; length up to 1.8 m/6 ft. (Family: Scianidae.) >> bass

sea bream Any of several deep-bodied fish widespread in tropical to temperate seas; length up to 50 cm/20 in; head bluntly rounded; pinkish red, with a large dark spot above the pectoral fin; also called **porgy**. (Family: Sparidae.) >> fish [i]

sea canary >> **beluga** (mammal)

sea cow A term used for any mammal of the order Sirenia (manatees and the dugong); formerly used also for the walrus and the hippopotamus. >> dugong; manatee

sea cucumber A typically sausage-shaped, soft-bodied marine invertebrate (echinoderm); mouth at one end surrounded by up to 30 tentacles; found on or in the seabed. (Class: Holothuroidea.) >> echinoderm [i]

sea elephant >> **elephant seal**

seagull >> **gull**

sea horse A distinctive small fish, widely distributed; body with segmented armour and slender prehensile tail, length 4–30 cm/$1\frac{1}{2}$–12 in; snout prolonged into a horse-

Sea horse

like head; swims upright in water, using delicate membranous fins. (Genus: *Hippocampus*. Family: Syngnathidae.) >> fish [i]

seakale A perennial (*Crambe maritima*) native to the Atlantic coasts of Europe; fleshy root; large, bluish, cabbage-like leaves; white, cross-shaped flowers. The shoots are eaten as a vegetable. (Family: Cruciferae.)

seal (biology) A marine mammal of the family Phocidae, called the **true seal**, **earless seal**, or **hair seal** (19 species); has fur and a thick layer of blubber; no external ears; cannot turn rear flippers forwards; moves on land by shuffling body horizontally along the ground. >> crabeater / elephant seal; mammal [i]; sea-lion

seal (substance) A blob of wax, or other adhesive substance, bearing an impression, and attached to a document as evidence of its authenticity; also the engraved or carved object (the *matrix* or *die*) used to make the impression. The study of seals, which are found from the oldest times, is known as **sigillography**. >> wax

sea level datum >> **Ordnance Datum**

sea-lion A marine mammal of the family Otariidae, called **eared seals** (14 species); resembles the true seal, but has small external ears and, on land, turns long hind flippers forwards under its body, and moves rapidly with body raised from the ground; some (**fur seals**) have a thick undercoat of soft fur, and have been hunted commercially. >> seal (biology)

SEALS >> **SBS**

Sealyham terrier [**seel**iam] A breed of dog, developed in the 19th-c on the Sealyham estate, Haverfordwest, Wales; long body with short legs; short erect tail; long head with eyebrows, moustache, and beard; short pendulous ears; thick pale wiry coat. >> dog; terrier

Seaman, David (1963–) Footballer, born in Rotherham, South Yorkshire. A goalkeeper, he played for Peterborough, Birmingham, and Queens Park Rangers, before moving to Arsenal in 1989. He established himself as the England goalkeeper, and by mid-1998 had won 39 caps.

seance A meeting of one or more persons, generally with a spiritualist medium, for the purpose of contacting the deceased. A seance, sometimes referred to as a 'sitting', may involve apparently paranormal phenomena, such as the medium supposedly receiving communications from deceased people, or the apparent control of the medium by an alleged spirit (a *spirit guide* or *control*). Seances may also involve physical mediumship, such as materializations, and psychokinetic activity (raps, movement of objects, etc). They are also frequently associated with the fraudulent production of phenomena of this kind. >> medium (parapsychology); spiritualism

sea otter A mammal native to N Pacific coasts (*Enhydra lutris*); lives mostly in the water; broader body than freshwater otters; front feet small, not webbed; floats on its back with a stone on its chest, and breaks prey open on the stone. (Family: Mustelidae.) >> Mustelidae; otter

Sea Peoples An assortment of marauders, probably from the Mycenaean world, who destroyed the Hittite empire in Anatolia c.1200 BC. They penetrated as far south as Egypt before being checked and dispersed. >> Hittites; Mycenaean civilization

sea perch Small, deep-bodied fish (*Morone americana*) found in fresh, brackish, and coastal marine waters of the W North Atlantic; length up to 35 cm/14 in; silver with greenish-grey upper surface. (Family: Serranidae.) >> fish [i]

seaplane An aircraft capable of taking off and landing upon water using a specially shaped body or floats. The most famous seaplanes were those that took part in the Schneider Trophy races of the late 1920s and early 1930s, when the trophy was finally won by a British Supermarine S6B at a speed of 655 kph/407 mph. >> aircraft [i]; Schneider Trophy

Search for Extraterrestrial Intelligence (SETI) A NASA research programme, aimed at using large radio telescopes to detect artificially generated radio signals coming from interstellar space. The search is conducted in the quiet region of the electromagnetic spectrum – the 'microwave window' between 1000 and 10 000 mHz frequency. First proposed in 1959, 30 very limited searches have already been undertaken. A new programme was initiated in 1992 and was cancelled by the US Congress in 1993, but work has continued under private sponsorship. >> electromagnetic radiation [i]; NASA; telescope [i]

Searle, Ronald (William Fordham) [serl] (1920–) Artist, born in Cambridge, Cambridgeshire. After the war he became widely known as the creator of the macabre schoolgirls of 'St Trinian's'.

Sears Tower The national headquarters of Sears, Roebuck and Co in Chicago, IL, USA; the second tallest office building in the world (as of 1999). Built in 1970–4, it has 110 storeys and reaches a height of 443 m/1454 ft. >> Chicago; skyscraper

seascape painting A genre of painting which flourished in the Netherlands in the 17th-c, reflecting the importance of overseas trade for the Dutch economy. A later master was Turner, whose great shipwrecks are among the highest achievements of 19th-c English art. >> landscape painting; Turner, J M W

seasickness >> **travel sickness**

sea slug A marine slug-like mollusc, often brightly coloured and of an elaborate shape, with various projections along its body; shell absent. (Class: Gastropoda. Order: Nudibranchia.) >> gastropod; mollusc; slug (biology)

sea snake A venomous snake of family Hydrophiidae (50 species), sometimes included in family Elapidae; inhabits warm coastal waters in the Pacific and Indian oceans; small head, thick body, tail flattened; eats fish and fish eggs; venom very powerful. >> krait; snake

seasonal affective disorder (SAD) A form of 'winter depression', due to lack of light, which is accompanied by fatigue and lethargy, with a craving for carbohydrates which often results in weight gain. People are often affected during winter months, since light affects the body's biological rhythms through substances released by the pineal gland. The best cure for SAD is natural sunlight, but sitting for 4–6 hours per day in front of a high intensity artificial 'light box' relieves symptoms for many patients. >> pineal gland

sea spider A long-legged, small-bodied marine arthropod, found on the seabed; most are predators; contains c.1000 species. (Subphylum: Chelicerata. Class: Pycnogonida.) >> arthropod

SEATO >> **South East Asia Treaty Organization**

Seattle [seeatl] 47°36N 122°20W, pop (1995e) 591 000. City in WC Washington, USA; industrial, financial, and cultural centre of the Pacific NW; founded, 1851; developed rapidly after the 1897 Alaskan gold rush and the opening of the Panama Canal; main port serving Alaska; airport; railway; monorail; two universities (1861, 1892); Space Needle, a tower 183 m/600 ft high with a revolving restaurant and observation deck; professional teams, Mariners (baseball), Supersonics (basketball), Seahawks (football). >> Panama Canal; Washington (state)

sea urchin A typically hollow, globular, marine invertebrate (echinoderm); body formed by fused skeletal plates bearing movable spines; anus usually on upper surface, mouth on lower surface; complex jaw apparatus known as 'Aristotle's lantern'; contains c.5000 fossil and 950 living species. (Phylum: Echinodermata. Class: Echinoidea.) >> echinoderm [i]

seaweed A common name for any large marine alga belonging to families Chlorophyceae (**green seaweeds**), Phaeophyceae (**brown seaweeds**), and Rhodophyceae (**red seaweeds**). >> agar; algae; brown algae; kelp

sebaceous glands >> **skin** [i]

Sebastian, St (?–288) Martyr, a native of Narbonne, France. He was a captain of the praetorian guard, and secretly a Christian. When his belief was discovered, Diocletian ordered his death. Feast day 20 January. >> Christianity; Diocletian

Sebastiano del Piombo [**pyom**boh], originally **Sebastiano Luciano** (c.1485–1547) Venetian painter, called *del Piombo* ('of the Seal') from his appointment in 1523 as sealer of briefs to Pope Clement VII. His masterpiece is 'The Raising of Lazarus' (1519, National Gallery, London).

Sebastopol [se**bas**topol], Russ **Sevastopol** 44°36N 33°31E, pop (1995e) 369 000. Port in Ukraine; founded, 1783; besieged in the Crimean War (1854); rail terminus; naval base; seaside resort; health resorts nearby. >> Crimea; Crimean War; Ukraine [i]

SECAM [**see**kam] Acronym for **Séquentiel Couleur à Mémoire**, a coding system for colour television developed in France in the 1960s and later adopted in the USSR, Eastern Europe, and some Middle East countries. The two colour difference signals are not phase-separated, but transmitted on alternate lines of the picture. >> colour television [i]; NTSC; PAL

Secombe, Sir Harry (Donald) [**see**km] (1921–) Comedian, singer, and media personality, born in Swansea, SC Wales. An exuberant comic, he achieved fame as a member of *The Goons* (1951–9). His stage appearances include *Humpty Dumpty* (1959) and *Pickwick* (1963), and his films include *Oliver!* (1968) and *Song of Norway* (1970). A professional singer with dozens of albums to his credit, he hosted the religious television series *Highway* (1983–93). >> Goons, The

second Base SI unit of time; symbol *s*; defined as the duration of 9 192 631 770 periods of the radiation corresponding to the transition between the two hyperfine levels of the ground state of the caesium-133 atom. Formerly defined as 1/86 400 of the mean solar day, the atomic definition is now the basis of universal time. >> time

secondary education The phase of education following the primary stage, beginning in most countries at the age of 11 or 12. Usually the style of education moves towards more specialized work in key subjects. Secondary education usually ends at some point between the age of 15 and 19, this varying in different countries, and culminates in most cases in some kind of public leaving-examination. >> high school; middle school; primary education

secondary modern school A school in those parts of the UK which operate a selective system. Intake consists of those children who were not successful in gaining entry to a grammar school, or who did not wish to attend it. >> comprehensive / grammar school

secondary store >> **auxiliary store**

second-generation computers >> **computer generations**

Second World >> **Three Worlds theory**

Second World War >> **World War 2**

Secretariat, UN >> **United Nations**

secretary bird A large, ground-dwelling bird of prey (*Sagittarius serpentarius*) native to S Africa; long stilt-like legs; head with an untidy crest of long feathers (resembling pens held behind the ear of a secretary). (Family: Sagittariidae.) >> bird of prey

secretary of state The title of most UK government ministers who preside over a department, as distinct from junior ministers. It has increasingly replaced the title of *minister*. In the USA, the term refers to the head of the state department in charge of foreign affairs, a senior member of the administration.

secret service >> **intelligence service**

sect A separately organized group, usually religious, which rejects established religious or political authorities, and claims to adhere to the authentic elements of the wider tradition from which it has separated itself. It is distinctive and exclusive, claiming to possess true belief, correct ritual, and warranted standards of conduct. Membership takes precedence over all other allegiances. >> Christadelphians; Druze; Nichiren Buddhism; religion

section A term used to describe a two-dimensional view in an architectural or engineering drawing, which reveals the internal structure of the subject of the drawing. The object is drawn as if cut through by an imaginary plane with the part between the observer and the cutting plane removed. >> axonometric [i]

secular Christianity A mid-20th-c theology which acknowledged the secularization of W civilization and sought to present a 'religionless' Christianity, with the emphasis on human freedom and responsibility. >> Bonhoeffer; Christianity; 'death of God' theology

securities A general term for financial assets, such as stocks, shares, and bonds. >> bond; shares; stocks

Securities and Exchange Commission (SEC) A body set up in 1934 in the USA during the Great Depression to regulate and control the issue of shares by corporations. It generally regulates the way US stock markets operate. >> shares; stocks

Securities and Investments Board (SIB) An agency set up in 1985 to regulate the activities of investment business in the UK. It has power, under the Financial Services

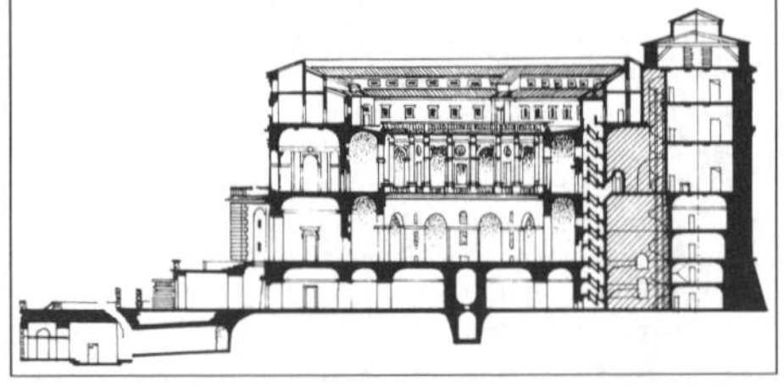

Section – A section of the Palazzo Farnese, Caprarola (1559 onwards), architect G B da Vignola

Act (1986), to oversee the activities of various self-regulatory organizations which have been set up to control aspects of the UK's financial markets, such as the Investment Management Regulatory Board (IMRO). >> investment

Security Council >> **United Nations**

sedative A drug used to calm anxious patients without actually causing sleep; also known as **tranquillizer**. *Phenobarbitone* was previously the most commonly used sedative, but it has been replaced for this purpose by drugs such as the safer *benzodiazepines* (eg *diazepam*). >> barbiturates; benzodiazepines; thalidomide

Seddon, Richard John, nickname **King Dick** (1845–1906) New Zealand statesman and prime minister (1893–1906), born in Eccleston, Lancashire, UK. As prime minister he led a Liberal Party government remembered for its social legislation, such as introducing old-age pensions. >> New Zealand ℹ

sedge A name applied to many members of the family Cyperaceae, but especially to *Carex*, a huge genus (1500–2000 species) found almost everywhere, but especially common in alpine and marshy, subarctic habitats; perennial; tufts of grass-like leaves; flowers tiny; males and females usually in separate spikes which resemble those of grasses; characteristic fruit oval, 3-sided. (Family: Cyperaceae.) >> grass ℹ

sedimentary rock Consolidated deposits composed of material laid down by water, wind, ice, or gravity, or by chemical precipitation. >> coal; limestone; sandstone; shale; stratigraphy

sedimentation The process of deposition of rock fragments suspended in water on to the floor of an ocean, sea, lake, or river floodplain. The unconsolidated sediment may become compacted, dewatered, and cemented together, ultimately forming a sedimentary rock. >> sedimentary rock

seed The mature, fertilized ovule of a plant, containing the embryo and a food store to sustain the seedling during germination, enclosed within a protective coat, the *testa*. In gymnosperms the seeds lie exposed on the cone scales; in flowering plants they are protected within the ovary. Some seeds are very large and are produced in small numbers (eg the coconut); others are very small and are produced in prodigious numbers (eg the orchid). >> flowering plants; fruit; gymnosperms; nut; reproduction; seed plant

seed plant Any plant reproducing by seeds. All flowering plants and gymnosperms are included. In some classifications these together form the division Spermatophyta. >> flowering plants; gymnosperms; seed

Seeger, Pete(r) (1919–) Folk singer, songwriter, guitarist, and banjo player, born in New York City. Several of his songs became popular hits in the 1960s, such as 'If I Had a Hammer' and 'Where Have All the Flowers Gone?', and he co-wrote the lyrics for 'We Shall Overcome'. He is an activist on issues of ecology, politics, and individual liberties.

Seghers, Hercules [**say**gerz] (c.1589–c.1635) Painter, born in Haarlem, The Netherlands. He was author of some of the most romantic mountain landscapes of the 17th-c (influencing Rembrandt, who collected his work), yet fewer than 15 pictures survive. >> landscape painting; Rembrandt

segmented worm >> **annelid**

Segovia, Andrés [se**goh**via] (1894–1987) Guitarist, born in Linares, Spain. He evolved a revolutionary guitar technique permitting the performance of a wide range of music, and many modern composers wrote works for him. >> guitar

Segovia [se**goh**via] 40°57N 4°10W, pop (1995e) 54 600. City in NWC Spain; altitude c.1000 m/3000 ft; bishopric; railway; Roman aqueduct and old town, a world heritage site; cathedral (16th-c). >> Spain ℹ

segregation The cultural, political, organizational, and typically geographical separation of one group of people from another. It is often based on perceived ethnic or racial divisions, an extreme example being apartheid (literally 'separateness') in South Africa, where physical segregation between whites and blacks was most apparent (eg in public transport, washrooms, housing, sport). >> apartheid; civil rights; Jim Crow Laws; racial discrimination

Seiber, Mátyás [**shiy**ber] (1905–60) Composer, born in Budapest. He gained only belated recognition as a composer, his works including chamber music, piano pieces, and songs.

seiche [saysh] An oscillation or sloshing of water in a partially confined body of water such as a bay or an estuary. The period of time required for the oscillation is determined by the physical size and shape of the basin. >> wave (oceanography)

Seifert, Jaroslav [**siy**fert] (1901–86) Poet, born in Prague. His major works include *Postovni holub* (1929, The Carrier Pigeon) and *Zhasnête svêtla* (1938, Put out the Lights), and with his postwar volume *Přílba hlíny* (1945, A Helmet of Earth) he was established as the national poet. He was awarded the Nobel Prize for Literature in 1984.

Seine, River [sen] River in NC France, rising in the Langres plateau; flows past Paris and Rouen to enter the English Channel; length 776 km/482 mi; third longest river in France. >> France ℹ; Paris

seismic zone A belt of intense earthquake activity which occurs at the boundaries between crustal plates. >> earthquake; plate tectonics ℹ

seismograph The data collected by a **seismometer**, an instrument that records and measures the arrival of seismic waves from distant earthquakes, or from movement caused by explosions in the Earth's crust. >> earthquake

seismology The study of earthquakes and the propagation of seismic waves through the Earth. By studying the velocity of seismic waves, the structure of the Earth and the discontinuities which define its core, mantle, and crust have been discovered. >> earthquake; seismograph

seismometer >> **seismograph**

Sejanus [se**jay**nus] (?–31) Prefect of the Praetorian Guard (14–31), and all-powerful at Rome after the Emperor Tiberius's retirement to Capri (26). When his ambitions were made known to Tiberius, his fall from grace was sudden and spectacular. >> Praetorian Guard; Tiberius

Sekmet >> **Sakhmet**

Sekondi-Takoradi 4°59N 1°43W, pop (1995e) 121 000. Major seaport in S Ghana; founded by the Dutch, 16th-c; Sekondi expanded after construction of railway to Tarkwa (1898–1903), and merged with Takoradi, 1946; important supply base during World War 2. >> Ghana ℹ

selaginella [selaji**nel**a] A member of a large genus of mostly tropical spore-bearing plants related to clubmosses and quillworts. It is one of the few living members of the ancient class Lycopsida. (Genus: *Selaginella*, 700 species. Family: Selaginellaceae.) >> clubmoss; quillwort

Selangor [say**lang**gaw(r)] pop (1995e) 2 227 000; area 7997 sq km/3087 sq mi. State in W Peninsular Malaysia; British protectorate, 1874; capital, Shah Alam. >> Malaysia ℹ

Selcraig, Alexander >> **Selkirk, Alexander**

select committee Members of a legislature whose task is to inquire into matters that come within its competence, usually as prescribed by the government. Two main types may be distinguished: *ad hoc*, which normally ceases to exist when its task is completed; and *permanent* or *standing*, which normally lasts for an electoral term and which investigates particular policy areas or the actions of government departments. Membership is usually based on party composition in the legislature.

selective school >> **comprehensive school; grammar school**

Selene [se**lee**nee] In Greek mythology, the goddess of the Moon. She was depicted as a charioteer. >> Artemis; Endymion; Phoebe (mythology)

selenium [se**leen**ium] Se, element 34. A metalloid in the oxygen group, found as a minor constituent of sulphide ores, and mainly produced from the residue of copper refinement. Mainly important for its electrical properties, selenium can be used to convert light to electric current (in photocells) and alternating current to direct current (in rectifiers). >> chemical elements; metalloids; RR0136

Seles, Monica [**sel**esh] (1973–) Tennis player, born in Yugoslavia. In 1990 she became the youngest woman to win a 'Grand Slam' singles title this century, winning the French Championship at 16 years 169 days (a record broken by Hingis in 1997). Before she reached 18 she had won three out of four Grand Slam singles titles. In 1993 she was unable to play for some months following an incident on court in which she was stabbed by a deranged fan of Steffi Graf. Later successes include the 1996 Australian Open title. She became a US citizen in 1994. >> Graf; tennis [i]

Seleucids [se**loo**sidz] The Greek dynasty descended from Alexander the Great's general, Seleucus (c.358–281 BC). They ruled a vast empire stretching from Asia Minor to NW India, but were suppressed by Rome in 63 BC. >> Alexander the Great

self-regulatory organization (SRO) A body which manages its own affairs and has its own rules of conduct, eliminating the need for government legislation. Lloyd's and the London Stock Exchange are two such bodies. >> Lloyd's; Securities and Investments Board; stock exchange

Selfridge, Harry Gordon (c.1864–1947) Merchant, born in Ripon, WI, USA. While visiting London in 1906, he bought a site in Oxford Street, and built upon it the large store which bears his name (opened 1909).

Seljuqs / Seljuks A family of Turkish mercenary soldiers that rose to prominence and conquered much of Asia Minor in the 11th–12th-c. They were converted to the Muslim faith, and became established as sultans in the area of present-day Syria and E Turkey. >> Islam

Selkirk, Alexander, also spelled **Selcraig** (1676–1721) Sailor, born in Largo, Fife, whose story suggested that of Defoe's Robinson Crusoe. He joined the South Sea buccaneers, quarrelled with his captain, and at his own request was put ashore on Juan Fernández I, (1704). He lived there alone until 1709, when he was discovered and brought back to Britain. >> Defoe

Sellafield, formerly **Windscale** 54°38N 3°30W. Nuclear power plant in Cumbria, NW England; processes nuclear waste; nearby Calder Hall gas-cooled, moderated nuclear reactors, commercial operation 1956–9. >> Cumbria; nuclear reactor [i]

Sellers, Peter (1925–80) Actor and comedian, born in Southsea, Hampshire. His meeting with Spike Milligan heralded *The Goon Show* (1951–9), which revolutionized British radio comedy. One of the stalwarts of British film comedy, *Lolita* (1962) and *Dr Strangelove* (1963) established his international reputation. His popularity was unrivalled as the incompetent Inspector Clouseau in a series that began with *The Pink Panther* (1963). He received an Oscar nomination for *Being There* (1980). >> Goons, The

Selten, Reinhard [**zel**ten] (1930–) Economist, born in Wrocław, Poland (formerly Breslau, Prussia). He shared the Nobel Prize for Economics in 1994 for his contribution to the analysis of equilibria in the theory of non-co-operative games.

selva The Portuguese term for the tropical rainforest of the Amazon Basin. Its use has been extended to cover similar vegetation types elsewhere. >> rainforest

Selwyn-Lloyd, (John) Selwyn (Brooke) Lloyd, Baron [**sel**win **loyd**] (1904–78) British Conservative statesman, born in Liverpool, Merseyside. His posts include minister of defence (1955); foreign secretary (1955–60), defending Eden's policy on Suez; Chancellor of the Exchequer, introducing the 'pay pause' (1960–2); and Speaker of the House of Commons (1971–6). >> Conservative Party; Eden

Selznick, David O(liver) (1902–65) Film producer, born in Pittsburgh, PA. He founded his own company in 1937, which at its peak made *Gone with the Wind* (1939). Among the stars he created was Jennifer Jones, to whom he was married from 1949.

semantics The study of the meaning system of a language. The word *meaning* has itself many meanings, and semantic approaches vary widely. In one view, meaning is the relationship between language and the external world (*referential* or *denotative* meaning), between a word and the concept it stands for. In another, it involves the mental state of the speaker, as reflected in a range of personal and emotional overtones (*affective* or *connotative* meaning). A considerable part of the present-day subject is devoted to the study of the meanings of expressions in terms of formal systems of analysis, or calculi (**formal semantics**). >> etymology; linguistics; synonym

semaphore A code and signalling apparatus for visual communication. It consists of one or two mechanically-operated arms attached to an upright post, or two hand-held flags at arm's length, which are moved in a vertical plane to a sequence of positions. Each position represents a different letter of the alphabet, numeral, or punctuation feature. The system was widely used in visual telegraphy, before the advent of electricity.

Semele [**sem**ilee] In Greek mythology, the daughter of Cadmus, and mother by Zeus of Dionysus. She asked Zeus to appear in his glory before her, and was consumed in fire, but it made her son immortal. >> Dionysus

semen Yellow-white fluid ejaculated from the penis at orgasm. It consists of spermatozoa, and secretions from the accessory sex glands which assist in the nourishment and motility of the spermatozoa. >> AIDS; artificial insemination; infertility; penis [i]

semicircular canals >> **vestibular apparatus**

semiconductor A substance whose electrical conductivity is between that of an insulator and a conductor at room temperature. The conductivity can be made to vary with temperature and the impurities in the semiconductor crystal. Typical semiconductor devices such as diodes and transistors each have a different arrangement of impurities in the crystal. >> doping; electrical conduction; thyristor; transistor

semiconductor laser A tiny laser, crucial to optical fibre communications and compact disc players. A current flowing across the junction between two regions of semiconductor (eg gallium arsenide) doped in different ways causes electron transitions in the material. >> laser [i]; optical fibres [i]; optoelectronics

Seminole [**se**minohl] A Muskogean-speaking North American Indian group of SE USA. They eventually moved to reservations in Oklahoma, now numbering c.14 000 (1990 census).

semiology >> **semiotics**

semiotics The study of signs, sign systems, and the social production of meaning, also known as **semiology**. A fundamental notion is the arbitrary nature of communication systems (written and spoken language, gestures, dress, etc). Meaning is largely produced by relationships and differences between individual signs, organized in codes, rather than by simple reference to external reality. >> Peirce; pragmatics; Saussure; semantics; syntax

Semipalatinsk [semipa**la**tinsk], formerly **Semipalatka** 50°26N 80°16E, pop (1995e) 358 000. River port in Kazakhstan, on R Irtysh; founded as a fortress, 1718; airport; railway. >> Kazakhstan

semi-precious stones >> **gemstones**

Semiramis [se**mi**ramis] (9th-c BC) In Greek mythology, the daughter of the goddess Derceto, who became Queen of Assyria. She founded many cities, including Nineveh and Babylon, and is probably based on the historical Sammuramat (c.810–805 BC).

Semites A group of peoples found in SW Asia. In antiquity they included the Ammonites, Amorites, Assyrians, Babylonians, Canaanites, and Phoenicians; today the most prominent Semitic peoples are the Jews and the Arabs. >> Assyria; Babylonia; Phoenicia

Semitic alphabets The writing systems of the Semitic languages spoken in the Middle East, in which only consonants are registered, the vowels being optionally marked by diacritics. The earliest known alphabet was North Semitic, developed from the second millennium BC in Palestine and Syria. >> alphabet ℹ; graphology

Semitic languages >> **Afro-Asiatic languages**

semolina A heated solution of the flour of hard wheat. It is used to make pasta and milk puddings. >> durum

Sen, Amartya (Kumar) (1933–) Economist, born in Bengal, India. He worked at New Delhi University, the London School of Economics, and Oxford, moving in 1988 to Harvard. Noted for his work on the nature of poverty and famine, and, and he was awarded the 1998 Nobel Prize for Economics for his contributions to welfare economics.

Senate (Roman) An advisory body, first to the kings, then the consuls, finally the emperor. By the end of the Republic its resolutions had come to have the force of law. >> consul 1; Roman history ℹ

Senate (USA) One of the two houses of the US Congress, consisting of two senators from each State (100 in all), chosen by the people to serve for six years; a third are chosen every two years. It has powers of 'advice and consent' on presidential treaties and appointments. Much of its work is done through committees rather than on the floor. >> Congress; House of Representatives

Sendai [sen**da**ee] 38°16N 140°52E, pop (1995e) 943 000. City in NE Honshu, Japan; airport; railway; university (1907). >> Honshu

Sendero Luminoso [sen**dai**roh loomi**noh**soh] (Span 'Shining Path') A rural guerrilla movement of uncompromisingly revolutionary character, which began operating in the Peruvian C Andes during the 1980s. >> Peru ℹ; terrorism

Seneca, Lucius Annaeus [**sen**eka], known as **the Elder** (c.55 BC–c.AD 40) Roman rhetorician, born in Córdoba, Spain. Besides a history of Rome, now lost, he wrote several works on oratory. >> rhetoric

Seneca, Lucius Annaeus [**sen**eka], known as **Seneca the Younger** (c.5 BC–AD 65) Roman philosopher, statesman, and author, born in Córdoba, Spain, the son of Seneca the Elder. He was the tutor of Nero, but his high moral aims gradually incurred the emperor's displeasure. Drawn into conspiracy, he was condemned, and committed suicide. The publication of his *Tenne Tragedies* in 1581 was a major influence on Elizabethan drama. >> Nero

Seneca [**sen**eka] An Iroquois-speaking North American Indian group, who settled in present-day W New York State and E Ohio. A member of the Iroquois League, they supported the British during the American Revolution. They were settled on reservations in 1797. >> American Indians; Iroquois Confederacy

Senefelder, Aloys [**zay**nefelder, **a**lohis] (1771–1834) Inventor, born in Prague. He accidentally discovered the technique of lithography by using a grease pencil on limestone (1796). >> lithography ℹ

Senegal [**sen**egawl], **Sénégal**, official name **Republic of Senegal**, Fr **République du Sénégal** pop (1995e) 8 314 000; area 196 790 sq km/75 729 sq mi. Country in W Africa; capital, Dakar; timezone GMT; chief ethnic groups, Wolof (44%), Fulani (23%), Serer (14%); chief religions, Islam (91%), local beliefs (3%); official language, French; unit of currency, the franc CFA; extensive low-lying basin of savannah and semi-desert vegetation to the N; S rises to around 500 m/1640 ft; tropical climate with a rainy season (Jun–Sep); part of the Mali Empire, 14th–15th-c; French established a fort at Saint-Louis, 1658; incorporated as a territory within French West Africa, 1902; autonomous state within the French community, 1958; joined with French Sudan as independent Federation of Mali, 1959; withdrew in 1960 to become a separate independent republic; joined with The Gambia to form the Confederation of Senegambia, 1982–9; unstable relationships with Mauritania (open conflict, 1989–90); secessionist movement growing in S (Casamance), 1992; negotiations with separatists ongoing, 1999; governed by a president, prime minister, and National Assembly; economy mainly agricultural, employing c.75% of the workforce. >> Dakar; Gambia, The ℹ; Mali ℹ; Senegambia, Confederation of; RR1021 political leaders

Sénégal, River River in W Africa; rises in the Fouta Djallon massif (Guinea); enters the Atlantic Ocean; length, 1635 km/1016 mi. >> Senegal ℹ

Senegambia, Confederation of [sene**gam**bia] An association between The Gambia and Senegal, begun in 1982, designed to integrate military, economic, communications, and foreign policies, while preserving independence and sovereignty. It was ended by mutual agreement in 1989. >> Gambia, The ℹ; Senegal ℹ

senescence A series of changes in the body which are related to increasing mortality with increasing age. Modern views hold that it is essentially a continuing and increasing failure of adaptability to environmental varia-

tions, due ultimately to errors in the replication of DNA in cell division and/or errors in the production of proteins and enzymes by cells. >> DNA ℹ; genetics ℹ

senile dementia >> **dementia**

senna A drug obtained from the pods and dried leaves of certain species of *Cassia*, a large group of trees and shrubs native to Africa and Arabia. It is noted for its laxative properties. (Genus: *Cassia*. Family: Leguminosae.)

Senna, Ayrton, in full **Ayrton Senna da Silva** (1960–94) Motor racing driver, born in São Paulo, Brazil. He became World Formula One champion 1988, 1990, and 1991, and had 41 Grand Prix victories (second only to Alain Prost). He was killed during the 1994 San Marino Grand Prix. >> motor racing; Prost

Sennacherib [se**nak**erib] (8th–7th-c BC) King of Assyria (704–681 BC), the son of Sargon II. His fame rests mainly on his conquest of Babylon (689 BC) and his rebuilding of Nineveh. >> Assyria; Nineveh

Sennett, Mack, originally **Michael** or **Mikall Sinnott** (1880–1960) Film producer, born in Richmond, Quebec, Canada. He made hundreds of shorts, establishing a tradition of knockabout slapstick under the name of Keystone Komics (1912) and later the Sennett Bathing Beauties (1920). He was given an Academy Award in 1937.

sensitive plant A perennial, prickly-stemmed herb (*Mimosa pudica*), growing to 90 cm/3 ft, native to South America; a common weed in tropical areas, and in cooler climates often cultivated as a novelty in hothouses. It is exceedingly sensitive, exhibiting nastic movement, closing up at night. This response can also be triggered at greater speed by a shock stimulus such as a touch. (Family: Leguminosae.)

sentence In law, the decision of a court imposed on a person convicted of a crime, such as a fine, a period of imprisonment, a period of supervision, the death sentence in certain jurisdictions, or an absolute discharge. >> community service order; detention centre; parole; probation; suspended sentence; young offender institution

Seoul or **Sŏul** [sohl] 37°30N 127°00E, pop (1995e) 11 115 000. Capital of Korea; founded, 14th-c; called Hanyang until the 20th-c; seat of the Yi dynasty government 1392–1910; badly damaged in Korean War; airport; railway; 17 universities; Kyongbok-kung Palace (14th-c, rebuilt 1867); Ch'angdŏ-kung palace (1405, rebuilt 1611); location of 1988 Olympic Games. >> Korea ℹ

sepal [**se**pl] One of the outermost whorl of flower parts, collectively termed the *calyx*. Usually green, free, or sometimes fused together, they protect the flower in bud. >> flower ℹ

separation, judicial An order granted by a court in the UK where either marriage partner presents a petition supported by one of the facts necessary for a divorce. The parties remain married, however. In the USA, legal separation also changes the parties' financial obligations to each other, especially in community property jurisdictions. >> divorce

separatism The demand for separation by a particular group or area from the territorial and political sovereignty of the state of which they are a part. Examples of separatist movements are the Basques in Spain and the Tamils in Sri Lanka.

Sephardim [se**fah(r)**dim] Descendants of Jews who lived in Spain and Portugal before 1492, but who were then expelled for not accepting Christianity. They migrated to N Europe and the Americas, where they kept distinct from other Jews. >> Diaspora; Judaism

sepiolite >> **meerschaum**

septicaemia / septicemia [septi**seem**ia] The occurrence and multiplication of bacteria in the blood stream; more commonly known as **blood poisoning**. It is usually a serious complication of infection. >> blood

Septuagesima [septyua**je**sima] In the Western Christian Church, the third Sunday before Lent, apparently so called by analogy with *Quinquagesima* which is two Sundays later. (Latin *septuagesimus*, 'seventieth'). >> Lent

Septuagint [**sep**tyuajint] A translation into Greek of the Hebrew Bible, obtaining its name (meaning 'translation of the 70') from a legend in the *Letter of Aristeas* (2nd-c BC) about its composition as the work of 72 scholars, six from each of the 12 tribes of Israel. The translation was begun c.3rd-c BC to meet the need of Greek-speaking Jews in the Diaspora. When it was adopted by Christians as their preferred version of the Old Testament, it lost favour among the Jews. >> Bible; Diaspora; Old Testament

sequence 1 From c.850 to c.1000, a non-biblical Latin text added to a long portion of chant originally sung to one syllable at the end of the Alleluia; later, a similar syllabic chant specially composed. >> plainchant **2** A musical phrase immediately repeated at a different pitch. The opening of Beethoven's Fifth Symphony furnishes a familiar example.

Sequoia (California) [se**kwoy**a] National park in E California, USA, in the Sierra Nevada; contains the enormous, ancient sequoia trees; area 1631 sq km/630 sq mi. >> California; coast redwood

Sequoia (leader) or **Sequoyah** [se**kwoy**a], also known as **George Gist** or **Guest** (c.1770–1843) Cherokee Indian leader, born in Taskigi, NC. He was a major figure behind the decision of the Cherokee to adopt as much as possible of white culture, while retaining their own identity. >> Cherokee

sequoia [se**kwoy**a] >> **coast redwood**

seraphim [**ser**afim] Heavenly beings mentioned in Jewish Scriptures only in the vision in *Isa* 6, where they are described as having six wings and being stationed above the throne of God. >> cherubim; God

Serbia [**ser**bia], formerly spelled **Servia**, Serbo-Croatian **Srbija** pop (1995e) 9 910 000; area 88 361 sq km/ 34 107 sq mi. Mountainous republic in Yugoslavia; land rises to the Dinaric Alps (W) and Stara Planina (E); capital, Belgrade; Serbian state founded, 6th-c; overrun by Turks, 1389; kingdom, 1882; incorporated into Yugoslavia, including the autonomous regions of Vojvodina (N) and Kosovo (S), 1918; constituent republic, 1946; confrontation with Croatia over disputed border areas and status of Serbian minority led to civil war, 1991; UN sanctions imposed in an effort to alleviate conflict in former Yugoslav republics, 1992; part of Federal Republic of Yugoslavia, 1992; fighting continued in Bosnia until 1995, when a peace agreement established a Bosnian Serb republic alongside a Muslim-Croat Federation; confrontation with NATO over Serbian intervention in Kosovo, March 1999, followed by air-strikes against military targets throughout Serbia. >> Belgrade; Kosovo; Yugoslavia ℹ; Yugoslavian Civil War

serenade Originally, music to be played or sung in the evening, especially for courting. The term is now most widely applied to works for full or string orchestra in several movements, which are lighter in style and less ambitious than a symphony. >> symphony

Serengeti [sereng**ge**tee] area 14 763 sq km/5698 sq mi. National park in N Tanzania; a world heritage site; established in 1951; average elevation c.1500 m/5000 ft; noted for its wildlife. >> Tanzania ℹ

serfdom The condition of peasants lacking personal freedom, especially of movement and the disposal of property, and liable to arbitrary obligations; an intermediate position between slavery and freedom. Characteristic of mediaeval times, the condition persisted in E Europe – in Russia until 1861. >> feudalism; villein

sergeant at arms In the UK, the officer of the House of Commons responsible for maintaining order and for internal administration. He also has certain ceremonial functions, particularly that of carrying the Speaker's mace in procession to the Chair at the beginning of the day's business. >> Commons, House of

serialism A method of composing music in which a series (or 'row' or 'set') of different notes is used, in accordance with certain strict practices, as the basis of a whole work. The most common type is 12-note serialism, in which the 12 pitches of the chromatic scale are re-ordered to form one of a possible 479 001 600 different series. Schoenberg arrived at 12-note serialism in 1923, as a means of structuring atonal music; his method was adopted, in very different ways, by his pupils Berg and Webern. Some later composers have applied serial methods to such other elements of composition as rhythm, dynamics, and articulation. >> atonality; chromaticism; scale 🛈; Berg; Schoenberg; Webern

serial killing A class of murder which, though known to have existed for centuries, has become increasingly prominent during the latter part of the 20th-c. Serial killing involves a succession of at least two but usually more murders committed as discrete episodes over a substantial period of time, often months or years. This is in contrast to a mass murder or mass killing, where a number of people are killed over a short period of time, such as a few hours, as part of a single continuous act. >> Jack the Ripper; murder; Sutcliffe, Peter

serin >> **canary**

Sermon on the Mount or **Plain** A collection of Jesus's ethical teaching, depicted in *Matt* 5–7 as preached on a mountain early in Jesus's ministry. It contains the Beatitudes, teaching about true adherence to God's law. >> Beatitudes; Jesus Christ

serology [se**rol**ojee] A branch of medicine which specializes in the analysis of serum. In particular it looks for evidence of infection, by the detection of antibodies or micro-organisms. >> medicine; serum

serotonin [sero**toh**nin] A widely distributed chemical substance (a monoamine), particularly found in the blood, brain, and certain cells of the gut; it is also known as **5-hydroxytryptamine (5-HT)**. It is involved in sleep, emotional disposition (mood), prolactin secretion, and circadian rhythms. >> amines; biological rhythm

Serpens (Lat 'serpent') A constellation of the equatorial region of the sky. It is unique, because it is bisected (by Ophiuchus) into two distinct sections: **Serpens Caput** ('head') and **Serpens Cauda** ('body'). >> constellation; Ophiuchus; RR968

serpent >> **snake**

serpentine A hydrous magnesium silicate ($Mg_3Si_2O_5(OH)_4$) occurring in two main forms: **chrysotile** (an asbestos variety) and **antigorite**. It is soft, green to black, and used in decorative carving. >> talc

SERPS >> **pension**

serum The residue of any animal liquid after the separation and removal of the more solid components. It is specifically used to refer to human blood serum, which is a clear, yellowish fluid separated from clotted blood plasma. Serum with appropriate antibodies protects against specific diseases. >> blood; serology

serval [**ser**vl] A nocturnal member of the cat family (*Felis serval*) native to S Africa; slender, with long neck and short tail; pale with small or large dark spots (small-spotted type formerly called **servaline cat**). >> Felidae

Servetus, Michael [ser**vay**tus] (1511–53) Theologian and physician, born in Tudela, Spain. His theological writings denied the Trinity and the divinity of Christ, and he was burnt at Geneva for heresy. While studying medicine he discovered the pulmonary circulation of the blood. >> Trinity

service club A group of men and women organized to perform volunteer community service. The first such club, for business and professional men, was formed in 1905 by US lawyer Paul Harris (1868–1947) in Chicago, IL, using the name *Rotary* (because the meetings took place at each member's office in turn). This grew into Rotary International, whose motto 'Service above Self' embodies the ideals of all service clubs. Women were admitted for the first time in 1987. *Kiwanis International* began in 1915 in Detroit, MI, and the *International Association of Lions Clubs* was formed in Dallas, TX in 1917.

service industry An industry which does not manufacture a product, but provides a service. It is a fast-growing sector in most Western nations; activities range from banking and other financial services to tourism, hotels, and catering. >> gross domestic product

service tree The name given to two species of *Sorbus*, native to Europe, both deciduous trees with white flowers in large, flat clusters. The wild service tree or **chequerberry** (*Sorbus torminalis*) has lobed leaves and brown berries, used for preserves and drinks. (Family: Rosaceae.)

Servile Wars The collective name for the official attempts to suppress the slave uprisings of the late 2nd-c and early 1st-c BC in Sicily and S Italy. The most serious was the revolt led by Spartacus (73–71 BC). >> Spartacus

servo system A system controlled by a servomechanism: a high-power output device is controlled with a command signal from a low-input device. Power-assisted braking or steering are servo systems. >> control engineering

sesame [**ses**amee] An annual (*Sesamum indicum*) growing to 60 cm/2 ft, probably native to SE Asia; flowers white, usually marked with purple or yellow; fruit an oblong capsule. It is cultivated in warmer countries for its seeds, which are used for baking and as a source of oil in margarine, soap manufacture, and cosmetics. (Family: Pedaliaceae.)

Sessions, Roger (Huntingdon) (1896–1985) Composer, born in New York City. His compositions include eight symphonies, a violin concerto, piano and chamber music, and operatic works.

set In mathematics, a well-defined class of elements, ie a class where it is possible to tell exactly whether any one element does or does not belong to it. We can have the set of all even numbers, as every number is either even or not even, but we cannot have the set of all large numbers, as we do not know what is meant by 'large'. The **empty set** θ is the set with no elements. The **universal set** $\mathscr{E}$ or $\mathscr{U}$ is the set of all elements. The **intersection** of two sets A and B (written $A \cap B$) is the set of all elements in both A and B. The **union** of two sets A and B (written $A \cup B$) is the set of all elements in either A or B or both. >> Cantor; Venn diagram 🛈

Set or **Seth** An ancient Egyptian god, depicted with the head of an animal with a long muzzle. The brother and enemy of Osiris, he was associated with evil forces and rebellion. >> Osiris

Seth, Vikram (1952–) Novelist, poet, and travel-writer, born in Calcutta, India. He became widely known after his novel *A Suitable Boy* (1993), one of the longest works of fiction in English. His other writing includes the travel book *From Heaven Lake* (1983), the poetry collection *Mappings* (1980), and *An Equal Music* (1999).

Seton, St Elizabeth Ann [**see**tn], *née* **Bayley** (1774–1821) The first native-born saint of the USA, born in New York City. In 1809 she founded the USA's first religious order, the Sisters of Charity. She was beatified by Pope John XXIII in 1963, and canonized in 1975. Feast day 4 January.

setter A long-haired sporting dog which belongs to one of several breeds performing the same function as a pointer;

probably developed by breeding spaniels with pointers. >> Irish setter; pointer; spaniel; sporting dog

Settlement, Act of An important British statute of 1701 which determined the succession of the English throne after the death of Queen Anne and her heirs, if any. It excluded the Catholic Stuarts from the succession, which was to pass to the Electress Sophia of Hanover, descendant through the female line of James I. >> Anne; Stuarts

Setúbal [se**too**bal] 38°30N 8°58W, pop (1995e) 83 200. Industrial seaport in S Portugal; at the mouth of R Sado; railway. >> Portugal ℹ

Seurat, Georges (Pierre) [soerah] (1859–91) Artist, born in Paris. He became known for such works as 'Une Baignade' (A Bather, 1883–4, Tate, London), painted in a Divisionist style. His main achievement was the marrying of an Impressionist palette to classical composition. >> Divisionism; Impressionism (art)

Seuss, Dr, pseudonym of **Theodor Seuss Geisel**, other pseudonyms **Theo LeSieg** and **Rosetta Stone** (1904–91) Writer and illustrator of children's books, born in Springfield, MA. His famous series of 'Beginner Books' started with *The Cat in the Hat* (1957) and *Yertle the Turtle* (1958). By 1970, 30 million copies had been sold in the USA, and Seuss had become synonymous with learning to read.

Seven against Thebes In Greek legend, seven champions who attacked Thebes to deprive Eteocles of his kingship, led by his brother Polynices. They were defeated by another seven champions at the seven gates of Thebes. Later the sons of the Seven, the Epigoni, succeeded in destroying the city. >> Creon; Eteocles; Polynices

Seven Days' Battles (26 Jun–2 Jul 1862) The final conflict in the Peninsular Campaign during the American Civil War, fought below Richmond. The battles ended with a Confederate withdrawal. >> American Civil War; Peninsular Campaign

seven deadly sins The fundamental vices thought, in Christian tradition, to underlie all sinful actions. They are pride, covetousness, lust, envy, gluttony, anger, and sloth. >> Christianity; sin

Seven Sisters >> **Pleiades** (astronomy)

Seven Sleepers of Ephesus In mediaeval legend, seven persecuted Christians who fled into a cave at the time of the Emperor Decius (AD 250); they slept for 200 years, emerging in 447 at the time of Theodosius II.

Seven Wonders of the Ancient World The most renowned artificial structures of the ancient world: the Pyramids of Egypt; the Hanging Gardens of Babylon; the Tomb of Mausolus at Halicarnassus; the Temple of Artemis at Ephesus; the Colossus of Rhodes; the Statue of Zeus at Olympia; and the Pharos of Alexandria. >> Babylon; Colossus of Rhodes; Ephesus; Mausolus, Tomb of; Pharos of Alexandria; pyramid; Zeus, statue of

Seven Years' War (1756–63) A major European conflict rooted in the rivalry between Austria and Prussia and the imminent colonial struggle between Britain and France in the New World and the Far East. Hostilities in North America (1754) pre-dated the Diplomatic Revolution in Europe (1756), which created two opposing power blocs: Austria, France, Russia, Sweden, and Saxony against Prussia, Britain, and Portugal. British maritime superiority countered Franco-Spanish naval power, and prevented a French invasion. >> Paris, Treaties of 1

Severn, River River in SE Wales and W England; rises on Plynlimon, C Wales; wide estuary into the Bristol Channel; length 354 km/220 mi; known for the **Severn bore** (tidal wave c.2 m/6 ft); railway tunnel (completed 1885); **Severn Bridge**, suspension bridge carrying M4 motorway (988 m/3240 ft), completed 1966; **Severn Bridge II** (456 m/1496 ft) completed 1996. >> Bristol Channel

Severnaya Zemlya [**say**vernaya zem**lya**], formerly **Zemlya Imperatora**, Eng **North Land** or **Nicholas II Land** area 37 000 sq km/14 300 sq mi. Uninhabited archipelago in the Arctic Ocean. >> Russia ℹ

Severus, Lucius Septimius [**se**verus] (c.146–211) Roman emperor (193–211) and founder of the Severan dynasty (193–235). He proved to be an able administrator, effecting many reforms. His final years were spent in Britain, trying unsuccessfully to restore order in the N of the province.

Sévigné, Madame de [sayveenyay], *née* **Marie de Rabutin-Chantal** (1626–96) Writer, born in Paris. Her letters, lasting over 25 years, recount the inner history of her time in great detail, and in a natural, colloquial style.

Seville [se**vil**], Span **Sevilla**, ancient **Hispalis** 37°23N 6°00W, pop (1995e) 664 000. River-port in Andalusia, S Spain; on R Guadalquivir; Moorish cultural centre, 8th–13th-c; archbishopric; airport; railway; university (1502); birthplace of Velásquez and Murillo; cathedral (15th-c), largest Gothic church in the world, with tomb of Columbus; Moorish citadel and Archivo de Indias, a world heritage site. >> Andalusia; Columbus, Christopher; Giralda; Murillo; Spain ℹ; Velásquez

Sèvres porcelain [sevr] The French royal porcelain factory, founded c.1745 to produce soft- and hard-paste luxury porcelain. The factory's speciality became items with exquisitely painted vignettes against richly coloured plain grounds with elaborate gilding. >> porcelain

sewage Waste matter, especially human excrement, carried away from houses by special conduits (**sewers**). The use of water-borne sewage disposal became established in the 1870s, the sewers being linked either directly to the sea through an outfall, if a suitable one was available, or to a **sewage farm**. A sewage farm uses beds of sand to grow and support a gelatinous bacterial film which develops as the true filter, removing almost all solids. Other precipitation treatments remove substances in solution. >> bacteria; gelatin

Seward Peninsula Peninsula in Alaska, USA; the most W point of the North American continent. >> Alaska

Sewell, Anna [**syoo**el] (1820–78) Novelist, born in Yarmouth, Norfolk. Her *Black Beauty* (1877), the story of a horse, was written as a plea for the more humane treatment of animals.

sewellel [se**wel**el] >> **mountain beaver**

Sexagesima [seksa**je**sima] The second Sunday before Lent, apparently so called by analogy with *Quinquagesima*, the following Sunday. (Lat *sexagesimus*, 'sixtieth'). >> Lent

sex hormones Steroid hormones produced and secreted mainly by the gonads, necessary for sexual development and the control of reproductive function. In humans the most important are certain androgens (testosterone and dihydrotestosterone) found predominantly in males, and progestogens (progesterone) and certain oestrogens (oestradiol, oestrone, and oestriol) found predominantly in females. >> androgens; gonad; hormones; oestrogens; progesterone; steroid

sexism A set of preconceived assumptions about the 'proper' roles, attitudes, and characteristics (especially physical) that men and women should have, typically working to the advantage of men over women; for example, the assumption that 'a woman's place is in the home'. >> feminism

Sex Pistols, The British rock band, formed in London in 1975, consisting at first of **Johnny Rotten** (originally **John Lydon**, 1956– , vocals), **Steve Jones** (1955– , guitar and vocals), **Glen Matlock** (1956– , bass guitar), and **Paul Cook** (1956– , drums); Matlock was replaced by **Sid Vicious** (originally **John Simon Ritchie**, 1957–79). They gained notoriety in the late 1970s as the best-known exponents of British 'punk rock'. The band had broken up by the end of the decade. >> punk rock; rock music

Sextans (Lat 'sextant') A very faint equatorial constellation between Leo and Hydra. >> constellation; Hydra (astronomy); Leo; RR968

sextant An optical instrument for measuring angular distances; in particular, the elevation of the Sun above the horizon at noon, for determining latitude. The observer views the horizon through a telescope, and simultaneously (through a mirror attached to an arm on a graduated arc) the Sun. >> latitude and longitude ℹ

sex therapy Treatment for sexual problems of psychological origin, which may arise as a result of a mental reaction to physical illness by the affected individual or partner, or to psychological attitudes themselves, either of which imperil normal sexual relations. An assessment of the individual or couple's problem is followed by simple counselling or, in the event of failure, by referral to specially trained sex therapists, who generally advise a graduated programme of tasks which the couple pursue at home.

sexually transmitted diseases >> **AIDS; gonorrhoea; syphilis; venereal disease**

Seychelles [say**shelz**], official name **Republic of Seychelles** pop (1995e) 71 100; land area 455 sq km/175 sq mi. Island group in the SW Indian Ocean, N of Madagascar, comprising 115 islands scattered over 1 374 000 sq km/530 000 sq mi between 4° and 5°S; largest, Mahé (153 sq km/59 sq mi); capital, Victoria (on Mahé); timezone GMT +4; population largely descended from 18th-c French colonists and their freed African slaves; chief religion, Roman Catholicism (90%); unit of currency, the Seychelles rupee; chief languages, Creole, French, English; islands fall into two main groups; a compact group of 41 mountainous islands rising steeply from the sea, highest point 906 m/2972 ft on Mahé; to the SW, a group of low-lying coralline islands and atolls; tropical climate; colonized by the French, 1768; captured by Britain, 1794; incorporated as a dependency of Mauritius, 1814; separate colony, 1903; independent republic within the Commonwealth, 1976; governed by a president, a Council of Ministers, and a unicameral National Assembly; expanding tourist industry; diversifying small industry. >> Mauritius ℹ; Victoria (Seychelles); RR1021 political leaders

Seyfert, Carl [**say**fert] (1911–60) US astronomer, who first drew attention (1943) to the existence of galaxies with brilliant nuclei. >> galaxy; quasar

Seymour, Jane [**see**moor] (c.1509–37) Third queen of Henry VIII, the mother of Edward VI, and the sister of Protector Somerset. She was a lady-in-waiting to Henry's first two wives, and married him 11 days after the execution of Anne Boleyn. She died soon after the birth of her son. >> Boleyn; Edward VI; Henry VIII (of England)

Sezession [set**ses**yohn] (Ger 'secession') The name adopted by a number of groups of modern artists in Germany between c.1890 and World War 1, who seceded from the orthodox academic bodies to form their own exhibiting societies. >> Art Nouveau; *Brücke, die*

Sfax [sfaks] 34°45N 10°43E, pop (1995e) 283 000. Seaport in E Tunisia; second largest city of Tunisia; built on the site of Roman and Phoenician settlements; occupied by Sicilians (12th-c) and Spaniards (16th-c); airfield; railway. >> Tunisia ℹ

SGML >> **Standard Generalized Mark-up Language**

sgraffito or **graffito** A technique in art in which one colour is laid over another and a design scratched through. Mediaeval and Renaissance buildings were sometimes decorated with two layers of plaster – one white, one coloured – and scratched decoration applied.

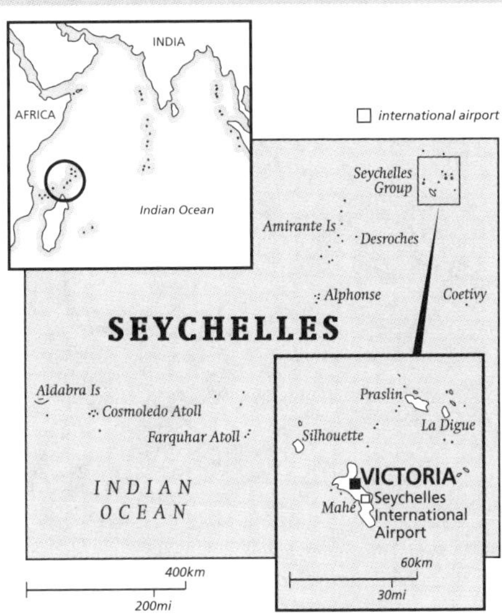

Shabbat >> **sabbath**

Shabuoth or **Shavuot(h)** [sha**voo**-oth, -ot] The Jewish Feast of Weeks, observed in May or June (6 or 7 Sivan) in commemoration of God's giving of the Law to Moses on Mt Sinai (*Ex* 19); also known as **Pentecost**. >> Moses; RR982

Shackleton, Sir Ernest Henry (1874–1922) Explorer, born in Kilkee, Co Kildare, Ireland. He was a junior officer in Scott's National Antarctic Expedition (1901–3), and nearly reached the South Pole in his own expedition of 1909. In 1915 his ship *Endurance* was crushed in the ice. He died at South Georgia during a fourth expedition. >> Antarctica ℹ; Scott, R F

shad Small herring-like fish (*Alosa sapidissima*) native to the Atlantic seaboard of North America but now widespread on the Pacific coast also; live in large schools; length up to 75 cm/30 in; silver with greenish-blue upper surface. (Family: Clupeidae.) >> herring

shaddock A citrus fruit (*Citrus grandis*) resembling grapefruit, 10–25 cm/4–10 in diameter; globose or pear-shaped, with greenish-yellow rind and sweet pink or yellow pulp. It is grown mainly in the tropics. (Family: Rutaceae.) >> citrus

shadow-mask tube A cathode-ray tube for the display of colour video images. Electron beams from three separate guns modulated by the red, green, and blue signals are deflected by a scanning system through holes in a plate to fall on minute phosphor dots of the appropriate colour comprising the screen. These dots glow according to the intensity of the beam reaching them and appear as additive colour hues. >> cathode-ray tube; colour television ℹ; *see illustration on p. 778*

shadow puppets Puppets which are manipulated in performance so as to cast a shadow on a screen. There are two major traditions. In one, the sticks operating the two-dimensional figures are worked from below, as with Balinese and Javanese shadow theatre. In the other, the sticks are operated from behind, as with Chinese and Turkish shadow theatre. >> puppetry

Shadwell, Thomas (c.1642–92) Playwright, born in Brandon, Norfolk. He found success with his first satirical comedy, *The Sullen Lovers* (1668), and such later 'comedies of manners' as *Epsom-Wells* (1672). He succeeded Dryden as poet laureate in 1689. >> Dryden

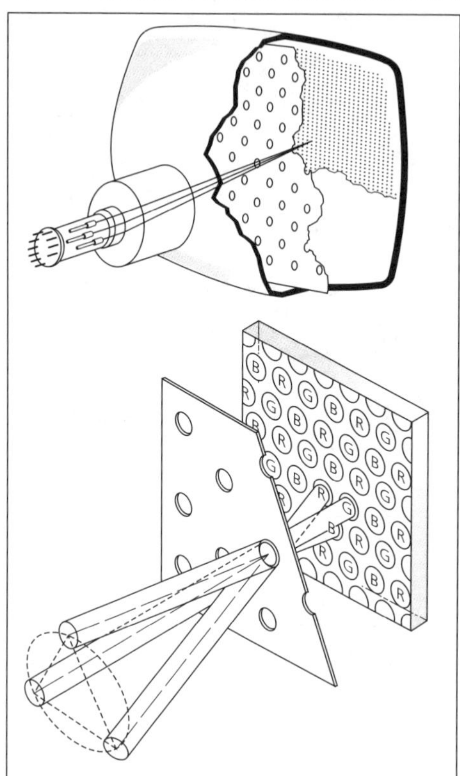

Shadow-mask tube – modulated electron beams from three separate guns pass through holes in the mask plate to fall on the individual colour phosphor dots which comprise the screen. (Lower illustration a magnified detail.)

Shaftesbury, Anthony Ashley Cooper, 1st Earl of [**shahfts**bree] (1621–83) English statesman, born in Wimborne St Giles, Dorset. He became a member of the Short Parliament (1640) and of the Barebones Parliament (1653), and was made one of Cromwell's Council of State, but from 1655 was in opposition. At the Restoration he became Chancellor of the Exchequer (1661–72), a member of the Cabal (1667), and Lord Chancellor (1672–3). >> Barebones Parliament; Cabal; English Civil War; Restoration

Shaftesbury, Anthony Ashley Cooper, 3rd Earl of [**shahfts**bree] (1671–1713) Moral philosopher, born in London, the grandson of the 1st Earl of Shaftesbury. He is best known for his essays, collected as *Characteristics of Men, Manners, Opinions, Times* (1711). He was one of the leading English deists. >> deism

Shaftesbury, Anthony Ashley Cooper, 7th Earl of [**shahfts**bree] (1801–85) Factory reformer and philanthropist, born in London. He became the main spokesman of the factory reform movement, and a leader of the evangelical movement within the Church of England. >> evangelicalism

shag >> **cormorant**

Shah Jahan [ja**hahn**] (1592–1666) Mughal Emperor of India (1628–58), born in Lahore, Pakistan. His reign saw two wars in the Deccan, 1636, 1655, the subjugation of Bijapur and Golconda, 1636, and attacks on the Uzbegs and Persians. His buildings included the Taj Mahal (1632–54). >> Mughal Empire; Taj Mahal

Shaka [**shah**ka] (c.1788–1828) African ruler, born near Melmoth, KwaZulu Natal, South Africa. He was a highly successful military ruler, who intensified the centralization of Zulu power, adapted the weapons and tactics of local warfare, and set about the incorporation of neighbouring peoples. He was killed by his half-brother, Dingane. >> Zulu

Shakers The popular name for members of the United Society for Believers in Christ's Second Appearing, founded in England under the leadership of Ann Lee (1736–87), who led them to America in 1774. They are communitarian and pacifist, and their ecstatic dancing gave rise to their popular name. Their acceptance of strict celibacy has led to their disappearance, with the death in 1992 of Ethel Hudson, aged 96, the last Shaker sister at Canterbury Shaker Valley. >> Christianity; millenarianism

Shakespeare, William (1564–1616) Playwright and poet, the greatest English writer, born in Stratford-upon-Avon, Warwickshire, the son of **John Shakespeare**, a glover, and **Mary Arden**, of farming stock. He married **Anne Hathaway**, from a local farming family, in 1582, who bore him a daughter, Susanna, in 1583, and twins Hamnet and Judith in 1585. He moved to London, possibly in 1591, and became an actor. His sonnets, known by 1598, though not published until 1609, fall into two groups: 1 to 126 are addressed to a fair young man, and 127 to 154 to a 'dark lady' who holds both the young man and the poet in thrall. The first evidence of his association with the stage is in 1594, when he was acting with the Lord Chamberlain's company of players. When the company built the Globe Theatre S of the Thames in 1597, he became a partner. He returned to Stratford c.1610, living as a country gentleman at his house, New Place. His will was made in March 1616, and he was buried at Stratford. The modern era of Shakespeare scholarship has been marked by an enormous amount of investigation into the authorship, text, and chronology of the plays, in particular the different quarto editions, and the first collected works, the First Folio of 1623. The authorship of such plays as *Titus Andronicus*, *Two Noble Kinsmen*, and *Henry VI*, part I, is still a matter of controversy, as is Shakespeare's part in the writing of *Timon of Athens*, *Pericles*, and *Henry VIII*. It is conventional to group the plays into early, middle, and late periods, and to distinguish comedies, tragedies, and histories, recognizing other groups that do not fall neatly into these categories. Details of these groups are shown in the panel on p. 779.

shale Sedimentary rock predominantly formed from consolidated and compacted clay deposits. Oil shale contains sufficient decayed organic matter that an oil can be extracted from it by destructive distillation. >> clay minerals; sedimentary rock

shallot [sha**lot**] A variety of onion with clusters of small, oval bulbs, widely grown as a vegetable. >> allium; onion

shaman [**shay**man, **shah**man] A person thought to possess special powers to communicate with and influence the spirits by dissociating his soul from his body. Shamans are found among Siberian and Asian peoples; similar practitioners are found in many other religions, under other names.

Shamir, Yitzhak [sha**meer**], originally **Yitzhak Jazernicki** (1915–) Zionist leader and prime minister of Israel (1983–4, 1986–92), born in Ruzinoy, Poland. He was foreign minister (1980–3), before taking over the leadership of the right-wing Likud Party, and becoming prime minister. From 1984 he shared an uneasy coalition with the Labour leader Shimon Peres, and was re-elected in 1988,

Shakespeare: the Plays

Early comedies	Written	Well-known characters
The Comedy of Errors	1590–94	Antipholus, Dromio, Andriana
Love's Labour's Lost	1590–94	Armado, Berowne, Costard
The Two Gentlemen of Verona	1592–3	Proteus, Valentine, Julia, Sylvia
The Taming of the Shrew	1592	Petruchio, Katharina, Sly
Histories		
Henry VI Part I	1589–90	Henry, Talbot, Joan of Arc
Henry VI Part II	1590–91	Henry, Margaret, Jack Cade
Henry VI Part III	1590–91	Henry, Margaret, Richard of Gloucester
Richard III	1592–3	Richard, Margaret, Clarence, Anne
King John	1595–7	John, Constance, Arthur, Bastard
Richard II	1595	Richard, John of Gaunt, Bolingbroke
Henry IV Part I	1596	Henry, Hal, Hotspur, Falstaff
Henry IV Part II	1597	Henry, Hal, Falstaff, Mistress Quickly
Henry V	1599	Henry (formerly Hal), Pistol, Nym, Katherine
Henry VIII	1613	Henry, Katherine, Wolsey
Middle comedies		
A Midsummer Night's Dream	1595	Oberon, Titania, Puck, Bottom
The Merchant of Venice	1596–8	Bassanio, Portia, Shylock, Jessica
The Merry Wives of Windsor	1597	Falstaff, Mistress Quickly, Shallow
As You Like It	1599	Rosalind, Orlando, Touchstone, Jacques
Twelfth Night	1600–2	Orsino, Olivia, Viola, Malvolio, Feste, Sir Andrew Aguecheek
Dark comedies		
Much Ado About Nothing	1598	Beatrice, Benedick, Dogberry, Verges
All's Well That Ends Well	1602–3	Bertram, Helena, Parolles
Measure for Measure	1604–5	Duke, Angelo, Isabella, Mariana
Tragedies		
Romeo and Juliet	1595–6	Romeo, Juliet, Mercutio, the Nurse
Hamlet	1600–1	Hamlet, Ophelia, the Ghost, the Grave-Digger
Othello	1604	Othello, Desdemona, Iago, Cassio
King Lear	1605–6	Lear, Cordelia, the Fool, Kent, Edgar/Poor Tom
Macbeth	1605–6	Macbeth, Lady Macbeth, Banquo/Ghost, the Three Witches
Greek and Roman plays		
Titus Andronicus	1590–94	Andronicus, Aaron, Lavinia
Julius Caesar	1599	Caesar, Brutus, Cassius, Antony
Troilus and Cressida	1601–2	Troilus, Cressida, Pandarus
Timon of Athens	1605–9	Timon, Apemantus
Antony and Cleopatra	1606–7	Antony, Cleopatra, Enobarbus
Coriolanus	1607–8	Coriolanus, Volumnia
Late comedies		
Pericles	1607–8	Pericles, Marina
Cymbeline	1609–10	Innogen, Iachimo
The Winter's Tale	1611	Leontes, Perdita, Florizel, Autolycus
The Tempest	1613	Prospero, Miranda, Ferdinand, Ariel, Caliban

but lost his position when Labour under Rabin won the 1992 election. >> Peres; Rabin

Shammai [**sha**miy] (c.1st-c BC–AD 1st-c) A Jewish scholar and Pharisaic leader, head of a famous school of Torah scholars, whose interpretation of the Law was often in conflict with the equally famous school led by Hillel. Both are often referred to in the Mishnah. >> Hillel I; Judaism; Mishnah; Pharisees; Torah

shamrock The name applied to several different plants with leaves divided into three leaflets, including **wood sorrel** (*Oxalis acetosella*) and various species of **clover** (*Trifolium*). It has been adopted as the national emblem of Ireland, and is worn each year on 17 March to commemorate St Patrick. It is a slender annual growing to 25 cm/10 in; flowers yellow, petals later turning dark brown; native to Europe, N Africa, and the W African islands (Macaronesia). (Family: Leguminosae.) >> clover; trefoil

Shang or **Yin dynasty** (1523–1028 BC) The earliest historical Chinese dynasty (the dates are disputed). Evidence is found in the Zhou and Han periods, and in 200 000 Shang period oracle bones which yield detail of daily life, as well as royal and ministerial chronologies. Its capital (from 1300 BC) was at Anyang, N of the Yellow River. >> Han / Zhou dynasty; oracle bones

Shanghai 31°13N 121°25E; pop (1995e) 8 806 000; administrative region 13 341 896; municipality area 5800 sq km/ 2239 sq mi. Port in E China, on Huangpu and Wusong Rivers; largest city in China; developed in the Yuan period as a cotton centre; trading centre in the 17th–18th-c; opened to foreign trade, 1842; two airports; two airfields; rail and sea links to other cities; university (1895) and several other higher education institutions; Longhua Temple (c.7th-c); Yu Yuan (Garden of Happiness), 1577, the basis for 'willow pattern' chinaware. >> China ⓘ; Opium Wars; willow pattern

Shankar, Ravi [**shangk**ah(r)] (1920–) Sitar player, born in Benares, India. Through his foreign tours and recordings, he has done much to make Indian classical music better known abroad. >> sitar ⓘ

Shanklin >> **Sandown**

Shankly, Bill, popular name of **William Shankly** (1913–81) Footballer and manager, born in Scotland. As a manager, he found fame with Liverpool (1959–74), creating a team which was highly successful in Britain and Europe. >> football ⓘ; Liverpool

Shannon, Ir **Rineanna** 52°42N 8°57W, pop (1995e) 7900. Town in Clare county, W Ireland; duty-free airport. >> Clare; Ireland (republic) ⓘ

Shannon, River River in Ireland, rising in Co Cavan, Ulster, and flowing c.385 km/240 mi to Limerick Bay. >> Ireland (republic) ⓘ

SHAPE >> **NATO**

Shapur or **Sapor II** [**sha**poor], known as **the Great** (309–79) King of Persia (309–79), who ruled with the help of regents until the age of 16. Under him the Sassanian Empire reached its zenith. >> Sassanids

sharefarming A form of tenure in which the landlord provides the land, fixed equipment, and often a proportion of the variable inputs, in exchange for an agreed proportion of the final crop.

shares Certificates of part ownership of a company, which represent equal amounts of money invested in the company. The **shareholders** provide the original capital for the company and are its residual owners. They are entitled to any profits made, either as dividends or as a capital distribution if the company is sold or wound up. If the company makes losses they may lose their money, hence the term **risk capital**, though if the company has limited liability they cannot lose more than they put in. >> company; dividend; equity (economics); investment; preference shares

Sharia [sha**ree**a] The sacred law of Islam, embracing all aspects of a Muslim's life. It has four sources: the *Quran* (Koran), the *sunna* or 'practice' of the Prophet Mohammed, *ijma* or 'consensus of opinion', and *qiyas* or 'reasoning by analogy'. >> Islam; Koran

Sharif, Omar [sha**reef**], originally **Michael Shalhouz** (1932–) Film actor, born in Alexandria, Egypt. He attracted international attention following his role in *Lawrence of Arabia* (1962), and starred in *Doctor Zhivago* (1965). Later films include *Funny Girl* (1968), *The Tamarind Seed* (1974), and *The Mirror has Two Faces* (1996). He is also a renowned bridge player.

Sharjah [**shah(r)**ja], or **Shariqah** pop (1995e) 354 000; area 2600 sq km/1000 sq mi. Third largest of the United Arab Emirates; capital, Ash Sharjah; offshore oil production began in 1974. >> United Arab Emirates ⓘ

shark Any of a large group of active, predatory, cartilaginous fishes belonging to 19 separate families, such as the Alopiidae (thresher sharks), Cetorhinidae (basking sharks), and Chlamydoselachidae (frilled sharks). >> basking / blue / hammerhead / thresher / tiger / whale / white shark; cartilaginous fish; dogfish; tope

Sharman, Helen (Patricia) (1963–) Britain's first astronaut, born in Sheffield, South Yorkshire. In 1989 she responded to an advertisement for trainee astronauts, and was eventually selected to be the British member of the Russian scientific space mission, Project Juno (1991), spending eight days in space. She has since become known as a lecturer in science education; her book *The Space Place* appeared in 1997.

Sharpe, Tom, popular name of **Thomas Ridley Sharpe** (1928–) Novelist, born in London. He was a lecturer in history (1963–71) before turning to full-time writing, beginning with *Riotous Assembly* (1971). Later novels include *Indecent Exposure* (1973), *Porterhouse Blue* (1974), a series introducing the character of Wilt (from 1976), and *The Midden* (1996).

Sharpe, William F (1934–) Economist, born in Cambridge, MA. He shared the 1990 Nobel Prize for Economics for his contributions to the corporate finance field. >> Markowitz; Miller, Merton

Sharpeville [**shah(r)p**vil] 26°40S 27°52E, pop (1995e) 134 000. Black African township in NE South Africa; scene of the Sharpeville massacre (1960); inauguration of the new constitution took place here in December 1996. >> Sharpeville massacre; South Africa ⓘ

Sharpeville massacre (21 Mar 1960) A major incident in the black African township of Sharpeville in South Africa, when police opened fire on a crowd demonstrating against the laws restricting non-white movements and requiring non-whites to carry identification (the *pass laws*); 69 people were killed and 180 wounded. The massacre produced an international outcry, and made black nationalism in South Africa increasingly radical. >> apartheid; Black Consciousness Movement; civil rights; South Africa ⓘ

Shastri, Lal (Bahadur) [**shas**tree] (1904–66) Indian statesman and prime minister (1964–6), born in Mughalsarai, Uttar Pradesh, India. He succeeded Nehru as premier, but died of a heart attack in Tashkent, Uzbekistan, the day after signing a 'no war' agreement with Pakistan. >> Nehru

Shatner, William (1931–) Actor and director, born in Montreal, Canada. He became internationally known following the cult success of the *Star Trek* television series (1966–9), in which he played Captain James T(iberius) Kirk. He reprised the role in several feature film sequels, directing as well as acting in *Star Trek V: The Final Frontier* (1989).

Shatt al-Arab [**shat** al **a**rab] Tidal river formed by the union of the Tigris and Euphrates Rivers, SE Iraq; flows 192 km/119 mi to enter the Persian Gulf; part of the Iraq–Iran border in its lower course; wide delta, containing the world's largest date-palm groves; international commission in 1935 gave control to Iraq, but disputes over navigational rights were one of the issues that led to the outbreak of the Gulf War. >> Gulf War 1; Iraq ⓘ

Shavuot(h) >> **Shabuoth**

Shaw, Anna Howard (1847–1919) Minister and feminist, born in Newcastle upon Tyne, Tyne and Wear. Her family emigrated to the USA in 1851. She became president of the National American Women's Suffrage Association in 1904, holding office until 1915. >> women's liberation movement

Shaw, George Bernard (1856–1950) Playwright, essayist, and pamphleteer, born in Dublin. In 1882 he turned to Socialism, joined the committee of the Fabian Society, and became known as a journalist. He began to write plays in 1885, and among his early successes were *Arms and the Man* (1894), *Candida* (1897), and *The Devil's Disciple* (1897). Later plays included *Man and Superman* (1905), *Major Barbara* (1905), *The Doctor's Dilemma* (1906), *Pygmalion* (1913, adapted as a musical play, *My Fair Lady*, in 1956, filmed in 1964), and *Saint Joan* (1923). He wrote over 40 plays, and continued to write them even in his 90s. He was also passionately interested in the question of spelling reform. In 1925 he was awarded the Nobel Prize for Literature. >> Fabian Society; spelling reform

Shawnee [shaw**nee**] North American Algonkin Indians who originally settled in Ohio, but were pushed out of the area by the Iroquois. They eventually settled in Oklahoma. >> Iroquois

Shearing, George (1919–) Jazz pianist, bandleader, and composer, born in London. Blind from birth, he moved to the USA in the late 1940s. His compositions include 'Lullaby of Birdland' and 'September in the Rain'. >> jazz

shear modulus A measure of a material's resistance to twisting; symbol *G*, units Pa (pascal); also called the **modulus of rigidity** or **torsion modulus**. It is defined as shear stress divided by shear strain, and is applicable only to solids. >> strain; stress; torsion

shearwater A petrel with a long slender bill; plumage dark above, dark or pale beneath. The name is also used for skimmers. >> muttonbird; petrel; skimmer

sheathbill A white, pigeon-like shorebird, native to the Antarctic and sub-Antarctic; short, stout bill with horny cover at base; the only native Antarctic bird without webbed feet. (Family: Chionididae, 2 species.)

Sheba, Queen of [**shee**ba] (c.10th-c BC) Monarch mentioned in the Bible (1 *Kings* 10 and 2 *Chron* 9). She is said to have journeyed to Jerusalem to test the wisdom of Solomon and exchange gifts. >> Solomon (Hebrew Bible)

sheep A grazing mammal of family Bovidae; eight species in genus *Ovis* (seven wild species and the domestic sheep, *Ovis aries*); male with large spiralling horns; female with small or absent horns; wild sheep have a coarse outer coat and a fleecy underlayer which grows only in winter; domesticated breeds have only the underlayer, which is thick and grows continuously; male called a *ram* or *tup*, female a *ewe*, young a *lamb*. >> aoudad; argali; bighorn; Bovidae; merino

sheepdog Any working dog used to guard sheep from wild animals or to assist in herding; also any dog belonging to a breed formerly used for this purpose. >> collie; dog; kelpie (zoology); non-sporting dog; Old English sheepdog

Sheffield 53°23N 1°30W, urban area pop (1995e) 536 000. City in South Yorkshire, N England; on the R Don; developed as a cutlery-manufacturing town in the early 18th-c and as a steel town in the 19th-c; city status in 1893; major rebuilding after World War 2 bombing; universities, (1905, 1992); railway; cathedral (12th-c); Crucible Theatre; football league teams, Sheffield United (Blades), Sheffield Wednesday (Owls). >> Hillsborough; Yorkshire, South

Sheffield Shield A silver trophy purchased from a donation of £150 by Lord Sheffield to promote Australian cricket. It has been the object of annual cricket competitions between the colonies (to 1900) and the states (after 1900) since 1892–3. >> cricket (sport) ℹ; RR1049

Shelburne, William Petty Fitzmaurice, 2nd Earl of (1737–1805) British statesman and prime minister (1782–3), born in Dublin. Made premier on the death of Rockingham, he resigned when outvoted by the coalition between Fox and North. >> Fox, Charles James; North, Frederick; Rockingham, Marquess of

sheldgoose A South American goose of the genus *Chloephaga* (5 species); eats grass (4 species) or seaweed (the **kelp goose**, *Chloephaga hybrida*); nests on ground. (Subfamily: Anatinae. Tribe: Tadornini.) >> goose

sheldrake >> **shelduck**

shelduck A goose-like duck, native to the Old World (except the far N); nests in burrows or holes; also known as a **sheldrake**. (Genus: *Tadorna*, 7 species. Subfamily: Anatinae. Tribe: Tadornini.) >> duck; goose

shell The mineralized outer covering of a variety of invertebrate animals, such as molluscs and brachiopods; usually containing a large amount of calcium. The calcareous shell of a bird's egg is a secondary egg membrane secreted by the genital duct of the mother bird. >> brachiopod; calcium; egg; mollusc

shellac A resin generally obtained from a secretion from the insect *Tachardia lacca*. Solutions of shellac are used as varnishes and French polish. >> resin

Shelley, Mary (Wollstonecraft), *née* **Godwin** (1797–1851) Writer, born in London, the daughter of William Godwin and Mary Wollstonecraft. She eloped with Shelley in 1814, and married him two years later. She wrote several novels, notably *Frankenstein, or the Modern Prometheus* (1818). >> Godwin, William; Shelley, Percy Bysshe; Wollstonecraft, Mary

Shelley, Percy Bysshe [bish] (1792–1822) Poet, born in Horsham, West Sussex. He married Harriet Westbrook in London, and settled in Keswick, where he wrote his revolutionary poem *Queen Mab* (1813). He formed a liaison with Mary Godwin, with whom he eloped (1814) and whom he later married. From 1818 he lived in Italy, where he wrote the bulk of his poetry, including the verse drama *Prometheus Unbound* (1818–19). He was drowned near Livorno. >> Byron; Romanticism

shellfish An informal name for edible molluscs and crustaceans collectively; includes groups such as shrimps, crabs, lobsters, clams, bivalves, whelks, and mussels. >> crustacean; mollusc

Shelter (National Campaign for the Homeless) In the UK, a charity founded in 1966 to provide help for the homeless and to campaign on their behalf. Its income comes principally from donations.

Sheltie >> **Shetland pony**

Shem Biblical character, the eldest son of Noah, brother of Ham and Japheth. He is depicted as the legendary father of 'Semitic' peoples, meant to include the Hebrews. >> Noah

Shema [she**mah**] (Heb 'hear') A well-known ancient Jewish prayer, beginning 'Hear, O Israel: the Lord our God, the Lord is one'. It introduces the Jewish morning and evening prayers. >> Amidah; Judaism; tefillin

Shenandoah River [shenuhn**doh**uh] River in West Virginia and Virginia, USA; formed at the junction of the North Fork and South Fork Rivers; flows 88 km/55 mi NE to meet the Potomac R. >> Virginia

Shenyang [shuhnyahng], formerly **Mukden** 41°50N 123°26E, pop (1995e) 5 006 000. Largest industrial city in NE China; capital of Manchu state, 1625; invasion by Japanese, 1931, which led to the establishment of Manchukuo; occupied by Nationalists, 1945; taken by Communists, 1948; renamed, 1949; airfield; railway; university; Imperial Palace (1625–36). >> China ℹ; Manchukuo

Shepard, Alan B(artlett) (1923–98) The first US astronaut, born in East Derry, NH. His sub-orbital flight in a Mercury space capsule ('Freedom 7') took place on 5 May 1961, reached an altitude of 185 km/116 mi, and lasted 15 min. He was also a member of the Apollo 14 crew which landed on the Moon in 1971. >> Apollo programme; astronaut; Mercury programme

Shepherd, Cybill (1950–) Film actress, born in Memphis, TN. She made an acclaimed film debut in *The Last Picture Show* (1971), following this with *The Heartbreak Kid* (1973) and *Taxi Driver* (1976). Television work includes the series *Moonlighting* (1985–9), with Bruce Willis, and *Cybill* (1995–). >> Willis, Bruce

shepherd moons Small natural moons whose gravitational fields serve to confine narrow rings around some of the outer planets. For example, the 'F' Ring of Saturn discovered by Pioneer 11 is a ribbon c.100 km/60 mi wide; its 'braided' structure was observed by Voyager spacecraft. >> Pioneer programme; Saturn (astronomy); Voyager project ℹ

Shepparton 36°25S 145°26E, pop (1995e) 26 700. City in N Victoria, Australia; railway; International Village, featuring worldwide tourist information. >> Victoria (Australia)

sherardizing [**she**rah(r)diyzing] A steel protection process named after English inventor Sherard Osborn Cowper-Coles (1866–1935). The outermost layer of the finished product is zinc, which grades into an adherent iron/zinc alloy. It is very corrosion resistant, and good for surface painting. >> steel

Sheraton, Thomas (1751–1806) Cabinet maker, born in Stockton-on-Tees, Durham. He produced a range of Neo-classical designs which had a wide influence on contemporary taste in furniture. >> Neoclassicism (art and architecture)

Sheridan, Philip H(enry) (1831–88) US general, born in Albany, NY. In 1864 he was given command of the Army of the Shenandoah, defeating General Lee, and was active in the final battles which led to Lee's surrender. >> American Civil War; Lee, Robert E

Sheridan, Richard Brinsley (Butler) (1751–1816) Playwright, born in Dublin, Ireland. In 1775 appeared the highly successful comedy of manners, *The Rivals*, and this was followed by several other comedies, notably *The School for Scandal* (1777).

sheriff Originally, the king's representative in the English shires responsible for legal, administrative, and military matters. Since the Middle Ages the office has largely declined in importance in England and Wales, and the sheriff's duties are now largely ceremonial and administrative. In Scotland, however, since 1946, sheriffs have been judges with a wide civil and criminal jurisdiction. In the USA, sheriffs are generally elected in each of the 3000 or more counties. They are responsible for law enforcement principally in rural areas, though many of their duties have been transferred to local or state police. >> civil / criminal law; police

Sheringham, Teddy (1966–) Footballer, born in Walthamstow, Greater London. A forward, he played for Millwall, Aldershot, Nottingham Forest, and Tottenham Hotspurs, signing for Manchester United in 1997. By mid-1998 he had won 33 caps playing for England.

Sherman, William Tecumseh (1820–91) US general in the Union army during the Civil War, born in Lancaster, OH. His most famous campaign was in 1864, when he captured Atlanta, and commenced his famous 'March to the Sea', which divided the Confederate forces. >> American Civil War

Sherpa A mountain people of Sikkim State and Nepal, India. They are famous as mountain traders and porters in the Himalayas. >> Nepal [i]; Sikkim

Sherrington, Sir Charles Scott (1857–1952) Physiologist, born in London. His research on the nervous system constituted a landmark in modern physiology, and he shared the Nobel Prize for Physiology or Medicine in 1932. >> Adrian; nervous system

sherry A white wine, fortified with brandy; named after Jerez de la Frontera in the Andalusian region of Spain. *Fino* is dry, light-coloured, of a high quality, and usually drunk young; *amontillado* is darker and moderately dry; *oloroso* is fuller and dark, the sweetest available. >> brandy; wine

Sherwood Forest An area of heath and woodland, mainly in Nottinghamshire, UK, where mediaeval kings hunted deer. It is famed for being the home of Robin Hood. >> Robin Hood

Shetland, also called **The Shetlands**, formerly **Zetland** pop (1995e) 22 900; area 1433 sq km/553 sq mi. Group of c.100 islands off coast of NE Scotland; 80 km/50 mi NE of Orkney Is; c.20 inhabited; chief islands, Mainland, Unst, Yell, Fetlar, Whalsay; low-lying, highest point Ronas Hill in N Mainland (450 m/1476 ft); capital, Lerwick, on Mainland; annexed by Norway in 9th-c; annexed by Scotland, 1472; cattle and sheep raising, knitwear, fishing, oil services at Lerwick and Sandwick, oil terminal at Sullom Voe; several prehistoric remains. >> Orkney; Scotland [i]; Shetland pony

Shetland pony The strongest of all breeds of horse (can pull twice its own weight), developed on the Scottish Shetland and Orkney Is; height, 9 hands/0·9 m/3 ft; stocky, with short legs; long mane and tail; also known as **Sheltie** or **Shelty**. >> horse [i]; Shetland

Shevardnadze, Eduard Amvrosiyevich [sheve**rnad**ze] (1928–) Georgian head of state (1992–) and former Soviet statesman, born in Mamati, Georgia. A member of the USSR Politburo, in 1985 he was appointed foreign minister. He resigned in 1990, expressing concern over some of Gorbachev's decisions, and warning of dictatorship. He was elected Chairman of the State Council of Georgia in 1992, but was unable to prevent the country's slide into civil war. >> Georgia (republic) [i]; Gorbachev

shiatsu [sheeatsoo] (Jap 'finger pressure') A form of massage in which pressure is applied to acupuncture points and meridians using the fingers, thumbs, and sometimes elbows, knees, hands, and feet. It is designed to release blockages and balance the flow of energy, and healing energy may also be transmitted from the practitioner to the patient. >> traditional Chinese medicine

shield A geological term for a large region of stable continental crust, usually Precambrian in age and forming the core of a continental land mass. >> Baltic Shield; Canadian Shield; Precambrian era

shield bug A typically shield-shaped true bug; c.5000 species, including some pests of economically important crops. (Order: Heteroptera. Family: Pentatomidae.) >> bug (entomology)

shielding >> **screening**

Shih-chia-chuang >> **Shijiazhuang**

Shih Tzu [shee tsoo] A toy breed of dog of Tibetan or Chinese origin; similar to the Pekinese in shape; thick straight coat; hair cascades to cover eyes and ears. >> dog; Pekinese

Shiites [**shee**iyts] A minority division, representing c.10% of Islam, which holds that legitimacy derives from the descendants of the Prophet Mohammed. Shiites venerate the lineal descendants of Ali, the fourth caliph, as infallible *imams*. Three main groups are distinguished: the Zaydis of Yemen; the Ismailis of India and East Africa; and the Imamis, or 'twelvers', who recognize twelve *imams*, the last of which disappeared in the 9th-c and whose return as the *Mahdi* is expected to usher in an age of justice. Shiism is the state religion of the Islamic Republic in Iran. >> Ali; imam 3; Islam; Ismailis

Shijiazhuang or **Shih-chia-chuang** [shoejiahjwahng] 38°04N 114°28E, pop (1995e) 1 490 000. City in N China; a major railway junction; mining (coal, iron ore, limestone, marble); China's largest pharmaceutical plant. >> China [i]

Shikoku [shi**koh**koo] pop (1995e) 4 287 000; area 18 795 sq km/7255 sq mi. Smallest of the four main islands of Japan; subtropical climate; mountainous and wooded interior; chief towns, Matsuyama, Takamatsu. >> Japan [i]

Shilluk An E Sudanic-speaking people living along the Nile S of Khartoum in the Sudan Republic. They are farmers, with many cattle. >> Sudan [i]

Shiloh [**shiy**loh] The site of an ancient city in C Palestine; noted as the central sanctuary of the tribes of Israel during the settlement of Palestine under the tribal judges. It was destroyed c.1050 BC. >> Judaism

Shiloh, Battle of [**shiy**loh] (1862) An engagement in the American Civil War in SW Tennessee between Union forces under General Grant and Confederate forces under Albert Sidney Johnston (1803–62). Losses were heavy on both sides. >> Grant, Ulysses S

shingles A condition arising from the re-activation of the chickenpox virus which lies latent in the ganglia of sensory somatic nerves; also known as **herpes zoster**. It causes pain and a blister-like rash over the segmental distribution of a sensory nerve. >> chickenpox; nervous system; virus

Shinkansen [shingkansen] The Japanese New Tokaido Line, a standard gauge line from Tokyo to Osaka for high speed trains (commonly known as 'bullet trains'), completed in 1964. The network is being extended to cover all main Honshu routes. >> locomotive ℹ; railway

Shinto [**shin**toh] The indigenous religion of Japan. It emerged from the nature-worship of Japanese folk religions, reflected in ceremonies appealing to the mysterious powers of nature for protection. By the 8th-c, divine origins were ascribed to the imperial family, and in time it became the basis for State Shintoism and its obedience to the Emperor. There were nearly 3 million Shintoists in 1999. >> Buddhism; jinja

shinty A twelve-a-side stick-and-ball game originating in Ireland more than 1500 years ago, and now popular in the Scottish Highlands. The playing pitch is up to 155 m/170 yd long and 73 m/80 yd wide. The object is to score goals by using the stick to propel the ball.

Shinwell, Emmanuel Shinwell, Baron, popularly known as **Manny Shinwell** (1884–1986) British statesman, born in London. In the postwar Labour government he was minister of fuel and power (1946), secretary of state for war (1947), and minister of defence (1950–1). Well known for his party political belligerence, in his later years he mellowed into a backbench 'elder statesman'. >> Labour Party; socialism

ship A sea-going vessel of considerable size. At the time of Queen Hatshepsut (c.1500 BC) an expedition to E Africa was mounted using vessels of about 20 m/60 ft in length. These are the first sea-going ships of which there are reliable pictorial records. Greeks and Romans built galleys relying on oars, a square sail coming into use when the wind was favourable. Chinese ships were making voyages of over a year by the 1st-c AD. Roman merchant vessels 28–56 m/90–180 ft long were propelled by a large square sail hung from a single mast. Viking ships varied in length from 20 m/70 ft to 40 m/120 ft, and were propelled by a large square-rigged sail and oars. By the 15th-c the Portuguese had developed the lateen-rigged caravel into a three- or four-masted ocean-going craft. Out of this grew the carrack, where lateen sails gradually gave way to square sails. US influence dates from 1845, with the clipper ship. In 1802 the first viable steamship, the *Charlotte Dundas*, was used as a tug on the Forth–Clyde canal. The first continuous steam crossing of the Atlantic was achieved by the British-owned packet vessel, the 700-ton *Sirius*, in 1838. Brunel's *Great Britain* (1844) was the first screw-propelled, double-bottomed, iron-hulled transatlantic passenger ship. The diesel engine, patented in 1892, won ocean-going acceptance in the 5000-gross-ton *Selandia* in 1912. Nuclear-fuelled vessels provide an alternative means of generating the heat to provide steam to drive turbines. This method is used in government vessels such as ice-breakers, aircraft carriers, and missile-carrying submarines, but it has proved to be uneconomical for merchant vessels. >> brig; caravel ℹ; carrack; clipper ship; container ship; cutter; dredger; galleon; icebreaker; longship; obo; reefer; ro-ro; sailing rig ℹ; schooner; Ship of Cheops; Sutton Hoo ship burial; tanker; trawler; trireme ℹ; warships ℹ; *see illustration on p. 784*

Ship of Cheops [**kee**ops] An ancient Egyptian funeral ship found dismantled at Giza in 1954 in one of five boat pits around the Pyramid of Cheops (2551–2528 BC). Reconstructed, the ship measures 44 m/143 ft long with a beam of 6 m/19 ft, and carried six pairs of oars 6.5–8.5 m/21–28 ft long. >> pyramid

Shiraz [shee**raz**] 29°38N 52°34E, pop (1995e) 1 110 000. City in SW Iran; capital of Persia, 1750–79; fifth largest city in Iran; airfield; university (1945). >> Iran ℹ

shire The largest breed of horse, developed in England from war-horses used to carry knights in armour; used for farm work; height, 17–18 hands/1.7–1.8 m/5 ft 8 in–6 ft; black or brown and white; long legs with hair covering hooves. >> horse ℹ

Shiva [**shee**va] One of the three principal deities of the Hindu triad (*Trimurti*) – a god of contrasting features: creation and destruction, good and evil, fertility and asceticism. >> Hinduism; Trimurti

Shkodër [**shkoh**der], Ital **Scutari**, ancient **Scodra** 42°05N 19°30E, pop (1995e) 89 000. Market town in NW Albania; former capital of Albania; railway; citadel (14th-c), cathedral. >> Albania ℹ

shock A term used by the lay public to denote the psychological state of fear or grief that follows a sudden accident, calamity, or bereavement. Its medical use refers to a clinical state in which the blood pressure and circulation is insufficient to maintain the functioning of the brain or other organs. >> blood vessels ℹ

Shockley, William B(radford) (1910–89) Physicist, born in London. In 1947 he helped to devise the point-contact transistor, then devised the junction transistor, which heralded a revolution in radio, TV, and computer circuitry. He shared the Nobel Prize for Physics in 1956. >> Bardeen; transistor

shock therapy A term sometimes used as a synonym for **electroconvulsive therapy**, but also for **electrosleep**, in which a weak rhythmically-repeated pulse of electric current is applied to the brain for the treatment of anxiety, insomnia, and a variety of other medical conditions with a psychological component. >> electroconvulsive therapy; sleep

shoddy Products made from reprocessed old wool. Strictly the term applies only to the loose fibre, but it is commonly used to describe the products made from shoddy. >> wool

shoebill A large, grey, stork-like bird with a large head (*Balaeniceps rex*); bill extremely wide and deep, shaped like a broad shoe; inhabits marshes in C Africa; nocturnal; also known as the **shoe-billed stork** or **whale-headed stork**. (Family: Balaenicipidae.) >> stork

Shoemaker, Willie, popular name of **William Lee Shoemaker**, nickname **the Shoe** (1931–) Jockey and trainer, born in Fabens, TX. He won more races than any other jockey – nearly 9000 winners between 1949 and his retirement in 1989. >> horse racing

Shoemaker–Levy 9 [shoomaker-**lee**vee] The name given to a comet (estimated to have been c.2 km/1.2 mi in diameter) which crashed into the planet Jupiter in 1994; jointly discovered by US astronomer Carolyn (Spellman) Shoemaker (1929–), her husband, astrogeologist Eugene (Merle) Shoemaker (1928–97), and amateur astronomer David Levy (1948–). Over 20 fragments made spectacular impacts into the planet during the period 16–22 July, leaving dark markings observable by infrared telescopes. >> comet; Jupiter

shogi [shohgee] A Japanese form of chess, believed to have originated in India. It is played on a squared board, each player having 20 pieces. >> chess

shogun [**shoh**gn] A Japanese general, the head of a system of government which dates from 1192. Most important were the Tokugawa Shoguns (1603–1868), who ruled as military dictators, the emperor remaining a figurehead, without power. The system ended in 1868. >> Meiji Restoration; Tokugawa

Egyptian ship, c.1480 BC, length 21 m/70 ft

Roman merchantman, AD 200, length 27 m/90 ft

Viking longship, AD 800, length 24 m/80 ft

Portuguese carrack, 1490, length 24 m/80 ft

American clipper, *Flying Cloud*, length 64 m/209 ft

Great Britain, 1844, length 98 m/322 ft

Mauretania, 1907, length 232 m/762 ft

Queen Elizabeth 2, 1968, length 293.5 m/963 ft

Not to scale

Ships

Sholem Aleichem [a**lay**khem], also spelled **Sholom** or **Shalom** (Hebrew, 'peace unto you'), pseudonym of **Solomon J Rabinowitz** (1859–1916) Writer, born in Pereyaslev, Ukraine. The pogroms of 1905 drove him to the USA, where he worked as a playwright for the Yiddish theatre. The musical *Fiddler on the Roof* is based on his stories. >> Yiddish

Sholes, Christopher Latham [shohlz] (1819–90) Inventor,

born in Mooresbury, PA. A printer in his early years, he went on to develop the typewriter (1868).

Sholokhov, Mikhail Alexandrovich [**sho**lokhof] (1905–84) Novelist, born near Veshenskaya, Russia. Best known for his novel tetralogy *Tikhy Don* (1928–40, trans Quiet Flows the Don), he received the Nobel Prize for Literature in 1965.

Shona [**sho**na] A cluster of Bantu-speaking agricultural peoples of E Zimbabwe who formed a powerful state during the 13th–15th-c. Their members dominate ZANU, the ruling party of Zimbabwe. >> Zimbabwe [i]

shooting The use of firearms for pleasure, hunting, sport, or in battle. The first reference to the gun was in 1326, and it soon became the chief weapon of war. It developed as a sport in the 15th-c, the first shooting club being formed at Lucerne, Switzerland, in 1466. In competitive shooting, the most popular weapons are the standard pistol, small bore rifle, full bore rifle, air rifle, and air pistol. Several tournaments are held, such as those organized by the National Rifle Association (founded, 1871) in the USA. >> biathlon; clay pigeon shooting; pistol; rifle; RR1060

shooting star >> **meteor**

shop stewards Workers appointed by their fellows within a trade union to represent them on matters relevant to their pay and conditions. In some instances the post is a full-time job. >> trade union

Short, Clare (1946–) British stateswoman. She became an MP in 1983, joined the shadow cabinet in 1995, and was spokesperson on transport (1995–6) and overseas development (1996–7). She became secretary-of-state for international development in the 1997 Labour government.

Short, Nigel (1965–) Chess player, born in Atherton, Lancashire. He became the UK's youngest ever grandmaster in 1984, and in 1993 the first UK grandmaster to qualify for a World Championship match, but was defeated by Gary Kasparov. He resigned from FIDE (the international chess organization) in 1993 and with Kasparov formed the Professional Chess Association. >> chess; Kasparov

shorthand A method of writing at speed to take verbatim records of speech, also known as **stenography**. Shorthand systems variously use symbols which are abbreviations of words (as in *speedwriting*), representations of speech sounds, or arbitrary symbols which the user has to memorize. Much used in commerce and industry, and in courts of law, in recent years its popularity has lessened with the advent of dictating machines.

shorthorn A type of domestic cattle with short horns. In 18th-c England, Charles and Robert Colling improved the type, leading to such breeds as the **Durham** (the *shorthorn* of the American ranchers) and the **Teeswater**. >> cattle

short-sightedness >> **eye** [i]

short story A prose fiction of not more than some 10 000 words. Beyond this lie the similarly imprecise categories 'long short story', 'novella', and 'short novel'. There are many rudimentary forms of short story, including myths, fables, legends, and parables; but the modern short story began in the mid-19th-c with Edgar Allan Poe, and was confirmed as a major genre by Maupassant in France and Turgenev and Chekhov in Russia. >> novel; novella; Chekhov; Maupassant; Poe; Turgenev

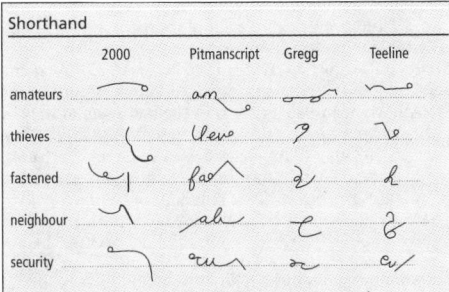

Shorthand

	2000	Pitmanscript	Gregg	Teeline
amateurs				
thieves				
fastened				
neighbour				
security				

Five words transcribed in Pitman 2000, Pitmanscript, Gregg and – a relative newcomer – Teeline, a combination of shorthand and speed-writing that became increasingly popular in the 1980s.

Short Take-Off and Landing >> **STOL**

Shoshoni [shoh**shoh**nee] North American Indians who once lived in California, Nevada, Utah, and Wyoming; semi-nomadic hunter-gatherers. They now live mainly on reservations. >> hunter-gatherers

Shostakovich, Dmitri Dmitriyevich [shosta**koh**vich] (1906–75) Composer, born in St Petersburg, Russia. His music was at first highly successful, but his operas and ballets were later criticized by the government for some years for a failure to observe the principles of 'Soviet realism'. He wrote 15 symphonies; violin, piano, and cello concertos; chamber music; and choral works.

shotgun A smooth-bore weapon firing cartridges filled with small lead or steel pellets (*shot*), which spread in flight to broaden their destructive effects; widely used by farmers and sportsmen.

shot put An athletics field throwing event. The shot is a brass or iron sphere weighing 7.3 kg/16 lb for men and 3.6 kg/8 lb 13 oz for women. It is propelled, using only one hand, from a starting position under the chin. The thrower must not leave the 2.1 m/7 ft diameter throwing circle. The current world record for men is 23.12 m/75 ft 10 in, achieved by Randy Barnes (USA) in 1990 at Los Angeles, CA; for women it is 22.63 m/74 ft 3 in, achieved by Natalya Lisovskaya (Russia) in 1987 at Moscow. >> athletics

shou >> **red deer**

shoulder Commonly used to refer to the rounded region at the top of the arm passing towards the neck and upper back; more specifically, in anatomy, the articulation between the humerus and the scapula. It is an extremely mobile joint, at the expense of some joint stability. >> scapula

shove-halfpenny; shovelboard >> **shuffleboard**

shoveller / shoveler A dabbling duck, native to South America (1 species), S Africa (1 species), Australia and New Zealand (1 species), and the N hemisphere (1 species); nests in reed beds; also known as the **spoonbill**. (Genus: *Anas*, 4 species.)

showboat A paddle-wheel river steamer complete with theatre and its own repertory company. They were mainly used along the Mississippi in the 19th-c.

show jumping Horse jumping over a course containing a variety of strategically placed fences. Those who clear the fences and incur no penalty points are then involved in a 'jump-off' against the clock, where speed as well as accuracy is important. Points are incurred for knocking down a fence, or for refusing to jump a fence. >> equestrianism

show trials Originally a series of trials held in Moscow in the late 1930s under Stalin. It refers to any political trial where the accused make a public confession of their 'crimes', although their guilt is often open to doubt. >> Stalinism

Shrapnel, Henry (1761–1842) British artillery officer. In c.1793 he invented the **shrapnel shell**, an anti-personnel device which exploded while in flight, scattering lethal lead shot and other material.

shrew A widespread mammal of family Soricidae (246 species); an insectivore; mouse-like with a longer pointed snout and small eyes. >> insectivore; tree shrew

Shrewsbury [**shrooz**bree, **shrohz**bree], Anglo-Saxon **Scrobesbyrig** 52°43N 2°45W, pop (1995e) 62 600. County town of Shropshire, WC England; on the R Severn; Roman city of Uriconium to the E; site of Battle of Shrewsbury (1403); railway; castle (11th-c); football league team, Shrewsbury Town (Shrews). >> Shropshire

shrike A bird mainly of the Old World, especially Africa; strong bill with hooked tip; grasping, clawed feet. The **red-backed shrike** (*Lanius collurio*) is also called the **butcher-bird**. (Family: Laniidae, c.72 species.) >> woodchat

shrimp An aquatic crustacean; females typically carry eggs on abdominal legs until ready to hatch into swimming larvae (*zoeae*); many species of economic importance as food. (Class: Malacostraca. Order: Decapoda.) >> prawn

shrimp plant A bushy perennial (*Beloperone guttata*) growing to 1 m/3¼ ft, native to Mexico, named for the flower spikes which fancifully resemble crustacea; flowers hooded, white. (Family: Acanthaceae.) >> crustacean

Shropshire, sometimes abbreviated **Salop** pop (1995e) 417 000; area 3490 sq km/1347 sq mi. County in WC England; county town, Shrewsbury; Wrekin a unitary authority from 1998; Ironbridge Gorge open-air museum. >> England ℹ; Ironbridge; Shrewsbury

Shroud of Turin >> **Holy Shroud**

Shrove Tuesday In the UK, the day before the beginning of Lent, so called because traditionally on that day Christians went to confession and were 'shriven' (absolved from their sins). Shrove Tuesday is often known as **Pancake Day** from the custom of making pancakes on that day. >> Lent; Mardi Gras

shrub A woody perennial plant, usually differentiated from a **tree** by being smaller and having a trunk which produces branches at or near the base; but the distinction is far from clear-cut, and some large shrubs are essentially small trees. >> tree ℹ

shuffleboard A game in which discs are sent moving by hand or with an implement along a board or court, so that they come to a halt within a predetermined area. Today, a version of the game, also called **shovelboard**, is a popular deck sport aboard ship. Another version of the game, known as **shove-halfpenny**, is played on a small board in English pubs, where coins or small discs must be pushed so as to stop between narrowly ruled lines.

Shull, Clarence G (1915–) Physicist, born in Pittsburgh, PA. He shared the Nobel Prize for Physics in 1994 for his work in the field of neutron scattering.

Shultz, George P(ratt) (1920–) US secretary of state (1982–9), born in New York City. He was named secretary of labor by President Nixon (1969), and went on to hold a number of high governmental posts before returning to private life in 1974. In 1982 President Reagan made him secretary of state. >> Nixon, Richard M; Reagan, Ronald

Shute, Nevil, pseudonym of **Nevil Shute Norway** (1899–1960) Writer, born in Ealing, Greater London. After World War 2, he emigrated to Australia, which became the setting for most of his later books, notably *A Town Like Alice* (1949), and *On the Beach* (1957).

shuttle 1 In spinning, a spindle-shaped device holding a bobbin, used to carry the crosswise threads (*weft*) through the lengthwise threads (*warp*) during weaving. >> spinning **2** >> space shuttle

Shwe Dagon Pagoda An important Buddhist pilgrimage site in Yangon (Rangoon), Myanmar. It consists of a magnificent gold-plated shrine (*stupa*) 98 m/326 ft high. >> Buddha; Yangon

Shwezigon Pagoda A pagoda erected in the 11th-c near Pagan, Myanmar, as a reliquary shrine for a tooth and a bone of the Buddha. >> Buddha

sial [**siy**al] The silica and alumina-rich upper part of the Earth's crust which makes up the bulk of the continents and overlies the sima. >> alumina; Earth ℹ; silica; sima

Sialkot [**syal**koht] 32°29N 74°35E, pop (1995e) 445 000. City in E Pakistan; railway; mausoleum of Sikh apostle Nanak. >> Pakistan ℹ

Siam >> **Thailand** ℹ

siamang [**siy**amang] A gibbon (*Hylobates syndactylus*) native to Malaysia and Sumatra; the largest gibbon (armspan of 1.5 m/5 ft); throat with large red balloon-like vocal sac. >> gibbon

Siamese cat A domestic cat of the *foreign short-haired* variety; many breeds, some called **Siamese** in Britain, **short-hair** in the USA; lean, with a triangular face and blue eyes; coat pale with darker *points* (ie face, legs, and tail). >> cat

Siamese twins A fault in embryological development in which identical twins are born physically joined together. The deformity ranges from one in which the twins may merely share one umbilical cord to one in which heads or trunks are joined together and cannot be separated. The name derives from the first twins in whom the condition was recognized in modern times, Chang and Eng (1811–74), born in Siam (modern Thailand). >> embryology

Sian >> **Xian**

Sibelius, Jean (Julius Christian) [si**bay**lius] (1865–1957) Composer, born in Tavastehus, Finland. A passionate nationalist, he wrote a series of symphonic poems based on episodes in the Finnish epic *Kalevala*. His major works include seven symphonies (he destroyed his eighth), symphonic poems – notably *Finlandia* (1899) – and a violin concerto. >> Kalevala

Siberia area c.7 511 000 sq km/2 900 000 sq mi. Vast geographic region of Asiatic Russia, comprising the N third of Asia; **W Siberian Lowlands** stretch over 1500 km/1000 mi from the Ural Mts (W) to the R Yenisey (E); **C Siberian Plateau** lies between the R Yenisey (W) and the R Lena (E); **E Siberian Highlands**, including the Altay Mts, rise to 4506 m/14 783 ft at Gora Belukha; rivers include the Ob, Yenisey, Lena; extreme continental climate; average winter temperatures generally below −18°C; tundra extends c.320 km/200 mi inland along the Arctic coast; chief cities (Novosibirsk, Omsk, Krasnoyarsk, Irkutsk, Khabarovsk, Vladivostok) lie on the Trans-Siberian Railway; used as a penal colony and place of exile for political prisoners; dramatic economic development under the 5-year plans, relying heavily on forced labour and population resettlement to establish mining, industrial, and agricultural installations. >> Asia; Kamchatka; Russia ℹ; Trans-Siberian Railway; tundra

Sibyl or **Sibylla** In Roman legend, a prophetess who uttered mysterious wisdom. The **Sybilline Books** were nine books of prophecy offered by the Sybil to Tarquinus Priscus. >> Apollo

Sicilian Vespers The wholesale massacre of the French in Sicily which began the Sicilian revolt against Charles of Anjou. It was so called because the first killings occurred in a church outside Palermo at vespers (evensong) on Easter Monday, 1282. >> Angevins

Sicily, Ital **Sicilia** pop (1995e) 5 010 000; area 25 708 sq km/9923 sq mi. Largest and most populous island in the Mediterranean, separated from the mainland of Italy by the narrow Strait of Messina; length 288 km/179 mi; width 192 km/119 mi; settled by the Greeks, 8th-c BC; province of Rome, 2nd-c BC; Norman conquest, 11th-c; conquest by Aragon, 1282; Kingdom of the Two Sicilies, 1815; conquest by Garibaldi, 1860, and unification with Italy; capital, Palermo; mountainous, average height 450 m/1450 ft; large earthquake zone on E coast, culminating in Mt Etna (3390 m/11 122 ft), highest point; an under-developed area, with considerable poverty; intensive vegetable growing, fruit, wine in fertile coastal areas; arable and pastoral farming in dry interior. >> Etna,

Mount; Garibaldi; Italy ℹ; Mafia; Messina, Strait of; Palermo; Sicilian Vespers

Sickert, Walter (Richard) (1860–1942) Artist, born in Munich, Germany. The Camden Town Group (later the London Group) was formed under his leadership c.1910, and he became a major influence on later English painters. >> Camden Town Group

sickle cell disease An inherited chemical abnormality of haemoglobin, in which the red cells contain haemoglobin S instead of the normal haemoglobin A. As a result the cells become sickle-shaped in place of their normal biconcave circular form. Such cells do not survive as long in the circulation, and anaemia is common. The disease is common in Africa. >> haemoglobin

Siddons, Sarah, *née* **Kemble** (1755–1831) Actress, born in Brecon, Powys, the eldest child of Roger Kemble. A member of her father's theatre company from childhood, she became the unquestioned queen of the stage, unmatched as a tragic actress. >> Kemble

side drum A shallow drum with a skin at each end, the upper one struck with a pair of wooden sticks, the lower fitted with *snares* (strings of metal or gut) which, when engaged, give the tone a rasping edge. It is worn slightly to one side when marching (hence the name). >> drum; percussion ℹ; tabor

sidereal time Time measured by considering the rotation of the Earth relative to the distant stars (rather than to the Sun, which is the basis of civil time). >> solar time; time

sidewinder A snake which moves by pushing its head forward onto the ground, then winding the body forwards and sideways until it lies stretched out to one side; meanwhile the head is moved forward again. Repeating this behaviour allows the snake to move rapidly over soft sand. *Crotalus cerastes* (the North American horned rattlesnake) usually uses sidewinding, and is commonly called the **sidewinder**.

Sidi bel Abbès [**si**dee bel a**bes**] 35°15N 0°39W, pop (1995e) 227 000. Town in N Algeria; headquarters of the French Foreign Legion until 1962; railway. >> Algeria ℹ

Sidmouth (of Sidmouth), Henry Addington, 1st Viscount [**sid**muhth] (1757–1844) British Tory statesman and prime minister (1801–4), born in London. His administration negotiated the Peace of Amiens (1802). He later became home secretary under Liverpool (1812–21). >> Liverpool, Earl of; Napoleonic Wars

Sidney, Algernon (1622–83) English Whig politician, born in Penshurst, Kent. An extreme Republican, he fought in the Civil War, and after the Restoration lived on the Continent for some years. In 1683, he was implicated in the Rye House Plot, and beheaded. >> English Civil War; Rye House Plot; Whigs

Sidney, Sir Philip (1554–86) Poet, born in Penshurst, Kent. His literary work, written 1578–82, was not published until after his death. It includes the unfinished pastoral romance *Arcadia*, the *Defence of Poesie*, and a sonnet cycle, *Astrophel and Stella*. >> pastoral

Sidon [**siy**dn] 33°32N 35°22E, pop (1995e) 28 900. Seaport in W Lebanon; founded in the third millennium BC; once noted for its glass and purple dyes; railway; Crusader castle. >> Lebanon ℹ

Siegfried Line [**zeeg**freed] Name given by the Allies in World War 2 to a fortified line of pill boxes and minefields set up in the 1930s along the W frontier of Germany. It provided respite to retreating German forces in 1944, but was breached by the Allies in 1945, and totally dismantled after the war. >> World War 2

siemens [**see**mnz] SI unit of electrical conductance; symbol *S*; defined as 1 divided by resistance as measured in ohms. >> resistance; Siemens

Siemens, (Ernst) Werner von [**zee**mens] (1816–92) Engineer, born in Lenthe, Germany. He developed the telegraphic system in Prussia, devised several forms of galvanometer, and determined the electrical resistance of different substances. His brother **(Karl) Wilhelm Siemens** (1823–83, known as **(Charles) William**, upon moving to England in 1844), invented a new steel-making technique in 1861. >> blast furnace ℹ; siemens

Siena [**syay**na], ancient **Suene Julia** 43°19N 11°19E, pop (1995e) 64 900. City in Tuscany, C Italy; founded by the Etruscans; centre of the Ghibelline faction and a rival of Florence, 12th-c; influential centre of mediaeval art; archbishopric; university (1240); major tourist city; cathedral (12th–14th-c); town hall (13th-c) with tower, Torre del Mangia (14th-c). >> Catherine of Siena, St; Ghibellines; Sienese School; Tuscany

Sienese School A school of art which flourished in Siena in the 14th-c and early 15th-c. It has deep roots in the Gothic and Byzantine traditions. >> Duccio di Buoninsegna; Lorenzetti; Martini; Siena

Sierra Club A US private, non-profit conservation organization. It was founded by the US naturalist and writer, John Muir (1838–1914) in 1892. >> conservation (earth sciences)

Sierra Leone [**sye**ra lee**ohn**], official name **Republic of Sierra Leone** pop (1995e) 4 719 000; area 71 740 sq km/ 27 692 sq mi. Coastal republic in W Africa; capital, Freetown; timezone GMT; population chiefly African (eg Mende, Temne); chief religions, Islam (60%), local beliefs (30%); official language, English, with Krio widely spoken; unit of currency, the leone; length, 322 km/200 mi; width 290 km/180 mi; low narrow coastal plain; highest point, Loma Mansa (1948 m/6391 ft); equatorial climate, with a rainy season (May–Oct); first visited by Portuguese navigators and British slave traders; land bought from local chiefs by English philanthropists who established settlements for freed slaves, 1780s; British Crown Colony, 1808; hinterland declared a British protectorate, 1896; independence, 1961; republic, 1971; referendum, 1991, in favour of multiparty democracy; governed by a president, cabinet, and

House of Representatives; military coup, 1992; further military coup, 1997, overturned 1998; renewed fighting in early 1999; mining is the most important sector of the economy; diamonds represent c.60% of exports; over 70% of the population involved in subsistence agriculture. >> Freetown; slave trade; RR1021 political leaders

Sierra Nevada (Spain) [**sye**ra nay**vah**tha] Mountain range in Andalusia, S Spain, rising to 3478 m/11 411 ft at Mulhacén, the highest peak in continental Spain. >> Spain ℹ

Sierra Nevada (USA) [**sye**ra ne**vah**da] Mountain range in W USA, mainly in E California; extends 725 km/450 mi between the Cascade and Coastal Ranges; highest point in the USA outside Alaska, Mt Whitney (4418 m/14 495 ft). >> California

Sierra Nevada de Mérida [**sye**ruh nay**vah**thuh thay **may**reethuh] Mountain range in W Venezuela; length, 500 km/300 mi; rises to 5007 m/16 427 ft at Pico Bolívar, highest peak in Venezuela. >> Venezuela ℹ

sievert [**see**vert] In radioactivity, the SI unit of dose equivalent, equal to absorbed dose multiplied by the relative biological effectiveness; symbol *Sv*; it is used in radiation safety measurements. >> radioactivity units ℹ

Sieyès, Emmanuel Joseph, comte de (Count of) [syayes], also known as **Abbé Sieyès** (1748–1836) French political theorist and clergyman, born in Fréjus, France. He became a member of the National Convention, the Committee of Public Safety (1795) and the Directory. In 1799, he helped to organize the revolution of 18th Brumaire, becoming a member of the Consulate. He was exiled at the Restoration (1815), returning to Paris after the July Revolution. >> French Revolution ℹ; July Revolution

sifaka [si**fa**ka] A leaping lemur; long silky hair and long tail; small gliding membranes from arms to sides of body; can leap 10 m/33 ft between trees. (Genus: *Propithecus*, 2 species.) >> lemur

sigillography >> **seal** (communication)

Signac, Paul [seenyak] (1863–1935) Artist, born in Paris. With Seurat he developed Divisionism (but using mosaic-like patches of pure colour rather than Seurat's pointillist dots), mainly in seascapes. >> Divisionism; Seurat

sign language A communication system in which manual signs are used to express a corresponding range of meanings to those conveyed by spoken or written language. The most widely used are those which have developed naturally in a deaf community, such as the American, British, French, and Swedish Sign Languages. Contrary to popular belief, such languages are not mutually intelligible, as they use different signs and rules of sentence structure. >> American Sign Language; dactylology

Signorelli, Luca [seenyaw**rel**ee], also known as **Luca da Cortona** (c.1441–1523) Painter, born in Cortona, Italy. The cathedral at Orvieto contains his greatest work, the frescoes of 'The Preaching of Anti-Christ' and 'The Last Judgment' (1500–4). >> fresco

Sigurd [**see**gerd] In Norse mythology, the son of Sigmund the Volsung, who kills Fafnir the dragon and wins Brunhild. Virtually the same story is told of **Siegfried** [**zeeg**freed] in German legends. >> Nibelungen

Sihanouk, Prince Norodom [**see**anook] (1922–) Cambodian leader, born in Phnom Penh. He was King of Cambodia (1941–55), chief of state (1960–70, and of the Khmer Republic 1975–6), prime minister on several occasions between 1952 and 1968, president of the government in exile (1970–5, 1982–91), president (1991–3), and once again king (1993–). His return to Cambodia in 1991 followed the signing of the peace treaty ending 13 years of civil war, and he was crowned king under the new constitution in 1993. >> Cambodia ℹ; Pol Pot

sika [**see**ka] A true deer (*Cervus nippon*) native to E Asia; brown (with pale spots in summer) with white rump; white spot halfway down rear leg; long antlers; also known as **Japanese deer**. >> deer

Sikhism [**seek**izm] A religion founded by the Guru Nanak (1469–1539) in the Punjab area of N India. It is called a religion of the gurus, and seeks union with God through worship and service. God is the true Guru, and his divine word has come to humanity through the 10 historical gurus. The line ended in 1708, since when the Sikh community is called guru. The Adi Granth, their sacred scripture, is also called a guru. There were over 23 million Sikhs in 1999. >> Adi Granth; guru; Punjab (India); religion

Sikh Wars [seek] Two campaigns (1845–6, 1848–9) between the British and the Sikhs which led to the British conquest and annexation of the Punjab, NW India (Mar 1849).

Sikkim [**sik**im] pop (1995e) 439 000; area 7300 sq km/2817 sq mi. State in NE India, in the E Himalayas; part of British Empire, 1866–1947; protectorate of India, 1950; voted to become a state, 1975; capital, Gangtok; governed by an Assembly; inhabited mostly by Lepchas, Bhutias, and Nepalis; state religion, Mahayana Buddhism, but many of the population are Hindu. >> India ℹ

Sikorski, Władysław (Eugeniusz) [si**kaw(r)**skee] (1881–1943) Polish general, statesman, and prime minister (1922–3), born in Galicia. In World War 2, he became commander of the Free Polish forces and from 1940 premier of the Polish government in exile in London. A national hero, his body was returned to Poland in 1993, and given a state funeral. >> Piłsudski; Poland ℹ

Sikorsky, Igor (Ivan) [si**kaw(r)**skee] (1889–1972) Aeronautical engineer, born in Kiev, Ukraine. He built and flew the first four-engined aeroplane (1913), and in 1939 produced the first successful helicopter. >> aeronautics

silage A fodder made from grass, maize, or other leafy material, and preserved in an airtight tower-silo or silage pit. Initial fermentation creates organic and amino acids, which act as preservatives. >> fermentation

Silbury Hill An artificial chalk mound, 40 m/130 ft high, erected c.2700 BC near Avebury, Wiltshire, in S England. Probably prehistoric Europe's largest barrow, it was an estimated 18 million man-hours in construction. >> Avebury

Silchester One of the three main Belgic towns of pre-Roman Britain, situated SW of Reading, S England. It was a prosperous place in Roman times until its mysterious abandonment at an unknown date.

Silenus [siy**lee**nuhs] In Greek mythology, a demi-god, who fostered and educated Dionysus. He is represented as a festive old man, usually quite drunk. >> Dionysus

Silesia [si**lee**zha], Czech **Slezsko**, Polish **Śląsk**, Ger **Schlesien** Region of EC Europe on both banks of the R Oder in SW Poland, N Czech Republic, and SE Germany; disputed area between Austria and Prussia, 17th–18th-c; divided into Upper and Lower Silesia, 1919; greater part granted to Poland, 1945; a largely industrial region. >> Czech Republic ℹ; Poland ℹ

silhouette A technique of paper cut-out picture popularized by French finance minister Etienne de Silhouette (1709–67) and used for cheap miniature portraits until the rise of photography in the mid-19th-c. The term is often extended to cover any type of dark image against a light background, or light on dark, as in Greek vase-painting.

silica Silicon dioxide (SiO_2), the main constituent of the Earth's crust, occurring in nature as pure minerals or combined with other elements in silicate minerals. >> chalcedony; opal; quartz; sial; silicate minerals; sima

silicate minerals A group of minerals constituting about 95% of the Earth's crust, and containing silicon and oxygen combined with one or more other elements. They are classified according to the degree of polymerization, from silicates containing isolated SiO_4 groups (eg olivines, gar-nets) to rings (eg beryl) to chain silicates (eg pyroxenes), sheets (eg micas, clays), and three-dimensional frameworks (eg quartz, feldspars). >> polymerization; silicon

silicon Si, element 14, melting point 1 410°C. A grey solid non-metal, the second most common element, 26% by weight, it is the second element in the carbon group, and like carbon it forms mainly covalent compounds, with a valence of 4. It does not occur uncombined in nature. Very pure silicon is widely used in electronic devices. It is also doped with controlled amounts of aluminium, phosphorus, and other elements to alter its conductivity. Silicates are the main constituents of brick, stone, cement, and glass. >> carbon; chemical elements; silicon carbide; silicone; RR1036

silicon carbide SiC. A compound produced by fusing a mixture of carbon and silica; also known as **carborundum**. It is high-melting and hard, and is used mainly as an abrasive. >> carbon; silica

silicon chip A very small slice of silicon, a few millimetres square, on which many electronic circuits containing many components are built; also called an **integrated circuit**. Silicon chips are reliable and cheap to produce in large numbers, and they are now used in computers, calculators, many modern programmed household appliances, and in most electronic applications. >> computer; integrated circuit; silicon

silicone An open-chain or cyclic polymer containing the repeating unit $-SiR_2-O-$. Odourless, colourless, insoluble in and unreactive with water, and having high flashpoints, silicones are used in high-temperature lubricants, hydraulic fluids, and varnishes. >> polymerization; silicon

Silicon Valley Santa Clara County, W California, USA, between Palo Alto and San José; a world centre for electronics, computing, and database systems. >> California; microelectronics; silicon

silicosis [sili**koh**sis] An industrial disease of such occupations as mining, stone dressing, and sand blasting, and of the ceramics industry. It results from the inhalation of fine particles of silica which induce scarring of the lungs. >> occupational diseases; silica

silk A very fine fibre obtained from the cocoons of silkworms. The rearing of silkworms (**sericulture**) originated in China before 1100 BC; and Japan and China now provide most of the high-quality cultivated silk. The fabrics are renowned for their lustre, drape, and handle. >> fibre; silkworm

Silk Road Ancient trade route from E China to C Asia and Europe; in exchange for silk, China received grapes, cotton, chestnuts, lucerne, and pomegranates; Chinese techniques for silkworm breeding, iron-smelting, paper-making, and irrigation spread W. >> China ℹ; Ferghana; silk

silk-screen >> **screen-process printing**

silkworm The larva of the common silk moth, *Bombyx mori*, which spins the silk cocoon from which commercial silk is derived. The cocoon is unwound mechanically, after softening, and each may contain up to 3 km/2 mi of silk. (Order: Lepidoptera. Family: Bombycidae.) >> larva; moth; silk

sill A sheet-like body of igneous rock that has been intruded between layers of sedimentary rock. It is usually composed of medium-grained rock, typically dolerite. Examples include the Whin Sill in N England. >> dolerite; igneous rock; intrusive rock

Sillitoe, Alan [**sil**itoh] (1928–) Novelist, born in Nottingham, Nottinghamshire. His first and most popular novel was *Saturday Night and Sunday Morning* (1958), followed by *The Loneliness of the Long Distance Runner* (1959, filmed 1962). Later novels include *Leonard's War* (1991), *Snowdrop* (1993), and *Leading the Blind* (1995). An autobiography, *Life Without Armour*, appeared in 1995.

Silone, Ignazio [si**loh**nay], pseudonym of **Secondo Tranquilli** (1900–78) Novelist, born in Aquilo, Italy. His books include *Fontamara* (1933), *Pane e vino* (1937, Bread and Wine), and *Il seme sotto la neve* (1941, The Seed Beneath the Snow).

silt The aggregate of fine mineral particles produced by the erosion and weathering of rock, in size intermediate between clay and sand. Silt deposits are laid down by water, and may consolidate to form the sedimentary rock **siltstone**. >> clay; sand

Silurian period [siy**loo**rian] The third of the geological periods of the Palaeozoic era, extending from c.435 to 408 million years ago. The earliest land plants appeared. >> geological time scale; Ordovician period; Palaeozoic era; RR976

Silvanus or **Sylvanus** [sil**vay**nus, sil**vah**nus] In Roman religion, the god of uncultivated land, especially woodland. He was therefore strange, and dangerous, like Pan. >> Pan

silver Ag (Lat *argentum*), element 47, melting point 961°C. A lustrous transition metal, relatively rare, but occurring uncombined in nature. Of all elements, it is the best conductor of electricity. Long used extensively in coinage, it has now become too expensive for that purpose. Much used in jewellery and medals, its compounds are also used in photography. >> chemical elements; metal; RR1036

silver birch A slender, elegant, short-lived species of birch (*Betula pendula*) reaching 15–18 m/50–60 ft, with distinctive silvery-white bark. Native to Europe, it is often planted for ornament. (Family: Betulaceae.) >> birch

silver fir An evergreen conifer native to the temperate N hemisphere; foliage often silvery or bluish; needles leathery; widely grown for timber and as ornamentals; its resin yields *Canada balsam*. (Genus: *Abies*, 50 species. Family: Pinaceae.) >> conifer; evergreen plants; resin

silverfish A tapering, primitively wingless insect covered with silvery white scales; tail 3-pronged; commonly found in houses; active at night, moves swiftly. (Order: Thysanura. Family: Lepismatidae.) >> insect ℹ

silver fox >> **red fox**

silver Persian >> **chinchilla cat**

silver plate A term applied to goods made of silver of sterling standard, established by law in England in the 13th-c. Hallmarking was introduced from 1300. It should not be confused with the various 19th-c techniques of **silver plating**, which involved a thin skin of sterling silver applied to base metal. >> hallmarks ℹ; silver

silverpoint A technique used by artists for drawing on paper, popular in the Renaissance, but afterwards superseded by the invention of the graphite pencil. The paper is coated with Chinese white paint and the drawing made with a slim metal point (silver, gold, copper, or lead).

Silves [**seel**vish] 37°11N 8°26W, pop (1995e) 10 600. Town in the Algarve, S Portugal; on R Arade; former Moorish capital; Moorish castle, cathedral (12th–13th-c). >> Algarve

sima [**siy**ma] The silica and magnesia-rich lower part of the crust which underlies the sial of the continents and forms the bulk of the oceanic crust. >> Earth ℹ; magnesium; sial; silica

Simbirsk [sim**birsk**], formerly **Ulyanovsk** (1924–91) 54°19N 48°22E, pop (1995e) 675 000. River port in WC European Russia; founded as a fortress, 1648; airfield; railway; birthplace of Lenin; renamed after his family name, Ulyanov. >> Lenin; Russia ℹ

Simenon, Georges (Joseph Christian) [**see**menõ] (1903–89) Crime novelist, born in Liège, Belgium. He revolutionized detective fiction with his tough, morbidly psychological Inspector Maigret series, beginning in 1933.

Simeon Stylites, St [stiy**liy**teez] (387–459) The earliest of the Christian ascetic 'pillar' saints. Revered as a miracle-worker, he separated himself from the people c.420 by establishing himself on top of a pillar c.20 m/70 ft high at Telanessa, near Antioch, where he spent the rest of his life preaching to crowds. He had many imitators, known as *stylites*. Feast day 5 January (W), September (E).

simile >> **metaphor**

Simla [**sim**la] 31°07N 77°09E. Hill station in N India; altitude c.2200 m/7100 ft; established in 1819 as former summer capital of British India. >> India [i]

Simmons, Jean (1929–) Film actress, born in London. She made her film debut in 1942, and moved to Hollywood in 1950. Her films include *The Robe* (1953), *Guys and Dolls* (1955), and *Spartacus* (1960), and during the 1980s she appeared in several television productions, including *The Thorn Birds* (1983).

Simnel, Lambert (c.1475–c.1535) English imposter, a joiner's son, who in 1487 was set up in Ireland, first as a son of Edward IV, and then as the Duke of Clarence's son, Edward, Earl of Warwick (1475–99), who was imprisoned in the Tower. Crowned at Dublin as 'Edward VI' (1487), he landed in Lancashire with 2000 German mercenaries, and was defeated at Stoke, Nottinghamshire. >> Edward IV; Henry VII

Simon, Claude (Eugène Henri) [seemõ] (1913–) Novelist, born in Antananarivo, Madagascar. His novels include *Le Vent* (1957, The Wind), *L'Herbe* (1958, The Grass), and *Le Palace* (1962, The Palace). He received the Nobel Prize for Literature in 1985.

Simon (of Stackpole Elidor), John (Allsebrook) Simon, 1st Viscount (1873–1954) British Liberal statesman and lawyer, born in Manchester. He was home secretary (1915–16), before resigning in opposition to conscription. He formed the Liberal National Party, supporting MacDonald's coalition governments, and became foreign secretary (1931–5), home secretary (1935–7), Chancellor of the Exchequer (1937–40), and Lord Chancellor (1940–5). >> Churchill, Winston; Liberal Party (UK); MacDonald, Ramsey

Simon, (Marvin) Neil (1927–) Playwright, born in New York City. His first Broadway Show, *Catch a Star!*, opened in 1955, and a series of long-running successes followed in the 1960s, including *The Odd Couple* (1965). His later work includes *Biloxi Blues* (1985, Tony), *Lost in Yonkers* (1991, Pulitzer, Tony), and *London Suite* (1995).

Simon, Paul (1941–) Singer, songwriter, and guitarist, born in Forest Hills, NY. He teamed up with Art Garfunkel at the age of 15. Their first big hit, 'The Sound Of Silence' (1964), was followed in 1968 by the film *The Graduate*, with songs written by Simon, and they had a major success with the album *Bridge Over Troubled Water* (1970). His solo career, using Third-World choirs and percussionists, led to one of the most successful albums of the 1980s, *Graceland* (1986). >> Garfunkel; pop music

Simon Magus [**may**gus], Eng **Simon the Magician** (1st-c) Practitioner of magic arts, who appears in Samaria c.37 well known for his sorceries. His offer to buy the gift of the Holy Ghost was condemned by Peter. The term *simony* derives from his name. >> Peter, St; simony

Simon Peter >> **Peter, St**

simony [**sim**onee] The practice of giving or acquiring some sacred object, spiritual gift, or religious office for money, or carrying on a trade in such matters. The practice was most notorious in the mediaeval practice of trading in indulgences. >> indulgences; Simon Magus

Simplon Pass, Ital **Passa del Sempione** Mountain pass between Brig, Switzerland and Domodossola, Italy, over the S Bernese Alps; height, 2006 m/6581 ft; built on the orders of Napoleon, 1801–5; rail tunnel (20 km/12 mi) opened in 1906.

Simpson, N(orman) F(rederick) (1919–) Playwright, born in London. The success of *A Resounding Tinkle*, a zany disruption of middle-class normality, brought him to prominence. His absurdist approach is also seen in *One-Way Pendulum* (1959).

Simpson Desert Desert in SE Northern Territory and SW Queensland, C Australia; area c.77 000 sq km/30 000 sq mi; first crossed in 1939 by Cecil Madigan. >> Australia [i]

simulator A mechanical, electromechanical, or computer device for producing a realistic representation of an event or system. It is used where the real thing is very expensive and inaccessible, and to train operators (eg aircraft pilots) in safety. Computers are also used to simulate complex phenomena where there are many variables, such as in atmospheric circulation studies. >> computer

simultaneity >> **special relativity** [i]

sin A religious term signifying purposeful disobedience to the known will of God or an action offensive to God. The Hebrew Bible represents sin as a constant element in the experience of Israel. There is an emphasis upon human responsibility, and this is carried over into Christian doctrine, where it is joined with the idea of the inevitability of sin in the concept of **original sin**. Islam identifies two types of sin: inadvertent or accidental sins and wilful transgressions. Unlike Christianity, Islam does not have a concept of original sin. >> Bible; Christianity; God; Islam; Judaism; original sin

Sinai [**siy**niy] pop (1995e) 226 000; area 60 174 sq km/23 227 sq mi. Desert peninsula in NE Egypt; bounded by Israel and Gulf of Aqaba (E) and Egypt and Gulf of Suez (W); N coastal plain rises S to mountains reaching 2637 m/8651 ft at Mt Catherine, Egypt's highest point, and Mt Sinai, 2286 m/7500 ft; capital, al-Arish; taken by Israel, 1967; returned to Egypt following the peace agreement, 1984. >> Arab–Israeli Wars; Egypt [i]; Sinai, Mount

Sinai, Mount [**siy**niy] Mountain of uncertain location, traditionally placed in the S Sinai peninsula, but sometimes located in Arabia E of the Gulf of Aqaba; also called **Horeb** in the Hebrew Bible. According to the Book of Exodus, this is where God revealed himself to Moses, and made a covenant with Israel. >> Moses; Sinai; Ten Commandments

Sinanthropus [sin**an**thropus] >> **Peking Man**

Sinatra, Frank, popular name of **Francis Albert Sinatra** (1915–98) Singer and actor, born in Hoboken, NJ. One of the greatest singers of popular songs, he began in the 1940s, made several hit records, and starred on radio and in movies. His appeal disappeared for some years, then was revived by his memorable acting in the movie *From Here to Eternity* (1953). He produced his masterworks in a series of recordings (1956–65), especially the albums *Songs for Swinging Lovers*, *Come Fly With Me*, and *That's Life*. His personal life always proved noteworthy, with turbulent marriages to Ava Gardner and Mia Farrow, among others, and alleged Mafia connections.

Sinclair, Upton (Beall) (1878–1968) Novelist, born in Baltimore, MD. He found success with his novel exposing meat-packing conditions in Chicago, *The Jungle* (1906). Later novels, such as *King Coal* (1917), became increasingly moulded by his socialist beliefs. >> socialism

Sind pop (1995e) 28 029 000; area 140 914 sq km/54 393 sq mi. Province in SE Pakistan; capital, Karachi; fertile land dissected by the R Indus; arrival of Islam, 8th-c; part of the Chandragupta Ganges Empire and the Delhi Empire; under British rule, 1843; autonomous province, 1937; province of Pakistan, 1947; agricultural economy. >> Pakistan [i]

sinfonietta An orchestral piece, usually in several movements but on a smaller scale than a symphony. The term is also used for a chamber orchestra, such as the London Sinfonietta (founded 1968). >> symphony

Singapore, official name **Republic of Singapore** pop (1995e) 2 963 000; area 618 sq km/238 sq mi. Republic at the S tip of the Malay Peninsula, SE Asia; consists of the island of Singapore and about 50 adjacent islets; capital, Singapore City; timezone GMT +8; ethnic groups include Chinese (77%), Malay (15%); Chinese mainly Buddhists, Malays mainly Muslims; chief languages, English, Malay, Chinese, Tamil; unit of currency, the Singapore dollar of 100 cents; Singapore I, c.42 km/26 mi by 22 km/14 mi at its widest points; low-lying, rising to 177 m/581 ft at Bukit Timah; deep-water harbour (SE); equatorial climate; high humidity; originally part of the Sumatran Srivijaya kingdom; leased by the British East India Company from the Sultan of Johore, 1819; Singapore, Malacca, and Penang incorporated as the Straits Settlements, 1826; British Crown Colony, 1867; occupied by the Japanese, 1942–5; self-government, 1959; part of the Federation of Malaya, 1963; independence, 1965; governed by a president, primeministe, and single-chamber parliament; major transshipment centre. >> Malaysia ℹ; Raffles; Singapore City; RR1021 political leaders

Singapore City 1°20N 103°50E. Seaport capital of Singapore; one of the world's busiest ports; third largest oil refining centre; distribution base for many international companies; first container port in SE Asia, 1972; airport; railway; two universities (1953, 1964). >> Singapore ℹ

Singer, Isaac Bashevis (1904–91) Yiddish writer, born in Radzymin, Poland. He sets his books among the Jews of Poland, Germany, and America, such as *The Family Moskat* (1950) and *The Magician of Lublin* (1960). He was awarded the Nobel Prize for Literature in 1978. >> Yiddish

Singer, Isaac (Merritt) (1811–75) Inventor and manufacturer of sewing machines, born in Pittstown, NY. At Boston in 1852 he devised an improved single-thread, chain-stitch sewing machine. His company became the largest producer of sewing machines in the world.

Singer, Peter (Albert David) (1946–) Philosopher, born in Melbourne, Victoria, Australia. His writing focuses on ethics, particularly in relation to animals and the environment. Also known as a political activist, his best known works, *Animal Liberation* (1977) and *Practical Ethics* (1979), were still exercising influence in the 1990s.

single lens reflex (SLR) A popular and versatile design of camera, with a surface-silvered mirror behind the lens angled at 45° to reflect the image onto a focusing screen. The camera lens is used both for the viewfinder system and for taking the photograph. Focusing is precise, and framing is free from parallax, so that 'what you see is what you get' in the picture. >> camera; lens

Singspiel [**zing**shpeel] A German opera with spoken dialogue. Mozart's *Die Zauberflöte* (The Magic Flute) is a famous example. >> Mozart; opera

Sinhalese [singga**leez**] The dominant ethnic group (74%) of Sri Lanka; descended from N Indians who came to the area in the 5th-c BC. They are predominantly Buddhist. >> Sri Lanka ℹ

Sinitic languages >> **Chinese**

Sinn Féin [shin **fayn**] (Gaelic 'Ourselves Alone') An Irish political party founded in 1900 by Arthur Griffith in support of Irish independence from Britain. It formed a separate assembly from the UK parliament, and succeeded in creating the Irish Free State (1922). It split to form the two main Irish parties, and in 1970 it split again into official and provisional wings. It has remained active in Northern Ireland, and has close contacts with the Irish Republican Army. Sinn Féin obtained a high profile for its role in relation to the IRA ceasefire (1994), but conflict with the UK government over its attitude to the resumption of the IRA campaign (1996) led to its being excluded from all-party talks that year. The party was eventually invited to join the talks following the resumption of the IRA ceasefire (1997), and has since been fully involved in the negotiations over the new Assembly. >> Adams, Gerry; Fianna Fáil; Fine Gael; IRA; McGuinness

Sino-Japanese War (1894–5) A longstanding conflict between Chinese and Japanese interests in Korea. China suffered a humiliating defeat. **2** (1937–45) A war which broke out in 1937 with the Japanese invasion of Tianjin and Beijing, but this was only the ultimate phase of Japan's territorial designs on China, following the occupation of Manchuria in 1932. Most of N China came under Japanese control. The war ended with Japan's surrender in 1945. >> Manchukuo; United Fronts; World War 2

Sinope [siy**noh**pee] The outermost natural satellite of Jupiter, discovered in 1914; distance from the planet 23 700 000 km/14 727 000 mi; diameter 40 km/25 mi. >> Jupiter (astronomy); RR964

Sino-Tibetan languages A family of languages spoken in China, Tibet, and Myanmar (Burma). There are some 300 languages in the family. >> Chinese; Tibetan

sintering One of the techniques of powder metallurgy. Metal parts are made by forming a shape in metal powder and then holding it for several hours just below the melting point of the metal. It is an economical process for making small parts, and is necessary for metal which has so high a melting point that it cannot easily be cast. >> powder metallurgy

Sintra [**seen**tra], formerly **Cintra** 38°47N 9°25W, pop (1995e) 20 700. Small resort town in C Portugal; former summer residence of the Portuguese royal family; railway; National Palace (14th–15th-c), Moorish castle. >> Portugal ℹ

sinus [**siy**nuhs] In anatomy, a space within the head or elsewhere in the body. The air-filled **paranasal sinuses** all communicate with the nasal cavity, at the front of the face. The blood-filled **intracranial sinuses** are generally found between the layers of the outer membrane which surrounds the brain (the *dura mater*). >> brain ℹ; nose; sinusitis

sinusitis [siynyu**siy**tis] Infection of the lining of one or more sinuses around the nose and in the bones of the face. It sometimes arises from infection of the upper respiratory passages, and results in severe pain over the sinus, or headache with fever. >> sinus

Sion (Jerusalem) [**ziy**on] >> **Zion**

Sion (Switzerland) [syõ], Ger **Sitten** 46°14N 7°22E, pop (1995e) 26 300. Town in SW Switzerland; bishopric since the 6th-c; market town for the Rhône valley; brewing; railway;

former cathedral (10th–13th-c), bishop's fortress (1294). >> Switzerland [i]

Sioux [soo] or **Dakota** A cluster of Siouan-speaking North American Indian groups belonging to the Plains Indian culture. They were involved in clashes with advancing White settlers, and were finally defeated at Wounded Knee (1890). They now number c.103 000 (1990 census), living mostly on reservations. >> Plains Indians

Sioux Falls [soo] 43°33N 96°44W, pop (1995e) 106 000. City in SE South Dakota, USA, on Big Sioux R; largest city in the state; established, 1857; city status, 1883; airfield; railway; commercial centre in a livestock farming region. >> South Dakota

siphon / syphon A means of transferring liquid from one level to a lower level, relying on a liquid-filled tube, the siphon. Liquid moves through the pipe under the influence of gravity at a rate proportional to the difference in levels. >> fluid mechanics; gravitation

Siphonaptera [siyfon**ap**tera] >> **flea**

Siraj-ud-Daula [**si**raj ud **dow**la], originally **Mirza Muhammad** (c.1732–57) Ruler of Bengal under the nominal suzerainty of the Mughal Empire. He forced the British to surrender at Calcutta, which led to the infamous Black Hole, for which he was held responsible. Defeated at Plassey in 1857, he was captured and executed. >> Black Hole of Calcutta; Mughal Empire

siren A salamander native to SE North America; dark, eel-like body; length, up to 90 cm/36 in; no hind legs; tiny front legs; feathery gills. (Family: Sirenidae, 3 species.) >> salamander [i]

Sirens In Greek mythology, deceitful creatures, half-woman and half-bird, who lured sailors to death by their singing. Odysseus was able to sail past their island by stopping the ears of his crew with wax; and by having himself bound to the mast, was restrained when he heard their song. >> Odysseus

si-rex [**siy**reks] >> **rex**

Sirhan, (Bishara) Sirhan [sir**hahn**] >> **Kennedy, Robert F**

Sirius [**si**rius] The brightest star in our sky, and sixth nearest; also known as the **dog star**. It has a faint companion star, which was the first white dwarf star to be recognized as such. >> white dwarf; RR965

Sirocco / Scirocco [si**ro**koh] A wind similar to the Khamsin in origin, blowing from the Sahara Desert. As it crosses the Mediterranean Sea it picks up moisture, and arrives in S Europe as a moist, oppressive, warm wind. >> Khamsin; wind [i]

Sirte, Gulf of [**seer**tay], Arabic **Khalij Surt** Gulf in the Mediterranean Sea off the coast of N Libya; access is an area of dispute between Libya and the USA. >> Libya [i]

siskin A finch, found worldwide; eats seeds and insects. (Genus: *Carduelis*, 16 species, or *Serinus*, 2 species. Family: Fringillidae.) >> finch

Sisley, Alfred [seeslay] (1839–99) Impressionist painter and etcher, born in Paris. He painted landscapes almost exclusively, particularly in the valleys of the Seine, Loire, and Thames. >> Impressionism (art); landscape painting

Sistine Chapel [**sis**teen] A chapel in the Vatican, built in 1475–81 for Pope Sixtus IV. It is remarkable for a series of frescoes executed on its ceiling and altar wall by Michelangelo. >> Michelangelo; Vatican City

Sisyphus [**si**sifus] In Greek mythology, a Corinthian king who was a famous trickster. In the Underworld he was condemned to roll a large stone up a hill from which it always rolled down again.

sitar [si**tah(r)**] A large Indian lute, with a gourd resonator and a long fretted neck. The modern concert sitar is about 122 cm/4 ft long, with usually seven strings plucked with a wire plectrum. >> lute; plectrum; string instrument 2

Sites of Special Scientific Interest (SSSIs) Areas designated by English Nature for the purposes of conservation, including some of the UK's best examples of particular wildlife habitats, interesting geological features, and habitats for rare plants and animals. >> conservation (earth sciences); English Nature

Sitka National monument on W Baranof I, SE Alaska, USA; Indian stockade, totem poles, Russian blockhouse; established, 1910; town and naval base of Sitka nearby. >> Alaska

Sitting Bull, Sioux name **Tatanka Iyotake** (1834–90) Warrior and chief of the Dakota Sioux, born near Grand River, SD. He was a leader in the Sioux War of 1876–7, after which he escaped to Canada, but surrendered in 1881. He later toured with Buffalo Bill's Wild West Show. >> Cody, William F; Sioux

Sitwell, Dame Edith (1887–1964) Poet, born in Scarborough, North Yorkshire, the sister of Osbert and Sacheverell Sitwell. Her experimental poetry was controversially received with *Façade* (1922), which (with Walton's music) was given a stormy public reading in London. She became a Catholic in 1955, after which her works reflect a deeper religious symbolism, as in *The Outcasts* (1962). >> Walton, William

Sitwell, Sir Osbert (1892–1969) Writer, born in London, the brother of Edith and Sacheverell Sitwell. He acquired notoriety with his satirical novel of the Scarborough social scene, *Before the Bombardment* (1927). He is best known for his five-volume autobiographical series, beginning with *Left Hand: Right Hand* (1944).

Sitwell, Sir Sacheverell [sa**shev**erel] (1897–1988) Poet and art critic, born in Scarborough, North Yorkshire, the brother of Edith and Osbert Sitwell. His books on art and architecture include *Southern Baroque Art* (1924). His many volumes of poetry cover a period of over 30 years, from *The People's Palace* (1918) to *An Indian Summer* (1982).

SI units >> **RR1032**

Six, Les [lay **sees**] A group of composers united for about six years after 1917 to further the cause of modern French music. It comprised Germaine Tailleferre (1892–1983), Georges Auric, Louis Durey (1888–1979), Arthur Honegger, Darius Milhaud, and Francois Poulenc. >> Auric; Honegger; Milhaud; Poulenc

Six Day War >> **Arab–Israeli Wars**

sixth-form college A college in the UK for pupils over the age of 16 and up to 18 or 19. It specializes in A-level work, but other forms of examination and qualification may also be offered.

Sizewell Nuclear power station in Suffolk, E England; gas-cooled, graphite-moderated reactors came into operation

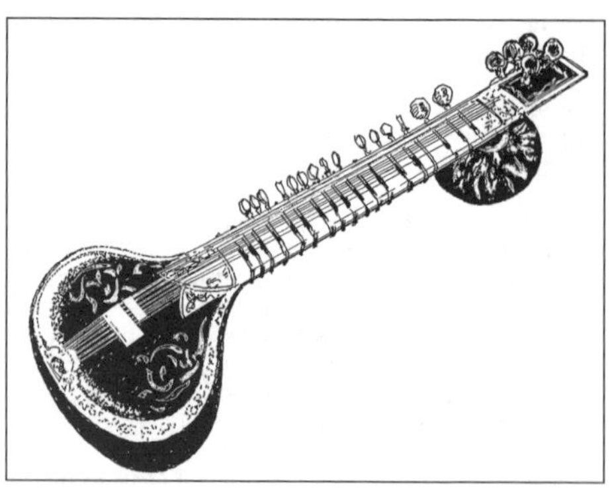

Sitar

in 1966; site of the first UK pressurized light-water-moderated and cooled reactor (**Sizewell B**). >> nuclear reactor ℹ; Suffolk

Sjælland [**shel**ahn] area 7500 sq km/2900 sq mi. Group of islands in Danish territorial waters, between Jutland and S Sweden. >> Denmark ℹ; Zealand

Skagerrak [**ska**gerak] Arm of the Atlantic Ocean linking the North Sea with the Baltic Sea; bounded (N) by Norway and (S) by Denmark; 240 km/150 mi long and 135 km/84 mi wide.

skaldic poetry (Old Norse *skaldr* 'poet') Poetry composed and recited by recognized individuals in Iceland and the Scandinavian countries between 800 and 1100. After this time, written versions made the *skaldr* redundant.

Skanda [**skahn**da] The Hindu god of War, the 'Attacker'. He is also responsible for the demons who bring diseases. >> Hinduism

Skanderbeg [**skan**derbek], nickname of **George Castriota** or **Kastrioti** (1405–68) Albanian patriot. In 1443 he drove the Turks from Albania, and for 20 years maintained Albanian independence. >> Albania ℹ

Skara Brae [**skah**ra **bray**] An exceptionally preserved Neolithic village of c.3100–2500 BC on the Bay of Skaill, Orkney, Scotland. It was exposed below sand dunes by storms in 1850. >> Three Age System

skate Any of several bottom-living rays of the family Rajidae; includes the large European species, *Raja batis*; length up to 2.5 m/8 ft, upper surface greenish-brown with lighter patches; fished commercially. >> ray

skateboarding Riding on land on a single flexible board, longer and wider than the foot, fixed with four small wheels on the underside. It developed as an alternative to surfing, and became very popular in the USA during the 1960s and in the UK during the 1970s and late 1980s.

skating >> **ice hockey; ice skating; roller skating**

Skegness [skeg**nes**] 53°10N 0°21E, pop (1995e) 18 800. Resort town in Lincolnshire, EC England; railway. >> Lincolnshire

skeleton The hardened tissues forming the supporting framework of plants and animals. In vertebrates it usually refers to the assembly and arrangement of bones. The **appendicular skeleton** comprises the bones of the limbs and the pelvic and pectoral girdles, while the **axial skeleton** comprises the bones of the vertebral column, skull, ribs, and sternum. >> bone; orthopaedics; osteopathy; Paget's disease

Skelton, John (c.1460–1529) Satirical poet, born in Norfolk. Court poet to Henry VII, and tutor to Prince Henry (VIII), he became known for his satirical vernacular poetry, such as *Colyn Cloute* (1522).

skepticism >> **scepticism**

sketchphone A system, linked to the telephone network, by which line drawings and sketches can be transmitted long distances to suitable receiving equipment. An electronic touch-sensitive screen sends sketches via a computer and the telephone line to a receiver. >> telephone

Skiathos [**skee**athos] area 48 sq km/18 sq mi. Island of the N Dodecanese, Greece; chief town, Skiathos; a popular holiday resort. >> Greece ℹ

Skiddaw [ski**daw**] 54°40N 3°08W. Mountain in the Lake District of Cumbria, NW England; rises to 928 m/3045 ft. >> Lake District

skiffle A type of popular music of the 1950s in which the washboard provided a distinctive timbre. It emanated from the USA, but the best-known singer was the Scot, Lonnie Donegan (1931–).

skiing The art of propelling oneself along on snow while standing on skis, and with the aid of poles, named from the Norwegian word *ski*, 'snow shoe'. **Alpine skiing** consists of the downhill and slaloms (zig-zag courses through markers), which are races against the clock. **Nordic skiing** incorporates cross-country skiing, the biathlon, and ski jumping. >> biathlon; RR1060

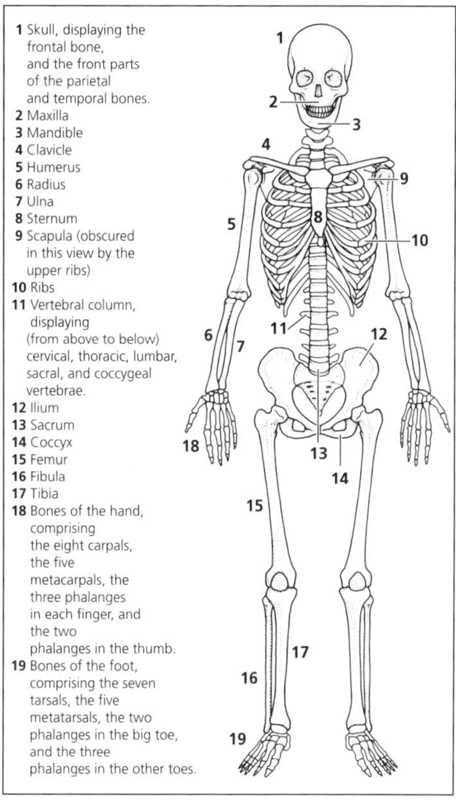

Skeleton

skimmer A bird inhabiting tropical freshwater and coasts; lower bill longer and narrower than upper; catches fish by flying low with lower bill cutting water surface; also known as the **shearwater**, **sea-dog**, or **scissorbill**. (Family: Rhynchopidae, 3 species.) >> shearwater

skin The tough, pliable, waterproof covering of the body, blending with the mucous membranes of the mouth, nose, eyelids, and urogenital and anal openings. It is the largest single organ in the body – approximately 1·8 sq m/19·4 sq ft in the adult human and 1–2 mm/0·04–0·08 in thick. As well as a surface covering, it is also a sensory organ providing sensitivity to touch, pressure, changes in temperature, and painful stimuli. Its waterproofing function prevents fluid loss from the body, but it also has an absorptive function when certain drugs, vitamins, and hormones are applied to it in a suitable form. It is usually loosely applied to underlying tissues, so that it is easily displaced. When subjected to continuous friction, it responds by increasing the thickness of its superficial layers. When wounded, it responds by increased growth and repair. Skin is composed of a superficial layer (the *epidermis*) and a deeper layer (the *dermis*). The epidermis consists of many cell layers, many sensory nerve endings, but no blood vessels. The dermis is the deeper interlacing feltwork of collagen and elastic fibres containing blood and lymphatic vessels, nerves and sensory nerve endings, a

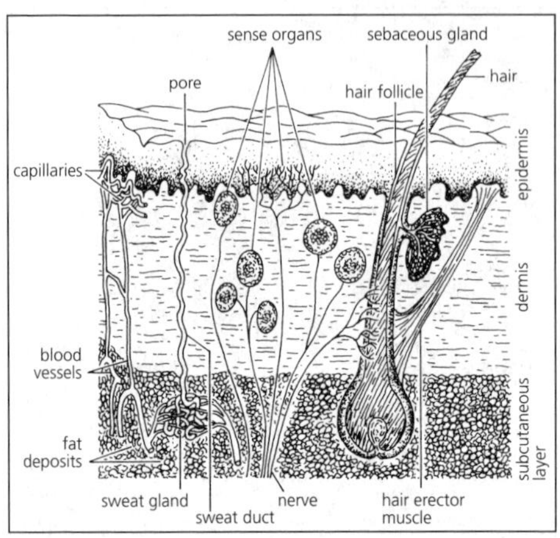

Magnified section through the skin of a mammal

small amount of fat, hair follicles, sweat and sebaceous glands, and smooth muscle. It is firmly anchored to the subcutaneous connective tissue. Skin colour depends on the presence of pigment (*melanin*) and the vascularity of the dermis. In response to sunlight, skin increases its degree of pigmentation, making it appear darker. >> acne; burn; dandruff; dermatitis; dermatology; erysipelas; impetigo; itch; keloid; keratin; mange; melanins; mole; prickly heat; psoriasis; urticaria; wart

skin cancer >> **keratosis; melanoma**

skin-diving A form of underwater swimming, popularized in the 1930s. Until the advent of the scuba, skin-divers used only goggles, face mask, flippers, and a short breathing tube, or *snorkel*. >> scuba diving

skink A lizard of the family Scincidae (1275 species), worldwide in tropical and temperate regions; usually with a long thin body and short legs (some species without legs); head often with large flat scales. >> lizard [i]

Skinner, B(urrhus) F(rederic) (1904–90) Psychologist, born in Susquehanna, PA. A behaviourist, he was a proponent of operant conditioning and inventor of the *Skinner box* for facilitating experimental observations. His main scientific works included *The Behavior of Organisms* (1938) and *Verbal Behavior* (1957). >> behaviourism; conditioning

skipjack Small species of tuna fish (*Katsuwonus pelamis*) widespread in offshore waters of tropical to temperate seas; body length up to about 1 m/3¼ ft; upper surface blue, sides silver with darker banding. (Family: Scombridae.) >> fish [i]

skipper A butterfly with relatively short wings and a large head and body; antennae often club-shaped. (Order: Lepidoptera. Family: Hesperiidae, c.3100 species.) >> butterfly

Skiros [**skee**ros] pop (1995e) 2950; area 209 sq km/ 81 sq mi. Largest island of the N Dodecanese, Greece; length 36 km/22 mi; maximum width 14 km/9 mi; tourism. >> Dodecanese; Greece [i]

skittles A game played in several different forms, all of which have the same objective: to knock down nine pins with a ball. The most popular forms are **alley skittles**, played in long alleys, and **table skittles**, played indoors on a specially constructed table with a swivelled ball attached to a mast by means of a chain. The pins are much smaller than those used in ten-pin bowling. >> bowling

Skopje [**skop**ye], or **Skoplje**, Turkish **Usküp**, ancient **Scupi** 42°00N 21°28E, pop (1995e) 570 000. Industrial capital of the Former Yugoslav Republic of Macedonia, on R Vardar; capital of Serbia, 14th-c; largely destroyed by earthquake, 1963; airport; railway; university (1949). >> Macedonia, Former Yugoslav Republic of [i]

Skorzeny, Otto [skaw(r)**tsay**nee] (1908–75) Soldier, born in Vienna. He was noted for his commando-style operations in World War 2. He freed Mussolini from internment in a mountain hotel on the Gran Sasso Range (1943), abducted Horthy, the Regent of Hungary (1944), but failed to capture Tito. He was tried at Nuremberg as a war criminal, but was acquitted (1947). >> Horthy; Mussolini; World War 2

Skou, Jens C [skoh] (1918–) Chemist, born in Denmark. He studied at Aarhus University, where he went on to teach. He shared the 1997 Nobel Prize for Chemistry for the discovery of an ion-transporting enzyme, Na+, K+-ATPase.

Skraelings [**skray**lingz] (Old Norse *skraelingr* 'pitiful wretch') The name given by the Vikings to the native peoples – principally Beothuk Indians and Inuit – they encountered in Greenland and North America. >> Vikings; Vínland

skua A large, gull-like seabird; usually dark plumage, fleshy band at base of bill; central tail feathers longest; also known as the **jaeger** or **bonxie**. (Family: Stercorariidae, 7 species.) >> gull

skull The skeleton of the head and face, composed of many individual bones closely fitted together. It consists of a large cranial cavity, which encloses the brain; and the bones of the face, which complete the walls of the *orbits* (eye sockets), nasal cavity, and roof of the mouth. The lower jaw (*mandible*) may also be included as part of the skull. The top of the skull is relatively smooth and rounded, while the underside is irregular, having many openings for the passage of nerves and vessels. The major bony parts (the number present is shown in parentheses) are the *frontal* (1), *parietal* (2), *occipital* (1), *temporal* (2), *maxillary* (2), *ethmoid* (1), and *zygomatic* (2) bones. >> bone; brain [i]; cephalic index; skeleton [i]; trepanning

skull-cap A very widespread perennial; flowers 2-lipped, often with upturned tube. Many species have brightly coloured flowers, and are cultivated for ornament. Others are medicinal, used for nerve tonics. (Genus: *Scutellaria*, 300 species. Family: Labiatae.)

skunk A mammal of family Mustelidae, native to the New World; long black and white coat; squirts foul-smelling fluid as defence. >> Mustelidae; polecat

skydiving Falling from an aircraft and freefalling down to a height of 600 m/2000 ft, when the parachute must be opened, before gliding to the ground. The sport is often called simply **freefalling**. >> parachuting

Skye Island in Highland, W Scotland; largest island of the Inner Hebrides, area 1665 sq km/643 sq mi; pop (1995e) 12 200; Cuillin Hills in SW, rising to 1008 m/3307 ft at Sgurr Alasdair; chief towns, Portree, Broadford, Dunvegan; Dunvegan castle, Dunsgiath castle; Skye Bridge completed, 1995. >> Hebrides; Scotland [i]

Skylab project The first US space station, launched on a Saturn V vehicle in May 1973. It was operated in low Earth orbit for 171 days by three successive three-man crews. The station re-entered the atmosphere in July 1979, the source of worldwide attention because there were fears of debris impacting Earth's surface (some pieces were in fact recovered from the Australian desert). >> launch vehicle [i]; space station

skylark A lark native to the Old World N hemisphere; inhabits grassland, farmland, salt marshes, and sand dunes; sings during ascending and descending fluttering flight. (Genus: *Alauda*, 2 species.) >> lark

skyscraper A multi-storey building of great height, typically using a steel frame and curtain wall construction, the floors being accessed via high-speed lifts. The term was first used in the USA at the end of the 19th-c. At 451·9 m/1483 ft, the Petronas Twin Towers (1996), is currently the world's tallest building; but perhaps the most famous skyscrapers are those of the 1920s, such as the Empire State Building (1930–1). >> CN Tower; Petronas Twin Towers; Sears Tower

Slade, Felix (1790–1868) Antiquary and art collector, born in Halsteads, Yorkshire. The Slade School of Fine Art, London, is named after him.

slander A defamatory statement made in some transient form – sounds (not necessarily words) or gestures. The term is not recognized by all jurisdictions (eg in Scotland). >> defamation; libel; tort

slate A fine-grained metamorphic rock having a perfect cleavage because of the parallel alignment of mica crystals. Split into thin sheets it is used for roofing, being durable and light. Well-known occurrences are in N Wales and the Vosges, France. >> metamorphic rock; micas

slavery A system of social inequality in which some people are treated as items of property belonging to other individuals or social groups. At one extreme, slaves might be worked to death, as in the Greek mining camps of the 5th-c and 4th-c BC. At the other, slaves were used less as chattels and more as servants, working in households, and to an extent even administering them, and acting as tutors to young children. >> American Civil War; slave trade

slave trade A trade in Africa which started in ancient times. The scale of the trade built up with the arrival of the Portuguese in Africa and the development of the labour-intensive plantation system in the colonies. The Portuguese dominated the trade in the 16th-c, the Dutch in the early 17th-c, while the late 17th-c was a period of intense competition with the French, British, Danes, and Swedes joining the early practitioners. The British abolished the slave trade in 1807, and the institution of slavery in 1833. There have been various estimates of the number of slaves removed from Africa, the most reliable figure being c.12.5 million between 1650 and 1850. >> slavery; Wilberforce

Slavic or **Slavonic languages** The NE branch of the Indo-European languages, normally divided into **South Slavic** (eg Bulgarian), **West Slavic** (eg Polish), and **East Slavic** (eg Russian). There are written records of Old Church Slavonic from the 9th-c, and its modern form, Church Slavonic, is used as a liturgical language in the Eastern Orthodox Church. The Baltic and Slavic languages between them have c.300 million mother-tongue speakers, more than half of whom speak Russian. Russian is also spoken by a further 120 million as a second language, throughout the republics of the former USSR. Polish is spoken by c.44 million in Poland and surrounding areas, as well as by emigrants in several parts of the world. Serbian (7·5 million) and Croatian (4·8 million) are spoken chiefly in Yugoslavia and Croatia, respectively. Czech is spoken in the Czech Republic by c.12 million. All the East Slavic languages, and some others, are still written in Cyrillic script. >> Indo-European languages; Cyrillic alphabet

Slavs The largest group of European peoples sharing a common ethnic and linguistic origin, consisting of Russians, Ukrainians, Byelorussians, Poles, Czechs, Slovaks, Bulgarians, Serbs, Croats, Montenegrins, and Macedonians. >> Slavic languages

sleep An unconscious state where the subject shows little responsiveness to the external world. There are two phases of sleep which alternate throughout the night. In deep sleep, the brain activity (EEG) shows slow delta waves (**slow wave sleep**, or **SWS**). This is interrupted every 90 minutes or so by 30 minutes of **rapid eye movement (REM) sleep**. Here the muscles are completely relaxed, but the closed eyes show rapid movements. Dreaming occurs in REM sleep, and perhaps also in SWS. >> brain [i]; electro-encephalogram

sleeping sickness >> **trypanosomiasis**

sleep-walking or **somnambulism** A state in which a sleeping individual rises from the bed and walks about for a variable period. It is unrelated to dream activity, and occurs particularly when an individual is subject to stress. It is most common in children. The most important aspect of management is ensuring that the sleep-walker has a safe environment (eg blocking off access to a flight of stairs). >> sleep

sleet A form of precipitation found in near-freezing surface air. In the UK the term is used for partially melted snow which reaches the ground, or a mixture of snow and rain. In the USA it describes raindrops which have frozen into ice pellets, and then partially thawed before reaching the ground. >> precipitation; rainfall; snow

slepton >> **supersymmetry**

slide A still picture transparency mounted for projection. The modern form is a colour photograph 36 × 24 mm in a standard mount 50 mm/2 in square. Slides are widely used as illustrations in educational and commercial presentations, in audio-visual shows, and as inserts in television news and current affairs programmes. >> audio-visual aids; multi-media (projection)

Sliema [**slee**ma] 35°55N 14°31E, pop (1995e) 14 200. Residential and resort town on N coast of main island of Malta; largest town in Malta. >> Malta [i]

Sligo [**sliy**goh], Ir **Sligeach** pop (1995e) 54 300; area 1795 sq km/693 sq mi. County in Connacht province, W Ireland; Ox Mts to the W; capital, Sligo, pop (1995e) 17 800; associated with W B Yeats. >> Ireland (republic) [i]; Yeats

Slim (of Yarralumia and of Bishopston), William (Joseph) Slim, 1st Viscount (1891–1970) British field marshal, born in Bristol. In World War 2, his greatest achievement was to lead his reorganized forces, the famous 14th 'Forgotten Army', to victory over the Japanese in Burma. He was also Governor-General of Australia (1953–60). >> World War 2

slime mould A primitive micro-organism resembling a fungus, but with an amoeba-like colony stage in its life cycle. (Class: Myxomycota.) >> amoeba; clubroot; fungus

slipped disc >> **prolapsed intervertebral disc**

Sloane, Sir Hans (1660–1753) Physician, born in Killyleagh, Co Down. His museum and library of 50 000 volumes and 3560 manuscripts formed the nucleus of the British Museum. >> British Museum

sloe >> **blackthorn**

sloop A single-masted, fore-and-aft rigged sailing vessel with only one headsail. In World War 2, it referred to an anti-submarine vessel superior to a corvette in speed and equipment. >> corvette; ship [i]

sloth A South American mammal of family Megalonychidae (**two-toed sloths**, 2 species) or of family Bradypodidae (**three-toed sloths**, 3 species); two-toed sloths actually have two fingers (all sloths have three toes); an edentate; hangs upside down in trees using huge claws. >> Edentata

Slough [slow] 51°31N 0°36W, pop (1995e) 103 000. Town and unitary authority (from 1998) in S England; railway; London Heathrow airport nearby. >> Berkshire

Slovakia >> **Slovak Republic**

Slovak Republic or **Slovakia**, Slovak **Slovenská Republika** pop (1995e) 5 381 000; area 49 035 sq km/18 927 sq mi. Republic in C Europe; capital, Bratislava; timezone GMT +1; major ethnic groups, Slovak (87%), Hungarian (11%),

Czech (1%), with German, Polish, and Ukrainian minorities; religions, Roman Catholic (60%), Protestant (8%), Orthodox (3%); languages, Slovak (official), with Czech and Hungarian widely spoken; currency, the Slovak koruna of 100 halura; landlocked state, dominated by the Carpathian Mts, rising to Gerlachovsky (2655 m/8711 ft); main rivers, the Danube, Vah, Hron; continental climate, with warm, humid summers and cold, dry winters; average annual temperature −4°C (Jan), 18°C (Jul) in Bratislava; average annual rainfall 500–650 mm/20–30 in; settled in 5th–6th-c by Slavs; part of Great Moravia, 9th-c; part of Magyar Empire from 10th-c; became part of Kingdom of Hungary, 11th-c; united with Czech lands to form state of Czechoslovakia, 1918; under German control, 1938–9; became a separate republic under German influence, 1939; Czechoslovakia regained independence, 1945; under communist rule following 1948 coup; attempt at liberalization by Dubček terminated by intervention of Warsaw Pact troops, 1968; from 1960s, revived efforts to gain recognition for Slovak rights; fall from power of Communist Party, 1989; 1992 agreement to divide Czechoslovakia into its constituent republics, effective January 1993; governed by a president, prime minster, Council of Ministers, and National Council; agricultural region, especially cereals, wine, fruit; steel production in Košice; heavy industry suffering, as previously dependent on state subsidies. >> Czech Republic 🛈; RR1021 political leaders

Slovenes A Slavonic people, concentrated in the NW corner of the Balkan peninsula; overwhelmingly Roman Catholic. Most live in the republic of Slovenia, though c.100 000 continue to inhabit Italy and c.80 000 Austria. >> Habsburgs; Slovenia

Slovenia [slohveenia], Slovene **Slovenija** pop (1995e) 2 002 000; area 20 251 sq km/7817sq mi. Republic in the Balkan Peninsula, SE Europe; capital, Ljubljana; timezone GMT +1; major ethnic group, Slovene (90%); religions, Roman Catholic, Protestant, some Eastern Orthodox; languages, Slovene, Croatian; currency, the Slovene tolar of 100 paras; mountainous region, Slovenian Alps rising to 2863 m/9393 ft at Triglav; rivers include the Sava, Savinja, Drava; continental climate, more Mediterranean in W; colder upland climate with winter snow; average annual temperature −1°C (Jan), 19°C (Jul) in Ljubljana; average annual rainfall 1600 mm/63 in; settled by Slovenians, 6th-c; later controlled by Slavs and Franks; part of the Austro-Hungarian Empire until 1918; people's republic within Yugoslavia, 1946; declaration of independence, 1991, initially opposed by central government; brief period of fighting upon the intervention of the Federal Army, which then withdrew, 1991; governed by a president, prime minister, and bicameral National Assembly, consisting of a State Assembly and a State Council; agriculture, with maize, wheat, sugar beet, potatoes, livestock; timber, lignite, textiles, vehicles, steel; coal, lead, mercury mining in W; tourism, especially winter sports. >> Slovenes; Yugoslavia 🛈; RR1021 political leaders

Slovo, Joe [slohvoh] (1926–95) South African political leader, born in Lithuania. He moved to South Africa as a child, and became one of the most influential white South Africans associated with the national liberation movement. He held high office in both the Communist Party and the African National Congress, and played a major role in the negotiations for a new dispensation. In 1994 he was appointed minister for housing in Mandela's first cabinet. >> African National Congress; First

slow-worm A legless lizard (*Anguis fragilis*) native to Europe, NW Africa, and SW Asia; grey or brown; also known as **blindworm**. (Family: Anguidae.) >> lizard 🛈

slug A terrestrial snail with an elongate body and usually a small external shell, or no shell at all; typically two pairs of tentacles on its head, the upper pair bearing the eyes; common in moist environments. (Class: Gastropoda. Subclass: Pulmonata.) >> sea slug; snail

slug >> **RR1032**

slump >> **depression** (economics)**; recession**

Sluter, Claus or **Claes** [slooter] (c.1350–c.1405) Sculptor, probably born in Haarlem, The Netherlands. His chief works are the porch sculptures of the Carthusian house of Champmol near Dijon, and the tomb of Philip the Bold. >> sculpture

Smalley, Richard E (1943–) Chemist, born in Akron, OH. He shared the Nobel Prize for Chemistry in 1996 for his contribution to the discovery of fullerenes (1985).

smallpox A highly infectious viral disease. As a result of a World Health Organization programme including vaccination, smallpox was declared in 1979 to have been completely eradicated. >> virus

smart bomb >> **bomb**

smelt Slender-bodied marine and freshwater fish belonging to either the N hemisphere family Osmeridae or the

Australasian family Retropinnidae; several species migrate into fresh water to breed.

smelting Obtaining a metal from its ore by heating, using fuel which will simultaneously remove other components of the ore, and a flux to promote the removal of impurities. Copper was probably the first metal to be obtained from an ore, and tin, lead, and silver were also smelted in early times. Charcoal was the universal fuel and reducing agent until the use of coke in the 18th-c. >> Bessemer process; charcoal; coke; flux (technology); open-hearth process

Smetana, Bedřich [**smet**ana] (1824–84) Composer, born in Litomyšl, Czech Republic. His compositions, intensely national in character, include nine operas, notably *Prodaná nevěsta* (1866, The Bartered Bride), and many chamber and orchestral works, including the series of symphonic poems *Má vlast* (1874–9, My Country).

smew A small bird, a species of merganser (*Mergus albellus*) native to the N Old World; untidy crest on back of head; male white with black back and tail; female mainly brown. >> merganser

Smiles, Samuel (1812–1904) Writer and social reformer, born in Haddington, East Lothian, Scotland. His main work was a guide to self-improvement, *Self-Help* (1859), with its short lives of great men and the admonition 'Do thou likewise'.

Smith, Adam (1723–90) Economist and philosopher, born in Kirkcaldy, Fife. In 1776 he published *An Inquiry into the Nature and Causes of the Wealth of Nations* (1776), the first major work of political economy. >> laissez-faire; political economy

Smith, Bessie, nickname **Empress of the Blues** (c.1898–1937) Blues singer, born in Chattanooga, TN. She recorded her first sides in New York City in 1923, and received her nickname after highly successful sales of her early songs. >> blues

Smith, Dodie, pseudonym **C L Anthony** (1896–1990) Playwright, novelist, and theatre producer, born in Whitefield, Greater Manchester. Among her best known works are the play *Dear Octopus* (1938) and the children's book *The Hundred and One Dalmatians* (1956, filmed 1961 and 1996).

Smith, Florence Margaret >> **Smith, Stevie**

Smith, Ian (Douglas) (1919–) Prime minister of Rhodesia (1964–79), born in Selukwe, Zimbabwe. As premier, in 1965 he unilaterally declared independence, which resulted in the imposition of increasingly severe economic sanctions. After formal independence (1980), he continued to be a vigorous opponent of the one-party state under Mugabe's government. >> Mugabe; Zimbabwe ℹ

Smith, John (1580–1631) Adventurer, born in Willoughby, Lincolnshire. He joined an expedition to colonize Virginia (1607), where his energy in dealing with the Indians led to his being elected president of the colony (1608–9). >> Pocahontas

Smith, John (1938–94) British politician, born in Dalmally, Argyll and Bute. He held various posts in government and in Opposition, becoming shadow Chancellor of the Exchequer in 1988. He succeeded Neil Kinnock as Labour leader after the 1992 general election. A highly respected figure, his unexpected death after a heart attack in May 1994 caused an unusually strong sense of national loss. >> Kinnock; Labour Party (UK)

Smith, Joseph (1805–44) Founder of the Church of Jesus Christ of Latter-day Saints (the Mormons), born in Sharon, VT. He received his first 'call' as a prophet in 1820, and in 1827 received the *Book of Mormon* on a hill near Palmyra, NY. He founded Nauvoo, IL in 1840, becoming mayor. Imprisoned for conspiracy, he was killed by a mob which broke into Carthage jail. >> Mormons

Smith, Maggie, popular name of **Dame Margaret Natalie Smith** (1934–) Actress, born in Ilford, E Greater London. Her films include *The Prime of Miss Jean Brodie* (1969, Oscar) and *California Suite* (1978, Oscar), and her stage work includes *Lettice and Lovage* (1988, Tony).

Smith, Stevie, pseudonym of **Florence Margaret Smith** (1902–71) Writer, born in Hull. She acquired a reputation principally as an eccentrically humorous poet on serious themes, illustrated by 'Not Waving but Drowning' (1957).

Smithfield An area just outside the walls of the City of London, in former times the scene of tournaments, trials, fairs, and cattle markets. The main London meat market has been located here since the mid-19th-c. >> London

Smithsonian Institution A foundation for the promotion of knowledge, endowed in 1826 by the English scientist James Smithson (1765–1829), and opened in Washington, DC in 1855. It administers a number of art, history, and science museums, and scientific research centres. >> National Gallery of Art

smog A form of air pollution with several sources. In Britain before the mid-20th-c, the smogs of industrial cities were a form of radiation fog, in which soot and smoke acted as condensation nuclei, and gases such as sulphur dioxide (SO_2) and carbon monoxide (CO) were unable to escape. At lower latitudes, photochemical smogs (*heat hazes*) occur. Emissions of hydrocarbons and oxides of nitrogen from industrial processes and vehicle exhausts react with sunlight. >> acid rain ℹ; fog

smoked foods The preservation of food using the ancient method of exposing it over a period of time to wood smoke. The preservation is achieved partly through drying and partly through the effects of chemicals in the smoke. >> food preservation

smoking The practice of inhaling the fumes from burning tobacco leaves, generally using cigarettes, cigars, or pipes, introduced into Europe from the Americas by early explorers. The practice is habit-forming, and is known to be a causative factor in the development of several diseases, notably lung cancer, throat cancer, and heart and respiratory conditions. >> cigarette; nicotine; passive smoking; tobacco ℹ

Smolensk [smo**lensk**] 54°49N 32°04E, pop (1995e) 353 000. River port in WC European Russia, on the upper Dnepr R; part of Russia, 1654; severely damaged in World War 2; railway; cathedral (12th-c). >> Russia ℹ

Smollett, Tobias (George) (1721–71) Novelist, born in Cardross, Argyll and Bute. He achieved success with his first works, the picaresque novels *The Adventures of Roderick Random* (1748) and *The Adventures of Peregrine Pickle* (1751). His masterpiece was *Humphry Clinker* (1771). >> picaresque novel

Smuts, Jan (Christiaan) (1870–1950) South African general, statesman, and prime minister (1919–24, 1939–48), born in Malmesbury, Cape Colony. A member of the Imperial War Cabinet in World War 1, he was a significant figure at Versailles, and was instrumental in the founding of the League of Nations in 1919. His coalition with the Nationalists in 1934 produced the United Party, and he became premier again in 1939. >> League of Nations

Smyrna >> **Izmir**

Smythe, Pat(ricia), married name **Koechlin** (1928–96) Show jumper, born in Switzerland. She won the European championship four times on 'Flanagan' (1957, 1961–3), and in 1956 was the first woman to ride in the Olympic Games. >> equestrianism

Snagge, John (Derrick Mordaunt) (1904–96) British broadcaster. He became a BBC announcer in 1928, especially known for his commentary on the Oxford and Cambridge Boat Race (1931–80). He retired in 1965, his voice having come to represent the traditional values of the BBC. >> BBC

snail A common name for many types of gastropod mollusc, but sometimes used more specifically for members of subclass Pulmonata; predominantly terrestrial or freshwater forms; usually possess a spirally coiled external shell. (Class: Gastropoda.) >> abalone; conch; gastropod; limpet; mollusc; murex; periwinkle (marine biology); shell; triton shell; wentletrap; whelk

snake A reptile believed to have evolved c.135 million years ago; also known as **serpent**; c.2400 living species, found worldwide except in very cold regions and on some islands; separate jaw bones connected by ligaments; these bones can move apart, allowing prey much wider than the snake's head to be swallowed; eats animals (or eggs); cannot chew (swallows prey whole); long cylindrical scaly body; no limbs or eyelids; skin moulted several times each year; c.300 venomous species; more than 50 dangerous to humans. (Suborder: Serpentes or Ophidia. Order: Squamata.) >> flying / mangrove / sea snake; adder; asp; boa; cobra; diamondback; krait; lizard ℹ; mamba; python; reptile; taipan; viper ℹ

snake-necked turtle A side-necked turtle, native to South America and Australasia; very long slender neck; called *tortoise* in Australia; also known as **long-necked turtle**. (Family: Chelidae, 36 species.) >> turtle (biology)

snake plant >> **mother-in-law's-tongue**

Snake River River in NW USA; rises in NW Wyoming; joins the Columbia R; length c.1600 km/1000 mi. >> Hell's Canyon; United States of America ℹ

snapdragon A short-lived, slightly bushy perennial (*Antirrhinum majus*), growing to 80 cm/30 in, native to Europe; flowers have two lips, with a projection forming a landing platform for bumble-bees, the only insects with sufficient strength to part the lips and reach the nectar within. The flowers of the wild plants are reddish purple, with cultivars in a range of colours. (Family: Scrophulariaceae.)

snapper Deep-bodied fish of the family Lutjanidae (4 genera, 300 species), widespread and locally common in tropical seas; name derives from the long conical front teeth and highly mobile jaws. >> fish ℹ

snare drum >> **side drum**

Snead, Sam(uel Jackson), nickname **Slammin' Sammy** (1912–) Golfer, born in Hot Springs, VA. He won the (British) Open in 1946, the US PGA Championship in 1942, 1949, and 1951, and the US Masters in 1949, 1952, and 1954.

Snapdragon – inset shows bee parting lips of flower

snipe A sandpiper, found worldwide; mottled brown plumage; shortish legs and long straight bill. (Genus: *Gallinago*, 17 species, or *Coenocorypha*, 1 species.) >> sandpiper

snooker A popular indoor game played with cues on a standard English billiards table by two (sometimes four) players. 22 balls are placed at specific positions on the table: one white, 15 reds, and six coloured balls (yellow, green, brown, blue, pink, and black). The object is to use the cue to hit the white ball to send ('pot') the other balls into any of six pockets around the table, according to certain rules. The coloured balls have an ascending points value of 2–7, while each red is worth one point. The game ends when the black is finally potted; and the winner is the player with most points. Snooker was invented by army officers serving in the Devonshire Regiment in India in 1875, who developed it from Black Pool. >> RR1060

Snorri Sturluson >> **Sturluson, Snorri**

snow A type of solid precipitation which forms at temperatures below the freezing point of water. At very cold temperatures, single ice crystals may fall as snow. At higher temperatures, ice crystals aggregate into geometrical forms called **snow flakes**. >> precipitation; sleet; whiteout

Snow, C(harles) P(ercy) Snow, Baron (1905–80) Novelist and physicist, born in Leicester, Leicestershire. He was the author of a cycle of successful novels portraying English life from 1920 onwards, starting with *Strangers and Brothers* (1940), and including *Corridors of Power* (1964). His controversial *Two Cultures and the Scientific Revolution* (Rede lecture, 1959) discussed the dichotomy between science and literature. He married the novelist Pamela Hansford Johnson in 1950. >> Johnson, Pamela Hansford

Snowdon, Welsh **Yr Wyddfa** 53°04N 4°05W. Mountain with five peaks rising to 1085 m/3560 ft in Gwynedd, NW Wales, UK; highest peak in England and Wales; rack railway from Llanberis to main peak. >> Gwynedd

Snowdon, Antony Armstrong-Jones, 1st Earl of (1930–) Photographer and designer, who married Princess Margaret in 1960 (divorced 1978). A freelance photojournalist since 1951, he designed the Aviary of the London Zoo in 1965, and in recent years has worked a great deal with the handicapped. >> Margaret, Princess

snowdrop A bulb often flowering in late winter (*Galanthus nivalis*) native to Europe and W Asia; flowers on long stalks, solitary, drooping, white. (Family: Amaryllidaceae.)

snow leopard A rare big cat (*Panthera uncia*) native to the mountains of SC Asia, living near the snow line; thick pale grey coat with dark rings (sometimes enclosing small spots); also known as **ounce**. >> Felidae

Snowy Mountains Scheme A massive construction project in SE Australia carried out 1949–72. The object was to divert the Snowy R inland into the Murrumbidgee R to provide hydroelectricity and irrigation. >> irrigation

snuff Any drug prepared as a fine powder which is administered by sniffing; it is absorbed through the nasal mucous membranes. More commonly, snuff is synonymous with tobacco snuff, taken for its nicotine content. >> nicotine; tobacco ℹ

Snyders, Frans (1579–1657) Painter, born in Antwerp. He specialized in still life and animals, and is well known for his hunting scenes.

Soane, Sir John (1753–1837) Architect, born in Goring, Oxfordshire. His designs include the Bank of England (1792–1833, now rebuilt) and Dulwich Picture Gallery (1811–14).

soap The salt of a fatty acid, usually stearic (octadecanoic) or palmitic (hexadecanoic) acids. Commercial soaps for toilet use are usually the sodium or potassium salts; insoluble calcium soaps are used as lubricants. >> detergent; napalm; palmitic acid; stearic acid

soapstone >> talc

Sobers, Gary [**soh**berz], popular name of **Sir Garfield St Aubrun Sobers** (1936–) Cricketer, born in Barbados. A great all-rounder, he is the only man to score 8000 Test runs and take 200 wickets. During his career (1953–74) he scored 28 315 runs in first-class cricket (average 54.87) and took 1043 wickets (average 27.74). >> cricket (sport) i

Sobukwe, Robert Mangaliso [soh**book**way] (1924–78) African nationalist leader, born in Graaff-Reinet, South Africa. He was co-founder and first president of the Pan African Congress, the main rival to the African National Congress (ANC) as opponent of the apartheid regime. He was jailed in 1960, and detained on Robben I (1963–9) under legislation (nicknamed the 'Sobukwe clause') used only against him. >> African National Congress; apartheid

soccer >> **football** 1 i

soccerene >> **buckminsterfullerene**

Social and Liberal Democratic Party (SLDP) >> **Liberal Party** (UK)

social anthropology >> **anthropology**

social contract or **social compact** The voluntary, unwritten agreement between a society's members to act in a mutually responsible manner, accepting the authority of the state which in turn guarantees certain moral principles. This philosophy was first propounded by Hobbes, Locke, and Rousseau, and has been an important feature of much liberal political theory in recent years. The concept was also seen in the UK in 1975, when the Labour government under Wilson arrived at a consensus with the Trades Union Council on the broad social and economic policies that the government should pursue. However, in 1978 no agreement could be reached, and the system lapsed. >> Hobbes; Locke, John; Rousseau, Jean Jacques; trade union; Wilson, Harold

Social Darwinism A school of thought which developed within 19th-c sociology based on the belief that social evolution depended on society adapting most efficiently to its environment. >> eugenics; Galton; sociology

social democracy A section of the socialist movement which emerged in the late 19th-c after the break-up of the First International, and which advocates achieving social change through reformist rather than revolutionary means. Some political parties that have adopted the social democratic label in the latter part of the 20th-c are, however, moderate centrist parties. >> International; Social Democratic Party; socialism

Social Democratic Party (SDP) A UK political party formed in 1981 by a 'gang of four', comprising David Owen, Shirley Williams, Roy Jenkins, and Bill Rogers (1928–). They broke away from the Labour Party, forming an electoral pact with the Liberals in 1981, but failed to break the two-party 'mould' of British politics. The SDP merged with the Liberal Party in 1988, becoming the **Social and Liberal Democratic Party** (later known as the **Liberal Democrats**), although a rump, led by David Owen, continued in existence as the SDP until 1990. >> Labour Party; Liberal Party (UK); Jenkins, Roy; Owen, David; Williams, Shirley

socialism A wide-ranging political doctrine which first emerged in Europe during industrialization in the 18th-c. Most socialists would agree that social and economic relationships play a major part in determining human possibilities, and that the unequal ownership of property under capitalism creates an unequal and conflictive society. The removal of private property or some means of counterbalancing its power, it is held, will produce a more equal society where individuals enjoy greater freedom and are able to realize their potential more fully. Possibly the major division within socialism is between those who believe that to bring it about revolution is necessary, and those who believe change can be achieved through reforms within democratic politics. >> anarchism; Maoism; Marxism; Marxism-Leninism; New Left; social democracy; syndicalism

Socialist Labor Party The longest-lasting socialist party in the USA. It nominated its first presidential candidate in 1892 and has existed ever since. >> socialism

Socialist Realism In literature and art, the official style of the former Soviet Union and of other socialist states, intended to appeal to the masses, and typically representing ordinary workers going about their mundane tasks. The Hungarian critic Georg Lukács was a major proponent, and Russian self-exile Andrei Sinyavsky (1925–97) a noted antagonist. >> Lukács; Realism; Sholokhov; social realism

Socialist Revolutionary (SR) Party A neo-populist revolutionary party in Russia, founded in 1902 and led by Victor Chernov (1873–1952). Their 'fighting detachments' carried out a number of spectacular political assassinations between 1902 and 1918. >> radicalism; Russian revolution

social medicine >> **community medicine**

social psychology The study of the behaviour of groups of individuals. Social psychologists might record anything from fine-grained details of the body posture of an individual to large-scale characteristics of crowd behaviour. They are also concerned with concepts that necessarily involve more than one individual, such as leadership, friendship, and persuasion. >> psychology

social realism A term current in art criticism since World War 2, referring to pictures which treat 'real life' subjects in a way that challenges the values of 'bourgeois' society. Courbet's 'Stonebreakers' (1849) may have been the first great social realist picture. >> Ashcan School; Courbet; Realism; Socialist Realism

social science A general term designating a number of disciplines, such as sociology, economics, political science, and geography, which have explored various aspects of society – such as social structure, the market, power, and spatial relations – through methods which are conventionally understood to be 'scientific'. There is still debate over whether these disciplines can be truly 'scientific', given that they are measuring patterns of human behaviour rather than the material of the natural and physical sciences. >> economics; geography; political science; sociology

social security 1 In the USA, a tax on wages and salaries imposed to pay for retirement benefits, disability insurance, and hospital insurance. The tax is an important part of all Federal revenues (around 40%), and is the equivalent of British **national insurance**. >> national insurance **2** In the UK, the provision of financial aid by the state to reduce poverty, financed out of taxation. It comprises a wide range of benefits (covering such matters as housing and family allowances) which are available to those in need.

social stratification A system of social inequality in which social groups occupy different positions (or *strata*) based on their unequal access to and ownership of material, political, and cultural (eg educational) resources. >> class; slavery

social studies A range of disciplines within the arts, humanities, and social sciences, including sociology, history, economics, and geography, whose principal concern is the study of various aspects of society. The term is less favoured today and more likely to be replaced by **social sciences**. >> social science

social work A term which is usually understood to refer to the occupational activities of the social-work profession, ie the provision of social services to the 'needy', including counselling, care, and the general administration of the benefits of the state.

Society Islands, Fr **Archipel de la Société** pop (1995e) 178 000; area 1535 sq km/592 sq mi. One of the five archipelagoes of French Polynesia, comprising the Windward Is (including Tahiti) and the Leeward Is; two clusters of volcanic and coral islands in a 720 km/450 mi chain stretching NW–SE; visited by Captain Cook in 1769, and named by him after the Royal Society; French protectorate, 1844; French colony, 1897; capital, Papeete (Tahiti). >> Leeward Islands (French Polynesia); Windward Islands (French Polynesia)

Socinus, Laelius [so**siy**nus], Ital **Lelio (Francesco Maria) Sozini** (1525–62) Protestant reformer, born in Siena, Italy. His anti-Trinitarian views were developed by his nephew **Faustus Socinus** (1539–1604) into a doctrine known as **Socinianism**. >> Protestantism; Reformation; Trinity

sociobiology The integrated study of the biological basis of social behaviour, based on the assumption that all behaviour is adaptive. Emphasis is placed on social systems as ecological adaptations, and explanations are given in terms of evolutionary theory. >> biology; ecology; evolution; sociology

sociogram >> **sociometry**

sociolinguistics The study of the relationships between language and the society which uses it. The subject has a wide range, encompassing the use of standard and non-standard forms; the language of different social class and caste groups; the differences between male and female speech; and the character of multilingual societies. >> dialectology; ethnolinguistics; linguistics; stylistics

sociology The study of patterned social behaviour which constitutes a social system or society, a term originally coined by French social theorist Auguste Comte. Sociologists explore the way in which social structures are continually modified as a result of social interaction, and thereby seek to explain the development of new institutions or new types of society. Certain areas of study have gained most attention, such as crime, the family, gender, the media, science and technology, medicine, and systems of inequality. >> Comte; ethnomethodology; Social Darwinism; social studies

sociometry A technique for mapping social networks. The networks are based on respondents ranking those people they find more and those less desirable. A graphical representation of a network of social relationships is known as a **sociogram**. >> social psychology

sockeye Species of salmon (*Oncorhynchus nerka*), widespread in the N Pacific Ocean and adjacent rivers; length up to 80 cm/32 in; also known as **red salmon**. (Family: Salmonidae.) >> salmon

Socrates [**sok**rateez] (469–399 BC) Greek philosopher, born in Athens. By Plato's account, he devoted his last 30 years to convincing the Athenians that their opinions about moral matters could not bear the weight of critical scrutiny. His technique, the so-called **Socratic method**, was to ask for definitions of such morally significant concepts as piety and justice, and to elicit contradictions from the responses, thus exposing the ignorance of the responder and motivating deeper enquiry into the concepts. He was tried on charges of impiety and corruption of the youth by zealous defenders of a restored democracy in Athens. Found guilty, he was put to death by drinking hemlock. His personality and his doctrines were immortalized in Plato's dialogues. >> Plato

soda >> **sodium**

soda bread A type of bread which uses sodium bicarbonate to provide the necessary carbon dioxide. In contrast to yeast-risen bread, it is easier and quicker to prepare. >> bicarbonate; bread

Soddy, Frederick (1877–1956) Radiochemist, born in Eastbourne, East Sussex. In 1913 he discovered forms of the same element with identical chemical qualities but different atomic weights (*isotopes*), for which he received the Nobel Prize for Chemistry in 1921. >> isotopes

sodium Na (Lat *natrium*), element 11, melting point 97.8°C. A very soft and reactive alkali metal, not found free in nature, but always in the form of one of its salts. These occur in salt deposits, but **sodium chloride** (common salt, or NaCl) can also be extracted from ocean water, of which it makes up about 3.5%. The metal is a very strong reducing agent, widely used in organic reactions and for the production of **sodium cyanide** (NaCN) and **sodium cyanamide** (Na_2CN_2), used in metallurgy and fertilizers. **Sodium carbonate** and **bicarbonate** (Na_2CO_3 and $NaHCO_3$), also called *washing soda* and *baking soda*, are important industrial chemicals, as is **sodium hydroxide** (NaOH), also called *caustic soda* or *lye*, used in soap making. >> alkali; chemical elements; metal; salt; RR1036

Sodom and Gomorrah [**sod**om, go**moh**ra] Two of five 'cities of the plain' in ancient Palestine, perhaps now submerged under the S end of the Dead Sea or located to the SE of the Dead Sea. The people were legendary for their wickedness, especially their sexual perversity. >> Lot

Soekarno, Achmad >> **Sukarno**

Sofia [so**fee**a], Bulgarian **Sofiya**, Lat **Serdica** 42°40N 23°18E, pop (1995e) 1 254 000. Capital of Bulgaria since 1878; Roman town 1st–4th-c; under Byzantine rule 6th–9th-c; under Turkish rule 1382–1878; airport; railway; university (1888); Alexander Nevsky memorial cathedral. >> Bulgaria [i]

softball A smaller version of baseball, played on a diamond-shaped infield with bases 60 ft (18.3 m) apart. The object, as in baseball, is to score runs by completing a circuit of the diamond before being put out. The principal differences between the two sports are that the softball field is smaller, the ball is bigger, the pitcher throws the ball underarm, and the game lasts seven innings (not nine). Slow-pitch softball is played ten (not nine) a side. >> baseball [i]; RR1061

software The suite of all computer programs, including operating system, compilers, packages, and user programs, which enable a particular computer centre to operate. The notion is contrasted with the **hardware** and the **liveware**. **Software engineering** is a methodology for developing computer software with the objective of ensuring that the software is efficient, does the job for which it is intended, and is produced within cost and on time. >> computer; computer program; firmware; hardware

Sogne Fjord [**song**nuh **fyaw(r)d**], Norwegian **Sognefjorden** Inlet on W coast of Norway; extends 204 km/127 mi; largest Norwegian fjord; average width, 5 km/3 mi. >> fjord; Norway [i]

soil The top layer of the Earth's surface, comprising a mixture of fine weathered rock particles and organic matter. The finest particles form clay; the less fine, silt; and the coarsest, sand. Provided moisture is available, soils generally support vegetation, and provide a habitat for a wide range of soil flora and fauna. >> soil science

soil science The study of soil, its information, and its management as a medium for plant growth. It includes both the physical management of soil, through cultivation, drainage, and irrigation, and the chemical management of soil, through the control of nutrient status, acidity, and salinity. >> agronomy; chernozem; humus; loam; pedology; soil

soja >> **soya bean**

solar cell A device for converting light directly into electrical power. Cells using single crystals of silicon are efficient (converting c.14% of incident energy to electricity) but expensive; other materials are cheaper, such as germanium arsenide and amorphous silicon. Solar cells are used to provide electrical power in remote places, such as buoys and space satellites. >> electricity; photovoltaic effect

solar constant The total radiation of all frequencies falling on the Earth from the Sun, as measured for an average Earth–Sun distance; symbol S, value 1367 W/m^2 (watt per metre squared). >> electromagnetism; radiometry; Sun

solar flare A violent release of energy in the vicinity of an active region on the Sun, emitting energetic particles, X-rays, and radio waves. It causes notable auroral displays in our upper atmosphere. >> aurora; Sun

solar power Energy radiating from the Sun, exploited to provide energy for heat and electricity generation. **Solar panels** or **collectors** (a black metal absorber) can be used to extract heat from the warmth of sunshine to heat water or air in pipes contained in or beneath the panels. Collectors can also be focused onto a small area of water to heat it, producing steam for electricity generation. In many developing countries solar power has great potential, especially as it is a renewable energy resource. By the early 1980s, solar collectors were producing energy equivalent to 0·01% of the world's total oil consumption. >> alternative energy; energy; renewable resources

solar prominence Flame-like clouds of matter in the solar chromosphere, sometimes triggered by solar flares, reaching heights of 1 000 000 km/600 000 mi at extremes. >> chromosphere; solar flare

Solar System The Sun and its associated, gravitationally bound, system of nine known planets, their 61 known satellites, the c.5000 asteroids, the comets, and interplanetary dust. The planets – Mercury, Venus, Earth, Mars (the four 'inner planets'), Jupiter, Saturn, Uranus, Neptune (the four outer 'gas giants') and Pluto – and asteroids orbit approximately in the plane of the Sun's equator, and rotate about the Sun in the same direction (counterclockwise when viewed from a N polar direction). The inner planets are comparatively small and dense, and are composed of high-temperature condensates (chiefly iron and metal silicates), while the four outer planets are much larger, and mainly composed of low-temperature condensates (chiefly gases and ices); Pluto is unique and poorly known. It is thought that the planetary system was formed 4·6 thousand million years ago as a by-product of the Sun's formation, which resulted from the gravitational collapse of an accumulation of gas and dust in this region of the Milky Way galaxy. >> asteroids; comet; Galaxy; interplanetary matter; Oort Cloud; planet; Sun; RR964

solar time Time measured by considering the rotation of the Earth relative to the Sun. **Mean solar time** is established by reference to the mean Sun, and was established as the fundamental measure of clock time before it was realized that the Earth has variable rotation. **Apparent solar time** is time shown by a sundial. >> sidereal time; sundial; universal time

solar wind A stream of charged particles (*plasma*) emanating from the upper atmosphere (corona) of the Sun and expanding continuously into the interplanetary medium with a velocity of 400–800 km/s (250–500 mi/s). The plasma interacts with planetary environments as it flows by them, notably by shaping the magnetospheres of those planets with magnetic fields. >> magnetosphere; Solar System; Sun

solder An alloy which will melt easily at a moderate temperature, and so provide a bond between two metal surfaces. It usually consists of tin and lead, when used for joining copper, brass, or iron with tin-plate. As distinct from **welding**, soldering only fills in interstices in the juxtaposed metals, and does not fuse into them. >> alloy

soldier beetle An elongate beetle; wing cases usually parallel-sided; adults commonly found on flowers and vegetation. (Order: Coleoptera. Family: Cantharidae, c.5000 species.) >> beetle

sole Any of the flatfish in the family Soleidae, widespread in shallow continental shelf waters of tropical to temperate seas; includes the common European sole, or **Dover sole** (*Solea solea*); length up to 50 cm/20 in; both eyes on right side of body; very popular food fish. >> flatfish

Solemn League and Covenant An alliance between the English Parliament and the Scottish rebels against Charles I, agreed in September 1643. The pact facilitated parliamentary victory in the first Civil War, but although it was part of the bargain, Presbyterianism was never fully implemented in England. >> English Civil War; Presbyterianism

solenodon [so**lee**nodon] A mammal native to Cuba, Haiti, and the Dominican Republic; an insectivore, resembling a very large shrew (length, up to 33 cm/13 in), with longer legs; has a venomous bite. (Family: Solenodontidae, 2 species.) >> insectivore; shrew

solenoid A coil of wire, usually cylindrical, partially surrounding a movable iron core. When a current flows in the coil, a magnetic field is produced which makes the core move. A solenoid converts electrical energy into mechanical energy, as in operating a switch or circuit breaker. >> electricity; magnetism

Solent, the A channel separating the I of Wight from mainland England; a major shipping route from Southampton; yacht racing. >> Southampton; Wight, Isle of

sol-fa, tonic >> **tonic sol-fa**

solicitor A lawyer whose responsibilities involve giving legal advice to clients. In order to practise, solicitors in the UK require a practising certificate from the appropriate Law Society. Most are concerned with advice on criminal law, family law, landlord and tenant law, and debt disputes. Solicitors also instruct barristers or advocates appearing for a client in either the lower or superior courts. The distinction between solicitors and barristers does not exist in the USA. A hybrid form of lawyer, a **solicitor advocate**, was introduced in Scotland in 1993. >> barrister; Law Society

solicitor general In the UK, one of the government's law officers, who is a member of the House of Commons and junior to the attorney-general. There is also a solicitor general for Scotland, who holds a similar position. >> attorney general

solid A dense form of matter characterized by its ability to transmit twisting forces and its inability to flow; virtually incompressible; tends to retain shape when stressed; described as rigid, the atoms generally not being free to move from point to point. Solids are divided into *crystals*, comprising ordered arrays of atoms; *amorphous solids*, which are disordered arrays; and *polymers* and *rubbers*, which comprise long chain-like molecules. >> ceramics; crystals; ice; phases of matter [i]; polymerization; solid-state physics

Solidarity (Polish *Solidarność*). An organization established in Poland (Sep 1980) as the National Committee of Solidarity to co-ordinate the activities of the emerging independent trade union following protracted industrial unrest, notably in the Lenin shipyard in Gdańsk. Its first president was Lech Wałesa. It organized a number of strikes in early 1981 for improved wages and conditions, and became a force for major political reform. It was made illegal, but came back into the political arena in mid-1988. Following its successes in the 1989 elections, Solidarity entered into a coalition government with the communists, with one of its members (Tadeusz Mazowiecki) eventually becoming prime minister. >> Poland ℹ; trade union; Walesa

solid-state device A device in which an electric signal flows through a solid material rather than a vacuum. Most are made from solid semiconductor materials, such as transistors and thyristors. They are much smaller and lighter than the traditional vacuum tubes, use less power, last longer, are more dependable, and cost less. >> electricity; semiconductor; thyristor; transistor

solid-state physics The study of all properties of matter in the solid state; a sub-branch of condensed matter physics, which includes liquids and solids. Traditionally it focuses on crystal structure, more recently embracing more complex systems such as alloys, ceramics, amorphous solids, and surfaces. >> materials science; physics; solid

Solihull [**sol**ihuhl] 52°25N 1°45W, pop (1995e) 95 200. Town in West Midlands, C England; a suburb of SE Birmingham; National Exhibition Centre; railway. >> West Midlands

soliloquy A stage device whereby a character talks aloud but alone, as it were confiding in the audience. The soliloquies of Richard III and Hamlet are famous examples in Shakespeare. There are similarities with the interior monologue or 'voice-over' in film. >> stream of consciousness

Solingen [**zoh**lingn] 51°10N 7°05E, pop (1995e) 168 000. Industrial city in Germany; in the Ruhr valley; badly bombed in World War 2. >> Germany ℹ

solipsism In philosophy, the theory that 'I' alone exist and that the 'outside world' exists only in my consciousness. The thesis proves hard to refute from within theories such as Descartes', which makes introspection and immediate experience the ultimate source of factual knowledge. >> Descartes

solitaire An extinct dodo-like bird. The name is also used for the **Hawaiian honeycreeper** (*Viridonia sagittirostris*) and New World thrushes of the genera *Myadestes* (7 species) and *Entomodestes* (2 species). >> dodo; thrush (bird)

soliton A moving, solitary, stable wave having a well-defined position and constant amplitude. They can be observed in water in shallow channels, such as tidal bore waves. >> wave motion ℹ

solo One of the family of trick-taking card games, similar to bridge. Players have to declare how many tricks they will win before each game. Tricks are won as in whist, but the declarer plays without a partner (hence the name), and there is an auction. >> bridge (recreation); whist

Solomon (Hebrew Bible) (10th-c BC) King of Israel, the second son of David and Bathsheba. His outwardly splendid reign saw the expansion of the kingdom and the building of the great Temple in Jerusalem. He was credited with extraordinary wisdom, and his name became attached to several Biblical and extra-canonical writings. >> David; Proverbs, Book of; Solomon, Psalms of; Song of Solomon; Wisdom of Solomon

Solomon (music), professional name of **Solomon Cutner** (1902–88) Pianist, born in London. He won a high reputation as a performer of the works of Beethoven, Brahms, and some of the modern composers.

Solomon, Psalms of A book of the Old Testament Pseudepigrapha, consisting of 18 psalms, probably written c.1st-c BC in response to the Roman occupation of Jerusalem. >> Pseudepigrapha; Solomon (Hebrew Bible)

Solomon Islands pop (1995e) 367 000; land area 27 556 sq km/10 637 sq mi. Archipelago of several hundred islands in the SW Pacific Ocean, stretching c.1400 km/870 mi between Papua New Guinea (NW) and Vanuatu (SE); capital, Honiara; timezone GMT +11; chief ethnic group, Melanesians (93%); chief religion, Christianity (95%); official language, English, with pidgin English widely spoken; unit of currency, the Solomon Island dollar of 100 cents; the large islands have forested mountain ranges and coastal belts; highest point, Mt Makarakomburu (2477 m/8126 ft) on Guadalcanal, the largest island; equatorial climate; high humidity; visited by the Spanish, 1568; S Solomon Is placed under British protection, 1893; outer islands added to the protectorate, 1899; scene of fierce fighting in World War 2; independence, 1978; British monarch is represented by a governor-general; prime minister leads a single-chamber parliament; economy based on agriculture. >> Guadalcanal; Honiara; RR1021 political leaders

Solomon Sea >> **Coral Sea**

Solon [**soh**lon] (7th–6th-c BC) Athenian statesman, lawgiver, and poet. As chief archon, he enacted many reforms, and paved the way for the development of democracy at Athens, and her emergence as a great trading state.

solstice An event when the Sun is at its furthest point from the Equator, resulting in the longest day and shortest night (the **summer solstice**) in one hemisphere and the shortest day and longest night (the **winter solstice**) in the other. In the N hemisphere, the summer solstice is on 21 or 22 June and the winter solstice on 21 or 22 December. >> midnight sun

Solti, Sir Georg [**shol**tee] (1912–97) Conductor, born in Budapest. He became director at the Munich Staatsoper (1946–52) and later at Frankfurt (1952–61) and Covent Garden, London (1961–71). He was also artistic director of the Salzburg Easter Festival (1992–3).

solubility The extent to which one substance dissolves in another. It is expressed as the mass/number of moles of a solute which will dissolve in a given volume/mass/number of moles of solvent. >> mole (physics); solution

solution A uniform phase, generally liquid, containing more than one component. When one component is present in excess, it is called the **solvent**; minor components are called **solutes**. >> solvent; titration

Solutrian [solyu**tree**an] In European prehistory, a short division of the Upper Palaeolithic Age, named after the site at La Solutré, Saône et Loire, C France, discovered in 1866. >> Three Age System

Solvay process or **ammonia–soda process** A technique for the production of sodium carbonate (an important industrial alkali), devised in 1865 by Belgian chemist Ernest Solvay (1838–1922), and improved by Ludwig Mond in 1870. Sodium chloride is treated with ammonia and then with carbon dioxide. >> Mond

solvent The major component of a solution. Water is often described as the 'universal solvent', but the term is also applied specifically to volatile organic materials such as acetone and ethyl acetate, used in paints and adhesives. >> solution

Solway Firth Inlet of the Irish Sea, separating Cumbria, England, from Dumfries and Galloway, Scotland; length c.65 km/40 mi; width at mouth, c.40 km/25 mi. >> Irish Sea

Solzhenitsyn, Alexander (Isayevich) [solzhe**nit**sin] (1918–) Writer, born in Kislovodsk, Russia. His first novel, *Odin den iz zhizni Ivana Denisovicha* (1962, One Day in the Life of Ivan Denisovich), set in a prison camp, was acclaimed both in the USSR and the West; but his denunciation of Soviet censorship led to the banning of his later, semi-autobiographical novels, *Rakovy korpus* (1968, Cancer Ward) and *V kruge pervom* (1968, The First Circle). He was awarded the Nobel Prize for Literature in 1970 (received in 1974). His later books include *Arkhipelag Gulag* (1973–8, The Gulag Archipelago), a factual account of the

Stalinist terror, for which he was arrested and exiled (1974). He lived in the USA for 20 years, returning to Russia in 1994.

Somali [so**mah**lee] A Cushitic-speaking people of Somalia and parts of Kenya, Ethiopia, and Djibouti. Roughly two-thirds are transhumant herders (the Samaal) living inland, with farmers and traders along the coast (the Saab). >> Somalia

Somalia [soh**mah**leeuh], official name **Somali Democratic Republic**, Arabic **Jamhuriyadda Dimugradiga Somaliya** pop (1995e) 8 565 000; area 637 357 sq km/246 201 sq mi. NE African republic; capital, Mogadishu; timezone GMT +3; chief ethnic group, Somali (85%); chief religion, Islam (Sunni); official language, Somali; unit of currency, the Somali shilling; occupies the E Horn of Africa, where a dry coastal plain broadens to the S, and rises inland to a plateau at nearly 1000 m/3300 ft; mountains on the Gulf of Aden coast rise to 2416 m/7926 ft at Mt Shimbiris; considerable variation in climate, with more rainfall (Apr–Sep) on E coast; average daily maximum temperatures 28–32°C; persistent threat of drought; settled by Muslims, 7th-c; Italian, French, and British interests after the opening of the Suez Canal, 1869; after World War 2, Somalia formed by the amalgamation of Italian and British protectorates; independence, 1960; from the 1960s, territorial conflict with Ethiopia (which has a large Somali population); military coup, 1969; new constitution approved, 1990; NE region seceded as Somaliland Republic, 1991; UN-sponsored truce, 1992, and UN-directed peace-keeping force despatched to secure food and aid distribution; killing of US soldiers led to withdrawal of US forces, and those of several other countries, 1993; peace agreement, 1994; withdrawal of UN peacekeeping force, 1995; civil war ongoing between different factions, with no national government in place, 1996; National Salvation Council formed, 1997; further peace accord signed by 26 of the country's 28 factions, 1997, but discord ongoing into 1999; a largely nomadic people (50%) raising cattle, sheep, goats, camels; cultivation practised close to rivers; difficult communications within the country, helped by a major road-building programme. >> Ethiopia [i]; Mogadishu; RR1021 political leaders

Somaliland Republic >> **Somalia**

Somers (of Evesham), John Somers, Baron [**suhm**erz] (1651–1716) English Whig statesman, born in Worcester, Hereford and Worcester. He held several posts under William III, culminating as Lord Chancellor (1697), and was president of the Privy Council under Anne (1708–14). >> Whigs; William III

Somerset [**suhm**erset] pop (1995e) 485 000; area 3451 sq km/1332 sq mi. County of SW England; uplands in the W include Exmoor and the Brendon and Quantock Hills; Mendip Hills in NE, Blackdown Hills in S; county town, Taunton; Cheddar Gorge. >> England [i]; Exmoor; Taunton

Somme, Battle of the [som] (1916) A major British offensive against German troops in NW France (1 Jul–19 Nov) which developed into the bloodiest battle in world history, with more than a million casualties. >> Somme, River; World War 1

Somme, River [som] River in N France, rising near St-Quentin; enters the English Channel; length 245 km/152 mi; scene of some of the worst fighting in World War 1 (1916). >> France [i]; Somme, Battle of the

somnambulism >> **sleep-walking**

Somoza (García), Anastasio [so**moh**za] (1896–1956) Nicaraguan dictator, born in San Marcos, Nicaragua. He established himself in supreme power in the early 1930s, and retained power until assassinated. His sons **Luis Somoza Debayle** (1923–67) and **Anastasio Somoza Debayle**

(1925–80) continued dynastic control of Nicaragua until the 1979 revolution. >> Nicaragua [i]

sonar Acronym for **sound navigation and ranging**, a means of detecting underwater vessels and objects, shoals of fish, and seabed features. The device emits pulsed bursts of sound underwater and listens for reflected echoes (**active sonar**), or simply listens for the sounds that a target may itself make (**passive sonar**). >> submarine

sonata A musical composition, usually for keyboard (harpsichord, piano, organ) or for another instrument with keyboard. The main Baroque type, however, was the trio sonata for two solo instruments (usually violins) and continuo. The 550 or so keyboard sonatas of Domenico Scarlatti are nearly all single-movement works, but the classical sonatas of Haydn, Mozart, and Beethoven are mostly in three or four movements. >> Baroque (music); continuo; Scarlatti, Domenico

sonatina A sonata of modest proportions, often not difficult to play. >> sonata

Sonderbund [**zon**derbunt] A political and military league of seven Swiss Catholic cantons formed in 1845 to resist liberal plans for centralization. The 25-day Sonderbund War (1847) ended with their defeat, and the creation of a Federal State (1848). >> Switzerland [i]

Sondheim, Stephen (Joshua) [**sond**hiym] (1930–) Composer, born in New York City. He earned his first success with his lyrics for Bernstein's *West Side Story* (1957). His own highly successful musicals include *A Funny Thing Happened on the Way to the Forum* (1962) and *Sweeney Todd* (1979). Later works include *Passion* (1994). >> Bernstein, Leonard

songbird A bird of the passerine sub-order Oscines. This sub-order includes most birds renowned for their singing ability. >> babbler; lark; passerine; sparrow; starling; sunbird; swallow; tanager; thickhead; thrush (bird); tit; treecreeper; wagtail; warbler; waxbill; waxwing; weaverbird; white-eye; whydah; wren

song cycle A sequence of separate songs united by some common theme or narrative thread. The earliest was perhaps Beethoven's *An die ferne Geliebte* (1816, To the Distant Beloved). >> *Lied*

Song or **Sung dynasty** (960–1279) A Chinese dynasty established by Taizu (r.960–76), which re-unified China after post-Tang confusion. The period is famed for its art, literature, and historical writing, besides important agrarian, financial, industrial, scientific, and technological progress. There were two dynastic phases: the Northern Song (960–1126) had its capital at Kaifeng on the Yellow River; later all N China was lost, and the Southern Song relocated to Hangzhou, S of the Yangtze. The dynasty fell to the Mongols under Kublai Khan. >> China ℹ

Songhai [**song**giy] A W African state which rose to power in the second half of the 15th-c, commanding the trade routes of the Sahara. Songhai peoples still control much of the Saharan caravan trade. >> Mali ℹ

Song of Solomon, Song of Songs, or **Canticles** A book of the Hebrew Bible/Old Testament, probably a collection of love songs, although sometimes considered a single poem or drama. The collection is usually dated c.3rd-c BC on linguistic grounds. >> allegory; Old Testament; poetry; Solomon (Hebrew Bible)

sonic boom A pressure shock wave created by aircraft travelling at supersonic speeds. The shock wave is produced continually, and travels outwards from the aircraft. Where it meets the ground it is perceived as a loud bang. A sonic boom was also produced when the British car *ThrustSSC* broke the land speed sound barrier in 1997. >> aerodynamics ℹ

sonnet (Ital *sonnetto* 'little song') A poem of 14 lines, usually in iambic pentameter, and with a structural balance between the first 8 lines (*octave*) and the last 6 (*sestet*). It was introduced in 13th-c Italy. >> metre (literature)

Soper, Donald (Oliver) Soper, Baron [**soh**per] (1903–98) Methodist minister, born in London. Widely known for his open-air speaking on London's Tower Hill, he wrote many books on Christianity and social questions. >> Methodism

sopherim >> **scribe**

Sophia (1630–1714) Electress of Hanover, born in The Hague, the youngest daughter of Elizabeth Stuart (daughter of James I of England) and Frederick, Elector Palatine, also elected King of Bohemia, 1618. Her son George, Elector of Hanover, became George I of Great Britain.

Sophists [**so**fists] Itinerant teachers (literally 'experts') in 5th-c Greece who, for a fee, offered professional training in rhetoric, and other skills to aspiring public figures. They are vividly portrayed in the dialogues of Plato, usually as dialectical opponents of Socrates. Among the best known was Protagoras. >> Protagoras; Socrates

Sophocles [**so**fokleez] (c.496–406 BC) Greek tragic playwright, born in Colonus Hippius. He wrote 123 plays, of which only seven survive: *Ajax*, *Electra*, *Women of Trachis*, *Philoctetes*, and his three major plays *Oedipus Rex*, *Oedipus at Colonus*, and *Antigone*.

Sophonias [sofo**niy**as] >> **Zephaniah, Book of**

Sopwith, Sir Thomas (Octave Murdoch) (1888–1989) Aircraft designer and sportsman, born in London. He built many of the aircraft used in World War 1, such as the Sopwith Camel. >> aircraft ℹ

sorbic acid A permitted food preservative which can inhibit the growth of moulds. It is obtained from the unripe fruits of the mountain ash. >> food preservation; rowan

Sorbonne [saw(r)**bon**] >> **Paris, University of**

sorcery >> **witchcraft**

sorghum [**saw(r)**guhm] A cereal resembling maize in general appearance, but with dense heads of small grains. The most important is *Sorghum vulgare*, also called **kaffir corn** or **guinea corn**, cultivated as a staple food in much of Africa and parts of Asia, and in America and Australia for animal feed. (Genus: *Sorghum*, 60 species. Family: Gramineae.) >> cereals; grass ℹ; maize

sororate >> **levirate**

sorority >> **fraternity and sorority**

Soros, George [**saw**ros] (1930–) Financier, born in Budapest. He joined a merchant bank in London, then worked as a financial analyst in New York City. In 1969 he set up the Quantum Fund, which grew rapidly from his daring speculations, and in 1979 he began to establish a network of Soros Foundations, mainly in Eastern Europe, to advance opportunities in education and business.

sorrel Any of several species of dock, native to Europe, usually with spear-shaped, acid-tasting leaves used as vegetables or in salads. (Genus: *Rumex*. Family: Polygonaceae.) >> dock

sort and merge A computer package designed to sort or re-sort files of computer data, and to combine two distinct files into a single sorted file. >> computer package; mailmerge; utility

sorus [**saw**ruhs] A plant structure formed from a number of sporangia. It is usually associated with ferns, where they are arranged in distinctive patterns on the undersides of the fronds. The lid-like flap of tissue protecting the sorus in some ferns is known as the *indusium*. >> fern; sporangium

Sotheby, John [**suh**thebee] (1740–1807) Auctioneer and antiquarian. In 1780 he became a director of the the first sale room in Britain exclusively for books, manuscripts, and prints.

Sotho–Tswana A cluster of Sotho-speaking peoples of Botswana, Lesotho, the Transvaal, Orange Free State, and N Cape. >> Botswana ℹ; Lesotho ℹ; South Africa ℹ

soul (music) A strongly emotional type of popular music which followed on from rhythm and blues in the 1960s, and drew on other types of pop music. It is associated primarily with black US singers, such as Aretha Franklin (1942–). >> Charles, Ray; gospel music; rhythm and blues

soul (religion) Usually, the principle of life, the ultimate identity of a person, or the immortal constituent of the self. In Christian thought, the concept is fused with the idea of the resurrection of the body. >> atman; Christianity; mind; resurrection

Soult, Nicolas Jean de Dieu [soolt] (1769–1851) French marshal, born in Saint-Amans-La-Bastide, France. He led the French armies in the Peninsular War (1808–14), and was Napoleon's chief-of-staff at Waterloo. Exiled until 1819, he presided over three ministries of Louis Philippe (1832–4, 1839–4, 1840–7). >> Louis Philippe; Peninsular War

sound A wave motion comprising a sequence of pressure pulses passing through some medium, typically air. The source of sound is a mechanical oscillator in a medium. It can be detected aurally, or using microphones or transducers. The speed of sound in air is 332 m/s. >> acoustics; sonar; sound intensity level ℹ; supersonic; wave motion ℹ

Sound, The, Danish **Øresund** Strait between Zealand I, Denmark, and S Sweden, connecting the Kattegat with the Baltic Sea; width of narrowest section, 6 km/4 mi. >> Denmark ℹ

sound barrier >> **aerodynamics** ℹ

sound film Cinema pictures with synchronized sound. A photographic sound record is printed by the side of the picture as a continuous track in which sound modulations are represented by variations of either its density or its width. By 1930, sound film had become universal in cinemas. >> cinematography; Movietone

sound intensity level Symbol L_I, units db (decibel); noise level relative to the faintest audible sound, which is rated as 0 db. It is related to sound intensity I, units W/m^2, the power per unit area of the sound wave. >> decibel; sound

sound navigation and ranging >> sonar

sound recording The conversion of sound into a storage medium from which it can later be reproduced. At first, sound signals were stored by direct mechanical conversion into grooves in a cylinder or disc, and reproduced using a phonograph or gramophone. In **digital recording**, the signal converted into corresponding electrical vibrations is represented numerically. With the *compact disc*, these digits are then directly decoded in the reproducing device, giving a recording that suffers no distortion as a result of the transmission process. >> compact disc; digital recording; Dolby system; magnetic tape 1; stereophonic sound; tape recorder

Sousa, John Philip [**soo**za] (1854–1932) Composer and bandmaster, born in Washington, DC. He became known as the composer of over 100 rousing military marches, and the inventor of the sousaphone. >> sousaphone

sousaphone [**soo**zafohn] A musical instrument resembling a tuba, but with the tubing encircling the player's body. It was designed by John Philip Sousa to be played while marching, and was first made in 1898. >> brass instrument [i]; Sousa; tuba

souslik [**soos**lik] or **suslik** [**suhs**lik] A squirrel native to Asia, Europe, and North America; coat may be striped or spotted; also known as **ground squirrel**. (Genus: *Spermophilus*, 32 species.) >> gopher; rodent; squirrel

Sousse [soos] 35°50N 10°38E, pop (1995e) 102 000. Port in NE Tunisia; founded by the Phoenicians, 9th-c BC; destroyed by the Vandals, AD 434; railway. >> Tunisia [i]

South Africa, official name **Republic of South Africa**, Afrikaans **Republiek van Suid-Afrika** pop (1996e) 37 900 000; area 1 233 404 sq km/476 094 sq mi. Southern African republic, divided into the nine provinces of Northern Cape, Western Cape, Eastern Cape, KwaZulu Natal, Orange Free State, North-West, Northern Transvaal, Eastern Transvaal, and Gauteng; Lesotho is landlocked within its borders; administrative capital, Pretoria; judicial capital, Bloemfontein; legislative capital, Cape Town; largest city, Johannesburg; timezone GMT +2; population is 77% black African, 12% white, 2.5% Asian, and 8.5% coloured; most whites and coloureds and c.60% of Africans are Christian, c.60% of Asians are Hindu, and c.20% are Muslim; 11 official languages, with 1996 population estimates – Zulu (22·4%), Xhosa (17·5%), Afrikaans (15·1%), Pedi (9·8%), English (9·1%), Tswana (7·2%), Sotho (6·9%), Tsonga (4·2%), Swati (2·6%), Venda (1·7%), Ndebele (1·5%); unit of currency, the rand of 100 cents; occupies the S extremity of the African plateau, fringed by fold mountains and a lowland coastal margin to the W, E, and S; N interior comprises the Kalahari Basin; Great Escarpment rises E to 3482 m/11 424 ft at Thabana Ntlenyana; subtropical climate in the E; dry moistureless climate on W coast; desert region further N; originally inhabited by Khoisan tribes; many Bantu-speaking tribes from the N after c.300; Portuguese reached the Cape of Good Hope, late 15th-c; settled by Dutch, 1652; arrival of British, 1795; British annexation of the Cape, 1806; Great Trek by Boers NE across the Orange R to Natal, 1836; first Boer republic founded, 1839; Natal annexed by the British 1843, but independence of the Boer republics of Transvaal (1852) and Orange Free State (1854) was recognized; Zulu War, 1879; South African Wars, 1880–1, 1899–1902; Transvaal, Natal, Orange Free State, and Cape Province joined as the Union of South Africa, a dominion of the British Empire, 1910; sovereign state within the Commonwealth, 1931–61; independent republic, 1961; politics dominated by treatment of non-white majority following the apartheid policy, 1948; continuing racial violence and strikes led to a state of emergency in 1986–90, and several countries imposed economic and cultural sanctions; progressive dismantling of apartheid system by de Klerk from 1990; African National Congress unbanned, 1990; all remaining apartheid legislation abolished, 1991; internal peace accord, 1991; Convention for a Democratic South Africa, 1991–2; constitutional agreement signed by de Klerk and Mandela, 1993; government of national unity, under a president, two vice-presidents, and a Cabinet; the national parliament consists of a 400-seat National Assembly and a 90-seat Council of Provinces; and the nine new provinces each have their their own premiers and legislatures; Mandela elected president, 1994; rejoined the Commonwealth and UNESCO, 1994; Truth and Reconciliation Committee appointed, 1995; new constitution approved, 1996; industrial growth as a result of 19th-c gold and diamond discoveries; world's largest producer of gold (about half the country's export income), platinum, chromium, vanadium, manganese, and aluminium silicates; produces nearly 40% of the world's chrome and cermiculite; cheap African labour used for new products and technologies. >> apartheid; Bloemfontein; Boer Wars; Bophuthatswana; Cape Coloured / provinces / Town; Ciskei; Great Trek; Johannesburg; Khoisan; KwaZulu Natal; Pretoria; Transkei; Transvaal; Venda; RR1021 political leaders

South African Native National Congress >> **African National Congress**

South America The fourth largest continent, extending c.7500 km/5000 mi from 12°25N to 56°S; area c.18 million sq km/7 million sq mi; linked to North America (NW) by the isthmus of Panama; bounded N by the Caribbean Sea, E by the Atlantic Ocean, and W by the Pacific Ocean; includes Argentina, Bolivia, Brazil, Chile, Colombia, Ecuador, Guyana, Paraguay, Peru, Suriname, Uruguay, and Venezuela; outlying islands include the Falkland Is, Galápagos Is, and Tierra del Fuego; the Andes run almost the full W length, rising to 6969 m/22 834 ft at Aconcagua; largest lake, Titicaca; major river basins, the Orinoco, Paraná, and Amazon (containing the world's largest tropical rainforest); considerable evidence of early Indian kingdoms, notably the Incas, destroyed by Spanish

and Portuguese invaders during the 16th-c; most countries achieved independence following wars in the early 19th-c. >> Amazon, River; Andes; Incas; Spanish–American Wars of Independence

Southampton, Lat **Clausentum**, Anglo-Saxon **Hamwih** 50°55N 1°25W, pop (1995e) 211 000. Port city and (from 1997) unitary authority in Hampshire, S England; on Southampton Water; major UK port handling container traffic and passenger ships; four tides daily; site of both Roman and Saxon settlements; city status (1964); railway; ferries to the I of Wight and N Europe; university (1952); St Michael's Church (1070); 15th-c Guildhall; football league team, Southampton (Saints). >> Hampshire

Southampton, Henry Wriothesley, 3rd Earl of [**roth**slee] (1573–1624) Courtier, born in Cowdray, Sussex. He was known as a patron of poets, notably of Shakespeare, who dedicated to him both *Venus and Adonis* (1593) and *The Rape of Lucrece* (1594). >> Shakespeare [i]

South Australia pop (1995e) 1 481 000; area 984 000 sq km/ 379 900 sq mi. State in S Australia; established as a British Crown Colony 1836; became a state, 1901; included most of Northern Territory, 1863–1901; largely desert, notably the Great Victoria Desert and Nullarbor Plain; fertile land in the SE corner irrigated by the Murray R; dry salt lakes inland; Flinders and Mt Lofty Ranges in the E; highest point, Mt Woodroffe (1440 m/4724 ft); Woomera Prohibited Area (weapons-testing range); 9600 km/ 6000 mi-long Dingo Fence protects S grazing sheep; capital, Adelaide; supplies 95% of world's opals; oranges and other citrus fruit; almost half of Australia's wine produced from the Barossa Valley N of Adelaide. >> Adelaide; Australia [i]; dingo; Great Victoria Desert; Nullarbor Plain

South Carolina pop (1995e) 3 784 000; area 80 580 sq km/ 31 113 sq mi. State in SE USA; the 'Palmetto State'; settled by the French at Port Royal, 1562; included in the Carolina grant in 1663, but returned to the Crown in 1729; brought under American control after the battle of Guilford Courthouse, 1781; eighth of the original 13 states to ratify the Constitution, 1788; the first state to secede from the Union, 1860; slavery abolished, 1865; re-admitted to the Union, 1868; capital, Columbia; Blue Ridge Mts in the extreme NW; highest point Mt Sassafras (1085 m/3560 ft); flat and (in the S) swampy coastland, cut by numerous rivers and creeks to form the Sea Islands, a major tourist centre; ground rises inland towards the rolling Piedmont, the agricultural and manufacturing centre; textiles and clothing, using the large cotton crop. >> American Civil War; Columbia; United States of America [i]; RR994

South China Sea area c.3 685 000 sq km/1 423 000 sq mi. W arm of the Pacific Ocean; subject to violent typhoons; main arms, Gulfs of Tongkin and Kompong; deep basin in NE, reaching 5490 m/18 012 ft. >> Pacific Ocean

Southcott, Joanna (c.1750–1814) Religious fanatic, born in Dorset. In c.1792 she declared herself to be the woman in *Rev* 12 who would give birth to the second Prince of Peace. She obtained a great following, but died soon after the predicted date of the birth. >> Revelation, Book of

South Dakota [da**koh**ta] pop (1995e) 732 000; area 199 723 sq km/77 116 sq mi. State in NC USA; the 'Coyote State'; part of the USA as a result of the Louisiana Purchase, 1803; included in Dakota Territory, 1861; population swelled when gold was discovered in the Black Hills, 1874; separated from North Dakota and became the 40th state of the Union, 1889; capital, Pierre; the Black Hills rise in the SW corner of the state; highest point, Mt Harney Peak (2207 m/7241 ft); W of Missouri R is a semi-arid, treeless plain, one-third owned by Sioux Indians; severe erosion has formed the barren Bad Lands; E of the R Missouri are rich, fertile plains; town of Lead in the Black Hills is the nation's leading gold-mining centre; second largest gold and beryllium producer in the USA; Mt Rushmore (in the Black Hills). >> Louisiana Purchase; Pierre; Sioux; United States of America [i]; RR994

South Downs Way Long-distance footpath following the South Downs of East and West Sussex, S England; stretches from Eastbourne to Harting; length 130 km/ 80 mi. >> Downs

South East Asia Treaty Organization (SEATO) An organization founded mainly to provide collective defence in the case of an attack against any one of the eight signatories to the treaty: Australia, France, New Zealand, Pakistan, the Philippines, Thailand, UK, and USA. SEATO's headquarters is in Bangkok. By 1992 it was inactive.

Southend [sowth**end**], in full **Southend-on-Sea** 51°33N 0°43E, pop (1995e) 173 000. Resort town and unitary authority (from 1998) in Essex, SE England; on the R Thames estuary; famous pier, 2 km/1¼ mi long; railway; airfield; football league team, Southend United (Shrimpers). >> Essex

Southern Alps Mountain range in WC South Island, New Zealand; length c.320 km/200 mi NE–SW; contains New Zealand's highest peaks, Mt Cook (3764 m/12 349 ft), Mt Tasman (3497 m/11 472 ft), and Mt Dampier (3440 m/ 11 286 ft). >> New Zealand [i]; South Island

Southern Cross >> **Crux**

Southern Ocean >> **Antarctic Ocean**

southernwood An aromatic shrub (*Artemisia abrotanum*) growing to 1 m/3½ ft; flower-heads globular, florets dull yellow. Its sweetly aromatic leaves are used for flavouring. (Family: Compositae.)

Southey, Robert [**suh**thee] (1774–1843) Writer, born in Bristol. Although made poet laureate in 1813, his poetry did not become as well known as his prose works, such as his life of Nelson, and his letters.

South Georgia 54°30S 37°00W; area c.3750 sq km/ 1450 sq mi. Barren, mountainous, snow-covered island in the S Atlantic, about 500 km/300 mi E of the Falkland Is; a British overseas territory administered from the Falkland Is; length, 160 km/100 mi; discovered by the London merchant De la Roche, 1675; landing by Captain Cook, 1775; British annexation, 1908 and 1917; invaded by Argentina and recaptured by Britain, April 1982; sealing and whaling centre until 1965; burial place of Ernest Shackleton. >> Falkland Islands [i]; Falklands War; Shackleton

South Glamorgan pop (1995e) 415 000; area 416 sq km/ 161 sq mi. Former county in S Wales, UK; created in 1974, and replaced in 1996 by Cardiff and Vale of Glamorgan counties. >> Wales [i]

South Korea >> **Korea** [i]

South Orkney Islands, Span **Orcadas del Sur** area 620 sq km/239 sq mi. Group of islands in the S Atlantic; used by British and US whalers since 1821; uninhabited, apart from scientific research; claimed by Argentina. >> British Antarctic Territory

South Pacific Forum An organization founded in 1971 to provide a setting where the heads of government of independent and self-governing Pacific island states could meet to discuss their common political concerns with each other and with Australia and New Zealand. It had 16 members in 1999.

South Pole >> **Poles**

Southport 53°39N 3°01W, pop (1995e) 88 800. Coastal resort town in Merseyside, NW England; the original 'garden city'; a notable golfing area (Birkdale); railway; annual flower show. >> Merseyside

South Sandwich Islands 56°18S–59°25S 26°15W. Group

of small, uninhabited islands in the S Atlantic, c.720 km/450 mi SE of South Georgia; a British overseas territory administered from the Falkland Is; discovered by Captain Cook, 1775; annexed by Britain, 1908 and 1917. >> Falkland Islands

South Sea Bubble A financial crisis in Britain (1720) arising out of speculation mania generated by Parliament's approval of the South Sea Company's proposal to take over three-fifths of the National Debt. Many investors were ruined in the aftermath.

South Shetland Islands area 4622 sq km/1784 sq mi. Group of mountainous islands in the S Atlantic; discovered in 1819; occasionally used for scientific bases. >> British Antarctic Territory

Southwark [suhtherk] 51°30N 0°06W, pop (1995e) 228 000. Borough of C Greater London, England; S of the R Thames; formerly famous for its inns and Elizabethan theatres (site of Globe Theatre); railway; 13th-c Southwark Cathedral, Dulwich College (1621), Guy's Hospital (1721), Imperial War Museum. >> London

Southwell, Robert (1561–95) Poet and martyr, born in Horsham, Norfolk. Beatified in 1929, he is known for his devotional lyrics, and for several prose treatises and epistles. >> Reformation

Southwest Africa >> **Namibia** ℹ

Southwest Africa People's Organization (SWAPO) A nationalist organization in Southwest Africa (Namibia), which opened a guerrilla campaign against South African rule in Namibia in 1969. Frontline states and the Organization of African Unity gave their support, and Angola provided bases for its liberation movement. At the end of 1988, an international agreement was reached in Geneva linking arrangements for the future independence of Namibia with the withdrawal of Cuban troops from Angola, and the cessation of South African attacks on that country and its support for the UNITA rebels. >> Angola ℹ; Namibia ℹ; Organization of African Unity

Southwest Indians North American Indian groups living in the SW states of New Mexico, Utah, Colorado, and Texas, and in Mexico. Many prehistoric remains provide evidence of early settlement, dating back to possibly 10 000 years ago. The largest Indian groups in North America currently live in the area. >> American Indians; Apache; Hopi; Navajo; Pueblo; Zuni

South Yorkshire >> **Yorkshire, South**

Soutine, Chaim [sooteen, khiym] (1893–1943) Artist, born in Smilovich, Belarus. He became known for his paintings of carcasses, and for his series of 'Choirboys' (1927). He was later recognized as a leading Expressionist painter. >> Expressionism

sovereign A British gold coin originally worth £1, but since the abolition of the gold standard worth considerably more. Sovereigns can now be purchased, their price varying with the price of gold. >> currency

sovereignty The capacity to determine conduct within the territory of a nation-state without external legal constraint. Where legal limits are placed upon the organs of government by the constitution, as in the USA, sovereignty is claimed to reside with the people.

soviet Originally, a workers' council established in Russia after the 1905 revolution. They re-appeared as workers' and soldiers' councils, important instruments of the 1917 revolution. Members of soviets were elected by popular vote.

Soviet space programme A dominant element in the exploration of space after the launch of Sputnik in 1957 until the demise of the Soviet Union in 1990. It was formally replaced by the Russian Space Agency in 1992. >> cosmonaut; Luna / Mars / Venera programme; Progress / Soyuz / Vostok spacecraft; Mir / Salyut space station; space exploration; Sputnik; VEGA project

Soviet Union, official name **Union of Soviet Socialist Republics (USSR)**, Russ **Soyuz Sovyetskikh Sotsialisticheskikh Republik** (Cyrillic alphabet, **CCCP**) pop (1990) 290 122 000; area 22 402 076 sq km/8 647 201 sq mi. Former federation of 15 republics, comprising most of E Europe and N and C Asia, which until its dissolution (1991) jointly formed the world's largest sovereign state; capital, Moscow; ethnic groups included Russian (52%), Ukrainian (16%), and over 100 others; chief religion, Russian Orthodox (18%), with 70% atheist; official language, Russian; unit of currency, the rouble of 100 kopeks; Union Republics were usually known as **Soviet Socialist Republics (SSR)**; there were in addition 20 **Autonomous Soviet Socialist Republics (ASSR)**, and several smaller divisions (6 *krays*, 123 *oblasts*, 8 *autonomous oblasts*, 10 *autonomous okrugs*); formed in 1922 following the October Revolution (1917) and the subsequent Civil War; first Soviet government headed by Lenin; vigorous socialist reform begun by Stalin in the 1920s, including the collectivization of agriculture and rapid industrialization; territories extended in the W after World War 2, with a corridor of communist-dominated countries between USSR and W Europe; period of Cold War following World War 2; intervention to suppress Hungarian uprising (1956) and Czech programme of liberalization (1968); invasion of Afghanistan, 1979–88; series of disarmament agreements in 1980s, with new approach to international relations under Gorbachev; constitutional reforms implemented in 1989 instituted a new Congress of the USSR People's Deputies, which elected from its ranks a 542-member Supreme Soviet; major internal changes in 1991, following the emerging independence of several republics and the reduced role of the Communist Party; failure of an attempted coup (Aug 1991), with resistance led by Yeltsin, resulted in the process of radical reform, liberalization, and recognition of independence movements in the constituent republics; recognition of Estonia, Latvia, and Lithuania (1990–1) was followed by the abolition of the Communist Party and ultimately the country's dissolution (Dec 1991); most of the constituent republics then formed the Commonwealth of Independent States. >> Armenia ℹ; Azerbaijan ℹ; Belarus ℹ; Commonweath of Independent States ℹ; communism; Estonia ℹ; Georgia ℹ; Gorbachev; Kazakhstan ℹ; Kyrgyzstan ℹ; Latvia ℹ; Lithuania ℹ; Moldova ℹ; Moscow; Russia ℹ; Russian history; Tajikistan ℹ; Turkmenistan ℹ; Ukraine ℹ; Uzbekistan ℹ; Yeltsin; RR1025 political leaders

sow >> **pig**

Soweto [sohwetoh] 26°15S 27°52E, pop (1995e) 1 008 000. Black African township in South Africa; the name derives from the official title of South-West Township; linked by rail (8 km/5 mi) to industrial W Johannesburg; student riots in 1976, when several hundred people were killed. >> South Africa ℹ

soya bean A bushy, reddish-haired annual (*Glycine max*), growing to 2 m/6¼ ft; pea-flowers rather inconspicuous, violet, pink, or white; pods up to 8 cm/3 in long, hairy; also called **soja** or **soy bean**. The edible seeds (**soya beans**), rich in protein, are eaten as a vegetable and used in the production of flour, margarine and cooking oils, artificial meat, and food for livestock. There are also numerous industrial uses, such as in enamels, paints, and varnishes. (Family: Leguminosae.) >> vegetable

Soyinka, Wole [soyingka, wolay], popular name of **Akinwande Oluwole Soyinka** (1934–) Writer, born near Abeokuta, Nigeria. His writing is deeply concerned with the tension between old and new in modern Africa. His poetic collection *A Shuttle in the Crypt* (1972) appeared after his release in 1969 from two years political detention. His first novel, *The Interpreters* (1965), was called the first really modern African novel. He was awarded the Nobel Prize for Literature in 1986. *The Open Sore of a Continent* appeared in 1996.

Soyuz ('Union') spacecraft A Soviet basic space capsule, consisting of three modules, and carrying a crew of one to three. It has been flown on several dozen missions, and is capable of precision targeting to soft-land in C Asia. The first flight was in 1967, when its pilot, V Komarov, was killed in a landing accident. Soyuz 19 docked with the Apollo spacecraft in Earth orbit after its rendezvous (1975). >> Soviet space programme; RR970

Spaak, Paul Henri (1899–1972) Belgian statesman and prime minister (1938–9, 1946, 1947–9), born in Schaerbeek, Belgium. He became president of the first General Assembly of the United Nations (1946), foreign minister (1954–7, 1961–8), and secretary-general of NATO (1957–61). >> NATO; United Nations

spacecraft Vehicles designed to operate in the vacuum–weightlessness–high radiation environment of space; used to convey human crew, to acquire scientific data, to conduct utilitarian operations (eg telecommunications), and to conduct research (eg microgravity experiments). The first spacecraft (Sputnik 1) was launched by the USSR in 1957 (4 Oct). >> Explorer 1; Progress / Soyuz / Vostok spacecraft; space exploration; Sputnik

space exploration An era which began with the first artificial satellite (Sputnik, 1957) and the first manned flight (Gagarin, 1961), with subsequent rapidly evolving capabilities in Earth orbit and Solar System exploration (initiated by Mariner 2, 1962). There has been reconnaissance as far as Neptune, in-depth exploration of Mars and Venus, and detailed study of the Moon. Human activity has been demonstrated to the point of crewed lunar landings (Apollo programme, 1969–72) and continuing space station occupancy (Salyut and Mir space stations), but remains dangerous and costly. Launch vehicle advances have achieved a re-usable crewed orbiter (US space shuttle), but inexpensive, reliable transportation is still in the future. Space physiological effects on humans are likely to limit the rate at which future exploration proceeds. >> Apollo programme; launch vehicle; Solar System; space station

Spacelab A research facility flown in the cargo bay of the NASA space shuttle; designed by the European Space Agency. It consists of a pressurized experiment module for scientist–astronaut activities, and one or more pallets upon which telescopes and Earth remote-sensing experiments are mounted. >> European Space Agency; space shuttle ⓘ

space shuttle A re-usable crewed launch vehicle. The first-generation US shuttle launched in April 1981; it carries up to seven crew, and is capable of launching a 27 000 kg/60 000 lb payload into low Earth orbit; missions are up to 9 days' duration. It comprises a delta-winged lifting body orbiter with main engines, a jettisonable external fuel tank, and two auxiliary solid rocket boosters. The fleet comprised four vehicles: *Columbia*, *Challenger*, *Discovery*, and *Atlantis*. The *Challenger* explosion on the 25th flight (28 Jan 1986) 73 sec after launch caused the loss of the crew. The first reflight took place in September 1988, and a replacement fourth orbiter, *Endeavour*, became operational in 1992. >> launch vehicle ⓘ; spacecraft; RR970; *see illustration on p. 809*

space station A long-lived crewed spacecraft in low Earth orbit; examples are US Skylab and USSR Mir. It is used for biomedical research, astronomy, Earth observations, and microgravity experiments. Eventually, it will be used as a transportation node for human planetary missions. The US space station programme underwent a major redesign in 1993 to incorporate substantial participation by Russia and to aim at full operational status by 2001. >> Mir / Salyut space station; Skylab project

space–time A fundamental concept in the special and general theories of relativity. Einstein showed that a complete description of relative motion required equations including time as well as the three spatial dimensions. The form in which time is expressed gives it the mathematical property of a fourth co-ordinate, or dimension. >> Einstein; general relativity

spadefoot toad A frog native to Europe, Asia, and North America; sharp projections (*spades*) on hind feet; burrows in dry sandy areas. (Family: Pelobatidae, 54 species.) >> frog

spadix [**spay**diks] A specialized type of inflorescence in which the usually tiny flowers are crowded on a fleshy, cylindrical axis, generally enveloped by a large bract – the *spathe*. It is typical of the arum family (Araceae). >> arum lily; bract; inflorescence ⓘ

spaghetti Western A motion picture drama following the themes and settings of the American 'Western', but cheaply produced by European companies on locations in Spain and Italy. The first of this genre was *A Fistful of Dollars* (1964), directed by Sergio Leone and starring Clint Eastwood.

Spain, Span **España**, ancient **Iberia**, Lat **Hispania**, official name **Kingdom of Spain**, Span **Reino de España** pop (1995e) 38 734 000; area of mainland 492 431 sq km/190 078 sq mi; total area 504 750 sq km/194 833 sq mi. Country in SW Europe, occupying four-fifths of the Iberian Peninsula, and including the Canary Is, Balearic Is, and several islands off the coast of N Africa, as well as the Presidios of Ceuta and Melilla in N Morocco; capital, Madrid; timezone GMT +1; chief religion, Roman Catholicism (95%); official language, Spanish, with Catalan, Galician, and Basque also spoken in certain regions; unit of currency, the peseta of 100 céntimos; mostly a furrowed C plateau (the Meseta, average height 700 m/2300 ft) crossed by mountains; Andalusian or Baetic Mts (SE) rise to 3478 m/11 411 ft at Mulhacén; continental climate in the Meseta, with hot summers, cold winters; S Mediterranean coast has the warmest winter temperatures on the European mainland; early inhabitants included Iberians, Celts, Phoenicians, Greeks, and Romans; Muslim domination from the 8th-c; Christian reconquest completed by 1492; a monarchy since the unification of the Kingdoms of Castile, León, Aragón, and Navarre, largely achieved by 1572; 16th-c exploration of the New World, and the growth of the Spanish Empire; period of decline after the Revolt of the Netherlands 1566–1648, and the defeat of the Spanish Armada in 1588; War of the Spanish Succession, 1701–13; Peninsular War against Napoleon, 1808–14; war with the USA in 1898 led to the loss of Cuba, Puerto Rico, and remaining Pacific possessions; dictatorship under Primo de Rivera (1923–30), followed by exile of the king and establishment of the Second Republic (1931); military revolt headed by Franco in 1936 led to civil war and a Fascist dictatorship; Prince Juan Carlos of Bourbon nominated to succeed Franco, 1969; acceded, 1975; governed by a king, prime minister, and bicameral parliament (*Cortes*) comprising a Congress of Deputies and a Senate; since 1978 there has been a move towards local government autonomy with the creation of 17 self-governing regions; traditionally agricultural economy gradually being supplemented by varied industries; a member of the European Community from 1986. >> Bourbons; Castile; Franco; Peninsular War; Revolt of the Netherlands; Spanish–American War; Spanish Armada

The orbiter structure is divided into nine major sections: the forward fuselage, which consists of upper and lower sections that fit clamlike around a pressurized crew compartment; wings; midfuselage; payload bay doors; aft fuselage; forward reaction control system; vertical tail; orbital manoeuvring system / reaction control system pods; and body flap. The majority of the sections are constructed of conventional aluminium and protected by re-usable surface insulation. The forward fuselage structure is composed of 2024 aluminium alloy skin-stringer panels, frames and bulkheads. The crew compartment is supported within the forward fuselage at four attachment points, and is welded to create a pressure-tight vessel. The three-level compartment has a side hatch for normal passage, and hatches in the airlock to permit extravehicular and intravehicular activities. The side hatch can be jettisoned.

All measurements are given in feet, with metric equivalents in parentheses.

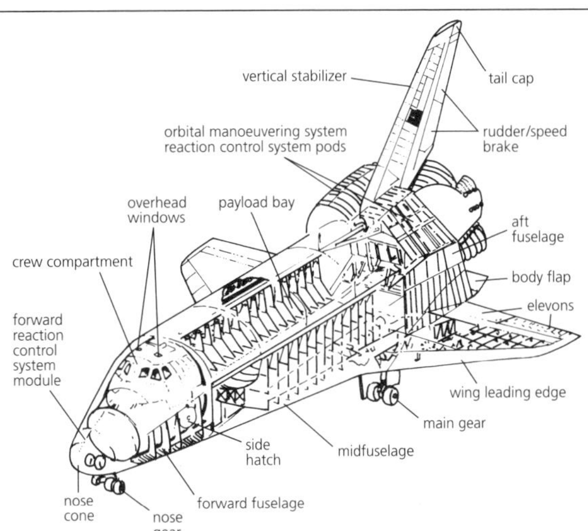

Minimum Ground Clearances	ft	(m)
body flap	12.07	(3.7)
main gear door	2.85	(0.87)
nose gear door	2.95	(0.89)
wing tip	11.92	(3.6)

Orbiter weight in lb/kg (approximate)

Orbiter vehicle (OV)	Total dry weight with three space shuttle main engines	Total dry weight without three space shuttle main engines
OV-102 Columbia	178 289/80 872	157 289/71 346
OV-103 Discovery	171 419/77 756	151 419/68 684
OV-104 Atlantis	171 205/77 659	151 205/68 587

Solid rocket booster weights in lb/kg (approximate)

1 300 000/590 000 each at launch (propellant weight 1 100 000/500 000 each). Inert weight 192 000/87 000 each

External tank weight in lb/kg (approximate)

1 655 600/750 000 with propellants. Inert weight 66 000/30 000

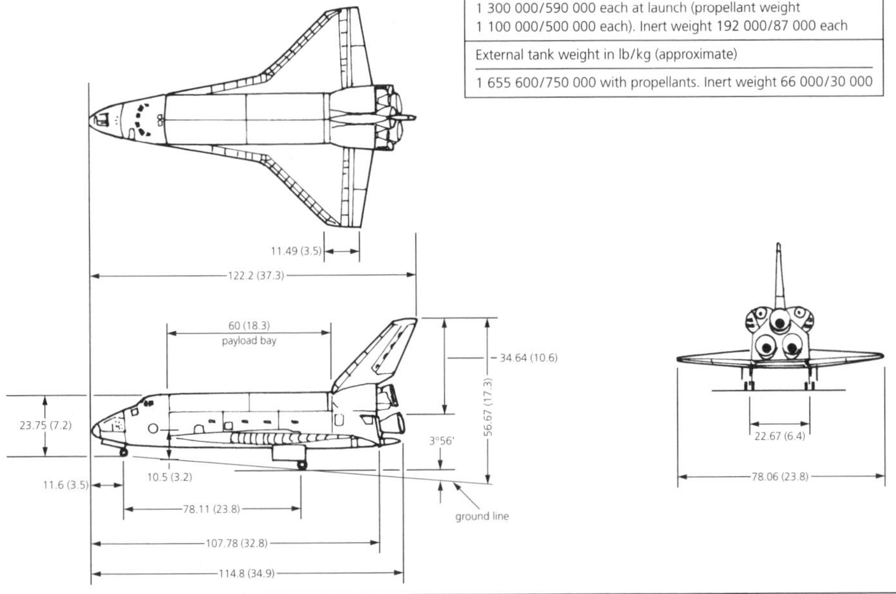

Space shuttle

/ Civil War; Spanish Succession, War of the; RR1022 political leaders; *see illustration on p. 810*

spaniel A sporting dog belonging to one of several breeds originally developed to assist hunters; usually small, affectionate, with long pendulous ears; now popular pets. >> cocker / King Charles / springer spaniel; Maltese (zoology); retriever; sporting dog

Spanish >> **Romance languages**

Spanish–American War (1898) A brief conflict growing out of US intervention in the Cuban revolution for independence, effectively ended by the destruction of the Spanish fleet. The war resulted in Cuban independence under US suzerainty, and in US acquisition of Puerto Rico and the Philippines.

Spanish–American Wars of Independence (1810–26) Wars fought in South America, following Napoleon's invasion of Spain (1808): reformers in the major South American colonies set up semi-independent governments (1810). The ensuing wars were fought in two main theatres: Venezuela, New Granada and Quito, where Simón Bolívar was the leading patriot general, and Argentina and Chile, from where General José de San Martín mounted an invasion of the Viceroyalty of Peru (1820–1). The final liberation of Peru was effected in 1824 by Bolívar. The last Spanish garrisons in South America surrendered in 1826. >> Bolívar; San Martín

Spanish Armada A fleet of 130 Spanish ships sent by Philip II of Spain to invade England in 1588. The invasion was in retaliation for English support of Protestant rebels in the Netherlands, the execution of Mary, Queen of Scots (1587), and raids on Spanish shipping. The fleet was routed by English attacks off Gravelines (28–29 Jul); 44 ships were lost in battles and during the flight home around Scotland and Ireland. >> Drake; Elizabeth I; Philip II (of Spain)

Spanish Civil War (1936–9) The conflict between supporters and opponents of the Spanish Republic (1931–6). The 'Republicans' included moderates, socialists, communists, and Catalan and Basque regionalists and anarchists. The 'Nationalist' insurgents included monarchists, Carlists, conservative Catholics, and fascist Falangists. The armed forces were divided. The Nationalist victory was due to the balance of foreign aid; to 'non-intervention' on the part of the Western democracies; and to greater internal unity, achieved under the leadership of General Franco. The Nationalists initially (Jul 1936) seized much of NW Spain and part of the SW, then (autumn 1936) advanced upon but failed to capture Madrid. They captured Málaga (Mar 1937) and the N coast (Mar–Oct 1937); advanced to the Mediterranean, cutting Republican Spain in two (Apr 1938); overran Catalonia (Dec 1938–Feb 1939); and finally occupied Madrid and SE Spain (Mar 1939). >> Basques; Catalonia; Falange; fascism; Franco; International Brigades; Spain [i]

Spanish fly A slender, metallic-green beetle which exudes acrid yellow fluid from its joints; wing cases formerly collected as a source of blistering agent (*cantharidin*) and as a counter-irritant; more popularly (but spuriously) used as an aphrodisiac, where its high toxicity has led to many cases of fatal poisoning. (Order: Coleoptera. Family: Meloidae.) >> aphrodisiacs; beetle

Spanish Main The mainland area of Spanish South America, known until the 19th-c for its pirates. It extends from Panama to the Orinoco R estuary in Venezuela. >> buccaneers

Spanish Riding School A school of classical horsemanship situated in Vienna, founded in the late 16th-c. The school is famous for its Lipizzaner horses, bred especially for *haute école* (Fr 'high school') riding, and originally imported from Spain. >> equestrianism; Lipizzaner

Spanish Succession, War of the (1701–13) A conflict fought in several theatres – the Netherlands, Germany, Spain, the Mediterranean, and the Atlantic – between the Grand Alliance (headed by Britain, the Dutch, and the Habsburg emperor) and Louis XIV of France, supported by Spain. Hostilities arose after the death of the last Habsburg King of Spain, Charles II. The war was concluded by the Treaties of Utrecht. >> Eugene, Prince; Habsburgs; Leopold I (Emperor); Louis XIV; Marlborough, Duke of; Philip V; Queen Anne's War

Spanish Town 17°59N 76°58W, pop (1995e) 96 100. Second largest city in S Jamaica; on the R Cobre; capital, 1535–1872; railway; serves a rich agricultural area; cathedral (1655). >> Jamaica [i]

Spark, Dame Muriel (Sarah) (1918–) Writer, born in Edinburgh. She is best known for her novels, notably *Memento Mori* (1959), *The Prime of Miss Jean Brodie* (1961), *The Mandelbaum Gate* (1965, James Tait Black), *The Driver's Seat* (1970), and *Reality and Dreams* (1996).

spark ignition engine An internal combustion engine which initiates the combustion of its air/fuel mixture by means of a spark, usually generated by a sparking plug.

This type of engine is most commonly found in motor cars. >> four-stroke engine [i]; internal combustion engine

sparrow A small songbird, native to the Old World; plumage usually brown/grey. (Family: Ploceidae, c.37 species; but some authorities place the sparrow in a separate family Passeridae.) >> accentor; bunting; finch; house sparrow; songbird

sparrowhawk A hawk (Genus: *Accipiter*, 24 species), native to the Old World, and to Central and South America; eats birds, other small vertebrates, and insects. >> falcon; hawk

sparrow-weaver >> **weaverbird**

Sparta (city-state) [**spah(r)**ta] One of the two leading city-states of ancient Greece, the other being Athens. Her defeat of Athens in 404 BC put her centre stage, but she played her role so badly that the other city-states combined against her. Thebes delivered the final blow at Leuctra in 371 BC. >> Lycurgus; Peloponnesian War; Thebes

Sparta (town) [**spah(r)**ta], Gr **Spartí** 37°05N 22°25E, pop (1995e) 15 900. Town in S Greece; on the R Evrotas; refounded on an ancient site in 1834. >> Greece [i]

Spartacists A left-wing revolutionary faction (the *Spartakusbund*), led by Rosa Luxemburg and Karl Liebknecht (1871–1919) in 1917, which supported the Russian Revolution, and advocated a German socialist revolution. Luxemburg and Liebknecht were murdered in disturbances in Berlin during the period following the Kaiser's abdication in 1918. >> Luxemburg

Spartacus [**spah(r)**takus] (?–71 BC) Thracian-born slave and gladiator at Capua, who led the most serious slave uprising in the history of Rome (73–71 BC). With a huge army of slaves and dispossessed, he inflicted numerous defeats on the Roman armies sent against him, until defeated and killed by Crassus. >> Crassus; Servile Wars

Spartakiad [spah(r)**tak**iad] Sporting games held every four years in the former Soviet Union, until 1979 for nationals only. They were named after the ancient Greek city of Sparta, which placed great emphasis on physical fitness.

spastic >> **cerebral palsy**

spathe [spayth] A large sheathing bract which surrounds the specialized inflorescence called a *spadix*. The spathe is often brightly coloured. >> bract; inflorescence [i]; spadix

Speaker The officer who presides over a legislative chamber. The post originated in 14th-c England, where one member of the Commons was designated to speak to the king. In the UK, the Speaker presides over the House of Commons, maintains order, and interprets its rules and practice. He or she is a constituency MP elected by fellow members, but must sever party connections and be entirely impartial. In the US House of Representatives, the Speaker is a leader of the majority party, and expected to assist in securing the passage of his party's legislation. >> Commons, House of; House of Representatives

spearmint >> **mint**

Special Air Service >> **SAS**

Special Boat Service >> **SBS**

Special Branch A branch of the British police force principally responsible for investigating offences against the state, including terrorism, sedition, treason, and contravention of the Official Secrets Act. It was formed in 1883. >> police; Scotland Yard

special education The provision of education to children who have special educational needs. They may be pupils who suffer from some kind of physical or mental handicap, who have learning or emotional difficulties, or whose needs cannot otherwise be catered for within the normal provision. In many cases the pattern is to provide special schools, but the trend in some countries has been for such children to be taught in ordinary schools.

Special Operations Executive (SOE) An organization set up with British War Cabinet approval in July 1940 in response to Churchill's directive to 'set Europe ablaze'. It promoted and co-ordinated resistance activity in enemy-occupied territory until the end of World War 2. >> Churchill, Winston; Maquis; World War 2

special relativity A system of mechanics applicable at high velocities (approaching the velocity of light) in the absence of gravitation; a generalization of Newtonian mechanics, due almost entirely to Albert Einstein (1905). Its fundamental postulates are that the velocity of light, *c*, is the same for all observers, no matter how they are moving; that the laws of physics are the same in all inertial frames; and that all such frames are equivalent. On this basis, no object may have a velocity in excess of the velocity of light; and two events which appear simultaneous to one observer need not be so for another. The system gives laws of mechanics which reproduce those of 'common sense' Newtonian mechanics at low velocities, and is well supported experimentally, especially in particle physics. Generalized special relativity, incorporating gravitation, is called **general relativity**. >> Einstein; mass–energy relation; Michelson; Newton, Isaac; tachyon; *see illustration on p. 812*

species A group of organisms, minerals, or other entities formally recognized as distinct from other groups. In biology, the species is a group of actually or potentially interbreeding natural populations, reproductively isolated from other similar groups such that exchange of genetic material cannot occur (the **species barrier**). >> fossil; morphology (biology); prion disease; reproduction; systematics; taxonomy

specific gravity >> **relative density**

specific heat capacity >> **heat capacity**

speckle interferometry A technique used in optical and infrared astronomy to produce high-resolution images. It processes numerous short exposures in a way which removes the effects of erratic motions (twinkling) caused by turbulence in the Earth's atmosphere. >> astronomy

spectacles A frame which supports lenses held in front of each eye, designed to correct abnormalities of refraction, such as long or short sight, and *astigmatism* (asymmetry of the cornea). **Bifocal spectacles** have lenses where the upper and lower parts have different curvatures, enabling the wearer to focus on distant and near objects respectively. >> eye [i]

Spector, Phil (1940–) Record producer, born in New York City. In the 1960s he developed a distinctive 'wall of sound' style using echo-effects and other innovative recording techniques, with hits by such groups as the Ronettes and the Crystals. His *Christmas Album* remains a festive classic.

spectroscopy The study of energy levels in atoms or molecules, using absorbed or emitted electromagnetic radiation. Inner atomic electrons give spectra in the X-ray region; outer atomic electrons give visible light spectra; the rotation and vibration of molecules give infrared spectra; the precession of nuclear magnetic moments gives radio-wave spectra. >> atomic spectra [i]; mass spectrometer; spectrum

spectrum The distribution of electromagnetic energy as a function of wavelength or frequency. A common example is the spectrum of white light dispersed by a prism to produce a rainbow of constituent colours. For white light the colours are red, orange, yellow, green, blue, and violet in order of decreasing wavelength. Individual atoms can emit and absorb radiation only at particular wavelengths corresponding to the transitions between energy levels in the atom. The spectrum of a given atom (or element) therefore consists of a series of emission or absorption lines. The device for displaying a spectrum is called a

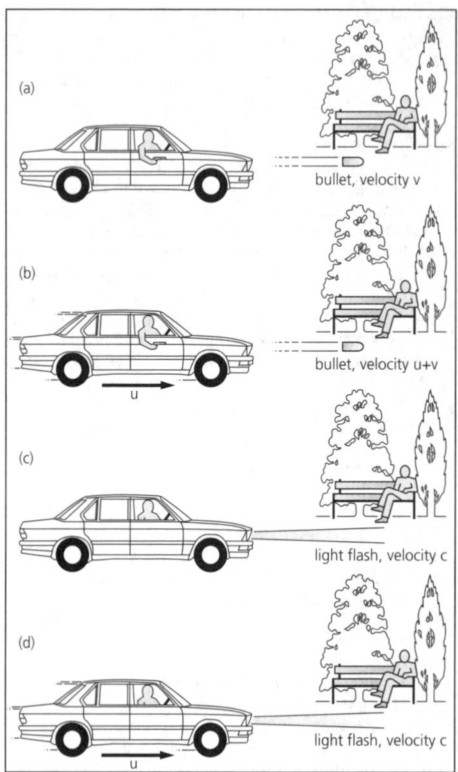

Special relativity – in (a) a bullet with velocity v is fired from a stationary car; in (b) a car is moving with velocity u, with a similar bullet fired in the same direction as the motion of the car; as seen by an observer, the bullet has velocity u + v. In (c) a flash of light sent by a stationary car is measured by an observer as c, the standard velocity of light; in (d) a flash of light is sent from a car moving at velocity u; the observer measures the velocity of the flash and finds that it too is c, not c + u. The velocity of light is always the same.

spectrograph. >> atomic spectra ℹ; electromagnetic radiation ℹ; light; optics ℹ; spectroscopy

speech pathology The study and treatment of all forms of clinically abnormal linguistic behaviour; also known as **(speech and) language pathology**. In several countries (eg the USA), the designation **speech pathologist** applies to professionals concerned with the treatment of language-handicapped people; in others (eg the UK) the equivalent profession is that of **speech and language therapist**. >> aphasia; apraxia; cluttering; dyslexia; stuttering

speech therapy >> **speech pathology**

Speed, John (1552–1629) Antiquary and cartographer, born in Cheshire. He published his 54 *Maps of England and Wales* in 1608–10. >> cartography

speed (drug) >> **amphetamine**

speed (physics) The rate of change of distance with time; symbol *v*, units m/s; a scalar quantity. Speed is the magnitude of velocity, but unlike velocity specifies no direction. >> velocity

speed of light >> **velocity of light**

speedometer An instrument fitted in a vehicle to show its speed. Usually a cable from the vehicle road-drive rotates a magnet, which induces an eddy current in a non-magnetic conductor attached to a pointer. >> magnetism; tachometer

speedway A form of motorcycle racing on machines with no brakes and only one gear. Other forms include **long track racing** and **ice speedway**. The sport originated in the USA in 1902. >> motorcycle racing; RR1061

speedwell An annual or perennial, some agricultural weeds, native to N temperate regions; flowers solitary or in spikes, blue or white, with a short tube and four petals, upper largest, lower smallest. (Genus: *Veronica*, 300 species. Family: Scrophulariaceae.)

Speenhamland system [**speen**uhmland] The most famous of many local expedients in Britain to improve the operation of the old poor laws at a time of crisis. The name was taken from the Berkshire parish whose magistrates in 1795 introduced scales of relief for labourers dependent both on the prevailing price of bread and the size of labourers' families. >> Poor Laws

Speer, Albert [shpeer] (1905–81) Architect and Nazi government official, born in Mannheim, Germany. He became minister of armaments in 1942. Always more concerned with technology and administration than ideology, he openly opposed Hitler in the final months of the war. He was imprisoned for 20 years in Spandau. >> Nazi Party

Speke, John Hanning (1827–64) Explorer, born in Bideford, Devon. He and Burton discovered L Tanganyika (1858), then Speke travelled on alone, finding the lake he named Victoria. His claims to have discovered the source of the Nile were doubted, so a second expedition set out (1860–3). He died before he was able to defend his discovery. >> Burton, Richard (Francis); Nile, River

speleology / spelaeology The scientific exploration and study of caves and other underground features, surveying their extent, physical history and structure, and natural history. When cave-exploring is taken up as a hobby, it is known as **spelunking** (US) or **potholing** (UK), where people descend through access points (potholes) to follow the course of underground rivers and streams. >> RR972

spelling reform A movement to regularize a language's spelling system. In English, for example, the spelling system is widely perceived as being irregular, because of a relatively small but frequently used number of striking inconsistencies between sounds and letters. This has led to calls for reform – sometimes for the complete replacement of existing symbols (as in Shaw's proposal for a new alphabet), more usually for a 'standardizing system', in which the existing alphabet is used in a way which more consistently reflects the correspondence between sound and symbol. The vested interests of the publishing world, allied to general public conservatism, have so far militated against the widespread adoption of any new system. >> i.t.a.

spelunking >> **speleology**

Spence, Sir Basil (Urwin) (1907–76) Architect, born in Mumbai (Bombay), India. He emerged as the leading postwar British architect; examples of his work include the pavilion for the Festival of Britain (1951) and the new Coventry Cathedral (1951).

Spencer, Herbert (1820–1903) Evolutionary philosopher, born in Derby, Derbyshire. His main work is the nine-volume *System of Synthetic Philosophy* (1862–93). He was a leading advocate of 'Social Darwinism'. >> Darwin, Charles; Social Darwinism

Spencer, Sir Stanley (1891–1959) Artist, born in Cookham, Windsor and Maidenhead. He produced many purely realistic landscapes, but his main works interpret the Bible in terms of everyday life, such as 'Resurrection: Port Glasgow' (1950, Tate, London).

Spencer-Churchill, Baroness >> **Churchill, Sir Winston**

Spender, Sir Stephen (Harold) (1909–95) Poet and critic, born in London. He became in the 1930s one of the group of 'modern poets' with Auden and Day-Lewis. His *Collected Poems, 1928–85* were published in 1985. >> Auden; Day-Lewis

Spengler, Oswald [**shpeng**gler] (1880–1936) Philosopher of history, born in Blankenburg, Germany. *Der Untergang des Abendlandes* (1918–22, 2 vols, The Decline of the West) argues that all cultures are subject to the same cycle of growth and decay in accordance with predetermined 'historical destiny'. >> Nazi Party

Spenser, Edmund (?1552–99) Poet, born in London. His first original work was a sequence of pastoral poems, *The Shepheards Calendar* (1579). His major work, *The Faerie Queene*, uses a nine-line verse pattern which later came to be called the 'Spenserian stanza'. >> pastoral

sperm The male gamete of animals: also called **spermatozoa**. It is typically a small motile cell which locates and penetrates the female gamete (*ovum*). It contains little cytoplasm. >> cytoplasm; gamete; semen

spermaceti [sperma**see**tee] A waxy oil found in the head of sperm whales (almost 2000 litres/440 UK galls/530 US galls per whale in *Physeter catodon*); solidifies in air; function unclear; formerly used as a lubricant, and in ointments and candles. >> sperm whale

sperm whale A toothed whale, widespread in tropical and temperate seas; bulbous head contains spermaceti organ; three species; **sperm whale** or **cachalot** (*Physeter catodon*) is the largest toothed mammal (length up to 20 m/65 ft), grey-black, head up to one-third length of body. (Family: Physeteridae.) >> ambergris; spermaceti; whale ⓘ

sphalerite [**sfal**eriyt] A zinc sulphide (ZnS) mineral, also known as **zinc blende**. It is the principal ore of zinc. >> zinc

sphere In mathematics, the locus in space of all points equidistant from a fixed point (the centre). The distance of each point from the centre is the radius *r* of the sphere. The surface area of a sphere is $4\pi r^2$; the volume of a sphere is $\frac{4}{3}\pi r^3$. >> geometry

sphinx [sfingks] In ancient Greece a mythological monster with a human head and a recumbent animal body (usually a lion's). Originating in the east, probably Egypt, it is found throughout the Levant and E Mediterranean.

sphygmomanometer [sfigmoma**nom**iter] A device for measuring blood pressure. An inflatable rubber cuff is used round a limb (usually the arm), and inflated until the pulse (heard through a stethoscope) can no longer be detected. The cuff is then slowly deflated until the sound of the pulse can be heard again. The first sound heard reflects the pressure of blood in the arteries as the heart actively contracts (*systole*). As the deflation of the cuff continues, a second sound is heard, reflecting the resting pressure (*diastole*) within the arteries. The pressure is read off either electronically or direct from a column of mercury. >> blood pressure

Spica [**spiy**ka] >> **Virgo**

spice A pungent-tasting plant used to flavour or preserve food. The term is used particularly when referring to hard parts, such as dry fruits and seeds, but it can include parts such as flower buds. >> allspice; caraway; cardamom; cinnamon; clove tree; coriander; cumin; fenugreek; ginger; herb; mace; nutmeg; pepper 2

Spice Girls, The British pop singing group, with members **Victoria ('Vicki') Addams**, known as 'Posh Spice' (1975–), born in Hertfordshire; **Melanie Jayne Chisholm**, or 'Mel(anie) C', known as 'Sporty Spice' (1975–), born in Liverpool; **Melanie Janine Brown**,or 'Mel(anie) B', known as 'Scary Spice' (1975–), born in Yorkshire; **Emma Lee Bunton**, or 'Emma', known as 'Baby Spice' (1976–), born in Finchley, N London; and **Geri Estelle Halliwell**, or 'Geri', known as 'Ginger Spice' (1972–), born in Watford, Hertfordshire. From earlier careers as dancers, singers, or models, they came together in 1996, their first record, 'Wannabe!', becoming a number 1 hit in the UK. Later hits 'Say You'll Be There' (1996), '2 Become 1' (1996), and 'Who Do You Think You Are' (1997). The group made a feature film, *Spiceworld – the Movie*, in 1997. Geri left the group in mid-1998, and was appointed Goodwill Ambassador for the UN Population Fund later that year.

Spice Islands >> **Moluccas**

spider A predatory, terrestrial arthropod; body divided into head (*prosoma*) and abdomen (*opisthosoma*) joined by slender waist; prosoma with 2–8 simple eyes, four pairs of slender legs, and a pair of fangs used to inject poison into prey; opisthosoma bears respiratory organs and usually three pairs of silk-spinning organs. (Class: Arachnida. Order: Araneae, c.35 000 species.) >> Arachnida; arthropod; black widow / funnel-web / money / sun / trapdoor / water spider; tarantula

spider crab A slow-moving crab with a small slender body and long legs; leg span up to 4 m/13 ft in the giant species. (Class: Malacostraca. Order: Decapoda.) >> crab; Hydrozoa

spider monkey A New World monkey; slender with extremely long legs and tail; thumbs small or absent. (Genus: *Ateles*, 4 species.) >> New World monkey

Spielberg, Steven [**speel**berg] (1947–) Film director, born in Cincinnati, OH. He achieved a blockbuster success with the monster film *Jaws* (1975), and followed this with science fiction in *Close Encounters of the Third Kind* (1977) and *ET, The Extra-Terrestrial* (1982). Later films include *Indiana Jones and the Temple of Doom* (1984), *Gremlins* (1984), *The Color Purple* (1986), and (with Disney Studios) *Who Framed Roger Rabbit?* (1988), *Jurassic Park* (1993, 1997), *Schindler's List* (1993, 2 Oscars, 2 BAFTAs), and *Saving Private Ryan* (1998, Oscar).

spikelet A structure peculiar to the inflorescence of grasses, consisting of one or several reduced flowers enclosed in a series of small bracts. The spikelets can be arranged in several ways to form the inflorescence. >> bract; grass ⓘ; inflorescence ⓘ

Spillane, Mickey [spi**layn**], pseudonym of **Frank Morrison Spillane** (1918–) Popular novelist, born in New York City. His novels often feature the private detective Mike Hammer. *Kiss Me Deadly* (1952) is a typical example of his work, in its representation of sadism, cheap sex, and casual violence.

spin A vector attribute of sub-atomic particles, having a precise meaning only in quantum theory, but modelled on classical mechanical spin; symbol *S*. It may be thought of as a particle spinning on its axis, with a higher spin number corresponding to a faster rotation. In the quantum case, only certain values of spin are possible. Electrons and protons have spin $\frac{1}{2}$; photons have spin 1. >> quantum mechanics; quantum numbers

spina bifida [**spiy**na **bif**ida] A congenital defect of one or more vertebrae, in which the arch of a vertebra fails to develop. As a result the spinal cord is unprotected and may be damaged. It usually affects the lower back, and when severe may cause paralysis of the lower limbs. Antenatal diagnosis can be made by detecting an abnormal protein (*alfa-fetoprotein*) in amniotic fluid, or by ultrasonography. >> congenital abnormality; vertebral column

spinach beet >> **beet**

spinal cord That part of the vertebrate central nervous system contained within and protected by the vertebral column, continuous with the medulla oblongata of the brain. It is essentially a long, thick cable formed by thousands of parallel-running axons surrounding a central H-shaped core of grey matter. It has a minute central canal (containing cerebrospinal fluid) which is continuous with the ventricles of the brain. In the human adult it is approximately 45 cm/18 in long; it gives rise to 31 pairs of spinal nerves, which process motor and sensory information. >> nervous system; neurone ℹ; poliomyelitis; vertebral column

spine >> **vertebral column**

spinel [spi**nel**] The name given to a group of minerals which are double oxides of divalent and trivalent metals. Its principal members are *chromite* ($FeCr_2O_4$), the chief source of chromium, *magnetite* (Fe_3O_4), and *spinel* ($MgAl_2O_4$), which may be valuable as a gemstone. >> chromium; gemstones

spinet A keyboard instrument resembling a harpsichord, but with a single set of strings running diagonally to the keyboard. It was particularly popular in 17th-c England. >> harpsichord; keyboard instrument; virginals

spinifex A coarse, spiny-leaved grass, native to E Asia and Australasia. The spikelets are massed to form globular heads which break off and act as tumbleweeds before breaking up. (Genus: *Spinifex*, 3 species. Family: Gramineae.) >> grass ℹ; tumbleweed

spinning The conversion of fibres into yarns. Two main types of yarn were traditionally produced: in *woollen* yarns, the fibres are randomly arranged; in *worsted* types, the fibres lie parallel to the length of the yarn. >> wool

Spinoza, Baruch or **Benedictus de** [spi**noh**za] (1632–77) Philosopher and theologian, born in Amsterdam. His major works include the *Tractatus theologico-politicus* (1670), and *Ethica* (published posthumously, 1677). He is regarded as one of the great Rationalist thinkers of the 18th-c.

spiraea / spirea [spiy**ree**a] A deciduous, sometimes suckering shrub, native to the temperate N hemisphere; flowers 5-petalled, white or pink, in dense clusters. (Genus: *Spiraea*, 100 species. Family: Rosaceae.)

spirit control >> **seance**

spiritism >> **spiritualism**

spirits Alcoholic beverages produced by distilling ethanol from a fermentation of mash from various sources, such as barley for whisky, sugar cane for rum, and potatoes for vodka. Some are blended with wines to produce such drinks as port, a blend of brandy and wine. >> brandy; gin; rum; vodka; whisky

spiritualism An organized religion which believes that spirits of the deceased survive bodily death and communicate with the living, usually via a medium by means of messages, or apparently paranormal physical effects. While many different cultures believe in **spiritism** (the ability of spirits of the deceased to communicate with the living), spiritualism is primarily a Western religion, most commonly found in North America and in Europe, arising in the mid-1800s. It maintains that, through communications with the deceased, people may come to better understand the laws of God. It is frequently criticized for having at least some members who use trickery to produce its phenomena. >> medium (parapsychology)

spirochaete [**spiy**rohkeet] A motile, spiral-shaped bacterium. Spirochaetes include the causative agents of such diseases as syphilis and relapsing fever. (Kingdom: Monera. Family: Spirochaetaceae.) >> bacteria ℹ

Spirogyra [spiyro**jiy**ra] A genus of filament-like green algae found in freshwater; chloroplast a spiral, ribbon-like band extending along the cell. (Class: Chlorophyceae. Order: Zygnematales.) >> algae; chloroplast

spiroplasm A motile, spiral-shaped mycoplasm, parasitic in insects and plants. It includes the causative agent of yellow disease in plants. (Kingdom: Monera. Class: Mollicutes.) >> mycoplasma

spit A ridge of sand and gravel stretching out along a coastline, deposited by longshore drift and often forming a lagoon on the landward side. A spit which links an island to the mainland is termed a **tombolo**.

Spitalfields An area in the East End of London, which flourished as a centre of silk-weaving from the late 17th-c until the late 19th-c. It lies on the site of a 12th-c spittle-house, or hospital, from which its name derives. >> East End; Huguenots

Spitsbergen >> **Svalbard**

spittlebug >> **froghopper**

spitz [spits] (Ger 'pointed') A dog belonging to a group of breeds, characterized by a curled tail usually held over the back, pointed ears and muzzle, and (usually) a thick coat. >> Alaskan malamute; basenji; corgi; dog; elkhound; husky; keeshond; Pomeranian; Samoyed (zoology)

Spitz, Mark (Andrew) (1950–) Swimmer, born in Modesto, CA. He earned worldwide fame at the 1972 Olympics by winning seven gold medals, all in world record time. >> swimming

spleen A soft, delicate, relatively mobile organ which is responsible for clearing the body of bacteria, protozoa, and non-living particles; the destruction of red blood cells; and the metabolism of iron, fats, and proteins. It is situated under cover of the rib-cage on the left side of the body towards the midline. It can be ruptured by severe blows to the lower left part of the thoracic cage. In adults, the loss of the spleen does not cause any ill effects. >> anatomy ℹ; blood; malaria; thorax

spleenwort A member of a large and widespread genus of perennial ferns, found especially in the temperate N hemisphere. (Genus: *Asplenium*, 650 species. Family: Polypodiaceae.) >> fern

Split, Ital **Spalato** 43°31N 16°28E, pop (1995e) 194 000 . Seaport and city in W Croatia; railway; car ferries to Italy and Turkey; university (1974); Diocletian's palace (3rd-c), a world heritage site; cathedral. >> Croatia ℹ

Spock, Benjamin (McLane), popular name **Dr Spock** (1903–98) Paediatrician, born in New Haven, CT. In 1946 he published his best-selling *Common Sense Book of Baby and Child Care*. He was a People's Party candidate for the US presidency in 1972 and the vice-presidency in 1976.

Spode, Josiah [spohd] (1755–1827) Potter, born in Stoke-on-Trent, Staffordshire. In 1770 he founded a firm which manufactured pottery, porcelain, and stoneware, and became the foremost china manufacturer of his time. >> porcelain; pottery; stoneware

Spohr, Louis [shpohr], originally **Ludwig Spohr** (1784–1859) Composer, violinist, and conductor, born in Brunswick, Germany. He is remembered chiefly as a composer for the violin, for which he wrote 17 concertos.

spoils system The US practice of filling public offices on the basis of loyalty to the party in power: 'to the victors belong the spoils'. It was said to have originated with De Witt Clinton, governor of New York (1817–23), and was in common use during the 19th-c. >> mugwump

Spokane [spoh**kan**] 47°40N 117°24W, pop (1995e) 203 000. City in E Washington, USA, on the Spokane R; founded, 1872; city status, 1891; airfield; railway; university (1887); commercial centre for inland farming, forestry, and mining areas; two cathedrals. >> Washington (state)

Spoleto [spo**lay**toh], Lat **Spoletium** 42°44N 12°44E, pop (1995e) 20 600. Town in Umbria, C Italy; cathedral (11th-c), basilica (4th-c), Roman remains; Festival of Two Worlds (Jun–Jul). >> Umbria

spondylosis [spondi**loh**sis] Degeneration of the vertebral bodies and of the joints between them. It especially affects the cervical and lumbar vertebrae (ie the spine in the neck and lower back). >> vertebral column

sponge A multicellular animal with a body that lacks

organization into tissues and organs; body perforated by a complex system of internal canals through which flagellate cells propel water; mostly marine, found from inter-tidal zone to deep sea; sometimes freshwater. (Phylum: Porifera.) >> flagellum

spoonbill An ibis-like bird, native to Old World (Genus: *Platalea*, 5 species) or Central and South America (*Ajaia ajaja*); bill straight and broadly flattened at tip. (Family: Threskiornithidae.) >> ibis; shoveller

Spooner, William Archibald (1844–1930) Anglican clergyman and educationist. His name is associated with a nervous tendency to transpose initial letters or half-syllables in speech, the **spoonerism** (eg 'a half-warmed fish' for 'a half-formed wish').

spoonworm An unsegmented, soft-bodied marine worm; body cylindrical or sac-like, bearing an extendable tube (*proboscis*) used for food collection and respiration. (Phylum: Echiura, c.140 species.) >> worm

sporangium [spo**ran**jium] The organ in which spores are formed in certain types of plant. In algae and fungi they are unicellular; in bryophytes and ferns they are multicellular. >> spore

spore A plant reproductive cell capable of developing into a new individual, either directly or after fusion with another spore. Spores typically function as a means of dispersal. A spore does not contain an embryo, and is thus distinct from a **seed**. >> plant; reproduction; seed

sporophyte [**spoh**rofiyt] The asexual (spore-producing or *diploid*) generation in the life cycle of a plant, produced by the fusion of two haploid gametes. In ferns and flowering plants it is the dominant part of the life cycle. >> gamete; spore

Sporozoa [sporo**zoh**a] A class of parasitic protozoans found in animal hosts. Several species cause serious diseases in humans and domesticated animals. (Phylum: Apicomplexa.) >> parasitology; Protozoa

sporting dog A dog belonging to a group of breeds developed to assist in field sports; includes pointers, setters, retrievers, spaniels (these four also called **gundogs**); used occasionally to include terriers and hounds. >> dog; hound; pointer; retriever; setter; spaniel; terrier

sprain Injury to a joint without fracture or displacement of bones. It is usually the result of a twisting movement, in which muscle and tendon attachments are torn. >> joint

sprat Small, slender-bodied fish (*Sprattus sprattus*) widespread and locally common in large shoals in coastal waters from Norway to the Mediterranean; length up to 15 cm/6 in; silver with upper surface green; young fish sold as whitebait. (Family: Clupeidae.) >> brisling

spreadsheets Computer programs which allow data, numbers, or text to be presented in a rectangular matrix. Data can be manipulated in a variety of different ways defined by the user; for example, columns or rows of numbers can be added, interchanged, or multiplied by constants. Spreadsheets provide a powerful means of analyzing numeric data, and are widely used in the commercial world. >> computer program

springbok or **springbuck** A gazelle (*Antidorcas marsupialis*) native to S Africa; reddish-brown with white rump and thick dark line along side; short lyre-shaped horns with inturned tips; may leap 3·5 m/11½ ft into the air when alarmed. >> gazelle

springer spaniel A medium-sized spaniel with thick coat; ears shorter and more highly set than in cocker spaniels; two breeds, white and brown (or black) **English springer spaniel**, and older, shorter-eared, white and red-brown **Welsh spaniel** or **Welsh springer spaniel**. >> cocker spaniel; spaniel

Springfield, Dusty, originally **Mary O'Brien** (1939–99) Pop singer, born in London. Originally part of The Springfields, her debut solo single 'I Only Want To Be With You' (1964) was a UK hit, as was her debut album, *A Girl Called Dusty* (1964). In the 1990s she acquired something of a cult following, as part of the renewed interest in music of the 1960s.

Springfield (Illinois) 39°48N 89°39W, pop (1995e) 110 000. Capital of state in C Illinois, USA; settled, 1818; city status, 1840; home and burial place of President Lincoln; railway; major commercial centre. >> Illinois; Lincoln, Abraham

Springfield (Massachusetts) 42°06N 72°35W, pop (1995e) 158 000. City in SW Massachusetts, USA, on the Connecticut R; railway; game of basketball devised at Springfield College. >> Massachusetts

Springfield (Missouri) 37°13N 93°17W, pop (1995e) 146 000. City in SW Missouri, USA; established, 1829; railway; university; industrial, trade and shipping centre; tourist centre for Ozark Mts. >> Missouri; Ozark Mountains

springhaas [**spring**hahs] A nocturnal squirrel-like rodent (*Pedetes capensis*), native to S Africa; superficially resembles a small kangaroo (length, less than 1 m/3¼ ft) with bushy black-tipped tail; digs burrows; also known as **springhare** or **jumping hare**. (Family: Pedetidae.) >> kangaroo; rodent; squirrel

Springsteen, Bruce (1949–) Rock singer, guitarist, and songwriter, born in Freehold, NJ. In 1973 he released his first recording amid unprecedented hype, being featured on the front covers of both *Time* and *Newsweek* in the same week. His hits, which include 'Born to Run' (1976) have led to his current position as one of the leading rock performers. >> rock music

springtail A blind, primitively wingless insect often extremely abundant in soils or leaf litter; leaps by means of a forked spring organ folded up on underside of abdomen. (Order: Collembola, c.2000 species.) >> insect i

spring tide An especially large tidal range occurring twice monthly, produced by the tidal forces of the Sun and Moon acting in conjunction. These maximum monthly tides occur during new and full moon. >> neap tide; tide

spruce An evergreen conifer native to the temperate N hemisphere, especially E Asia; leaves needle-like; cones pendulous, ripe after one year. It is a widespread forestry tree, grown for timber and for its turpentine-yielding resin. (Genus: *Picea*, 50 species. Family: Pinaceae.) >> conifer; Norway spruce; resin

sprue >> **malabsorption**

spurge A member of a large worldwide genus of diverse, latex-producing plants, annuals or perennials, sometimes shrubs. Some from arid regions look like cacti, and when not in flower can be distinguished from cacti only by the presence of latex. (Genus: *Euphorbia*, 2000 species. Family: Euphorbiaceae.) >> cactus i; latex

Sputnik [**sput**nik] (Russ 'travelling companion') The world's first artificial satellite. **Sputnik 1** was launched by the USSR (4 Oct 1957) from Tyuratam launch site; weight 84 gk/185 lb; it transmitted a radio signal for 21 days. **Sputnik 2** was launched in November 1957; weight 508 kg/1120 lb; it carried the dog 'Laika', killed by injection after 7 days of returning biomedical data. >> Explorer 1; Soviet space programme; RR970

squall A sudden increase in wind speed. For at least one minute, minimum velocity must increase by at least 8 m/s (26 ft/s), and reach 11 m/s (36 ft/s) before declining rapidly. >> wind i

Square Deal The popular name for the domestic policies of US President Theodore R Roosevelt, especially the enforcement of the Antitrust Acts. The term was coined by Roosevelt during a speaking tour in the summer of 1902. >> Roosevelt, Theodore

squark >> **supersymmetry**

squash Any of several species of the cucumber family (*Cucurbita maxima / mixta / moschata / pepo*), native to America; all trailing or climbing vines with tendrils; large, yellow, funnel-shaped flowers; fruits of various shapes and colours. **Summer squashes** are eaten before becoming ripe and fibrous; **winter squashes** are eaten ripe and can be stored through winter. (Family: Cucurbitaceae.) >> cucumber; marrow (botany); pumpkin

squash rackets (UK) / **squash racquets** (US) A popular indoor racket-and-ball court game, usually called **squash**. It is played by two players on an enclosed court 32 ft (9·75 m) long by 21 ft (6·4 m) wide. Each hits the ball against a front wall alternately. The object is to play a winning shot by forcing your opponent to fail to return the ball. >> rackets; RR1061

squid A carnivorous marine mollusc with a streamlined body bearing fins towards the back; eight arms and two tentacles around mouth, used to catch prey. (Class: Cephalopoda. Order: Teuthoidea.) >> Cephalopoda ℹ; mollusc; octopus

squill A perennial native to Europe, Asia, and S Africa; flowers star- or bell-shaped, sometimes drooping, blue or purple. (Genus: *Scilla*, 80 species. Family: Liliaceae.)

squint A defect in the alignment of the eyes, most commonly affecting movement in the horizontal plane; also known as **strabismus**. It is usually congenital in origin, and may be associated with an abnormality in focusing. >> eye ℹ

squirrel A rodent of family Sciuridae (267 species), virtually worldwide except Australasia; fine fur and bushy tail; range from small tree-dwelling squirrels to cat-sized ground-dwelling squirrels, which live in extensive burrows, and may hibernate for up to nine months. >> chipmunk; flying squirrel; marmot; prairie dog; red squirrel; rodent; souslik

squirrel monkey A New World monkey; small, lively, with long black-tipped tail; white face with black tip to muzzle; coat short, greyish. (Genus: *Saimiri*, 2 species.) >> New World monkey

Sri Jayawardenapura-Kotte [sree jiyahwah(r)dnapoora] 6°55N 79°52E, pop (1995e) 116 000. Capital of Sri Lanka since 1983; located in an E suburb of Colombo; relocation ongoing during the 1990s. >> Colombo; Sri Lanka ℹ

Sri Lanka [sree **lang**ka], formerly **Ceylon**, official name **Democratic Socialist Republic of Sri Lanka** pop (1995e) 18 100 000; area 65 610 sq km/25 325 sq mi. Island state in the Indian Ocean; legislative capital (since 1983), Sri Jayawardenapura-Kotte, a suburb of the administrative capital, Colombo; timezone GMT +5½; ethnic groups include Sinhalese (83%), Tamils (9%); chief religions, Buddhism (69%), Hinduism (15%), Christianity (8%), Islam (8%); official languages, Sinhala, Tamil; unit of currency, the Sri Lankan rupee of 100 cents; a pear-shaped island, 440 km/273 mi long, 220 km/137 mi wide; low-lying areas in N and S, surrounding SC uplands; highest peak, Pidurutalagala (2524 m/8281 ft); nearly half the country is tropical monsoon forest or open woodland; high temperatures and humidity in the N plains; visited by the Portuguese, 1505; taken by the Dutch, 1658; British occupation, 1796; British colony, 1802; Tamil labourers brought in from S India during colonial rule, to work on coffee and tea plantations; Dominion status, 1948; independent republic, 1972; governed by a president and a National State Assembly; acute political tension exists between the Buddhist Sinhalese majority and the Hindu Tamil minority, who wish to establish an independent state in the N and E; considerable increase in racial violence in the area during the 1980s, with offensives by the Liberation Tigers of Tamil Eelam; Indian troops sent in, 1987, but withdrawn 1989–90 without quelling violence; cease-fire agreed (1995), but conflict soon resumed, still continuing in 1999; agriculture employs c.40% of the labour force. >> Colombo; Sri Jayawardenapura-Kotte; Tamil; RR1022 political leaders

Srinagar [**sree**nagah(r)] 34°08N 74°50E, pop (1995e) 644 000. Summer capital of Jammu-Kashmir state, N India, on R Jhelum; founded, 6th-c; capital status, 1948; airfield. >> Jammu-Kashmir

SS Abbreviation of **Schutzstaffel** (Ger 'protective squad'), a Nazi organization founded in Germany in 1925 as Hitler's personal bodyguard. Within the Third Reich it became an independent organization, controlling a dominant repressive apparatus, and responsible for concentration camps and racial policy. >> Himmler; Nazi Party; World War 2

stabilizers A device which limits rolling in a ship, usually in the form of movable fins. They were first fitted successfully in the P & O liner *Chusan* in 1950.

Staël, Madame de [stahl], popular name of **Anne Louise Germaine Necker, Baroness of Staël-Holstein** (1766–1817) Writer, born in Paris, the daughter of the financier Jacques Necker. Both before and after the French Revolution, her *salon* became a centre of political discussion. She is known for her *Lettres* (1788, Letters) on Rousseau, her romantic novel, *Corinne* (1807), and her major work, *De L'Allemagne* (1813, Germany). >> Necker

Stafford 52°48N 2°07W, pop (1995e) 64 500. County town of Staffordshire, C England; railway; 11th-c castle, destroyed in the Civil War; birthplace of Izaak Walton. >> English Civil War; Staffordshire; Walton, Izaak

Staffordshire pop (1995e) 1 058 000; area 2716 sq km/1049 sq mi. County in C England; county town, Stafford; Stoke-on-Trent a new unitary authority from 1997; Potteries. >> England ℹ; Potteries, the; Stafford

Staffordshire bull terrier A medium-sized terrier developed in Britain as a fighting dog or guard dog; thick-set muscular body with a short coat, broad head, long muzzle, soft ears. >> bull terrier; terrier

stag beetle A large, dark-coloured beetle; males up to 66 mm/2½ in long, typically with large, antler-like processes on head, formed from mandibles. (Order: Coleoptera. Family: Lucanidae, c.1200 species.) >> beetle

stagecoach A type of horse-drawn coach that appeared c.1640 offering carriage to the public on predetermined routes and stages, usually running between provincial towns and London. The coming of the railways in the 1830s and 1840s ended the dominating role of stagecoaches within public transport. In the USA, the first mail stagecoaches ran between Boston and New York in 1784, but the main period of their use was from 1800 to 1840.

staghound >> **deerhound**

stained glass Pieces of different coloured glass mounted in lead framing to form a pictorial image. It was introduced from Byzantine art for the windows of European buildings in the late 12th-c, and flourished most splendidly in Western Romanesque and Gothic churches. It was revived in the 19th-c. >> Burne-Jones; Gothic architecture; Matisse; Rouault

stainless steels A group of steels which resist rusting and chemical attack through the addition of nickel and chromium. They are used to make utensils, cutlery, and chemical reaction vessels. >> chromium; nickel; steel

stakeholder economy >> **New Labour**

stalactites and stalagmites Icicle-like deposits of limestone formed by precipitation from slowly dripping water from the ceilings of caves. **Stalactites** grow from the ceiling, while **stalagmites** form on the floor and grow upwards at a rate of less than half a millimetre per year. >> limestone

Stalin, Joseph (1879–1953) Georgian Marxist revolutionary and later virtual dictator of the Soviet Union (1928–53), born in Gori, Georgia. As a leading Bolshevik he played an active role in the October Revolution (1917), and in 1922 became general secretary of the Party Central Committee, a post he held until his death. After Lenin's death (1924) he pursued a policy of building 'socialism in one country', and gradually isolated and disgraced his political rivals, notably Trotsky. In 1928 he launched the campaign for the collectivization of agriculture during which millions of peasants perished, and the first 5-year plan for the forced industrialization of the economy. Between 1934 and 1938 he inaugurated a massive purge of the party, government, armed forces, and intelligentsia in which millions of so-called 'enemies of the people' were imprisoned, exiled, or shot. He took part in the conferences of Teheran, Yalta, and Potsdam which resulted in Soviet military and political control over the liberated countries of postwar E and C Europe. From 1945 his foreign policies contributed to the Cold War between the Soviet Union and the West. He was posthumously denounced by Khrushchev at the 20th Party Congress (1956) for crimes against the Party and for building a 'cult of personality'. Under Gorbachev many of Stalin's victims were rehabilitated, and the whole phenomenon of 'Stalinism' officially condemned. >> Cold War; Gorbachev; Khrushchev; Lenin; October Revolution; Stalinism; Trotsky; World War 2

Stalingrad, Battle of (1942–3) One of the great battles of World War 2, fought between Nazi German and Soviet troops in and around Stalingrad (now Volgograd) on the R Volga during the winter of 1942–3. After savage fighting, which cost 70 000 German lives, the German 6th Army surrendered. The battle is regarded as a major turning-point in the Allied victory over Germany. >> World War 2

Stalinism A label used pejoratively outside the USSR to refer to the nature of the Soviet regime 1929–53. It refers to a tightly disciplined and bureaucratic system, with the party hierarchy having a monopoly of political and economic power. It also encompasses the total subservience of society and culture to political ends, suppression of political opponents, and the promotion of an individual above the party. >> communism; Stalin

Stallone, Sylvester [sta**lohn**] (1946–) Film actor, born in New York City. He became known as an action-film hero through the success of his first film *Rocky* (1976, 2 Oscars), which he also wrote. Later films include the *Rocky* sequels (1979, 1982, 1985, 1990), *First Blood* (1981), *Rambo* and its sequel (1985, 1988), and *The Hunter* (1997).

stamen The male organ of a flower, consisting of a stalk-like *filament* bearing sac-like *anthers* containing pollen. The number and arrangement is often diagnostic for plant families. >> flower [i]; pollen

Stamitz, Johann (Wenzel Anton) [**shtam**its] (1717–57) Violinist and composer, born in Havličkův Brod, Czech Republic. His works include 74 symphonies, several concertos, chamber music, and a Mass. His school of symphonists had a profound influence on Mozart. >> Mozart

stammering >> **stuttering**

Stamp Act A British Act passed in 1765 by the administration of George Grenville (1712–70), which levied a direct tax on all papers required in discharging official business in the American colonies. It was the first direct tax levied without the consent of the colonial assemblies, and caused much discontent in the colonies. It was withdrawn in 1766. >> American Revolution; Grenville, Baron; Townshend Acts

Standard Generalized Mark-up Language (SGML) A standard for coding documents so that they can be stored in a document database and presented on an output medium in the correct form for that medium. For example, if the output were to be printed it would appear in one form; if it were to be presented on a computer screen it would be in a different form; but in each case the presentation would be what was appropriate for that document. A development in the 1990s for generating World Wide Web pages is the **Hypertext Mark-up Language (HTML)**.

standard language The variety of a language which has greatest social and political prestige within a speech community. It cuts across regional differences in usage, and functions as a linguistically 'neutral' norm for use in the media and education. >> sociolinguistics

standard of living The level of welfare achieved by a nation or group; usually measured in terms of food, clothing, housing, and other material benefits. A simple measure for comparative purposes is gross national product per head of population. This shows a very fast rate of growth in W Europe and the USA, and a very wide gap between the richest nations and the poorest. >> gross domestic product

standard time The officially established local time adopted by a region or country, + or – so many hours from Greenwich Mean Time. The Earth can be divided into 24 time zones each based on sections of 15° of longitude. In each of these, standard time is calculated from the position of the Sun at a central point within the zone. In the USA there are seven standard time zones and in continental Europe two (+1 hour and +2 hours from GMT). Zones differ generally by a whole hour, although there are a few cases of half-hour zones (eg South Australia, India). >> Date Line; Greenwich Mean Time; RR977

Standish, Myles (c.1584–1656) Colonist, probably born in Ormskirk, Lancashire. He sailed with the *Mayflower* in

1620, and became military head of the first American settlement at Plymouth, MA, and treasurer of the colony (1644–9). >> Mayflower

Stanford, Sir Charles (Villiers) (1852–1924) Composer, born in Dublin. He wrote several major choral works, six operas, seven symphonies, and a great deal of chamber music, songs, and English church music.

Stanhope, James Stanhope, 1st Earl [**stan**uhp] (1675–1721) British soldier and statesman, born in Paris. He commanded in Spain during the War of the Spanish Succession (1701–13), was secretary of state for foreign affairs under George I, and became his chief minister in 1717. >> George I; Spanish Succession, War of the

Stanislavsky [stanis**lav**skee], originally **Konstantin Sergeyevich Alexeyev** (1863–1938) Actor, theatre director, and teacher, born in Moscow. In 1898 he helped to found the Moscow Arts Theatre. His teaching on acting remains the basis of much Western actor-training and practice.

Stanisław I Leszczyński [**stan**islav le**shin**skee] (1677–1766) King of Poland (1704–9, 1733–5), born in Lvov, Ukraine (formerly Poland. After his election in 1704, he was driven out by Peter the Great. Re-elected in 1733, he lost the War of the Polish Succession, and formally abdicated in 1736. >> Peter I

Stanley 51°45S 57°56W, pop (1995e) 1600. Port and capital of the Falkland Is, on the E coast of East Falkland; airport. >> Falkland Islands 🅘

Stanley, Sir Henry Morton, originally **John Rowlands** (1841–1904) Explorer and journalist, born in Denbigh, Denbighshire. In 1867 he joined the *New York Herald*, and in 1869 was told to 'find Livingstone' in Africa. In 1871 he left Zanzibar for Tanganyika and encountered Livingstone at Ujiji. In later expeditions, he explored L Tanganyika, traced the Congo to the sea, founded the Congo Free State, and went to the aid of Emin Pasha in the Sudan. >> Livingstone

Stanleyville >> **Kisangani**

Stannaries Former tin-mining districts of Cornwall, UK, lying within the lands of the Duchy of Cornwall. The tin miners of the Stannaries held special privileges, including the right to send representatives to the Stannary Parliament and to administer their own courts. >> Duchy of Cornwall

Stanton, Elizabeth, *née* **Cady** (1815–1902) Feminist, born in Johnstown, NY. She involved herself in the anti-slavery and temperance movements, and was personally responsible for the emergence of women's suffrage as a public issue. >> civil rights; slave trade; women's liberation movement

stapelia [sta**pee**lia] A perennial native to arid areas of tropical and S Africa, superficially resembling cacti, and similarly drought-adapted; fleshy, green stems swollen with water-storage tissue; large carrion flowers mottled red or maroon produce an overpowering smell of rotten meat. (Genus: *Stapelia*, 75 species. Family: Asclepiadaceae.) >> cactus 🅘

Staphylococcus [stafiloh**kok**us] A spherical bacterium c.1 micron in diameter, commonly occurring in clusters, and requiring oxygen for growth. It can cause superficial abscesses, and chronic to fatal systemic infections. (Kingdom: Monera. Family: Micrococcaceae.) >> bacteria 🅘

Staples, The >> **Farne Islands**

star A sphere of matter held together entirely by its own gravitational field, and generating energy by means of nuclear fusion reactions in its deep interior. The important distinguishing feature of a star is the presence of a natural nuclear reactor in its core, where the pressure of the overlying mass of material is sufficient to cause nuclear reactions, principally the conversion of hydrogen to helium. >> binary / circumpolar / double / dwarf / neutron / variable star; electromagnetic radiation 🅘; globular cluster; gravitation; pulsar; quasar; star cluster; supergiant; supernova; RR965

starch $(C_6H_{10}O_5)_n$. A carbohydrate; a condensation polymer of glucose, and isomeric with cellulose, found as a reserve material in living cells. Its non-food uses include adhesives, pill fillers, and paper sizing. >> carbohydrate; glucose; hydrolysis

Star Chamber, Court of the The royal prerogative court in Britain for hearing subjects' petitions and grievances, increasingly prominent under the Tudors and early Stuarts. It became notorious for its oppressive methods, and was abolished by the Long Parliament in 1641. >> Long Parliament; Stuarts

star cluster A group of stars physically associated in space. Dense, globular clusters are spherical, have hundreds of thousands of stars distributed in a halo around a galaxy, and are thousands of millions of years old. >> galaxy; globular cluster; gravitation; star

starfish A typically 5-armed, star-shaped marine invertebrate (echinoderm); most species omnivorous, feeding as scavengers or predators; contains c.1500 living species; also called **sea star**. (Phylum: Echinodermata. Subclass: Asteroidea.) >> echinoderm 🅘

starling A songbird, native to the Old World, with some introduced to the Americas; plumage often with metallic sheen, usually dark but sometimes colourful; flocks often a major nuisance on city buildings and large structures. (Family: Sturnidae, 92 species.) >> grackle; magpie; mynah; oriole; songbird

Star of Bethlehem A star mentioned in *Matt* 2.1–12, depicted as heralding Jesus's birth and guiding magi from the East to the birthplace in Bethlehem. Although sometimes considered a comet (Halley's comet, c.11 BC), a supernova, or a conjunction of Jupiter and Saturn in the constellation Pisces (c.7 BC), it is doubtful that these can explain the sustained presence or movement that is described. >> Jesus Christ; Magi

star-of-Bethlehem A perennial with a small bulb (*Ornithogalum umbellatum*), native to S Europe and the Mediterranean region; leaves narrow, grooved, with a white stripe down the centre; six narrow petals, white with a green stripe on the back. (Family: Liliaceae.)

Star of David or **Magen David** ('Shield of David') A six-pointed star, consisting of two crossed equilateral triangles, which in the last two centuries has come to symbolize Judaism. It appears on Israel's national flag today as a blue design against white. >> David; Judaism

Starr, Kenneth (1946–) Lawyer, born in Vernon, TX. He rose rapidly as a Republican lawyer, becoming solicitor general. He became nationally known as the Independent Prosecutor chosen to investigate the alleged misdemeanours of President Clinton, first with reference to the Whitewater affair, then in relation to Paula Jones and Monica Lewinsky. The 'Starr Report' into the latter appeared towards the end of 1998, and he himself gave evidence before a Congressional judiciary committee set up to consider the question of impeachment. >> Clinton; Lewinsky; Whitewater affair

Starr, Ringo >> **Beatles, The**

START [stah(r)t] Acronym for **Strategic Arms Reduction Talks**, held between the USA and USSR in 1982 and 1983, adjourned, then resumed at the end of the decade between Presidents Reagan and Bush and General Secretary Gorbachev. **START 1** (the first **Strategic Arms Reduction Treaty**) was signed in 1991, and aimed to cut the overall number of nuclear warheads held by the two super-powers by between 25% and 30%. In 1992, a second treaty (**START 2**) was agreed between Presidents Bush and Yeltsin, by which the USA and Russia agreed to cut by two-thirds their stocks of long range, land-based missiles with multiple warheads.

Star Trek US science-fiction television series created by Gene Roddenberry. Although only 72 episodes were made before its withdrawal by NBC because of poor ratings in 1969, the adventures of the starship *Enterprise*, boldly going where no man had gone before, and led by Captain James T Kirk (William Shatner) and the half-Vulcan/half-human Mr Spock (Leonard Nimoy) inspired great loyalty and affection among thousands of fans (*Trekkies*). Three other series were produced in the 1990s: *Star Trek: The Next Generation* and *Deep Space Nine*, with Captain Jean-Luc Picard (Patrick Stewart); and *Star Trek: Voyager*, with Captain Kathryn Janeway (Kate Mulgrew). By 1998 there had been nine *Star Trek* feature films. >> Roddenberry; science fiction

Star Wars >> **SDI**

State Department The oldest department of the US government, established by the fourth Act of Congress (Jul 1789), responsible to the president for the conduct of foreign affairs. It is headed by a secretary of state, and is regarded as the most senior department of government. >> Congress

Staten Island [**stat**n] pop (1995e) 386 000; area 153 sq km/ 59 sq mi. Borough of New York City, USA; separated from Long Island by the Narrows; first settled in 1641; named by early Dutch settlers after the *Staaten* or States General of 17th-c Holland. >> New York City

states' rights A US Constitutional doctrine that the separate states enjoy areas of self-control which cannot be breached by the federal government. The doctrine flourished among white Southerners between Reconstruction and the Civil Rights Movement, and amounted to a code term for white supremacy. >> civil rights

static electricity Electric charge which does not flow. Objects can acquire a static charge by rubbing against one another (eg by combing hair or rubbing a toy balloon on wool), which transfers electrons from one object to the other. >> electricity; electrostatics; van de Graaff generator

Stations of the Cross A popular form of devotion in the Roman Catholic and some Anglican Churches. It consists of meditating on a series of 14 pictures or carvings recalling the passion of Christ from his condemnation to his burial. >> Jesus Christ; Roman Catholicism

statistical mechanics A branch of physics which provides a link between large-scale phenomena involving many atoms or molecules, and the microscopic properties and interactions of individual atoms and molecules. The subject is essential in understanding critical phenomena and the thermodynamic properties of solids. >> physics

statistics The branch of mathematics which deals with the collection and analysis of numerical data. Numbers commonly found useful are those representative of a set of data – 'averages', such as *mean*, *median*, and *mode*, and those indicating variation in the data, describing the spread or dispersion, such as *range* and *standard deviation*. >> mean; median; mode; Galton; Gauss; Poisson

Statue of Liberty >> **Liberty, Statue of**

status The social position a person occupies, and the rank or esteem it enjoys. Systems of social stratification may be based on a strong status order, as in traditional caste systems, or status may be just one dimension of a more complex social hierarchy. >> caste; social stratification; Weber, Max

statute A particular law passed by the legislature, such as an act of parliament. A statute has a short title by which it is generally known, eg the Housing Act (1985). >> legislature; parliament

Stauffenberg, Claus, Graf von (Count of) [**shtow**fnberg] (1907–44) German soldier, born in Jettingen, Germany. A colonel on the German general staff in 1944, he placed the bomb in the unsuccessful attempt to assassinate Hitler at Rastenburg (20 Jul 1944). He was shot next day. >> Hitler

Stavanger [sta**vang**er] 58°58N 5°45E, pop (1995e) 101 000. Seaport in SW Norway; founded, c.8th-c; airport; rail terminus; important North Sea oil centre; cathedral (12th-c). >> Norway ℹ

steady-state theory One of two rival theories of cosmology (the other is the 'big bang'), proposed in 1948. It asserts that the universe is infinitely old, and contains the same density of material (on average) at all points and at all times. From the mid-1960s this model fell out of favour. >> 'big bang'; cosmology

steam The vapour phase of water (H_2O); also called **live steam**, to distinguish it from **dead steam**, visible droplets of recondensed vapour. >> water

steam engine An external combustion engine, in which the engine's working fluid (steam) is generated in a boiler outside the engine. The steam is brought into the engine by valves, and through its pressure and expansive properties a piston is made to oscillate within a cylinder. This oscillatory motion is then converted into rotary motion by means of a crankshaft mechanism. >> engine; locomotive ℹ

steamship >> **ship** ℹ

stearic acid [stee**ar**ik] $C_{17}H_{35}COOH$, IUPAC **octadecanoic acid**, melting point 71°C. A waxy solid, the commonest of the fatty acids obtained from the saponification of animal fat. It is used in soap and candle manufacture. >> carboxylic acids; IUPAC

stearin(e) [**stee**arin] The name used to describe fats derived from stearic acid, and also for a mixture of stearic and palmitic acids used in candle manufacture. >> fat; palmitic acid; stearic acid

steatite [**stee**uhtiyt] >> **talc**

steel The chief alloy of iron, and the most used of all metals. It consists of iron hardened by the presence of a small proportion of carbon. Most steel used today is a simple **carbon steel**, but there exist many special steels formed by the addition of other metals, such as high alloy steels for tools, and **stainless steel** (with nickel and chromium). >> alloy; Bessemer process; carbon; iron

Steel (of Aikwood), David (Martin Scott), Lord (1938–) British politician and leader of the Liberal Party (1976–88), born in Kirkcaldy, Fife. He sponsored a controversial bill to reform the laws on abortion (1966–7), and was active in the anti-apartheid movement. In 1981 he led the party into an Alliance with the Social Democratic Party, and following successful merger negotiations between the two parties (1987–8) was the last leader of the Liberal Party. >> Liberal Party (UK); Thorpe

steel band An ensemble, native to Trinidad, consisting mainly of steel drums – tuned percussion instruments made from used oildrums. Steel bands are typically heard at West Indian Carnivals and other community festivities. >> percussion ℹ

Steele, Sir Richard (1672–1729) Essayist, playwright, and politician, born in Dublin. He is best known for the satirical, political, and moral essays which formed much of the content of the new periodicals *The Tatler* (1709–11), which he founded, and *The Spectator* (1711–12), which he co-founded with Addison. >> Addison, Joseph

Steen, Jan (Havickszoon) [stayn] (1626–79) Painter, born in Leyden, The Netherlands. His best works were genre pictures of social and domestic scenes depicting the everyday life of ordinary folk, as in 'The Music Lesson' (National Gallery, London). >> genre painting

steenbok or **steinbok** A dwarf antelope (*Raphicerus campestris*) native to Africa S of the Sahara; reddish-brown with white underparts; large ears with white insides; short vertical horns. >> antelope

steeplechase 1 A form of National Hunt horse racing in which the horses have to negotiate fixed fences normally 3–4 ft (0·9–1·2 m) high. The first steeplechase was in Ireland in 1752, between Buttevant Church and St Mary's, Doneraile.>> Grand National; horse racing **2** A track athletics event over 3000 m. The competitors have to negotiate 28 hurdles and seven water jumps. Each obstacle is 3 ft (0·9 m) high. >> athletics

Stegodon [**steg**odon] An extinct, elephant-like mammal known from the Pliocene epoch of India; upper tusks long and very closely placed together. (Order: Proboscidea.) >> elephant; mammal ⓘ; Pliocene epoch

Stegosaurus [stego**saw**rus] A large dinosaur attaining a length of 9 m/30 ft; characterized by two rows of plates along back from skull to tail; four-legged, but forelimbs shorter than hindlimbs; known from the Upper Jurassic period of Colorado. (Order: Ornithischia.) >> dinosaur ⓘ; Jurassic period; Ornithischia

Steiger, Rod(ney Stephen) [**stiy**ger] (1925–) Film actor, born in Westhampton, NY. An exponent of the Method, he became known following his role in *On the Waterfront* (1954). Later films include *Al Capone* (1958), *Dr Zhivago* (1965), *The Pawnbroker* (1965), *In the Heat of the Night* (1967, Oscar), and *Incognito* (1997). >> Method, the

Stein, Gertrude [stiyn] (1874–1946) Writer, born in Allegheny, PA. Her main works include *Three Lives* (1908), *Tender Buttons* (1914), and her most widely-read book, *The Autobiography of Alice B Toklas* (1933). Her home became a salon for artists and writers between the two World Wars.

Stein, (Heinrich Friedrich) Karl, Freiherr (Baron) **von** [shtiyn] (1757–1831) Prussian statesman, born in Nassau, Germany. As chief minister (1807–8), he carried out important reforms in the army, economy, and both national and local government. >> Prussia

Steinbeck, John (Ernst) [**stiyn**bek] (1902–68) Novelist, born in Salinas, CA. His first novel of repute was *Tortilla Flat* (1935), and soon after came his major work, *The Grapes of Wrath* (1939). Other books include *Of Mice and Men* (1937), *East of Eden* (1952), and the humorous *Cannery Row* (1945). He received the Nobel Prize for Literature in 1962.

steinbok >> **steenbok**

Steiner, George [**stiyn**er] (1929–) Critic and scholar, born in Paris. He is a leading exponent of comparative literature, his publications including *The Death of Tragedy* (1961), *After Babel* (1975), and *No Passion Spent* (1996).

Steiner, Rudolf [**shtiyn**er] (1861–1925) Social philosopher, the founder of anthroposophy, born in Kraljevec, Croatia. In 1912 he established his first 'school of spiritual science', at Dornach in Switzerland. His aim was to integrate the psychological and the practical dimensions of life into an educational, ecological, and therapeutic basis for spiritual and physical development. Many schools and research institutions arose from his ideas, notably the **Rudolf Steiner Schools**, focusing on the development of the whole personality of the child. >> Goethe; theosophy

Steinway, Henry (Engelhard) [**stiyn**way], originally **Heinrich Engelhardt Steinweg** (1797–1871) Piano-maker, born in Wolfshagen, Germany. He established a piano factory in Brunswick in 1835, later transferring the business to the USA.

stele [**stee**lee, -liy] (plural **stelai**) In ancient Greece, a carved or inscribed upright rectangular stone which could be used as a gravestone, a boundary marker on property, or a permanent display board for public laws and documents.

stem (botany) The main axis of a plant, usually but not always above ground, and bearing the buds, leaves, and reproductive organs. It contains a vascular system: this conducts water and nutrients from the roots to the leaves, and the products of photosynthesis from the leaves to all other parts of the plant. In woody species, the stem is strengthened with additional supporting tissues, and protected by bark and cork layers. >> bulb; corm; photosynthesis; rhizome; tuber

stem (linguistics) >> **root** (linguistics)

Stendhal [sten**dahl**], pseudonym of **Marie-Henri Beyle** (1783–1842) Writer, born in Grenoble, France. He is best known for his novels, notably *Le Rouge et le noir* (1831, Scarlet and Black) and *La Chartreuse de Parme* (1839, The Charterhouse of Parma).

Sten gun The standard submachine-gun of the British Army from 1942 onwards. Its name derives from its designers Stephard and Turpin, and the Enfield factory where it was made. >> submachine-gun

Stenmark, Ingemar (1956–) Swedish skier, born in Tärnaby, Sweden, 100 mi S of the Arctic Circle. Overall champion three times (1976–8), he won 15 slalom/giant slalom titles, and five world titles. He retired in 1989. >> skiing

Steno, Nicolaus [**stee**noh], Lat name of **Niels Steensen** (1638–86) Anatomist and geologist, born in Copenhagen. He discovered the duct of the parotid gland and explained the function of the ovaries. He was also the first to explain the structure of the Earth's crust. >> fossil; ovary

stenography >> **shorthand** ⓘ

stenotype >> **palantype**

stephanotis [stefa**noh**tis] A twining, evergreen perennial (*Stephanotis floribunda*), native to Madagascar; a clustered wax flower; stems to 3 m/10 ft or more; flowers tubular with five spreading lobes, white, strongly fragrant; also called **Madagascar jasmine**. (Family: Asclepiadaceae.) >> wax plant

Stephen (c.1090–1154) Last Norman king of England (1135–54), and son of Stephen, Count of Blois, and Adela, daughter of William the Conqueror. He had sworn to accept Henry I's daughter, Empress Matilda, as queen, but seized the English crown and was recognized as Duke of Normandy on Henry's death in 1135. After 18 years of virtually continuous warfare, he was forced in 1153 to accept Matilda's son, the future Henry II, as his lawful successor. >> Angevins; Henry I / II

Stephen I, St (c.975–1038) The first king of Hungary (997–1038). He received from the pope the title of 'Apostolic King' and, according to tradition, St Stephen's Crown, now a Hungarian national treasure. He was canonized in 1083. Feast day 16 August.

Stephen, St (1st-c) According to the Acts of the Apostles (6–7), the first Christian martyr. He was charged by the Jewish authorities for speaking against the Temple and the Law, and stoned to death by the crowds in Jerusalem. Feast day 26 December. >> Acts of the Apostles; Christianity

Stephen, Sir Ninian (Martin) (1923–) Judge, born in England. Appointed Governor-General of Australia (1982–9), he retired from the position when he was made Australia's first ambassador for the environment, a non-political role from which he retired in 1991.

Stephenson, George (1781–1848) Railway engineer, born in Wylam, Northumberland. His most famous engine, the 'Rocket', running at 58 km/36 mi an hour, was built in 1829. >> locomotive ⓘ

Stephenson, Robert (1803–59) Civil engineer, born in Willington Quay, Northumberland, the son of George Stephenson. He attained independent fame through his tubular design for the Britannia Bridge over the Menai Straits in Wales (1846–9), and for bridges at

Conwy, Montreal, Newcastle upon Tyne, and elsewhere. >> Stephenson, George

Stephenson, Sir William, known as **Intrepid** (1896–1989) Secret intelligence chief, born in Point Douglas, near Winnipeg, Canada. In 1940 he was appointed British intelligence chief in North and South America. The novelist Ian Fleming, a member of his wartime staff, is said to have adopted Stephenson as the model for the character 'M' in the James Bond books.

steppe The extensive grassland, treeless region of Eurasia. It extends from the Ukraine through SE European and C Asian Russia to the Manchurian plains. Large areas are important for wheat growing. >> pampa(s); prairie

steradian [ste**ray**dian] SI unit of solid angle; symbol *sr*; an area drawn on the surface of a sphere equal to the square of the radius of the sphere subtends a solid angle of 1 steradian at the centre of the sphere; the total area of a sphere subtends a solid angle of 4π sr at the centre. >> geometry

stere >> **RR1032**

stereochemistry The study of the spatial relationships between atoms in molecules, especially the configuration of the atoms bonded to a central atom and the occurrence of geometrical and optical isomers. >> chemistry; isomers; molecule

stereolithography >> **lithography** ℹ

stereophonic sound The recording and transmission of sound which, when reproduced, appears to the listener to come from different directions and to reproduce a sound field similar to that where the sound was originally recorded. It normally uses two microphones, and two loudspeakers to reproduce the sound which has been recorded on two separate channels. Two-track stereo tape recordings appeared in 1954. >> sound recording

stereoscopic photography, also termed **3-D** (three-dimensional) **films** The recording and presentation of paired images to give the viewer an impression of solidity and depth. The basic system, developed from 1845, is to photograph the scene with two cameras whose lenses are 65 mm/$2\frac{1}{2}$ in apart, the normal separation of human eyes, and view the results in a device (such as a pair of special spectacles) which allows each eye to see only its appropriate right-eye or left-eye record. >> photography

sterilization 1 A surgical operation to render the individual unable to conceive. In the male the simplest procedure is to sever each vas deferens, a procedure known as *vasectomy*. In the female, obliteration of the Fallopian tubes is the simplest approach. >> contraception; uterine tubes **2** >> asepsis

sterling The name of the currency of Britain, usually used to distinguish the British pound from other currencies (**pound sterling**). The name derives from the Norman coin known as a *steorling*, which had a star on one face. >> currency

Stern, Howard (1954–) Radio disc-jockey and television talk-show host, born in New York City. He built a reputation as a 'shock jock', developing a flamboyant style and explicit programme content, in various 'Howard Stern' shows on radio and television during the 1990s. His best-selling book *Private Parts* (1993) was later issued as a recording and filmed (both 1997).

Sternberg, Josef von [**shtern**berg], originally **Jonas Stern** (1894–1969) Film director, born in Vienna. His most famous film was *Der blaue Engel* (1930, The Blue Angel) with Marlene Dietrich. His autocratic methods and aloof personality made him unpopular in the studios, and his later career was erratic. >> Dietrich

Sterne, Laurence (1713–68) Novelist, born in Clonmel, Co Tipperary, Ireland. In 1759 he wrote the first two volumes of his comic novel, *The Life and Opinions of Tristram Shandy*, which was very well received in London, and the remaining volumes appeared between 1761 and 1767.

sternum An elongated, almost flat bone lying in the midline of the front wall of the thorax; also known as the **breastbone**. It articulates with the clavicle and the ribs, and gives some protection to the heart. >> bone; clavicle; skeleton ℹ; thorax

steroid Any of several natural products, including many hormones, bile acids, and the *sterols*, derived from the non-glyceride portion of fats, the best known of which is cholesterol. Steroids are responsible for maintaining many vital functions, including sexual characteristics, salt and water balance, and muscle and bone mass. >> anabolic steroids; androgens; cholesterol; corticosteroids; hormones; oestrogens; progesterone; testosterone

Stevenage [**steev**nij] 51°55N 0°14W, pop (1995e) 74 600. Town in Hertfordshire, SE England; the first 'new town', 1946; railway. >> Hertfordshire

Stevens, Wallace (1879–1955) Poet, born in Reading, PA. He was over 40 when his first volume, *Harmonium* (1923), was published, and his *Collected Poems* appeared in 1954.

Stevenson, Adlai (Ewing) [**ad**liy] (1900–65) US Democratic politician, born in Los Angeles, CA. He helped to found the United Nations (1946), stood twice against Eisenhower as presidential candidate (1952, 1956), and was the US delegate to the UN in 1961–5. >> Eisenhower; United Nations

Stevenson, Robert Louis (Balfour) (1850–94) Writer, born in Edinburgh. The romantic adventure story *Treasure Island* brought him fame in 1883, and entered him on a course of romantic fiction which included *Kidnapped* (1886), *The Strange Case of Dr Jekyll and Mr Hyde* (1886), *The Master of Ballantrae* (1889), and the unfinished *Weir of Hermiston* (1896), considered his masterpiece.

Stevenson screen A shelter for meteorological instruments, particularly thermometers, providing protection from solar radiation. It is a white, wooden box with louvred sides to give ventilation. It was invented by Thomas Stevenson (1818–87), the father of Robert Louis Stevenson. >> meteorology; radiation

Stewart, Alec J (1963–) Cricketer, born in Merton, Greater London. He began playing for Surrey in 1981, made his Test debut in 1990, and by mid-1998 had played in 75 Tests. He took over as England captain in 1998.

Stewart, Jackie, popular name of **John (Young) Stewart** (1939–) Motor-racing driver, born in Milton, West Dunbartonshire. He won 27 world championship races between 1965 and 1973, and was world champion in 1969 (driving a Matra), 1971, and 1973 (both Tyrrell). He retired at the end of 1973. Since 1996 he has been chairman of Stewart Grand Prix >> motor racing; Prost

Stewart, James (Maitland) (1908–97) Film actor, born in Indiana, PA. He won an Oscar for his role in *The Philadelphia Story* (1940, Oscar). Later films include a series of outstanding Westerns (1950–5), and two successes for Hitchcock, *Rear Window* (1954) and *Vertigo* (1958). Later films included *Fools' Parade* (1971) and *Right of Way* (1982). He received an honorary Oscar in 1985.

Stewart, Patrick (1940–) Actor and playwright, born in Mirfield, West Yorkshire. He is best known for his role as Captain Jean-Luc Picard in the follow-up series of *Star Trek: The Next Generation* (1987). Later films include *Star Trek: First Contact* (1996) and *Star Trek: Insurrection* (1998).

Stewart, Rod(erick David) (1945–) Singer and songwriter, born in London. He began a career as a soloist, and also joined The Faces (1969–75). His numerous hit songs include 'Maggie May' (1971) and 'Sailing' (1975). Albums include *Every Picture Tells A Story* (1971), *Every Beat of My Heart* (1986), and *Unplugged and Seated* (1993).

Stewart Island pop (1995e) 708; area 1735 sq km/670 sq mi. Island of New Zealand, to the S of South Island; highest point, Mt Anglem (977 m/3205 ft); a refuge for animal and bird life. >> New Zealand ℹ

Stewarts >> **Stuarts**

stibine [**sti**been] SbH_3. A highly poisonous gas formed by the reduction of antimony compounds. >> antimony

stibnite An antimony sulphide (Sb_2S_3) mineral found in low-temperature hydrothermal veins, lead-grey in colour. It is the chief ore of antimony. >> antimony

stick insect A large, twig-like insect with an elongate body and legs; up to 30 cm/12 in long; also known as **walking sticks**. (Order: Phasmida. Family: Phasmatidae, c.2000 species.) >> insect ℹ

stickleback Small marine or freshwater fish of the family Gasterosteidae (5 genera), common throughout the N hemisphere; body typically elongate with a number of strong dorsal spines; length up to 6 cm/2½ in. >> fish ℹ

Stieglitz, Alfred [**steeg**lits] (1864–1946) Photographer, born in Hoboken, NJ. He founded in 1902 the American Photo-Secession Group with Edward Steichen (1879–1973) and consistently influenced the development of creative photography as an art form through his magazine *Camera Work* (1903–17) and his gallery of modern art in New York City.

stigma In flowering plants, the part of the carpel receptive to pollen. Sticky secretions, corrugated surfaces, or hairs may help collect and retain pollen grains. The stigma, and often the style, may through physiological means operate a complex compatibility system which accepts only pollen of the correct type. >> carpel; flowering plants; style

stigmata [**stig**mata, stig**mah**ta] Marks or wounds appearing on the human body, similar to those of the crucified Jesus. They may be temporary (related to ecstasy or revelation) or permanent, and are alleged to be a sign of miraculous participation in Christ's passion. >> Jesus Christ

stilbestrol / stilboestrol >> **DES**

Stilicho, Flavius [**sti**likoh] (?–408) Roman general who was virtual ruler of the W Roman Empire (395–408) under the feeble Emperor Honorius. His greatest achievements were his victories over Alaric and the Visigoths in N Italy at Pollentia (402) and Verona (403). >> Alaric I; Honorius

still life In art, the representation of objects such as books, candles, cooking utensils, musical instruments, fruit, flowers, etc. In W Europe it flourished above all in the Netherlands in the 17th-c. >> painting

Stilwell, Joseph W(arren), nickname **Vinegar Joe** (1883–1946) US general, born in Palatka, FL. In 1942 he commanded US forces in China, Burma, and India. Recalled after a dispute with Jiang Jieshi (Chiang Kai-shek) in 1944, he commanded the US 10th Army in the Pacific until the end of the war. >> World War 2

stimulants Drugs such as amphetamine, which produce feelings of wakefulness, alertness, elation, and an increased capacity to concentrate. Caffeine is a mild stimulant. >> amphetamine; caffeine; drug addiction

stimulated emission >> **laser** ℹ

Sting, originally **Gordon Matthew Sumner** (1951–) Singer, songwriter, and actor, born in London. Former vocalist and lyricist of The Police, his albums include *The Dream of the Blue Turtles* (1985), *Soul Cages* (1991), and *Mercury Falling* (1996). His films include *Quadrophenia* (1978), *Dune* (1984), and *The Grotesque* (1995). He has also been much associated with campaigns to do with the environment and with Amnesty International.

stinging nettle A perennial with creeping rhizomes (*Urtica dioica*) often forming large patches, native or introduced throughout temperate regions. The whole plant is covered in stinging hairs, each with a bulbous base containing acid, and a brittle, needle-like tip. When touched, the tip pierces the skin and breaks off, while pressure on the base injects acid, causing a sting and subsequent rash. The leaves are used as a vegetable and for tea; the stems yield tough fibres for cloth. (Family: Urticaceae.) >> deadnettle; rhizome

stingray Any of several bottom-living rays (Families: Dasyatidae, Potamotrygonidae, Urolophidae) in which the tail is whip-like and armed with one or more sharp poison spines; body length up to 2·5 m/8 ft. >> ray

stinkhorn The fruiting body of some fungi of the order Phallales; cap dissolves into putrid slime, containing spores that are dispersed by flies attracted over great distances by the fetid odour. (Subdivision: *Basidiomycetes*.) >> Basidiomycetes; fungus

stipendiary magistrate In England and Wales, a salaried and legally qualified magistrate. Such magistrates may sit alone when trying cases, unlike lay magistrates, and are found in London and other large towns. >> justice of the peace

Stirling 56°07N 3°57W, pop (1995e) 30 000. Capital of Stirling council, C Scotland, on S bank of R Forth; railway; university (1967); Stirling castle (12th-c); scene of Bruce's parliament (1326). >> Bruce, Robert; Scotland ℹ

Stirling Range Mountain range in SW Western Australia; extends 64 km/40 mi parallel with SW coast; rises to 1109 m/3638 ft at Bluff Knoll. >> Western Australia

stitchwort Either of two species of bluish-green perennials with brittle stems native to woodlands in Europe, N Africa, and Asia Minor; flowers white, 5-petalled. (Genus: *Stellaria*. Family: Caryophyllaceae.)

stoat A mammal of family Mustelidae, native to Europe, Asia, and North America (*Mustela erminea*); in summer, resembles a large weasel (length, 50 cm/20 in) with black tip to tail; winter coat (*ermine*) white, with black tail tip. >> Mustelidae; weasel

stock An annual or perennial, growing to 80 cm/30 in, native to Europe and Asia; leaves greyish; flowers in spikes, purple, red or white, cross-shaped. It includes **garden stock** or **gilliflower** (*Matthiola incana*) and **night-scented stock** (*Matthiola bicornis*). (Genus: *Matthiola*, 55 species. Family: Cruciferae.)

stock-car racing A type of motor racing which takes different forms in the USA and UK. In the USA, highly supercharged production cars race around banked concreted tracks. In the UK, 'bangers' (old cars) race against each other on a round or oval track with the intention of being the last car still moving at the end of the race. >> motor racing

stock exchange An institution through which stocks, shares, and bonds are traded under standard rules. The London Stock Exchange deals in some 7000 securities. Until 1986, business was carried out on 'the floor of the House', ie in the Stock Exchange itself. Individuals and institutions wishing to buy or sell securities would contact a *stockbroker*, who would place the order with a *jobber* (a trader on the floor). 27 October 1986 was the date of the 'Big Bang' when the distinction between brokers and jobbers was abolished and a computerized system was introduced for share trading. Most capital cities in the West have a stock exchange, Wall Street in New York City being the largest. >> shares; Stock Exchange Automated Quotations; stock market; stocks

Stock Exchange Automated Quotations (SEAQ) A system introduced in 1986 in the London stock market for trading securities. It is a computerized market-making activity which enables member firms to buy and sell and quote prices for specific securities. >> stock exchange

Stockhausen, Karlheinz [**shtok**howzn] (1928–) Composer, born in Mödrath, Germany. In 1953 he helped to found the electronic music studio at Cologne. He has written orchestral, choral, and instrumental works, including some which combine electronic and normal sonorities, such as *Kontakte* (1960). >> electronic music

Stockholm 59°20N 18°03E, pop (1995e) 699 000. Seaport and capital of Sweden; on a group of islands and the adjacent mainland; founded, 1255; important trading centre of the Hanseatic League; capital, 1436; bishopric; airport; railway; underground railway; university (1878); Drottningholm Palace (royal family residence). >> Hanseatic League; Sweden ℹ

Stockholm syndrome The unnatural close relationship that occasionally develops between a hostage of a criminal or terrorist and his or her captor. It was first described in a woman held hostage in a bank in Sweden who remained faithful to the thief during his imprisonment.

stock market The system of buying and selling stocks and shares; also, a building in which these transactions take place (the *stock exchange*). A stock market 'crash' refers to a situation when the prices of stocks fall dramatically, resulting in many bankruptcies. The most famous case was the Wall Street crash of 1929; a less dramatic crash also occurred in October 1987 in most world stock markets. >> bear market; Dow Jones Index; stock exchange

Stockport 53°25N 2°10W, pop (1995e) 136 000. Town in Greater Manchester, NW England; railway; Manchester airport nearby; football league team, Stockport County. >> Manchester, Greater

stocks In economics, a term used in two main senses, both of which refer to amounts at a given moment; opposed to **flows**, which refer to changes over time. **1** Stocks of goods (or **inventories**): raw materials, fuels, or unsold products in store at a given date. **2** Financial assets: in the UK, for example, government debt is called **government stock**, and is traded on the stock exchange; in the USA, company shares are called **common stocks**. >> equity (economics); shares

Stockton >> **Macmillan, Sir Harold**

Stockton-on-Tees 54°34N 1°19W, pop (1995e) 89 600. Town in NE England, on the R Tees estuary; unitary authority, 1996 (pop (1995e) 178 000); developed with the opening of the Stockton–Darlington railway in 1825. >> England ℹ

Stoicism A philosophical movement which flourished in the Hellenistic Roman period from c.320 BC–AD 200, founded by Zeno of Citium. They believed in a rational, materialistic, and deterministic universe in which virtue consisted in understanding natural necessity and then cheerfully accepting it; the individual soul is literally a part of a larger cosmos, into which it is absorbed. >> Zeno of Citium

Stoke-on-Trent 53°00N 2°10W, pop (1995e) 252 000. Industrial city and (from 1997) unitary authority in Staffordshire, C England; part of the Potteries urban area; on the R Trent; railway; University of Keele (1962) nearby, Staffordshire University (1992); clayware (largest producer in the world); birthplace of Josiah Wedgwood and Arnold Bennett; Alton Towers theme park nearby; football league teams, Stoke City (Potters), Port Vale. >> Bennett, Arnold; ceramics; Staffordshire; Wedgwood, Josiah

Stoker, Bram, popular name of **Abraham Stoker** (1847–1912) Writer, born in Dublin. Among several books, he is remembered for the classic horror tale *Dracula* (1897), which has occasioned a whole series of film adaptations.

Stokes' law In physics, a law expressing the viscous drag force F acting on a spherical object of radius r moving with velocity v through a fluid of viscosity η as $F = 6\pi\eta rv$; stated in 1845 by British physicist George Stokes (1819–1903). >> viscosity

Stokowski, Leopold (Antonin Stanislaw Boleslawawicz) [sto**kof**skee] (1882–1977) Conductor, born in London. He conducted the orchestras of Philadelphia (1912–36), New York (1946–50), and Houston (1955–60), and in 1962 founded the American Symphony Orchestra in New York City.

STOL [**es**tol] Acronym used for a fixed-wing aircraft specially designed for **Short Take-Off and Landing**. These aircraft usually accomplish their function by special aerodynamic devices providing high lift. >> aerodynamics ℹ; aircraft ℹ; VTOL

stolon A long shoot which bends under its own weight to the ground, and roots at the tip or at the nodes to form new plants. >> stem (botany)

stomach A digestive pouch between the oesophagus and the duodenum, which stores food, secretes gastric juice and, by wave-like contractions, churns and releases its contents into the duodenum at a controlled rate. It is divided into the *cardiac* region around the *cardiac orifice* (where the oesophagus opens into the stomach), the *fundus* (the region above the level of the cardiac orifice), the *body*, and the *pylorus*, which opens into the duodenum at the *pyloric orifice*. >> duodenum; gastritis; oesophagus; peptic ulcer

Stone, Oliver (1946–) Film director and scriptwriter, born in New York City. He won an Oscar for his screenplay of *Midnight Express* (1978). *Platoon* (1987) brought him a Best Director Oscar, and he received another for *Born On The Fourth Of July* (1989). Later films include *The Doors* (1991), *JFK* (1991), and *Nixon* (1995).

Stone Age >> **Three Age System**

stonebass >> **wreckfish**

stone carving >> **sculpture**

stonechat A thrush (*Saxicola torquata*) native to most of the Old World; male with dark head, white neck spots and pale reddish breast. >> thrush (bird)

stone circles Circular or near-circular rings of prehistoric standing stones found, particularly in Britain and Ireland, in the Late Neolithic and Early Bronze Age. They most probably functioned as temples in which celestial events, the passing of the seasons, and the fertility of the land and people could be celebrated. >> Avebury; megalith; Stonehenge; Three Age System

stonecrop A member of a large genus of succulents, mostly perennials, native to N temperate regions; flowers 5-petalled, starry, mainly white, yellow, or red. (Genus: *Sedum*, 300 species. Family: Crassulaceae.) >> succulent

stonefish Grotesque fish found in shallow inshore waters of the Indo-Pacific region; body strongly camouflaged in shape and colour; length 30–60 cm/12–24 in; dorsal fin armed with sharp poison spines that can inflict extremely painful stings. (Genus: *Synanceia*. Family: Synanceiidae.) >> fish ℹ

stonefly A primitive, winged insect typically found among stones along river banks; adults are poor fliers that run and hide when disturbed. (Order: Plecoptera, c.2000 species.) >> insect ℹ

Stonehenge A prehistoric monument near Amesbury, Wiltshire, S England, 130 km/80 mi W of London; a world heritage site. It was constructed in three major phases within the Middle–Late Neolithic period: 2950–2900 BC, a circular ditch with low inner and outer banks, c.110 m/360 ft in diameter, and a circle of pits known as 'Aubrey Holes' which perhaps held timber posts; 2900–2400 BC, posts were set up inside the earthwork, and cremations were placed in the Aubrey Holes; the third phase, 2550–1600 BC, is that of the surviving stone monument, when a 30 m/100 ft diameter lintelled circle and inner horseshoe of 80 dressed sarsen (sandstone) blocks, each weighing 20–50 tonnes, were erected, and bluestones from South Wales were set up in a circle and horseshoe. Alignment on the midsummer sunrise/midwinter sunset implies prehistoric use for seasonal festivals, but the association with the druids dates only from 1905, and has no historical basis. The theory that the pillars had been transported by land on wooden rollers from South Wales to Salisbury Plain has now been superseded by the view that they were carried to the area by glaciers. >> Avebury; stone circles

Stone Mountain Memorial A memorial carving on the exposed face of Stone Mountain in NW Georgia, USA. The work, which was completed in 1972, depicts Confederate leaders Jefferson Davis, Robert E Lee, and 'Stonewall' Jackson. It was executed by sculptors Gutzon Borglum, Augustus Lukeman, and Walter Kirtland Hancock, who worked on it in succession over a period of 50 years. >> Davis, Jefferson; Jackson, Thomas Jonathon; Lee, Robert E

stoneware A type of ceramic midway between pottery and porcelain, made of clay and a fusible stone. It is fired to a point where partial vitrification renders it impervious to liquids, but unlike porcelain it is seldom more than slightly translucent. >> porcelain; pottery

Stooges, The Three Comedy trio, originally the **Horwitz** (later **Howard**) brothers, **Samuel** (b.1895), **Moses** (b.1897), and **Jerome (Jerry)** (b.1911), they were known by their respective nicknames of Shemp, Moe, and Curly (with the bald head). Shemp left for a career of his own, and was replaced by **Larry Fine** (originally **Feinberg**), with the wild wavy hair. Their films were characterized by anarchic knockabout humour, with sound effects perfectly synchronized with their blows. Later, Shemp returned, replacing Jerry, and in turn was replaced by **Joe Besser**. In the late 1950s, **Joe de Rita** (b.1909) replaced Besser as the new Curly. Moe and Larry died in 1975, and Joe in 1993.

stoolball An 11-a-side bat-and-ball game resembling cricket and rounders. The batter defends his wicket, a 1 ft (30 cm) square wooden board 4 ft 8 in (1·4 m) from the ground, which the underarm bowler attempts to hit. >> cricket (sport) ℹ; rounders

Stopes, Marie (Charlotte Carmichael) [stohps] (1880–1958) Pioneer advocate of birth control, suffragette, and palaeontologist, born in Edinburgh. Alarmed at the unscientific way in which men and women embarked upon married life, she wrote a number of books on the subject, of which *Married Love* (1918) caused a storm of controversy. She later founded the first birth control clinic in N London (1921). >> contraception; women's liberation movement

stop–go policy A government economic policy in which action taken to boost the economy (**go**) results in inflation or exchange rate problems. Action is then taken to cure these problems, which results in a slow-down of the economy (**stop**). >> prices and incomes policy

Stoppard, Miriam, *née* **Stern** (1937–) British physician, writer, and broadcaster. She is well known for her television series, especially *Miriam Stoppard's Health and Beauty Show* (1988–). She married Tom Stoppard in 1972 (divorced, 1992). >> Stoppard, Tom

Stoppard, Sir Tom, originally **Tom Straussler** (1937–) Playwright, born in Zlín, Czech Republic. He made his name in 1967 with *Rosencrantz and Guildenstern are Dead*. Other plays include the philosophical satire *Jumpers* (1972), *Travesties* (1974), *The Real Thing* (1982), and *The Invention of Love* (1997). He was married to Miriam Stoppard (divorced, 1992). >> Stoppard, Miriam

Storey, David (Malcolm) (1933–) Novelist and playwright, born in Wakefield, West Yorkshire. His novels include *This Sporting Life* (1960) and *Saville* (1976); and his plays *The Changing Room* (1972) and *Stages* (1992).

stork A large bird, native to warm regions worldwide; long legs, neck, and long stout bill; flies with neck and legs outstretched. The **white stork** (*Ciconia ciconia*) is the stork of fable, a summer visitor to Europe, which prefers to nest on buildings. (Family: Ciconiidae, 17 species.) >> adjutant; ibis; jabiru; marabou

storksbill An annual or perennial native to temperate regions; flowers white, pink, or purple; fruit with a long point resembling a bird's beak. (Genus: *Erodium*, 90 species. Family: Geraniaceae.)

storm An intense meteorological disturbance, categorized on the Beaufort scale as force 10 (storm) or force 11 (violent storm). Wind speeds range from 25–32 m/s (55–72 mph). >> Beaufort Scale; thunderstorm; wind ℹ

Stormer, Horst L (1949–) Physicist, born in Frankfurt-am-Main, Germany. He graduated from Stuttgart University in 1977, joined Columbia University, NY, and shared the 1998 Nobel Prize for Physics for his contribution to the discovery of a new form of quantum fluid with fractionally charged excitations.

Stormont A suburb of Belfast, Northern Ireland, in which are situated Parliament House (built in 1932 to house the parliament of Northern Ireland, then the home of the Northern Ireland Assembly), Stormont House, and Stormont Castle. >> Belfast

storm petrel A petrel, worldwide, found at sea unless breeding. Some (Subfamily: Oceanitinae) 'walk' across the water surface in flight; others (Subfamily: Hydrobatinae) swoop over the water. (Family: Hydrobatidae, 22 species.) >> petrel

storm surge A localized rise in sea level produced by onshore winds and reduced atmospheric pressure caused by large storms. Much of the flood damage produced by hurricanes, typhoons, and other major storms is the result of storm surge.

Stornoway 58°12N 6°23W, pop (1995e) 8400. Port capital of Western Isles council, NW Scotland, on E coast of Lewis; airfield. >> Scotland ℹ; Western Isles

Stoss or **Stozz, Veit** [shtohs] (c.1447–1533) Woodcarver and sculptor, born in Nuremberg, Germany. He worked mainly in Kraków (1477–96), where he carved the high altar of the Marienkirche.

stout >> **beer** ℹ

Stowe, Harriet (Elizabeth) Beecher [stoh], *née* **Beecher** (1811–96) Novelist, born in Litchfield, CT. She became famous through her *Uncle Tom's Cabin*, which immediately focused anti-slavery sentiment in the North. Her other novels include *Dred* (1856) and *The Minister's Wooing* (1859).

Strabane [stra**ban**], Ir **An Srath Ban** 54°49N 7°27W, pop (1995e) 11 900. Market town in Tyrone, W Northern Ireland; on the Mourne and Finn Rivers; Irish border town. >> Tyrone

strabismus >> **squint**

Strabo [**stray**boh] (Gr 'squint-eyed') (c.64 BC–c.AD 23) Geographer and historian, born in Amasia, Pontus. Only a few fragments remain of his 47-volume historical work, but his *Geographica* in 17 books has survived almost complete.

Strachey, (Giles) Lytton [**stray**chee] (1880–1932) Biographer, born in London. He began his writing career as a critic, but turned to biography, creating a literary bombshell with his *Eminent Victorians* (1918). Later works included *Queen Victoria* (1921) and *Elizabeth and Essex* (1928). >> biography; Bloomsbury group

Stradivari or **Stradivarius, Antonio** [stradi**vah**rius] (c.1644–1737) Violin maker, born in Cremona, Italy. His best instruments are thought to be unsurpassed in quality. He made over a thousand violins, violas, and violoncellos between 1666 and his death; about 650 of these still exist. >> violin

Strafford, Thomas Wentworth, 1st Earl of (1593–1641) English statesman, born in London. In 1632 he was Lord Deputy of Ireland, where he imposed firm rule, and in 1639 became the king's principal adviser. His suppression of the rebellion in Scotland failed, and he was impeached by the Long Parliament. Despite a famous defence at Westminster, he was executed. >> Charles I (of England); Long Parliament

strain The fractional change in the dimensions of some object subjected to stress, expressed as a number. For force acting along the axis of a rod, **linear strain** is the change in length divided by the original length. **Volume strain** is the fractional change in volume for an object pressured on all sides. **Shear strain** measures the effectiveness of a twisting force. >> stress (physics)

Straits Settlements The name given to the former British crown colony which consisted of Singapore, Malacca, the Dindings, Penang, and Province Wellesley. All became part of Malaysia in 1963, and Singapore became independent in 1965. >> Malaysia ℹ

strangeness In particle physics, an internal additive quantum number conserved in strong and electromagnetic interactions, but not in weak interactions; symbol *S*. It was introduced during the 1930s to explain 'strange' reactions observed in cosmic ray experiments. >> particle physics; quantum numbers; quark

Stranraer [stran**rah(r)**] 54°54N 5°02W, pop (1995e) 10 000. Port in Dumfries and Galloway, SW Scotland; at the head of Loch Ryan; railway; ferries to N Ireland. >> Dumfries and Galloway; Scotland ℹ

Strasberg, Lee, originally **Israel Strassberg** (1901–82) Theatre director, actor, and teacher, born in Budzanow, Austria. In 1931 he was involved in the formation of the Group Theatre, evolving a technique (influenced by Stanislavsky) which became known everywhere as 'the Method'. He exercised great influence as director of the Actors' Studio (1949–82), his pupils including Marlon Brando, Anne Bancroft, and Paul Newman. >> Actors' Studio; Method, the; Stanislavsky

Strasbourg [**straz**berg], Fr [straz**boor**], Ger **Strassburg** [**shtras**boork], ancient **Argentoratum** 48°35N 7°42E, pop (1995e) 260 000. Industrial and commercial city in NE France; on the R Ill; sixth largest city and largest riverport in France; part of a bishopric since 1003; free imperial city in 13th-c; ceded to France, 1697; taken by Germany, 1871; returned to France, 1918; railway junction; university (founded 1537); seat of the Council of Europe, European Parliament, European Commission of Human Rights, and European Science Foundation; printing developed here by Gutenberg; tourist centre of Alsace; congress and conference centre; Gothic cathedral (begun 1015, with noted 14th-c astronomical clock). >> Alsace; Council of Europe; European Parliament; Gutenberg

Strategic Arms Limitation Treaty >> **SALT**

Strategic Arms Reduction Talks >> **START**

Strategic Defense Initiative >> **SDI**

strategic studies The academic study of the military, political, economic, and technological factors which affect the relations between nations. As distinct from military science, which concerns itself with the deployment of personnel and material in war, strategic studies looks at the continuous process of military relations between nations in war and peace. >> military science

Stratford-upon-Avon 52°12N 1°41W, pop (1995e) 23 700. Town in Warwickshire, C England; on the R Avon; birthplace of William Shakespeare; railway; Royal Shakespeare Theatre; Anne Hathaway's Cottage. >> Shakespeare ℹ; Warwickshire

Strathclyde [strath**kliyd**] pop (1995e) 2 270 000; area 13 537 sq km/5225 sq mi. Former region in W and C Scotland, established in 1975, and replaced in 1996 by 10 local councils: Argyll and Bute, West Dunbartonshire, East Dunbartonshire, Renfrewshire, Inverclyde, City of Glasgow, East Renfrewshire, North Ayrshire, East Ayrshire, South Ayrshire. >> Scotland ℹ

stratification A geological term for the formation of layers in sedimentary rock in which breaks in the deposition or changes in the nature of the deposited material define visible bedding planes. >> sedimentary rock; stratigraphy

stratigraphy A branch of geology concerned with the study of sequences of layers of rock, usually sedimentary. It aims to unravel changes in their depositional environment, and to correlate rocks of the same age in different places by their rock type and fossil content. >> sedimentary rock

Strato or **Straton of Lampsacus** [**stray**toh, **stray**ton] (?–c.270 BC) Greek philosopher, the successor to Theophrastus as the third head of the Lyceum (from c.287 to c.269 BC). His writings are lost, but he seems to have worked mainly to revise Aristotle's physical doctrines. >> Lyceum

stratocumulus clouds [stratoh**kyoom**yuluhs] Low layer clouds with a distinct cumulus or rounded shape; layers of cloud are rolled into rounded forms. They are white or grey in colour, and are found at c.500–2000 m/1600–6500 ft. Cloud symbol: Sc. >> cloud ℹ; cumulus clouds; stratus clouds

stratosphere The layer of the Earth's atmosphere at a height of c.15–50 km/10–30 mi, separated from the troposphere below by the tropopause, and from the mesosphere above by the stratopause. It contains the ozone layer. >> atmosphere ℹ; mesosphere; ozone layer; troposphere

Stratton, Charles (Sherwood), nickname **General Tom Thumb** (1838–83) Midget showman, born in Bridgeport, CT. He stopped growing at 6 months of age, and stayed 63 cm/25 in until his teens, eventually reaching 101 cm/40 in. Barnum displayed him in his museum from the age of 5, under the name of **General Tom Thumb**, and he became famous throughout the USA and Europe. >> Barnum; dwarfism

stratus clouds [**strat**uhs] The lowest layer of clouds in the atmosphere. They are composed of water droplets, and result in dull, overcast, and often drizzly conditions associated with the warm sector of a depression. They are found up to c.500 m/1600 ft. >> altostratus / cirrostratus / nimbostratus clouds; cloud ℹ; depression (meteorology) ℹ

Strauss, Johann [strows], known as **the Elder** (1804–49) Violinist, conductor, and composer, born in Vienna. He founded, with Josef Lanner, the Viennese Waltz tradition, and toured widely in Europe with his own orchestra. He composed several marches, notably the *Radetzky* (1848), and numerous waltzes. >> Strauss, Johann (the Younger); waltz

Strauss, Johann [strows], known as **the Younger** (1825–99) Violinist, conductor and composer, born in Vienna, the son of Johann Strauss (the Elder). He wrote over 400 waltzes, notably *The Blue Danube* (1867) and *Tales from the Vienna Woods* (1868), as well as polkas, marches, several operettas, including *Die Fledermaus* (1874, The Bat), and a favourite concert piece, *Perpetuum Mobile*. >> waltz

Strauss, Richard [strows] (1864–1949) Composer, born in Munich, Germany. He is best known for his symphonic poems, such as *Till Eulenspiegels lustige Streiche* (1894–5, Till Eulenspiegel's Merry Pranks) and *Also sprach Zarathustra* (1895–6, Thus Spoke Zarathustra), and his operas, notably *Der Rosenkavalier* (1911). >> symphonic poem

Stravinsky, Igor (Fyodorovich) [stra**vin**skee] (1882–1971) Composer, born near St Petersburg, Russia. He became famous with his music for the Diaghilev ballets *The Firebird* (1910), *Petrushka* (1911), and *The Rite of Spring* (1913).

Essentially an experimenter, after World War 1 he devoted himself to Neoclassicism, as in the opera-oratorio *Oedipus Rex* (1927) and the choral *Symphony of Psalms* (1930). Other major compositions include the *Symphony in C major* (1940), the opera *The Rake's Progress* (1951), and such later works as *Requiem Canticles* (1966), in which he adopted serialism. >> Diaghilev; Neoclassicism (music); serialism

Straw, Jack, popular name of **John Whitaker Straw** (1946–) British statesman. He became an MP in 1979, and went on to join the shadow cabinet as spokesman on education (1987–92), environment and local government (1992–3), local government (1993–4), and home affairs (1994–7). He became home secretary in the 1997 Labour government.

strawberry A perennial with arching runners rooting at nodes to form new plants, native to North and South America, Europe (N as far as Ireland), and Asia; flowers 5-petalled, white; false fruit consisting of swollen, fleshy, red receptacle bearing brown, dry, achenes (the 'seeds') on the surface. (Genus: *Fragaria*, 15 species. Family: Rosaceae.) >> achene; receptacle

strawberry tree An evergreen shrub or small tree (*Arbutus unedo*), native to the Mediterranean and W Europe north to Ireland; leaves reddish, leathery; flowers white, bell-shaped, in drooping clusters; fruits red, spherical, covered with soft warts. (Family: Ericaceae.)

streaming Putting children into higher or lower groups according to their general ability, as opposed to teaching them in *mixed ability* (also known as 'heterogeneous') groups, or *mixed age* (also called 'vertical' or 'family') groups. If this is done on the basis of their competence in a particular subject, the process is known as **setting** or (US) **tracking**.

streamlining A condition of fluid flow such that no turbulence occurs. Streamlining refers to the design of the shape of machinery or apparatus (eg automobiles, aircraft) so that turbulence is reduced to a minimum.

stream of consciousness A term introduced by William James in his *Principles of Psychology* (1890) to describe the continuous, random activity of the mind. It has been adopted by writers and critics to refer to the techniques used to register this inner experience in writing. >> James, William; Joyce, James

Streep, Meryl (Louise) (1949–) Actress, born in Summit, NJ. She made her film debut in *Julia* (1977). She gained Oscars for *Kramer v Kramer* (1979) and *Sophie's Choice* (1982), and critical acclaim for *The French Lieutenant's Woman* (1981), *Out of Africa* (1985), *Heartburn* (1986), and *Postcards From the Edge* (1990). Later films include *Dancing at Lughnasa* (1998).

street dance Forms of competitive dance that started in the early 1970s among gangs of youths in New York. **Break dancing** aims to develop control and co-ordination to perform acrobatic and athletic feats either solo, with a partner, or in a group. **Body popping** is a jerky articulation of isolated parts of the body creating a chain of movement. **Robotics** is a form where mime and puppet movements are important. A mechanical effect is created by tense muscles in a stiff body. >> modern dance

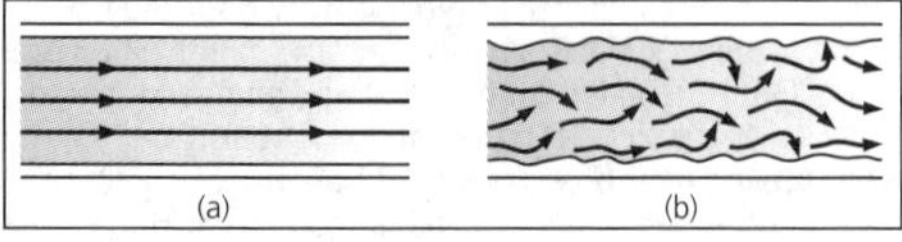

Streamlining – streamline flow (a); turbulent flow (b)

Streisand, Barbra [**striy**sand], originally **Barbara Joan Streisand** (1942–) Actress and singer, born in New York City. She played the lead in the Broadway show *Funny Girl*, which she repeated in the 1968 film version to win an Oscar. Later films included *Hello, Dolly* (1969) and *A Star is Born* (1976). She scripted, composed, directed, and starred in *Yentl* (1983), and co-produced and directed *Prince of Tides* (1991), and *The Mirror Has Two Faces* (1996).

Streptococcus [streptoh**kok**us] A spherical to ovoid bacterium which occurs in chains. Some species are useful in dairy fermentations; others are found in animal intestinal tracts and may be disease-causing. It includes the causative agents of scarlet fever and pneumonia. (Kingdom: Monera. Family: Streptococcaceae.) >> bacteria ℹ

streptomycin [strepto**miy**sin] An antibiotic discovered in 1944 which became the first clinically effective drug for the treatment of tuberculosis. Although drug resistance developed during its first years of use, it is still occasionally used in a cocktail of several drugs for treating tuberculosis. >> antibiotics; tuberculosis

stress (physics) A force per unit area which acts on an object attempting to deform it. A force F applied along the axis of a bar of cross section A produces a **linear stress** of F/A, units Pa (pascal). Such a force is involved in attempts to pull apart layers of atoms (**tensile stress**) or to push them together (**compressive stress**). A twisting force causes **shear stress**, which tries to slide layers of atoms over one another. >> strain

stress (psychology) In psychology, effects arising when certain external circumstances (**stressors**) lead to a stereotyped non-specific response from a person (the **stress response**). Stressors may be physical (noise, heat) or psychological (bereavement, unemployment), but their effect depends on their interpretation by the recipient. Response symptoms include attentional selectivity, memory loss, and autonomic activity (eg sweating).

strike A form of industrial action, where a group of workers stop work in protest at some action by their employer, or because of a failure of collective bargaining to achieve the desired results. An **official strike** is one which has been formally agreed by the members of the union. Since the passing of the Trade Union Act (1984), unions in the UK have to hold a secret ballot of members before strike action is formally declared. >> industrial action; trade union

Strindberg, (Johan) August (1849–1912) Playwright, born in Stockholm. He first achieved fame with the novel *Röda Rummet* (1879, The Red Room), followed by several plays. His plays *Fadren* (1887, The Father) and *Fröken Julie* (1888, Miss Julie) brought him to the forefront as the exponent of naturalistic drama.

string instrument 1 bowed Musical instruments in which the sound is produced by drawing a bow (made of horsehair) across one or more taut strings. Gut, metal, and (more recently) nylon are the materials most often needed for the strings themselves. The bowed string instruments of the modern orchestra – violin, viola, cello, and double bass – all have four strings (some double basses have five). The strings can be plucked as well as bowed. >> baryton; cello; chordophone; crwth; double bass; hurdy-gurdy; kit; string quartet; viola; viola da gamba; violin **2 non-bowed** Musical instruments in which the sound is produced by plucking or striking one or more strings. Many are fitted with keyboards; others are played with sticks or hammers, or are plucked or strummed with fingers or plectra. A large number are folk instruments, the only one commonly found in the modern orchestra being the harp. >> aeolian harp; balalaika; banjo; bouzouki; chitarrone; chordophone; cimbalom; cittern; dulcimer; gittern; guitar; harp; Hawaiian guitar; keyboard instrument;

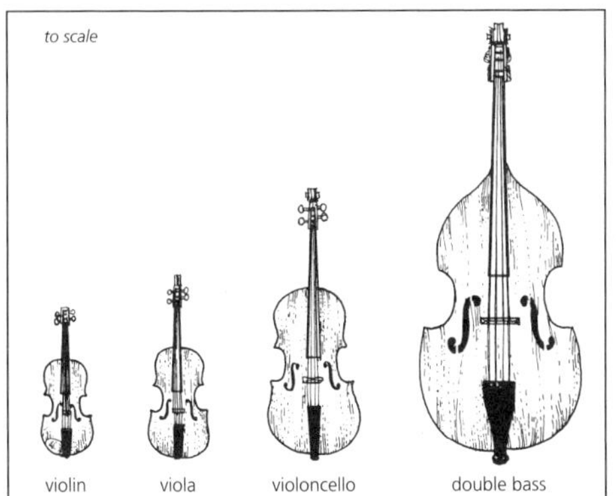

String instruments

kinnor; kithara ℹ; koto; lute; lyre; mandolin; pipa; plectrum; sitar ℹ; theorbo; ud; ukulele; zither

string quartet An ensemble of two violins, viola, and cello; also, a piece of music for such an ensemble. The first important composer of string quartets was Haydn, who established the four-movement structure and wrote some of the earliest masterpieces in the form. >> Haydn; string instrument 1 ℹ

strobilus [stro**biy**lus] A cone-shaped group of leaves or leaf-like structures bearing sporangia and found in spore-bearing vascular plants. In gymnosperms it has become the woody cone. >> gymnosperms; sporangium

stroboscope A device for producing a succession of short pulses of light, usually using light from a mercury arc lamp. The pulse frequency is variable, with several thousand flashes per second possible. In photography, it may be used to produce several images of a moving object in a single picture.

Stroessner, Alfredo [**stres**ner] (1912–) Paraguayan dictator, born in Encarnación, Paraguay. He became president in 1954, and was re-elected at regular intervals, but he was forced to stand down after a coup in 1989. He now lives in Brazil. >> Chaco War; Paraguay ℹ

Stroheim, Erich (Oswald) von [**stroh**hiym] (1886–1957) Film director and actor, born in Vienna. His first success as film director was with *Blind Husbands* (1919), followed by the classic film *Greed* (1923). Later he returned to film acting, often playing the roles of German officers, as in *Desert Fox* (1951).

stroke A sudden interference with the blood supply to the brain which results in the death of nerve tissue followed by varying degrees of disability. It may be caused by the rupture of an artery, by the clotting of blood within an artery (*thrombosis*), or by an embolism. >> aphasia; blood vessels ℹ; cerebral haemorrhage; embolism

Strong, Sir Roy (Colin) (1935–) Art historian and museum director, born in London. He became assistant keeper at the National Portrait Gallery, London, in 1959, and its director in 1967. He was also director of the Victoria and Albert Museum (1974–87).

strong interaction The strong short-range force binding together protons and neutrons in atomic nuclei, and quarks in protons and neutrons; also called **strong nuclear force**. It is independent of and stronger than electromagnetic force, and governs nuclear fission, fusion, and alpha decay. >> particle physics; quantum chromodynamics

strong nuclear force >> **strong interaction**

strontium Sr, element 38, melting point 769°C. A very reactive metal, very similar to calcium, and also an alkaline earth element; not found uncombined. Its main importance is that it will replace calcium in most crystals. One isotope, strontium-90, is an important product of nuclear fission, with a half-life of 28 years. >> calcium; chemical elements; metal; nuclear fission; RR1036

structuralism A theory which attempts to define the general properties of cultural systems, including language, mythology, art, and social organization; the approach derives from the work of the Swiss linguist Ferdinand de Saussure and the French anthropologist Claude Lévi-Strauss. The fundamental thesis is that individual terms or phenomena can be understood only in relationship to other elements of the same system, and that each system is built up using a limited set of contrasts. >> Barthes; Lévi-Strauss; linguistics; Saussure; semiotics

structure plan A requirement of UK planning law. Each planning authority has to produce a structure plan which is approved by the secretary of state for the environment. It forms the basis for policies of development (eg land use, traffic management) in the authority's area.

strychnine A poisonous alkaloid present in members of the genus *Strychnos*, thorny trees or climbing shrubs with hook-like tendrils, native to the tropics. *Strychnos nux vomica* was introduced into Germany in the 16th-c as a rat poison (and is still used for this purpose). (Genus: *Strychnos*, 200 species. Family: Loganiaceae.) >> alkaloids; curare

Stuart >> **Alice Springs**

Stuart or **Stewart, Prince Charles Edward (Louis Philip Casimir)**, known as **the Young Pretender** and **Bonnie Prince Charlie** (1720–88) Claimant to the British crown, born in Rome, Italy, the son of James Francis Edward Stuart. In 1745, he landed with seven followers at Eriskay in the Hebrides (Jul 1745) and raised his father's standard. The clansmen flocked to him, Edinburgh surrendered, and he kept court at Holyrood. Victorious at Prestonpans, he invaded England, but was routed at Culloden Moor (1746). With the help of Flora Macdonald he escaped to the Continent. He then lived in France and Italy, where (after his father's death in 1766) he assumed the title of Charles III of Great Britain. >> Forty-five Rebellion; Jacobites; Macdonald, Flora; Stuarts

Stuart or **Stewart, Prince James (Francis Edward)**, also known as **the Old Pretender** (1688–1766) Claimant to the British throne, born in London, the only son of James II of England and his second wife, Mary of Modena. In 1715 he landed at Peterhead, Aberdeenshire during the Jacobite rising, but left Scotland some weeks later. Thereafter he lived mainly in Rome. >> Fifteen Rebellion; Jacobites; James II (of England); Stuarts

Stuart, John McDouall (1815–66) Explorer, born in Dysart, Fife. He accompanied Captain Charles Sturt's expedition (1844–6), and in 1860 traversed Australia from S to N. Mt Stuart is named after him. >> Sturt

Stuarts, earlier spelled **Stewarts** A Scottish royal family, commencing with Robert II (r. 1371–90), which succeeded to the English throne in 1603 with the accession of James VI and I, the great-grandson of Henry VIII's sister, Margaret. James I (1603–25) and Charles II (1649–85) were both successful politicians; but Charles I (1625–49) and James II (1685–8) were not, and both lost their thrones. The Stuart line ended in 1714 with the death of Queen Anne, although pretenders laid claim to the throne as late as 1745. >> Anne; Charles I / II (of England); James I / II (of England); Mary II; Robert II; Stuart, Charles Edward; RR1026

Stubbs, George (1724–1806) Anatomist, painter, and engraver, born in Liverpool, Merseyside. He was best known for his sporting pictures, and excelled in painting horses.

stucco [**stu**koh] A good quality plaster often used in classical architecture for low relief ornamental carvings and mouldings. It is also employed as an inexpensive render which can replace or resemble stone. >> gypsum

stump-jump plough An Australian-designed plough (patented 1881) with shears that work independently of each other, allowing the cultivation of land with roots or large stones. Ordinary ploughs break under such conditions. >> plough [i]

stupa [**stoo**pa] An Indian cairn or mound originally constructed over the ashes of an emperor or some other great person, such as the Buddha. Later they were used to house the ashes of Buddhist monks and holy relics. >> Buddhism; pagoda

sturgeon Any of a group of large, primitive fish found in the N hemisphere; body elongate, armed with rows of heavy bony scales; head tapering, underside mouth with long barbels; body length 1–5 m/3–16 ft; eggs sold as caviar. (Family: Acipenseridae, 4 genera, 25 species.) >> beluga (fish); caviar

Sturluson, Snorri [**stur**luson] (1179–1241) Icelandic poet and historian. His main works were the *Prose Edda* and *Heimskringla* ('the Circle of the World'), a series of sagas of the Norwegian kings down to 1177. >> saga

Sturm und Drang [**shtoorm** unt **drang**] (Ger 'storm and stress') A revolutionary literary movement in late-18th-c Germany, which rejected classical values in favour of subjective feeling and artistic creativity. An important tributary of the Romantic movement, it influenced Goethe, Schiller, and Herder. >> Goethe; Herder; Romanticism; Schiller

Sturt, Charles (1795–1869) British explorer, born in Bengal, India. He went as an army captain to Australia, and headed three important expeditions (1828–45), discovering the Darling (1828) and the lower Murray Rivers (1830). >> Darling River

stuttering A disorder of fluency in the use of language; also called **stammering**. There is difficulty in controlling the rhythm and timing of speech, and a failure to communicate easily, rapidly, and continuously. Individual sounds may be abnormally repeated, lengthened, or fail to be released. The cause is unknown, but several physiological, genetic, and psychological factors have been implicated. >> cluttering; speech pathology

Stuttgart [**shtut**gah(r)t] 48°47N 9°12E, pop (1995e) 588 000. City in Germany; on the R Neckar; founded, 10th-c; former capital of the kingdom of Württemberg; badly bombed in World War 2; railway, airport; two universities (1967); notable mineral springs; major fruit and wine area; birthplace of Hegel; castle (originally 13th-c, much rebuilt). >> Germany [i]; Hegel

Stuyvesant, Peter [**stiy**vesant] (1592–1672) Dutch administrator, born in Scherpenzeel, The Netherlands. In 1646 he directed the New Netherland colony, doing much for the commercial prosperity of New Amsterdam until his reluctant surrender to the English in 1664. >> New Netherland

stye A localized infection in a gland or around a hair follicle in the eyelid. It causes a small, painful swelling in the eyelid, and is best treated by an appropriate antibiotic. >> eye [i]

style In flowering plants, the upper part of the carpel, separating the ovary and stigma. It may be elongated in order to better present the stigma to receive pollen. >> carpel; ovary; stigma

stylistics The systematic study of style, using the principles and procedures of linguistics. 'Style' here includes the features of language which identify an individual (as in 'Shakespeare's style') as well as those which identify major occupational groups (as in 'legal style', 'scientific style'). In **stylometry** or **stylostatistics**, a quantitative analysis is made of a text, to determine its statistical structure. Such studies are particularly important in plotting historical changes in style, or in investigating questions of disputed authorship. >> sociolinguistics

Stylites, Simeon >> **Simeon Stylites, St**

stylometry >> **stylistics**

Styne, Jule (1905–94) Songwriter, born in London. For three decades he wrote dozens of memorable melodies for films and Broadway musicals, among them 'Diamonds are a Girl's Best Friend' (1949), 'Three Coins in the Fountain' (1954, Oscar), and 'People' (1964). >> musical

styrene C_6H_5–CH=CH_2, boiling point 145°C, **phenylethene** or **vinylbenzene**. A colourless liquid, which undergoes addition polymerization to a glassy resin called **polystyrene**. 'Expanded' polystyrene, made porous with trapped gas, is widely used as a thermally-insulating packing material. >> polymerization; resin

styrene butadiene rubber >> **rubber**

Styx [stiks] In Greek mythology, a principal river of the Underworld; the name means 'hateful'. It was also the name of a river in Arcadia, which passes through a gloomy gorge. >> Charon (mythology); Hades

subatomic particles A general term for all particles smaller than atoms. It refers to electrons, protons, and neutrons, which directly constitute atoms, and to other particles including composite particles, resonances, and fundamental particles. All sub-atomic particles are either bosons (force particles) or fermions (matter particles). >> atom; boson; fermions; fundamental particles; particle physics

subconscious >> **unconscious**

subduction zone A region in which one crustal plate of the Earth is forced down (**subducted**) beneath another, and moves down into the mantle where it is eventually assimilated. Present-day subduction zones occur around the margins of the Pacific Ocean at the sites of deep ocean trenches, and are associated with earthquake and volcanic activity and the formation of island arcs such as Japan and the Aleutian Is. >> earthquake; plate tectonics [i]

sublimation Passing directly from solid to vapour without an intermediate liquid phase. Substances which sublime at normal pressures include solid carbon dioxide ('dry ice') and iodine. >> phases of matter [i]

subliminal advertising Advertising designed to be imperceptible to the conscious mind of audiences. It mostly involves split-second projections of brand names or commands ('Eat Popcorn'), screened in the cinema or on television, or sound messages at frequencies beyond the range of human hearing. It is now banned in most countries, though its actual extent and effectiveness is still disputed.

submachine-gun A small-arm midway in size between a pistol and a rifle, capable of firing a burst of automatic fire. First developed around 1918, it was used extensively during World War 2, but has been replaced in most modern armies by the assault rifle. >> machine-gun; rifle; Sten gun

submarine A vessel capable of remaining submerged for a considerable period of time. Since the advent of nuclear-armed, submarine-launched ballistic missiles, such as Polaris, submarines have become the most powerfully armed and strategically important of all warships, playing two distinct roles. They can act as an attack vessel, armed with torpedoes and missiles to attack other ships (including other submarines) at sea; and they can act as a floating platform for long-range missiles. >> ballistic missile; depth charge; sonar; torpedo; U-boat; warships [i]

Subotica [**soo**botitsa], Hung **Szabadka** 46°04N 19°41E, pop (1995e) 101 000. Town in NW Serbia republic, Yugoslavia; railway. >> Serbia; Yugoslavia [i]

subpoena [suh**pee**na] (Lat 'under penalty') An order to a person to attend court to give evidence or produce relevant documents. Failure to comply with the order is a contempt of court. The term is not used in Scottish law. >> contempt of court

subsistence agriculture A form of farming where the land provides most of the necessities of life – food, fuel, and shelter. Tools and other items which cannot be generated in this way are acquired through trading surplus commodities. >> crofting

succinic acid [suhk**sin**ik] HOOC–CH_2–CH_2–COOH, IUPAC **butanedioic acid**, melting point 188°C. A colourless solid, occurring in sugar cane, and also formed during fermentation. >> acid; sugar cane

Succoth >> **Sukkoth**

succubus [**suhk**yubuhs] >> **incubus**

succulent A plant in which the stems and leaves are fleshy and swollen with water-storage tissues. It is common in arid regions and other places where water is present, but not easily available. >> bromeliad; cactus [i]

Suchow >> **Suzhou**

sucker A shoot growing from a root, usually at some distance from the parent. It eventually develops its own root system and becomes independent of the parent plant. >> root (botany)

Suckling, Sir John (1609–42) Poet and playwright, born in Whitton, Greater London. His plays (*Aglaura*, 1637) are austere, but his lyrics are acclaimed. They were published in *Fragmenta aurea* (1646).

Sucre [**soo**kray], originally **Charcas**, also known as **Ciudad Blanca** 19°05S 65°15W, pop (1995e) 121 000. City in SC Bolivia; altitude 2790 m/9153 ft; official judicial and legal capital of Bolivia; founded 1538; revolutionary centre against Spain in 18th-c; airfield; railway; university (1624); cathedral (17th-c). >> Bolivia [i]

Sucre, Antonio José de [**soo**kray] (1793–1830) South American soldier-patriot, born in Cumaná, Venezuela. He was Bolívar's lieutenant, who defeated the Spaniards at Ayacucho (1824), and became the first president (1826) of Bolivia. >> Bolívar; Colombia [i]; Spanish–American Wars of Independence

sucrose [**soo**krohs] $C_{12}H_{22}O_{11}$, the best-known sugar – a disaccharide made up of a glucose molecule joined to a fructose molecule. It is digested in the small intestine to produce equal proportions of the monosaccharides glucose and fructose, which are then absorbed. Sucrose is the sugar of table sugar, icing sugar, and castor sugar, and may be obtained from either sugar beet or sugar cane. >> caries; disaccharide; sugar cane; sugars

Sudan [soo**dan**], official name **Republic of Sudan**, Arabic **Jamhuryat es-Sudan** pop (1995e) 31 173 000; area 2 505 870 sq km/967 243 sq mi. NE African republic; capital, Khartoum (executive), Omdurman (legislative); timezone GMT +2; chief ethnic groups, Nilotic, Negro, Nubian, Arab; chief religions, Islam (Sunni, 70%), local beliefs (20%); official language, Arabic; unit of currency, the Sudanese dinar, replacing Sudanese pound; largest country on the African continent, astride the middle reaches of the R Nile; E edge formed by the Nubian Highlands and an escarpment rising to over 2000 m/6500 ft on the Red Sea; Imatong Mts (S) rise to 3187 at Kinyeti; White Nile flows N to meet the Blue Nile at Khartoum; desert conditions in NW; christianized, 6th-c; Muslim conversion from 13th-c; Egyptian control of N Sudan, early 19th-c; Mahdi unified W and C tribes in a revolution, 1881; fall of Khartoum, 1885; combined British–Egyptian offensive in 1898, leading to a jointly administered condominium; independence, 1956; drought and N–S rivalry have contributed to years of instability and several coups; National Assembly dissolved, and constitution suspended; subsequent civil war; national constitutional conference to discuss reform, 1992; peace talks begun, 1993; new constitution, 1998; governed by a president and a 300-seat Transitional National Assembly; economy dominated by agriculture, employing over 75% of the people; large-scale irrigation schemes, fed by dams; major famines, especially 1984–5, 1990–91; commercial farming (N) and livestock farming (S); gum arabic (80% of world supply); development hindered by poor transport system and civil war. >> Khartoum; Mahdi; RR1022 political leaders

sudden infant death syndrome (SIDS) The sudden, unexpected death of an infant for which no adequate cause can be found on clinical or post-mortem examination; also known as **cot death**. Current theories include the cessation of breathing (*apnoea*) as a result of an unusually prolonged spell of respiratory irregularity; smoking by parents and others in the household; an exaggerated neural response to the drawing up of a small amount of stomach contents into the respiratory tract; obstruction to the airways as a result of temporary closure of the structures below the pharynx; increased vulnerability to toxins of respiratory bacteria that are normally harmless; the presence of harmful chemicals in mattresses; and disturbance of body temperature control related to a cold environment or to excessive covering with bedding. >> respiration

Sudeten or **Sudetenland** [soo**day**tenland] Mountainous territory on Polish–Czech border, comprising the Sudetic Mts rising to 1603 m/5259 ft at Sněžka; during World War 2, the name also applied to the parts of Bohemia and Moravia occupied by German-speaking people; invaded by Germany in 1938, and restored to Czechoslovakia in 1945. >> Czech Republic [i]

Sue, Eugène [sü], pseudonym of **Marie Joseph Sue** (1804–57) Novelist, born in Paris. He wrote a vast number of Byronic novels idealizing the poor, such as *Les Mystères de Paris* (1843, The Mysteries of Paris), which was a major influence on Hugo. >> Byron; Hugo

Suetonius [swe**toh**nius], in full **Gaius Suetonius Tranquillus** (75–160) Roman biographer and antiquarian. His best-known work is *De vita Caesarum* (The Lives of the First

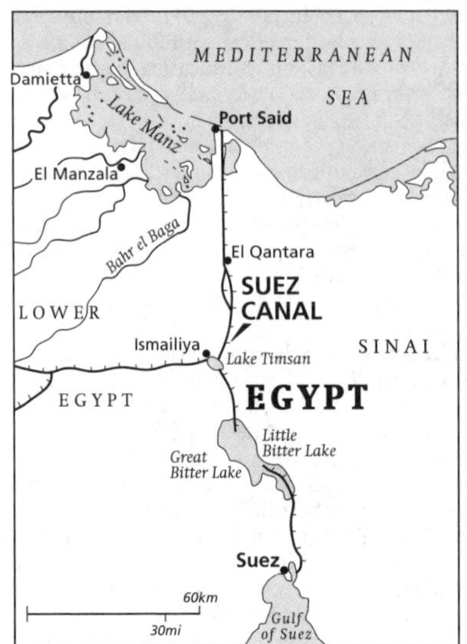

Twelve Caesars). Only fragments survive of his other writings.

Suez [**soo**iz], Arabic **al-Suweis** 29°59N 32°33E, pop (1995e) 431 000. Seaport in E Egypt; at S end of Suez Canal; railway. >> Egypt [i]; Suez Canal

Suez Canal Canal connecting the Mediterranean and Red Seas, in NE Egypt; built by Ferdinand de Lesseps, 1859–69; length 184 km/114 mi, including 11 km/7 mi of approaches to Suez (S end) and Port Said (N end); minimum width, 60 m/197 ft; minimum draught, 16 m/52 ft; open to vessels of any nation (except in wartime); controlled by British, 1882–1956; nationalized by Egypt, 1956; blocked by Egypt during war with Israel, 1967; re-opened, 1975. >> Arab–Israeli Wars; Egypt [i]; Lesseps; Suez Crisis

Suez Crisis A political crisis focused on the Suez Canal in 1956. When Egypt's President Nasser bought armaments from the Soviet block, the USA withdrew its support for the building of the Aswan Dam, whose financing collapsed. To remedy this, Nasser nationalized the Suez Canal, so that the Canal might pay for the Dam. Given the strategic interests of Britain and France in the Canal, they sought first to overturn Nasser's decision by appeal to the International Court, which instead confirmed the legality of the Egyptian government's move; thereafter, Britain and France worked to overthrow Nasser himself. While excluding the USA from their planning, they drew Israel in to provoke a conflict which would serve as a pretext for Anglo-French intervention. Israel invaded the Sinai in October 1956, followed by French and British forces in the cities of the Canal Zone. Diplomatic action by the USA and the USSR forced Britain and France to withdraw, and Israel to relinquish the Sinai. >> Arab–Israeli Wars; Eden; Nasser

Suffolk [**suhf**uhk] pop (1995e) 631 000; area 3797 sq km/ 1466 sq mi. County of E England; county town, Ipswich. >> England [i]; Ipswich

suffragette A woman identified with the late 19th–early 20th-c movement in the UK and USA to secure voting rights for women. The vote was won after the end of World War 1 in 1918, though it was limited to those women of 30 years of age or over. In England it was not until 1929 that women over 21 achieved the right to vote. >> Pankhurst; women's liberation movement

Sufism An Islamic mystical movement which represented a move away from the legalistic approach in Islam to a more personal relationship with God. The word comes from Arabic *suf* 'wool', because the early story-tellers from whom Sufism evolved wore woollen garments. >> Islam

sugar beet >> **beet**

sugar cane A bamboo-like grass but with soft canes 3–8 m/10–26 ft high, 3·5–5 cm/1½–2 in diameter; white to yellowish-green, red, or purplish; cultivated in tropical and sub-tropical environments. The cane is cut, chopped, and soaked in water to extract the sugar (*sucrose*), and the sugary solution is filtered, clarified, and dried. Sucrose crystallizes out, leaving *molasses* behind. The raw sugar is brown, and can be further purified to yield white sugar. (*Saccharum officinarum*. Family: Gramineae.) >> bamboo; grass [i]; molasses; sucrose; sugars

sugar palm A tree growing to 12 m/40 ft, native to Malaysia (*Arenga sacchifera*); leaves 1–1·5 m/3¼–5 ft, feathery, silver beneath; also called **gomuti palm**. Sugar is obtained from the sap. (Family: Palmae.) >> palm

sugars A group of sweet-tasting carbohydrates, chemically classified into single-unit (*monosaccharide*) and double-unit (*disaccharide*) types. Most people take *sugar* to mean *sucrose*; however, many other sugars are present in our diet, although not to the same levels as sucrose. These include *lactose*, the sugar of milk, and free *glucose* and *fructose* in fruits and honey. >> disaccharide; honey; sucrose; sugar cane

Suharto [soo**hah(r)**toh] (1921–) Indonesian soldier, statesman, and president (1968–98), born in Kemusu, Java. Educated for service in the Dutch colonial army, in 1965 he became Indonesia's chief of the army staff. Following civil unrest under Sukarno, he assumed power in 1967, becoming titular president the following year. He was forced to step down in 1998 following an economic crisis and civil disturbance.

suicide The act of deliberate self-destruction. Up to 1961 in the UK, attempted suicide was considered to be a crime, and it is still illegal in some US states. Since then it has been accepted as a terminal symptom of an abnormal mental state. It is a recognized complication of severe depressive illness or psychosis in which the individual suffers from inconsolable moods of despair, guilt, and self-blame. In other cases death results unintentionally from a conscious attempt to manipulate a situation, or from an impulse to obtain redress of circumstances which cause distress. This act is sometimes referred to as **parasuicide**. In some societies, suicide in certain circumstances is socially acceptable, and in ancient Greece and Rome, it was offered to the privileged as an alternative to execution. Recent years have seen the emergence of such groups as the Hemlock Society in the USA, and other societies which represent the 'right to die'. >> depression (psychiatry); euthanasia; psychosis

Sui dynasty [swee] (581–618) A two-reign dynasty which began the second great imperial phase of Chinese history (590–907). The crown was seized by Yang Jian, who took the reign name Wendi (590–604). He was followed by Yang Guang (Yangdi, 604–18). The Sui dynasty conquered the S and reunited China (590), fell to Northern insurrection, and was replaced by the Tang dynasty. >> Han / Tang dynasty

suite In Baroque music, a set of dances, all in the same key, perhaps preceded by a prelude; the terms *partita* and *ordre* are also used. Since the 19th-c the term has been used for a sequence of separate but connected pieces (as in Holst's *The Planets*) and for an orchestral selection from an opera, ballet, or other long work. >> Baroque (music); prelude

Sukarno or **Soekarno, Achmed** [su**kah(r)**noh] (1902–70) Indonesian statesman and first president of Indonesia (1945–66), born in Surabaya, Java. He formed the

Indonesia National Party in 1927, and became president when Indonesia was granted independence in 1945. An abortive communist coup (1965) led to a takeover by the army, his powers gradually devolving onto General Suharto (1921–). Sukarno finally retired in 1968.

sukiyaki [sukeeyakee] A Japanese beef dish. Thinly sliced beef is cooked with suet in an iron pan in the middle of the table. Sauce is added, made of *shoyu*, beaten raw egg, sugar, and *mirin* (a type of sweet saké). >> saké

Sukkoth or **Succoth** [**suh**kohth, -koht] The Jewish Feast of Tabernacles or Booths, celebrated in September or October (15–21 Tishri) as a festival of thanksgiving. Light temporary shelters are constructed in homes and in synagogues, in memory of the tents used by the Israelites in the desert after leaving Egypt (*Exodus* 13). >> RR982

Sukkur [**suk**oor], also **Sakhar** 27°42N 68°54E, pop (1995e) 284 000. City in Pakistan; on E bank of R Indus; Sukkur (Lloyd) Barrage built 1928–32 (dam 58 m/190 ft high); railway junction. >> Pakistan [i]

Sulaiman or **Suleyman I** [sülay**man**], known as **the Magnificent** (1494–1566) Ottoman Sultan (1520–66), who added to his dominions by conquest Belgrade, Budapest, Rhodes, Tabriz, Baghdad, Aden, and Algiers. His system of laws regulating land tenure earned him the name *Kanuni* ('lawgiver'), and he was a great patron of arts and architecture. >> Ottoman Empire

Sulawesi [sula**way**see] Island in Indonesia, off E Borneo; formerly **Celebes**; pop (1995e) 13 756 000; area 189 216 sq km/73 037 sq mi; chief towns Ujung Pandang, Palu, Kendari, Manado. >> Indonesia [i]

Suleyman >> **Sulaiman**

sulfur >> **sulphur**

Sulla, Lucius Cornelius, nickname **Felix** ('Lucky') (138–78 BC) Ruthless and enigmatic Roman politician of the late Republic, whose bitter feud with Marius twice plunged Rome into civil war in the 80s BC. Appointed 'Dictator' in 82 BC, he enacted a number of measures to boost the authority of the Senate. >> Marius

Sullivan, Sir Arthur (Seymour) (1842–1900) Composer, born in London. From 1871 he was known for his collaboration with W S Gilbert in such comic operas as *HMS Pinafore* (1878) and *The Pirates of Penzance* (1879). He also composed a grand opera, *Ivanhoe* (1891), cantatas, ballads, a *Te Deum*, and hymn tunes. >> Gilbert, W S

Sullivan, Louis (Henry) (1856–1924) Architect, born in Boston, MA. His experimental, functional skeleton constructions of skyscrapers and office blocks, particularly the Gage building and stock exchange, Chicago, IL, earned him the title 'Father of Modernism'.

Sully, Maximilien de Béthune, duc de (Duke of) [sülee] (1560–1641) French Huguenot soldier, financier, and statesman, born in Rosny, France. Instrumental in arranging Henry of Navarre's marriage to Marie de Médicis (1600), he became the king's trusted counsellor. His major achievement was the restoration of the economy after the civil wars. >> Huguenots; Religion, Wars of

Sully-Prudhomme [sülee prü**dom**], pseudonym of **René François Armand Prudhomme** (1839–1907) Poet, born in Paris. A leader of the Parnassian movement, which tried to restore elegance and control to poetry in reaction against Romanticism, he was awarded the first Nobel Prize for Literature in 1901. >> Romanticism

sulphonamides / sulfonamides [suhl**fon**amiydz] The first drugs to be used for the prevention and cure of bacterial infections in humans; their introduction in the late 1930s resulted in a sharp decline in deaths from infectious diseases. >> antibiotics

sulphur / sulfur S, element 16, a non-metal occurring in nature in yellow molecular crystals of S_8, also called **brimstone**. The solid melts at 113°C and boils at 440°C. It shows a great variety of oxidation states, giving rise to compounds called **sulphides**, **sulphites**, and **sulphates**. By far the most important use is oxidation to sulphuric acid. >> chemical elements; sulphuric acid; RR1036

sulphuric / sulfuric acid H_2SO_4, boiling point 330°C. A strong dibasic acid, a colourless oily liquid, formerly known as **oil of vitriol** or simply **vitriol**. It is one of the most important industrial chemicals, used in the production of almost all other acids, and in the manufacture of fertilizers, fabrics, dyestuffs, and detergents. >> acid; oxidation; sulphur

sumac or **sumach** [**soo**mak] Any of several species of a genus which includes poison ivy and the turpentine tree, many causing skin damage or dermatitis. (Genus: *Rhus*. Family: Anacardiaceae.) >> dermatitis; poison ivy; turpentine tree

Sumatra [su**mah**tra], Indonesian **Sumatera** pop (1995e) 40 343 000; area 473 606 sq km/182 812 sq mi. Island in W Indonesia, S of the Malay Peninsula; 1760 km/1094 mi long and 400 km/250 mi wide; centre of Buddhist kingdom of Sri Vijaya, 7th–13th-c; separatist movement followed Indonesian independence, 1949; major cities include Medan, Padang, Bukit Barisan range (W) rises to 3805 m/12 483 ft at Gunung Kerinci. >> Indonesia [i]; Palembang

Sumer [**soo**mer] The name given to the part of Lower Mesopotamia between Babylon and the Persian Gulf. It is the place where the world's first urban civilization evolved. >> Eridu; Mesopotamia; Ur; Uruk

summary trial A trial in a court of summary jurisdiction, in England and Wales in the magistrates' court, and in Scotland in either the Sheriff Court without a jury or in district courts. A number of offences may be tried on either a summary or indictable basis and certain ones such as theft are regularly tried in courts of summary jurisdiction. The decision about mode of trial largely rests with the prosecutor, although in England and Wales the defence have a right in certain circumstances to demand a trial on indictment before a jury. Such a right does not exist in Scotland. >> indictment; justice of the peace; stipendiary magistrate

Summers, Anne (Fairhurst) (1945–) Academic, journalist, and bureaucrat, born in Deniliquin, New South Wales, Australia. In 1987 she became editor-in-chief of the influential American feminist magazine *Ms*, and was its editor-at-large (1990–2). Adviser on women's affairs to Prime Minister Paul Keating in 1992, she returned to journalism as editor of the *Sydney Morning Herald* and (until 1997) *The Age*'s colour supplement. >> feminism; Keating, Paul

Summer Time >> **Daylight Saving Time**

summit diplomacy A term first used in the 1950s for negotiations between heads of state and governments with the intention of resolving disagreements; also known as **summitry**. Since the 1960s it has been applied to any special meeting between national leaders, with a symbolic and formal content.

sumo wrestling A Japanese national sport steeped in history and tradition. Competition takes place in a 12 ft (3·66 m) diameter circle, the object being to force one's opponent out of the ring or to the ground. Sumo wrestlers are very large and eat vast amounts of food to increase their weight and body size. >> wrestling

Sun The central object of our Solar System and the nearest star to the Earth. Its average distance from Earth is 150 million km/93 million mi, and on account of this proximity it is studied more than any other star. The source of its energy is nuclear reactions in the central core (temperature 15 million K, relative density 155) extending to a quarter of the solar radius and including half the mass.

Our Sun is nearly 5000 million years old, and is about halfway through its expected life cycle. >> solar constant / flare / prominence / time / wind; Solar System; sunspot

sun bear The smallest bear (length, 1.3 m/4 ft), native to SE Asia; short black coat with pale snout and yellow crescent on chest; also known as **honey bear**, **Malay bear**, or **bruang**. (*Helarctos malayanus*.) >> bear

sunbird A small songbird, native to the Old World tropics and the Middle East; slender curved bill and tubular tongue. (Family: Nectariniidae, 106 species.) >> songbird

sunburn Damage to the skin caused by strong sunlight, especially in people with fair complexions. Short exposure results in redness and itch. More prolonged exposure causes pain, swelling of the skin, and blistering, accompanied by fever, headache, and nausea. >> heat stroke; keratosis; melanoma: ultraviolet radiation

Sunda Islands [**soon**da] Island group in Indonesia, comprising the **Greater Sunda Is** of Java, Sumatra, Borneo, and Sulawesi, with their small adjacent islands, and **Nusa Tenggara**, formerly the **Lesser Sunda Is** of Bali, Lombok, Sumba, Sumbawa, Flores, and Timor, with their small islands. >> Indonesia [i]

Sun Dance An annual summer ceremony of the Plains Indians of North America. Participants are subject to a demanding discipline including ceremonial dancing while gazing at the Sun. >> Plains Indians

Sundance Kid, popular name of **Harry Longabaugh** or **Langbaugh** (1870–?1909) Outlaw, born in Phoenixville, PA. He teamed up with Butch Cassidy, and drifted throughout North and South America robbing banks, trains, and mines. His date and place of death is uncertain, but it is generally held that he was fatally shot by a cavalry unit in Bolivia.

Sundanese A people from the highlands of W Java, Indonesia, but now also living in other parts of Java and Sumatra. One of three main groups on the island, they converted to Islam in the 16th-c. >> Java (country)

Sunday The day of the week set aside by the Christian religion for divine worship, mainly in commemoration of Christ's resurrection. In 1971 the UK ratified the recommendation of the International Standardization Organization that Monday replace Sunday as the first day of the week. >> Christianity; Sabbath

Sunday School Classes for the religious education of children, usually linked to worship services, in Protestant Churches. They derive from the Sunday charity school, instituted in London in 1780, for the basic education of children of the poor. >> Protestantism

Sunderland, formerly **Wearmouth** 54°55N 1°23W, pop (1995e) 197 000. Port town in Tyne and Wear, NE England; at the mouth of the R Wear; site of monastery (674); railway; university (1992); football league team, Sunderland (Black Cats). >> Tyne and Wear

sundew A carnivorous plant, usually a small perennial, native in most tropical and temperate regions, especially Australasia and S Africa; flowers 5-petalled, in slender spikes. The long hairs of the leaves are tentacle-like, and secrete a sticky substance which traps insects. (Genus: *Drosera*, 100 species. Family: Droseraceae.) >> carnivorous plant

sundial A device for showing the passage of time by the shadow cast on a graduated scale by a *gnomon* (some solid object, such as a rod or triangular plate attached to the dial). The earliest-known sundial dates from c.300 BC.

Sundsvall [**suns**val] 62°22N 17°20E, pop (1995e) 96 800. Seaport and commercial town in SE Sweden; important trading centre from the 6th-c; charter, 1624; railway. >> Sweden [i]

sunfish Large and very distinctive fish (*Mola mola*) widespread in open waters of tropical to temperate seas; body compressed, almost circular; length typically 1–2 m/$3\frac{1}{4}$–$6\frac{1}{2}$ ft, but up to 4 m/13 ft; mouth small, teeth fused into a sharp beak; also called **trunkfish**. (Family: Molidae.) >> fish [i]

sunflower A large annual (*Helianthus annuus*) growing to 3 m/10 ft, a native of North America; usually a solitary drooping flower-head up to 30 cm/12 in across; outer ray florets golden yellow. Several varieties are cultivated for the edible and rich oil-yielding seeds. (Family: Compositae.)

Sung dynasty >> **Song dynasty**

sungrabe >> **finfoot**

Sung Tsu-wen >> **Song Ziwen**

Sunnis [**su**neez] The predominant form of Islam, which bases its legitimacy on the sayings and actions, or *sunnah*, of the Prophet Mohammed. Representing c.85% of Muslims in the world, the Sunnis are considered the orthodoxy of Islam. >> Islam; Koran

sunscreen The use of barrier creams to reduce the penetration of ultraviolet rays to the skin. A number of substances are used, including para-aminobenzoic acid and zinc. >> sunburn

sun spider A long-legged, predatory arthropod found mostly in deserts and arid habitats; fangs massive; first pair of legs slender, used as feelers; also known as **wind scorpions**. (Class: Arachnida. Order: Solpugida, c.900 species.) >> Arachnida; arthropod

sunspot An apparently dark region on the solar photosphere, the central part termed the *umbra*. They are caused by an intense magnetic field erupting from within the Sun, and follow a cycle of growth and decay over c.11 years. >> photosphere; Sun

sunstroke >> **heat stroke**

Sun Yixian [sun yeeshan], or **Sun Yatsen**, originally **Sun Wen** (1866–1925) Founder and early leader of China's Nationalist Party, born in Xiangshan, Guangdong, China. He helped to organize risings in S China, but after the 1911 Wuhan rising, realized that he would not be widely acceptable as president, and voluntarily handed over the office to Yuan Shikai. Civil war ensued (1913), and he set up a separate government at Guangzhou (Canton). He was widely accepted as the true leader of the nation. >> Guomindang; Yuan Shikai

superbowl >> **football** 2 [i]; RR1044

Superconducting Super Collider (SSC) A huge particle accelerator planned at Waxahachie, near Dallas, TX. The accelerator, inside an 87-km/54-mi oval tunnel, would have collided protons on protons, and been the most powerful subatomic particle accelerator in the world. Construction began in 1990, but the project was terminated by Congress in 1993. >> particle accelerators

superconductivity The property of zero electrical resistance, accompanied by the expulsion of magnetic fields, exhibited by certain metals, alloys, and compounds when cooled to below some critical temperature, typically less than −260°C. An electrical current established in a superconducting ring of material will continue indefinitely while the low temperature is maintained. High temperature superconductivity, for temperatures in excess of −250°C, was first observed in 1986 by Argentinian physicist Alex Müller (1943–) and German physicist Georg Bednorz (1950–), using a ceramic of copper oxide containing barium and lanthanum. Superconductors are currently used in large magnets, such as those required by nuclear magnetic resonance spectrometers and particle accelerators. >> ceramics; electrical conduction; resistance; superfluidity

superfluidity The property of zero resistance to flow (ie zero viscosity), exhibited by liquid helium at temperatures below −271°C. Superfluid helium exhibits unusual properties, including the ability to creep out of a container apparently in defiance of gravity, and the inability to be set spinning in the way a solid object can. >> cryogenics; helium; superconductivity; viscosity

supergiant A rare type of star, very massive, and the most luminous known. Examples include Polaris, Betelgeuse (in Orion), and Canopus. They are 10–60 solar masses, 10 000 times brighter than the Sun, and thus visible at great distances. >> star

supergravity A speculative quantum theory incorporating gravity, electromagnetic force, and nuclear force. It is a gauge theory based on supersymmetry, postulating gravitons and gravitinos as carriers of the gravitational force. Theoretically attractive, it lacks experimental support. >> supersymmetry

superheterodyne [sooper**het**erodiyn] The most common technique used in radio reception. The incoming radio frequency signal is converted into a lower intermediate frequency by mixing it with a signal generated inside the receiver, called the *local oscillator*. >> frequency modulation; oscillation; radio

Superior, Lake Largest of the Great Lakes, and the largest freshwater lake in the world; part of US–Canadian bound ary; length 563 km/350 mi; breadth 257 km/160 mi; maximum depth 405 m/1329 ft; area 82 103 sq km/ 31 692 sq mi, 35% in Canada; connected with L Huron (SE) via St Mary's R (the Soo canals). >> Great Lakes

supernatural >> **paranormal**

supernova A rare and spectacular explosion resulting in the destruction of a massive star. Light emission is temporarily 100 million times brighter than the Sun, and the star can be seen for up to two years. Well-known examples are the supernova of 1054 (Crab Nebula), 1604 (seen by Kepler), and 1987 in the Large Magellanic Cloud. >> star

superovulation syndrome A condition which occasionally results when infertile women are given human gonadotrophic hormone and/or the synthetic drug clomiphene to stimulate ovulation. Several ova may be simultaneously released and fertilized, with consequential multiple births. >> pregnancy ℹ

superphosphates Fertilizers containing phosphate as the $H_2PO_4^{2-}$ ion. They are so called because, for a given weight, $Ca(H_2PO_4)_2$ contains more phosphorus than does $CaHPO_4$. >> fertilizer; phosphate

Superrealism >> **Photorealism**

supersonic In fluid mechanics, fluid flow which is faster than the velocity of sound in that fluid, either in the case of an object moving through the fluid, or a fluid moving around a stationary object. Supersonic aircraft fly faster than the speed of sound in air. >> aerodynamics ℹ; fluid mechanics; sound

superstition A derogatory description of any behaviour, usually traditional in origin, that has lost its rationale though still betraying a fear of the unknown. An example is 'touching wood' when mentioning one's good fortune, a hidden reference to the cross on which Christ was crucified. In Ancient Roman religion, *superstition* referred to an act or attitude of excessive piety; the term was later applied by Christian clergy to religious or quasi-religious acts which they regarded as pagan or corrupt, such as ringing church bells to avert thunderstorms. >> folklore; taboo

superstrings A speculative quantum theory, embracing all the forces of nature, which may avoid the difficulties encountered by early unification schemes involving gravity; proposed by British physicist Michael Green and US physicist John Schwartz in 1984. It is based on a fundamental extended submicroscopic string in place of the usual point particle, plus supersymmetry. >> forces of nature ℹ; supersymmetry

supersymmetry In particle physics, a symmetry relation linking particles of different spins. Theories incorporating supersymmetry predict particles that are partners to observed particles, having the same mass but different spin. No such supersymmetric partners (squark, slepton, photino, and others) have been observed. >> superstrings; supergravity

supply and demand An economic concept which states that the price of an article (or 'good') will move to the level where the quantity demanded by purchasers equals the quantity that suppliers are willing to sell.

supply-side economics The view that the main contribution of policy to promoting the growth of incomes is through measures to improve the supply of goods and services and the working of markets. The approach contrasts with the Keynesian view, which puts more weight on managing the economy so as to increase demand. >> economics; Keynes; prices and incomes policy

suprarenal glands >> **adrenal glands**

Suprematism A form of modern art based on four simple shapes: rectangle, circle, triangle, and cross. The movement was started in Russia c.1913 by Kazimir Malevich (1878–1935). >> abstract / Minimal / modern art

Supreme Court In the USA, the highest federal court established under the constitution, members of which are appointed by the president with the advice and consent of the Senate. In addition to its jurisdiction relating to appeals, the court also exercises oversight of the constitution through the power of judicial review of the acts of state, federal legislatures, and the executive. >> Chief Justice; Constitution of the United States

Supreme Headquarters Allied Expeditionary Force (SHAEF) An organization formally established (1944) under General Eisenhower, with Air Chief Marshal Tedder as deputy supreme commander, to mount the Allied invasion of occupied Europe and strike at the heart of Germany. >> D-Day; Eisenhower; Tedder; World War 2

Supreme Soviet >> **soviet**

Surabaya [soora**bah**ya] or **Surabaja** 7°14S 112°45E, pop (1995e) 2 726 000. Industrial seaport in E Java, Indonesia, at mouth of R Kali Mas; Indonesia's second largest city; important trading centre since the 14th-c; airfield; railway; university (1954); naval base. >> Java (country)

Surat [**soo**rat] 21°12N 72°55E, pop (1995e) 1 620 000. Port in Gujarat, W India; rich trading centre of Mughal Empire, 17th–18th-c; first English trading post in India, 1612; headquarters of British East India Company until 1687; railway; university (1967). >> Gujarat

Sûreté [süruhtay], in full **Sûreté nationale** (Fr 'National Security') One of four police forces existing in France, which are largely independent of each other. Founded in the early 19th-c, it is responsible for criminal investigations, corresponding roughly to the CID in Britain and the FBI in the USA. >> CID; Federal Bureau of Investigation; police

surf Wind-generated waves that have broken upon encountering shallow water. Waves become unstable and 'break' typically in water depth of about 1·3 times the wave height. Once a wave has broken, the water particles move laterally towards the shore, and are known as surf. >> beach; wave (oceanography)

surface active agent >> **surfactant**

surface physics The study of the electronic and structural properties of the surface of matter, ie the outermost layer of atoms. Surface properties are important in several domains, including catalysis, corrosion, the emission of electrons from surfaces, optical properties, and friction. >> solid-state physics; surface tension ℹ; tribology

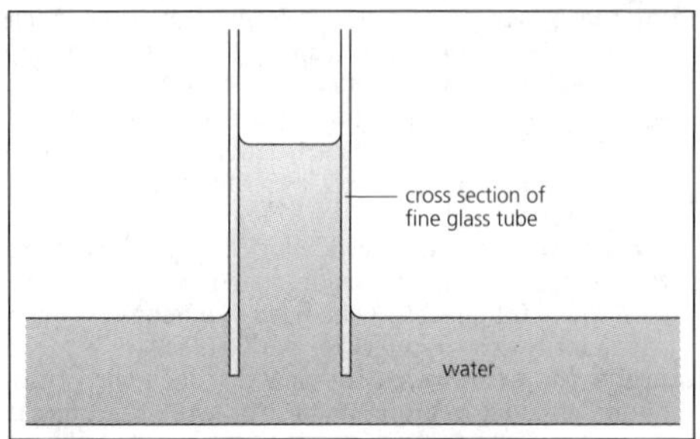

Surface tension – water rises up a narrow pipe by capillarity, a surface tension effect which can be explained in terms of pressure differences across a curved air-liquid boundary. The curved liquid is called the *meniscus*.

surface tension A property of the surface of a liquid. It is a tensioning force due to the inward attraction of molecules at the surface. Because of surface tension, liquid surfaces appear elastic, as observed in bubbles and soap films. >> capillarity

surfactant Any substance that strongly influences the surface properties of a material; also called a **surface active agent**. It is often applied to soaps and detergents, whose cleaning powers depend on the surfactant's ability to increase the spreading and wetting power of water. >> surface tension ℹ

surgeonfish Any of the family Acanthuridae of colourful deep-bodied fish widespread in tropical seas; name refers to the sharp movable spine on sides of tail which can be erected for defence; body length typically 10–40 cm/4–16 in; also called **tang**. >> fish ℹ

surgery The branch of medicine which treats diseases and conditions by operating on the patient. Early surgical operations were limited to those near the surface of the body, such as hernia repair and amputation. With modern anaesthesia, all parts of the body have become accessible, and surgery is now routine in such areas as the lungs, heart, and brain. Organ transplantation, and the development of artificial body parts are major modern developments. >> asepsis; medicine; plastic surgery; trepanning; transplantation

Suriname [**soo**rinam], also **Surinam**, official name **Republic of Suriname**, **Republiek Suriname** pop (1995e) 414 000; area 163 265 sq km/63 020 sq mi. Republic in NE South America; capital, Paramaribo; timezone GMT −3; major ethnic groups, Creoles (35%), Indo-Pakistan (33%), Javanese (16%), Bush Negro (10%); wide range of religious groups; official language, Dutch, with Surinamese widely spoken; unit of currency, the Suriname guilder; diverse natural regions, ranging from coastal lowland through savannah to mountainous upland; highland interior (S) overgrown with dense tropical forest; tropically hot and humid, two rainy seasons (May–Jul, Nov–Jan); sighted by Columbus, 1498; first settled by the British, 1651; taken by the states of Zeeland, 1667; captured by the British, 1799; restored to the Netherlands, 1818; independent republic, 1975; emigration of c.40% of population to The Netherlands, following independence; military coup, 1980; 1987 constitution provides for a National Assembly and president; guerrilla warfare from 1986, with peace accord in 1989; Shankar elected president, 1988; deposed by military, 1990; elections for new National Assembly, 1991; lack of foreign exchange has hindered development of the economy, which is based on agriculture and mining, bauxite mining provides c.80% of export income; vast timber resources. >> Netherlands, The ℹ; Paramaribo; RR1022 political leaders

Surrealism (Fr 'over' or 'intense' realism) An important movement in modern art and literature which flourished between the World Wars, mainly in France. The first Surrealist manifesto of André Breton (1924) proposed the subversion of 19th-c Realism by the three related means of humour, dream, and counter-logic (the absurd). The basic idea was to free the artist from the demands of logic, and to penetrate beyond everyday consciousness to the 'super-reality' that lies behind. Freud's theory of the subconscious was appealed to, and many pictures by Dali, Magritte, and Tanguy seek to recreate the fantasy world of dreams. In literature, the movement is illustrated by the work of Ionesco, Beckett, and Genet. Luis Buñuel guaranteed its impact on the cinema. >> absurdism; Dada; modern art; Realism; Arp; Beckett; Breton, André; Buñuel; Chirico; Dali; Duchamp; Ernst; Ionesco; Klee; Magritte; Picabia; Picasso

Surrey pop (1995e) 1 046 000; area 1679 sq km/648 sq mi. County in SE England; crossed E–W by the North Downs, rising to 294 m/964 ft at Leith Hill; county town, Guildford; largely residential; Box Hill, Runnymede, Royal Botanic Gardens (Kew). >> Downs; England ℹ; Guildford

Surrey, Henry Howard, Earl of (c.1517–47) Courtier and poet, born in Hunsdon, Hertfordshire. He is remembered for his love poetry, influenced by the Italian tradition, in which he pioneered the use of blank verse and the Elizabethan sonnet form. >> blank verse; sonnet

Surtees, John (1934–) Racing driver and motor-cyclist, born in Westerham, Kent, the only man to win world titles on two and four wheels. He won the 350 cc motor cycling world title in 1958–60, and the 500 cc title in 1956, 1958–60 (all on an MV Augusta). He then won the 1964 world title driving a Ferrari. >> motor cycle racing

Surtsey Island [**sert**see] area 1·9 sq km/0·7 sq mi. Volcanic island off S coast of Iceland; one of the Westman Is; erupted and formed in 1963. >> Westman Islands

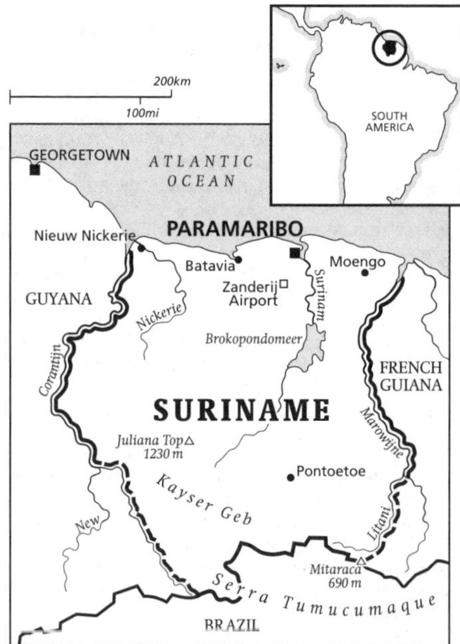

surveying The accurate measurement and collection of data, such as relief, for a given area in order to make a map. It has traditionally been based on fieldwork, using equipment such as chains, plane tables, and theodolites, used to measure the distance, elevation, and angle of an object from an observation point. **Geodetic surveying** is the measurement of the size and shape of the Earth, and the determination of the position of places on its surface. >> aerial photography; cartography; geodesy; map; remote sensing

Surveyor programme A series of robotic soft-lander missions to the Moon undertaken by NASA (May 1966–Jan 1968) in preparation for the manned Apollo landings. It was highly successful, with five of the seven spacecraft landing as planned. >> Apollo programme; Moon; NASA; RR970

Surya [**soor**ya] The Sun-god in Hindu mythology. He was the son of Indra, the pre-eminent god of the Rig-Veda. >> Hinduism; Veda

Susa [**soo**za] The Greek name for **Shushan**, in antiquity, the main city of Elam and the capital of the Achaemenid empire under Darius I and his successors. It is the site of the world's best preserved ziggurat. >> Elam; Persian Empire; ziggurat i

Susanna, Book of A book of the Old Testament Apocrypha, or Chapter 13 of the Book of Daniel in Catholic versions of the Bible; an addition of uncertain date or provenance. >> Apocrypha, Old Testament; Daniel, Book of

suslik >> **souslik**

Suslov, Mikhail Andreyevich [**sus**lof] (1902–82) Soviet politician, born in Shakhovskoye, Russia. He opposed Khrushchev's 'de-Stalinization' measures, economic reforms, and foreign policy, and was instrumental in unseating him in 1964. >> Khrushchev; Stalin

suspended sentence A sentence of imprisonment which is not activated immediately, but may be imposed should the offender commit a further offence during the period of suspension, in addition to any penalty the later court imposes. Suspended sentences may operate in conjunction with supervision by a probation officer. They are not available in all jurisdictions (eg in Scotland). >> sentence

suspension A mixture in which particles (of solid or liquid) are dispersed through another phase (liquid or gas) without dissolving in it. Suspensions are not indefinitely stable, and will eventually settle into separate phases. >> colloid

Sussex Former county of England; divided into East Sussex and West Sussex in 1974, West Sussex gaining part of S Surrey. >> Sussex, East; Sussex, West

Sussex, East pop (1995e) 736 000; area 1795 sq km/693 sq mi. County of SE England; South Downs parallel to the coast, part of the Weald to the N; county town, Lewes; Brighton and Hove a unitary authority (from 1997); major tourist area on S coast; castles at Bodiam, Hastings, Lewes, Pevensey; site of Battle of Hastings. >> Downs; England i; Hastings, Battle of; Lewes; Weald, the

Sussex, Kingdom of A kingdom of the Anglo-Saxon heptarchy, situated between Kent and Wessex, and founded probably by c.500. It was annexed to Wessex in the 9th-c. >> Anglo-Saxons; Wessex

Sussex, West pop (1995e) 713 000; area 1989 sq km/768 sq mi. County of S England; South Downs parallel to the coast; county town, Chichester; Arundel and Bramber castles. >> Chichester; England i

sustainable agriculture A system of crop cultivation which does not impair the manurial or humus content of the soil. Such systems contrast with many systems of crop cultivation, particularly those used in the tropics, in which the mineral content and water-holding capacity of the soil is continually reduced. >> agriculture; agroforestry; humus; manure

Sutcliffe, Peter, known as **the Yorkshire Ripper** (1946–) Convicted murderer, born in Bingley, West Yorkshire. He murdered 13 women over five years in N England and the Midlands, the first body being found in 1975. A routine check on a car registration led to his arrest in 1981.

Sutherland, Donald (1934–) Film actor, born in St John, New Brunswick, Canada. He became known for his role in *The Dirty Dozen* (1967), following this with *M.A.S.H* (1970) and *Klute* (1971). Among his later films are *A Time To Kill* (1996) and *Shadow Conspiracy* (1997).

Sutherland, Graham (Vivian) (1903–80) Artist, born in London. He was an official war artist (1941–5), and later produced several memorable portraits, including 'Sir Winston Churchill' (1955). His large tapestry, 'Christ in Majesty', was hung in the new Coventry Cathedral in 1962.

Sutherland, Dame Joan (1926–) Operatic soprano, born in Sydney, New South Wales, Australia. She made her debut at Sydney in 1947, moved to London in 1951, and joined the Royal Opera, becoming resident soprano at Covent Garden. In 1990 she gave her final performance at the Sydney Opera House. >> coloratura

Sutlej, River [**sut**lej] River of Asia; the longest of the five rivers of the Punjab; rises in Tibet (Xizang); meets the Indus; length 1370 km/850 mi. >> Punjab (India, Pakistan)

suttee >> **sati**

Sutton Hoo ship burial The grave of an Anglo-Saxon king, probably Raedwald of East Anglia (c.600–624/5), discovered beneath a barrow near Woodbridge, E England, in 1939. Amidships in a 40-oar open rowing boat (4.25 m/14 ft in beam and 27 m/89 ft long) stood a wooden burial chamber containing silver plate, gold jewellery, and coins, weapons, and domestic equipment (now in the British Museum).

Suva [**soo**va] 18°08S 178°25E, pop (1995e) 76 200. Chief port and capital of Fiji, on SE coast of Viti Levu I; city since 1953; university (1968). >> Fiji i; Viti Levu

Suwon [soo**wuhn**] or **Suweon** 37°16N 126°59E, pop (1995e) 675 000. Industrial city in NW Korea; subway from Seoul; agricultural college; reconstructed fortress walls and gates. >> Korea i

Suzhou [soo**joh**] or **Suchow** 31°21N 120°40E, pop (1995e) 946 000. Town in E China, on the banks of the Grand Canal; first settled c.1000 BC; capital, Kingdom of Wu, 518 BC; railway; over 150 ornamental gardens (a world heritage site). >> China i; Grand Canal

Suzman, Helen, *née* **Gavronsky** (1917–) South African politician, born in Germiston, Transvaal, South Africa. Elected to parliament in 1953, she gained the respect of the black community and, for years the sole MP of the Progressive Party, proved to be a fierce opponent of apartheid. In 1978 she received the UN Human Rights Award. >> apartheid

Svalbard [**sval**bah(r)d] pop (1995e) 3360; area 62 000 sq km/23 932 sq mi. Island group in the Arctic Ocean, c.650 km/400 mi N of the Norwegian mainland; four large and several smaller islands; islands include Spitsbergen; discovered, 1596; formerly an important whaling centre; incorporated in Norway, 1925; administrative centre, Longyearbyen; wide range of minerals. >> Norway i

Sverdlovsk [sverd**lofsk**] >> **Yekaterinburg**

Svevo, Italo [**zvay**voh], pseudonym of **Ettore Schmitz** (1861–1928) Novelist, born in Trieste, Italy. He had a considerable success with *La coscienza di Zeno* (1923, The Confessions of Zeno), a psychological study of inner conflicts.

Swabia A SW mediaeval German duchy, extending from the R Rhine in the W to the Alps in the S, Bavaria in the E, and Franconia in the N, containing the cities of Strasbourg, Constance, and Augsberg. >> Peasants' War

Swabian League An alliance of 22 imperial German cities, clerical lords, and princes, with a league of knights of Swabia (1488), to support the Holy Roman Empire. It was active in suppressing rebellions in 1523–5, but declined because of religious divisions caused by the Reformation. >> Holy Roman Empire; Reformation

Swahili [swa**hee**lee] A cluster of Bantu-speaking peoples of the coast and islands of E Africa, an amalgam of African groups and Arab immigrants entering the area continually since ancient times. By the 15th-c they were at the height of their power as a trading nation. The Swahili language probably replaced Arabic from about the 13th-c, and is today spoken by c.30 million as a lingua franca throughout E Africa. >> lingua franca; Niger-Congo languages

swallow A small songbird, found worldwide; dark blue/green above, pale below; tail long, forked; inhabits open country near fresh water; eats small insects caught in flight; temperate populations migrate; nests in holes or mud nests on cliffs, buildings, etc. The name is also used for several unrelated birds. (Family: Hirundinidae, 57 species.) >> martin; songbird; swift

swamp A permanently flooded area of land with thick vegetation of reeds or trees. **Mangrove swamps** are common along river mouths in tropical and subtropical areas. In the Carboniferous period, marine swamps were common, and are the origin of present-day coal deposits. >> Carboniferous period; Everglades; mangrove

swamp cypress A deciduous or semi-evergreen conifer, native to the SE USA and Mexico; also called **bald cypress**. (Genus: *Taxodium*, 3 species. Family: Taxodiaceae.) >> conifer; cypress

swan A large water-bird of the duck family; found worldwide; usually white; neck very long; male called *cob*, female *pen*. (Tribe: Anserini. Genus: *Cygnus*, 10 species, and *Coscoroba*, 2 species. Subfamily: Anserinae.) >> black swan; duck; waterfowl

Swan River Major watercourse of SW Australia; rises in the hills near Corrigin; flows past Perth, entering the Indian Ocean at Fremantle; length 386 km/240 mi; the Swan River Settlement (1829) was the first colonial settlement in Western Australia. >> Perth (Australia)

Swanscombe skull The partial skull of an archaic form of *Homo sapiens* found at Swanscombe near London in 1935–6, and 1955. Its possible age is 250 000 years. >> *Homo* ℹ

Swansea, Welsh **Abertawe** 51°38N 3°57W, pop (1995e) 173 000. Port city and (from 1996) unitary authority (pop (1995e) 230 900), SC Wales, UK; at the mouth of the R Neath; chartered, 1158–84; airfield; railway; university college (1920); national vehicle licensing centre; Norman castle; football league team, Swansea City (Swans). >> Wales ℹ

swastika [**swos**tika] A symbol consisting of a cross with its four arms bent at right angles, either clockwise or anticlockwise. Found in ancient Hindu, Mexican, Buddhist, and other traditions, possibly representing the Sun, it is now tainted since its appropriation by the Nazi party as its official emblem. The name derives from the Sanskrit *svasti* + *ka*, meaning a mystical cross used to denote good luck.

Swazi A Bantu-speaking agricultural and pastoral people living in Swaziland and adjoining parts of S Africa. They are one of the Nguni cluster of peoples, formed into a kingdom in the early 19th-c. >> Nguni; Swaziland ℹ

Swaziland [**swah**zeeland], official name **Kingdom of Swaziland** pop (1995e) 900 000; area 17 363 sq km/ 6702 sq mi. Constitutional monarchy in SE Africa; capital, Mbabane; timezone GMT +2; chief ethnic group, Swazi; chief religions, Christianity (57%), local beliefs; official languages, English (government business), Siswati; unit of currency, the lilangeni (plural, emalangeni); small country, 192 km/119 mi N–S and 144 km/ 89 mi E–W; highest point Emblembe (1862 m/6109 ft); humid, near-temperate climate in the E; tropical in the W, susceptible to drought; arrival of Swazi in the area, early 19th-c; boundaries with the Transvaal decided, and independence guaranteed, 1881; British High Commission territory, 1903; independence as a constitutional monarchy, 1968; governed by a bicameral parliament consisting of a National Assembly and Senate; the king chooses a cabinet and a prime minister to advise him; Mswati III crowned, 1986; agriculture employs 70% of the population. >> Mbabane; Transvaal; RR1023 political leaders

sweat A dilute solution of salts (mainly sodium chloride) and other small molecules (eg urea, lactic acid, and ammonia) actively secreted by sweat (*sudoriferous*) glands present in the skin of mammals. It is particularly important in humans with respect to temperature regulation. >> prickly heat

swede A biennial vegetable (*Brassica napus*, variety *napobrassica*), related to rape, with a taproot and stem base forming a fleshy tuber. (Family: Cruciferae.) >> brassica; rape (botany); tuber; vegetable

Sweden, Swed **Sverige**, official name **Kingdom of Sweden**, Swed **Konungariket Sverige** pop (1995e) 8 889 000; area 411 479 sq km/158 830 sq mi. Kingdom of N Europe, occupying the E side of the Scandinavian peninsula; capital, Stockholm; timezone GMT +1; population mainly of Teutonic descent; chief religion, Lutheran Protestantism (93%); official language, Swedish, with Finnish and Lapp also spoken in the N; unit of currency, the Swedish krona of 100 øre; large amount of inland water (9%); many coastal islands, notably Gotland and Öland; Kjölen Mts (W) form much of the boundary with Norway; highest peak, Kebnekaise (2111 m/6926 ft); typically continental climate, with considerable range of temperature between summer and winter, except in the SW, where winters warmer; formed from the union of the kingdoms of the Goths and Svears, 7th-c; Danes continued to rule in the

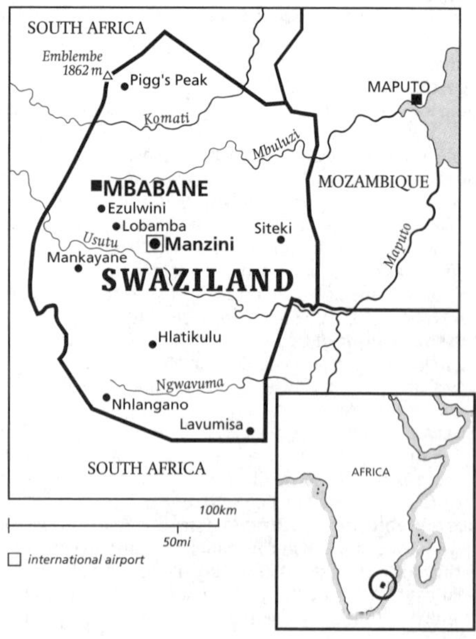

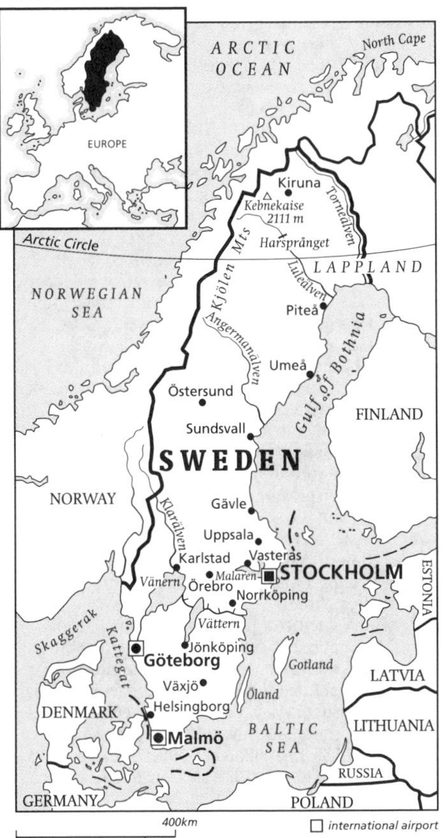

extreme S (Skåne) until 1658; united with Denmark and Norway under Danish leadership, 1389; union ended in 1527, following revolt led by Gustavus Vasa; Sweden acquired Norway from Denmark, 1814; union with Norway dissolved, 1905; a neutral country since 1814; a representative and parliamentary democracy, with a monarch as head of state; governed by a prime minister and single-chamber parliament; joined European Union, 1995; gradual shift in the economy from the traditional emphasis on raw materials (timber and iron ore) to advanced technology; hydroelectricity provides 70% of power. >> Gustavus Vasa; Kalmar Union; Stockholm; RR1023 political leaders

Swedenborg, Emanuel [**swee**dnbaw(r)g], originally **Emanuel Swedberg** (1688–1772) Mystic and scientist, born in Stockholm. In 1734 he published his monumental *Opera philosophica et mineralia* (Philosophical and Logical Works), a mixture of metallurgy and metaphysical speculation on the creation of the world. He expounded his spiritual doctrines in such works as *The New Jerusalem* (1758), and in 1787 his followers (known as Swedenborgians) formed the Church of the New Jerusalem. >> mysticism; New Jerusalem, Church of the

Swedish >> **Germanic / Scandinavian languages**

Sweet, Henry (1845–1912) Philologist, born in London. His works include Old and Middle English texts, primers, and dictionaries, and a historical English grammar. He was the probable source for Professor Higgins in Shaw's *Pygmalion*. >> English; phonetics; Shaw, George Bernard

sweet alyssum [**al**isuhm] A low, bushy annual or perennial (*Lobularia maritima*) native to the Mediterranean; flowers very numerous, white or blue, cross-shaped. It is one of the most popular garden bedding plants, often referred to simply as 'alyssum'. (Family: Cruciferae.) >> alyssum

sweet bay An evergreen shrub or tree (*Laurus nobilis*), growing to 20 m/65 ft, but often less, native to the Mediterranean; male and female flowers yellow or white, 4-lobed; berry black; often referred to simply as **bay**. It is the 'laurel' of poets and victors in classical times. (Family: Lauraceae.) >> laurel

sweet briar >> **eglantine**

sweet cherry >> **cherry**

sweet chestnut A deciduous tree (*Castanea sativa*) growing to 30 m/100 ft, native to the Mediterranean and W Asia; long catkins have green female flowers below yellow males; nuts shiny, brown, three enclosed in a densely spiny case; also called **Spanish chestnut**. The nuts are the familiar roast chesnuts. (Family: Fagaceae.) >> horse chestnut

sweet cicely A perennial (*Myrrhis odorata*) growing to 2 m/6½ ft, smelling strongly of aniseed, native to Europe; divided, fern-like leaves; tiny white flowers, in clusters; also called **garden myrrh**. It is cultivated as a seasoning. (Family: Umbelliferae.)

sweet corn >> **maize**

sweeteners >> **additives**

sweet gum A deciduous tree native to North America, Asia Minor, and China; leaves turning bright red in autumn; flowers tiny, in separate, globular heads. It yields storax, a fragrant amber-coloured gum used in adhesives and perfumes. (*Liquidambar*, 6 species. Family: Styracaceae.) >> storax

sweet pea An annual climber, a native of S Italy and Sicily; stems growing to 2 m/6½ ft or more; flowers sweetly scented. The wild plants are purple-flowered, but cultivars now exist in a wide range or combination of colours. (*Lathyrus odoratus*. Family: Leguminosae.)

sweet potato A tuberous perennial with trailing or climbing stems (*Ipomoea batatas*); flowers large, purple, funnel-shaped. It is unknown in the wild, but numerous different strains are cultivated throughout warm regions as a staple food. The edible tubers, sometimes wrongly called *yams*, resemble large potatoes. (Family: Convolvulaceae.) >> potato; tuber; yam

sweet sop >> **custard apple**

sweet william A biennial (*Dianthus barbatus*) native to S Europe; flowers in dense, compact heads; five petals, dark red or pink, in garden forms also white, and often spotted or barred. (Family: Caryophyllaceae.) >> pink

Sweyn or **Svein** [svayn], known as **Forkbeard** (?–1014) King of Denmark (987–1014) and England (1013–14), the son of Harold Blue-tooth, and the father of Canute. He first attacked England in 994, and during his final campaign in 1013 established mastery over the whole country. >> Canute

swift A swallow-like bird of the worldwide family Apodidae (**true swifts**, 78 species) or the SE Asian Hemiprocnidae (**crested swifts**, 4 species); spends most of its life flying. >> parakeet; swallow

Swift, Graham (1949–) Novelist and short-story writer, born in London. His books include the novels *The Sweet Shop Owner* (1980) and *Last Orders* (1996, Booker Prize), as well as two collections of stories (1982, 1985).

Swift, Jonathan (1667–1745) Clergyman and satirist, born in Dublin. He attacked religious dissension in *A Tale of a Tub* (1704), and produced a wide range of political and religious essays and pamphlets. His world-famous satire, *Gulliver's Travels*, appeared in 1726. In later years he wrote a great deal of light verse, and several essays on such topics as language and manners.

swimming The act of propelling oneself through water without any mechanical aids. There are four strokes: the *breast stroke*, developed in the 16th-c, and the *front crawl* (freestyle), *backstroke*, and *butterfly*, developed in the 20th-c. In competitions there are also relays, involving four swimmers, and medley races, which are a combination of all four strokes. Race lengths range from 50 m/55 yd to 1500 m/1640 yd. >> channel swimming; scuba diving; skin-diving; RR1062

Swinburne, Algernon Charles (1837–1909) Poet and critic, born in London. He achieved success with his play *Atalanta in Calydon* (1865), and the first of his series of *Poems and Ballads* (1866) took the public by storm. >> Pre-Raphaelite Brotherhood

Swindon 51°34N 1°47W, pop (1995e) 148 000. Old market town in Thamesdown (unitary authority from 1997), Wiltshire, S England; developed into a modern industrial town with the arrival of the Great Western Railway in the 19th-c; Great Western Railway museum (1962); football league team, Swindon Town (Robins). >> Wiltshire

swine >> **pig**

swine fever The name used for two highly contagious viral infections of pigs. An infection of the intestines is called *hog cholera*, and an infection of the lungs is called *swine plague*. >> pig

Swiss cheese plant >> **monstera**

Swiss Guards The papal police corps, originally instituted by Pope Julius II (r. 1503–13) and recruited from the mercenaries of the cantons of the Swiss confederacy, whose reputation as infantrymen was established after their victories over the Burgundian cavalry in 1476. >> pope

Swiss lake dwellings Prehistoric settlements around the Swiss lakes, first identified in 1854 at Obermeilen, L Constance, by Swiss archaeologist Ferdinand Keller (1800–81). Over 200 comparable Neolithic sites preserved by waterlogging were subsequently revealed (1860–75). >> Three Age System

Swithin or **Swithun, St** (?–862) English saint and theologian, adviser to Egbert. When in 971 the monks exhumed his body to bury it in the rebuilt cathedral of Winchester, the removal, which was to have taken place on 15 July, is said to have been delayed by violent rains. Hence the current belief that if it rains on that day, it will rain for 40 days more. Feast day 15 July. >> Anglo-Saxons; Egbert

Switzerland, Fr **La Suisse**, Ger **Schweiz**, Ital **Svizzera**, ancient **Helvetia**, official name **Swiss Confederation**, Fr **Confédération Suisse**, Ger **Schweizerische Eidgenossenschaft**, Ital **Confederazione Svizzera** pop (1995e) 6 990 000; area 41 228 sq km/15 914 sq mi. Landlocked European republic, divided into 23 cantons; federal capital, Bern; judicial capital, Lausanne; largest city, Zürich; timezone GMT +1; chief religions, Roman Catholicism, Protestantism; chief languages, German (64%), French (19%), Italian (8%), Romansch (0.6%); unit of currency, the Swiss franc of 100 centimes; Alps run roughly E–W in the S; highest peak, Dufourspitze (4634 m/15 203 ft); Jura Mts run SW–NW; mean altitude of C plateau, 580 m/1900 ft, fringed with great lakes; c.3000 sq km/1160 sq mi of glaciers, notably the Aletsch; temperate climate, varying greatly with relief and altitude; warm summers, with considerable rainfall; the Föhn, a warm wind, noticeable in late winter and spring in the Alps; part of the Holy Roman Empire, 10th-c; Swiss Confederation created in 1291; centre of the Reformation, 16th-c; Swiss independence and neutrality recognized under the Treaty of Westphalia, 1648; conquered by Napoleon, who instituted the Helvetian Republic, 1798; organized as a confederation of cantons, 1815; federal constitution, 1848; neutral in both World Wars; governed by a parliament comprising a Council of States and a National Council; president elected yearly; increased specialization and development in high-technology products; a major financial centre; headquarters of many international organizations; all-year tourist area. >> Alps; Bern; Föhn wind; Napoleon I; Sonderbund; RR1023 political leaders

sword dance A ceremonial form of dance. In Scotland individuals or groups perform jigs over crossed swords placed on the floor. In England the dancers are linked together by metal or wooden swords, and perform intertwining figures without breaking the circle.

swordfish Large, agile, and very distinctive fish (*Ziphias gladius*) found worldwide in temperate and warm temperate seas; length up to 5 m/16 ft; upper jaw prolonged into a flattened blade or 'sword', teeth absent. (Family: Xiphiidae.) >> fish [i]

swordtail Small, colourful, freshwater fish (*Xiphophorus helleri*) native to streams and swamps of Central America; length up to c.12 cm/5 in; green with orange side stripe; lower edge of tail fin in male prolonged to form the 'sword'; a popular aquarium fish. (Family: Poeciliidae.) >> fish [i]

sycamore A spreading deciduous tree (*Acer pseudoplatanus*), growing to 35 m/115 ft, native to C and S Europe and W Asia; leaves palmately divided into five toothed lobes; flowers yellowish, lacking petals, in pendulous clusters; winged seeds fused in pairs. (Family: Aceraceae.) >> maple; palmate

Sydenham's chorea [**sid**nuhmz ko**ree**a] Irregular, jerking, and unpredictable movements of the limbs, and sometimes of the whole body. The condition is related to streptococcal infection and rheumatic fever. It is named after English physician Thomas Sydenham (1624–89). >> chorea; rheumatic fever; *Streptococcus*

Sydney 33°55S 151°10E, pop (1995e) 3 741 000. Port and state capital of New South Wales, Australia; largest city in Australia; founded as the first British settlement, 1788; airport; railway; five universities (1850, 1949, 1964, 1989, 1990); two cathedrals; two major harbours (Sydney, Port Botany); commercial, cultural, and financial centre; State Parliament House. >> Botany Bay; New South Wales; Sydney Harbour Bridge; Sydney Opera House

Sydney Harbour Bridge One of Australia's best-known landmarks, and the widest and heaviest arch bridge in the world, built 1923–32; length of main arch 503 m/1651 ft; highest point 134 m/440 ft above sea-level. A harbour tunnel was opened in 1992. >> New Guard; Sydney

Sydney Opera House Australia's best-known contemporary building. Its imaginative design came from an international competition, won in 1956 by the Danish architect Joern Utzon (1918–) in 1956. It was completed in 1973. >> Sydney

syenite [**siy**eniyt] A coarse-grained igneous rock containing feldspar and hornblende as essential minerals, with some biotite. >> feldspar; hornblende; igneous rock

syllabary A writing system in which the basic units (*graphemes*) correspond to syllables, normally representing a sequence of consonant and vowel. An example is found in Japanese *kana*, where the graphemes correspond to such spoken sequences as *ka*, *ga*, and *no*. >> graphology

syllogism In logic, a deductive argument containing two premisses. For example, 'Some dogs are chihuahuas, All chihuahuas are small; *therefore* Some dogs are small'. >> logic; premiss

Sylvanus >> **Silvanus**

symbiosis [simbi**oh**sis] A general term for the living together of two dissimilar organisms, usually to their mutual benefit. It is commonly used to describe all the different types of relationship between the members of two different and interacting species. >> parasitology

symbolic logic >> **logic**

Symbolism In general terms, the belief that ideas or emotions may be objectified in terms which make them communicable, whether in words, music, graphics, or plastic forms. This belief may be traced back to Plato, and is clearly active in much Romantic poetry. The systematic invocation of a transcendental world in poetry was practised by several French poets in the mid-19th-c, who came to be known as Symbolists. >> Symbolists

Symbolists A group of mid-19th-c French poets, including Baudelaire, Mallarmé, Verlaine, and Rimbaud. Their general aim was to invoke rather than to describe reality, by subliminal means. In art, there was a reaction against Realism and Impressionism; leading artists included Denis and Puvis de Chavannes. >> *Nabis, Les*; Realism; Symbolism; Baudelaire; Denis, Maurice; Mallarmé; Puvis de Chavannes; Rimbaud; Verlaine

sympathetic nervous system >> **autonomic nervous system**

symphonic poem A single-movement orchestral work in which a composer seeks to express the emotional, pictorial, or narrative content of a poem, story, painting, etc. It was developed by Liszt from the programmatic concert overture and taken up by other Romantic composers. >> overture; programme music; Romanticism; Liszt

symphony An orchestral work originating in the 18th-c, although the term had been used earlier with different meanings. The classical symphony of Haydn, Mozart, Beethoven, and Schubert was mostly in four movements: a fast movement in sonata form; a slow movement; a minuet or scherzo; and a finale, often in sonata form like the first movement. In the 19th-c the structure was varied a good deal, and programmatic or descriptive intentions were often present, as in the five-movement *Symphonie fantastique* of Berlioz. >> minuet; movement; programme music; scherzo; sinfonietta; symphonic poem

Symplegades [sim**play**gadeez] In Greek mythology, the Clashing Rocks, situated at the entrance to the Black Sea, through which the *Argo* had to pass. >> Argonauts

synagogue (Gr 'congregation', 'meeting') The local Jewish institution for instruction in the Torah and worship, the religious focal point of individual Jewish communities. At first applied to the congregation, the term was eventually used of the buildings in which the people met. In Orthodox synagogues, men and women have traditionally separated; but in non-Orthodox synagogues, they now sit together. >> elder (religion) 1; Judaism; rabbi; Torah

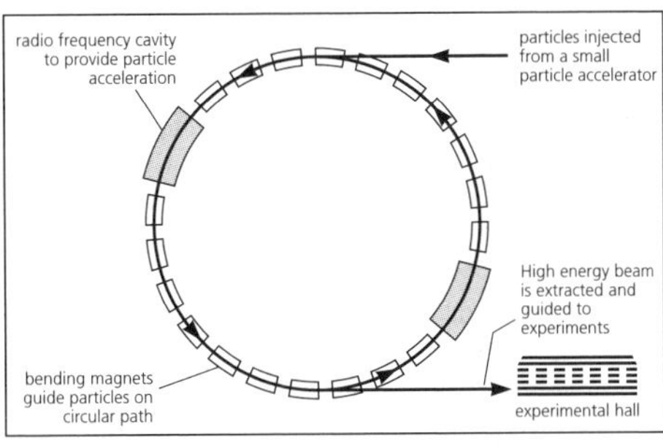

A synchrotron particle accelerator. The bending magnets may number a few hundred, and the complete machine may be several kilometres across. The particle beam travels inside an evacuated pipe, itself inside a tunnel.

synapse [**siy**naps] The specialized junction between two neurones, present in the nervous system of all animals. Nerve impulses at the axon terminals of one neurone are transmitted across the junction either chemically (by neurotransmitters) or electrically (by local currents). >> neurone [i]

synchrotron A machine for accelerating subatomic particles, usually protons or electrons. The particles are guided through an evacuated pipe in a circular path by magnets, accelerated by radio-frequency (rf) electric fields. Synchrotrons are a major experimental tool in particle physics. >> particle accelerators

syncline A geological fold structure in the form of a trough or inverted arch, produced by the downfolding of stratified rocks. It is the opposite of an anticline. >> stratification

syncope [**sing**kopee] >> **fainting**

syndicalism A revolutionary socialist doctrine that emphasized workers taking power by seizing the factories in which they worked; developed in the 1890s, and common in France, Italy, and Spain in the early 20th-c. By 1914 it had lost its political force. >> anarchism; socialism

Synge, J(ohn) M(illington) [sing] (1871–1909) Playwright, born near Dublin. He settled among the people of the Aran Is, who provided the material for his plays, notably *The Playboy of the Western World* (1907). He was a director of the Abbey Theatre from 1904. >> Abbey Theatre

synodic period The average time taken by a planet to return to the same position in its orbit relative to the Earth. For the Moon this is 29·53 days, the interval between successive new moons. >> Moon; planet

synonym A word which is similar enough in meaning to another word for it to be usable as a substitute in some contexts, such as *illuminate* and *light*. An **antonym** is a word which has the opposite meaning to another, such as *light* and *dark*. A **hyponym** is a word whose meaning is included within that of another, such as *horse* and *animal*. The study of sense relations of this kind is part of the subject of semantics. >> semantics

synoptic gospels A term applied to three New Testament Gospels (Matthew, Mark, Luke), so called because of the striking amount of common material that they contain. Most of Mark's Gospel, for example, is reproduced in

Matthew and Luke, and the correspondence often extends to the order of passages and wording. >> Gospels, canonical

synovitis [siynoviytis] Inflammation of the synovial membranes that enclose tendons or cover surfaces within and around the joints. It arises from persistent injury (eg from sports), or from bacterial or immunological inflammation, when it takes the form of arthritis. >> arthritis; joint; tendon

synroc [sinrok] An artificial ceramic material used to store high-level radioactive waste. The waste is added to mixed powdered metal oxides from which the ceramic is formed by heat and compression. It is under development as an alternative to storage using glass. >> ceramics; radioactivity

syntax In linguistics, the study of sentence structure; alternatively, the study of how words can be combined into larger grammatical units. A syntax for a language specifies a set of grammatical categories (such as verb, noun phrase, and sentence) and a set of rules which define the ways in which these categories relate to each other. >> grammar; semantics

synthesizer An electronic apparatus for generating musical sounds, usually fitted with one or more keyboards and loudspeakers. One of the earliest and best known was developed in 1964 by Robert A Moog (1934–). Modern digital types, based on microprocessors, are virtually unlimited in the number and range of sounds they can produce. >> electrophone; keyboard instrument

syphilis [sifilis] A chronic infection caused by *Treponema pallidum*; a sexually transmitted disease in which a primary lesion appears on the genitalia or anus. This is followed in several weeks by a skin rash and features of generalized infection and fever. These features subside, and the condition may then remain latent for 10 or more years. Thereafter the heart, aorta, and brain may become affected. The causative organism is sensitive to penicillin treatment. >> meningitis; penicillin; penis 🅘; vagina; venereal disease

syphon >> **siphon**

Syracuse (Italy) [sirakyooz], Ital **Siracusa** 37°04N 15°18E, pop (1995e) 123 000. Seaport in Sicily, Italy; founded by Greek settlers, 734 BC; leading cultural centre, 5th-c BC; taken by the Romans, 212 BC; railway; birthplace of Archimedes, Theocritus; cathedral (640), Greek theatre (3th-c BC), Roman remains. >> Archimedes; Sicily; Theocritus

Syracuse (USA) [sirakyooz] 43°03N 76°09W, pop (1995e) 167 000. City in C New York, USA; developed during the 1780s; city status, 1848; airfield; railway; university (1870). >> New York (state)

Syria, Arabic **Suriya**, official name **Syrian Arab Republic**, Arabic **Al-Jumhuriyah al-Arabiyah as-Suriyah** pop (1995e) 14 325 000; area 185 180 sq km/71 479 sq mi. Republic in the Middle East; capital, Damascus; timezone GMT +2; population mainly Arab (90%); chief religions, Islam (74% Sunni Muslim, 16% Alawite Druze and other sects), Christianity (10%); official language, Arabic; unit of currency, the Syrian pound; narrow Mediterranean coastal plain; Anti-Lebanon range (SW) rises to 2814 m/9232 ft at Mt Hermon; open steppe and desert to the E; coastal Mediterranean climate, with hot, dry summers and mild, wet winters; desert or semi-desert climate in 60% of country; part of the Phoenician Empire; Islam introduced, 7th-c; conquered by Turks, 11th-c; scene of many Crusader battles in Middle Ages; part of Ottoman Empire, 1517; brief period of independence, 1920, then made a French mandate; independence, 1946; merged with Egypt to form the United Arab Republic, 1958; re-established itself as independent state under present name, 1961; Golan Heights region seized by Israel, 1967; governed by a president, a prime minister, and People's Council; since 1974, oil has been the most important source of export revenue; Euphrates dam project (begun 1978) supplies 97% of domestic electricity demand. >> Arab–Israeli Wars; Crusades 🅘; Damascus; Islam; khamsin; Phoenicia; RR1023 political leaders

Syriac >> **Aramaic**

syringa [siringga] >> **lilac; mock orange**

Syrinx [siringks] In Greek mythology, a nymph pursued by Pan. She called on the Earth to help, and so sank down into it and became a reed-bed. Pan cut some of the reeds, and made the panpipes. >> Pan

syrinx [siringks] The voice-producing organ of birds; situated in the windpipe where this divides into two. Its structure and position has been used in bird classification to indicate the relationships of groups. >> trachea

system Any biological, mechanical, or organizational entity which carries out a specific function, receiving inputs from its surroundings and sending outputs to its surroundings. In computing, the word is used to refer to a part of the information processing of an organization which might be appropriate for implementation by a computer, such as the handling of a payroll. Today, **systems analysts** are just as concerned about the human organizational systems as the clerical processing systems. >> software; systems analysis

systematics The classification of organisms into a hierarchical series of groups which emphasizes their presumed evolutionary interrelationships. The main categories of modern classifications are (in order of increasing generality) species, genus, family, order, class, phylum (animals), division (plants), and kingdom. >> binomial nomenclature; genus; kingdom; phylum; species; taxonomy

systemic lupus erythematosus (SLE) [loopus erithematohsus] A generalized disorder affecting connective tissue throughout the body. It tends to affect 30–40-year-old females. It causes arthritis and skin rashes, and the kidneys, heart, and brain may be involved. The condition is ameliorated by immuno-suppressive drugs, but may lead to death in some cases. >> arthritis; immunosuppression

systems analysis In computing, the techniques involved in the intimate understanding, design, and optimization of computer systems. **Systems analysts** are responsible

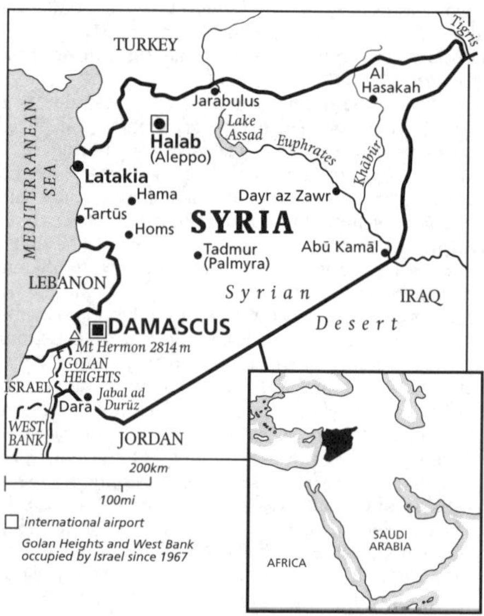

for the precise definition and implementation of a computer system in business, research, and other contexts. >> computer

systole [**sis**tolee] Phases of the cardiac cycle when the atria (**atrial systole**) and especially the ventricles (**ventricular systole**) contract forcibly, ejecting the blood into the aorta (from the left ventricle) and pulmonary trunk (from the right ventricle). >> diastole; heart ℹ

syzygy [**siz**ijee] An astronomical situation which occurs when the Sun, Earth, and Moon are roughly in a straight line. Eclipses are likely when the Moon is at syzygy. >> eclipse

Szczecin [**shche**cheen], Ger **Stettin** 53°25N 14°32E, pop (1995e) 419 000. Industrial river port in NW Poland; on R Oder; largest Baltic trading port; urban status, 1243; member of the Hanseatic League, 1360; Prussian rule, 1720–1945; badly damaged in World War 2; ceded to Poland, 1945; airfield; railway; maritime college; medical academy; technical university (1946); cathedral, castle (16th-c), 13th–14th-c city walls. >> Poland ℹ

Szeged [**se**ged] 46°16N 20°10E, pop (1995e) 173 000. River port in S Hungary, on R Tisza; railway; university (1872, refounded 1921); railway; cultural centre of the S Alföld; medicinal baths; castle (1242). >> Hungary ℹ

Székely [**say**kel] A Magyar-speaking people, since the 11th-c inhabiting the SE Transylvanian region of post-1918 Romania. In both the interwar and the contemporary periods, the position of the Székely has given rise to disputes between the Romanian and Hungarian states.

Székesfehérvár [**say**keshfeheervah(r)], Ger **Stuhlweissenburg**, ancient **Alba Regia** 47°15N 18°25E, pop (1995e) 107 000. City in WC Hungary; ancient capital of Hungarian kingdom; badly damaged in World War 2; market centre for tobacco, wine, fruit; cathedral. >> Hungary ℹ

Szell, George [sel] (1897–1970) Conductor and pianist, born in Budapest. From 1946 he was musical director and conductor of the symphony orchestra in Cleveland, OH.

Szilard, Leo [**zil**ah(r)d] (1898–1964) Physicist, born in Budapest. Earlier than most physicists, he saw (in 1934) the possibility of large-scale energy generation by nuclear fission, and initiated the idea of an atomic bomb. >> atomic bomb; Fermi; nuclear fission

Szombathely [**som**bot-hay], Ger **Steinamanger**, ancient **Sabaria** 47°14N 16°38E, pop (1995e) 84 100. City in W Hungary, on R Gyöngyös; bishopric; railway; cathedral. >> Hungary ℹ

Szymborska, Wislawa [sim**baw(r)**ska] (1923–) Poet and critic, born in Bnin (now part of Kornik), Poland. Her first collections of poetry appeared in 1952 and 1954, but were subject to the censorship of the era, and she now recognizes only her work published after 1957. English-language collections include *People on a Bridge* (1990) and *Sounds, Feelings, Thoughts* (1996). She received the Nobel Prize for Literature in 1996.

Tabari, al- [ta**bah**ree], in full **Abu Jafar Mohammed Ben Jarir al-Tabari** (839–923) Historian, born in Amol, Persia. He wrote a major commentary on the Koran, and a history of the world from creation until the early 10th-c. >> Koran

Tabarley, Eric (1931–98) French yachtsman. He was twice winner of the single-handed trans-Atlantic race, in 1964 in *Pen Duick II*, and in 1976 in *Pen Duick VI*. >> sailing

tabasco sauce [ta**bas**koh] A red sauce rich in chillis and hot red peppers, originating in the Mexican state of Tabasco. It is made from the fruit of the plant *Capsicum frutescens*.

Tabernacle A movable sanctuary or tent; in early Israelite religion, the shelter for the Ark of the Covenant during the desert wanderings. >> Ark of the Covenant; Atonement, Day of; Holy of Holies

Tabernacles, Feast of >> **Sukkoth**

tablature A system of musical notation tailored to a particular instrument or group of instruments and indicating the keys, frets, etc to be used rather than the pitch to be sounded. It is used today for the ukulele and the guitar: the notation conveys a diagrammatic indication of finger-placings.

Table Mountain 33°58S 18°25E. Mountain in SW South Africa; height 1086 m/3563 ft; a flat-topped central massif; Cape Town at the foot. >> Cape Town; South Africa ℹ

table tennis An indoor bat-and-ball game played by two or four players on a table measuring 9 ft (2·75 m) by 5 ft (1·52 m). The centre of the table has a net 6 in (15·25 cm) high stretched across it. The ball must be hit over the net and into the opposing half of the table. The object is to force one's opponent not to return the ball successfully. The winner is the first to reach 21 points with at least a two-point lead. Known as **ping pong** in the early part of the 20th-c, it is very popular in China and Korea. >> RR1062

taboo A prohibited form of conduct; from a Polynesian word, *tapu*. A wide variety of actions may be *tapu* – for example, a chief's *tapu* may prevent him being allowed to carry burdens, or children may be prohibited from touching seagoing canoes. Breaching a *tapu* may result directly in sickness or death, or may provoke physical punishment. The term is now used more generally, especially with reference to any subject-matter (eg death, politics) or language (eg swearing, obscenity) which people on occasion avoid.

tabor A small double-headed side drum with snares, known from mediaeval times. It was often played with one stick, the player at the same time blowing a three-holed pipe to accompany dancing. >> side drum

Tabriz [ta**breez**], ancient **Tauris** 38°05N 46°18E, pop (1995e) 1 301 000. Fourth largest city in Iran; often severely damaged by earthquakes; airport; railway; university (1949); industrial and commercial centre. >> Iran ℹ

Tachisme >> **action painting**

tachometer [ta**kom**eter] An instrument for measuring the speed of rotation. There are many methods; a typical modern device rotates a magnet near a non-magnetic conductor, exerting a force through the field produced by eddy currents. It is widely used to monitor the driving practices of lorry-drivers and bus-drivers. >> magnetism

tachyon [**tak**yon] A hypothetical elementary particle having imaginary mass (ie m^2 less than 0), and able to travel faster than the velocity of light without violating special relativity. >> particle physics; special relativity ℹ

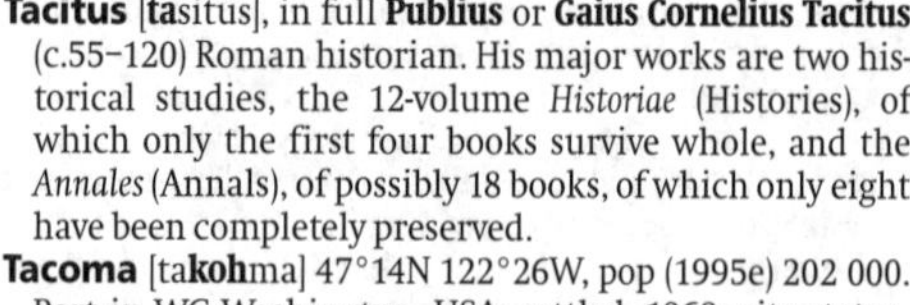

Tacitus [**tas**itus], in full **Publius** or **Gaius Cornelius Tacitus** (c.55–120) Roman historian. His major works are two historical studies, the 12-volume *Historiae* (Histories), of which only the first four books survive whole, and the *Annales* (Annals), of possibly 18 books, of which only eight have been completely preserved.

Tacoma [ta**koh**ma] 47°14N 122°26W, pop (1995e) 202 000. Port in WC Washington, USA; settled, 1868; city status, 1875; railway; university (1888); air force base; major NW Pacific container port. >> Washington (state)

Tadmur or **Tadmor**, ancient **Palmyra** 34°36N 38°15E, pop (1995e) 24 300. Ancient city in C Syria, a world heritage site; financial capital of the E world, 1st–2nd-c; on ancient caravan route from Persian Gulf to Mediterranean Sea; rail terminus. >> Syria ℹ

tadpole The larva of an amphibian, especially a frog or toad; largest 25 cm/10 in long; usually a short spherical body, feathery gills, large tail; with age, gills and tail shrink, legs appear, larvae become carnivorous. >> amphibian; frog

Taegu [tiy**goo**] 35°52N 128°36E, pop (1995e) 2 331 000. City in SE Korea; largest inland city after Seoul; market town at centre of apple-growing area; railway; university (1946); Haeinsa temple (802). >> Korea ℹ

Taejon [tiy**jon**] 36°20N 127°26E, pop (1995e) 1 111 000. City in C Korea; badly damaged in Korean War; railway; university (1952); agricultural centre. >> Korea ℹ

taekwondo [tiy**kwon**doh] A martial art developed in Korea by General Choi Hong Hi. The International Taekwondo Federation was founded in 1966. >> martial arts

Taft, William Howard (1857–1930) US statesman and 27th president (1909–13), born in Cincinnati, OH. He secured an agreement with Canada that meant relatively free trade. His son **Robert Alphonso Taft** (1889–1953) became a Republican leader (1939–53), but was defeated as a candidate for presidential nomination on three occasions. >> Republican Party

Taganrog [tagan**rok**] 47°14N 38°55E, pop (1995e) 297 000. Seaport in S European Russia; on the Sea of Azov; founded as a fortress and naval base, 1698; rail terminus; birthplace of Chekhov. >> Chekhov; Russia

Tagore, Rabindranath [ta**gaw(r)**] (1861–1941) Poet and philosopher, born in Calcutta, India. He is best known for his poetic works, notably *Gitanjali* (1912, Song Offering), and short stories, such as *Galpaguccha* (1912, A Bunch of Stories). He received the Nobel Prize for Literature in 1913, the first Asian writer to do so, and was knighted in 1915 – an honour which he resigned in 1919 as a protest against British policy in the Punjab.

Tagus, River [**tay**guhs], Span **Río Tajo**, Port **Río Tejo** River rising in the Sierra de Albarracín, Spain; enters Lisbon Bay; length, 1007 km/626 mi. >> Portugal ℹ; Spain ℹ

Tahiti [ta**hee**tee], Fr **Archipel de Tahiti [taeetee]** 17°37S 149°27W; pop (1995e) 151 000; area 1042 sq km/402 sq mi. Largest island of French Polynesia; length, 48 km/30 mi; French colony, 1880; capital, Papeete; rises to 2237 m/7339 ft in the volcanic peak of Mt Orohena. >> French Polynesia; Papeete

Tai, Mount [tiy], Chin **Taishan** The most revered of China's five sacred mountains, in Shandong province; a world heritage site. Evidence of settlement dates back 400 000 years. >> China ℹ

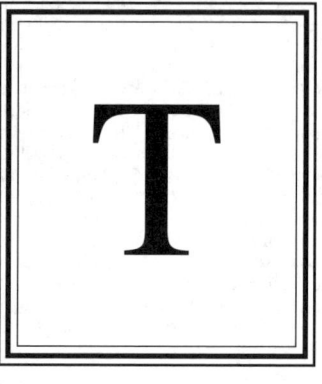

Taibei or **Taipei** [tiybay], also **T'ai-pei** 25°05N 121°32E, pop (1995e) 2 808 000. Capital of Taiwan; one of the fastest-growing cities in Asia; occupied by the Japanese, 1895–1945; seat of the Nationalist Government, 1949; airport; airfield; railway; three universities (1927, 1928, 1946). >> Taiwan ℹ

tai chi chuan [tiy chee chwan] A Chinese martial art said to date from the 13th-c, when a Taoist monk, Chang San Feng, observed a fight between a snake and a crane and devised a series of postures based on the movements of these animals from which the present forms are developed. The foundation of the art is the practice of 'the form', a series of 108 movements in a slow, continuous sequence, which is used as a method of meditation to harmonize the mind, body, and spirit. >> alternative medicine; martial arts

Taif, at- [at **tiy**f] 21°05N 40°27E, pop (1995e) 404 000. Summer resort town in WC Saudi Arabia; altitude, 1158 m/3799 ft; unofficial seat of government during the summer; airfield; centre of fruit-growing district. >> Saudi Arabia ℹ

taiga [**tiy**ga] A Russian term for the open coniferous forest zone intermediate between the boreal forest and tundra regions. Open areas are usually poorly drained muskeg. >> boreal forests; conifer; muskeg; tundra

Tailang >> **Mon**

tailorbird An Old World warbler (Family: *Sylviidae*) native to India and SE Asia; nest formed by folding a large leaf and 'sewing' the edges together with separate stitches of wool, silk, or spider's web. (Genus: *Orthotomus*, 9 species. >> warbler

Taimyr, Lake >> **Taymyr, Lake**

Tainan or **T'ai-nan** [tiynahn] 23°01N 120°14E, pop (1995e) 713 000. Oldest city in Taiwan; capital, 1684–7; university (1971). >> Taiwan ℹ

Taine, Hippolyte (Adolphe) [ten] (1828–93) Critic, historian, and positivist philosopher, born in Vouziers, France. His greatest work, *Les Origines de la France contemporaine* (1875–94, The Origins of Contemporary France) constituted a strong attack on the Revolution. >> positivism

taipan [**tiy**pan] A venomous snake (*Oxyuranus scutellatus*), native to NE Australia and New Guinea; one of the world's most deadly snakes; length up to 4 m/13 ft; brown with paler head. (Family: Elapidae.) >> snake

Taiping Rebellion (1850–64) A major uprising against the Qing dynasty in China, led by Hong Xiuquan (1814–64). Its programme aimed at ushering in a 'Heavenly Kingdom of Great Peace' (*Taiping Tian Guo*). The rebels took Nanjing (Nanking) in 1853, but the Qing forces under Zeng Guofan (1811–72) eventually brought about the downfall of the movement. >> Qing dynasty

Taiwan [tiy**wan**], official name **Republic of China, formerly** Formosa pop (1995e) 21 419 000; area 36 000 sq km/ 13 896 sq mi. Island republic consisting of Taiwan I and several smaller islands; c.130 km/80 mi off the SE coast of China; capital, Taipei; timezone GMT +8; population mainly Han Chinese (98%); several religions practised; official language, Mandarin Chinese; unit of currency, the new Taiwan dollar; c.395 km/245 mi long, 100–145 km/ 60–90 mi wide; mountain range runs N–S, covering two-thirds of the island; highest peak, Yu Shan (3997 m/ 13 113 ft); low-lying land mainly in the W; crossed by the Tropic of Cancer; tropical monsoon-type climate; hot and humid summers; mild and short winters; visited by the Portuguese, 1590; conquered by Manchus, 17th-c; ceded to Japan, 1895; returned to China, 1945; Jiang Jieshi (Chiang Kai-shek) moved the Nationalist government here, 1949; ongoing tension with China over political status; governed by a president, prime minister, National Assembly, and Legislative *Yuan*; economy has changed from agriculture to industry since the 1950s. >> Chinese; Guomindang; Jiang Jieshi; Taipei; RR1024 political leaders

Taiyuan or **T'ai-yüan** [tiyyüan] 37°50N 112°30E, pop (1995e) 2 199 000. Capital of Shanxi province, NEC China; founded during W Zhou dynasty; railway. >> China ℹ; Zhou dynasty

Taizé [**tay**zay] An ecumenical community founded near Lyon, France, by members of the French Reformed Church in 1940. Members observe a rule similar to most monastic orders. Their aim is the promotion of Christian unity, particularly between Protestants and Catholics. >> ecumenism; monasticism; Reformed Churches; Roman Catholicism

Taizhong or **T'ai-chung** [tiychung] 24°09N 120°40E, pop (1995e) 803 000. Third largest city in Taiwan; economic, cultural, and commercial centre of C Taiwan; designated an export processing zone. >> Taiwan ℹ

Tajikistan [tajiki**stahn**], official name **Republic of Tajikistan**, also spelled **Tadzhikistan**, Tajik **Jumhurii Tojikistan** pop (1995e) 5 367 000; area 143 100 sq km/ 55 200 sq mi. Republic in SE Middle Asia; capital, Dushanbe; timezone GMT +3; major ethnic groups, Tajik (64%), Uzbek (24%), Russian (7%); religion, Sunni Muslim; languages, Tajik (official), Russian; currency, the Tajik rouble; Tien Shan, Gissar-Alai, and Pamir ranges cover over 90% of the area; Communism Peak reaches 7495 m/24 590 ft; R Amudarya flows E–W along the S border; largest lake, L Kara-Kul; continental climate; subtropical valley areas; annual mean temperature −0.9°C (Jan), 27°C (Jul); average annual rainfall (lowlands) 150–250 mm/ 6–10 in, (highlands) about half of these totals; incorporated into Turkmenistan, 1918; part of Uzbek SSR, 1924; became a Soviet Socialist Republic, 1929; declaration of independence, 1991; governed by a president, prime minister, and National Assembly; republican Communist Party remained in power until start of civil war, 1992; several rounds of peace talks, finally agreed in 1997; oil, natural gas, coal, lead, zinc, machinery, metalworking,

chemicals, food processing; cotton, wheat, maize, vegetables, fruit; hot mineral springs and health resorts. >> Commonwealth of Independent States 🅘; Dushanbe; RR1024 political leaders

Taj Mahal [**tahj** ma**hahl**] A renowned monument to love constructed (1632–54) at Agra in Uttar Pradesh, India, as a mausoleum for Mumtaz Mahal, the favourite wife of Shah Jahan. Built of white marble and inlaid with semi-precious stones and mosaic work, it is a masterpiece of Mughal architecture, and a world heritage site. >> Shah Jahan

take all A parasitic disease (*Gauemannomyces graminis*) which attacks the roots of wheat, barley, and rye, causing severe losses when susceptible crops are grown successively on the same land. The disease causes death (*take all*) or premature ripening (*whiteheads*) of the crop. (Order: Ascomycetes.) >> barley; fungus; parasitic plant; rye; wheat

talapoin [**tal**apoyn] The smallest Old World monkey, from W Africa (*Miopithecus talapoin*); greenish with pale underparts; round head and long tail; partly webbed hands and feet; swims well; also known as **pygmy guenon**. >> guenon; Old World monkey

Talbot, William Henry Fox (1800–77) Pioneer of photography, born in Melbury Abbas, Dorset. In 1838 he succeeded in making photographic prints on silver chloride paper, which he termed 'photogenic drawing', and later developed the Calotype process. >> photography

talc A hydrous magnesium silicate mineral ($Mg_3Si_4O_{10}(OH)_2$), formed in metamorphic rocks as light-grey soft masses; also known as **steatite** or **soapstone**. It is used in cosmetics (talcum powder) and in the paper, paint, rubber, and textile industries. >> magnesium; silicate minerals

Talca [**tal**ka] 35°25S 71°39W, pop (1995e) 197 000. City in C Chile; founded, 1692; destroyed by earthquake, 1742 and 1928, then completely rebuilt; Chilean independence declared here, 1818; railway; greatest wine-producing area in Chile. >> Chile 🅘

Talcahuano [talka-**hwa**noh] 36°40S 73°10W, pop (1995e) 266 000. Industrial port in C Chile; best harbour in Chile, containing main naval base and dry docks; railway. >> Chile 🅘

Taliesin [tal**ye**sin] (6th-c) Welsh bard, possibly mythical. He is known only from a collection of poems, *The Book of Taliesin*, written in the late 13th-c.

Tallahassee [tala**ha**see] (Muskogean 'town-old') 30°27N 84°17W, pop (1995e) 138 000. Capital of state in NW Florida, USA; state capital, 1824; railway; two universities (1857, 1887). >> Florida

Talleyrand (-Périgord), Charles Maurice de [talayrã] (1754–1838) French statesman, born in Paris. Elected to the States General, he was made president of the Assembly (1790), but lived in exile until after the fall of Robespierre. As foreign minister under the Directory (1797–1807), he helped to consolidate Napoleon's position; but alarmed by Napoleon's ambitions, he resigned in 1807. He became foreign minister under Louis XVIII, representing France with great skill at the Congress of Vienna (1814–15), and was Louis Philippe's chief adviser at the July Revolution. >> French Revolution 🅘; July Revolution; Louis XVIII; Louis Philippe; Napoleon I

Tallien, Jean Lambert [talyĩ] (1767–1820) French revolutionary politician, born in Paris. As president of the Convention (1794), he was denounced by Robespierre, but conspired with Barras and Fouché to bring about the former's downfall. >> Barras; Fouché; French Revolution 🅘; Robespierre

Tallinn [ta**lin**], formerly Ger **Revel** or **Reval** (to 1917) 59°22N 24°48E, pop (1995e) 475 000. Seaport capital of Estonia, on S coast of the Gulf of Finland; member of the Hanseatic League; taken by Russia, 1710; occupied by Germany in World War 2; airfield; railway; extensive military and naval installations; citadel (13th-c), cathedral (13th–15th-c); old town a world heritage site. >> Estonia 🅘; Hanseatic League

Tallis, Thomas (c.1505–85) English musician, 'the father of English cathedral music'. One of the greatest contrapuntists of the English School, he wrote much church music, including a motet in 40 parts, *Spem in alium*. >> counterpoint

Talmud [**tal**mud] (Heb 'study') An authoritative, influential compilation of rabbinic traditions and discussions about Jewish life and Laws. It includes the Mishnah of Rabbi Judah (c.200), accompanied by a commentary (the *Gemara*), in versions dating from the 4th–5th-c. >> Gemara; Judaism; Mishnah; Torah

talus >> **scree**

Tamale [ta**ma**le] 9°26N 0°49W, pop (1995e) 178 000. Capital of Northern region, Ghana; airfield; educational centre. >> Ghana 🅘

tamandua [taman**doo**a] >> **anteater**

tamaraw or **tamarau** >> **water buffalo**

tamarin [**tam**arin] A marmoset of genus *Saguinus* (10 species); lower canine teeth longer than incisors; also known as **long-tusked marmoset**. >> marmoset

tamarisk A slender shrub or tree, native to the Mediterranean and Asia; deciduous small twigs with scaly leaves giving a feathery appearance; flowers in spikes, 4–5 petals, pink or white. (Genus: *Tamarix*, 54 species. Family: Tamaricaceae.) >> manna

Tambo, Oliver (1917–93) South African politician, born in Bizana, South Africa. He became deputy president of the African National Congress (ANC) in 1958, and when the ANC was banned in 1960, he left South Africa to set up an external wing. He became acting ANC president in 1967, and president in 1977. >> African National Congress; Mandela, Nelson

tambourine A small frame drum fitted with jingles, and covered on one side with parchment or plastic. It may be shaken, tapped, or stroked, to produce various effects, mostly while accompanying dancing. >> drum; membranophone

Tambov [tam**bof**] 52°44N 41°28E, pop (1995e) 338 000. City in SC European Russia; founded as a fortress, 1636; airfield; railway. >> Russia ℹ

Tamburlaine >> **Timur**

Tamerlane >> **Timur**

Tamil A Dravidian-speaking people of S India and Sri Lanka, living as traders and seafarers. Predominantly Hindu, they were instrumental in diffusing Indian culture to many parts of SE Asia in the 11th-c. Tamil is now the major Dravidian language of S India, with written records dating from the 3rd-c BC. >> Dravidian languages; Hinduism

Tamil Nadu [**ta**mil **nah**doo], formerly **Madras** pop (1995e) 60 225 000; area 130 069 sq km/50 207 sq mi. State in S India; part of the Chola Empire, 10th–13th-c; first British trading settlement, 1611; boundaries of Mysore state altered in 1956 and 1960; renamed Tamil Nadu, 1968; capital, Madras; governed by a Legislative Council and a Legislative Assembly; population mainly Hindu (c.90%). >> India ℹ; Madras

Tamil Tigers A Tamil separatist guerrilla movement in Sri Lanka. It emerged in the early 1970s, protesting against the second-class status of Sri Lanka's minority Tamils, who represent 18% of its predominantly Singhalese population. By the mid-1980s, the 'Tigers' had several armies of liberation, with bases in the S Indian state of Tamil Nadu. Their relations with the Indian government deteriorated from 1987, when Rajiv Gandhi's peace accord with President Jayawardene brought the Indian army into Sri Lanka and thereafter into collision with the Tigers. >> Gandhi, Rajiv; Jayawardene; Sri Lanka ℹ; Tamil

Tammany Hall The most powerful of the four Democratic Party Committees in New York City; originally a club (the Society of Tammany) founded in 1789, which in the late 19th-c and early 20th-c was notorious for its political corruption. >> Democratic Party; Tweed Ring

Tammerfors >> **Tampere**

Tammuz or **Thammuz** [**tam**uz] A Babylonian god of vegetation who was beloved by Ishtar (in Syria by Astarte). He returns from the dead and dies again each year. >> Adonis; Ishtar

Tampa 27°57N 82°27W, pop (1995e) 311 000. Port in W Florida, USA; developed around a military post, 1824; later a cigar-making centre, then a resort; airport; railway; university (1931); processing and shipping centre for citrus fruit and phosphates; professional team, Buccaneers (football). >> Florida

Tampere [**tam**pere], Swed **Tammerfors** 61°32N 23°45E, pop (1995e) 176 000. Second largest city in Finland; established, 1779; developed as industrial centre in 19th-c; airfield; railway; university (1966); technological institute (1965); cathedral (20th-c). >> Finland ℹ

Tampico [tam**pee**koh] 22°18N 97°52W, pop (1995e) 301 000. Seaport in NE Mexico; airport; railway. >> Mexico ℹ

tam-tam >> **gong**

Tana, Lake, Amharic **Tana Hāyk** Lake in NWC Ethiopia; area 3600 sq km/1400 sq mi; altitude 1830 m/6000 ft; source of the Blue Nile; notable for its 40 monasteries on islands in the lake. >> Blue Nile; Ethiopia ℹ

tanager [**tan**ajer] A songbird, native to the New World tropics; plumage usually brightly coloured; wings short, rounded. (Family: Thraupidae, c.239 species.) >> magpie; songbird

Tananarive >> **Antananarivo**

Tancred [**tang**kred] (c.1076–1112) Norman crusader, the grandson of Robert Guiscard. He went on the First Crusade, and was given the principality of Tiberias (1099). He also ruled at Edessa and Antioch. >> Crusades ℹ; Normans

tang >> **surgeonfish**

Tanga [**tang**ga] 6°10S 35°40E, pop (1995e) 226 000. Seaport in NE Tanzania; occupied by the British, 1916; centre of an agricultural area. >> Tanzania ℹ

Tanganyika, Lake [tanggan**yee**ka] Freshwater lake in EC Africa; length, 645 km/400 mi NNW–SSE; the longest, deepest (over 1400 m/4600 ft), and second largest lake (after L Victoria) in Africa; width, 25–80 km/15–50 mi; altitude, 772 m/2533 ft; European discovery in 1858 by John Speke and Richard Burton. >> Africa; Burton, Richard; Speke

Tang or **T'ang dynasty** (618–907) A Chinese dynasty founded by Li Yuan with its capital at Changan (modern Xian). It is generally regarded as the golden age of Chinese poetry. It was also a major period for printing, porcelain, technology (eg gunpowder), medicine, education, and science. >> China ℹ

tangent A line (usually a straight line) which touches a curve at a point *P* with the same gradient as the curve at *P*. The tangent to a circle at a point *P* is perpendicular to the radius of the circle through *P*. >> geometry

tangerine A citrus fruit (*Citrus reticulata*); a variety of mandarin with bright orange rind. (Family: Rutaceae.) >> citrus; mandarin

Tangier or **Tangiers** [tan**jeer(z)**], ancient **Tingis** 35°48N 5°45W, pop (1995e) 355 000. Seaport in N Morocco; at W end of the Strait of Gibraltar; occupied by the Portuguese in 1471, and later by the Spanish, English, and Moors; established as an international zone, 1923; Spanish occupation in World War 2; part of Morocco, 1959; free port status restored, 1962; airport; railway; university (1971); royal summer residence. >> Morocco ℹ

Tangshan or **T'angshan** 39°37N 118°05E, pop (1995e) 1 627 000. City in N China; railway; coal mining, heavy industry. >> China ℹ

Tanizaki, Junichiro [tani**za**kee] (1886–1965) Novelist, born in Tokyo. He became known in the West only after the translation in 1957 of his long novel *Sasameyuki* (1943–8, The Makioka Sisters), a notable example of descriptive realism.

tank An armoured fighting vehicle, typically equipped with tracks enabling it to manoeuvre across broken ground, and armed by a high velocity gun in a rotating turret. The first practical tanks were used in action in 1916 by the British. In the years before 1939, they were developed into fast-moving, hard-hitting machines, and emerged as the most important land weapon of World War 2. Modern vehicles show a great deal of electronic sophistication, with advanced night vision devices, laser range-finders, and fire control computers. >> armoured fighting vehicle; blitzkrieg; Panzer

tanker A vessel designed to carry liquid in bulk in a number of tanks, each of which is an integral part of the hull structure.The vessel with the largest gross tonnage is the Norwegian-registered oil tanker *Jahre Viking* of 260 851 gross tonnes and a deadweight capacity of 564 739 tonnes. Previously known as the *Seawise Giant*, she is the largest ship ever built. >> ship ℹ

tanning The process of turning raw animal hide or skin into a permanent, durable, flexible form. Cleaned skin is soaked in solutions of vegetable extracts containing tannins (eg oak bark) or, since the 19th-c, chrome salts. >> leather

tannins A mixture of derivatives of polyhydroxybenzoic acid from various plants, notably tea. They are water-soluble, with a bitter and astringent taste, and have long been used in the tanning of leather and in dyeing. >> tea

Tantalus [**tan**talus] In Greek mythology, a king of Sipylos in Lydia, who committed terrible crimes. He stole the food of the gods, so becoming immortal. As punishment, he sits in a pool which recedes when he bends to drink, and the grapes over his head elude his grasp.

tantra [**tan**tra] A type of Hindu or Buddhist ritual text, and the practice of its instruction. They include spells, mantras, meditative practices, and rituals to be performed. >> Buddhism; Hinduism; mantra

Tanzania [tanza**nee**a], official name **United Republic of Tanzania** pop (1995e) 31 363 000; area 945 087 sq km/364 900 sq mi. E African republic; includes the islands of Zanzibar, Pemba, and Matia; capital, Dodoma; former capital, Dar es Salaam; timezone GMT +3; population mainly of Bantu origin; chief religion on the mainland, Christianity (40%), on Zanzibar, almost entirely Islam; official languages, English, Swahili; unit of currency, the Tanzanian shilling; largest E African country, just S of the Equator; rises towards a C plateau, average elevation 1000 m/3300 ft; Rift Valley branches round L Victoria (N), where there are several high volcanic peaks, notably Mt Kilimanjaro (5895 m/19 340 ft); extensive Serengeti plain to the W; W branch of Rift Valley includes L Tanganyika and L Rukwa; hot, humid, tropical climate on coast and offshore islands; hot and dry on the C plateau; Swahili culture developed, 10th–15th-c; Zanzibar capital of the Omani empire, 1840s; exploration of the interior by German missionaries and British explorers, mid-19th-c; Zanzibar a British protectorate, 1890; German East Africa established, 1891; British mandate to administer Tanganyika, 1919; first E African country to gain independence, 1961; republic with Julius Nyerere as president, 1962; Zanzibar given independence as a constitutional monarchy with the Sultan as head of state; Sultan overthrown in 1964, and Act of Union between Zanzibar and Tanganyika led to the United Republic of Tanzania; plans for a multi-party democracy, 1992; governed by a president, cabinet, and National Assembly; economy largely based on agriculture; most of the world's market in cloves; tourism especially relating to Mt Kilimanjaro, national parks, and game reserves. >> Dodoma; Nyerere; Rift Valley; Serengeti; Zanzibar (island); RR1024 political leaders

Taoism or **Daoism** [**tow**izm] Chinese philosophical tradition, initially based on the ideas of 'Laozi' (Lao-tzu, ?6th-c BC) and Zhuangzi (Chuang-tzu, 369–286 BC). The *Tao* is the 'way' governing all human existence, which in Taoist terms lies in harmony between the individual and the natural world. Appropriate conduct arises from such harmony. From these origins as a life-philosophy, Taoism developed (1st-c BC) as a cult, its idealized dream-world readily absorbing primitive mystical and shamanistic beliefs. Favoured as a court religion under the Sui and Tang dynasties (590–906), Taoism came into conflict with Buddhism, and the latter was suppressed (845). In 1281, Taoism itself was suppressed by Kublai Khan, but rose again to favour under Ming emperors (1368–1644). >> Buddhism; Laozi; Ming / Sui / Tang dynasty; traditional Chinese medicine

tape recorder Equipment for storing sound and other information on magnetic tape; also used to play back these recordings. The sound to be recorded is turned into an electrical signal by a microphone, and fed to the recording head. Magnetic tape passes over this head, and a record of the original sound is imprinted in magnetic signals on the tape. >> magnetic tape 1; sound recording

tapestry A heavy decorative textile, hand-woven with multi-colour pictorial designs, and often of large size. Oriental in origin, tapestries were used for wall hangings, furniture, and floor coverings. Some tapestries were not woven but were embroidered – the Bayeux Tapestry being a famous example. >> Bayeux Tapestry

tapeworm A parasitic flatworm; adults commonly found in intestines of vertebrates; life cycle usually includes a larval stage found in a different intermediate host that is eaten by the final host. (Phylum: Platyhelminthes. Class: Cestoda.) >> flatworm; larva; parasitology

tapioca [tapi**oh**ka] A starchy preparation derived from the root crop cassava. It is used in puddings and as a thickening agent in liquid food. >> cassava

tapir [**tay**per] A nocturnal mammal native to Central and South America and SE Asia; resembles a small, smooth-skinned, hornless rhinoceros, with a short smooth coat, and a snout extended as a short trunk; the only perissodactyl with four toes on front feet. (Family: Tapiridae, 4 species.) >> perissodactyl [i]; rhinoceros

tar The liquid product of heating coal in the absence of air (**coal tar**). It contains many important substances, useful in the chemical industry (benzene, phenol, pyridine, etc). **Wood tar** is the first product of the destructive distillation of wood. Further distillation yields *creosote* and a variety of organic compounds depending on the wood; for example, resinous woods yield turpentine. The residue is *pitch*. >> coal

Tara A prehistoric hillfort, 40 km/23 mi NW of Dublin. It is the supposed site of St Patrick's conversion of Lóegaire in the 5th-c, and the traditional seat of the kings of Ireland. >> Patrick, St

tarantella [taran**tel**a] A lively folk-dance from S Italy, named after the town of Taranto. It was said to cure (or in some legends to be induced by) the bite of the tarantula. >> tarantula

Tarantino, Quentin (Jerome) [taran**tee**noh] (1963–) Film director, producer, actor, and screenwriter, born in Knoxville, TN. He sold his first screenplays, *True Romance* (1987, released 1993) and *Natural Born Killers* (released 1994), to enable him to start production of *Reservoir Dogs* (1992), in which he was director, screenwriter, and actor. The success of this film, and its successor *Pulp Fiction* (1994, Oscar), brought him celebrity status. Later films include *Four Rooms* (1995) and *From Dusk Till Dawn* (1996).

tarantula Any of the large hairy spiders of the family Therophosidae; rather sluggish spiders with a strong bite which may be venomous; hairs can cause rash when handled. (Order: Araneae.) >> spider

Tarawa 1°30N 173°00E, pop (1995e) 28 200. Capital town of Kiribati; airport; scene of US–Japanese battle in 1943. >> Kiribati ℹ

Tarbes [tah(r)b], ancient **Bigorra** 43°15N 0°03E, pop (1995e) 51 800. Industrial and commercial city in S France; on left bank of R Adour; originally a Roman settlement; ancient capital of province of Bigorre; road and rail junction; cathedral (12th–14th-c). >> France ℹ

Tardigrada [tah(r)**di**grada] >> **water bear**

tare >> **vetch**

targum [**tah(r)**gum] (Heb 'translation') An Aramaic translation of the Hebrew Scriptures or parts thereof, probably originally composed orally (c.1st-c BC) when the Torah was read aloud in the synagogues, then written in the rabbinic period. Best known is the *Targum Onkelos*. >> Aramaic; Judaism; Old Testament; rabbi; Torah

tariff A tax on goods entering a country. Tariffs may be intended mainly to raise revenue, particularly in less developed countries. They may also be aimed at reducing imports in general, or designed to promote the domestic production of goods. Tariffs generally harm other countries, and are the subject of various international agreements. >> devaluation; European Economic Community; General Agreement on Tariffs and Trade; taxation

Tarim Basin, Chin **Talimu Pendi** Largest inland basin in China; area 530 000 sq km/205 000 sq mi; rich in salt and non-ferrous metals; nuclear testing in the region. >> China ℹ

Tarkenton, Fran(cis Asbury) (1940–) Player of American football, born in Richmond, VA. He played for the Minnesota Vikings and New York Giants (1961–78), and gained 47 003 yds passing, a National Football League record. >> football ℹ

taro [**ta**roh] A perennial (*Colocasia esculenta*) native to SE Asia; also called **dasheen**. It is cultivated commercially in the tropics for its large corms. (Family: Araceae.) >> corm

tarot [**ta**roh] A pack of playing cards used chiefly in fortune-telling. It consists of 22 picture cards of the *major arcana* (*arcana* 'secret') and 56 cards in suits of the *minor arcana* – staves (or wands), cups, swords, and coins. Their design was influenced by occult features, and some designs relate to ancient religions. >> divination; occultism; playing cards

tarpan A wild horse native to the steppes of SE Europe; grey-brown with dark stripe along spine, occasionally with stripes on front legs; stiff, erect mane. >> horse ℹ

tarpon Large fish (*Tarpon atlanticus*) widespread in open waters of the Atlantic Ocean; length up to 2·4 m/8 ft; mouth oblique, lower jaw prolonged; dorsal fin small with long posterior fin ray. (Family: Megalopidae.)

Tarquinius Superbus, Lucius [tah(r)**kwin**ius soo**per**bus] (6th-c BC) Tyrannical king of Rome, whose overthrow (510 BC) marked the end of monarchy at Rome, and the beginning of the Republic. >> Lucretia; Roman history ℹ

tarragon An aromatic perennial (*Artemisia dracunculus*) growing to 120 cm/4 ft, native to Asia; flower-heads globular, yellowish, drooping. It is widely cultivated as a culinary herb, and for seasoning vinegar. (Family: Compositae.) >> herb

Tarragona [tara**go**na], Lat **Tarraco** 41°05N 1°17E, pop (1995e) 111 000. Port in Catalonia, NE Spain; archbishopric; airport; railway; cathedral (12th–13th-c). >> Catalonia; Spain ℹ

tarsier [**tah(r)**sier] A nocturnal primate native to Indonesia and the Philippines; large eyes, long hind legs; long naked tail with tuft of hairs at the tip. (Family: Tarsiidae, 3 species.) >> primate (biology)

Tarski, Alfred (1902–83) Logician, born in Warsaw. He made pioneering contributions to the study of formal semantics, especially to the definition of 'truth', and to several branches of mathematics and mathematical logic. >> logic; semantics

Tarsus [**tah(r)**suhs] 36°52N 34°52E, pop (1995e) 163 000. Town in S Turkey, on R Pamuk; important ancient city of Asia Minor; birthplace of St Paul; railway; agricultural trade centre. >> Turkey ℹ

tartan A fabric of a twill structure, made from variously coloured warp and weft yarns, using checkered designs which are almost always symmetrical. Tartans are mainly associated with the Scottish clans, in a tradition of dress dating from the 17th-c. >> twill

Tartar >> **Tatar**

tartaric acid [tah(r)**ta**rik] IUPAC **2,3-dihydroxybutanedioic acid**, $C_4H_6O_6$. Potassium hydrogen tartrate is used as an acid in baking powder, and is called **cream of tartar**. **Tartar emetic** is a double salt of potassium and antimony. >> isomers; IUPAC

Tartarus [**tah(r)**tarus] In Greek mythology, the name of the part of the Underworld where those who offended the gods were punished. >> Ixion; Sisyphus; Tantalus

tartrazine An artificial yellow colouring permitted for use in foods. It has been associated with hypersensitivity reactions among urticaria sufferers and asthmatics. >> asthma; colouring agents; urticaria

Tashkent [tash**kent**] 41°16N 69°13E, pop (1995e) 2 307 000. Capital city of Uzbekistan; oldest city of C Asia, known in the 1st-c BC; taken by Russia, 1865; virtually rebuilt after earthquake damage, 1966; airport; railway; university (1920). >> Uzbekistan ℹ

Tasman, Abel Janszoon [**taz**mn] (1603–c.59) Navigator, born near Groningen, The Netherlands. In 1642 he discovered the area he named Van Diemen's Land (now Tasmania) and New Zealand, followed by Tonga and Fiji (1643). He made a second voyage (1644) to the NW coast of Australia. >> Tasmania

Tasmania, formerly **Van Diemen's Land** (to 1856) pop (1995e) 479 000; area 67 800 sq km/26 200 sq mi. Island state of Australia, separated from the mainland by the Bass Strait; includes the main island of Tasmania, and several smaller islands; European discovery by Abel Tasman, 1642; first European settlement, 1803 (a British dependency of New South Wales); became a separate colony, 1825; mountainous interior, with a Central Plateau rising to 1617 m/5305 ft at Mt Ossa; temperate maritime climate; the most fertile regions along the NW and E coasts and along the river valleys; capital, Hobart; first Aborigines settled here 25 000 years ago; numerous unique plants and animals. >> Australia ℹ; Hobart; Tasman

Tasmanian devil An Australian carnivorous marsupial (*Sarcophilus harrisii*); the largest dasyure (length, up to 1·1 m/3·6 ft); bear-like in shape, with large powerful head and long bushy tail. >> dasyure; marsupial ℹ

Tasmanian tiger / wolf >> **thylacine** ℹ

Tasman Sea [**taz**mn] Part of the Pacific Ocean separating E Australia and Tasmania from New Zealand; named for the Dutch explorer Abel Tasman. >> Pacific Ocean; Tasman

TASS [tas] Acronym for **Telegrafnoe Agentsvo Sovetskovo Soyuza** ('Telegraph Agency of the Soviet Union'), the national news agency of the former USSR. Established in 1935, its headquarters was in Moscow. >> news agency

Tasso, Torquato (1544–95) Poet, born in Sorrento, Italy. His epic masterpiece on the capture of Jerusalem during the first crusade, *Gerusalemme Liberata* (1581, Jerusalem Liberated), was later rewritten, in response to criticisms, as *Gerusalemme Conquistata* (1593, Jerusalem Conquered).

taste buds Small sensory organs located on the tongue and palate, which recognize four primary tastes: sweet, sour, salt, and bitter. The tip of the tongue is sensitive to salt and sweet stimuli, the back to bitter stimuli, and the edges to sour and salt. >> tongue

tatami [ta**tah**mee] Traditional Japanese floor matting, made of layers of rushes, edged with narrow strips of black cloth. Tatami are standard size, equivalent to one sleeping space, and rooms are described as '6 mat, 8 mat', etc. >> futon

Tatar or **Tartar** A Turkic-speaking people living in Russia. Sunni Muslims since the 14th-c, they were a highly stratified mediaeval society. Their fierce reputation is the source of the modern word 'tartar'.

Tate, Sir Henry (1819–99) Sugar magnate, art patron, and philanthropist, born in Chorley, Lancashire. He attained great wealth as a Liverpool sugar refiner. The Tate Gallery was founded by him. >> Tate Gallery

Tate, James (1943–) Poet, born in Kansas City, KS. He taught at the University of Massachusetts, publishing his first collection, *The Lost Pilot*, in 1967. In 1992 he won the Pulitzer Prize for his *Selected Poems* (1991).

Tate, Nahum [**nay**uhm] (1652–1715) Poet and playwright, born in Dublin. He is known for his 'improved' versions of Shakespeare's tragedies, substituting happy endings to suit the popular taste. He became poet laureate in 1692. >> Shakespeare ℹ

Tate Gallery A London gallery housing the nation's chief collection of British art and modern foreign art. It was opened in 1897 as a branch of the National Gallery, and became fully independent in 1955. There is also now a Tate Gallery at the Albert Dock development in Liverpool. >> London; National Gallery; Tate, Henry

Tati, Jacques [tatee], popular name of **Jacques Tatischeff** (1908–82) Actor and film producer, born in Le Pecq, France. He made his reputation as the greatest film comedian of the postwar period, notably in *Les Vacances de Monsieur Hulot* (1953, Mr Hulot's Holiday) and *Mon Oncle* (1958, My Uncle), which won several awards.

Tatra Mountains [**tah**tra], Czech **Tatry** Mountain group in C Carpathian Mts, rising to 2655 m/8711 ft at Gerlachovský Štít. >> Carpathian Mountains

Taung skull The partial skull and brain case of a young *Australopithecus africanus*, found at Taung, S Africa, in 1924. This was the first discovery of these small-brained early hominids. >> *Homo* ℹ

Taunton [**tawn**tn] 51°01N 3°06W, pop (1995e) 56 100. County town in Somerset, SW England; on the R Tone; founded in 705; Duke of Monmouth crowned king here, 1685; 12th-c castle hall, where Bloody Assizes held (1685); railway. >> Bloody Assizes; Monmouth, James, Duke of

Taupo, Lake [**tow**poh] area 606 sq km/234 sq mi. Lake in C North Island, New Zealand, filling an old volcanic crater; length 40 km/25 mi, width 27 km/17 mi; largest New Zealand lake. >> New Zealand ℹ

tauraco >> **turaco**

Taurus [**taw**rus] (Lat 'bull') A prominent N constellation of the zodiac, including the Pleiades and Hyades clusters and the Crab Nebula. It lies between Aries and Gemini. Its brightest star is the red giant, Aldebaran. Distance: 21 parsec. >> Pleiades (astronomy); RR968

Taurus Mountains [**taw**rus], Turkish **Toros Dağlari** Mountain chain of S Turkey; highest peak, Ala Dağlari (3910 m/12 828 ft); its NW extension is called the **Anti-Taurus**. >> Turkey ℹ

Tavener, John (Kenneth) (1944–) Composer, born in London. His music is predominantly religious, and includes the cantata *The Whale* (1966) and a sacred opera *Therese* (1979). His *Song for Athene* (1993), written to commemorate the death of a family friend, Athene Hariades, in a cycling accident, became nationally known when it was chosen as part of the funeral ceremony for Princess Diana in 1997. >> cantata; Diana, Princess of Wales

tawny owl A typical owl (*Strix aluco*) native to Europe, Asia, and N Africa; mottled brown with black eyes and no ear tufts. >> owl

taxation The means by which a government raises money to finance its activities. **Direct taxes** are paid by individuals (eg income tax, national insurance contributions) and companies (eg corporation tax). **Indirect taxes** are those levied on goods and services (eg value-added tax, sales tax). >> capital gains tax; corporation tax; customs and excise; estate duty; excise tax; income tax; inheritance tax; purchase tax; sales tax; tax-haven; turnover tax; VAT

tax-haven A country where tax rates are particularly low. Companies or individuals may choose to reside there to avoid paying high rates of tax in their own home country. The Isle of Man, the Channel Is, and some West Indian countries are current examples. >> taxation

taxis [**tak**sis] A directed movement or orientation reaction of an organism to a stimulus. Taxis is usually used with a prefix to indicate the nature of the stimulus, for example *chemotaxis* (for a chemical stimulus), *phototaxis* (for a light stimulus), and *thermotaxis* (for a temperature stimulus). >> ethology; tropism

taxol A substance which occurs naturally in the bark of the evergreen Pacific yew tree (*Taxus brevifolia*), and which has shown promising activity against certain forms of cancer. It requires the bark of 12 000 trees to produce 2·5 kg of taxol, and strenuous efforts are being made to synthesize it artificially. >> cancer; yew

taxonomy The theory and practice of describing, naming, and classifying organisms. It is divided into *alpha taxonomy*, the description and designation of species typically on the basis of morphological characters; *beta taxonomy*, the arrangement of species into hierarchical systems of higher categories; and *gamma taxonomy*, the study of the evolutionary relationships between groups (*taxa*) and of variation within and between populations. >> binomial nomenclature; morphology (biology); systematics

Tay, River Longest river in Scotland; length 192 km/119 mi; rises on Ben Lui in the Grampians; enters the Firth of Tay. >> Scotland ℹ

Taylor, Elizabeth (Rosemond) (1932–) Film star, born in London. Her films include *Cat on a Hot Tin Roof* (1958), *Butterfield 8* (1960, Oscar), and *Cleopatra* (1962), which provided the background to her well-publicized romance with her co-star Richard Burton, with whom she made several films, including *Who's Afraid of Virginia Woolf?* (1966, Oscar). She has been married eight times, her husbands including the actor Michael Wilding, film producer Michael Todd, and Richard Burton (twice). She received a BAFTA honorary fellowship in 1999. >> Burton, Richard (Jenkins)

Taylor, Zachary (1784–1850) US general, statesman, and 12th president (1849–50), born in Montebello, VA. In the Mexican War (1846–8) he won a major victory at Buena Vista, though heavily outnumbered. The main issue of his presidency was the status of the new territories, and the extension of slavery there. >> Mexican War

Taymyr or **Taimyr, Lake** [tiy**meer**] area 4560 sq km/1760 sq mi. Lake in N Siberian Russia; length, 250 km/155 mi. >> Russia ℹ

Tayside pop (1995e) 401 000; area 7493 sq km/2893 sq mi. Former region in E Scotland, created in 1975 and replaced in 1996 by Angus, Perth and Kinross, and Dundee City councils. >> Scotland ℹ

Tbilisi [tbi**lee**see], formerly **Tiflis** (to 1936) 41°43N 44°48E, pop (1995e) 1 295 000. Capital city of Georgia, on the R Kura; founded, 5th-c; airport; railway junction; university (1918); cathedral (6th–7th-c). >> Georgia (republic) ℹ

Tchad >> **Chad** ℹ

Tchaikovsky or **Tschaikovsky, Piotr Ilyich** [chiy**kofs**-kee] (1840–93) Composer, born in Kamsko-Votkinsk, Russia. Among his greatest works are the ballets *Swan Lake* (1876–7), *The Sleeping Beauty* (1890), and *The Nutcracker* (1892), the last three of his six symphonies, two piano concertos, and several tone poems, notably *Romeo and Juliet* and *Capriccio Italien*.

tea A small evergreen tree (*Camellia sinensis*) growing to c.4 m/13 ft in the wild, but only a small shrub in cultivation; native to Myanmar and Assam, but cultivated in China since early times, with Japan, India, and Sri Lanka now also major producers. The shoot tips with the first two leaves are picked, allowed to wither, then rolled, fermented, and dried; when infused with boiling water they make the well-known beverage containing the stimulants tannin and caffeine. (Family: Theaceae.) >> camellia

Teacher of Righteousness The religious leader and founder of the Qumran community, probably in the mid-2nd-c BC. He was apparently a Zadokite priest who opposed the Hasmoneans, and led his followers into exile near the Dead Sea. >> Qumran, community of; Zadokites

Teagarden, Jack, popular name of **Weldon John Teagarden** (1905–64) Jazz trombonist and singer, born in Vernon, TX. He joined the orchestras of Ben Pollack and Paul Whiteman before leading his own orchestra (1939–46). He was also a member of Louis Armstrong's All Stars (1947–51). >> Armstrong, Louis

teak A large evergreen tree (*Tectona grandis*), growing to 45 m/150 ft, native to S India and SE Asia; flowers small, white, 5-lobed bells. It is a source of high-quality, durable, water-resistant timber. (Family: Verbenaceae.)

teal A small dabbling duck (Genus: *Anas*, 16 species), found worldwide; eats water-weeds and invertebrates. (Subfamily: Anatinae.) >> duck

Teamsters' Union The **International Brotherhood of Teamsters, Chauffeurs, Warehousemen and Helpers of America**, the largest US labour union, with over 1½ million members. >> trade union

teasel A large, stiff, and prickly biennial (*Dipsacus fullonum*), growing to 2 m/6½ ft, native to Europe and the Mediterranean; flowers tiny, white or mauve, in heads the size and shape of an egg. The prickly heads of the cultivated **fuller's teasel** (subspecies *sativus*) were used for raising the nap on cloth (**teasing**). (Family: Dipsacaceae.)

Tebbit (of Chingford), Norman (Beresford) Tebbit, Baron (1931–) British Conservative statesman, born in Enfield, Greater London. He was employment secretary (1981–3), and secretary for trade and industry (1983–5), but his career was interrupted in 1984 when both he and his wife were badly hurt during the IRA bombing of the Grand Hotel at Brighton. In 1985 he became chairman of the party, but following policy disagreements with Mrs Thatcher he retired to the backbenches in 1987. He was made a life peer in 1992. >> Conservative Party; IRA; Thatcher, Margaret

Technicolor The trademark of a colour cinematography process internationally dominant between 1935 and 1955. Shooting involved special three-strip cameras. >> cinematography

technology The use of tools, machines, materials, techniques, and sources of power to make work easier and more productive. Whereas science is concerned with understanding how and why things happen, technology deals with making things happen; it can be subdivided into many specializations, such as medical, military, and nuclear. >> automation; machine i

tectonics The study of the structure of the Earth's crust, particularly such processes as the movement of rocks during folding and faulting. >> Earth i; orogeny; plate tectonics i

Tecumseh [te**kum**suh] (c.1768–1813) American Indian chief of the Shawnees, who joined his brother, 'The Prophet', in a rising against the whites, suppressed in 1811. He commanded the Indian allies in the War of 1812. >> War of 1812

Tedder (of Glenguin), Arthur William Tedder, Baron (1890–1967) Marshal of the Royal Air Force, born in Glenguin, Stirling, Scotland. He became deputy supreme commander of the Allied Expeditionary Force under Eisenhower (1943–5). >> World War 2

Tees, River [teez] River of NE England; rises on Cross Fell, Cumbria and flows 128 km/79 mi to the North Sea; upper river valley known as **Teesdale**. >> Teesside; Tyne, River

Teesside Urban area surrounding the R Tees estuary in NE England; includes Stockton-on-Tees, Redcar, Thornaby, Middlesbrough. >> Tees, River

teeth Small, bone-like structures of the jaws used for the biting and chewing of food. Each tooth consists of a core of *pulp* surrounded by *dentine*, which is covered in its upper part by enamel and in its lower part by cement (the *root*). The *crown* is the enamel-covered part that projects beyond the gums; it may have one or more projections called *cusps*. In many mammals, different types of teeth can be identified: *incisors* for cutting, *canines* for cutting and tearing, and *premolars* and *molars* for grinding. In humans the first set of teeth (*deciduous* or *milk* teeth) usually appears between 6 and 24 months of age, there being 20 deciduous teeth in all (2 incisors, 1 canine, and 2 molars in each half-jaw). These gradually become replaced (from about age 6) by the *permanent* teeth, with the addition of 3 more teeth in each half-jaw giving a total complement of 32. The third molar is often referred to as the *wisdom tooth*, because of its time of eruption. Not all of the teeth may appear. >> caries; dentistry; fluoridation of water; gums; jaw; *see panel below*

tefillin [tef**ileen**] Jewish phylacteries or frontlets, consisting of two black leather cubes with leather straps, bound over the head and arm, and worn during Jewish morning prayers, except on sabbaths and festivals. The cubes contain scriptural texts. >> Judaism

Tegucigalpa [taygoosi**galpa**] 14°05N 87°14W, pop (1995e) 736 000. Capital city of Honduras; founded, 1524; altitude 975 m/3200 ft; capital, 1880; airport; university (1847); cathedral (18th-c); devastated by hurricane Mitch in 1998. >> Honduras i

Tehran or **Teheran** [tair**ahn**] 35°44N 51°30E, pop (1995e) 7 883 000. Capital city of Iran; altitude 1 200–1700 m/

The approximate times of eruption and shedding of the various teeth in humans

	Eruption	Shed
Milk		
incisor 1	6 months	6–7 years
incisor 2	8 months	7–8 years
canine 1	18 months	10–12 years
molar 1	1 year	9–11 years
molar 2	2 years	10–12 years
Permanent		
incisor 1	7–8 years	
incisor 2	8–9 years	
canine 1	10–12 years	
premolar 1	10–11 years	
premolar 2	11–12 years	
molar 1	6–7 years	
molar 2	12 years	
molar 3	17–21 years	

Note: the lower teeth usually appear before the upper equivalent teeth.

4000–5500 ft; capital of Persia, 1788; airport; road and rail junction; six universities (oldest, 1935); Shahyad Tower, symbol of modern Iran. >> Iran ℹ

Tehran Conference [tair**ahn**] The first inter-allied conference of World War 2, attended by Stalin, Roosevelt, and Churchill, held at Tehran in 1943. >> Churchill, Winston; Roosevelt, Franklin D; Stalin; Tehran; World War 2

Teilhard de Chardin, Pierre [**tay**ah duh **shah(r)**dĩ] (1881–1955) Geologist, palaeontologist, Jesuit priest, and philosopher, born in Sarcenat, France. His unorthodox ideas led to a Church ban on his teaching and publishing. His major work, *Le Phénomène humain* (written 1938–40, The Phenomenon of Man) was posthumously published; it argues that humanity is in a continuous process of evolution towards a perfect spiritual state. >> Jesuits

Te Kanawa, Dame Kiri [tay **kah**nawa] (1944–) Operatic soprano, born in Gisborne, New Zealand. She made her debut with the Royal Opera Company in 1970, and has since taken a wide range of leading roles. In 1981 she sang at the wedding of the Prince and Princess of Wales.

tektite A rounded, flat, and glassy meteorite ranging in diameter from submillimetre size up to c.10 cm/4 in. >> meteorite

Tel Aviv–Yafo 32°05N 34°46E, pop (1995e) 407 000. Twin cities in W Israel, a commercial port on the Mediterranean Sea; Tel Aviv founded in 1909 as a garden suburb of Yafo (Jaffa), today an artists' centre; former capital (to 1950) of Israel; airport; railway; two universities (1953, 1974). >> Israel ℹ

telebanking A system which enables banking transactions to be carried out via a communications network. This is usually through a viewdata system or an interactive computer link. >> teleshopping; viewdata

telecine [**tel**eesinee] Equipment for converting motion picture film to video for broadcast television or videotape recording. Developments in digital scanning allow special effects to be introduced during transfer. >> telerecording

telecommunications The transmission of data-carrying signals, often between two widely separated points; it includes radio, telegraphy, telephones, television, and computer networks. Telecommunications in the modern sense began in the 19th-c: the Great Western Railway telegraph lines from Paddington to Slough, England, opened in 1843; telephones for commercial use were installed in Boston and Cambridge, MA, in 1877; radio telegraphy became a commercial success after Marconi founded the Wireless, Telegraph and Signal Co in London in 1897. During the 20th-c, first radio (from the 1920s) and then television (from the 1950s) became important for communication over distance. In 1962 the US Telstar 1 satellite was launched to relay communications signals, and large numbers of *geostationary* satellites now provide day-long international links for telephony and television transmissions. The use of optical fibre links in telephone cables enables hundreds of simultaneous conversations to be transmitted. >> Marconi; mobile communications; optical fibres ℹ; radio; satellite; telegraphy; telephone; television

teleconferencing The connection of several locations by television links to provide continuous intercommunication of sound and sight. In some applications, the picture is presented as a rapidly changing series of stills, rather than in continuous motion, in order to reduce the bandwidth required in transmission. >> television

telegraphy Communication at a distance of written, printed, or pictorial matter, by the transmission of electrical signals along wires. Modern examples of this are telex and fax. In **radiotelegraphy** the message is carried by radio waves rather than along a wire. >> fax; radio; telecommunications; telex

telekinesis >> **psychokinesis**

Tel el-Amarna [**tel** el a**mah(r)**na] The ancient Akhetaten ('the horizon of Aten'), a short-lived Egyptian city on the E bank of the R Nile, founded c.1350 BC by the heretic pharoah Akhenaton and demolished after his death. >> Akhenaton

Telemachus [te**le**makus] In the *Odyssey*, the son of Odysseus and Penelope. He sets out to find his father, and helps Odysseus fight Penelope's suitors. >> Odysseus

Telemann, Georg Philipp [**tay**leman] (1681–1767) Composer, born in Magdeburg, Germany. A prolific composer, his works include church music, 46 passions, over 40 operas, oratorios, many songs, and instrumental music.

telemarketing A marketing system which uses the telephone, handling responses to advertisements which carry telephone numbers. It also involves making calls to prospective clients on behalf of marketing outlets. >> telephone

teleology A view which maintains that some phenomena can be explained fully only by citing the functions they perform ('a function of the liver is to secrete bile') or the purposes for which the activity was undertaken ('Iago lied in order to provoke Othello').

teleost [**tel**iost, **tee**liost] Any of a large group of ray-finned fishes (Actinopterygii) in which the tail is symmetrical, without an upturned body axis; comprises the great majority of extant species of true bony fishes. >> bony fish; fish ℹ

telephone A device for transmitting speech sounds over a distance. In 1876 Alexander Graham Bell was granted a patent to develop such an instrument, and his induction receiver, along with Thomas Edison's carbon transmitter, form the basis of the modern telephone. In the mouthpiece, a carbon microphone translates sound vibrations into a varied electric current which is relayed through wires to the receiver, where it is converted back into sound waves by a diaphragm and an electromagnet. Amplifiers (repeaters) placed at intervals along a line make long-distance telephoning possible. Modern telephone instruments are largely electronic, with keypads replacing dials, and the addition of such 'smart' features as last-number recall. Developments of the 1990s include the growth in use of cordless telephones, the worldwide introduction of mobile phones, and the first digital videophones. >> Bell, Alexander Graham; Edison; loudspeaker ℹ; microphone ℹ; telecommunications

telephoto lens A camera lens of long focal length but comparatively short overall dimensions, giving increased magnification for a limited angle of view. In 35 mm still cameras, focal lengths of 100–300 mm are usual, but for special purposes such as news work, sports and natural history 500–1000 mm may be employed. >> camera; lens

telerecording The transfer of a video programme to motion picture film. Since the interval between successive video frames is very short, a film camera with extremely rapid movement from one frame to the next is essential. >> cinematography; telecine; video

telescope An optical instrument for producing magnified images of distant objects. The earliest devices were made c.1608 by Lippershey and Galileo. **Refracting telescopes** use a lens to bring light rays to a focus, a technique first applied to astronomy by Galileo. **Reflecting telescopes** use a mirror to bring the light rays to a focus, a technique first applied to astronomy by Newton. The largest telescopes today are all reflectors. For special purposes, such as photography, there may be a combination of mirror and lens, as in the Schmidt camera. **Radio telescopes** collect and analyze cosmic radio emission from celestial sources. The basic type consists of a steerable, paraboloidal collecting dish with a central detector connected to amplifiers. Telescopes for other types of radiation (eg infrared, ultraviolet, X-rays) are also used, sometimes above the Earth's atmosphere. >> altazimuth; binoculars; coelostat; electromagnetic radiation [i]; Galileo; Herschel; Newton, Isaac; Very Large Array; Australia / Cassegrain / Hubble Space Telescope

Telescopium [tele**skohp**ium] (Lat 'telescope') A small, faint S constellation delineated by Lacaille in honour of the astronomical telescope. >> constellation; Lacaille

teleshopping A system for shopping from home, using a communications network such as a public videotex system; also called **on-line shopping**. A list of food and goods available to the shopper is displayed on the television screen, and these can be ordered directly over the communications link. >> telebanking

Telesto [te**les**toh] The 13th natural satellite of Saturn, discovered in 1980; distance from the planet 295 000 km/ 183 000 mi; diameter 30 km/19 mi. >> Saturn (astronomy); RR964

Teletex A service, provided by a posts, telegraph and telephones authority, which offers computer-based facilities such as electronic mail to a subscriber. >> electronic mail

teletext An information service of alpha-numerical data and simple diagrams transmitted as individual pages in digitally coded form during a TV broadcast signal. The constantly updated results, typically news headlines, football scores, weather maps, etc, can be displayed on any domestic receiver equipped with a decoder and page-selection keyboard. In the UK, the services Ceefax (BBC) and Oracle (IBA) were introduced in the 1970s. >> Ceefax; field; Oracle; television; viewdata

teletype A rather old form of keyboard printer-based terminal used for linking into a computer. Teletypes were slow and unreliable, and have been replaced almost everywhere by a combination of visual display unit and (where hard copy is required) attached printer. >> computer terminal; visual display unit

television The transmission and reproduction of moving pictures and associated sound by electronic means; developed in the late 19th-c and early 20th-c, with the first pictures presented by Baird in 1926. The image of a scene in a TV camera is analyzed by scanning along a series of horizontal lines, the variations of brightness along each line being converted into a train of electrical signals for transmission or recording. At the receiver the picture is reconstituted on the fluorescent screen of a cathode- ray tube by an electron beam scanning a precisely similar pattern. The number of scanning lines and the picture frequency vary in different systems, the American standard having 525 lines with 30 pictures per second (pps) and the European 625 lines at 25 pps. >> Baird; cable / high-definition / satellite television; camera; eidophor

television camera >> **camera**

telex An international telegraphic system in which telephone lines transmit printed messages, using devices which convert typed words into electrical signals and vice versa (*teleprinters*); the name is an acronym of 'teletypewriter exchange service'. Subscribers to the system have their own call sign and number. The system is relatively cheap, and has been much used by commercial organizations, but has largely been overtaken by fax and e-mail. >> e-mail; fax; telecommunications; telegraphy

Telford 52°42N 2°28W. A new town in Shropshire, WC England, designated in 1963, comprising three previous urban areas: **Telford Dawley**, pop (1995e) 30 300; **Telford North**, pop (1995e) 56 100; **Telford South**, pop (1995e) 24 600; on the R Severn; railway. >> Shropshire

Telford, Thomas (1757–1834) Engineer, born near

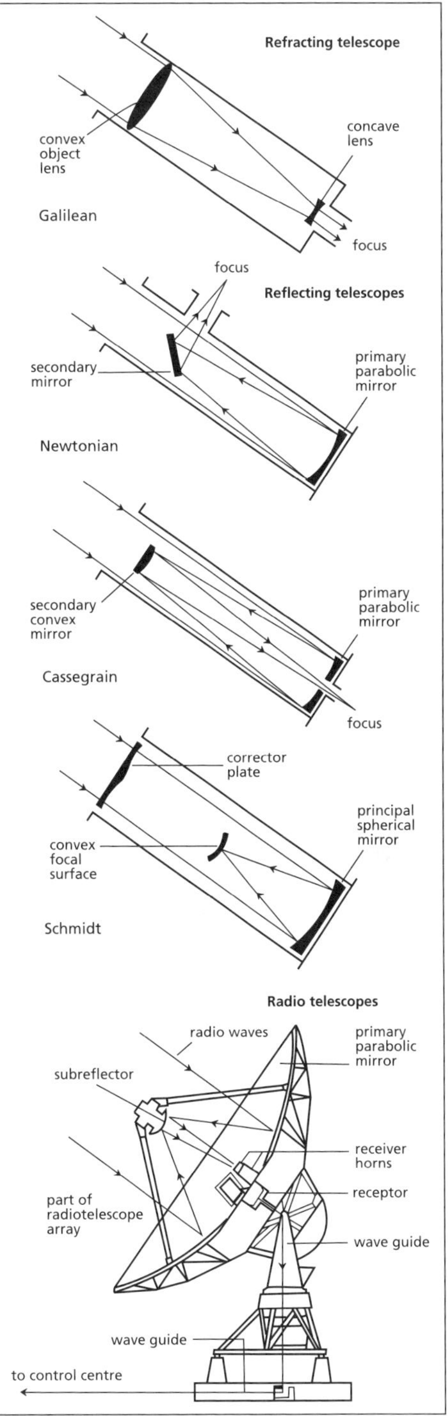

Telescope – section through five types

Langholm, Dumfries and Galloway. His works include the Ellesmere (1793–1805) and Caledonian (1803–23) canals, and the road from London to Holyhead, with the Menai Suspension Bridge (1826). >> civil engineering

tell An Arabic 'mound' or 'hill', in archaeological usage, an artificial mound formed through the long-term accumulation of mud brick from houses successively levelled and rebuilt. >> Çatal Hüyük; Jericho

Tell, Wilhelm, Eng **William Tell** (13th–14th-c) Legendary Swiss patriot and crossbow marksman of Bürglen in Uri. According to tradition, he was compelled by the tyrannical Austrian governor to shoot an apple off his own son's head from a distance of 80 paces. Later, Tell slew the tyrant, and so initiated the movement which secured the independence of Switzerland. >> Switzerland 🛈

Tellus >> **Gaea**

Telugu [**tel**uhgoo] The Dravidian language associated particularly with the state of Andhra Pradesh in S India. It has some 73 million speakers. >> Dravidian languages

Tempe [**tem**pee] 33°25N 111°56W, pop (1995e) 159 000. Health resort in SC Arizona, USA; settled, 1872; railway; university (1885). >> Arizona

tempera [**tem**pera] A method of painting with powdered pigment mixed with egg-yolk and water, usually on specially prepared wooden panels. This technique was normal in the Middle Ages. >> paint

temperance movement A response to the social evils caused by the alcoholism so widespread in the 18th-c and 19th-c. Temperance societies were organized first in the USA, then in Britain and Scandinavia. >> prohibition

temperature Measurement related to heat flow between objects. It is measured using thermometers, thermocouples, and pyrometers, and is controlled using thermostats. The Kelvin temperature scale is used in physics (an SI unit), fixed by the triple point of water, 273·16 K. Other temperature scales include the Celsius (°C), also called Centigrade, Fahrenheit (°F) and Rankine (°R). >> pyrometer; Réaumur; thermocouple; thermometer; RR1033

Templars The Poor Knights of Christ and of the Temple of Solomon; an international religious-military order, whose members were subject to monastic vows. The order was founded c.1120 chiefly to protect pilgrims to the Holy Land; its name derives from the location of its headquarters – near the site of the Jewish Temple in Jerusalem. It developed into a great army, and was suppressed by Pope Clement V in 1312. >> Crusades 🛈

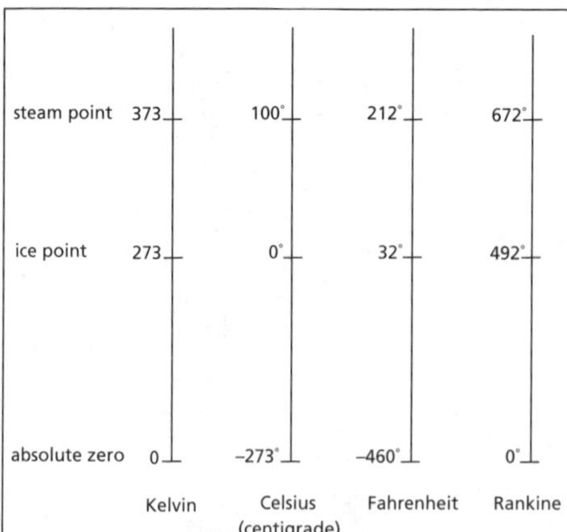

Temperature scales

Temple, Shirley, married name **Black** (1928–) Child film star, born in Santa Monica, CA. During 1934–8 she appeared in more than 20 feature films, such as *Stand Up and Cheer* (1934) and *Bright Eyes* (1934), and was consistently the top US movie star. In her married status as **Mrs S T Black** she entered politics, and was US Ambassador to Ghana (1974–6), and Czechoslovakia (1989–93).

Temple, Sir William (1628–99) Diplomat and essayist, born in London. He negotiated the Triple Alliance (1668) against France, and helped to bring about the marriage of the Prince of Orange to the Princess Mary. His essay style was a major influence on 18th-c writers, including Swift, who was his secretary. >> Swift; William III

Temple, William (1881–1944) Anglican churchman, born in Exeter, Devon. He became Archbishop of York (1929–42) and Archbishop of Canterbury (1942–4). An outspoken advocate of social and Church reform, he was a leader in the ecumenical movement. >> Church of England; ecumenism

Temple A group of buildings, including the 12th-c Temple church, in Fleet St, London. They were established on land once owned by the Knights Templar. >> Inns of Court; London; Templars

Temple, Jerusalem The central shrine of Jewish worship and its priesthood since its establishment under Solomon. It was first destroyed by Nebuchadnezzar in c.587 BC, but rebuilt later in the 6th-c BC after the return from exile. Extended on an elaborate scale by Herod the Great, beginning c.20 BC, it was barely renewed before its destruction under Titus during the Jewish revolt of AD 70. Still unrestored today, its site is now partly occupied by the Muslim mosque, the Dome of the Rock, built in the late 7th-c. >> Herod the Great; Holy of Holies; Judaism; Solomon (Hebrew Bible); Tabernacle

Temple Bar A site at the junction of the Strand and Fleet St, London, where from 1301 a gateway marked the boundary of the Cities of London and Westminster. It is now marked by a statue of a griffin. >> London

Temple of Heaven A group of buildings in Beijing, in which the emperors formerly conducted their devotions. The complex was laid out in 1406–20. >> Beijing

Temple of the Tooth The Dalada Maligawa, an important Buddhist pilgrimage site in Kandy, Sri Lanka. The shrine was built to house one of the Buddha's teeth. >> Buddha; Kandy

Templeton, Sir John Marks (1912–) Businessman and philanthropist, born in Winchester, TN. He started on Wall Street in 1937, and went on to found several major investment funds. He is widely known for the establishment in 1972 of the Templeton Prize for Progress in Religion. >> Templeton Prize

Templeton Prize A prize for progress in religion, created in 1972, and awarded annually by the Templeton Foundation, New York City. It is the world's largest money award, whose total passed $1 million dollars for the first time in 1992. Its aim is to increase sensitivity to the diversity of religious thought and work. >> Templeton; RR1042

tempura [tem**pu**ra] Japanese fritters, probably originating with the Portuguese in 16th-c Japan. They are served crisp, with diluted soy sauce mixed with grated radish to balance the oil.

tench Freshwater fish (*Tinca tinca*) native to slow rivers and lakes of Europe and W Asia, but now more widespread; length up to 60 cm/2 ft; body stout, fins rounded; mouth with pair of thin barbels; dark green to brown. (Family: Cyprinidae.)

Ten Commandments or **Decalogue** The fundamental laws of the Jews; in the Bible, said to have been given to

Moses on Mt Sinai. One tradition declares that God inscribed them on two tablets of stone which were then deposited in the Ark of the Covenant (*Deut* 9). The well-known 'ethical' decalogue contains the commands: (1) the God of Israel shall be acknowledged as one and unique, (2) worship of images is prohibited, (3) misuse of the Lord's name is prohibited, (4) the Sabbath must be observed, (5) one's parents must be honoured, (6–10) murder, adultery, theft, false testimony, and coveting one's neighbour's goods are prohibited. >> Ark of the Covenant; covenant; God; Sinai, Mount; Torah

tendon An extremely strong fibrous cord or sheet of connective tissue (bundles of collagen fibres), continuously attaching muscle to bone or cartilage. >> bone; cartilage; muscle [i]; synovitis

tendril An organ with which climbing plants attach themselves to supports; most coil around the support but some end in sticky, sucker-like pads. >> climbing plant; sucker

Tenerife >> **Canary Islands**

Teng Hsiao-p'ing >> **Deng Xiaoping**

Teniers, David [te**neerz**], known as **the Elder** (1582–1649) Baroque genre painter, born in Antwerp, Belgium. His son, **David Teniers the Younger** (1610–90), executed c.700 paintings, and is best known for his scenes of peasant life, in the tradition of Brueghel. >> Baroque (art and architecture); genre painting

Ten Lost Tribes of Israel Ten tribes of Israel taken captive by Assyria in 721 BC and merged (hence 'lost') with the Assyrians. >> Israel, tribes of

Tennant Creek 19°31S 134°15E, pop (1995e) 3680. Town in Northern Territory, Australia; airfield; an important gold mining centre since the 1930s. >> Northern Territory

Tennessee pop (1995e) 5 254 000; area 109 149 sq km/ 42 144 sq mi. State in SEC USA; the 'Volunteer State'; ceded by France, 1763; explored by Daniel Boone, 1769; temporary state of Franklin formed in 1784, after the War of Independence; Federal government created the Territory South of the Ohio, 1790; admitted as the 16th state to the Union, 1796; seceded, 1861; the scene of many battles during the Civil War; slavery abolished, 1865; re-admitted to the Union, 1866; highest point, Clingmans Dome (2025 m/6644 ft); in the E lie the Great Smoky Mts, Cumberland Plateau; fertile 'bluegrass' country in the C, ideal for livestock and dairy farming; in the W is a rich floodplain where most of the state's cotton is grown; capital, Nashville; nation's largest producer of zinc and pyrites. >> American Civil War; Boone; Nashville–Davidson; United States of America [i]; RR994

Tennessee River River in SE USA; formed by the confluence of the French Broad and Holston Rivers; joins the Ohio R at Paducah; length (including the French Broad) 1398 km/869 mi; used for irrigation, flood-control, and hydroelectric power (the Tennessee Valley Authority, 1933). >> United States of America [i]

Tenniel, Sir John [te**neel**] (1820–1914) Artist, born in London. He became known as a book illustrator, notably in his work for *Alice's Adventures in Wonderland* (1865) and *Through the Looking-glass* (1872). >> Carroll

tennis A racket-and-ball game for two or four players developed from real tennis. It is played on a rectangular court measuring 78 ft (23.77 m) long by 27 ft (8.23 m) wide for singles, or 36 ft (10.97 m) wide for doubles. A net 3 ft (0.9 m) high at the centre is stretched across the width of the court. Playing surface varies, and can be grass, clay, shale, concrete, wood, or other suitable artificial materials. >> Davis Cup; platform tennis; real tennis; Wightman Cup; RR1063

tennis elbow Pain in the external aspect of the elbow following repetitive trauma, such as may occur in playing tennis. It may possibly result from small tears in the muscles in the region. >> elbow

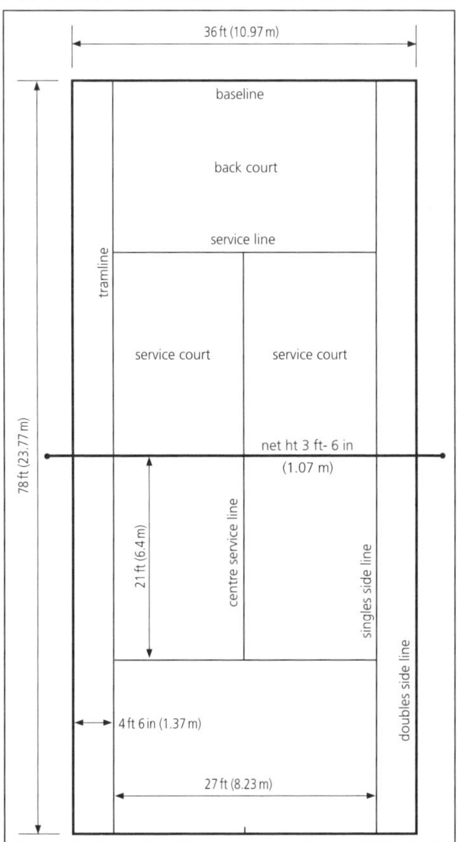

Tennis court – dimensions

Tennyson, Alfred Tennyson, Baron [**te**nison], known as **Alfred, Lord Tennyson** (1809–92) Poet, born in Somersby, Lincolnshire. His major poetic achievement was the elegy mourning the death of his friend, Arthur Hallam, *In Memoriam* (1850); and in the same year he succeeded Wordsworth as poet laureate. In 1859–85 he published a series of poems on the Arthurian theme, *Idylls of the King* (1859). >> Wordsworth, William

Tenochtitlan [te**nok**titlahn] The island capital of L Texcoco, now beneath Mexico City, from which the Aztecs dominated Mexico from c.1344–5 to the Spanish Conquest in 1519. >> Aztecs

ten-pin bowling >> **bowling**

tenrec [**ten**rek] A mammal of family Tenrecidae (31 species), native to Madagascar; an insectivore; species can resemble hedgehogs, moonrats (but lack tails), shrews, or moles. >> insectivore

tensile strength The stretching stress at which a material breaks; symbol σ, units Pa (pascal). >> fracture (physics)

Ten Years' War The name usually given to the unsuccessful Cuban insurrection against Spanish colonial rule. >> Cuba [i]; Spain [i]

Tenzing Norgay, known as **Sherpa Tenzing** (1914–86) Mountaineer, born in Tsa-chu near Makalu, Nepal. In 1953 he succeeded in reaching the Everest summit with

Edmund Hillary, for which he was awarded the George Medal. >> Everest, Mount; Hillary

Teotihuacán [tayo**tee**wakahn] A great city, 30 km/20 mi NE of Mexico City, flourishing c.450–650, but destroyed and burnt in c.700; a world heritage site. >> Mexico [i]

tepal >> **perianth**

teratorn A condor-like vulture with a wingspan exceeding 4 m/13 ft; the largest flying bird ever to have lived, now extinct; known from Pleistocene fossils. (Genus: *Teratornia*.) >> Pleistocene epoch; vulture

Terborch or **Terburg, Gerard** [ter**baw(r)kh**] (1617–81) Painter, born in Zwolle, The Netherlands. He worked mostly on a small scale, producing genre pictures and fashionable portraits, but is best known for his painting of 'The Peace of Munster' (1648, National Gallery, London). >> genre painting

Terbrugghen, Hendrik [tair**brook**hen] (c.1588–1629) Painter, born in Deventer, The Netherlands. He excelled in chiaroscuro effects, and in the faithful representation of physiognomical details and drapery, as in his 'Jacob and Laban' (1627, National Gallery, London). >> chiaroscuro

terebinth >> **turpentine tree**

Terence, in full **Publius Terentius Afer** (c.190–159 BC) Latin comic poet, born in Carthage, N Africa. His surviving six comedies are Greek in origin and scene, directly based on Menander. Many of his conventions were later used by European dramatists. >> Menander

Terengganu [tereng**gah**noo] pop (1995e) 847 000; area 12 928 sq km/4990 sq mi. State in NE Peninsular Malaysia; ceded to Britain, 1909; capital, Kuala Terengganu. >> Malaysia [i]

Teresa of Ávila, St (1515–82) Saint and mystic, born in Ávila, Spain. Famous for her ascetic religious exercises and sanctity, in 1562 she re-established the ancient Carmelite rule, with additional observances. She was canonized in 1622; feast day 15 October. >> Carmelites

Teresa (of Calcutta), Mother, originally **Agnes Gonxha Bojaxhiu** (1910–97) Christian missionary in India, born in Skopje, Former Yugoslav Republic of Macedonia. Her sisterhood, the Missionaries of Charity, started in 1950, and in 1957 she started work with lepers and in many disaster areas of the world. She was awarded the Pope John XXIII Peace Prize in 1971, and the Nobel Peace Prize in 1979.

Teresa of Lisieux >> **Theresa of Lisieux**

Tereshkova, Valentina [te**resh**kova] (1937–) Cosmonaut and the first woman to fly in space, born in Maslennikovo, Russia. She was a solo crew member of the 3-day Vostok 6 flight launched on 16 June 1963. >> cosmonaut; Soviet space programme; Vostok

Terfel, Bryn [**ter**vel, brin], originally **Bryn Terfel Jones** (1965–) Bass baritone, born in Pant-glas, Caernarfonshire, Wales. He became known after winning the Lieder Prize in the Cardiff Singer of the World competition in 1989. In 1993 he received the Newcomer of the Year International Classic Music Award, and has since appeared at many of the world's leading opera houses.

Terkel, Studs, popular name of **Louis Terkel** (1912–) Writer and oral historian, born in New York City. He became a radio commentator and television host, and travelled worldwide conducting interviews with the famous and the anonymous. His publications include *The Good War: an Oral History of World War Two* (1984, Pulitzer).

Terme [**tair**may] The national museum of Rome, containing one of the world's most important collections of Greek and Roman art. It is housed in the ancient Diocletian Baths.

terminal >> **computer terminal**

Terminus The Roman god of boundary marks, where his statue or bust was sometimes placed. His festival (**Terminalia**) was on 23 February.

termite A small, social insect that constructs nests in rotten wood or makes earth mounds which may measure several metres across; workers mostly sterile, blind, and with soft white cuticle (known as **white ants**); adults winged; c.2000 species, causing great economic problems in the tropics, damaging timber buildings and crops. (Order: Isoptera.) >> ant; insect [i]

tern A small, gull-like seabird, found worldwide; plumage usually pale with black cap and forked tail; head with partly erectile crest (**crested tern**) or smooth. (Family: Laridae, 42 species; some authors put the tern in a separate family, Sternidae.) >> Arctic tern; gull; skimmer

terpene A class of natural products, also known as **essential oils**, based upon the oligomerization of isoprene, having formulae closely related to $(C_5H_8)_n$. Common examples are pinene, limonene, menthol, and carotene. >> essential oils; isoprene; oligomer

Terpsichore [terp**si**kawree] In Greek mythology, one of the Muses, usually associated with dancing or lyric poetry. >> Muses

terracotta Clay, modelled into sculpture or tiles and fired in a kiln, becoming hard and brittle but very permanent. Examples survive from ancient times and from all over the world. >> sculpture; Xian

Terracotta Army >> **Mount Li** [i]

terrapin [**te**rapin] A reptile of the family Emydidae, found in fresh or brackish water or on land; also known as **pond turtle**. (Order: Chelonia.) >> Chelonia [i]; reptile

terrier A small hardy domestic dog, bred for hunting (especially foxes); originally sent into burrows after prey; traditionally aggressive, tenacious, fearless; many modern breeds. >> Airedale / Border / Boston / bull / fox / Irish / Lakeland / Scottish / Sealyham / Staffordshire bull / Yorkshire terrier; Dandie Dinmont; dog; Jack Russell; schnauzer; sporting dog

Territorial Army, in full **Territorial and Voluntary Reserve Army (TAVRA)** A British reserve military force, first formed in 1908, each battalion being attached to a battalion of the regular army. The 'Terriers' (known as the Territorial Force to 1920, the Territorials thereafter) fought with distinction in the two world wars. They receive continuous training on a part-time basis. The **Voluntary Reserve** consists of ex-regular soldiers who commit themselves to reserve service for a fixed period. >> militia

territory In US history, political status prior to the attainment of statehood. Hawaii and Alaska were the last two places to have territorial status. >> Ordinance of 1787

terrorism Coercive and violent behaviour undertaken to achieve or promote a particular political objective or cause, often involving the overthrow of established order. Terrorist activity is designed to induce fear through its indiscriminate, arbitrary, and unpredictable acts of violence. It may be 'official', as under Stalin, or 'unofficial', as employed by various opposition or underground movements. Such movements are usually minority groups who feel there are no other means available to them of achieving their objectives. Terrorism may have an international dimension, manifest in hijackings and hostage-taking. >> Baader-Meinhof; IRA; PLO; Red Brigades

Terry, Dame (Alice) Ellen (1847–1928) Actress, born in Coventry, West Midlands, a member of a large family of actors. She became the leading Shakespearean actress in London, dominating the English and US theatre (1878–1902) in partnership with Henry Irving. In 1903 she went into theatre management. >> Irving

Terry-Thomas, originally **Thomas Terry Hoar Stevens** (1911–90) Film actor, born in Finchley, Greater London. He was the gap-toothed villain in dozens of post-World War 2 comedies, satirizing and eventually personifying the upper-class bounder in such films as *I'm All Right Jack* (1959) and *School for Scoundrels* (1960).

Tertiaries Members of the Third Order of religious life. Normally, these are lay people striving after Christian perfection in life in the world under the guidance of a religious Order. A **Regular Tertiary** is a member of a community bound by vows. >> Christianity; Orders, Holy; monasticism

tertiary education Post-secondary education. It is often used to refer to further and higher education, but in the UK it can also refer to attendance at a **tertiary college**, which is a college for all those over 16 wishing to pursue academic or vocational courses. >> further education

Tertiary period The earlier of the two geological periods of the Cenozoic era, extending from c.65 to 2 million years ago. It is divided into five epochs: the Palaeocene, Eocene, Oligocene, Miocene, and Pliocene. >> Cenozoic era; geological time scale; orogeny; RR970

Tertullian [ter**tul**ian], in full **Quintus Septimus Florens Tertullianus** (c.160–220) Christian theologian, born in Carthage. His opposition to worldliness in the Church culminated in his becoming a leader of the Montanist sect (c.207). He was the first to produce major Christian works in Latin. >> Christianity; Montanism

Tesla, Nikola [**tes**la] (1856–1943) Inventor, born in Smiljan, Croatia. His inventions included improved dynamos, transformers, and the high-frequency coil which now bears his name. >> magnetic flux; tesla

tesla SI unit of magnetic flux density; symbol *T*; defined as a magnetic flux of 1 weber per square metre; named after US inventor Nikola Tesla. >> magnetic flux; Tesla

tessera >> **mosaic**

tessitura [tessi**too**ra] That part of a vocal compass in which the most demanding passages in a piece of music are concentrated. An aria, operatic role, etc may be said to demand a high tessitura.

Test Act A British Act passed in 1673 by a parliament anxious to curb Catholic influence at Charles II's court. Every office holder had to take Oaths of Supremacy and Allegiance, and to take Communion according to the rites of the Church of England. The Act remained in force until 1828. >> Catholic Emancipation; Charles II (of England); Church of England

testis (plural **testes**) The essential reproductive gland (*gonad*) of male animals, producing spermatozoa; also known as the **testicle**. In vertebrates the testis also synthesizes and secretes sex hormones (*androgens*). In mammals (eg humans), there are usually two, lying suspended within the scrotum, oval and flattened in shape. >> androgens; castration; gonad; penis [i]; scrotum

testosterone [tes**tos**terohn] The male sex hormone, produced in the testes, and responsible for the development of the primary sex organs, secondary sex characteristics (eg facial hair), and sexual behaviour. >> hormones; testis

test-tube baby The lay term to indicate *in vitro* fertilization and embryo replacement (**IVF**). Infertile women are given drugs that stimulate ovulation. Several ova are then retrieved from the surface of the ovaries by a technique known as *laparoscopy* and placed in a suitable culture medium to which spermatozoa are added. The fertilized egg (4–8 cells in size) is transferred to the uterus via the vagina and cervix. Successful pregnancy occurs in about 10–20% of cases. >> infertility; pregnancy [i]; uterine tubes

tetanus [**te**tanuhs] A disease resulting from infection with *Clostridium tetani*, which exists in the soil and in the gut of humans and other animals; also known as **lockjaw**. Infection enters the body through wounds in the skin caused by a nail or splinter. The bacteria produce a toxin which affects motor nerve cells in the spinal cord, and induces convulsions and muscle spasms. The disease can be prevented by active vaccination. >> nervous system; penicillin

Tethys [**tee**this] The third natural satellite of Saturn, discovered in 1684; distance from the planet 295 000 km/ 183 000 mi; diameter 1050 km/650 mi; orbital period 1·888 days. >> Saturn (astronomy); RR964

Tétouan or **Tetuán** [tay**twahn**] 35°34N 5°22W, pop (1995e) 267 000. City in NE Morocco; settled by Moorish exiles from Spain, 15th-c; captured by Spanish, 1860; airfield; Medina a world heritage site. >> Morocco [i]

tetra Any of many small colourful freshwater fish (family Characidae), from South and Central America; length typically 3–10 cm/1¼ in.

tetracyclines [tetra**siy**klinz] A class of antibiotics obtained from *Streptomyces*, a genus of organisms intermediate between bacteria and fungi, active against a broad spectrum of infections. The first was produced in 1948. >> antibiotics

tetraethyl lead $Pb(C_2H_5)_4$. An organometallic compound made by the reaction of lead chloride with a Grignard reagent, used as an additive to petrol to control 'knocking'. Its hazardous properties are leading to its progressive disuse. >> Grignard; knocking; lead; petrol

Tetragrammaton >> **Yahweh**

Teutonic Knights Members of the Order of St Mary of the Germans, a religious-military order founded c.1190 and inspired by crusading ideals. By the 14th-c they controlled the E Baltic lands of the Livonian Knights, Prussia, and E Pomerania. >> Crusades [i]; Prussia

tex >> **count** (textiles)

Texas pop (1995e) 18 709 000; area 691 003 sq km/ 266 807 sq mi. State in SW USA; the 'Lone Star State'; second largest state in the USA; first settled by the Spanish in the late 1600s; first American settlement, 1821; declared independence, defeated by Santa Anna at the Alamo, 1836; Mexican army then defeated by Sam Houston at San Jacinto, 1836; independence of Texas recognized; admitted to the Union as the 28th state, 1845; US–Mexican War, 1846–8; joined the Confederate states in the Civil War; readmitted to the Union, 1870; discovery of extensive oil deposits (1901) transformed the economy; Rio Grande forms the state's entire international border with Mexico; highest point, Guadalupe Peak (2667 m/8750 ft); Gulf coastal plains around Houston heavily industrialized; SC plains and Edwards Plateau have vast wheat and cotton farms and cattle ranches; capital, Austin; nation's leading producer of oil and natural gas; large Spanish-speaking population. >> Alamo; Austin; Dallas; Houston; Mexican War; United States of America [i]; RR994

Thackeray, William Makepeace (1811–63) Novelist, born in Calcutta. His major novels were *Vanity Fair* (1847–8), *Pendennis* (1848), *Henry Esmond* (1852), and *The Newcomes* (1853–5), several published as monthly serials.

Thaddeus, St >> **Jude, St**

Thai [tiy] The official language of Thailand, spoken by c.30 million people. There is written evidence of the language from the 13th-c. >> Thailand [i]

Thailand [**tiy**land], Thai **Muang Thai**, formerly **Siam**, official name **Kingdom of Thailand** pop (1995e) 60 100 000; area 513 115 sq km/198 062 sq mi. Kingdom in SE Asia; capital, Bangkok; timezone GMT +7; ethnic groups include Thai (75%), Chinese (14%); chief religion, Buddhism; official language, Thai; unit of currency, the baht; C agricultural region dominated by the floodplain of the Chao Praya R; NE plateau rises above 300 m/1000 ft and covers a third of the country; mountainous N region rising to 2595 m/8514 ft at Doi Inthanon; covered in tropical rainforest; equatorial climate in the S; tropical monsoon

climate in the N and C; evidence of Bronze Age communities, 4000 BC; Thai nation founded, 13th-c; occupied by the Japanese in World War 2; king is head of state; governed by a prime minister and bicameral National Assembly; military coup, 1991; new constitution, 1991, and general election, 1992, followed by political unrest and constitutional amendments; agriculture is the most important economic activity; tin (world's third largest supplier), tungsten (world's second largest supplier). >> Bangkok; Thai; RR1024 political leaders

thalamus >> **diencephalon**

thalassaemia / thalassemia [thala**seem**ia] An inherited disease of the blood in which there is impaired formation of normal haemoglobin-A, with resulting anaemia. It occurs in SE Asia and in the Mediterranean area. >> anaemia; haemoglobin

Thales [**thay**leez] (c.620–c.555 BC) Greek natural philosopher, traditionally regarded as the first philosopher, born in Miletus. None of his writings survive. >> Aristotle

Thalia or **Thaleia** [tha**liy**a] In Greek mythology, the Muse of comedy and idyllic poetry. >> Muses

thalidomide A sedative introduced in West Germany in 1956, in the UK in 1958, and subsequently in some other countries. It became widely used because of its particular safety, but when it was found to cause congenital abnormalities, it was withdrawn; approximately 20% of babies whose mothers had taken thalidomide during early pregnancy suffered absence of limbs or part of limbs. >> sedative

Thallophyta [tha**lo**fita] A collective name formerly used for all lower plant-like organisms that lack differentiation into root, stem, and leaf; sometimes treated as a subkingdom of plants comprising the eucaryotic algae and fungi; also known as **Thallobionta**. >> algae; eucaryote; fungus; plant

Thames, River [temz], Lat **Tamesis** River rising in the Cotswold Hills, SE Gloucestershire, England; flows 352 km/219 mi E and SE through Greater London to enter the North Sea in a long, wide estuary; navigable as far as London by large ships; Thames Conservancy Board established in 1857; tidal barrier built across approach to London to reduce risk of floods (completed 1983). >> London

Thanet, Isle of Urban area in E Kent, SE England, originally an island; contains the towns of Margate, Broadstairs, and Ramsgate; railway. >> Kent

Thanksgiving Day A day set apart for a public acknowledgment of God's goodness and mercy; in Canada the second Monday in October, and in the USA the fourth Thursday of November, both public holidays. The occasion dates from 1621, when the new American settlers celebrated their first harvest. In modern times, the day is especially important for family reunions.

Thanlwin, River, formerly **Salween** River in SE Asia, rising in SW China; enters the Andaman Sea; length 2815 km/1750 mi. >> Myanmar [i]

Thant, U [oo **tant**] (1909–74) Burmese diplomat, born in Pantanaw, Myanmar. As secretary-general of the UN (1962–71), he played a major diplomatic role during the Cuban crisis, formulated a plan to end the Congolese Civil War (1962), and mobilized a UN peace-keeping force in Cyprus (1964). >> Cuban Missile Crisis; United Nations

Thar Desert [tah] or **(Great) Indian Desert** area c.320 000 sq km/125 000 sq mi. Arid region in NW India and E Pakistan, S Asia; 800 km/500 mi long and 400 km/250 mi wide. >> desert; India [i]; Pakistan [i]

Thatcher (of Kesteven), Margaret (Hilda) Thatcher, Baroness, *née* **Roberts** (1925–) British Conservative prime minister (1979–90), born in Grantham, Lincolnshire. She became minister of education (1970–4), and in 1975 replaced Edward Heath as Leader of the Conservative Party to become the first woman party leader in British politics. Her government instituted the privatization of nationalized industries and national utilities, tried to institute a market in state-provided health care and education, and reduced the role of local government as a provider of services. She resigned in 1990, following her opposition to full economic union with Europe, having become the longest serving premier of the 20th-c. She was created a life peer in 1992. >> Conservative Party; European Monetary System; Heath, Edward; right wing

theatre / theater Derived from the Greek for 'seeing place', the term originally signified the area occupied by spectators. It now describes the whole building and the social art form it houses. >> Actors' Studio; Berliner Ensemble; Broadway; Comédie Française, La; *commedia dell'arte*; Fringe, the; masque; music hall; Provincetown Players; Royal Shakespeare Company; theatre in the round; Theatre Workshop; Abbey / Globe / Living Theatre / Theater; Tony

theatre / theater in the round A theatre in which the auditorium surrounds a central stage and both performer and audience share the same acoustic space. Also known as an **arena stage**, the form demands that the actors project in all directions simultaneously. >> theatre

Theatre Workshop An English theatre company founded in Manchester by Joan Littlewood in 1945. From 1953 onwards it was based in London at the Theatre Royal, Stratford East, and is best remembered for its vigorous ensemble acting exemplified by such shows as *Oh, What a Lovely War* (1963). >> Littlewood

Thebe [**thee**bee] A tiny natural satellite of Jupiter, discovered in 1979 by Voyager 2; distance from the planet 222 000 km/138 000 mi; diameter 100 km/60 mi. >> Jupiter (astronomy); Voyager project [i]; RR964

Thebes [theebz] **1** The ancient capital of Upper Egypt, and the location of many magnificent temples and tombs, such as Tutankhamen's; a world heritage site. It was situated on the R Nile, where the town of Luxor now stands. >> Luxor; Tutankhamen **2** In ancient Greece, the most powerful city-state in Boeotia; now a market town for a rich agricultural region in SE Greece; pop (1995e) 19 900. >> Boeotia

theft The taking or appropriation of property belonging to another person without consent, with the intention of permanently depriving that person of the property. Borrowing is not theft, but it may sometimes be the subject of another criminal sanction: the temporary taking of a motor-car without the owner's consent is a criminal offence. Most US jurisdictions divide theft into **petty theft** (usually involving thefts of property worth less than $400) and **grand theft** (all other property). >> criminal law; robbery

thegn [thayn] (Old English 'one who serves') In Anglo-Saxon England, a member of the noble class. Until the Norman Conquest, thegns were indispensable to effective royal control of the localities. >> Anglo-Saxons

theine [**thee**in] >> **caffeine**

theism Belief in a single divine being, transcendent and personal, who created the world and, although involved with and related to the creation, is distinct from it. It is a feature of Jewish and Islamic as well as Christian faith. >> agnosticism; atheism; deism; pantheism

theme park An entertainment centre based on a particular theme, the most popular being wildlife parks. Many are also amusement parks. The first theme park was Disneyland, at Anaheim, CA, USA, opened in 1955, based on the Walt Disney cartoon characters.

Themis [**the**mis] In Greek mythology, the goddess of established law and justice. As a consort of Zeus, she is the mother of the Horae and the Moerae. >> Moerae

Themistocles [the**mis**tokleez] (c.523–c.458 BC) Athenian general and visionary politician. He made possible the great Athenian naval victory at Salamis (480 BC), and laid the foundations of their maritime empire. >> Persian Wars; Salamis

Theocritus [thee**ok**ritus] (c.310–250 BC) Greek pastoral poet, probably born in Syracuse. His short poems dealing with pastoral subjects, and representing a single scene, came to be called 'idylls' (*eidullia*). Tennyson was deeply influenced by him. >> pastoral; Tennyson

theodolite [thee**od**oliyt] An optical surveying instrument for measuring vertical or (more importantly) horizontal angles. It is a small telescope, with cross wires, movable over horizontal and vertical graduated circular scales. It is usually seen mounted on a stable tripod. >> surveying

Theodorakis, Mikis [thayodo**rah**kees] (1925–) Composer, born in Khios, Greece. His prolific musical output includes oratorios, ballets, song cycles, and music for film scores, the best known of which was *Zorba the Greek* (1965).

Theodore of Mopsuestia (c.350–428) Christian theologian, born in Antioch. His views on the Incarnation were condemned by the fifth ecumenical council in 553. >> Christianity; Incarnation

Theodoric or **Theoderic** [thee**od**orik], known as **the Great** (?–526) King of the Ostrogoths (471–526), who invaded Italy in 489, defeating the barbarian ruler, Odoacer. His long reign secured for Italy tranquillity and prosperity. >> Odoacer; Ostrogoths

Theodosius I [theeo**doh**shus], known as **the Great** (c.346–95) Roman emperor of the East (379–95). His title comes from his vigorous championship of orthodox Christianity. >> Theodosius II

Theodosius II [theeo**doh**shus] (401–50) Roman emperor (408–50), the grandson of Theodosius I and, like him, a staunch champion of orthodox Christianity. He is chiefly remembered for his codification of the Roman law in 438 (the **Theodosian Code**).

theology Literally, the science of the divine, or of discourse about God. In Christianity, it is understood as the systematic critical clarification of the historical beliefs of the Church. It has been divided into **natural theology**, that which can be known about God from nature or by reason alone, and **revealed theology**, that which can only be known through the self-disclosure of God. >> Christianity; God

Theophrastus [theeoh**fras**tus] (c.372–286 BC) Greek philosopher, born in Eresus, Lesbos. He became head of the Peripatetic school after Aristotle's death. >> Aristotle

theorbo [thee**aw(r)**boh] A large lute with six strings above a fretted fingerboard, and seven or eight additional bass strings which are not stopped and have a separate pegbox. It was widely used in the 17th-c as a continuo instrument. >> continuo; lute; string instrument 2 ℹ

theorem A proposition proved by logical deduction from one or more initial premises. Although geometrical theorems are the most widely known, theorems exist in all branches of mathematics. A theorem which has already been proved and is then used towards the proof of another theorem is known as a *lemma*.

theosophy [thee**os**ofee] Any system of philosophical or theological thought based on the direct and immediate experience of the divine. It has been especially used to describe the principles of the Theosophical Society founded in 1875 by Madame Blavatsky (1831–91) and H S Olcott (1832–1907) in New York City. >> Blavatsky

Thera [**thee**ra] >> **Santorini**

Therapsida [the**rap**sida] An order of fossil reptiles including the direct ancestors of the mammals; known mainly from the Permian and Triassic periods. (Subclass: Synapsida.) >> Dicynodon; Permian period; reptile; Triassic period

Theravada [thera**vah**da] The form of Buddhism commonly found in S Asia. It is generally distinguished from the later **Mahayana** Buddhism in its rejection of the theory of bodhisattvas. >> bodhisattva; Buddhism; Mahayana

Theresa, Mother >> **Teresa, Mother**

Theresa of Lisieux, St [leesyoe], originally **(Marie Françoise) Thérèse Martin**, also known as **the Little Flower** and **St Theresa of the Child Jesus** (1873–97) Saint, born in Alençon, France. She entered the Carmelite convent of Lisieux in Normandy at the age of 15, where she remained until her death from tuberculosis nine years later. Her account of her life was published posthumously as *Histoire d'une âme* (1898, Story of a Soul). She was canonized in 1925, and made a doctor of the Church in 1997. Feast day 1 October. >> Carmelites

therm >> **British thermal unit**

thermal conduction The transfer of heat through a substance without bulk movement of the substance; thermal conductivity symbol k, units W/(m.K) (watt per metre.kelvin). >> heat; thermal insulation

thermal efficiency In thermodynamics, the ratio of useful work derived from a heat engine to the heat absorbed by it; symbol e, a number between 0 and 1. It represents a theoretical maximum possible efficiency. >> heat engine; thermodynamics

thermal insulation Shielding whose function is to reduce heat flow. Heat loss by conduction is stemmed using layers of material having low thermal conductivity. Loss by convection is reduced by preventing the movement of fluids around the object. Loss by heat radiation is reduced using reflective coatings. >> screening; thermal conduction

thermal printer A type of printer which generally uses thermally sensitive paper and produces characters using a set of electrically heated wires. Although thermal printers are relatively inexpensive, the special paper they use is not. >> computer printer

thermic lance A torch-like cutting device for resistant steel and alloys, which depends on the fact that iron will burn in oxygen. A main nozzle for a jet of oxygen has a subsidiary nozzle for acetylene, which preheats the metal to the temperature at which it will begin to burn in the stream of oxygen. >> alloy; iron; steel

Thermidor coup [**ther**midaw(r)] The *coup d'état* of 16–27 July 1794 (8–9 Thermidor Year II), when Robespierre and his supporters were overthrown, ending the most radical phase of the French Revolution. >> French Republican calendar; Robespierre

thermionics The study of the processes involved in thermionic emission, ie the emission of electrons from a metal surface caused by applying heat to that surface. The effect was discovered by Thomas Edison in 1883. >> Edison; electron; thermionic valve

thermionic valve An electronic device (an *electron tube*) containing two or more electrodes, which are used to regulate the flow of electrons in an electric current. Thermionic valves were used in all types of electronic circuit, but have now largely been replaced by semiconductor devices such as the transistor. >> diode; semiconductor; transistor

thermistor A temperature sensor constructed from semiconductor material whose electrical resistance falls rapidly as the temperature rises. It is used in electronic circuits measuring or controlling temperature, and in time-delay circuits. >> electricity; resistance; semiconductor

thermite A mixture of aluminium and iron oxide which, if ignited, undergoes a fierce chemical reaction producing a high temperature (c.2400°C) and yielding molten iron. The process is useful for the preparation of intractable metals, or in welding, and has been used for incendiary bombs. >> aluminium; bomb; iron

thermochemistry The study of the energy changes accompanying chemical reactions. These changes are widely used in determining the energy value of foods. >> chemistry

thermocouple A type of thermometer that allows the direct electronic monitoring of temperature. >> thermoelectric effects; thermometer

thermodynamics The study of heat and heat-related phenomena, based on four fundamental laws. *Zeroth Law* If two systems are in thermodynamic equilibrium with a third, they will be in thermodynamic equilibrium with one another. For example, two objects left to stand a while in a still room will be the same temperature as the room and therefore as each other. *First Law* The sum of the energy changes occurring in some isolated process is zero, which is equivalent to the statement that total energy is conserved. For example, a battery may be used to raise the temperature of some water electrically, in which case chemical energy from the battery is converted into heat; but the total energy of the complete system before and after the circuit is switched on is the same. *Second Law* A law giving direction to thermodynamic processes in time, and thus forbidding some which would otherwise be allowed by the First Law. For example, no heat engine can have a thermal efficiency of 100%, ie it is impossible to convert heat totally into mechanical work. *Third Law* Absolute zero can never be reached. Expressing the thermodynamic properties of systems on the assumption that they are composed of large numbers of distinct atoms is termed *statistical mechanics*. >> Carnot; energy; heat; heat engine; Kelvin; Rumford; statistical mechanics

thermoelectric effects A general expression for temperature-dependent electrical properties of matter. Thermocouples use a potential difference resulting from the difference in temperature between two junctions of dissimilar metals – the **Seebeck effect**, discovered in 1821 by German physicist Thomas Seebeck (1770–1831). The **Peltier effect**, discovered in 1834 by French physicist Jean Peltier (1785–1845), is the reverse of the Seebeck effect, and may be used to make refrigerators having no moving parts. >> thermocouple

thermography A detection technique which converts invisible heat energy into a visible picture. Objects radiate varying amounts of infrared (IR) heat energy, depending on their temperature. Inside a thermograph, a solid-state detector 'sees' the IR, even in the dark or smoke. TV-style pictures show temperatures by variations in brightness or colour. >> solid-state device

thermoluminescence dating A method of dating ancient pottery by measuring the energy accumulated in the crystal lattice of its inclusions of quartz, through the breakdown over time of naturally occurring uranium. >> archaeology; quartz; uranium

thermometer A device for measuring temperature. In household alcohol and mercury thermometers, heat causes the liquid in a reservoir to expand, forcing some of the liquid up a graduated tube. The graduations are fixed by calibration against known markers of chosen temperature scale. The first reliable mercury-in-glass thermometer was invented by German physicist Gabriel Fahrenheit in 1714. >> Fahrenheit; pyrometer; temperature [i]

thermonuclear bomb >> **hydrogen bomb** [i]

thermoplastic A class of resin which softens and hardens reversibly on heating and cooling any number of times. >> plastics; resin

Thermopylae [ther**mop**ilee] A pass between mountains and sea in C Greece. The failure of the Greeks to hold it in 480 BC enabled the Persians to capture Athens and sack the Acropolis. >> Acropolis; Leonidas; Persian Wars

thermoset A class of resin which sets irreversibly on heating. Examples include epoxy resins such as Araldite. >> epoxy resin; plastics

thermosphere The upper atmospheric layer above the mesopause (c.80 km/50 mi) in which atmospheric densities are very low. The lower part is composed mainly of nitrogen (N_2) and oxygen in molecular (O_2) and atomic (O) forms, whereas above 200 km/125 mi atomic oxygen predominates over N_2 and N. >> atmosphere [i]; ionosphere; mesosphere

Theroux, Paul (Edward) [the**roo**] (1941–) Novelist and travel writer, born in Medford, MA. His novels include *Waldo* (1969), *Picture Palace* (1978, Whitbread), the highly acclaimed *The Mosquito Coast* (1981, James Tait Black), *The Pillars of Hercules* (1995), and *Kowloon Tong* (1997). He first reached a wide public through his rail journeys, such as *The Great Railway Bazaar* (1975) – a genre which he has continued with *Travelling the World* (1990) and other books.

Theseus [**thee**syoos] A legendary king and national hero of Athens. With Ariadne's help he killed the Minotaur. He conquered the Amazons, and married their queen; later, he married Phaedra. >> Ariadne; Minotaur

Thessalonians, Letters to the New Testament writings of Paul to the church he founded in the capital of the Roman province of Macedonia, although his authorship of the second letter is disputed. >> New Testament; Paul, St

Thessaloníki [thesalo**nee**kee] >> **Salonica**

Thessaly [**the**salee], Gr **Thessalía** pop (1995e) 749 000; area 14 037 sq km/5418 sq mi. Fertile agricultural region of E

Greece; annexed by Greece, 1881; capital, Larisa; major cereal region. >> Greece ℹ

Thetis [**the**tis] In Greek mythology, a nereid destined to bear a son greater than his father. This was the secret known to Prometheus. She was married to Peleus, and was the mother of Achilles. >> Achilles; nereid; Peleus; Prometheus

thiamine A water-soluble vitamin (B_1) which acts as an enzyme co-factor in the oxidation of glucose. A deficiency leads to beri-beri, a disease once common, especially in SE Asia. >> beriberi; enzyme; glucose; vitamins ℹ

thiazole [**thiy**azohl] C_3H_3NS, boiling point 117°C. A five-membered ring compound; a colourless liquid, the basis for a range of dyestuffs. >> ring

thickhead A songbird, native to E India, SE Asia, and Australia; rounded head and strong bill; also known as **whistler**. (Family: Pachycephalidae, 46 species.) >> songbird

thick-knee A plover-like bird, widespread; legs with swollen ankles (not knees); plumage mottled; eyes large, yellow; mainly nocturnal. (Family: Burhinidae, 9 species.) >> plover

Thiers, (Louis) Adolphe [tyair] (1797–1877) French statesman, historian, and first president of the Third Republic (1871–3), born in Marseille, France. After the collapse of the Second Empire he became chief of the executive power in the provisional government, suppressed the Paris Commune, and was elected president. His most ambitious literary work was the 20-volume *L'histoire du consulat et de l'empire* (1845–62, History of the Consulate and the Empire). >> Commune of Paris

Thimphu [**thim**poo] or **Thimbu**, also **Tashi Chho Dzong** 27°32N 89°43E, pop (1995e) town, 12 900. Official capital of Bhutan, on R Raidak; founded, 1581; fortified town, a major monastery; capital since 1962; air strip. >> Bhutan ℹ

Thingvellir [theeng**vet**lir] 64°15N 21°06W. National shrine of Iceland, at the N end of Thingvalla Water; the Icelandic *Althing*, oldest parliament in the world, was founded here in 930. >> Iceland ℹ

Thíra [**thee**ra] >> **Santorini**

third-generation computers >> **computer generations**

third stream A type of music which aims to combine the styles of Western art music with those of jazz or various ethnic traditions. Among composers associated with it are John Lewis (1920–) and Günther Schuller (1925–). >> jazz

Third World >> **Three Worlds theory**

Thirteen Colonies The American provinces that revolted against British rule and declared independence in 1776. From N to S they were New Hampshire, Massachusetts, Rhode Island, Connecticut, New York, New Jersey, Pennsylvania, Delaware, Maryland, Virginia, North Carolina, South Carolina, and Georgia. Fourteen states actually declared independence, because Vermont separated from New York at the same time. >> American Revolution

thirty-eighth parallel The boundary line proposed for the partition of Korea at the Potsdam Conference in 1945, after the defeat of Japan (which had annexed Korea in 1910). It now forms the line of division between North and South Korea. >> Korea ℹ; Korea, North ℹ

Thirty-nine Articles A set of doctrinal formulations for the Church of England, finally adopted by the Convocation of 1571. They do not comprise a creed, but rather a general Anglican view on a series of contentious matters in order to maintain the unity of the Anglican Communion. They concern matters such as the presence of Christ in the Eucharist and the authority of Scriptures and the Councils. Church of England clergy have been required since 1865 to affirm these principles in general terms. >> Anglican Communion

Thirty Tyrants The Spartan-backed clique which seized power in Athens towards the end of the Peloponnesian War (404 BC), overthrew the democracy, and instituted a reign of terror. They were overthrown in 403 BC and the democracy was restored. >> Peloponnesian War; Sparta (Greek history)

Thirty Years' War (1618–48) A complex phase, specifically German in origin, of a long and intermittent power struggle between the kings of France and the Habsburg rulers of the Holy Roman Empire and Spain (1491–1715). With the Elector Frederick V's defeat (1620) and intervention by other powers, the conflict intensified, spreading to other theatres. Isolated as Spain collapsed, the emperor opened negotiations (1643–8) which ended the German war at the Peace of Westphalia. >> Habsburgs; Holy Roman Empire

thistle The name applied to several spiny plants of the daisy family, many belonging to the genera *Cirsium* and *Carduus*. All have leaves with spiny margins, flower heads often almost globular, solitary or in clusters; florets reddish, purple, or white; the national emblem of Scotland. (Family: Compositae.) >> bract; daisy

Thistle, Most Ancient and Most Noble Order of the A Scottish order of chivalry, probably instituted by James III of Scotland. There are 16 members under the sovereign (though royal knights may be additional to this number). The motto of the order is *Nemo me impune lacessit* (Lat 'No-one provokes me with impunity'); the ribbon is dark green.

Thomas, St (1st-c) A disciple of Jesus, most prominent in John's Gospel, where he is also called *Didymus* (Gr 'the Twin'), and where he is portrayed as doubting the resurrection until he touches the wounds of the risen Christ (*John* 20). Early church traditions describe him subsequently as a missionary to the Parthians or a martyr in India. Feast day 21 December. >> apostle; Jesus Christ

Thomas, Clarence (1948–) Jurist, born in Savannah, GA. He studied at Yale, and in 1992 was named by President Bush as the second black American to sit in the Supreme Court. His Senate confirmation hearings attracted widespread attention due to allegations of sexual misconduct brought by a former colleague. >> Marshall, Thurgood; Supreme Court

Thomas, D(onald) M(ichael) (1935–) Novelist, poet, and translator, born in Redruth, Cornwall. A former teacher and lecturer, he became known after his controversial novel *The White Hotel* (1981). Other novels include his first, *The Flute Player* (1979), *Lying Together* (1990), and *Flying into Love* (1992). He has also translated major literary works from Russian.

Thomas, Dylan (Marlais) (1914–53) Poet, born in Swansea, SC Wales. He established himself with the publication of *Eighteen Poems* in 1934. His *Collected Poems* appeared in 1953, and he then produced the radio 'play for voices', *Under Milk Wood* (1954). An alcoholic in later years, he died in New York City during a lecture tour.

Thomas, (Philip) Edward, pseudonym **Edward Eastaway** (1878–1917) Poet and critic, born in London. He wrote most of his work during active service between 1915 and his death at Arras, France.

Thomas, R(onald) S(tuart) (1913–) Poet, born in Cardiff. He was ordained in 1936 and became a rector in the Church of Wales. His collections include *Poetry for Supper* (1958), and *No Truth with the Furies* (1995).

Thomas, Terry >> **Terry-Thomas**

Thomas à Becket >> **Becket, Thomas**

Thomas à Kempis >> **Kempis, Thomas à**

Thomas Aquinas >> **Aquinas, St Thomas**

Thomism [**toh**mizm] In Christian philosophical theology, the name given to the doctrines of Thomas Aquinas, and to later schools claiming descent from him. >> Aquinas; Christianity

Thompson, Sir Benjamin, Graf (Count) **von Rumford**, known as **Count Rumford** (1753–1814) Administrator and scientist, born in Woburn, MA. In 1784 he entered the service of Bavaria, where he carried out military, social, and economic reforms, for which he was made a count of the Holy Roman Empire. He first showed the relation between heat and work, a concept fundamental to modern physics. In 1799 he returned to London, and founded the Royal Institution.

Thompson, Daley, popular name of **Francis Morgan Thompson** (1958–) Athlete, born in London. An outstanding decathlete, he was world champion (1983), European champion (1982, 1986), and Olympic champion (1980, 1984). >> athletics

Thompson, Emma (1959–) Actress, born in London. In 1989 she appeared in the film of *Henry V*, directed by Kenneth Branagh, whom she married the same year (separated, 1995). With her husband she went on to make *Dead Again* (1991) and *Much Ado About Nothing* (1993). Her other films include *Howards End* (1992, Oscar), *Remains of the Day* (1993), *Sense and Sensibility* (1996, BAFTA), and *Primary Colors* (1998). >> Branagh

Thompson, Francis (1859–1907) British poet, born in Preston, Lancashire. His later work was mainly religious in theme; it includes the well-known 'The Hound of Heaven'.

Thompson, John T(alafierro) (1860–1940) US inventor, born in Newport, KY. In 1918 he originated the Thompson gun, one of the world's first effective submachine guns. The 'Tommy gun' became infamous as a favourite weapon of the gangsters of prohibition America. >> submachine gun

Thomson, James (1700–48) Poet, born in Ednam, Scottish Borders. He is best known for his four-part work, *The Seasons* (1730), the first major nature poem in English; his ode 'Rule, Britannia' (1740); and the Spenserian allegory, *The Castle of Indolence* (1748). >> Spenser

Thomson, Sir J(oseph) J(ohn) (1856–1940) Physicist, born in Cheetham Hill, Greater Manchester. He showed in 1897 that cathode rays were rapidly moving particles, and deduced that these 'corpuscles' (electrons) must be nearly 2000 times smaller in mass than the lightest known atomic particle, the hydrogen ion. He received the Nobel Prize for Physics in 1906. >> nuclear physics

Thomson (of Fleet), Roy (Herbert) Thomson, Baron (1894–1976) Newspaper and television magnate, born in Toronto, Ontario, Canada. He started several radio stations, and bought many Canadian and US newspapers. He settled in Edinburgh on acquiring his first British paper, *The Scotsman* (1952), bought the Kemsley newspapers in 1959 (including the *Sunday Times*, to which he added the first colour supplement in 1962), and in 1966 took over *The Times*.

Thomson, Virgil (1896–1989) Composer and critic, born in Kansas City, KS. He is best known for his operas with libretti by Gertrude Stein, *Four Saints in Three Acts* (1934) and *The Mother of Us All* (1947). He also wrote symphonies, ballets, and choral, chamber, and film music. >> Stein, Gertrude

Thomson, Sir William >> **Kelvin, 1st Baron**

Thor In Norse mythology, the god of thunder, son of Odin and Frigga. His hammer is called Miolnir. He is the strongest of the gods, and protects them. >> Ragnarok

thorax That part of the body between the neck and the abdomen enclosed by the thoracic part of the vertebral column, the ribs, and the sternum, and separated from the abdomen by the diaphragm; also known as the **thoracic cage** or **chest**. Roughly cone-shaped, it surrounds and protects the lungs, heart, and great vessels. >> anatomy [i]; diaphragm; rib; sternum; vertebral column

Thoreau, Henry (David) [tho**roh**] (1817–62) Essayist and poet, born in Concord, MA. In c.1839 he began the walks and studies of nature which became his major occupation, recorded in a daily journal. His writings include *Walden, or Life in the Woods* (1854).

thorn-apple An evil-smelling annual weed (*Datura stramonium*) found throughout most of the N hemisphere; up to 1 m/3¼ ft high; flowers trumpet-shaped, white to blue; fruit a spiny, ovoid capsule containing poisonous seeds; also called **jimson weed**. (Family: Solanaceae.)

thornbill A warbler, native to Australia and New Guinea; also known as the **thornbill warbler**. (Genus: *Acanthiza*, 12 species. Family: Acanthizidae.) >> warbler

Thorndike, Edward L(ee) (1874–1949) Psychologist, born in Williamsburg, MA. As a result of studying animal intelligence, he formulated his 'law of effect', which states that a given behaviour is learned by trial-and-error, and is more likely to occur if its consequences are satisfying. >> learning

Thorndike, Dame (Agnes) Sybil (1882–1976) Actress, born in Gainsborough, Lincolnshire. In 1924 she played the title role in the first performance of Shaw's *Saint Joan*, and during World War 2 was a notable member of the Old Vic Company. She married the actor Lewis Casson (1875–1969) in 1908.

Thornhill, Sir James (1675–1734) Baroque painter, born in Melcombe Regis, Dorset. He executed paintings for the dome of St Paul's Cathedral, Blenheim Palace, and other public buildings, and in 1718 was made history painter to the king. >> Baroque (art and architecture)

thoroughbred The fastest breed of horse (over 65 kph/40 mph), developed in England for racing; height, 16 hands/1·6 m/5 ft 4 in; also known as **English thoroughbred** or **racehorse**. >> falabella; horse [i]

Thorpe, (John) Jeremy (1929–) British politician, born in London. Elected Leader of the Liberal Party in 1967, he resigned the leadership in 1976 following allegations of a previous homosexual relationship with Norman Scott. In 1979 he was acquitted of charges of conspiracy and incitement to murder Mr Scott. >> Liberal Party (UK)

Thorvaldsen, Bertel [**tor**valsn] (c.1768–1844) Neoclassical sculptor, born in Copenhagen. His best-known pieces include 'Christ and the Twelve Apostles' at Copenhagen, and the Cambridge statue of Byron. >> Neoclassicism (art)

Thoth [thoht, toht] An ancient Egyptian Moon-god, sometimes depicted with the head of an ibis, sometimes as a baboon. The god of words, magic, and scribes, in the Underworld he records the souls of the dead.

Thothmes III >> **Thutmose III**

Thousand, Expedition of the (1860) A military campaign led by Garibaldi, originally involving 1146 men, which formed a crucial stage in the Italian Risorgimento. Sailing from Genoa, they seized Sicily, crossed to the mainland, and four months later had liberated the Kingdom of Naples. >> Garibaldi; Risorgimento

Thrace [thrays], Gr **Thráki** pop (1995e) 346 000; area 8578 sq km/3311 sq mi. NE region of Greece; area now divided between Turkey, Greece, and Bulgaria; capital, Komotini; region of fertile plains. >> Greece [i]

threadfin Any of the tropical marine and estuarine fish in the family Polynemidae (3 genera); long free pectoral fin rays which serve in part as sensitive feelers; body length may reach over 1·5 m/5 ft. >> fish [i]

Three Age System The chronological division of Old World prehistory into three successive ages of **Stone**, **Bronze**, and **Iron**. The subdivision of the Stone Age into the **Palaeolithic** (**Old Stone Age**), characterized by chipped stone, and the **Neolithic** (**New Stone Age**), characterized by polished stone tools, was made in the 1860s, and the term **Mesolithic** (**Middle Stone Age**), covering the five millennia following the end of the last glaciation, also dates from then. The term **Chalcolithic** for the **Copper** or earliest Bronze Age belongs to more recent times. >> archaeology; Aurignacian; Beaker culture; Gravettian; Hallstatt; Kurgan culture; La Tène; Magdalenian; Maglemosian; Mousterian; Natufian; Solutrian

three-day event A combined training competition comprising the three main equestrain disciplines: dressage, showjumping, and cross-country. >> equestrianism; horse

three-D (3-D) films >> **stereoscopic photography**

Three Emperors' League, Ger **Dreikaiserbund** An entente (1873) between emperors William I of Germany, Francis Joseph of Austria–Hungary, and Alexander II of Russia. It was designed by Bismarck to protect Germany by isolating France and stabilizing SE Europe. It lapsed in 1887. >> Bismarck

Three Worlds theory A theory that sees the world as being divided into three main blocs of countries, defined by their economic status. These are the developed capitalist economies (the **First World**), the developed communist countries (the **Second World**), and underdeveloped countries (the **Third World**), covering most of Latin America and recently independent African and Asian states. Some (including the United Nations) recognize a 'Fourth World', of the 25 poorest nations. The collapse of the Communist states after 1989 makes the typology somewhat redundant, although the term *Third World* is likely to persist due to its extensive usage. >> capitalism; communism

thresher shark Large surface-living shark (*Alopias vulpinus*), widespread in tropical to temperate seas; easily recognized by the long upper lobe of tail fin which may exceed half its body length; tail lobe used to round up shoals of fish by thrashing the water surface; body length up to 6 m/20 ft. (Family: Alopiidae.) >> fish ℹ; shark

thrift A densely tufted perennial (*Armeria maritima*), woody at base, native to Europe; leaves grass-like, bluish-green; flowers pink, scented, in long-stalked, hemispherical heads; also called **sea pink**; a mainly coastal plant. (Family: Plumbaginaceae.)

thrip A minute insect in which the wings, when present, are slender with a long fringe of hairs; mouthparts specialized for piercing and sucking. (Order: Thysanoptera, c.5000 species.) >> insect ℹ

thrombophlebitis >> **phlebitis**

thrombosis [throm**boh**sis] The formation of a blood clot within a blood vessel, resulting in a partial or complete blockage. Its basis is the formation of the protein, fibrin, which forms a mesh in which platelets and red blood cells are trapped, and produces a plug to the flow of blood. >> blood vessels ℹ

thrush (bird) A medium-sized songbird, widespread, inhabiting diverse regions from tropical rainforests to deserts; some species called **chats**. (Family: Turdidae, c.300 species.) >> blackbird; bluebird; chat; fieldfare; nightingale; ouzel; redwing; robin; solitaire; songbird; stonechat; wheatear; whinchat

thrush (disease) >> **candidiasis**

ThrustSSC British jet-powered car, driven by Andrew Green, which broke the world land speed record at the Black Rock site, Great Basin, USA, in 1997, and became the first car to travel at supersonic speed. It achieved a speed of 1227·95 kph/763·035 mph (Mach 1·020). >> car

Thucydides [thyoo**sid**ideez] **1** (c.460–c.400 BC) Athenian aristocratic historian of the Peloponnesian War. >> Peloponnesian War **2** (5th-c BC) Athenian politician, leader of the opposition to Pericles until ostracized in 443 BC. >> ostracism; Pericles

Thuggee [**thuh**gee] An Indian cult which combined robbery and ritual murder (usually by strangling) in the name of Kali (the Hindu goddess of destruction). Vigorous steps were taken to eradicate the problem in the 19th-c. >> Hinduism; Kali

thuja [**thoo**ja] >> **arbor vitae**

Thule [**thyoo**lee] 77°30N 69°29W. Eskimo settlement in NW Greenland; founded as a Danish trading post in 1910; scientific installations; name also given by the ancients to the most northerly land of Europe, an island described c.310 BC by the Greek navigator, Pytheas. >> Greenland ℹ

Thumb, General Tom >> **Stratton, Charles**

Thummim >> **Urim and Thummim**

Thun [toon], Fr **Thoune** 46°46N 7°38E, pop (1995e) 39 300. Town in Switzerland, on the R Aare near L Thun; gateway to the Bernese Oberland; railway junction; castle (1191). >> Switzerland ℹ

Thunder Bay 48°27N 89°12W, pop (1995e) 121 000. Resort and port in S Ontario, Canada, on NW shore of L Superior; created in 1970 by the union of Fort William and Port Arthur; airfield; railway; university (1965); grain storage and shipping point. >> Ontario; Superior, Lake

thunderstorm A storm of heavy rain, thunder, and lightning which occurs when cumulonimbus clouds develop in unstable, humid conditions. As air rises, condensation releases latent heat, and this increases the available energy, reinforcing the rising tendency of the air. An electric charge builds up at the base of the cloud, and when large enough, is discharged in the form of lightning. >> cloud ℹ; cumulonimbus clouds; lightning; rainfall

Thurber, James (Grover) (1894–1961) Writer and cartoonist, born in Columbus, OH. His drawings first appeared in his book *Is Sex Necessary?* (1929), and there are several anthologies of his work, such as *Thurber's Dogs* (1955). He was also the creator of the fantasizing character Walter Mitty.

Thuringia [thu**ring**ia] A historic area of Germany, including the Harz Mts and Thuringian Forest. It was divided between Saxony, Hesse-Kassel, and others from 1485–1920, then became part of East Germany, and is now a province within united Germany. >> Germany ℹ

Thurso 58°35N 3°32W, pop (1995e) 8600. Port town in N Scotland; on N coast, at head of R Thurso; car ferry service to Orkney from Scrabster. >> Highland; Scotland ℹ

Thutmose III [thut**moh**suh], also **Thothmes** or **Tuthmosis** (?–1450 BC) Egyptian pharaoh (c.1504–1450 BC), one of the greatest of Egyptian rulers, who re-established Egyptian control over Syria and Nubia. He built the temple of Amon at Karnak, and erected many obelisks, including those now known as 'Cleopatra's Needle'.

Thyestes [thi**yes**teez] In Greek mythology, a son of Pelops, who inherited the curse upon that house. His brother Atreus set before him a dish made of the flesh of Thyestes' children.

thylacine [**thiy**lasiyn] An Australian marsupial, probably extinct since the 1930s; length, up to 1·6 m/5¼ ft; sandy brown with dark vertical stripes over back and hindquarters; female with short backward-facing pouch; also known as the **Tasmanian wolf** or **tiger**. (Family: Thylacinidae.) >> marsupial ℹ; *see illustration on p. 862*

thyme A small spreading aromatic shrub, often only a few cm high, native to Europe and Asia; flowers 2-lipped, usually pink or mauve, in crowded whorls forming spikes or heads. It is widely cultivated as a culinary herb. (Genus: *Thymus*, c.400 species. Family: Labiatae.) >> herb

thymine [**thiy**meen] $C_5H_6N_2O_2$. One of the pyrimidine bases in DNA, usually paired with adenine. >> DNA ℹ; pyrimidines

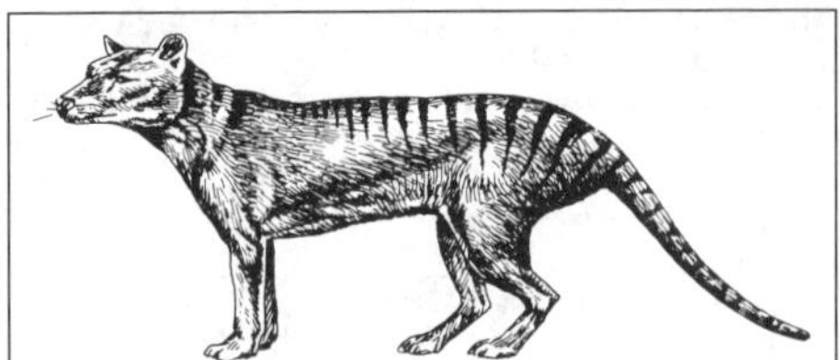

Thylacine

thymus A lymphoid gland of vertebrates, which in mammals lies in the upper part of the chest close to the great vessels and the heart. Its presence is essential in the newborn for the development of lymphoid tissue and immunological competence. In early life, cells migrate from bone marrow into the thymus, where they mature to become T-lymphocytes (*T-cells*) responsible for cellular immunity. >> gland; lymphocyte

thyristor [thiy**ris**ter] A semiconductor device that acts as a switch; also called a **silicon-controlled rectifier**. Thyristors are replacing gas-filled electronic valves. >> rectifier; semiconductor; solid-state device

thyroid gland An endocrine gland of vertebrates situated in the region of the neck, overlying the lower part of the larynx and the upper part of the trachea. It secretes thyroid hormone and calcitonin (from C-cells). >> larynx; thyroid hormone

thyroid hormone A collective term for iodine-containing amine hormones secreted from vertebrate thyroid glands. In humans and other mammals, the principle hormones are thyroxine (T_4) and trilodothyronine (T_3), which have important roles in fetal development and throughout life in the control of metabolism. >> cretinism; dwarfism; goitre; hormones; hyperthyroidism; myxoedema; thyroid gland

Thysanoptera [thiysan**op**tera] >> **thrip**

Tiananmen Square [tianahnmen] or **T'ien-an-men Square** The largest public square in the world, covering 40 ha/98 acres and lying before the gate to the Imperial Palace in C Beijing. In June 1989, it was the scene of mass protests by students and others against the Chinese government, crushed by troops of the Chinese Army with an undisclosed number of dead. >> Beijing; Forbidden City

Tianjin, Tientsin, or **T'ien-chin** [tianjin] 39°08N 117°12E; pop (1995e) 6 277 000; administrative region 8 758 402; municipality area 4000 sq km/1500 sq mi. Port city in E China; China's largest artificial harbour, built during Japanese occupation, 1937–45, completed 1952; founded in Warring States period, 403–221 BC; attacked by British and French in 1860; badly damaged by earthquake, 1976; airport; railway; two universities; designated a special economic zone. >> China ℹ; Opium Wars

Tian Shan or **T'ien Shan** Mountain range in C Asia, on border of Russia and China; length, 2500 km/1500 mi; rises to 7439 m/24 406 ft at Tomur (Pobedy) peak. >> China ℹ

Tiber, River [**tiy**ber], Ital **Tevere**, ancient **Tiberis** Third longest river of Italy, rising in the Etruscan Apennines; length 405 km/252 mi; enters the Tyrrhenian Sea near Ostia. >> Italy ℹ

Tiberias [tiy**beer**ias], Hebrew **Tevarya** 32°48N 35°32E, pop (1995e) 40 100. Holiday resort town in N Israel, on L Tiberias; named after the Roman emperor, Tiberius; medicinal hot springs; one of the four holy cities of the Jews. >> Israel ℹ

Tiberias, Lake or **Sea of Galilee** [tiy**beer**ias], Hebrew **Yam Kinneret**, ancient **Sea of Chinnereth** area 166 sq km/64 sq mi. Lake in NE Israel, in the Jordan valley; 210 m/689 ft below sea-level; length 22·5 km/14 mi; width 12 km/7½ mi; maximum depth 46 m/150 ft; fed and drained by the R Jordan; Israel's largest reservoir; many centres around the lake of historic and scriptural interest, especially connected with the life of Jesus. >> Israel ℹ; Jesus Christ

Tiberius [tiy**beer**ius], in full **Tiberius Julius Caesar Augustus** (42 BC–AD 37) Roman emperor (14–37), the son of Livia, and stepson and successor of the Emperor Augustus. The suspicious death of his heir Germanicus (19), followed by the excesses of his chief henchman, Sejanus, and the reign of terror that followed Sejanus's downfall (31), made him widely hated. >> Agrippina the Elder; Germanicus; Livia; Sejanus

Tibesti Mountains [tee**bes**tee] Mountain range in NC Africa, largely in NW Chad; area 100 000 sq km/38 600 sq mi, length 480 km/300 mi; highest peak, Emi Koussi (3415 m/11 204 ft). >> Chad ℹ; Sahara Desert

Tibet, Chin **Xizang** [shitsang] pop (1995e) 2 354 000; area 1 221 600 sq km/471 500 sq mi. Autonomous region in SW China; Tibet Plateau, average altitude 4000 m/13 000 ft; Himalayas in the S, rising to 8848 m/29 028 ft at Mt Everest; Kunlun Shan range in the N; major farming area in S valleys; capital, Lhasa; dominated by Buddhist lamas since 7th-c AD until departure of Dalai Lama into exile, 1959; conquered by Mongols, 1279–1368; controlled by Manchus, 18th-c; Chinese rule restored in 1951, and full control asserted after revolt in 1959; most monasteries and temples now closed or officially declared historical monuments, but many people still worship daily; further uprising in 1993. >> Buddhism; China ℹ; Dalai Lama; Manchus; Tibet Plateau

Tibetan One of the major languages in the Sino-Tibetan group; probably 3–4 million speakers. Written records, mainly to do with the Buddhist religion, date from the 8th-c. >> Sino-Tibetan languages

Tibet Plateau or **Qinghai–Tibet Plateau**, Chinese **Xizang Gaoyuan** Plateau in W and SW China; average altitude, 4000 m/13 000 ft; area 2.3 million sq km/0.9 million sq mi; bounded S by the Himalayas; major farming region in S, with warm, humid climate; C and N are cold and dry. >> China ℹ; Tibet

tibia >> **leg**

Tibullus, Albius [ti**bul**us] (c.54–19 BC) Latin poet, considered by Quintilian to be the greatest elegaic writer. He is known for his books of love poetry, but several works under his name are probably by other authors.

tic An involuntary non-rhythmic motor movement or vocal production which serves no apparent purpose. It occurs most famously in *Gilles de la Tourette syndrome*, where the patient may suddenly utter a sound like a bark, or swear without an intention to do so.

tick A large mite specialized as a blood-feeding, external parasite of terrestrial vertebrates; fangs modified for cutting skin; can transmit diseases of humans and domesticated animals. (Order: Acari. Family: Ixodidae.) >> mite

tidal wave The extremely long-period waves driven by the forces producing the tides. The term is often popularly used to refer to tsunamis, which are not related to tides. >> tide; tsunami; wave (oceanography)

tide The regular, periodic rise and fall of the surface of the sea. The tides are produced by differences in gravitational forces acting on different points on the Earth's surface, and affect all bodies of water to some extent. These so-called tidal forces are produced primarily by the Sun and Moon. >> bore; gravitation; spring tide; tidal wave

T'ien-ching >> **Tianjin**

Tientsin >> **Tianjin**

Tiepolo, Giovanni Battista [**tyay**poloh] (1696–1770) Artist, born in Venice, Italy. The last of the great Venetian painters, he became renowned as a decorator of buildings throughout Europe. >> Baroque (art and architecture); Venetian School

Tiergarten [**teer**gah(r)tn] A park covering 255 ha/630 acres in Berlin. Originally a royal hunting ground, it was landscaped in the 18th-c and opened to the public. >> Berlin

Tierra del Fuego [**tye**ra thel **fway**goh] pop (1995e) 73 400; area 73 746 sq km/28 473 sq mi. Island group at the extreme S of South America; E side (about one third) belongs to Argentina, remainder belongs to Chile; boundary agreed in 1881; highest point, Monte Darwin (2438 m/ 7999 ft); discovered by Magellan 1520; capital (Argentina), Ushuaia; capital (on Chile mainland), Punta Arenas; dispute over islands at E end of Beagle Channel, resolved in 1985 in favour of Chile. >> Argentina i; Chile i; Magellan

tiger A member of the cat family (*Panthera tigris*) native to S and SE Asia; reddish brown with dark vertical stripes; swims well; eats mainly large mammals; several subspecies: **Bengal**, **Indochinese**, **Chinese**, **Sumatran**, **Siberian** (the largest known cat), and possibly extinct **Caspian**, **Bali**, and **Javan** tigers. >> Felidae; liger

tiger fish Large predatory freshwater fish with strong fang-like teeth, widespread in rivers and lakes of Africa; length up to 1·8 m/6 ft. (Genus: *Hydrocynus*. Family: Characidae.) >> fish i

tiger-moth A medium-sized, typically colourful moth; may be an important pest causing damage to tree foliage. (Order: Lepidoptera. Family: Arctiidae.) >> cinnabar (entomology); moth

tiger shark Large and very dangerous shark (*Galeocerda cuvier*) widely distributed in tropical and warm temperate seas; length up to 5 m/16 ft; grey to brown, with darker vertical stripes and patches. (Family: Carcharhinidae.) >> shark

tigon [**tiy**gn] >> **liger**

Tigray or **Tigre** [**tee**gray] pop (1995e) 3 307 000; area 64 921 sq km/40 575 sq mi. Region in NE Ethiopia; low-lying E half, with large section below sea-level at centre of Danakil Depression; capital, Mekele; one of the areas most severely affected by the drought in the 1980s, and a centre of resistance to the government; Tigray people are Semitic-speaking, mostly nomadic herders in the N, agriculturalists in the S. >> Afro-Asiatic languages; Ethiopia i

tigrillo >> **ocelot**

Tigris, River [**tiy**gris], Arabic **Shatt Dijla**, Turkish **Dicle** River in SE Turkey and Iraq; rises in EC Turkey; joins the Euphrates to form the Shatt al-Arab; length 1850 km/ 1150 mi; several ancient cities along its banks, eg Nineveh, Seleucia. >> Iraq i; Shatt al-Arab

Tijuana [tee**hwah**na] 32°32N 117°02W, pop (1995e) 824 000. Border town in NW Mexico; airfield; resort town with casinos and nightclubs. >> Mexico i

Tikal [tee**kahl**] An ancient Mayan city in N Guatemala, settled by 250 BC, at its peak in the 7th–8th-c AD, but abruptly abandoned c.900; a world heritage site. >> Mayas

Tilburg [**til**berkh] 51°31N 5°06E, pop (1995e) 164 000. Industrial city in S Netherlands; railway; major business and cultural centre in the S. >> Netherlands, The i

Tilbury 51°28N 0°23E, pop (1995e) 12 000. Town in Essex, SE England; on the R Thames estuary; railway; major port and docks for London and the SE. >> Essex

till or **boulder clay** A geological term for sediment or drift consisting of an unstratified and unsorted deposit of clay, sand, gravel, and boulders left behind after the retreat of glaciers and ice-sheets. **Tillite** is till which has consolidated into solid rock. >> glaciation; moraine; stratification

Tillett, Ben(jamin) (1860–1943) Trade union leader, born in Bristol. He achieved prominence as leader of the great dockers' strike (1889), and of the transport workers' strike in London (1911). >> trade union

Till Eulenspiegel >> **Eulenspiegel, Till**

Tilley, Vesta, stage name of **Matilda Alice, Lady de Frece**, *née* **Powles** (1864–1952) Music-hall entertainer, born in Worcester, Hereford and Worcester. She became a celebrated male impersonator, her many popular songs including 'Burlington Bertie'.

Tillich, Paul (Johannes) [**til**ikh] (1886–1965) Protestant theologian, born in Starzeddel, Germany. A Lutheran pastor, he was dismissed by the Nazis in 1933, and moved to the USA. His major work was *Systematic Theology* (1953–63, 3 vols).

Tilly, Johann Tserclaes, Graf (Count) **von** (1559–1632) Flemish soldier, born in Tilly, Belgium. He successfully commanded the forces of the Catholic League in the Thirty Years' War, gaining decisive victories at the White Mountain and Prague (1620). He was routed by Gustavus Adolphus at Breitenfeld (1631). >> Gustavus II; Thirty Years' War

timbre The sound quality of a voice or musical instrument, which depends on the prominence or otherwise of upper harmonics (*partials*) in the notes produced. The timbre of a flute or recorder, for example, is weak in upper harmonics compared with that of the much brighter violin or trumpet. >> harmonic

Timbuktu [timbuhk**too**], Fr **Tombouctou** 16°49N 2°59W, pop (1995e) 27 600. Town in N Mali; settled in the 11th-c; a chief centre of Muslim learning; taken by the French, 1893; airfield; several mosques (from 13th-c). >> Mali i

time That which distinguishes sequential events from simultaneous events; symbol *t*, units s (second); the fourth dimension, in addition to the three spatial dimensions. It allows the assignment of cause and effect, and, according to our perception, the assignment of past, present, and future. In Newtonian mechanics, time is absolute, meaning that a second as measured by one observer is the same as a second measured by any other observer in the universe. Relativity explains that this view of the nature of time is false. >> Daylight Saving Time; entropy; general relativity; light year; month; second; sidereal / solar / standard / universal time; space–time; special relativity i

time and motion study The technique of job analysis to discover how tasks are actually carried out; more usually known now as **work study** or **industrial engineering**. Its aim is to find the most efficient way of performing a task, in order to raise productivity. >> productivity

time code A series of digitally coded signals appearing sequentially on the magnetic tape of a video or audio recording, and sometimes on film, to provide specific identification for each frame in editing and post-production. In its simplest form it denotes Hours, Minutes, Seconds, and Frames. >> tape recorder

time-lapse photography A series of photographs taken at regular intervals from the same viewpoint to record the development of a subject, for example, plant growth or traffic flow. When filmed as successive single frames, projection at normal speed provides a rapid presentation of slow changes. >> photography

Time of Troubles A period of intense social and political turmoil in Russia (1598–1613), involving a series of successive crises, civil war, famines, Cossack and peasant revolts, foreign invasions, and widespread material destruction. >> Cossacks

time-sharing (computing) A means of providing simultaneous access by several users to the same computer. Each user, in turn, is assigned full use of the central processing unit for a very small duration, making it appear that each user has continuous access. >> real-time computing

time-sharing (leisure) The joint ownership of holiday accommodation by a consortium. Depending upon the number of shares acquired, each share holder is entitled to a specific period of use.

Times Square The area in New York City formed by the intersection of Broadway, 42nd Street, and 7th Avenue. It is at the centre of the city's theatre district. >> Broadway; New York City

Timişoara [timi**shwah**ra], Hung **Temesvár** 45°45N 21°15E, pop (1995e) 322 000. City in W Romania; ceded to Romania, 1919; violent suppression of a pro-Hungarian demonstration there in December 1989 sparked a more general uprising against the Ceauşescu regime; railway; university (1962); technical university (1920); fine arts academy; two cathedrals; Hunyadi Castle (15th-c). >> Romania ℹ

Timor [**tee**maw(r)] pop (1995e) 1 772 000; area 33 912 sq km/ 13 090 sq mi. Mountainous island in SE Asia, in the Sunda group; divided between Portugal and Holland, 1859; **West Timor** (former Dutch Timor) included in Indonesia at independence; capital, Kupang; former Portuguese territory of **East Timor** declared itself independent as the Democratic Republic of East Timor, 1975; invaded by Indonesian forces and annexed, the claim not recognized by the United Nations; considerable local unrest (1989–90), and mounting international concern over civilian deaths; independence movement (Fretilin) largely suppressed by 1993; UN-sponsored talks, 1993; ongoing conflict, mid-1990s; fresh proposals for special status, 1998; area 14 874 sq km/5 741 sq mi; pop (1995e) 818 000; capital, Dili. >> Indonesia ℹ; Sunda Islands

Timoshenko, Semyon Konstantinovich [timoh**shengk**oh] (1895–1970) Russian general, born in Furmanka, Ukraine. In 1940 he smashed Finnish resistance during the Russo-Finnish War, then commanded in the Ukraine, but failed to stop the German advance (1942). >> Russo-Finnish War; World War 2

Timothy, Letters to Two of the Pastoral Letters in the New Testament, for which Pauline authorship is often disputed today. Both letters are purportedly addressed to Paul's close companion Timothy. >> Pauline letters

timpani [**tim**panee] (singular **timpano**) Drums made from large copper bowls (hence the English name **kettledrum**), with heads of calfskin or plastic, which can be tuned to various pitches by means of hand-screws or, in modern instruments, pedals. They are normally played with two felt-headed sticks. >> drum; percussion ℹ

Timur [ti**moor**], known as **Timur Lenk** (Turk 'Timur the Lame'), English **Tamerlane** or **Tamburlaine** (1336–1405) Tatar conqueror, born near Samarkand, Uzbekistan. He subdued nearly all Persia, Georgia, and the Tatar empire, conquered all the states between the Indus and the lower Ganges (1398), and defeated the Turks at Angora (1402), taking Sultan Bajazit prisoner. >> Bajazit I

tin Sn (Lat *stannum*), element 50, melting point 232°C, density 7.3 g/cm^3. A white metal in the carbon group of elements, occurring in nature mainly as the oxide (SnO_2). It is used as a plating for other metals because of its corrosion resistance. >> chemical elements; corrosion; metal; oxide; RR1036

tinamou [**tin**amoo] A partridge-like bird, native to the New World tropics; eggs incubated by male. (Family: Tinamidae, c.50 species.) >> partridge

Tinbergen, Jan [**tin**bergen] (1903–94) Economist, born in The Hague, the brother of Nikolaas Tinbergen. His major contribution was the econometric modelling of cyclical movements in socio-economic growth. In 1969 he shared the first Nobel Prize for Economics. >> Frisch, Ragnar; Tinbergen, Nikolaas

Tinbergen, Nikolaas [**tin**bergen] (1907–88) Ethologist, born in The Hague, the brother of Jan Tinbergen. His major concern was with the patterns of animal behaviour in nature, showing that many are stereotyped. He shared the Nobel Prize for Physiology or Medicine in 1973. >> ethology; Lorenz; Tinbergen, Jan

Tindale >> **Tyndale, William**

tineid moth [**tin**eeid] A small, drab moth of the family Tineidae; c.3500 species, including the clothes moths, and other pests of stored products. (Order: Lepidoptera.) >> moth

Tinian [**tin**ian] pop (1995e) 2200; area 101 sq km/39 sq mi. One of the N Mariana Is; length 18 km/11 mi; four long runways built by the USA during World War 2. >> Mariana Islands

tinnitus [**tin**itus] A ringing or hissing sound heard within the ear, which may arise from almost any disorder of the ear or its nerve supply. In many cases, the disorder is intractable. >> ear ℹ

Tin Pan Alley A nickname coined c.1900 for the popular music-publishing centre of New York City situated on 28th Street and 6th Avenue, and later on Broadway near 49th Street. >> New York City

tinplate A thin steel sheet coated with tin by dipping or electrolytic deposition, used for light robust containers and protective constructions. After the invention of canning in the early 19th-c, it attained worldwide industrial importance. >> electrolysis; tin

Tintoretto [tinto**re**toh], originally **Jacopo Robusti** (1518–94) Venetian painters, probably born in Venice, the son of a dyer (*tintore*). His major works include 'The Last Supper' (1547, Venice), 'The Last Judgment' (c.1560, Venice) and the 'Paradiso' (1588, Venice), famous for its great size. >> Venetian School

Tipperary [tipuh**rair**ee], Ir **Thiobrad Arann** County in Munster province, SC Ireland; divided into **North Riding** (pop (1995e) 57 400; area 1996 sq km/770 sq mi) and **South Riding** (pop (1995e) 74 400; area 2258 sq km/ 872 sq mi); capital, Clonmel; rich dairy-farming area; centre for horse and greyhound breeding. >> Clonmel; Ireland (republic) ℹ

Tippett, Sir Michael (Kemp) (1905–98) Composer, born in London. His oratorio, *A Child of our Time* (1941), reflecting the problems of the 1930s and 1940s, won him wide recognition. His other works include the operas *The Midsummer Marriage* (1952) and *King Priam* (1961), four symphonies, a piano concerto, and string quartets.

Tippoo Sultán [ti**poo**], also known as **Tippoo Sahib** (1749–99) Sultan of Mysore (1782–99), born in Devanhalli, India, the son of Haidar Ali. He continued his father's policy of opposing British rule, but was defeated by Cornwallis and had to cede half his kingdom. >> Cornwallis; Haidar Ali

Tiranë [tee**rah**na], Ital **Tirana** 41°20N 19°50E, pop (1995e) 264 000. Capital town of Albania; founded by Turks in the early 17th-c; made capital in 1920; university (1957); railway; airport. >> Albania ℹ

Tiresias [tiy**reez**ias] In Greek mythology, a blind Theban prophet, who takes a prominent part in Sophocles' plays about Oedipus and Antigone. >> Sophocles

Tirol or **Tyrol** [ti**rohl**] pop (1995e) 653 000; area 12 647 sq km/ 4882 sq mi. Federal state of W Austria; capital, Innsbruck; leading state for tourism, especially winter sports. >> Austria ℹ; Innsbruck

Tirpitz, Alfred (Friedrich) von [**teer**pits] (1849–1930) German admiral, born in Kostrzyn, Poland (formerly Küstrin, Prussia). As secretary of state for the imperial navy (1897–1916), he raised a fleet to challenge British supremacy of the seas, and acted as its commander 1914–16. >> World War 1

Tirso de Molina [**teer**soh, mo**lee**na], pseudonym of

Gabriel Téllez (c.1571–1648) Playwright, born in Madrid. He wrote many comedies and religious plays, but is best known for his treatment of the Don Juan legend in *El burlador de Sevilla* (1635, The Seducer of Seville).

Tirthankara [teer**tang**kara] (Sanskrit, 'ford-maker') A title used by Jains of the 24 great heroes of their tradition who, by their teaching and example, taught them the way to cross the stream from the bondage of physical existence to freedom from rebirth. >> Jainism

Tiruchchirappalli [tiroochira**pah**lee] or **Trichinopoly** [triki**nop**olee] 10°45N 78°45E, pop (1995e) 770 000. City in Tamil Nadu, S India, on the Kaveri R; airfield; railway; educational, religious, and commercial centre, noted for its gold, silver, and brass working. >> Tamil Nadu

Tiryns [**teer**inz] An ancient Greek town in the Argolid near Mycenae, famous for the remains of its fortified Bronze Age palace. >> Mycenae

Tissot, James Joseph Jacques [**tee**soh] (1836–1902) Painter, born in Nantes, France. He painted highly accomplished scenes of Victorian life in London, and produced a series of the life of Christ in watercolour.

Tisza, River [**ti**sa], Czech **Tisa**, Russian **Tissa** Longest tributary of the R Danube in E Europe; rises in the Carpathian Mts; enters the Danube SW of Belgrade; length 962 km/598 mi. >> Hungary ℹ

tit A small, lively, acrobatic songbird, native to the N hemisphere and Africa; also known as the **titmouse**; includes the **chickadees** of North America. (Family: Paridae, 46 species.) >> bluetit; chickadee; songbird

Titan (astronomy) [**tiy**tn] Saturn's largest satellite, discovered in 1655; distance from the planet 1 222 000 km/759 000 mi; diameter 5150 km/3200 mi; orbital period 15·945 days. It is the second-largest moon in the Solar System, and the only satellite with a substantial atmosphere, principally composed of nitrogen and methane. >> Saturn (astronomy); Voyager project ℹ; RR964

Titan (mythology) [**tiy**tn] In Greek mythology, a member of the older generation of gods, the children of Uranus and Gaia. After Zeus and the Olympians took power, the Titans made war on them; but they were defeated and imprisoned in Tartarus. >> Cronus; Greek gods ℹ; Hyperion (mythology); Iapetus (mythology); Mnemosyne; Oceanus; Phoebe (mythology); Prometheus; Rhea (mythology)

Titania (astronomy) The largest satellite of Uranus, discovered in 1787 by Herschel; distance from the planet 436 000 km/271 000 mi; diameter 1580 km/980 mi. It has an icy, cratered surface. >> Herschel; Uranus (astronomy); RR964

Titania (mythology) In Greek mythology, a female Titan, identified with the Moon. In Shakespeare's *A Midsummer Night's Dream* she is the queen of the fairies. >> Oberon; Titan

Titanic [tiy**tan**ik] British 46 329-gross-tonnes passenger liner, belonging to White Star Line, which collided with an iceberg in the N Atlantic on her maiden voyage in April 1912. Lifeboat capacity was inadequate, and just over 700 people were saved, while 1500 went down with the ship. The vessel was rediscovered in 1985, explored, and photographed on the seabed. An Oscar-winning film of the tragedy, directed by James Cameron, was released in 1997.

titanium Ti, element 22, melting point 1660°C. A lustrous, white metal, with a relatively low density of 4.5 g/cm^3. It is found widely distributed in nature, never uncombined, and usually as an oxide (TiO_2). The metal, produced by magnesium reduction, is used in some alloys, especially for aircraft. >> alloy; chemical elements; metal; RR1036

titanothere [tiy**tan**otheer] A medium to large plant-eating mammal; known as fossils from the early Tertiary period of North America and E Asia; some stood 2·5 m/8 ft at the shoulder. (Order: Perissodactyla.) >> herbivore; mammal ℹ; Tertiary period

Titchmarsh, Alan (Fred) (1949–) Gardener, broadcaster, and writer, born in Ilkley, West Yorkshire. He became a BBC household name for his expert advice on gardening matters, in 1996 becoming presenter of the popular radio series, *Gardener's World*.

tithes Offerings of a proportion (literally 'the tenth part') of one's property or produce to God, often given to the priesthood of temples; customary among peoples since ancient times. Civil tithes were replaced in England by a rent charge in 1836, and even this was abolished in 1936.

titi or **tee-tee** [**tee**tee] A New World monkey of genus *Callicebus* (3 species); thick coat and long tail; characteristically crouches on a branch with all four feet together, tail hanging vertically. >> New World monkey

Titian [**tish**an], Ital **Tiziano Vecellio** (c.1490–1576) Venetian painter, born in Pieve di Cadore, Italy. For the Duke of Ferrara he painted three great mythological subjects, 'The Feast of Venus' (c.1515–18), 'Bacchanal' (c.1518, both Prado, Madrid), and the richly-coloured 'Bacchus and Ariadne' (c.1523, National Gallery, London). Later works include his famous 'Ecce Homo' (1543, Vienna) and 'Christ Crowned with Thorns' (c.1570, Munich). >> Venetian School

Titicaca, Lake [teetee**ka**kuh] Lake in SE Peru and W Bolivia; largest lake in South America (area 8290 sq km/3200 sq mi) and highest large lake in world (3812 m/12 506 ft); length 177 km/110 mi; width 56 km/35 mi; maximum depth 475 m/1558 ft; steamers run from Guaqui (Bolivia) to Puno (Peru); hunting, fishing, yachting; statue of Virgin de Copacabana (1576) on SW shore, place of pilgrimage. >> Bolivia ℹ; Incas

titmouse >> **tit**

Tito [**tee**toh], known as **Marshal Tito**, originally **Josip Broz** (1892–1980) Yugoslav president (1953–80), born in Kumrovec, Croatia. In 1941 he organized partisan forces against the Axis conquerors, and after the war became the country's first communist prime minister (1945). He broke with the Cominform in 1948, developing Yugoslavia's independent style of communism (**Titoism**). >> Axis Powers; Chetniks; communism

Titograd >> **Podgorica**

titration A technique for finding the volume of one solution chemically equivalent to a given volume of another, usually by adding the first solution slowly until equivalence is reached. This can be detected by the addition of a small amount of an indicator material. >> solution

Titus [**tiy**tus], in full **Titus Flavius Vespasianus** (39–81) Roman emperor (79–81), the elder son of Vespasian. Popular with the Romans, he is execrated in Jewish tradition for his destruction of Jerusalem (70) and suppression of the Jewish Revolt. His brief reign was marred by many natural calamities, notably the eruption of Vesuvius (79). >> Pompeii; Vesuvius

Titus, St [**tiy**tus] (1st-c) In the New Testament, a Gentile companion of the apostle Paul. Ecclesiastical tradition makes him the first Bishop of Crete. Feast day 6 February (W), 23 August (E). >> Paul, St; Titus, Letter to

Titus, Letter to One of the Pastoral Letters in the New Testament, for which Pauline authorship is usually disputed today. The letter addresses problems of church order and false teachers. >> New Testament; Pauline Letters

Tiv An agricultural people of C Nigeria, living along the Benue R. They speak a Niger–Congo language. >> Niger–Congo languages; Nigeria ℹ

Tiwi [**tee**wee] The Aboriginal inhabitants of Melville and Bathurst Islands, off Darwin, Northern Territory, Australia. Cut off from the mainland for 5000 or more years, they developed a distinctive culture. >> Aborigines

Tlapanek >> **Hokan languages**

Tlemcen [tlem**sen**], ancient **Pomaria** 34°53N 1°21W, pop (1995e) 302 000. Town in NW Algeria; capital of major Moroccan dynasties (12th–16th-c); railway; Almovarid Great Mosque (1135). >> Algeria ℹ; Almoravids

Tlingit A North American Indian group of the Pacific NW coast who lived mainly by fishing and hunting, c.14 000 (1990 census). They are famed for their art. >> Northwest Coast Indians

TNT The abbreviation for **trinitrotoluene**, $C_7H_5N_3O_6$. A high explosive made by the nitration of toluene with nitric and sulphuric acids; a solid melting at 82°C. It is one of the most effective of the military high explosives. >> explosives

toad >> **frog**

toadfish Robust bottom-living fish of the family Batrachoididae (6 genera), found in inshore waters of tropical to temperate seas; body typically elongate, tapering to a small tail, dorsal and anal fins long; eyes placed on top of flattened head, mouth large with strong teeth.

toadflax An annual or perennial, native to the N hemisphere, especially the Mediterranean region; flowers in a variety of colour combinations; tube spurred and 2-lipped, with a projection closing the tube, so that pollinators must part the lips to reach nectar held in the spur. (Genus: *Linaria*, 150 species. Family: Scrophulariaceae.)

toadstool An informal name for many typically umbrella-shaped fungal fruiting bodies, especially those that are poisonous or inedible. >> fungus; mushroom

Toamasina, also **Tamatave** 18°10S 49°23E, pop (1995e) 171 000. Port on the E coast of Madagascar, on the Indian Ocean; popular tourist resort; airfield; railway. >> Madagascar ℹ

tobacco An annual or shrubby perennial, native to warm parts of the New World and Australasia; tubular flowers, greenish, yellow, pink, or reddish. The dried, slightly fermented leaves of various species, principally *Nicotiana tabacum*, are used for smoking, chewing, and snuff, and contain the powerful alkaloid *nicotine*. (Genus: *Nicotiana*, 66 species. Family: Solanaceae.) >> alkaloids; nicotine; smoking

Tobago [to**bay**goh] pop (1995e) 51 800; area 300 sq km/ 116 sq mi. Island in the West Indies; part of the Republic of Trinidad and Tobago; chief town, Scarborough; united with Trinidad in 1889; airport; luxury hotel-conference centre at Rocky Point; tourist complex at Minster Point. >> Trinidad and Tobago ℹ

Tobacco plant

Tobin, James [**toh**bin] (1918–) Economist, born in Champaign, IL. He is best known for his work on portfolio choice under uncertainty, in which he clarifies the trade-off between risk and yield. He was awarded the Nobel Prize for Economics in 1981. >> Keynesian; portfolio theory

Tobit or **Tobias, Book of** [**toh**bit] A book of the Old Testament Apocrypha named after its hero, Tobit, written perhaps c.3rd–2nd-c BC by an unknown author. >> Apocrypha, Old Testament; Judaism

tobogganing >> **bobsledding**

Tobruk or **Tubruq** [tu**bruk**] 32°06N 23°56E, pop (1995e) 127 000. Seaport in N Libya; occupied by the Italians, 1911; important battle site in World War 2; taken by Australians (Jan 1941), then changed hands several times until finally taken by the British (late 1942). >> Libya ℹ; Rommel

Toby jug A pottery jug in the form of a seated figure, usually a stout man smoking a pipe and wearing a tricorn hat which forms the pouring lip. Such jugs seem to have been introduced in N Staffordshire c.1770. >> pottery

Toc H A Christian fellowship founded in 1915 as a club for British soldiers serving in Belgium. Its name derives from its location in Talbot House (named after Lt Gilbert Talbot (1891–1915)), the initials of which were 'pronounced' by army signallers as 'Toc H'. The club now engages in a wide range of social work in the English-speaking world. >> Christianity

tocopherol A naturally occurring E vitamin, inhibiting rancidity in oils rich in polyunsaturated fatty acids. It is widely distributed in foods, but its highest levels are found in vegetable oils. >> antioxidants; polyunsaturated fatty acids; vitamins ℹ

Tocqueville, Alexis (Charles Henri Maurice Clérel) de [**tok**veel] (1805–59) Historian and political scientist, born in Verneuil, France. His political study, *De la Démocratie en Amerique* (1835, Democracy in America) gave him a European reputation. After Louis Napoleon's coup, he wrote the first volume of *L'Ancien Régime et la Révolution* (1856, The Old Regime and the Revolution), but died before it could be completed. >> Napoleon III

Todaiji [toh**diy**jee] Buddhist shrine at Nara, Japan. Founded in 743, it contains a huge Buddha, 16 m/53 ft high, made of 450 000 kg/1 million lb of bronze, on a base 20 m/68 ft across. >> Buddhism; Horyuji; Nara; Toshodaishi

Todd, Mike, popular name of **Michael Todd**, originally **Avrom Hirsch Goldbogen** (1909–58) Showman, born in Minneapolis, MN. He sponsored the 'TODD-AO' wide-screen process, used for his greatest film, *Around the World in Eighty Days* (1956, Oscar). He married his third wife, Elizabeth Taylor, in 1957, but was killed the next year in an aircrash. >> Taylor, Elizabeth

Todi, Jacopone da [**toh**dee, jako**poh**nay] (c.1230–1306) Religious poet, born in Todi, Italy. To him is ascribed the authorship of the *Stabat Mater*; and he wrote *laudi spirituali* ('spiritual praises'), important in early Italian drama.

tog A unit for measuring the 'warmth' rating in bedding textiles. The tog rating is a measure of thermal resistance: the higher the value, the better its performance.

Togo [**toh**goh], official name **Republic of Togo**, Fr **République Togolaise** pop (1995e) 4 074 000; area 56 790 sq km/ 21 921 sq mi. Republic in W Africa; capital, Lomé; timezone GMT; chief ethnic groups, Hamitic (N) and Ewe (S); chief religions, local beliefs (70%), Christianity (20%); official language, French, with many local languages spoken; unit of currency, the franc CFA; land rises from the lagoon coast of the Gulf of Guinea, to the Atakora Mts running in the N; highest peak, Pic Baumann (986 m/

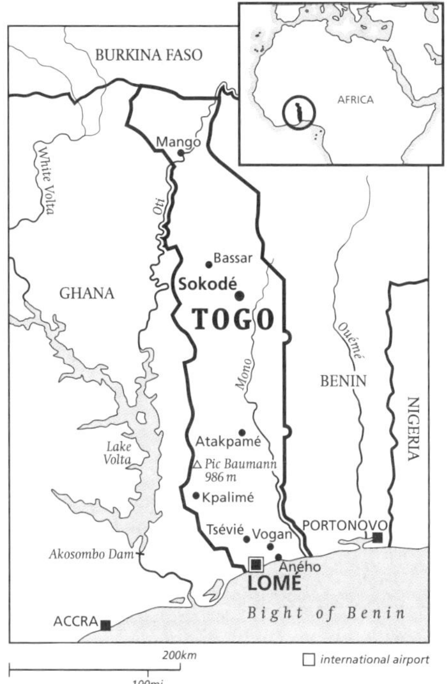

3235 ft); tropical climate; formerly part of the Kingdom of Togoland; German protectorate, 1884–1914; mandate of the League of Nations in 1922, divided between France (French Togo) and Britain (part of British Gold Coast); trusteeships of the United Nations, 1946; French Togo became an autonomous republic within the French Union, 1956; British Togoland voted to join the Gold Coast (Ghana), 1957; independence, 1960; military coups, 1963, 1967; return to civilian rule, 1980; governed by a president, prime minister, and National Assembly; largely agricultural economy. >> Ghana ℹ; Lomé; mandates; RR1024 political leaders

Tojo, Hideki [**toh**joh] (1885–1948) Japanese general, statesman, and prime minister (1941–4), born in Tokyo. During World War 2 he was minister of war (1940–1) and premier. He was hanged as a war criminal in Tokyo. >> World War 2

tokamak [**tok**amak] A machine used in nuclear fusion research. A complex system of magnetic fields confines the plasma of reactive charged particles in a hollow chamber, where it is then heated to temperatures in excess of 10^8°C. >> Joint European Torus; nuclear fusion; plasma (physics)

tokay gecko [**toh**kay **ge**koh] A large gecko (*Gekko gekko*) (length, almost 30 cm/12 in), native to India and SE Asia; mottled coloration; nocturnal; also known as **common gecko**. >> gecko

Tokelau [tohke**low**], formerly **Union Islands** 8–10°S 171–173°W; pop (1995e) 1500; area 10.1 sq km/3.9 sq mi. Island territory consisting of three small atolls in the S Pacific Ocean, c.3500 km/2200 mi N of New Zealand; chief settlement, Nukunonu; timezone GMT −11; ethnic group, Polynesian; chief languages, Tokelauan, English; inhabitants are citizens of New Zealand; Western Samoa and New Zealand currencies in use; British protectorate in 1877; annexed in 1916, and included with the Gilbert and Ellice Islands Colony; returned to separate status in 1925, under administrative control of New Zealand, but substantially self-governing at local level; principal revenue earners are copra, stamps, souvenir coins, and handicrafts. >> New Zealand ℹ

tokonama [tokonahma] A Japanese alcove, in Japanese-style houses the place for scroll painting, flower arrangement, and art objects, especially at New Year. At home or in a restaurant the most honoured place for the guest is next to the *tokonama*.

Tok Pisin [tok **pi**zhin] An English-based pidgin, spoken by c.750 000 people in Papua New Guinea. It is now spoken by some as a mother-tongue, and has thus become a creole. >> creole; pidgin

Tokugawa, Ieyasu [tokugahwa] (1542–1616) The third of the three great historical unifiers of Japan; a noble from E Japan. He founded the Tokugawa shogunate (1603–1868), completed Edo Castle as his headquarters, and instituted a centralized control of Japanese life. >> Meiji Restoration; Shogun

Tokyo 35°40N 139°45E, pop (1995e) 8 103 000 (metropolitan district). Seaport capital of Japan, E Honshu; on R Sumida; founded as village of Edo, 12th-c; headquarters of the Tokugawa shogunate, 1603; imperial capital, 1868; severe earthquake damage, 1923; heavily bombed in World War 2; airport; railway; over 100 universities; dense pollution and traffic congestion; Tokyo Tower (1958), tallest metal tower in the world; Ginza shopping district, 17th-c Imperial Palace, Meiji Shrine, Sensai Temple, Yasukuni Shrine; Disneyland (1983), 10 km/6 mi SE. >> Japan ℹ; Tokugawa

Toledo (Spain) [to**lay**t͟ho], Lat **Toletum** 39°50N 4°02W, pop (1995e) 60 000. City in Spain, on R Tagus; former capital of Visigothic kingdom; railway; noted for its swords and knives; Moorish citadel, cathedral (13th–17th-c), El Greco's house; old city is a world heritage site. >> Greco, El; Spain ℹ; Visigoths

Toledo (USA) [to**lee**doh] 41°39N 83°33W, pop (1995e) 346 000. Port in NW Ohio, USA, at the W end of L Erie; formed by the union of two settlements, 1833; involved in the 'Toledo War', 1835–6, a boundary dispute between Ohio and Michigan; railway; university (1872); one of the country's largest rail centres. >> Ohio

Tolkien, J(ohn) R(onald) R(euel) [**tol**keen] (1892–1973) Philologist and writer, born in Bloemfontein, South Africa. His interest in language and saga led to his books about a fantasy world in which the beings have their own language and mythology, notably *The Hobbit* (1937), *The Lord of the Rings* (3 vols, 1954–5), and *The Silmarillion* (1977).

Tolpuddle martyrs Agricultural labourers at Tolpuddle, Dorset, who were organized in 1833 into a trade union by a local Methodist preacher, George Loveless (1796–1874), convicted of taking illegal oaths, and transported. The action provoked substantial protests, and the labourers were eventually pardoned. >> trade union

Tolstoy, Count Leo Nikolayevich (1828–1910) Russian writer, moralist, and mystic, born at Yasnaya Polyana, Russia. He became known for his short stories, then wrote his epic story of Russia during the Napoleonic Wars, *Voyna i mir* (1865–9, War and Peace), followed by *Anna Karenina* (1875–7). He experienced a spiritual crisis which culminated in such works as *Ispoved* (written 1879, A Confession) and *V chyom moya vera* (1883, What I Believe). He made over his fortune to his wife and lived poorly as a peasant under her roof. Leaving home secretly, he died of pneumonia some days later at Astopovo railway station. His doctrines founded a sect, and Yasnaya Polyana became a place of pilgrimage.

Toltecs [**tol**teks] A people (or peoples) who controlled most of C Mexico between AD c.900 and AD 1150; the last such dominant culture prior to the Aztecs. Their capital was at

Tula, 80 km/50 mi N of Mexico City. >> Chichén Itzá; Mexico ℹ

Toluca or **Toluca de Lerdo** [to**loo**ka] 19°17N 99°39W, pop (1995e) 541 000. City in C Mexico; altitude 2675 m/ 8776 ft; founded, 1535; university (1956). >> Mexico ℹ

toluene [**tol**yooeen] $C_6H_5CH_3$, IUPAC **methylbenzene**, boiling point 111 °C. A colourless liquid with a characteristic odour, widely used as an organic solvent, being substantially less toxic than benzene. It is obtained from coal tar. >> picric acid; TNT

tomatillo An annual native to tropical America (*Physalis ixocarpa*); flowers bright yellow with dark basal spots; berry 5 cm/2 in, yellow to purple. It is a locally important food crop. (Family: Solanaceae.) >> physalis

tomato A bushy annual (*Lycopersicon esculentum*) native to Pacific South America, but now cultivated on a commercial scale throughout the world; flowers in short sprays, yellow, with five reflexed petals; berry bright red, fleshy, edible; originally called **love apple** and regarded as an aphrodisiac. (Family: Solanaceae.)

Tombaugh, Clyde W(illiam) [**tom**bow] (1906–97) Astronomer, born in Streator, IL. He discovered the planet Pluto in 1930 as a result of a systematic search. >> Gemini; Pluto (astronomy)

tombolo [**tom**bohloh] >> **spit**

Tommy gun >> **submachine-gun; Thompson, John T**

tomography [toh**mo**grafee] A technique using X-rays or ultrasound in which a clear image of structures in a single plane of body tissues at a particular depth is achieved. >> ultrasound; X-rays

Tompion, Thomas (c.1639–1713) Clock-maker, born in Northill, Bedfordshire. He made watches, table clocks, and long-case clocks with greatly improved timekeeping, and is acknowledged as the greatest English maker. >> clock; watch

Tomsk 56°30N 85°05E, pop (1995e) 509 000. River port in WC Siberian Russia, on R Tom; founded, 1604; airfield; railway; university (1888). >> Russia ℹ

Tom Thumb >> **Stratton, Charles**

tomtit >> **bluetit**

tom-tom A cylindrical, double-headed, high-pitched drum, played with sticks in sets of two or more in Western dance bands and jazz groups. >> drum

tonality The property of music which is written 'in a key', ie with a particular pitch as a point of aural reference towards which other key centres gravitate. The theoretical corner-stones of tonality are the diatonic major and minor scales, in which pitches are related to a **tonic**, or key note, so that the intervals between any two degrees of the scale remain the same whichever note serves as the tonic. Tonality admits only two modes (major and minor), but each of these may be expressed in 12 possible keys. Tonality gradually replaced modality in the 16th–17th-c, and served as the main structural basis for musical work of the next 250 years. In the 20th-c several alternatives were proposed. >> atonality; bitonality; chromaticism; modulation; scale ℹ; serialism; transposition

Tone, (Theobald) Wolfe (1763–98) Irish nationalist, born in Dublin. He helped to organize the United Irishmen, and had to flee to the USA and to France (1795). He induced France to invade Ireland, was captured, and committed suicide. >> nationalism

tone In music, **1** the interval (equal to two semitones) between, for example, the first two notes of a diatonic scale, or *doh* and *ray* in tonic sol-fa. >> scale ℹ **2** The timbre of a voice or instrument. >> timbre **3** US usage for *note* (pitch) in such contexts as '12-tone music', 'tone cluster', and 'tone row'.

tone cluster >> **tone 3**

tone language A language in which the pitch level (**tone**) carried by a word is an essential signal of its meaning. In one variety of Chinese, for example, the word *ma* means 'mother' with a level tone, and 'horse' with a falling-rising tone. >> prosody

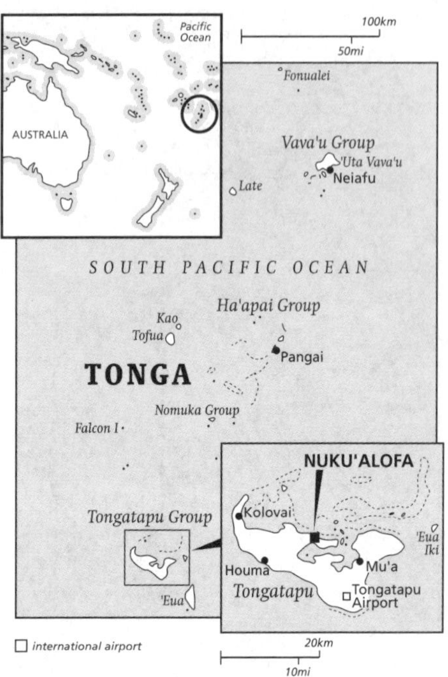

tone poem >> **symphonic poem**

Tonga, official name **Kingdom of Tonga**, Tongan **Pule'anga Fakatu'i 'o Tonga**, formerly **Friendly Islands** pop (1995e) 105 000; area 646 sq km/249 sq mi. Island group in the SW Pacific Ocean, 2250 km/1400 mi NE of New Zealand; capital, Nuku'alofa; timezone GMT +13; population mainly Polynesian (98%); chief religion, Christianity; official languages, English, Tongan; unit of currency, the pa'anga; largest island is Tongatapu, with two-thirds of the population, area 260 sq km/100 sq mi; W islands mainly volcanic; highest point, extinct volcano of Kao (1014 m/3327 ft); semi-tropical climate; British protectorate in 1899, under its own monarchy; independence, 1970; governed by a sovereign, Privy Council, and a unicameral Legislative Assembly; economy largely based on agriculture; tourism and cottage handicrafts are growing industries. >> Nuku'alofa; RR1024 political leaders

Tongariro [tongga**ree**roo] 39°08S 175°42E; area 765 sq km/ 295 sq mi. Active volcano rising to 1968 m/6457 ft in SWC North Island, New Zealand; winter skiing resort; many historical Maori sites. >> New Zealand ℹ

Tongeren [**tong**eren], Fr **Tongres** 50°47N 5°28E, pop (1995e) 29 800. Rural market town in Belgium, on R Jeker; oldest town in Belgium, founded 1st-c AD; basilica of Our Lady. >> Belgium ℹ

Tongres [tõgr] >> **Tongeren**

tongue A highly mobile, muscular structure vital for the digestive functions of chewing, taste, and swallowing. In humans it is also important in speech, being essential for the production of all vowels and most consonants. It consists of a free front part within the mouth, containing numerous taste buds, and a more fixed back part in the oropharynx, which has accumulations of lymphoid tissue associated with it (the *lingual tonsil*). The two parts are separated by a V-shaped furrow on the upper surface, with its apex directed backwards. The muscles of the tongue are grouped into those which change its shape (the *intrinsic* muscles) and those which change its position within the mouth (the *extrinsic* muscles). >> mouth; pharynx; tonsils

tonic sol-fa A system of musical notation devised by John Curwen, who based it on the solmization system of Guido d'Arezzo, anglicizing the pitch names to *doh, ray, me, fah, soh, la, te*. >> Curwen; scale ℹ

Tonkin or **Tongking, Gulf of** [tong**kin**] Gulf in Indo-China, situated E of Vietnam and W of Hainan I, China; an inlet of the South China Sea.

Tonlé Sap [**ton**lay **sap**], Eng **Great Lake** Freshwater lake in WC Cambodia; area 2850 sq km/1100 sq mi during the dry season; linked to the Mekong R; area almost tripled during the wet season. >> Cambodia ℹ

tonnage and poundage British mediaeval customs duties: tonnage was collected on tuns of imported wine; poundage at a rate of 3d per £ of the value of imports. They were incorporated into the civil list in 1697. >> civil list

tonne >> **kilogram**

tonsillitis Acute or chronic inflammation of the tonsils, usually due to infection with streptococci. Removal of the tonsils (**tonsillectomy**) is now rarely required, and only when the tonsils are greatly enlarged and the infection deep-seated. >> *Streptococcus*; tonsils

tonsils Accumulations of lymphoid tissue found at the entrance to the respiratory and digestive tracts. The **palatine** tonsils (also referred to simply as 'the tonsils') are found at the entrance to the oropharynx. The **lingual** tonsils are under the back part of the tongue. The **tubal** tonsils are in the nasopharynx. The **pharyngeal** tonsils are behind the nasal cavity; they are also known as the **adenoids**. The four pairs of tonsils form a protective ring of tissue whose primary function is to combat airborn infections entering the body. >> adenoids; pharynx; quinsy; tonsillitis

tonsure The shaving of all or part of the head, to denote clerical or monastic status. It is still compulsory for certain monks and priests. >> monasticism

Tony An annual award for theatrical achievement in New York City; named after US actress and director Antoinette Perry (1888–1946). It recognizes several categories within plays and musicals, including acting, direction, music, choreography, and design, as well as best play, best musical, and best revival. >> theatre

Tooke, John Horne [tuk], originally **John Horne** (1736–1812) Radical politician, born in London. In 1771 he formed the Constitutional Society, supporting the American colonists and parliamentary reform. *The Diversions of Purley* (1786) was written while in prison for supporting the American cause. >> American Revolution

tool Any implement which is used to carry out a task. Early man made the first axes by sharpening flint. Stone tools were replaced around 4000 BC by metal tools, which were used to build instruments and simple machines. The Industrial Revolution saw the introduction of machine tools, and mass production of goods became a possibility. >> machine ℹ; machine tools

Toole, John Kennedy (1937–69) Novelist, born in New Orleans, LA. His novel *A Confederacy of Dunces* (1980), published 11 years after he committed suicide, won critical acclaim, and was awarded the 1981 Pulitzer Prize. *The Neon Bible* was published in 1989.

tooth >> **teeth** ℹ

toothwort A parasitic perennial (*Lathraea sqaumaria*), native to Europe and Asia; stem white; flowers tinged dull purple, forming a 1-sided spike. (Family: Scrophulariaceae.) >> broomrape; parasitic plant

Toowoomba 27°35S 151°54E, pop (1995e) 85 600. City in Queensland, Australia; airfield; railway; university, 1989; commercial centre for the rich agricultural Darling Downs area. >> Queensland

topaz An aluminium silicate mineral ($Al_2SiO_4(OH,F)_2$), occurring in acid igneous rocks, pegmatites, and veins, with a colour range including colourless, yellow, and blue. It may be used as a gemstone. >> aluminium; gemstones; silicate minerals

tope [tohp] Slender-bodied grey shark common (*Galeorhinus galeus*) in inshore waters of the E North Atlantic; length up to c.2 m/6½ ft. (Family: Carcharhinidae.) >> shark

Topeka [to**pee**ka] 39°03N 95°40W, pop (1995e) 125 000. Capital of state in E Kansas, USA, on Kansas R; settled by anti-slavery colonists, 1854; capital, 1861; railway; university (1865); marketing centre for agricultural products, particularly cattle and wheat; centre for psychiatric research. >> Kansas

topi [**toh**pee] An African ox-antelope (*Damaliscus lunatus*) with a long face; lyre-shaped horns ringed with ridges; coat with large dark patches on rich chestnut-red; fastest of all hoofed mammals (over 70 kph/40 mph). >> antelope

topography The study of the physical characteristics of the Earth's surface (eg relief, soils, vegetation). A topographical map portrays information such as elevation and gradient through the use of symbols and special shading to show contours and spot heights. >> map

topology A generalization of geometry which studies the properties of shapes and space that are independent of distance. The usual map of the London Underground is an example of a topological diagram, for it shows the lines joining various stations, yet is not to scale. >> geometry; Möbius strip ℹ

tor A mound of weathered, well-jointed, resistant, bare rocks. The rock is usually crystalline, and is exposed when surrounding and overlying rocks are stripped away by agents of erosion. Similar features in the tropics are known as **kopjes**. >> crystals; erosion

Torah [**toh**ra] (Heb 'instruction') The Jewish Law, most narrowly considered the Priestly Code found in the Pentateuch and said to have been given to Moses by God. The term was also often applied to the Pentateuch as a whole. This written Torah was eventually supplemented in Pharisaic and rabbinic tradition by the Oral Torah, an elucidation of the Written Torah by sages of various periods. >> Judaism; Mishnah; Old Testament; Pentateuch; rabbi

Torfaen [**to(r)**viyn] pop (1995e) 90 600; area 126 sq km/49 sq mi. County (unitary authority from 1996) in SE Wales, UK; administrative centre, Pontypool; other chief town, Cwmbran. >> Wales ℹ

Tories The British political party which emerged in 1679–80 as the group opposed to the exclusion of James, Duke of York, from succession to the throne. The name was taken from 17th-c Irish outlaws who plundered and killed English settlers. The party developed as the supporters of the divine right of monarchy, and had particular support from the country squirearchy and most sections of the Anglican church. It went into decline after the Hanoverian succession, but revived under the younger Pitt as the leading opposition to French Revolutionary ideology in the 1790s. Toryism developed into Conservatism under Peel, but survived as a nickname for the Conservatives. >> Conservative Party; Peel; Whigs

torii [**toh**ree] A Shinto gateway in Japan, the traditional arch at the entrance to the sacred grounds of Shinto shrines. It is generally orange-red in colour, but sometimes unpainted, giving the name of the deity.

tormentil [**taw(r)**mentil] Any of various species of *Potentilla*, with 4-petalled, yellow flowers. (Family: Rosaceae.) >> potentilla

tornado A column of air rotating rapidly (up to 100 m/s, c.225 mph) around a very low pressure centre. Over the Great Plains of the USA, they are common in spring and early summer, and resemble a dark funnel extending from the cloud base to the ground. Although short-lived, and usually only a few hundred metres in diameter, they can be very destructive in restricted areas. >> waterspout; whirlwind

Toronto 43°42N 79°25W, pop (1995e) 674 000, (metropolitan area) 3 183 000. Capital of Ontario province, Canada, on N shore of L Ontario, at the mouth of the Don R; largest city in Canada; French fort, 1749; occupied by the British, 1759; settled by migrants from the American Revolution, 1793; named York; capital of Upper Canada, 1796; city and modern name, 1834; capital of Ontario, 1867; two airports; railway; subway; two universities (1827, 1959); leading commercial and cultural centre; professional teams, Blue Jays (baseball), Maple Leafs (ice hockey); Toronto Symphony Orchestra; Fort York (1793, restored 1934). >> American Revolution; C N Tower; Ontario

torpedo A munition of naval warfare, in essence a guided underwater missile, equipped with a motor to propel it through the water and an explosive charge fused to detonate on impact with its target. The first practical torpedo dates from the middle of the 19th-c. Modern torpedoes are equipped with sonar-seeking heads which track underwater sounds, and computerized guidance systems. >> missile, guided; sonar; submarine

torpedo ray >> **electric ray**

Torquay [taw(r)**kee**] 50°28N 3°30W, pop (1995e) 60 700. Resort town in Torbay unitary authority, Devon, SW England; centre for recreational sailing; railway; Torr Abbey (12th-c); football league team, Torquay United (Gulls). >> Devon

torque In mechanics, the ability of a force to cause rotation. Torque equals the product of the force with the perpendicular distance between the rotation axis and the line of action of the force; symbol Γ; units Nm (newton.metre). >> mechanics; moment

Torquemada, Tomás de [taw(r)kay**mah**tha] (1420–98) First Inquisitor-General of Spain, born in Valladolid, Spain. As Grand Inquisitor from 1483, he displayed great cruelty, and was responsible for an estimated 2000 burnings. >> Ferdinand (of Castile); Inquisition

torr Unit of pressure; symbol *torr*; named after Evangelista Torricelli; defined via atmospheric pressure; 1 torr equals the pressure of a column of mercury 1 mm high; 1 torr = 133.3 Pa (pascal, SI unit). >> pascal; Torricelli

Torrens, Lake Salt lake in SC South Australia, W of the Flinders Ranges; 240 km/150 mi long; 65 km/40 mi wide; area 5775 sq km/2229 sq mi. >> South Australia

Torres Strait [**to**rez] Channel to the N of Cape York, Queensland, Australia; c.130 km/80 mi wide; discovered by Spanish explorer Luis Vaez de Torres, 1606; contains **Torres Strait Islands**, which may be remains of a land bridge linking Asia and Australia; annexed by Queensland in 19th-c; pop (1995e) 6500. >> Queensland

Torricelli, Evangelista [tori**chel**ee] (1608–47) Physicist and mathematician, born in Faenza, Italy. He discovered the effect of atmospheric pressure on water in a suction pump, and gave the first description of a barometer, or 'Torricellian tube' (1643). >> barometer; Galileo; torr

Tórshavn [**tors**-hown], also **Thorshavn** 62°02N 6°47W, pop (1995e) 16 000. Seaport capital of the Faeroe Is; on SE coast of Strømø I; commerce and fishing. >> Faeroe Islands

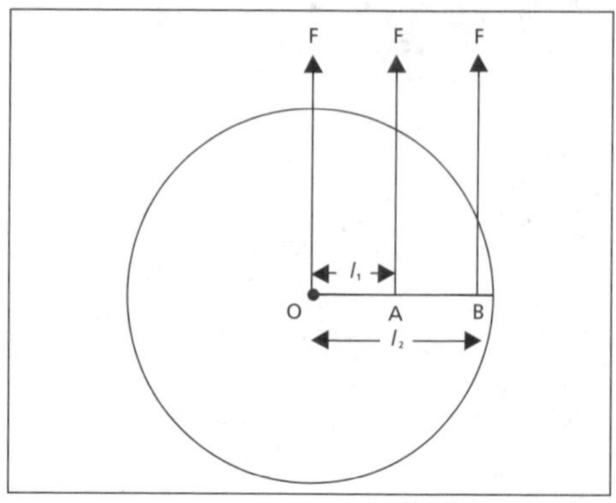

Torque – force F acting through a fixed centre O will not cause the disc to rotate, whereas the force applied at points A and B will. Applied at point B, a given force produces torque $\Gamma = Fl_2$ larger than the torque Fl_1 at A. A force applied at the outer edge of a disc thus sets the disc spinning more rapidly than the same force applied closer to the centre.

torsion The application of twisting force. *Torsional forces* cause shear strain. *Torsion balances* measure forces by detecting the degree of twist. >> shear modulus; torque ℹ

tort A wrong actionable in the civil courts of England and Wales. The usual remedies are damages and/or an injunction. Individual torts include negligence, trespass, and nuisance. The term is also used in the USA. **Delict** is the analogous term in Scots law. >> damages; injunction; negligence

Tortelier, Paul [taw(r)**tel**yay] (1914–90) Cellist, born in Paris. One of the leading soloists of the instrument. His son **Yan Pascal Tortelier** (1947–) and daughter **Maria de la Pau Tortelier** (1950–) are highly gifted players of the violin and piano respectively.

tortoise A land-dwelling reptile of order Chelonia; feet short, round, with short claws; toes not webbed; used especially for 41 species of family Testudinidae; native to tropical and subtropical regions (except Australasia); usually vegetarian. >> Chelonia ℹ; Galápagos giant tortoise ℹ; reptile; turtle (biology)

tortoiseshell butterfly A colourful butterfly; wings reddish with dark patches, and with blue patches on both wings or on hindwings. (Order: Lepidoptera. Family: Nymphalidae.) >> butterfly

tortoiseshell cat A British short-haired domestic cat; mottled coat of black, dark red, and light red (with no white); also known as **calimanco cat** or **clouded tiger**. >> cat

Toruń [to**roon**], Ger **Thorn** 53°01N 18°35E, pop (1995e) 205 000. Industrial river port in NC Poland, on R Vistula; railway; university (1945); birthplace of Copernicus; Church of St John (13th-c), castle (13th-c); medieval town, a world heritage site. >> Poland ℹ

torus >> **Joint European Torus**

Torvill and Dean Figure skaters **Jayne Torvill** (1957–) and **Christopher Dean** (1958–), both from Nottingham, Nottinghamshire. They were world ice dance champions 1981–4, and Olympic champions in 1984. They turned professional in 1984, but returned to international competition in 1993, winning the gold medal in the 1994 European Championships. However, after achieving only a bronze medal in the 1994 Winter Olympics, they once again retired. >> ice skating

Toscanini, Arturo [toska**nee**nee] (1867–1957) Conductor, born in Parma, Italy. He conducted at La Scala, Milan (1898–1908), the Metropolitan Opera House, New York (1908–15), and the New York Philharmonic (1926–36), and brought into being the Orchestra of the National Broadcasting Corporation of America (1937–53).

Tosefta or **Tosephta** [toh**sef**ta] (Aramaic 'supplement') A large collection of rabbinic traditions and discussions which supplement the teachings of the Mishnah, but are usually considered of lesser authority. It was perhaps compiled AD c.4th–5th-c. >> Mishnah; rabbi; Talmud

totalitarianism In its modern form, a political concept first used to describe the USSR's communist regime and Italy and Germany's fascist regimes during the period between the two World Wars. The leadership claims exclusive rights to govern, usually on behalf of the party and its ideology; all aspects of life are controlled by the state apparatus; political opposition is suppressed; and decision-making is highly centralized. >> communism; dictator; fascism

Totalizator A method of placing bets at horse race or greyhound meetings, commonly known as the **Tote**. All money invested is returned to winning punters, less expenses and taxes.

totem A word of North American Indian origin, widely used by social anthropologists and others to describe an animal or plant to which a particular clan or tribe has a special attachment. Attachment to the totem, or **totemism**, has been regarded as a key aspect of primitive religion. >> totem pole

totem pole An elaborately carved pole about 20 m/65 ft high, erected in front of houses, made by Pacific NW Coast American Indians. The tradition dates back to the mid-19th-c, when huge trees were cut down. It is a symbol of prestige, lacking any religious meaning. >> Northwest Coast Indians

toucan A largish bird with an enormous bill, native to the New World tropics; brightly coloured; bare coloured skin around eye; long tail. (Family: Ramphastidae, 42 species.)

touch-me-not >> **balsam**

touch screen A form of screen on a computer display which can sense any point at which it is touched and communicate the co-ordinates of that point to the computer. This is used in situations where the computer can display a set of options and the operator touches the screen at the option which is to be selected. >> computer terminal

Toulon [toolõ], Lat **Tilio Martius** 43°10N 5°55E, pop (1995e) 173 000. Fortified naval port in SE France; major naval station in World War 1; railway; episcopal see; cathedral (11th–12th-c). >> World War 2

Toulouse [toolooz], ancient **Tolosa** 43°37N 1°27E, pop (1995e) 370 000. City in S France; on R Garonne; capital of former province of Languedoc; fourth largest city in France; road and rail junction; archbishopric; cultural and economic centre of S France; university (1229); Catholic Institute of Toulouse (1877); Church of St-Sernin (11th–12th-c), cathedral (11th–17th-c). >> Languedoc

Toulouse-Lautrec (-Monfa), Henri (Marie Raymond) de [too**looz** loh**trek**] (1864–1901) Painter and lithographer, born in Albi, France. Physically frail, at the age of 14 he broke both his legs, which then ceased to grow. He settled in Montmartre, where he painted and drew the cabaret stars, prostitutes, barmaids, clowns, and actors of that society, as in 'The Bar' (1898, Zürich) and 'At the Moulin Rouge' (1892, Chicago). He also depicted fashionable society, as in 'At the Races' (1899, Albi), and produced several portraits.

touraco >> **turaco**

Touraine [tooren] Former province in C France; known for its Huguenot silk-weaving trade; chief town, Tours. >> Huguenots; Tours

Tour de France [toor duh **frãs**] The world's most gruelling bicycle race, first held in 1903. Riders have to cover approximately 4800 km/3000 mi of French countryside during a 3-week period each July.

tourmaline [**toor**maleen] A complex borosilicate mineral found in igneous and metamorphic rocks. It forms hard, dense, prismatic crystals, and may be used as a gemstone. >> gemstones; silicate minerals

Tournai [toornay], Flemish **Doornik**, ancient **Tornacum** 49°52N 5°24E, pop (1995e) 68 500. Administrative and cultural town in Belgium, on the R Scheldt; bishopric; founded AD 275; railway; cathedral (11th–12th-c, restored 19th-c). >> Belgium ℹ

Tourneur, Cyril [**ter**ner] (c.1575–1626) English playwright. He is known for his two plays, *The Revenger's Tragedy* (1607, sometimes assigned to Webster or Middleton), and *The Atheist's Tragedy* (1611).

Tours [toor], ancient **Caesarodunum** or **Turoni** 47°22N 0°40E, pop (1995e) 133 000. Industrial and commercial city in WC France; episcopal see, 3rd-c; grew up around tomb of St Martin (died in 397), becoming a place of pilgrimage; Huguenot silk industry in 15th–16th-c; airport; road and rail junction; birthplace of Balzac; university (1970); cathedral (12th–16th-c). >> Balzac; Huguenots; Martin, St; Touraine

Toussaint l'Ouverture [toosĩ loover**tür**], originally **François Dominique Toussaint** (1746–1803) Black revolutionary leader, born a slave in Saint Domingue (Haiti, from 1804). In 1791, he joined the insurgents, and by 1797 was effective ruler of the former colony. Following an expedition sent by Napoleon to restore slavery, Toussaint was arrested, and died in a French prison. His surname comes from his bravery in once making a breach in the ranks of the enemy. >> Haiti; Napoleon I

Tower Bridge The easternmost bridge on the R Thames, London, which can open to allow large ships in and out of the Pool of London. It was opened in 1894. >> Thames, River

Tower of London A palace-fortress started by the Normans in the 11th-c, and a state prison from the 15th-c to the 18th-c. It is now Britain's most popular tourist attraction, and the depository of the royal coronation regalia. >> crown jewels; London; Normans

Townes, Charles H(ard) (1915–) Physicist, born in Greenville, SC. He shared the 1964 Nobel Prize for Physics for his work on the development of the maser, and later the laser. >> laser ℹ; maser

town hall clock >> **moschatel** ℹ

Townsend, Sue (1946–) Novelist and playwright, born in Leicester, Leicestershire. She made her name through a series of novels introducing the character of Adrian Mole, beginning with *The Secret Diary of Adrian Mole Aged 13¾* (1982). Her plays include *Bazaar and Rummage* (1982) and *The Queen and I* (1992).

Townshend (of Rainham), Charles Townshend, 2nd Viscount [**town**zend], known as **Turnip Townshend** (1674–1738) British Whig statesman, born in Raynham, Norfolk. Made secretary of state by George I (1714–16, 1721–30), he acquired his nickname for his proposal to use turnips in crop rotation. >> George I

Townshend Acts (1767) Taxes imposed by the British parliament on five categories of goods imported into the American colonies. Following resistance, four categories were repealed in 1770. The fifth, on tea, remained in effect until the Boston Tea Party. The Acts are named after the British Chancellor of the Exchequer, Charles Townshend (1725–67), who sponsored them. >> American Revolution; Stamp Act

Townsville 19°13S 146°48E, pop (1995e) 92 300. Industrial port and resort in Queensland, Australia; founded, 1864; Australian Institute of Marine Science; airport; railway; university (1970); army and air-force bases. >> Queensland

toxicology The study of the adverse effects of chemicals on living systems. Toxicology allows prediction of the risks likely to be associated with a particular chemical or drug.

toxin A poison produced by a micro-organism, which causes certain diseases or disorders. Toxins from *Salmonella typhi* cause typhoid fever; toxins from *Pasteurella pestis* cause bubonic plague; toxins from *Shigella dysenteriae* cause dysentery. >> botulism; toxicology

toxocariasis [toksohka**riy**asis] Infection with the ova of *Toxocara canis* (carried by dogs). They cause allergic features such as asthma, and sometimes also a lesion of the eye. >> allergy

toxoplasmosis [toksohplaz**moh**sis] Infection with the protozoan *Toxoplasma gondi*. It is often harmless, but may be transmitted by an infected mother to the fetus, with involvement of the brain, eyes, heart, and lungs. >> Protozoa

toy dog >> **non-sporting dog**

Toynbee, Arnold (Joseph) [**toyn**bee] (1889–1975) Historian, born in London. His major work was the multi-volume *Study of History* (1933–61).

Toynbee, Polly, popular name of **Mary Louisa Toynbee** (1946–) British journalist and broadcaster. She became a reporter and feature writer with *The Observer* (1968–71, 1972–7), then a columnist on *The Guardian* (1977–88), BBC social affairs editor (1988–95), and associate editor and columnist on *The Independent* (from 1995).

Toynbee Hall The first university settlement (institutions through which universities provide support to deprived inner city communities), founded in E London in 1885. It was named after the social reformer and economist Arnold Toynbee (1852–83).

trabeated construction >> **post and lintel** ⓘ

trace elements >> **nutrients**

tracer bullet A bullet containing a charge of chemical compound (such as phosphorus) which glows brightly as it flies through the air, indicating the 'trace' of the bullet's path, and thus its efficacy in reaching the target.

tracery The ornamental stone pattern work used in the upper part of a window, screen, panel, or other building element. It is usually associated with Gothic architecture. >> Gothic architecture

trachea [tra**kee**a] A tube connecting the larynx with the principal bronchi; also known as the **windpipe**. In the human adult it is 9–15 cm/3.5–6 in long. In cases of respiratory distress the trachea can be surgically opened between the cartilage rings within the lower part of the neck to provide a passage for air (**tracheostomy**). >> anatomy ⓘ; bronchi; cartilage; croup; larynx; respiration

trachoma [tra**koh**ma] Infection with a *Chlamydia* bacterium that affects the eyes, leading to conjunctivitis and blindness. Vast numbers of people living in the tropics and subtropics are affected. >> blindness; chlamydia; conjunctivitis

Tractarianism >> **Oxford Movement**

tractor A self-propelled vehicle found on farms or similar places of work, and normally used for towing and powering various agricultural machines. Tractors do not usually have a frame or springs, but use the engine and transmission housing to provide structural rigidity, with the tyres to provide cushioning.

Tracy, Spencer (Bonadventure) (1900–67) Actor, born in Milwaukee, WI. He received Academy Awards for *Captains Courageous* (1937) and *Boys' Town* (1938). In the 1940s and 1950s he played opposite Katherine Hepburn in eight outstanding comedies. Later films included *Judgment at Nuremberg* (1961) and *Guess Who's Coming to Dinner* (1967), again with Hepburn.

trade association >> **employers' association**

trade cycle The pattern of changing levels of activity in an economy over a period of time. Cycles have varied in length from four to ten years, but some economists have claimed to detect longer cycles in activity, with periods of up to 70 years. >> fiscal policy; recession

trademark A symbol placed on an article to show that it has been made by a certain company. When the mark is registered, its unauthorized use is illegal. In the USA, trademarks often include the sign ™, signifying that the mark has been registered.

tradescantia [trades**kan**tia] A succulent perennial with jointed, often trailing stems, native to the New World; flowers 3-petalled, often white or blue, in small terminal clusters; named after John Tradescant, botanist to Charles I of England. (Genus: *Tradescantia*, 60 species. Family: Commelinaceae.) >> succulent; wandering Jew / sailor

Trades Union Congress (TUC) A voluntary association of trade unions in the UK, founded in 1868. It meets annually in September to decide policy, and representation at the Conference is based on one delegate per 5000 members. There are 74 affiliated unions, representing 6·8 million members. >> trade union

trade union An association of people, often in the same type of business, trade, or profession, who have joined together to protect their interests and improve their pay and working conditions. The trade union movement developed in the early years of the 19th-c, growing rapidly after the repeal of the Combination Acts (declaring unions illegal) in 1824–5. In the UK there are almost 100 such bodies, half of them supporting the Labour Party. They are often organized into branches, with local 'shop' representation in the form of a *shop steward*. In the USA, the American Federation of Labor (AFL) was established in 1886 among skilled workers, and rapidly developed into a widespread and powerful movement. In the 1930s, the Congress of Industrial Organizations (CIO) was formed as a means of providing union membership for unskilled workers, such as in the steel and automobile industries. The two organizations merged in 1955. >> industrial action; shop stewards; Teamsters' Union; Trades Union Congress; World Federation of Trade Unions

trade winds Winds blowing from areas of high pressure, centred on the Tropics of Cancer (23.5°N) and Capricorn

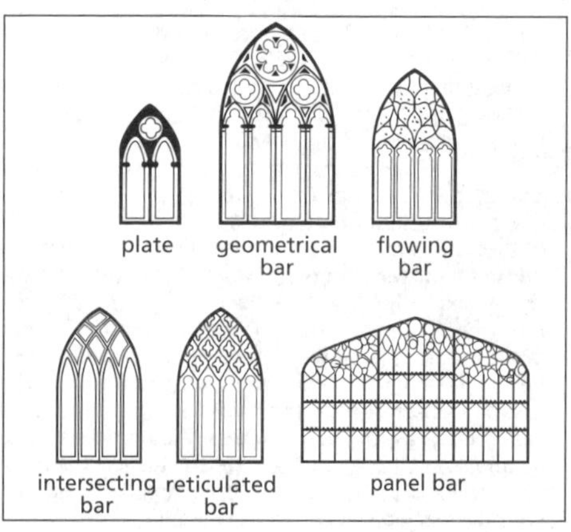

Tracery in windows

(23.5°S), towards the Intertropical Convergence Zone at the Equator. >> wind ℹ

traditional Chinese medicine (TCM) A system of medicine based on Taoist principles and texts, dating back more than 2000 years. It views health as a state in which the mind, body, and spirit are in harmony, and there is a perfect balance of yin and yang energy. Disease is due to an imbalance of energy, blockage of energy flow, and the influence of internal or external 'perverse energies', which are described according to the climatic conditions that they resemble (eg wind, heat, and damp). >> acupuncture; herbalism; shiatsu; Taoism; yin and yang

Trafalgar, Battle of (21 Oct 1805) The most famous naval engagement of the Napoleonic Wars, which destroyed Napoleon's hopes of invading England. Fought off Cape Trafalgar, Spain, between the British and Franco-Spanish fleets, the British triumph was marred by the death of Nelson. >> Napoleonic Wars; Nelson, Horatio

tragedy A play which presents the occurrence and the effects of a great misfortune suffered by an individual, and reverberating in society. Earlier, this required a great person as protagonist, but modern writers have attempted to confer tragic status on ordinary people. The fundamental purpose of tragedy (reminding us of its origins in religious ritual) was claimed by Aristotle to be the 'awakening of pity and fear', of a sense of wonder and awe at human potential, including the potential for suffering; it makes or implies an assertion of human value in the face of a hostile universe. >> Aeschylus; Corneille; Racine; Shakespeare ℹ

tragopan A pheasant, native to SE Asia; nests in tree. (Genus: *Tragopan*, 5 species.) >> pheasant

Traherne, Thomas [tra**hern**] (1637–74) Mystical writer, born in Hereford, Hereford and Worcester. The manuscripts of his *Poetical Works* (1903) and *Centuries of Meditations* (1908) were discovered by chance on a London street bookstall in 1896.

Trajan [**tray**jn], in full **Marcus Ulpius Trajanus** (c.53–117) Roman emperor (98–117), the first after Augustus to expand the Roman Empire significantly. In Rome he constructed a new forum, library, and aqueduct.

Tralee [tra**lee**], Ir **Tráighlí** 52°16N 9°42W, pop (1995e) 17 700. Capital of Kerry county, SW Ireland; railway; technical college. >> Ireland (republic) ℹ; Kerry

tram A passenger vehicle normally propelled by an electric motor fed from overhead lines, designed to run on rails set into public roads. The tram is still a major means of transport in several US and European cities (eg New Orleans, Cologne), in the UK there is a tourist service in Blackpool and in the 1990s new services began in Manchester and Sheffield. >> trolley bus

trampolining The art of performing acrobatics on a sprung canvas sheet stretched across a frame, first used at the turn of the 20th-c as a circus attraction. It was developed into a sport in 1936. >> RR1064

tranquillizer >> **benzodiazepines**

transaction processing A form of computer processing of data, through the use of a terminal, in which the operation is carried out as a sequence of transactions. At each transaction the computer poses a question via the terminal, and the terminal operator gives a response. For example, to book an airline seat the computer asks which flight, then which class, then whether smoking or nonsmoking, etc. >> batch / on-line / processing; real-time computing

Transalpine Gaul >> **Gaul**

Transcaucasia Region extending S from the Greater Caucasus to the Turkish and Iranian frontiers; comprises the republics of Georgia, Azerbaijan, and Armenia, which in 1922–36 formed the Transcaucasian SFSR. >> Caucasus Mountains

transcendentalism In philosophy, the theory, particularly associated with Kant, that the world of experience is conditioned by and logically dependent on the organizing structure of principles and concepts common to all rational minds. The term applies to a movement in 19th-c New England led by Emerson and Thoreau, which exalted the ideals of self-knowledge, self-reverence, and individual autonomy. >> Kant; Thoreau

transcendental meditation (TM) A meditation technique taught by Maharishi Mahesh Yogi, based in part on Hindu meditation. It has been widely practised in the West since the 1960s, when he 'converted' the Beatles. >> Beatles, The; maharishi

transducer Any device which converts one form of energy into another. A microphone is an acoustic transducer, converting sound waves into electrical signals. >> loudspeaker ℹ; microphone ℹ; turbine

transept The part of a cruciform-planned church that projects out at right angles to the main body of the building, usually between nave and chancel. >> chancel; choir; church ℹ; nave

transference In psychiatry, the unconscious attachment of feelings originally associated with significant early figures in one's life (eg parents) to others (particularly to the psychotherapist). In psychotherapy this allows for the exploration of a patient's early difficulties which have remained unresolved. >> psychotherapy

Transfiguration An event described in the synoptic gospels when Jesus was temporarily changed in appearance on a mountain in front of his disciples Peter, James, and John. The revelation of glory is described as accompanied by an appearance of Elijah and Moses, and a heavenly voice similar to that at Jesus's baptism. Feast day 6 August. >> Elijah; Jesus Christ; Moses; Peter, St; synoptic gospels

transformational grammar >> **generative grammar**

transformer A device which transfers an alternating current (AC) from one circuit to one or more other circuits, usually with a change of voltage. It is usually used for converting the high voltage from AC power supplies to the normal domestic supply voltage. >> electricity

transhumance The transfer of livestock, usually cattle and sheep, between winter and summer pastures. It is characteristic of some mountainous regions, where whole families may move, with their flocks, up to the high-altitude pastures.

transistor A solid-state device, made by joining semiconductors with different electrical characteristics, which can be used as an amplifier or a rectifier. Small, robust, and safe (since they need low voltage), transistors have replaced thermionic valves, and have revolutionized the construction of electronic circuits. >> electronics; rectifier; semiconductor; solid-state device; thermionic valve

transition elements Chemical elements in which an incomplete electron shell other than the valence level is being filled. They are all metals, and include the elements with atomic numbers 21 (scandium) to 29 (copper) and their groups. >> chemical elements; metal; vanadium; RR1036

transition state In a chemical reaction, an unstable arrangement of atoms characteristic of the highest energy through which the atoms must pass during the reaction. >> chemical reaction

Transkei [tranz**kiy**] Former independent black homeland in SE South Africa; capital, Umtata; traditional territory of the Xhosa; self-government, 1963; granted independence by South Africa (not recognized internationally), 1976; military coup, 1987; incorporated into Eastern Cape province in the South African constitution of 1994. >> apartheid; Eastern Cape; South Africa [i]; Xhosa

translation The conversion of one language into another; often used specifically with reference to written texts, as opposed to the **interpretation** of spoken language. **Word-for-word translation**, in which each word is found an equivalent, often makes little sense; **literal translation** adheres to the linguistic structure of the original, but transposes it into the appropriate grammatical conventions of the target language; **free translation** translates the 'sense' of the text, and seeks an idiomatic equivalent.

transliteration The written representation of a word in the closest corresponding characters of a different language. The process is commonly seen at work in loanwords, as in the Welsh *miwsig* from 'music', *bws* from 'bus'.

transmission The system fitted to an engine that transmits the power generated by the engine to the point at which it is required. Normally this system is composed of mechanical components such as gears, shafts, clutches, and chains, but other methods using hydraulic and electrical means can also be used. >> clutch; engine; gear

transpiration The loss of water vapour from a plant. The process cools and prevents damage to the leaves in hot weather, and helps draw water up from the roots to other parts of the plant. >> leaf [i]

transplantation The transfer of an organ or tissue from one person to another. Unless the recipient is an identical twin, such a graft sets up an immunological reaction of variable severity which may destroy the transplanted tissue. This reaction may be partially or completely controlled by the use of immunosuppressive drugs. Tissues that have been transplanted successfully include bone marrow, undertaken for leukaemia, and the kidney and heart, carried out for severe kidney and heart failure. >> Barnard; bone marrow; cornea; heart [i]; immunosuppression; kidneys

transportation Sentence of banishment from England for those convicted of certain offences, introduced in 1597. Increasingly large numbers of English convicts were shipped to North America in the 17th-c and 18th-c; but in 1788, after the US War of Independence, the inflow was stopped. As a result, the British government turned their attention to Australia: 162 000 convicts were transported to Australia from 1788 to 1868.

transposing instrument A musical instrument which sounds at a higher or lower pitch than that at which its music is notated. In the modern orchestra the main transposing instruments are as follows (sound level above/below written pitch is shown in parentheses): piccolo (one octave above), cor anglais (a perfect 5th below), clarinet in A (a minor 3rd below), clarinet in B♭ (a major 2nd below), horn in F (a perfect 5th below), trumpet in B♭ (a major 2nd below), celesta (one octave above), and double bass (one octave below). >> transposition

Transputer A one-chip computer which has been designed specifically to allow parallel processing involving large numbers of Transputers working together. This technique can provide very fast, powerful computers. >> parallel processing

transsexual A person who has changed behaviour, physical appearance, and body (by surgery and/or the consumption of hormones) to that of the opposite sex. >> gender

Trans-Siberian Railway An important rail route extending across Siberia, originally between terminals at Chelyabinsk in the Urals and Vladivostok on the Pacific. It was constructed 1891–1905, with an extension around L Baykal completed in 1916. The journey from Moscow to Vladivostok (9311 km/5786 mi) takes 7 days. >> Siberia

transubstantiation The Roman Catholic doctrine of the Eucharist (Mass), affirming the belief that the bread and wine used in the sacrament are converted into the body and blood of Christ, who is therefore truly present. The doctrine, rejected by 16th-c Reformers, was reaffirmed by the Council of Trent. >> consubstantiation; Eucharist; Mass; Roman Catholicism

transuranic elements [tranzyu**ran**ik] >> **actinides**

Transvaal [tranz**vahl**] Former province in South Africa; settled by the Boers after the Great Trek of 1836; independence, 1852, recognized by Britain; known as the South African Republic; annexed by Britain, 1877; Boer rebellion in 1880–1 led to restoration of the republic; annexed as a British colony, 1900; self-government, 1906; joined Union of South Africa, 1910; in the 1994 constitution, divided into Northern Province and Mpumalanga. >> Boer Wars; Great Trek; Northern Province; South Africa [i]

transverse wave >> **wave motion** [i]

transvestism The recurrent practice of dressing in the clothes of the opposite sex, normally for sexual excitement. It usually begins in adolescence.

Transylvania [transil**vay**nia], Hung **Erdély**, Ger **Siebenbürgen** Geographical region and province of N and C Romania; a former Hungarian principality that became part of the Austro-Hungarian Empire; incorporated into Romania, 1918; chief towns, Cluj-Napoca and Braşov. >> Romania [i]

trapdoor spider A spider that lives in a silk-lined tube constructed in a burrow in the ground, closed off by a silk lid; passing insects are attacked and pulled into the tube with great speed; found in Africa, the Americas, and Australia. (Order: Araneae.) >> spider

Trappists The popular name of the Cistercians of the More Strict Observance, centred on the monastery of La Trappe, France, until 1892. The Order continues throughout the world, devoted to divine office, and noted for its austerity (eg perpetual silence). >> Cistercians; monasticism

trap shooting >> **clay pigeon shooting**

travel sickness Nausea and vomiting induced by the motion of ships, cars, and aeroplanes in a proportion of healthy individuals. The motion disturbs the function of the semicircular canals in the inner ear, and causes a reflex stimulation of the vomiting centre in the brain stem. Psychological factors and fear of sickness play a part in some people. >> ear [i]

Traven, B [**tray**vn], pseudonym of **Benick Traven Torsvan** (?1882/90–1969) Writer of adventure stories, whose reclusive character left many details of his early life unclear. In Mexico in the 1920s he wrote several novels and short stories, notably *Der Schatz der Sierra Madre* (1927, The Treasure of the Sierra Madre), on which the celebrated film (1947) by John Huston is based. >> Huston

Travers, Ben(jamin) (1886–1980) Playwright, born in London. He became famous for the farces which played in the Aldwych Theatre, London, continuously from 1922 until 1933. He was still writing in his nineties.

travertine [**tra**vertin] A type of limestone formed by precipitation from springs or streams rich in dissolved calcium carbonate. It is extensively mined in Tuscany, Italy, and used as a paving stone. >> limestone

Travolta, John [tra**vol**ta] (1954–) Film actor, born in Englewood, NJ. He joined the Broadway cast of *Grease*, and became well known for his role in the TV series *Welcome Back Koter*. His major films include *Saturday Night Fever* (1977), *Grease* (1978), *Pulp Fiction* (1994), *Get Shorty* (1995, Golden Globe), *Michael* (1997), and *Primary Colors* (1998).

trawler A vessel designed to drag a large bag-shaped net along or near the bottom of the sea to catch fish. Modern trawlers equipped with echo-sounder fish-finders and refrigeration to preserve their catch may be as big as 4000 gross tonnes. >> ship [i]

treacle A product obtained from molasses, used to sweeten and darken cakes and puddings. During the refining process, the molasses darkens from a richly golden syrup to a black treacle, also known as **blackstrap molasses** in the USA. >> molasses; sugar cane

treason The crime of failing to pay proper allegiance to a government or monarch. In the UK, for example, it includes conspiring or inciting to kill the monarch, and levying war against the monarch in his or her realm (*insurrection*). In the USA, treason is defined and limited in Article III, section (3) of the Constitution, and conviction requires the testimony of at least two witnesses or a confession in open court as well as wrongful intent and an overt act.

treasury In business and accounting, the function of managing finance, especially its provision and use. In UK government terms, the **Treasury** is the name of the department responsible for managing the nation's finances, headed by the Chancellor of the Exchequer, who is responsible to the prime minister (the First Lord of the Treasury). In the USA, it is known as the **Department of Treasury**, and elsewhere usually as the **Ministry of Finance**.

treasury bills Bills sold at a discount over a three-month period by the Bank of England on behalf of the government. The bills are issued to discount houses at below their face value, and are redeemed at face value. These bills are frequently used by the government as a form of short-term borrowing. >> discount houses

treaty ports >> **Opium Wars**

Trebizond, Turk **Trabzon** A city on the Black Sea coast of present-day Turkey, former capital of the Christian empire (1204–1461), It was founded by Alexius Comnenus. >> Alexius Comnenus

Tree, Sir Herbert (Draper) Beerbohm (1853–1917) Actor-manager, born in London. He built His Majesty's theatre (1897), where he rivalled Irving's productions at the Lyceum. He founded the Royal Academy of Dramatic Art in 1904. >> Irving, Henry

tree A large, perennial plant with a single, woody, self-supporting stem (the *trunk* or *bole*) extending to a considerable height above the ground before branching to form the leafy *crown*. Trees exhibit a wide variety of shapes, and may be evergreen or deciduous. Dicotyledonous and gymnosperm trees grow in height by extension of the shoots, and in girth by the addition of internal tissue layers; monocotyledonous trees achieve their full girth as seedlings, and subsequently increase in height only. >> annual ring; deciduous plants; dicotyledons; evergreen plants; gymnosperms; monocotyledons; perennial; shrub; tree fern; *see illustration on p.876*

treecreeper Either of two families of songbirds of the N hemisphere: the **treecreeper** (US **creeper**) (Certhiidae, 6 species); and the **Australian treecreeper** (Climacteridae, 6 species), native to Australia and New Guinea. >> songbird

tree fern The name applied to members of two fern families with a trunk-like stem reaching 25 m/80 ft, the fronds forming a crown. It is native to much of the tropics and subtropics. (Families: Cyatheaceae, Dicksoniaceae.) >> fern

tree frog A frog adapted to live in trees; flat with sucker-like discs on fingers and toes; two families: **true tree frogs** (Hylidae, 637 species) and **Old World tree frogs** (Rhacophoridaea, 184 species). >> frog

treehopper A small, hopping insect that feeds by sucking the sap of trees and shrubs; mainly in warm dry regions. (Order: Homoptera. Family: Membracidae, c.2500 species.) >> insect [i]

tree kangaroo A kangaroo of genus *Dendrolagus* (7 species); hind legs not longer than front legs; hands and feet with long claws; inhabits rainforests; may jump to ground from heights of 18 m/60 ft. >> kangaroo

tree shrew A small SE Asian mammal, rodent-like with a long tail and long thin shrew-like muzzle; tail bushy or with tufted tip; lives in trees and on ground. (Order: Scandentia. Family: Tupaiidae, 16 species.) >> shrew

trefoil A member of either of two groups of plants belonging to the pea family, Leguminosae. Genus *Trifolium* comprises yellow-flowered species of clovers. Genus *Lotus* includes a widely distributed group of annual or perennial herbs; pea-like flowers, small, often yellow or reddish-coloured. >> bird's-foot trefoil; clover; pea; shamrock

Trekkies >> ***Star Trek***

Tremain, Rose [tre**mayn**] (1943–) Novelist and short-story writer, born in London. She published her first novel, *Sadler's Birthday*, in 1976. Later books include *The Cupboard* (1981) and *Sacred Country* (1992, James Tait Black). Her books of short stories include *Evangelista's Fan* (1994), and she has also written for children.

Trematoda [trema**toh**da] A class of parasitic flatworms; body flattened and covered with a horny layer (cuticle); contains c.8000 species, including the monogenetic and digenetic flukes. (Phylum: Platyhelminthes.) >> flatworm; fluke; parasitology

Trenchard (of Wolfeton), Hugh Montague Trenchard, 1st Viscount (1873–1956) Marshal of the RAF, born in Taunton, Somerset. He commanded the Royal Flying Corps in World War 1, helped to establish the RAF (1918), and became the first Chief of Air Staff (1918–29). >> Royal Air Force

Trent, Council of (1545–63) A Council of the Roman Catholic Church, held at Trento, Italy. It was called to combat Protestantism and to reform the discipline of the Church, and spear-headed the Counter-Reformation. >> Councils of the Church; Counter-Reformation

Trent, River River rising in N Staffordshire, C England; flows 275 km/171 mi to meet the Humber estuary. >> England [i]

Trento, Ger **Trent** 46°04N 11°08E, pop (1995e) 100 000. City in N Italy, on the left bank of the R Adige; archbishopric; railway; cathedral (11th–12th-c). >> Italy [i]

Trenton 40°14N 74°46W, pop (1995e) 90 400. State capital of New Jersey, USA, on the Delaware R; settled by English Quakers in the 1670s; city status, 1792; scene of a British defeat by George Washington, 1776; railway; research and development centre. >> New Jersey; Washington, George

trepanning One of the earliest surgical operations: the removal of a rectangle or disc of bone from the vault of the skull, commonly to alleviate pressure on the brain caused by skull fracture; also known as **trephination**. The instrument involved (now called a **trephine**) is still commonly used in neurosurgical operations. >> skull

trephination >> **trepanning**

trespass Unlawful entry onto the property of another. It includes entry below the land (eg mining) and within a reasonable distance above the land (eg shooting a bullet). Historically, the notion includes any unlawful act which interferes with another's property or rights.

Tretyakov Gallery [tretya**kof**] One of the world's largest art galleries, located in Moscow, and housing exhibits of Russian painting and sculpture from the 11th-c to the present. The museum building was erected in 1901–2. >> Moscow

Treurnicht, Andries Petrus [**troy**ernikht] (1921–93) South African politician, born in Piketberg, South Africa. He became Transvaal provincial National Party leader in 1978, and held a succession of posts in the cabinets of P W

Trees

Botha from 1979. He and his colleagues resigned from the party in 1982 to form the new, right-wing Conservative Party. >> apartheid; Botha, P W

Trevelyan, G(eorge) M(acaulay) [tre**vel**yan] (1876–1962) Historian, born in Welcombe, Warwickshire. He is best known as a pioneer social historian. His *English Social*

History (1944) was a companion volume to his *History of England* (1926).

Trèves >> **Trier**

Trevithick, Richard [**tre**vithik] (1771–1833) Engineer and inventor, born in Illogan, Cornwall. In 1796–1801 he invented a steam carriage, which ran between Camborne and Tuckingmill, and which in 1803 ran from Leather Lane to Paddington by Oxford Street. >> steam engine

triad The Western name given to a Chinese secret society (because of the importance of the triangle, representing the harmony of Earth, Heaven, and Man, in the initiation ceremonies). These societies originated in response to Qing suppression of Ming loyalists in the later 17th-c, were active in revolutionary movements, and are now reputedly prominent in organized crime, especially international drug trafficking. They have similarities with the Chinese protection associations (*tongs*) which developed in the USA in the second half of the 19th-c. >> Qing dynasty

triangle (mathematics) A plane figure bounded by three straight lines (*sides*). If all three are equal, the triangle is said to be *equilateral*; if two are equal, it is said to be *isosceles*. The sum of the angles of a triangle was proved by the Greeks to be equal to two right angles. If the largest angle in a triangle is less than a right angle, the triangle is called *scalene*; if the largest angle is greater than a right angle the triangle is *obtuse-angled*; if the largest angle is a right angle, the triangle is called *right-angled*, and the subject of Pythagoras's theorem. >> Pythagoras's theorem

triangle (music) A musical instrument of great antiquity, made from a steel rod in the form of a triangle, with one corner left open. It is struck with a short metal beater to produce a high, silvery sound of indefinite pitch. >> percussion ℹ

Triangulum (Lat 'triangle') A small but distinctive N constellation between Aries and Andromeda. There is also a prominent S constellation **Triangulum Australe** ('southern triangle'). >> constellation; RR968

Trianon, Grand / Petit >> **Versailles**

Triassic period [triy**as**ik] The earliest of the periods of the Mesozoic era, extending from c.248 to 213 million years ago. It was characterized by the first appearance of dinosaurs and small mammals. >> dinosaur ℹ; geological time scale; Mesozoic era; RR976

triathlon A three-part sporting event consisting of sea swimming (3.8 km/2.4 mi), cycling (180 km/112 mi), and marathon running (42·2 km/26·2 mi). The events take place in sequence on a single occasion.

tribology [triy**bol**ojee] The study of phenomena involving the sliding of one surface over another. It includes friction, lubrication, and wear. >> friction; rheology; surface physics

tribunal An official body exercising functions of a quasi-judicial nature. In the UK, tribunals frequently deal with matters where the citizen is in conflict with a government department. They tend to be specialized, governing such issues as employment rights, mental health, and taxation. The proceedings of a tribunal may be subject to judicial review. >> judicial review

tribunes In late Republican Rome, 10 annually elected officials whose function was to defend the lives and property of ordinary citizens. The office was part of the hierarchy of offices (the *cursus honorum*), coming between the quaestorship and praetorship.

Triceratops [**triy**seratops] The largest ceratopsian dinosaur, known from the Cretaceous period of North America; heavily built, reaching 9 m/30 ft in length; four-legged; bony frill at back of skull relatively short; paired nasal horns above eyes well developed; plant-eating. (Order: Ornithischia.) >> Ceratopsia; Cretaceous period; dinosaur ℹ; herbivore; Ornithischia

Trichina [tri**kiy**na] A small roundworm (*Trichinella spiralis*), parasitic in the small human intestine; infection usually results from eating raw or undercooked pork. (Phylum: Nematoda.) >> nematode; parasitology

Trichinopoly [triki**nop**olee] >> **Tiruchchirappalli**

trichomoniasis [trikomo**niy**asis] Infestation of the mucous membrane of the vagina with a flagellated protozoan. It causes irritation and vaginal discharge, and may be passed to the male urethra during sexual contact. >> Protozoa

trick or treat >> **Hallowe'en**

Trident missile The US Navy's third-generation submarine-launched ballistic missile (SLBM) system, following on from the earlier Polaris and Poseidon missiles. The first version, Trident C-4, became operational in 1980. The larger Trident D-5 was tested with the US Navy in 1989, and entered service with the British Royal Navy in the mid-1990s. The missile has a very long range (11 000 km/7000 mi), and carries up to 14 individually targetable re-entry vehicles (MIRVs). >> ballistic missile; MIRV; Polaris missile; submarine

Trier [treer], Fr **Trèves**, Eng **Treves** [treevz], ancient **Augusta Treverorum** 49°45N 6°39E, pop (1995e) 101 000. River port in Germany; on the R Moselle; bishopric since the 4th-c; centre of wine production and trade; railway; university (1970); Roman Catholic Theological College; birthplace of Marx; Porta Nigra (2nd-c), cathedral (4th-c, 11th–12th-c), and Roman basilica, world heritage sites. >> Germany ℹ; Marx

Trieste [tree-**est**] 45°39N 13°47E, pop (1995e) 256 000. Port in NE Italy, on the Adriatic coast; capital of Free Territory of Trieste, established by the United Nations in 1947, divided in 1954 between Italy and Yugoslavia; airport; railway; university (1938); cathedral (14th-c), castle (14th–17th-c). >> Italy ℹ

triggerfish Deep-bodied fish with a spiny first dorsal fin; large front spine, locked in upright position by a second smaller spine, serving to wedge the fish in rock crevices. (Family: Balistidae, 5 genera.) >> fish ℹ

triglyceride The major chemical compound found in dietary fats and storage fat in adipose tissue. A glycerol molecule ($C_3H_8O_3$) combines with three fatty acids, mostly of chain length 14–20. >> polyunsaturated fatty acids

trigonometry The branch of mathematics mainly concerned with relating the sides and angles of a triangle, based on triangles being similar if they have one right angle and one other angle equal. The **trigonometric functions** can be defined as the ratio of sides of a right-angled triangle, the commonest being.

$$\text{sine} = \frac{\text{opposite}}{\text{hypotenuse}},\ \text{cosine} = \frac{\text{adjacent}}{\text{hypotenuse}},\ \text{tangent} = \frac{\text{opposite}}{\text{adjacent}}$$

>> triangle (mathematics)

trilobite An extinct primitive marine arthropod, characterized by two grooves along its body producing a tri-lobed appearance; diverse and widespread from the Cambrian to the Permian periods; ranged from minute to 1 m/3 ft long. (Phylum: Arthropoda. Class: Trilobita, c.4000 species.) >> arthropod; Cambrian period; Permian period; RR976

trimaran [**triy**maran] A vessel with a narrow hull and large outriggers or floats giving the appearance of a three-hulled craft. The design gives great stability, thus permitting a large sail area which produces relatively high speed. >> catamaran; yacht ℹ

Trimble, David (1944–) Northern Ireland politician. A former university lecturer, he became MP for Upper Bann in 1990, and leader of the Ulster Unionist Party in 1995. He came to prominence for his role in the peace negotiations of the mid-1990s, and shared the 1998 Nobel Peace Prize with John Hume for his efforts. He became first minister of the new National Assembly in 1998. >> Hume, John

Trimurti [tri**moor**tee] (Sanskrit, 'having three forms') The Hindu triad, manifesting the cosmic functions of the Supreme Being, as represented by Brahma, Vishnu, and Shiva. Brahma is the balance between the opposing principles of preservation and destruction, symbolized by Vishnu and Shiva respectively. >> Brahma; Hinduism; Shiva; Vishnu

Trincomalee or **Trinkomali** [tringkoma**lee**] 8°44N 81°13E, pop (1995e) 52 400. Seaport in Sri Lanka; at the mouth of the R Mahaweli; taken by the British, 1795; principal British naval base during World War 2 after the fall of Singapore; ruins of Temple of a Thousand Columns (3rd-c BC). >> Sri Lanka ℹ

Trinidad and Tobago, official name **Republic of Trinidad and Tobago** pop (1995e) 1 270 000; area 5128 sq km/1979 sq mi. Southernmost islands of the Lesser Antilles chain, SE Caribbean; capital, Port of Spain; timezone GMT −4; population mainly of East Indian or African descent; chief religions, Protestantism (30%), Roman Catholicism (29%), Hinduism (24%); official language, English; unit of currency, the Trinidad and Tobago dollar; island of Trinidad (4828 sq km/1864 sq mi) roughly rectangular in shape; separated from Venezuela (S) by the 11 km/7 mi-wide Gulf of Paria; N range includes El Cerro del Aripo (940 m/3084 ft); Tobago lies 30 km/19 mi NE (area 300 sq km/116 sq mi); Main Ridge extends along most of the island, rising to 576 m/1890 ft; tropical climate, annual average temperature of 29°C; visited by Columbus, 1498; Trinidad settled by Spain, 16th-c; ceded to Britain, 1802; Tobago a British colony, 1814; joint British Crown Colony, 1899; independent member of the Commonwealth, 1962; republic, 1976; governed by a prime minister and bicameral parliament, comprising a Senate and House of Representatives; economy based on the oil and gas industry; industrial complex on W coast of Trinidad; main tourist centre on Tobago. >> Antilles; Caribbean; West Indies; RR1024 political leaders

trinitrotoluene [triyniytro**tol**yooeen] >> **TNT**

Trinity A distinctively Christian doctrine that God exists in three persons, Father, Son, and Holy Spirit. The unity of God is maintained by insisting that the three persons or modes of existence of God are of one substance. The functions of the persons of the Trinity, and the relationship between them, has been the subject of much controversy (eg the split between Eastern and Western Churches on the *Filioque* clause), but the trinitarian concept is reflected in most Christian worship. >> Christianity; Filioque; God; Holy Spirit; Jesus Christ

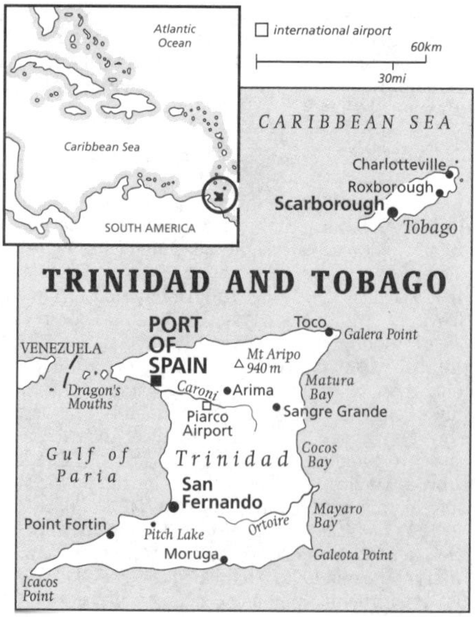

Atlantic Ocean
international airport
60km
30mi
Caribbean Sea
SOUTH AMERICA
CARIBBEAN SEA
Charlotteville
Roxborough
Scarborough
Tobago
TRINIDAD AND TOBAGO
PORT OF SPAIN
Toco
Galera Point
VENEZUELA
Mt Aripo 940 m
Dragon's Mouths
Caroni
Arima
Matura Bay
Piarco Airport
Sangre Grande
Gulf of Paria
Trinidad
Cocos Bay
San Fernando
Mayaro Bay
Point Fortin
Pitch Lake
Ortoire
Moruga
Galeota Point
Icacos Point

Trinity House The lighthouse authority for England and Wales, the Channel Islands, and Gibraltar. It is one of the principal pilotage authorities, and also supervises the maintenance of navigation marks carried out by local harbour authorities.

Trinity Sunday In the Christian Church, the Sunday after Whitsunday, observed in honour of the Trinity. It was introduced by Pope John XXII in 1334. >> Trinity; Whitsunday

trio 1 An ensemble of three singers or instrumentalists, or a piece of music for such an ensemble. The **string trio** is normally composed of violin, viola, and cello; in the **piano trio**, a piano replaces the viola. >> chamber music **2** The central section of a minuet or scherzo, which in the earliest examples often employed a three-part texture. >> minuet; scherzo

triode An electronic valve having three electrodes; a positive anode, an electron-emitting cathode, and a negatively biased control grid. A triode can be used as an amplifier or oscillator. >> anode; oscillator; diode; thermionic valve

tripe The fore-stomach of a ruminant, used as food – both the rumen (*plain tripe*) and the reticulum (*honeycomb tripe*). In France and the UK it is traditionally stewed with onions, vegetables, and herbs, although recipes differ. >> ruminant ℹ

Triple Alliance, War of the or **Paraguayan War** (1864–70) A devastating war fought by Paraguay against the combined forces of Brazil, Argentina and Uruguay (the **Triple Alliance**). The eventual victory of the Allies was achieved at the cost of reducing the male population of Paraguay by nine-tenths. >> Paraguay ℹ

Triple Crown A term used in many sports to describe the winning of three major events. In British horse racing it is the Derby, 2000 Guineas, and St Leger; in US racing, the Preakness Stakes, Kentucky Derby, and Belmont Stakes. In British Rugby Union it is the beating of the other three Home countries in the International Championship.

triple jump An athletics field event, which takes place in the same area as the long jump. Competitors, after completing their run-up, must take off and hop on the same foot. The second phase is a step onto the other foot, followed by a jump. The event was previously called the **hop, step, and jump**. The current world record for men is 18·29 m/60 ft $0\frac{1}{4}$ in, achieved by Jonathan Edwards (1966–) of Great Britain, in 1995 at Gothenburg, Sweden; for women, it is 15·50 m/50 ft $10\frac{1}{4}$ in, achieved by Inessa Kravets (1966–) of Ukraine, in 1995 at Gothenburg, Sweden. >> athletics; long jump; RR1045

Tripoli (Lebanon) [**tri**polee], Arabic **Trablous**, Gr **Tripolis**, ancient **Oea** 34°27N 35°50E, pop (1995e) 203 000. Seaport in NW Lebanon; trade centre for N Lebanon and NW Syria; mostly occupied by Sunni Muslims; two Palestinian refugee camps nearby; railway; 12th-c Crusader Castle of St Gilles. >> Lebanon ℹ; Sunnis

Tripoli (Libya) [**tri**polee], Arabic **Tarabulus** or **Tarabulus al-Gharb**, ancient **Oea** 32°54N 13°11E, pop (1995e) 721 000. Seaport capital of Libya; founded by the Phoenicians, and developed by the Romans; important Axis base in World War 2; bombed, 1941–2, and occupied by the British, 1943; bombed by US Air Force in response to alleged terrorist activities, 1986; airport; railway; university (1973); old city partly surrounded by Byzantine and mediaeval walls. >> Axis Powers; Libya ℹ

Tripolitania [tripoli**tayn**ia] Region of N Africa, lying between Tunis and Cyrenaica; under Turkish control from the 16th-c until 1911; under Italian control until 1943; British control until 1952. >> Libya ℹ

Tripp, Linda >> **Lewinsky, Monica**

triptych >> **altarpiece**

Tripura [**tri**pura] pop (1995e) 2 971 000; area 10 477 sq km/ 4044 sq mi. State in E India; became a state of India, 1949; status changed to union territory, 1956; reverted to a state, 1972; capital, Agartala; governed by a Legislative Assembly; tribal shifting cultivation gradually being replaced by modern farming methods. >> India ℹ

trireme [**triy**reem] A Mediterranean war galley of Greek origin propelled by three banks of oars. It was fitted with a square sail, and a strong projection fixed to the bow below the waterline, used to ram other ships. >> bireme; ship ℹ

Tristan da Cunha [**tri**stan da **kun**ya] 37°15S 12°30W; pop (1990e) 350; area 110 sq km/42 sq mi. Small volcanic island in the S Atlantic; volcanic cone rises to 2060 m/ 6758 ft; inhabitants are the descendants of a British garrison established in 1816 during Napoleon's exile in St Helena; became a dependency of St Helena, 1922; chief settlement, Edinburgh; islanders evacuated in 1961 after a volcanic eruption, but returned in 1963. >> Napoleon I; St Helena

Tristram or **Tristan** [**tri**stram] In the Arthurian legends, a knight who was sent to woo Iseult the Fair (Isolde) on behalf of his uncle, King Mark of Cornwall. He fell in love with her himself, then fled to Brittany. >> Arthur

triticale [triti**kay**lee] An artificial hybrid (*Triticosecale*), derived from wheat (*Triticum*) and rye (*Secale*), giving yields and grain quality approaching those of wheat in cold climates where only rye could be grown previously. Its cultivation is expanding rapidly in Poland and Russia. (Family: Gramineae.) >> rye; wheat

tritium [**tri**tium] A heavy isotope of hydrogen, in which the nucleus comprises one proton and two neutrons rather than a single proton (as for common hydrogen). It is radioactive, with a half-life of 12.3 years. It is an important ingredient of nuclear fusion reactions and hydrogen bombs. >> deuterium; hydrogen; isotopes; nuclear fusion

Triton (astronomy) [**triy**tn] The principal natural satellite of Neptune, discovered in 1846; distance from the planet 355 000 km/221 000 mi; diameter 2720 km/1690 mi, orbital period 5·9 days. Uniquely, for a large moon, its orbit is retrograde about Neptune. The encounter by Voyager 2 (1989) showed that it has a thin atmosphere of nitrogen. >> Neptune (astronomy); Voyager project ℹ; RR964

Triton (mythology) [**triy**tn] In Greek mythology, the son of Poseidon and Amphitrite. He is depicted in art as a fish from the waist down, and blowing a conch-shell.

triton shell [**triy**tn] A large marine snail found in the Indo-Pacific region; one of the world's largest snails, length up to 36 cm/14 in. (Class: Gastropoda. Order: Mesogastropoda.) >> gastropod; snail

triumvirate Literally Lat, 'a group of three men'; in ancient Rome **1** the name given to any publicly appointed administrative board of three; **2 First Triumvirate** the name commonly applied to the unofficial coalition between Caesar, Pompey, and Crassus in 60 BC; **3 Second Triumvirate** the name given to the joint rule from 43 BC of Antonius, Octavian (Augustus), and Lepidus. >> Roman history ℹ

Trivandrum or **Trivandram** [tri**van**druhm] 8°31N 77°00E, pop (1995e) 894 000. Capital of Kerala state, SW India; on the Malabar coast; airfield; railway; university (1937); commercial and cultural centre; noted for its wood and ivory carving. >> Kerala

trivium >> ***quadrivium***

Trobriand Islander A Melanesian people of the scattered Trobriand Is, off New Guinea. They were studied by Malinowski from 1915, and their way of life described in several monographs. >> Malinowski; Melanesia

trogon [**troh**gn] A bird native to the New World tropics, Africa, and SE Asia; plumage soft, brightly coloured; tail long. (Family: Trogonidae, c.40 species.) >> quetzal

Troilus [**troh**ilus, **troy**lus] In Greek legend, a prince of Troy, the son of Priam and Hecuba, who was killed by Achilles. In mediaeval stories, he is the lover of Cressida. >> Cressida

Trojan asteroids Asteroids which have orbits very similar to Jupiter, positioned 60° ahead or behind the planet, where they are trapped in a stable configuration. About 230 are known. >> asteroids; Jupiter (astronomy)

Trojan Horse A huge wooden horse left behind on the beach by the Greeks, who had pretended to give up the siege of Troy. Told by Sinon that it was an offering to Athena, the Trojans broke down their city wall to bring it

Trireme

inside. At night, warriors emerged and captured the city. >> Trojan War

Trojan War In Greek legend, the 10-year conflict between the Greeks and Trojans, which began when Paris carried off Helen, the wife of Menelaus, and ended in the sacking of Troy. The story was the subject of Homer's *Iliad*, and is tentatively dated on the basis of archaeology to c.1260 BC. >> Achilles; Agamemnon; Menelaus; Trojan Horse; Troy

troll [trohl] In early Scandinavian mythology a huge ogre, in later tradition a mischievous dwarf, the guardian of treasure, inhabiting caves and mountains and skilled with his hands. >> mythology

trolley bus A type of bus popular in the UK until the 1960s, using an electric motor rather than an internal combustion engine as its motive power. Electricity was provided by overhead cables, with the electricity being conducted from the wires by means of trailing wiper arms. The trolley bus differed from the tram in not running on tracks. They were used in the USA and several European cities, but were generally replaced by the motor bus, with its freer road movement. However, their avoidance of noise and air pollution have renewed the attractiveness of the concept in the environmentally-aware 1990s. >> tram

Trollope, Anthony [**trol**uhp] (1815–82) Novelist, born in London. His first novel in the Barsetshire series, *The Warden*, appeared in 1855, and was followed by such successful books as *Barchester Towers* (1857). His later novels include *Phineas Finn* (1869) and *The Way We Live Now* (1875).

Trollope, Joanna (1943–) Writer and novelist, born in Gloucestershire. She became an English teacher and freelance writer, before publishing her first novel, *Eliza Stanhope* (1978). Later books include *The Rector's Wife* (1991) and *Next of Kin* (1996). She has also written novels as **Caroline Harvey**, including *Legacy of Love* (1992) and *The Steps of the Sun* (1996).

trombone A musical instrument made from brass tubing, mainly cylindrical, which expands to a bell at one end and is fitted with a cup-shaped mouthpiece at the other. A slide is used to vary the length, and therefore the fundamental pitch, of the instrument. Its history dates back to the 15th-c; until c.1700 it was known as the **sackbut**. >> brass instrument ℹ

Tromp, Maarten (Harpertszoon) (1598–1653) Dutch Admiral, born in Briel, The Netherlands. In 1639 he defeated a superior Spanish fleet off Gravelines, and won the Battle of the Downs. His encounter with Blake in 1652 started the first Anglo-Dutch War. Victorious off Dover, he was defeated off Portland, and finally off Terhejide, near Schevingen, where he was killed. >> Blake, Robert; Dutch Wars

trompe l'oeil [trõp **loe**ee] (Fr 'deceive the eye') A painting which may have little aesthetic value, but which is cleverly designed to trick the spectator into thinking the objects represented are really there. >> Naturalism (art)

Tromsø [**trom**soe] 69°42N 19°00E, pop (1995e) 53 300. Seaport in N Norway; founded, 13th-c; charter, 1794; largest town in N Norway; base for expeditions to the Arctic; bishopric; university (1972). >> Norway ℹ

Trondheim [**trond**hiym], formerly **Nidarøs** 63°36N 10°23E, pop (1995e) 142 000. Seaport in C Norway, at the mouth of the R Nidelv (Nea); former capital of Norway during the Viking period; occupied by the Germans, 1940–5; bishopric; airport; railway; university (1968); cathedral (1066–93). >> Norway ℹ; Vikings

Troödos Mountains [**troh**uhthos] Mountain range in C Cyprus; rises to 1951 m/6400 ft at Mt Olympus. >> Cyprus ℹ

Troon 55°32N 4°40W, pop (1995e) 14 300. Town and golf resort in South Ayrshire, W Scotland; railway. >> Scotland ℹ

Trooping the Colour In the UK, originally the display of the regimental standard to the troops; now usually taken to refer to the annual ceremony on Horse Guards Parade, London, when the monarch reviews one of the five battalions of the Guards regiment and its flag, or **colour**, is presented. The ceremony takes place to mark the monarch's official birthday, and is currently in June.

tropical year The time taken for the Earth to complete one revolution round the Sun relative to the vernal equinox: 365·24219 mean solar days. >> equinox

tropics A climatic zone located between the Tropics of Cancer (23.5°N) and Capricorn (23.5°S). The N tropic is so called because the Sun at the summer solstice (when it is vertically over that tropic) enters the zodiacal sign of Cancer; the S tropic is named for a similar reason. Temperatures are generally high, such as a mean monthly temperature greater than 20°C. >> rainforest; savannah; zodiac ℹ

tropism [**troh**pizm] A plant response by directional movement towards (**positive tropism**) or away from (**negative tropism**) a sustained external stimulus. **Phototropism** is a response to light; **geotropism** to gravity; and **chemotropism** to chemicals. >> growth hormone

troposphere The lowest layer of the Earth's atmosphere, within which the weather is active because of the continual motion of the air and a steadily decreasing temperature with height. >> atmosphere ℹ

Trotsky, Leon, pseudonym of **Lev Davidovich Bronstein** (1879–1940) Russian Jewish revolutionary, born in Yanovka, Ukraine. He joined the Bolsheviks and played a major role in the October Revolution. In the Civil War he was Commissar for War, and created the Red Army. After Lenin's death (1924) he was ousted from the Party by Stalin, and expelled from the Soviet Union (1929). He finally found asylum in Mexico, but was assassinated there by one of Stalin's agents. >> Bolsheviks; Lenin; October Revolution; Stalin; Trotskyism

Trotskyism A development of Marxist thought by Leon Trotsky. Essentially a theory of permanent revolution, Trotskyism stressed the internationalism of socialism, avoided co-existence, and encouraged revolutionary movements abroad; this conflicted with Stalin's ideas of 'socialism in one country'. >> communism; Marxism–Leninism; Stalinism; Trotsky

troubadours [**troo**badoor] (Provençal, 'inventor') Court poet-musicians (some known by name, such as Guillaume d'Acquitaine) who flourished in the S of France 1100–1350. They wrote (in the S dialect *langue d'oc*) mainly love poems, and had an important influence on the development of the European lyric. Their equivalent in the N (writing in the N dialect *langue d'oil*) were the **trouvères**, who also wrote *chansons de geste*. >> Blondel; chansons de geste

trout Any of several species of the family Salmonidae, existing in two forms: the **brown trout**, confined to fresh water, and the migratory and much larger **sea trout**; an excellent food fish. >> salmon

trouvères [troovair] >> **troubadours**

Trowbridge [**troh**brij] 51°20N 2°13W, pop (1995e) 30 500. County town of Wiltshire, S England; railway. >> Wiltshire

Troy, Turk **Truva**, also ancient **Ilium** Ancient ruined city in W Turkey; the archaeological site lies S of the Dardanelles, near Hisarlik; from the Stone Age to Roman times, over a period of 4000 years, the city was rebuilt on the same site nine times; excavated by Heinrich Schliemann in the 1870s, the occupation level known as Troy VIIa is thought to be the city of the Greek legend. >> Homer; Schliemann; Trojan War; Turkey ℹ

Troyes [trwah], ancient **Augustobona Tricassium** 48°19N 4°03E, pop (1995e) 62 600. City in NE C France; on channel of the R Seine; bishopric, 4th-c; capital of old province of

Champagne; railway; centre of hosiery trade; cathedral (13th–16th-c). >> Champagne-Ardenne

Trucial States The former name of the United Arab Emirates. The name derives from a truce signed between the ruling sheiks and Great Britain in 1820. In 1892 they accepted British protection. >> United Arab Emirates ℹ

Trudeau, Pierre (Elliott) [**troo**doh] (1919–) Canadian statesman and Liberal prime minister (1968–79, 1980–4), born in Montreal, Quebec, Canada. His term of office as prime minister saw the October Crisis (1970) in Quebec, the introduction of the Official Languages Act, federalist victory during the Quebec Referendum (1980), and the introduction of Canada's constitution (1982). >> Canada ℹ

Trueman, Freddy, popular name of **Frederick Sewards Trueman** (1931–) Cricketer and broadcaster, born in Stainton, South Yorkshire. A Yorkshire fast bowler for 19 years (1949–68), he played in 67 Tests for England between 1952 and 1965, and took a record number of 307 wickets, three times taking 10 wickets in a match. He has worked as a cricket writer and commentator since he retired. >> cricket (sport) ℹ

Truffaut, François [**troo**foh] (1932–84) Film critic and director, born in Paris. In 1959 he made his first feature, *Les Quatre Cents Coups* (The 400 Blows), effectively launching the French 'Nouvelle Vague' movement, followed by *Tirez sur le Pianiste* (1960, Shoot the Pianist), *Jules et Jim* (1962), and *Fahrenheit 451* (1966). *La Nuit américaine* (1972, trans Day for Night) brought him an Oscar. >> Nouvelle Vague

truffle The underground fruiting body of fungi belonging to the genus *Tuber*; may be fleshy or waxy; much sought after as a delicacy. (Subdivision: Ascomycetes. Order: Tuberales.) >> Ascomycetes; fungus

Trujillo [troo**heel**yoh] 8°06S 79°00W, pop (1995e) 580 000. City in NW Peru; founded by Pizarro, 1536; airfield; railway; university (1824); cathedral. >> Peru ℹ

Truk or **Chuuk** pop (1995e) 57 300; area 127 sq km/ 49 sq mi. One of the Federated States of Micronesia, W Pacific, comprising 11 high volcanic islands and numerous outlying atolls; capital, Weno (formerly Moen). >> Micronesia, Federated States of

Truman, Harry S (1884–1972) US Democratic statesman and 33rd president (1945–53), born in Lamar, MO. His decisions included the dropping of two atom bombs on Japan, the postwar loan to Britain, and the sending of US troops to South Korea. He promoted the policy of giving military and economic aid to countries threatened by Communist interference (the **Truman Doctrine**). At home, he introduced a *Fair Deal* of economic reform. >> Democratic Party; Fair Deal

trumpet A musical instrument made from cylindrical brass (or other metal) tubing, fitted with a cup-shaped mouthpiece, and widening at the other end to a flared bell. It was traditionally used for signalling, and since the 17th-c as an orchestral and solo instrument. The modern trumpet has three valves and is a transposing instrument pitched in B♭. >> brass instrument ℹ; transposing instrument

Truro 50°16N 5°03W, pop (1995e) 20 500. City and county town of Cornwall, SW England; on R Truro; railway; cathedral (1880–1910), Pendennis Castle (1543). >> Cornwall

trust An arrangement whereby a person (the **trustee**) holds property for the benefit of another (the *beneficiary*). The terms of the settlement or will creating the trust are binding on the trustees. >> equity

Trusteeship >> **Trust Territory**

Trusteeship Council >> **United Nations**

Trust Territory A non-self-governing area, the administration of which is supervised by the United Nations established after World War 2. The origins of the system lay in the need to administer colonial territories taken from powers defeated in World War 1. Most such areas are now independent, with the exception of a small number of Pacific islands. >> United Nations

Truth, Sojourner, originally **Isabella Van Wagener** (c.1797–1883) Abolitionist, born into slavery in Ulster County, NY. She joined the abolitionist movement, became an effective anti-slavery speaker, and remained active in the causes of black and women's rights until her death. >> slave trade; women's liberation movement

Truth and Reconciliation Commission A committee established in South Africa in November 1995 to investigate the abuses of the apartheid era. Its hearings, under the chairmanship of Archbishop Desmond Tutu, achieved an international profile, though the value of the exercise as a means of achieving better race relations was frequently questioned within the country. Its report was published in October 1998. >> apartheid; Tutu

trypanosomiasis [tripanohso**miy**asis] Any of several diseases caused by infection with one of the trypanosomes that live on the skin of rodents, armadilloes, and domestic animals. African trypanosomiasis is transmitted to humans by bites from tsetse flies; it is also known as **sleeping sickness**. Fever may be severe and prolonged, and the liver, spleen, lungs, and heart may be involved; drowsiness and coma can occur. American trypanosomiasis occurs widely in South and Central America; also known as **Chagas' disease**, after the Brazilian physician Carlos Chagas (1879–1934). >> Protozoa

tsar or **czar** The title used by the rulers of Russia from 1547 to 1721; derived from Latin *Caesar*. It remained in common use until the Revolution (1917), although the official title of the ruler from 1721 was *Emperor*.

Tschaikovsky, Piotr Ilyich >> **Tchaikovsky**

tsetse fly [**tet**see, **tsee**tsee] A small biting fly found in tropical Africa; feeds on blood of vertebrates; of great medical and veterinary importance as the carrier of sleeping sickness (in humans) and nagana (in cattle). (Order: Diptera. Family: Glossinidae.) >> trypanosomiasis

Tsinan >> **Jinan**

Tsiolkovsky, Konstantin Eduardovich [tseeol**kof**skee] (1857–1935) Physicist and rocketry pioneer, born in Izhevsk, Russia. From 1911 he developed the basic theory of rocketry, and also multi-stage rocket technology (1929). Much earlier (1881), unaware of Maxwell's work, he independently developed the kinetic theory of gases. >> Goddard; Maxwell, James Clerk; rocket

Tsui, Daniel C [tsooee] (1939–) Physicist, born in Henan, China, but holding posts in the USA since the 1960s. He shared the 1998 Nobel Prize for Physics for his contribution to the discovery of a new form of quantum fluid with fractionally charged excitations.

tsunami [tsu**nah**mee] Long-period ocean waves produced by movements of the sea floor associated with earthquakes, volcanic explosions, or landslides. Tsunamis may cross entire ocean basins at speeds as great as 800 km/ 500 mi per hour, and strike coastal regions with devastating force, reaching heights in excess of 30 m/100 ft. They are also referred to as **seismic sea waves**, and in popular (but not technical oceanographic) use as **tidal waves**. >> wave (oceanography); RR975

Tswana >> **Sotho–Tswana**

Tuamotu Archipelago [tow**moh**too] 135–143°W 14–23°S; pop (1995e) 12 400; area 826 sq km/319 sq mi. Island group of French Polynesia; largest group of coral atolls in the world; area used for nuclear testing by the French since 1962. >> French Polynesia

Tuareg [**twah**reg] A Berber pastoral people of the C Sahara and the N Sahel zone of W Africa. About half the Tuareg population are no longer nomads, and demands for their own homeland increased during the early 1990s. >> Berber; pastoralism

tuatara [tooa**tah**ra] A rare lizard-like reptile (*Sphenodon punctatus*), native to islands off the coast of New Zealand; the only remaining member of the order Rhyncocephalia; green or orange-brown; length, up to 65 cm/26 in; male with crest of tooth-like spines along back; nocturnal. >> lizard 🅘; reptile

tuba A musical instrument made from brass tubing curved elliptically, with usually three valves, a mouthpiece set at right angles, and a wide bell pointing upwards. It is the largest and lowest in pitch of all brass instruments. >> brass instrument 🅘; euphonium; saxhorn; sousaphone

tubenose A marine bird found worldwide; nostrils long and tubular on long, grooved, hooked bill; also known as **petrel**. (Order: Procellariiformes, or Tubinares.) >> albatross; fulmar; petrel; shearwater

tuber An underground organ storing food for the next season's growth. **Stem tubers** are distinguished by the presence of buds or 'eyes'; **root tubers** bear no buds.

tuberculosis (TB) A disease almost always caused in humans by infection with *Mycobacterium tuberculosis*. The organisms enter the body via the respiratory or the gastro-intestinal tract. Any organ in the body may be affected, but pulmonary TB is the most common. The outlook of patients has been transformed with the development of specific antibiotics, but in recent years new strains showing resistance to traditional antibiotics have emerged, and are causing concern. In 1998 the World Health Organization reported that TB is killing more people worldwide than any other infectious disease. >> BCG; Koch, Robert; lungs; lupus vulgaris; Mantoux test; scrofula

Tubifex [**tyoo**bifeks] A genus of freshwater annelid worms, found part buried in mud on river beds; red in colour because of haemoglobin in blood; commonly used to feed aquarium fishes. (Class: Oligochaeta. Order: Haplotaxida.) >> annelid; haemoglobin

Tübingen [**tü**bingen] 48°32N 9°04E, pop (1995e) 82 600. City in Germany; on R Neckar; railway; university (1477). >> Germany 🅘

Tubman, Harriet (1820–1913) Abolitionist and rescuer of slaves, born in Dorchester Co, MD. She escaped from slavery in Maryland (1849), and from then until the Civil War was active on the slave escape route (the 'Underground Railroad'). >> American Civil War; slave trade

Tubruq >> **Tobruk**

Tubuai Islands [too**bwiy**] or **Austral Islands**, Fr **Iles Tubuai** pop (1995e) 8200; area 137 sq km/53 sq mi. Volcanic island group of French Polynesia; chief settlement, Mataura (on Tubuai). >> French Polynesia

tubular bells A set of metal tubes tuned to different pitches and suspended in a large frame. They are struck with a short mallet to produce bell sounds in orchestral and operatic music. >> percussion 🅘

TUC >> **Trades Union Congress**

Tucana [too**kah**na] (Lat 'toucan') A faint S constellation, which includes the prominent Small Magellanic Cloud. >> constellation; Magellanic Clouds; RR968

Tucker, Albert Lee (1914–) Painter, born in Melbourne, Victoria, Australia. He is known as a pioneer of Surrealism in Australia, and for his paintings of harsh Australian landscape as well as for his self-portraits. >> Expressionism; Surrealism

Tucson [too**son**] 32°13N 110°58W, pop (1995e) 453 000. City in SE Arizona, USA, on the Santa Cruz R; founded, 1776; ceded to the USA, 1853; city status, 1883; state capital, 1867–77; airport; railway; university (1885); distributing centre for cotton, livestock, and nearby mines; major tourist and health resort. >> Arizona

Tucumán >> **San Miguel de Tucumán**

Tudor, Owen >> **Henry VII**

Tudors A N Wales gentry family, one of whose scions married a Plantagenet in the early 15th-c. The dynasty began when Henry, 2nd Earl of Richmond and son of Margaret Beaufort (a Lancastrian claimant to the crown) overthrew Richard III in 1485. It ended with the death of Elizabeth I in 1603. >> Edward VI; Elizabeth I; Henry VII; Henry VIII; Mary I; RR1026

tuff >> **pyroclastic rock**

tug of war An athletic event of strength involving two teams who pull against each other from opposite ends of a long, thick rope. A team normally consists of eight members. With sheer strength and determination they have to pull their opponents over a predetermined mark. >> RR1064

tui [**too**ee] A honeyeater (*Prosthemadera novaeseelandiae*) native to the New Zealand area; dark plumage with small knot of white feathers on throat, and collar of delicate white filaments; also known as **parson bird**. >> honeyeater

Tuileries [**twee**leree(z)] Formal gardens laid out in the 17th-c by Le Nôtre in Paris. They are all that remain of the former Tuileries Palace built for Catherine de' Medici in the 16th-c, and destroyed by fire in 1871. >> Le Nôtre; Paris

Tula (Mexico) [**too**la] An ancient Meso-American city, from which the Toltecs dominated C Mexico AD c.900–1150. It developed from AD c.750, and was destroyed c.1168. >> Toltecs

Tula (Russia) [**too**la] 54°11N 37°38E, pop (1995e) 549 000. Industrial city in NC European Russia; on R Upa; Imperial Small Arms Factory founded here by Peter the Great, 1712; railway; airfield; cathedral (1762–4). >> Peter I; Russia 🅘

tulip A bulb native to Europe and Asia, especially the steppe regions; flowers solitary, occasionally 2–6, in a variety of shapes and colours but usually large and showy, with six segments. A huge industry is built around several thousand named cultivars, especially in Holland. (Genus: *Tulipa*, 100 species. Family: Liliaceae.) >> bulb; cultivar

tulip tree A deciduous tree (*Liriodendron tulipifera*) reaching 35 m/115 ft, native to North America; flowers with six greenish-yellow petals, resembling the tulip in size and shape. It is a valuable timber tree, known commercially as **Canary** or **American whitewood**; also called **tulip poplar** in North America. (Family: Magnoliaceae.) >> tulip

Tull, Jethro (1674–1741) Agriculturist, born in Basildon, West Berkshire. He introduced several new farming methods, including the invention of a seed drill which planted seeds in rows (1701).

Tullamore [tuhla**maw(r)**], Ir **Tulach Mhór** 53°16N 7°30W, pop (1995e) 9400. Capital of Offaly county, Leinster, C Ireland; railway; abbey at Durrow founded by St Columba. >> Ireland (republic) 🅘; Offaly

Tulip tree – flower and leaves

Tulsa [**tuhl**sa] 36°10N 95°55W, pop (1995e) 387 000. City in NE Oklahoma, USA; port on the Arkansas R; settled in the 1830s; developed in the 1880s with the coming of the railway; airport; university (1894); major national centre of the petroleum industry. >> Oklahoma

tumbleweed The name given to various bushy plants which, at the end of the growing season, break off at ground level and are blown and rolled considerable distances by the wind, simultaneously scattering their seeds. >> spinifex

tumour A swelling of any kind in any part of the body. The term is often used to refer to a **neoplasm** (a benign or malignant new growth); but swellings caused by infection or by the growth of a cyst are also often referred to as tumours. >> abscess; cancer; cyst; polyp

tuna Any of several large fast-swimming predatory fish (especially the *Thunnus* species) found in surface ocean waters; belong with the mackerels to the family Scombridae; body adapted for power and speed; many heavily exploited commercially. >> albacore; yellowfin tuna

Tunbridge Wells or **Royal Tunbridge Wells** 51°08N 0°16E, pop (1995e) 59 700. Spa town in Kent, SE England; iron-rich springs discovered in 1606; fashionable health resort in 17th–18th-c; 'Royal' since 1909, a legacy of visits made by Queen Victoria; railway. >> Kent

tundra The treeless vegetation zone found polewards of the taiga of North America, Europe, and Asia. Often underlain by permafrost, the vegetation is dominated by mosses, lichens, herbaceous perennials, dwarf shrubs, and grasses. >> muskeg; permafrost; taiga

tungsten W (from Ger *wolfram*), element 74, density 20 g/cm^3, melting point 3410°C. A grey metal, difficult to work, occurring mainly with other elements in oxide ores. The metal is used extensively for lamp filaments, because of its high melting point and general lack of reactivity. **Tungsten carbide** (WC), is very hard, and is used in cutting and grinding tools. >> chemical elements; metal; RR1036

Tunguska event An explosion of enormous force low in the atmosphere over the Siberian wilderness area of Tunguska R valley (30 Jun 1908), thought to have resulted from the impact of a small comet nucleus or asteroid. It levelled 3000 sq km/1200 sq mi of forest. >> asteroids; comet; meteor; Meteor Crater; meteorite

tunicate [**tyoo**nikuht] A marine invertebrate chordate; may be solitary or in colonies, base-attached or free-swimming; adult body enclosed in leathery tunic; c.1250 species, including sea squirts, salps, and larvaceans. (Phylum: Chordata. Subphylum: Tunicata.) >> Chordata

tuning fork A two-pronged metal instrument, invented in 1711 by English trumpeter John Shore (c.1662–1752), which is made to vibrate and then pressed down on a wooden surface to produce a note (virtually free from upper harmonics) to which voices or instruments can adjust their pitch. >> idiophone

Tunis [**tyoo**nis] 36°50N 10°13E, pop (1995e) 727 000. Seaport capital of Tunisia; Phoenician origin, later dominated by Carthage; capital status, 1236; captured by Turks, 1533; occupied by French, 1881; airport; railway; university (1960); Great Mosque of Zitouna (9th-c); Medina of Tunis is a world heritage site. >> Phoenicia; Tunisia ℹ

Tunisia [tyoo**ni**zia], official name **Republic of Tunisia**, Arabic **al-Jumhuria at-Tunisia** pop (1995e) 8 902 000; area 164 150 sq km/63 362 sq mi. N African republic; capital, Tunis; timezone GMT +1; population mainly Arabic (98%); chief religion, Islam (98%); official language, Arabic, but French widely spoken; unit of currency, the dinar of 1000 millimes; Atlas Mts (NW) rise to 1544 m/5065 ft at Chambi; dry, sandy upland to the S; Mediterranean climate on coast; further S, rainfall decreases and temperatures can be extreme; variously ruled by Phoenicians, Carthaginians, Romans, Byzantines, Arabs, Spanish, and Turks; French protectorate, 1883; independence, 1956; monarchy abolished and republic declared, 1957; governed by a president, prime minister, and National Assembly, elected every five years; agriculture employs 50% of the population, but of declining importance; world's fourth largest producer of olive oil; fifth largest producer of phosphates. >> Atlas Mountains; Tunis; RR1024 political leaders

Tunja [**toon**kha] 5°33N 73°23W, pop (1995e) 111 000. City in EC Colombia; altitude 2819 m/9249 ft; university (1953); one of the oldest cities in Colombia; refounded as a Spanish city, 1539; decisive battle of Boyacá, 1818. >> Colombia ℹ

tunnel An artificial underground passage constructed for a variety of purposes, such as roads, railways, canals, mining, or conducting water. Tunnels are constructed either by cutting away the material above and then covering the tunnel over (the *cut and cover* method), or by driving through the ground using hand tools, a tunnelling shield, or rock drills as appropriate. The longest tunnel in the world is the Delaware Aqueduct in New York (169 km/105 mi), which is used for water supply.

tunny >> **tuna**

tup >> **sheep**

Tupamaros [toopa**mah**ros] An Uruguayan urban guerrilla movement founded by Raúl Sendic in 1963, named after the 18th-c Peruvian Indian rebel, Túpac Amaru. The movement was suppressed by the military-controlled government of 1972–85. >> Uruguay ℹ

tupelo [**tyoo**peloh] A deciduous tree (*Nyssa sylvatica*) native to the swamps of eastern North America; inconspicuous flowers, small, greenish; edible fruit, oval, blue-black; also called **black gum** and **pepperidge**. (Family: Nyssaceae.)

Tupolev, Andrey Nikolayevich [**too**polef] (1888–1972) Aircraft designer, born in Pustomezovo, Russia. He produced over 100 types of aircraft, including the first Soviet civil jet, the Tu-104 (1955), and in 1968 completed the first test flight of a supersonic passenger aircraft, the Tu-144.

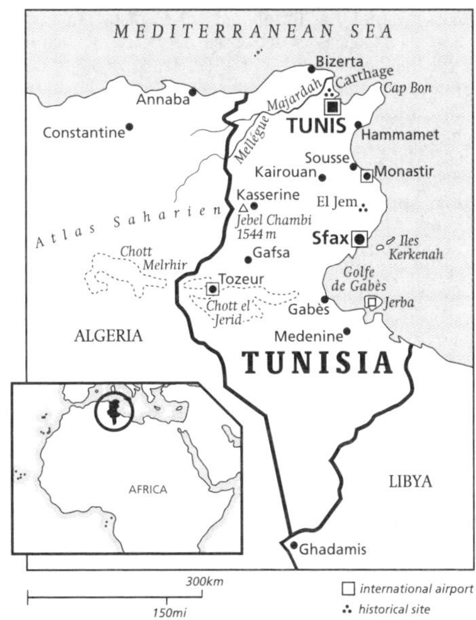

Tupungato, Cerro [tupun**gah**toh] 33°22S 69°50W. Mountain on the border between Argentina and Chile, rising to 6800 m/22 309 ft. >> Andes

tur >> **goat**

turaco [**toor**akoh] A large African bird; tail long; head usually with crest; also known as the **touraco**, **tauraco**, (in S Africa) **lourie** or **loerie**, and (in W Africa) **plantain-eater**. (Family: Musophagidae, 24 species.)

turbine A balanced wheel having at its rim a large number of small radiating blades of aerofoil cross section. When an axial flow of fluid is made to pass over the blades, the turbine rotates about its shaft. If the fluid is steam, the engine is called a **steam turbine**; if water, a **water turbine**. In a **turbo-jet** aircraft, the thrust is derived directly from the rearward expulsion of exhaust gases. In a **turbo-prop** aircraft, the exhaust gases drive a turbine fixed to a propeller. >> aerodynamics i; engine; gas turbine; jet engine i

turbo-jet; turbo-prop >> **turbine**

turbot European flatfish (*Scophthalmus maximus*) widespread on gravel bottoms of inshore waters of the E North Atlantic; length up to 1 m/3¼ ft; light brown with darker spots and patches. (Family: Scophthalmidae.) >> flatfish

Turenne, Henri de la Tour d'Auvergne, vicomte de (Viscount of) [tü**ren**] (1611–75) French marshal, born in Sedan, France. In the Thirty Years' War he fought with distinction for the armies of the Protestant alliance. In the Franco-Spanish war he conquered much of the Spanish Netherlands after defeating Condé at the Battle of the Dunes (1658), and won fame for his campaigns in the United Provinces during the Dutch War (1672–5). >> Condé; Dutch Wars; Thirty Years' War

Turgenev, Ivan (Sergeyevich) [toor**gyay**nyef] (1818–83) Novelist, born in Orel province, Russia. His greatest novel, *Fathers and Sons* (1862), was badly received in Russia, but a particular success in England. He also wrote poetry, plays, short stories, and tales of the supernatural.

Turgot, Anne Robert Jacques [**toor**goh] (1727–81) French statesman and economist, born in Paris. Appointed comptroller-general of finance by Louis XVI (1774), he embarked on a comprehensive scheme of national economic reform, but the opposition of the privileged classes to his Six Edicts led to his overthrow (1776), and his reforms were abandoned. >> Louis XVI

Turin [tyoo**rin**], Ital **Torino**, ancient **Augusta Taurinorum** 45°04N 7°40E, pop (1995e) 996 000. City in Piedmont, NW Italy, on left bank of R Po; Roman colony under Augustus; capital of Kingdom of Sardinia, 1720; centre of the 19th-c Risorgimento; first capital of the Kingdom of Italy until 1865; airport; railway; archbishopric; university (1404); cathedral (15th-c). >> Italy i; Piedmont; Risorgimento

Turin, Shroud of >> **Holy Shroud**

Turing, Alan (Mathison) [**toor**ing] (1912–54) Mathematician, born in London. He provided a mathematical characterization of computability, and introduced the theoretical notion of an idealized computer (since called a **Turing machine**), laying the foundation for the field of artificial intelligence. >> artificial intelligence

Turkana, Lake [toor**kah**na], formerly **Lake Rudolf** (to 1979) area 6405 sq km/2472 sq mi. Lake in NW Kenya and Ethiopia, E Africa; length 290 km/180 mi; width 56 km/35 mi; depth c.70 m/230 ft; The lake is surrounded by extensive Plio-Pleistocene deposits covering the last 3–4 million years. Many important hominid fossils have been recovered. >> Kenya i; Leakey

Turkestan Historical area of C Asia occupying parts of modern Kazakhstan, Kyrgyzstan, Tajikistan, Turkmenistan, Uzbekistan, and Xinjiang, including the great trading centres of Samarkand and Tashkent. It was traversed by the E–W Silk Road, and was thus of great economic importance to China, especially from the 2nd-c BC onwards. >> China i; Silk Road

turkey A large pheasant-like bird, native to C and S North America; head naked; male with pendulous fold of skin at base of bill, and prominent spur on each leg; plumage dark, mottled; a popular poultry bird, especially in the USA at Thanksgiving and the UK at Christmas. (Family: Meleagrididae, 2 species.) >> pheasant

Turkey, Turkish **Türkiye**, official name **Republic of Turkey**, Turkish **Türkiye Cumhuriyeti** pop (1995e) 62 964 000; area 779 452 sq km/300 868 sq mi. Republic lying partly in Europe and partly in Asia; W area (Thrace), E area (Anatolia); capital, Ankara; timezone GMT +2; chief ethnic groups, Turkish (85%) and Kurd (12%); chief religion, Islam; official language, Turkish; unit of currency, the lira; Turkish Straits (Dardanelles, Sea of Marmara, Bosporus) connect the Black Sea (NE) and Mediterranean Sea (SW); mountainous, average height 1100 m/3700 ft; Taurus Mts cover the entire S part of Anatolia; highest peak Mt Ararat (5165 m/16 945 ft); typically Mediterranean climate on Aegean and Mediterranean coasts, with hot, dry summers and warm, wet winters; Seljuk sultanate replaced by the Ottoman in NW Asia Minor, 13th-c; Turkish invasion of Europe, first in the Balkans, 1375; fall of Constantinople, 1453; empire at its peak under Sulaiman the Magnificent, 16th-c; Young Turks seized power, 1908; Balkan War, 1912–13; allied with Germany during World War 1; republic followed Young Turk revolution, led by Kemal Atatürk, 1923; policy of westernization and economic development; neutral throughout most of World War 2, then sided with Allies; military coups, 1960, 1980; strained relations with Greece, and invasion of Cyprus, 1974; governed by a president, prime minister, and single-chamber Grand National Assembly; agriculture employs c.40% of the workforce; many Turks find work in Europe, especially Germany. >> Ankara; Atatürk; Cyprus i; Istanbul; Ottoman Empire; Seljuks; Sulaiman; Young Turks; RR1024 political leaders

Turkish >> **Altaic**

Turkmenistan [terkmeni**stahn**], official name **Republic of Turkmenistan**, formerly **Turkmenia**, Turkmen **Türkmenistan Jumhuriyäti** pop (1995e) 4 322 000; area 488 100 sq km/188 400 sq mi. Republic in SW Middle Asia; capital, Ashgabad (Ashkhabad); timezone GMT +5; major ethnic groups, Turkmen (72%), Russian (10%), with

□ international airport 1 Antakya (Antioch) 2 Iskenderun (Alexandretta) 3 Ataturk Dam 4 Keban Dam

Uzbek, Kazakh, and Ukrainian minorities; religion, Sunni Muslim; languages, Turkmenian (official), other Turkic languages, Russian; currency, the manat of 100 gapik; Kara-Kum desert occupies c.80% of the country; people live mainly around oases; foothills of mountain ranges in S; chief rivers, the Amu Darya and Murghab; continental climate, with great temperature variation; range in Kara-Kum, −33°C (Jan), 50°C (Jul); average annual rainfall 120–250 mm/5–10 in; from 15th-c under rule of Persian and Uzbek Khanates; forceably taken by Russian Empire, 1895; declared independence, 1918; proclaimed a Soviet Socialist Republic, 1924; declaration of independence, 1991; governed by a president, prime minister, and parliament (*Majlis*); mineral resources of oil, natural gas, sulphur, salt; oil refining and gas extraction are major industries; chemicals, food processing, rugs, machinery; cotton, silk; noted for camels, Turkoman horses, Karakul sheep. >> Commonwealth of Independent States ℹ; Kara-Kum; Soviet Union; RR1025 political leaders

Turks and Caicos Islands [**kay**kos] pop (1995e) 13 900; area 500 sq km/200 sq mi. Two island groups comprising c.30 islands and cays forming the SE archipelago of the Bahamas chain; a British overseas territory; capital, Grand Turk; timezone GMT −5; population mainly of African descent; chief religion, Christianity; official language, English; unit of currency, the US dollar; Turks Is and Caicos Is separated by 35 km/22 mi; subtropical climate; visited by the Spanish, 1512; linked formally to the Bahamas, 1765; transferred to Jamaica, 1848; British Crown Colony, 1972; internal self-government, 1976; British sovereign represented by a governor, who presides over a Council; tourism is a rapidly expanding industry. >> Caicos Islands

Turku [**toor**koo], Swed **Åbo** 60°27N 22°15E, pop (1995e) 162 000. Seaport in SW Finland; on R Aurajoki; third largest city in Finland; established, 11th-c; capital of Finland until 1812; airport; railway; ferries to Sweden and Åland Is; two universities (Swedish 1918, Finnish 1920). >> Finland ℹ

turmeric [**ter**merik] A perennial native to India (*Curcuma longa*), related to ginger and East Indian arrowroot; flowers with a yellow lip, borne in a dense spike with white and pink bracts. It is cultivated for the fleshy, aromatic rhizomes, ground to provide the smell and colour of curry powder. It also produces a yellow dye. (Family: Zingiberaceae.) >> arrowroot; bract; ginger; rhizome

Turnbull, Malcolm (Bligh) (1954–) Merchant banker, lawyer, and republican, born in Sydney, New South Wales, Australia. He became known for successfully defending Peter Wright in the *Spycatcher* trial. In 1993 he was appointed chairman of the Republic Advisory Committee. >> Australian republicanism; intelligence service

Turner, J(oseph) M(allord) W(illiam) (1775–1851) Landscape artist and watercolourist, born in London. He spent three years in collaboration with Girtin producing watercolours. He then took to oils, his early works including 'Frosty Morning' (1813) and 'Crossing the Brook' (1815). Later works include 'The Fighting Téméraire' (1839) and 'Rain, Steam and Speed' (1844); all in the National Gallery, London. >> Impressionism (art); landscape painting

Turner, Kathleen (1954–) Actress, born in Springfield, MO. She made her film debut in *Body Heat* (1981), and went on to star in such popular films as *Romancing the Stone* (1984). She received a Best Actress Oscar nomination for her role in *Peggy Sue Got Married* (1986), and provided the husky voice for Jessica Rabbit in the film *'Who Framed Roger Rabbit?* (1988).

Turner, Nat (1800–31) Slave insurrectionist, born in Southampton Co, VA. Leading a force of eight, he succeeded in killing 51 whites, but the revolt quickly collapsed. Captured after six weeks in hiding, he was hanged at Jerusalem, VA. >> slave trade

Turner, Tina, originally **Annie May Bullock** (1939–) Pop singer, born in Nutbush, TN. She achieved considerable success in the rhythm-and-blues vocal duo, Ike and Tina Turner, before their marriage and professional partnership ended in 1976. Her solo hits include 'Let's Stay Together' (1983) and 'Private Dancer' (1985), and she recorded the title song for the James Bond film *Goldeneye* (1996).

Turner Prize Britain's most prestigious prize for contemporary art, awarded to a British artist under 50 for an outstanding exhibition in the previous year. An initiative of the Tate Gallery, London, it was first awarded in 1984, and has since attracted considerable controversy for its choice of winners, regularly forcing a public debate on the question of 'Is it art?'. >> Tate Gallery; RR1042

turnip An annual or biennial vegetable (*Brassica rapa*), 1 m/3¼ ft high; yellow, cross-shaped flowers. The cultivated turnip (subspecies *rapa*) has an edible tuberous taproot, and is widely grown as a vegetable and for fodder. (Family: Cruciferae.) >> brassica; vegetable

turnkey system A method of acquiring a system of computer hardware and software as a whole from a single supplier. Buying a turnkey system removes the need for carrying out a full systems analysis and design exercise. >> computer; hardware; software

turnover tax A tax levied at several stages in the progression from materials to finished goods, or when certain services are provided. For example, a miller pays turnover tax on wheat from the farmer; the baker pays it on the flour; and the customer pays it on the bread. >> taxation

turnpike A gate across a road to stop the passage of vehicles or persons until a toll is paid. The roads were known as **turnpike roads**, and were common during the 18th–19th-c.

turpentine tree A deciduous shrub or small tree (*Pistacia terebinthus*), growing to 10 m/30 ft, native to the Mediterranean region and SW Asia; flowers tiny; fruits coral-red; also called **terebinth**. It produces a resin which yields turpentine. (Family: Anacardiaceae.) >> sumac

Turpin, Dick, popular name of **Richard Turpin** (1706–39) Robber, born in Hempstead, Essex. He was hanged at York for horse stealing and murder. His legendary ride to York upon Black Bess belongs (if to anyone) to 'Swift John Nevison', who in 1676 is said to have robbed a sailor at

Gadshill at 4 am, and to have established an 'alibi' by reaching York at 7.45 pm.

turquoise A hydrated aluminium phosphate mineral formed by the surface alteration of aluminium-rich rock, with bright-blue to green-blue masses or veins, opaque with a waxy lustre. It is valued as a semi-precious stone. >> aluminium; gemstones

turtle (biology) A reptile of order Chelonia; in the USA, includes all species; in the UK, only the marine species with the legs modified as paddles (**sea turtles**, 7 species in families Chelonidae and Dermochelyidae). >> Chelonia [i]; leatherback / snake-necked turtle; matamata [i]; reptile; terrapin; tortoise

turtle (computing) An electromechanical computer drawing device. The precise movements of the turtle are sent to it by the computer. The device is normally associated with the computer programming language LOGO, used in elementary educational environments. >> computer graphics; mouse (computing)

turtle-dove A dove native to Europe, W Asia, and N Africa (*Streptopelia turtur*); eye with dark ring; breast pink, wing feathers with reddish edges. >> dove

Tuscan order The simplest of the five main orders of classical architecture, probably derived from Etruscan-type temples. It closely resembles the Doric order, but with a plain base, shaft, and entablature. >> entablature; orders of architecture [i]

Tuscany, Ital **Toscana** pop (1995e) 3 614 000; area 22 989 sq km/8874 sq mi. Region of Italy; capital, Florence; mountainous with fertile valleys; industry mainly in the Arno valley; important agricultural area; home of Chianti wine; tourism focused on traditional centres of art, notably Florence, Siena, Pisa. >> Florence; Italy [i]

Tuskeegee Institute US institution dedicated to black education. It was founded by Booker T Washington in 1881, and since then has specialized in vocational and technical education. >> Washington, Booker T

Tussaud, Marie [tuh**sawd**], Fr [tüsoh], *née* **Grosholtz** (1761–1850) Modeller in wax, born in Strasbourg, France. She toured Britain with her life-size portrait waxworks, and in 1835 set up a permanent exhibition in London. The exhibition still contains her own handiwork, notably of Marie Antoinette, Napoleon, and Burke and Hare in the Chamber of Horrors. >> wax

Tutankhamen or **Tut'ankhamun** [tootan**kah**men, tootangka**moon**] (14th-c BC) Egyptian pharaoh of the XVIIIth dynasty (1361–1352 BC), the son-in-law of Akhenaton. He came to the throne at the age of 12, and is famous only for his magnificent tomb at Thebes, which was discovered intact in 1922 by Lord Carnarvon and Howard Carter. >> Akhenaton

Tuthmosis >> **Thutmose III**

Tutsi >> **Hutu and Tutsi**

Tutu, Desmond (Mpilo) (1931–) Anglican clergyman, born in Klerksdorp, South Africa. He became Bishop of Lesotho (1977), Bishop of Johannesburg (1984), and Archbishop of Cape Town (1986), retiring in 1996. A fierce critic of the apartheid system, he advocated international sanctions against South Africa, but condemned the use of violence by its opponents. He was awarded the Nobel Peace Prize in 1984, and was appointed chair of the Truth and Reconciliation Commission in 1995. >> apartheid; South Africa [i]

Tutuola, Amos [tu**twoh**la] (1920–97) Novelist, born in Abeokuta, Nigeria. He was celebrated in the West as the author of *The Palm-Wine Drinkard* (1952), a transcription in pidgin English prose of an oral tale of his own invention. >> pidgin

Tuvalu [toova**loo**], formerly **Ellice Is** (to 1976) 5–11°S 176–180°E; pop (1995e) 10 100; area 26 sq km/10 sq mi. Island group in the SW Pacific, 1050 km/650 mi N of Fiji; capital, Funafuti; timezone GMT +12; chief ethnic group, Polynesian; chief religion, Christianity; chief languages, Tuvaluan, English; unit of currency, the Australian dollar; comprises nine low-lying coral atolls, running NW–SE in a chain 580 km/360 mi long; hot and humid climate; invaded by Samoans, 16th-c; British protectorate, as the Ellice Is, 1892; administered as a colony jointly with the Gilbert Is (now Kiribati), 1915; separate constitution, following 1974 referendum; independence, 1978; British monarch represented by a governor-general; governed by a prime minister, cabinet, and unicameral parliament. >> Funafuti; Kiribati [i]; RR1025 political leaders

Twain, Mark, pseudonym of **Samuel Langhorne Clemens** (1835–1910) Writer, born in Florida, MO. *The Innocents Abroad* (1869) established his reputation as a humorist. His two masterpieces, *Tom Sawyer* (1876) and *Huckleberry Finn* (1884), drawn from his own boyhood experiences, are firmly established among the world's classics. Widely known as a lecturer, he developed a great popular following.

twayblade An orchid (*Listera ovata*) native to cool and arctic regions of Europe and Asia; flowers green with a yellowish 2-lobed lip. Any insect visiting the flower triggers an explosion of sticky liquid which glues the pollen grains to the insect's head. (Family: Orchidaceae.) >> orchid [i]

tweed A coarse, heavy, wool, outerwear fabric, first made in S Scotland, manufactured in several distinctive weave patterns. Often mistakenly associated with the R Tweed, the name originates from *tweel*, a Scottish word for twill fabrics. >> twill

Tweed, River River in SE Scotland and NE England; rises at Tweed's Well; enters the North Sea at Berwick-upon-Tweed; length, 155 km/96 mi.

Tweed Ring US 19th-c political scandal. Led by William Marcy 'Boss' Tweed (1823–78), the ring ruled New York City in the 1860s and 1870s. Its headquarters, Tammany Hall, became synonymous with urban corruption. >> Tammany Hall

Twelfth Night The evening of 5 January, the last evening of the 12 days of the traditional Christmas festival. It was formerly marked by particularly boisterous and anarchic festivities before the return to sober normality on **Twelfth Day** (Epiphany, 6 Jan).

Twelve, the >> **apostle**

twelve-tone music Music based on the 12 notes of the chromatic scale arranged in a predetermined order. >> serialism; tone 3

Twiggy, professional name of **Lesley Lawson**, *née* **Hornby** (1949–) Fashion model, actress, and singer, born in London. A modelling superstar almost overnight at the age of 17, she was a symbol of the 'swinging sixties' in London's Carnaby Street. Her films include *The Boy Friend* (1971) and *Blues Brothers* (1981).

twilight The interval of time shortly after sunset or just before sunrise. **Civil twilight** begins or ends when the Sun is 6° below the local horizon; **nautical twilight** 12° below the horizon; and **astronomical twilight** 18° below the horizon.

twill A type of woven fabric characterized by a pattern of diagonal lines. Many variations are possible, such as *herringbone* twills, where the pattern zigzags across the cloth. Twill weaves produce strong, hard-wearing fabrics, often employed in sports and work-wear situations. >> denim; tartan

twinning The linking of two towns or cities in different countries, so that they may have a 'special relationship' and foster cultural exchanges. For example, Edinburgh is twinned with Munich, Nice, Florence, Dunedin, San Diego, Vancouver, and Xian.

twins A pair of offspring produced at the same birth. **Fraternal** (or *dizygotic*) twins are derived from two separate fertilized eggs. **Identical** (or *monozygotic*) twins are derived from a single fertilized egg, and are thus genetically identical. >> pregnancy ⓘ; zygote

twist The winding together of fibres, which gives added strength to yarns. The twist level affects other factors than strength, including stretch and softness. >> yarn

twitch grass >> **couch grass**

two-stroke engine A practical engine cycle with one in two strokes of the piston being the power stroke. This type of engine is frequently used to drive light motorcycles. >> Carnot cycle; engine; motorcycle

Tyan Shan >> **Tian Shan**

Tyche [**tiy**kee, **tiy**kay] The Greek goddess of chance or luck, prominent in the Hellenistic period. She is usually depicted as blind. >> Fortuna; Hellenistic Age

Tyler, John (1790–1862) US statesman and 10th president (1841–5), born in Charles City Co, VA. He became president on the death of Harrison, only a month after his inauguration. His administration was marked by the annexation of Texas. >> Harrison, William Henry

Tyler, Wat (?–1381) English leader of the Peasants' Revolt (1381). The rebels of Kent, after taking Rochester Castle, chose him as captain, and marched to London. The Mayor of London, William Walworth, had him beheaded. >> Peasants' Revolt; Richard II

Tynan, Kenneth [**tiy**nan] (1927–80) Theatre critic, born in Birmingham, West Midlands. He was drama critic for several publications, notably *The Observer* (1954–63), literary manager of the National Theatre (1963–9), and writer of the controversial revue *Oh! Calcutta* (1969).

Tyndale or **Tindale, William** [**tin**dayl] (?–1536) Translator of the Bible, probably born in Slymbridge in Gloucestershire. He completed his translation of the New Testament into English in Cologne in 1525. In 1531 he went to Antwerp, where he continued to work on an Old Testament translation, but was accused of heresy, and executed. >> Bible; humanism

Tyne, River [tiyn] River of NE England; formed by confluence of North Tyne and South Tyne; flows 48 km/30 mi E to meet the North Sea; South Tyne rises on Cross Fell, E Cumbria; North Tyne rises in the Cheviot Hills, and is dammed to form Kielder Water reservoir. >> Kielder Water; Tees, River

Tyne and Wear [weer] pop (1995e) 1 148 000; area 540 sq km/208 sq mi. County of NE England, created in 1974; administrative centre, Newcastle upon Tyne; a highly industrialized area; now designated a special development area, with considerable diversification of industries; metropolitan council abolished in 1986. >> England ⓘ; Newcastle (UK); Tyne, River; Tyneside

Tyneside Urban area in NE England; towns include Newcastle upon Tyne, Gateshead, Jarrow, Wallsend, and North and South Shields; airport; railway. >> Tyne and Wear

typewriter A hand-operated machine for producing printed letters and other symbols on paper. Traditionally, characters mounted on rods are made to hit an inked ribbon against paper by pressing on keys; the paper is automatically moved when a key is struck. The machine was invented by Christopher Sholes in 1867, and developed by the Remington firm soon after. Later developments include electric typewriters, in which the keys need only to be touched; the 'golf-ball' typewriter, using replaceable spheres with additional symbols and typefaces; and electronic typewriters, with memory, screen, fast printing, and many of the editing and storage features of word processors. >> Sholes; word processor

typhoid fever An infectious disease caused by *Salmonella typhi*, also known as **enteric fever**. The disease spreads by way of infected water, milk, or food, or by carriers of the disease employed in food preparation. The condition is now readily treated with antibiotics. >> immunization; paratyphoid fever; salmonella

typhoon >> **hurricane**

typhus Any of several illnesses caused by infection with a strain of *Rickettsia*, carried by lice, fleas, and ticks; also known as **spotted fever**. A specific serological test, the Weil–Felix reaction, is the basis of diagnosis. The infections respond to the appropriate antibiotic. >> flea; louse; tick; rickettsia

typography The design of letterforms for use as typefaces, and the selection of typefaces for typeset documents. Typefaces are designed and used for a multitude of purposes (eg books, newspapers, handbills) and for use on various kinds of typesetting equipment, in both print and non-print media (such as film and television). Typefaces are chosen for their appeal, appropriateness, and legibility, and vary immensely in their appearance. They can be divided into two major classes: the *serif* faces, with short cross-strokes at the ends of the letters (eg Times), and the *sans-serif* faces, which lack these cross-strokes (eg Helvetica). Times New Roman, designed by Stanley Morrison in 1932 for the redesigned *Times* newspaper, has been called the most important type design of the 20th-c. >> graphic design

tyramine [**tiy**ramin] A chemical compound derived from the amino acid tyrosine, which occurs in foods such as cheese and wine, sometimes in large quantities. Migraine headaches may be associated with excess amine production aggravated by a high intake of tyramine. >> amines; migraine

Tyrannosaurus rex [tirano**saw**rus reks] The largest terrestrial flesh-eating animal of all time; known from the Cretaceous period; a dinosaur reaching 12 m/40 ft in length; skull massive with short, deep jaws bearing dagger-like teeth; tail heavy and muscular; forelimbs tiny; slow-moving, with a top speed of about 4 kph/$2\frac{1}{2}$ mph.

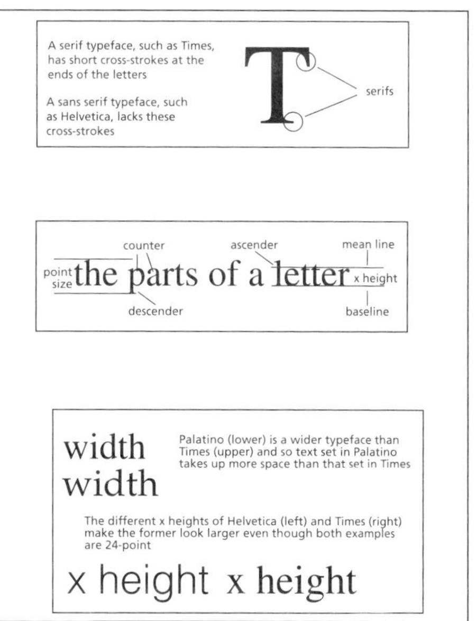

Typography

(Order: Saurischia.) >> Cretaceous period; dinosaur [i]; Saurischia

tyrant In Greek city-states of the 7th-c and 6th-c BC, a neutral term describing an absolute ruler who had seized power illegally. Only later (5th-c BC) did it acquire its present meaning – a cruel and oppressive ruler.

Tyre [tiyr], Arabic **Sour** 33°12N 35°11E, pop (1995e) 16 200. Mediterranean fishing port, SW Lebanon; railway; ancient city was the most important commercial centre in the E Mediterranean, noted for silk, glass, and Tyrean purple dye; several Roman remains; a world heritage site. >> Lebanon [i]

tyre / tire A circular cushion fixed to the rim of a wheel, which absorbs variations in the road surface, so providing an easier ride to the vehicle. Most tyres are *pneumatic*, being flexible tubes stiffened by high-pressure air, and are made of a combination of rubber compounded with other chemicals and fabric, usually nylon or polyester. The inventor of the pneumatic tyre was Robert William Thomson, who patented a design for application to coaches in 1845. >> bicycle; Dunlop; Michelin

Tyrol >> **Tirol**

Tyrone [tiy**rohn**], Ir **Tir Eoghain** pop (1995e) 165 000; area 3136 sq km/1210 sq mi. County in W Northern Ireland; hilly, with the Sperrin Mts rising (N) to 683 m/2241 ft at Mt Sawel; county town, Omagh. >> Northern Ireland [i]; Omagh

Tyrrhenian Sea [tiy**reen**ian] Arm of the Mediterranean Sea; bounded by the Italian Peninsula, Sicily, Sardinia, and Corsica. >> Mediterranean Sea

Tyson, Mike, popular name of **Michael (Gerald) Tyson** (1966–) Boxer, born in New York City. He beat Trevor Berbick (1952–) for the World Boxing Council version of the world heavyweight title in 1986, and added the World Boxing Association title in 1987, when he beat James Smith (1954–). Later that year he became the first undisputed champion since 1978, when he beat Tony Tucker (1958–). He won 41 of 42 decisions before losing the title in 1990. He was later convicted of rape, and jailed (1992–5). He regained the WBC heavyweight title in 1996, then vacated it soon afterwards . >> boxing [i]

Tyumen [tyoo**mayn**] 57°11N 65°29E, pop (1995e) 500 000. City in SW Siberian Russia, on R Tura; founded, 1585; formerly an important centre of trade with China; railway junction; university. >> Russia [i]

Tzu-po >> **Zibo**

U

U and non-U Terms coined by English linguist Alan Ross (1907–80) in an effort to capture the essentials of class-based variation in English usage. The features claimed to mark **upper-class** (U) and **non-upper-class** (non-U) usage are most noticeable in vocabulary, such as U *luncheon* and *pudding* for non-U *dinner* and *sweet*. >> class

Ubangi, River [oo**bang**gee], Fr **Oubangui** Major tributary of R Congo, in N and WC Africa; length, including longest headstream (R Uele), 2250 km/1400 mi. >> Zaire, River

U-boat An abbreviation of *Unterseeboat* (Ger 'submarine'). The German Navy launched large-scale submarine offensives in both World Wars. >> submarine

Ucayali, River [ookiy**al**ee] River in E Peru; one of the Amazon's main headstreams; length c.1600 km/1000 mi. >> Amazon, River; Peru ℹ

Uccello, Paolo [oo**chel**oh], originally **Paolo di Dono** (1397–1475) Painter, born in Pratovecchio, Italy. He applied the principles of perspective to his paintings, such as in 'The Flood' (1447–8, Florence), where his use of foreshortening gives a sternly realistic effect.

ud [ood] An Arabian lute, known since the 7th-c, with usually five courses of strings, played with a plectrum or with the fingers of both hands. It is the ancestor of the European lute. >> lute; plectrum; string instrument 2 ℹ

udad >> **aoudad**

Udall, Nicholas [**yoo**dal] (1504–56) Playwright, born in Southampton, Hampshire. He is chiefly remembered as the author of the first major comedy in English, *Ralph Roister Doister* (c.1563, published 1567).

Udine [**oo**deenay] 46°04N 13°14E, pop (1995e) 102 000. Industrial town in NE Italy; suffered severe bombing in World War 2; archbishopric; railway; castle (16th-c), cathedral. >> Italy ℹ

UEFA (Union of European Football Associations) [yoo**ay**fa] A football organization founded in 1954, and by 1999 consisted of 51 member associations. It is responsible for organizing the three major European club tournaments: the Champions' Cup, the Cup Winners' Cup, and the UEFA Cup. They also run their own European Championship. >> football ℹ

Ufa [oo**fa**] 54°45N 55°58E, pop (1995e) 1 109 000. City in E European Russia; in the Ural Mts, on the R Ufa; founded as a fortress, 1586; airport; railway; university (1957). >> Russia ℹ

Uffizi [oo**feet**see] A museum in Florence, Italy, housing one of the world's greatest collections of works by Italian masters. The Renaissance palace, designed by Vasari in 1560, was opened to the public in the 17th-c. >> Vasari

Uganda [yoo**gan**da], official name **Republic of Uganda** pop (1995e) 21 368 000; area 241 038 sq km/150 645 sq mi. E African republic; capital, Kampala; timezone GMT +3; chief ethnic group, Bantu, with Nilotic and Hamitic minorities; chief religion, Christianity (66%); official languages, English, Swahili; unit of currency, the Uganda shilling; landlocked country, mainly plateau, height 900–1000 m/3000–3250 ft; dry savannah or semi-desert in the N; population concentrated in the fertile L Victoria basin; Margherita Peak (5110 m/16 765 ft), highest point in Uganda and Democratic Republic of Congo; main lakes include Victoria (SE), George (SW), Edward (SW), Albert (W), Kwania (C), Kyoga (C), and Bisina (formerly L Salisbury, E); the two main rivers are upper reaches of the R Nile, the Victoria Nile and the Albert Nile; visited by Arab traders in the 1840s; explored by Speke in the 1860s; granted to the British East Africa Company, 1888; Kingdom of Buganda became a British protectorate, 1893; other territory included by 1903; independence, 1962; Dr Milton Obote assumed all powers, 1966; coup led by General Idi Amin Dada, 1971; Amin's regime overthrown, 1979; further coup in 1985; transitional military regime, with a ban on political activity; elections to Constituent Assembly, 1994; new constitution, 1995; agriculture is the main economic activity. >> Amin; Kampala; Nile, River; Speke; Victoria Nile; RR1025 political leaders

Uganda Martyrs A group of 22 African youths, converted to Roman Catholicism, killed for their faith in Uganda between 1885 and 1887. They were canonized in 1964. >> Roman Catholicism

Ugarit [ooga**reet**] A flourishing Canaanite city on the coast of N Syria, which in the late Bronze Age (c.1450–1200 BC) enjoyed wide contacts with the Egyptians, the Hittites, and the Mycenaeans. It was destroyed by the Sea Peoples c.1200 BC. >> Canaan; Sea Peoples

UHT milk An abbreviation of **ultra-high-temperature milk**; milk heated to a temperature of 132°C for one second, and subsequently packed in an airtight container. It will then have a shelf-life of six months at room temperature. >> milk; pasteurization

Uighurs [**wee**goorz] One of China's national minorities, mostly settled in Xinjiang. They are a people of Turkic origin who emerged as an independent force in the 7th-c. They were brought into the Chinese empire in the 18th-c.

Ujung Padang [oo**joong** pa**dang**], formerly **Makassar** or **Macassar** (to 1973) 5°09S 119°28E, pop (1995e) 1 031 000. Seaport in Indonesia; in SW corner of Sulawesi I; important trade centre, established by the Dutch in 1607; free port, 1848; airfield; university (1956). >> Sulawesi

UK Athletics The governing body for athletics in England and Wales. It was set up following the financial demise of the British Athletic Association in 1998. Its headquarters is in Birmingham. >> British Athletic Association

ukiyo-e [oo**kee**yoh ay] (Jap 'pictures of the floating world') In Japanese painting and printmaking, a movement that flourished in the 16th–19th-c. Favourite themes included theatrical subjects, actors, prostitutes, and landscapes. >> Hiroshige; Hokusai

Ukraine [yoo**krayn**], official name **Republic of Ukraine**, Ukrainian **Ukrayina** pop (1995e) 52 570 000; area 603 700 sq km/233 028 sq mi. Republic in SE Europe; capital, Kiev; timezone GMT +2; major ethnic groups, Ukrainian (73%), Russian (22%), with Moldovan, Bulgarian, and Polish minorities; religions, Orthodox (Autocephalous and Russian) (76%), Roman Catholic (14%), with other Christian and Muslim minorities; languages, Ukrainian (official), Russian; currency, the hryvna of 100 kopijka; generally a highly fertile plain with high elevations in the W, S and SE; Ukrainian Carpathians (W) rise to 2061 m/6762 ft at Mt Goverla; borders Black Sea and Sea of Azov (S); chief rivers, the Dnepr, Dnestr, Severskiy Donets, Prut; many reservoirs and lakes; continental climate, with average annual temperatures −3°C (Jan), 23°C (Jul); average annual rainfall in Crimea 400–610 mm/16–24 in; conquered by Mongols, 1240; dominated by Poland, 13th–16th-c; applied to Moscow for help fighting Poland in return for sovereignty, 1654; declared independence from Russia, 1918; became a member of the Soviet Union, 1922; great devastation in World War 2; declaration of independence, 1991; conflict over autonomy movement in Crimea, 1993–5; new constitution, 1996; governed by a president, prime minister, and Supreme Council; contains the Donets coalfield (area 25 900 sq km/10 000 sq mi); iron ore, metallurgy, machinery, fertilizers, fibres, synthetic resins, plastics, dyes, rubber products, food processing, natural gas, oil refining; major grain-exporting republic; wheat, sugar beet, sunflower, cotton, flax, tobacco, soya, hops, fruit, vegetables. >> Commonwealth of Independent States 🛈; Cossacks; Kiev; Soviet Union; RR1025 political leaders

ukulele [yookuhl**lay**lee] A Hawaiian musical instrument, resembling a small guitar, with four gut or nylon strings that are strummed with the fingernails and fingertips. Since the 1920s it has been a favourite instrument for popular music in the USA. >> guitar; string instrument 2 🛈

Ulaanbaatar [**oo**lahn **bah**taw(r)], formerly **Ulan Bator**, **Urga** (to 1924) 47°54N 106°52E, pop (1995e) 627 000. Capital of Mongolia; founded as Urga in 1639, centre of Lamaistic religion in Mongolia; trading centre on caravan routes between Russia and China, 18th-c; capital, 1921; university (1942). >> Mongolia

Ulanova, Galina Sergeyevna [oo**lah**nova] (1910–98) Ballerina, born in St Petersburg, Russia. She became the leading ballerina of the Soviet Union and was four times a Stalin prizewinner.

Ulan-Ude [oo**lan** oo**day**], formerly **Verkhneudinsk** (to 1934) 51°45N 107°40E, pop (1995e) 363 000. City in SE Siberian Russia; on R Selenga; founded, 1666; airfield; railway junction; cathedral (1741–85). >> Russia 🛈

Ulbricht, Walter (Ernst Karl) [**ul**brikht] (1893–1973) East German statesman, born in Leipzig, Germany. In 1945 he became deputy premier of the German Democratic Republic and general secretary of the Communist Party in 1950. He was largely responsible for the 'sovietization' of East Germany, and built the Berlin wall in 1961. >> communism; Germany 🛈

ulcer A break in the surface of the skin or mucous membrane, which may be acute in onset and short-lived or persistent. Ulcers may also occur in the mouth, oesophagus, and gastro-intestinal tract, in which trauma or other factors are responsible. >> duodenal / peptic ulcer

Uleåborg >> **Oulu**

Ulfilas or **Wulfila** [**ul**filas, **wul**fila] (c.311–83) Gothic missionary bishop. He devised the Gothic alphabet, and carried out the first translation of the Bible into a Germanic language (c.350). >> Bible; Gothic

Ullapool [**uhl**apool] 57°54N 5°10W, pop (1995e) 1350. Port town in Highland, NW Scotland; ferry service to Stornoway, I of Lewis; tourist resort. >> Highland; Scotland 🛈

Ullswater Second largest lake in England; length 12 km/7 mi; width 1 km/¾ mi; depth 64 m/210 ft. >> Lake District

Ulm [oolm] 48°24N 10°00E, pop (1995e) 114 000. Industrial and commercial city in Germany; on R Danube; scene of Napoleon's defeat of Austria, 1805; railway; university (1967); birthplace of Einstein; Gothic Minster (1377–1529), with the world's highest spire (161 m/528 ft). >> Einstein; Germany 🛈; Gothic architecture; Napoleonic Wars

ulna >> **arm**

Ulster [**uhl**ster] pop (1995e) 230 000; area 8012 sq km/3093 sq mi. Province in Ireland; comprising counties of Cavan, Donegal, and Monaghan; Donegal separated by part of Connacht, lying W of Northern Ireland; Cavan and Monaghan lie to the S of Northern Ireland; chief towns include Donegal, Letterkenny, Cavan, and Monaghan; a former kingdom; land confiscated by the English Crown, and distributed to Protestant English and Scots settlers in the 17th-c; partitioned in 1921 into the present-day division. The name is used as an alternative for **Northern Ireland**. >> Ireland (republic) 🛈; Northern Ireland 🛈

Ultra A British security classification (the very highest) given during World War 2 to intelligence gathered from the breaking of the key German military codes used with their 'Enigma' encryption device. 'Ultra' intelligence was available to the British high command from the outset of the war. >> cryptography

Ultramontanism [uhltramon**tayn**izm] Literally, 'beyond the mountains'; a movement, deriving from France, asserting the centralization of the authority and power of the Roman Catholic Church in Rome and the pope. It reached its high point with the First Vatican Council (1870) and the declaration of papal infallibility. >> infallibility; pope; Roman Catholicism

ultrasound Sound of a frequency greater than 20 000 Hz; inaudible to humans, but certain animals such as dogs and bats can hear some ultrasonic signals. Pulses of very high frequency sound are reflected back to different extents by different materials. If such a 'sonar' device is connected to a computer, accurate representations of the structure of the material can be made. Ultrasound is widely used in medical scanning (eg in the examination of a fetus) and also in engineering (eg detecting cracks in railway lines). >> sonar; sound; transducer

ultraviolet astronomy The analysis of radiation from celestial sources in the wavelength range 50–320 nm. The hottest stars emit most of their radiation in this waveband, which is accessible only from rockets and satellites. >> astronomy; spectroscopy; ultraviolet radiation

ultraviolet radiation Electromagnetic radiation of wavelength a little shorter than visible light, between 3.9×10^{-7} m and 10^{-8} m; discovered in 1801 by German physicist Johann Ritter (1776–1810). Invisible to the naked eye, it is produced by electron transitions in atoms, such as in mercury discharge lamps. >> electromagnetic radiation i; sunburn

Uluru [oo**loo**roo] National park in Northern Territory, C Australia; area c.1325 sq km/500 sq mi; an area of cultural and religious significance to the Aboriginal people; a world heritage site. >> Aborigines; Ayers Rock; Northern Territory

Ulysses >> **Odysseus**

Ulysses project A joint ESA-NASA space exploration mission, launched in 1990, to observe the Sun and solar wind from a high solar latitude perspective. It requires the spacecraft to fly on a trajectory which passes over the poles of the Sun, using a boost from Jupiter's gravity field. >> European Space Agency; NASA; Sun

U-matic The trade name for the first helical-scan videotape cassette recorder introduced by Sony in 1970, initially for the professional non-broadcast market. It uses $\frac{3}{4}$-in (19 mm) tape at a speed of 9·53 cm/3$\frac{3}{4}$ in per second in a large cassette with a playing time of up to 1 hour. >> videotape recorder

Umayyad Mosque [u**miy**ad] The great mosque at Damascus in Syria, built (705–15) on the site of a Christian church to John the Baptist, and believed to incorporate the reliquary shrine of the saint's head. >> John the Baptist, St

Umayyads [u**miy**adz] A Damascus-based dynasty, founded by the Muslim general Muawiya ibn Abi-Sufyan (c.605–80), which ruled until 750. It replaced the era of the four Medina-based caliphs, of whom the last, Ali, was murdered in 661. >> Ali

umbel A type of inflorescence, typical of the carrot family Umbellifereae, in which all the flower-stalks arise from the top of the stem, the outermost stalks longest, giving a flat-topped, umbrella-shaped cluster of flowers. >> carrot; inflorescence i

Umberto II [um**bair**toh] (1904–83) Last king of Italy (1946), born in Racconigi, Italy. He succeeded to the throne after the abdication of his father, Victor Emmanuel III, but himself abdicated a month later, after a national referendum had declared for a republic. In 1947 he and his descendants were banished from Italy. >> Italy i

umbilical cord A solid flexible cord which connects the developing fetus of some mammals (eg humans and dogs) to the placenta within the uterus. The average length in humans is 60 cm/24 in. It allows the fetus to float freely in the fluid of the uterus (the *amniotic cavity*) and to obtain nutrition from the placenta, as well as to eliminate waste products, by the flow and return of blood through the vessels within it. At birth it is severed close to the infant's front abdominal wall, leaving a scar (the **umbilicus** or *navel*). >> placenta (anatomy); uterus i

umbra >> **sunspot**

umbrella bird A large cotinga; males with dark plumage and umbrella-like crest covering head and bill; breast with inflatable air sac and pendant feathered fold of skin. (Genus: *Cephalopterus*, 3 species.) >> cotinga

Umbria [**um**bria] pop (1995e) 826 000; area 8456 sq km/3265 sq mi. Region of C Italy; capital, Perugia; prosperous farming region; industry around Terni, Narni, and Foligno; textiles and crafts in Perugia and Spoleto; Umbrian school of painting during the Renaissance (eg Raphael); Basilica of St Francis in Assisi severely damaged by earthquake, 1997. >> Italy i; Perugia

Umbriel [**uhm**briel] The fourth largest satellite of Uranus, discovered in 1851, distance from the planet 266 000 km/165 000 mi; diameter 1170 km/730 mi; orbital period 4.1 days. >> Ariel; Uranus (astronomy); RR964

Umeå [**ü**mayaw] 63°50N 20°15E, pop (1995e) 95 300. Seaport in N Sweden; at the mouth of the R Ume; seat of the Provincial Appeal Court; railway; university (1963). >> Sweden i

Umm al-Qaiwain [**oom** al kiy**wiyn**] pop (1995e) 38 400; area 750 sq km/290 sq mi. Member state of the United Arab Emirates; capital, Umm al-Qaiwain. >> United Arab Emirates i

Un-American Activities Committee A committee of the House of Representatives established in 1938 to consider the loyalty of federal government employees. Supposedly concerned with identifying communists, it was notorious for harassing individuals whose political opinions offended committee members. It was abolished in 1975. >> McCarthy, Joseph

Unamuno (y Jugo), Miguel de [oona**moo**noh] (1864–1936) Philosopher and writer, born in Bilbao, Spain. His main philosophical work is *Del sentimiento trágico de la vida en los hombres y en los pueblos* (1913, The Tragic Sense of Life in Men and Peoples). As rector of Salamanca, he defied the forces of Franco in the Civil War.

unconscious When used psychoanalytically, the collection of feelings, drives, memories, and emotional conflicts which individuals are not aware of, but which influence their mental processes and behaviour, such as dreams and slips of the tongue indicating true feelings. In contrast, the **subconscious** is used colloquially to describe memories about which an individual is only dimly aware, but which can be recalled if focused upon. >> psychoanalysis

underground A complete railway system designed to operate underground in tunnels or tubes, also known as the **tube**, **subway**, or **metro**. Traction is supplied almost exclusively by electric motor. Due to their high cost of construction, undergrounds are normally used only for passenger traffic within large cities. The first practical underground railway was the City and South London Railway, which opened for traffic in 1890. The world's largest system (in terms of number of stations, 468) is the New York City subway (383 km/238 mi). London Underground in 1999 had 392 km/243 mi of track, with 267 stations, and a further 10 scheduled for completion (the Jubilee Line extension) that year. >> railway

Underground Railroad A network of safe houses, hiding places, and routes to aid escaped American slaves to reach freedom in the N or Canada. It was active as early as 1786, but was most widespread after 1830. >> slavery

underwriter In business or insurance, a person or company that guarantees payment if a certain event should occur. In insurance, the underwriter pays in the event of fire or theft. In finance, an underwriter of a share issue guarantees that they will buy at a pre-arranged price any shares not 'taken up' (ie bought) by others. >> insurance; Lloyd's

undulant fever >> **brucellosis**

unemployment A situtation where a person able and willing to do work is not employed. **Demand-deficiency** or **Keynesian unemployment** is where there is simply insufficient demand. In **classical unemployment**, the lowest pay that workers will accept is above what employers think their labour is worth. **Frictional unemployment** is where workers and employers exist whose offers are mutually acceptable, but who are looking for and have not yet located each other. **Mismatch** occurs when the vacant jobs and unemployed workers differ in skill or location. Possible cures include expanding effective demand, lowering wages, improving the mechanics of matching workers and vacancies, and assisting mobility and the acquisition of skills. >> depression (economics); Neo-Keynesianism; redundancy; supply-side economics

UNESCO [yoo**nes**koh] Acronym for **United Nations Educational, Cultural and Scientific Organization**, founded in 1946 with the objective of contributing to peace and security by promoting collaboration among nations through education, science, and culture. Its headquarters is in Paris. In the mid-1980s, there emerged serious concern among the non-communist industrialized countries over the organization's administrative inefficiency and its allegedly inappropriate political aims. In consequence the USA left in 1985, which had a major impact on UNESCO's finances. The UK and Singapore subsequently withdrew, but the UK rejoined in 1997. In 1999 there were 186 member states, while the USA retained observer status along with the Vatican.

Ungaretti, Giuseppe [ungga**ret**ee] (1888–1970) Poet, born in Alexandria, Egypt. His poems, characterized by symbolism, compressed imagery, and modern verse structure, became the foundation of the *hermetic* movement.

Ungava–Quebec Crater >> **Chubb Crater**

ungulate A mammal in which toes end in hooves rather than claws; includes *artiodactyls* (**even-toed ungulates**) and *perissodactyls* (**odd-toed ungulates**); also the **primitive ungulates** (elephant, hyrax, aardvark); usually large and herbivorous. >> artiodactyl; herbivore; mammal [i]; perissodactyl [i]

unicameral system A legislature which has only one chamber. This uncommon system tends to be found in countries with relatively small populations, where there would be problems in maintaining a dual system of representation. New Zealand, Israel, and Denmark are examples. >> bicameral system

UNICEF The **United Nations Children's Fund**, formerly known as the **United Nations International Children's Emergency Fund**, established in 1946 to provide help for children left destitute after Word War 2, and now concerned with children in need everywhere. It was given a permanent role within the UN in 1953. In 1998, UNICEF was supporting programmes in over 160 countries in relation to child health, nutrition, water and sanitation, or education, and also providing emergency aid in many parts of the world. Funded entirely by voluntary contributions from the general public and governments, and with national committees in most industrialized countries, it is unique in the UN system. >> United Nations

unicorn A fabulous creature, a horse with a single horn on its forehead; probably based on stories of the rhinoceros.

Unification Church >> **Moonies**

Uniformity, Acts of A series of acts passed by the English parliament in 1549, 1552, 1559, and 1662. They sought to impose religious uniformity by requiring the use of the Church of England liturgy as contained in the Book of Common Prayer. >> Book of Common Prayer

union >> **trade union**

union >> **set**

Union, Acts of The Acts which joined England in legislative union with Scotland (1707) and Ireland (1800). The 1800 Act created the United Kingdom of Great Britain and Ireland, which came into effect in 1801, and lasted until 1922. >> United Kingdom [i]

Union Islands >> **Tokelau**

Unionist >> **Conservative Party**

Union Movement A party formed by Sir Oswald Mosley in 1948 as a successor to his New Party (1931) and the British Union of Fascists (1932). The party's main plank was opposition to immigration. The movement died out by the end of the 1960s. >> fascism; Mosley

Union of European Football Associations >> **UEFA**

Union of Soviet Socialist Republics >> **Soviet Union**

Uniramia [yooni**ray**mia] A group of arthropods characterized by their 1-branched (*uniramous*) limbs, and by jaws that bite transversely at the tip; comprises the insects (*Insecta*), centipedes (*Chilopoda*), millipedes (*Diplopoda*), and velvet worms (*Onychophora*); sometimes treated as a separate phylum at the arthropodan level of organization. >> arthropod; centipede; insect [i]; millipede; systematics; velvet worm

Unitarians A religious group which, although in many ways akin to Christianity, rejects the doctrines of the Trinity and the divinity of Christ. As an organized group, it dates back to the 16th-c Protestant Reformation, first in parts of S Europe, and from the 18th-c in Britain and America. >> Anabaptists; Trinity

United Arab Emirates, Arabic **al-Arabiyah al-Muttahida**, formerly **Trucial States** pop (1995e) 2 181 000; area 83 600 sq km/32 300 sq mi. Federation comprising seven internally self-governing emirates, EC Arabian Peninsula; capital, Abu Dhabi; timezone GMT +4; major ethnic groups Emirian (19%), other Arabs (23%), S Asian (50%); chief religion, Islam; official language, Arabic; unit of currency, the dirham; located along the S shore (Trucial Coast) of the Persian Gulf; al-Fujairah has a coastline along the Gulf of Oman; barren desert and gravel plain inland; Hajar Mts in Al Fujairah rise to over 1000 m/ 3000 ft; hot climate with limited rainfall; sandstorms common; peace treaty with Britain signed by rulers of the Trucial States, 1820; new state formed by six emirates, 1971; Ras al-Khaimah joined, 1972; governed by a Supreme Council comprising the hereditary rulers of the seven emirates, advised by a Federal National Council; an important commercial and trading centre; economy based on oil and gas, Abu Dhabi the major producer, followed by Dubai; saline water supplies have restricted agriculture to the oases and the irrigated valleys of the Hajar Mts. >> Abu Dhabi; Ajman; Dubai; Fujairah, al-; Ras al-Khaimah; Sharjah; Umm al-Qaiwain; RR1025 political leaders; *see illustration on p. 893*

United Church of Christ A Christian denomination formed in the USA in 1961 by the union of the Congregational and Christian Churches with the Evangelical and Reformed Church. >> Congregationalism; Reformed Churches

United Fronts Two attempts to promote co-operation between the Chinese Communist and Nationalist Parties in the face of Japanese aggression in the late 1930s. Clashes between Nationalist and Communist forces led to its virtual disintegration by 1941.

United Irishmen, Society of A society formed in Belfast in 1791 by Protestant lawyer Wolfe Tone, which supported the French Revolution and espoused both religious equality and parliamentary reform. The Society was instrumental in organizing French support for the unsuccessful Irish rebellion of 1798, and afterwards went into decline. >> French Revolution ⓘ; Tone

United Kingdom (UK), also **United Kingdom of Great Britain and Northern Ireland** or **Great Britain** pop (1995e) 58 541 000; area 244 755 sq km/94 475 sq mi. Kingdom of W Europe, comprising the kingdoms of England and Scotland, the principality of Wales, and Northern Ireland; population 81·5% English, 9·6% Scottish, 2·4% Irish, 1·9% Welsh, and 2% West Indian, Asian, and African; chief religion, Christianity; official language, English, with Welsh and Gaelic spoken by minorities; unit of currency, the pound sterling of 100 pence; Wales was effectively joined to England in 1536, Scotland in 1603 (Act of Union 1707), and Ireland in 1801 (the United Kingdom of Great Britain and Ireland); present name dates from 1922, following the establishment of the Irish Free State; a kingdom with a monarch as head of state; governed by a bicameral parliament, comprising an elected 650-member House of Commons and a House of Lords; a Cabinet is appointed by the prime minister. >> England ⓘ; Northern Ireland ⓘ; Scotland ⓘ; Wales ⓘ; RR1026 political leaders and monarchs

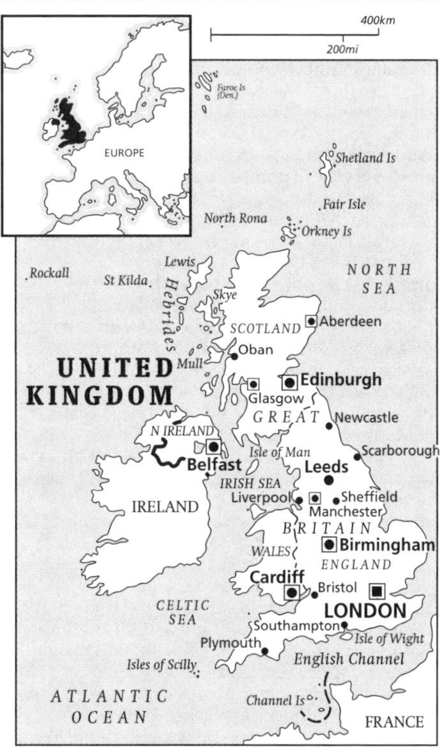

major international airport

United Kingdom Atomic Energy Authority An authority set up by the Atomic Energy Authority Act in 1954. It has prime responsibility for research and the development of nuclear power in the UK on behalf of the government. >> International Atomic Energy Agency; nuclear reactor ⓘ

United Nations (UN) An organization formed to maintain world peace and foster international co-operation, formally established on 24 October 1945 with 51 founder countries; there were 185 members in early 1999. The **General Assembly** is the plenary body which controls much of the UN's work, and debates major issues of international affairs. The 15-member **Security Council** is dominated by the five permanent members (China, France, UK, Russia, and USA) who each have the power of veto over any resolutions; the remaining 10 are elected for 2-year periods. The primary role of the Council is to maintain international peace and security; its decisions, unlike those of the General Assembly, are binding on all other members. The **Secretariat**, under the secretary-general, employs some 16 000 at the UN's headquarters in New York City and 50 000 worldwide. The secretary-general is often a significant person in international diplomacy and is able to take independent initiatives. The **International Court of Justice** consists of 15 judges appointed by the Council and the Assembly. As only states can bring issues before it, its jurisdiction depends on the consent of the states who are a party to a dispute. The **Economic and Social Council** is elected by the General Assembly; it supervises the work of various committees, commissions, and expert bodies in the economic and social area, and co-ordinates the work of UN specialized agencies. The **Trusteeship Council** (suspended at the end of 1994) oversaw the transition of Trust Territories to self-government. In addition, there is a range of subsidiary agencies, many with their own constitutions and membership, and some pre-dating the UN. >> RR993, RR1027 political leaders

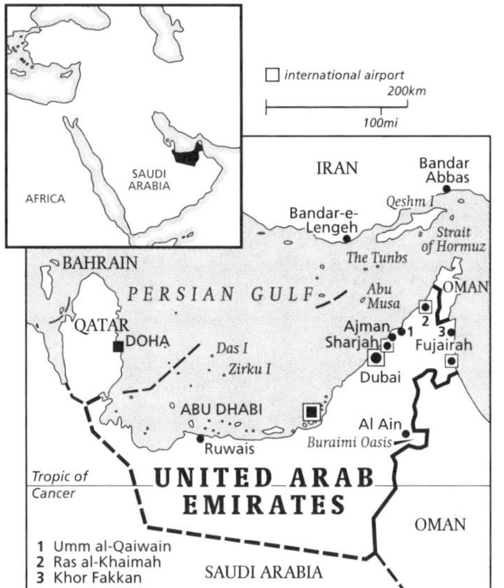

United Nations Conference on Trade and Development (UNCTAD) An organ of the UN, established by the 1964 General Assembly, which meets irregularly to consider ways of increasing international trade and promoting economic development. >> United Nations

United Nations Educational, Cultural and Scientific Organization >> UNESCO

United Provinces of the Netherlands Seven sovereign states of the Dutch Republic, roughly comprising the present kingdom of The Netherlands, which achieved independence from the Spanish crown (1568–1609). The republic declined in the 18th-c, collapsing during the Revolutionary Wars (1795). >> French Revolutionary Wars; Netherlands, Austrian and Spanish

United Service Organizations (USO) Founded in the USA in 1941, it is an association of agencies, such as the YMCA, the YWCA, and the Salvation Army, whose aims are to care for the recreational needs of the Armed Forces. >> Young Men's Christian Association

United States military academies Federal training institutions for people who want to become officers in the US armed forces. The **United States Air Force (USAF) Academy** was formed by Act of Congress in 1948, and is located near Colorado Springs, CO. The **United States Military Academy** was founded in 1802, and is now at West Point on the Hudson R, NY. The **United States Naval Academy** was founded in 1845, and is at Annapolis, MD. The **United States Coast Guard (USCG) Academy** was founded in 1876, and has been located at New London, CT since 1936.

United States of America (USA), also called **United States**, and often **America** pop (1995e) 262 693 000; area 9 160 454 sq km/3 535 935 sq mi. A federal republic of North America; includes the detached states of Alaska and Hawaii; timezones GMT −5 (E coast) to −8 (Pacific Coast), Alaska GMT −9, Hawaii GMT −10; capital, Washington; ethnic groups, white (84%, including 10% Hispanic), black (12%), Asian and Pacific (3.3%), Native American, Eskimo, and Aleut (0.7%); religion mainly Christianity (85%); chief language English, with a sizeable Spanish-speaking minority; currency is the US dollar of 100 cents; E Atlantic coastal plain is backed by the Appalachian Mts from the Great Lakes to Alabama; Great Plains to the W; further W, Rocky Mts rise to over 4500 m/14 750 ft (highest point in USA, Mt McKinley, Alaska, 6194 m/20 321 ft); permanent risk of earthquakes along W coast (notable events, 1906, 1964, 1994); climate varies from conditions found in hot tropical deserts (in the SW) to those typical of Arctic continental regions; wide temperature variation in the Great Plains; smaller range on the W coast; gradual increase in winter temperatures southwards on E coast; hurricanes and tornadoes on Gulf coast; first settled by groups who migrated from Asia across the Bering land-bridge over 25 000 years ago; explored by the Spanish (16th-c), who settled in Florida and Mexico; in the 17th-c, settlements by the British, French, Dutch, Germans, and Swedish; many black Africans introduced as slaves to work on the plantations; British control during the 18th-c; revolt of the English-speaking colonies in the War of Independence, 1775–83, with the creation of the United States of America; Louisiana sold to the USA by France in 1803 (the Louisiana Purchase) and the westward movement of settlers began; Florida ceded by Spain in 1819, and further Mexican states joined the Union between 1821 and 1853; 11 Southern states left the Union over the slavery issue, and formed the Confederacy, 1860–1; Civil War, 1861–5, ended in victory for the North, and the Southern states later rejoined the Union; Alaska purchased from Russia, 1867; Hawaiian Is annexed, 1898; several other islands formally associated with the USA, such as Puerto Rico, American Samoa, and Guam; in the 19th-c, arrival of millions of immigrants from Europe and the Far East; more recently, arrival of large numbers of Spanish-speaking people, mainly from Mexico and the West Indies; now the chief industrial nation in the world, with vast mineral and agricultural resources, a highly diversified economy, and an advanced system of communications and transportation; a leader in the space exploration programme of the 1970s; entered World War 1 on the side of the Allies in 1917, and again in World War 2 in 1941; after that, the chief world power opposed to communism, a policy which led to major military involvements in Korea and Vietnam; campaign for black civil rights developed here in the 1960s, accompanied by much civil disturbance; Congress consists of a 435-member House of Representatives elected for 2-year terms, and a 100-member Senate elected for 6-year terms; a president, elected every 4 years by a college of state representatives, appoints an executive cabinet responsible to Congress; divided into 50 federal states and the District of Columbia, each state having its own two-body legislature and governor. >> American Civil War / Revolution; civil rights; Congress; federalism; Washington (DC); World War 1 / 2; RR994 list of states; RR1027 political leaders; *see also illustration on p. 895*

United States Trust Territory of the Pacific Islands 1–22°N 142–172°E; pop (1990e) 40 000; area 1854 sq km/716 sq mi. Group of c.2000 islands in the W Pacific Ocean,

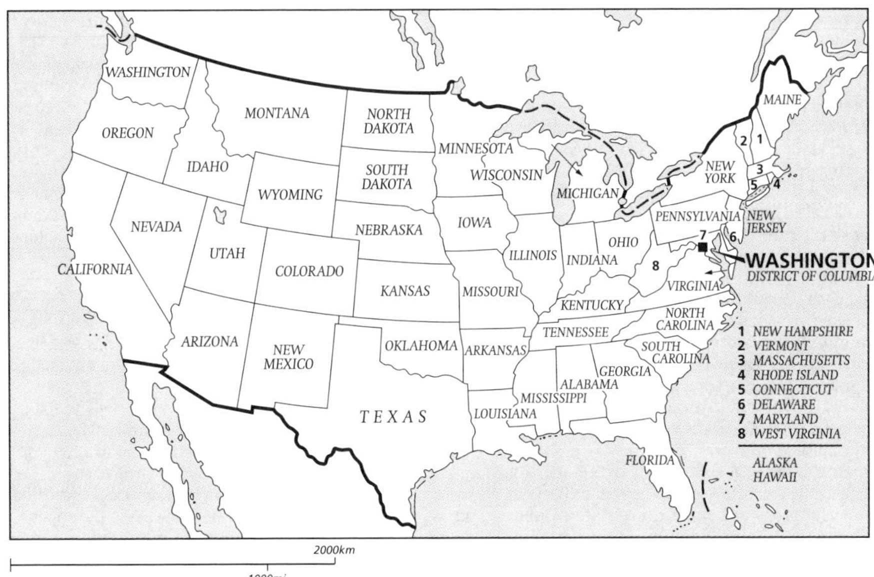

N of Papua New Guinea; until 1990, comprised the Commonwealth of the N Mariana Is, the Federated States of Micronesia, the Republic of Belau, and the Marshall Is; population mostly Micronesian, with some Polynesian; official language, English; islands mainly of volcanic origin, few rising above 120 m/400 ft; administered by Japan in the inter-war years; placed under UN trusteeship, 1947; trust status ended (except for Belau), 1990; economy based on agriculture, fisheries, tourism. >> Belau; Mariana Islands, Commonwealth of the Northern; Marshall Islands; Micronesia, Federated States of; Pacific Ocean

United States Virgin Islands >> **Virgin Islands, United States**

units (scientific) Most quantities in science are expressed using the International System of units, abbreviated to **SI units**, introduced in 1960. The most fundamental are called **base units**: the metre, kilogram, second, ampere, kelvin, candela, and mole. There are two **supplementary units**: the radian and steradian. All quantities of interest can be expressed in terms of these units. Certain combinations which appear often are called **derived units** and have special names, eg the newton. Many other units exist, either for historical reasons or for convenience; examples are the parsec and calories. Other systems of units have been used in the past: these include the old FPS British system, based on foot, pound, and second; the CGS system, based on centimetre, gram, and second; and the MKSA system, based on metre, kilogram, second, and ampere. SI units are an extension of MKSA units. >> natural units; RR1031–2

unit trust A form of investment. The trust buys shares in a number of companies, and offers the public an opportunity to buy a unit of the portfolio. It is a means of spreading risk. >> investment

universalism The religious belief that all people will be saved. It implies rejection of the traditional Christian belief in hell. A feature of much contemporary Protestant theology, it is motivated by moral doubts concerning eternal punishment, and by a recognition of the validity of other non-Christian world faiths. >> Christianity; hell; Protestantism

universal time The precise system of time measurement used for all practical purposes. Formerly based on *mean solar time*, it has since 1972 been based on *international atomic time*, a uniform time derived from the frequencies of selected transitions within atoms. >> Greenwich Mean Time; solar time

universe In modern astronomy, everything that is in the cosmos and that can affect us by means of physical forces. The definition excludes anything that is in principle undetectable physically, such as regions of space–time that were, are, or will be irreversibly cut off from our own space–time. >> 'big bang'; microwave background radiation

university An institution of higher education which offers study at degree level. Courses may be taken leading to bachelor, master, or doctoral level. Both academic and vocational courses are followed, leading to qualifications in such professions as medicine, teaching, engineering, and the law, sometimes in conjunction with professional bodies. Research is given a high priority. The earliest European universities date from Bologna (10th-c), Paris (1170), Oxford (1249), and Cambridge (1284). The first Chinese university was established in 124 BC. >> Cambridge ℹ / London ℹ / Open / Oxford ℹ / Paris University; Ivy League ℹ; New / Red-brick / Scottish universities ℹ

Unix An operating system developed by AT&T Laboratories in the USA which has become widely adopted, particularly in educational centres, and is seen as a suitable operating system to form the basis of open systems interconnection. The Open Software Foundation is seeking to develop Unix as a standard operating system for this purpose. >> open systems interconnection; operating system

Unknown Soldier or **Warrior** An unnamed soldier, taken as representative of all those who died in World War 1, whose grave is a memorial to all war dead. Several countries have such a memorial: in France beneath the Arc de Triomphe; in the UK in Westminster Abbey; in the USA in Arlington National Cemetery. >> World War 1

Unleavened Bread, Feast of >> **Passover**

Unrepresented Nations and Peoples' Organization A body established in 1991 to represent ethnic and minority groups unrecognized by the United Nations, with the aim of defending the right of self-determination of oppressed peoples. The body had 47 members in 1999.

Unsworth, Barry (Forster) (1930–) British novelist. His works include *The Greeks Have a Word for It* (1967), *Mooncranker's Gift* (1973), *Pascali's Island* (1980, filmed 1988), *Sacred Hunger* (1992, co-winner Booker Prize), and *After Hannibal* (1996).

Unter den Linden [**un**ter den **lin**dn] A boulevard running between Marx–Engels Platz and the Brandenburg Gate, in the heart of Berlin, Germany. Formerly a stately avenue lined with lime trees and historic buildings, much of its character was destroyed during World War 2. >> Berlin

untouchables >> **caste**

Upanishads [oo**pan**ishadz] The last section of the Hindu scriptures (the Veda), composed in Sanskrit between 800 and 400 BC. The name, meaning 'to sit near', refers to the secret transmission of these teachings by gurus. >> Hinduism; Veda

upas tree [**yoo**pas] An evergreen tree (*Antiaris toxicaria*) native to Malaysia; flowers tiny, green; milky latex makes a powerful arrow-poison. In the 18th-c, misunderstanding led to the belief that poisonous emanations from the tree killed all life for miles around. (Family: Moraceae.) >> latex

Updike, John (Hoyer) (1932–) Writer, born in Shillington, PA. His novels, exploring human relationships in contemporary US society, include *Rabbit, Run* (1960), *Rabbit is Rich* (1981, Pulitzer), *Rabbit at Rest* (1990, Pulitzer), and *The Witches of Eastwick* (1984, filmed 1987), and he has published several collections of short stories.

Up-Helly-Aa [uhp heli **ah**] A festival held annually in Lerwick in the Shetland Islands, UK, on the last Tuesday in January, ending in the burning of a replica Viking longship.

Upper Volta >> **Burkina Faso**

Uppsala [**up**sala] 59°55N 17°38E, pop (1995e) 176 000. City in E Sweden; archbishopric; railway; educational centre, with university (1477) and many other academic institutions; cathedral (13th–15th-c), with tombs of Gustavus Vasa and other kings; castle (16th-c). >> Gustavus Vasa; Sweden [i]

Ur [oor] The early home of the Jewish patriarch Abraham, an ancient Sumerian city-state lying to the SE of Babylon. At its zenith in the third millennium BC, it was destroyed by Elam c.2000 BC, and finally abandoned in the 4th-c BC. >> Abraham; Elam; Sumer

uraemia / uremia [yoo**ree**mia] A rise in the concentration of urea in the blood, one of the first chemical abnormalities to be detected in kidney failure. >> blood

Uralic languages A family of languages descended from an ancestor spoken in the region of the N Ural Mts over 7000 years ago. The major languages are Finnish, Estonian, and Lapp, with an isolated member, Magyar, in Hungary. Numerous other languages are scattered through N Russia. >> Lapp; Magyar; Slavic languages

Ural Mountains [**yoo**ral(z)] or **The Urals**, Russ **Uralskiy Khrebet** Mountain range in Russia, forming the traditional boundary between Europe and Asia, and separating the E European Plain (W) from the W Siberian Lowlands (E); extends 1750 km/1100 mi S; generally 200–1000 m/ 700–3300 ft high; N Urals contain the highest peak, Mt Narodnaya (1894 m/6214 ft); heavily forested; rich mineral deposits. >> Russia [i]

Urania [yoo**ray**nia] In Greek mythology, the Muse of astronomy. >> Muses

uraninite >> **pitchblende**

uranium U, element 92, density 19 g/cm^3, melting point 1132°C. The heaviest of the naturally occurring elements. It has no stable isotopes, but the commonest (^{238}U) has a half-life of more than 10^9 years. Uranium compounds are now used almost exclusively for conversion to plutonium in nuclear fuel applications. >> chemical elements; nuclear reactor [i]; plutonium; RR1036

uranium–lead dating A method of radiometric dating for old rocks, using the fact that the radioactive isotope uranium-238 decays with a known half-life to give lead-206 and another isotope of uranium, uranium-235, decays to give lead-207. The amount of each isotope in a rock can be used to determine its absolute age. >> radiometric dating

Uranus (astronomy) [**yoo**ranuhs, yu**ray**nuhs] The seventh planet from the Sun, discovered by William Herschel in 1781; a smaller 'gas giant' than Jupiter or Saturn, and a near-twin to Neptune. It has the following characteristics: mass 8·7 × 10^{25} kg; radius 25 500 km/15 800 mi; mean density 1·3 g/cm^3; rotational period 84·01 years; orbital period 17·2 hours; eccentricity of orbit 0·047; inclination of equator 82°; mean distance from the Sun 2·87 × 10^9 km/ 1·78 × 10^9 mi. Composed mainly of hydrogen and helium, like Jupiter and Saturn, Uranus has a larger percentage of ammonia and methane. Methane gas in the upper atmosphere accounts for the planet's greenish hue. It is highly unusual in having a rotation axis tilted, so that the poles lie almost in the ecliptic, and its equatorial plane with rings and moons lies almost perpendicular to the ecliptic. It was observed at close range for the first time by Voyager 1 in 1986, which discovered two new rings to add to the nine already observed telescopically. There are five major moons (Miranda, Ariel, Umbriel, Titania, Oberon) in synchronous rotation; 10 additional small moons were discovered by Voyager. >> ammonia; methane; planet; shepherd moons; Solar System; Voyager project [i]; RR964

Uranus (mythology) [**yoo**ranuhs, yu**ray**nuhs] or **Ouranus** In Greek mythology, the earliest sky-god, who was the father of the Titans. He is equivalent to Roman **Caelus**, 'the heavens'. >> Titan (mythology)

Urdu >> **Indo-Aryan languages**

urea [yu**ree**a] $H_2N–CO–NH_2$, melting point 135°C. A colourless solid, manufactured by heating ammonia and carbon dioxide under pressure: also called **carbamide**. It is used as an animal feed additive as well as a fertilizer, and is the starting material for urea resins. >> ammonia; resin; urine

urethritis [yoore**thriy**tis] Inflammation of the urethra, caused by one of several organisms such as *Neisseria gonorrhoeae* and *Chlamydia*. The symptoms include a burning sensation on passing urine, and frequency of urination. >> urinary system

Urey, Harold C(layton) [**yoo**ree] (1893–1981) Chemist and pioneer in the study of the Solar System, born in Walkerton, IN. In 1932 he isolated heavy water and discovered deuterium, for which he received the Nobel Prize for Chemistry in 1934. His work on lunar and planetary formation laid the scientific foundation for the space age exploration of the Solar System. >> deuterium

Urfé, Honoré d' [**ür**fay] (1568–1625) Writer, born in Marseille, France. He was the author of the pastoral romance, *Astrée* (1610–27), regarded as the first French novel. >> pastoral

uric acid [**yoo**rik] An acid derived from purine, $C_5H_4N_4O_3$; like urea, used by animals as a means of excreting nitrogen. Deposits of crystals of uric acid and its salts cause pain in gout and rheumatism. >> purines; urine

Urim and Thummim [**oo**rim, **thuh**mim] Objects of uncertain description, kept in the breastplate and vestments of the Israelite high priest. They were apparently used to discern God's answer to 'yes'-or-'no' questions put to him. >> Judaism; oracle

urinary stones The formation of calculi within the kidney substance and pelvis, ureter, and bladder. They commonly consist of salts of calcium, magnesium, ammonium phosphate, carbonate, and oxalate. Factors predisposing to their formation include working in hot climates, high dietary calcium and oxalate intake, and familial factors. >> calculi; kidneys

urinary system The physiological system involved in the production, storage, and excretion of urine. In mammals it consists of a pair of kidneys each connected to a muscular sac (the *bladder*) by a narrow fibromuscular tube (the *ureter*); a single *urethra* links the bladder to the exterior. >> bladder; kidneys; penis ⓘ; pyelonephritis; urine

urine A liquid or semi-solid solution produced by the kidneys in vertebrates (eg humans), Malpighian tubules in some invertebrates (eg insects), and nephridia in most invertebrates (eg annelids, molluscs). It consists of water, the end-products of metabolism (eg urea, uric acid, hydrogen ions), dietary constituents taken in excess (eg salts, vitamins), and foreign substances (eg drugs), or their derivatives. The expulsion of urine from the bladder is often referred to as *micturition*. >> diuretics; kidneys; urinary system

Ursa Major [**er**sa **may**jer] (Lat 'great bear') A huge and conspicuous constellation, containing the Plough. It is mentioned extensively in literature from the earliest times, and is the one constellation that most people in the N hemisphere can locate without difficulty. >> constellation; Plough, the; Polaris; RR968

Ursa Minor [**er**sa **miy**ner] (Lat 'little bear') The constellation around the N celestial pole. Its brightest star is Polaris. >> constellation; Polaris; RR968

Ursulines Worldwide congregations of sisters engaged in the education of girls. The principal and oldest congregation was founded in 1535 by St Angela Merici as the Company of St Ursula, after the 4th-c legendary saint and martyr. >> nun

urticaria [erti**kair**ia] A rash due to the release of histamine, resulting in the formation of weals and blisters in the skin; also known as **nettle rash** or **hives**. The commonest form results from allergy. >> histamine; skin ⓘ

Uruguay [**yoo**ruhgwiy], official name **Oriental Republic of Uruguay**, Span **República Oriental del Uruguay** pop (1995e) 3 187 000; area 176 215 sq km/68 018 sq mi. Republic in E South America; capital, Montevideo; timezone GMT −3; population mainly European (90%); chief religion, Roman Catholicism (66%); official language, Spanish; unit of currency, the nuevo peso of 100 centésimos; grass-covered plains (S) rise N to a high sandy plateau; R Negro flows SW to meet the R Uruguay on the Argentine frontier; temperate climate with warm summers and mild winters; originally occupied by Charrúas Indians; visited by the Spanish, 1515; part of the Spanish Viceroyalty of Río de la Plata, 1726; province of Brazil, 1814–25; independence, 1828; unrest caused by Tupamaro guerrillas in late 1960s and early 1970s; military rule until 1985; a president is advised by a Council of Ministers; bicameral legislature consists of a Senate and Chamber of Deputies; economy traditionally based on livestock and agriculture. >> Montevideo; Tupamaros; RR1027 political leaders

Uruguay, River (Span **Río**), Port **Rio Uruguai** South American river; rises in S Brazil, joins the R Paraná to form the R Plate; length c.1600 km/1000 mi. >> Argentina ⓘ

Uruk [**oo**ruk] One of the greatest city-states of Sumer, lying to the NW of Ur. The home of the legendary Gilgamesh, it is also the site of the earliest writing ever found. It survived well into the Parthian period (3rd-c AD). >> Sumer; Ur

Ürümqi [urum**chee**], **Urumchi**, or **Wulumuqi**, also spelled **Wu-lu-mu-ch'i** 43°43N 87°38E, pop (1995e) 1 305 000. City in NW China; airfield; railway; eight universities; two medical schools; agricultural college (1952); communist base in 1930s and 1940s. >> China ⓘ

urus [**yoo**rus] >> **aurochs**

USA >> **United States of America** ⓘ

Usborne, Mount 51°35S 58°57W. Mountain on the island of East Falkland; highest point in the Falkland Is, rising to 705 m/2313 ft. >> Falkland Islands ⓘ

USENET A computer network established by those computer centres running the Unix operating system. It has become worldwide, offering electronic mail and bulletin boards. >> bulletin board; computer network; electronic mail

Usher >> **Ussher**

Uspallata [uspa**yah**ta] 32°50S 70°04W. Pass in the Andes between Mendoza (Argentina) and Santiago (Chile); rises to 3900 m/12 795 ft; statue of Christ of the Andes (1904). >> Andes

Ussher or **Usher, James** (1581–1656) Clergyman, born in Dublin. His major work was the *Annales veteris et novi testamenti* (1650–4, Annals of the Old and New Testament), which gave a long-accepted chronology of Scripture, and fixed the Creation at 4004 BC. >> Bible; Cromwell, Oliver

USSR >> **Soviet Union**

Ustinov, Sir Peter (Alexander) [**yus**tinof] (1921–) Actor and playwright, born in London, the son of White Russian parents. A prolific playwright, his works include *The Love of Four Colonels* (1951), *Romanoff and Juliet* (1956), and *Overheard* (1981). He has made over 50 films, and in recent years has established a considerable reputation as a raconteur.

Ustinov >> **Izhevsk**

Usumacinta, River [oosuma**seen**ta] River in Guatemala and Mexico, enters the Gulf of Mexico; length (with the Chixoy, which rises in Guatemala) c.965 km/600 mi. >> Guatemala; Mexico

US War of Independence >> **American Revolution**

Utah [**yoo**taw] pop (1995e) 1 957 000; area 219 880 sq km/ 84 899 sq mi. State in W USA, the 'Beehive State'; first white exploration by the Spanish, 1540; acquired by the USA through the Treaty of Guadalupe Hidalgo, 1848; arrival of the Mormons, 1847; Utah Territory organized, 1850; antagonism between Mormon Church and Federal law led to the 'Utah War', 1857–8; joined the Union as the 45th state, 1896; capital, Salt Lake City: contains the Great Salt Lake in the NW; the Wasatch Range runs N–S; highest point, Kings Peak (4123 m/13 527 ft); mountainous and sparsely inhabited E region; major cities (containing four-fifths of the population) lie along W foothills of the Wasatch Range; Great Basin further W; arid Great Salt Lake Desert in the NW. >> Guadalupe Hidalgo, Treaty of; Mormons; Salt Lake City; United States of America ℹ; RR994

Utamaro, (Kitagawa) [ootamahroh], originally **Kitagawa Nebsuyoshi** (1753–1806) Painter and master of the colour print, born in Edo (modern Tokyo). He came to specialize in portraits of court ladies, painted flowers, birds and fish, and carried the technique of the *ukiyo-e* to its highest artistic level. >> ukiyo-e

uterine tubes A pair of long ducts passing outwards from the upper part of the uterus towards the ovary, also known as the **Fallopian tubes**, after Italian anatomist Gabriele Fallopius (1523–62). >> ovarian follicle; pregnancy ℹ; uterus ℹ

uterus [**yoo**teruhs] A pear-shaped, thick-walled muscular organ of females which projects upwards and forwards above the bladder from the upper part of the vagina; also known as the **womb**. It consists of a *fundus* (the region of the body above the level of entrance of the uterine tubes), a *body*, and the *cervix* (separated from the body by a slight narrowing). In the human female the non-pregnant uterus is c.7·5 cm/3 in in length and weighs 40 g/1·4 oz. During pregnancy it increases in size to become c.30 cm/ 12 in in length and can weigh as much as 1 kg/2·2 lb by the eighth month. >> Caesarian section; cervix; dilation and curettage; gynaecology; hysterectomy; menstruation; uterine tubes; vagina

Uther Pendragon [**yoo**ther pen**dra**gn] In the Arthurian legends, a king of Britain, who was the father of King Arthur by Ygraine, the wife of Duke Gorlois of Cornwall. >> Arthur

utilitarianism In ethics, the theory that all actions are to be judged by their consequences for the general welfare; 'the greatest happiness of the greatest number' is the sole criterion of moral choice. It flourished particularly in the 19th-c. >> Bentham; Hume, David

utility In computing, a term used for a computer program which carries out a specific function needed by a computer centre, but which is not sufficiently extensive to justify the development of a computer package. Normally a function such as sort and merge is provided as a utility. >> computer package; sort and merge

Utopia (Gr 'nowhere') A name for a fictional republic, invented by Sir Thomas More in *Utopia* (1516); hence, any imaginary (and by implication, unattainable) ideal state. The term **dystopia** refers to the reverse, a nightmare state such as in Orwell's *Nineteen Eighty Four* (1949). >> More, Thomas; utopianism

utopianism A general term to describe a political philosophy distinguished by its belief in an ideal future state of global social harmony. Its supporters work to establish the basis for the **utopia** of the future. >> political science; Utopia

Utrecht [yoo**trekt**], Dutch [**oo**trekht], Lat **Trajectum ad Rhenum** 52°06N 5°07E, pop (1995e) 238 000. City in W Netherlands; political and cultural centre; Union of Utrecht, 1579; Treaties of Utrecht, 1713–14; archbishopric; railway; university (1634); cathedral (1254). >> Netherlands, The ℹ

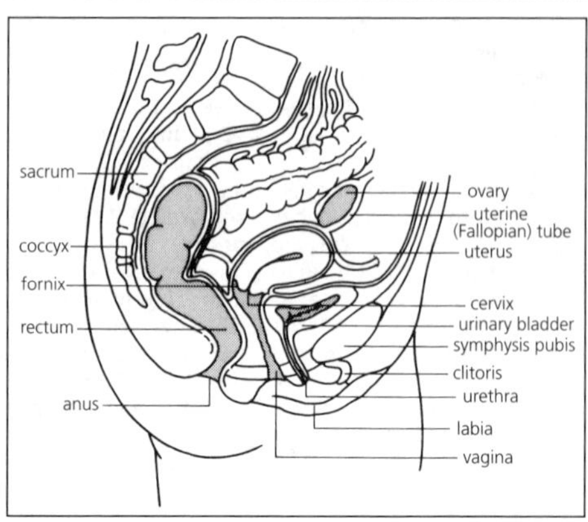

Main female organs of reproduction, and surrounding structures

Utrecht, Treaties of (1713–14) The peace settlement ending the War of the Spanish Succession, a series of agreements between France, Spain, Britain, Holland, and the League of Augsburg. The Bourbons made considerable concessions, but Louis XIV's grandson, Philip V, retained the throne of Spain. >> Philip V; Spanish Succession, War of the

Utrecht School A group of Dutch painters who went to Rome early in the 17th-c and were deeply influenced by Caravaggio. >> Caravaggio; Honthorst; Terbrugghen

Utrillo, Maurice [oo**treel**oh] (1883–1955) Painter, born in Paris. He was a prolific artist, producing picture-postcard views of the streets of Paris, particularly old Montmartre.

Uttar Pradesh [**oo**tar pra**daysh**] pop (1995e) 150 492 000; area 294 413 sq km/113 643 sq mi. State in NC India; known as the Bengal Presidency until 1833, then divided into provinces of Agra and Oudh; under one administration, 1877; called United Provinces of Agra and Oudh, 1902; renamed as United Provinces, 1935; adopted present name in 1950; capital, Lucknow; governed by a Legislative Council and Legislative Assembly; official language, Hindi; largest producer of foodgrains in India. >> India ℹ

Uttley, Alison (1884–1976) Writer of children's stories, born on a farm in Derbyshire. *The Country Child* (1931) was followed by a series of books, mainly for children, which revealed her knowledge of the countryside.

uvula [**yoo**vyula] The conical, midline muscular extension of the soft palate, of variable length in humans (5–20 mm/0·2–0·8 in). It is elevated in swallowing, and is occasionally used in the production of speech sounds (eg the French 'uvular r'). >> palate

Uxmal [oosh**mahl**] An ancient Mayan city in the Yucatan peninsula, Mexico. It flourished AD c.600–1000, and was finally abandoned c.1450. >> Mayas

Uzbekistan [uzbeki**stahn**], official name **Republic of Uzbekistan**, Uzbek **Ozbekistan Jumhuriyäti** pop (1995e) 21 669 000; area 447 400 sq km/172 696 sq mi. Republic in C and N Middle Asia; capital, Tashkent; timezone GMT +5; major ethnic groups, Uzbek (71%), Russian (8%), Tajik (5%), Kazakh (4%); language, Uzbek; religion, Sunni Muslim; currency, the som; large area occupied by the

Kyzyl-Kum desert; 80% of the area is flat sandy plain; Turan Plain (NW) rises near Aral Sea to 90 m/300 ft above sea level; Pskem Mts (E) rise to 4299 m/14 104 ft at Beshtor Peak; chief rivers, the Amu Darya, Syr Darya, Chirchik; dry, continental climate; average annual temperature in S −12°C (Jan), 32–40°C (Jul); low rainfall; conquered by Alexander the Great, 4th-c BC; invaded by Mongols under Genghis Khan, 13th-c; converted to Islam, 14th-c; part of Timur's empire, 16th-c; conquered by Russia, mid-19th-c; proclaimed a Soviet Socialist Republic, 1925; declaration of independence, 1991; President Karimov resigned after supporting coup against Gorbachev, 1991, but re-elected president after joining CIS; new constitution, 1992; governed by a president, prime minister, and 250-member Supreme Assembly; deposits of coal, natural gas, oil, gold, lead, copper, zinc; oil refining, metallurgy, fertilizers, machinery, cotton, silk, food processing; orchards and vineyards; intensive cultivation with the aid of irrigation; third largest cotton-growing area in the world. >> Commonwealth of Independent States [i]; Soviet Union; Tashkent; RR1027 political leaders

Vaal River [vahl] River in South Africa; length 1200 km/750 mi; a major tributary of the Orange R. >> South Africa ⓘ

Vaasa [**vah**sa], Swed **Vasa**, formerly **Nikolainkaupunki** 63°06N 21°38E, pop (1995e) 54 500. Seaport in SW Finland; established, 1606; destroyed by fire, 1852; rebuilt on present site, c.1860; airfield; railway; shortest ferry route between Finland and Sweden. >> Finland ⓘ

Vac [vats] 47°49N 19°10E, pop (1995e) 34 700. River port and summer resort town in NC Hungary; on R Danube; bishopric; railway; cathedral. >> Hungary ⓘ

vaccination A medical procedure which derives its name from *vaccinia* or cowpox, serum from which was used by Jenner in 1795 to protect against smallpox. Today, the term is used in a more general sense, equivalent to **immunization**. >> immunization; Jenner

vacuum Any space in which no matter is present. In the laboratory, near vacuum is achieved by pumping out air from an enclosed chamber. A perfect vacuum can never be attained; the closest is interstellar space. >> physics; vacuum technology

vacuum technology A technology which produces and uses pressures from a thousand to one million million times less than the atmosphere. Thin coatings (metal or non-metal) are made by evaporation in a vacuum, and used in optical instruments or the electronics industry. The technology is used to provide vacuums inside television tubes, X-ray tubes, particle accelerators, and for dehydration at low temperatures ('freeze drying'). >> vacuum

Vadim, Roger [va**dim**], originally **Roger Vadim Plemiannikov** (1928–) Film director, born in Paris. His *Et Dieu créa la femme* (1956, And God Created Woman), starring his wife Brigitte Bardot as a sex-kitten, was a massive box-office success, and paved the way for further sex-symbol presentations of his later wives, Annette Stroyberg in *Les Liaisons dangereuses* (1959, Dangerous Liaisons), Jane Fonda in *Barbarella* (1968), and his lover, Catherine Deneuve, in *La Vice et la vertue* (1962, Vice and Virtue). >> Bardot

Vaduz [**vah**doots] 47°08N 9°32E, pop (1995e) 5200. Capital of Liechtenstein, in the R Rhine valley; 12th-c castle (rebuilt, 20th-c). >> Liechtenstein

vagina A variable-sized fibro-muscular tube, open at its lower end, which communicates at its upper end with the cavity of the uterus. In virgins the lower opening is partly closed by a thin crescent-fold (the *hymen*). >> cervix; uterus ⓘ

vagus [**vay**guhs] The 10th cranial nerve. It descends in the neck, supplying the muscles of the larynx and pharynx; in the thorax it supplies the oesophagus, trachea, lungs, heart, and great vessels; in the abdomen it supplies the stomach, the small and part of the large intestine, the pancreas, and the liver. >> nervous system

valence or **valency** [**vay**lens, **vay**lensee] The combining power of an atom expressed either as (1) the **covalence**, or net number of bonds an atom makes, weighting double bonds as two, etc, or (2) the **electrovalence**, essentially equivalent to the oxidation state. >> atom; chemical bond

Valencia (Spain) [va**len**sia], Span [va**len**thia] pop (1995e) 3 862 000; area 23 260 sq km/8978 sq mi. Autonomous region of E Spain, occupying a narrow coastal area from the Ebro delta to R Segura; a former Moorish kingdom, under Spanish rule from 1238; includes tourist resorts on the Costa Blanca and Costa del Azahar; chief town, Valencia, pop (1995e) 759 000, on R Turia; third largest city in Spain; archbishopric; airport; railway; car ferries to Balearics and Canary Is; university (1500); cathedral (13th–15th-c). >> Costa Blanca; Costa del Azahar; El Cid; Spain ⓘ

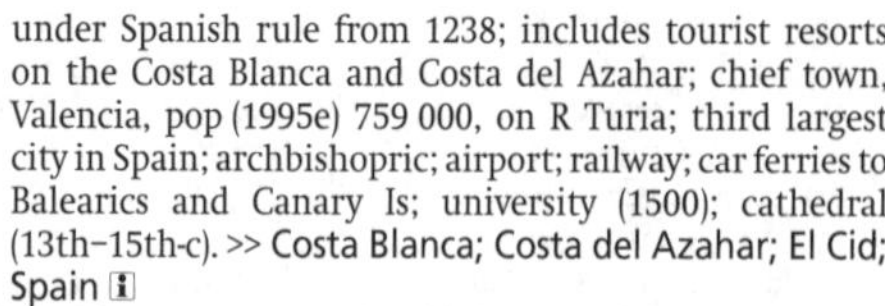

Valencia (Venezuela) [va**len**sia] 10°11N 67°59W, pop (1995e) 1 007 000. Third largest city in Venezuela; on R Cabriales; railway; university (1852); cathedral (18th-c); noted for its oranges. >> Venezuela ⓘ

valentine >> **St Valentine's Day**

Valentino [valen**tee**noh], popular name of **Valentino Garavani** (1933–) Fashion designer, born in Rome. He opened his own house in Rome in 1959, but achieved worldwide recognition with his 1962 show in Florence.

Valentino, Rudolph [valen**tee**noh] (1895–1926) Film actor, born in Castellaneta, Italy. His performances in *The Sheikh* (1921), *Blood and Sand* (1922), and other silent film dramas made him the leading 'screen lover' of the 1920s.

Vale of Glamorgan, Welsh **Bro Morgannwg** pop (1995e) 119 200; area 337 sq km/130 sq mi. County (unitary authority from 1996) in S Wales, UK; administrative centre, Barry; tourism at Barry I. >> Wales ⓘ

Valera, Eamon de >> **de Valera, Eamon**

valerian A perennial herb native to Europe and Asia; flowers pink, in dense terminal heads; fruits with a parachute of feathery hairs. (Family: Valerianaceae.)

Valéry, (Ambroise) Paul (Toussaint Jules) [valayree] (1871–1945) Poet and critic, born in Sète, France. After writing a great deal of poetry he relapsed into a 20 years' silence, taken up with mathematics and philosophical speculations, later published as *Cahiers* (29 vols, 1957–60). He emerged in 1917 with a new Symbolist poetic outlook and technique. >> Symbolism

Valetta >> **Valletta**

Valhalla [val**hal**a] In Norse mythology, a great hall built by Odin to house warriors who die bravely in battle. >> Odin; Ragnarok

Valium >> **benzodiazepines**

Valkyries [val**kee**reez, **val**kireez] (Old Norse 'choosers of the slain') In Norse and German mythology, the Maidens of Odin. They rode out to collect warriors killed in battle for Valhalla. >> Odin; Valhalla

Valladolid [valyado**leeth**] 41°38N 4°43W, pop (1995e) 331 000. City in NWC Spain; on R Pisuerga; archbishopric; airport; railway; Columbus died here; university (1346); cathedral (16th-c). >> Spain ⓘ

Valle d'Aosta [**val**ay da**os**ta], Fr **Val d'Aoste** pop (1995e) 118 000; area 3263 sq km/1259 sq mi. Autonomous region of Italy (1948), bounded W by France and N by Switzerland; population mostly French-speaking; access route to the Great and Little St Bernard Passes. >> Alps; Italy ⓘ

Valles Marineris [**val**ez mari**nair**is] A vast, complex system of interconnected canyons stretching for c.4000 km/2500 mi around Mars. Generally the canyons are over 3 km/1½ mi deep and over 100 km/60 mi wide. They were discovered by Mariner 9 orbiter in 1972, and studied in detail by Viking orbiters. >> Mariner programme; Mars (astronomy); Viking project

Valletta or **Valetta** [va**let**a] 35°54N 14°32E, pop (1995e) 9600. Capital of Malta; a world heritage site; founded by

the Knights of St John, 1566; airport; university (1769); cathedral (16th-c). >> Malta ℹ

valley An elongated trough in the Earth's surface, most commonly formed by the erosional action of rivers over a long period of time. It may also be carved out by a glacier, in which case it is U-shaped rather than (as in a river valley) V-shaped. >> glacier; rift valley ℹ; river ℹ

Valley Forge National historical park in Pennsylvania, USA, 7 km/4 mi SE of Phoenixville; winter headquarters of George Washington, 1777–8; renowned for the endurance and loyalty shown by the troops during the severe winter. >> American Revolution; Pennsylvania

Valley of the Kings A remote limestone wadi on the W bank of the R Nile at Luxor, 650 km/400 mi S of Cairo. Cut into its walls are the tombs of the Egyptian kings of the New Kingdom (XVIII–XX Dynasties, 1550–1070 BC), such as Rameses VI and Tutankhamun. >> Egyptian history, Ancient ℹ; Luxor; pharaoh

Valois [**val**wah] A ruling dynasty of France from the accession of Philip VI, Count of Valois (1328), to the death of Henry III (1589). >> Henry III (of France); Orleans, House of; Philip VI

Valois, Dame Ninette de [**val**wah], originally **Edris Stannus** (1898–98) Dancer, born in Blessington, Co Wicklow, Ireland. In 1931 she founded the Sadler's Wells Ballet, continuing as its artistic director until 1963. She is regarded as the pioneer of British ballet, both in her own choreography and in the development of a school and two major companies. >> Royal Ballet

Valparaíso [valpara**ee**soh] 33°03S 71°07W, pop (1995e) 315 000. Chile's main port and a major commercial centre; founded, 1536; most old buildings destroyed by earthquakes; railway; cathedral; Naval Academy; two universities (1926, 1928). >> Chile ℹ; Viña del Mar

value-added tax >> **VAT**

valve >> **thermionic valve**

vampire In Slavic and Greek folklore a dead person of either sex whose body does not decompose after burial as expected. Vampires, like other ghosts, seek to take living people with them into the after-life. Typically, they rise at night to prey on and suck the blood of the living. Like other ghosts too, vampires are repelled by crucifixes, garlic, and daylight, and can be destroyed by being beheaded or pierced through the heart with a wooden stake. Bram Stoker's *Dracula* (1897) popularized and distorted the myth.

vampire bat A bat of family Desmodontidae, native to the New World tropics; makes shallow incision with incisors (prey usually not disturbed) and laps blood; bat's saliva prevents blood clotting; three species. >> bat

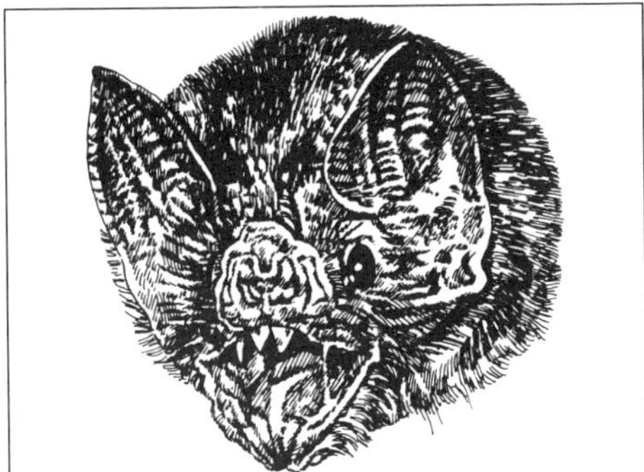

Vampire bat

Van, Lake, Turk **Van Gölü** area 3173 sq km/1225 sq mi. Salt lake in mountainous E Anatolia, Turkey; length, 120 km/75 mi; width, 80 km/50 mi; home of the ancient Armenian civilization. >> Turkey ℹ

vanadium [va**nay**dium] V, element 23, density 6.1 g/cm^3, melting point 1890°C. A transition metal, not occurring free in nature, and often replacing phosphorus as an impurity in phosphate rocks. Its main uses are in steel production, usually in combination with chromium. >> chemical elements; phosphorus; transition elements; RR1036

Van Allen radiation belts Two rings of high-energy-charged particles surrounding the Earth, probably originating in the Sun and trapped by the Earth's magnetic field. The lower, more energetic belt is at c.300 km/185 mi from the Earth's surface; the outer belt at c.16 000 km/10 000 mi. They were discovered in 1958 by US physicist James Van Allen (1914–) from satellite data. >> geomagnetic field; magnetosphere

Vanbrugh, Sir John [**van**bruh] (1664–1726) Playwright and Baroque architect, born in London. He scored a success with his comedies *The Relapse* (1696) and *The Provok'd Wife* (1697), and became a theatre manager with Congreve. As architect, he designed Castle Howard, Yorkshire (1699–1726). >> Baroque (art and architecture); Congreve

Van Buren, Martin (1782–1862) US statesman and eighth president (1837–41), born in Kinderhook, NY. In 1824 he was a member of the group which founded the Democratic Party. Arriving in office during the financial panic of 1837, his measure introducing a treasury independent of private banks created opposition, and he was overwhelmingly defeated in 1840. >> Democratic Party

Vance, Cyrus (Roberts) (1917–) Lawyer and statesman, born in Clarksburg, WV. He served as secretary of state under President Carter, resigning in 1980 over the handling of the crisis when US diplomats were being held hostage in Iran. He worked with Lord Owen for the UN Security Council as the secretary-general's representative during the Yugoslavian conflict, and was instrumental in drawing up the unsuccessful Vance–Owen peace initiative (1992–3). >> Carter, Jimmy; Vance–Owen plan

Vance–Owen plan A set of proposals for a solution to the Bosnia-Herzegovina civil war, presented to the UN general peace conference in early 1993, under the chairmanship of Cyrus Vance and Lord Owen. The plan proposed the reorganization of the country into 10 provinces, a set of constitutional principles which would give the provinces a level of autonomy, and a ceasefire. The plan was rejected by the Bosnian Serb Assembly, to widespread international criticism. >> Bosnia and Herzegovina ℹ; Owen, David; Vance

Vancouver 49°13N 123°06W, pop (1995e) 501 000; (Greater Vancouver) 1 391 000. Seaport in SW British Columbia, Canada; third largest city in Canada; settled c.1875, named Granville; reached by railway, 1886; city and modern name, 1886; airport; two universities (1908, 1963); professional teams, Vancouver Canucks (ice hockey), BC Lions (football); Chinatowns, second largest Chinese community in North America. >> British Columbia

Vandals A Germanic people, originally perhaps from the Baltic area, who settled in the Danube valley in the 4th-c. They invaded Gaul (406), crossed into Spain, conquered Roman Africa (429–39), and sacked Rome (455). >> Gaul

Van de Graaff, Robert (Jemison) (1901–67) Physicist, born in Tuscaloosa, AL. He constructed an improved type of electrostatic generator (later called the **Van de Graaff generator**), and developed this into the **Van de Graaff**

accelerator, which became a major tool of atomic and nuclear physicists. >> particle accelerators

Vanderbilt, Cornelius (1794–1877) Financier, born on Staten I, NY. By age 40 he had become the owner of steamers running to Boston and up the Hudson; and in 1849, during the gold rush, he established a route to California. At 70 he became a railroad financier.

van der Post, Sir Laurens (Jan) [post] (1906–96) Writer, born in Philippolis, South Africa. He was best known for his books in the mixed genres of travel, anthropology, and metaphysical speculation, such as *Venture to the Interior* (1951) and *The Lost World of the Kalahari* (1958).

van der Waals, Johannes Diderik [vahlz] (1837–1923) Physicist, born in Leyden, The Netherlands. He extended the classical 'ideal' gas laws (of Boyle and Charles) to describe the behaviour of real gases, deriving the **van der Waals equation of state** in 1873. He was awarded the Nobel Prize for Physics in 1910. >> gas laws

Van Diemen's Land >> **Tasmania**

van Dyck, Sir Anthony [diyk] (1599–1641) Painter, born in Antwerp, Belgium. He travelled widely in Italy, where he painted portraits and religious subjects, and in 1632 went to London, where he was knighted by Charles I and made painter-in-ordinary. His work greatly influenced the British school of portraiture in the 18th-c, and left a thoroughly romantic glimpse of the Stuart monarchy. >> Stuarts

Van Dyke, Dick (1925–) Popular entertainer, born in West Plains, MO. His television series, *The Dick Van Dyke Show* (1961–6), was highly popular, and won him Emmies in 1962, 1964, and 1965. His film career includes *Mary Poppins* (1964) and *Chitty, Chitty, Bang, Bang* (1968), and he returned to the screen as Fletcher in *Dick Tracy* (1990).

Vane, Sir Henry (1613–62) English statesman, born in Hadlow, Kent. He helped to impeach Strafford, promoted the Solemn League and Covenant, supported the parliamentary cause in the Civil War, and during the Commonwealth became one of the Council of State (1649–53). At the Restoration, he was imprisoned and executed. >> English Civil War; Solemn League and Covenant; Strafford

Vänern, Lake [**ve**nern] area 5585 sq km/2156 sq mi. Lake in SW Sweden; length, 146 km/91 mi; maximum depth, 98 m/321 ft. >> Sweden ℹ

van Gogh, Vincent (Willem) [hokh], Br Eng [gof], US Eng [goh] (1853–90) Painter, born in Groot-Zundert, The Netherlands. At Nuenen he painted his first masterpiece, a domestic scene of peasant poverty, 'The Potato Eaters' (1885, Amsterdam). At Arles, the Provençal landscape gave him many of his best subjects, such as 'Sunflowers' (1888, Tate, London) and 'The Bridge' (1888, Cologne). He showed increasing signs of mental disturbance and, after some time in an asylum, he committed suicide. One of the pioneers of Expressionism, he used colour primarily for its emotive appeal, and profoundly influenced the Fauves and other experimenters of 20th-c art. >> Expressionism; Fauvism

vanilla An evergreen climbing orchid (*Vanilla planifolia*), native to Central America. The large green flowers are followed by slender pods up to 15 cm/6 in long, which turn black when dried and contain the essence *vanillin*, used as flavouring. (Family: Orchidaceae.) >> orchid ℹ

van Meegeren, Han or **Henricus** [**may**geren] (1889–1947) Artist and forger, born in Deventer, The Netherlands. In 1945 he was accused of selling art treasures to the Germans. To clear himself, he confessed to having forged the pictures, and also the famous 'Supper at Emmaus', which had been 'discovered' in 1937 and was widely accepted to be by Vermeer. In 1947 he was imprisoned, and died a few weeks later. >> Vermeer

Vannes [van], ancient **Dariorigum** 47°40N 2°47W, pop (1995e) 49 900. Port in NW France; railway; picturesque Old Town, cathedral (13th–19th-c). >> Brittany

Vanua Levu [va**noo**a **lay**voo] area 5556 sq km/2145 sq mi. Mountainous volcanic island in SW Pacific Ocean; second largest of the Fiji Is; length 176 km/109 mi; chief town, Labasa. >> Fiji ℹ

Vanuatu [vanoo**ah**too], official name **Republic of Vanuatu**, formerly **New Hebrides** pop (1995e) 167 000; area 14 763 sq km/5698 sq mi. An irregular Y-shaped island chain in the SW Pacific Ocean, 400 km/250 mi NE of New Caledonia; 12 islands and 60 islets, the largest being Espiritu Santo (3947 sq km/1523 sq mi); capital, Vila (on Efate); timezone GMT +11; population mainly Melanesian (95%); chief religion, Christianity (70%); national language, Bislama; official languages, English, French; unit of currency, the vatu; mainly volcanic and rugged, with raised coral beaches fringed by reefs; highest peak (on Espiritu Santo) rises to 1888 m/6194 ft; several active volcanoes; tropical climate, with a hot and rainy season (Nov–Apr) when cyclones may occur; visited by the Portuguese, 1606; under Anglo-French administration as the condominium of the New Hebrides, 1906; independence as the Republic of Vanuatu, 1980; governed by a president, prime minister, and Assembly; wide range of tropical agriculture; tourism rapidly increasing, especially from cruise ships. >> Melanesia; Pacific Ocean; Vila; RR1027 political leaders

Van Vleck, John H(asbrouck) (1899–1980) Physicist, born in Middletown, CT. He founded the modern theory of magnetism based on quantum theory, and also devised theories of magnetic behaviour in crystals. He shared the Nobel Prize for Physics in 1977. >> crystals; magnetism; quantum mechanics

Varanasi >> **Benares**

variable star Any star with a luminosity that is not constant. The variation can be regular or irregular. The principal types are Cepheid variables, RR Lyrae stars, and the long-period Mira variables. >> Cepheid variable; Mira; star

variations A type of musical composition in which a theme is presented a number of times in different guises or with fresh embellishments. The theme itself may be the composer's own (eg Haydn's *Variations in F minor* for piano), or someone else's (eg Brahm's *Variations on a Theme of Paganini*), or a folksong (eg Delius's *Brigg Fair*). >> chaconne; partita; passacaglia; rhapsody

varicose veins Distended veins which result from obstruction to the flow of blood within them or incompetence of their valves. They may occur anywhere in the body, but the veins in the legs are most often affected. When severe, they lead to pain and swelling. >> phlebitis; vein

Varna, formerly **Stalin** (1949–56), Lat **Odessus** 43°13N 27°56E, pop (1995e) 306 000. Resort in E Bulgaria; site of defeat by the Turks (1444); third largest town and largest harbour in Bulgaria; airport; railway; Roman thermae and baths. >> Bulgaria ℹ

varnish A liquid which dries to a hard protective transparent or decorative film, consisting of a solution of gums in oil with a thinner such as turpentine. **Spirit varnishes** have resins (such as, notably, shellac) dissolved in alcohol (industrial or methylated spirit). Modern varieties have polymers such as polyurethane in solvents. >> lacquer; polymerization; resin

varnish tree >> **lacquer tree**

Varro, Marcus Terentius (116–27 BC) Roman scholar and author, born in Reate, Italy. He wrote over 600 books, covering a wide range of subject matter; only his work on agriculture and part of his book on Latin survive.

varve dating A method of dating the ages of Pleistocene shales, by counting the layers (**varves**) found in the fine lake sediments deposited by the water flowing from glaciers. The layered arrangement arises from the alternation of fine and coarser material from winter to summer. >> Pleistocene epoch; shale

Vasa (Finland) >> **Vaasa**

Vasa (Sweden) A royal dynasty that provided all Swedish monarchs from 1523 to 1818, with only two exceptions. It was founded by Gustavus I (r. 1523–60), who led the country's conversion to the Lutheran Reformation and ousted foreign powers. >> Gustavus I; Gustavus II; Luther, Martin

Vasarely, Viktor [vaza**ray**lee] (1908–97) Painter, born in Pecs, Hungary. His particular kind of geometrical-abstract painting, which he began to practise c.1947, pioneered the visually disturbing effects that were later called Op Art. >> Op Art

Vasari, Giorgio [va**zah**ree] (1511–74) Art historian, born in Arezzo, Italy. He was an architect and painter, best known for his design of the Uffizi in Florence, but today his fame rests on his *Lives of the Most Eminent Italian Architects, Painters, and Sculptors* (1550), which remains the major source of information on its subject. >> Renaissance; Uffizi

vascular plant Any plant possessing xylem and phloem, distinct conducting tissues which together make up the vascular system; they include flowering plants, gymnosperms, ferns, clubmosses, and horsetails, and in some classifications form the division Tracheophyta. Additional differences between vascular plants and the non-vascular bryophytes and algae are the presence of stomata, and the sporophyte as the dominant generation. >> clubmoss; flowering plants; gymnosperms; horsetail; phloem; sporophyte; xylem

vasectomy >> **sterilization 1**

vassal A freeman who had acknowledged the lordship of a superior by giving homage and swearing fealty, normally in return for a fief. The lord's default, especially in giving protection, rendered the relationship void, as did the disobedient vassal's withholding of military assistance and general support. >> feudalism

VAT Acronym for **value-added tax**, an indirect tax levied on products or services as a percentage of their value. The customer pays VAT in addition to the normal price. The seller pays VAT on the value of sales, less VAT on purchased inputs. VAT is used in many countries; in the UK it was introduced in 1973, replacing purchase tax. Some goods, such as food in the UK, or businesses below a minimum turnover, are exempt. >> customs and excise; sales tax

Vatican City, Ital **Stato della Città del Vaticano** pop c.1000; area 44 ha/109 acres. Papal sovereign state in Rome, on the W bank of the R Tiber; created in 1929 by the Lateran Treaty; timezone GMT +1; includes St Peter's, the Vatican Palace and Museum, several buildings in Rome, and the pope's summer villa at Castel Gandolfo; issues its own stamps and coinage. >> Lateran Treaty; pope; Sistine Chapel; RR1029–30

Vatican Councils Two councils of the Roman Catholic Church. The **First Vatican Council** (1869–70) was called by Pope Pius IX to deal with doctrine, discipline and canon law, foreign missions, and the relationship between Church and state. It is best remembered for the decree on papal infallibility (1870). The **Second Vatican Council** (1962–5) was called by Pope John XXIII, with the task of renewing religious life and bringing up-to-date the belief, structure, and discipline of the Church (*aggiornamento*). >> aggiornamento; Council of the Church; ecumenism; John XXIII; Pius IX; Roman Catholicism; Ultramontanism

Vättern, Lake [**vet**ern], also **Vetter** or **Wetter** area 1912 sq km/738 sq mi. Lake in S Sweden; extends 130 km/81 mi; maximum width 30 km/19 mi. >> Sweden ℹ

Vauban, Sebastien le Prestre de [vohbã] (1633–1707) French soldier and military engineer, born in Saint Léger. He brought about a revolution in siege warfare and fortification, directing siege operations throughout Louis XIV's campaigns, and surrounding the kingdom with a cordon of fortresses (1667–88). >> Louis XIV

vaudeville In the USA, a variety show tradition stemming from the family entertainments created by Tony Pastor from 1881 onwards. In France, the term was originally used for the dumb shows with songs of the Paris fairs, and later for the light satirical songs popular in 18th-c theatres. >> music hall

Vaughan, Henry [vawn] (1622–95) Religious poet, born in Newton-by-Usk, S Wales. His best-known works are the pious meditations, *Silex scintillans* (1650) and the prose devotions *The Mount of Olives* (1652). >> metaphysical poetry

Vaughan Williams, Ralph [vawn] (1872–1958) Composer, born in Down Ampney, Gloucestershire. He developed a national style of music which derived from English choral tradition, especially of the Tudor period, and folksong. His works include nine symphonies, the opera *The Pilgrim's Progress* (1948–9), and scores for stage and cinema, such as *The Wasps* (1909) and *Scott of the Antarctic* (1948).

vault An arched covering over any building; usually built of stone or brick, and sometimes imitated in wood or plaster. Various configurations exist, including the barrel, cross, domical, fan, and rib vaults. >> arch ℹ; Gothic architecture

Vavilov, Nikolay Ivanovich [**va**vilof] (1887–1943) Plant geneticist, born in Moscow. In 1930 he was appointed by Lenin to direct Soviet agricultural research, and established 400 institutes, and a collection of 26 000 varieties of wheat. His reputation was challenged by Lysenko, who denounced him at a genetics conference in 1937. Vavilov was arrested in 1940, and is thought to have died in a Siberian concentration camp. >> genetics; Lysenko

VDU >> **visual display unit**

Veblen, Thorstein (Bunde) [**veb**len] (1857–1929) Economist and social scientist, born in Manitowoc Co, WI. His best-known work is *The Theory of the Leisure Class* (1899), in which he attempted to apply an evolutionary approach to the study of economics. >> economics

vector (mathematics) In mathematics, a quantity having magnitude and direction. Vector quantities include position (showing the position of one point relative to another), displacement (the distance in a certain direction), velocity, acceleration, force, and momentum. They contrast with the *scalar* quantities of distance, time, mass, energy, etc, which have magnitude only. >> scalar

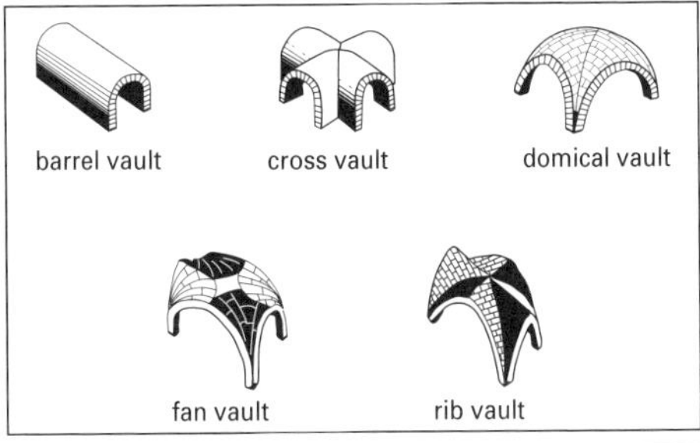

Types of vault

vector (medicine) An organism, commonly an arthropod, which acts as an intermediary agent in transferring a pathogenic micro-organism from one host to another. Examples are ticks in typhus, and mosquitoes in malaria. >> arthropod

Veda [**vay**da] The 'sacred knowledge' of the Hindus, dating from c.1500 BC, contained in the four collections called the *Vedas*, the *Brahmanas* appended to them, and the *Aranyakas* and *Upanishads* which serve as an epilogue or conclusion. Originally the Veda consisted of the **Rig-veda** (sacred songs or hymns of praise), **Sama-veda** (melodies and chants used by priests during sacrifices), and **Yajur-veda** (sacrificial formulae); to which was later added the **Athara-veda** (spells, charms, and exorcistic chants). >> Brahma; Hinduism; Upanishads; Vedanta

Vedanta (Sanskrit 'conclusion of the Veda') Originally the teachings of the Upanishads; later, a trend in Indian philosophy advocating the identity of the individual self, *atman*, with a transindividual super-self, *brahman*, an undifferentiated being-and-consciousness considered the single source of cognition and action. >> atman; Hinduism; Upanishads

Vega [**vay**ga] >> **Lyra**

Vega (Carpio), Lope (Félix) de [vay**ga**] (1562–1635) Playwright and poet, born in Madrid. He first made his mark as a ballad writer, and after 1588 produced a wide range of historical and contemporary dramas – about 2000 plays and dramatic pieces, of which over 400 still survive.

vegan >> **vegetarianism**

VEGA project [**vay**ga] A highly successful Soviet mission to Venus and Halley's Comet undertaken 1984–6; the name is an acronym based on the Russian equivalents for 'Venus' and 'Halley'. Two spacecraft each deployed a lander and a balloon at Venus (Jun 1985), then used a Venus gravity assist to fly on to intercept Halley's Comet (6 and 9 Mar 1986), Vega 2 passing within 8900 km/5530 mi of its nucleus. The balloons were deployed at 54 km/34 mi altitude and tracked for two days by an international network of antennas. The mission also provided the first close-up view of the comet's nucleus, and the first measurements of gas and dust properties, before becoming nonoperational. >> Halley's comet; Soviet space programme; Venus (astronomy)

vegetable In a broad sense, anything of or concerning plants; but commonly referring to a plant or its parts, other than fruits and sometimes seeds, used for food. The term is often qualified by reference to the particular parts eaten (eg leaf vegetable, root vegetable). A number of foods often called vegetables are actually fruits, such as the tomato. >> aubergine; bean; brassica; cabbage; carrot; celery; courgette; fruit; globe artichoke; haricot bean; Jerusalem artichoke; kohlrabi; leek; legume; lentil; lettuce; marrow (botany); onion; pea; pulse (botany); radish; runner bean; seakale; soya bean; swede; turnip

vegetarianism The practice of eating a diet devoid of meat. People who follow a diet containing dairy products and eggs are known as **ovo-lacto-vegetarians**. Those who shun all animal foods are known as **vegans**. The vegetarian diet may be healthier than that of the omnivore, since it is likely to contain less fat and more fibre. There are few nutritional disadvantages, the only possible problem being in the low availability of iron in vegetable foods. Veganism, however, does pose problems, with low dietary intakes of available calcium, iron, and zinc, and little or no dietary intake of vitamin B_{12}, which is not found in plants. >> diet; omnivore; vitamins [i]

vein A vessel usually conveying deoxygenated blood from tissues back to the heart. **Deep veins** accompany arteries; **superficial veins** lie in the subcutaneous tissue, and often appear as blue channels just below the skin (eg at the wrist and on the forearm). Blood flow in veins is slower and at a lower pressure than in arteries; consequently veins are often larger and their walls are thinner. >> artery; circulation; phlebitis; varicose veins

Vejle [**viy**luh] 55°43N 9°30E, pop (1995e) 51 900. Seaport and manufacturing town in E Jutland, Denmark; railway; church (13th-c). >> Denmark [i]

Vela [**vee**la] (Lat 'sails') A S constellation in the Milky Way whose four brightest stars form a near quadrilateral. It includes the Vela pulsar. >> constellation; RR968

Velázquez, Diego (Rodriguez de Silva) [vay**las**keth] (1599–1660) Painter, born in Seville, Spain. He produced several domestic genre pieces and court portraits, but is best known for his three late masterpieces, 'Las Meniñas' (1655, The Maids of Honour; Madrid), 'Las Hilanderas' (c.1657, The Tapestry Weavers; Madrid), and 'Venus and Cupid', known as 'The Rokeby Venus' (c.1658, National Gallery, London).

Velde, Henry (Clemens) van de [**vel**duh] (1863–1957) Architect, born in Antwerp, Belgium. He established the famous Weimar School of Arts and Crafts (1906) from which developed the Bauhaus. >> Art Nouveau; Bauhaus

Velde, Willem van de [**vel**duh], known as **the Elder** (c.1611–93) Marine painter, born in Leyden, The Netherlands. He came to England in 1657, and painted large pictures of sea battles for Charles II and James II. His son, **Willem van de Velde, the Younger** (1633–1707) became court painter to Charles II (of England) in 1674. A second son, **Adriaen van de Velde** (1636–72), was a landscape painter.

veld(t) [velt] The undulating plateau grassland of S Africa, primarily in Zimbabwe and the Republic of South Africa. It can be divided into the **high veld** (over 1500 m/c.5000 ft), **middle veld** (900–1500 m/c.3000–5000 ft) and **low veld** (under 900 m/c.3000 ft). >> grass [i]

Veliko Turnovo [**vel**ikuh **toor**novuh] 43°04N 25°39E, pop (1995e) 61 900. City in NEC Bulgaria; on the R Yantra; capital of the second Bulgarian kingdom (1187–1393); airport; railway; Tsarevets Hill. >> Bulgaria [i]

Velingrad 42°01N 23°59E, pop (1995e) 23 800. Spa town in S Bulgaria; a therapeutic centre, with 70 thermal springs; railway. >> Bulgaria [i]

vellum >> **parchment**

velocity For *linear motion*, the rate of change of distance with time in a given direction; velocity v, units m/s. For *rotational motion*, it is the rate of change of angle with time; **angular velocity** ω, units radian/s. Both are vector quantities. >> acceleration; mechanics; momentum; speed (physics); vector (mathematics); velocity of light

velocity of light A universal constant, the same value for all observers and all types of electromagnetic radiation; symbol c, value 2.998×10^8 m/s (approximately 186 000 mi/s). >> light; special relativity [i]

Velvet Underground US rock band, formed in 1966, originally with **Lou Reed** (1944– , vocals, songwriter), **John Cale** (1940– , vocals, various instruments, songwriter), **Sterling Morrison** (bass guitar), **Maureen Tucker** (drums), and (slightly later) **Nico** (1940– , vocals). Their albums *The Velvet Underground and Nico* (1967) and *White Heat/White Light* (1968) have since become rock classics. The band broke up in 1970. >> rock music; Warhol

velvet worm A primitive terrestrial arthropod; body cylindrical, segmented, length up to 150 mm/6 in; head with a pair of antennae and a pair of jaws; c.70 species, mostly nocturnal. (Phylum: Arthropoda. Subphylum: Onychophora.) >> arthropod; *Peripatus*

Venables, Terry, popular name of **Terence Frederick Venables** (1943–) Football player, manager, and coach, born in London. He played with Chelsea (1958–66), Tottenham Hotspur (1966–8) and Queens Park Rangers

(1968–73), then managed Crystal Palace (1976–80), Queens Park Rangers (1980–4), Barcelona (1984–7), and Tottenham Hotspur (1987–93), where he was also chief executive (1991–3) until a much publicized conflict with club chairman Alan Sugar. Venables later became the English national team coach (1994–6), then coach to the Australian national soccer team.

Venda [**ven**da] Former independent black homeland in NE South Africa; self-government, 1973; granted independence by South Africa (not recognized internationally), 1979; military coup, 1990; incorporated into Northern Province in the South African constitution of 1994. >> apartheid; Northern Province; South Africa ℹ

Vendée, Wars of the [vãday] French counter-revolutionary insurrections in the W provinces against the central government in Paris. The brutal rising in La Vendée (1793), when priests and nobles encouraged the conservative peasantry to rebel against the Convention's conscription and anticlerical policies, was a precedent for other provincial revolts in 1795, 1799, 1815, and 1832. >> French Revolution ℹ

Vendôme, Louis Joseph, duc de (Duke of) [vãdohm] (1654–1712) French general, born in Paris, the great-grandson of Henry IV. He commanded in Italy and Flanders during the War of the Spanish Succession (1701–13), was victorious at Cassano (1705) and Calcinato (1706), but defeated at Oudenaarde by Marlborough (1708). >> Spanish Succession, War of the

Venera Programme [ve**nair**a] A highly successful evolutionary series of Soviet space missions to Venus 1961–83. Its highlights include: the first complete descent to the surface (Venera 5, 1969); the first TV pictures from the surface (Venera 9, 1975); and the first balloons deployed and tracked in the atmosphere (VEGA, 1985). >> Soviet space programme; VEGA project; Venus (astronomy)

venereal disease (VD) A range of infectious diseases usually transmitted by sexual contact and occasionally in other ways. There is no specific treatment for AIDS or hepatitis B virus infection. Syphilis, gonorrhoea, and chancroid are treated with appropriate antibiotics. >> AIDS; chancroid; gonorrhoea; hepatitis; syphilis

Venetian School The art associated with Venice, beginning with the building of the Basilica of St Mark in the 11th-c. Painting developed from the 14th-c onwards, leading masters including Bellini, Giorgione, Titian, Veronese, and Tintoretto. The Baroque period saw the building of magnificent churches such as Sta Maria della Salute, and the 18th-c saw a final flowering in painting, with Tiepolo, Canaletto, and Guardi. >> Florentine school; Bellini; Canaletto; Giorgione; Guardi; Tiepolo; Tintoretto; Titian; Veronese

Venezuela [venez**way**la], official name **Republic of Venezuela**, Span **República de Venezuela** pop (1995e) 21 547 000; area 912 050 sq km/352 051 sq mi. Most northerly country in South America; capital, Caracas; timezone GMT –4; chief ethnic groups, mestizo (69%), European (20%), black (9%); chief religion, Roman Catholicism (92%); official language, Spanish; unit of currency, the bolívar of 100 céntimos; Guiana Highlands (SE) cover over half the country; Venezuelan Highlands in the W and along the coast, reaching heights of over 5000 m/16 000 ft; generally hot and humid climate; one rainy season (Apr–Oct); originally inhabited by Caribs and Arawaks; seen by Columbus, 1498; Spanish settlers, 1520; frequent revolts against Spanish colonial rule; independence movement under Bolívar, leading to the establishment of the State of Gran Colombia (Colombia, Ecuador, Venezuela), 1821; independent republic, 1830; governed by an elected two-chamber National Congress, comprising a Senate and a Chamber of Deputies; a president is advised by a Council of Ministers; largely an agricultural country until the 1920s, when the development of oil from Maracaibo transformed the economy (75% of tax revenues); 4% of the land is under cultivation. >> Bolívar; Caracas; RR1028 political leaders

Venice, Ital **Venezia**, Lat **Venetia** 45°26N 12°20E, pop (1995e) 319 000. Seaport in NE Italy, at the head of the Adriatic Sea; 4 km/2 mi from the Italian mainland in a salt-water lagoon; built on 118 small islands, and crossed by numerous canals, notably the Grand Canal, the main traffic artery; the houses and palaces are built on piles; connects with the mainland by a road and rail causeway, and by ferries; patriarch-archbishopric; airport; railway; a major tourist area; St Mark's Cathedral (remodelled 11th-c) and Campanile (97 m/319 ft-high bell-tower, rebuilt 1905–12), Doge's Palace (14th–15th-c), Bridge of Sighs (c.1595), Church of Saints John and Paul (13th-c); fresh anxiety since the 1980s over the risk to the city from flooding and pollution; Venice and the lagoon are world heritage sites. >> Bridge of Sighs; Doge's Palace; Italy ℹ; Rialto Bridge; St Mark's Cathedral

Venn diagram In mathematics, a diagram illustrating the relations between sets, devised by the English logician, John Venn (1834–1923). For example, the diagram shows that Set *A* is a subset of *B*, and *B* does not contain any elements of *C*, ie *B* and *C* are disjoint. >> set; union

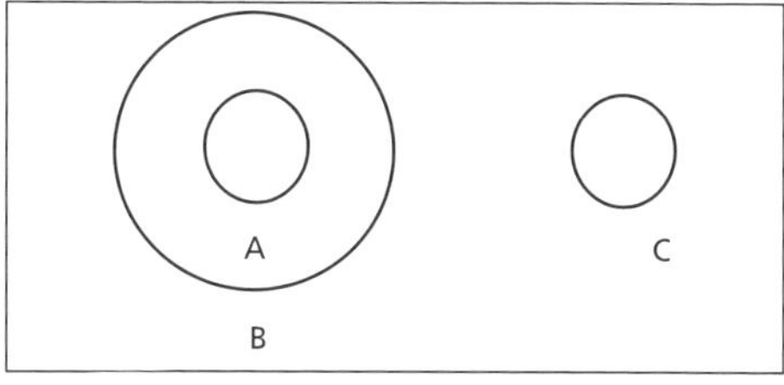

Venn diagram

ventricles 1 The chambers of the heart which eject blood into the pulmonary trunk (right ventricle) or the aorta (left ventricle). >> heart 🅘 **2** The spaces within the brain where cerebrospinal fluid (CSF) is produced. There are four ventricles, below which a central canal extends into the spinal cord. >> brain 🅘; cerebrospinal fluid; hydrocephalus; skull

Ventris, Michael (George Francis) (1922–56) Linguist, born in Wheathampstead, Hertfordshire. He investigated Minoan scripts found on tablets excavated at palace sites in Crete (Linear B), and in 1952 announced that the language was early Greek, a conclusion later confirmed by other scholars. >> Evans, Arthur; Linear B

Ventura Publisher [ven**tyoo**ra] A desk-top publishing package developed by Xerox for the preparation of large textual documents such as scientific papers and books. >> desk-top publishing

Venturi tube [ven**too**ree] A device for measuring the amount of fluid flowing in a tube; named after the Italian physicist Giovanni Battista Venturi (1746–1822). The tube is constricted to form a throat, and pressure is measured on either side, the pressure difference indicating the rate of flow. >> fluid mechanics

Venus (astronomy) The second planet from the Sun, attaining the greatest brilliancy in the night sky, outshining all the stars, hence its poetic names 'morning/evening star'. There are no natural satellites. It has the following characteristics: mass $4{\cdot}87 \times 10^{24}$ kg; radius 6051 km/3760 mi; mean density $5{\cdot}2$ g/cm^3; equatorial gravity 860 cm/s^2; rotational period 243 days (retrograde); orbital period 224·7 days; obliquity 0°; orbital eccentricity 0·007; mean distance from the Sun $108{\cdot}2 \times 10^6$ km/$67{\cdot}2 \times 10^6$ mi. It is a near twin to Earth in size and density, but with a radically different atmosphere of mainly carbon dioxide, 90 times denser than our own, and with surface temperatures near 460°C. The thick atmosphere and cloud cover create a greenhouse effect that maintains high temperatures. There is no observable magnetic field. About 85% consists of volcanic plains marked by thousands of individual volcanic constructs and relatively few impact craters. >> greenhouse effect; Magellan project; Mariner / Pioneer / Venera programme; planet; Solar System

Venus (mythology) Originally an obscure Italian deity of the vegetable garden, she was identified with Aphrodite, and, as a Roman goddess, took over the latter's mythology and attributes. >> Aphrodite; Cupid; Psyche

Venus's fly trap A small carnivorous perennial (*Dionaea muscipula*), native only to the pine barrens of SE USA. Each leaf is divided into a lower, winged portion and an upper portion (the trap) formed by two lobes each bearing three trigger hairs and fringed with teeth. Stimulation of these hairs by an insect causes the lobes to snap shut, the teeth crossing to trap the prey. (Family: Droseraceae.) >> carnivorous plant

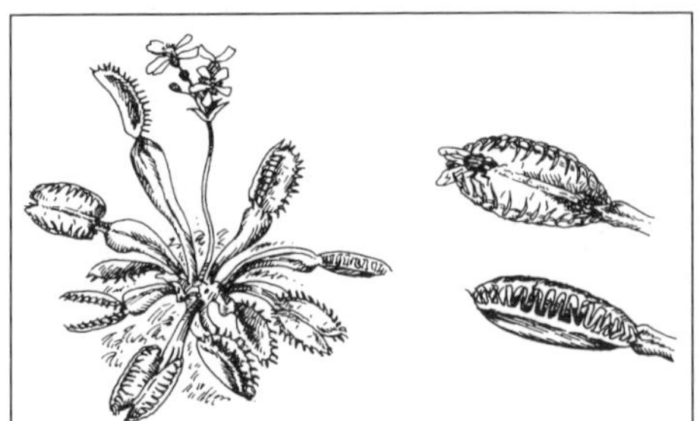

Venus's fly trap

Veracruz [vayra**kroos**] 19°11N 96°10W, pop (1995e) 363 000. Seaport in E Mexico; site of Cortés landing, 1519; airport; railway; principal port of entry for Mexico; Castle of San Juan de Ulúa (1565). >> Mexico 🅘

verbena >> **vervain**

Verdi, Giuseppe (Fortunino Francesco) [**vair**dee] (1813–1901) Composer, born in Le Roncole, Italy. His first major success was *Nabucco* (1842). *Rigoletto* (1851), *Il Trovatore* (1853), and *La Traviata* (1853) established him as the leading Italian operatic composer of the day. His spectacular *Aïda* was commissioned for the new opera house in Cairo, built in celebration of the Suez Canal (1871). Apart from the *Requiem* (1874), there was then a lull in output until, in his old age, he produced *Otello* (1887) and *Falstaff* (1893).

verdigris [**ver**digree] Basic copper carbonate, approximately $Cu_3(CO_3)_2(OH)_2$, formed in the atmospheric corrosion of copper surfaces. It is green in colour. >> copper; corrosion

Verdun >> **World War 1**

Vereeniging, Peace of [ve**ray**niging] (1902) The peace treaty which ended the Boer War, signed at Pretoria. The Boers won three important concessions: an amnesty for those who had risen in revolt within the Cape Colony; a promise that the British would deny the franchise to Africans until after the Boer republics were returned to representative government; and additional financial support for reconstruction. >> Boer Wars

Vergil >> **Virgil**

verificationism In philosophy, the criterion of significance applied by logical positivists. A statement or principle was said to be meaningful only if it was analytical or if it could in principle be verified by empirical observation. The effect, and the intention, was to discriminate in favour of science, logic, and mathematics and against metaphysics, theology, and normative ethics. >> Ayer; logical positivism

Verlaine, Paul (Marie) [verlen] (1844–96) Poet, born in Metz, France. He mixed with the leading Parnassian writers, and achieved success with his second book of poetry, *Fêtes galantes* (1869). He travelled in Europe with the young poet Rimbaud, but their friendship ended in Brussels (1873) when Verlaine, drunk and desolate at Rimbaud's intention to leave, shot him in the wrist. While in prison he wrote *Romances sans paroles* (1874, Songs Without Words). Later works include critical studies, notably *Les Poètes maudits* (1884), short stories, and sacred and profane verse. >> Rimbaud

Vermeer, Jan [ver**mayr**] (1632–75) Painter, born in Delft, The Netherlands. He painted small, detailed domestic interiors, notable for their use of perspective and treatment of the various tones of daylight. Forty of his paintings are known, among them the 'Allegory of Painting' (c.1665, Vienna) and 'Woman Reading a Letter' (c.1662, Amsterdam).

vermiculite [ver**mik**yuliyt] A group of clay minerals formed by the alteration of micas. They consist of porous and flaky particles which expand to about 20 times their volume when heated, producing low-density, thermally insulating, and inert material. This is used in plaster, insulation, and packing material, and as a medium for raising plants from seed. >> clay minerals; micas

vermilion >> **mercury**

Vermont [ver**mont**] pop (1995e) 580 000; area 24 899 sq km/9614 sq mi. New England state in NE USA; the 'Green Mountain State'; explored by Champlain, 1609; first settlement established at Fort Dummer, 1724; 14th state admitted to the Union, 1791; capital, Montpelier; the

Green Mts run N–S through the C; highest point, Mt Mansfield (1339 m/4393 ft); forestry and timber products, arable farming, dairy products, maple syrup, marble and granite. >> Champlain; Montpelier; United States of America ℹ; RR994

vermouth A fortified red or white wine. Pure alcohol is used for the fortification, up to the same alcohol level as sherry, and various herbs and spices are added for flavour. >> sherry; wine

vernal equinox >> **equinox**

Verne, Jules (1828–1905) Writer, born in Nantes, France. He developed a new vein in fiction, exaggerating and anticipating the possibilities of science. His best-known books are *Voyage au centre de la terre* (1864, Journey to the Centre of the Earth), *Vingt mille lieues sous les mers* (1870, Twenty Thousand Leagues under the Sea), and *Le Tour du monde en quatre-vingts jours* (1873, Around the World in Eighty Days). Several successful films have been made from his novels.

Vernon, Edward, nickname **Old Grog** (1684–1757) British admiral. In 1739, during the War of Jenkins' Ear, his capture of Portobello made him a national hero. He was nicknamed 'Old Grog', from his grogram coat, and in 1740 ordered the dilution of navy rum with water, the mixture being thereafter known as 'grog'. >> Jenkins' Ear, War of

Verona [ve**roh**na] 45°26N 11°00E, pop (1995e) 265 000. City in N Italy, on the R Adige; important communications centre; railway; agricultural market centre; many Roman and mediaeval remains; cathedral (12th–15th-c). >> Italy ℹ

Veronese, Paolo [vayro**nay**zay], originally **Paolo Caliari** (c.1528–88) Venetian decorative painter, born in Verona, Italy. His major paintings include 'The Marriage Feast at Cana' (1562–3, Louvre), 'The Adoration of the Magi' (1573, National Gallery, London), and 'Feast in the House of the Levi' (1573, Venice), which brought him before the Inquisition for trivializing religious subjects. >> Tintoretto; Titian; Venetian School

Verrazano-Narrows Bridge A major steel suspension bridge across the entrance to New York harbour; constructed in 1959–64; length of main span 1298 m/4260 ft; Narrows named after the Italian explorer, Giovanni da Verrazano (1485–1528). >> New York City

Verrocchio, Andrea del [ve**roh**kioh], originally **Andrea del Cione** (c.1435–88) Sculptor, painter, and goldsmith, born in Florence, Italy. He is best known for his magnificent equestrian statue of Colleoni at Venice.

verruca [vuh**roo**ka] >> **wart**

Versace, Gianni [ver**sa**chee] (1946–97) Fashion designer, born in Reggio di Calabria, Italy. He launched his own ready-to-wear collection in 1978, and became known for his glamorous styles, producing a range of siren dresses that became his trademark, and often using innovative materials and techniques. He was shot dead by an assassin outside his home in Miami Beach, Florida.

Versailles [vair**siy**] A chateau built for Louis XIII at the village of Versailles, 23 km/14 mi SW of Paris in the 17th-c, and transformed under Louis XIV to create a palace, unequalled in its display of wealth, in which to house the entire court. Later extensions were the Grand Trianon (a smaller residence in the palace grounds) and the Petit Trianon (added by Louis XV). The palace was ransacked during the French Revolution, but has been restored to its original state, and is now a world heritage site. >> chateau; Le Brun; Le Nôtre; Louis XIV; Versailles, Treaty of

Versailles, Treaty of [vair**siy**] A peace treaty drawn up in 1919 between Germany and the Allied powers at Paris. Germany and her allies were made responsible for reparation payments. Germany lost all overseas colonies, and considerable territory to Poland in the E. The Rhineland was demilitarized and occupied by Allied troops, and German armed forces were strictly limited. >> Paris Peace Conference; World War 1

verse A single line of poetry, a stanza, or poetry in general ('English verse'). *Versification* refers to the technical characteristics of a given poetic form, and also to the exploitation of these by a given poet. *Verse* also has a special use in biblical contexts, where it refers to a traditional division of the text of a chapter. >> metre (literature); poetry

vertebra >> **vertebral column**

vertebral column The backbone of all vertebrates: a series of bony elements (**vertebrae**) separated by **intervertebral discs**, and held together by ligaments and muscles. In the majority of vertebrates the column lies horizontally, being supported by hindlimbs and forelimbs. In humans it is held erect and supported by the hindlimbs only. It carries and supports the thorax, and gives attachment to many muscles; it surrounds and protects the spinal cord from mechanical trauma; it acts as a shock-absorber (by virtue of its curvatures and the presence of the invertebral discs); and it can transmit forces from one part of the body to another. In humans it is 72–75 cm/28–30 in long (c.40% of an individual's height) and consists of 7 cervical, 12 thoracic, 5 lumbar, 5 fused sacral, and 4 fused coccygeal vertebrae. Each intervertebral disc consists of a central gelatinous core surrounded by rings of fibrous tissue. During the course of the day the discs gradually lose water and become thinner; consequently at the end of the day an individual is not as tall as first thing in the morning (the difference may be as large as 2 cm/0·8 in. Similarly, with increasing age the discs also lose water, so that an individual's height may decrease in later life. >> coccyx; epidural anaesthesia; lumbago; lumbar puncture; prolapsed invertebral disc; skeleton ℹ; spina bifida; spinal cord; spondylosis

Vertebrata >> **Chordata**

Vertical Take-Off and Landing >> **VTOL**

Verulamium [veryu**lay**mium] A Belgic town in Roman Britain which stood on the site of present-day St Albans. Completely destroyed in the Revolt of Boadicea (Boudicca) in AD 60, it was later rebuilt and became a focal point for the Romanization of the province.

vervain A tough-stemmed perennial (*Verbena officinalis*), growing to 60 cm/2 ft, native to Europe, Asia, and N Africa; flowers lilac, in slender spikes. (Family: Verbenaceae.)

vervet monkey A guenon (*Cercopithecus aethiops*) native to Africa S of the Sahara; yellow-brown with a black face surrounded by white whiskers. >> guenon

Verwoerd, Hendrik (Frensch) [fer**voort**] (1901–66) South African statesman and prime minister (1958–66), born in Amsterdam, The Netherlands. His administration was marked by the highly controversial policy of apartheid, and the establishment of South Africa as a Republic (1962). He was assassinated in Cape Town. >> apartheid; South Africa ℹ

Very, Edward Wilson [**veer**ee] (1847–1910) US ordnance expert and inventor. In 1877 he invented chemical flares (**Very lights**) for signalling at night.

Very Large Array The world's most elaborate full synthesis radio telescope at Socorro, NM, consisting of 27 antennae arranged on rail tracks forming a Y. It is used to investigate the structure of gaseous nebulae in our Galaxy, and of remote radio galaxies and quasars. >> telescope ℹ

very large scale integration (VLSI) A technique of manufacturing integrated circuits with a very high number of individual components. It is usually defined to refer to integrated circuits containing more than 100 000 components in one chip. >> chip; integrated circuit

Vesalius, Andreas [vezaylius], Lat name of **Andries van Wesel** (1514–64) Anatomist, born in Brussels. His major work was *De humani corporis fabrica libri septem* (1543, The Seven Books on the Structure of the Human Body), which greatly advanced the science of anatomy with its detailed descriptions and drawings. >> anatomy [i]

Vespasian [vespayzhn], in full **Titus Flavius Vespasianus** (9–79) Roman emperor (69–79), the founder of the Flavian dynasty (69–96). He ended the civil wars that had been raging since Nero's overthrow, and put the state on a sound financial footing. Among his many lavish building projects was the Colosseum. >> Nero

Vespers The evening hour of the divine office of the Western Church. In monastic, cathedral, and collegiate churches in the Roman Catholic Church it is sung daily between 3 and 6 pm. >> liturgy; Roman Catholicism

Vespucci, Amerigo [vespoochee] (1454–1512) Explorer, born in Florence, Italy. He promoted a voyage to the New World in the track of Columbus, and explored the coast of Venezuela. His name was given to America through an inaccurate account of his travels, in which he is represented as having discovered the mainland in 1497. >> Columbus, Christopher

Vesta (astronomy) The fourth asteroid discovered (1807). It is one of the few that can be seen with the unaided eye, mainly on account of its high reflectivity. >> asteroids

Vesta (mythology) Roman goddess of the hearth. Her sacred fire, and a shrine containing sacred objects, were kept in a round building, and tended by the **Vestal Virgins**. >> Hestia

vestibular apparatus [vestibyuler] The part of the internal ear concerned with balance, consisting of a series of spaces and tubes within the temporal bone of the skull. It contains the *saccule* and *utricle*, which convey information regarding head position by responding to linear and tilting movements, and three *semicircular canals*, which convey information about rotatory and angular movements of the head. >> ear [i]

vestments Special and distinctive garments worn by clergy in religious worship and liturgy of the Christian Church. >> liturgy; mitre; *see panel*

Vestris, Madame, popular name of **Lucia Elizabeth Vestris** or **Mathews**, *née* **Bartolozzi** (1797–1856) Actress, born in London. She appeared at Drury Lane in 1820, becoming famous in a wide range of roles, was lessee of the Olympic Theatre for nine years, and later managed Covent Garden and the Lyceum.

Vesuvius [vesoovius], Ital **Vesuvio** 40°49N 14°26E. Active volcano in S Italy, 15 km/9 mi SE of Naples; height 1277 m/4190 ft; crater circumference, 1400 m/4593 ft, depth 216 m/709 ft; first recorded eruption AD 79, overwhelming Pompeii, Herculaneum, and Stabiae; last eruption, 1944. >> Pompeii; volcano

vetch A member of a large group of annuals or perennials, often climbing or scrambling, native to N temperate regions and South America; also called **tare**; generally of little economic importance, and sometimes an agricultural pest. (Genus: *Vicia*, 140 species. Family: Leguminosae.)

Veterans' Day A public holiday in the USA (Nov 11), held to honour veterans of all wars; originally instituted as **Armistice Day** after World War 1, by which name it was known until 1954. >> Armistice Day

veterinary science The science concerned with the diseases of animals, especially their treatment or their avoidance. It is applied primarily to domesticated animals, or to captive animals in zoos. Most countries have a national veterinary association, such as the **British Veterinary Association (BVA)** and the **American Veterinary Medical Association (AVMA)**. Internationally veterinary matters are dealt with by the **World Veterinary Association (WVA)**, founded in 1863. The international aspects of companion animal veterinary medicine come under the **World Small Animal Veterinary Association (WSAVA)**, founded in 1958. >> bovine spongiform encephalopathy; cat flu; feline immunodeficiency virus; feline infectious enteritis; kennel cough; scrapie

Religious vestments

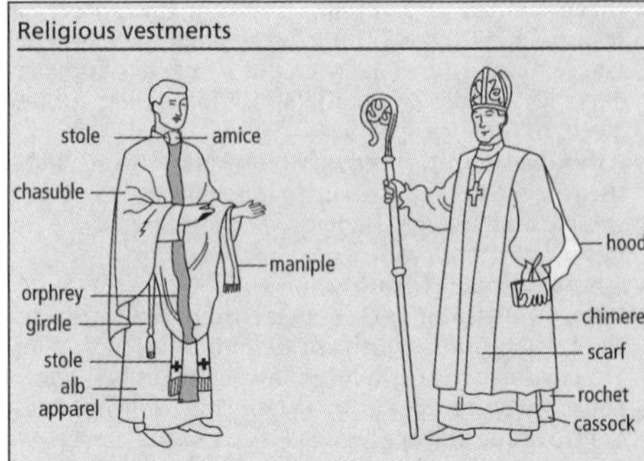

alb A long white garment reaching to the ankles; derived from an ancient tunic.
amice A linen square worn round the back to protect the other vestments; formerly a neckcloth.
apparels Ornamental panels at the foot of the alb, front and back, and on the amice.
cassock The long black gown worn under other vestments: formerly, the daily working costume of the clergy.
chasuble Outer sleeveless vestment worn by a priest or bishop when celebrating Holy Communion; derived from the commonest outdoor garment of classical times.
chimere Worn by bishops over the rochet; of black or scarlet, open in front.
cope In the pre-Christian era, a long cloak; now a costly embroidered vestment, semi-circular in shape, worn by bishops and priests on special occasions.
cotta similar to the surplice, but shorter, especially in the sleeves; sometimes used by clergy and servers in place of the surplice.
hood Worn by clergy at choir offices; a mediaeval head-dress, now worn hanging down the back; denotes a university degree.
maniple Worn over the left arm by bishops, priests, and deacons at the Eucharist; originally a napkin.
orphreys The embroidered strips, customarily cross-shaped, on a chasuble.
rochet Worn by bishops, similar to an alb, but used without girdle or apparels.
stole Once a napkin or towel carried by servants on the left shoulder; now folded and narrow, worn over both shoulders.
surplice Of white linen, reaching to the knees; worn by choir and servers as well as clergy.

Vézelay church [vayzelay] The 12th-c abbey church of St Madeleine, a world heritage site at Vézelay, France.

VHS (Video Home Service) The trade name for a videotape cassette recorder introduced in 1975 by JVC/Matsushita for the domestic market, and widely adopted by other manufacturers. It uses $\frac{1}{2}$ in (12·7 mm) tape at a speed of 2·34 cm/$\frac{15}{16}$ in per second in a cassette $189 \times 104 \times 25$ mm/$7\frac{1}{2} \times 4 \times 1$ in. It has a playing time of up to 4 hours, and has proved to be the most internationally popular home VTR system. **Super-VHS** is an improved version with separate luminance and chrominance signals, using metal particle tape to give higher picture definition and colour quality. >> videotape recorder

Viagra® Trade-name of an anti-impotence drug developed by the Pfizer Corporation in the USA, made available in 1998. Its action, increasing blood flow to the male genitals, was first noted as part of research into treatment for heart disease. >> impotence

Vian, Boris [veeã] (1920–59) Playwright, novelist and poet, born in Ville d'Avray, France. He won a cult following for such tragi-comic novels such as *L'Ecume des jours* (1947, trans Froth on the Daydream) and *L'Arrache-coeur* (1953, trans Heartsnatcher).

Viborg [**vee**baw(r)] 56°28N 9°25E, pop (1995e) 29 500. Ancient city in NC Jutland, Denmark; railway; Gothic cathedral (12th-c, restored 1864–76). >> Denmark 🛈

vibraphone A musical instrument resembling a xylophone, but with metal bars and resonators fitted with electrically operated vanes, producing a vibrating, tremolo effect. It is usually played with soft beaters. >> percussion 🛈; xylophone

vibration >> **oscillation**

Vibrio A genus of straight or curved rod-shaped bacteria, typically with flagella at one end. They are found in aquatic environments and animal intestines, and include the causative agent of cholera. (Kingdom: Monera. Family: Vibrionaceae.) >> bacteria 🛈; cholera

viburnum >> **guelder rose**

vicar (Lat *vicarius*, 'substitute') Literally, one who takes the place of another; for example, the pope is said to be the Vicar of Christ. In Anglican Churches, the term applies technically to the priest acting for the rector, but is widely used for any parish priest or minister. >> Church of England

Vicente, Gil [vee**sen**tay] (c.1470–c.1537) Portuguese playwright and poet. He wrote on religious, national, and social themes, as well as farces, and pastoral and romantic plays, all with great lyricism and a predominantly comical spirit.

Vicenza [vi**chen**tsa], ancient **Vicetia** 45°33N 11°33E, pop (1995e) 114 000. City in NE Italy; railway junction; cathedral (15th-c). >> Italy 🛈

Vichy [**vee**shee] The informal name of the French political regime between 1940 and 1945, a client regime of Germany; officially **l'Etat Français** ('the French State'). Established at the spa town of Vichy following Germany's defeat of France (1940), its head of state was Marshal Philippe Pétain. >> Laval, Pierre; Pétain; World War 2

Vickers test >> **hardness**

Vickrey, William (1914–96) Economist, born in Victoria, British Columbia, Canada. He shared the Nobel Prize for Economics in 1996 for his work in analyzing the consequences of incomplete financial information.

Vicksburg 32°21N 90°53W, pop (1995e) 21 700. Port in W Mississippi, USA; on the Mississippi R; settled, 1791; captured by Union forces during the Civil War (1863) after a long siege (the 'Vicksburg Campaign'); national cemetery nearby; railway; important processing and shipping centre for cotton, timber, and livestock area. >> American Civil War; Mississippi

Vicky, pseudonym of **Victor Weisz** (1913–66) Political cartoonist, born in Berlin. He emigrated to Britain in 1935, and established himself as the leading left-wing political cartoonist of the period.

Vico, Giambattista [**vee**koh] (1668–1744) Historical philosopher, born in Naples, Italy. In his *Scienza nuova* (1725, New Science), he attempted to systematize the humanities into a single human science in a cyclical theory of the growth and decline of societies.

Victor Emmanuel III (1869–1947) King of Italy (1900–46), born in Naples, Italy. He initially ruled as a constitutional monarch, but defied parliamentary majorities by bringing Italy into World War 1 on the side of the Allies in 1915, and in 1922 when he offered Mussolini the premiership. The fascist government then reduced him to a figurehead. He abdicated in 1946. >> fascism; Mussolini

Victoria (Australia) pop (1995e) 4 487 000; area 227 600 sq km/87 900 sq mi. State in SE Australia; named by Captain Cook, 1770; Melbourne settled, 1835; separated from New South Wales, 1851; gold discovered at Ballarat, 1851; E is the Great Dividing Range, known in this region as the Australian Alps; highest point Mt Bogong (1986 m/6516 ft); about 36% of the land occupied by forest; SW region known as Gippsland; several inland lakes, mostly very saline; contains 25% of the Australian population concentrated into 3% of the land; capital, Melbourne; major contribution to Australia's agricultural output; coal mining (Latrobe Valley one of the world's largest deposits of brown coal); oil and natural gas fields in the Gippsland Basin and Bass Strait. >> Australia 🛈; Cook, James; Melbourne

Victoria (Canada) 48°25N 123°22W, pop (1995e) 75 600. Capital of British Columbia, Canada, at SE end of Vancouver I; founded as fur-trading post, 1843; colonial capital, 1866; airfield; railway; university (1963). >> British Columbia

Victoria (Seychelles) 4°37S 55°28E, pop (1995e) 24 500. Seaport capital of the Seychelles, Indian Ocean; on the NE coast of Mahé I. >> Seychelles 🛈

Victoria (Queen), in full **Alexandrina Victoria** (1819–1901) Queen of Great Britain (1837–1901) and (from 1876) Empress of India, born in London, the only child of George III's fourth son, Edward, and Victoria Maria Louisa of Saxe-Coburg. Taught by Lord Melbourne, her first prime minister, she had a clear grasp of constitutional principles and the scope of her own prerogative, which she resolutely exercised in 1839 by setting aside the precedent which decreed dismissal of the current ladies of the bedchamber, thus causing Peel not to take up office as prime minister. In 1840 she married Prince Albert of Saxe-Coburg and Gotha, and had four sons and five daughters. Strongly influenced by her husband, after his death (1861) she went into lengthy seclusion, which brought her unpopularity; but with her recognition as Empress of India, and the celebratory golden (1887) and diamond (1897) jubilees, she increased the prestige of the monarchy. >> Albert, Prince; Melbourne, Viscount; Peel

Victoria, Tomás Luis de, Ital **Vittoria, Tommaso Ludovico da** (c.1548–1611) Composer, born in Ávila, Spain. He wrote only religious music, his 180 works including several books of motets and over 20 Masses.

Victoria, Lake area 69 500 sq km/26 827 sq mi. Lake in E Africa; largest lake on the African continent; altitude 1300 m/4265 ft; 400 km/250 mi long; 240 km/150 mi wide; contains several islands, notably the Sese archipelago; European discovery by John Speke, 1858; extensively explored by Stanley, 1875; originally called Ukewere, renamed in honour of Queen Victoria. >> Africa; Speke

Victoria and Albert Mùseum A museum of fine and applied arts, opened in London in 1852 as the Museum of Manufactures. In 1899, when Queen Victoria laid the foundation stone of the present building, she requested that it be renamed the Victoria and Albert.

Victoria Cross (VC) In the UK, the highest military decoration, instituted by Queen Victoria in 1856 and awarded 'for conspicuous bravery in the face of the enemy'. The medal is inscribed 'For valour'; the ribbon is crimson.

Victoria Desert >> **Great Victoria Desert**

Victoria Falls, indigenous name **Mosi oa Tunya** ('the smoke that thunders') Waterfalls on the Zambezi R; height, 61–108 m/200–354 ft; width, 1688 m/5538 ft; European discovery by Livingstone, 1855; named after Queen Victoria; major tourist attraction. >> Livingstone, David

Victoria Island Island in Northwest Territories, Canada, in the Arctic Ocean; area 217 290 sq km/83 874 sq mi; 515 km/320 mi long; 274–595 km/170–370 mi wide; named for Queen Victoria; sparse population. >> Northwest Territories

Victoria Nile Upper reach of River Nile in NW Uganda; flows from the N end of L Victoria; ends in a swampy delta at the NE end of L Albert; length 420 km/260 mi. >> Nile, River

Victoria Peak 22°18N 114°08E. Principal peak on Hong Kong Island, SE Asia; height, 554 m/1818 ft; named after Queen Victoria; Peak Tramway (opened 1888). >> Hong Kong ℹ

***Victory*, HMS** Nelson's flagship at the battle of Trafalgar (1805). She is now in permanent dry dock, but still flies the white ensign as flagship to the commander-in-chief, Portsmouth. >> Nelson, Horatio

vicuña [vi**ku**nya] A wild member of the camel family (*Vicugna vicugna*), native to high grassland in the C Andes; resembles a llama, but smaller; produces the finest wool in the world. >> alpaca; artiodactyl; Camelidae; llama

Vidal, Gore (Eugene Luther, Jr) [vi**dal**] (1925–) Writer, born in West Point, NY. His many novels include several satirical comedies, such as *Myra Breckinridge* (1968) and *Duluth* (1983), and the historical trilogy, *Burr* (1973), *1876* (1976), and *Lincoln* (1984). His fictional history of America reaches the 20th-c with *Empire* (1987).

video Strictly, that part of the television signal which carries the picture information, as distinct from the audio signal carrying the sound; but by extension the term has become generally accepted to cover the electronic recording and reproduction of combined picture and sound, especially in its non-broadcast application. >> videotape recorder

videoconferencing The use of computer networks and virtual reality to enable groups in separate locations to conduct a conference with the impression that they are all in the same room. The use of computer networks allows the participants to have shared access to computer files and programs. >> computer network; groupware; virtual reality

video disc A reproduction medium in which both picture and sound are recorded as an extremely fine spiral track on a flat circular disc. A series of pits in a reflective surface is optically scanned with a helium-neon laser, and the reflected beam read by a photo-diode to produce the signal. A 30 cm/12 in diameter disc can contain an hour's programme, and access from one part of the programme to another can be very rapid. >> videotape

video games >> **electronic games**

videogram A complete programme recorded as a videotape cassette or video disc for distribution by sale or hire. >> video disc; videotape

videotape A high-quality magnetic coating on a flexible polyester base for recording and reproducing video signals. It has been made in widths of 2 in (50·8 mm, now obsolete), 1 in (25·4 mm), $\frac{3}{4}$ in (19 mm), $\frac{1}{2}$ in (12·7 mm), $\frac{1}{3}$ in (8 mm), and $\frac{1}{4}$ in (6·3 mm); the latter two widths are used for domestic applications. >> videotape recorder

videotape recorder (VTR) A device for recording the picture and sound signals from a television camera on magnetic tape. To obtain a writing speed sufficient for the very high frequencies of a television signal, the recording head must travel rapidly across the moving magnetic tape. Modern VTRs use a narrow tape with helical scanning, each diagonal track recording a single TV field, with audio and control on the edges. Several systems are available, including U-matic, Betamax, and VHS, all incompatible; U-matic was preferred for professional production and VHS for domestic use. In the 1980s two more helical systems for high-quality production and broadcast were introduced, Betacam in 1981 and M-II in 1986. In 1987–8, digital recording on videotape (DVTR) became available in the D1 and D2 formats, and soon after, the first digital recorders using solid-state storage chips. >> Betacam; Betamax; helical scan ℹ; U-matic; VHS; videotape

videotex An interactive information service using a telephone link between the user and a central computer, such as PRESTEL, run by British Telecom in the UK. It can be used for home banking, armchair shopping, ticket ordering, and other such functions. >> PRESTEL; teletext

videowall A rectangular grouping of a number of separate video monitor screens, from 3 × 3 units upwards. They can be programmed for the display of individual single, multiple, or combination images with a sound track from videotape or disc recordings. >> video

Vidor, King (Wallis) [**vee**daw(r)] (1894–1982) Film director, born in Galveston, TX. He made the silent classics *The Big Parade* (1925) and *The Crowd* (1928); later films included *Northwest Passage* (1940) and the big screen epic *Solomon and Sheba* (1959).

Vienna, Ger **Wien** 48°13N 16°22E, pop (1995e) 1 589 000. Capital city of Austria; on the R Danube; C area surrounded by the monumental buildings and gardens of the Ringstrasse, developed 1859–88; badly damaged in World War 2, and occupied by the Allies, 1945–55; UNO-City, conference and office complex (opened 1979); archbishopric; university of technology (1815); university (1873–84); Spanish Riding School; associations with many composers in 18th–19th-c; cathedral, Schottenkirche (12th-c, rebuilt 1638–48); Ruprechtskirche (12th–13th-c); Palace of Schönbrunn; Opera House; Prater. >> Albertina; Austria ℹ; Danube, River; Schönbrunn Palace

Vienna, Congress of (1814–15) A European assembly convened at the instigation of the four victorious Powers to redefine the territorial map of Europe after the defeat of Napoleon. >> Napoleonic Wars

Vienna Circle A group of philosophers, scientists, and mathematicians centred on Vienna University in the 1920s and 1930s. It was founded by Schlick, and had among its associates Gödel, Neurath, and Carnap. It became an international focus for logical positivism. >> Carnap; Gödel; logical positivism; Neurath, Otto; Schlick

Vientiane [vyen**tyan**], Lao **Viangchan** 17°59N 102°38E, pop (1995e) 493 000. Capital city of Laos, SE Asia; port on R Mekong; airport; university (1958). >> Laos ℹ

Viet Cong or **Vietcong** ('Vietnamese Communists') The name given by the South Vietnamese government in 1959 to all the guerrilla forces that fought them during the Vietnam War. In 1960 they formed the National Liberation Front. >> Vietnam War

Viet Minh or **Vietminh** The abbreviation of **Viet Nam Doc Lap Dong Minh** ('League for the Independence of Vietnam'), a politico-military organization formed by Ho Chi-minh in 1941. In 1945 it formed a government in Hanoi, and its army defeated the French at Dien Bien Phu in 1954. >> Ho Chi-minh; Vietnam War

Vietnam, official name **Socialist Republic of Vietnam**, Vietnamese **Cong Hoa Xa Hoi Chu Nghia Viet Nam** pop (1995e) 73 655 000; area 329 566 sq km/127 212 sq mi. Independent socialist state in SE Asia; capital, Hanoi; timezone GMT +7; chief ethnic group, Vietnamese; chief religions, Buddhism, Confucianism, Taoism, Roman Catholicism; official language, Vietnamese; unit of currency, the dông; occupies a narrow strip along the coast of the Gulf of Tongking and the South China Sea; highest peak, Fan Si Pan (3143 m/10 311 ft); tropical monsoon-type climate; temperatures high in the S, cooler in the N (Oct–Apr); under the influence of China since Han period; regions of Tongking (N), Annam (C), and Cochin-China (S) united as Vietnamese Empire, 1802; French protectorates established in Cochin-China, 1867, and in Annam and Tongking, 1884; formed the French Indo-Chinese Union with Cambodia and Laos, 1887; occupied by the Japanese in World War 2; communist Viet-Minh League under Ho Chi-minh formed after the War, not recognized by France; Indo-Chinese War, resulting in French

withdrawal, 1946–54; 1954 armistice divided the country between the communist 'Democratic Republic' in the N and the 'State' of Vietnam in the S; civil war led to US intervention on the side of South Vietnam, 1964; fall of Saigon, 1975; reunification as the Socialist Republic of Vietnam, 1976; large numbers of refugees tried to find homes in the W in the late 1970s; Chinese invasion of Vietnam in 1979 greatly increased the number attempting to leave the country by sea ('boat people'), many returning since 1980s; new constitution, 1992; governed by a president, prime minister, and National Assembly; over 70% of the workforce employed in agriculture; Vietnam War brought depopulation of the countryside, and considerable destruction of forest and farmland; towns overcrowded with refugees have since contributed to the economic problems, as have natural disasters caused by typhoons and flooding. >> boat people; Hanoi; Ho Chi-minh; Vietnam War; RR1028 political leaders

Vietnamese An Austro-Asiatic language, spoken in Vietnam, Laos, and Cambodia by over 50 million people. A Latin-based alphabet, called *Quoc-ngu* (national language) was introduced in the 17th-c. >> Austro-Asiatic languages; Vietnam ⓘ

Vietnam War (1946–75) Hostilities between communist North Vietnam and non-communist South Vietnam, and others, also known as the **First** and **Second Indo-Chinese Wars**. The first began in 1946 after the breakdown of negotiations between France and the Viet Minh under Ho Chi-minh, and ended with the defeat of the French at Dien Bien Phu in 1954. The subsequent Geneva settlement left North Vietnam under communist rule. From 1961, US aid to the South increased considerably. From 1964, US aircraft bombarded the North, and by 1968 over 500 000 US troops were involved. These troops were withdrawn in 1973, and hostilities ceased in 1975, when the North's victory was completed with the capture of Saigon (renamed Ho Chi Minh City). >> My Lai incident; Viet Cong; Viet Minh; Vietnam ⓘ

viewdata >> **videotex**

Vignola, Giacomo (Barozzi) da [vee**nyoh**la] (1507–73) Architect, born in Vignola, Italy. In Rome he designed the Villa di Papa Giulio and the Church of the Gesú, which had a great influence on French and Italian church architecture.

Vigny, Alfred Victor, comte de (Count of) [**vee**nyee] (1797–1863) Romantic writer, born in Loches, France. His best-known works include the historical novel, *Cinq-Mars* (1826), a volume of exhortatory tales, *Stello* (1832), and the Romantic drama, *Chatterton* (1835). >> Romanticism

Vigo [**vee**goh] 42°12N 8°41W, pop (1995e) 277 000. Naval and commercial port in Galicia, NW Spain; airport; boat services to the Canary Is; watersports; castle. >> Galicia; Spain ⓘ

Viking project The first successful landing mission to Mars, consisting of two highly instrumented orbiter-lander spacecraft. Launched in 1975 by NASA, the first landing (20 Jul 1976) was on Chryse Planitia and the second (3 Sep 1976) on Utopia Planitia. Although evidence for life was not found, data from other lander and orbiter experiments have provided the basis for continuing intensive research on Martian evolution and climate. >> Mars (astronomy); NASA; RR970

Vikings Raiders, traders, and settlers from Norway, Sweden, and Denmark, who between the late 8th-c and the mid-11th-c conquered and colonized large parts of Britain (from 787), Normandy, and Russia; attacked Spain, Morocco, and Italy; traded with Byzantium, Persia, and India; discovered and occupied Iceland and Greenland; and reached the coast of North America (c.1000). As sea-borne raiders they gained a deserved reputation for destructiveness, but as merchants and settlers they played an influential role in the development of mediaeval Europe. >> Canute; Danelaw; Normans; Rollo; Vínland

Vila [**vee**la], also **Port-Vila** 17°45S 168°18E, pop (1995e) 22 400. Port and capital town of Vanuatu, on the SW coast of Efate I; airport. >> Vanuatu

Vila Real [**vee**la ray**al**] 41°17N 7°48W, pop (1995e) 15 400. Town in N Portugal; on R Corgo, 77 km/48 mi NE of Oporto; airfield; Mateus wine produced nearby; cathedral. >> Portugal ⓘ

Villa, Pancho [**vee**yah], also known as **Francisco Villa**, originally **Doroteo Arango** (1878–1923) Mexican revolutionary, born in Hacienda de Río Grande, Mexico. In a fierce struggle for control of the Mexican Revolution, he was defeated by Venustiano Carranza, and eventually made peace with the government (1920). >> Mexico ⓘ

Villahermosa [**veel**ya-air**moh**sa] 18°00N 92°53W, pop (1995e) 433 000. River port in SE Mexico, on the R Grijalva; university (1958). >> Mexico ⓘ

Villa-Lobos, Heitor [**vee**la **loh**bush] (1887–1959) Composer and conductor, born in Rio de Janeiro, Brazil. His many compositions include 12 symphonies, as well as operas, large-scale symphonic poems, concertos, ballets, and the nine suites *Bachianas Brasileiras* (1930–45), in which he treats Brazilian-style melodies in the manner of Bach.

Villars, Claude Louis Hector, duc de (Duke of) [veelah(r)] (1653–1734) Marshal under Louis XIV, born in Moulins, France. In the War of the Spanish Succession (1701–13) he inflicted heavy losses on Marlborough at Malplaquet (1709), and defeated the British and Dutch at Denain (1712). >> Marlborough, Duke of; Spanish Succession, War of the

Villas-Boas Brothers A family of brothers – **Orlando Villas-Boas** (1916–), **Claudio Villas-Boas** (1918–98), and **Leonardo Villas-Boas** (1920–61) – who have devoted their lives to the care and welfare of the Indians living around the Xingu R, Matto Grosso, Brazil, previously unknown tribes whom they met during a military expedition to the interior in 1943. They have twice been nominated for the Nobel Peace Prize. >> Xingu

Villehardouin, Geoffroi de [veelah(r)dwĩ] (c.1160–c.1213) Mediaeval chronicler, born near Bar-sur-Aube, France. He took part in the Fourth Crusade, and described the events from 1198 to 1207, including the capture of Constantinople in 1204. >> Crusades ℹ

villein [vilayn] In mediaeval England, a legally unfree peasant or serf who was tied to the manor, liable to arbitrary obligations (including labour services on the lord's estate), denied control over goods and property, and wholly bound to the lord's jurisdiction. >> manor; serfdom

Villeneuve, Jacques [veelnoev] (1971–) Motor-racing driver, born in Quebec, Canada. In 1995 he became the youngest driver to win the PPG Indy Car World Series title. He joined Formula One in 1996, driving for the Williams-Renault team, finished second in the World Driver's Championship, and won the Championship in 1997.

Villeneuve, Pierre (Charles Jean Baptiste Sylvestre) de [veelnoev] (1763–1806) French admiral, born in Valensole, France. In 1805 he was in charge of the French fleet at Trafalgar, where he was taken prisoner. >> Trafalgar, Battle of

Villiers de L'Isle Adam, comte (Count) **(Philippe) Auguste (Mathias)** [veelyay duh leel adã] (1840–89) Writer, born in St-Brieuc, France. A pioneer of the Symbolist movement, he wrote many poems, short stories (eg *Contes cruels*, 1883, Cruel Tales), novels (eg *Isis*, 1862), and plays (eg *La Révolte*, 1870, The Revolt). >> Symbolism

Villon, François [veeyõ], pseudonym of **François de Montcorbier** (1431–?) Poet, born in Paris. His works include *Le Lais* (The Legacy, also known as *Le Petit Testament*), and his long poetic sequence, *Le Grand Testament* (1461). He is known to have taken part in several crimes, and in 1463 received a death sentence, commuted to banishment.

Vilnius [veelnius], formerly **Wilno** (1920–39) 54°40N 25°19E, pop (1995e) 597 000. Capital city of Lithuania, on R Vilnya; one of the largest industrial centres of the Soviet Baltic region; formerly part of Poland; ceded to Russia, 1795; occupied by Germany in World War 2; airport; railway junction; university (1579); cathedral (1777–1801), castle. >> Lithuania ℹ

Vimy Ridge [veemee] An escarpment 8 km/5 mi NE of Arras, a strongly held part of the German defence line on the Western Front in World War 1. It was successfully stormed by the Canadian Corps of the British 1st Army (1917). >> World War 1

Viña del Mar [veenya thel mah(r)] 33°02S 71°35W, pop (1995e) 332 000. Seaside town in Valparaíso province, C Chile; residential suburb and popular South American resort. >> Chile ℹ; Valparaíso

Vincent de Beauvais [vĩsã duh bohvay], Lat **Vincentius Bellovacensis** (c.1190–c.1264) French Dominican priest and encyclopedist. He compiled his *Speculum majus* (Great Mirror) on a wide range of natural, doctrinal, and historical subjects.

Vincent de Paul, St (c.1580–1660) Priest and philanthropist, born in Pouy, France. He formed associations for helping the sick, and in 1625 founded the Congregation of Priests of the Missions (or 'Lazarists', from their priory of St Lazare) and (1634) the Sisterhood of Charity. He was canonized in 1737. Feast day 27 September. >> Lazarists

Vincentians >> **Lazarists**

Vinci, Leonardo da >> **Leonardo da Vinci**

vine >> **climbing plant; grapevine**

vinegar A sour liquid used as a food preservative or domestic flavour enhancer. It derives from the oxidization of alcohol by bacteria, the ethanol being converted to acetic acid. >> ethanol; food preservation

Vingt, les [lay vĩ] A group of 20 modern painters, including Ensor, founded in Brussels in 1884. For 10 years they held exhibitions showing pictures by leading Postimpressionists. >> modern art; Postimpressionism; Ensor

vingt-et-un >> **pontoon**

Vínland [veenland] A generalized Norse name meaning 'Berry Land' or 'Vine Land', applied to the E coast of North America from the time of its first sighting by the Viking Leif Eriksson AD c.985. Accounts of the Norse discovery of America in Icelandic sagas are confirmed by archaeological evidence. >> L'Anse aux Meadows; Leif Eriksson; Skraelings; Vikings

Vinson Massif Highest peak in Antarctica, rising to 5140 m/16 863 ft in the Ellsworth Mts. >> Antarctica ℹ

vinyl An important organic chemical grouping (CH_2=CH–). Many types of polymer are based on it. >> polyvinylacetate; polyvinylchloride

viola A bowed string instrument, in all essential respects like a violin but slightly larger and tuned a fifth lower. >> string instrument 1 ℹ; string quartet; violin

viola da gamba Strictly speaking, any member of the viol family – bowed string instruments held upright on the knees, or between the legs, of the player; more generally, the bass instrument of that family, loosely resembling a cello but with sloping shoulders, a flat back, six strings, and a fretted fingerboard like a guitar's. >> cello; string instrument 1 ℹ

violet An annual or perennial native to most temperate regions, many being alpine species; flowers 5-petalled, blue, yellow, white, or these colours combined, sometimes fragrant. It includes the species and varieties commonly known as **pansies**. (*Viola*, 500 species. Family: Violaceae.) >> heartsease; pansy

violin The most widespread of all bowed string instruments. The four-string violin was developed in the 16th-c from earlier three-string types, and reached its highest point of perfection between 1650 and 1730 in the hands of Stradivari and the Amati and Guarneri families. The other regular members of the violin family are the viola, cello, and double bass. >> kinnor; kit; string instrument 1 ℹ; string quartet; viola; Guarneri; Stradivari

Viollet-le-Duc, Eugène (Emmanuel) [vyohlay luh dük] (1814–79) Architect and archaeologist, born in Paris. His restorations included the cathedrals of Notre Dame, Amiens, and Laon, and the Château de Pierrefonds.

violoncello >> **cello**

viper A venomous snake of family Viperidae (187 species), worldwide except Australia; thick body; head usually triangular, broad; fangs attached to front of upper jaw. >> asp; pit viper ℹ; snake; *see illustration on p. 913*

Virgil or **Vergil**, in full **Publius Vergilius Maro** (70–19 BC) Latin poet, born in Andes, Italy. His works include *Eclogues* (37 BC), the *Georgics*, or *Art of Husbandry* (36–29 BC), and for the rest of his life he worked at the request of the emperor on the *Aeneid*. >> Aeneas

virginals A keyboard instrument with a mechanism similar to that of the harpsichord, but with strings set at right angles to the keys (as in the clavichord). It was widely used from the 15th-c to the 17th-c. >> clavichord; harpsichord; keyboard instrument

Virgin Birth The Christian belief that Jesus Christ had no human father, but was conceived through the power of the Holy Spirit without his mother, Mary, losing her virginity. >> Jesus Christ; Mary (Mother of Jesus)

Virginia pop (1995e) 6 672 000; area 105 582 sq km/ 40 767 sq mi. State in E USA; 'Old Dominion'; first permanent British settlement in America (at Jamestown, 1607); named after Elizabeth I (the 'Virgin Queen'); one of the first colonies to move for independence; scene of the British surrender at Yorktown, 1781; 10th of the original 13 states to ratify the Constitution, 1788; scene of several major battles in the Civil War (Richmond was the Confederacy capital); re-admitted to the Union, 1870; highest point, Mt Rogers (1743 m/5718 ft); flat and swampy coastal area (the Tidewater region); to the W, land rises into the rolling, fertile Piedmont, interrupted further W by the Blue Ridge Mts; W of these lies a series of beautiful valleys (the Valley of Virginia), notably the Shenandoah; capital, Richmond; tobacco (chief agricultural crop); the area's scenery and history make tourism a major state industry. >> American Civil War; Richmond (USA); United States of America [i]; RR994

Virginia Resolutions >> **Kentucky and Virginia Resolutions**

Virgin Islands, British pop (1995e) 13 000; area 153 sq km/ 59 sq mi. Island group at the NW end of the Lesser Antilles chain, E Caribbean; British overseas territory; capital, Road Town (on Tortola I); timezone GMT −4; population mainly of African or mixed descent; chief religion, Protestantism; official language, English; unit of currency, the US dollar; comprises four large islands and over 30 islets and cays; only 16 islands inhabited; highest point, Sage Mt (540 m/1772 ft) on Tortola I; subtropical climate; Tortola colonized by British planters, 1666; constitutional government, 1774; part of the Leeward Is, 1872; separate Crown Colony, 1956; governor represents the British sovereign; Executive Council and Legislative Council; tourism. >> Antilles; Leeward Islands (Caribbean); Road Town

Virgin Islands, United States, official name **Virgin Islands of the United States**, formerly **Danish West Indies** (to 1917) pop (1995e) 113 000; area 342 sq km/132 sq mi. A group of more than 50 islands in the Lesser Antilles, Caribbean Sea; capital, Charlotte Amalie; timezone GMT −4; chief religion, Protestantism; official language, English; unit of currency, the US dollar; three main inhabited islands, St Croix, St Thomas, St John; volcanic origin; highest peak, Crown Mt (474 m/1555 ft) on St Thomas; Denmark colonized St Thomas and St John in 1671, and bought St Croix from France in 1733; purchased by the USA, 1917; now an unincorporated territory of the USA; a governor heads a unicameral legislature; chief industry is tourism; badly damaged by hurricane Hugo in 1989. >> Charlotte Amalie; St Croix; St John (US Virgin Is); St Thomas

Virgo (Lat 'virgin') A constellation of the zodiac, which contains the first quasar to be recognized as such, 3C 273, and one of the largest galaxies known, M87. Its brightest star is Spica. Virgo lies on the celestial equator, between Leo and Libra. >> constellation; galaxy; quasar; RR968

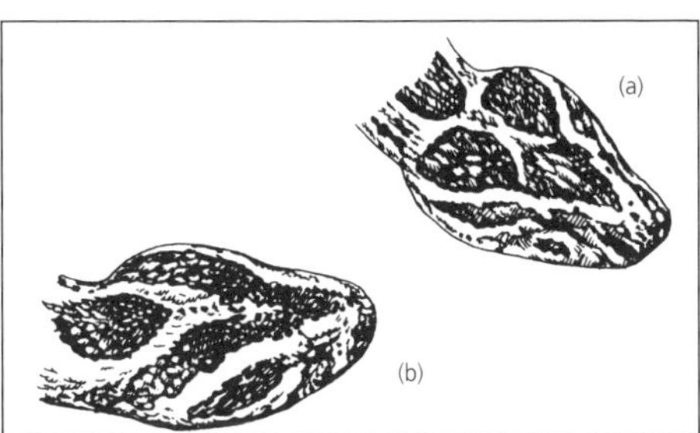

Viper heads showing the 'V' marking – Palestinian viper (a); Russell's viper (b)

viroid A fragment of infectious nucleic acid that resembles a virus. It typically consists of a small loop of ribonucleic acid not enclosed within a protein shell. >> RNA; virus

virtual reality A computing technique in which the computer user sees only a computer output screen, and all the movements and sounds from the user are recorded by the computer. This allows the computer to simulate another environment in which users might well believe they are wholly involved. Virtual reality is used in a wide range of contexts, such as flight simulators for training pilots, videoconferencing suites, and computer games. >> computer game; videoconferencing

virus The smallest infectious particle, 10–300 nm in diameter. Viruses infect other micro-organisms such as bacteria, fungi, and algae, as well as higher plants and animals. The genetic material of each virus is present as a molecule of either ribonucleic acid or deoxyribonucleic acid, encased inside a protein shell. Viruses replicate only in living cells, their nucleic acid directing the host cell to synthesize material required for producing more virus. The study of viruses is known as **virology**. >> DNA [i]; RNA; viroid

Visayan Islands [vi**siy**an] area 61 991 sq km/23 928 sq mi. Island group in the C Philippines; chief islands include Cebu, Bohol, Panay, Leyte, Samar, Negros, Masbate. >> Philippines [i]

viscacha [vis**ka**cha] A cavy-like rodent from South America; resembles a large chinchilla; four species in genera *Lagostomus* and *Lagidium*. (Family: Chinchillidae.) >> cavy; chinchilla; rodent

Visconti, Luchino [vis**kon**tee] (1906–76) Stage and film director, born in Milan, Italy. His first film, *Ossessione* (1942, Obsession), took Italy by storm, with its strict realism and concern with social problems. Later films included *Il gattopardo* (1963, The Leopard) and *Morte a Venezia* (1971, Death in Venice).

viscose The solution of cellulose from which regenerated cellulose fibre (rayon) is produced. Discovered in 1892, the viscose process is still the basis of most rayon manufacturing. >> cellulose; rayon

viscosity [vis**kos**itee] A measure of a fluid's reluctance to flow, corresponding to internal friction in the fluid as one portion of the fluid seeks to slide over another; symbol η, units Pa.s (pascal.second), but a more common unit is *poise*, P (1P = 0·1/10 Pa.s). It is defined as the ratio of shear stress to the rate of change of shear strain. >> fluid mechanics; friction; rheology

viscount (Lat *vice-comes* 'deputy of a count') In the UK, the second lowest rank of the peerage, often the second title of an earl or marquess bestowed as a courtesy title on his eldest son. >> peerage

Vishinsky >> **Vyshinsky, Andrei**

Vishnu [**vish**noo] A major Hindu deity, second in the triad (*Trimurti*) of gods manifesting the cosmic functions of the Supreme Being. The preserver of the universe and the embodiment of goodness and mercy, he is believed to have assumed visible form in nine descents (*avataras*), of which his appearances as Rama and Krishna are the most important. >> avatar; Hinduism; Krishna; Trimurti

visibles >> **invisibles**

Visigoths A Germanic people who fled from the Huns in 376 into the Roman Empire, and eventually founded the Visigothic kingdom, embracing at its height in the 7th-c Portugal, virtually all Spain, and part of S Gaul. It was extinguished by the Arab conquest of 711. >> Gaul; Goths; Huns

Vistula, River [vistyula], Pol **Wisła** Longest river in Poland; rises in the Carpathians and flows for 1047 km/651 mi to meet the Baltic Sea at Gdańsk. >> Poland ℹ

visual display unit (VDU) The screen attached to a computer. Most VDUs are based on cathode-ray-tube technology similar to that used in television sets, and both single colour and full colour versions are used. An increasing number of VDUs are being based on liquid crystal displays, particularly in portable computer applications. >> cathode-ray tube; liquid crystals

vitamins Organic substance present in minute quantities in natural foods that are essential for health, classified as either **water-soluble** or **fat-soluble**. Specific abnormalities result if they are absent from the diet or present in insufficient amounts. >> antivitamin factors; ascorbic acid; biotin; cyanocobalamin; folic acid; megavitamin therapy; pyridoxine; retinol; riboflavin; tocopherol; vegetarianism; *see panel below*

Viti Levu [veetee layvoo] area 10 429 sq km/4026 sq mi. Largest and most important island of Fiji; length 144 km/89 mi; width 104 km/65 mi; mountainous interior, rising to 1324 m/4344 ft at Tomaniivi (Mt Victoria); capital, Suva; airport. >> Fiji ℹ

vitriol >> **sulphuric acid**

Vitruvius [vitroovius], in full **Marcus Vitruvius Pollio** (1st-c) Roman architect and military engineer. He wrote the 10-volume *De architectura* (On Architecture), the only extant Roman treatise on this subject.

Vittoria, Tommasso Ludovica da >> **Victoria, Tomás Luis de**

Vittoria [veetohria], Span **Vitoria** 42°51N 2°40W, pop (1995e) 207 000. Basque city in N Spain; scene of French defeat in the Peninsular War, 1813; bishopric; airport; railway; old and new cathedrals. >> Basque Provinces; Peninsular War; Spain ℹ

Vittorino da Feltre [vitoreenoh da feltray], originally **Vittorino dei Ramboldini** (c.1378–1446) Educationist, born in Feltre, Italy. In Mantua he founded a school for both rich and poor children (1425), in which he devised new methods of instruction, integrating the development of mind and body through the study of the Classics and Christianity.

Vivaldi, Antonio (Lucio) [vivaldee] (1678–1741) Violinist and composer, born in Venice, Italy. *L'estro armonico* (1712) gave him a European reputation and *The Four Seasons* (1725), an early example of programme music, proved highly popular; he also wrote operas, sacred music, and over 450 concertos.

Vivekananda [vivaykananda], also known as **Swami Vivekananda**, originally **Narendranath Datta** or **Dutt** (1862–1902) Hindu philosopher, born in Calcutta, India. After meeting Ramakrishna, he became his leading disciple, establishing the headquarters of the Ramakrishna Order at Belur Math on the Ganges, near Calcutta. He attempted to combine Indian spirituality with Western materialism, and became the main force behind the Vedanta movement in the West. >> Ramakrishna

Viverridae [viveridee] A family of small to medium-sized carnivores native to the S Old World; 72 species; long thin body, long tail, pointed muzzle, short legs; coat often spotted or banded. >> binturong; carnivore ℹ; civet; ichneumon (mammal); mongoose; *see illustration on p. 915*

Vivés, Juan Luis [veevays], Lat **Ludovicus Vives** (1492–1540) Philosopher and humanist, born in Valencia, Spain. His writings include *Adversus Pseudodialecticos* (1570, Against the Pseudo-Dialecticians), and several other works on educational theory and practice.

viviparity [viviparitee] In animals, the production of live young rather than eggs. The embryos grow within the mother's body, which provides nourishment via a pla-

The main types of vitamin

Fat soluble vitamins

Vitamin	Chemical name	Precursor	Main symptom of deficiency	Dietary source
A	retinol	ß-carotene	xerophthalmia (eye disease)	*retinol:* milk, butter, cheese, egg yolk, liver, and fatty fish *carotene:* green vegetables, yellow and red fruits and vegetables, especially carrots
D	cholecalciferol	UV-activated 7-dehydro-cholesterol	rickets, osteomalacia	liver oils of fatty fish, margarine, some fortified milks, and breakfast cereals
K	phytomenadione		haemorrhagic problems	green leafy vegetables and liver
E	tocopherols		multiple effects	vegetable oils

Water soluble vitamins

Vitamin	Chemical name	Main symptom of deficiency	Dietary source
C	ascorbic acid	scurvy	citrus fruits, potatoes, green leafy vagetables
B-vitamins			
B_1	thiamine	beriberi	seeds and grains; widely distributed
B_2	riboflavin	failure to thrive	liver, milk, cheese, yeast, leafy vegetables
–	nicotinic acid	pellagra	meat, fish, wholemeal cereals, pulses
B_6	pyridoxine	dermatitis; neurological disorders	cereals, liver, meat, fruits, leafy vegetables
B_{12}	cyanocobalamin	anaemia	meat, milk, liver, egg yolk
–	folic acid	anaemia	liver, green vegetables, nuts
–	pantothenic acid	dermatitis	widespread
–	biotin	dermatitis	liver, kidney, yeast extracts

Viverridae – banded linsang

centa or similar structure. In plants, it refers to the production of seeds that germinate within the fruit while still attached to the parent plant. >> placenta (anatomy); reproduction

vivisection The practice of dissecting live animals for experimental purposes. Research includes experiments which look for the effects of new drugs, food additives, cosmetics, and a wide range of chemicals on the body tissue and behaviour of such animals as guinea pigs, rabbits, rats, and monkeys, as an alternative to using human subjects. Such research is now strictly controlled by legislation in most Western nations, but nonetheless can provoke considerable public opposition, including the use of violence against scientists by animal rights extremists.

Vlaanderen [**vlan**deren] >> **Flanders**

Vladimir I, St, in full **Vladimis Svyatoslavich**, known as **the Great** (956–1015) Grand Prince of Kiev (c.978–1015). One of ancient Russia's most illustrious rulers, in 988 he was converted to Christianity, and adopted the Greek Orthodox rite as the official religion of Russia. He was later canonized. Feast day 27 September.

Vladivostok [vladi**vos**tok] 43°10N 131°53E, pop (1995e) 655 000. Seaport in Russia, on the Sea of Japan; chief Soviet port on the Pacific Ocean (kept open in winter by ice-breakers); base for fishing and whaling fleets; founded, 1860; terminus of the Trans-Siberian Railway; university (1920); naval base. >> Russia 🛈; Trans-Siberian Railway

Vlaminck, Maurice de [**vla**mĩk] (1876–1958) Artist, born in Paris. By 1905 he was one of the leaders of the *Fauves*, using typically brilliant colour, then painted more realist landscapes (1908–14), and later developed a more sombre Expressionism. >> Expressionism; Fauvism

Vlissingen >> **Flushing**

Vlorë or **Vlora** [**vlo**ruh], Ital **Valona**, ancient **Aulon** 40°27N 19°30E, pop (1995e) 80 300. Seaport in SW Albania; a 5th-c bishopric; independence proclaimed here in 1912; railway. >> Albania 🛈

VLSI >> **very large scale integration**

Vltava, River [**vuhl**tava], Ger **Moldau** River in the Czech Republic, formed in the Bohemian Forest; meets the R Elbe; length 427 km/265 mi. >> Czech Republic 🛈

VOA >> **Voice of America**

vocal cords Two muscular folds in the larynx, behind the Adam's apple. They are brought together to impede the airflow during speech, when they vibrate and produce voice, used in the articulation of vowels and many consonants. They are also used to vary the pitch of the voice and in the production of several distinctive tones of voice. >> intonation; larynx

vocational education Education which is aimed at the preparation of students for employment. Often undertaken in colleges of further education, it can also take place on the job in the workplace itself. A wide range of vocational qualifications is usually available, some from chartered award-giving institutions, others from professional organizations. >> further education; polytechnic

vodka A colourless spirit produced from potatoes, the national drink of Poland and Russia. It is almost tasteless, and is thus used in many mixed drinks, such as the 'Bloody Mary' (vodka and tomato juice). >> spirits

Voice of America (VOA) The external broadcasting service of the US Information Agency, founded in 1942. By the early 1990s, the VOA was broadcasting worldwide in English and 45 other languages. >> broadcasting

Volans [**voh**lanz] (Lat 'flying fish') A tiny and inconspicuous S constellation near the Large Magellanic Cloud. >> constellation; Magellanic Clouds; RR968

volcano A vent or fissure in the Earth's crust where molten lava is erupted onto the surface. Most volcanoes are confined to the zones along boundaries between crustal plates, and are closely associated with earthquakes, as in the circum-Pacific 'ring of fire'; but there are notable exceptions, such as the Hawaiian Is, which have formed on a 'hot spot' in the Earth's crust. The scientific study of volcanoes is known as **vulcanology**. >> earthquake; igneous rock; plate tectonics 🛈; ring of fire; RR973

Volcanus >> **Vulcan** (mythology)

vole A mouse-like rodent native to Asia, Europe, and North America; most species with large head, blunt snout, and short tail; closely related to lemmings. (Tribe: Microtini, 96 species.) >> lemming; mouse (zoology); rodent; water vole

Volga, River, ancient **Rha** Longest river of Europe, in C European Russia; rises in the Valdai Hills; enters the Caspian Sea in a broad delta; length, 3531 km/2194 mi. >> Russia 🛈

Volgograd [**vol**gograd], formerly **Tsaritsyn** (to 1925), **Stalingrad** (1925–61) 48°45N 44°30E, pop (1995e) 1 011 000. City in SE European Russia, on R Volga; founded, 16th-c; largely destroyed in World War 2; airport; railway. >> Russia 🛈

volleyball An indoor court game, played by two teams of six-a-side. Players hit a large ball with their hands or arms over a raised net in the hope of forcing an error, and thus score points. It was invented in 1895 by William G Morgan at the YMCA, Holyoke, MA, USA. >> RR1064

Volsungasaga [**vol**sunga**sah**ga] A 13th-c German epic deriving in part from the Norse *Edda*. It tells the story of the dynasty of the Volsungs, which is linked to that of the Nibelungs. >> Edda; Nibelungen

volt SI unit of electrical potential difference; symbol *V*; named after Alessandro Volta; if the power dissipated between two points along a wire carrying a current of 1 amp is 1 watt, then the potential difference between the two points equals 1 volt. >> potential difference; Volta

Volta, Alessandro (Giuseppe Antonio Anastasio) [**vol**ta] (1745–1827) Physicist, born in Como, Italy. He experimented on current electricity, and invented an electric battery which gave the first reliable supply. >> battery (electricity); electricity; volt

voltage >> **potential difference**

Voltaire [vol**tair**], pseudonym of **François Marie Arouet** (1694–1778) Writer, the embodiment of the 18th-c Enlightenment, born in Paris. His tragedy *Oedipe* brought him fame, but he gained enemies at court, and was forced to go into exile for a time. He later wrote plays, poetry, historical and scientific treatises, and his *Lettres Philosophiques* (1734, Philosophical Letters). From 1762 he produced a range of anti-religious writings and the *Dictionnaire philosophique* (1764, Philosophical Dictionary). >> Enlightenment

voltmeter An instrument used for measuring potential difference or electromotive force between points in a circuit. Most voltmeters consist of an ammeter connected in line with a high resistance, and calibrated in volts. >> electricity

Voluntary Reserve >> **Territorial Army**

Voluntary Service Overseas (VSO) A British charity founded in 1958 to send skilled volunteers to work for two-year periods in developing countries. The host government provides a living allowance and accommodation; VSO provides briefing, air fare, and a grant. >> Peace Corps

von Braun, Wernher >> **Braun, Wernher von**

V-1 The abbreviation of *Vergeltungswaffe-1* (Ger 'revenge weapon 1'); small, winged, pilotless aircraft powered by a pulse jet motor, developed by the Luftwaffe. They carried a tonne of high explosive at a speed of c.800 kph/500 mph. Between 1944 and 1945, 5823 were launched against Britain. From the noise of their motors, they were also known as **buzz-bombs**. >> bomb; Luftwaffe; V-2

Vonnegut, Kurt, Jr [**von**eguht] (1922–) Novelist, born in Indianapolis, IN. His novels are satirical fantasies, usually cast in the form of science fiction, as in *Player Piano* (1952) and *Galapagos* (1985). He is best known for *Slaughterhouse Five* (1969).

Von Neumann, John [**noy**man], originally **Johann von Neumann** (1903–57) Mathematician, born in Budapest. His mathematical work on high-speed calculations for H-bomb development contributed to the development of computers, and he also introduced game theory (1944), which was a major influence on economics.

voodoo The popular religion of Haiti, also found in the West Indies and parts of South America. A blending of Roman Catholicism with W African religion, its followers attend both the church and the voodoo temple, where a voodoo priest or priestess leads a ritual invoking of the spirits of the voodoo world through magical diagrams, songs, and prayer. >> Haiti; magic; Roman Catholicism

Voortrekkerse >> **Afrikaners; Great Trek**

Voronezh [vo**ron**yesh] 51°40N 39°10E, pop (1995e) 902 000. River port in EC European Russia, on R Voronezh; founded as a fortress, 1586; airport; railway; university (1918). >> Russia [i]

Voroshilov, Kliment Yefremovich [voro**sheel**of] (1881–1969) Soviet marshal, statesman, and president (1953–60), born near Dniepropetrovsk, Ukraine. He played a military rather than a political role in the 1917 Revolution, and as commissar for defence (1925–40) was responsible for the modernization of the Red Army. He became head of state after Stalin's death. >> Red Army (USSR); Russian Revolution; Stalin

Voroshilovgrad >> **Lugansk**

Vorster, John [**faw(r)**ster], originally **Balthazar Johannes Vorster** (1915–83) South African statesman, prime minister (1966–78), and president (1978–9), born in Jamestown, South Africa. He was minister of justice under Verwoerd (1961), whom he succeeded, maintaining the policy of apartheid. >> apartheid; South Africa [i]; Verwoerd

vortex A rotational form of fluid flow. Lines of flow are curved, and may even form closed loops. Examples of vortices are whirlpools, tornadoes, and the circulating eddies caused by obstructions in rivers. >> fluid mechanics

Vorticism A modern art movement started in England in 1913, partly inspired by the Futurists. Leading members included Wyndham Lewis, C R W Nevinson (1889–1946), and Henri Gaudier-Brzeska. >> Cubism; Futurism; Gaudier-Brzeska; modern art; Lewis, Wyndham

Vortigern [**vaw(r)**tijern] (fl.425–50) Semi-legendary British king. According to Bede, he recruited Germanic mercenaries led by Hengist and Horsa to help fight off the Picts after the final withdrawal of the Roman administration from Britain (409). >> Angles; Bede; Jutes; Picts; Saxons

Vosges Mountains [vohzh], ancient **Vosegus** area 7425 sq km/2866 sq mi. Range of hills in NE France; highest point, Ballon de Guebwiller (1423 m/4669 ft), length, 250 km/155 mi. >> Jura Mountains

Vostok [**vos**tok] ('East') **spacecraft** The first generation of Soviet crewed spacecraft, carrying a single member. Vostok 1 carried the first human into space (12 Apr 1961) – Yuri Gagarin, who orbited Earth once on a flight of 118 min. The last Vostok flight carried Valentina Tereshkova, the first woman to fly in space (Vostok 6, 16 Jun 1963). **Voskhod** ('Sunrise') was an intermediate-generation Soviet-crewed spacecraft following Vostok and preceding Soyuz; it made only two flights, in 1964 and 1965. >> Gagarin; Soviet space programme; spacecraft; Tereshkova

vowel One of the two main categories of speech sound (the other being **consonant**). It is produced when the air flows freely through the mouth without constriction from the pharynx, tongue, or lips; it also forms the nucleus of the syllable, and (unlike a consonant) can stand alone (as in such words as *I* and *a* in English).

Voyager project A multiple outer-planet flyby mission undertaken by NASA to make the first detailed exploration beyond Mars, and designed to take advantage of a rare (every 175 years) celestial alignment of Jupiter, Saturn, Uranus, and Neptune. Twin spacecraft in the Mariner series were launched in 1977. They flew through the Jovian system (Mar, Jul 1979) and, with a boost from Jupiter's gravity, flew on to Saturn (encounters Nov 1980, Aug 1981). Voyager 2 used Saturn's gravity to fly on to the historic encounters with Uranus (1986) and Neptune (1989). >> NASA; Solar System; RR970; *see illustration on p. 917*

voyeurism A repeated tendency to observe others engaging in intimate, including sexual, behaviour. Sexual excitement often occurs in anticipation of the voyeuristic act, which may be accompanied by masturbation.

Voznesensky, Andrey Andreyevich [vozhne**shen**skee] (1933–) Poet, born in Moscow. His best-known volume *Antimiry* (Antiworlds) appeared in 1964, and the more difficult poems of *Soblazn* (Temptation) in 1979.

VSO >> **Voluntary Service Overseas**

VTOL [**vee**tol] Acronym used for a fixed-wing aircraft specially designed for **Vertical Take-Off and Landing**. The most successful aircraft of this type is the Hawker Siddeley Harrier, which can deflect the thrust from its jet engine from the vertical to the horizontal while in flight. >> aircraft [i]; jet engine [i]; STOL

V-2 The abbreviation of *Vergeltungswaffe-2* (Ger 'revenge weapon 2'); a guided ballistic missile developed by the German army, which began rocket experiments under the direction of Wernher von Braun in 1937. It was unstoppable, but wildly inaccurate. Between September 1944 and March 1945, 1054 fell on Britain. >> ballistic missile; Braun, Wernher von; V-1

Vuillard, (Jean) Edouard [vweeyah(r)] (1868–1940) Painter and printmaker, born in Cuiseaux, France. One of the later Impressionists, a member of *Les Nabis*, he executed mainly flower pieces and simple interiors, painted with a great sense of light and colour. >> Impressionism (art); *Nabis, Les*

Vulcan, also **Vulcanus** or **Volcanus** The Roman god of fire, sometimes called **Mulciber**. He was identified with the Greek Hephaestus. >> Hephaestus

vulcanite or **ebonite** A hard black material made by the vulcanization of rubber with a high proportion of sulphur (2:1). It was important as an insulator before the coming of modern synthetics. >> rubber; vulcanization

vulcanization The modification of the properties of rubber by chemical treatment, mainly with sulphur. The technique, which originated in 1839, improves tensile strength, elasticity, and abrasion resistance. >> rubber; vulcanite

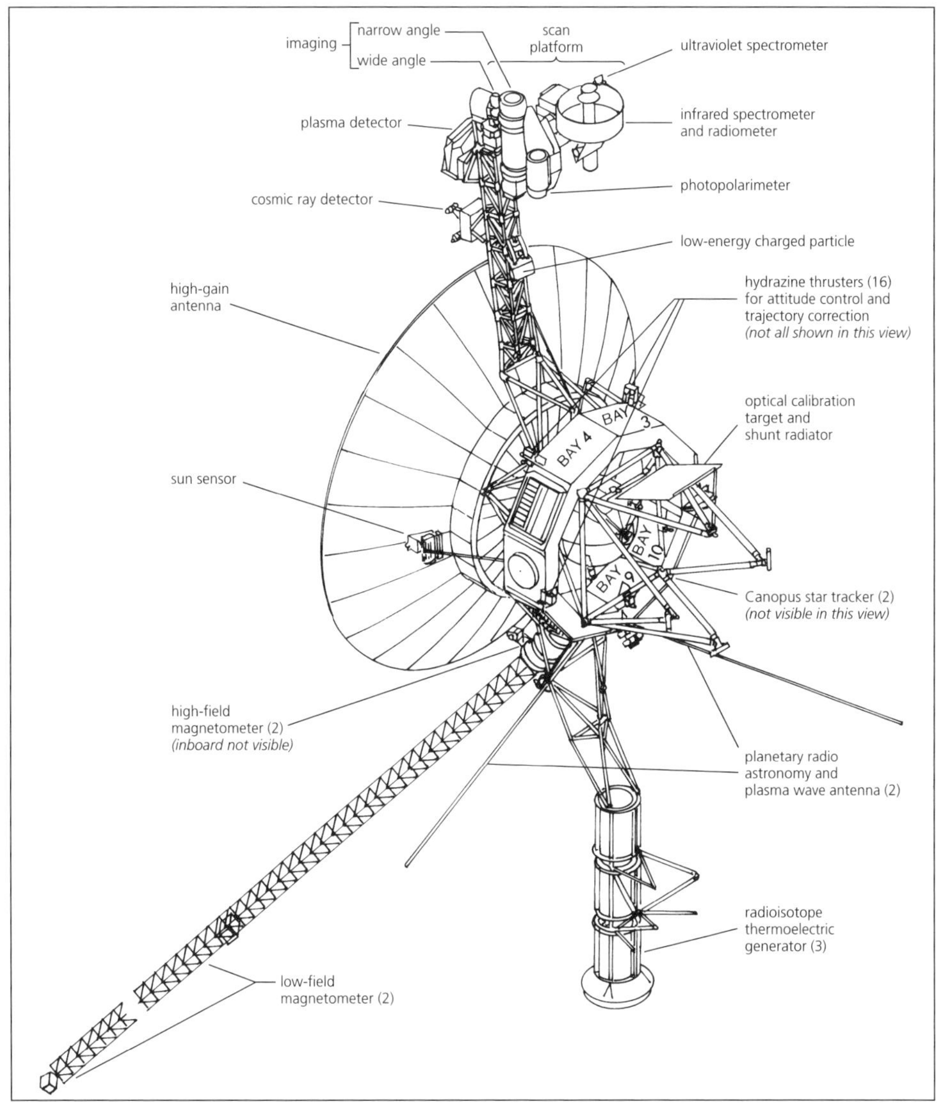

Voyager spacecraft (shown without thermal blankets, for clarity), giving the locations of most of the external science and engineering instrumentation

vulcanology >> **volcano**

Vulgate [**vuhl**gayt] The Latin translation of the Christian Bible, originating with Jerome (c.405). It emerged in Western Christianity as the favourite Latin version (*vulgate* meaning the 'common' edition), and in 1546 the Council of Trent recognized it as the official Latin text of the Roman Catholic Church. >> Bible; Jerome, St; Roman Catholicism

Vulpecula [vul**pek**yula] (Lat 'little fox') A small N constellation in the Milky Way. >> constellation; Milky Way; RR968

vulture A bird of prey specialized to feed on carrion; head often lacking long feathers. There are two groups. **Old World vultures** (Family: Accipitridae, 14 species) were formerly worldwide but now absent from the Americas; no sense of smell. **New World** or **cathartid vultures** (Family: Cathartidae, 7 species) are now restricted to the Americas. >> bird of prey; condor; griffon; lammergeier

Vygotsky, Lev Semenovich [vi**got**skee] (1896–1934) Psychologist, born in Orsha, Belarus. His writings, such as *Thought and Language* (1934–62) and *Mind in Society* (1978), have had a major influence on Russian and (since the 1960s) Western psychology.

Vyshinsky, Andrey Yanuaryevich [vi**shin**skee] (1883–1954) Jurist and politician, born in Odessa, Ukraine. He was the public prosecutor at the state trials (1936–8) which removed Stalin's rivals, and later became the Soviet delegate to the United Nations (1945–9, 1953–4), and foreign minister (1949–53). >> Stalin

Waddington, C(onrad) H(al) (1905–75) Embryologist and geneticist, born in Evesham, Hereford and Worcester. He introduced important concepts into evolutionary theory, and also helped to popularize science in such general books as *The Ethical Animal* (1960). >> genetics

wadi [**wod**ee] A desert ravine or steep-sided gorge formed during flash floods, but generally containing water only during rainy seasons.

Wagga Wagga 35°07S 147°24E, pop (1995e) 56 500. Town in New South Wales, Australia; centre of a rich agricultural area; railway; airfield; university, 1989. >> New South Wales

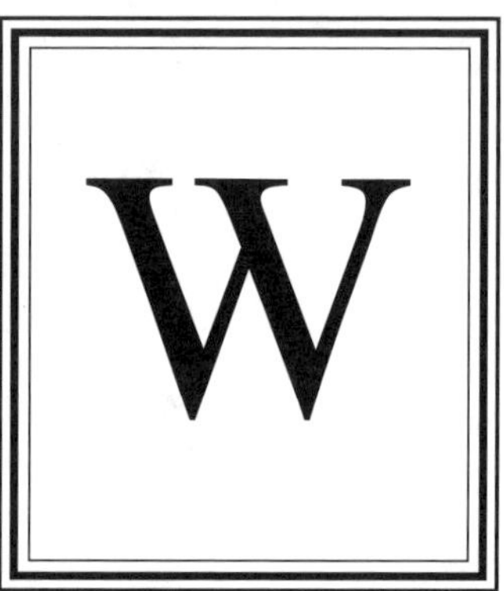

Wagner, Otto [**vahg**ner] (1841–1918) Architect and teacher, born in Penzing, Austria. The founder of the Vienna School, he became an important advocate of purely functional architecture, notably through his book *Modern Architecture* (1895). >> International Style **2**

Wagner, (Wilhelm) Richard [**vahg**ner] (1813–83) Composer, born in Leipzig, Germany. His *Rienzi* (1842) was a great success at Dresden, but his next operas, including *Tannhäuser* (1845), were failures. In 1853 he began to write *Das Rheingold* (The Rhinegold), followed by *Die Walküre* (1856, The Valkyries) and the first two acts of *Siegfried* (1857). In 1864 he was saved from ruin by the eccentric young King of Bavaria, Ludwig II, who became a fanatical admirer of his work. His first wife, Minna, having died in 1866, Wagner then married Cosima von Bülow, the wife of his musical director, after her divorce. *Die Meistersinger* was completed in 1867, and *Götterdämmerung* in 1874. He opened the now famous theatre at Bayreuth in 1876 with a performance of the whole *Ring* cycle. *Parsifal*, his last opera, was staged in 1882. His son **Siegfried Wagner** (1869–1930) was director of the Bayreuth theatre from 1909. His grandson **Wieland Wagner** (1917–66) took over the directorship in 1951, followed by Wieland's brother, **Wolfgang Wagner** (1919–).

wagtail A small, ground-dwelling songbird, found worldwide; plumage usually bold, black-and-white, yellow, or green (dull species are called **pipits**); long tail which wags vertically. (Family: Motacillidae, 48 species.) >> fantail; flycatcher; pipit; songbird

Wahhabis [**wa**habeez] An 18th-c Islamic movement which derives from Mohammed ibn Abd al-Wahhab, a religious reformer, and Mohammed ibn Saud, the ancestor of the present rulers of Saudi Arabia. It maintains that legal decisions must be based exclusively on the Koran and the *Sunna*. The original Wahhabis banned music, dancing, poetry, silk, gold, and jewellery, and in the 20th-c have attacked the telephone, radio, and television. >> Islam; Saudi Arabia [i]

Waikato, River [wiy**ka**toh] River in North Island, New Zealand; length 425 km/264 mi; rises in L Taupo; enters the Tasman Sea. >> New Zealand [i]

Waikiki Beach [wiykee**kee**] Resort beach in SE Honolulu on the Pacific island of Oahu, Hawaii state, USA; surfing popular on the reef. >> Hawaii (state)

Wain, John (Barrington) [wayn] (1925–94) Writer and critic, born in Stoke-on-Trent, Staffordshire. His novels include *Hurry on Down* (1953) and *The Contenders* (1958), and his poetry includes *Weep Before God* (1961). Among his later books are *Young Shoulders* (1982, Whitbread) and *Comedies* (1990). >> Angry Young Men

Waitangi, Treaty of [wiy**tang**ee] A compact signed by Maori representatives and Governor William Hobson at Waitangi (6 Feb 1840) on the occasion of the British annexation of New Zealand. Waitangi Day is the national day of New Zealand. >> New Zealand [i]

Waite, Terry [wayt], popular name of **Terence (Hardy) Waite** (1939–) Adviser to the Archbishop of Canterbury on Anglican Communion Affairs since 1980, born in Cheshire. As the Archbishop's special envoy, he was particularly involved in negotiations to secure the release of hostages held in the Middle East. He was himself kidnapped in Beirut in January 1987, and not released until November 1991. A volume of memoirs, *Taken on Trust* was published in 1993. >> Anglican Communion

Waitz, Grete [viyts], *née* **Andersen** (1953–) Athlete, born in Oslo. She was the world's leading female road athlete, the world marathon champion in 1983, the Olympic silver medallist in 1984, and on four occasions set world best times for the marathon. >> athletics

Wajda, Andrzej [**viy**da] (1926–) Film director, born in Suwałki, Poland. He is best known outside Poland for *Czlowiek z marmary* (1977, Man of Marble), dealing with the Stalinist era, and *Czlowiek z zelaza* (1981, Man of Iron). >> Solidarity

Wakefield 53°42N 1°29W, pop (1995e) 76 800. Administrative centre of West Yorkshire, N England; on the R Calder; a woollen centre since the 16th-c; railway; site of Battle of Wakefield (1460) in Wars of the Roses. >> Yorkshire, West

Wakefield settlements Settlements of British migrants organized according to Edward Gibbon Wakefield's (1796–1862) ideas of 'systematic colonization'. The aim was to maintain traditional standards of order and refinement by transplanting a cross-section of English society, and restricting land ownership to the wealthy. The settlements were Adelaide, in Australia; and Wellington, Wanganui, New Plymouth, Nelson, Otago, and Canterbury in New Zealand.

Wake Islands 19°18N 166°36E; pop (1995e) 200; area 10 sq km/4 sq mi. Horseshoe-shaped coral atoll enclosing three islands in C Pacific Ocean; annexed by USA, 1898; seaplane base opened, 1935; under control of US Air Force since 1972. >> Pacific Ocean

Walachia >> **Moldavia and Wallachia**

Walburga, Walpurga, or **Walpurgis, St** >> **Walpurga**

Walcott, Derek [**wol**kot] (1930–) Poet and playwright, born in St Lucia. He founded the Trinidad Theatre Workshop in 1959, and his *Collected Poems* was published in 1986. He was awarded the Nobel Prize for Literature in 1992.

Waldenses or **Waldensians** A small Christian community originating in a reform movement initiated by Peter Waldo at Lyon, France, in the 12th-c. They rejected the authority of the pope, prayers for the dead, and veneration of the saints. After the Reformation, as Protestants, they continued mainly in N Italy. >> Reformation

Waldheim, Kurt [**valt**hiym] (1918–) Austrian statesman and president (1986–), born near Vienna. He was Austrian representative at the United Nations (1964–8, 1970–1), foreign minister (1968–70), and UN secretary-general (1972–81). His presidential candidature was controversial, because of claims that he had lied about his wartime activities, and been involved in anti-Jewish and other atrocities, but he denied the allegations. >> Austria [i]; United Nations

Wales, Welsh **Cymru** [kuhm**ree**] pop (1995e) 2 916 000; area 20 761 sq km/8014 sq mi. Principality on the W coast of the UK, divided into 22 unitary authorities (from 1996); includes the island of Anglesey; nearly 20% of the population speak Welsh, mainly in the N; capital, Cardiff; rises to 1085 m/3560 ft at Snowdon (NW); also, Cambrian Mts (C), Brecon Beacons (S); industrialized S valleys and coastal plain, based on local coal; tourism in N and NW, with seaside resorts and mountains; ferries to Ireland at Holyhead, Fishguard; important source of water for England; Royal Mint at Llantrisant; Rhodri Mawr united Wales against Saxons, Norse, and Danes, 9th-c; Edward I of England established authority over Wales, building several castles, 12th–13th-c; Edward I's son created first Prince of Wales (1301); 14th-c revolt under Owen Glendower; politically united with England at Act of Union, 1536; centre of Nonconformist religion since 18th-c; University of Wales, 1893, with constituent colleges; political nationalist movement (Plaid Cymru), returned first MP in 1966; Welsh television channel; 1979 referendum opposed devolution; 1997 referendum for Welsh Assembly in 2000 successful; national day, 1 March (St David's Day). >> Cardiff; Glendower, Owen; Nonconformists; Plaid Cymru; Snowdon; Welsh; RR998

Wałesa, Lech [va**wen**sa] (1943–) Polish trade unionist and president (1990–5), born in Popowo, Poland. A former Gdańsk shipyard worker, he became leader of the independent trade union, Solidarity, which challenged the Polish government's policies. He was detained by the authorities in 1981, but released in 1982, and awarded the Nobel Peace Prize in 1983. He continued to be a prominent figure in Polish politics, was much involved in the negotiations which led to Solidarity being involved in government in 1989, and was elected president the following year but defeated by Alexander Kwasniewski in 1995. >> Poland ℹ; Solidarity

Walker, Alice (Malsenior) (1944–) Novelist and poet, born in Eatonville, GA. She is best known for her novels, notably *The Color Purple* (1982, Pulitzer), later made into a successful film. She has also written volumes of short stories and essays. >> Goldberg

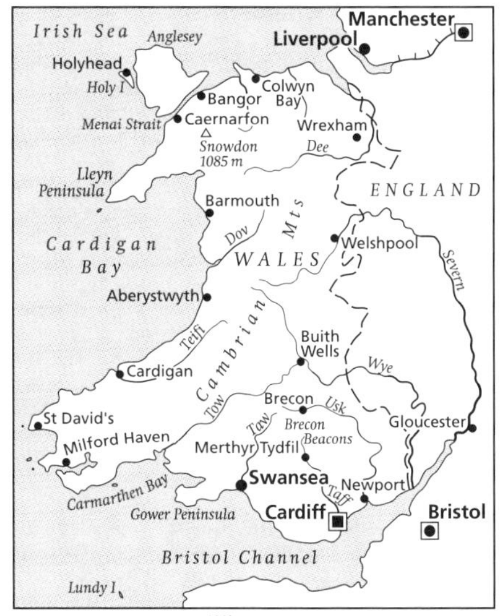

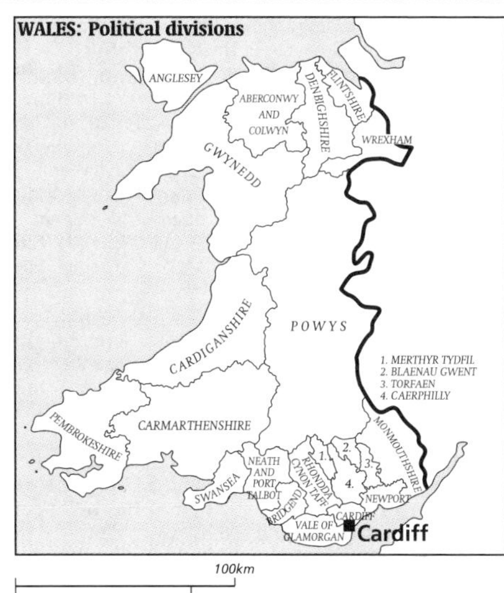

Walker, John E (1941–) Chemist, born in Halifax, West Yorkshire. He studied at Oxford, then worked at the Molecular Biology Laboratory in Cambridge. He shared the 1997 Nobel Prize for Chemistry for his contribution towards the elucidation of the enzymatic mechanism underlying the synthesis of adenosine triphosphate.

walking Either a leisurely pursuit or a competitive sport. As a sport, both road and track walking are popular. The rules governing the use of the feet are strict: one foot must be touching the ground at all times, and the lead leg must be straight as it passes under the torso. It has been an Olympic event since 1956, over distances of 20 km (12.4 mi) and 50 km (31 mi). >> RR1064

wallaby >> **kangaroo**

Wallace, Alfred Russel (1823–1913) Naturalist, born in Usk, Monmouthshire. He contributed greatly to the scientific foundations of zoogeography, including his proposal for the evolutionary distinction between the fauna of Australia and Asia ('Wallace's line'). >> Darwin, Charles; zoogeography

Wallace, (Richard Horatio) Edgar (1875–1932) Writer, born in London. He wrote over 170 novels and plays, and is best remembered for his crime novels, such as *The Clue of the Twisted Candle*.

Wallace, Lew(is) (1827–1905) Writer and soldier, born in Brookville, IN. He was author of the successful religious novel *Ben Hur* (1880), which has twice formed the subject of a spectacular film (1927, 1959).

Wallace, Sir William (c.1270–1305) Scottish knight and champion of the independence of Scotland, probably born in Elderslie, Renfrewshire. He routed the English army at Stirling (1297), and took control of the government of Scotland as 'Guardian', but was defeated by Edward I at Falkirk (1298), and executed in London. >> Edward I

Wallachia [wo**lay**kia] >> **Moldavia and Wallachia**

Wallenstein or **Waldstein, Albrecht (Wenzel Eusebius), Herzog von** (Duke of) [**wol**enstiyn], Ger [**val**enshtiyn] (1583–1634) Bohemian general, born in Heřmanice, Czech Republic. During the Thirty Years' War he became commander of the Imperial armies and won a series of victories (1625–9), but was defeated by Gustavus Adolphus at Lützen (1632). His intrigues led to an Imperial proclamation of treason, resulting in his assassination. >> Gustavus II; Thirty Years' War

Waller, Edmund (1606–87) Poet, born in Coleshill, Buckinghamshire. In 1643 he plunged into a conspiracy (**Waller's plot**) against parliament, was arrested, and banished, but returned to England in 1651. His collected poems were published in 1645. >> English Civil War

Waller, Fats, popular name of **Thomas Wright Waller** (1904–43) Jazz pianist, organist, singer, and songwriter, born in New York City. Among his many hits are 'Ain't Misbehavin' (1929) and 'Keepin' Out of Mischief Now' (1932).

walleye Large freshwater fish (*Stizostedion vitreum*) related to the zander, found in rivers and lakes of E North America; length up to 90 cm/3 ft. (Family: Percidae.) >> zander

wallflower A perennial reaching 20–60 cm/8–24 in (*Cheiranthus cheiri*), native to the E Mediterranean; flowers yellow to orange-red, fragrant. (Family: Cruciferae.)

Wallis, Sir Barnes (Neville) (1887–1979) Aeronautical engineer and inventor, born in Ripley, Derbyshire. His many successes include the design of the Wellington bomber, and the 'bouncing bombs' which destroyed the Mohne and Eder dams. In the 1950s he designed the first swing-wing aircraft. >> aircraft ℹ

Wallis, John (1616–1703) Mathematician, born in Ashford, Kent. His *Arithmetica infinitorum* (1655, The Arithmetic of Infinitesimals) anticipated calculus, and he also wrote on proportion, mechanics, grammar, logic, theology, and the teaching of the deaf. >> calculus

Wallis and Futuna Islands, official name **Territory of the Wallis and Futuna Islands** pop (1995e) 14 500; area 274 sq km/106 sq mi. Island group in the SC Pacific Ocean, NE of Fiji; a French overseas territory comprising the Wallis Is and the Hooru Is, 230 km/140 mi apart; capital, Matu Utu on Uvéa; chief ethnic group, Polynesian; chief religion, Roman Catholicism; unit of currency, the franc; Wallis Is (area 159 sq km/61 sq mi) include Uvéa, rising to 145 m/476 ft at Mt Lulu; Hooru Is (115 sq km/44 sq mi) include Futuna and Alofi, mountainous and volcanic; warm and damp climate; French protectorate, 1842; overseas territory of France, 1961; governed by an administrator, assisted by a Territorial Assembly. >> France ℹ; Pacific Ocean

Wallonia French-speaking region of S Belgium; pop (1995e) 3 230 000. Walloons (36% of Belgian population). >> Belgium ℹ; Fleming and Walloon

Walloon >> **Fleming and Walloon**

Wall Street A street in Manhattan, New York City, where the New York Stock Exchange is located. The road follows what once was the walled N boundary of the original Dutch colony. >> New York City

walnut A deciduous, spreading tree (*Juglans regia*,) growing to 30 m/100 ft, native to the Balkans; fruit 4–5 cm/$1\frac{1}{2}$–2 in, smooth, green. The wrinkled woody seed is the familiar walnut. The timber is used commercially, especially for furniture. (Family: Juglandaceae.) >> nut

Walpole, Horace (or **Horatio**), **4th Earl of Orford** (1717–97) Writer, born in London, the fourth son of Sir Robert Walpole. He produced a number of literary collections and a Gothic novel, *The Castle of Otranto* (1764). >> Gothic novel; Walpole, Robert

Walpole, Sir Hugh (Seymour) (1884–1941) Writer, born in Auckland, New Zealand. His many novels were very popular during his lifetime, and include *The Secret City* (1919), *The Cathedral* (1922), and the four-volume family saga, *The Herries Chronicle* (1930–3).

Walpole, Sir Robert, 1st Earl of Orford (1676–1745) English statesman and leading minister (1721–42) of George I and George II, born in Houghton, Norfolk. Sent to the Tower for alleged corruption during the Tory government (1712), he was recalled by George I, and made a privy councillor and (1715) Chancellor of the Exchequer. He was Chancellor again in 1721 and widely recognized as 'prime minister'. Regarded as indispensable by both George I and George II, his period in office is widely held to have increased the influence of the House of Commons in the Constitution. >> George I / II (of Great Britain)

walrus A marine mammal (*Odobenus rosmarus*) of family Odobenidae; resembles a large sea-lion with a broad bristly snout; canine teeth enormous, forming tusks; skin with little hair; inhabits coastal Arctic waters. >> sea-lion

Walsingham, Sir Francis [**wol**singam] (c.1530–90) English statesman, secretary of state to Elizabeth I (1573–90), born in Chislehurst, Kent. A strong opponent of the Catholics, he developed a complex system of espionage at home and abroad, enabling him to reveal the plots of Throckmorton and Babington against the Queen. >> Babington; Elizabeth I

Walter, Bruno [**val**ter], originally **Bruno Walter Schlesinger** (1876–1962) Conductor, born in Berlin. He directed the Munich Opera (1913–22) and the Berlin Opera (1925–9), conducted at Leipzig (1929–33), then settled in the USA, where he conducted the New York Philharmonic and other orchestras.

Walter, Hubert (c.1140–1205) English clergyman and statesman, who accompanied Richard I on the Third Crusade (1190–3). He was appointed Archbishop of Canterbury in 1193, and justiciar of England, responsible for all the business of government until his resignation in 1198. On John's accession (1199), he became chancellor. >> Crusades ℹ; John; Richard I

Walter, John (1739–1812) Printer and newspaper publisher, born in London. In 1785 he founded *The Daily Universal Register* newspaper, which in 1788 was renamed *The Times*.

Walther von der Vogelweide [**val**ter fon der **foh**glviyduh] (c.1170–1230) German lyric poet. In 1204 he outshone his rivals in the great contest at the Wartburg.

Walton, Izaak (1593–1683) Writer, born in Stafford, Staffordshire. Best known for his treatise on fishing and country life, *The Compleat Angler* (1653), he also wrote several biographies.

Walton, Sir William (Turner) (1902–83) Composer, born in Oldham, Lancashire. He became known through his instrumental setting of poems by Edith Sitwell, *Façade* (1923). His works include two symphonies, concertos for violin, viola, and cello, the biblical cantata *Belshazzar's Feast* (1931), and the opera *Troilus and Cressida* (1954). >> Sitwell, Edith

waltz A dance in triple time which became the most popular ballroom dance in 19th-c Europe – despite the initial shock caused by the requirement that the man should grasp his female partner at the waist. Austrian composer Joseph Lanner (1801–43) and the Strauss family established the style in Vienna. >> Strauss, Johann (the Elder)

Walvis Bay [**wol**vis], Afrikaans **Walvisbaai** 22°59S 14°31E, pop (1995e) 32 700. Seaport in WC Namibia; Walvis Bay enclave (area 1124 sq km/434 sq mi) formerly administered by South Africa as part of Cape Province; annexed by the Dutch, 1792; taken by Britain, 1878; incorporated into Cape Colony, 1884; a South African enclave after Namibian independence; transferred to Namibia, 1994; airfield; railway terminus; handles most of Namibia's trade. >> Namibia ℹ; South Africa ℹ

wampum [**wom**puhm] Beads used as a form of exchange, mnemonic devices, and guarantees of promises by certain Iroquois-speaking North American Indian groups. They were made of bits of seashells cut, drilled, and strung into belts or strands. >> Iroquois

wandering Jew A species of tradescantia (*Tradescantia fluminensis*) with variegated leaves. (Family: Commelinaceae.) >> tradescantia

Wandering Jew A character in Christian legend who taunted Christ as he carried his cross, and was condemned to wander the Earth until the end of the world or until Christ's second coming. >> Jesus Christ

wandering sailor A species of tradescantia (*Tradescantia blossfeldiana*), with leaves maroon on undersides. (Family: Commelinaceae.) >> tradescantia

Wanganui, River [wanga**noo**ee] River in W North Island, New Zealand; rises NW of L Taupo; enters the Tasman Sea; length 290 km/180 mi; town of Wanganui near the mouth, pop (1995e) 43 700. >> New Zealand

Wankel engine [**vang**kl] A particular form of internal combustion engine whose piston rotates about a horizontal axis in a specially shaped combustion chamber, rather than oscillating within a cylinder, as in a conventional internal combustion engine. It is named after its designer, German engineer Felix Wankel (1902–88). >> internal combustion engine

wapiti [**wop**itee] >> **red deer**

Warbeck, Perkin (c.1474–99) Pretender to the English throne, born in Tournai, Belgium. In 1492 he professed to be Richard, Duke of York, the younger of Edward's two sons who were murdered in the Tower. He made an ineffectual landing in Kent (1495), then landed in Cornwall (1497), but was captured and executed. >> Edward IV

warble fly A small, robust fly; larvae live as parasites under the skin of mammals, causing swellings (*warbles*). (Order: Diptera. Family: Oestridae, c.60 species.) >> fly; larva

warbler A songbird of the families Sylviidae (**Old World warblers**, 350 species), Parulidae (**American warblers** or **wood warblers**, 114 species), Acanthizidae (**Australian warblers**, 65 species), or Maluridae (**Australian wren-warblers**, 26 species). >> tailorbird; thornbill; wren

Ward, Artemus >> **Browne, Charles Farrar**

Ward, Dame Barbara (Mary), Baroness Jackson of Lodsworth (1914–81) Journalist, economist, and conservationist, born in York, North Yorkshire. A prolific and popular writer on politics, economics, and ecology, her books included *Spaceship Earth* (1966) and *Only One Earth* (1972). >> ecology

wardship proceedings Proceedings whereby the custody of a person under the age of 18 living in England and Wales, or an English subject living outside the jurisdiction of the English courts, is transferred to the Family Division of the High Court. Being made a **ward of court** results in all major decisions in a child's life being subject to the approval of the court. The wardship may be ended by a court order or on the child becoming 18. Wardship proceedings do not exist in all jurisdictions. >> custody

warfarin >> **anticoagulants**

Warhol, Andy [**waw(r)**hohl], originally **Andrew Warhola** (1927–87) Artist and film-maker, born in Pittsburgh, PA. He was a pioneer in 1961 of Pop Art, with his brightly-coloured exact reproductions of familiar everyday objects such as the famous soup-can label. His films include the 3-hour silent observation of a sleeping man, *Sleep* (1963). In the 1960s he also turned to music, founding a rock revue called The Exploding Plastic Inevitable (1966–7). The Andy Warhol Museum opened in Pittsburgh in 1994. >> Pop Art

warlords Chinese provincial military rulers who engaged in a bitter power struggle and civil war after the death of Yuan Shikai in 1916. They were eventually subdued by Jiang Jieshi in 1927. >> Yuan Shikai

Warlpiri The dominant language of the central desert of Australia. Warlpiri country was colonized by cattle stations (ranches) during the early 20th-c, and some cattle stations are now Aboriginal-owned. >> Aborigines

Warner, Jack, originally **Jack Leonard Eichelbaum** (1892–1978) Film producer, born in London, Ontario, Canada. He was the youngest of the four **Warner Brothers** (the others being **Harry**, **Albert**, and **Sam**) who set up studios in 1923. Warners were the first to introduce sound into their films, and had a major success with *The Jazz Singer* (1927). Jack's later productions included *My Fair Lady* (1964) and *Camelot* (1967).

Warnock (of Weeke), (Helen) Mary Warnock, Baroness, *née* **Wilson** (1924–) British philosopher and educationist. A fellow and tutor in philosophy at St Hugh's College, Oxford (1949–66, 1976–84), she has chaired several important committees of inquiry into such topics as special education (1974–8), animal experiments (1979–85), higher education (1984), teaching quality (1990), and bioethics (1992–4).

War of 1812 (1812–14) A war between Britain and the USA, declared by the latter on the basis of British conduct towards neutral US shipping during the Napoleonic Wars. It brought the British capture of Washington, DC, and the bombardment of Baltimore. US victories in several sea duels and at New Orleans (fought after the Treaty of Ghent had restored peace) became central elements in the US military self-image.

War of Independence, US >> **American Revolution**

War of the Pacific A war fought by Chile with Peru and Bolivia (in alliance since 1873) and arising out of Chilean grievances in the Atacama desert, then Bolivian-held. Chile made large territorial gains. >> Bolivia [i]; Chile [i]; Peru [i]

warranty >> **condition**

Warren, Earl (1891–1974) US Republican politician and judge, born in Los Angeles, CA. He became chief justice in 1954, and was responsible for the epochal decision in *Brown* v. *Board of Education of Topeka, KS* (1954), outlawing school segregation. He was chairman of the federal commission that investigated the assassination of President Kennedy. >> civil rights; Kennedy, John F

Warren, Robert Penn (1905–89) Writer, born in Guthrie, KY. He established an international reputation with his novel, *All the King's Men* (1943, Pulitzer; filmed 1949).

Warrington 53°24N 2°37W, pop (1995e) 87 600. Town in Cheshire, NWC England; on the R Mersey; designated a 'new town' in 1968; unitary authority from 1998; railway. >> Cheshire

Warsaw, Polish **Warszawa** 52°15N 21°00E, pop (1995e) 1 665 000. River-port capital of Poland, on R Vistula; city centre is a world heritage site; established, 13th-c; capital of the Duchy of Mazovia, 1413; capital of Poland, 1596; occupied by Germany in both World Wars; Jewish ghetto established in 1940, with uprising and death of most residents in 1943; largely destroyed in World War 2; post-war reconstruction of the mediaeval old town followed the pre-war street pattern; airport; railway; Polish Academy of Sciences; two universities (1818, 1945); cathedral (14th-c, restored), royal castle. >> Poland [i]

Warsaw Pact The countries which signed the East European Mutual Assistance Treaty in Warsaw in 1955: Albania, Bulgaria, Czechoslovakia, East Germany, Hungary, Poland, Romania, and the USSR. Albania withdrew in 1968. The pact established a unified military command for the armed forces of all the signatories. It was a communist response, in part, to the formation of NATO by the West, and was formally dissolved in 1991. >> NATO

warships Vessels designed for use in wartime. Navies of the world still employ a vast range of warships, but the use of highly sophisticated guided-missile weaponry has

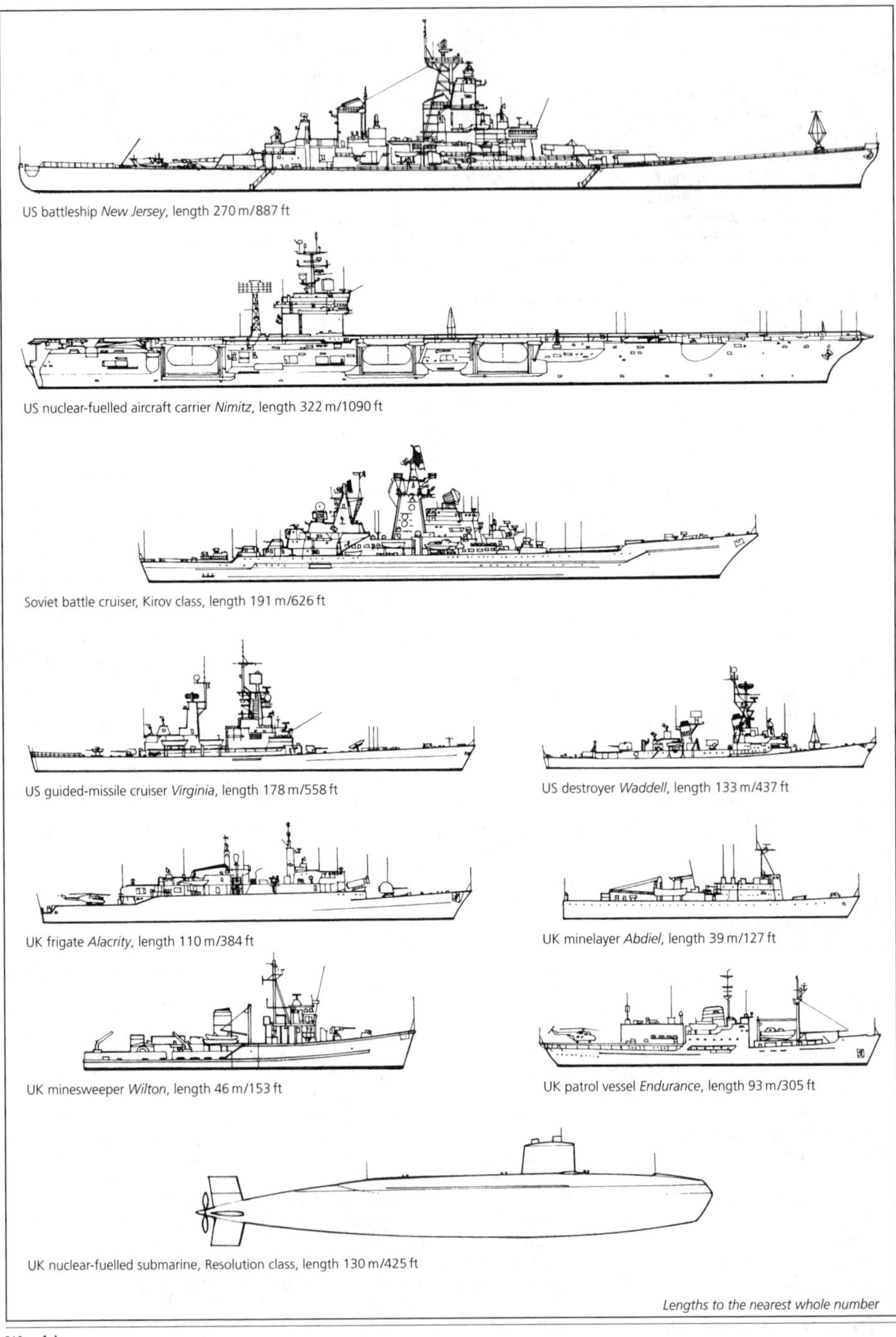
US battleship *New Jersey*, length 270 m/887 ft

US nuclear-fuelled aircraft carrier *Nimitz*, length 322 m/1090 ft

Soviet battle cruiser, Kirov class, length 191 m/626 ft

US guided-missile cruiser *Virginia*, length 178 m/558 ft

US destroyer *Waddell*, length 133 m/437 ft

UK frigate *Alacrity*, length 110 m/384 ft

UK minelayer *Abdiel*, length 39 m/127 ft

UK minesweeper *Wilton*, length 46 m/153 ft

UK patrol vessel *Endurance*, length 93 m/305 ft

UK nuclear-fuelled submarine, Resolution class, length 130 m/425 ft

Lengths to the nearest whole number

Warships

made their roles less easily defined than those of the World War 2 period. >> aircraft carrier; battleship; corvette; cruiser; destroyer; frigate; ironclad; Jane; minesweeper; ship ①; submarine

wart A small benign overgrowth in the outer layer of the skin, arising from a virus infection; also known as a **verruca**. It is common in children, and unpredictable in occurrence. >> skin ①; virus

wart disease A disease (*Synchytrium endobioticum*) causing excessive cell division in the tubers of potatoes, resulting in the growth of soft warty tissues which destroy their economic value. All new European varieties are now officially tested, and only those showing immunity are released for cultivation. (Order: Chytridiales.) >> immunity; potato; tuber

warthog A wild pig native to Africa S of the Sahara (*Phacochoerus aethiopicus*); sparse covering of shaggy hair; face broad, flattened, with four wart-like knobs of thickened skin; large curved tusks. >> pig

Warwick [**wo**rik] 52°17N 1°34W, pop (1995e) 23 100. County town of Warwickshire, C England; on the R Avon; founded in 914; railway; university (1965); 14th-c castle. >> Warwickshire

Warwick, Richard Neville, Earl [**wo**rik], also known as **Warwick the Kingmaker** (1428–71) English soldier and politician, who exercised great power during the first phase of the Wars of the Roses. He championed the Yorkist cause, captured Henry VI at Northampton, and had his cousin, Edward of York, proclaimed king as Edward IV (1461). When Edward tried to assert his independence, Warwick joined the Lancastrians, and restored Henry VI to the throne (1470). He was killed by Edward IV at the Battle of Barnet. >> Edward IV; Henry VI; Roses, Wars of the

Warwickshire [**wo**riksheer] pop (1995e) 501 000; area 1981 sq km/765 sq mi. County of C England; county town, Warwick; castles at Kenilworth and Warwick; Shakespeare industry at Stratford. >> England ℹ; Shakespeare ℹ; Warwick

Wasa [**vah**sa] A four-masted Swedish warship of 1628 which foundered on her maiden voyage. She was salvaged in 1961 and preserved in dry dock in Stockholm. >> *Mary Rose*

Wash, The Shallow inlet of the North Sea on E coast of England; between Norfolk (S) and Lincolnshire (W and N). >> Fens, the

Washington (DC, city) 38°54N 77°02W, pop (1995e) 694 000. Capital of the USA, co-extensive with the District of Columbia; on the E bank of the Potomac R; the US legislative, administrative, and judicial centre: the Federal Government provides most of the city's employment; occupied by the Federal Government, 1800; sacked and burned by the British, 1814; two airports; railway; five universities; professional teams, Bullets (basketball), Capitals (ice hockey), Redskins (football). >> Capitol; Gallaudet College; Library of Congress; Lincoln Memorial; National Gallery of Art; Smithsonian Institution; Washington Monument; White House

Washington (state) pop (1995e) 5 568 000; area 176 473 sq km/68 139 sq mi. State in NW USA; the 'Evergreen State'; first settled in the late 18th-c, part of Oregon Territory; Britain and the USA quarrelled over the region until the international boundary was fixed by treaty to lie along the 49th parallel, 1846; became a territory, 1853; joined the Union as the 42nd state, 1889; Seattle an important outfitting point during the Alaskan gold rush, 1897–9; Olympic Mts in the NW; Puget Sound to the E, extending c.160 km/ 100 mi inland, with numerous bays and islands; Cascade Range runs N–S through the middle of the state; mountainous and forested in the W; dry and arid in the E; highest point, Mt Rainier (4395 m/14 419 ft); Mt St Helens volcano in the S (erupted May 1980); North Cascades National Park; capital, Olympia; apples (nation's largest crop); wide range of minerals; major tourist area; substantial Indian population and several reservations. >> Olympia (USA); St Helens, Mount; Seattle; United States of America ℹ; RR994

Washington, Booker T(aliaferro) (1856–1915) Black leader and educationist, born a slave in Franklin Co, VA. In 1881 he was appointed principal of the newly-opened Tuskegee Institute, Alabama, and built it up into a major centre of black education. He was the foremost black leader in late 19th-c USA, but his policies were repudiated by the 20th-c civil rights movement. >> civil rights; Tuskegee Institute

Washington, George (1732–99) Commander of American forces and first president of the USA, born in Bridges Creek, VA. He represented Virginia in the first (1774) and second (1775) Continental Congresses, and was given command of the American forces, where he displayed great powers as a strategist and leader. He inflicted notable defeats on the enemy at Trenton and Princeton (1777), then suffered defeats at the Brandywine and Germantown, but held his army together through the winter of 1777–8 at Valley Forge, and forced the surrender of Cornwallis at Yorktown in 1781. In 1787 he became president, remaining neutral while political parties were formed, but eventually joining the Federalist Party. >> American Revolution; Constitutional Convention; Continental Congress; Cornwallis; Mount Vernon

Washington Monument A marble column in honour of George Washington, designed by Robert Mills (1781–1855) and erected (1848–84) in Washington, DC. The tower is 169 m/555 ft high. >> Washington, George

wasp The common name of several different types of solitary and social insects of the order Hymenoptera. Social wasps (mainly in the family Vespidae) are usually banded black and yellow; females inflict painful stings. >> gall wasp; hornet; ichneumon (insect)

Wasserman, August Paul von [**va**serman] (1866–1925) Bacteriologist, born in Bamberg, Germany. He discovered a blood-serum test for syphilis in 1906 (the **Wasserman reaction**). >> syphilis

waste disposal The disposal of waste from domestic, industrial, and agricultural sources; a major environmental concern. Methods commonly used include burial in landfill sites and at sea, incineration (sometimes for power generation), and the production of refuse-derived fuel pellets which can be used as an energy source. >> biogas; hazardous substances; pollution; radioactive waste; recycling

watch A small timepiece for wear or in the pocket. Watches have been made ever since the invention of the mainspring (c.1500) made portable clocks possible. In recent times electrical movements have been much used, a small battery replacing the mainspring as a source of energy. The traditional analogue display (by rotation of hands) is often replaced by a digital display using a liquid crystal display (LCD) face. >> clock ℹ; liquid crystals

water H_2O. The commonest molecular compound on Earth; a liquid, freezing to ice at 0°C and boiling to steam at 100°C. It covers about 70% of the Earth's surface, and dissolves almost everything to some extent. However, it is a poor solvent for substances which are found in solution

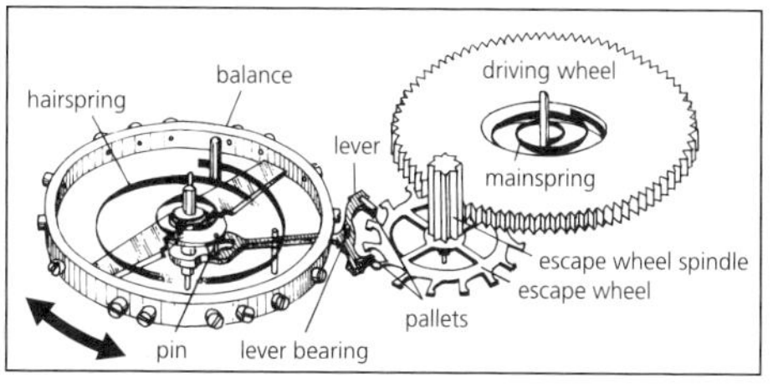

Watch – Drive mechanism (lever escapement)

as molecules (eg oxygen, methane). It is essential to life, and occurs in all living organisms. Unusually, the solid is less dense than the liquid; this results in ice floating, and accounts for the destructiveness of continued freezing and thawing. Water containing substantial concentrations of calcium and magnesium ions is called 'hard', and is 'softened' by replacing these ions with sodium or potassium, which do not form insoluble products with soaps. >> hydrate; ice

water avens >> **avens**

water bear A microscopic animal possibly related to the arthropods; body short, bearing four pairs of stumpy legs usually armed with claws; c.400 species, found in surface water-films on mosses, lichens, algae, plant litter, and soil. (Phylum: Tardigrada.) >> arthropod

water beetle A dark, shiny beetle up to 40 mm/1½ in long; silvery in appearance underwater; abundant in the tropics. (Order: Coleoptera. Family: Hydrophilidae, c.2000 species.) >> beetle

water birth A technique in which a mother gives birth to her baby while seated in a pool of warm water. There are well documented reductions in the requirement for analgesia, duration of labour, incidence of tears in the vagina, need for episiotomy, and incidence of fetal distress. Some psychotherapists also believe that the birth of a baby into a warm and quiet environment avoids the trauma of delivery, and thus reduces the incidence of psychological problems in later life. >> labour; natural childbirth; pregnancy ℹ

water boatman A predatory aquatic bug that swims upside-down in water, using its paddle-like hindlegs; distributed worldwide. (Order: Heteroptera. Family: Notonectidae, c.200 species.) >> bug (entomology)

water buffalo A SE Asian member of the cattle family; lives near water; closely related to the anoa; two species: *Bubalis bubalis* (**Asian water buffalo**, **carabao**, or **arni** – widely domesticated), and *Bubalis mindorensis* (**tamaraw** or **tamarau**). >> anoa; Bovidae

water chestnut A free-floating aquatic annual (*Trapa natans*), native to warm parts of Europe, Asia, and Africa; flowers white, 4-petalled; fruits woody, triangular with 2–4 spiny horns. Fast-growing, it forms thick, floating mats which can block waterways. The fruit, rich in starch and fat, forms a staple food in much of Asia. (Family: Trapaceae.) >> sedge

watercolour Any form of painting in which the pigment is mixed with a water-soluble medium such as gum arabic. Watercolour was used in ancient Egypt and China, and mediaeval manuscripts were illuminated with water-based paint. The great masters of watercolour were all English. >> Cotman; Girtin; Turner, J M W

watercress A semi-aquatic perennial (*Nasturtium officinale*), native to Europe and Asia; flowers small, white, cross-shaped. It has been cultivated since the 19th-c as a salad plant rich in vitamin C. Its peppery tasting leaves stay green in the autumn. (Family: Cruciferae.) >> cress; vitamins ℹ

water-crowfoot An aquatic species of buttercup, growing in still or slow-moving water. The predominantly white flowers project above the water. (Genus: *Ranunculus* subgenus *Batrachium*, c.30 species. Family: Ranunculaceae.) >> buttercup

water deer A deer native to China and Korea (*Hydropotes inermis*), and introduced in UK and France; the only true deer without antlers; also known as **Chinese water deer**. >> antlers ℹ; deer

water flea A small aquatic crustacean; characterized by a jerky swimming motion using large antennae for propulsion; body short; c.450 species, most in fresh water. (Class: Branchiopoda. Order: Cladocera.) >> crustacean

Waterford, Ir **Phort Láirge** pop (1995e) 90 000; area 1839 sq km/710 sq mi. County in Munster province, S Ireland; Knockmealdown Mts in the W; popular resorts on S coast; capital, Waterford, pop (1995e) 41 500; on R Suir; cathedral (1793), priory (1226); known for its glassware. >> Ireland (republic) ℹ

waterfowl Aquatic birds, especially ducks, geese, and swans; also known as **wildfowl**. The name *waterfowl* is often used for populations kept in captivity; *wildfowl* for wild birds, especially those hunted. >> duck; swan

water gas A gas produced by passing steam over hot coke to give hydrogen and carbon monoxide. This process yields a gas of high energy content. >> coke; gas 2 ℹ

Watergate (1972–4) A political scandal that led to the first resignation of a president in US history (Richard Nixon, in office 1968–74). The actual 'Watergate' is a hotel and office complex in Washington, DC, where the Democratic Party had its headquarters. During the presidential campaign of 1972, a team of burglars was caught inside Democratic headquarters, and their connections were traced to the White House. Investigations revealed that high officials very close to President Nixon were implicated, and that Nixon himself was aware of illegal measures to cover up that implication. A number of officials were eventually imprisoned. Nixon himself left office when it became clear that he was likely to be impeached. >> Bernstein, Carl; Irangate; Nixon, Richard M

water glass A concentrated aqueous solution of sodium silicate (Na_2SiO_3), which sets to a hard, transparent layer, and is used as a waterproofing agent and a preservative. >> silica; sodium

Waterhouse, Alfred (1830–1905) Architect, born in Liverpool, Merseyside. He built the romanesque Natural History Museum in London (1873–81), and from his great use of red brick came the name 'red-brick university'.

water hyacinth A free-floating perennial aquatic plant (*Eichhornia speciosa*), native to South America; flowers funnel-shaped, violet. It grows and spreads rapidly, and is probably the world's most troublesome aquatic weed. (Family: Pontederiaceae.)

waterlily An aquatic perennial found in still or very slow-moving water; large, floating, or slightly emergent leaves and flowers; flowers bowl-shaped with numerous petals and stamens. (Family: Nymphaeaceae.)

Waterloo, Battle of (18 Jun 1815) The final defeat of Napoleon, ending the French Wars and the emperor's last bid for power in the Hundred Days. It was a hard-fought battle, in which Blücher's Prussian force arrived at the climax to support Wellington's mixed Allied force. >> Blücher; Hundred Days; Napoleon I; Wellington, Duke of

Waterloo Cup >> **bowls; coursing**

water-melon A trailing vine with (*Citrullus lanatus*) tendrils, native to the Mediterranean, Africa, and tropical Asia; flowers yellow, funnel-shaped; fruit up to 60 cm/2 ft long, ovoid, rind dark green, leathery; black seeds embedded in red flesh. It is cultivated for fruit, especially in the USA. (Family: Cucurbitaceae.) >> melon

water milfoil A submerged aquatic perennial, found almost everywhere; leaves feathery; flowers small, in slender spikes above water, reddish or yellowish. (Genus: *Myriophyllum*, 45 species. Family: Halagoraceae.)

water polo Developed in Britain in 1869, and played by teams of seven-a-side in a swimming pool. The object is to score goals by propelling the ball into the opposing team's goal at the end of the pool. >> football ℹ; polo; RR1064

water rat A term used generally for many unrelated rats which inhabit the edge of bodies of water. Some species have webbed hind feet and waterproof fur. >> muskrat; rat; water vole

water scorpion An aquatic bug that lives submerged, breathing through a tubular tail that reaches the surface; c.200 species, found in still or slow-moving waters. (Order: Heteroptera. Family: Nepidae.) >> bug (entomology)

water spider The only spider that lives permanently submerged; breathes by means of air film over body surface; bite venomous, causing vomiting and fever. (Order: Araneae. Family: Agelenidae.) >> crustacean; spider

water-spout The marine equivalent of a tornado; a rapidly rotating funnel of air which extends from the cloud base to the water surface, picking up water. >> tornado; whirlwind

water table The surface below which the ground is saturated with water. The position of the water table varies with the topography and amount of rainfall; where it intersects the surface, springs are formed. >> hydrology

water vole A vole of genus *Arvicola*; three species, from NW North America, from Europe, and Asia; also known as **bank vole**. >> vole

Watling Street >> **Roman roads** 🛈

Watson, James (Dewey) (1928–) Geneticist, born in Chicago, IL. He helped to discover the molecular structure of DNA, for which he shared the 1962 Nobel Prize for Physiology or Medicine. >> Crick; DNA 🛈

Watson, Tom, popular name of **Thomas (Sturges) Watson** (1949–) Golfer, born in Kansas City, MO. He has won the (British) Open five times (1975, 1977, 1980, 1982–3), the US Open (1982), and the Masters (1977, 1981). >> golf; Nicklaus

Watt, James (1736–1819) Inventor, born in Greenock, Inverclyde. He studied steam as a motive force, went into partnership with Matthew Boulton (1728–1809), and manufactured a new engine at Birmingham in 1774. Several other inventions followed, including the design of a steam locomotive (1784). The SI unit of power is named after him. >> Industrial Revolution; steam engine; watt

watt SI unit of power; symbol *W*; named after James Watt; the production of 1 joule of energy per second corresponds to a power of 1 watt; commonly used as **kilowatts** (*kW*, 10^3 W) or **megawatts** (*MW*, 10^6 W). >> kilowatt-hour; power; Watt

Watteau, (Jean) Antoine [**va**toh] (1684–1721) Rococo painter, born in Valenciennes, France. The mythological 'L'Embarquement pour l'île de Cythère' (Embarkation for the island of Cythera, 1717, Louvre) won him membership of the Academy. He is also known for his 'Fêtes galantes' (Scenes of Gallantry), quasi-pastoral idylls in court dress which became fashionable in high society. >> Rococo

wattle Any of a large group of mainly trees or shrubs, native to many tropical and subtropical areas, but notably Australia where (together with the eucalypts) they form the dominant tree vegetation; flowers mostly yellow, very small but numerous, in clusters. Many are useful timber trees, producing very hard tough wood. The bark and pods are employed for tanning. Some yield gum arabic. Commonly cultivated species include the **blue-leaved wattle** (*Acacia cyanophylla*) from W Australia, a small tree growing to 10 m/30 ft, and the **silver wattle** (*Acacia dealbata*) from SE Australia and Tasmania, a tree growing to 30 m/100 ft. >> gum arabic / tree; shrub

wattle and daub A framework of interlaced twigs and rods plastered with mud or clay. The walls of timber-framed houses were often made in this way, and when protected from the weather by good overhanging eaves, could last for hundreds of years.

wattmeter An instrument for measuring electric power. Many types are used, the most common being the **electro-dynamic wattmeter** which depends on the interaction of fields in two sets of coils. >> electricity; watt

Watts, George Frederick (1817–1904) Painter, born in London. He became known for his penetrating portraits of notabilities, 150 of which he presented to the National Portrait Gallery in 1904.

Watts Towers A group of sculptures incorporating metal, stone, cement, tiles, glass, and waste materials, in the Watts district of Los Angeles, CA. The towers were completed in 1954, having been constructed over a period of 35 years by Simon Rodin (1879–1965). >> Los Angeles

Waugh, Evelyn (Arthur St John) [waw] (1903–66) Writer, born in London. His social satirical novels include *Decline and Fall* (1928), *Vile Bodies* (1930), and *Scoop* (1938). He became a Catholic in 1930, and his later books display a more serious attitude, as seen in the religious theme of *Brideshead Revisited* (1945), and his war trilogy, beginning with *Men at Arms* (1952). His son **(Alexander) Auberon Waugh** (1939–) became a novelist and journalist, known for his critical reviews and essays.

wave (oceanography) In oceanography, a disturbance moving under or along the surface of the water. Most ocean surface waves are generated by the wind blowing over the surface of the sea, imparting energy to the water. They can be transmitted over thousands of miles of ocean, often losing little energy until they break upon a shore. >> bore; seiche; tidal wave; tide; tsunami; wind 🛈

wave (physics) >> **wave motion**

wavelength The distance between two successive crests of a wave along the direction of propagation; symbol λ, units m (metres). The wavelength of light is 390–780 nm; the wavelength of sound, 16 mm–16 m. >> wave motion 🛈

Wavell, Archibald Percival Wavell, 1st Earl [**way**vl] (1883–1950) British field marshal, born in Winchester, Hampshire. In 1939 he was given the Middle East Command, defeated the Italians in N Africa, but failed against Rommel, and in 1941 was transferred to India, where he became viceroy (1943). >> Allenby; Rommel; World War 2

wave motion A disturbance from equilibrium which propagates in time from one place to another. **Longitudinal waves** occur when the displacement is in the same direction as the wave propagation (eg sound waves). **Transverse waves** correspond to a displacement perpendicular to the direction of wave propagation (eg ripples on water). **Standing waves** (also called **stationary waves**) result from interference between waves travelling in opposite directions (eg on a guitar string). **Periodic waves** (ie waves produced by some regular repeating motion) are described by amplitude *A*, frequency *f* or period *T*, and wavelength λ (see illustration on p. 926); wave velocity $v = f\lambda$ m/s. **Sine waves** may be expressed as $y = A\sin 2\pi(ft - x/\lambda)$. Complicated periodic waves can be expressed as sums of sine waves using Fourier analysis. >> amplitude; frequency; interference; phase; polarization; quantum mechanics; wavelength

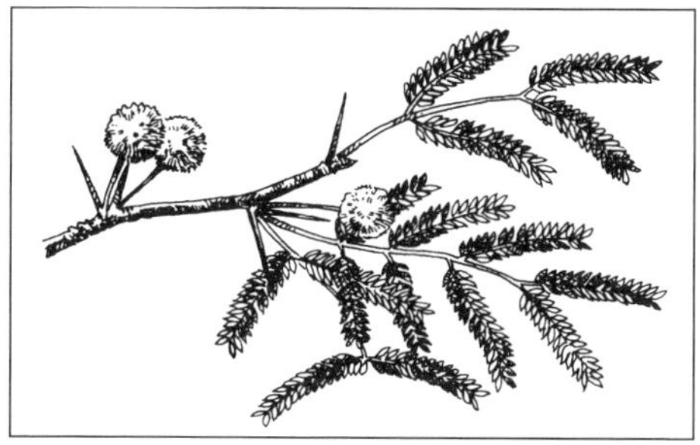

Wattle – Leaves, flower and thorn

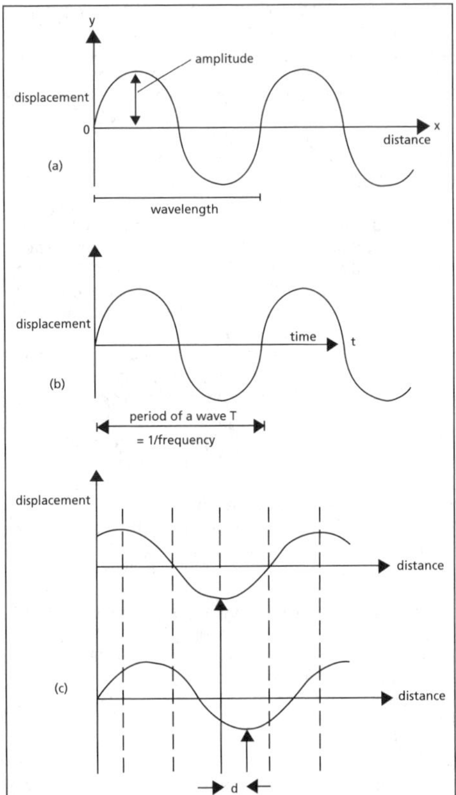

Wave – Sine wave at a fixed time, displaying amplitude and wavelength (a); sine wave at a fixed position, displaying period T (b); two sine waves out of phase, ie one leads the other, with a phase difference ϕ given by $\phi = 2\pi d/\lambda$ (c)

wax A substance of a firm but plastic solid consistency, with a low coefficient of friction, and water-repellant. **Mineral waxes**, notably **paraffin wax**, are hydrocarbons of high molecular weight with a microcrystalline structure. **Plant** and **animal waxes** are esters of fatty acids, which fulfil a mainly protective function (as **beeswax** in the honeycomb). Beeswax has a long history as a preferred material for candles and polishes, and as a medium for modelling. >> hydrocarbons; paraffin wax

waxbill A songbird of the weaver-finch family Estrildidae (17 species); native to Africa, Arabia, and S Asia to N Australia. >> finch; songbird; weaver-finch

wax flower >> **wax plant**

wax plant An evergreen climbing perennial (*Hoya carnosa*), reaching 6 m/20 ft or more, native to Australia; leaves elliptical, glossy and rather fleshy; flowers in drooping heads, fragrant, 5-petalled, waxy-white with red centre; also called **wax flower**. (Family: Asclepiadaceae.) >> climbing plant; stephanotis

waxwing A songbird of the N hemisphere; grey-brown with black tail; head with crest; some individuals with red, wax-like tips to some wing feathers. (Family: Bombicillidae, 3 species.) >> songbird

Wayland In Norse, German, and Old English legends, a clever inventor, also known as **Wayland the Smith**. Many heroes carry swords made by him; his 'Smithy' is a dolmen on the Berkshire Downs, UK.

Wayne, Anthony, known as **Mad Anthony** (1745–96) Revolutionary soldier, born in Easttown, PA. He commanded at Ticonderoga until 1777, when he joined Washington in New Jersey. He fought at Brandywine (1777), led the attack at Germantown, captured supplies for the army at Valley Forge, carried Stony Point, and saved Lafayette in Virginia (1781). >> American Revolution

Wayne, John, originally **Marion Michael Morrison**, nickname **the Duke** (1907–79) Film actor, born in Winterset, IA. He achieved stardom as the Ringo Kid in *Stagecoach* (1939), and went on to make over 80 films, typically starring as a tough but warm-hearted gunfighter or lawman. He was awarded an Oscar for his role in *True Grit* (1969).

weak interaction The feeble short-range force responsible for radioactive beta decay, characterized by the presence of a particle called the neutrino; also known as **weak nuclear force**. It is mediated by W and Z particles. >> beta decay; neutrino; particle physics

weak nuclear force >> **weak interaction**

Weald, The [weeld] Area in Kent, Surrey, and Sussex, SE England, between North and South Downs; fertile agricultural area. >> Downs

weasel A small carnivorous mammal with a long thin body, short legs, and small head; tail usually half length of body; brown with pale underparts (may be all white in winter). (Genus: *Mustela*, 9 species. Family: Mustelidae.) >> carnivore [i]; Mustelidae

weather The atmospheric processes operating at a location at a particular time: for example, day-to-day conditions of temperature, precipitation, atmospheric pressure, and wind; the scientific study of weather is *meteorology*. Weather differs from climate in that it is concerned with short-term meteorological events, whereas climate encompasses all the weather characteristics of a place, and is concerned with the long-term behaviour of atmospheric processes. >> climate; meteorology; weather satellite

weather balloon >> **radiosonde balloon**

weather satellite A satellite used to record global weather patterns. It contains several remote sensing instruments, and measurements are made of atmospheric energy fluxes, atmospheric and surface temperatures, cloud cover, and amounts of water vapour. >> meteorology; remote sensing; weather

weaver >> **weaverbird**

Weaver, Sigourney (1949–) Film actress, born in New York City. She became well known through her role as astronaut Ripley in the film *Aliens* (1979). Later films include *Ghostbusters* (1984), the three *Aliens* sequels, and *The Ice Storm* (1997).

weaverbird A finch-like songbird, also known as **weaver**. Many (not all) species weave nests suspended from branches. The group sometimes includes **weaver-finches**. >> finch; grosbeak; songbird; whydah

weaver-finch A finch-like bird, also known as the **estrildid finch** or (sometimes) the **waxbill**; native to the Old World tropics. (Family: Estrildidae, c.130 species.) >> finch; waxbill; whydah

weaving An ancient craft in which fabric is produced by interlacing *warp* (lengthwise) and *weft* (crosswise) threads on machines called *looms*. Hand looms are known from very early times. They developed little until the Industrial Revolution, when the flying shuttle was invented by John Kay, in association with Richard Arkwright, in 1733, followed later in the century by Cartwright's power loom (1785). >> Arkwright; Cartwright; spinning

Webb Social reformers, historians, and economists: **Sidney James Webb** (1859–1947) and **(Martha) Beatrice Webb**, *née* **Potter** (1858–1943), born in London and Standish,

Gloucestershire, respectively, and married in 1892. They began a joint life of service to Socialism and trade unionism, publishing their classic *History of Trade Unionism* (1894), *English Local Government* (9 vols, 1906–29), and other works. They also started the *New Statesman* (1913). >> Fabian Society; socialism

Webb, Karrie (1974–) Golfer, born in Ayr, Queensland, Australia. She won the women's Open title in the UK in 1995, the youngest ever winner, and won it again in 1997.

Webber, Andrew Lloyd >> **Lloyd Webber, Andrew**

Weber, Carl (Maria Friedrich) von [**vay**ber] (1786–1826) Composer and pianist, born in Eutin, Germany. He is known as the founder of German romantic opera, notably in *Der Freischütz* (1821, The Freeshooter), *Euryanthe* (1823), and *Oberon* (1826), and he also wrote several orchestral works, piano, chamber, and church music, and many songs.

Weber, Max [**vay**ber] (1864–1920) Economist, born in Erfurt, Germany. His best-known work is *Die protestantische Ethik und der Geist des Kapitalismus* (1904, The Protestant Ethic and the Spirit of Capitalism), which was a major influence on sociological theory.

weber [**vay**ber] SI unit of magnetic flux; symbol *Wb*; named after German scientist Wilhelm Weber (1804–91); defined as the amount of flux which, when allowed to decrease steadily to zero in 1 second, will produce 1 volt of electromotive force in the loop of wire through which the flux passes. >> magnetic flux

Webern, Anton (Friedrich Ernst von) [**vay**bern] (1883–1945) Composer, born in Vienna. He studied under Schoenberg, and became one of his first musical disciples, making wide use of 12-tone techniques. His works include a symphony, cantatas, chamber music, a concerto for nine instruments, and songs. >> Schoenberg; twelve-tone music

Webster, Daniel (1782–1852) US statesman, born in Salisbury, NH. He helped found the Whig Party, was twice secretary of state (1841–3, 1850–2), and was instrumental in arranging a political compromise over slavery between North and South in 1850. >> slavery

Webster, John (c.1580–c.1625) English playwright. He collaborated with several other writers, especially Dekker, but is best known for his two tragedies, *The White Devil* (1612) and *The Duchess of Malfi* (1623). >> Dekker

Webster, Noah (1758–1843) Lexicographer, born in Hartford, CT. He achieved fame with the first part (later known as 'Webster's Spelling Book') of *A Grammatical Institute of the English Language* (1783). He is best known for his *American Dictionary of the English Language* (2 vols, 1828), which was a major influence on US dictionary practice. >> dictionary

Webster–Ashburton Treaty (1842) An agreement between Britain and the USA which established the present-day boundary between NE USA and Canada. The parties involved were US secretary of state Daniel Webster and Alexander Baring, Baron Ashburton.

Weddell Sea Arm of the Atlantic Ocean, SE of Argentina; named after James Weddell (1787–1834), who claimed to have discovered the sea in 1823. >> Atlantic Ocean

Wedekind, Frank [**vay**dekint] (1864–1918) Playwright, born in Hanover, Germany. He is best known for his unconventional tragedies, in which he anticipated the Theatre of the Absurd, such as *Die Büchse der Pandora* (1903, Pandora's Box). >> absurdism

Wedgwood, Dame Cicely (Veronica) (1910–97) Historian, born in Stocksfield, Northumberland. Her books include *Oliver Cromwell* (1939), *William the Silent* (1944), and *The Thirty Years' War* (1938).

Wedgwood, Josiah (1730–95) Potter, born in Burslem, Staffordshire. Inspired by antique models, he invented

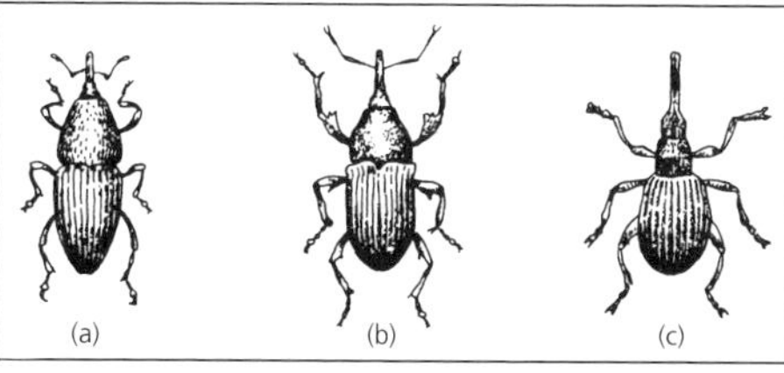

Weevils – Grain (a); cotton ball (b); clover and seed (c)

unglazed black basalt ware and blue jasper ware with raised designs in white. His concern over social welfare led him to build a village for his workmen at Etruria, Staffordshire. >> pottery

Weeks, Feast of >> **Shabuoth**

Weelkes, Thomas (c.1575–1623) Madrigal composer, probably born in Elsted, Surrey. Nearly 100 of his madrigals have survived, as well as some instrumental music, and fragments of his sacred music. >> madrigal

weeping willow Any of several species of willow, all making quite large trees, with the smaller branches pendulous, often reaching the ground. Many are ornamentals, and arose in cultivation. (Family: Salicaceae.) >> willow

weever Bottom-dwelling fish with powerful poison spines on first dorsal fin and gill covers; eyes large and placed on top of head, mouth oblique. (Genus: *Trachinus*. Family: Trachinidae.)

weevil A robust beetle with a characteristic snout on the front of the head; wing cases often sculptured and toughened; antennae club-like, with elbow joint; species include many important pests such as the grain weevil and cotton boll weevil. (Order: Coleoptera. Family: Curculionidae, c.60 000 species.) >> beetle; boll weevil

Wegener, Alfred (Lothar) [**vay**gener] (1880–1930) Explorer and geophysicist, born in Berlin. His theory of continental drift is named after him (**Wegener's hypothesis**), and is the subject of his main publications. >> continental drift

Weigel, Helene [**viy**gl] (1900–71) Actress-manager, born in Austria. She married Bertolt Brecht in 1929, and became a leading exponent of his work. She took control of the Berliner Ensemble after Brecht's death in 1956. >> Berliner Ensemble; Brecht

weigela [wiy**jel**a] A small deciduous shrub native to E Asia; flowers trumpet-shaped, 5-lobed, pink or crimson, in clusters. (Genus: *Weigela*, 12 species. Family: Caprifoliaceae.)

weight The downwards force on an object due to the gravitational attraction of the Earth; symbol *G*, units N (newton); distinct from mass. Weight decreases with altitude. >> force; mass

weightlifting A test of strength by lifting weights attached to both ends of a metal pole (*barbell*). Weightlifting formed part of the Ancient Olympic Games. It was introduced as a sport c.1850, and held its first world championship in 1891. Competitors have to make two successful lifts: the *snatch*, taking the bar directly above the head, and the *clean and jerk*, taking the bar onto the chest then above the head with outstretched arms. Another form of weightlifting is **powerlifting**, which calls for sheer strength as opposed to technique. This takes three forms: the *squat*, *dead lift*, and *bench press*. >> RR1065

Weil, Simone [vay] (1909–43) Philosophical writer and mystic, born in Paris. Her posthumously published works include *La Pesanteur et la grâce* (1946, Gravity and Grace) and *Attente de Dieu* (1950, Waiting for God).

Weill, Kurt [viyl] (1900–50) Composer, born in Dessau, Germany. He is best known for his collaboration with Brecht in *Die Dreigroschenoper* (1928, The Threepenny

Opera), its best-known song, 'Mack the Knife', becoming an international classic. >> Brecht

Weil's disease [viyl] An infectious disease caused by *Leptospira icterohaemorrhagiae*, commonly carried by rodents; also known as **leptospirosis**. Associated with muscle pain and jaundice, the condition carries a mortality of c.20%. It is named after German physician Adolf Weil (1848–1916). >> infection; jaundice

Weimar [**viy**mah(r)] 50°59N 11°20E, pop (1995e) 67 100. City in S Germany, on R Ilm; railway; colleges of technology, music, and architecture; associations with Schiller, Goethe, Liszt; castle. >> Bauhaus; Germany [i]; Goethe; Liszt; Schiller; Weimar Republic

Weimar Republic [**viy**mah(r)] The name by which the German federal republic of 1919–33 is known. In 1919 a National Constituent Assembly met at Weimar, and drew up a constitution for the new republic. It was suspended by Hitler in 1933. >> Hitler; Weimar

Weinberger, Caspar (Willard) [**wiyn**berger] (1917–) US statesman, born in San Francisco, CA. He served in the Nixon and Ford administrations, then became secretary of defense after Reagan's election victory in 1980. >> Reagan

Weissmuller, Johnny [**wiyz**muhler], popular name of **(Peter) John** (originally **Jonas**) **Weissmuller** (1904–84) Swimmer, born in Freidorf, Romania. In 1922 he made history by becoming the first person to swim 100 m (109 yd) in under one minute. He starred in 12 Tarzan films between 1932 and 1948. >> swimming

Weizmann, Chaim (Azriel) [**viyts**man, khiym] (1874–1952) Jewish statesman and president of Israel (1949–52), born near Pinsk, Russia. President of the Zionist Organization (1920–30, 1935–46), and of the Jewish Agency (from 1929), he played a major role in the establishment of the state of Israel (1948), and was its first president. >> Israel [i]; Zionism

Welch, Raquel, originally **Raquel Tejada** (1940–) Actress, born in Chicago, IL. She made her film debut in 1964, and was launched as a sex symbol after her scantily-clad appearance in *One Million Years BC* (1966). She received a Best Actress Golden Globe Award for *The Three Musketeers* (1973).

weld A biennial, native to Europe, W Asia, and N Africa (*Reseda luteola*); stem in second year growing to 1·5 m/5 ft; flowers small, yellowish, 4-petalled in long spike; fruit a 3-lobed capsule; also called **dyer's rocket**. It was once cultivated as a source of bright yellow dye. (Family: Resedaceae.) >> dyestuff

Weldon, Fay (1933–) Writer, born in Alvechurch, Worcestershire. Her work deals with contemporary feminist themes, as in *Female Friends* (1975), and caustic satires of male-dominated society, as in *Darcy's Utopia* (1989). Later books include *Wicked Women* (1995) and *Worst Fears* (1996).

Welensky, Sir Roy [we**len**skee] (1907–91) Rhodesian statesman, born in Salisbury, Zimbabwe (formerly Southern Rhodesia). From 1956 to its break-up in 1963 he was prime minister of the Federation of Rhodesia and Nyasaland. His handling of the constitutional crisis in 1959 aroused much controversy. >> Zimbabwe [i]

welfare state A system of government whereby the state assumes responsibility for protecting and promoting the welfare of its citizens in such areas as health, income maintenance, unemployment, and pensions. A comprehensive system was established in the UK following World War 2, funded out of national insurance contributions and taxation. In recent years concern has been expressed about the proportion of the budget consumed by welfare services. >> Beveridge

Welland, Colin (Williams) (1934–) British actor and playwright. In 1970, 1973, and 1974 he was voted best television playwright in Britain, his work including *Roll on Four O'Clock* (1970) and *Bank Holiday* (1977). His screenplays include *Chariots of Fire* (1981) and *Twice in a Lifetime* (1987).

Welland Ship Canal Canal in Ontario, E Canada, linking L Erie and L Ontario, bypassing Niagara Falls; first canal opened, 1829; modern canal, 1932; length 61 km/38 mi. >> Great Lakes

Welles, (George) Orson (1915–85) Film director and actor, born in Kenosha, WI. In 1938 his radio production of Wells's *War of the Worlds* was so realistic that it caused panic in the USA. In 1941, he wrote, produced, directed, and acted in the film *Citizen Kane*, a revolutionary landmark in cinema technique, and this was followed by *The Magnificent Ambersons* (1942). He played a variety of memorable stage and film roles, the most celebrated being that of Harry Lime in *The Third Man* (1949).

Wellesley, Arthur >> **Wellington, 1st Duke of**

Wellesley (of Norragh), Richard (Colley) Wellesley, 1st Marquess (1760–1842) Colonial administrator, born in Dangan, Co Meath, Ireland, the brother of Arthur Wellesley. While he was Governor-General of India (1797–1805), British rule in India became supreme: the influence of France was extinguished, and the power of the princes reduced by the crushing of Tippoo Sahib (1799) and the Marathas (1803). >> Tippoo Sahib

Wellington 41°17S 174°47E, pop (1995e) 338 000. Capital city of New Zealand, on S coast of North Island; founded, 1840; capital, 1865; airport; railway; ferry to South Island; university (1899); Government Building, Parliament Buildings (1922, 1980), cathedral (1866). >> New Zealand [i]

Wellington, Arthur Wellesley, 1st Duke of (1769–1852) British general, statesman, and prime minister (1828–30), born in Dublin, Ireland, the brother of Richard Wellesley. He defeated the Danes during the Copenhagen expedition (1807), and in the Peninsular War drove the French out of Portugal and Spain, gaining victories at Talavera (1809), Salamanca (1812), and Toulouse (1814). After Napoleon's escape from Elba, he routed the French at Waterloo (1815). His period as prime minister significantly weakened the Tory Party, which split over the question of Catholic emancipation, and was further weakened by disagreements over trade and reform. >> Napoleonic Wars; Peninsular War; Tories; Waterloo, Battle of

wellingtonia >> **mammoth tree**

Wells, H(erbert) G(eorge) (1866–1946) Writer, born in Bromley, Kent. He achieved fame with scientific fantasies such as *The Time Machine* (1895) and *War of the Worlds* (1898), and wrote a range of comic social novels which proved highly popular, notably *Kipps* (1905) and *The History of Mr Polly* (1910). A member of the Fabian Society, he also wrote several socio-political works dealing with the role of science and the need for world peace. >> Fabian Society

wels Large nocturnal freshwater catfish (*Silurus glanis*) found in large rivers and lakes of E Europe; length up to 3 m/10 ft; body devoid of scales, mouth with long barbels, anal fin long. (Family: Siluridae.) >> catfish

Welsh The Celtic language spoken in Wales, assigned equal status with English in all legal and administrative affairs. Of all the extant Celtic languages, Welsh enjoys the most vibrant literary scene, which continues a tradition dating from the epic poem *Taliesin* (c.6th-c), and the prose tales of the *Mabinogi*, preserved in mediaeval manuscripts. Its high point is the annual, week-long, high-culture festival, the National Eisteddfod, which has become the focal point of Welsh identity for many. A Welsh-language television channel has broadened the range of information and entertainment sources in the media. There are about 500 000 speakers. >> Celtic languages

Welsh corgi >> **corgi**

Welsh Nationalist Party >> Plaid Cymru

welwitschia [wel**wich**ia] A peculiar gymnosperm (*Welwitschia mirabilis*) found only in the deserts of SW Africa. Its turnip-like stem produces just two strap-shaped leaves several metres long, which grow throughout the plant's life of over a century. (Family: Gnetaceae.) >> gymnosperms

Welwyn Garden City [**we**lin] 51°48N 0°13W, pop (1995e) 41 500. Town in Hertfordshire, SE England; founded in 1919 by Ebenezer Howard; designated a 'new town' in 1948; railway. >> Hertfordshire; Howard, Ebenezer

Wembley Stadium One of the most famous football stadiums in the world, built at Wembley in NE London in 1923, with a capacity of 92 000. It is now used for a wide range of sports and other occasions, such as pop concerts and religious meetings. >> London

Wenceslaus or **Wenceslas, St** [**wen**seslas], known as **Good King Wenceslas** (c.903–935) Duke and patron of Bohemia, born in Stochov, Czech Republic. He encouraged Christianity in Bohemia, against the wishes of his mother, and was murdered by his brother Boleslaw. He became the patron saint of Bohemia and Czechoslovakia. Feast day 28 September. >> Christianity

Wentworth, Thomas >> **Strafford, Earl of**

Wentworth, W(illiam) C(harles) (1790–1872) Australian landowner and politician, born on Norfolk I. He was a staunch champion of self-government for Australia, which he made the policy of his newspaper *The Australian* (established 1824). >> Australia ℹ

werewolf In traditional belief, a person assuming the form of a wolf, usually involuntarily and temporarily. There are traces of the belief in Ancient Greek religion, and it existed in much of Europe, but especially in the Balkans. It seems to be related to some kind of initiation rite, in which youths wore animal skins. >> folklore; lycanthropy

Wergeland, Henrik Arnold [**ver**geland] (1808–45) Poet, playwright, and patriot, born in Kristiansand, Norway. He is best known for his poetry, notably his Creation epic, *Skabelsen, Mennesket, og Messias* (1830, Creation, Humanity, and Desire). He became Norway's national poet.

Wesak [**we**sahk] A Buddhist festival held in May to celebrate the birth, enlightenment, and death of the Buddha. >> Buddha; Buddhism

Weser, River [**vay**zer], ancient **Visurgis** Major river in Germany, formed by the confluence of the Werra and Fulda Rivers; enters the North Sea; length 440 km/273 mi. >> Germany ℹ

Wesker, Arnold (1932–) Playwright, born in London. The Kahn family trilogy, *Chicken Soup with Barley*, *Roots*, and *I'm Talking about Jerusalem* (1958–60), echo the march of events, pre- and post-World War 2, in a left-wing family. Later plays include *Chips with Everything* (1962), *Caritas* (1981), and *Tokyo* (1994). >> Centre 42

Wesley, John (1703–91) Evangelist and founder of Methodism, born in Epworth, Lincolnshire. He became leader of a small group which had gathered round his brother **Charles Wesley** (1707–88), nicknamed the Methodists. In 1738, at a meeting in London, he experienced an assurance of salvation which led him to preach, but his zeal alarmed most of the parish clergy, who closed their pulpits against him. This drove him into the open air at Bristol (1739), where he founded the first Methodist chapel, and then the Foundry at Moorfields, London, which became their headquarters. His many writings included collections of hymns, sermons and journals, and a magazine. >> evangelicalism; Methodism; Whitefield, George

Wessex A kingdom of the Anglo-Saxon heptarchy, with its main centres at Winchester and Hamwic (Southampton). Under Alfred, Wessex – by then incorporating Kent and Sussex – was the only English kingdom to withstand the onslaughts of the Vikings. >> Alfred; Anglo-Saxons; Vikings

West, Benjamin (1738–1820) Painter, born in Springfield, PA. He settled in London in 1763. The representation of modern instead of classical costume in his best-known picture, 'The Death of General Wolfe' (c.1771), was an innovation in British historical painting.

West, Mae (1893–1980) Actress, born in New York City. Throughout the 1930s a series of racy comedies exploited her voluptuousness, although under much pressure from censorship. Her name was given to an airman's pneumatic life-jacket which, when inflated, was considered to give the wearer the generous bosom for which she was noted.

West, Nathanael, pseudonym of **Nathan Wallenstein Weinstein** (1903–40) Novelist, born in New York City. He wrote four short fantasy novels, of which the best known are *Miss Lonelyhearts* (1933) and his satire on Hollywood, *The Day of the Locust* (1939).

West, Dame Rebecca, pseudonym of **Cicily Isabel Andrews**, *née* **Fairfield** (1892–1983) Novelist and critic, born in London. She is best known for her studies arising out of the Nuremberg war trials: *The Meaning of Treason* (1947) and *A Train of Powder* (1955). Her novels include *The Thinking Reed* (1936) and *The Birds Fall Down* (1966). >> Nuremberg Trials

West Bank Region of the Middle East W of the R Jordan and the Dead Sea; part of the former mandate of Palestine, administered by Jordan, 1949–67; seized by Israel in the 1967 War, and remained under Israeli occupation; area includes Old (East) Jerusalem, as well as Bethlehem, Jericho, Hebron, and Nablus; a focus of territorial aspirations by the Palestine Liberation Organization; scene of an uprising (*intifada*) against the Israelis since early 1988; focus of Israeli–PLO peace agreement (1993) for recognition of Palestine. >> Arab–Israeli Wars; East Bank; Israel ℹ; Jordan ℹ; Palestine; PLO

West Bengal [beng**gawl**] pop (1995e) 73 587 000; area 87 853 sq km/33 911 sq mi. State in NE India; created in 1947; capital, Calcutta; governed by a Legislative Assembly. >> Calcutta; India ℹ

westerlies The prevailing winds found at mid-latitudes, between 30° and 60°N and S of the Equator. Westerlies in the S hemisphere are stronger because there is a smaller land mass, and are known as the **Roaring Forties**, from the latitudes at which they occur. >> wind ℹ

Western Australia pop (1995e) 1 678 000; area 2 525 500 sq km/975 000 sq mi. State in W Australia; Dutchman Dirk Hartog landed here in 1616, and Englishman William Dampier in 1688; Britain's first non-convict settlement on the Swan R, 1829; governed at first by New South Wales; separate colony, 1890; a third of the total area of Australia; over 90% occupied by the Great Plateau (mean altitude 600 m/2000 ft); highest point, Mt Meharry (1245 m/4085 ft); Great Sandy Desert, Gibson Desert, Great Victoria Desert, Nullarbor Plain in the E; capital, Perth. >> Australia ℹ; Perth (Australia)

Western Cape One of the nine new provinces established by the South African constitution of 1994, in SW South Africa; capital, Cape Town (also legislative capital of South Africa); pop (1996e) 4 118 000; area 129 386 sq km/ 49 943 sq mi; chief languages, Afrikaans (63%), English (20%), Xhosa; tourism (Table Mountain, Robben I, Cape of Good Hope, Cape Agulhas); South Africa's richest province. >> Cape Provinces; Cape Town; South Africa

Western European Union An organization of 10 W European nations, founded in 1954 to co-ordinate defence and other policies, replacing the defunct European

Defence Community, and reactivated in the 1980s; its members include Belgium, France, Germany, Greece, Italy, Luxembourg, The Netherlands, Portugal, Spain, and the UK. Several E European countries are linked to it under the heading of Associate Partners. >> Council of Europe; NATO

Western Isles pop (1995e) 29 200; area 2898 sq km/1119 sq mi. Administrative region in Scotland; group of islands off the W coast (Outer Hebrides); main islands, Lewis, North Uist, Benbecula, South Uist, Barra; c.210 km/130 mi N–S; capital, Stornoway, on Lewis; Harris tweed; name often used to refer to both Inner and Outer Hebrides. >> Hebrides; Lewis with Harris; Scotland ℹ; Stornoway

Western Reserve Territory in NW Ohio successfully claimed by the state of Connecticut in 1786, during the final settlement of interstate boundary disputes that dated from the colonial era. >> Connecticut

Western Sahara pop (1995e) 215 000; area 252 126 sq km/97 321 sq mi. Former Spanish province in NW Africa, between Morocco (N) and Mauritania (S); chief town, al-Aioun, pop (1995e) 122 000; desert area, rich in phosphates; partitioned by Morocco and Mauritania after its Spanish status ended in 1975; withdrawal of Mauritania, 1979; now administered by Morocco; named the **Democratic Saharan Republic** by the independence movement, *Frente Polisario*, which has set up a 'government in exile'; UN peace resolution, 1991; renewed fighting, 1993; agreement to UN proposal for a referendum, 1994, but implementation repeatedly postponed. >> Mauritania ℹ; Morocco ℹ

Western Samoa >> **Samoa**

Western Wall The only surviving part of the Second Temple of Jerusalem and, as such, the most sacred of Jewish sites. Traditionally a place of prayer and lamentation during the dispersion of the Jews, it was formerly often referred to as the **Wailing Wall**. >> Temple, Jerusalem; Judaism

West Germany >> **Germany** ℹ

West Indies Federation (1958–1962) An unsuccessful attempt to establish a single government for the English-speaking West Indies. >> Caribbean Sea

Westinghouse, George (1846–1914) Engineer, born in Central Bridge, NY. In 1863 he invented an air-brake for railways, and founded a company (now a corporation) for the manufacture of this and other appliances. He founded the Westinghouse Electrical Co in 1886.

West Irian >> **Irian Jaya**

Westman Islands, Icelandic **Vestmannaeyjar** pop (1995e) 5400; area 21 sq km/8 sq mi. Group of 15 islands and 30 reefs off the S coast of Iceland; island of Surtsey was formed during eruptions in 1963–6. >> Iceland ℹ; Surtsey Island

Westmeath [**west**meeth], Ir **na h-Iarmhidhe** pop (1995e) 61 400; area 1764 sq km/681 sq mi. County in Leinster province, C Ireland; capital, Mullingar. >> Ireland (republic) ℹ; Mullingar

West Midlands pop (1995e) 2 631 000; area 899 sq km/347 sq mi. County of C England; adminstrative centre, Birmingham; metropolitan council abolished in 1986. >> Birmingham; England ℹ

Westminster, City of 51°30N 0°09W, pop (1995e) 191 000. Borough of C Greater London, England; N of the R Thames; administrative centre of the UK; includes the major tourist area from Westminster Bridge through Trafalgar Square to the West End. >> Big Ben; Buckingham Palace; Downing Street; Hyde Park; Houses of Parliament; National / National Portrait / Tate Gallery; St James's Palace; Westminster Abbey; Whitehall

Westminster, Palace of >> **Houses of Parliament**

Westminster, Statutes of Part of a comprehensive legislative programme undertaken by Edward I to reform English law and administration. Three Statutes were passed, in 1275, 1285, and 1290. >> Edward I

Westminster Abbey The church of St Peter in Westminster, London. The first recorded abbey church, consecrated in 1065, was replaced from 1245 by the present building in early English Gothic style. It serves as a coronation church and national shrine, with many memorials to those who have shaped the country's history and culture. >> London

Westminster Assembly A body of clerics and laymen convened by the English Long Parliament in 1643 to arrange a religious settlement to replace the Church of England. Dominated by Presbyterians, it produced a directory of public worship to replace the Prayer Book, and the Westminster Confession of Faith. >> Church of England; Long Parliament; Presbyterianism

Westminster Confession of Faith The main Presbyterian Confession of Faith, adopted by the Westminster Assembly, England, in 1643. It became the major confessional influence among Reformed Churches of the English-speaking world. >> confession 1; Reformed Churches

Westmorland Former county of NW England; part of Cumbria since 1974.

Westphalia NW German principality, first settled by Saxons c.700, later forming part of the Lower Rhine–Westphalian Circle of the Empire (1512). >> Holy Roman Empire

West Point A US military academy founded by Act of Congress in 1802 at the West Point military station on the Hudson R in the state of New York. >> New York (state)

West Sussex >> **Sussex, West**

West Virginia pop (1995e) 1 842 000; area 62 758 sq km/24 232 sq mi. State in E USA; the 'Mountain State'; part of Virginia until the Civil War, when the area remained loyal to the Union, and split from Confederate East Virginia, 1861; 35th state admitted to the Union as West Virginia, 1863; capital, Charleston; Allegheny Mts dominate the E; highest point Mt Spruce Knob (1481 m/4859 ft); a rugged, hilly state, most of which is in the Allegheny Plateau; 65% forested; nation's leading producer of bituminous coal; major producer of natural gas; both summer and winter tourism. >> American Civil War; Charleston (West Virginia); United States of America ℹ; Virginia; RR994

wet rot A type of timber decay caused by the cellar fungus, *Coniophora puteana*; found only in wood with a high moisture content. >> fungus

Wexford, Ir **Loch Garman** pop (1995e) 101 000; area 2352 sq km/908 sq mi. County in Leinster province, SE Ireland; Wicklow Mts (N), Blackstairs Mts (W); capital, Wexford, pop (1995e) 15 300; main seaport, Rosslare; rich farmland (cattle) and resort area. >> Ireland (republic) ℹ

Weyden, Rogier van der [**viy**dn] (c.1400–64) Religious painter, born in Tournai, Belgium. He executed many portraits and altarpieces, and among his best-known works are 'The Descent from the Cross' (c.1435–40, Madrid) and the 'Last Judgment' altarpiece (c.1450, Beaune). >> altarpiece

whale An aquatic mammal of worldwide order Cetacea (79 species); resembles fish in shape (although tail blades – *flukes* – are horizontal, not vertical); breathes air through opening(s) on top of head; has insulating layer of oily blubber under skin; two major groups: **toothed whales** (5 families with 69 species, including the sperm whale, killer whale, dolphin, and porpoise); larger **baleen whales** (3 families with 10 species, including rorquals, grey whales, and right whales). >> baleen ℹ; blue / killer / pilot / sperm whale; dolphin; grampus; mammal ℹ; narwhal; rorqual; whaling; *see illustration on p. 931*

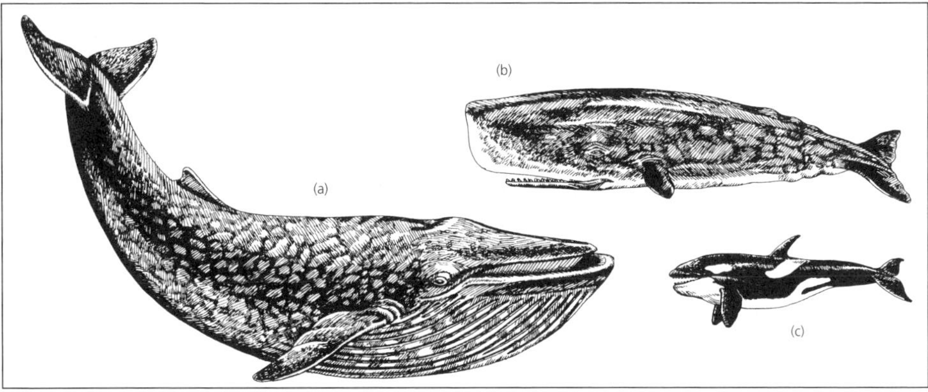

Whales – Blue whale (a); sperm whale (b); killer whale (c)

whalebone >> **baleen** ℹ

whale shark The largest of all fishes (*Rhincodon typus*), widely distributed in surface waters of tropical seas; length up to 18 m/60 ft; weight up to 20 tonnes. (Family: Rhincodontidae.) >> shark

whaling The hunting of whales for oil, meat, and blubber, which has resulted in a serious decline in whale populations and the near-extinction of several species. The International Whaling Commission, set up in 1946, exists to regulate the industry, but overfishing has continued. >> whale ℹ

Wharton, Edith (Newbold), *née* **Jones** (c.1861–1937) Novelist, born in New York City. She wrote mainly about upper-class New York society, and is best known for her novels, *The House of Mirth* (1905), *Ethan Frome* (1911), and *The Age of Innocence* (1920, Pulitzer).

wheat A cereal second only to rice in importance, originating in the Middle East but cultivated throughout temperate regions of the world. The various species yield different qualities of flour, such as **bread wheat** (*Triticum aestivum*) and **durum wheat** (*Triticum durum*) from which pasta is made. Wheat is the most suitable for making bread, because of the presence of the elastic protein gluten. (Genus: *Triticum*, 20 species. Family: Gramineae.) >> bread; cereals; durum; gluten; oats

wheatear A thrush native to the N hemisphere and S Africa; the name is a corruption of 'white arse' (after white rump). (Genus: *Oenanthe*, 20 species.) >> thrush (bird)

Wheatley, Denis (Yates) (1897–1977) Novelist, born in London. He produced an enormously popular mix of satanism and historical fiction. Indicative titles in a lurid oeuvre are *The Devil Rides Out* (1935), *The Scarlet Impostor* (1942), and *The Sultan's Daughter* (1963).

Wheatstone, Sir Charles (1802–75) Physicist, born in Gloucester, Gloucestershire. He invented the concertina (1829), took out a patent for an electric telegraph (1837), and invented a sound magnifier for which he introduced the term *microphone*. **Wheatstone's bridge**, a device for the comparison of electrical resistances, was brought to notice (though not invented) by him. >> microphone ℹ; resistance

wheel One of the most important innovations in human material culture, allowing continuous rotary motion, and the continuous conversion of rotary motion into linear motion, and vice versa. The earliest wheels are found c.3500 BC; the earliest with spokes c.2000 BC. Other improvements were the separate axle, the reinforced hub, which could be lubricated, and the metal tyre, which strengthened the rim.

Wheeler, Sir (Robert Eric) Mortimer (1890–1976) Archaeologist, born in Glasgow. He carried out notable excavations in Britain at Verulamium (St Albans) and Maiden Castle, and from 1944–7 was director-general of archaeology in India. He was well known for spirited popular accounts of his subject, in books and on television. >> archaeology; Maiden Castle

wheel window >> **rose window** ℹ

whelk A marine snail with a spirally coiled external shell; aperture closed off by a chitinous covering once head and body are drawn inside. (Class: Gastropoda. Order: Neogastropoda.) >> chitin; gastropod; snail

Whichcote, Benjamin (1609–83) Philosopher and theologian, born in Stoke, Shropshire. He became Provost of King's College, Cambridge (1644–60), and is regarded as the spiritual founder of the Cambridge Platonists. >> Cambridge Platonists

Whicker, Alan (Donald) [**wi**ker] (1925–) British broadcaster and journalist, born in Cairo. He began his *Whicker's World* documentary series in 1958, and became British television's most travelled man.

whidah >> **whydah**

Whig Party One of two major US political parties during the decades prior to the Civil War. The name was adopted in 1834 to signify opposition to 'King' Andrew Jackson (president, 1829–37). The Whigs stood for greater governmental intervention in the economy than did the Democrats, who followed Jackson, but both parties agreed on the necessity of keeping the slavery issue out of politics. The Whigs collapsed in 1854, precisely because the slavery issue could no longer be contained. >> Jackson, Andrew; slave trade

Whigs A British political party which emerged in 1679–80 as the group agitating for the exclusion of James, Duke of York, on the grounds of his Catholicism. The name was probably a contraction of 'Whiggamores' – militant Scottish Presbyterians. During its long period of dominance in British politics after 1714, it drew much strength from defending 'the principles of 1688', which included limited monarchy and the importance of parliament. Most of its leaders were great landowners who used political patronage to create family-based groupings in parliament. Whig fortunes waned in the late 18th-c, and Whigs became leading members of the new Liberal party from the mid-19th-c. >> Liberal Party (UK); Presbyterianism; Tories

whimbrel A curlew (*Numenius phaeopus*) which breeds in the N hemisphere on tundra and moors; migrates to shores in the S hemisphere; striped head; also known as the **seven whistler**. >> curlew

whinchat A bird of the thrush family Murcicapidae, native to Europe, N Africa, and W Asia (*Saxicola rubetra*); mottled above, pale beneath, with light 'eyebrow' line. >> thrush (bird)

whip A party official in a legislative chamber responsible for ensuring that members attend and vote in accordance with party policy; the name derives from the jargon of hunting, a 'whipper in'.

whippet A small slender breed of dog developed in Britain by cross-breeding small greyhounds with terriers. >> greyhound; terrier

Whipple, George H(oyt) (1878–1976) Pathologist, born in Ashland, NH. He shared the Nobel Prize for Physiology or Medicine in 1934 for the discovery of the lifesaving liver therapy against pernicious anaemia. >> anaemia; Minot; Murphy, William P

whip-poor-will A North American bird (a goatsucker, *Caprimulgus vociferus*); inhabits open woodland.

whip scorpion A nocturnal, predatory arthropod; body scorpion-like, up to 75 mm/3 in long, ending in a long whip-like tail; found in the tropics and subtropics. (Class: Arachnida. Order: Uropygi, c.85 species.) >> Arachnida; arthropod; scorpion

whirligig A dark, shiny beetle that lives in groups on the surface of ponds; fast-moving, typically swimming in small circles; eyes divided for vision above and below water surface. (Order: Coleoptera. Family: Gyrinidae.) >> beetle

whirlwind A column of air rotating rapidly around a localized centre of low pressure. It is caused by local surface heating, which results in instability and convectional uprising. >> tornado

whiskey >> **whisky**

Whiskey Rebellion (1794) An insurrection of farmers in W Pennsylvania, USA, against the excise tax imposed by the federal government on whisky, which they made in large quantities from their crops of grain. It was suppressed by government forces.

whisk fern A member of a group of only 10 living species plus various fossil forms, considered the most primitive of vascular plants and possible ancestors of the ferns. Fossil forms date mainly from the Devonian period, the most famous being *Rhynia*. (Class: Psilophyta.) >> Devonian period; fern

whisky (Ireland/US **whiskey**) A spirit distilled from fermented grain, such as barley, rye, or wheat; the main spirit produced and consumed in Ireland and Scotland. Whiskies can be single malt, a product of a single distillate, or a blend of several batches. >> bourbon; scotch whisky

whist A non-gambling card game, normally played with four people in pairs. Each player receives 13 cards, and the object is to win more tricks than the opposing pair. Trumps are decided before each game, and at **whist drives** trumps are normally played in the following order; hearts, clubs, diamonds, spades. A round of 'no trumps' is also common. >> bridge (recreation)

Whistler, James (Abbott) McNeill (1834–1903) Artist, born in Lowell, MA. He is best known for his evening scenes ('nocturnes'), such as 'Old Battersea Bridge' (c.1872–5, Tate, London), and for the famous portrait of his mother (1871–2, Musée d'Orsay).

Whistler, Rex (John) (1905–44) British artist. He excelled in the rendering of 18th-c life, ornament, and architecture, particularly in book illustration, murals, and designs for the theatre and ballet.

Whitby, Synod of A meeting in Britain in 663 when the differences in organization between Roman and Celtic Christianity were debated. Roman concepts of church order prevailed. >> Christianity

White, Gilbert (1720–93) Clergyman and naturalist, born in Selborne, Hampshire. His *Natural History and Antiquities of Selborne* (1789) has become an English classic.

White, Patrick (Victor Martindale) (1912–90) Writer, born in London. His first novel, *Happy Valley*, appeared in 1939, and he has since written several novels, short stories, and plays, achieving international success with *The Tree of Man* (1954). He received the Nobel Prize for Literature in 1973.

White, T(erence) H(anbury) (1906–64) Novelist, born in Mumbai (Bombay), India. With the exception of the largely autobiographical *The Goshawk* (1951), his best work was in the form of legend and fantasy, especially his sequence of novels about King Arthur, beginning with *The Sword in the Stone* (1937).

white ant >> **termite**

White Australia Policy The unofficial national policy of Australia from 1901 to the 1960s, designed to exclude non-European migrants; it was particularly aimed at Asians, Pacific Islanders, and Africans who, it was feared, might come to dominate Europeans. In the late 1960s, the policy was progressively dismantled.

whitebait Small silvery fish found abundantly in shallow coastal waters and estuaries; includes the N Atlantic first-year herrings, *Clupea harengus*, and young sprats, *Sprattus sprattus*. >> herring; sprat

whitebeam A spreading, deciduous tree or shrub (*Sorbus aria*), native to Europe; flowers white, in clusters; berries red. (Family: Rosaceae.)

white bryony A perennial with a large, white, tuber-like base (*Bryonia dioica*,) native to Europe, W Asia, and N Africa; flowers greenish-white, 5-petalled; berry changing from green through white and orange to red. (Family: Cucurbitaceae.)

White Canons >> **Premonstratensians**

white cedar A species of *arbor vitae* (*Thuja occidentalis*), native to E North America, which provides white or yellowish timber. (Family: Cupressaceae.) >> arbor vitae

white currant >> **red currant**

white dwarf A small, dim star in the final stages of its evolution. White dwarfs are defunct stars, collapsed to about the diameter of the Earth, at which stage they stabilize, with their electrons forming a degenerate gas, the pressure of which is sufficient to balance gravitational force. >> dwarf star

white-eye A small songbird, native to Old World tropical regions; white ring around eye. (Family: Zosteropidae, c.85 species.) >> songbird

Whitefield, George [**whit**feeld] (1714–70) Methodist evangelist, born in Gloucester, Gloucestershire. Associated with the Wesleys at Oxford, he founded no distinct sect, but many of his adherents followed the Countess of Huntingdon in Wales, and formed the Calvinistic Methodists. He made several visits to America, where he played an important role in the Great Awakening. >> Calvinism; Great Awakening; Huntingdon, Countess of; Methodism

whitefish Any of a small group of freshwater and brackish-water fishes widespread in lakes and large rivers of the N hemisphere; species include the vendace, cisco, and houting. (Genus: *Coregonus*. Family: Salmonidae.) >> fish [i]

whitefly A small, sap-sucking bug; adults active fliers; bodies and wings covered with a waxy, white powder; commonly produces honeydew, and attended by ants. (Order: Homoptera. Family: Aleyrodidae, c.1200 species.) >> bug (entomology)

White Friars >> **Carmelites**

Whitehall A wide thoroughfare lying between Parliament and Trafalgar Squares in London, and by association the offices of central government which line it. >> London

Whitehead, A(lfred) N(orth) (1861–1947) Mathematician and philosopher, born in Ramsgate, Kent. He collaborated with his former pupil, Bertrand Russell, in writing the *Principia Mathematica* (1910–13). Other more popular works include *Adventures of Ideas* (1933) and *Modes of Thought* (1938). >> Russell, Bertrand

Whitehorse 60°41N 135°08W, pop (1995e) 19 000. Capital of Yukon territory, NW Canada; on the R Lewes; founded during Klondike gold rush, 1900. >> Yukon

White Horse, Vale of the Site in Oxfordshire, England, of a stylized representation of a horse, carved on the chalk hillside about 3000 years ago. Perhaps originally a cult object for the local Celtic tribe, the Belgae, it has inspired many imitations. >> Celts; Three Age System

White House The official residence of the US president, situated on Pennsylvania Avenue in Washington, DC. The 132-room Neoclassical mansion was built (1793–1801) from the designs of James Hoban (1762–1831), who also supervised its reconstruction (1814–29) after it was burnt down by the British in 1814. >> Neoclassicism (art and architecture); Washington (DC)

Whitelaw, William (Stephen Ian) Whitelaw, 1st Viscount, popularly known as **Willie Whitelaw** (1918–) British Conservative statesman, born in Nairn, Highland. His posts include secretary of state for Northern Ireland (1972–3) and for employment (1973–4), and home secretary (1979–83). He was Leader of the House of Lords until 1988. >> Conservative Party

Whiteman, Paul (1890–1967) Jazz bandleader, composer, and arranger, born in Denver, CO. Known in his early days as 'the King of Jazz', he was the most popular bandleader of the 1920s and early 1930s, before the swing era. >> Gershwin, George; jazz

White Nile or **Bahr El Ablad** Upper reach of R Nile in S and E Sudan; a continuation of the Albert Nile; joined at Khartoum by the Blue Nile, forming the R Nile proper; length 1900 km/1180 mi. >> Nile, River

whiteout A condition which occurs when there is a scattering of light between the base of low cloud and a bright snow surface, making it difficult to locate the horizon. The term is also used for blizzard conditions in which it is difficult to determine direction. >> snow

white paper In the UK, a government publication setting out its policy and legislative intentions in a specific area. Different degrees of scope exist for consultation before the proposals are put into effect. >> green paper

White Russia >> **Belarus**

White Russians The name collectively given to counterrevolutionary forces led by ex-tsarist officers, which fought unsuccessfully against the Bolshevik Red Army during the Russian Civil War (1918–22). >> Bolsheviks

White Sands An area of white gypsum sand dunes in S New Mexico, USA, designated a national monument in 1933. The first nuclear explosion took place here in July 1945. >> atomic bomb; New Mexico

White Sea, Russian **Beloye More** area c.95 000 sq km/ 36 670 sq mi. Arm of the Arctic Ocean and inlet of the Barents Sea, NW European Russia; ice-breakers keep some sea channels open in winter. >> Arctic Ocean

white shark Large and extremely aggressive shark (*Carcharodon carcharias*), considered the most dangerous of all sharks; widespread in tropical to temperate seas; length up to 6 m/20 ft; grey to brown above, underside white; teeth large and finely serrated; many attacks on humans. (Family: Lamnidae.)

Whitewater affair A series of allegations of financial misconduct levelled against Bill and Hillary Clinton, relating to a commercial land development in the 1980s. Whitewater was the name of an Arkansas property development corporation in which (at the time) Governor Clinton and his wife (a member of a local law firm) were partners. The allegations surfaced in the media following Clinton's inauguration as president in 1993, but Republican calls for an official enquiry were largely overtaken by events associated with the Lewinsky scandal. >> Clinton; Lewinsky; Starr

white whale >> **beluga** (mammal)

Whitgift, John (c.1530–1604) Clergyman, born in Grimsby, North East Lincolnshire. He became Archbishop of Canterbury (1583) and a Privy Councillor (1586). A champion of conformity, he vindicated the Anglican position against the Puritans. >> Puritanism

whiting European codfish (*Merlangius merlangus*) widely distributed in shallow shelf waters from N Norway to the Black Sea; length up to 70 cm/28 in. (Family: Gadidae.) >> cod

Whiting, John (Robert) (1917–63) Playwright, born in Salisbury, Wiltshire. His best-known work was *The Devils* (1961), a dramatization of Huxley's *The Devils of Loudon*.

Whitlam, (Edward) Gough [gof] (1916–) Australian statesman and Labor prime minister (1972–5). He ended conscription and relaxed the policy on non-white immigrants. He was dismissed by the governor-general after the opposition blocked his money bills in the upper house of the Senate – the first time that the crown had so acted against an elected prime minister. >> Australian Labor Party

Whitman, Walt(er) (1819–92) Poet, born in West Hills, Long Island, NY. An outstanding proponent of free verse, his major poetic work was *Leaves of Grass* (1855). His later prose works include *Democratic Vistas* (1871) and *Specimen Days and Collect* (1882–3). >> free verse

Whitney, Eli (1765–1825) Inventor, born in Westborough, MA. He devised the cotton-gin (patented in 1793), and in 1798 developed a new system of mass-production for the manufacture of firearms. >> cotton [i]

Whitsunday or **Whit Sunday** In the Christian Church, the seventh Sunday after Easter, commemorating the day of Pentecost. The name Whit ('white') Sunday derives from the white robes traditionally worn by those baptized on this day. >> Pentecost

Whittier, John Greenleaf (1807–92) Quaker poet and abolitionist, born near Haverhill, MA. He published a collection of poems and stories, *Legends of New England*, in 1831. Later works include *In War Time* (1864) and *At Sundown* (1892).

Whittington, Dick, popular name of **Richard Whittington** (c.1358–1423) English merchant, who set out at 13 for London, where he found work as an apprentice, and in 1397 became Lord Mayor of London. The legend of his cat is an accepted part of English folklore.

Whittle, Sir Frank (1907–96) Inventor and aviator, born in Coventry, Warwickshire. He successfully developed the jet engine for aircraft (1941), and became government technical adviser on engine design (1946–8). >> jet engine [i]; turbine

Whitworth, Kathy, popular name of **Kathrynne Ann Whitworth** (1939–) Golfer, born in Monahans, TX. The most successful woman golfer of all time, she has won all the women's 'Majors' except the US Open. She turned professional in 1958. >> golf

WHO >> **World Health Organization**

whooping cough A highly infectious disease which results from *Bordetella pertussis*, mainly affecting children; also known as **pertussis**. Upper respiratory catarrh is followed by a series of short sharp coughs followed by a deep inspiration (the 'whoop'). The condition carries a high mortality in infants, and active immunization is highly desirable. >> immunization

whortleberry >> **bilberry**

Whovian >> **Doctor Who**

whydah [**wi**duh] A songbird of the genus *Vidua* (8 species), treated variously as a weaver-finch or weaverbird, and sometimes put in a separate family (Viduidae); finch-like; male with very long tail; also known as **whidah** or **widow finch**. >> finch; songbird; weaverbird; weaver-finch

Whymper, Edward (1840–1911) Wood-engraver and mountaineer, born in London. During 1860–9 he conquered several hitherto unscaled peaks of the Alps, including the Matterhorn (1865).

Wichita [**wich**itaw] 37°42N 97°20W, pop (1995e) 318 000. City in S Kansas, USA, on the Arkansas R; settled, 1866; city status, 1870; airport; railway; two universities (1892, 1898); chief commercial and industrial centre in S Kansas; Cow Town (1870s replica). >> Kansas

Wicklow, Ir **Cill Mhantáin**, nickname **the Garden of Ireland** pop (1995e) 96 500; area 2025 sq km/782 sq mi. County in Leinster province, E Ireland; Wicklow Mts (W); capital, Wicklow (pop (1995e) 5200); agriculture; resort towns (eg Bray). >> Ireland (republic) ℹ

wide area network (WAN) >> **local area network**

widgeon >> **wigeon**

Widor, Charles Marie (Jean Albert) [weedaw(r)] (1844–1937) Composer, born in Lyon, France. He composed 10 symphonies for the organ, as well as a ballet, chamber music, and other orchestral works.

widow bird / finch >> **whydah**

Wieland, Christoph Martin [**vee**lant] (1733–1813) Writer, born near Biberach, Germany. He made the first German translation of Shakespeare (1762–6), and wrote a number of popular romances, notably *Agathon* (1766–7). His best-known work is the heroic poem *Oberon* (1780).

Wien [veen] >> **Vienna**

Wiener, Norbert [**ween**er] (1894–1964) Mathematical logician, the founder of cybernetics, born in Columbia, MO. His study of the handling of information by electronic devices, based on the feedback principle, encouraged comparison between these and human mental processes in *Cybernetics* (1948) and other works. >> cybernetics

Wiesbaden [**veez**bahdn] 50°05N 8°15E, pop (1995e) 267 000. City in Germany; on the R Rhine; railway; popular health resort; traditional wine centre. >> Germany ℹ; wine

Wieschaus, Eric F [**vee**shows] (1947–) Developmental biologist, born in South Bend, IA. He shared the Nobel Prize for Physiology or Medicine in 1995 for his research into how genes control early development of the human embryo.

Wigan 53°33N 2°38W, pop (1995e) 90 100. Town in Greater Manchester, NW England; a borough since 1246; railway; Wigan Pier, now a museum, made famous by George Orwell, in *The Road to Wigan Pier* (1932); football league team, Wigan Athletic (Latics). >> Manchester, Greater; Orwell

wigeon or **widgeon** A dabbling duck of the genus *Anas*; includes the **European wigeon** (*Anas penelope*), from Eurasia and N Africa, and the **North American wigeon** or **baldpate** (*Anas americana*).

Wiggin, Kate Douglas, *née* **Smith** (1856–1923) Novelist and kindergarten educator, born in Philadelphia, PA. She led the kindergarten movement in the USA, but is best remembered for her children's novels, notably *Rebecca of Sunnybrook Farm* (1903).

Wight, Isle of, Lat **Vectis** pop (1995e) 123 000; area 381 sq km/147 sq mi. Island county off the S coast of England, a unitary authority from 1995; in the mouth of Southampton Water, separated from Hampshire by the Solent and Spithead; imposing cliffs of the vertical sandstone Needles near Alum Bay; county town, Newport; ferry services from Portsmouth, Southampton, Lymington; tourism; yachting (especially Cowes Regatta Week). >> England ℹ; Newport (Isle of Wight)

Wightman Cup An annual lawn tennis competition involving professional women's teams from the USA and UK. It was first held in 1923, and named after the former US player Hazel Wightman (*née* Hotchkiss) (1886–1974). It was scrapped in 1992. >> tennis, lawn ℹ

Wigman, Mary, originally **Marie Wiegmann** (1886–1973) Dancer, choreographer, and teacher, born in Hanover, Germany. She opened a school in Dresden in 1920, and created numerous solo and group dances which typified German expressionist dancing. >> choreography; modern dance

Wilberforce, William (1759–1833) British politician, evangelist, and philanthropist, born in Hull. In 1788 he began the movement which resulted in the abolition of the slave trade in the British West Indies in 1807. He died one month before the Slavery Abolition Act was passed in parliament. >> slave trade

Wilbur, Richard (Purdy) (1921–) Poet, born in New York City. Based in Cummington, MA, he has won acclaim for his translations as well as for his own lyrical poetry, as in *New and Collected Poems* (1988). He was named poet laureate of the USA in 1987.

Wilbye, John (1574–1638) Madrigal composer, born in Diss, Norfolk. He is known for only 66 madrigals, but these are renowned for his careful setting of literary texts, and for several translations of Italian poems. >> madrigal

wild boar A wild ancestor (*Sus scrofa*) of the domestic pig, native to Europe, NW Africa, and S Asia; thick dark hair; male with tusks; domesticated in SE Asia 5–10 000 years ago. >> pig

wild cat A member of the cat family (*Felis silvestris*), found from N Europe to Africa and India; ancestor of the domestic cat, but larger, with a shorter, thicker tail. >> cat; Felidae

Wilde, Oscar (Fingal O'Flahertie Wills) (1854–1900) Writer, born in Dublin. Celebrated for his wit and flamboyant manner, he became a leading member of the 'art for art's sake' movement. His early work included his *Poems* (1881), the novel *The Picture of Dorian Gray* (1891), and several comic plays, notably *Lady Windermere's Fan* (1892) and *The Importance of being Earnest* (1895). *The Ballad of Reading Gaol* (1898) and *De profundis* (1905) reveal the effect of two years' hard labour for homosexual practices. >> art for art's sake

wildebeest [**wil**duhbeest, **vil**duhbeest] An African grazing antelope; sturdy, with a large convex face; short horns spread sideways with upturned tips; long mane; long fringe of hairs along throat; also known as **gnu**. (Genus: *Connochaetes*, 2 species.) >> antelope

Wilder, Billy, originally **Samuel Wilder** (1906–) Film director and scriptwriter, born in Sucha, Austria. His films include *The Lost Weekend* (1945, Oscar), *Sunset Boulevard* (1950), and *The Apartment* (1960, Oscar).

Wilder, Gene, originally **Jerome Silberman** (1935–) Film actor, writer, and director, born in Milwaukee, WI. He received a Best Supporting Actor Oscar nomination for *The Producers* (1968), later films including *Blazing Saddles* (1974) and *Young Frankenstein* (1974). Known also as a screenwriter and director, he returned to the stage in 1996, starring in the London production of *Laughter on the 23rd Floor*.

Wilder, Thornton (Niven) (1897–1975) Writer, born in Madison, WI. His first novel, *The Cabala* (1926), was followed by the very successful *The Bridge of San Luis Rey*

(1927), and the plays *Our Town* (1938) and *The Skin of Our Teeth* (1942), which all won Pulitzer Prizes.

Wilderness Campaign 1 (1864) An indecisive conflict in the American Civil War between the Union army under General Grant and the Confederate army under General Lee, fought in the Wilderness area of Virginia. >> Grant, Ulysses S; Lee, Robert E **2** (1755) The term **Battle of the Wilderness** is also used for a conflict in Western Pennsylvania, in which Indians and French troops decimated a larger British army under General Edward Braddock.

Wilderness Road The early route across the S Appalachian Mts, from the Holston R through Cumberland Gap to Boonesborough on the Kentucky R. It was constructed in 1775 by a party led by Daniel Boone. >> Appalachian Mountains; Boone

wildlife refuge An area set aside for the protection and conservation of wildlife (eg Serengeti National Park, Tanzania, and Australia's Great Barrier Reef). Ideally, it should be a wilderness area large enough to sustain its plant and animal population. >> endangered species; National Park; Nature Reserve

Wildlife Trusts >> **Royal Society for Nature Conservation**

Wiles, Andrew (John) (1953–) Mathematician, born in Cambridge, Cambridgeshire. In 1993 he announced that he had solved one of mathematics' oldest mysteries, Fermat's last theorem, and acceptance of his proposal followed in 1994. >> Fermat's last theorem

Wilfrid or **Wilfrith, St** (634–709) Monk and bishop, born in Northumbria, England. As Bishop of York (c.665), he was involved in controversy over the organization of the Church in Britain, and was the first churchman to appeal to Rome to settle the issue. Feast day 12 October. >> Whitby, Synod of

Wilhelmina (Helena Pauline Maria) [wiluh**mee**na] (1880–1962) Queen of The Netherlands (1890–1948), born in The Hague. During World War 2, though compelled to seek refuge in Britain, she steadfastly encouraged Dutch resistance to the German occupation. In 1948, she abdicated in favour of her daughter **Juliana**. >> Juliana

Wilkes, John (1727–97) British politician and journalist, born in London. He became an MP (1757), and attacked the ministry in his weekly journal, *North Briton* (1762–3), for which he was expelled from the house. Re-elected on several occasions, and repeatedly expelled, he came to be seen as a champion of liberty, and an upholder of press freedom. He finally gained admission to parliament in 1774.

Wilkes Land Area of Antarctica between Queen Mary Land (W) and Terre Adélie, lying mostly between 105° and 135° E. >> Antarctica i

Wilkie, Sir David (1785–1841) Painter, born in Cults, Fife. His fame mainly rests on his genre painting, but he also painted portraits, and in his later years sought to emulate the richness of colouring of the old masters, choosing more elevated subjects. >> genre painting

Wilkins, Sir George (Hubert) (1888–1958) Polar explorer, born in Mt Bryan East, Australia. He flew from England to Australia (1919), explored the Antarctic with Shackleton (1920–2), and made a pioneer flight from Alaska to Spitsbergen over polar ice (1928). >> Poles; Shackleton

Wilkins, Maurice (Hugh Frederick) (1916–) Biophysicist, born in Pongaroa, New Zealand. With Crick and Watson he shared the Nobel Prize for Physiology or Medicine in 1962 for work on the structure of DNA. >> biophysics; DNA i

Wilkins, Roy (1910–81) Journalist and civil rights leader, born in St Louis, MO. He edited the newspapers of the National Association for the Advancement of Colored People (1934–49), and was then appointed the organization's executive secretary, retiring in 1977. >> civil rights

will A document in which a person (the *testator* or *testatrix*) sets out the way in which his or her property (the *estate*) is to be distributed to beneficiaries after death. In order to be valid, a will must comply with certain requirements (which vary between jurisdictions): for example, in the UK it must be signed in the presence of two witnesses, both of whom are present at the same time. If a person dies without making a will (dies *intestate*), statutory rules in some jurisdictions govern the distribution of property. >> probate

Willandra Lakes A world heritage site covering c.6000 sq km/2300 sq mi in the Murray R Basin in New South Wales, Australia. The region provides a remarkable 'fossil landscape', generally unmodified since the end of the Pleistocene ice age. >> Murray River; Pleistocene epoch

Willard, Emma, *née* **Hart** (1787–1870) Educator, born in Berlin, CT. As founder of the Troy (NY) Female Seminary in 1821 (now the Emma Willard School), she was instrumental in the emergence of intellectually demanding secondary education for American women. >> Stanton; women's liberation movement

Willemstad [**vil**emstaht] 12°12N 68°56W, pop (1995e) 51 300. Capital town of the Netherlands Antilles, on SW coast of Curaçao I; established by the Dutch as a trading centre, mid-17th-c; airport; free port; inner city and harbour, a world heritage site. >> Netherlands Antilles i

Willendorf [**vil**endaw(r)f] A prehistoric site near Krems, lower Austria, with Gravettian occupation dated c.32–28 000 BC. It is celebrated for the 'Willendorf Venus', a limestone statuette, 11 cm/4⅜ in high, painted with red ochre, which presumably served as a fertility or house goddess. >> Gravettian

William I (of England), known as **the Conquerer** (c.1028–1087) Duke of Normandy (1035–87) and the first Norman king of England (1066–87), the illegitimate son of Duke Robert of Normandy. Edward the Confessor most probably designated him as future King of England in 1051. When Harold Godwinson took the throne as Harold II, William invaded with the support of the papacy, defeated and killed Harold at the Battle of Hastings, and was crowned king on Christmas Day 1066. By the time of the Domesday Book (1086), the leaders of Anglo-Saxon society S of the Tees had been almost entirely replaced by a new ruling class of Normans, Bretons, and Flemings, who were closely tied to William by feudal bonds. >> Domesday Book; Edward the Confessor; Harold II; Norman Conquest

William I (of Germany), Ger **Wilhelm** (1797–1888) King of Prussia (1861–88) and first German emperor (1871–88), born in Berlin, the second son of Frederick William III. He placed Bismarck at the head of the ministry, and was victorious against Denmark (1864), Austria (1866), and France (1871). The rapid rise of socialism in Germany led to severe repressive measures, and he survived several attempts at assassination. >> Bismarck; Prussia; Roon

William I (of the Netherlands), **Prince of Orange**, known as **William the Silent** (1533–84) First of the hereditary stadholders of the United Provinces of the Netherlands (1572–84), born in Dillenburg, The Netherlands. In 1568 he took up arms against the Spanish crown, and became stadholder of the Northern provinces, united in the Union of Utrecht (1579). He was assassinated by a Spanish agent. His byname comes from his ability to keep secret Henry II's scheme to massacre all the Protestants of France and the Netherlands, confided to him when he was a French hostage in 1559. >> Henry II (of France); Philip II (of Spain); United Provinces of the Netherlands

William I (of Scotland), known as **William the Lion** (c.1142–1214) King of Scots (1165–1214), the brother and successor of Malcolm IV. In 1173–4 he invaded Northumberland during the rebellion against Henry II, but was defeated at Alnwick. He was nevertheless able to make Scotland a much stronger kingdom. >> Henry II (of England)

William II (of England), known as **William Rufus** (c.1056–1100) King of England (1087–1100), the second surviving son of William the Conqueror. His main goal was the recovery of Normandy from his elder brother Robert Curthose, and from 1096, when Robert departed on the First Crusade, William ruled the duchy as *de facto* duke. He also led expeditions to Wales (1095, 1097), and came to exercise a controlling influence over Scottish affairs. He exploited his rights over the Church and the nobility, and quarrelled with Anselm, Archbishop of Canterbury. He was killed by an arrow while hunting in the New Forest. >> Anselm, St; Crusades [i]; Henry I (of England)

William II (of Germany), Ger **Wilhelm**, known as **Kaiser Wilhelm** (1859–1941) German Emperor and King of Prussia (1888–1918), born in Potsdam, Germany, the eldest son of Frederick III and Victoria, daughter of Britain's Queen Victoria. He dismissed Bismarck (1890), and began a long period of personal rule, displaying a bellicose attitude in international affairs. During World War 1 he became a mere figurehead, and when the German armies collapsed, he abdicated. >> Bismarck; World War 1

William III, known as **William of Orange** (1650–1702) Stadtholder of the United Provinces (1672–1702) and King of Great Britain (1689–1702), born in The Hague, the son of William II of Orange by Mary, the eldest daughter of Charles I of England. In 1677 he married his cousin, **Mary** (1662–94), the daughter of James II by Anne Hyde. Invited to redress the grievances of the country, he landed at Torbay in 1688 with an English and Dutch army, and forced James II to flee. He defeated James's supporters at Dunkeld (1689) and at the Boyne (1690), then concentrated on the War of the League of Augsburg against France (1689–97), in which he was finally successful. >> James II (of England)

William IV, known as **the Sailor King** (1765–1837) King of Great Britain and Ireland, and King of Hanover (1830–7), born in London, the third son of George III. He was the last monarch to use prerogative powers to dismiss a ministry with a parliamentary majority when he sacked Melbourne in 1834. >> Melbourne, Viscount

William of Malmesbury [**mahmz**bree] (c.1090–c.1143) English chronicler and Benedictine monk, the librarian of Malmesbury Abbey, Wiltshire. His main works include *Gesta regum anglorum*, a general history of England from the coming of the Anglo-Saxons. >> Anglo-Saxons; Benedictines

William of Ockham or **Occam** [**ok**am] known as **the Venerable Inceptor** (c.1285–c.1349) Philosopher and theologian, born in the village of Ockham, Surrey. He became involved in a dispute between the Franciscans and Pope John XXII over apostolic poverty. He is especially known for his use of the principle of parsimony (**Ockham's razor**): 'Do not multiply entities beyond necessity' – a theory should not propose the existence of anything more than is needed for its explanations.

William of Tyre (c.1130–86) Chronicler and churchman, born in Palestine of French parents. He was appointed Archbishop of Tyre in 1175. His main work, *Historia rerum in partibus transmarinis gestarum* (History of Deeds in Foreign Parts), deals with the history of Palestine from 614 to 1184. >> Crusades [i]

William of Wykeham or **Wickham** [**wik**am] (1324–1404) English statesman and clergyman, born in Wickham, Hampshire. He was appointed Bishop of Winchester (1367), and was twice Chancellor of England (1367–71, 1389–91). >> Edward III

Williams, (George) Emlyn (1905–87) Playwright and actor, born in Mostyn, Flintshire. He achieved success as a dramatist with *A Murder has been Arranged* (1930) and the psychological thriller, *Night Must Fall* (1935). He featured in several films, and gave widely acclaimed readings from the works of Dickens, Dylan Thomas, and Saki.

Williams, Hank, popular name of **Hiram King Williams** (1923–53) Influential country singer and songwriter, born in Georgetown, AL. His many hits include 'Lovesick Blues', 'Jambalaya', and 'Hey Good Lookin''. His son, **Hank Williams Jr** (1949–), continues as a successful country singer and songwriter. >> country and western

Williams, Jody (1950–) US activist, born in Putney, VT, the campaign coordinator for the International Campaign to Ban Landmines. She shared the 1997 Nobel Peace Prize along with the organization for their work towards the banning and clearing of anti-personnel mines. >> International Campaign to Ban Landmines

Williams, John (Christopher) (1942–) Guitarist, born in Melbourne, Australia, but resident in England since 1952. Several classical composers have written works for him, and he founded a rock group known as Sky (1979–84). >> guitar; Segovia

Williams, J(ohn) P(eter) R(hys) (1949–) Rugby union player, born in Bridgend, S Wales. He is the most capped Welshman, with 55 appearances, and the game's most capped fullback (54). >> rugby football

Williams, Robin (1952–) Film actor and entertainer, born in Chicago, IL. He starred in the television series *Mork and Mindy* (1978–82), made his film debut in *Popeye* (1981), and became known for his versatile and energetic performances. He earned Oscar nominations for *Good Morning Vietnam* (1987) and *Dead Poets Society* (1989), and a Best Supporting Actor Oscar for *Good Will Hunting* (1997).

Williams, Roger (c.1604–83) Colonist who founded Rhode Island, born in London. He became an extreme Puritan, and emigrated to New England in 1630. He purchased lands from the Indians, and founded the city of Providence (1636), allowing full religious toleration. >> Puritanism; Rhode Island

Williams (of Crosby), Shirley (Vivien Teresa Brittain) Williams, Baroness, *née* **Catlin** (1930–) British stateswoman, born in London. She became a Labour MP in 1964, and was secretary of state for prices and consumer protection (1974–6), and for education and science (1976–9). She became a co-founder of the Social Democratic Party in 1981, and the party's first elected MP later that year. She lost her seat in the 1983 general election, but remained as the SDP's president (1982–7). She later moved to the USA, but remains involved in British politics, and was made a life peer in 1993. >> Labour / Liberal Party (UK); Social Democratic Party

Williams, Tennessee, pseudonym of **Thomas Lanier Williams** (1911–83) Playwright, born in Columbus, MS. He achieved success with *The Glass Menagerie* (1944). His later plays, almost all set in the Deep South against a background of decadence and degradation, include *A Streetcar Named Desire* (1947, Pulitzer), *Cat on a Hot Tin Roof* (1955, Pulitzer), *Suddenly Last Summer* (1958), and *Night of the Iguana* (1961). He also wrote short stories, essays, poetry, memoirs, and two novels.

Williams, William Carlos (1883–1963) Poet and novelist, born in Rutherford, NJ. He developed a distinctly American style for his shorter lyrics, which commanded attention from *Spring and All* (1923), and he adapted this for his 'personal epic', *Paterson* (1946–51). He also wrote plays, essays, a trilogy of novels, and criticism, including *In The American Grain* (1925).

Williamsburg 37°17N 76°43W, pop (1995e) 12 400. City in SE Virginia, USA; settled, 1633 (as Middle Plantation, renamed 1699); state capital, 1699–1780; Colonial Williamsburg is a major building restoration scheme; College of William and Mary (1693). >> Virginia; William III

Williamson, Malcolm (Benjamin Graham Christopher) (1931–) Composer, born in Sydney, New South Wales, Australia. His compositions include the operas *Our Man in Havana* (1963) and *The Red Sea* (1972), as well as a wide variety of orchestral, vocal, choral, and other works. He was made Master of the Queen's Musick in 1975.

Willis, Bruce (1955–) Film actor, born in West Germany, but moved to the USA as a young child. He became widely known in the television series *Moonlighting* (1985–9), and achieved star status for his role in the *Die Hard* series (1988, 1990, 1995). Later films include *Death Becomes Her* (1992), *Pulp Fiction* (1994), *12 Monkeys* (1995), and *The Siege* (1998).

will o' the wisp >> **ignis fatuus**

willow A member of a large genus of mostly N temperate deciduous trees and shrubs; flowers in separate male and female catkins; seeds plumed with silky hairs for wind dispersal. Willows show a wide range of form, from low, creeping arctic species to large trees, many growing in or near water. They are a source of withies for basketwork, and cricket bats. (Genus: *Salix*, 500 species. Family: Salicaceae.) >> osier; sallow; tree ℹ; weeping willow

willow-herb A member of a somewhat variable genus of mostly perennials, native throughout temperate and arctic regions; flowers with four rose, purple, sometimes white petals on top of a long, purplish ovary; fruit a capsule containing numerous white-plumed seeds. (Genus: *Epilobium*, 215 species. Family: Onagraceae.) >> ovary

willow pattern A decorative scene used on pottery tablewares, showing a Chinese landscape, with figures, buildings, and a bridge, carried out in blue transfer-printing on white. It was first engraved by Thomas Minton c.1780, and widely copied by many factories. >> Minton ceramics

Wills, Helen (Newington), married names **Moody** and **Roark** (1905–98) Tennis player, born in Berkeley, CA. She won the Wimbledon singles title eight times in nine attempts (1927–30, 1932–3, 1935, 1938), and in all won 31 Grand Slam events. >> tennis ℹ

Wilmington 39°45N 75°33W, pop (1995e) 77 900. Port in N Delaware, USA; founded by the Swedes as Fort Christina, 1638; taken by the British and renamed Willington, 1731; renamed Wilmington, 1739; city status, 1832; largest city in the state; airfield; railway; chemicals ('the chemical capital of the world'); home of several large corporations. >> Delaware

Wilmot Proviso (1846) A motion introduced in the US Congress by David Wilmot (Democrat, Pennsylvania) to forbid the expansion of slavery into territory acquired during the Mexican War. It passed the House of Representatives but not the Senate. >> Mexican War; slave trade

Wilson, Sir Angus (Frank Johnstone) (1913–91) Writer, born in Bexhill, East Sussex. His works include the novels *Anglo-Saxon Attitudes* (1956) and *The Old Men at the Zoo* (1961), the play *The Mulberry Bush* (1955), and two volumes of short stories.

Wilson, C(harles) T(homson) R(ees) (1869–1959) Pioneer of atomic and nuclear physics, born in Glencorse, Midlothian. His major achievement was to devise the cloud chamber method for observing the track of alpha particles and electrons. In 1927 he shared the Nobel Prize for Physics. >> cloud chamber; Compton, Arthur

Wilson, Colin (Henry) (1931–) Novelist and writer on philosophy, sociology, and the occult, born in Leicester, Leicestershire. His books include *The Mind Parasites* (1966), *Poltergeist!* (1981), *Written in Blood* (1989), and *From Atlantis to the Sphinx* (1996). His psychic interests brought him status as a cult figure in the 1980s.

Wilson, Edmund (1895–1972) Literary and social critic, born in Red Bank, NJ. He was a prolific author, producing several studies on aesthetic, social, and political themes, as well as verse, plays, travel books, and historical works.

Wilson, Edward (Osborne) (1929–) Biologist, born in Birmingham, AL. His book *Sociobiology: the New Synthesis* (1975) virtually founded the subject of sociobiology. >> sociobiology

Wilson (of Rievaulx), (James) Harold Wilson, Baron (1916–95) British statesman and prime minister (1964–70, 1974–6), born in Huddersfield, West Yorkshire. He was President of the Board of Trade (1947–51), and in 1963 succeeded Gaitskell as Leader of the Labour Party. His economic plans were badly affected by a balance of payments crisis, leading to severe restrictive measures. He was also faced with the problem of Rhodesian independence, and opposition to Britain's proposed entry into the European Economic Community. Following his third general election victory, he resigned as Labour leader in 1976. >> Gaitskell; Labour Party; prices and incomes policy

Wilson (of Libya and of Stowlangtoft), Henry Maitland Wilson, Baron (1881–1964) British field marshal, born in London. He led the initial British advance in Libya (1940–1) and the unsuccessful Greek campaign (1941), and became commander-in-chief Middle East (1943) and supreme allied commander in the Mediterranean theatre (1944). >> World War 2

Wilson, Richard (1714–82) Landscape painter, born in Penygroes, Powys. He began as a portrait painter, but after a visit to Italy (1752–6) turned to landscapes. >> landscape painting

Wilson, (Thomas) Woodrow (1856–1924) US statesman and 28th president (1913–21), born in Staunton, VA. Elected Democratic president in 1912 and 1916, his administration saw the prohibition and women's suffrage amendments to the constitution, America's participation in World War 1, his peace plan proposals (the *Fourteen Points*), and his championship of the League of Nations. He received the Nobel Peace Prize in 1919. >> Democratic Party; Fourteen Points; League of Nations; World War 1

Wiltshire pop (1995e) 602 000; area 3481 sq km/1344 sq mi. County of S England; chalk downland of Salisbury Plain at the centre; county town, Trowbridge; Thamesdown a unitary authority from 1997; many ancient prehistoric remains, such as Stonehenge; Marlborough Downs, Savernake Forest, Longleat House. >> Avebury; England ℹ; Salisbury Plain; Silbury Hill; Stonehenge; Trowbridge

Wimbledon Residential district in Merton borough, S Greater London, England; headquarters of the All England Tennis Club; annual lawn tennis championships (Jun–Jul). >> London; tennis, lawn ℹ; RR1063

Winchester, Lat **Venta Belgarum**, Anglo-Saxon **Wintanceaster** 51°04N 1°19W, pop (1995e) 38 700. City and county town in Hampshire, S England; on the R Itchen; Roman settlement the fifth largest in Britain; capital of Wessex in 519, and capital of England in 827; Domesday Book compiled here; railway; longest Gothic cathedral N of the Alps (11th–16th-c); Winchester College (1382), oldest public school in England; 12th-c St Cross Hospital; 13th-c castle hall, containing a mediaeval 'replica' of Arthur's Round Table. >> Arthur; Domesday Book; Hampshire; William I (of England)

Winckelmann, Johann (Joachim) [**vingk**elman] (1717–68) Archaeologist and art historian, born in Stendal, Germany. His works include the pioneering study, *Geschichte der Kunst des Alterthums* (1764, History of the Art of Antiquity).

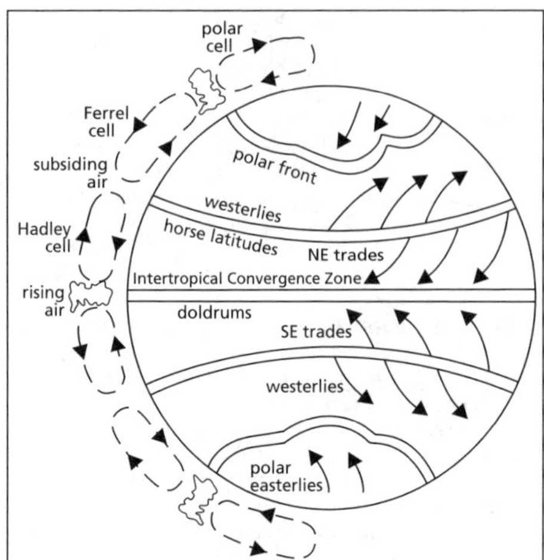

Wind – the three cell general circulation model of the atmosphere

wind The movement of air along the pressure gradient from areas of high to lower pressure; one of the basic elements of weather. Pressure gradients develop through the unequal cooling or heating of a layer of atmosphere. The steeper the gradient, the stronger the wind. In the N hemisphere the Coriolis force deflects wind to the right, and in the S hemisphere to the left. At low altitudes, the frictional force of the Earth's surface reduces the influence of the Coriolis force, diverting the wind towards the centre of the low pressure area. >> anemometer [i]; Beaufort scale; Coriolis force [i]; Föhn / Foehn wind; Harmattan; isobar; Khamsin; Mistral; Sirocco; squall; trade winds; westerlies

wind chill An effect of wind decreasing the apparent temperature felt by a human body. Strong winds increase the heat loss from exposed flesh, and so at low temperatures may induce hypothermia at a higher air temperature than would occur in calm conditions. For example, an air temperature of −18°C with no wind would be equivalent to −38°C at 7 m/23 ft/s. >> hypothermia

Windermere 54°23N 2°54W, pop (1995e) 8300. Lakeside resort town in Cumbria, NW England; on L Windermere; railway; major tourist centre; Rydal Mount (10 km/6 mi NW), Wordsworth's home from 1813 to 1850; Brantwood, home of Ruskin. >> Cumbria; Lake District; Ruskin; Wordsworth, William

Windermere, Lake Largest lake in England, in the Lake District; extending 18 km/11 mi S from Ambleside; largest island, Belle Isle. >> Lake District; Windermere

Windhoek [**vint**huk] 22°34S 17°06E, pop (1995e) 185 000. Capital of Namibia; altitude, 1650 m/5413 ft; occupied by South African forces, 1915; capital of German South-West Africa, 1922; airport; railway; cathedral. >> Namibia [i]

wind instrument >> **aerophone**

windmill A mill worked by the action of wind on sails. Windmills have been used principally for grinding corn, cleansing (*fulling*) cloth, and for drainage. There are three types: **post mills**, where the mill itself revolves on a central post to face the wind, and **tower mills** (built of brick) and **smock mills** (built of timber), where only the cap revolves. Windmills were in common use until the end of the 19th-c, when they were largely superseded by the advent of steam power.

windows A form of graphic user interface in which the computer presents on a screen a set of sub-screens (windows), each sub-screen corresponding to a different program running in the computer. The sub-screens can be moved about, placed one on top of another, or temporarily shrunk in order to minimize the amount of information presented on the screen at any time, and to allow different programs to pass files between them. *Windows* is also the name of a registered trade mark of a multitasking operating environment for MS-DOS. >> operating system

windpipe >> **trachea**

Windscale >> **Sellafield**

Windsor (Canada) 42°18N 83°00W, pop (1995e) 203 000. Town in S Ontario, Canada, on Detroit R, opposite Detroit, MI; founded, 1835; rapid industrial growth in 19th-c; railway; university (1857). >> Detroit; Ontario

Windsor (UK) 51°30N 0°38W, pop (1995e) 32 600. Town linked with Eton in Windsor and Maidenhead unitary authority, S England; on R Thames; railway; Windsor Castle, Eton College (1440); Royal Windsor Horse Show (May). >> Berkshire; Windsor Castle

Windsor, Duke of >> **Edward VIII**

Windsor, House of The name of the British royal family since 1917. This unequivocally English name resulted from a Declaration by George V, a member of the House of Saxe-Coburg-Gotha. It was felt that a Germanic surname for the British monarchy was inappropriate, especially during a war against Germany. >> George V

Windsor Castle The largest of England's castles, situated on the R Thames at Windsor, S England. It was founded by William I and first used as a royal residence by Henry I. It was severely damaged by fire in 1992. Restoration work was completed in 1997. >> castle; Windsor

wind tunnel >> **aerodynamics** [i]

Windward Islands (Caribbean) Island group of the Lesser Antilles in the Caribbean Sea; S of the Leeward Is, from Martinique (N) to Grenada (S), excluding Trinidad and Tobago; so called because of their exposure to the prevailing NE trade winds; formerly the name of a British colony comprising Dominica, St Lucia, St Vincent, and Grenada. >> Antilles; Leeward Islands (Caribbean)

Windward Islands (French Polynesia), Fr **Iles du Vent** pop (1995e) 151 000. Island group of the Society Is, French Polynesia; comprises Tahiti, Moorea, and the smaller Mehetia, Tetiaroa, and Tubuai Manu Is; capital, Papeete. >> Papeete; Society Islands; Tahiti

wine The alcoholic beverage produced from the fermentation of grapes or other fruits. The alcohol content varies, but is usually 12%, the point at which fermentation stops. A wine's taste is determined by the type of grape used, the soil in which it is grown, and the local climate. It may be white, red, or rosé, dry or sweet, still or sparkling. White wine can be made from red (or black) grapes as well as white (or green): the final colour depends on whether the skins are left to ferment with the juice. Sweet wine is taken from the vat before fermentation has finished, while some sugar remains; dry wine is left to ferment until all the sugar has been converted to alcohol. Sparkling wine is produced by bottling it before the fermentation process is completed, so that fermentation continues in the bottle. Fermentation is stopped by the addition of alcohol (eg brandy) to produce fortified wines (eg sherry and port). Known since ancient times, viniculture was taken to Italy by the Greeks, and by the Romans to Gaul. France has long been regarded as the producer of the greatest wines, in Bordeaux (claret) and Burgundy. France and Italy are the leading producers, with Spain and Germany also traditional centres. The 20th-c has seen the development of vineyards all over the world. >> alcohol; fermentation; grapevine; phylloxera

Winfrey, Oprah [**win**free] (1954–) Television talk-show host, actor, and producer, born in Kosciusko, MS. She launched the highly successful *Oprah Winfrey Show* (3 Emmies) in 1986. She established Harpo Productions in Chicago, her films including *The Color Purple* (1985, Oscar nomination). She is also known for her exercise and dieting programmes, and as an activist in support of children's rights.

Wingate, Orde (Charles) (1903–44) British general, born in Naini Tal, India. He served in the Sudan (1928–33) and Palestine (1936–9), where he helped create a Jewish defence force, and in the Burma theatre (1942) organized the Chindits. >> Chindits; World War 2

Winkler, Hans-Günther [**vingk**ler] (1926–) Show jumper, born in Wuppertal-Barmen, Germany. He is the only man to have won five Olympic gold medals (for West Germany) at show jumping: the team golds in 1956, 1960, 1964, and 1972, and the individual title on *Halla* in 1956. >> equestrianism

Winnipeg 49°53N 97°10W, pop (1995e) 655 000. Capital of Manitoba province, C Canada, on the Red R; established 1738 as Fort Rouge; fur-trading post, 1806; modern name, 1873; expansion after arrival of railway, 1881; airport; universities (1877, 1967); professional teams, Winnipeg Jets (ice hockey), Winnipeg Blue Bombers (football); Centennial Arts Centre, Civic Auditorium (home of Winnipeg Symphony Orchestra), Royal Winnipeg Ballet. >> Manitoba

Winnipeg, Lake Lake in SC Manitoba province, S Canada; length 386 km/240 mi; breadth 88 km/55 mi; area 24 390 sq km/9414 sq mi. >> Manitoba

Winston-Salem 36°06N 80°15W, pop (1995e) 155 000. City in NC North Carolina, USA; Winston founded in 1849, Salem in 1766; towns united, 1913; Wake Forest University (1834); railway; the nation's chief tobacco manufacturer. >> North Carolina

wintergreen A member of a family of small evergreen perennials, native to N temperate and arctic regions; flowers drooping, bell-shaped, 5-petalled, pink or white. (Family: Pyrolaceae.)

Winterhalter, Franz Xaver [**vin**terhalter] (1806–73) Painter, born in Menzenschwand, Germany. In 1834 he went to Paris, where he became the fashionable artist of his day, painting many royal figures.

Winter Palace >> **Hermitage**

Winterthur [**vin**tertoor] 47°30N 8°45E, pop (1995e) 88 700. Town in Switzerland; near the R Töss, NE of Zürich; railway junction. >> Switzerland [i]

Winter War >> **Russo-Finnish War**

Winthrop, John (1588–1649) Colonist, born in Edwardstone, Suffolk, UK. He was appointed governor of Massachusetts colony in 1629, and was a major influence in forming the political institutions of the Northern states of America. >> Massachusetts

wire service >> **news agency**

wireworm >> **click beetle**

Wisconsin [wis**kon**sin] pop (1995e) 5 185 000; area 145 431 sq km/56 153 sq mi. State in N USA; the 'Badger State'; first settled by French traders, 1670; surrendered to the British, 1763; ceded to the USA, 1783 (part of the Northwest Territory); Territory of Wisconsin formed, 1836; 30th state to join the Union, 1848; c.26 000 sq km/10 000 sq mi of L Michigan lie within the state boundary; capital, Madison; highest point, Timms Hill (595 m/1952 ft); glaciated terrain in the N and W, largely forested; over 8500 lakes; produces more milk, butter, and cheese than any other state; over a third of the nation's cheese production; heavy industry in the Milwaukee area. >> Madison; Michigan, Lake; United States of America [i]; RR994

Wisdom, Book of >> **Wisdom of Solomon**

wisdom literature In the Hebrew Bible/Old Testament, a group of writings, usually including Proverbs, Ecclesiastes, the Song of Songs, and Job. Among the Apocrypha, it also includes Ecclesiasticus and the Wisdom of Solomon. The literature is usually traced to a special class of sages in Israel who sought to draw lessons for life from general human experience rather than from revealed religious truths. >> Old Testament; Wisdom of Solomon

Wisdom of Solomon or **Book of Wisdom** A book of the Old Testament Apocrypha, purportedly from Solomon, but usually attributed to an unknown Alexandrian Jew c.1st-c BC. >> Apocrypha, Old Testament; Solomon (Hebrew Bible)

Wise, Ernie >> **Morecambe, Eric**

Wiseman, Nicholas (Patrick Stephen), Cardinal (1802–65) Roman Catholic churchman, born in Seville, Spain. His appointment as the first Archbishop of Westminster and a cardinal (1850) called forth a storm of religious excitement, which led to the passing of the Ecclesiastical Titles Assumption Act. >> Roman Catholicism

Wise Men >> **Magi**

wisent [**vee**zent] >> **bison**

Wishart, George [**wish**ert] (c.1513–46) Reformer and martyr, born in Pitarrow, Aberdeenshire. He preached the Lutheran doctrine in several towns, and was arrested and burned at St Andrews. One of his converts was John Knox. >> Knox, John; Lutheranism

wisteria A deciduous climbing shrub from E Asia and North America; pea-flowers fragrant, lilac, violet, or white, in long pendulous clusters. It is often grown for ornament. (Genus: *Wisteria*, 6 species. Family: Leguminosae.) >> climbing plant

witan or **witenagemot** (Old English 'meeting of wise men') The council of the Anglo-Saxon kings, once regarded as the first English 'parliament'. >> Anglo-Saxons

witchcraft The alleged possession and exercise of magical or psychic powers, especially involving the manipulation of natural objects or events; often called *black magic* if harmful to people, *white magic* if helpful. In Europe the Christian Church began persecuting witches in the 14th-c, alleging that witches consciously made a pact with Satan. Contemporary witchcraft in the West sees itself as an alternative religion, celebrating gods drawn from various European pre-Christian religions, and exercising its magical powers in beneficial ways. >> magic; Salem (Massachusetts); voodoo

witch hazel A deciduous shrub or small tree, native to E Asia and eastern North America; flowers in short-stalked clusters, each with four long strap-shaped yellow petals. The bark yields an astringent lotion. (Genus: *Hamamelis*, 6 species. Family: Hamamelidaceae.) >> dowsing

witchweed A higher plant parasite (*Striga hermonthica*) causing severe damage to the roots of sorghum, millet, sugar cane, and other tropical grain crops, and also occasionally attacking pigeon pea and other legumes. It is most serious in Africa and the drier parts of India, but has also been reported from North America. (Family: Scrophulariaceae.) >> legume; millet; parasitic plant; sorghum; sugar cane

withdrawal syndrome Symptoms which occur when an addictive substance is no longer available to someone who has become addicted to it; they include nausea, vomiting, stomach cramps, anxiety, panic attacks, palpitations, headaches, hallucinations, sweating, shaking, and possibly convulsions. The treatment of drug dependency involves replacing the body's biochemical requirement for the drug with a similar but less addictive substance. Diminishing doses of the substance are given until eventually all medication can be withdrawn. >> drug addiction

Witt, Katerina [vit] (1965–) Figure skater, born in Karl-Marx-Stadt, Germany. She was world champion in 1984–5 and 1987–8, and Olympic champion in 1984 and 1988. >> ice skating

Wittenberg [**vit**nberg] 51°53N 12°39E, pop (1995e) 55 700. Town in EC Germany; on R Elbe; associated with the beginning of the Reformation, 1517; part of Prussia, 1814; railway; university (1817); Schlosskirche, to the doors of which Luther nailed his 95 theses. >> Germany i; Luther; ninety-five theses; Reformation

Wittgenstein, Ludwig (Josef Johann) [**wit**genstiyn], Ger [**vit**genshtiyn] (1889–1951) Philosopher, born in Vienna. He produced major works on the philosophy of language, notably *Tractatus logico-philosophicus* (1921) and the posthumously-published *Philosophische Untersuchungen* (1953, Philosophical Investigations), in which he studies the 'language games' whereby language is given its meaning in actual *use*.

Witwatersrand [wit**waw**terzrand], Afrikaans [vuht**vah**ter-srant] or **The Rand, ('white water's reef')** Region centred on a ridge of gold-bearing rock in South Africa; length 100 km/60 mi; width 40 km/25 mi; Johannesburg located near its centre; the power house of the South African economy; gold discovered in 1886 (produces over half the world's supply). >> South Africa i

woad A biennial or perennial (*Isatis tinctoria*) with numerous yellow, cross-shaped flowers and pendulous, purplish capsules. The blue dye used by Ancient Britons (and still produced until the 19th-c) is made by exposing part-dried, crushed leaves to the air. (Family: Cruciferae.)

Wodehouse, Sir P(elham) G(renville) [**wud**hows] (1881–1975) Novelist, born in Guildford, Surrey. He established his reputation with the creation of Bertie Wooster and his 'gentleman's gentleman' Jeeves. A prolific writer, he produced a succession of novels, short stories, sketches, and librettos.

Woden >> **Odin**

Wogan, Terry [**woh**gn], popular name of **Michael Terence Wogan** (1938–) Broadcaster and writer, born in Limerick, Ireland. He began as a radio announcer in Ireland, and joined the BBC in 1965. His television shows include *Blankety Blank* (1977–81), the annual Eurovision Song Contests, and an early evening chat-show (1982–92). The recipient of many broadcasting 'personality of the year' awards, he returned to radio work in 1993.

Wöhler, Friedrich [**voe**ler] (1800–82) Chemist, born near Frankfurt, Germany. He isolated aluminium (1827) and beryllium (1828). His synthesis of urea from ammonium cyanate in 1828 was a turning point for organic chemistry. >> aluminium; beryllium; organic chemistry

Wojtyła, Karol Jozef >> **John Paul II**

Wolf, Hugo (Philipp Jakob) [volf] (1860–1903) Composer, born in Windischgraz, Austria. From 1888 he composed c.300 songs, settings of poems by Goethe and others, and wrote an opera, *Der Corregidor* (1895), and other works.

wolf A member of the dog family; two species: the **grey** (or **timber**) **wolf** (*Canis lupus*), the largest wild dog and ancestor of the domestic dog, native to forests throughout the temperate N hemisphere (distribution now patchy); and the rare **red wolf** (*Canis rufus*) of E USA. >> Canidae; dog

Wolfe, Charles (1791–1823) Poet, born in Dublin. He is remembered for his poem 'The Burial of Sir John Moore' (1817), which caught the admiration of the public. >> Moore, John

Wolfe, James (1727–59) British soldier, born in Westerham, Kent. In 1758 he was prominent in the capture of Louisburg, and commanded in the famous capture of Quebec (1759), where he was killed. >> Abraham, Plains of; Seven Years' War

Wolfe, Thomas (Clayton) (1900–38) Novelist, born in Asheville, NC. He wrote several plays, but found success with novels, notably *Look Homeward, Angel* (1929) and *Of Time and the River* (1935).

Wolfe, Tom, popular name of **Thomas Kennerley Wolfe** (1931–) Journalist, pop-critic, and novelist, born in Richmond, VA. A proponent of New Journalism, his books include *The Electric Kool-Aid Acid Test* (1968) and the best selling novel, *The Bonfire of the Vanities* (1988).

Wolfenden, John (Frederick) Wolfenden, Baron [**wulf**enden] (1906–85) Educationist, born in Halifax, West Yorkshire. He was best known for his government investigation of homosexuality and prostitution (the **Wolfenden Report**, 1957).

Wolf-Ferrari, Ermanno [volf fe**rah**ree] (1876–1948) Composer, born in Venice, Italy. His best-known works are *I quattro rusteghi* (1906, trans The School for Fathers) and *Il segreto di Susanna* (1909, Susanna's Secret). He also composed choral and chamber works, and music for organ and piano.

wolffia A tiny floating freshwater herb (*Wolffia arhiza*) consisting only of a minute green body 0·5–1 mm/0·02–0·04 in across, with a budding pouch from which new plants are produced. It is the smallest flowering plant in the world. (Family: Lemnaceae.) >> flowering plants

Wölfflin, Heinrich [**voel**flin] (1864–1945) Art historian, born in Winterthur, Switzerland. He was one of the founders of modern art history, as seen in such works as *Principles of Art History* (1915).

wolfhound >> **borzoi; Irish wolfhound**

Wolfit, Sir Donald [**wulf**it] (1902–68) Actor-manager, born in Newark, Nottinghamshire. He formed his own company in 1937, and became known for his Shakespeare performances. He also appeared in several films.

wolfram [**wul**fram] >> **tungsten**

wolframite [**wul**framiyt] An iron manganese tungstate mineral ($(Fe,Mn)WO_4$), found in pegmatites and hydrothermal veins as tabular crystals or brown masses. It is the principal ore of tungsten. >> scheelite; tungsten

Wolfram von Eschenbach [**volf**ram fon **esh**enbakh] (c.1170–c.1220) Poet, born near Ansbach, Germany. He is best known for his epic *Parzival* (c.1200–10), which introduced the theme of the Holy Grail into German literature.

Wolfsburg [**volfs**boork] 52°27N 10°49E, pop (1995e) 131 000. City in Germany; founded, 1938; railway; known as the 'Volkswagen town' (site of car factory). >> Germany i

Wolfson, Sir Isaac (1897–1991) Businessman, born in Glasgow. In 1955 he set up the **Wolfson Foundation** for the advancement of health, education, and youth activities in the UK and the Commonwealth.

Wollongong [wolon**gong**] 34°25S 150°52E, pop (1995e) 184 000. Urban centre in SE New South Wales, Australia; railway; university (1975). >> New South Wales

Wollstonecraft, Mary [**wul**stonkraft], married name **Godwin** (1759–97) Feminist and educationist, born in London. In 1792 she wrote *Vindication of the Rights of Woman*, advocating equality of the sexes. She married William Godwin in 1797. >> Godwin, William

Wolof [**wol**of] A West Atlantic-speaking agricultural people of Senegal and Gambia. They are traditionally grouped into a state with elaborate hierarchical distinctions.

Wolpe, Joseph [**vol**pay] (1915–97) Psychiatrist, born in Johannesburg, South Africa. He founded the field of behavioural therapy, widely used in the treatment of neurotic disorders. >> behaviour therapy; neurosis

Wolseley, Garnet (Joseph) Wolseley, 1st Viscount [**wulz**lee] (1833–1913) British field marshal, born in Golden Bridge, Co Dublin, Ireland. He served in campaigns in many parts of the world, including the Crimea, India, China, and Canada, and led the attempted rescue of General Gordon at Khartoum. As army commander-in-chief (1895–1901), he carried out several reforms, and mobilized forces for the Boer War (1899–1902). >> Gordon

Wolsey, Thomas, Cardinal [**wul**zee] (c.1475–1530) English cardinal and statesman, born in Ipswich, Suffolk. Under Henry VIII, he became Archbishop of York (1514) and a cardinal (1515). Made Lord Chancellor (1515–29), he was Henry VIII's leading adviser. When he failed to persuade the pope to grant Henry's divorce, he was arrested, and died while travelling to London. >> Henry VIII

Wolverhampton [wulver**hamp**tn] 52°36N 2°08W, pop (1995e) 245 000. Industrial town in West Midlands, C England; collegiate church founded here in 994; railway; university, 1992; football league team, Wolverhampton Wanderers (Wolves). >> West Midlands

wolverine A mammal of family Mustelidae, native to the N forests and tundra of Scandinavia, Asia, and North America; stocky (length, 1 m/3¼ ft), pointed muzzle, bushy tail; dark brown, often pale on face and sides; also known as **glutton**. (*Gulo gulo*.) >> Mustelidae

womb >> **uterus** ℹ

wombat A nocturnal Australian marsupial; length, up to 1·3 m/4 ft; bear-like, with a stout body, very small tail; round head, blunt muzzle with a large nose pad; digs burrows. (Family: Vombatidae, 3 species.) >> marsupial ℹ; *see illustration below*

Women's Institutes, National Federation of (WI) A women's voluntary organization, started in Canada in 1897 by Adelaide Hoodless to provide classes in domestic science and home-making. The WI spread to Britain in 1915, and to other Commonwealth countries later.

women's liberation movement A broad cultural and political movement initiated by women to improve their social position by freeing themselves from the constraints and disadvantages of a society said to be dominated by men. 'Women's lib' has very strong roots in the USA and Europe, and has been politicized, especially by radical feminists who claim the continued existence of male dominance in capitalist societies. >> feminism; women's studies

Women's Royal Voluntary Service (WRVS) In the UK, an organization founded in 1938 (designated Royal in 1966), made up of unpaid helpers who do community work. They pioneered the first home help scheme (1944), and run the 'meals on wheels' service for the housebound elderly, as well as providing voluntary workers for day centres, hospitals, playgroups, prison visiting, and rural transport. >> Reading, 1st Marquess of

women's services Military organizations in which women enlist for non-combatant duty. In Britain, there are separate corps for army, navy, and air force. The **Women's Royal Army Corps (WRAC)** was founded in 1949, directly succeeding the Auxiliary Territorial Service (ATS) within which large numbers of women had served during World War 2. British women had served during World War 1 in the **Women's Auxiliary Army Corps (WAAC)** formed in 1917. The **Women's Royal Naval Service (WRNS)**, popularly known as 'the Wrens', was first formed in 1917. The **Women's Royal Air Force (WRAF)** was formed in 1918, and later became known as the **Women's Auxiliary Air Force (WAAF)**. In the USA, the **Women's Army Corps (WAC)** was established in 1948, and dissolved in 1978.

Wombat

women's studies The study of the history and contemporary role of girls and women. More available in further and higher education than in schools, it is favoured by feminist groups, who feel that girls and women are disadvantaged and that the nature of this disadvantage is often not mentioned in education. >> feminism; gender; women's liberation movement

Wonder, Stevie, originally **Steveland Judkins** (1951–) Soul singer, songwriter, and instrumentalist, born in Saginaw, MI. He was blind from birth, played the harmonica, drums, keyboards, and guitar from an early age, and was signed to Motown Records in 1961. His first album *Little Stevie Wonder: the 12-Year-Old Genius* was an immediate success. Later albums include *Songs In The Key Of Life* (1976) and *Hotter Than July* (1980). >> Motown; soul (music)

wood The bulk of the tissue making up the trunk and branches of trees and shrubs. For commercial purposes, it is divided into two types: **softwoods**, derived from gymnosperms, and **hardwoods**, which have a less regular grain and are derived from flowering plants. The terms are misleading, as some softwoods are very hard and durable. >> flowering plants; gymnosperms; xylem

Wood, Sir Henry (Joseph) (1869–1944) Conductor, born in London. In 1895 he helped to found the Promenade Concerts which he conducted annually until his death. He composed operettas and an oratorio, but his international reputation was gained as a conductor.

wood alcohol >> **methanol**

wood avens >> **avens**

woodbine >> **honeysuckle**

wood block A percussion instrument (also known as a **Chinese block**) in the form of a hollowed rectangular or spherical block of wood, with one or more slits in the surface, which is struck with a wooden stick. >> percussion ℹ

woodchat A shrike native to Europe, Africa, and W Asia (*Lanius senator*); top of head and neck chestnut-brown; breast white; also known as **woodchat shrike**. >> shrike

woodchuck A marmot native to North America (*Marmota monax*); large (length, 80 cm/30 in), aggressive; may dig a den in woodland for the winter months; also known as **groundhog**. >> marmot

woodcock A short-legged sandpiper, native to the Old World and E North America; mottled brown; bill long, straight. (Genus: *Scolopax*, 6 species.) >> sandpiper

woodcreeper A bird native to the New World tropics; tail stiffened as in woodpeckers; many shapes of bill; also known as a **woodhewer**. (Family: Dendrocolaptidae, 47 species; sometimes placed in family Furnariidae.) >> woodpecker

woodcut One of the simplest and oldest methods of relief-printing. The design is gouged into the smooth surface of a block of wood, and sticky ink rolled over the top. The cut-away areas print as white patches, the rest as solid black. >> relief printing

Woodhenge Prehistoric site in Wiltshire, S England; 3 km/1¾ mi NE of Stonehenge; discovered by aerial reconnaissance in 1926. It apparently consisted of a number of concentric ovals of wooden pillars oriented for the same ritualistic forms as were in use at Stonehenge. >> Stonehenge

woodhewer >> **woodcreeper**

Woodland culture A generic term for the Indian culture of the E USA as far W as the Great Plains, c.700 BC–AD 1500. It is characterized archaeologically by burial mounds, cord-impressed pottery, and tobacco smoking. >> Cahokia; Hopewell

woodlouse A terrestrial crustacean found under stones, in litter and soil; abdominal limbs modified for aerial breathing and for reproduction; thoracic legs adapted for walking. (Order: Isopoda, c.3500 species.) >> crustacean; louse

woodpecker A bird of the family Picidae (198 species); clings to tree trunks; tail stiff and presses against tree for support except in small **piculets** (Subfamily: Picumninae, 27 species) and **wrynecks**. >> woodcreeper; wryneck; yellowhammer

wood pigeon A pigeon native to Europe, N Africa, and W Asia (*Columba palumbus*); plumage dark grey with white patch on neck; also known as **ringdove**. >> pigeon

woodrush A tufted perennial, found almost everywhere; leaves grass-like, fringed with long, colourless hairs. (Genus: *Luzula*, 80 species. Family: Juncaceae.)

Woods, Tiger, popular name of **Eldrick Woods** (1976–) Golfer, born in Cypress, CA. He turned professional in 1996, and shot to fame after winning the US Masters at Augusta in 1997 at the age of 21.

Woodstock Small town in Ulster Co, SE New York; tourist centre, in the foothill of the Catskill Mts; noted for its artists' colony; became world famous for the 3-day rock festival held nearby as part of the Woodstock Music and Art Fair in 1969, the largest rock festival of the 1960s, recorded in the film *Woodstock* (1970).

Woodward, Bob >> **Bernstein, Carl**

woodwind instrument A musical instrument made principally from wood (or, in the case of the saxophone and some flutes, from metal), in which a column of air is activated by the player blowing across a mouth-hole (as in the flute or piccolo), through a duct (as in the recorder), or against a single or double reed (as in the bassoon, cor anglais, oboe, and clarinet). >> aerophone; bassoon; clarinet; cor anglais; cornett; didgeridoo; fife; flageolet; flute; oboe; ocarina; panpipes; piccolo; recorder; reed instrument

woodworm >> **furniture beetle**

woody nightshade A scrambling woody perennial (*Solanum dulcamara*), native to Europe, Asia, and N Africa; flowers with five purple petals, and a cone of yellow stamens; berries oval, green turning yellow and finally red when ripe, mildly poisonous; also called **bittersweet**. (Family: Solanaceae.)

Wookey Hole Limestone caves near the village of Wookey in Somerset, SW England; on the SW slopes of the Mendip Hills. >> Somerset

wool The fibre obtained from the fleeces of sheep. There are many qualities of wool, from fine soft wools obtained from the merino sheep of Australia, South Africa, and Argentina to coarse fibres which come from sheep in the cooler climates of New Zealand, Europe, and North America. Medium quality wools are used in clothing, including knitwear of the Shetland type; coarse wools are used mainly for carpets and other furnishings. >> merino; shoddy

Woolf, (Adeline) Virginia, *née* **Stephen** (1882–1941) Novelist, born in London. A leading member of the Bloomsbury Group, she made a major contribution to the development of the novel, in such works as *Mrs Dalloway* (1925), *To the Lighthouse* (1927), and *The Waves* (1931), noted for their impressionistic style. Publication of her *Diary* (5 vols, 1977–84) and *Letters* (6 vols, 1975–80) has further enhanced her reputation. >> Bloomsbury Group; stream of consciousness

Woolley, Sir (Charles) Leonard (1880–1960) Archaeologist, born in London. He directed the important excavations (1922–34) at Ur in Mesopotamia, and wrote several popular accounts of his work, notably *Digging up the Past* (1930). >> archaeology; Ur

woolly monkey A New World monkey; large round head, long grasping tail; short dense woolly coat; plain dark colour; also known as **barrigudo**. (Genus: *Lagothrix*, 2 species.) >> New World monkey

woolly rhinoceros An extinct rhinoceros (*Coelodonta antiquitatis*), once native to Europe and N Asia; length, 3·5 m/11 ft; thick coat of long hair; snout with two horns. >> rhinoceros

woolsack A large red cushion filled with wool that the Lord Chancellor sits on in the UK House of Lords. It is said to represent the authority of the Lord Chancellor who presides over the proceedings of the House. >> Lords, House of

Woolworth, Frank W(infield) (1852–1919) Merchant, born in Rodman, NY. In 1879 he opened a store in Utica, NY, for 5-cent goods only; this failed, but a second store, in Lancaster, PA, selling also 10-cent goods, was successful.

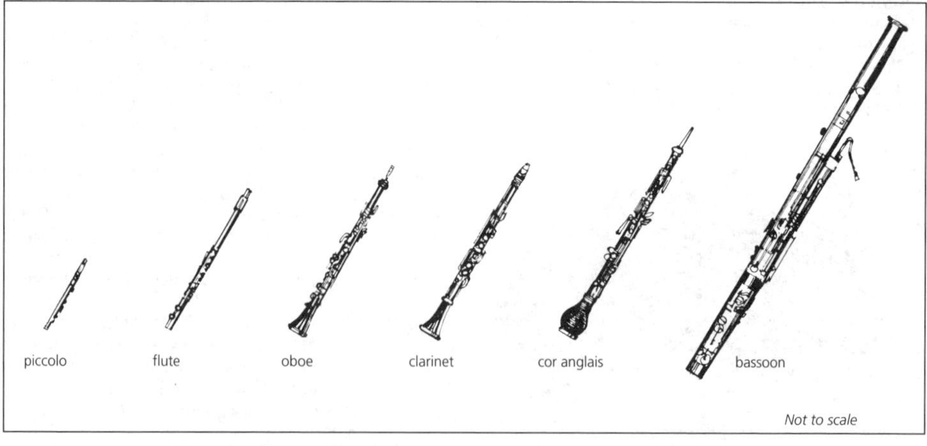

Woodwind instruments

He then built a chain of similar stores, setting up the F W Woolworth Company in 1905.

Wootton (of Abinger), Barbara Frances Wootton, Baroness (1897–1988) Social scientist, born in Cambridge, Cambridgeshire. She is best known for her work, *Testament for Social Science* (1950), in which she attempted to assimilate the social to the natural sciences.

Worcester [**wus**ter], Anglo-Saxon **Wigorna Ceaster** 52°11N 2°13W, pop (1995e) 90 700. County town of Hereford and Worcester, WC England; on the R Severn; founded AD c.680; site of Cromwell's victory in Civil War; railway; cathedral (14th-c); Worcester porcelain, from 1751; Three Choirs Festival in rotation with Hereford and Gloucester (Sep). >> English Civil War; Hereford and Worcester

word class A group of words which share several grammatical properties, such as the same kind of inflection or position in sentence structure; also known as **part of speech**. The grouping of words into classes was first carried out by the Greeks, and the main classes (noun, verb, etc) have since been universally used in language description.

Worde, Wynkyn de [werd] (?–?1535) London printer, born in Holland or in Alsace. He was a pupil of Caxton, and in 1491 succeeded to his stock-in-trade. He made great improvements in printing and typecutting. >> Caxton; printing ℹ

word processor A computer program, normally running on a personal computer, which allows the computer to be used as a sophisticated typewriter. Documents can be held as whole documents; they can be fully edited before they are printed; and they can be repeatedly updated. >> computer program; personal computer; typewriter

Wordsworth, Dorothy (1771–1855) Writer born in Cockermouth, Cumbria, the sister of William Wordsworth. Her *Journals* show a keen sensibility and acute observation of nature. >> Coleridge; Wordsworth, William

Wordsworth, William (1770–1850) Poet, born in Cockermouth, Cumbria. Following travels in Europe, he set up house at Racedown, Dorset, with his sister, Dorothy, where he began to write poetry exploring the lives of humble folk living in close contact with nature. *Lyrical Ballads* (1798), written with Coleridge, was the first manifesto of the new Romantic poetry. He later moved to Dove Cottage, Grasmere, married Mary Hutchinson in 1802, and wrote much of his best work, including his poetic autobiography, *The Prelude* (1805, published posthumously in 1850). He succeeded Southey as poet laureate in 1843. >> Coleridge; Romanticism; Wordsworth, Dorothy

work The product of force and distance; symbol W, units J (joule). Applying a force F to an object over a distance d means work $W = Fd$ is done, equal to the object's increase in kinetic energy. The rate of doing work is *power*. >> force; kinetic energy; power (physics)

workfunction The minimum energy which must be supplied to extract an electron from a solid; symbol Φ, units J (joule), or more often eV (electronvolt). It is a measure of how tightly electrons are bound to a material. >> electron

work-hardening An alteration in the properties of a metal by repeated hammering, rolling, or other forming processes. The process may be deleterious, in producing brittleness, or advantageous, in increasing strength. >> annealing; metal

workhouse A building used for the accommodation, and often employment, of the unemployed poor in Britain. Workhouses gained special notoriety after the Poor Law Amendment Act (1834), when the policy was to increase their number and place as many able-bodied paupers as possible in them. This policy was much criticized by reformers, who unearthed many 'workhouse scandals'. Workhouses survived until the later 1920s. >> Poor Laws

Working Men's Clubs and Institutes Union In the UK, clubs that provide education and recreation for working men; originally founded as an alternative to the public house. The Union was created in 1862, the inspiration of the Rev Henry Solly; initially the clubs did not serve alcohol, but now provide it at a lower price than in public houses, which helps to contribute to their popularity.

Works Projects Administration (WPA) (1935–43) A US federal agency established under President Roosevelt to combat unemployment during the Great Depression. Originally called the **Works Progress Administration**, it built transportation facilities, parks, and buildings. >> Great Depression; Roosevelt, Franklin D

work study >> **time and motion study**

work-to-rule >> **industrial action**

World Bank >> **International Bank for Reconstruction and Development**

World Commission on Environment and Development An independent body established by the UN in 1983 to formulate 'a global agenda for change'. Its purpose is to propose strategies for sustainable development by the year 2000, to promote co-operation between nations at different stages of economic development, and to consider ways by which the international community can deal with environmental concerns. It published the Brundtland Report, *Our Common Future*, in 1987, and convened the Earth Summits in 1992 and 1997. >> biodiversity; Brundtland; Earth Summit

World Council of Churches An interdenominational council of Churches, formed in Amsterdam in 1948. Originating in the ecumenical movement of the early 20th-c, its main task is to seek the unity of the Church. It comprises most of the main-line Christian denominations with the exception of the Roman Catholic Church, with which it keeps close contact. Its headquarters is in Geneva. >> Christianity; ecumenism

World Court >> **International Court of Justice**

World Cup A term used to describe an international sporting competition. The soccer World Cup is the best known, first contested in Uruguay in 1930; and skiing, athletics, rugby union, cricket and several other sports have inaugurated World Cup competitions. >> football ℹ

World Federation of Trade Unions (WFTU) An association of world trade union federations, set up in 1945. The democratic unions of W Europe and North America broke away in 1949, after disagreements with communist members. In the 1990s it contained some 55 affiliated national trade union federations, mainly from E Europe. >> International Confederation of Free Trade Unions

World Health Organization (WHO) A specialized agency formed in 1948 within the United Nations to advance international co-operation for the improvement in health of peoples in all countries. It is primarily concerned with the control of epidemic diseases, vaccination and other programmes, worldwide sanitation, and water supplies. There were 191 member countries in 1999. >> medicine; United Nations

world heritage site A site (natural or cultural) recognized by the international community (in the shape of the World Heritage Convention founded by the General Conference of UNESCO in 1972) as possessing universal value, and thus coming under a collective responsibility. A country nominates a site to the Convention, and a decision on whether to include it in the world heritage list is made by an international 21-member committee. In early 1999 there were 582 sites in 118 states. >> conservation; environment; UNESCO

World Series >> **baseball** ℹ

World Trade Center A complex of buildings occupying 6·5 ha/16 acres in Manhattan, New York City. Its two 110-storey skyscrapers were the world's tallest buildings from their completion in 1973 until topped by the Sears Tower a year later. >> New York City; skyscraper

World Trade Organization (WTO) A permanent body created in 1994 at the conclusion of the GATT Uruguay Round of talks to succeed GATT in monitoring international trade and resolve disputes. It began work in 1995, with headquarters in Geneva. It meets every two years, and is overseen by a General Council. It had 134 members in early 1999. >> General Agreement on Tariffs and Trade

World War 1 (1914–18) A war whose origins lay in the reaction of other great powers to the ambitions of the German Empire after 1871. The assassination of the heir to the Habsburg throne, Franz Ferdinand, at Sarajevo in Bosnia (28 Jun 1914), triggered the war. Austria declared war on Serbia (28 Jul); Russia mobilized in support of Serbia (29–30 Jul); and Germany declared war on Russia (1 Aug), and on France (3 Aug). The German invasion of neutral Belgium (4 Aug) brought the British into the war on the French side. Japan joined Britain, France, and Russia under the terms of an agreement with Britain (1902, 1911), and Italy joined the Allies in May 1915. Turkey allied with Germany (Nov 1914), and they were joined by Bulgaria (Oct 1915). Military campaigning centred on France and Belgium in W Europe, and on Poland and W Russia in E Europe. The British Expeditionary Force and French army prevented the Germans, at the first battle of Ypres, from reaching the Channel ports. By the end of 1914, a static defence line had been established from the Belgian coast to Switzerland. The Allies attempted to break the stalemate by a campaign in Gallipoli (Apr 1915–Jan 1916), but failed. For 3 years, an Allied army was involved in a Macedonian campaign, and there was also fighting in Mesopotamia against Turkey. The Allies organized a large offensive for the W front in 1916, but were forestalled by the Germans, who attacked France at Verdun (Feb–Jul). To relieve the situation, the Battle of the Somme was launched, but proved indecisive. The Germans then unleashed unrestricted submarine warfare (Jan 1917) to cripple Britain economically. The USA declared war (2 Apr 1917) when British food stocks were perilously low, and the German submarine menace was finally overcome by the use of convoys. In the spring of 1918, the Germans launched a major attack in the W, but were driven back, with the USA providing an increasing number of much-needed troops. By November, when the armistice was signed, the Allies had recaptured E Belgium and nearly all French territory. >> ANZAC; Central Powers; Fourteen Points; Gallipoli campaign; Marne / Passchendaele / Somme / Vimy Ridge / Ypres, Battle of; Paris Peace Conference 1; Versailles, Treaty of

World War 2 (1939–45) A war whose origins lay in three different conflicts which merged after 1941: Germany's desire for European expansion; Japan's struggle against China; and a resulting conflict between Japanese ambitions and US interests in the Pacific. After the German invasion of Czechoslovakia (Mar 1939), Britain and France pledged support to Poland. Germany concluded an alliance with Russia (Aug 1939), and then invaded Poland (1 Sep). Britain and France declared war on Germany (3 Sep), but could not prevent Poland from being overrun in four weeks. For six months there was a period of 'phoney war', when little fighting took place, but the Germans then occupied Norway and Denmark (Apr 1940), and Belgium and Holland were invaded (10 May). There followed the Battle of Britain, in which Germany tried to win air supremacy over Britain, but failed. Germany launched submarine attacks against British supply routes, but then moved E and invaded Greece and Yugoslavia (Apr 1941). British military efforts were concentrated against Italy in the Mediterranean and N Africa. Rommel was sent to N Africa with the Afrika Corps, and campaigning continued here for three years until Allied troops finally ejected German and Italian forces in mid-1943, invaded Sicily and then Italy itself, and forced Italy to make a separate peace (3 Sep 1943). In June 1941, Germany invaded her ally Russia along a 2000 mi front. After spectacular early successes, from November 1942 they were gradually driven back, and were finally driven out of Russia in August 1944. Leningrad (now St Petersburg) was under siege for nearly $2\frac{1}{2}$ years (until Jan 1944). A second front was launched against Germany by the Allies (Jun 1944), through the invasion of Normandy, and Paris was liberated (25 Aug). The Allies advanced into Germany (Feb 1945) and linked with the Russians on the R Elbe (28 Apr). The Germans surrendered unconditionally at Reims (7 May 1945). In the Far East, Japan's desire for expansion led to her attack on Pearl Harbor and other British and US bases (7 Dec 1941), and the USA declared war against Japan the next day. In reply Japan's allies, Germany and Italy, declared war on the USA (11 Dec). Within four months, Japan controlled SE Asia and Burma. Not until June 1942 did naval victories in the Pacific stem the advance. Bitter fighting continued until 1945, when, with Japan on the retreat, the USA dropped two atomic bombs on Hiroshima and Nagasaki (6 and 9 Aug). Japan then surrendered (14 Aug). >> Afrika Corps; Anschluss; Atlantic Charter; Atlantic Wall; Axis Powers; blitzkrieg; Chindits; D-Day; Desert Rats; Free French; Gestapo; Holocaust; Home Guard; kamikaze; Lend-Lease Agreement; Maginot Line; Munich Agreement; Normandy Campaign; Nuremberg Trials; Pearl Harbor; Special Operations Executive; SS; Atlantic / Britain / Bulge, the / El Alamein / Stalingrad, Battle of; Casablanca / Paris Peace 2 / Potsdam / Tehran / Yalta Conference

World Wide Fund for Nature (WWF) An international voluntary organization, founded in 1961 as the **World Wildlife Fund**, with its headquarters in Switzerland; international president, the Duke of Edinburgh. It aims to create awareness of the need for conservation of endangered wild animals, plants, and places, and promote the wise use of the world's natural resources. In 1999 its global network was active in some 100 countries.

World Wildlife Fund >> **World Wide Fund for Nature**

worm The common name for a wide range of long-bodied, legless invertebrate animals. >> annelid; earthworm; fanworm; flatworm; guinea worm; leech; lugworm; nematode; ribbon worm; spoonworm; tapeworm

Worms [vorms], Eng [wermz], Lat **Borbetomagus** 49°38N 8°23E, pop (1995e) 78 500. River port in Germany; on R Rhine; one of the oldest towns in Germany; capital of kingdom of Burgundy, 5th-c; scene of many Imperial Diets; badly bombed in World War 2; railway; centre of the wine trade (notably for Liebfraumilch); cathedral (11th–12th-c). >> Burgundy; Diet, Imperial; Germany [i]; Worms, Diet of

Worms, Diet of Meetings of the estates of the German empire in 1521 and 1545, which sealed the religious fate of 16th-c Germany. At the first, Luther was condemned, following papal declarations of heresy; at the second, an attempt to heal the religious divisions between Catholics and Lutherans failed. >> Lutheranism; Roman Catholicism; Worms

wormwood An aromatic perennial (*Artemisia absinthium*) growing to 90 cm/3 ft, native to Europe and Asia; flower-heads numerous, yellow, drooping. It is cultivated as a flavouring, and also used in the preparation of absinthe liqueur. (Family: Compositae.)

Worrall, Denis John (1935–) South African politician, born in Benoni, South Africa. He established the Independent Party, which in 1989 merged with other white Opposition parties to form the reformist Democratic Party. A co-leader of this party, he was elected to parliament in 1989.

Worthing 50°48N 0°23W, pop (1995e) 97 600. Resort town in West Sussex, S England; railway. >> Sussex, West

Wotan >> **Odin**

Wounded Knee The site in S Dakota of the final defeat of Sioux Indians (29 Dec 1890). The 'battle' was in fact a massacre by US troops.

woundwort An annual or perennial, found almost everywhere; flowers 2-lipped, usually white to pink or purple with darker spots, in whorls. It had an old herbal use in salves for treating cuts. (Genus: *Stachys*, 300 species. Family: Labiatae.) >> herb

Wouwerman, Philips [**vow**verman], also found as **Wouwermans** (c.1619–68) Painter of battle and hunting scenes, born in Haarlem, The Netherlands. His pictures are mostly small landscapes, with several figures in energetic action. He had two brothers, also painters, **Peter Wouwerman** (1623–82) and **Jan Wouwerman** (1629–66), who chose similar subjects.

W particle A particle that carries weak nuclear force; symbol W; mass 81 GeV; charge +1 (W^+) or −1 (W^-); spin 1; decays to an electron or muon plus neutrino; discovered in 1983. >> fundamental particles

WRAC >> **women's services**

Wrangel, Ferdinand Petrovich, Baron von [**vrang**gl] (1794–1870) Explorer, born in Pskov, Russia. He travelled in Arctic waters and on Siberian coasts, and made valuable surveys and observations.

Wrangel Island [**vran**gl], Russ **Ostrov Vrangelya** area 5180 sq km/2000 sq mi. Tundra-covered island in the W Chukchi Sea; length, 120 km/75 mi; width, 72 km/45 mi; rises to 1097 m/3599 ft; ceded to Russia, 1924; small settlements of Chukchi and Eskimo. >> Russia [i]; Wrangel

wrasse [ras] Any of a large group of mostly small colourful fishes widespread in tropical to temperate seas; length typically 10–30 cm/4–12 in. (Family: Labridae, 15 genera.) >> fish [i]

wreckfish Large heavy-bodied fish (*Polyprion americanus*) found mainly in the tropical Atlantic; length up to 2 m/$6\frac{1}{2}$ ft; also called **stonebass**. (Family: Serranidae.) >> fish [i]

Wren, Sir Christopher (1632–1723) Architect, born in East Knoyle, Wiltshire. After the Great Fire of London (1666), he drew designs for rebuilding the whole city, but his scheme was never implemented. In 1669 he designed the new St Paul's (building begun 1675) and many other public buildings in London, such as the Greenwich Observatory.

Wren, P(ercival) C(hristopher) (1885–1941) Popular novelist, born in Devon. He joined the French Foreign Legion, and this provided him with the background of several novels of adventure, notably *Beau Geste* (1924) and *Beau Sabreur* (1926).

wren A small songbird of the New World family Troglodytidae (**wrens**, c.65 species, one extending to the N Old World); name also used for Maluridae (**Australian wrens/wren-warblers**, 26 species, including the **fairy** or **blue wrens**, **grasswrens**, and **emu-wrens**); Xenicidae, sometimes called Acanthisittidae (**New Zealand wrens**, 3 species); and for many small birds of other families. >> emu wren; goldcrest; rifleman; songbird; warbler

wren babbler A small babbler, found from India to SE Asia; inhabits woodland; eats mainly insects, some snails, possibly seeds. (Tribe: Pomatorhinini, 22 species.) >> babbler

wren-warbler >> **emu wren; warbler**

wrestling The sport of one man fighting against another, but without the use of fists. In most cases the object is to fell your opponent to the ground. Many forms exist, the most popular amateur forms being **freestyle** and **Graeco-Roman**. In the latter, holds below the waist and the use of the legs are prohibited. Other forms include **Sambo**, which originated in Russia; **Sumo**, the national sport of Japan; British variations **Cumberland and Westmoreland** and **Devon and Cornwall**; and **Yagli**, the national sport of Turkey. Women's wrestling has also developed in recent years. >> judo; sumo wrestling; RR1065

Wrexham [**rek**sm], Welsh **Wrecsam** pop (1995e) 123 400; area 499 sq km / 193 sq mi. County (unitary authority from 1996) in NE Wales, UK; administrative centre, Wrexham; Wrexham cathedral, Church of St Giles (15th-c); football league team, Wrexham (Robins). >> Wales [i]

Wright, Frank Lloyd (1867–1959) Architect, born in Richland Center, WI. He became known for his low-built, prairie-style residences, but soon launched out into more controversial designs, and is regarded as the leading designer of modern private dwellings, planned in conformity with the natural features of the land. Among his larger works is the Guggenheim Museum of Art in New York City. >> architecture

Wright, Judith (Arundel) (1915–) Poet, born near Armidale, New South Wales. She was one of the first white writers to recognize Aboriginal claims, in *The Moving Image (1946)*. Her *Collected Poems: 1942–1985* appeared in 1994.

Wright, Peter >> **intelligence service**

Wright, Richard (1908–60) Novelist, born in Natchez, MS. He is most widely known for *Native Son* (1940), the first substantial novel of US black revolt, and for his autobiography *Black Boy* (1945).

Wright, Sewall (1889–1988) Geneticist and statistician, born in Melrose, MA. He drew attention to random fluctuations in gene frequencies in small populations, and the possibility that alleles could be lost or fixed by chance rather than by natural selection. This concept of genetic drift (the **Sewall Wright effect**) was strongly criticized at the time, but is now widely accepted. >> allele

Wright brothers Aviation pioneers: **Orville Wright** (1871–1948), born in Dayton, OH, and **Wilbur Wright** (1867–1912), born near Millville, IN. They were the first to fly in a heavier-than-air machine (17 Dec 1903), at Kitty Hawk, NC. >> aeronautics; aircraft [i]

wrist A region of the upper limb between the forearm and the hand, consisting of eight *carpal* bones arranged in two rows. The rows make an arch forming part of a tunnel (the *carpal tunnel*), which transmits nearly all the structures entering the hand. >> arm; hand

writing systems >> **alphabet [i]; cuneiform [i]; epigraphy; graphology; hieroglyphics [i]; ideography; logography; pictography [i]; syllabary**

Wrocław [**vrots**waf], Ger **Breslau** 51°05N 17°00E, pop (1995e) 651 000. River port in W Poland, on R Oder; capital of lower Silesia; founded, 10th-c; badly damaged in World War 2; airport; railway junction; technical university (1945); cathedral (13th-c). >> Poland [i]

wrought iron A form of iron, of very low carbon content, once much used by blacksmiths, but now mostly replaced by steel. It is less brittle than cast iron. Famous wrought iron structures were the SS *Great Britain* (1856) and the Eiffel Tower (1889). It is not much used now, except for decorative purposes. >> carbon; cast iron

WRVS >> **Women's Royal Voluntary Service**

wrybill A small plover, native to New Zealand (*Anarhynchus frontalis*); bill straight when seen from side, but tip bends to right; inhabits river beds and sand flats. >> plover

wryneck A short-billed, uncharacteristic woodpecker, native to Europe, Asia, and Africa; mottled brown. (Genus: *Jynx*, 2 species. Subfamily: Jynginae.) >> woodpecker

Wu, Empress, in full **Wu Zhao** (?625–?706) Empress of China, the only woman ever to rule China in her own name. A concubine of Emperor Taizong, she married his son, Emperor Gaozong. After his death (683) she first ruled through her own sons, then after a reign of terror she seized the title *emperor* in 690 with the dynastic name Zhou (Chou). She was forced to abdicate in 705. >> Lü

Wuhan or **Wu-han** [woo**han**], **Han-kow**, or **Han-kou** 30°35N 114°19E, pop (1995e) 4 331 000. Inland port in EC China; at confluence of Han Shui and Yangtze Rivers; commercial centre of C China; airfield; railway; university (1913); Central China Engineering Institute; Guiyuan Buddhist Temple (c.1600), now a museum. >> China 🛈

Wulfila >> **Ulfilas**

Wuppertal [**vup**ertahl] 51°15N 7°10E, pop (1995e) 392 000. Industrial city in Germany; on R Wupper in the Ruhr valley; includes the former towns of Barmen, Elberfeld, and Vohwinkel; university (1972). >> Germany 🛈; Ruhr, River

Würzburg [**vürts**boork] 49°48N 9°57E, pop (1995e) 135 000. Industrial city in Germany; on R Main; railway; centre of wine production and trade in Franconia; university (1582); cathedral (11th–13th-c), Marienberg (fortress, 13th-c); Würzburg Residence (episcopal palace built by Balthasar Neumann, 1719–44), a world heritage site. >> Germany 🛈; Neumann, Balthasar

Wyatt, James (1746–1813) Architect, born in Burton Constable, Staffordshire. He achieved fame with his Neoclassical design for the London Pantheon (1772). His best-known work is the Gothic Revival Fonthill Abbey (1796–1807), which largely collapsed in the 1820s. >> Gothic Revival

Wyatt, Sir Thomas, known as **the Elder** (1503–42) Courtier and poet, born in Allington, Kent. In 1557 his poems, published in *Tottel's Miscellany*, helped to introduce the Italian sonnet and other forms into English literature. >> sonnet

Wycherley, William [**wich**erlee] (c.1640–1716) Playwright, born in Clive, Shropshire. He wrote several satirical comedies, notably *The Country Wife* (1675) and *The Plain Dealer* (1677), both based on plays by Molière. >> Molière

Wycliffe or **Wicliffe, John** [**wik**lif], also spelled **Wyclif, Wycliff** (c.1330–84) Religious reformer, born near Richmond, Yorkshire. He attacked the Church hierarchy, priestly powers, and the doctrine of transubstantiation, wrote many popular tracts in English (as opposed to Latin), and issued the first English translation of the Bible (1380). His followers were known as Lollards, and the influence of his teaching was widespread in England, in many respects anticipating the Reformation. >> Bible; Lollards; Reformation; transubstantiation

Wye, River 1 River rising on Plynlimon, C Wales; flows 208 km/129 mi to meet the R Severn estuary; notable for its valley scenery. **2** River rising in Buckinghamshire, SC England; flows 15 km/9 mi to meet the R Thames. **3** River rising near Buxton in Derbyshire, C England; flows 32 km/20 mi SE to meet the R Derwent. >> England 🛈

Wyler, William [**wiy**ler] (1902–81) Film director, born in Mulhouse, France (formerly Germany). In 1935 his association with the producer Sam Goldwyn resulted in several successes, including *Mrs Miniver* (1942, Oscar), *The Best Years of Our Lives* (1946), *Ben Hur* (1959, Oscar), and *Funny Girl* (1968).

Wyndham, John [**wind**am], pseudonym of **John Wyndham Parkes Lucas Beynon Harris** (1903–69) Science-fiction writer, born in Knowle, West Midlands. His novels include *The Day of the Triffids* (1951), *The Kraken Wakes* (1953), and *The Midwich Cuckoos* (1957). He has also published collections of short stories, such as *The Seeds of Time* (1969).

Wynkyn de Worde >> **Worde, Wynkyn de**

Wyoming [wiy**oh**ming] pop (1995e) 484 000; area 253 315 sq km/97 809 sq mi. State in W USA; the 'Equality State'; most of the region acquired by the USA from France in the Louisiana Purchase, 1803; total American jurisdiction, 1848; Wyoming Territory established, 1868; first territory or state to adopt women's suffrage, 1869; admitted to the Union as the 44th state, 1890; conflicts between cattle and sheep ranchers in the 1890s; contains the Wind River Indian reservation; a sparsely populated state; several ranges of the Rocky Mts (largely forested); highest point, Gannett Peak (4201 m/13 782 ft); eroded 'badlands' in the extreme NE; capital, Cheyenne; ranching and farming on the fertile Great Plains (E); an important mining state; very little manufacturing; major tourist area; national parks at Grand Teton and Yellowstone. >> Cheyenne; Louisiana Purchase; Rocky Mountains; United States of America 🛈; Yellowstone; RR994

WYSIWYG [**wiz**eewig] Acronym for **what you see is what you get**, used to refer to those computer systems, usually word processors or desktop publishing systems, where the display on the screen exactly mimics the final result produced by the printer. >> desktop publishing; word processor

Wyss, Johann Rudolf [vees] (1781–1830) Writer, born in Berne. He is best known for his completion and editing of *Der Schweizerische Robinson* (1812–13, trans The Swiss Family Robinson), written by his father, **Johann David** (1743–1818).

Wyszyński, Stefan, Cardinal [vi**shin**skee] (1901–81) Polish cardinal, born in Zuzela. Following his indictment of the Communist campaign against the Church, he was imprisoned (1953). Freed in 1956, he agreed to a reconciliation between Church and state under the Gomułka regime, but relations remained uneasy. >> communism; Gomułka

wytch elm >> **elm**

Xanthophyceae [zanthuh**fiy**see-ee] >> **yellow-green algae**

Xavier, Francis, St >> **Francis Xavier, St**

Xenakis, Iannis [ze**nah**kees] (1922–) Composer, born in Braila, Romania. He developed a highly complex style which incorporated mathematical concepts of chance and probability (so-called *stochastic music*), as well as electronic techniques. >> electronic music

Xenocrates [ze**no**kratees] (c.395–314 BC) Greek philosopher and scientist, born in Chalcedon on the Bosphorus. He was a pupil of Plato, and in 339 BC succeeded Speusippus as head of the Academy which Plato had founded. >> Plato

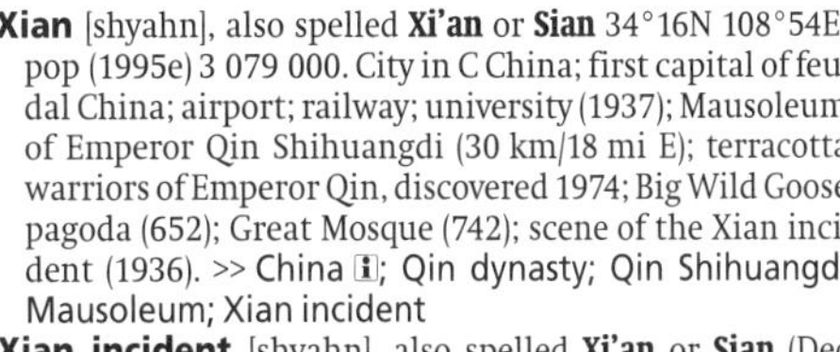

xenoglossia [zeno**glos**ia] >> **glossolalia**

xenon [**ze**non] Xe, element 54, boiling point –107°C. The fifth of the noble gases recovered from the atmosphere, of which it makes up only 0·000009%. Like the other noble gases, it is used in gas discharge tubes. >> chemical elements; noble gases; RR1036

Xenophanes [ze**no**faneez] (c.570–c.480 BC) Greek philosopher, born in Colophon, Ionia. He attacked traditional Greek conceptions of the gods, arguing against anthropomorphism and polytheism. >> polytheism

Xenophon [**ze**nofon] (c.435–354 BC) Athenian historian, essayist, and soldier, born in Attica. In 401 BC he served with a group of 10 000 Greek mercenaries under Persian Prince Cyrus. After Cyrus was killed, the Greeks were isolated over 1500 km/900 mi from home, but under Xenophon the group successfully fought their way back to the Black Sea. This heroic feat formed the basis of his major work, *Anabasis Kyrou* (The Expedition of Cyrus).

xerographic printer In computing, a printer which uses electrostatic techniques to provide text and/or graphics. Most photocopiers are of this type. Laser printers generally use this basic technology, which has the advantage of being silent, and capable of very high quality reproduction. >> computer printer; xerography ℹ

xerography [ze**ro**grafee] The most widely used method of photocopying, first devised in the late 1930s by US physicist Chester F Carlson, but not developed commercially until the 1950s. A photoconductive surface is charged and exposed to the image to be copied; the charge is lost except in the image areas. The secondary image so produced is developed with a charged pigment which is transferred to copy paper and fixed by heat. >> electrostatics; photoconductivity; photocopying

Xerxes I [**zerk**seez] (c.519–465 BC) Achaemenid king of Persia (485–465 BC), the son of Darius I. He is remembered in the West mainly for the failure of his forces against the Greeks in the Second Persian War. >> Darius I; Persian Wars

Xhosa [**khoh**sa] A cluster of Bantu-speaking peoples of the Transkei and Ciskei, South Africa. Xhosa is the most widely spoken African language in South Africa. >> Nguni

Xiamen, Hsia-men, or **Amoy** [shyahmuhn] 24°26N 118°07E, pop (1995e) 710 000. Subtropical port city in SE China; on island in Taiwan Strait; connected to mainland by 5 km/3 mi-long causeway (1949); first settled during S Song dynasty (1127–1279); made an open port, 1842; designated a special economic zone, 1981; new harbour; airfield; railway; university (1921); centre of growing unofficial trade between China and Taiwan. >> China ℹ; Opium Wars; Taiwan ℹ

Xian [shyahn], also spelled **Xi'an** or **Sian** 34°16N 108°54E, pop (1995e) 3 079 000. City in C China; first capital of feudal China; airport; railway; university (1937); Mausoleum of Emperor Qin Shihuangdi (30 km/18 mi E); terracotta warriors of Emperor Qin, discovered 1974; Big Wild Goose pagoda (652); Great Mosque (742); scene of the Xian incident (1936). >> China ℹ; Qin dynasty; Qin Shihuangdi Mausoleum; Xian incident

Xian incident [shyahn], also spelled **Xi'an** or **Sian** (Dec 1936) an incident in which Jiang Jieshi (Chiang Kai-shek) was held hostage in Xian by one of his own commanders, the 'young marshal' Zhang Xueliang, who demanded an anti-Japanese united front. He was released only on the intervention of Zhou Enlai. A united front of Communist and Nationalist forces resulted. >> United Fronts; Xian

Xingu [**sheeng**goo] National park in WC Brazil; crossed by branches of the Xingu R (length c.1980 km/1230 mi), a S tributary of the Amazon; created in 1961 by the Villas-Boas brothers to protect the Indian tribes, but in recent years it has suffered from property developers. >> Brazil ℹ

Xinhua [shinwah] The national news agency of the People's Republic of China, with headquarters in Beijing. Established as the communist Red China News Agency in 1929, and renamed *Hsin Hua* in 1937 (Xinhua since 1979), it is sometimes known nowadays as the New China News Agency. >> news agency

Xining [sheening], **Hsi-ning**, or **Sining** 36°35N 101°55E, pop (1995e) 748 000. City in WC China; airfield; railway. >> China ℹ

Xizang >> **Tibet**

X-ray astronomy A general term for the study of the X-rays from cosmic sources. It needs satellite-borne instruments, because X-rays do not penetrate our atmosphere. >> astronomy; X-rays

X-ray diffraction An interference effect in which atoms in a material scatter X-rays to give a pattern of spots or concentric rings. These may be detected photographically, and their position and intensity can be used to determine the material's structure. The technique was discovered in 1912 by German physicist Max von Laue (1879–1960). >> diffraction; X-rays

X-rays Invisible electromagnetic radiation having a much shorter wavelength than light, between 10^{-8} and 3×10^{-11}

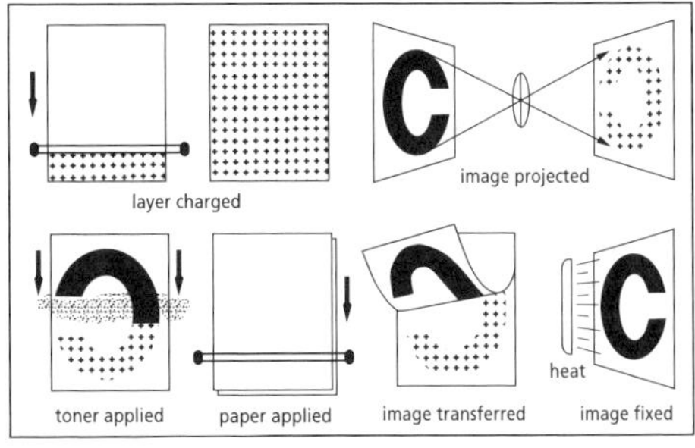

Stages in the xerographic process

metres; discovered by Wilhelm Röntgen in 1895, and originally called **Röntgen rays**. They are produced by the transitions of electrons in the inner levels of excited atoms, or by the rapid deceleration of charged particles. X-rays are useful in medicine, since different components of the body absorb X-rays to a different extent, but enough radiation passes through the body to register on a photograhic plate beyond. >> electromagnetic radiation 🅘; exposure; Röntgen, Wilhelm; X-ray astronomy / diffraction

xylem [**zi**lem] A tissue composed of several types of conducting cells and supporting fibres which transports water and minerals up from the roots to all other parts of a plant. It forms the 'wood' of woody plants. >> wood

xylophone A percussion instrument known in various forms since the 14th-c. The modern orchestral instrument has two rows of wooden bars arranged like a piano keyboard, with a compass of $3\frac{1}{2}$–4 octaves. These are mounted over tubular resonators and played with hard wooden sticks. >> marimba; percussion 🅘

X–Y plotter A form of pen recorder where one or more pens can be placed anywhere on the drawing surface. This allows complicated drawings and text to be produced. >> computer graphics

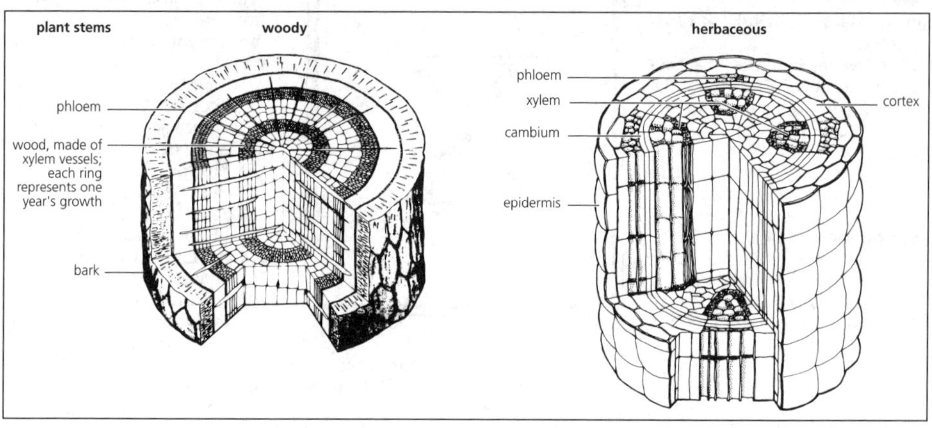

Xylem

yacht A sailing or power-driven vessel used for the pleasure of the owner. The first known yacht race was between Charles II and his brother James in 1661 from Greenwich to Gravesend and back. Yachting increased steadily in popularity throughout the 19th-c, and received a great boost from the continuing interest of Edward, Prince of Wales and other royals. >> America's Cup; sailing; RR1065

Yahweh [**yah**way] or **YHWH** The name of the God of Israel, usually taken to mean 'He is/will be', 'He comes to be/creates', or 'He causes to fall'. The unvocalized YHWH (known as the **Tetragrammaton**) is considered by Jews too sacred to pronounce aloud, and is usually replaced orally by *Adonai* ('Lord') when it is read from the Bible. Christians erroneously vocalized it as 'Jehovah'. >> Bible; Elohim; God; Holy of Holies; Jehovah

Y

yak A member of the cattle family, native to the high Tibetan Plateau; thick shaggy brown coat; white muzzle; widely spread upturned horns; females crossbred with male domestic cattle or zebu; hybrid offspring (a *dzo*) economically important as draught animals. (*Bos mutus*.) >> Bovidae; cattle; ox; zebu

Yakut A Turkic-speaking Mongoloid people of NE Siberia, and the main group in the area. They are sedentary cattle and reindeer herders, and fishermen. >> Siberia

yakuza [**ya**kuza] A Japanese gangster. The 90 000 yakuza belong to recognized groups, cultivate a pseudo-samurai loyalty, and are proud of their traditions. Like the Mafia, they are widely involved in such activities as gambling, extortion, and racketeering. >> Mafia; pachinko; samurai

Yale University >> **Ivy League** ℹ

Yalow, Rosalyn S(ussman) [**ya**loh] (1921–) Medical physicist, born in New York City. In the 1950s she devised the technique of radio-immunoassay, and shared the Nobel Prize for Physiology or Medicine in 1977. >> radio-immunoassay

Yalta Conference A meeting at Yalta, in the Crimea, during World War 2 (4–11 Feb 1945), between Churchill, Stalin, and Roosevelt. Among matters agreed were the disarmament and partition of Germany, the Russo-Polish frontier, and the establishment of the United Nations. >> Churchill, Winston; Curzon Line; Roosevelt, Franklin D; Stalin; World War 2

Yalu, River [ya**loo**] River forming the N border between North Korea and NE China; rises in the Changbai Shan range; flows into Korea Bay; length 790 km/490 mi. >> Korea, North ℹ

yam A tuberous perennial, native to tropical and subtropical regions. Some 60 species are important food plants, especially in SE Asia, W Africa, and South America, where they are cultivated for the starchy tubers. In recent years some species have become important as a source of a steroid-type chemical used in oral contraceptives. (Genus: *Dioscorea*. Family: Dioscoreaceae.) >> steroid; sweet potato; tuber

International Racing Yacht Classes

class	crew	type of craft
Finn	1	centre board dinghy
Flying Dutchman	2	centre board dinghy
International 470	2	centre board dinghy
International Soling	3	keel boat
International Star	2	keel boat
International Tornado	2	catamaran
Windglider	1	single board

Yamoussoukro [yamoo**soo**kroh] 6°49N 5°17W, pop (1995e) 174 000. Capital of Côte d'Ivoire; weekend resort town; presidential residence. >> Abidjan; Côte d'Ivoire ℹ

Yamuna or **Jumna, River** [**yah**muna] River of NW India; rises in the Himalayas; joins the R Ganges; length 1370 km/850 mi; confluence with the Ganges is one of the most sacred Hindu places. >> Hinduism; India ℹ

yang >> **yin and yang**

Yangchow >> **Yangzhou**

Yangon, formerly (to 1989) **Rangoon** 16°47N 96°10E, pop (1995e) 3 190 000. Chief port and capital of Myanmar; on R Yangon; settlement in 6th-c; capital, 1886; large Indian and Chinese population; airport (Mingaladon); railway; university (1920); Sule and Botataung Pagodas (both over 2000 years old), Shwedagon Pagoda (height 99·4 m/326 ft). >> Myanmar ℹ

Yangtze River [**yangk**see] or **Yangtse-kiang**, Chin now normally **Chang Jiang** Longest river in China and third longest in the world; length c.6300 km/3900 mi; rises in the Tanggula Shan range; enters the E China Sea; provides c.40% of China's electricity; Three Gorges dam project, begun in 1994 (completion scheduled, 2011); major transportation artery between E and W China; densely populated river basin contains about a quarter of China's cultivated land. >> China ℹ

Yangzhou or **Yangchow** [yahngjoh] 32°25N 119°26E, pop (1995e) 489 000. City in E China, on Yangtze and Hua Rivers; first settled during Spring and Autumn Period, 770–476 BC; largest multiple-purpose water control project in China (1961–75); artistic centre for crafts, lacquerware screens, jade carving and printing. >> China ℹ

Yao (Africa) [yow] A cluster of agricultural Bantu-speaking peoples of Tanzania, Malawi, and Mozambique. The majority are Muslims.

Yao (Asia) A mountain village people of SE Asia, dispersed and culturally diverse. They live chiefly in China, with some also in Thailand, Vietnam, and Laos.

Yaoundé or **Yaundé** [ya**oon**day] 3°51N 11°31E, pop (1995e) 973 000. Capital of Cameroon, W Africa; established as military post by Germans in 1899; occupied by Belgian colonial troops, 1915; capital of French Cameroon, 1921; airport; railway to the coast (Douala); university (1962). >> Cameroon ℹ

Yap pop (1995e) 14 800; area 119 sq km/46 sq mi. One of the Federated States of Micronesia, W Pacific; comprises four large islands with some 130 outer islands; airport; capital, Colonia. >> Micronesia, Federated States of

yapok [ya**pok**] A marsupial native to Central and South America (*Chironectes minimus*); slender with long legs, pointed head, long naked tail; the only truly semiaquatic marsupial; hind feet webbed; also known as **water opossum**. (Family: Didelphidae.) >> marsupial ℹ

yarn The spun thread from which woven, knitted, and other fabrics are manufactured. Yarns vary widely in their properties, depending upon fibre content, count, and the spinning process used. >> count (textiles); twist

Yaroslavl [yaro**slafl**] 57°34N 39°52E, pop (1995e) 643 000. River port in E European Russia; founded c.1024; railway; university (1971); monastery (12th-c). >> Russia ℹ

yarrow A perennial (*Achillea millefolium*) growing to 60 cm/2 ft, native to Europe and W Asia; flower-heads numerous, in dense, flat-topped clusters; also called **milfoil**. It was formerly employed extensively in herbal medicine. (Family: Compositae.) >> herb

Yates, Dornford, pseudonym of **Cecil William Mercer** (1885–1960) Novelist, born in London. He achieved great popularity with an entertaining series of fanciful escapist adventure fiction, such as *Berry and Co* (1921).

Yavneh [yavne] >> **Jabneh**

yawl >> **ketch** 🅘

yaws An infectious disease of tropical regions caused by the bacterium *Treponema pertenue*. It is largely confined to eruptions in the skin. >> bacteria 🅘

yeast A fungus that can occur as single cells; typically reproduces by budding or by fission; used in fermentation processes in the brewing and baking industries. (Subdivision: Ascomycetes. Order: Endomycetales.) >> Ascomycetes; fungus

Yeats, W(illiam) B(utler) [yayts] (1865–1939) Poet and playwright, born near Dublin. In 1888 he published *The Wanderings of Oisin*, a long narrative poem that established his reputation. His three most popular plays were *The Countess Cathleen* (1892), *The Land of Heart's Desire* (1894), and *Cathleen ni Houlihan* (1903), and he wrote several others for the Abbey Theatre, which he helped to found in 1904. Many of his best-known poems appeared in *The Tower* (1928), *The Winding Stair* (1929), and *A Full Moon in March* (1935). He received the Nobel Prize for Literature in 1923. >> Abbey Theatre

Yekaterinburg or **Ekaterinburg** [yekatuhrinberg], formerly **Sverdlovsk** (1924–91) 56°52N 60°35E, pop (1995e) 1 386 000. Industrial city in E European Russia; on R Iset; founded as a military stronghold and trading centre, 1723; tsar and his family shot here, 1917; airport; on the Trans-Siberian Railway; university (1920). >> Russia 🅘; Trans-Siberian Railway

yellow fever An infection caused by a virus which infests monkeys and is transmitted to humans from them by mosquitoes. It is often a mild short-lived feverish illness, but may become severe, with liver and kidney failure. It occurs in Africa and South America. >> virus

yellowfin tuna Species of tuna fish (*Thunnus albacares*) widespread in surface waters of tropical and warm temperate seas; length up to 2 m/6½ ft; golden band along side of body, dorsal and anal fins yellow; heavily exploited commercially. (Family: Scombridae.) >> tuna

yellow-green algae Aquatic algae containing the photosynthetic pigments chlorophyll *a* and *c*, and various carotenoids which produce the yellow-green colour of the chloroplasts; they vary in form from single cells to filaments. (Class: Xanthophyceae.) >> algae; chloroplast; photosynthesis

yellowhammer (Ger *ammer*, 'bunting') A bird, a species of bunting (*Emberiza citronella*), native to NW regions of the Old World; black and yellow streaked plumage with chestnut rump; also known as the **yellow bunting**. The name is used in the USA for the woodpecker, *Colaptes auratus*. >> bunting; woodpecker

Yellowknife 62°30N 114°29W, pop (1995e) 16 100. Capital of North West Territories, Canada, on NW shore of Great Slave Lake at mouth of Yellowknife R; founded, 1935; capital, 1967. >> Northwest Territories

Yellow River, Chin **Huang Ho** or **Huang He** Second longest river in China; length 5464 km/3395 mi; rises in Bayan Har Shan Range; enters the Bo Hai Gulf; flooding now increasingly controlled by dykes; several conservancy projects on upper and middle reaches. >> China 🅘

Yellow Sea, Chin **Hwang Hai** Inlet of the Pacific Ocean, bounded by China (N, W) and by N and S Korea (E); maximum width c.650 km/400 mi; maximum depth c.150 m/500 ft; named for its colour, because of the silt brought down by its rivers. >> Pacific Ocean

Yellowstone Largest US national park, and the world's first, mainly in NW Wyoming; contains over 3000 hot springs and geysers, including Old Faithful, a geyser that spurts water at regular intervals; area 8992 sq km/3472 sq mi. >> National Park; Wyoming

yellow wood A member of a large genus of evergreen conifers found in the mountains of warm temperate and tropical regions of the S hemisphere. They are important forest trees, especially in Australasia, yielding valuable timber. (Genus: *Podocarpus*, 100 species. Family: Pinaceae.) >> conifer

Yeltsin, Boris (Nikolayevich) (1931–) Russian president, born in Butka, Russia. Inducted into the Central Committee in 1981 by Gorbachev, he was appointed Moscow party chief, and set about renovating the corrupt 'Moscow machine'. In 1987, after he had bluntly criticized party conservatives for sabotaging *perestroika*, he was downgraded to a lowly administrative post. He returned to public attention in 1989 as a member of the new Congress of USSR People's Deputies, and in 1990 was elected president of the Russian Federation. Following the attempted coup to oust Gorbachev in 1991, his political standing greatly increased when he led the protestors who defeated the coup, and following the break-up of the Soviet Union he remained in power as president. He has continued to press for reform, but has met increasing resistance from more conservative elements in the parliament. Although successful in the 1996 elections, continuing ill health was causing him major difficulties. >> Gorbachev; perestroika; Russia 🅘; Soviet Union

Yemen, official name **Republic of Yemen**, Arabic **al-Jumhurijah al-Yemenijah** pop (1995e) 13 510 000; area 531 570 sq km/205 186 sq mi. Republic occupying the SW corner of the Arabian peninsula, formed in 1990 from the merging of North and South Yemen; political capital, Sana; commercial capital, Aden; timezone GMT +3; population mainly Arab; chief religion, Islam; official language, Arabic; units of currency, the rial; narrow coastal plain, backed by mountains rising to 3500 m/11 500 ft; dry and arid Rub al Khali, NE; hot and humid on coastal

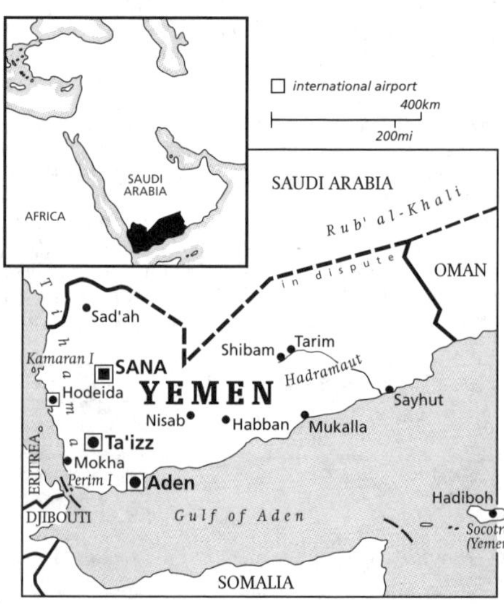

strip. Former *People's Democratic Republic of South Yemen*: fishing port of Aden occupied by Britain, 1839; British protectorate, 1937; part of Federation of South Arabia, 1963; overrun by the National Liberation Front, British troops withdrawn, and republic proclaimed, 1967; border disputes with Oman and North Yemen in 1970s. Former *Yemen Arab Republic (North Yemen)*: Turkish occupation, 1872–1918; rule of Hamid al-Din dynasty until 1962; fighting between royalists and republicans until 1967, when republican regime recognized; border clashes with South Yemen. *Republic of Yemen* (from 1990): increasing economic and political tensions between N and S areas resulted in South Yemen declaring independence as Democratic Republic of Yemen, and civil war, 1994, won by North Yemen; governed by a president, prime minister, and House of Representatives; largely agriculture and light industry; millet, wheat, barley, pulses, fruit, vegetables, dates, cotton, coffee, gat; textiles, cement, aluminium products, soft drinks, handicrafts, oil refining, salt, fishing. >> Aden; Sana; RR1028 political leaders

Yenisey or **Yenisei, River** [yeni**say**] River in C Siberian Russia; rises in the E Sayanskiy Khrebet; enters the Kara Sea; length, 3487 km/2167 mi. >> Russia i

yeoman A person in late mediaeval England qualified, by holding freehold worth 40 shillings or more, to serve on juries and vote for knights of the shire. In the early modern period, the name is used for the better-off freeholders or tenant-farmers who were often dominant in village life and administration.

Yeomen of the Guard The oldest of the four corps of the British sovereign's personal bodyguard, known also as **Beefeaters**, supposedly in tribute to their healthy appearance. They are called out for special duties only, when they wear their basically Tudor uniforms. The same uniforms are worn by the **Yeomen Warders** of the Tower of London. >> Tower of London

Yerevan or **Erivan** [yere**van**] 40°10N 44°31E, pop (1995e) 1 364 000. Capital city of Armenia; on R Razdan; altitude of highest part, 1042 m/3419 ft; one of the world's most ancient cities; ceded to Russia, 1828; airfield; railway; university. >> Armenia i

Yesenin, Sergey [ye**say**nin] (1895–1925) Poet, born in Yesenino (formerly Konstantino), Russia to a peasant family. He gained literary success with his first volume *Radunitsa* (1916, Mourning for the Dead). His suicide in St Petersburg prompted a wave of imitative suicides in Russia.

yeti A supposed ape-like creature said to live at the edge of the snow-line in high valleys of the Himalayan Mts; generally described as large, covered in brown hair, and walking upright like a human; first reported in 1889; footprints of length 15–30 cm/6–12 in have been photographed, but various expeditions have failed to find it; also known as **abominable snowman**. >> ape; Bigfoot; hominid

Yevtushenko, Yevegeny (Alexandrovich) [yevtu**sheng**koh] (1933–) Poet, born in Zima, Russia. His early poetry, such as *The Third Snow* (1955), made him a spokesman for the young post-Stalin generation. Major poems include *Stantsiya Zima* (1956, Zima Junction), considering issues raised by the death of Stalin, and *Babi Yar* (1962) which attacked anti-Semitism. In 1960 he began to travel abroad to give readings of his poetry. Among later works are *Pre-morning* (1995). His first major stage piece, *Under the Skin of the Statue of Liberty*, was a huge success in 1972.

yew A small evergreen tree or shrub, native to the western N hemisphere; leaves narrow, flattened, spreading in two horizontal rows. The foliage and seeds are highly poisonous. Popular for cemeteries, topiary, and mazes, yews were once the source of the finest longbows. (Genus: *Taxus*, 10 species. Family: Taxaceae.) >> taxol; tree i

Yiddish A language used by E European Jews, developed from Old High German in the 9th-c, and written using the Hebrew alphabet. It flourished as a medium of literature in the 19th-c, but its literary use has diminished following the establishment of Hebrew as the official language of Israel. >> Aleichem; Germanic languages; Hebrew

yield The interest paid on a stock, share, or bond in relation to its current market value, in percentage terms. If a company pays a dividend of 20p a share, before tax is deducted, and the share price is 400p, then the dividend yield is 5%. >> dividend

yield stress The lowest stretching stress at which a material undergoes an irreversible plastic deformation, producing what is called a 'permanent set' in the material; symbol σ_y, units Pa (pascal). >> stress (physics)

yin and yang The Chinese concept that everything is explicable in terms of two complementary but opposing principles. Yang represents heaven, and is the positive, male force which is characteristically aggressive, stimulating, light, hot, and dry. Yin is seen as the negative, female force, which is characteristically cold, dark, heavy, and damp. Yang people are active, alert, energetic, and precise, but suffer with problems of anxiety, stress, tension, irritability, and inability to relax. Yin people are calm, relaxed, peaceful, and creative, but are prone to laziness, depression, and lethargy. Representing all experience in a dynamic framework, the yin–yang concept has underpinned Chinese cyclical views of history, and was developed in a sophisticated form by Han times (3rd-c BC–AD 3rd-c). >> Book of Changes; macrobiotics; numerology; Taoism; traditional Chinese medicine

Yinchuan or **Yinch'uan** [yinchwahn] 38°30N 106°19E, pop (1995e) 538 000. Capital of Ningxia autonomous region, N China; airfield; commercial centre; centre of agricultural trade; Muslims are a third of the population. >> China i

ylang-ylang [eelang **ee**lang] An evergreen tree (*Cananga odorata*) growing to 25 m/80 ft, native to Malaysia and the Philippines; flowers 6-petalled, dull yellow, fragrant. Ylang-ylang or macassar oil from the flowers is used in perfumes. (Family: Annonaceae.) >> oil (botany)

YMCA Abbreviation of **Young Men's Christian Association**, a charity founded in London in 1844 to promote the spiritual, social, and physical welfare of boys and young men. In the 1990s it was active in over 130 countries, with over 100 000 centres and 30 million people participating in its activities. >> YWCA

yoga In Indian religious tradition, any of various physical and contemplative techniques designed to free the superior, conscious element in a person from involvement with the inferior material world. More narrowly, Yoga is a school of Hindu philosophy. >> Hinduism

yogurt or **yoghurt** A product, originating in the Balkans, obtained by fermenting milk with the bacteria *Lactobacillus bulgaricus* and *Streptococcus acidophilus*. Various sweetenings and flavourings may be added. >> fermentation; lactose; milk

Yogyakarta [yagya**kah(r)**ta] or **Yogya** 7°48S 110°24E, pop (1995e) 516 000. City in SC Java, Indonesia; cultural centre of Java; airfield; railway; two universities (1945, 1949); ancient temples of Borobudur and Prambanan. >> Java (country)

Yokohama [yohkoh**hah**ma] 35°28N 139°28E, pop (1995e) 3 292 000. Port in C Honshu, Japan; second largest city in Japan, handling 15% of foreign trade; first port to be opened to foreign trade, 1859; linked to Tokyo by first Japanese railway, 1872; largely destroyed by earthquake in 1923, and by bombing in 1945; railway; two universities (1949). >> Honshu; Tokyo

Yolngu The Aboriginal people and language of NE Arnhem Land; sometimes called **Murngin**. Three Yolngu clans were the plaintiffs in a land rights case in 1968, and their failure to secure legal recognition led directly to the introduction of the first Australian land rights legislation in 1976. >> Aborigines

Yom Kippur [**yohm** kipoor, **yom ki**pur] The Day of Atonement, a Jewish holy day (10 Tishri) coming at the end of 10 days of penitence which begin on Rosh Hashanah; a day devoted to fasting, prayer, and repentance for past sins. >> Judaism

Yom Kippur War >> **Arab–Israeli Wars**

yoni [**yoh**nee] >> **lingam**

Yonkers 40°56N 73°54W, pop (1995e) 191 000. Town in SE New York, USA; a residential suburb on the Hudson R; railway; St Andrews golf course (first course in the USA). >> New York (state)

York, Lat **Eboracum** 53°58N 1°05W, pop (1995e) 102 000. City in North Yorkshire, N England; unitary authority from 1996 (pop (1995e) 174 000); Roman settlement founded in AD 71 as capital of the Roman province of Britannia; thereafter a royal and religious centre, capital of Anglo-Saxon Northumbria; captured by the Danes, 867, known as **Jorvík**; Archbishop of York bears the title Primate of England; expanded rapidly in the 19th-c as a railway centre; university (1963); 14th-c city walls; York Minster (12th–15th-c), south transept badly damaged by fire in 1984, since restored; National Railway Museum; Jorvik Viking Centre (1984); football league team, York City. >> Danelaw; Yorkshire, North

York, Alvin (Cullum) (1887–1964) US soldier and popular hero, born in Pall Mall, TN. While in France during World War 1, he led a small detachment against a German machine-gun emplacement, in which he killed 25 of the enemy, inducing 132 Germans to surrender. Gary Cooper portrayed him in the movie *Sergeant York* (1941). >> American Legion; World War 1

York, Duke of In the UK, a title often given to the second son of the sovereign. It is currently held by Andrew, the second son of Queen Elizabeth.

York, House of The younger branch of the Plantagenet dynasty, founded by Edmund of Langley, the fourth son of Edward III and first Duke of York (1385–1402), whence came three kings of England: Edward IV (1461–83), who usurped the Lancastrian king Henry VI; Edward V (1483); and Richard III (1483–5) killed at Bosworth Field. >> Edward IV / V; Plantagenets; Richard III; Roses, Wars of the

Yorkshire, North pop (1995e) 731 000; excluding York, 556 000; area 8309 sq km/3207 sq mi. County in N England, created in 1974; largest county in England; York a unitary authority from 1996; Pennines in the W; Vale of York, North Yorkshire Moors, Cleveland Hills in the E; county town, Northallerton; Rievaulx Abbey, Yorkshire Dales national park, Castle Howard, York Minster, Fountains Abbey. >> England [i]; Fountains Abbey; York

Yorkshire, South pop (1995e) 1 312 000; area 1560 sq km/602 sq mi. Area of N England, created in 1974, divided into four metropolitan borough councils: Sheffield, Rotherham, Doncaster, Barnsley. >> England [i]

Yorkshire, West pop (1995e) 2 119 000; area 2039 sq km/787 sq mi. County of N England; administrative centre, Wakefield; metropolitan council abolished in 1986; Ilkley Moor, Haworth Parsonage (home of the Brontës), Peak District National Park. >> Brontë; England [i]; Wakefield

Yorkshire Dales National park in North Yorkshire and Cumbria, England; area 1761 sq km/680 sq mi; established in 1954; limestone scenery, popular with potholers and fell walkers. >> Cumbria; Yorkshire, North

Yorkshire terrier A British toy terrier; very small, with long fine brown and blue-grey hair; coat reaches ground; head with large erect ears and very long hair. >> terrier

Yorktown 37°14N 76°30W. Town in SE Virginia, USA, at the mouth of the York R; settled, 1631; now in Colonial National Historical Park; besieged during the Revolution, 1781, and the Civil War, 1862. >> American Civil War / Revolution; Virginia; Yorktown Campaign

Yorktown Campaign (30 Aug–19 Oct 1781) The final campaign of the US War of Independence, ending with the entrapment at Yorktown, VA, of the British army under Lord Cornwallis by troops under Washington and a French fleet under Admiral de Grasse (1722–88). >> American Revolution; Cornwallis; Washington, George

Yoruba [**yo**ruhba] A cluster of Kwa-speaking peoples of SW Nigeria and Benin. Their dominant state in the 17th–18th-c was the kingdom of Oyo. >> Benin [i]; Nigeria [i]

Yosemite [yoh**sem**itee] ('grizzly bear') National park in E California, USA, in the Sierra Nevada; rises to 3990 m/13 090 ft in Mt Lyell; Yosemite Falls (highest in North America); area 3083 sq km/1189 sq mi. >> California

Young, Andrew (Jackson), Jr (1932–) Civil rights activist, Protestant minister, and public official, born in New Orleans, LA. As a minister, he joined the Southern Christian Leadership Conference in 1960, and came to be one of the closest associates of Martin Luther King, Jr. He later became US representative to the UN, but was forced to resign after it was revealed that he had met secretly with members of the PLO. >> civil rights; King, Martin Luther

Young, Brigham (1801–77) Mormon leader, born in Whitingham, VT. Converted in 1832, he became president of the Church upon the death of Joseph Smith in 1844. He led the Mormons to Utah (1847), where they founded Salt Lake City. He established over 300 towns and settlements, and had (according to one estimation) 27 wives and 56 children. >> Mormons; Salt Lake City; Smith, Joseph

Young, Cy, popular name of **Denton True Young** (1867–1955) Baseball pitcher, born in Gilmore, OH. One of the first of baseball's greats, during his career he threw 749 and won 511 games, both records. National and American League's leading pitchers win the **Cy Young Award** every year. >> baseball [i]

Young, Lester (Willis), nickname **Prez** (1909–59) Influential and much-imitated jazz musician, born in Woodville, MI. Originally a drummer, he became a master of the tenor and alto saxophones, becoming known in the 1930s and 1940s. Billie Holiday gave him his nickname, short for 'President'. >> Holiday; jazz

Young, Thomas (1773–1829) Physicist, physician, and egyptologist, born in Milverton, Somerset. He established the wave theory of light, and made a fundamental contribution to the deciphering of the inscriptions on the Rosetta Stone. >> light; Rosetta Stone; Young's modulus

Young Ireland An Irish protest movement, founded in 1840, arguing for repeal of the Act of Union. It set up an Irish Confederation in 1847, which returned several nationalists to parliament. >> nationalism; O'Connell; Union, Acts of

Young Italy An Italian patriotic organization which played an important role in the early stages of the Risorgimento, founded in Marseille (1833) by Mazzini. It played a significant part in the revolutions of 1848. >> Mazzini; Risorgimento

Young Men's Christian Association >> **YMCA**

Young Men's / Women's Hebrew Association (YMHA/YWHA) In the USA, an organization to promote health, social activities, and Jewish culture. The first

YMHA was founded in 1854, and the first independent YWHA in 1902. >> Judaism

young offender institution An institution in the UK where adolescent and young adult offenders between 16 and 21 (between 15 and 21 for male offenders, in England and Wales) may be detained either on remand or following a sentence of the court. In the USA, detention centres for both male and female offenders are often known as *juvenile halls*, *youth camps*, or *youth authorities*. >> juvenile court

Young's modulus Linear stress divided by linear strain, a constant for a given material; symbol *E*, units Pa (pascal); also called the **modulus of elasticity** or the **elastic modulus**; named after British physicist Thomas Young. A high Young's modulus means that material is stiffer. >> elasticity; strain; stress (physics); Young, Thomas

Young Turks The modernizing and westernizing reformers in the early 20th-c Ottoman Empire. With the support of disaffected army elements under Enver Pasha, they rebelled against Sultan Abd-ul-Hamid II in 1908, and deposed him in 1909. >> Enver Pasha; Ottoman Empire

Young Women's Christian Association >> **YWCA**

Yourcenar, Marguerite [**yer**senah(r)], pseudonym of **Marguerite de Crayencour** (1903–87) Novelist, born in Brussels. She is best known for her historical novel *Mémoires d'Hadrien* (1951, Memoirs of Hadrian), and for being the first woman to be elected to the Académie Française.

youth court A court introduced in England and Wales in 1991 to replace the existing juvenile courts. Youth courts deal with most young offenders from the age of criminal responsibility (10 in England and Wales) up to the age of 18. >> criminal law; juvenile court

Youth Hostels Association (YHA) >> **International Youth Hostel Association**

Ypres [eepr], Flemish **Ieper** 50°51N 2°53E, pop (1995e) 35 600. Town in W Belgium, close to the French border; long associated with the cloth trade; devastated in World War 1; Menin Gate (Menenpoort) memorial, graveyards, and Garden of Peace provide a place of pilgrimage; railway; cloth hall (13th-c); cathedral. >> Belgium [i]; Ypres, Battles of

Ypres, Battle of [eepr] **1** (Oct–Nov 1914) In World War 1, the halting of a German offensive to outflank the British Expeditionary Force. It left Ypres (Belgium) and its salient dominated on three sides by German-occupied heights. >> World War 1 **2** (Apr–May 1915) A series of German attacks, using poison gas (chlorine) for the first time in warfare. It forced the British to shorten their defence line in the Ypres salient. >> chlorine **3** (Jul–Nov 1917) >> Passchendaele, Battle of

Ysselmeer >> **Ijsselmeer**

yttrium [**yit**rium] Y, element 39, density 4·5 g/cm^3, melting point 1522°C. A relatively rare element occurring in ores of the lanthanide elements, many of whose properties it shares. It is a constituent of many superconducting ceramics. >> chemical elements; lanthanides; superconductivity; RR1036

Yuan dynasty [yooan] or **Mongol dynasty** (1279–1368) A Chinese dynasty founded by Kublai Khan (1264), who took the name Yuan in 1271 and conquered the Song dynasty in 1279. There were significant developments in astronomy, medicine, shipbuilding, and technology; and a vernacular literary genre evolved, with new dramatic forms. The dynasty was eventually overthrown by a Chinese uprising led by Zhu Yuanzhang, the first Ming emperor. >> Kublai Khan

Yuan Shikai [yüan sheekiy], also spelled **Yuan Shih-k'ai** (1859–1916) Chinese statesman and soldier, born in Xiancheng, Henan, China, the first president of the Republic established in 1912. He lost support by procuring the murder of the parliamentary leader of the Nationalists, making war on them, and proclaiming himself emperor (1915), and he was forced to abdicate. >> Qing dynasty

Yucatán [yuka**tahn**] pop (1995e) 1 512 000; area 38 402 sq km/14 823 sq mi. State in SE Mexico, on the N Yucatán peninsula; capital, Mérida; numerous Mayan ruins, including Chichén Itzá and Uxmal; the name also often given to the whole peninsula. >> Chichén Itzá; Mayas; Mexico [i]; Palenque; Uxmal

yucca An evergreen perennial native to the USA, Mexico, and the Caribbean; somewhat palm-like in appearance, trunk short, thick; leaves sword-shaped; flowers night-scented, white, bell-shaped and hanging, in spikes. (Genus: *Yucca*, 40 species. Family: Agavaceae.)

Yugoslavia or **Jugoslavia** [yoogoh**slah**via], official name **Federal Republic of Yugoslavia**, Serbian **Savezna Republika Jugoslavija** pop (prior to 1991) 23 860 000, (1995e) 10 494 000; area (prior to 1991) 256 409 sq km/98 974 sq mi, (since 1991) 102 173 sq km/39 438 sq mi. Federal republic in the Balkan peninsula of SE Europe, now consisting of the republics of Serbia and Montenegro, but before 1991 also consisting of Bosnia and Herzegovina, Croatia, Macedonia, and Slovenia; capital, Belgrade (also capital of Serbia); timezone GMT +2; chief ethnic groups, Serb (62%), Albanian (17%); chief religions, Serbian Orthodox; chief languages, Serbian (Serbo-Croatian), with Albanian and Hungarian also spoken; unit of currency, the Yugoslav dinar of 100 paras; Julian and Karawanken Alps rise (N) to 2863 m/9393 ft at Triglav; Adriatic fringed by the Dinaric Alps; Mediterranean climate on Adriatic coast; continental climate in the N and NE; Serbs, Croats, and Slovenes united under one monarch, 1918; country renamed Yugoslavia, 1929; civil war between Serbian royalists (Chetniks), Croatian nationalists, and Communists; occupied by Germans during World War 2; Federal People's Republic established under Tito, 1945; revised constitution in 1974 instituted a rotating leadership, with the prime minister elected annually; governed by a bicameral Federal Assembly, comprising a Federal Chamber and a Chamber of Republics and Provinces; following a break with the USSR in 1948, the country followed an independent form of communism and a general policy of nonalignment; at the end of the 1980s political disagreement between the federal republics increased; Slovenian unilateral declaration of independence in 1989, followed by Macedonian and Croatian declarations in 1991, considered illegal by central government, leading to civil war (see separate entry); Federal Republic of Yugoslavia declared, 1992, consisting of only two of the republics which made up former Yugoslavia (Serbia, Montenegro); Serbian policy of 'ethnic cleansing' in Kosovo, with mass displacement of ethnic Albanian population and widespread reports of human rights violations, led to NATO intervention (Mar 1999), with bombing of military targets throughout Yugoslavia; industrial base extended since World War 2; agriculture, especially wheat, maize, sugar beet, livestock; economy badly affected by civil war. >> Belgrade; Bosnia and Herzegovina; communism; Croatia; Kosovo; Macedonia, Former Yugoslav Republic of [i]; Montenegro; Serbia; Slovenia; Tito; Yugoslavian Civil War; RR1028 political leaders; *see illustrations on p. 954*

Yugoslavian Civil War (1991–5) Declaration of independence by Slovenia, Macedonia, and Croatia considered illegal by central Yugoslav government. Confrontation between Croatia and Serb-dominated national army developed into civil war. Croatian independence was internationally recognized in 1991, but fighting continued between Croats and Muslims in Bosnia, and between Croats and Serb guerrillas in Krajina (a Serb-dominated

enclave in Croatia), who wished to see the area as part of a 'Greater Serbia'. UN recognition of Bosnia-Herzegovina independence in 1992 opposed by Serbs. UN sanctions imposed on Yugoslavia (and suspension from the UN) following its support of Serb guerrillas in Bosnia and the Serbian policy of 'ethnic cleansing' (driving Muslims from areas shared with ethnic Serbs). Croatian-dominated Western Herzegovina proclaimed itself autonomous, raising the possibility of a 'Greater Croatia'. Internationally sponsored plan introduced 'safe areas' for Muslims in Bosnia, to be monitored by a UN Protection Force. Serb attacks on Sarajevo, 1994, led to NATO ultimatum, imposition of a 'no-fly' zone, and NATO bombing of Serb forces in response to attacks on safe areas. Serbs captured Muslim safe-area enclave of Srebrenica, which brought reports of major atrocities. Successful Croatian offensive in Krajina and NW Bosnia restored territorial balance in the area. Serb attack on Sarajevo led to NATO/UN attacks on Bosnian Serb targets, and Serb withdrawal. A peace treaty, signed in Dayton, OH, left Bosnia as a single state, made up of the Bosnian-Croat Federation and the Bosnian Serb Republic, with a united Sarajevo, and the establishment of a NATO peace implementation force. >> Yugoslavia i

Yukon [**yoo**kon] pop (1995e) 29 500; area 483 450 sq km/186 660 sq mi. Territory in NW Canada; capital, Whitehorse; area of plateaux and mountain ranges, rising to 5950 m/19 521 ft at Mt Logan; tundra in N; several lakes; Hudson's Bay Company fur-trading post, 1842; gold prospectors from 1873; district of Northwest Territories, 1895; separate territory when Klondike gold rush at its height, 1898; governed by an Executive Council appointed from a Legislative Assembly. >> Canada i; Hudson's Bay Company; Logan, Mount; tundra; Whitehorse

Yukon River Major river in North America, in Yukon territory and Alaska; rises in the Rocky Mts, enters the Bering Sea; length to the head of the longest headstream (the Nisutlin) 3185 km/1979 mi; ice-bound most of the year (Oct–Jun). >> Alaska; Yukon

Yunupingu, Mandawuy [yunu**ping**goo, **man**dawoy] (1956–) Singer, born in Yirrkala, a former Methodist mission in NE Arnhem Land, Australia. A member of one of the leading families in the Gumatj clans, in 1986 he established the group *Yothu Yindi* ('mother–child' in Yolngu-matha). In 1993 he was made Australian of the Year, an honour also bestowed on his brother **Galarrwuy** in 1978. >> Aborigines

Yurak >> **Nenets**

YWCA Abbreviation of **Young Women's Christian Association**, a charity formed in London in 1877 by the joining of a prayer union and a home for nurses travelling to and from the Crimean War. It is now active in over 80 countries. >> YMCA

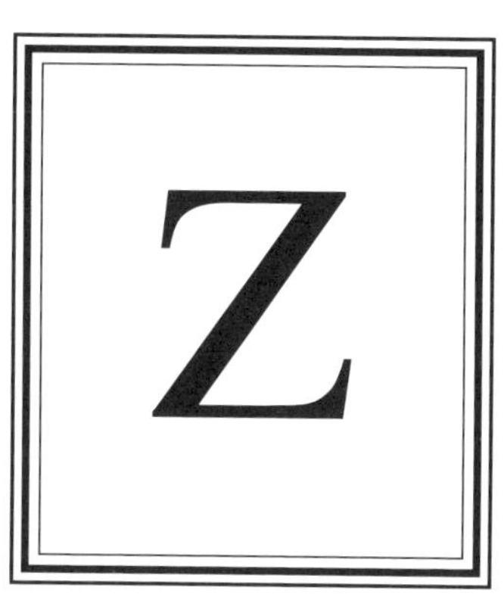

Zabrze [**zab**uhrzhe], Ger **Hindenburg** 50°18N 18°47E, pop (1995e) 202 000. Mining and industrial city in S Poland; second largest city in upper Silesian industrial region; railway. >> Poland ℹ

Zacharias >> **Zechariah, Book of**

Zacynthus [**za**kinthus], Gr **Zákinthos**, ancient **Zante** pop (1995e) 33 500; area 406 sq km/157 sq mi. Third largest of the Ionian Is, W Greece; length 40 km/25 mi; capital, Zacynthus; devastated by earthquakes in 1953. >> Greece ℹ; Ionian Islands

Zadar [**za**dah(r)], Ital **Zara** 44°07N 15°14E, pop (1995e) 124 000. Seaport and resort town in Croatia, on the Adriatic; conquered by Venice, 1000; passed to Austria, 1797; enclave of Italy, 1920–47; airfield; railway; car ferries to Ancona (Italy); cathedral. >> Croatia ℹ

Zadkine, Ossip [**zad**keen] (1890–1967) Sculptor, born in Smolensk, Russia. He developed an individual Cubist style, making effective use of the play of light on concave surfaces, as in 'The Three Musicians' (1926) and 'Destroyed City' (1952, Rotterdam). >> Cubism

Zadokites [**zay**dokiyts] Descendants of Zadok, a priest apparently of Aaronic lineage who was appointed high priest, serving in Solomon's temple. His family continued to hold this office until Jerusalem fell in 587 BC, and again later in the Second Temple period. The Qumran community continued to look for a renewal of the Zadokite priesthood. >> Aaron; Qumran, community of; Solomon (Hebrew Bible)

Zagreb [**zag**reb], Ger **Agram**, Hung **Zágráb**, ancient **Andautonia** 45°48N 15°58E, pop (1995e) 721 000. Capital city of Croatia; on R Sava; Croat cultural centre; airport; railway; university (1669); cathedral. >> Croatia ℹ

Zaharias, Babe >> **Disrikson, Babe**

Zaire >> **Congo, Democratic Republic of**

Zaire, River >> **Congo, River**

zakat [**zak**at] The alms tax obligatory on all Muslims, and the third of the five 'pillars' of Islam. Traditionally, it consisted of a 2·5% annual levy on income and capital.

Zambezi [zam**bee**zee] or **Zambesi, River**, Port **Zambeze** River in SE Africa, flowing through Angola, Zimbabwe, Zambia, Namibia, and Mozambique; length c.2700 km/1700 mi; rises in NW Zambia; Victoria Falls, L Kariba, and Kariba Dam; enters the Mozambique Channel as a marshy delta; middle course explored by Livingstone in the early 1850s. >> Africa; Kariba Dam

Zambia [**zam**bia], official name **Republic of Zambia**, formerly **Northern Rhodesia** (to 1964) pop (1995e) 9 846 000; area 752 613 sq km/290 509 sq mi. S African republic; capital, Lusaka; timezone GMT +2; chief ethnic groups, Bembo (34%), Tonga (16%), Malawi (14%), Lozi (9%); chief religions, Christianity (over 50%), local beliefs; official language, English, with local languages widely spoken; unit of currency, the kwacha of 100 ngwee; high plateau, altitude 1000–1400 m/3300–4600 ft; highest point, 2067 m/6781 ft, SE of Mbala; Zambezi R rises in the N; warm-temperate climate on upland plateau; tropical climate in lower river valleys; European influence followed Livingstone's discovery of the Victoria Falls, 1855; administered by the British South Africa Company under Cecil Rhodes; area declared a British sphere of influence, 1889–90; North-Eastern and North-Western Rhodesia amalgamated as Northern Rhodesia, 1911; Northern Rhodesia became British Crown Colony, 1924; joined with Southern Rhodesia and Nyasaland as the Federation of Rhodesia and Nyasaland, 1953; Federation dissolved, 1963; independence in 1964, with Kenneth Kaunda as first president; new constitution, 1991; governed by a president and National Assembly; economy based on copper and cobalt, which provide over half the national income. >> Copperbelt; Kaunda; Livingstone, David; Lusaka; Rhodes, Cecil; Zambezi, River; RR1029 political leaders

Zamboanga or **Zamboanga City** [sambo**hang**ga] 6°55N 122°05E, pop (1995e) 493 000. Seaport in W Mindanao, Philippines; founded, 1635; airfield. >> Philippines ℹ

Zamenhof, L(azarus) L(udwig) [**za**menof], pseudonym **Doktoro Esperanto** (1859–1917) Physician and oculist, the inventor of Esperanto, born in Białystok, Poland. His aims were to promote international tolerance and world peace, which he hoped to achieve through the use of an artificial language. >> auxiliary language; Esperanto

Zamyatin, Yevgeny Ivanovich [zam**ya**tin], also spelled **Zamiatin** (1884–1937) Writer, born in Lebedyan, Russia. In 1921 he was a founder member of the Modernist group, the Serapion Brothers. He is best known for the novel *My* (1920, We). >> Bolsheviks; Modernism

zander Freshwater fish (*Stizostedion lucioperca*) found in large rivers and lakes of E Europe; length up to c.1 m/$3\frac{1}{4}$ ft; greenish-grey on back, underside white; a voracious predator; also called **pikeperch**. (Family: Percidae.) >> fish ℹ

Zante [**zan**tay] >> **Zacynthus**

Zanuck, Darryl F(rancis) [**za**nuhk] (1902–79) US film producer, born in Wahoo, NE. He became a co-founder of Twentieth-Century Pictures (later Twentieth-Century Fox) in 1933. Among his many successful films are *The Jazz Singer* (1927), *The Longest Day* (1962), and *The Sound of Music* (1965).

Zanzibar [**zan**zibah(r)] pop (1995e) 447 000; area 1554 sq km/971 sq mi. Island region of Tanzania; separated from the

mainland by the 40 km/25 mi-wide Zanzibar Channel; length, 85 km/53 mi; width, 39 km/24 mi; highest point, 118 m/387 ft; capital, Zanzibar; largely Islamic since the 10th-c; developed under Omani Arab rule into the commercial centre of the W Indian Ocean, 17th-c; now a world centre of clove production; annexed by Germany, 1885; British protectorate, 1891; independence, 1963; ruling Sultanate overthrown in 1964, and the People's Republic of Zanzibar created; joined with Tanganyika, Zanzibar, and Pemba, now forming Tanzania; later the United Republic of Tanzania. >> Tanzania ℹ

Zapata, Emiliano [sa**pah**ta] (1879–1919) Mexican revolutionary, born in Anencuilio, Mexico. After the onset of the Mexican Revolution, he mounted a land distribution programme in areas under his control. >> Mexico ℹ; Villa

Zaporozhye [zapuh**rozh**ye], formerly **Aleksandrovsk** (to 1921) 47°50N 35°10E, pop (1995e) 908 000. River port in Ukraine, on R Dnepr; founded as a fortress, 1770; airfield; railway; major industrial and energy-producing centre. >> Ukraine ℹ

Zapotecs A pre-Columbian Middle American Indian civilization of S Mexico (300 BC–AD 300), influenced by Olmec culture. It was centred on Monte Albán. >> Olmecs

Zappa, Frank, popular name of **Francis Vincent Zappa** (1940–93) Avant-garde rock musician and composer, born in Baltimore, MD. He led the satirical 'underground' band The Mothers of Invention in the 1960s and 1970s, making inventive and often scabrous albums such as *Freak-Out!* (1966) and *We're Only in it for the Money* (1967). >> rock music

Zarathustra >> **Zoroaster**

Zaria [**za**ria] 11°01N 7°44E, pop (1995e) 367 000. Town in SW Nigeria; founded, 16th-c; airfield; railway junction; university (1962). >> Nigeria ℹ

Zarqa [**zah(r)**ka] 32°04N 36°05E, pop (1995e) 608 000. Industrial town in N Jordan; large phosphate reserves nearby; airfield; railway. >> Jordan ℹ

zarzuela [thah(r)**thway**la] A type of popular Spanish opera with spoken dialogue. The name derives from the palace near Madrid (now the king's residence) where the genre was first staged in the 17th-c. >> opera

Zatopek, Emil [**za**topek] (1922–) Athlete, born in Kopřivnice, Czech Republic. He won the 10 000 m title at the London Olympics in 1948, subsequently breaking 13 world records, and winning the 5000 m, 10 000 m, and the marathon at the 1952 Olympics. >> athletics

Zealand, Dan **Sjælland**, Ger **Seeland** area 7000 sq km/2700 sq mi. Largest of the islands of Denmark; separated from Sweden by The Sound; length 128 km/80 mi; rises to 126 m/413 ft; chief towns include Copenhagen. >> Denmark ℹ; Sjælland

Zealots [**zel**ots] A militant Jewish sect which came into prominence in Palestine in the 1st-c AD. Its aim was to cast off the Roman yoke, using violence if necessary.

zebra An African wild horse; stocky with bold black and white stripes; three species: *Equus grevyi* (**Grevy's zebra**, **imperial zebra**, or **hippotigris**) with narrow stripes; *Equus zebra* (**mountain zebra**) with short crosswise stripes on top of hindquarters; and *Equus burchelli* (**common zebra**, **plains zebra**, or **Burchell's zebra**) with variable markings. >> horse ℹ; quagga

zebra fish Small, colourful fish (*Therapon jarbua*) common in shallow inshore waters of the Indian Ocean and W Pacific; length up to 30 cm/1 ft; grey to silver with dark horizontal banding. (Family: Theraponidae.) >> fish ℹ

zebrass An animal resulting from the mating of a male zebra and a female ass. >> ass; zebra

zebu [**zee**boo] S Asian domestic cattle; usually pale with upturned horns; fatty hump on shoulders; heavy hanging skin along throat; traditionally considered sacred in India; also known as **Brahman cattle** or **humped cattle**. (*Bos taurus*, sometimes called *Bos indicus*.) >> Bovidae; cattle; yak

Zechariah or **Zacharias, Book of** [zeka**riya**] One of 12 so-called 'minor' prophetic writings of the Hebrew Bible/Old Testament, attributed to Zechariah, writing c.520–518 BC after returning to Jerusalem from exile. >> Haggai, Book of; Old Testament

Zeebrugge [**zay**bruguh] 51°20N 3°12E. Belgian ferry port, the scene of a major shipping disaster in March 1987, when the Townsend Thoresen ferry, *Herald of Free Enterprise*, foundered just outside the harbour, with the loss of 193 lives. The accident resulted from the main car deck doors having been left open to the sea.

Zeeland [**zay**lant] pop (1995e) 367 000; land area 1786 sq km/689 sq mi. Province in West Netherlands; capital, Middelburg; entire area reclaimed from the sea by artificial dykes, and mostly below sea-level; scene of major flooding in 1953. >> Netherlands, The ℹ

Zeffirelli, Franco [zefi**rel**ee] (1923–) Stage, opera, and film director, born in Florence, Italy. His major films include *The Taming of the Shrew* (1966), *Romeo and Juliet* (1968), and the television *Jesus of Nazareth* (1977), and film versions of the operas *La traviata* (1983) and *Otello* (1986), and of *Jane Eyre* (1996).

Zeiss, Carl [tsiys] (1816–88) Optician, born in Weimar, Germany. In 1846 he established a factory at Jena which became noted for the production of lenses, microscopes, and other optical instruments. >> lens; microscope

Zen Buddhism [zen **bud**izm] A meditation school of Buddhism introduced into Japan by monks returning from China in the 12th-c. Zen stresses the personal experience of enlightenment based on a simple life lived close to nature, and upon methods of meditation which avoid complicated rituals and abstruse thought. >> Buddhism

zener diode [**zee**ner **diy**ohd] A semiconductor junction diode which produces a sharply increased reverse current when the reverse bias voltage reaches a certain value; named after US physicist Clarence Zener (1905–93).

zenith >> **nadir**

Zeno of Citium [**zee**noh, **sish**ium] (c.336–c.265 BC) Greek philosopher, the founder of Stoicism, born in Citium, Cyprus. He opened a school at the *Stoa poikile* ('painted colonnade'), from which the name of his philosophy derives. >> Stoicism

Zeno of Elea [**zee**noh, **eel**ia] (c.490–c.420 BC) Greek philosopher and mathematician, a native of Elea, Italy. He became known for a series of paradoxes, many of which denied the possibility of spatial division or motion. The best known is 'Achilles and the Tortoise', whose conclusion is that no matter how fast Achilles runs, he cannot overtake a tortoise, if the tortoise has a head start.

zeolites [**zee**oliyts] A group of hydrous aluminosilicate minerals containing sodium, potassium, calcium, and barium, and formed by the alteration of feldspars. They are characterized by structures into which gases, ions, and molecules can easily diffuse, and hence they are used as molecular sieves and ion exchangers for water softening. >> feldspar; silicate minerals

Zephaniah, Book of [zefa**niya**] One of 12 so-called 'minor' prophetic writings of the Hebrew Bible/Old Testament, attributed to Zephaniah, son of Cushi and descendant of Hezekiah, active in Josiah's reign (7th-c BC), but unknown apart from this work. >> Josiah; Old Testament; prophet

Zeppelin, Ferdinand (Adolf August Heinrich), Graf von (Count of) (1838–1917) German army officer, born in Konstanz, Germany. In 1897–1900 he constructed his first airship, setting up a factory for their construction at Freidrichshafen. >> airship

Zermatt [**zer**mat] 46°01N 7°45E, pop (1995e) 4750. Fashionable skiing resort and popular mountaineering centre in the Pennine Alps, S Switzerland. >> Switzerland ℹ

zero-emission vehicle (ZEV) A type of motor vehicle with no tailpipe pollutants. During the 1980s, approaches using alternative fuels made progress towards this goal, but only specially designed vehicles powered by electricity seem likely to achieve it. >> alternative fuel; electric car

Zeus [zyoos] In Greek mythology, the supreme god, equivalent to Jupiter. He is usually depicted with thunderbolt and eagle, and associated with the oak-tree. >> aegis; Cronus; Jupiter (mythology); Prometheus

Zeus, statue of [zyoos] A colossal statue, wrought in ivory and gold over a core of wood, formerly located in the Temple of Zeus at Olympia. It was one of the foremost works of the great Athenian sculptor, Phidias. >> Olympia; Seven Wonders of the Ancient World

Zeuxis [**zyook**sis] (5th-c BC) Greek painter, born in Heraclea. He excelled in the representation of natural objects.

ZEV >> **zero-emission vehicle**

Zhdanov >> **Mariupol**

Zhengzhou, **Chengchow**, or **Cheng-chou** [juhngjoh] 34°35N 113°38E, pop (1995e) 1 926 000. Capital of Henan province, NC China; major market and transportation centre first settled before 1000 BC; airfield; railway junction. >> China ℹ

Zhenjiang, **Chen-chiang**, or **Chinkiang** [juhnjiahng] 32°08N 119°30E, pop (1995e) 531 000. River port in E China, at confluence of Yangtze R and Grand Canal; founded, 545 BC; railway; scenic area; Jinshan Temple (4th-c). >> China ℹ; Grand Canal

Zhitomir or **Jitomir** [zhi**to**myir] 50°18N 28°40E, pop (1995e) 302 000. City in WC Ukraine; on R Teterev; founded, 9th-c; railway junction. >> Ukraine ℹ

Zhou or **Chou dynasty** [joh] (1027–256 BC) The second historical Chinese dynasty. Accounts of its origins are a mixture of history and legend. Its capital was at Hao (near Xi'an) until 771 BC, and at Luoyi (near Luoyang) until its occupation by the Qin in 256 BC. A form of feudal monarchy, the Zhou saw the first flowering of Chinese historical, philosophical, and literary writing. >> China ℹ

Zhou Enlai [joh enliy], also spelled **Chou En-lai** (1898–1975) One of the leaders of the Communist Party of China, and prime minister of the Chinese People's Republic from its inception in 1949 until his death. As minister of foreign affairs (and concurrently prime minister) he vastly increased China's international influence. Perhaps his greatest triumph of mediation was during the Cultural Revolution, when he worked to preserve national unity against the forces of anarchy. >> China ℹ; Cultural Revolution

Zhu De [joo de], also spelled **Chu-teh** (1886–1976) Chinese communist general, born in Yilong, Sichuan, China. He joined Mao Zedong to found the Jiangxi Soviet and together they built the Red Army. With Mao he led the Long March in 1934, and from 1949 he was commander-in-chief of the Chinese armed forces. >> Long March; Mao Zedong; Red Army (China)

Zhu Jiang, Chu-chiang, or **Chu-kiang** [joo jiahng], Eng **Pearl River** River in S China; forms wide estuary between Hong Kong and Macao; length 2197 km/1365 mi; densely populated, fertile river valley. >> China ℹ

Zhukov, Giorgiy Konstantinovich [**zhoo**kof] (1896–1974) Soviet marshal, born in Strelkovka, Russia. He became army chief-of-staff (1941), lifted the siege of Moscow, and in 1943 his counter-offensive was successful at Stalingrad. In 1944–5 he captured Warsaw, conquered Berlin, and accepted the German surrender. >> Stalingrad, Battle of; World War 2

Zhu Rongji (1929–) Chinese politician and prime minister (1998–). Exiled twice under Mao Zedong, he became mayor of Shanghai (1988–91), known for his peaceful resolution of student protests there in 1989. He was appointed vice premier in 1991, and in his role as the government's chief economic policy maker (1993–8) introduced a successful austerity programme. >> Cultural Revolution; Mao Zedong

Zia ul-Haq, Muhammad [**zee**a ul **hak**] (1924–88) Pakistani general and president (1978–88), born near Jullundhur, Punjab, India. He led a bloodless coup in 1977, imposed martial law, banned political activity, and introduced an Islamic code of law. Despite international protest, he sanctioned the hanging of former President Bhutto in 1979. >> Bhutto; Pakistan ℹ

Ziaur Rahman [zeea**oor** ra**mahn**] (1935–81) Bangladeshi soldier and president (1977–81). Appointed chief of army staff after the assassination of Mujibur Rahman (1975), he became the dominant figure within the military. He survived many attempted coups, but was finally assassinated in Dhaka. >> Bangladesh ℹ; Rahman

Zibo [tsoeboh] or **Tzu-po** 36°51N 118°01E, pop (1995e) 2 663 000. Industrial city in Shandong province, E China; railway. >> China ℹ

zidovudine >> **AZT**

Ziegfeld, Florenz [**zeeg**feld] (1869–1932) Theatre manager, born in Chicago, IL. His *Follies of 1907* was the first of an annual series that continued until 1931 and made his name synonymous with extravagant theatrical production.

Ziegler, Karl [**zeeg**ler] (1898–1973) Chemist, born in Helsa, Germany. With Italian chemist Giulio Natta (1903–79) he was awarded the 1963 Nobel Prize for Chemistry for his research into long-chain polymers leading to new developments in industrial materials, such as polypropylene. >> polymerization

ziggurat [**zig**urat] A temple tower, in the shape of a mountain, found throughout ancient Sumeria and the adjacent region of Elam. It consisted of a high, pyramidal mound, constructed in stages and surmounted by a shrine. Access to the shrine was by a series of external stairways or ramps. >> Elam; Sumer

Zimbabwe [zim**bab**way], official name **Republic of Zimbabwe**, formerly **Southern Rhodesia** (to 1979) pop (1995e) 11 365 000; area 390 759 sq km/150 873 sq mi. Landlocked S African republic; capital, Harare; timezone GMT +2; chief ethnic groups, Bantu (97%), mainly Shona and Ndebele; chief religions, Christianity and local beliefs; official language, English; unit of currency, the Zimbabwe dollar; high plateau country, altitude 900–1200 m/3000–3900 ft; mountains on E frontier rise to 2592 m/8504 ft at Mt Inyangani; generally subtropical climate, strongly influenced by altitude; mediaeval Bantu-speaking kingdom, 12th–16th-c, with capital at

The ziggurat at Ur

Great Zimbabwe; visited by Livingstone in the 1850s; Southern Rhodesia under British influence in the 1880s as the British South Africa Company under Cecil Rhodes; divided into North Eastern and North-Western Rhodesia, amalgamated into Northern Rhodesia, 1911; Southern Rhodesia became a self-governing British colony, 1923; Northern and Southern Rhodesia and Nyasaland formed a multi-racial federation, 1953; independence of Nyasaland and Northern Rhodesia, 1963; opposition to the independence of Southern Rhodesia under African rule resulted in a Unilateral Declaration of Independence (UDI) by the white-dominated government, 1965; economic sanctions and internal guerrilla activity forced the government to negotiate with the main African groups, the Zimbabwe African People's Union (ZAPU), led by Joshua Nkomo, the Zimbabwe African National Union (ZANU), led by Robert Mugabe, and the United African National Council (UANC), led by Bishop Abel Muzorewa; independence as Zimbabwe in 1980, with Robert Mugabe as first prime minister; bicameral legislature replaced in 1990 by a new single chamber parliament, the House of Assembly; an executive president combines the posts of head of state and head of government; agriculture involves 70% of the population; rich mineral resources; tourism to the national parks. >> Harare; Livingstone, David; Mugabe; Muzorewa; Nkomo; Rhodes, Cecil; Zimbabwe, Great; RR1029 political leaders

Zimmer walking frame A self-standing metal frame consisting of two double legs joined together by a bar in front; the name derives from the US orthopaedic company which manufactures it. It is used to assist walking by elderly persons, or those with pain or weakness in the legs. >> orthopaedics

zinc Zn, element 30, density 7 g/cm^3, melting point 420°C. An active, silvery-blue metal, never occurring uncombined, but found in many minerals, especially as a sulphide. It has been used from earliest times as an alloy with copper (*brass*). It owes its corrosion resistance to an adherent oxide coating, and is used as a plating to protect iron (*galvanizing*). It is also used in primary batteries as an anode. **Zinc oxide** (ZnO) is used as a pigment, filler, and mild antiseptic in cosmetics, pharmaceuticals, paints, and plastics. **Zinc sulphide** (ZnS) is used in luminous screens. >> alloy; brass; chemical elements; metal; RR1036

zinc blende >> **sphalerite**

Zinjanthropus [zin**jan**thropus] The former name of *Australopithecus boisei*. >> *Homo* ℹ

Zinkernagel, Rolf M [**zing**kernahgel] (1944–) Immunologist, born in Basel, Switzerland. He shared the Nobel Prize for Physiology or Medicine in 1996 for his contribution to the discovery of how the immune system recognizes virus-infected cells – research which was first reported in 1974.

zinnia An annual, perennial, or small shrub, distributed throughout the USA and S into South America, but predominantly Mexican; chrysanthemum-like flower-heads, showy. (Genus: *Zinnia*, 22 species. Family: Compositae.) >> chrysanthemum

Zinoviev, Grigoriy Yevseyevich [zin**ov**yef], originally **Grigoriy Yevseyevich Radomyslskiy** (1883–1936) Russian Jewish revolutionary and politician, born in the Ukraine. Charged with organizing terrorist activities, he was executed following the first of Stalin's Great Purge trials in Moscow. The so-called **Zinoviev letter** urging British Communists to incite revolution in Britain contributed to the downfall of the Labour government in the 1924 general elections; fresh research reported in 1999 confirmed the view that this letter was a forgery. >> Stalin

Zinzendorf, Nicolaus Ludwig, Graf von (Count of) [**tsin**tsendaw(r)f] (1700–60) Religious leader, born in Dresden, Germany. He invited the persecuted Moravians to his estates, and there founded for them the colony of *Herrnhut* ('the Lord's keeping'). He later became Bishop of the Moravian Brethren. >> Moravian Brethren

Zion or **Sion** [**ziy**on] (Heb probably 'fortress' or 'rock') Term used in the Hebrew Bible and Jewish literature in various ways: for one of the hills in Jerusalem; for the mount on which the Temple was built; for the Temple itself; and symbolically for Jerusalem or even Israel as a whole. Today 'Mount Zion' usually denotes the SW hill in Jerusalem just S of the city wall. >> Temple, Jerusalem; Zionism

Zionism The movement which sought to recover for the Jewish people their historic Palestinian homeland (the *Eretz Israel*) after centuries of dispersion. The modern movement arose in the late 19th-c with plans for Jewish colonization of Palestine, and under Theodor Herzl also developed a political programme. Its objectives were supported by the British Balfour Declaration in 1917, as long as rights for non-Jews in Palestine were not impaired. Zionism is still active, as a movement encouraging diaspora Jews to immigrate to and take an interest in the Jewish state. >> Herzl; Israel ℹ; Zion

zircon [**zer**kn] A zirconium silicate ($ZrSiO_4$) mineral commonly occurring in very small amounts in a wide variety of rocks. It is very hard, and is used as a gemstone. It is the principal source of zirconium. >> gemstones

Ziska, John [**zhish**ka] or **Žižka, Jan** (c.1370–1424) Bohemian Hussite leader, born in Trocznov, Czech Republic. During the Civil War he was chosen leader of the popular party, captured Prague (1421), and erected the fortress of Tabor, his party coming to be called Taborites. He continued to lead his troops in a series of victories, compelling Emperor Sigismund to offer the Hussites religious liberty. >> Huss

zither A musical instrument consisting of a box strung with five fretted and about 30 open (unfretted) strings. The fretted strings are stopped by the fingers of the left hand and plucked with a plectrum worn on the right thumb; the right-hand fingers pluck the open strings. >> dulcimer; plectrum; string instrument 2 ℹ

zodiac A zone of fixed stars, approximately 16° in width, which marks the apparent courses of the Sun, Moon, and planets (apart from Pluto) about the Earth. Early astronomers projected patterns on to this area of sky, creating 12 groupings or constellations. The **tropical zodiac** takes the equinoxial position as a starting point, irrespective of the underlying constellation. On the 21st of each month (approximately) the Sun appears to change sign in the tropical zodiac, from Aries through Taurus, Gemini, Cancer, Leo, Virgo, Libra, Scorpius (Scorpio), Sagittarius, Capricorn, Aquarius and Pisces. The disposition of the planets within the signs of the zodiac furnishes important information to the astrologer. >> astrology; constellation; equinox; New Age

zodiacal light A permanent glow of light, readily visible in the tropics after sunset as a cone of light extending from the horizon. It is sunlight reflected from dust in interplanetary space. >> interplanetary matter

Zoffany, John or **Johann** [**tsof**anee] (1734–1810) Portrait painter, born in Frankfurt (am Main), Germany. His speciality was the conversation piece. >> conversation piece

Zog I [zohg], originally **Ahmed Bey Zogu** (1895–1961) Albanian prime minister (1922–4), president (1925–8), and king (1928–39), born in Burgajet, Albania. He formed a republican government in 1922, and after a period in exile became president, later proclaiming himself king. When Albania was overrun by the Italians (1939), he fled to Britain, and formally abdicated in 1946. >> Albania ℹ

Zohar [**zoh**hah(r)] The main text of the Jewish Kabbalah. Discovered in Spain in the late 13th-c, it was said to be the mystical teachings of Rabbi Simeon bar Yochai and his followers, who lived in Palestine in the 2nd–3rd-c. There have always been doubts about its authenticity. >> Judaism; Kabbalah

zokor >> **mole rat**

Zola, Emile [**zoh**la] (1840–1902) Novelist, born in Paris. After his first major novel, *Thérèse Raquin* (1867), he began the long series called *Les Rougon-Macquart*, a sequence of 20 books described in the subtitle as 'the natural and social history of a family under the Second Empire', including such acclaimed studies as *Nana* (1880), *Germinal* (1885), and *La Bête humaine* (1890, trans The Beast in Man). In 1898 he espoused the cause of Dreyfus in his open letter *J'accuse*. >> Dreyfus

Zola, Gianfranco (1966–) Footballer, born in Oliena, Sardinia, Italy. He played for Parma, then joined Chelsea in 1996. He was also a member of the Italy national team in the Euro '96 championships.

Zollverein [**tsol**veriyn] A German customs union, based on the enlarged Prussia of 1814, and officially constituted in 1834. It represented an important stage in the German unification process. >> customs union; Prussia

zoogeography [zohuhji**og**rafee] The study of the past and present geographical distribution of animals and animal communities. >> biogeography; phytogeography; zoology

zoology The branch of biology dealing with the study of animals. It includes their anatomy, behaviour, ecology, evolution, genetics, and physiology. >> biological sciences

zoom A visual effect in motion pictures or video, enlarging or diminishing the image as though rapidly approaching or receding. Originally made by actual camera movement, it is now provided by a **zoom lens** whose focal length, and hence its magnification, can be continuously varied. >> camera; lens

zooplankton >> **plankton**

zoosemiotics [zohohsemi**ot**iks] The science of animal communication. Combining semiotics and ethology, this interdisciplinary field seeks to understand the many complex systems of meaning employed by animals, such as bird calls, bee-dancing, and grasshopper signals. >> bee dancing; ethology; semiotics

zorilla [tho**reel**ya] An African mammal (*Ictonyx striatus*) of family Mustelidae; long coat and long brush-like tail; black with white markings on face, long white stripes along body; superficially resembles the skunk; also known as **striped polecat**. >> Mustelidae; polecat; skunk

Zorn, Anders (Leonhard) (1860–1920) Etcher, sculptor, and painter, born in Mora. His paintings deal mainly with Swedish peasant life. He achieved European fame as an etcher, known for his series of nudes, and for his portraits. >> etching

Zoroaster [zoroh**as**ter], Greek form of **Zarathustra** (6th-c BC) Iranian prophet and founder of the ancient Parsee religion which bears his name. He appears as a historical person only in the earliest portion of the Avesta. >> Avesta; Zoroastrianism

Zoroastrianism [zoroh**as**trianizm] The worship of a supreme God, Ahura Mazda, in Iran during the first millennium BC. Rites of worship were performed by priests (*Magi*), and there was a body of scriptures called *Avesta*, the earliest part of which was made up of hymns attributed to a religious teacher, Zoroaster. Today it is practised by Parsees. >> Ahura Mazda; Avesta; Parseeism; Zoroaster

Z particle A particle that carries weak nuclear force; symbol *Z*; mass 94 GeV; charge zero; spin 1; decays to an

Signs of the zodiac

electron plus positron, or a muon plus antimuon; it was discovered in 1983. >> fundamental particles

Zuccarelli, Francesco [tsuka**ray**lee] (1702–88) Painter, born in Pitigliano, Italy. His pastoral landscapes, populated by shepherds and maidens and painted in a soft Rococo style, were very popular, especially in England. >> Rococo

Zuccari or **Zuccaro, Taddeo** [tsu**kah**ree] (1529–66) Painter, born in Vado, Italy, who executed several frescoes and easel pieces. His brother **Federigo Zuccari** (c.1543–1609) painted portraits and frescoes, and became an influential art theorist. The two brothers were leaders of the Roman late Mannerist school. >> fresco; Mannerism

zucchini [zu**kee**nee] >> **courgette**

Zuckerman (of Burnham Thorpe), Solly Zuckerman, Baron (1904–93) Zoologist, born in Cape Town, South Africa, and chief scientific adviser to the British government (1964–71). He carried out extensive research into primates, publishing such classic works as *The Social Life of Monkeys and Apes* (1932). >> primate (biology)

Zug [tsug] 47°10N 8°31E, pop (1995e) 22 300. Town in C Switzerland; railway junction; noted for its local kirsch; Gothic church (15th–16th-c). >> Switzerland ℹ

Zugspitze [**tsuk**shpitsuh] 47°25N 11°00E. Mountain in S Germany, rising to 2962 m/9718 ft on the Wettersteingebirge of the Bavarian Alps. >> Bavarian Alps

Zuider Zee >> **Ijsselmeer**

Zukofsky, Louis [zu**kof**skee] (1904–78) Poet, born in New York City. A leading experimentalist after Pound, his works appear in *An Objectivist Anthology* (1932) and *All: The Collected Short Poems* (1965, 1967). >> Pound, Ezra

Zulu A Bantu-speaking agricultural and cattle people of Natal, South Africa; one of the Nguni group. Formed into a kingdom in the early 19th-c, they became a formidable fighting force; but were conquered by the Boers and British, and much of their territory annexed. They have retained a strong self-identity, and are organized politically into the modern Inkatha movement under their leader Chief Mangosuthu Buthelezi. Their territory, greatly contracted, became one of the 'Homelands' of South Africa during the apartheid period: KwaZulu. >> Buthelezi; Inkatha; KwaZulu Natal; Nguni; Xhosa

Zuni [**zoo**nyee] A North American Indian group of the American SW, living in New Mexico and Arizona; one of the Pueblo peoples. Many are now assimilated to US culture. >> Pueblo; Southwest Indians

Zurbarán, Francisco de [thoorba**ran**] (1598–1664) Religious painter, born in Fuente de Cantos, Spain. Apart from a few portraits and still-life studies, his main subjects were monastic and historical, and he came to be called 'the Spanish Caravaggio'. >> altarpiece; Caravaggio

Zürich [**zoo**rikh], Ger [**tsü**reekh] 47°22N 8°32E, pop (1995e) 353 000. Financial centre in N Switzerland; on R Limmat, at NW end of L Zurich; largest city in Switzerland; Swiss Federal Institute of Technology (1855); joined Swiss Confederation, 1351; airport; railway; university (1833); Swiss Federal Institute of Technology (1855); Grossmünster (11th–14th-c), Fraumünster (13th-c, restored). >> Switzerland ℹ

Zweig, Arnold [tsviyk] (1887–1968) Writer, born in Glogau, Germany. He is best known for his pacifist novel, *Der Streit um den Sergeanten Grischa* (1928, The Case of Sergeant Grischa).

Zweig, Stefan [tsviyk] (1881–1942) Writer, born in Vienna. His best-known work was his set of historical portraits, *Sternstunden der Menschheit* (1928, trans The Tide of Fortune).

Zwickau [**tsvi**kow] 50°43N 12°30E, pop (1995e) 124 000. Mining and industrial city in S Germany; on R Mulde; a free imperial city, 1290–1323; railway; birthplace of Schumann. >> Germany ℹ; Schumann, Robert

Zwingli, Huldrych or **Ulrich** [**tsving**glee], Lat **Ulricus Zuinglius** (1484–1531) Protestant reformer, born in Wildhaus, Switzerland. In 1518, he opposed the selling of indulgences, and espoused the Reformed doctrines, but in 1524 split with Luther over the question of the Eucharist. >> Eucharist; indulgences; Luther; Reformation

zwitterion [**tsvit**eriyon] A molecule containing both a positive and a negative charge simultaneously. It is the predominant form of an amino acid in solution. >> amino acid

Zwolle [**zvol**uh] 52°31N 6°06E, pop (1995e) 99 200. City in E Netherlands; railway; canal junction; major cattle market; St Michaelskerk (15th-c). >> Netherlands, The ℹ

Zworykin, Vladimir (Kosma) [**tsvo**rikin] (1889–1982) Physicist, born in Murom, Russia. In 1923–4 he patented an all-electronic television system using a scanned camera-tube (the *iconoscope*), in 1929 demonstrated a cathode-ray display (the *kinescope*), and in later years contributed to the development of colour television and the electron microscope. He is regarded as 'the father of modern television'. >> electron microscope ℹ; television

zygomorphic flower A flower which is bilaterally symmetrical, so that it can be divided into equal halves in one plane only. It is often found in the more advanced plant families. >> flower ℹ

zygote [**ziy**goht] The fertilized egg of a plant or animal, formed by the fusion of male (*sperm*) and female (*ovum*) gametes. It is usually diploid (possessing a double chromosome set), having received a haploid chromosome set from each gamete. >> chromosome ℹ; fertilization; gamete; twins

THE CAMBRIDGE PAPERBACK ENCYCLOPEDIA

READY REFERENCE SECTION

Index

The Earth in Space

PLANETARY DATA

Planet	Distance from sun maximum		minimum		Sidereal period	Axial rotation (equatorial)	Diameter (equatorial)	
	million km	million mi	million km	million mi			km	mi
Mercury	69.4	43.0	46.8	29.0	88 d	58 d 16h	4 878	3 031
Venus	109.0	67.6	107.6	66.7	224.7 d	243 d	12 104	7 521
Earth	152.6	94.6	147.4	91.4	365.26 d[1]	23 h 56 m	12 756	7 927
Mars	249.2	154.5	207.3	128.5	687 d	24 h 37 m 23 s	6 794	4 222
Jupiter	817.4	506.8	741.6	459.8	11.86 y	9 h 50 m 30 s	142 800	88 800
Saturn	1 512	937.6	1 346	834.6	29.46 y	10 h 14 m	120 000	74 600
Uranus	3 011	1 867	2 740	1 699	84.01 y	16–28 h[2]	51 000	31 600
Neptune	4 543	2 817	4 466	2 769	164.79 y	18–20 h[2]	49 500	30 800
Pluto	7 364	4 566	4 461	2 766	248.5 y	6 d 9 h	2 300	1 430

[1] 365 d 5 h 48 m 46 s.

[2] Different latitudes rotate at different speeds.

y: years d: days h: hours m: minutes s: seconds km: kilometres mi: miles

PLANETARY SATELLITES

	Year discovered	Distance from planet km	Distance from planet mi	Diameter km	Diameter mi
Earth					
Moon	—	384 000	238 850	3 476	2 155
Mars					
Phobos	1877	938 000	583 000	27	17
Deimos	1877	2 346 000	1 458 000	15	9
Jupiter					
Metis	1979	127 000	79 000	40	25
Adrastea	1979	129 000	80 000	24	15
Amalthea	1892	180 000	112 000	270	168
Thebe	1979	222 000	138 000	100	60
Io	1610	422 000	262 000	3 630	2 260
Europa	1610	671 000	417 000	3 140	1 950
Ganymede	1610	1 070 000	665 000	5 260	3 270
Callisto	1610	1 883 000	1 170 000	4 800	3 000
Leda	1974	11 100 000	6 900 000	20	12
Himalia	1904	11 480 000	7 134 000	186	110
Lysithea	1938	11 720 000	7 283 000	40	25
Elara	1905	11 740 000	7 295 000	80	50
Ananke	1951	21 200 000	13 174 000	30	19
Carme	1938	22 600 000	14 044 000	40	25
Pasiphae	1908	23 500 000	14 603 000	50	30
Sinope	1914	23 700 000	14 727 000	40	25
Saturn					
Pan	1990	134 000	83 000	10	6
Atlas	1980	138 000	86 000	40	25
Prometheus	1980	139 000	86 000	100	60
Pandora	1980	142 000	88 000	100	60
Epimetheus	1980	151 000	94 000	140	90
Janus	1966	151 000	94 000	200	120

	Year discovered	Distance from planet km	Distance from planet mi	Diameter km	Diameter mi
Saturn					
Mimas	1789	186 000	116 000	390	240
Enceladus	1789	238 000	148 000	500	310
Calypso	1980	295 000	183 000	30	19
Telesto	1980	295 000	183 000	24	15
Tethys	1684	295 000	183 000	1 050	650
Dione	1684	377 000	234 000	1 120	700
Helene	1980	378 000	235 000	36	22
Rhea	1672	527 000	327 000	1 530	950
Titan	1655	1 222 000	759 000	5 150	3 200
Hyperion	1848	1 481 000	920 000	400	250
Iapetus	1671	3 560 000	2 212 000	1 460	910
Phoebe	1898	12 950 000	8 047 000	220	137
Uranus					
Miranda	1948	130 000	81 000	480	300
Ariel	1851	191 000	119 000	1 160	720
Umbriel	1851	266 000	165 000	1 170	730
Titania	1787	436 000	271 000	1 600	1 000
Oberon	1787	583 100	362 000	1 600	1 000

A further ten satellites at distances from 50 000 to 86 000 km, and with diameters 15–170 km, were discovered in 1986.

	Year discovered	Distance from planet km	Distance from planet mi	Diameter km	Diameter mi
Neptune					
Triton	1846	355 000	221 000	3 800	2 400
Nereid	1949	5 510 000	3 424 000	300	190

A further six satellites at distances from 48 000 to 118 000 km, and with diameters 50–400 km, were discovered in 1989.

	Year discovered	Distance from planet km	Distance from planet mi	Diameter km	Diameter mi
Pluto					
Charon	1978	19 100 000	11 900 000	1 200	745

THE NEAREST STARS

Star	Distance (light years)
Proxima Centauri	4.24
Alpha Centauri A	4.34
Alpha Centauri B	4.34
Barnard's Star	5.97
Wolf 359 (CN Leonis)	7.80
Lalande 21185	8.19
UV Ceti A	8.55
UV Ceti B	8.55
Sirius A	8.67
Sirius B	8.67
Ross 154	9.52
Ross 248 (HH Andromedae)	10.37
Epsilon Eridani	10.63
Ross 128 (FI Virginis)	10.79
L 789–6	11.12
GX Andromedae	11.22
GQ Andromedae	11.22
61 Cygnus A	11.22
61 Cygnus B	11.22
HD 173739	11.25
Epsilon Indi	11.25
Tau Ceti	11.41

STARS OF THE FIRST MAGNITUDE

Star	Proper name	Magnitude	Distance (light years)
Alpha Canis Majoris	Sirius	–1.47	8.7
Alpha Carinae	Canopus	–0.72	98
Alpha Centauri	Rigil Kentaurus	–0.29	4.3
Alpha Boötis	Arcturus	–0.04	36
Alpha Lyrae	Vega	0.03	26
Alpha Aurigae	Capella	0.08	45
Beta Orionis	Rigel	0.12	815
Alpha Canis Minoris	Procyon	0.34	11
Alpha Orionis	Betelgeuse	0.50(v)	520
Alpha Eridani	Achernar	0.50	118
Beta Centauri	Hadar	0.60(v)	490
Alpha Crucis	Acrux	0.76	370
Alpha Aquilae	Altair	0.77	16
Alpha Tauri	Aldebaran	0.85(v)	68
Alpha Scorpii	Antares	0.96(v)	520
Alpha Virginis	Spica	0.98(v)	220
Beta Geminorum	Pollux	1.15	35
Alpha Piscis Austrini	Fomalhaut	1.16	23
Beta Crucis	Mimosa	1.20(v)	490
Alpha Cygni	Deneb	1.25	1600
Alpha Leonis	Regulus	1.35	85

(v) = variable

ANNUAL MAJOR METEOR SHOWERS

Name	Dates of maximum	Hourly rate
Quadrantids	3–4 January	100
Lyrids	21–22 April	10
Eta Aquarids	5–6 May	35
Delta Aquarids	28–29 July	20
Perseids	12–13 August	75
Orionids	22 October	25
Taurids	4 November	10
Leonids	17–18 November	10
Geminids	13–14 December	75

TOTAL SOLAR ECLIPSES 2000–2020

Date		Visible from parts of[1]
21 June	2001	S America, S Atlantic, C & S Africa
4 December	2002	S Africa, Australia
23 November	2003	Antarctica
8 April	2005	S & C Pacific, C America
29 March	2006	C Atlantic, W & N Africa, C Asia
1 August	2008	Greenland, N & C Asia
22 July	2009	S Asia, C Pacific
11 July	2010	S Pacific
13 November	2013	N Australia, S Pacific
20 March	2015	N Atlantic, Arctic
9 March	2016	Indonesia, C Pacific
21 August	2017	N Pacific, N America, N Atlantic
2 July	2019	S Pacific, S America
14 December	2020	S Pacific, S America, S Atlantic

[1] The eclipse begins in the first area named.

THE NEAR SIDE OF THE MOON

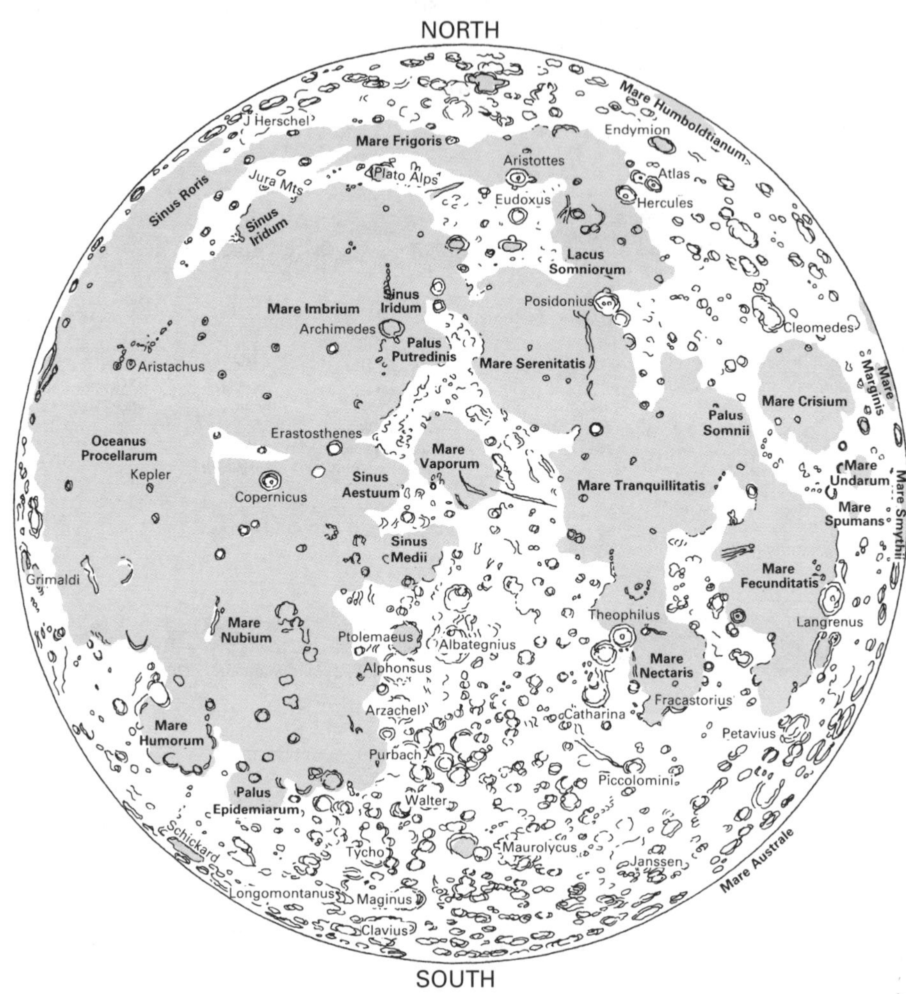

THE LUNAR 'SEAS'

Latin name	*English name*
Lacus Somniorum	Lake of Dreams
Mare Australe	Southern Sea
Mare Crisium	Sea of Crises
Mare Fecunditatis	Sea of Fertility
Mare Frigoris	Sea of Cold
Mare Humboldtianum	Humboldt's Sea
Mare Humorum	Sea of Humours
Mare Imbrium	Sea of Showers
Mare Ingenii	Sea of Geniuses
Mare Marginis	Marginal Sea
Mare Moscoviense	Moscow Sea
Mare Nectaris	Sea of Nectar
Mare Nubium	Sea of Clouds
Mare Orientale	Eastern Sea
Mare Serenitatis	Sea of Serenity
Mare Smythii	Smyth's Sea
Mare Spumans	Foaming Sea
Mare Tranquillitatis	Sea of Tranquillity
Mare Undarum	Sea of Waves
Mare Vaporum	Sea of Vapours
Oceanus Procellarum	Ocean of Storms
Palus Epidemiarum	Marsh of Epidemics
Palus Putredinis	Marsh of Decay
Palus Somnii	Marsh of Sleep
Sinus Aestuum	Bay of Heats
Sinus Iridum	Bay of Rainbows
Sinus Medii	Central Bay
Sinus Roris	Bay of Dew

THE FAR SIDE OF THE MOON

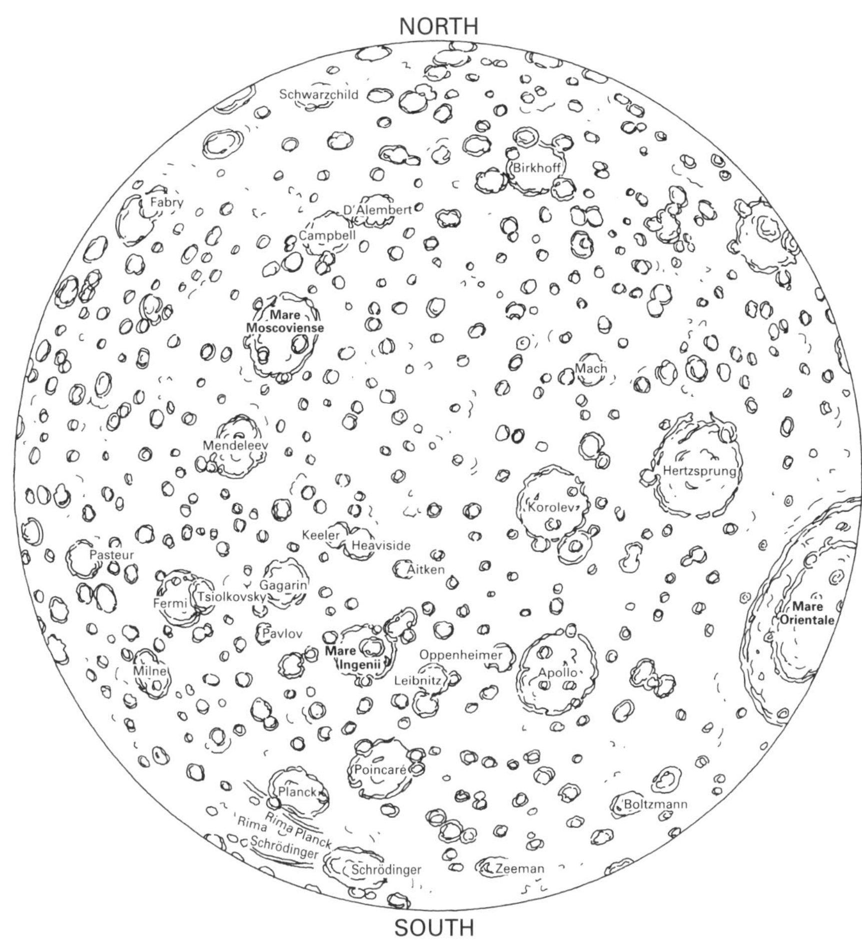

LUNAR ECLIPSES 2000–2010

Date		Type	Time of mid-eclipse (Universal Time)
21 January	2000	Total	04.43
16 July	2000	Total	13.56
9 January	2001	Total	20.21
5 July	2001	Partial[u]	14.55
30 December	2001	Partial	10.29
26 May	2002	Partial	12.03
24 June	2002	Partial	21.27
20 November	2002	Partial	01.46
16 May	2003	Total	03.40
9 November	2003	Total	01.18
4 May	2004	Total	20.30
28 October	2004	Total	03.04
24 April	2005	Partial	09.55
17 October	2005	Partial[u]	12.03
14 March	2006	Partial	23.47
7 September	2006	Partial[u]	18.51
3 March	2007	Total	23.21
28 August	2007	Total	10.37
21 February	2008	Total	03.26
16 August	2008	Partial[u]	21.10
9 February	2009	Partial	14.38
7 July	2009	Partial	09.38
6 August	2009	Partial	00.39
31 December	2009	Partial[u]	19.23
26 June	2010	Partial[u]	11.38
21 December	2010	Total	08.17

[u] Umbral; all others are penumbral

THE CONSTELLATIONS

Latin name	English name
Andromeda	Andromeda
Antlia	Air Pump
Apus	Bird of Paradise
Aquarius (Z)	Water Bearer
Aquila	Eagle
Ara	Altar
Aries (Z)	Ram
Auriga	Charioteer
Boötes	Herdsman
Caelum	Chisel
Camelopardalis	Giraffe
Cancer (Z)	Crab
Canes Venatici	Hunting Dogs
Canis Major	Great Dog
Canis Minor	Little Dog
Capricornus (Z)	Sea Goat
Carina	Keel
Cassiopeia	Cassiopeia
Centaurus	Centaur
Cepheus	Cepheus
Cetus	Whale
Chamaeleon	Chameleon
Circinus	Compasses
Columba	Dove
Coma Berenices	Berenice's Hair
Corona Australis	Southern Crown
Corona Borealis	Northern Crown
Corvus	Crow
Crater	Cup
Crux	Southern Cross
Cygnus	Swan
Delphinus	Dolphin
Dorado	Goldfish
Draco	Dragon
Equuleus	Little Horse
Eridanus	River Eridanus
Fornax	Furnace
Gemini (Z)	Twins
Grus	Crane
Hercules	Hercules
Horologium	Clock
Hydra	Sea Serpent
Hydrus	Water Snake
Indus	Indian
Lacerta	Lizard

(Z) Found in the Zodiac

THE NORTHERN SKY

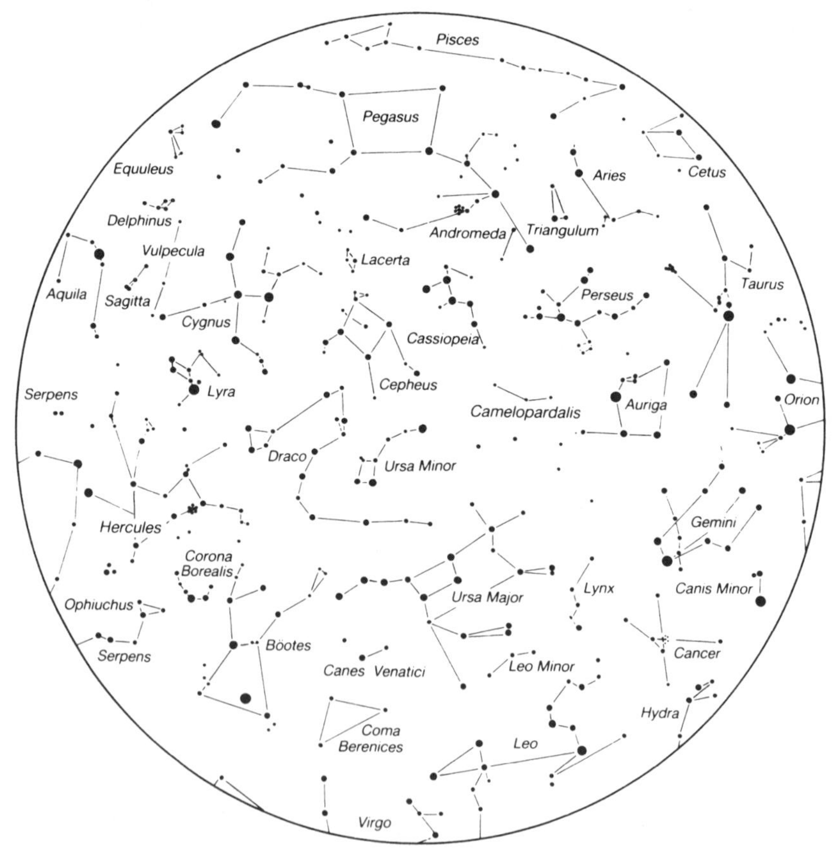

THE CONSTELLATIONS (continued)

Latin name	English name
Leo (Z)	Lion
Leo Minor	Little Lion
Lepus	Hare
Libra (Z)	Scales
Lupus	Wolf
Lynx	Lynx
Lyra	Harp
Mensa	Table
Microscopium	Microscope
Monoceros	Unicorn
Musca	Fly
Norma	Level
Octans	Octant
Ophiuchus	Serpent Bearer
Orion	Orion
Pavo	Peacock
Pegasus	Winged Horse
Perseus	Perseus
Phoenix	Phoenix
Pictor	Easel
Pisces (Z)	Fishes
Piscis Austrinus	Southern Fish
Puppis	Ship's Stern
Pyxis	Mariner's Compass
Reticulum	Net
Sagitta	Arrow
Sagittarius (Z)	Archer
Scorpius (Z)	Scorpion
Sculptor	Sculptor
Scutum	Shield
Serpens	Serpent
Sextans	Sextant
Taurus (Z)	Bull
Telescopium	Telescope
Triangulum	Triangle
Triangulum Australe	Southern Triangle
Tucana	Toucan
Ursa Major	Great Bear
Ursa Minor	Little Bear
Vela	Sails
Virgo (Z)	Virgin
Volans	Flying Fish
Vulpecula	Little Fox

THE SOUTHERN SKY

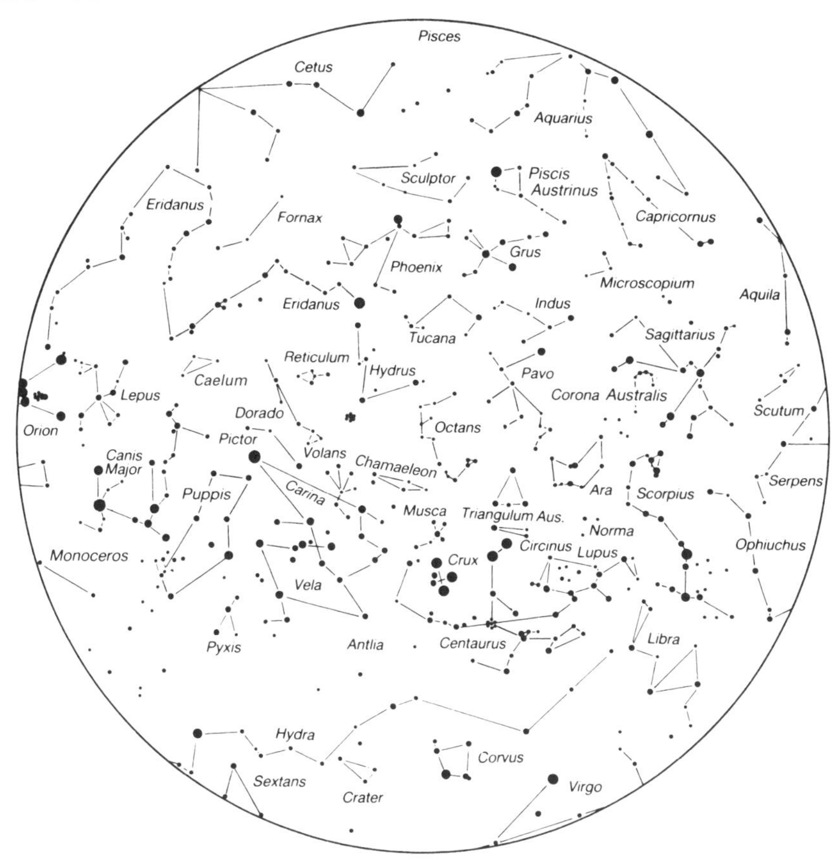

Space Exploration

MAJOR SPACE ASTRONOMY EVENTS 1957-99

Name of event/mission	*Country/agency*	*Launch*	*Event description*
Sputnik 1	USSR	4 Oct 1957	First Earth satellite
Sputnik 2	USSR	3 Nov 1957	Biosatellite
Explorer 1	USA	31 Jan 1958	Discovery of Earth's radiation belts
Luna 1	USSR	2 Jan 1959	Escaped Earth gravity; discovery of the solar wind
Vanguard 2	USA	17 Feb 1959	First Earth photo
Luna 2	USSR	12 Sep 1959	Lunar impact
Luna 3	USSR	4 Oct 1959	First lunar photo (dark side)
Sputnik 5	USSR	19 Aug 1960	Orbited animals
Vostok 1	USSR	12 Apr 1961	First manned orbital flight (Yuri Gagarin)
Mercury	USA	20 Feb 1962	First US manned orbital flight (John Glenn)
Mariner 2	USA	26 Aug 1962	Venus flyby
Mars 1	USSR	1 Nov 1962	Mars flyby
Vostok 6	USSR	16 June 1963	First woman in orbit
Ranger 7	USA	28 Jul 1964	First close-up TV pictures of lunar surface
Mariner 4	USA	28 Nov 1964	Mars flyby pictures
Voskhod 2	USSR	18 Mar 1965	First spacewalk (AA Leonov)
Venera 3	USSR	16 Nov 1965	Venus impact
Luna 9	USSR	31 Jan 1966	Lunar soft landing; first picture from the lunar surface
Gemini 8	USA	16 Mar 1966	Manned docking
Luna 10	USSR	31 Mar 1966	Lunar orbiter
Surveyor 3	USA	17 Apr 1967	Lunar surface sampler
Cosmos 186/188	USSR	22/28 Oct 1967	Automatic docking
Zond 5	USSR	14 Sep 1968	Animals moon orbit
OAO 2	USA	1968	First orbiting astronomical observatory
Apollo 8	USA	21 Dec 1968	Manned lunar orbit
Apollo 11	USA	16 Jul 1969	First person on the moon (Neil Armstrong)
Copernicus	USA	1970	First far ultra-violet observatory
Venera 7	USSR	17 Aug 1970	Venus soft landing
Mars 3	USSR	28 May 1971	Mars soft landing
Pioneer 10	USA	3 Mar 1972	Jupiter flyby; crossed Pluto orbit; escaped Solar System
Skylab	USA	1973	High resolution images of solar corona in X-rays
Pioneer 11	USA	6 Apr 1973	Saturn flyby
Mariner 10	USA	3 Nov 1973	First detailed picture of Mercury
Venera 9	USSR	8 Jun 1975	Venus orbit; first picture of Venusian surface
Apollo/Soyuz	USA/USSR	15 Jul 1975	First manned international cooperative mission
Viking 1, 2	USA	Aug/Sep 1975	First pictures taken on the Martian surface
Voyager 1, 2	USA	Aug/Sep 1977	First images of Jupiter, Saturn, Uranus and Neptune
IUE	USA/UK/ESA	1978	First international space observatory
ISEE C	USA	12 Aug 1978	Comet intercept
STS 1	USA	12 Apr 1981	First launch of *Columbia* space shuttle
STS 6	USA	4 Apr 1983	First launch of *Challenger*
Soyuz T 9	USSR	27 Jun 1983	Construction in space
STS 9	USA	28 Nov 1983	First flight of the ESA spacelab
STS 41 D	USA	30 Aug 1984	First launch of *Discovery*
STS 51 A	USA	8 Nov 1984	Recovery of satellites 'Westar 6' and 'Palapa B2'
Vega 1	USSR	15 Dec 1984	Halley flyby
STS 51 J	USA	3 Oct 1985	First launch of *Atlantis*
Giotto	ESA	1986	First high resolution image of Halley's nucleus
Magellan	USA	5 May 1989	Global radar map of Venus
STS 34	USA	18 Oct 1989	*Galileo* launch
Muses A	Japan	24 Jan 1990	Two satellites placed in orbit round the moon
STS 31	USA/ESA	24 Apr 1990	Launch of Hubble Space Telescope
STS 41	USA/ESA	6 Oct 1990	Launch of *Ulysses*; first flight above the solar poles
STS 47	USA	7 May 1992	First launch of *Endeavour*
STS 49	USA/ESA	31 Jul 1992	Launch of *Eureca* (European recoverable carrier)
STS 59	USA	2 Dec 1993	Hubble Space Telescope repaired in space
STS 69	USA/Russia	29 Jun 1995	Atlantis docked with Mir space station
Mars Pathfinder	USA	4 Dec 1996	Mars Pathfinder mission, with Sojourner surface rover
Cassini	USA	15 Oct 1997	Cassini Orbiter to Saturn, with Huygens probe to Titan
DSI	USA	24 Oct 1998	Deep Space 1, first technology demonstration probe

(ESA = European Space Agency)

Earth: General Data

There are no universally agreed estimates of the natural phenomena given in this section. Surveys make use of different criteria for identifying natural boundaries, and use different techniques of measurement. The sizes of continents, oceans, seas, deserts, and rivers are particularly subject to variation.

Age 4 500 000 000 years (accurate to within a small percentage of possible error)
Area 509 600 000 km²/197 000 000 sq mi
Mass 5976×10^{24} kg
Land surface 148 000 000 km²/57 000 000 sq mi (*c.* 29% of total area)
Water surface 361 600 000 km²/140 000 000 sq mi (*c.* 71% of total area)
Circumference at equator 40 076 km/24 902 mi
Circumference of meridian 40 000km/24 860 mi

CONTINENTS

Name	*Area*		*% of total*	*Lowest point below sea level*			*Highest elevation*		
	km²	*sq mi*			*m*	*ft*		*m*	*ft*
Africa	30 293 000	11 696 000	20.2	Lake Assal, Djibouti	156	512	Kilimanjaro, Tanzania	5 895	19 340
Antarctica	13 975 000	5 396 000	9.3	Bently subglacial trench	2 538	8 327	Vinson Massif	5 140	16 864
Asia	44 493 000	17 179 000	29.6	Dead Sea, Israel/Jordan	400	1 312	Mt Everest, China/Nepal	8 848	29 028
Oceania	8 945 000	3 454 000	6	Lake Eyre, S Australia	15	49	Puncak Jaya (Ngga Pulu), Indonesia	5 030	16 500
Europe	10 245 000	3 956 000	6.8	Caspian Sea, Russia	29	94	Elbrus, Russia	5 642	18 510
North America	24 454 000	9 442 000	16.3	Death Valley, California	86	282	Mt McKinley, Alaska	6 194	20 320
South America	17 838 000	6 887 000	11.9	Peninsular Valdez, Argentina	40	131	Aconcagua, Argentina	6 959	22 831

OCEANS

Name	*Area*		*% of total*	*Av depth*		*Greatest depth*		
	km²	*sq mi*		*m*	*ft*		*m*	*ft*
Arctic	13 986 000	5 400 000	3	1 330	4 300	Eurasia Basin	5 122	16 804
Atlantic	82 217 000	32 000 000	24	3 700	12 100	Puerto Rico Trench	8 648	28 372
Indian	73 426 000	28 350 000	20	3 900	12 800	Java Trench	7 725	25 344
Pacific	181 300 000	70 000 000	46	4 300	14 100	Marianas Trench	11 040	36 220

LARGEST SEAS

Name	*Area**		*Name*	*Area**	
	km²	*sq mi*		*km²*	*sq mi*
Coral Sea	4 791 000	1 850 200	Arafura Sea	1 037 000	400 000
Arabian Sea	3 863 000	1 492 000	Philippine Sea	1 036 000	400 000
S China (Nan) Sea	3 685 000	1 423 000	Sea of Japan	978 000	378 000
Caribbean Sea	2 515 000	971 000	E Siberian Sea	901 000	348 000
Mediterranean Sea	2 510 000	967 000	Kara Sea	883 000	341 000
Bering Sea	2 304 000	890 000	E China Sea	664 000	256 000
Bay of Bengal	2 172 000	839 000	Andaman Sea	565 000	218 000
Sea of Okhotsk	1 590 000	614 000	North Sea	520 000	201 000
Gulf of Mexico	1 543 000	596 000	Black Sea	508 000	196 000
Gulf of Guinea	1 533 000	592 000	Red Sea	453 000	175 000
Barents Sea	1 405 000	542 000	Baltic Sea	414 000	160 000
Norwegian Sea	1 383 000	534 000	Celebes Sea	280 000	110 000
Gulf of Alaska	1 327 000	512 000	Persian Gulf	240 000	93 600
Hudson Bay	1 232 000	476 000	St Lawrence Gulf	238 300	92 000
Greenland Sea	1 205 000	465 000			

Oceans are excluded.

*Areas are rounded to nearest 1000 km²/sq mi.

LARGEST LAKES

Name/location	*Area**	
	km²	*sq mi*
Caspian Sea, Iran/Russia	371 000	143 200[1]
Superior, USA/Canada	82 260	31 760[2]
Victoria, E Africa	62 940	24 300
Aral Sea, Kazakhstan	62 000	24 180[1]
Huron, USA/Canada	59 580	23 000[2]
Michigan, USA	58 020	22 400
Tanganyika, E Africa	32 000	12 350
Baikal, Russia	31 500	12 160
Great Bear, Canada	31 330	12 100
Great Slave, Canada	28 570	11 030
Erie, USA/Canada	25 710	10 030[2]
Winnipeg, Canada	24 390	9420
Malawi/Nyasa, E Africa	22 490	8680
Balkhash, Kazakhstan	17 000–22 000	6500–8500[1]
Ontario, Canada	19 270	7440[2]
Ladoga, Russia	18 130	7000
Chad, W Africa	10 000–26 000	4000–10 000
Maracaibo, Venezuela	13 010	5020[3]
Patos, Brazil	10 140	3920[3]
Onega, Russia	9800	3800
Rudolf, Kenya	9100	3500
Eyre, Australia	8800	3400[3]
Titicaca, Peru/Bolivia	8300	3200

[1]Salt lakes
[2]Average of areas given by Canada and USA
[3]Salt lagoons
*Areas are given to the nearest 10 km²/sq mi. The Caspian and Aral Seas, being entirely surrounded by land, are classified as lakes.

LONGEST RIVERS

Name	Outflow	Length*	
		km	mi
Nile–Kagera–Ruvuvu–Ruvusu–Luvironza	Mediterranean Sea (Egypt)	6 690	4 160
Amazon–Ucayali–Tambo–Ene–Apurimac	Atlantic Ocean (Brazil)	6 570	4 080
Mississippi–Missouri–Jefferson–Beaverhead–Red Rock	Gulf of Mexico (USA)	6 020	3 740
Chang Jiang (Yangtze)	E China Sea (China)	5 980	3 720
Yenisey–Angara–Selenga–Ider	Kara Sea (Russia)	5 870	3 650
Amur–Argun–Kerulen	Tartar Strait (Russia)	5 780	3 590
Ob–Irtysh	Gulf of Ob, Kara Sea (Russia)	5 410	3 360
Plata–Parana–Grande	Atlantic Ocean (Argentina/Uruguay)	4 880	3 030
Huang Ho (Yellow)	Yellow Sea (China)	4 840	3 010
Congo (Zaire)–Lualaba	Atlantic Ocean (Angola–Zaïre)	4 630	2 880
Lena	Laptev Sea (Russia)	4 400	2 730
Mackenzie–Slave–Peace–Finlay	Beaufort Sea (Canada)	4 240	2 630
Mekong	S China Sea (Vietnam)	4 180	2 600
Niger	Gulf of Guinea (Nigeria)	4 100	2 550

*Lengths are given to the nearest 10 km/mi, and include the river plus tributaries comprising the longest watercourse.

HIGHEST WATERFALLS

Name	Height		Location
	m	ft	
Angel (upper fall)	807	2 648	Venezuela
Itatinga	628	2 060	Brazil
Cuquenan	610	2 000	Guyana/Venezuela
Ormeli	563	1 847	Norway
Tysse	533	1 749	Norway
Pilao	524	1 719	Brazil
Ribbon	491	1 612	USA
Vestre Mardola	468	1 535	Norway
Roraima	457	1 500	Guyana
Cleve-Garth	450	1 476	New Zealand

Distances are given for individual leaps.

LARGEST ISLANDS

Name	Area*	
	km²	sq mi
Australia	7892300	3078000
Greenland	2131600	831300
New Guinea	790000	305000
Borneo	737000	285000
Madagascar	587000	228900
Baffin, Canada	507000	196000
Sumatra	473600	184700
Honshu (Hondo), Japan	228000	88000
Great Britain	219000	84400
Vancouver I, Canada	217300	83900
Ellesmere, Canada	196000	75800
Sulawesi (Celebes)	174000	67400
South Is, New Zealand	151000	58200
Java	129000	50000
North Is, New Zealand	114000	44200
Newfoundland, Canada	109000	42000
Cuba	105000	40500
Luzon, Philippines	105000	40400
Iceland	103000	39700
Mindanao, Philippines	94600	36500
Novaya Zemlya (two Is), Russia	90600	35000
Ireland	84100	32500
Hokkaido, Japan	78500	30300
Hispaniola	77200	29800
Sakhalin, Russia	75100	29000
Tierra del Fuego	71200	27500
Tasmania, Australia	67900	26200

*Areas are rounded to the nearest three significant digits.

DEEPEST CAVES

Name/location	Depth	
	m	ft
Jean Bernard, France	1 494	4 900
Snezhnaya, Russia	1 340	4 397
Puertas de Illamina, Spain	1 338	4 390
Pierre-Saint-Martin, France	1 321	4 334
Sistema Huautla, Mexico	1 240	4 067
Berger, France	1 198	3 930
Vqerdi, Spain	1 195	3 921
Dachstein–Mammuthöhle, Austria	1 174	3 852
Zitu, Spain	1 139	3 737
Badalona, Spain	1 130	3 707
Batmanhöhle, Austria	1 105	3 626
Schneeloch, Austria	1 101	3 612
GES Malaga, Spain	1 070	3 510
Lamprechtsofen, Austria	1 024	3 360

HIGHEST MOUNTAINS

Name	Height*		Location
	m	ft	
Mt Everest	8850	29030	China/Nepal
K2 (Mt Godwin-Austen)	8610	28250	Kashmir–Jammu
Kangchenjunga	8590	28170	India/Nepal
Lhotse	8500	27890	China/Nepal
Kangchenjunga, S Peak	8470	27800	India/Nepal
Makalu I	8470	27800	China/Nepal
Kangchenjunga, W Peak	8420	27620	India/Nepal
Llotse E Peak	8380	27500	China/Nepal
Dhaulagiri	8170	26810	Nepal
Cho Oyu	8150	26750	China/Nepal
Manaslu	8130	26660	Nepal
Nanga Parbat	8130	26660	Kashmir–Jammu
Annapurna I	8080	26500	Nepal
Gasherbrum I	8070	26470	Kashmir–Jammu
Broad-highest	8050	26400	Kashmir–Jammu
Gasherbrum II	8030	26360	Kashmir–Jammu
Gosainthan	8010	26290	China
Broad-middle	8000	26250	Kashmir–Jammu
Gasherbrum III	7950	26090	Kashmir–Jammu
Annapurna II	7940	26040	Nepal
Nanda Devi	7820	25660	India
Rakaposhi	7790	25560	Kashmir
Kamet	7760	25450	India
Ulugh Muztagh	7720	25340	Tibet
Tirich Mir	7690	25230	Pakistan
Muz Tag Ata	7550	24760	China
Communism Peak	7490	24590	Tajikistan
Pobedy Peak	7440	24410	Kyrgyzstan
Aconcagua	6960	22830	Argentina
Ojos del Salado	6910	22660	Argentina/Chile

*Heights are given to the nearest 10 m/ft.

LARGEST DESERTS

Name/location	Area* km²	sq mi
Sahara, N Africa	8 600 000	3 320 000
Arabian, SW Asia	2 330 000	900 000
Gobi, Mongolia/NE China	1 166 000	450 000
Patagonian, Argentina	673 000	260 000
Great Basin, SW USA	492 000	190 000
Chihuahuan, Mexico	450 000	175 000
Great Sandy, NW Australia	450 000	175 000
Great Victoria, SW Australia	325 000	125 000
Sonoran, SW USA	310 000	120 000
Kyzyl-Kum, Kazakhstan/Uzbekistan	300 000	115 000
Takla Makan, N China	270 000	105 000
Kalahari, SW Africa	260 000	100 000
Kara-Kum, Turkmenistan	260 000	100 000
Kavir, Iran	260 000	100 000
Syrian, Saudi Arabia/Jordan/Syria/Iraq	260 000	100 000
Nubian, Sudan	260 000	100 000
Thar, India/Pakistan	200 000	77 000
Ust'-Urt, Kazakhstan/Uzbekistan	160 000	62 000
Bet-Pak-Dala, Kazakhstan	155 000	60 000
Simpson, C Australia	145 000	56 000
Dzungaria, China	142 000	55 000
Atacama, Chile	140 000	54 000
Namib, SE Africa	134 000	52 000
Sturt, SE Australia	130 000	50 000
Bolson de Mapimi, Mexico	130 000	50 000
Ordos, China	130 000	50 000
Alashan, China	116 000	45 000

*Desert areas are very approximate, because clear physical boundaries may not occur.

MAJOR VOLCANOES

Name/location	Height m	ft	Major eruptions (years)	Last eruption (year)
Aconcagua (Argentina)	6 960	22 831	Extinct	
Ararat (Turkey)	5 198	16 915	Extinct	Holocene
Awu (Sangir Is, Indonesia)	1 327	4 355	1711, 1856, 1892, 1968	1992
Bezymianny (Kamchatka, Russia)	2 800	9 186	1955–6	1984
Coseguina (Nicaragua)	847	2 780	1835	1835
El Chichón (Mexico)	1 349	4 430	1982	1982
Erebus (Antarctica)	4 023	13 200	1947, 1972, 1986	1991
Etna, (Italy)	3 236	10 905	AD 122, 1169, 1329, 1536, 1669, 1928, 1964, 1971, 1986, 1992	1994
Fuji (Japan)	3 776	12 388	1707	1707
Galunggung (Java)	2 180	7 155	1822, 1918	1982
Hekla (Iceland)	1 491	4 890	1693, 1845, 1947–8, 1970, 1981	1991
Helgafell (Iceland)	215	706	1973	1973
Jurullo (Mexico)	1 330	4 360	1759–74	1774
Katmai (Alaska)	2 298	7 540	1912, 1920, 1921, 1931	1974
Kilauea (Hawaii)	1 247	4 090	1823–1924, 1952, 1955, 1960, 1967–8, 1968–74, 1983–7, 1988, 1991–2	1994
Kilimanjaro (Tanzania)	5 930	19 450	Extinct	Pleistocene
Kluychevskoy (Kamchatka, Russia)	4 850	15 910	1700–1966, 1984–5	1993
Krakatoa (Sumatra)	818	2 685	1680, 1883, 1927, 1952–3, 1969	1980
La Soufrière (St Vincent)	1 232	4 040	1718, 1812, 1902, 1971–2	1979
Laki (Iceland)	500	1 642	1783	1784
Lamington (Papua New Guinea)	1 780	5 840	1951	1956
Lassen Peak (USA)	3 186	10 453	1914–15	1921
Mauna Loa (Hawaii)	4 172	13 685	1859, 1880, 1887, 1919, 1950, 1984	1987
Mayon (Philippines)	2 462	8 075	1616, 1766, 1814, 1897, 1968, 1978	1993
Nyamuragira (Zaïre)	3 056	10 026	1921–38, 1971, 1980, 1984, 1988	1991
Paricutin (Mexico)	3 188	10 460	1943–52	1952
Pelée (Martinique)	1 397	4 584	1902, 1929–32	1932
Pinatubo (Philippines)	1 758	5 770	1391, 1991	1992
Popocatepetl (Mexico)	5 483	17 990	1920	1943
Rainer, Mt (USA)	4 392	14 410	1st-c BC, 1820	1882
Ruapehu (New Zealand)	2 796	9 175	1945, 1953, 1969, 1975, 1986, 1995	1996
St Helens, Mt (USA)	2 549	8 364	1800, 1831, 1835, 1842–3, 1857, 1980, 1987	1991
Santorini/ Thera (Greece)	556	1 824	1470 BC, 197 BC, AD 46, 1570–3, 1707–11, 1866–70	1950
Stromboli (Italy)	931	3 055	1768, 1882, 1889, 1907, 1930, 1936, 1941, 1950, 1952, 1986, 1990	1994
Surtsey (Iceland)	174	570	1963–7	1967
Taal (Philippines)	1 448	4 752	1911, 1965, 1969, 1977	1988
Tambora (Sumbawa, Indonesia)	2 868	9 410	1815	1880
Tarawera (New Zealand)	1 149	3 770	1886	1973
Vesuvius (Italy)	1 289	4 230	AD 79, 472, 1036, 1631, 1779, 1906	1944
Vulcano (Italy)	502	1 650	Antiquity, 1444, 1730–40, 1786, 1873, 1888–90	1890

MAJOR EARTHQUAKES 1600–1999

All magnitudes on the Richter scale[1]

Location	Country	Year	Magnitude	Deaths
Armenia	Colombia	1999	6.0	2 000+
Rostaq	Afghanistan	1998	7.1	2 000
Khorasan	Iran	1997	7.1	4 000
Takhar	Afghanistan	1998	6.1	4 000
Lijiang, Yunan	China	1996	7.0	250
Biak I	Indonesia	1996	7.5	100
Neftegorsk	Russia	1995	7.6	1989
Kobe	Japan	1995	7.2	5 378
Los Angeles	USA	1994	6.8	5.7
Maharashtra	India	1993	6.5	9 748
Cairo	Egypt	1992	5.9	500
Erzincan	Turkey	1992	6.2	2 000
Uttar Pradesh	India	1991	6.1	1 000
Costa Rica/Panama		1991	7.5	80
Georgia		1991	7.2	100
Hindu Kush Mts	Afghanistan/Pakistan	1991	6.8	1 300
Cabanatuan, Luzon	Philippines	1990	7.7	1 653
Caspian Sea area	Iran	1990	7.7	40 000
Moyobamba	Peru	1990	5.8	90
Carpathian Mts	Romania	1990	6.6	70
Luzon Island	Philippines	1990	7.7	1 600
San Francisco	USA	1989	6.9	100
Armenia	CIS	1988	7.0	25 000
Mexico City	Mexico	1985	8.1	7 200
Naples	Italy	1980	7.2	4 500
Tabas	Iran	1978	7.7	25 000
Tangshan	China	1976	8.2	242 000
Guatemala City	Guatemala	1976	7.5	22 778
Kashmir	Pakistan	1974	6.3	5 200
Managua	Nicaragua	1972	6.2	5 000
Tehran	Iran	1972	6.9	5 000
El Asnam	Algeria	1980	7.3	5 000
Agadir	Morocco	1960	5.8	12 000
Ashkhabad	USSR	1948	7.3	19 800
Erzincan	Turkey	1939	7.9	23 000
Chillan	Chile	1939	7.8	30 000
Quetta	India	1935	7.5	60 000
Gansu	China	1932	7.6	70 000
Nan-Shan	China	1927	8.3	200 000
Kanto	Japan	1923	8.3	143 000
Gansu	China	1920	8.6	180 000
Avezzano	Italy	1915	7.5	30 000
Messina	Italy	1908	7.5	120 000
Valparaiso	Chile	1906	8.6	20 000
San Francisco	USA	1906	8.3	500
Calabria	Italy	1783		50 000
Lisbon	Portugal	1755		70 000
Calcutta	India	1737		300 000
Hokkaido	Japan	1730		137 000
Catania	Italy	1693		60 000

[1]The Richter scale is a logarithmic scale, devised in 1935 by geophysicist Charles Richter, for representing the energy released by earthquakes. A figure of 2 or less is barely perceptible, while an earthquake measuring over 5 may be destructive. More relevant as a measure of earthquake strength is the intensity, for which the modified Mercalli scale is widely used.

EARTHQUAKE SEVERITY

Modified Mercalli intensity scale (1956 revision)

Intensity value

- **I** Not felt; marginal and long-period effects of large earthquakes.
- **II** Felt by persons at rest, on upper floors or favourably placed.
- **III** Felt indoors; hanging objects swing; vibration like passing of light trucks; duration estimated; may not be recognized as an earthquake.
- **IV** Hanging objects swing; vibration like passing of heavy trucks, or sensation of a jolt like a heavy ball striking the walls; standing cars rock; windows, dishes, doors rattle; glasses clink; crockery clashes; in the upper range of IV, wooden walls and frames creak.
- **V** Felt outdoors; direction estimated; sleepers wakened; liquids disturbed, some spilled; small unstable objects displaced or upset; doors swing, close, open; shutters, pictures move; pendulum clocks stop, start, change rate.
- **VI** Felt by all; many frightened and run outdoors; persons walk unsteadily; windows, dishes, glassware break; knick-knacks, books, etc, fall off shelves; pictures off walls; furniture moves or overturns; weak plaster and masonry D crack; small bells ring (church, school); trees, bushes shake visibly, or heard to rustle.
- **VII** Difficult to stand; noticed by drivers; hanging objects quiver; furniture breaks; damage to masonry D, including cracks; weak chimneys broken at roof line; fall of plaster, loose bricks, stones, tiles, cornices, also unbraced parapets and architectural ornaments; some cracks in masonry C; waves on ponds, water turbid with mud; small slides and caving in along sand or gravel banks; large bells ring; concrete irrigation ditches damaged.
- **VIII** Steering of cars affected; damage to masonry C and partial collapse; some damage to masonry B; none to masonry A; fall of stucco and some masonry walls; twisting, fall of chimneys, factory stacks, monuments, towers, elevated tanks; frame houses move on foundations if not bolted down; loose panel walls thrown out; decayed piling broken off; branches broken from trees; changes in flow or temperature of springs and wells; cracks in wet ground and on steep slopes.
- **IX** General panic; masonry D destroyed; masonry C heavily damaged, sometimes with complete collapse; masonry B seriously damaged; general damage to foundations; frame structures, if not bolted, shift off foundations; frames racked; serious damage to reservoirs; underground pipes break; conspicuous cracks in ground; in alluviated areas sand and mud ejected, earthquake fountains, sand craters.
- **X** Most masonry and frame structures destroyed with their foundations; some well-built wooden structures and bridges destroyed; serious damage to dams, dikes, embankments; large landslides; water thrown on banks of canals, rivers, lakes, etc; sand and mud shifted horizontally on beaches and flat land; rails bent slightly.
- **XI** Rails bent greatly; underground pipelines completely out of service.
- **XII** Damage nearly total; large rock masses displaced; lines of sight and level distorted; objects thrown into the air.

Note

Masonry A Good workmanship, mortar and design; reinforced, especially laterally, and bound together by using steel, concrete etc; designed to resist lateral forces. *Masonry B* Good workmanship and mortar; reinforced, but not designed in detail to resist lateral forces. *Masonry C* Ordinary workmanship and mortar; no extreme weakness like failing to tie in at corners, but neither reinforced nor designed against horizontal forces. *Masonry D* Weak materials, such as adobe; poor mortar; low standards of workmanship; weak horizontally.

MAJOR TSUNAMIS

Location of source	Year	Height m	ft	Location of deaths/damage	Deaths
West Sepik	1998	10	32	Papua New Guinea	3 000
Mindoro	1994	15	49	Philippine Is	60
Banyuwangi	1994	5	16	Indonesia	200
Sea of Japan	1983	15	49	Japan, Korea	107
Indonesia	1979	10	32	Indonesia	187
Celebes Sea	1976	30	98	Philippine Is	5 000
Alaska	1964	32	105	Alaska, Aleutian Is, California	122
Chile	1960	25	82	Chile, Hawaii, Japan	1 260
Aleutian Is	1957	16	52	Hawaii, Japan	0
Kamchatka	1952	18.4	60	Kamchatka, Kuril Is, Hawaii	many
Aleutian Is	1946	32	105	Aleutian Is, Hawaii, California	165
Nankaido (Japan)	1946	6.1	20	Japan	1 997
Kii (Japan)	1944	7.5	25	Japan	998
Sanriku (Japan)	1933	28.2	93	Japan, Hawaii	3 000
E Kamchatka	1923	20	66	Kamchatka, Hawaii	3
S Kuril Is	1918	12	39	Kuril Is, Russia, Japan, Hawaii	23
Sanriku (Japan)	1896	30	98	Japan	27 122
Sunda Strait	1883	35	115	Java, Sumatra	36 000
Chile	1877	23	75	Chile, Hawaii	many
Chile	1868	21	69	Chile, Hawaii	25 000
Hawaii Is	1868	20	66	Hawaii Is	81
Japan	1854	6	20	Japan	3 000
Flores Sea	1800	24	79	Indonesia	400–500
Ariake Sea	1792	9	30	Japan	9 745
Italy	1783	?	?	Italy	30 000
Ryukyu Is	1771	12	39	Ryukyu Is	11 941
Portugal	1775	16	52	W Europe, Morocco, W Indies	60 000
Peru	1746	24	79	Peru	5 000
Japan	1741	9	30	Japan	1 000+
SE Kamchatka	1737	30	98	Kamchatka, Kuril Is	?
Peru	1724	24	79	Peru	?
Japan	1707	11.5	38	Japan	30 000
W Indies	1692	?	?	Jamaica	2 000
Banda Is	1629	15	49	Indonesia	?

METEOROLOGICAL SEA AREAS

WIND FORCE AND SEA DISTURBANCE

Beaufort number	Windspeed kph	mph	Wind name	Observable wind characteristics
0	<1	<1	Calm	Smoke rises vertically
1	1–5	1–3	Light air	Wind direction shown by smoke drift but not by wind vanes
2	6–11	4–7	Light breeze	Wind felt on face; leaves rustle; vanes moved by wind
3	12–19	8–12	Gentle breeze	Leaves and small twigs in constant motion; wind extends light flag
4	20–28	13–18	Moderate	Raises dust, loose paper; small branches moved
5	29–38	19–24	Fresh	Small trees begin to sway; crested wavelets on inland waters
6	39–49	25–31	Strong	Large branches in motion; whistling heard in telegraph wires; difficult to use umbrellas
7	50–61	32–38	Near gale	Whole trees in motion; difficult to walk against wind
8	62–74	39–46	Gale	Breaks twigs off trees; impedes progress
9	75–88	47–54	Strong gale	Slight structural damage occurs
10	89–102	55–63	Storm	Trees uprooted; considerable damage occurs
11	103–17	64–72	Violent storm	Widespread damage
12–17	≥118	≥73	Hurricane	

Sea disturbance number	Average wave ht m	ft	Observable sea characteristics
0	0	0	Sea like a mirror
0	0	0	Ripples like scales, without foam crests
1	0.3	0–1	More definite wavelets, but crests do not break
2	0.3–0.6	1–2	Large wavelets; crests beginning to break; scattered white horses
3	0.6–1.2	2–4	Small waves becoming longer; fairly frequent white horses
4	1.2–2.4	4–8	Moderate waves with longer form; many white horses; some foam spray
5	2.4–4	8–13	Large waves forming; more white foam crests; spray
6	4–6	13–20	Sea heaps up; streaks of white foam blown along
6	4–6	13–20	Moderately high waves of greater length; well-marked streaks of foam
6	4–6	13–20	High waves; dense streaks of foam; sea begins to roll; spray affects visibility
7	6–9	20–30	Very high waves with overhanging crests; generally white appearance of surface; heavy rolling
8	9–14	30–45	Exceptionally high waves; long white patches of foam; poor visibility; ships lost to view behind waves
9	14	>45	Air filled with foam and spray; sea completely white; very poor visibility

GEOLOGICAL TIME SCALE

Eon	Era	Period	Epoch	Million years before present	Geological events	Sea life	Land life
Phanerozoic	Cenozoic	Quaternary	Holocene	0.01	Glaciers recede. Sea level rises. Climate becomes more equable.	As now.	Forests flourish again. Humans acquire agriculture and technology.
			Pleistocene	2.0	Widespread glaciers melt periodically, causing seas to rise and fall.	As now.	Many plant forms perish. Small mammals abundant. Primitive humans established.
		Tertiary	Pliocene	5.1	Continents and oceans adopting their present form. Present climatic distribution established. Ice caps develop.	Giant sharks extinct. Many fish varieties.	Some plants and mammals die out. Primates flourish.
			Miocene	24.6	Seas recede further. European and Asian land masses join. Heavy rain causes massive erosion. Red Sea opens.	Bony fish common. Giant sharks.	Grasses widespread. Grazing mammals become common.
			Oligocene	38.0	Seas recede. Extensive movements of Earth's crust produce new mountains (eg Alpine–Himalayan chain).	Crabs, mussels, and snails evolve.	Forests diminish. Grasses Pachyderms, canines, and felines develop.
			Eocene	54.9	Mountain formation continues. Glaciers common in high mountain ranges. Greenland separates. Australia separates.	Whales adapt to sea.	Large tropical jungles. Primitive forms of modern mammals established.
			Palaeocene	65	Widespread subsidence of land. Seas advance again. Considerable volcanic activity. Europe emerges.	Many reptiles become extinct.	Flowering plants widespread. First primates. Giant reptiles extinct.
	Mesozoic	Cretaceous	Late Early	97.5 144	Swamps widespread. Massive alluvial deposition. Continuing limestone formation. S America separates from Africa. India, Africa and Antarctica separate.	Turtles, rays, and now-common fish appear.	Flowering plants established. Dinosaurs become extinct.
		Jurassic	Malm Dogger Lias	163 188 213	Seas advance. Much river formation. High mountains eroded. Limestone formation. N America separates from Africa. Central Atlantic begins to open.	Reptiles dominant.	Early flowers. Dinosaurs dominant. Mammals still primitive. First birds.
		Triassic	Late Middle Early	231 243 248	Desert conditions widespread. Hot climate slowly becomes warm and wet. Break up of Pangea into supercontients Gondwana (S) and Laurasia (N).	Ichthyosaurs, flying flying fish, and crustaceans appear.	Ferns and conifers thrive. First mammals, dinosaurs, and flies.
	Palaeozoic	Permian	Late Early	258 286	Some sea areas cut off to form lakes. Earth movements form mountains. Glaciation in southern hemisphere.	Some shelled fish become extinct.	Deciduous plants. Reptiles dominant. Many insect varieties.
		Carbon-iferous	Pennsylvanian Mississippian	320 360	Sea-beds rise to form new land areas. Enormous swamps. Partly-rotted vegetation forms coal.	Amphibians and sharks abundant.	Extensive evergreen forests. Reptiles breed on land. Some insects develop wings.
		Devonian	Late Middle Early	374 387 408	Collision of continents causing mountain formation (Appalachians, Caledonides, and Urals). Sea deeper but narrower. Climatic zones forming. Iapetus ocean closed.	Fish abundant. Primitive sharks. First amphibians.	Leafy plants. Some invertebrates adapt to land. First insects.
		Silurian	Pridoli Ludlow Wenlock Llandovery	414 421 428 438	New mountain ranges form. Sea level varies periodically. Extensive shallow sea over the Sahara.	Large vertebrates.	First leafless land plants.
		Ordovician	Ashgill Caradoc Llandeilo Llanvirn Arenig Tremadoc	448 458 468 478 488 505	Shore lines still quite variable. Increasing sedimentation. Europe and N America moving together.	First vertebrates. Coral reefs develop.	None.
		Cambrian	Merioneth St David's Caerfai	525 540 590	Much volcanic activity, and long periods of marine sedimentation.	Shelled invertebrates. Trilobites.	None.
Proterozoic	Precambrian	Vendian		650	Shallow seas advance and retreat over land areas. Atmosphere uniformly warm.	Seaweed. Algae and invertebrates.	None.
		Riphean	Late Middle Early	900 1300 1600	Intense deformation and metamorphism.	Earliest marine life and fossils.	None.
		Early Proterozoic		2500	Shallow shelf seas. Formation of carbonate sediments and 'red beds'.	First appearance of stromatolites.	None.
Arch-aean		Archaean (Azoic)		4600	Banded iron formations. Formation of the Earth's crust and oceans.	None.	None.

Times and Distances

INTERNATIONAL TIME DIFFERENCES

The time zones of the world are conventionally measured from longitude 0 at Greenwich Observatory (Greenwich Mean Time, GMT).

Each 15° of longitude east of this point is one hour ahead of GMT (eg when it is 2pm in London it is 3pm or later in time zones to the east). Hours ahead of GMT are shown by a plus sign, eg +3, +4/8.

Each 15° west of this point is one hour behind GMT (2pm in London would be 1pm or earlier in time zones to the west). Hours behind GMT are shown by a minus sign, eg –3, –4/8.

Some countries adopt time zones that vary from standard time. Also, during the summer, several countries adopt Daylight Saving Time (or Summer Time), which is one hour ahead of the times shown below.

>> Date Line, Daylight Saving Time.

Country	GMT
Afghanistan	+4½
Albania	+1
Algeria	+1
Angola	+1
Antigua	–4
Argentina	–3
Australia	+8/10
Austria	+1
Bahamas	–5
Bahrain	+3
Bangladesh	+6
Barbados	–4
Belgium	+1
Belize	–6
Benin	+1
Bermuda	–4
Bolivia	–4
Botswana	+2
Brazil	–2/5
Brunei	+8
Bulgaria	+2
Burkina Faso	0
Burundi	+2
Cambodia	+7
Cameroon	+1
Canada	–3/9
Cape Verde	–1
Central African Republic	+1
Chad	+1
Chile	–4
China	+8
Colombia	–5
Comoros	+3
Congo	+1
Costa Rica	–6
Côte d'Ivoire	0
Cuba	–5
Cyprus	+2
Czech Republic	+1
Denmark	+1
Djibouti	+3
Dominica	–4
Dominican Republic	–4
Ecuador	–5
Egypt	+2
El Salvador	–6
Equatorial Guinea	+1
Estonia	+3
Ethiopia	+3
Falkland Islands	–4
Fiji	+12
Finland	+2
France	+1
Gabon	+1
Gambia, The	0
Germany	+1
Ghana	0
Gibraltar	+1
Greece	+2
Greenland	–3
Grenada	–4
Guatemala	–6
Guinea	0
Guinea–Bissau	0
Guyana	–3
Haiti	–5
Honduras	–6
Hong Kong	+8
Hungary	+1
Iceland	0
India	+5½
Indonesia	+7/9
Iran	+3½
Iraq	+3
Ireland	0
Israel	+2
Italy	+1
Jamaica	–5
Japan	+9
Jordan	+2
Kenya	+3
Kiribati	–12
Korea, North	+9
Korea, South	+9
Kuwait	+3
Laos	+7
Latvia	+3
Lebanon	+2
Lesotho	+2
Liberia	0
Libya	+1
Liechtenstein	+1
Lithuania	+3
Luxembourg	+1
Madagascar	+3
Malawi	+2
Malaysia	+8
Maldives	+5
Mali	0
Malta	+1
Mauritania	0
Mauritius	+4
Mexico	–6/8
Monaco	+1
Morocco	0
Mozambique	+2
Myanmar (Burma)	+6½
Namibia	–2
Nauru	+12
Nepal	+5¾
Netherlands	+1
New Zealand	+12
Nicaragua	–6
Niger	+1
Nigeria	+1
Norway	+1
Oman	+4
Pakistan	+5
Panama	–5
Papua New Guinea	+10
Paraguay	–4
Peru	–5
Philippines	+8
Poland	+1
Portugal	+1
Qatar	+3
Romania	+2
Russia	+2/13
Rwanda	+2
St Christopher and Nevis	–4
St Lucia	–4
St Vincent	–4
Samoa	–11
San Marino	+1
São Tomé	0
Saudi Arabia	+3
Senegal	0
Seychelles	+4
Sierra Leone	0
Singapore	+8
Slovak Republic	+1
Solomon Is	+11
Somalia	+3
South Africa	+2
Spain	+1
Sri Lanka	+5½
Sudan	+2
Suriname	–3
Swaziland	+2
Sweden	+1
Switzerland	+1
Syria	+2
Taiwan	+8
Tanzania	+3
Thailand	+7
Togo	0
Tonga	+13
Trinidad and Tobago	–4
Tunisia	+1
Turkey	+2
Tuvalu	+12
Uganda	+3
United Arab Emirates	+4
UK	0
Uruguay	–3
USA	–5/10
Vanuatu	+11
Venezuela	–4
Vietnam	+7
Yemen	+3
Yugoslavia	+1
Zaïre	+1/2
Zambia	+2
Zimbabwe	+2

INTERNATIONAL TIME ZONES

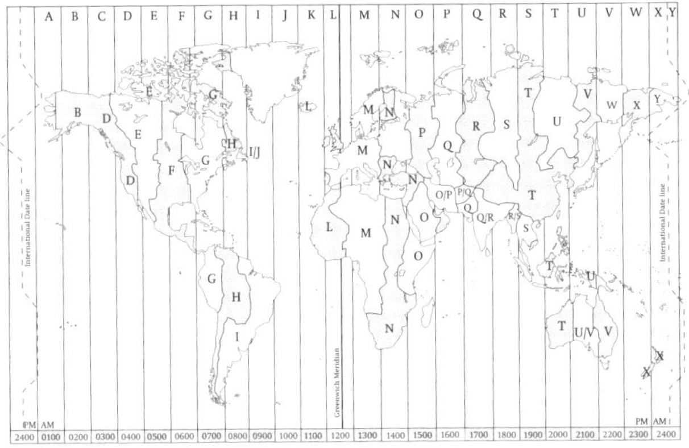

World times at 12 noon GMT

Some countries have adopted half-hour time zones which are indicated on the map as a combination of two coded zones. For example, it is 1730 hours in India at 1200 GMT. The standard times shown are subject to variation in certain countries where Daylight Saving/Summer Time operates for part of the year.

AIR DISTANCES

Air distances between some major cities, given in statute miles. To convert to kilometres, multiply number given by 1.6093.

* Shortest route.

	Amsterdam	Anchorage	Beijing	Buenos Aires	Cairo	Chicago	Delhi	Hong Kong	Honolulu	Istanbul	Johannesburg	Lagos	London	Los Angeles	Mexico City	Montreal	Moscow	Nairobi	Paris	Perth	Rome	Santiago	Sydney	Tokyo
Anchorage	4475																							
Beijing	6566	4756																						
Buenos Aires	7153	8329	12000																					
Cairo	2042	6059	6685	7468																				
Chicago	4109	28	7599	5587	6135																			
Delhi	3985	8925	2368	8340	2753	8119																		
Hong Kong	5926	5063	1235	3124	5098	7827	2345																	
Honolulu	8368	2780	6778	8693	9439	4246	7888	5543																
Istanbul	1373	6024	4763	7783	764	5502	2833	5998	9547															
Johannesburg	5606	1042	10108	5725	4012	8705	6765	6728	12892	4776														
Lagos	3161	7587	8030	4832	2443	7065	5196	7541	10367	3207	2854													
London	217	4472	5054	6985	2187	3956	4169	5979	7252	1552	5640	3115												
Los Angeles	5559	2333	6349	6140	7589	1746	8717	7231	2553	6994	10443	7716	5442											
Mexico City	5724	3751	7912	4592	7730	1687	9806	8794	4116	7255	10070	7343	5703	1563										
Montreal	3422	3100	7557	5640	5431	737	7421	8564	4923	4795	8322	5595	3252	2482	2307									
Moscow	1338	4291	3604	8382	1790	5500	2698	4839	8802	1089	6280	4462	1550	6992	6700	4393								
Nairobi	4148	8714	8888	7427	2203	8177	4956	7301	11498	2967	1809	2377	4246	9688	9949	7498	3951							
Paris	261	4683	5108	6892	1995	4140	4089	5987	7463	1394	5422	2922	220	5633	5714	3434	1540	4031						
Perth	9118	8368	4987	9734	7766	11281	5013	3752	7115	7846	5564	10209	9246	9535	11098	12402	8355	7373	12587					
Rome	809	5258	5306	6931	1329	4828	3679	5773	8150	852	4802	2497	898	6340	6601	5431	1478	3349	688	8309				
Santiago	7714	7919	13622	710	8029	5328	12715	3733	8147	10109	5738	6042	8568	5594	4168	5551	10118	7547	461	15129	7548			
Sydney	1039	8522	5689	7760	9196	9324	6495	4586	5078	9883	7601	11700	10565	7498	9061	9980	9425	9410	10150	2037	10149	13092		
Tokyo	6006[a]	3443	1313	13100	6362	6286	3656	1807	3831	5757	8535	9130[a]	6218	5451	7014	6913	4668	8565	6208[a]	4925	6146	11049	4640	
Washington	3854	3430	7930	6097	5859	590	7841	8385	4822	5347	8199	5472	3672	2294	1871	493	4884	7918	3843	11829	4495	5061	9792	6763

FLYING TIMES

Approximate flying times between some major cities. Times quoted (in hours and minutes) are 'flying time' only. In many cases, in order to travel between two points, it is necessary to change aircraft one or more times. Time between flights has not been included.

	Amsterdam	Anchorage	Beijing	Buenos Aires	Cairo	Chicago	Delhi	Hong Kong	Honolulu	Istanbul	Johannesburg	Lagos	London	Los Angeles	Mexico City	Montreal	Moscow	Nairobi	Paris	Perth	Rome	Santiago	Sydney	Tokyo
Anchorage	9.00																							
Beijing	16.50	11.45																						
Buenos Aires	17.45	10.48	28.31																					
Cairo	4.20	13.20	13.15	20.40																				
Chicago	8.35	5.44	15.15	15.40	18.40																			
Delhi	8.15	16.50	6.40	26.20	7.00	20.05																		
Hong Kong	15.15	11.40	3.00	29.35	10.55	17.05	6.05																	
Honolulu	16.42	5.44	10.55	19.00	22.50	9.25	16.50	13.05																
Istanbul	3.15	12.15	15.40	18.45	2.00	12.20	7.35	17.35	21.05															
Johannesburg	13.15	19.50	20.10	12.30	8.55	21.40	23.45	14.55	30.25	16.30														
Lagos	6.40	14.55	22.35	9.55	8.20	14.55	14.55	22.30	23.40	8.05	6.55													
London	1.05	8.30	18.05	16.35	5.35	8.30	10.35	16.05	17.15	3.50	13.10	6.25												
Los Angeles	11.15	6.13	15.25	13.45	21.00	5.00	19.30	15.50	5.15	14.50	24.10	17.25	11.00											
Mexico City	12.27	10.49	18.45	10.25	16.47	5.15	20.42	19.10	8.35	15.42	25.42	19.07	14.35	3.20										
Montreal	7.40	7.91	27.30	16.00	12.35	2.20	17.35	23.05	12.50	10.15	20.10	13.25	7.00	6.40	4.45									
Moscow	3.15	12.15	8.40	22.05	5.25	12.15	7.35	18.00	21.00	4.40	13.30	10.10	3.45	14.45	18.10	10.45								
Nairobi	8.15	17.00	16.00	24.55	4.55	17.00	10.45	12.45	25.45	7.15	3.45	6.20	8.30	19.30	20.42	15.30	12.50							
Paris	1.10	9.00	16.35	15.35	5.05	9.00	10.45	16.40	18.05	3.10	15.50	7.45	1.05	12.50	13.25	6.25	4.00	9.20						
Perth	20.35	17.25	11.15	25.20	17.10	23.00	9.30	8.15	17.25	15.25	14.20	25.55	19.30	19.30	22.50	26.30	19.40	23.00	21.40					
Rome	2.20	12.00	16.10	14.40	3.25	11.35	8.50	15.10	19.13	2.35	12.25	6.55	2.25	14.35	5.35	8.10	4.10	7.20	1.55	20.00				
Santiago	20.50	19.13	22.34	2.10	25.10	17.15	29.05	19.15	8.35	21.00	19.55	24.25	21.55	16.00	12.00	14.50	24.05	29.05	19.45	26.00	18.50			
Sydney	23.05	16.35	16.15	20.45	17.20	21.10	13.50	10.35	11.50	18.40	31.50	28.35	21.55	18.10	18.05	24.50	19.40	31.35	25.05	4.35	23.50	24.30		
Tokyo	11.40	7.20	3.50	28.30	19.40	12.55	9.45	4.20	7.05	14.05	25.00	18.40	11.50	11.55	16.25	18.55	9.25	19.55	16.45	10.05	17.40	27.55	9.15	
Washington	8.55	7.25	25.50	11.00	14.20	1.45	20.10	24.15	10.55	11.25	21.20	14.45	8.10	5.25	7.50	2.50	12.30	17.10	9.25	22.45	12.40	17.40	23.35	12.40

US AIR DISTANCES

Air distances between US cities, given in statute miles. To convert to kilometres, multiply number given by 1.6093.

	Atlanta	Boston	Chicago	Dallas	Denver	Detroit	Houston	Kansas City	Los Angeles	Miami	Minneapolis	New Orleans	New York	Oklahoma City	Omaha	Philadelphia	Phoenix	Pittsburgh	Portland	St Louis	Salt Lake City	San Antonio	San Francisco	Seattle
Boston	946																							
Chicago	606	867																						
Dallas	721	1555	796																					
Denver	1208	1767	901	654																				
Detroit	595	632	235	982	1135																			
Houston	689	1603	925	217	864	1095																		
Kansas City	681	1254	403	450	543	630	643																	
Los Angeles	1946	2611	1745	1246	849	1979	1379	1363																
Miami	595	1258	1197	1110	1716	1146	964	1239	2342															
Minneapolis	906	1124	334	853	693	528	1046	394	1536	1501														
New Orleans	425	1367	837	437	1067	936	305	690	1671	674	1040													
New York	760	187	740	1383	1638	509	1417	1113	2475	1090	1028	1182												
Oklahoma City	761	1505	693	181	500	911	395	312	1187	1223	694	567	1345											
Omaha	821	1282	416	585	485	651	793	152	1330	1393	282	841	1155	418										
Philadelphia	665	281	678	1294	1569	453	1324	1039	2401	1013	980	1094	94	1268	1094									
Phoenix	1587	2300	1440	879	589	1681	1015	1043	370	1972	1270	1301	2143	833	1037	2082								
Pittsburgh	526	496	412	1061	1302	201	1124	769	2136	1013	726	918	340	1010	821	267	1814							
Portland	2172	2537	1739	1637	985	1959	1834	1492	834	2700	1426	2050	2454	1484	1368	2411	1009	2148						
St Louis	484	1046	258	546	781	440	667	229	1592	1068	448	604	892	462	342	813	1262	553	1708					
Salt Lake City	1589	2105	1249	1010	381	1489	1204	919	590	2088	991	1428	1989	865	839	1932	507	1659	630	1156				
San Antonio	875	1764	1041	247	793	1215	191	697	1210	1143	1097	495	1587	407	824	1502	843	1277	1714	786	1086			
San Francisco	2139	2704	1846	1476	956	2079	1636	1498	337	2585	1589	1911	2586	1383	1433	2521	651	2253	550	1735	599	1482		
Seattle	2182	2496	1720	1670	1019	1932	1874	1489	954	2725	1399	2087	2421	1520	1368	2383	1109	2124	132	1709	689	1775	678	
Washington, DC	532	414	590	1163	1464	385	1189	927	2288	919	909	969	229	1158	1000	136	1956	184	2339	696	1839	1361	2419	2307

UK ROAD DISTANCES

Road distances between British centres are given in statute miles, using routes recommended by the Automobile Association based on the quickest travelling time. To convert to kilometres, multiply number given by 1.6093.

	Aberdeen	Birmingham	Bristol	Cambridge	Cardiff	Dover	Edinburgh	Exeter	Glasgow	Holyhead	Hull	Leeds	Liverpool	Manchester	Newcastle	Norwich	Nottingham	Oxford	Penzance	Plymouth	Shrewsbury	Southampton	Stranraer	York
Birmingham	430																							
Bristol	511	85																						
Cambridge	468	101	156																					
Cardiff	532	107	45	191																				
Dover	591	202	198	121	234																			
Edinburgh	130	293	373	337	395	457																		
Exeter	584	157	81	233	119	248	446																	
Glasgow	149	291	372	349	393	490	45	444																
Holyhead	457	151	232	246	209	347	325	305	319															
Hull	361	136	227	157	246	278	229	297	245	215														
Leeds	336	115	216	143	236	265	205	288	215	163	59													
Liverpool	361	98	178	195	200	295	222	250	220	104	126	72												
Manchester	354	88	167	153	188	283	218	239	214	123	97	43	34											
Newcastle	239	198	291	224	311	348	107	361	150	260	121	91	170	141										
Norwich	501	161	217	62	252	167	365	295	379	309	153	173	232	183	258									
Nottingham	402	59	151	82	170	202	268	222	281	174	92	73	107	71	156	123								
Oxford	497	63	74	82	109	148	361	152	354	218	188	171	164	153	253	144	104							
Penzance	696	272	195	346	232	362	561	112	559	419	411	401	366	355	477	407	265	265						
Plymouth	624	199	125	275	164	290	488	45	486	347	341	328	294	281	410	336	328	193	78					
Shrewsbury	412	48	128	142	110	243	276	201	272	104	164	116	64	69	216	205	724	113	315	242				
Southampton	571	128	75	133	123	155	437	114	436	296	253	235	241	227	319	192	471	67	227	155	190			
Stranraer	241	307	386	361	406	503	130	457	88	332	259	232	234	226	164	393	1048	371	572	502	287	447		
York	325	128	221	153	241	274	191	291	208	190	38	24	100	71	83	185	2108	185	406	340	144	252	228	
London	543	118	119	60	155	77	405	170	402	263	215	196	210	199	280	115	1157	56	283	215	162	76	419	209

EUROPEAN ROAD DISTANCES

Road distances between some European cities, given in kilometres. To convert to statute miles, multiply number given by 0.6214.

	Athens	Barcelona	Brussels	Calais	Cherbourg	Cologne	Copenhagen	Geneva	Gibraltar	Hamburg	Hook of Holland	Lisbon	Lyons	Madrid	Marseilles	Milan	Munich	Paris	Rome	Stockholm
Barcelona	3313																			
Brussels	2963	1318																		
Calais	3175	1326	204																	
Cherbourg	3339	1294	583	460																
Cologne	2762	1498	206	409	785															
Copenhagen	3276	2218	966	1136	1545	760														
Geneva	2610	803	677	747	853	1662	1418													
Gibraltar	4485	1172	2256	2224	2047	2436	3196	1975												
Hamburg	2977	2018	597	714	1115	460	460	1118	2897											
Hook of Holland	3030	1490	172	330	731	269	269	895	2428	550										
Lisbon	4532	1304	2084	2052	1827	2290	2971	1936	676	2671	2280									
Lyons	2753	645	690	739	789	714	1458	158	1817	1159	863	1778								
Madrid	3949	636	1558	1550	1347	1764	2498	1439	698	2198	1730	668	1281							
Marseilles	2865	521	1011	1059	1101	1035	1778	425	1693	1479	1183	1762	320	1157						
Milan	2282	1014	925	1077	1209	911	1537	328	2185	1238	1098	2250	328	1724	618					
Munich	2179	1365	747	977	1160	583	1104	591	2565	3805	851	2507	724	2010	1109	331				
Paris	3000	1033	285	280	340	465	1176	513	1971	877	457	1799	471	1273	792	856	821			
Rome	817	1460	1511	1662	1794	1497	2050	995	2631	1751	1683	2700	1048	2097	1011	586	946	1476		
Stockholm	3927	2868	1616	1786	2196	1403	650	2068	3886	949	1500	3231	2108	3188	2428	2187	1754	1827	2707	
Vienna	1991	1802	1175	1381	1588	937	1455	1019	2974	1155	1205	2935	1157	2409	1363	898	428	1249	1209	2105

MAP OF EUROPE

YEAR EQUIVALENTS

Jewish[1]	(AM)	*Islamic*[2]	(H)	*Hindu*[3]	(SE)
5759	(21 Sep 1998 – 10 Sep 1999)	1419	(28 Apr 1998 – 17 Apr 1999)	1920	(22 Mar 1998 – 21 Mar 1999)
5760	(11 Sep 1999 – 29 Sep 2000)	1420	(18 Apr 1999 – 5 Apr 2000)	1921	(22 Mar 1999 – 21 Mar 2000)
5761	(30 Sep 2000–17 Sep 2001)	1421	(6 Apr 2000–25 Mar 2001)	1922	(22 Mar 2000–21 Mar 2001)
5762	(18 Sep 2001–6 Sep 2002)	1422	(26 Mar 2001–14 Mar 2002)	1923	(22 Mar 2001–21 Mar 2002)
5763	(7 Sep 2002–26 Sep 2003)	1423	(15 Mar 2002–3 Mar 2003)	1924	(22 Mar 2002–21 Mar 2003)
5764	(27 Sep 2003–15 Sep 2004)	1424	(4 Mar 2003–21 Feb 2004)	1925	(22 Mar 2003–21 Mar 2004)

Gregorian equivalents are given in parentheses and are AD (= Anno Domini).

[1] Calculated from 3761 BC, said to be the year of the creation of the world. AM = Anno Mundi.

[2] Calculated from AD 622, the year in which the Prophet went from Mecca to Medina. H = Hijra.

[3] Calculated from AD 78, the beginning of the Saka era (SE), used alongside Gregorian dates in Government of India publications since 22 Mar 1957. Other

MONTH EQUIVALENTS

Gregorian equivalents to other calendars are given in parentheses; the figures refer to the number of solar days in each month.

Gregorian (Basis: Sun)	*Jewish* (Basis: Moon)	*Islamic* (Basis: Moon)	*Hindu* (Basis: Moon)
January (31)	Tishri (Sep–Oct) (30)	Muharram (Sep–Oct) (30)	Caitra (Mar–Apr) (29 or 30)
February (28 or 29)	Heshvan (Oct–Nov) (29 or 30)	Safar (Oct–Nov) (29)	Vaisakha (Apr–May) (29 or 30)
March (31)	Kislev (Nov–Dec) (29 or 30)	Rabi I (Nov–Dec) (30)	Jyaistha (May–Jun) (29 or 30)
April (30)	Tevet (Dec–Jan) (29)	Rabi II (Dec–Jan) (29)	Asadha (Jun–Jul) (29 or 30)
May (31)	Shevat (Jan–Feb) (30)	Jumada I (Jan–Feb) (30)	Dvitiya Asadha *certain leap years*
June (30)	Adar (Feb–Mar) (29 or 30)	Jumada II (Feb–Mar) (29)	Svrana (Jul–Aug) (29 or 30)
July (31)	Adar Sheni *leap years only*	Rajab (Mar–Apr) (30)	Dvitiya Sravana *certain leap years*
August (31)	Nisan (Mar–Apr) (30)	Shaban (Apr–May) (29)	Bhadrapada (Aug–Sep) (29 or 30)
September (30)	Iyar (Apr–May) (29)	Ramadan (May–Jun) (30)	Asvina (Sep–Oct) (29 or 30)
October (31)	Sivan (May–Jun) (30)	Shawwal (Jun–Jul) (29)	Karttika (Oct–Nov) (29 or 30)
November (30)	Tammuz (Jun–Jul) (29)	Dhu al-Qadah (Jul–Aug) (30)	Margasirsa (Nov–Dec) (29 or 30)
December (31)	Av (Jul–Aug) (30)	Dhu al-Hijjah (Aug–Sep) (29 or 30)	Pausa (Dec–Jan) (29 or 30)
	Elul (Aug–Sep) (29)		Magha (Jan–Feb) (29 or 30)
			Phalguna (Feb–Mar) (29 or 30)

MONTHS: ASSOCIATIONS

In many Western countries, the months are traditionally associated with gemstones and flowers. There is considerable variation. The following combinations are widely recognized in North America and the UK.

Month	*Gemstone*	*Flower*
January	Garnet	Carnation, Snowdrop
February	Amethyst	Primrose, Violet
March	Aquamarine, Bloodstone	Jonquil, Violet
April	Diamond	Daisy, Sweet Pea
May	Emerald	Hawthorn, Lily of the Valley
June	Alexandrite, Moonstone, Pearl	Honeysuckle, Rose
July	Ruby	Larkspur, Water Lily
August	Peridot, Sardonyx	Gladiolus, Poppy
September	Sapphire	Aster, Morning Glory
October	Opal, Tourmaline	Calendula, Cosmos
November	Topaz	Chrysanthemum
December	Turquoise, Zircon	Holly, Narcissus, Poinsettia

THE SEASONS

N hemisphere	*S hemisphere*	*Duration*
Spring	Autumn	From vernal/autumnal equinox (*c.* 21 Mar) to summer/winter solstice (*c.* 21 Jun)
Summer	Winter	From summer/winter solstice (*c.* 21 Jun) to autumnal/spring equinox (*c.* 23 Sept)
Autumn	Spring	From autumnal/spring equinox (*c.* 23 Sept) to winter/summer solstice (*c.* 21 Dec)
Winter	Summer	From winter/summer solstice (*c.* 21 Dec) to vernal/autumnal equinox (*c.* 21 Mar)

WEDDING ANNIVERSARIES

In many Western countries, different wedding anniversaries have become associated with gifts of different materials. There is some variation between countries.

1st	Cotton	10th	Tin	30th	Pearl
2nd	Paper	11th	Steel	35th	Coral
3rd	Leather	12th	Silk, Linen	40th	Ruby
4th	Fruit, Flowers	13th	Lace	45th	Sapphire
5th	Wood	14th	Ivory	50th	Gold
6th	Sugar	15th	Crystal	55th	Emerald
7th	Copper, Wool	20th	China	60th	Diamond
8th	Bronze, Pottery	25th	Silver	70th	Platinum
9th	Pottery, Willow				

CHINESE ANIMAL YEARS AND TIMES 1948-2007

Chinese	*English*	*Years*					*Time of day (hours)*
Shu	Rat	1948	1960	1972	1984	1996	2300–0100
Niu	Ox	1949	1961	1973	1985	1997	0100–0300
Hu	Tiger	1950	1962	1974	1986	1998	0300–0500
T'u	Hare	1951	1963	1975	1987	1999	0500–0700
Lung	Dragon	1952	1964	1976	1988	2000	0700–0900
She	Serpent	1953	1965	1977	1989	2001	0900–1100
Ma	Horse	1954	1966	1978	1990	2002	1100–1300
Yang	Sheep	1955	1967	1979	1991	2003	1300–1500
Hou	Monkey	1956	1968	1980	1992	2004	1500–1700
Chi	Cock	1957	1969	1981	1993	2005	1700–1900
Kou	Dog	1958	1970	1982	1994	2006	1900–2100
Chu	Boar	1959	1971	1983	1995	2007	2100–2300

MAJOR HINDU FESTIVALS

S = Sukla, 'waxing fortnight'.
K = Krishna 'waning fortnight'.

Caitra	*S* 9	Ramanavami (Birthday of Lord Rama)
Asadha	*S* 2	Rathayatra (Pilgrimage of the Chariot at Jagannath)
Sravana	*S* 11–15	Jhulanayatra ('Swinging the Lord Krishna')
Sravana	*S* 15	Rakshabandhana ('Tying on lucky threads')
Bhadrapada	*K* 8	Janamashtami (Birthday of Lord Krishna)
Asvina	*S* 7–10	Durga-puja (Homage to Goddess Durga) (*Bengal*)
Asvina	*S* 1–10	Navaratri (Festival of 'Nine Nights')
Asvina	*S* 15	Lakshmi-puja (Homage to Goddess Lakshmi)
Asvina	*K* 15	Diwali, Dipavali ('String of lights')
Kartikka	*S* 15	Guru Nanak Jananti (Birthday of Guru Nanak)
Magha	*K* 5	Sarasvati-puja (Homage to Goddess Sarasvati)
Magha	*K* 13	Maha-sivaratri (Great Night of Lord Shiva)
Phalguna	*S* 14	Holi (Festival of fire)
Phalguna	*S* 15	Dolayatra (Swing Festival) (*Bengal*)

MAJOR ISLAMIC FESTIVALS

1	Muharram	New Year's Day; starts on the day which celebrates Mohammed's departure from Mecca to Medina in AD 622
12	Rabi I	Birthday of Mohammed (Mawlid al-Nabi) AD 572; celebrated throughout month of Rabi I
27	Rajab	'Night of Ascent' (Laylat al-Mi'raj) of Mohammed to Heaven
1	Ramadan	Beginning of month of fasting during daylight hours
27	Ramadan	'Night of Power' (Laylat al-Qadr); sending down of the Koran to Mohammed
1	Shawwal	'Feast of breaking the Fast' ('Id al-Fitr); marks the end of Ramadan
8–13	Dhu-l-Hijja	Annual pilgrimage ceremonies at and around Mecca; month during which the great pilgrimage (Hajj) should be made
10	Dhu-l-Hijja	Feast of the Sacrifice ('Id al-Adha)

MAJOR JEWISH FESTIVALS

For Gregorian Calendar equivalents, see RR000

1–2	Tishri	Rosh Hashana (New Year)
3	Tishri	Tzom Gedaliahu (Fast of Gedaliah)
10	Tishri	Yom Kippur (Day of Atonement)
15–21	Tishri	Sukkoth (Feast of Tabernacles)
22	Tishri	Shemini Atzeret (8th Day of the Solemn Assembly)
23	Tishri	Simhat Torah (Rejoicing of the Law)
25	Kislev – 1–2 Tevet	Hanukkah (Feast of Dedication)
10	Tevet	Asara be-Tevet (Fast of 10th Tevet)
13	Adar	Taanit Esther (Fast of Esther)
14–15	Adar	Purim (Feast of Lots)
15–22	Nisan	Pesach (Passover)
27	Nisan	Holocaust Remembrance day
5	Iyar	Israel Independence Day
18	Iyar	Lag B'Omer (Counting of barley sheaves)
6–7	Sivan	Shavuoth (Feast of Weeks)
17	Tammuz	Shiva Asar be-Tammuz (Fast of 17th Tammuz)
9	Av	Tisha be-Av (Fast of 9th Av)

MAJOR JAPANESE FESTIVALS

1–3	Jan	Oshogatsu (New Year)
3	Mar	Ohinamatsuri (Doll *or* Girls' Festival)
5	May	Tango no Sekku (Boys' Festival)
7	Jul	Hoshi matsuri *or* Tanabata (Star Festival)
13–15	Jul	Obon (Buddhist All Souls)
(*or* 13–15	Aug)	

MAJOR IMMOVABLE CHRISTIAN FEASTS

1 Jan	Solemnity of Mary, Mother of God
6 Jan	Epiphany
7 Jan	Christmas Day (*Eastern Orthodox*)[1]
11 Jan	Baptism of Jesus
25 Jan	Conversion of Apostle Paul
2 Feb	Presentation of Jesus (*Candlemas Day*)
22 Feb	The Chair of Peter, Apostle
25 Mar	Annunciation to the Virgin Mary (*Lady Day*)
24 Jun	Birth of John the Baptist
6 Aug	Transfiguration
15 Aug	Assumption of the Virgin Mary
22 Aug	Queenship of Mary
8 Sep	Birthday of the Virgin Mary
14 Sep	Exaltation of the Holy Cross
2 Oct	Guardian Angels
1 Nov	All Saints
2 Nov	All Souls
9 Nov	Dedication of the Lateran Basilica
21 Nov	Presentation of the Virgin Mary
8 Dec	Immaculate Conception
25 Dec	Christmas Day
28 Dec	Holy Innocents

[1] Fixed feasts in the Julian calendar fall 13 days later than the Gregorian calendar date.

MOVABLE CHRISTIAN FEASTS, 1999–2010

Year	*Ash Wednesday*	*Easter*	*Ascension*	*Whit Sunday*	*First Sunday in Advent*	*Trinity Sunday*	*Corpus Christi*
1999	17 Feb	4 Apr	13 May	23 May	28 Nov	30 May	3 Jun
2000	8 Mar	23 Apr	1 Jun	11 Jun	3 Dec	18 Jun	22 Jun
2001	28 Feb	15 Apr	24 May	3 Jun	2 Dec	10 Jun	14 Jun
2002	13 Feb	31 Mar	9 May	19 May	1 Dec	26 May	30 May
2003	5 Mar	20 Apr	29 May	8 Jun	30 Nov	15 Jun	19 Jun
2004	25 Feb	11 Apr	20 May	30 May	28 Nov	6 Jun	10 Jun
2005	9 Feb	27 Mar	5 May	15 May	27 Nov	22 May	26 May
2006	1 Mar	16 Apr	25 May	4 Jun	3 Dec	11 Jun	15 Jun
2007	21 Feb	8 Apr	17 May	27 May	2 Dec	3 Jun	7 Jun
2008	6 Feb	23 Mar	1 May	11 May	30 Nov	18 May	22 May
2009	25 Feb	12 Apr	21 May	31 May	29 Nov	7 Jun	11 Jun
2010	17 Feb	4 Apr	13 May	23 May	28 Nov	30 May	3 Jun

Ash Wednesday, the first day of Lent, can fall at the earliest on 4 Feb and at the latest on 10 Mar.

Palm (Passion) Sunday is the Sunday before Easter; Good Friday is the Friday before Easter; Holy Saturday (often referred to as Easter Saturday) is the Saturday before Easter; Easter Saturday, in traditional usage, is the Saturday following Easter.

Easter Day can fall at the earliest on 22 Mar and at the latest on 25 Apr. Ascension Day can fall at the earliest on 30 Apr and at the latest on 3 Jun. Whit Sunday can fall at the earliest on 10 May and at the latest on 13 Jun, it commemorates the day of Pentecost. There are not fewer than 22

PERPETUAL CALENDAR 1821–2020

The calendar for each year is given under the corresponding letter below.

1821 C	1841 K	1861 E	1881 M	1901 E	1921 M	1941 G	1961 A	1981 I	2001 C
1822 E	1842 M	1862 G	1882 A	1902 G	1922 A	1942 I	1962 C	1982 K	2002 E
1823 G	1843 A	1863 I	1883 C	1903 I	1923 C	1943 K	1963 E	1983 M	2003 G
1824 J	1844 D	1864 L	1884 F	1904 L	1924 F	1944 N	1964 H	1984 B	2004 J
1825 M	1845 G	1865 A	1885 I	1905 A	1925 I	1945 C	1965 K	1985 E	2005 M
1826 A	1846 I	1866 C	1886 K	1906 C	1926 K	1946 E	1966 M	1986 G	2006 A
1827 C	1847 K	1867 E	1887 M	1907 E	1927 M	1947 G	1967 A	1987 I	2007 C
1828 F	1848 N	1868 H	1888 B	1908 H	1928 B	1948 J	1968 D	1988 L	2008 F
1829 I	1849 C	1869 K	1889 E	1909 K	1929 E	1949 M	1969 G	1989 A	2009 I
1830 K	1850 E	1870 M	1890 G	1910 M	1930 G	1950 A	1970 I	1990 C	2010 K
1831 M	1851 G	1871 A	1891 I	1911 A	1931 I	1951 C	1971 K	1991 E	2011 M
1832 B	1852 J	1872 D	1892 L	1912 D	1932 L	1952 F	1972 N	1992 H	2012 B
1833 E	1853 M	1873 G	1893 A	1913 G	1933 A	1953 I	1973 C	1993 K	2013 E
1834 G	1854 A	1874 I	1894 C	1914 I	1934 C	1954 K	1974 E	1994 M	2014 G
1835 I	1855 C	1875 K	1895 E	1915 K	1935 E	1955 M	1975 G	1995 A	2015 I
1836 L	1856 F	1876 N	1896 H	1916 N	1936 H	1956 B	1976 J	1996 D	2016 L
1837 A	1857 I	1877 C	1897 K	1917 C	1937 K	1957 E	1977 M	1997 G	2017 A
1838 C	1858 K	1878 E	1898 M	1918 E	1938 M	1958 G	1978 A	1998 I	2018 C
1839 E	1859 M	1879 G	1899 A	1919 G	1939 A	1959 I	1979 C	1999 K	2019 E
1840 H	1860 B	1880 J	1900 C	1920 J	1940 D	1960 L	1980 F	2000 N	2020 H

A

January
S M T W T F S
1 2 3 4 5 6 7
8 9 10 11 12 13 14
15 16 17 18 19 20 21
22 23 24 25 26 27 28
29 30 31

February
S M T W T F S
1 2 3 4
5 6 7 8 9 10 11
12 13 14 15 16 17 18
19 20 21 22 23 24 25
26 27 28

March
S M T W T F S
1 2 3 4
5 6 7 8 9 10 11
12 13 14 15 16 17 18
19 20 21 22 23 24 25
26 27 28 29 30 31

April
S M T W T F S
1
2 3 4 5 6 7 8
9 10 11 12 13 14 15
16 17 18 19 20 21 22
23 24 25 26 27 28 29
30

May
1 2 3 4 5 6
7 8 9 10 11 12 13
14 15 16 17 18 19 20
21 22 23 24 25 26 27
28 29 30 31

June
1 2 3
4 5 6 7 8 9 10
11 12 13 14 15 16 17
18 19 20 21 22 23 24
25 26 27 28 29 30

July
1
2 3 4 5 6 7 8
9 10 11 12 13 14 15
16 17 18 19 20 21 22
23 24 25 26 27 28 29
30 31

August
1 2 3 4 5
6 7 8 9 10 11 12
13 14 15 16 17 18 19
20 21 22 23 24 25 26
27 28 29 30 31

September
1 2
3 4 5 6 7 8 9
10 11 12 13 14 15 16
17 18 19 20 21 22 23
24 25 26 27 28 29 30

October
1 2 3 4 5 6 7
8 9 10 11 12 13 14
15 16 17 18 19 20 21
22 23 24 25 26 27 28
29 30 31

November
1 2 3 4
5 6 7 8 9 10 11
12 13 14 15 16 17 18
19 20 21 22 23 24 25
26 27 28 29 30

December
1 2
3 4 5 6 7 8 9
10 11 12 13 14 15 16
17 18 19 20 21 22 23
24 25 26 27 28 29 30
31

B (leap year)

January
S M T W T F S
1 2 3 4 5 6 7
8 9 10 11 12 13 14
15 16 17 18 19 20 21
22 23 24 25 26 27 28
29 30 31

February
S M T W T F S
1 2 3 4
5 6 7 8 9 10 11
12 13 14 15 16 17 18
19 20 21 22 23 24 25
26 27 28 29

March
S M T W T F S
1 2 3
4 5 6 7 8 9 10
11 12 13 14 15 16 17
18 19 20 21 22 23 24
25 26 27 28 29 30 31

April
S M T W T F S
1 2 3 4 5 6 7
8 9 10 11 12 13 14
15 16 17 18 19 20 21
22 23 24 25 26 27 28
29 30

May
1 2 3 4 5
6 7 8 9 10 11 12
13 14 15 16 17 18 19
20 21 22 23 24 25 26
27 28 29 30 31

June
1 2
3 4 5 6 7 8 9
10 11 12 13 14 15 16
17 18 19 20 21 22 23
24 25 26 27 28 29 30

July
1 2 3 4 5 6 7
8 9 10 11 12 13 14
15 16 17 18 19 20 21
22 23 24 25 26 27 28
29 30 31

August
1 2 3 4
5 6 7 8 9 10 11
12 13 14 15 16 17 18
19 20 21 22 23 24 25
26 27 28 29 30 31

September
1
2 3 4 5 6 7 8
9 10 11 12 13 14 15
16 17 18 19 20 21 22
23 24 25 26 27 28 29
30

October
1 2 3 4 5 6
7 8 9 10 11 12 13
14 15 16 17 18 19 20
21 22 23 24 25 26 27
28 29 30 31

November
1 2 3
4 5 6 7 8 9 10
11 12 13 14 15 16 17
18 19 20 21 22 23 24
25 26 27 28 29 30

December
1
2 3 4 5 6 7 8
9 10 11 12 13 14 15
16 17 18 19 20 21 22
23 24 25 26 27 28 29
30 31

C

January
S M T W T F S
1 2 3 4 5 6
7 8 9 10 11 12 13
14 15 16 17 18 19 20
21 22 23 24 25 26 27
28 29 30 31

February
S M T W T F S
1 2 3
4 5 6 7 8 9 10
11 12 13 14 15 16 17
18 19 20 21 22 23 24
25 26 27 28

March
S M T W T F S
1 2 3
4 5 6 7 8 9 10
11 12 13 14 15 16 17
18 19 20 21 22 23 24
25 26 27 28 29 30 31

April
S M T W T F S
1 2 3 4 5 6 7
8 9 10 11 12 13 14
15 16 17 18 19 20 21
22 23 24 25 26 27 28
29 30

May
1 2 3 4 5
6 7 8 9 10 11 12
13 14 15 16 17 18 19
20 21 22 23 24 25 26
27 28 29 30 31

June
1 2
3 4 5 6 7 8 9
10 11 12 13 14 15 16
17 18 19 20 21 22 23
24 25 26 27 28 29 30

July
1 2 3 4 5 6 7
8 9 10 11 12 13 14
15 16 17 18 19 20 21
22 23 24 25 26 27 28
29 30 31

August
1 2 3 4
5 6 7 8 9 10 11
12 13 14 15 16 17 18
19 20 21 22 23 24 25
26 27 28 29 30 31

September
1
2 3 4 5 6 7 8
9 10 11 12 13 14 15
16 17 18 19 20 21 22
23 24 25 26 27 28 29
30

October
1 2 3 4 5 6
7 8 9 10 11 12 13
14 15 16 17 18 19 20
21 22 23 24 25 26 27
28 29 30 31

November
1 2 3
4 5 6 7 8 9 10
11 12 13 14 15 16 17
18 19 20 21 22 23 24
25 26 27 28 29 30

December
1
2 3 4 5 6 7 8
9 10 11 12 13 14 15
16 17 18 19 20 21 22
23 24 25 26 27 28 29
30 31

D (leap year)

January
S M T W T F S
1 2 3 4 5 6
7 8 9 10 11 12 13
14 15 16 17 18 19 20
21 22 23 24 25 26 27
28 29 30 31

February
S M T W T F S
1 2 3
4 5 6 7 8 9 10
11 12 13 14 15 16 17
18 19 20 21 22 23 24
25 26 27 28 29

March
S M T W T F S
1 2
3 4 5 6 7 8 9
10 11 12 13 14 15 16
17 18 19 20 21 22 23
24 25 26 27 28 29 30
31

April
S M T W T F S
1 2 3 4 5 6
7 8 9 10 11 12 13
14 15 16 17 18 19 20
21 22 23 24 25 26 27
28 29 30

May
1 2 3 4
5 6 7 8 9 10 11
12 13 14 15 16 17 18
19 20 21 22 23 24 25
26 27 28 29 30 31

June
1
2 3 4 5 6 7 8
9 10 11 12 13 14 15
16 17 18 19 20 21 22
23 24 25 26 27 28 29
30

July
1 2 3 4 5 6
7 8 9 10 11 12 13
14 15 16 17 18 19 20
21 22 23 24 25 26 27
28 29 30 31

August
1 2 3
4 5 6 7 8 9 10
11 12 13 14 15 16 17
18 19 20 21 22 23 24
25 26 27 28 29 30 31

September
1 2 3 4 5 6 7
8 9 10 11 12 13 14
15 16 17 18 19 20 21
22 23 24 25 26 27 28
29 30

October
1 2 3 4 5
6 7 8 9 10 11 12
13 14 15 16 17 18 19
20 21 22 23 24 25 26
27 28 29 30 31

November
1 2
3 4 5 6 7 8 9
10 11 12 13 14 15 16
17 18 19 20 21 22 23
24 25 26 27 28 29 30

December
1 2 3 4 5 6 7
8 9 10 11 12 13 14
15 16 17 18 19 20 21
22 23 24 25 26 27 28
29 30 31

E

January
S M T W T F S
1 2 3 4 5
6 7 8 9 10 11 12
13 14 15 16 17 18 19
20 21 22 23 24 25 26
27 28 29 30 31

February
S M T W T F S
1 2
3 4 5 6 7 8 9
10 11 12 13 14 15 16
17 18 19 20 21 22 23
24 25 26 27 28

March
S M T W T F S
1 2
3 4 5 6 7 8 9
10 11 12 13 14 15 16
17 18 19 20 21 22 23
24 25 26 27 28 29 30
31

April
S M T W T F S
1 2 3 4 5 6
7 8 9 10 11 12 13
14 15 16 17 18 19 20
21 22 23 24 25 26 27
28 29 30

May
1 2 3 4
5 6 7 8 9 10 11
12 13 14 15 16 17 18
19 20 21 22 23 24 25
26 27 28 29 30 31

June
1
2 3 4 5 6 7 8
9 10 11 12 13 14 15
16 17 18 19 20 21 22
23 24 25 26 27 28 29
30

July
1 2 3 4 5 6
7 8 9 10 11 12 13
14 15 16 17 18 19 20
21 22 23 24 25 26 27
28 29 30 31

August
1 2 3
4 5 6 7 8 9 10
11 12 13 14 15 16 17
18 19 20 21 22 23 24
25 26 27 28 29 30 31

September
1 2 3 4 5 6 7
8 9 10 11 12 13 14
15 16 17 18 19 20 21
22 23 24 25 26 27 28
29 30

October
1 2 3 4 5
6 7 8 9 10 11 12
13 14 15 16 17 18 19
20 21 22 23 24 25 26
27 28 29 30 31

November
1 2
3 4 5 6 7 8 9
10 11 12 13 14 15 16
17 18 19 20 21 22 23
24 25 26 27 28 29 30

December
1 2 3 4 5 6 7
8 9 10 11 12 13 14
15 16 17 18 19 20 21
22 23 24 25 26 27 28
29 30 31

F (leap year)

January
S M T W T F S
1 2 3 4 5
6 7 8 9 10 11 12
13 14 15 16 17 18 19
20 21 22 23 24 25 26
27 28 29 30 31

February
S M T W T F S
1 2
3 4 5 6 7 8 9
10 11 12 13 14 15 16
17 18 19 20 21 22 23
24 25 26 27 28 29

March
S M T W T F S
1
2 3 4 5 6 7 8
9 10 11 12 13 14 15
16 17 18 19 20 21 22
23 24 25 26 27 28 29
30 31

April
S M T W T F S
1 2 3 4 5
6 7 8 9 10 11 12
13 14 15 16 17 18 19
20 21 22 23 24 25 26
27 28 29 30

May
1 2 3
4 5 6 7 8 9 10
11 12 13 14 15 16 17
18 19 20 21 22 23 24
25 26 27 28 29 30 31

June
1 2 3 4 5 6 7
8 9 10 11 12 13 14
15 16 17 18 19 20 21
22 23 24 25 26 27 28
29 30

July
1 2 3 4 5
6 7 8 9 10 11 12
13 14 15 16 17 18 19
20 21 22 23 24 25 26
27 28 29 30 31

August
1 2
3 4 5 6 7 8 9
10 11 12 13 14 15 16
17 18 19 20 21 22 23
24 25 26 27 28 29 30
31

September
1 2 3 4 5 6
7 8 9 10 11 12 13
14 15 16 17 18 19 20
21 22 23 24 25 26 27
28 29 30

October
1 2 3 4
5 6 7 8 9 10 11
12 13 14 15 16 17 18
19 20 21 22 23 24 25
26 27 28 29 30 31

November
1
2 3 4 5 6 7 8
9 10 11 12 13 14 15
16 17 18 19 20 21 22
23 24 25 26 27 28 29
30

December
1 2 3 4 5 6
7 8 9 10 11 12 13
14 15 16 17 18 19 20
21 22 23 24 25 26 27
28 29 30 31

PERPETUAL CALENDAR 1821–2020 (continued)

G

January

S	M	T	W	T	F	S
			1	2	3	4
5	6	7	8	9	10	11
12	13	14	15	16	17	18
19	20	21	22	23	24	25
26	27	28	29	30	31	

February

S	M	T	W	T	F	S
						1
2	3	4	5	6	7	8
9	10	11	12	13	14	15
16	17	18	19	20	21	22
23	24	25	26	27	28	

March

S	M	T	W	T	F	S
						1
2	3	4	5	6	7	8
9	10	11	12	13	14	15
16	17	18	19	20	21	22
23	24	25	26	27	28	29
30	31					

April

S	M	T	W	T	F	S
		1	2	3	4	5
6	7	8	9	10	11	12
13	14	15	16	17	18	19
20	21	22	23	24	25	26
27	28	29	30			

May

S	M	T	W	T	F	S
				1	2	3
4	5	6	7	8	9	10
11	12	13	14	15	16	17
18	19	20	21	22	23	24
25	26	27	28	29	30	31

June

S	M	T	W	T	F	S
1	2	3	4	5	6	7
8	9	10	11	12	13	14
15	16	17	18	19	20	21
22	23	24	25	26	27	28
29	30					

July

S	M	T	W	T	F	S
		1	2	3	4	5
6	7	8	9	10	11	12
13	14	15	16	17	18	19
20	21	22	23	24	25	26
27	28	29	30	31		

August

S	M	T	W	T	F	S
					1	2
3	4	5	6	7	8	9
10	11	12	13	14	15	16
17	18	19	20	21	22	23
24	25	26	27	28	29	30
31						

September

S	M	T	W	T	F	S
	1	2	3	4	5	6
7	8	9	10	11	12	13
14	15	16	17	18	19	20
21	22	23	24	25	26	27
28	29	30				

October

S	M	T	W	T	F	S
			1	2	3	4
5	6	7	8	9	10	11
12	13	14	15	16	17	18
19	20	21	22	23	24	25
26	27	28	29	30	31	

November

S	M	T	W	T	F	S
						1
2	3	4	5	6	7	8
9	10	11	12	13	14	15
16	17	18	19	20	21	22
23	24	25	26	27	28	29
30						

December

S	M	T	W	T	F	S
	1	2	3	4	5	6
7	8	9	10	11	12	13
14	15	16	17	18	19	20
21	22	23	24	25	26	27
28	29	30	31			

H (leap year)

January

S	M	T	W	T	F	S
			1	2	3	4
5	6	7	8	9	10	11
12	13	14	15	16	17	18
19	20	21	22	23	24	25
26	27	28	29	30	31	

February

S	M	T	W	T	F	S
						1
2	3	4	5	6	7	8
9	10	11	12	13	14	15
16	17	18	19	20	21	22
23	24	25	26	27	28	29

March

S	M	T	W	T	F	S
1	2	3	4	5	6	7
8	9	10	11	12	13	14
15	16	17	18	19	20	21
22	23	24	25	26	27	28
29	30	31				

April

S	M	T	W	T	F	S
			1	2	3	4
5	6	7	8	9	10	11
12	13	14	15	16	17	18
19	20	21	22	23	24	25
26	27	28	29	30		

May

S	M	T	W	T	F	S
					1	2
3	4	5	6	7	8	9
10	11	12	13	14	15	16
17	18	19	20	21	22	23
24	25	26	27	28	29	30
31						

June

S	M	T	W	T	F	S
	1	2	3	4	5	6
7	8	9	10	11	12	13
14	15	16	17	18	19	20
21	22	23	24	25	26	27
28	29	30				

July

S	M	T	W	T	F	S
			1	2	3	4
5	6	7	8	9	10	11
12	13	14	15	16	17	18
19	20	21	22	23	24	25
26	27	28	29	30	31	

August

S	M	T	W	T	F	S
						1
2	3	4	5	6	7	8
9	10	11	12	13	14	15
16	17	18	19	20	21	22
23	24	25	26	27	28	29
30	31					

September

S	M	T	W	T	F	S
		1	2	3	4	5
6	7	8	9	10	11	12
13	14	15	16	17	18	19
20	21	22	23	24	25	26
27	28	29	30			

October

S	M	T	W	T	F	S
				1	2	3
4	5	6	7	8	9	10
11	12	13	14	15	16	17
18	19	20	21	22	23	24
25	26	27	28	29	30	31

November

S	M	T	W	T	F	S
1	2	3	4	5	6	7
8	9	10	11	12	13	14
15	16	17	18	19	20	21
22	23	24	25	26	27	28
29	30					

December

S	M	T	W	T	F	S
		1	2	3	4	5
6	7	8	9	10	11	12
13	14	15	16	17	18	19
20	21	22	23	24	25	26
27	28	29	30	31		

I

January

S	M	T	W	T	F	S
				1	2	3
4	5	6	7	8	9	10
11	12	13	14	15	16	17
18	19	20	21	22	23	24
25	26	27	28	29	30	31

February

S	M	T	W	T	F	S
1	2	3	4	5	6	7
8	9	10	11	12	13	14
15	16	17	18	19	20	21
22	23	24	25	26	27	28

March

S	M	T	W	T	F	S
1	2	3	4	5	6	7
8	9	10	11	12	13	14
15	16	17	18	19	20	21
22	23	24	25	26	27	28
29	30	31				

April

S	M	T	W	T	F	S
			1	2	3	4
5	6	7	8	9	10	11
12	13	14	15	16	17	18
19	20	21	22	23	24	25
26	27	28	29	30		

May

S	M	T	W	T	F	S
					1	2
3	4	5	6	7	8	9
10	11	12	13	14	15	16
17	18	19	20	21	22	23
24	25	26	27	28	29	30
31						

June

S	M	T	W	T	F	S
	1	2	3	4	5	6
7	8	9	10	11	12	13
14	15	16	17	18	19	20
21	22	23	24	25	26	27
28	29	30				

July

S	M	T	W	T	F	S
			1	2	3	4
5	6	7	8	9	10	11
12	13	14	15	16	17	18
19	20	21	22	23	24	25
26	27	28	29	30	31	

August

S	M	T	W	T	F	S
						1
2	3	4	5	6	7	8
9	10	11	12	13	14	15
16	17	18	19	20	21	22
23	24	25	26	27	28	29
30	31					

September

S	M	T	W	T	F	S
		1	2	3	4	5
6	7	8	9	10	11	12
13	14	15	16	17	18	19
20	21	22	23	24	25	26
27	28	29	30			

October

S	M	T	W	T	F	S
				1	2	3
4	5	6	7	8	9	10
11	12	13	14	15	16	17
18	19	20	21	22	23	24
25	26	27	28	29	30	31

November

S	M	T	W	T	F	S
1	2	3	4	5	6	7
8	9	10	11	12	13	14
15	16	17	18	19	20	21
22	23	24	25	26	27	28
29	30					

December

S	M	T	W	T	F	S
		1	2	3	4	5
6	7	8	9	10	11	12
13	14	15	16	17	18	19
20	21	22	23	24	25	26
27	28	29	30	31		

J (leap year)

January

S	M	T	W	T	F	S
				1	2	3
4	5	6	7	8	9	10
11	12	13	14	15	16	17
18	19	20	21	22	23	24
25	26	27	28	29	30	31

February

S	M	T	W	T	F	S
1	2	3	4	5	6	7
8	9	10	11	12	13	14
15	16	17	18	19	20	21
22	23	24	25	26	27	28
29						

March

S	M	T	W	T	F	S
	1	2	3	4	5	6
7	8	9	10	11	12	13
14	15	16	17	18	19	20
21	22	23	24	25	26	27
28	29	30	31			

April

S	M	T	W	T	F	S
				1	2	3
4	5	6	7	8	9	10
11	12	13	14	15	16	17
18	19	20	21	22	23	24
25	26	27	28	29	30	

May

S	M	T	W	T	F	S
						1
2	3	4	5	6	7	8
9	10	11	12	13	14	15
16	17	18	19	20	21	22
23	24	25	26	27	28	29
30	31					

June

S	M	T	W	T	F	S
		1	2	3	4	5
6	7	8	9	10	11	12
13	14	15	16	17	18	19
20	21	22	23	24	25	26
27	28	29	30			

July

S	M	T	W	T	F	S
				1	2	3
4	5	6	7	8	9	10
11	12	13	14	15	16	17
18	19	20	21	22	23	24
25	26	27	28	29	30	31

August

S	M	T	W	T	F	S
1	2	3	4	5	6	7
8	9	10	11	12	13	14
15	16	17	18	19	20	21
22	23	24	25	26	27	28
29	30	31				

September

S	M	T	W	T	F	S
			1	2	3	4
5	6	7	8	9	10	11
12	13	14	15	16	17	18
19	20	21	22	23	24	25
26	27	28	29	30		

October

S	M	T	W	T	F	S
					1	2
3	4	5	6	7	8	9
10	11	12	13	14	15	16
17	18	19	20	21	22	23
24	25	26	27	28	29	30
31						

November

S	M	T	W	T	F	S
	1	2	3	4	5	6
7	8	9	10	11	12	13
14	15	16	17	18	19	20
21	22	23	24	25	26	27
28	29	30				

December

S	M	T	W	T	F	S
			1	2	3	4
5	6	7	8	9	10	11
12	13	14	15	16	17	18
19	20	21	22	23	24	25
26	27	28	29	30	31	

K

January

S	M	T	W	T	F	S
					1	2
3	4	5	6	7	8	9
10	11	12	13	14	15	16
17	18	19	20	21	22	23
24	25	26	27	28	29	30
31						

February

S	M	T	W	T	F	S
	1	2	3	4	5	6
7	8	9	10	11	12	13
14	15	16	17	18	19	20
21	22	23	24	25	26	27
28						

March

S	M	T	W	T	F	S
	1	2	3	4	5	6
7	8	9	10	11	12	13
14	15	16	17	18	19	20
21	22	23	24	25	26	27
28	29	30	31			

April

S	M	T	W	T	F	S
				1	2	3
4	5	6	7	8	9	10
11	12	13	14	15	16	17
18	19	20	21	22	23	24
25	26	27	28	29	30	

May

S	M	T	W	T	F	S
						1
2	3	4	5	6	7	8
9	10	11	12	13	14	15
16	17	18	19	20	21	22
23	24	25	26	27	28	29
30	31					

June

S	M	T	W	T	F	S
		1	2	3	4	5
6	7	8	9	10	11	12
13	14	15	16	17	18	19
20	21	22	23	24	25	26
27	28	29	30			

July

S	M	T	W	T	F	S
				1	2	3
4	5	6	7	8	9	10
11	12	13	14	15	16	17
18	19	20	21	22	23	24
25	26	27	28	29	30	31

August

S	M	T	W	T	F	S
1	2	3	4	5	6	7
8	9	10	11	12	13	14
15	16	17	18	19	20	21
22	23	24	25	26	27	28
29	30	31				

September

S	M	T	W	T	F	S
			1	2	3	4
5	6	7	8	9	10	11
12	13	14	15	16	17	18
19	20	21	22	23	24	25
26	27	28	29	30		

October

S	M	T	W	T	F	S
					1	2
3	4	5	6	7	8	9
10	11	12	13	14	15	16
17	18	19	20	21	22	23
24	25	26	27	28	29	30
31						

November

S	M	T	W	T	F	S
	1	2	3	4	5	6
7	8	9	10	11	12	13
14	15	16	17	18	19	20
21	22	23	24	25	26	27
28	29	30				

December

S	M	T	W	T	F	S
			1	2	3	4
5	6	7	8	9	10	11
12	13	14	15	16	17	18
19	20	21	22	23	24	25
26	27	28	29	30	31	

L (leap year)

January

S	M	T	W	T	F	S
					1	2
3	4	5	6	7	8	9
10	11	12	13	14	15	16
17	18	19	20	21	22	23
24	25	26	27	28	29	30
31						

February

S	M	T	W	T	F	S
	1	2	3	4	5	6
7	8	9	10	11	12	13
14	15	16	17	18	19	20
21	22	23	24	25	26	27
28	29					

March

S	M	T	W	T	F	S
		1	2	3	4	5
6	7	8	9	10	11	12
13	14	15	16	17	18	19
20	21	22	23	24	25	26
27	28	29	30	31		

April

S	M	T	W	T	F	S
					1	2
3	4	5	6	7	8	9
10	11	12	13	14	15	16
17	18	19	20	21	22	23
24	25	26	27	28	29	30

May

S	M	T	W	T	F	S
1	2	3	4	5	6	7
8	9	10	11	12	13	14
15	16	17	18	19	20	21
22	23	24	25	26	27	28
29	30	31				

June

S	M	T	W	T	F	S
			1	2	3	4
5	6	7	8	9	10	11
12	13	14	15	16	17	18
19	20	21	22	23	24	25
26	27	28	29	30		

July

S	M	T	W	T	F	S
					1	2
3	4	5	6	7	8	9
10	11	12	13	14	15	16
17	18	19	20	21	22	23
24	25	26	27	28	29	30
31						

August

S	M	T	W	T	F	S
	1	2	3	4	5	6
7	8	9	10	11	12	13
14	15	16	17	18	19	20
21	22	23	24	25	26	27
28	29	30	31			

September

S	M	T	W	T	F	S
				1	2	3
4	5	6	7	8	9	10
11	12	13	14	15	16	17
18	19	20	21	22	23	24
25	26	27	28	29	30	

October

S	M	T	W	T	F	S
						1
2	3	4	5	6	7	8
9	10	11	12	13	14	15
16	17	18	19	20	21	22
23	24	25	26	27	28	29
30	31					

November

S	M	T	W	T	F	S
		1	2	3	4	5
6	7	8	9	10	11	12
13	14	15	16	17	18	19
20	21	22	23	24	25	26
27	28	29	30			

December

S	M	T	W	T	F	S
				1	2	3
4	5	6	7	8	9	10
11	12	13	14	15	16	17
18	19	20	21	22	23	24
25	26	27	28	29	30	31

M

January

S	M	T	W	T	F	S
						1
2	3	4	5	6	7	8
9	10	11	12	13	14	15
16	17	18	19	20	21	22
23	24	25	26	27	28	29
30	31					

February

S	M	T	W	T	F	S
		1	2	3	4	5
6	7	8	9	10	11	12
13	14	15	16	17	18	19
20	21	22	23	24	25	26
27	28					

March

S	M	T	W	T	F	S
		1	2	3	4	5
6	7	8	9	10	11	12
13	14	15	16	17	18	19
20	21	22	23	24	25	26
27	28	29	30	31		

April

S	M	T	W	T	F	S
					1	2
3	4	5	6	7	8	9
10	11	12	13	14	15	16
17	18	19	20	21	22	23
24	25	26	27	28	29	30

May

S	M	T	W	T	F	S
1	2	3	4	5	6	7
8	9	10	11	12	13	14
15	16	17	18	19	20	21
22	23	24	25	26	27	28
29	30	31				

June

S	M	T	W	T	F	S
			1	2	3	4
5	6	7	8	9	10	11
12	13	14	15	16	17	18
19	20	21	22	23	24	25
26	27	28	29	30		

July

S	M	T	W	T	F	S
					1	2
3	4	5	6	7	8	9
10	11	12	13	14	15	16
17	18	19	20	21	22	23
24	25	26	27	28	29	30
31						

August

S	M	T	W	T	F	S
	1	2	3	4	5	6
7	8	9	10	11	12	13
14	15	16	17	18	19	20
21	22	23	24	25	26	27
28	29	30	31			

September

S	M	T	W	T	F	S
				1	2	3
4	5	6	7	8	9	10
11	12	13	14	15	16	17
18	19	20	21	22	23	24
25	26	27	28	29	30	

October

S	M	T	W	T	F	S
						1
2	3	4	5	6	7	8
9	10	11	12	13	14	15
16	17	18	19	20	21	22
23	24	25	26	27	28	29
30	31					

November

S	M	T	W	T	F	S
		1	2	3	4	5
6	7	8	9	10	11	12
13	14	15	16	17	18	19
20	21	22	23	24	25	26
27	28	29	30			

December

S	M	T	W	T	F	S
				1	2	3
4	5	6	7	8	9	10
11	12	13	14	15	16	17
18	19	20	21	22	23	24
25	26	27	28	29	30	31

N (leap year)

January

S	M	T	W	T	F	S
						1
2	3	4	5	6	7	8
9	10	11	12	13	14	15
16	17	18	19	20	21	22
23	24	25	26	27	28	29
30	31					

February

S	M	T	W	T	F	S
		1	2	3	4	5
6	7	8	9	10	11	12
13	14	15	16	17	18	19
20	21	22	23	24	25	26
27	28	29				

March

S	M	T	W	T	F	S
			1	2	3	4
5	6	7	8	9	10	11
12	13	14	15	16	17	18
19	20	21	22	23	24	25
26	27	28	29	30	31	

April

S	M	T	W	T	F	S
						1
2	3	4	5	6	7	8
9	10	11	12	13	14	15
16	17	18	19	20	21	22
23	24	25	26	27	28	29
30						

May

S	M	T	W	T	F	S
	1	2	3	4	5	6
7	8	9	10	11	12	13
14	15	16	17	18	19	20
21	22	23	24	25	26	27
28	29	30	31			

June

S	M	T	W	T	F	S
				1	2	3
4	5	6	7	8	9	10
11	12	13	14	15	16	17
18	19	20	21	22	23	24
25	26	27	28	29	30	

July

S	M	T	W	T	F	S
						1
2	3	4	5	6	7	8
9	10	11	12	13	14	15
16	17	18	19	20	21	22
23	24	25	26	27	28	29
30	31					

August

S	M	T	W	T	F	S
		1	2	3	4	5
6	7	8	9	10	11	12
13	14	15	16	17	18	19
20	21	22	23	24	25	26
27	28	29	30	31		

September

S	M	T	W	T	F	S
					1	2
3	4	5	6	7	8	9
10	11	12	13	14	15	16
17	18	19	20	21	22	23
24	25	26	27	28	29	30

October

S	M	T	W	T	F	S
1	2	3	4	5	6	7
8	9	10	11	12	13	14
15	16	17	18	19	20	21
22	23	24	25	26	27	28
29	30	31				

November

S	M	T	W	T	F	S
			1	2	3	4
5	6	7	8	9	10	11
12	13	14	15	16	17	18
19	20	21	22	23	24	25
26	27	28	29	30		

December

S	M	T	W	T	F	S
					1	2
3	4	5	6	7	8	9
10	11	12	13	14	15	16
17	18	19	20	21	22	23
24	25	26	27	28	29	30
31						

Nations of the World

GENERAL DATA

For detailed information about each country, see the entries and maps located alphabetically in the main body of the encyclopedia.

In the case of countries that do not use the Roman alphabet (such as the Arabic countries), there is variation in the spelling of names and currencies, depending on the system of transliteration used.

Where more than one language is shown with a country, the status of the languages may not be equal. Some languages have a 'semi-official' status, or are used for a restricted set of purposes, such as trade or tourism.

Population census estimates are for 1995 or later.

English name	*Local name*	*Official name (in English)*	*Capital (English name in parentheses)*	*Official language(s) (in English)*	*Currency*	*Population*
Afghanistan	Afghānestān	Republic of Afghanistan	Kābul	Dari, Pushtu	1 Afghani (Af) = 100 puls	21 017 000
Albania	Shqipërisë	Republic of Albania	Tiranë (Tirana)	Albanian	1 Lek (L) = 100 qintars	3 549 000
Algeria	Al-Jazā'ir (Arabic); Algérie (French)	Democratic and Popular Republic of Algeria	El Djazair (Algiers)	Arabic	1 Algerian Dinar (AD, DA) = 100 centimes	28 513 000
Andorra	Andorra	Principality of Andorra; the Valleys of Andorra	Andorra La Vella	Catalan, French	1 French Franc (Fr) = 100 centimes; 1 Peseta (Pta) = 100 céntimos	67 900
Angola	Angola	People's Republic of Angola	Luanda	Portuguese	1 New Kwanza (kw, kz) = 100 lweis	11 539 000
Antigua and Barbuda	Antigua and Barbuda	Antigua and Barbuda	St John's	English	1 East Caribbean Dollar (EC$) = 100 cents	63 900
Argentina	Argentina	Argentine Republic	Buenos Aires	Spanish	1 Peso = 100 centavos	34 513 000
Armenia	Armenia	Republic of Armenia	Yerevan	Armenian	1 Dram (Drm) = 100 loumas	3 671 000
Australia	Australia	Commonwealth of Australia	Canberra	English	1 Australian Dollar ($A) = 100 cents	19 089 000
Austria	Österreich	Republic of Austria	Vienna	German	1 Schilling (S, Sch) = 100 Groschen	8 097 000
Azerbaijan	Azerbaijchan	Republic of Azerbaijan	Baku	Azeri	1 Manat = 100 gapik	7 500 000
Bahamas	Bahamas	Commonwealth of the Bahamas	Nassau	English	1 Bahamian Dollar (BA$, B$) = 100 cents	274 000
Bahrain	Al-Baḥrayn	State of Bahrain	Al-Manāmah (Manama)	Arabic	1 Bahrain Dinar (BD) = 1000 fils	555 000
Bangladesh	Bangladesh	People's Republic of Bangladesh	Dhaka (Dacca)	Bengali	1 Taka (TK) = 100 poisha	117 372 000
Barbados	Barbados	Barbados	Bridgetown	English	1 Barbados Dollar (Bds$) = 100 cents	261 000
Belarus	Belarus	Republic of Belarus	Mensk (Minsk)	Belorussian	1 Belorussian Rouble (R) = 100 kopecks	10 424 000
Belgium	Belgique (French); België (Flemish)	Kingdom of Belgium	Bruxelles (Brussels)	Flemish, French, German	1 Belgian Franc (BFr) = 100 centimes	10 099 000
Belize	Belize	Belize	Belmopan	English	1 Belize Dollar (Bz$) = 100 cents	212 000
Benin	Bénin	Republic of Benin	Porto Novo	French	1 CFA Franc (CFAFr) = 100 centimes	5420 000

GENERAL DATA (continued)

English name	*Local name*	*Official name (in English)*	*Capital (English name in parentheses)*	*Official language(s) (in English)*	*Currency*	*Population*
Bhutan	Druk-Yul	Kingdom of Bhutan	Thimbu/ Thimphu	Dzongkha	1 Ngultrum (Nu) = 100 chetrum	1 622 000
Bolivia	Bolivia	Republic of Bolivia	La Paz/Sucre	Spanish, Aymará, Quechua	1 Boliviano (Bs) = 100 centavos	8 120 000
Bosnia-Herzegovina	Bosnai Hercegovina	Republic of Bosnia-Herzegovina	Sarajevo	Serbo-Croat	Convertible Mark (KM)	4 470 000
Botswana	Botswana	Republic of Botswana	Gaborone	English, Setswana	1 Pula (P, Pu) = 100 thebes	1 540 000
Brazil	Brasil	Federative Republic of Brazil	Brasília	Portuguese	1 Cruzeiro real (Cr$) = 100 centavos	159 233 000
Brunei	Brunei	State of Brunei, Abode of Peace	Bandar Seri Begawan	Malay, English	1 Brunei Dollar (Br$) = 100 cents	293 000
Bulgaria	Bǎlgarija	Republic of Bulgaria	Sofija (Sofia)	Bulgarian	1 Lev (Lv) = 100 stotinki	8 670 000
Burkina Faso	Burkina Faso	Burkina Faso	Ouagadougou	French	1 CFA Franc (CFAFr) = 100 centimes	10 328 000
Burma see Myanmar						
Burundi	Burundi	Republic of Burundi	Bujumbura	French, (Ki) Rundi	1 Burundi Franc (BuFr, FBu) = 100 centimes	6 131 000
Cambodia	Cambodia	State of Cambodia	Phnom Pénh (Phnom Penh)	Khmer	1 Riel (CRI) = 100 sen	9 629 000
Cameroon	Cameroun	Republic of Cameroon	Yaoundé	English, French	1 CFA Franc (CFAFr) = 100 centimes	13 986 000
Canada	Canada	Canada	Ottawa	English, French	1 Canadian Dollar (C$, Can$) = 100 cents	28 972 000
Cape Verde	Cabo Verde	Republic of Cape Verde	Praia	Portuguese	1 Escudo (CVEsc) = 100 centavos	394 000
Central African Republic	République Centrafricaine	Central African Republic	Bangui	French	1 CFA Franc (CFAFr) = 100 centimes	3 422 000
Chad	Tchad	Republic of Chad	N'djamena	Arabic, French	1 CFA Franc (CFAFr) = 100 centimes	6 424 000
Chile	Chile	Republic of Chile	Santiago	Spanish	1 Chilean Peso (Ch$) = 100 centavos	14 263 000
China	Zhongguo	People's Republic of China	Beijing/Peking	Mandarin Chinese	1 Renminbi Yuan (RMBY, $, Y) = 10 jiao = 100 fen	1 215 293 000
Colombia	Colombia	Republic of Colombia	Bogotá	Spanish	1 Colombian Peso (Col$) = 100 centavos	35 021 000
Comoros	Comores	Federal Islamic Republic of the Comoros	Moroni	Arabic, French	1 Comorian Franc (CFAFr) = 100 centimes	600 000
Congo	Congo	Republic of Congo	Brazzaville	French	1 CFA Franc (CFAFr) = 100 centimes	2 954 000
Congo, Democratic Republic of	République Democratique du Congo	Democratic Republic of Congo	Kinshasa	French	1 Zaire (Z) = 100 makuta (sing. likuta)	41 837 000
Costa Rica	Costa Rica	Republic of Costa Rica	San José	Spanish	1 Costa Rican Colón (CR¢) = 100 céntimos	3 383 000
Côte d'Ivoire	Côte d'Ivoire	Republic of Côte d'Ivoire	Yamoussoukro	French	1 CFA Franc (CFAFr) = 100 centimes	14 651 000

GENERAL DATA (continued)

English name	*Local name*	*Official name (in English)*	*Capital (English name in parentheses)*	*Official language(s) (in English)*	*Currency*	*Population*
Croatia	Hrvatska	Republic of Croatia	Zagreb	Serbo-Croat	1 Kuna (K) = 100 lipa	4 876 000
Cuba	Cuba	Republic of Cuba	La Habana (Havana)	Spanish	1 Cuban Peso (Cub$) = 100 centavos	11 089 000
Cyprus	Kypriaki (Greek); Kibris (Turkish)	Republic of Cyprus	Levkosia (Nicosia)	Greek, Turkish	1 Cyprus Pound (£C) = 100 cents	600 000
Czech Republic	Česká Republika	Czech Republic	Praha (Prague)	Czech	1 Koruna (Kčs) = 100 haléř	10 411 000
Denmark	Danmark	Kingdom of Denmark	København (Copenhagen)	Danish	1 Danish Krone (Dkr) = 100 øre	5 188 000
Djibouti	Djibouti	Republic of Djibouti	Djibouti	Arabic, French	1 Djibouti Franc (DF, DjFr) = 100 centimes	607 000
Dominica	Dominica	Commonwealth of Dominica	Roseau	English	1 East Caribbean Dollar (EC$) = 100 cents	83 900
Dominican Republic	República Dominicana	Dominican Republic	Santo Domingo	Spanish	1 Dominican Peso (RD$, DR$) = 100 centavos	7 994 000
Ecuador	Ecuador	Republic of Ecuador	Quito	Spanish	1 Sucre (Su, S/.) = 100 centavos	11 423 000
Egypt	Misr	Arab Republic of Egypt	Al-Qāhirah (Cairo)	Arabic	1 Egyptian Pound (E£, LE) = 100 piastres	60 284 000
El Salvador	El Salvador	Republic of El Salvador	San Salvador	Spanish	1 Colón (ES/C) = 100 centavos	5 811 000
Equatorial Guinea	Guinea Ecuatorial	Republic of Equatorial Guinea	Malabo	Spanish	1 CFA Franc (CFAFr) = 100 centimes	427 000
Eritrea	Eritrea	Eritrea	Asmara	Arabic, English	1 Ethiopian birr (Br) = 100 cents	3 955 000
Estonia	Eesti	Republic of Estonia	Tallinn	Estonian	1 Kroon (EEK) = 100 centts	1 568 000
Ethiopia	Ityopiya	People's Democratic Republic of Ethiopia	Adis Abeba (Addis Ababa)	Amharic	1 Ethiopian Birr (Br) = 100 cents	57 919 000
Federated States of Micronesia	Federated States of Micronesia	Federated States of Micronesia	Palikir, on Ponape	English	1 US Dollar (US $) = 100 cents	119 000
Fiji	Fiji	Sovereign Democratic Republic of Fiji	Suva	English	1 Fijian Dollar (F$) = 100 cents	775 000
Finland	Suomi (Finnish); Finland (Swedish)	Republic of Finland	Helsingfors (Helsinki)	Finnish, Swedish	1 Markka (FMk) = 100 penni	5 110 000
France	France	Republic of France	Paris	French	1 French Franc (Fr) = 100 centimes	58 333 000
Gabon	Gabon	Gabonese Republic	Libreville	French	1 CFA Franc (CFAFr) = 100 centimes	1 379 000
Gambia, The	Gambia	Republic of the Gambia	Banjul	English	1 Dalasi (D, Di) = 100 butut	1 053 000
Georgia	Sakartvelos	Georgia	Tbilisi	Georgian	1 Rouble (R) = 100 kopecks	5 481 000
Germany	Bundesrepublik Deutschland	Federal Republic of Germany	Berlin	German	1 Deutsche Mark (DM) = 100 pfennig	82 235 000
Ghana	Ghana	Republic of Ghana	Accra	English	1 Cedi (¢) = 100 pesewas	17 086 000
Greece	Ellás	Hellenic Republic	Athinai (Athens)	Greek	1 Drachma (Dr) = 100 lepta	10 513 000
Grenada	Grenada	Grenada	St George's	English	1 East Caribbean Dollar (EC$) = 100 cents	91 900
Guatemala	Guatemala	Republic of Guatemala	Guatemala City	Spanish	1 Quetzal (Q) = 100 centavos	10 557 000
Guinea	Guinée	Republic of Guinea	Conakry	French	1 Guinea Franc (GFr) = 100 cauris	6 543 000
Guinea-Bissau	Guiné-Bissau	Republic of Guinea-Bissau	Bissau	Portuguese	1 CFA Franc (CFAFr) = 100 centimes	1 070 000
Guyana	Guyana	Co-operative Republic of Guyana	Georgetown	English	1 Guyana Dollar (G$) = 100 cents	750 000

GENERAL DATA (continued)

English name	Local name	Official name (in English)	Capital (English name in parentheses)	Official language(s) (in English)	Currency	Population
Haiti	Haïti	Republic of Haiti	Port-au-Prince	French	1 Gourde (G, Gde) = 100 centimes	6 472 000
Holland see Netherlands, The						
Honduras	Honduras	Republic of Honduras	Tegucigalpa	Spanish	1 Lempira (L, La) =100 centavos	5 628 000
Hungary	Magyarország	Republic of Hungary	Budapest	Magyar	1 Forint (Ft) = 100 fillér	10 220 000
Iceland	Ísland	Republic of Iceland	Reykjavík	Icelandic	1 Krónur (IKr, ISK) = 100 aurar	268 000
India	Bharat (Hindi)	Republic of India	New Delhi	Hindi, English	1 Indian Rupee (Re, Rs) = 100 paise	944 157 000
Indonesia	Indonesia	Republic of Indonesia	Jakarta	Bahasa Indonesia	1 Rupiah (Rp) = 100 sen	194 956 000
Iran	Īrān	Islamic Republic of Iran	Tehrān (Tehran)	Farsi	1 Iranian Rial (Rls, Rl) = 100 dinars	65 127 000
Iraq	Al-'Irāq	Republic of Iraq	Baghdād (Baghdaad)	Arabic	1 Iraqi Dinar (ID) = 1000 fils	20 645 000
Ireland	Éire (Gaelic); Ireland (English)	Republic of Ireland	Baile ́Atha Cliath (Dublin)	Irish, English	1 Irish Pound/Punt (I£, IR£) = 100 pence	3 499 000
Israel	Yisra'el (Hebrew); Isrā'īl (Arabic)	State of Israel	Yerushalayim (Jerusalem)	Hebrew, Arabic	1 New Israeli Shekel (NIS) = 100 agorot	5 843 000
Italy	Italia	Italian Republic	Roma (Rome)	Italian	1 Italian Lira (L, Lit) = 100 centesimi	57 333 000
Ivory Coast see Côte d'Ivoire						
Jamaica	Jamaica	Jamaica	Kingston	English	1 Jamaican Dollar (J$) = 100 cents	2 519 000
Japan	Nihon	Japan	Tōkyō (Tokyo)	Japanese	1 Yen (=Y, Y) = 100 sen	124 641 000
Jordan	Al'Urdunn	Hashemite Kingdom of Jordan	'Ammān (Amman)	Arabic	1 Jordanian Dinar = 1000 fils	4 565 000
Kampuchea see Cambodia						
Kazakhstan	Kazakhstan	Republic of Kazakhstan	Astana	Kazakh	1 Tenge	17 155 000
Kenya	Kenya	Republic of Kenya	Nairobi	Swahili, English	1 Kenyan Shilling (KSh) = 100 cents	29 520 000
Kiribati	Kiribati	Republic of Kiribati	Bairiki	English, Gilbertese	1 Australian Dollar ($A) = 100 cents	79 700
Korea, North	Choson Minjujuui In'min Konghwaguk	Democratic People's Republic of Korea	P'yongyang (Pyongyang)	Korean	1 Won (NKW) = 100 chon	23 518 000
Korea, South	Taehan-Min'guk	Republic of Korea	Sŏul (Seoul)	Korean	1 Won (W) = 100 chon	44 853 000
Kuwait	al-Kuwayt	State of Kuwait	al-Kuwayt (Kuwait City)	Arabic	1 Kuwaiti Dinar (KD) = 1000 fils	1 019 000
Kyrgyzstan	Kyrgyzstan	Republic of Kyrgyzstan	Bishkek (formerly Frunze)	Kyrgyz	1 Som = 100 kopecks	4 694 000
Laos	Lao	Lao People's Democratic Republic	Viangchan (Vientiane)	Lao	1 Kip (Kp) = 100 at	4 791 000
Latvia	Latvija	Republic of Latvia	Riga	Latvian	1 Lat (Ls) = 100 santims	2 620 000
Lebanon	al-Lubnān	Republic of Lebanon	Bayrut (Beirut)	Arabic	1 Lebanese Pound/Livre (LL, £L) = 100 piastres	2 919 000
Lesotho	Lesoto	Kingdom of Lesotho	Maseru	English, Sesotho	1 Loti (pl Maloti) (M, LSM) = 100 lisente	2 017 000
Liberia	Liberia	Republic of Liberia	Monrovia	English	1 Liberian Dollar (L$) = 100 cents	3 029 000
Libya	Lībiyā	Socialist People's Libyan Arab Jamahiriya	Tarābulus (Tripoli)	Arabic	1 Libyan Dinar (LD) = 1000 millemes	4 848 000
Liechtenstein	Liechtenstein	Principality of Liechtenstein	Vaduz	German	1 Swiss Franc (SFr, SwF) = 100 centimes	31 000

GENERAL DATA (continued)

English name	*Local name*	*Official name (in English)*	*Capital (English name in parentheses)*	*Official language(s) (in English)*	*Currency*	*Population*
Lithuania	Lietuva	Republic of Lithuania	Vilnius	Lithuanian	1 Litas (Lt) = 100 centas	3 775 000
Luxembourg	Lëtzebuerg (Letz.); Luxembourg (French); Luxemburg (German)	Grand Duchy of Luxembourg	Luxembourg	Luxemburgish French, German	1 Luxemburgish Franc (FL or Flux) = 100 centimes	402 000
Macedonia	Makedonija	(Former Yugoslav) Republic of Macedonia	Skopje	Macedonian	1 Dinar (D, din) = 100 paras	1 937 000
Madagascar	Madagasikara	Democratic Republic of Madagascar	Antananarivo	Malagasy, French	1 Malagasy Franc (FMG, MgFr) = 100 centimes	13 456 000
Malawi	Malaŵi (Chewa)	Republic of Malawi	Lilongwe	Chichewa, English	1 Kwacha (MK) = 100 tambala	10 753 000
Malaysia	Malaysia	Malaysia	Kuala Lumpur	Malay	1 Malaysian Dollar/Ringgit (M$) = 100 cents	20 004 000
Maldives	Maldive; Divehi Jumhuriya	Republic of Maldives	Malé	Dhivehi	1 Rufiyaa (MRf, Rf) = 100 laaris	251 000
Mali	Mali	Republic of Mali	Bamako	French	1 CFA Franc (CFAFr) =100 centimes	10 173 000
Malta	Malta	Republic of Malta	Valletta	English, Maltese	1 Maltese Lira (LM) = 100 cents	370 000
Marshall Islands	Marshall Islands	Republic of the Marshall Islands	Dalap-Uliga -Darrit	Marshallese (Kahjin-Majol)	1 US Dollar ($, US $) = 100 cents	56 600
Mauritania	Mauritanie (French); Mūritāniyā	Islamic Republic of (Arabic)	Nouakchott Mauritania	Arabic	1 Ouguija (U, UM) = 5 khoum	2 295 000
Mauritius	Mauritius	Mauritius	Port Louis	English	1 Mauritius Rupee (MR, MauRe) = 100 cents	1 141 000
Mexico	México	United Mexican States	Ciudad de México (Mexico City)	Spanish	1 Mexican Peso (Mex$) = 100 centavos	89 872 000
Moldova	Moldova	Republic of Moldova	Kishinev	Moldovan, Ukranian	1 Leu	4 367 000
Monaco	Monaco	Principality of Monaco	Monaco	French	1 French Franc (F) = 100 centimes	30 600
Mongolia	Mongol Ard Uls	Mongolian People's Republic	Ulaanbaatar (Ulan Bator)	Khalkha	1 Tugrik (Tug) = 100 möngö	2 302 000
Morocco	Al-Magrib	Kingdom of Morocco	Rabat	Arabic	1 Dirham (DH) = 100 centimes	28 010 000
Mozambique	Moçambique	Republic of Mozambique	Maputo	Portuguese	1 Metical (Mr, MZM) = 100 centavos	18 138 000
Myanmar	Pyidaungsu Myanma Naingngandaw	Union of Myanmar	Yangon	Burmese (Rangoon)	1 Kyat (K) = 100 pyas	46 398 000
Namibia	Namibia	Republic of Namibia	Windhoek	Afrikaans, English	1 Nambian Dollar = 100 cents	2 156 000
Nauru	Naeoro (Nauruan); Nauru (English)	Republic of Nauru	Yaren District	Nauruan, English	1 Australian Dollar ($A) = 100 cents	9 900
Nepal	Nepāl	Kingdom of Nepal	Kathmandu	Nepali	1 Nepalese Rupee (NRp, NRs) = 100 paise/pice	20 827 000
Netherlands, The	Nederland	Kingdom of the Netherlands	Amsterdam/ 's-Gravenhage	Dutch (The Hague)	1 Dutch Guilder (Gld)/Florin (f) = 100 cents	15 499 000

GENERAL DATA (continued)

English name	*Local name*	*Official name (in English)*	*Capital (English name in parentheses)*	*Official language(s) (in English)*	*Currency*	*Population*
New Zealand	New Zealand (English); Aotearoa (Maori)	New Zealand	Wellington	English, Maori	1 New Zealand Dollar ($NZ) = 100 cents	3 560 000
Nicaragua	Nicaragua	Republic of Nicaragua	Managua	Spanish	1 Córdoba Oro (C$) = 100 centavos	4 553 000
Niger	Niger	Republic of Niger	Niamey	French	1 CFA Franc (CFAFr) = 100 centimes	9 050 000
Nigeria	Nigeria	Federal Republic of Nigeria	Abuja	English	1 Naira (N, =N) = 100 kobo	96 171 000
Norway	Norge	Kingdom of Norway	Oslo	Norwegian	1 Norwegian Krone (NKr) = 100 øre	4 345 000
Oman	'Umān	Sultanate of Oman	Masqat (Muscat)	Arabic	1 Omani Rial (RO) = 1000 baizas	1 845 000
Pakistan	Pākistān	Islamic Republic of Pakistan	Islāmābād (Islamabad)	Urdu	1 Pakistan Rupee (PRs, Rp) = 100 paisas	141 783 000
Panama	Panamá	Republic of Panama	Panamá (Panama City)	Spanish	1 Balboa (B, Ba) = 100 cents	2 669 000
Papua New Guinea	Papua New Guinea	Independent State of Papua New Guinea	Port Moresby	English, Tok Pīsin Hi-i Motu	1 Kina (K) = 100 toea	4 093 000
Paraguay	Paraguay	Republic of Paraguay	Asunción	Spanish	1 Guaraní (/G) = 100 céntimos	4 896 000
Peru	Perú	Republic of Peru	Lima	Spanish, Quechua	1 New Sol = 100 céntimos	23 407 000
Philippines	Filipinas	Republic of the Philippines	Manila	English, Pilipino	1 Philippine Peso (PP, –P) = 100 centavos	67 900 000
Poland	Polska	Republic of Poland	Warszawa (Warsaw)	Polish	1 Z/loty (Zl) = 100 groszy	39 003 000
Portugal	Portugal	Republic of Portugal	Lisboa (Lisbon)	Portuguese	1 Escudo (Esc) = 100 centavos	9 793 000
Puerto Rico	Puerto Rico	Commonwealth of Puerto Rico	San Juan	Spanish, English	1 US Dollar (US$) = 100 cents	3 683 000
Qatar	Qatar	State of Qatar	Ad-Dawhah (Doha)	Arabic	1 Qatar Riyal (QR) = 100 dirhams	597 000
Romania	Romania	Republic of Romania	Bucure,sti (Bucharest)	Romanian	1 Leu (pl lei) = 100 bani	23 033 000
Russia	Rossiyskaya	Russian Federation	Moskva (Moscow)	Russian	1 Rouble (R) = 100 kopecks	149 899 000
Rwanda	Rwanda	Republic of Rwanda	Kigali	Kinyarwanda, French	1 Rwanda Franc (RF)=100 centimes	8 430 000
Saint Kitts and Nevis	Saint Christopher/ Kitts and Nevis	Federation of Saint Christopher and Nevis	Basseterre	English	1 East Caribbean Dollar (EC$) = 100 cents	42 800
Saint Lucia	Saint Lucia	Saint Lucia	Castries	English	1 East Caribbean Dollar (EC$) = 100 cents	140 000
Saint Vincent and the Grenadines	Saint Vincent and the Grenadines	Saint Vincent and the Grenadines	Kingstown	English	1 East Caribbean Dollar (EC$) = 100 cents	120 000
Samoa	Samoa (English) Samoa i Sisifo (Samoan)	Independent State of Samoa	Apia	Samoan, English	1 Tala (WS$) = 100 sene	193 000

GENERAL DATA (continued)

English name	*Local name*	*Official name (in English)*	*Capital (English name in parentheses)*	*Official language(s) (in English)*	*Currency*	*Population*
San Marino	San Marino	Most Serene Republic of San Marino	San Marino	Italian	1 Italian Lira (L, Lit) = 100 centesimi 1 San Marino Lira = 100 centesimi	24 500
São Tomé and Príncipe	São Tomé e Príncipe	Democratic Republic of São Tomé and Príncipe	São Tomé	Portuguese	1 Dobra (Db) = 100 centimos	135 000
Saudi Arabia	al-'Arabīyah as-Saʿūdīyah	Kingdom of Saudi Arabia	Ar-Riyād (Riyadh)	Arabic	1 Saudi Arabian Riyal (SAR, SRls) = 100 halalah	17 124 000
Senegal	Sénégal	Republic of Senegal	Dakar	French	1 CFA Franc (CFAFr) = 100 centimes	8 314 000
Seychelles	Seychelles	Republic of Seychelles	Victoria	Creole French, English, French	1 Seychelles Rupee (SR) = 100 cents	71 100
Sierra Leone	Sierra Leone	Republic of Sierra Leone	Freetown	English	1 Leone (Le) = 100 cents	4 719 000
Singapore	Singapore	Republic of Singapore	Singapore City	Chinese, English, Malay, Tamil	1 Singapore Dollar/Ringgit (S$) = 100 cents	2 963 000
Slovak Republic	Slovenská Republika	Slovak Republic	Bratislava	Slovak	1 Slovak Crown = 100 halér	5 381 000
Slovenia	Slovenija	Republic of Slovenia	Ljubljana	Slovene, Serbo-Croat	1 Slovene Tolar = 100 paras	2 002 000
Solomon Islands	Solomon Islands	Solomon Islands	Honiara	English	1 Solomon Island Dollar (SI$) = 100 cents	367 000
Somalia	Somaliya	Somali Democratic Republic	Muqdisho (Mogadishu)	Somali	1 Somali Shilling (SoSh) = 100 cents	8 565 000
South Africa	South Africa (English); Suid-Afrika (Afrikaans)	Republic of South Africa	Pretoria/Cape Town	Afrikaans, English	1 Rand (R) = 100 cents	40 720 000
Spain	España	Kingdom of Spain	Madrid	Spanish	1 Peseta (Pta, Pa) = 100 céntimos	38 734 000
Sri Lanka	Sri Lanka	Democratic Socialist Republic of Sri Lanka	Sri Jayawardenapura/ Colombo	Sinhala, Tamil, English	1 Sri Lankan Rupee (SLR, SLRs) = 100 cents	18 100 000
Sudan	As-Sūdān	Republic of the Sudan	Al-Khartum (Khartoum)	Arabic	1 Sudanese Dinar (SD) = 100 piastres	31 173 000
Suriname	Suriname	Republic of Suriname	Paramaribo	Dutch	1 Suriname Guilder/Florin (SGld, F) = 100 cents	414 000
Swaziland	Swatini	Kingdom of Swaziland	Mbabane	English, Siswati	1 Lilangeni (pl Emalangeni) (Li, E) = 100 cents	900 000
Sweden	Sverige	Kingdom of Sweden	Stockholm	Swedish	1 Swedish Krona (Skr) = 100 øre	8 889 000
Switzerland	Schweiz (German); Suisse (French); Svizzera (Italian)	Swiss Confederation	Bern (Berne)	French, German, Italian, Romansch	1 Swiss Franc (SFr, SwF) = 100 centimes	6 990 000
Syria	As-Sūrīyah	Syrian Arab Republic	Dimashq (Damascus)	Arabic	1 Syrian Pound (LS, Syr) = 100 piastres	14 325 000
Taiwan	T'ai-Wan	Republic of China	T'aibei (Taipei, T'ai-pei)	Mandarin Chinese	1 New Taiwan Dollar (NT$) = 100 cents	21 419 000
Tajikistan (Tadzhikistan)	Tajikistan	Republic of Tajikistan	Duschanbe	Tajik	1 Rouble (R) = 100 kopecks	5 367 000

GENERAL DATA (continued)

English name	*Local name*	*Official name (in English)*	*Capital (English name in parentheses)*	*Official language(s) (in English)*	*Currency*	*Population*
Tanzania	Tanzania	United Republic of Tanzania	Dar es Salaam	Swahili, English	1 Tanzanian Shilling (TSh) = 100 cents	31 363 000
Thailand	Muang Thai	Kingdom of Thailand	Krung Thep (Bangkok)	Thai	1 Baht (B) = 100 satang	60 100 000
Togo	Togo	Republic of Togo	Lomé	French	1 CFA Franc (CFAFr) = 100 centimes	4 074 000
Tonga	Tonga	Kingdom of Tonga	Nuku'alofa	English, Tongan	1 Pa'anga/Tongan Dollar (T$) = 100 seniti	105 000
Trinidad and Tobago	Trinidad and Tobago	Republic of Trinidad and Tobago	Port of Spain	English	1 Trinidad and Tobago Dollar (TT$) = 100 cents	1 270 000
Tunisia	Tunis (Arabic); Tunisie (French)	Republic of Tunisia	Tunis	Arabic	1 Tunisian Dinar (TD, D) = 1000 millimes	8 902 000
Turkey	Türkiye	Republic of Turkey	Ankara	Turkish	1 Turkish Lira (TL) = 100 kurus	62 964 000
Turkmenistan	Turkmenostan	Republic of Turkmenistan	Ashkhabad	Turkmenian	1 Manat = 100 gapik	4 322 000
Tuvalu	Tuvalu	Tuvalu	Funafuti	English	1 Australian Dollar = 100 cents	10 000
Uganda	Uganda	Republic of Uganda	Kampala	English	1 Uganda Shilling = 100 cents	21 368 000
Ukraine	Ukraina	Ukraine	Kiev	Ukrainian	1 Karbovanet = 100 kopijka	52 570 000
United Arab Emirates	Ittiḥād al-Imārāt al-'Arabīyah	United Arab Emirates	AbūẒabi (Abu Dhabi)	Arabic	1 Dirham (DH) = 100 fils	2 181 000
United Kingdom	United Kingdom/ (Great) Britain	United Kingdom of Great Britain and Northern Ireland	London	English	1 Pound Sterling (£) = 100 new pence	58 541 000
United States of America	United States of America (USA)	United States of America	Washington, DC	English	1 US Dollar ($, US$) = 100 cents	262 693 000
Uruguay	Uruguay	Oriental Republic of Uruguay	Montevideo	Spanish	1 Uruguayan New Peso (NUr$, UrugN$) = 100 centésimos	3 187 000
Uzbekistan	Ozbekistan Republikasy	Republic of Uzbekistan	Tashkent	Uzbek	1 Som	21 669 000
Vanuatu	Vanuatu	Republic of Vanuatu	Port Vila	English, French, Bislama	1 Vatu (VT) = 100 centimes	167 000
Venezuela	Venezuela	Republic of Venezuela	Caracas	Spanish	1 Bolívar (B) = 100 céntimos	21 547 000
Vietnam	Viêt-nam	Socialist Republic of Vietnam	Ha-noi (Hanoi)	Vietnamese	1 Dông = 10 hao = 100 xu	73 655 000
Western Samoa see Samoa						
Yemen	Al-Yaman	Republic of Yemen	Sana/Aden	Arabic	1 Yemeni Rial (YR, YRI) = 100 fils; 1 Yemeni Dinar (YD) = 1000 fils	13 510 000
Yugoslavia see Bosnia-Herzegovina, Croatia, Macedonia, Slovenia						
Zaire see Congo, Democratic Republic of						
Zambia	Zambia	Republic of Zambia	Lusaka	English	1 Kwacha (K) = 100 ngwee	9 846 000
Zimbabwe	Zimbabwe	Republic of Zimbabwe	Harare	English	1 Zimbabwe Dollar (Z$) = 100 cents	11 365 000

UNITED NATIONS MEMBERSHIP

Grouped according to year of entry.

1945 Argentina, Australia, Belgium, Belorussian SSR (Belarus, 1991), Bolivia, Brazil, Canada, Chile, China (Taiwan to 1971), Colombia, Costa Rica, Cuba, Czechoslovakia (to 1993), Denmark, Dominican Republic, Ecuador, Egypt, El Salvador, Ethiopia, France, Greece, Guatemala, Haiti, Honduras, India, Iran, Iraq, Lebanon, Liberia, Luxembourg, Mexico, Netherlands, New Zealand, Nicaragua, Norway, Panama, Paraguay, Peru, Philippines, Poland, Saudi Arabia,South Africa, Syria, Turkey, Ukranian SSR (Ukraine, 1991), UK, Uruguay, USA, USSR, Venezuela, Yugoslavia
1946 Afghanistan, Iceland, Sweden, Thailand
1947 Pakistan, Yemen (N, to 1990)
1948 Burma (Myanmar, 1989)
1949 Israel
1950 Indonesia
1955 Albania, Austria, Bulgaria, Ceylon (Sri Lanka, 1970), Finland, Hungary, Ireland, Italy, Jordan, Kampuchea (Cambodia), Laos, Libya, Nepal, Portugal, Romania, Spain
1956 Japan, Morocco, Sudan, Tunisia
1957 Ghana, Malaya (Malaysia, 1963)
1958 Guinea
1960 Cameroon, Central African Republic, Chad, Congo, Côte d'Ivoire Zaire, Cyprus, Dahomey (Benin, 1975), Gabon, Madagascar, Mali, Niger, Nigeria, Senegal, Somalia, Togo, Upper Volta (Burkina Faso, 1984),Democratic Republic of Congo (formerly Zaire)
1961 Mauritania, Mongolia, Sierra Leone, Tanganyika (within Tanzania, 1964)
1962 Algeria, Burundi, Jamaica, Rwanda, Trinidad and Tobago, Uganda
1963 Kenya, Kuwait, Zanzibar (within Tanzania, 1964)
1964 Malawi, Malta, Tanzania, Zambia
1965 Maldives, Singapore, The Gambia
1966 Barbados, Botswana, Guyana, Lesotho
1967 Yemen (S, to 1990)
1968 Equatorial Guinea, Mauritius, Swaziland
1970 Fiji
1971 Bahrain, Bhutan, China (Peoples' Republic), Oman, Qatar, United Arab Emirates
1973 Bahamas, German Democratic Republic (within GFR, 1990), German Federal Republic
1974 Bangladesh, Grenada, Guinea-Bissau
1975 Cape Verde, Comoros, Mozambique, Papua New Guinea, São Tomé and Principe, Suriname
1976 Angola, Seychelles, Samoa (formerly Western Samoa)
1977 Djibouti, Vietnam
1978 Dominica, Solomon Islands
1979 St Lucia
1980 St Vincent and the Grenadines, Zimbabwe
1981 Antigua and Barbuda, Belize, Vanuatu
1983 St Christopher and Nevis
1984 Brunei
1990 Liechenstein, Namibia, Yemen (formerly N Yemen and S Yemen)
1991 Estonia, Federated States of Micronesia, Latvia, Lithuania, Marshall Islands, N Korea, Russia (formerly USSR), S Korea
1992 Armenia, Azerbaijan, Bosnia-Herzegovina, Croatia, Georgia, Kazakhstan, Kyrgysztan, Moldova, San Marino, Slovenia, Tajikistan, Turkmenistan, Uzbekistan
1993 Andorra, Czech Republic, Eritrea, Former Yugoslav Republic of Macedonia, Monaco, Slovak Republic

SPECIALIZED AGENCIES OF THE UNITED NATIONS

Abbreviated form	*Full title/location*	*Area of concern*
ILO	International Labour Organization, Geneva	Social justice
FAO	Food and Agriculture, Rome	Improvement of the production and distribution of agricultural products
UNESCO	United Nations Educational, Scientific and Cultural Organization, Paris	Stimulation of popular education and the spread of culture
ICAO	International Civil Aviation Organization, Montreal	Encouragement of safety measures in international flight
IBRD	International Bank for Reconstruction and Development, Washington	Aid of development through investment
IMF	International Monetary Fund, Washington	Promotion of international monetary cooperation
UPU	Universal Postal Union, Berne	Uniting members within a single postal territory
WHO	World Health Organization, Geneva	Promotion of the highest standards of health for all people
ITU	International Telecommunication Union, Geneva	Allocation of frequencies and regulation of procedures
WMO	World Meteorological Organization, Geneva	Standardization and utilization of meteorological observations
IFC	International Finance Corporation, Washington	Promotion of the international flow of private capital
IMCO	Inter-governmental Maritime Consultative Organization, London	The coordination of safety at sea
IDA	International Development Association, Washington	Credit on special terms to provide assistance for less-developed countries
WIPO	World Intellectual Property Organization, Geneva	Protection of copyright, designs, inventions, etc
IFAD	International Fund for Agricultural Development, Rome	Increase of food production in developing countries by the generation of grants or loans
UNIDO	United Nations Industrial Development Organization, Vienna	Promotion of industrialization of developing countries with special emphasis on manufacturing sector

AMERICAN STATES

Time zones: two sets of figures indicate that different zones operate in a state. The second figure refers to Summer Time (Apr–Oct, approximately). **2** Aleutian/Hawaii Standard Time; **3** Alaska Standard Time; **4** Pacific Standard Time; **5** Mountain Standard Time; **6** Central Standard Time; **7** Eastern Standard Time

Name	*Area* km²	sq mi	*Capital*	*Time zone*	*Population (1995est.)*	*Nickname(s)*
Alabama (AL)	133 911	51 705	Montgomery	7/8	4 283 000	Camellia State, Heart of Dixie
Alaska (AK)	1 518 748	586 412	Juneau	3/4	647 000	Mainland State, The Last Frontier
Arizona (AZ)	295 249	114 000	Phoenix	5	4 097 000	Apache State, Grand Canyon State
Arkansas (AR)	137 403	53 187	Little Rock	6/7	2 473 000	Bear State, Land of Opportunity
California (CA)	411 033	158 706	Sacramento	4/5	32 601 000	Golden State
Colorado (CO)	269 585	104 091	Denver	5/6	3 753 000	Centennial State
Connecticut (CT)	12 996	5 018	Hartford	7/8	3 272 000	Nutmeg State, Constitution State
Delaware (DE)	5 296	2 045	Dover	7/8	725 000	Diamond State, First State
District of Columbia (DC)	174	67	Washington	7/8	563 000	
Florida (FL)	151 934	58 664	Tallahassee	6/7, 7/8	14 355 000	Everglade State, Sunshine State
Georgia (GA)	152 571	58 910	Atlanta	7/8	7 184 000	Empire State of the South, Peach State
Hawaii (HI)	16 759	6 471	Honolulu	2	1 243 000	Aloha State
Idaho (ID)	216 422	83 564	Boise	4/5, 5/6	1 164 000	Gem State
Illinois (IL)	145 928	56 345	Springfield	6/7	11 937 000	Prairie State, Land of Lincoln
Indiana (IN)	93 716	36 185	Indianapolis	6/7, 7/8	5 841 000	Hoosier State
Iowa (IA)	145 747	56 275	Des Moines	6/7	2 865 000	Hawkeye State, Corn State
Kansas (KS)	213 089	82 277	Topeka	5/6, 6/7	2 591 000	Sunflower State, Jayhawker State
Kentucky (KY)	104 658	40 410	Frankfort	6/7, 7/8	3 864 000	Bluegrass State
Louisiana (LA)	123 673	47 752	Baton Rouge	6/7	4 389 000	Pelican State, Sugar State, Creole State
Maine (ME)	86 153	33 265	Augusta	7/8	1 245 000	Pine Tree State, Lumber State
Maryland (MD)	27 090	10 460	Annapolis	7/8	5 105 000	Old Line State, Free State
Massachusetts (MA)	21 455	8 284	Boston	7/8	6 062 000	Bay State, Old Colony
Michigan (MI)	151 579	58 527	Lansing	6/7, 7/8	9 654 000	Wolverine State, Great Lake State
Minnesota (MN)	218 593	84 402	St Paul	6/7	4 642 000	Gopher State, North Star State
Mississippi (MS)	123 510	47 689	Jackson	6/7	2 676 000	Magnolia State
Missouri (MO)	180 508	69 697	Jefferson City	6/7	5 309 000	Bullion State, Show Me State
Montana (MT)	380 834	147 046	Helena	5/6	863 000	Treasure State, Big Sky Country
Nebraska (NE)	200 342	77 355	Lincoln	5/6, 6/7	1 649 000	Cornhusker State, Beef State
Nevada (NV)	286 341	110 561	Carson City	4/5	1 539 000	Silver State, Sagebrush State
New Hampshire (NH)	24 032	9 279	Concord	7/8	1 114 000	Granite State
New Jersey (NJ)	20 167	7 787	Trenton	7/8	7 878 000	Garden State
New Mexico (NM)	314 914	121 593	Santa Fe	5/6	1 685 000	Sunshine State, Land of Enchantment
New York (NY)	127 185	49 108	Albany	7/8	18 317 000	Empire State
North Carolina (NC)	136 407	52 699	Raleigh	7/8	7 176 000	Old North State, Tar Heel State
North Dakota (ND)	180 180	69 567	Bismarck	5/6, 6/7	631 000	Flickertail State, Sioux State
Ohio (OH)	107 040	41 330	Columbus	7/8	11 193 000	Buckeye State
Oklahoma (OK)	181 083	69 919	Oklahoma City	6/7	3 313 000	Sooner State
Oregon (OR)	251 409	97 073	Salem	4/5	3 192 000	Sunset State, Beaver State
Pennsylvania (PA)	117 343	45 308	Harrisburg	7/8	12 200 000	Keystone State
Rhode Island (RI)	3 139	1 212	Providence	7/8	1 008 000	Little Rhody, Plantation State
South Carolina (SC)	80 579	31 113	Columbia	7/8	3 784 000	Palmetto State
South Dakota (SD)	199 723	77 116	Pierre	5/6, 6/7	732 000	Sunshine State, Coyote State
Tennessee (TN)	109 149	42 144	Nashville	6/7, 7/8	5 254 000	Volunteer State
Texas (TX)	691 003	266 807	Austin	5/6, 6/7	18 709 000	Lone Star State
Utah (UT)	219 880	84 899	Salt Lake City	5/6	1 957 000	Mormon State, Beehive State
Vermont (VT)	24 899	9 614	Montpelier	7/8	580 000	Green Mountain State
Virginia (VA)	105 582	40 767	Richmond	7/8	6 672 000	Old Dominion State, Mother of Presidents
Washington (WA)	176 473	68 139	Olympia	4/5	5 568 000	Evergreen State, Chinook State
West Virginia (WV)	62 758	24 232	Charleston	7/8	1 842 000	Panhandle State, Mountain State
Wisconsin (WI)	145 431	56 153	Madison	6/7	5 185 000	Badger State, America's Dairyland
Wyoming (WY)	253 315	97 809	Cheyenne	5/6	484 000	Equality State

Inhabitant	*Flower*	*Tree*	*Bird*	*Animal*	*Fish*	*Gemstone*
Alabamian	Camellia	Southern Pine	Yellowhammer		Tarpon	
Alaskan	Forget-me-not	Sitka Spruce	Willow Ptarmigan		King Salmon	Jade
Arizonan	Giant Cactus	Paloverde	Cactus Wren			Turquoise
Arkansan	Apple Blossom	Pine	Mockingbird			Diamond
Californian	Golden Poppy	California Redwood	California Valley Quail	California Grizzly Bear	South Fork Golden Trout	
Coloradan	Columbine	Blue Spruce	Lark Bunting	Rocky Mountain Bighorn Sheep		Aquamarine
Nutmegger	Mountain Laurel	White Oak	American Robin			Garnet
Delawarean	Peach Blossom	American Holly	Blue Hen Chicken			
Washingtonian	American Beauty Rose	Scarlet Oak	Woodthrush			
Floridian	Orange Blossom	Sabal Palm	Mockingbird			Agatized Coral
Georgian	Cherokee Rose	Live Oak	Brown Thrasher			
Hawaiian	Hibiscus	Kukui	Nene			
Idahoan	Syringa	Western White Pine	Mountain Bluebird			Idaho Star Garnet
Illinoisan	Butterfly Violet	White Oak	Cardinal			
Hoosier	Peony	Tulip Tree	Cardinal			
Iowan	Wild Rose	Oak	Eastern Goldfinch			
Kansan	Native Sunflower	Cottonwood	Western Meadowlark	Bison		
Kentuckian	Goldenrod	Kentucky Coffee Tree	Cardinal			
Louisianian	Magnolia	Bald Cypress	Eastern Brown Pelican			
Downeaster	White Pine Cone and Tassel	Eastern White Pine	Chickadee			Tourmaline
Marylander	Black-eyed Susan	White Oak	Baltimore Oriole		Striped Bass	
Bay Stater	Mayflower	American Elm	Chickadee			
Michigander	Apple Blossom	White Pine	Robin		Trout	Chlorastrolik
Minnesotan	Moccasin Flower	Red Pine	Loon		Walleye	Lake Superior Agate
Mississippian	Magnolia	Magnolia	Mockingbird			
Missourian	Hawthorn	Dogwood	Bluebird			
Montanan	Bitterroot	Ponderosa Pine	Western Meadowlark			Sapphire, Agate
Nebraskan	Goldenrod	Cottonwood	Western Meadowlark			Blue Agate
Nevadan	Sagebrush	Single-leaf Piñon	Mountain Bluebird			
New Hampshirite	Purple Lilac	White Birch	Purple Finch			
New Jerseyite	Purple Violet	Red Oak	Eastern Goldfinch			
New Mexican	Yucca	Piñon	Roadrunner	Black Bear	Cutthroat trout	Turquoise
New Yorker	Rose	Sugar Maple	Bluebird			Garnet
North Carolinian	Dogwood	Longleaf Pine	Cardinal	Grey Squirrel	Channel Bass	Emerald
North Dakotan	Wild Prairie Rose	American Elm	Western Meadowlark		Northern Pike	Teredo petrified wood
Ohioan	Scarlet Carnation	Buckeye	Cardinal			
Oklahoman	Mistletoe	Redbud	Scissor-tailed Flycatcher			
Oregonian	Oregon Grape	Douglas Fir	Western Meadowlark	Beaver	Chinook Salmon	Thunder Egg
Pennsylvanian	Mountain Laurel	Hemlock	Ruffed Grouse	Whitetail Deer		
Rhode Islander	Violet	Red Maple	Rhode Island Red			
South Carolinian	Yellow Jessamine	Cabbage Palmetto	Carolina Wren	Whitetail Deer	Striped Bass	
South Dakotan	Pasque	Black Hills Spruce	Ring-necked Pheasant	Coyote		Fairburn Agate
Tennessean	Iris	Tulip Poplar	Mockingbird	Raccoon		Pearl
Texan	Bluebonnet	Pecan	Mockingbird			Topaz
Utahn	Sego Lily	Blue Spruce	Sea Gull			Topaz
Vermonter	Red Clover	Sugar Maple	Hermit Thrush	Morgan Horse		
Virginian	Dogwood	Flowering Dogwood	Cardinal			
Washingtonian	Western Rhododendron	Western Hemlock	Willow Goldfinch		Steelhead Trout	Petrified Wood
West Virginian	Big Rhododendron	Sugar Maple	Cardinal	Black Bear		
Wisconsinite	Wood Violet	Sugar Maple	Robin	Badger	Muskellunge	
Wyomingite	Indian Paintbrush	Cottonwood	Meadowlark			Jade

WORLD POPULATION ESTIMATES

Date (AD)	Millions
1	200
1000	275
1250	375
1500	420
1700	615
1800	900
1900	1625
1920	1860
1930	2070
1940	2295
1950	2500
1960	3050
1970	3700
1980	4450
1990	5246
1992	5480
2000	6100
2050	11000

Estimates for 2000 and 2050 are United Nations 'medium' estimates. They should be compared with the 'low' estimates for these years of 5400 and 8500, and 'high' estimates of 7000 and 13500, respectively.

AUSTRALIAN STATES

Name	Area km²	sq mi	State capital
Australian Capital Territory	2400	930	Canberra
New South Wales	801400	309400	Sydney
Northern Territory	1346200	519800	Darwin
Queensland	1727200	666900	Brisbane
South Australia	984000	379900	Adelaide
Tasmania	67800	26200	Hobart
Victoria	227600	87900	Melbourne
Western Australia	2525500	975000	Perth

CANADIAN PROVINCES AND TERRITORIES

Name	Area km²	sq mi	Capital
Alberta	661190	255285	Edmonton
British Columbia	947800	365945	Victoria
Manitoba	649950	250945	Winnipeg
New Brunswick	73440	28355	Fredericton
Newfoundland	405720	156648	St John's
Northwest Territories	3426320	1322902	Yellowknife
Nova Scotia	55490	21424	Halifax
Ontario	1068580	412578	Toronto
Prince Edward Is	5660	2185	Charlottetown
Quebec	1540680	594856	Quebec City
Saskatchewan	652380	251883	Regina
Yukon Territory	483450	186660	Whitehorse

SOUTH AFRICAN PROVINCES

Name	Area km²	sq mi	State capital
Eastern Cape	170616	65858	Bisho
Free State	129437	49963	Bloemfontein
Gauteng	18760	7241	Johannesburg/Pretoria
Kwazulu Natal	91481	35312	Pietermaritzburg *or* Ulundi (*to be confirmed*)
Mpumalanga	81816	31581	Nelspruit
North-West	118710	45822	Mmabatho
Northern Cape	363389	140268	Kimberley
Northern Transvaal	119606	46168	Pietersburg
Western Cape	129386	49943	Cape Town

NATIONAL PARKS IN THE USA

Park (Date authorized)	Location	Area hectares	acres
American Samoa (1988)	American Samoa	3642	9000
Arcadia (1916)	SE Maine	77038971	38971
Arches (1929)	E Utah	29695	73379
Badlands (1929)	SW South Dakota	98461	243302
Big Bend (1935)	W Texas	286565	708118
Biscayne (1968)	SE Florida	72900	180128
Bryce Canyon (1923)	SW Utah	14502	35835
Canyonlands (1964)	SE Utah	136610	337570
Capitol Reef (1937)	S Utah	97895	214904
Carlsbad Caverns (1923)	SE New Mexico	18921	46755
Channel Islands (1938)	S California	100910	249354
Crater Lake (1902)	SW Oregon	64869	160290
Denali (1917)	S Alaska	1645248	4065493
Everglades (1934)	S Florida	566075	1398800
Gates of the Arctic (1978)	N Alaska	2854000	7052000
Glacier (1910)	NW Montana	410188	1013595
Glacier Bay (1925)	SE Alaska	1569481	3878269
Grand Canyon (1908)	NW Arizona	493059	1218375
Grand Teton (1929)	NW Wyoming	125661	310516
Great Smoky Mountains (1926)	N Tennessee	210550	520269
Guadalupe Mountains (1966)	W Texas	30875	76293
Haleakala (1916)	Hawaii	11956	28655
Hawaii Volcanoes (1916)	Hawaii	92745	229177
Hot Springs (1832)	Central Arkansas	2358	5826
Isle Royale (1931)	NW Michigan	231398	571796
Katmai (1918)	SW Alaska	1792810	4430125
Kenai Fjords (1978)	S Alaska	229457	567000
Kings Canyon (1940)	E California	186211	460136
Kobuk Valley (1978)	N Alaska	692000	1710000
Lake Clark (1978)	S Alaska	987000	2439000
Lassen Volcanic (1907)	N California	43047	106372
Mammoth Cave (1926)	Central Kentucky	21230	52452
Mesa Verde (1906)	SW Colorado	21078	52085
Mount Rainier (1899)	SW Washington	95265	235404
North Cascades (1968)	N Washington	204277	504781
Olympic (1909)	NW Washington	370250	914890
Petrified Forest (1906)	E Arizona	37835	93493
Redwood (1915)	NW California	44280	109415
Rocky Mountain (1915)	Central Colorado	106762	263809
Sequoia (1890)	E California	162885	402488
Shenandoah (1926)	Virginia	78845	194826
Theodore Roosevelt (1947)	W North Dakota	28497	70416
Virgin Islands (1956)	Virgin Islands	5947	14695
Voyageurs (1971)	N Minnesota	88678	219128
Wind Cave (1903)	SW South Dakota	11449	28292
Wrangell-St Elias (1978)	SE Alaska	3297000	8147000
Yellowstone (1872)	Idaho, Montana, Wyoming	898350	2219823
Yosemite (1890)	E California	307932	760917
Zion (1909)	SW Utah	59308	146551

COUNTIES OF ENGLAND

County	Area km²	Area sq mi	Population (1995 e)	Admin. Centre
Avon	1 346	520	980 000	Bristol
Bedfordshire	1 235	477	550 000	Bedford
Berkshire	1 259	486	774 000	Reading
Buckinghamshire	1 883	727	665 000	Aylesbury
Cambridgeshire	3 409	1 316	704 000	Cambridge
Cheshire	2 328	899	970 000	Chester
Cleveland	583	225	562 000	Middlesbrough
Cornwall	3 564	1 376	480 000	Truro
Cumbria	6 810	2 629	493 000	Carlisle
Derbyshire	2 631	1 016	959 000	Matlock
Devon	6 711	2 591	1 064 000	Exeter
Dorset	2 654	1 025	676 000	Dorchester
Durham	2 436	941	611 000	Durham
Essex	3 672	1 418	1 584 000	Chelmsford
Gloucestershire	2 643	1 020	548 000	Gloucester
Greater London	1 579	610	6 946 000	–
Greater Manchester	1 287	497	2 591 000	–
Hampshire	3 777	1 458	1 607 000	Winchester
Hereford and Worcester	3 926	1 516	705 000	Worcester
Hertfordshire	1 634	631	1 012 000	Hertford
Humberside	3 512	1 356	895 000	Beverley
Isle of Wight	381	147	123 000	Newport
Kent	3 730	1 440	1 543 000	Maidstone
Lancashire	3 063	1 183	1 426 000	Preston
Leicestershire	2 553	986	927 000	Leicester
Lincolnshire	5 915	2 284	615 000	Lincoln
Merseyside †	652	252	1 433 000	Liverpool
Norfolk	5 368	2 073	774 000	Norwich
Northamptonshire	2 367	914	601 000	Northampton
Northumberland	5 032	1 943	309 000	Morpeth
Nottinghamshire	2 164	836	1 041 000	Nottingham
Oxfordshire	2 608	1 007	607 000	Oxford
Shropshire	3 490	1 347	417 000	Shrewsbury
Somerset	3 451	1 332	485 000	Taunton
Staffordshire	2 716	1 049	1 058 000	Stafford
Suffolk	3 797	1 466	631 000	Ipswich
Surrey	1 679	648	1 046 000	Kingston upon Thames
Sussex, East	1 795	693	736 000	Lewes
Sussex, West	1 989	768	713 000	Chichester
Tyne and Wear †	540	208	1 148 000	Newcastle upon Tyne
Warwickshire	1 981	765	501 000	Warwick
West Midlands †	899	347	2 631 000	Birmingham
Wiltshire	3 481	1 344	602 000	Trowbridge
Yorkshire, North	8 309	3 208	736 000	Northallerton
Yorkshire, South	1 560	602	1 312 000	Barnsley
Yorkshire, West †	2 039	787	2 119 000	Wakefield

† County status abolished in 1986

NEW LOCAL GOVERNMENT AUTHORITIES

County	New unitary authority	Commencement year
Avon[a]	Bath and NE Somerset	1996
	Bristol	1996
	South Gloucestershire	1996
	NW Somerset	1996
Bedfordshire[b]	Luton	1997
Berkshire	Windsor and Maidenhead	1998
	Wokingham	1998
	Reading	1998
	Slough	1998
	West Berkshire	1998
	Bracknell Forest	1998
Buckinghamshire[b]	Milton Keynes	1997
Cambridgeshire[b]	Peterborough	1998
Cheshire[b]	Warrington	1998
	Halton	1998
Cleveland[a]	Hartlepool	1996
	Redccar and Cleveland	1996
	Middlesbrough	1996
	Stockton-on-Tees	1996
Derbyshire[b]	Derby	1997
Devon[b]	Plymouth	1998
	Torbay	1998
Dorset[b]	Bournemouth	1997
	Poole	1997
Durham[b]	Darlington	1997
Essex[b]	Southend	1998
	Thurrock	1998
Hampshire[b]	Portsmouth	1997
	Southampton	1997
Hereford and Worcester[b]	Herefordshire	1998
Humberside[a]	East Riding of Yorkshire	1996
	Hull	1996
	North Lincolnshire	1996
	North East Lincolnshire	1996
Isle of Wight	Isle of Wight	1995
Kent[b]	Medway	1998
Lancashire[b]	Blackpool	1998
	Blackburn	1998
Leicestershire[b]	Leicester	1997
	Rutland	1997
Nottinghamshire[b]	Nottingham	1998
Shropshire[b]	Wrekin	1998
Staffordshire[b]	Stoke-on-Trent	1997
Sussex, East[b]	Brighton and Hove	1997
Wiltshire[b]	Thamesdown	1997
Yorkshire, North[b]	York	1996

[a] These counties disappeared on 1 April 1996. [b] Rest of county continues with two-tier government.

LOCAL COUNCILS OF SCOTLAND

Name	Area km²	Area sq mi	Population (1995e)	Admin. centre
Aberdeen City	186	72	218 220	Aberdeen
Aberdeenshire	6 318	2 439	223 630	Aberdeen
Angus	2 181	842	111 020	Forfar
Argyll and Bute	6 930	2 675	90 550	Lochgilphead
Clackmannanshire	157	61	48 660	Alloa
Dumfries and Galloway	6 439	2 485	147 900	Dumfries
Dundee City	65	25	153 710	Dundee
East Ayrshire	1 252	483	123 820	Kilmarnock
East Dunbartonshire	172	66	110 220	Kirkintilloch
East Lothian	6 778	2 616	85 640	Haddington
East Renfrewshire	173	67	86 780	Giffnock
Edinburgh, City of	262	101	441 620	Edinburgh
Falkirk	299	115	142 610	Falkirk
Fife	1323	511	132 256	Glenrothes
Glasgow, City of	175	68	623 850	Glasgow
Highland	25 784	9 953	206 900	Inverness
Inverclyde	162	63	89 990	Greenock
Midlothian	356	137	79 910	Dalkeith
Moray	2 238	864	86 250	Elgin
North Ayrshire	884	341	139 020	Irvine
North Lanarkshire	474	183	326 750	Motherwell
Orkney	992	383	19 760	Kirkwall
Perth and Kinross	5 311	2 050	130 470	Perth
Refrewshire	261	101	17 970	Paisley
Scottish Borders	4 734	1827	105 300	Newtown St Boswells
Shetland	1438	555	22 830	Lerwick
South Ayrshire	1202	464	113 960	Ayr
South Lanarkshire	1771	684	307 100	Hamilton
Stirling	2 196	848	81630	Stirling
West Dunbartonshire	162	63	97 790	Dumbarton
Western Isles	3133	1209	29 410	Stornoway
West Lothian	425	164	146 730	Livingston

WALES UNITARY AUTHORITIES[a]

Name	Area km²	Area sq mi	Population (1995e)	Admin. centre
Aberconwy and Colwyn	1130	436	110 700	Colwyn Bay
Anglesey	719	277	68 500	Llangefni
Blaenau Gwent	109	42	73 300	Ebbw Vale
Bridgend	246	95	130 900	Bridgend
Gwynedd	2 548	983	117 000	Caernarfon
Caerphilly	279	108	171 000	Hengoed
Cardiff	139	54	306 600	Cardiff
Cardiganshire	1797	694	69 700	Aberystwyth
Carmarthenshire	2 398	926	169 000	Carmarthen
Denbighshire	844	326	91 300	Ruthin
Flintshire	437	169	145 300	Mold
Merthyr Tydfil	111	43	59 500	Merthyr Tydfil
Monmouthshire	851	328	84 200	Cwmbran
Neath and Port Talbot	422	171	140 100	Port Talbot
Newport	191	74	137 400	Newport
Pembrokeshire	1590	614	113 600	Haverfordwest
Powys	5204	2009	121 800	Llandrindod Wells
Rhondda, Cynon, Taff	424	164	239 000	Cardiff (temporary)
Swansea	378	146	230 900	Swansea
Torfaen	126	49	90 600	Pontypool
Vale of Glamorgan	337	130	119 200	Barry
Wrexham	499	193	123 500	Wrexham

[a] From 1 April 1996

DISTRICTS OF NORTHERN IRELAND

District	Area km²	Area sq mi	Population (1995 est.)	Admin. centre	Formerly part of
Antrim	563	217	44 300	Antrim	Antrim
Ards	369	142	67 200	Newtownards	Down
Armagh	672	259	51 600	Armagh	Armagh
Ballymena	638	246	57 200	Ballymena	Antrim
Ballymoney	419	162	25 000	Ballymoney	Antrim
Banbridge	444	171	34 000	Banbridge	Down
Belfast	140	54	283 000	Belfast	Antrim
Carrickfergus	87	34	34 700	Carrickfergus	Antrim
Castlereagh	85	33	53 100	Belfast	Antrim, Down
Coleraine	485	187	51 600	Coleraine	Antrim
Cookstown	623	240	31 500	Cookstown	Tyrone
Craigavon	382	147	77 000	Craigavon	Antrim, Down, Armagh
Derry	382	147	101 000	Derry	Londonderry
Down	646	249	62 400	Downpatrick	Down
Dungannon	779	301	49 400	Dungannon	Armagh, Tyrone
Fermanagh	1 676	647	53 600	Enniskillen	Fermanagh
Larne	338	131	30 100	Larne	Antrim
Limavady	587	227	23 500	Limavady	Londonderry
Lisburn	444	171	102 000	Lisburn	Antrim, Down
Magherafelt	573	221	37 100	Magherafelt	Londonderry
Moyle	495	191	14 800	Ballycastle	Antrim
Newry & Mourne	895	346	74 900	Newry	Armagh, Down
Newtownabbey	152	59	77 100	Newtownabbey	Antrim
North Down	73	28	73 800	Bangor	Down
Omagh	1 129	436	47 400	Omagh	Tyrone
Strabane	870	336	37 000	Strabane	Tyrone

OTHER BRITISH ISLANDS

Name	Area km²	Area sq mi	Population (1995 est.)	Admin. centre
Channel Islands				
Alderney	8	3	2 280	St Anne's
Guernsey	63	24	59 400	St Peter Port
Jersey	116	45	87 200	St Helier
Sark	4	2	632*	
Isle of Man	572	221	73 800	Douglas

* Unofficial estimate. Sark no longer takes part in any official estimate.

COUNTIES OF IRELAND

County	Area km²	Area sq mi	Population (1995 est.)	Admin. centre
Carlow	896	346	40 600	Carlow
Cavan	1 891	730	52 400	Cavan
Clare	3 188	1 231	90 200	Ennis
Cork	7 459	2 880	407 000	Cork
Donegal	4 830	1 865	127 000	Lifford
Dublin	922	356	1 018 000	Dublin
Galway	5 939	2 293	179 000	Galway
Kerry	4 701	1 815	121 000	Tralee
Kildare	1 694	654	122 000	Naas
Kilkenny	2 062	796	73 100	Kilkenny
Laoighis (Leix)	1 720	664	51 900	Portlaoise
Leitrim	1 526	589	23 400	Carrick
Limerick	2 686	1 037	161 000	Limerick
Longford	1 044	403	30 100	Longford
Louth	821	317	90 000	Dundalk
Mayo	5 398	2 084	110 000	Castlebar
Meath	2 339	903	105 000	Trim
Monaghan	1 290	498	50 800	Monaghan
Offaly	1 997	771	58 100	Tullamore
Roscommon	2 463	951	51 500	Roscommon
Sligo	1 795	693	54 300	Sligo
Tipperary	4 254	1 642	131 000	Clonmel
Waterford	1 839	710	90 000	Waterford
Westmeath	1 764	681	61 400	Mullingar
Wexford	2 352	908	101 000	Wexford
Wicklow	2 025	782	96 500	Wicklow

Political Rulers & Leaders 1900–99

Countries and organizations are listed alphabetically. Rulers are named chronologically since 1900 or (for new nations) since independence. For the major English-speaking nations, relevant details are also given of pre-20th-century rulers, along with a note of any political affiliation.

The list does not distinguish successive terms of office by a single ruler.

There is no universally agreed way of transliterating proper names in non-Roman alphabets; variations from the spellings given are therefore to be expected, especially in the case of Arabic rulers.

Minor variations in the titles adopted by Chiefs of State, or in the name of an administration, are not given; these occur most notably in countries under military rule.

Listings complete to March 1999.

AFGHANISTAN

Afghan Empire

Monarch

1880–1901 Abdur Rahman Khan
1901–19 Habibullah Khan
1919–29 Amanullah Khan
1929 Habibullah Ghazi
1929–33 Mohammed Nadir Shah
1933–73 Mohammed Zahir Shah

Republic of Afghanistan

Prime Minister

1973–8 Mohammad Daoud Khan

Democratic Republic of Afghanistan

Revolutionary Council – President

1978–9 Nur Mohammad Taraki
1979 Hafizullah Amin

Soviet Invasion

1979–86 Babrak Karmal
1986–7 Haji Mohammad Chamkani *Acting*
1987 Mohammed Najibullah

General-Secretary

1978–86 *As President*
1986–7 Mohammed Najibullah

Islamic Republic of Afghanistan

President

1987–92 Mohammad Najibullah
1992 Seghbatullah Mujjaddedi
1992–6 Burhanuddin Rabbani

Interim Council

1996– Mohammad Rabbani (*Chairman*)

Prime Minister

1929–46 Sardar Mohammad Hashim Khan
1946–53 Shah Mahmoud Khan Ghazi
1953–63 Mohammad Daoud
1963–5 Mohammad Yousef
1965–7 Mohammad Hashim Maiwandwal
1967–71 Nour Ahmad Etemadi
1972–3 Mohammad Mousa Shafiq
1973–9 *As President*
1979–81 Babrak Karmal
1981–8 Sultan Ali Keshtmand

Republic of Afghanistan from 1987

1988–9 Mohammad Hasan Sharq
1989–90 Sultan Ali Keshtmand
1990–2 Fazl Haq Khaleqiar
1992–3 Abdul Sabur Fareed
1993–4 Gulbardin Hekmatyar
1994– Arsala Rahmani *Acting*

Chairman of the Provisional Government

1996– Mohammad Rabbani

ALBANIA

Monarch

1928–39 Zog I (Ahmed Zogu)
1939–44 *Italian rule*

People's Socialist Republic of Albania

President

1944–85 Enver Hoxha
1985–92 Ramiz Alia
1992–7 Sali Berisha
1997 Rexhep Mejdani

Prime Minister

1914 Turhan Pashë Permëti
1914 Esad Toptani
1914–18 Abdullah Rushdi
1918–20 Turhan Pashë Permëti
1920 Sulejman Deluina
1920–1 Iljaz Bej Vrioni
1921 Pandeli Evangeli
1921 Xhafer Ypi
1921–2 Omer Vrioni
1922–4 Ahmed Zogu
1924 Iljaz Bej Vrioni
1924–5 Fan Noli
1925–8 Ahmed Zogu
1928–30 Koço Kota
1930–5 Pandeli Evangeli
1935–6 Mehdi Frashëri
1936–9 Koço Kota
1939–41 Shefqet Verlaci
1941–3 Mustafa Merlika-Kruja
1943 Eqrem Libohova
1943 Maliq Bushati
1943 Eqrem Libohova
1943 *Provisional Executive Committee* (Ibrahim Biçakçlu)
1943 *Council of Regents* (Mehdi Frashëri)
1943–4 Rexhep Mitrovica
1944 Fiori Dine
1944–54 Enver Hoxha
1954–81 Mehmed Shehu
1981–91 Adil Carcani

Republic of Albania

1991 Ylli Bufi
1991–2 Vilson Ahmeti
1992–7 Aleksander Meksi
1997 Baskim Fino
1997–8 Fatos Nano
1998– Pandeli Majko

ALGERIA

President

1962–5 Ahmed Ben Bella
1965–78 Houari Boumédienne
1978–92 Chadli Benjedid
1992 Mohamed Bondiaf
1992–4 Ali Kafi
1994–9 Lamine Zeroual
1999 Abdelaziz Bouteflika

Prime Minister

1977–84 Mohammed Ben Ahmed Abdelghani
1984–8 Abdelhamid Brahimi
1989–91 Mouloud Hamrouche
1991–2 Sid Ahmed Ghozali
1992 Belaid Abdessalam
1992–4 Redha Malek
1994–5 Mokdad Sifi
1995–8 Ahmed Ouyahia
1998– Ismail Hamdani

ANGOLA

President

1975–9 Antonio Agostinho Neto
1979– José Eduardo Dos Santos

Prime Minister

1992–6 Marcolino José Carlas Moco
1996–9 Fernando José França Van Dúnem

ANTIGUA AND BARBUDA

Prime Minister

1981–94 Vere Cornwall Bird
1994– Lester Bird

ARGENTINA

President

1898–1904 Julio Argentino Roca
1904–6 Manuel Quintana
1906–10 José Figueroa Alcorta
1910–14 Roque Sáenz Peña
1914–16 Victorino de la Plaza
1916–22 Hipólito Yrigoyen
1922–8 Marcelo T de Alvear
1928–30 Hipólito Yrigoyen
1930–2 José Félix Uriburu
1932–8 Augustin Pedro Justo
1938–40 Roberto M Ortiz
1940–3 Ramón S Castillo
1943–4 Pedro P Ramírez
1944–6 Edelmiro J Farrell
1946–55 Juan Perón
1955–8 Eduardo Lonardi
1958–62 Arturo Frondizi
1962–3 José María Guido
1963–6 Arturo Illia
1966–70 Juan Carlos Onganía
1970–1 Roberto Marcelo Levingston
1971–3 Alejandro Agustin Lanusse
1973 Héctor J Cámpora

1973–4 Juan Perón
1974–6 Martínez de Perón
1976–81 *Military junta* (Jorge Rafaél Videla)
1981 *Military junta* (Roberto Eduardo Viola)
1981–2 *Military junta* (Leopoldo Galtieri)
1982–3 Reynaldo Bignone
1983–8 Raúl Alfonsín Foulkes
1988– Carlos Saúl Menem

ARMENIA

President
1991–8 Levon Ter-Petrosian
1998– Robert Kocharyan
Prime Minister
1991–2 Gagik Arutynyan
1992–3 Khasrov Haroutunian
1993–7 Hrand Bagratian
1997–8 Robert Kocharyan
1998– Armen Darpinyan

AUSTRALIA

Chief of State: British monarch, represented by Governor-General
Prime Minister
1901–3 Edmund Barton *Prot*
1903–4 Alfred Deakin *Prot*
1904 John Christian Watson *Lab*
1904–5 George Houston Reid *Free Prot**
1905–8 Alfred Deakin *Prot*
1908–9 Andrew Fisher *Lab*
1909–10 Alfred Deakin *Fusion*
1910–13 Andrew Fisher *Lab*
1913–14 Joseph Cook *Lib*
1914–15 Andrew Fisher *Lab*
1915-16 William Morris Hughes *Lab*
1916–17 William Morris Hughes *Nat Lab*
1917–23 William Morris Hughes *Nat*
1923–9 Stanley Melbourne Bruce *Nat/Co**
1929–32 James Henry Scullin *Lab*
1932-8 Joseph Aloysius Lyons *UAP*
1938-9 Joseph Aloysins Lyons *UAP/Co**
1939 Earle Christmas Page *Co*/UAP**
1939–40 Robert Gordon Menzies *UAP*
1940-1 Robert Gordon Menzies *UAP/Co**
1941 Arthur William Fadden *Co/UAP**
1941–5 John Joseph Curtin *Lab*
1945 Francis Michael Forde *Lab*
1945–9 Joseph Benedict Chifley *Lab*
1949–66 Robert Gordon Menzies *Lib/Co**
1966–7 Harold Edward Holt *Lib/Co**
1967–8 John McEwen *Lib/Co**
1968–71 John Grey Gorton *Lib/Co**
1971–2 William McMahon *Lib/Co**
1972–5 Edward Gough Whitlam *Lab*
1975–83 John Malcolm Fraser *Lib/Co**
1983–91 Robert James Lee Hawke *Lab*
1991–6 Paul Keating *Lab*
1996– John Howard *Lib*
Co Country
Free Free Trade
Lab Labor
Lib Liberal
Nat Nationalist
Nat Lab National Labor
Prot Protectionist
UAP United Australian Party
**coalition*

AUSTRIA

President
1918–20 Karl Sätz
1920–8 Michael Hainisch
1928–38 Wilhelm Miklas
1938–45 *German rule*
1945–50 Karl Renner
1950–7 Theodor Körner
1957–65 Adolf Schärf
1965–74 Franz Jonas
1974–86 Rudolf Kirchsläger
1986–92 Kurt Waldheim
1992– Thomas Klestil
Chancellor
1918–20 Karl Renner
1920–1 Michael Mayr
1921–2 Johann Schober
1922 Walter Breisky
1922 Johann Schober
1922–4 Ignaz Seipel
1924–6 Rudolph Ramek
1926–9 Ignaz Seipel
1929–30 Ernst Streeruwitz
1930 Johann Schober
1930 Carl Vaugoin
1930–1 Otto Ender
1931–2 Karl Buresch
1932–4 Engelbert Dollfus
1934–8 Kurt von Schuschnigg
1938–45 *German rule*
1945 Karl Renner
1945–53 Leopold Figl
1953–61 Julius Raab
1961–4 Alfons Gorbach
1964–70 Josef Klaus
1970–83 Bruno Kreisky
1983–6 Fred Sinowatz
1986–97 Franz Vranitzky
1997– Viktor Klima

AZERBAIJAN

President
1991–2 Ayaz Mutalibov
1992–3 Abulfaz Elchibey
1993– Geidar Aliyev
Prime Minister
1991–3 Hassan Hasanov
1993–4 Panakh Guseinov
1994–5 Surat Guseinov
1995–6 Fuad Guliyev
1996– Artur Rasizade

THE BAHAMAS

Chief of State: British monarch, represented by Governor-General
Prime Minister
1973–92 Lynden O Pindling
1992– Hubert Alexander Ingraham

BAHRAIN

Emir
1869–1935 Isa I
1923–42 Hamad
1942–61 Salman II
1961–99 Isa II Bin Sulman al-Khalifa
1999– Hamad II Bin Isa al-Khalifa
Prime Minister
1971– Khalifa Bin Sulman al-Khalifa

BANGLADESH

President
1971–2 Sayed Nazrul Islam *Acting*
1972 Mujibur Rahman
1972–3 Abu Saeed Chowdhury
1974–5 Mohammadullah
1975 Mujibur Rahman
1975 Khondaker Mushtaq Ahmad
1975–7 Abu Saadat Mohammad Sayem
1977–81 Zia Ur-Rahman
1981–2 Abdus Sattar
1982–3 Abdul Fazal Mohammad Ahsanuddin Chowdhury
1983–90 Hossain Mohammad Ershad
1990–1 Shehabuddin Ahmed
1991–6 Abdur Rahman Biswas
1996– Shehabuddin Ahmed
Prime Minister
1971–2 Tajuddin Ahmed
1972–5 Mujibur Rahman
1975 Mohammad Monsur Ali
1975–9 *Martial Law*
1979–82 Mohammad Azizur Rahman
1982–4 *Martial Law*
1984–5 Ataur Rahman Khan
1986–8 Mizanur Rahman Chowdhury
1988–9 Moudud Ahmed
1989–91 Kazi Zafar Ahmed
1991–6 Begum Khaleda Zia
1996– Hasina Wajed

BARBADOS

Prime Minister
1966–76 Errol Walton Barrow
1976–85 J M G (Tom) Adams
1985–6 H Bernard St John
1986–7 Errol Walton Barrow
1987–94 L Erskine Sandiford
1994– Owen Arthur

BELARUS

Chairman of the Supreme Soviet
1991–4 Stanislav Shushkevich
1994–6 Mechislav Grib
1996– Syamyon Sharetski
President
1994 Alexander Lukashenko
Prime Minister
1991–4 Vyacheslav Kebich
1994–6 Mikhail Chigir
1996– Syargey Ling

BELGIUM

Monarch
1865–1909 Leopold II
1909–34 Albert I
1934–50 Leopold III
1950–93 Baudoin I
1993– Albert II

Prime Minister

1899–1907 Paul de Smet de Nayer
1907–8 Jules de Trooz
1908–11 Frans Schollaert
1911–18 Charles de Broqueville
1918 Gerhard Cooreman
1918–20 Léon Delacroix
1920–1 Henri Carton de Wiart
1921–5 Georges Theunis
1925 Alois van de Vyvere
1925–6 Prosper Poullet
1926–31 Henri Jaspar
1931–2 Jules Renkin
1932–4 Charles de Broqueville
1934–5 Georges Theunis
1935–7 Paul van Zeeland
1937–8 Paul Émile Janson
1938–9 Paul Spaak
1939–45 Hubert Pierlot
1945–6 Achille van Acker
1946 Paul Spaak
1946 Achille van Acker
1946–7 Camille Huysmans
1947–9 Paul Spaak
1949–50 Gaston Eyskens
1950 Jean Pierre Duvieusart
1950–2 Joseph Pholien
1952–4 Jean van Houtte
1954–8 Achille van Acker
1958–61 Gaston Eyskens
1961–5 Théodore Lefèvre
1965–6 Pierre Harmel
1966–8 Paul Vanden Boeynants
1968–72 Gaston Eyskens
1973–4 Edmond Leburton
1974–8 Léo Tindemans
1978 Paul Vanden Boeynants
1979–81 Wilfried Martens
1981 Marc Eyskens
1981–92 Wilfried Martens
1992– Jean-Luc Dehaene

BELIZE

Chief of State: British monarch, represented by Governor-General

Prime Minister

1981–4 George Cadle Price
1985–9 Manuel Esquivel
1989–93 George Cadle Price
1993–8 Manuel Esquivel
1998– Said Musa

BENIN

President

Dahomey

1960–3 Hubert Coutoucou Maga
1963–4 Christophe Soglo
1964–5 Sourou Migan Apithy
1965 Justin Tométin Ahomadegbé
1965 Tairou Congacou
1965–7 Christophe Soglo
1967–8 Alphonse Amadou Alley
1968–9 Émile Derlin Zinsou
1969–70 *Presidential Committee* (Maurice Kouandete)
1970–2 (Hubert Coutoucou Maga)
1972–5 Mathieu Kerekou

Republic of Benin

1990–1 Ahmed Kerekou
1991–6 Nicéphore Soglo
1996– Ahmed Kérékou

People's Republic of Benin

1975–90 Mathieu (*from 1980* Ahmed) Kerekou

Prime Minister

1958–9 Sourou Migan Apithy
1959–60 Hubert Coutoucou Maga
1960–4 *As President*
1964–5 Justin Tométin Ahomadegbé
1965–7 *As President*
1967–8 Maurice Kouandete
1968–96 *As President*
1996–8 Adrien Houngbedji

BHUTAN

Monarch (Druk Gyalpo)

1907–26 Uggyen Wangchuk
1926–52 Jigme Wangchuk
1952–72 Jigme Dorji Wangchuk
1972– Jigme Singye Wangchuk

BOLIVIA

President

1899–1904 José Manuel Pando
1904–9 Ismael Montes
1909–13 Heliodoro Villazón
1913–17 Ismael Montes
1917–20 José N Gutiérrez Guerra
1920–5 Bautista Saavedra
1925–6 José Cabina Villanueva
1926–30 Hernando Siles
1930 Roberto Hinojusa *President of Revolutionaries*
1930–1 Carlos Blanco Galindo
1931–4 Daniel Salamanca
1934–6 José Luis Tejado Sorzano
1936–7 David Toro
1937–9 Germán Busch
1939 Carlos Quintanilla
1940–3 Enrique Peñaranda y del Castillo
1943–6 Gualberto Villaroel
1946 Nestor Guillen
1946–7 Tomas Monje Gutiérrez
1947–9 Enrique Hertzog
1949 Mamerto Urriolagoitía
1951–2 Hugo Ballivián
1952 Hernán Siles Suazo
1952–6 Victor Paz Estenssoro
1956–60 Hernán Siles Suazo
1960–4 Victor Paz Estenssoro
1964–5 René Barrientos Ortuño
1965–6 René Barrientos Ortuño *and* Alfredo Ovando Candía
1966 Alfredo Ovando Candía
1966–9 René Barrientos Ortuño
1969 Luis Adolfo Siles Salinas
1969–70 Alfredo Ovando Candía
1970 Rogelio Mirando
1970–1 Juan José Torres Gonzales
1971–8 Hugo Banzer Suárez
1978 Juan Pereda Asbún
1978–9 *Military junta* (David Padilla Arericiba)
1979 Walter Guevara Arze
1979–80 Lydia Gueiler Tejada
1980–1 *Military junta* (Luis García Meza)
1981–2 *Military junta* (Celso Torrelio Villa)
1982 Guido Vildoso Calderón
1982–5 Hernán Siles Suazo
1985–9 Victor Paz Estenssoro
1989–93 Jaime Paz Zamora
1993–7 Gonzalo Sánchez de Lozada
1997– Hugo Bánzer Suárez

BOSNIA-HERZEGOVINA

President

1992–6 Aliya Izetbegovic

Collective Presidency (Chairman)

1996–8 Aliya Izetbegovic
1998– Zivko Radisic

Prime Minister

1992 Jure Pelivan
1992–3 Mile Akmadzic
1993–6 Haris Silajdzic

Republic of Herzegovina

1996 Hasan Muratovic
1996–8 Grojko Klickovic
1998–9 Boro Bosic
1999– Svetozar Mihajlovic

Federation of Bosnia-Herzegovina

1996–8 Izudin Kapetanovic
1998– Haris Silajdzic

BOTSWANA

President

1966–80 Seretse Khama
1980–98 Quett K J Masire
1998– Festus Mogae

BRAZIL

President

1898–1902 Manuel Ferraz de Campos Sales
1902–6 Francisco de Paula Rodrigues Alves
1906–9 Alfonso Pena
1909–10 Nilo Peçanha
1910–14 Hermes Rodrigues da Fonseca
1914–18 Venceslau Brás Pereira Gomes
1918–19 Francisco de Paula Rodrigues Alves
1919–22 Epitácio Pessoa
1922–6 Artur da Silva Bernardes
1926–30 Washington Luís Pereira de Sousa
1930–45 Getúlio Dorneles Vargas
1945–51 Eurico Gaspar Dutra
1951–4 Getúlio Dorneles Vargas
1954–5 João Café Filho
1955 Carlos Coimbra da Luz
1955–6 Nereu de Oliveira Ramos
1956–61 Juscelino Kubitschek de Oliveira
1961 Jânio da Silva Quadros
1961–3 João Belchior Marques Goulart
1963 Pascoal Ranieri Mazilli
1963–4 João Belchior Marques Goulart
1964 Pascoal Ranieri Mazilli
1964–7 Humberto de Alencar Castelo Branco
1967–9 Artur da Costa e Silva
1969–74 Emílio Garrastazu Médici

1974–9 Ernesto Geisel
1979–85 João Baptista de Oliveira Figueiredo
1985–90 José Sarney
1990–2 Fernando Collor de Mello
1992–5 Itamar Franco
1995– Fernando Henrique Cardoso

BRUNEI

Monarch (Sultan)
1885–1906 Hashim Jalil al 'Alam Akam-ud-Din
1906–24 Muhammad Jamal al 'Alam II
1924–50 Ahmad Taj-ud-Din
1950–67 'Umar 'Ali Sa'if-ud-Din III
1967– Muda Hassan al Bolkiah Mu'iz-ud-Din Waddaulah

BULGARIA

Monarch
1887–1908 Ferdinand *Prince*
1908–18 Ferdinand I
1918–43 Boris III
1943–6 Simeon II

Chairman of the Presidium of the National Assembly
1946–7 Vasil Kolarov
1947–50 Mincho Naichev
1950–8 Georgi Damianov
1958–64 Dimitar Ganev
1964–71 Georgi Traikov

Chairman of the State Council
1971–89 Todor Zhivkov
1989–90 Petar Mladenov

President
1991–6 Zhelyu Zhelev
1996– Petar Stoyanov

Premier
1946–9 Georgi Dimitrov
1949–50 Vasil Kolarov
1950–6 Vulko Chervenkov
1956–62 Anton Yugov
1962–71 Todor Zhivkov
1971–81 Stanko Todorov
1981–6 Grisha Filipov
1986–90 Georgy Atanasov
1990 Andrei Lukanov
1990–1 Dimitar Popov
1991–2 Filip Dimitrov
1992–4 Lyuben Berov
1994–5 Reneta Indzhova
1995–7 Zhan Videnov
1997 Nicolay Dobrev
1997 Stefan Safianki
1997– Ivan Kostov

First Secretary
1946–53 Vulko Chervenkov
1953–89 Todor Zhivkov
1989–90 Petar Mladenov
1990–1 Alexander Lilov
1991–6 Zhan Videnov
1996 Georgi Parvanov

BURKINA FASO

President

Upper Volta
1960–6 Maurice Yaméogo
1966–80 Sangoulé Lamizana
1980 Saye Zerbo

People's Salvation Council
1982–3 Jean-Baptiste Ouedraugo *Chairman*

National Revolutionary Council
1983–4 Thomas Sankara *Chairman*

Burkina Faso
1984–7 Thomas Sankara *Chairman*
1987– Blaise Compaoré

Prime Minister
1992–4 Youssouf Ouedraogo
1994–6 Roch Christian Kabore
1996– Kadre Desire Ouedraogo

BURUNDI

Monarch
1962–6 Mwambutsa II
1966– Ntare V

President
1966–77 Michel Micombero
1977–87 Jean-Baptiste Bagaza
1987–93 *Military Junta* (Pierre Buyoya)
1993–4 Melchoir Ndadaye
1994 Cyprien Ntaryamina
1994–5 Sylvestre Ntibantunganya
1996– Pierre Buyoya *(Military coup)*

Head of Government
1993–4 Sylvie Kinigi
1994–5 Anatole Kanyenkiko
1995–6 Antoine Nduwayo
1996– Pascal-Firmin Ndimira

CAMBODIA (Kampuchea)

Monarch
1941–55 Norodom Sihanouk I
1955–60 Norodom Suramarit

Chief of State
1960–70 Prince Norodom Sihanouk

Khmer Republic
1970–2 Cheng Heng *Acting*
1972–5 Lon Nol
1975–6 Prince Norodom Sihanouk
1976–81 Khieu Samphan
1981–91 Heng Samrin

Government in exile

President
1970–5 Prince Norodom Sihanouk
1982–91 Prince Norodom Sihanouk

Interim Government

Chairman of the Supreme National Council
1991–3 Prince Norodom Sihanouk

Kingdom of Cambodia

Monarch
1993– Norodom Sihanouk II *Restored*

Prime Minister

Kingdom of Cambodia
1945–6 Son Ngoc Thanh
1946–8 Prince Monireth
1948–9 Son Ngoc Thanh
1949–51 Prince Monipong
1951 Son Ngoc Thanh
1951–2 Huy Kanthoul
1952–3 Norodom Sihanouk II
1953 Samdech Penn Nouth
1953–4 Chan Nak
1954–5 Leng Ngeth
1955–6 Prince Norodom Sihanouk
1956 Oum Chheang Sun
1956 Prince Norodom Sihanouk
1956 Khim Tit
1956 Prince Norodom Sihanouk
1956 Sam Yun
1956–7 Prince Norodom Sihanouk
1957–8 Sim Var
1958 Ek Yi Oun
1958 Samdech Penn Nouth *Acting*
1958 Sim Var
1958–60 Prince Norodom Sihanouk
1960–1 Pho Proung
1961 Samdech Penn Nouth
1961–3 Prince Norodom Sihanouk
1963–6 Prince Norodom Kantol
1966–7 Lon Nol
1967–8 Prince Norodom Sihanouk
1968–9 Samdech Penn Nouth
1969–72 Lon Nol

Khmer Republic (1970)
1972 Sisovath Sivik Matak
1972 Son Ngoc Thanh
1972–3 Hang Thun Hak
1973 In Tam
1973–5 Long Boret
1975–6 Samdech Penn Nouth
1976–9 Pol Pot
1979–81 Khieu Samphan 1981–5 Chan Si
1985–91 Hun Sen

Government in exile
1970–3 Samdech Penn Nouth
1982–91 Son Sann

Interim Government
1991–3 *No Prime Minister*

Kingdom of Cambodia
1993–7 Norodom Ranariddh
1993–8 Hun Sen *(Joint)*
1997–8 Ing Huot *(joint)*
1998– Hun Sen

CAMEROON

President
1960–82 Ahmadou Ahidjo
1982– Paul Biya

Prime Minister
1991–2 Sadou Hayatou
1992–6 Simon Achidi Achu
1996– Peter Mafany Musonge

CANADA

Chief of State: British monarch, represented by Governor-General

Prime Minister
1896–1911 Wilfrid Laurier *Lib*
1911–20 Robert Borden *Con*
1920–1 Arthur Meighen *Con*
1921–6 William Lyon Mackenzie King *Lib*
1926 Arthur Meighen *Con*
1926–30 William Lyon Mackenzie King *Lib*
1930–5 Richard Bedford Bennett *Con*

1935–48 William Lyon Mackenzie King *Lib*
1948–57 Louis St Laurent *Lib*
1957–63 John George Diefenbaker *Con*
1963–8 Lester Bowles Pearson *Lib*
1968–79 Pierre Elliott Trudeau *Lib*
1979–80 Joseph Clark *Con*
1980–4 Pierre Elliott Trudeau *Lib*
1984 John Napier Turner *Lib*
1984–93 Brian Mulroney *Con*
1993 Kim Campbell *Con*
1993– Jean Chrétien *Lib*
Con Conservative
Lib Liberal

CAPE VERDE

President
1975–91 Arístides Pereira
1991– Antonio Mascarenhas Monteiro
Prime Minister
1975–91 Pedro Pires
1991– Carlos Veiga

CENTRAL AFRICAN REPUBLIC

President
1960–6 David Dacko
1966–79 Jean Bédel Bokassa (*from 1977*, Emperor Bokassa I)
1979–81 David Dacko
1981–93 André Kolingba
1993– Ange-Félix Patasse
Prime Minister
1991–2 Edouard Frank
1992–3 Thimothée Malendoma
1993 Enoch Derant Lakoue
1993–5 Jean-Luc Mandaba
1995–6 Gabriel Koyambounou
1996–7 Jean-Paul Ngoupandé
1997–9 Michel Gbezera-Bria
1999 Anicet Georges Dologuélé

CHAD

President
1960–75 François Tombalbaye
1975–9 *Supreme Military Council* (Félix Malloum)
1979 Goukouni Oueddi
1979 Mohammed Shawwa
1979–82 Goukouni Oueddi
1982–90 Hissène Habré
1990– Idriss Déby
Prime Minister
1991–2 Jean Alingue Bawoyeu
1992–3 Joseph Yodemane
1993 Fidèle Moungar
1994–5 Delwa Kassire Koumakoye
1995–7 Koibla Djimasta
1997– Nassour Ouidou Guelendouksia

CHILE

President
1900–1 Federico Errázuriz Echaurren
1901 Aníbal Zañartu *Vice President*
1901–3 Germán Riesco
1903 Ramón Barros Luco *Vice President*
1903–6 Germán Riesco
1906–10 Pedro Montt
1910 Ismael Tocornal *Vice President*
1910 Elías Fernández Albano *Vice President*
1910 Emiliano Figueroa Larraín *Vice President*
1910–15 Ramón Barros Luco
1915–20 Juan Luis Sanfuentes
1920–4 Arturo Alessandri
1924–5 *Military Juntas*
1925 Arturo Alessandri
1925 Luis Barros Borgoño *Vice President*
1925–27 Emiliano Figueroa
1927–31 Carlos Ibáñez
1931 Pedro Opaso Letelier *Vice President*
1931 Juan Esteban Montero *Vice President*
1931 Manuel Trucco Franzani *Vice President*
1931–2 Juan Estaban Montero
1932 *Military Juntas*
1932 Carlos G Dávila *Provisional President*
1932 Bartolomé Blanche *Provisional President*
1932 Abraham Oyanedel *Vice President*
1932–8 Arturo Alessandri Palma
1938–41 Pedro Aguirre Cerda
1941–2 Jerónimo Méndez Arancibia *Vice President*
1942–6 Juan Antonio Ríos Morales
1946–52 Gabriel González Videla
1952–8 Carlos Ibáñez del Campo
1958–64 Jorge Alessandri Rodríguez
1964–70 Eduardo Frei Montalva
1970–3 Salvador Allende Gossens
1973–90 Augusto Pinochet Ugarte
1990–4 Patricio Aylwin Azócar
1994– Eduardo Frei Ruíz-Tagle

CHINA

Qing dynasty
Emperor
1875–1908 Guangxu (Kuang-hsü)
1908–12 Xuantong (Hsüan-t'ung)
Prime Minister
1901–3 Ronglu (Jung-lu)
1903–11 Yikuang (I-k'uang), Prince Qing (Ch'ing)
1912 Lu Zhengxiang (Lu Cheng-hsiang)
1912 Yuan Shikai (Yüan Shih-k'ai)
Republic of China
President
1912 Sun Yat-sen (Sun Wen, Sun Yixian) *Provisional*
1912–16 Yuan Shikai (Yüan Shih-k'ai)
1916–17 Li Yuanhong (Li Yüan-hung)
1917–18 Feng Guozhang (Feng Kuo-chang)
1918–22 Xu Shichang (Hsü Shih-ch'ang)
1921–5 Sun Yat-sen *Guangzhou (Canton) Administration*
1922–3 Li Yuanhong
1923–4 Cao Kun (Ts'ao K'un)
1924–6 Duan Qirui (Tuan Ch'i-jui)
1926–7 *Civil disorder*
1927–8 Zhang Zuolin (Chang Tso-lin)
1928–31 Chiang K'ai-shek (Jiang Jieshi, Chiang Chieh-shih)
1931–2 Cheng Mingxu (Ch'eng Ming-hsü) *Acting*
1932–43 Lin Sen (Lin Sen)
1940–4 Wang Jingwei (Wang Ching-wei) *In Japanese-occupied territory*
1943–9 Chiang Kai-shek
1945–9 *Civil war*
1949 Li Zongren (Li Tsung-jen)
Premier
1912 Tang Shaoyi (T'ang Shao-i)
1912–13 Zhao Bingjun (Chao Ping-chün)
1912–13 Xiong Xiling (Hsiung Hsi-ling)
1914 Sun Baoyi (Sun Pao-i, Pao-chi)
1914–15 Xu Shichang (Hsü Shih-ch'ang)
1915–16 *no Premier*
1916–17 Duan Qirui (Tuan Ch'i-jui)
1917–18 Wang Shizhen (Wang Shih-chen)
1918 Duan Qirui (Tuan Ch'i-jui)
1918–19 Qian Nengxun (Ch'ien Neng-hsün)
1919 Gong Xinzhan (Kung Hsin-chan)
1919–20 Jin Yunpeng (Chin Yün-p'eng)
1920 Sa Zhenbing (Sa Chen-ping)
1920–1 Jin Yunpeng
1921–2 Liang Shiyi (Liang Shih-i)
1922 Zhou Ziqi (Chou Tzu-ch'i) *Acting*
1922 Yan Huiqing (Yen Hui-ch'ing, W W Yen)
1922 Wang Chonghui (Wang Ch'ung-hui)
1922–3 Wang Daxie (Wang Ta-hsieh)
1923 Zhang Shaozeng (Chang Shao-tseng)
1923–4 Gao Lingwei (Kao Ling-wei)
1924 Sun Baoyi (Sun Pao-i, Pao-ch'i)
1924 Gu Weijun (Ku Wei-chün, W W Wellington Ku) *Acting*
1924 Yan Huiqing
1924 Huang Fu (Huang Fu) *Acting*
1924–5 Duan Qirui
1925–6 Xu Shiying (Hsü Shih-ying)
1926 Jia Deyao (Chia Te-yao)
1926 Hu Weide (Hu Wei-te)
1926 Yan Huiqing
1926 Du Xigui (Tu Hsi-kuei) *Acting*
1926–7 Gu Weijun
1927 *Civil disorder*
President of the Executive Council
1928–30 Tan Yankai (T'an Yen-k'ai)
1930 T V Soong (Song Ziwen, Sung Tzu-wen) *Acting*
1930 Wang Jingwei (Wang Ching-wei)
1930–1 Chiang K'ai-shek
1931–2 Sun Fo (Sun Fo)
1932–5 Wang Jingwei
1935–7 Chiang K'ai-shek
1937–8 Wang Chonghui (Wang Ch'ung-hui) *Acting*
1938–9 Kong Xiangxi (K'ung Hsiang-hsi)
1939–44 Chiang K'ai-shek
1944–7 T V Soong
1945–9 *Civil war*
1948 Wang Wenhao (Wong Wen-hao)
1948–9 Sun Fo
1949 He Yingqin (Ho Ying-ch'in)
1949 Yan Xishan (Yen Hsi-shan)
People's Republic of China
President
1949–59 Mao Zedong (Mao Tse-tung)
1959–68 Liu Shaoqi (Liu Shao-ch'i)

1968–75 Dong Biwu (Tung Pi-wu)
1975–6 Zhu De (Chu Te)
1976–8 Song Qingling (Sung Ch'ing-ling
1978–83 Ye Jianying (Yeh Chien-ying)
1983–8 Li Xiannian (Li Hsien-nien)
1988–93 Yang Shangkun (Yang Shang-k'un)
1993– Jiang Zemin

Prime Minister

1949–76 Zhou Enlai (Chou En-lai)
1976–80 Hua Guofeng (Huo Kuo-feng)
1980–7 Zhao Ziyang (Chao Tzu-yang)
1987–98 Li Peng (Li P'eng)
1998– Zhu Rongji

Communist Party

Chairman

1935–76 Mao Zedong
1976–81 Hua Guofeng
1981–2 Hu Yaobang (Hu Yao-pang)

General Secretary

1982–7 Hu Yaobang
1987–9 Zhao Ziyang
1989– Jiang Zemin (Chiang Tse-min)

COLOMBIA

President

1900–4 José Manuel Marroquín *Vice President*
1904–9 Rafael Reyes
1909–10 Ramón González Valencia
1910–14 Carlos E Restrepo
1914–18 José Vicente Concha
1918–21 Marco Fidel Suárez
1921–2 Jorge Holguín *President Designate*
1922–6 Pedro Nel Ospina
1926–30 Miguel Abadía Méndez
1930–4 Enrique Olaya Herrera
1934–8 Alfonso López
1938–42 Eduardo Santos
1942–5 Alfonso López
1945–6 Alberto Lleras Camargo *President Designate*
1946–50 Mariano Ospina Pérez
1950–3 Laureano Gómez
1953–7 Gustavo Rojas Pinilla
1957 *Military Junta*
1958–62 Alberto Lleras Camargo
1962–6 Guillermo León Valencia
1966–70 Carlos Lleras Restrepo
1970–4 Misael Pastrana Borrero
1974–8 Alfonso López Michelsen
1978–82 Julio César Turbay Ayala
1982–6 Belisario Betancur
1986–90 Virgilio Barco Vargas
1990–4 César Gaviria Trujillo
1994–8 Ernesto Samper
1998– Andrés Pastrana Arango

COMMONWEALTH

Secretary General

1965–75 Arnold Smith
1975–90 Shridath S Ramphal
1990–9 Emeka Anyaoku
1999– Don McKinnon

COMOROS

President

1976–8 Ali Soilih
1978–89 Ahmed Abdallah Abderemane
1989–96 Said Mohammed Djohar
1996–8 Mohammed Taki Abdoulkarim
1998–9 Majidine ben Said Massonde
1999– *Military coup* (Azali Assoumani)

Prime Minister

1990-2 Said Ali Kemal
1992 Mohammed Taki Abdoulkarim
1992-3 Ibrahim Abderamane Halidi
1993 Said Ali Mohammed
1993-4 Ahmed ben Cheikh Attoumane
1994 Mohammed Abdou Mahdi
1994–5 Halifa Houmadi
1995–6 Caabi el Yachroutou Mohamed
1996 Majidine ben Said
1996–7 Ahmed Abdou
1997–8 Nourdine Bourhane
1998–9 Abbass Djoussuf

CONGO

1960–3 Abbé Fulbert Youlou
1963–8 Alphonse Massemba-Debat
1968 Marien Ngouabi
1968 Alphonse Massemba-Debat
1968–9 Alfred Raoul
1969–77 Marien Ngouabi
1977–9 Joachim Yhomby Opango
1979–92 Denis Sassou-Nguesso
1992–7 Pascal Lissouba
1997– Denis Sassou-Nguesso

Head of Government

1992–3 Claude Antonio Dacosta
1993–6 Jacques-Joachim Yhambi-Opango
1996–7 Charles David Ganoa
1997– Bernard Kolelas

CONGO, DEMOCRATIC REPUBLIC OF

President

1960–5 Joseph Kasavubu
1965–97 Mobuto Sese Seko (*formerly* Joseph Mobutu)
1997– Laurent Kabila

Prime Minister

1960 Patrice Emergy Lumumba
1960 Joseph Ileo
1960–1 *College of Commissioners*
1961 Joseph Ileo
1961–4 Cyrille Adoula
1964–5 Moise Tshombe
1965 Evariste Kimba
1965–6 Mulamba Nyungu wa Kadima
1966–77 *As President*
1977–80 Mpinga Kasenga
1980 Bo-Boliko Lokonga Monse Mihambu
1980–1 Nguza Karl I Bond
1981–3 Nsinga Udjuu
1983–6 Kengo wa Dondo
1986–8 *No Prime Minister*
1988 Sambura Pida Nbagui
1988–9 Kengo wa Dondo
1989–1 Lunda Bululu
1991 Mulumba Lukeji
1991 Etienne Tshisekedi
1991–2 Bernardin Mungul Diaka
1992–3 Etienne Tshisekedi
1993–4 Fouistin Birindwa *Acting*
1994–7 Kengo wa Dondo
1997 Etienne Tshisekedi
1997– Likulia Bolongo

COSTA RICA

President

1894–1902 Rafael Yglesias y Castro
1902–6 Ascención Esquivel Ibarra
1906–10 Cleto González Víquez
1910–12 Ricardo Jiménez Oreamuno
1912–14 Cleto González Víquez
1914–17 Alfredo González Flores
1917–19 Federico Tinoco Granados
1919 Julio Acosta García
1919–20 Juan Bautista Quiros
1920–4 Julio Acosta García
1924–8 Ricardo Jiménez Oreamuno
1928–32 Cleto González Víquez
1932–6 Ricardo Jiménez Oreamuno
1936–40 León Cortés Castro
1940–4 Rafael Ángel Calderón Guardia
1944–8 Teodoro Picado Michalski
1948 Santos Léon Herrera
1948–9 *Civil Junta* (José Figueres Ferrer)
1949–52 Otilio Ulate Blanco
1952–3 Alberto Oreamuno Flores
1953–8 José Figueres Ferrer
1958–62 Mario Echandi Jiménez
1962–6 Francisco José Orlich Bolmarcich
1966–70 José Joaquín Trejos Fernández
1970–4 José Figueres Ferrer
1974–8 Daniel Oduber Quirós
1978–82 Rodrigo Carazo Odio
1982–6 Luis Alberto Monge Alvarez
1986–90 Oscar Arias Sánchez
1990–4 Rafael Angel Calderón Fournier
1994–8 José Mariá Figueres
1998– Miguel Angel Rodríguez Echeverría

CÔTE D'IVOIRE

President

1960–93 Félix Houphouët-Boigny
1993– Henri Bedie

Prime Minister

1990–3 Alassane Dramane Ouattara
1993– Daniel Kablan Duncan

CROATIA

President

1991– Franjo Tudjman

Prime Minister

1991–2 Franjo Greguric
1992–3 Hrvoje Sarinic
1993– Nikica Valentic

CUBA

President

1902–6 Tomas Estrada Palma

1906–9 *US rule*
1909–13 José Miguel Gómez
1913–21 Mario García Menocal
1921–5 Alfredo Zayas y Alfonso
1925–33 Gerardo Machado y Morales
1933 Carlos Manuel de Céspedes
1933–4 Ramón Grau San Martín
1934–5 Carlos Mendieta
1935–6 José A Barnet y Vinagres
1936 Miguel Mariano Gómez y Arias
1936–40 Federico Laredo Bru
1940–4 Fulgencio Batista
1944–8 Ramón Grau San Martín
1948–52 Carlos Prío Socarrás
1952–9 Fulgencio Batista
1959 Manuel Urrutia
1959–76 Osvaldo Dorticós Torrado
1959–76 Fidel Castro Ruz *Prime Minister and First Secretary*
1976– Fidel Castro Ruz *President*

CYPRUS

President
1960–77 Archbishop Makarios III
1977–88 Spyros Kyprianou
1988–93 Georgios Vassiliou
1993– Glafkos Clerides

CZECHOSLOVAKIA

President
1918–35 Tomáš Garrigue Masaryk
1935–8 Edvard Beneš
1938–9 Emil Hácha
Occupation
1938–45 Edvard Beneš *Provisional President*
1939–45 Emil Hácha *State President*
1939–45 Jozef Tiso *Slovak Republic President*
Post-war
1945–8 Edvard Beneš
1948–53 Klement Gottwald
1953–7 Antonín Zápotocký
1957–68 Antonín Novotný
1968–75 Ludvík Svoboda
1975–89 Gustáv Husák
1989–92 Václav Havel
Prime Minister
1918–9 Karel Kramář
1919–20 Vlastimil Tusar
1920–1 Jan Černý
1921–2 Edvard Beneš
1922–6 Antonín Švehla
1926 Jan Černý
1926–9 Antonín Švehla
1929–32 František Udržal
1932–5 Jan Malypetr
1935–8 Milan Hodža
1938 Jan Syrový
1938–9 Rudolf Beran
1940–5 Jan Šrámek *in exile*
1945–6 Zdeněk Fierlinger
1946–8 Klement Gottwald
1948–53 Antonín Zápotocký
1953–63 Viliam Široký
1963–8 Josef Lenárt
1968–70 Oldřich Černík
1970–88 Lubomír Štrougal
1988–9 Ladislav Adamec
1989–92 Marian Čalfa
1992– Jan Strasky
First Secretary
1948–52 Rudolf Slánský
1953–68 Antonín Novotný
1968–9 Alexander Dubček
1969–87 Gustáv Husák
1987–9 Míloš Jakeš
1989 Karel Urbánek
1989–92 Ladislav Adamec

CZECH REPUBLIC

President
1993– Václav Havel
Prime Minister
1993–7 Václav Klaus
1997–8 Josef Tosovsky
1998– Miloš Zeman

DENMARK

Monarch
1863–1906 Christian IX
1906–12 Frederik VIII
1912–47 Christian X
1947–72 Frederik IX
1972– Margrethe II
Prime Minister
1900–1 H Sehested
1901–5 J H Deuntzer
1905–8 J C Christensen
1908–9 N Neergaard
1909 L Holstein-Ledreborg
1909–10 C Th Zahle
1910–13 Klaus Berntsen
1913–20 C Th Zahle
1920 Otto Liebe
1920 M P Friis
1920–4 N Neergaard
1924–6 Thorvald Stauning
1926–9 Th Madsen-Mygdal
1929–42 Thorvald Stauning
1942 Wilhelm Buhl
1942–3 Erik Scavenius
1943–5 *No government*
1945 Wilhelm Buhl
1945–7 Knud Kristensen
1947–50 Hans Hedtoft
1950–3 Erik Eriksen
1953–5 Hans Hedtoft
1955–60 Hans Christian Hansen
1960–2 Viggo Kampmann
1962–8 Jens Otto Krag
1968–71 Hilmar Baunsgaard
1971–2 Jens Otto Krag
1972–3 Anker Jorgensen
1973–5 Poul Hartling
1975–82 Anker Jorgensen
1982–93 Poul Schlüter
1993– Poul Nyrop Rasmussen

DJIBOUTI

President
1977–9 Hassan Gouled Aptidon
1999– Ismail Omar Guelleh
Prime Minister
1977–8 Abdallah Mohammed Kamil
1978– Barkat Gourad Hamadou

DOMINICA

President
1977 Frederick E Degazon
1978–9 Louis Cods-Lartigue *Interim*
1979–80 Lenner Armour *Acting*
1980–4 Aurelius Marie
1984–93 Clarence Augustus Seignoret
1993–8 Crispin Sorhaindo
1998– Vernon Shaw
Prime Minister
1978–9 Patrick Roland John
1979–80 Oliver Seraphine
1980–95 Mary Eugenia Charles
1995– Edison James

DOMINICAN REPUBLIC

President
1899–1902 Juan Isidro Jiménez
1902–3 Horacio Vásquez
1903 Alejandro Wos y Gil
1903–4 Juan Isidro Jiménez
1904–6 Carlos Morales
1906–11 Ramon Cáceres
1911–12 Eladio Victoria
1912–13 Adolfo Nouel y Bobadilla
1913–14 José Bordas y Valdés
1914 Ramon Báez
1914–16 Juan Isidro Jiménez
1916–22 *US occupation* (Francisco Henríquez y Carrajal)
1922–4 (Juan Batista Vicini Burgos)
1924–30 Horacio Vásquez
1930 Rafael Estrella Urena
1930–8 Rafael Leónidas Trujillo y Molina
1938–40 Jacinto Bienvenudo Peynado
1940–2 Manuel de Jesus Troncoso de la Concha
1942–52 Rafael Leónidas Trujillo y Molina
1952–60 Hector Bienvenido Trujillo
1960–2 Joaquín Videla Balaguer
1962 Rafael Bonnelly
1962 *Military Junta* (Huberto Bogaert)
1962–3 Rafael Bonnelly
1963 Juan Bosch Gavino
1963 *Military Junta* (Emilio de los Santos)
1963–5 Donald Reid Cabral
1965 Elias Wessin y Wessin
1965 Antonio Imbert Barreras
1965 Francisco Caamaño Deñó
1965–6 Héctor García Godoy Cáceres
1966–78 Joaquín Videla Balaguer
1978–82 Antonio Guzmán Fernández
1982–6 Salvador Jorge Blanco
1986–96 Joaquín Videla Balaguer
1996– Leonel Fernandez Reyna

ECUADOR

President
1895–1901 Eloy Alfaro

1901–5	Leónides Plaza Gutiérrez
1905–6	Lizardo García
1906–11	Eloy Alfaro
1911	Emilio Estrada
1911–12	Carlos Freile Zaldumbide
1912–16	Leónides Plaza Gutiérrez
1916–20	Alfredo Baquerizo Moreno
1920–4	José Luis Tamayo
1924–5	Gonzálo S de Córdova
1925–6	*Military Juntas*
1926–31	Isidro Ayora
1931	Luis A Larrea Alba
1932–3	Juan de Dios Martínez Mera
1933–4	Abelardo Montalvo
1934–5	José María Velasco Ibarra
1935	Antonio Pons
1935–7	Federico Páez
1937–8	Alberto Enriquez Gallo
1938	Manuel María Borrero
1938–9	Aurelio Mosquera Narváez
1939–40	Julio Enrique Moreno
1940–4	Carlos Alberto Arroya del Río
1944–7	José María Velasco Ibarra
1947	Carlos Mancheno
1947–8	Carlos Julio Arosemena Tola
1948–52	Galo Plaza Lasso
1952–6	José María Velasco Ibarra
1956–60	Camilo Ponce Enríquez
1960–1	José María Velasco Ibarra
1961–3	Carlos Julio Arosemena Monroy
1963–6	*Military Junta*
1966	Clemente Yerovi Indaburu
1966–8	Otto Arosemena Gómez
1968–72	José María Velasco Ibarra
1972–6	Guillermo Rodríguez Lara
1976–9	*Military Junta*
1979–81	Jaime Roldós Aguilera
1981–4	Oswaldo Hurtado Larrea
1984–8	León Febres Cordero Rivadeira
1988–92	Rodrigo Borja Cevallos
1992–6	Sixto Durán Ballén
1996–7	Abdala Bucaram
1997	Rosalia Arteaga
1997–8	Fabian Alarcón Rivero
1998–	Jamil Mahuad Witt

EGYPT

Monarch

1922–36	Fouad I
1936–7	Farouk *Trusteeship*
1937–52	Farouk I

Republic of Egypt

President

1952–4	Mohammed Najib
1954–70	Gamal Abdel Nasser
1970–81	Mohammed Anwar el-Sadat
1981–	Mohammed Hosni Mubarak

Prime Minister

1895–1908	Mustafa Fahmy
1908–10	Butros Ghali
1910–14	Mohammed Said
1914–19	Hussein Rushdi
1919	Mohammed Said
1919–20	Yousuf Wahba
1920–1	Mohammed Tewfiq Nazim
1921	Adli Yegen
1922	Abdel Khaliq Tharwat
1922–3	Mohammed Tewfiq Nazim
1923–4	Yehia Ibrahim
1924	Saad Zaghloul
1924–6	Ahmed Zaywan
1926–7	Adli Yegen
1927–8	Abdel Khaliq Tharwat
1928	Mustafa an-Nahass
1928–9	Mohammed Mahmoud
1929–30	Adli Yegen
1930	Mustafa an-Nahass
1930–3	Ismail Sidqi
1933–4	Abdel Fattah Yahya
1934–6	Mohammed Tewfiq Nazim
1936	Ali Maher
1936–7	Mustafa an-Nahass
1937–9	Mohammed Mahmoud
1939–40	Ali Maher
1940	Hassan Sabri
1940–2	Hussein Sirry
1942–4	Mustafa an-Nahass
1944–5	Ahmed Maher
1945–6	Mahmoud Fahmy El-Nuqrashi
1946	Ismail Sidqi
1946–8	Mahmoud Fahmy El-Nuqrashi
1948–9	Ibrahim Abdel Hadi
1949–50	Hussein Sirry
1950–2	Mustafa an-Nahass
1952	Ali Maher
1952	Najib el-Hilali
1952	Hussein Sirry
1952	Najib el-Hilali
1952	Ali Maher

Republic of Egypt

1952–4	Mohammed Najib
1954	Gamal Abdel Nasser
1954	Mohammed Najib
1954–62	Gamal Abdel Nasser
1958–61	*United Arab Republic*
1962–5	Ali Sabri
1965–6	Zakariya Mohyi Ed-Din
1966–7	Mohammed Sidqi Soliman
1967–70	Gamal Abdel Nasser
1970–2	Mahmoud Fawzi
1972–3	Aziz Sidki
1973–4	Mohamed Anwar el-Sadat
1974–5	Abdel Aziz Hijazy
1975–8	Mamdouh Salem
1978–80	Mustafa Khalil
1980–1	Mohamed Anwar el-Sadat
1981–2	Hosni Mubarak
1982–4	Fouad Monyi Ed-Din
1984	Kamal Hassan Ali
1985–6	Ali Lotfi
1986–96	Atef Sidqi
1996–	Kamal Ahmed Ganzouri

EL SALVADOR

President

1898–1903	Tomás Regalado
1903–7	Pedro José Escalon
1907–11	Fernando Figueroa
1911–13	Manuel Enrique Araujo
1913–14	Carlos Meléndez *Designate*
1914–15	Alfonso Quiñónez Molina *President Designate*
1915–18	Carlos Meléndez
1918–19	Alfonso Quiñónez Molina *Vice President*
1919–23	Jorge Meléndez
1923–7	Alfonso Quiñónez Molina
1927–31	Pio Romero Bosque
1931	Arturo Araujo
1931	*Military Administration*
1931–4	Maximiliano H Martinez *Vice President*
1934–5	Andrés I Menéndez *Provisional*
1935–44	Maximiliano H Martinez
1944	Andrés I Menéndez *Vice President*
1944–5	Osmin Aguirre y Salinas *Provisional*
1945–8	Salvador Castaneda Castro
1948–50	*Revolutionary Council*
1950–6	Oscar Osorio
1956–60	José María Lemus
1960–1	*Military Junta*
1961–2	*Civil-Military Administration*
1962	Rodolfo Eusebio Cordón *Provisional*
1962–7	Julio Adalberto Rivera
1967–72	Fidel Sánchez Hernández
1972–7	Arturo Armando Molina
1977–9	Carlos Humberto Romero
1979–82	*Military Juntas*
1982–4	*Government of National Unanimity* (Alvaro Magaña)
1984–9	José Napoleón Duarte
1989–94	Alfredo Cristiani
1994–9	Armando Calderón Sol
1999–	Francisco Flores

EQUATORIAL GUINEA

President

1968–79	Francisco Macias Nguema
1979–	Teodoro Obiang Nguema Mbasogo

Prime Minister

1993–6	Silvestre Siale Bileka
1996–	Angel Serafin Seriche Dougan

ERITREA

President

1993–	Issais Afewerki

ESTONIA

President

1938–40	Konstantin Päts
1940–91	*Russian rule*
1991–2	Arnold Rüütel
1992–	Lennart Meri

Prime Minister

1918–19	Konstantin Päts
1919	Otto Strandmann
1919–20	Jaan Tonisson
1920–21	Ants Piip
1921–2	Konstantin Päts
1922–3	Juhan Kukk
1923–4	Konstantin Päts
1924	Friedrich Akel
1924–5	Jüri Jaakson
1925–7	Jaan Teemant
1927–8	Jaan Tonisson

1928–9	August Rei
1929–31	Otto Strandmann
1931–2	Konstantin Päts
1932	Jaan Teemant
1932	Kaarel Einbund
1932–3	Konstantin Päts
1933	Jaan Tonisson
1933–8	Konstantin Päts
1938–9	Kaarel Eenpalu (Einbund)
1939–40	Jüri Uluots
1940–91	*Russian rule*
1991–2	Edgar Savisaar
1992	Tiit Vahi
1992–4	Mart Laar
1994–7	Andres Tarand
1997–9	Mart Siiman
1999–	Mart Laar

ETHIOPIA

Monarch

1889–1911	Menelik II
1911–16	Lij Iyasu (Joshua)
1916–28	Zawditu
1928–74	Haile Selassie *Emperor from 1930*

Provisional Military Administrative Council

Chairman

1974–7	Teferi Benti
1977–87	Mengistu Haile Mariam

People's Democratic Republic

President

1987–91	Mengistu Haile Mariam
1991–5	Meles Zenawi (*Interim*)
1995–	Negaso Gidada

Prime Minister

1991	Tesfaye Dinka
1991–5	Tamirat Layne
1995–	Meles Zenawi

EUROPEAN UNION (EU)

European Commission

President

1967–70	Jean Rey
1970–2	Franco M Malfatti
1972–3	Sicco L Mansholt
1973–7	Francois-Xavier Ortoli
1977–81	Roy Jenkins
1981–5	Gaston Thorn
1985–94	Jacques Delors

European Union

1994	Jacques Delors
1995–	Jacques Santer

FEDERATED STATES OF MICRONESIA

President

1991–6	Bailey Olter
1996–9	Jacob Nena
1999–	Leo Falcam

FIJI

Chief of State: British monarch, represented by Governor-General

Prime Minister

1970–87	Kamisese Mara
1987	Timoci Bavadra

Interim Administration

Governor-General

1987	Penaia Ganilau
1987–	*Military* (Sitiveni Rabuka)

Republic

Chairman

1987	Sitiveni Rabuka

President

1987–93	Penaia Ganilau
1993–	Kamisese Mara

Prime Minister

1987–92	Kamisese Mara
1992–9	Sitiveni Rabuka
1999–	Mahendra Chaudhry

FINLAND

President

1919–25	Kaarlo Juho Ståhlberg
1925–31	Lauri Kristian Relander
1931–7	Pehr Evind Svinhufvud
1937–40	Kyösti Kallio
1940–4	Risto Ryti
1944–6	Carl Gustaf Mannerheim
1946–56	Juho Kusti Paasikivi
1956–81	Urho Kaleva Kekkonen
1982–94	Makino Koivisto
1994–	Martti Ahtisaarsi

Prime Minister

1917–18	Pehr Evind Svinhufvud
1918	Juho Kusti Paasikivi
1918–19	Lauri Johannes Ingman
1919	Kaarlo Castrén
1919–20	Juho Vennola
1920–1	Rafael Erich
1921–2	Juho Vennola
1922	Aino Kaarlo Cajander
1922–4	Kyösti Kallio
1924	Aino Kaarlo Cajander
1924–5	Lauri Johannes Ingman
1925	Antti Agaton Tulenheimo
1925–6	Kyösti Kallio
1926–7	Väinö Tanner
1927–8	Juho Emil Sunila
1928–9	Oskari Mantere
1929–30	Kyösti Kallio
1930–1	Pehr Evind Svinhufvud
1931–2	Juho Emil Sunila
1932–6	Toivo Kivimäki
1936–7	Kyösti Kallio
1937–9	Aino Kaarlo Cajander
1939–41	Risto Ryti
1941–3	Johann Rangell
1943–4	Edwin Linkomies
1944	Andreas Hackzell
1944	Urho Jonas Castrén
1944–5	Juho Kusti Paasikivi
1946–8	Mauno Pekkala
1948–50	Karl August Fagerholm
1950–3	Urho Kekkonen
1953–4	Sakari Tuomioja
1954	Ralf Törngren
1954–6	Urho Kekkonen
1956–7	Karl August Fagerholm
1957	Väinö Johannes Sukselainen
1957–8	Rainer von Fieandt
1958	Reino Iisakki Kuuskoski
1958–9	Karl August Fagerholm
1959–61	Väinö Johannes Sukselainen
1961–2	Martti Miettunen
1962–3	Ahti Karjalainen
1963–4	Reino Ragnar Lehto
1964–6	Johannes Virolainen
1966–8	Rafael Paasio
1968–70	Mauno Koivisto
1970	Teuvo Ensio Aura
1970–1	Ahti Karjalainen
1971–2	Teuvo Ensio Aura
1972	Rafael Paasio
1972–5	Taisto Kalevi Sorsa
1975	Keijo Antero Liinamaa
1975–7	Martti Miettunen
1977–9	Taisto Kalevi Sorsa
1979–82	Mauno Koivisto
1982–7	Taisto Kalevi Sorsa
1987–91	Harri Holkeri
1991–5	Esko Aho
1995–	Paavo Lipponen

FRANCE

President

Third Republic

1899–1906	Emile Loubet
1906–13	Armand Fallières
1913–20	Raymond Poincaré
1920	Paul Deschanel
1920–4	Alexandre Millerand
1924–31	Gaston Doumergue
1931–2	Paul Doumer
1932–40	Albert Lebrun

Fourth Republic

1947–54	Vincent Auriol
1954–8	René Coty

Fifth Republic

1958–69	Charles de Gaulle
1969–74	Georges Pompidou
1974–81	Valéry Giscard d'Estaing
1981–95	François Mitterrand
1995–	Jacques René Chirac

Prime Minister

Third Republic

1899–1902	Pierre Waldeck-Rousseau
1902–5	Emile Combes
1905–6	Maurice Rouvier
1906	Jean Sarrien
1906–9	Georges Clemenceau
1909–11	Aristide Briand
1911	Ernest Monis
1911–12	Joseph Caillaux
1912–13	Raymond Poincaré
1913	Aristide Briand
1913	Jean Louis Barthou
1913–14	Gaston Doumergue
1914	Alexandre Ribot
1914–15	René Viviani
1915–17	Aristide Briand
1917	Alexandre Ribot
1917	Paul Painlevé
1917–20	Georges Clemenceau
1920	Alexandre Millerand
1920–1	Georges Leygues

1921–2 Aristide Briand
1922–4 Raymond Poincaré
1924 Frédéric François-Marsal
1924–5 Édouard Herriot
1925 Paul Painlevé
1925–6 Aristide Briand
1926 Édouard Herriot
1926–9 Raymond Poincaré
1929 Aristide Briand
1929–30 André Tardieu
1930 Camille Chautemps
1930 André Tardieu
1930–1 Théodore Steeg
1931–2 Pierre Laval
1932 André Tardieu
1932 Édouard Herriot
1932–3 Joseph Paul-Boncour
1933 Édouard Daladier
1933 Albert Sarrault
1933–4 Camille Chautemps
1934 Édouard Daladier
1934 Gaston Doumergue
1934–5 Pierre-Étienne Flandin
1935 Fernand Bouisson
1935–6 Pierre Laval
1936 Albert Sarrault
1936–7 Léon Blum
1937–8 Camille Chautemps
1938 Léon Blum
1938–40 Édouard Daladier
1940 Paul Reynaud
1940 Philippe Pétain

Vichy Government

1940–4 Philippe Pétain

Provisional Government of the French Republic

1944–6 Charles de Gaulle
1946 Félix Gouin
1946 Georges Bidault

Fourth Republic

1946–7 Léon Blum
1947 Paul Ramadier
1947–8 Robert Schuman
1948 André Marie
1948 Robert Schuman
1948–9 Henri Queuille
1949–50 Georges Bidault
1950 Henri Queuille
1950–1 René Pleven
1951 Henri Queuille
1951–2 René Pleven
1952 Edgar Faure
1952–3 Antoine Pinay
1953 René Mayer
1953–4 Joseph Laniel
1954–5 Pierre Mendès-France
1955–6 Edgar Faure
1956–7 Guy Alcide Mollet
1957 Maurice Bourgès-Maunoury
1957–8 Félix Gaillard
1958 Pierre Pflimin
1958–9 Charles de Gaulle

Fifth Republic

1959–62 Michel Debré
1962–8 Georges Pompidou
1968–9 Maurice Couve de Murville
1969–72 Jacques Chaban Delmas
1972–4 Pierre Mesmer
1974–6 Jacques Chirac
1976–81 Raymond Barre
1981–4 Pierre Mauroy
1984–6 Laurent Fabius
1986–8 Jacques Chirac
1988–91 Michel Rocard
1991–2 Edith Cresson
1992–3 Pierre Bérégovoy
1993–5 Édouard Balladur
1995–7 Alain Juppé
1997 Lionel Jospin

GABON

President

1960–7 Léon M'ba
1967– Omar (Albert-Bernard *to 1973*) Bongo

Prime Minister

1960–75 *As President*
1975–90 Léon Mébiame (Mébiane)
1990–4 Casimir Oyé M'ba
1994–9 Paulin Obame Nguema
1999– Jean-François Ntoutoume-Emane

THE GAMBIA

President

1965–94 Dawda Kairabu Jawara

Military Rule

1994- Yayeh Jameh (Chairman)

GEORGIA

President

1991–2 Zviad Gamsakhurdia
1992 *Military Council* (Tengiz Kitovani, Dzhaba Ioseliani)
1992– Eduard Shevardnadze *Chair of the Supreme Soviet*

Prime Minister

1992–3 Tengiz Sigua
1993–5 Otar Patsarsia

Minister of State

1995–8 Nikoloz Lekishvili
1998– Vazha Lortkipanidze

GERMANY

German Empire

Monarch

1881–1918 Wilhelm I

Chancellor

1900–9 Bernhard Heinrich, Prince von Bülow
1909–17 Theobald von Bethmann Hollweg
1917–18 Georg von Hefling
1918 Prince Max of Baden

Weimar Republic

Chancellor

1918 Friedrich Ebert
1919–20 Philipp Scheidemann
1920–1 Konstantin Fehrenbach
1921–2 Karl Joseph Wirth
1922–3 Wilhelm Cuno
1923 Gustav Stresemann
1923–5 Wilhelm Marx
1925–6 Hans Luther
1926–8 Wilhelm Marx
1928–9 Herman Müller
1929–32 Heinrich Brüning
1932–3 Franz von Papen
1933–45 Adolf Hitler (from 1934 *Führer*)

German Democratic Republic (East Germany)

President

1949–60 Wilhelm Pieck

Chairman of the Council of State

1960–73 Walter Ernst Karl Ulbricht
1973–6 Willi Stoph
1976–89 Erich Honecker
1989 Egon Krenz
1989–90 Gregor Gysi *General Secretary as Chairman*

Premier

1949–64 Otto Grotewohl
1964–73 Willi Stoph
1973–6 Horst Sindermann
1976–89 Willi Stoph
1989–90 Hans Modrow
1990 Lothar de Maizière

German Federal Republic (until 1990 West Germany)

President

1949–59 Theodor Heuss
1959–69 Heinrich Lübke
1969–74 Gustav Heinemann
1974–9 Walter Scheel
1979–84 Karl Carstens
1984–94 Richard von Weizsäcker
1994–9 Roman Herzog
1999– Johannes Rau

Chancellor

1949–63 Konrad Adenauer
1963–6 Ludwig Erhard
1966–9 Kurt Georg Kiesinger
1969–74 Willy Brandt
1974–82 Helmut Schmidt
1982–98 Helmut Kohl
1998– Gerhard Schröder

GHANA

President

1960–6 Kwame Nkrumah

National Liberation Council

Chairman

1966–9 Joseph Arthur Ankrah
1969 Akwasi Amankwa Afrifa
1969–70 *Presidential Committee*

President

1970–2 Edward Akufo-Addo

Chairman

1972–8 *National Redemption Council* (Ignatius Kuti Acheampong)
1978–9 *Supreme Military Council* (Fred W Akuffo)
1979 *Armed Forces Revolutionary Council* (Jerry John Rawlings)

President

1979–81 Hilla Limann

Provisional National Defence Council

Chairman

1981–92 Jerry John Rawlings

President

1992– Jerry John Rawlings

Prime Minister

1960–9 *As President*
1969–72 Kufi Abrefa Busia
1972–8 *As President*
1978– *No Prime Minister*

GREECE

Monarch

1863–1913 Georgios I
1913–17 Konstantinos I
1917–20 Alexandros
1920–2 Konstantinos I
1922–3 Georgios II
1923–4 Pavlos Koundouriotis *Regent*

Republic

President

1924–6 Pavlos Koundouriotis
1926 Theodoros Pangalos
1926–9 Pavlos Koundouriotis
1929–35 Alexandros T Zaïmis

Monarch

1935 Georgios Kondylis Regent
1935–47 Georgios II
1947–64 Pavlos I
1964–7 Konstantinos (Constantine) II
1967–73 *Military Junta*
1973 Georgios Papadopoulos *Regent*

Republic

President

1973 Georgios Papadopoulos
1973–4 Phaedon Gizikis
1974–5 Michael Stasinopoulos
1975–80 Konstantinos Tsatsos
1980–5 Konstantinos Karamanlis
1985–90 Christos Sartzetaki
1990–5 Konstantinos Karamanlis
1995– Kostas Stephanopoulos

Prime Minister

1899–1901 Georgios Theotokis
1901–2 Alexandros Thrasyboulos Zaïmis
1902–3 Theodoros Deligiannis
1903 Georgios Theotokis
1903 Dimitrios Georgios Rallis
1903–4 Georgios Theotokis
1904–5 Theodoros Deligiannis
1905 Dimitrios Georgios Rallis
1905–9 Georgios Theotokis
1909 Dimitrios Georgios Rallis
1909–10 Kyriakoulis P Mavromichalis
1910 Stephanos Nikolaos Dragoumis
1910–15 Eleutherios K Venizelos
1915 Dimitrios P Gounaris
1915 Eleutherios K Venizelos
1915 Alexandros Thrasyboulos Zaïmis
1915–16 Stephanos Skouloudis
1916 Alexandros Thrasyboulos Zaïmis
1916 Nikolaos P Kalogeropoulos
1916–17 Spyridon Lambros
1917 Alexandros Thrasyboulos Zaïmis
1917–20 Eleutherios K Venizelos
1920–1 Dimitrios Georgios Rallis
1921 Nikolaos P Kalogeropoulos
1921–2 Dimitrios P Gounaris
1922 Nikolaos Stratos
1922 Petros E Protopapadakis
1922 Nikolaos Triandaphyllakos
1922 Sotirios Krokidas
1922 Alexandros Thrasyboulos Zaïmis
1922–3 Stylianos Gonatas
1924 Eleutherios K Venizelos
1924 Georgios Kaphandaris
1924 Alexandros Papanastasiou
1924 Themistocles Sophoulis
1924–5 Andreas Michalakopoulos
1925–6 Alexandros N Chatzikyriakos
1926 Theodoros Pangalos
1926 Athanasius Eftaxias
1926 Georgios Kondylis
1926–8 Alexandros Thrasyboulos Zaïmis
1928–32 Eleutherios K Venizelos
1932 Alexandros Papanastasiou
1932 Eleutherios K Venizelos
1932–3 Panagiotis Tsaldaris
1933 Eleutherios K Venizelos
1933 Nikolaos Plastiras
1933 Alexandros Othonaos
1933–5 Panagiotis Tsaldaris
1935 Georgios Kondylis
1935–6 Konstantinos Demertzis
1936–41 Yanni Metaxas
1941 Alexandros Koryzis
1941 *Chairman of Ministers* Georgios (George) II
1941 *German occupation* (Emmanuel Tsouderos)
1941–2 Georgios Tsolakoglou
1942–3 Konstantinos Logothetopoulos
1943–4 Ioannis Rallis

Government in exile

1941–4 Emmanuel Tsouderos
1944 Sophocles Venizelos
1944–5 Georgios Papandreou

Post-war

1945 Nicholaos Plastiras
1945 Petros Voulgaris
1945 Damaskinos, Archbishop of Athens
1945 Panagiotis Kanellopoulos
1945–6 Themistocles Sophoulis
1946 Panagiotis Politzas
1946–7 Konstantinos Tsaldaris
1947 Dimitrios Maximos
1947 Konstantinos Tsaldaris
1947–9 Themistocles Sophoulis
1949–50 Alexandros Diomedes
1950 Ioannis Theotokis
1950 Sophocles Venizelos
1950 Nicholaos Plastiras
1950–1 Sophocles Venizelos
1951 Nicholaos Plastiras
1952 Dimitrios Kiousopoulos
1952–5 Alexandros Papagos
1955 Stephanos C Stephanopoulos
1955–8 Konstantinos Karamanlis
1958 Konstantinos Georgakopoulos
1958–61 Konstantinos Karamanlis
1961 Konstantinos Dovas
1961–3 Konstantinos Karamanlis
1963 Panagiotis Pipinellis
1963 Stylianos Mavromichalis
1963 Georgios Papandreou
1963–4 Ioannis Paraskevopoulos
1964–5 Georgios Papandreou
1965 Georgios Athanasiadis-Novas
1965 Elias Tsirimokos
1965–6 Stephanos C Stephanopoulos
1966–7 Ioannis Paraskevopoulos
1967 Panagiotis Kanellopoulos
1967–74 *Military junta*
1967 Konstantinos Kollias
1967–73 Georgios Papadopoulos
1973 Spyridon Markezinis
1973–4 Adamantios Androutsopoulos
1974–80 Constantine Karamanlis
1980–1 Georgios Rallis
1981–9 Andreas Georgios Papandreou
1989 Tzannis Tzannetakis
1989–90 Xenofon Zolotas
1990–3 Konstantinos Mitsotakis
1993–6 Andreas Papandreou
1996– Kostas Simitis

GRENADA

Chief of State: British monarch, represented by Governor-General

Prime Minister

1974–9 Eric M Gairy
1979–83 Maurice Bishop
1983–4 Nicholas Brathwaite *Chairman of Interim Council*
1984–9 Herbert A Blaize
1989–90 Ben Jones *Acting*
1990–5 Nicholas Brathwaite
1995 George Brizan
1995– Keith Mitchell

GUATEMALA

President

1898–1920 Manuel Estrada Cabrera
1920–2 Carlos Herrera y Luna
1922–6 José María Orellana
1926–30 Lázaro Chacón
1930 Baudillo Palma
1930–1 Manuel María Orellana
1931 José María Reyna Andrade
1931–44 Jorge Ubico Castañeda
1944 Federico Ponce Vaidez
1944–5 Jacobo Arbenz Guzmán
1945–51 Juan José Arévalo
1951–4 Jacobo Arbenz Guzmán
1954 *Military Junta* (Carlos Díaz)
1954 Elfego J Monzón
1954–7 Carlos Castillo Armas
1957 *Military Junta* (Oscar Mendoza Azurdia)
1957 Luis Arturo González López
1957–8 *Military Junta* (Guillermo Flores Avendaño)
1958–63 Miguel Ydígoras Fuentes
1963–6 *Military Junta* (Enrique Peralta Azurdia)
1966–70 Julio César Méndez Montenegro
1970–4 Carlos Araña Osorio
1974–8 Kyell Eugenio Laugerua García
1978–82 Romeo Lucas García
1982 Angel Aníbal Guevara

1982–3 Efraín Rios Montt
1983–6 Oscar Humberto Mejía Victores
1986–91 Marco Vinicio Cerezo Arévalo
1991–3 Jorge Serrano Elias
1993–6 Ramiro de Léon Carpio
1996– Alvaro Arzú Irigoyen

GUINEA

President
1961–84 Ahmed Sékou Touré
1984– Lansana Conté

Prime Minister
1958–72 Ahmed Sékou Touré
1972–84 Louis Lansana Beavogui
1984–5 Diarra Traore
1985–96 *No Prime Minister*
1996–9 Sidia Toure
1999– Lamine Sidime

GUINEA-BISSAU

President
1974–80 Luis de Almeida Cabral
1980–4 *Revolutionary Counci* (João Bernardo Vieira)
1984–99 João Bernardo Vieira
1999– Malam Bacai Sanhá (*Acting*)

Prime Minister
1992–4 Carlos Correia
1994–7 Manuel Saturnino da Costa
1997–8 Carlos Correia
1998– Francisco Fadul

GUYANA

President
1970– Edward A Luckhoo
1970–80 Arthur Chung
1980–5 (Linden) Forbes (Sampson) Burnham
1985–92 (Hugh) Desmond Hoyte
1992–7 Cheddi Bharrat Jagan
1997 Samuel Hinds
1997– Janet Jagan

Prime Minister
1966–85 (Linden) Forbes (Sampson) Burnham
1985–92 Hamilton Green
1992–7 Samuel Hinds
1997 Janet Jagan
1997– Samuel Hinds

HAITI

President
1896–1902 P A Tirésias Simon Lam
1902 Boisrond Canal
1902–8 Alexis Nord
1908–11 Antoine Simon
1911–12 Michel Cincinnatus Leconte
1912–13 Tancrède Auguste
1913–14 Michael Oreste
1914 Oreste Zamor
1914–15 Joseph Davilmare Théodore
1915 Jean Velbrun-Guillaume
1915–22 Philippe Sudre Dartiguenave
1922–30 Joseph Louis Bornó
1930 Étienne Roy
1930–41 Sténio Joseph Vincent
1941–6 Élie Lescot
1946 *Military Junta* (Frank Lavaud)
1946–50 Dumarsais Estimé
1950 *Military Junta* (Frank Lavaud)
1950–6 Paul E Magloire
1956–7 François Sylvain
1957 *Military Junta*
1957 Léon Cantave
1957 Daniel Fignolé
1957 Antoine Kebreau
1957–71 François Duvalier ('Papa Doc')
1971–86 Jean-Claude Duvalier ('Baby Doc')
1986–8 Henri Namphy
1988 Leslie Manigat
1988 Henri Namphy
1988–90 Prosper Avril
1990 Ertha Pascal-Trouillot *Interim*
1990–1 Jean Bertrand Aristide
1991–2 Joseph Nerette *Interim*
1992–4 Marc Bazin
1994–6 Jean Bertrand Aristide
1996– René Préval

Prime Minister
1992–3 Marc Bazin
1993–4 Robert Malval
1994–5 Smarck Michel
1995–6 Claudette Werleigh
1996–7 Rosny Smart
1997–8 *No Prime Minister*
1998– Jacques Edouard Alexis

HONDURAS

President
1900–3 Terencio Sierra
1903 Juan Angel Arias
1903–7 Manuel Bonilla Chirinos
1907–11 Miguel E Dávila
1911–12 Francisco Bertrand
1912–13 Manuel Bonilla Chirinos
1913–19 Francisco Bertrand
1919–24 Rafael López Gutiérrez
1924–5 Vicente Tosta Carrasco
1925–8 Miguel Paz Barahona
1929–33 Vicente Mejía Clindres
1933–49 Tiburcio Carías Andino
1949–54 Juan Manuel Gálvez

Head of State
1954–6 Julio Lozano Diaz
1956–7 *Military Junta*

President
1958–63 José Ramón Villeda Morales

Head of State
1963–5 Oswaldo López Arellano

President
1965–71 Oswaldo López Arellano
1971–2 Ramón Ernesto Cruz

Head of State
1972–5 Oswaldo López Arellano
1975–8 Juan Alberto Melgar Castro
1978–80 Policarpo Paz García

President
1982–6 Roberto Suazo Córdova
1986–90 José Azcona Hoyo
1990–4 Rafael Callejas Romero
1994–7 Carlos Roberto Reina
1997– Carlos Roberto Flores Facussé

HUNGARY

Monarch
1900–1916 Franz Josef I
1916–18 Charles IV

President
1919 Mihály Károlyi
1919 *Revolutionary Governing Council* (Sándor Garbai)
1920–44 Miklós Horthy *Regent*
1944–5 *Provisional National Assembly*
1946–8 Zoltán Tildy
1948–50 Arpád Szakasits
1950–2 Sándor Rónai
1952–67 István Dobi
1967–87 Pál Losonczi
1987–8 Károly Németh
1988–9 Brunó Ferenc Straub
1989–90 Mátyás Szúrös
1990– Árpád Göncz

Premier
1899–1903 Kálmán Széll
1903 Károly Khuen-Héderváry
1903–5 István Tisza
1905–6 Géza Fejérváry
1906–10 Sándor Wekerle
1910–12 Károly Khuen-Héderváry
1912–13 László Lukács
1913–17 István Tisza
1917 Móric Esterházy
1917–18 Sándor Wekerle
1918–19 Mihály Károlyi
1919 Dénes Berinkey
1919 *Revolutionary Governing Council*
1919 Gyula Peidl
1919 István Friedrich
1919–20 Károly Huszár
1920 Sándor Simonyi-Semadam
1920–1 Pál Teleki
1921–31 István Bethlen
1931–2 Gyula Károlyi
1932–6 Gyula Gömbös
1936–8 Kálmán Darányi
1938–9 Béla Imrédy
1939–41 Pál Teleki
1941–2 László Bárdossy
1942–4 Miklós Kállay
1944 Döme Sztójay
1944 Géza Lakatos
1944 Ferenc Szálasi
1944–5 *Provisional National Assembly* (Béla Miklós Dálnoki)
1945–6 Zoltán Tildy
1946–7 Ferenc Nagy
1947–8 Lajos Dinnyés
1948–52 István Dobi
1952–3 Mátyás Rákosi
1953–5 Imre Nagy
1955–6 András Hegedüs
1956 Imre Nagy
1956–8 János Kádár
1958–61 Ferenc Münnich
1961–5 János Kádár
1965–7 Gyula Kállai
1967–75 Jenö Fock
1975–87 György Lázár

1987–8	Károly Grosz
1988–90	Miklós Németh
1990–3	József Antall
1993–4	Peter Boros
1994–8	Gyula Horn
1998–	Viktor Orban

First Secretary

1949–56	Mátyás Rákosi
1956	Ernö Gerö
1956–88	János Kádár
1988–9	Károly Grósz

ICELAND

President

1944–52	Sveinn Björnsson
1952–68	Ásgeir Ásgeirsson
1968–80	Kristján Eldjárn
1980–96	Vigdís Finnbogadóttir
1996–	Olafur Ragnar Grimsson

Prime Minister

1900–1	C Goos
1901–4	P A Alberti
1904–9	Hannes Hafstein
1909–11	Björn Jónsson
1911–12	Kristján Jónsson
1912–14	Hannes Hafstein
1914–15	Sigurdur Eggerz
1915–17	Einar Arnórsson
1917–22	Jón Magnússon
1922–4	Sigurdur Eggerz
1924–6	Jón Magnússon
1926–7	Jon Porláksson
1927–32	Tryggvi Pórhallsson
1932–4	Ásgeir Ásgeirsson
1934–42	Hermann Jónasson
1942	Ólafur Thors
1942–4	Björn Pórdarsson
1944–7	Ólafur Thors
1947–9	Stefán Jóhann Stefánsson
1949–50	Ólafur Thors
1950–3	Steingrímur Steinpórsson
1953–6	Ólafur Thors
1956–8	Hermann Jónasson
1958–9	Emil Jónsson
1959–61	Ólafur Thors
1961	Bjarni Benediktsson
1961–3	Ólafur Thors
1963–70	Bjarni Benediktsson
1970–1	Jóhann Hafstein
1971–4	Ólafur Jóhannesson
1974–8	Geir Hallgrímsson
1978–9	Ólafur Jóhannesson
1979	Benedikt Gröndal
1980–3	Gunnar Thoroddsen
1983–7	Steingrímur Hermannsson
1987–8	Thorsteinn Pálsson
1988–91	Steingrímur Hermannsson
1991–	David Oddsson

INDIA

President

1950–62	Rajendra Prasad
1962–7	Sarvepalli Radhakrishnan
1967–9	Zakir Husain
1969	Varahagiri Venkatagiri *Acting*
1969	Mohammed Hidayatullah *Acting*
1969–74	Varahagiri Venkatagiri
1974–7	Fakhruddin Ali Ahmed
1977	B D Jatti *Acting*
1977–82	Neelam Sanjiva Reddy
1982–7	Giani Zail Singh
1987–92	Ramaswami Venkataraman
1992–7	Shankar Dayal Sharma
1997–	K R Narayanan

Prime Minister

1947–64	Jawaharlal Nehru
1964	Gulzari Lal Nanda *Acting*
1964–6	Lal Bahadur Shastri
1966	Gulzari Lal Nanda *Acting*
1966–77	Indira Gandhi
1977–9	Morarji Ranchhodji Desai
1979–80	Charan Singh
1980–4	Indira Gandhi
1984–9	Rajiv Gandhi
1989–90	Vishwanath Pratap Singh
1990–1	Chandra Shekhar
1991–6	P V Narasimha Rao
1996	Atal Bihari Vajpayee
1996–7	Deve Gowda
1997–8	Inder Kumar Gujral
1998–	Atal Bihari Vajpayee

INDONESIA

President

1945–9	Ahmed Sukarno

Republic

1949–66	Ahmed Sukarno
1966–98	Thojib N J Suharto
1998–	Bacharuddin Jusuf Habibie

Prime Minister

1945	R A A Wiranatakusumah
1945–7	Sutan Sjahrir
1947–8	Amir Sjarifuddin
1948	Mohammed Hatta
1948–9	Sjarifuddin Prawiraranegara
1949	Susanto Tirtoprodjo
1949	Mohammed Hatta
1950	Dr Halim
1950–1	Mohammed Natsir
1951–2	Sukiman Wirjosandjojo
1952–3	Dr Wilopo
1953–5	Ali Sastroamidjojo
1955–6	Burhanuddin Harahap
1956–7	Ali Sastroamidjojo
1957–9	Raden Haji Djuanda Kurtawidjaja
1959–63	Ahmed Sukarno
1963–6	S E Subandrio
1966–	*No Prime Minister*

IRAN (PERSIA)

Shah

1896–1907	Muzaffar-ud-Din
1907–9	Mohammed 'Ali
1909–25	Ahmad Mirza
1925–41	Reza Khan
1941–79	Mohammed Reza Pahlavi

Republic

Leader of the Islamic Revolution

1979–89	Ruhollah Khomeini
1989–	Seyed Ali Khamenei

President

1980–1	Abolhassan Bani-Sadr
1981	Mohammed Ali Rajai
1981–9	Sayed Ali Khamenei
1989–97	Ali Akbar Hashemi Rafsanjani
1997–	Sayed Mohammad Khatami

Prime Minister

1979	Shahpur Bakhtiar
1979–80	Mehdi Bazargan
1980–1	Mohammed Ali Rajai
1981	Mohammed Javad Bahonar
1981	Mohammed Reza Mahdavi-Kani
1981–9	Mir Hossein Moussavi
1989–	*No Prime Minister*

IRAQ

Monarch

1921–33	Faisal I
1933–9	Ghazi I
1939–58	Faisal II (*Regent 1939–53* Abdul Illah)

Republic

Commander of the National Forces

1958–63	Abdul Karim Qassem

Head of Council of State

1958–63	Mohammed Najib ar-Rubai

President

1963–6	Abdus Salaam Mohammed Arif
1966–8	Abdur Rahman Mohammed Arif
1968–79	Said Ahmad Hassan al-Bakr
1979–	Saddam Hussein (at-Takriti)

IRELAND

Governor-General

1922–7	Timothy Michael Healy
1927–32	James McNeill
1932–6	Donald Buckley

President

1938–45	Douglas Hyde
1945–59	Sean Thomas O'Kelly
1959–73	Éamon de Valera
1973–4	Erskine Hamilton Childers
1974–6	Carroll Daly
1976–90	Patrick J Hillery
1990–7	Mary Robinson
1997–	Mary McAleese

Prime Minister (Taoiseach)

1919–21	Éamon de Valera
1922	Arthur Griffiths
1922–32	William Cosgrave
1932–48	Éamon de Valera
1948–51	John Aloysius Costello
1951–4	Éamon de Valera
1954–7	John Aloysius Costello
1957–9	Éamon de Valera
1959–66	Sean Lemass
1966–73	John Lynch
1973–7	Liam Cosgrave
1977–9	John Lynch
1979–82	Charles Haughey
1982–7	Garrett FitzGerald
1987–92	Charles Haughey
1992–4	Albert Reynolds
1994–7	John Bruton
1997–	Bertie Aherne

ISRAEL

President

1948–52	Chaim Weizmann
1952–63	Itzhak Ben-Zvi
1963–73	Zalman Shazar
1973–8	Ephraim Katzair
1978–83	Yitzhak Navon
1983–93	Chaim Herzog
1993–	Ezer Weizmann

Prime Minister

1948–53	David Ben-Gurion
1954–5	Moshe Sharett
1955–63	David Ben-Gurion
1963–9	Levi Eshkol
1969–74	Golda Meir
1974–7	Itzhak Rabin
1977–83	Menachem Begin
1983–4	Yitzhak Shamir
1984–6	Shimon Peres
1986–92	Yitzhak Shamir
1992–5	Itzhak Rabin
1995–6	Shimon Peres
1996–9	Binyamin Netanyahu
1999–	Ehud Barak

ITALY

Kingdom of Italy

Monarch

1900–46	Victor-Emmanuel III

Italian Republic

President

1946–8	Enrico de Nicola
1948–55	Luigi Einaudi
1955–62	Giovanni Gronchi
1962–4	Antonio Segni
1964–71	Giuseppe Saragat
1971–8	Giovanni Leone
1978–85	Alessandro Pertini
1985–92	Francesco Cossiga
1992–9	Oscar Luigi Scalfaro
1999–	Carlo Azeglio Campi

Kingdom of Italy

Prime Minister

1900–1	Giuseppe Saracco
1901–3	Giuseppe Zanardelli
1903–5	Giovanni Giolitti
1905–6	Alessandro Fortis
1906	Sydney Sonnino
1906–9	Giovanni Giolitti
1909–10	Sydney Sonnino
1910–11	Luigi Luzzatti
1911–14	Giovanni Giolitti
1914–16	Antonio Salandra
1916–17	Paolo Boselli
1917–19	Vittorio Emmanuele Orlando
1919–20	Francesco Saverio Nitti
1920–1	Giovanni Giolitti
1921–2	Ivanoe Bonomi
1922	Luigi Facta
1922–43	Benito Mussolini
1943–4	Pietro Badoglio
1944–5	Ivanoe Bonomi
1945	Ferrucio Parri
1945	Alcide de Gasperi

Italian Republic

1946–53	Alcide de Gasperi
1953–4	Giuseppe Pella
1954	Amintore Fanfani
1954–5	Mario Scelba
1955–7	Antonio Segni
1957–8	Adone Zoli
1958–9	Amintore Fanfani
1959–60	Antonio Segni
1960	Fernando Tambroni
1960–3	Amintore Fanfani
1963	Giovanni Leone
1963–8	Aldo Moro
1968	Giovanni Leone
1968–70	Mariano Rumor
1970–2	Emilio Colombo
1972–4	Giulio Andreotti
1974–6	Aldo Moro
1976–8	Giulio Andreotti
1979–80	Francisco Cossiga
1980–1	Arnaldo Forlani
1981–2	Giovanni Spadolini
1982–3	Amintore Fanfani
1983–7	Bettino Craxi
1987	Amintore Fanfani
1987–8	Giovanni Goria
1988–9	Ciriaco de Mita
1989–92	Giulio Andreotti
1992–3	Giuliano Amato
1993–4	Carlo Azeglio Ciampi
1994–5	Silvio Berlusconi
1995–6	Lamberto Dini
1996–8	Romano Prodi
1998–	Massimo D'Alema

JAMAICA

Chief of State: British monarch, represented by Governor-General

Prime Minister

1962–7	William Alexander Bustamante
1967	Donald Burns Sangster
1967–72	Hugh Lawson Shearer
1972–80	Michael Norman Manley
1980–9	Edward Philip George Seaga
1989–92	Michael Norman Manley
1992–	Percival J Patterson

JAPAN

Emperor (Era name)

1867–1912	Mutsuhito (Meiji)
1912–26	Yoshihito (Taishō)
1926–89	Hirohito (Shōwa)
1989–	Akihito (Heisei)

Prime Minister

1900–1	Hirobumi Itō
1901–6	Tarō Katsura
1906–8	Kimmochi Saionji
1908–11	Tarō Katsura
1911–12	Kimmochi Saionji
1912–13	Tarō Katsura
1913–14	Gonnohyōe Yamamoto
1914–16	Shigenobu Ōkuma
1916–18	Masatake Terauchi
1918–21	Takashi Hara
1921–2	Korekiyo Takahashi
1922–3	Tomosaburō Katō
1923–4	Gonnohyōe Yamamoto
1924	Keigo Kiyoura
1924–6	Takaaki Katō
1926–7	Reijirō Wakatsuki
1927–9	Giichi Tanaka
1929–31	Osachi Hamaguchi
1931	Reijirō Wakatsuki
1931–2	Tsuyoshi Inukai
1932–4	Makoto Saitō
1934–6	Keisuke Okada
1936–7	Kōki Hirota
1937	Senjūrō Hayashi
1937–9	Fumimaro Konoe
1939	Kiichirō Hiranuma
1939–40	Nobuyuki Abe
1940	Mitsumasa Yonai
1940–1	Fumimaro Konoe
1941–4	Hideki Tōjō
1944–5	Kuniaki Koiso
1945	Kantarō Suzuki
1945	Naruhiko Higashikuni
1945–6	Kijūrō Shidehara
1946–7	Shigeru Yoshida
1947–8	Tetsu Katayama
1948	Hitoshi Ashida
1948–54	Shigeru Yoshida
1954–6	Ichirō Hatoyama
1956–7	Tanzan Ishibashi
1957–60	Nobusuke Kishi
1960–4	Hayato Ikeda
1964–72	Eisaku Satō
1972–4	Kakuei Tanaka
1974–6	Takeo Miki
1976–8	Takeo Fukuda
1978–80	Masayoshi Ōhira
1980–2	Zenkō Suzuki
1982–7	Yasuhiro Nakasone
1987–9	Noburu Takeshita
1989	Sasuke Uno
1989–91	Toshiki Kaifu
1991–3	Kiichi Miyazawa
1993–4	Morihiro Hosokawa
1994	Tsutomu Hata
1994–5	Tomiichi Murayama
1995–8	Ryutaro Hashimoto
1998–	Keizo Obuchi

JORDAN

Monarch

1949–51	Abdullah ibn Hussein
1951–2	Talal I
1952–99	Hussein ibn Talal
1999–	Abdullah ibn Hussein

Prime Minister

1921	Rashid Tali
1921	Muzhir Ar-Raslan
1921–3	Rida Ar-Riqabi
1923	Muzhir Ar-Raslan
1923–4	Hassan Khalid
1924–33	Rida Ar-Riqabi
1933–8	Ibrahim Hashim
1939–45	Taufiq Abul-Huda
1945–8	Ibrahim Hashim
1948–50	Taufiq Abul-Huda
1950	Said Al-Mufti
1950–1	Samir Ar-Rifai

1951–3 Taufiq Abul-Huda
1953–4 Fauzi Al-Mulqi
1954–5 Taufiq Abul-Huda
1955 Said Al-Mufti
1955 Hazza Al-Majali
1955–6 Ibrahim Hashim
1956 Samir Ar-Rifai
1956 Said Al-Mufti
1956 Ibrahim Hashim
1956–7 Suleiman Nabulsi
1957 Hussein Fakhri Al-Khalidi
1957–8 Ibrahim Hashim
1958 Nuri Pasha Al-Said
1958–9 Samir Ar-Rifai
1959–60 Hazza Al-Majali
1960–2 Bahjat Talhuni
1962–3 Wasfi At-Tall
1963 Samir Ar-Rifai
1963–4 Sharif Hussein Bin Nasir
1964 Bahjat Talhuni
1965–7 Wasfi At-Tall
1967 Sharif Hussein Bin Nasir
1967 Saad Jumaa
1967–9 Bahjat Talhuni
1969 Abdul Munem Rifai
1969–70 Bahjat Talhuni
1970 Abdul Munem Rifai
1970 *Military Junta* (Mohammed Daud)
1970 Mohamed Ahmed Tuqan
1970–1 Wasfi At-Tall
1971–3 Ahmad Lozi
1973–6 Zaid Rifai
1976–9 Mudar Badran
1979–80 Sherif Abdul Hamid Sharaf
1980 Kassem Rimawi
1980–4 Mudar Badran
1984–5 Ahmad Ubayat
1985–9 Zaid Ar-Rifai
1989 Sharif Zaid Bin Shaker
1989–91 Mudar Badran
1991 Taher Al-Masri
1991–3 Sharif Zaid Bin Shaker
1993–6 Abdul Salam Majali
1996–7 Abdul Karim Kabariti
1997–8 Abdul Salim al-Majali
1998–9 Fayez Tarawneh
1999– Abdul-Raouf Rawabdeh

KAZAKHSTAN

President
1991– Nursultan A Nazarbayev
Prime Minister
1991–4 Sergei Tereshchenko
1994–7 Kazhageldin Akezhan Magzhan Ulu
1997– Nurlan Balgimbayev

KENYA

President
1963–78 Mzee Jomo Kenyatta
1978– Daniel arap Moi

KIRIBATI

President
1979–91 Ieremia T Tabai
1991–4 Teatao Teannaki
1994– Teburoro Tito

DEMOCRATIC PEOPLE'S REPUBLIC OF KOREA (North Korea)

President
1948–57 Kim Doo-bong
1957–72 Choi Yong-kun
1972–94 Kim Il-sung
1994– Kim Jong-il
Prime Minister
1948–76 Kim Il-sung
1976–7 Park Sung-chul
1977–84 Li Jong-ok
1984–6 Kang Song-san
1986–8 Yi Kun-mo
1988–92 Yon Hyong-muk
1992–7 Kang Song-san
1997– Hong Song-nam

REPUBLIC OF KOREA (South Korea)

President
1948–60 Syngman Rhee
1960 Ho Chong *Acting*
1960 Kwak Sang-hun *Acting*
1960 Ho Chong *Acting*
1960–3 Yun Po-sun
1963–79 Park Chung-hee
1979–80 Choi Kyu-hah
1980 Park Choong-hoon *Acting*
1980–8 Chun Doo-hwan
1988–93 Roh Tae-woo
1993–7 Kim Young-sam
1997– Kim Dae Jung
Prime Minister
1948–50 Lee Pom-sok
1950 Shin Song-mo *Acting*
1950–1 John M Chang
1951–2 Ho Chong *Acting*
1952 Lee Yun-yong *Acting*
1952 Chang Taek-sang
1952–4 Paik Too-chin
1954–6 Pyon Yong-tae
1956–60 Syngman Rhee
1960 Ho Chong
1960–1 John M Chang
1961 Chang To-yong
1961–2 Song Yo-chan
1962–3 Kim Hyun-chul
1963–4 Choe Tu-son
1964–70 Chung Il-kwon
1970–1 Paik Too-chin
1971–5 Kim Jong-pil
1975–9 Choi Kyu-hah
1979–80 Shin Hyun-hwak
1980 Park Choong-hoon *Acting*
1980–2 Nam Duck-woo
1982 Yoo Chang-soon
1982–3 Kim Sang-hyup
1983–5 Chin Lee-chong
1985–8 Lho Shin-yong
1988 Lee Hyun-jae
1988–90 Kang Young-hoon
1990–1 Ro Jai-bong
1991–2 Chung Won-shik
1992–3 Hyung Soong-jang
1993 Hwang In-sung
1993–4 Lee Hoi-chang
1994 Lee Yung-duk
1994–5 Lee Hong-koo
1995–7 Lee Soo-sung
1997–8 Koh Kun
1998– Kim Jong-pil

KUWAIT

Emir
Family name: al-Sabah
1896–1915 Mubarak
1915–17 Jabir II
1917–21 Salim al-Mubarak
1921–50 Ahmed al-Jaber
1950–65 'Abdullah III al-Salim
1965–77 Sabah III al-Salim
1977– Jabir III al-Ahmed al-Jaber
Prime Minister
1962–3 Abdallah al-Salem
1963–5 Sabah al-Salem
1965–78 Jaber al-Ahmed al-Jaber
1978– Saad al-Abdallah al-Salim al-Sabah

KYRGYZSTAN

President
1991– Askaar Akayev
Prime Minister
1991–3 Tursunbek Chyngyshev
1993–8 Apas Jumagulov
1998 Kubanychbek Djumaliev
1998–9 Jumabek Ibraimov
1999– Amangeldy Muraliev

LAOS

Monarch
1904–59 Sisavang Vong
1959–75 Savang Vatthana
Lao People's Republic
President
1975–87 Souphanouvong
1987–91 Phoumi Vongvichit
1991–2 Kaysone Phomvihane
1992–8 Nouhak Phoumsavan
1998– Khamtay Siphandon
Prime Minister
1951–4 Souvanna Phouma
1954–5 Katay Don Sasorith
1956–8 Souvanna Phouma
1958–9 Phoui Sahanikone
1959–60 Sunthone Patthamavong
1960 Kou Abhay
1960 Somsanith
1960 Souvanna Phouma
1960 Sunthone Patthamavong
1960 Quinim Pholsena
1960–2 Boun Oum Na Champassac
1962–75 Souvanna Phouma
Lao People's Democratic Republic
1975–91 Kaysone Phomvihane
1991– Khamtay Siphandon

LATVIA

President

1918–27 Janis Cakste
1927–30 Gustavs Zemgals
1930–6 Alberts Kviesis
1934–40 Kārlis Ulmanis
1940–91 *Russian rule*
1991–3 Anatolijs Gorbunovs
1993– Guntis Ulmanis

Prime Minister

1918–21 Kārlis Ulmanis
1921–3 Zigfrīds Meierovics
1923 Jānis Pauluks
1923–4 Zigfrīds Meierovics
1924 Voldemārs Zāmuēls
1924–5 Hugo Celmiņš
1925–6 Kārlis Ulmanis
1926 Artūrs Alberings
1926–8 Margers Skujenieks
1928 Pēteris Juraševskis
1928–31 Hugo Celmiņš
1931 Kārlis Ulmanis
1931–3 Margers Skujenieks
1933–4 Ādolfs Bīodnieks
1934–40 Kārlis Ulmanis
1940–91 *Russian rule*
1991–3 Ivars Godmanis
1993–4 Valdis Birkvs
1994–5 Maris Gailis
1995–7 Andris Skele
1997–8 Guntar Krasts
1998– Vilis Kristopans

LEBANON

President

1943–52 Bishara Al-Khoury
1952–8 Camille Shamoun
1958–64 Fouad Shehab
1964–70 Charle Hilo
1970–6 Suleiman Frenjieh
1976–82 Elias Sarkis
1982 Bachir Gemayel
1982–8 Amin Gemayel
1988–9 *No President*
1989 Rene Muawad
1989–98 Elias Hrawi
1998– Emile Lahou

Prime Minister

1943 Riad Solh
1943–4 Henry Pharaon
1944–5 Riad Solh
1945 Abdul Hamid Karame
1945–6 Sami Solh
1946 Saadi Munla
1946–51 Riad Solh
1951 Hussein Oweini
1951–2 Abdullah Yafi
1952 Sami Solh
1952 Nazem Accari
1952 Saeb Salam
1952 Fouad Chehab
1952–3 Khaled Chehab
1953 Saeb Salam
1953–5 Abdullah Yafi
1955 Sami Solh
1955–6 Rashid Karami
1956 Abdullah Yafi
1956–8 Sami Solh
1958–60 Rashid Karami
1960 Ahmad Daouq
1960–1 Saeb Salam
1961–4 Rashid Karami
1964–5 Hussein Oweini
1965–6 Rashid Karami
1966 Abdullah Yafi
1966–8 Rashid Karami
1968–9 Abdullah Yafi
1969–70 Rashid Karami
1970–3 Saeb Salam
1973 Amin al-Hafez
1973–4 Takieddine Solh
1974–5 Rashid Solh
1975 Noureddin Rifai
1975–6 Rashid Karami
1976–80 Selim al-Hoss
1980 Takieddine Solh
1980–4 Chafiq al-Wazan
1984–8 Rashid Karami
1988–90 Michel Aoun/Selim al-Hoss
1990 Selim al-Hoss
1990–2 Umar Karami
1992 Rashid al-Solh
1992–8 Rafiq al-Hariri
1998– Selim al-Hoss

LESOTHO

Monarch

1966–90 Moshoeshoe II
1990–4 Letsie III *Abdicated*
1994–6 Moshoeshoe II
1996– Letsie III

Prime Minister

1966–86 Leabua Jonathan
1986–93 *No Prime Minister*

Chairman of Military Council

1986–91 Justin Metsing Lekhanya
1991–3 Elias Tutsoane Ramaema

Prime Minister

1993–8 Ntsu Mokhehle
1998– Bethuel Pakalitha Mosisili

LIBERIA

President

1900–4 Garretson Wilmot Gibson
1904–12 Arthur Barclay
1912–20 Daniel Edward Howard
1920–30 Charles Dunbar Burgess King
1930–43 Edwin J Barclay
1943–71 William V S Tubman
1971–80 William Richard Tolbert

People's Redemption Council

Chairman

1980–6 Samuel Kanyon Doe

President

1986–90 Samuel Kanyon Doe
1990–94 Amos Sawyer *Acting*

Council of State

Chairman

1994–5 David Kpormakor
1995–6 Wilton Sankawulo
1995–7 Ruth Perry

President

1997– Charles Taylor

LIBYA

Monarch

1951–69 Mohammed Idris Al-Mahdi Al-Senussi

Revolutionary Command Council

Chairman

1969–77 Muammar al-Gaddafi

General Secretariat

Secretary General

1977–9 Muammar al-Gaddafi
1979–84 Abdul Ati al-Ubaidi
1984–6 Mohammed az-Zaruq Rajab
1986–90 Omar al-Muntasir
1990–7 Abu Zaid Omar Dourda
1997– Muhammad Ahmad al-Mangoush

Leader of the Revolution

1969– Muammar al-Gaddafi

LIECHTENSTEIN

Prince

1858–1929 Johann II
1929–38 Franz von Paula
1938–89 Franz Josef II
1989– Hans Adam II

Prime Minister

1928–45 Franz Josef Hoop
1945–62 Alexander Friek
1962–70 Gérard Batliner
1970–4 Alfred J Hilbe
1974–8 Walter Kieber
1978–93 Hans Brunhart
1993 Markus Büchel
1993– Mario Frick

LITHUANIA

President

1919–20 Anatas Smetona
1920–6 Aleksandras Stulginskis
1926 Kazys Grinius
1926–40 Anatas Smetona
1940–91 *Russian rule*
1991–3 Vytautas Landsbergis
1993–8 Algirdas Brazauskas
1998 Valdas Adamkus

Prime Minister

1918 Augustinas Voldemaras
1918–19 Mykolas Šleževičius
1919 Pranas Dovydailus
1919 Mykolas Šleževičius
1919–20 Ernestas Galvanauskas
1920–2 Kazys Grinius
1922–4 Ernestas Galvanauskas
1924–5 Antanas Tumenas
1925 Vytautas Petrulis
1925–6 Leonas Bistras
1926 Mykolas Šleževičius
1926–9 Augustinas Voldemaras
1929–38 Juozas Tubelis
1938–9 Vladas Mironas

	Joans Cernius
	Antanas Merkys
	Russian rule
	Gediminas Vagnorius
	Aleksandras Abisala
3	Bronislovas Lubys
–6	Adolfas Šleževičius
6	Laurynas Stankevicius
96–9	Gediminas Vagnorius
999–	Irena Degutiene (*Acting*)

LUXEMBOURG

Grand Dukes and Duchesses

1905–12	William IV
1912–19	Marie-Adelaide
1919–64	Charlotte *in exile 1940–4*
1964–	Jean

Prime Minister

1915	Mathias Mongenast
1915–16	Hubert Loutsch
1916–17	Victor Thorn
1917–18	Léon Kaufmann
1918–25	Emil Reuter
1925–6	Pierre Prum
1926–37	Joseph Bech
1937–53	Pierre Dupong *in exile 1940–4*
1953–8	Joseph Bech
1958–9	Pierre Frieden
1959–74	Pierre Werner
1974–9	Gaston Thorn
1979–84	Pierre Werner
1984–95	Jacques Santer
1995–	Jean-Claude Juncker

MACEDONIA, FORMER YUGOSLAV REPUBLIC OF

President

1991–	Kiro Gligorov

Prime Minister

1991–2	Branko Crvenkovski
1992–6	Petar Gosev
1996–8	Branko Crvenkovski
1998–	Ljubco Georgievski

MADAGASCAR

President

1960–72	Philibert Tsiranana
1972–5	Gabriel Ramanantsoa
1975	Richard Ratsimandrava
1975	Gilles Andriamahazo
1975–93	Didier Ratsiraka
1993–6	Albert Zafy
1996	Norbert Ratsirahonana
1996–	Didier Ratsiraka

Prime Minister

1960–75	*As President*
1975–6	Joël Rakotomala
1976–7	Justin Rakotoriaina
1977–88	Désiré Rakotoarijaona
1988–91	Victor Ramahatra
1991–3	Guy Willy Razanamasy
1993–5	Francisque Ravony
1995–6	Emmanuel Rakotovahiny
1996–7	Norbert Ratsirahonana
1997–8	Pascal Rakotomavo
1998–	Tantely Andrianarivo

MALAWI

President

1966–94	Hastings Kamuzu Banda
1994–	Bakili Muluzi

MALAYSIA

Chief of State (Yang di-Pertuan Agong)

1957–63	Abdul Rahman
1963–5	Sayyid Harun Putra Jamal-ul-Lail
1965–70	Isma'il Nasir-ud-Din Shah
1970–5	'Abdul-Halim Mu'azzam Shah
1975–9	Yahya Petra Ibrahim
1979–84	Ahmad Shah al-Musta'in
1984–9	Mahmud Iskandar Shah
1989–4	Azlan Muhibbuddin Shah
1994–9	Ja'afar ibn Abdul Rahman
1999–	Salehuddin Abdul Aziz Shah

Prime Minister

Malaya

1957–63	Abdul Rahman Putra Al-Haj

Malaysia

1963–70	Abdul Rahman Putra Al-Haj
1970–6	Abdul Razak bin Hussein
1976–9	Haji Hussein bin Onn
1979–	Mahathir bin Mohamad

MALDIVES

Monarch (Sultan)

1954–68	Muhammad Farid Didi

Republic

President

1968–78	Ibrahim Nasir
1978–	Maumoon Abdul Gayoom

MALI

President

1960–8	Modibo Keita
1969–92	Moussa Traoré
1992–	Alpha Oumar Konare

Prime Minister

1986–8	Mamadou Dembelé
1988–91	*No Prime Minister*
1991–2	Soumana Sacko
1992–3	Younoussi Touré
1993–4	Abdoulaye Sekou Sow
1994–	Ibrahim Boubakar Keita

MALTA

President

1974–6	Anthony Mamo
1976–81	Anton Buttigieg
1982–7	Agatha Barbara
1987–9	Paul Xuereb *Acting*
1989–94	Vincent Tabone
1994–9	Ugo Mifsud Bonnici
1999–	Guido de Marco

Prime Minister

1962–71	G Borg Olivier
1971–84	Dom Mintoff
1984–7	Carmelo Mifsud Bonnici
1987–96	Edward Fenech Adami
1996–8	Alfred Sant
1998–	Edward Fenech Adami

MARSHALL ISLANDS

President

1979–	Amata Kabua

MAURITANIA

President

1961–78	Mokhtar Ould Daddah
1979	Mustapha Ould Mohammed Salek
1979–80	Mohammed Mahmoud Ould Ahmed Louly
1980–4	Mohammed Khouna Ould Haydalla
1984–	Moaouia Ould Sidi Mohammed Taya

Prime Minister

1991–6	Mohammed Ould Boubaker
1996–7	Cheikh el Avia Ould Mohamed Khouna
1997–8	Mohamed Lemine Ould Guig
1998–	Cheikh el Avia Ould Mohamed Khouna

MAURITIUS

President

1992	Veerasamy Ringadoo
1992–	Cassum Uteem

Prime Minister

1992–5	Anerood Jugnauth
1995–	Navin Ramgoolam

MEXICO

President

1876–1911	Porfirio Diaz
1911	Francisco León de la Barra
1911–13	Francisco I Madero
1913–14	Victoriano Huerta
1914	Francisco Carvajal
1914	Venustiano Carranza
1914–15	Eulalio Gutiérrez *Provisional*
1915	Roque González Garza *Provisional*
1915	Francisco Lagos Chazaro *Provisional*
1917–20	Venustiano Carranza
1920	Adolfo de la Huerta
1920–4	Alvaro Obregón
1924–8	Plutarco Elías Calles
1928–30	Emilio Portes Gil
1930–2	Pascual Ortíz Rubio
1932–4	Abelardo L Rodríguez
1934–40	Lazaro Cardenas
1940–6	Manuel Avila Camacho
1946–52	Miguel Alemán
1952–8	Adolfo Ruiz Cortines
1958–64	Adolfo López Mateos
1964–70	Gustavo Díaz Ordaz
1970–6	Luis Echeverría
1976–82	José López Portillo
1982–8	Miguel de la Madrid Hurtado
1988–94	Carlos Salinas de Gortari
1994–	Ernesto Zedillo

MOLDOVA

President

1991–6	Mircea Snegur
1996–	Petru Lucinschi

Prime Minister

1991–2 Valeriu Muravschi
1992–7 Andrei Sangeli
1997–9 Ion Cabuc
1999– Ion Sturza

MONACO

Head of state

1889–1922 Albert
1922–49 Louis II
1949– Rainier III

Minister of State

1991–4 Jacques Dupont
1994–7 Paul Dijoud
1997– Michel Lévêque

MONGOLIA

Prime Minister

1924–8 Tserendorji
1928–32 Amor
1932–6 Gendun
1936–8 Amor
1939–52 Korloghiin Choibalsan
1952–74 Yumsjhagiin Tsedenbal

Chairman of the Praesidium

1948–53 Gonchighlin Bumatsende
1954–72 Jamsarangiin Sambu
1972–4 Sonomyn Luvsan
1974–84 Yumsjhagiin Tsedenbal
1984–90 Jambyn Batmunkh

President

1990–7 Punsalmaagiyn Ochirbat
1997 Natsagiyn Bagabandi

Premier

1974–84 Jambyn Batmunkh
1984–90 Dumaagiyn Sodnom
1990–2 Dashiyn Byambasuren
1992–6 Puntsagiyn Jasray
1996–8 Mendsayhany Enhsayhan
1998 Tsakhiagiin Elbegdovj
1998 Rinchinnyamiin Amarjargal
1998– Janlaviyn Narantsatsralt

MOROCCO

Monarch

1957–61 Mohammed V
1961– Hassan II

Prime Minister

1955–8 Si Mohammed Bekkai
1958 Ahmad Balfrej
1958–60 Abdullah Ibrahim
1960–3 *As Monarch*
1963–5 Ahmad Bahnini
1965–7 *As Monarch*
1967–9 Moulay Ahmed Laraki
1969–71 Mohammed Ben Hima
1971–2 Mohammed Karim Lamrani
1972–9 Ahmed Othman
1979–83 Maati Bouabid
1983–6 Mohammed Karim Lamrani
1986–92 Azzedine Laraki
1992–4 Karim Lamrani
1994–8 Abdellatif Filali
1998– Abderrahmane el-Yousifi

MOZAMBIQUE

President

1975–86 Samora Moïses Machel
1986– Joaquim Alberto Chissanó

Prime Minister

1986–94 Mario da Graça Machungo
1994– Pascoal Mocumbi

MYANMAR (BURMA)

President

1948–52 Sao Shwe Thaik
1952–7 Agga Maha Thiri Thudhamma Ba U
1957–62 U Wing Maung
1962 Sama Duwa Sinwa Nawng

Revolutionary Council

1962–74 Ne Win

State Council

1974–81 Ne Win
1981–8 U San Yu
1988 U Sein Lwin
1988 Maung Maung
1988–92 Saw Maung
1992– Than Shwe

Prime Minister

1947–56 Thakin Nu
1956–7 U Ba Swe
1957–8 U Nu
1958–60 Ne Win
1960–2 U Nu
1962–74 Ne Win
1974–7 U Sein Win
1977–8 U Maung Maung Ka
1988 U Tun Tin
1988–92 Saw Maung
1992– Than Shwe

NAMIBIA

President

1990– Sam Daniel Nujoma

Prime Minister

1990– Hage Geingob

NAURU

President

1968–86 Hammer de Robурt
1986 Kennan Adeang
1986–9 Hammer de Roburt
1989 Kenas Aroi
1989–97 Bernard Dowiyogo
1997–8 Kinza Clodumar
1998– Bernard Dowiyogo

NEPAL

Monarch

1881–1911 Prithvi Bir Bikram Shah
1911–55 Tribhuvana Bir Bikram Shah
1956–72 Mahendra Bir Bikram Shah
1972– Birendra Bir Bikram Shah

Prime Minister

1885–1901 Bir Sham Sher J B Rama
1902 Dev Sham Sher J B Rama
1903–29 Chandra Sham Sher J B Rana
1929–31 Bhim Cham Sham Sher J B Rana
1931–45 Juddha Sham Sher Rana
1945–8 Padma Sham Sher J B Rana
1948–51 Mohan Sham Sher J B Rana
1951–2 Matrika Prasad Koirala
1952–3 Tribhuvana Bir Bikram Shah
1953–5 Matrika Prasad Koirala
1955–6 Mahendra Bir Bikram Shah
1956–7 Tanka Prasad Acharya
1957–9 *King also Prime Minister*
1959–60 Sri Bishawa Prasad Koirala
1960–3 *No Prime Minister*
1963–5 Tulsi Giri
1965–9 Surya Bahadur Thapa
1969–70 Kirti Nidhi Bista
1970–1 *King also Prime Minister*
1971–3 Kirti Nidhi Bista
1973–5 Nagendra Prasad Rijal
1975–7 Tulsi Giri
1977–9 Kirti Nidhi Bista
1979–83 Surya Bahadur Thapa
1983–6 Lokendra Bahadur Chand
1986–90 Marich Man Singh Shrestha
1990 Lokendra Bahadur Chand
1990–1 Krishna Prasad Bhattarai
1991–4 Girija Prasad Koirala
1994–5 Man Mohan Adhikari
1995–7 Sher Bahadur Deupa
1997 Lokendra Bahadur Chand
1997–8 Surya Bahadur Thapa
1998– Girija Prasad Koirala

THE NETHERLANDS

Monarch

1890–1948 Wilhelmina
1948–80 Juliana
1980– Beatrix

Prime Minister

1897–1901 Nicholas G Pierson
1901–5 Abraham Kuyper
1905–8 Theodoor H de Meester
1908–13 Theodorus Heemskerk
1913–18 Pieter W A Cort van der Linden
1918–25 Charles J M Ruys de Beerenbrouck
1925–6 Hendrikus Colijn
1926 Dirk J de Geer
1926–33 Charles J M Ruys de Beerenbrouck
1933–9 Hendrikus Colijn
1939–40 Dirk J de Geer
1940–5 Pieter S Gerbrandy *in exile*
1945–6 Willem Schemerhorn/ Willem Drees
1946–8 Louis J M Beel
1948–51 Willem Drees/Josephus R H van Schaik
1951–8 Willem Drees
1958–9 Louis J M Beel
1959–63 Jan E de Quay
1963–5 Victor G M Marijnen
1965–6 Joseph M L T Cals
1966–7 Jelle Zijlstra
1967–71 Petrus J S de Jong
1971–3 Barend W Biesheuvel
1973–7 Joop M den Uyl
1977–82 Andreas A M van Agt
1982–94 Ruud Lubbers
1994– Wim Kok

EALAND

ate: British monarch, represented by -General

Minister

	Henry Sewell
	William Fox
6–61	Edward William Stafford
61–2	William Fox
862–3	Alfred Domett
1863–4	Frederick Whitaker
1864–5	Frederick Aloysius Weld
1865–9	Edward William Stafford
1869–72	William Fox
1872	Edward William Stafford
1873	William Fox
1873–5	Julius Vogel
1875–6	Daniel Pollen
1876	Julius Vogel
1876–7	Harry Albert Atkinson
1877–9	George Grey
1879–82	John Hall
1882–3	Frederick Whitaker
1883–4	Harry Albert Atkinson
1884	Robert Stout
1884	Harry Albert Atkinson
1884–7	Robert Stout
1887–91	Harry Albert Atkinson
1891–3	John Ballance
1893–1906	Richard John Seddon *Lib*
1906	William Hall-Jones *Lib*
1906–12	Joseph George Ward *Lib/Nat*
1912	Thomas Mackenzie *Nat*
1912–25	William Ferguson Massey *Ref*
1925	Francis Henry Dillon Bell *Ref*
1925–8	Joseph Gordon Coates *Ref*
1928–30	Joseph George Ward *Lib/Nat*
1930–5	George William Forbes *Un*
1935–40	Michael Joseph Savage *Lab*
1940–9	Peter Fraser *Lab*
1949–57	Sidney George Holland *Nat*
1957	Keith Jacka Holyoake *Nat*
1957–60	Walter Nash *Lab*
1960–72	Keith Jacka Holyoake *Nat*
1972	John Ross Marshall *Nat*
1972–4	Norman Eric Kirk *Lab*
1974–5	Wallace Edward Rowling *Lab*
1975–84	Robert David Muldoon *Nat*
1984–9	David Russell Lange *Lab*
1989–90	Geoffrey Winston Russell Palmer *Lab*
1990	Michael Kenneth Moore *Lab*
1990–7	James Brendan Bolger *Nat*
1997–	Jenny Shipley *Nat*
Lab	Labour
Lib	Liberal
Nat	National
Ref	Reform
Un	United

NICARAGUA

President

1893–1909	José Santos Zelaya
1909–10	José Madriz
1910–11	José Dolores Estrada
1911	Juan José Estrada
1911–17	Adolfo Díaz
1912	Luis Mena *Rival President*
1917–21	Emiliano Chamorro Vargas
1921–3	Riego Manuel Chamorro
1923–4	Martínez Bartolo
1925–6	Carlos Solórzano
1926	Emiliano Chamorro Vargas
1926–8	Adolfo Díaz
1926	Juan Bautista Sacasa *Rival President*
1928–32	José Marcia Moncada
1933–6	Juan Bautista Sacasa
1936	Carlos Brenes Jarquin
1937–47	Anastasio Somoza García
1947	Leonardo Argüello
1947	Benjamin Lascayo Sacasa
1947–50	Victor Manuel Román y Reyes
1950–6	Anastasio Somoza García
1956–63	Luis Somoza Debayle
1963–6	René Schick Gutiérrez
1966–7	Lorenzo Guerrero Gutiérrez
1967–72	Anastasio Somoza Debayle
1972–4	*Triumvirate*
1974–9	Anastasio Somoza Debayle
1979–84	*Government Junta of National Reconstruction*
1984–90	Daniel Ortega Saavedra
1990–6	Violeta Barrios de Chamorro
1996–	Arnoldo Aleman Lacayo

NIGER

President

1960–74	Hamani Diori
1974–87	Seyni Kountché
1987–93	Ali Saibou
1993–6	Mahamane Ousmane
1996–9	Ibrahim Barre Mainassara
1999–	Daouda Malam Wanke (*Acting*)

Prime Minister

1990–1	Aliou Mahamidou
1991–3	Amadou Cheiffou
1993–4	Mahamdou Issoufou
1994–5	Abdoulaye Souley
1995–6	Hama Amadou
1996	Boukary Adji
1996–7	Amadou Boubacar Cisse
1997–	Ibrahim Assane Mayaki

NIGERIA

President

1960–6	Nnamdi Azikiwe

Prime Minister

1960–6	Abubakar Tafawa Balewa

Military Government

1966	J T U Aguiyi-Ironsi
1966–75	Yakubu Gowon
1975–6	Murtala R Mohamed
1976–9	Olusegun Obasanjo

President

1979–83	Alhaji Shehu Shagari

Military Government

1983–4	Mohammadu Buhari
1985–93	Ibrahim B Babangida
1993	Ernest Adegunle Shonekan *Interim*
1993–8	Sanni Abacha
1998–9	Abdusalem Abubakar

President

1999–	Olusegun Obasanjo

NORWAY

Monarch

1872–1905	Oscar II *union with Sweden*
1905–57	Haakon VII
1957–91	Olaf V
1991–	Harald V

Prime Minister

1898–1902	Johannes Steen
1902–3	Otto Albert Blehr
1903–5	George Francis Hagerup
1905–7	Christian Michelsen
1907–8	Jørgen Løvland
1908–10	Gunnar Knudsen
1910–12	Wollert Konow
1912–13	Jens Bratlie
1913–20	Gunnar Knudsen
1920–1	Otto Bahr Halvorsen
1921–3	Otto Albert Blehr
1923	Otto Bahr Halvorsen
1923–4	Abraham Berge
1924–6	Johan Ludwig Mowinckel
1926–8	Ivar Lykke
1928	Christopher Hornsrud
1928–31	Johan Ludwig Mowinckel
1931–2	Peder L Kolstad
1932–3	Jens Hundseid
1933–5	Johan Ludwig Mowinckel
1935–45	Johan Nygaardsvold
1945–51	Einar Gerhardsen
1951–5	Oscar Torp
1955–63	Einar Gerhardsen
1963	John Lyng
1963–5	Einar Gerhardsen
1965–71	Per Borten
1971–2	Trygve Bratteli
1972–3	Lars Korvald
1973–6	Trygve Bratteli
1976–81	Odvår Nordli
1981	Gro Harlem Brundtland
1981–6	Kåre Willoch
1986–9	Gro Harlem Brundtland
1989–90	Jan P Syse
1990–6	Gro Harlem Brundtland
1996–7	Thorbjoern Jagland
1997–	Kjell Magne Bondevik

OMAN

Sultan

1888–1913	Faisal Bin Turki
1913–32	Taimur Bin Faisal
1932–70	Said III Bin Taimur
1970–	Qaboos Bin Said

PAKISTAN

President

1956–8	Iskander Mirza
1958–69	Mohammad Ayub Khan
1969–71	Agha Mohammad Yahya Khan
1971–3	Zulfikar Ali Bhutto
1973–8	Fazal Elahi Chawdry

1978–88 Mohammad Zia Ul-Haq
1988–93 Gulam Ishaq Khan
1993–7 Farooq Ahmed Leghan
1997– Mohammad Rafiq Tara

Prime Minister

1947–51 Liaquat Ali Khan
1951–3 Khawaja Nazimuddin
1953–5 Mohammad Ali
1955–6 Chawdry Mohammad Ali
1956–7 Hussein Shahid Suhrawardi
1957 Ismail Chundrigar
1957–8 Malik Feroz Khan Noon
1958 Mohammad Ayoub Khan
1958–73 *No Prime Minister*
1973–7 Zulfikar Ali Bhutto
1977–85 *No Prime Minister*
1985–8 Mohammad Khan Junejo
1988 Mohammad Aslam Khan Khattak
1988–90 Benazir Bhutto
1990 Ghulam Mustafa Jatoi
1990–3 Nawaz Sharif
1993–6 Benazir Bhutto
1996–7 Malik Meraj Khalid
1997– Mian Mohammad Nawaz Sharif

PANAMA

President

1904–8 Manuel Amador Guerrero
1908–10 José Domingo de Obaldia
1910 Federico Boyd
1910 Carlos Antonio Mendoza
1910–12 Pablo Arosemena
1912 Rodolfo Chiari
1912–16 Belisario Porras
1916–18 Ramón Maximiliano Valdés
1918 Pedro Antonio Diaz
1918 Cirilo Luis Urriola
1918–20 Belisario Porras
1920 Ernesto T Lefevre
1920–4 Belisario Porras
1924–8 Rodolfo Chiari
1928 Tomás Gabriel Duque
1928–31 Florencio Harmodio Arosemena
1931 Harmodio Arias
1931–2 Ricardo Joaquín Alfaro
1932–6 Harmodio Arias
1936–9 Juan Demóstenes Arosemena
1939 Ezequiel Fernández Jaén
1939–40 Augusto Samuel Boyd
1940–1 Arnulfo Arias Madrid
1941 Ernesto Jaén Guardia
1941 José Pezet
1941–5 Ricardo Adolfo de la Guardia
1945–8 Enrique Adolfo Jiménez Brin
1948–9 Domingo Diaz Arosemena
1949 Daniel Chanis
1949 Roberto Francisco Chiari
1949–51 Arnulfo Arias Madrid
1951–2 Alcibiades Arosemena
1952–5 José Antonio Remón
1955 José Ramón Guizado
1955–6 Ricardo Manuel Arias Espinosa
1956–60 Ernesto de la Guardia
1960–4 Roberto Francisco Chiari
1964–8 Marco A Robles
1968 Arnulfo Arias Madrid
1968 *Military Junta*
1968–9 Omar Torrijos Herrera
1969–78 Demetrio Basilio Lakas
1978–82 Aristides Royo
1982–4 Ricardo de la Esoriella
1984 Jorge Enrique Illueca Sibauste
1984–5 Nicolás Ardito Barletta
1985–8 Eric Arturo Delvalle
1988–9 Manuel Solís Palma
1989–4 Guillermo Endara Gallimany
1994–9 Ernesto Pérez Balladares
1999– Mireya Moscoso

PAPUA NEW GUINEA

Prime Minister

1975–80 Michael T Somare
1980–2 Julius Chan
1982–5 Michael T Somare
1985–8 Paias Wingti
1988–92 Rabbie Namiliu
1992–4 Paias Wingti
1994–7 Julius Chan
1997 John Giheno
1997 Julius Chan
1997– Bill Skate

PARAGUAY

President

1898–1902 Emilio Aceval
1902 Hector Carballo
1902–4 Juan Antonio Escurra
1904–5 Juan Gaona
1905–6 Cecilio Báez
1906–8 Benigno Ferreira
1908–10 Emiliano González Navero
1910–11 Manuel Gondra
1911 Albino Jara
1911 Liberato Marcial Rojas
1912 Pedro Peña
1912 Emiliano González Navero
1912–16 Eduardo Schaerer
1916–19 Manuel Franco
1919–20 José P Montero
1920–1 Manuel Gondra
1921 Félix Paiva
1921–3 Eusebio Ayala
1923–4 Eligio Ayala
1924 Luis Alberto Riart
1924–8 Eligio Ayala
1928–31 José Particio Guggiari
1931–2 Emiliano González Navero
1932 José Particio Guggiari
1932–6 Eusebio Ayala
1936–7 Rafael Franco
1937–9 Félix Paiva
1939–40 José Félix Estigarribia
1940–8 Higino Moriñigo
1948 Juan Manuel Frutos
1948–9 Juan Natalicio González
1949 Raimundo Rolón
1949 Felipe Molas López
1949–54 Federico Chaves
1954 Tomás Romero Pareira
1954–89 Alfredo Stroessner
1989–93 Andrés Rodríguez
1993–8 Juan Carlos Wasmosy
1998–9 Raúl Cubas Grau
1999– Luis Gonzalez Macchi

PERU

President

1899–1903 Eduardo López de la Romaña
1903–4 Manuel Candamo
1904 Serapio Calderón
1904–8 José Pardo y Barreda
1908–12 Augusto B Leguía
1912–14 Guillermo Billinghurst
1914–15 Oscar R Benavides
1915–19 José Pardo y Barreda
1919–30 Augusto B Leguía
1930 Manuel Ponce
1930–1 Luis M Sánchez Cerro
1931 Leoncio Elías
1931 Gustavo A Jiménez
1931 David Samanez Ocampo
1931–3 Luis M Sánchez Cerro
1933–9 Oscar R Benavides
1939–45 Manuel Prado
1945–8 José Luis Bustamante y Rivero
1948–56 Manuel A Odría
1956–62 Manuel Prado
1962–3 *Military Junta*
1963–8 Fernando Belaúnde Terry
1968–75 *Military Junta* (Juan Velasco Alvarado)
1975–80 *Military Junta* (Francisco Morales Bermúdez)
1980–5 Fernando Belaúnde Terry
1985–90 Alan García Pérez
1990– Alberto Keinya Fujimori

Prime Minister

1991–2 Alfonso de los Heros
1992–3 Oscar de la Puente Raygada
1993–4 Alfonso Bustamente y Bustamente
1994–5 Efrain Goldenberg Schreiber
1995–6 Dante Córdoba Blanco
1996–8 Alberto Pandolfi Arbulu
1998 Javier Valle Riestra
1998– Alberto Pandolfi Arbulu

PHILIPPINES

President

Commonwealth

1935–44 Manuel Luis Quezon

Japanese Occupation

1943–4 José P Laurel

Commonwealth

1944–6 Sergio Osmeña

First Republic

1946–8 Manuel A Roxas
1948–53 Elpidio Quirino
1953–7 Ramon Magsaysay
1957–61 Carlos P Garcia
1961–5 Diosdado Macapagal
1965–72 Ferdinand E Marcos

Martial Law

1972–81 Ferdinand E Marcos

New Republic

1981–6 Ferdinand E Marcos
1986–92 Corazon Aquino

…del Ramos
…osep Arap Estrada

…ND

… State

… Bolesław Bierut *Acting*
…2 Bolesław Bierut
…64 Aleksander Zawadzki
…-8 Edward Ochab
…68–70 Marian Spychalski
…970–2 Józef Cyrankiewicz
1972–85 Henryk Jabłonski
1985–90 Wojciech Jaruzelski *President 1989*

President

1990–5 Lech Wałesa
1995– Alexander Kwasniewski

Premier

1947–52 Józef Cyrankiewicz
1952–4 Bolesław Bierut
1954–70 Józef Cyrankiewicz
1970–80 Piotr Jacoszewicz
1980 Edward Babiuch
1980–1 Józef Pinkowski
1981–5 Wojciech Jaruzelski
1985–8 Zbigniew Messner
1988–9 Mieczysław Rakowski
1989 Czesław Kiszczak
1989–91 Tadeusz Mazowiecki
1991 Jan Krzysztof Bielecki
1991–2 Jan Olszewski
1992 Waldemar Pawlak
1992–3 Hanna Suchocka
1993–5 Waldemar Pawlak
1995–6 Jozef Oleksy
1996–7 Włodzimierz Cimoszewicz
1997– Jerzy Buzek

First Secretary

1945–8 Władysław Gomułka
1948–56 Bolesław Bierut
1956 Edward Ochab
1956–70 Władysław Gomułka
1970–80 Edward Gierek
1980–1 Stanisław Kania
1981–9 Wojciech Jaruzelski
1989–90 Mieczysław Rakowski

PORTUGAL

President

First Republic

1910–11 Teófilo Braga
1911–15 Manuel José de Arriaga
1915 Teófilo Braga
1915–17 Bernardino Machado
1917–18 Sidónio Pais
1918–19 João do Canto e Castro
1919–23 António José de Almeida
1923–5 Manuel Teixeira Gomes
1925–6 Bernardino Machado **New State**
1926 *Military Junta* (José Mendes Cabeçadas)
1926 *Military Junta* (Manuel de Oliveira Gomes da Costa)
1926–51 António Oscar Fragoso Carmona
1951–8 Francisco Craveiro Lopes
1958–74 Américo de Deus Tomás

Second Republic

1974 *Military Junta* (António Spínola)
1974–6 *Military Junta* (Francisco da Costa Gomes)

Third Republic

1976–86 António dos Santos Ramalho Eanes
1986–96 Mário Soares
1996 Jorge Sampaio

Prime Minister

1932–68 António de Oliveira Salazar
1968–74 Marcelo Caetano
1974 Adelino da Palma Carlos
1974–5 Vasco Gonçalves
1975–6 José Pinheiro de Azevedo
1976–8 Mário Soares
1978 Alfredo Nobre da Costa
1978–9 Carlos Alberto de Mota Pinto
1979 Maria de Lurdes Pintasilgo
1980–1 Francisco de Sá Carneiro
1981–3 Francisco Pinto Balsemão
1983–5 Mário Soares
1985–95 Aníbal Cavaço Silva
1995– António Guterres

QATAR

Emir

Family name: Al-Thani
1876–1905 Ahmad I
1905–13 Qasim
1913–49 Abdullah
1949–60 Ali
1960–72 Ahmad Bin Ali
1972–95 Khalifah Bin Hamad
1995– Hamad bin Khalifa

Prime Minister

1995– Abdulla bin Khalifa

ROMANIA

Monarch

1881–1914 Carol I
1914–27 Ferdinand I
1927–30 Michael *Prince*
1930–40 Carol II
1940–7 Michael I

Republic

President

1947–8 Mihai Sadoveanu *Interim*
1948–52 Constantin I Parhon
1952–8 Petru Groza
1958–61 Ion Georghe Maurer
1961–5 Georghe Gheorghiu-Dej
1965–7 Chivu Stoica
1967–89 Nicolae Ceausescu
1989–96 Ion Iliescu
1996– Emil Constantinescu

General Secretary

1955–65 Georghe Gheorghiu-Dej
1965–89 Nicolae Ceausescu

Prime Minister

1900–1 Petre P Carp
1901–6 Dimitrie A Sturdza
1906–7 Gheorge Grigore Cantacuzino
1907–9 Dimitrie A Sturdza
1909 Ionel Brătianu
1909–10 Mihai Pherekyde
1910–11 Ionel Brătianu
1911–12 Petre P Carp
1912–14 Titu Maiorescu
1914–18 Ionel Brătianu
1918 Alexandru Averescu
1918 Alexandru Marghiloman
1918 Constantin Coandă
1918 Ionel Brătianu
1919 Artur Văitoianu
1919–20 Alexandru Vaida-Voevod
1920–1 Alexandru Averescu
1921–2 Take Ionescu
1922–6 Ionel Brătianu
1926–7 Alexandru Averescu
1927 Ionel Brătianu
1927–8 Vintila I C Brătianu
1928–30 Juliu Maniu
1930 Gheorghe C Mironescu
1930 Juliu Maniu
1930–1 Gheorghe C Mironescu
1931–2 Nicolae Iorga
1932 Alexandru Vaida-Voevod
1932–3 Juliu Maniu
1933 Alexandru Vaida-Voevod
1933 Ion G Duca
1933–4 Constantin Angelescu
1934–7 Gheorghe Tătărescu
1937 Octavian Goga
1937–9 Miron Cristea
1939 Armand Călinescu
1939 Gheorghe Argeșanu
1939 Constantine Argetoianu
1939–40 Gheorghe Tătărescu
1940 Ion Gigurtu
1940–4 Ion Antonescu
1944 Constantin Sănătescu
1944–5 Nicolas Rădescu
1945–52 Petru Groza
1952–5 Gheorghe Gheorghiu-Dej
1955–61 Chivu Stoica
1961–74 Ion Gheorghe Maurer
1974–80 Manea Mănescu
1980–3 Ilie Verdet
1983–9 Constantin Dăscălescu
1989–91 Petre Roman
1991–2 Theodor Stolojan
1992–6 Nicolae Vacaroiu
1996–8 Victor Ciorbea
1998– Radu Vasile

RUSSIA

President

1991– Boris Yeltsin

Prime Minister

1992–8 Viktor Chernomyrdin
1998 Sergei Kiriyenko
1998–9 Yevgeny Primakov
1999– Sergey Stepashin

RWANDA

President

1962–73 Grégoire Kayibanda

1973–94 Juvénal Habyarimana
1994–5 Théodore Sindikubwabo *Interim*
1995– Pasteur Bizimunga

Prime Minister

1991–2 Sylvestre Nsanzimana
1992–3 Dismas Nsengiyaremye
1993–4 Agathe Uwilingiymana
1994–5 Jean Kambanda *Acting*
1995– Pierre-Celestin Rwigyema

SAINT CHRISTOPHER AND NEVIS

Chief of State: British monarch, represented by Governor-General

Prime Minister

1983–95 Kennedy Alphonse Simmonds
1995– Denzil Douglas

SAINT LUCIA

Chief of State: British monarch, represented by Governor-General

Prime Minister

1979 John Compton
1979–81 Allan Louisy
1981–3 Winston Francis Cenac
1983–96 John George Melvin Compton
1996–7 Vaughan Lewis
1997– Kenny Anthony

SAINT VINCENT AND THE GRENADINES

Chief of State: British monarch, represented by Governor-General

Prime Minister

1979–84 Milton Cato
1984– James Fitzallen Mitchell

SAMOA

President

1962–3 Tupua Tamesehe Mea'ole *and* Malietoa Tanumafili II *Joint Presidents*
1963– Malietoa Tanumafili II

Prime Minister

1962–70 Fiame Mata'afa Faumiuna Mulinu'u II
1970–6 Tupua Tamasese Leolofi IV
1976–82 Tupuola Taisi Efi
1982 Va'ai Kolone
1982 Tupuola Taisi Efi
1982–6 Tofilau Eti
1986–8 Va'ai Kolone
1988–99 Tofilau Eti Alesana
1999– Tuila'epa Sa'ilele Malielegaoi

SAN MARINO

1986– Gabriele Gatti

SÃO TOMÉ AND PRINCIPE

President

1975–91 Manuel Pinto da Costa
1991– Miguel Trovoada

Prime Minister

1992–4 Noberto Costa Alegre
1994 Evaristo do Espirito Santo Carvalho
1994–5 Carlos da Graça
1995–6 Armindo Vaz d'Almeida
1996–9 Raul Bragança Neto
1999– Guilherme Posser da Costa

SAUDI ARABIA

Monarch

Family name: al-Saud

1932–53 Abdulaziz Bin Abdur-Rahman
1953–64 Saud Bin Abdulaziz
1964–75 Faisal Bin Abdulaziz
1975–82 Khalid Bin Abdulaziz
1982–96 Fahd Bin Abdulaziz
1996 Abdullah ibn Abdulaziz (*Acting*)
1996– Fahd bin Abdulaziz

SENEGAL

President

1960–80 Léopold Sédar Senghor
1981– Abdou Diouf

Prime Minister

1991–8 Habib Thiam
1998– Mamadou Lamine Loum

SEYCHELLES

President

1976–7 James R Mancham
1977– France-Albert René

SIERRA LEONE

President

1971 Christopher Okero Cole
1971–85 Siaka Probin Stevens
1985–92 Joseph Saidu Momoh

Chairman

1992–6 Valentine Strasser
1996 *Military Rule*

President

1996–7 Ahmad Tejan Kabbah
1997–8 Johnny Paul Koroma
1998– Ahmad Tejan Kabbah

Prime Minister

Commonwealth

1961–4 Milton Margai
1964–7 Albert Michael Margai
1967 Siaka Stevens
1967 David Lansana
1967 Ambrose Genda
1967–8 *National Reformation Council* (Andrew Saxon-Smith)
1968 John Bangura
1968–71 Siaka Stevens

Republic

1971–5 Sorie Ibrahim Koroma
1975–8 Christian Alusine Kamara Taylor
1978– *No Prime Minister*

SINGAPORE

President (Yang di-Pertuan Negara)

1959–70 Yusof bin Ishak
1970–81 Benjamin Henry Sheares
1981–5 Chengara Veetil Devan Nair
1985–93 Wee Kim Wee
1993– Ong Teng Cheong

Prime Minister

1959–90 Lee Kuan Yew
1990– Goh Chok Tong

SLOVAK REPUBLIC

President

1993–8 Michal Kovac
1998–9 *No head of state*

Prime Minister

1993–4 Vladimir Mečiar
1994–7 Jozef Moravcik
1997–8 Vladimír Mečiar
1998– Mikuláš Dzurinda

SLOVENIA

President

1991– Milan Kučan

Prime Minister

1991–2 Lozje Peterle
1992– Janez Drnovšek

SOLOMON ISLANDS

Chief of State: British monarch, represented by Governor-General

Prime Minister

1978–82 Peter Kenilorea
1982–4 Solomon Mamaloni
1984–6 Peter Kenilorea
1986–9 Ezekiel Alebua
1989–93 Solomon Mamaloni
1993–4 Francis Billy Hilly
1994–7 Solomon Mamaloni
1997– Bartholomew Ulufa'alu

SOMALIA

President

1961–7 Aden Abdallah Osman
1967–9 Abdirashid Ali Shermarke

Supreme Revolutionary Council

1969–80 Mohammed Siad Barre

Republic

1980–91 Mohammed Siad Barre
1991– Ali Mahdi Mohammed

Prime Minister

1961–4 Abdirashid Ali Shermarke
1964–7 Abdirizak Haji Hussein
1967–9 Mohammed Haji Ibrahim Egal
1987–90 Mohammed Ali Samater
1990–1 Mohammed Hawadie Madar
1991–8 Umar Arteh Ghalib
1998– Hussein Mohamed Aidid

SOUTH AFRICA

Governor-General

1910–14 Herbert John, Viscount Gladstone
1914–20 Sydney, Earl Buxton
1920–4 Arthur, Duke of Connaught
1924–31 Alexander, Earl of Athlone
1931–7 George Herbert Hyde Villiers
1937–43 Patrick Duncan
1943–5 Nicolaas Jacobus de Wet
1945–51 Gideon Brand Van Zyl
1951–9 Ernest George Jansen
1959 Lucas Cornelius Steyn
1959–61 Charles Robberts Swart

Republic

President

1961–7	Charles Robberts Swart
1967	Theophilus Ebenhaezer Dönges
1967–8	Jozua François Nandé
1968–75	Jacobus Johannes Fouché
1975–8	Nicolaas Diederichs
1978–9	Balthazar Johannes Vorster
1979–84	Marais Viljoen
1984–9	Pieter Willem Botha
1989–94	Frederick Willem de Klerk
1994–9	Nelson Mandela
1999–	Thabo Mbeki (*in waiting*)

Prime Minister

1910–19	Louis Botha *SAf*
1919–24	Jan Christiaan Smuts *SAf*
1924–39	James Barry Munnick Hertzog *Nat*
1939–48	Jan Christiaan Smuts *Un*
1948–54	Daniel François Malan *Nat*
1954–8	Johannes Gerardus Strijdom *Nat*
1958–66	Hendrik Frensch Verwoerd *Nat*
1966–78	Balthazar Johannes Vorster *Nat*
1978–84	Pieter Willem Botha *Nat*
1984–	*No Prime Minister*
Nat	National
SAf	South African Party
Un	United

SPAIN

Monarch

1886–1931	Alfonso XIII

Second Republic

President

1931–6	Niceto Alcalá Zamora y Torres
1936	Diego Martínez Barrio *Acting*

Civil War

1936–9	Manuel Azaña y Díez
1936–9	Miguel Cabanellas Ferrer

Nationalist Government

Chief of State

1936–75	Francisco Franco Bahamonde

Monarch

1975–	Juan Carlos I

Prime Minister

1900–1	Marcelo de Azcárraga y Palmero
1901–2	Práxedes Mateo Sagasta
1902–3	Francisco Silvela y Le-Vielleuze
1903	Raimundo Fernández Villaverde
1903–4	Antonio Maura y Montaner
1904–5	Marcelo de Azcárraga y Palmero
1905	Raimundo Fernández Villaverde
1905	Eugenio Montero Ríos
1905–6	Segismundo Moret y Prendergast
1906	José López Domínguez
1906	Segismundo Moret y Prendergast
1906–7	Antonio Aguilar y Correa
1907–9	Antonio Maura y Montaner
1909–10	Segismundo Moret y Prendergast
1910–12	José Canalejas y Méndez
1912	Alvaro Figueroa y Torres
1912–13	Manuel García Prieto
1913–15	Eduardo Dato y Iradier
1915–17	Alvaro Figueroa y Torres
1917	Manuel García Prieto
1917	Eduardo Dato y Iradier
1917–18	Manuel García Prieto
1918	Antonio Maura y Montaner
1918	Manuel García Prieto
1918–19	Álvaro Figueroa y Torres
1919	Antonio Maura y Montaner
1919	Joaquín Sánchez de Toca
1919–20	Manuel Allendesalazar
1920–1	Eduardo Dato y Iradier
1921	Gabino Bugallal Araujo *Acting*
1921	Manuel Allendesalazar
1921–2	Antonio Maura y Montaner
1922	José Sánchez Guerra y Martínez
1922–3	Manuel García Prieto
1923–30	Miguel Primo de Rivera y Oraneja
1930–1	Dámaso Berenguer y Fusté
1931	Juan Bautista Aznar-Cabañas
1931	Niceto Alcalá Zamora y Torres
1931–3	Manuel Azaña y Díez
1933	Alejandro Lerroux y García
1933	Diego Martínez Barrio
1933–4	Alejandro Lerroux y García
1934	Ricardo Samper Ibáñez
1934–5	Alejandro Lerroux y García
1935	Joaquín Chapaprieta y Terragosa
1935–6	Manuel Portela Valladares
1936	Manuel Azaña y Díez
1936	Santiago Casares Quiroga
1936	Diego Martínez Barrio
1936	José Giral y Pereyra
1936–7	Francisco Largo Caballero
1937–9	Juan Negrín

Chairman of the Council of Ministers

1939–73	Francisco Franco Bahamonde

Prime Minister

1973	Torcuato Fernández Miranda y Hevía *Acting*
1973–6	Carlos Arias Navarro
1976–81	Adolfo Suárez
1981–2	Calvo Sotelo
1982–96	Felipe González Márquez
1996–	José Maria Aznar

SRI LANKA

President

1972–8	William Gopallawa
1978–89	Junius Richard Jayawardene
1989–93	Ranasinghe Premadasa
1993–4	Dingiri Banda Wijedunga
1994–	Chandrika Bandanaraike Kumaratunga

Prime Minister

Ceylon

1947–52	Don Stephen Senanayake
1952–3	Dudley Shelton Senanayake
1953–6	John Lionel Kotelawela
1956–9	Solomon West Ridgway Dias Bandaranaike
1960	Dudley Shelton Senanayake
1960–5	Sirimavo Ratwatte Dias Bandaranaike
1965–70	Dudley Shelton Senanayake

Sri Lanka

1970–7	Sirimavo Bandaranaike
1977–89	Ranasinghe Premadasa
1989–93	Dingiri Banda Wijetunga
1993–4	Ranil Wickremasinghe
1994–	Sirimavo R D Bandanaraike

THE SUDAN

Chief of State

1956–8	*Council of State*
1958–64	Ibrahim Abboud
1964–5	*Council of Sovereignty*
1965–9	IsmailAl-Azhari
1969–85	Gaafar Mohamad Nimeiri (*President from 1971*)

Transitional Military Council

Chairman

1985–6	Abd al-Rahman Siwar al-Dahab

Supreme Council

Chairman

1986–9	Ahmad al-Mirghani
1989–93	Omar Hassan Ahmed al-Bashir

President

1993–	Omar Hassan Ahmed al-Bashir

Prime Minister

1955–6	Ismail al-Azhari
1956–8	Abdullah Khalil
1958–64	*As President*
1964–5	Serr al-Khatim al-Khalifa
1965–6	Mohammed Ahmed Mahjoub
1966–7	Sadiq al-Mahdi
1967–9	Mohammed Ahmed Mahjoub
1969	Babiker Awadalla
1969–76	*As President*
1976–7	Rashid al-Tahir Bakr
1977–85	*As President*
1985–6	*Transitional Millitary Council* (al-Jazuli Dafallah)
1986–9	Sadiq al-Mahdi *Military Council, Prime Minister*
1989–	Omar Hassan Ahmed al-Bashir

SURINAME

President

1975–80	J H E Ferrier
1980–2	Henk Chin-a-Sen
1982–8	L F Ramdat-Musier *Acting*
1988–90	Ramsewak Shankar
1990–1	Johan Kraag
1991–6	Ronald Ventiaan
1996–	Jules Wijdenbosch

National Military Council

Chairman

1980–7	Désiré (Desi) Bouterse

Prime Minister

1975–80	Henk Arron
1980	Henk Chin-a-Sen
1980–2	*No Prime Minister*
1982–3	Henry Weyhorst
1983–4	Errol Alibux
1984–6	Wim Udenhout
1986–7	Pretaapnarian Radbakishun
1987–8	Jules Wijdenbosch
1988–90	Henk Arron

1990–1	Jules Wijdenbosch
1991–6	Jules Ajodhia
1996–	Pretaapnarain Radhakishun

SWAZILAND

Monarch

1967–82	Sobhuza II *Chief since 1921*
1983	Dzeliwe *Queen Regent*
1983–6	Ntombi *Queen Regent*
1986–	Mswati III

Prime Minister

1967–78	Prince Makhosini
1978–9	Prince Maphevu Dlamini
1979–83	Prince Mbandla Dlamini
1983–6	Prince Bhekimpi Dlamini
1986–9	Sotsha Dlamini
1989–93	Obed Dlamini
1993–6	Jameson Mbilini Dlamini
1996–	Sibusiso Barnabus Dlamini

SWEDEN

Monarch

1872–1907	Oskar II
1907–50	Gustav V
1950–73	Gustav VI Adolf
1973–	Carl XVI Gustaf

Prime Minister

1900–2	Fredrik von Otter
1902–5	Erik Gustaf Boström
1905	Johan Ramstedt
1905	Christian Lundeberg
1905–6	Karl Staaf
1906–11	Arvid Lindman
1911–14	Karl Staaf
1914–17	Hjalmar Hammarskjöld
1917	Carl Swartz
1917–20	Nils Edén
1920	Hjalmar Branting
1920–1	Louis De Geer
1921	Oscar Von Sydow
1921–3	Hjalmar Branting
1923–4	Ernst Trygger
1924–5	Hjalmar Branting
1925–6	Rickard Sandler
1926–8	Carl Gustaf Ekman
1928–30	Arvid Lindman
1930–2	Carl Gustaf Ekman
1932	Felix Hamrin
1932–6	Per Albin Hansson
1936	Axel Pehrsson-Branstorp
1936–46	Per Albin Hansson
1946–69	Tage Erlander
1969–76	Olof Palme
1976–8	Thorbjörn Fälldin
1978–9	Ola Ullsten
1979–82	Thorbjörn Fälldin
1982–6	Olof Palme
1986–91	Ingvar Carlsson
1991–4	Carl Bildt
1994–6	Ingvar Carlsson
1996–	Goran Persson

SWITZERLAND

President

1900	Walter Hauser
1901	Ernst Brenner
1902	Joseph Zemp
1903	Adolf Deucher
1904	Robert Comtesse
1905	Marc-Emile Ruchet
1906	Ludwig Forrer
1907	Eduard Müller
1908	Ernst Brenner
1909	Adolf Deucher
1910	Robert Comtesse
1911	Marc-Emile Ruchet
1912	Ludwig Forrer
1913	Eduard Müller
1914	Arthur Hoffmann
1915	Guiseppe Motta
1916	Camille Decoppet
1917	Edmund Schulthess
1918	Felix Calonder
1919	Gustave Ador
1920	Giuseppe Motta
1921	Edmund Schulthess
1922	Robert Haab
1923	Karl Scheurer
1924	Ernest Chuard
1925	Jean-Marie Musy
1926	Heinrich Häberlin
1927	Giuseppe Motta
1928	Edmund Schulthess
1929	Robert Haab
1930	Jean-Marie Musy
1931	Heinrich Häberlin
1932	Giuseppe Motta
1933	Edmund Schulthess
1934	Marcel Pilet-Golaz
1935	Rudolf Minger
1936	Albert Meyer
1937	Giuseppe Motta
1938	Johannes Baumann
1939	Philipp Etter
1940	Marcel Pilet-Golaz
1941	Ernst Wetter
1942	Philipp Etter
1943	Enrico Celio
1944	Walter Stampfli
1945	Eduard von Steiger
1946	Karl Kobelt
1947	Philipp Etter
1948	Enrico Celio
1949	Ernst Nobs
1950	Max Petitpierre
1951	Eduard von Steiger
1952	Karl Kobelt
1953	Philipp Etter
1954	Rodolphe Rubattel
1955	Max Petitpierre
1956	Markus Feldmann
1957	Hans Streuli
1958	Thomas Holenstein
1959	Paul Chaudet
1960	Max Petitpierre
1961	Friedrich Wahlen
1962	Paul Chaudet
1963	Willy Spühler
1964	Ludwig von Moos
1965	Hans Peter Tschudi
1966	Hans Schaffner
1967	Roger Bonvin
1968	Willy Spühler
1969	Ludwig von Moos
1970	Hans Peter Tschudi
1971	Rudolf Gnägi
1972	Nello Celio
1973	Roger Bonvin
1974	Ernst Brugger
1975	Pierre Graber
1976	Rudolf Gnägi
1977	Kurt Furgler
1978	Willi Ritschard
1979	Hans Hürlimann
1980	Georges-André Chevallaz
1981	Kurt Furgler
1982	Fritz Honegger
1983	Pierre Aubert
1984	Leon Schlumpf
1985	Kurt Furgler
1986	Alphons Egli
1987	Pierre Aubert
1988	Otto Stich
1989	Jean-Pascal Delamuraz
1990	Arnold Koller
1991	Flavio Cotti
1992	Réné Felber
1993	Adolf Ogi
1994	Otto Stich
1995	Kasper Villiger
1996	Jean-Pascal Delamuraz
1997	Arnold Koller
1998	Flavio Cotti
1999	Ruth Dreifuss

SYRIA

President

1943–9	Shukri Al-Quwwatli
1949	Husni Az-Zaim
1949–51	Hashim Al-Atasi
1951–4	Adib Shishaqli
1954–5	Hashim Al-Atasi
1955–8	Shukri Al-Quwwatli
1958–61	*Part of United Arab Republic*
1961–3	Nazim Al-Qudsi
1963	Luai Al-Atassi
1963–6	Amin Al-Hafiz
1966–70	Nureddin Al-Atassi
1970–1	Ahmad Al-Khatib
1971–	Hafez Al-Assad

Prime Minister

1946–8	Jamil Mardam Bey
1948–9	Khalid Al-Azm
1949	Husni Az-Zaim
1949	Muhsi Al-Barazi
1949	Hashim Al-Atassi
1949	Nazim Al-Qudsi
1949–50	Khalid Al-Azm
1950–1	Nazim Al-Qudsi
1951	Khalid Al-Azm
1951	Hassan Al-Hakim
1951	Maruf Ad-Dawalibi
1951–3	Fauzi As-Salu
1953–4	Adib Shishaqli

1954 Shewqet Shuqair
1954 Sabri Al-Asali
1954 Said Al-Ghazzi
1954–5 Faris Al-Khuri
1955 Sabri Al-Asali
1955–6 Said Al-Ghazzi
1956–8 Sabri Al-Asali
1958–61 *Part of United Arab Republic*
1961 Abd Al-Hamid As-Sarraj
1961 Mamun Kuzbari
1961 Izzat An-Nuss
1961–2 Maruf Ad-Dawalibi
1962 Bashir Azmah
1962–3 Khalid Al-Azm
1963 Salah Ad-Din Al-Bitaar
1963 Sami Al-Jundi
1963 Salah Ad-Din Al-Bitaar
1963–4 Amin Al-Hafez
1964 Salah Ad-Din Al-Bitaar
1964–5 Amin Al-Hafez
1965 Yousif Zeayen
1966 Salah Ad-Din Al-Bitaar
1966–8 Yousif Zeayen
1968–70 Nureddin Al-Atassi *Acting*
1970–1 Hafez Al-Assad
1971–2 Abdel Rahman Khleifawi
1972–6 Mahmoud bin Saleh Al-Ayoubi
1976–8 Abdul Rahman Khleifawi
1978–80 Mohammed Ali Al-Halabi
1980–7 Abdel Rauof Al-Kasm
1987– Mahmoud Zubi

TAIWAN

President
1950–75 Chiang Kai-shek
1975–8 Yen Chia-kan
1978–88 Chiang Ching-kuo
1988– Lee Teng-hui

President of Executive Council
1950–4 Ch'eng Ch'eng
1954–8 O K Yui
1958–63 Ch'eng Ch'eng
1963–72 Yen Chia-ken
1972–8 Chiang Ching-kuo
1978–84 Sun Yun-suan
1984–9 Yu Kuo-hwa
1989–90 Lee Huan
1990–3 Hau Pei-tsun
1993–6 Lien Chan
1996– Vincent Siew

TAJIKISTAN

President
1991–2 Rakhman Nabiyev
1992 Akbarsho Iskandrov *Chair of the Supreme Soviet*
1992– Imamoli Rakmanov

Chairman of the Council of Ministers
1991–2 Akbar Mirzoyev
1992–3 Abdumalik Abdulladjanov
1993–4 Abduljalil Samadov
1994–6 Jamshed Karimov
1996– Yahya Azimov

TANZANIA

President
1964–85 Julius Kambarage Nyerere
1985–95 Ndugu Ali Hassan Mwinyi
1995– Benjamin Mkapa

Prime Minister
1964–72 Rashid M Kawawa *Vice President*
1972–7 Rashid M Kawawa
1977–80 Edward M Sokoine
1980–3 Cleopa D Msuya
1983–4 Edward M Sokoine
1984–5 Salim A Salim
1985–90 Joseph S Warioba
1990–4 John Malecela
1994–5 Cleopa Msuya
1995– Frederick Sumaye

THAILAND

Monarch
1868–1910 Chulalongkorn, Rama V
1910–25 Rama VI
1925–35 Rama VII
1935–9 Rama VIII (Ananda Mahidol)
1939–46 Nai Pridi Phanomyong *Regent*
1946– Rama IX (Rangsit of Chainat *Regent 1946–50*)

Prime Minister
1932–3 Phraya Manopakom
1933–8 Phraya Phahon Phonphahuyasena
1938–44 Luang Phibun Songgram
1945 Thawi Bunyaket
1945–6 Mom Rachawongse Seni Pramoj
1946 Nai Khuang Aphaiwong
1946 Nai Pridi Phanomyong
1946–7 Luang Thamrong Nawasawat
1947–8 Nai Khuang Aphaiwong
1948–57 Luang Phibun Songgram
1957 Sarit Thanarat
1957 Nai Pote Sarasin
1957–8 Thanom Kittikatchom
1958–63 Sarit Thanarat
1963–73 Thanom Kittikatchom
1973–5 Sanya Dharmasaki
1975–6 Mom Rachawongse Kukrit Pramoj
1976 Seni Pramoj
1976–7 Thanin Kraivichien
1977–80 Kriangsak Chammanard
1980–7 Prem Tinsulanonda
1987–91 Chatichai Choonhavan
1991–2 Anand Panyarachun
1992 Suchinda Kraprayoon
1992–5 Chuan Leekpai
1995–6 Banharn Silpa-Arche
1996–7 Chavalit Yongchaiyudh
1997– Chuan Leekpai

TOGO

President
1960–3 Sylvanus Olympio
1963–7 Nicolas Grunitzky
1967–91 Gnassingbé Eyadéma

Prime Minister
1991–4 Joseph Koukou Koffigoh
1994–6 Edem Kodjo
1996– Kwasi Klutse

TONGA

Monarch
1893–1918 George Tupou II
1918–65 Salote Tupou III
1965– Taufa'ahau Tupou IV

Prime Minister
1970–91 Fatafehi Tu'ipelehake
1991– Baron Vaea

TRINIDAD AND TOBAGO

President
1976–87 Ellis Emmanuel Clarke
1987–97 Noor Mohammed Hassanali
1997– Arthur Napoleon Raymond Robinson

Premier
1956–62 Eric Williams

Prime Minister
1962–81 Eric Williams
1981–6 George Chambers
1986–92 Arthur Napoleon Raymond Robinson
1992–5 Patrick Manning
1995– Basdeo Panday

TUNISIA

Bey
1882–1902 'Ali Muddat
1902–6 Muhammad IV al-Hadi
1906–22 Muhammad V an-Nadir
1922–9 Muhammad VI al-Habib
1929–42 Ahmad II
1942–3 Muhammad VII al-Munsif
1943–57 Muhammad VIII al-Amin

President
1957–87 Habib Bourguiba
1987– Zine al-Abidine bin Ali

Prime Minister
1956–7 Habib Bourguiba
1957–69 *No Prime Minister*
1969–70 Bahi Ladgham
1970–80 Hadi Nouira
1980–6 Mohammed Mezali
1986–7 Rashid Sfar
1987 Zine Al-Abidine Bin Ali
1987–9 Hadi Baccouche
1989– Hamed Karoui

TURKEY

Sultan of the Ottoman Empire
1876–1909 Abdülhamit
1909–18 Mehmet Resat
1918–22 Mehmet Vahideddin

Turkish Republic

President
1923–38 Mustafa Kemal Atatürk
1938–50 Ismet Inönü
1950–60 Celâl Bayar
1961–6 Cemal Gürsel
1966–73 Cevdet Sunay
1973–80 Fahri S Korutürk
1982–9 Kenan Evren
1989–93 Turgut Özal
1993– Süleyman Demirel

Prime Minister
1923–4 Ismet Paza Inönü
1924–5 Ali Fethi Okyar
1925–37 Ismet Paza Inönü

1937–9 Celâl Bayar
1939–42 Refik Saydam
1942–6 Sükrü Saracoglu
1946–7 Recep Peker
1947–9 Hasan Saka
1949–50 Semseddin Günaltay
1950–60 Adnan Menderes
1960–1 *Military Junta*
1961–5 Ismet Paza Inönü
1965 Fuat Hayri Ürgüplü
1965–71 Suleyman Demirel
1971–2 Nihat Erim
1972–3 Ferit Melen
1973 Naim Télu
1973–4 Bülent Ecevit
1974–7 Suleyman Demirel
1978–9 Bülent Ecevit
1979–80 Suleyman Demirel
1980–3 Bülent Ulusu
1983–9 Turgut Özal
1989–91 Yildirim Akbulut
1991 Mesut Yilmaz
1991–3 Süleyman Demirel
1993–6 Tansu Çiller
1996 Mesut Yilmaz
1996–7 Necmettin Erbakan
1997–8 Mesut Yilmaz
1998– Bulent Ecevit

TURKMENISTAN

President
1991– Saparmurad Niyazov
Prime Minister
1991–2 Khan Akhmedov
1992– *As President*

TUVALU

Chief of State: British monarch, represented by Governor-General
Prime Minister
1978–81 Toalipi Lauti
1981–9 Tomasi Puapua
1989–93 Bikenibeu Paeniu
1993–6 Kamuta Laatasi
1996–9 Bikenibeu Paeniu
1999– Ionatana Ionatana

UGANDA

President
1962–6 Edward Muteesa II
1967–71 Apollo Milton Obote
1971–9 Idi Amin
1979 Yusufu Kironde Lule
1979–80 Godfrey Lukongwa Binaisa
1981–5 Apollo Milton Obote
1985–6 *Military Council* (Tito Okello Lutwa)
1986– Yoweri Kaguta Museveni
Prime Minister
1962–71 Apollo Milton Obote
1971–81 *No Prime Minister*
1981–5 Eric Otema Alimadi
1985 Paulo Muwanga
1985–6 Abraham N Waliggo
1986–91 Samson B Kisekka
1991–4 George Cosmas Adyebo
1994–9 Kintu Musoke
1999– Apolo Ngibambi

UKRAINE

President
1990–4 Leonid M Kravchuk
1994– Leonid Kuchma
Prime Minister
1991–2 Vitold P Fokin
1992–3 Leonid Kuchma
1993 Yukhim Zvyagilsky
1994–5 Vitali Masol
1995–6 Yevhenii Marchuk
1996–7 Pavlo Lazarenko
1997 Vasyl Durdynets
1997– Valery Pustovoytenko

UNITED ARAB EMIRATES

President
1971– Zayed bin Sultan al-Nahyan
Prime Minister
1971–9 Maktoum bin Rashid al-Maktoum
1979–90 Rashid bin Said al-Maktoum
1990– Maktoum bin Rashid al-Maktoum

Abu Dhabi
Tribe: Al Bu Falah or Al Nahyan (Bani Yas)
Family name: al-Nahyan
Shaikh
1855–1909 Zayed
1909–12 Tahnoun
1912–22 Hamdan
1922–6 Sultan
1926–8 Saqr
1928–66 Shakhbout
1966– Zayed

Ajman
Tribe: Al Bu Kharayban (Naim)
Family name: al-Nuaimi
Shaikh
1900–10 Abdel-Aziz
1910–28 Humaid
1928–81 Rashid
1981– Humaid

Dubai
Tribe: Al Bu Flasah (Bani Yas)
Family name: al-Maktoum
Shaikh
1894–1906 Maktoum
1906–12 Butti
1912–58 Said
1958–90 Rashid
1990– Maktoum

Fujairah
Tribe: Sharqiyyin
Family name: al-Sharqi
Shaikh
1952–75 Mohammed
1975– Hamad

Ras Al-Khaimah
Tribe: Huwalah
Family name: al-Qasimi
Shaikh
1900–9 Khaled
1921–48 Sultan
1948– Saqr

Sharjah
Tribe: Huwalah
Family name: al-Qasimi
Shaikh
1883–1914 Saqr
1914–24 Khaled
1924–51 Sultan
1951–65 Saqr
1965–72 Khaled
1972–87 Sultan
1987 Abdel-Aziz
1987– Sultan

Umm Al-Qaiwain
Tribe: al-Ali
Family name: al-Mualla
Shaikh
1873–1904 Ahmad
1904–22 Rashid
1922–3 Abdullah
1923–9 Hamad
1929–81 Ahmad
1981– Rashid

UNION OF SOVIET SOCIALIST REPUBLICS

President
1917 Leo Borisovich Kamenev
1917–19 Yakov Mikhailovich Sverlov
1919–46 Mikhail Ivanovich Kalinin
1946–53 Nikolai Shvernik
1953–60 Klimentiy Voroshilov
1960–4 Leonid Brezhnev
1964–5 Anastas Mikoyan
1965–77 Nikolai Podgorny
1977–82 Leonid Brezhnev
1982–3 Vasily Kuznetsov *Acting*
1983–4 Yuri Andropov
1984 Vasily Kuznetsov *Acting*
1984–5 Konstantin Chernenko
1985 Vasily Kuznetsov *Acting*
1985–8 Andrei Gromyko
1988–90 Mikhail Gorbachev
Executive President
1990–1 Mikhail Gorbachev
Chairman (Prime Minister)
Council of Ministers
1917 Georgy Evgenyevich Lvov
1917 Aleksandr Fyodorovich Kerensky
Council of People's Commissars
1917–24 Vladimir Ilyich Lenin
1924–30 Aleksei Ivanovich Rykov
1930–41 Vyacheslav Mikhailovich Molotov
1941–53 Josef Stalin
Council of Ministers
1953–5 Georgiy Malenkov
1955–8 Nikolai Bulganin
1958–64 Nikita Khrushchev
1964–80 Alexei Kosygin
1980–5 Nikolai Tikhonov
1985–90 Nikolai Ryzhkov
1990–1 Yuri Maslyukov *Acting*

1991	Valentin Pavlov

General Secretary

1922–53	Josef Stalin
1953	Georgiy Malenkov
1953–64	Nikita Khrushchev
1964–82	Leonid Brezhnev
1982–4	Yuri Andropov
1984–5	Konstantin Chernenko
1985–91	Mikhail Gorbachev

UNITED KINGDOM

Monarch

West Saxon Kings

802–39	Egbert
839–58	Æthelwulf
858–60	Æthelbald
860–5	Æthelbert
866–71	Æthelred
871–99	Alfred the Great
899–924	Edward (the Elder)
924–39	Athelstan
939–46	Edmund I
946–55	Edred
955–9	Edwy
959–75	Edgar
975–8	Edward (the Martyr)
978–1016	Æthelred II (the Unready)
1016	Edmund II (Ironside)

Danish Kings

1016–35	Cnut (Canute the Great)
1035–7	Harold *Regent*
1037–40	Harold I (Harefoot)
1040–2	Harthacnut
1042–66	Edward (the Confessor)
1066	Harold II

House of Normandy

1066–87	William I (the Conqueror)
1087–1100	William II (Rufus)
1100–35	Henry I

House of Blois

1135–54	Stephen

House of Plantagenet

1154–89	Henry II
1189–99	Richard I (Coeur de Lion)
1199–1216	John
1216–72	Henry III
1272–1307	Edward I
1307–27	Edward II
1327–77	Edward III
1377–99	Richard II

House of Lancaster

1399–1413	Henry IV
1413–22	Henry V
1422–61	Henry VI

House of York

1461–70	Edward IV

House of Lancaster

1470–1	Henry VI

House of York

1471–83	Edward IV
1483	Edward V
1483–5	Richard III

House of Tudor

1485–1509	Henry VII
1509–47	Henry VIII
1547–53	Edward VI
1553–8	Mary I
1558–1603	Elizabeth I

House of Stuart

1603–25	James I (VI of Scotland)
1625–49	Charles I

Commonwealth and Protectorate

1649–53	*Council of State*
1653–8	Oliver Cromwell *Lord Protector*
1658–9	Richard Cromwell *Lord Protector*

House of Stuart *(restored)*

1660–85	Charles II
1685–8	James II
1689–94	William III *(jointly with* Mary II)
1694–1702	William III (*alone*)
1702–14	Anne

House of Hanover

1714–27	George I
1727–60	George II
1760–1820	George III
1820–30	George IV
1830–7	William IV
1837–1901	Victoria

House of Saxe-Coburg

1901–10	Edward VII

House of Windsor

1910–36	George V
1936	Edward VIII
1936–52	George VI
1952–	Elizabeth II

Prime Minister

1721–42	Robert Walpole *Whig*
1742–3	Spencer Compton, Earl of Wilmington *Whig*
1743–54	Henry Pelham *Whig*
1754–6	Thomas Pelham (Pelham-Holles), Duke of Newcastle *Whig*
1756–7	William Cavendish, 1st Duke of Devonshire *Whig*
1757–62	Thomas Pelham (Pelham-Holles), Duke of Newcastle *Whig*
1762–3	John Stuart , 3rd Earl of Bute *Tory*
1763–5	George Grenville *Whig*
1765–6	Charles Watson Wentworth, 2nd Marquis of Rockingham *Whig*
1766–7	William Pitt, 1st Earl of Chatham *Whig*
1767–70	Augustus Henry Fitzroy, 3rd Duke of Grafton *Whig*
1770–82	Frederick, 8th Lord North *Tory*
1782	Charles Watson Wentworth, 2nd Marquis of Rockingham *Whig*
1782–3	William Petty, 2nd Earl of Shelburne *Whig*
1783	William Henry Cavendish, Duke of Portland *Coal*
1783–1801	William Pitt *Tory*
1801–4	Henry Addington, 1st Viscount Sidmouth *Tory*
1804–6	William Pitt *Tory*
1806–7	William Wyndham Grenville, 1st Baron Grenville *Whig*
1807–9	William Henry Cavendish, Duke of Portland *Coal*
1809–12	Spencer Perceval *Tory*
1812–27	Robert Banks Jenkinson, 2nd Earl of Liverpool *Tory*
1827	George Canning *Tory*
1827–8	Frederick John Robinson, 1st Earl of Ripon *Tory*
1828–30	Arthur Wellesley, 1st Duke of Wellington *Tory*
1830–4	Charles Grey, 2nd Earl Grey *Whig*
1834	William Lamb, 2nd Viscount Melbourne *Whig*
1834–5	Robert Peel *Con*
1835–41	William Lamb, 2nd Viscount Melbourne *Whig*
1841–6	Robert Peel *Con*
1846–52	Lord John Russell, 1st Earl Russell *Lib*
1852	Edward Geoffrey Smith Stanley, 14th Earl of Derby *Con*
1852–5	George Hamilton-Gordon, 4th Earl of Aberdeen *Peelite*
1855–8	Henry John Temple, 3rd Viscount Palmerston *Lib*
1858–9	Edward Geoffrey Smith Stanley, 14th Earl of Derby *Con*
1859–65	Henry John Temple, 3rd Viscount Palmerston *Lib*
1865–6	Lord John Russell, 1st Earl Russell *Lib*
1866–8	Edward Geoffrey Smith Stanley, 14th Earl of Derby *Con*
1868	Benjamin Disraeli, 1st Earl of Beaconsfield *Con*
1868–74	William Ewart Gladstone *Lib*
1874–80	Benjamin Disraeli, 1st Earl of Beaconsfield *Con*
1880–5	William Ewart Gladstone *Lib*
1885–6	Robert Arthur Talbot Gascoyne-Cecil, 3rd Marquis of Salisbury *Con*
1886	William Ewart Gladstone *Lib*
1886–92	Robert Arthur Talbot Gascoyne-Cecil, 3rd Marquis of Salisbury *Con*
1892–4	William Ewart Gladstone *Lib*
1894–5	Archibald Philip Primrose, 5th Earl of Rosebery *Lib*
1895–1902	Robert Arthur Talbot Gascoyne-Cecil, 3rd Marquis of Salisbury *Con*
1902–5 *Con*	Arthur James, 1st Earl of Balfour
1905–8	Henry Campbell-Bannerman *Lib*
1908–15	Herbert Henry Asquith, 1st Earl of Oxford and Asquith *Lib*
1915–16 *Coal*	Herbert Henry Asquith, 1st Earl of Oxford and Asquith
1916–22 *Coal*	David Lloyd-George, 1st Earl Lloyd-George of Dwyfor
1922–3	Andrew Bonar Law *Con*
1923–4	Stanley Baldwin, 1st Earl Baldwin of Bewdley *Con*
1924	James Ramsay MacDonald *Lab*
1924–9	Stanley Baldwin, 1st Earl Baldwin of Bewdley *Con*
1929–31	James Ramsay MacDonald *Lab*
1931–5	James Ramsay MacDonald *Nat*
1935–7	Stanley Baldwin, 1st Earl Baldwin of Bewdley *Nat*
1937–40	(Arthur) Neville Chamberlain *Nat*
1940–5	Winston Leonard Spencer Churchill *Coal*
1945–51	Clement Richard Attlee, 1st Earl Attlee *Lab*

1951–5 Winston Leonard Spencer Churchill *Con*
1955–7 (Robert) Anthony Eden, 1st Earl of Avon *Con*
1957–63 (Maurice) Harold Macmillan, 1st Earl of Stockton *Con*
1963–4 Alexander Frederick (Alec) Douglas-Home, Baron Home of the Hirsel *Con*
1964–70 (James) Harold, Baron Wilson *Lab*
1970–4 Edward Richard George Heath *Con*
1974–6 (James) Harold, Baron Wilson *Lab*
1976–9 (Leonard) James, Baron Callaghan *Lab*
1979–90 Margaret Hilda Thatcher *Con*
1990–7 John Major *Con*
1997– (Anthony Charles Lynton) Tony Blair

Coal Coalition
Con Conservative
Lab Labour
Lib Liberal

UNITED NATIONS

Secretary General
1946–53 Trygve Lie *Norway*
1953–61 Dag Hammarskjöld *Sweden*
1962–71 U Thant *Burma*
1971–81 Kurt Waldheim *Austria*
1982–92 Javier Pérez de Cuéllar *Peru*
1992–7 Boutros Boutros Ghali *Egypt*
1997– Koffi Annan *Ghana*

UNITED STATES OF AMERICA

President
Vice President in parentheses

1789–97 George Washington (1st) (John Adams)
1797–1801 John Adams (2nd) *Fed* (Thomas Jefferson)
1801–9 Thomas Jefferson (3rd) *Dem-Rep* (Aaron Burr, 1801–5) (George Clinton, 1805–9)
1809–17 James Madison (4th) *Dem-Rep* (George Clinton, 1809–12) *No Vice President 1812–13* (Elbridge Gerry, 1813–14) *No Vice President 1814–17*
1817–25 James Monroe (5th) *Dem-Rep* (Daniel D Tompkins)
1825–9 John Quincy Adams (6th) *Dem-Rep* (John C Calhoun)
1829–37 Andrew Jackson (7th) *Dem* (John C Calhoun, 1829–32) *No Vice President 1832–3* (Martin van Buren, 1833–7)
1837–41 Martin van Buren (8th) *Dem* (Richard M Johnson)
1841 William Henry Harrison (9th) *Whig* (John Tyler)
1841–5 John Tyler (10th) *Whig* *No Vice President*
1845–9 James Knox Polk (11th) *Dem* (George M Dallas)
1849–50 Zachary Taylor (12th) *Whig* (Millard Fillmore)
1850–3 Millard Fillmore (13th) *Whig* *No Vice President*
1853–7 Franklin Pierce (14th) *Dem* (William R King, 1853) *No Vice President 1853–7*
1857–61 James Buchanan (15th) *Dem* (John C Breckinridge)
1861–5 Abraham Lincoln (16th) *Rep* (Hannibal Hamlin, 1861–5) (Andrew Johnson, 1865)
1865–9 Andrew Johnson (17th) *Dem-Nat* *No Vice President*
1869–77 Ulysses Simpson Grant (18th) *Rep* (Schuyler Colfax, 1869–73) (Henry Wilson, 1873–5) *No Vice President* 1875–7
1877–81 Rutherford Birchard Hayes (19th) *Rep* (William A Wheeler)
1881 James Abram Garfield (20th) *Rep* (Chester A Arthur)
1881–5 Chester Alan Arthur (21st) *Rep* *No Vice President*
1885–9 Grover Cleveland (22nd) *Dem* (Thomas A Hendricks, 1885) *No Vice President 1885–9*
1889–93 Benjamine Harrison (23rd) *Rep* (Levi P Morton)
1893–7 Grover Cleveland (24th) *Dem* (Adlai E Stevenson)
1897–1901 William McKinley (25th) *Rep* (Garret A Hobart, 1897–9) *No Vice President 1899–1901* (Theodore Roosevelt, 1901)
1901–9 Theodore Roosevelt (26th) *Rep* *No Vice President 1901–5* (Charles W Fairbanks, 1905–9)
1909–13 William Howard Taft (27th) *Rep* (James S Sherman, 1909–12) *No Vice President 1912–3*
1913–21 Woodrow Wilson (28th) *Dem* (Thomas R Marshall)
1921–3 Warren Gamaliel Harding (29th) *Rep* (Calvin Coolidge)
1923–9 Calvin Coolidge (30th) *Rep* *No Vice President 1923–5* (Charles G Dawes, 1925–9)
1929–33 Herbert Clark Hoover (31st) *Rep* (Charles Curtis)
1933–45 Franklin Delano Roosevelt (32nd) *Dem* (John N Garner, 1933–41) (Henry A Wallace, 1941–5) (Harry S Truman, 1945)
1945–53 Harry S Truman (33rd) *Dem* *No Vice President 1945–9* (Alben W Barkley, 1949–53)
1953–61 Dwight David Eisenhower (34th) *Rep* (Richard M Nixon)
1961–3 John Fitzgerald Kennedy (35th) *Dem* (Lyndon B Johnson)
1963–9 Lyndon Baines Johnson (36th) *Dem* *No Vice President 1963–5* (Hubert H Humphrey, 1965–9)
1969–74 Richard Milhous Nixon (37th) *Rep* (Spiro T Agnew, 1969–73) *No Vice President Oct–Dec 1973* (Gerald R Ford, 1973–4)
1974–7 Gerald Rudolph Ford (38th) *Rep* *No Vice President Aug-Dec 1974* (Nelson A Rockefeller, 1974–7)
1977–81 Jimmy Carter (39th) *Dem* (Walter F Mondale)
1981–9 Ronald Wilson Reagan (40th) *Rep* (George H W Bush)
1989–93 George Herbert Walker Bush (41st) *Rep* (J Danforth Quayle)
1993– William Jefferson Clinton (42nd) *Dem* (Alfred Gore)

Dem Democrat *Fed* Federalist
Nat National Union *Rep* Republican

URUGUAY

President
1899–1903 Juan Lindolfo Cuestas
1903–7 José Batlle y Ordóñez
1907–11 Claudio Williman
1911–15 José Batlle y Ordóñez
1915–19 Feliciano Viera
1919–23 Baltasar Brum
1923–7 José Serrato
1927–31 Juan Capisteguy
1931–8 Gabriel Terra
1938–43 Alfredo Baldomir
1943–7 Juan José de Amézaga
1947 Tomás Berreta
1947–51 Luis Batlle Berres
1951–5 Andrés Martínez Trueba

National Government Council (1955–67)
1955–6 Luis Batlle Berres
1956–7 Alberto F Zubiría
1957–8 Alberto Lezama
1958–9 Carlos L Fischer
1959–60 Martín R Etchegoyen
1960–1 Benito Nardone
1961–2 Eduardo Víctor Haedo
1962–3 Faustino Harrison
1963–4 Daniel Fernández Crespo
1964–5 Luis Giannattasio
1965–6 Washington Beltrán
1966–7 Alberto Heber Usher
1967 Oscar Daniel Gestido
1967–72 Jorge Pacheco Areco
1972–6 Juan María Bordaberry Arocena
1976–81 Aparicio Méndez
1981–4 Gregorio Conrado Alvarez Armelino
1984–90 Julio María Sanguinetti Cairolo
1990–5 Luis Alberto Lacalle Herrera
1995– Julio María Sanguinetti

UZBEKISTAN

President
1991– Islam A Karimov

Prime Minister
1991–5 Abdulhashim Mutalov
1995– Otkir Sultonov

VANUATU

President
1980–9 George Sokomanu (*formerly* Kalkoa)
1989–94 Frederick Timakata
1994–9 Jean-Marie Leye
1999– John Barnard Bani

Prime Minister
1980–91 Walter Hadaye Lini
1991–2 Donald Kalpokas
1992–5 Maxime Carlot Korman

1995–6 Serge Vohor
1996 Maxime Carlot Korman
1996–8 Serge Vohor
1998– Donald Kalpokas

VENEZUELA

President

1899–1908 Cipriano Castro
1908–36 Juan Vicente Gomez
1936–41 Eleazar Lopez Contreras
1941–5 Isaias Medina Angarita
1945–7 *Military Junta* (Romulo Betancourt)
1947–8 Romulo Gallegos
1948–50 *Military Junta* (Carlos Delgado Chalbaud)
1950–9 *Military Junta* (Marcos Perez Jimenez)
1959–64 Romulo Betancourt
1964–9 Raul Leoni
1969–74 Rafael Caldera Rodriguez
1974–9 Carlos Andres Pérez
1979–84 Luis Herrera Campins
1984–9 Jaime Lusinchi
1989–93 Carlos Andres Pérez
1993 Ramón José Velásquez *Interim*
1993–8 Rafael Caldera Rodríguez
1998– Hugo Chavez Frías

VIETNAM

Democratic Republic of Vietnam

President

1945–69 Ho Chi-Minh
1969–76 Ton Duc Thang

State of Vietnam

1949–55 Bao Dai

Republic of Vietnam

1955–63 Ngo Dinh Diem
1963–4 Duong Van Minh
1964 Nguyen Khanh
1964–5 Phan Khac Suu
1965–75 Nguyen Van Thieu
1975 Tran Van Huong
1975 Duong Van Minh
1975–6 *Provisional Revolutionary Government* (Huynh Tan Phat)

Socialist Republic of Vietnam

1976–80 Ton Duc Thang
1980–1 Nguyen Hun Tho *Acting*
1981–7 Truongh Chinh
1987–92 Vo Chi Cong
1992– Le Duc Anh

Democratic Republic of Vietnam

Prime Minister

1955–76 Pham Van Dong

State of Vietnam

1949–50 Nguyen Van Xuan
1950 Nguyen Phan Long
1950–2 Tran Van Huu
1952 Tran Van Huong
1952–3 Nguyen Van Tam
1953–4 Buu Loc
1954–5 Ngo Dinh Diem

Republic of Vietnam

1955–63 Ngo Dinh Diem
1963–4 Nguyen Ngoc Tho
1964 Nguyen Khan
1964–5 Tran Van Huong
1965 Phan Huy Quat
1965–7 Nguyen Cao Ky
1967–8 Nguyen Van Loc
1968–9 Tran Van Huong
1969–75 Tran Thien Khiem
1975 Nguyen Ba Can
1975–6 Vu Van Mau

Socialist Republic of Vietnam

Premier

1976–87 Pham Van Dong
1987–8 Pham Hung
1988 Vo Van Kiet *Acting*
1988–91 Do Muoi
1991–7 Vo Van Kiet
1997– Phan Van Khai

General Secretary

1960–80 Le Duan
1986 Truong Chinh
1986–91 Nguyen Van Linh
1991–7 Do Muoi
1997– Le Kha Phieu

YEMEN

Yemen Arab Republic (North Yemen)

Monarch

1918–48 Yahya Mohammed Bin Mohammed
1948–62 Ahmed Bin Yahya
1962–70 Mohammed Bin Ahmed
1962 *Civil War*

President

1962–7 Abdullah al-Sallal
1967–74 Abdur Rahman al-Iriani
1974–7 *Military Command Council* (Ibrahim al-Hamadi)
1977–8 Ahmed bin Hussein al-Ghashmi
1978–90 Ali Abdullah Saleh

Prime Minister

1964 Hamud al-Jaifi
1965 Hassan al-Amri
1965 Ahmed Mohammed Numan
1965 *As President*
1965–6 Hassan al-Amri
1966–7 *As President*
1967 Muhsin al-Aini
1967–9 Hassan al-Amri
1969–70 Abd Allah Kurshumi
1970–1 Muhsin al-Aini
1971 Abdel Salam Sabra *Acting*
1971 Ahmed Mohammed Numan
1971 Hassan al-Amri
1971–2 Muhsin al-Aini
1972–4 Qadi Abdullah al-Hijri
1974 Hassan Makki
1974–5 Muhsin al-Aini
1975 Abdel Latif Deifallah *Acting*
1975–90 Abdel-Aziz Abdel-Ghani

People's Democratic Republic of Yemen (South Yemen)

President

1967–9 Qahtan Mohammed al-Shaabi
1969–78 Salim Ali Rubai
1978 Ali Nasir Mohammed Husani
1978–80 Abdel Fattah Ismail
1980–6 Ali Nasir Mohammed Husani
1986–90 Haider Abu Bakr al-Attas

Prime Minister

1969 Faisal Abd al-Latif al-Shaabi
1969–71 Mohammed Ali Haithem
1971–85 Ali Nasir Mohammed Husani
1985–6 Haidar Abu Bakr al-Attas
1986–90 Yasin Said Numan

Republic of Yemen

President

1990– Ali Abdullah Saleh

Head of Government

1990–4 Haider Abu Bakr al-Attas
1994–7 Abdel Aziz Abdel-Ghani
1997–8 Faraj Said ben Ghanem
1998– Abdul Karim al-Iriani

YUGOSLAVIA

Monarch

1921–34 Aleksandar II
1934–45 Petar II *in exile from 1941*

Republic

National Assembly

Chairman

1945–53 Ivan Ribar

President

1953–80 Josip Broz Tito

Collective Presidency

1980 Lazar Koliševski
1980–1 Cvijetin Mijatović
1981–2 Serghei Kraigher
1982–3 Petar Stambolić
1983–4 Mika Spiljak
1984–5 Veselin Duranović
1985–6 Radovan Vlajković
1986–7 Sinan Hasani
1987–8 Lazar Mojsov
1988–9 Raif Dizdarević
1989–90 Janez Drnovsek
1990–1 Borisav Jovic
1991–2 Stipe Mesic

Federal Republic of Yugoslavia

1992–3 Dobrica Cosic
1993–7 Zoran Lilic
1997– Slobodan Milosevic

Prime Minister

1929–32 Pear Živkovic
1932 Vojislav Marinković
1932–4 Milan Srškić
1934 Nikola Uzunović
1934–5 Bogoljub Jevtić
1935–9 Milan Stojadinović
1939–41 Dragiša Cvetković
1941 Dušan Simović

Government in exile

1942 Slobodan Jovanović
1943 Miloš Trifunović
1943–4 Božidar Purić
1944–5 Ivan Šubašić
1945 Drago Marušić

Home government

1941–4 Milan Nedić
1943–63 Josip Broz Tito
1963–7 Petar Stambolić
1967–9 Mika Špiljak
1969–71 Mitja Ribičič
1971–7 Džemal Bijedić
1977–82 Veselin Duranović
1982–6 Milka Planinc
1986–9 Branko Mikulić
1989–92 Ante Marković

Federal Republic of Yugoslavia

1992–3 Milan Panic
1993–8 Radoje Kontic
1998– Momir Bulatovic

Communist Party

First Secretary

1937–52 Josip Broz Tito

League of Communists

1952–80 Josip Broz Tito

League of Communists Central Committee

President

1979–80	Stevan Doronjski *Acting*
1980–1	Lazar Mojsov
1981–2	Dušan Dragosavac
1982–3	Mitja Ribičič
1983–4	Dragoslav Marković
1984–5	Ali Sukrija
1985–6	Vidoje Žarkovic
1986–7	Milanko Renovica
1987–8	Boško Krunić
1988–9	Stipe Suvar
1989–90	Milan Pancevski
1990	Miomir Grbovic

ZAMBIA

President

1964–91	Kenneth David Kaunda
1991–	Frederick Chiluba

Prime Minister

1964–73	Kenneth David Kaunda
1973–5	Mainza Chona
1975–7	Elijah Mudenda
1977–8	Mainza Chona
1978–81	Daniel Lisulu
1981–5	Nalumino Mundia
1985–9	Kebby Musokotwane
1989–91	Malimba Masheke
1991–4	Levy Mwanawasa
1994–	Godfrey Miyanda

ZIMBABWE

President

1980–7	Canaan Sodindo Banana
1987–	Robert Gabriel Mugabe

POPES

Antipope refers to a pontiff set up in opposition to one asserted to be canonically chosen.

until c. 64	Peter
c. 64–c. 76	Linus
c. 76–c. 90	Anacletus
c. 90–c. 99	Clement I
c. 99–c. 105	Evaristus
c. 105–c. 117	Alexander I
c. 117–c. 127	Sixtus I
c. 127–c. 137	Telesphorus
c. 137–c. 140	Hyginus
c. 140–c. 154	Pius I
c. 154–c. 166	Anicetus
c. 166–c. 175	Soter
175–89	Eleutherius
189–98	Victor I
198–217	Zephyrinus
217–22	Calixtus I
217–c. 235	Hippolytus Antipope
222–30	Urban I
230–5	Pontian
235–6	Anterus
236–50	Fabian
251–3	Cornelius
251–c. 258	Novatian Antipope
253–4	Lucius I
254–7	Stephen I
257–8	Sixtus II
259–68	Dionysius
269–74	Felix I
275–83	Eutychianus
283–96	Caius
296–304	Marcellinus
308–9	Marcellus I
310	Eusebius
311–14	Miltiades
314–35	Sylvester I
336	Mark
337–52	Julius I
352–66	Liberius
355–65	Felix II Antipope
366–84	Damasus I
366–7	Ursinus Antipope
384–99	Siricius
399–401	Anastasius I
402–17	St Innocent I
417–18	St Zosimus
418–22	Boniface I
418–19	Eulalius Antipope
422–32	Celestine I
432–40	Sixtus III
440–61	Leo I 'the Great'
461–8	Hilarus
468–83	Simplicius
483–92	Felix III (II)
492–6	St Gelasius I
496–8	Anastasius II
498–514	(Coelius) Symmachus
498, 501–5	Laurentius Antipope
514–23	Hormisdas
523–6	John I
526–30	Felix IV (III)
530–2	Boniface II
530	Dioscorus Antipope
533–5	John II
535–6	Agapetus I
536–7	Silverius
537–55	Vigilius
556–61	Pelagius I
561–74	John III
575–9	Benedict I
579–90	Pelagius II
590–604	St Gregory I 'the Great'
604–6	Sabinianus
607	Boniface III
608–15	Boniface IV
615–18	Deusdedit or Adeodatus I
619–25	Boniface V
625–38	Honorius I
640	Severinus
640–2	John IV
642–9	Theodore I
649–55	St Martin I
654–7	St Eugenius I[1]
657–72	Vitalian
672–6	Adeodatus II
676–8	Donus
678–81	Agatho
682–3	Leo II
684–5	Benedict II
685–6	John V
686–7	Cono
687	Theodore Antipope
687–92	Paschal Antipope
687–701	Sergius I
701–5	John VI
705–7	John VII
708	Sisinnius
708–15	Constantine
715–31	St Gregory II
731–41	St Gregory III
741–52	St Zacharias
752	Stephen II (not consecrated)
752–7	Stephen II (III)
757–67	Paul I
767–9	Constantine II Antipope
768	Philip Antipope
768–72	Stephen III (IV)
772–95	Adrian I
795–816	Leo III
816–17	Stephen IV (V)
817–24	Paschal I
824–7	Eugenius II
827	Valentine
827–44	Gregory IV
844	John Antipope
844–7	Sergius II
847–55	Leo IV
855–8	Benedict III
855	Anastasius Bibliothecarius Antipope
858–67	St Nicholas I 'the Great'
867–72	Adrian II
872–82	John VIII
882–4	Martin II (Marinus I)
884–5	Adrian III
885–91	Stephen V (VI)
891–6	Formosus
896	Boniface VI
896–7	Stephen VI (VII)
897	Romanus
897	Theodore II
898–900	John IX
900–3	Benedict IV
903	Leo V
903–4	Christopher Antipope
904–11	Sergius III
911–13	Anastasius III
913–14	Lando
914–28	John X
928	Leo VI
928–31	Stephen VII (VIII)
931–5	John XI
936–9	Leo VII
939–42	Stephen IX
942–6	Martin III (Marinus II)
946–55	Agapetus II
955–64	John XII (Octavian)
963–5	Leo VIII
964–6	Benedict V
965–72	John XIII
973–4	Benedict VI
974, 984–5	Boniface VII Antipope
974–83	Benedict VII
983–4	John XIV
985–96	John XV
996–9	Gregory V

POPES (continued)

997–8	John XVI Antipope
999–1003	Sylvester II
1003	John XVII
1004–9	John XVIII
1009–12	Sergius IV
1012–24	Benedict VIII
1012	Gregory Antipope
1024–32	John XIX
1032–44	Benedict IX
1045	Sylvester III
1045	Benedict IX (second reign)
1045–6	Gregory VI
1046–7	Clement II
1047–8	Benedict IX (third reign)
1048	Damasus II (Poppo)
1048–54	Leo IX (Bruno of Toul)
1055–7	Victor II (Gebhard of Hirschberg)
1057–8	Stephen IX (X) (Frederick of Lorraine)
1058–9	Benedict X (John of Tusculum) Antipope
1059–61	Nicholas II (Gerard of Burgundy)
1061–73	Alexander II (Anselm of Lucca)
1061–72	Honorius II (Peter Cadalus) Antipope
1073–85	Gregory VII (St Hildebrand)
1080, 1084–1100	Clement III (Guibert of Ravenna) Antipope
1086–7	Victor III (Desiderius)
1088–99	Urban II (Odo of Chatillon)
1099–1118	Paschal II (Raneiro da Bieda)
1100–2	Theodoric Antipope
1102	Albert Antipope
1105–11	Sylvester IV Antipope
1118–19	Gelasius II (John of Gaeta)
1118–21	Gregory VIII (Maurice of Braga) Antipope
1119–24	Callistus II (Guy of Burgundy)
1124–30	Honorius II (Lamberto dei Fagnani)
1124	Celestine II Antipope
1130–43	Innocent II (Gregory Parareschi)
1130–8	Anacletus II Antipope
1138	Victor IV[2] Antipope
1143–4	Celestine II (Guido di Castello)
1144–5	Lucius II (Gherardo Caccianemici)
1145–53	Eugenius III (Bernardo Paganelli)
1153–4	Anastasius IV (Corrado della Subarra)
1154–9	Adrian IV (Nicholas Breakspear)
1159–81	Alexander III (Orlando Bandinelli)
1159–64	Victor IV[2] (Ottaviano di Monticelli) Antipope
1164–8	Paschal III (Guido of Crema) Antipope
1168–78	Calixtus III (John of Struma) Antipope
1179–80	Innocent III (Lando da Sessa)
1181–5	Lucius III (Ubaldo Allucingoli)
1185–7	Urban III (Uberto Crivelli)
1187	Gregory VIII (Alberto di Morra)
1187–91	Clement III (Paolo Scolari)
1191–8	Celestine III (Giacinto Boboni-Orsini)
1198–1216	Innocent III (Lotario de'Conti)
1216–27	Honorius III (Cancio Savelli)
1227–41	Gregory IX (Ugolino di Segni)
1241	Celestine IV (Goffredo Castiglione)
1243–54	Innocent IV (Sinibaldo de' Fieschi)
1254–61	Alexander IV (Rinaldo di Segni)
1261–4	Urban IV (Jacques Pantaléon)
1265–8	Clement IV (Guy le Gros Foulques)
1271–6	Gregory X (Tebaldo Visconti)
1276	Innocent V (Pierre de Champagni)
1276	Adrian V (Ottoboni Fieschi)
1276–7	John XXI[3] (Pietro Rebuli-Giuliani)
1277–80	Nicholas III (Giovanni Gaetano Orsini)
1281–5	Martin IV (Simon de Brie)
1285–7	Honorius IV (Giacomo Savelli)
1288–92	Nicholas IV (Girolamo Masci)
1294	Celestine V (Pietro di Morrone)
1294–1303	Boniface VIII (Benedetto Caetani)
1303–4	Benedict XI (Niccolo Boccasini)
1305–14	Clement V (Raymond Bertrand de Got)
1316–34	John XXII (Jacques Duèse)
1328–30	Nicholas V (Pietro Rainalducci) Antipope
1334–42	Benedict XII (Jacques Fournier)
1342–52	Clement VI (Pierre Roger de Beaufort)
1352–62	Innocent VI (Étienne Aubert)
1362–70	Urban V (Guillaume de Grimoard)
1370–8	Gregory XI (Pierre Roger de Beaufort)
1378–89	Urban VI (Bartolomeo Prignano)
1378–94	Clement VII (Robert of Geneva) Antipope
1389–1404	Boniface IX (Pietro Tomacelli)
1394–1423	Benedict XIII (Pedro de Luna) Antipope
1404–6	Innocent VII (Cosmato de' Migliorati)
1406–15	Gregory XII (Angelo Correr)
1409–10	Alexander V (Petros Philargi) Antipope
1410–15	John XXIII (Baldassare Cossa) Antipope
1417–31	Martin V (Oddone Colonna)
1423–9	Clement VIII (Gil Sanchez Muños) Antipope
1425–30	Benedict XIV (Bernard Garnier) Antipope
1431–47	Eugenius IV (Gabriele Condulmer)
1439–49	Felix V (Amadeus VIII of Savoy) Antipope
1447–55	Nicholas V (Tommaso Parentucelli)
1455–8	Calixtus III (Alfonso de Borja)
1458–64	Pius II (Enea Silvio de Piccolomini)
1464–71	Paul II (Pietro Barbo)
1471–84	Sixtus IV (Francesco della Rovere)
1484–92	Innocent VIII (Giovanni Battista Cibo)
1492–1503	Alexander VI (Rodrigo Borgia)
1503	Pius III (Francesco Todoeschini-Piccolomini)
1503–13	Julius II (Giuliano della Rovere)
1513–21	Leo X (Giovanni de' Medici)
1522–3	Adrian VI (Adrian Dedel)
1523–34	Clement VII (Giulio de' Medici)
1534–49	Paul III (Allessandro Farnese)
1550–5	Julius III (Gianmaria del Monte)
1555	Marcellus II (Marcello Cervini)
1555–9	Paul IV (Giovanni Pietro Caraffa)
1559–65	Pius IV (Giovanni Angelo Medici)
1566–72	Pius V (Michele Ghislieri)
1572–85	Gregory XIII (Ugo Buoncompagni)
1585–90	Sixtus V (Felice Peretti)
1590	Urban VII (Giambattista Castagna)
1590–1	Gregory XIV (Niccolo Sfondrati)
1591	Innocent IX (Gian Antonio Facchinetti)
1592–1605	Clement VIII (Ippolito Aldobrandini)
1605	Leo XI (Alessandro de' Medici-Ottaiano)
1605–21	Paul V (Camillo Borghese)
1621–3	Gregory XV (Alessandro Ludovisi)
1623–44	Urban VIII (Maffeo Barberini)
1644–55	Innocent X (Giambattista Pamfili)
1655–67	Alexander VII (Fabio Chigi)
1667–9	Clement IX (Julio Rospigliosi)
1670–6	Clement X (Emilio Altieri)
1676–89	Innocent XI (Benedetto Odescalchi)
1689–91	Alexander VIII (Pietro Vito Ottoboni)
1691–1700	Innocent XII (Antonio Pignatelli)
1700–21	Clement XI (Gian Francesco Albani)
1721–4	Innocent XIII (Michelangelo dei Conti)
1724–30	Benedict XIII (Pietro Francesco Orsini)
1730–40	Clement XII (Lorenzo Corsini)
1740–58	Benedict XIV (Prospero Lambertini)
1758–69	Clement XIII (Carlo Rezzonico)
1769–74	Clement XIV (Lorenzo Ganganelli)
1775–99	Pius VI (Giovanni Angelo Braschi)
1800–23	Pius VII (Luigi Barnaba Chiaramonti)
1823–9	Leo XII (Annibale della Genga)
1829–30	Pius VIII (Francesco Saven Castiglioni)
1831–46	Gregory XVI (Bartolomeo Alberto Capellari)
1846–78	Pius IX (Giovanni Maria Mastai Ferretti)
1878–1903	Leo XIII (Vincenzo Gioacchino Pecci)
1903–14	Pius X (Giuseppe Sarto)
1914–22	Benedict XV (Giacomo della Chiesa)
1922–39	Pius XI (Achille Ratti)
1939–58	Pius XII (Eugenio Pacelli)
1958–63	John XXIII (Angelo Giuseppe Roncalli)
1963–78	Paul VI (Giovanni Battista Montini)
1978	John Paul I (Albino Luciani)

[1] Elected during the banishment of Martin I [2] Different individuals [3] There was no John XX

Measurement

SI CONVERSION FACTORS

This table gives the conversion factors for many British and other units which are still in common use, showing their equivalents in terms of the International System of Units (SI). The column labelled 'SI equivalent' gives the SI value of one unit of the type named in the first column, eg 1 calorie is 4.187 joules. The column labelled 'Reciprocal' allows conversion the other way, eg 1 joule is 0.239 calories. (All values are to three decimal places.) As a second example, 1 dyne is 10 μN = 10 $\times 10^{-6}$ N = 10^{-5} N; so 1 newton is $0.1 \times 10^{+6} = 10^5$ dyne. Finally, 1 torr is 0.133 kPa = 0.133 $\times 10^3$ Pa; so 1 Pa is 7.501×10^{-3} torr.

Unit name	*Symbol*	*Quantity*	*SI equivalent*	*Unit*	*Reciprocal*
acre		area	0.405	hm^2	2.471
ångström*+	Å	length	0.1	nm	10
are	a	area	100	m	.01
astronomical unit*	AU	length	0.150	Tm	6.684
atomic mass unit*	amu	mass	1.661×10^{-27}	kg	6.022×10^{26}
bar*+	bar	pressure	0.1	MPa	10
barn+	b	area	100	fm^2	0.01
barrel (US) = 42 US gal	bbl	volume	0.159	m^3	6.290
British thermal unit*	btu	energy	1.055	kJ	0.948
calorie*	cal	energy	4.187	J	0.239
cubic foot	cu ft	volume	0.028	m^3	35.315
cubic inch	cu in	volume	16.387	cm^3	0.061
cubic yard	cu yd	volume	0.765	m^3	1.308
curie*+	Ci	activity of radionuclide	37	GBq	0.027
degree = 1/90 rt angle	°	plane angle	π/180	rad	57.296
degree Celsius*	°C	temperature	1	K	1
degree Centigrade*	°C	temperature	1	K	1
degree Fahrenheit*	°F	temperature	5/9	K	1.8
degree Rankine	°R	temperature	5/9	K	1.8
dyne	dyn	force	10	μN	0.1
electronvolt*	eV	energy	0.160	aJ	6.241
erg	erg	energy	0.1	μJ	10
fathom (6ft)		length	1.829	m	0.547
fermi	fm	length	1	fm	1
foot	ft	length	30.48	cm	0.033
foot per second	fts	velocity	0.305	m/s	3.281
			1.097	km/h	0.911
gal	Gal	acceleration due to gravity	.01	ms	100
gallon (UK)	gal	volume	4.546	litre (dm^3)	0.220
gallon (US) = 231in³	gal	volume	3.785	litre (dm^3)	0.264
gallon (UK) per mile		consumption	2.825	litre (dm^3)/km	0.354
gauss	Gs, G	magnetic flux density	100	μT	0.01
grade = 0.01 rt angle	rt angle	plane angle	π/200	rad	63.662
grain	gr	mass	0.065	g	15.432
hectare+	ha	area	1	hm^2	1
horsepower*	hp	power	0.746	kW	1.341
inch	in	length	2.54	cm	0.394
kilogram-force	kgf	force	9.807	N	0.102
knot+		velocity	1.852	km h^{-1}	0.540
light year*	ly	length	9.461×10^{15}	m	1.057×10^{-16}
litre*	l	volume	1	dm^3	1
Mach number*	Ma	velocity	1193.3	km h^{-1}	8.380×10^{-4}
maxwell	Mx	magnetic flux	10	nWb	0.1
metric carat		mass	0.2	g	5
micron*	μ	length	1	μm	1
mile (nautical)+		length	1.852	km	0.540
mile (statute)		length	1.609	km	0.621
miles per hour (mph)	mph	velocity	1.609	km/h	0.621
minute = (1/60)°	′	plane angle	π/10 800	rad	3 437.75
oersted	Oe	magnetic field strength	1/(4π)	kA/m	4π
ounce (avoirdupois)	oz	mass	28.349	g	0.035
ounce (troy) = 480 gr		mass	31.103	g	0.032
parsec*	pc	length	30 857	Tm	0.0000324
phot	ph	illuminance	10	klx	0.1
pint (UK)	pt	volume	0.568	litre (dm^3)	1.760
poise*	P	viscosity	0.1	Pa s	10
pound	lb	mass	0.454	kg	2.205
pound force	lbf	force	4.448	N	0.225
pound force/per sq in		pressure	6.895	kPa	0.145
poundal	pdl	force	0.138	N	7.233
rad*+	rad	absorbed dose	0.01	Gy	100

SI CONVERSION FACTORS

Unit name	*Symbol*	*Quantity*	*SI equivalent*	*Unit*	*Reciprocal*
rem*+	rem	dose equivalent	0.01	Sv	100
right angle = $\pi/2$ rad		plane angle	1.571	rad	0.637
röntgen*+	R	exposure	0.258	mC/kg	3.876
second = (1/60)′	″	plane angle	$\pi/648$	mrad	206.265
slug		mass	14.594	kg	0.068
solar mass	M	mass	1.989×10^{30}	kg	5.028×10^{-31}
square foot	sq ft	area	9.290	dm^2	0.108
square inch	sq in	area	6.452	cm^2	0.155
square mile (statute)	sq mi	area	2.590	km^2	0.386
square yard	sq yd	area	0.836	m^2	1.196
standard acceleration of gravity	g_n	acceleration	9.807	m/s^2	0.102
standard atmosphere	atm	pressure	0.101	MPa	9.869
stere	st	volume	1	m^3	1
stilb	sb	luminance	10	kcd/m^2	0.1
stokes	St	viscosity	1	cm^2/s^{-1}	1
therm = 10^5	btu	energy	0.105	GJ	9.478
ton = 2240 lb		mass	1.016	tonne (Mg)	0.984
ton-force	tonf	force	9.964	kN	0.100
ton-force per sq in		pressure	15.444	MPa	0.065
tonne	t	mass	1	Mg	1
torr* / mmHg	torr	pressure	0.133	kPa	7.501
X unit		length	0.100	pm	10
yard	yd	length	0.914	m	1.093

*See also main text entry. +In temporary use with SI.

SI PREFIXES

Factor	*Prefix*	*Symbol*	*Factor*	*Prefix*	*Symbol*	*Factor*	*Prefix*	*Symbol*
10^{18}	exa	E	10^2	hecto	h	10^{-6}	micro	µ
10^{15}	peta	P	10^1	deca	da	10^{-9}	nano	n
10^{12}	tera	T	10^{-1}	deci	d	10^{-12}	pico	p
10^9	giga	G	10^{-2}	centi	c	10^{-15}	femto	f
10^6	mega	M	10^{-3}	milli	m	10^{-18}	atto	a
10^3	kilo	k						

COMMON MEASURES

Metric units

		Imperial equivalent
Length		
	1 millimetre	0.03937 in
10 mm	1 centimetre	0.39 in
10 cm	1 decimetre	3.94 in
100 cm	1 metre	39.37 in
1000 m	1 kilometre	0.62 mi
Area		
	1 square millimetre	0.0016 sq in
	1 square centimetre	0.155 sq in
100 cm^2	1 square decimetre	15.5 sq in
10 000 cm^2	1 square metre	10.76 sq ft
10 000 m^2	1 hectare	2.47 acres
Volume		
	1 cubic centimetre	0.016 cu in
1 000 cm^3	1 cubic decimetre	61.024 cu in
1 000 dm^3	1 cubic metre	35.31 cu ft, 1.308 cu yds
Liquid volume		
	1 litre (dm^3)	1.76 pt
100 litres	1 hectolitre	22 gal
Weight		
	1 gram	0.035 oz
1 000 g	1 kilogram	2.2046 lb
1 000 kg	1 tonne	0.0842 ton

Imperial units

		Metric equivalent
Length		
	1 inch	2.54 cm
12 in	1 foot	30.48 cm
3 ft	1 yard	0.9144 m
1 760 yd	1 mile	1.6093 km
Area		
	1 square inch	6.45 cm^2
144 sq in	1 square foot	0.0929 m^2
9 sq ft	1 square yard	0.836 m^2
4 840 sq yd	1 acre	0.405 ha
640 acres	1 square mile	259 ha
Volume		
	1 cubic inch	16.3871 cm^2
1 728 cu in	1 cubic foot	0.028 m^2
27 cu ft	1 cubic yard	0.765 m^2
Liquid volume		
	1 pint	0.57 l
2 pt	1 quart	1.14 l
4 qt	1 gallon	4.55 l
Weight		
	1 ounce	28.3495 g
16 oz	1 pound	0.4536 kg
14 lb	1 stone	6.35 kg
8 st	1 hundredweight	50.8 kg
20 cwt	1 ton	1.016 t

CONVERSION FACTORS

Imperial to metric

		Multiply by		
Length	inches	→	millimetres	25.4
	inches	→	centimetres	2.54
	feet	→	metres	0.3048
	yards	→	metres	0.9144
	statute miles	→	kilometres	1.6093
	nautical miles	→	kilometres	1.852
Area	square inches	→	square centimetres	6.4516
	square feet	→	square metres	0.0929
	square yards	→	square metres	0.8361
	acres	→	hectares	0.4047
	square miles	→	square kilometres	2.5899
Volume	cubic inches	→	cubic centimetres	16.3871
	cubic feet	→	cubic metres	0.0283
	cubic yards	→	cubic metres	0.7646
Capacity	UK fluid ounces	→	litres	0.0284
	US fluid ounces	→	litres	0.0296
	UK pints	→	litres	0.5682
	US pints	→	litres	0.4732
	UK gallons	→	litres	4.546
	US gallons	→	litres	3.7854
Weight	ounces (avoirdupois)	→	grams	28.3495
	ounces (troy)	→	grams	31.1035
	pounds	→	kilograms	0.4536
	tons (long)	→	tonnes	1.016

Metric to imperial

		Multiply by		
Length	millimetres	→	inches	0.0394
	centimetres	→	inches	0.3937
	metres	→	feet	3.2808
	metres	→	yards	1.0936
	kilometres	→	statute miles	0.6214
	kilometres	→	nautical miles	0.54
Area	square centimetres	→	square inches	0.155
	square metres	→	square feet	10.764
	square metres	→	square yards	1.196
	hectares	→	acres	2.471
	square kilometres	→	square miles	0.386
Volume	cubic centimetres	→	cubic inches	0.061
	cubic metres	→	cubic feet	35.315
	cubic metres	→	cubic yards	1.308
Capacity	litres	→	UK fluid ounces	35.1961
	litres	→	US fluid ounces	33.8150
	litres	→	UK pints	1.7598
	litres	→	US pints	2.1134
	litres	→	UK gallons	0.2199
	litres	→	US gallons	0.2642
Weight	grams	→	ounces (avoirdupois)	0.0353
	grams	→	ounces (troy)	0.0322
	kilograms	→	pounds	2.2046
	tonnes	→	tons (long)	0.9842

OVEN TEMPERATURES

Gas mark	*Electricity*		*Rating*	*Gas mark*	*Electricity*		*Rating*
	°C	°F			°C	°F	
½	120	250	Slow	5	190	375	
1	140	275		6	200	400	Hot
2	150	300		7	220	425	
3	170	325		8	230	450	Very hot
4	180	350	Moderate	9	260	500	

TEMPERATURE CONVERSION

To convert	*To*	*Operation*
°Fahrenheit	°Celsius	–32, ×5, ÷9
°Fahrenheit	°Rankine	+459.67
°Fahrenheit	°Réaumur	–32, ×4, ÷9
°Celsius	°Fahrenheit	×9, ÷5, +32
°Celsius	Kelvin	+273.16
°Celsius	°Réaumur	×4, ÷5
Kelvin	°Celsius	–273.16
°Rankine	°Fahrenheit	–459.67
°Réaumur	°Fahrenheit	×9, ÷4, +32
°Réaumur	°Celsius	×5, ÷4

Carry out operations in sequence.

PETROL CONSUMPTION

Use UK table and US table independently.

per UK gal		*per litre*		*per US gal*		*per litre*	
mi	*km*	*mi*	*km*	*mi*	*km*	*mi*	*km*
30	48	6.6	10.61	30	48	7.9	12.78
35	56	7.7	12.38	35	56	9.3	14.91
40	64	8.8	14.15	40	64	10.6	17.04
45	72	9.9	15.92	45	72	11.9	19.17
50	80	11	17.69	50	80	13.2	21.30

TYRE PRESSURES

psi	*kg/cm²*	*psi*	*kg/cm²*
10	0.7	26	1.8
15	1.1	28	2
20	1.4	30	2.1
24	1.7	40	2.8

INTERNATIONAL CLOTHING SIZES

Size equivalents are approximate, and may display some variation between manufacturers..

Women's suits/dresses

UK	USA	UK/Continent
8	6	36
10	8	38
12	10	40
14	12	42
16	14	44
18	16	46
20	18	48
22	20	50
24	22	52

Women's hosiery

UK/USA	UK/Continent
8	0
8½	1
9	2
9½	3
10	4
10½	5

Men's shirts

UK/USA	UK/Continent
12	30–31
12½	32
13	33
13½	34–35
14	36
14½	37
15	38
15½	39–40
16	41
16½	42
17	43
17½	44–45

Men's suits/overcoats

UK/USA	Continental
36	46
38	48
40	50
42	52
44	54
46	56

Men's socks

UK/USA	UK/Continent
9½	38–39
10	39–40
10½	40–41
11	41–42
11½	42–43

Adults' shoes

UK	USA (ladies)	UK/ Continent
4	5½	37
4½	6	38
5	6½	38
5½	7	39
6	7½	39
6½	8	40
7	8½	41
7½	8½	42
8	9½	42
8½	9½	43
9	10½	43
9½	10½	44
10	11½	44
10½	11½	45
11	12	46

Children's shoes

UK/USA	UK/Continent
0	15
1	17
2	18
3	19
4	20
5	22
6	23
7	24
8	25
8½	26
9	27
10	28
11	29
12	30
13	32

INTERNATIONAL PATTERN SIZES

Size	Bust cm	Bust in	Waist cm	Waist in	Hip cm	Hip in	Back waist length cm	Back waist length in
Young junior/teenage								
5/6	71	28	56	22	79	31	34.5	13½
7/8	74	29	58	23	81	32	35.5	14
9/10	78	30½	61	24	85	33½	37	14½
11/12	81	32	64	25	89	35	38	15
13/14	85	33½	66	26	93	36½	39	15⅜
15/16	89	35	69	27	97	38	40	15¾
Misses								
6	78	30½	58	23	83	32½	39.5	15½
8	80	31½	61	24	85	33½	40	15¾
10	83	32½	64	25	88	34½	40.5	16
12	87	34	67	26½	92	36	41.5	16¼
14	92	36	71	28	97	38	42	16½
16	97	38	76	30	102	40	42.5	16¾
18	102	40	81	32	107	42	43	17
20	107	42	87	34	112	44	44	17¼

Size	Bust cm	Bust in	Waist cm	Waist in	Hip cm	Hip in	Back waist length cm	Back waist length in
Half-size								
10½	84	33	69	27	89	35	38	15
12½	89	35	74	29	94	37	39	15¼
14½	94	37	79	31	99	39	39.5	15½
16½	99	39	84	33	104	41	40	15¾
18½	104	41	89	35	109	43	40.5	15⅞
20½	109	43	96	37½	116	45½	40.5	16
22½	114	45	102	40	122	48	41	16⅛
24½	119	47	108	42½	128	50½	41.5	16¼
Women's								
38	107	42	89	35	112	44	44	17¼
40	112	44	94	37	117	46	44	17⅜
42	117	46	99	39	122	48	44.5	17½
44	122	48	105	41½	127	50	45	17⅝
46	127	50	112	44	132	52	45	17¾
48	132	52	118	46½	137	54	45.5	17⅞
50	137	54	124	49	142	56	46	18

INTERNATIONAL PAPER SIZES

A series

	mm	in
A0	841×1189	33.11×46.81
A1	594×841	23.39×33.1
A2	420×594	16.54×23.29
A3	297×420	11.69×16.54
A4	210×297	8.27×11.69
A5	148×210	5.83×8.27
A6	105×148	4.13×5.83
A7	74×105	2.91×4.13
A8	52×74	2.05×2.91
A9	37×52	1.46×2.05
A10	26×37	1.02×1.46

B series

	mm	in
B0	1000×1414	39.37×55.67
B1	707×1000	27.83×39.37
B2	500×707	19.68×27.83
B3	353×500	13.90×19.68
B4	250×353	9.84×13.90
B5	176×250	6.93×9.84
B6	125×176	4.92×6.93
B7	88×125	3.46×4.92
B8	62×88	2.44×3.46
B9	44×62	1.73×2.44
B10	31×44	1.22×1.73

C series

	mm	in
C0	917×1297	36.00×51.20
C1	648×917	25.60×36.00
C2	458×648	18.00×25.60
C3	324×458	12.80×18.00
C4	229×324	9.00×12.80
C5	162×229	6.40×9.00
C6	114×162	4.50×6.40
C7	81×114	3.20×4.50
DL	110×220	4.33×8.66
C7/6	81×162	3.19×6.38

A1
A2
A4
A3
A6
A5
A7 A7

All sizes in these series have sides in the proportion of 1: $\sqrt{2}$.
A series is used for writing paper, books and magazines.
B series for posters.
C series for envelopes.

SIGNS AND SYMBOLS

MATHEMATICAL SIGNS AND SYMBOLS

+	plus; positive; underestimate
−	minus; negative; overestimate
±	plus or minus; positive or negative; degree of accuracy
∓	minus or plus; negative or positive
×	multiplies (colloq. 'times') (6×4)
·	multiplies (colloq. 'times') (6·4); scalar product of two vectors (**A**·**B**)
÷	divided by (6÷4)
/	divided by; ratio of (6/4)
-	divided by; ratio of (6/4)
!	factorial (4!=4×3×2×1)
=	equals
≠, ≠	not equal to
≡	identical with
≢, ≢	not identical with
≙	corresponds to
:	ratio of (6:4)
::	proportionately equals (1 : 2 : : 2 : 4)
≈	approximately equal to; equivalent to; similar to
>	greater than
≫	much greater than
≯	not greater than
<	less than
≪	much less than
≮	not less than
⩾, ≧, ⋝	equal to or greater than
⩽, ≦, ⋜	equal to or less than
∝	directly proportional to
( )	parentheses
[ ]	brackets
{ }	braces
—	vinculum: division $\overline{a-b}$; chord of circle or length of line ($\overline{AB}$); arithmetic mean ($\overline{X}$)
∞	infinity
→	approaches the limit
√	square root
∛, ∜	cube root, fourth root, etc.
%	per cent
′	prime; minute(s) of arc; foot/feet
″	double prime; second(s) of arc; inch(es)
⌒	arc of circle
°	degree of arc
∠, ∠^{s}	angle(s)
⩝	equiangular
⊥	perpendicular
∥	parallel
○, Ⓢ	circle(s)
△, △ (s)	triangle(s)
□	square
▭	rectangle
▱	parallelogram
≅	congruent to
∴	therefore
∵	because
≞	measured by
Δ	increment
Σ	summation
Π	product
∫	integral sign
∇	del: differential operator
∪	union
∩	intersection
∈	is an element of
⊂	strict inclusion
⊃	contains
⇒	implies
⇐	implied by
⇔	implies and is implied by

HAZARD SYMBOLS

harmful / irritant

toxic

radioactive

flammable

corrosive

oxidising / supports fire

explosive

CLOTHES CARE

Do not iron

Can be ironed with *cool* iron (up to 110°C)

Can be ironed with *warm* iron (up to 150°C)

Can be ironed with *hot* iron (up to 200°C)

Hand wash only

Can be washed in a washing machine. The number shows the most effective washing temperature (in °C)

Reduced (medium) washing conditions

Much reduced (minimum) washing conditions (for wool products)

Do not wash

Can be tumble dried (one dot within the circle means a low temperature setting; two dots for higher temperatures)

Do not tumble dry

Do not dry clean

Dry cleanable (letter indicates which solvents can be used)
A: all solvents

Dry cleanable
F: white spirit and solvent 11 can be used

Dry cleanable
P: perchloroethylene (tetrachloroethylene), white spirt, solvent 113 and solvent 11 can be used

Dry cleanable, if special care taken

Chlorine bleach may be used with care

Do not use chlorine bleach

TABLE OF ELEMENTS

1	2											3	4	5	6	7	8
1 H Hydrogen 1.00794																1 H Hydrogen 1.00794	2 He Helium 4.00260
3 Li Lithium 6.941	4 Be Beryllium 9.01218											5 B Boron 10.81	6 C Carbon 12.011	7 N Nitrogen 14.0067	8 O Oxygen 15.9994	9 F Fluorine 18.998403	10 Ne Neon 20.179
11 Na Sodium 22.98977	12 Mg Magnesium 22.98977	*Transition series*										13 Al Aluminium 26.98154	14 Si Silicon 28.0855	15 P Phosphorus 30.97376	16 S Sulphur 32.06	17 Cl Chlorine 35.453	18 Ar Argon 39.948
19 K Potassium 39.0983	20 Ca Calcium 40.08	21 Sc Scardium 44.9559	22 Ti Titanium 47.88	23 V Vanadium 50.9415	24 Cr Chromium 51.996	25 Mn Manganese 54.9380	26 Fe Iron 55.847	27 Co Cobalt 58.9332	28 Ni Nickel 58.69	29 Cu Copper 63.546	30 Zn Zinc 65.38	31 Ga Gallium 69.72	32 Ge Germanium 72.59	33 As Arsenic 74.9216	34 Se Selenium 78.96	35 Br Bromine 79.904	36 Kr Krypton 83.80
37 Rb Rubidium 85.4678	38 Sr Strontium 87.62	39 Y Yttrium 88.9059	40 Zr Zirconium 91.22	41 Nb Niobium 92.9064	42 Mo Molybdenum 95.94	43 Tc Technetium (98)	44 Ru Ruthenium 101.07	45 Rh Rhodium 102.9055	46 Pd Palladium 106.42	47 Ag Silver 107.8682	48 Cd Cadmium 112.41	49 In Indium 114.82	50 Sn Tin 118.69	51 Sb Antimony 121.75	52 Te Tellenum 127.60	53 I Iodine 126.9045	54 Xe Xenon 131.29
55 Cs Caesium 132.9054	56 Ba Barium 137.33	57–71 Lathanide series (rare earth elements) ★	72 Hf Hafnium 178.49	73 Ta Tantalum 180.7479	74 W Tungsten 180.7479	75 Re Rhenium 186.207	76 Os Osmium 190.2	77 Ir Iridium 192.2	78 Pt Platinum 195.08	79 Au Gold 196.9665	80 Hg Mercury 200.59	81 Tl Thallium 204.383	82 Pb Lead 207.2	83 Bi Bismuth 208.9804	84 Po Polonium (209)	85 At Astatine (210)	86 Rn Radon (222)
87 Fr Francium (223)	88 Ra Radium 226.0254	89–103 Actinide series (radioactive rare earth elements) ☆	104 Unq Unnilquadium (261)	105 Unp Unnilpentium (262)	106 Unh Unnilhexium (263)	107 Uns Unnilseptium (262)		108 Une Unnilennium (266)									

Atomic number — 86
Rn — Symbol
Element name — Radon
(222) — Atomic weight (most stable isotope of radioactive elements in parentheses)

★	57 La Lanthanum 138.9055	58 Ce Cerium 140.12	59 Pr Praseodymium 140.9077	60 Nd Neodymium 144.24	61 Pm Promethium (145)	62 Sm Samarium 150.36	63 Eu Europium 151.96	64 Gd Gadolinium 157.25	65 Tb Terbium 158.9254	66 Dy Dysprosium 162.50	67 Ho Holmium 164.9304	68 Er Erbium 167.26	69 Tm Thulium 168.9342	70 Yb Ytterbium 173.04	71 Lu Lutetium 174.967
☆	89 Ac Actinium 227.0278	90 Th Thorium 232.0381	91 Pa Protactinium 231.0359	92 U Uranium 238.0289	93 Np Neptunium 237.0482	94 Pu Plutonium (244)	95 Am Americium (243)	96 Cm Curium (247)	97 Bk Berkelium (247)	98 Cf Californium (252)	99 Es Einsteinium (254)	100 Fm Fermium (257)	101 Md Mendelevium (258)	102 No Nobelium (259)	103 Lr Lawrencium (260)

RELIGIOUS SYMBOLS

The Trinity

Equilateral triangle

Triangle in circle

Circle within triangle

Trefoil

Triquetra

Triquetra and circle

Interwoven circles

God the Father

All-seeing eye

Hand of God

Hand of God

Lamb of God

Fish

Dove descending

Sevenfold flame

Old Testament

Menorah (seven branch candlestick)

Abraham

The Ten Commandments

Pentateuch (The Law)

Marked doorposts and lintel (Passover)

Twelve tribes of Israel

Star of David

Crosses

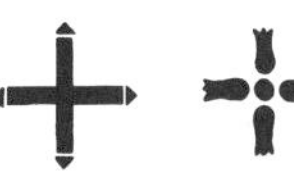
Aiguisée

Avellane

Barbée

Trefly

Canterbury

Celtic

Cercelée

Cross crosslet

Crux ansata

Entrailed

Fleurée

Globical

Graded (Calvary)

Greek

Iona

Jerusalem

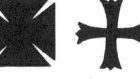

Latin

Maltese

Millvine

Papal

Patée

Patée formée

Patonce

Patriarchal (or Lorraine)

Pommel or Pommée

Potent

Raguly or Ragulée

Russian Orthodox

St Andrew's (Saltire)

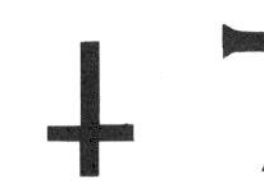
St Peter's

Tau (St Anthony's)

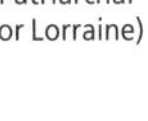
IHC (Latin form) (from Gk IHCOYC 'Jesus')

Chi Rho (from Gk XPICTOC 'Christ')

The Christian Church Year

Advent

Christmas

Epiphany

Lent

Maundy Thursday

Good Friday

Easter Day

Ascension

Pentecost

Other symbols

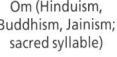

Ankh (Egyptian)

Yin-yang Tao symbol of harmony

Torii (Shinto)

Om (Hinduism, Buddhism, Jainism; sacred syllable)

Ik-onkar (Sikhism; symbol of God)

Swastika (originally symbol of the Sun)

Yantra: Sri Cakra (wheel of fortune)

CHESS NOTATION

QR QN QB Q K KB KN KR

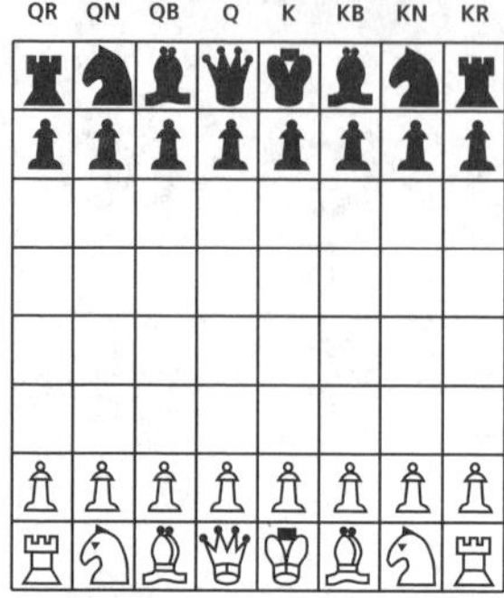

QR QN QB Q K KB KN KR

The opening position

Abbreviations

B	Bishop
K	King
KB	King's bishop
KN	King's knight
KR	King's rook
N	Knight
P	Pawn
Q	Queen
QB	Queen's bishop
QN	Queen's knight
QR	Queen's rook
R	Rook

Black

QR1 QR8	QN1 QN8	QB1 QB8	Q1 Q8	K1 K8	KB1 KB8	KN1 KN8	KR1 KR8
QR2 QR7	QN2 QN7	QB2 QB7	Q2 Q7	K2 K7	KB2 KB7	KN2 KN7	KR2 KR7
QR3 QR6	QN3 QN6	QB3 QB6	Q3 Q6	K3 K6	KB3 KB6	KN3 KN6	KR3 KR6
QR4 QR5	QN4 QN5	QB4 QB5	Q4 Q5	K4 K5	KB4 KB5	KN4 KN5	KR4 KR5
QR5 QR4	QN5 QN4	QB5 QB4	Q5 Q4	K5 K4	KB5 KB4	KN5 KN4	KR5 KR4
QR6 QR3	QN6 QN3	QB6 QB3	Q6 Q3	K6 K3	KB6 KB3	KN6 KN3	KR6 KR3
QR7 QR2	QN7 QN2	QB7 QB2	Q7 Q2	K7 K2	KB7 KB2	KN7 KN2	KR7 KR2
QR8 QR1	QN8 QN1	QB8 QB1	Q8 Q1	K8 K1	KB8 KB1	KN8 KN1	KR8 KR1

White

Descriptive notation

Each file is named by the piece on the first rank; ranks are numbered 1–8 away from the player.

x	captures (Q x P = Queen takes Pawn)
—	moves to (Q-KB4)
ch	check (R-QB3 ch)
dis ch	discovered check
dbl ch	double check
e.p.	en passant
mate	checkmate
0–0	castles, King's side
0–0–0	castles, Queen's side
!	good move (PxR!)
!!	very good move
!!!	outstanding move
?	bad move
!?	good or bad move (depends on response of the other player)

Black

a8	b8	c8	d8	e8	f8	g8	h8
a7	b7	c7	d7	e7	f7	g7	h7
a6	b6	c6	d6	e6	f6	g6	h6
a5	b5	c5	d5	e5	f5	g5	h5
a4	b4	c4	d4	e4	f4	g4	h4
a3	b3	c3	d3	e3	f3	g3	h3
a2	b2	c2	d2	e2	f2	g2	h2
a1	b1	c1	d1	e1	f1	g1	h1

White

Algebraic notation

Each square is named by a combination of file letter and rank number.

Chess pieces in other languages

French

B fou (fool)
K roi (king)
N cavalier (horseman)
P pion (pawn)
Q dame (lady), reine (queen)
R tour (tower)

German

B Läufer (runner)
K König (king)
N Springer (jumper)
P Bauer (peasant)
Q Königin (queen)
R Turm (tower)

INTERNATIONAL CAR INDEX MARKS

A	Austria
ADN	former Yemen PDR
AFG	Afghanistan
AL	Albania
AND	Andorra
AUS	Australia*
B	Belgium
BD	Bangladesh*
BDS	Barbados*
BG	Bulgaria
BH	Belize
BR	Brazil
BRN	Bahrain
BRU	Brunei•
BS	Bahamas*
BUR	Myanmar (Burma)
C	Cuba
CDN	Canada
CH	Switzerland
CI	Côte d'Ivoire
CL	Sri Lanka*
CO	Colombia
CR	Costa Rica
CS	Czech Republic
CY	Cyprus*
D	Germany
DK	Denmark
DOM	Dominican Republic
DY	Benin
DZ	Algeria
E	Spain
EAK	Kenya*
EAT	Tanzania*
EAU	Uganda*
EAZ	Zanzibar*
EC	Ecuador
ES	El Salvador
ET	Egypt
ETH	Ethiopia
F	France
FJI	Fiji*
FL	Liechtenstein
FR	Faroe Is
GB	UK*
GBA	Alderney*
GBG	Guernsey*
GBJ	Jersey*
GBM	Isle of Man*
GBZ	Gibraltar
GCA	Guatemala
GH	Ghana
GR	Greece
GUY	Guyana*
H	Hungary
HK	Hong Kong*
HKJ	Jordan
I	Italy
IL	Israel
IND	India*
IR	Iran
IRL	Ireland*
IRQ	Iraq
IS	Iceland
J	Japan*
JA	Jamaica*
K	Kampuchea
KWT	Kuwait
L	Luxembourg
LAO	Laos PDR
LAR	Libya
LB	Liberia
LR	Latvia
LS	Lesotho*
M	Malta*
MA	Morocco
MAL	Malaysia*
MC	Monaco
MEX	Mexico
MS	Mauritius•
MW	Malawi*
N	Norway
NA	Netherlands Antilles
NIC	Nicaragua
NL	Netherlands
NZ	New Zealand*
P	Portugal
PA	Panama
PAK	Pakistan*
PE	Peru
PL	Poland
PNG	Papua New Guinea*
PY	Paraguay
RA	Argentina
RB	Botswana*
RC	Taiwan
RCA	Central African Republic
RCB	Congo
RCH	Chile
RH	Haiti
RI	Indonesia*
RIM	Mauritania
RL	Lebanon
RM	Madagascar
RMM	Mali
RN	Niger
RO	Romania
ROK	Korea, Republic of
ROU	Uruguay
RP	Philippines
RSM	San Marino
RU	Burundi
RWA	Rwanda
S	Sweden
SD	Swaziland*
SF	Finland
SGP	Singapore*
SME	Suriname*
SN	Senegal
SU	former USSR
SWA	Namibia*
SY	Seychelles*
SYR	Syria
T	Thailand*
TG	Togo
TN	Tunisia
TR	Turkey
TT	Trinidad and Tobago*
USA	USA
V	Vatican City
VN	Vietnam
WAG	Gambia
WAL	Sierra Leone
WAN	Nigeria
WD	Dominica*
WG	Grenada*
WL	St Lucia*
WS	W Samoa
WV	St Vincent & the Grenadines•
YU	Yugoslavia
YV	Venezuela
Z	Zambia*
ZA	South Africa*
ZRE	Zaïre
ZW	Zimbabwe*

*Countries in which the rule of the road is drive on the left; in other countries, drive on the right.

BRITISH CAR INDEX MARKS

AA	Bournemouth
AB	Worcester
AC	Coventry
AD	Gloucester
AE	Bristol
AF	Truro
AG	Hull
AH	Norwich
AJ	Middlesbrough
AK	Sheffield
AL	Nottingham
AM	Swindon
AN	Reading
AO	Carlisle
AP	Brighton
AR	Chelmsford
AS	Inverness
AT	Hull
AU	Nottingham
AV	Peterborough
AW	Shrewsbury
AX	Cardiff
AY	Leicester
BA	Manchester
BB	Newcastle upon Tyne
BC	Leicester
BD	Northampton
BE	Lincoln
BF	Stoke-on-Trent
BG	Liverpool
BH	Luton
BJ	Ipswich
BK	Portsmouth
BL	Reading
BM	Luton
BN	Manchester
BO	Cardiff
BP	Portsmouth
BR	Newcastle upon Tyne
BS	Aberdeen
BT	Leeds
BU	Manchester
BV	Preston
BW	Oxford
BX	Haverfordwest
BY	London NW
CA	Chester
CB	Manchester
CC	Bangor
CD	Brighton
CE	Peterborough
CF	Reading
CG	Bournemouth
CH	Nottingham
CJ	Gloucester
CK	Preston
CL	Norwich
CM	Liverpool
CN	Newcastle upon Tyne
CO	Exeter
CP	Huddersfield
CR	Portsmouth
CS	Glasgow
CT	Lincoln
CU	Newcastle upon Tyne
CV	Truro
CW	Preston
CX	Huddersfield
CY	Swansea
DA	Birmingham
DB	Manchester
DC	Middlesbrough
DD	Gloucester
DE	Haverfordwest
DF	Gloucester
DG	Gloucester
DH	Dudley
DJ	Liverpool
DK	Manchester
DL	Portsmouth
DM	Chester
DN	Leeds
DO	Lincoln
DP	Reading
DR	Exeter
DS	Glasgow
DT	Sheffield
DU	Coventry
DV	Exeter
DW	Cardiff
DX	Ipswich
DY	Brighton
EA	Dudley
EB	Peterborough
EC	Preston
ED	Liverpool
EE	Lincoln
EF	Middlesbrough
EG	Peterborough
EH	Stoke-on-Trent
EJ	Haverfordwest
EK	Liverpool
EL	Bournemouth
EM	Liverpool
EN	Manchester
EO	Preston
EP	Swansea
ER	Peterborough
ES	Dundee
ET	Sheffield
EU	Bristol
EV	Chelmsford
EW	Peterborough
EX	Norwich
EY	Bangor
FA	Stoke-on-Trent
FB	Bristol
FC	Oxford
FD	Dudley
FE	Lincoln
FF	Bangor
FG	Brighton
FH	Gloucester
FJ	Exeter
FK	Dudley
FL	Peterborough
FM	Chester
FN	Maidstone
FO	Gloucester
FP	Leicester
FR	Preston
FS	Edinburgh
FT	Newcastle upon Tyne
FU	Lincoln
FV	Preston
FW	Lincoln
FX	Bournemouth
FY	Liverpool
GA	Glasgow
GB	Glasgow
GC	London SW
GD	Glasgow
GE	Glasgow
GF	London SW
GG	Glasgow
GH	London SW
GJ	London SW
GK	London SW
GL	Truro
GM	Reading
GN	London SW
GO	London SW
GP	London SW
GR	Newcastle upon Tyne
GS	Luton
GT	London SW
GU	London SE
GV	Ipswich
GW	London SE
GX	London SE
GY	London SE
HA	Dudley
HB	Cardiff
HC	Brighton
HD	Huddersfield
HE	Sheffield
HF	Liverpool
HG	Preston
HH	Carlisle
HJ	Chelmsford
HK	Chelmsford
HL	Sheffield
HM	London Central
HN	Middlesbrough
HO	Bournemouth
HP	Coventry
HR	Swindon
HS	Glasgow
HT	Bristol
HU	Bristol
HV	London Central
HW	Bristol
HX	London Central
HY	Bristol
JA	Manchester
JB	Reading
JC	Bangor
JD	London Central
JE	Peterborough
JF	Leicester
JG	Maidstone
JH	Reading
JJ	Maidstone
JK	Brighton
JL	Lincoln
JM	Reading
JN	Chelmsford
JO	Oxford
JP	Liverpool
JR	Newcastle upon Tyne
JS	Inverness
JT	Bournemouth
JU	Leicester
JV	Lincoln
JW	Birmingham
JX	Huddersfield
JY	Exeter
KA	Liverpool
KB	Liverpool
KC	Liverpool
KD	Liverpool
KE	Maidstone
KF	Liverpool
KG	Cardiff
KH	Hull
KJ	Maidstone
KK	Maidstone
KL	Maidstone
KM	Maidstone
KN	Maidstone
KO	Maidstone
KP	Maidstone
KR	Maidstone
KS	Edinburgh
KT	Maidstone
KU	Sheffield
KV	Coventry
KW	Sheffield
KX	Luton
KY	Sheffield
LA	London NW
LB	London NW
LC	London NW
LD	London NW
LE	London NW
LF	London NW
LG	Chester
LH	London NW
LJ	Bournemouth
LK	London NW
LL	London NW
LM	London NW
LN	London NW
LO	London NW
LP	London NW
LR	London NW
LS	Edinburgh
LT	London NW
LU	London NW
LV	Liverpool
LW	London NW
LX	London NW
LY	London NW
MA	Chester
MB	Chester
MC	London NE
MD	London NE
ME	London NE
MF	London NE
MG	London NE
MH	London NE
MJ	Luton
MK	London NE
ML	London NE
MM	London NE
MN	*not used*
MO	Reading
MP	London NE
MR	Swindon
MS	Edinburgh
MT	London NE
MU	London NE
MV	London SE
MW	Swindon
MX	London SE
MY	London SE
NA	Manchester
NB	Manchester
NC	Manchester
ND	Manchester
NE	Manchester
NF	Manchester
NG	Norwich
NH	Northampton
NJ	Brighton
NK	Luton
NL	Newcastle upon Tyne
NM	Luton
NN	Nottingham
NO	Chelmsford
NP	Worcester
NR	Leicester
NS	Glasgow
NT	Shrewsbury
NU	Nottingham
NV	Northampton
NW	Leeds
NX	Dudley
NY	Cardiff
OA	Birmingham
OB	Birmingham
OC	Birmingham
OD	Exeter
OE	Birmingham
OF	Birmingham
OG	Birmingham
OH	Birmingham
OJ	Birmingham
OK	Birmingham
OL	Birmingham
OM	Birmingham
ON	Birmingham
OO	Chelmsford
OP	Birmingham
OR	Portsmouth
OS	Glasgow
OT	Portsmouth
OU	Bristol
OV	Birmingham
OW	Portsmouth
OX	Birmingham
OY	London NW
PA	Guildford
PB	Guildford
PC	Guildford
PD	Guildford
PE	Guildford
PF	Guildford
PG	Guildford
PH	Guildford
PJ	Guildford
PK	Guildford
PL	Guildford
PM	Guildford
PN	Brighton
PO	Portsmouth
PP	Luton
PR	Bournemouth
PS	Aberdeen
PT	Newcastle upon Tyne
PU	Chelmsford
PV	Ipswich
PW	Norwich
PX	Portsmouth
PY	Middlesbrough

BRITISH CAR INDEX MARKS (continued)

RA Nottingham
RB Nottingham
RC Nottingham
RD Reading
RE Stoke-on-Trent
RF Stoke-on-Trent
RG Newcastle upon Tyne
RH Hull
RJ Manchester
RK London NW
RL Truro
RM Carlisle
RN Preston
RO Luton
RP Northampton
RR Nottingham
RS Aberdeen
RT Ipswich
RU Bournemouth
RV Portsmouth
RW Coventry
RX Reading
RY Leicester

SA Aberdeen
SB Glasgow
SC Edinburgh
SD Glasgow
SE Aberdeen
SF Edinburgh
SG Edinburgh
SH Edinburgh
SJ Glasgow
SK Inverness
SL Dundee
SM Carlisle
SN Dundee
SO Aberdeen
SP Dundee
SR Dundee
SS Aberdeen
ST Inverness
SU Glasgow
SV *spare*
SW Carlisle
SX Edinburgh
SY *spare*

TA Exeter
TB Liverpool
TC Bristol
TD Manchester
TE Manchester
TF Reading
TG Cardiff
TH Swansea
TJ Liverpool
TK Exeter
TL Lincoln
TM Luton
TN Newcastle upon Tyne
TO Nottingham
TP Portsmouth
TR Portsmouth
TS Dundee
TT Exeter
TU Chester
TV Nottingham
TW Chelmsford
TX Cardiff
TY Newcastle upon Tyne

UA Leeds
UB Leeds
UC London Central
UD Oxford
UE Dudley
UF Brighton
UG Leeds
UH Cardiff
UJ Shrewsbury
UK Birmingham
UL London Central
UM Leeds
UN Exeter
UO Exeter
UP Newcastle upon Tyne
UR Luton
US Glasgow
UT Leicester
UU London Central
UV London Central
UW London Central
UX Shrewsbury
UY Worcester

VA Peterborough
VB Maidstone
VC Coventry
VD *series withdrawn*
VE Peterborough
VF Norwich
VG Norwich
VH Huddersfield
VJ Gloucester
VK Newcastle upon Tyne
VL Lincoln
VM Manchester
VN Middlesbrough
VO Nottingham
VP Birmingham
VR Manchester
VS Luton
VT Stoke-on-Trent
VU Manchester
VV Northampton
VW Chelmsford
VX Chelmsford
VY Leeds

WA Sheffield
WB Sheffield
WC Chelmsford
WD Dudley
WE Sheffield
WF Sheffield
WG Sheffield
WH Manchester
WJ Sheffield
WK Coventry
WL Oxford
WM Liverpool
WN Swansea
WO Cardiff
WP Worcester
WR Leeds
WS Bristol
WT Leeds
WU Leeds
WV Brighton
WW Leeds
WX Leeds
WY Leeds

XA–
XY *spare index marks*

YA Taunton
YB Taunton
YC Taunton
YD Taunton
YE London Central
YF London Central
YG Leeds
YH London Central
YJ Brighton
YK London Central
YL London Central
YM London Central
YN London Central
YO London Central
YP London Central
YR London Central
YS Glasgow
YT London Central
YU London Central
YV London Central
YW London Central
YX London Central
YY London Central

PRIZES AND AWARDS

NOBEL PRIZES 1979–98

Year	Peace	Literature	Economic Science	Chemistry	Physics	Physiology/Medicine	Year
1979	Mother Theresa	Odysseus Elytis	Arthur Lewis Theodore W Schultz	Herbert C Brown Georg Wittig	Steven Weinberg Sheldon L Glashow Abdus Salam	Allan M Cormack Godfrey N Hounsfield	1979
1980	Adolfo Pérez Esquivel	Czesław Miłosz	Lawrence R Klein	Paul Berg Walter Gilbert Frederick Sanger	James W Cronin Val L Fitch	Baruj Benacerraf George D Snell Jean Dausset	1980
1981	Office of the UN High Commissioner for Refugees	Elias Canetti	James Tobin	Kenichi Fukui Roald Hoffmann	Nicolaas Bloembergen Arthur L Schawlow Kai M Siegbahn	Roger W Sperry David H Hubel Torsten N Wiesel	1981
1982	Alfonso García Robles Alva Myrdal	Gabriel García Márquez	George J Stigler	Aaron Klug	Kenneth G Wilson	Sune K Bergström Bengt I Samuelsson John R Vane	1982
1983	Lech Wałesa	William Golding	Gerard Debreu	Henry Taube	Subrahmanyan Chandrasekhar William A Fowler	Barbara McClintock	1983
1984	Desmond Tutu	Jaroslav Seifert	Richard Stone	Robert B Merrifield	Carlo Rubbia Simon van der Meer	Niels K Jerne Georges J F Köhler César Milstein	1984
1985	International Physicians for the Prevention of Nuclear War	Claude Simon	Franco Modigliani	Herbert Hauptman Jerome Karle	Klaus von Klitzing	Joseph L Goldstein Michael S Brown	1985
1986	Elie Wiesel	Wole Soyinka	James M Buchanan	Dudley R Herschbach Yuan Tseh Lee John C Polanyi	Gerd Binnig Heinrich Rohrer Ernst Ruska	Stanley Cohen Rita Levi-Montalcini	1986
1987	Oscar Arias Sánchez	Joseph Brodsky	Robert M Solow	Charles Pedersen Donald Cram Jean-Marie Lehn	George Bednorz Alex Müller	Susumu Tonegawa	1987
1988	UN Peacekeeping Forces	Naguib Mahfouz	Maurice Allais	Johann Deisenhofer Robert Huber Hartmut Michel	Leon Lederman Melvin Schwartz Jack Steinberger	James Black Gertrude Elion George Hitchings	1988
1989	Tenzin Ciyatso (Dalai Lama)	Camilo José Cela	Trygve Haavelmo	Sydney Altman Thomas Cech	Hans Dehmelt Wolfgang Pauli Norman Ramsay	J Michael Bishop Harold E Varmus	1989
1990	Mikhail Gorbachev	Octavio Paz	Harry M Markovitz Merton Miller William Sharpe	Elias James Corey	Jerome Friedman Henry Kendall Richard Taylor	Joseph E Murray E Donnall Thomas	1990
1991	Aung San Suu Kyi	Nadine Gordimer	Ronald Coase	Richard R Ernst	Pierre-Gilles de Gennes	Erwin Neher Bert Sakmann	1991
1992	Rigoberta Menchú	Derek Walcott	Gary S Becker	Rudolph Marcus	Georges Charpak	Edmund H Fisher Edward K Krebs	1992
1993	Nelson Mandela F W de Klerk	Toni Morrison	Douglas C North Robert W Fogel	Kary Mullis Michael Smith	Joseph Taylor Russell Hulse	Richard R Roberts Phillip A Sharp	1993
1994	Yitzhak Rabin Yasser Arafat Shimon Peres	Kenzaburo Oe	John Nash Reinhard Selten John Harsanyi	George A Olah	Bertram N Brockhouse Clifford G Shull	Alfred G Gilman Martin Rodbell	1994
1995	Joseph Rotblat Pugwash Conferences	Seamus Heaney	Robert E Lucas Jr	Paul Crutzen Mario Molina Sherwood Rowland	Martin Perl Frederick Reines	Edward B Lewis Christiane Nüesslein-Volhard Eric F Wieschaus	1995
1996	Carlos Felipe Belo Jose Ramos-Horta	Wislawa Szymborska	James Mirlees William Vickrey	Harold Kroto Robert Curl Richard Smalley	Douglas Osheroff David Lee Robert Richardson	Peter Doherty Rolf Zinkernagel	1996
1997	Jody Williams International Campaign to Ban Landmines	Dario Fo	Myron Scholes Robert Merton	Jen Skou John Walker Paul Boyer	Steven Chu Claude Cohen-Tannoudji William D Phillips	Stanley Prusiner	1997
1998	John Hume David Trimble	Jose Saramago	Amartya Sen	Walter Kohn John A Pople	Robert B Laughlin Horst L Stormer Daniel C Tsui	Robert Furchgott Louis J Ignarro	1998

LITERARY PRIZES

Booker Prize (UK)

1976 David Storey *Saville*
1977 Paul Scott *Staying On*
1978 Iris Murdoch *The Sea The Sea*
1979 Penelope Fitzgerald *Offshore*
1980 William Golding *Rites of Passage*
1981 Salman Rushdie *Midnight's Children*
1982 Thomas Keneally *Schindler's Ark*
1983 J M Coetzee *Life and Times of Michael K*
1984 Anita Brookner *Hotel du Lac*
1985 Keri Hulme *The Bone People*
1986 Kingsley Amis *The Old Devils*
1987 Penelope Lively *Moon Tiger*
1988 Peter Carey *Oscar and Lucinda*
1989 Kazuo Ishiguro *The Remains of the Day*
1990 A S Byatt *Possession*
1991 Ben Okri *The Famished Road*
1992 Barry Unsworth *Sacred Hunger*
Michael Ondaatje *The English Patient*
1993 Roddy Doyle *Paddy Clarke Ha Ha Ha*
1994 James Kelman *How Late it Was, How Late*
1995 Pat Barker *The Ghost Road*
1996 Graham Swift *Last Orders*
1997 Arundhati Roy *The God of Small Things*
1998 Ian McEwan *Amsterdam*

Prix Goncourt (France)

1977 Didier Decoin *John L'Enfer*
1978 Patrick Modiano *Rue des boutiques obscures*
1979 Antonine Maillet *Pelagie-la-Charrette*
1980 Yves Navarre *Le Jardin d'acclimation*
1981 Lucien Bodard *Anne Marie*
1982 Dominique Fernandez *Dans la Main de l'ange*
1983 Frédérick Tristan *Les Égarés*
1984 Marguerite Duras *L'Amant*
1985 Yann Queffelec *Les Noces barbares*
1986 Michel Host *Valet de Nuit*
1987 Tahar ben Jalloun *La Nuit sacrée*
1988 Erik Orsenna *L'Exposition coloniale*
1989 Jean Vautrin *Un Grand Pas vers le Bon Dieu*
1990 Jean Rouaud *Les Champs d'Honneur*
1991 Pierre Combescot *Les Filles du Calvaire*
1992 Patrick Chamoiseau *Texaco*
1993 Amin Malouf *Le Rocher de Tanois*
1994 Didier van Cauwelaert, *Un Aller simple*
1995 Andrei Makine *Le Testament française*
1996 Pascole Roze *Chasseur Zéro*
1997 Patrick Ramboud *La Bataille*
1998 Paule Constant *Confidence Pour Confidence*

Pulitzer Prize (USA)

1979 John Cheever *The Stories of John Cheever*
1980 Norman Mailer *The Executioner's Song*
1981 John Kennedy Toole *A Confederacy of Dunces*
1982 John Updike *Rabbit is Rich*
1983 Alice Walker *The Color Purple*
1984 William Kennedy *Ironweed*
1985 Alison Lurie *Foreign Affairs*
1986 Larry McMurtry *Lonesome Dove*
1987 Peter Taylor *A Summons to Memphis*
1988 Toni Morrison *Beloved*
1989 Anne Tyler *Breathing Lessons*
1990 Oscar Hijuelos *The Mambo Kings Play Songs of Love*
1991 John Updike *Rabbit at Rest*
1992 Jane Smiley *A Thousand Acres*
1993 Robert Olen Butler *A Good Scent from a Strange Mountain*
1994 E Annie Proulx *The Shipping News*
1995 Carol Shields *The Stone Diaries*
1996 Richard Ford *Independence Day*
1997 Steven Millhauser *Martin Dressler: The Tale of an American Dreamer*
1998 Phillip Roth *American Pastoral*

POETS LAUREATE

1617 Ben Jonson*
1638 Sir William Davenant*
1668 John Dryden
1689 Thomas Shadwell
1692 Nathum Tate
1715 Nicholas Rowe
1718 Laurence Eusden
1730 Colley Cibber
1757 William Whitehead
1785 Thomas Warton
1790 Henry Pye
1813 Robert Southey
1843 William Wordsworth
1850 Alfred, Lord Tennyson
1896 Alfred Austin
1913 Robert Bridges
1930 John Masefield
1968 Cecil Day Lewis
1972 Sir John Betjeman
1984 Ted Hughes
1999 Andrew Motion

* The post was not officially established until 1668.

THE TEMPLETON PRIZE FOR PROGRESS IN RELIGION

1977 Chiara Lubich, Italy
1978 Rev Prof Thomas F Torrance, UK
1979 Nikkyo Niwano, Japan
1980 Prof Ralph Wendell Burhoe, USA
1981 Dame Cecily Saunders, UK
1982 Rev Dr Billy Graham, USA
1983 Alexander Solzhenitsyn, Soviet Union
1984 Rev Michael Bourdeaux, UK
1985 Sir Alister Hardy, UK
1986 Rev Dr James I McCord, USA
1987 Rev Prof Stanley L Jaki, Hungary/USA
1988 Dr Inamullah Khan, Pakistan
1989 (jointly) Very Rev Lord Macleod of Fiunary, UK Prof Carl Fredrich von Weizsäcker, Germany
1990 (jointly) Baba Amte, India
Prof L Charles Birch, Austrailia
1991 Rt Hon Lord Jakobovits, UK
1992 Dr Kyung-Chik Han, South Korea
1993 Charles W Colson, USA
1994 Michael Novak, USA
1995 Prof Paul Charles William Davies, UK
1996 William ("Bill") Bright, USA
1997 Pandurang Shastri Athavale, India
1998 Sir Sigmund Sternberg, Hungary

TURNER PRIZE

Awarded to a British artist under 50 for an outstanding exhibition in the preceding 12 months.

1988 Tony Cragg
1989 Richard Long
1990 *Prize suspended*
1991 Anish Kapoor
1992 Grenville Davey
1993 Rachel Whiteread
1994 Anthony Gormley
1995 Damien Hirst
1996 Douglas Gordon
1997 Gillian Wearing
1998 Chris Ofili

MOTION PICTURE ACADEMY AWARDS

Best film	*Best actor*	*Best actress*
1983 *Terms of Endearment* (James L Brooks)	Robert Duval, *Tender Mercies*	Shirley MacLaine, *Terms of Endearment*
1984 *Amadeus* (Milos Forman)	F Murray Abraham, *Amadeus*	Sally Field, *Places in the Heart*
1985 *Out of Africa* (Sydney Pollack)	William Hurt, *Kiss of the Spider Woman*	Geraldine Page, *The Trip to Bountiful*
1986 *Platoon* (Oliver Stone)	Paul Newman, *The Color of Money*	Marlee Matlin, *Children of a Lesser God*
1987 *The Last Emperor* (Bernardo Bertolucci)	Michael Douglas, *Wall Street*	Cher, *Moonstruck*
1988 *Rain Man* (Barry Levinson)	Dustin Hoffman, *Rain Man*	Jodie Foster, *The Accused*
1989 Driving Miss Daisy (Bruce Beresford)	Daniel Day Lewis, *My Left Foot*	Jessica Tandy, *Driving Miss Daisy*
1990 Dances with Wolves (Kevin Kostner)	Jeremy Irons, *Reversal of Fortune*	Kathy Bates, *Misery*
1991 The Silence of the Lambs (Jonathan Demme)	Anthony Hopkins, *The Silence of the Lambs*	Jodie Foster, *The Silence of the Lambs*
1992 Unforgiven (Clint Eastwood)	Al Pacino, *Scent of a Woman*	Emma Thompson, *Howard's End*
1993 *Schindler's List* (Steven Spielberg)	Tom Hanks, *Philadelphia*	Holly Hunter, *The Piano*
1994 *Forrest Gump* (Robert Zemeckis)	Tom Hanks, *Forrest Gump*	Jessica Lange, *Blue Sky*
1995 *Braveheart* (Mel Gibson)	Nicolas Cage, *Leaving Las Vegas*	Susan Sarandon, *Dead Man Walking*
1996 *The English Patient* (Anthony Minghella)	Geoffrey Rush, *Shine*	Frances McDormand, *Fargo*
1997 *Titanic* (James Cameron)	Jack Nicholson, *As Good As It Gets*	Helen Hunt, *As Good As It Gets*
1998 *Shakespeare in Love* (John Madden)	Roberto Benigni, *Life is Beautiful*	Gwyneth Paltrow, *Shakespeare in Love*

Competitive Sports and Games

OLYMPIC GAMES

First modern Olympic Games took place in 1896, founded by Frenchman Baron de Coubertin; held every four years; women first competed in 1900. First separate Winter Games celebration in 1924.

Venues

	Summer Games	*Winter Games*
1896	Athens, Greece	–
1900	Paris, France	–
1904	St Louis, USA	–
1908	London, UK	–
1912	Stockholm, Sweden	–
1920	Antwerp, Belgium	–
1924	Paris, France	Chamonix, France
1928	Amsterdam, Holland	St Moritz, Switzerland
1932	Los Angeles, USA	Lake Placid, New York, USA
1936	Berlin, Germany	Garmisch-Partenkirchen, Germany
1948	London, UK	St Moritz, Switzerland
1952	Helsinki, Finland	Oslo, Norway
1956	Melbourne, Australia	Cortina, Italy
1960	Rome, Italy	Squaw Valley, California, USA
1964	Tokyo, Japan	Innsbruck, Austria
1968	Mexico City, Mexico	Grenoble, France
1972	Munich, West Germany	Sapporo, Japan
1976	Montreal, Canada	Innsbruck, Austria
1980	Moscow, USSR	Lake Placid, New York, USA
1984	Los Angeles, USA	Sarajevo, Yugoslavia
1988	Seoul, South Korea	Calgary, Canada
1992	Barcelona, Spain	Albertville, France
1994		Lillehammer, Norway
1996	Atlanta, USA	
1998		Nagano, Japan
2000	Sydney, Australia	
2002		Salt Lake City, USA

*As from 1994, the Winter Games take place at the midway point between the Summer Games.

Olympic Games were also held in 1906 to commemorate the 10th anniversary of the birth of the modern Games.

The 1956 equestrian events were held at Stockholm, Sweden, due to quarantine laws in Australia.

Leading medal winners

Summer Games 1996	*Gold*	*Silver*	*Bronze*	*Total*
1 USA	44	32	25	101
2 Russia	26	21	16	63
3 Germany	20	18	27	65
4 China	16	22	12	50
5 France	15	7	15	37
6 Italy	13	11	12	35
7 Australia	9	9	22	40
8 Cuba	9	8	8	25
9 Ukraine	9	2	12	23
10 South Korea	7	15	5	27
Winter Games 1998				
1 Germany	12	9	8	29
2 Norway	10	10	5	25
3 Russian Federation	9	6	3	18
4 Canada	6	5	4	15
5 USA	6	3	4	13
6 Netherlands	5	4	2	11
7 Japan	5	1	4	10
8 Austria	3	5	9	17
9 Korea	3	1	2	6
10 Italy	2	6	2	10

COMMONWEALTH GAMES

First held as the British Empire Games in 1930; take place every four years and between Olympic celebrations; became the British Empire and Commonwealth Games in 1954; the current title adopted in 1970.

Venues

1930	Hamilton, Canada	1970	Edinburgh, Scotland
1934	London, England	1974	Christchurch, New Zealand
1938	Sydney, Australia	1978	Edmonton, Canada
1950	Auckland, New Zealand	1982	Brisbane, Australia
1954	Vancouver, Canada	1986	Edinburgh, Scotland
1958	Cardiff, Wales	1990	Auckland, New Zealand
1962	Perth, Australia	1994	Victoria, Canada
1966	Kingston, Jamaica	1998	Kuala Lumpur

Leading medal winners

Nation	*Gold*	*Silver*	*Bronze*	*Total*
1 Australia	564	486	432	1482
2 England	467	459	471	1417
3 Canada	357	374	466	1197
4 New Zealand	107	144	200	451
5 Scotland	65	79	127	271
6 South Africa	71	59	67	197
7 Wales	42	51	74	167
8 India	50	57	46	153
9 Kenya	49	34	45	127
10 Nigeria	30	38	39	107

AEROBATICS

World championships

First held in 1960 and every two years since then except 1974 and 1992.

Recent winners: men

1980 Leo Loudenslager (USA)
1982 Viktor Smolin (USSR)
1984 Petr Jirmus (Czechoslovakia)
1986 Petr Jirmus (Czechoslovakia)
1988 Henry Haigh (USA)
1990 Claude Bessière (France)
1994 Xavier de Lattarent (France)
1996 Victor Chmal (Russia)
1998 Patrick Paris (France)

Recent winners: women

1980 Betty Stewart (USA)
1982 Betty Stewart (USA)
1984 Khalide Makagonova (USSR)
1986 Liubov Nemkova (USSR)
1988 Catherine Maunoury (France)
1990 Natalya Sergeeva (USSR)
1994 Christine Genin (France)
1996 Svetlana Kapanina (Russia)
1998 Svetlana Kapanina (Russia)

AMERICAN FOOTBALL

Superbowl

First held in 1967 between champions of the National Football league (NFL) and the American Football League (AFL); takes place each January; since 1971 an end of season meeting between the champions of the AFC and the NFC.

1989 San Francisco 49ers (NFC)
1990 San Francisco 49ers (NFC)
1991 New York Giants (NFC)
1992 Washington Redskins (NFC)
1993 Dallas Cowboys (NFC)
1994 San Francisco 49ers (NFC)
1995 Dallas Cowboys (NFC)
1996 Green Bay Packers (NFC)
1997 Denver Broncos (AFC)
1998 Denver Broncos (AFC)
1999 Denver Broncos (AFC)

Most wins: (5) San Francisco 49ers 1982, 1985, 1989–90, 1994.

ANGLING

World freshwater championship

First held in 1957; takes place annually.

Recent individual winners

1988 Jean-Pierre Fouquet (France)
1989 Tom Pickering (England)
1990 Bob Nudd (England)
1991 Bob Nudd (England)
1992 David Wesson (Australia)
1993 Mario Barras (Portugal)
1994 Bob Nudd (England)
1995 Pierre Jean (France)
1996 Alan Scotthorne (England)
1997 Alan Scotthorne (England)
1998 Alan Scotthorne (England)

Recent team winners

1990 France
1991 England
1992 Italy
1993 Italy
1994 England
1995 France
1996 Italy
1997 Italy
1998 England

Most wins: Individual (3), Robert Tesse (France) 1959–60, 1965; Bob Nudd (England) as above; Alan Scotthorne (England) as above. Team (12), France, 1959, 1963–4, 1966, 1968, 1972, 1974–5, 1978–9, 1981, 1995.

World fly-fishing championship

First held in 1981; takes place annually.

Recent individual winners

1990 Franciszek Szajnik (Poland)
1991 Brian Leadbetter (England)
1992 Pierluigi Cocito (Italy)
1993 Russell Owen (Wales)
1994 Pascal Cognard
1995 Jeremy Hermann (England)
1996 Pierluigi Cocito (Italy)
1997 Pascal Cognard (France)
1998 Tomas Starychsojtu (Czech Republic)

Recent team winners

1990 Czechoslovakia
1991 New Zealand
1992 Italy
1993 England
1994 Czech Republic
1995 England
1996 Czech Republic
1997 France
1998 Czech Republic

Most wins: Individual (2) Brian Leadbetter (England) 1987 and as above; Pierluigi Cocito (Italy); Pascal Cognard (France) as above. Team (5), Italy, 1982–4, 1986, 1992.

ARCHERY

World championships

First held in 1931; took place annually until 1959; since then, every two years.

Recent individual winners: men

1979 Darrell Pace (USA)
1981 Kysti Laasonen (Finland)
1983 Richard McKinney (USA)
1985 Richard McKinney (USA)
1987 Vladimir Yesheyev (USSR)
1989 Stanislav Zabrodsky (USSR)
1991 Simon Fairweather (Australia)
1993 Kyung-Mo Park (Korea)
1995 Gary Broadhead (Cuba)
1997 Kyung-ho Kim (South Korea)

Recent team winners: men

1973 USA
1975 USA
1977 USA
1979 USA
1981 USA
1983 USA
1985 South Korea
1987 South Korea
1989 USSR
1991 South Korea
1993 France
1995 USA
1997 South Korea

Most wins: Individual (4), Hans Deutgen (Sweden) 1947–50. Team (15), USA 1957–83, 1995.

Recent individual winners: women

1977 Luann Ryon (USA)
1979 Jin-Ho Kim (South Korea)
1981 Natalia Butuzova (USSR)
1983 Jin-Ho Kim (South Korea)
1985 Irina Soldatova (USSR)
1987 Ma Xiagjun (China)
1989 Kim Soo-nyung (South Korea)
1991 Kim Soo-nyung (South Korea)
1993 Kim Hyo Jung (South Korea)
1995 Angela Moscarelly (USA)
1997 Du-ri Kim (South Korea)

Recent team winners: women

1977 USA
1979 South Korea
1981 USSR
1983 South Korea
1985 USSR
1987 USSR
1989 South Korea
1991 South Korea
1993 South Korea
1995 USA
1997 South Korea

Most wins: Individual (7), Janina Kurkowska (Poland) 1931–4, 1936, 1939, 1947. Team (9), USA 1952, 1957–9, 1961, 1963, 1965, 1977, 1995.

ASSOCIATION FOOTBALL

FIFA World Cup

Association Football's premier event; first contested for the Jules Rimet Trophy in 1930; Brazil won it outright after winning for the third time in 1970; since then teams have competed for the FIFA (*Fédération Internationale de Football Association*) World Cup; held every four years.

Post-war winners

1958 Brazil
1962 Brazil
1966 England
1970 Brazil
1974 W Germany
1978 Argentina
1982 Italy
1986 Argentina
1990 W Germany
1994 Brazil
1998 France

Most wins: (4), Brazil, as above.

European Champions Cup

The leading club competition in Europe; open to the League champions of countries affiliated to UEFA (Union of European Football

Associations); commonly known as the 'European Cup'; inaugurated in the 1955–6 season; played annually.

Recent winners

1988 PSV Eindhoven (Holland)
1989 AC Milan (Italy)
1990 AC Milan (Italy)
1991 Red Star Belgrade (Yugoslavia)
1992 Barcelona (Spain)
1993 AC Milan (Italy)[a]
1994 AC Milan (Italy)
1995 Ajax (Holland)
1996 Juventus (Italy)
1997 Borussia Dortmund (Germany)
1998 Real Madrid (Spain)
1999 Manchester United

Most wins: (7), Real Madrid (Spain), 1956–60, 1966, 1998.

[a] Replacing Olympique Marseilles (France), who lost the title after allegations of bribery.

South American championship

First held in 1916, for South American national sides; discontinued in 1967, but revived eight years later; now played every two years.

Recent winners

1959* Argentina
1959* Uruguay
1963 Bolivia
1967 Uruguay
1975 Peru
1979 Paraguay
1983 Uruguay
1987 Uruguay
1989 Brazil
1991 Argentina
1993 Argentina
1995 Uruguay
1997 Brazil

* There were two tournaments in 1959.

Most wins: (14), Uruguay, 1916–17, 1920, 1923–4, 1926, 1935, 1942, 1956, 1959, 1967, 1983, 1987, 1997.

Football Association Challenge Cup

The world's oldest club knockout competition (the 'FA cup'), held annually; first contested in the 1871–2 season; first final at the Kennington Oval on 16 March 1872; first winners were The Wanderers.

Recent winners

1988 Wimbledon
1989 Liverpool
1990 Manchester United
1991 Tottenham Hotspur
1992 Liverpool
1993 Arsenal
1994 Manchester United
1995 Everton
1996 Manchester United
1997 Chelsea
1998 Arsenal
1999 Manchester united

Most wins: (10), Manchester United, 1909, 1948, 1963, 1977, 1983, 1985 and as above.

Football League

The oldest league in the world, founded in 1888; consists of four divisions, since 1992 the Premier League and League divisions 1, 2, and 3; the current complement of 92 teams achieved in 1950.

Recent league champions

1989–90 Liverpool
1990–1 Arsenal
1991–2 Leeds United
1992–4 Manchester United
1994–5 Blackburn Rovers
1995–7 Manchester United
1997–8 Arsenal
1998–9 Manchester United

Most wins: (18), Liverpool, 1901, 1906, 1922–3, 1947, 1964, 1966, 1973, 1976–7, 1979–80, 1982–4, 1986, 1988, 1990.

ATHLETICS

World championships

First held in Helsinki, Finland in 1983; take place every two years from 1993; held in Sweden in 1995, Athens 1997.

Event	*Winners: men*
1995	
100 m	Donovan Bailey (Canada)
200 m	Michael Johnson (USA)
400 m	Michael Johnson (USA)
800 m	Wilson Kipketer (Denmark)
1500 m	Noureddine Morceli (Algeria)
5000 m	Ismael Kurui (Kenya)
10000 m	Haile Gebresilassie (Ethiopia)
Marathon	Martin Fizz (Spain)
110 m hurdles	Allen Johnson (USA)
400 m hurdles	Derrick Atkins (USA)
3000 m steeplechase	Moses Kiptanui (Kenya)
20 km walk	Michele Didoni (Italy)
50 km walk	Valentin Kononen (Finland)
4×100 m relay	Canada
4×400 m relay	USA
High jump	Troy Kemp (Bahamas)
Long jump	Ivan Pedroso (Cuba)
Pole vault	Sergey Bubka (USSR)
Triple jump	Jonathon Edwards (UK)
Shot	John Godina (USA)
Discus	Lars Reidel (Germany)
Javelin	Jan Zelezny (Czech Republic)
Hammer	Andrei Abduvaliyev (Tajikistan)
Decathlon	Dan O'Brien (USA)
1997	
100 m	Maurice Greene (USA)
200 m	Ato Boldon (Jamaica)
400 m	Michael Johnson (USA)
800 m	Wilson Kipketer (Denmark)
1500 m	Hicham El Guerrouj (Morocco)
5000 m	Daniel Komen (Kenya)
10000 m	Haile Gebresilassie (Ethopia)
Marathon	Abel Anton (Spain)
3000 m steeplechase	Wilson Kipketer (Denmark)
110 m hurdles	Allen Johnson (USA)
400 m hurdles	Stéphane Diagana (France)
High jump	Javier Sotomayor (Cuba)
Pole vault	Sergei Bubka (Ukraine)
Long jump	Ivan Pedroso (Cuba)
Triple jump	Yoelvis Quesada (Cuba)
Shot	John Godina (USA)
Discus	Lars Reidel (Germany)
Hammer	Heinz Weis (Germany)
Javelin	Marius Corbett (South Africa)
Decathlon	Tomas Dvorak (Czech Republic)
20 km walk	Daniel Garcia (Mexico)
50 km walk	Robert Korzeniowski (Poland)

Event	*Winners: women*
1995	
100m	Gwen Torrence (USA)
200m	Merlene Ottey (Jamaica)
400m	Marie-Jose Perec (France)
800m	Ana Fedelia Quirot (Cuba)
1500m	Hassiba Boulmerka (Algeria)
5000m	Sonia O'Sullivan (Ireland)
10000m	Fernanda Ribeiro (Portugal)
Marathon	Manuela Machado (Portugal)
100m hurdles	Gail Devers (USA)
400m hurdles	Kim Batten (USA)
10km walk	Irina Stankina (Russia)
4×100m relay	USA
4×400m relay	USA
High jump	Stefka Kostadinova (Bulgaria)
Long jump	Fiona May (Italy)
Shot	Astrid Kumbernuss (Germany)
Discus	Ellina Svereva (Belarus)
Javelin	Natalya Shikolenka (Belarus)
Heptathlon	Ghada Shouaa (Syria)
1997	
100 m	Marion Jones (USA)
200 m	Zhanna Pintussevich (Ukraine)
400 m	Cathy Freeman (Australia)
800 m	Ana Fidelia Quirot (Cuba)
1500 m	Carla Sacramento (Portugal)
5000 m	Gabriela Szabo (Romania)
10000 m	Sally Barsosio (Kenya)
Marathon	Hiromi Suzuki (Japan)
100 m hurdles	Ludmila Enquist (Sweden)
400 m hurdles	Nezha Bidouane (Morocco)
High jump	Hanne Haugland (Norway)
Long jump	Lyudmilla Galkina (Russia)
Shot	Astrid Kumbernuss (Germany)
Discus	Beatrice Faumuina (New Zealand)
Javelin	Trini Hattestad (Norway)
Heptathlon	Saubine Braun (Germany)
10 km walk	Annarita Sidoti (Italy)

AUSTRALIAN RULES FOOTBALL

Australian Football League

The top prize is the annual VFL Premiership Trophy; first contested in 1897 and won by Essendon. Known as the Victoria Football League until 1987.

Recent winners

1988 Hawthorn
1989 Hawthorn
1990 Collingwood
1991 Hawthorn
1992 West Coast Eagles
1993 Essendon

1994 West Coast Eagles
1995 Carlton
1996 North Melbourne
1997 Adelaide Crows
1998 Adelaide Crows
Most wins: (15), Carlton, 1906–8, 1914–15, 1938, 1945, 1947, 1968, 1970, 1972, 1979, 1981–2, 1987, 1995.

BADMINTON

World championships

First held in 1977; initially took place every three years; since 1983 every two years.

Recent singles winners: men
1989 Yang Yang (China)
1991 Zhao Jianhua (China)
1993 Joko Suprianto (Indonesia)
1995 Heryanto Arbi (Indonesia)
1997 Peter Rasmussen (Denmark)
1999 Sun Jun (China)
Recent singles winners: women
1989 Li Lingwei (China)
1991 Tang Jiuhong (China)
1993 Susi Susanti (Indonesia)
1995 Ye Zhaoying (China)
1997 Ye Zhaoying (China)
1999 Camilla Martin (Denmark)
Most titles: (4), Park Joo Bong (South Korea), men's doubles 1985, 1991, mixed doubles 1989, 1991.

Thomas Cup

An international team event for men's teams; inaugurated 1949, now held every two years.

Recent winners
1979 Indonesia
1982 China
1984 Indonesia
1986 China
1988 China
1990 China
1992 Malaysia
1994 Indonesia
1996 Indonesia
1998 Indonesia
Most wins: (11), Indonesia, 1958–61, 1964, 1970–9, 1984, 1994, 1996, 1998.

Uber Cup

An international event for women's teams; first held in 1957; now held every two years.
Recent winners
1972 Japan
1975 Indonesia
1978 Japan
1981 Japan
1984 China
1986 China
1988 China
1990 China
1992 China
1994 Indonesia
1996 Indonesia
1998 China
Most wins: (6), China, as above.

All-England championship

Badminton's premier event prior to the inauguration of the World Championships; first held in 1899.

Recent singles winners: men
1988 Ib Frederikson (Denmark)
1989 Yang Yang (China)
1990 Zhao Jianhua (China)
1991 Ardi Wiranata (Indonesia)
1992 Liu Jun (China)
1993 Heryanto Arbi (Indonesia)
1994 Heryanto Arbi (Indonesia)
1995 Poul-Erik Hoyer Larsen (Denmark)
1996 Poul-Erik Hoyer Larsen (Denmark)
1997 Dong Jiong (China)
1998 Sun Jun (China)
1999 Peter Gade Christensen (Denmark)

Recent singles winners: women
1988 Gu Jiaming (China)
1990 Susi Susanti (Indonesia)
1991 Susi Susanti (Indonesia)
1992 Tang Jiuhong (China)
1993 Susi Susanti (Indonesia)
1994 Susi Susanti (Indonesia)
1995 Lin Xiao Qing (Sweden)
1996 Bang Soo-Hyun (South Korea)
1997 Ye Zhaoying (China)
1998 Ye Zhaoying (China)
1999 Ye Zhaoying (China)
Most titles: (21): 4 singles, 9 men's doubles, 8 mixed doubles), George Thomas (England) 1903–28.

BASEBALL

World Series

First held in 1903; takes place each October, the best of seven matches; professional Baseball's leading event, the end-of-season meeting between the winners of the two major baseball leagues in the USA, the National League (NL) and American League (AL).

Recent winners
1988 Los Angeles Dodgers (NL)
1989 Oakland Athletics (AL)
1990 Cincinnati (NL)
1991 Minnesota Twins (AL)
1992 Toronto Blue Jays (AL)
1993 Toronto Blue Jays (AL)
1994 *not held*
1995 Atlanta Braves (NL)
1996 New York Yankees (AL)
1997 Florida Marlins (NL)
1998 New York Yankees (AL)
Most wins: (24), New York Yankees (AL), 1923, 1927–8, 1932, 1936–9, 1941, 1943, 1947, 1949–53, 1956, 1958, 1961–2, 1977–8, 1996, 1998.

World amateur championship

Instituted in 1938; since 1974 held every two years.

Recent winners
1978 Cuba
1980 Cuba
1982 South Korea
1984 Cuba
1986 Cuba
1988 Cuba
1990 Cuba
1992 Cuba
1994 Cuba
1996 Cuba
1998 Cuba
Most wins: (24), Cuba, 1939–40, 1942–3, 1950, 1952–3, 1961, 1969–73, 1976–80, 1984–6, 1988, 1990–8.

BASKETBALL

World championship

First held 1950 for men, 1953 for women; usually takes place every four years.

Winners: men
1963 Brazil
1967 USSR
1970 Yugoslavia
1974 USSR
1978 Yugoslavia
1982 USSR
1986 USA
1990 Yugoslavia
1994 USA
1998 Yugoslavia
Most wins: (4), USSR and Yugoslavia, as above.

Winners: women
1967 USSR
1971 USSR
1975 USSR
1979 USA
1983 USSR
1987 USA
1991 USA
1994 Brazil
1998 USA
Most wins: (6), USSR 1998, USA 1959, 1964 and as above.

National Basketball Association championship

First held in 1947; the major competition in professional basketball in the USA, end-of-season NBA Play-off involving the champion teams from the Eastern Conference (EC) and Western Conference (WC).

Recent winners
1987 Los Angeles Lakers (WC)
1988 Los Angeles Lakers (WC)
1989 Detroit Pistons (EC)
1990 Detroit Pistons (EC)
1991 Chicago Bulls (EC)
1992 Chicago Bulls (EC)
1993 Chicago Bulls (EC)
1994 Houston Rockets (WC)
1995 Houston Rockets (WC)
1996 Chicago Bulls (EC)
1997 Chicago Bulls (ED)
1998 Chicago Bulls (EC)
Most wins: (16), Boston Celtics, 1957, 1959–66, 1968–9, 1974, 1976, 1981, 1984, 1986.

BIATHLON

World championship

First held in 1958; take place annually; the Olympic champion is the automatic world champion in Olympic years; women's championship first held in 1984.

20 km

1983 Frank Ullrich (East Germany)
1984 Peter Angerer (West Germany)
1985 Yuriy Kashkarov (USSR)
1986 Valeriy Medvetsev (USSR)
1987 Frank-Peter Rötsch (East Germany)
1988 Frank-Peter Rötsch (East Germany)
1989 Eric Kvalfoss (Norway)
1990 Valeriy Medvetsev (USSR)
1991 Mark Kirchner (Germany)
1992 Yevgeriy Redkine (CIS)
1993 Franz Zingerle (Austria)
1994 Sergei Tarasov (Russia)
1995 Tomaz Sikora (Poland)
1996 Sergei Tarasov (Russia)
1997 Ricco Gross (Germany)
1998 Halvard Hanevold (Norway)

Most individual titles: (6), Frank Ullrich (East Germany), as above plus 1978 10km.

Recent individual winners: women

10km (15km since 1988)

1984 Venera Chernyshova (USSR)
1985 Kaya Parva (USSR)
1986 Eva Korpela (Sweden)
1987 Sanna Gronlid (Norway)
1988 Anne-Elinor Elvebakk (Norway)
1989 Petra Schaaf (West Germany)
1990 Svetlana Davydova (USSR)
1991 Petra Schaaf (Germany)
1992 Antje Misersky (Germany)
1993 Petra Schaaf (Germany)
1994 Myriam Bedard (Canada)
1995 Corrine Miogret (France)
1996 Emmanuelle Claret (France)
1997 Magdalena Forsberg (Sweden)
1998 Ekaterina Dafovska (Bulgaria)

Most individual wins: (3) Anne-Elinor Elvebakk (Norway), and Petra Schaaf (West Germany) as above.

BILLIARDS

World professional championship

First held in 1870, organized on a challenge basis; became a knockout event in 1909; discontinued in 1934; revived in 1951 as a challenge system; reverted to a knockout event in 1980.

Recent winners

1989 Mike Russell (England)
1990 *not held*
1991 Mike Russell (England)
1992 Geet Sethi (India)
1993 Geet Sethi (India)
1994 Peter Gilchrist (England)
1995 Geet Sethi (India)
1996 Mike Russell (England)
1997 Mike Russell (England)
1998 Geet Sethi (India)
1999 Mike Russell (England)

Most wins: (knockout) (6), Tom Newman (England), 1921–2,1924–7, (challenge) (8), John Roberts, Jr (England), 1870–85.

BOBSLEIGHING AND TOBOGGANING

World championships

First held in 1930 (four-man) and in 1931 (two-man); Olympic champions automatically become world champions.

Recent winners: two-man

1989 Wolfgang Hoppe/Bogdan Musiol (East Germany)
1990 Gustav Weder/Bruno Gerber (Switzerland)
1991 Rudi Lochrer/Marcus Zimmermann (Germany)
1992 Gustav Weder/Donat Acklin (Switzerland)
1993 Christoph Langan/Peer Joechel (Germany)
1994 Gustav Weder/Donat Acklin (Switzerland)
1995 Cristoph Langen/Olaf Hampel (Germany)
1996 Cristoph Langen/Markus Zimmermann (Germany)
1997 Reto Goetschi/Guido Acklin (Switzerland)
1998[a] Pierre Lueders/David MacEachern (Canada) Günther Huber/Antonio Tartaglia (Italy)
1999 Günther Huber/Ubaldo Ranzi (Italy)

[a] shared medal

Recent winners: four-man

1988 Switzerland
1989 Switzerland
1990 Switzerland
1991 Germany
1992 Austria
1993 Switzerland
1994 Switzerland
1995 Germany
1996 Germany
1997 Germany
1998 Germany
1999 France

Most wins: Two-man (8), Eugenio Monti (Italy) 1957–61, 1963, 1966, 1968. Four-man (15), Switzerland, 1939, 1947, 1954–5, 1957, 1971, 1973, 1975, 1982–3, 1986–9, 1994.

Luge world championships

First held in 1955; annually until 1981, then every two years; Olympic champions automatically become world champions.

Recent winners: men's single-seater

1985 Michael Walter (East Germany)
1987 Markus Prock (Austria)
1988 Jens Müller (East Germany)
1989 Georg Hackl (West Germany)
1990 Georg Hackl (West Germany)
1991 Arnold Huber (Italy)
1992 Georg Hackl (Germany)
1993 Wendel Suckow (USA)
1994 Georg Hackl (Germany)
1995 Armin Zoggeler (Italy)
1997 Georg Hackl (Germany)
1998 Georg Hackl (Germany)
1999 Armin Zoggeler (Italy)

Most wins: (6), Georg Hackl (West Germany and Germany), as above.

Recent winners: women's single-seater

1988 Steffi Walter (née Martin) (East Germany)
1989 Susi Erdmann (East Germany)
1990 Gabriele Kohlisch (East Germany)
1991 Susi Erdmann (Germany)
1992 Doris Neuner (Austria)
1993 Gerda Weissensteiner (Italy)
1994 Gerda Weissensteiner (Italy)
1995 Gabriele Kohlisch (Germany)
1997 Susi Urdmann (Germany)
1998 Silke Kraushaar (Germany)
1999 Sonja Wiedemann (Germany)

Most wins: (5), Margrit Schumann (East Germany), 1973–7.

BOWLS

World championships

Instituted for men in 1966 and for women in 1969; held every four years.

Men's singles

1972 Malwyn Evans (Wales)
1976 Doug Watson (South Africa)
1980 David Bryant (England)
1984 Peter Bellis (New Zealand)
1988 David Bryant (England)
1992 Tony Allcock (England)
1996 Tony Allcock (England)

Men's pairs

1972 Hong Kong
1976 South Africa
1980 Australia
1984 USA
1988 New Zealand
1992 Scotland
1996 Ireland

Men's triples

1972 USA
1976 South Africa
1980 England
1984 Ireland
1988 New Zealand
1992 Israel
1996 Scotland

Men's fours

1972 England
1976 South Africa
1980 Hong Kong
1984 England
1988 Ireland
1992 Scotland
1996 England

Leonard Trophy

Team award, given to the nation with the best overall performances in the men's World Championship.

Winners
1972 Scotland
1976 South Africa
1980 England
1984 Scotland
1988 England
1992 Scotland
1996 Scotland
Most wins: (6), David Bryant (singles 1966 and as above, plus Triples and Team 1980, 1988).

Women's singles
1973 Elsie Wilke (New Zealand)
1977 Elsie Wilke (New Zealand)
1981 Norma Shaw (England)
1985 Merle Richardson (Australia)
1988* Janet Ackland (Wales)
1992 Margaret Johnston (Ireland)
1996 Carmen Johnston (Norfolk Island)

Women's pairs
1973 Australia
1977 Hong Kong
1981 Ireland
1985 Australia
1988* Ireland
1992 Ireland
1996 Ireland

Women's triples
1973 New Zealand
1977 Wales
1981 Hong Kong
1985 Australia
1988* Australia
1992 Scotland
1996 South Africa

Women's fours
1973 New Zealand
1977 Australia
1981 England
1985 Australia
1988* England
1992 Scotland
1996 Australia

Women's team
1973 New Zealand
1977 Australia
1981 England
1985 Australia
1988* England
1992 Scotland
1996 South Africa
Most wins: (3), Merle Richardson (Fours 1977; Singles and Pairs 1985).
* The women's event was advanced to Dec 1988 (Australia).

World indoor championships

Men's competition first held in 1979; Women's in 1988; both held annually.

Men's singles
1989 Richard Corsie (Scotland)
1990 John Price (Wales)
1991 Richard Corsie (Scotland)
1992 Ian Shuback (Australia)
1993 Richard Corsie (Scotland)
1994 Richard Corsie (Scotland)
1995 Andrew Thompson (England)
1996 David Gourly Jr (Scotland)
1997 Hugh Duff (Scotland)
1998 Paul Foster (Scotland)
1999 Alex Marshall (Scotland)
Most wins: (3), David Bryant (England), 1979–81.

Women's singles
1992 Sarah Gourlay (Scotland)
1993 Kate Adams (Scotland)
1994 Jan Woodley (Scotland)
1995 Joyce Lindoores (Scotland)
1996 Sandy Hazell (England)
1997 Norma Shaw (England)
1998 Caroline McAllister (Scotland)

Waterloo Handicap

First held in 1907 and annually at Blackpool's Waterloo Hotel; the premier event of Crown Green Bowling. Women's event inaugurated in 1988.

Recent winners: men
1988 Ingham Gregory
1989 Brian Duncan
1990 John Bancroft
1991 John Eccles
1992 Brian Duncan
1993 Alan Broadhurst
1994 Bill Hilton
1995 Ken Strutt
1996 Lea Heaton
1997 Andrew Cairns
1998 Michael Jagger
Most wins: (5), Brian Duncan, 1979 and as above.

Winners: women
1993 Sheila Smith
1994 Veronica Lyons
1995 Joyce Foxcroft
1996 Lynn Pritchett
1997 Karen Johnson
1998 Lynn Pritchett

BOXING

World heavyweight champions

The first world heavyweight champion under Queensbury rules with gloves was James J Corbett in 1892.

Champions since 1985		*Recognizing body*
1985	Michael Spinks (USA)	IBF
1985	Tony Tubbs (USA)	WBA
1986	Tim Witherspoon (USA)	WBA
1986	Trevor Berbick (Canada)	WBC
1986	Mike Tyson (USA)	WBC
1986	James Smith (USA)	WBA
1987	Tony Tucker (USA)	IBF
1987	Mike Tyson (USA)	WBA/WBC
1987	Mike Tyson (USA)	UND
1989	Francesco Damiani (Italy)	WBO
1990	James (Buster) Douglas (USA)	WBA/WBC/IBF
1990	Evander Holyfield (USA)	WBA/WBC/IBF
1991	Ray Mercer (USA)	WBO
1992	Riddick Bowe (USA)	WBA/WBC/IBF
1992	Michael Mourer (USA)	WBO
1992	Lennox Lewis (Great Britain)	WBC
1994	Oliver McCall (UK)	WBC
1994	George Foreman (USA)	IBF/WBA
1995	Frank Bruno (UK)	WBC
1996	Mike Tyson (USA)	WBC
1996	Henry Akinwande (UK)	WBO
1996	Evander Holyfield (USA)	WBA
1996	Michael Moorer (USA)	IBF
1997	Lennox Lewis (UK)	WBC
1997	Herbie Hide (UK)	WBO
1997	Evander Holyfield (USA)	WBA/IBF
1998	Lennox Lewis (UK)	WBC

IBF = International Boxing Federation
WBA = World Boxing Association
WBC = World Boxing Council
WBO = World Boxing Organization
UND = Undisputed champion

CANOEING

Olympic Games

The most prestigious competition in the canoeing calendar, included at every Olympic celebration since 1936; the Blue Riband event in the men's competition is the Kayak Singles over 1000 m, and in the women's the Kayak Singles over 500 m.

Single kayak: men
1948 Gert Fredriksson (Sweden)
1952 Gert Fredriksson (Sweden)
1956 Gert Fredriksson (Sweden)
1960 Erik Hansen (Denmark)
1964 Rolf Peterson (Sweden)
1968 Mihaly Hesz (Hungary)
1972 Aleksandr Shaparenko (USSR)
1976 Rüdiger Helm (East Germany)
1980 Rüdiger Helm (East Germany)
1984 Alan Thompson (New Zealand)
1988 Greg Barton (USA)
1992 Clint Robinson (Australia)
1996 Oliver Fix (Germany)

Single kayak: women
1952 Sylvi Saimo (Finland)
1956 Elisaveta Dementyeva (USSR)
1960 Antonina Seredina (USSR)
1964 Lyudmila Khvedosyuk (USSR)
1968 Lyudmila Pinayeva (USSR)
1972 Yulia Ryabchinskaya (USSR)
1976 Carola Zirzow (East Germany)
1980 Birgit Fischer (East Germany)
1984 Agneta Andersson (Sweden)
1988 Vania Guecheva (USSR)
1992 Birgit Schmidt (Germany)
1996 Stepanka Hilgertova (Czech Republic)
Most wins: Men (3), Gert Fredriksson, as above. No woman has won more than one title.

CHESS

World champions

World champions have been recognized since 1888; first women's champion recognized in 1927. A split between the World Chess

Federation (FIDE) and the new Professional Chess Association (PCA) resulted in two championship matches in 1993.

Champions: men
1963–9 Tigran Petrosian (USSR)
1969–72 Boris Spassky (USSR)
1972–5 Bobby Fischer (USA)
1975–85 Anatoly Karpov (USSR)
1985– Gary Kasparov (USSR/Russia (PCA))
1993 Anatoly Karpov (Russia) (FIDE)

Longest reigning champion: 27 years, Emanuel Lasker (Germany) 1894–1921.

Champions: women
1950–3 Lyudmila Rudenko (USSR)
1953–6 Elizaveta Bykova (USSR)
1956–8 Olga Rubtsova (USSR)
1958–62 Elizaveta Bykova (USSR)
1962–78 Nona Gaprindashvili (USSR)
1978–92 Maya Chiburdanidze (USSR)
1992–5 Xie Jun (China)
1996 Zsusza Polgar (Hungary)
Longest reigning champion: 17 years, Vera Menchik-Stevenson (UK), 1927–44.

CONTRACT BRIDGE

World team championship

The game's biggest championship; men's contest (The Bermuda Bowl) first held in 1951, and now takes place every two years; women's contest (The Venice Cup) first held in 1974, and since 1985 is concurrent with the men's event.

Recent winners: men
1977 USA
1979 USA
1981 USA
1983 USA
1985 USA
1987 USA
1989 Brazil
1991 Iceland
1993 Netherlands
1995 USA
1997 France
Most wins: (13), Italy, 1957–9, 1961–3, 1965–7, 1969, 1973–5.

Recent winners: women
1976 USA
1978 USA
1981 UK
1983 *not held*
1985 UK
1987 Italy
1989 USA
1991 USA
1993 USA
1995 Germany
1997 USA
Most wins: (7), USA, 1974–8, 1989–93, 1997.

World Team Olympiad

First held in 1960; since then, every four years.

Winners: men
1964 Italy
1968 Italy
1972 Italy
1976 Brazil
1980 France
1984 Poland
1988 USA
1992 France
1996 France

Winners: women
1964 UK
1968 Sweden
1972 Italy
1976 USA
1980 USA
1984 USA
1988 Denmark
1992 Austria
1996 USA
Most wins: Men (4), France 1960, 1980, 1992, 1996.

CRICKET

World Cup

First played in England in 1975; held every four years; the 1987 competition was the first to be played outside England, in India and Pakistan.

Winners
1979 West Indies
1983 India
1987 Australia
1992 Pakistan
1996 Sri Lanka

County championship

The oldest cricket competition in the world; first won by Sussex in 1827; not officially recognized until 1890, when a proper points system was introduced.

Recent winners
1988 Worcestershire
1989 Worcestershire
1990 Middlesex
1991 Essex
1992 Essex
1993 Middlesex
1994 Warwickshire
1995 Warwickshire
1996 Leicestershire
1997 Glamorgan
1998 Leicestershire
Most outright wins: (29), Yorkshire, 1893, 1896, 1898, 1900–2, 1905, 1908, 1912, 1919, 1922–5, 1931–3, 1935, 1937–9, 1946, 1959–60, 1962–3, 1966–8.

AXA Equity and Law league

First held in 1969; known as the John Player League 1969–86; then as Refuge Assurance League until 1991.

Recent winners
1984 Essex
1985 Essex
1986 Hampshire
1987 Worcestershire
1988 Worcestershire
1989 Lancashire
1990 Derbyshire
1991 Nottinghamshire
1992 Middlesex
1993 Glamorgan
1994 Warwickshire
1995 Kent
1996 Surrey
1997 Warwickshire
1998 Lancashire
Most wins: (4), Kent, 1972–3, 1976, 1995; Lancashire 1969–70, 1989, 1998.

NatWest Bank trophy

First held in 1963; known as the Gillette Cup until 1981.

Recent winners
1988 Middlesex
1989 Warwickshire
1990 Lancashire
1991 Hampshire
1992 Northamptonshire
1993 Warwickshire
1994 Worcestershire
1995 Warwickshire
1996 Lancashire
1997 Essex
1998 Lancashire
Most wins: (7), Lancashire, 1970–2, 1975, 1990, 1996, 1998.

Benson and Hedges Cup

First held in 1972.

Recent winners
1988 Hampshire
1989 Nottinghamshire
1990 Lancashire
1991 Worcestershire
1992 Hampshire
1993 Derbyshire
1994 Warwickshire
1995 Lancashire
1996 Lancashire
1997 Surrey
1998 Essex
Most wins: (4), Lancashire 1984, 1990, 1995, 1996.

Sheffield Shield

Australia's leading domestic competition; contested inter-state since 1891.

Recent winners
1987 Western Australia
1988 Western Australia
1989 Western Australia
1990 Western Australia
1991 Victoria
1992 Western Australia
1993 New South Wales
1994 New South Wales
1995 Queensland
1996 South Australia
1997 Queensland
1998 Western Australia
Most wins: (41), New South Wales, 1896–7, 1900, 1902–7, 1909, 1911–12, 1914, 1920–1, 1923, 1926, 1929, 1932–3, 1938, 1940, 1949–50, 1952, 1954–62, 1965–6, 1983, 1985–6, 1990, 1992, 1994.

CROQUET

McRobertson Shield

Croquet's leading tournament; held spasmodically since 1925; contested by teams from Great Britain, New Zealand and Australia.

Winners
1928 Australia
1930 Australia
1935 Australia
1937 Great Britain
1950 New Zealand
1956 Great Britain
1963 Great Britain
1969 Great Britain
1974 Great Britain
1979 New Zealand
1982 Great Britain
1986 New Zealand
1990 Great Britain
1993 Great Britain
1996 Great Britain
Most wins: (10), Great Britain, 1925 and as above.

CROSS-COUNTRY RUNNING

World championships

First international championship held in 1903, but only included runners from England, Ireland, Scotland and Wales; recognized as an official world championship from 1973; first women's race in 1967.

Recent individual winners: men
1988 John Ngugi (Kenya)
1989 John Ngugi (Kenya)
1990 Khalid Skah (Morocco)
1991 Khalid Skah (Morocco)
1992 John Ngugi (Kenya)
1993 William Sigei (Kenya)
1994 William Sigei (Kenya)
1995 Paul Tergat (Kenya)
1996 Paul Tergat (Kenya)
1997 Paul Tergat (Kenya)
1998 Paul Tergat (Kenya)
1999 Paul Tergat (Kenya)

Recent team winners: men
1989 Kenya
1990 Kenya
1991 Kenya
1992 Kenya
1993 Kenya
1994 Kenya
1995 Kenya
1996 Kenya
1997 Kenya
1998 Kenya
1999 Kenya
Most wins: Individual (5), John Ngugi (Kenya), 1986–7 and as above; Paul Tergat (Kenya) as above. Team (44), England, between 1903 and 1980.

Recent individual winners: women
1988 Ingrid Kristiansen (Norway)
1989 Annette Sergent (France)
1990 Lynn Jennings (USA)
1991 Lynn Jennings (USA)
1992 Lynn Jennings (USA)
1993 Albertina Dïas (Portugal)
1994 Helen Chepngeno (Kenya)
1995 Derartu Tulu (Ethiopia)
1996 Gete Wami (Ethiopia)
1997 Derartu Tulu (Ethiopia)
1998 Sonia O'Sullivan (Ireland)
1999 Gete Wami (Ethiopia)

Recent team winners: women
1990 USSR
1991 Ethiopia and Kenya (tied)
1992 Kenya
1993 Kenya
1994 Portugal
1995 Kenya
1996 Kenya
1997 Ethiopia
1998 Kenya
1999 France
Most wins: Individual (5), Doris Brown (USA), 1967–71; Greta Waitz (Norway), 1978–81, 1983. Team (8), USA, 1968–9, 1975, 1979, 1983–5, 1987.

CURLING

World championships

First men's championship held in 1959; first women's championship in 1979; takes place annually.

Recent winners: men
1988 Norway
1989 Canada
1990 Canada
1991 Scotland
1992 Switzerland
1993 Canada
1994 Canada
1995 Canada
1996 Canada
1997 Sweden
1998 Canada
1999 Scotland

Recent winners: women
1988 West Germany
1989 Canada
1990 Norway
1991 Norway
1992 Sweden
1993 Canada
1994 Canada
1995 Canada
1996 Canada
1997 Canada
1998 Sweden
1999 Sweden
Most wins: Men (24), Canada, 1959–64, 1966, 1968–72, 1980, 1982, 1983, 1984–7 and as above. Women (10), Canada, 1980, 1984–7 and as above.

CYCLING

Tour de France

World's premier cycling event; first held in 1903.

Recent winners
1988 Pedro Delgado (Spain)
1989 Greg LeMond (USA)
1990 Greg LeMond (USA)
1991 Miguel Indurain (Spain)
1992 Miguel Indurain (Spain)
1993 Miguel Indurain (Spain)
1994 Miguel Indurain (Spain)
1995 Miguel Indurain (Spain)
1996 Bjarne Riis (Denmark)
1997 Jan Ullrich (Germany)
1998 Marco Pantani (Italy)
Most wins: (5), Jacques Anquetil (France), 1957, 1961–4; Eddy Merckx (Belgium), 1969–72, 1974; Bernard Hinault (France), 1978–9, 1981–2, 1985; Miguel Indurain (Spain), as above.

World road race championships

Men's race first held in 1927; first women's race in 1958; takes place annually.

Recent winners: professional men
1988 Maurizio Fondriest (Italy)
1989 Greg LeMond (USA)
1990 Rudy Dhaemens (Belgium)
1991 Gianni Bugno (Italy)
1992 Gianni Bugno (Italy)
1993 Lance Armstrong (USA)
1994 Luc Le Blanc (France)
1995 Abraham Olano (Spain)
1996 Johan Museeuw (Belgium)
1997 Laurent Brochard (France)
1998 Oscar Camenzind (Switzerland)

Recent winners: women
1984 *not held*
1988 Jeannie Longo (France)
1989 Jeannie Longo (France)
1990 Catherine Marsal (France)
1991 Leontien van Moorsel (Netherlands)
1992 Leontien van Moorsel (Netherlands)
1993 Leontien van Moorsel (Netherlands)
1994 Monica Valvik (Norway)
1995 Jeannie Longo (France)
1996 Jeannie Longo (France)
1997 Alessandra Cappelloto (Italy)
1998 Diana Ziliute (Lithuania)
Most wins: Men (3), Alfredo Binda (Italy), 1927, 1930, 1932; Rik Van Steenbergen (Belgium), 1949, 1956–7; Eddy Merckx (Belgium), 1967, 1971, 1974; Gianno Bugno (Italy), as above. Women (5), Jeannie Longo (France), 1985–7 and as above.

CYCLO-CROSS

World championships

First held in 1950 as an open event; separate professional and amateur events since 1967; both events combined from 1994 to form the open; since 1995 called the Elite.

Recent winners: professional
1987 Klaus-Peter Thaler (West Germany)
1988 Pascal Richard (Switzerland)
1989 Danny De Bie (Belgium)
1990 Henk Baars (Netherlands)
1991 Radomir Simunek (Czechoslovakia)
1992 Mike Kluge (Germany)
1993 Dominique Arnaud (France)

Recent winners: amateur
1987 Mike Kluge (West Germany)
1988 Karol Camrola (Czechoslovakia)
1989 Ondrej Glaja (Czechoslovakia)
1990 Andreas Buesser (Switzerland)
1991 Thomas Frischknecht (Switzerland)
1992 Daniele Pontoni (Italy)
1993 Henrik Djernis (Denmark)

Recent winners:open elite
1994 Paul Hrijes (Belgium)
1995 Dieter Runkel (Switzerland)
1996 Adri van de Poel (Netherlands)
1997 Daniele Pontoni (Italy)
1998 Mario De Clercq (Belgium)
1999 Mario De Clercq (Belgium)
Most wins: Professional (7), Eric de Vlaeminck (Belgium), 1966, 1968–73. Amateur (5), Robert Vermiere (Belgium), 1970–1, 1974–5, 1977.

DARTS

World professional championship

First held at Nottingham in 1978; known as the Embassy World Championships.

Recent winners
1987 John Lowe (England)
1988 Bob Anderson (England)
1989 Jocky Wilson (Scotland)
1990 Phil Taylor (England)
1991 Dennis Priestley (England)
1992 Phil Taylor (England)
1993 John Lowe (England)
1994 John Part (Canada)
1995 Richie Burnett (Wales)
1996 Steve Beaton (England)
1997 Les Wallace (Scotland)
1998 Raymond Barneveld (Netherlands)
1999 Raymond Barneveld (Netherlands)
Most wins: (5), Eric Bristow, 1980–1, 1984–6.

World Cup

A team competition first held at Wembley in 1977; takes place every two years.

Recent team winners
1987 England
1989 England
1991 England
1993 England
1995 England
1997 Wales

Recent individual winners
1987 Eric Bristow (England)
1989 Eric Bristow (England)
1991 John Lowe (England)
1993 Roland Schollen (Denmark)
1995 Martin Addams (England)
1997 Raymond Barneveld (Netherlands)
Most wins: Team (9), England 1979, 1981–95. Individual (4), Eric Bristow (England) 1983–9.

DRAUGHTS

World championship

Held on a challenge basis.

Winners
1979–90 M Tinsley (USA)
1990–4 D Oldbury (Great Britain)
1994– R King (Barbados)

British Open championship

The leading championship in Britain; first held in 1926; now takes place every two years.

Recent winners
1976 A Huggins (Great Britain)
1978 J McGill (Great Britain)
1980 T Watson (Great Britain)
1982 T Watson (Great Britain)
1984 A Long (USA)
1986 H Devlin (Great Britain)
1988 D E Oldbury (Great Britain)
1990 T Watson (Great Britain)
1992 H Devlin (Great Britain)
1994 W J Edwards (Great Britain)
1996 W J Edwards (Great Britain)

EQUESTRIAN EVENTS

World championships

Show jumping championships first held in 1953 (for men) and 1965 (for women); since 1978 they have competed together and on equal terms; team competition introduced in 1978. Three Day Event and Dressage championships introduced in 1966; all three now held every four years.

Show jumping winners: men
1953 Francisco Goyoago (Spain)
1954 Hans-Günter Winkler (West Germany)
1955 Hans-Günter Winkler (West Germany)
1956 Raimondo D'Inzeo (Italy)
1960 Raimondo D'Inzeo (Italy)
1966 Pierre d'Oriola (France)
1970 David Broome (Great Britain)
1974 Hartwig Steenken (West Germany)

Show jumping winners: women
1965 Marion Coakes (Great Britain)
1970 Janou Lefèbvre (France)
1974 Janou Tissot (née Lefèbvre) (France)

Show jumping winners: individual
1986 Gail Greenough (Canada)
1990 Eric Navet (France)
1994 Franke Slloothaak (Germany)
1998 Rodrigo Pessoa (Brazil)

Show jumping winners: team
1990 France
1994 Germany
1998 Germany

Three-day event winners: individual
1978 Bruce Davidson (USA)
1982 Lucinda Green (Great Britain)
1986 Virginia Leng (Great Britain)
1990 Blyth Tait (New Zealand)
1994 Vaugh Jefferis (New Zealand)
1998 Blyth Tait (New Zealand)

Three-day event winners: team
1978 Canada
1982 Great Britain
1986 Great Britain
1990 New Zealand
1994 Great Britain
1998 New Zealand

Dressage winners: individual
1978 Christine Stückelberger (Switzerland)
1982 Reiner Klimke (West Germany)
1986 Anne Grethe Jensen (Denmark)
1990 Nicole Uphoft (West Germany)
1994 Isabelle Werth (Germany)
1998 Isabelle Werth (Germany)

Dressage winners: team
1978 West Germany
1982 West Germany
1986 West Germany
1990 West Germany
1994 Germany
1998 Germany

FENCING

World championships

Held annually since 1921 (between 1921–35, known as European Championships); not held in Olympic years.

Foil: men – individual

Recent winners
1989 Alexander Koch (West Germany)
1990 Philippe Omnès (France)
1991 Ingo Weissenborn (Germany)
1993 Alexander Koch (Germany)
1994 Rolando Tucker (Cuba)
1995 Dimitriy Chevtchenko (Russia)
1997 Sergey Golubitsky (Ukraine)
1998 Sergey Golubitsky (Ukraine)

Foil: men – team

Recent winners
1989 USSR
1990 Italy
1991 Cuba
1993 Germany
1994 Italy
1995 Cuba
1997 France
1998 Poland
Most wins: Individual (5), Alexander Romankov (USSR), 1974, 1977, 1982–3. Team (15), USSR (between 1959–89).

Foil: women – individual

Recent winners
1989 Olga Velitchko (USSR)
1990 Anja Fichtel (West Germany)
1991 Giovanna Trillini (Italy)
1993 Francesca Bortolozzi (Italy)
1994 Reka Szabo-Lazar (Romania)
1995 Laura Badea (Romania)
1997 Giovanna Trillini (Italy)
1998 Sabine Bau (Germany)

Foil: women – team

Recent winners
1989 West Germany
1990 Italy
1991 Italy
1993 Germany
1994 Romania
1995 Italy
1997 Italy
1998 Italy
Most wins: Individual (3), Helène Mayer (Germany), 1929, 1931, 1937; Ilona Elek (Hungary), 1934–5, 1951; Ellen Müller-Preiss (Austria), 1947, 1949, 1950 (*shared*); Cornelia Hanisch, 1979–81, and as above. Team (15), USSR (between 1956–86).

Epée: men – individual
Recent winners
1989 Manuel Pereira (Spain)
1990 Thomas Gerull (West Germany)
1991 Andrey Shuvalov (USSR)
1993 Pavel Kolobkov (Russia)
1994 Pavel Kolobkov (Russia)
1995 Eric Srecki (France)
1997 Eric Srecki (France)
1998 Hugues Obry (France)

Epée: men – team
Recent winners
1989 Italy
1990 Italy
1991 USSR
1993 Italy
1994 Germany
1995 Germany
1997 Cuba
1998 Hungary
Most wins: Individual (3), Georges Buchard (France), 1927, 1931, 1933; Alexei Nikanchikov (USSR), 1966–7, 1970. Team (12), Italy (between 1931–58, and as above).

Epée: women – individual
Recent winners
1993 Oksana Emakova (Estonia)
1994 Laura Chiesa (Italy)
1995 Joanna Jakimiuk (Poland)
1997 Miraide Garcia-Soto (Cuba)
1998 Laura Flessel (France)

Epée: women – team
Recent winners
1994 Spain
1995 Hungary
1997 Hungary
1998 France

Sabre: men – individual
Recent winners
1989 Grigory Kirienko (USSR)
1990 György Nébald (Hungary)
1991 Grigory Kirienko (USSR)
1993 Grigory Kirienko (Russia)
1994 Felix Becker (Germany)
1995 Grigoriy Kirienko (Russia)
1997 Stanislav Pozdnyakov (Russia)
1998 Luigi Tarantino (Italy)

Sabre: men – team
Recent winners
1989 USSR
1990 USSR
1991 Hungary
1993 Hungary
1994 Russia
1995 Italy
1997 France
1998 Hungary
Most wins: Individual (4), Grigoriy Kirienko (Russia), 1989, 1991, 1993, 1995. Team (18), Hungary (between 1930–74, and as above).

GAELIC FOOTBALL

All-Ireland Championship

First held 1887; takes place in Dublin on the third Sunday in September each year.

Recent winners
1987 Meath
1988 Meath
1989 Cork
1990 Cork
1991 Down
1992 Donegal
1994 County Derry
1995 Dublin
1996 Meath
1997 Kerry
1998 Galway
Most wins: (31), Kerry, 1903–4, 1909, 1913–14, 1924, 1926, 1929–32, 1937, 1939–41, 1946, 1953, 1955, 1959, 1962, 1969–70, 1975, 1978–81, 1984–6, 1997.

GLIDING

World championships

First held in 1937; current classes are Open, Standard and 15 metres; the Open class is the principal event, held every two years until 1978 and again since 1981.

Recent winners
1978 George Lee (Great Britain)
1981 George Lee (Great Britain)
1983 Ingo Renner (Australia)
1985 Ingo Renner (Australia)
1987 Ingo Renner (Australia)
1989 Robin May (Great Britain)
1991 Janusz Centka (Poland)
1993 Andy Davis (Great Britain)
1995 Raymond Lynskey (New Zealand)
1997 Gerard Lherm (France)
Most wins: (3), George Lee, 1976, 1978, 1981; Ingo Renner, as above.

GOLF

Open

First held at Prestwick in 1860, and won by Willie Park; takes place annually; regarded as the world's leading golf tournament.

Recent winners
1988 Severiano Ballesteros (Spain)
1989 Mark Calcavecchia (USA)
1990 Nick Faldo (Great Britain)
1991 Ian Baker-Finch (Australia)
1992 Nick Faldo (Great Britain)
1993 Greg Norman (Australia)
1994 Nick Price (Zimbabwe)
1995 John Daley (USA)
1996 Tom Lehman (USA)
1997 Justin Leonard (USA)
1998 Mark O'Meara (USA)
Most wins: (6), Harry Vardon (Great Britain), 1896, 1898–9, 1903, 1911, 1914.

United States Open

First held at Newport, Rhode Island in 1895, and won by Horace Rawlins; takes place annually.

Recent winners
1987 Scott Simpson (USA)
1988 Curtis Strange (USA)
1989 Curtis Strange (USA)
1990 Hale Irwin (USA)
1991 Payne Stewart (USA)
1992 Tom Kite (USA)
1993 Lee Janzen (USA)
1994 Ernie Els (South Africa)
1995 Cory Pavin (USA)
1996 Steve Jones (USA)
1997 Ernie Els (South Africa)
1998 Lee Janzen (USA)
Most wins: (4), Willie Anderson (USA), 1901, 1903–5; Bobby Jones (USA), 1923, 1926, 1929–30; Ben Hogan (USA), 1948, 1950–1, 1953; Jack Nicklaus (USA), 1962, 1967, 1972, 1980.

US Masters

First held in 1934; takes place at the Augusta National course in Georgia every April.

Recent winners
1989 Nick Faldo (Great Britain)
1990 Nick Faldo (Great Britain)
1991 Ian Woosnam (Great Britain)
1992 Fred Couples (USA)
1993 Bernhard Langer (Germany)
1994 José María Olázabal (Spain)
1995 Ben Crenshaw
1996 Nick Faldo (Great Britain)
1997 Tiger Woods (USA)
1998 Mark O'Meara (USA)
1999 José María Olázabal (Spain)
Most wins: (6), Jack Nicklaus (USA), 1963, 1965–6, 1972, 1975, 1986.

United States PGA championship

The last of the season's four 'Majors'; first held in 1916, and a match-play event until 1958; takes place annually.

Recent winners
1988 Jeff Sluman (USA)
1989 Payne Stewart (USA)
1990 Wayne Grady (Australia)
1991 John Daly (USA)
1992 Nick Price (Zimbabwe)
1993 Paul Azinger (USA)
1994 Nick Price (Zimbabwe)
1995 Steve Elkington (Australia)
1996 Mark Brooks (USA)
1997 Davis Love III (USA)
1998 Vijay Singh (Fiji)
Most wins: (5), Walter Hagen (USA), 1921,

1924–7; Jack Nicklaus (USA), 1963, 1971, 1973, 1975, 1980.

Ryder Cup

The leading international team tournament; first held at Worcester, Massachusetts, in 1927; takes place every two years between teams from the USA and Europe (Great Britain 1927–71; Great Britain and Ireland 1973–7).

Recent winners

1977 USA 12½–7½
1979 USA 17–11
1981 USA 18½–9½
1983 USA 14½–13½
1985 Europe 16½–11½
1987 Europe 15–13
1989 Drawn 14–14
1991 USA 15–13
1993 USA 15–13
1995 Europe 14½–13½
1997 Europe 14½–13½

Wins: (22), USA between 1927 and 1991. (3), Great Britain, 1929, 1933, 1957. (4), Europe, 1985, 1987, 1995, 1997. (2), Drawn, 1969, 1989.

GREYHOUND RACING

Greyhound Derby

The top race of the British season, first held in 1927; run at the White City every year (except 1940) until its closure in 1985; since then all races run at Wimbledon.

Recent winners

1987 Signal Spark
1988 Hit the Lid
1989 Lartigue Note
1990 Slippy Blue
1991 Ballinderry Ash
1992 Farloe Melody
1993 Arfur Daley
1994 Ringa Hustle
1995 Moaning Lad
1996 Shanless Slippy
1997 Some Picture
1998 Toms The Best

Most wins: (2), Mick the Miller, 1929–30; Patricia's Hope, 1972–3.

GYMNASTICS

World championships

First held in 1903; took place every four years, 1922–78; since 1979, every two years.

Recent individual winners: men

1985 Yuri Korolev (USSR)
1987 Dmitri Belozerchev (USSR)
1989 Igor Korobichensky (USSR)
1991 Grigoriy Misutin (USSR)
1993 Vitaly Scherbo (Belarus)
1994 Ivan Ivankov (Belarus)
1995 Li Xiaoshuang (China)
1997 Ivan Ivankov (Belarus)

Recent team winners: men

1981 USSR
1983 China
1985 USSR
1987 USSR
1989 USSR
1991 USSR
1994 China
1995 China
1997 China

Most wins: Individual (2), Marco Torrès (France), 1909, 1913; Peter Sumi (Yugoslavia), 1922, 1926; Yuri Korolev (USSR), 1981, 1985; Dmitri Belozerchev (USSR) 1983, 1987; Ivan Ivankov (Belarus), as above. Team (8), USSR, as above, plus 1954, 1958.

Recent individual winners: women

1981 Olga Bitcherova (USSR)
1983 Natalia Yurchenko (USSR)
1985 Yelena Shoushounova (USSR) and Oksana Omeliantchuk (USSR)
1987 Aurelia Dobre (Romania)
1989 Svetlana Boginskaya (USSR)
1991 Kim Zmeskal (USA)
1993 Shannon Miller (USA)
1994 Shannon Miller (USA)
1995 Lilia Podkopayeva (Ukraine)
1997 Svetlana Khorkina (Russia)

Recent team winners: women

1985 USSR
1987 Romania
1989 USSR
1991 USSR
1994 Romania
1995 Romania
1997 Romania

Most wins: Individual (2), Vlasta Dekanová (Czechoslovakia), 1934, 1938; Larissa Latynina (USSR), 1958, 1962; Vera Caslavska, 1962, 1966; Ludmila Tourischeva, 1970, 1974; Shannon Miller (USA) 1993, 1994. Team (10), USSR, 1954, 1958, 1974, 1978, 1981 and as above.

HANDBALL

World championships

First men's championships held in 1938, both indoors and outdoors (latter discontinued in 1966); first women's outdoor championships in 1949, (discontinued in 1960); first women's indoor championships in 1957.

Winners: indoors – men

1958 Sweden
1961 Romania
1964 Romania
1967 Czechoslovakia
1970 Romania
1974 Romania
1978 West Germany
1982 USSR
1986 Yugoslavia
1990 Sweden
1993 Russia
1995 France
1997 Russia

Most wins: (4), Romania, as above.

Winners: indoors – women

1965 Hungary
1971 East Germany
1973 Yugoslavia
1975 East Germany
1979 East Germany
1982 USSR
1986 USSR
1990 USSR
1993 Germany
1995 Germany
1997 Denmark

Most wins: (3), E Germany and USSR, as above.

HANG GLIDING

World championships

First held officially in 1976; since 1979, take place every two years.

Individual winners: class 1

1981 Pepe Lopez (Brazil)
1983 Steve Moyes (Australia)
1985 John Pendry (Great Britain)
1987 Rich Duncan (Australia)
1989 Robert Whittall (Great Britain)
1991 Tomás Suchanek (Czechoslovakia)
1993 Tomás Suchanek (Czech Republic)
1995 Tomás Suchanek (Czech Republic)
1997 Guido Gehrmann (Germany)
1998 Guido Gehrmann (Germany)

Team winners

1985 Great Britain
1987 Australia
1989 Great Britain
1991 Great Britain
1993 USA
1995 Austria
1997 Austria
1998 Austria

Most wins: Individual, Tomás Suchanek (Czech Republic), as above. Team (4), Great Britain, 1981 and as above; Austria, as above

HOCKEY

World Cup

Men's tournament first held in 1971, and every four years since 1978; women's tournament first held in 1974, and now takes place every three years.

Recent winners: men

1978 Pakistan
1982 Pakistan
1986 Australia
1990 Netherlands
1994 Pakistan
1998 Netherlands

Most wins: (4), Pakistan, as above, plus 1971.

Recent winners: women

1978 Netherlands
1981 West Germany
1983 Netherlands
1986 Netherlands
1990 Netherlands
1994 Australia
1998 Australia

Most wins: (6), Netherlands, 1974 and as above.

Olympic Games

Regarded as hockey's leading competition; first held in 1908; included at every celebration since 1928; women's competition first held in 1980.

Post-war winners: men
1952 India
1956 India
1960 Pakistan
1964 India
1968 Pakistan
1972 W Germany
1976 New Zealand
1980 India
1984 Pakistan
1988 Great Britain
1992 Germany
1996 Netherlands

Winners: women
1984 Netherlands
1988 Australia
1992 Spain
1996 Australia

Most wins: Men (8), India, 1928, 1932, 1936, 1948 and as above. Women (2) Australia 1988, 1996.

HORSE RACING

The Derby

The 'Blue Riband' of the Turf; run at Epsom over 1.5 miles; first run in 1780.

Recent winners
Horse (Jockey)
1987 Reference Point (Steve Cauthen)
1988 Kahyasi (Ray Cochrane)
1989 Nashwan (Willie Carson)
1990 Quest for Fame (Pat Eddery)
1991 Generous (Alan Munro)
1992 Dr Devious (John Reid)
1993 Commander-In-Chief (Michael Kinane)
1994 Erhaab (Willie Carson)
1995 Lammtarra (Walter Swinburn)
1996 Shaamit (Michael Hills)
1997 Benny The Dip (Willie Ryan)
1998 High Rise (Olivier Peslier)

Most wins: Jockey (9), Lester Piggott, 1954, 1957, 1960, 1968, 1970, 1972, 1976–7, 1983.

The Oaks

Raced at Epsom over 1.5 miles; for fillies only; first run in 1779.

Recent winners
Horse (Jockey)

1987 Unite (Walter Swinburn)
1988 Diminuendo (Steve Cauthen)
1989 Aliysa (Walter Swinburn)
1990 Salsabil (Willie Carson)
1991 Jet Ski Lady (Christy Roche)
1992 User Friendly (George Duffield)
1993 Intrepidity (Michael Roberts)
1994 Balanchine (Lanfranco Dettori)
1995 Moonshell (Lanfranco Dettori)
1996 Lady Carla (Pat Eddery)
1997 Reams of Verse (Kieren Fallon)
1998 Shahtoush (Michael Kinane)

Most wins: Jockey (9), Frank Buckle, 1797–9, 1802–3, 1805, 1817–18, 1823.

One Thousand Guineas

Run over 1 mile at Newmarket; for fillies only; first run in 1814.

Recent winners
Horse (Jockey)
1988 Ravinella (Gary Moore)
1989 Musical Bliss (Walter Swinburn)
1990 Salsabil (Willie Carson)
1991 Shadayid (Willie Carson)
1992 Hatoof (Walter Swinburn)
1993 Sayyedati (Walter Swinburn)
1994 Las Meninas (John Reid)
1995 Harayir (Richard Hills)
1996 Bosra Sham (Pat Eddery)
1997 Sleepytime (Kieren Fallon)
1998 Cape Verde (Lanfranco Dettori)
1999 Wince (Kieren Fallon)

Most wins: Jockey (7), George Fordham, 1859, 1861, 1865, 1868–9, 1881, 1883.

Two Thousand Guineas

Run at Newmarket over 1 mile; first run in 1809.

Recent winners
Horse (Jockey)
1988 Doyoun (Walter Swinburn)
1989 Nashwan (Willie Carson)
1990 Tiroi (Michael Kinane)
1991 Mystiko (Michael Roberts)
1992 Rodrigo de Triano (Lester Piggott)
1993 Zafonic (Pat Eddery)
1994 Mister Baileys (Jason Weaver)
1995 Pennekamp (Thierry Jarnet)
1996 Mark of Esteem (Lanfranco Dettori)
1997 Entrepreneur (Michael Kinane)
1998 King of Kings (Michael Kinane)
1999 Island Sands (Frankie Dettori)

Most wins: Jockey (9), Jem Robinson, 1825, 1828, 1831, 1833–6, 1847–8.

St Leger

The oldest of the five English classics; first run in 1776; raced at Doncaster annually over 1 mile 6 furlongs 127 yards.

Recent winners
Horse (Jockey)
1988 Minster Son (Willie Carson)
1989 Michelozzo (Steve Cauthen)
1990 Snurge (Richard Quinn)
1991 Toulon (Pat Eddery)
1992 User Friendly (George Duffield)
1993 Bob's Return (Philip Robinson)
1994 Moonax (Pat Eddery)
1995 Classic Cliche (Lanfranco Dettori)
1996 Shantou (Lanfranco Dettori)
1997 Silver Patriarch (Pat Eddery)
1998 Nedawi (John Reid)

Most wins: Jockey (9), Bill Scott, 1821, 1825, 1828–9, 1831, 1846.

Grand National

Steeplechasing's most famous race; first run at Maghull in 1836; at Aintree since 1839, wartime races at Gatwick 1916–18.

Recent winners
Horse (Jockey)
1988 Rhyme 'N' Reason (Brendan Powell)
1989 Little Polveir (Jimmy Frost)
1990 Mr Frisk (Marcus Armytage)
1991 Seagram (Nigel Hawke)
1992 Party Politics (Carl Llewellyn)
1993 *Race void due to false starts*
1994 Minnehoma (Richard Dunwoody)
1995 Royal Athlete (Jason Titley)
1996 Rough Quest (Mick Fitzgerald)
1997 Lord Gyllene (Tony Dobbin)
1998 Earth Summit (Carl Llewellyn)
1999 Bobbyjo (Paul Carberry)

Most wins: Jockey (5), George Stevens, 1856, 1863–4, 1869–70. Horse (3), Red Rum 1973–4, 1977.

Prix de l'Arc de Triomphe

The leading end of season race in Europe; raced over 2400 metres at Longchamp; first run in 1920.

Recent winners
Horse (Jockey)
1988 Tony Bin (John Reid)
1989 Caroll House (Michael Kinane)
1990 Saumarez (Gerald Mosse)
1991 Suave Dancer (Cash Asmussen)
1992 Subotica (Thierry Jarnet)
1993 Urban Sea (Eric Saint-Martin)
1994 Carnegie (Sylvan Guillot)
1995 Lammtarra (Lanfranco Dettori)
1996 Helissio (Olivier Peslier)
1997 Peintre Celebre (Olivier Peslier)
1998 Sagamix (Oliver Peslier)

Most wins: Jockey (4), Jacko Doyasbere, 1942, 1944, 1950–1; Freddy Head, 1966, 1972, 1976 1979; Yves Saint-Martin, 1970, 1974 1982, 1984; Pat Eddery. Horse (2), Ksar, 1921–2; Motrico, 1930, 1932; Corrida, 1936–7; Tantième, 1950–1; Ribot, 1955–6; Alleged 1977–8.

HURLING

All-Ireland championship

First contested in 1887; played on the first Sunday in September each year.

Recent winners
1988 Galway
1989 Tipperary
1990 Cork
1991 Tipperary
1992 Limerick
1993 Kilkenny
1994 Offaly
1995 Clare
1996 Wexford
1997 Clare
1998 Offaly

Most wins: (27), Cork, 1890, 1892–4, 1902–3, 1919, 1926, 1928–9, 1931, 1941–4, 1946, 1952–4, 1966, 1970, 1976–8, 1984, 1986, 1990.

ICE HOCKEY

World championship

First held in 1930; takes place annually (except 1980); up to 1968 Olympic champions also regarded as world champions.

Recent winners
1988 USSR
1989 USSR
1990 USSR
1991 Sweden
1992 Sweden
1993 Russia
1994 Canada
1995 Finland
1996 Czech Republic
1997 Canada
1998 Sweden
1999 Czech Republic
Most wins: (24), USSR, 1954, 1956, 1963–71, 1973–5, 1978–9, 1982–4, 1986 and as above.

Stanley Cup

The most sought-after trophy at club level; the end-of-season meeting between the winners of the two conferences in the National Hockey League in the USA and Canada.

Recent winners
1987 Edmonton Oilers
1988 Edmonton Oilers
1989 Calgary Flames
1990 Edmonton Oilers
1991 Pittsburgh Penguins
1992 Pittsburgh Penguins
1993 Montreal Canadiens
1994 New York Rangers
1995 New Jersey Devils
1996 Colorado Avalanche
1997 Detroit Red Wings
1998 Detroit Red Wings
Most wins: (24), Montreal Canadiens, 1916, 1924, 1930–1, 1944, 1946, 1953, 1956–60, 1965–6, 1968–9, 1971, 1973, 1976–9, 1986, 1993.

ICE SKATING

World championships

First men's championships in 1896; first women's event in 1906; pairs first contested in 1908; ice dance officially recognized in 1952.

Recent winners: men
1988 Brian Boitano (USA)
1989 Kurt Browning (Canada)
1990 Kurt Browning (Canada)
1991 Kurt Browning (Canada)
1992 Viktor Petrenko (Unified Team)
1993 Kurt Browning (Canada)
1994 Aleksei Urmanov (Russia)
1995 Elvis Stojko (Canada)
1996 Todd Eldredge (USA)
1997 Elvis Stojko (Canada)
1998 Alexei Yagudin (Russia)
1999 Alexei Yagudin (Russia)
Most wins: (10), Ulrich Salchow (Sweden), 1901–5, 1907–11.

Recent winners: women
1988 Katarina Witt (East Germany)
1989 Midori Ito (Japan)
1990 Jill Trenary (USA)
1991 Kristi Yamaguchi (USA)
1992 Kristi Yamaguchi (USA)
1993 Oksana Baiul (Ukraine)
1994 Oksana Baiul (Ukraine)
1995 Lu Chen (China)
1996 Michelle Kwan (USA)
1997 Tara Lipinski (USA)
1998 Michelle Kwan (USA)
1999 Maria Butyrskaya (Russia)
Most wins: (10), Sonja Henie (Norway), 1927–36.

Recent winners: pairs
1990 Yekaterina Gordeeva/Sergey Grinkov (USSR)
1991 Natalya Mishkutienko/Artur Dmitriev (USSR)
1992 Natalya Mishkutienko/Artur Dmitriev (Unified Team)
1993 Isabelle Brasseur/Lloyd Eisler (Canada)
1994 Yekaterina Gordeeva/Sergey Grinkov (Russia)
1995 Radka Kovarikova/Rene Novotny (Czech Republic)
1996 Marina Eltsova/Andrey Bushkov (Russia)
1997 Mandy Woetzel/Ingo Steuer (Germany)
1998 Elena Berzhnaya/Anton Sikharulidze (Russia)
1999 Elena Berzhnaya/Anton Sikharulidze (Russia)
Most wins: (10), Irina Rodnina (USSR), 1969–72 (with Aleksey Ulanov), 1973–8 (with Aleksander Zaitsev).

Recent winners: ice dance
1987 Natalya Bestemianova/Andrey Bukin (USSR)
1988 Natalya Bestemianova/Andrey Bukin (USSR)
1989 Marina Klimova/Sergey Ponomarenko (USSR)
1990 Marina Klimova/Sergey Ponomarenko (USSR)
1991 Isabelle and Paul Duchesnay (France)
1992 Marina Klimova/Sergey Ponomarenko (Unified Team)
1993 Maia Usova/Aleksander Zhulin (Unified team)
1994 Oksana Grichtchuk/Yevgeny Platov (Russia)
1995 Oksana Grichtchuk/Yevgeny Platov (Russia)
1996 Oksana Grichtchuk/Yevgeny Platov (Russia)
1997 Oksana Grichtchuk/Yevgeny Platov (Russia)
1998 Anjelika Krylova/Oleg Ovsyannikov (Russia)
1999 Anjelika Krylova/Oleg Ovsyannikov (Russia)
Most wins: (6), Lyudmila Pakhomova/Aleksander Gorshkov (USSR), 1970–4, 1976.

JUDO

World championships

First held in 1956, now contested every two years; current weight categories established in 1979; women's championship instituted in 1980.

Recent winners: open class – men
1987 Naoyo Ogawa (Japan)
1989 Naoyo Ogawa (Japan)
1991 Naoya Ogawa (Japan)
1993 Rafael Kubacki (Poland)
1995 David Douillet (France)
1997 Rafael Kubacki (Poland)

Recent winners: over 95kg – men
1987 Grigori Vertichev (USSR)
1989 Naoyo Ogawa (Japan)
1991 Sergei Kosorotov (USSR)
1993 David Douillet (France)
1995 David Douillet (France)
1997 David Douillet (France)

Recent winners: under 95kg – men
1987 Hitoshi Sugai (Japan)
1989 Koba Kurtanidze (Japan)
1991 Stéphane Traineau (France)
1993 Antal Kovacs (Hungary)
1995 Pawel Nastula (Poland)
1997 Pawel Nastula (Poland)

Recent winners: under 86kg – men
1987 Fabien Canu (France)
1989 Fabien Canu (France)
1991 Hirotaka Okada (Japan)
1993 Yoshio Yakumura (Japan)
1995 Ki-young Chun (South Korea)
1997 Ki-young Chun (South Korea)

Recent winners: under 78kg – men
1987 Hirotaka Okada (Japan)
1989 Byung-ju Kim (South Korea)
1991 Daniel Lascau (Germany)
1993 Ki-yung Chun (South Korea)
1995 Toshihiko Koga (Japan)
1997 Cho-in Chul (South Korea)

Recent winners: under 71kg – men
1987 Mike Swain (USA)
1989 Toshihiko Koga (Japan)
1991 Toshihiko Koga (Japan)
1993 Chung-hoon Yung (South Korea)
1995 Daisuke Hideshima (Japan)
1997 Kenzo Nakamura (Japan)

Recent winners: under 65kg – men
1987 Yosuke Yamamoto (Japan)
1989 Drago Becanovic (Yugoslavia)
1991 Udo Quellmalz (Germany)
1993 Yukimasa Nakamura (Japan)
1995 Udo Quellmalz (Germany)
1997 Hyuk Kim (South Korea)

Recent winners: under 60 kg – men
1989 Amiran Totikashvili (USSR)
1991 Tadanori Koshino (Japan)
1993 Ryuji Sonoda (Japan)
1995 Nikolai Ojeguine (Russia)
1997 Tadahiro Nomura (Japan)
Most titles: (4), Yashiro Yamashita (Japan), 1981 (Open), 1979, 1981, 1983 (over 95kg);

Shozo Fujii (Japan), 1971, 1973, 1975 (under 80 kg), 1979 (under 78 kg); David Douillet (France), 1995 (open), 1993–7 (over 95 kg).

Recent winners: open class – women
1987 Fenglian Gao (China)
1989 Estela Rodriguez (Cuba)
1991 Zhuang Xiaoyan (China)
1993 Beata Maksumow (Poland)
1995 Monique Van Der Lee (Netherlands)
1997 Diana Beltran (Cuba)

Recent winners: over 72 kg – women
1987 Fenglian Gao (China)
1989 Fenglian Gao (China)
1991 Moon Ji-yoon (South Korea)
1993 Johanna Hagen (Germany)
1995 Angelique Seriese (Netherlands)
1997 Christine Cicot (France)

Recent winners: under 72 kg – women
1987 Irene de Kok (Netherlands)
1989 Ingrid Berghmans (Belgium)
1991 Kim Mi-jung (South Korea)
1993 Cheng Huileng (China)
1995 Diadenis Luna (Cuba)
1997 Noriko Anno (Japan)

Recent winners: under 66 kg – women
1989 Emanuela Pierantozzi (Italy)
1991 Emanuela Pierantozzi (Italy)
1993 Cho Min-Sun (South Korea)
1995 Cho Min-sun (South Korea)
1997 Kate Howey (Great Britain)

Recent winners: under 61 kg – women
1987 Diane Bell (Great Britain)
1989 Catherine Fleury (France)
1991 Frauke Eickoff (Germany)
1993 Gella van de Caveye (Belgium)
1995 Young Sung-sook (South Korea)
1997 Servenr Vendenhende (France)

Recent winners: under 56 kg – women
1987 Catherine Arnaud (France)
1989 Catherine Arnaud (France)
1991 Miriam Blasco (Spain)
1993 Nicola Fairbrother (Great Britain)
1995 Driulis Gonzalez (Cuba)
1997 Isabel Fernandez (Spain)

Recent winners: under 52 kg – women
1987 Sharon Rendle (Great Britain)
1989 Sharon Rendle (Great Britain)
1991 Alessandra Giungi (Italy)
1993 Rodriguez Verdecia (Cuba)
1995 Marie-Claire Restoux (France)
1997 Marie-Claire Restoux (France)

Recent winners: under 48 kg – women
1987 Z Li (China)
1989 Karen Briggs (Great Britain)
1991 Cécile Nowak (France)
1993 Ryoko Tamura (Japan)
1995 Ryoko Tamura (Japan)
1997 Ryoko Tamura (Japan)
Most titles: (6), Ingrid Berghmans (Belgium), 1980, 1982, 1984, 1986 (Open), 1984, 1989 (both under 72 kg).

KARATE

World championships

First held in Tokyo 1970; takes place every two years since 1980, when women first competed; there is a team competition plus individual competitions – Kumite (seven weight categories for men and three for women) and Kata. Separate men and women's teams started in 1992.

Team winners: men
1992 Spain
1994 France
1996 France
Team winners: women
1992 Great Britain
1994 Spain
1996 Great Britain

LACROSSE

World championships

First held for men in 1967; for women in 1969; taken place every four years since 1974; since 1982 the women's event has been called the World Cup.

Winners: men
1978 Canada
1982 USA
1986 USA
1990 USA
1994 USA
1998 USA
Most wins: (7), USA, 1974 and as above.

Winners: women
1974 USA
1978 Canada
1982 USA
1986 Australia
1989 USA
1993 USA
1994 USA
1998 USA
Most wins: (6), USA, as above.

Iroquois Cup

The sport's best known trophy; contested by English club sides annually since 1890.

Recent winners
1987 Stockport
1988 Mellor
1989 Stockport
1990 Cheadle
1991 Cheadle
1992 Cheadle
1993 Heaton Mersey
1994 Cheadle
1995 Cheadle
1996 Stockport
1997 Mellor
1998 *not played*
Most wins: (18), Stockport, 1897–1901, 1903, 1905, 1911–13, 1923–4, 1926, 1928, 1934, 1987, 1989, 1996.

MODERN PENTATHLON

World championships

Held annually since 1949 with the exception of Olympic years, when the Olympic champions automatically become world champions.

Recent individual winners: men
1987 Joel Bouzou (France)
1988 Janos Martinek (Hungary)
1989 Laszlo Fabien (Hungary)
1990 Gianluca Tiberti (Italy)
1991 Arkadiusz Skrzypaszek (Poland)
1992 Arkadiusz Skrzypaszek (Poland)
1993 Richard Phelps (Great Britain)
1994 Dimitriy Svatkovskii (Russia)
1995 Dimitriy Svatkovski (Russia)
1996 Alexander Parygin (Kazakhstan)
1997 Sebastien Deleigne (France)

Recent team winners: men
1987 Hungary
1988 Hungary
1989 Hungary
1990 USSR
1991 USSR
1992 Poland
1993 Hungary
1994 France
1995 Poland
1996 Poland
1997 Hungary
Most wins: Individual (6), Andras Balczo (Hungary), 1963, 1965–9, 1972. Team (18), USSR, 1956–9, 1961–2, 1964, 1969, 1971–4, 1980, 1982–3, 1985, 1990, 1991.

Recent individual winners: women
1987 Irina Kisselyeva (USSR)
1988 Dorota Idzi (Poland)
1989 Lori Norwood (USA)
1990 Eva Fjellerup (Denmark)
1991 Eva Fjellerup (Denmark)
1992 Iwona Kowalewska
1993 Eva Fjellerup (Denmark)
1994 Eva Fjellerup (Denmark)
1995 Kerstin Danielsson (Sweden)
1996 Janna Dolgacheva-Shubenok (Russia)
1997 Elisavet Suvorova (Russia)

Recent team winners: women
1984 USSR
1985 Poland
1986 Poland
1987 USSR
1988 Poland
1989 Poland
1990 Poland
1991 Poland
1992 Poland
1993 Russia
1994 Italy
1995 Poland
1996 Russia
1997 Italy

MOTOR CYCLING

World championships

First organized in 1949; current titles for 500 cc, 250 cc, 125 cc, 80 cc and Sidecar; Formula One and Endurance world championships also held annually; the most prestigious title is the 500 cc category.

Recent winners: 500 cc

1988 Eddie Lawson (USA)
1989 Eddie Lawson (USA)
1990 Wayne Rainey (USA)
1991 Wayne Rainey (USA)
1992 Wayne Rainey (USA)
1993 Kevin Schwantz (USA)
1994 Michael Doohan (Australia)
1995 Michael Doohan (Australia)
1996 Michael Doohan (Australia)
1997 Michael Doohan (Australia)
1998 Michael Doohan (Australia)

Most wins: (8), Giacomo Agostini (Italy), 1966–72, 1975.
Most world titles: (15), Giacomo Agostini, 500 cc, 350 cc, 1968–74.

Isle of Man TT Races

The most famous of all motor cycle races; takes place each June; first held 1907; principal race is the Senior TT.

Recent winners: senior TT

1987 Joey Dunlop (Ireland)
1988 Joey Dunlop (Ireland)
1989 Steve Hislop (Great Britain)
1990 Carl Fogarty (Great Britain)
1991 Steve Hislop (Great Britain)
1992 Steve Hislop (Great Britain)
1993 Nigel Davies (Great Britain)
1994 Steve Hislop (Great Britain)
1995 Joey Dunlop (Ireland)
1996 Phil McCallen (Ireland)
1997 Phil McCallen (Ireland)
1998 Ian Simpson (Scotland)

Most Senior TT wins: (7), Mike Hailwood (Great Britain), 1961, 1963–7, 1979.

MOTOR RACING

World Championship

A Formula One drivers' world championship instituted in 1950; constructor's championship instituted in 1958.

Winners

1988 Ayrton Senna (Brazil) *McLaren*
1989 Alain Prost (France) *McLaren*
1990 Ayrton Senna (Brazil) *McLaren*
1991 Ayrton Senna (Brazil) *McLaren*
1992 Nigel Mansell (Great Britain) *Williams-Renault*
1993 Alain Prost (France) *Williams-Renault*
1994 Michael Schumacher (Germany) *Benetton-Ford*
1995 Michael Schumacher (Germany) *Benetton-Ford*
1996 Damon Hill (Great Britain) *Williams-Renault*
1997 Jacques Villeneuve (Canada) *Williams-Renault*
1998 Mika Hakkinen (Finland) *McLaren-Mercedes*

Most wins: Driver (5), Juan Manuel Fangio (Argentina), 1951, 1954–7; Constructor (8) Ferrari, 1961, 1964, 1975–7, 1979, 1982–3.

Le Mans 24-Hour Race

The greatest of all endurance races; first held in 1923.

Recent winners

1989 Jochen Mass (West Germany)/ Manuel Reuter (West Germany)/ Stanley Dickens (Sweden)
1990 John Nielson (Denmark)/Martin Brundle (Great Britain)/Price Cobb (USA)
1991 Volker Weidler (Germany)/ Johnny Herbert (Great Britain) / Bertrand Gachot (Belgium)
1992 Derek Warwick (Great Britain)/ Mark Blundell (Great Britain)/ Yannick Dalmas (France)
1993 Geoff Brabham (Australia)/ Christophe Bouchut (France)/ Eric Helary (France)
1994 Yannick Dalmas (France)/Mauro Baldi (Italy)/Hurley Haywood(USA) *pseudonym
1995 Yannick Dalmas (France)/JJ Lehto (Finland)/Masanori Sekiya (Japan)
1996 Manuel Reuter (Germany)/Davey Jones (USA)/Alexander Würz (Austria)
1997 Michele Alboreto (Italy)/Stefan Johansson (Sweden)/Tom Kristensen (Denmark)
1998 Allan McNish (Great Britain)/Laurent Aiello (France)/Stéphane Ortelli (France)

Most wins: (6), Jacky Ickx (Belgium), 1969, 1975–7, 1981–2.

Indianapolis 500

First held in 1911; raced over the Indianapolis Raceway as part of the Memorial Day celebrations at the end of May each year.

Recent winners

1987 Al Unser (USA)
1988 Rick Mears (USA)
1989 Emerson Fittipaldi (Brazil)
1990 Arie Luyendyk (Netherlands)
1991 Rick Mears (USA)
1992 Al Unser Jr (USA)
1993 Emerson Fittipaldi (Brazil)
1994 Al Unser Jr (USA)
1995 Jacques Villeneuve (Canada)
1996 Buddy Lazier (USA)
1997 Arie Luydendyk (Netherlands)
1998 Eddie Cheever Jr (USA)

Most wins: (4), A J Foyt (USA), 1961, 1964, 1967, 1977; Al Unser (USA), 1970–1, 1978, 1987; Rick Mears (USA), 1979, 1984, 1988, 1991.

Monte Carlo Rally

The world's leading rally; first held in 1911.

Recent winners

1985 Ari Vatanen (Finland)
1986 Henri Toivonen (Finland)
1987 Mikki Biasion (Italy)
1988 Bruno Saby (France)
1989 Miki Biasion (Italy)
1990 Didier Auriol (France)
1991 Carlos Sainz (Spain)
1992 Didier Auriol (France)
1993 Didier Auriol (France)
1994 François Delecour (France)
1995 Carlos Sainz (Spain)
1996 Patrick Bernardini (France)
1997 Piero Liatti (Italy)
1998 Carlos Sainz (Spain)
1999 Tommi Makinen (Finland)

Most wins: (4), Sandro Munari (Italy), 1972, 1975–7; Walter Röhrl (West Germany), 1980, 1982–4.

NETBALL

World championships

First held in 1963, then every four years.

Winners

1967 New Zealand
1971 Australia
1975 Australia
1979 Australia, New Zealand, Trinidad & Tobago (*shared*)
1983 Australia
1987 New Zealand
1991 Australia
1995 Australia

Most wins: (7), Australia, 1963 and as above.

ORIENTEERING

World championships

First held in 1966; takes place every two years (to 1978, and since 1979).

Individual winners: men

1970 Stig Berge (Norway)
1972 Age Hadler (Norway)
1974 Bernt Frilen (Sweden)
1976 Egil Johansen (Norway)
1978 Egil Johansen (Norway)
1979 Oyvin Thon (Norway)
1981 Oyvin Thon (Norway)
1983 Morten Berglia (Norway)
1985 Kari Sallinen (Finland)
1987 Kent Olsson (Sweden)
1989 Peter Thoresen (Norway)
1991 Jörgen Mårtensson (Sweden)
1993 Allan Mogensen (Denmark)
1995 Jörgen Mårtensson (Sweden)
1997 Peter Thoresen (Norway)

Individual winners: women

1976 Lia Veijalainen (Finland)
1978 Anne Berit Eid (Norway)
1979 Outi Bergonstrom (Finland)
1981 Annichen Kringstad (Norway)
1983 Annichen Kringstad Svensson (Norway)
1985 Annichen Kringstad Svensson (Norway)
1987 Arja Hannus (Sweden)
1989 Marita Skogum (Sweden)
1991 Katalin Olah (Hungary)
1993 Marita Skogum (Sweden)

1995 Katalin Olah (Hungary)
1997 Hanne Staff (Norway)

Most wins: Men (2), Age Hadler (Norway), 1966, 1972; Egil Johansen (Norway), Oyvin Thon (Norway), Peter Thoresen (Norway), Jörgen Mårtensson (Sweden) as above. Women (3), Annichen Kringstad (Norway), as above.

Relay winners: men

1970 Norway
1972 Sweden
1974 Sweden
1976 Sweden
1978 Norway
1979 Sweden
1981 Norway
1983 Norway
1985 Norway
1987 Norway
1989 Norway
1991 Switzerland
1993 Norway
1995 Switzerland
1997 Denmark

Relay winners: women

1970 Sweden
1972 Finland
1974 Sweden
1976 Sweden
1978 Finland
1979 Finland
1981 Sweden
1983 Sweden
1985 Sweden
1987 Norway
1989 Sweden
1991 Sweden
1993 Sweden
1995 Finland
1997 Sweden

Most wins: Men (8), Norway, as above. Women (11) Sweden, 1966 and as above.

POLO

Cowdray Park Gold Cup

First held in 1956, replacing the Champion Cup; the British Open Championship for club sides; so named because played at Cowdray Park, Sussex.

Recent winners

1988 Tramontana
1989 Tramontana
1990 Hildon
1991 Tramontana
1992 Black Bears
1993 Alcatel
1994 Ellerston Blacks
1995 Ellerston White
1996 CS Brooks
1997 Labegorce
1998 Ellerston White

Most wins: (5), Stowell Park, 1973–4, 1976, 1978, 1980; Tramontana, 1986–7 and as above.

POWERBOAT RACING

World championships

Instituted in 1982; held in many categories, with Formula One and Formula Two being the principal competitions; Formula One discontinued in 1986; Formula Two became known as Formula Grand Prix, then reverted to Formula One in 1990.

Formula One winners

1990 John Hill (Great Britain)
1991 Jonathan Jones (Great Britain)
1992 Fabrizio Bocca (Italy)
1993 Guido Capellina (Italy)
1994 Guido Capellina (Italy)
1995 Guido Capellina (Italy)
1996 Guido Capellina (Italy)
1997 Scott Gillman (USA)
1998 Scott Gillman (USA)

Most wins: (4), Guido Capellina (Italy), as above.

Formula Two/Formula Grand Prix winners

1982 Michael Werner (West Germany)
1983 Michael Werner (West Germany)
1984 John Hill (Great Britain)
1985 John Hill (Great Britain)
1986 Jonathan Jones (Great Britain) and Buck Thornton (USA) (*shared*)
1987 Bill Seebold (USA)
1988 Chris Bush (USA)
1989 Jonathan Jones (Great Britain)
1990 John Hill (Great Britain)
1991 Jonathan Jones (Great Britain)

Most wins: (3), John Hill (Great Britain), as above; Jonathan Jones (Great Britain), as above.

RACKETS

World championship

Organized on a challenge basis, the first champion in 1820 was Robert Mackay (Great Britain).

Recent winners

1973–4 Howard Angus (Great Britain)
1975–81 William Surtees (USA)
1981–4 John Prenn (Great Britain)
1984–6 William Boone (Great Britain)
1986–8 John Prenn (Great Britain)
1988–9 James Male (Great Britain)
1999– Neil Smith (Great Britain)

Longest reigning champion: 18 years, Geoffrey Atkins (1954–72).

REAL TENNIS

World championship

Organized on a challenge basis; the first world champion was M Clerge (France) c.1740, regarded as the first world champion of any sport. Women's championship first held in 1985, and then every two years.

Recent winners: men

1957–9 Albert Johnson (Great Britain)
1959–69 Northrup Knox (USA)
1969–72 Pete Bostwick (USA)
1972–5 Jimmy Bostwick (USA)
1976–81 Howard Angus (Great Britain)
1981–7 Chris Ronaldson (Great Britain)
1987–94 Wayne Davies (Australia)
1994– Robert Fahey (Australia)

Longest reigning champion: 33 years, Edmond Barre (France), 1829–62.

Winners: women

1985 Judy Clarke (Australia)
1987 Judy Clarke (Australia)
1989 Penny Fellows (Great Britain)
1991 Penny Lumley (née Fellows) (Great Britain)
1993 Sally Jones (Great Britain)
1995 Penny Lumley (Great Britain)
1997 Penny Lumley (Great Britain)

Most wins: (4), Penny Fellows Lumley (Great Britain), as above.

ROLLER SKATING

World championships

Figure skating world championships were first organized in 1947.

Recent winners: men – combined

1987 Kevin Carroll (USA)
1988 Sandro Guerra (Italy)
1989 Sandro Guerra (Italy)
1990 Samo Kokorovec (Italy)
1991 Sandro Guerra (Italy)
1992 Sandro Guerra (Italy)
1993 Samo Kokorovec (Italy)
1994 Steven Finlay (USA)
1995 Jason Sutcliffe (Australia)
1996 Francesco Ceresola (Italy)
1997 Mauro Mazzoni (Italy)
1998 Daniele Tofani (Italy)

Most wins: (5), Karl-Heinz Losch (West Germany), 1958–9, 1961–2, 1966.

Recent winners: women – combined

1987 Chiara Sartori (Italy)
1988 Rafaella Del Vinaccio (Italy)
1989 Rafaella Del Vinaccio (Italy)
1990 Rafaella Del Vinaccio (Italy)
1991 Rafaella Del Vinaccio (Italy)
1992 Rafaella Del Vinaccio (Italy)
1993 Letitia Tinghi (Italy)
1994 April Dayney (USA)
1995 Letitia Tinghi (Italy)
1996 Giusy Loncani (Italy)
1997 Sabrini Tommasini (Italy)
1998 Christine Bartolozzi (Italy)

Most wins: (5), Rafaella Del Vinaccio (Italy), as above.

Recent winners: pairs

1984 John Arishita/Tammy Jeru (USA)
1985 John Arishita/Tammy Jeru (USA)
1986 John Arishita/Tammy Jeru (USA)
1987 Fabio Trevisani/Monica Mezzardi (Italy)
1988 Fabio Trevisani/Monica Mezzardi (Italy)
1989 David De Motte/Nicky Armstrong (USA)
1990 Larry McGrew/Tammy Jeru (USA)
1991 Larry McGrew/Tammy Jeru (USA)

1992 Patrick Venerucci/Maura Ferri (Italy)
1993 Patrick Venerucci/Maura Ferri (Italy)
1994 Patrick Venerucci/Beatrice Pallazzi Rossi (Italy)
1995 Patrick Venerucci/Beatrice Pallazzo Rossi (Italy)
1996 Patrick Venerucci/Beatrice Pallazzo Rossi (Italy)
1997 Patrick Venerucci/Beatrice Pallazzo Rossi (Italy)
1998 Patrick Venerucci/Beatrice Pallazzo Rossi (Italy)
Most wins: (7), Patrick Venerucci, as above.

Recent winners: dance
1983 David Golub/Angela Famiano (USA)
1984 David Golub/Angela Famiano (USA)
1985 Martin Hauss/Andrea Steudte (West Germany)
1986 Scott Myers/Anna Danks (USA)
1987 Rob Ferendo/Lori Walsh (USA)
1988 Peter Wulf/Michela Mitzlaf (West Germany)
1989 Greg Goody/Jodee Viola (USA)
1990 Greg Goody/Jodee Viola (USA)
1991 Greg Goody/Jodee Viola (USA)
1992 Doug Wait/Deanna Monaham (USA)
1993 Doug Wait/Deanna Monaham (USA)
1994 Tim Patten/Lisa Friday (USA)
1995 Tim Patten/Lisa Friday (USA)
1996 Axel Haber/Swansi Gebauer (Germany)
1997 Axel Haber/Swansi Gebauer (Germany)
1998 Roland Bren/Candy Powderly (USA)
Most wins: (3), Jane Puracchio (USA), 1973, 1975–6; Dan Littel/Florence Arsenault, 1977–9; Greg Goody/Jodee Viola (USA), as above.

ROWING

World championships

First held for men in 1962 and for women in 1974; Olympic champions assume the role of world champion in Olympic years; principal events are the single sculls.

Recent single sculls winners: men
1988 Thomas Lange (East Germany)
1989 Thomas Lange (East Germany)
1990 Yuri Janson (USSR)
1991 Thomas Lange (Germany)
1992 Thomas Lange (Germany)
1993 Derek Porter (Canada)
1994 Andre Willms (Germany)
1995 Iztok Cop (Slovenia)
1996 Xeno Müller (Switzerland)
1997 James Koven (USA)
1998 Rob Waddell (New Zealand)
Most wins: (5), Thomas Lange (Germany), as above.

Recent sculls winners: women
1988 Jutta Behrendt (East Germany)
1989 Elisabeta Lipa (Romania)
1990 Brigit Peter (East Germany)
1991 Silke Laumann (Canada)
1992 Elisabeta Lipa (Romania)
1993 Jana Phieme (Germany)
1994 Trine Hansen (Denmark)
1995 Maria Brandin (Sweden)
1996 Yekaterina Khodotovich (Belarus)
1997 Yekaterina Khodotovich (Belarus)
1998 Irina Fedotova (Russia)
Most wins: (5), Christine Hahn (née Scheiblich) (East Germany), 1974–8.

University Boat Race

An annual contest between the crews from the Oxford and Cambridge University rowing clubs; first contested in 1829; the current course is from Putney to Mortlake.

Recent winners
1987 Oxford
1988 Oxford
1989 Oxford
1990 Oxford
1991 Oxford
1992 Oxford
1993 Cambridge
1994 Cambridge
1995 Cambridge
1996 Cambridge
1997 Cambridge
1998 Cambridge
1999 Cambridge
Wins: 76, Cambridge; 68, Oxford; 1 dead-heat (1877).

Diamond Sculls

Highlight of Henley Royal Regatta held every July; first contested in 1884.

Recent winners
1983 Steve Redgrave (Great Britain)
1984 Chris Baillieu (Great Britain)
1985 Steve Redgrave (Great Britain)
1986 Bjarne Eltang (Denmark)
1987 Peter-Michael Kolbe (West Germany)
1988 Hamish McGlashan (Australia)
1989 Vaclav Chalupa (Czechoslovakia)
1990 Eric Verdonk (New Zealand)
1991 Wim van Belleghem (Belgium)
1992 Rorie Henderson (Great Britain)
1993 Thomas Lange (Germany)
1994 Xeno Muller (Switzerland)
1995 Juri Jannson (Estonia)
1996 Merlin Verroom (Netherlands)
1997 Greg Saarle (Great Britain)
1998 James Koven (USA)
Most wins: (6), Stuart Mackenzie (Great Britain), 1957–62, Guy Nickalls (Great Britain), 1888–91, 1893–4.

RUGBY LEAGUE

Challenge Cup Final

First contested in 1897 and won by Batley; first final at Wembley Stadium in 1929.

Recent winners
1988 Wigan
1989 Wigan
1990 Wigan
1991 Wigan
1992 Wigan
1993 Wigan
1994 Wigan
1995 Wigan
1996 St Helens
1997 St Helens
1998 Sheffield
1999 Leeds
Most wins: (16), Wigan, 1924, 1929, 1948, 1951, 1958–9, 1965, 1985, and as above.

Premiership Trophy

End-of-season knockout competition involving the top eight teams in the first division; first contested at the end of the 1974–5 season. It was replaced by the Superleague Grand Final in 1998.

Recent winners
1983 Widnes
1984 Hull Kingston Rovers
1985 St Helens
1986 Warrington
1987 Wigan
1988 Widnes
1989 Widnes
1990 Widnes
1991 Hull
1992 Wigan
1993 Wigan
1994 Wigan
1995 Wigan
1996 Wigan
1997 Wigan
Most wins: (7), Wigan as above.

Superleague Grand Final

1998 Wigan

RUGBY UNION

World Cup

The first Rugby Union World Cup was staged in 1987.

Recent winners
1987 New Zealand
1991 Australia
1995 South Africa

Five Nations championship

A round-robin competition involving England, Ireland, Scotland, Wales and France; first contested in 1884.

Recent winners
1988 France and Wales
1989 France
1990 Scotland
1991 England
1992 England
1993 France
1994 Wales
1995 England
1996 England
1997 France
1998 France
1999 Scotland
Most outright wins: (22), Wales, 1893, 1900, 1902, 1905, 1908–9, 1911, 1922, 1931, 1936, 1950, 1952, 1956, 1965–6, 1969, 1971, 1975–6, 1978–9, 1994.

County championship

First held in 1889.

Recent winners
1989 Durham
1990 Lancashire
1991 Cornwall
1992 Lancashire
1993 Lancashire
1994 Yorkshire
1995 Warwickshire
1996 Gloucestershire
1997 Cumbria
1998 Cheshire
1999 Cornwall
Most wins: (16), Gloucestershire, 1910, 1913, 1920–2, 1930–2, 1937, 1972, 1974–6, 1983–4, 1996.

Tetley's Bitter Cup

An annual knockout competition for English club sides; first held in the 1971–2 season. Known as the John Player Special Cup until 1988 and the Pilkington Cup until 1997.

Recent winners
1989 Bath
1990 Bath
1991 Harlequins
1992 Bath
1993 Leicester
1994 Bath
1995 Bath
1996 Bath
1997 Leicestershire
1998 Saracens
1999 Wasps
Most wins: (10), Bath, 1984–7 and as above.

SWALEC Cup

The knockout tournament for Welsh clubs; first held in 1971–2.

Recent winners
1988 Llanelli
1989 Neath
1990 Neath
1991 Llanelli
1992 Llanelli
1993 Llanelli
1994 Cardiff
1995 Swansea
1996 Pontypridd
1997 Cardiff
1998 Llanelli
1999 Swansea
Most wins: (10), Llanelli, 1973–6, 1985 and as above.

SHOOTING

Olympic Games

The Olympic competition is the highlight of the shooting calendar; winners in all categories since 1980 are given below.

Free pistol: men
1988 Sorin Babil (Romania)
1992 Konstantin Loukachik (Unified Team)
1996 Boris Kokorev (Russia)

Rapid fire pistol: men
1988 Afanasi Kouzmine (USSR)
1992 Ralf Schumann (Germany)
1996 Ralf Schumann (Germany)

Small bore rifle: three position – men
1988 Malcolm Cooper (Great Britain)
1992 Grachya Petikiane (Unified Team)
1996 Jean-Pierre Amat (France)

Running game target: men
1992 Michael Jakosits (Germany)
1996 Yang Ling (China)

Small bore rifle: prone – men
1988 Miroslav Varga (Czechoslovakia)
1992 Lee Eun-chul (South Korea)
1996 Christian Klees (Germany)

Air rifle: men
1992 Yuri Fedkin (Unified Team)
1996 Artem Khadzhibekov (Russia)

Air pistol: men
1992 Wang Yifu (China)
1996 Robert Di Donna (Italy)

Trap: men and women
1988 Dmitri Monakov (USSR)
1992 Petr Hrdlicka (Czeckoslovakia)
1996 Michael Diamond (Australia)

Double Trap: men
1996 Mark Russell (Australia)

Double Trap: women
1996 Kim Rhodes (USA)

Skeet: men
1992 Zhang Shan (China)
1996 Ennion Falco (Italy)

Sport pistol: women
1992 Marina Logvinenko (Unified Team)
1996 Li Duihong (China)

Air rifle: women
1988 Irina Chilova (USSR)
1992 Yeo Kab-soon (South Korea)
1996 Renata Mauer (Poland)

Small bore rifle: women
1988 Silvia Sperber (West Germany)
1992 Launi Melli (USA)
1996 Alexandra Ivosev (Yugoslavia)

Air pistol: women
1992 Marina Logvinenko (Unified Team)
1996 Olga Klochneva (Russia)

SKIING

World Cup

A season-long competition first organized in 1967; champions are declared in downhill, slalom, giant slalom and super-giant slalom, as well as the overall champion; points are obtained for performances in each category.

Recent overall winners: men
1989 Marc Girardelli (Luxembourg)
1990 Pirmin Zurbriggen (Switzerland)
1991 Marc Girardelli (Luxembourg)
1992 Paul Accola (Swiatzerland)
1993 Marc Girardelli (Luxembourg)
1994 Kaetel Andre Aamodt (Norway)
1995 Alberto Tomba (Italy)
1996 Lasse Kjus (Norway)
1997 Luc Alphand (France)
1998 Hermann Maier (Austria)
1999 Lasse Kjus (Norway)

Recent overall winners: women
1989 Vreni Schneider (Switzerland)
1990 Petra Kronberger (Austria)
1991 Petra Kronberger (Austria)
1992 Petra Kronberger (Austria)
1993 Anita Wachter (Austria)
1994 Vreni Schneider (Switzerland)
1995 Vreni Schneider (Switzerland)
1996 Katja Seizinger (Germany)
1997 Pernilla Wiberg (Sweden)
1998 Katja Seizinger (Germany)
1999 Alexandra Meissnitzer (Austria)
Most wins: Men (5), Marc Girardelli (Luxembourg), as above. Women (6), Annemarie Moser-Pröll (Austria), 1971–5, 1979.

Olympic Games

Gold medal winners, 1998
Men's Alpine Combination
Mario Reiter (Austria)
Women's Alpine Combination
Katja Seizinger (Germany)

SNOOKER

World Professional Championship

Instituted in the 1926–7 season; a knockout competition open to professional players who are members of the World Professional Billiards and Snooker Association; played at the Crucible Theatre, Sheffield.

Recent winners
1990 Stephen Hendry (Scotland)
1991 John Parrott (England)
1992 Stephen Hendry (Scotland)
1993 Stephen Hendry (Scotland)
1994 Stephen Hendry (Scotland)
1995 Stephen Hendry (Scotland)
1996 Stephen Hendry (Scotland)
1997 Ken Doherty (Ireland)
1998 John Higgins (Scotland)
1999 Stephen Hendry (Scotland)
Most wins: (15), Joe Davis (England), 1927–40, 1946.

Benson & Hedges Masters

The most important non-ranking tournament.

Winners
1989–93 Stephen Hendry (Scotland)
1994 Alan McManus (Scotland)
1995 Ronnie O'Sullivan (England)
1996 Stephen Hendry (Scotland)
1997 Steve Davis (England)
1998 Mark Williams (Wales)
1999 John Higgins (Scotland)
Most wins: (7), Stephen Hendry (Scotland), as above.

Ranking tournaments

Preston Grand Prix
Originally the Professional Players Tournament;

under present name since 1998; a ranking tournament since its inauguration.

Winners
1987 Stephen Hendry (Scotland)
1988–9 Steve Davis (England)
1990–1 Stephen Hendry (Scotland)
1992 Jimmy White (England)
1993 Jimmy White (England)
1994 John Higgins (Scotland)
1995 Stephen Hendry (Scotland)
1996 Mark Williams (Wales)
1997 Dominic Dale (Wales)
1998 Stephen Lee (England)
Most wins: (3), Steve Davis (England), 1985 and as above.

Regal Scottish Open
A ranking tournament since 1984. International Open to 1997. Originally the Mercantile Credit Classic.

Winners
1987–8 Steve Davis (England)
1989 Doug Mountjoy (Wales)
1990 Steve James (England)
1991 Jimmy White (England)
1992 Steve Davis (England)
1993 Stephen Hendry (Scotland)
1994 John Parrott (England)
1995 John Higgins (Scotland)
1996 John Higgins (Scotland)
1997 Stephen Hendry (Scotland)
1998 Ronnie O'Sullivan (England)
1999 Stephen Hendry (Scotland)
Most wins: (5), Steve Davis (England), 1980 and as above.

Liverpool Victoria UK Championship
A ranking tournament since 1984; under present name since 1998.

Winners
1991 John Parrott (England)
1992 Jimmy White (England)
1993 Jimmy White (England)
1994 Ronnie O'Sullivan (England)
1995 Stephen Hendry (Scotland)
1996 Stephen Hendry (Scotland)
1997 Ronnie O'Sullivan (England)
1998 John Higgins (Scotland)
Most wins: (6), Steve Davis (England), 1980-1, 1984–7.

British Open
A ranking tournament since 1985.

Winners
1987 Jimmy White (England)
1988 Stephen Hendry (Scotland)
1989 Tony Meo (England)
1990 Bob Chaperon (Canada)
1991 Stephen Hendry (Scotland)
1992 Jimmy White (England)
1993 Steve Davis (England)
1994 Ronnie O'Sullivan (England)
1995 John Higgins (Scotland)
1996 Nigel Bond (England)
1997 Mark Williams (Wales)
1998 John Higgins (Scotland)
1999 Fergal O'Brien (Ireland)
Most wins: (5), Steve Davis (England), 1981–2, 1984, 1986 and as above.

World Amateur Championship

First held in 1963; originally took place every two years, but annual since 1984.

Recent winners
1989 Ken Doherty (Ireland)
1990 Stephen O'Connor (Ireland)
1991 Noppodol Noppachorn (Thailand)
1992 Neil Moseley (England)
1993 Neil Moseley (England)
1994 Mohammed Yusuf (Pakistan)
1995 Sackai Sim-ngan (Thailand)
1996 Stuart Bingham (England)
1997 Marco Fu (Hong Kong)
1998 Luke Simmonds (England)
Most wins: (2), Gary Owen (England), 1963, 1966; Ray Edmonds (England), 1972, 1974; Paul Mifsud (Malta), as above; Neil Mosley (England), as above.

SOFTBALL

World championships

First held for women in 1965 and for men the following year; now held every four years.

Winners: men
1968 USA
1972 Canada
1976 Canada, New Zealand, USA (*shared*)
1980 USA
1984 New Zealand
1988 USA
1992 Canada
1996 New Zealand
Most wins: (5), USA, 1966 and as above.

Winners: women
1974 USA
1978 USA
1982 New Zealand
1986 USA
1990 USA
1994 USA
1998 USA
Most wins: (6), USA, as above.

SPEEDWAY

World championships

Individual championships inaugurated in 1936; team championship instituted in 1960; first official pairs world championship in 1970 (threes from 1991); (became the World Team Cup in 1994).

Recent winners
1988 Erik Gundersen (Denmark)
1989 Hans Nielsen (Denmark)
1990 Per Jonsson (Sweden)
1991 Jan Pedersen (Denmark)
1992 Gary Havelock (England)
1993 Sam Ermolenko (USA)
1994 Tony Rickardsson (Sweden)
1995 Hans Nielsen (Denmark)
1996 Billy Hamill (USA)
1997 Greg Hancock (USA)
1998 Tony Rickardsson (Sweden)
Most wins: (6), Ivan Mauger (New Zealand), 1968–70, 1972, 1977, 1979.

Recent pairs winners
1989 Erik Gundersen/Hans Nielsen (Denmark)
1990 Hans Nielsen/Jan Pedersen (Denmark)
1991 Hans Nielsen/Jan Pedersen/Tommy Knudsen (Denmark)
1992 Greg Hancock/Sam Ermolenko/ Ronnie Correy (USA)
1993 Tony Rickardsson/Henrik Gustafsson (Sweden)
1994 (World Team Cup) Per Gustafsson/Tony Rickardsson (Sweden)
1995 Hans Nielsen/Tommy Knudsen/Brian Carger (Denmark)
1996 Tomasz Gollob/Piotr Protasiewicz/ Slawomir Drabik (Poland)
1997 Hans Nielsen/Tommy Knudsen/Jesper Jensen (Denmark)
1998 Greg Hancock/Billy Hamill/Sam Ermolenko (USA)
Most wins: (9), Hans Nielsen (Denmark) 1979, 1986–8 as above.

Recent team winners
1986 Denmark
1987 Denmark
1988 Denmark
1989 England
1990 USA
1991 Denmark
1992 USA
1993 USA
1994 Sweden
1995 Denmark
1996 Poland
1997 Denmark
1998 USA
Most wins: (10), Denmark, 1981, 1983–8, 1991, 1995, 1997.

SQUASH

World Open championship

First held in 1976; takes place annually for men, every two years for women.

Winners: men
1988 Jahangir Khan (Pakistan)
1989 Jansher Khan (Pakistan)
1990 Jansher Khan (Pakistan)
1991 Rodney Martin (Australia)
1992 Jansher Khan (Pakistan)
1993 Jansher Khan (Pakistan)
1994 Jansher Khan (Pakistan)
1995 Jansher Khan (Pakistan)
1996 Jansher Khan (Pakistan)
1997 Rodney Eyles (Australia)
1998 Jonathon Power (Canada)
Most wins: (8), Jansher Khan (Pakistan), 1987 and as above.

Winners: women
1992 Sue Devoy (New Zealand)

1993 Michelle Martin (Australia)
1994 Michelle Martin (Australia)
1995 Michelle Martin (Australia)
1996 Sarah Fitzgerald (Australia)
1997 Sarah Fitzgerald (Australia)
1998 Sarah Fitzgerald (Australia)
Most wins: (5), Sue Devoy (New Zealand), 1985, 1990–1, and as above.

SURFING

World professional championship

A season-long series of Grand Prix events; first held in 1970.

Recent winners: men
1987 Damien Hardman (Australia)
1988 Barton Lynch (Australia)
1989 Martin Potter (Great Britain)
1990 Tommy Curren (USA)
1991 Damien Hardman (Australia)
1992 Kelly Slater (USA)
1993 Derek Ho (Hawaii)
1994 Kelly Slater (USA)
1995 Kelly Slater (USA)
1996 Kelly Slater (USA)
1997 Kelly Slater (USA)

Recent winners: women
1987 Wendy Botha (South Africa)
1988 Frieda Zamba (USA)
1989 Wendy Botha (South Africa)
1990 Pam Burridge (Austrialia)
1991 Wendy Botha (Australia, ex-South Africa)
1992 Wendy Botha (Australia)
1993 Pauline Menczer (Australia)
1994 Lisa Anderson (USA)
1995 Lisa Anderson (USA)
1996 Lisa Anderson (USA)
1997 Lisa Anderson (USA)
Most wins: Men (5), Mark Richards (Australia), 1975, 1979–83; Kelly Slater (USA), as above. Women (4), Wendy Botha (Australia), as above.

SWIMMING AND DIVING

World championships

First held in 1973, the World Championships have since taken place in 1975, 1978, 1982, 1986, 1991, 1994 and 1998.

1998 World champions: men

50m freestyle Phil Pilczuk (USA)
100m freestyle Alexander Popov (Russia)
200m freestyle Michael Klim (Australia)
400m freestyle Ian Thorpe (Australia)
1500m freestyle Grant Hackett (Australia)
100m backstroke Lenny Krayzelburg (USA)
200m backstroke Lenny Krayzelburg (USA)
100m breaststroke Fred de Burghgraeve (Belgium)
200m breaststroke Kurt Grote (USA)
100m butterfly Michael Klim (Australia)
200m butterfly Denys Sylantyev (Ukraine)
200m individual medley Marcel Wouda (Netherlands)
400m individual medley Tom Dolan (USA)
1m springboard diving Zhuocheng Yu (China)
Platform diving Dimitri Sautin (Russia)

1998 World champions: women

50m freestyle Amy Van Dyken (USA)
100m freestyle Jenny Thompson (USA)
200m freestyle Claudia Poll (Costa Rica)
400m freestyle Chen Yan (China)
800m freestyle Brooke Bennett (USA)
100m backstroke Lee Maurer (USA)
200m backstroke Roxanna Maracineanu (France)
100m breaststroke Kristy Kowal (USA)
200m breaststroke Agnes Kovacs (Hungary)
100m butterfly Jenny Thompson (USA)
200m butterfly Susan O'Neill (Australia)
200m individual medley Wu Yanyan (China)
400m individual medley Chan Yen (China)
1m springboard diving Irina Lashko (Russia)
Platform diving Olena Zhupyna (Ukraine)
Synchronized swimming, solo Olga Sedakova (Russia)
Synchronized swimming, duet Olga Sedakova/Olga Brusnikina (Russia)

Olympic Games

1996 Gold medal winners: men

50m freestyle Alexander Popov (Russia)
100m freestyle Alexander Popov (Russia)
200m freestyle Danyon Loader (New Zealand)
400m freestyle Danyon Loader (New Zealand)
1500m freestyle Keiren Perkins (Australia)
100m breaststroke Fredde Burghgraeve (Belgium)
200m breaststroke Norbert Rozsa (Hungary)
100m butterfly Denis Pankratov (Russia)
200m butterfly Denis Pankratov (Russia)
100m backstroke Jeff Rouse (USA)
200m backstroke Brad Bridgewater (USA)
200m individual medley Attila Czene (Hungary)
400m individual medley Tom Dolan (USA)

1996 Gold medal winners: women

50m freestyle Amy Van Dyken (USA)
100m freestyle Jingyi Le (China)
200m freestyle Claudia Poll (Costa Rica)
400m freestyle Michelle Smith (Ireland)
100m breaststroke Penelope Heyns (South Africa)
200m breaststroke Penelope Heyns (South Africa)
100m backstroke Beth Botsford (USA)
200m backstroke Krisztina Egerszegi (Hungary)
100m butterfly Amy Van Dyken (USA)
200m butterfly Susan O'Neill (Australia)
200m individual medley Michelle Smith (Ireland)
400m individual medley Michelle Smith (Ireland)

TABLE TENNIS

World championships

First held in 1926 and every two years since 1957.

Recent winners: Swaythling cup – men's team
1977 China
1979 Hungary
1981 China
1983 China
1985 China
1987 China
1989 Sweden
1991 Sweden
1993 Sweden
1995 China
1997 China

Recent winners: Corbillon Cup – women's team
1977 China
1979 China
1981 China
1983 China
1985 China
1987 China
1989 China
1991 South Korea
1993 China
1995 China
1997 China
Most wins: Swaythling Cup (12), Hungary, 1926, 1928–31, 1933 (twice), 1935, 1938, 1949, 1952, 1979. Corbillon Cup (12), China, 1965, 1975, 1977, 1979, 1981, 1983, 1985, 1987, 1989, 1993, 1995, 1997.

Recent winners: men's singles
1977 Mitsuru Kohno (Japan)
1979 Seiji Ono (Japan)
1981 Guo Yuehua (China)
1983 Guo Yuehua (China)
1985 Jiang Jialiang (China)
1987 Jiang Jialiang (China)
1989 Jan-Ove Waldner (Sweden)
1991 Jorgen Persson (Sweden)
1993 Jean-Philippe Gatien (France)
1995 Kong Ling-hui (China)
1997 Jan-Ove Waldner (Sweden)
Most wins: (5), Viktor Barna (Hungary), 1930, 1932–5.

Recent winners: women's singles
1977 Pak Yung-sun (North Korea)
1979 Ge Xinai (China)
1981 Ting Ling (China)
1983 Cao Yanhua (China)
1985 Cao Yanhua (China)
1987 He Zhili (China)
1989 Qiao Hong (China)
1991 Deng Yaping (China)
1993 Hyun Jung-hwa (South Korea)
1995 Deng Yaping (China)
1997 Deng Yaping (China)
Most wins: (6), Angelica Rozeanu (Romania), 1950–55.

Recent winners: men's doubles
1977 Li Zhenshi/Liang Geliang (China)
1979 Dragutin Surbek/Anton Stipancic (Yugoslavia)
1981 Cai Zhenhua/Li Zhenshi (China)
1983 Dragutin Surbek/Zoran Kalinic (Yugoslavia)
1985 Mikael Applegren/Ulf Carlsson (Sweden)
1987 Chen Longcan/Wei Quinguang (China)
1989 Joerg Rosskopf/Stefen Fetzner (West Germany)
1991 Peter Karlson/Thomas von Scheele (Sweden)
1993 Wang Tao/Lu Lin (China)
1995 Wang Tao/Lu Lin (China)
1997 Kong Linghui/Liu Guoliang (China)
Most wins: (8), Viktor Barna (Hungary/England), 1929–33 (two titles 1933), 1935, 1939.

Recent winners: women's doubles
1975 Maria Alexandru (Romania)/ Shoko Takashima (Japan)
1977 Pak Yong-Lok (North Korea)/Yang Yin (China)
1979 Zhang Li/Zhang Deying (China)
1981 Zhang Deying/Cao Yanhua (China)
1983 Shen Jianping/Dai Lili (China)
1985 Dai Lili/Geng Lijuan (China)
1987 Yang Young-ja/Hyun Jung-hwa (South Korea)
1989 Qiao Hong/Deng Yaping (China)
1991 Chen Zhie/Gao Jun (China)
1993 Liu Wen/Qiao Yunping (China)
1995 Deng Yaping/Qiao Hong (China)
1997 Deng Yaping/Yang Ying (China)
Most wins: (7), Maria Mednyanszky (Hungary), 1928, 1930–5.

Recent winners: mixed doubles
1977 Jacques Secretin/Claude Bergeret (France)
1979 Liang Geliang/Ge Xinai (China)
1981 Xie Saike/Huang Junqun (China)
1983 Guo Yuehua/Ni Xialian (China)
1985 Cai Zhenua/Cao Yanhua (China)
1987 Hui Jun/Geng Lijuan (China)
1989 Yoo Nam-Kyu/Hyun Jung-Hwa (South Korea)
1991 Wang Tao/Liu Wei (China)
1993 Wang Tao/Liu Wei (China)
1995 Wang Tao/Liu Wei (China)
1997 Liu Guoliang/Wu Na (China)
Most wins: (6), Maria Mednyanszky (Hungary), 1927–8, 1930–1, 1933 (two titles).

TENNIS (LAWN)

Wimbledon championships

The All-England Championships at Wimbledon are Lawn Tennis's most prestigious championships; first held in 1877.

Recent winners: men's singles
1987 Pat Cash (Australia)
1988 Stefan Edberg (Sweden)
1989 Boris Becker (West Germany)
1990 Stefan Edberg (Sweden)
1991 Michael Stich (Germany)
1992 Andre Agassi (USA)
1993 Pete Sampras (USA)
1994 Pete Sampras (USA)
1995 Pete Sampras (USA)
1996 Richard Krajicek (Netherlands)
1997 Pete Sampras (USA)
1998 Pete Sampras (USA)
Most wins: (7), William Renshaw (Great Britain), 1881–6, 1889.

Recent winners: women's singles
1987 Martina Navratilova (USA)
1988 Steffi Graf (West Germany)
1989 Steffi Graf (West Germany)
1990 Martina Navratilova (USA)
1991 Steffi Graf (Germany)
1992 Steffi Graf (Germany)
1993 Steffi Graf (Germany)
1994 Conchita Martinez (Spain)
1995 Steffi Graf (Germany)
1996 Steffi Graf (Germany)
1997 Martina Hingis (Switzerland)
1998 Jana Novotná (Czech Republic)
Most wins: (9), Martina Navratilova (USA), 1978, 1979, 1982–7, 1990.

Recent winners: men's doubles
1989 John Fitzgerald (Australia)/ Anders Jarryd (Sweden)
1990 Rick Leach/Jim Pugh (USA)
1991 John Fitzgerald (Australia)/ Anders Jarryd (Sweden)
1992 John McEnroe (USA)/Michael Stich (Germany)
1993 Todd Woodbridge/Mark Woodforde (Australia)
1994 Todd Woodbridge/Mark Woodforde (Australia)
1995 Todd Woodbridge/Mark Woodforde (Australia)
1996 Todd Woodbridge/Mark Woodforde (Australia)
1997 Todd Woodbridge/Mark Woodforde (Australia)
1998 Jacco Eltingh/Paul Haarhuis (Netherlands)
Most wins: (8), Lawrence Doherty/Reg Doherty (Great Britain), 1897–1901, 1903–5.

Recent winners: women's doubles
1989 Jana Novotná/Helena Sukova (Czechoslovakia)
1990 Jana Novotná/Helena Sukova (Czechoslovakia)
1991 Larissa Savchenko/Natalya Zvereva (USSR)
1992 Gigi Fernandez (USA)/Natalya Zvereva (Belarus)
1993 Gigi Fernandez (USA)/Natalya Zvereva (Belarus)
1994 Gigi Fernandez (USA)/Natalya Zvereva (Belarus)
1995 Jana Novotná (Czech Republic)/Arantxa Sánchez Vicario (Spain)
1996 Helen Sukova (Czech Republic)/Martina Hingis (Switzerland)
1997 Gigi Fernandez/Natalya Zvereva (USA)
1998 Jana Novotná (Czech Republic)/Martina Hingis (Switzerland)
Most wins: (12), Elizabeth Ryan (USA), 1914, 1919–23, 1925–7, 1930, 1933–4.

Recent winners: mixed doubles
1990 Zina Garrison/Rick Leach (USA)
1991 Elizabeth Smylie/John Fitzgerald (Australia)
1992 Larissa Savchenko (Latvia)/Cyril Suk (Czech Republic)
1993 Martina Navratilova (USA)/ Mark Woodforde (Australia)
1994 Helena Suková (Czech Republic)/ Todd Woodbridge (Australia)
1995 Martina Navratilova/Jonathan Stark (USA)
1996 Helen Sukova/Cyril Suk (Czech Republic)
1997 Helen Sukova/Cyril Suk (Czech Republic)
1998 Serena Williams (USA)/Max Mirnyi (Belarus)
Most wins: (7), Elizabeth Ryan (USA), 1919, 1921, 1923, 1927–8, 1930, 1932.

United States Open

First held in 1881 as the United States Champion-ship; became the United States Open in 1968.

Winners: men's singles
1988 Mats Wilander (Sweden)
1989 Boris Becker (West Germany)
1990 Pete Sampras (USA)
1991 Stefan Edberg (Sweden)
1992 Stefan Edberg (Sweden)
1993 Pete Sampras (USA)
1994 Andre Agassi (USA)
1995 Pete Sampras (USA)
1996 Pete Sampras (USA)
1997 Patrick Rafter (Australia)
1998 Patrick Rafter (Australia)

Winners: women's singles
1988 Steffi Graf (West Germany)
1989 Steffi Graf (West Germany)
1990 Gabriela Sabatini (Argentina)
1991 Monica Seles (Yugoslavia)
1992 Monica Seles (Yugoslavia)
1993 Steffi Graf (Germany)
1994 Arantxa Sanchez Vicario (Spain)
1995 Steffi Graf (Germany)
1996 Steffi Graf (Germany)
1997 Martina Hingis (Switzerland)
1998 Lindsay Davenport (USA)
Most wins: Men (7), Richard D Sears (USA), 1881–7; Bill Larned (USA), 1901–2, 1907–11; Bill Tilden (USA), 1920–5, 1929. Women (7), Molla Mallory (née Bjurstedt) (USA), 1915–16, 1918, 1920–2, 1926; Helen Wills-Moody (USA), 1923–5, 1927–9, 1931.

Davis Cup

International team competition organized on a knockout basis; first held in 1900; contested on a challenge basis until 1972.

Recent winners
1987 Sweden
1988 W Germany
1989 W Germany
1990 USA
1991 France
1992 USA
1993 Germany
1994 Sweden
1995 USA
1996 France
1997 Sweden
1998 Sweden
Most wins: (37), USA, 1900, 1902, 1913, 1920–6, 1937–8, 1946–9, 1954, 1958, 1963, 1968–72, 1978–9, 1981–2, and as above.

TENPIN BOWLING

World championships

First held in 1923 by the International Bowling Association; since 1954 organized by the Federation Internationale des Quillieurs (FIQ); since 1963, when women first competed, held every four years.

Recent individual winners: men
1967 David Pond (Great Britain)
1971 Ed Luther (USA)
1975 Bud Staudt (USA)
1979 Ollie Ongtawco (Philippines)
1983 Armando Marino (Colombia)
1987 Rolland Patrick (France)
1991 Ma Ying-chei (Thailand)
1995 Marc Doi (Canada)

Recent individual winners: women
1967 Helen Weston (USA)
1971 Ashie Gonzales (Puerto Rico)
1975 Annedore Haefker (West Germany)
1979 Lita de la Roas (Philippines)
1983 Lena Sulkanen (Sweden)
1987 Edda Piccini (Italy)
1991 Martina Beckel (Germany)
1995 Debby Ship (Canada)
Most wins: No one has won more than once.

TRAMPOLINING

World championships

First held in 1964 and annually until 1968; since then, every two years.

Recent individual winners: men
1978 Yevgeni Yanes (USSR)
1980 Stewart Matthews (Great Britain)
1982 Carl Furrer (Great Britain)
1984 Lionel Pioline (France)
1986 Lionel Pioline (France)
1988 Vadim Krasnoshapka (USSR)
1990 Alexander Mosalenko (USSR)
1992 Alexander Mosalenko (Russia)
1994 Alexander Mosalenko (Russia)
1996 Dimitri Poliarauch (Belarus)
1998 German Khnivchev (Russia)
Most wins: (3), Alexander Mosalenko (USSR/Russia), as above.

Recent individual winners: women
1980 Ruth Keller (Switzerland)
1982 Ruth Keller (Switzerland)
1984 Sue Shotton (Great Britain)
1986 Tatyana Lushina (USSR)
1988 Rusadan Khoperia (USSR)
1990 Yelena Merkulova (USSR)
1992 Yelena Merkulova (Russia)
1994 Irina Karavaeva (Russia)
1996 Tatyana Kovaleva (Russia)
1998 Irina Karavaeva (Russia)
Most wins: (5), Judy Wills (USA), 1964–8.

TUG OF WAR

World championships

Instituted in 1975, held every two years; contested at 560 kg from 1982.

Winners

	720 kg	*640 kg*	*560 kg*
1978	England	England	–
1980	England	England	–
1982	England	Ireland	Switzerland
1984	Ireland	Ireland	England
1985	Switzerland	Switzerland	Switzerland
1986	Ireland	Ireland	England
1988	Ireland	England	England
1990	Ireland	Ireland	Switzerland
1992	Switzerland	Switzerland	Spain
1994	Switzerland	Switzerland	Spain
1996	Netherlands	Switzerland	Spain
1998	Netherlands	England	Spain

Most titles: (16), England, 1975–7 and as above.

VOLLEYBALL

World championships

Inaugurated in 1949; first women's championships in 1952; now held every four years, but Olympic champions are also world champions in Olympic years.

Recent winners: men
1980 USSR
1982 USSR
1984 USA
1986 USA
1988 USA
1990 Italy
1992 Brazil
1994 Italy
1996 Netherlands
1998 Italy

Recent winners: women
1980 USSR
1982 China
1984 China
1986 China
1988 USSR
1990 USSR
1992 Cuba
1994 Cuba
1996 Cuba
1998 Cuba
Most wins: Men (9), USSR, 1949, 1952, 1960, 1962, 1964, 1968, and as above. Women (9), USSR, 1952, 1956, 1960, 1968, 1970, 1972, and as above.

WALKING

Lugano Trophy

The principal road walking trophy; contested every two years by men's national teams; first held in 1961.

Recent winners
1979 Mexico
1981 Italy
1983 USSR
1985 East Germany
1987 USSR
1989 USSR
1991 Italy
1993 Mexico
1995 Mexico
1997 Russia
Most wins: (5), E Germany, 1965, 1967, 1970, 1973, 1985.

Eschborn Cup

The women's equivalent of the Lugano Trophy; first held in 1979; takes place every two years.

Winners
1985 China
1987 USSR
1989 USSR
1991 USSR
1993 Italy
1995 China
1997 Russia
Most wins: (4), USSR, 1981 and as above.

WATER POLO

World championship

First held in 1973, and every four years since 1978; included in the world swimming championships; since 1991 has been held separately. First women's event held in 1986.

Winners: men
1978 Italy
1982 USSR
1986 Yugoslavia
1991 Yugoslavia
1994 Italy
1998 Spain

Winners: women
1994 Hungary
1998 Italy
Most wins: Men (2), USSR, 1975, 1982 Yugoslavia, Italy as above.

World Cup

Inaugurated in 1979 and held every two years; women's event unofficial until 1989.

Winners: men
1983 USSR
1985 W Germany
1987 Yugoslavia
1989 Yugoslavia

1991 USA
1993 Italy
1995 Hungary
1997 USA
Most wins: (2), USSR 1981, 1983, Yugoslavia, as above.

WATER SKIING

World championships

First held in 1949; take place every two years; competitions for Slalom, Tricks, Jumps and the Overall Individual title.

Recent overall winners: men
1977 Mike Hazelwood (Great Britain)
1979 Joel McClintock (Canada)
1981 Sammy Duvall (USA)
1983 Sammy Duvall (USA)
1985 Sammy Duvall (USA)
1987 Sammy Duvall (USA)
1989 Patrice Martin (France)
1991 Patrice Martin (France)
1993 Patrice Martin (France)
1995 Patrice Martin (France)
1997 Patrice Martin (France)
Most wins: (5), Patrice Martin (France), as above.

Recent overall winners: women
1977 Cindy Todd (USA)
1979 Cindy Todd (USA)
1981 Karin Roberge (USA)
1983 Ana-Maria Carrasco (Venezuela)
1985 Karen Neville (Australia)
1987 Deena Brush (USA)
1989 Deena Mapple (née Brush) (USA)
1991 Karen Neville (Australia)
1993 Natalia Rumiantseva (Russia)
1995 Judy Messer (Canada)
1997 Elena Milakova (Russia)
Most wins: (3), Willa McGuire (née Worthington) (USA), 1949–50, 1955; Liz Allan-Shetter (USA), 1965, 1969, and as above.

WEIGHTLIFTING

World championships

First held in 1898; 11 weight divisions; the most prestigious is the 110kg plus category (formerly known as Super Heavyweight); in 1993 the weight for this category was changed to 108 kg plus; Olympic champions are automatically world champions in Olympic years.

Recent champions: over 110kg
1986 Antonio Krastev (Bulgaria)
1987 Alexander Kurlovich (USSR)
1988 Alexander Kurlovich (USSR)
1989 Alexander Kurlovich (USSR)
1990 Leonid Taranenko (USSR)
1991 Alexander Kurlovich (USSR)
1992 Alexander Kurlovich (Unified Team)
1993 Ronnie Weller (Germany)
1994 Alexander Kurlovich (Belarus)
1995 Alexander Kurlovich (Belarus)
1996 Andrei Chermerkin (Russia)
1997 Andrei Chermerkin (Russia)
1998 Andrei Chermerkin (Russia)
Most titles (all categories): (8), John Davies (USA), 82.5kg 1938; 82.5+kg 1946–50; 90+kg 1951–2; Tommy Kono (USA), 67.5kg 1952; 75 kg 1953, 1957–9; 82.5 kg 1954–6; Vasiliy Alexseyev (USSR), 110+kg 1970–7.

WRESTLING

World championships

Graeco-Roman world championships first held in 1921; first freestyle championships in 1951; each style contests 10 weight divisions, the heaviest being the 130kg (formerly over 100 kg) category; Olympic champions become world champions in Olympic years.

Recent winners: super-heavyweight/over 100kg
Freestyle

1988 David Gobedzhishvilli (USSR)
1989 Ali Reiza Soleimani (Iran)
1990 David Gobedzhishvilli (USSR)
1991 Andreas Schroder (Germany)
1992 Bruce Baumgartner (USA)
1993 Mikael Ljunberg (Sweden)
1994 Mahmut Demir (Turkey)
1995 Bruce Baumgartner (USA)
1996 Mahmut Demir (Turkey)
1997 Zekeriya Güglü (Turkey)
1998 Alexis Rodriguez (Cuba)

Graeco-Roman
1988 Alexander Karelin (USSR)
1989 Alexander Karelin (USSR)
1990 Alexander Karelin (USSR)
1991 Alexander Karelin (USSR)
1992 Alexander Karelin (Unified Team)
1993 Alexander Karelin (Russia)
1994 Alexander Karelin (Russia)
Most titles (all weight divisions): *Freestyle* (10), Alexander Medved (USSR), 90kg 1962–4, 1966; 100kg 1967–8; over 100kg 1969–72. *Graeco-Roman* (11), Alexander Karelin (Russia); Over 100kg as above.

YACHTING

America's Cup

One of sport's famous trophies; first won by the schooner *Magic* in 1870; now held approximately every four years, when challengers compete in a series of races to find which of them races against the holder; all 25 winners up to 1983 were from the United States.

Recent winners
Winning yacht (Skipper)
1967 *Intrepid* (USA) (Emil Mosbacher)
1970 *Intrepid* (USA) (Bill Ficker)
1974 *Courageous* (USA) (Ted Hood)
1977 *Courageous* (USA) (Ted Turner)
1980 *Freedom* (USA) (Dennis Conner)
1983 *Australia II* (Australia) (John Bertrand)
1987 *Stars & Stripes* (USA) (Dennis Conner)
1988 *Stars & Stripes* (USA) (Dennis Conner)*
1992 *America 3* (USA) (Bill Koch)
1995 Black Magic (New Zealand) (Russell Coutts)
* *Stars & Stripes* won a special challenge match but on appeal the race was awarded to *New Zealand* skippered by Davis Barnes. However, after much legal wrangling, the cup was retained by *Stars & Stripes*.
Most wins: (Skipper) (3), Charlie Barr (USA), 1899, 1901, 1903; Harold Vanderbilt (USA), 1930, 1934, 1937; Dennis Conner (USA), as above.

Admiral's Cup

A two-yearly series of races in the English Channel, around Fastnet rock and at Cowes; national teams of three boats per team; first held in 1957.

Recent winners
1977 Great Britain
1979 Australia
1981 Great Britain
1983 West Germany
1985 West Germany
1987 New Zealand
1989 Great Britain
1991 France
1993 Germany
1995 Italy
1997 USA
Most wins: (9), Great Britain, 1957, 1959, 1963, 1965, 1971, 1975, 1977, 1981, 1989.

Common Abbreviations

This section includes all the abbreviations used in the body of the Cambridge Paperback Encyclopedia, along with a number of related notions in widespread contemporary use.

A

AA Alcoholics Anonymous
AA Automobile Association
AA(A) anti-aircraft (artillery)
AAA Amateur Athletics Association
AAA American Automobile Association
AAU Amateur Athletic Union (USA)
ABA Amateur Boxing Association
ABA American Broadcasting Association
ABC Australian Broadcasting Corporation
ABM antiballistic missile
ABTA Association of British Travel Agents
AC alternating current
ACAS Advisory, Conciliation and Arbitration Service
ACLU American Civil Liberties Union
ACT Australian Capital Territory
ACTH adrenocorticotrophic hormone
ACTU Australian Council of Trade Unions
ACU Auto Cycle Union
ACV air cushion vehicle
AD anno Domini (in the year of Our Lord)
A-D analog-to-digital (in computing)
ADH antidiuretic hormone
ADP adenosine diphosphate
AEA Atomic Energy Authority (UK)
AEC Atomic Energy Commission (USA)
AFC American Football Conference
AFL/CIO American Federation of Labor/Congress of Industrial Organizations
AFP Agence France Presse
AFV armoured fighting vehicle
AGM annual general meeting
AGR advanced gas-cooled reactor
AH anno Hegirae (in the year of the Hegira)
AHF antihaemophilic factor
AI artificial intelligence
AIBA International Amateur Boxing Federation
AID artificial insemination by donor
AIDS acquired immune deficiency syndrome
AIF Australian Imperial Force
AIH artificial insemination by husband
ALCM air-launched cruise missile
ALGOL algorithmic language
ALP Australian Labor Party
ALU arithmetic and logic unit
AM amplitude modulation
AMA American Medical Association
amu atomic mass unit
ANC African National Congress
ANS autonomic nervous system
ANSI American National Standards Institute
ANZAC Australian and New Zealand Army Corps
ANZUS Australia, New Zealand and the United States
AOB any other business
AONB Area of Outstanding Natural Beauty
AP Associated Press
APEX Association of Professional, Executive, Clerical and Computer Staff
APL A Programming Language
APR annual percentage rate
APRA Alianza Popular Revolutionaria Americana (American Popular Revolutionary Alliance)
AR aspect ratio
ARCIC Anglican–Roman Catholic International Commission
A/S Advanced/Supplementary
ASA Amateur Swimming Association
ASA American Standards Association
ASCII American Standard Code for Information Interchange
ASDIC Admiralty Submarine Detection Investigation Committee
ASEAN Association of South-East Asian Nations
ASL American Sign Language
ASLEF Associated Society of Locomotive Engineers and Firemen
ASLIB Association of Special Libraries and Information Bureaux
ASM air-to-surface missile
ASPCA American Society for the Prevention of Cruelty to Animals
ASTMS Association of Scientific, Technical and Managerial Staffs
ATM automated teller machine
ATP adenosine triphosphate
ATS Auxiliary Territorial Service
ATV Associated Television
AU astronomical unit
AV audio-visual
AVMA American Veterinary Medical Association
AWACS Airborne Warning and Control System
AWU Australian Workers' Union

B

B&W black and white
BAF British Athletics Federation
BAFTA British Academy of Film and Television Arts
BALPA British Airline Pilots' Association
BASIC Beginners All-purpose Symbolic Instruction Code
BASIC British American Scientific International Commercial (English)
BBC British Broadcasting Corporation
BC before Christ
BCD binary coded decimal
BCG bacille (bacillus) Calmette–Guérin
BCS Bardeen, Cooper & Schrieffer (theory)
BDO British Darts Organisation
BEF British Expeditionary Force
BEV Black English vernacular
BHP Broken Hill Proprietary Company
BIA Bureau of Indian Affairs
BIS Bank for International Settlements
BLAISE British Library Automated Information Service
BMA British Medical Association
BOSS Bureau of State Security (South Africa)
BP blood pressure
BSE bovine spongiform encephalopathy
BSI British Standards Institution
BST British Summer Time
btu British thermal unit
BUF British Union of Fascists
BUPA British United Provident Association
BVA British Veterinary Association

C

CAB Citizen's Advice Bureau
CACM Central American Common Market
CAD computer-aided design
CAI computer-aided instruction
CAL computer-aided learning
CAM computer-aided manufacture
CAP Common Agricultural Policy
CARICOM Caribbean Community
CARIFTA Caribbean Free Trade Area
CASE computer-aided software engineering
CATV cable television
CB citizen's band (radio)
CBE Commander of the (Order of the) British Empire
CBI Confederation of British Industry
CBL computer-based learning
CCD charge-coupled device
CCK cholecystokinin-pancreozymin
CCR camera cassette recorder

COMMON ABBREVIATIONS (continued)

CCTA Central Computer and Telecommunications Agency
CCTV closed circuit television
CD Civil Defence
CD compact disc
CDC Centers for Disease Control
CDC Commonwealth Development Corporation
CD-ROM compact disc read-only memory
CDU Christian Democratic Union
CENTO Central Treaty Organization
CERN Organisation Européene pour la recherche nucléaire (formerly, Conseil Européen pour la recherche nucléaire)
cgs centimetre-gram-second
CGT capital gains tax
CGT Confédération générale du travail
CH Companion of Honour
CHAPS Clearing House Automated Clearing System
CHIPS Clearing House Interbank Payments System
CIA Central Intelligence Agency
CID Criminal Investigation Department
CIM computer-integrated manufacture
CIO Congress of Industrial Organizations
CM Congregation of the Mission
CMG Companion of (the Order of) St Michael & St George
CNAA Council for National Academic Awards
CND Campaign for Nuclear Disarmament
CNES Centre national d'éspace
CNR Canadian National Railway
CNS central nervous system
COBE Cosmic Background Explorer
COBOL Common Business Oriented Language
COMAL Common Algorithmic Language
COMECON Council for Mutual Economic Assistance
CORE Congress of Racial Equality
CP Congregation of the Passion
CPI Consumer Price Index
CP/M control program monitor
CPR Canadian Pacific Railway
CPR cardio-pulmonary resuscitation
CPU central processing unit
CRO cathode-ray oscilloscope
CRT cathode-ray tube
CSCW computer-supported co-operative work
CSE Certificate of Secondary Education
CSF cerebrospinal fluid
CSIRO Commonwealth Scientific and Industrial Research Organization
CSO colour separation overlay
CT computed tomography
CTC city technology college
CTT capital transfer tax
CV cultivar
CVO Commander of the Royal Victorian Order
CVS chorionic villus sampling
CWA County Women's Association
CWS Co-operation Wholesale Society

D

D-A digital-to-analog
D&C dilatation and curettage
DALR dry adiabatic lapse rate
DAT digital audio tape
DBE Dame Commander of the (Order of the) British Empire
DBMS database management system
DBS direct broadcasting from satellite
dc direct current
DCF discounted cash flow
DCMG Dame Commander Grand Cross of (the Order of) St Michael and St George
DCVO Dame Commander of the Royal Victorian Order
DDT dichloro-diphenyl-trichloroethane
DES Department of Education and Science
DES diethylstilboestrol
DFC Distinguished Flying Cross
DHA District Health Authority
DIA Defence Intelligence Agency
DLP Democratic Labor Party (Australia)
DMSO dimethyl sulphoxide
DNA deoxyribonucleic acid
DOS Disk Operating System
DSC Distinguished Service Cross
DSN Deep Space Network
DSO Distinguished Service Order
DST daylight saving time
DTP desk-top publishing

E

EAC European Atomic Commission
EAR entity–attribute–relationship model
EARM electronically alterable read-only memory
EBCDIC extended binary-coded decimal interchange code
EBU European Boxing Union
EBU European Broadcasting Union
EC European Community
ECA European Commission on Agriculture
ECF extracellular fluid
ECG electrocardiograph
ECM European Common Market
ECO European Coal Organization
ECOSOC Economic and Social Council (of the United Nations)
ECOWAS Economic Community of West African States
ECSC European Coal and Steel Community
ECT electroconvulsive therapy
ECTG European Channel Tunnel Group
ECU European currency unit
ED extra-low dispersion
EDC European Defence Community
EDF European Development Fund
EDI electronic data interchange
EDVAC Electronic Discrete Variable Automatic Computer
EEOC Equal Employment Opportunity Commission
EFA European Fighter Aircraft
EFC European Forestry Commission
EFTA European Free Trade Association
EFTPOS electronic funds transfer at point of sale
EGF epidermal growth factor
EI Exposure Index
EKG electrocardiogram (in USA)
ELDO European Launcher Development Organization
ELF Eritrea Liberation Front
emf electromotive force
EMS European Monetary System
emu electromagnetic units
ENIAC Electronic Numeral Indicator and Calculator
EOKA Ethniki Organosis Kipriakou Agonos (National Organization of Cypriot Struggle)
EP European Parliament
EPA Environmental Protetection Agency
EPR Einstein–Podolsky–Rosen (paradox)
EPR electron paramagnetic resonance
EPROM electronically programmable read-only memory
ERNIE Electronic Random Number Indicator Equipment
ERW enhanced radiation weapon
ESA Environmentally Sensitive Area
ESA European Space Agency
ESC electronic stills camera
ESCU European Space Operations Centre
ESO European Southern Observatory
ESP extra-sensory perception
ESPRIT European Strategic Programme for Research and Development in Information Technology
ESRO European Space Research Organization
ESTEC European Space Research and Technology Centre
ETU Electricians Trade Union
EU European Union
EUFA European Union Football Associations

COMMON ABBREVIATIONS (continued)

EURATOM European Atomic Energy Community

F

FA Football Association
FAA Federal Aviation Administration
FAO Food and Agriculture Organization
FBI Federal Bureau of Investigation
FCA Farm Credit Administration
FCC Federal Communications Commission
FDA Food and Drug Administration
FDDI fibre distributed data interface
FDIC Federal Deposit Insurance Corporation
FEI International Equestrian Federation
FeLV feline leukaemia virus
FIA International Automobile Association
FIAC International Amateur Cycling Federation
FIBA International Basketball Federation
FIBT International Bobsleigh and Tobogganing Federation
FIC International Canoeing Federation
FIDE International Chess Federation
FIE feline infectious enteritis
FIE International Fencing Federation
FIV feline immunodeficiency virus
FIFA Fédération internationale de football association (International Association Football Federation)
FIG International Gymnastic Federation
FIH International Hockey Federation
FILA International Amateur Wrestling Federation
FIM International Motorcycling Federation
FIMBRA Financial Intermediaries, Managers and Brokers Regulatory Association
FINA International Amateur Swimming Federation
FIQ International Bowling Federation
FIRA International Amateur Rugby Federation
FIS International Ski Federation
FIT International Trampoline Federation
FITA International Archery Federation
FIVB International Volleyball Federation
FLN Front de libération nationale
fm frequency modulation
FORTRAN formula translation
fps foot-pound-second
FRELIMO Frente de Libertação de Moçambique
FSH follicle-stimulating hormone
FTC Federal Trade Commission

G

GAA Gaelic Athletic Association
GAR Grand Army of the Republic
GATT General Agreement on Tariffs and Trade
GBE Knight/Dame Grand Cross of (the Order of the) British Empire
GC George Cross
GCC Gulf Co-operation Council
GCE General Certificate of Education
GCHQ Government Communications Headquarters
GCMG Knight/Dame Grand Cross of (the Order of) St Michael and St George
GCSE General Certificate Secondary Education
GCVO Knight/Dame Grand Cross of the Royal Victorian Order
GDI gross domestic income
GDP gross domestic product
GEO geosynchronous Earth orbit
GESP generalized extra-sensory perception
GH growth hormone
GIFT gamete intrafallopian transfer
GLC gas-liquid chromatography
GLCM ground-launched cruise missile
GM George Medal
GMC General Medical Council
GMT Greenwich Mean Time
GNP gross national product
GnRH gonadotrophin-releasing hormone
GP General Practitioner
GPSS General Purpose System Simulator
GUI graphic user interface
GUT grand unified theory

H

HCG human chorionic gonadotrophin
HE His/Her Excellency
HEP hydro-electric power
HF high frequency
HGV heavy goods vehicle
HIH His/Her Imperial Highness
HIM His/Her Imperial Majesty
HIV human immunodefiency virus
HLA human leucocyte antigen
HM His/Her Majesty
HMG His/Her Majesty's Government
HMI His/Her Majesty's Inspectorate
HMO Health Maintenance Organization
HMS His/Her Majesty's Ship/Service
HMSO His/Her Majesty's Stationery Office
HNC Higher National Certificate
HND Higher National Diploma
hp horsepower
HR House of Representatives
HRH His/Her Royal Highness

I

IAAF International Amateur Athletic Federation
IAEA International Atomic Energy Agency
IBA International Baseball Association
IBF International Badminton Federation
IBF International Boxing Federation
IBRD International Bank for Reconstruction and Development
IBSF International Billiards and Snooker Federation
ICAO International Civil Aviation Organization
ICC International Cricket Council
ICF International Curling Federation
ICFTU International Confederation of Free Trade Unions
ICI Imperial Chemical Industries
IDA International Development Agency
IFAD International Fund for Agricultural Development
IFC International Finance Corporation
IHF International Handball Federation
IIHF International Ice Hockey Federation
IJF International Judo Federation
ILP Independent Labour Party
ILO International Labour Organization
IMCO Intergovernmental Maritime Consultative Organization
IMF International Monetary Fund
INLA Irish National Liberation Army
INRI Iesus Nazarenus Rex Iudeorum (Jesus of Nazareth, King of the Jews)
IOC International Olympic Committee
IPA International Phonetic Alphabet
IPSS international packet switching service
IQ intelligence quotient
IR infrared
IRA Irish Republican Army
IRB Irish Republican Brotherhood
IRBM intermediate-range ballistic missile
IRFB International Rugby Football Board
ISBN international standard book number
ISDN Integrated Services Digital Network
ISO International Organization for Standardization
ISRF International Squash Rackets Federation
ISSN international standard serial number
ISU International Skating Union
ita initial teaching alphabet
ITCZ intertropical convergence zone
ITF International Tennis Federation
ITN Independent Television News
ITT International Telephone and Telegraph Corporation
ITTF International Table Tennis Federation

COMMON ABBREVIATIONS (continued)

ITU International Telecommunication Union
ITV Independent Television
IUCN International Union for the Conservation of Nature and Natural Resources
IUD intra-uterine (contraceptive) device
IUPAC International Union of Pure and Applied Chemistry
IUPAP International Union of Pure and Applied Physics
IVF in vitro fertilisation
IVR International Vehicle Registration
IWF International Weightlifting Federation
IWSF International Water Ski Federation
IWW Industrial Workers of the World
IYRU International Yacht Racing Union

J

JANET Joint Academic Network
JET Joint European Torus
JP Justice of the Peace
JPL Jet Propulsion Laboratory

K

KADU Kenya African Democratic Union
KANU Kenya African National Union
KB Knight Bachelor; Knight of the (Order of the) Bath
KBE Knight Commander of the (Order of the) British Empire
KC King's Counsel
KCB Knight Commander of the (Order of the) Bath
KCMG Knight Commander Grand Cross of (the Order of) St Michael and St George
KCVO Knight Commander of The Royal Victorian Order
KG Knight of the (Order of the) Garter
KGB Komitet Gosudarstvennoye Bezhopaznosti (Committee of State Security)
KKK Ku Klux Klan
KMT Kuomintang
kpc kiloparsec
KT Knight of the (Order of the) Thistle

L

LAFTA Latin American Free Trade Association
LAN local area network
LAUTRO Life Assurance and Unit Trust Regulatory Organization
LCD liquid-crystal display
LDC less-developed country
LEA Local Education Authority
LED light-emitting diode
LEO low Earth orbit
LFA less favoured area
LH luteinizing hormone
LHRH luteinizing-hormone-releasing hormone
LIFFE London International Financial Futures Exchange
LISP list processing
LMS London Missionary Society
LPG liquefied petroleum gas
LPGA Ladies Professional Golfers' Association
LSD lysergic acid diethylamide
LSI large-scale integration
LTA Lawn Tennis Association
LVO Lieutenant of the Royal Victorian Order

M

MAC multiplexed analog component
MAN Metropolitan Area Network
MAO monoamine oxidase
MATV Master Antenna Television
MBE Member of the (Order of the) British Empire
MC Military Cross
MCA monetary compensation amount
MDMA methylenedioxymethamphetamine
ME myalgic encephalomyelitis
MH Medal of Honor
MHD magnetohydrodynamics
MICR magnetic ink character recognition
Mired micro reciprocal degrees
MIRV multiple independently targeted re-entry vehicle
mksa metre-kilogram-second-ampere
MLR minimum lending rate
mmf magnetomotive force
MMI man–machine interaction
MOH Medal of Honor
Mpc megaparsec
MPS marginal propensity to save
MPTP methylphenyltetrahydropyridine
MRA Moral Rearmament
MRI magnetic resonance imaging
MSC Manpower Services Commission
MSG monosodium glutamate
MSH melanocyte-stimulating hormone
MVD Ministerstvo Vnutrennykh Del (Ministry for Internal Affairs)
MVO Member of the Royal Victorian Order

N

NAACP National Association for the Advancement of Coloured People
NAFTA North American Free Trade Association
NANC non-adrenergic, non-cholinergic
NASA National Aeronautics and Space Administration
NASDA National Space Development Agency
NATO North Atlantic Treaty Organisation
NBA National Basketball Association (USA)
NBC National Broadcasting Corporation
NCAA National Collegiate Athletic Association (USA)
NDE near-death experience
NDP New Democratic Party
NEDO National Economic Development Office
NEP new economic policy
NF National Front
NFC National Football Conference
NFL National Football League (USA)
NGC new general catalogue
NGF nerve growth factor
NHL National Hockey League (USA)
NHS National Health Service
NIH National Institute of Health
NKVD Narodnyi Komissariat Vnutrennikh Del (People's Commissariat of Internal Affairs)
NLRB National Labor Relations Board
NOW National Organization for Women
NPT non-proliferation treaty
NRA National Recovery Administration
NRAO National Radio Astronomy Observatory
NSF National Science Foundation
NSPCC National Society for the Prevention of Cruelty to Children
NTSC National Television System Commission
NUM National Union of Mineworkers
NUT National Union of Teachers
NVC non-verbal communication

O

OAPEC Organization of Arab Petroleum Exporting Countries
OAS Organisation de l'armée secrète (Secret Army Organization)
OAS Organization of American States
OAU Organization of African Unity
OB Order of the Bath
OB outside broadcast
OBE Officer of the (Order of the) British Empire
OCarm Order of the Brothers of the Blessed Virgin Mary of Mount Carmel
OCart Order of Carthusians
OCR optical character recognition/reader
OCSO Order of the Reformed Cistercians of the Strict Observance
OD ordnance datum
ODA Overseas Development Administration
ODC Order of Discalced Carmelites
ODECA Organizacion de estados Centro Americanos (Organization of Central American States)
OECD Organization for Economic Co-operation and Development

COMMON ABBREVIATIONS (continued)

OEEC Organization for European Economic Co-operation
OEM original equipment manufacturer
OFM Order of Friars Minor
OFMCap Order of Friars Minor Capuchin
OFMConv Order of Friars Minor Conventual
OGPU Otdelenie Gosudarstvenni Politcheskoi Upravi (Special Government Political Administration)
OM Order of Merit
OMCap Order of Friars Minor of St Francis Capuccinorum
OOBE out-of-body experience
OP Order of Preachers
OPEC Organization of Petroleum Exporting Countries
OSA Order of the Hermit Friars of St Augustine
OSB Order of St Benedict
OSF Open Software Foundation
OSFC Order of Friars Minor of St Francis Capuccinorum
OSI open systems interconnection
OTC over-the-counter (stocks and shares, drugs)
OTEC ocean thermal energy conversion
OU Open University
OXFAM Oxford Committee for Famine Relief

P

PAC Pan-African Congress
PAC political action committee
PAL phase alternation line
PAYE pay as you earn
pc parsec
PC personal computer
PC Poor Clares
PC Progressive Conservative Party
PCP phenylcyclohexylpiperidine
PDGF platelet-derived growth factor
PDR precision depth recorder
PEN International Association of Poets, Playwrights, Editors, Essayists, and Novelists
PEP Political and Economic Planning
PF Patriotic Front
PGA Professional Golfers' Association
PH Purple Heart
PIN personal identification number
PK psychokinesis
PKU phenylketonuria
PLA People's Liberation Army
plc public limited company
PLO Palestine Liberation Organization
PM of F Presidential Medal of Freedom
PNLM Palestine National Liberation Movement
POS point of sale
POW prisoner of war
PPI plan position indicator
PQ Parti Québecois
PR proportional representation
PRO Public Record Office
PRO public relations officer
PROM programmable read-only memory
PSBR public sector borrowing requirement
PSTN public switched telephone network
PTA parent–teacher association
PTFE polytetrafluorethylene
PTT Posts, Telegraph and Telephones Authority
PVA polyvinyl acetate
PVC polyvinyl chloride
PWA Public Works Administration
PWR pressurized-water reactor
PYO pick-your-own

Q

QALY quality adjusted life year
QC Queen's Counsel
QCD quantum chromodynamics
QED quantum electrodynamics

R

RA Royal Academy
R&A Royal & Ancient Golf Club of St Andrews
RAAF Royal Australian Air Force
RACE Research in Advanced Communications in Europe
RADA Royal Academy of Dramatic Art
RAF Royal Air Force
RAM read-and-write memory
RAM Royal Academy of Music
RAN Royal Australian Navy
R&D research and development
RDA recommended daily allowance
REM rapid eye movement
RFLP restriction fragment length polymers
RFU Rugby Football Union
RGB red, green and blue (colour television)
RHA Regional Health Authority
RISC reduced instruction set computer
RKKA Rabochekrest'yanshi Krasny (Red Army of Workers and Peasants)
RL Rugby League
RM Royal Marines
rms root-mean-square
RN Royal Navy
RNA ribonucleic acid
RNLI Royal National Lifeboat Institution
ROM read-only memory
RP received pronunciation
RPI retail price index
RPM resale price maintenance
rpm revolutions per minute
RS Royal Society
RSPB Royal Society for the Protection of Birds
RSPCA Royal Society for the Prevention of Cruelty to Animals
RTG radio-isotope thermo-electric generator
RVO Royal Victorian Order

S

SA Sturm Abteilung (Storm Troopers)
SAD seasonal affective disorder
SALR saturated adiabatic lapse rate
SALT Strategic Arms Limitation Talks
SAS Special Air Service
SAT Standard Assessment Task
SBR styrene butadiene rubber
SBS Special Boat Service
SCID severe combined immuno-deficiency
SCLC Southern Christian Leadership Conference
SDI selective dissemination of information
SDI Strategic Defense Initiative
SDP Social Democratic Party
SDR special drawing rights
SDS Students for a Democratic Society
SDU Social Democratic Union
SEAQ Stock Exchange Automated Quotations
SEATO South-East Asia Treaty Organization
SEC Securities and Exchange Commission
SECAM Séquence électronique couleur avec mémoire (Electronic colour sequence with memory)
SERPS state earnings-related pension scheme
SGML standard generalized mark-up language
SHAEF Supreme Headquarters Allied Expeditionary Force
SHAPE Supreme Headquarters Allied Powers, Europe
SHF super-high frequency
SI système internationale (International System)
SIB Securities and Investments Board
SIOP single integrated operation plan
SJ Society of Jesus
SLBM submarine-launched ballistic missile
SLCM sea-launched cruise missile
SLDP Social and Liberal Democratic Party
SLE systemic lupus erythematosus

COMMON ABBREVIATIONS (continued)

SLR single-lens reflex
SNCC Student Non-Violent Co-ordinating Committee
SNOBOL string-oriented symbolic language
SNP Scottish National Party
SOCist Cistercians of Common Observance
SOE Special Operations Executive
SONAR sound navigation and ranging
SPSS statistical package for the social sciences
SQL structured query language
SQUID superconducting quantum interference device
SRO self-regulatory organization
SRO single-room occupancy
SS Schutzstaffel (Protective Squad)
SSADM structured systems analysis and design methodology
SSSI Site of Special Scientific Interest
START strategic arms reduction talks
STD sexually-transmitted disease
STOL short take-off and landing
SWAPO South-West Africa People's Organization
SWS slow wave sleep

T

TAB Totalisator Agency Board
TARDIS time and relative dimensions in space
TASS Telegrafnoe Agentsvo Sovetskovo Soyuza (Telegraph Agency of the Soviet Union)
TAVRA Territorial and Voluntary Reserve Army
TCCB Test and County Cricket Board
TCDD tetrachlorodibenzo-p-dioxin
TCM traditional Chinese medicine
TEFL teaching English as a foreign language
TESL teaching English as a second language
TGWU Transport and General Workers Union
TM transcendental meditation
TNT trinitrotoluene
TT Tourist Trophy
TTL through the lens
TUC Trades Union Congress
TV television
TVA Tennessee Valley Authority

U

UAE United Arab Emirates
UAP United Australia Party
UCAR Union of Central African Republics
UCCA University Central Council on Admissions
UDA Ulster Defence Association
UDI Unilateral Declaration of Independence
UEFA Union of European Football Associations
UFO unidentified flying object
UHF ultra-high frequency
UHT ultra-high temperature
UIPMB International Union of Modern Pentathlon and Biathlon
UIT International Shooting Union
UK United Kingdom
UN United Nations
UNCED United Nations Conference on Environment and Development
UNCTAD United Nations Conference on Trade and Development
UNDC United Nations Disarmament Commission
UNDP United Nations Development Programme
UNEP United Nations Environment Programme
UNESCO United Nations Educational, Scientific and Cultural Organization
UNFAO United Nations Food and Agriculture Organization
UNGA United Nations General Assembly
UNHCR United Nations High Commissioner for Refugees
UNHRC United Nations Human Rights Commissioner
UNICEF United Nations Children's Fund (formerly UN International Children's Emergency Fund)
UNIDO United Nations Industrial Development Organization
UNO United Nations Organization
UNRWA United Nations Relief and Works Agency for Palestine Refugees in the Near East
UNSC United Nations Security Council
UNSG United Nations Secretary General
UNTT United Nations Trust Territory
UPU Universal Postal Union
USA United States of America
USAF United States Air Force
USCG United States Coast Guard
USGA United States Golf Association
USIS United States Information Service
USPGA United States Professional Golfers' Association
USSR Union of Soviet Socialist Republics

V

VA Veterans Administration
VAN value-added network
VAT value-added tax
VC Victoria Cross
VCR video cassette recorder
VD venereal disease
VDU visual display unit
VHF very high frequency
VHS video home system
VIP vasoactive intestinal polypeptide
VLF very low frequency
VLSI very large scale interpretation
VOA Voice of America
VRC visible record computer
VSEPR valence shell electron pair repulsion
VSO Voluntary Service Overseas
VTOL vertical take-off and landing
VTR video tape recorder

W

WAAC Women's Auxiliary Army Corps
WAAF Women's Auxiliary Air Force
WAC Women's Army Corps
WASP White Anglo-Saxon Protestant
WBA World Boxing Association
WBC World Boxing Council
WBO World Boxing Organisation
WCC World Council of Churches
WEA Workers' Educational Association
WFTU World Federation of Trade Unions
WHO World Health Organization
WI (National Federation of) Women's Institutes
WIPO World Intellectual Property Organization
WMO World Meteorological Organization
WPA Work Projects Administration
WPBSA World Professional Billiards and Snooker Association
WRAC Women's Royal Army Corps
WRAF Women's Royal Air Force
WRNS Women's Royal Naval Service
WRVS Women's Royal Voluntary Service
WTO World Trade Organization
WVA World Veterinary Association
WVS Women's Voluntary Service
WWF Worldwide Fund for Nature
WWSU World Water Skiing Union

Y

YHA Youth Hostels Association
YMCA Young Men's Christian Association
YMHA Young Men's Hebrew Association
YWCA Young Women's Christian Association
YWHA Young Women's Hebrew Association